CONTEMPORARY
ARTISTS

CONTEMPORARY ARTS SERIES

Contemporary Artists
Contemporary Architects
Contemporary Photographers
Contemporary Designers
International Contemporary Arts Directory

CONTEMPORARY
ARTISTS

THIRD EDITION

Editor:
Colin Naylor

Advisers:
Jean-Christophe Ammann, Szymon Bojko
Melvin N. Day, Jorge Glusberg
Klaus Honnef, Arthur McIntyre
Joan Murray, Frank Popper
Peter Selz, Tazmi Shinoda
Heinz Spielmann, Tommaso Trini
Marina Vaizey

St J

ST. JAMES PRESS
CHICAGO AND LONDON

Front cover: Horst Antes—maquette for *Der Ring*, 1987.

© 1989 by St. James Press
All rights reserved. For information, write:

ST. JAMES PRESS
233 East Ontario Street
Chicago 60611, U.S.A.
or
3 Percy Street
London W1P 9FA, England

First Published in the U.S.A. and U.K. in 1989

British Library Cataloguing in Publication Data

Contemporary artists—3rd ed.
  1. Visual arts—Biographies
  I. Naylor, Colin, *1944–*
  709′ .2′2

  ISBN 0-912289-96-1

Printed and bound in Great Britain by
Butler & Tanner Ltd, Frome and London
Typeset at BookMasters, Ashland, Ohio

CONTENTS

EDITOR'S NOTE

The selection of entrants in this third edition of *Contemporary Artists* is based on the recommendations of the Advisers whose names are listed on page ix. Guidelines for selection proposed that all entrants should have worked as professional artists for at least five years, have exhibited their work in several individual exhibitions at important galleries, and have been included in large-scale museum survey shows—and be represented in the permanent collections of major museums throughout the world. In the case of young—and perhaps lesser-known—artists, one important criterion was that they should have already attracted serious critical attention in the current art media. The inclusion of deceased artists is dependent upon the continuing influence of their work on current art activity—though, for general purposes, no artist deceased prior to 1960 has been included.

Entries include: a biography; a list of individual exhibitions; a selection of up to 10 group exhibitions; a listing of those public galleries and museums that have the work of the entrant in their permanent collection (again, up to a limit of 10); and a bibliography of books and articles by and about the entrant. As well, living entrants have been invited to make a statement on their work or on contemporary art in general, and to choose a photograph of a representative work. Critical texts have been provided by 125 contributors.

Most of the information in the entries on living artists was supplied by the entrants themselves. Research was carried out mainly in the libraries of the Tate Gallery, London, the Museum of Modern Art, New York, and the Art Institute of Chicago: we are grateful to the staff at all three institutions for their unfailing co-operation and courtesy.

ADVISERS/CONTRIBUTORS

Advisers

Jean-Christophe Ammann, Szymon Bojko
Melvin N. Day, Jorge Glusberg, Klaus Honnef
Arthur McIntyre, Joan Murray, Frank Popper
Peter Selz, Tazmi Shinoda, Heinz Spielman
Tommaso Trini, Marina Vaizey

Contributors

Daniel Abadie, Albrecht D., Lawrence Alloway
Jean-Christophe Ammann, Ban Andras

Carrie Barker, D. C. Barrett, Konstantin Bazarov
Jane Bell, Carmine Benincasa, Maurice Berger
Florent Bex, Willard Bohn, Szymon Bojko
Achille Bonito Oliva, Jean-Luc Bordeaux
David Bourdon, David Brown, William Burroughs

Massimo Carboni, Gary Catalano, Barbara Cavaliere
Ronny Cohen, Michael Compton, Lynne Cooke
Barbara Cortright, Fenella Crichton

Melvin N. Day, Gillo Dorfles

Mary Ellis, Muriel Emanuel

Zdenek Felix, Michael Alastair Findlay
Andrew Forge, Claude Fournet, Alison Fraser
B. H. Friedman, Kenneth S. Friedman, Gerolf Fritsch

Peggy Gale, Edda Gazzero, Ron Glowen
Jorge Glusberg, Janet Goleas, Olle Granath

James Harithas, Dick Higgins, John H. Holloway
Klaus Honnef

Jill Johnston

Paul J. Karstorm, Victoria Keller, Jane Kelly
Alicja Kepinska, Joshua Kind, April Kingsley
Helena Kontova, Richard Kostelanetz, Udo Kultermann

Roberto G. Lambarelli, Sharon Lancer, Elise La Rose
Lavina Learmont, Dominique Linquois, Marco Livingstone
Norbert Lynton

Alastair Mackintosh, Andrée Marechal-Workman
Henry Martin, Carine Maurice, Cecile N. McCann
Arthur McIntyre, Marco Meneguzzo, Thomas Messer
Gunter Metken, Tamon Miki, Alan Moore
Barbara Moore, Lynda Morris, Joan Murray
Italo Mussa

Yusuke Narahara, Roald Nasgaard, Michael Newman
Percy North

Harold Osborne

Demetrio Paparoni, Loredana Parmesani
Ralph Pomeroy, Frank Popper

George Rickey, John Roberts, John Robinson
Marlee Robinson

Merle Schipper, Werner Schulze-Reimpell
Dieter Schwarz, Peter Selz, Michael Shepherd
Tazmi Shinoda, Dagmar Sinz, Katharine Smith
Charles Spencer, Heinz Spielmann, Ryszard Stanislawski
Mary Stofflet, Marie Luise Syring

Daniel Thomas, Yoshiaki Tono
H.J.A.M. van Haaren, Radu Varia, Luca Venturi
Giorgio Verzotti, Monika von Zitzewitz

A.F. Wagemans, John A. Weil, G. S. Whittet
Karen Wilkin, Sheldon Williams, Adina Wingate

Chryssa Zacharea

CONTEMPORARY
ARTISTS

Magdalena Abakanowicz
Ivor Abrahams
Marina Abramovic
Vito Acconci
Valerio Adami
Nicholas Africano
Afro
Yaacov Agam
Vincenzo Agnetti
Josef Albers
Ivan Albright
Pierre Alechinsky
Terry Allen
Laurie Anderson
Carl Andre
Michael Andrews
Giovanni Anselmo
Horst Antes
Eleanor Antin
Stephen Antonakos
Richard Anuskiewicz
Siegfried Anzinger
Karel Appel
Shusaku Arakawa
Arman
Kenneth Armitage
John Armleder
Robert Arneson
Eduardo Arroyo
Richard Artschwager
Michael Asher
David Askevold
Conrad Atkinson
Gabor Attalai
Bernard Aubertin
Frank Auerbach
Alice Aycock
Ay-O

Francis Bacon
Jo Baer
Olle Baertling
Enrico Baj
John Baldessari
Balthus
Walter Darby Bannard
Clive Barker
Robert Barry
Jennifer Bartlett
Gianfranco Baruchello
George Baselitz
Leonard Baskin
Carlo Battaglia
Herbert Bayer
Jean Bazaine
Jack Beal
Romare Bearden
Bernhard and Hilla Becher
Robert Bechtle
Bill Beckley
Larry Bell
Hans Bellmer
Luis Benedit
Lynda Benglis
Billy Al Bengston
Jan Berdyszak
Jaap Berghuis
Henryk Berlewi
Antonio Berni
Bertholin
Jake Berthot
Harry Bertoia
Jean-Pierre Bertrand
Joseph Beuys
Charles Biederman
Max Bill
Isabel Bishop
James Bishop
Ronald Bladen
Peter Blake
Bernhard-Johannes Blume
Peter Blume
Mel Bochner
Alighiero E. Boetti

Mari Boeyen
Marinus Boezem
Ilya Bolotowsky
Christian Boltanski
Lee Bontecou
Peter Booth
Jon Borofsky
Jean François Bory
Derek Boshier
Fernando Botero
Martha Boto
Theo Botschuyver
Louise Bourgeois
Arthur Boyd
Mark Boyle
Erich Brauer
Claudio Bravo
George Brecht
Robert G. Breer
K.P. Brehmer
Stuart Brisley
Marcel Broodthaers
James Brooks
Stanley Brouwn
Günter Brus
Tadeusz Brzozowski
Stephen Buckley
Edward Bullmore
Chris Burden
Daniel Buren
Victor Burgin
Edward Burra
Alberto Burri
Pol Bury
Jack Bush
Michael Buthe
Reg Butler
Deborah Butterfield

Paul Cadmus
John Cage
Alexander Calder
Antonio Calderara
Pier Paolo Calzolari
Peter Campus
Louis Cane
Rafael Canogar
Guiseppe Capogrossi
Anthony Caro
Ian Carr-Harris
Nicola Carrino
Pietro Cascella
Enrico Castellani
Luciano Castelli
Jorge Castillo
Patrick Caulfield
Alik Cavaliere
Mario Ceroli
Cesar
Lynn Chadwick
Marc Chagall
John Chamberlain
Alan Charlton
Sandro Chia
Giuseppe Chiari
Judy Chicago
Eduardo Chillida
Christo
Chryssa
Roman Cieslewicz
Lygia Clark
John Clem Clarke
Francesco Clemente
Chuck Close
Bernard Cohen
Tony Coleing
James Coleman
James Collins
Gianni Colombo
Alex Colville
Bruce Conner
Pietro Consagra
Ron Cooper
William Nelson Copley

Corneille
Joseph Cornell
Claudio Costa
Robert Cottingham
Tony Cragg
Michael Craig-Martin
Leonardo Cremonini
Roberto Crippa
Carlos Cruz-Diez
Enzo Cucchi
José Luis Cuevas
Greg Curnoe
Roger Cutforth

Dado
K.F. Dahmen
Walter Dahn
Salvador Dali
Ken Danby
Nassos Daphnis
Hanne Darboven
Allan D'Arcangelo
Ben D'Armagnac
Alan Davie
John Davies
Douglas Davis
Gene Davis
John Davis
Ronald Davis
Richard Deacon
John De Andrea
Sergio de Camargo
Giorgio de Chirico
Gino de Dominicis
George Deem
Roy De Forest
Raoul de Keyser
Ad Dekkers
Ger Dekkers
Willem de Kooning
Lucio Del Pezzo
Paul Delvaux
Hugo Demarco
Nicola De Maria
Walter De Maria
Agnes Denes
José de Riva
Marc Devade
Paul de Vree
Herman De Vries
Jean Dewasne
Daniel Dezeuze
Antonio Dias
Jan Dibbets
Richard Diebenkorn
Hans-Jürgen Diehl
Erik Dietmann
Braco Dimitrijevic
Jim Dine
Mark Di Suvero
Jiri Georg Dokoupil
Noël Dolla
César Domela
Piero Dorazio
Russell Drysdale
Jean Dubuffet
Marcel Duchamp
Natalia Dumitresco
David Dye
Friedel Dzubas

Don Eddy
Benni Efrat
Franz Eggenschwiler
Pieter Engels
Max Ernst
Errò
Richard Estes
Maurice Esteve
Philip Evergood

Luciano Fabro
Oyvind Fahlstrom
Wojciech Fangor

Murray Favro
Edgar Fernhout
Jackie Ferrara
Rafael Ferrer
Rainer Fetting
Robert Filliou
Ian Hamilton Finlay
Eric Fischl
Joel Fisher
Barry Flanagan
Dan Flavin
Lucio Fontana
Llyn Foulkes
Terry Fox
Sam Francis
Helen Frankenthaler
Donald Hamilton Fraser
Lucian Freud
Elisabeth Frink
Terry Frost
Günter Fruhtrunk
Ernst Fuchs
Hamish Fulton
John Furnival
Klaus Fussmann

Marco Gastini
Yves Gaucher
Winfred Gaul
Johannes Geccelli
General Idea
Juan Genoves
Isa Genzken
Karl Gerstner
Franz Gertsch
Jochen Gerz
Alberto Giacometti
Wim Gijzen
Gilbert and George
Sam Gilliam
Bruno Gironcoli
Fritz Glarner
Domenico Gnoli
Mathias Goeritz
Ralph Goings
Leon Golub
Joe Goode
Robert Goodnough
Ron Gorchov
Robert Gordy
Ludwig Gosewitz
Adolph Gottlieb
Dan Graham
Robert Graham
Gotthard Graubner
Josep Grau Garriga
Morris Graves
Nancy Graves
Emilio Greco
Alan Green
Gloria Greenberg
Balcomb Greene
Giorgio Griffa
Victor Grippo
Red Grooms
Nancy Grossman
Robert Grosvenor
Johannes Grützke
Philip Guston
Renato Guttuso
Brion Gysin

Hans Haacke
Raymond Hains
Etienne Hajdu
Nigel Hall
Richard Hamilton
Duane Hanson
David Hare
Helen Harrison
Newton Harrison
Grace Hartigan
Hans Ernst Hartung
Erich Hauser

Stanley William Hayter
Tim Head
Erwin Heerich
Bernhard Heiliger
Michael Heizer
Al Held
Jean Hélion
Geoffrey Hendricks
Maurice Henry
Barbara Hepworth
Patrick Heron
Eva Hesse
Sheila Hicks
Dick Higgins
Anthony Hill
John Hilliard
Roger Hilton
David Hockney
Howard Hodgkin
Rudolf Hoflehner
Tom Holland
Nancy Holt
Jenny Holzer
Gottfried Honegger
Rebecca Horn
Dom Sylvester Houedard
John Hoyland
Alfred Hrdlicka
Douglas Huebler
Friedensreich Hundertwasser
Bryan Hunt
Richard Hunt
Paul Huxley

Dorothy Iannone
Taka Iimura
Jorg Immendorff
Robert Indiana
Will Insley
Jean Ipousteguy
Robert Irwin

Christian Jaccard
Alain Jacquet
Horst Janssen
Valerie Jaudon
Paul Jenkins
Neil Jenney
Alfred Jensen
Luis Jimenez
Jasper Johns
Lester Johnson
Ray Johnson
Joan Jonas
Allen Jones
Asger Jorn
Michel Journiac
Donald Judd

Horst Egon Kalinowski
Stephen Kaltenbach
Howard Kanovitz
Tadeusz Kantor
Anish Kapoor
Allan Kaprow
Alex Katz
Craig Kauffman
Tatsuo Kawaguchi
On Kawara
Ellsworth Kelly
Michael Kenny
Anselm Kiefer
Edward Kienholz
Phillip King
William King
Alain Kirili
Per Kirkeby
R.B. Kitaj
Yoshihisa Kitatsuji
Konrad Klapheck
Milan Knížák
Alison Knowles
John Koch
Pyke Koch

J.H. Kocman
Oscar Kokoschka
Jiri Kolar
Gyula Kosice
Leon Kossoff
Joseph Kosuth
Fritz Köthe
Jannis Kounellis
Piotr Kowalski
Joyce Kozloff
Lee Krasner
Norbert Kricke
Dieter Krieg
Richard Kriesche
Barbara Kruger
Nicolas Krushenick
Tetsumi Kudo
Gary Kuehn
Yayoi Kusama
Robert Kushner
Tadaaki Kuwayama

Gerald Lang
Laszlo Lakner
Wilfredo Lam
David Lamelas
Lois Lane
Nikolaus Lang
Ellen Lanyon
Berto Lardera
John Latham
Bob Law
Jan Lebenstein
Louis Le Brocquy
Jean Le Gac
Ian Lenica
Thomas Lenk
Julio Le Parc
Alfred Leslie
Barry Le Va
David Leverett
Les Levine
Marilyn Levine
Sol LeWitt
Alexander Liberman
Roy Lichtenstein
Liliane Lijn
Richard Lindner
Christian Lindow
Bengt Lindström
Richard Lippold
Seymour Lipton
Frank Lobdell
Richard Paul Lohse
Richard Long
Antonio Lopez Garcia
Roelof Louw
Reinier Lucassen
Sven Lukin
Evert Lundquist
Ana Lupas
Markus Lupertz
Urs Lüthi
Len Lye

George Maciunas
Heinz Mack
René Magritte
Leopoldo Maler
Alfred Manessier
Robert Mangold
Sylvia Mangold
Man Ray
Giacomo Manzù
Conrad Marca-Relli
Brice Marden
Marino Marini
Tom Marioni
Marisol
Agnes Martin
Kenneth Martin
Ron Martin
John Mason
André Masson

Georges Mathieu
Yutaka Matsuzawa
Roberto Matta
Gordon Matta-Clark
Fabio Mauri
Ann McCoy
John McCracken
James McGarrell
John D. McLaughlin
Bruce McLean
F.E. McWilliam
Bernard Meadows
David Medalla
Christian Megert
Fausto Melotti
John Meredith
Richard Merkin
Mario Merz
E.L.T. Mesens
Annette Messager
Gustav Metzger
Henri Michaux
Tomio Miki
Manolo Millares
Keith Milow
Antoni Miralda
Joan Miró
Joan Mitchell
Manfred Mohr
Guido Molinari
Pierre Molinier
Jacques Monory
Nicholas Monro
Jeremy Moon
Henry Moore
Giorgio Morandi
Francois Morellet
Malcolm Morley
Ennio Morlotti
Michael Morris
Robert Morris
Wilfred Moser
Ed Moses
Olivier Mosset
Robert Motherwell
Tania Mouraud
Otto Muehl
Robert Muller
Bruno Munari
Henry Mundy
Catherine Murphy
Elizabeth Murray
Robert Murray

Hidetoshi Nagasawa
Peter Nagel
Hitoshi Nakazato
Maurizio Nannucci
David Nash
Bruce Nauman
Paul Neagu
Edgar Negret
Ernst Neizvestny
Lowell Nesbitt
Joshua Neustein
Louise Nevelson
Barnett Newman
Ben Nicholson
Mario Nigro
Minoru Niizuma
Hermann Nitsch
Constantino Nivola
Isamu Noguchi
Sidney Nolan
Kenneth Noland
Richard Nonas
Maria Nordman
Gastone Novelli
Jim Nutt

Helio Oiticica
Georgia O'Keeffe
Claus Oldenburg
Jules Olitski

Nathan Oliveira
Claudio Olivieri
Toshinobu Onosato
Luigi Ontani
Roman Opalka
Julian Opie
Dennis Oppenheim
Meret Oppenheim
Alfonso Ossorio

Robin Page
Nam June Paik
Mimmo Paladino
Pablo Palazuelo
Palermo
Panamarenko
Gina Pane
Giulio Paolini
Eduardo Paolozzi
Claudio Parmiggiani
Mike Parr
David Partridge
Ed Paschke
Victor Pasmore
Philip Pearlstein
Alicia Penalba
A.R. Penck
Giuseppe Penone
Beverly Pepper
Achille Perilli
Irving Petlin
Peter Phillips
Tom Phillips
Pablo Picasso
Roland Piché
Otto Piene
Edouard Pignon
John Piper
Vettor Pisani
Michelangelo Pistoletto
Anne and Patrick Poirier
Sigmar Polke
Arnaldo Pomodoro
Gio Pomodoro
Larry Poons
Stephen Posen
Richard Pousette-Dart
Lucio Pozzi
Mario Prassinos
Mark Prent
Kenneth Price
Patrick Procktor

Mario Radice
Markus Raetz
Joseph Raffael
Arnulf Rainer
Tomas Rajlich
Mel Ramos
Robert Rauschenberg
Jean Pierre Raynaud
Martial Raysse
Paul Rebeyrolle
Ad Reinhardt
Edda Renouf
Erich Reusch
Hans Peter Reuter
Gerhard Richter
George Rickey
Bridget Riley
Klaus Rinke
Jean-Paul Riopelle
Larry Rivers
Dorothea Rockburne
Osvaldo Romberg
Ulrike Rosenbach
James Rosenquist
Charles Ross
Theodore Roszak
Mimmo Rotella
Dieter Roth
Susan Rothenberg
Mark Rothko
Ulrich Ruckriem

Allen Ruppersberg
Edward Ruscha
Reiner Ruthenbeck
Robert Ryman

Niki de Saint-Phalle
Yoshishige Saito
David Salle
Lucas Samaras
Fred Sandback
Michael Sandle
Jean-Michel Sanejouand
Alan Saret
Sarkis
Paul Sarkisian
Peter Saul
Antonio Saura
Angelo Savelli
Henry Saxe
Emilio Scanavino
Italo Scanga
Salvatore Scarpitta
Christian Schad
Miriam Schapiro
Mario Schifano
Julius Schmidt
Julian Schnabel
Carolee Schneemann
Nicolas Schöffer
Jan J. Schoonhoven
HA Schult
Bernard Schultze
Emil Schumacher
Tim Scott
William Scott
Peter Sedgley
George Segal
Nobuo Sekine
Colin Self
Richard Serra
Pablo Serrano
Michel Seuphor
Ben Shahn
Joel Shiparo
Jeffrey Shaw
Alan J. Shields
Mieko Shiomi
Katharina Sieverding
Charles Simonds
David Smith

Richard Smith
Tony Smith
Robert Smithson
Kenneth Snelson
Michael Snow
K.R.H. Sonderborg
Alan Sonfist
Keith Sonnier
Peter Sorge
Jesus Rafael Soto
Pierre Soulages
Giangiacomo Spadari
Giuseppe Spagnulo
Nancy Spero
Daniel Spoerri
Klaus Staeck
Theodoros Stamos
Peter Stämpfli
Richard Stankiewicz
Robert Stanley
Henryk Stazewski
Jeffrey Steele
Saul Steinberg
Frank Stella
Ian Stephenson
Harold Stevenson
John Stezaker
Clyfford Still
Michelle Stuart
Kishio Suga
Kumi Sugai
George Sugarman
Graham Sutherland
Philip Sutton

Emilio Tadini
Shinkichi Tajiri
Jiro Takamatsu
Takis
Pierre Tal-Coat
Rufino Tamayo
Antoni Tapiès
Ernesto Tatafiore
Hervé Télémaque
Paul Thek
Wayne Thiebaud
Imants Tillers
Sidney Tillim
Joe Tilson
David Tindle

Jean Tinguely
Gerard Titus-Carmel
Mark Tobey
Henryk Tomaszewski
Niele Toroni
Endre Tot
Claude Tousignant
Goran Trbuljak
David Tremlett
Julian Trevelyan
Rosemarie Trockel
David Troostwyk
Antonio A. Trotta
Clovis Trouille
Anne Truitt
Costas Tsoclis
Albert Tucker
William Tucker
Giulio Turcato
William Turnbull
Jim Turrell
Richard Tuttle
Cy Twombly
Jack Tworkov

Günther Uecker
Timm Ulrichs
Giuseppe Uncini
Ken Unsworth
Janos Urban
Nicolas Uriburu

DeWain Valentine
Jiri Valoch
Woody van Amen
Richard Van Buren
J.C.J. van der Heyden
Ger Van Elk
Rob Van Koningsbruggen
Jan van Munster
Bram Van Velde
Victor Vasarely
Keith Vaughan
Ben Vautier
Emilio Vedova
Vladimir Velickovic
Bernar Venet
Claude Viallat
Vieira da Silva
Dario Villalba

Jacques de la Villegle
Carel Visser
Maurice de Vlaminck
Gerhard von Graevenitz
David Von Schlegell
Jan Voss
Wolf Vostell
Peter Voulkos

Robert Wade
Jaap Wagemaker
John Walker
Brian Wall
Franz Erhard Walther
Andy Warhol
Robert Marshall Watts
William Wegman
Lawrence Weiner
Roger Welch
Günter Weseler
Tom Wesselmann
Co Westerik
H.C. Westermann
Doug Wheeler
Robert Whitman
Joyce Wieland
William T. Wiley
Stephen Willats
John Willenbecher
Robert M. Wilson
Gerd Winner
Rolf Winnewisser
Jacqueline Winsor
Krzysztof Wodiczko
Derrick Woodham
Bill Woodrow
Paul Wunderlich
Andrew Wyeth

Masaaki Yamada
Takeo Yamaguchi
Richard Yokomi
Kenji Yoshida
Fumio Yoshimura
Peter Young
Jack Youngerman
Adja Yunkers

Gianfranco Zappettini
Gilberto Zorio

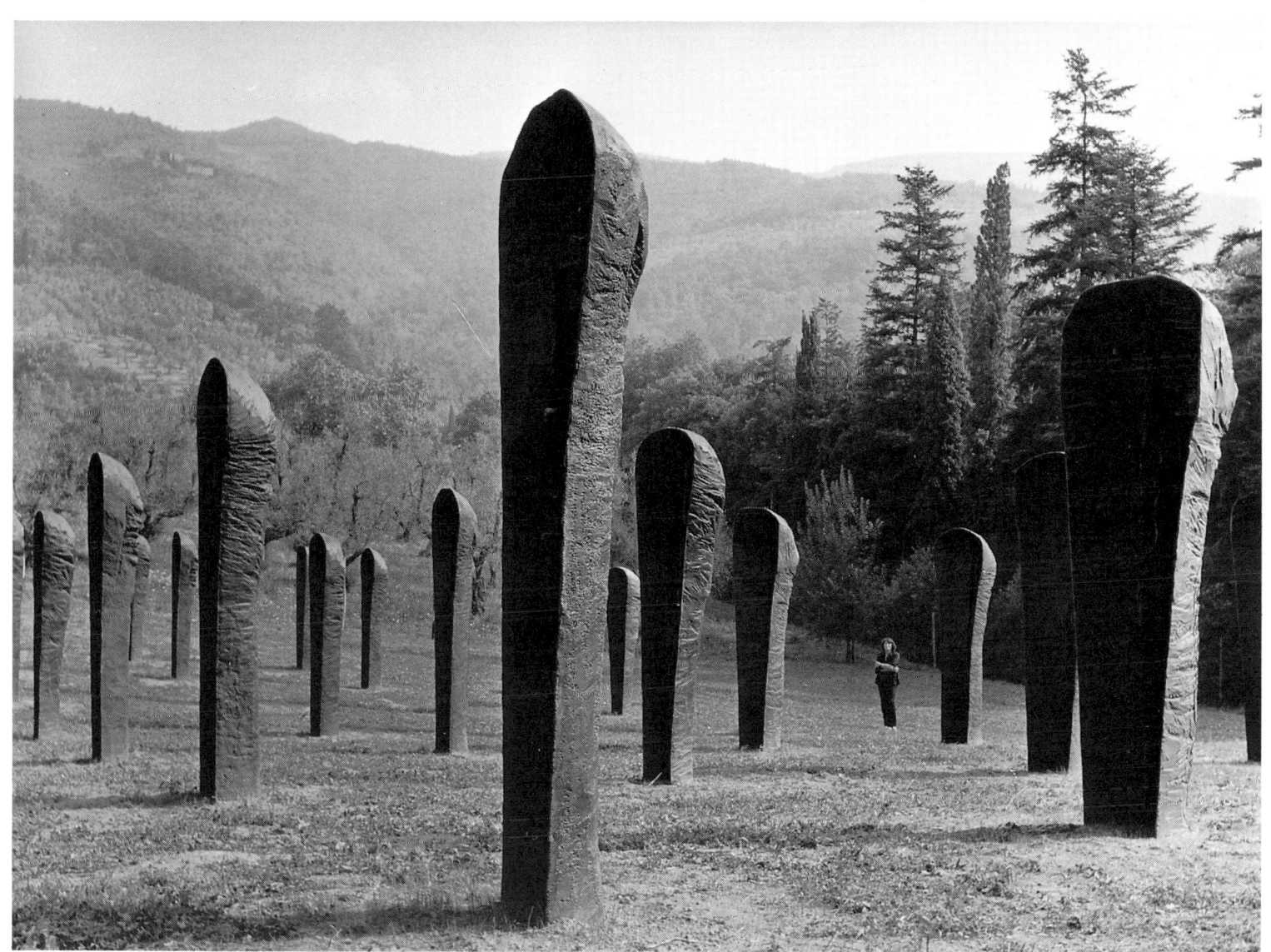

Magdalena Abakanowicz: *Katarsis*, Santomato di Pistoia, Italy, 1985

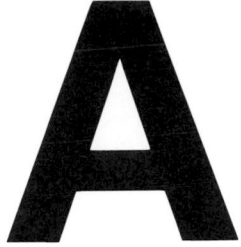

ABAKANOWICZ, Magdalena.

Polish. Born in Falenty, 20 June 1930. Educated at the School of Fine Arts, Sopot, 1949, and at the Academy of Fine Arts, Warsaw, 1950-55, M.A. 1955. Married Jan Kosmowski in 1956. Independent artist, Warsaw, since 1956; has concentrated on woven constructions and sculptures since 1961. Instructor, 1965-74, Associate Professor, 1974-79, and since 1979 Professor, State College of Arts, Poznan. Member, Z.A.I.K.S. Union of Polish Artists, Writers and Composers, Warsaw, 1965. Recipient: State Travel Fellowship to France, Warsaw, 1962; 1st Prize, Ministry of Culture, 1965; Gold Medal, Polish Artists' Union, 1965; Gold Medal, *Bienal*, Sao Paulo, 1965; Grand Prize of the Ministry for Foreign Affairs, 1970; State Prize of the Polish Folk Republic, Warsaw, 1972; Grand Prize, World Crafts' Council, New York, 1974; Golden Cross of Merit, Polish Folk Republic, Poznan, 1974; Special Professor's Prize, State College of Art, Poznan, 1975; Gottfried-von-Herder Prize, Vienna 1979; Cross of Polonia Restituta, Warsaw, 1980; Jurzykowski Foundation Award, New York, 1983. Honorary doctorate: Royal College of Art, London, 1974. Chevalier, Ordre des Arts et Lettres, France, 1985. Agent: Galerie Alice Pauli, 6 Avenue Rumine, 1005 Lausanne, Switzerland. Address: A1. Stanow Zjednoczonych 16/53, 03-947 Warsaw, Poland.

Individual Exhibitions:

1960	Kordegarda, Warsaw
1962	Galerie Dautzenberg, Paris
1963	Galerie Sztuki Nowoczesnej, Warsaw
1965	Galerie Zacheta, Warsaw
	Biuro Wystaw Artystycznych, Zakopane, Poland
1966	Biuro Wystaw Artystycznych, Zielona Gora, Poland
1967	Galerie Alice Pauli, Lausanne
	Galeria Wspolczesna, Warsaw
	Kunstindustrimuseet, Oslo (travelled to Vestlandske Kunstindustrimuseum, Bergen; the Stavanger Kunstforening; and the Trondheim Kunstforening)
1968	Van Abbemuseum, Eindhoven, Netherlands (travelled to the Frans Halsmuseum, Haarlem; Groninger Museum, Groningen; and the Stedelijk Museum, Schiedam)
	Helmhaus, Zurich
1969	Galerie Alice Pauli, Lausanne
	Tapisserien und Raumliche Texturen, Kunsthalle, Mannheim
	Stedelijk Museum, Arnhem, Netherlands
1970	Nationalmuseum, Stockholm
	Textil Skulptur/Textil Environment, Konsthall, Sodertalje, Sweden
1971	Galerie Alice Pauli, Lausanne
	Galeria Pryzmat, Cracow
	Galeria Wspolczesna, Warsaw
	Pasadena Art Museum, California
1972	Aberdeen Art Gallery, Scotland
	Textile Strukturen und Konstruktionen, Environments, Kunstverein für die Rheinlande und Westfalen, Dusseldorf
1973	Arnolfini Gallery, Bristol
	Galerie Alice Pauli, Lausanne (with Jagoda Buic)
	Galerie des Beaux-Arts, Bordeaux

1974	Museum Sztuki, Lodz, Poland
1975	Galerie Alice Pauli, Lausanne
	Galerie Zacheta, Warsaw
	Whitechapel Art Gallery, London
1976	Art Gallery of New South Wales, Sydney (travelled to the National Gallery of Victoria, Melbourne)
1977	Galerie Alice Pauli, Lausanne
	Konsthalle, Malmo, Sweden
	Sonja Henie-Niel Onstadt Kunstsenter, Oslo
1978	Biuro Wystaw Artystyczynch, Lodz, Poland
	Biuro Wystaw Artystyczynch, Bydogoszczy, Poland
1979	Galerie Alice Pauli Lausanne (retrospective)
1980	Polish Pavilion, at the *Biennale*, Venice
1981	Galerie Alice Pauli, Lausanne
1982	ARC/Musée d'Art Moderne de la Ville, Paris
	Galerie Jeanne Bucher, Paris
	Walter Phillips Gallery, The Banff Centre, Alberta, Canada
	Museum of Contemporary Art, Chicago (toured the United States and Canada)
1983	De Cordova Museum, Lincoln, Massachusetts (retrospective)
	National Academy of Sciences, Washington, D.C.
	Musée d'Art Contemporain, Montreal
	Visual Arts Centre of Alaska, Anchorage
1984	Dallas Museum of Arts, Texas
	University of California, Los Angeles
	Portland Art Museum, Oregon
1985	Galerie Alice Pauli, Lausanne
	Virginia Museum of Fine Arts, Richmond
	Xavier Fourcade Inc., New York
1986	Catholic University Art Gallery, Lublin, Poland
	McIntosh-Drysdale Gallery, Washington, D.C.
1987	BWA Muzeum Chemitex-Stilon, Gorzow Wielkopolski, Poland
	Muku Gallery, Hiroshima, Japan

Selected Group Exhibitions:

1962	*Biennale Internationale de la Tapisserie*, Musée Cantonal des Beaux-Arts, Lausanne (regularly until 1979)
1965	*Bienal*, Sao Paulo
1968	*Wall Hangings*, Museum of Modern Art, New York
1979	*Sculpture Polonaise*, Musée d'Art Moderne de la Ville, Paris
1980	*Biennale*, Venice
1981	*Malmoe*, Konsthall, Malmo, Sweden
1982	*Kunst Wirt Material*, Nationalgalerie, Berlin
1984	*Recent Painting and Sculpture*, Museum of Modern Art, New York
1986	*Eva und die Zukunft*, Kunsthalle, Hamburg
1987	*Avant-Garde in the Eighties*, Los Angeles County Museum of Art

Collections:

Muzeum Narodow, Warsaw; Muzeum Sztuki, Lodz, Poland; Stedelijk Museum, Amsterdam; Nationalmuseum, Stockholm; Henie-Onstad Kunstsenter, Oslo; Centre Georges Pompidou, Paris; Museu de Arte Moderna, Sao Paulo; National Museum of Modern Art, Kyoto; Australian Gallery of Art, Canberra; Museum of Modern Art, New York.

Publications:

On ABAKANOWICZ: books—*Abakanowicz*, exhibition catalogue, with text by André Kuenzi. Lausanne 1967; *Magdalena Abakanowicz: Tapisserien und Raumliche Texturen*, exhibition catalogue, with text by Heinz Fuchs, Mannheim 1969; *Magdalena Abakanowicz: Textil Skulptur/Textil Environment*, exhibition catalogue, with text by Eje Hogestatt and Danuta Wroblewska, Sodertalje, Sweden 1970; *Beyond Craft: The Art Fabric* by Mildred Constantine and Jack Lenor Larsen, New York 1972; *Magdalena Abakanowicz: Textile Strukturen und Konstruktionen, Environments*, exhibition catalogue, with text by Karl-Heinz Hering and Jasia Reichardt, Dusseldorf 1972; *La Nouvelle Tapisserie* by André Kuenzi, Geneva 1974; *Biennale di Venezia '80: Magdalena Abakanowicz*, exhibition catalogue, with text by Aleksander Wojciechowski, Warsaw 1980; films—*Abakany*, 1969; *Abakanowicz in Australia* 1976; *Division of Space*, 1976; *Abakanowicz*, 1976.

From the very beginning man has created myths out of his longing for the lost state of balance, for prehistoric existence called paradise which was a state without consciousness. He tried to find in religion the explanation of himself, to compensate his defects by its commandments, to justify the suffering of life by giving them purpose as does Christianity. In the practice of Tantra and yoga, man attempted to gain control over his instincts. This struggle of man with himself for control over his own nature, a struggle with a lack of internal norms of behaviour is reflected in the whole mythology, and ultimately in the vision of man seeking balance and perfection from the remotest time of the Assyrian poem "Gilgamesh" to the circular shape described by Plato of the first human being, to Balzac's book about Serafit the only one of Balzac's works not based on reality, or in Goethe's considerations about the Demon as the creator of life in his poem "Faust".

While reading about the structure and functioning of the human brain, which is formed of interdependent parts, but originating in different periods of evolution, I discovered how contradictory the factors determining behaviour are, how deeply rooted are sources of this permanent struggle. To all the most ancient fears of man I add my own. These can perhaps be glimpsed in my art as a story of the same anxieties and pains which have accompanied human existence as well as mine.

I once observed mosquitoes swarming. In gray masses. Host upon a host. Little creatures in slew of other little creatures. In incessant motion. Each preoccupied with its own spoor. Each different, distinct in details of shape. A horde emitting a common sound. Were they mosquitoes or people?

I feel overawed by quantity where counting no longer makes sense. By irrepeatabiliy within such a quantity. By creatures of nature gathered in herds, droves, species, in which each individual while subservient to the mass retains some distinguishing features. A crowd of people or birds, insects or leaves, is a mysterious assemblage of variants of certain prototype. A riddle of nature's abhorrence of exact repetition or inability to produce it. Just as a human hand cannot repeat its own gesture I invoke this disturbing law, switching my own immobile herds into that rhythm.

—Magdalena Abakanowicz

The manipulation of fiber into thread and the weaving of those threads into intricately constructed forms and surfaces are skills that can be counted among human-kind's earliest and most enduring accomplishments. Those same techniques, which for all these thousands of years have produced shelters, utilitarian artifacts and garments to warm and protect human bodies, are the means by which Magdalena Abakanowicz shapes hauntingly eloquent and powerful sculptures. Many of these take possession of the spaces in which they are placed, sometimes seeming to become themselves architectural elements of the structures that enclose them; other groups of work assume more specific ref-erential form.

In her first exhibitions Abakanowicz presented highly abstract environmental aspects, binding fibers into long, attenuated hawsers, shaping large organic forms and weaving stiff, heavy hangings or huge dark cocoons of rough jute. The alleyways and mazes cre-ated by these installations simultaneously functioned as enclosures and as impediments to free movement; their dark rough textures were pleasant to see but harsh to touch. A viewer walking among the forms could experience their impressive strengths, which offered a comforting but somewhat intimidating envi-ronment, suggesting a reference to the experience of individuals who find themselves cared for, and op-pressed by, the unresponsive structures of a socialist state.

The cultural implications of Abakanowicz's work have become more explicit since the early 1970's. Burlap sacking, impregnated with glue and molded into the plaster cast of a seated male figure, became shell-like fragments, as if these were the broken, emptied husks of human bodies. Installed in mute throngs or lined up in poignant queues, they silently protested all authoritarian and suppressive regimes. A sequence of very large wrapped heads succeeded the figures, followed later by groups of hollow, burlap-covered ovoid forms, some intact and some fractured, in a wide range of sizes.

The imagery with which Abakanowicz works is as universal as her materials and techniques. It speaks to emotional responses which are even more basic and instinctive than the techniques which shape her forms. Since its earliest exhibitions, her work has been a provocative stimulus to other artists, revolu-tionizing our contemporary conceptions of fiber art.

—Cecile N. McCann

ABRAHAMS, Ivor.

British. Born in Wigan, Lancashire, in January 1935. Studied sculpture, St. Martin's School of Art, Lon-don 1952–53; under Karl Vogel, Camberwell School of Art, London 1953–57. Married; sons: Saul and Etienne. Worked as display artist, London, 1956–60. Full-time artist, London, since 1960. Visiting Lec-turer in Sculpture, Royal College of Art, London, Goldsmith's College, London. Slade School of Art, London, and Edinburgh College of Art. Agent: Mayor Gallery, London. Address: c/o Mayor Gallery, 22a Cork Street, London W1, England.

Individual Exhibitions:

1962	Gallery One, London
1970	Richard Feigen Gallery, New York
	Axiom Gallery, London
1971	Arnolfini Gallery, Bristol
1972	Felicity Samuel Gallery, London
	Mappin Art Gallery, Sheffield
	Aberdeen Art Gallery
1973	Environments, Skulpturen, Zeichnungen, Komplette Graphiken, Kunstverein, Cologne
	Lijnbaan Centrum, Rotterdam
	Galerie von Loeper, Hamburg

1974	Bernard Jacobson Gallery, London
	Private Gallery, Munich
	Galerie de la Clautre, Perigeaux, France
	Galerie T., Amsterdam
	Galerie Richard Foncke, Ghent
	Galeria Quince, Madrid
	Galerie Marzona, Bielefeld, West Germany
	Natalie Stern Gallery, London
	Galleri Ahlner, Stockholm
	Galerie Laurent, Geneva
1975	Galerie Kummel, Cologne
	Aktionsgalerie, Berne
	Galleria del Cavallino, Venice
	Bernard Jacobson Gallery, London
	Galleri Ahlner, Stockholm
	Galerie Bonnier, Geneva
1976	Mayor Gallery, London
	Galleria Vinciana, Milan
	Ikon Gallery, Birmingham
	Galleri Nordenhake, Malmo, Sweden
	Galerie Bonnier, Geneva
1977	Galleri Malgram, Gothenburg, Sweden
	Galerie Ann von Horrenbeck, Brussels
	Galerie Manfred Schonbrun, Frankfurt
1978	Drol-Kolbert Gallery, New York
	Mayor Gallery, London
	Hobson Gallery, Cambridge
1979	Sculpture and Works on Paper, Bernard Jacobson Gallery, London
	Effigies du Pays d'Oc: Oeuvres de 1979, Galerie Bonnier, Geneva
	Ferens Art Gallery, Hull England (toured Britain)
1980	St. Enoch's Gallery, Glasgow
	Mayor Gallery, London
1981	Hobson Gallery, Cambridge
1982	Bernard Jacobson Ltd., Los Angeles
	Warwick Arts Trust, London
1983	Mayor Gallery, London
1984	Bolton Museum and Art Gallery, Lancashire
	Bluecoat Gallery, Liverpool, Merseyside
	Bernard Jacobson Ltd., Los Angeles
	Galerie Bonnier, Geneva
	Galerie Engelberts, Geneva
	Yorkshire Sculpture Park, Wakefield
1986	Bernard Jacobson Gallery, London
	Mayor Gallery, London
1987	Galerie Albrecht, Munich

Selected Group Exhibitions:

1961	La Joven Escultura Inglesa, Salas des Exposiciones del Ateneo, Madrid
1964	MICA Sculpture Exhibition, City Art Gallery, Man-chester
1968	From Life, Camden Arts Centre, London
1970	Print Loan Show, Museum of Modern Art, New York
1971	Road Show, at the Bienal, Sao Paulo
1973	La Peinture Anglaise Aujourd'hui, Musée d'Art Mo-derne de la Ville, Paris
1976	Arte Inglese Oggi 1960–76, Palazzo Reale, Milan
1979	Museum of Drawers, Kunsthaus, Zurich
1982	Symbol and Imagination 1957–80, Whitechapel Art Gallery, London
1988	Figure It Out: Visual Body Language, Helander Gal-lery, Palm Beach, Florida

Collections:

Victoria and Albert Museum, London; Arts Council of Great Britain, London; British Council, London; Museum Boymans-van Beuningen, Rotterdam; Wilhelm-Lehmbruck-Museum, Duisburg, West Germany; Museum of Modern Art, New York; Princeton University, New Jersey; Vassar College, Poughkeepsie, New York; Norton College of Art, Miami; National Gallery of Australia, Canberra.

Publications:

By ABRAHAMS: books—Oxford Garden: A Sketchbook, London 1977.

On ABRAHAMS: books—The New Sculpture by Udo Kulter-man, London 1966; Bienal de Sao Paulo: Gran Bretanha—Road Show, exhibition catalogue, London 1971; 14 Big Prints, with a foreword by Bernard Jacobson, London 1972; La Peinture Anglaise Aujourd'hui, exhibition catalogue with texts by Jacques Lassaigne and Edward Lucie Smith, Paris 1973; Ivor Abrahams: Environments, Skulpturen, Zeich-nungen, Komplette Graphiken, exhibition catalogue, with an interview by R. J. Rees, and texts by W. Herzongenrath, M. S. Bibble and others, Cologne 1973; Ivor Abrahams, ex-hibition catalogue, with text by Richard Shone, London 1978; Ivor Abrahams: Sculpture and Works on Paper, exhibi-tion catalogue, with text by Richard Shone, London 1979; Ivor Abrahams: Effigies du Pays d'Oc: Oeuvres de 1979 exhi-bition catalogue, Geneva 1979; Ivor Abrahams: The Garden Image Prints and Related Sculpture 1969–79, exhibition cata-logue with foreword by John McEwen, London 1984; Ivor Abrahams: Models for Projects 1986, exhibition catalogue with introduction by Bryan Robertson, London 1986.

The meeting of man and nature; the meeting of form and atmosphere; the meeting of popular art and for-mal art; the meeting of the present with what endures from the past—all these together sound like a great but well-nigh impossible task for 20th-century art. Add to that, a way of being English and also Euro-pean. However, Ivor Abrahams has found a sly, tan-gential, subtle angle of approach with which to encompass all these themes, in works which give great delight. His basic ingredients are vegetation, space, and the implicit hand of man, partly able, partly unable, to control and plan. Since this em-braces activities from the ordinary, vulgar and popu-lar passion for "gardening", to the most refined and ambitious landscaping design, and from the most formally-disintegrating romantic situations, to the most severely classic, formal or even rigid, Abra-hams' scope is potentially tremendous. At the same time, his actual realizations of these perceptions, ranging from glass fibre sprayed with bright green flock, with its "pop" associations, to bronzes which tend to compete with the formal and monumental which they themselves comment on, allows Abra-hams a wide range of mood—comic, witty, ironic or detached. His effective drawings and lithographs should also be noted. There are many things to enjoy in Abrahams' art, from the way he catches our own childhood memories of secret corners in public parks, to elegiac and formal allusions which speak of the Europe of earlier centuries. His early training as a display artist has stood him in good stead; and his wide reading among the treatises on gardening, from popular to grand, enables him to include concept as well as precept. He is in the broadest sense an "ob-server"; and an observer of society as much as art: "I'm interested in the rules behind the rules," he has said; and the Brechtian "alienation effect" is impor-tant to him in his detached view of this "public aes-thetic given concrete form." He has been singularly successful in making, out of passively truthful obser-vation of man's relationship to nature, creative and witty realizations—in his earlier work, more literal, and in the later work more sculptural. One side effect of his art is that he has created a relationship between "pop" and "popular" art, and also reminded us that gardening is a real example of popular art, involving ordinary people in aesthetic judgments from blatant to subtly civilized.

—Michael Shepherd

ABRAMOVIC, Marina.

Yugoslav. Born in Belgrade in 1946. Studied at Acad-emy of Fine Arts, Belgrade. Independent perfor-mance artist, Belgrade, from 1972; currently lives and works in Amsterdam. Address: Brouwersgracht 196, Amsterdam, Netherlands.

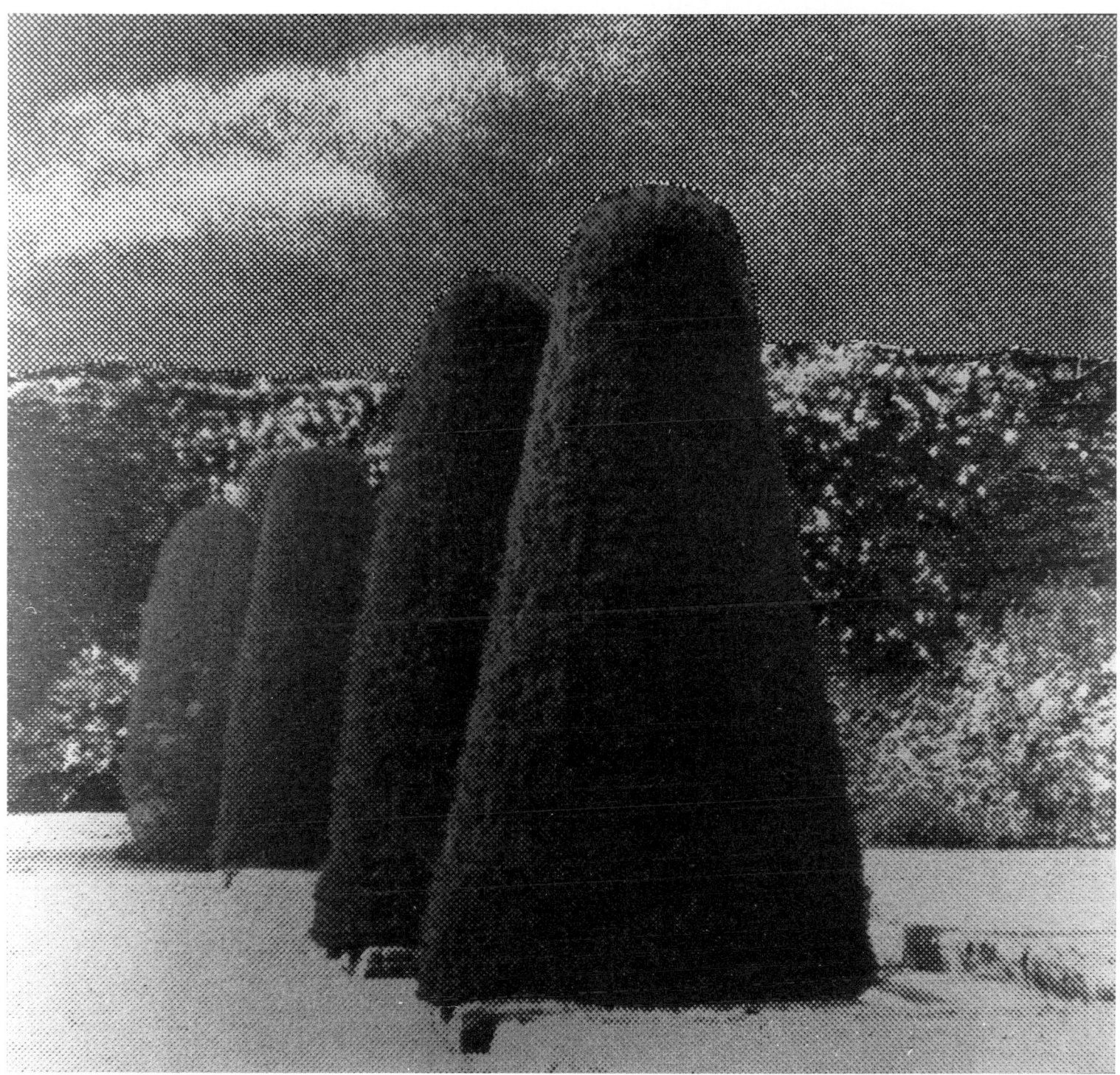

Ivor Abrahams: image from *Garden Suite*, 1970

Individual Exhibitions:

1974   Galerija Suvremene umjetnosti, Zagreb
        Galleria Diagramma, Milan
1975   Studio Morra, Naples
1987   Centre d'Art Contemporain, Paris

Selected Group Exhibitions:

1970   *April Meeting,* Student Cultural Centre, Belgrade
        (and 1971, 1972)
1972   *Young Artists and Young Critics,* Museum of Modern
        Art, Belgrade
1973   *Post-Object Trends in Yugoslav Art,* Museum of
        Modern Art, Belgrade
        8 Yugoslav Artists, Richard Demarco Gallery, Edin-
        burgh
1974   *Contemporanea,* Parcheggio Villa Borghese, Rome

1975   *Contemporary Yugoslav Art,* Richard Demarco
        Gallery/Fruit Market Gallery, Edinburgh (toured
        the U.K.)
1979   *Expansion: International Biennale für Graphik und
        Visuelle Kunst,* Stadtpark, Vienna
1980   *ROSC '80,* University College, Dublin
1987   *Avant-Garde in the Eighties,* Los Angeles County
        Museum of Art

Publications:

By ABRAMOVIC: books—*Relation Work and Detour: First
Complete Works,* Nijmegen, Netherlands 1980; videotapes—
Television Is a Machine, 1972; *Rhythm 4,* 1974; *Smaile,*
1975; *I Won't . . . ,* 1975.

On ABRAMOVIC: books—*Marina Abramovic,* exhibition
catalogue, with text by Davor Maticevic, Zagreb 1974; *Contemporary Yugoslav Art,* exhibition catalogue, with text by

Richard Demarco and others, Edinburgh 1975; *Expansion:
Internationale Biennale für Graphik und Visuelle Kunst,* ex-
hibition catalogue, with text by Horst Gerhard Haberl, Georg
F. Schwarzbauer and others, Vienna 1979.

Before they met in 1975 Marina Abramovic and Ulay
were both engaged in the performance of a kind of
radical Body Art that took them to the limits of danger and physical resistance; that was while one of
them was working in Belgrade unknown to the other,
who was working in Amsterdam.

In their very first work together, the performance
called "Relation in Movement" at the 1976 Venice
Biennale, the couple expressed the special idea of
performance based on interaction, the reciprocal exchange of energy effected both actually and symbolically. Their work, like their lives at that time, began
to grow closer and to unite, until they became inseparable. Thus, in their performances and in their daily

life, they began to develop the possibilities of releasing and controlling their mind through forms of asceticism, creating situations of physical suffering. "You have to nearly break your body before you can free the mind," Ulay declared after one of their most punishing performances, during which both of them went without food for several days.

But unlike the ascetics, Abramović and Ulay use the structures and elements of art, one of which is the geometric pattern, linear or circular, used to coordinate their movements. This is an idea derived from abstract art, or rather from minimal art, which in the real sense, in performance that is, suggests the concentration of energy. The circle is also a symbol of meeting and may be thought of as possessing magic powers. Each element is thus used in a number of senses. The repetitiveness of their movements or the staticness of their performances allow them to be easily interpreted in photography, video or film, media which they do in fact use for documentary purposes. Recently, in some static performances, these artists have created the illusion of a picture, almost a Tableau Vivant.

Moving as they do on the frontier between illusion and reality, between the physical and the metaphysical, Abramović and Ulay show that our empirical world is far vaster than we can usually perceive, but that by certain practices our minds can be freed from many of its limitations.

—Helena Kontova

ACCONCI, Vito.

American. Born in New York City, 25 January 1940. Studied literature at Holy Cross College, Worcester, Massachusetts, B.A. 1962; University of Iowa, 1962–64, M.F.A. 1964. Independent poet and writer, New York, 1965–69; independent visual artist, concentrating on performance and environment works, New York, since 1969. Lecturer in Art Theory, School of Visual Arts, New York 1968–71; Instructor in post-studio art, California Institute of Art, Valencia, 1976. Formerly, Co-Editor, *0 to 9* magazine, New York. Agent: Sonnabend Gallery, 420 West Broadway, New York, New York 10013. Address: 39 Pearl Street, Brooklyn, New York 11201, U.S.A.

Individual Exhibitions:

1969	Rhode Island School of Design, Providence
	Emanu-eul Midtown Y.M./Y.W.H.A., New York
	Architectural League of New York
	Far Broadway, New York
1970	Gain Ground Gallery, New York
	Art Institute of Chicago
	Nova Scotia College of Art and Design, Halifax
1971	74 Grand Street, New York
	A Space, Toronto, Ontario (2 shows)
	93 Grant Street, New York
	Trappings, Kunstmuseum, Mönchengladbach, West Germany
	Protetch-Rivkin Gallery, Washington, D.C.
	Rhode Island School of Design, Providence
	Museum of Conceptual Art, San Francisco
	John Gibson Gallery, New York
	Wisconsin State University at Whitewater
	Sonnabend Gallery, New York
1972	California Institute of the Arts, Valencia
	Sonnabend Gallery, New York
	Galerie Sonnabend, Paris
	Galleria L'Attico, Rome
1973	Modern Art Agency, Naples, Italy
	Galerie D. Brussels
	Galleria Schema, Florence
1974	Galleria Forma, Genoa
	Galleria Alessandra Castelli, Milan

1975	Sonnabend Gallery, New York
	Portland Center for the Visual Arts, Oregon
	And/Or Gallery, Seattle
	Carp Gallery, Los Angeles
	Museum of Conceptual Art, San Francisco
	Hallwalls Gallery, Buffalo, New York
	Fine Arts Building, New York
	Whitney Museum, New York
1976	The Kitchen, New York
	Lerner-Heller Gallery, New York
	Anthology Film Archives, New York
	Sonnabend Gallery, New York
1977	Ohio State University, Columbus
	School of Visual Arts, New York
	University of Massachusetts, Amherst
	Anthology Film Archives, New York
	Sonnabend Gallery, New York
	Modern Art Agency, Naples
	Galerie D, Brussels
	Institute of Art and Urban Resources, New York
	Centre d'Art Contemporain, Geneva
	Galeria Stampa, Basle
1978	Studio Ala, Milan
	San Francisco Museum of Modern Art
	Galerie Nachst St. Stephan, Vienna
	International Cultureel Centrum, Antwerp, Belgium
	The Kitchen, New York
	Kunstmuseum, Lucerne
	Stedelijk museum, Amsterdam (retrospective)
	Galleria Mario Diacono, Bologna
	Tampa Bay Art Center, Florida
1979	Young-Hoffman Gallery, Chicago
	Sonnabend Gallery, New York
	Galerie De Appel, Amsterdam (toured the Netherlands)
	University of Rhode Island, Kingston
	Galerie Sonnabend, Paris
1980	Muhlenberg College, Allentown, Pennsylvania
	Vito Acconci: A Retrospective 1969 to 1980, Museum of Contemporary Art, Chicago (retrospective)
1981	Machineworks: Vito Acconci, Alice Aycock, Dennis Oppenheim, Institute of Contemporary Art, Philadelphia
	Museum of Fine Arts, Montreal
	Indianapolis Museum of Art, Indiana
1981	Young-Hoffman Gallery, Chicago
	Institute of Contemporary Art, Philadelphia (with Alice Aycock and Dennis Oppenheim)
1982	Virginia Museum of Fine Arts, Richmond
	Portland Center for the Visual Arts, Oregon
	San Diego State University, California
	University of Massachusetts, Amherst
1983	Miami-Dade Community College, Florida
	Whitney Museum, New York
	Williams College, Williamstown, Massachusetts
1984	Gallery Nature Morte, New York
	University of Nebraska, Omaha
	Zone Center for the Arts, Springfield, Massachusetts
1985	University of North Carolina, Chapel Hill
	Carpenter and Hochmann Gallery, New York
	City Hall Park, New York
	Rhona Hoffman Gallery, Chicago
	Brooklyn Museum, New York
	Wadsworth Atheneum, Hartford, Connecticut
1986	Kent State University, Ohio
	The Palladium, New York
	University of South Florida, Tampa
	Zone Gallery, New York
1987	International Center of Photography, New York
	International with Monument, New York
	La Jolla Museum of Contemporary Art, California

Selected Group Exhibitions:

1969	Language 3, Dwan Gallery, New York
1970	Software, Jewish Museum, New York (traveled to the Smithsonian Institution, Washington, D.C.)
1971	Biennale, Musée d'Art Moderne, Paris
1972	Documenta 5, Kassel, West Germany (and Documenta 7, 1982)
1973	Aspects de l'Art Actuel, Musée Galliera, Paris
1974	Art and Image in Recent Art, Art Institute of Chicago
1976	Biennale, Venice
1978	Performance Art Festival, Vienna
1981	Italians and American Italians, Crown Point Gallery, Oakland, California
1982	Metaphor: New Projects by Contemporary Sculptors, Hirshhorn Museum, Washington D.C.
1985	Promenades, Parc Lullin, Genthod, Geneva
1987	Concrete Crisis: Urban Images of the 80s, Exit Art, New York

Collections:

Museum of Modern Art, New York; Los Angeles County Museum of Art, California; Musée National d'Art Moderne/Centre Georges Pompidou, Paris.

Publications:

By ACCONCI: books—*Four Book*, New York 1968; *Transference: Roget's Thesaurus*, New York 1969; *Notes Toward the Development of a Show*, Hamburg 1972; *Leap/Think/Rethink/Fall*, Dayton, Ohio 1979; Films—*3 Frame Studies*, 1970; *2 Inceptions, 3 Adaption Studies*, 1970; *2 Clearance Studies*, 1970; *Openings*, 1970; *Hand and Mouth*, 1970; *Twin Cover Studies*, 1970; *4 Studies for a Meditation Chamber* 1970; *Three Relationship Studies*, 1970; *See-Through Rubbings*, 1970; *Applications*, 1970; *Watch*, 1971; *Second Hand*, 1971; *Control Room*, 1971; *Zone*, 1971; *Combination*, 1971; *Pickup*, 1971; *Storage*, 1971; *Waterways*, 1971; *Conversions 1, 2, 3*, 1971; *Training Ground*, 1971; *Trappings*, 1971; *Dress Up*, 1971; *Directions*, 1971; *Seedbed Transference Zone*, 1972; *Supply Room*, 1972; *Cross Fronts*, 1972; *Anchors*, 1972; *Reception Room*, 1972; *Air Time*, 1972; *My Reticence*, 1972; video—*Corrections*, 1970; *Pryings*, 1971; *Centers*, 1971; *Feelers*, 1971; *Claim*, 1971; *Passes*, 1971; *Association Area*, 1971; *Trials*, 1971; *Contacts*, 1971; *Pull*, 1971; *Sound Barrier*, 1971; *Waiting Room*, 1971; *Filles*, 1971; *Focal Points*, 1971; *2 Track*, 1971; *Eyespots*, 1971; *Sounding Board*, 1971; *Remote Control*, 1971; *Projections*, 1972; *Supply Room*, 1972; *Undertone*, 1973; *Face Off*, 1973; *Home Movies*, 1973; *Walk-Over*, 1973; *Theme Song*, 1973; *Full Circle*, 1973; *Stages*, 1973.

On ACCONCI: books—*Software*, exhibition catalogue, with introduction by Jack Burnham, New York 1970; *Conceptual Art* by Ursula Meyer, New York 1972; *Documenta 5*, exhibition catalogue, edited by Harald Szeemann and others, Kassel, West Germany 1972; *Pop Art et Cie* by Francois Pluchart, Paris 1972; *6 Years: The Dematerialization of the Art Object from 1966 to 1972* by Lucy R. Lippard, London and New York 1973; *Art and Image in Recent Art*, exhibition catalogue, with text by Anne Rorimer, Chicago 1974; *Senza Titolo* by Germano Celant, Milan 1974; *Il Corpo come Linguaggio* by Lea Vergine, Milan 1974; *Vito Acconci* by Mario Diacono, New York 1976; *Vito Acconci*, exhibition catalogue, with text and interview by Martin Kunz, Lucerne 1978; *Vito Acconci: A Retrospective 1969 to 1980* exhibition catalogue, with texts by John Hallmark Neff and Judith Russi Kirshner, Chicago 1980; *Machineworks: Vito Acconci, Alice Aycock, Dennis Oppenheim*, exhibition catalogue, with texts by Janet Kardon and Kay Larson, Philadelphia 1981; *Italians and American Italians: Etchings by Francisco Clemente, Jannis Klunellis, Italo Scanga, Tom Marioni, Vito Acconci*, exhibition catalogue, with an introduction by Kathan Brown, Oakland 1981; *Metaphor: New Projects by Contemporary Sculptors*, exhibition catalogue, with text by Howard N. Fox, Washington, D.C. 1982; *Vito Acconci: Domestic Trappings*, exhibition catalogue with essay by Ronald J. Onorato, La Jolla 1987.

For many artists in the 1960s who sought to evade the cul de sac of formalism and its concomitant obsession with the art object, the continued aesthetization of art became untenable. The institutions of painting and sculpture were surpassed by other forms of advanced art and especially by photography, which offered new possibilities for a generation who grew up surrounded by the imagery of television. The artist Vito Acconci both identified and defined the very terms of his art of the 1970s—his investigations of the self within the broad scope of conceptual art—in the photographic and cinematic medium of video.

The video projects Acconci produced in the late

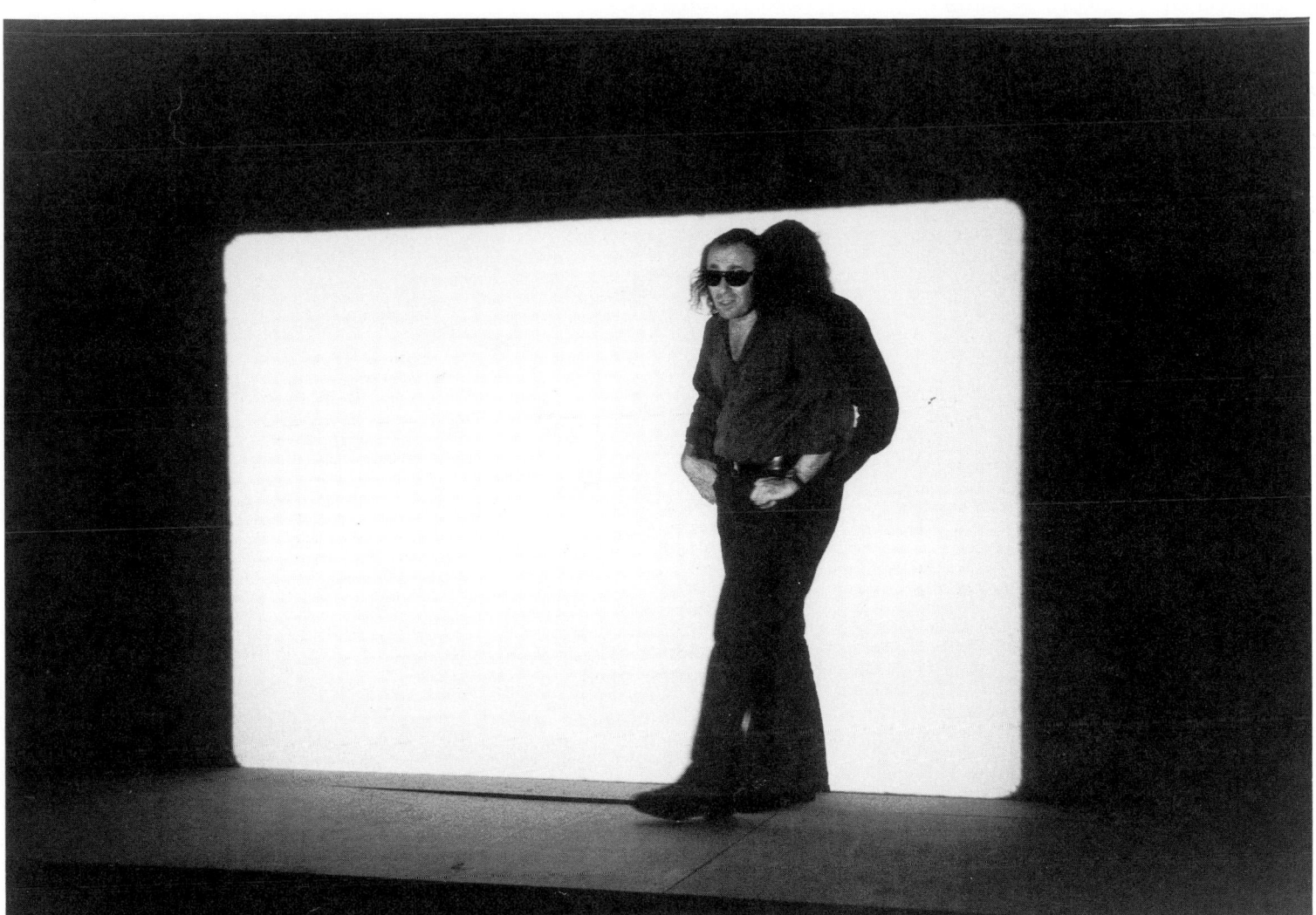

Vito Acconci: Performance at *Aspects de l'Art Actuel*, Paris, 1973

1960s and early '70s sought to transpose the aesthetic and philosophical terms of Minimalism and Process Art, both explorations of self-referential, temporal, and phenomenological conditions. Similar to the temporal/physical passage from one state to another experienced in Process Art, video permitted the artist to further intensify a dismantling of the myth of the subject as something given and preconstructed.

Minimalism's disavowal of structural closure and the myths of universal meaning became for Acconci a positive, liberating force. In his full-length video *The Red Tapes*, 1976–77—a trilogy reflecting the full range of his social, political and semiotic concerns—the artist, in fact, perpetuates the '60s revolutionary spirit with just such a message: "Let's make the symbols our own." Challenging the origin of the work of art in memory and *a priori* assumptions, the temporal experience of Minimalism tended to decenter our perception of the object. Attempting to exceed that movement's primary interest in formal concerns, Acconci began to exploit the dominant Minimalist aesthetic—temporal manipulations and the concomitant loss of self—as analogous to the fractured nature of consciousness as it is reproduced in video. Despite the proliferation of cultural types immediately accessible during the media-oriented '60s, a period fascinated by social change, Acconci was aware that the cooption of the self by the political economy of late-capitalism would render hopeless any search for a "new" or fixed identity.

Mirroring the reflexive nature of consciousness, video's electronic feedback allowed both the artist and viewer to dialectically explore the self as object and subject. Such a process suggested the distinction experienced by the patient in psychoanalysis between a subjectivity experienced and the conceptual projec-tion of the self as object. Acconci contrasted one's identity as felt with one's own seen/heard projection, for example, in *Air Time*, 1973, in which the artist faces a mirror and for 35 minutes engages his own reflection in a monologue. In *Centers*, 1971, in which the artist filmed himself pointing at the center of a television monitor for 20 minutes, Acconci moved toward a condition of self-enclosure in an effort to constitute or encapsulate a self—a particularly ironic exercise, during a cultural period of sexual and psychological openness, of disillusioning futility.

It was, however, this fundamental conjunction (and consequent diffusion) of the personal by a subsuming public "other" that connects Acconci's earlier video and performance work with his more recent furniture-like sculpture. Throughout most of the last two decades, he has transgressed convention, continually challenging our standards of normalcy by relentlessly blurring the categories (landscape, architecture, site) that define the spaces we live in. Acconci's strategy of representation, based on the pragmatics of language, hinges on the latter's arbitrariness. In order to combat the rigidity of our lives, Acconci's recent work increasingly has assumed the status of "play." The notion of play—with its irreverent collapse of convention and constant assertion of new rules—is manifest in many of the artist's recent fantasy-rooted works. Pieces such as *Garden Chair* [1986], *Bad Dream House* [1984] or *Sleeping Dog Couch* [1984] have permitted Acconci to create a deceptively simple fusion of form and content, one which is *engaging* rather than alienating.

—Mason Klein

ADAMI, Valerio (Romani).
Italian. Born in Bologna, 17 March 1935. Studied painting, under A. Funi, at the Accademia de Brera, Milan, 1951–54. Married Camilla Adami in 1962. Independent painter and graphic artist since 1955, working in Milan, 1955–61, in London, 1957, 1961–62, and in Arona, Italy, since 1961, and in Paris 1962, 1963, 1964. Agent: Galerie Lelong, 13 rue de Teheran, 75008 Paris. Address: Villa Cantoni, via San Carlo 56, 28041 Arona, Italy.

Individual Exhibitions:

1958	Galleria San Fedele, Milan
1959	Galleria del Naviglio, Milan
1960	Galerie Art Bremen, Bremen, West Germany
1961	Galleria L'Attico, Rome
	Salone Annunciata, Milan
1962	Institute of Contemporary Arts, London
1963	*Disegni e Parole*, Galleria del Naviglio, Milan
1964	Galleria del Cavallino, Venice
1965	Galeria Ad Libitum, Antwerp
	Galleria Schwarz/Studio Marconi, Milan
	Galleria L'Attico, Rome
1966	Galleria Il Punto, Turin
	Galerie Aujourd'hui, Brussels
	Galleria Schwarz/Studio Marconi, Milan
1967	Studio Marconi, Milan
	Galleria L'Attico, Rome
	Galerie Aujourd'hui, Brussels
	Galleria Schwarz/Studio Marconi, Milan
1968	Institute of Contemporary Art, Boston
	Deson Gallery, Chicago
	Fondacion Mendoza, Caracas
	Privacy, Galerie B. Mommaton, Paris

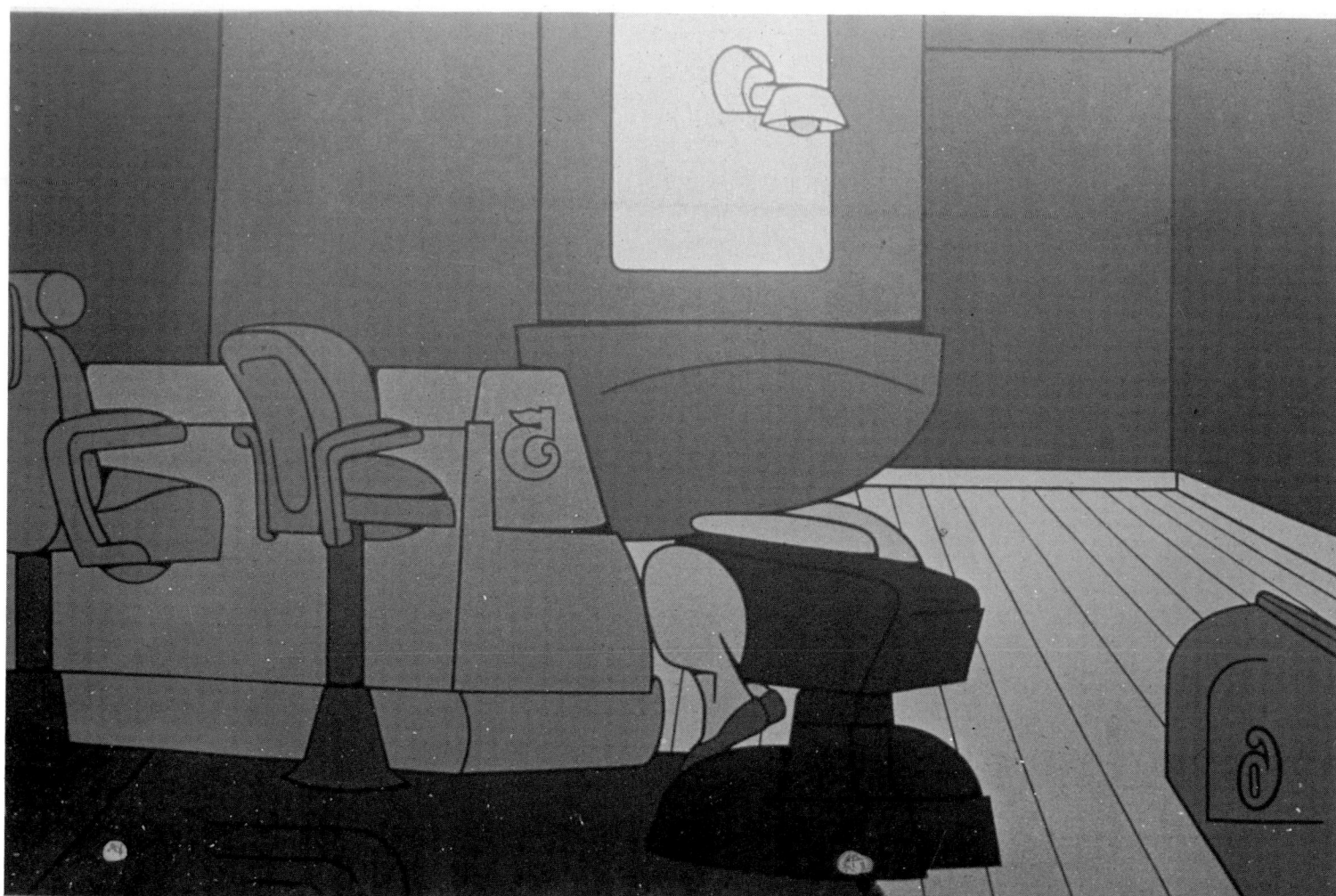

Valerio Adami: *Interno Pubblico*, 1969

Galerie Withofs, Brussels
Institute of Contemporary Arts, London
1969 Museo de Bellas Artes, Caracas
Galleria Schwarz, Milan
Studio Marconi, Milan
Galerie Withofs, Brussels
1970 Hansen Gallery, San Francisco
Musée d'Art Moderne de la Ville, Paris
Kunstverein, Ulm, West Germany
Galerie Maeght, Paris
62 Elsworthy Road, London
Galerie Wunsche, Bonn
Studio Marconi, Milan
1971 Museo de Bellas Artes, Caracas
1972 Galerie Schmela, Dusseldorf
Galerie Maeght, Zurich
Galleri Lowenadler, Stockholm
Galerie Maeght, Paris
Galerie Wunsche, Bonn
1973 Galerie Jacqueline Storme, Lille, France
Kunstverein, Hamburg
Galerie Maeght, Paris
Galerie Wunsche, Hamburg
1974 University of Wisconsin, Madison
1975 Bijou Galerie, Grenoble, France
Galerie Karl Flinker, Paris
Galerie Maeght, Paris
1976 Galerie Jacqueline Storme, Lille, France
Centre d'Arts Plastiques Contemporains, Bordeaux
Pinturas, Dibuixos, Aquarelles 1970–1975, Galeria
Maeght, Barcelona
Galerie Maeght, Paris
Galerie Maeght, Zurich
1977 Musée Cantini, Marseilles
1978 Palais des Beaux-Arts, Charleroi, Belgium
Abbaye de Fontevraud, France
Galerie Maeght, Zurich

1980 Musée de Grenoble, France
1981 Galerie Maeght, Zurich
Judith Posner Gallery, Milwaukee, Wisconsin
1982 Lens Fine Art, Antwerp
Centre d'Animation Culturelle, Mulhouse, France
Galleria Stamparte, Bologna, Italy
1983 Galleria Giulia, Rome
Galerie Maeght, Paris
Fùji Television Gallery, Tokyo
Goldman Kraft Gallery, Chicago
1984 Marisa del Re Gallery, New York
Galeria Alencon, Madrid
Museo de Bellas Artes de Asturias, Oviedo, Spain
1985 Musée de la Ville, Vitry, France
Galerie Il Punto, Monte Carlo
Centre Georges Pompidou, Paris
Palazzo Reale, Milan
Galerie Les Cordeliers, Chateauroux, France
Galerie A.C.A.P., Le Touquet, France

Selected Group Exhibitions:

1956 *Premio Marzotto*, Milan
1959 *Possibilita di Relazione*, Galleria L'Attico, Rome
1960 *Young Italian Painters*, Museum of Kamakura, Japan
1962 *Italian New Figurative Painters*, Piccadilly Gallery,
London
1969 *Maler und Modell*, Staatliche Kunsthalle, Baden-
Baden, West Germany
1971 *Radical Realists*, D. M. Gallery, London
1977 *La Traccia del Racconto*, Villa Comunale Ormond,
Sanremo, Italy
1982 *Arte Italiana 1960–82*, Hayward Gallery, London
1983 *Bonjour Monsieur Manet*, Centre Georges Pompidou, Paris
1985 *Il Cinema*, Galleria Gastaldelli, Milan

Collections:

Galleria d'Arte Moderna, Milan; Musée National d'Art Moderne, Paris; Kunstverein, Ulm, West Germany; Museo de Bellas Artes, Caracas; Rhode Island School of Design, Providence.

Publications:

By ADAMI: book—*Dix Lecons sur le Reich*, with Helmut Heissenbuttel, Munich and Paris 1974; film—*Vacances dans le Desert*, with Giancarlo Adami, 1970; record—*Concerto per un quadro di Adami*, with Henry Martin, 1970.

On ADAMI: books—*Valerio Adami: disegni e parole*, exhibition catalogue, with text by Enrico Crispolti, Milan 1963; *Le Pop Art* by Enrico Crispolti, Milan 1966; *Painting in the 20th Century* by Werner Haftmann, New York 1967; *Art of Our Time* by Will Grohmann, London 1967; *Pop Art* by Lucy R. Lippard, London 1967; *Righe per Adami* by Carlos Fuentes, Venice 1968; *Adami: Privacy*, exhibition catalogue, with text by Gerald Gassiot-Talabot and Henry Martin, Paris 1968; *Adami*, exhibition catalogue, with text by Carlos Franqui, Milan 1969; *Adami*, exhibition catalogue, with texts by Pierre Gaudibert, Henry Martin, Carlos Fuentes and others, Paris 1970; *Art Without Boundaries 1950–1970*, edited by Gerald Wood, Philip Thompson and John Williams, London 1972; *Valerio Adami*, exhibition catalogue, with texts by Hans Gerd Tuchel, Castor Seibel and Jacques Dupin, Hamburg 1973; *Adami* by Hubert Damisch and Henry Martin, Paris 1974; *Adami: pinturas, dibuixos, aquarelles 1970–1975*, exhibition catalogue, with text by Xavier Rubert de Ventos, Barcelona 1976; *Valerio Adami*, exhibition catalogue, with text by Nicolas and Elena Calas, Charleroi, Belgium 1978; *Valerio Adami*, exhibition catalogue, with text by Italo Calvino, Zurich 1981; *Valerio Adami*, exhibition catalogue, with text by Pietro Bonfiglioli, Bologna 1982; *Adami, presence contemporaine*, exhibition catalogue with texts by Nicolas and Elena Calas, Marc Le Bot and others, Aix-en-Provence, France 1984.

Arturo Schwarz of Milan lists Valerio Adami as one of the top International Avant-garde. He is certainly crisp in the Pop Art sense of the world, but he is also blessed with a tight ingredient of irony which slots comfortably into his unusual dislocated imagery. His flat colours vary between primaries and interesting tints, and generally every colour has a black edge to it.

Adami, armed with his personal style, is able to make wry comments upon sex and eroticism, intellectualism, psychology, social conditions, and art itself (as for instance in the "Surrealist Map of the World" 1972). What change there has been in his works has been a gradual drift from curious abstractions to a more formal figuration which began to take place in the late 1960's. Yet although the figuration may become steadily more and more recognizable to the unsophisticated eye, the colours continue their wayward direction; the woodwork or metal of a chair can be white, but the upholstery is straight green, the cushion red. It all sounds normal enough, but the talent of Adami transforms the three into the abstract colours of a flag or a trademark. These colours are bright, never gaudy; their message is immediate, magnetic.

In very different moods this painter has things in common with two such disparate artists as Jean-Pierre Raynaud and Tom Wesselmann. In his jigsaw-style interiors he sometimes introduces bourgeois fixtures that Raynaud might employ as adjuncts for his "objects" (one thinks of the lavatory—impersonalised by Raynaud, but sharply ludicrous in an Adami painting) or that Wesselman interpolates into his visions of "the American way-of-life." Of course the climates in the works of all three artists are entirely different but, just because their imagery can overlap at times, they can, however disconnected, be seen to belong to their own special era.

—Sheldon Williams

AFRICANO, Nicholas.

American. Born in Kankakee, Illinois, in 1948. Studied at Illinois State University, B.A. in English literature 1970, M.A. in painting, 1974, M.F.A. in painting 1975. Agent: Holly Solomon Gallery, New York. Address: c/o Holly Solomon Gallery, 724 Fifth Avenue, New York, New York 10019, U.S.A.

Individual Exhibitions:

1976   University of Illinois, Urbana
        Nancy Lurie Gallery, Chicago
1977   Sheldon Memorial Art Gallery, University of Nebraska, Lincoln
        Daddy's Old, Holly Solomon Gallery, New York
        New Concepts Gallery, University of Iowa, Iowa City
        Insulin, Holly Solomon Gallery, New York
        University of Rhode Island, Kingston
        Personal Information, Nancy Lurie Gallery, Chicago
1978   *The Man Who Lived in a Hat,* Walker Art Center, Minneapolis
1979   *The Battered Woman,* Holly Solomon Gallery, New York
        Battered Woman Series, Mayor Gallery, London
        Asher/Faure Gallery, Los Angeles
        Galerie Farideh Cadot, Paris
1980   Holly Solomon Gallery, New York
        Galerie 't Venster, Rotterdam
1981   *The Girl of the Golden West,* Holly Solomon Gallery, New York
        The Girl of the Golden West, Middendorf/Lane Gallery, Washington, D.C.
        The Girl of the Golden West, Asher/Faure Gallery, Los Angeles
1982   *The Girl of the Golden West,* Dart Gallery, Chicago
        The Girl of the Golden West, Greenberg Gallery, St. Louis
1983   Asher/Faure Gallery, Los Angeles
1984   North Carolina Museum of Art, Raleigh

Nicholas Africano: *A Passionate Man,* 1980

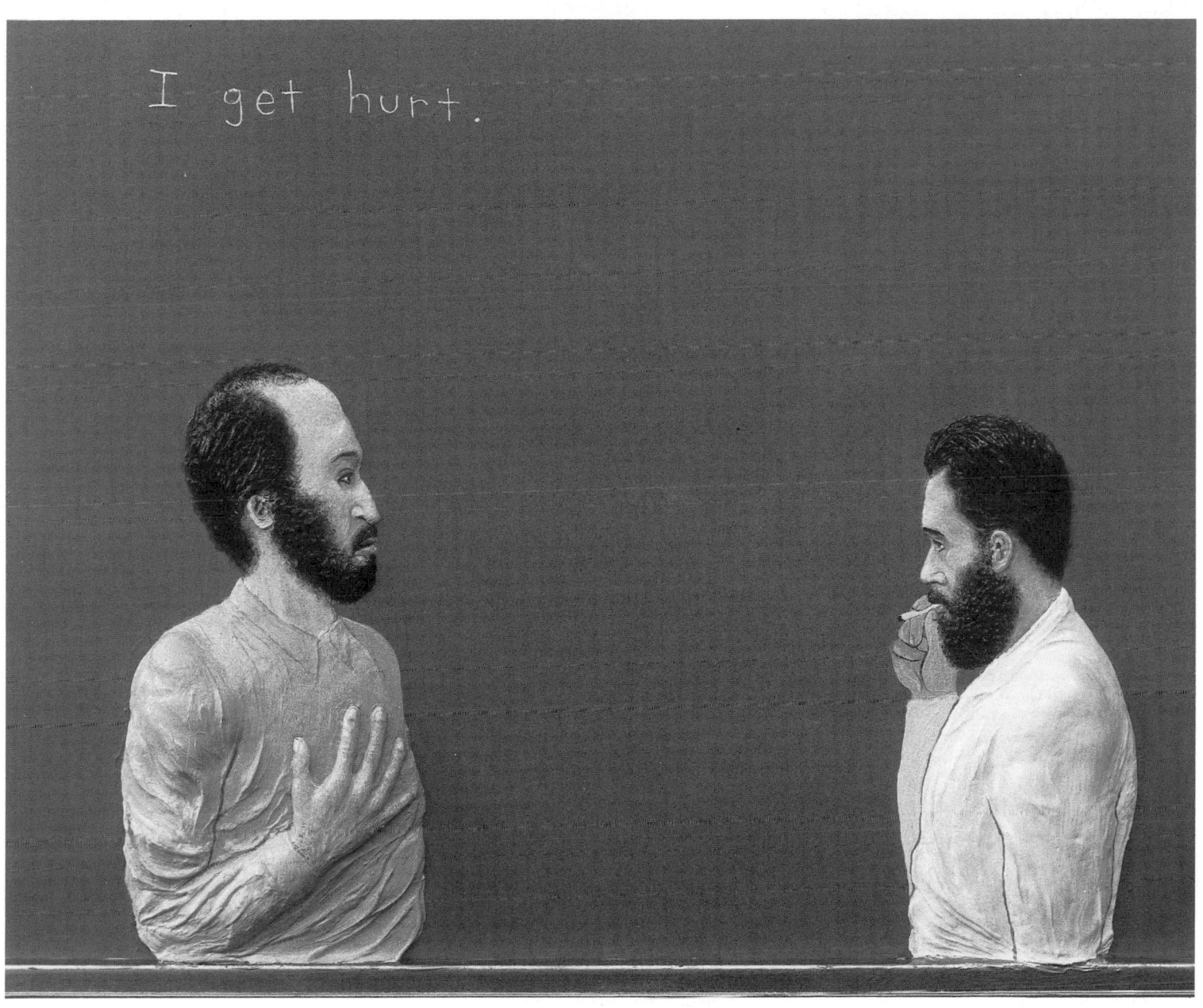

Selected Group Exhibitions:

1976 *Chicago Connection*, E. B. Crocker Gallery, Sacramento, California
1977 *American Painting '75, '76, '77*, Sarah Lawrence College, Bronxville, New York (travelled to the Museum of the American Foundation for the Arts, Miami, and the Contemporary Arts Center, Cincinnati, Ohio)
1978 *Narration*, Institute of Contemporary Art, Boston
1979 *New Image Painting*, Whitney Museum, New York
       American Portraits of the 60's and 70's, Aspen Center for the Visual Arts, Colorado
1980 *The Pluralist Decade*, at the *Biennale*, Venice (toured Europe, 1980–81)
       Chicago/Chicago, Contemporary Arts Center, Cincinnati, Ohio
1981 *Contemporary Drawings in Search of an Image*, University of California Art Museum, Santa Barbara
1982 *New York Now*, Kestner-Gesellschaft, Hannover
1984 *The Human Condition*, San Francisco Museum of Modern Art

Publications:

On AFRICANO: book—*Nicholas Africano: Paintings 1976–1983*, exhibition catalogue with essay by Mitchell D. Kahan, Raleigh 1983; articles—"Nicholas Africano" by Peter Frank in *The Village Voice* (New York), 7 November 1977; "Nicholas Africano" by Harold Olejarz in *Arts Magazine* (New York), April 1979; "Nicholas Africano: Responsible Relevance" by Dupuy Reed in *Arts Magazine* (New York), June 1979; "Nicholas Africano's Primitivism" by Howard Singerman in *Artweek* (Oakland, California), 29 September 1979; "New York, New York: Nicholas Africano" by Valentin Tatransky in *Flash Art* (Milan), March/April 1979; "Rodney Ripps and Nicholas Africano" by John Russell in the *New York Times*, 16 May 1980; "Art (Nicholas Africano/Rodney Ripps)" by Kay Larson in *The Village Voice* (New York), 26 May 1980; "Nicholas Africano Parables" by Joan Hugo in *Artweek* (Oakland, California), 16 May 1981.

Nicholas Africano places one or two tiny figures, molded in lumpy bas-relief, close to center in large monochrome fields or sometimes directly on the wall. His pictorial methodology makes us draw closer to focus in on the mini-people who are unattractively lumpy and primitivizing and marked by a cartoony flavor relating them with the Chicago-based group "The Hairy Who," particularly with Jim Nutt's bizarre and theatrical figures.

Africano's kind of "knowing" naiveté and true grit encourages an attitude of uncomfortable empathy toward his intimately scaled object of attention, who is characteristically poised during a moment of tension, facing some basic psychological state with tentative indecision. The ambiguously portrayed drama borders on the narrative but is never quite elaborated in specific terms. Trained as a writer, Africano wants to evade the formal element and concentrate on evoking meaning. The pictorial elements, however, are used quite effectively to lead to underlying content. Africano's uses of proportion and location place the figure at an introspective removal from the world at large, and his use of densely modeled form lends his figures a sense of physicality in their vulnerability. The primitivizing quality lies somewhere in between Africano's regard for the Italian primitives and for the cartoonist's satire. He starts, in fact, with a series of sketches like the frames of the cartoon format.

During the late 1970's, Africano produced a number of works in the autobiographical vein, such as "Nicholas Waiting" (1976, oil, acrylic, wax, linoleum shelf), which concentrated on the bearded figure of the artist himself. His 1978 series, "Battered Woman," moves away from the autobiographical, coming closer to a narrative of social implications. In a series of 10 canvases, Africano portrays the dilemmas faced by the "battered woman" in question, who is going through a set of psycho-sociological situations with an aura of dread understandable to any sympathetic viewer. The fifth in the series, "The

Door," exemplifies Africano at his more effective moments. The miniaturized victim stands facing a simply rendered door, leading to the unknown, whether within or without. The moment of poignant vulnerability is captured with a rugged sensitivity which avoids sentimental melodrama successfully, though precariously.

Africano is creating humane stage settings of a contemporary tragi-comic order, locating himself on the borderline between the real and the surreal and on the fragile tightrope which aims at avoiding the literally illusionistic while realistically evoking the basic alienation felt by the young in today's society, whether they be artists or not. His is a youthful, quirky expression, and it remains to be seen how well it will serve in his future development.

—Barbara Cavaliere

AFRO (Basaldella).
Italian. Born in Udine, 4 March 1912. Educated in Florence and Venice. Served in Italian Army, 1933–34, 1940–44. Independent artist, Milan, 1930–33, 1935–36, in Rome, 1936–40, 1945–76: associated with new generation of painters, including Birolli and Morlotti, Milan, 1930–36; worked with sculptor Arturo Martini, 1932; member, Gruppo degli Otto artists' group, Rome, 1952. Guest Lecturer, Mills College, Oakland, California, 1958. Recipient: Regional Grand Prize for Painting, Udine, 1929; Prize, 1952, 1954, and Grand Prize, 1956, *Biennale*, Venice; International Painting Prize, *Bienal*, Sao Paulo, 1955. *Died* (in Zurich) 24 July 1976.

Individual Exhibitions:

1932 Galleria del Milione, Milan
1936 Galleria La Cometa, Rome
1940 Galleria Mediterranea, Palermo
1942 Galleria Roma, Rome
1944 Galleria del Sindicato Belle Arti, Udine
1946 Galleria dello Zodiaco, Rome
       Galleria Lo Scorpione, Trieste
1947 Galleria Il Camino, Milan
1948 Galleria La Saletta, Modena
       Galleria dell'Obelisco, Rome
1950 Catherine Viviano Gallery, New York
       Galleria del Milione, Milan
1951 Studio d'Arte Palma, Rome
1952 Catherine Viviano Gallery, New York
1953 Galleria dell'Obelisco, Rome
1955 Catherine Viviano Gallery, New York
       Galleria dell'Obelisco, Rome
1956 Italian Pavilion, at the *Biennale*, Venice
1957 Catherine Viviano Gallery, New York
1959 Catherine Viviano Gallery, New York
1960 Galleria La Tartaruga, Rome
       Galleria Schneider, Rome
       Italian Pavilion, at the *Biennale*, Venice
       Catherine Viviano Gallery, New York
       Massachusetts Institute of Technology, Cambridge
1961 Galleria Blu, Milan
       Galerie de France, Paris
1962 Galleria Toninelli, Milan
       AMIT Gallery, Boston
1963 Catherine Viviano Gallery, New York
1964 Galerie im Erker, St. Gallen, Switzerland
       Catherine Viviano Gallery, New York
1965 Galerie Rabner, Lucerne
       Galerie Ricke, Kassel, West Germany
       Galerie Günther Franke, Munich
       Galleria La Medusa, Rome
1966 University of South Florida, Tampa
1967 Palazzina Vitelli, Città di Castello, Italy
1968 Galleria Toninelli, Milan
       Catherine Viviano Gallery, New York
       Galleria Michaud, Florence
       Galleria Narciso, Turin

1969 Nationalgalerie, West Berlin
       Kunstverein, Darmstadt
       Galleria Civca d'Arte Moderna, Ferrara, Italy
1970 Centro Culturale Nuove Frontiere, Gaviarate, Italy
       Galleria D4, Alessandria, Italy
       Galleria Moretto, Brescia, Italy
       Galleria Forni, Bologna
1973 Galleria Editalia, Rome
1974 Galleria del Milione, Milan
1975 Galleria 2RC, Rome
1978 Galleria Nazionale d'Arte Moderna, Rome (retrospective; travelled to the Villa Manin di Passariano, Udine)
1981 *Retrospektive 1912–1976*, Staatsgalerie Moderner Kunst, Munich (travelled to the Wilhelm-Hack-Museum, Ludwigshafen, West Germany)
1987 Palazzo Rosari Spada, Spoleto, Italy

Selected Group Exhibitions:

1936 *Quadriennale di Roma*, Galleria d'Arte Moderna, Rome
1949 *Afro/Cagli/Guttuso/Morlotti/Pizzinato*, Catherine Viviano Gallery, New York
1951 *Exhibition of Italian Art*, Museum of Modern Art, New York
1952 *Biennale*, Venice (and 1954)
1953 *Bienal*, Sao Paulo (and 1955)
1955 *The New Decade*, Museum of Modern Art, New York
1959 *Carnegie International*, Carnegie Institute, Pittsburgh
1971 *New Italian Art 1953–1971*, Walker Art Gallery, Liverpool

Collections:

Galleria Nazionale d'Arte Moderna, Rome; Museo Civico, Turin; Nationalgalerie, West Berlin; Musée des Beaux-Arts, La Chaux de Fonds, Switzerland; Tate Gallery, London; Museum of Modern Art, New York; Guggenheim Museum, New York; Museum of Fine Arts, Boston; Los Angeles County Museum of Art; Museum of Fine Arts, Montreal, Quebec.

Publications:

On AFRO: books—*Afro*, exhibition catalogue, with text by L. de Libero, Rome 1946; *Afro*, exhibition catalogue, with text by Luca Venturi, New York 1955; *Afro*, exhibition catalogue, with text by Marco Valescchi, Milan 1961; *Afro*, exhibition catalogue, with text by Cesare Brandi, New York 1963; *Afro*, exhibition catalogue, with text by Hans Platte, Munich 1965; *Afro*, exhibition catalogue, with text by Maurizio Calvesi, Rome 1965; *Afro*, exhibition catalogue, with text by Lamberto Vitali, Milan 1968; *Afro*, exhibition catalogue, with text by Werner Haftmann, and Bernd Krimmel, West Berlin 1969; *Afro*, exhibition catalogue, by Hans G. Sperlich and Bernd Krimmel, Darmstadt 1969; *New Italian Art 1953–1971*, exhibition catalogue, with text by Giovanni Caradente, Liverpool 1971; *Afro*, exhibition catalogue, with text by Cesare Brandi, Rome 1973; *Afro*, by Cesare Brandi, Rome 1977; *Afro*, exhibition catalogue with text by B. Mantura, Rome 1978; *Afro: Retrospektive 1912–1976*, exhibition catalogue, with texts by Guido Ballo, and Carla Schulz-Hoffmann, Munich 1981; *Afro*, by Alessandra Borgogelli, Milan 1986.

After completing his artistic studies in Venice, Afro moved to Rome in 1933 where he visited Corrado Cagli and the group known as the Roman School. Two years later, he participated in the Rome Quadriennale, the capital's most important public show. Included in this exhibition were the figurative paintings that were characteristic of Afro's work up to the outbreak of World War II. In 1937 he had his first one-man show at the Galleria La Cometa, which had taken on the best of the young artists.

Afro's work of the late 1930s had become luminous and baroque, as can be seen in a still life of 1937 where the picture is enriched by a surreal use of carnival masks. He frequently used such motifs to explore problems of tonality. The early 1940s brought his first expressionist works; feeling now predominated over formal or decorative qualities, expressive pathos becoming the primary mood of the picture, as Afro profoundly felt the horror of war.

In 1944 he began his first neo-cubist works. With the end of a world conflict, a new cultural ferment swept through Italian art. Artists working with abstraction offered the possibility of international dialogue; Afro meanwhile continued exhibiting in several European Countries and in the United States while developing a new approach. In this, the form and colour are still those of his neo-cubist phase, but the composition is decidedly different. The style which was to give Afro his international status was already here in embryo. In 1952 he exhibited with the Gruppo degli Otto. The art critic and historian Lionello Venturi, co-ordinator of the group, wrote of their work: "They have adopted a pictorial language which emerges from those traditions of the period around 1910, incorporating the ideas of the cubists, expressionists and abstract artists."

Afro also took part in the show *Five Italian Painters* at the Catherine Viviano Gallery in New York in 1952, with Cagli, Guttuso, Morlotti and Pizzinato. Contact with the cultural ambiance of New York was a positive influence, leading to a series of works strongly inspired by American abstract expressionism. These works bear a strong resemblance to those of Arshile Gorky, while maintaining Afro's characteristic use of vibrant and transparent colour. For example, *Balletto*, a work of 1953, with its vertical organization arrangement of the motifs, creates a line which constructs the image and its range of blue tones. These elements are maintained unaltered throughout Afro's most extreme period of expressionism when all naturalistic references had been abandoned.

By the end of the 1960s, Afro had developed his particular style of abstraction by reducing the composition to a colossal smudge of saturated hues. The colour is now sombre, expressing the dark sentiment of the night, of the end of existence.

Afro died in Zurich in 1976.

—Roberto Lambarelli

AGAM, Yaacov.

Israeli. Born Jacob (Yaacov) Gipstein in Rishon Letzion, Palestine, now Israel, 11 May 1928; adopted name "Agam," Paris, 1953. Studied art at the Bezalel School, Jerusalem, 1947–48; architecture, under Siegfrid Giedion, at the Kunstgewerbeschule, Zurich, 1949; and art at the Atelier d'Art Abstrait, Paris, 1951. Married Clila Agam in 1956; children: Ron, Orram and Orrit. Independent artist, in Paris, since 1951; first transformable paintings, 1951; first polyphonic paintings, 1953; first sound paintings, 1961; stainless steel sculptures, from 1968. Guest Instructor, Illinois Institute of Technology, Chicago, 1961; Visiting Lecturer, Harvard University, Cambridge, Massachusetts 1968. Recipient: Painting Prize, *International Festival of Painting*, Cagnes-sur-Mer, France 1970. Agent: Galerie Denise René, 124 rue La Boetie, 75008 Paris. Address: 45 rue Castagnary, 75015 Paris, France.

Individual Exhibitions:

1953   Galerie Craven, Paris
1954   Galerie Furstenberg, Paris
1955   Doris Meltzer Gallery, New York
        Galerie Denise René, Paris (with Soto and Abner)
1956   Galerie Denise René, Paris
1958   Galerie Aujourd'hui, Brussels
        Tel-Aviv Museum
        Galerie Denise René, Paris

1959   *Transformable Painting/Painting in Movement*, Drian Gallery, London
        Galerie Suzanne Bollag, Zurich
        Städtisches Museum, Leverkusen, West Germany
1962   *Peinture Transformable, Peinture Polyphonique, Peinture et Mouvement*, Galerie Suzanne Bollag, Zurich
1966   Marlborough-Gerson Gallery, New York
1969   Whitechapel Art Gallery, London (with Lifshitz and Zaritzky)
1971   *Transformables*, Galerie Denise René, New York
1972   Musée d'Art Moderne, Paris (travelled to the Stedelijk Museum, Amsterdam; Städtisches Museum, Dusseldorf; and the Tel-Aviv Museum, 1972–73)
1975   *Selected Suites*, Jewish Museum, New York
1980   Guggenheim Museum, New York

Selected Group Exhibitions:

1954   *Salon des Réalités Nouvelles*, Musée d'Art Moderne, Paris
1958   *Carnegie International*, Carnegie Institute, Pittsburgh
1961   *Bewogen Beweging*, Stedelijk Museum, Amsterdam
1963   *7th Bienal*, Sao Paulo
1965   *The Responsive Eye*, Museum of Modern Art, New York
1967   *Art and Movement*, National Gallery of Canada, Ottawa (toured Canada)
1970   *International Festival of Painting*, Cagnes-sur-Mer, France
1972   *12 Ans d'Art Contemporain en France*, Grand Palais, Paris
1973   *The Non-Objective World 1914-1955*, Annely Juda Fine Art, London (travelled to the University of Texas, Austin)

Collections:

Centre Georges Pompidou, Paris; Kaiser-Wilhelm-Museum, Krefeld, West Germany; Kunstmuseum, Dusseldorf; Julliard School, Lincoln Center, New York.

Publications:

By AGAM: films—*Recherches et Inventions*, with I. Mambush, 1956; *Le Desert Chante, Microsalon*, with I. Mambush, 1957.

On AGAM: books—*Agam: Transformable Painting/Painting in Movement*, exhibition catalogue, with texts by Michel Ragon and Eugene Kolb, London 1959; *Yaacov Agam: Peinture Transformable, Peinture Polyphonique, Peinture et Mouvement*, exhibition folder, with text by Siegfried Giedion, Zurich 1962; *Yaacov Agam* by Jasia Reichardt, London 1966; *Yaacov Agam*, exhibition catalogue, with texts by Haim Gamzu and Jasia Reichardt, New York 1966; *Neue Dimensionen der Plastik* by Udo Kultermann, Tübingen 1967; *New Tendencies in Art* by Aldo Pellegrini, London 1967; *Beyond Modern Sculpture* by Jack Burnham, New York 1968; *Origins and Development of Kinetic Art* by Frank Popper, London and New York 1968; *Movements in Art since 1945* by Edward Lucie Smith, London 1969; *Op Art* by Cyril Barrett, London 1969; *Yaacov Agam: Transformables*, exhibition catalogue, with texts by Haim Gamzu and Jean-Jacques Leveque, New York 1971; *Agam*, exhibition catalogue, with texts by Jean Leymarie, Blaise Gautier, Germain Viatte and others, Paris 1972; *Yaacov Agam: Peintures, Sculptures* exhibition catalogue with text by Haim Gamzu, Tel-Aviv 1973; *Yaacov Agam: Selected Suites*, exhibition catalogue, with text by Paul Kaniel, New York 1975; *Agam* by Frank Popper, New York 1976, 1980; *Yaacov Agam* by Günter Metken, London 1977.

Agam is one of the pioneers of Kinetic Art and in particular of the trend which is concerned with the participation of the spectator. Having begun with paintings, reliefs, play objects and sculptures, he then experimented with the forces of light, air, water and fire before reaching a stage where his works are developed on the environmental scale, sometimes with the aid of the newest technological means.

But it is impossible to dissociate Agam's plastic

achievements from the metaphysical implications of his research, his religious and cosmological beliefs. Agam's search for the perceptible absence of the image, his demonstration of the irreversibility of time, and the simultaneity of significant happenings which can be found in most of his works have a biblical and epistemological origin.

All of Agam's works are "transformable," since a time sequence is implicit in their structure. But this term is reserved by the artist himself for works in which the basis of transformation lies in the possibility of modifying the pictorial structure, a research begun back in the early 1950s which has given rise to a great number of statements ranging from "polyphonic" pictures destined for the interior or the exterior of private dwellings to environmental installations like the "Salon de l'Elysée" in Paris, "Agam Space" at the Forum in Leverkusen or the "Aenaitral Tower" and the "Panoramagam" created for the artist's one-man show at the Guggenheim Museum in New York in 1980. All these transformable pictorial statements imply the spectator's participation since their chromatic structures are revealed only through his movements.

However, the movable structures and play objects of the early 50s which preceded the Tactile works and which were followed by a great variety of small-and large-scale metal sculptures provoked a still more complete participation of the spectator who was induced to freely exercise his creative powers.

The multiplicity of the pursuits of Agam and the great diversity of his works can only be measured if one also mentions his graphic works and inventions, ranging from the single print to the holograph by way of multigraphs, polymorph graphics, interspaceographs, environmental graphics, prismographics, and video graphics. Agam's other achievements include constructions with artificial light, water-fire sculptures, monumental mixed media works such as the Fountain at the Défence complex near Paris, and incursions into other domains like the theatre as well as many technological experiments and pedagogical projects.

All these endeavours show clearly the tendency of Agam's thought: his entirely optimistic and dynamic interpretation and celebration of the force of life in art and his total faith in the participation of the public in the creative process.

—Frank Popper

AGNETTI, Vincenzo.

Italian. Born in Milan, 14 September 1926. Studied at the Academy of Dramatic Art, Milan; Liceo Artistico, Accademia di Brera, Milan. Married Bruna Soletti in 1949 (divorced); daughter: Germana. Worked as actor, Piccolo Teatro, Milan, 1949–51. Concentrated on "informal painting," Milan, 1953–61; settled in Buenos Aires, 1961–67; returned to Milan, 1967–81; spent year in Rome, 1969–70; visited New York frequently, 1977–81. Lecturer in Art, Accademia di Brera, Milan; Guest Lecturer, in Art and Architecture, Universities of Rome, Milan and New York, 1974–81. Recipient: Premio Pascali, Rome, 1972. Agent: Bruna Soletti, Piazza S. Alesandro, 6 Milan. *Died* (in Milan) *1 September 1981*.

Individual Exhibitions:

1967   Palazzo dei Diamanti, Ferrara, Italy
1968   Galleria Visualità, Milan
1971   Galleria La Tartaruga, Rome
1972   Galleria Lambert, Milan
        Galleria Martano, Turin
        Galleria Schema, Florence
        Galleria Toselli, Milan

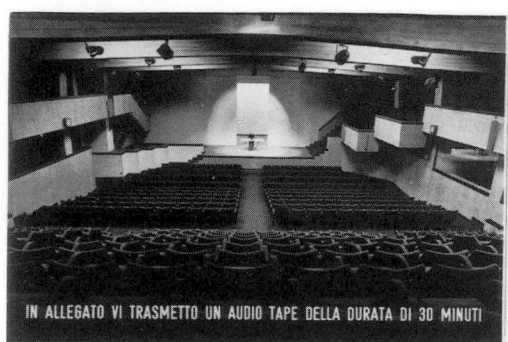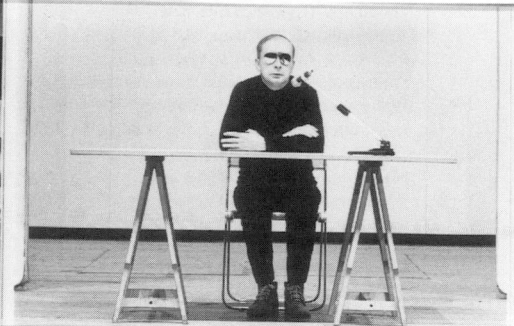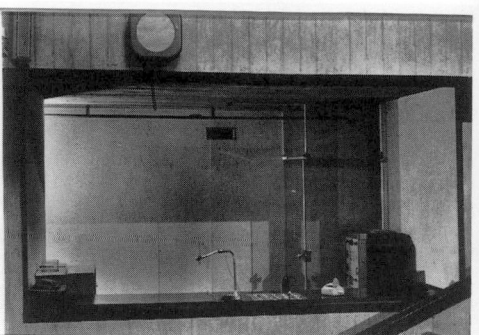

IN ALLEGATO VI TRASMETTO UN AUDIO TAPE DELLA DURATA DI 30 MINUTI

Vincenzo Agnetti: *Monolog in an Empty Theatre*, 1973

<table>
<tr><td>1973</td><td>Galerie Annemarie Verna, Zurich</td></tr>
<tr><td></td><td>Galleria Rumma, Naples</td></tr>
<tr><td></td><td>San Fedele Teatro, Milan</td></tr>
<tr><td></td><td>Galleria Marilena Bonomo, Bari, Italy</td></tr>
<tr><td></td><td>Galleria Nazionale d'Arte Moderna, Rome</td></tr>
<tr><td></td><td>Galleria Forma, Genoa</td></tr>
<tr><td>1974</td><td>Galleria Seconda Scala, Rome</td></tr>
<tr><td></td><td>Bolaffi Arte, Turin</td></tr>
<tr><td></td><td>Galleria Alessandra Castelli, Bergamo, Italy</td></tr>
<tr><td></td><td>Museum am Ostwall, Dortmund, West Germany</td></tr>
<tr><td></td><td>Galleria Allesandra Castelli, Milan</td></tr>
<tr><td>1975</td><td>Ronald Feldman Fine Arts, New York</td></tr>
<tr><td></td><td>Studio Canaviello, Rome</td></tr>
<tr><td></td><td>Sonnabend Galerie, Paris</td></tr>
<tr><td></td><td>Art in Progress, Munich</td></tr>
<tr><td>1976</td><td>Galleria La Tartaruga, Rome</td></tr>
<tr><td></td><td>Mercato del Sale, Milan</td></tr>
<tr><td>1977</td><td>Israel Museum, Jerusalem</td></tr>
<tr><td></td><td>Studio Guiliana de Crescenzo, Rome</td></tr>
<tr><td></td><td>Galleria Civica d'Arte Moderna, Castello di Porto-
fino, Italy</td></tr>
<tr><td>1978</td><td>Ronald Feldman Fine Arts, New York</td></tr>
<tr><td></td><td>Galerie Wintersberg, Cologne</td></tr>
<tr><td></td><td>Arta Studio, Milan</td></tr>
<tr><td>1979</td><td>Ronald Feldman Fine Arts, New York</td></tr>
<tr><td></td><td>Palazzo Grassi, Venice</td></tr>
<tr><td>1980</td><td>Ronald Feldman Fine Arts, New York</td></tr>
<tr><td></td><td>Galleria Toselli, Milan</td></tr>
<tr><td></td><td>Padiglione d'Arte Contemporanea, Milan</td></tr>
<tr><td>1981</td><td>Galleria Bruna Soletti, Milan</td></tr>
<tr><td>1982</td><td>Galleria Comunale d'Arte Moderna, Bologna</td></tr>
<tr><td></td><td>Galleria Il Luogo di Gauss, Milan</td></tr>
</table>

Selected Group Exhibitions:

<table>
<tr><td>1969</td><td>Principia, Historical Archives, Biennale, Venice</td></tr>
<tr><td>1970</td><td>Vitality of the Negative, Palazzo delle Esposizione,
Rome</td></tr>
<tr><td>1972</td><td>Documenta 5, Kassel, West Germany</td></tr>
<tr><td>1973</td><td>Bienal, Sao Paulo</td></tr>
<tr><td>1976</td><td>Artists and Photograph, Israel Museum, Jerusalem</td></tr>
<tr><td>1986</td><td>Aspects of Italian Art 1960–85, Kunstverein, Frank-
furt</td></tr>
</table>

Collections:

Galleria Nazionale d'Arte Moderna, Rome; Galleria d'Arte Moderna, Parma, Italy; Raccolte Civiche d'Arte, Milan; Galleria d'Arte Moderna, Livorno, Italy; Galleria d'Arte Moderna, Cagliari, Italy.

Publications:

By AGNETTI: books—*Intorno alla,* Milan 1967; *Obsoleto,* Milan 1967; *Rigoree Utopia,* Milan 1968; *Tesi,* Milan 1968; *Ciclostile,* Milan 1969; *Spazio perduto e Spazio Costruito,* Marcerata, Italy 1972; *Progetto per un Amieto Politico,* Genoa 1973; *Tradotto azzerato presentato,* Milan 1974; *Image of an Exhibition,* Milan and New York 1974; *Machiavelli 30,* Milan 1978; *Lettre dal Deserto,* Milan 1981; articles— "Intervento" in *Tavole di Accertamento* by Piero Manzoni, Milan 1958; "Intervento" in *Linea* by Piero Manzoni, Milan 1959; "Non commettere atti Impuri" in *Azimuth* (Milan), 1959; "Indulgentia" in *Nuova Corrente* (Milan), March

1968; "Copia dal Vero Numero Primo" in *Domus* (Milan), nos. 495–498, 1971; "Utopia" in *Ricerca Contemporanea* (Milan), nos. 1–3, 1971; "High Fidelity" in *Documenta 5,* exhibition catalogue, Kassel, West Germany 1972; interview, with Mario Peruzzi, in *Corriere della Sera* (Milan), February 1972; video tapes—*Vobulazione e Bioloquenza: NEG,* with G. Colombo, 1970; *Documentario No. 2,* Centro Diffusione Grafica, Florence 1973; *Machiavelli 30,* with Licitra, Roselli and Pagano, 1978.

On AGNETTI: books—*Manzoni* by Germano Celant, Rome 1971; *Territorio Magico* by Achille Bonita Oliva, Florence 1972; articles—by Tommaso Trini and Pierre Restany in *Domus* (Milan), February 1973; "The Why of Things and Gestures" by Jane Bell in *Arts Magazine* (New York), October 1974; "Arte e Critica dopo l'Avanguardia" by Maurizio Calvesi in *Corriere della Sera* (Milan), February 1975; "Torniami alle Armi" by Pierre Restany in *Vincenzo Agnetti,* exhibition catalogue, Bologna 1982.

Milanese conceptual artist Vincenzo Agnetti emerged from a thoroughly European tradition, that which finds its roots in the image of the "Renaissance Man." Agnetti's studies in film, theater, philosophy, and applied engineering not only weave in and out of his work as esoteric references, but also serve as a solid foundation for his complex *oeuvre,* both visual and linguistic. This "intervention" (i.e., conscious interdisciplinary approach to an entire system) was from the beginning crucial to his work, although in no way can he be dismissed as another "multimedia" artist. Only by understanding this precept can the work be at all accessible.

There are certain obvious parallels to other artists using the conceptual mode; like *Art-Language,* Agnetti used verbal structures; like Hanna Darboven, he based a good deal of his work on numerical anti-systems; and, like Beuys, whom he most closely resembles, he used the tape-recorded dialogue format. But he attempted to carry out the conceptual premise further still, away from tautologies and freedom from (or negation of) content. In his 1975 New York exhibition he demonstrated post-Duchampian irony combined with a serious investigation of perceptual distortions, primarily of Time and Space. His work is as complex, although less formal and more free-wheeling, as that of his conceptual colleagues. What concerns him in such works as "Herewith I Transmit a 30-Minute Tape Recording," "Architecture Translated for all the Peoples of the World," and "1870–1974," is a quest for anti-meaning, a meaning which transcends that of pure gesture, into a fundamentally eccentric world of paradox and imaginative constructs. The disciplines that he chose (whether electronic, photographic, or apparently mathematical) became catalytic tools, replacing, as he said himself, "the how it is done" by "the why it is done." Apparently analytic in method, Agnetti's work is not, in fact, analytic in intent. It differs also from other conceptual work in the fact that it is not hermetic; it is not only unselfconscious, but rarely self-absorbed. What concerned him is the *behavior* of phenomena and mental processes themselves.

Much of the value in Agnetti's investigations, perhaps best exemplified by "A's Median Age," a "translation" of a woman's face taken from photographs

from different stages of her life culminating in a composite, very nearly ideational construct, lies in his critical and even admittedly prejudiced approach to his subjects. The work is in the nature of speculation, as a search for conclusions, even if he would occasionally perform an entirely unexpected about-face and negate those same conclusions; this method is used to great effect in his "Architecture Translated for all the Peoples in the World," in which his final conclusion (after an impeccably, apparently inevitably reached solution) negates his initial premise.

Agnetti's *oeuvre* is thus a combination of rigorous but potentially pliable thought and an intuitively formal elegance, concerned with the whole culture, and not simply with the strictly visual arts. As he wrote in 1974, "I am only an intuitive creator of signs who makes paintings out of philosophy by searching out shape and design in the dialogue, by looking for forms in the culture that has crystallized our common experience." It is this common experience, or what Henry Martin has termed the "*universalization* of culture and experience," that underscores the importance of Agnetti's ironic speculations.

—Jane Bell

ALBERS, Josef.
American. Born in Bottrop, Westphalia, Germany, 19 March 1888; emigrated to the United States, 1935; naturalized, 1939. Educated at Teachers College, Buren, Germany, 1905–08; studied at the Königliche Kunstschule, Berlin, 1913–15 (qualified as art teacher, 1915); Kunstgewerbeschule, Essen, 1916–19; Kunstakademie, Munich, 1919–20; Bauhaus, Weimar, 1920–23. Married Anni Fleischmann in 1925. Taught in public schools in Bottrop, 1908–13 and 1915–19; organized glass workshop and designed stained glass windows and developed one-pane glass paintings at the Bauhaus, Weimar, 1922, and conducted course in design, at the invitation of Gropius, 1923, then became Lecturer, 1923–25, Professor, 1925–33, Assistant Director, 1930, and Director of the Furniture Workshop, at the Bauhaus, Weimar, Dessau and Berlin (developed sandblasted glass painting, and designed glass, metal and wood furniture containers, Dessau, 1926). Lecturer, International Congress for Art Education, Prague, 1928; Chairman, Art Department, Black Mountain College, Beria, North Carolina, 1933–49; Head of the Art School, 1950–58, and Visiting Professor, 1958–60, Yale University, New Haven, Connecticut (also developed special teaching methods, for basic design, drawing and color, Yale Art School, during the 1960's). Recipient: William A. Clark Prize, Corcoran Gallery, Washington, D.C., 1954; Ada S. Garrett Prize, Art Institute of Chicago, 1954; Courant von Goesch Prize, 1958; Ford Foundation Fellowship, 1959; Penwalphra Museum College of Art Award, 1962; Medal of the Year, American Institute of Graphic Arts, 1964; National Institute of Arts and Letters Award, 1968; Grand Prize, North Rhein-Westphalia, Germany, 1968; Citation, National Asso-

ciation of Schools of Art, 1971; Citation, College Art Association, 1973; Akademie der Künste Award, Berlin, 1974; Fine Arts Medal, *American Institute of Arts Convention,* Atlanta, 1975; D.F.A.: University of Hartford, Connecticut, 1957; Yale University, 1962. Benjamin Franklin Fellow, Royal Society, London, 1970; Honorary Citizen, Bottrop, West Germany, 1970. Fellow, American Academy of Arts and Sciences, 1973. Albers Museum opened in Bottrop, 1983. *Died (in Orange, Connecticut) 24 March 1976.*

Individual Exhibitions:

1948	*Josef Albers/Hans Arp/Max Bill,* Herbert Hermann Gallery, Stuttgart
1949	Cincinnati Art Museum, Ohio
	Yale University Art Gallery, New Haven, Connecticut
	Museum of Fine Arts, Richmond, Virginia
	Sidney Janis Gallery, New York
1950	J. B. Speed Art Museum, Louisville
1951	Contemporary Art Society, Sydney
1952	Sidney Janis Gallery, New York
	Arts Club of Chicago (with Naum Gabo)
1953	Museum of Art, San Francisco
	Josef and Anni Albers, Wadsworth Atheneum, Hartford, Connecticut
1954	Academy of Art, Honolulu
1955	Sidney Janis Gallery, New York
	Massachusetts Institute of Technology, Cambridge
1956	Yale University Art Gallery, New Haven, Connecticut
	Kunsthaus, Zurich (with Fritz Glarner and Friedrich Vordemberge-Gildewart)
1957	Galerie Denise René, Paris
	Museum der Stadt, Ulm, West Germany
	Karl Ernst Osthaus Museum, Hagen, West Germany
1958	Sidney Janis Gallery, New York
	Kunstverein, Freiburg im Breisgau, West Germany
	Landesmuseum, Münster, West Germany
1959	Sidney Janis Gallery, New York
	Museum am Ostwall, Dortmund
1961	Stedelijk Museum, Amsterdam
	Sidney Janis Gallery, New York
	Gimpel Fils, London
1963	Sidney Janis Gallery, New York
	Galerie Hybler, Copenhagen
	Kunsthaus, Hamburg
	Folkwangmuseum, Essen
	Art Museum, Dallas
1964	Sidney Janis Gallery, New York
	Museum of Modern Art, New York
	Museum of Art, San Francisco
1965	Galleria Toninelli, Milan
	Galerie Gimpel-Hanover, Zurich
	Morgner-Haus, Soest, West Germany

Josef Albers: *Homage to the Square—Pale Autumn,* **1963** Courtesy Museum of Contemporary Art, Chicago

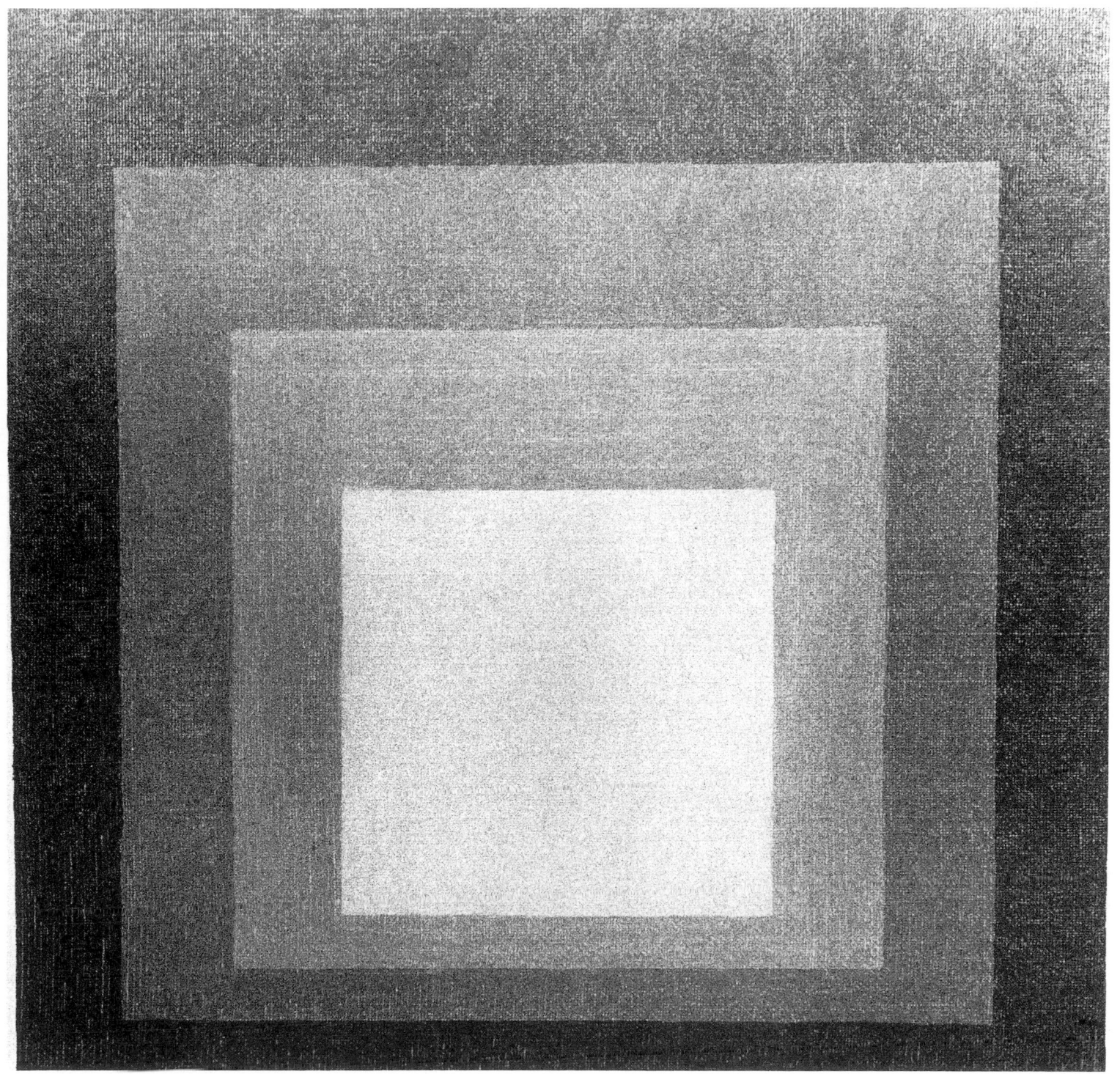

Gallery of Modern Art, Washington, D.C.
Museum of Modern Art, New York (toured South America, Mexico and the United States, 1965–67)
1968 Landesmuseum, Münster, West Germany (toured Germany and Switzerland, 1968–69)
Sidney Janis Gallery, New York
Galerie Denise René, Paris
1969 Kestner Gesellschaft, Hannover
Sonia Henie-Niels Onstad Foundation, Oslo
1970 Sidney Janis Gallery, New York
Kunsthalle, Hamburg
Kunstverein, Munich
Städtische Kunsthalle, Dusseldorf
1971 London Arts Gallery
University Art Museum, Princeton University, New Jersey
Metropolitan Museum of Art, New York
1973 Landesmuseum, Münster, West Germany
Kestner Gesellschaft, Hannover
Galerie Beyeler, Basle
Kunsthaus, Zurich
Galerie Gmurzynska, Cologne
Galerie Melki, Paris
Heslington Hall, York University, England
1976 Busch-Reisinger Museum, Harvard University, Cambridge, Massachusetts
1980 Galerie Christel, Stockholm
1981 Montclair Art Museum, New Jersey
1983 Josef Albers Museum, Bottrop, West Germany
1984 Sidney Janis Gallery, New York
1986 Galerie Teufel, Cologne
Sidney Janis Gallery, New York
1987 Galeria Theo, Madrid

Group Exhibitions:

1929 *Bauhaus Masters*, Kunsthalle, Basle (travelled to the Kunsthalle, Zurich)
1939 *American Abstract Artists*, Riverside Museum, New York
1951 *Contemporary American Painting*, University of Illinois, Champaign
1962 *Geometric Abstraction in America*, Whitney Museum, New York
1965 *The Responsive Eye*, Museum of Modern Art, New York
1967 *2 Decades of American Painting*, Museum of Modern Art, New York (toured Japan, India and Australia)
1972 *Geometric Abstraction 1926–42*, Museum of Fine Art, Dallas
1973 *Futurism: A Modern Focus*, Guggenheim Museum, New York
1983 *Modern Art in the West*, Metropolitan Art Museum, Tokyo
1986 *Seven Artists in Depth: The Creative Process*, San Francisco Museum of Modern Art

Collections:

Metropolitan Museum of Art, New York; Guggenheim Museum, New York; Museum of Modern Art, New York; Museum des 20. Jahrhunderts, Vienna; Centre Georges Pompidou, Paris; Bauhaus Archiv, Darmstadt; Stedelijk Museum, Amsterdam; Moderna Museet, Stockholm; Kunstmuseum, Basle; Kunsthaus, Zurich.

Publications:

By ALBERS: books—*Zeichnungen: Drawings*, New York 1956; *Poems and Drawings*, New Haven, Connecticut 1958; *Poems and Drawings: Gedichte und Zeichnungen*, New York 1961; *Despite Straight Lines*, New Haven, Connecticut 1961; *The Interaction of Color*, New Haven, Connecticut 1963; *Search Versus Re-Search: 3 Lectures by Josef Albers at Trinity College April 1965*, New Haven, Connecticut 1969; *Formulation: Articulation*, New York 1972; articles—"Werklicher Formunterricht" in *Bauhaus 2*, Dessau, Germany 1928; "Concerning Art Instruction" in *Black Mountain College Bulletin* (Beria, North Carolina), no. 2, 1934; "Modular Brick Wall Partition" in *Art in Modern Architecture* by Eleanor Bitterman, New York 1952; "Homage to the

Square" in *Artnews* (New York), October 1961; "Op Art and/or Perceptual Effects" in the *Yale Scientific Magazine* (New Haven, Connecticut), November 1965; "My Courses at the Hochschule für Gestaltung at Ulm" in *Form* (Opladen, West Germany), no. 4, 1967; "Selected Writings" in *Origin* (Kyoto, Japan), January 1968; statement in *Futurism: A Modern Focus*, exhibition catalogue, New York 1973.

On ALBERS: books—*Staatliches Bauhaus: Weimar 1919-23*, Munich 1923, *Die Kunst des 19. und 20. Jahrhunderts* by Hans Hildebrandt, Potsdam 1924; *Bauhaus 1919–28* by Herbert Bayer and Walter and Ilse Gropius, New York 1938; *Erinnerungen an Sturm und Bauhaus* by Lothar Schreyer, Munich 1956; *Josef Albers, Despite Straight Lines: An Analysis of His Graphic Constructions* by Francois Bucher, New Haven, Connecticut 1961; *The Artist's Voice: Talks with 17 Artists*, New York 1962; *Josef Albers* by Eugen Gomringer, New York 1968; *The Bauhaus: Weimar, Dessau, Berlin, Chicago* by Hans Maria Wingler, Cambridge, Massachusetts 1969; *Josef Albers* by Werner Spies, London 1971; *Josef Albers 1888-1976*, exhibition catalogue with essay by Francois Boucher, Cologne 1986; *Albers*, exhibition catalogue with text by Kelly Feeney, New York 1986.

*

The works of Josef Albers (1888–1976) span much of the 20th century and, although seminal in generating considerable similar output by others, bear unmistakably the stamp of his strong individuality. They are part of his evolving quest for simplicity and understanding. His practical background, son of a Westphalian furniture manufacturer, gave him experience with wood, glass and other construction materials. Indeed, among his numerous interests during his early Bauhaus years was furniture design, where woodgrain and natural whorled patterns were (frustratingly?) bounded and constrained by simple rectangular shapes. His pieces feature studies in contrast (light vs. dark oak, flat-back painted vs. natural wood surfaces), as well as economy of design and rationing of decoration. Perhaps an early portent of his colored squares to come are to be found on an Albers-designed set of four hand-painted glass-topped stacking tables.

Moving from 3-dimensional to 2-dimensional artistry, for a time (1930–1950) his graphics exhibit preoccupation with the contrast between, and the not obviously reconcilable superposition of, grain patterns and geometric designs. Also evident is a struggle between and attempts at fusion of curved boundaries and straight-edged objects. With the eventual rejection of the former, which implies also a disposal of most of the demands for emotional analysis of his productions, Albers' works came to feature primarily the seemingly simple rectangle and square. The realization that even these exhibit intriguing and non-trivial complexities led to a search for simplification, to separation into studies of the effects of geometry and those of color and shading.

Albers' studies of simple lined black and white planar objects led to numerous examples of interactions of lines and of the trickery encountered when the eye views 2-dimensional information and the brain attempts a 3-dimensional interpretation of it. Here, for example, he produced a massive output of interwoven box-figures, each interpretable in multi-variate readings.

Simultaneously his quest for successful analysis and understanding and his long career in teaching led him to study interaction of colors, whereupon he produced a monumental and still much-discussed book on the topic, *The Interaction of Color* (1963). A primary idea was the use of squares of colors to minimize as much as possible the intrusion of shape and of associative, descriptive or emotional context. His celebrated series of hundreds of paintings "Homage to the Square" yields clear examples of what the physical scientist has also come to realize, that scientific method to focus on the simplest possible system is rewarding but has ultimate limitations, in that the surroundings and the presence of the observer can never be completely eliminated. Albers' Squares, and their more elaborate cousins, entitled "Variants," amply demonstrate that identical colors in different settings are perceived to be different by different observers, in different lighting, at different times.

Whatever his final place in art history, Josef Albers was a charming and exciting man; a teacher who felt that "good teaching is more a giving of right questions than a giving of right answers," a lifelong student whose "main concern [was] to remain a student looking for further problems to be solved and working for [his] own development," and an artist who produced superficially impersonal images but images which echoed the pithy quality of his written statements. His aims were simple "My painting is meditative, is restful. . . . I seek no quick effects. . . . You see, this is what I want to create: meditation pictures of the 20th century."

—John A. Weil and John H. Holloway

ALBRIGHT, Ivan (Le Lorraine).

American. Born in North Harvey, Illinois, near Chicago, 20 February 1897. Educated at New Trier High School, Evanston, Illinois, 1911–15; Northwestern University, Evanston, 1915–16; University of Illinois, Urbana, 1916–17; Ecole des Beaux-Arts, Nantes, France, 1919; School of the Art Institute of Chicago, 1920–23, B.F.A. 1923; Pennsylvania Academy of Fine Arts, Philadelphia, 1923; National Academy of Design, New York, 1924. Served in the United States Army, 1917–18: did medical drawings at Base Hospital No. 11, Nantes, France, 1918–19. Married Josephine Medill Patterson Reeve in 1946; children: Adam Medill and Blandina Van Etten. Worked at architectural offices of Dwight Heald Perkin and did color work for advertising at Alfred Pick and Company, Chicago, 1919; independent artist, 1924 until his death in 1983: travelled to Laguna Beach and La Jolla, California, Camelback, Arizona, and Old Laguna, New Mexico, 1924–25; established studio on Cherry Street, Philadelphia, 1925–26; and in Balboa Park, California, 1927; settled in Warrenville, Illinois and established studio (also built twin studios with brother Malvin Marr Albright), 1927–46; spent summers in Maine, 1939–41; worked for Metro-Goldwyn-Mayer film studios painting a portrait for the film *The Picture of Dorian Gray*, Hollywood 1943–44; returned to Chicago in 1946; moved to New England, 1971. Visiting Artist, Dartmouth College, Hanover, New Hampshire 1971–74. Recipient: Temple Gold Medal, Pennsylvania Academy of Fine Arts, Philadelphia, 1942; First Prize and Purchase Prize (refused), *The Artists for Glory Exhibition*, Metropolitan Museum of Art, New York, 1942; Watson F. Blair Prize, Art Institute of Chicago, 1949; Centennial Award, Northwestern University, 1951; Silver Medal, Corcoran *Biennial*, Washington, D.C., 1955; Benjamin Altman Figure Prize, National Academy of Design, 1961; Award, *Dunn International Exhibition*, Beaverbrook Art Gallery, Fredericton, New Brunswick, Canada, 1963; Governor of Vermont Award for Excellence in the Arts, 1975. D.H.L.: Mundelein College, Chicago, 1969; D.F.A.: Lake Forest College, Illinois, 1972, Columbia College, Chicago, 1974, and School of the Art Institute of Chicago, 1977. Associate Academician, 1942, and Academician, 1950, National Academy of Design. Member, National Institute of Arts and Letters, 1957. Agent: Kennedy Galleries, 40 West 57th Street, New York, New York 10019. *Died* (in Woodstock, Vermont) *13 November 1983*.

Individual Exhibitions:

1930 Walden Books Shop, East Walton Place, Chicago
1931 Art Institute of Chicago
1935 Old White Art Gallery, White Sulphur Springs, West Virginia
1945 Associated American Artists Galleries, New York (with Malvin Marr Albright)
1946 Associated American Artists Galleries, Chicago (with Malvin Marr Albright)

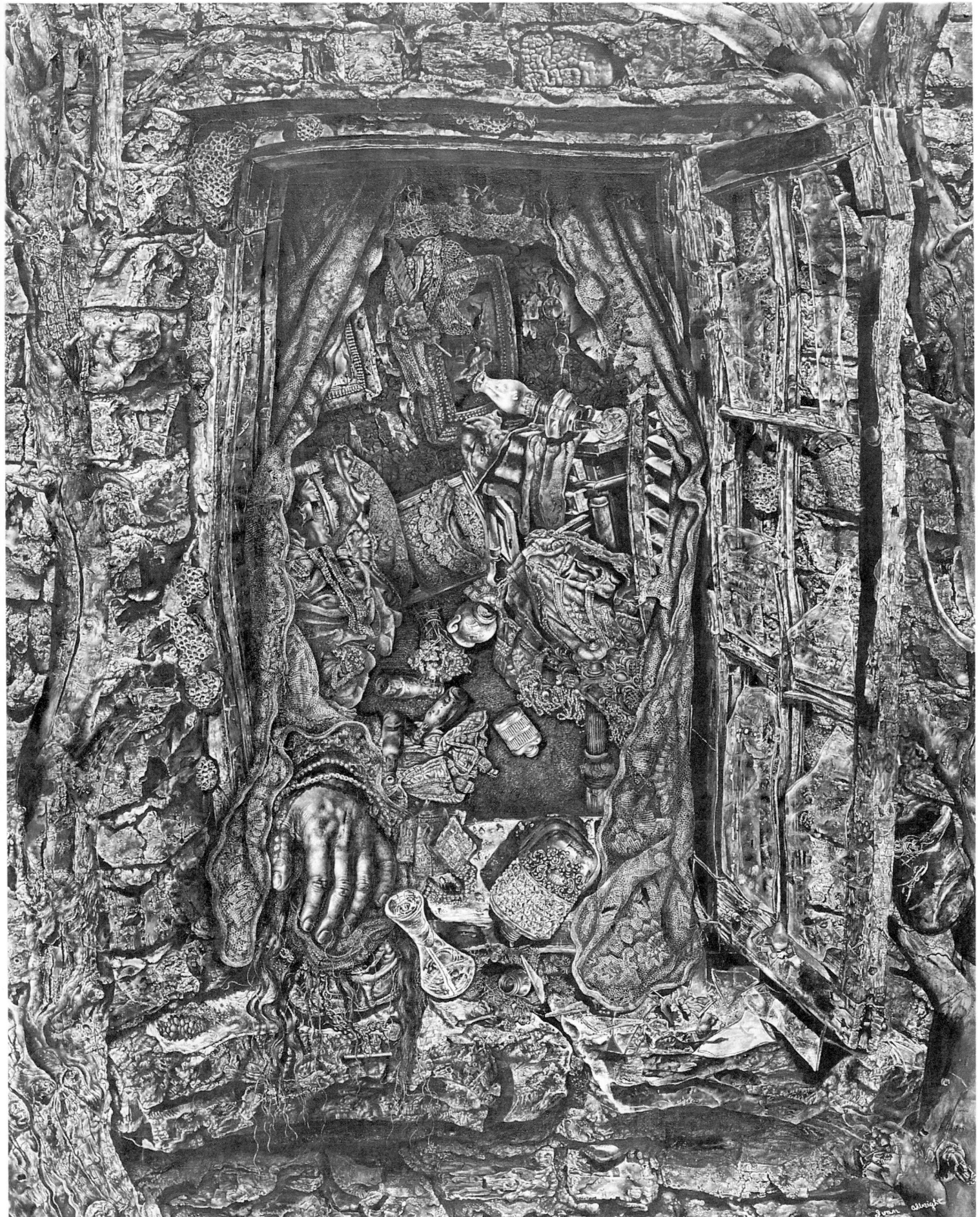

Ivan Albright: *Poor Room . . .*, c. 1961

1964 Roosevelt University, Chicago
      Art Institute of Chicago (retrospective; travelled to
         the Whitney Museum, New York, 1965)
1972 *Medical Drawings,* Galleries of the Renaissance Society, University of Chicago
1975 *Ivan Albright: The Vermont Farmer,* Dartmouth College, Hanover, New Hampshire
1978 Art Institute of Chicago
      Graven Image: The Prints of Ivan Albright 1931–1977, Lake Forest College, Illinois

Selected Group Exhibitions:

1923 *Annual Chicago Exhibition,* Art Institute of Chicago
1926 *Annual American Exhibition,* Art Institute of Chicago
1942 *Artists for Victory,* Metropolitan Museum of Art, New York
1963 *Dunn International Exhibition,* Beaverbrook Arts Gallery, Fredericton, New Brunswick, Canada
1975 *Selected Works from the L. Marshall Pucci Collection,* Mt. Vernon, Illinois

Collections:

Metropolitan Museum of Art, New York; Art Institute of Chicago.

Publications:

By ALBRIGHT: recorded interview—"Interview, Woodstock, Vermont" with Paul Cummings, in *Archives of American Art,* February 1972.

On ALBRIGHT: books—*For Art's Sake* by Adam Emory Albright, Chicago 1953; *The Artist's Voice: Talks with Seventeen Artists,* New York 1962; *American Realists and Magic Realists,* edited by Dorothy C. Miller and Alfred H. Barr, Jr., with statements by artists, and an introduction by Lincoln Kirstein, New York 1963; *Ivan Albright,* exhibition catalogue, by Frederick A. Sweet, with commentary by Jean Dubuffet, Chicago 1964; *Medical Drawings by Ivan Le Lorraine Albright,* exhibition pamphlet, with an introduction by Harold Haydon, Chicago 1972; *Readings in American Art 1900–1975,* edited by Barbara Rose, New York, 1975; *Selected Works from the L. Marshall Pucci Collection,* exhibition catalogue, Mt. Vernon, Illinois 1975; *Graven Image: The Prints of Ivan Albright 1931–1977,* exhibition catalogue, compiled and edited by Gael Grayson, with an introduction by Michael Croydon, Lake Forest, Illinois 1978; *Ivan Albright* by Michael Croydon, New York 1978; film—*Unfinished Portrait of an Artist* by Lester Weinrott, Chicago 1963.

Man is not an individual
Nothing is individual in the world
Man is not a separate identity
Man is a fragment of the whole
Everything in existence makes the whole
The whole is one—and the one includes all
Man cannot be separated from his surroundings
Out doors he is part of the trees the grass the flowers
He is not separate from them—he is part of them
In—doors he is part of the room the window—the door—the chair the table—the fork—the spoon—
All that man sees becomes part of him
There is no separation of parts in the universe
Everything is part of everything else
The whole is one
Man is no more an individual than a blade of grass or a pebble
Man cannot hold onto a minute of time
And life
If life were life there would be no death
There is only light and motion in this world
And they are life
As fragments I am in you and you are in Me
And we are One
And the One is the whole.
          —Ivan Albright(1982)

World wide, Albright may at present still be considered *the* Chicago artist, even as a succession of Chicago artists' groups and individuals have achieved renown since World War II. And Albright's idiosyncratic spirit might be argued as adrift in these more recent artists—of course through primitivizing, Surreal, Pop and abstract modes far removed from his expressionist realism. If he has been a "father figure," then it is not in paint quality or disposition of subject matter, but rather in his life-long absorption with an unhurried pace to produce an utterly personal if not obsessional personal art. Albright's larger works appear as a concretion of his daily life experience in time—e.g. *The Poor Room* (1962) was in his studio for 21 years (and he worked from a full-size model of a brick-surrounded window frame).

Outwardly a cheerful if shy person, Albright's pace came about partially no doubt through his life-patterns. Left a life-long income by the investments of his artist-father (as was also his twin brother Malvin Marr, an exhibiting artist who took the pseudonym 'Zsissley' so that he might be alone at the far end of an exhibition catalog), Albright married only in later middle age. Josephine Reeve was an heiress, daughter of the founder of the *New York Daily News,* and Albright expanded his subject matter to coincide with his new residences in Vermont, Wyoming, and Georgia.

All this anxiety-free existence notwithstanding, ironically there is omnipresent in perhaps all of his large scale work, in both their figures and object-world, a literal depiction of decay—the dissolution of the physicality of matter. (The older U.S. general public may still associate the Albright brothers with a well-publicized episode in Hollywood in 1943 when they painted the images used in a movie version of *The Portrait of Dorian Gray:* audiences shrieked when they were shown). But Albright's profound sense of being alive in time—perhaps with some influence from Cezanne—also moved him to dislocate elements of an image with a slight bend or twist, the more clearly to emphasize personal feeling if not moreso the transiency of art and artist. Because of his absorption with minutiae, and his long involvement with individual works, there is often still found, left over no doubt from older catalogs, his label as Magic Realist. Yet seen close, his surface touch is brusque and whatever optical presence it has, occurs only in smaller scale reproduction.

It may also be said that he practiced—however self-consciously—two manners. In his use of oils, through the layered build-up of paint in his laborious process, the constant touch returning to every part of the canvas, there appears a diminishment of the overt quality of his inherent naivete. (He had a lengthy academic training which concluded at the Pennsylvania Academy of Fine Art, where his father had been a student of Thomas Eakins.) However in his drawings and watercolors, such technique is not possible, and so the halting quality of his attack is more readily revealed. Albright's almost ingenuous earnestness, his yearning for some means to translate his sense of the melancholy immediacy of his perception, is often found in his characteristic statements such as: "After all, there is no sorrow like existence, but the thought of anything existing is so marvelous that I doubt its reality." It is no coincidence that Jean Dubuffet who was very much after some similar quality of existential actuality which would dissolve the abstraction of visual creative process, was deeply moved by Albright's work.

Many of the artist's important works are in the collections of Art Institute of Chicago, donated by Albright himself.

          —Joshua B. Kind

ALECHINSKY, Pierre.
Belgian. Born in Brussels, 19 October 1927. Educated in Brussels, also studied clarinet there; studied book illustration and typography, at the Ecole Nationale Supérieure d'Architecture et des Arts Décoratifs, La Cambre, Brussels, 1944–48, and engraving, under S. W. Hayter, at Atelier 17, Paris 1952. Married Michele (Micky) Dendal in 1949; sons: Ivan and Nicolas. Painter, designer and illustrator, in Brussels, 1947–51, in Paris, since 1951. Member, Jeune Peinture Belge group, Brussels, 1947–51; Founder-Member, Les Ateliers du Marais community studios, Brussels, 1949–51; Founder-Member, with Karel Appel, Corneille, Asger Jorn, Constant, Pedersen, etc., COBRA (Copenhagen-Brussels-Amsterdam) group, 1949–51. Committee Member, October Salon, Paris 1953; Organizer, *Autour de S. W. Hayter* touring exhibition, Amsterdam, Brussels, Copenhagen and Florence, 1953; Member, Management Committee, *Salon du Mai,* Paris, 1958–70; Contributor, *Daily Bul,* La Louvière, Belgium, 1957, and *The Situationist Times* and *La Breche,* Paris 1963. Recipient: Prix Helene Jacquet, La Louvière, 1950; Prix Jeune Peinture Belge, Brussels, 1950; Special Award, *Festival du Film d'Art,* Bergamo, Italy, 1957; Hallmark Prize, New York, 1960; Diploma of Honour, *Festival of Cultural Film,* Tokyo, 1961; First Prize, *Triennale de la Gravure en Belgique,* Brussels 1966; First Prize, *Biennale Internationale de la Gravure,* Cracow 1966; Premio Marzotto, Valdagno, Italy, 1968; Andrew W. Mellon Prize, Carnegie Institute, Pittsburgh, 1976. Agent: Lefebre Gallery, 47 East 77th Street, New York, New York 10021, U.S.A. Address: 2 bis rue Henri Barbusse, 78 Bougival, Paris, France.

Individual Exhibitions:

1947 Galerie Lou Cosyn, Brussels
1948 Galerie Apollo, Brussels
1953 Kunsthandel Martinet, Amsterdam (with Shinkichi Tajiri)
1954 Galleria Schwarz, Milan
      Galerie Nina Dausset, Paris
1955 Palais des Beaux-Arts, Brussels
      Nabis Gallery, Tokyo
1956 Galerie du Dragon, Paris
1957 Galerie Espace, Haarlem, Netherlands
      Galerie Aujourd'hui, Brussels
      Galerie Michael Warren, Paris
1958 Institute of Contemporary Arts, London
1960 Galerie Benador, Geneva
1961 Carnegie Institute, Pittsburgh
      Stedelijk Museum, Amsterdam (with Reinhoud; travelled to the Kunstkring, Rotterdam)
      Galerie Van de Loo, Munich
1962 Galerie de France, Paris
      Lefebre Gallery, New York
1963 Stedelijk Van Abbemuseum, Eindhoven, Netherlands
      Librairie-Galerie La Hune, Paris
      Stedelijk Museum, Amsterdam
      Lefebre Gallery, New York
1964 Galerie Birch, Copenhagen
      Galerie Espace, Amsterdam
      Galleria Il Punto, Turin
      Instituto Torcuato di Tella, Buenos Aires (with Reinhoud)
1965 Lefebre Gallery, New York
      Arts Club of Chicago (travelled to University of Minnesota, Minneapolis; and the Jewish Museum, New York)
1966 Galerie de France, Paris
      Stedelijk Museum, Amsterdam
      Galleria La Medusa, Rome
1967 Museum of Fine Arts, Houston
      Lefebre Gallery, New York
      Librairie-Galerie La Hune, Paris
      Galerie La Balance, Brussels
      20 Jahre Impressionen, Galerie Van de Loo, Munich
1968 Galerie de France, Paris
      Museum voor Schone Kunsten, Ghent
      Staatliche Kunstgalerie, Bochum, West Germany (travelled to the Kunstverein, Freiburg)

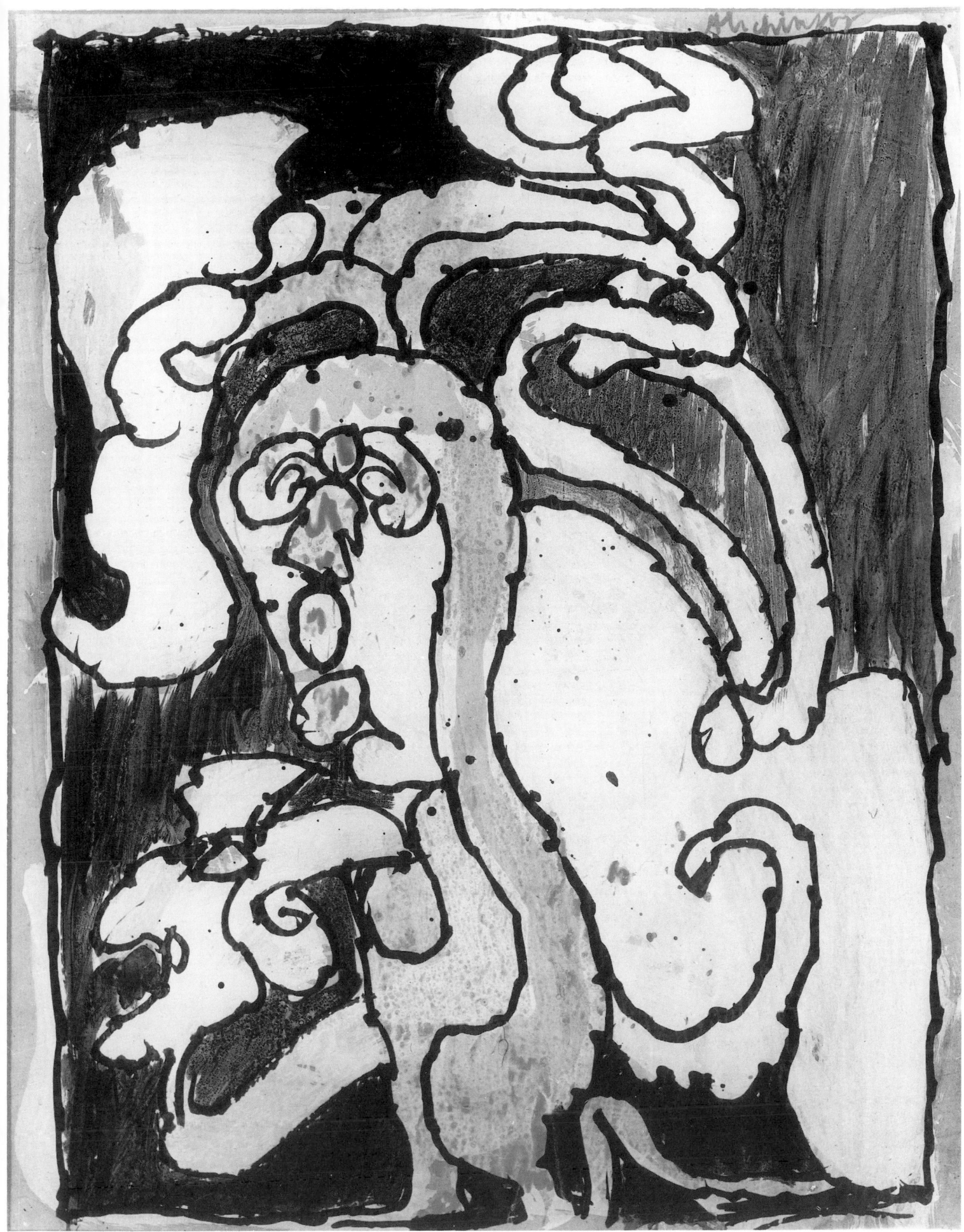

Pierre Alechinsky: *Monsieur Hune*, 1974

Galerie Birch, Copenhagen
Lefebre Gallery, New York
Galleri Moderne, Silkeborg, Denmark
APIAW, Liège, Belgium
Kaleidoscoop Galerie, Ghent
1969 Palais des Beaux-Arts, Brussels
Louisiana Museum, Humlebaek, Denmark
Kunstverein, Dusseldorf
Kunsthalle, Bremen, West Germany
Galerie La Taille Douce, Brussels
International School, Brussels
Dom Galerie, Cologne
Nielsen Gallery, Boston
Galerie de Montreal
J. L. Hudson Gallery, Detroit
1970 London Arts Gallery, London
Librairie-Galerie La Hune, Paris
Israel Museum, Jerusalem
Galleria Rotta, Milan
Lefebre Gallery, New York
Galerie Birch, Copenhagen
Chez Stephane Janssen, Brussels
1971 Galerie de France, Paris
Galleri Haaken, Oslo
Galerie Espace, Amsterdam
Galerie du Fleuve, Bordeaux
Lens Fine Art, Antwerp
Grand Rapids Art Museum, Michigan (with Reinhoud)
1972 Maison des Jeunes et de la Culture, Annecy, France (toured France)
Lefebre Gallery, New York
Galerie de l'Auditorium, Brussels
Galerie Benador, Geneva
Galerie in der Blutgasse, Vienna
Galleria San Sebastianello, Rome
1973 Lefebre Gallery, New York
Galerie de France, Paris
Galerie Birch, Copenhagen
Galleria del Milione, Milan
Palazzo Municipale, Asolo, Italy
Galerie Vega, Liège, Belgium
Galerie Stephane Janssen, Brussels
Librairie-Galerie La Hune, Paris
Lens Fine Art, Antwerp
Musée d'Art Moderne, Brussels
1974 Le Miroir d'Encre, Brussels
Galerie Espace, Amsterdam
Mathildenhoehe, Darmstadt (toured Europe)
1975 Galerie Birch, Copenhagen
Galeria Turner, Madrid
Galeria 42, Barcelona
Musée Cantini Marseilles
Galerie Van de Loo, Munich
Galerie Stephane Janssen, Basle
Librairie-Galerie La Hune, Paris
Graphica Club, Milan
1976 Lefebre Gallery, New York
Maison de la Culture, Chalon-sur-Saône, France (toured Europe)
Galeria Aele, Madrid
Galerie Birch, Copenhagen
La Maison Bleue, Strasbourg
1977 Galerie Fleuve Trois, Bordeaux
Galeria Aele, Madrid
Herzog Galerie, Orleans, France
Galeria Ponce, Madrid
Halifax University, Nova Scotia
Le Miroir d'Encre, Brussels
Galerie de France, Paris (with Reinhoud)
Paintings and Writings, Carnegie Institute, Pittsburgh (retrospective; travelled to the Art Gallery of Ontario, Toronto)
Lens Fine Art, Antwerp
Lefebre Gallery, New York
Riis Gallery, Trondheim, Norway
Librairie-Galerie La Hune, Paris
1978 *Les Dessins d'Alechinsky*, Centre Georges Pompidou, Paris
Galerie de France, Paris (with Karel Appel; toured Europe)
Galerie Van de Loo, Munich (travelled to Galerie Rolf Ohse, Bremen)

1979 Lefebre Gallery, New York
Le Miroir d'Encre, Brussels
1980 Museo de Arte Moderno, Mexico City
Galerie Maeght, Paris
Galerie Maeght, Zurich
Kaneko Gallery, Tokyo
Kestner-Gesellschaft, Hannover (retrospective)
Museum of Modern Art, New York (print retrospective)
1981 Lefebre Gallery, New York
1982 Galerie Moderne, Silkeborg, Denmark
Galerie Birch, Copenhagen
1983 Galerie M, Hannover
1984 Kaneko Art Gallery, Tokyo
Lefebre Gallery, New York
Galerie Maeght Lelong, Paris
1985 Galerie Le Mejan, Arles, France
Galerie Birch, Copenhagen
Gand Gallery, Seoul, Korea
Musée d'Art et d'Histoire, Metz, France
Galerie Van de Loo, Munich
1986 Lefebre Gallery, New York
Artcurial, Paris
Galerie La Hune, Paris
Galerie Maeght Lelong, Paris
1987 Lefebre Gallery, New York
Isselbacher Gallery, New York
Guggenheim Museum, New York

Selected Group Exhibitions:

1948 *Les Mains Eblouies*, Galerie Maeght, Paris
1949 *Cobra: 1st Exhibition of Experimental Art*, Stedelijk Museum, Amsterdam
1959 *European Art Today*, Minneapolis Institute of Art
1968 *Painting in France 1900–1967*, National Gallery of Art, Washington, D.C. (toured the United States)
1976 *Daily Bul & Co.*, Fondation Maeght, St. Paul de Vence, France (travelled to Studio du Passage 44, Brussels)
1978 *Cobra 1948–78*, Statens Museum for Konst, Copenhagen
1980 *L'Affiche en Belgique*, Musée d'Affiche, Paris
1983 *Informele Kunst 1945–60*, Rijksmuseum Twenthe, Enschede, Netherlands
1985 *Painterly Visions 1945–85*, Guggenheim Museum, New York
1987 *Galerie Espace 1956–86*, Galerie Espace, Amsterdam

Collections:

Musées Royaux des Beaux-Arts de Belgique, Brussels; Centre Georges Pompidou, Paris; Stedelijk Museum, Amsterdam; Museum der Stadt, Darmstadt,; Galleria Nazionale d'Arte Moderna, Rome; Guggenheim Museum, New York; Museum of Modern Art, New York; Carnegie Institute, Pittsburgh; Musée d'Art Contemporain, Montreal, Quebec; Israel Museum, Jerusalem.

Publications:

By ALECHINSKY: books and portfolios—*Trades*, 9 etchings, with text by Luc de Heusch, Brussels 1948; *Les Poupées de Dixmunde*, Brussels 1950; *Bites*, etchings portfolio, Milan 1962; *Titres et Pains Perdus*, Paris 1965; *Ideotraces*, Paris 1966; *Le Test du Titre*, Paris 1967; *Minutes*, Venice 1967; *Indivisible Prints*, with Arman, text by Joyce Mansour, London 1969; *Vulcanologies*, lithos portfolio, Paris 1970; *Roue Libre*, Geneva 1971; *L'Avenir de la Propriété*, Paris and Geneva 1972; *Les Estampes: Pierre Alechinsky 1946– 1972*, Paris 1972; *Krach*, engravings portfolio, Paris 1973; *Au Fil du Bois*, woodcuts portfolio, Paris 1973; *Blindly*, etchings portfolio, Rome 1974; *Serpent*, engravings portfolio, Paris 1977; *Far Rockaway*, Montpellier 1977; *Monument Tobacco*, with text by Marcel and Gabriel Piqueray, Paris 1978; *Encres à Deux Pinceaux*, with Karel Appel, text by Hugo Claus, Paris 1978; *Papiers Traites*, 6 lithographs, Paris 1978; *La Vie comme elle Tourne*, drawings portfolio, with text by André Frenaud, Paris 1979; books illustrated—*Le Sens des Tarots* by Marcel Lecomte, Brussels 1948; *Zonder Vorm van Proces* by Hugo Claus, Brussels 1950; *La Reine des Murs* by Christian Dotremont, Paris 1960; *Les Tireurs de Lange* by Amos

Kenan, Turin 1961; *Moi Qui J'Avais* by Christian Dotremont, Paris 1961; *A la Gare* by Amos Kenan, Milan 1962; *One Cent Life* by Walasse Ting, Zurich 1964; *Carre Blanc* by Joyce Mansour, Paris 1965; *De la Mort* by Francois Nourissier, Brussels 1967; *Le Bleu des Fonds* by Joyce Mansour, Paris 1968; *Tourmente* by Michel Butor, with Bernard Dufour and Jacques Herold, Montpellier 1968; *Au Demeurant* by Achille Chavee, La Louvière, Belgium 1969; *Hoire-Voirie* by Michel Butor, Milan 1970; *Pointes* by Louis Scutenaire, Paris 1972; *Laborinthe* by Jean-Clarence Lambert, Paris 1973; *Un Mannequin sur le Trottoir* by Roger Caillois, Paris 1974; *Reve de l'Ammonite* by Michel Butor, Montpellier 1975; *Par Experience* by Yves Bonnefoy, Paris 1976; *Vacillations* by A. M. Cloran, Montpellier 1980; film—*Japanese Calligraphy*, with Francis Haar, Roger Blin and others, 1956.

On ALECHINSKY: books—*The COBRA Library: Alechinsky* by Luc de Heusch, Copenhagen 1950; *Ink* by Jean Cleinge, Paris 1963; *Pierre Alechinsky: 20 Jahre Impressionen*, exhibition catalogue, Munich 1967; *Alechinsky* by Jacques Putman, Milan and Paris 1967; *Alechinsky* by Alain Bosquet, Paris 1971; *Alechinsky à la Ligne: catalogue raisonne*, edited by Yves Riviere, Paris 1973; *Pierre Alechinsky*, exhibition catalogue, with text by Bernd Krimmel, Darmstadt 1974; *Kunstpocket no. 3: Alechinsky* by Freddy de Vree, Schelderode 1976; *Pierre Alechinsky: Paintings and Writings*, exhibition catalogue, with texts by Leon A. Arkus and Eugene Ionesco, Pittsburgh 1977; *Les Dessins d'Alechinsky*, exhibition catalogue, with text by Pierre Georgel, Paris 1978; *Pierre Alechinsky eine retrospektive*, exhibition catalogue, with text by Carl Haenlein, Hannover 1980; *Pierre Alechinsky: Bouches et Grilles*, exhibition catalogue with essay by Pierre Descargues, Paris 1986; *Pierre Alechinsky: Margin and Centre*, exhibition catalogue with texts by Michael Gibson and Octavio Paz, New York 1987.

A great debate has raged for years about what values training at an art school can bestow upon an artist in embryo. Sometimes the experience provides full knowledge of useful techniques, sometimes the bonus amounts to little more than the chance to take advantage of important contacts that will reduce the teething pains of starting an art career.

Pierre Alechinsky belongs to the first category. At the Ecole Nationale Supérieure d'Architecture et des Arts Décoratifs in Brussels he mastered "book illustration" which involves wide knowledge and experience of all kinds of graphic printing, including typography.

Today he is recognized as one of the prime graphic artists. As early as 1948 he was able to design a set of tarot cards for the Belgian surrealist Marcel Lecomte and he also made the pictures for "Les Metiers" by Luc de Heusch.

In Paris Alechinsky made contact with the surrealist movement through Max Ernst. He was also recognized by Dubuffet who saw in his works a flavour of *Art Brut*.

In 1949 he joined the COBRA group with Appel, Corneille, Constant, Dotremont, Jorn and Pedersen, and a few years later he went to work at S. W. Hayter's Atelier 17 in order to still further improve his graphic techniques. But perhaps the greatest influence he received came when he visited Japan (1955) and made a careful and professional study of the art of that country, particularly as it applied to the printed image and to calligraphy (about which he made a prize-winning film).

It is tempting to concentrate upon his graphic works because of his confident expertise in this wide field, but it should not be overlooked that Alechinsky is a good painter and an attractive collagist.

In all his works he retains his own version of COBRA imagery. Strange beasts, strange people, strange flowers; but he is also adept in the storytelling which inspires his own fantasy comicstrips—a genre he exploits both in his painting and in his prints. Good examples of this narrative painting are found in large canvases like "The Voyeur Seen," "Stars and Disasters" and "Central Park".

Whilst his colours are not those of Jorn or Appel, and certainly not those of Pedersen, they are rich with COBRA tints and toning. The rusts and cerulean blues are particularly appealing. But, as with every painting, there is always more than just the colour scheme. Alechinsky's imagery, whether solid or in line, has a rangy-ness that makes the eye restless, makes it search for inner meanings. The composition also arouses this tatters-in-the-wind sensation (when it is not volcanic). Even so, his early experience as an illustrator has given him a well-defined sense of balance.

—Sheldon Williams

ALLEN, Terry.

American. Born in Wichita, Kansas, 7 May 1943; raised in Lubbock, Texas. Studied at Chouinard Art Institute, Los Angeles, B.F.A. 1966. Independent artist since 1968, working in a wide variety of modes including musical and theatrical performance, sculpture, painting and video. Taught drawing classes at Chouinard Art Institute, Los Angeles, 1968–69; Guest Artist, University of California at Berkeley, 1971; on faculty of California State University at Fresno, 1971–79. Recipient: National Endowment for the Arts Fellowship, 1972, 1979; Guggenheim Fellowship, New York, 1986; Bessie Award, New York, 1986. Agent: Wanda Hansen, 615 Main Street, Sausalito, California 94965. Address: 735 East Fedora, Fresno, California 93704, U.S.A.

Individual Exhibitions:

1966   Gallery 66, Los Angeles
1968   Michael Walls Gallery, San Francisco

Terry Allen: *The Magic Kingdom*, 1986

        Pasadena Art Museum, California
1970 Michael Walls Gallery, San Francisco
1971 Mizuno Gallery, Los Angeles
        Museum of Contemporary Art, Chicago
1973 Michael Walls Gallery, Los Angeles
1974 Michael Walls Gallery, New York
1975 *Juarez Series*, Contemporary Art Museum, Houston
1976 Claire S. Copley Gallery, Los Angeles
        Morgan Art Gallery, Kansas City, Kansas
1978 Hansen-Fuller Gallery, San Francisco
        Nancy Lurie Gallery, Chicago
        Landfall Press Gallery, Chicago
1979 Lubbock Lights Gallery, Texas
        Morgan Art Gallery, Kansas City, Kansas
        Miami-Dade Community College, Florida
1980 Baxter Art Gallery, California Institute of Technology, Pasadena
1981 Portland Center for the Visual Arts, Oregon
        Ring, Nelson Gallery/Atkins Museum, Kansas City, Missouri
        The Southern Voice: Terry Allen, Vernon Fisher, Ed McGowin, Fort Worth Art Museum, Texas
1983 *Rooms and Stories*, La Jolla Museum of Contemporary Art, California
        University of California, San Diego
        Morgan Art Gallery, Kansas City, Missouri
1984 *Sprawl/Prowl/Growl*, Espace Lyonnais d'Art Contemporain, Lyon, France
        Barbara Gladstone Gallery, New York
1985 Betty Moody Gallery, Houston
        China Night, Fresno Art Center, California
1986 *Revelations*, Southwest Center for Arts and Crafts, San Antonio, Texas
        Ohio, Wright State University, Dayton, Ohio
        John Weber Gallery, New York
        Gallery Paule Anglim, San Francisco
1988 L. A. Louver Gallery, Venice, California
        Santa Barbara Contemporary Arts Forum, California

        Pittsburgh Center for the Arts, Pennsylvania
        Moore College of Art, Philadelphia
        Institute of Contemporary Arts, Boston
        Madison Art Center, Wisconsin
        Gallery Paule Anglim, San Francisco

Selected performances: plays and occurrences—*Dialogues in Drag . . . a Satire*, Lucille Street Theatre, Los Angeles, 1968; *The 20th Century Pronto, Arrived*, Lucille Street Theatre, Los Angeles, 1968; *The Levels* (performance for Robert Irwin), University of California at Berkeley, 1970; *The Embrace . . . Advanced to Fury*, Spinoza Arena/Theatre, Houston, 1978; *Anterabbit Bleeder (a biography)*, La Jolla Museum of Contemporary Art, 1983; *Face to Face/Back to Back*, California State University, Fullerton, 1984; *Pedal Steel*, Brooklyn Academy of Music, New York, 1985; *Leonce and Lena*, Walker Art Center, Minneapolis, 1987; music—since 1964, Allen has made numerous appearances as a solo performer in both country and western music venues and in galleries and museums; since 1978 he has frequently appeared with the Panhandle Mystery Band.

Selected Group Exhibitions:

1973 *Extraordinary Realities*, Whitney Museum, New York
1976 *The Great American Rodeo Show*, Fort Worth Art Museum, Texas
        Painting and Sculpture in California: The Modern Era, San Francisco Museum of Modern Art (travelled to the National Collection of Fine Arts, Smithsonian Institution, Washington, D.C.).
1977 *10th Biennale de Paris*
        The Record as Artwork, Fort Worth Art Museum, Texas (toured the United States and Canada)
1979 *Image & Object in Contemporary Sculpture*, Detroit Institute of Arts (travelled to P.S. 1, New York)

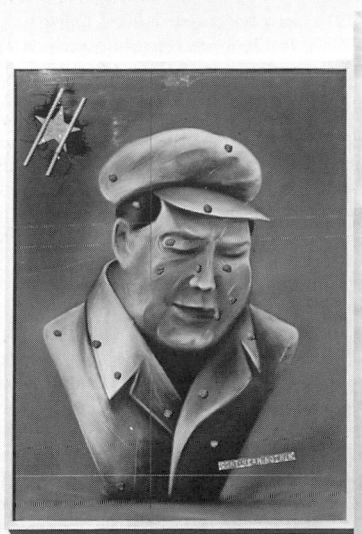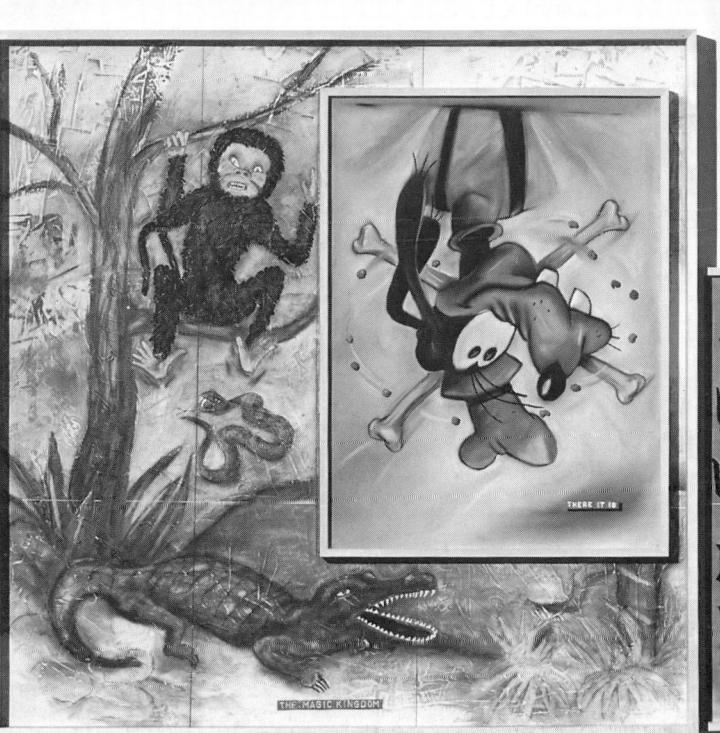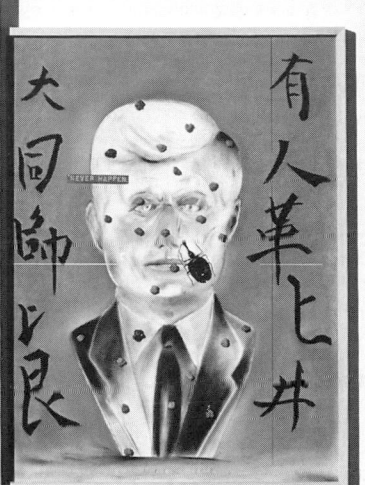

1982   *Sydney Biennale*, Art Gallery of New South Wales, Australia
1984   *Content: A Contemporary Focus 1978–84*, Hirshhorn Museum, Washington, D.C.
1986   *The Texas Landscape 1900–86*, Museum of Fine Arts, Houston
1987   *Avant Garde in the Eighties*, Los Angeles County Museum of Art

Collections:

Museum of Modern Art, New York; Fort Worth Art Museum, Texas; Detroit Institute of Arts; University Art Museum, Berkeley, California; Nelson Gallery/Atkins Museum, Kansas City, Missouri; La Jolla Museum of Contemporary Art, California; The Stuart Collection, La Jolla California; Los Angeles County Museum of Art; Metropolitan Museum of Art, New York.

Publications:

By ALLEN: books—*China Night*, with Roxy Gordon, Fresno, California 1985; *Terry Allen's "Ohio"*, with essay by Dave Hickey, Dayton, Ohio 1986; recordings—"Gonna California" and "Color Book" (single), Bale Creek Records, Los Angeles 1968; *Juarez* (album), Landfall Press, Chicago 1975 (re-released by Fate Records, Chicago 1980); *Lubbock (on everything)* (album), Fate Records, Chicago 1978; "Cajun Roll" and "Whatever Happened to Jesus (and Maybeline)?" (single), Fate Records, Chicago 1979; *Smokin the Dummy* (album), Fate Records, Chicago 1980; "The Arizona Spiritual" (single), 1983; *Bloodlines* (album), 1984; "Cocktail Desperado" (single), 1986.

On ALLEN: books—*Juarez Series: Terry Allen*, exhibition catalogue, by Paul Shimmel, Michael Walls and Dave Hickey, Houston 1975; *Performance Anthology*, edited by Carl Loeffler and Darlene Tong, San Francisco 1980; *Ring: Terry Allen*, exhibition catalogue, by Marcia Tucker and Sherry Cromwell-Lacy, Kansas City, Missouri 1981; *Rooms and Stories by Terry Allen*, exhibition catalogue, by Dave Hickey, Robert McDonald and Lynda Forsha, La Jolla, California 1983; *Sprawl/Prowl/Growl: A Geographic Survey of Works by Terry Allen* by Thierry Raspail, Marcia Tucker and others, Lyon, France 1984; *Terry Allen: Visual and Aural Mythologies* by Ron Gleason and Val Greenfield, Calgary, Alberta 1985; *KaChina Night* by Craig Adcock, Tallahassee, Florida 1986; articles—"Earthscapes, Landworks and Oz" by Dave Hickey in *Art in America* (New York), September/October 1971; "The Ironic L.A. Artist" by Sandy Ballatore in *Artweek* (Oakland, California), 2 November 1974; "Terry Allen's C & W Imagery at CAM" by Charlotte Moser in the *Houston Chronicle*, 16 November 1975; "The Art of Terry Allen: A Personal Evaluation" by Claire Copley in *Journal* (Los Angeles), October/November 1976; "Terry Allen's Narratives" by Robert McDonald in *Artweek* (Oakland, California), 22 April 1978; "Wrestling with Human Relationships" by Janice Ross in *Artweek* (Oakland, California), 4 November 1978; "Objecting to Image" by Kay Larson in the *Village Voice* (New York), 14 January 1980; "Dallas/Ft. Worth You Can Go Home Again" by Janet Kutner in *Artnews* (New York), December 1981; "West Texas Dada" by Jonathan Crary in *Art in America* (New York), September 1983; "Terry Allen: The Return of Vietnam" by Gregory Galligan in *Arts Magazine* (New York), April 1987.

Terry Allen is a musician and songwriter, storyteller and visual artist hailing from none other than Lubbock, Texas. Though he's spent most of his adult life in southern California, he retains his "southernness" most obviously in his compositions (a little rock 'n roll, a little country western) which tell the tale of waitresses, truckers, mobile home life, card playing and drinking whiskey on their own down home surface. It is underneath the surface, however, that Allen's writing as well as his visuals become more dense, more circuitous. In his visual art of every conceivable medium, all of the above ambitions fuse to create cryptic narratives which meander somewhat autobiographically around the conflicts and passages of his heroes and heroines.

The installations themselves combine such dramas as murder, denial, anger, love, alcoholism and confusion (to name very few) which are represented by an odd assortment of everyday objects doubling as loaded symbols which address his perplexing soap operas. Crows, playing cards, male and female silhouettes, high heels, books and rocks combine with an infinite array of materials ranging from live birds to typewritten notes to videotape and much, much more. The viewer, inevitably disoriented by these intricate tales must tug at and dig through each revolving metaphor to cull out whatever drama may reside in these abstruse worlds of passion and intrigue.

Like a scavenger, the viewer picks and pulls at details both visual and "verbal" which are certainly no exercise in futility, lead to no plot and no resolution. But Allen is more than merely a perpetrator of tricky labyrinths. His circular stories catapult the viewer into a world which defines the very stuff they're made of. Each phrase, while leading into another, also confirms or denies its own identity within the context of the myth as a whole and the separate components which reveal it. There is so much happening in Allen's work at any given moment that it is difficult to assign any specific or literal "meaning" to it.

Perhaps his most renowned piece, "Ring" is a four-section, four year work of individual but ideologically connected installations, a videotape (theatre occurrence, as Allen would say) written by Allen (he does not perform in these) and several smaller pieces. The installations ("The Evening Gorgeous George Died" and "Messages from Wrestlers in Hell") include both two and three dimensional elements as well as varying typewritten narratives which partially illuminate an obscure relationship between the stars, HE and SHE. Intricate details of these participants' lives are revealed through their discussions of marriage, drinking, affairs and fantasies. Though these characters lead and acknowledge their complex existences as more than simple fictions, they remain only shadows on the wall—emblems of Allen's ruminations and not their own. Their identity is that of mythical situations rather than actual folks.

Clearly, in his work, Allen develops a mysterious dialogue in which the skeletons of a private saga are uncloaked for us all. But still, we must excavate the obscure threads with which these tales are woven to reveal the humour, intensity and reality of their games.

—Janet Goleas

ANDERSON, Laurie.
American. Born in Wayne, Illinois, in 1942. Educated at Barnard College, New York, B.A. 1969 (magna cum laude with honors in art history; Phi Beta Kappa); studied sculpture at Columbia University, New York, M.F.A. 1972. Performance artist, New York, since 1972. Instructor in art history, City College, New York, 1973–75. Recipient: New York State Council on the Arts grant, 1974, 1977; National Endowment for the Arts grant, 1974, 1977, 1979; Villager Award, 1981. Honorary doctorate: San Francisco Art Institute, 1980; Guggenheim Fellowship, New York, 1983. Agent (for visual works): Holly Solomon Gallery Inc., 724 Fifth Avenue, New York, New York 10019. Address: 530 Canal Street, New York New York 10013, U.S.A.

Individual Exhibitions:

1970   Barnard College, New York
1973   Harold Rivkin Gallery, Washington, D.C.
1974   Artists Space, New York
1977   Holly Solomon Gallery, New York
       Hopkins Center, Dartmouth College, Hanover, New Hampshire
1978   And/Or Gallery, Seattle
       Projects Gallery, Museum of Modern Art, New York
       Matrix Gallery, Hartford Atheneum, Connecticut

1979   University of California Art Museum, Berkeley
1980   *Dark Dogs, American Dreams*, Holly Solomon Gallery, New York
1981   *Scenes from 'United States,'* Holly Solomon Gallery, New York
1982   *Retrospective*, Institute of Contemporary Arts, London
1983   Institute of Contemporary Art, Philadelphia (travelled to Los Angeles; Houston; Flushing, New York)
1984   Laforet Museum, Akasaka, Tokyo
       Nihon Seinehkau, Tokyo
       Sankei Hall, Osaka, Japan
       Kyoto Kaikan, Tokyo

Performances: *Automotive*, Town Green, Rochester, Vermont, 1972; *O-Range*, Lewisohn Stadium, City College of New York, 1973; Artists Space, New York, 1974; The Clocktower, Institute for Urban Resources, New York, 1974; Projects Gallery, Boston, 1974; *Duets on Ice*, 5 New York City locations, 1974; *How to Yodel*, The Kitchen, New York, 1974; music, Whitney Museum Downtown Branch, New York, 1975; *Songs and Stories for the Insomniac*, Artists Space, New York, 1975; *Songs and Stories for the Insomniac . . . Continued*, Oberlin College, Ohio, 1975; *Out of the Blue*, University of Massachusetts, Amherst, 1975; *Dearreader*, Holly Solomon Gallery, New York, 1975; *Dearreader-2*, Sarah Lawrence College, Bronxville, New York, 1975; *Dearreader-3*, Rhode Island School of Design, Providence, Rhode Island, 1975; From *"For Instants,"* Whitney Museum, New York, 1976; From *"For Instants,"* Brockport College, New York, 1976; *Fast Food*, Artist Space, New York, 1976; From *"For Instants,"* Skidmore College, Saratoga, New York, 1976; From *"For Instants 3,"* Philadelphia College of Art, 1976; From *"For Instants,"* California Institute of the Arts, Valencia, 1976; From *"For Instants-4,"* University of California at San Diego, 1976; From *"For Instants-4,"* Museum of Contemporary Art, La Jolla, California, 1976; *Stereo Stories*, M. L. D'Arc Gallery, New York, 1976; *Engli-SH*, Akademie der Kunst, Berlin, 1976; *Engli-SH*, Louisiana Museum, Humlebaek, Denmark, 1976; *Road Songs*, St. Mark's Poetry Center, New York 1976; *Songs*, New School, New York, 1976; *For Instants-5: Songs for Lines, Songs for Waves*, The Kitchen, New York, 1977; *Audio Talk*, School of Visual Arts, New York, 1977; De Appel, Amsterdam, 1977; From *"For Instants,"* at Arte Fiera, Bologna, 1977; *Some Songs*, International Cultural Center, Brussels, 1977; *That's Not the Way I Heard It*, at Documenta, Kassel, West Germany, 1977; *On Dit*, at the *Biennale*, Paris, 1977; *That's Not the Way I Heard It-2*, Galleria Salvatore Ala, Milan, 1977; *For Instants—Continued*, Otis Art Gallery, Los Angeles, 1978; *Some Songs*, And/Or Gallery, Seattle, 1978; *Like a Stream*, The Kitchen, New York, 1978; reading, The Ear Inn, New York; *Like a Stream-3*, with St. Paul Chamber Orchestra, at Walker Art Center, Minneapolis, 1978; *Down Here*, Texas Opry House, Houston (sponsored by Contemporary Art Museum, Houston), 1978; *Some Songs*, Mills College, Oakland, California, 1978; *Some Songs-2*, Portland Center for the Visual Arts, Oregon, 1978; *For Instants-6*, DC Space, Washington, D.C., 1978; *A Few Are . . .* , Art Gallery of Ontario, Toronto, 1978; *Songs for Self-Playing Violin*, Contemporary Art Center, Cincinnati, Ohio, 1978; *Songs for Self-Playing Violin*, Real Art Ways, Hartford, Connecticut, 1978; *Some Are . . .* , benefit for Hallwalls, Buffalo, New York, 1978; *Americans on the Move—Preview*, Carnegie Recital Hall, New York, 1979; *Americans on the Move*, The Kitchen, New York, 1979; at *Theatre of Nations Festival*, Hamburg, 1979; Groningen Museum, Netherlands, 1979; International Cultural Center, Brussels, 1979; Dany Keller Gallery, Munich; Cultural Center, Bonn, 1979; CAPC, Bordeaux, 1979; Stadtparkforum, Graz, Austria, 1979; Modern Art Gallery, Vienna, 1979; Aspen Center for the Visual Arts, Colorado, 1979; *Blue Horn File*, with David van Tieghem and Peter Gordon, Mudd Club, New York, 1979; *Commerce*, with Peter Gordon, U.S. Customs House, New York, 1979; at *Cabrillo Festival*, California, 1979; at *Autumn Festival*, Paris, 1979; at *OGGImusica Festival*, Lugano, Switzerland, 1979; Real Art Ways, Hartford, Connecticut, 1979; San Francisco Art Institute, 1979; Mills College, Oakland, California, 1979; Thorne Hall, Northwestern University, Chicago, 1979; University of Virginia, Richmond, 1979; Glenbow Museum, Calgary, Alberta, 1979; *Für Augen und Ohren*, Akademie der Kunst,

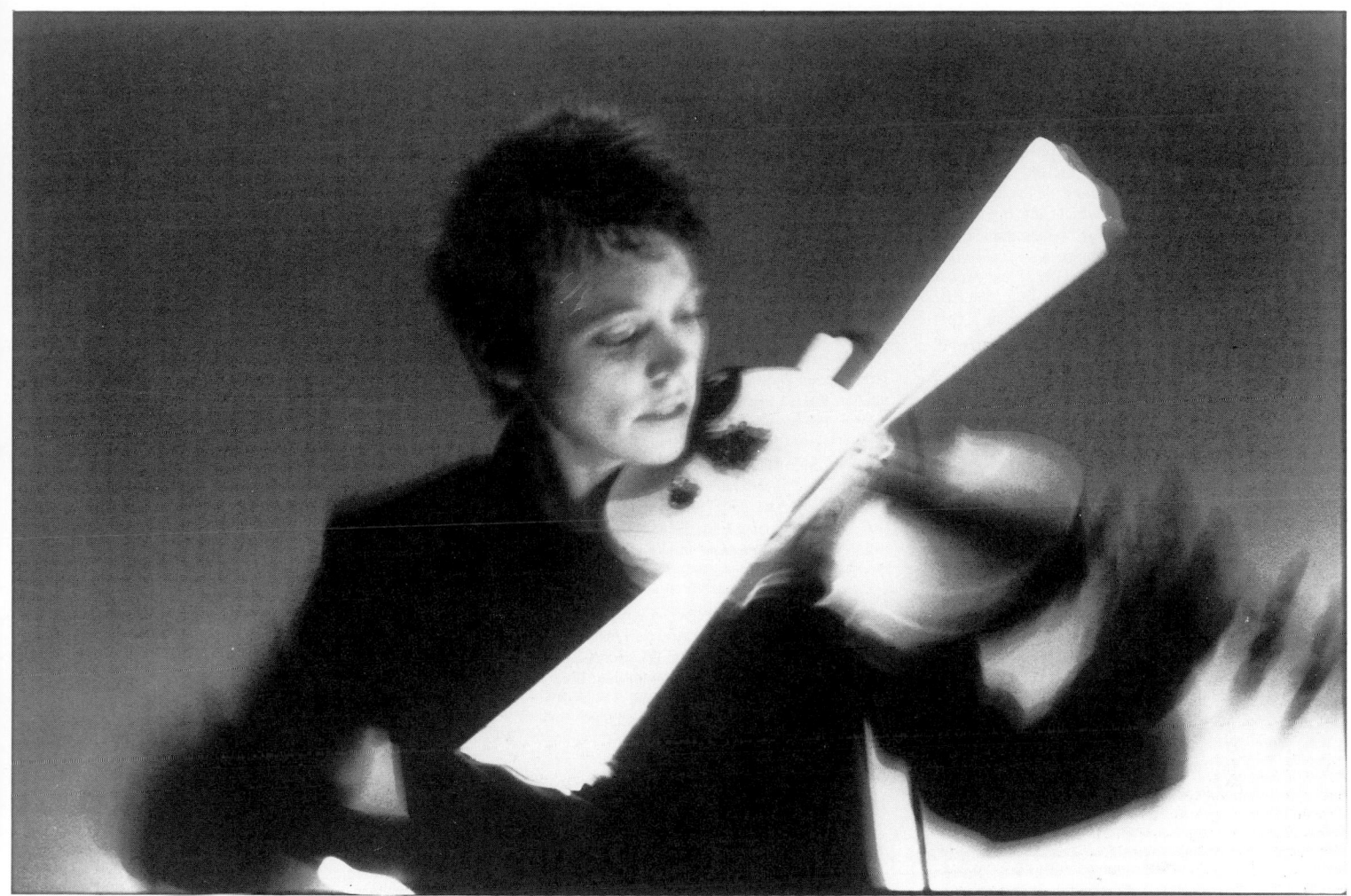

Laurie Anderson photo by Chris Harris

Berlin, 1980; Santa Barbara Museum of Art, California, 1980; at *Per-for-mance Festival*, Florence, 1980; Harvard University, Cambridge, Massachusetts, 1980; at *Rome Performance Festival*, 1980; *New Music America,*Walker Art Center, Minneapolis, 1980; Parachute Magazine Performance Series, Montreal, 1980; University of Northern Iowa, Cedar Falls, 1980; Levande, Gothenburg, Sweden, 1980; Paul Klee Kunstmuseum, Berne, 1980; Kunstmuseum, Zurich, 1980; Mixage International, Rotterdam, 1980; Rust/Roost, Middleburg, Netherlands, 1980; at *ROSC,* Dublin, 1980; Benefit for Volume Magazine, Irving Plaza, New York, 1980; Lenbachhaus, Munich, 1980; Paramount Theatre, with Oakland Youth Symphony, California, 1980; Orpheum Theatre, New York (sponsored by the Kitchen), 1980; Glenbow Museum, Calgary, Alberta, 1981; Western Front, Vancouver, 1981; York University, Toronto, 1981; Kunstmuseum, Basel, 1981; Cirque Divers, Liège, Belgium, 1981; Pension Building, Washington, D.C. (sponsored by DC Space and WPA), 1981; Detroit Institute of Arts, 1981; Institute of Contemporary Art, Philadelphia, 1981; University of California at San Diego, 1981; University of California at Davis, 1981; *Privates,* New York (sponsored by Franklin Furnace), 1981; *Bonds* (sponsored by The Kitchen), New York, 1981; Riverside Studios, London, 1981; Pension Building, Washington, D.C., 1981; *It's Cold Outside,* Alice Tully Hall, New York (commissioned by American Composers Concerts), 1981; *United States,* Moore Theatre, Seattle, 1982; *United States I-IV,* Park West, Chicago (sponsored by the Museum of Contemporary Art, Chicago), 1982; *Mister Heartbreak,* toured the United States, Canada and Japan, 1984–85.

Selected Group Exhibitions:

1973   *Thought Structures*, Pace University, New York
1976   *New Work, New York*, Fine Arts Gallery, California
         State University at Los Angeles

1977   *Surrogates/Self-Portraits*, Holly Solomon Gallery, New York
         Words at Liberty, Museum of Contemporary Art, Chicago
1978   *American Narrative Story Art*, Contemporary Art Museum, Houston (travelled to the University of California Art Museum, Berkeley)
1979   *10 Artists: Artists' Space*, Neuberger Museum, State University of New York at Purchase (travelled to the New Museum, New York)
1980   *Drawings: The Pluralist Decade*, at the *Biennale*, Venice (toured Europe; American version shown at Institute for Contemporary Art, Philadelphia)
1987   *Avant-Garde in the Eighties*, Los Angeles County Museum of Art

Publications:

By ANDERSON: books—*The Package*, New York 1971; *October*, New York 1972; *Transportation Transportation*, New York 1973; *The Rose and the Stone*, New York 1974; *Notebook*, 1976; *Typisch Frau*, Regensburg, West Germany 1981; *Artifacts at the End of a Decade*, with an essay by John Perreault, 1981; articles—"From 'For Instants' " in *Individuals*, edited by Alan Sondheim, New York 1977; "From 'Americans on the Move' " in *October* (New York), Spring 1979; interview, with Robin White, in *View* (Oakland, California), vol. II, no. 8, 1980, "Dark Dogs American Dreams" in *Hotel*, New York 1980; "Laurie Anderson: Interview," with David Sparkman, in *Washington Review*, October/November 1981; films—*14 Americans*, 1979; *Film du Silence*, 1981; records—*It's Not the Bullet That Kills You, It's the Hole*, 1977; *Airwaves*, 1977; *New Music for Electronic and Recorded Media*, 1978; *Big Ego*, 1979; *Walk the Dog, O Superman*, 1981.

On ANDERSON: book—*Variants: Drawings by Contemporary Sculptors*, exhibition catalogue, Houston 1981;

articles—"Laurie Anderson" by Robert Pincus-Witten in *Art Rite* (New York), April 1974; 5–11 November 1980; "Laurie Anderson Grows as a Performance Artist" by John Rockwell in the *New York Times*, 27 October 1980; "Laurie Anderson: American on the Move: Touching, Funny, Vivid, Assured" by Gregory Sandow in the *Village Voice* (New York) 5–11 November 1980; "The United States of Laurie Anderson" in *Soho News* (New York), 5–11 November 1980; "Amplifications: Laurie Anderson" by Craig Owens in *Art in America* (New York), March 1981; "Laurie Anderson: Ephemeral turns Permanent" by Robert Palmer in the *New York Times*, 21 April 1982.

During her art historical training at Barnard College in New York, performance artist Laurie Anderson explored the proliferating critical discourse of the 1970s—the semiological and structuralist theories that formed the basis of Minimal and Conceptual Art. Anderson's early Minimalist sculpture was influenced by Process Art (especially the work of Eve Hesse), an art that questioned the non-objectivity of materials whose intrinsic qualities could elicit a range of psycho-sexual responses and whose installations often created a theatrical effect. The static modernist art object, with its authoritative ideologies that sustained belief in the universality of meaning vested in form, was no longer tenable. Moreover, a Minimalism rooted in phenomenological rather than cultural conditions precluded textual, postmodern and, most importantly, feminist discourse, ideas important to Anderson.

After a number of one-person performances, invariably accompanied by a mechanically enhanced violin, Anderson, beginning with *Americans on the Move* in 1979, enlarged her production. At first, she increased her musical accompaniment to five musicians playing electronic instruments, eventually introducing film and photographic imagery into her performances. In her seven-hour, four-part opus, *United States* ("Transportation," "Politics," "Money" and "Love," 1979-83), the artist transcended the personal and autobiographical tone of her earlier work in favor of a multimedia examination of the social codes and mythologies that pervade popular culture. With *United States*, she arrived at a basic theme in her oeuvre—a questioning of the linguistic and semiological systems by which information is transmitted and received and their concomitant ideologies. In whole or in part based on songs from *United States*, her two albums *Big Science* [1982] and *Mister Heartbreak* [1984]—the latter resulting in an international tour that formed the basis for Anderson's first movie *Home of the Brave* [1986]—allowed Anderson to reach an even larger audience.

Anderson's imagery—generalized depictions of cityscapes, highways and newscasts culled from advertising and the media—is a veritable field of semiotic signs in the form of maps, clocks, airplanes, roads and hands. Such a panoply of urban images is, of course, foreboding, and is aggressively compounded by the use of a cold, corporate voice speaking the demands of "big brother," by a radical plurality of altered voices and characters, and by a constant sense of temporal and geographic dislocation. Further denuding herself of a stable identity through the use of parody and quotation, Anderson acts as an electronic magician who both controls and receives the messages of a technocratic society.

Despite the multitude of technological and theatrical effects, which both augment her performance works and diffuse her personality, the focus rarely shifts from Anderson's finely honed persona. Exchanging the rarified aesthetics of the modernist art object for the temporal and confrontational medium of performance (in an age when the music video was first being launched), Anderson's complex media-driven persona reveals the relative purity of the Minimalist performances of Yvonne Rainer, Robert Morris and Simone Forti. In an age of cultural icons inflated by the media, Anderson presents herself in order to wryly comment on the cultural and textual nature of postmodernism.

—Mason Klein

ANDRE, Carl.

American. Born in Quincy, Massachusetts, 16 September 1935. Educated in Quincy Public Schools, 1941-50; Phillips Academy, Andover, Massachusetts, with Patrick and Maude Morgan, Hollis Frampton, Michael Chapman, Frank Stella and Harry Curtis, 1951-53. Served in the United States Army, in North Carolina, 1955-56. Married Rosemarie Castoro (divorced). Freelance artist. Worked for the Boston Gear Works, Quincy, and travelled in England and France, 1954; moved to New York, 1957; worked as an editorial assistant, New York, 1957-58; freight brakeman and conductor, Pennsylvania Railroad, 1960-64. Member, Art Workers Coalition, New York, 1967-72. Agents: Paula Cooper Inc., 155 Wooster Street, New York, New York 10012; Konrad Fischer, Platanestrasse 7, 4 Dusseldorf, West Germany. Address: Post Office Box 1001, Cooper Station, New York, New York 10003, U.S.A.

Individual Exhibitions:

1965	Tibor de Nagy Gallery, New York
1966	Tibor de Nagy Gallery, New York
1967	Dwan Gallery, New York
	Dwan Gallery, Los Angeles
	Konrad Fischer Gallery, Dusseldorf
1968	Stadtisches Museum, Monchengladbach, West Germany

Heiner Friedrich Gallery, Munich
Wide White Space, Antwerp
Irving Blum Gallery, Los Angeles

1969	Dwan Gallery, New York
	Konrad Fischer Gallery, Dusseldorf
	Wide White Space, Antwerp
	Haagsgemeentemuseum, The Hague
	Galleria Gian Enzo Sperone, Turin
1970	Guggenheim Museum, New York
	Ace Gallery, Los Angeles
1971	St. Louis Art Museum
	Dwan Gallery, New York
	Konrad Fischer Gallery, Dusseldorf
	Locksley-Shea Gallery, Minneapolis
	Galerie Yvon Lambert, Paris
	Wide White Space, Antwerp
	Heiner Friedrich Gallery, Munich
1972	John Weber Gallery, New York
	Konrad Fischer Gallery, Dusseldorf
	Friends of Contemporary Art, Denver
	Janie C. Lee Gallery, Dallas
	Lisson Gallery, London
1973	John Weber Gallery, New York
	Thayer Academy, Braintree, Massachusetts
	Galleria Gian Enzo Sperone, Turin
	Portland Center for the Visual Arts, Oregon
	Addison Gallery, Phillips Academy, Andover, Massachusetts
	Institute for Contemporary Art, Boston
	Museum of Modern Art, New York
	Konrad Fischer Gallery, Dusseldorf
	Max Protetch Gallery, Washington, D.C.
1974	Wide White Space, Antwerp
	Konrad Fischer Gallery, Dusseldorf
	Ace Gallery, Vancouver
1975	Barbara Cusak Gallery, Houston
	Ace Gallery, Vancouver
	Lisson Gallery, London
	Galleria Sperone, Rome
	Sperone Westwater Fischer Gallery, New York
	Dan Weinberg Gallery, San Francisco
	Museum of Modern Art, Oxford
	Sculpture 1958-1974, Kunsthalle, Berne
	John Weber Gallery, New York
1976	Barbara Cusak Gallery, Houston
	John Weber Gallery, New York
	Ace Gallery, Venice, California
	Ace Gallery, Los Angeles
	Konrad Fischer Gallery, Dusseldorf
	Galerie Yvon Lambert, Paris
	Carl Andre/Richard Long/Barry LeVa, Corcoran Gallery, Washington, D.C.
	Davidson Art Center, Wesleyan University, Middletown, Connecticut
	The Clocktower, New York
	Detroit Institute of Arts
	Kabinet für Aktuele Kunst, Bremerhaven, West Germany
	Minneapolis College of Art and Design
1977	Sperone Westwater Fischer Gallery, New York
	Joseloff Gallery, Hartford Art School, Connecticut
	Otis Art Institute, Los Angeles
1978	*Sculpture 1959-1977*, Sperone Westwater Fischer Gallery, New York
	Sculpture 1959-78, Whitechapel Art Gallery, London
	Laguna Gloria Art Museum, Austin, Texas
	Contemporary Arts Center, Cincinnati
	Albright-Knox Art Gallery, Buffalo, New York
	Art Institute of Chicago
1979	La Jolla Museum of Contemporary Art, California
	University of California Art Museum, Berkeley
	Museum of Fine Arts, Dallas
	Musée d'Art Contemporaine, Montreal
	Musée d'Art Moderne de la Ville de Paris
1980	Institute of Contemporary Arts, Boston
	Paula Cooper Gallery, New York
	Lopoukhine Nayduch Gallery, Boston
	David Bellman Gallery, Toronto
	National Gallery of Canada, Ottawa
	Portland State University, Oregon
	Galerie Konrad Fischer, Dusseldorf
1981	Susan Caldwell Gallery, New York

Seagram Plaza, New York
Wurttembergischer Kunstverein, Stuttgart
Anthony D'Offay Gallery, New York
Museum Haus Lange, Krefeld, West Germany
Graeme Murray Gallery, Edinburgh

1982	Susan Caldwell Gallery, New York
	Galerie Konrad Fischer, Dusseldorf
	Alberta College of Art, Calgary
	University of New Mexico, Albuquerque
	Colorado State University, Fort Collins
	University of Wyoming, Laramie
	Galerie Hans Mayer, Basel
	University of Miami, Coral Gables
1983	Galerie Konrad Fischer, Zurich
	Paula Cooper Gallery, New York
	Heath Gallery, Atlanta, Georgia
	Galerie Daniel Templon, Paris
	Nouveau Musee, Lyon, France
	Le Coin du Miroir, Dijon, France
	The Clocktower, New York
	Flow Ace Gallery, Venice, California
	Galerie Plus-Kerns, Brussels
1984	Broward Community College, Fort Lauderdale, Florida
	Richland College, Dallas
	Westfalischer Kunstverein, Munster, West Germany
	Galerie Konrad Fischer, Dusseldorf
	Galleria Primo Piano, Rome
	Galerie im Kornerpark, Berlin-Neukolln
	State University of New York at Stony Brook
	Galerie Plus-Kern, Brussels
	Galerie Andre, West Berlin
1985	Paula Cooper Gallery, New York
	Galerie Daniel Templon, Paris
	Kunstraum Munchen, Munich
	Galerie Konrad Fischer, Dusseldorf
	Galleria Gian Enzo Sperone, Rome
1986	Galerie Plus-Kern, Brussels
	Galerie Konrad Fischer, Dusseldorf
1987	Van Abbemuseum, Eindhoven, Netherlands
	Haags Gemeentemuseum, The Hague
	Museo d'Arte Contemporanea, Castello di Rivoli, Italy

Selected Group Exhibitions:

1964	*Eight Young Artists*, Hudson River Museum, Yonkers, New York (and Bennington College, Vermont)
1968	*Minimal Art*, Gemeentemuseum, The Hague (travelled to Dusseldorf and Berlin)
1970	*Unitary Forms: Minimal Sculpture*, San Francisco Museum of Art
1974	*Andre / Broodthaers / Buren / Burgin / Gilbert and George / On Kawara / Long / Richter*, Palais des Beaux-Arts, Brussels
1975	*The Condition of Sculpture: A Selection of Recent Sculpture by Younger British and Foreign Artists*, Hayward Gallery, London
1976	*Drawing Now*, Museum of Modern Art, New York (toured West Germany, Israel and Norway)
1977	*Paris—New York*, Musée d'Art Moderne, Centre Georges Pompidou, Paris
1980	*Andre/Judd/Morris: Sculpture Minimal*, Galleria Nazionale d'Arte Moderna, Rome
1985	*Transformations in Sculpture*, Guggenheim Museum, New York
1987	*A Century of Modern Sculpture*, Dallas Museum of Art, Texas (and National Gallery of Art, Washington, D.C.)

Collections:

Museum of Modern Art, New York; Albright-Knox Art Gallery, Buffalo, New York; Walker Art Center, Minneapolis; National Gallery of Canada, Ottawa; Tate Gallery, London; Stedlijk Museum, Amsterdam; Kunstmuseum, Basel; Hessisches Landesmuseum, Darmstadt; Wallraf-Richartz Museum, Cologne.

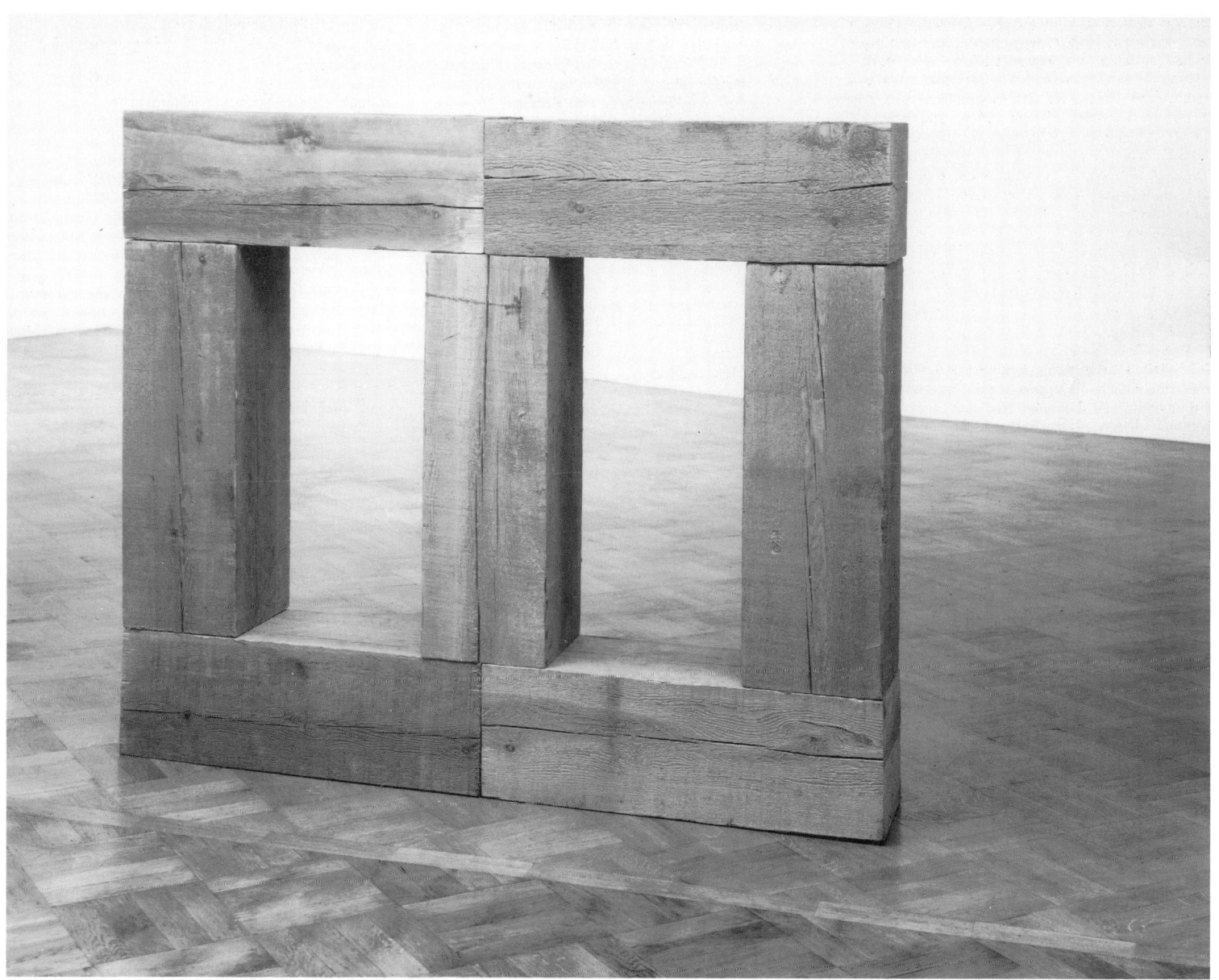

Carl Andre: *Hellgate,* 1981 Courtesy Anthony D'Offay Gallery, London

Publications:

By ANDRE: books—*First 5 Poems,* New York 1961; *The Xerox Book,* with others, New York 1968; *7 Books of Poetry: Passport, Shape and Structure, A Theory of Poetry, 100 Sonnets, American Drill, 3 Operas, Lyrics and Odes,* New York 1969; *Attica Book,* with others, edited by Benny Andrews and Rudolf Barabik, New York 1972; *Quincy Book,* Andover, Massachusetts 1973; *144 Blocks and Stones,* Portland, Oregon 1973; *11 Poems,* Turin 1974; *Wood/Carl Andre,* with additional text by R. H. Fuchs, Eindhoven, Netherlands 1978; *12 Dialogues: 1962-1963,* with Hollis Frampton, New York and Halifax, Nova Scotia 1980; articles—"Frank Stella" in *Allen Memorial Art Museum Bulletin* (Oberlin, Ohio), vol. 17, no. 1, Fall 1959; "Preface to Stripe Painting (Frank Stella)" in *16 Americans,* exhibition catalogue, New York 1959; "beam . . . room" in *Primary Structures: Younger American and British Sculptors,* exhibition catalogue, New York 1966; "Art Is What We Do/Culture Is What Is Done to Us" in "Sensibility of the 60's" in *Art in America* (New York), January/February 1967; "New in New York: Line Work" in *Arts Magazine* (New York), May 1967; "Artist Interviews Himself" in *Carl Andre,* exhibition catalogue, Monchengladbach, West Germany 1968; "Flags: An Opera for 3 Voices" in *Studio International* (London), April 1969; "Carl Andre: Form, Structure, Place" in *Arts Magazine* (New York), May 1969; "A Reasonable and Practical Proposal for Artists Who Wish to Remain Free Men in These Terrible Times" in *Open Hearing: Art Workers Coalition,* New York 1969; "Questions et Responses" in *VH101* (Paris), Spring 1970; "An Interview with Carl Andre," with Phyllis Tuchman in *Artforum* (New York), June 1970; statement in "The Artist and Politics: A Symposium" in *Artforum* (New York), September 1970; "Carl Andre," interview with Jeanne Siegel, in *Studio International* (London), November 1970; "Carl Andre," interview with Willoughby Sharp, in *Avalanche* (New York), Fall 1970; "A Juror's Statement" in *Centennial Exhibition,* exhibition catalogue, San Francisco 1971; "Letters" in *Artforum* (New York), March 1972; "Interview with Carl Andre," with Achille Bonito Oliva, in *Domus* (Milan), October 1972; "A Note on Bernhard and Hilla Becher" in *Artforum* (New York), December 1972; statement in *Deurle 11/7/73,* exhibition catalogue, Brussels 1973; "Dialogues with Carl Andre," with Andrea Gould, in *Arts Magazine* (New York), May 1974; "Carl Andre," interview with Irmeline Lebeer in *L'Art Vivant* (Paris), June 1974; "Against Duchamp" in *Praxis* (Chicago), Spring 1975; "The Role of the Artist in Today's Society" in *Art Journal* (New York), Summer 1975; "8 Statements (on Matisse): in *Art in America* (New York), July/August 1975; "Versions of Witness: A Note on Sculpture and Scholarship" in *Art Journal* (New York), Winter 1975-76; "An Interview with Carl Andre," with Michael Ballou and George Morgenstern, in *Minneapolis College of Art and Design* newspaper, 1976; Billy Builder, or, The Painful Machine," chapters I–IV, in *Tracks* (New York), Spring 1976; "Public Notice" in *Artforum* (New York), April 1976; statement in "Views from the Studio" by Henry Gerrit in *Art News* (New York), May 1976; "Correspondence" in *Studio International* (London), May/June 1976; "Commodity and Contradiction; or, Contradiction as Commodity," with Jeremy Gilbert-Rolfe, in *October* (New York), Summer 1976; "Billy Builder; or, The Painful Machine," chapters V–XI, in *Tracks* (New York), Fall 1976; notes in *Bienal,* exhibition catalogue, Sao Paulo 1977; "Questions, Public? Sculpture? For Münster?" in *Skulptur Ausstellung in Münster,* exhibition catalogue, Münster, West Germany 1977; "Billy Builder, or, The Painful Machine," chapters XII–XVI, in *Tracks* (New York), Spring 1977; statement in "The 20th-Century Artists Most Admired by Other Artists" in *Art News* (New York), November 1977; interview in *Artists in Their Own Words* by Paul Cummings, New York 1979; "Interview with Carl Andre," with Ida Panicelli, in *Neue Kunst in Europa* (Munich), January/February 1985.

On ANDRE: books—*8 Young Artists,* exhibition catalogue, by C. E. Goossen, Yonkers, New York 1964; *Carl Andre,* exhibition catalogue, Monchengladbach, West Germany 1968; *Carl Andre,* exhibition catalogue, by Enno Develing, The Hague 1969; *Unitary Forms: Minimal Sculpture by Carl Andre, Don Judd, John McCracken, Tony Smith,* exhibition catalogue, by Suzanne Foley, San Francisco 1970; *Carl Andre,* exhibition catalogue, by Diane Waldman, New York 1970; *the New Avant-Garde* by Gregoire Müller, New York 1972; *Carl Andre: Sculpture 1958-1974,* exhibition catalogue, by Angela Westwater, Berne 1975; *Carl Andre: Sculpture 1959-78,* exhibition catalogue, with an essay by Nicholas Serota, London 1978; *Carl Andre: Sculpture 1959-1977,* exhibition catalogue, by David Bourdon, with a foreword by Barbara Rose, New York 1978; *Carl Andre: Sculpture 1983,* exhibition catalogue, with essay by John Howett, Atlanta, Georgia 1983; *Carl Andre* (catalogue raisonne), The Hague 1987; articles—"Carl Andre: Poems 1958-74" by Lynda Morris in *Studio International* (London), September/October 1975; "An Andre Is What It Is, Not Another Thing" by John Russell in the *New York Times,* 20 February 1976; editorial in *Studio International* (London), March/April 1976; "Carl Andre: Art Versus Talk" by Jeff Perrone in *Artforum* (New York), May 1976; "Carl Andre Has the Floor" by Thomas Hess in *New York,* 7 June 1976; "Carl Andre on

Work and Politics" by Sandy Ballatore in *Artweek* (Oakland, California), 3 July 1976; "Trivialization of Art by the Press" by Pat Gilmour in *Arts Review Yearbook,* London 1977; "Minimalism and Critical Response" by Phyllis Tuchman in *Artforum* (New York), May 1977; "Carl Andre" by David Bourdon in *Arts Magazine* (New York), December 1977; "Background of a Minimalist: Carl Andre" by Phyllis Tuchman in *Artforum* (New York), March 1978; "Andre in Retrospect" by Kenneth Baker in *Art in America* (New York), April 1980; "Bricklaying with Andre" by Waldemar Januszczak in *The Guardian* (London), 12 December 1985.

My works are not the embodiments of ideas or conceptions. My works are, in the phrase of William Blake, "Lineaments of gratified desire."

—Carl Andre

Carl Andre's minimalist work of the 1960s participated in a radical disruption of the reverential condition of traditional sculpture. His early work, wooded columns influenced by Brancusi's totemic figures, eventually yielded to austere, floorbound arrangements of ordinary, prefabricated materials such as brick, metal plates or ribbon, and wood. The promotion of a minimal esthetic, exemplified by Andre's work of the late 60s, represented a prolonged reaction against abstract Expressionism and the spiritual and utopian program of modernism in general. Andre's disenchantment with the antigravitational illusionism of 20th century sculpture led him to explore the possibilities of earthworks, stating that the "ideal piece of sculpture is a road." The artist's interest in the idea of passage, perhaps related to his employment in the early 1960s as a freight brakeman and conductor for the Pennsylvania Railroad, resulted in a rejection of the conventional model of sculpture as a closed and sanctified object. "Spill" (1968), a scatter-piece in which 800 identical plastic blocks were flung to the gallery floor, further emphasized this rejection. While "Spill" has been tenuously compared to Jackson Pollock's overall compositions, it is, on the contrary, antithetical to Pollock's painting in its tacit repudiation of the modernist preoccupation with internal paradox, structural balance, and artistic control. Instead, Andre's floorbound arrangements of magnesium, lead, copper, or steel plates aim for a continuity with their ambient space: "FORM = STRUCTURE = PLACE" Andre has written in a kind of theoretical formula for his work. Rather than possessing internal or metaphoric content, these minimalist pieces function at the level of externality; it is the temporal experience—the act of passage itself—that is at the core of Andre's work.

Engaged in a subtle dialogue with modernism, Andre's minimalist pieces, therefore, cannot be seen as entirely ahistorical. "Lever" (1966), an early and generative work composed of a single row of unattached firebricks, marked an auspicious beginning for the artist's offensive against sculptural convention. Andre's position toward modernism is suggested in a remark made in relation to "Lever": " . . . all I am doing is putting Brancusi's 'Endless Column' on the ground instead of in the air. . . . The engaged position is to run along the earth." Toppled from its "pedestal," "Lever" is representative of the postmodernist attack against the sanctity of the art object. The underlying principles of modernism, as Andre's statement indicates, were not entirely rejected; rather, they were brought to the threshold of something radical and new.

—Maurice Berger

ANDREWS, Michael.

British. Born in Norwich, Norfolk, in 1928. Educated at City of Norwich School; studied at evening classes, Norwich Art School; studied at the Slade School of Fine Art, London, 1949-53. Served in British Army, in Bicester, Oxfordshire and in Egypt, 1946-49. Painter, in London, 1953-77, and in Norfolk since 1977; participated in Lorenza Mazzetti's films *Metamorphosis,* 1952, and with Eduardo Paolozzi, *q.v.,* in *Together,* 1954. Lecturer, Norwich Art School, 1959; Chelsea School of Art, London, 1960, and Slade School of Fine Art, London, 1963-66. Recipient: Rome Scholarship in Painting, 1953; Gulbenkian Purchase Award, 1961. Agent: Anthony D'Offay, London. Address: c/o Anthony D'Offay, 9 Dering Street, London W1, England.

Individual Exhibitions:

1958   Beaux-Arts Gallery, London
1963   Beaux-Arts Gallery, London
1964   Norfolk Contemporary Arts Society, Norwich (with Bernard Meadows)
1974   Anthony D'Offay Gallery, London
1978   *Paintings 1977-78,* Anthony D'Offay Gallery, London
1980   Hayward Gallery, London (travelled to the Fruit Market Gallery, Edinburgh; and the Whitworth Art Gallery, Manchester)
1986   Anthony D'Offay Gallery, London

Selected Group Exhibitions:

1952   *Young Painters,* Institute of Contemporary Arts, London
1954   *Drawings for Pictures,* Arts Council Gallery, London
1960   *Modern British Portraits,* Arts Council Gallery, London
1964   *British Painting in the 60's,* Whitechapel Art Gallery, London
1966   *Figurative Art,* Camden Arts Centre, London
1971   *The Slade 1871-1971,* Royal Academy of Arts, London
1979   *Narrative Painting,* Institute of Contemporary Arts, London
1981   *8 Figurative Painters,* Yale Center for British Art, New Haven, Connecticut (travelled to the Santa Barbara Museum of Art, California)
1984   *Hard-Won Image,* Tate Gallery, London
1987   *A School of London,* Kunstnernes Hus, Oslo (travelled Humlebaek, Denmark; Dusseldorf)

Collections:

Tate Gallery, London; Victoria and Albert Museum, London; Arts Council of Great Britain, London; Gulbenkian Foundation, London; Slade School of Fine Art, University College, London; Norwich Castle Museum, Norfolk; Australian National Gallery, Canberra; National Gallery of Victoria, Melbourne.

Publications:

By ANDREWS: articles—"Notes and Pre-occupations" in *X: A Quarterly Review* (London), vol. 1, no. 1, 1960-61; statement in *Survey 66: Figurative Art,* exhibition catalogue, London 1966.

On ANDREWS: books—*Modern English Painters, volume III: Wood to Hockney* by John Rothenstein, London 1974; *Michael Andrews: Paintings 1977-78,* exhibition catalogue, with text by Anne D'Offay, London 1978; *Michael Andrews,* exhibition catalogue, with text by Lawrence Gowing, London 1980; *8 Figurative Painters,* exhibition catalogue, with texts by Andrew Forge and Lawrence Gowing, New Haven, Connecticut 1981; *A Partial Testament* by Helen Lessore, London 1986; articles—"Stranded Dinosaurs" by William Feaver in *London Magazine* July/August 1970; "Painter of Fact and Feeling" by Lawrence Gowing in the *Sunday Times Magazine* (London), October 1980; "Michael Andrews: Recent Paintings" by Peter Fuller in *Burlington Magazine* (London), July 1986.

At the very beginning of his career Michael Andrews was dubbed Britain's most interesting young artist by Britain's leading contemporary painter; recently it has been said of him that "he paints hardly anything but masterpieces." Yet even in this time when individuality is said to be so highly prized, there are individual artists, even of Andrews' stature, who escape attention; and it was not until his retrospective of 1980 that the general public—and much of the art public—"discovered" Andrews. This can be variously attributed to his slowish production, his figurative content, and his subtle, expansive and unfashionable preoccupations; among artists, his equal ability (shared with Bacon) with broad summary brushwork and exquisitely judged sprays and washes has incited partisan envy.

The title of one of Andrews' earliest paintings, made on passing out of the Slade School of Art in 1952, affords a valuable clue to his interests: "A Man Who Suddenly Fell Over." The individual human ego and its relation to society and to public "image"—as well as its "staying power"—has constantly preoccupied him, and one can imagine both Rembrandt and Hals being fascinated by Andrews' perceptions of the psychological undercurrents that make up a single face, or one of his several group scenes. (It reminds us how rare this once common theme, of community, has become.) His figure studies, and his studies of spatial effects such as fish in water, would grace any public gallery or museum; yet he is one of those artists whose work is best appreciated when seen in sequence. The almost oriental allusiveness of that haunting image of the *shadow* only of a balloon seen against the sand of a deserted beach with a scribble of seaweed—the equivalent of a Japanese *haiku* poem—can be recognised as a superb aesthetic achievement, vibrant with emotional meaning; but a knowledge of Andrews' earlier paintings of the ego as expanding or shrinking balloon adds to its appreciation.

British art is constantly in danger of yielding to a predominantly literate culture; but in Andrews we have an artist who can set a scene like a playwright, a novelist or a poet, yet whose exceptional skills in rapid brushwork plus refined manipulation of paint, and in condensed imagery, open a huge area of life to his potential observation, whose paintings give pleasures both popular and refined. And there is always the feeling that he could move in any direction for his subject-matter—one awaits every new painting from him with eager anticipation.

—Michael Shepherd

ANSELMO, Giovanni.

Italian. Born in Borgofranco d'Ivrea, 5 August 1934. Lives and works in Turin. Agent: Galleria Christian Stein, 206 Piazza San Carlo, 10121 Turin. Address: Via Massena 68, 10128 Turin, Italy.

Individual Exhibitions:

1968   Galleria Sperone, Turin
1969   Galleria Sperone, Turin
       Galerie Sonnabend, Paris
1970   Galleria Sperone, Turin
       Galleria Toselli, Milan
1971   Galleria Sperone, Turin
       Galleria Multipli, Turin
1972   Galleria Sperone, Turin
       John Weber Gallery, New York
1973   Galerie MTL, Brussels
       Kunstmuseum, Lucerne
1974   Galleria Marilena Bonomo, Bari, Italy
       Galleria Sperone-Fischer, Rome
       Studio d'Arte L. Rumma, Naples
       Galleria Sperone, Turin
       Galerie Foksal, Warsaw

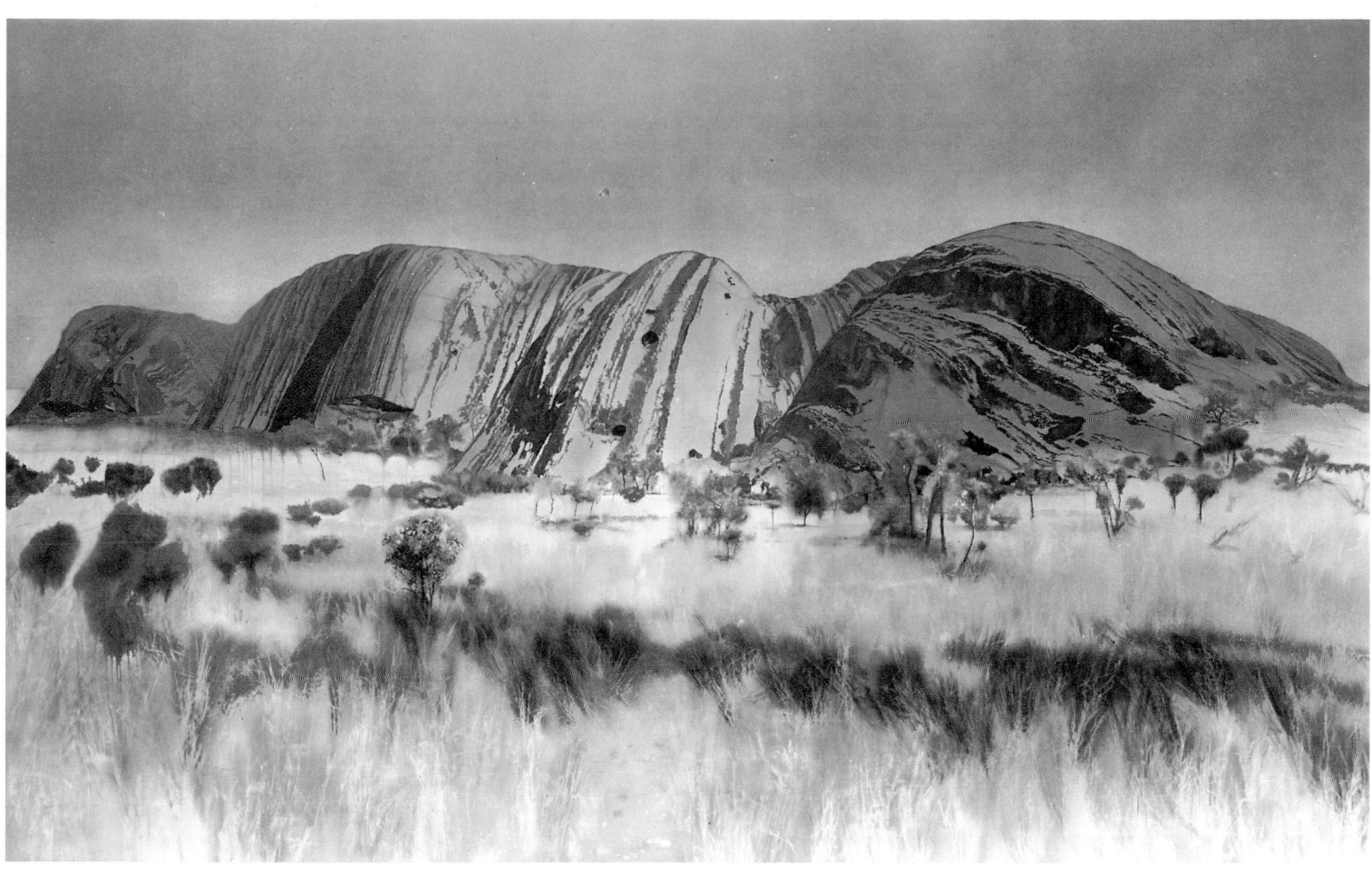

Michael Andrews: *The Cathedral* (*Ayres Rock*), **1987** Courtesy Anthony D'Offay Gallery, London

1975	Galleria Sperone, Turin
	Galleria Sperone, Rome
	Galleria Area, Florence
	Saman Galleria, Genoa
	Kabinett für Aktuelle Kunst, Bremerhaven, West Germany
1976	Galleria Ghiringelli-Sperone, Milan
	Sam Galleria, Genoa
	Nuovi Strumenti, Brescia, Italy
1977	Galleria Sperone, Rome
	Kabinett für Aktuelle Kunst, Bremerhaven, West Germany
	Galleria Il Tritone, Biella, Italy
	Galleria G. de Crescenzo, Rome
1978	Galleria Salvatore Ala, Milan
	Studio Tucci Russo, Turin
	Galerie Paul Maenz, Cologne
	Galerie Durand-Dessert, Paris
	Sperone-Westwater-Fischer Gallery, New York
1979	Kunsthalle, Basle
	Galerie Rudiger Schöttle, Munich
	Galleria Emilio Mazzoli, Modena
1980	Stedelijk van Abbemuseum, Eindhoven
	Galerie Helen van der Meij, Amsterdam
	Forum Kunst, Rottweil, West Germany
	Musée de Grenoble, France
	Galleria Sperone, Turin
1981	Salvatore Ala Gallery, New York
1982	Galleria Christian Stein, Turin
	Galerie Durand-Dessert, Paris
	Galerie Helen van der Meij, Amsterdam
1983	Galleria Christian Stein, Turin
1984	Marian Goodman Gallery, New York
	Galerie Michele Szwacjer, Antwerp
	Castello di Rivoli, Turin
1985	ARC/Musee d'Art Moderne de la Ville, Paris
1986	Kunstnernes Hus, Oslo
	Galleria Christian Stein, Milan
1987	Galerie Tanit Kunigk und Mollier, Munich

Selected Group Exhibitions:

1967	*Group Exhibition*, Galleria Sperone, Turin
1968	*9 at Castelli*, Leo Castelli Warehouse, New York
1969	*When Attitude Becomes Form*, Kunsthalle, Berne (travelled to the Museum Haus Lange, Krefeld, West Germany, and the Institute of Contemporary Arts, London)
1970	*Vitalita del Negativo nell'Arte Italiana 1960–1970*, Palazzo delle Esposizioni, Rome
1972	*Documenta 5*, Kassel, West Germany
1974	*Art and Image in Recent Art*, Art Institute of Chicago
1978	*Words*, Kunstmuseum, Bochum, West Germany (travelled to the Palazzo Ducale, Genoa)
1981	*Identite Italienne: L'Ari en Italie depuis 1959*, Centre Georges Pompidou, Paris
1983	*Presence Discrete*, Musee des Beaux-Arts, Dijon, France
1985	*The European Iceberg*, Art Gallery of Ontario, Toronto

Collections:

Stedelijk van Abbemuseum, Einhoven; Stedelijk Museum, Amsterdam; Rijksmuseum, Kroller-Muller, Otterlo, Netherlands; Groninger Museum, Groningen, Netherlands; Australian National Gallery, Canberra.

Publications:

By ANSELMO: books—*Leggere*, Turin 1972; *116 Particolari Visibili e Misurabili di Infinito*, Turin 1975.

On ANSELMO: books—*Anselmo*, exhibition catalogue, by Maurizio Fagiolo, Turin 1968; *Giovane Scultura Italiana* by Germano Celant, Casabella, Italy 1968; *Arte Povera* by Germano Celant, Salerno/Milan/Tübingen/New York 1969; *Giovanni Anselmo*, exhibition catalogue, by Jean-Christophe Ammann, Lucerne 1973; *Giovanni Anselmo*, exhibition catalogue, by Jean-Christophe Ammann and Rudi Fuchs, Basle 1979; *Giovanni Anselmo*, exhibition catalogue, by Thierry Raspail, Grenoble, France 1980; *Anselmo*, exhibition catalogue with text by Suzanne Page, Paris 1985.

By the time Giovanni Anselmo had held his first one-man show at the Galleria Sperone in Milan in 1968, the group known as Arte Povera, of which he was a member, had already been formed. In this exhibition of his work, with its balanced cubes, floating bubbles, suspended sheets of plexiglass and hanging chains, Anselmo had abandoned the traditional picture plane in an attempt to create a more direct representation of the themes of gravity and movement. He was striving for an immediate relation to the real world, both visible and invisible.

In 1966 he had made a work consisting of a small cube above which was fixed a slender baton. The work was labeled *Untitled,* but the materials employed were precisely noted: iron, wood and the force of gravity. A work of 1967/68, *Direzione,* is made of a heavy triangular granite block containing a small compass. The stone is oriented to the north as indicated by the compass needle. Anselmo thus commented on the magnetic forces residing in all natural objects.

Torsione of 1968 is made of cowhides partially embedded in a block of concrete. The lengths of hide emerging from the cement block are stretched out and secured by a sturdy piece of wood piercing and keeping the hides in tension from its position leaning against the wall.

Anselmo's work makes play with the themes of infinity and energy, and the notion that the artist intervenes in a natural order, impressing his own definition of reality on the materials at his disposal.

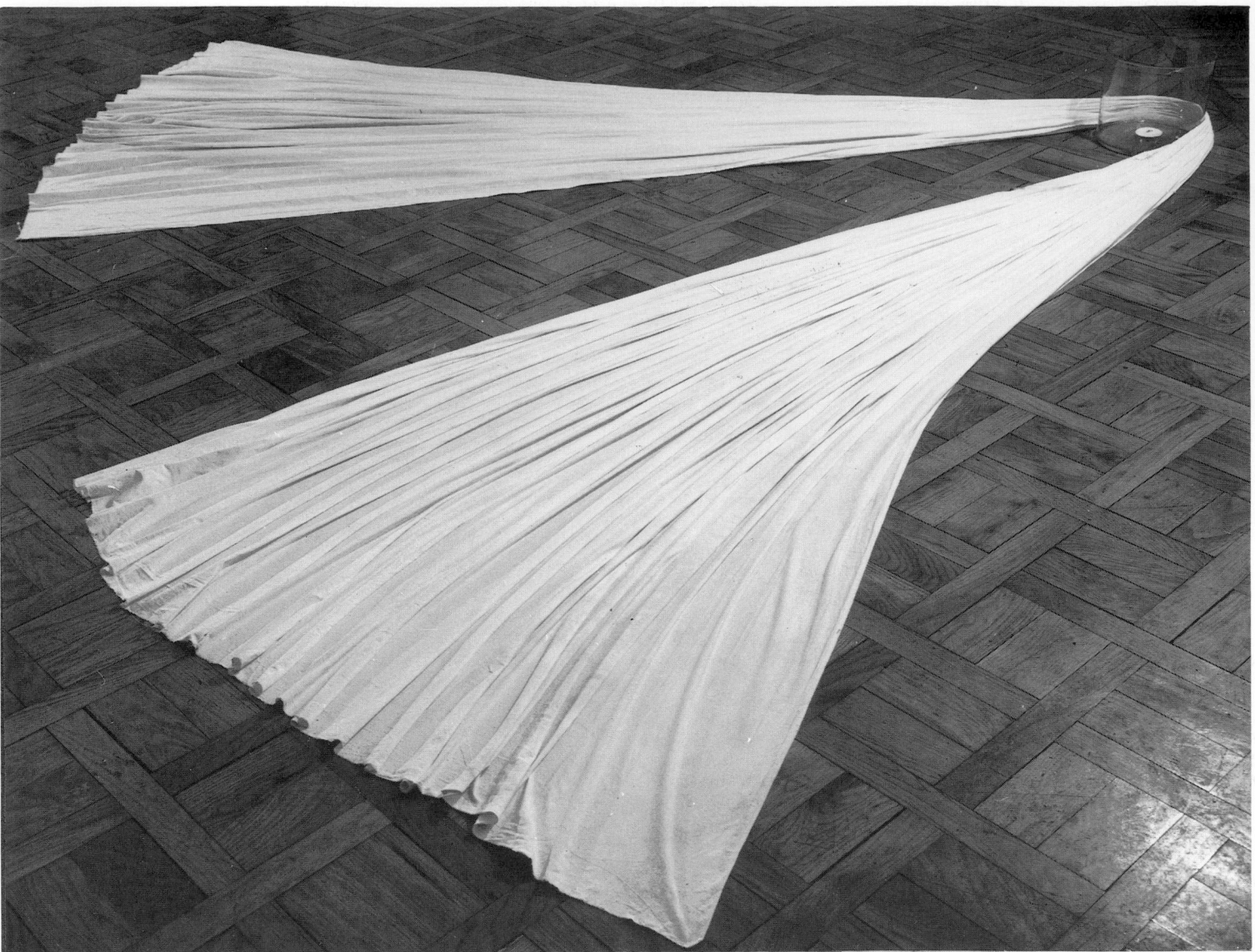

Giovanni Anselmo: *Direzione*, 1968

From 1970 onwards he began using projected slides together with parallelopiped prism shapes made of lead onto which words were engraved. *Infinito* is a work of 1971 in which Anselmo uses a projection, focused to infinity of the word "Infinito." In other works he projects the word "particolare" (detail) onto a wall to distinguish it from the remainder of the unlit surface. In *Invisibile,* the projection focuses the word "visibile" into an empty space so that the word *is* genuinely invisible. He uses the same idea when he engraves a parallelopiped of lead with the word "visibile": the space in which we would expect to find the prefix "in-" is missing, and all that remains is "visibile".

The different ways in which Anselmo pursues these ideas are all aimed at establishing an appropriate expressive rapport between the energies of the invisible and the infinite. His work is thus intended to be a part, or fragment, which indicates an invisible totality.

—Roberto Lambarelli

ANTES, Horst.
German. Born in Heppenheim, 28 October 1936. Educated at primary school in Heppenheim, 1942–47,

and Heppenheim College, 1948–57; studied at the Staatliche Akademie der Bildenden Künste, under H. A. P. Grieshaber, Karlsruhe, 1957–59. Married Dorothea Grossman in 1961; children: Aaron and Salomea. Lived in Florence, 1962; in Rome, 1963; now lives and works in Karlsruhe. Professor of Art, Staatliche Akademie der Bildenden Künste, Karlsruhe, 1965–73; Guest Professor of Art, Academy of Fine Arts, Berlin, 1967–68. Recipient: Kunstpreis, Hannover, 1959; Pankofer prize, 1959; Stipendium des Kulturkreises im Bundesverband der Deutschen Industrie, 1960; Junger Western Fellowship, Recklinghausen, 1961; André Malraux Prize, *Biennale,* Paris, 1961; Villa Romana Prize, Florence, 1962; Villa Massimo Fellowship, Rome, 1963; Guggenheim Award, 1964; Aldegrever-Gesellschaft Fellowship, Münster, 1966; Unesco Prize, *Biennale,* Venice, 1966; Premio Marzotto-Europa, Valdango, 1968. Agents: Galerie Brusberg, Kurfürstendamm 213, 1000 Berlin 15 (West), Germany; Galerie Gunzenhauser, Maximilianstrasse 10, 8000 Munich 22, West Germany; Nishimura Gallery, 4-3-13 Ginza, Chuo-ku, Tokyo 104, Japan. Address: 11 Hohenbergstrasse, 75000 Karlsruhe 41, West Germany.

Individual Exhibitions:

1960	Galerie der Spiegel, Cologne
	Galerie Richentor, Basle
	Galerie Boukes, Wiesbaden, West Germany
	Galerie 61, Freiburg, West Germany
1961	Kellergalerie im Schloss, Darmstadt
	Galerie Baier, Mainz, West Germany
	Studio for Neue Kunst, Wuppertal, West Germany
1962	Stadtheater, Remscheid, West Germany
1963	Galerie der Spiegel, Cologne
	Galerie N., Bremen, West Germany
	Musée d'Art Moderne, Paris
	Städtisches Museum, Ulm, West Germany
1964	Städtisches Galerie, Munich
	Freie Galerie, Berlin
	Kurbuchhandlung and Galerie Krohn, Badenweiler, West Germany
	Galerie d'Eendt, Amsterdam
	Galerie Schmucking, Braunschweig, West Germany
	Kleiner Raum Clasing, Münster, West Germany
1965	Deutsche Bibliothek, Brussels
	Galerie der Spiegel, Cologne
	Galerie Stangl, Munich
1966	Galerie Altes Theater, Ravensburg, West Germany
	Kunstverein, Ulm, West Germany
	Galerie Valentien, Stuttgart
	Galerie Maercklin, Stuttgart
	Galerie Schmucking, Braunschweig, West Germany
	Städtische Kunsthalle, Mannheim
	Galerie Defet, Nuremberg, West Germany
1967	Lefebre Gallery, New York
	Studentenhaus, Universität Tübingen, West Germany
	Kunstkabinett am Institut für Lehrerweiterbildung, Berlin-Pankow
	Bundesgartenschau, Karlsruhe (travelled to the Badischer Kunstverein, Karlsruhe)

Kurbuchhandlung and Galerie Krohn, Badenweiler, West Germany
Städtischer Kunstpavillon, Soest, West Germany
Kleiner Raum Clasing, Münster, West Germany
Kunstmuseum, Basle
Galerie d'Eendt, Amsterdam (with Hans Andreus)
Galerie Gimpel and Hanover, Zurich
Staatliche Kunsthalle, Baden-Baden, West Germany
Freunde Mainfränkischer Kunst und Geschicht, Wurzburg, West Germany
1968 Gimpel Fils, London
Kunstverein, Braunschweig, West Germany
Galleria d'Art del Naviglio, Milan
Galerie Lochte, Hamburg
Galerie Junge Generation, Innsbruck
Arts Studeo, Aarhus, Denmark
Galerie Junge Generation, Vienna
Worpsweder Kunsthalle, Bremen, West Germany
Galerie Stangl, Munich
Galerie Forum 67, Linz, Austria
Theater Stadt Nordhorn, West Germany
1969 Lefebre Gallery, New York
Galerie Prisma, Copenhagen
Tatkreis Kunst der Ruhr, Essen
Galerie Trost, Lippstadt, West Germany
Galerie Regio, Lorrach, Switzerland
Goethe Institut, Marseilles
Galleria d'Arte del Cavallino, Venice
1970 Galerie Valentien, Stuttgart
Sitzende Figur mit Scheibe und Ei, Gimpel and Hanover Galerie, Zurich
Gimpel Fils, London
Galerie Jesse, Bielefeld, West Germany
1971 Galerie Muchow, Freiburg, West Germany
Galerie Walther, Dusseldorf
Kunsthalle, Kiel, West Germany
Städtische Verkehrsamt, Offenburg, West Germany
Galerie Schmucking, Braunschwieg, West Germany
Bilder und Skulpturen 1965–1971, Kunsthalle, Baden-Baden, West Germany (travelled to the Gesellschaft der Kunstfreunde, Lindau; Kunsthalle, Berne; Kunsthalle, Bremen; and the Frankfurter Kunstverein)
Antes in der Sammlung Wolf und Ursula Hermann, Kabinett 2, Graphisches Kabinett, Bremen, West Germany
1972 Galerie Hoeppner, Hamburg
Kunsthalle, Wilhelmshaven, West Germany
Lefebre Gallery, New York
Kunstverein Gentofte, Copenhagen
Nordjutland Museum, Aalborg, Denmark
Galerie Stangl, Munich
Galerie Pudelko, Bonn
Galerie Defet, Nuremberg, West Germany
1973 Goethe Institut, Rome
Theater der Stadt, Schweinfurt, West Germany
Gimpel Fils, London
Gimpel and Hanover Galerie, Zurich
Kunstkreis Hameln, West Germany
1974 Ulmer Museum, West Germany
Städtisches Galerie, Rosenheim, West Germany
Lefebre Gallery, New York
Galerie Orek, Constance, West Germany
Librairie et Galerie La Hune, Paris
P and P Galerie, Zug, Switzerland
1975 Galerie Stangl, Munich
Lippische Gesellschaft für Kunst, Detmold, West Germany
1976 Gimpel Fils Gallery, London
Lefebre Gallery, New York
Arts Club of Chicago
1978 Gimpel-Hanover-André Emmerich Galleries, Zurich
Lefebre Gallery, New York
1980 Lefebre Gallery, New York
1981 Galerie Valentien, Stuttgart
Nishimura Gallery, Tokyo
1982 Galerie Brusberg, Hannover
Galerie Schloss Hardenberg, Velbert-Neviges, West Germany
Galerie Rehklau, Augsburg, West Germany
Kreissparkasse, Reutlingen, West Germany
Galerie Der Spiegel, Cologne
Galerie Schaefer, Giessen, West Germany

Galerie Bernd Lutze, Friedrichshafen, West Germany
Lefebre Gallery, New York
1983 Galerie von Loe, Konigstein, West Germany
Galerie Brusberg, West Berlin
Kunsthalle, Bremen, West Germany
Stadtische Galerie, Frankfurt
Kunstmuseum, Hannover
Galerie Gunzenhauser, Munich
Stadthalle, Weiden, West Germany
Goethe-Institut, Athens
Dada Art Gallery, Athens
Wilhelm-Hack-Museum, Ludwigshafen, West Germany
Kunstverein, Ludwigshafen, West Germany
1984 Goethe-Institut, Cairo
Goethe-Institut, Nicosia, Cyprus
Freilichtgalerie, Ludwigsburg, West Germany
Villa Franck, Ludwigsburg, West Germany
Galerie Der Spiegel, Cologne
Galerie Ilverich, Meerbusch-Ilverich, West Germany
Galerie Albrecht, Kaltern/Bozen, West Germany
Lefebre Gallery, New York
Guggenheim Museum, New York
Galerie Hor, Nuremberg, West Germany
Nishimura Gallery, Tokyo
Galerie Defet, Nuremberg, West Germany
1985 Lefebre Gallery, New York
Galerie Krohn, Badenweiler, West Germany
Kupferstichkabinett, Dresden, East Germany
Galerie Michael Neumann, Dusseldorf
Kunstverein, Bayreuth, West Germany
1986 Lefebre Gallery, New York
Kunstbuchhandlung Art Service, Karlsruhe-Durlach, West Germany
Stadtsparkasse, Gladbeck, West Germany
Galerie Reichard, Frankfurt
Galerie Funck, Mannheim, West Germany
Taimei Gallery, Tokyo
Galerie Schmucking, Archsum/Sylt, West Germany
Galerie Gunzenhauser, Munich
1987 Galerie Holbein, Lindau, West Germany
Galerie Wilbrand, Cologne
Stadtische Galerie, Villingen-Schwenningen, West Germany (and Kunstverein Hochrhein, Bad Sackingen)
Galerie K. G. Schafer, Frankfurt
Galerie Ilverich, Meerbusch-Ilverich, West Germany
Galerie Gunzenhauser, Munich

Selected Group Exhibitions:

1959 *1st Biennale des Jeunes Artistes*, Musée d'Art Moderne, Paris
1961 *Carnegie International*, Pittsburgh
1964 *Documenta 3*, Kassel, West Germany
1966 *Biennale*, Venice
1968 *European Painters Today*, Musée des Arts Décoratifs, Paris (toured the United States)
1971 *2nd Triennale of India*, New Delhi
1974 *From Picasso to Lichtenstein*, Tate Gallery, London
1982 *Torso als Prinzip*, Kunstverein, Kassel, West Germany
1985 *Kunst in der Bundesrepublik 1945–85*, Nationalgalerie, West Berlin
1987 *Fifty Years of Collecting*, Guggenheim Museum, New York

Collections:

Kunstmuseum, Basle; Neue Nationalgalerie, Berlin; Städtische Kunstsammlungen, Bonn; Wallraf-Richartz, Cologne; Musée Royaux des Beaux-Arts, Brussels; Centre Georges Pompidou, Paris; Gemeentemuseum, The Hague; museum Boymans-van Beuningen, Rotterdam; Museum des 20. Jahrhunderts, Vienna; Guggenheim Museum, New York.

Publications:

By ANTES: articles—"Interview mit Horst Antes," with Otmar Engel, in *Civis* (Bonn), no. 9-10, 1963; *Deutsche Kunst: Eine Neue Generation* by Rolf-Günter Dienst, Cologne 1970; *Noch Kunst—Neuestes aus deutschen Ateliers* by Rolf-Günter Dienst, Dusseldorf 1970; *Horst Antes: Sitzende Figur mit Scheibe und Ei*, exhibition catalogue, by Willy Rotzler and Mark Rothko, Zurich 1970; *Antes in der Sammlung Wolf und Ursula Hermann*, exhibition catalogue, Bremen, West Germany 1971; *Horst Antes*, exhibition catalogue, by Willy Rotzler, Zurich and London 1973.

On ANTES: books—*Horst Antes*, exhibition catalogue, with text by Herbert Pee, Ulm, West Germany 1963; *Vortrag zur Eroffnung der Ausstellung Horst Antes—Das graphische Werk 1959–1967* by Günther Gercken, Baden-Baden, West Germany 1967; *Kunst unserer Zeit* by Will Grohmann, Cologne 1970; *Bis Heute* by Karin Thomas, Cologne 1971; *Horst Antes: Bilder and Skulpturen 1965–1971*, exhibition catalogue, by Carlo Huber, Berne 1971; *Contemporary Prints* by Riva Castleman, New York 1973; *Antes*, exhibition catalogue, by Wolf Hermann, Rosenheim, West Germany 1974; *Horst Antes Poggibonsi 1979–1980* by Klaus Gallwitz, Frankfurt 1980; *Horst Antes Votives*, exhibition catalogue, with texts by Werner Haftmann and Thomas Messer, New York 1984; *Horst Antes—Dreiundfunfzig Bilder, Dreiunddreissig Sammler aus Suddeutschland*, edited by Volker Huber, Offenbach am Main 1987.

*   *   *

Though he studied at Karlsruhe and returned there to teach at the Academy of Fine Arts from 1965 to 1973, Horst Antes could be described as the explorer of a territory known only to himself, an anthropologist specialising in creatures discovered in his own imaginative experience.

His early paintings in the late 1950's were strong, highly coloured works deriving partly from the Expressionism of the previous generations of German painters and partly from the example of his professor H. A. P. Grieshaber. They were a variant of the New Figuration that was popular among German artists at the time. Antes then developed his own figuration in his "Gnome" people, massive beings who presented their profiles impassively on the canvas. Bright synthetic colours heightened the surrealist effect of these strange personages, often crippled or distorted so that a head would surmount two legs without a trunk, one arm waving in futility. Large in scale, these brooding heads sometimes with eyes set vertically one above the other recall such visual twists by Picasso while a landscape of a deserted classic temple beneath floating white clouds takes on the atmosphere of a naive Chirico.

Within a year of leaving the Karlsruhe Academy Antes had his first one-man show at the Spiegel Gallery, Cologne, and since then he has shown continuously in Europe and the U.S.A. In 1962 and 1963 he lived in Italy and now spends much of his time in Tuscany. His interest in the paintings of the Italian Primitives had its effect on his work which became more pure and simplified in colour.

Antes's "family" of art figures possess formidable sculptural elements often truncated and disjointed and painted in monochrome. On two facing figures prehensile toes of equal length and stylised hands assume schematic patterns akin to the hieratic reliefs of Assyrian wall sculpture.

The severe iconography of the pictures, their economy of colour and simplicity of motives demand a concentration upon meaning that is never clarified. Deliberate malformation of humanity carries with it some of the ominous messages transmitted by Bacon but in more mechanistic effigy and at the same time carrying something of the haunting masks of primitive societies.

Man as mask is likewise suggested in other connotations such as "Portrait with Slide" where a man looks out from the apertures in his helmet of skin. Affinities with Leger seem superficial; in the projected puzzle there is more of the early surreal drama of Max Ernst and the prehistoric imagery of Easter Island gods.

Iconic and personal, the paintings and prints of Horst Antes illustrate not a phase of art history but the concrete externalisation of community dreams. He has created the identifiable hero of contemporary myth, conveying in each successive work satisfaction of a curiosity aroused in all sagas: what happens next? He maintains the strength of his figurative concepts by involving the spectator in the funambulist contest of his rudimentary compositions.

—G. S. Whittet

ANTIN, Eleanor.

American. Born Eleanor Fineman in New York City, 27 February 1935. Studied at the Tamara Daykarhanova School for the Stage, New York; studied creative writing at the College of the City of New York. Married the poet David Antin in 1961; child: Blaise. Worked as a professional actress, 1955–58; now a full-time artist, living and working in California. Visiting Lecturer, University of California at Irvine, 1974–75. Assistant Professor, 1975–78, Associate Professor, 1978–79, and since 1979 Professor of Visual Arts, University of California at San Diego. Recipient: National Endowment for the Arts grant, 1979; Vesta Award for Performance, 1985. Agent: Ronald Feldman Fine Arts, 31 Mercer Street, New York, New York 10013. Address: Post Office Box 1147, Del Mar, California 92014, U.S.A.

Individual Exhibitions:

1968   Long Island University, Brooklyn, New York
1970   *California Lives*, Gain Ground Gallery, New York
1971   *Library Science*, Brand Library Art Center, Los Angeles
      Portraits of 8 New York Women, Chelsea Hotel, New York
1972   *Traditional Art*, Henri Gallery, Washington, D.C.
      Library Science, California Institute of the Arts, Valencia, California
      Library Science, University of California at San Diego
      Library Science, Austin Peay State University, Clarksville, Tennessee
      Traditional Art, Orlando Gallery, Los Angeles
1973   *100 BOOTS*, Museum of Modern Art, New York
      Part of an Autobiography, Portland Center for the Visual Arts, Oregon
      More Traditional Art, Northwood Experimental Art Institute, Dallas
      I Dreamed I was a Ballerina, Orlando Gallery, Los Angeles
1974   *Several Selves*, Everson Museum, Syracuse, New York
      The Ballerina and the King, Galleria Forma, Genoa
      Black Is Beautiful, University of California at Irvine
1975   The Kitchen, New York (video exhibition)
      2 Transformations, Stefanotty Gallery, New York
1976   *Eleanor Antin, R.N.*, The Clocktower, New York
1977   *The Angel of Mercy*, D'Arc Gallery, New York
      The Angel of Mercy, La Jolla Museum of Contemporary Art, California
      The Nurse and the Hijackers, Ronald Feldman Fine Arts Gallery, New York
      100 BOOTS Once Again and Choreographies, Wadsworth Atheneum, Hartford, Connecticut
1978   *The Ballerina*, Whitney Museum, New York
      The Nurse and the Hijackers, Long Beach Museum of Art, California
      Ballerina, Los Angeles Institute of Contemporary Art
1979   *Before the Revolution*, Ronald Feldman Fine Arts Gallery, New York
      100 BOOTS: Transmission and Reception, Franklin Furnace, New York
      The Black Ballerina, Marianne Deson Gallery, Chicago
1980   *Recollections of My Life with Diaghilev*, Ronald Feldman Fine Arts Gallery, New York

1981   *Angel of Mercy*, Los Angeles Institute of Contemporary Art
      Nova Gallery, Vancouver
      Early Works, Palomar College, California
1982   *Recollections of My Life with Diaghilev*, Minneapolis College of Art and Design, Minnesota
      La Mamelle, San Francisco
      Rutgers University, New Brunswick, New Jersey
1983   *El Desdichado*, Ronald Feldman Fine Arts, New York
      Recollections of My Life with Diaghilev, Tortue Gallery, Los Angeles
1986   *Loves of a Ballerina*, Ronald Feldman Gallery, New York

Performances: *The Ballerina Goes to the Big Apple*, Woman's Building, Los Angeles, 1974; *Eleanor 1954*, Woman's Building, Los Angeles, 1974; *The King's Meditations*, Center for Music Experiment, University of California at San Diego, 1975; *The Ballerina Goes to the Big Apple*, Stefanotty Gallery, New York, 1975; *The Battle of the Bluffs*, Fine Arts Gallery, San Diego, 1975; *The Battle of the Bluffs*, Palace of Fine Arts, San Francisco, 1975; *Escape*, Palace of the Legion of Honor, San Francisco, 1975; *The Battle of the Bluffs*, The Clocktower, New York, 1976; *The Battle of the Bluffs*, Los Angeles Institute of Contemporary Art, 1976; *The Battle of the Bluffs*, at the *Biennale*, Venice, 1976; *The Battle of the Bluffs*, at the *American Theatre Association Convention*, Los Angeles, 1976; *Escape from the Tower*, The Clocktower, New York, 1976; *It's Still the Same Old Story*, The Clocktower, New York, 1976; *The Angel of Mercy*, D'Arc Gallery, New York, 197; *The Angel of Mercy*, La Jolla Museum of Contemporary Art, California, 1977; *The Battle of the Bluffs*, Museum of Contemporary Art, Chicago, 1978; *The Battle of the Bluffs*, Contemporary Arts Museum, Houston, 1978; *The Battle of the Bluffs*, Center for Music Experiment, University of California at San Diego, 1978; *Before the Revolution*, Kitchen Center for Music, Video and Dance, New York, 1979; *Before the Revolution*, Santa Barbara Museum of Art, California, 1979; *Recollections of My Life with Diaghilev*, Ronald Feldman Fine Arts Gallery, New York, 1980; *Recollections of My Life with Diaghilev*, 80 Langton Street, San Francisco, 1980; *The Battle of the Bluffs*, at the *National Women's Caucus for Art*, New Orleans, 1980; *The Battle of the Bluffs*, performed at the Ford Theatre, at the *11th Annual International Sculpture Conference*, Washington, D.C., 1980; *Battle of the Bluffs*, College of Art, Calgary, Alberta, 1980; *The Battle of the Bluffs*, Western Front, Vancouver, 1981; *Battle of the Bluffs*, Concordia University, Montreal, 1981; *Battle of the Bluffs*, Newport Harbor Art Museum, California, 1981; *Angel of Mercy*, Los Angeles Institute of Contemporary Art, 1981; *Recollections of My Life with Diaghilev*, Contemporary Arts Museum, Houston, 1981; *Recollections of My Life with Diaghilev*, School of the Art Institute of Chicago, 1981; *Recollections of My Life with Diaghilev*, University of Regina, Saskatchewan, 1981; *Battle of the Bluffs*, La Mamelle, San Francisco, 1982; *Recollections of My Life with Diaghilev*, Oklahoma City Museum of Fine Arts, 1982; *Battle of the Bluffs*, Hofstra University, Hempstead, New York, 1982; *Recollections of My Life with Diaghilev*, California State University, Chico, 1983; *Recollections of My Life with Diaghilev*, Institute of Contemporary Art, Boston, 1984; *Student Days in Paris*, Radio Station WGBH, Boston, 1984; *Recollections of My Life with Diaghilev*, Laguna Beach Museum of Art, California, 1985; *Help! I'm in Seattle*, L.A.C.E., Los Angeles, 1986; *Help! I'm in Seattle*, Franklin Furnace, New York, 1987; *Who Cares About a Ballerina*, Bowery Theatre, San Diego, California, 1987.

Selected Group Exhibitions:

1969   *Language 3*, Dwan Gallery, New York
1975   *Video Art U.S.*, at the *Bienal*, Sao Paulo
1976   *Autobiographical Fantasies*, Los Angeles Institute of Contemporary Art
1977   *American Narrative/Story Art 1967-1977*, Contemporary Arts Museum, Houston (travelled to the Fine Arts Museum, New Orleans; Fine Arts Museum, Vancouver; University of California Museum of Art, Berkeley; and the University of California at Santa Barbara)

1979   *Directions*, Hirshhorn Museum and Sculpture Garden, Smithsonian Institution, Washington, D.C.
1981   *Persona*, New Museum, New York
1984   *Content: A Contemporary Focus*, Hirshhorn Museum, Washington, D.C.
      Revising Romance: New Feminist Video, Institute of Contemporary Art, Boston (toured the United States, 1984–86)
1985   *From the Collection of Sol LeWitt*, California State University, Long Beach (toured the United States)
1986   *Photography as performance*, The Photographers' Gallery, London

Collections:

Museum of Modern Art, New york; Wadsworth Atheneum, Hartford, Connecticut; San Francisco Museum of Modern Art; Long Beach Museum of Art, California; Walker Art Center, Minneapolis.

Publications:

By ANTIN: books—*Before the Revolution*, Santa Barbara, California 1979; *Being Antinova*, Los Angeles 1983; *The Antinova Plays*, Los Angeles 1987; articles—"Women Without Pathos" in *Artnews* (New York), January 1971, reprinted in *Art and Sexual Politics*, edited by Elizabeth Baker and Thomas Hess, New York 1973; "Out of the Box" in *Art Gallery* (Ivoryton, Connecticut), June 1972; "Reading Ruscha" in *Art in America* (New York), September/October 1973; "Recollections of My Life with Diaghilev" in *Artweek* (Oakland, California), 27 October 1973; "Letter to a Young Woman Artist" in *Anonymous Was A Woman*, Valencia, California 1974; "Video as a Medium" in *Art-Rite* (New York), October 1974; photo-texts of "Ballerina and the Bum" and "Little Match Girl Ballet" in *Video Art*, edited by Ira Schneider and Beryl Korot, New York 1976; interview, with Leo Rubenfein, in *Art in America* (New York), September/October 1978; "Interview with Eleanor Antin," with Dinah Portner, in *Journal: Southern California Art Magazine* (Los Angeles), February/March 1980; interview, with Nancy Bowen, in *Profile: Eleanor Antin*, publication of the Video Data Bank, School of the Art Institute of Chicago, 1981; "Pocahontas" in *Skew* (Tucson), no. 1, 1981; "Revolutions Per Minute," interview, with Carter Ratcliff, in *Inter-View* (New York), September 1982.

On ANTIN: books—*6 Years: The Dematerialization of the Art Object from 1966-72* by Lucy Lippard, New York 1973; *Art Talk* by Cindy Nemser, New York 1975; *Angel of Mercy*, exhibition catalogue, with essays by Jonathan Crary and Kim Levin, La Jolla, California 1977; *Originals: American Women Artists* by Eleanor Munro, New York 1979; *Directions*, exhibition catalogue, with an essay by Howard Fox, Washington, D.C. 1979; *Performance Anthology: Source Book for a Decade of California Performance Art*, edited by Carl Loefler and Darlene Tong, San Francisco 1980; *The Amazing Decade: Women and Performance Art in America 1970-1980*, edited by Moira Roth, Los Angeles 1983; articles—review by Lawrence Alloway in *The Nation* (New York), 23 February 1970; "Los Angeles 1971" by Elizabeth Baker in *Artnews* (New York), September 1971; "The Post Perceptual Portrait" by Amy Goldin in *Art in America* (New York), January/February 1975; "4 Artists of Sensuality" by Cindy Nemser in *Arts Magazine* (New York), March 1975; "When Greatness is a Box of Wheaties" by Carol Duncan in *Artforum* (New York), October 1975; "Eleanor Antin: Wishes, Lies and Dreams" by Peter Frank in *Soho Evening News* (New York), 19 February 1976; "Eleanor Antin's Historical Daydream" by John Russell in the *New York Times*, 23 January 1977; "The Nurse and the Dandy" by John Perreault in the *Soho Evening News* (New York), 27 January 1977; "Life/Art/Life: Quentin Crisp and Eleanor Antin: Notes on Performance in the 70's" by John R. Clarke in *Arts Magazine* (New York), February 1979; "Entries: Maximalism" by Robert Pincus-Witten in *Arts Magazine* (New York), February 1981; "Antin/Antinova: The Self as Art Medium" by Sanda Agalidi in *Michigan Quarterly Review* (Ann Arbor), Winter 1984; "Antinova Dances Again" by Henry Sayre in *Artweek* (Oakland, California), 31 May 1986.

For some time I have been considering my art as an exploration of the self, which means that I have been attempting to define my self by moving out to its frontiers, where knowledge of what I cannot and will not be gradually helps shape what I am.

Apparently I have an action or acting theory of the

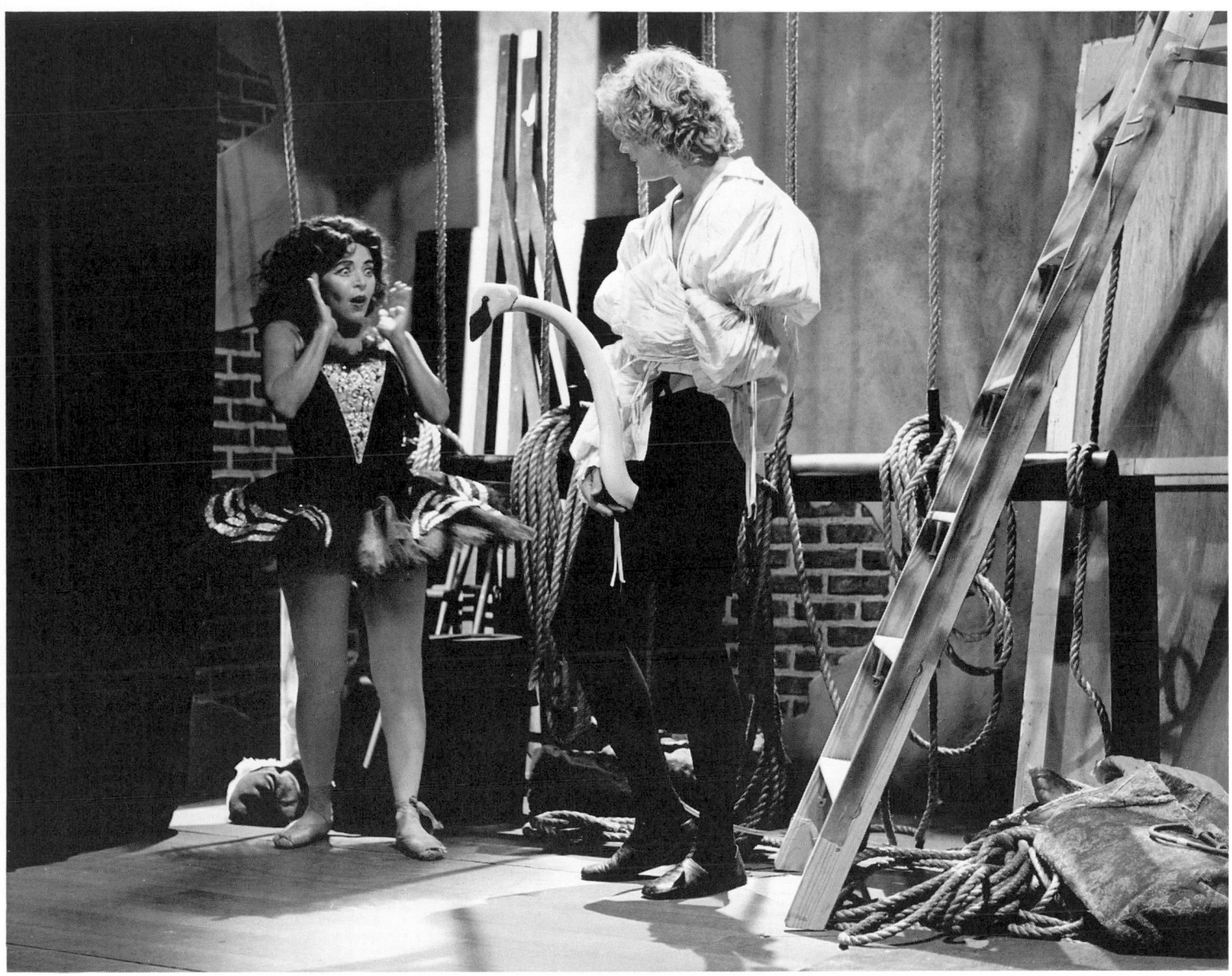

Eleanor Antin: image from the film *Swan Lake*, 1986

self, because I tend to think of the self as a collection of possible characteristic roles that wait in the wings for their chance to play. No actor can play all roles. A good one can play at most three or four fundamental ones, which he or she can, with effort and talent, bend, stretch and transform to satisfy the casting demands life makes on him or her. The inferior actor—the impoverished self—can play only one role over and over again, no matter what demands life makes on him. This boring and impoverished performance is considered sincerity by an equally boring and impoverished criticism, which supposes one life, one truth. I have never accepted such a trivial truth, and I have determined by empirical investigation of my soul that I am by nature typecast as a King, a Ballerina, a Nurse, and a color—Black. A King must rule or try to rule, a Ballerina must star, a Nurse must help, and as all of my selves turn Black, I transform my eccentric Blackness in a white culture into a virtue and a power.

My work has taken the course through drawing, painting, writing, photography, video and performance—of allowing these figures of my soul to play out their roles and answer to all the demands that life makes on me—an artist, a woman, an American in the last quarter of the 20th century.

—Eleanor Antin

Eleanor Antin is a small woman who looks remark-

ably kingly in the cape and beard she wears during performances as the King of Solana Beach. The King visits the people of Solana Beach (where Antin happens to live) and discusses politics while participating in daily activities. The real life encounters are documented in black and white slides which become part of performances such as the *Battle of the Bluffs*. The King feels that Solana Beach is a small but natural kingdom "for no kingdom should extend further than a King can walk on any given day." Although Antin is not interested in having Solana Beach revert to the 17th century, a time more familiar to a King dressed like a Van Dyck portrait, the emphasis on naturalness is significant. The "battle" refers to a confrontation between real estate developers and a band of young skateboarders and elderly citizens with shuffleboard sticks who are organized by the King to stop excessive construction in the small California beach town. There are arrests, and the King escapes down a cliff to travel around the country and alert others. "The world restored will have trees and homegrown food," says the King.

Antin's performance work is autobiographical, yet it has historical and art historical roots. As the King, Antin is pleased with her resemblance to Charles I as painted by Van Dyck, finding him to be "a very small man, like me, a stubborn romantic, and all in all, an impossible person. . . . I recognized all these things in myself. So I knew what sort of man I was, and that he was my political self because a king rules a coun-

try." As Eleanora Antinova, she presents herself as a black dancer with Diaghilev's troupe, reminiscing over her triumphs and failures. As a nurse, she occasionally uses material from the life of Florence Nightingale. At all times Antin is completely immersed not only in her part but in many parts. The *Battle of the Bluffs* is done as a narrative, and although Antin wears the King's costume and performs in front of slides of the King's activities in Solana Beach, she provides the voices for all the characters, lending a charming story hour at the library ambiance to the work.

Autobiography blends with historical allusions and the real history of Antin's characters, documented for performance in slides, or, for Eleanora Antinova, photographs of the ballerina in her greatest roles. Antin's self, therefore, manifests itself in several characters and across several centuries. She is in a position of power as the King, and in a position of powerlessness as the black dancer whose career is thwarted. She controls the performance, yet she is always a vulnerable character. As King, she travels on foot, unprotected, through her kingdom in a manner no one expects of leaders or royalty. By mingling her own vision and experiences with the past, she gives clues to the self of Eleanor Antin in a context which redefines not only the artist but some concepts about power and traditional roles for women. While she has not abandoned any of her characters, Antin has focused on Eleanora Antinova, the black ballerina, in the 1980s. In 1983 she published *Being Antinova*, a detailed account of the twenty-day buildup and letdown of transforming herself from a performance artist living in California to Antinova, dancer in New York. The milieu is the contemporary New York art world, with an astonishing quantity of frank comments and gossip, but the artist's familiarity as a native New Yorker enables her to provide a wide-ranging commentary on class and race consciousness in the Big Apple past and present. Antinova resurfaced in 1986 in *Help! I'm in Seattle*, a performance wherein she hits the skids as a performer in vaudeville houses in the 1930s, and mourns her past with Diaghilev. Once again Antin poses seemingly unsolveable questions about the relation between theater and performance art, couching them in Antinova's own dilemma.

—Mary Stofflet

ANTONAKOS, Stephen.

American. Born in St. Nickolas, Gythion, Greece, 1 November 1926; settled with his family in the United States, 1930. Studied at the Brooklyn Community College, New York. Independent artist, New York, since 1950. Instructor in Painting, Brooklyn Museum Art School, 1965–67; Instructor, University of North Carolina, Greensboro, 1967, 1969; Artist-in-Residence, Viterbo College, LaCrosse, Wisconsin, 1968; Instructor, Yale University, New Haven, Connecticut, 1968; Instructor in Sculpture, Brooklyn College, 1970; Artist-in-Residence, University of Wisconsin, Madison, and Fresno State College, California, 1971. Recipient: Creative Artists Public Service Program Grant, New York, 1972; National Endowment for the Arts grant, 1973. Lives and works in New York. Address: 435 West Broadway, New York, New York 10012, U.S.A.

Individual Exhibitions:

1958   Avant-Garde Gallery, New York
        University of Maine Art Gallery, Orono
1964   Byron Gallery, New York
        Schram Galleries, Fort Lauderdale, Florida
        Miami Museum of Modern Art
1967   Fischbach Gallery, New York
1968   Fischbach Gallery, New York
1970   Fort Worth Art Center Museum, Texas
        Fischbach Gallery, New York
1971   Madison Art Center, Wisconsin
        Fischbach Gallery, New York
        Allen Priebe Art Gallery, Wisconsin State University, Oshkosh
        Contemporary Arts Museum, Houston
1972   Fischbach Gallery, New York
        Fresno State College Art Gallery, California
1973   State University of New York Art Galleries, Albany (toured the United States)
1974   *Drawings*, Rosa Esman Gallery, New York
        4 Neon Sculptures, John Weber Gallery, New York
        Recent Drawings and Sculptures, Albright-Knox Art Gallery, Buffalo, New York
        Discussions: Works/Words, The Clocktower, New York
        4 Incomplete Square Neons, Cusack Gallery, Houston
        10 Outdoor Neons, Fort Worth Art Museum, Texas
1975   *Incomplete Blue Neon Circles*, Galleria Marilena Bonomo, Bari, Italy
        Incomplete Red Neon Circles, Galerie 26, Paris
        Incomplete Green Squares, Galleriaforma, Genoa
        Neon for Wright State, Wright State University Art Gallery, Dayton, Ohio
        Incomplete Neon Squares/Incomplete Neon Circles, John Weber Gallery, New York

1976   *Incomplete Neon Circles*, Galerie December, Dusseldorf
        Packages Meant to Be Opened/Packages Meant Never to Be Opened, John Weber Gallery, New York
        Incomplete Circles, Neons and Drawings, Art and Project, Amsterdam
        Incomplete Circle Neons, Galerie Bonnier, Geneva
        Incomplete Neon Squares/Incomplete Neon Circles, Nancy Lurie Gallery, Chicago
1977   *Neons—Stockholm—1977*, Galerie Aronowitsch, Stockholm
        Neons—New York—1977, John Weber Gallery, New York
        Neons-Athens—1977, Jean and Karen Bernier, Athens
1978   *Outdoor and Indoor Neons*, University of Massachusetts Art Gallery, Amherst
        Drawings, Galerie Tanit, Munich
        Neons/Drawings/Chicago/1978, Young Hoffman Gallery, Chicago
1979   *Neons/Paris/1979*, Galerie Nancy Gillespie/Elisabeth de Laage, Paris
1980   *Neons, Drawings, Collages, München, 1980*, Galerie Tanit, Munich
        3 Neon Walls, Lowe Art Museum, Miami
1982   *New Works/1982*, Nassau County Museum of Art, Roslyn, New York
1983   *Neon for Nevers*, Maison de Culture, Nevers, France
        Three Neons, Le Coin du Miroir, Dijon, France
        New York/1983, Bonnier Gallery, New York
        Neons, Jean Bernier Gallery, Athens
1984   *Neons and Works on Paper*, La Jolla Museum of Contemporary Art, California
1985   Sandpiper Gallery, Tacoma, Washington
        Neons, Davenport Art Gallery, Iowa
1986   *Neons and Drawings*, Brandeis University, Waltham, Massachusetts
        Neon Room for the Elvehjem Museum of Art, University of Wisconsin, Madison (installation)
1987   *Neons and Drawings*, Burnett Miller Gallery, Los Angeles
        Neons, Drawings and Prints, Dalsheimer Gallery, Baltimore, Maryland

Selected Group Exhibitions:

1975   *Painting, Drawing and Sculpture of the 60's and 70's from the Dorothy and Herbert Vogel Collection*, Institute of Contemporary Art, Philadelphia
1976   *Soho—Downtown Manhattan*, at the *Fall Arts Festival*, West Berlin
1977   *Documenta 6*, Kassel, West Germany
1978   *A Shade of Light*, San Francisco Museum of Modern Art
1979   *Minimal Tradition*, Aldrich Museum of Contemporary Art, Ridgefield, Connecticut
1980   *Aspects of the 70's: Site Work*, Jewett Arts Center, Wellesley College Museum, Massachusetts
1981   *Summer Light*, Museum of Modern Art Penthouse, New York
1983   *Elektra*, Musee d'Art Moderne de la Ville, Paris
1984   *Intermedia Space*, Aldrich Museum of Contemporary Art, Ridgefield, Connecticut
1987   *XIX Bienal de Sao Paulo*, Brazil

Collections:

Whitney Museum, New York; Museum of Modern Art; New York; Finch College Museum of Art, New York; Newark Museum, New Jersey; Aldrich Museum of Contemporary Art, Ridgefield, Connecticut; Milwaukee Art Center; Miami Museum of Modern Art; Weatherspoon Art Gallery, University of North Carolina, Greensboro; Phoenix Art Museum, Arizona; La Jolla Museum of Contemporary Art, California.

Permanent public installations: Federal Building, Dayton, Ohio; Crown Center, Hampshire College, Amherst, Massachusetts; University of Massachusetts, Amherst; Hartsfield International Airport, Atlanta; 42nd Street, between Ninth and Tenth Avenues, New York; Charles Center Mass Transit Station, Baltimore; Center Resident Theatre; Seattle; York College, New York; Southwestern Bell Texas Headquarters,

Dallas; Columbus Museum of Art, Ohio; Tacoma Dome, Washington.

Publications:

On ANTONAKOS: books—*New Forms/New Media*, exhibition catalogue, by Lawrence Alloway and Allan Kaprow, New York 1960; *Minimal Art: A Critical Anthology*, edited by Gregory Battcock, New York, 1968; *The Magic Theatre* by Ralph T. Coe, Kansas City, Missouri 1970; *Stephen Antonakos: Six Corner Neons*, exhibition catalogue, with essay by Naomi Spector, New York 1973; *Stephen Antonakos*, exhibition catalogue, with texts by Xavier Douroux, Franck Gautherot and Naomi Spector, Dijon 1983; *Neons and Works on Paper*, exhibition catalogue, with essay by Sally Yard, La Jolla 1984; articles—"New Talent" by Larry Aldrich in *Art in America* (New York), July/August 1966; "Stephen Antonakos: 5 Neons for the San Francisco Show" by Naomi Spector in *Data* (Milan), Autumn 1973; "Stephen Antonakos" by Lawrence Campbell in *Artnews* (New York), April 1974; "Stephen Antonakos" by Ellen Lubell in *Arts Magazine* (New York), April 1974; "Stephen Antonakos at the Fort Worth Art Museum" by Janet Kutner in *Art in America* (New York), September/October 1975; "Stephen Antonakos' Neons" by Hugh Davies in *Arts Magazine* (New York), January 1979; "Lights of the Night" by Michael Webb in *Sky* (New York), February 1984; "Creations in Neon" by William Zimmer in the *New York Times*, 15 March 1987.

My work concerns light, color and space: neon used in relation to architectural sites, painted canvases, and painted wood panels. My drawings, prints, books, and other projects are also very important to me in working out my ideas about placing elements in relation to each other.

Neon is endless. Its ability to change and be changed by various elements—alone, or in combination—is a continuing source of inspiration to me.

I am interested in a direct visual experience which will allow the viewer to participate fully, which will provide a feeling of heightened consciousness, or excitement.

—Stephen Antonakos

Stephen Antonakos' work has never been a search for new technical possibilities. His concern for light as a means of expression is the sole impetus for his perserverance with a potentially dated art form, neon. Yet he is no "light artist," but a sculptor and a painter. His search is rather for new ways of commanding ever more intense and refined statements from his formal vocabulary.

Born in southern Greece, Antonakos immigrated to the United States in 1930. He graduated from the New York Institute of Applied Arts and Sciences in 1947, then worked two years as a commercial artist until becoming frustrated by the restrictions of drawing in black and white. After assisting Umberto Romano in 1951, Antonakos spent nine months in Europe visiting galleries and museums. During that period he formulated an individual approach to painting in colour.

Nearly all of Antonakos' work contains the leitmotif of incompletion. In the late 40s and early 50s he developed a complicated vocabulary of forms and a penchant for natural and found materials and colours. The result was a composition of found objects and fragments glued, pinned, or sewn to the canvas called "sewlages." He devoted his energies in the late 50s to freestanding, wooden assemblages. Beginning in September 1962, Antonakos conceived all of the renowned "Pillow" series in one intense 14 month period. The pillows communicate in words, in forms, in materials, in symbols, and with real objects. They deliver themes of interruption, chaos, loss and pain, offering riddles, promising revelations, and ultimately define the struggle of an identity unable to reconcile what it wants to be with what it really is. The pillows tell a story of how they must overcome being ripped open, sewn up, and nailed down to achieve understanding and to reach wholeness.

The focus of his work shifted again in 1962 as he developed a regime of light as environment. The first

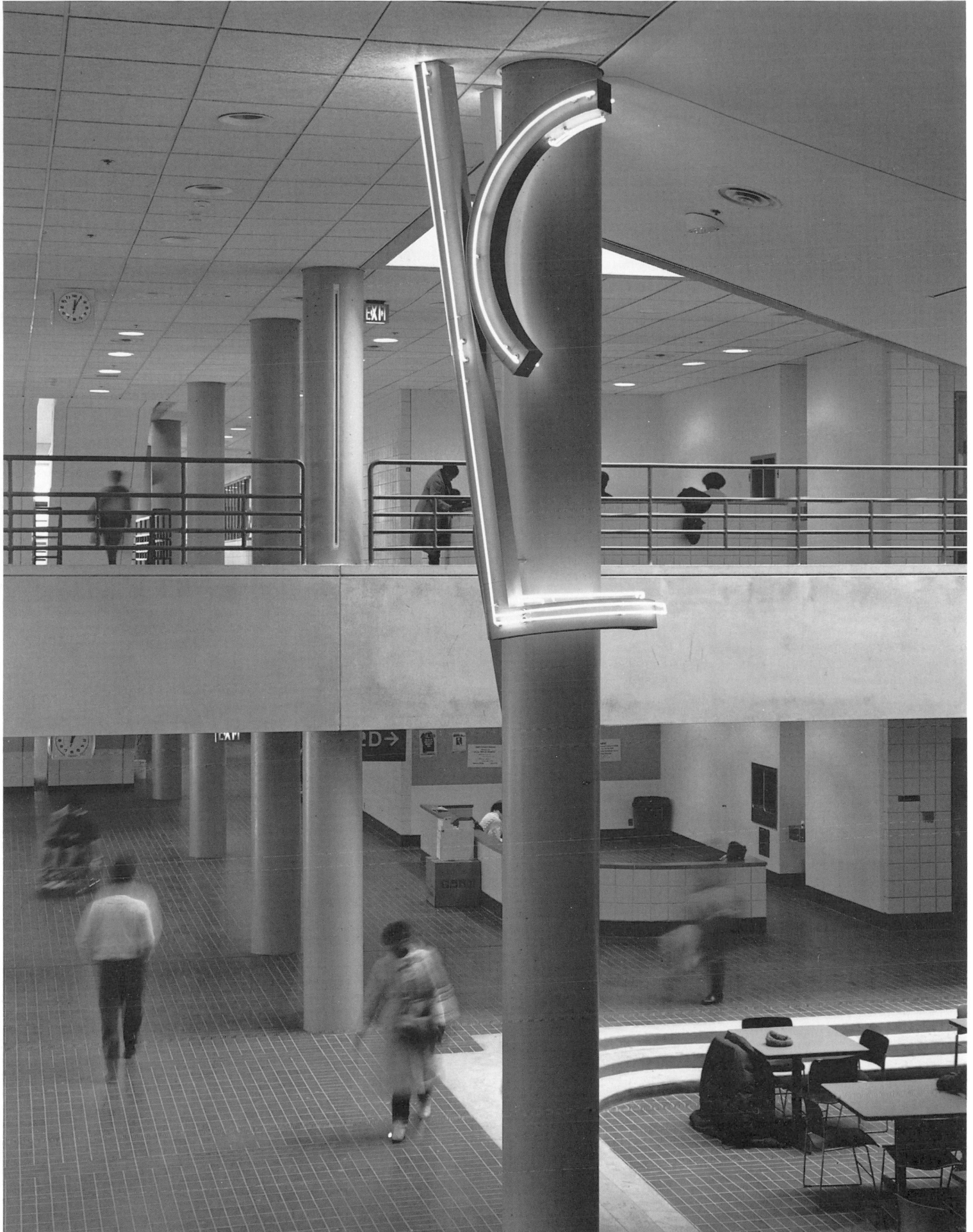

Stephen Antonakos: *Neon for New York College,* **1986**

neons were fully three-dimensional sculpture forms, traditional pedestal objects whose constituent tubes emitted intense coloured light and were programmed to turn on and off in series. With the advent of environmental art during the decade following, Antonakos persistently exploited the full potential of a medium which projects colour and creates volume without sculptural mass.

The three-dimensional forms gradually evolved into neons which conspicuously hugged the plane of the wall. In this sense his work has progressed from assertively sculptural to architectural and finally to environmental painting. The latter is characterised by a dramatic increase in scale, as many neon elements are arranged across the entire two-dimensional surface in mural fashion. The painting's actual dimensions are obfuscated by deliberate perspectival distortions: the bright neon elements establish a flat plane, although the neon itself appears to float, making the depth of the rear supporting wall ambiguous.

Recently Antonakos discovered that painting the supporting walls in colours compliments the neons they entertain. Background colour defines the boundaries of the work and alters the ambient light. He reiterates his original leit-motif by painting the walls in fragments of squares or circles, incomplete shapes that suggest the language of minimalism.

Yet his work seems to adhere to no single identifiable group. Being conspicuously versatile it satisfies dogmatists of most spheres: technological utopianism, geometric reduction, grammatical vision. Because neon is so direct it seems uncomplicated at first, but even in the same piece it can be completely different in meaning: it is quiet and inconspicuous in the daylight, more alert and assertive at dusk, progressively more dominating and abstract at night. From different points of view it is a series of illusions which succeeds as an architectural statement both indoors and out.

The power of these neons rests undeniably in their ability to excite and evoke. Antonakos is particularly sensitive to the warmth and ambiance of colour—mostly reds, blues and greens—and rhythm. When the light goes off, the tubes often seem to become immaterial, and when they burst back on, the shock is extremely effective, especially in rhythmic repetition. This rhythmic quality is one of his most crucial elements. From the beginning the forms—especially the linear ones—appear in repetitive patterns hinting at rhythms of various sorts.

While the emanation of ambient light and the resulting environmental command it bears resemble artists like Flavin, the colour and composition of his neon paintings echo the works of Matisse. Indeed his work bears comparison to a range of artists and dogmas, although the constant evolution in Antonakos's work continues to avoid type-casting.

—Carrie Barker

ANUSKIEWICZ, Richard (Joseph).

American. Born in Erie, Pennsylvania, 23 May 1930. Studied at the Cleveland Institute of Art, 1948–53, B.F.A. 1953; School of Art and Architecture, Yale University, New Haven, Connecticut, 1953–55 (studied with Josef Albers), M.F.A. 1955; Kent State University, Ohio, B.S. in Education 1956. Independent artist known for hard-edge non-objective paintings and prints. Instructor, Cooper Union, New York, 1963–65; Artist-in-Residence, Dartmouth College, Hanover, New Hampshire, 1967; Visiting Artist, University of Wisconsin, Madison, Cornell University, Ithaca, New York, and Visiting Artist, Kent State University, Ohio, 1968; instructor in painting, School of Visual Arts, New York, since 1983. Recipient: Pulitzer Travelling Scholarship, National Academy of Design, 1953; Purchase Prize, Flint Institute of Arts, Michigan, 1966. Agent: Sidney Janis Gallery, 110 West 57th Street, New York, New York 10019. Address: 76 Chestnut Street, Englewood, New Jersey 07631, U.S.A.

Individual Exhibitions:

1955	Butler Art Institute, Youngstown, Ohio
1960	The Contemporaries, New York
1961	The Contemporaries, New York
1963	The Contemporaries, New York
1965	Sidney Janis Gallery, New York
1966	Cleveland Museum of Art
1967	Sidney Janis Gallery, New York
	Hopkins Art Center, Dartmouth College, New Hampshire
1968	Kent State University, Ohio
1969	Sidney Janis Gallery, New York
1971	Sidney Janis Gallery, New York
1972	DeCordova Museum, Lincoln, Massachusetts
	Jacksonville Art Museum, Florida
1973	Sidney Janis Gallery, New York
1974	Andrew Crispo Gallery, New York
1975	Andrew Crispo Gallery, New York
	Ulrich Museum of Art, Wichita, Kansas
1976	Andrew Crispo Gallery, New York
	La Jolla Museum of Contemporary Art, California
1977	University of California Art Museum, Berkeley
	Columbus Gallery of Fine Arts, Ohio
1978	Ringling Museum, Sarasota, Florida
	Allentown Art Museum, Pennsylvania
1979	Alex Rosenberg Gallery, New York
	Clark Art Institute, Williamstown, Massachusetts
1980	Brooklyn Museum, New York
	Carnegie Institute, Pittsburgh
1981	University Fine Arts Galleries, Tallahassee, Florida
	Museum of Fine Arts, St. Petersburg, Florida
	Lowe Art Museum, Coral Gables, Florida
	Hokin Gallery, Bay Harbor Islands, Florida
1984	Butler Art Institute, Youngstown, Ohio
	Heckscher Museum, Huntington, New York
	Pembroke Gallery, Houston, Texas
1985	Hokin-Kaufman Gallery, Chicago
	Schweyer-Galdo Galleries, Pontiac, Michigan
1986	Tampa Museum, Florida

Selected Group Exhibitions:

1962	*Geometric Abstraction in America*, Whitney Museum, New York (toured the United States)
1965	*The Responsive Eye*, Museum of Modern Art, New York
1967	*American Painting Now*, Institute of Contemporary Art, Boston
1968	*Documenta 4*, Kassel, West Germany
1971	*Color Structure*, Whitney Museum, New York
1974	*Opening Exhibition*, Hirshhorn Museum, Smithsonian Institution, Washington, D.C.
1975	*34th Biennial of Contemporary American Painting*, Corcoran Gallery, Washington, D.C.
1976	*30 Years of American Printmaking*, Brooklyn Museum
1979	*2 Decades of Printmaking*, Museum of Modern Art, New York
1980	*5 in Florida: Anuszkiewicz/Chamberlain/Olitski/Rauschenberg/Rosenquist*, University of South Florida, Tampa

Collections:

Metropolitan Museum of Art, New York; Museum of Modern Art, New York; Whitney Museum, New York; Albright-Knox Art Gallery, Buffalo, New York; Yale University Art Gallery, New Haven, Connecticut; Corcoran Gallery of Art, Washington, D.C.; Smithsonian Institution, Washington, D.C.; Art Institute of Chicago; Detroit Institute of Arts; Philadelphia Museum of Art.

Publications:

On ANUSKIEWICZ: books—*The New Art: A Critical Anthology*, edited by Gregory Battcock, New York 1966; *Pur-*

poses of Art by Albert Elsen, New York 1967; *Constructivism: Origins and Evolution* by George Rickey, New York 1967; *Optical Art: Theory and Practice* by Rene Parola, New York 1969; *Op Art* by Cyril Barrett, New York 1970; articles—"A Theology of Hard Edge" by Edouard Roditi in *Arts Magazine* (New York), December 1963; "Art That Pulses, Quivers and Fascinates" by John Canaday in the *New York Times*, February 1965; "Anuskiewicz Sets Legs in Motion" by Bernadine Morris in the *New York Times*, May 1965; "Richard Anuskiewicz: "It's Baffling" by John Canaday in the *New York Times*, April 1969; "Graphics '70: Richard Anuskiewicz" by Donald Karshan in *Art in America* (New York), March 1970; "Trays by 10 Artists" by Mario Amaya in *Art in America* (New York), January 1971; "Portrait of the Artist: Richard Anuskiewicz" by Jay Jacobs in *Art Gallery* (Ivoryton, Connecticut), March 1971; "At Lincoln: Anuskiewicz Acrylics" by Susan Drysdale in the *Christian Science Monitor* (Boston), March 1972.

Born in 1930 of Polish emigrant parents, Richard Anuskiewicz is one of the most outstanding exponents of colorism, the movement which developed from abstract expressionism, and pop art. At first, Anuskiewicz leaned towards realism. The change took place as a result of meeting Albers at Yale while he was studying there. Albers opened his eyes to the way colours behave and to their mutual influence on each other which causes "everything to depend on everything else."

In spite of all his respect for the master, Anuskiewicz rejects total acceptance of Albers' theory. Other theories of colour also interest him—that of Paul Klee, in particular. He has found Klee less pedantic and more poetic in his perception of the world of colour.

Anuskiewicz was one of the first American painters to be interested in creating space in a picture, introducing the effect of vibrations on a flat surface. He was a pioneer in applying the technique of mixing colours optically—i.e., instead of physically mixing colours on a palette, he achieves the same impression on the retina. This, of course, was nothing new; the process had been in use since divisionism. Developed now, in terms of non-representational art, based on geometric form—it brought a new element to painting. Anuskiewicz's painting, while exploiting 19th century colour physics, Chevreul's and Helmholtz's theories of colour, also makes use of new technology. This kind of painting distinguishes itself by a specific atmosphere. Created as it is under warm light conditions, it ideally needs to be viewed in a similar light. The intensity of colour, the precision of its optical limits, the technical elegance of coloured surfaces, by rays or a regular network, the juxtaposition of complementary colours which causes after-images—all form a tight, logical system.

This system, recalling Albers' theoretical assumptions, is inherent in the structure of the square. The square forms an unlimited collection of alternatives; divisions into quadrilateral compartments are filled with ever greater or ever smaller fields of squares. These, in turn, yield not only diagonal rhombuses, networks, screens, modules, cuboid spatial variants covered by a network of lines giving the impression of being concave or convex, but also deformations of perspective. Optical illusions also arise on a flat, square surface. If a geometric shape is given by the grouping or separation of lines, the space between them is formed by a subtle gradation of chromatic shades of equal intensity.

The construction of complicated linear and interlinear structures (both inside and outside the modulated squares) has become possible from a technological point of view, thanks to industrial innovations. The fact is that, at the beginning of the 1960's, fast-drying paints (acrylics) appeared as did masking tapes—adhesive and varying in width from 0.2 cm—used hitherto in technical projects. When stuck to the surface of a painting, the tapes cover the parts already painted, thus protecting them from being covered by the next layer of paint. When the tapes are removed, the outline of the resulting image appears. Thanks to the tapes, the business of masking can be carried out with ideal precision, impossible with any other technique. Even the thinnest lines have sharp, well-defined edges. But that is not the artist's goal. "What I am trying to do," Anuskiewicz has said, "is to achieve a soft effect by means of so-called hard media." That is why his paintings, in spite of his emphasis on geometry, differ from classical geometrical abstraction by a softness, blurred forms and a chromatic subduing, despite a simultaneously bright palette. They also differ from op-art—although articles about him usually refer to Anuskiewicz as an op-artist. This kind of classification is not wholly wrong. Artists interested in optics, optical illusion and kinetics are also called perpetuators of the Bauhaus and Constructivist traditions. Thus Anuskiewicz, Vasarely, Riley and others all share a common antecedent.

Anuskiewicz proclaimed his particular view of painting in the United States, but maintained a certain independence from other American artists, retaining his own vision during two decades, the 1960's and 70's. Nothing augurs a change in his artistic attitude.
—Szymon Bojko

ANZINGER, Siegfried.

Austrian. Born in Weyer, in 1953. Educated in Steyr, until 1971; studied art, under Professor Melcher, Akademie der bildenden Kunste, Vienna, 1971–77. Married the painter Marie-Luise Lebschik. Independent painter, Vienna, since 1977, and in Cologne, since 1981. Address: Neusser Strasse 27/29, 5000 Cologne 1, West Germany.

Individual Exhibitions:

1976	Galerie Herzog, Vienna
1978	Galerie Ariadne, Vienna
1979	Osterreichische Hochschulerschaft, Vienna
1980	Galerie und Edition Sigrid Friedrich/Sabine Knust, Munich
	Galerie Krinzinger, Innsbruck
	Galerie Ariadne, Vienna
1981	Galerie und Edition Sigrid Friedrich/Sabine Knust, Munich
	Perspektive, at Art 12, '81, Basel
1982	Galerie Buchmann, St. Gallen, Switzerland
	Galerie t'Venster, Rotterdam (with Hubert Schmalix)
	Galerie Bitterlin, Basel (with Hubert Schmalix)
	Galerie Krinzinger, Innsbruck
	Galerie Nachst St. Stephan, Vienna
	Galerie Thaddaus J. Ropac, Lienz, Austria
1983	Galerie Sigrid Friedrich, Munich
	Galeria Heinrich Ehrhardt, Madrid (with Hubert Schmalix)
	Galerie Vera Munro, Hamburg
	Galerie Albert Baronian, Brussels
	Galerie Gugu Ernesto, Cologne
1984	Galerie Farideh Cadot, Paris (with Hubert Schmalix and Alois Mosbacher)
	Holly Solomon Gallery, New York (with Hubert Schmalix)
	Studio Cannaviello, Milan
	Galerie Bleich-Rossi, Graz, Austria
1985	Kunstmuseum, Basel
	Galerie Buchmann, Basel
	ORF, Graz, Austria
	Galerie Gugu Ernesto, Cologne
	Burnette Mille Gallery, Los Angeles (with Hubert Schmalix)
	Galerie Six Friedrich, Munich
	Museum für Gegenwartskunst, Basel (travelled to Bonn and Linz 1985–86)
1986	Neue Galerie Graz, Austria
	Kunsthalle, Hamburg
	Galerie Krinzinger, Vienna
	Kunstverein, Frankfurt
	Galerie Sigma, Bregenz, Austria

Selected Group Exhibitions:

1977	*Interkunst*, Palais Liechtenstein, Vienna
1980	*Malerei 80*, Galerie Annasaule, Innsbruck
1981	*Neue Malerei in Ostereich*, Landesgalerie Joanneum, Graz, Austria
1982	*Documenta 7*, Museum Fridericianum, Kassel, West Germany
1983	*Einfach gute Malerei*, Museum des 20. Jahrhunderts, Vienna
1987	*Arco 87*, Madrid

Collections:

Kupferstichkabinett, Basel; Neue Galerie der Stadt Linz, Austria.

Publications:

By ANZINGER: books—*Laokoon Ubt*, with introduction by Peter Weiermair, Innsbruck and Vienna 1986.

On ANZINGER: books—*Siegfried Anziner: Malerei, Gouachen, Zeichnungen*, exhibition catalogue, with introduction by Dieter Ronte, Vienna and Munich 1982; *Siegfried Anzinger: Werke auf Papier 1977-1985*, exhibition catalogue with text by Dieter Koepplin, Basel 1985; *Siegfried Anzinger: Zeichnung, Malerei, Skulpture*, exhibition catalogue, by Dieter Koepplin, Innsbruck 1986.

APPEL, Karel.

Dutch. Born in Amsterdam, 25 April 1921. Educated at the Royal Academy of Fine Arts, Amsterdam, 1940–43. Met Corneille, Louis Van Lint, and Marc Mendeksin, 1946; Co-Founder of the Dutch experimental artists group "Reflex" (known as "COBRA" in Paris), Amsterdam, 1948; moved to Paris, 1950, and officially ended "COBRA"; met the avant-garde art critic Michel Tapie, Paris, 1951; first travelled to America and Mexico, 1957; established studios at the Chateau de Molesmes, Auxerre, France, 1964–72; now lives in Monaco and New York. Recipient: Unesco Prize, *Biennale*, Venice, 1954; Prize at the *Premio Lissone*, Italy, 1957; Graphics Prize, *Biennale*, Ljubljana, 1957; International Prize for Painting, *Sao Paolo Bienal*, 1959; First Prize from the Netherlands Committee, and First Prize for Painting, *Guggenheim International Exhibition*, New York, 1960. Honorary Citizen, Hamilton, Ontario, 1977. Knight of Orange Nassau, Netherlands, 1968. Agent: Marisa del Re Gallery, New York. Address: c/o Marisa del Re Gallery, 41 East 57th Street, New York, New York 10022, U.S.A.

Individual Exhibitions:

1946	Beerenhuis, Groningen, The Netherlands
1947	Guildhall, Amsterdam
1948	Santee Landweer, Amsterdam
1951	Van Lier Gallery, Amsterdam
1952	Het Venster Gallery, Rotterdam
1953	Palais des Beaux-Arts, Brussels
	Bennewitz Gallery, The Hague
1954	Martha Jackson Gallery, New York
	Studio Fachetti, Paris
1955	Bennewitz Gallery, The Hague
	Galerie Rive Droite, Paris
	Cultural Center, Schiedam, Netherlands
	Stedelijk Museum, Amsterdam
1956	Galleria dell'Ariete, Milan
1957	Institute of Contemporary Arts, London
	Galerie Espace, Haarlem, The Netherlands
	Galleria Tartaruga, Rome
	Martha Jackson Gallery, New York
1958	Galerie Claude Bernard, Paris
	Galerie Anna Abels, Cologne
	Palais des Beaux-Arts, Brussels

1959	Galerie Espace, Haarlem, The Netherlands
	Gimpel Fils, London
	Charles Lienhard Gallery, Zurich
	Gendai Gallery, Tokyo
	Musée d'Art, Neuchâtel, Switzerland
1960	Martha Jackson Gallery, New York
	Gimpel Fils, London
	Galleria Lorenzelli, Bergamo, Italy
	Nova Gallery, Boston
	Fairweather-Hardin Gallery, Chicago
	Rudolf Zwirner, Essen
	Esther Robles Gallery, Los Angeles
	David Anderson Gallery, New York
	Galerie Rive Droite, Paris
1961	Esther Robles Gallery, Los Angeles
	David Anderson Gallery, New York
	Gallery Espace, Amsterdam
	Galerie d'Art Moderne, Basel
	Stedelijk Van Abbe Museum, Eindhoven
	Haags Gemeentemuseum, The Hague
	Irving Gallery, Milwaukee
	Tirca Karlis Gallery, Provinceton, Massachusetts
	Galleria Le Medusa, Rome
	Gallery Moos, Toronto
	Gres Gallery, Washington, D.C.
	Galleria Blu, Milan
	Museum of Art, San Francisco (retrospective)
	Pasadena Art Museum, California (retrospective)
	Phoenix Art Museum, Arizona (retrospective)
	Santa Barbara Art Museum, California (retrospective)
1962	Galerie Rive Droite, Paris
	Gallery Moos, Toronto
	La Jolla Art Museum, California
	Gimpel Fils, London
	Galleria dell'Ariete, Milan
	Gallery Charles Lienhard, Zurich
	Galerie Agnes Lefort, Montreal
	Stephen Hahn Gallery, New York
	Martha Jackson Gallery, New York
	James Goodman Gallery, New York
	Park Gallery, Detroit
	Anderson-Mayer Galerie, Paris
	Esther Robles Gallery, Los Angeles
1964	Gimpel Fils, London
	Martha Jackson Gallery, New York
	Stephen Hahn Gallery, New York
	American Art Gallery, Copenhagen
	Gallery Krikhaar, Amsterdam
1965	Kunsthallen, Göteborg, Sweden
	Palais des Beaux-Arts, Brussels
	Donald Morris Gallery, Detroit
	Gallery Leger, Malmo, Sweden
	Stedelijk Museum, Amsterdam (retrospective)
	City Museum, Copenhagen (retrospective)
	Moderna Museet, Stockholm (retrospective)
	Museum of Bochum, West Germany (retrospective)
1966	Stedelijk Museum, Breda, Netherlands (retrospective)
1967	Martha Jackson Gallery, New York
	Redfern Gallery, London
	Galerie Agnes Lefort, Montreal
1968	Centre National d'Art Contemporain, Paris
	Stedelijk Museum, Amsterdam
1969	Martha Jackson Gallery, New York
	Galerie Gimpel und Hanover, Zurich
	Gallery Gimpel, London
	Galerie Krikhaar, Amsterdam
	Kunsthalle, Basel
	Palais des Beaux-Arts, Brussels
1970	Centraal Museum, Utrecht (retrospective)
	Galleria La Medusa, Rome
	Winterhur, Lucerne
	Richard Gray Gallery, Chicago
	Gallery Moos, Toronto
	Galerie Nova, Spectra, The Hague
1971	Galerie Nova, Spectra, The Hague
	Galerie Ariel, Paris
	Martha Jackson Gallery, New York (thrice)
	Galerie Teatre, Brussels
	Nantensi Gallery, Tokyo (twice)
	Kunstgalleri, Aarhus, Denmark
	London Arts Gallery, Detroit
	London Arts Gallery, London

e Arts, Philadelphia
Rinaldo Rotta, Milan
llery, Detroit
Gallery, Jamaica, New York
all Mall, Toronto (retrospective)
Gallery, Stratford, Ontario (retro-

Contemporain, Montreal (retrospec-

f Greater Victoria, British Columbia
e)
Gallery, Alberta (retrospective)
Gallery, Manitoba (retrospective)
1973   Art Gallery f Ontario, Toronto (retrospective)
    Martha on Gallery, New York
    Dalhousie University Art Gallery, Halifax, Nova Scotia (retrospective)
    London Public Library and Art Museum, London, Ontario (retrospective)
    Art Gallery of Hamilton, Ontario (retrospective)
    New York Cultural Center, New York (retrospective)
    Miami Art Center (retrospective)
    Gallery Moos, Toronto
1974   Oklahoma Art Center, Oklahoma City (retrospective)
    Ft. Lauderdale Museum, Florida (retrospective)
    Phoenix Art Museum, Arizona (retrospective)
    Galleria La Medusa, Rome
    Galerie Ariel, Paris
    Gimpel Fils, London
    Gimpel and Weitzenhoffer, New York
    Court Gallery, Copenhagen
    Gloria Lauria Gallery, Miami
1975   Gimpel and Weitzenhoffer, New York
    Galerie Nova Spectra, The Hague
    David Gallery, Pittsford, New York
    Aberbach Fine Arts, New York
    Wildenstein Gallery, London
1976   Galerie Nova Spectra, The Hague
    Gallery Moos, Toronto
    Modern Master Tapestries Inc., New York
1977   Galerie Ariel, Paris
    Galerie Krikhaar, Amsterdam
    Museo de Arte Moderno, Mexico City (retrospective)
    Hamilton Museum, Ontario
    Museum Terneuzen, The Netherlands
    Museum 'Slot Zeist, The Netherlands
    Palm Springs Desert Museum, California
    Gallery Collection d'Art, Amsterdam
    Lillian Heidenberg Gallery, New York
1978   Galerie Nova Spectra, The Hague
    Galerie Krikhaar, Amsterdam
    Museo de Bellas Artes, Caracas (retrospective)
    Museo de Arte Moderno, Bogota (retrospective)
    Moderne Galerie Saarlandmuseum, Saarbrucken, West Germany
    Museum Van Bommel, Van Dam, Venlo, The Netherlands
    Cultureel Centrum Hasselt, Belgium
    Brewster Gallery, New York
1979   Vienna Museum, Austria (retrospective)
    Bonn Museum, West Germany (retrospective)
    Janus Gallery, Washington, D.C.
    6 Scandinavian Museums (retrospective; tour)
1980   Galerie Daniel Templon, Paris
    Janus Gallery, Washington, D.C.
    State University of New York, Binghamton
    Bede Gallery, Jarrow, County Durham
    Museum Wilhelmshafen, West Germany
1981   Galerie Ariel, Paris
    Gimpel Fils, London
    Kunstforum, Schelderode, Belgium
    Stedelijk Museum, Amsterdam
    Fame Gallery, Houston, Texas
    London Arts Gallery, Detroit
    Fundacao Gulbenkian, Lisbon
    Museu de Arte Moderna, Rio de Janeiro
    Museu de Arte Moderna, Sao Paulo
1982   Biblioteca Nacional, Madrid
    Gemeentemuseum, The Hague
    Museum Boymans-van Beuningen, Rotterdam
    Galerie Collection d'Art, Amsterdam
    Staatliche Kunsthalle, Baden-Baden, West Germany

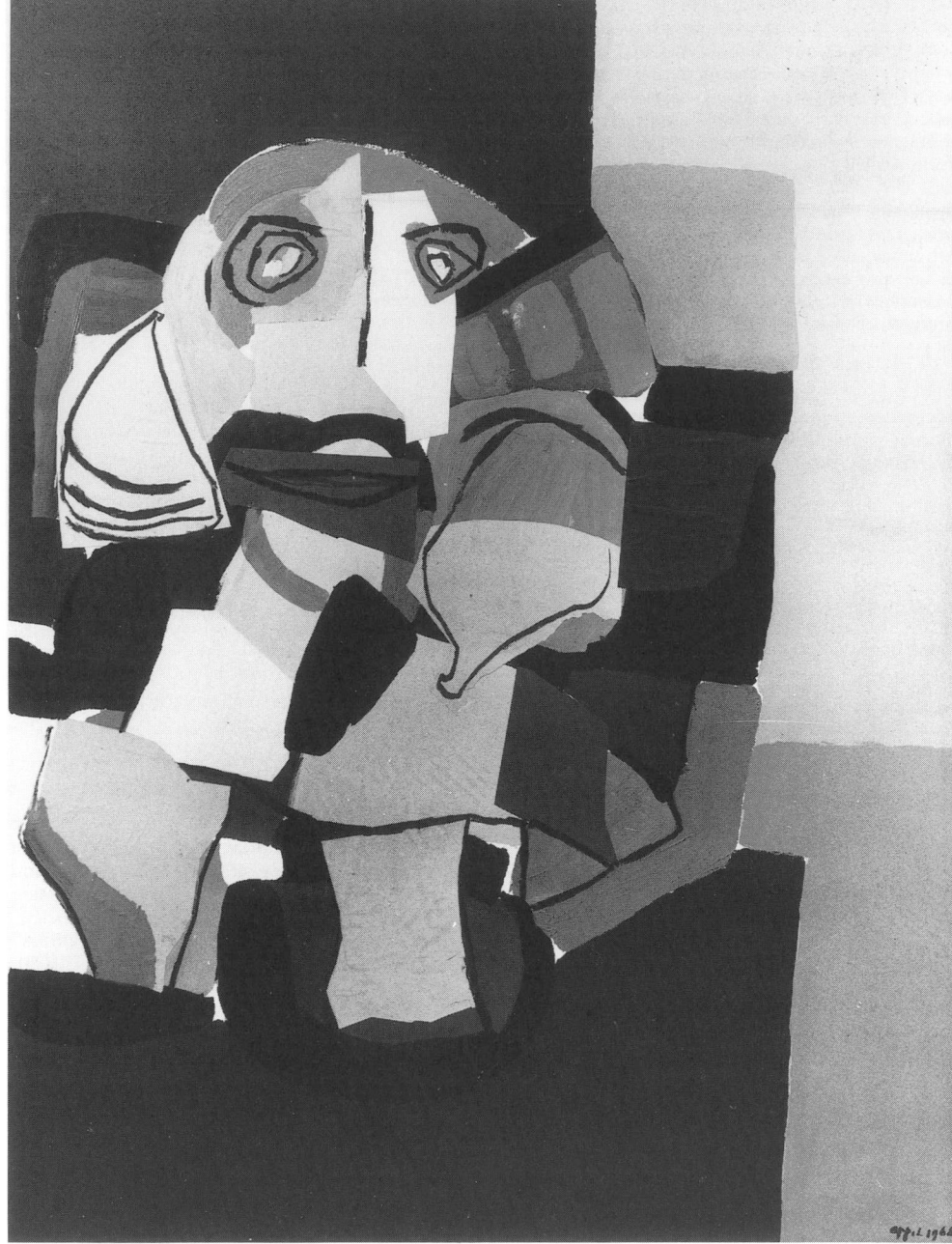

Karel Appel: *Donna Cubista*, 1968

1984   Kunstforening, Copenhagen
    National Gallery of Iceland, Reykjavik
    Palais des Beaux-Arts, Brussels
    Galerie Collection d'Art, Amsterdam
1985   Palazzo di Medici, Florence
1986   Arnolfini Gallery, Bristol, Avon
    Marisa del Re Gallery, New York
    Fort Lauderdale Museum of Art, Florida
    Virginia Miller Gallery, Coral Gables, Florida
1987   Galerie d'Art Contemporain, Nice, France
    Douglas Hyde Gallery, Dublin
    Marisa del Re Gallery, New York
1988   Galerie Beyeler, Basle

Selected Group Exhibitions:

1946   *Salon de Mai*, Paris (regularly until 1971)
1951   *2nd COBRA International*, Palais des Beaux-Arts, Liege, Belgium
1953   *2nd Biennial*, Museum of Modern Art, Sao Paolo
1955   *Expressionism 1900–1955*, Walker Art Center, Minneapolis (toured the United States)
1959   *50 Years of Research*, Stedelijk Museum, Amsterdam
1964   *Documenta 3*, Kassel, West Germany

1969   *Portraits in Contemporary Art*, Museum of Modern Art, New York
1972   *Humor, Satire, Irony*, New School for Social Research, New York
1973   *25th Anniversary Exhibition of COBRA*, Court Gallery, Copenhagen
1982   *On The Road: The Jack Kerouac Exhibit*, Boulder Center for the Visual Arts, Colorado

Collections:

Stedelijk Museum, Amsterdam; Stedelijk Van Abbe Museum, Eindhoven, Netherlands; Musée Royal des Beaux-Arts, Brussels; Centre National d'Art Contemporain, Paris; Tate Gallery, London; National Museet, Copenhagen; Museum of Modern Art, New York; Guggenheim Museum, New York; Museum of Fine Arts, Boston; Los Angeles County Museum; Hamilton Museum, Ontàrio; Art Gallery of Ontario, Toronto; Montreal Museum of Fine Arts.

Publications:

By APPEL: books—*A Beast-Drawn Man*, portfolio, with Bert Schierbeek, Paris 1962; *Karel Appel over Karel Appel*, with a foreword by Albert Rikmans, Amsterdam 1971; *En-*

cres à Deux Pinceaux et Leurs Poemes par Hugo Claus, with Pierre Alechinsky, Paris 1978; Forty Years of Paintings, Sculptures and Drawings, Paris 1987; Nocturne de San Ildefonso, with poems by Octavio Paz, Paris 1987.

On APPEL: books—Art since 1945 by Marcel Brion and Samuel Hunter, New York 1958; Karel Appel: Painter by Hugo Claus, New York 1962; Karel Appel: Nudes, exhibition catalogue, by Bert Schiebeek, New York 1964; Karel Appel: Reliefs 1964–1968, exhibition catalogue, by Julien Alvard, Paris 1968; Appel by Peter Bellew, Milan 1968; Het Tidschrift Cobra by Anne Choisez, Brussels 1970; Appel's Oogappels, exhibition catalogue, by Simon Vinkenoog, Utrecht 1970; Appel's Appels, exhibition catalogue, by Luke Rombout, Toronto 1972; Karel Appel: The Early 50's, exhibition catalogue, New York 1973; Opere di Karel Appel by Armondo Nocentini, Florence 1973; Karel Appel: Recent Works, exhibition catalogue, New York 1973; Cobra + Contrasts, exhibition catalogue, by Willem Sandberg, Detroit 1974; Appel, exhibition catalogue, by Herbert Read, London 1975; Karel Appel: Pintor de Insolita Expresividad, exhibition catalogue, by Antonio Rodriguez, Mexico City 1977; Visages-Payages, exhibition catalogue, Paris 1977; Karel Appel by Peter Berger, Venlo, Netherlands 1977; Pierre Alechinsky, by the Artist by Pierre Alechinsky, New York 1977; Het Gezicht van Appel by Nico Koster and Edward Wingen, Venlo, Netherlands 1977; Eloge de la Folie by Jean-Clarence Lambert, Paris 1977; 30 Years of Painting by Appel by Edward Wingen, Venlo, Netherlands 197; Karel Appel, exhibition catalogue, Bogota 1978; Karel Appel: Works on Paper by Jean-Clarence Lambert, with a foreword by Marshall McLuhan, New York 1980; Karel Appel by Alfred Frankenstein, New York 1980; Karel Appel: Paintings 1980–85, exhibition catalogue with introduction by Rupert Martin, Dublin and Bristol 1986; Karel Appel: Recent Paintings, exhibition catalogue with text by Sam Hunter, New York 1986; Karel Appel: Recent Paintings and Sculpture, exhibition catalogue with text by Donald Kuspit, New York 1987.

*

Over the years my work has changed, and the philosophy behind my thinking about my work has changed too, and still is changing today. I mean by this, that painting is always a fight with yourself and the material. The most difficult thing is the concentration and tension to be "one" with myself, my painting and my materials. It's an inner fight, and inner fight means the inner evolution that the artist can see in his work—in his paint, in his image, in his expression, in his color—that means his *inner* evolution is going on.

Take television, for instance. Television is something like the artist—a reality of our planet. The only difference is that television shows only reality and I show the future. I work on the future, and that is the most important thing for me, and thus the reason why my work started changing after the war.

When we started to paint seriously, we formed the *Cobra* group and we met people, other artists, who were busy with the same phenomena, problems and concerns. We made good comrades. *Cobra* was the only real new movement after the War in Europe. A real movement like Dada, Surrealism, Tachism and so on. All these movements existed before the War and there was nothing new about them. But the Cobra group started new, and first of all we threw away all these things we had known and started afresh, like a child—fresh and new. Sometimes my works look very childish, or child-like, schizophrenic or stupid, you know. But that was the good thing for me. Because, for me, the material is the paint itself. The paint expresses itself. In the mass of paint, I find my imagination and go on to paint it. I paint the imagination I find in the material I paint.

Karel Appel

*

During his COBRA period Karel Appel stood out together with the Dane Asger Jorn and the Belgian Corneille as the most extreme representatives of a wild and uncontrolled Expressionism which had more in common with the vehement impetuosity of the traditional Dutch and Flemish Expressionism than with the more sober classicism of the French. Working in very thick impasto, Appel produced swirling abstract masses of vigorously contrasting colours and clusters of contorted linear scribbling stamped with the imprint of sweeping brush-strokes. The effect was one of apparently unrestrained spontaneity which, as

H. H. Arnason has said, was at first sight reminiscent of Ruskin's remark about Whistler—a pot of paint thrown in the face of the public. Or, to quote Herbert Read, when looking at Appel's pictures one has the impression of "a spiritual tornado that has left the images of its passage." Relying heavily on the evocative power of the materials when moulded into abstract shapes, his work anticipated "art informel" and represented a violent reaction from the principles of order and harmony which dominated de Stijl. In its largely automatic procedures, spontaneous brushstrokes and excited linear gestures it represented an early European parallel to American Action Painting. The aim was direct expression unguided by the intellect. Associations were aroused and the mechanism of the unconscious was set in motion by the act of painting itself. Like his fellow-countryman De Kooning in America, Appel did not eschew figuration, but his aim was to stimulate associations and set in motion the unconscious phantasy by the dramatic power and evocative force of his waves of speaking colour—as is evidenced, for example, by "Red Nude" (1960) and "Angry Landscape" (1967). His later, post-COBRA, work displayed no radical change although the pigment became somewhat more fluid and the facture smoother, while the images often emerged more explicitly as the strange faces in "Two Times" (1974) which in the words of Arnason possess "a wonderful quality of childlike madness." Appel's images are in the tradition of Bosch and Ensor: distorted vestiges of human or animal bodies, grimacing masks, strange demonic figures reminiscent of Nordic mythology and folklore. His portraits were often composed of contorted clusters of spiky lines and masses of spontaneous colour without apparent figuration, as in his "Portrait of Willem Sandberg" (1956).

In 1968 Appel began to do relief paintings, and from this he progressed to sculpture in painted wood and polychrome polyester. Of this work he said: "These materials open for me more possibilities to work in space—which is the feeling I want to achieve in my paintings." He then worked in aluminum sheet and made sculptures with movable parts, of which he said: "I hinge the ears so that you can play with them, and they move in the wind as well, which changes the whole shape of the sculpture. The toy principle, you know."

In an exhibition catalogue Herbert Read summed up the painting of Appel: "Violent as they are, I do not find terror in his images; as Christian Dotrement has said, he captures the beast but does not kill it. He then identifies himself with its animal vitality. One must always distinguish between vitality and violence. Though Appel's paintings may be said to stream with the blood of animals, they are not patches on the floor of an abattoir: they represent the physical substance of life itself. Their colors are living, moving, never coagulated or faded. They stream through the field of vision as natural forces, conveying life to hearts that are invisible only because they are hidden within our own breasts." In less poetic vein Appel himself said of the change that took place in his work: "Around 1957–58 my painting was a fight. I did not paint—I hit! . . . My red, for instance, was blood. Now my red is space. . . . My work was a war, was a fight . . . little by little I have gone over more to a magic space feeling. . . . I set my frame of mind in a child-like feeling or toy feeling. My work is like a toy for adults. I believe that through the coming atomic age there will be more time for people to express themselves and to express their own desires as a play element in life. This being the same feeling of inner joy as a child gets with its toys. This is one of the feelings I project as a sound of the future in my work."

—Harold Osborne

ARAKAWA, Shusaku.
Japanese. Born in Nagoya, 6 July 1936. Studied medicine and mathematics, in Tokyo, 1954–58. Has lived in New York since 1961. Recipient: DAAD Fellowship, West Berlin, 1972. Agent: Ronald Feldman Fine Arts, 31 Mercer Street, New York, New York 10013. Address: 124 West Houston Street, New York, New York 10012, U.S.A.

Individual Exhibitions:

1958	Museum of Modern Art, Tokyo
1961	Mudo Gallery, Tokyo
1963	Galerie Schmela, Dusseldorf
1964	Dwan Gallery, Los Angeles
	Palais des Beaux-Arts, Brussels
1965	Galerie Schmela, Dusseldorf
	Minami Gallery, Tokyo
	Galleria dell'Ariete, Milan
1966	Dwan Gallery, New York
	Dwan Gallery, Los Angeles
	Minami Gallery, Tokyo
	Galerie Schmela, Dusseldorf
	Wide White Space, Antwerp
	Württembergischer Kunstverein, Stuttgart
	Stedelijk van Abbemuseum, Eindhoven, Netherlands
1967	Von der Heydt Museum, Wuppertal, West Germany
	Dwan Gallery, New York
	Dwan Gallery, Los Angeles
	Galleria Schwarz, Milan
	Galerie Seyfried, Monaco
1968	Dwan Gallery, New York
	Galerie Lauter, Mannheim
1969	Galerie Yvon Lambert, Paris
	Galleria Schwarz, Milan
	Dwan Gallery, New York
	Minami Gallery, Tokyo
	Whitney Museum, New York (film)
1970	Musée d'Art Moderne de la Ville, Paris
	Kunstverein, Hannover
	Badischer Kunstverein, Karlsruhe
	Biennale, Venice
1971	Fendrick Gallery, Washington, D.C.
	Harcus-Krakow Gallery, Boston
	Galerie Yvon Lambert, Paris
	Galleria Schwarz, Milan
	Angela Flowers Gallery, London
	ROSC, Dublin
	CAYC, Buenos Aires
	Whitney Museum, New York (films)
1972	Kunsthalle, Hamburg National Galerie, Berlin
	Lenbachhaus, Munich
	Kunstverein, Frankfurt
	Kunsthalle, Berne
	Art in Progress, Zurich
	Galleria Bertesca, Genoa
	Ronald Feldman Fine Arts, New York
1973	Daytons Gallery 12, Minneapolis
	Margo Leavin Gallery, Los Angeles
1974	Alessandra Castelli Gallery, Milan
	Museum of Modern Art, New York
	University of Wisconsin at Eau Claire
	Ronald Feldman Fine Arts, New York
	University of Missouri-Rolla
	University of Oklahoma, Norman
	Moorhead State College, Minnesota
	Multiples Gallery, New York
	Louisiana Museum, Humleback Denmark
1975	Galerie Art in Progress, Dusseldorf
	Galerie Aronowitsch, Stockholm
	Galerie Yvon Lambert, Paris
	Isy Brachot, Brussels
	Pasquale Trisorio, Naples
	Henie Onstad Museum, Oslo
	Michael Berger Gallery, Pittsburgh
	Carl Solway Gallery, Cincinnati
1976	Ronald Feldman Fine Arts, New York
	Multiples, New York
	Galeria 42, Barcelona
	Art Gallery of Ontario, Toronto
	Rubicon Gallery, Los Altos, California
	Margo Leavin Gallery, Los Angeles
	Delahunty Gallery, Dallas

Grupo Quince, Madrid
Galerie Art in Progress, Munich
Dorothy Rosenthal Gallery, Chicago
ICC, Antwerp
University of Wisconsin Art History Gallery, Milwaukee
Stadtische Kunsthalle, Dusseldorf
Galerie Maeght, Paris
Galerie Art in Progress, Dusseldorf
Museo de Arte Moderno, Bogota
1978 Gallery Takagi, Nagoya, Japan
Stedelijk Museum, Amsterdam
Margo Leavin Gallery, Los Angeles
Galerie Maeght, Paris
Neue Galerie am Landesmuseum Johanneum, Graz, Austria
1979 Stadtische Kunstsammlungen, Ludwigshafen, West Germany
Seibu Museum of Art, Tokyo
Austrian Landesmuseum, Graz
National Museum, Osaka
Ronald Feldman Fine Arts, New York
Minneapolis Institute of Arts
Gallery Takagi, Nagoya, Japan
Dorothy Rosenthal Gallery, Chicago
1980 John Stoller and Company, Minneapolis
Gallery Luria, Palm Beach, Florida
Gallery Takagi, Nagoya, Japan
Galerie Maeght, Zurich
1981 Ronald Feldman Fine Arts, New York

Selected Group Exhibitions:

1975 *View of Japanese Contemporary Art,* Seibu Museum of Art, Tokyo
1976 *Artist-Immigrants of America 1876–1976,* Hirshhorn Museum, Washington, D.C.
1977 *Documenta 6,* Kassel, West Germany
Words: A Look at the Use of Language in Art, Whitney Museum Downtown, New York
1978 *Art about Art,* Whitney Museum, New York
Drawings of the 70's, Art Institute of Chicago
1980 *Lettres et Chiffres,* Galerie Beyeler, Basel
1981 *American Prints and Printmaking 1956–1981,* Pratt Graphics Center, New York

Collections:

Museum of Modern Art, New York; Walker Art Center, Minneapolis; Kunsthalle, Berne; Kunstmuseum, Basel; National Galerie, West Berlin; Musée d'Art Modern, Paris; Stedelijk Museum, Amsterdam; National Museum of Modern Art, Tokyo.

Publications:

By ARAKAWA: books—*Mechanismus der Bedeutung,* with Madeline H. Gins, Munich 1971; *For Example (A Critique of Never),* with Madeline H. Gins, Milan 1974; *The Mechanism of Meaning,* with Madeline H. Gins, New York 1979; article—"Forgettance (Exhaustion Exhumed)" in *Arts Magazine* (New York), 1975; "Some Words" in *Arakawa,* exhibition catalogue, Dusseldorf 1977.

On ARAKAWA: books—*Icons and Images* by Nicolas Calas, New York 1971; *Prints of the 20th Century: A History* by Riva Castleman, New York 1976; *Constructive Concepts: A History of Constructive Art from Cubism to the Present* by Willy Rotzler, Zurich 1977; *Arakawa,* exhibition catalogue, Dusseldorf 1977; *Arakawa,* exhibition catalogue, Tokyo 1979; articles—"Arakawa's Paintings: A Reading" by Lawrence Alloway in *Arts Magazine* (New York), November 1969; "Arakawa: The Mechanism of Meaning" by Lawrence Alloway in *Art International* (Lugano), November 1972; "Art: The Universe of Arakawa" by John Russell in the *New York Times,* 7 September 1974; "Playing in the Surd" by John Loring in *Arts Magazine* (New York), February 1975; "ReTurning Points and Revolutions" by John Loring in *Print Collector's Newsletter* (New York), May/June 1977; special issue of *Derrière le Miroir* (Paris), no. 223, 1977; "Traces of the Unimaginable: On Arakawa's Recent Work" by Rolf-Dieter Hermann in *Arts Magazine* (New York), April 1978; "Arakawa" by Brian Wallis in *Arts Magazine* (New York), September 1979; "The Flourishing Art of the Print" by Ann

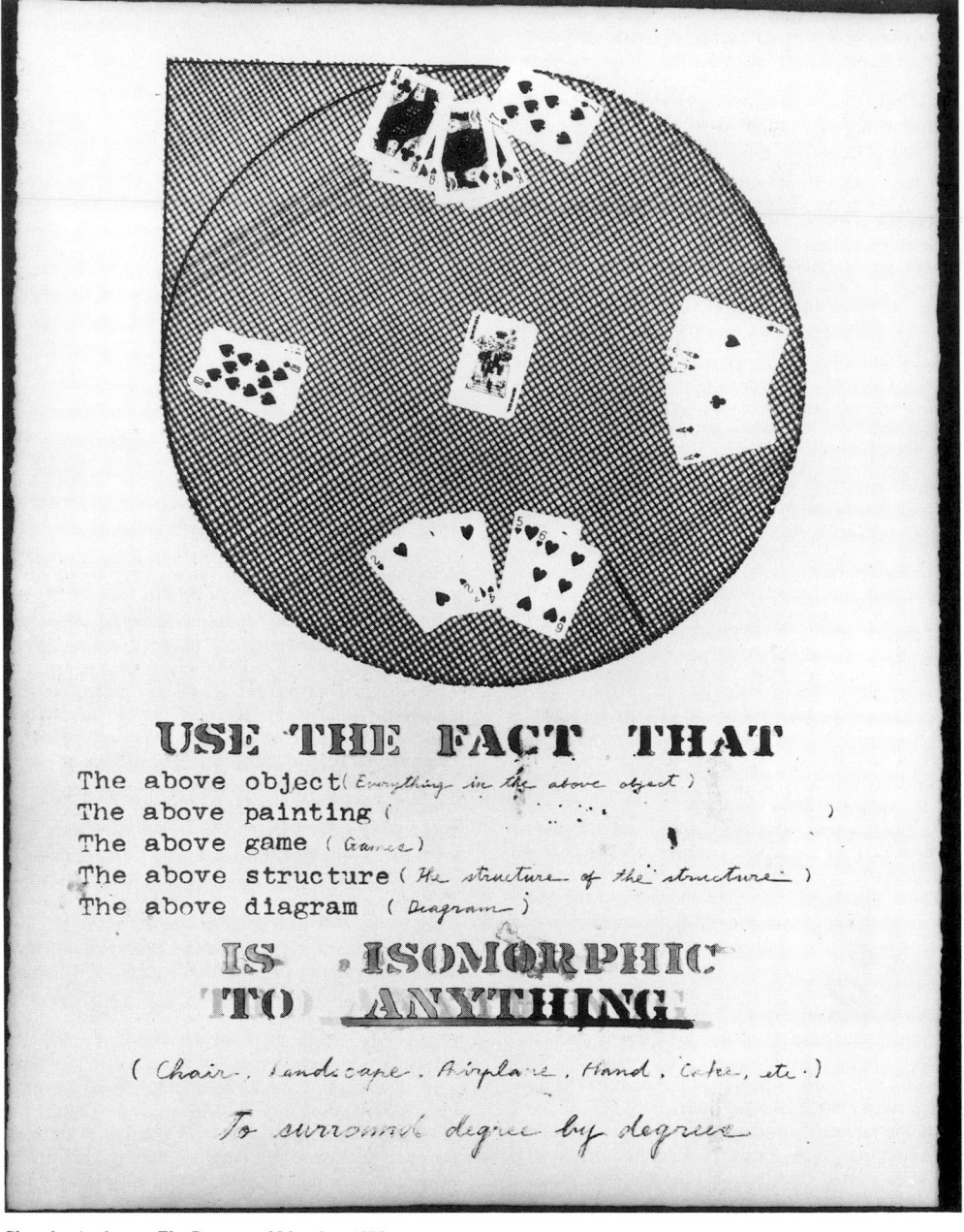

Shusaku Arakawa: *The Degrees of Meaning,* 1973

Barry in the *New York Times,* 10 February 1980; "Arakawa: 'I Am Looking for a New Definition of Perfection' " by Paul Gardner in *Art News* (New York), May 1980; " 'Some Place Enormously Movable'—The Collaboration of Arakawa and Madeline H. Gins" by Robert Creeley in *Artforum* (New York), Summer 1980.

Born in Nagoya in 1936, Shusaku Arakawa left Tokyo's Musashino College of Art before completing his studies. In 1958 he began submitting paintings to the Yomiuri Independent exhibitions, and in 1960 joined the Neo-Dada Organizers group. In a happening, by placing himself in a pitchblack room in a "feigned state of death," he experimented with the physical bounds of man. In his "Box" series, which in one instance consisted of a glob of cement and cotton placed on a blanket and called "Foetus," he gave expression to fear and madness. This work attracted attention as being an original expression of the contemporary spirit of the times. In 1962 he went to the United States, and abandoned work in the "Boxes" series in favor of a new series, "Diagram." In this series of paintings on canvas he juxtaposed silhouettes of such things as tennis rackets, combs, footprints, arrows, circles and other symbols, to depict structurally the "relationship" of man to the material world.

After participating in a group show at the Sidney

Janis Gallery in New York, in 1963, Arakawa had a number of one-man shows, at the Dwan Gallery in Los Angeles, at the Alfred Schmela Gallery in Dusseldorf, and elsewhere. He won the grand prize at the *Contemporary Art Exhibition of Japan* in 1968, and also showed his work at the Venice *Biennale* in 1970. From about this time, even the "silhouettes" disappeared from his paintings, and almost all his paintings were given simple names such as "Window Place" and "Room," and Arakawa painted words on the canvas. By this means, words, which are symbols of images and things, themselves became the objects painted, and the image evoked by the words was assigned a secondary place.

His new development is a series called "Mechanisms of Meaning." In 1969 he made a full-length film, *Why Not: A Serenade of Eschatological Ecology,* which became a sensation because of the way he depicted the relationship between man and object within a lifeless domain of sex. A sequel, *For Instance,* was completed in 1971. Although Arakawa's concept remains unchanged throughout the 1970s up to the present, his large paintings in the 1980s reveal more and more intricate diagrammatic vertigo with multi-directional arrow signs, indicating a conceptual relationship between the physical presence and the metaphysical contemplations.

—Yoshiaki Tono

ARMAN.

American. Born Armand Fernandez in Nice, France, 17 November 1928; relinquished surname in 1947; adopted name Arman, as a result of printing error, 1958; emigrated to the United States; naturalized, 1972. Educated at Cours Poisat School, 1934–40; studied at the Ecole du Louvre and Ecole Nationale des Arts Décoratifs, Paris. Served in the French Army, 1952. Hitch-hiked with Yves Klein and Claude Pascall in Europe, 1947; concentrated on Zen Buddhism and astrology, 1947–53; lived in New York, 1963; worked on series of assemblages in collaboration with Renault Car Company, Paris, 1967. Artist-in-Residence, University of California at Los Angeles, 1967–68. Recipient: Prize, *International Biennale, Exhibition of Prints,* Tokyo, 1964; Second Prize, Premio Marzotto, 1966. Commander, Order of Arts and Letters, France, 1984. Agent: Marisa Del Re Gallery, 41 East 57th Street, New York, New York 10022. Address: 430 Washington Street, New York, New York 10013, U.S.A.

Individual Exhibitions:

1956   Galerie du Haut Pave, Paris
1957   Galerie La Roue, Paris
1958   Galerie Iris Clert, Paris
1959   Galleria Apollinaire, Milan
       Galerie St. Germain, Paris
1960   Galerie Iris Clert, Paris
       Galerie Schmela, Dusseldorf
1961   Galleria Schwarz, milan
       Cordier and Warren Gallery, New York
1962   Galerie Saggarah, Gstaad, Switzerland
       Dwan Gallery, Los Angeles
       Galerie Aujourd'hui, Brussels
       Galerie Lawrence, Paris
1963   Galleria Schwarz, Milan
       Galerie Lawrence, Paris
       Sidney Janis Gallery, New York
       Galerie ad Libitum, Antwerp
       Galerie Schmela, Dusseldorf
1964   Walker Art Center, Minneapolis
       Stedelijk Museum, Amsterdam
       Museum Haus Lange, Krefeld, West Germany (retrospective)
       Sidney Janis Gallery, New York
1965   Richard Feigen Gallery, Chicago
       Galerie Bonnier, Lausanne, Switzerland
       Galerie Lawrence, Paris
       Galleria del Leone, Venice
1966   Galerie Saggarah, Gstaad, Switzerland
       Svensk-Franska Konstgalleriet, Stockholm
       Palais des Beaux-Arts, Brussels (retrospective)
       Galerie La Vieille Echoppe, Saint-Paul-de-Vence, France
       Musée de la Ville, Saint-Paul-de-Vence, France
1967   Galerie Ileana Sonnabend, Paris
       Galleria Il Punto, Turin
       Galerie Françoise Meyer, Brussels
       Galerie des Ponchettes, Nice
       Galleria La Bussola, Turin
       Galleria Sperone, Turin
       Palazzo Grassi, Venice
1968   Galleria Schwarz, Milan
       Sidney Janis Gallery, New York
       Biennale, Venice
1969   Galerie Bonnier, Lausanne, Switzerland
       Arman: Verk från 1964–1969, Svensk-Franska Konstgalleriet, Stockholm
       Accumulations Renault, Musée des Arts Décoratifs, Paris (toured Europe)
       Galerie Ileana Sonnabend, Paris
       Galerie Mathias Fels, Paris
1970   Galerie Ileana Sonnabend, Paris
       Städtische Kunstsammlungen, Ludwigshafen, West Germany
       Ace Gallery, Los Angeles (travelled to the Ace Gallery, Vancouver)
       Galerie der Spiegel, Cologne
       Galleria dell'Ariete, Milan
       Studio Sant'Andrea, Milan

       Galerie Lambert-Monet, Geneva
       Galerie Bonnier, Geneva
       Galerie Jacqueline Soisson, Nice
       Lawrence Rubin Gallery, New York
1971   Galerie Bonnier, Geneva
       Galerie de la Salle, Saint-Paul-de-Vence, France
       Lawrence Rubin Gallery, New York
       Galerie Bischofberger, Zurich
       Galerie Semiha Huber, Zurich
       Galleria Arte Borgogna, Milan
       Galerie Venise, Casablanca
1972   Galleria del Leone, Venice
       Galleria Arte Borgogna, Basle
       Galleria Sanluca, Bologna
       Galerie Guillaume Campo, Antwerp
       Galerie de l'Oeil, Paris
1973   Galerie Kriwin, Brussels
       Le Tas de Echanges, Galerie Entre, Paris
       Arman: Selected Activities, John Gibson Gallery, New York
       Galerie Aronovich, Stockholm

       White Gallery, Lausanne, Switzerland
       Galleria Arte Bologna, Milan
       Rosa Esman Gallery, New York
       Concrete Lyrics, Andrew Crispo Gallery, New York
1974   Andrew Crispo Gallery, New York
       Musée d'Arles, France
       Galerie Daniel Templon, Paris
       Arman: Selected Works 1958–1974, La Jolla Museum of Contemporary Art, California (travelled to Henry Art Gallery, University of Washington, Seattle; Fort Worth Art Museum, Texas; Des Moines Art Center, Iowa; and Albright-Knox Art Museum, Buffalo, New York, 1974–75)
       Dartmouth College, Hanover, New Hampshire
1975   Musée d'Art Moderne de la Ville, Paris
       Galerie Bonnier, Geneva
       Galerie Tchou, Paris
       John Gibson Gallery, New York
       Lyrical Surfaces, Andrew Crispo Gallery, New York
1976   Andrew Crispo Gallery, New York
       Musée d'Art Moderne de la Ville, Paris

Arman: *End of Romanticism,* 1973

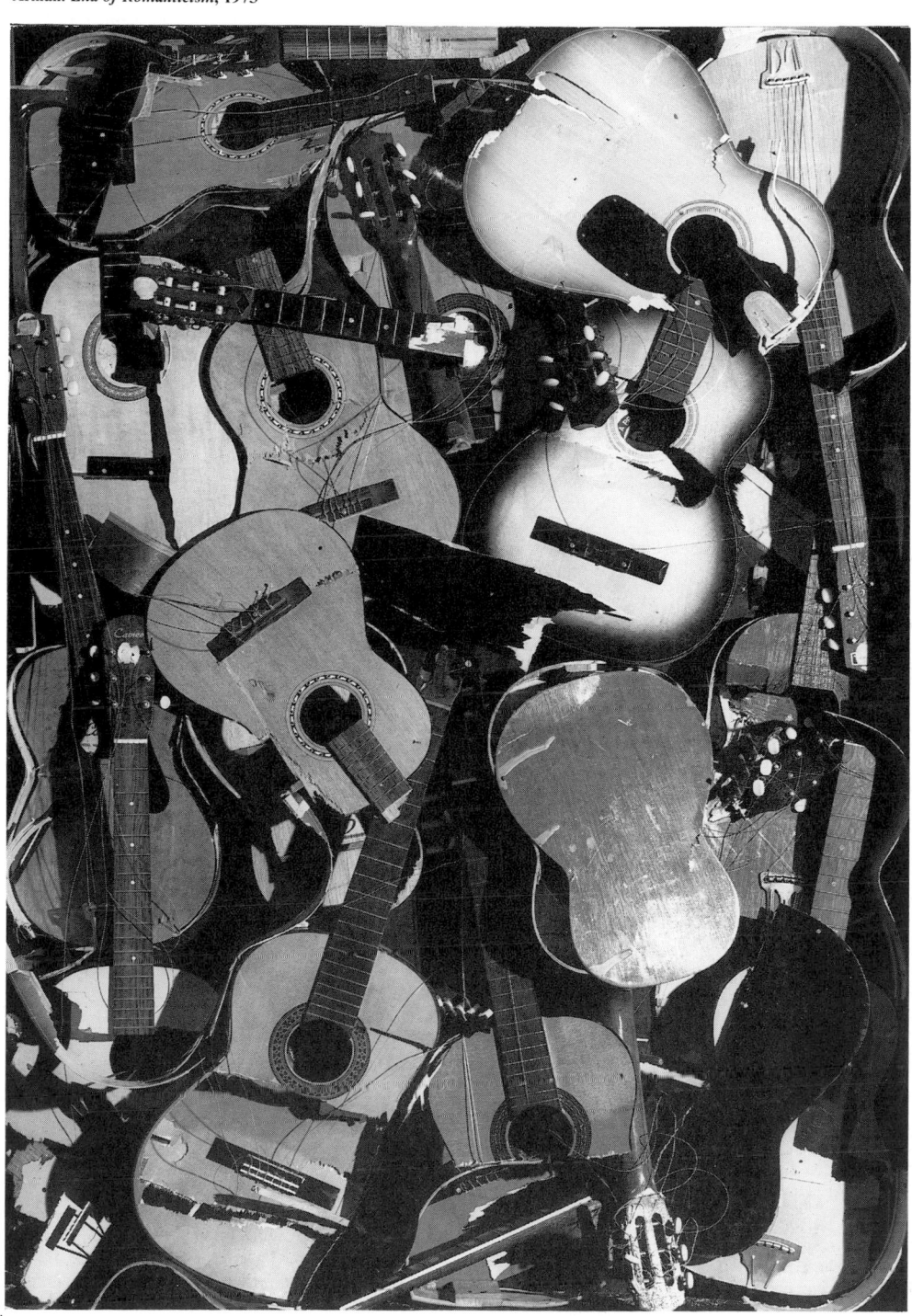

1979 André Emmerich Gallery, New York
1980 Amano Gallery, Osaka, Japan
Satani Gallery, Tokyo
1981 Galerie Beaubourg, Paris
Grand Palais, Paris
1982 Galerie Sapone, Nice, France
Galerie Beaubourg, Paris
Solomon Gallery, Dublin
1983 Goldman's Gallery, Haifa, Israel
Galerie Beaubourg, Paris
1984 Gloria Luria Gallery, Bay Harbor Islands, Florida
Galerie Reckermann, Cologne
Galerie Rene Ziegler, Zurich
Marisa Del Re Gallery, New York
1985 Seibu Museum of Art, Tokyo
1986 Marisa Del Re Gallery, New York
1988 Galerie de Poche, Paris

Selected Group Exhibitions:

1964 *International Biennale Exhibition of Prints*, Tokyo
1967 *Expo '67*, Montreal
1968 *Documenta 4*, Kassel, West Germany
1970 *Expo '70*, Osaka, Japan
1980 *From Reinhardt to Christo*, Allen Memorial Museum, Oberlin, Ohio
1984 *Salvaged: Altered Everyday Objects*, Project Studio One, Long Island City, New York

Collections:

Museum of Modern Art, New York; Albright-Knox Art Museum, Buffalo, New York; Walker Art Center, Minneapolis; Stedelijk Museum, Amsterdam; Musée Royal des Beaux-Arts, Brussels; Musée d'Art Moderne, Ghent; Louisiana Museum of Art, Humlebaek, Denmark; Museum Haus Lange, Krefeld, West Germany; Centre Georges Pompidou, Paris; Musée des Arts Décoratifs, Paris.

Publications:

By ARMAN: articles—"Interview d'Arman," with Michel Ragon, in *Chorus*, nos. 5/6/1970; "Arman Qualité Quantité," interview, with Catherine Millet, in *Art Press* (Paris), December/January 1974.

On ARMAN: books—*Arman*, exhibition pamphlet, with text by Pierre Restany, Los Angeles 1962; *Arman*, exhibition catalogue, with text by Alain Jouffroy, Milan 1963; *Arman*, exhibition catalogue, with text by Pierre Restany, and Claude Pascal, with statement by Arman, Amsterdam 1964; *Arman*, exhibition catalogue, Stockholm 1966; *Arman*, exhibition catalogue, with texts by Otto Hahn, Pierre Restany, and Michael Sonnabend, Paris 1967; *Arman*, exhibition catalogue, with text by John Ashbery, New York 1968; *Arman*, exhibition catalogue, with text by Pierre Restany, Milan 1968; *Arman: Accumulations Renault*, exhibition catalogue, with text by François Mathey, and interview of Arman with Claude Renard, Paris 1969; *Arman: Verk from 1964–1969*, exhibition catalogue, Stockholm 1969; *Arman*, exhibition catalogue, Milan 1970; *Arman*, exhibition pamphlet, with introduction by Pierre Restany, Antwerp 1972; *Arman: Ateliers d'Aujourd'hui* by Otto Hahn, Paris 1972; *Arman: Selected Activities*, exhibition catalogue, with texts by Peter Schjeldahl and Jan van der Marck, New York 1973; *Arman* by Henry Martin, New York 1973; *Arman: Concrete Lyrics*, exhibition catalogue, with text by Andrew Crispo, New York 1974; *Arman: Selected Works 1958–1974*, exhibition catalogue, with an introduction by Jan van der Marck, La Jolla, California 1974; *Arman: Lyrical Surfaces*, exhibition catalogue, New York 1975; *Arman: Objets Armés 1971–74*, exhibition catalogue, with text by Jacques Lassaigne, Paris 1975; *From Reinhardt to Christo*, exhibition catalogue, Oberlin, Ohio 1980; *Arman* by Jan van der Marck, New York 1984; *Arman*, exhibition catalogue, with text by Masashi Miura, Tokyo 1985; *Arman: Gods and Goddesses*, exhibition catalogue with essay by Henry Geldzahler, New York 1986.

Of all the "New Realists" who appeared at various places in Europe at the beginning of the 1960's, Arman ranks surely as the purest poet of the object, but he's also the artist of the group with the clearest commitment to a concept of significant form, and the power of his work depends on an almost relentless classicism. He is never sentimental. Even though he seems to allow the objects he deals with to speak entirely by themselves, he also allows his procedures a very similar sort of privilege, and it's the procedures of the artist rather than the objects of reality that finally hold the upper hand. The object is almost always reduced to a statuesque icon or an element of an all-over pattern, and the excitement of these configurations lies in the way we are invited to deal both with what the objects that go into them used to be and as well as with what they have since become. Arman keeps us spell-bound by creating an almost palpable tension between things we know with our intellect and things we see with our eyes.

Arman first came into his own around 1955 when he ceased to be what Pierre Restany has called a "Sunday painter" dedicated to " 'nice' painting in the taste of the period, a post-Cubism at first figurative and later on abstract." That was the moment at which he invented the first of a whole series of new and entirely personal genres. He began to make works that consisted of repeated stampings of the same rubber stamp (his *cachets*); he then went on to making tracings (*allures*) of objects other than rubber stamps by inking them and sending them scudding across sheets of paper or canvas; he then decided that the object itself can be a trace of itself and put a definitive end to his work with rubber stamps by sealing them all into a box and this was the beginning of the *accumulations*, which were also later to become accumulations of trash called *poubelles* (trash cans). Later still he began to work with the possibility of smashing, burning, and sectioning objects (often musical instruments, and especially violins) and these became his *coleres* (rages). He has made accumulations of everything from dollar bills to crucifixes, machine-gun bullets, dolls, Kodak brownie cameras, sewing machines, cigarette butts, trombones, chess men, tea pots, gas burners from old kitchen stoves, guns, parts of automobiles, cogs and wheels for watches, tennis shoes, pencils and squeezed tubes of artist's oil paint; his way of dealing with these accumulated objects is sometimes to weld them together, at other times to nail them to a board or simply to heap them into a glass-covered box; still other accumulations, like many of the destroyed violins, are drowned in polyester or embedded in cement. With his *coleres*, he has been known to take an axe to quarry as large as a grand piano and to dynamite a sports car. He once went before an audience and destroyed the entirety of the contents of a fully furnished three-room middle-class apartment that had been set up for him in a New York art gallery.

Arman's work, finally, simply isn't understood at all unless it's understood to be an always on-going ritual. He is always bending the object to his entirely personal and purely arbitrary will as though to tell us that will is what we are most truly made of; the utilitarian objects in which will is codified and limited are destroyed or accumulated into almost purely visual pattern as though to tell us that we must know how to look beyond them if we're to see the essence of the human capacity that went into pulling them into existence in the first place.

—Henry Martin

ARMITAGE, Kenneth.

British. Born in Leeds, Yorkshire, 18 July 1916. Studied at the Leeds College of Art, 1934–37; Slade School of Fine Art, London, 1937–39. Served in the British Army, 1939–46. Independent sculptor, since 1946. Visited Caracas; formed workshop, together with other Venezuelan sculptors, 1964; lived in Berlin, 1967–69. Chairman, Sculpture Department, Bath Academy of Art, Crosham, 1946–56; Visiting Professor, Boston University, 1970. Visiting Tutor, Royal College of Art, London, since 1974. Recipient: Gregory Fellowship in Sculpture, Leeds University, York-shire, 1953–55; First Prize International War Memorial Competition, Krefeld, West Germany, 1956; David E. Bright Foundation Award, *Biennale*, Venice 1958; Prize, *International Drawing and Engraving Exhibition*, Lugano, Switzerland, 1958; Berlin Arts Programme Fellowship, 1967–69. C.B.E. (Commander of the Order of the British Empire), 1969. Address: 22a Avonmore Road, London W14 8RR, England.

Individual Exhibitions:

1952 Gimpel Fils, London
1954 Bertha Schaefer Gallery, New York
1956 Bertha Schaefer Gallery, New york
1957 Gimpel Fils, London
1958 Paul Rosenberg Gallery, New York
Musée Nationale d'Art Moderne, Paris
Biennale, Venice (with Stanley William Hayter and William Scott; toured Europe)
1959 Whitechapel Art Gallery, London
British Council World Tour (until 1976)
1960 Kestner Gesellschaft, Hannover (with Lynn Chadwick; toured Europe and Japan, 1960–61)
1962 Paul Rosenberg Gallery, New York
Marlborough Fine Art, London
Galerie Suvremene Umjetnosti, Zagreb
1963 Galerie Charles Linehard, Zurich
Galerie Wilhelm Groshennig, Dusseldorf
Galleria Blu, Milan
1965 Marlborough Fine Art, London
Arnolfini Gallery, Bristol
1972 Castle Museum, Norwich (toured the U.K., 1972–73)
1974 Hester van Royen Gallery, London
Gallery Kasahara, Osaka
1975 New Art Centre, London
1978 Fuji Television Gallery, Tokyo (travelled to the Galerie Humanite, Nagoya, and the Gallery Kasahara, Osaka)
1980 Gimpel Fils, London
1981 City Museum and Art Gallery, Stoke-on-Trent, Staffordshire
1982 Sala Mendoza, Caracas
Taranman Gallery, London
1985 Artcurial, Paris (retrospective)

Selected Group Exhibitions:

1952 *Biennale*, Venice
1953 *Open Air Sculpture Exhibition*, Middleheim Park, Antwerp
1955 *The New Decade*, Museum of Modern Art, New York
1957 *Bienal*, Sao Paulo
1959 *New Images of Man*, Museum of Modern Art, New York
1962 *British Sculpture Today*, San Francisco Museum of Art (toured the United States)
1967 *Guggenheim International Sculpture Exhibition*, Guggenheim Museum, New York
1972 *British Sculptors 72*, Royal Academy of Art, London
1982 *British Sculpture of the 20th Century, Parts I and II*, Whitechapel Art Gallery, London
1987 *British Art of the 20th Century*, Royal Academy of Arts, London (travelled to Staatsgalerie, Stuttgart)

Collections:

Tate Gallery, London; Arts Council, London; Victoria and Albert Museum, London; Middleheim Museum, Antwerp; Musée Royale des Beaux-Arts, Brussels; Centre Georges Pompidou, Paris; Kunsthalle, Hamburg; Galleria Nazionale d'Arte Moderna, Rome; Albright-Knox Art Gallery, Buffalo, New York; Museum of Modern Art, New York.

Publications:

On ARMITAGE: books—*Artists of our Time, No. 7: Kenneth Armitage* by Sir Roland Penrose, Amriswil, Switzerland

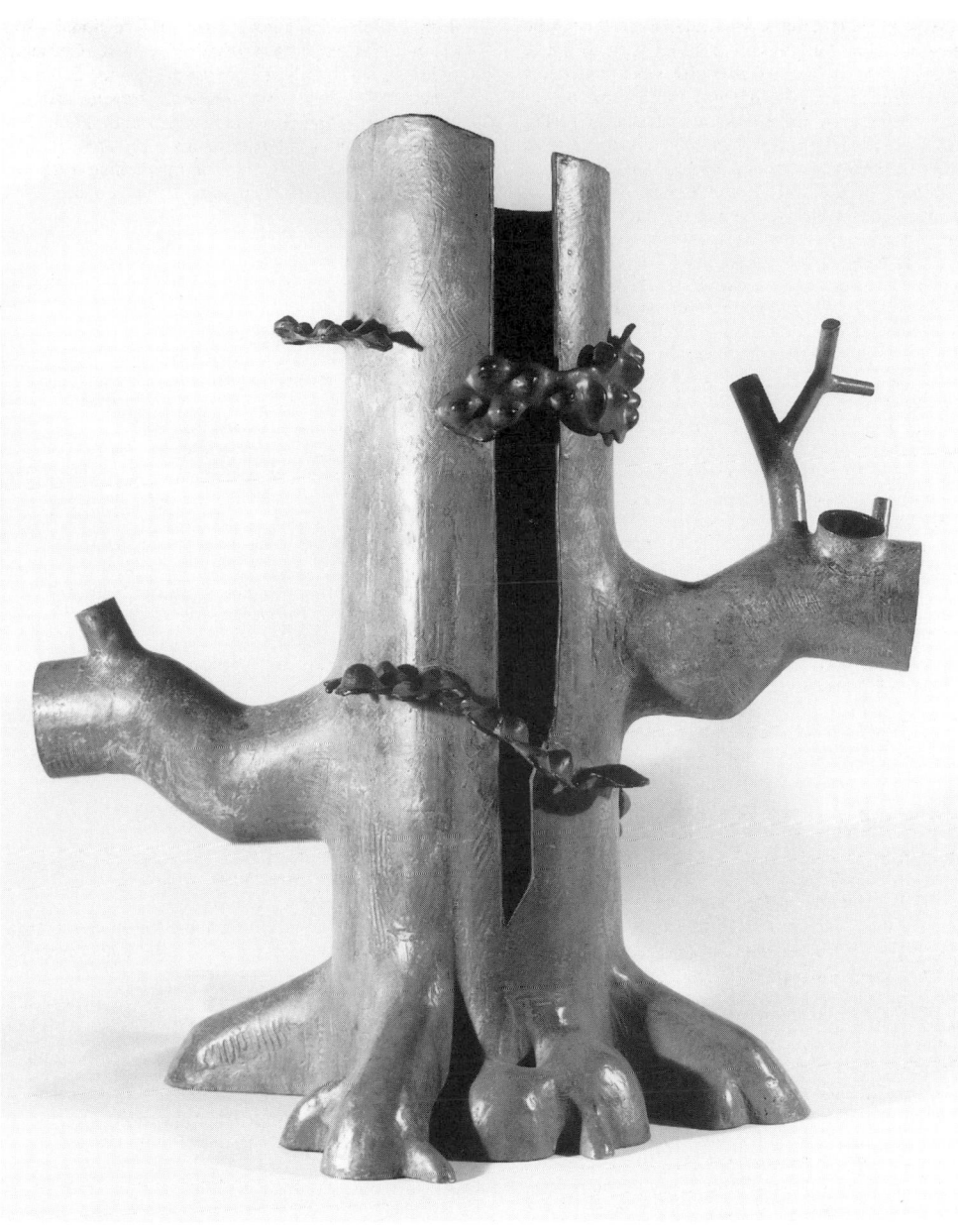

Kenneth Armitage: *Blasted Oak*, 1986

Read rhetorically dubbed artists of this self-consciously angst-ridden post-war era the "geometry of fear" sculptors, but unlike many of the others Armitage stuck to the human figure rather than employing bestial or insect hybrids to serve at metaphors for the human condition. Moreover, Armitage's figures were not loaded with a tragic import; they were depicted in low-key casual situations, as seen in "People in a Wind." Their scale was usually small, the observations modest and delivered sotto voce. In these respects his work owed more to artists like Giacometti and Picasso than to Surrealism and Moore.

When he adopted a larger scale and a more public manner in such works of the later 50's as "Diarchy," Armitage invested his figures with a hieratic monumentality: the torsos are flattened into plaques or tablets from which protrude the architectonic limbs. They are static and silent images, with a rare grandeur that is free from bombast and posturing.

During the 60's he experimented with various new figurative subjects and new materials, including resins and aluminum, but recently he has returned to bronze, long his favorite material. A new richness of color and material is evident in his series of Richmond Oaks from the late 70's. Armitage has always made drawings, both sketches and presentation works; they act as aids to observation but not as blueprints for sculptures. Once again numerous studies, this time of trees in Richmond Park, accompany this group of new works. Characteristically, these sculptures are modest in scale and statement, but no less powerful for that. Armitage has abandoned the figure almost for the first time in his career, yet he never anthropomorphizes his oaks, and that elusive sense of poetic metaphor which inhabits his best works is found here too.

—Lynne Cooke

1960; *Arts in Progress: Kenneth Armitage* by Norbert Lynton, London 1962; *Kenneth Armitage* by Charles Spencer, London 1973; *Kenneth Armitage: Sculptures and Drawings*, exhibition catalogue, with foreword by Roland Penrose, Tokyo 1978; *Kenneth Armitage: Richmond Oaks and Other Works*, exhibition catalogue, with introduction by John McEwen, London 1980; *Kenneth Armitage: New Sculptures and Collages*, exhibition catalogue, with introduction by John McEwen, London 1982; articles—"Kenneth Armitage" by John Glaves-Smith in *Artscribe* (London), no. 16, 1979; "Artists' Dialogue" by Connie Glenn in *Architectural Digest* (Los Angeles) February 1982; films—*Kenneth Armitage*, directed by John Read, BBC Television, London 1960; *5 British Sculptors Work and Talk*, directed by Warren Forma, 1964; *Armitage in Berlin*, Berlin 1969.

The character of my work divides into periods, some short, others long-lasting, in the way we tend to wear different clothes at different times. For example, the Oak Tree love affair in Richmond Park lasted non-stop from 1975 to 1986 with one or two large versions yet to be made. Others, like the attempts to combine drawing and sculpture, went no further than five or six pieces, although a ten-foot relief combining both has now started, and a residual of black pubic and head hair still occurs, The series called *Chair* (based on my bedroom chair) lasted only through four versions, Then, a time-lag can exist between forming an idea and testing it in one or several

maquettes—and the full-scale realization perhaps not until several years later. Or I can finish something started long ago, like the big *Arm* made in Berlin in 1968 and cast temporarily in white resin and shown like that in Japan and London, is now receiving attention with a sprayed camouflage design based on drawings made in 1968 but never used until now. I regard it all as a body of work without much care for what was done when, and where nothing is final. A lifetime is so very short anyway, and the time-scale of art enormous. I sometimes look at a small engraving on a reindeer antler fragment in the British Museum with an age estimated at 11,000 BC—which might have been made by a good artist last week. We often hear people on television say, "way back in (say) 1985," when an Irish sense of time can range over centuries as though it was only recent. This easy communication across race, language and vast spans of time is comforting in an age when indifference to art seems general.

—Kenneth Armitage

Although he gained his international laurels as one of that group of young British sculptors that included Butler, Chadwick and Paolozzi, which showed at the Venice *Biennale* in 1952, Kenneth Armitage has generally stood aside from the prevailing ethos. Herbert

ARMLEDER, John M(ichael).
Swiss. Born in Geneva, 24 June 1948. Studied at the Ecole des Beaux-Arts, Geneva, 1966–67; with John Epstein, Glamorgan Summer School, Wales, 1969. Associated with the Groupe Luc Bois artists' group, Geneva, 1963; independent artist, from 1969; founder, with Patrick Lucchini and Claude Rychner, Groupe Ecart, Geneva, 1969; Galerie Ecart, Geneva, from 1973; Ecart Publications, Geneva, 1972; Ecart Performance Group, Geneva, 1974; Ecart/Books, Geneva, 1975; International Institutions Register, Geneva, 1976; Leathern Wing Scribble Press, 1977; Laboratorio artists' co-operative, Milan, 1977. Recipient: Graphics Prize, *Xylon VI* exhibition, Geneva, 1972; Kiefer-Hablitzel-Stipendium, Geneva, 1972, 1974, 1976; Eidgenossische Kunststipendium, Geneva, 1977, 1978, 1979; Prize of the Banque Hypothecaire du Canton de Geneve, 1986. Agents: Ecart Books, rue Philippe, Plantamour 6, 1211 Geneva; Galerie Marika Malacorda, rue de l'Eveche 1, 1204 Geneva; Galerie Toni Gerber, Gerechtigkeitsgasse 74, 3011 Berne. Address: 3 rue des Paquis, P.O.B. 253, 1211 Geneva, Switzerland.

Individual Exhibitions:

1973   Galerie Ecart, Geneva
          Palais de l'Athenee, Geneva
          Galerie Ecart, Geneva (with Patrick Lucchini)
1975   Galerie Gaetan, Carouge, Switzerland
1976   Palais de l'Athenee, Geneva
1977   Galerie Marika Malacorda, Geneva
1980   Rue Vignier, Geneva
          Kunstmuseum, Basle
          C Space, New York (with Helmut Federle and Christoph Gossweiler)

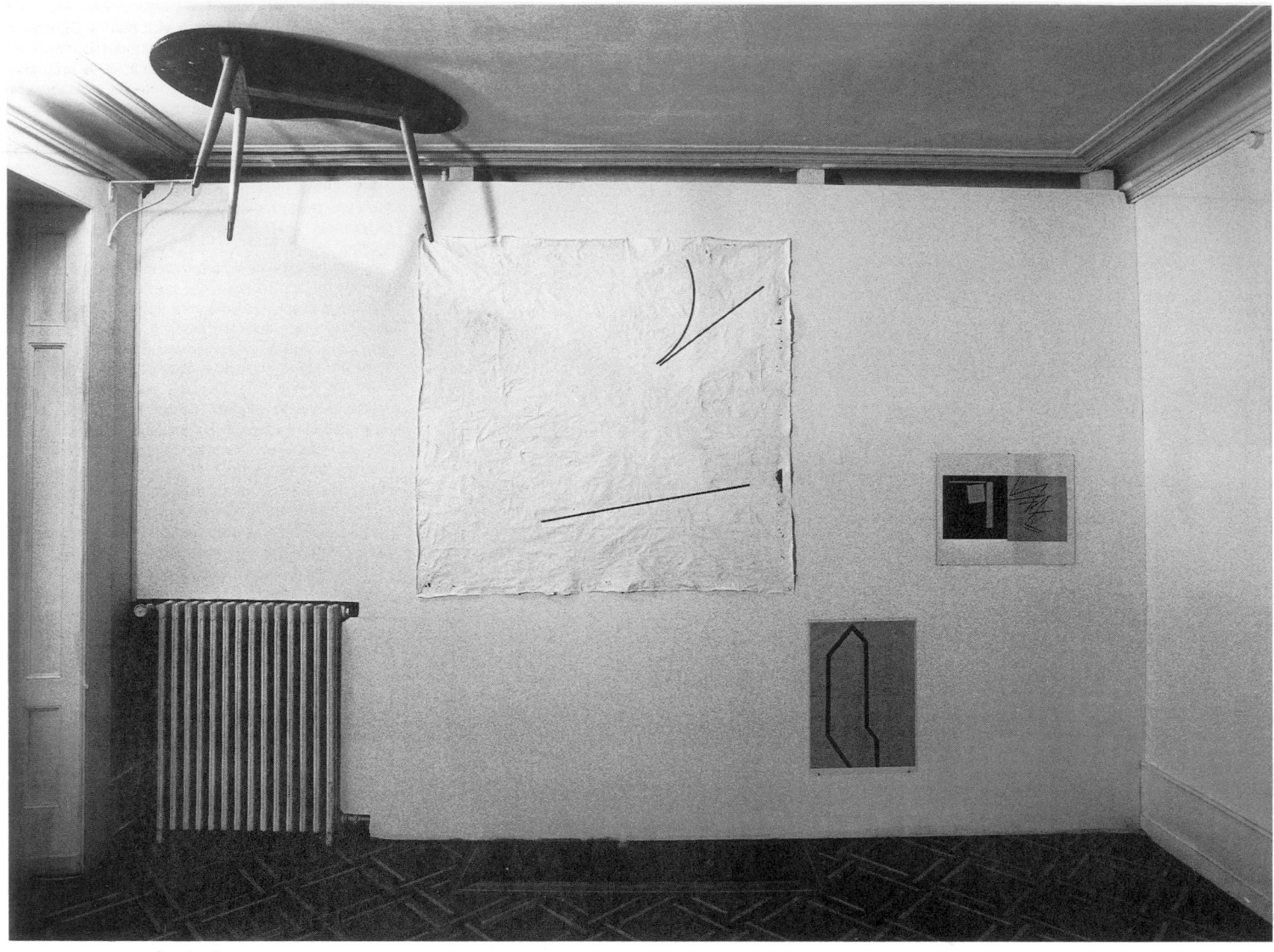

John Armleder: *1681*, installation at the Centre d'Art Contemporain, Geneva, 1981

1981	Centre d'Art Contemporain, Geneva (with Martin Disler and Helmut Federle)		
!982	Musee d'Art et d'Histoire, Fribourg, Switzerland		
	Gangurinn/The Corridor, Reykjavik		
	Galerie Toni Gerber, Berne		
	Galerie Marika Malacorda, Geneva		
	Vitrine Fri-Art, Fribourg, Switzerland		
	Nylistasafnid/The Living Arts Museum, Reykjavik		
1983	Kunstmuseum, Solothurn, Switzerland		
	Gymnase Cantonal du Bugnon, Lausanne		
	Galerie Grita Insam, Vienna		
	Galerie Rivolta, Lausanne		
	Galerie Susanna Kulli, St. Gallen, Switzerland		
	Le Consortium, Dijon, France		
1984	Galerie Marika Malacorda, Geneva		
	John Gibson Gallery, New York		
	Galerie Claudia Knapp, Chur, Switzerland		
	Galerie Filiale, Basle (with Christian Floquet)		
1985	Galerie Marika Malacorda, Geneva		
	John Gibson Gallery, New York		
	Galerie Media, Neuchatel, Switzerland		
	Galerie und Lager Rudolf Zwirner, Cologne		
1986	Galerie Susanna Kulli, St. Gallen, Switzerland		
	Ecole Nationale d'Art Decoratif, Limoges, France		
	Galerie Rivolta, Lausanne		
	John Gibson Gallery, New York		
	Galerie Tanit, Munich		
	Swiss Pavilion, *Biennale*, Venice		
	Galerie Catherine Issert, St. Paul-de-Vence, FRance		
	Galerie Toni Gerber, Berne		
	Galerie Bama, Paris		
	Lisson Gallery, London		
	Musee d'Art et d'Histoire, Geneva		

Verein Kunsthalle, Zurich (with Helmut Federle and Olivier Mosset)

Stadtische Galerie, Regensburg, West Germany (with Olivier Mosset)

1987 Galleria Piero Cavellini, Milan
Galerie Munro, Hamburg
Galerie Daniel Buchholz, Cologne
Galerie Nachst St. Stephan, Vienna
Galerie Susanna Kulli, St. Gallen, Switzerland
Galerie Jean-Francois Dumont, Bordeaux, France
Kunstmuseum, Winterthur, Switzerland (travelled to Paris, Dusseldorf, and West Berlin)
John Gibson Gallery, New York
Pat Hearn Gallery, New York
Daniel Newburg Gallery, New York
Musee de Peinture et de Sculpture, Grenoble, France
Galerie Marika Malacorda, Geneva
Galerie Tanit, Munich
Hoffman Borman Gallery, Santa Monica, California
Galerie Joost Declercq, Ghent, Belgium
Kunstverein, Aachen, West Germany
Maison de la Culture, St. Etienne, France (with Olivier Mosset; travelled to Nevers)

1988 Galerie Tanit Kunigk und Moller, Munich

Selected Group Exhibitions:

1972 *Xylon VI*, Musee d'Art et d'Histoire, Geneva
1974 *Ambiente 74: 28 Schweizer Kunstler*, Kunstmuseum, Winterthur, Switzerland (travelled to Geneva and Lugano)

1976 *Rubber Stamp Exhibition*, La Mamelle Arts Center, San Francisco
1978 *Artwords and Bookworks*, Los Angeles Institute of Contemporary Art
1981 *CH '70–'80*, Kunstmuseum, Lucerne (travelled to Bologna, Genoa, Bonn and Graz)
1982 *Zwitserse Avant-Garde*, Galerie Nouvelles Images, The Hague
1984 *Peinture Abstraite*, Galerie Ecart, Geneva
1986 *Tableaux Abstraits*, Villa Arson, Nice, France
1987 *Documenta 8*, Museum Fridericianum, Kassel, West Germany

Collections:

Kunstmuseum, Basle; Kunstmuseum, Lucerne; Musee d'Art et d'Histoire, Geneva; Cabinet des Estampes, Geneva; Kunsthaus,Zurich; Kunstmuseum, Winterthur; Staatsgalerie, Stuttgart; Musee Saint-Pierre, Lyon; Musee d'Art et d'Industrie, Saint-Etienne; Musee de Grenoble.

Publications:

By ARMLEDER: books—*Lezards Sauvages*, Geneva 1973; *Ayacotl*, with Patrick Lucchini, Geneva 1973; *Ayacotl-Excerpts*, Geneva 1973; *12 Portes + 1*, with Patrick Lucchini, Geneva 1973; *Correspondances avec John Armleder*, with Endre Tot, Geneva 1974; *Niente, Purtroppo*, Geneva 1975; *John Armleder*, with texts by Heinz Breloh, Jochen Gerz and others, Geneva 1975; *The John Armleder Is A Vegetarian Book*, Geneva 1975; *Une Pluie d'Etoiles Filantes*, Geneva 1975; *Dictionnaire Moderne Francais-Arabe*, Geneva

1975; *Dieu Expulse du Paradis*, with Claude Rychner, Geneva 1976; *3 x (2 x 1): A Chhjlnoruxy Production*, with Patrick Lucchini and Claude Rychner, Lucerne and Geneva 1977; *Hall*, with Dougal, Geneva 1977; *Sketches to Higgins' Intermedia Object No. 1*, with Patrick Lucchini, Geneva 1977; *Lezards Sauvages IIA: Egouttes*, Geneva 1979; *Titles Untitled*, Geneva 1979; *The D. S. Lick Nets*, with Helgi Thorgils Fridjonsson, Reykjavik 1982; *The Geneva Pond Bubbles*, with Arni Ingolfsson and others, Reykjavik 1982; *The Rex-Headed Master*, with Dadi Gudbjornsson and others, Reykjavik 1982; *One Year Lick*, with Dadi Gudbjornsson and Helgi Thorgils Fridjonsson, Reykjavik and Geneva 1983; *One Year Net*, with Helgi Thorgils Fridjonsson and Thor Vigfusson, Reykjavik and Geneva 1983; *Ecrits et Etretiens*, with Helmut Federle and Olivier Mosset, St. Etienne and Grenoble 1987; *Furniture Sculpture 1979-1986*, with texts by Nena Dimitrijevic and Christoph Schenker, Dudweiler 1987.

On ARMLEDER: books—*AMAM: Premieres Acquisitions et Donations*, exhibition catalogue with text by Rainer Michael Mason, Geneva 1976; *John M. Armleder: 891 und weitere Stucke*, exhibition catalogue with text by Dieter Koepplin, Basle 1980; *John M. Armleder/Martin Disler/Helmut M. Federle*, exhibition catalogue with texts by Christoph Schenker, Dieter Schwarz and others, Geneva 1982; *John M. Armleder: Arbeiten auf Papier 1962-83*, exhibition catalogue with texts by André Jamber and Ben Vautier, Solothurn 1983; *John Armleder*, exhibition catalogue with text by Jean-Hubert Martin, Dijon 1983; *John Armleder: Paintings and Furniture Sculpture*, exhibition catalogue with text by Stuart Morgan, London 1986; *John M. Armleder*, exhibition catalogue with text by Maurice Besset and Dieter Schwarz, Winterthur 1987.

For about seven years now the public has been seeing pictures and articles of furniture by John Armleder, an artist who had previously made a name for himself via graphics and performance art. If his first pictures still owed something to graphics, Armleder was soon elaborating a working style which, although it could not have been described as 'painterly,' was nevertheless clearly distinct from the poetic refinements of work on paper. These next works, rather than embodying a specifically subjective style, offered a neutral stage for the representation of various techniques; the drawings might incorporate traces of 'happening-activities' or they might equally follow paraconstructive lines (to use Armleder's terminology); simple designs might appear alongside designs based on complex random methods. Armleder was already playing with a variety of referents which would be evident to the acute observer: references to compositions by Cage, to graffiti, but also to Balla, Picabia and the Russian Constructivists. If there seemed to be a connection between these works and the Swiss graphic mentality of the seventies this was as a result of the intimacy of the medium rather than of a deliberate strategy. In contrast to his colleagues, Armleder was concerned with deconstructing a closed poetic universe rather than with a steady materialisation of the same; his pictures and furniture now confirm that beyond doubt.

In 1984 Armleder exhibited a large number of pictures for the first time, putting on a one-man exhibition in Geneva and contributing a selection of his work to a group exhibition which he himself had organised under the title *Peinture abstraite*. This exhibition, whose title, in a period when figurative art was in retreat, almost took on the quality of a manifesto, contained a mixture of abstract pictures of a geometric type in which Armleder's own works were completely at home. The choice of works by foreign artists was determined by circumstances and by the pressure towards improvisation; it demonstrated, not historical continuity, but abstraction as the icon of modernity. That in this exhibition concrete artists of the Zurich School (Loewensberg) hung beside Americans of the most diverse provenance (Held, Motherwell and Ryman on the one hand, minimal artists such as Lewitt and Mangold on the other), in combination with younger artists like Merz, Mosset and Armleder himself, was a clear indication that Armleder was concerned, not with a precise stylistic definition of his work, but with a practical blurring of the boundaries which the various schools of abstract art have erected. From the various processes of abstraction Armleder takes up for his own use only certain elements which point to the modernistic tradition without representing it in all its consequences.

Armleder's pictures are not painterly in the first instance, because it is not his aim to carry on working through the problems of an art radicalised by the modern approach. He avoids the formalistic tradition, which continues to preoccupy artists such as Toroni or Mosset, and concerns himself with the concept of 'modernism' as hypostatised by the avant-garde in the first half of the century. Consequently, he is not caught up in an exclusively geometric approach but takes as his theme the historical representation of this method: a rhetoric which establishes itself in an idealised sphere beyond mediation, seduction and expropriation. By distancing himself, however, from the geometric approach, Armleder has not shifted to a new form of representation. In this, he differs from artists like Schuyff or Taaffe who produce pictures which either verbally cite models from the '60s or use the geometric approach as a means to the production of a, yet again, illusionistic field of vision. In contrast too to Halley, for whom the geometric elements serve as pretext for a symbolical scenery, Armleder extracts from his simple polka dots the possibility for a dissolution of content. In denying the significance of an isolated picture and concentrating instead on its contextualisation, he abandons the sphere of pure painting. An example of this is to be found in the group exhibition Armleder organised, and also in his one-man exhibitions: each of his dot pictures relates first to the other dot pictures present, which differ from one another according to their physical composition, the materials used and variations in the organisation of the ground plan, and secondly to the whole range of dot and scanning patterns in modernist art. The dots are especially relevant to Armleder's purpose, since on the one hand they mark out a simple latticework distribution of the picture's surface, but on the other, in contrast to a quadratic arrangement, they disturb any uninterrupted perception of that surface.

In his combination of pictures and objects Armleder finds further possibilities for contextualisation. The objects, be they old pieces of furniture or newly produced consumer articles, are set, as anonymously produced decorative elements, over and against painting itself. It is not by chance that Armleder began with old drawing room furniture, sofas and dressing tables, more recently replaced by musical instruments. If the furniture devalues the picture (which furnishes the background to conversation) as part of the furnishings, the canvases on the other hand, often hung in place of mirrors, reflect the narcissistic position of the subjectively determined abstract painting, which was suppressed in the modernistic tradition by the concept of the autonomy of the painting. The musical instruments for their part repeat a popular still-life motif (compare, for example, the guitar employed by the Cubists), at the same time shifting the pictures out of the painterly tradition and into association with the contemporary entertainments industry.

Pictures and objects are not parts of a continuum. Picture and object react one upon the other: the pictorial composition turns to account formal qualities of the neighbouring object and the object defines the picture's real location. They do not interreact like parts of a surrealistic montage in which the alienating co-existence of objects very different to one another provides the key note. In contrast to Rauschenberg with his *Combine Paintings*, Armleder is not interested in the graduation of planes between painting, reproduction and real object. His so-called *Furniture Sculptures* intervene in painting, treating the picture no longer as an autonomous object but as a commodity and presenting commodities as possible extensions of painting.

—Dieter Schwarz

ARNESON, Robert.

American. Born in Benicia, California, 4 September 1930. Educated at Benicia High School, 1945-49; Marin College, Kenfield, California, 1949-51; studied art education at California College of Arts and Crafts, Oakland, 1952-54, B.A. 1954; studied art, under Antonio Prieto, Mills College, Oakland, 1957-58, M.F.A. 1958. Married Jeanette Jensen in 1955 (divorced, 1972); sons: Leif, Derek, and Kirk; married Sandra Shannonhouse in 1973. Sports cartoonist, *Benicia Herald*, 1949-52. Independent artist, since 1958; established studio with Richard McLean, East Oakland, 1961-62; lived in Doylestown, Pennsylvania and shared New York loft studio with former student Stephen Kaltenbach, 1967; established and maintains studio in old saloon, Benicia, California, since 1975; travelled to major museums in France, Belgium, Holland, and Switzerland, 1978. Art Teacher, Menlo-Atherton High School, Atherton, California, 1954-57, Santa Rosa Junior College, California, 1958-59, and Fremont High School, Oakland, 1959-60; Instructor in Design and Crafts, Mills College, Oakland, 1960-62. Assistant Professor of Art and Design, 1962-68, Associate Professor of Art, 1968-73, and Professor, since 1973, University of California at Davis. Recipient: Creative Arts Grant, University of California, 1967; Artists' Fellowship Grant, 1971, and Apprentice Fellowship Grant, 1978, National Endowment for the Arts; National Council on Education for the Ceramic Arts Award, 1979; D.F.A.: Rhode Island School of Design, Providence, 1985. Agents: Fuller-Goldeen Gallery, 228 Grant Avenue, San Francisco, California 94108; Allen Frumkin Gallery, 50 West 57th Street, New York, New York 10022. Address: c/o Art Department, University of California at Davis, Davis, California 95616, U.S.A.

Individual Exhibitions:

1960　Oakland Art Museum, California (with Tony De-Lap)
1962　M. H. de Young Memorial Museum, San Francisco
　　　Barrios Gallery, Sacramento, California
1963　Richmond Art Center, California
1964　Cellini Gallery, San Francisco
　　　Home Economics Building, University of California at Davis
　　　Allan Stone Gallery, New York
1967　San Francisco Museum of Art
1968　Hansen-Fuller Gallery, San Francisco
1969　Hansen-Fuller Gallery, San Francisco
　　　Bob and Roy Ceramics, Esther Robles Gallery, Los Angeles (with Roy De Forest)
　　　Candy Store Gallery, Folsom, California
1970　*Recent Art Works in Porcelain*, Hansen-Fuller Gallery, San Francisco
　　　Bob and Roy Ware, Candy Store Gallery, Folsom, California (with Roy De Forest)
　　　Fresno State College of Art Gallery, California
1971　Hansen-Fuller Gallery, San Francisco
　　　Candy Store Gallery, Folsom, California
　　　Manolides Gallery, Seattle (with William T. Wiley)
　　　University of Calgary, Alberta
1972　Hansen-Fuller Gallery, San Francisco
　　　Miami-Dade Junior College, Florida
1973　Hansen-Fuller Gallery, San Francisco
　　　Church Fine Arts Gallery, University of Nevada, Reno
1974　Hansen-Fuller Gallery, San Francisco
　　　Deson-Zaks Gallery, Chicago
　　　Museum of Contemporary Art, Chicago (retrospective; travelled to the San Francisco Museum of Art)
　　　Candy Store Gallery, Folsom, California
1975　Allan Frumkin Gallery, New York
　　　Hansen-Fuller Gallery, San Francisco
　　　Ruth Schaffner Gallery, Los Angeles
　　　Dootson/Calderhead Gallery, Seattle
1976　Hansen-Fuller Gallery, San Francisco
　　　Fendrick Gallery, Washington, D.C.
　　　Memorial Union Art Gallery, University of California at Davis

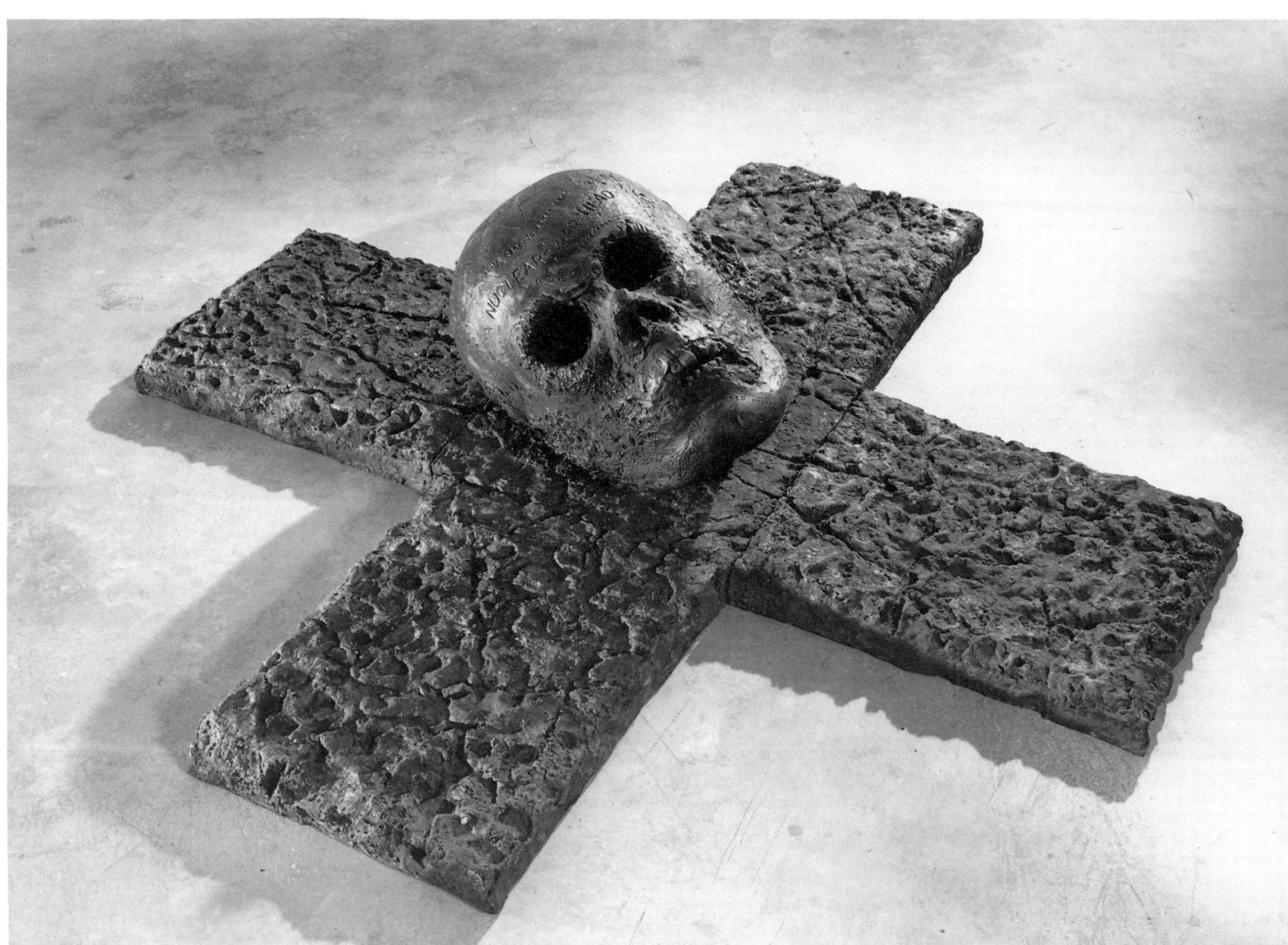

Robert Arneson: *Ground Zero*, **1984**

Allan Frumkin Gallery, Chicago
National Collection of Fine Arts, Smithsonian Institution, Washington, D.C.
1977 Hansen-Fuller Gallery, San Francisco
Allan Frumkin Gallery, New York
1978 *Works on Paper,* Allan Frumkin Gallery, New York
Allan Frumkin Gallery, Chicago
1979 *Heroes and Clowns,* Allan Frumkin Gallery, New York
Self-Portraits 1965–1978, Moore College of Art, Philadelphia
Allan Frumkin Gallery, New York
1980 Hansen-Fuller-Goldeen Gallery, San Francisco
Frumkin and Struve Gallery, Chicago
1981 Allan Frumkin Gallery, New York
1982 Foster Goldstrom Gallery, San Francisco
University of California, Davis
Fuller-Goldeen Gallery, San Francisco
1983 Allan Frumkin Gallery, New York
Landfall Press Inc., Chicago (travelled to Beloit, Wisconsin; Saginaw, Michigan; Springfield, Missouri; Tulsa, Oklahoma; Shawnee Mission, Kansas; Muncie, Indiana)
Yares Gallery, Scottsdale, Arizona
Crocker Art Museum, Sacramento, California
Triton Museum of Art, Santa Clara, California (travelled to Sacramento, California; Fresno, California; Portland, Oregon)
1984 Allan Frumkin Gallery, New York
Fuller-Goldeen Gallery, San Francisco

Frumkin and Struve Gallery, Chicago
1985 Fuller-Goldeen Gallery, San Francisco

Selected Group Exhibitions:

1964 *Ceramic National,* Everson Museum of Art, Syracuse, New York (toured the United States, 1964–66)
1967 *Funk Art,* University of California Art Museum, Berkeley
1968 *Dada-Surrealism and Their Heritage,* Museum of Modern Art, New York
1970- *Teacups, Teapots and Gorillas,* Moore College of Art, Philadelphia (with Ron Nagle, David Gilhooly, and Michael Frimkess)
1972 *A Decade of Ceramic Art 1962–1972,* San Francisco Museum of Art
1976 *Painting and Sculpture in California: The Modern Era,* San Francisco Museum of Art (travelled to the National Gallery, Smithsonian Institution, Washington, D.C., 1977)
1978 *American Art since 1950,* Whitney Museum, New York
1981 *Ceramic Sculpture: Six Artists,* Whitney Museum, New York (travelled to San Francisco Museum of Modern Art, 1982)
1982 *100 Years of California Sculpture,* Oakland Art Museum, California
1984 *California Sculpture Show,* University of Southern

California, Los Angeles (travelled to Bordeaux, France; Mannheim, West Germany; West Bretton, Yorkshire; Hovikodden, Norway)

Collections:

Whitney Museum, New York; Museum of Contemporary Crafts, New York; Hirshhorn Museum and Sculpture Garden, Smithsonian Institution, Washington, D.C.; Philadelphia Museum of Art; University of California at Berkeley; San Francisco Museum of Modern Art; Oakland Museum, California; E. B. Crocker Art Gallery, Sacramento, California; Stedelijk Museum, Amsterdam; Australian National Gallery, Canberra.

Publications:

By ARNESON: book—*My Head in Ceramics,* exhibition catalogue, San Francisco, 1972; articles—"About Arneson, Art and Ceramics," interview, with Cecile N. McCann, in *Artweek* (Oakland, California), 26 October 1974; "Robert Arneson in Conversation with Gwen Stone" in *Visual Dialog* (Los Altos, California), vol. 2, no. 1, 1977.

On ARNESON:books—*A Decade of Ceramic Art 1962–1972,* exhibition catalogue, with text by Suzanne Foley, San Francisco 1972; *Robert Arneson,* exhibition catalogue, with texts by Suzanne Foley and Stephen Prokopoff, Chicago 1974; *American Sculpture in Process 1930–1976* by Wayne Anderson, New York 1975; *Tradition and Change: The*

American Craftsman by Julie Hall, New York 1977; *Painting and Sculpture in California: The Modern Era*, exhibition catalogue, San Francisco 1977; *History of American Ceramics: The Studio Potter* by Paul S. Donhauser, Dubuque, Iowa 1978; *Heroes and Clowns*, exhibition catalogue, with text by Michael McTwigan, New York 1979; *Robert Arneson: Self-Portraits 1965-1978*, exhibition catalogue, with text by Beth Coffelt, Philadelphia, 1979; *A Century of Ceramics in the United States 1878-1978*, exhibition catalogue, with texts by Garth Clark and Margie Hughto, New York 1979; articles—"Sweet Land of Funk" by Harald Paris in *Art In America* (New York), March/April 1967; "Arneson, Richardson" by Cecile N. McCann in *Artweek* (Oakland, California), 23 May 1970; "Sacramento!" by John FitzGibbon in *Art in America* (New York), November/December 1971; "Crock Art" By Douglas Davis in *Newsweek* (New York), 5 July 1971; "Arneson, Moses—Study in Contrasts" by Cecile N. McCann in *Artweek* (Oakland, California), 14 October 1972; "Arneson and Towbridge" by Cecile N. McCann in *Artweek* (Oakland, California), 20 October 1973; "Robert Arneson's Feats of Clay" by Dennis Adrian in *Art in America* (New York), September/October 1974; "Bob Arneson: Take Notice" by David Van Houten in *Artweek* (Oakland, California), 25 January 1975; "Arneson's Landscape" by R. F. Stepan in *Artweek* (Oakland, California), 24 January 1976; "The Ceramic Sculpture of Robert Arneson, Transformation of Craft into Art" by Alfred Frankenstein in *Artnews* (New York), January 1976; "Sculpture—From Boring to Brilliant" by Hilton Kramer in the *New York Times*, 15 May 1977; "Robert Arneson at Frumkin" by Sarah McFadden in *Art in America* (New York), July 1977; "A Modern Way with Clay" by Bill Marvel in *Horizon* (New York), September 1978; "57,500 Ceramics Commission" in *Ceramics Monthly* (Athens, Ohio), May 1981; "Arneson's Bust" by Robert Sommer in *Arts and Architecture* (Los Angeles), 1 August 1982; "A Monumental Side to Arneson" by Dennis Adrian in *San Francisco Chronicle*, 22 February 1984; "Arneson's Outrage" by Donald Kuspit in *Art in America* (New York), May 1985.

I think I've always been a social political artist. My art is accessible. Recently, I've done a body of work on the nuclear issue. *Ground Zero* (1984) is a typical example. It visualizes targeting of mankind through a nuclear holocaust. It's not fun to look at, but I wanted to bring my concern of the dangers of nuclear proliferation to an expanded art audience—the museum and gallery visitor—to let them know that art and life were inseparable.

—Robert Arneson

Robert Arneson's explicitly autobiographical sculptures confront his pleasures and embarrassments with a wry, self-deprecating humor that touches a responsive chord for most viewers. It is easy to identify with the blissful face that surveys a table loaded with festive foods or the ceramic head which shows the sculptor on the receiving end of a gob of clay—mud in his eye, or perhaps a metaphor for critical barbs occasionally flung at his work.

Beyond the clearly personal comments, the work contains wide-ranging art-historical references. Arneson has so thoroughly studied the history of ceramics that he has made both the concepts and techniques of the past accessible for his own uses. At one time he created a series of irreverent small sculptures that used imagery resembling fruit stand souvenirs, and made them of exquisitely finished, celadon-glazed porcelain as seductive as a Sung bowl. One homage to ancient Rome took the form of a self portrait bust set head-high on an accurately reproduced classical column, the calm austerity of the piece punctured by male genitals protruding from the smooth cylinder at the appropriate position and bare toes peeking at the column's base as if it were the hem of a toga. Pomposity and self-importance are not permitted to linger in this artist's work.

More recently Arneson has preferred low-fire white ware as a medium, indulging his painter's eye in the pleasures of skillfully handled color only possible with the brilliance of low-temperature glazes. The self-portraits continue, their good-natured jocularity reflecting the pleasanter aspects of Arneson's daily life. If the cheerfulness at times seems over-insistent, perhaps this has some connection with the long, sustained effort necessary to produce a sculpture. In the

immediacy of watercolors and drawings, Arneson occasionally records darker thoughts and grim self-images, as if to purge them from his mind and let happier moods return. Happy or sad, it is himself and the small concerns that define a personality which Arneson records with detailed accuracy.

—Cecile N. McCann

ARROYO, Eduardo.

Spanish. Born in Madrid, 26 February 1937. Educated at Lycée Francais, Madrid, 1949-53; studied journalism at the Ecole Supérieure de Journalisme, Madrid, 1956-57; mainly self-taught in painting, from 1949. Served in the Spanish Infantry, 1956-57. Worked as freelance journalist, Madrid, 1957; as independent painter, Paris, 1958-68; in Milan, 1968-72; in West Berlin, 1975-76; permanently in Paris, since 1973. Instructor, Atelier Populaire, Ecole des Beaux-Arts, Paris, 1968. Worked as freelance theatre, set and costumer designer, in Milan, Bremen, Dusseldorf, Frankfurt, Berlin, and Paris, 1969-76. Recipient: Deutscher Akademischer Austauschdienst (D.A.A.D.) Grant, Berlin, 1975-76. Agent: Galerie Karl Flinker, 25 rue de Tournon, 75006 Paris. Address: 2 Passage Dantzig, 75015 Paris, France.

Individual Exhibitions:

1961	Galerie Claude Levin, Paris
1962	Crane Kalman Gallery, London
1963	Galleria Biosca, Madrid
1964	Galerie 20, Amsterdam
	Galerie 20, Arnhem, Netherlands
	Galerie Bernheim Jeune, Paris
1965	Galerie André Schoeller Jr., Paris
	Galerie 20, Amsterdam
1967	Galleria de'Foscherari, Bologna
	Galleria Mendoza, Caracas
	Galleria Il Fante di Spade, Rome
1968	Studio Marconi, Milan
	Studio Bellini, Milan
	Galleria Il Canale, Venice
	Galleria La Chiocciola, Padua
1969	Galleria La Bussola, Turin
	Galleria La Robinia, Palermo
	Galerie André Weill, Paris
1970	Galerie Withofs, Brussels
	Galleria Il Fante di Spade, Rome
	Galleria Aldina, Rome
	Galleria Arte Borgogna, Milan
	Galleria San Michele, Brescia
1971	*30 Jahre Danach*, Kunstverein, Frankfurt (travelled to the Musée d'Art Moderne de la Ville, Paris)
	Museum Hedendaagse Kunst, Utrecht
	Kunstverein, Munich
	Kunstverein, Berlin
	Palazzo del Gobernatore, Parma
	Galleria People, Turin
1972	Galerie 9, Paris
	Städtische Kunsthalle, Düsseldorf
	Galerie d'Eendt, Amsterdam
1973	Galleria d'Arte Borgogna, Milan
	Gastaldelli Arte Contemporanea, Milan
	Galleria Nuove Muse, Bologna
1974	*Portraits*, Galerie Karl Flinker, Paris
	Studio P. L., Milan
1975	Galerie Fred Lanzenberg, Brussels
	Galleria L'Aprodo, Turin
1976	D.A.A.D. Akademie der Künste, Berlin (with Grazia Eminente)
	Galerie Leger, Malmo, Sweden
1977	Galeria Maeght, Barcelona
	Galeria Juana Mordo, Madrid
	Galeria Val y 30, Valencia
1978	Fondation Nationale des Artes Graphiques et Plastiques, Paris
	Galerie Karl Flinker, Paris
1979	Galerie Karl Flinker, Basle
	Gallery Art Package, Highland Park, Illinois
1980	Galerie Maeght, Zurich
	Städtische Galerie im Lenbachhaus, Munich
	Galerie Michael Hasenclever, Munich
1981	Galerie Karl Flinker, Paris
1982	Modern Art Museum, Madrid
	Centre Georges Pompidou, Paris
	Eva Cohen Gallery, Highland Park, Illinois
1983	Leonard Hutton Galleries, New York
1984	Galerie Levy, Hamburg
	Guggenheim Museum, New York (retrospective)

Selected Group Exhibitions:

1960	*Salon de la Jeune Peinture*, Paris
1964	*Neue Realisten und Pop Art*, Akademie der Künste, Berlin
1965	*Pop Art: Nouveaux Réalistes*, Palais des Beaux-Arts, Brussels
1970	*Kunst und Politik*, Kunstmuseum, Karlsruhe, West Germany
1971	*Peintures et Objets*, Musée Galliera, Paris
1972	*Immagini per la Città*, Palazzo Reale, Genoa
1974	*L'Arte contre il Fascismo*, Palazzo della Loggia, Brescia
1976	*Realidada Social 1936-76*, at the *Biennale*, Venice
1979	*1968-79: Tendances de l'Art en France II*, Musée d'Art Moderne de la Ville, Paris
1980	*L'Art et le Sport*, Centre Culturel, Boulogne-Billancourt, France

Collections:

Musée d'Art Moderne de la Ville, Paris; Centre Georges Pompidou, Paris; Ministère de la Culture et de la Communication, Paris; Fondation Maeght, St. Paul de Vence, France; Musée des Beaux-Arts, Lausanne; National Galerie, Berlin; Hirshhorn Museum, Washington, D.C.

Publications:

By ARROYO: book—*"Panama" Al Brown 1902-1951*, Paris 1982.

On ARROYO: books—*Kunst und Politik*, exhibition catalogue, Karlsruhe 1970; *Eduardo Arroyo: 30 Jahre Danach*, exhibition catalogue, with text by Gerard Gassiot-Talabot, Frankfurt 1971; *Arroyo: Portraits*, exhibition catalogue, with text by Michel Tournier, Paris 1974; *Eduardo Arroyo*, exhibition catalogue, with text by Gilbert Lascault, Paris 1978; *Eduardo Arroyo: Blinde Maler und Exit*, exhibition catalogue, with text by Armin Zweite, Munich 1980; *Arroyo* by Pierre Astier, Paris 1982; *Eduardo Arroyo*, exhibition catalogue with texts by Dominique Bozo and Werner Spies, New York 1983.

There has always been an element of nakedness about Eduardo Arroyo's imagery. Even in early times, when the paint of his pictures was a little thicker, it was present. This is the surface effect, but below it lies an active conscience that dictates imagery. Not the sort of artist who can live comfortably in the cloying atmosphere of a dictatorship. This Spaniard with his direct approach tinted with character is a fine example of *engagierte kunst*. The Buonaparte paintings he showed in Paris made this very plain. But even politics as an inspiration for artists has not necessarily got eternal appeal.

Some of his later work has been concerned with the boxing ring, especially with coloured fighters. In these new works he is able to give a fresh and wholly unexpected dimension to the promotional side of "commercial art," although in Arroyo's case it is fine art, not the product of advertising nor some hybrid hyperrealist artist that is under consideration.

Arroyo's paint is flat. The subject (at one time he even divided his canvases into sections like a comic strip, although hardly in the same vein as those of CPLY's) is painted sparingly with the minimum of chiaroscuro. Colours tend to be block, and there is

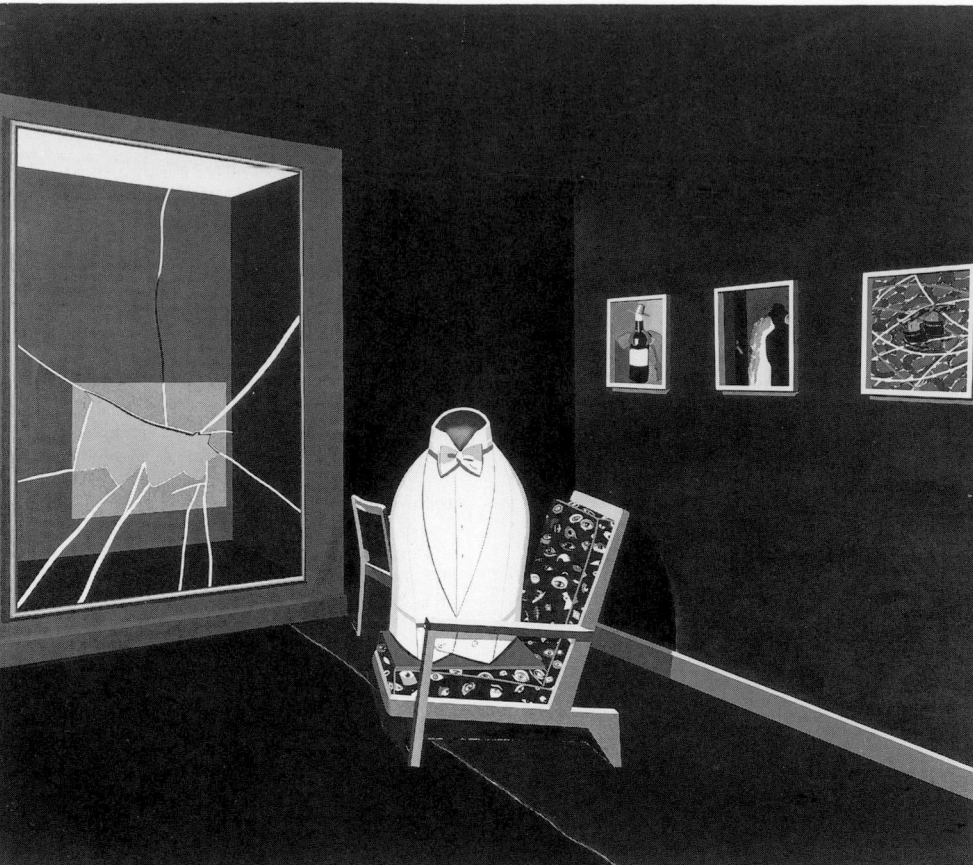

Eduardo Arroyo: *A la Tate Gallery, José Maria Blanco White est Surveillé*, 1979

virtually no tinting. All of his pictures have a careful, even traditional, sense of composition. Carried out by another artist, they might even have been associated with the pop image.

—Sheldon Williams

ARTSCHWAGER, Richard (Ernst).

American. Born in Washington, D.C., 26 December 1924. Studied chemistry and mathematics at Cornell University, Ithaca, New York, 1943–44, 1946–48, B.A. 1948; studied art with Amedee Ozenfant, New York, 1950. Served in the United States Army, 1944–46. Married Elfriede Wejmelka in 1947 (divorced, 1971); daughter: Eva; married Catherine Kord in 1972. Worked as a baby photographer for Stork Diaper Service, New York; lathe operator for Efrem Natkin Flexible Couplings, New York; and in export/import department, Colonial Trust Company, New York, 1950–55; operated a furniture factory, New York, 1955–65. Full-time artist, New York, since 1970. Recipient: Cassandra Award, New York, 1969; National Endowment for the Arts grant, 1973. Agent: Leo Castelli Gallery, 4 West 77th Street, New York, New York 10021. Address: 158 South Oxford Street, Brooklyn, New York 11217, U.S.A.

Individual Exhibitions:

1965 Leo Castelli Gallery, New York
1967 Leo Castelli Gallery, New York
1968 Galerie Konrad Fischer, Dusseldorf
1969 Galerie Ricke, Cologne
1970 Lo Guidice, Chicago
Eugenia Butler Gallery, Los Angeles
Onnasch Galerie, Berlin
1972 Leo Castelli Gallery, New York
Galerie Ricke, Cologne

1973 Leo Castelli Gallery, New York
Dunkelman Gallery, Toronto
Museum of Contemporary Art, Chicago
1974 Daniel Weinberg Gallery, San Francisco
Galerie Ileana Sonnabend, Geneva
1975 Leo Castelli Gallery, New York
Daniel Weinberg Gallery, San Francisco
Jared Sable Gallery, Toronto
Galerie Neuendorf, Hamburg
Galerie Sonnabend, Paris
1976 Walter Kelly Gallery, Chicago
Castelli Graphics, New York
1977 Sable-Castelli Gallery, Toronto
1978 Texas Gallery, Houston
Clocktower, New York
Institute for Art and Urban Resources, New York
Morgan Gallery, Shawnee Mission, Kansas
Kunstverein, Hamburg
1979 Leo Castelli Gallery, New York
Albright-Knox Art Gallery, Buffalo, New York
Institute of Contemporary Art, University of Pennsylvania, Philadelphia
1980 La Jolla Museum of Contemporary Art, California
Young-Hoffman Gallery, Chicago
1982 Leo Castelli Gallery, New York
1985 Kunstverein, Basel
Leo Castelli Gallery, New York
1986 CAPC Musée d'Art Contemporain, Bordeaux, France
1988 Whitney Museum, New York

Selected Group Exhibitions:

1964 *Boxes*, Dwan Gallery, Los Angeles
1966 *Primary Structures*, Jewish Museum, New York
1967 *The 1960's*, Museum of Modern Art, New York
1968 *Documenta 4*, Kassel, West Germany
1969 *When Attitudes Become Form*, Kunsthalle, Berne (toured Germany and Great Britain)
1972 *Documenta 5*, Kassel, West Germany
1974 *American Pop Art*, Whitney Museum, New York
1976 *200 Years of American Sculpture*, Whitney Museum, New York

1977 *Improbable Furniture*, Institute of Contemporary Art, University of Pennsylvania, Philadelphia
1987 *Documenta 8*, Museum Fridericianum, Kassel, West Germany

Collections:

Museum of Modern Art, New York; Whitney Museum, New York; Wadsworth Atheneum, Hartford, Connecticut; Kansas City Museum, Missouri; Detroit Institute of Arts; La Jolla Museum of Contemporary Art, California; Art Institute of Chicago; Rotterdam Museum; Wallraf-Richartz Museum, Cologne; Kunstmuseum, Basel.

Publications:

By ARTSCHWAGER: books—*Leo Castelli: 20 Years*, pamphlet, New York 1977; articles—"The Hydraulic Door Check" in *Arts Magazine* (New York), November 1967; "Statements on Art: in *N.A.M.E. Gallery, Book I*, edited by Donald Sultan and Nancy Davidson, Chicago 1977; "Actual Art" in *Skira Annual 79*, Geneva 1979; "Parade in the Face of Death: Robert Stanley" in *Galleries Magazine* (New York), September 1987.

On ARTSCHWAGER: books—*Direction I: Options*, exhibition catalogue, with introduction by Lawrence Alloway, Milwaukee 1968; *Documenta 5*, exhibition catalogue, Kassel, West Germany 1972; articles—"The Object: Still Life" by Jan McDevitt in *Craft Horizons* (New York), September/October 1965; "Artschwager's Mental Furniture" by Elizabeth C. Baker in *Art News* (New York), January 1968; "Richard Artschwager" by William Zimmer in *Arts Magazine* (New York), June 1975; "Richard Artschwager" by Noel Frackman in *Arts Magazine* (New York), January 1977; "Die Graue Tarnhulle der Wirklichkeit" by Peter Winter in *Frankfurter Allgemeine Zeitung* (Frankfurt), 2 October 1978; "The Elastic Vision of Richard Artschwager" in *Art in America* (New York), May/June 1978; article by John Russell in the *New York Times*, 8 July 1979; "The Artschwager Enigma" by Roberta Smith in *Art in America* (New York), October 1979.

It has been known since the Renaissance that art is produced by artists, and the notion has been available for more than a century that art is internal to the recipient; in a sense, "made" by the recipient. The first notion has tended to block off the availability of the second, and I think my contribution has been to make it not only available but Necessary, i.e., to force the issue of the context or, to put it in more old-fashioned terms, to make art that has no boundaries. At the beginning (around 1962) this was worked out in two steps: first make something which is "art," then insert it into a demanding, absorbent context, like inserting a garlic sliver into a joint of mutton. I have done some other things, but this certainly got the ball rolling!

—Richard Artschwager

Artschwager studied cell biology at Cornell University, with an interruption for military service, between 1941–48. In 1949–50 he studied in New York with Amadee Ozenfant. In 1953 he took up cabinet making and by 1956 he was massproducing simple furniture.

With the encouragement of his first wife he turned his energies towards actively being an artist by the early 1960s. He began to produce his 'infactory' works which were Constructivist in tone with identical sheets of plywood cut-offs joined into stacks, fans and baffles. By the mid 1960s, (when he began to exhibit with Leo Castelli Gallery), his work had become more like highly simplified furniture shapes frequently with formica or laminated surfaces. This neo-Dada type work came to be classified as "Minimalist." Barbara Rose, wrote in 1965 on Minimalist Art: "It is part of the irony of the works . . . and irony plays a large part in them—that they blatantly assert their unsaleability and functionlessness. Some, like Artschwager's pseudofurniture or Warhol's Brillo boxes, are not too unwieldy to be sold, but since they approximate real objects with actual uses, they begin to raise questions about the utility of art, and its ambiguous role in our culture."

At the same time as he was producing the 'pseudo-furniture,' Artschwager was making grisaille pictures, frequently of highrise apartment blocks, by grid-enlarging photos and reproducing them with acrylic on celotex. In 1967 he developed an object which he termed a Blp and which he used as a kind of installation piece that could be installed anywhere, (a gallery wall, or on the sidewalk). The Blp was a long flat oval of any size, painted black. The name Blp came from a military expression Artschwager had learned during the war; it is an object connected with a sound as it moves on a radar screen.

In the late 1960s there came a lapse into pure Surrealism when Artschwager produced hair boxes and wall reliefs. The acrylic on celotex pictures, primarily of architectural interiors, lasted well into the 1970s.

By the early 1980s, Artschwager had become one of the sculptors involved in the U.S. government's General Services Administration's 'Art in Architecture' programme. This partnership has had a high profile with the Battery Park City development in southwestern Manhattan, where Artschwager's work will be sited.

—Victoria Keller

Richard Artschwager: *Chair,* 1963

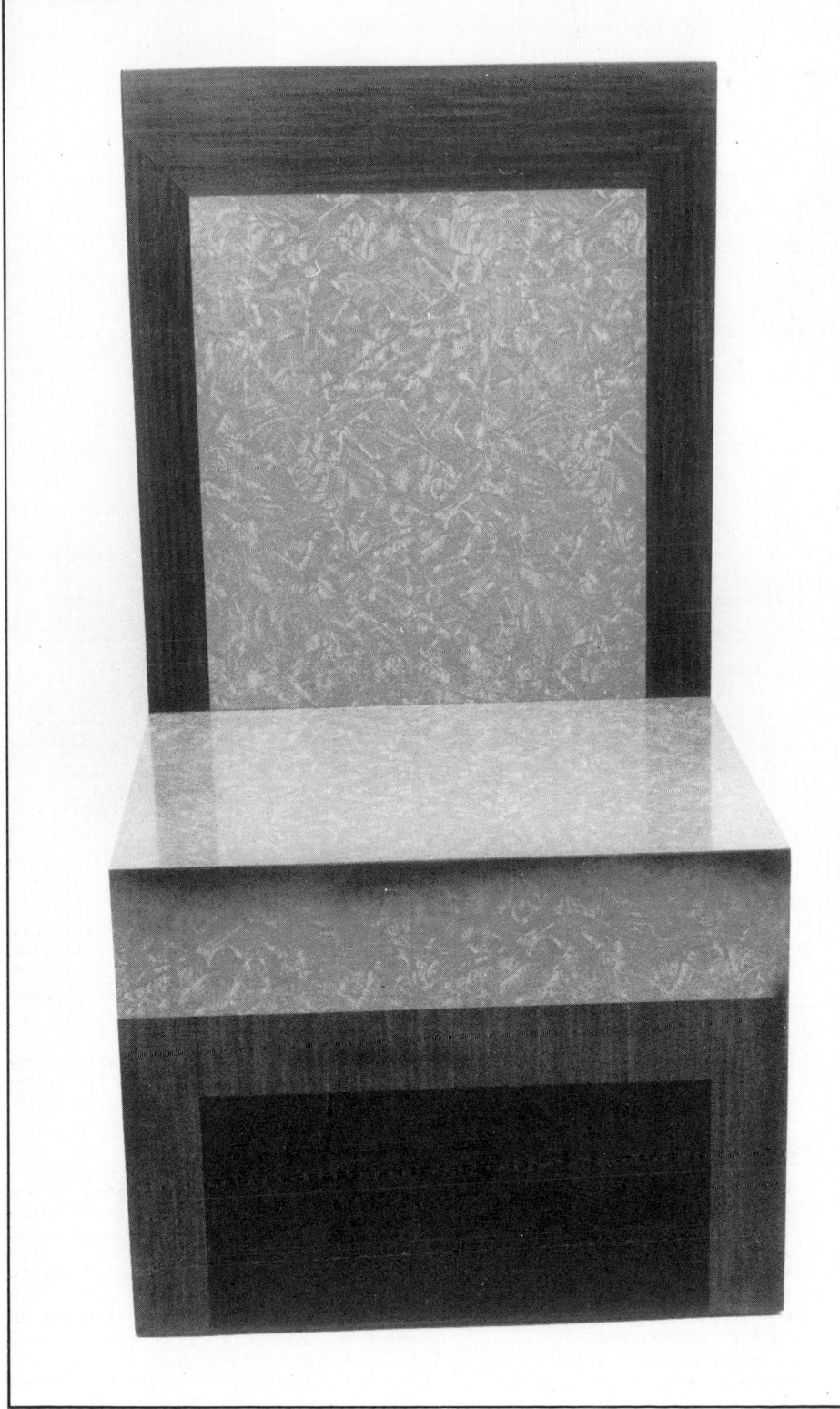

ASHER, Michael.

American. Born in Los Angeles, California, 15 July 1943. Studied liberal arts and sciences at Orange Coast College, Costa Mesa, California, 1961–63; anthropology and art, University of New Mexico, Albuquerque, 1963–64; New York Studio School, 1964–65; fine arts, University of California at Irvine, 1965–67, B.A. 1966. Worked as advertising sales representative for West Coast Industries, New York, 1964; worked as research assistant for use of cardboard materials in furniture, Los Angeles. Independent sculptor and environmental artist, Los Angeles, since 1966. Assistant Instructor in Sculpture, 1966–67, and Painting Instructor, 1967–68, University of California at Irvine; Instructor in Art, California Institute of Arts, Valencia, 1976. Artist-in-Residence, University of California at Irvine, 1973, California Institute of the Arts, Valencia, 1973, Nova Scotia College of Art and Design, 1974, and Otis Art Institute, Los Angeles, 1975. Recipient: Purchase Award, Contemporary Art Council, Los Angeles County Museum of Art, 1967; Short-Term Activities Fellowship Grant, National Endowment for the Arts, 1973; Guggenheim Fellowship, 1974; Artists Fellowship Grant, National Endowment for the Arts, 1975. Address: 262 Carmelina Avenue South, Apt. 6, Los Angeles, California 90291, U.S.A.

Individual Exhibitions:

1969   La Jolla Museum of Art, California
1970   Gladys K. Montgomery Art Center, Pomona College, Claremont, California
1972   Market Street Program, Venice, California
1973   Gallery A 402, California Institute of the Arts, Valencia
      Cambridge School, Weston, Massachusetts
      Lisson Gallery, London
      Galerie Heiner Friedrich, Cologne
      Galleria Toselli, Milan
1974   Claire S. Copley Gallery, Los Angeles
      Anna Leonowens Gallery, Nova Scotia College of Art and Design, Halifax
1975   Otis Art Institute, Los Angeles
1976   The Clocktower, New York
      The Floating Museum, San francisco
1977   Van Abbemuseum, Eindhoven, Netherlands
1980   *Exhibitions in Europa 1972–1977,* Van Abbemuseum, Eindhoven, Netherlands
1984   Hofhour Gallery, Albuquerque, New Mexico
1986   Hofhour Gallery, Albuquerque, New Mexico

Selected Group Exhibitions:

1967   *I Am Alive,* Los Angeles County Museum of Art
1969   *Anti-Illusion: Procedures: Materials,* Whitney Museum, New York
      Plane und Projekte als Kunst, Kunsthalle, Berne (travelled to Aktionsraum I, Munich, and the Kunsthaus, Hamburg)
1970   *Art in the Mind,* Allen Art Museum, Oberlin College, Ohio
1971   *24 Young Los Angeles Artists,* Los Angeles County Museum of Art
1972   *Documenta 5,* Kassel, West Germany
1973   *3D into 2D: Drawings for Sculpture,* New York Cultural Center
1975   *University of California, Irvine, 1965–75,* La Jolla Museum of Contemporary Art, California
1976   *Ambiente,* at *Biennale,* Venice
1977   *Skulptur,* Westfälische Landesmuseum, Münster, West Germany

Publications:

By ASHER: book—Commentary in *Michael Asher: Exhibitions in Europa 1972–1977,* exhibition catalogue, Eindhoven, Netherlands, 1980.

On ASHER: book—*Anti-Illusion: Procedures: Materials,* exhibition catalogue, with texts by James Monte and Marcia

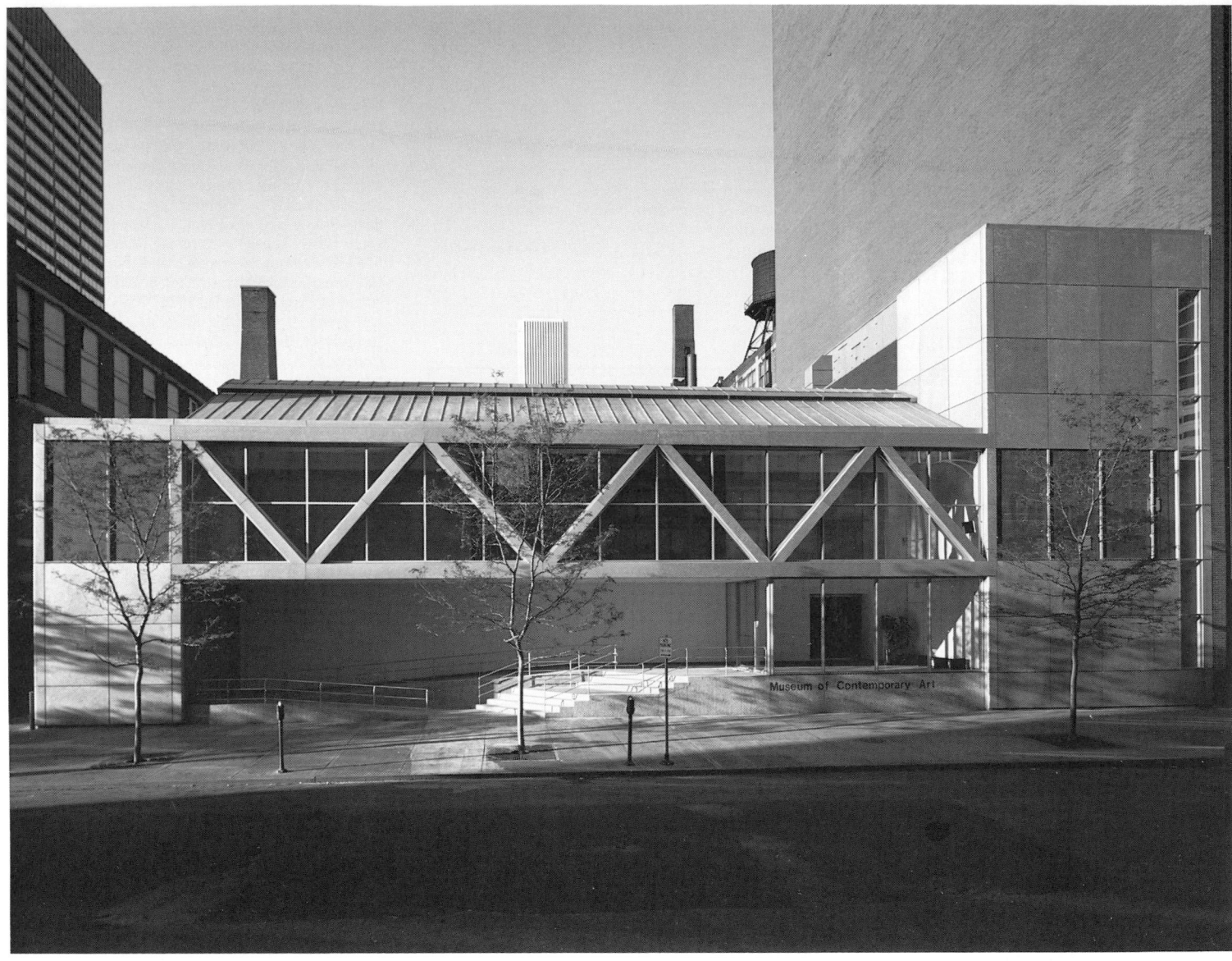

Michael Asher: *Untitled*, installation at the Museum of Contemporary Art, Chicago, 1979

Tucker, New York 1969; *8e Biennale de Paris,* exhibition catalogue, with texts by J. Cahen-Salvador, and others, Paris 1973; *Michael Asher: Exhibitions in Europa 1972–1977,* exhibition catalogue, with essays by R. H. Fuchs and B. H. D. Buchloh, Eindhoven, Netherlands 1980; articles—"Michael Asher: La Jolla Art Museum" by T. H. Garver in *Artforum* (New York), January 1970; "Michael Asher: An Environmental Project" by B. Munger in *Studio International* (London), October 1970; "The Art of Existence: 3 Extravisual Artists, Works in Progress" by Robert Morris in *Artforum* (New York), January 1971; "Michael Asher: The Thing of It Is . . ." by Peter Plagens in *Artforum* (New York), April 1972.

I feel it is implicit, yet perhaps not immediately recognised through background information, that those activities which pertain to my art and those activities which pertain to me in general, are determined by one another.

—Michael Asher

ASKEVOLD, David.

American. Born in Conrad, Montana, 30 March 1940. Educated at University of Montana, Missoula; Brooklyn Museum School of Art, New York; Art Institute of Kansas City, Missouri. Taught at Nova Sco-

tia College of Art and Design, Halifax, 1968–75; University of California at Irvine, 1976–77; and California Institute of the Arts, Valencia, 1977–78; instructor, Art Center College of Design, Pasadena, California, 1980–81; lecturer, York University, Downsview, Ontario, 1981–82. Agents: Studio Cannaviello, Piazza Beccaria 10, 20122 Milan, Italy; Galerie Paul Maenz, Bismarckstrasse 50, 5000 Cologne 1, West Germany. Address: P.O. Box 898, Big Sky, Montana 59716, U.S.A.

Individual Exhibitions:

1970 Nova Scotia College of Art and Design, Halifax
1971 Anna Leonowens Gallery, Nova Scotia College of Art and Design, Halifax
1972 Anna Leonowens Gallery, Nova Scotia College of Art and Design, Halifax
      Galerie Paul Maenz, Cologne
      Galerie Yvon Lambert, Paris
      Galleria Françoise Lambert, Milan
      Jack Wendler Gallery, London
1973 John Gibson Gallery, New York
1974 Anna Leonowens Gallery, Nova Scotia College of Art and Design, Halifax
      Galerie Paul Maenz, Cologne
      Galleria Françoise Lambert, Milan
1975 Galerie Yvon Lambert, Paris
      John Gibson Gallery, New York
      Art Metropole, Toronto

1976 Fine Arts Gallery, University of California at Irvine
1977 John Gibson Gallery, New York
1978 Thomas Lewallen Gallery, Los Angeles
      Foundation for Art Resources, Los Angeles (with Michael Kelley)
1980 Van Abbemuseum, Eindhoven, Netherlands
      Cannaviello Studio d'Arte, Milan
1981 Jancar Kuhlenschmidt Gallery, Los Angeles

Selected Group Exhibitions:

1974 Palais des Beaux-Arts, Brussels
1976 Daniel Templon Galerie, Paris
      The Artist and the Photograph, Israel Museum, Jerusalem
1977 *Documenta,* Kassel, West Germany
1978 *Story, Narrative Art,* Contemporary Art Museum, Houston (travelling exhibition)
1979 *Narrative Art,* Groningen Museum, Netherlands
      Text/Visual, Commune di Milano, Milan
1980 *Camerie Incantate,* Commune de Milano, Milan
      Artist and Camera, Arts Council of Great Britain (travelling exhibition)

Collections:

Van Abbemuseum, Eindhoven, Netherlands; Museum of Contemporary Art, Houston, Texas.

Publications:

By ASKEVOLD: book—*Extra,* Cologne, April 1975; articles—"Liberal Art University Experiences: David Askevold in Conversations with Paul McMahon" in *Studio International* (London), April 1972; article in *Video by Artists,* edited by Peggy Gale, Toronto 1976; radio broadcast—17 Minute Tuning Fork Music Concert, K.P.F.A. Radio, Berkeley, California, April 1971.

On ASKEVOLD: books—*6 Years: The Dematerialization of the Art Object* by Lucy Lippard, New York 1973; *Individuals: Post Movement Art in America,* edited by Alan Sondheim, New York 1977; *The Artist and the Photograph #2,* exhibition catalogue No. 55, Jerusalem 1977; *Narrative Art,* exhibition catalogue, Groningen, Netherlands 1979; articles—"Artist as Film-Maker" by Annabel Nicholson in *Art and Artists* (London), December 1972; review in *Arts* (New York), February 1974; article in *Kunst Magazine* (Munich), March 1974; article in *Artforum* (New York), September 1974; article by Ronald Shuebrook in *Artscanada* (Toronto), December 1974; article in *Data* (Milan) nos. 16/17, 1975; articles in *Artweek* (Oakland, California), 4 February 1977, and 14 July 1979; article in *Kunstforum* (Cologne), Fall 1979; article in *Artweek* (Oakland, California), 13 February 1979; article in *Artforum* (New York), May 1981.

David Askevold is perhaps one of the most prolific and experimental of all the artists associated with the school of Narrative Art. In many ways he differs from them wildly: unlike Bill Beckley, he has never remained with one primary medium (the large glossy color photograph and short, pithy text); and unlike French artist Jean Le Gac, he is not concerned with the gentler aspect of a series of banal incidents and certainly does not invest his narrative with mild or startling humor. Rather, Askevold steers his work through a variety of mediums and even concerns, depending upon their appropriateness at a given time. He has, of course, made many still works (the conventional Narrative device of visual sign and quasi-expository text), but he has also made discrete films and videotapes, and ambitious film, video, and slide installations. Furthermore, these are frequently and deliberately obscure, and therefore do not share with other work in the genre an immediate and engaging sensibility.

This is not to say that there is not an active and linking sensibility throughout Askevold's oeuvre. This takes the form of a complex approach and an occasionally sinister iconography. First of all, Askevold rarely if ever follows the structural pattern of several of his colleagues, in which image and text deliberately diverge (i.e., the texts meandering while the images form a logical dramatic sequence). Instead, the combination of word and sign create, as Filiberto Menna has pointed out in a catalogue essay, "a perfect parallelism between the two terms, so that the text accompanies and comments upon the horizontal concatenation of the images . . . " (This, of course, applies specifically to Askevold's more conventionally Narrative pieces, such as "Elektra," a series of eleven photos and text, completed in 1974.) Secondly, Askevold has never felt restricted by the convention of his chosen genre, and on several occasions has used an extraordinary ambitious formal structure, as in his installation "Four Notes Through a Wall and Into the Grass" (1972-73) which used a series of 80 color slides, audiotape, drawing, and super-8 film. And, as far as Askevold's iconography is concerned, it has involved a frequent use of snakes (as in the previously mentioned "Four Notes" and "Kepler's Music of the Spheres to Be Played by Six Snakes," (1971-73), as well as paradigms from algebra and physics, and quasi-psychological experiments.

In one of his most major sequences, "Dream of Descartes," Askevold takes a theme through several media: in his still version, he uses four photographs and a number of versions of a nearly identical text (with phrases added or deleted), as well as a 16 millimeter color film, and later, a fairly ambitious installation using two super-8 film projections and scored music, combined with Kepler's "Music of the Spheres." Askevold's is, in a sense, an art of re-trieval, both physical and conceptual, never linear or progressive, but continually evolving both backwards and forwards, borrowing from and expanding upon itself.

—Jane Bell

ATKINSON, Conrad.

British. Born in Cleator Moor, Cumbria, 15 June 1940. Educated in Cumbria primary schools; studied painting at the Carlisle College of Art, 1957-61, Liverpool College of Art, 1961-62, and the Royal Academy of Art Schools, London, under William Townsend, 1962-65. Married Margaret Harrison in 1967; daughter: Sophie. Printmaking Adviser, the Royal Academy of Art Schools, London, 1963-65; Exhibition Organizer, Northern Arts Gallery, Newcastle upon Tyne, 1975-76. Since 1978, Lecturer, Slade School of Fine Art, London. Member, Art Science Working Party, University of London, 1971; Member, National Committee, British Society for Social Responsibility on Science, 1972; Chairman, Artists' Union, London, 1974; Member, Visual Arts Panel, Northern Arts, Newcastle upon Tyne, 1975-76; Member, Tyneside Trade Unionists for Socialist Arts, Newcastle upon Tyne, 1975-76. Recipient: National Book League Prize, 1955; Second Prize, Northern Young Artists, Middlesborough, 1965; Leverhulme Award, 1965; Abbey Travelling Scholarship, 1965; Granada Fellowship, 1967; Churchill Fellowship, 1972. Associate, School of Advanced Studies, Manchester, 1968; Fellow in Fine Arts, Northern Arts Association, Newcastle upon Tyne, 1974-76. Agent: Ronald Feldman Fine Arts, 31 Mercer Street, New York, New York 10013, U.S.A. Address: 172 Erlanger Road, London SE14, England. Address: 96 Lyndhurst Grove, London SE15, England.

Individual Exhibitions:

1967	*2 Painters,* City Art Gallery, Manchester (with Gerald Park)
1972	Institute of Contemporary Arts, London
1974	Institute of Contemporary Arts, London (toured the U.K.)
1975	Northern Ireland's Arts Council Gallery, Belfast
1976	Art Net Gallery, London
1977	Northern Arts Gallery, Newcastle upon Tyne
1978	Serpentine Gallery, London
1979	Ronald Feldman Fine Arts, New York
	The Craft of Art, Walker Fine Art Gallery, Liverpool
1980	Chapter House Gallery, Cardiff
	1975-1980: Work about the North, Pentonville Gallery, London
	Project Gallery, Dublin
	Carlisle Museum and Art Gallery
1981	Institute of Contemporary Arts, London
	Sunderland Arts Centre
1983	Power Gallery, Sydney
1985	Art Institute of Chicago
1987	Artangel Trust, London

Selected Group Exhibitions:

1965	*Northern Young Artists,* City Art Gallery, Middlesborough
1968	*Royal Academy Bicentenary,* Royal Academy of Art, London
1970	*Garbage Strike,* Sigi Krauss Gallery, London
1973	*Critics' Choice,* Tooth Gallery, London
1975	*Biennale de Paris*
1977	*British Art 77,* Newcastle upon Tyne
1978	*Art for Society,* Whitechapel Gallery, London
1979	*Un Certain Art Anglais,* Musée National d'Art Moderne, Paris

1980	*Photography into Print,* Victoria and Albert Museum, London
1981	*Landscape,* Tate Gallery, London

Collections:

City Art Gallery, Manchester; William Morris Housing Estate, Cleator Moor, Cumbria.

Publications:

By ATKINSON: books—*A Shade of Green: An Orange Edge,* exhibition catalogue, with John Hewitt and Caroline Tisdall, Belfast 1975; *Newcastle Writings,* Newcastle upon Tyne 1977; *Art for Whom,* exhibition catalogue, London 1978; statement in *The Craft of Art,* exhibition catalogue, by Edward Lucie Smith, Liverpool 1979; *Shamrock's Truth: The 1st Casualty: The British Media and Northern Ireland,* 1979; articles—"Conrad Atkinson: An Interview," with Richard Cork in *Studio International* (London), March/April 1976; "Capitalist Realism or Socialism in One Person" in *Skira Annual,* Geneva 1977; introduction to *Conrad Atkinson 1975-1980: Work about the North,* exhibition catalogue, London 1980.

On ATKINSON: books—*The Craft of Art,* exhibition catalogue, by Edward Lucie Smith, Liverpool 1979; *Art in the 70's* by Edward Lucie Smith, Oxford 1980; *Conrad Atkinson: Picturing the System,* edited by Caroline Tisdall and Sandy Nairne, London 1981; articles—"Tribute to a strike" by Laurie Flynn in *the Socialist Worker* (London), June 1972; "The Art of Work" by Caroline Tisdall in *The Guardian* (London), April 1974; "A Struggling Artist" by Bobby Campbell in *The Morning Star* (London), April 1974; "Atkinson in Northern Ireland" by Caroline Tisdall in *The Guardian* (London), 1976; film—*Atkinson,* BBC Television, 1981.

To deal with living situations and forces is obviously a difficult undertaking for an artist, fraught with pitfalls. It is an era unexplored by artists since the 1920's, and it is one in which attitudes to both form and content have a vast and unexplored potential.

One of the main problems for any artist is the necessity to isolate sections of our perceptions in order to examine and express them. Yet we have to maintain a sense of total relationships. The uneasy tug of war between these two conflicting necessities is the battleground on which the specialist and the generalist fight. In this difficult question of isolating an area of research without alienating oneself from overall problems, there is a tension which creates new solutions.

Most of my works have a potency and an impact on the social dynamic of their communities which artists trained as academic easel painters might well enjoy in its immediacy, its utilization within its community and its context. This is where art touches base. The relevance of this art is central to the philosophies and ideologies which it supports and in some cases advances. All societies lay down rules the main function of which is naturally to preserve those societies and hopefully to develop their aims and ideas. These rules tend to operate as mechanisms for preserving the status quo. Most of the citizens of societies understandably go along with these rules and laws, and artists, contrary to popular opinion, are in general no exception. Nevertheless, no matter what sort of society is involved, the values and aspirations of that society need to be constantly either affirmed, probed, developed or denied; to analyse and create a picture for these purposes is one of the important functions of art.

Artists, I think, have had a dialogue with themselves and with other artists for far too long during the course of the 20th century. I believe one must start from a belief that art is not about art, but that art is about anything which is not art, and my work should be seen as an attempt to relate to the aims and aspirations of the mass of the people, the opposite in fact to the popular view of the artist as an isolated individual committed to the exploration of his own psyche. It then follows that a whole range of subjects become open to investigation for artists from regional development to the EEC, from wage differentials to

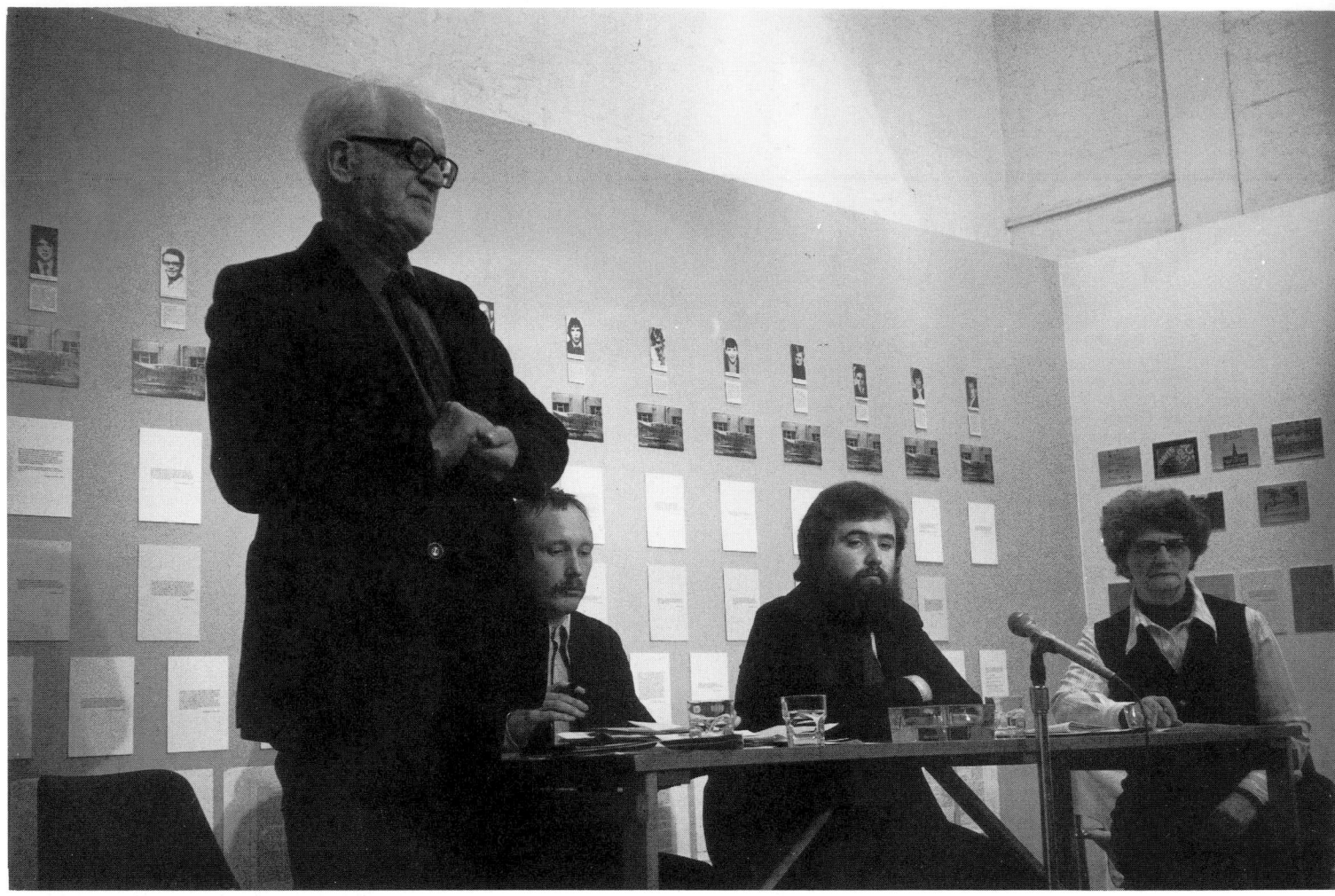

Conrad Atkinson: Meeting at Art Net, London, 1968 (Atkinson second from left)

strikes, from minority rights to profits, from property to politics, from education to pensions, housing, factories, leisure—any human activity becomes a possible subject and open to the artist in a different way than hitherto. In this way, the artist can move towards a more central position in society, a position from which real issues, real analyses, real dialogue and real gains can be made.

It may be that art has a problem for all solutions. If that is the case, then artists in their relationship to society may reconsider another famous slogan in the attempt to break art from the magic hedonism of current art forms: "If you are not part of the solution, you must be part of the problem."

—Conrad Atkinson

Conrad Atkinson is an artist who works in a radical tradition of politics and social reality. This is, in large measure, due to his background and the formative influences of his birth and upbringing in Cleator Moor, a small mining village in a depressed industrial area which lies in a narrow strip on the western coast of Cumbria. Previously a place of heavy industry, as the coal and iron ore were exhausted a pall of unemployment and poverty enveloped the community and the men were driven away to find work. Thus the young Conrad was faced with the basic problems of life from his earliest years. During the 1950's there was a brief period of boom during the building of the nuclear power station known as Calder Hall, later to bear the ominous name of Windscale and now known as Sellafield. Atkinson himself worked for a short time for British Nuclear Fuels. The mining industry had always taken its toll annually in injuries and deaths from its workers but after the opening of the nuclear power station the local population had to

learn to live with persistent and disquieting anxieties about radioacative fallout.

Conrad Atkinson studied art first at the nearby School of Art at Carlisle and then at the Royal Academy Schools in London but he has never distanced himself from the place where he was born and its people. In his art he shows his deep involvement by creating telling images of the bitter contrast between the depressed west coast industrial wasteland and the Lakeland National Park. The latter he has described as a "middle class, high income bracket, outdoor museum and playground, 'The English Lake District' in which the workers are 'invisible' or 'hidden' as were the workers in Engel's Manchester . . . "

In a major work entitled "For Wordsworth, For West Cumbria," (1980) which has since been acquired by the Tate Gallery, London, he shows these concerns in an imaginative assemblage of sixteen panels displayed in two rows of eight. They are in a mixed media of photography, acrylic, iron ore and coal. The images reveal how passionately he feels but the treatment in this cool, documentary mode creates a tension between subject matter and manner which reinforces their impact.

The upper row of eight panels which is mainly photographic are all of an outstretched hand and a daffodil flower. This row is bright and inviting with its pale yellow and pale green lettering superimposed which invites the viewer to draw nearer and read the quotation from Wordsworth, the Lakes Poet. The outstretched hand represents 'man' and the yellow daffodil stands for 'nature' and changes in scale tell of a changing imbalance between the two. The lower row is bleaker to look at; a photograph of a picket line in a long drawn out strike has a superimposed picture postcard 'scenic' view of the Lakes; a contour map of the Lake District has a tracery of the dangers and

perils to which workers in the area have been and are exposed; one panel shows a lump of iron ore between two excerpts from a poem by an immigrant worker forced to leave Cleator when the iron ore and the work ran out; the record of the first acknowledged death from exposure to radioactive waste which caused a young worker to contract leukemia; disused mining machinery with nature encroaching; and under words from Wordsworth after the loss of his brother at sea in 1805 a panel commemorates the drowning of six local men in the wreck of an oil rig onto which unemployment had driven them to work.

Wordsworth is important to Atkinson who said he only really discovered him after he had grown up and realised the relevance of Wordsworth and the Romantic poets, through their commitment politically and economically, to social issues and the crucial relationship between man and the landscape—a landscape which man both helps to create and preserve and also to destroy and which may, in its turn, destroy him. Atkinson points up vividly the harsh choice that so many West Cumbrian workers have had to make between 'life and livelihood' both from the perils of mining and the unseen, insidious dangers of nuclear power. In his work Atkinson skillfully avoids the dangers inherent in strongly polemical and controversial issues of becoming either shrill or hectoring and presents his arguments with thoughtful sensitivity.

—Mary Ellis

ATTALAI, Gabor.

Hungarian. Born in Budapest, 20 November 1934. Educated at Applied Arts University, Budapest, 1953–58. Married Maria Nemes in 1961; daughter: Nora. Served as corporal in the Hungarian Infantry, in Nagykanisz and Mezotur, 1955–1956. Designer, Imparmuveszeti Vallat Company, Budapest, since 1958. Recipient: Magyar Nepkoztarsaasag Muveszeti Alap (Prize for experimental art), Budapest, 1970; Fellowship of the Neue Galerie, Graz, 1973; Yorkshire Arts Association Prize, England, 1974; Prize of the Galerie d'Art Contemporain, Zagreb, 1974. Address: Groza rkp. 11, Budapest 1013, Hungary.

Individual Exhibitions:

1963   Petrigalla Room, Budapest
1966   Modern Nordisk Konst Gallery, Gothenburg, Sweden
1970   Bank of Danube, Budapest
1972   KKI Galerie, Budapest
       International Artists' Cooperation, Oldenburg, Germany
       Central Administration of Artistic Environment Defence, Bad Salzdetfurth, Germany
1973   Veste Sagrada Organizacao Criativa, Rio de Janeiro
       Sum Gallery, Reykjavik
1974   Galerie Remont, Warsaw
       New Reform Gallery, Antwerp
1975   New Reform Gallery, Aalst, Belgium
1976   Galerie Sztuki Najnowszej, Wroclaw, Poland
       Galleria Banco, Brescia
       Galleria Diagramma, Milan
1977   Galerie Loa, Haarlem, Netherlands
1978   Pecsi Galerie, Pecs, Hungary
       Galerie Sudurgata, Reykjavik
1979   Echnaton Gallery, Cairo

Selected Group Exhibitions:

1960   *Debrenci Tarlat,* Deryne Museum, Debrecen, Hungary
1964   *Forma '64,* Veszpremi Muzeum, Veszprem, Hungary
1969   *Plans and Projects as Art,* Kunsthalle, Berne
1970   *Mozgds,* Janus Pannonius Museum, Pecs, Hungary
1971   *"Land Art,"* Aktionsraum, Munich
1972   *3rd International Graphics Biennale,* Rijeka Museum, Rijeka, Yugoslavia
1973   *Omaha Flow Systems,* Joslyn Art Museum, Omaha, Nebraska
1974   *4th British International Print Biennale,* Cartwright Hall, Bradford
1982   *International Photo Biennale,* Vienna

Collections:

Dery Museum, Debrecen, Hungary; Iparmuveszeti Museum, Budapest; Janus Pannonius Museum, Pecs, Hungary; Saveria Museum, Szombathely, Hungary; Neue Galerie, Graz, Austria; National Museum, Stockholm; Modern Art Museum, Zagreb; Bradford City Council, England.

Publications:

By ATTALAI: books—*Future,* Budapest 1972; *Identifications,* Budapest 1972; *Time Book,* Oldenburg, Germany 1973; *Without Instruments,* Aalst, Belgium 1974; *11 Textiles,* Budapest 1978; *Photographie als Kunst,* Vienna 1979; *Texts,* Munster 1979; *Del Libro artista,* Geneva 1979; *Muveszet,* Budapest 1979–80; *Mozgo Vilag,* Budapest 1981; *Objektek szituaciok Ellenpontok Lagy anyagokkal* Budapest 1981; article—essay in *Aktuelle Kunst in Osteuropa,* edited by Klaus Groh, Cologne 1972.

On ATTALAI: books—*Mugyujto* by Janos Frank, Budapest 1972; *Gabor Attalai und die "society art"* by Klaus Groh, Nuremberg 1972; articles—"Report" by Janos Frank in *Elet Es Irodalom* (Budapest), March 1969; "Die Ungarische Avantgarde" by Jurgen Weighardt in *Nordwest Zeitung* (Oldenburg, Germany), no. 15, 1969; "Concept Makers" by A.

Merckx in *Newspaper* (Brussels), February 1972; "Objects from Felt" by Gyula Rozsa in *Nepszabadsag* (Budapest), June 1972; "Andere Kreative Production in Osteurope" by Klaus Groh in *Osteurope* (Stuttgart), no. 11, 1972; review in *+-0* (Genval-Lac, Belgium), no. 9, 1975.

*

In the last five years I have created paintings, environments and photographs to an idea: "Red-y Made," which is the counterpoint of Duchampian Ready-Made. Red-y Mades are paintings. Yellow-y Mades are also.

—Gabor Attalai

AUBERTIN, Bernard

French. Born in Fontenay-aux-Roses, 29 July 1934. Initially self-taught in painting, studying cubist and futurist works, until 1951; studied at the Ecole des Metiers d'Art, and the Ecole du Professorat de Dessin, Paris, 1952–54. Served in the French Army, 1957–58. Married the artist Denise Demaldent in 1955; sons: Vincent and Frederic; lived with Joelle Fontaine, 1975–86; children: Julien and Solene. Painter, influenced initially by Yves Klein, Paris, since 1957; first monochrome red paintings, 1958; rednail-paintings, 1960–71; fire-paintings, 1961; burned-book works, 1962. Lived in Brest, Finistere, 1975–86. Agents: Galerie Beaubourg, 23 rue de Renard, 75004 Paris; Galerie Cical-Lefebre, 30 rue Mazarine, 75006 Paris; Galerie Spiess, 4 Avenue de Messine, 75008 Paris; Espace J. et J. Donguy, 57 rue de la Roquette, 7501 Paris. Address: 14 Villa St. Jacques, 75014 Paris, France.

Individual Exhibitions:

1962   Galerie Wulfengasse 14, Klagenfurt, Austria
1967   Galerie Weiller, Paris
       Galerie M. E. Thelen, Essen
1968   Galerie des Quatre Vents, Paris
       Galerie Riquelme, Paris
       Kleine Galerie, Frankfurt
1969   Galerie Senatore, Stuttgart
1971   Galerie Ursula Lichter, Frankfurt
1972   Centre National d'Art Contemporain, Paris (retrospective; with Fred Deux and Otto Dumel)
1973   Galerie Toni Brechbuhl, Grenchen, Switzerland
       Musée de l'Abbaye Sainte-Croix, Les Sables-d'Olonne, France
       Galerie Seebacher, Vorarlberg, Austria
1974   Galerie 2, Stuttgart
       Studio Brescia, Brescia, Italy
       Galleria Banco, Brescia, Italy
       Studio Firenze, Florence
       Galleria dei Mille, Bergamo, Italy
       Galleria Delta, Salerno, Italy
       Studio F. 22, Palazzolo, Italy
       Galleria Il Canale, Venice
1975   Studio Brescia, Brescia, Italy
       Galleria Il Canale, Venice
       Galleria Il Punto, Turin
1977   Galleria Rebus, Florence
1978   Palazzetto dello Sport, Abano Terme, Italy
       Galerie 44, Kaarst bei Dusseldorf, West Germany
1979   Galerie Weiller, Paris
1983   Galerie J. et J. Donguy, Paris
       Galerie Toni Brechbuhl, Grenchen, Switzerland
1986   Galerie Charley Chevalier, Paris
1987   Galerie Beatrix Wilhelm, Stuttgart

Selected Group Exhibitions:

1961   *Zero,* Galerie Dato, Frankfurt
1965   *Zero Avant-Garde,* Atelier de Fontana, Milan
1967   *Luminism,* George Washington Hotel, New York
1968   *Cinetisme,* Maison de la Culture, Grenoble, France

1969   *Dynamozero 1959–1969,* Galerie Ursula Lichter, Frankfurt
1971   *Sammlung Cremer: Kunst der 60er Jahre,* Kunstverein, Heidelberg
1972   *Douze Ans d'Art Contemporain en France,* Grand Palais, Paris
1976   *Kunst der 60er und 70er Jahre,* Kunstmuseum, Bonn
1985   *Eine Europaische Bewegung,* Museum Carolino Augusteum, Salzburg
1987   *Ephemerite,* Chapelle St. Louis de la Salpetriere, Paris

Collections:

Centre National d'Art Contemporain, Paris; Mobilier National, Paris,; Musée de l'Abbaye Sainte-Croix, Les Sables-d'Olonne, France; Musée de Grenoble, France; Kunstmuseum, Dusseldorf, Kunsthalle, Tübingen, West Germany; Landesmuseum Joanneum, Graz, Austria.

Publications:

By AUBERTIN: books—*Bernard Aubertin: 6 Textes,* Paris 1962; *Bernard Aubertin: 9 Textes,* Paris 1968; *Aubertin Pyromane,* Paris 1969; *Aubertin par Aubertin pour Aubertin,* Brest, France 1985; articles—"Esquisse de la situation picturale du rouge dans un concept spatial" in *Zero* (Dusseldorf), no. 3, 1961; "La Monochromie" in *Nul=0* (Arnhem, Netherlands), no. 1, 1962; "La Couleur" in *Nul=0* (Arnhem, Netherlands), no. 2, 1963; "Je suis un realiste" in *Integration* (Arnhem, Netherlands), no. 4, 1965; "L'Art dans la Société Capitaliste d'Aujourd'hui" in *Integration* (Arnhem, Netherlands), no. 7–8, 1967; "Sur Pierre Manzoni" in *Robho* (Paris), no. 3, 1968; "Yves le bleu vu par Bernard le rouge" in *La Galerie des Arts* (Paris), no. 64, 1969; "La Cage Rouge de Fumée . . . " in *Robho* (Paris), no. 5–6, 1971; "A Propos de mes Nouvelles Sculptures" in *Integration* (Eschenau, Netherlands), no. 13–14, 1972.

On AUBERTIN: books—*Bernard Aubertin,* exhibition catalogue, with text by Udo Kultermann, Essen, West Germany 1967; *Douze Ans d'Art Contemporain en France,* exhibition catalogue, with texts by F. Mathey, V. Huchard, D. Cordier and others, Paris 1972; *Aubertin/Deux/Schauer,* exhibition catalogue, with texts by Hans Haacke, Bernard Rancillac, Udo Kultermann and others, Paris 1972; *Factotum Book 5: Bernard Aubertin,* with text by Egidio Mucci, Padua 1978; *Bernard Aubertin: Le Point Zero de la Peinture,* exhibition catalogue, edited by Charley Chevalier, Paris 1986; *Bernard Aubertin,* exhibition catalogue, with essay by Gabriele Kubler, Stuttgart 1987.

*

I started painting in my 21st year after having studied two years in an artist's studio preparing to enter the State schools of decoration. On receiving admission I disdained returning there: I wanted to dedicate myself to painting, my vocation. Until the age of 23 I painted portraits, landscapes, still-lifes, and above all did plenty of drawing. The figurative or abstract painting I saw in the galleries did not satisfy me. In 1957 I met Yves Klein and this meeting was for me, of major importance. Under his influence I completed about 15 canvases, which were monochrome, red and very structured. I used to do this with every type of painter's knife, even the prongs of a fork, the round back of a spoon, etc. The whole painted surface was a unity composed of repeated structures. These structures didn't give me entire satisfaction: they weren't specific enough for my taste. One day I threw a handful of nails into the red colour spread on the canvas. Accidentally, I had just discovered in the nail the structure which corresponded to that precision which I was looking for. From here the idea of planting the nails one by one in the support, rather than scattering them at random on it, followed naturally. I was recreating the unity of the surface by filling it with nails. My work on nail-pictures divides into two periods: 1) the picture presents the nail head-outwards; 2) the picture presents the point of the nail, the head of the nail being the picture.

I soon had the idea of using elements other than nails in series: screws, pitons, matches. With matches, I invented fire-painting. All my researches

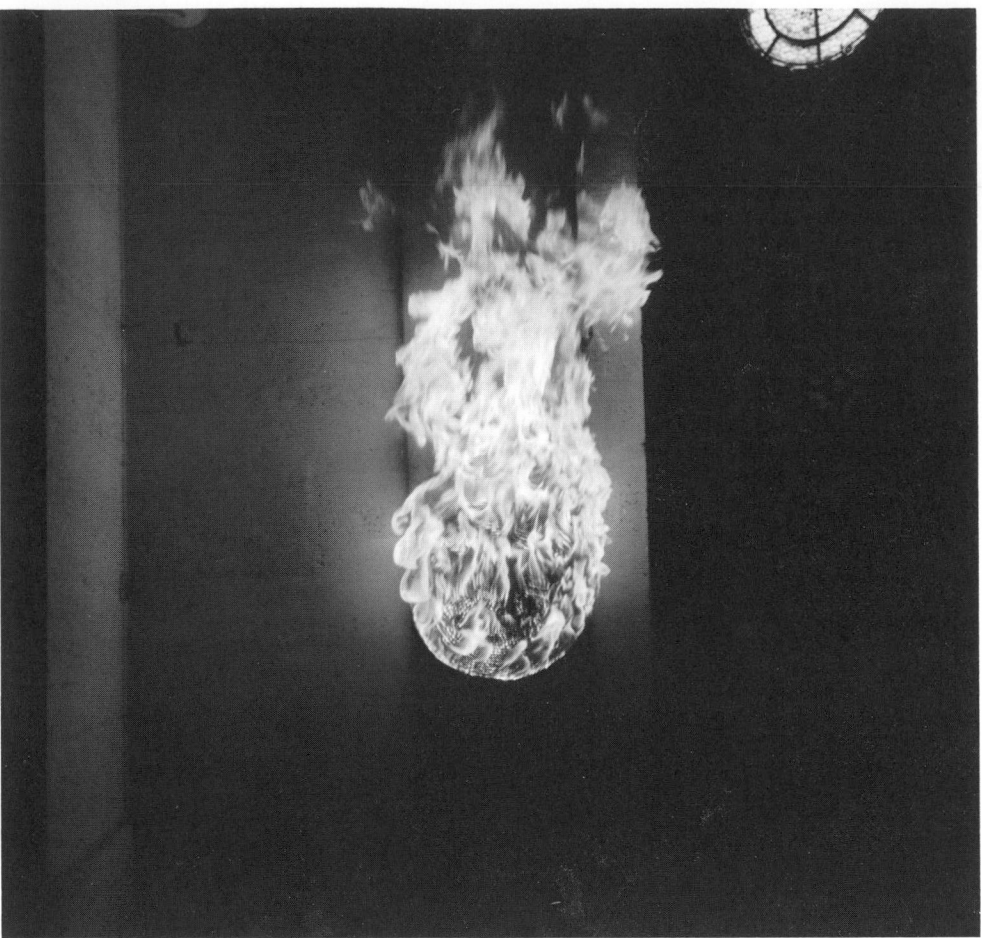

Bernard Aubertin: Rotating Fire Disk from *Ephemerité*, 1987

are inspired by one ideal: to humanise. From my own observation of what is going on in the culture of our present-day world, I have acquired the opinion that our present art expresses, for the most part, the impossibility, for man, of communicating harmoniously with his fellows. Our present art is founded on a therapy on the level of the individual, without any message for other men concerning the transformation of human nature demanded of humanity. It is the statement of the misery of a humanity in conflict with itself, dehumanised: it is journalism, news in brief; it offers itself up to the caprices of fashion, creates it, and finally reveals itself as completely incapable of exerting a vaguely spiritual influence.

The truth is that it is incumbent upon the artist, aware of the always dehumanised state of society, to base art first of all on man.

Art, in my sense, can not be envisaged except as a therapy on the collective level, which brings about the fraternisation of men and ennobles the dose of therapy inherent in all art. Our role as artists is to lead to the TOTALITY, shorn of all contradictions, of human nature. In this way, man will always be in a position to foresee the needs of humanity and to reply to them. In acting for collectivity, we liberate ourselves from nature and from our own natures.

That is why, in the field of the realisation of a plastic work, I find it necessary to reduce the role of manual execution to its dominant function: the hand is nothing else than a manufacturing tool; to entrust it with the responsibility of fixing the various tensions—emotive, instinctive, animal even—accumulated in the soul, is an error.

We must strive to take distance in comparison with nature, if we want to realise ourselves as a specific human species. The creation of a distance in the execution is the means that one finds to take distance in comparison with nature and with our own natures.

Thus, to fill the surface regularly with the help of nails, screws, pitons, matches etc. signifies, in my case, the creation of this distance in the execution. If

form in art is limitation, if it corresponds, in the plastic arts, to the natural and social order in which we live (we all know that man is determined), it must not be unchanging. On the contrary, it must be constructed by means of the relief which catches the light and modifies it naturally. (Form can be rendered mobile by many other means; I'm talking here of what I do myself.) The distribution of the light on the reliefs of my pictures changes according to the times of day. In this way, the picture is never completely the same.

I am seeking to obtain greater precision in the definition of human nature. In this sense, I think I have the right to say: I am a realist.

—Bernard Aubertin

Where does Bernard Aubertin begin? One would like to reply: at the stake stripped of all its witches. To ignite things like this, by vocation, at least with a "flash in the pan" of the metaphors, would not easily resolve that linguistic impression that the world is an artifice—hence this determination to strike things which, from the blow, take fire with a mad hope: to illuminate the art of ashes.

The technique is simple: fire. The proposition "water propagates, fire reduces" is thus articulated in this way: the machinery of fire, as play of flames, starting from propositions reduced to homothetic multiplications (matches) forms a system. Hence the difficulty of any extraneous propositions: water does not extinguish fire. For the pyromaniac who Aubertin demands of himself is substituted a flamboyant fireman.

The Aubertin rises again from his ashes and explains himself historically. Use of the time where the history of art stores away its recipes. It's practically everything (the question at least, since there must be a "reader" or a "spectator" which is *the question itself,* posed to Aubertin.)

Therefore an obstinate question situated at *his* origin, towards a first glance, in a gesture which does not lack antecedents: Heraclitus the hydropic marking

the rhythm of the first (philosophical) cadence, Empedocles and Etna—but this time with matches: another Ulysses, of the time of Mr. Bloom, whom one meets in the tobacconist, carrying out his provision of combustibles.

This symbol is clear (he is lighting things up); in it one forgets that "reality" does not invent itself. That it suffices to "trap" it with the means at hand: means which are objective, existing, taken as given—the setting fire as "act" not justifying an investment, but the operation which results from an excessive confrontation: burning as radicalization setting ablaze as opening out. In such a way that escaping from subjectivism comes back to risking any gesture (any breath) in a given matter. Aubertin excels at explaining it, and there is no reason not to read it. What he is showing passes beyond the fabrication of what he is applying. One can see in it what one wills: broaching the subject, as sufficient reason, when all is allowed: it suffices to know where.

In the titles first of all—for once explicit: fire-pictures, monochromes dedicated, as he writes, to the dynamism of colour. More exactly a trajectory of flame, from red to black, from burning to burnt. A brief, momentary act from which there is no reconversion. What has been used once has been used for good—in the sense that the work with fire measures its adequacy in igniting as much as possible to consume as surely as possible. Nevertheless the object resists. There are thus unexpected versions: the remains stick to the ash, support it. A new limit is shown, a new route can be hazarded. When Aubertin partially burns telephone books (which are difficult to burn, he acknowledges), "using" the debris (of the phone books) to construct his "avalanches," to constitute "series" where he arranges other fragments, the reference he is making is to the geography of an act begun more than 10 years ago. In the same way the red monochromes and the nail-pictures *imagine* the flame and the work in fire: I mean that they determine the place of an act which symbolically unites all these acts. The symbolic place, for the artist (in this case Aubertin, as will have been guessed . . .), reducing itself to a machinery where chance (including Aubertin) tests the states; the works only correspond to stratificatory moments which never add up to the entirety of the researches. In this sense, no "master works," no over-meaningful points, but a series of connotations, "object-arts," "fabrication-routes," in the very judgement which presents them as works.

One understands that Aubertin asserts himself (with obstinacy) as a realist. He is so to the scandal of all dogmatism. Because "reality" does not stop, it does not copy itself, it does not depict itself. Either it does work or it doesn't work. And it always works differently in the sense that the principal of identity, so dear to a certain rationalism, in art, designates its imposture. It is therefore to a "lesson in reality" that we invite Aubertin with all the ardour which is wasting away there.

—Claude Fournet

AUERBACH, Frank.
British. Born in Berlin, 29 April 1931; emigrated to England in 1939; naturalized, 1947. Educated in Kent primary schools; attended art classes at Hampstead Garden Suburb Institute, London, 1947; Borough Polytechnic, under David Bomberg, London, 1947–48; St. Martin's School of Art, London, 1948–52; Royal College of Art, London, 1952–55 (Silver Medal, 1955). Married Julia Wolstenholme in 1958; one son. Independent painter, London, since 1955. Lecturer, art schools in Sidcup, Kent, and London Boroughs: Ealing, Bromley and Camberwell; and Slade School of Fine Art, London, 1956–58. Recipient: Golden Lion Award, *42nd Biennale*, Venice, 1986. Agent: Marlborough Fine Art, London. Ad-

dress: c/o Marlborough Fine Art, 6 Albemarle Street, London W1X 4BY, England.

Individual Exhibitions:

1956	Beaux Arts Gallery, London
1959	Beaux Arts Gallery, London
1961	Beaux Arts Gallery, London
1962	Beaux Arts Gallery, London
1963	Beaux Arts Gallery, London
1965	Marlborough Fine Art, London
1967	Marlborough Fine Art, London
1969	Marlborough Gerson Gallery, New York
1971	Marlborough Fine Art, London
	Villiers Art Gallery, Sydney
	Municipal Gallery, Dublin
1972	Toorak Gallery, Melbourne
1973	University of Essex, Colchester
	Galleria Bergamini, Milan
1974	Marlborough Fine Art, London
	Municipal Gallery of Modern Art, Dublin
1976	Marlborough Fine Art, London (with Francis Bacon)
	Marlborough Galerie, Zurich
1978	Hayward Gallery, London (travelled to the Fruit Market Gallery, Edinburgh)
1979	Bernard Jacobson, New York
1982	*Recent Paintings and Drawings*, Marlborough Gallery, New York
1983	Marlborough Fine Art, London
	Anne Berthoud Gallery, London
1986	Kunstverein, Hamburg
1987	Marlborough Fine Art, London
	Museum Folkwang, Essen, West Germany
	Centro de Arte Reina Sofia, Madrid

Selected Group Exhibitions:

1958	*Critics' Choice*, Arthur Tooth and Sons, London
1961	*Pittsburgh International*, Carnegie Institute, Pittsburgh
1967	*Stuyvesant Foundation Exhibition*, London and Zurich
1970	*Painting and Perception*, MacRobert Centre Art Gallery, University of Stirling, Scotland
1972	*Immagine per la Città*, Palazzo dell'Accademia and Palazzo Reale, Genoa
1977	*British Painting 1952-1977*, Royal Academy of Art, London
1979	*This Knot of Life: Paintings and Drawings of British Artists*, Louver Gallery, Venice, California
1981	*A New Spirit in Painting*, Royal Academy of Art, London
1984	*The British Art Show*, City Art Gallery, Birmingham (and Ikon Gallery, Birmingham; travelled to Edinburgh, Sheffield and Southampton)
1987	*A London School*, Louisiana Museum, Humlebaek, Denmark (travelled to Oslo, Venice and Dusseldorf)

Collections:

British Museum, London; Tate Gallery, London; Scottish National Gallery of Modern Art, Edinburgh; National Gallery of Australia, Canberra; National Gallery of Victoria, Melbourne; Metropolitan Museum of Art, New York; Museum of Modern Art, New York; Los Angeles County Museum of Art; Tamayo Museum, Mexico City; Museo de Art Moderna da Bahia, Salvador, Brazil.

Publications:

By AUERBACH: articles—"7 Portraits" in *Ark 23* (London), 1958; "Fragments from a Conversation" *X Quarterly* (London), 1959; "Reply to a Letter from Michael Peppiatt" in *Cambridge Opinion*, January 1964; "Frank Auerbach Talks to Christopher Battye" in *Art and Artists* (London), January 1971; statement in *European Painting in the 70's*, exhibition catalogue, Los Angeles 1975; statement in *Frank Auerbach*, exhibition catalogue, Zurich 1976; "Conversation with Frank Auerbach," with Catherine Lampert, in *Frank Auerbach*, ex-hibition catalogue, London 1978; foreword to *Late Sickert Paintings*, exhibition catalogue, London 1981.

On AUERBACH: books—*Frank Auerbach*, exhibition catalogue, by William Feaver, Zurich 1976; *Frank Auerbach*, exhibition catalogue, by Leon Kossoff and Catherine Lampert, London 1978; *Frank Auerbach: Recent Paintings and Drawings*, exhibition catalogue, by Stephen Spender, New York 1982; *Frank Auerbach: XLII Venice Biennale*, exhibition catalogue, by Catherine Lampert, London 1986; articles—"A Stick in the Dark" by John Berger in *New Statesman* (London), April 1961; "Titian and Auerbach" by Richard Wollheim in *The Listener* (London), October 1973.

*   *   *

Frank Auerbach came to England from Berlin at the age of 8. In retrospect it is difficult to believe that he had been anywhere else than in the London in which he works and whose portrait he has painted so many times. Even harder to understand is how he somehow absorbed and subsequently recorded in his painting an Englishness that has been a kind of national art accent right through the Bloomsbury period of British culture. The scenes are right. Even the friendly contact with the subjects of the portraits is right. And so is the ungainly sprawl of nudes who seem to have come out of an age when central heating never functioned properly. The penny-in-the-slot gas fire epoch.

None of these remarks relates to the way in which Auerbach paints. They have been made because the mood or moods which invade his paintings must be accepted as "English" in a very strong way. Specially English. This anglicization is almost unique, unless one counts David Bomberg as British.

Auerbach is famous for his thick pigment. No one past maturity should attempt to lift any but the smallest canvases. If this heavy paint has not been of quite the same density in recent years, that is not to suggest that it is still not laid onto the picture like pâté. The result is a dour sort of late expressionism whose temperament is occasionally lightened by swathes of bright colour.

Where Auerbach succeeds is in his extraordinarily effective control of so much viscous material. How successful he may seem to have been with each picture may depend upon the character of the viewer. Some may reject some of the paintings as being too lumbering or opaque, while others will recognize in them the uncanny skill with which he makes the paint not only do his bidding but also turn *itself* into whatever figuration he seeks.

—Sheldon Williams

Frank Auerbach: *Head of Julia*, 1987

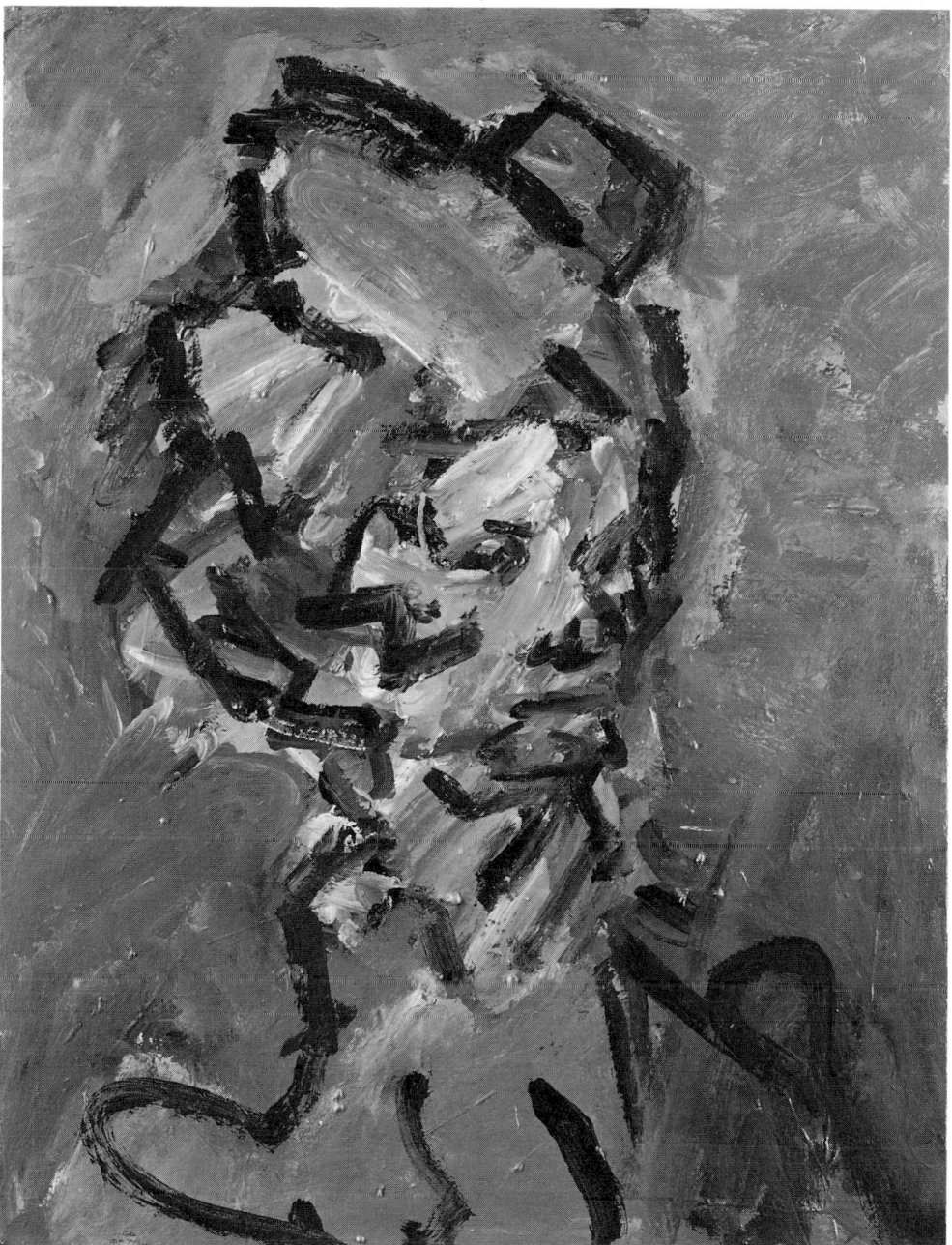

AYCOCK, Alice.

American. Born in Harrisburg, Pennsylvania, 20 November 1946. Educated at Douglass College, New Brunswick, New Jersey, 1964-68, B.A. 1968; Hunter College, New York (studied under Robert Morris), 1968-71, M.A. 1971. Married Mark Segal in 1968. Independent sculptor and installation artist, since 1972, known for large-scale semi-architectural and machine-like projects. Adjunct Lecturer in Art, Hunter College, 1972-73; Visiting Sculptor and Teacher, Rhode Island School of Design, Providence, 1977; taught foundation and advanced sculpture courses at the School of Visual Arts, New York, 1977-78; Visiting Sculptor and Teacher, Princeton University, New Jersey, 1979; Visiting Sculptor and Teacher, San Francisco Art Institute, 1979. Since 1979, teacher at the School of Visual Arts, New York. Artist-in-Residence, Williams College, Williamstown, Massachusetts, 1974. Recipient: National Endowment for the Arts Fellowship, 1975, 1980, 1986; New York State Creative Artists Public Service Grant, 1976. Agent: John Weber Gallery, 142 Greene Street, New York, New York 10012. Address: 62 Greene Street, New York, New York 10012, U.S.A.

Individual Exhibitions:

1972	Nova Scotia College of Art and Design, Halifax
1974	112 Greene Street Gallery, New York
	Project inc., Cambridge, Massachusetts
	Williams College Museum of Art, Williamstown, Massachusetts
1976	Wheaton College, Norton, Massachusetts
1977	Projects Room, Museum of Modern Art, New York
1978	Portland Center for the Visual Arts, Oregon
	John Weber Gallery, New York
	University of Rhode Island, Kingston
	Salvatore Ala, Milan
	Projects for PCA, Philadelphia College of Art
	Cranbook Academy of Art, Bloomfield Hills, Michigan
	Projects and Proposals, Muhlenberg College, Allentown, Pennsylvania
1979	*Flights of Fancy,* San Francisco Art Institute
	The Contemporary Art Center, Cincinnati, Ohio
	Machinations, Protetch-McIntosh Gallery, Washington, D.C.
	The Large Scale Disintegration of Microelectronic Memories, Art on the Beach, Battery Park Landfill, New York
	Collected Ghost Stories From the Workhouse from the series *How to Catch and Manufacture Ghosts,* University of South Florida, Tampa
1980	*The Miraculating Machine in the Garden,* Douglass College, New Brunswick, New Jersey
1981	*The Savage Sparkler,* New York State University at Plattsburgh
	Machineworks: Vito Acconci/Alice Aycock/Dennis Oppenheim, Institute of Contemporary Art, Philadelphia
	John Weber Gallery, New York
1982	*Drawings,* Locus Solus, Genoa
	Lawrence Oliver Gallery, Philadelphia
	New Work, John Weber Gallery, New York
1983	Museum of Contemporary Art, Chicago
	Protetch McNeil Gallery, New York
	Wurttembergischer Kunstverein, Stuttgart (retrospective; travelled to Cologne, Marl, The Hague and Lucerne)
1984	*New Work,* John Weber Gallery, New York
1985	Humanic Corporation Gallery, Graz, Austria
	Serpentine Gallery, London
	New Drawings, Insam Gallery, Vienna
1986	Sculpture Park, St. Louis, Missouri
	John Weber Gallery, New York
	Tel Aviv Museum, Israel
1987	Central Park, New York
	Galerie Walter Storms, Munich

Selected Group Exhibitions:

1972	*Untitled V,* Museum of Modern Art, New York

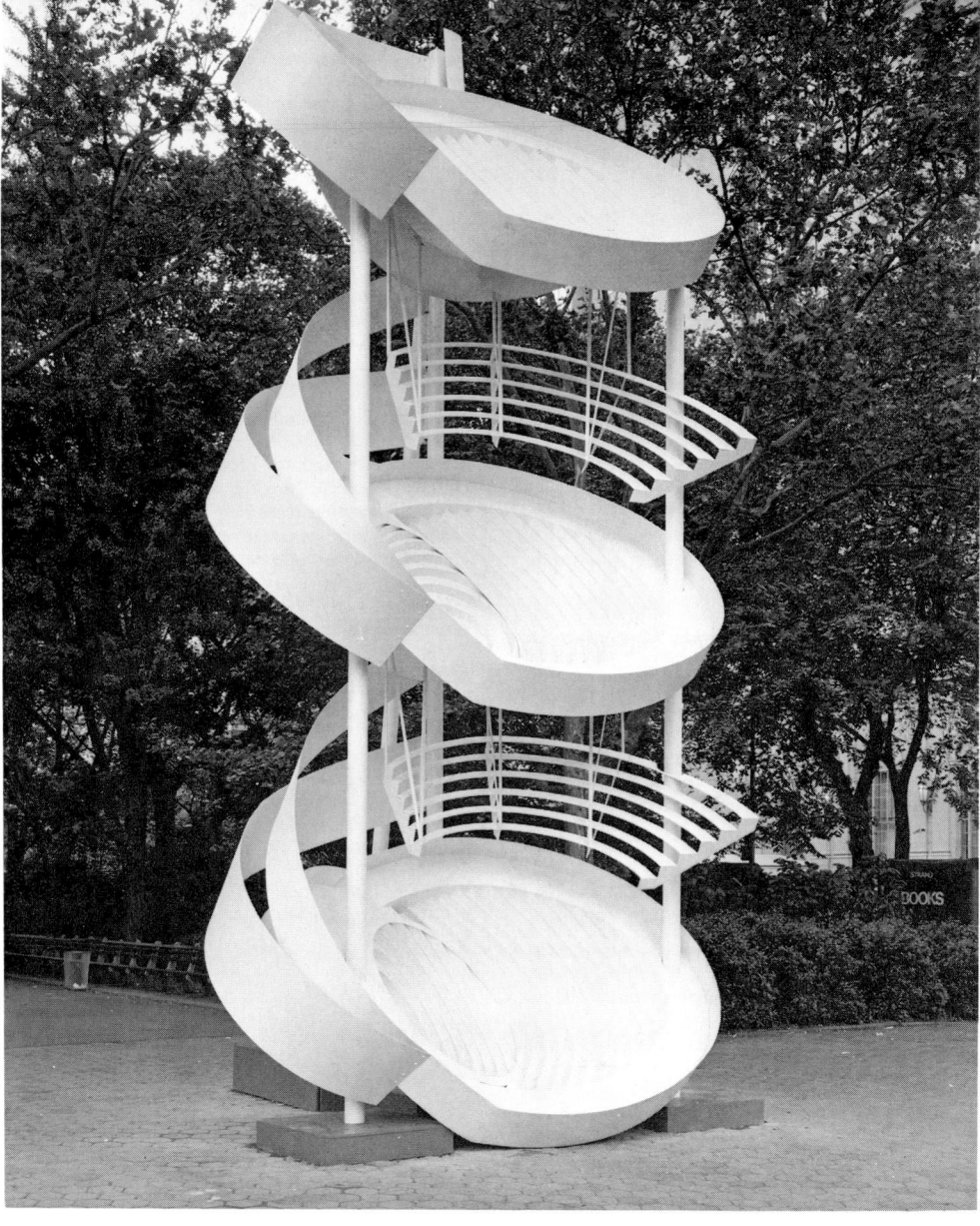

Alice Aycock: *Three-Fold Manifestation II,* 1987

1974	*Interventions in Landscape,* Massachusetts Institute of Technology, Cambridge
1977	*Documenta 6,* Kassel, West Germany
1978	*Biennale,* Venice
1979	*Whitney Biennial,* Whitney Museum, New York
1980	*International Sculpture Conference,* Washington, D.C.
1981	*Mythos & Ritual in der Kunst der 70er Jahre,* Kunsthaus, Zurich
1984	*Land Marks,* Bard College, Annandale-on-Hudson, New York
1985	*Modern Machines: Recent Kinetic Sculpture,* Whitney Museum, New York
1987	*Avant-Garde in the Eighties,* Los Angeles County Museum of Art

Collections:

Museum of Modern Art, New York; Guggenheim Museum, New York; Hirshhorn Museum, Washington, D.C.; Whitney Museum, New York.

Publications:

By AYCOCK: books—*Project Entitled "The Beginnings of a Complex . . . ,"* New York 1977; *After Years of Ruminating on the Events That Led Up to This Misfortune, Alice Aycock—Projects and Proposals,* with essays by Stuart Morgan and Edward Fry, Allentown, Pennsylvania 1978; *Alice Aycock Projects 1979-1981,* with an introduction by Edward Fry, Tampa 1981; *Alice Aycock: Retrospective of Projects and ideas 1972-1983,* exhibition catalogue, Stuttgart 1983; articles—"Four 36-38 Exposures" in *Avalanche* (New York), Spring 1972; "5 Semi-Architectural Projects" in *c. 7500,* Valencia, California 1973; "New York City Orientations" in *Triquarterly* (Evanston, Illinois), Winter 1975; "Notes on Project for a Simple Network of Underground Wells and Tunnels" in *Projects in Nature,* Far Hills, New Jersey 1975; "Interviews with Some Modern Mazemakers—Interview with Alice Aycock" by Janet Kardon in *Art International* (Lugano, Switzerland), April/May 1976; "Work 1972-1974" in *Individuals: Post-Movement Art in America,* edited by Alan Sondheim, New York 1977; "Projects for My Body" in *17 Lotus International* (New York), December 1977; "An Interview with Alice Aycock" in *D.A.A. Journal* (Cincinnati, Ohio), no. 1, 1980; "2 Fantasies of a Mythical Waterworks," with James Freed, in *Artists and Architects Collaboration,* edited by Barbaralee Diamonstein, New York 1981; "A Conversation with Alice Aycock," interview with Aimee Price Brown, in *Architectural Digest* (Los Angeles), April 1983; video—*Alice Aycock,* interview with Kate Horsfield, Video Data Bank, School of the Art Institute of Chicago, 1977.

On AYCOCK: books—*6 Years: The Dematerialization of the Art Object* by Lucy R. Lippard, New York 1972; *From the Center* by Lucy R. Lippard, New York 1976; *Unbuilt America,* by Alison Sky and Michelle Stone, New York 1976;

Metaphor: New Projects by Contemporary Sculptors, by Howard N. Fox, Washington, D.C. 1982; *Avant-Garde in the Eighties,* exhibition catalogue, with introduction by Howard Fox, Los Angeles 1987; articles—"Aligned with the Nazca" by Robert Morris in *Artforum* (New York), October 1975; "Projects in Nature" by Jonathan Crary in *Arts Magazine* (New York), December 1975; "Labyrinths, Philadelphia College of Art" by April Kingsley in *Artforum* (New York), February 1976; "The Modern Maze" by Ronald Onorato in *Art International* (Lugano, Switzerland), April/May 1976; " 'Sculpture Sited' at the Nassau County Museum" by Lucy Lippard in *Arts In America* (New York), March/April 1977; "American Women Architects" by John Lobell in *Artforum* (New York), Summer 1977; "Mystery Under Construction" by Margaret Sheffield in *Artforum* (New York), September 1977; "6 Women at Work in the Landscape" by April Kingsley in *Arts Magazine* (New York), April 1978; "Alice Aycock: A Certain Image of Something I Like Very Much" by Stuart Morgan in *Arts Magazine* (New York), March 1978; "The Present Tense of Space" by Robert Morris in *Art in America* (New York), January/February 1978; "Women of the Fourth Wave; Humboldt's Daughters" by Eleanor Munro in *Originals: American Women Artists,* New York 1979; "Discovery of the Sources: Model of History" by Jean-Luc Daval in *Art Actuel: Skira Annual '79,* Geneva 1979; "Complexes: Sculpture in Nature" by Lucy Lippard in *Art in America* (New York), January/February 1979; "Ancient Places and Personal Spaces: Homage to Alice Aycock" by Elter, McCormick, McKeon and Reynolds, "Alice Aycock's Explanation, An, of Spring and the Weight of Air" by Jonathan Kamholtz, and "The Work of Alice Aycock: A Pictorial Section" in *D.A.A. Journal* (Cincinnati, Ohio), no. 1, 1980; "Aycock's Dream Houses" by Donald Kuspit in *Art in America* (New York), September 1980; "Beyond Revivalism and the Bauhaus: A New Partnership in the Arts" by Jonathan Barnett in *Artists and Architects Collaboration,* New York 1981; "Alice in Duchamp-Land" by Kay Larson in *New York,* 25 May 1981; "The Poetic Machines of Alice Aycock" by Edward Fry in *Portfolio* (Boulder, Colorado), November–December 1981; "Alice Aycock" by Antje von Graevenitz in *Museumjournaal* (Amsterdam), no. 27, 1982.

AY-O.

Japanese. Born Takao Iijima in Ibaraki Prefecture, Japan, 19 May 1931. Educated at Kyoiku University, Tokyo, B.A. 1954. Married Ikuko Yoshida in 1955; child: Hanako. Independent artist: began as engraver and lithographer, then expanded work to include painting, sculpture, environments, and happenings; joined "Demokrato" avant-garde artists group, 1954, lived in New York, 1958–66; joined "Flux" avant-garde artists group, 1962; travelled in Europe and India before returning to Japan, 1966; has concentrated on producing rainbow-hued silk-screens, since mid-1960's; again lived in New York, 1968–71; returned to Japan, 1971; travelled in Britain, Europe, and Nepal, 1973. Visiting Professor of Painting, University of Kentucky, Lexington, 1968–69. Recipient: Special Prize, *Vancouver International Prints Biennial,* 1967; Grand Prize, 1969, and Minister of Foreign Affairs Award, 1971, *Japan Art Festival;* Award, *Mainichi Modern Art Exhibition,* National Museum of Modern Art, Kyoto; Brazil Bank Prize, *Bienal,* Sao Paulo, 1969; Prize, *Tokyo International Print Biennial,* National Museum of Modern Art, Tokyo,

1970; Bridgestone Museum Prize, *Mainichi modern Art Exhibition,* Japan, 1971; Prize, *Exposition International de Dessins Originaux,* Rijeka, Yugoslavia, 1973; Grand Prize, Listowele Print Biennial, 1980; Zagreb Contemporary Art Gallery Prize, Original Drawings Exhibition, Rijeka, Yugoslavia, 1982; Warsaw National Museum Prize, International Drawing Triennale, Wroclaw, 1982. Agent: Suzuki Graphics Inc., 797 Madison Avenue, New York, New York 10021, U.S.A. Address: 2-6-38 Matsuyama, Kiyoseshi, Tokyo 100–31, Japan.

Individual Exhibitions:

1955	Takemiya Gallery, Tokyo
1956	Forme Gallery, Tokyo
1962	Gordon's Fifth Avenue Gallery, New York
1963	Gordon's Fifth Avenue Gallery, New York
1964	Smolin Gallery, New York
1965	Smolin Gallery, New York
1966	Gordon's Fifth Avenue Gallery, New York
	Minami Gallery, Tokyo
1967	Gallery 669, Los Angeles
1969	Melida Gallery, Louisville, Kentucky
	Hank Baum Gallery, San Francisco
1971	Minami Gallery, Tokyo
1972	Nantenshi Gallery, Tokyo
	Suzuki Graphics Gallery, New York
	Hank Baum Gallery, San Francisco
1973	Suzuki Graphics Gallery, New York
	Museum of Modern Art, New York
1974	Suzuki Graphics Gallery, New York
1975	Suzuki Graphics Gallery, New York
1976	Suzuki Graphics Gallery, New York
	Nantenshi Gallery, Tokyo
	Hank Baum Gallery, San Francisco
	Bonino Gallery, New York
1977	Minami Gallery, Tokyo
1978	Hank Baum Gallery, San Francisco
1979	Ikeda Museum of Contemporary Art, Japan
1980	Graphics Gallery, San Francisco
	Wako Hall, Tokyo
	Hank Baum Gallery, San Francisco
	Suzuki Graphics Gallery, New York
1982	Fuji Television Gallery, New York
!985	Fuji Television Gallery, Tokyo

Selected Group Exhibitions:

1964	*Rainbow Happening: Flux-Orchestra Concert,* Carnegie Recital Hall, New York
	Rainbow-Happening: "The Tart" by Dick Higgins, Sunny-Side Garden, New York
1965	*Rainbow Happening: Flux Concert,* Carnegie Recital Hall, New York
1966	*Rainbow Tactile Room,* at the *Biennale,* Venice
1967	*Annual Avant-Garde Festival,* New York (and 1968, 1972, 1977, 1980)
1969	*Tactile Rainbow Room,* at *Expo 70,* Tokyo (travelled to the Cincinnati Art Museum, Ohio, and the University of Kentucky, Lexington)
	Modern Japanese Art, National Museum of Art, Kyoto

1971	*Bienal,* Sao Paulo
1973	*Japanese Artists in the Americas,* National Museum of Modern Art, Kyoto
1987	*FIAC '87,* Grand Palais, Paris

Collections:

National Museum of Modern Art, Tokyo; National Museum of Modern Art, Kyoto; Museum of Modern Art, New York; Metropolitan Art Museum, Tokyo; National Museum, Warsaw; Cincinnati Art Museum, Ohio; Stedelijk Museum, Amsterdam; British Museum, London.

Publications:

By AY-O: book—*Rainbow Prints: Catalogue Raisonne 1954–1979,* compiled by Sadajiro Kubo, Tokyo 1979.

On AY-O: books—*FLUXshoe,* exhibition catalogue, edited by David Mayor and Felipe Ehrenberg, Cullompton, England 1972; *Japanese Artists in the Americas,* exhibition catalogue, by T. Ogura, Kyoto 1973; *Ay-O: Arc-en-ciel,* exhibition catalogue, with introduction by Akira Asahi, Paris 1987; article—"Tokyo Letter" by J. P. Love in *Art International* (Lugano, Switzerland), March 1971.

Ay-O has nearly magical power by which he metamorphoses objects which are a part of everyday life into metaphysical, tactile objects which demand to be sensually experienced. His 1961 "Ay-O's Box," exemplifies this. It consists of a series of cubical wooden boxes snugly fitting into an attaché chase; each box has a hole through which an unexpected sensory experience is obtained by inserting a forefinger into the holes. The rainbow series on which he has been working since 1964 is nothing less than the creation of versicolored environments, of walls, furniture, utensils and other ordinary articles used in daily life. One work in this series, "Rainbow Tactile Room," was exhibited at the 1966 Venice *Biennale.*

Born Takao Iijima in Ibaraki Prefecture in 1931, the artist graduated from the art department of Tokyo's University of Arts and Science in 1954. He started as an engraver and lithographer and gradually expanded his scope of activity to include painting, sculpture, environments and happenings. In 1966 he returned to Japan after nine years overseas, and had a show at Minami Gallery, Tokyo. Since 1962 he has often been among the Japanese artists exhibiting in the Tokyo *International Biennale Exhibition of Prints.* Ay-O was awarded the JAFA Prize in the 1969 Japan Art Festival. The same year, he won the Kyoto National Museum of Modern Art Prize at the Ninth Modern Japanese Art Exhibition.

Ay-O was a member of the Fluxus movement in New York in the early 1960s, making a lot of performance events with George Maciunas and other Fluxus artists. His recent manifestation was on the Eiffel Tower in Paris. A truly astonishing effect was created in 1987 by a 300-meter long banner in rainbow colour flowing down to the ground from the tower's observation platform.

—Yoshiaki Tono

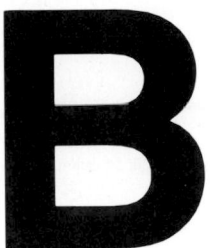

B

BACON, Francis.
British. Born, of English parents, in Dublin, Ireland, 28 October 1909. Mainly self-taught in art, from 1927. Served in Civil Defence Corps, London 1942–45. Worked in an office, London 1925; visited Berlin and Paris, 1926–27; worked as an interior decorator, London 1928–31. Independent painter, London 1929–46, Monte Carlo, 1946–50 and again in London since 1950; study-travels in South Africa 1950, in Italy 1954, with Peter Lacey in Tangier, 1956–59; visited New York and Rome, 1968; death of friend and model George Dyer, in Paris, 1971. Recipient: Painting Prize, *Carnegie International*, Pittsburgh, 1966; Rubenspreis, Siegen, West Germany 1967. Agent: Marlborough Fine Art, London. Address: c/o Marlborough Fine Art, 6 Albemarle Street, London W1X 4BY, England.

Individual Exhibitions:

1930	Bacon Studio, London (with Roy Le Maistre)
1934	Transition Gallery, London
1949	Hanover Gallery, London
1950	Hanover Gallery, London
1951	Hanover Gallery, London
1952	Hanover Gallery, London
1953	Durlacher Gallery, New York
	Beaux-Arts Gallery, London
1954	Hanover Gallery, London
1955	Institute of Contemporary Arts, London
	Hanover Gallery, London (with William Scott and Graham Sutherland)
1957	Galerie Rive Droite, Paris
	Hanover Gallery, London
1958	Galleria Galatea, Turin, Italy (travelled to the Galleria dell'Ariete, Milan and the Galleria dell'Obelisco, Rome)
	Victoria Art Gallery, Bath, Avon (with Matthew Smith and Victor Pasmore; toured Britain)
1959	Richard Feigen Gallery, Chicago
	British section, at the *5th Bienal*, Sao Paulo
	Hanover Gallery, London
1960	Marlborough Fine Art, London
	University of California at Los Angeles (with Hyman Bloom)
1961	University of Nottingham
1962	Galleria Galatea, Milan
	Tate Gallery, London (travelled to Mannheim, Turin and Zurich)
1963	Galleria Il Centro, Naples (with Graham Sutherland)
	Galleria La Loggia, Bologna (with Graham Sutherland)
	Granville Gallery, New York
	Marlborough Fine Art, London
	Guggenheim Museum, New York (travelled to Art Institute of Chicago, and the Houston Contemporary Arts Association)
1965	Kunsthalle, Hamburg (travelled to the Moderna Museet, Stockholm, and the Museum of Modern Art, Dublin)
	Marlborough Fine Art, London
1966	Galleria Toninelli, Milan
	Galerie Maeght, Paris (travelled to Marlborough Fine Art, London)
1967	Oberes Schloss, Siegen, West Germany
1968	Marlborough-Gerson Gallery, New York
1970	Galleria Galatea, Turin
1971	Grand Palais, Paris (travelled to the Kunsthalle, Dusseldorf)
1972	Galleria del Milione, Milan
1975	Metropolitan Museum of Art, New York
	Marlborough Galerie, Zurich
1976	Musée Cantini, Marseilles
1977	Galerie Claude Bernard, Paris
	Museo de Arte Moderna, Mexico City (travelled to the Museo de Arte Contemporaneo, Caracas)
1978	Fundación Juan March, Madrid (travelled to the Fundación Joan Miró, Barcelona)
1980	Marlborough Gallery, New York
	Städtische Kunsthalle, Mannheim
1983	National Museum of Modern Art, Tokyo (travelled to Kyoto and Nagoya)
	Marlborough Fine Art, London
1984	Galerie Maeght/Lelong, Paris
	Marlborough Gallery, New York
1985	Marlborough Fine Art, London
	Tate Gallery, London (travelled to Stuttgart and West Berlin)
1987	Marlborough Gallery, New York
	Galerie Beyeler, Basel
	Galerie Lelong, Paris

Selected Group Exhibitions:

1937	*Young British Painters*, Agnew Gallery, London
1945	*Recent Paintings: Bacon/Hodgkins/Moore/Smith/Sutherland*, Lefevre Gallery, London
1973	*Cuatro Maestros Contemporaneos: Giacometti, Dubuffet, De Kooning, Bacon*, Museo de Bellas Artes, Caracas (travelled to Sao Paulo and Rio de Janeiro)
1977	*Englische Kunst der Gegenwart*, Kunstlerhaus, Bregenz, Austria
1981	*A New Spirit in Painting*, Royal Academy of Art, London
1983	*Modern Art in the West*, Metropolitan Museum, Tokyo
1985	*Painterly Visions 1940–85*, Guggenheim Museum, New York
1987	*A School of London*, Kunstnernes Hus, Oslo (travelled to Copenhagen, Venice and Dusseldorf)

Collections:

Tate Gallery, London; Ulster Museum, Belfast; Centre Georges Pompidou, Paris; Nationalgalerie, West Berlin; Musée des Beaux-Arts, Brussels; Museum of Modern Art, New York; Guggenheim Museum, New York; Art Institute of Chicago; National Gallery of Canada, Ottawa; National Gallery of Australia, Canberra.

Publications:

On BACON: books—*Art Now* by Herbert Read, London 1933; *Francis Bacon*, exhibition catalogue, with text by M. Clarac Serou, London 1955; *Francis Bacon*, exhibition catalogue, with text by Helen Lessore, Nottingham 1961; *Francis Bacon*, exhibition catalogue, with text by John Rothenstein, London 1962; *Francis Bacon*, exhibition catalogue, with texts by Thomas Messer and Lawrence Alloway, New York 1963; *The Masters: Francis Bacon* by John Rothenstein, London and Milan 1963, Paris 1967; *Francis Bacon* (catalogue raisonne), by John Rothenstein and Ronald Alley, London 1964; *Francis Bacon* by John Russell, London, Paris and Berlin 1971; *Francis Bacon*, exhibition catalogue, with text by Michel Leiris, Paris 1971; *The Age of the Avant-Garde: An Art Chronicle of 1956–1972* by Hilton Kramer, New York and London 1974; *Interviews with Francis Bacon* by David Sylvester, London and New York 1975; *Francis Bacon* by Lorenza Trucchi, Milan and New York 1975, London 1976, rev. ed. Milan 1984; *Francis Bacon: Logique de la Sensation* by Gilles Deleuze, Paris 1981, 1984; *Francis Bacon: Full Face and in Profile* by Michel Leiris, London, New York, Paris and Munich 1983; *Francis Bacon* by Dawn Ades and Andrew Forge, London and Berlin 1985; *Francis Bacon: Vier Studien zu einem Portrait* by Wieland Schmied, Berlin 1985; *Francis Bacon: Kreuzigung* by Jorg Zimmermann, Frankfurt 1986; *Francis Bacon* by Hugh Davies and Sally Yard, New York 1986.

The two biggest names Britain has bestowed upon the contemporary art world are Moore and Bacon. Moore has moved steadily and unhesitatingly forward in world esteem, but Francis Bacon, ever since Herbert Read reproduced his "Crucifixion" (1933) in the first issue of *Art Now,* has shot up and, in recent years, with meteoric velocity.

Bacon, from being a one-time designer of "modern furniture" (actually reviewed in the *Studio* magazine, 1930), proved himself in 1966 one of the only British artists able in those days to beat Parisian chauvinism. Against all forecasts by experienced pundits his exhibition at the Galerie Maeght was a sell-out. But by then he had already made his reputation in Italy, the U.S., Brazil, Germany, Sweden, Switzerland and Ireland. The following year brought him the coveted Rubens International Prize.

Contemporary Bacon began 25 years ago. It was at that point that his style became identifiably his own. Since then he has passed through a number of specific phases and enthusiasms. Once he had overcome his fascination for the umbrella (although it certainly re-occurred), he turned to other categories like the series of near-monochrome business men (in expensive if shadowy suits), his portraits of the popes at peace or screaming, the oil collection of pictures he made based upon studies by the photographic pioneer Muybridge, the Van Gogh self-portraits, animals and sphynxes—especially the lonely dog caught in some kind of proto-Chirico piazza, and so on to the nudes like butchers' cadavers splayed or jumbled up after they have been defrozen and have been taken off the hook. Hypodermics, narcotics, addicts, all the sub-life of the seedy 60's.

How is Bacon now, compared with then?

During all this time when he has been establishing a world reputation, his style has become steady and consistent, but he has also acquired a kind of personal painterly finesse which is particularly evident in the portraits (especially the portrait studies). The brush-strokes in these display a kind of skilful instantaneous ease remote from the tortured and heavy impasto that clad many of his earlier paintings. It is as if the food has been cooked with greater expertise and experience, but has the strange exoticism of the meal lived up to the mysterious quality of those in the past? The

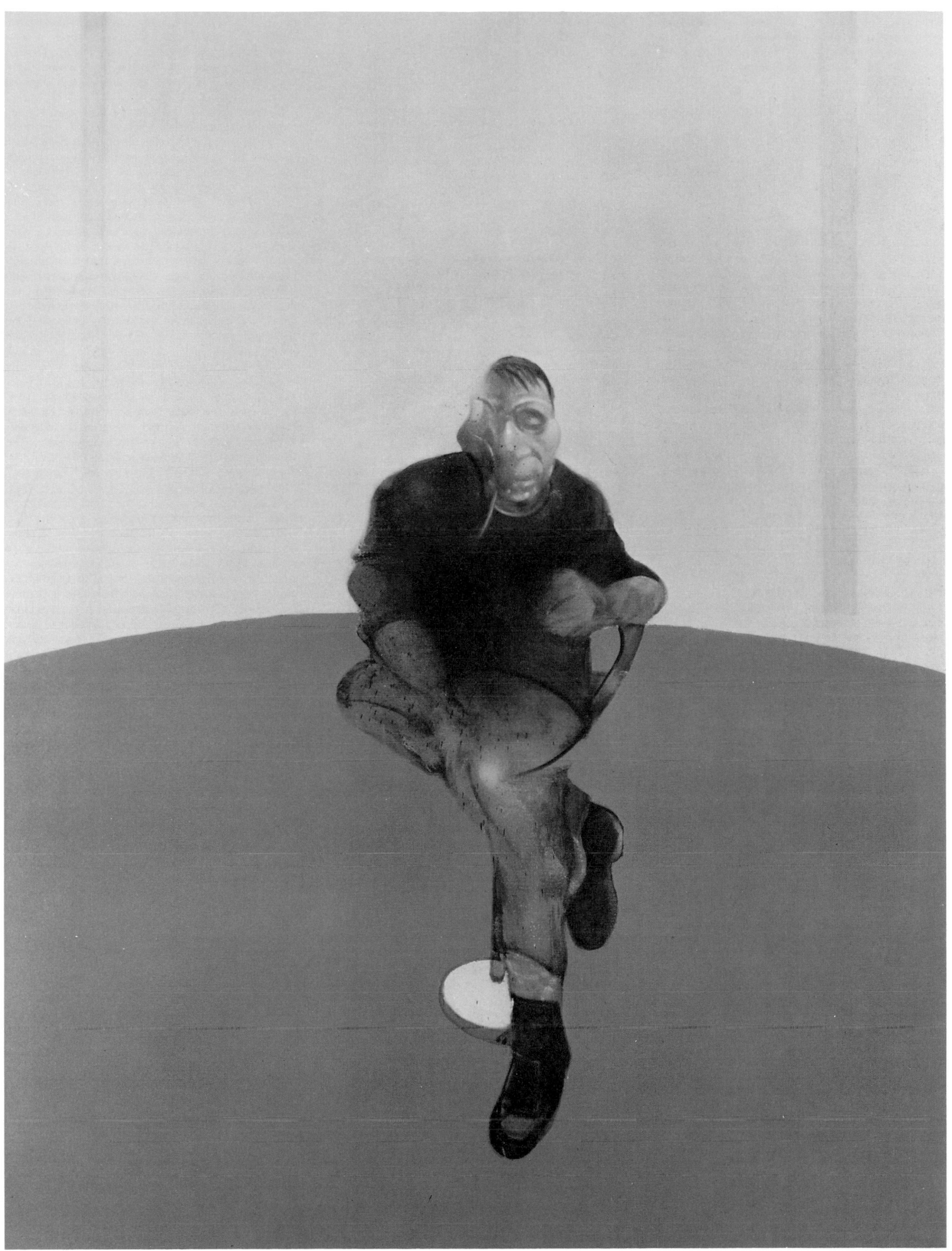

Francis Bacon: *Study for Self-Portrait Triptych*, 1986

world seems to think so. There will be many more Bacon Crucifixions (although nowadays they seem to spread into enormous triptychs), but will they ever revive the visual shriek of the one that Herbert Read picked to illustrate in *Art Now* more than 40 years ago?

—Sheldon Williams

BAER, Jo.

American. Born Josephine Gail Kleinberg in Seattle, Washington, 7 August 1929. Studied biology and art at the University of Washington, Seattle, 1946–49. Married television writer Richard Baer in 1953; son: Joshua; married John Wesley in 1960. Painter: worked in kibbutz in Israel, then moved to New York, 1950; worked with Graduate Faculty in Physiological Psychology, New School for Social Research, New York, 1952; moved to Los Angeles, 1953; associated peripherally with the Ferus Gallery run by Walter Hopps and Ed Kienholz, 1957; returned to New York, 1960, changing painting style from Abstract-Expressionist to a reductive, hard-edge style; began first "mature" series of work, 1962. Instructor, School of Visual Arts, New York 1969–70. Recipient: National Endowment for the Arts Grant, 1969. Agent: John Weber Gallery, 420 West Broadway, New York, New York 10012. Address: Art Galaxy, 262 Mott Street, New York, New York 10012, U.S.A.

Individual Exhibitions:

1966	Fischbach Gallery, New York
1967	*Jo Baer/David Judd/Peter Young*, Noah Goldowsky Gallery, New York
1968	*Jo Baer and Al Leslie*, Noah Goldowsky Gallery, New York
1969	Galerie Rolf Ricke, Cologne
1970	Galerie Rolf Ricke, Cologne
	Gordon Locksley-Shea Gallery, Minneapolis
	Noah Goldowsky Gallery, New York
1971	*Paintings from '62-'63*, School of Visual Arts, New York
1972	Lo Guidice Gallery, New York
1973	Galerie Rolf Ricke, Cologne
	Nicholas Wilder Gallery, Los Angeles
1974	Galleria Toselli, Milan
	Paintings 1962–1972, Daniel Weinberg Gallery, San Francisco
1975	Whitney Museum, New York

Selected Group Exhibitions:

1964	*11 Artists*, Kaymar Gallery, New York
1966	*Systematic Painting*, Guggenheim Museum, New York
1967	*Annual Exhibition of Contemporary American Painting*, Whitney Museum, New York (and 1969)
1968	*Documenta 4*, Kassel, West Germany
1969	*Eine Tendenz Zeitgenössischer Malerei*, Kölnischer Kunstverein, Cologne
1971	*Drawings*, Art Institute of Chicago
1973	*Options and Alternatives*, Yale University of Art Gallery, New Haven, Connecticut
1974	*5 Artists: A Logic of Vision*, Museum of Contemporary Art, Chicago
1975	*14 Artists*, Baltimore Museum of Art
	Hand Colored Prints, travelling exhibition organized by Brooke Alexander, Inc., New York

Collections:

Museum of Modern Art, New York; Guggenheim Museum, New York; Albright-Knox Art Museum, Buffalo, New York; University of North Carolina at Greensboro; University of Texas at Austin; Kölnischer Kunstverein, Cologne; Suermondt Museum, Aachen, West Germany; Australian National Gallery, Canberra.

Publications:

By BAER: book—*Cardinations*, portfolio of 9 screenprints, New York 1974; articles—"Letters" in *Artforum* (New York), September 1967; "Edward Kienholz: A Sentimental Journeyman" in *Art International* (Lugano, Switzerland), April 1968; "Letters" in *Artforum* (New York), April 1969; "The Artist and Politics: A Symposium" in *Artforum* (New York), September 1970; "Mach Bands: Art and Vision: and "Xerography and Mach Bands: Instrumental Model" in *Aspen Magazine* (Colorado), Fall/Winter 1970; "Art and Politics" and "On Painting" in *Flash Art* (Milan), November 1972.

On BAER: books—*Systematic Painting*, exhibition catalogue, with text by Lawrence Alloway, and statement by Baer, New York 1966; *Minimal Art: A Critical Anthology*, edited by Gregory Battcock, New York 1968; *American Art of the 20th Century* by Sam Hunter, New York 1972; *5 Artists: A Logic of Vision*, exhibition catalogue, with an introduction by Stephen Prokopoff, Chicago 1974; *American Art since 1900* by Barbara Rose, revised edition, New York 1975; *Jo Baer*, exhibition catalogue, with text by Barbara Haskell, New York 1975; *Hand Colored Prints*, exhibition catalogue, with an introduction by Carter Ratcliff, New York 1975; articles—"Jo Baer" by Will Insley in *Art International* (Lugano, Switzerland), 20 February 1969; "Diversity in Unity: Recent Geometricizing Styles in America" by Lucy Lippard in *Abstract Art since 1945*, New York 1971; "Jo Baer: Playing on the Senses" by Peter Schjeldahl in the *New York Times*, 14 May 1972; "Once More with Feeling" by Carter Ratcliff in *Artnews* (New York), Summer 1972; "Baer's Painterly Elegance" by Elena Karina Canavier in *Artweek* (Oakland, California), 28 April, 1973; "Jo Baer: Peintre Traditionel et 'Radical' " by Serge Guilbaut and Michael Sgan-Cohen in *Art Press* (Paris), May 1974.

Jo Baer began her career, in the 1950's, as an abstract expressionist. But with the advent of hard-edge abstraction in the 1960's she found a style more to her liking. The brand of hard-edge abstraction which she adopted came to be called "minimal," as practised by Judd and Le Witt. The principle was reductionist—less is more. It is no coincidence that at the time she came under the influence of Samuel Beckett, whose work, always reductive, was then reaching the *ne plus ultra* of reductionism, as in *Come and Go*, where three female characters literally come and go, and hardly a word is spoken. (It was my pleasure to open Jo Baer's exhibition on the occasion of the inauguration of the Douglas Hyde Gallery, Trinity College, Dublin, which, appropriately, contains a Beckett room.)

It might be said that Baer did for painting what Beckett did for drama, that is, pare everything down to an absolute minimum, so exiguous that with one more stroke there would be nothing left.

Even in her abstract expressionist days she had been interested in contrasts of light and darkness. This contrast persists in her minimal paintings. There is black round the edges and white or grey in the centre. Some are completely surrounded by black, like mortuary cards; others, of a somewhat later vintage, on the vertical sides only (given the equestrian name "Doublebar"). They are square or rectangular; sometimes vertical (V), sometimes horizontal (H). In the earlier works there is often a contrasting lightly coloured motif, like art deco decoration, which makes them even more like mortuary cards. They are usually arranged in groups of two (diptychs) or three (triptychs). And, most important of all, there is always a thin band of colour in or beside the black border.

It is this band of colour—blue, orange, green, lavender, red and aluminum being the favourite colours—which gives the richness and vibrancy to her work: the more added to the less. Where the thin line of colour is in the black, a reaction takes place which enhances the colour; where the colour is on the boundary of the black and white, the reaction is ambiguous, since the black tends to enhance and the white to bleach the band of light colour; but the result is always an effect of vibrancy. Further complexities are introduced by juxtaposing canvases, whether vertical or horizontal, into groups of diptychs or triptychs. In this way the blacks, whites and coloureds not only react with each other internally within a canvas, but react with their neighbours in the juxtaposed canvases.

It should, perhaps, be mentioned that Baer studied physiological and Gestalt psychology, and, in particular, the work of the 19th century physicist Ernst Mach (famous for his work on the relationship of a projectile to the speed of sound). She refers to the bands of colour in relationship to the black and white as "Mach Bands"; they, as it were, break the colour barrier by a sudden acceleration of light intensity.

While other minimalists, such as Judd and Le Witt, abandoned the flat surface in favour of the third dimension, on the grounds that two dimensional painting is allusionistic, Baer, who disagreed, quite rightly persisted in painting flat surfaces. However, in the late 1960's, she succumbed. At first she merely distanced the canvas from the wall by deepening the stretcher. But she soon evolved what she called "Wraparounds" in which the bands continue round the side of the stretcher. At the same time the severity of the bands of black was eased by making them taper and by breaking them up or making them intersect. By the early 1970's the black was replaced by bands of colour and the rectilinear shapes by curved ones. They even took on an Art Deco appearance. The white central area had been invaded. She also gave them invented Latin names such as "Pandurata," "Eutopicus," "Orbitaster" and "Arcuata" (extended, twisted, curved) derived from the names of orchids, a flower particularly dear to Jo Baer.

By the end of the 1970's the curve had become dominant and Jo Baer's painting underwent a radical change. From being starkly and geometrically abstract, it became figurative, sensual and, at times, erotic; from being ordered and closely knit, it became fragmented: drawings of anatomical parts, predominantly, human and animal buttocks, studies of seated nudes, etc. These latest "drawings," mostly in black on white (still the contrast), look like entries in a sketchbook or the fragmented drawings on caves. The drawings are sensitive in line; colour, when it is used, is sensuous. In spite of the fragmented appearance of these works, they are highly, if covertly, ordered.

It is hard, as yet, to assess these works in relation to the earlier ones, but one thing is certain: Jo Baer is among the most perspective of contemporary artists, one who makes demands on the perceptive powers of those who look at her work. Even her description of her work—"percepts become precepts, precepts become percepts"—might elude the casual or superficial reader.

—D. C. Barrett

BAERTLING, Olle.

Swedish. Born in Halmstead, 6 December 1911. Educated at State Secondary Grammar School, Halmstead, 1922–28; studied business administration at the School of Economics and Trade, Stockholm, 1928–29; also studied English, French and German, 1929–40; studied painting, under André Lhote and Fernand Léger, Paris, 1948. Married Lisa Maria von Roxendorff in 1939. Worked as branch manager and publicity manager, Skandinaviska Enskilda Banken, Stockholm, 1929–47, and part time, 1949–55; independent artist, in Paris and Stockholm, 1949–81:associated with painter Auguste Herbin, Paris from 1950; Member, Réalités Nouvelles artists group, Paris, 1950–56; Co-Founder, Groupe Espace, Paris, 1952–59. Recipient: Painting Prize, *Bienal*, Sao Paulo, 1963; National Swedish Art Award, 1964. *Died* (in Stockholm) *2 May 1981*.

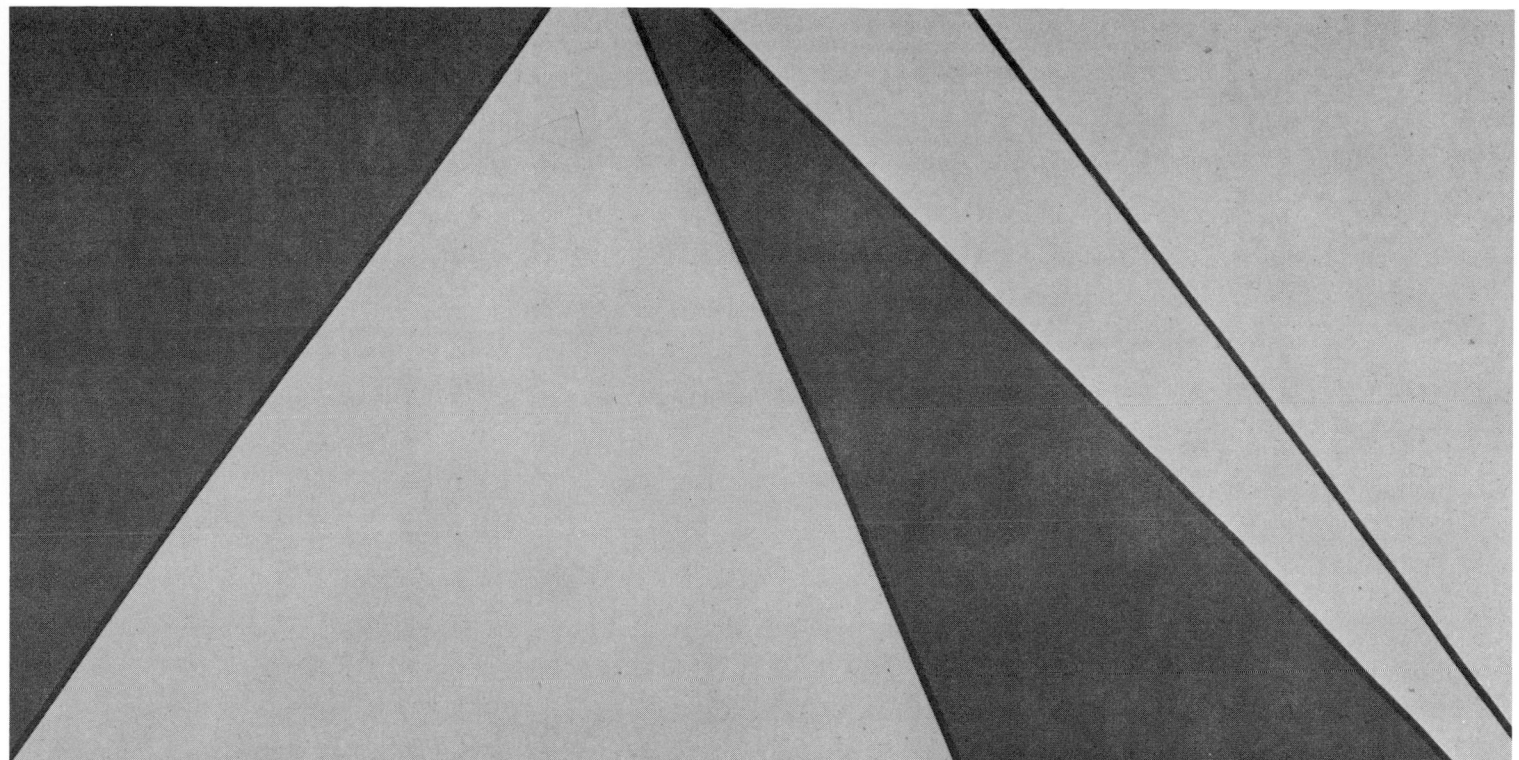

Ölle Baertling: *Yoyan*, 1970

Individual Exhibitions:

1949 Galerie Samlaren, Stockholm
1951 Galerie Brinken, Stockholm (with Auguste Herbin)
1952 Galerie Birch, Copenhagen
1953 Konsthall, Uppsala, Sweden
1954 Galerie Denise René, Paris (with Breer and Bitran)
     Galerie Samlaren, Stockholm (open-air exhibition)
1955 Galerie Samlaren, Stockholm
     Skanska Konstmuseum, University of Lund, Sweden
       (with Mortensen)
1956 Liljevalchs Konsthall, Stockholm (with Jacobsen and
       Mortensen)
     Royal Academy of Fine Art, Copenhagen (with Ja-
       cobsen and Mortensen)
1957 Galerie Samlaren, Stockholm (3 exhibitions)
1958 *Dramaturge des Formes*, Galerie Denise René, Paris
     Musée des Beaux-Arts, Liège, Belgium (with
       Matisse and Kylberg)
1960 Galerie Samlaren, Stockholm
     Konstnarshuset, Stockholm (retrospective)
1961 Galerie Samlaren, Stockholm (with Matisse and
       Léger)
1962 Galerie Denise René, Paris
     Galerie Observatorium, Stockholm
1963 Galerie Hybler, Copenhagen
     Swedish Pavilion, at the *Bienal*, Sao Paulo
1964 Galerie Samlaren, Stockholm
     Columbia University, New York (retrospective;
       toured the United States and Sweden, 1964–66)
1966 Galerie Samlaren, Stockholm
1967 Rose Fried Gallery, New York (retrospective)
     S.D. Gallery, New York
     Galerie Lowendahl, Uppsala, Sweden
1968 Galerie Aronowitsch, Stockholm (retrospective)
     Galerie Bleue, Stockholm
     Musée des Arts Décoratifs/Palais du Louvre, Paris
1969 Galerie Plus-Kern, Ghent
     Royal Academy of Fine Arts, Stockholm (retrospec-
       tive)
     New York University (retrospective)
     Esther Robles Gallery, Los Angeles (retrospective)
1970 Rose Fried Gallery, New York (retrospective)
     Axiom Gallery, London (retrospective)
1971 Galerie Larsson, Gavle, Sweden, (retrospective)
1972 Galerie Denise René, Paris (retrospective)
     Galerie 66–H. G. Krupp, Hofheim/Taunus, West
       Germany

Obrebro Museum, Sweden (retrospective)
Norrkoping Museum, Sweden (retrospective)
1973 Vasteras Museum, Sweden (retrospective)
     Galerie Samlaren, Stockholm
     University of Stockholm (Baertling Collection)
     Le Disque Rouge, Brussels
     Galleria Lorenzelli, Milan (retrospective)
1974 Galleria della Trinita, Rome
     Galerie Samlaren, Stockholm
     Galerie Denise René, Paris (retrospective)
     Galerie Ferm, Malmo, Sweden
1975 Galerie Denise René, Paris
     Galleriet, Lund, Sweden
     Baertling: Creator of Open Form, Junior Galerie,
       Copenhagen (travelled to the Junior Galerie, Zu-
       rich)
1976 Contemporary Royale, Vancouver
     Galerie Denise René, Paris
     Galerie Denise René Rive Gauche, Paris
     Galerie Royal, Calgary, Alberta
     Galerie Nordenhake, Malmo, Sweden
     Konstsalongen Samlaren, Stockholm
     Galerie Fabian Carlsson, Gothenburg, Sweden
1977 Nordenhaken Rykken Galleri, Oslo
     Gemalde, Skulpturen 1950–1975, Kunsthalle, Dus-
       seldorf
     Galerie Karsten Greve, Cologne (retrospective)
1978 Galerie Karin Fesel, Wiesbaden, West Germany (ret-
       rospective)
     Galerie von Bartha, Basle (retrospective)
     Galleri Christel, Helsinki
1979 Galerie von Bartha, at the *Internationale Kunst-
       messe*, Basel (retrospective)
1981 *Baertling 1911–1981: Creator of Open Form*, Kons-
       thall, Malmo, Sweden (travelled to Moderna Mu-
       seet, Stockholm)
     Galerie Nordenhake, Malmo, Sweden
     Galerie Bel'Art, Stockholm
1982 Henie-Onstad Kunstsenter, Hovikodden, Norway
     Galerie Konstruktiv Tendens, Stockholm
     Moderna Museet, Stockholm

Selected Group Exhibitions:

1950 *Salon des Réalités Nouvelles*, Musée d'Art Moderne
     Paris

1960 *Construction and Geometry in Painting*, Galerie
       Chalette, New York (toured the United States)
1967 *Art et Mouvement*, Musée d'Art Contemporain,
       Montreal
1972 *Swedish Art 1972*, Museum of Modern Art, Tokyo
       (travelled to the Museum of Modern Art, Kyoto)
1974 *Konstruktivt 1974*, Moderna Museet, Stockholm
       (travelled to the Amos Andersonin Taidemuseo,
       Helsinki)
1976 *Creative Sweden*, Northwestern National Bank of
       Minnesota, Minneapolis
1978 *Museo Nacional de la Resistencia Salvador Allende*,
       Moderna Museet, Stockholm
1979 *Constructivism and the Geometric Tradition*,
       Albright-Knox Art Gallery, Buffalo, New York
       (toured the United States)
1980 *Dansk-Svensk Grafik*, Jonkopings Lans Museum,
       Sweden
1981 *Hommage à Baertling*, Liljevalchs Konsthall, Stock-
       holm

Collections:

National Museum, Stockholm; Konsthall, Malmo, Sweden;
Tate Gallery, London; Centre Georges Pompidou, Paris; Gal-
leria Nazionale d:Arte Moderna, Rome; Nationalgalerie,
West Berlin; Stedelijk Museum, Amsterdam; Museum of
Modern Art, Tokyo; Museum of Modern Art, New York;
Hirshhorn Museum, Washington, D.C.

Publications:

By BAERTLING: books—*Document-Aspect-61*, exhibition
catalogue, with others, Stockholm 1961; *Nytt Svenskt
Konstnarsgalleri*, exhibition catalogue, with others, Malmo,
Sweden 1966; *Baertling: precurseur de la Forme Ouverte*,
exhibit catalogue, with others, Paris 1968; *The Angles of
Baertling*, exhibition catalogue, New York 1969; *Baertling:
precurseur de la forme ouverte*, with others, Stockholm,
Paris and New York 1971, 1974; *Olle Baertling*, exhibition
catalogue, with others, Milan 1973; *Open Form*, Stockholm
1978; articles—"Mortensen" in *Aujourd'hui* (Paris), March
1955; "Konkret Realism", in *Konstperspektiv* (Gothenburg,
Sweden), February 1956; "Den aktuella konstens proble-
matik" in *Konstperspektiv* (Gothenburg, Sweden), January
1958; "Angreppet ar ovasentglit" in *Fonstret* (Stockholm),
July 1959; "Estetisk rum—immateriell rymd" in *Konstperspektiv* (Gothenburg, Sweden), February 1960; "Om den

konstruktiva konsten" in *Svenska Dagbladet* (Stockholm), 4 March 1963; "Konstruktive konst—framtids miljo" in *Arkitektur* (Stockholm), June 1965; "Aben Form—uendligt rum" in *Kunst* (Odense), November 1969.

On BAERTLING: books—*Baertling: Dramaturge des Formes*, exhibition catalogue, with text by Oscar Reutersvard, Paris 1958; *Abstract Painting: 50 Years of Accomplishment from Kandinsky to the Present* by Michel Seuphor, New York 1961; *History of Modern Art: Painting, Sculpture, Architecture* by H. H. Arnason, New York 1969; *Aesthetics: An Introduction* by Ruth Saw, New York 1971; *Alla Trinita—Baertling*, exhibition catalogue, with text by Lorenza Trucchi, Rome 1974; *Another Light: Swedish Art since 1945* by Olle Granath, Stockholm 1975; *Baertling: Creator of Open Form*, exhibition catalogue, with text by Teddy Brunius, Copenhagen 1975; *Konstruktive Konsepte: Eine Geschichte der Konstruktivier Kunst von Kubismus bis Heute* by Willy Rotzler, Zurich 1977; *Olle Baertling: Gemalde, Skulpturen 1950-1975*, exhibition catalogue, with text by Karl-Heinz Heing, Teddy Brunius and Oscar Reutersvard, Dusseldorf 1977; *Olle Baertling*, exhibition catalogue, with text by Friedrich W. Heckmanns, Wiesbaden, West Germany 1978; *Baertling 1911-1981: Creator of Open Form*, exhibition catalogue, with texts by Teddy Brunius, Oscar Reutersvard and Gunnar Berefelt, Malmo and Stockholm 1981.

In 1953, Olle Baertling introduced into a vertical-horizontal world (of landscape, of gravity, of architects, of the written or printed page, of the reference co-ordinates of human measurement of space, of Mondrian) images of great clarity, positiveness, and vitality, made up entirely of diagonal lines which marked out acutely tapered triangles. For three decades Baertling continued to reveal this diagonal world, a little at a time, not to ingratiate or to win confidence or friends, but to create and populate a world of his own, not comfortable in its topography, not ingratiating in the colors of its landscape, but hard and real and challenging to the explorer.

Baertling's lines made space—in two senses: the *space between* rigid dividers (whether in his sculpture of his painting) and the *space generated* behind and in front of the picture plane by illusion, through the perspective effect of converging lines and the advance-recession stimulus of flat colors in combination. Using both these kinds of space as a plastic material, modelled and modified by a knowing mind and eye and a powerful and decisive hand, he developed what he called "open form." This was a modest label, for the forms Baertling opened were not the blooming of a flower but an explosion which burst through the frame of the painting.

Between the lines there are his colors. In maps only enough are used to give each country a chromatic autonomy. Three will do. Baertling's economical linear assertions succeed with black and a single color. He often used only two colors, rarely three and almost never four. Color, especially when it is unmodulated, separates and emphasizes; any distinguishable hues suffice. But Baertling knew that color is sensation and aesthetic in its fundamental meaning of "feeling." He used it to provide sensation, but not necessarily pleasure. He used it for visibility, for stimulus, for impact. His colors are as awkward as his discordant, unbalanced triangles, and as forceful. So in the face of a strong personality, we modify our aesthetics and begin to take pleasure in these colors. As so often happens in art we come to like those qualities which at first we most disliked.

In Baertling's world we find confirmed that rules are made *by* works of art not *for* them. To allow converging lines to meet at or near the picture's edge used to be compositional blunder; it is Baertling's principal compositional theme. Directing diagonals into the corner of a picture was worse; it drew the eye away from the center of interest; it caused visual traffic jams. Such traffic jams at the edge, or even projected outside the center of the painting, are precisely what Baertling wanted to confront us with. Concomitant with these hard, sharp, punching vertices are the unadjusted, unmodulated, disharmonious, blatant colors. Having got to know them, one can miss them like a departed friend, with whom one liked to argue.

Baertling repeated himself. He took from his small

bundle of lines, from his bundle of narrow, sharp, scalene triangles, from his tiny handful of sharp colors, only what he needed for each successive painting; and for his sculptures, he took only the lines. The repertoire is small; the performance is in a long, narrow rectangular space, two by one or two and half by one. Over and over again he played out the variations in that squeezed space, with vertices spilling out of it. Like a conscientious detective story writer, he had certain rules for himself. Not only did diagonals never cross inside the rectangle but also he never allowed an island to establish itself in his space; nor would he allow a compositional idea to complete itself within his frame—the action was always resolved off stage.

The effect of this repetition has been that each painting, each sculpture, reasserted and at the same time expanded, by a small increment, the world which Baertling had made his own and had ruled without compromise.

—George Rickey

BAJ, Enrico.

Italian. Born in Milan, 31 October 1924. Educated in Milan: studied law, 1937-39; painting, at the Accademia de Brera, 1945-48. Married Gigliola Olivieri in 1954; daughter; Lucilla; married Roberta Cerini de Castegnate in 1966; children: Angelo, Andrea, Pietro and Marianna. Independent painter, writer and graphic artist, since 1948. Founder Member, with Sergio Dangelo, Nuclear Art Movement, Milan, 1951; Founder, with Asger Jorn, International Movement for an Imaginary Bauhaus, Albissola, Italy, 1953; Founder Editor, with Sergio Dangelo, *Il Gesto* magazine, Milan, 1955-1959; produced first collages and assemblages, Milan, 1956; contributed regularly to avant-garde magazines *Phases, Boa, Edda, Direzioni* and *Bokubi*, Milan, 1956-60; associated with the Nouveau Realiste group, Milan, 1959; Founder, with Raymond Queneau, Institute of Pataphysics, Milan, 1963; friendly with Max Ernst, Marcel Duchamp and André Breton, Paris, 1963-66; produced first pointilliste works, Milan, 1971. Spazio Baj permanent exhibition centre established by the city of Milan, 1987. Agent: Studio Marconi, Milan. Address: Via delle Ville 18, 21029 Vergiate, Italy.

Individual Exhibitions:

1951	Galleria San Fedele, Milan (with Sergio Dangelo)
1954	Galleria l'Asterisco, Rome
	Galleria Schettini, Milan
1956	Galleria Schettini, Milan
	Kunstkredsen, Copenhagen
1957	Gallery One, London
	Galleria Il Prisma, Turin
1958	Galleria Gruppo, Bergamo (with Lucio Fontana and Piero Manzoni)
	Galerie Daniel Cordier, Paris
1959	Gallery One, London
	Galerie Rive Gauche, Paris
1960	Galleria del Naviglio, Milan
1961	Galerie Raymond Cordier, Paris
	Galeria du Fleuve, Paris
	Galleria Schwarz, Milan
1962	Sevenarts Gallery, London
	Galerie Berggruen, Paris
1963	Cordier and Ekstrom Gallery, New York
1964	Galerie Alice Pauli, Lausanne
	Palazzo Reale, Milan
1965	Galerie Pierre, Stockholm
	Castello Spagnolo, L'Aquila, Italy
	Galerie Berggruen, Paris
1966	Galleria Odyssia, Rome
	Arts Club of Chicago

1967	Studio Marconi, Milan
	Gemeentemuseum, The Hague
	Museum voor Schone Kunsten, Ghent
	Galerie Francoise Mayer, Brussels
	Galleria del Minotauro, Brescia, Italy
1968	Studio Condotti, Rome
1969	Studio Marconi, Milan
	Galerie Creuzevault, Paris
1970	Studio Condotti, Rome
	Galerie Georges Moos, Geneva
1971	Musée de l'Athénée, Geneva
	Palazzo Grassi, Venice
	Museum of Contemporary Art, Chicago
1972	Galleria Michaud, Florence
1973	Museum Boymans-van-Beuningen, Rotterdam
	Moderna Museet, Stockholm
	Kunsthalle, Dusseldorf
1974	Koninklijk Museum voor Schone Kunsten, Antwerp
	Palazzo Reale, Milan (travelled to the Kunsthalle, Dusseldorf, and the Palais des Beaux-Arts, Brussels)
	Musée d'Art et d'Histoire, Cabinet des Estampes, Geneva
	Galleria Spagnoli, Florence
	Galerie Spectrum, Vienna
1975	Galleria San Benedetto, Brescia, Italy
	Studio Marconi, Milan
	Centre Design, Lugano, Switzerland
	Galerie Christel, Helsinki (toured Sweden)
	Museo Progressivo d'Arte Contemporanea, Livorno, Italy
	Galleria della Piazza, Varese, Italy (with Lucio Del Pezzo and Emilio Scanavino)
1976	Galleria Il Centro, Naples
	Galerie Friebe, Cologne (travelled to Galerie Volker Huber, Frankfurt)
	Arras Gallery, New York
	Arte Contacto, Caracas
	Galleria Pancheri, Rovereto, Italy
	Gallerie Ostermalm, Stockholm
	Castello Sforzesca, Milan
1977	Arras Gallery, New York
	Galerie Actu-Art, Helsingor, Denmark
	Palazzo dei Diamanti, Ferrara, Italy
	Centro Congressi La Sera, Ivrea, Italy
	Galeria Gerhild Grolitsch, Munich
1978	Galleria Schettini, Milan
	Arras Gallery, New York
	Indianapolis Museum of Art
	Palais de l'Europe, Menton, France
1979	Studio Marconi, Milan
	Dartmouth College, Hanover, New Hampshire
1980	Galerie l'Ile de France, Paris
1981	Studio Marconi, Milan
1982	Palazzo della Ragione, Mantua, Italy
1983	Studio Marconi, Milan
1985	Center of Fine Art, Miami, Florida
	Castello di Bard, Val d'Aosta, Italy
	FIAC, Paris
1987	Palazzo Bellini, Comacchio, Italy

Selected Group Exhibitions:

1952	*Arte Nucleare*, Amici della Francia, Milan
1957	*Phasen*, Stedelijk Museum, Amsterdam
1961	*The Art of Assemblage*, Museum of Modern Art, New York
1963	*Schrift en Beeld*, Stedelijk Museum, Amsterdam
1968	*Recent Italian Painting and Sculpture*, Jewish Museum, New York
1971	*Metamorphase de l'Objet*, Palais des Beaux-Arts, Brussels
1977	*Italienische Druckgraphic des 20. Jahrhunderts*, Kunsthalle, Darmstadt
1980	*Arte Nucleare 1951-1957*, Galleria San Fedele, Milan
1984	*Primitivism in 20th Century Art*, Museum of Modern Art, New York
1987	*Lo specchio e il doppio*, Mole Antonelliana, Turin

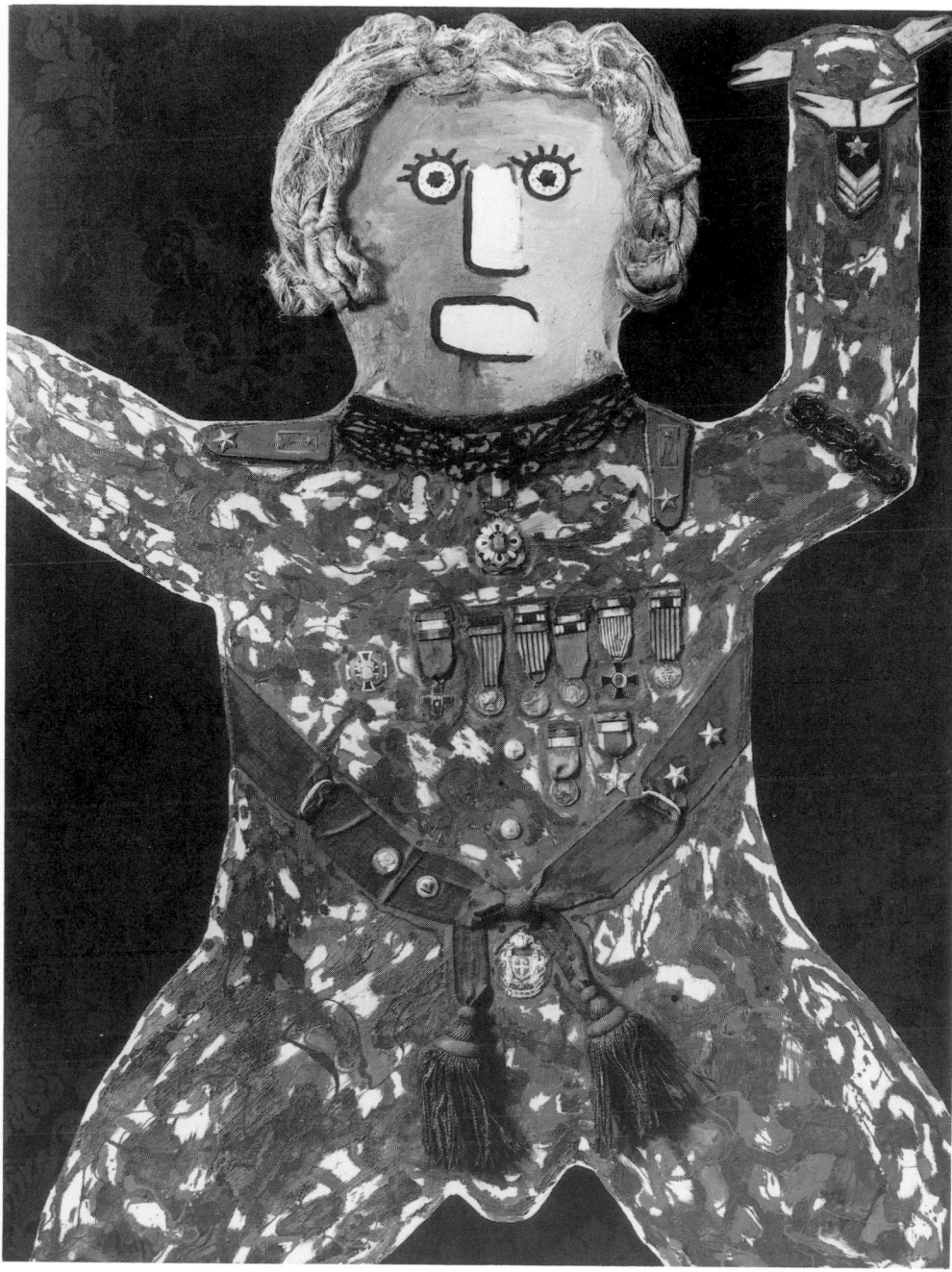

Enrico Baj: *Generale "Generale"*, 1961

Collections

Centre Georges Pompidou, Paris; Museum Boymans-van Beuningen. Rotterdam; Stedelijk Museum, Amsterdam; Moderna Museet, Stockholm; Museum des 20. Jahrhunderts. Vienna; Tate Gallery, London; Lodz Museum, Poland; Galleria d'Arte Moderná, Milan; Museum of Contemporary Art, Chicago; National Gallery, Washington, D.C.

Publications:

By BAJ: books—*Manifeste de la Peinture Nucleaire*, with Sergio Dangelo, Brussels 1952; *Contro lo Stile*, with others, Milan 1957; *Arte Interplanetaria*, with others, Pianeta Terra, Italy 1959; *Manifeste de Naples*, with others, Naples 1959; *A Proposito de Coesistenza e Modificazione*, Naples 1959; *Pittura e Realtà*, Milan 1959; *Alternativi Attuali*, exhibition catalogue, L'Aquila, Italy 1962; *Testa a Testa*, with Umberto Geo, Padua 1980; *Autodanse*, Bologna 1980; articles—"Pop Napoli" in *Marcatre* (Milan), June 1965; "Milano Caves" in *Marcatre* (Milan), December 1965; "La Vita e l'Uomo" in *Del Pezzo*, exhibition catalogue, Milan 1966; "Parigi: FON 2104" in *Marcatre* (Milan), April 1966; "Ho visto Dio" in *Marcatre* (Milan), June 1966; "L'affaire des Generaux" in *L'Ultimo dei Generali*, Gallarate, Italy 1968; "Deflorando" in *Guido Biasi*, exhibition catalogue, Turin 1969; "L'Austra-lia ha sete" in *Corriere della Sera* (Milan), May 1969; "Da Breton alla Luna" in *Corriere della Sera* (Milan), August 1969; "Baj da San Francisco" in *Flash Art* (Milan), no. 13, 1969; "Lattuga a Porno" in *Corriere della Sera* (Milan), October 1970; "Buzzati sexpittore" in *Dino Buzzati: Un Caso a Porte*, Rome, 1971; "Milano Cinquanta" in *Milano 70/70 Un Secolo d'Arte*, Milan 1972; "Sonnenstern" in *Multiplicata Internationale*, Stockholm and Zurich 1972; "Venne la Crisi e fu la Catastrofe" in *Corriere della Sera* (Milan), 25 May 1975; "Signorno all Autoritarismo" in *Doppiovu* (Milan), December 1976; "Pompidou chez Baj: Baj chez Pompidou" in *La Nuova Rivista Europea* (Trento, Italy), September / October 1977; "Baj on Baj," interview with Ellen Wardwell Lee in *Baj*, exhibition catalogue, by Joanne Muller Kuebler, Indianapolis 1978.

On BAJ: books—*Baj* by Jan van der Marck, Milan 1962; *Baj: Catalogue de l'Oeuvre et des Multiples*, 2 vols., by Jean Petit, Geneva 1970, 1974; *Baj* by Alain Jouffroy, Paris 1972; *Catalogo Generale Bolaffi Opere di Baj* by Enrico Crispolti, Turin 1973; *Enrico Baj, Dada Impressionist* by Herbert Lust, Turin 1973; *Enrico Baj, Apocalisse*, edited by Umberto Eco, Milan 1979; *Enrico Baj* by Jean Baudrillard, Paris 1980; *Testa a Testa* by Umberto Eco, Padua 1980; *Baj, dal generale al particolare* by Italo Calvino, Gerard G. Lemaire and Jan van der Marck, Milan 1985; *Baj: graphic works—catalogue raisonné*, edited by Roberto Sanesi and Jan van der Marck, Milan 1986; *Baj, nostalgia del futuro* by J. Baudrillard, P Bellasi and others, Milan 1987.

On other occasions, I have put forward a distinction between art-as-invention, i.e. art capable of affecting the current vision of things, and art-as-representation—which is to say, art which simply records and is more or less descriptive or analytical. At the ultimate level of ignominy is to be found commemorative art, seen without question in the art so dear to Stalin and Hitler, and at the Museum of Modern Art when engaged in the defence of Campbell's Soup or Coca-Cola. Celebrative art is art that does not content itself with merely representing power or is extreme in it homogenising degenerations, but even glorifies with marble monuments and kitsch imagery the commandant-bosses and / or the flavour of the month—be it neon lights, cartoons and plastic packages or any of the variety of junk with which we identify our finer feelings.

Today, more than ever, in our landscape made of conditioned and computerised responses, art as invention anticipates the new systems of communication in new visual languages capable of confronting an all-embracing robotization.

The spaces of the gallery Studio Marconi in Milan lend themselves to this type of research. There, space, which is everything for the painter, allows the exhibition of large canvases and the organization of the exhibit as the manifestation of different states of mind. I do have a system for filling such spaces—in fact, for some time I returned wholeheartedly to the technique of the 'fifties: action painting, dripping, gesture and sign. These methods of mine between 1951 and 1959 were constrained within the walls of small (not to say minimal) studio spaces in Milan; the constraints of the place inhibited my gesture and my dance around the canvas placed on the floor.

Living now in the countryside and the open air, I have recovered a completely different dimension. Onto a fine green meadow—a green I've always loved—I lay out a fresh canvas (which looks like an airport runway) and there my action begins, my own way of making pictures, which is the ultimate in the exultation, continuation and mega-inflation of painting 'au plein air'. Man must return to nature. Never again should he fight it, if he is to survive! This is the message of Georgescu Roegen and the message of the hope of a solar civilization. A new message and a new hope—new because they are given to us in highly philosophical and scientific terms, and not just to satisfy a naturalistic urge. At times, I work only with black on a white canvas, and I retrieve signs, symbols and scribbles reminiscent of the famous Rorschach test. At other times, I have abandoned black to give myself over to the manic and overwhelming joy of colour, I grind it, splash it, dilute it with turpentine and various solvents, or allow it to coagulate in the sun until concentrated, stringy and viscous to the touch before using it to create contrasts with other chromatic dilutions. Sometimes, I work with a kind of abstract drawing or pointillism, attracting me into a vacuum made up of a thousand colours. On other occasions, mindful of the cultural revolution of May 1968, when everybody spraycanned on walls the slogan of his own political failures, I try to produce ancestral languages and figures precisely in spraypaint, a sign language similar to the man of Altamira. The feelings we experience, the messages we intercept, the materials at our disposal are by now extremely varied, manifold and often contradictory, so that my exhibition will include a dual series of watercolours and drawings. The watercolours are reminiscent of a kind of cubo-futurism I practised at the time of my Manifesto for Static Futurism. Pastel drawings, on the other hand, emerged together with my use of the big spray green canvases. Finally, other canvases incorporate the symbolic transposition of bits and pieces of wood collected off the ground during the construction of my new studio.

Such wooden fragments, due to their humble, ephemeral and weathered look, have a charge which I would define as archaeological. They imply an ancient discourse redolent of the gesture of the carpenter's or bricklayer's art. Effectively, our houses are already archaeological. We live in archaeology as is demonstrated by the continual restoration of old farm houses and decaying city centres. Today, the streets where brothels operated, the Fossati cinema building and the industrial premises are precious relics that we should clean up and restore.

Some of the canvases with wooden fragments are used to represent my family, whereas another is freely inspired by Pythaogras' theorem. One is a study for Voltaire's Micromegas. The famous conversation between the inhabitants of Sirio and Saturno reverberates in my latest works, as in the Citta del Sole for which I am indebted to another great Utopianist (T. Campanella).

'Megalizzazione' and 'miniaturizzazione' face one another in everyday life. It should not be difficult to understand that, faced with grand general projects (and their frequent failure), we opt for the cure of the particular.

—Enrico Baj

What we might regard as a new iconology, combining the influence of popular and of cultured iconology and reviving the mytho-poetical qualities of present-day man, has always been present in Enrico Baj's work. Ever since 1951—the time of the *Movimento Nucleare*, of which he was a member—Baj has understood the importance of those mocking creatures that fill the popular horizon and in the end can be heard breathing within the "cultured" painting, and he has press-ganged them into his paintings and *assemblages*. Thus we have seen the first clumsy sketches of the "ultrabodies" or of the flying saucers, and after them those of the Generals and the Dames: a whole gallery teeming with people and events which are beginning to be organized and which the artist has used as a background against which to compose his pictures.

In Baj's case, in addition to the readymade material constituted by the *objet trouvé*, used just as it is as an emotional and fanciful starting point, there is always the desire to give life to the shapeless, to find the right relationship between forms and colours. Ever since his first grotesque drawings, the artist has been able to combine his sense of humour with his feeling for experiment, his narrative ability with his eagerness for research into materials; thus he has worked with stained cloth from mattresses or tapestries, for use as background to his "monsters"; he has borrowed our grandfathers' looking-glasses, but in order to create an ambiguous medium that would reflect the image of the past and that of the future together.

While almost all American and British pop art used "found objects" as symbols of everyday life, Baj took a completely opposite line. The wide use he made of old, out-of-date materials, of old 19th-century trimmings, of ancient medals, of our great-grandparents' ribbons and lace, tells us how the artist has pointed out the importance of creating a "kingdom of memory," haunted by the ghosts of an age already far away from us but in which we can still recognize our origins. When Baj invented his "Dames" and "Generals," the Pop adventure was still a long way off; it was too easy, later, to lump his pictures together with those of other masters of United States pop.

If, then, we want to analyse the signs and symbols in some of Baj's figures and collages, we must notice the subtle metaphorical game that he plays with the heteroclitic materials he uses; we must notice that it is no accident that the discs he uses for eyes are buttons, the nipples are skittles, the sexes are rough brushes.

There are too many examples to quote here, but they show us how there nearly always exists in these works a Concept side by side with an Object; a linguistic search (for a visual-verbal metaphor) side by side with a plastic search. And it is this that, in the last years, has enabled Baj to tackle the great socio-political themes depicted in some of his gigantic works like "Watergate," "The Anarchic Pinelli" and "The Apocalypse," in which the same humorous elements from the past have been used for a more exact-ing, more austere purpose: to put in relief the sins of our civilization and draw attention to the threats that supreme political power can exert on present and future society.

—Gillo Dorfles

BALDESSARI, John.

American. Born in National City, California, 17 June 1931. Educated at Sweetwater High School, National City, 1945–49; studied painting at San Diego State College, California, 1949– 53, 1954–57, B.A. 1953, M.A. 1957. Married Carol Wixom in 1962; children: Anna Marie and Antonio. Professional artist since 1957. Instructor, Fine Arts Gallery, San Diego, 1953–54, San Diego city schools, 1956–57, San Diego State College, 1956, 1959–61, and Southwestern College, Chula Vista, California, 1962–68; Assistant Professor of Art, University of California at San Diego, 1968–70; also, Instructor, La Jolla Museum of Art, California, 1966–70. Professor, California Institute of Arts, Los Angeles, since 1970. Visiting Instructor, Hunter College, New York, 1971. Recipient: National Endowment for the Arts Grant, 1973, 1974–75. Agents: Sonnabend Gallery, New York; and James Corcoran Gallery, 8223 Santa Monica Boulevard, Los Angeles, California 90046. Lives and works in Santa Monica, California. Address: c/o Sonnabend Gallery, 420 West Broadway, New York, New York 10012, U.S.A.

Individual Exhibitions:

1960	La Jolla Museum of Art, California
1962	Southwestern College, Chula Vista, California (and 1964)
1966	La Jolla Museum of Art, California
1968	Molly Barnes Gallery, Los Angeles
1970	Richard Feigen Gallery, New York
	Eugenia Butler Gallery, Los Angeles
1971	Galerie Konrad Fischer, Dusseldorf
	Art and Project, Amsterdam
	Nova Scotia College of Art and Design, Halifax
1972	Galerie MTL, Brussels
	Art and Project, Amsterdam
	Galleria Franco Toselli, Milan
	Jack Wendler Gallery, London
1973	Sonnabend Gallery, New York
	Galerie Sonnabend, Paris
	Galleria Schema, Florence
	Galerie Konrad Fischer, Dusseldorf
1974	Galerie Folker Skulima, West Berlin
	Jack Wendler Gallery, London
	Galleria Franco Toselli, Milan
	Art and Project/Galerie MTL, Antwerp
1975	Galerie Felix Handschin, Basle
	Galerie MTL, Brussels
	Saman Gallery, Genoa
	Sonnabend Gallery, New York
	Stedelijk Museum, Amsterdam
	Modern Art Agency, Naples
	Galerie Sonnabend, Paris
	Southwestern College, Chula Vista, California
	The Kitchen, New york
	University of California at Irvine
1976	Ewing Gallery, University of Melbourne, Australia
	Auckland Art Gallery, New Zealand
	University of Akron, Ohio
	Ohio State University, Columbus
	Cirrus Editions Gallery, Los Angeles
	James Corcoran Gallery, Los Angeles
1977	Galleria Massimo Valsecchi, Milan
	Matrix, Hartford Atheneum, Connecticut
	John Baldessari: Films, Fox Venice Theatre, Venice, California
	Robert Self Gallery, London
	Julian Pretto Gallery, New York
1978	Portland Center for the Visual Arts, Oregon
	Sonnabend Gallery, New York
	Recent Films, Theatre Vanguard, Los Angeles
	Films by Baldessari, Artists' Space, New York
	3 Films, Pacific Film Archives, Berkeley, California
	Baldessari: New Films, Whitney Museum, New York
1979	Halle für Internationale Neue Kunst, Zurich
1980	*Fugitive Essays*, Sonnabend Gallery, New York
1981	*Werken 1966–1981*, Stedelijk Van Abbemuseum, Eindhoven, Netherlands
	John Baldessari/Deborah Turbeville, Sonnabend Gallery, New York
	Wright State University, Dayton, Ohio
1982	Stedelijk Van Abbemuseum, Eindhoven, Netherlands
	Museum Folkwang, Essen, West Germany
	CEPA Gallery, Buffalo, New York
	Albright-Knox Art Gallery, Buffalo, New York
	Galerie Rudiger Schottle, Munich
	Sonnabend Gallery, New York
	Samangallery, Genoa, Italy
	Contemporary Art Center, Cincinnati
	Wright State University, Dayton, Ohio
	Contemporary Arts Museum, Houston, Texas
1983	Galerie Stampa, Basle
	Marian Deson Gallery, Chicago
	Galerie Arte Viva, Basle
1984	Sonnabend Gallery, New York
	Margo Leavin Gallery, Los Angeles
	Galerie Peter Pakesch, Vienna
	Galerie Gillespie-Laage-Salomon, Paris
1985	Le Consortium Centre d'Art Contemporain, Dijon, France
	De Vleeshal, Middelburg, Netherlands
1986	Sonnabend Gallery, New York
	University of California, Berkeley
	University of California, Santa Barbara
	Margo Leavin Gallery, Los Angeles

Selected Group Exhibitions:

1960	*The Uncommon Denominator: 13 San Diego Painters*, La Jolla Art Center, California (toured the United States)
1969	*Pop Art Redefined*, Hayward Gallery, London
1976	*Painting and Sculpture in California: The Modern Era*, San Francisco Museum of Modern Art (travelled to the National Collection of Fine Arts, Smithsonian Institution, Washington, D.C.)
1977	*Photography as Means*, Center for Photographic Art, La Jolla, California
1978	*Narration*, Institute of Contemporary Art, Boston
	Art about Art, Whitney Museum, New York
1979	*American Photography in the 70's*, Art Institute of Chicago
1981	*Westkunst*, Messehallen, Cologne
1985	*Extending the Perimeters of 20th Century Art*, San Francisco Museum of Modern Art
1987	*Avant-Garde in the Eighties*, Los Angeles County Museum of Art

Collections:

Museum of Modern Art, New York; Los Angeles County Museum of Art; La Jolla Museum of Art, California; Wallraf-Richartz Museum, Cologne; Stedelijk Museum, Amsterdam; Kunstmuseum, Basle.

Publications:

By BALDESSARI: books—*Ingres and Other Parables*, London 1972; *Choosing: Green Beans*, Milan 1972; *Throwing 3 Balls in the Air to Get a Straight Line (Best of 36 Attempts)*, Milan 1973; *Throwing a Ball Once to Get 3 Melodies and 15 Chords*, Irvine, California 1975; *4 Events and Reactions*, Amsterdam 1975; *Artists and Photographers*, portfolio, with others, New York 1975; *Raw Prints*, portfolio, Los Angeles 1976; *Brutus Killed Caesar*, Akron, Ohio 1976; *A Sentence of 13 Parts (with 12 Alternative Verbs) Ending in Fable*, Hamburg 1977; articles—"Photography and Language," interview, in *John Baldessari*, exhibition catalogue, Los Angeles

John Baldessari: *Vanitas Series—With Hair and Bubbles*, 1981

1976; "John Baldessari: Interview," with Diane Spodarek, in *Detroit Artists' Monthly,* June 1976; interview with Leo Rubinfein in *Art in America* (New York), September/October 1978; also, interview for the Video Data Bank, School of the Art Institute of Chicago, 1973.

On BALDESSARI: books—*Pop Art Redefined* by John Russell and Suzi Gablik, London and New York 1969; *Conceptual Art* by Ursula Meyers, New York 1971; *Video Visions: A Medium Discovers Itself* by Jonathan Price, New York 1972; *Video Art* by Ira Schneider and Beryl Korot, New York 1976; *John Baldessari,* exhibition catalogue, with texts by Marcia Tucker and Robert Pinsuc-Witten, and an interview by Nancy Drew, Dayton, Ohio 1981; articles—"John Baldessari, Sonnabend Gallery" by Nancy Foote in *Artforum* (New York), September 1976; "When Is a Book Not a Book?" by Grace Glueck in the *New York Times,* 18 March 1977; "Pictures and Picture Books" by April Kingsley in the *Soho Weekly News* (New York), 21 April 1977; "John Baldessari and Daniel Buren" by Jeff Perrone in *Artforum* (New York), September 1977; "Making Light of Heavy Art" by Kenneth Baker in the *Boston Phoenix,* 10 January 1978; review by Paul Stimson in *Art in America* (New York), March/April 1979; "John Baldessari's Blasted Allegories" by Hal Foster in *Artforum* (New York), October 1979; "Well Hung" by Ben Lifson in the *Village Voice* (New York), 5 November 1980; review by Joan Casademont in *Artforum* (New York), January 1981.

WHAT THINKS ME NOW.

I want to re-enchant and remythologize.
   I want to drill a hole deep-down in art to discover the mythic infrastructure.
(I am less interested in the form art takes than the meaning an image evokes.)
(I am interested in myth as a way of knowing.)
I want to express myself in archetypal imagery.
I want to stand at the edge rather than the center.
I want to recall what I always knew. (I am interested in what thinks me.)
(I would rather discover the memory of the soul than to be correct in thought.)

I want to move away from racial amnesia.
I want to produce images that startle one into recollection.
I want to think of history so that it is not a record of events but is a method of release.
I want to see the world as something else than serial progression.
I want to know the matrix of events in history.
(What appears to be trivial in a fairy tale, etc. could be the lingering remnant of the memory of the soul.)
I want to engage in the spiritualization of matter and the materialization of the spirit.
I want to think of time as synchronic.
I want to see all variants of a myth in a single imaginary space w/o regard to historical context.
I want to sift information from noise.
I want to avoid the tedium of sectarianism and dogma.
I want to consider language as an articulation of the limited to express the unlimited.
I want to be at home with the paradoxical, the ambiguous, and the random.
I want to eroticize time, consciousness, and human culture.
I want to blur the boundaries between truth and fiction.

—John Baldessari

Baldessari is a Californian who—like his long-time friend William Wegman—rejected a '60s modernism become too self-important and aloofly formalist. He will for long be known for his declaration *I will not make any more boring art,* and the burning in 1970 of his earlier work, the ashes ending up in a book-shaped urn marked with his name and the dates 1953–1967. Although Baldessari is more broadly classed a conceptual artist and has worked with photography, video, film and texts, through his use of media imagery, he can be held a pioneer "image ap-

propriator." (Salle and Brauntuch number among his students.) His work harbors ambiguity, yet its mystery is not that of modernist symbolism and ego-centered stream-of-consciousness. Instead Baldessari can be said to be a post-modernist in his casual and good-natured didacticism; and thus a post-structuralist in his dissection of signs and their information bearing dimensions. His pervasive flavor has then been an enigmatic conjunction of imagery, often with text to influence the nature of the viewer's perception, and most often pointing to some semantic issue: the cliches of perception a constant focus. Such an overriding philosophical reflection in his work bespeaks his long-time absorption with spiritual relationships in the world, perhaps evinced by his church membership into early adulthood. While in his earliest such work, in the later 1960s and on into the following decade, the construct was achieved through his own photography, he then became a collector of literature and images. When he turned to the popular media, and for instance came to use television imagery as a major source, he positioned three cameras to face three soundless TV screens; within the past decade, his most important source came to be still photographic scenes from the history of film, thus tacitly acknowledging their ready availability and his residence in Los Angeles. Through his wit and intelligence, Baldessari has not permitted himself to become a mere illustrator of theoretical premises—he retains his position as major representative of a cerebral-founded visual art.

—Joshua B. Kind

BALTHUS.

French. Born Comte Balthazar Klowssowski de Rola, of Polish parents, in Paris, 29 February 1908. Studied in Paris in 1924, but mainly self-taught in art. Served in the French Army in Morocco, 1929–33; recalled, Paris, 1939, but demobilized shortly thereafter because of ill health. Married in 1937. First book of drawings published, Geneva, 1920; worked on frescoes, Church of Beatenburg, Bernese Oberland, 1928; designed sets and costumes for *The Cenci* by Antonin Artaud, Paris, 1935; during Occupation, lived in Switzerland; returned to Paris, 1945; designed sets and costumes for *Cosi fan Tutti,* Aix-en-Provence, 1950; settled in Morvan, France, 1954. Director, French Academy, Rome, since 1961. Recipient: Premio Via Condotti, Rome, 1983. Address: Viale Trinite dei Monti 1, Villa Medicis, 00187 Rome, Italy.

Individual Exhibitions:

1934	Galerie Pierre, Paris
1938	Pierre Matisse Gallery, New York
1943	Galerie Moos, Geneva
1946	Wildenstein Galerie, Paris
1949	Pierre Matisse Gallery, New York
1952	Lefevre Gallery, London
1956	Wildenstein Galerie, Paris
	Museum of Modern Art, New York
1961	Galleria Civica d'Arte Moderna, Turin
1962	Pierre Matisse Gallery, New York
1963	E. V. Thaw and Company, New York
1964	Arts Club of Chicago
	Massachusetts Institute of Technology, Cambridge
1966	Casino Municipal, Knokke-le-Zoute, Belgium
	Pierre Matisse Gallery, New York
	Musée des Arts Decoratifs, Paris
	Galerie Henriette Gomes, Paris
1967	Pierre Matisse Gallery, New York
1968	Tate Gallery, London
1969	Donald Morris Gallery, Detroit
1971	*Dessins et Aquarelles,* Galerie Claude Bernard, Paris
1973	Musée Cantini, Marseilles
1977	Pierre Matisse Gallery, New York

1978 Pierre Matisse Gallery, New York
1980 Scuola Grande di San Giovanni Evangelista, Venice
1982 Museo d'Arte, Spoleto, Italy
1983 Musée d'Art Moderne, Paris

Selected Group Exhibitions:

1976 *Group Exhibition*, Galerie Jacques Benador, Geneva
1980 *Biennale*, Venice
1981 *The New Spirit in Painting*, Royal Academy of Arts, London
1982 *A Century of Modern Drawing*, British Museum, London

Collections:

Centre National d'Art Contemporain, Paris; Tate Gallery, London; Museum of Modern Art, New York; Hirshhorn Museum and Sculpture Garden, Smithsonian Institution, Washington, D.C.; Wadsworth Atheneum, Hartford, Connecticut; Institute of Art, Minneapolis; Art Institute of Chicago; National Gallery of Victoria, Melbourne.

Publications:

On BALTHUS: books—*Balthus,* exhibition catalogue, by James Thrall Soby, New York 1938; *Balthus,* exhibition catalogue, by Albert Camus, New York 1949; *Balthus and a Selection of French Paintings* by Cyril Connolly, London 1952; *Balthus,* exhibition catalogue, by James Thrall Soby, New York 1956; *Balthus,* exhibition catalogue, by John Russell, London 1968; *Balthus: Dessins et Aquarelles,* exhibition catalogue, by Jean Leymarie, Paris 1971.

Nearly unique in this century in his allegiance to the traditions of figurative art, Balthus has worked aloof from the torrents of abstraction. He has contributed at least three great portraits to those traditions—of the painters Derain and Miró and of the art patron Marie Laure, Vicomtesse de Noilly. He has added luminous, direct landscapes as well, and, perhaps most importantly of all, a series of narrative compositions centering on young girls.

If the portraits contain a little of the doll-like quality sometimes produced by Goya, the large compositions of Paris streets recall the arrested drama that charges the frozen figures of Seurat—also, in another way, doll-like. And of course these unexplained, "plotless" dramas raise many questions, chiefly: who are these people? and what are they doing? We are made uneasy in the presence of gesturing orientals, misshapen children, streets without traffic, forms smoothed down as though carved from wood. The isolation of each figure—though caught forever in reaction to others—reminds us of Piero della Francesca. Like that painter, Balthus stops time, "correcting reality" to use the marvellous phrase Camus once wrote in an essay about him.

Again and again it is evident how much Balthus has learned from the painters of the past. Even the "awkwardly" posed adolescents—forever at their games, or reading, sprawled on couch or floor for which he is most famous—can be seen echoed, say, in the posture of Noah, passed-out, in "The Drunkenness of Noah" by Giovani Bellini. And yet the formal power of these paintings, with their close-value browns, greys and reds, their light-struck whites, and their elaborate design, cannot displace the force of their subject matter: young nudes with heads thrown back in Mannerist transport; girls with legs raised in invitation, arms behind their heads provocatively; girls kneeling uncomfortably over books; girls arched over chairs—all, usually, occupying rooms of stifling respectability and often accompanied by disturbing, unclear—in the sense of who or what they are—dwarf-like figures busy pulling back curtains or lighting fires. Many compositions feature a cipher cat sometimes sitting sphinx-like, sometimes actively involved wearing a cunning, even satanic expression.

It is all a bit like the world of Lewis Carroll taken several extreme steps further. No wonder Balthus has been able to create a superbly apt set of illustrations for *Wuthering Heights* and that Picasso, a master of erotic games, kept one of Balthus' paintings nearby until his death.

—Ralph Pomeroy

BANNARD, Walter Darby.

American. Born in New Haven, Connecticut, 23 September 1934. Educated at Phillips Exeter Academy, Exeter, New Hampshire, 1950–52; Princeton University, New Jersey, 1952–56, B.A. 1956. Married Mya Hay in 1977; son: William. Independent artist, Princeton, since 1956. Visiting Critic, Columbia University Art School, New York, 1968; Visiting Professor, Princeton University Creative Arts Program, 1974; Visiting Artist, Kent State University, Ohio, 1974; Visiting Artist and Lecturer, University of Texas at Austin, 1975; Visiting Critic, Brooklyn Museum Art School, New York, 1975; Instructor in Painting, San Francisco Art Institute, 1979. Contributing Editor, *Artforum,* New York, 1973–74. Juror, Davidson National Print and Drawing Competition, North Carolina, 1974; Adviser, *The Flowering of American Folk Art,* exhibition at the Whitney Museum, New York, 1974; Curator, *Hans Hofmann* exhibition, Hirshhorn Museum, Washington, D.C., 1976. Member, Art Advisory Committee, Phillips Exeter Academy, since 1977; Co-Chairman, International Panel on the Visual Arts, National Endowment for the Arts, Washington, D.C., since 1979. Recipient: Guggenheim Fellowship, 1968; National Endowment for the Arts Award, 1968; Purchase Award, New Jersey State Museum, 1971; Francis J. Greenburger Foundation Award, 1986. Agent: Knoedler Contemporary Art, 19 East 70th Street, New York, New York 10021. Address: Box 1157, Princeton, New Jersey 08540, U.S.A.

Individual Exhibitions:

1965 Tibor de Nagy Gallery, New York
     Kasmin Gallery, London
1966 Tibor de Nagy Gallery, New York (twice)
     Richard Feigen Gallery, Chicago
1967 Nicholas Wilder Gallery, Los Angeles
     Tibor de Nagy Gallery, New York
1968 Kasmin Gallery, London
     Tibor de Nagy Gallery, New York
1969 Kasmin Gallery, London
     Tibor de Nagy Gallery, New York
     New Gallery, Bennington College, Vermont
     David Mirvish Gallery, Toronto
1970 David Mirvish Gallery, Toronto
     Lawrence Rubin Gallery, New York
     Joseph Helman Gallery, St. Louis
1971 Neuendorf Gallery, Cologne
1972 Lawrence Rubin Gallery, New York
     Newport Harbor Art Museum, Newport Beach, California
     Kasmin Gallery, London
     David Mirvish Gallery, Toronto
1973 Lawrence Rubin Gallery, New York
     Pasadena Art Museum
     Walter Darby Bannard, 1957–1973, Baltimore Art Museum (retrospective; toured the United States)
     Tibor de Nagy Gallery, Houston (opening show)
1974 Knoedler Contemporary Art, New York (twice)
1975 Tibor de Nagy Gallery, Houston
     Douglas Drake Gallery, Kansas City, Kansas
     David Mirvish Gallery, Toronto
     Olympia Gallery, Philadelphia
     Knoedler Contemporary Art, New York
1976 Knoedler Contemporary Art, New York
1977 Knoedler Contemporary Art, New York
     Watson/de Nagy Gallery, Houston (twice)
     Lamont Gallery, Phillips Exeter Academy, New Hampshire

     Greenberg Gallery, St. Louis
1978 Knoedler Contemporary Art, New York
     David Mirvish Gallery, Toronto
1979 Knoedler Contemporary Art, New York
     Watson/de Nagy Gallery, Houston
     Miami University, Oxford, Ohio
1980 Knoedler Contemporary Art, New York
     Douglas Drake Gallery, Kansas City, Kansas
     Ulrich Art Museum, Wichita
     State University of Kansas, Wichita
     Gallery 700, Milwaukee
     Knoedler Gallery, New York
     Wichita State University, Kansas
     Douglas Drake Gallery, Kansas City, Kansas
     Gallery 700, Milwaukee, Wisconsin
1981 Watson/de Nagy Gallery, New York
     Knoedler Gallery, New York
1982 Martin Gerard Gallery, Edmonton, Alberta
     Knoedler Gallery, New York
     Watson/de Nagy Gallery, New York
     James Madison University, Harrisonburg, Virginia
     Clayworks Studio Workshop, New York
     Virginia Technical University, Blacksburg
1983 Mint Museum of Art, Charlotte, North Carolina
     Martin Gerard Gallery, Edmonton, Alberta
     Edmonton Art Gallery, Alberta
1984 Knoedler Gallery, New York
     Watson/de Nagy Gallery, New York
1986 Salander-O'Reilly Galleries, New York
1987 St. Lawrence University, Canton, New York

Selected Group Exhibitions:

1965 *The Responsive Eye,* Museum of Modern Art, New York (toured the United States)
1968 *Art of the Real,* Museum of Modern Art, New York (toured the United States and Europe)
1970 *Color and Field 1890–1970,* Albright Knox Art Gallery, Buffalo, New York (toured the United States)
1974 *The Great Decade of American Abstraction: Modernist Art 1960 to 1970,* Museum of Fine Arts, Houston
1977 *Private Images: Photographs by Painters,* Los Angeles County Museum of Art
1979 *Art in America After World War II,* Guggenheim Museum, New York
1980 *Aspects of the 70's: Painterly Abstracolor,* Brockton Art Museum, Massachusetts
1983 *Touch,* Laguna Gloria Art Museum, Austin, Texas
1985 *PrePostmodern,* St. Lawrence University, Canton, New York
1987 *Luminous Impressions,* Mint Museum of Art, Charlotte, North Carolina

Collections:

Guggenheim Museum, New York; Metropolitan Museum of Art, New York; Whitney Museum, New York; Museum of Modern Art, New York; Albright-Knox Art Gallery, Buffalo, New York; Princeton University, New Jersey; Newark Museum, New Jersey; Fogg Art Museum, Cambridge, Massachusetts; Baltimore Museum of Art; Museum of Fine Arts, Houston; University of Texas at Austin.

Publications:

By BANNARD: books—*The Structure of Color,* exhibition catalogue, New York 1971; *Hans Hofmann,* exhibition catalogue, Washington D.C. 1976; articles—"Color, Paint and Present-Day Painting" in *Artforum* (New York), April 1966; "Present-Day Art and Ready-Made Styles" in *Artforum* (New York), December 1966; "Cubism, Abstract Expressionism and David Smith" in *Artforum* (New York), April 1968; "Willem de Kooning's Retrospective at the Museum of Modern Art" in *Artforum* (New York), April 1969; review of *Beyond Modern Sculptures* by Jack Burnham, in *Artforum* (New York), May 1969; "Hofmann's Rectangles" in *Artforum* (New York), Summer 1969; "Notes on American Painting of the 60's" in *Artforum* (New York), January 1970; "Color Painting and the Map Problem" in *Artforum* (New York), March 1970; "The Artist and Politics" in *Artforum* (New York), September 1970; "Notes on An Auction" in *Artforum* (New York), September 1970; "Touch and Scale:

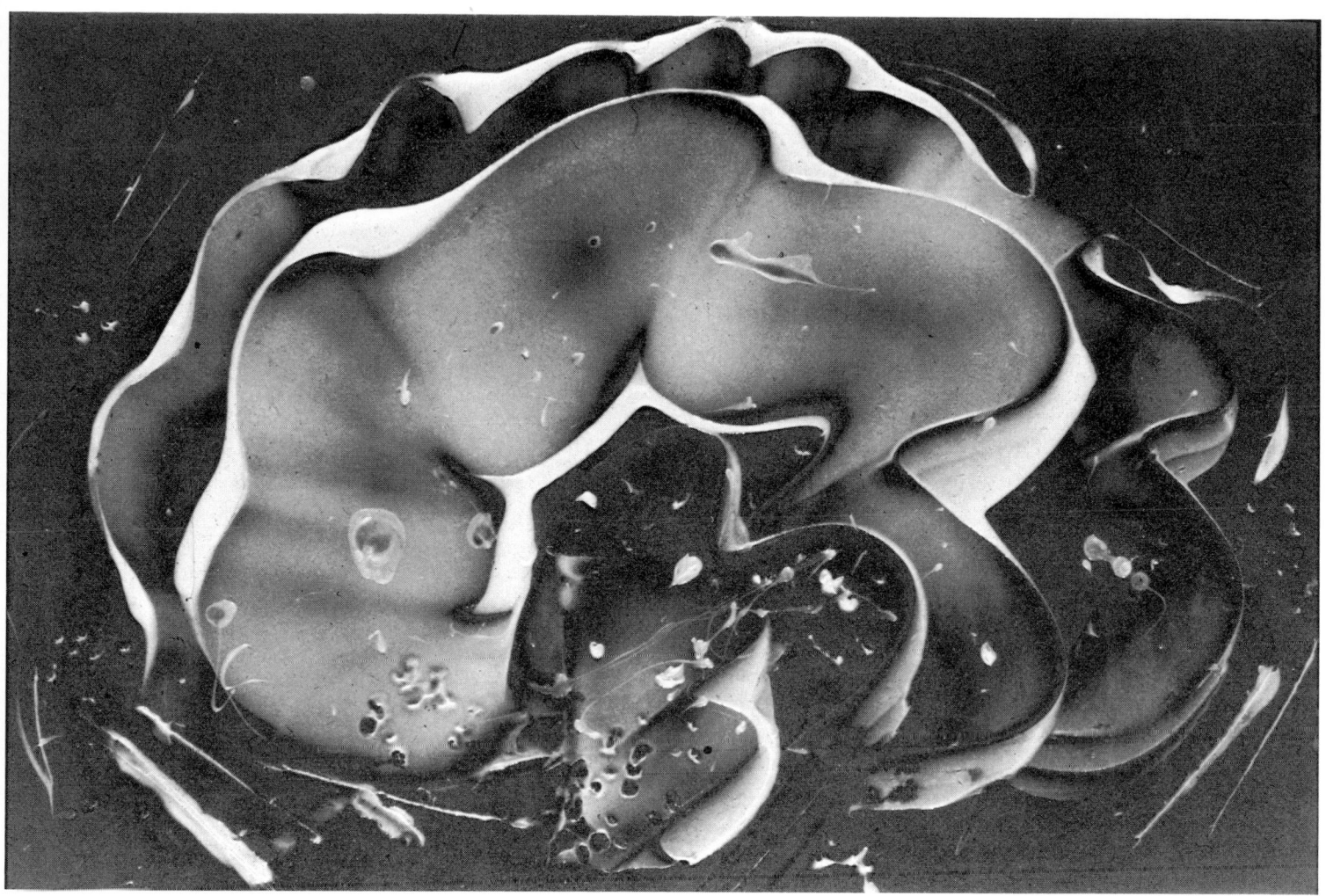

Walter Darby Bannard: *The Flurry*, 1982

Cubism, Pollock, Newman and Still" in *Artforum* (New York), September 1970; review of Michael Fried's *Morris Lewis* in *The Print Collector's Newsletter* (New York), July/August 1971; "Noland's New Paintings" in *Artforum* (New York), November 1971; *The Structure of Color*, exhibition catalogue (New York), June 1972; review of Thomas B. Hess' *Barnett Newman*, in the *Paint Collector's Newsletter* (New York), July/August 1972; "The War Against the Good in Art" in the *New York Times*, 6 August 1972; "Quality, Style and Olitski" in *Artforum* (New York), October 1972; statement in *Walter Darby Bannard*, exhibition catalogue, Newport Beach, California 1972; "He Comes to Praise the Net" in the *New York Times*, 1 July 1973; "Morris Louis and the Restructured Picture" in *Studio International* (London), July/August 1974; "The Museum and the Living Artist," essay in *On Understanding Art Museums*, New York 1974; "Art Quality and the Formalist Controversy" in *Quadrille* (Vermont), Fall 1974; "On Postmodernism" in *Arts* (New York), February 1984; "The Art Glut" in *Arts* (New York), December 1986.

On BANNARD: books—*The Development of Modern Painting: Jackson Pollock to the Present*, exhibition catalogue, with text by R. T. Buck Jr., St. Louis 1969; *The Structure of Color*, exhibition catalogue, with an essay by Marcia Tucker, New York 1971; *6 Painters*, exhibition catalogue, by G. Smith, New York 1971; *Walter Darby Bannard*, exhibition catalogue, with an essay and interview by J. H. Cone, Baltimore 1973; *Walter Darby Bannard*, exhibition catalogue, with text by Terry Fenton, Edmonton, Alberta 1983; articles—"Darby Bannard: The Possibilities of Color" by David Bourdon in *Art International* (New York), May 1967, "London Commentary: Bannard at Kasmin" by J. Mashek in *Studio International* (London), November 1969; "Walter Bannard at Kasmin Gallery" by John Eiderfeld in *Studio International* (London), November 1972; "Walter Darby Bannard at the Baltimore Museum" by David Bourdon in *Art in America* (New York), March/April 1974; "Third Generation Abstraction" by K. Carpenter in *Arts Magazine* (New York), February 1975; "The Impasto World of Walter Darby Bannard" by V. Raynor in the *New York Times*, 29 May 1981; "Walter Darby Bannard's New Pictures" by J. Walsh in *Arts* (New York), September 1982; "Walter Darby Bannard" by J. Link in *Arts* (New York), October 1986.

Like everybody else, I just keep working and try to do the best I can.

—Walter Darby Bannard

Walter Darby Bannard is probably as well known for his perceptive writings about art as he is for his economical abstract paintings. A frequent contributor to art journals, he is also the author of, among other essays, an important critical study of the work of Hans Hofmann. Bannard, however, considers himself first and foremost a painter and feels that being a practitioner gives him special insight as a critic.

His reputation was first established as a painter, soon after he turned 30, when he began to exhibit spare color abstractions that marked him as one of the most thoughtful and original young artists of the mid-60s. By then, Bannard had been painting seriously for about a decade, since his student days at Princeton. Frank Stella had been a fellow student and a friend, but the two young painters worked in quite different ways. Unlike Stella, Bannard was unaffected by the seductions of minimalism. His earliest paintings often seemed to allude, albeit distantly, to landscape motifs or floating figures, and while he soon radically simplified these pictures, it was to clarify what they were about, not to conform to theory.

During his first years of concentrated paintings, Bannard realized that his primary concern was color and stripped his imagery down to allow himself to focus on how colors affected one another when set side by side. Like many of the best young painters of the period, he arrived at simplified, clear formats that resolved, for the moment, issues of where to put color. Bannard's paintings from about 1959 through 1961 were usually symmetrical, often square, with narrow framing borders and centralized disc shapes. Thinly painted, with no sense of anything having been concealed, they demonstrated Bannard's opposition to the layered, gestural de Kooning-inspired version of Abstract Expressionism of the time. Yet even the most severe of his "band" and "framed circle" pictures of these years was conspicuously handmade and intuitive. Bannard may have dissected painting into what he saw as essential components of field, figure and edge, but he did so in the service of making color as eloquent as possible, not as a demonstration of a system.

In the 1960s and '70s, Bannard seemed primarily a colorist. His distinctive palette of odd, chalky pastels was unmistakeable and criticism of the time frequently praised him for having managed to detach cosmetic, candy hues from their conventional associations. Bannard, on the other hand, claims simply to have liked the colors and to have had no particular associations with them. His primary concern remained the unexpected juxtaposition of the disparate. The extreme close-valuing of his palette brought even the most unlikely pairings into tonal unity and at the same time, made the smallest nuances of differences in hue or surface of overmastering importance. Bannard's sensibility was so subtle that, on occasion, the chief distinction between areas of identical color could be the difference between mat and gloss.

Bannard has never hesitated to change the look of his pictures quite dramatically, in order to explore his changing ideas of what a painting could be. During the '60s and '70s, his compositions remained essentially geometric, but became increasingly complex, as though he had expanded his reach. The pared-down, centered band and framed circle layouts gave way to arrangements of hard-edged intersecting arcs and later to "checkerboards" and floating rectangles. He seemed to rely less on predetermined placement of colors or, at least, on predetermined *areas* in which to set colors, and by the late '60s, he seemed more willing to let the making of the picture dictate its structure rather than to rely on a simplified and preconceived format. His profound understanding of Hofmann's ability to construct with color is apparent in these paintings, particularly in a series that juxtaposed relatively solidly painted rectangles against multicolored grounds. They could be described as "Hofmann disembodied", a translation of Hofmannesque attitudes into then current notions about color as pure optical experience, richly evocative and expressive, but as detached from any material presence as possible.

Bannard's pictures of the late '60s and early '70s are remarkable for their complex structure: overlapping layers of color, repeated passes of a spreading tool, create intricate intersecting color shapes. Only Bannard's meticulous orchestration of pale values keeps these canvases unified and makes one's experience of them that of all-over painting rather than of violent polychromy. The tension between their deadpan surfaces—an overwhelming sense of a flat, uninterrupted expanse—and their notably broad color range—which breaks that expanse into smaller units—constitutes part of these pictures' strength and part of Bannard's originality.

Bannard's next series, made in the early '70s, appears, in retrospect, like a deliberate effort to explore completely opposite notions to those examined in the pale, flat color paintings of the previous few years. Each of the series has a single, dominant, startling hue—off-white, poison green or funky lavender, for example—distributed in thick, aggressively scraped strokes. Paint is piled and trowelled in broad bands that fold around one another; underlying colors are glimpsed between strokes. The act of moving the paint across the surface of the canvas is what *makes* the image, literally and metaphorically. It is a logical extension of the attitude that led to Bannard's checkerboards of the preceeding years, but all vestiges of preconception have been banished. The checkerboards and their fellows were made very directly, but still depended upon a tacit acknowledgement of the given vertical and horizontal dimensions of the canvas. In Bannard's best paintings of the series that followed, there is no sense of a preexisting rectangle's having been divided. Instead, the expanse and dimension of the painting seem to have been created by the momentary coalescence of the broad, juicy strokes of paint.

Bannard relaxed his innate sense of the geometric in his subsequent series, while giving free rein to his growing taste for materiality. Like many of his colleagues, he was fascinated with the expanded properties of the acrylic paints and gels beginning to be commonly available in the late '70s and early '80s: thickeners and additives that allowed greater surface advantage of these possibilities, exploiting gel-thickened acrylic's ability to retain the mark of a tool or the rhythm of a gesture. A group of pictures from the early '80s depended upon his typically surprising color sensibility, but presented in new ways; underlying layers of color were revealed by the pulling back of a superimposed layer of thicker, shinier paint in a contrasting hue. For the first time, drawing and surface inflection—here a playful scalloping—seemed as important as color itself. The danger was that Bannard's method could be a little insistent, but in the most successful of the series, inventive color and exuberant drawing made considerations of how the pictures were made seem irrelevant.

The next series was still more complex, as Bannard layered a variety of paint applications, masking and reexcavating buried courses of color. As surfaces grew more elaborate, however, color became more restrained, so that the series is characterized by a range of greys, silvers and unnameable neutrals. As if in reaction to the density and complexity of these pictures, Bannard's most recent paintings are as direct and pared down as those of 20 years ago. They are

once again transparent and made, apparently, by a single campaign of over-scaled sweeps and passes. The best seem to happen as we look, drawing, painting and structure having magically and instantaneously fused. Bannard has, for the moment, abandoned the high chroma that preoccupied him until a few years ago, but paradoxically, the subtle metallic greys, greens, sepias and the like of his 1987 pictures seem closer, in their clarity, to the pastels of his earlier palette than to the "off" shades of the thick, worked pictures that preceeded them. In the earlier, thickly painted canvases, neutral hues appeared to have been the result of many different colors' cancelling each other out; by contrast, Bannard's newer pictures have a limpid, monochrome transparency.

Of course, the monochrome, textured, all-over picture is not unique to Bannard, any more than paintings based on thinly applied and various colors were unique to him in the 1960s. He shares common attitudes with, for example, his older colleagues, Kenneth Noland and Jules Olitski, and his contemporary, Lawrence Poons. All take as their point of departure the assumption that a painting is a flat surface whose raw materials can be both expressive and communicative in themselves and the carriers of the painter's deepest feelings. In a period riddled with trend, dictated by fashion, Bannard takes his place among the uncompromising American artists who have remained faithful to these notions. In his more than 25 years of painting, Bannard's work has provided intense pleasure and, at the same time, it has been a rigorous examination of the implications of post-war abstraction. He has been described as a lyrical painter, but his lyricism depends on considerable toughness. The intelligence manifest in Bannard's writing is equally present in his art.

—Karen Wilkin

BARKER, Clive.

British. Born in Luton, Bedfordshire, 29 August 1940. Educated in Luton primary schools; studied at the Luton College of Technology and Art, 1951–56. Married the artist, Rose Bruen, in 1961; sons: Tad and Erasmus. Worked at Vauxhall Motors, Luton, 1960–61; as a pawnbroker, in London, 1962–64; began creating art objects, 1962; worked on series of 12 bronze studies of Francis Bacon, 1978; moved to Malvern, Worcestershire, 1978. Lecturer, Maidstone School of Art, Kent, 1965; Croydon School of Art, 1971. Recipient: Arts Council Purchase Prize, London, 1978; Elephant Trust Award, London, 1983. Address: 6 The Clock Tower, Heath Street, London NW3, England.

Individual Exhibitions:

1968   Robert Fraser Gallery, London
1969   Hanover Gallery, London
1974   Anthony d'Offay Gallery, London
1978   Felicity Samuel Gallery, London (with Francis Bacon)
1981   *Sculpture, Drawings and Prints,* Mappin Art Gallery, Sheffield (toured the U.K., 1981–82)
1983   Imperial War Museum, London
1985   Wolverhampton Art Gallery, Staffordshire
1987   National Portrait Gallery, London

Selected Group Exhibitions:

1962   *Young Contemporaries,* FBA Galleries, London
1968   *Young British Artists,* Museum of Modern Art, New York

1969   *Pop Art,* Hayward Gallery, London
1971   *Metamorphose de l'Objet,* Palais de Beaux-Arts, Brussels (toured Europe)
1975   *Bienal,* Sao Paulo
1977   *British Artists of the '60s,* Tate Gallery, London
1981   *British Sculpture in the 20th Century,* Whitechapel Art Gallery, London
1984   *British Pop Art,* Robert Fraser Gallery, London
1986   *Contrariwise Surrealism and Britain 1930–86,* Glynn Vivian Art Gallery, Swansea (travelled to Bath, Newcastle and Llandudno)
1987   *Pop Art—UK, USA,* Odakyu Grand Gallery, Tokyo (travelled to Osaka and Yokohama)

Collections:

Arts Council of Great Britain, London; Imperial War Museum, London; Victoria and Albert Museum, London; Tate Gallery, London; Kunsthalle, Mannheim; Smithsonian Institution, Washington, D.C.; National Portrait Gallery, London; Wolverhampton Art Gallery, Staffordshire; Ferens Art Gallery, Hull, Yorkshire.

Publications:

On BARKER: books—*Pop Art* by Christopher Finch, London 1968; *Pop Art Redefined* by John Russell, London 1969; *Image as Language* by Christopher Finch, London 1969; *Art in Britain 1969–1970* by Edward Lucie-Smith, London 1971; *Heads and Chariots,* exhibition catalogue, by Sir Roland Penrose, London 1974; *Clive Barker: Sculpture, Drawings and Prints,* exhibition catalogue, by George Melly, Sheffield, Yorkshire 1981; *Clive Barker: Portraits,* exhibition catalogue, with introduction by Norbert Lynton, London 1987.

Clive Barker initially made his name in the late 1960s with chromeplated sculptures of steel, bronze and brass both of objects from everyday life—including buckets, Coca Cola bottles, cowboy boots, a newspaper and even a set of false teeth—and of artefacts conceived as materializations from the work of famous painters such as Magritte, Picasso and Soutine. Of all these homages the most Pop in flavour were undoubtedly *Van Gogh's Chair* (chrome-plated bronze, 1966) and *Van Gogh's Sunflowers* (bronze, 1969), both of them devoted to images which had entered the public domain through an incessant reproduction by which the aura of the originals had been replaced by their status as icons of modern art. Barker's habit of coating his objects in a uniform shiny surface had the effect both of distancing them from reality and of creating for them a new identity as symbols of another level of experience. As Christopher Finch remarked in the catalogue to Barker's 1968 exhibition at the Robert Fraser Gallery, 'The banal is metamorphosed into the perfect . . . Their perfection is not an end in itself but acts as a foil for . . . an irony of affirmation. The perfection of an *objet d'art* is intrinsically prosaic since it contains no ambiguities . . . Barker's objects, by contrast, are lyrical in themselves—charged by the ambiguities that exist between banality and perfection.' The two *Art Boxes* that Barker produced in 1967—one in chrome-plated steel, the second in gold-plated brass—are quintessential Pop sculptures that bring together Barker's favoured theme of art about art with his innate feeling for objects. The irony of a sculptor producing a three-dimensional replica of the tools of a painter —rendering them passive and useless—is compounded by means of the simple tactic of casting actual brushes and tubes of paint. Although the human head has occupied Barker's attention at intervals since the early 1970s—notably in the threatening group of gas masks shown in 1974 and in a series of portraits of Francis Bacon, beginning with a life mask in 1969 and elaborated in a group of studies in 1978—it is from other art that he has continued to draw the most sustenance. *Venus Escargot* is his latest mutation of the Venus de Milo, that fragment of classical perfection which has exerted such a powerful hold over the collective imagination.

—Marco Livingstone

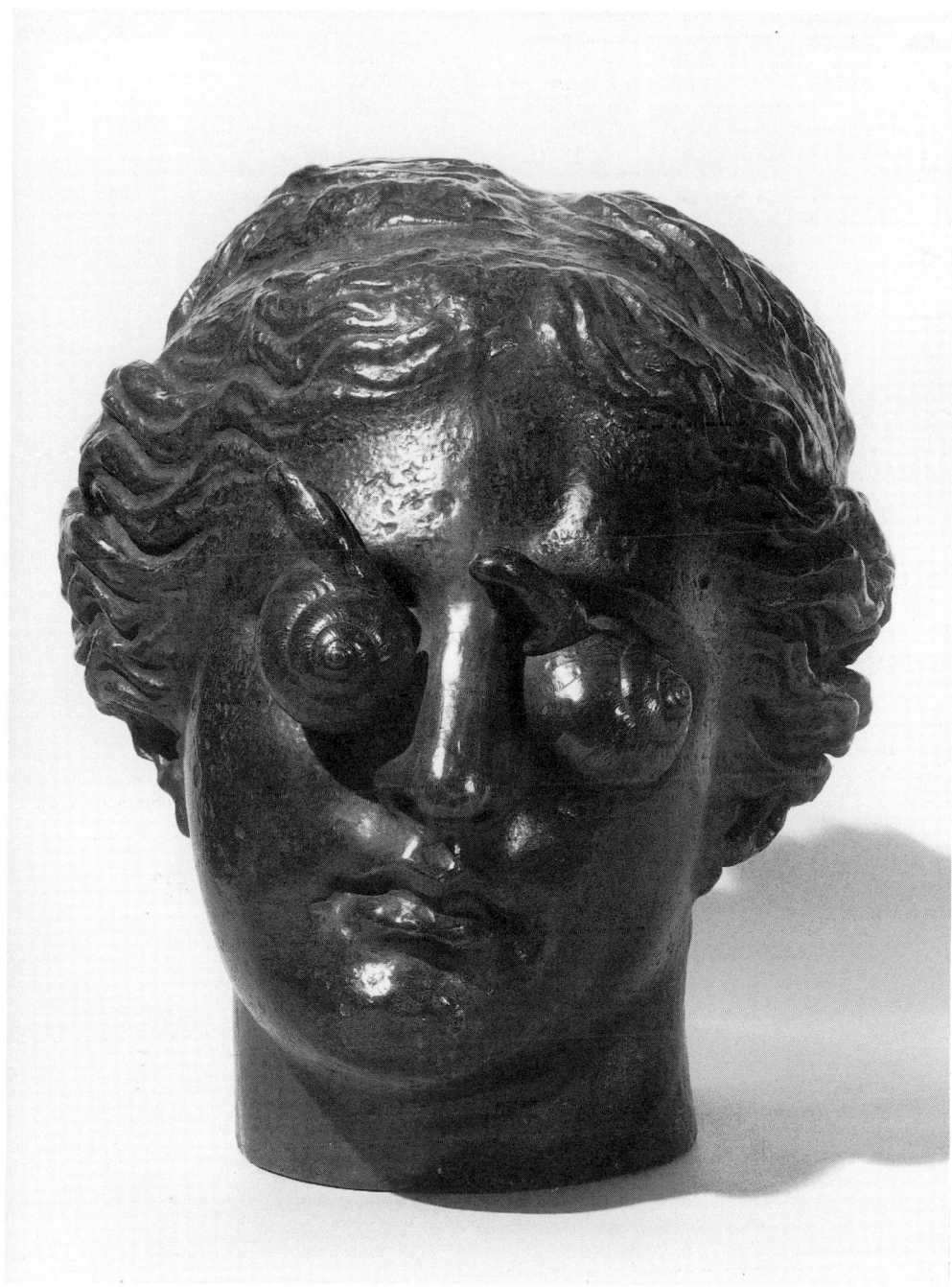

Clive Barker: *Venus Escargot,* 1987

BARRY, Robert.
American. Born in the Bronx, New York, 9 March 1936. Studied at Hunter College, New York, B.F.A., 1957, M.A. 1963. Agent: Sperone-Westwater-Fischer Inc., 142 Greene Street, New York, New York 10012. Address: c/o Hunter College, 695 Park Avenue, New York, New York 10021, U.S.A.

Individual Exhibitions:

1964	Westerly Gallery, New York
1969	Seth Siegelaub Gallery, Los Angeles
	Galleria Sperone, Turin
	Art and Project, Amsterdam
1970	Eugenia Butler Gallery, Los Angeles
	Galleria Sperone, Turin
1971	Galerie Yvon Lambert, Paris
	Galerie Paul Maenz, Cologne
	Leo Castelli Gallery, New York
	Galleria San Fedele, Milan
	Art and Project, Amsterdam
	Eugenia Butler Gallery, Los Angeles

1972	Galleria Toselli, Milan
	Jack Wendler Gallery, London
	Galerie M.T.L., Brussels
	Tate Gallery, London
	Galerie Paul Maenz, Cologne
	Leo Castelli Gallery, New York
	Art and Project, Amsterdam
1973	Galleria Sperone and Fischer, Rome
	Galeria Foksal, Warsaw
	Kabinett für Aktuelle Kunst, Bremerhaven, West Germany
1974	Galerie Yvon Lambert, Paris
	Leo Castelli Gallery, New York
	Jack Wendler Gallery, London
	Galerie Paul Maenz, Cologne
	Art and Project-M.T.L., Antwerp
	Kunstmuseum, Lucerne
	Stedelijk Museum, Amsterdam
1975	Gian Enzo Sperone Gallery, New York
	Cusack Gallery, Houston
1976	Leo Castelli Gallery, New York
	Galerie Rolf Preisig, Basle
	Galerie Paul Maenz, Cologne

	Galleria Enzo Sperone, Rome
	Portrait: Part I, Julian Pretto Gallery, New York
	Portrait: Part II, P.S. 1 Gallery, Long Island City, New York
1977	Stedelijk Van Abbemuseum, Eindhoven, Netherlands
	Robert Self Gallery, London
	Galerie Yvon Lambert, Paris
	Galerie Rudiger Schöttle, Munich
1978	Museum Folkwang, Essen
	Galerie M.T.L., Brussels
	Leo Castelli Gallery, New York
	Museum of Conceptual Art, San Francisco
	University of Colorado, Boulder
1979	Leo Castelli Gallery, New York
	Galleria François Lambert, Milan
	Galerie Rolf Preisig, Basle
	Galerie Paul Maenz, Cologne
1980	Joslyn Art Museum, Omaha, Nebraska
1987	Glynn Vivian Art Gallery, Swansea, Wales
	Camarthen Museum, Abergwili, Wales
	Oriel Gallery, Cardiff, Wales
	Galleria Christian Stein, Turin (with Lawrence Weiner)
1988	Galerie Schiessel, Munich

Selected Group Exhibitions:

1968	*8 New Artists,* Hudson River Museum, New York
1966	*Systematic Painting,* Guggenheim Museum, New York
1969	*Barry/Huebler/Kosuth/Weiner,* Seth Siegelaub Gallery, New York
	When Attitudes Become Form, Stedelijk Museum, Amsterdam (travelled to the Museum Folkwang, Essen)
1970	*Conceptual Art, Arte Povera, Land Art,* Galleria Civica d'Arte Moderna, Turin
	Nirvana, Kyoto Municipal Museum of Fine Arts, Japan
1971	*Artist, Theory and Work,* Kunsthalle, Nuremberg, West Germany
1973	*Documenta 5,* Kassel, West Germany
1974	*Concept Art,* Kunstverein, Braunschweig, West Germany
1980	*Music, Sound, Language, Theater: John Cage, Tom Marioni, Robert Barry, Joan Jonas,* Cowell College, University of California at Santa Cruz (toured the United States)

Publications:

By BARRY: books-*An Untitled Book,* Turin 1970; *One Billion Dots,* Turin 1971; *30 Pieces as of 14 June 1971,* Cologne 1971; *Two Pieces,* Turin 1972; *It Is . . . It Isn't . . . ,* Paris 1972; *Changes and Disappearences,* portfolio of 5 etchings, 1979; articles—interview, with Arthur Rose, in *Arts Magazine* (New York), February 1969; interview, with Achille Bonito Oliva, in *Domus* (Milan), August 1973; film—*Scenes 1967,* New York 1967.

On BARRY: books—*Systematic Painting,* exhibition catalogue, with text by Lawrence Alloway, New York 1966; *Arte Povera* by Germano Celant, Milan, 1969; *Conceptual Art* by Ursula Meyes, New York 1972; *6 Years: The De-Materialization of the Art Object from 1966 to 1972* by Lucy R. Lippard, New York 1973; *Idea Art* by Gregory Battcock, New York 1973; *Robert Barry,* exhibition catalogue, with text by Jean-Christophe Ammann, Lucerne 1974; *Robert Barry,* exhibition catalogue, Eindhoven, Netherlands 1977; *Robert Barry,* exhibition pamphlet, with text by Holliday T. Day, Omaha, Nebraska 1980; *Music, Sound, Language, Theater: John Cage, Tom Marioni, Robert Barry, Joan Jonas,* exhibition catalogue, edited by Robin White, with essays by Kathan Browne and others, Oakland, California 1980; articles—"Systematic Painting" by Robert Pincus-Witten in *Artforum* (New York), November 1966; "Painting Is Obsolete" by Gregory Battcock in *New York Free Press,* January 1969; "Impossible Art" by David Shirey in *Art in America* (New York), May/June 1969; "Art after Philosophy" by Joseph Kosuth in *Studio International* (London), November/December 1969; "Concept Art" by Klaus Honnef in *Kunst* (Mainz, West Germany), 1970; "Book as Artwork" by Germano Celant in *Data 1,* Milan 1971.

Jennifer Bartlett: *Squaring—2/4/16/256/65,536*, 1974

BARTLETT, Jennifer (Losch).
American. Born in Long Beach, California, 14 March 1941. Educated at Mills College, Oakland, California, 1961–63, B.A. 1963; Yale School of Art and Architecture, New Haven, Connecticut, with Jack Tworkov, James Rosenquist, Al Held and Jim Dine, 1963–65, B.F.S. 1964, M.F.A. 1965. Instructor, University of Connecticut, Storrs, 1968–72; Visiting Artist, Art Institute of Chicago, 1962. Instructor in Painting, School of Visual Arts, New York, 1972–77. Recipient: Creative Artist Public Services Fellowship, 1974; Harris Prize, Art Institute of Chicago, 1976; Lucas Visiting Lecture Award, Carleton College, Northfield, Minneapolis, 1979; Creative Arts Award, Brandeis University, Waltham, Massachusetts, 1983; American Institute of Arts and Letters Award, New York, 1983; Harris Prize and M. V. Konstamm Award, Art Institute of Chicago, 1986; American Institute of Architects Award, New York, 1986. Agent: Paula Cooper Gallery, New York. Address: c/o Paula Cooper Gallery, 155 Wooster Street, New York, New York 10012, U.S.A.

Individual Exhibitions:

1963	Mills College, Oakland, California
1970	119 Spring Street Gallery, New York
1972	Reese Palley Gallery, New York
1973	Jacob's Ladder, Washington D.C. (with Jack Tworkov)
1974	Paula Cooper Gallery, New York
	Saman Galleria, Genoa
1975	John Doyle Gallery, Chicago
	Garage, London (with Joel Shapiro)
1976	Paula Cooper Gallery, New York
	Dartmouth College, Hanover, New Hampshire

	Contemporary Art Center, Cincinnati, Ohio
1977	Wadsworth Atheneum, Hartford, Connecticut
	Paula Cooper Gallery, New York
1978	Saman Galleria, Genoa
	University of California at Irvine
	San Francisco Museum of Modern Art
	Hansen-Fuller Gallery, San Francisco
	Art Museum of South Texas, Corpus Christi
	Baltimore Art Museum
1979	Margo Leavin Gallery, Los Angeles
	The Clocktower, New York
	University of Akron, Ohio
	Carleton College, Northfield, Minnesota
	Heath Gallery, Atlanta
	Paula Cooper Gallery, New York
1980	Galerie Mukai, Tokyo
	Akron Art Institute, Ohio
	Hallwall, Buffalo, New York
	Albright-Knox Art Gallery, Buffalo, New York
1981	Paula Cooper Gallery, New York
	Margo Leavin Gallery, Los Angeles
1982	Joslyn Art Museum, Omaha
	Paula Cooper Gallery, New York
	Tate Gallery, London
	McIntosh/Drysdale Gallery, Houston
1983	Margo Leavin Gallery, Los Angeles
	Gloria Luria Gallery, Harbor Islands, Florida
	Heath Gallery, Atlanta, Georgia
	Paula Cooper Gallery, New York
1984	Brandeis University, Waltham, Massachusetts
	Long Beach Museum of Art, California
	University of California, Berkeley
1985	Paula Cooper Gallery, New York
	Lowe Art Museum, Coral Gables, Florida
	Knight Gallery, Charlotte, North Carolina
	Carpenter + Hochman Gallery, Dallas
	Hodges Taylor Gallery, Charlotte, North Carolina

	Walker Art Center, Minneapolis (travelled to Kansas City, Missouri; Brooklyn, New York; La Jolla, California; Pittsburgh)
1986	Cleveland Museum of Art, Ohio
	Greg Kucera Gallery, Seattle, Washington
1987	Harvard Graduate School of Design, Cambridge, Massachusetts
	Paula Cooper Gallery, New York

Selected Group Exhibitions:

1975	*37th Corcoran Biennial*, Corcoran Gallery, Washington, D.C.
1976	*The Liberation: 14 American Artists*, Aarhus Museum of Art, Denmark (toured Europe)
1977	*Documenta 6*, Kassel, West Germany
1978	*New Image Painting*, Whitney Museum, New York
1979	*Corner*, Hayden Gallery, Massachusetts Institute of Technology, Cambridge
1980	*Urban Encounters*, Institute of Contemporary Art, University of Pennsylvania, Philadelphia
	Printed Art: A View of 2 Decades, Museum of Modern Art, New York
1981	*Biennial Exhibition*, Whitney Museum, New York
1983	*Back to the U.S.A.*, Rheinisches Landesmuseum, Bonn (travelled to Lucerne and Stuttgart)
1987	*The Monumental Image*, Sonoma State University, Rohnert Park, California (toured the United States)

Collections:

Museum of Modern Art, New York; Metropolitan Museum of Art, New York; Whitney Museum, New York; Albright-Knox Gallery, Buffalo, New York; Yale University Art Gallery, New Haven, Connecticut; Philadelphia Museum of Art; Allen Memorial Art Museum, Oberlin, Ohio; Walker Art Center, Minneapolis; Museum of Fine Arts, Dallas.

Publications:

By BARTLETT: books—*Cleopatra I–IV,* poems, New York 1971; *Autobiography,* New York 1973; *History of the Universe* New York 1973; texts in *The World: Autobiography Issue,* edited by Lewis Warsh, New York 1973.

On BARTLETT: books—*Painting and Sculpture Today,* exhibition catalogue, Indianapolis 1972; *Arts Without Limits,* exhibition catalogue, by Ira Licht, New York 1972; *Painting: New Options,* exhibition catalogue, Minneapolis 1972; *Art in Evolution,* exhibition catalogue, by Anthony Sorce, New York 1973; *Jennifer Bartlett and Jack Tworkov,* exhibition catalogue, Washington, D.C. 1973; *34th Biennial of Contemporary American Painting,* exhibition catalogue, Paris 1975; *72nd American Exhibition,* exhibition catalogue, by Anne Rorimer, Chicago 1976; *New Work/New York,* exhibition catalogue, Los Angeles 1976; *Matrix* by Andrea Miller Keller, Hartford, Connecticut 1977; *Painting '75, '76, '77,* exhibition catalogue, New York 1977; *Documenta 6,* exhibition catalogue, Kassel, West Germany 1977; *Critics' Choice,* exhibition catalogue, New York 1977; *New Image Painting,* exhibition catalogue, New York 1978; *New York Now,* exhibition catalogue, Phoenix, Arizona 1979; *Corners,* exhibition catalogue, Cambridge, Massachusetts 1979; *Printed Art: A View of 2 Decades,* exhibition catalogue by Riva Castleman, New York 1980; *Extensions: Jennifer Bartlett/Lynda Benglis/Robert Longo/Judy Pfaff,* exhibition catalogue, Houston 1980; *Aspects of the 70's: Painterly Abstractions,* exhibition catalogue, by Marilyn Friedman Hoffman, Brockton, Massachusetts 1980; *Drawings: The Pluralist Decade,* exhibition catalogue, with an introduction by Janet Kardon, Philadelphia 1980; *Jennifer Bartlett: Selected Works,* exhibition catalogue, Buffalo, New York 1980; *20 Artists: Yale School of Art 1950–1970,* exhibition catalogue, New York 1981; articles—"Jennifer Bartlett" by Sally Webster in the *Feminist Art Journal* (Brooklyn, New York), Vol. 5, no. 3, 1976; "Jennifer Bartlett: Artist Who Keeps Pushing" by Caroline Drewes in the *San Francisco Examiner,* 24 May 1978; "The Abstract Image" by Roberta Smith in *Art in America* (New York), March/April 1979; "Les nouvelle images de la peinture Americaine" by Thomas B. Hess in *Art Press International* (Paris), May 1979; "Jennifer Bartlett" by Barbara Schreiber in *Atlanta Art Workers' Coalition,* January/February 1980; "Young Artists New Yorkers Are Talking About" by Lee Wohlfett in *Town and Country* (London), September 1980; "Adding Up Jennifer Bartlett" by Diane Bertolo in the *Buffalo Evening News,* 30 Novmeber 1980; "Bartlett's Pairs" by Kim Levin in the *Village Voice* (New York), 4 February 1981; "She's Got Style" by Jeff Perone in *Arts Magazine* (New York), April 1981.

"The series," Jennifer Bartlett has said, "permits a range of possibilities; it reminds us that things can change." Since 1968, the series has constituted the central theme of Bartlett's work. "Rhapsody" (1975–76), a series of 987 gridded, one-foot square enameled plates, represents a monumental exploration of serial structure. Like most of the artist's work, "Rhapsody" juxtaposes the raw and the cooked, examining the way the world is filtered through the human mind and is encoded into cultural conventions or sign systems. The work offers a succinct discourse on the strategies of representation: a sophisticated "botanical" drawing of a tree is matched with a naive rendering of the same subject, or a simple geometric form (a square or a triangle) is contrasted by a signifying one (a house). On another level, Bartlett locates the work historically, advancing a subtle commentary on the paradoxical situation of modernism (e.g. the integrity of abstraction over decoration). In the end, "Rhapsody" is about transition and stasis, continuity and discontinuity suspended in a matrix of resonant formal and intellectual values.

Mapped onto a field of facts, images, and associations, Bartlett's serial structure is often analogous to conventional systems for organizing the world. A "pointillist" map of the United States (from "Series XIV", 1971–72) is further subdivided into 15 parts, establishing a parallel relationship between the formal conditions of Bartlett's serial projection and cartographic apportionment based on real political boundaries. The artist's recurrent use of points, dot, or dashes to compose her imagery creates a situation in which each unit serves as a node within a network of scale systems. Bartlett's fascination with the series extends even to her large-scale public work "Swimmers Atlanta" (1979), a 9-painting series commissioned by the General Services Administration for the lobby of a federal court building in Georgia's capital city. While the obsessive interest in serial form has subsided in Bartlett's most recent work, the seemingly arbitrary scale relationships of "Up the Creek" and "To the Island" (1981–82), two 10-part multimedia works, appear to be governed by a personal, internal logic. Concentrating on problems of condition and place (the syntax of the present work hinges on locative prepositions), these paintings are neither fully autonomous nor serial; in their indecisiveness, they fail to obtain a convincing balance.

The historian Michel Foucault, in his brilliant *The Archaeology of Knowledge,* has explored the shift in historical methodologies from a continuous to a discontinuous view of events and monuments. As attention has turned away from "vast unities like 'periods' or 'centuries' to the phenomena . . . of discontinuity," Foucault argues that an internal organizing structure must come into play to make "relevant" an otherwise ungrouped mass of elements: "The problem now is to constitute series," he writes, "to define elements proper to each series, to fix its boundaries, to reveal its own specific type of relations, to formulate its laws, and beyond this, to describe the relations between different series." Postmodernism has produced a similar challenge for the artist at a time when the continuities of modernist thought have yielded to a more pluralistic attitude. In her most resolute exploration of the series, Jennifer Bartlett has clearly understood the dynamics of this challenge.

—Maurice Berger

BARUCHELLO, Gianfranco.

Italian. Born in Livorno, 29 August 1924. Studied in Rome. Married to Agnese Naldoni; daughter: Paolina. Lives and works in Rome. Agent: Galleria Schwarz, Via Gesu 17, 20121 Milan. Address: Via di Santa Cornelia, km. 6,5 (prima porta), Rome, Italy.

Individual Exhibitions:

1963	Galleria La Tartaruga, Rome
1964	Cordier and Ekstrom Gallery, New York
1965	Galleria Schwarz, Milan
1966	Galleria Il Punto, Turin
	Cordier and Ekstrom Gallery, New York
	IOIOMISS, Galleria Schwarz, Milan
1967	Palais des Beaux-Arts, Brussels
	Galerie Yvon Lambert, Paris
1968	Galleria Schwarz, Milan
	Galleria Roma, Chicago
1969	Studio Condotti 85, Rome
	Galerie Schmela, Dusseldorf
	Galerie Lauter, Mannheim
1970	Galleria Schwarz, Milan
1971	Galerie Buchholz, Munich
1972	Studio Condotti 85, Rome
	Centro d'Arte Europa, Naples
	Galleria La Bertesca, Genoa
1973	Galleria L'Uomo e L'Arte, Milan
	Galerie Der Spiegel, Cologne
	Galerie Craven, Paris
1975	Galleria Schwarx, Milan
	Galleria L'Arcipelago, Turin
	Galleria Etrusculudens, Rome
1976	Italian Pavilion, at the *Biennale,* Venice
	Galleria Valsecchi, Milan
	Galerie Fred Lansenberg, Brussels
	Galerie Gilbert Delorme, Paris
1977	Galleria Il Mercato del Sale, Milan
	Galleria Margherita, Rome

	Galerie Arta, Geneva
	Galerie Bama, Paris
1981	Galleria Milano, Milan
1983	Galerie Reckermann, Cologne
1987	Galleria Milano, Milan

Selected Group Exhibitions:

1962	*Collage et Objet,* Galerie du Cercle, Paris
1963	*4th Biennale,* San Marino (and *6th Biennale,* 1967)
1966	*European Drawings,* Guggenheim Museum, New York
1967	*Pictures to Be Read, Poetry to Be Seen,* Museum of Contemporary Art, Chicago
1968	*Le Collage,* Kunstverein, Frankfurt (travelled to the Kunstgewerbemuseum, Zurich)
1969	*Al di della Pittura,* Galleria Pilota, Modena, Italy
1970	*Il Cocodrillo,* Teatro dell'Opera, Rome (deoors for V. Bucchi opera)
1975	*Baruchello/Erro/Fahlstrom/Liebig,* Musée d'Art Moderne de la Ville, Paris
	Let's Mix All Feelings Together, Städtische Galerie im Lenbachhaus, Munich (travelled to Frankfurt and Paris)
1978	*La Traccia del Racconto,* Villa Comunal Ormond, Sanremo, Italy

Collections:

Museum of Modern Art, New York; Guggenheim Museum, New York.

Publications:

By BARUCHELLO: books—*Mi Vione in Mente,* Milan 1966; *Enonce Impossible,* Milan 1967; *In Cold Fact,* Milan 1968; *La Quindices,* Rome 1968; *Avventure nell'Armadio di Plexiglass,* Milan 1968; *Fragments of a Possible Apocalypse,* with Henry Martin, Milan 1978; *Agricola Cornelia S.P.A. 1973– 81,* Milan 1981; *Faraone dei Sentimenti,* Milan 1987; films and videos—*La Verifica Incerta,* with Alberto Grifi, 1964; *Costretto a Scomparire,* 1968; *Perforce,* 1968; *Complete di Colpa,* 1968; *Norme per gli Olocausti,* 1969; *Per una Giornata de Malumore Nazionale,* 1969; *Non Accaduto,* 1969; *Limbosigne,* 1969; *A Little More Paranoid,* 1969; *I Giorni di Lun,* 1969; *In Quarantasette Secondi,* 1969; *La de'Gringolade,* 1970; *Pietro Bessone en Renato Ghittoni, due gemme della Lotta di Liberazione,* 1970; *LAP,* 1971; *Deep Sea Show,* 1971; *Beaufort no. 2,* 1971.

On BARUCHELLO: books—*Gianfranco Baruchello,* exhibition catalogue, with text by Giorgio Manganelli, Milan 1965; *Gianfranco Baruchello: IOIOMISS,* exhibition catalogue, Milan 1966; *Gian Franco Baruchello,* exhibition catalogue, with text by Italo Calvino, New York 1966; *Baruchello,* exhibition catalogue, with interview by Arturo Schwarz, Milan 1968; *Introduzione a Baruchello* by Tomasso Trini, Milan 1975; *Let's Mix All Feelings Together,* exhibition catalogue, Munich 1975; *La Traccia del Racconto,* exhibition catalogue, Sanremo, Italy 1978.

Between 1959 and 1963 Gianfranco Baruchello's investigations into art moved through a series of widely differing but interconnected problems and experiences. His first works were a kind of super-cold abstract expressionism; these works were abandoned in favor of found objects that seem a little reminiscent of Dada; the found objects turned into assemblages or constructions and also furnished images for drawings that have the flavor of a harsh and expressive surrealism. These assemblages then simplified themselves and entered into a kind of New Realism while the drawings turned into paintings full of an internal debate about the relative weight and importance of paint quality and personally significant imagery. The decision went clearly, after not too long, to personally significant imagery, and Baruchello began to work on large squares of aluminum sheet metal, first primed white and then sprinkled with miniscule drawings of schematic trees, imaginary monsters, non-existent machines, arrows, words, sentences and paragraphs written in various languages, tiny representations of

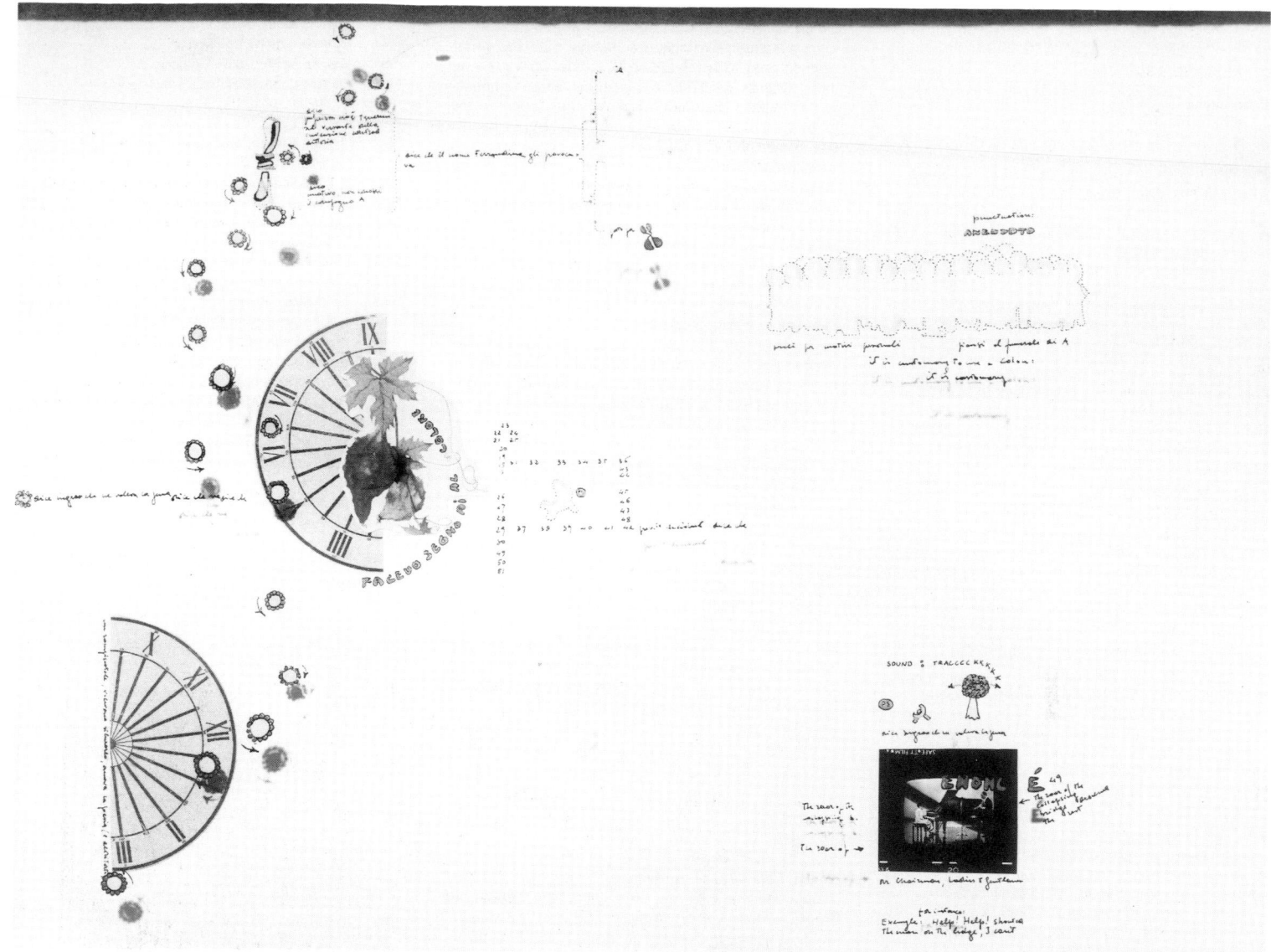

Gianfranco Baruchello: *The Roar of the Collapsing Bridge Drowned the Rest*, 1967

the various organs of the body, patches of hair, diagrams, articles of clothing, splotches of numbers, a veritable convention of erudite references to a host of personal mysteries at the point where they encounter public and political confusions.

And just as Baruchello's paintings have not always been what they are today, they are also a part of a vaster series of aesthetic activities that include objects, films, theater pieces, books, video tapes, stage sets, postal happenings, sound tracks, sculptures, narrative series of drawings, assemblages of odds and ends and cardboard cut-outs in plexiglass cases and wooden boxes, and he has also reported on the experience of running a farm as though it were a work of art. The relationship between the paintings and these other activities is a fairly curious relationship: the themes of these other activities frequently find their source in the paintings and the "results" of these activities are usually reintroduced into the paintings.

Painting for Baruchello is the Queen of the Sciences just as theology was the Queen of the Sciences for the Scholastics of the Middle Ages: his paintings always seem to want to do more than what any rigorously materialistic definition of the act of painting would allow him to do, and his excursions into other media help him to define more clearly the impossible tasks to which his paintings must be put. His paintings, for Baruchello, are what all of reality must be reduced to; they're the crucible in which reality, as Phoenix, is to be experimentally incinerated and then resurrected as myth. The intention is to deal with all of reality in a way that will make all of reality coherent, self-reflexive, and emotionally meaningful.

Baruchello's technique is to work by themes, each of which, as it exhausts itself, is responsible for spawning another. It's as though he were trying to discover the myth that's the source of all myth, and he is always interrogating the facts of his daily experience to see what sort of a place they can have within it.

—Henry Martin

BASELITZ, Georg.

German. Born Georg Dern in Deutschbaselitz, Saxony, now East Germany, 23 January 1938; adopted name "Baselitz" in 1956. Educated at Volksschule and Gymnasium, Kamenz, until 1955; studied art at the Kunstakademie, East Berlin, 1956–57; under Hann Trier, Akademie der Künste, West Berlin, 1957–64. Married Elke Kretzschmar in 1962; sons: Daniel and Anton. Painter, in West Berlin, 1964–66, in Osthofen bei Worms, 1966–70, in Forst, 1970–73, in Mussbach, 1973–75, in Derneburg, Lower Saxony, since 1975; associated with artist Ralf Winckler (A. R. Penck), West Berlin, 1961; published "Pandemonium" manifestos, with Eugen Schönebeck, West Berlin, 1961, 1962. Instructor, 1977–78, and Professor, 1978–83, Staatliche Akademie der bildenden Kunste, Karlsruhe; Professor, Hochschule der Kunste, West Berlin, since 1983. Recipient: Villa Romana Scholarship, Florence 1965; Kulturpreis der Deutsche Industrie, 1968; Kaiserring-Prize, City of Goslar, 1986; Kunstpreis der Nord/LB, Hannover, 1986. Agents: Galerie Neuendorf, Feldstrasse, Hoschhaus 1, Hamburg; Galerie Michael Werner, Friesenstrasse 50, Cologne. Address: Schloss Derneburg, 3201 Holle bei Hildesheim, West Germany.

Individual Exhibitions:

Staatliche Graphische Sammlung, Munich
Galerie Loehr, Frankfurt
Galerie im Goethe-Institut, Amsterdam
Galerie Rudolf Zwirner, Cologne
1973 *Bilder, Objekte, Filme, Konzepte,* Galerie Heiner Freidrich, Munich
Galerie Loehr, Frankfurt
Galerie Grunangergasse, Vienna
Ein neuer Typ, Galerie Neuendorf, Hamburg
1974 Galerie Heiner Friedrich, Cologne
Radierungen 1963–1974/Holzschnitte 1966–1967, Städtisches Museum Schloss Morsbroich, Leverkusen, West Germany
Städtisches Galerie Altes Theater, Ravensburg, West Germany
1975 Galerie Heiner Friedrich, Munich
Galerie Michael Werner, Cologne
Galerie Loehr, Frankfurt
1976 Staatsgalerie Moderner Kunst, Munich
Malerei, Handzeichnungen, Druckgraphik, Kunsthalle, Berne
Galerie Heiner Friedrich, Cologne
Kunsthalle, Cologne
1977 Galerie Heiner Friedrich, Cologne
Galerie Heiner Friedrich, Munich
1978 Galerie Helen van der Meij, Amsterdam
Galerie Heiner Friedrich, Cologne
1979 Galerie Gillespie/De Laage, Paris
Bilder 1977–78, Stedelijk van Abbenuseum, Eindhoven, Netherlands
32 Linolschnitte aus den Jahren 1976 bis 1979, Josef-Haubrich-Kunsthalle, Cologne
Tekeningen/Zeichnungen, Groninger Museum, Groningen, Netherlands
1980 Galerie Heiner Friedrich, Cologne
Galerie Gillespie/De Laage, Paris,
Galerie Rudolf Springer, West Berlin
Whitechapel Art Gallery, London (with Max Backmann)
Centre d'Arts Plastiques Contemporains, Bordeaux (with A. R. Penck and Joseph Beuys)
1981 Kastrupgardsamlingen, Kastrup, Denmark
Galerie Michael Werner, Cologne
Stedelijk van Abbemuseum, Eindhoven, Netherlands
Kunsthalle, Dusseldorf (with Gerhard Richter)
Kunstverein, Braunschweig, West Germany
Das Strassenbild, Stedelijk Museum, Amsterdam
Galerie Annemarie Verna, Zurich
Galerie Fred Jahn, Munich
Xavier Fourcade Inc., New York
1982 *Zeichnungen,* Galerie Michael Werner, Cologne
Sonnabend Gallery, New York
Waddington Galleries, London
Galerie Fred Jahn, Munich
Galerie Rudolf Zwirner, Cologne
Anthony D'Offay, London
Galerie Helen van der Meij, Amsterdam
Galerie Springer, West Berlin
Xavier Fourcade Inc., New York
Young Hoffman Gallery, Chicago
Galerie Nachst St. Stephan, Vienna
Kunstverein, Gottingen, West Germany
1983 Galerie Michael Werner, Cologne
CAPC Musee d'Art Contemporain, Bordeaux, France
Galerie Albert Baronian, Brussels
Galerie Springer, West Berlin
Galerie am Markt, Schwabisch Hall, West Germany
Galerie Gillespie-Laage-Salomon, Paris
Xavier Fourcade Inc., New York
Sonnabend Gallery, New York
Galerie Neuendorf, Hamburg (twice)
Akron Art Museum, Ohio (with Julian Schnabel)
Whitechapel Art Gallery, London
Galerie Folker Skulima, West Berlin
Galerie Fred Jahn, Munich
Los Angeles County Museum of Art
1984 Van Abbemuseum, Eindhoven, Netherlands (drawings retrospective)
University of California, Berkeley
Kunstmuseum, Basel
Kunsthalle, Basel
Mary Boone/Michael Werner Gallery, New York

Neue Pinakothek, Munich (graphics retrospective)
Galerie Borgmann, Cologne
Stadtische Kunstmuseum, Bonn
Mussee d'Art et d'Histoire, Geneva
Kunstverein, Freiburg, West Germany
Galerie Meyer-Ellinger, Frankfurt
Kunsthalle, Nuremberg, West Germany
Artotheque, Lyon, France
Waddington Galleries, London
Vancouver Art Gallery, British Columbia
Deweer Art Gallery, Zwevegem-Otegem, Belgium
Galerie Michael Werner, Cologne
1985 Galerie Fred Jahn, Munich
Stadtisches Museum Simeonstift, Trier, West Germany
DAAD-Galerie, West Berlin
Kunstverein, Hannover
Galerie Gillespie-Laage-Salomon, Paris
Bibliotheque Nationale, Paris (print and sculpture retrospective)
Galerie Collection d'Art, Amsterdam
Galerie-Lager Rudolf Zwirner, Cologne
Galerie Joachim Becker, Cannes, France
Anthony d'Offay, London
Haus am Waldsee, West Berlin
Kunsthalle, Bielefeld, West Germany
Galerie Thomas Borgmann, Cologne
Ernst Barlach Haus, Hamburg
Alpha Gallery, Boston

Kunstverein, Oldenburg, West Germany
1986 Kunstmuseum, Winterthur, Switzerland
Mary Boone/Michael Werner Gallery, New York
Galerie Beyeler, Basel
Muzej Savremene Umetnosti, Belgrade
Obalne Galerije, Piran, Yugoslavia
Galerija Loza, Koper, Yugoslavia
Cankarjev Dom, Liubliana, Yugoslavia
Galerija Grada, Zagreb, Yugoslavia
Galerija Suvremene Umjetnosti, Zagreb, Yugoslavia
Galerie Beuamont, Luxembourg
Galerie Thaddaeus Ropac, Salzburg, Austria
Galerie Chobot, Vienna
Sonja Henie/Nils Onstads Stifelser, Oslo
Monchehaus Museum fur moderne Kunst, Goslar, West Germany
Wiener Secession, Vienna
Galerie Heike Curtze, Vienna
Galerie Springer, West Berlin
1987 Maximilian Verlag/Sabine Knust, Munich
Meine kleine Galerie, Hildesheim, West Germany
Galleria Christian Stein, Milan
Galerie Collection d'Art, Amsterdam
Kestner-Gesellschaft, Hannover
Galerie Buchmann, Basel
Museum Ludwig, Cologne
Galerie Neuendorf, Frankfurt
Anthony D'Offay Gallery, London

Georg Baselitz: *Untitled,* **1967** Courtesy Anthony D'Offay Gallery, London

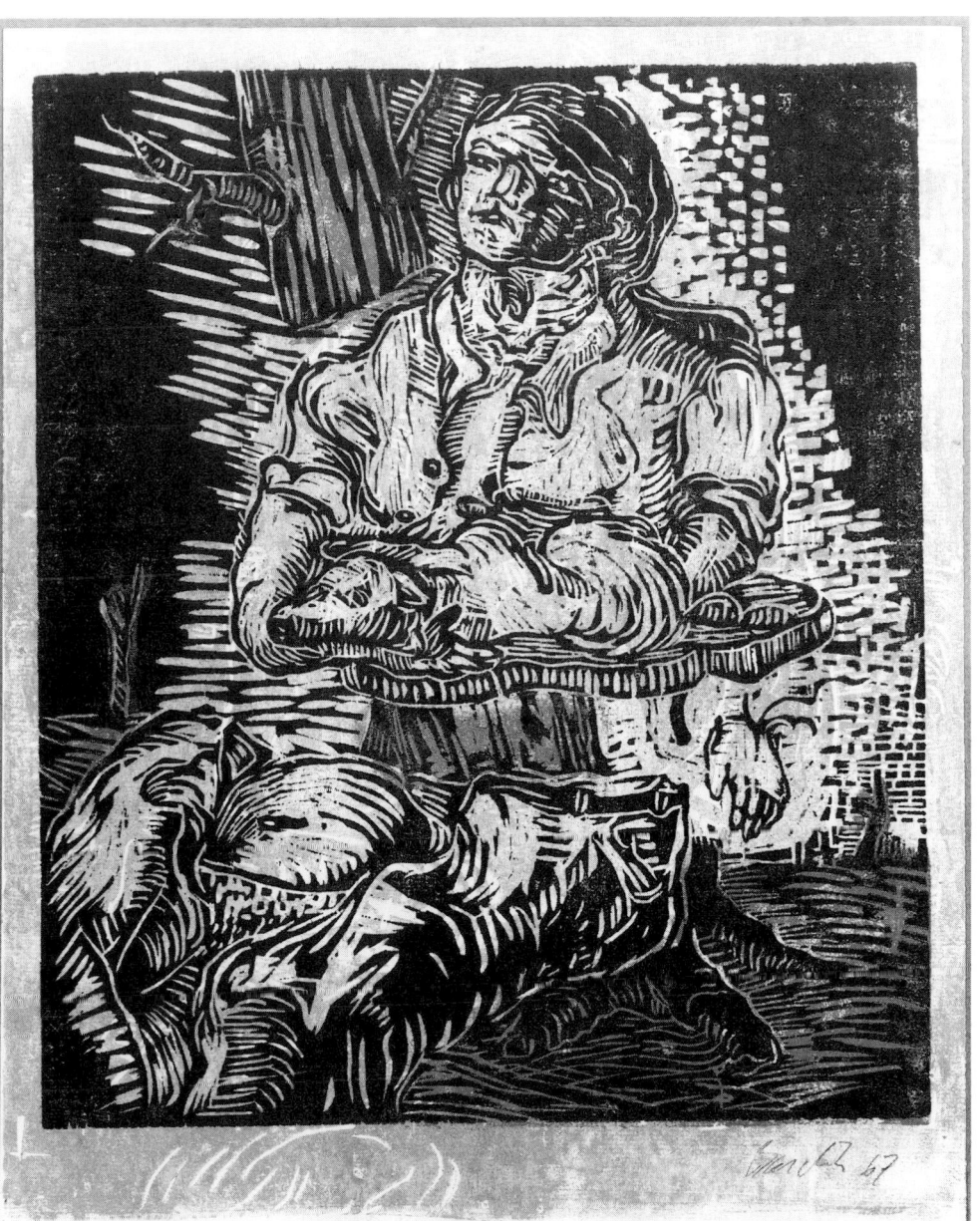

Selected Group Exhibitions:

1968   *14 x 14*, Kunsthalle, Baden-Baden, West Germany
1969   *Kunst und Kritik*, Städtisches Museum, Wiesbaden, West Germany
1971   *Zeichen und Farbe*, Staatsgalerie, Stuttgart
1972   *Documenta 5*, Kassel, West Germany (and *Documenta 7*, 1982)
1973   *Prospekt '73*, Städtische Kunsthalle, Dusseldorf
1975   *Bienal*, Sao Paulo
1980   *Biennale*, Venice
1981   *A New Spirit in Painting*, Royal Academy of Art, London
1985   *The European Iceberg*, Art Gallery of Ontario, Toronto
1987   *Berlinart 1961-87*, Museum of Modern Art, New York (travelled to San Francisco Museum of Modern Art)

Collections:

Kunsthalle, Hamburg; Städtisches Museum, Braunschweig, West Germany; Hessisches Landesmuseum, Darmstadt; Sammlung Ludwig, Cologne; Stedelijk Museum, Amsterdam; Museum Boymans-van Beuningen, Rotterdam; Centre Georges Pompidou, Paris.

Publications:

By BASELITZ: books and pamphlets—*Pandemonium: First Manifesto*, with Eugen Schönebeck, West Berlin 1961; *Pandemonium: Second Manifesto*, with Eugen Schönebeck, West Berlin 1962; *Warum das Bild 'Die grossen Freunde' ein gutes Bild ist*, manifesto and poster, West Berlin 1966; *Comte de Lautreamont: Die Gesange des Maldoror*, gouache illustrations, Munich 1976; articles—"Liber Herr W." in *Die Schastrommel* (Berlin/Bolzano), March 1972; "Vier Wande und Oberlicht" in *Kunstforum International* (Mainz), no. 4, 1979; "George Baselitz", special monograph issue of *Lo Spazio Umano* (Milan), January/March 1983.

On BASELITZ: books—*Baselitz*, exhibition catalogue, with text by Martin G. Butler, Herbert Read and Edouard Roditi, West Berlin 1963; *Baselitz: Zeichnungen*, exhibition catalogue, with text by Dieter Koeppplin, Antwerp 1970; *Georg Baselitz: Zeichnungen und Radierungen*, exhibition catalogue, with text by Herbert Poe, Munich 1972; *George Baselitz: Gemalde und Zeichnungen*, exhibition catalogue, with text by Heinz Fuchs, Mannheim 1972; *George Baselitz: Ein neuer Typ*, exhibition catalogue, with text by Günther Gercken, Hamburg 1973; *Bilder, Objekte, Filme, Konzepte*, exhibition catalogue, Munich 1973; *Georg Baselitz: Radierungen 1963-1974/Holzschnitte 1966-1967*, exhibition catalogue, with text by Rolf Wedewer, Fred Jahn and Mircea Eliade, Leverkusen, West Germany 1974; *13. Bienal de Sao Paulo: George Baselitz*, exhibition catalogue with text by Evelyh Weiss, Cologne 1975; *Baselitz: Malerei, Handzeichnungen, Druckgraphik*, exhibition catalogue, with text by Theo Kneubuhler, Berne 1976; *Georg Berlitz*, exhibition catalogue, with text by Carla Schulz-Hoffman, Günther Gercken and Johannes Gachnang, Munich 1976; *Georg Baselitz: Bilder 1977-78*, exhibition catalogue, with text by Rudi Ruchs, Eindhoven, Netherlands 1979; *Georg Baselitz: 32 Linolschnitte aus den Jahren 1976 bis 1979*, exhibition catalogue, with texts by Siegfried Gohr and Fred Jahn, Cologne 1979; *Georg Baselitz: Tekeningen/Zeichnungen*, exhibition catalogue with texts by Frans Haks and Johannes Gachnang, Groningen, Netherlands 1979; *Georg Baselitz: Biennale de Venezia 1980*, exhibition catalogue, with texts by Johannes Gachnang, Theo Kneubuhler and Klaus Gallwitz, Stuttgart 1980; *Georg Baselitz: Das Strassenbild*, exhibition catalogue, with text by A. van Grevenstein, Amsterdam 1981; *George Baselitz: Zeichnungen*, exhibition catalogue, with text by H. Heere, Cologne 1982; *Georg Baselitz: Holzplastiken*, exhibition catalogue, with texts by A. Franzke, R. H. Fuchs and S. Gohr, Cologne 1983; *Baselitz: Paintings 1960-83*, exhibition catalogue with texts by N. Serota and R. Calvocoressi, London 1983; *Georg Baselitz: Das malerische Werk 1960-83, Linolschnitte 1976-79*, exhibition catalogue, with texts by J. C. Ammann and R. Calvocoressi, Basel 1984; *Georg Baselitz: Selected Prints 1963-85*, exhibition catalogue, with text by J. E. Fink, Boston 1985; *Georg Baselitz: Baume*, exhibition catalogue, with texts by E. Kob, O. Rychlik and H. Hrachovec, Vienna 1986; *Georg Baselitz: Skulpturen und Zeichnungen 1979-1987*, exhibition catalogue, with texts by C. Haenlein, A. M. Hammacher and others, Hannover 1987.

From the end of the 1960's, in a search for a new equilibrium—new, but still within the dimension of painting, clarifying the control of the actual picture through well thought analytical premises—Georg Baselitz has continually explored the modalities of a procedure which, while making use of recognizable images, refutes the classical conceptions—the sense of space, composition, perspective, the idea of style, etc. What we see is thus the continuous and constant presentation of the negation of exposition, of meaning, of the subject-object relationship that makes reality manifest as if reflected in a mirror.

Baselitz's painting tends to confuse the viewer, distorting the organized mechanisms of visual perception. It repudiates sensuousness, the quality of traditionally accepted painting, the subject and all those other elements that show it to be a reference to something. The picture, the work, thus becomes just a picture, a work—an enquiry into painting filtered through a complex pre-established mental process and a play of arbitrary elaborations.

What is exceptional in Georg Baselitz's methods lies in the fact that his works repudiate "painting with images" by actually using recognizable images which are presented directly as themselves, with no suggestion of story or description. The picture thus has to be looked at, not as a mirror on the world, but as a world in itself, self-sufficient.

It is as if these works had been executed with a technique such as might be used to build a boat actually in the sea during a shipwreck. Painting that does not have to flirt with structuralism, but is rather looked at casually, establishes an equilibrium of its own; the boat will not sink provided there are eyes to be sure of being present at the shipwreck—that of the modern age. The artist is building rafts with his pictures, fragments at a time of the recent past which, despite everything, are still in our present time and fragments of the present projected into the next moment, fragments which together (deliberately or not, it matters little) build a bridge towards "that which has been."

—Demetrio Paparoni

BASKIN, Leonard.
American. Born in New Brunswick, New Jersey, 15 August 1922. Educated at a yeshiva, Brooklyn, New York, 1929-38; studied at New York University of School of Architecture and Allied Arts, 1939-40; Yale University School of Fine Arts, 1941-42; Académie de la Grande Chaumière, Paris, 1950; Accademia di Belle Arte, Florence, 1951. Served in the United States Navy, 1943-46. Independent artist active in sculpture, painting and printmaking as well as calligraphy, design and illustration. Instructor in Printmaking, Worcester Art Museum, Massachusetts, 1952. Has taught at Smith College, Northampton, Massachusetts, since 1953. Recipient: Honorable Mention for Sculpture, Prix de Rome, 1940; Tiffany Foundation Fellowship for Sculpture, 1947; Guggenheim Fellowship, 1953; Ohara Prize, National Museum of Tokyo, 1954; National Institute of Arts and Letters Grant, 1961; Mather Prize, Art Institute of Chicago, 1961; Widener Medal, Pennsylvania Academy of Fine Arts, 1965; Special Medal of Merit, American Institute of Graphic Arts, 1965; Medal, National Institute of Arts and Letters, 1969; Agent: Kennedy Galleries, New York. Address: c/o Kennedy Galleries, 40 West 57th Street, New York, New York 10019, U.S.A.

Individual Exhibitions:

1952   Mount Holyoke College, South Hadley, Massachusetts

1957   Worcester Art Museum, Massachusetts
1961   Museum Boymans-van Beuningen, Rotterdam
Le Centre Culturel Américain, Paris
University of Minnesota, Minneapolis
1962   Royal Watercolor Society Galleries, London
Bowdoin College Museum of Art, Brunswick, Maine
1963   Maxwell Galleries, San Francisco
1966   Peale House, Pennsylvania Academy of the Fine Arts, Philadelphia
1968   Stockholm National Museum (travelled to Oslo, Norway and Gothenburg, Sweden)
1970   *Leonard Baskin: The Graphic Work 1950-1970*, FAR Gallery, New York
Smithsonian Institution, Washington, D.C.
Illustrations for the Divine Comedy of Dante by Leonard Baskin, Yale University, New Haven, Connecticut
1971   Kennedy Galleries, New York
1972   *Indian Drawings*, Amon Carter Museum, Fort Worth, Texas
Brookhaven National Laboratory, Associated Universities, Upton, New York
1973   Kennedy Galleries, New York
1974   Kennedy Galleries, New York
Summit Art Center, New Jersey
Museum of Fine Arts, Springfield, Massachusetts
1975   Kennedy Galleries, New York
Watercolors for a Passover Haggadah, Fine Arts Museums of San Francisco
1976   Kennedy Galleries, New York
Indianapolis Museum of Art
Towson State College Art Gallery, Baltimore, Maryland
1977   Prince Arthur Galleries, Toronto
Port Washington Public Library, New York
Lockhaven Art Center, Orlando, Florida
1978   *Images of Man*, Washington University Gallery of Art, St. Louis
Recent Works, Kennedy Galleries, New York
1980   Kennedy Galleries, New York
1981   Cottage Gallery, London
Leonard Baskin's West, Amon Carter Museum, Forth Worth, Texas (toured the Western United States)
1982   *Sculpture and Watercolors*, Kennedy Galleries, New York

Selected Group Exhibitions:

1961   *Bienal*, San Paulo
1962   *American Paintings and Drawings from Michigan Collections*, Detroit Institute of Arts
1969   *The Figurative Tradition in Recent American Art*, at the *Biennale*, Venice (travelled to National Collection of Fine Arts, Washington, D.C. and Sheldon Gallery, University of Nebraska, Lincoln)
1979   *The American View*, MacNider Museum, Mason City, Iowa
1980   *Sculpture in the 70s: The Figure*, Pratt Manhattan Center Gallery, New York
A Penthouse Aviary, Museum of Modern Art, New York

Collections:

Museum of Modern Art, New York; Whitney Museum, New York; Hirshhorn Collection, Smithsonian Institution, Washington, D.C.; National Gallery of Art, Washington, D.C.; Museum of Fine Arts, Boston; Art Institute of Chicago; Detroit Institute of Arts; Amon Carter Museum of Art, Fort Worth, Texas; Vatican Museum, Rome.

Publications:

By BASKIN: books—*To Color Thought*, New Haven, Connecticut 1967; *Figures of Dead Men*, Amherst, Massachusetts 1968; *5 Addled Etchers*, Hanover, New Hampshire 1969; *Baskin: Sculpture, Drawings, Prints*, New York 1970; books illustrated—*Creatures of Darkness* by Esther Baskin, Boston 1962; *The Iliad of Homer*, translated by Richmond Lattimore, Chicago 1962; *The Poppy and Other Deadly*

Plants by Esther Baskin, New York 1967; *The Divine Comedy* by Dante Alighieri, translated by Thomas Bergin, New York 1969; *Hosie's Alphabet* by Hosea, Tobias and Lisa Baskin, New York 1972; *Selected Poems 1957–1967* by Ted Hughes, New York 1973; *A Passover Haggadah,* New York 1974; *Season Songs* by Ted Hughes, New York 1975; *Hosie's Aviary* by Tobias, Hosea, Lucretia and Lisa Baskin, New York 1979; *Chosen Days* by David Rosenberg, New York 1980; *Hosie's Zoo* by Tobias, Hosea, Lucretia and Lisa Baskin, New York 1981; *Under the North Star* by Ted Hughes, New York 1981; articles—"New Talent in the USA: with Note by the Artist" in *Art in America* (New York), February 1956; "The Necessity for the Image" in *Atlantic Monthly* (Boston), April 1961; "To Wear Blood Stain with Honor" in *Judaism* (New York), vol. 10, 1961; "On the Nature of Originality" in *Show* (New York), August 1963; "Of Roots and Veins: A Testament" in *Atlantic Monthly* (Boston), September 1964; "Studio Talk . . . Industrial Sand Casting in Bronze: An Interview with Leonard Baskin" in *Arts* (New York), February 1967.

On BASKIN: books—*Conversations with Artists* by Selden Rodman, New York 1961; *The Sculpture of Leonard Baskin* by Irma Jaffe, New York 1980; *Profiles of American Artists Represented by Kennedy Galleries* by Gloria-Gilda Deak, New York 1981; articles—"Art: Baskin's Foreboding Reflections" by Dore Ashton in the *New York Times*, 2 April 1958; "Nouvelles Images de L'Homme" by Peter Selz in *L'Oeil* (Paris), February 1960; "Leonard Baskin" by Brian O'Doherty in *Art in America* (New York), Summer 1962; "Leonard Baskin" by Brian O'Doherty in *Art in America* (New York), August 1963; "Baskin and the Sooty God" by John Canaday in the *New York Times*, 9 February 1964; "Leonard Baskin: Printer, Teacher, Affluent Artist—The Pleasant Pariah" by Jane Howard in *Life* (New York), 24 January 1964; "Leonard Baskin's Gehenna Press" by D. R. Roylance in *Art in America* (New York), November 1966; "Baskin—His Graphic Work" by J. T. Butler in *Connoisseur* (London), May 1970; "Art's Poet Laureate" by Douglas Davis in *Newsweek* (New York), 29 June 1970; "Images of Man" by Alfred Werner in *Art and Artists* (London), October 1976; "FDR Memorial: A Monument to Politics, Bureaucracy and the Art of Accommodation" by M. N. Carter in *Artnews* (New York), October 1978; "History and Fate in Leonard Baskin's Sculpture" by J. Deckert in *Arts* (New York), June 1980.

Leonard Baskin is one of those anomalies of contemporary art, though more complex than most. He belongs to the 20th century, to a certain extent is of it, yet repudiates it. He has not received the recognition he deserves, simply because he is not and does not want to be in the so-called mainstream of modern art. It is hard to say whether the neglect of this major artist is due to his own intransigence or to the myopia of art critics and art historians. There is another element: for me, at least, his output is uneven; that is, one could defend the neglect with reference to certain works. This makes an assessment of Baskin's achievement difficult.

Although his reputation rests on his sculpture, to my mind his chief title to fame is as a draughtsman and watercolourist and, secondly, as a printer, engraver, maker of wood-cuts and lithographs, in that order. His illustrations for Ted Hughes's poem *Crow* are masterly, the equal of any studies of birds by Picasso.

Even in his sculpture he is unfailingly successful in his treatment of birds, some pathetic, some menacing. His treatment of the human form is not quite so successful. Some works have the simplicity, if not the charm, of Barlach, whom Baskin much admired—he even did a head of Barlach in 1959; most impressive. His "Seated Woman" and "Seated Man with Owl" have the simple eloquence of the best of 20th century sculpture, well worthy of Barlach. Like Barlach, Baskin has been in search of humanistic, spiritual and religious values in sculpture which reach back beyond the Renaissance, to the late Middle Ages, to the simple expression of Tino do Camaino, particularly the sinister Counsellors of Pisa.

Baskin's themes are mostly drawn from the Bible and classical mythology, with some symbolic representations of abstract ideas—expulsion, thought, silence. The human figure, usually cast in bronze, sometimes nude, sometimes elaborately swathed in garments, is central to his work, as it was to the sculptors of the Renaissance and to Rodin, whom, in

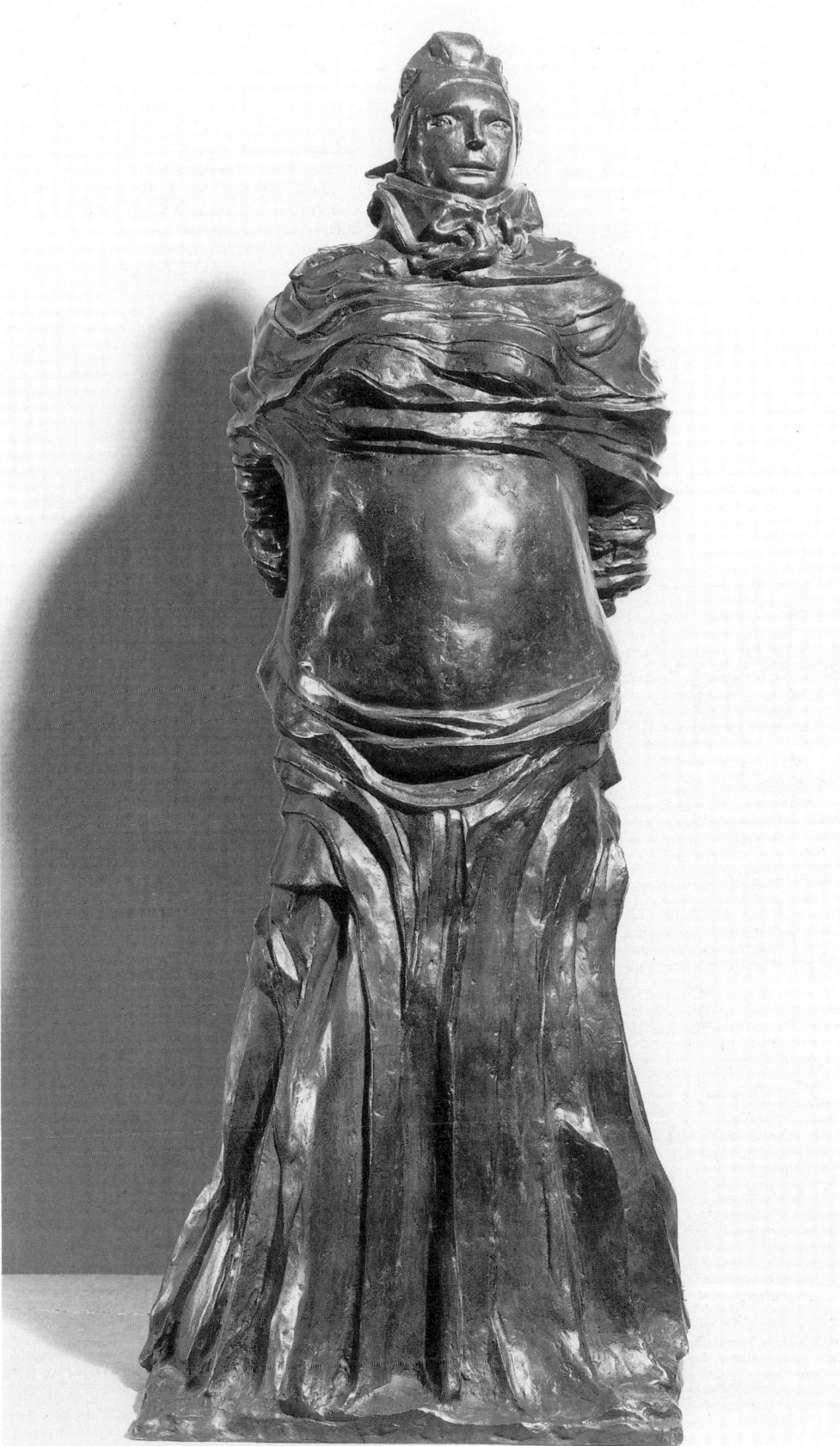

Leonard Baskin: *Medea*, 1980

his more elaborate works, he closely resembles—there is the same malleability of material, the sensuousness of moulding of garments, etc.

At his best Baskin can produce powerful and impressive sculptural images. But he has a tendency to over-dramatize and to be highly emotional, when restraint would have been more effective, as in his "Prodigal Son" (compare it with Barlach's version of the same subject). And, at times, his fantastical

works make very little impact and seem to belong to a private, eccentric vision, rather than to one which can be shared.

But his versatility, not only in the variety of media in which he is supremely competent, but also in the variety of visual ideas, is remarkable. I have mentioned his studies of birds (and other animal studies must be added); add his treatment of the human form, of legendary and symbolic subjects (to which one must add subjects from European and American literature, Dante, Shakespeare, etc), and his fantasies. There are also his portraits of artists (Géricault, Corot, Velasquez) and of literary figures (Melville, Blake, John Skelton). And there are excellent pastiches, such as his "Homage to August Saint-Gaudens."

Baskin will probably not be seen for what he is—an artist in the European tradition, who continued that tradition, while being open, in part, to new developments in the visual arts, artist of individual, original, if sometimes eccentric, vision—until the dust of 'modernism' settles.

—D. C. Barrett

BATTAGLIA, Carlo.

Italian. Born La Maddalena, Sardinia, 28 January 1933. Studied at the Accademia delle Belle Arti, Rome, 1952–57. Served in the Italian Air Force, 1958–59. Married Anna Paparetti in 1959 (divorced, 1962); married Carla Panicali in 1972. Designed scenery for *La Merce Esclusa* by Elio Pagliarani, at the Teatro Parioli, Rome, 1965. Visited New York, 1967. Assistant Professor of Scenography, Accademia delle Belle Arti, Rome, 1970–72. Lives alternately in Rome and New York, since 1980. Agent: Galleria L'Isola, Via Gregoriana 5, 00187 Rome. Address: Via di Monserrato 111, 00186 Rome, Italy.

Individual Exhibitions:

1964	Galleria La Salita, Rome
1965	Galleria La Metopa, Bari, Italy
1968	Galleria Salone Annunciata, Milan
1968	Galleria Editalia, Rome (with Nicola Carrino)
	Galleria Salone Annunciata, Milan
	Galleria Arco d'Alibert Rome
	Galleria Qui Arte Contemporanea, Rome
1969	Galleria Flori, Florence
	Galleria Qui Arte Contemporanea, Rome
	Galleria Editalia, Rome
1970	Galleria Salone Annunciata, Milan
	Biennale, Venice
1971	Deson-Zaks Gallery, Chicago
	Galleria Salone Annunciata, Milan
1972	Galleria Editalia, Rome
	Galleria Peccolo, Livorno
	Galleria Qui Arte Contemporanea, Rome
	Westend Galerie, Frankfurt
	Studio 3Bi, Bolzano, Italy
1973	Galleria Godel, Rome
	Galleria Nova Arte Moderna, Prato, Italy
1974	Galleria Salone Annunciata, Milan
	Elementi per Carlo Battaglia, Palazzo Grassi, Venice
	Studio Soldano, Milan
1975	Studio 3Bi, Bolzano, Italy
	Galleria Il Sole, Bolzano, Italy
	Galleria Il Segnapassi, Pesaro, Italy
	Galerie Daniel Templon, Paris
	Galleria La Bertesca, Genoa
1976	Galeria Arnessen, Copenhagen
	Galleria Salone Annunciata, Milan
	Galeria La Bertesca, Dusseldorf
	Palazzo dei Diamante, Ferrara
1977	Studio 3Bi, Bolzano, Italy
	Galleria Il Sole, Bolzano, Italy
	Galleria La Bertesca, Rome
	Studio Ennesse, Milan
1978	Galleria E Tre, Rome
	Kunsthalle, Dusseldorf
1980	Studio 3Bi, Bolzano, Italy
	Sergio Tosi, New York
	Galleria Civica, Alessandria, Italy
	Galleria E Tre, Rome

	Studio Grossetti, Milan
	Ann Jacob Gallery, Atlanta
	Biennale, Venice
	Galleria Il Sole, Bolzano, Italy
1981	Lo Spazio, Naples
1983	Galleria Il Sole, Bolzano, Italy
	Galeria Albrecht, Caldaro, Bolzano, Italy
	Galleria L'Isola, Rome
	Studio Carlo Grossetti, Milan
1984	Ann Jacob Gallery, Atlanta, Georgia
1985	Galleria Arte Duchamp, Cagliari, Italy
	Galleria L'Isola, Rome
1986	Galleria Forzani, Terni, Italy
	Museo Civico d'Arte Contemporanea, Gibellina, Italy
	Studio Marconi, Milan
1987	Galleria Ellequadro, Genoa, Italy

Selected Group Exhibitions:

1964	*Arte Nuova*, Konsthall, Lund, Sweden
1966	*Peintures Italiennes d'Aujourd'hui*, Teheran
1968	*6th Biennale Romana*, Palazzo Esposizioni, Rome
1972	*Proposta a Quattro*, Galleria del Milione, Milan
1975	*Tendensen Moderne Kunst*, Nordjylands Kunstmuseum, Aalborg, Denmark (travelled to Stifts Museum, Odense, Denmark)
1978	*Biennale*, Venice
1980	*Arte e Critice*, Museo Nazionale d'Arte Moderna, Rome
1982	*Arte Italiana 1960–82*, Hayward Gallery, London
1984	*Art from Italy*, Hirshhorn Museum, Washington, D.C.
1986	*Arte e Scienza-Colore*, at the *Biennale*, Venice

Carlo Battaglia: *Imbre*, 1986

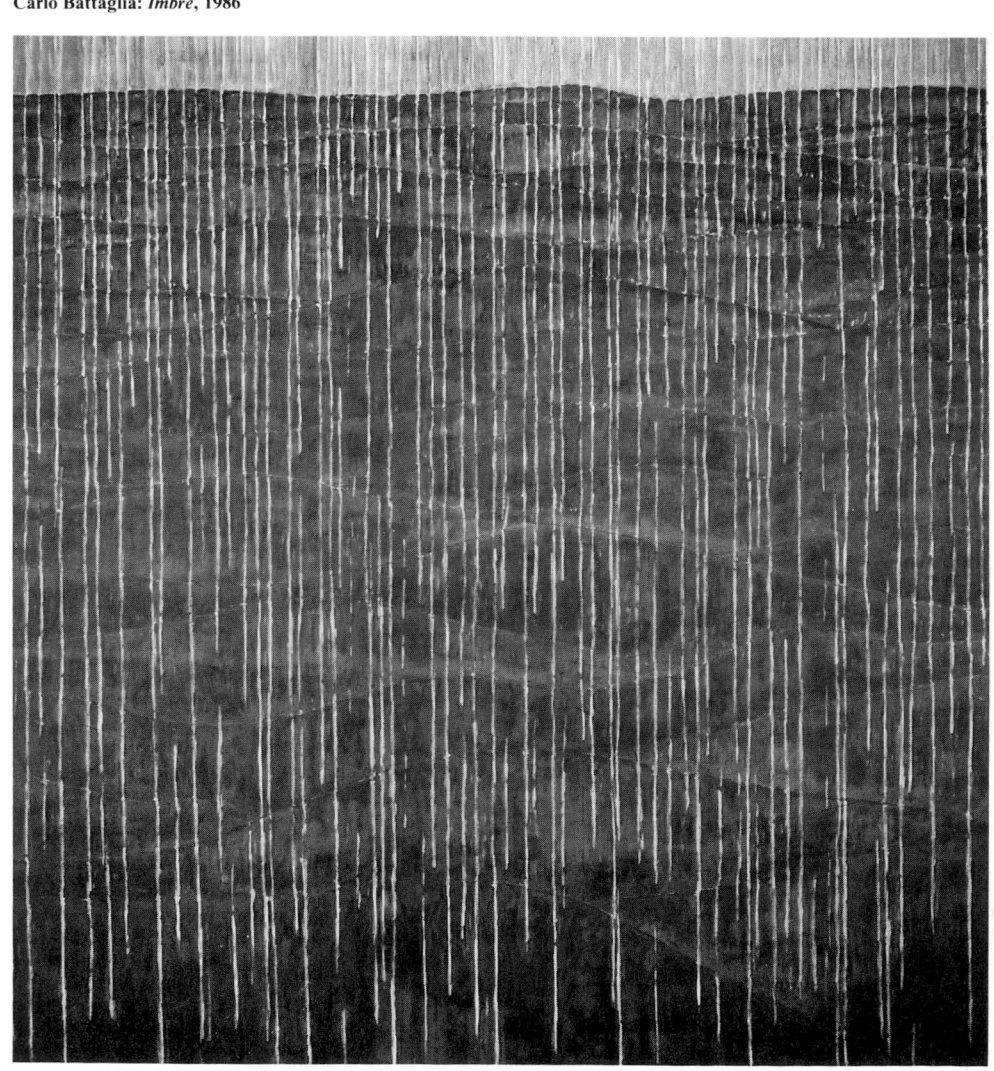

Collections:

Museo Nazionale d'Arte Moderna, Rome; Boymans-van Beuningen Museum, Rotterdam; Louisiana Museum, Humlebaek, Denmark; Museo Soto, Ciudad Bolivar, Venezuela; Hirshhorn Museum and Sculpture Garden, Smithsonian Institution, Washington, D.C.

Publications:

By BATTAGLIA: articles—statement in *Carlo Battaglia*, exhibition catalogue, Milan 1968; statement in *Flash Art* (Milan), February 1972; "3 Artists: Ryman, Marden and Bell" in *Qui Arte Contemporanea* (Rome), June 1973; "Come Dipingono," interview with Griffa Verna, in *Data* (Milan), Summer 1973; "La Pittura come Disciplina," with Maurizio Fagiolo, in *Bolaffi Arte* (Turin), April 1975; "L'Immagine parallela" in *L'Immagine parallela ed altre congetture*, Genoa 1976; "Dialogo tra Carlo Battaglia, Giampaolo Prearo e Nino Soldano" in *Casa Arredamento e Giardino* (Milan), April 1979; "Arshile Gorky al Guggenheim" in *Flash Art* (Milan), no. 105, 1981; "Marginalia" in *Carlo Battaglia*, exhibition catalogue, Rome 1985.

On BATTAGLIA: books—*Carlo Battaglia* by Tommaso Trini, Milan 1974; *Elementi per Carlo Battaglia*, exhibition catalogue, by Roberto Sanesi, Venice 1974; *Carlo Battaglia*, exhibition catalogue, by Filiberto Menna, Dusseldorf 1978; *Carlo Battaglia*, exhibition catalogue, by Dore Ashton, New York 1980; *Il corpo della pittura: critici e nuovi pittori in Italia 1972-76* by Claudio Caritelli, Turin 1986; articles—"La Pittura come Paesaggio" by Gabriella Otudi in *Data* (Milan), May 1972; "Carlo Battaglia: Ambiguita Visionaria" by Guido Ballo in *Arte Milano* (Milan), March 1973; "Carlo Battaglia" by Filiberto Menna in *Opus International* (Paris), September 1974; "Carlo Battaglia a Palazzo Grassi, Venezia" by Gianni Contessi in *Nac* (Milan), December 1974; "Il quadro di Carlo Battaglia" by Vittorio Fagone in *Data* (Milan), July / September 1976; "Incontro col pittore Carlo Battaglio" by Maurizio Fagiolo in *Il Messaggero* (Rome), 18 April 1977; "Carlo Battaglia, La metrica del mare" by Vito Apuleo in *l Messaggero* (Rome), 7 June 1983; "I paesaggi di Carlo Battaglia" by Enzo Bilardello in *Corriere della Sera* (Milan), 16 December 1985.

"My aspiration is to catch everyone's attention, even those people who know nothing about painting. The idea of landscapes, which obsesses me at the moment, could also be this: the vague discernment of a common need for contemplation. Contemplating is a fundamentally irrational act. I want to pursue this gratuitous impulse until I attain the mutable visionariness of landscapes which escapes the control of logic, but is conveyable by virtue of its very obviousness. I see the risks I am running: the idolatry of the mists of emotions or the unconditional surrender to popular banality. Two blind alleys for anyone who is tempted to nullify the enigma of expression. Except I have already made my choice, beyond the point of no return. I say so without hesitation.

This is an excerpt from an article by Gabriella Drudi about my work in 1972, entitled "Painting as Landscape," and article which, miming a series of conversations we had, put words into my mouth that are much more specific than I was able to formulate at that time. The result of that remote and still vague motive are these pictures. I don't know if I have surmounted those risks, doubt is always the only certainty, but I am relieved to know that I have carried out what I felt obliged to do: this is the only conceit I allow myself. Observation and love lie at the root of these paintings. Identification between painting and landscape, landscape as a place of memory, dreamy distance, timeless portrayal. The reflections in perpetual motion in the clear pure light of the archipelago, the shadows, mysterious abstract clippings, summon up memories, fragments, pictures loved to the point of becoming a part of me, presences, awareness. The "Madonna Enthroned with Child and Saints" at S. Zaccaria, the giddy interplay of countless sources of light, sublime challenge of the "Martyrdom of St. Lawrence" at the Jesuits, the gold ground no longer a flat emblematic surface but a glowing atmosphere of light-space in the polyptych of the Misericordia in Sansepolcro, the appearance of the city of Delft in Den Haag as the sudden, unexpected materialization of those islands suspended between cobalt blue and ultramarine, murky with green, haloed with pink and violet. An ancient landscape, the presence of the sacred in the absence of man, a landscape that already in itself is structure, archetype.

So I haven't painted rocks and shrubs as such. They are tokens, essential traits shaped by the age-old erosion of wind and sea, precious traces for re-inventing a pictorial structure free of imitation or representation, a "parallel code". I have sought to paint the air between object and object, island and island, foreground and distances inside a spherical space. The sea, crazed anamorphosis of a checkerboard. To pinpoint the eternal in the prime elements, earth, water, air. Not a specific landscape but the place of universal landscapes. I don't feel like, nor up to, giving theoretical explanations of my work. I am also aware of its probable unactuality was well as its ineluctability. What I can say is that I have attempted to do something that exists once and for all.

As to feelings, passions, expectations and dramas I choose not to speak of them. If I have been capable of expressing them they are contained in the pictures, hence visible to all.

—Carlo Battaglia

Carlo Battaglia's first one-man show was in 1964 at the La Salita gallery in Rome. At that time, his work was based on the rapport between space and colour. The show heralded a significant change in his work which, as noted by Milton Gendel in 1966, signified "the end of his research between the School of Paris and of New York". In *Spazio Ambiguo* of 1966, a

large rectangle occupies the central part of the canvas in the manner of a window across which an orthogonal takes on the character of a road moving to infinity until interrupted by a horizontal line.

From 1967 his painting changed, in accordance with that particular tendency characterised by Argan as the transition of Cubism from Mondrian to Constructivism. In this way, after a brief stay in Paris, Battaglia moved to New York for some time. The works of this period convey a strong geometric character. Between 1967 and 1968, he produced a series of works forming the cycle Misterioso in which he organized the picture plane in different perspectival planes to create an advancing and receding space. Our attention is directed around an ordered geometrical space of outlines and blocks of form to create a perspectival illusion.

The year 1969 was marked by a new departure. *Light Visionario* and *Solitario* both make their impact as large monochrome canvases with soft and hazy mood. Libertated from any geometric reference these works have become like large windows open to a sky of visionary light. In 1970, the year he took part in the Venice Biennale, Battaglia produced the first works based on two opposing characters, one geometric, and the other evocative and visionary. By now, he had arrived at his personal poetic style. The structure of the surface is abbreviated to horizontal marks or isolated strokes of geometric form overlaying the visionary field of colour and light. Out of this period come *Cadmus, Calypso, Renir, Spargi, Diaspro*—all works of 1970—that confirm the artist's declaration: "What I have sought to do is to imbue the picture with as much significance as possible, including signifiers whose origin seems quite obscure, to give force to this garden of images." Gradually, the geometric shapes give way to the colour-light field which has now assumed a dominant role. Having abandoned geometric rigour, Battaglia releases the picture, free to evoke a natural world.

Grande immagine parallela (1976), a large work of ten metres length, constitutes a poetic introduction to the work which will follow. In this parallel image of the natural world, Battaglia attempts to overcome the anachronistic dichotomy between figuration and abstraction, a position that is to become clearer in later work. Emblematic of this intention is *Grande Oceana Blu* of 1980 / 81. An area of sea (as evinced by the title) is painted as an arrangement of wavey marks in chiaroscuro. This work recalls those made ten years earlier which evoked a luminescent blue sky, while the most recent works, such as the series *Oltremare* (1982 / 83), the reference is to the ocean depths.

In this most recent work, references to the natural world are more pronounced. By means of a highly refined technique, Battaglia continually inserts an element of ambivalence, making the meaning difficult to grasp—as in *Gli dei a Gibellina* of 1985, where the landscape continually moves between land and sea. In this way Battaglia stresses his need to put in every significance possible.

—Roberto Lambarelli

BAYER, Herbert.
American. Born in Haag, Austria, 5 April 1900; emigrated to the United States, 1938; naturalized, 1944. Educated at gymnasium, Linz, Austria, 1911–17; apprentice in architecture and decorative arts, under architect George Schmidthammer, Linz, 1919; graphic design and typography assistant to architect Emanuel Margold, Darmstadt, Germany, 1920; studied mural painting and design, with Vasily Kandinsky, at the Staatliche Bauhaus, in Weimar, 1921–23, and in Dessau, 1925–28. Served in Infantry Regiment 14, Austrian Army, 1917–19. Married Irene Hecht in 1925 (divorced); daughter: Julia; married Joella Haweis Levy in 1944. Young Master of Typography and

Graphic Design, Staatliche Bauhaus, Dessau, 1925–28; Director, Dorland Studio of Design, and active as painter, photographer, graphic designer and exhibition architect, Berlin 1928–30; painter, photographer, graphic designer, and exhibition architect, New York, 1938–45; Director, Dorland International design company, New York, 1945; Consultant Designer, 1945–56, and Chairman of Department of Design, 1956–65, Container Corporation of America, Chicago. Consultant and Architect, Aspen Institute of Humanistic Studies, Colorado, 1946–85; Art and Design Consultant, Atlantic Richfield Company, Los Angeles, 1966–85. Visiting Artist, Jerusalem Foundation, 1977; Artist-in-Residence, American Academy, Rome, 1978. Recipient: First Prize, *Foreign Advertising Photography* exhibition, New York, 1931; Medal, City of Salzburg, Austria, 1936; Gold Medal, Art Directors Club of Philadelphia, 1961; Trustees Award, Aspen Institute for Humanistic Studies, Colorado, 1965; Ambassador's Award for Excellence, London, 1968; Kulturpreis for Photography, Cologne, 1969; Gold Medal, American Institute of Graphic Arts, 1970; Adalbert Stifter Preis für Bildende Kunst Verliehen, Linz, Austria, 1971; Austrian Cross of Honor for Art and Science, 1978. Honorary Doctorate: Technische Hochschule, Graz, Austria, 1973; D.F.A.: Philadelphia College of Art, 1974. Honorary Member, Alliance Graphique Internationale, 1975; Honorary Fellow, Royal Academy of Fine Art, The Hague, Netherlands, 1975. Fellow, American Academy of Arts and Sciences, 1979. Agent: Marlborough Gallery, 40 West 57th Street, New York, New York 10019. *Died* (in Montecito, California) 30 September 1985.

Individual Exhibitions:

1929	Kunstverein Marz, Linz, Austria
	Galerie Povolotsky, Paris
1931	Staatliche Bauhaus, Dessau, Germany
1936	Kunstverein, Salzburg, Austria
1937	London Gallery
1939	Black Mountain College, North Carolina
	P.M. Gallery, New York
1940	Yale University, New Haven, Connecticut
1943	Willard Gallery, New York
	North Texas State Teachers College, Denton
1944	Outline Gallery, Pittsburgh
1947	*The Way Beyond Art*, Brown University, Providence, Rhode Island (retrospective; toured the United States, 1947–49)
1952	Cleveland Institute of Art
1953	Hans Schaeffer Galleries, New York
1954	Kunstkabinett Klihm, Munich
	Galleria del Milione, Milan
1955	Aspen Institute for Humanistic Studies, Colorado
1956	*33 Years of Herbert Bayer's Work*, Germanisches Nationalmuseum, Nuremberg, West Germany (retrospective; travelled to Munich, Zurich, Berlin, Braunschweig and Vienna, 1956–57)
1957	Kunstkabinett Klihm, Munich
1958	*Recent Works*, Fort Worth Art Center, Texas (travelled to the Walker Art Center, Minneapolis)
1959	Kunstkabinett Klihm, Munich
1960	Städtische Kunsthalle, Dusseldorf
	Museum am Ostwall, Dortmund, West Germany
1961	Bauhaus Archiv, Darmstadt, West Germany
1962	Stadtisches Kunstmuseum, Duisberg, West Germany (retrospective; toured the United States, Germany and Italy)
1963	Andrew Morris Gallery, New York
	Neue Galerle, Linz, Austria
1964	Aspen Institute for Humanistic Studies, Colorado
	5207 Galleries, Oklahoma City
1965	Byron Gallery, New York
	Esther Robles Gallery, Los Angeles
	Boise Art Association, Idaho
1966	University of New Hampshire, Durham
1967	Galerie Klihm, Munich
	Galerie Conzen, Dusseldorf
	Philadelphia Art Alliance
1968	Marlborough New London Gallery

Herbert Bayer: *Aging Star*, **1968** Courtesy Museum of Contemporary Art, Chicago

1969   University of California at Santa Barbara
        Two Visions of Space: Herbert Bayer and Ingeborg ten Haeff, Hudson River Museum, Yonkers, New York
1970   Dunkelman Gallery, Toronto
        Germanisches Nationalmuseum, Nuremberg
        Galerie Conzen, Dusseldorf
1971   Marlborough Gallery, New York
        Centre Culturel Allemand, Paris
        Goethe-Institut, Paris
        Die Neue Sammlung, Munich
        Österreichisches Museum für Angewandte Kunst, Vienna
1972   Marlborough Gallery, Montreal
        Mer-Kup Galerias, Mexico City
1973   Landesbildstelle, Hamburg (travelled to Krefeld and Leverkusen)
        Saarland Museum, Saarbrücken
        Herbert Bayer: A Total Concept, Denver Art Museum (retrospective)
1974   Marlborough Galerie, Zurich
        Galerie Klihm, Munich
        Galerie Nächst St. Stephan, Vienna (travelled to Innsbruck and Graz)
        Marlborough Graphics, New York (toured the United States, 1974–75)
        Das Druckgrafische Werk bis 1971, Haus Deutscher Ring, Hamburg (retrospective; toured Germany, Switzerland, Portugal and Spain), 1974–76)
1975   Marlborough Gallery, Toronto
        Arte Contacto Galeria, Caracas
1976   *Beispiele aus dem Gesamtwerk 1919–1974*, Neue Galerie, Linx, Austria
        Graphics and Small Sculptures, Marlborough Gallery, New York
        Photomontages, Marlborough Gallery, New York
1977   Marian Locks Gallery, Philadelphia
        From Type to Landscape, Hopkins Center, Dart-

mouth College, Hanover, New Hampshire (American Federation of Art show; toured the United States)
        Photographic Works, Arco Center for Visual Art, Los Angeles (toured the United States)
1978   *Tapestries and Environmental Designs*, Galerie Klihm, Munich
        Museum Bochum, West Germany (retrospective)
1979   *Recent Works*, Marlborough Gallery, New York
        Photographic Exhibition, Galerie Breiting, West Berlin
1980   *Inaugural Exhibition of the Herbert Bayer Archive*, Denver Art Museum
        Neue Gallery, Linz, Austria
        Galerias Mer-Kup, Mexico City
1981   *A Selected Survey*, Grapestake Gallery, San Francisco
        Centre Georges Pompidou, Paris (with Umbo)
        University of California, Santa Barbara
1982   Bauhaus Archiv, West Berlin (travelled to Basle)
1983   Galerie Thomas, Munich
1984   Galerie Lopes, Zurich
        Saidenberg Gallery, New York
1986   Museum fur Gestaltung, West Berlin
1987   Quadrat Moderne Galerie, Bottrop, West Germany
        Kunsthaus, Zug, Switzerland
        Oberosterreichisches Landesmuseum, Linz, Austria

Selected Group Exhibitions:

1923   *Kunst and Technik: Eine neue Einheit*, Bauhaus und Staatliches Landesmuseum, Weimar
1929   *Film und Foto*, Stuttgart
1936   *Entartete Kunst*, Haus der Deutschen Kunst, Munich
1959   *V Bienal*, São Paulo
1964   *Documenta*, Kassel, West Germany
1966   *Les Années 25*, Musée des Art Décoratifs, Paris

1967   *50 Jahre Bauhaus*, Württembergische Kunstverein, Stuttgart (toured Europe, the United States, Canada, Argentina and Japan)
1978   *Paris-Berlin 1900–1933*, Centre Georges Pompidou, Paris
1980   *Avant-Garde Photography in Germany 1919–1939*, San Francisco Museum of Modern Art (toured the United States)
1985   *Das Aktfoto*, Fotomuseum im Stadtmuseum, Munich

Collections:

Museum of Modern Art, New York; Fogg Art Museum, Cambridge, Massachusetts; Denver Art Museum, Colorado (Archives); Santa Barbara Museum of Art, California; San Francisco Museum of Modern Art; Neue Galerie der Stadt Linz, Austria; Museum Folkwang, Essen; Bauhaus Archiv, Berlin; Nationalgalerie, Berlin; Nazionale d'Arte Moderna, Rome

Publications:

By BAYER: books—*Fotomontagen*, portfolio of 11 photomontages, Berlin 1932; *Fotoplastiken*, portfolio of 10 photos, Berlin 1937; *Bauhaus 1919–1928*, with Ise and Walter Gropius, New York 1938, 1959, 1975; *Seven Convolutions*, portfolio of lithographs, Colorado Springs 1948; *World Geo-Graphic Atlas*, Aspen, Colorado 1953; *Book of Drawings*, Chicago 1961; *Eight Monochrome Suite*, portfolio of lithographs, Los Angeles 1965; *Herbert Bayer: Paintings*, portfolio of reproductions, Chicago 1965; *Herbert Bayer: Painter/Designer/Architect*, New York, Ravensburg, London and Tokyo 1967; *Herbert Bayer*, portfolio of 6 silkscreens, with introduction by Dieter Honisch, Stuttgart 1968; articles—"Reflections from One of the Sculptors Who Contributed to the 'Route of Friendship' " in *Architecture Formes et Fonctions* (Lausanne), 1969; "Typography and Design" in *Concepts of the Bauhaus: Busch-Reisinger Museum Collection*, exhibition catalogue, Cambridge, Massachusetts 1971; foreward to *The Graphic Design of Yusaka Kamekura* by Masuro Katsumi, New York 1973; "Herbert Bayer," interview, in *Dialogue with Photography*, edited by Paul Hill and Thomas Cooper, London 1979; "Many Paths from the Bauhaus," interview, in *Darkroom Photography* (San Francisco), January/February 1981.

On BAYER: books—*The Way Beyond Art: The Work of Herbert Bayer* by Alexander Dorner, New York 1947; *Fotoauge Herbert Bayer*, exhibition catalogue, edited by Jan Tschichold, Munich 1967; *Herbert Bayer*, exhibition catalogue, with text by Ludwig Grote, London 1968; *50 Jahre Bauhaus*, exhibition catalogue, by Wulf Herzongenrath, Stuttgart and London 1968; *Two Visions of Space: Herbert Bayer and Ingeborg ten Haeff*, exhibition catalogue, with introduction by Carl Black, Jr., New York 1969; *The Bauhaus* by Hans M. Wingler, Cambridge, Massachusetts 1969; *Painters of the Bauhaus* by Eberhard Roters, New York 1969; *Bauhaus and Bauhaus People*, edited by Eckhard Neumann, New York 1970; *Herbert Bayer: A Total Concept*, exhibition catalogue, with introduction by Karl Otto Bach, Denver 1973; *Herbert Bayer: Das Druckgrafische Werk bis 1971*, with text by Hans M. Wingler and Peter Hahn, Berlin 1974; *Herbert Bayer*, exhibition catalogue, with introductions by Ida Rodriguez Prampolini, Zurich 1974; *Photographie als Kunstlerisches Experiment* by Willi Rotzler, Lucerne and Frankfurt 1974; *Herbert Bayer: Un Concepta Total* by Ida Rodriguez Prampolini, Mexico City 1975; *Beispiele aus dem Gesamtwerk 1919–1974*, exhibition catalogue, with introduction by Peter Baum, Linz 1976; *Photomontage* by Dawn Ades, London and New York 1976; *Herbert Bayer: From Type to Landscape*, exhibition catalogue, with text by Jan van der Marck, New York 1977; with text by Leland Rice and Beaumont Newhall, Los Angeles, 1977; *Kunstlerphotographie im XX. Jahrhundert*, exhibition catalogue, edited by Carl-Albrecht Haenlein, Hannover 1977; *Neue Sachlichkeit und German Realism of the Twenties*, exhibition catalogue, by Wieland Schmied and Ute Eskildsen, London 1978; *Das Experimentelle Photo in Deutschland 1918–1940* by Emilio Bertonati, Munich 1978; *Paris-Berlin 1900–1933*, exhibition catalogue, by Herbert Molderings, Werner Spies, Günter Metken and others, Paris 1978; *Photographen der 20er Jahre* by Karl Steinorth, Munich 1979; *Film und Foto der 20er Jahre*, exhibition catalogue, by Ute Eskildsen and Jan Christopher Horak, Stuttgart 1979; *Internationale Ausstellung des Deutschen Werkbundes "Film und Foto" 1929*, facsimile reprint, edited by Karl Steinorth, Stuttgart 1979; *Herbert Bayer: Recent Works*, exhibition catalogue, New York 1979; *Herbert Bayer: Das kunstlerische Werk 1918–1938*, exhibition catalogue, West Berlin 1982; *Herbert Bayer: The Complete Work* by Arthur A. Cohen, Cambridge, Massachusetts 1984.

I believe in a totality of art and design integrated with the life of our time. I have extensively collaborated with industry and other institutions toward the visual improvements in life.

—Herbert Bayer (1983)

Of all the artists who taught at the Bauhaus, Herbert Bayer was the most prone to the non-figurative-design way of life promoted by that institution. He himself was particularly active in the field of design, and much of what he produced at that time still influences the works of contemporary lay-out and functional design (and craft) as it is found in the notepaper, packaging and kindred requirements in bureaux of industry, commerce and trade today.

Something of this commercial "awareness" percolated through to his art works. Accuracy is exact. Almost over-exact. Techniques are manifold and he is the master of all of them. Neatness is the key-word to the entire oeuvre. The shapes and the compositions in which they find themselves cannot be faulted. Colours are chosen with unyielding care but not with love. Any one of Bayer's pictures could grace the boardroom without affront and without distracting attention from business. The words "modern art" would not pass through the head of any of the directors. Bayer is "safe," efficient, and burdened with good taste, a kind of glyptothek taste that wounds none, however up-to-date in accent.

Can he claim a place in the ranks of Contemporary Artists? As a stylist and one whose influence on design is far from moribund—Yes.

In the words of Will Grohmann, "Bayer was first and foremost a graphic designer, and secondly a painter who, with patterns and metal foil, succeeded in transcending reality."

—Sheldon Williams

BAZAINE, Jean.

French. Born in Paris, 21 December 1904. Educated in the Ile-de-France, 1914–20; studied sculpture with Landowski, Paris, 1920–24; mainly self-taught in painting, from 1924. Independent painter, Paris, since 1924; associated with artists Pierre Bonnard and Marcel Gromaire, from 1932; executed stained glass windows for church of Assy, 1943–47, for Chateau de la Chaux, Morvan, 1954, for church of Villaparisis 1958, and murals for church of Audincourt, 1951, Unesco Building, Paris, 1960, Maison de la Radio, Paris, 1963, and windows for Saint Severin, Paris, 1966. Recipient: Prix Blumenthal, Paris 1938; Grand Prix National des Arts, 1964. Address: c/o Editions de Seuil, 27 rue Jacob, 75006 Paris, France.

Individual Exhibitions:

1932	Galerie Van Leer, Paris
1934	Galerie Van Leer, Paris
1941	Galerie Jeanne Bucher, Paris
1945	Galerie Louis Carre, Paris (with Esteve and Lapicque)
1946	Stedelijk Museum, Amsterdam (with Esteve and Lapicque; travelled to the Statens Museum for Konst, Copenhagen, and the Foreningen for Nutida Konst, Stockholm)
1949	Galerie Maeght, Paris
1950	Galerie Blanche, Stockholm
1953	Galerie Maeght, Paris
1957	Galerie Maeght, Paris
1958	Galerie Benador, Geneva
1959	Kunsthalle, Berne, Switzerland (retrospective; travelled to Van Abbemuseum, Eindhoven, Netherlands, and the Stedelijk Museum, Amsterdam)
1963	Kestner-Gesellschaft, Hannover (retrospective; travelled to the Kunsthaus, Zurich, and the Kunstnernes Hus, Oslo)
1964	Galerie Blanche, Stockholm (travelled to the Konstmuseum, Gothenburg)
1965	Musée d'Art Moderne, Paris (retrospective)
	Galerie Louis Carre, Paris
1968	Galerie Maeght, Paris
1975	*Aquarelles*, Villand-Galanis, Paris
1976	Galerie Maeght, Zurich
1979	Galerie Moderner Kunst, Frankfurt
1980	*Paintings and Watercolours 1970–1979*, Talbot Rice Art Centre, Edinburgh (travelled to the Institut Francais, London)

Selected Group Exhibitions:

1937	*L'Art Indépendant: Maitres d'Aujourd'hui*, Petit Palais, Paris
1941	*20 Jeunes Peintres de Tradition Francaise*, Galerie Braun, Paris
1942	*Bazaine/Esteve/Lapicque/Villon*, Galerie Louis Carre, Paris
1948	*Biennale*, Venice
1951	*Bienal*, San Paulo
1952	*Biennale*, Venice
1953	*Bienal*, Sao Paulo
1955	*Documenta*, Kassel, West Germany
1958	*World's Fair*, Brussels
1959	*Documenta*, Kassel, West Germany

Collections:

Centre Georges Pompidou, Paris; Stedelijk Museum, Amsterdam

Publications:

By BAZAINE: books—*La Noce Noire*, illustrations to poem by André Frenaud, Paris 1947; *Notes sur la peinture d'aujourd'hui*, Paris 1948, 1953, 1960; *Hollande*, with text by Jean Tardieu, Paris 1962; *Entre Savoir et Croire*, illustrations to text by Pierre Lecomte du Nouy, Paris 1964.

On BAZAINE: books—*Bazaine, Esteve, Lapicque*, exhibition catalogue, with text by André Frenaud, Paris 1945; *Peintres d'Aujourd'hui* by Pierre Courthion, Geneva 1952; *Jean Bazaine* by Jean Leymarie, Paris 1959; *Jean Bazaine*, exhibition catalogue, with text by Franz Meyer, Berne 1959; *Jean Bazaine*, exhibition catalogue, with text by Ole Henrik Moe, Oslo 1963; *Jean Bazaine*, exhibition catalogue, with text by Werner Schmalenbach, Hannover and Zurich 1963; *Jean Bazaine*, exhibition catalogue, with text by Bernard Dorival, Paris 1965; *Bazaine: Aquarelles*, exhibition catalogue, with text by Jean-Claude Schneider, Paris 1975; *Bazaine: Paintings and Watercolours 1970–1979*, exhibition catalogue, with text by Jean-Claude Schneider, Edinburgh and London 1980.

During the 1930's Jean Bazaine painted in a manner of expressive Naturalism in which the impact of the late Impressionism of Monet and Bonnard combined with influences from the Naturalism of Gromaire. Always sensitive to the value of tradition, he acknowledged his debt to both Fauvism and Cubism although he was never a convert to either style. He painted still lifes and landscapes, striving to come ever closer to the expressive individuality of his theme as in the "Nageur dans les roseaux" of 1943. During the 1940's he became increasingly discontent with the reproduction of expressive appearances and made it his aim to present the mysterious inner reality which lies behind the visible and external, what he called the "interior geometry of forms"—the secret rhythms and structure which in his view unite each individual thing with the totality of things while at the same time endowing it with its separate particularity for human feeling. Thus he evolved a non-objective mode of expression which had little in common with the "psychic improvisation" of Wols and Hartung or with the "automatism" of Riopelle but brought him within the ambit of the group of artists around Roger Bissière who wished to display the expressive structure of things without fidelity to appearances. His style at this time had affinities with that of the Tachists Charles Lapique, Alfred Manessier and Jean le Moal.

His essay *Notes sur la peintre d'aujourd'hui*, first published in 1948, gives an illuminating insight into his own artistic outlook and is perhaps the best statement ever made of the philosophy which animated painters of this school. In it he says: "A tree, a landscape, even a human face, I see these through their complex network of directions, their lines of force." He denies that his work was abstract in any other sense than that in which all art is necessarily abstract, but claimed that "the object must disappear as object to find its justification as form" and that in painting "an essential quality of the object devours the object." He also said that it was his aim "to retrieve the essential by violent means, the passion for expression relying on the choice of elementary colours and forms." His work at this period consisted typically of a lattice of firm and criss-cross lines in glowing, semi-transparent colours on several planes and distantly reminiscent of the stained glass technique in which he also worked. An example is "La Messe de l'Homme armé" (1944, illustrated in colour in Bernard Dorival's *Les Peintres du Vingtième Siècle*).

It was because of his belief in the unity of the whole universe and man, the oneness of form and feeling, that he understood his own style to represent a continuation and culmination of the main tradition of French painting. "True sensibility," he wrote, "begins when the painter discovers that the eddies of a tree and the bark of the water are kin, that the stones and his own face are twins, and when as the whole world thus shrinks together he gradually sees arise under this rain of appearances those great essential signs which are at once his own truth and the truth of the universe. For more than half a century we have shared the efforts of French painting to give ever new shape to its incarnation, to realize this interpretation, this great common structure, this profound resemblance between man and the world without which no living form exists."

From the mid 1950's his style became somewhat less rectilinear, as in the painting "Rochetaillée" (1955, illustrated in colour in Marcel Brion: *Art Abstrait*) and more free in the manner of Robert Lapoujade or Pierre Dmitrienko, as in "The Sea at Noon" (1960, illustrated in colour in H. Osborne: *The Oxford Companion to Twentieth-Century Art*).

—Harold Osborne

BEAL, Jack.

American. Born in Richmond, Virginia, 25 June 1931. Educated at the Norfolk Division of William and Mary College, Virginia, 1950–53; studied at the Art Institute of Chicago, under Briggs Dyer, Isobel MacKinnon and Kathleen Blackshear, 1953–56; University of Chicago, 1955–56. Painter: lives and works in New York. Artist-in-Residence/Visiting Lecturer, University of Indiana, Bloomington, 1966; Purdue University, Lafayette, Indiana, 1967; University of Wisconsin, Madison, 1967; and Cooper Union, New York, 1968. Recipient: First Prize, *University of Chicago Arts Festival*, 1955; Wild Award, *70th American Exhibition*, Art Institute of Chicago, 1972; National Endowment for the Arts Grant, 1972. Agent: Allan Frumkin Gallery, 50 West 57th Street, New York, New York 10019. Address: 67 Vestry Street, New York, New York 10013; and 83-A Delhi Stage, Oneonta, New York 13820, U.S.A.

Individual Exhibitions:

1965	Allan Frumkin Gallery, New York (2 exhibitions)
1966	Allan Frumkin Gallery, Chicago

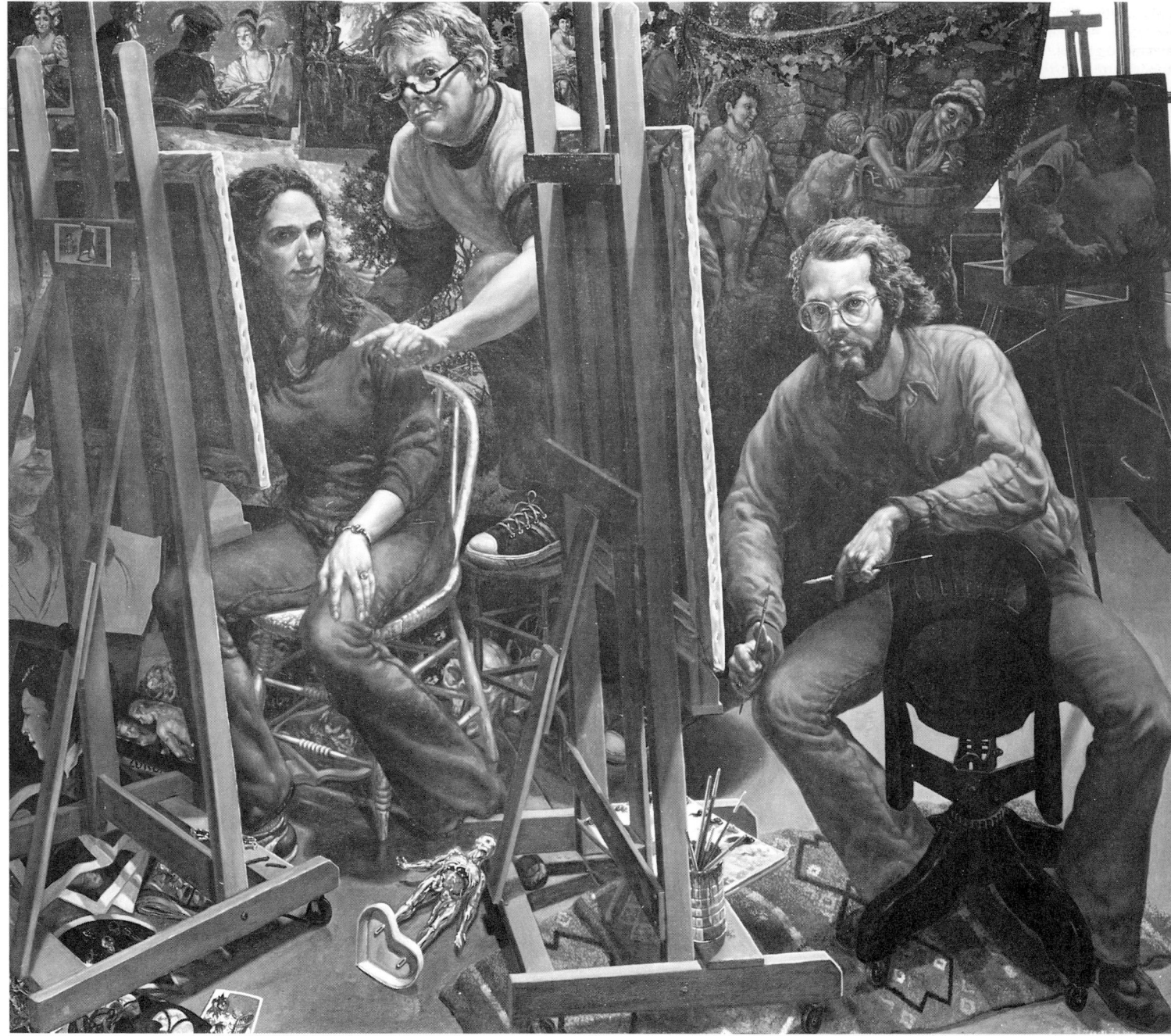

Jack Beal: *The Painting Lesson*, 1981

1967 Allan Frumkin Gallery, New York
1968 *Recent Paintings by Jack Beal*, Allan Frumkin Gallery, New York
1969 Allan Frumkin Gallery, Chicago
1970 Allan Frumkin Gallery, New York
1972 Allan Frumkin Gallery, New York
Miami-Dade Junior College, Florida
1973 Allan Frumkin Gallery, New York
Galerie Claude Bernard, Paris
Virginia Museum, Richmond (retrospective; travelled to Boston University, and the Museum of Contemporary Art, Chicago, 1974)
1974 Allan Frumkin Gallery, Chicago
1975 Allan Frumkin Gallery, New York
1978 Allan Frumkin Gallery, New York
1980 Allan Frumkin Gallery, New York
Reynolds' Minor Gallery, Richmond, Virginia

Selected Group Exhibitions:

1968 *Whitney Annual*, Whitney Museum, New York (and 1969)

1969 *Aspects of a New Realism*, Milwaukee Art Center (toured the United States)
1971 *New Realism*, Art Gallery of the State University of New York at Potsdam (travelled to the Delaware Art Museum, Wilmington)
1973 *American Realism: Post Pop*, Oakland University, Rochester, Michigan
1975 *Drawings: Techniques and Types*, William Benton Museum of Art, University of Connecticut, Storrs
Portrait Painting 1970–1975, Allan Frumkin Gallery, New York
1976 *America 1976*, United States Department of the Interior travelling Exhibition (toured the United States, 1976–78)
1979 *100 Artists/100 Years: Alumni of the School of the Art Institute of Chicago*, Art Institute of Chicago
1981 *Contemporary American Realism since 1960*, Pennsylvania Academy of Fine Arts, Philadelphia
1985 *American Realism*, San Francisco Museum of Modern Art (travelled to Lincoln, Massachusetts; Austin, Texas; Evanston, Illinois; Williamstown, Massachusetts; Akron, Ohio; Madison, Wisconsin)

Collections:

Whitney Museum, New York; Museum of Modern Art, New York; Neuberger Museum, Purchase, New York; University of Vermont, Burlington; Delaware Art Museum, Wilmington; University of North Carolina, Chapel Hill; Art Institute of Chicago; Minneapolis Institute of Art; Walker Art Center, Minneapolis; Museum of Modern Art, San Francisco.

Publications:

On BEAL: books—*Recent Painting by Jack Beal*, exhibition catalogue, with an introduction by R. C. Kenedy, New York 1968; *Aspects of a New Realism*, exhibition catalogue, with texts by Sidney Tillim and William Wilson, Milwaukee 1969; *22 Realists*, exhibition catalogue, New York 1970; *Jack Beal*, exhibition catalogue, with text by Mark Strand, Paris 1973; *Jack Beal*, exhibition catalogue, with text by Peter Schjeldahl, Norfolk, Virginia 1973; *Jack Beal*, exhibition catalogue, with text by Gerrit Henry, New York 1975; *100 Artists/100 Years: Alumni of the School of the Art Institute of Chicago*, Chicago 1979; articles—"Is Jack Beal Still a Figurative Painter?" by Scott Burton in *Art Scene* (Chicago), April 1969.

Make art like life—make life like art—that's become my motto. As a student my training was confined to modernist aesthetics and practices, which I finally found too restrictive. I began to paint from Life, and realized that I could use everything I had learned from modernism, *and* all that study of great representational art had taught me, to make paintings about the best of life as we live it. This purpose grew as I understood that the arts had influenced my own life at least as much as the experience of life itself had done. I hope to contribute to that tradition.

—Jack Beal

Among the diverse painters who arose during the late 1960's under the banner of 'New Realism,' Jack Beal lies somewhere towards the middle. Over the years his work has been more closely aligned with that of Philip Pearlstein and Alfred Leslie than that of the Photo-Realists. Beal concentrates on tightly controlled organization, structuring his complex composition with clarity of detail, intricate articulation of contour, color and light in a manner which implies the mentality of a post-Pop, post-formalist abstraction context. He is most noted for his compositions of the figure (many of them nudes) in interior environments filled with complexly patterned fabrics, which stress a dynamically diagonal thrust and a point of view slightly below eye level.

Among the best of these is Beal's "Danae" (1972) which skillfully incorporates flesh, figure, pattern and sharp light and shadow in an intimate interior, conveying a sense of presence yielded by its deliberately dispassionate ordering. Beal, like Pearlstein, stresses the objectivity of his analysis which treats the figure as one element among the many in the composition. Yet despite the sense of distancing and the anti-narrative leaning, there is always a psychological element which reads as content beyond the formal in Beal's pictoral analyses. It is evoked by the very openness of the forms whose blank, nonjudgmental qualities constitute a state of mind as concrete as it is aesthetic. The title, "Danae," is suggestive of Beal's involvement with Renaissance to Baroque themes and structures which have lately come even more into the forefront of his painting.

In 1977 Beal completed a series of four murals commissioned by the General Services Administration for the Department of Labor Building in Washington, D.C. on the given theme of the History of American Labor. For help in accomplishing this complex task, Beal turned to the art historical past, specifically to Caravaggio, the Italian Mannerists and Benjamin West, for various elements of dramatic realism, composition and figure drawing. The murals, titled "Settlement," "Colonization," "Industry" and "Technology," are 12 by 12 foot, monumental statements of a sweeping moral nature which have earned Beal the position of being called the most prominent Social Realist in America since the 1930's generation.

Although Beal continues to paint his more intimate studies of figures and textured surroundings, he has also produced works of a more directly traditional thematic kind. In a series titled "Vices and Virtues" (Envy, Sloth, Prudence, Avarice, Lust, Anger, Justice, Fortitude), Beal makes his contemporary models into allegorical figures who symbolize the traditionally moral themes. As always, the compositions are tight and complex, stressing diagonal motion which is more violent in the painting of "Anger" and more meditatively dynamic in "Fortitude." In his large paintings "The Farm" (1979) and "Harvest" (1980), Beal takes on a more bucolic subject matter. Painted on his farm in Oneonta, New York, these two pictures combine two figures in a rural setting which is highly idealized. The man and woman in "The Farm" are painting some pigs in the company of a dog/companion and in a setting filled with some flowers and sun and blue skies. People, animals, art and nature working in harmony, the details of which are given tender loving care which is reminiscent of the Hudson River School painters and, even more, of the

Pre-Raphaelite William Holman Hunt. However, there is the basic difference of context, relevance and artifice, and, although Beal is a master technician, the pictures come across as a kind of adaptation from the past which remains more in the realm of the formal than the social real or meaningful real, whether as art or as nature.

—Barbara Cavaliere

BEARDEN, Romare (Howard).

American. Born in Charlotte, North Carolina, 2 September 1914. Educated at Public School 139, New York, until 1925; Peabody High School, Pittsburgh, Pennsylvania, 1925–29; New York University, 1932–35, B.S. 1935; studied under George Grosz, at the Art Students League, New York, 1936–37; studied advanced mathematics at Columbia University, New York, 1943, and philosophy and art history at the Sorbonne, Paris, 1951. Served in the 372nd Infantry, United States Army, 1942–45. Married Nanette Rohan in 1954. Case Worker, New York City Department of Social Services, 1938–42, 1946–49, and 1952–66. Travelled in Italy, Switzerland, Algiers, and Morocco, 1950; concentrated on song writing, 1951–54; established studio on Canal Street, New York, 1956; Art Director, Harlem Cultural Council, New York, since 1964; Co-Founder, with Norman Lewis and Ernest Crichlow, Cinque Gallery in New York Public Theater, 1969; Set and Costume Designer for Alvin Ailey Ballet Company, New York, 1977. Artist-in-Residence, Spelman College, Atlanta, 1968; Visiting Lecturer in African and Afro-American Art, Williams College, Williamstown, Massachusetts, 1969; Artist-in-Residence, University of Delaware, Newark, 1970; Instructor, Yale College, New Haven, Connecticut, 1980. Recipient: American Academy of Arts and Letters Painting Award, 1966; National Institute of Arts and Letters Grant, 1966; Guggenheim Fellowship, 1970; Ford Foundation Fellowship, 1973; Medal of the State of North Carolina, 1976; Frederick Douglas Medal, New York Urban League, 1978; James Weldon Johnson Award, Atlanta Chapter of the National Association for the Advancement of Colored People (NAACP), 1978. Honorary Doctorates: Pratt Institute, New York, 1973; Carnegie Mellon University, Pittsburgh, 1975; Maryland Institute of Art, Baltimore, 1976; North Carolina Central University, Durham, 1977; Davidson College, North Carolina, 1978. Member, American Academy of Arts and Letters. Agent: Cordier and Ekstrom Inc., 980 Madison Avenue, New York, New York 10021. Address: 357 Canal Street, New York, New York 10013, U.S.A.

Individual Exhibitions:

1935	"G" Place Gallery, Washington, D.C.
1940	A. D. Bates Studio, New York
1944	*10 Hieroglyphic Paintings,* "G" Place Gallery, Washington, D.C.
1945	Galerie John Duvuloy, Paris (with Pietro Lazzari)
	"G" Place Gallery, Washington, D.C.
	Samuel Kootz Gallery, New York
1946	Samuel Kootz Gallery, New York
1947	Samuel Kootz Gallery, New York
1948	Niveau Gallery, New York
1955	Barone Gallery, New York
1960	Michel Warren Gallery, New York
1961	Cordier and Ekstrom Gallery, New York
1964	*Projections,* Cordier and Ekstrom Gallery, New York
1966	Carnegie Institute, Pittsburgh
	6 Panels on a Southern Theme, Bundy Art Gallery, Waitsfield, Vermont
	Corcoran Gallery, Washington, D.C.
1967	Fine Arts Building, Spelman College, Atlanta
	Collages, J. L. Hudson Gallery, Detroit
	Cordier and Ekstrom Gallery, New York
1968	*Paintings and Projections,* State University of New York at Albany
1969	Williams College, Williamstown, Massachusetts
	Iowa State University, Iowa City
1970	Cordier and Ekstrom Gallery, New York
	Tricia Karliss Gallery, Provincetown, Massachusetts
	The Prevalence of Ritual, Museum of Modern Art, New York (retrospective; toured the United States, 1971–72)
	Cordier and Ekstrom Gallery, New York
1973	Cordier and Ekstrom Gallery, New York
1974	Galerie Albert Loeb, Paris
	Madison Art Museum, Wisconsin
	Everson Museum, Syracuse, New York
	Of the Blues, Cordier and Ekstrom Gallery, New York
1976	Firehouse Gallery, Nassau College, New York
	Graphics Gallery, Toronto
	Cordier and Ekstrom Gallery, New York
1977	Union College, Cranford, New Jersey
	Odysseus: Collages, Cordier and Ekstrom Gallery, New York
1978	Cordier and Ekstrom Gallery, New York
	Davidson College, North Carolina
1980	*Retrospective: 1970–1980,* Mint Museum, Charlotte, North Carolina (travelled to the Mississippi Museum of Art, Jackson; Baltimore Museum of Art; and the Virginia Museum of Fine Arts, Richmond, 1981)
1981	*Collages: Profile: The 30's,* Cordier and Ekstrom Gallery, New York

Selected Group Exhibitions:

1945	*Annual Exhibition,* Whitney Museum, New York (and 1946, 1955, 1969)
1948	*6 American Painters,* Galerie Maeght, Paris
	Abstract and Surrealist American Art, Art Institute of Chicago
1951	*Survey of American Art,* Metropolitan Museum of Art, New York
1968	*30 Contemporary Black Artists,* Minneapolis Institute of Art (toured the United States, 1968–70)
1969	*New American Painting and Sculpture,* Museum of Modern Art, New York
1970	*5 Famous Black Artists,* Museum of the National Center of Afro-American Arts, Boston
1981	*6 Black Americans,* New Jersey State Museum, Trenton
	The Human Form, Maryland Institute College of Art, Baltimore
	24 Black American Artists, Goucher College, Baltimore

Collections:

Metropolitan Museum of Art, New York; Museum of Modern Art, New York; Whitney Museum, New York; Rochester Memorial Art Gallery, New York; Museum of Fine Arts, Boston; Princeton University, New Jersey; Newark Museum, New Jersey; Philadelphia Museum of Art; High Museum of Art, Atlanta; Madison Art Center, Wisconsin.

Publications:

By BEARDEN: books—*The Painter's Mind,* with Carl Holty, New York 1969; *6 Black Masters of American Art,* with Harry Henderson, New York 1972; *Prevalence of Ritual,* portfolio of 5 silkscreens, New York 1977; articles—"The Negro Artist and Modern Art" in *Opportunity,* December 1934; "Problems of the Negro Artists" in *Critique,* October 1948; "Rectangular Structure in My Montage Paintings" in *Leonardo* (Paris), January 1969; "The Artist and His Education" in *Harvard Art Review* (Cambridge, Massachusetts), Spring 1969.

On BEARDEN: books—*Romare Bearden: Paintings and Projections,* exhibition catalogue, with text by Ralph Ellison, Albany, New York 1968; *Romare Bearden: The Prevalence of Ritual,* exhibition catalogue, with an introduction by Carroll

Greene, New York 1971; *The Art of Romare Bearden* by John Williams and Bundie Washington, New York 1974; *Of the Blues*, exhibition catalogue, with text by Albert Murray, New York 1975; *Romare Bearden: Odysseus: Collages*, exhibition catalogue, with an introduction by Calvin Tomkins, New York 1977; *Romare Bearden: Collages: Profile: The 30's*, exhibition catalogue, edited by Albert Murray, New York 1981; articles—"Romare Bearden—Projections" by Dore Ashton in *Quadrum* (Brussels), no. 17, 1965; "Black Persephone" by Ralph Pomeroy in *Artnews* (New York), October 1967; "Romare Bearden—Paintings and Projections" by Ralph Ellison in *Crisis* (New York), March 1970; "Profile: by Calvin Tomkins in *New Yorker*, 28 November 1977; "Romare Bearden: 'I Paint Out of the Tradition of the Blues' " by Avis Berman in *Artnews* (New York), December 1980; "Romare Bearden" in *Vogue* (New York), February 1981; "Romare Bearden" in *Smithsonian* (Washington, D.C.), March 1981; "Romare Bearden" in *Newsweek* (New York), 30 March 1981; "Romare Bearden: Rites and Riffs" by M. S. Campbell in *Art in America* (New York), December 1981.

Part of Romare Bearden's originality lies in his application of the formal means discovered by the Cubist masters at the beginning of the century to the world of the American black. Negro himself, he simply rethought the subject matter that interested and involved him most in such a way that he was able to "distance" it as an artist and, instead of some negative form of protest, to take the history and life of his race and present it anew in works of high artistic sophistication. He has looked fully and found Aphrodite in a vegetable patch, "The Three Musicians" in the apartment next door.

His themes run to jazz and folk music, urban and rural Negro life, rituals of baptism and voodoo, home life and street action. He prefers the archetypal and the not-too-specific image. He combines fragments of photostats and torn and cut paper which he has painted and mounts them on canvas. Usually he draws the composition beforehand in charcoal in the traditional manner. There is something especially "right" about his large collages in their mix of African imagery with Cubist space—a moving backwards as it were through art history past the discoveries of African art that led to the invention of Cubism. It is this formal strength that sets Bearden apart from many of his contemporaries. He is not afraid of the strong traditional qualities in his pictures. In fact he strives for them. By being so much a part of something already established in terms of time he is able to surmount the merely fashionable and enter a larger span of time. It is also a way of placing at the proper distance whatever it is he wants to show us. His sense of the largeness of his themes enables him not only to equate a field hand with a god, but to mix the races: it is no surprise in his work to come upon, say, a hand that has both black and white fingers. This way he avoids being pinned down to the over-simplified and the over-stressed. Because he has taken unexpected routes, he has succeeded in arriving at new realms of dignity.

—Ralph Pomeroy

BECHER, Bernhard and Hilla.

German. Bernhard Becher born in Siegen, 20 August 1931; studied painting and lithography at the Staatlichen Kunstakademie, Stuttgart, 1953–56, and typography at the Staatlichen Kunstakademie, Dusseldorf, 1957–61. Hilla Becher born Hilla Wobeser in Potsdam 2 September 1934; studied photography in Potsdam, and painting at the Staatlichen Kunstakademie, Dusseldorf. Bernhard and Hilla Becher married in 1961; they have worked together as freelance photographic artists, concentrating on industrial photography, Dusseldorf, since 1959. Both are instructors in photography at the Staatlichen Kunstakademie, Dusseldorf. Recipients: British Council Photo Study Grant, 1966; Fritz-Thyssen-Stiftung grant, West Germany, 1967–68. Agents: Galerie Konrad Fischer, Platanenstrasse 7, Dusseldorf; Nigel Greenwood Inc., 4

New Burlington Street, London W1X 1FE, England; and Sonnabend Gallery, 420 West Broadway, New York, New York 10012, U.S.A. Address: Wittlauer 4, Am Muhlenkamp 16, Dusseldorf, West Germany.

Individual Exhibitions:

1963	Galerie Ruth Nohl, Siegen, West Germany
1965	Galerie Pro, Bad Godesburg, West Germany
1966	Staatliche Kunstakademie, Dusseldorf
1967	Staatliches Museum, Munich
	Technische Hochschule, Karlsruhe
	Bergbau-Museum, Bochum, West Germany
	Kunstakademie, Copenhagen
1968	Wachsman Institute, University of Southern California, Los Angeles
	Goethe Center, San Francisco
	Stedelijk Van Abbemuseum, Eindhoven, Netherlands
	Galerie Ruth Nohl, Siegen, West Germany
	Städtisches Museum, Monchengladbach, West Germany
1969	Städtische Kunsthalle, Dusseldorf
1970	Städtisches Museum, Ulm, West Germany
	Form genom Funktion, Moderna Museet, Stockholm
	Galerie Konrad Fischer, Dusseldorf
1971	Kabinett für Aktuelle Kunst, Bremerhaven, West Germany
	Gegenverkehr, Aachen, West Germany
1972	Sonnabend Gallery, New York
	Bennington College, Vermont
1973	Galleria Forma, Genoa
	Nigel Greenwood Inc., London
	Sonnabend Gallery, New York
1974	Institute of Contemporary Arts, London (toured the U.K.)
	LaJolla Museum of Contemporary Art, California
	Sonnabend Gallery, New York
1975	*Fotografien* 1957–1975, Rheinisches Landesmuseum, Bonn
	Galleria Castelli, Milan
	Museum of Modern Art, New York
	Sonnabend Gallery, New York
1976	Kunsthalle, Tübingen, West Germany
1977	Sonnabend Gallery, New York
1978	Sonnabend Gallery, New York
	Milwaukee Art Center, Wisconsin
	Von der Heydt Museum, Wuppertal, West Germany
1979	Galerie Sonnabend, Paris
	Kunstbibliothek Tranegarden, Copenhagen
	Galleria Massimo Valsecchi, Milan
	Kunstraum Munich
1981	Stedelijk Van Abbemuseum, Eindhoven, Netherlands (Retrospective)
	Kunstverein, Siegen, West Germany
	Sonnabend Gallery, New York
	Carl Taylor Gallery, Dallas
1982	Sonnabend Gallery, New York
1985	Museum Folkwang, Essen, West Germany
	Musée d'Art Moderne, Paris
	Musée d'Art Moderne, Liège, Belgium
1986	Architekturmuseum, Basle

Selected Group Exhibitions:

1969	*Prospekt '69*, Städtische Kunsthalle, Dusseldorf
1970	*Information*, Museum of Modern Art, New York
1974	*Art and Image in Recent Art*, Art Institute of Chicago
1975	*New Topographics: Photographs of a Man-Altered Landscape*, International Museum of Photography, George Eastman House, Rochester, New York (travelled to the Otis Art Institute, Los Angeles, and Princeton University Art Museum, New Jersey)
1977	*Documenta 6*, Museum Fridericianum, Kassel, West Germany
1979	*Photographie als Kunst 1879–1979/Kunst als Photographie 1949–1979*, Tiroler Landesmuseum Ferdinandeum, Innsbruck, Austria (travelled to the Neue Galerie am Wolfgang Gurlitt Museum,

Linz, Austria; Neue Galerie am Landesmuseum Joanneum, Graz, Austria; and Museum des 20. Jahrhunderts, Vienna)

	Concept, Narrative, Document, Museum of Contemporary Art, Chicago
1981	*Photos der 70er Jahre*, Galerie Wilde, Cologne
1983	*The Medium is Photography*, San Francisco Museum of Modern Art
1987	*Photography and Art 1946–86*, Los Angeles County Museum of Art

Collections:

Wallraf-Richartz Museum, Cologne; Moderna Museet, Stockholm; Tate Gallery, London; Museum of Modern Art, New York; Metropolitan Museum of Art, New York; Allen Memorial Art Museum, Oberlin College, Ohio; Art Gallery of Ontario, Toronto.

Publications:

By the BECHERS: books—*Anonyme Skulpturen: Eine Typologie Technische Bauten*, Dusseldorf 1970; *Die Architektur der Förder-und Wasser-Türme*, with text by W. Schoenberg, J. Werth and T. Aachen, Munich 1971; *Industrial Buildings*, portfolio of 14 photos, Munich 1975; *Framework Houses of the Siegen Industrial Region*, Munich 1977; articles—interview, with Lynda Morris, in *Berhard and Hilla Becher*, exhibition catalogue, London 1974; "Photographing Industrial Architecture," interview, with Angela Graverholz and Anne Ramsden, in *Parachute* (Montreal), Spring 1981.

On the BECHERS: books—*Bernhard och Hilla Becher: form genom Funktion*, exhibition catalogue, Stockholm 1970; *Visuelle Kommunikation*, edited by Hermann K. Ehmer, Cologne 1971; *Bernhard and Hilla Becher*, exhibition catalogue, edited by Lynda Morris, London, 1974; *Berhard and Hilla Becher*, exhibition catalogue, with text by Germano Celant, LaJolla, California 1974; *Bernhard and Hilla Becher: Fotografien 1957-1975*, exhibition catalogue, with text by Klaus Honnef, Bonn 1975; *New Topographics: Photographs of a Man-Altered Landscape*, exhibition catalogue, with text by William Jenkins, Rochester, New York 1975; *Documenta 6/Band 2*, edited by Klauf Honnef and Evelyn Weiss, Kassel and Cologne 1977; *Geschichte der Fotografie im 20. Jahrhundert/Photography in the 20th Century* by Petr Rausk, Cologne 1977, London 1980; *Typologien Industrieller Bau 1963-1975*, exhibition catalogue, Sao Paulo 1977; *Photographie als Kunst 1879-1979/Kunst als Photographie 1949-1979*, exhibition catalogue, 2 vols., by Peter Weiermair, Innsbruck, Austria 1979; *Bernd und Hilla Becher*, Exhibition catalogue, Essen 1985; *Photography and Art 1946-86*, exhibition catalogue by Andy Grundberg and Kathleen M. Gauss, Los Angeles 1987.

The age of industrialization brought with it vast collections of documentation which depicted all the elements of mechanical subjects in the clearest detail. Towards the 18th Century when smokestacks, factories and bridges became an almost inseparable part of the landscape, this documentation, once a singular expression of scientific reality, had also become a statement of new sociological and human realities. Since 1959 Hilla and Bernd Becher, upholding a tradition of archeological-industrial documentation, have salvaged testimonies of past developments for future cultural historians.

Their medium is photography, one that ignores every expressionistic component and concentrates on the real subject. The anonymous nature of photography gives the viewer the possibility of perceiving the reality of a rational and conceptual process, which produces two results: the first, the industrial monument, and the second, an artistic composition. This monument will derive a decorative value because it exists as a testimony of itself without the artists in any way adding a personal setting. It was with great perserverance that the Bechers traced a variety of objects, simply because they existed. They began photographing in Germany, then travelled to the industrial regions of Belgium, France, Luxemborg, Holland, England and the United States. Their artistic endeavours were propelled as much by their interest in the technical qualities of these areas as by the

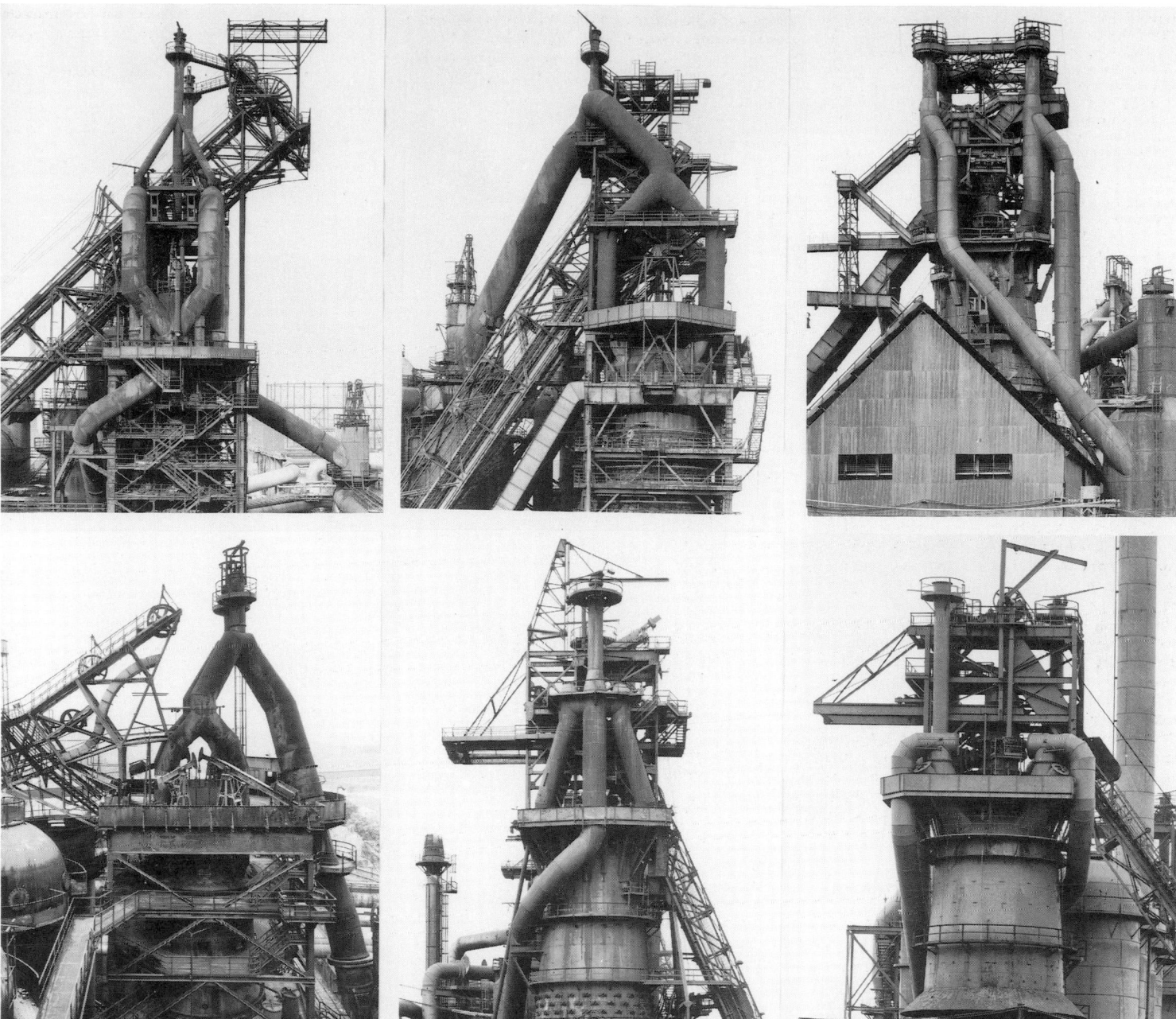

Bernhard and Hilla Becher: *Blast Furnaces*, 1970–1980

strange fascination of the "anonymous" buildings, many of which, having been recently demolished, remain only as a visual record.

To organise the overwhelming quantity of their work, the Bechers developed a consistent, methodological photographic approach. Irrespective of the photograph's subject, a certain legibility had to be maintained. The photographs had to be pure images rather than the artists' interpretation. Each shot was equal in light intensity: greyish, overcast, even skies, no dramatic cloud effects producing photographs at once factual and objective and simultaneously enhanced by the details unfolding around the subject. Equally important to the Bechers' approach was the concept of comparability, since the true character of an object gains explicitness when compared with other objects of the same kind. Thus by means of a comparison of all available structures of a particular type and by means of offering different angles and different points of view, they reveal their subject.

The visual association of the same subjects, specifically industrial monuments, provides a "reading system" for visual comparison, enabling artifacts of apparent anonymity and banality to be seen in terms of notable decorative and typological differences. The Bechers are chiefly interested in photographing a sequence of heavy drills, silos, gas tanks, water towers and other structures. Each structural "family" disposes itself throughout the sequences of illustrations to form typological catalogues whose variations are grouped according to their material and formal similarities. But these are presented in a way that offers contrasting images characterized by symbols and ornamentation of different styles. Thus the visual result (in the same category of object) glows with differences, paradoxes and contradictions, likening it to sculpture.

The Bechers' photographs, along with their other capabilities, underline environmental and social differences between the cultures. They show the industrial monuments of England as being cold, resolved to mere practical uses and devoid of aesthetic value. Those of Continental Europe, however, are quietly symbolic as if to negate their function by masquerading as buildings either Romanesque or Renaissance. The typological correlation of different structures of different periods or countries has become not just a source of information of different areas of knowledge (history, technology), but also a new kind of vision. In this sense Bernd and Hilla Becher are making significant visual and intellectual contributions to our knowledge of the environment.

—Carrie Barker

BECHTLE, Robert (Alan).

American. Born in San Francisco, California, 14 May 1932. Studied graphic design at the California College of Arts and Crafts, Oakland, 1950–54, 1956–58, B.A. 1954, M.F.A. 1958; education and literature, University of California at Berkeley, 1960–61. Served in the United States Army, 1954–56. Married Nancy Elizabeth Dalton in 1963; children: Max, Robert, and Anne Elizabeth. Worked part-time as Graphic Designer for Kaiser Industries, Oakland, California, 1956–59; travelled in Europe, 1961–62;

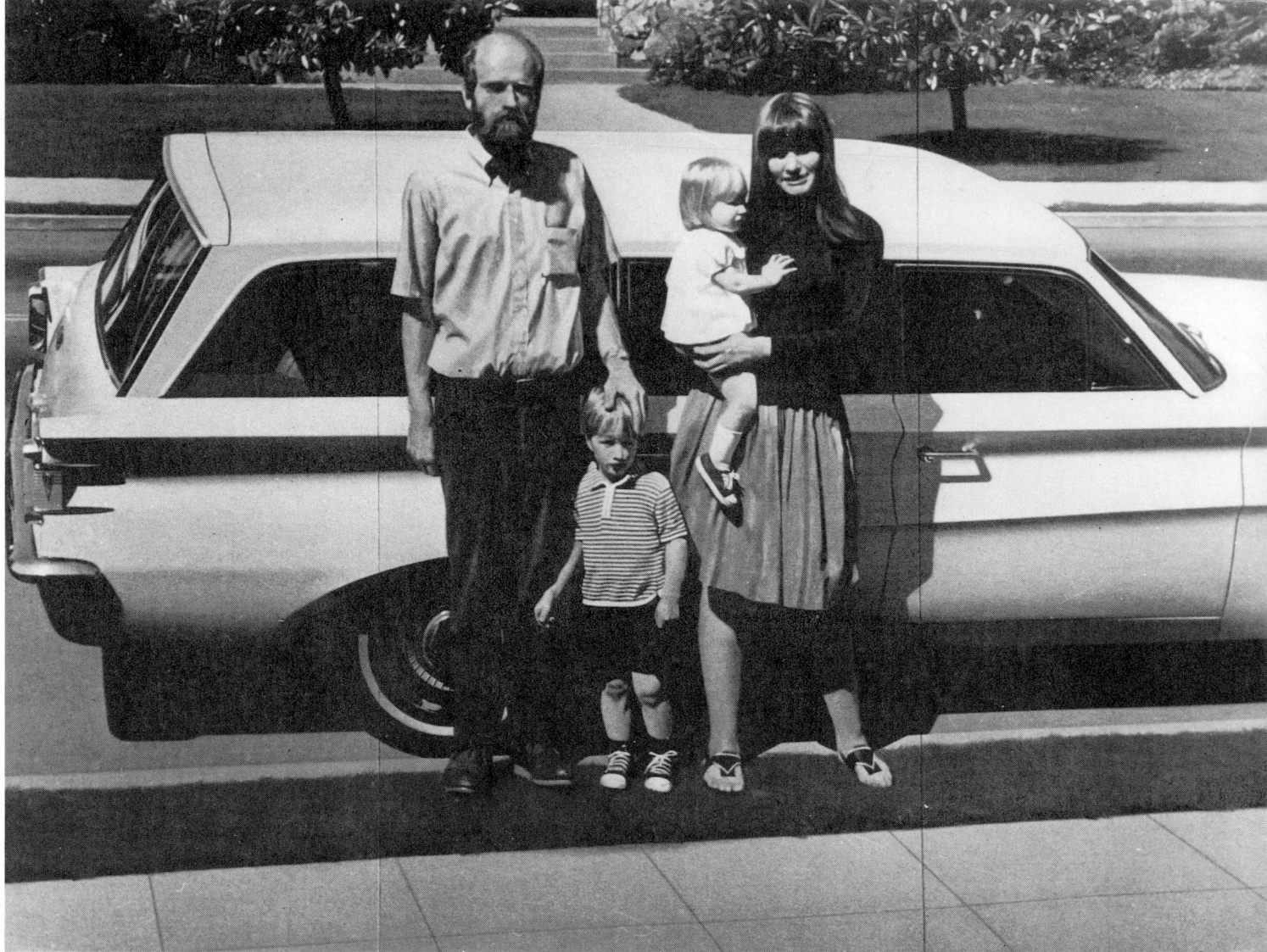

Robert Bechtle: *'61 Pontiac*, 1969

established studio in Oakland, 1966. Instructor, 1957–61, and Associate Professor, 1962–65, California College of Arts and Crafts, Oakland; Lecturer in Design, University of California at Berkeley, 1965–66; Associate Professor, San Francisco State University, now California State University, since 1968. Visiting Artist, University of California at Davis, 1967–68. Recipient: James D. Phelan Award for Painting, San Francisco, 1965; National Endowment for the Arts Grant, Washington, D.C., 1977, 1982. Agents: O. K. Harris Gallery, 383 West Broadway, New York, New York 10012; John Berggruen Gallery, 228 Grant Avenue, San Francisco, California 94108. Address: 4250 Horton Street, Apartment 14, Emeryville, California 94608, U.S.A.

Individual Exhibitions:

1959	Museum of Art, San Francisco
1965	Berkeley Gallery, San Francisco
	Richmond Art Center, California
1966	E. B. Crocker Art Gallery, Sacramento, California
1967	University of California at Davis
	Berkeley Gallery, San Francisco
	San Francisco Museum of Art
1969	Achenbach Foundation for Graphic Arts, San Francisco
1971	O. K. Harris Gallery, New York
1973	E. B. Crocker Art Gallery, Sacramento, California (retrospective; travelled to the Fine Arts Gallery, San Diego)

John Berggruen Gallery, San Francisco (retrospective; travelled to Jack Glenn Gallery, San Diego)

1974	O. K. Harris Gallery, New York
	O. K. Harris Gallery, New York
1977	O. K. Harris Gallery, New York
1980	Matrix Gallery, University of California Art Museum, Berkeley

Selected Group Exhibitions:

1968	*Realism Now*, Vassar College, Poughkeepsie, New York
1970	*22 Realists*, Whitney Museum, New York
1971	*Radical Realism*, Museum of Contemporary Art, Chicago
1972	*Documenta 5*, Kassel, West Germany
1975	*Image, Color and Form: Recent Paintings by Americans*, Toledo Museum of Art, Ohio
1976	*Super Realism*, Baltimore Museum of Art
1977	*30 Years of American Art 1945–1975*, Whitney Museum, New York
1980	*Photo-Realistic Painting in California: A Survey*, Santa Barbara Museum of Art
1985	*American Realism*, San Francisco Museum of Modern Art (travelled to Lincoln, Massachusetts; Austin, Texas; Evanston, Illinois; Williamstown, Massachusetts; Akron, Ohio; Madison, Wisconsin)
1988	*Figure It Out: Visual Body Language*, Helander Gallery, Palm Beach, Florida

Collections:

Guggenheim Museum, New York; Museum of Modern Art, New York; Chase Manhattan Bank, New York; Library of Congress, Washington, D.C.; Caollection of Fine Arts, Smithsonian Institution, Washington, D.C.; High Museum of Art, Atlanta; Oakland Museum, California; Mills College, Oakland; San Francisco Museum of Modern Art; Arts Council of Great Britain, London.

Publications:

By BECHTLE: articles—interview, with Brian O'Doherty, in *Art in America* (New York), November/December 1972; interview, with P. J. Karlstrom, in *Archives of American Art Journal* (Washington, D.C.), vol. 20, no. 2, 1980.

On BECHTLE: books—*Realism Now*, exhibition catalogue, with an introduction by Linda Nochlin, Poughkeepsie, New York 1968; *The Highway*, exhibition catalogue, with an introduction by Denise Scott Brown and Robert Venturi, Philadelphia 1970; *22 Realists*, exhibition catalogue, New York 1970; *Robert Bechtle: A Retrospective Exhibition*, catalogue, with text by Susan McKillop, Sacramento, California 1973; *Neue Formen des Realismus* by Peter Sager, Cologne 1973; *Super Realism* by Gregory Battcock, New York 1975; *Superrealist Painting and Sculpture* by C. Lindey, New York 1980.

I first started to work in a realistic manner as a way of avoiding many of the problems of style that were troubling me in the early 1960's. I was interested in the use of subject matter, and Realism, paradoxically, seemed the only direction that was relatively open and free of recent precedent. It offered the prospect of solving painting problems without being overly aware of how others had solved them or even knowing what the problems and possibilities might be.

My inclination toward the use of subject matter goes back to the Bay Area Figurative tradition of the late 50's. My drift to realism came partly as a reaction against the more obvious expressionist attitudes of the tradition and partly as an acceptance of the implications of using subject matter for its own sake.

It became important for me to try for a kind of neutrality or transparency that hides the more artful evidences of the painter's craft and that causes the subject to be the first thing encountered in the picture. Of course my painting is no more neutral than any other. It involves choice, decision, emotion, etc., but hopefully in a way that is not overly apparent. I choose to paint the things I do—cars, suburban street, etc., because they seem to offer the greatest opportunity of looking without reminding me of other art.

—Robert Bechtle

One of America's leading Photo-Realists, Robert Bechtle has systematically explored the possibilities of the realist style for more than two decades. Like many other young California art students in the late 1950's, he first experimented with Abstract Expressionism before coming under the influence of Bay Area figurative painters such as Richard Diebenkorn and Nathan Oliveira. During and immediately following a trip to Europe his interests became more objective and, as a consequence, his style tighter and less expressionistic. Stimulated by a growing desire to record the appearances of things, and his concurrent exposure to the work of Larry Rivers and the British Pop artists, Bechtle began to look with fresh eyes at his suburban California environment as a possible subject for serious painting.

By 1963 Bechtle had abandoned the Bay Area figurative style in a favor of a far more literal treatment of common-place subjects within the context of contemporary formalist issues. At the same time, he became interested in Pop Art's use of commercial art techniques—notably photography. Initially concentrating on objects within the studio—pictures, mirrors, furniture—depicted straight-forwardly but within a rigidly controlled format, he soon turned his attention outside to the still-life framed by the studio window. It was at this point that the parked automobile accidentally entered Bechtle's *oeuvre* in "'56 Plymouth" (1963). A subsequent painting depicting another car through a window, "'61 Pontiac" (1963), began the series of automobile portraits that occupied him through the mid-70's and for which he is probably best known. Typical and important examples are "'61 Pontiac," 1969 (Whitney Museum) and "'60 T-Bird," 1967-68 (University Art Museum, Berkeley).

Bechtle's approach to his subjects—parked automobiles, snapshot vignettes of middle-class life, abandoned streets in suburban neighborhoods, or family and friends gethered on decks and patios (e.g. "Stinson Beach Cookout," 1979)—is that of a sympathetic but neutral observer: sympathetic in that he is depicting the world in which he grew up and neutral in his lack of overt commentary. His frequently banal subjects are chosen precisely because they are unremarkable. Presented within a fine art context, they challenge the established ways we look at our surroundings. Above all, Bechtle (like most of his fellow Photo-Realists) strives to avoid symbolic and literary content. He selects familiar, nondescript objects to allow the viewer to respond directly to the painting without interference on the part of the artist. Bechtle's methodology involves the basic Photo-Realist practice of creating compositions from projected slides (the "models") with a minimum adjustment of elements. The practice is laborious, time-consuming, and far from spontaneous. Another area of Bechtle's creative activity, one in which he is an accomplished master, allows for the immediacy his large oil paintings deny him. Bechtle's watercolor

views of sunwashed stucco facades and neat suburban lawns convey the precise temperature and time of day in a manner that brings to mind Edward Hopper or even Winslow Homer. "Ingleside House" of 1975 (Oakland Museum) perfectly embodies the sensitive and contemplative observation which distinguishes Bechtle's softened Photo-Realism. Breathing life into sharp-focus literalism, he maintains a humanistic warmth missing in the glittering, reflective and artificial surfaces of many of his colleagues' more dramatic images. In Bechtle's paintings, humble and familiar subjects are skillfully transformed into convincing and imposing works of art.

—Paul J. Karlstrom

BECKLEY, Bill.

American. Born in Hamburg, Pennsylvania, 11 February 1946. Educated at Kutztown State College, Pennsylvania, 1964–68, B.A. 1968; studied under Italo Scanga and Steven Green, Temple University, Philadelphia, 1968–70, M.F.A. 1970. Instructor, School of Visual Arts, New York, since 1971. Committee Member, New York State Council of Arts Grants, 1975. Recipient: Creative Artists Program Service Grant, New York, 1972, 1973, 1974, 1975; National Endowment for the Arts Grant, Washington, D.C., 1979; New York Foundation of the Arts Grant, 1987. Agent: Hans Mayer, Grabbeplatz 2, 4000 Dusseldorf, West Germany. Address: 155 Wooster Street, New York, New York 10012, U.S.A.

Individual Exhibitions:

1969	Wabash Transit Gallery, Chicago
1971	93 Grand Street, New York (performance)
1972	98 Green Street, New York (performance)
	112 Green Street, New York (installation)
	Galerie Rudolf Zwirner, Cologne (performance)
	Galerie 20, Amsterdam
	Galleria Françoise Lambert, Milan
1973	John Gibson Gallery, New York
	Nigel Greenwood Gallery, London
	Galerie Conrad Fischer, Dusseldorf
1974	Galerie 20, Amsterdam
	Galleria François Lambert, Milan (performance)
	John Gibson Gallery, New York
1975	Galerie Yvon Lambert, Paris
	Galerie Patric Verelst/Marc Poitier, Antwerp
	Galleria François Lambert, Milan
	Steinway Hall, New York (performance)
	Galerie 20, Amsterdam
1976	Galleria d'Allessandro-Ferranti, Rome
	Narrational Imagery: Beckley, Ruscha, Warhol, University of Massachusetts, Amherst
	John Gibson Gallery, New York
	Galleria Lucio Amelio, Naples
1977	Nigel Greenwood Gallery, London
	Galerie Denise René/Hans Mayer, Dusseldorf
1978	Galerie Daniel Templon, Paris
1979	Museum of Modern Art, New York
1980	Hal Bromm Gallery, New York
	Bill Beckley and Philip Greenwood, Nigel Greenwood Gallery, London
1981	Annina Nosei Gallery, New York
	Marian Deson Gallery, Chicago
	Galerie Daniel Templon, Paris
	International Center of Photography, New York
1982	Studio Cannaviello, Milan
	Brownlow Gallery, New York
1983	John Gibson Gallery, New York
	Galerie Denise Rene/Hans Mayer, Dusseldorf
1984	Freidus/Ordover Gallery, New York
	Stadtisches Museum, Monchengladbach, West Germany (retrospective)
1986	Galerie Daniel Templon, Paris
	John Gibson Gallery, New York
	Galleria Pasquale Trisorio, Naples
1987	Toni Shafrazi Gallery, New York
	Galerie Hans Mayer, Dusseldorf

Selected Group Exhibitions:

1969	*Art in the Mind,* Allen Memorial Art Museum, Oberlin, Ohio
1971	*Projects Piers 18,* Museum of Modern Art, New York
1972	*Actualité d'un Bilan,* Galerie Yvon Lambert, Paris
1973	*"7",* Museum of Modern Art, New York
	Biennale, Paris
1976	*Biennale,* Venice
1977	*Documenta 6,* Kassel, West Germany
	Pier + Ocean, Hayward Gallery, London (travelled to the Rijksmuseum Kroller-Muller, Otterlo, Netherlands)
1983	*Kunst mit Photographie,* Nationalgalerie, West Berlin (travelled to Cologne, Munich and Kiel)
1985	*A New Beginning,* Hudson River Museum, Yonkers, New York
1987	*Large Scale Photography,* Los Angeles County Museum of Art

Collections:

Museum of Modern Art, New York; Guggenheim Museum, New York; Whitney Museum, New York; Kunstmuseum, Basel; Stadtisches Museum, Monchengladbach; Victoria and Albert Museum, London; La Jolla Art Museum, California; Cincinnati Art Museum, Ohio; Morton Neuman Collection, Chicago.

Publications:

On BECKLEY: books—*Art in the Mind,* exhibition catalogue, by Athena Spear, Oberlin, Ohio 1969; *Narrative Art,* exhibition catalogue, Brussels 1974; *In Progress 5,* exhibition catalogue, with text by Achille Bonita Oliva, Livorno, Italy 1975; *Modern Art* by Sam Hunter, New York 1979; *Bill Beckley,* exhibition catalogue, Monchengladbach, West Germany 1984; *Bill Beckley,* exhibition catalogue, Paris 1986; articles—"Story Art" by James Collins in *Artforum* (New York), September 1973; "Bill Beckley" in *Heute Kunst* (Dusseldorf), July/August 1973; "Bill Beckley" in *Interfunctionen* (Cologne), no. 10, 1973; "Bill Beckley" by M. Jochimsen in *Kunst* (Mainz, West Germany), September 1974; "Story Art" by James Collins in *New York Magazine,* October 1974; "Narrative Art" in *Arti* (Milan), January 1975; "Story Art" by Barbara Radice in *Data* (Milan), June 1975; "Narrative Art" by Peter Schjeldahl in *Domus* (Milan), February 1976; "Bill Beckley's Lies" by E. Cameron in *Artforum* (New York), February 1977; "Bill Beckley: L'Archeologie du Tableau" by Anne Dagbert in *Art Press* (Paris), June 1985.

Born in 1946, Bill Beckley is not only one of the youngest proponents of the new "Narrative Art," but also one who has produced one of the most solid bodies of work in a relatively short time. Like other artists whose work has been linked to the grass-roots "Story Art" movement, such as James Collins, William Wegman, and even John Baldessari, Beckley concerns himself with three interrelationships; time, relationships between objects, humans, animals and natural or urban phenomena, and process. Also like them, Beckley spices his technically brilliant, sleek series of photographs and texts with a gleeful wit ranging from the subtly self-deprecating to the patently absurd. As a result, his work tends to be more immediately accessible than, for example, David Askevold's or Peter Hutchinson's.

Formerly, Beckley presented his stories in a shaggy dog style, beginning and ending with deliberately pointless incidents—sometimes an encounter between a young man (the artist) and a groundhog, sometimes an erotic encounter more obviously based in fantasy than in reality, though the confessional spirit seems to be an underlying thematic device. Beckley's "shaggy dog stories" have been from his first shows immensely popular (though never populist), because they never propound theory but present faintly ridiculous incidents via one or two mysteriously selected photographs and a dead-pan, non-editorializing simple text. Because of this tersely poetic presentation, his stories frequently take on the characteristics of entertaining myths or children's tales once told to prove an otherwise, unpalatable point.

Beckley's work since 1975 shares this mythologizing aspect, but has become less accessible and perhaps consequently stronger in its formal aspects. It has become, in fact, a work hinging more directly on the manipulation of mood in a progressively more theatrical (or contrived) context. Beckley depends less on the unconscious and more on establishing a formal situation, while replacing the explicit story/subject with an implicit one. The "characters" in his stories—which rely almost entirely on large panels of color prints—now tend to be almost exclusively domestic objects, engaged in an anthropomorphic visual dialogue. Two color-coded faucets, for example, drip and meet in a single stream down a yellow drain; a broom relentlessly follows a dustball until it is, literally, swept "under the rug"; two equally lovely professional photographic models wordlessly enact the vainglorious theme of Snow White, in his panel, "The Fairest of Them All"; even a hamburger and its condiments are "actors" in a Beckley scenario. Because of the increased visualization of Beckley's narrations, the trick ending so frequently used to effect in his shaggy dog period has been deliberately sacrificed for a harder, more sophisticated statement; the slyly innocent inanities in the early work are making way for greater formal impact in the exquisite staging of objects photographed in lush flat colors, and an increasingly mysterious iconographic power.

—Jane Bell

BELL, Larry.

American. Born in Chicago, Illinois, 6 December 1939. Educated at Birmingham High School, Eureka, California, 1953–57; Chouinard Art Institute, Los Angeles, 1957–59. Married Gloria Jean Neilsen in 1967 (divorced, 1971); daughter: Zara Augusta; has lived with Janet Ruth Burns, since 1973. Worked as a bowling alley maintenance engineer, truck driver and picture framer, Los Angeles, 1957–59; general manager, The Unicorn saloon-cabaret, Hollywood, 1957–65. Full-time artist since 1965. Instructor, University of California, Berkeley, 1972, and University of South Florida, Tampa, 1973. Founder-Member, with Bob Irwin, Newton Harrison, Joshua Young, Ed Wirtz, and Frank Geary, Don Quixote Collective, California, 1974. Recipient: William Noma Copley Foundation Prize, 1963; Guggenheim Fellowship, 1969. Address: Box 4101, Taos, New Mexico 87571, U.S.A.

Individual Exhibitions:

1962	Ferus Gallery, Los Angeles
1963	Ferus Gallery, Los Angeles
1965	Ferus Gallery, Los Angeles
	Pace Gallery, New York
1967	Galerie Sonnabend, Paris
	Pace Gallery, New York
	Stedelijk Museum, Amsterdam
1969	Mizuno Gallery, Los Angeles
1970	Pace Gallery, New York
	Ace Gallery, Los Angeles
1971	Pace Gallery, New York
	Helman Gallery, St. Louis
	Mizuno Gallery, Los Angeles
	Ace Gallery, Los Angeles
	Galerie Rudolf Zwirner, Cologne
1972	Pace Gallery, New York

	Felicity Samuel Gallery, London
	Pasadena Art Museum, California
	Wilmaro Gallery, Denver
1973	Oakland Art Museum, California
	Pace Gallery, New York
	Bonython Gallery, Sydney
1974	Marlborough Galleria d'Arte, Rome (toured Italy)
	Galleria La Cittá, Verona
	Galleria Il Cavallino, Venice
	Salone Annunciata, Milan
1975	Marlborough Galleria d'Arte, Rome (toured Italy)
	Galleria Il Cavallino, Venice
	Tally Richards Gallery, Taos, New Mexico
	Recent Works, Fort Worth Art Museum, Texas
1976	Washington University, St. Louis
	Santa Barbara Museum of Art, California
	Art Museum of South Texas, Corpus Christi
1977	Hayden Gallery, Massachusetts Institute of Technology, Cambridge
	University of Massachusetts, Amherst
	Federal Reserve, Boston
	Fort Worth Art Museum, Texas (with Eric Orr)
1978	Multiples Gallery, New York
	Delahunty Gallery, New York
	Texas Gallery, Houston
	Erica Williams-Anne Johnson Gallery, Seattle
	University of New Mexico, Albuquerque
	Roswell Museum and Art Center, New Mexico
	Tally Richards Gallery, Taos, New Mexico
1979	Roswell Museum and Art Center, New Mexico
	Multiples Gallery, New York
	Sebastian-Moore Gallery, Denver
	Hill's Gallery of Contemporary Art, Santa Fe, New Mexico
	Hansen Fuller Gallery, San Francisco
	Tally Richards Gallery, Taos, New Mexico
	Janus Gallery, Venice, California
	Marian Goodman Gallery, New York
1980	Sebastian-Moore Gallery, Denver
	Hill's Gallery of Contemporary Art, Santa Fe, New Mexico
	Tally Richards Gallery, Taos, New Mexico
	Marion Goodman Gallery, New York
1981	Hudson River Museum, Yonkers, New York
	Marion Goodman Gallery, New York
	Ann Jacob Gallery, Atlanta, Georgia (with Eric Orr)
	L. A. Louver Gallery, Venice, California
	Wildine Galleries, Albuquerque, New Mexico
	Tally Richard Gallery, Taos, New Mexico
	University of Ohio, Athens
1982	Newport Harbor Art Museum, Newport Beach, California
	Marion Goodman/Multiples Gallery, New York
	Ruth S. Schaffner Gallery, Santa Barbara, California
	Erica Williams/Anne Johnson Gallery, Seattle, Washington
	Milwaukee Art Museum, Wisconsin
	Museum of Fine Arts, Santa Fe, New Mexico
	Tally Richards Gallery, Taos, New Mexico
	Detroit Institute of Arts, Michigan
1983	University of Nebraska, Lincoln
	Advanced Art Gallery, Riconada, New Mexico
	Arco Center for Visual Art, Los Angeles
	Wildine Gallery, Albuquerque, New Mexico
1984	Colorado springs Fine Arts Center, Colorado
	Museum of Contemporary Art, Los Angeles
	The Works Gallery, Long Beach, California
1985	Dord Fitz Gallery, Amarillo, Texas (with Lee Mullican)
	The Works Gallery, Long Beach, California
	L. A. Louver Gallery, Venice, California
1986	Braunstein Gallery, San Francisco
	Boise Gallery of Art, Idaho
	The New Gallery, Houston
	Amarillo Art Center, Texas
1987	Galerie Gilbert Brownstone, Paris
	Braunstein/Quay Gallery, San Francisco (with Peter Voulkos)

Selected Group Exhibitions:

1964	California Hard-Edge Painting, Pavilion Gallery, Balboa, California

1966	Primary Structures, Jewish Museum, New York
1972	USA West Coast, Kunstverein, Hamburg (travelled to Hannover, Cologne and Stuttgart)
1976	200 Years of American Sculpture, Whitney Museum, New York
1977	Painting and Sculpture in California: The Modern Era, Washington Collection of Fine Arts, Smithsonian Institution, Washington D.C.
1979	Contemporary Sculpture: Selections from the Collection of MOMA, Museum of Modern Art, New York
1980	Beyond Object, Aspen Center for the Visual Arts, Colorado
1982	One Hundred Years of California Sculpture, Oakland Museum, California
1984	Americans in Glass, Woodson Art Museum, Wausau, Wisconsin (toured Europe)
1987	Art and the West, University of Wyoming, Laramie

Collections:

Whitney Museum, New York; Guggenheim Museum, New York; Museum of Modern Art, New York; National Collection of Fine Arts, Smithsonian Institution, Washington, D.C.; Fort Worth Art Center, Texas; Museum of New Mexico, Santa Fe; Roswell Museum and Art Center, New Mexico; Los Angeles County Museum of Art; Norton Simon Art Museum, Pasadena, California; Tate Gallery, London; Stedelijk Museum, Amsterdam.

Publications

By BELL: articles—statement in "Saint Andy" by Philip Leider in Artforum (New York), 1965; statement in A New Esthetic, exhibition catalogue, Washington, D.C. 1967; interview in Los Angeles 6, exhibition catalogue, by John Coplans, Vancouver 1968; interview in Transparency, Reflection, Light, Space, exhibition catalogue, by Frederick S. Wight, Los Angeles 1971; "Larry Bell," interview with Alastair Mackintosh, in Art and Artists (London), January 1972; "The Iceberg" in Vision (Oakland, California), September 1975.

On BELL: books—Larry Bell, exhibition catalogue, with texts by Raphael Sorin and Annette Michelson, Paris 1967; American Art since 1900 by Barbara Rose, London 1967; 6 Artists: 6 Exhibitions, exhibition catalogue, Milwaukee 1968; West Coast 1945-1969, exhibition catalogue, by John Coplans, Pasadena, California 1969; Kompas IV-West Coast U.S.A., exhibition catalogue, Amsterdam 1969; Larry Bell, Robert Irwin, Doug Wheeler, exhibition catalogue, by M. Compton and N. Reid, London 1970; Larry Bell, exhibition catalogue, by Barbara Haskell, Pasadena, California 1972; USA West Coast, exhibition catalogue, Hamburg 1972; Possibilities for Glass Sculpture, exhibition catalogue, Sydney 1973; Larry Bell, exhibition catalogue, Rome 1974; Sunshine Muse: Contemporary Art on the West Coast by Peter Plagens, New York 1974; Readings in America Art 1900-1975, edited by Barbara Rose, New York 1975; Larry Bell: Recent Works, exhibition catalogue, Fort Worth, Texas 1975; Larry Bell: New Work, exhibition catalogue with introduction by Robert Creeley, New York 1981; articles—"A Lot of Talent . . ." by Henry J. Seldis in the Los Angeles Times, 21 October 1973; "American in Paris: 1974" by Melinda Wortz in Arts Magazine (New York), 1975; "Larry Bell" in Art News (New York), March 1975; "A Hotbed of Advanced Art" by E. Perlmutter in Art News (New York), January 1976; "Larry Bell on New York" by David Rush in Artweek (Oakland, California), 15 May 1976; "The Grip of the Iceberg" by Kenneth Baker in the Boston Phoenix, 8 February 1977; "A Glass Menagerie" by R. Talor in the Boston Globe, 16 June 1977; "Larry Bell and Eric Orr" by Gerrit Henry in Art News (New York), April 1978; article by Gerrit Henry in Art News (New York), May 1979; "Larry Bell" by Jon Meyer in Arts Magazine (New York), September 1982; "Art Vapor Made" by Jody Jacobs in the Los Angeles Times, 14 October 1985; "Larry Bell's Lights" by Kenneth Baker in the San Francisco Chronicle, 14 June 1986; film—A Video Portrait: Larry Bell, directed by John Hunt, Venice, California 1976.

I used to think that a person got what he wanted, and that was all he got, 'cause that's all there was. Everything was very simple. If you didn't know what you wanted, you still got what you set up for yourself, but you may not know that you got what you wanted. In a recent conversation with a friend, he suggested that

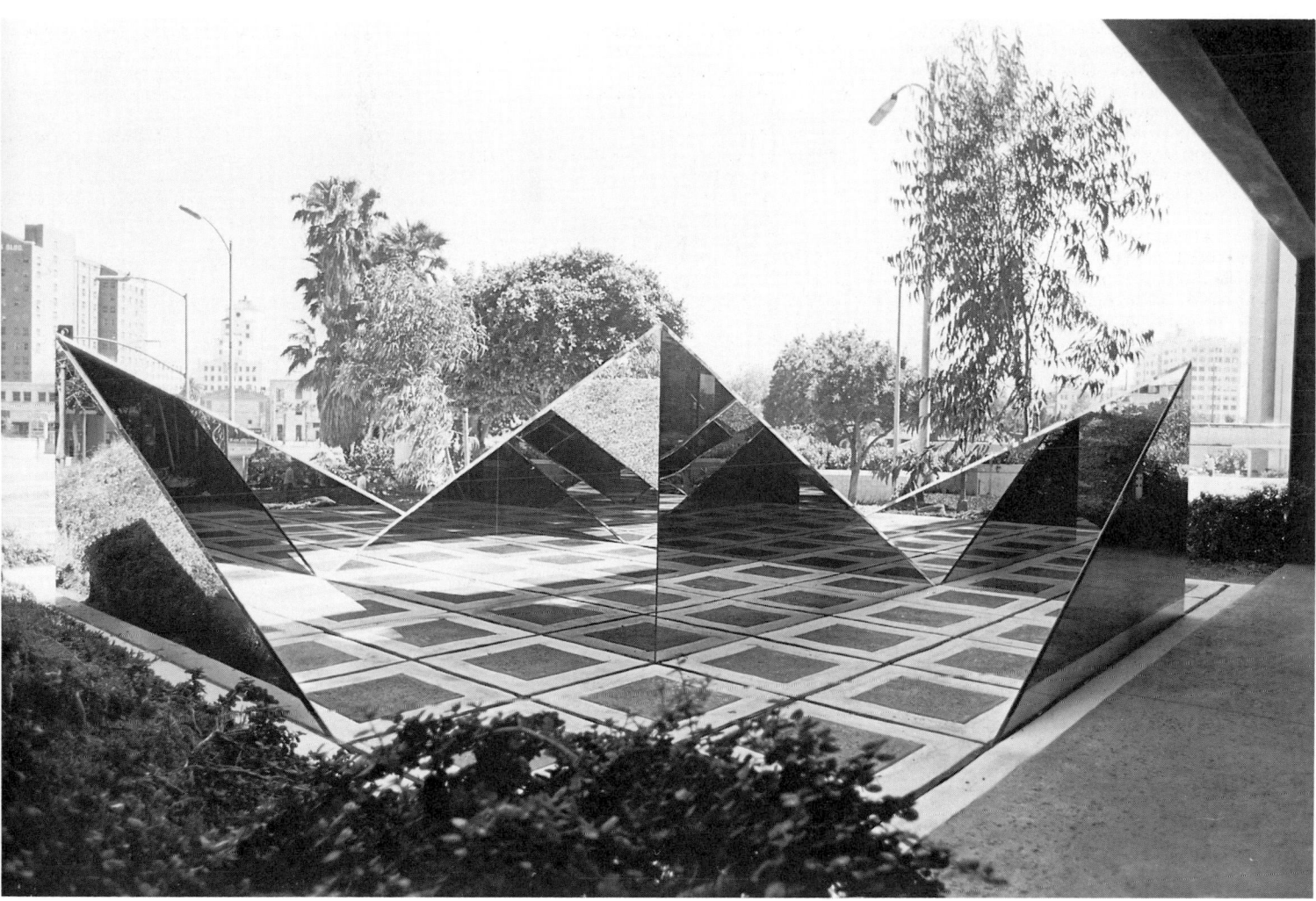

Larry Bell: *Triangles on Grid*, 1984

maybe you get what your character dictates, and you spend most of your life trying to make sense out of the chaos of your character; finding your rational explanation to yourself, of what it's all about. I like to look at it like this. And I am responsible for my acts, for the things I say and do, just like everybody else. My rational mind is fighting the same chaotic battle that everyone fights every day, who either thinks that they know what they want, or don't think about it at all. I think it's a terrible delusion to believe that a person is the master of his character.

—Larry Bell

In all the art capitals of the world, the artists jostle for their place in the hierarchy of reputation, eyeing the other contenders and marshalling their supporting forces of critics and other hangers-on: in all the capitals except Los Angeles, where Larry Bell is undisputed king.

There are of course many West Coast artists with high reputations and an international following, and it would be foolish to pretend at this stage of history that one could say who will or will not be remembered. Anyway, status has little to do with quality; it stems rather from the stance or image of the artist, and the consistency and self-confidence of the work.

Bell has achieved his position of pre-eminence by matching his work exactly to the ethos of Los Angeles. Art from New York tends to have an intellectual and slightly paranoid edge, that from San Francisco a colourful messiness associated with psychedelia—the art matches the city from whence it grows. L.A. is the blandest, least intellectual and most stylish of American cities, the worst place on earth to be poor. Economic extravagance is an aesthetic quality in

L.A., and nothing matters more than effect.

This may sound like a condemnation, but any quality can become a virtue in the hands of a skilful artist, and there is no denying Bell's skill. His art may depend on great technical ability based upon a high cost of production, but it is also successful. Who complains at the cost of a high budget movie as long as it succeeds at box office, and Bell's work has certainly done that.

His work, since it first became widely known in 1964, has all been variations on a single idea. The earlier examples were glass cubes with 15–30 cm sides, upon which were imposed pattersn by an aluminising process, which caused delicate interference when one side was seen against another. Soon, however, Bell was finding this technique too crude, and he switched to vacuum coating, which allowed him to introduce extremely subtle variations of transparent colour onto the surface of the glass. After experimenting with various colour effects, he settled mainly on the use of greys, some of which were so slight as to be almost non-existent.

The reductive quality of these works has led to Bell's being associated with minimalism, an essentially East Coast school of art. But the differences are far greater than the similarities. Minimalism is an intellectual system; art is reduced to the bare essentials for theoretical reasons and any visual impact is a subsidiary bonus. Bell's work is extremely sensuous and the reduction is made to increase the sensuality, not for any theoretical reason. It is minimal only in the sense that the whiteness of Jean Harlow's satin dresses is minimal, as an increase of visual impact.

In 1968, Bell started to work on a large scale, evolving techniques that would allow him to make pieces big enough for the viewer to walk through.

The equipment necessary to achieve this was very expensive, and this had a concomitant effect on Bell's prices. On the East Coast there is still a feeling that art should cost little to make (whatever price it is sold for) and that blatantly industrial techniques are somehow cheating; but in Los Angeles this attitude is considered absurd. In a city where you can buy a gold-plated toothbrush, vacuum coated sculpture is perfectly logical.

There is no denying that Bell's work is possibly the most sheerly beautiful and elegant of the post-war period. Its flawless finish combined with great simplicity makes it seductively attractive compared to the "unfinished" aesthetic of most contemporary art. Critics have tended to underrate Bell because there is no theory to his art for them to bite on; it is there, you look at it and that is that, and in a period where art is weighed down by the verbiage that surrounds it, this is a highly satisfactory quality.

Bell's best pieces are probably those constructed in the form of simple mazes. The sheets of glass, six feet high, are coated with grey, and this is further treated with a mirroring process which fades evenly top to bottom. The viewer finds himself in a web of reflections, sometimes seeing himself in a mirrorized part of the glass and sometimes seeing through the surface to a further series of reflections beyond. It is like entering a multiple exposure photograph. The effect is not at all disturbing, but rather of pure visual pleasure, in which the analytical part of the mind becomes servant to the sensuous, and problems of form and content do not exist; a Los Angeles aesthetic par excellence, and one that is perfectly legitimate for that.

—Alastair Mackintosh

BELLMER, Hans.

German. Born in Katowice, Silesia, Germany/Poland border (now in Poland), 13 March 1902. Studied engineering, Technische Hochschule, Berlin, 1923–24; drawing and perspective studies with artist George Grosz, Berlin, 1924. Married Margarete Bellmer in 1927 (died, 1937); 2 daughters; married again in 1942 (separated, 1946); twin daughters: Doraine and Beatrice; lived with poetess Nora Mitrani, 1946–51, and with writer Unica Zurn, 1953–70 (died, 1970). Worked as coal-miner, Katowice, 1920–23; designer, typographer and illustrator, for Malik Publishing Company, Berlin, 1924–25; independent painter and designer, Berlin, 1926–36, in Paris, 1936–39; interned in prison camp, Aix-en-Provence, France, 1940; independent painter and designer, Toulouse, France, 1941–45, and Paris, 1946 until his death, 1975; worked on photographs of puppet doll (Die Puppe), Berlin, 1934–36, and in Paris, 1936–39, 1946–75. Recipient: William and Noma Copley Foundation Prize, Chicago, 1958. *Died* (in Paris) *23 February 1975.*

Individual Exhibitions:

1943	Galerie Trentin, Toulouse
1945	Galerie du Luxembourg, Paris
1963	Galerie Daniel Cordier, Paris
1966	Robert Fraser Gallery, London
	Galerie Sydow, Frankfurt
	Robert Self Gallery, London
	Ulmer Museum, Ulm, West Germany
	Galerie Benador, Geneva
	Galerie Gmurzynska, Cologne
1967	Galerie A. F. Petit, Paris
	Kestner Gesellschaft, Hannover (retrospective)
	Galerie Wolfgang Ketterer, Munich
	Galleria d'Arte Moderna, Turin
	Galerie Thomas, Munich and Cologne
1969	Galerie A. F. Petit, Paris
1970	Stedelijk Museum, Amsterdam
	Galerie La Pochade, Paris
1971	Centre National d'Art Contemporain, Paris (retrospective)
	Von der Heydt Museum, Wuppertal, West Germany
1971	Lerner-Misrachi Gallery, New York
	Sidney Janis Gallery, New York
	Editions Graphiques, London
1974	Sidney Janis Gallery, New York
	Galerie Schindler, Berne
1975	Museum of Contemporary Art, Chicago
	Galerie A. F. Petit, Paris
1976	Galerie A. F. Petit, Paris
1980	*Les Jeux de la Poupée,* Vision Gallery, Boston
1983	Centre Georges Pompidou, Paris
1984	Kestner-Gesellschaft, Hannover
1985	Barbara Gladstone Gallery, New York

Selected Group Exhibitions:

1935	*Exposicion Surealista,* Galeria Ateneo, Tenerife, Canary Islands
1936	*International Surrealist Exhibition,* Museum of Modern Art, New York
1947	*Exposition Internationale du Surrealisme,* Galerie Maeght, Paris
1960	*Exposition Internationale du Surrealisme,* Galerie Daniel Cordier, Paris
1977	*Künstlerphotographien im 20. Jahrhundert,* Kestner Gesellschaft, Hannover
1978	*Dada and Surrealism Reviewed,* Hayward Gallery, London
1979	*Photographic Surrealism,* New Gallery of Contemporary Art, Cleveland, Ohio (travelled to Dayton Art Institute, Ohio; and Brooklyn Museum, New York)
1980	*Masks, Mannequins and Dolls,* Prakapas Gallery, New York
1981	*Germany: The New Vision,* Fraenkel Gallery, San Francisco

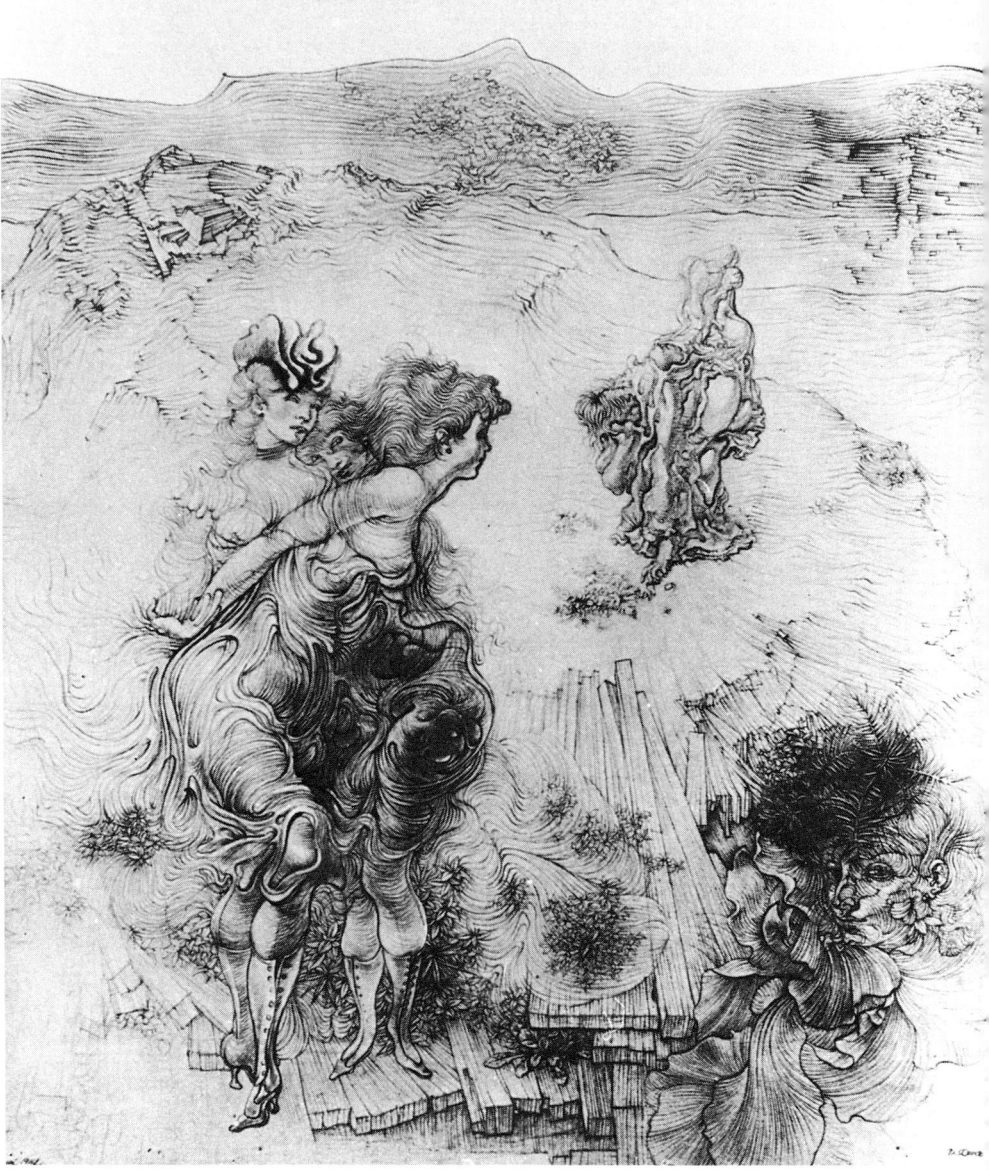

Hans Bellmer: *Pay-sage 1800,* 1942

1985	*L'Amour Fou: Photography and Surrealism,* Corcoran Gallery of Art, Washington, D.C., (travelled to San Francisco, Paris and London)

Collections:

Centre Georges Pompidou, Paris; Ulmer Museum, Ulm, West Germany; Galerie Brusberg, Hannover; Museum of Modern Art, New York; Institute for Sex Research, University of Indiana, Bloomington; Art Institute of Chicago.

Publications:

By BELLMER: books—*Die Puppe,* Karlsruhe 1934, Paris 1936, revised edition, Berlin 1962; *The Story of Eve,* with text by Georges Bataille, Paris 1944; *Les Jeux de la Poupée,* with text by Paul Eluard, Paris 1949; *L'Anatomie de l'Image,* Paris 1957; *A Sade,* Paris 1967; *Madame Edwarda,* with text by Georges Bataille, Paris 1965; *Mode d'Emploi,* Paris 1967.

On BELLMER: books—*Hans Bellmer* by Christian d'Orgeix, Paris 1950; *Hans Bellmer* by Alain Jouffroy, Chicago and London 1959; *Les Dessins de Hans Bellmer,* edited by Constantin Jelenski, Paris 1966; *Hans Bellmer: Oeuvre Gravé* by André Pieyre de Mandiargues, Paris 1969; *CNAC Archives I: Hans Bellmer,* exhibition catalogue, by Paul Eluard and others, Paris 1971; *The Drawings of Hans Bellmer,* edited by Alex Grall, London 1972, New York 1973; *Hans Bellmer* by Sarane Alexandrian, Paris 1972, New York 1973; *Photography as Art* by Volker Kahmen, London 1974; *The Erotic Arts* by Peter Webb, London 1975; *Künstlerphoto-graphien im XX. Jahrhundert,* exhibition catalogue, by Carl-Albrecht Haenlein, Hannover 1977; *Geschichte der Fotografie im 20. Jahrhundert/Photography in the 20th Century* by Petr Tausk, Cologne 1977, London 1980; *Dada and Surrealism Reviewed,* exhibition catalogue, by Dawn Ades, London 1978; *Le Trésor Cruel de Hans Bellmer* by André Pieyre de Mandiargues, Paris 1979; *Photographic Surrealism,* exhibition catalogue, by Nancy Hall-Duncan, Cleveland 1979; *Avant-Garde Photography in Germany 1919–39,* exhibition catalogue, by Van Deren Coke, Ute Eskildsen and Bernd Lohse, San Francisco 1980; *L'Amour Fou: Photography and Surrealism* by Rosalind Krauss and Jane Livingston, Washington, D.C. and New York 1985.

Hans Bellmer was the prince of image therapy. His dolls, reconditioned like pieces of fractured antique sculpture, were expertly reincarnated except that he re-assembled their parts according to the dictates of his own pleasure rather than as an archeologist would have attempted to make repairs in order to restore figurative realism. For Bellmer, time and erosion had nothing to do with it. He did his own disjointing and subsequent realignment. He made toys for grown-ups which could be accounted art products (whether they were exhibited in the forms in which he fashioned them, whether they were made the subject of alarming photographs—some of them crowding several poses into one frame, others enlarged to the extent of being over lifesize—or whether they were used as the inspirations for his pictures of physical reconstruction).

This artist had dual gifts of imagination and craft, both to an exceptional degree. Whatever he set out to achieve was so exquisitely made that even his most hysterical critics could not fail to be abashed. The same expertise that he employed in his portraits would also appear with identical accuracy in the pictures he made of carnal romps or sexual adventures.

Faced by such doughty accomplishment, moral censors find it difficult to make much of a case against Bellmer on grounds of erotic licence (or—for the most passionately outraged—pornography). Those who would like the portrayal of physical licentiousness to be kept under lock and key, or at least to be refrigerated, have always discovered themselves to be in an awkward position when the creator of what they are attacking is so obviously a consummate artist. One remembers Savonarola's problems with Botticelli, the unbreachable popularity of the Gavarni prints, Stanley Spencer's tangles with the Royal Academy and the Establishment in Britain.

Bellmer exhibited with the surrealists, and he was certainly on the best of terms with many of the movement's members, but his own art could never have been described as definitively surrealist. Nor could he be seen as some kind of contemporary descendant of Felicien Rops and clearly not as a companion of Horst Janssen. Sex as a subject for Bellmer is not so much a private investigation of adult personal habits (way-out habits even, in the instance of an artist like the Marquis von Bayros) as a corporeal re-creation which may suddenly burst into flame at the bureau desk of a secretary or, in another mood, captures the most venal recesses of thought in the mind of a little girl, secrets that even Graham Ovenden can scarcely have pondered upon. And talking of Ovenden, it is interesting to find Bellmer making his own "translation" of *Alice in Wonderland,* a new interpretation in that Alice has lifted the billows of her Edwardian skirt and petticoats in order to vaunt her unveiled sex.

Hans Bellmer saw the female body as raw material for creativity. Its natural configuration for him was no more than a chance series of juxapositions by Nature. Legs, arms, breasts, buttocks and primary sexual characteristics could find fresh patterns of relationship, and the way in which he made these rearrangements always seemed to have a biological and physical viability, however bizarre the resulting assembly. It would never, for instance, have occurred to Bellmer to embark upon cubist experiments in the manner of Picasso. The waistline might be discovered in an unexpected divorce from hips and belly, but eyes, nose and lips belonged to the face and Bellmer kept them there.

—Sheldon Williams

BENEDIT, Luis Fernando.

Argentinian. Born in Buenos Aires, Argentina, 12 July 1937. Educated at the Facultad de Arquitectura, Universidad de Buenos Aires, 1956–63, Diploma Arquitecto 1963; studied popular architecture, Instituto de Cultura Hispanica, Madrid, 1964–65; drawing and landscape, Facoltà d'Architettura, Rome, 1967–68. Served in the Argentine Air Force, Buenos Aires, 1958. Married Monica Prebisch in 1963; children: Juana, Pedro, Rosita, and Tomas. Architect, Estudio Prebisch, Buenos Aires, 1969–71. Recipient: Premio Ver y Estimar, Buenos Aires, 1962; Premio Rosa Galisteo, *Salón de Santa Fé,* Argentina, 1962; Premio en el Arte, San Isidro, Argentina, 1968; Premio de la Critica, *Salón Nacional,* Buenos Aires, 1968. Agents: Galeria Bonino, Marcelo T. de Alvear 636, Buenos Aires, Argentina; Spectrum Gallery, Leopoldstraat 10, 2000 Antwerp, Belgium; Galerie Buchholz, Maximilianstrasse 29, Munich 22, West Germany. Address: Ingeniero Huergo 1191, Buenos Aires, Argentina.

Individual Exhibitions:

1961	Galeria Lirolay, Buenos Aires
1962	Galeria Lirolay, Buenos Aires
1963	Galeria Rubbers, Buenos Aires
1964	Galeria Lirolay, Buenos Aires
1965	Galerie Europe, Paris
1966	Galerie La Balance, Brussels
1967	Galeria Rubbers, Buenos Aires
1968	Galeria Rubbers, Buenos Aires
1969	Pan American Union, Washington, D.C.
1972	*3-Labyrinthe von Luis F. Benediti Ein Versuch über der Displazierung,* Galerie Buchholz, Munich
1973	C.A.Y.C., Buenos Aires
1975	Spectrum Gallery, Antwerp
	Galeria Bonino, Buenos Aires
	Whitechapel Gallery, London
	Galerie Buchholz, Munich

Selected Group Exhibitions:

1961	*3 Nuevos Rostros,* Galeria Lirolay, Buenos Aires
1966	*Salón des Jeunes,* Musée d'Art Moderne, Paris
1967	*Surrealismo en la Argentina,* Instituto Di Tella, Buenos Aires
1968	*Materiales, Nuevas, Técnicas, Nuevas Expresiónes,* Museo de Bellas Artes, Buenos Aires
1969	*Biennale des Jeunes,* Musée de Arte Moderno, Buenos Aires
	Argentinische Kunst der Gegenwart, Kunsthalle, Basle (toured Europe)
1972	*Toys by Artists,* Musée des Arts Décoratifs, Paris (and world tour)
1975	*International Exhibition of Prints,* Museum of Modern Art, Tokyo

Collections:

Museo de Arte Moderno, Buenos Aires; Museo de Bellas Artes, Buenos Aires; Museo de Bellas Artes, La Plata, Argentina; Museo Rosa Galisteo de Rodrizuez, Santa Fé, Argentina; Museo de Bellas Artes, Tandil, Argentina; Museum of Modern Art, New York; Museum of Rhode Island, Providence; Museum of the Organization of American States, Washington, D.C.; Braniff Collection, University of Texas at Austin.

Publications:

By BENEDIT: article—prologue in *Bienal de Arte Coltejer,* exhibition catalogue, Medellin, Colombia 1970; film—editor, *4,000 Abejas en Venezia* by Pedro Roth, Venice, Italy 1970.

On BENEDIT: book—*3-Labyrinthe von Luis F. Benedit: Ein Versuch über die Kunst der Displazierung,* exhibition catalogue, by A. M. Battro, Munich 1972; article—"Intra-Functional Modules" by Jorge Glusberg in *Art and Artists* (London), July 1970.

I am interested in designing physical spaces which can be inhabited, explored or observed, and where the major evidence is a certain sort of behavior, individual or collective. I use persons, animals or physical phenomena simply as protagonists. My aim is to force culturally the aesthetic participant of my works: I consider my work justified if I am able to provoke just one reflection out of the daily routine about his inner self.

These works are *experiences* in the field of art, but if their mechanism is operated by a scientist they can be transformed into real *experiments* with consequences outside the field of aesthetics.

—Luis Benedit

Luis Benedit shows how every plant constitutes by itself a laboratory. By means of a process of osmosis their roots obtain the possibility of elaborating the food substances which could be either in the earth or in the inert substances in which they arrive; a nutritive solution. Furthermore, the roots separate out the acids which help out in the dissolution of the minerals existent in the earth or in the plastic material. The roots also serve as deposits of the assimilated products. The stem and the branches act as a system to transport the liquids, and the fibrovasculars work like small channels. It isn't until the food substances which have been absorbed by the roots and converted into sap (solutions which circulate inside the plants) get into the leaves that they can be utilized, by means of a process called chlorophyllous synthesis, in which by utilizing solar light the plant obtains the energy which it needs for its subsistence and reproduction.

In the works of Benedit the plants find the same environmental conditions which nature offers them, and the artificial nutritive solution is the basis of his experiment: with that system the artist models along

Luis Benedit: *Project Cancer Pagurus,* 1975

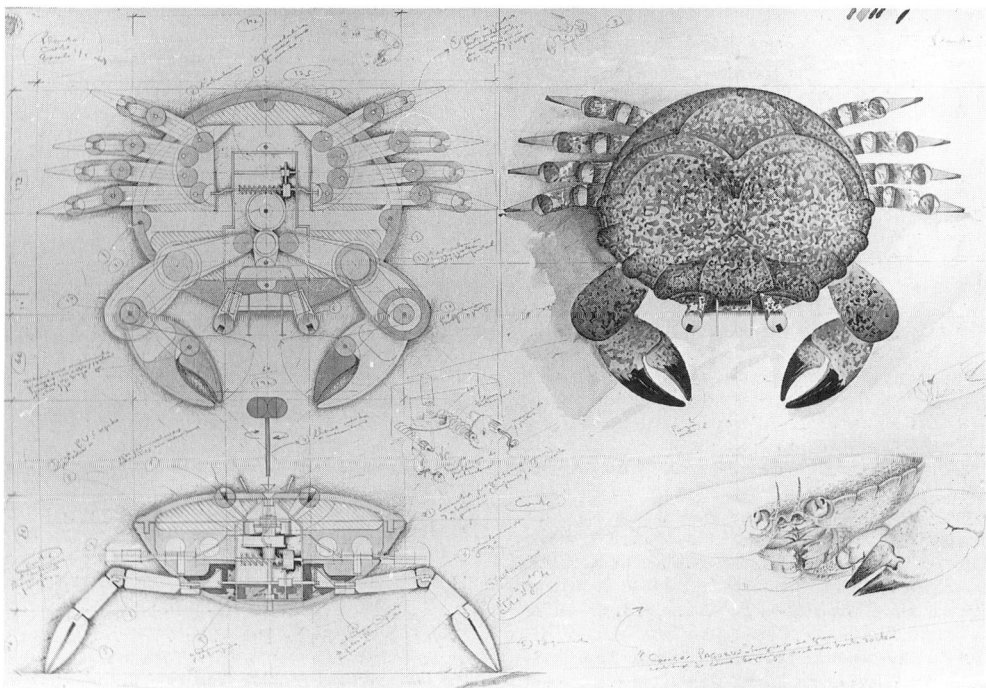

with the scientist the conditions which the earth offers to the vegetables.

The botanical experiments of Benedit, architect and painter, who studied the drawing of landscapes with the Italian master Francesco Fariello, are surely a result of the lessons he was allowed to enjoy from European gardens. The elements of landscape painting are precisely the plants, the birds, water and the sun, all of which are elements which Benedit utilizes in his investigations: the presentation of natural facts, their representation, the relation between the works of art and animals, their functions; without a scientific explanation, but simply showing what is observable.

From "Biotron," his most important work with animals (an experiment with 4,000 bees), Benedit went on to present the behaviour of plants, varying the parameters and conditioning them in accordance with scientific experiments, such as hydroponics.

In the "Phitotron" Benedit puts the spectator in front of a natural system of live organisms which develops, and modifies, allowing in addition a direct observation of the growth and change, during a determined length of time.

The proposal is not a direct scientific observation of the phenomenon, but rather the developments which could grow out of his proposal. Adhering to and developing the ideas of Duchamp, Benedit thinks that the observation of these natural phenomena, in terms of the different context in which he proposes them, produce a different effect in the spectator.

Every science not only uses models of other sciences, but also uses them on distinct levels of abstraction in order to anticipate kinds of happenings or realities. The models serve as objects of representation, as constructions which reproduce phenomena in such a way as to make them more accessible or easier to investigate.

In the case of Benedit's botanical experiments, the marks of reference elected are the investigations by means of vegetable models, a kind of scientific laboratory where collective behaviour in a vegetable community is studied. Benedit operates as a social anthropologist; he has elaborated a series of interesting models which, although exhibited as artistic facts, go beyond the purely descriptive or documental study. In August of 1968 Benedit made his first "Animal Habitat" in the Buenos Aires Fine Arts Museum; and in December of that year, in the Rubbers Gallery, he worked painstakingly with cats, lizards, fish, turtles, birds, a hive of bees in full activity and botanical experiments in fecundation and germination.

The objects of his studies are not industrial or folkloric structures, as are the objects of Marcel Duchamp; rather, they are located at a level in which the object nearly tends to disappear due to its being used, something like an object which carries its presence to the limit of perception. He does not establish a cultural dialogue with the spectator, but rather liberates activity and existence in the animal and vegetable world, in a process in which every possible intellectual intervention is reduced. He puts in the forefront the elements of reality and makes them react among themselves, in order to investigate their own expressive charges.

—Jorge Glusberg

BENGLIS, Lynda.
American. Born in Lake Charles, Louisiana, 25 October 1941. Educated at Newcomb College, New Orleans, with Zoltan Buki, Harold Carney, Ida Kolhmeyer, Patrick Trivigno, 1960–64, B.F.A. 1964; Yale Summer School, Norfolk, Connecticut, 1963; Brooklyn Museum Art Achool, Max Beckmann Scholarship Class, 1964–65. Assistant Professor of Sculpture, University of Rochester, New York, 1970–72; Assistant Professor, Hunter College, New York, 1972–73; Visiting Professor, California Institute of

the Arts, Valencia, 1974; Visiting Professor, Princeton University, New Jersey, 1975; Visiting Professor, California Institute of the Arts, Valencia, 1976; Visiting Artist, Kent State University, Ohio, 1977; Visiting Artist, Skowhegan School of Painting and Sculpture, Maine, 1979. Recipient: Guggenheim Fellowship, 1975; Artpack Grant, 1976; Australian Arts Council Award, 1976; National Endowment for the Arts Grant, 1979; Avery Distinguished Professor Award, Bard College, Annandale-on-Hudson, New York, 1987. Agent: Paula Cooper Gallery, 155 Wooster Street, New York, New York, 10012. Address: 222 Bowery, New York, New York, 10012, U.S.A.

Individual Exhibitions:

1969	University of Rhode Island, Kingston
1970	Paula Cooper Gallery, New York
	Janie C. Lee Gallery, Dallas
	Virginia Polytechnic Institute, Rockwell
1971	Kansas State University, Manhattan
	Paula Cooper Gallery, New York
	Hayden Gallery, Massachusetts Institute of Technology, Cambridge
1972	Hansen-Fuller Gallery, San Francisco
1973	Hansen-Fuller Gallery, San Francisco
	Portland Center for the Visual Arts, Oregon
	The Clocktower, New York
1974	Hansen-Fuller Gallery, San Francisco
	Texas Gallery, Houston
	Paula Cooper Gallery, New York
1975	Texas Gallery, Houston
	Physical and Psychological Monuments in Time, State University of New York, at Oneonta (retrospective)
	The Kitchen, New York
	Paula Cooper Gallery, New York
1976	Paula Cooper Gallery, New York
1977	Margo Leavin Gallery, Los Angeles
	Hansen-Fuller Gallery, San Francisco
	Douglas Drake Gallery, Kansas City
1978	Paula Cooper Gallery, New York
1979	Texas Gallery, Houston
	Dart Gallery, Chicago
	Real Art Ways, New Haven, Connecticut
	Hansen-Fuller Gallery, San Francisco
	Georgia State University, Atlanta
	Galerie Albert Baronian, Belgium
	Suzanne Hilberry Gallery, Birmingham, Michigan (with Ron Gorchov)
1980	Galerie Albert Baronia, Belgium
	Texas Gallery, Houston
	Lynda Benglis: 1968–1979, University of South Florida, Tampa
	Lowe Art Museum, Miami
	Margo Leavin Gallery, Los Angeles
	Portland Center for the Visual Arts, Oregon
	Paula Cooper Gallery, New York
	David Heath Gallery, Atlanta
	Chatham College, Pittsburgh
	Suzanne Hilberry Gallery, Birmingham, Michigan
1981	University of Arizona, Tucson
	Galerie Albert Baronian, Brussels
	Dart Gallery, Chicago
	Texas Gallery, Houston
	Jacksonville Art Museum, Florida
1982	Okun-Thomas Gallery, St. Louis, Missouri
	Margo Leavin Gallery, Los Angeles
	Paula Cooper Gallery, New York
	Fuller Goldeen Gallery, San Francisco
1983	Susan Hillbery Gallery, Birmingham, Michigan
	Dart Gallery, Chicago
1984	Paula Cooper Gallery, New York
	Texas Gallery, Houston
	Tilden-Foley Gallery, New Orleans
1985	Margo Leavin Gallery, Los Angeles
	Dart Gallery, Chicago
	Susan Hillbery Gallery, Birmingham, Michigan
	Heath Gallery, Atlanta, Georgia
1986	Fuller Goldeen Gallery, San Francisco
	Tilden-Foley Gallery, New Orleans
1987	Paula Cooper Gallery, New York

Selected Group Exhibitions:

1977	*Recent Acquisitions,* Guggenheim Museum, New York
1978	*Art at Work: Recent Art from Corporate Collections,* Whitney Museum, Downtown Branch, New York
1979	*Contemporary Sculpture: Selections from the Collection of The Museum of Modern Art,* Museum of Modern Art, New York
1980	*Extensions: Jennifer Bartlett/Lynda Benglis/Robert Longo/Judy Pfaff,* Contemporary Arts Museum, Houston
1981	*Decorative Sculpture,* Whitney Museum, New York
1982	*Postminimalism,* Aldrich Museum of Contemporary Art, Ridgefield, Connecticut
1983	*Back to the U.S.A.,* Rheinisches Landesmuseum, Bonn (travelled to Lucerne and Frankfurt)
1984	*American Art Since 1970,* Whitney Museum, New York
1985	*New York Now: Correspondences,* Laforet Museum, Tokyo (travelled to Tochigi and Kobe, Japan)
1986	*Between Geometry and Gesture,* Palacio de Velazquez, Madrid

Collections:

Museum of Modern Art, New York; Guggenheim Museum, New York; Philadelphia Museum of Art, Detroit Institute of Arts; Walker Art Center, Minneapolis; Milwaukee Art Center; National Gallery of Australia, Canberra.

Publications:

By BENGLIS: articles—"Interview 99/Lynda Benglis," with Karen Edwards, in the *Sunday Herald* (New York), 13 June 1971 "Lynda Benglis in Conversation with France Morin" in *Parachute* (Montreal), Spring 1977; videotapes—*Totem 1971,* New York, 1971; *Document 1972,* Castelli-Sonnabend exhibition catalogue, New York, 1972; *Collage,* Castelli-Sonnabend exhibition catalogue, New York, 1973; *Female Sensibility,* Castelli-Sonnabend exhibition catalogue, New York, 1974.

On BENGLIS: books—*Physical and Psychological Monuments in Time,* exhibition catalogue, by Robert Pincus-Witten, Oneonta, New York, 1975; *Video Art,* exhibition catalogue, with essays by David Antin, Lizzie Borden, Jack Burnham, and John McHale, Philadelphia 1975; *From the Center* by Lucy Lippard, New York, 1976; *American Artists '76: A Celebration,* exhibition catalogue, with an essay by Alice Simkins, San Antonio, Texas 1976; *The 1976 Biennale of Sydney,* exhibition catalogue, Sydney 1976; *Artculture* by Douglas Davis, New York, 1977; *Video-Visions: A Medium Discovers Itself* by Jonathan Price, New York 1977; *Postminimalism* by Robert Pincus-Witten, New York 1977; *5 from Louisiana,* exhibition catalogue, supplement to the *Times-Picayune* (New Orleans), 30 January 1977; *A View of a Decade* exhibition catalogue, Chicago 1977; *Made by Sculptors,* exhibition catalogue, Amsterdam 1978; *American Portraits of the 60's and 70's,* exhibition catalogue, Aspen, Colorado 1979; *Painting: 5 Views,* exhibition catalogue, Wayne, New Jersey 1979; *Contemporary Sculpture: Selections from the Collection of the Museum of Modern Art,* exhibition catalogue, New York 1979; *Extensions: Jennifer Bartlett/Lynda Benglis/Robert Longo/Judy Pfaff,* exhibition catalogue, Houston 1980; *Sculpture on the Wall* exhibition catalogue, Amherst, Massachusetts 1980; *Lynda Benlis: 1968–1979,* exhibition catalogue, Tampa, Florida 1980; *Current/New York,* exhibition catalogue, Syracuse, New York 1980; *Painting in Relief,* exhibition catalogue, New York 1980; *Painting in Environment,* exhibition catalogue, Milan 1980; *Drawing: The Pluralist Decade,* exhibition catalogue, introduction by Janet Kardon, Philadelphia 1980; *With Paper, About Paper,* exhibition catalogue, with an essay by Charlotta Kotik, Buffalo, New York 1980; *Lynda Benglis: Works in Glass,* exhibition catalogue, with essay by David Shapiro, Los Angeles, 1985; articles—"Lynda Benglis: The Frozen Gesture" by Robert Pincus-Witten in *Artforum* (New York), November 1974; "The New Sexual Frankness: Good-bye to Hearts and Flowers" by Dorothy Seiberling in *New York Magazine,* 17 February 1975; "Lynda Benglis: Sculptural Knots" by Suzanne Muchnic in *Artweek* (Oakland, California), 4 June 1977; "Artpeople" by John Russell in the *New York Times,* 17 February 1975; "Lynda Benglis" by Ellen Lubell in *Arts Magazine* (New York), January 1979; "Cosmetic Transcendentalism: Surface Light in John Torreano, Rodney Ripps and Lynda Benglis" by Donal Kuspit in *Artforum* (New York), October 1979; "Painting in New York: An Illustrated Guide"

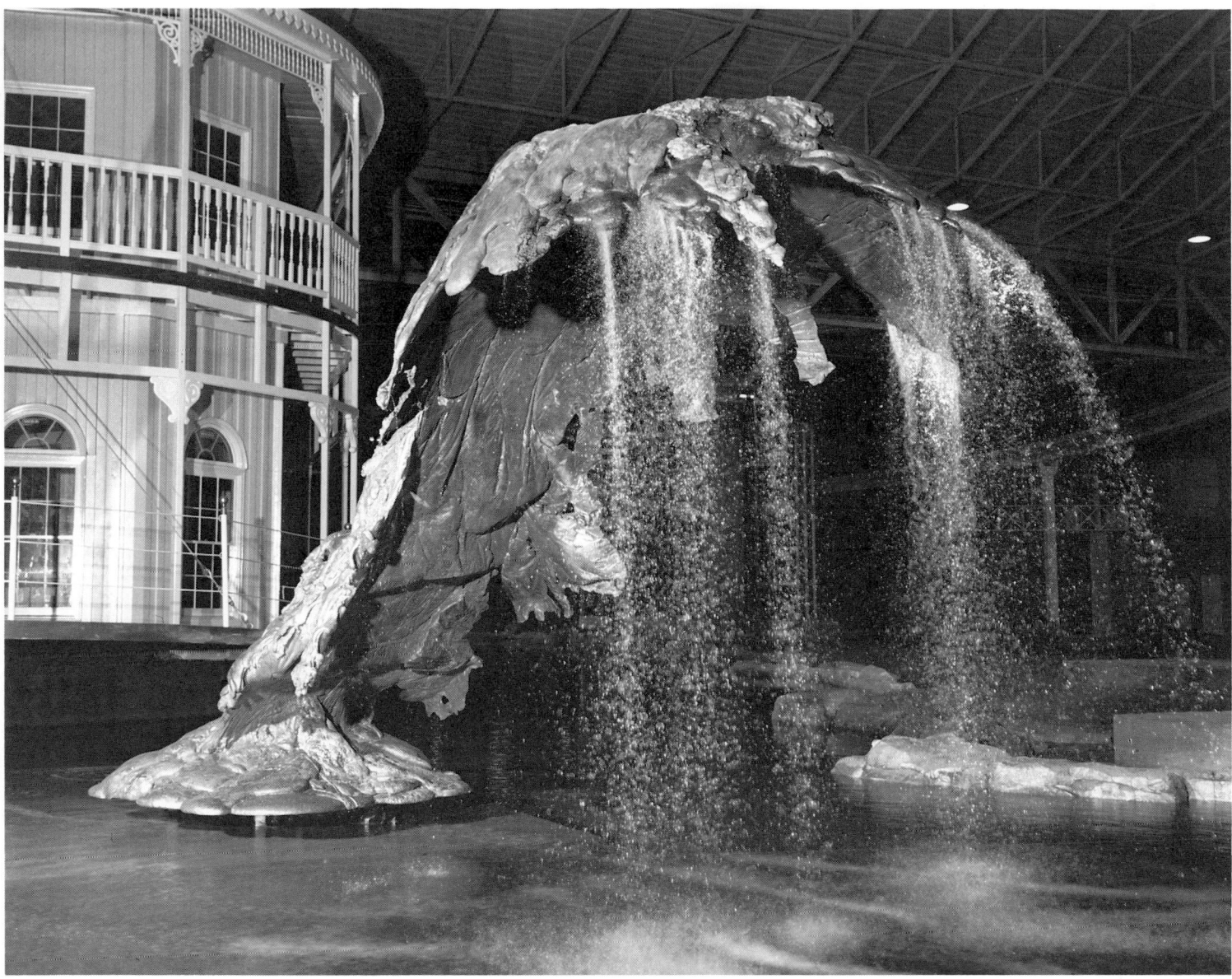

Lynda Benglis: *The Wave*, 1984

by Thomas Lawson in *Flash Art* (Milan), October/November 1979; "Women Artists" by John Gruen in *Working Women* (New York), July 1980; "Ramshackle Kennels Glimpsed by Moonlight" by John Ashbery in *New York Magazine*, 6 October 1980; "Lynda Benglis" by Douglas Welch in *Arts Magazine* (New York), November 1980; "Knot-Theme Sculptures by Lynda Benglis" by Vivien Raynor in the *New York Times*, 26 November 1982; "A Girl of the Zeitgeist" by Janet Malcolm in *The New Yorker*, 20 October 1986; "Lynda Benglis at Paula Cooper" by Holland Cotter in *Art in America* (New York), July 1987.

I am interested in work that depends on technology, that is visually exciting, and that hasn't been experienced in art or technology. Through genetic engineering, science is re-creating nature. Artists also do this. Only recently has science been able to understand nature in order to re-create it (e.g., using fusion research to create a star and genetic engineering to create new forms of life). Art ideas that are really inventive do not repeat each other. They re-create the nature of art.

The allusion to and the imitation of nature are the substance of art. I like to think that I mime the spirit of nature in re-creating it. Adjustments to gravity, weightlessness, hardness, softness, and motion are felt. Painting led me to sculpture; I wanted to free color of its flat form on canvas or board and to free form of much-used flat planes. I work with the probable and stretch it to the possible by using contradic-

tions in material and context. Each work exists in its right scale and motion within the contextual rules I've set up.

Perhaps these rules exist as I make them (that's my illusion), or perhaps they exist as they have always existed and I only allude to them. I am definitely bound by traditional concepts of classicism and beauty, while using technology, and wish to enter the contemporary spirit with this personal game.

—Lynda Benglis

Lynda Benglis' interests in a wide range of materials, structures and modes of presentation have produced some of the most sensuous and provocative sculpture in contemporary American art. With the first execution of the organic latex and foam floor pieces in the late 1960's that boasted blob-like and spreading structures and intensely garish colors, she began the explorations of an issue that proved to be a major concern of hers in the 1970's and that continues to occupy many artists in the 1980's: the relationship of painting and sculpture. Benglis created these works by pouring the liquid substances onto the floor and mixing in fluorescent tones; this method, by the late 1960's was associated with the "poured" paintings, say, of Morris Louis. In the early 1970's the forms moved off the floor onto the wall and took on more specific shapes. Made of various combinations of materials they offered a more concentrated experience of

color and form. Two examples are "Sparkle Totem" (1971–72), a narrow tube consisting of cotton bunting, plaster, pigment and sparkles; and "Valencia" (1972) a vertical bar with a corrugated surface of beeswax and damar resin on masonite. Staying on the wall, the works that followed explored various formats. Some of them continued to develop the narrow tubular shape; they include the cord-like "Zulu" (1970) a mixed mediums piece that features a central knot and the columnar-like "Volt" (1977), gold leaf and mixed mediums. Among the others that explored eccentric gestural shapes are "Pinto" (1971), the serial, polyurethane foam piece whose wing-like, curved appendages appear to fly-off-the-wall and penetrate the viewer's space, and "Omega" (1973), an asymmetrical multiple layered surface, containing folds and various protuberances.

In the middle 1970's Benglis also made videos in which she focused on female sexuality. Perhaps her most controversial statement on this subject was the announcement card she did for the May 1985 show she had at the Paula Cooper Gallery in New York. It featured a color photograph of the artist herself nude except for the jeans dropped to below her knees and a pair of platform shoes. With head turned toward the viewer and back-side aimed at the same, she is offering a provocative take-off on the "classic" pin-up pose.

Benglis is continuing to explore the issue of the female in the abstract relief sculptures she has done since the late 1970s. The sensual curves of the female body are brought to mind in a number of the gold leaf pieces whose volumetric sections swell out at top and bottom from a narrow center. Figure #2 (1978) is an example. In the cast metal pieces with repetitive elements reminiscent of pleats and fanning structures there is strong reference made to the tradition of the draped female figure in classical sculpture. In Essex (1986) and Lozier (1985) the vivid sensations of movement produced by the contrasting rhythms of each composition's dynamic parts are heightened by the intensely reflective metallic surfaces to give the illusion of glorious presence.

—Ronny Cohen

BENGSTON, Billy Al.

American. Born in Dodge City, Kansas, 7 June 1934. Educated at Los Angeles City College, 1953–54; Los Angeles State College, 1954–55; California College of Arts and Crafts, San Francisco, 1955–56; and Los Angeles County Art Institute, 1956–57. Independent Artist since 1957. Founder of Artist Studio, Venice, California, 1960. Instructor, Chouinard Art Institute, Los Angeles, 1961; Lecturer, University of California at Los Angeles, 1962–63; Guest Artist, University of Oklahoma, Norman, 1967; Guest Professor, University of Colorado, Boulder, 1969; Guest Instructor, in Ceramics and Painting, University of California at Irvine, 1973. Recipient: National Foundation for the Arts Grant, 1967; Tamarind Fellowship, Tamarind Lithography Workshop, Los Angeles, 1968, 1982; Guggenheim Fellowship, 1975. Agent: James Corcoran Gallery, 8223, Santa Monica Boulevard, Los Angeles, California 90046. Address: 100 Mildred Avenue, Venice, California 90291, U.S.A.

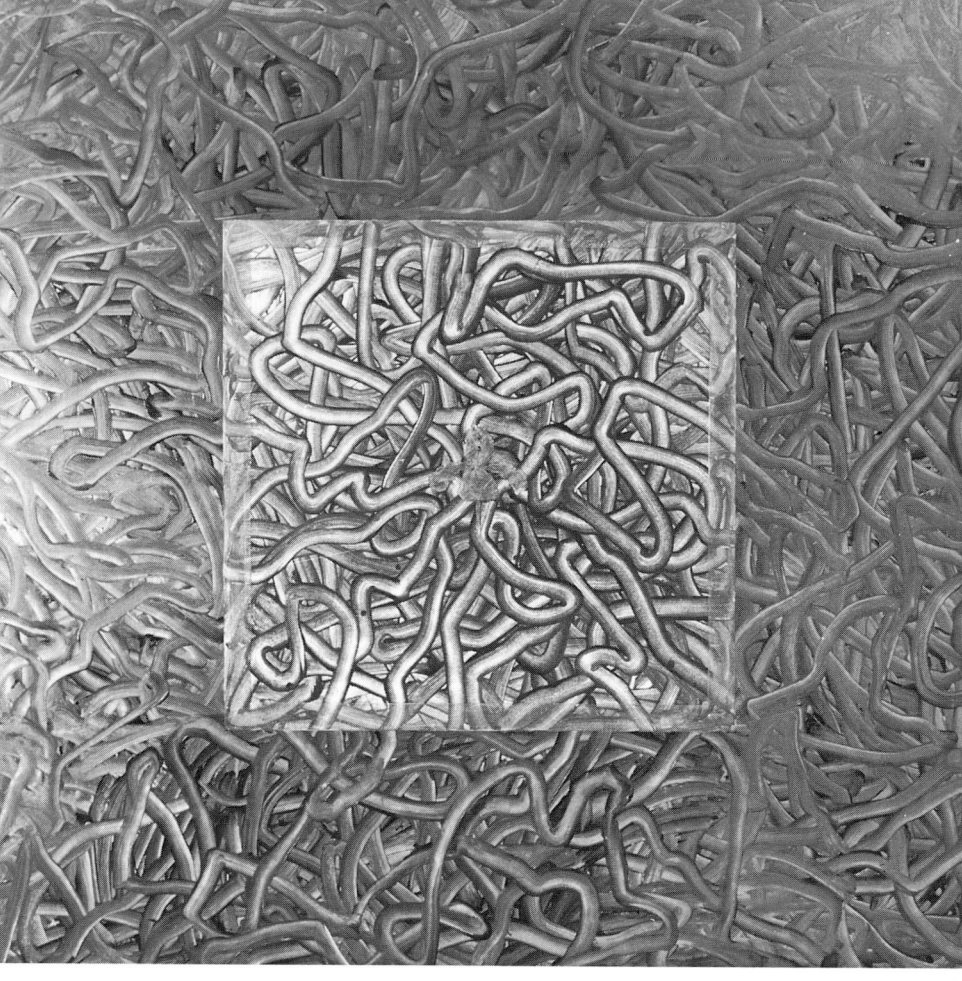

Billy Al Bengstom: *Bolognese Dracula (A. R.)*, 1972

Individual Exhibitions:

1958	Ferus Gallery, Los Angeles
1960	Ferus Gallery, Los Angeles
1961	Ferus Gallery, Los Angeles
1962	Martha Jackson Gallery, New York
	Ferus Gallery, Los Angeles
1963	Ferus Gallery, Los Angeles
1968	*Motel Dracula*, San Francisco Museum of Art (toured America and Canada)
1969	Utah Museum of Fine Arts, Salt Lake City
1970	Santa Barbara Museum of Art, California
	Mizuno Gallery, Los Angeles
	Galerie Neuendorf, Hamburg
	Galerie Neuendorf, Cologne
1971	Margo Leavin Gallery, Los Angeles
	La Jolla Museum of Art, California
	Contract Graphic Associates, Houston
	Galerie Neuendorf, Cologne
1972	Felicity Samuel Gallery, London
	Galerie Neuendorf, Hamburg
1973	Corcoran and Corcoran Gallery, Miami
	Nicholas Wilder Gallery, Los Angeles
	Pollock Gallery, Southern Methodist University, Dallas
	Contemporary Arts Museum, Houston
	Texas Gallery, Houston
1974	John Berggruen Gallery, San Francisco
	Jared Sable Gallery, Toronto
	Texas Gallery, Houston
	Nicholas Wilder Gallery, Los Angeles
1975	Pyramid Gallery, Washington, D.C.
	Seder/Creigh Gallery, Coronado, California
	Tortue Gallery, Santa Monica, California
	Dootson-Calderhead Gallery, Seattle
1976	Texas Gallery, Houston
	Dobrick Gallery, Chicago
	Portland Center for the Visual Arts, Oregon

1977	Texas Gallery, Houston
	University of Montana, Missoula
	James Corcoran Gallery, Los Angeles
1978	James Corcoran Gallery, Los Angeles
	Security Pacific Bank Building, Los Angeles
	John Berggruen Gallery, San Francisco
	Sarah Campbell Blaffer Gallery, University of Houston
	Texas Gallery, Houston
	Mizuno Ceramics Gallery, Los Angeles
1979	James Corcoran Gallery, Los Angeles
	Texas Gallery, Houston
	Conejo Valley Art Museum, Thousand Oaks, California
	Acquavella Contemporary Art Gallery, New York
	Cantor-Lemberg Gallery, Birmingham, Michigan
1980	James Corcoran Gallery, Los Angeles
	Malibu Art and Design, California
	Honolulu Academy of Arts
1981	Corcoran Gallery, Washington, D.C.
	Acquavella Contemporary Art, New York
	San Diego University, California
	Thomas Babeor Gallery, La Jolla, California
	James Corcoran Gallery, Los Angeles
	Texas Gallery, Houston
1982	James Corcoran Gallery, Los Angeles
	Thomas Babeor Gallery, La Jolla, California
	Linda Farris Gallery, Seattle, Washington
1983	James Corcoran Gallery, Los angeles
	John Berggruen Gallery, San Francisco
	Thomas Babeor Gallery, La Jolla, California
	Acquavella Contemporary Art, New York
1984	Smith Anderson Gallery, Palo Alto, California
	Douglas Drake Gallery, Kansas City, Kansas
	James Corcoran Gallery, Los Angeles
	Thomas Babeor Gallery, La Jolla, California
	Texas Gallery, Houston
1985	James Corcoran Gallery, Los Angeles

	Angles Gallery, Santa Monica, California
	Thomas Babeor Gallery, La Jolla, California
1986	James Corcoran Gallery, Los Angeles
	Thomas Babeor Gallery, La Jolla, California
	Smith Anderson Gallery, Palo Alto, California

Selected Group Exhibitions:

1957	*Los Angeles Annual*, Los Angeles County Museum of Art
1963	*Pop Art USA*, Oakland Art Museum, California
1969	*New Media: New Methods*, Museum of Modern Art, New York (toured the United States)
1972	*Working in California*, Albright-Knox Art Gallery, Buffalo, New York
1976	*The Last Time I Saw Ferus*, Newport Harbor Art Museum, Newport Beach, California
1979	*1979 Biennal Exhibition*, Whitney Museum, New York
1980	*Fabrications*, Lowe Art Museum, University of Miami
1983	*On and Off the Wall*, Oakland Museum, California (toured the United States)
1985	*Poly-Eclecticism*, Humano Institute, Tokyo
1986	*Tamarind Impressions: Recent Lithographs*, Tamarind Institute, Albuquerque, New Mexico

Collections:

Los Angeles County Museum of Art; Newport Harbor Art Museum, Newport Beach, California; La Jolla Museum of Contemporary Art, California; University of California at Los Angeles; San Francisco Museum of Modern Art; Guggenheim Museum, New York; Museum of Modern Art, New York; Whitney Museum, New York; Museum of Fine Arts, Houston; Art Institute of Chicago.

Publications:

By BENGSTON: book—*Business Cards,* with Ed Ruscha, Los Angeles 1968; articles—"Late 50's at the Ferus" in *Artforum* (New York), January 1969; "Los Angeles Artists' Studios" in *Art in America* (New York), November/December 1970; interview with William Robinson in *Art in America* (New York), March/April 1973; "Billy Al Bengsten Framed by Joan Quinn", interview, in *Interview* (New York), October 1979.

On BENGSTON: books—*Pop Art,* by Lucy Lippard, New York 1966; *Billy Al Bengston,* exhibition catalogue, by James Monte, Los Angeles 1968; *Sunshine Muse,* by Peter Plagens, New York 1974; *Billy Al Bengston,* exhibition catalogue, Los Angeles 1977; *Billy Al Bengston: Paintings of the 70's,* exhibition catalogue, by Fredericka Hunter, Los Angeles 1978; articles—"Billy Al Bengston" by John Coplans in *Artforum* (New York), June 1965; "Billy Al Bengston's Dentos" by Fidel Danieli in *Artforum* (New York), May 1967; "Bengston in Los Angeles" by James Monte in *Artforum* (New York), November 1968; "Billy Al Bengston, Vancouver Art Gallery" by Charlotte Townsend in *Artscanada* (Toronto), August 1969; "Billy Al Bengston, Felicity Samuel Gallery" by Peter Fuller in *Connoisseur* (London), December 1972; "Bengston's Recent Work" by R. H. MacDonald in *Artweek* (Oakland, California), March 1974; "Billy Al Bengston's New Paintings" by Peter Piagens in *Artforum* (New York), March 1975; "The Decorative Impulse" by Jeff Perrone in *Artforum* (New York), November 1979; "Billy Al Bengston" by Ruth Bass in *Artnews* (New York), November 1979; "Billy Al Bengston: Sensuality and Structure" by Susie Kahil in *Artweek* (Oakland), 22 December 1979; "Billy Al Bengston" by Elise Miller in *San Diego Magazine,* May 1981; "New Editions" in *Artnews* (New York), October 1983; "Los Angeles: The New Mecca" by Barnaby Conrad III in *Horizon* (New York), January/February 1987.

It's the best I can do.

—Billy Al Bengston

Undeservedly, there may yet hover about Bengston's works a "tough guy" image. If so, it remains from the textbook use, to illustrate early 1960s Pop art, of his paintings which prominently featured a centralized motif of chevron bars. Of course these were taken, as in *Buster* (1962) as military iconography. What was forgotten is that the chevrons were centered on a gently hazy sprayed lacquer surface surrounded by glowing balls of light. While Bengston himself is a physical person, with life-long interests in gymnastics, surfing, and motorcycle racing, his art has always been, like Los Angeles Pop art, easy-going and non-aggressive. His oeuvre may in fact be taken as almost a cliche of California Art: light-filled, vaporously-hued, Japanese influenced both in calligraphic concerns, and more importantly in the wider sense of elegant finesse. (His memory of the on-set of the chevron bar element is simply a personal fascination with the motif-pattern; and such thinking has permeated his art since, as he continues to fasten upon a particular shape or object—for no outward reason and with no intent to indicate and incisive daily life involvment.) And so there appear in his body of works, long series of paintings which show bars, circles, fish, the Iris, et. al. In their decorative, collaged-like flat pattern, his paintings in recent years have come to resemble silk-screened fabrics. Bengston clearly foreshadows the Pattern and Decoration movement and may be linked to those artists who coalesced that idiom through contact with the Art Department at the University of California at San Diego—M. Schapiro, Kushner, Zakanitch, and MacConnel.

—Joshua Kind

BERDYSZAK, Jan.

Polish. Born in Zawory, 15 June 1934. Educated at State College of Plastic Arts, Poznan, 1952-58, sculpture diploma 1958. Married Maria Mrozek in 1958; son: Marcin. Served as a Lieutenant in the Polish Army, 1953-56. Artist working in sculpture, painting, graphics, ephemeral media and stage design; lives in Poznan. Director of Sculpture, State Academy of Plastic Arts, Poznan, since 1965; Director, Department of Architecural Painting and Sculpture, since 1970. Recipient: Design Prize, *3rd International Puppet Theatre Exhibition,* Bucharest, 1965; Honorable Mention, *International Education Year Exhibition,* Unesco, Paris, 1970; Third Art Prize, Ministry of Culture and Art, Warsaw, 1971; First Prize, *International Triennale of Drawings,* Wroclaw, 1974; First Prize, *Art Biennale for Children,* Poland, 1977; Jan Cybis Prize, Warsaw 1978; Gold Medal, *Quadriennale,* Prague 1979; Third Prize, *Polish Print Exhibition,* Warsaw, 1981. Address: U1. Augustowska 17, 61–051 Poznan, Poland.

Individual Exhibitions:

1960	Klub Od Nowa, Poznan
	Klub Zwiazku Polskich Artystow Plastykow, Poznan
1962	Biuro Wystaw Artystycznych, Poznan
1964	Galerie Zwiazku Polskich Artystow Plastykow, Poznan
	Biuro Wystaw Artystycznich Arsenal, Poznan
1965	Galerie Krzystofory, Cracow
	Stowarzyszenie Polskich Artystow Muzykow, Warsaw
1966	Akiyama Gallery, Tokyo
	Biuro Wystaw Artystycznych Arsenal, Poznan
	State College of Plastic Arts, Poznan
1967	Galcrie in der Biberstrasse, Vienna
	Galerie A. Gniezno, Poland
1968	Panstowa Opera il Filharmonia Baltycka, Danzig
	Biuro Wystaw Artystycznych Arsenal, Poznan
1969	Central Biuro Wystaw Artystycznych Zacheta, Warsaw
	Galerie Od Nowa, Poznan
	Grabowski Gallery, London
	Galerie Krzysztofory, Cracow
1970	Biuro Wystaw Artystycznych, Sopot, Poland
1971	Biuro Wystaw Artystycznych Arsenal, Poznan
	House of Arts, Brno, Czechoslovakia
	Galerie 70, Zielona Gora, Poland
1972	Lengyel Kultura, Budapest
	Galerie Arkady, Cracow
	Klub Zwiaskow Tworczych, Wroclaw
1973	Krytykow, Lublin
1974	Muzeum Narodow, Poznan
1975	Galerie Teatru Studio, Warsaw
1976	Osrodek Propagandy Sztuki, Lodz
1977	Galerie Koregarda, Warsaw
	Galerie Sztuki Najnowszej, Wroclaw
1978	Biuro Wystaw Artystycznych, Poznan
	Galerie Kordegarda, Warsaw
	Biuro Wystaw Artystycznych, Radom, Poland
	Biuro Wystaw Artystycznych, Jelenia Gora, Poland
	Dom Artysty Plastyka, Warsaw
1979	Galerie Aut, Gdansk
	Biuro Wystaw Artystycznych, Szczecin, Poland
	Biuro Wystaw Artystycznych, Pila, Poland
1980	Galerie Foto, Medium Art, Wroclaw
	Galerie Krytykow, Warsaw
	Biuro Wystaw Artystycznych, Koszalin, Poland
	Galerie Zapiecek, Warsaw
1981	Biuro Wystaw Artystycznych, Lublin
	Galerie GN, Gdansk
	Galerie Krzysztofory, Cracow
	Galerie Foto, Medium Art, Wroclaw
	Biuro Wystaw Artystycznych, Bialystok, Poland
1982	Biuro Wystaw Artystycznych, Poznan
	Galerie Kubus, Hannover
	Galerie Tolerance, Hamburg
1983	Galerie ON, Poznan
	Biuro Wystaw Artystycznych, Jelenia Gora, Poland
1984	Galerie ON, Poznan
	Galerie MPiK, Torun, Poland
	Mala Galeria, Gorzow, Poland
1985	Biuro Wystaw Artystycznych, Leszno, Poland
	Galerie Wschodnia, Lodz
	Galerie Rysunku, Gdynia, Poland
	Biuro Wystaw Artystycznych, Lublin, Poland
1986	Biuro Wystaw Artystycznych, Torun, Poland
	Biuro Wystaw Artystycznych, Bydgoszcz, Poland
	Biuro Wystaw Artystycznych, Lodz

Selected Group Exhibitions:

1969	*Biennale,* Paris
1971	*3rd Triennale Rysunku,* Museum Architektury, Wroclaw
1972	*Modern Legnyel Muveszet,* Mucsarnok, Budapest
1973	*Polkst Moderne Kunst,* Nordyllands Kunstmuseum, Aalborg, Denmark
1974	*10th Biennale d'Art,* Palais de l'Europe, Menton, France
1975	*Polish Painting Today,* Mall Galleries, London
1978	*7th International Contemporary Art Exhibition,* New Delhi
1980	*International Print Biennale,* Cracow
1983	*Biennale der Europaischen Grafik,* Baden-Baden, West Germany
1985	*International Open-Air Sculpture Biennale,* Athens

Publications:

By BERDYSZAK: articles—"Calosc Monumentalna i synteyczna" in *Nurt* (Poznan), February 1968; "Kreaja Przestrzeni Spolecznej: Lagow wrzesien 1974," with Stefan Papp, in *Madodrze* (Zielona Gora), November 1975; "Emptiness as a Sense of Individual Creations" in *The Aspects of Polish Modern Arts,* exhibition catalogue, Warsaw 1975, "Pytanie o Poznanie" in *Jan Berdyszak,* exhibition catalogue, Wroclaw 1977; "Wieloobraz porownawczy" in *Berdyszak,* exhibition catalogue, Jelenia Gora, Poland 1978; "Varied Media . . ." in *Jan Berdyszak,* exhibition catalogue, Wroclaw 1980; "Obszary koncentrujace" in *Jan Berdyszak,* exhibition catalogue, Lublin 1981.

On BERDYSZAK: books—*Jan Berdyszak,* exhibition catalogue, Poznan 1964; *Jan Berdyszak,* exhibition catalogue, by Tadeusz Czrzanowski, Cracow 1965; *Jan Berdyszak,* exhibition catalogue, by Teresa Kostyrko, Griezno, Poland 1967; *Jan Berdyszak,* exhibition catalogue, by Bozena Kowalska, Sopot, Poland 1970; *Jan Bedryszak,* exhibition catalogue, with text by Bozena Kowalska, Frno, Czechoslovakia 1971; *Problemy Sztuki Wspolczesnei* by Teresa and Krzysztof Kostyrkowic, Poznan 1972; *Jan Berdyszak,* exhibition catalogue, by Adam Radajewski, Lublin 1973; *Katalogu Wystawy Jana Berdyszak,* exhibition catalogue, with text by Kazimierz Malinowski and Maria Berdyszakova, Poznan 1974; *Polska Awangarda Malarska 1945– 1970* by Bozena Kowalska, Warsaw 1975; *Jan Berdyszak,* exhibition catalogue, by Bozena Kowalska, Lodz 1976; *Jan Berdyszak,* exhibition catalogue, with text by Alicja Kepinska, Torun, Poland 1986.

Art, unlike philosophy, never allows the possibility of "arrangement." Art is natural; it remains a general value even when declaring, for example, some perceptible construction. Art has always aimed to be, was and is COGNITION. Cognition is contrary to recognition, regardless of whether it is based on an object, situation, happening, energy, plurality of reality, homogeneity of language, or analogous abstraction.

External order, then, is either distorted or tolerated by the necessary as long as it does not make creative needs impossible.

There is no order in cognition; there are wishful guesses. It seems to be most important to sense plurality without order, leading us to possibilities of forming "breaks" in our sense of reality, which, perhaps, will allow us to look at hitherto existing concepts and senses of existence and our fellow creatures in some other way. By "look at" I do not mean either seeing, saying or knowing but communication of self-communication from the area between naming and recognizability. Understanding is less; experiencing is more.

Experiencing, unlike experience, does not permit the repetition of phenomena, therefore does not resolve to elements, perceptible processes or values; at the same time, it is also impossible to define whole

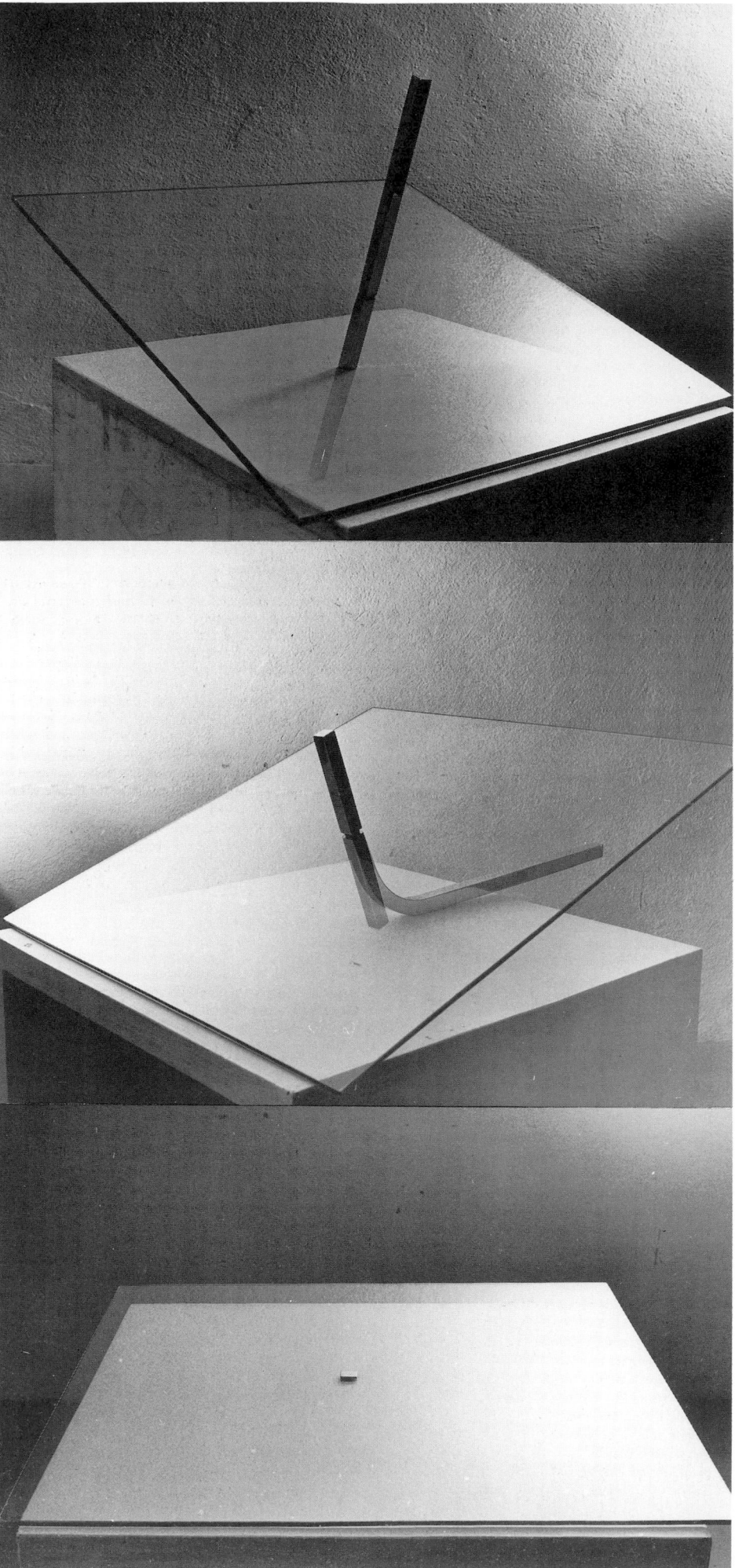

states and intervalues—supplementary values. Experiencing does not exist non-personally; it is not homogeneous, so inheres potentially.

Art is experiencing. Experiencing is a one-fold possibility, and I perceive one-foldedness as the most important feature of continuous eternity.

—Jan Berdyszak

For Jan Berdyszak art is a cognitive activity: cognition through art is a specific kind of active thought, a kind of total cognition, covering the whole experience—intuition and knowledge—of the creator, yet not "total" or "apart" or "complete." The artist calls it "cognition among cognitions," an awakening of the senses through art; simultaneously, it builds its own content.

This kind of act differs from other kinds of cognition—for example, academic—and gives rise to the question which provokes Berdyszak's attention: what conditions are necessary for the creation of art?

This is, at the same time, a question about the ontological status of art. It doesn't suggest a definitive answer but points to the possibility of an infinite number of approaches to the problem. Berdyszak builds successive models of approximation. Each model takes on the character of the cycle in the frame: as such, as a mutation of the end product, it becomes an instrument of cognition. In the process of examining the creative potential of the artist's imagination, he compares it with "emptiness," the primary state. It is a special area, referred to variously as "unknown place" or "area to question" or "area for contemplation" or "concentrated region" to be filled in and pondered in order that the reality of art may appear in the process. The boundaries of these regions are delineated with the help of the shape and colour of their shells, and as such are given the name "painting." The real picture, however, is the emptiness, that which does not exist.

This emptiness makes the existence of the "potential painting" possible: the onus is on the actual possibility of existence. These dealings simultaneously concern the whole history of the occurrence of "painting," revealing its basic construction, the "shell" (frame) and "that which is inside." Examples are "Models of the Value of a Picture" (1975), where the indispensable elements are maintained but always threatened by some process of disturbance. On the other hand, "Multi-Image" (1977), consisting of three paintings superimposed, shows three aspects of a painting: its "record," "statement" and "essence."

The delineation of the potential areas of construction of art which are so important to the artist sometimes takes place through the adaptation of the rule of uncertainty concerning the boundaries of the region. For example, there are "areas of reflection"—discs of metaplex covered with a thickening white substance that gradually blots out their transparency. Sheets of glass, also, are laid on top of each other until they lose their transparency.

The awareness of the unlimited potential of art causes the problem of infinity to be an important one in Berdyszak's work. The artist constructs various models of understanding of the infinite: one of them treats the infinite as that which is "apart"; another treats it as a centric value—i.e., conditioned by something. In the "Great" and the "Small Circle of Infinity," the object, which has been split up as far as possible, he tries to bring the actual concept of infinity closer to us. Infinity—a term used in mathematics and logic—also inheres in the idea of "boundary." In Berdyszak's work, this idea appears in two ways—in the sense of the boundary of regions that call forth the construction of art and as a question having to do with the possibility of filling these areas—their individual penetration.

The ever-present problem of "potential regions" appears in the cycle "Projects of Conception" (since 1977). Here, the artist poses the problem of his own

Jan Berdyszak: *Die Durchsichtige VI*, 1974

question. He ignores our conditioned response, that a question must necessarily involve awaiting an answer. In order to focus on the meaning of the actual question as a value in itself, he introduces the term "negative question." For example, in a number of works, "negative painting" is that which exists between "painting" and that which is no longer the painting and which can be called, for want of a better word, "space."

From the question so considered come "Studies After" from the period 1975–79. They are graphics obtained by the artist's throwing the shapes of old sculptures onto a lit offset plate. These statues are thought of as creating a picture of continuity; it is a way of proceeding "after" and not "to"—a question of the importance of what it was that follows man like a shadow.

In the 1980s, he rendered the series "Concentrating Areas", "Ontological Areas" and "Radical Wholes". All of them deal with the possibilities of existence rather than existence itself. In fact, Berdyszak's art evolves in the direction of seeking possibilities instead of fulfilment.

The artist ever more readily uses transparent material—panes of glass. Transparent planes do not close anything, do not remove anything from vision and do not define anything ultimately. On the other hand, placed on the floor, stood by the wall, suspended in the air, sticking from among rocks they show places where we can ponder over art, that is change our behavior. Therefore, these places become potential areas as they focus our attention and open themselves up to us, revealing ways to unexpected destination.

In recent years also the role of drawing has been growing in Berdyszak's art, as if in keeping with Bachelard's statement: "If a metaphysician did not draw, would he be able to think? Openings and closures become ideas for him".

The artist formulates his ideas also in his numerous texts. In one of them he writes: "Most doubts are raised whatever is determined and "recognized". The expressed springs from the hope called by uncertainty. Searching for the potential is an attempt to bring back the conscience of the beginning or to become aware of special states and forms of existence. Differentiation and discrimination of the potential makes one come closer to the pre-initial which as form is not to be replaced while approaching the beings and their personal experience."

—Alicja Kępińska

BERGHUIS, Jaap.

Dutch. Born in Smilde, 15 August 1945. Studied interior architecture at the Instituut voor Kunstnijverheidsonderwijs, Amsterdam, 1963–67; painting, at Atelier 63, Haarlem, 1969–71. Married Annette Fehrmann in 1971; son: Thomas. Worked as interior architect, Nielson and Spruit, Amsterdam, 1967–69, and with D. van Shedregt and J. Rietveld, Amsterdam, 1969. Independent artist, concentrating on painting, Amsterdam, since 1969. Recipient: Dutch Government Study Grant, 1968, 1976, 1979. Agent: Art and Project, Prinsengracht 785, Amsterdam. Addresses: Javastraat 126, 1094 HP Amsterdam; Wilhelminastraat 57, 1054 VW Amsterdam, Netherlands.

Individual Exhibitions:

1969 Galerie Siau 1, Amsterdam
1970 Galerie Booker, Amsterdam
1974 Art and Project, Amsterdam
1975 Kabinett für Aktuelle Kunst, Bremerhaven, West Germany
      Art and Project, Amsterdam

Westfälischer Kunstverein, Münster, West Germany (with Rajlich and Rous)
1976 Art and Project, Amsterdam
1977 Kabinett fur Aktuelle Kunst, Bremerhaven, West Germany
      Galleria La Bertesca, Genoa, Italy
      Galerie Waalkens, Finsterwolde, Netherlands
      Galleria La Bertesca, Dusseldorf
      Galleria La Bertesca, Milan
      Art and Project, Amsterdam
1979 Museum Fodor, Amsterdam
      Art and Project, Amsterdam (with J. Commandeur and T. Rajlich)
1980 Art and Project, Amsterdam
1981 Art and Project, Amsterdam (with A. Blom and J. Commandeur)
1982 Art and Project, Amsterdam

Selected Group Exhibitions:

1970 *Utrechtse Kring*, Neudeflat, Utrecht
1972 *Multiples*, Kunststichting, Amsterdam
1973 *Prospect 73*, Städtische Kunsthalle, Dusseldorf
1974 *Somer 74*, Art and Project, Amsterdam
1975 *Fundamentele Schilderkunst*, Stedelijk Museum, Amsterdam
1976 *Sovrastruttura e Metapittura*, University of Palermo, Sicily
1977 *Bilder ohne Bildhauer*, Rheinisches Landesmuseum, Bonn
1980 *Neue Malerei aus den Niderlanden*, Neue Galerie, Graz, Austria
1982 *Amsterdam 60–80*, Museum Fodor, Amsterdam

Collections:

Stedelijk Museum, Amsterdam; Frans Halsmuseum, Haarlem, Netherlands; Dienst voor Rijks Verspreide Kunstvoorwerpen, The Hague; Museum Boymans-van Beuningen, Rotterdam; PTT Collection, The Hague.

Publications:

By BERGHUIS: articles—texts in *Art and Project Bulletin* (Amsterdam), nos. 77, 78, 1974; interview, with Dorine Mignot, in *Fundamentele Schilderkunst*, exhibition catalogue, Amsterdam 1975; interview, with Gijs Van Tuyl, in *Elementarformen*, exhibition catalogue, Bonn 1975.

On BERGHUIS: books—*Berghuis/Rajlich/Rous*, exhibition catalogue, with text by Klaus Honnef, Münster, West Germany 1975; *Elementarformen*, exhibition catalogue, with texts by Hans Sizoo, Klaus Honnef and others, Bonn 1975; *Berghuis/Dibbets/van Elk*, exhibition catalogue with text by R. Hammacher-van den Brande, Belgrade 1977; articles—"Debuten" by Lambert Tegenbosch in *De Volkskrant* (Amsterdam), September 1969; "Erotiek en Humor" by Fanny Kelk in *Het Parool* (Amsterdam), October 1969; "Jaap Berghuis" by M. van Emde Boas in *NRC-Handelsblad* (Amsterdam), October 1969; "Seizoenbegin in de Amsterdamse Kunstzalen" by M. van Emde Boas in *NRC-Handelsblad* (Amsterdam), September 1970; "Anonymous—Art & Project" in *Flash Art* (Milan), December 1974; "Fordert zur Kunst aug" by Hannelore Ahorn in *Nordsee-Zeitung* (Bremerhaven, West Germany), January 1975; "Jaap Berghuis" by Klaus Honnef in *Art Press* (Paris), September 1975; "Jaap Berghuis" by Betty van Gerrel in *NRC Handelsblad* (Amsterdam), 29 October 1982.

BERLEWI, Henryk.

Polish. Born in Warsaw, 30 October 1894. Educated in schools in Warsaw; attended art classes, Warsaw, 1904–09, and Antwerp, 1909–10; studied at the Ecole des Beaux-Arts, Paris, 1911–12. Lived in Warsaw, 1913–21; settled in Berlin, 1921; participated in Group "G" with Hans Richter, Werner Graeff, Sacha Stone and Mies van der Rohe; Member, Novembergruppe, Berlin, 1922; experimented with Mecano-Faktura theory, publishing his manifesto, 1923–24; returned to Warsaw, 1923; Co-Founder, Blok, 1923; worked as a theatre designer and art critic, 1926; settled in Paris, 1928; returned to Mecano-Faktura theory, 1957; founded Archives of *Abstract Art and International Avant-Garde*, Paris, 1960; continued development of Mecano-Faktura theory; experimented with cinematographic representation, Akademie der Künste, Berlin, 1962. *Died* (in Paris) 2 August 1967.

Jaap Berghuis: *Pieces for Schumann VII*, 1980

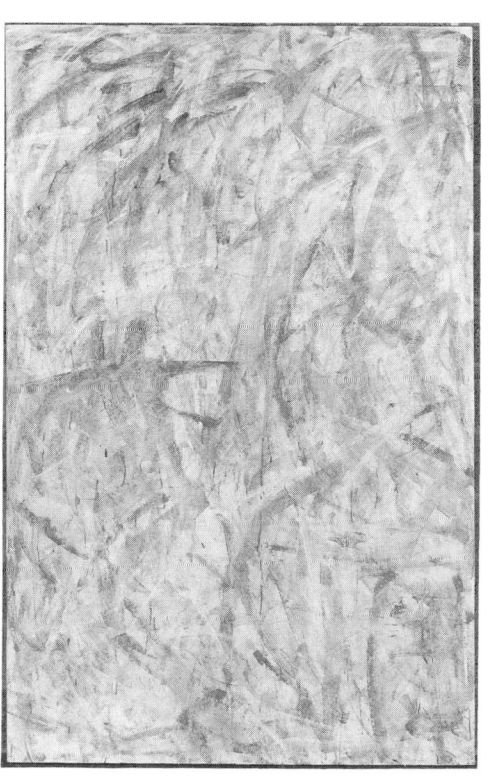

Individual Exhibitions:

1934	Austro-Daimler Automobilsalon, Warsaw
	Galerie der Sturm, Berlin
1950	Galerie Petrides, Paris
1963	Galerie Situationen 60, Berlin
1964	Maison de France, Berlin
1965	Centre d'Art Cybernetique, Paris
1966	Fine Art Society, Warsaw (toured Poland)
1967	Galerie Rewolle, Bremen
1978	Helen Serger, La Boetie, New York

Selected Group Exhibitions:

1914	*4th Jack of Diamonds*, Moscow
1915	*Zacheta*, Warsaw (and regularly until 1921)
1916	*Futurist Exhibition 0.10*, Petrograd
1923	*Novembergruppe*
1954	*Zeitgenossische Kunst aus Hannoverschem Prvatbesitz*, Kestner Gesellschaft, Hannover
1958	*De Renaissance der 20th Eeuw*, Stedelijk Museum, Amsterdam
1961	*The Art of Assemblage*, Museum of Modern Art, New York
1963	*Schrift und Bild*, Kunsthalle, Baden-Baden
1965	*Signale: Manifest: Proteste im 20 Jahrhundert*, Stadtische Kunsthalle, Recklinghausen
1966	*Von Impressionismus zum Bauhaus*, Kunstverein, Frankfurt

Collections:

Sztuki Museum, Lodz, Poland; Musée d'Art Moderne de la Ville, Paris.

Publications:

By BERLEWI: book—*Temoignages*, Paris 1965; articles—"Mecano Faktura Manifesto" in *Der Sturm* (Berlin), 1924; "Michel Larionov und Natalie Goncharova und der Rayonismus" in *Das Werk* (Winterthur, Switzerland), October 1961.

On BERLEWI: books—*Constructivism in Poland*, exhibition catalogue, Essen 1973; *Henryk Berlewi*, exhibition catalogue, by Helen Serger, New York 1978; article—"Berlewi et les Maccano-Factures" by C. Estienne in *XXe Siècle* (Paris), May 1966.

Henryk Berlewi's paintings of the 1960's give very little clue of how important this emigré Pole was to the development of non-figurative painting after his involvement with Dada during the First World War. It was in the early 1920's that his personal contribution to non-figurative art began. Through Lissitzky he was to become associated with the "New Poland," albeit at some distance removed. A year later he joined the Novembergruppe in Berlin and started his own version of abstract art which he called Mecano-Faktura (details of which were published in *Der Sturm* in 1924), ideas and theories which, however remote from the AR activities of Strzeminski and Kobro in Lodz, still made him eligible as an innovator in their eyes. In fact, so successful was Berlewi when he returned to Warsaw that he became the founder member of yet another group of abstract artists—Blok.

The Stalinist period in Poland meant that there was no room for artists like Berlewi, and he left his homeland yet again for the West. The absurd political interruption in the progress of contemporary Polish culture had a devastating effect upon a great number of Polish creative talents (in some cases actually lethal—after the culmination of the Nazi occupation during which men like the gifted artist Karol Hiller went to their deaths).

For Berlewi it meant the start of one more new life. The hard-edge perfection of geometricized Kandinsky (in pianissimo mood) in rich colours, all of which had passed comfortably from Mecano-Faktura to Blok, gave way to the old man's translations of the Mediterranean. Fine paintings, but not to be compared for quality with what had gone before.

—Sheldon Williams

BERNI, Antonio.

Argentinian. Born in Rosario, 14 May 1905. Educated in Roldan, Santa Fe Province, 1915, 1917–20; apprenticeship in a stained-glass workshop and drawing studies at the Catala Centre, Rosario, 1916; studied in Madrid, 1925, and under André Lhote and Othon Friesz at the Grand Chaumière, Paris, 1926 (on Santa Fé Government Scholarship). Married Paule Cazenave in 1930; daughter: Hélène; married Nelida Gerino in 1950; son: José Antonio. Lived with peasants in the Pampas, painting landscapes, 1921–24; lived in Madrid, 1925, in Paris, 1926, and in Arcueil, near Paris, also travelling to Italy, Belgium, and Holland, 1927–30; influenced by Surrealists and Marxists while in Europe, and began making photomontages, collages, drawings, and paintings in surrealistic style, 1929; returned to Argentina, 1930; worked as a municipal employee, Rosario, 1931; cofounder with other young painters of "New Realism" movement in Argentina, and organized group productions of larger canvases, Buenos Aires, 1932–40; travelled to the Pacific Coast, 1946; lived for long periods of time with cotton harvesters and woodcutters, and painting popular subjects, Santiago del Estero, 1947–56; resumed collage and assemblage techniques of the 1930's, 1957–60; concentrated on engravings, 1960–64. Instructor, National School of Fine Arts, Buenos Aires, 1935–45. Recipient: Prix, 1925, Premier Prix, 1940, and Grand Prix, 1943, *Salon Nacional*, Buenos Aires: Prix d'Honneur, *Salon Internacional*, Buenos Aires, 1960; Grand Prix International de la Gravure, *Biennale*, Venice, 1962; Prix de la Commission Culturelle, *Biennale Internacional de la Gravure*, Ljubljana, 1965; Prix, *Biennale Internationale de la Gravure*, Cracow, 1966; Prix Intergrafik, Berlin, 1967. *Died* (in Buenos Aires) *13 October 1981*.

Individual Exhibitions:

1928	Salon Nancy, Madrid
1932	Galeria Amigos del Arte, Buenos Aires (surrealistic works)
1938	Galeria Amigos del Arte, Montevideo
1952	Galeria Viau, Buenos Aires
1954	Teatro del Pueblo, Buenos Aires
1955	Galeria Creuze, Paris
1957	Galeria Witcomb, Buenos Aires
1958	Galeria Serra, Buenos Aires
1961	Galeria Peuser, Buenos Aires
	Galeria Witcomb, Buenos Aires
1963	Galeria du Passeur, Paris
	Museo de Arte Moderno, Buenos Aires
1964	Museo de Arte Moderno, Santiago de Chile (retrospective)
	Galeria Rubbers, Buenos Aires
1965	Instituto Di Tella, Buenos Aires (retrospective; travelled to Cordoba and Santa Fe)
1966	Galleria Due Mondi, Rome
1967	Galeria Rubbers, Buenos Aires
1968	Galeria Rubbers, Buenos Aires
1969	Galeria El Taller, Buenos Aires
1970	Galeria Exposhow, Buenos Aires
1971	ARC / Musée d'Art Moderne de la Ville, Paris
	Galeria Rubbers, Buenos Aires
1973	Atelier Jacob, Paris
	Galeria Rubbers, Buenos Aires
1974	Wells Gallery, Ottawa
	Galeria del Mar, Buenos Aires
	Galeria Imagen, Buenos Aires
	Galeria Rubbers, Buenos Aires
1975	Galleria Zunini, Rome
	Galeria Imagen, Buenos Aires
1976	Galeria Carmen Waugh, Buenos Aires
	Galeria Imagen, Buenos Aires
1977	Museo de Bellas Artes, Caracas (retrospective)
	Bonino Gallery, New York
1978	Galeria Bonino, Buenos Aires
	Galeria Imagen, Buenos Aires
1980	Galeria Arte Nuevo, Buenos Aires
	Fundacion San Telmo, Buenos Aires
	Museo de Arte Contemporaneo, Mar del Plata (retrospective)

Selected Group Exhibitions:

1955	*Hommage à Machado*, Maison de la Pensée, Paris
1962	*Biennale*, Venice
	Art Latino-Américain, Centre Georges Pompidou, Paris (and 1965)
1965	*Mythologies Quotidiennes*, Centre Georges Pompidou, Paris
	Biennale Internationale de la Gravure, Ljubljana, Yugoslavia
1967	*Le Monde en Question*, Musée d'Art Moderne de la Ville, Paris
	La Nature Moderne, Palais de Glace, Paris
1969	*Art et Cybernétique*, Galeria Bonino, Buenos Aires (travelled to Caracas, 1970)
1972	*Encuentro de Artistas Plasticas del Cono Sur*, Santiago de Chile
1980	*Biennale of Contemporary Art*, Tokyo

Collections:

Museo Nacional de Bellas Artes, Buenos Aires; Museo de Arte Moderno, Buenos Aires; Museum of Modern Art, New York; Musée Municipal, Saint-Denis, France.

Publications:

By BERNI: articles—"Siqueiros et l'Art des Masses" in *Nueva Revista* (Buenos Aires), 1935; "Le Peintre Colonial Melchor Perez de Holquin" in *Prensa* (Buenos Aires), 15 February 1942; "Goribar, Peintre de Quito" in *Prensa* (Buenos Aires), 31 May 1942; "La Culture de Quito a l'Epoque Coloniale" in *Prensa* (Buenos Aires), 25 April 1943; "El arte como experiencia" in *Continente* (Buenos Aires), 16 April 1952; "Persecucion a la Inteligencia" in *Propositos* (Buenos Aires) 18 December 1957; "El arte, su desarrollo, promocion y mercado" in *La Opinion* (Buenos Aires), 9 June 1972.

On BERNI: books—*Antonio Berni* by Geo-Dorival, Buenos Aires, 1944; *Antonio Berni* by Roger Pla, Buenos Aires 1945; *Biennale di Venezia*, exhibition catalogue with text by Jorge Romero Brest, Venice 1962; *Naissance d'un Art Nouveau* by Michel Ragon, Paris 1963; *Antonio Berni*, exhibition catalogue, with text by Gérald Gassiot-Talabot, Buenos Aires 1965; *Ramona Montiel* by E. Sabato and E. Schoo, Buenos Aires 1966; *Panorama de la Pintura Argentina Contemporanea* by Aldo Pellegrini, Buenos Aires 1967; *Berni* by Rafael Squirru, Montevideo 1968; *Vingt-Cinq Ans d'Art Vivant* by Michel Ragon, 1969; *A History of Latin American Art and Architecture* by Leopoldo Castedo, London 1969; articles—"Antonio Berni" by Rafael Squirru in *Journal of Inter-American Studies* (Washington, D.C.) July 1965; "Antonio Berni" by Gérald Gassiot-Talabot in *Depuis 45*, vol. 2, Brussels 1970; "Antonio Berni" by Michel Troche in *Opus International* (Paris), May 1971.

"The most thought-provoking human drama in Latin America in our century is that of those nations suffering under the yoke of colonialism with its burden of poverty and backwardness . . . . To seek to draw our artists away from the essential truth in order to direct them towards other secondary truths is equivalent to depriving them of all possibility of achieving the great art to which every man of progress aspires", wrote Antonio Berni in 1952, himself a fellow-traveller on this artistic journey dictated by political commitment. Eschewing all aesthetic and formal apriority, Berni's art is above all an art of the real, an art whose concern is to emphasise and denounce the excess of social injustices weighing down the Argentinian nation.

Berni was born in 1905 in Santa Fé. As in the case of the majority of his fellow Argentinians, many of his ancestors were Italian emigrés. Berni studied painting and drawing from an early age at the Centro Catala de Rosario, the capital of the province and second major city of Argentina. A scholarship from the Jockey Club gave him the opportunity to complete his studies in Europe. This trip, an inevitable 'return to one's roots' for any Latin American artist eager to seek out aesthetic models from the continent of his origin, took Berni first to Madrid, then to Paris, where he became familiar with various currents of avant-garde thinking. In 1926 he began studying painting at the Grande Chaumière under the direction of Othon Friesz and Andrè Lhote, but his taste for realism, intense colours and architectural decors was to find in De Chirico, rather than in the Cubists whom he nevertheless admired, a source of inspiration which accorded with his artistic sensibilities. This influence is manifest in the self-portrait of 1929 showing the painter in a garish light which accentuates the angular lines of the face and the austerity of a poverty-stricken urban environment. His meeting with the Surrealists in 1928, his relations with Max Jacob, Louis Aragon and various intellectuals of the period, far from seducing him into accepting the easy and frivolous life style of a certain Parisian intellectual milieu, were to drive him to take a stand against oppression and social injustice and to deepen his political convictions by familiarising himself with the theories of Marx, Lenin and Engels, theories which would form the mainstay henceforth of his artistic work.

On his return to Argentina in 1930 he exhibited a collection of works which were regarded as the first example of Surrealist art realised by an artist from the American continent. This series of paintings and collages, which have been described as 'fantastic metaphysical' art, present everyday objects with symbolical associations—keys, screws, locks, pins—invading neo-classic landscapes and architecture with their nightmarish presences abounding in references to torture, imprisonment and repression.

But this incursion into the world of objects and dreams, still conditioned by European influences, was to be suddenly invested with all the emotional force of a direct human crisis when Berni confronted the situation that had arisen in his own country. For he could not have remained indifferent to the particularly alarming political and economic crisis which overtook Argentina at the beginning of the 'thirties. During his 'realist period', which lasted approximately from 1934 to 1957, the Argentine artist introduced into his large pictorial compositions various aspects of the harsh existence endured by an urban rural proletariat which he daily frequented in Buenos Aires and during his numerous trips into the country. With their violent colours, massive outlines and the almost 'cinematographic' structure of the different parts of the image, Berni's paintings inevitably remind one of certain aspects of Mexican 'Muralismo' (Berni met the 'muralista' D. Alfaro Siqueiros during the latter's stay in Buenos Aires) and of Expressionism, but they exaggerate still further the dramatic intention, the working-class, specifically Third World, character of their themes by their pathetic rendering of faces, their choice of nuances and sordid accentuation of details. Painted from photographs or from straightforward observation, these scenes showing work in the fields, popular manifestations of anger or impotence in face of an inflexible social system, unemployment and poverty, function as political denunciations purely through the evocative power of the evidence contained in the choice of subject matter.

The Second World War produced a radical change in the formal orientation of Berni's work and the innovative character of his researches was soon to bring him international renown, crowned by the prize for engraving at the Venice Biennale in 1962. Although the social theme remained central to his work, Berni became absorbed in new technical processes based on assemblage, discovering the rich plasticity of reject materials and the naiveté of popular urban art. In his compositions the recycling of used objects, picked up in the streets of the Argentine capital or in the Parisian flea markets, seems to have nothing to do with either the 'cult of the object' in the manner of Pop Art, or with a fad for assembling disparate objects for its own sake, but, as Gerald Gassiot-Talabot supposes, tends to underline "the relationship which is established between the reject and the social organisation which has produced it". And, in order to denounce even more firmly the aberrations of the social organisation, Berni was to retrace in the course of his work the urban epic of the life of a small boy, Juanito

Laguna, a stereotype for the lives of all the thousands of inhabitants of those 'villa misérias', the shanty town homes sprawling on the periphery of Buenos Aires. In these large-format collages the decor, worked without attention to perspectives, is comprised of objects deriving from the very place they represent; the figures are set off and unified by the pictorial matter and their faces have coarse, roughly executed, almost caricatured faces which are movingly expressive.

These chapters of Juanito's life relate trivial incidents and scenes in the naive manner of children but in which the intrusion of elements symbolising progress or science (cosmonauts, the bomb . . .) only renders all the more insupportable the anachronistic situation in which the characters find themselves. Then, through Ramona Montiel, a woman torn between her romantic ideals and the sordid experience of prostitution, Berni describes the corrosive, degrading world of money, corruption and power. As if himself seduced by the charms of his Ramona, the artist deploys all his skill in assembling, all his engraving talents, to dress her in lace cut from cake wrappings, to coif her with buttons and artificial flowers, and to surround her with all the kitsch imagery of a shanty town Madame Bovary. So emotive are these works that the characters of Berni's 'pictorial novel' have been reintegrated into popular Argentinian culture, giving rise, for example, to numerous songs.

During the last years of his life Berni put together a collection of sculptural pieces: assemblages of three-dimensional objects characterised by a mixture of a baroque and the science fictional, the humorous and the horrific, in order to represent in the form of monsters and dragons nightmarish visions of maleficent powers, of death, vice, power and terror, in other words, all man's ancestral fears. Some of these sculptures were to inhabit 'Ramona's cavern', a huge site of a son et lumière, which was presented in 1968.

From his first Surrealist paintings to his final sculptures, via his realist period and the large series of assemblages which have often been associated—because of their chronological simultaneity and their political bias—with the 'Nouvelle Figuration' in Europe, Berni's oeuvre, which has achieved a formal diversity of astonishing richness (including painting, sculpture, engraving, xylography and collages), stands out above all for the commitment and acuteness of observation which puts it at the service not of the aesthetic demands of its age, but of a reality which, beneath its wretched exterior, is full of the tragic grandeur of the objects and feelings which are its offspring.

—Dominique Liquois

BERTHOLIN.

French. Born Maurice Bertholin in Granges-sur-Vologne, Vosges, 20 April 1936. Mainly self-taught in art, since 1952. Served in Service de Santé, French Army, in Nancy, France, 1956-58; Oran and Ain Sefra, Algeria, 1958. Married Francoise Andreux in 1959; children: Jacques, Veronique, Elisabeth. Nurse in Saint-Die Hospital, France, since 1959. Professor, Ecole des Beaux-Arts, since 1977. Agent: Galerie Baudoin Lebon, 34 rue des Archives, 75004 Paris, France. Address: 42 rue Eau de Robec, 76000 Rouen, France.

Individual Exhibitions:

1972	Galerie Sonnabend, Paris
	Galerie Handschin, Basle
1974	Musée d'Art Moderne de la Ville, Paris
1975	Galerie Maenz, Cologne
	Galerie Germain, Paris
	Galerie Art in Progress, Munich

1976	Galerie Isy Brachot, Brussels
	International Cultural Centrum, Antwerp
	Galerie Germain, Paris
	Galerie Paul Maenz, Cologne
1977	*La Matière Inavouable,* Musée de Saint-Etienne, France
	Galerie Germain, Paris
1978	*Bertholin-Objekte,* Bädischer Kunstverein, Karlsruhe
	Galerie Art Actuel, Nancy
	Stèles de Bertholin, Galerie Isy Brachot, Brussels
	Galerie Baudoin Lebon, Paris
1979	Kunst Forum, Rottweil, West Germany
	L'Infinito Intrattenimento con le Cose, Galleria Unimedia, Genoa
1980	Galleria Cenobio Visualita, Milan
	Ray Hughes Gallery, Brisbane
	Galerie Baudoin Lebon, Paris
	Galleria Il Gabbiano, La Spezzia, Italy
1981	Galleria Villa Romana, Florence
	Galleria Unimedia, Genoa
	Musée Départmental des Vosges, Epinal, France
1982	Musée du Fer, Jarville, Nancy, France
	Musée d'Art Moderne, Strasbourg, France
1983	ARC/Musée d'Art Moderne de la Ville, Paris
	Centre d'Art Contemporain, Chateauroux, France
1984	Espace Lyonnais d'Art Contemporain, Lyon, France
	Galerie Baudoin Lebon, Paris
1987	Musée de la Cohue, Vannes, France

Selected Group Exhibitions:

1971	*Biennale des Jeunes,* Paris
1972	*Salon de Mai,* Musée d'Art Moderne, Paris
1973	*5 Musées Personnels,* Musée de Grenoble, France
1974	*L'Art du 20th Siècle: Les Courants Historiques, Les Tendances de l'Art Actuel,* Musée d'Art Moderne, Paris
1975	*Today, Together,* Galerie Paul Maenz, Cologne
1977	*Documenta 6,* Kassel, West Germany
1978	*La Creazione Volgeva alla Fine,* Galleria Unimedia, Genoa
1984	*Les écritures dans la peinture,* Villa d'Arson, Nice, France
1985	*Livres d'Artistes,* Centre Georges Pompidou, Paris
1978	*Les Années Mémoire,* Centre d'Art Contemporain, Meymac, France

Collections:

Centre National d'Art Contemporain, Paris; Centre Georges Pompidou, Paris; Musée de Grenoble, France; Musée Cantini, Marseilles; Musée de Ceret, France; Musée de Strasbourg, France; Musée d'Epinal, France; Musée de Martiques, France; Queensland Art Gallery, Brisbane; Power Gallery of Contemporary Art, Sydney.

Publications:

By BERTHOLIN: books—*Impact II,* exhibition catalogue, Caret, France 1972; *5 Musees Personnels,* exhibition catalogue, Grenoble 1973; *Pour Mémoires,* exhibition catalogue, Bordeaux 1973; articles—article in *Flash Art* (Milan), July/August 1977; statement in *Documenta 6,* exhibition catalogue, Kassel, West Germany 1977; statement in *Bertholin-Objekte,* exhibition catalogue, Karlsruhe 1978; "Emtretien avec Eddy Devolder" in *Jalons et actualités des Arts* (Paris), May 1978; "On ne peut que parler dans l'ombre . . ." in *Cahier* (Paris), Autumn 1987.

On BERTHOLIN: books—*Bertholin et La Matière Inavouable,* exhibition catalogue, with text by Gilbert Lascault, Saint-Etienne 1977; *Bertholin-Objekte,* exhibition catalogue, with text by Andreas Franzke, Karlsruhe 1978; *Stèles de Bertholin,* exhibition catalogue, with text by André Jocou, Brussels 1978; *Bertholin: L'Infinito Intrattenimento con le Cose,* exhibition catalogue, with text by Antonio D'Avossa, Genoa 1979; *Bertholin,* exhibition catalogue, with text by Bernard Noel, Paris 1980; *Le Bout des Bordes: les choses pensantes de Bertholin* by Jean-Luc Parant, Paris 1980; *Bertholin: les choses mêmes,* exhibition catalogue by Philippe Lacoue-Lbarthe, Paris 1983; *Bertholin: Les choses, l'utopie,* exhibition catalogue by Alain Cueff, Lyon 1984;

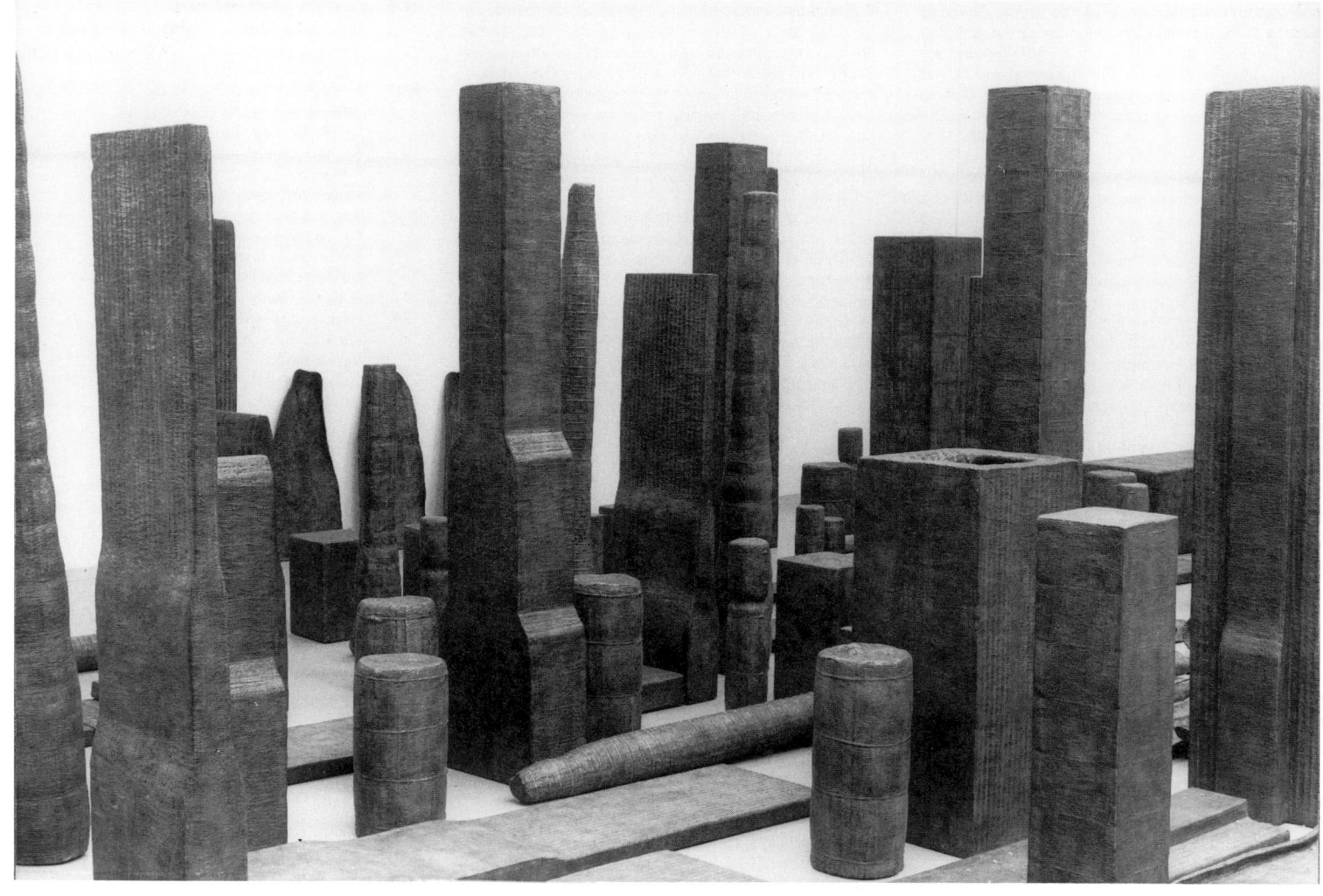

Bertholin: Works of 1971–1983 at the ARC, Paris, 1984

Bertholin—un fragmentaire qui s'assemble, exhibition catalogue by Valerie Chanut, Vannes 1987; articles—"Bertholin" by Bernard Borgeaud in *L'Art Vivant* (Paris), January 1972; "Fevrier à Paris" by Francois Pluchart in *Artitudes* (Saint Jeannet, France), March 1972; "Une Avant-Garde Clandestine" by Jean Clair in *L'Art Vivant* (Paris), September 1972; "Art en France: Une Nouvelle Generation" by Jean Clair in *Chêne* (Paris), 1973; "L'Art de Masse n'Existe Pas" by Jean Clair in *L'Art Vivant* (Paris), 1974; "Aux Entrepots de la Mémoire" by Pierre Schneider in *L'Express* (Paris), 30 September 1974; "Un Rituel Fétichiste" by Alain Macaire in *Artitudes* (Saint Jeannet, France), March 1976; "Bertholin" by Jacques Memis in *Libre Belgique* (Brussels), 19 May 1978; "Bertholin Aides-Mémoires" by Thierry Chabanne in *Art Press* (Paris), January 1979; "Bertholin et la Communication différée" in *Art Press* (Paris), December 1980; "Bertholin: Le papier est à l'intérieur" by Bernard Huin in *Kanal* (Paris), January 1985.

It was working out something very modest but definitely of my own that I was seized by a profound need to fabricate, using an artisan's method of working, some "things" which would possess something of the history of men and of myself.

Begotten like life itself at the price of infinite care, all these "things" are fashioned from the same material and retain the mark of fire and the trace of varied manipulations. This "substance" is transformed from several worn-out materials recovered from refuse consigned to destruction, so that in transmuting them into this new "paste" I tear them, momentarily, from their inexorable annihilation as if for an ultimate celebration of the perishable.

From the most complex pieces to the pellets formed in the hollows of my hand, all these "things"—tangible witness of the ephemeral activity of man—are in harmony with my intimate life or are disinterred from the furthest recesses of my memory of the world. If their form is, in the first instance, copied from objects from everyday life, it becomes, as the work is amplified and enlarged, more complex not to say even in certain cases fragmentary and destructured.

As for the dimensions of the pieces, they have sprung from two currents which co-exist in the work: on the one hand all those which can be held in the hand, on the other hand those which are to be proportions of the human body. It is according to the latter tendency that the dimensions are, more and more, copied from the height of my children or the size of a part of their body. If each piece becomes the witness of a moment of their growth, this aleatory—established through chance—system of measurement recalls that the origin of measurements is to be found in the measurements of the human body while thus transgressing the fixed systems of measurement imposed by societies.

It must be noted that a number of pieces present themselves as a sort of prolongation of the hand—rediscovery of the primordial tool—but where the place and the function of these "tools," like moreover the corporal gestures which accompany them, escape all elucidations.

Other pieces—the large chests for example—comparable to types of "furniture," can it seems contribute to the furnishing of a habitable place. In fact many pieces present surfaces which retain the mark of a wear and tear due to the work of man.

Each piece is repeated untiringly in order to take from it whatever it might conserve of the unique, the rare and the precious, but also to lead to a greater perfecting through gestures which have become familiar. This repetition is also felt as a need to win over this "thing," to seize from it its hidden forces and its relations with the world.

Nevertheless, it becomes more and more apparent that these works are the fruit of a visceral and organic activity in which are mixed the rational and the irrational, rigour and approximation, precision and imprecision. Work that is open, not allowing the loss of any "accident" or artefact (it is in looking for India that one finds America). This production—so to speak physiological—with its pulsations and its phantasms seeks not to exhaust but to maintain in me a certain power of invention. This process of auto-production—always on the edge of disaster—oscillates between memory and invention, imitation and creation, experiment and practice . . .

Each piece invokes another or its contrary, thus adding them to one another in an endless movement, a perpetually unfinished work—far from all references—and with almost infinite combinations.

In exile whatever the place which receives them, all these unindexed "things," without evident link between themselves, unless it be their epidermis, come to accumulate, letting one perceive that they derive from a coherent whole but one which would have existed far away. Nevertheless, it seems that each of these "things" only becomes clear by the relations which link it to the others, and one can not therefore decipher each piece except with regard to the whole, as one can not seize the whole except by starting out from each piece.

Thus, all these "vestiges" of the history of men and of myself have finally no meaning but that of allowing me to play a role in it.

With some stubborn materials and long manual work, this production becomes a function of life, a mania to produce to kill the anguish, an effort to escape from an unbearable solitude, a last bridge between man and the indistinct forces which surround him, an ultimate interrogation of the human condition and aesthetic practice, and, derisory though it may seem, a wish to leave some traces of my passing.

—Bertholin

BERTHOT, Jake.

American. Born in Niagara Falls, New York, 30 March 1939. Studied at the New School for Social Research, New York, 1960–61; Pratt Institute, Brooklyn, New York, 1960–62. Independent artist, New York, since 1962. Artist-in-Residence, Yale University, New Haven, Connecticut, 1982. Recipient: Guggenheim Fellowship, 1981. Agent: David McKee Gallery, 41 East 57th Street, New York, New York 10022. Address: 105 Bowery, New York, New York 10002, U.S.A.

Individual Exhibitions:

1970	O.K. Harris Gallery, New York
1971	Michael Walls Gallery, San Francisco
1972	O.K. Harris Gallery, New York
	Michael Walls Gallery, San Francisco
1973	Portland Center for the Visual Arts, Oregon
	Galerie de Gestlo, Hamburg
	Cunningham Ward Gallery, New York
1974	Locksley-Shea Gallery, Minneapolis
1975	O.K. Harris Gallery, New York
	Daniel Weinberg Gallery, San Francisco
1976	David McKee Gallery, New York
1977	Galerie de Gestlo, Hamburg
	Brandeis University, Waltham, Massachusetts
1978	David McKee Gallery, New York
1979	Nigel Greenwood Gallery, London
	Nina Nielsen Gallery, Boston
1982	David McKee Gallery, New York
1983	David McKee Gallery, New York
1984	University of California, Berkeley
	Nina Nielsen Gallery, Boston
1985	Southern Methodist University, Dallas
	David McKee Gallery, New York

Selected Group Exhibitions:

1972	*8 New York Painters*, University of California Art Museum, Berkeley
1974	*Recent Abstract Painting*, Pratt Institute, Brooklyn, New York
1976	*Critical Perspectives in American Art*, at the *Biennale*, Venice
1977	*8 Abstract Painters*, Institute of Contemporary Art, Philadelphia
1979	*New Painting/New York*, Hayward Gallery, London
1980	*L'Amerique aux Indépendents 1944-1980*, Grand Palais, Paris
1981	*New Works on Paper*, Museum of Modern Art, New York (travelled to the Museum of Fine Arts, Houston; La Jolla Art Museum, California; and the Art Museum of South Texas, Corpus Christi)
1984	*International Survey of Recent Painting and Sculpture*, Museum of Modern Art, New York
1985	*Landscape and Abstract Art*, Colby College, Waterville, Maine
1988	*Contemporary American Art*, Sara Hilden Art Museum, Tampere, Finland (travelled to Oslo)

Collections:

Museum of Modern Art, New York; Whitney Museum, New York; Guggenheim Museum, New York; Fogg Art Museum, Harvard University, Cambridge, Massachusetts; Museum of Art, Carnegie Institute, Pittsburgh; Philadelphia Museum of Art; High Museum of Art, Atlanta; Dallas Museum of Fine Arts; Australian National Gallery, Canberra.

Publications:

By BERTHOT: article—comment in "Points of View: A Taped Conversation with 4 Painters" by Willoughby Sharp in *Arts Magazine* (New York), December 1971.

On BERTHOT: books—*Jake Berthot*, exhibition catalogue, with text by Dore Ashton, Minneapolis 1974; *Painting Endures*, exhibition catalogue, Boston 1975; *Critical Perspectives in American Art*, exhibition catalogue, Venice 1976; *Jake Berthot*, exhibition catalogue, with text by Bonnie Saulnie, Waltham, Massachusetts 1977; *8 Abstract Painters*, exhibition catalogue, with text by Dore Ashton, Philadelphia 1977; *Silence and Slow Time*, exhibition catalogue, by Robin Karson, South Hadley, Massachusetts 1977; *New Painting/New York*, exhibition catalogue, with text by C. Lampert, London 1979; *New Works on Paper*, exhibition catalogue, New York 1981; *American Art Since 1945* by Dore Ashton, New York 1984; articles—"Jake Berthot Paints Quietness" by Dore Ashton in *Arts Magazine* (New York), November 1971; "Jake Berthot" by C. Beret in *Art Press* (Paris), September/October 1973; "Jake Berthot: Recent Works" by Stephen Kasher in *Artforum* (New York), September 1978; "Jake Berthot" by Dore Ashton in *Arts Magazine* (New York), January 1979; "Jake Berthot" by Oswell Blakeston in *Arts Review* (London), 27 April 1979; "Jake Berthot" by B. Lemarche-Vadel in *Artistes* (Paris), April 1981; "Jake Berthot's Order" by Dore Ashton in *Arts Magazine* (New York), March 1982; "Jake Berthot" by Grace Glueck in the *New York Times*, 25 November 1983; "A Return to the Basics: Jake Berthot's Recent Paintings" by John Yau in *Arts* (New York), March 1984.

BERTOIA, Harry.

American. Born in San Lorenzo, Udine, Italy, 10 March 1915; moved to the United States, 1930. Educated at Cass Technical High School, Detroit, 1932–36; studied, on scholarship, at the Society of Arts and Crafts, Detroit, 1936, and at the Cranbrook Academy of Art, Bloomfield Hills, Michigan, 1937–39. Married Brigitta Valentiner in 1943; children: Mara, Val, Celia. Set up metal shop and taught metalwork, Cranbrook Academy, 1939–43; produced molded plywood products for the war effort at the Evans Products Company, Venice, California, 1943–46 (later designed chairs with Charles Eames for the same company); did graphic work at the Point Loma Naval Electronics Laboratory, 1947–49; settled in Pennsylvania, 1950, setting up studio there, with support of Knoll Associates of New York: Bertoia Chair introduced by Knoll, 1952. Recipient: Fine Arts Medal, 1955, and Craftsmanship Medal, 1956, American Institute of Architects; Graham Foundation Grant, for European travel, 1957; Fine Arts Medal, American Institution of Architects, Pennsylvania Chapter, 1963, 1967; Gold Medal, American Institute of Architects, 1973. Honorary doctorate: Muhlenberg College, Allentown, Pennsylvania, 1971. Agent: Staempfli Gallery, 47 East 77th Street, New York, New York, U.S.A. *Died 6 November 1978.*

Individual Exhibitions:

1940	Karl Nierendorf Gallery, New York
1943	Karl Nierendorf Gallery, New York
	Museum of Non-Objective Art, New York
	Smithsonian Institution, Washington, D.C. (toured the United States)
1947	Karl Nierendorf Gallery, New York
1951	Knoll Associates, New York
1956	Fairweather-Hardin Gallery, Chicago
1959	Staempfli Gallery, New York
1961	Fairweather-Hardin Gallery, Chicago
	Staempfli Gallery, New York
1963	Staempfli Gallery, New York
1964	Knoll International, Paris
1967	Knoll International, Amsterdam
1968	Fairweather-Hardin Gallery, Chicago
	Staempfli Gallery, New York
	Knoll International, Zurich
1970	Staempfli Gallery, New York
1972	K.B. Gallery, Oslo
1974	*Sensations in Sculpture*, Wadsworth Atheneum, Hartford, Connecticut
1975	K.B. Gallery, Oslo
	Fairweather-Hardin Gallery, Chicago
	Art Institute of Chicago
	Sculpture and Graphics, Allentown Art Museum, Pennsylvania (restrospective)
1976	Staempfli Gallery, New York
1978	Staempfli Gallery, New York
1981	Staempfli Gallery, New York
1982	Robert Kidd Associates, Birmingham, Alabama
	Community College, Lancaster, Pennsylvania
1983	Benjamin Mangel Gallery, Philadelphia
1986	Allentown Art Museum, Pennsylvania
1987	Michigan State University, East Lansing

Selected Group Exhibitions:

1943	*Non-Objective Painting Exhibition*, Guggenheim Foundation, New York
1945	*Graphics*, San Francisco Museum of Art
1958	*World's Fair*, Brussels
1963	*London Triennial Exhibition of Sculpture in the Open Air*, Battersea Park, London
1970	*The Modern Chair 1918–70*, Whitechapel Art Gallery, London
1974	*Sensations in Sculpture*, Wadsworth Atheneum, Hartford, Connecticut
1983	*Design Since 1945*, Philadelphia Museum of Art

Collections:

Museum of Modern Art, New York; Albright-Knox Art Gallery, Buffalo, New York; Munson-Williams-Proctor Institute, Utica, New York; Massachusetts Institute of Technology, Cambridge; Virginia Museum of Fine Art, Richmond; Joslyn Art Museum, Omaha, Nebraska; Denver Art Museum; Colorado Springs Fine Art Center; Dallas Public Library; San Francisco Museum of Modern Art.

Numerous commissions in public buildings and plazas throughout the United States.

Publications:

On BERTOIA: books—*Form and Space: Sculpture in the 20th Century* by Eduard Trier, New York 1968; *The Sculptural Idea* by James J. Kelly, Minneapolis 1970; *Harry Bertoia: Sculptor* by June Kompass Nelson, Detroit 1970; *The Technique of Kinetic Art* by John Torvey, New York 1971; *Bertoia*, Copenhagen 1972; *Science and Technology in Art Today* by Jonathan Benthall, New York 1972; *Art and the Future: A History/Prophecy of the Collaboration Between Science, Technology and Art* by Douglas Davis, New York 1973; *Harry Bertoia: An Exhibition of His Sculpture and Graphics*, exhibition catalogue, by Beverly H. Twitchell, Allentown, Pennsylvania 1975; *Design Since 1945*, exhibition catalogue edited by Kathryn B. Hiesinger and George H. Marcus, Philadelphia 1983; articles—"Harry Bertoia" by Jules Langsner in *Arts and Architecture* (Los Angeles), January 1953; "Sculpture Alive" by John Canaday in the *New York Times*, 19 March 1961; "Song and Dance Man" in *Time* (New York), 31 March 1961; "Creative Casting" by Lawrence Campbell in *Craft Horizons* (New York), November/December 1963; article in *Art International* (Lugano), April 1973; "Harry Bertoia: An American Sculptor with an Extended Concept of His Art" by Stig Anderson in *Kunsteg Idag* (Oslo), no. 1, 1973; film—*Harry Bertoia's Sculpture* by Clifford B. West, 1965.

People sometimes ask me how I do it, how I get my ideas, and I tell them by working like hell. I'm in this studio every day from 9 to 5. I know that runs against people's notions of creativity—you know, the midnight bursts of inspiration—but I don't think there is such a thing as a moment of inspiration. You get an idea and you try it out and it doesn't work, so you try something else until you discover something which pleases you.

I believe I'm getting to something of great importance. I think of the excitement of Picasso, Braque

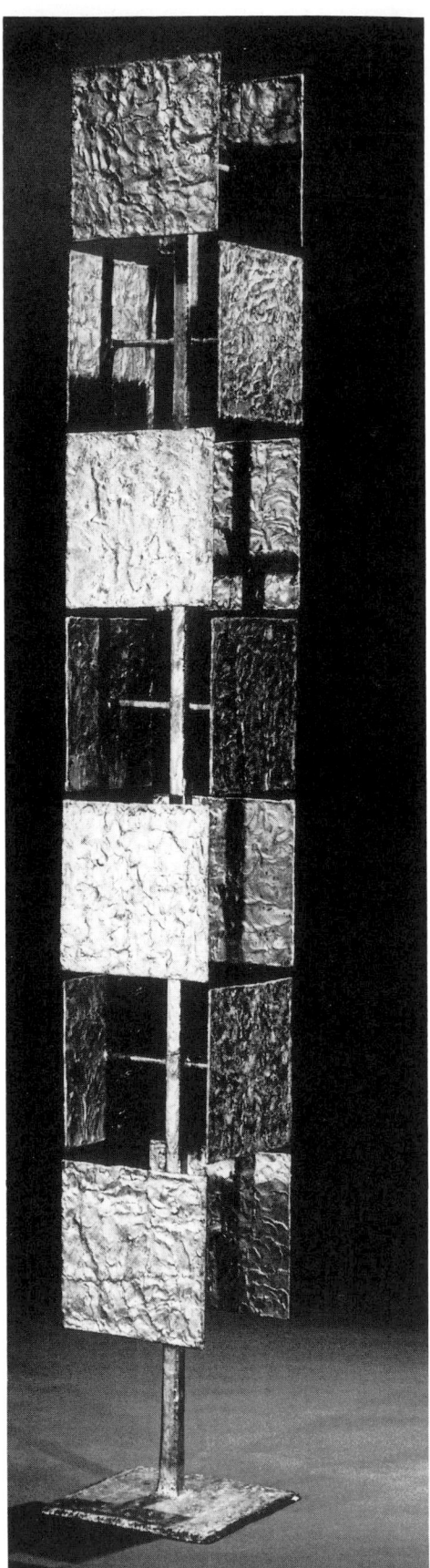

Harry Bertoia: *Metal Sculpture,* c. 1962

and Gris when they began their experiments in cubism. What they did was to introduce a new dimension into painting—the dimension of time—revealing all sides of an object simultaneously. I believe sound is a dimension which could have great consequences. I know it's more meaningful to me now than the dimensions of color intensity or spatial relations. I don't hold onto terms like music and sculpture anymore. Those old distinctions have lost their meaning.

If I had to sum up my 40 years as an artist I'd say my intent has always been the enrichment of life. I've avoided that which would depress man's mood or being. There's plenty in the newspapers of that. I want to show what's positive and joyful in the world. I like to see the beauty of a flower before I admit it will vanish in three days.

—Harry Bertoia (from the 1st edition)

Well known as the designer of the wire shell chair produced by Knoll Associates that bears his name. Harry Bertoia had a multifaceted career which included the production of woodcuts, monoprints, biomorphic shaped silver jewelry, kinetic sculpture he referred to as "sculptural soundings," stationary sculpture including fountains, and environmental metal screens that are a combination of sculpture and architecture.

Born in Italy, Bertoia came to the United States with his father during his adolescence and he studied art and design at Cranbrook Academy in Bloomfield Hills, Michigan. After graduation he taught in the department of metalcraft and graphic arts from 1939 to 1943. Bertoia's training at America's premier institution of design nurtured his conception of himself as a craftsman rather than as a fine artist, which conditioned his habit of leaving his works unsigned and largely untitled. Florence Knoll, one of his associates at Cranbrook, encouraged his turn to furniture design for her husband's firm, Knoll Associates. In 1952 Knoll Associates introduced the Bertoia chair, a grid of welded metal wires in a diamond shape with a curved indentation molded to fit the contours of a seated human form. Routinely upholstered or padded, the chair reflects modern industrial design technology adapted for domestic interiors to enhance comfort, utility, and durability.

Bertoia designed a high backed chair, an ottoman, a side chair, and bench by 1953 when he turned his attention to more monumental architectural projects. During the late 1940s Bertoia had begun welding abstract metal sculpture from metal rods and wire and this technique precipitated his initial architectural collaboration with his Cranbrook classmate Eero Saarinen. His first major welded metal work and the first of his numerous public commissions was designed for Saarinen's General Motors Technical Center in Warren, Michigan in 1953. To designate a division between an entryway and a cafeteria, Bertoia structured a screen wall from a series of layered metal rectangles that demonstrate an artistic use of the techniques and materials utilized in the company's car making facility. Two years later Saarinen and Bertoia worked together on a non-denominational chapel for Massachusetts Institute of Technology. Bertoia designed an altar screen of rectangular bits of metal welded to a row of thin metal wires to hang behind the altar. Illuminated from above by a skylight, the only natural lighting in the circular chapel, the irregular metal shapes appear to float in space and they reflect on the water in the moat surrounding the chapel lending it an especially mystical presence. For their final artistic association, Bertoia made a mural of poured bronze panels for Saarinen's Dulles Airport in Chantilly, Virginia that was installed in 1963 after the architect's death.

Bertoia's other major public screen sculptures can be found in the Dallas Public Library (1955), Lambert/St. Louis Airport (1955), and the Southdale Shopping Center in Minneapolis (1956). One of Bertoia's fountains of welded rods radiating from a central core that sprays water in a spherical patter is also in Minneapolis as is his only major sculpture to be

named. *Sunlit Straw,* a monumental sculpture comprised of brass coated steel rods hangs in the lobby of Minoru Yamasaki's National Life Insurance Company building.

During the 1960s Bertoia began exploring kinetic sculpture in his "sculptural soundings," made of bronze rods welded to a stationary base. When brushed against or activated by wind currents the rods resonate with ringing that expands into the surrounding space. For Bertoia welded metal was the material most representative of modern technology and he exploited its possibilities in sculpture, furniture, and interior design. His innovative range of creative endeavors designates him as a leading designer of his generation—a master of modern materials and environmental concerns.

—Percy North

BERTRAND, Jean-Pierre.

French. Born in Paris, 11 January 1937. Studied filmmaking at the Ecole Technique du Cinéma, Paris, 1955-57; mainly self-taught in drawing. Served in film section, French Army, in Senegal, Algeria and West Germany, 1958-60. Married Christa Anna Seidl in 1963 (divorced, 1975); daughter: Viana. Worked as cameraman in several film productions in France, 1960-63; television cameraman, O.R.T.F., Paris, 1963-69; freelance cameraman, in Buenos Aires, Rome, Hamburg and Madrid, 1969-72; independent artist, Paris, since 1972. Address: 27 rue Titon, 75011 Paris, France.

Individual Exhibitions:

Selected Group Exhibitions:

Collections:

Centre Georges Pompidou, Paris; Musée de Toulon, France.

Publications:

On BERTRAND: *Pour Memoires,* exhibition catalogue, with text by Jean Clair and others, Bordeaux 1974; *Jean-Pierre Bertrand,* exhibition catalogue, Toulon, France 1981;

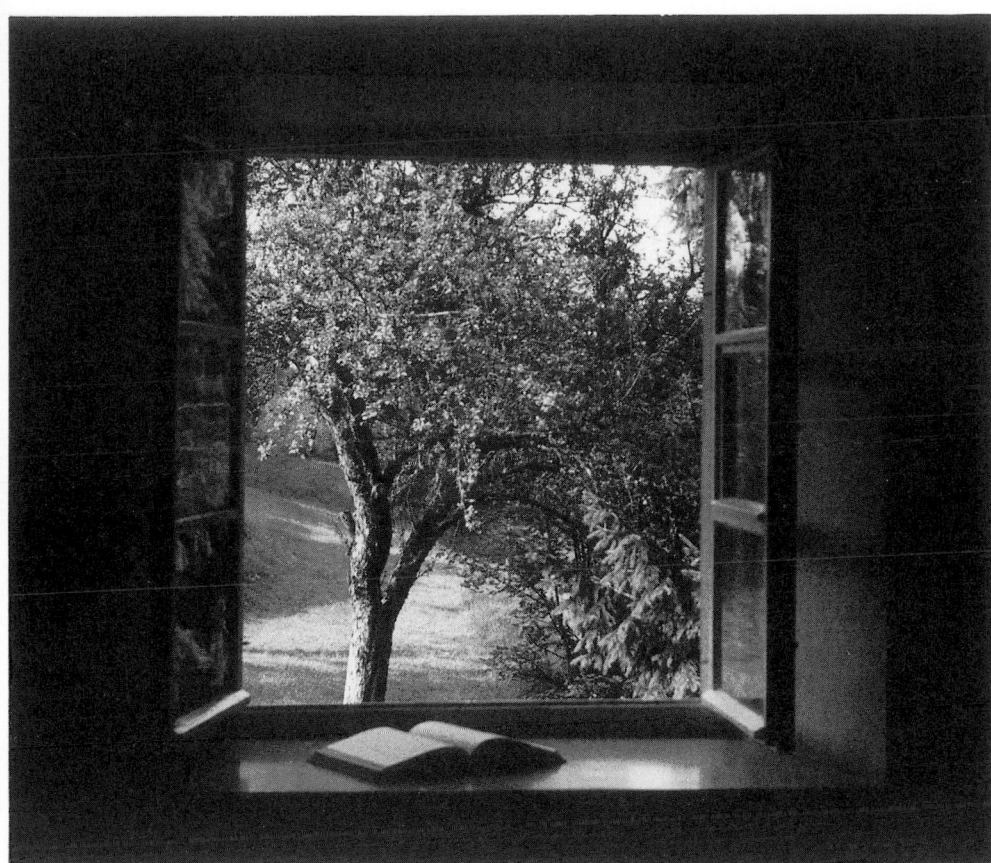

Jean-Pierre Bertrand: *The Fifty Four Days of Robinson Crusoe*, 1974

articles—"Jean-Pierre Bertrand" by C. Bouyere in *Opus International* (Paris), June 1974; "In Memoriam" by Effie Stephano in *Art and Artists* (London), July 1974; "L'obscure Clarté de J. P. Bertrand" by Michel Nuridsany in *Le Figaro* (Paris), 19 June, 1981; "Jean Pierre Bertrand in Milano" in *Domus* (Milan), June 1982.

Perhaps my work began during this summer morning when, entering in my room, I saw a book opened in front of the window, between outside and outside, sun and darkness. With the sun, the two pages seemed to be white for a short time I was in the whiteness; the magic world revealed in His absence-presence. The book was the memorandum of Robinson Crusoe in the island. During fifty-four days I began to copy each day a day of Crusoe at the present form (the original text is at past) and took each day a photo of the book opening more and more to the end laying by the window. A few years after I noticed that Crusoe left the island when he was fifty-four years old. My last show was a sentence of which Crusoe has a strange relation with my own life.

I try to be available and vigilant with the magic world. Sometimes art makes me wink. Sometimes I wink at art. As Defoe says "serious reflections during the life and surprising adventures of Robinson Crusoe." The solitary man is between the "real" man and his emblematic original.

—Jean-Pierre Bertrand

The art of Jean-Pierre Bertrand recalls attitudes typical of the 'seventies. This aspect of his work appears spontaneously and without inhibition in his choice of materials—a choice which ultimately makes way for the unpredictable and extra-artistic element. Objects, natural products, photographs, paper drawings or ready-mades all provide the ideal vehicle for the realization of Bertrand's concepts, through which the chemical components intrinsic to these materials find their expression.

Bertrand's works and installataions thus become a theatre of phenomena, revelations of nature and hidden decay, which at the same time are visualizations of the artist's attention to those materials through which he can find the most appropriate metaphor. Here we have honey or lemon juice sprinkled onto paper, and, in time, changing back to their original colour; salt placed in a metal box will corrode, or may be used to form a star on the floor of a room; a dark area drawn around the edge of a sheet of white paper, then covered by a pane of glass (which then protects it) takes on the character of the missing frames from around drawings in series of diptychs, and thus becomes a part of the work.

In certain respects, Bertrand's work has similarities to those processes typical of 'Arte Povera', in particular those of Gilberto Zorio, where the work is an event occurring within the duration of the time taken to construct it. In other respects, he recalls Beuys, who employed every means available, even his own body, to expound his own ideology and elaborate symbolism. Bertrand also institutes the symbolic language of the Cabala, which for this French artist redefines and renews specific aspects of Hebraic mysticism. This complex system transforms the work—canvases or performances—resulting in a freedom and sensibility which is essentially contemporary while contributing a timeless and precise significance.

—Giorgio Verzotti

BEUYS, Joseph.
German. Born in Krefeld, 12 May 1921. Educated in Rindern, near Kleve, 1930–39; preparatory medical studies, Kleve, 1940; studied art, under Joseph Enseling and Ewald Matare. Staatliche Kunstakademie, Dusseldorf, 1947–51. Served as a radio-operator and fighter pilot, German Air Force, in Posen, Erfurt and Pardobitz, 1940–45; injured in plane crash in Russia, 1943; prisoner-of-war, Cuxhaven, 1945. First concentrated on art, Kleve, 1946; independent artist, Dusseldorf and Kleve, 1951, until his death in 1986: first "actions" and contact with Fluxus artists, Dusseldorf, 1962–65. Professor of Sculpture, Staatliche Kunstakademie, Dusseldorf, 1961–72; Guest Professor, Hochschule für Bildende Kunste, Hamburg, 1974–75. Founder, German Students Party, Dusseldorf, 1967, and Non-Voting Free Referendum Party for Direct Democracy, Dusseldorf, 1970; Candidate, Joint Action Party for Independent Germans, Dusseldorf, 1976; Candidate for the Green Party, West Germany, 1979. Recipient: Lichtwark-Preis, Hamburg, 1977; Thorn-Prikker-Ehrenplakette, Krefeld, 1978; Kaiserring Award, Goslar, 1979; Honorary Citizen Award, Bolognano, 1984; Wilhelm-Lehmbruck Prize, Duisburg, 1986. Honorary doctorate, Nova Scotia College of Art and Design, 1976; Member, Akademie der Kunste, West Berlin, 1978; Member, Royal Academy of Fine Arts, Stockholm, 1980. *Died (in Dusseldorf) 23 January 1986.*

Individual Exhibitions:

1952   Kunstmuseum, Wuppertal, West Germany
1953   Kunstmuseum, Nijmegen, Netherlands
1961   Städtische Museum, Kleve, West Germany
1963   Staatliche Kunstakademie, Dusseldorf
       Haus van der Grinten, Kranenburg, West Germany
1965   Galerie Schmela, Dusseldorf
1966   *Joseph Beuys . . . mit Braunkreuz*, Galerie René Block, West Berlin
       Galerie St. Stephan, Vienna
       Galerie Schmela, Dusseldorf
1967   Galerie Franz Dahlem, Darmstadt
       Wide White Space Gallery, Antwerp
       Beuys und das weisse Kreuz von Malewitsch, Städtische Museum, Mönchengladbach, West Germany
1968   Stedelijk Van Abbemuseum, Eindhoven, Netherlands
       Kunstmuseum, Hamburg
       Neue Pinakothek, Munich
       Intermedia Galerie, Cologne
       Staatliche Kunstakademie, Dusseldorf
1969   Galerie Schmela, Dusseldorf
       Galerie René Block, West Berlin
       Nationalgalerie, West Berlin
       Akademie der Künste, West Berlin
       Städtisches Museum, Mönchengladbach, West Germany
       Werk aus der Sammlung Stroher, Kunstmuseum, Basle
1970   Galerie Nachst, St. Stephan, Vienna
       Herzog Anton-Ulrich Museum, Braunschweig, West Germany
       Louisiana Museum, Humlebaek, Denmark
       Kunsthalle, Dusseldorf
       Zeeuws Museum, Middleburg, Netherlands
       Kunstmuseum, Lucerne
       Kunstverein, Ulm, West Germany
1971   *Sammlung Hans und Franz Josef van der Grinten*, Galerie im Taxispalais, Innsbruck
       Zeichnungen und Objekte 1937-1970 aus der Sammlung van der Grinten, Moderna Museet, Stockholm
       Galerie Schellmann, Munich
       Von-der-Heydt Museum, Wuppertal, West Germany
       Kunsthalle, Kiel, West Germany
       Galerie Schmela, Dusseldorf
       Galerie Seebacher, Nuziders, Austria
1972   Staatliche Graphische Sammlung, Munich
       Galerie René Block, West Berlin
       Art Information Agency, Naples
       Harcus-Krakow Gallery, Boston
       Museum Folkwang, Essen
       Tate Gallery/Whitechapel Art Gallery, London
       "Friedenfeier," Mönchengladbach, West Germany
       Centro d'Informazione Alternativa, Rome
       Videogalerie Gerry Schum, Dusseldorf
       Galerie Schmela, Dusseldorf
       Hessisches Landesmuseum, Darmstadt
       Galleria L'Attico, Rome
       Tate Gallery, London

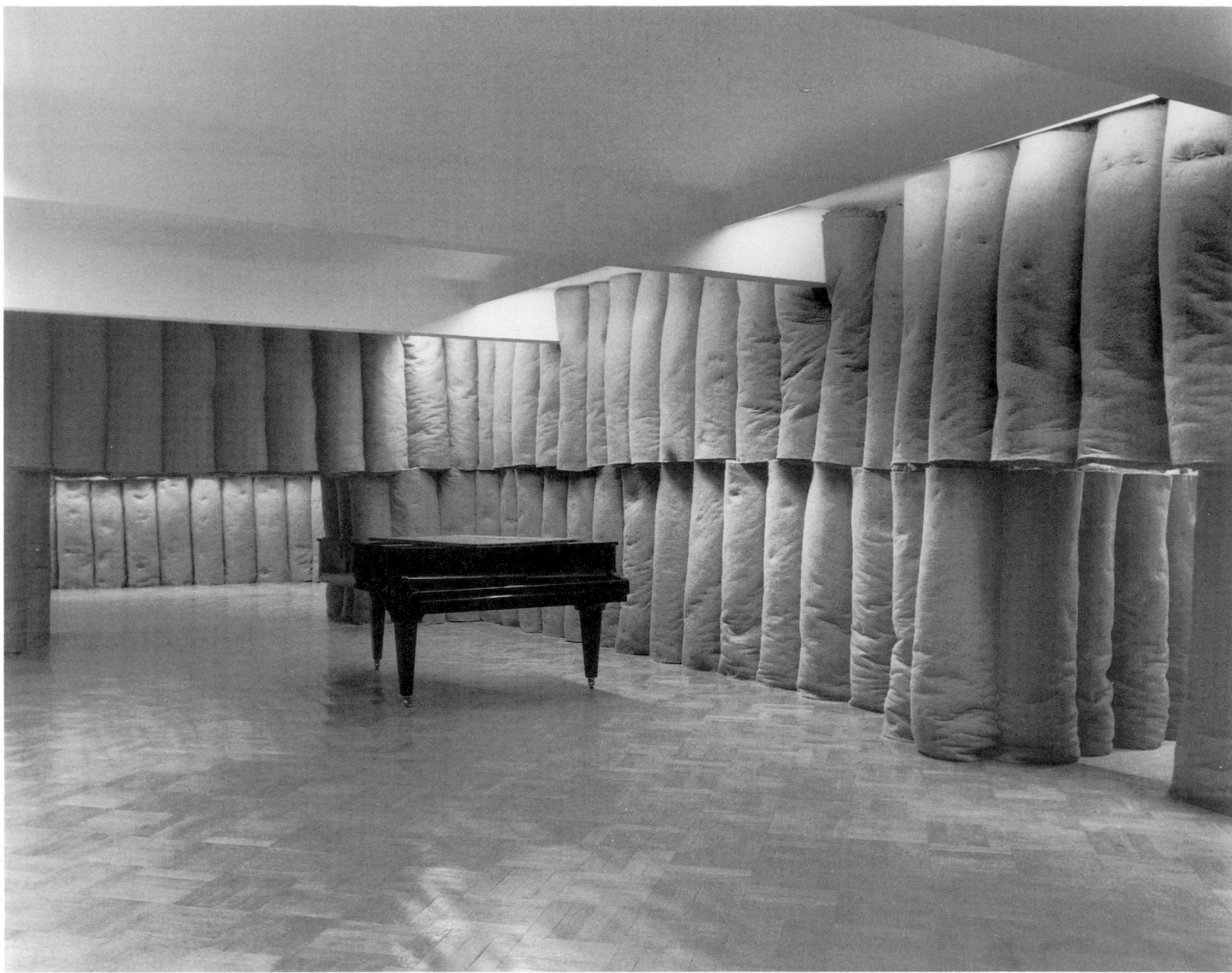

Joseph Beuys: *Plight* (detail), 1958–1985 Courtesy Anthony D'Offay Gallery, London

1973 Ronald Feldman Fine Art, New York
John Gibson Gallery, New York
Galerie Loehr, Frankfurt
Studio Marconi, Milan
Galerie Klein, Bonn
Galerie Grafikmeyer, Karlsruhe, West Germany
Eat-Art Galerie, Dusseldorf
Daytons Gallery 12, Minneapolis
Kaiser-Wilhelm-Museum, Krefeld, West Germany
Galerie René Block, West Berlin
1974 Ronald Feldman Fine Art, New York
René Block Gallery, New York
John Gibson Gallery, New York
Centre d'Art Contemporain, Bordeaux
The Secret Block for a Secret Person in Ireland, Museum of Modern Art, Oxford, (travelled to National Gallery of Modern Art, Edinburgh; Institute of Contemporary Arts, London; Municipal Gallery of Modern Art, Dublin; Arts Council Gallery, Belfast)
Zeichnungen 1946–1971, Museum Haus Lange, Krefeld, West Germany
Galerie Bama, Paris
Galleria Lucrezia De Domizio, Pescara, Italy
1975 Studio Brescia, Brescia, Italy
Galleria Lucrezia De Domizio, Pescara, Italy
René Block Gallery, New York
Ronald Feldman Fine Art, New York
Schwarzes Kloster, Freiburg, West Germany

Kestner-Gesellschaft, Hannover
Kunstverein, Kassel, West Germany
Fecoman Gallery, New York
1976 Kunstforum, Munich
Galerij Albert Baronian, Brussels
Kaiser-Wilhelm-Museum, Krefeld, West Germany
Wasserfarben 1936–1963, Kunstverein, Frankfurt
1977 Galerie Bama, Paris
Galleria Lucrezia De Domizio, Pescara, Italy
Museum Folkwang, Essen
Richtkrafte, Nationalgalerie, West Berlin
Kunstmuseum, Basle
Galerie Marika Malacorda, Geneva
Galerie Konrad Fischer, Dusseldorf
Galerie Schellmann und Kluser, Munich
Tekeningen, Aquarellen, Gouaches, Collages, Olieverven, Museum van Hedendaagse Kunst, Ghent
Galleria Saman, Genoa, Italy
1978 Kleine-Grafik-Galerie, Bremen, West Germany
Museo Diego Aragona Pignatelli Cortes, Naples
Galleria Ferrari, Verona, Italy
Kunstverein, Bremerhaven, West Germany
Galerie Polit-Art/o42, Nijmegen, Netherlands
University of California, Riverside
Studio Cavalieri, Bologna, Italy
Galerie Cuenca, Ulm, West Germany
Universitatsmuseum, Marburg, West Germany
Landesmuseum Joanneum, Graz, Austria

Galerie Schmela, Dusseldorf
1979 Galerie Nachst St. Stephan, Vienna
Kunstverein, Gottingen, West Germany
Galerie Puschel, Bielefeld, West Germany
Monchehaus-Museum, Goslar, West Germany
Galleri Per Sten, Copenhagen
Museum Boymans-van Beuningen, Rotterdam (travelled to Berlin, Bielefeld and Bonn)
Guggenheim Museum, New York
Galerie Schmela, Dusseldorf
1980 Galerie Schellmann and Kluser, Munich
Galleria Piero Cavellini, Brescia, Italy
Galleria Delta, Salerno, Italy
Anthony D'Offay Gallery, London
Richard Demarco Gallery, Edinburgh
Stadtisches Kunstmuseum, Bonn
Badischer Kunstverein, Karlsruhe, West Germany
Galerie Holtmann, Cologne
Stadtische Galerie, Erlangen, West Germany
1981 Ink Halle fur internationale Kunst, Zurich
Kunstverein, Mannheim, West Germany
Heath Gallery, Atlanta, Georgia
Kunstraum, Munich
Galleria del Cortile, Rome
Galleria Schellmann und Kluser, Munich
Stadtische Galerie im Lenbachhaus, Munich
Museum Commanderie van St. Jan, Nijmegen, Netherlands (travelled to Dusseldorf and Ulm)
Sammlung Ulbricht, East Berlin

1982   Ronald Feldman/Schellmann und Kluser, New York
        Galerie Durand-Dessert, Paris
        Forum fur aktuelle Kunst/Galerie Krinzinger, Innsbruck, Austria
        Henie-Onstad Kunstsenter, Hovikodden, Norway
        Galerie Klein, Bonn
1983   City Art Gallery, Leeds, Yorkshire (travelled to Cambridge and London)
        Galerie Konrad Fischer, Dusseldorf
        Galerie Schmela, Dusseldorf
        Europaisches Forum, Alpbach, Austria
        Stadelschen Kunstinsitut, Frankfurt
        Anthony D'Offay Gallery, London
        Galerie Stahlberger, Weil am Rhein, West Germany
        Musee Cantonal des Beaux-Arts, Lausanne (travelled to Winterthur; Calais; St. Etienne; Linz; Oslo; Marseille)
1984   Galerie Konrad Fischer, Dusseldorf
        Galerie Durand-Dessert, Paris
        Stadtsparkasse, Wuppertal, West Germany
        Galerie Schellmann und Kluser, Munich
        Mittelrhein-Museum, Mainz, West Germany
        Busch-Reisinger Museum, Harvard University, Cambridge, Massachusetts
        Seibu Museum of Art, Tokyo
        Kunsthalle, Tubingen, West Germany
        Kunstlerhaus Eisenturm, Mainz, West Germany
        Neue Galerie der Stadt Linz, Austria
        Stadtische Galerie, Wurzburg, West Germany
1985   Galerie Beaubourg, Paris
        Galerie Cuenca, Ulm, West Germany
        Edition Schellmannn, Munich
        Nassauischer Kunstverein, Wiesbaden, West Germany
        Museum und Museumsverein, Aachen, West Germany
        Commanderie van St. Jan, Nijmegen, Netherlands
        Suermondt-Ludwig-Museum, Aachen (travelled to Ratingen)
        Museum am Ostwall, Dortmund, West Germany
        John Gibson Gallery, New York
        Galerie Bernd Kluser, Munich
        Anthony D'Offay Gallery, London
        Edizione Lucio Amelio, Naples (travelled to New York)
        Fundacion Caja de Pensiones, Madrid
        Museo di Capodimonte, Naples
1986   Stadtische Galerie im Lenbachhaus, Munich
        Galerie Gogger und Murrer, Munich

Selected Group Exhibitions:

1963   *Festum Fluxorum Fluxus*, Staatliche Kunstakademie, Dusseldorf
1964   *Documenta 3*, Museum Fridericianum, Kassel, West Germany (and *Documenta 4*, 1968; *Documenta 5*, 1972; *Documenta 7*, 1982)
1973   *Contemporanea*, Parcheggio Villa Borghese, Rome
1974   *Projekt 74*, Kunsthalle, Cologne
1976   *Biennale*, Venice
1977   *Art of the 60s*. Städtisches Kunstmuseum, Bonn
1982   *Arte Povera et Anti-Form*, Centre d'Arts Plastiques Contemporains, Bordeaux
1983   *Museums by Artists*, Art Gallery of Ontario, Toronto
1985   *Kunst in der Bundesrepublik 1945-85*, Nationalgalerie, West Berlin
1987   *Berlinart 1961-87*, Museum of Modern Art, New York (travelled to San Francisco)

Collections:

Stroher Collection, Hessisches Landesmuseum, Darmstadt; Kaiser-Wilhelm-Museum, Krefeld, West Germany; Städtisches Museum, Mönchengladbach, West Germany; Louisiana Museum, Humlebaek, Denmark; Kunstmuseum, Basle; Centre Georges Pompidou, Paris.

Publications:

By BEUYS: books—*1 a gebraten Fischgrate*, West Berlin 1972; *Die Leute sind ganz prima in Foggia*, Naples 1973; *Lotta Poetica; 3 Pots Action, Edinburgh*, Brescia 1975; *Zeichnungen zu "Codices Madrid" von Leonardo da Vinci*, Stuttgart 1975; *Joseph Beuys: Series of 90 Paintings*, Munich 1976; articles—"Plastik und Zeichnung" in *Kunst* (Mainz), 1965; "Winterlager" in *Christ und Welt* (Dusseldorf), no. 37, 1968; "Direkte Demokratie: Joseph Beuys Talking at Documenta 5" in *Avalanche* (New York), 1972; "Joseph Beuys: Public Dialogue" in *Avalanche* (New York), May/June 1974.

On BEUYS: books—*Joseph Beuys . . . mit Braunkreuz*, exhibition catalogue, edited by René Block, West Berlin 1966; *Beuys und das weisse Kreuz von Malewitsch*, exhibition catalogue, with text by Johannes Cladders, Mönchengladbach, West Germany 1967; *Wat Bedoelt Beuys?* by Tom-Frenken, Eindhoven, Netherlands 1968; *Beuys' Boys* by Per Kirkeby, Copenhagen 1968; *Beuys*, exhibition catalogue, with text by Otto Maurer, Eindhoven, Netherlands 1968; *Joseph Beuys: Werk aus der Sammlung Stroher*, exhibition catalogue, with text by Dieter Koepplin, Basle 1969; *Joseph Beuys* by Gotz Adriani, Winfried Konnertz and Krain Thomas, Cologne, 1970; *La Rivoluzione siamo noi* by Achille Bonito Oliva, Naples 1971; *Joseph Beuys: Sammlung Hans und Franz Josef van der Grinten*, exhibition catalogue, with an introduction by Hans van der Grinten, Innsbruck 1971; *Uber Beuys* by Rolf Wedewer and Lothar Romain, Dusseldorf 1972; *Joseph Beuys: Zeichnungen 1947-1959*, with text by Hagen Lieberknecht, Cologne 1972; *Joseph Beuys: Bleistiftzeichnungen aus den Jahren 1946-1964* by Franz Josef and Hans van der Grinten, West Berlin 1973; *Tod im Leben, gedicht für Joseph Beuys* by Heiner Bastian, Munich 1972; *Joseph Beuys: Zeichnungen 1946-1971*, exhibition catalogue, with text by Paul Wember, Krefeld, West Germany 1974; *Joseph Beuys: The Secret Block for a Secret Person in Ireland*, exhibition catalogue, with foreword by Nick Serota, Oxford 1974; *Joseph Beuys, Jeder Mensch ein Kunstler* by Clara Bodenmann-Ritter, Frankfurt, West Berlin and Vienna 1975; *Joseph Beuys*, exhibition catalogue, with text by Paul Wember, Hannover 1975; *Ioseph Beuys: Wasserfarben 1936-1963*, exhibition catalogue, with text by Franz Josef and Hans van der Grinten, Frankfurt 1976; *Soziale Plastik, Materialen zu Joseph Beuys* by Volker Harlan, Rainer Rappmann and Peter Shata, Achberg 1976; *Joseph Beuys: Coyote*, with text by Caroline Tisdall, Munich 1976; *Joseph Beuys: Tekeningen, Aquarellen, Gouaches, Collages, Olieverven*, exhibition catalogue, with text by R. Vandenwege, Jan Hoct and Clair van Damme, Ghent 1977; *Prophete rechts, Prophete links: Joseph Beuys* by Ingrid Burgbacher-Krupka, Stuttgart 1977; *Joseph Beuys: Richtkrafte*, exhibition catalogue, West Berlin 1977; *Joseph Beuys: Multiples—catalogue raisonne*, Munich 1977; *Beuys tracce in Italia* by Germano Celant, Naples 1978; *Joseph Beuys: Spuren in Italien*, exhibition catalogue, with text by Martin Kunz, Lucerne 1979; *Joseph Beuys*, exhibition catalogue, with text by Caroline Tisdall, New York 1979; *Beuys/Burri*, exhibition catalogue, edited by Italo Tomassoni, Perugia, Italy 1980; *Joseph Beuys: Multiplizierte Kunst 1965- 1980* with text by Willi Bongard, Dusseldorf 1980; *Joseph Beuys: Zeichnungen Begleitende Texte*, with foreword by Ulrich Weisner, text by Heribert Heere, Bielefeld, West Germany 1980; *Joseph Beuys: Zeichnungen, Bildobjekte, Holzschnitte*, exhibition catalogue, with texts by Michael Schwarz and Dieter Koepplin, Karlsruhe 1980; *Joseph Beuys: Dernier Espace avec Introspecteur 1964-1982* by Caroline Tisdall, London 1982; *Joseph Beuys: Is It About A Bicycle?*, exhibition catalogue with text by Bernard Lamarche-Vadel, New York 1985.

Of all the hagiographies of 20th century art, none has seemed more secure than that of Marcel Duchamp. It has been argued that the style and subject matter of most post-war art can be traced to his influence, that he set up the pieces of the game which everybody else is now playing. To question Duchamp's status is like attacking the Pope if you're Catholic.

Yet Duchamp's influence has been largely negative. There was nothing forward looking in his art; rather, it was an attempt to close the book before the barbarians arrived. He belonged to the old European tradition of artists—elegant, sensitive, aristocratic. If the language of art were tainted, then the only thing a gentleman could do was lapse into enigmatic silence. Duchamp's art is one of defeat.

So it is apt that it was a barbarian who called this deadly silence. One thinks of Luther nailing his theses on the church door: enough of this southern pomp and circumstance, enough of this Frenchness. So the barbarian, dressed like a poacher, bearing the scars of a war that destroyed Duchamp's country writes in chalk across a blackboard:

THE SILENCE OF DUCHAMP
IS OVERRATED.

Joseph Beuys was not interested in enigma; come to that he was not interested in Dada, Happenings, Situations, Environments, Performances or any of that Latinate epicenity. I suspect he had suffered too much to think that art was anything else but a life and death matter.

Duchamp had destroyed the language of art; Beuys would create a new one; one that was based, as are all languages of art in their new born state, on the emotions used raw, on pain and pleasure, on the senses used as reasoning devices, on the mind used as a sense.

In Dusseldorf, he sat in a bar room, surrounded by the salient textures of his universe: felt, fat, wires, wood, cradling in his arms a dead hare. The piece was called "How to explain art to a Dead Hare." The urgent whispering shattered Duchamp's silence, and here, for those prepared to follow him was a solution; go back to your own experience, to your own agony if necessary, for there the fountainhead of art was still bubbling.

The art of Beuys then is, like all great developments, a move towards realism. In recent years, that word has been much in vogue, but it has usually been applied to painting of a clearly revisionist tendency, or to the rather shallow use of "real" objects à la Duchamp. Beuys used reality in the form of his favourite textures and objects, or his own body and personality—not for theoretical or stylistic reasons, but for honesty. They were important to him, as important as perspective was to Piero or chiaroscuro to Caravaggio, and I think he believed that they are important also to everyone else. We may not all be felt freaks or butter fetishists, but we all have our obsessions. Upon these, Beuys suggests, our humanity rests.

Robert Morris also uses felt in large rolls, but for their abstract, sculptural quality. Beuys reacts against abstraction; he used such materials because they made up his world, his real world, a world in which theory has become debased but in which real people still live and die, as happy or miserable as they have always done.

One must not hope to understand Beuys if one has seen him only in the centres of culture, the great museums, the private dealers. One had to catch him somewhere where people still talk to each other, still get drunk to forget, where they couldn't give a damn about modern art. There he made sense, there people would warm to him, but not in New York, Paris or London.

I saw him first in Scotland, home of last stands and hopeless causes. In a huge bare room he went through a series of motions, sitting, drawing, sticking globs of fat to a wall and picking them off again, finally standing motionless. The first day he spent three hours doing this, by the fifth and last the whole procedure took nearer five. Yet people looked in and stayed. He had the ability to convince one of the significance of his actions. Each of his moves seemed like an element of meaning and by putting them together he was creating a new syntax. The resulting sentence was not written in any existing syntax, and its meaning can not be exactly transcribed, but as far as I am able to put it into words, I would say that its basic ingredients were to do with passion, courage and nobility, not exactly words one would associate with most contemporary art.

There was a moment when it seemed as if Beuys was destined to become a cult figure with a pathetic band of imitators trailing behind him. He refused, however, to act in the way expected of him, and frequently offended his defenders by offering unfashionable views. He remains, though, the most avant-garde of artists, in the true sense of the word, the one who most convincingly forged a new language, and a new method. His real influence has been to suggest that artists must rely upon themselves rather than upon any one style. One cannot imitate Beuys, but one can follow his method.

—Alastair Mackintosh

BIEDERMAN, Charles.

American. Born in Cleveland, Ohio, 23 August 1906.
Educated at the Art Institute of Chicago, 1926–29;
has studied semantics privately, since 1938. Married
Mary K. Moore in 1941; daughter: Anna. Travelled
and lived in New York and Paris, 1930–37; now lives
and works in Minnesota. Member, Advisory Committee, Artists, Composers and Authors Caucus, Minnesota, 1972. Recipient: Sikkens Award, Sikkens Paint
Company, Amsterdam, 1962; Ford Foundation Purchase Award, 1964; Minnesota State Arts Council
Award, 1969; Fine Arts Award, Minnesota Branch,
American Institute of Architects, 1971; National Endowment for the Arts Award, 1973. D.F.A.: Minneapolis College of Art and Design, 1973. Agent:
Grace Borgenicht Gallery, 1018 Madison Avenue,
New York, New York 10021. Address: Route 2, Red
Wing, Minnesota 55066, U.S.A.

Individual Exhibitions:

1936	Pierre Matisse Gallery, New York
1941	Arts Club of Chicago
1954	St. Paul Gallery, Minnesota
1963	Columbia University School of Architecture, New York (toured the United States)
1965	Walker Art Center, Minneapolis (retrospective)
1967	Rochester Art Center, Minnesota
1969	Hayward Gallery, London (retrospective, toured England)
1971	Dayton's Gallery, 12, Minneapolis
1976	Minneapolis Institute of Arts (retrospective; toured the East Coast of America, 1976–77)
1980	Borgenicht Gallery, New York
1985	Borgenicht Gallery, New York

Selected Group Exhibitions:

1936	*5 Peintres Americains*, Galerie Pierre, Paris
1962	*Experiment in Constructie*, Stedelijk Museum, Amsterdam (travelled to Kunstgewerbemuseum, Zurich)
1964	*Mondrian, De Stijl and Their Impact*, Marlborough Gallery, London
1966	*Reliefs, Sculpture*, Marlborough New London Gallery, London
1968	*Relief/Construction/Relief*, Museum of Contemporary Art, Chicago (toured the United States)
1972	*Geometric Abstraction: 1926–42*, University Museum, University of Texas at Austin
1973	*The Non-Objective World 1914–1955*, Annely Juda Fine Art, London
1979	*Vanguard American Sculptors, 1913–1939*, Rutgers University Art Gallery, New Jersey
1983	*Abstract Painting and Sculpture in America 1927–1944*, Carnegie Institute, Pittsburgh
1987	*Twentieth Century Drawings*, Whitney Museum, New York

Collections:

Museum of Modern Art, New York; Whitney Museum, New
York; Metropolitan Museum of Art, New York; Albright-
Knox Art Gallery, Buffalo, New York; Art Institute of Chi-
cago; Dallas Museum; High Museum, Atlanta; Minneapolis
Institute of Art; Walker Art Center, Minneapolis; Tate Gal-
lery, London.

Publications:

By BIEDERMAN: books—*Art as The Evolution of Visual
Knowledge*, Red Wing, Minnesota 1948; *Letters on The New
Art*, Red Wing, Minnesota 1951; *The New Cezanne*, Red
Wing, Minnesota 1958; *An Art Credo*, Lanark, Scotland
1965; *Search for New Arts*, Red Wing, Minnesota 1979;
articles—"Art and Science as Creation" in *Parnas* (Amster-
dam), no. 5, 1956; "Nature and Art" in *Structure* (Amster-
dam), series 2, No. 2, 1957; "Symmetry, Nature and the
Plane" in *Structure* (Amsterdam), series 3, No. 1, 1960;
"Dialogue on Art as Imitation or Creation" in *Main Currents*
(New York), March/April 1962; "A Non-Aristotelian Crea-

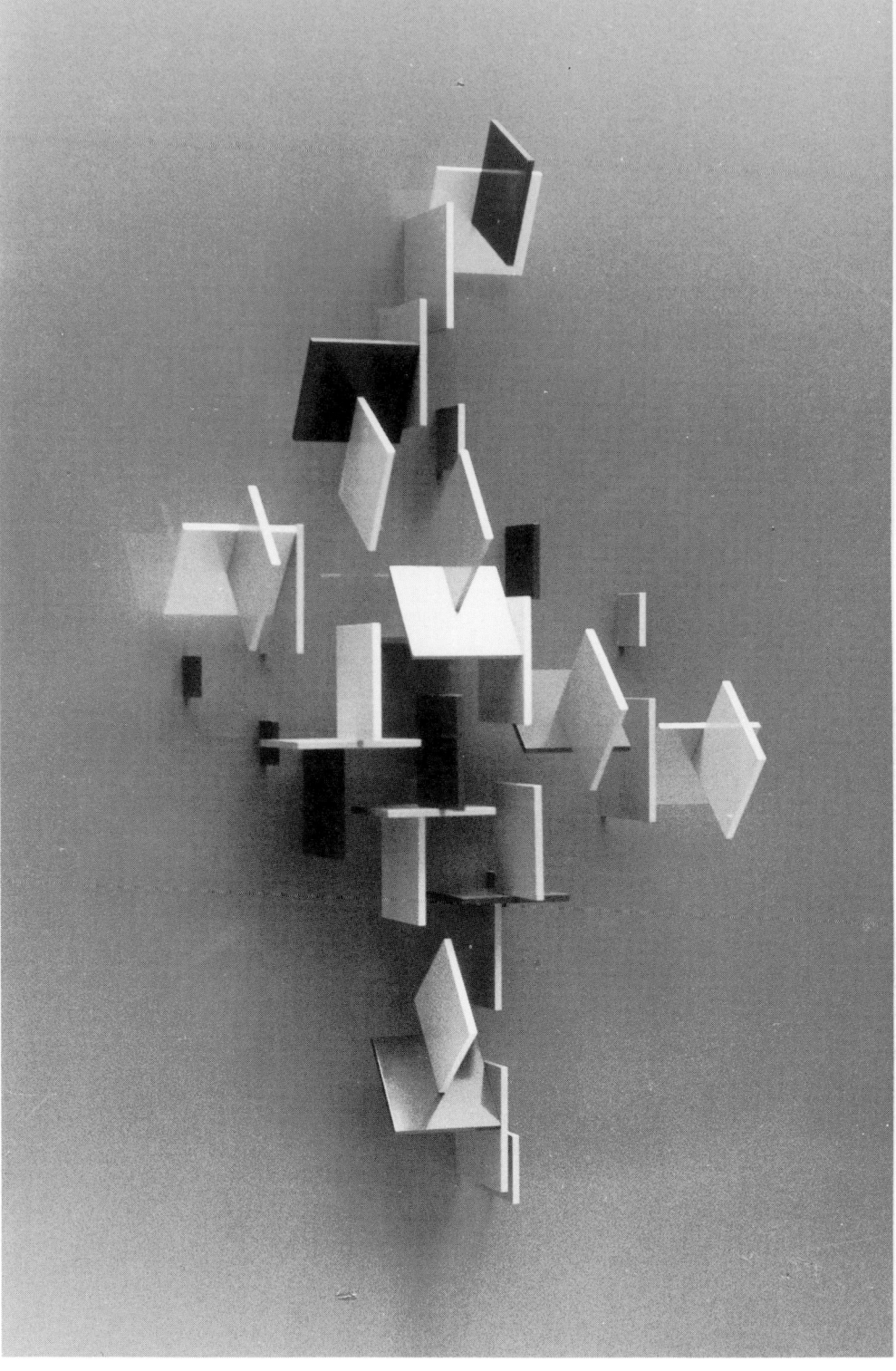

Charles Biederman: *Number 34*, 1972

tive Reality" in *Structure* (Amsterdam), series 4, No. 2,
1962; "The Sphere and The Cube" in *Structure* (Amsterdam), series 6, No. 1, 1964; "The Visual Revolution of
Structurist Art" in *Artforum* (New York), April 1965; "Art
in Crisis" in *Studies in the 20th Century*, Troy, New York
1968; "Dialogue II: Creative or Conditioned Vision" in
DATA (London), 1968; "Note on New Arts" in *Studio International* (London), 1970.

On BIEDERMAN: books—*Charles Biederman*, exhibition
catalogue, Minneapolis, 1965; *Charles Biederman: A Retrospective*, London 1969; *Experimental Painting* by Stephen
Bann, New York and London 1970; *Documents of 20th Century Art: The Tradition of Constructivism*, edited by Stephen
Bann, New York 1974; *Charles Biederman: A Retrospective*,
Minneapolis 1976; articles—"Biederman and the New Art"
by Frank Getlein in the *New Republic* (New York), February
1963; "Biederman's Structurism: Its Influence" by Leif Sjo-

berg in *Art International* (Lugano), March 1966; "Charles
Biederman and The Structurist Direction in Art" by Jan van
der Marck in *Feestbundel* (Amsterdam), 1966; "The Centrality of Charles Biederman" by Stephen Bann in *Studio International* (London), September 1969; "The Un-American
Activist" by Norbert Lynton in *The Guardian* (London), September 1969; "American Geometric Abstraction in the Late
30's" by John Elderfield in *Artforum* (New York), December
1972; "Biedermans Konst Och Evolution" by Leif Sjoberg in
Kunst Og Kuttur (Oslo), 1978; "Charles Biederman's Art of
Complicity" by David Craven in *Arts* (New York), April
1980; "Charles Biederman and the English Constructionists"
in *The Burlington Magazine* (London), February 1984.

After passing through the influence of nearly all the
major aspects of 20th century European art, I con-

cluded that the post-Cezannian condition of art (and architecture) has been one of confusion and desperation. I understood that all the much lauded "diversity" (Read) of modern art, purportedly exemplifying a great liberation, was simply a mask for the retreat of each artist to his own personal world. The artist had not only lost a coherent relation to the whole of the past human effort at art, but had sealed in his isolation completely by severing himself from the perceptual life of nature.

After many years I arrived at a view of new art that was not uniquely American, that is, not in the sense of the futile New York chauvinism, nor a uniquely European view, however that might be considered. Hence, European critics would note the "American" characteristics of my art and theory, while Americans (New York) regarded my work as "un-American." What escaped notice was that my art was the result of both America and Europe, but in the sense of the uniquely American temperament allowing for a wholly new perception of the uniquely European achievements.

The new art I pursue brings to a conclusion the "research" which Cezanne felt he would not live to "realize" and answers his hope for a "continuator" of his efforts. I realized this goal, not by "going back" to Cezanne, but rather by experiencing an American evolution in my art which opened the way for the continuance of Cezanne's extraordinary achievements in the spatial world of light. This became possible because, like Monet and Cezanne, I sought solutions in the visual study of nature, and like them was able to extend my perception of the structural process of nature. This permitted a truly genuine non-mimetic creation of the artist's art (bereft of confusion and compromise with the now obsolete vision of mimesis), according to the creative potentialities inherently given in the creative structural process of nature—the only structural possibilities available to the artist. The alternative is the artist's false assumption of superiority to nature, his denial of nature and his arrogant claim of being "his own nature." This alternative confuses and confounds the structural world of nature, and so art, by a naive appeal to an unlimited freedom purportedly residing in the subconscious.

It is precisely out of this attitude that the post-Cezannian chaos has arisen in which art is *reduced* to the "puny" (Cezanne) concern of revealing the questionable value of the artist's personal "inner world." The new art I advocate, in the line of Monet-Cezanne, acts in the very opposite way. That is, not "reducing" but extending the past evolution of human art by ceasing any form of imitating what nature has already created, ceasing the limitation of imitating light as in painting and ceasing the limited notion of form as in sculpture. The new art liberates the artist to create his own art in the full dimensions of the actualities of spatial reality. The artist is freed from conditioning to the biological creations of nature to adopt what is uniquely suited to human creation—geometric structuring. This mode of structuring, however, is submitted to the potentialities as given by the creative process of nature. It then becomes evident why neither the brush nor the chisel but rather the machine is now the ideal medium which enables the artist to engage the exactitude of geometric structuring in the spatial world of light and thus secure the full reality experience inherent in the new art of creation.

—Charles Biederman

To be an eminent theoretician and one who withdraws from the art scene of life in cities is to risk international obscurity. Charles Biederman has written extensively about his theory of "structurism," and his works have been read and to some extent heeded by a narrow echelon of cultured cognoscenti. In this wise his reputation has thrived, albeit to a limited capacity. He chose to live and work—since 1942—in Red Wing, Minnesota. It was in that remote area that he evolved his principles of "structurism," and it was at that address that he wrote and prepared his most famous book, *Art as the Evolution of Visual Knowledge,* which influenced the development of a number of artists—not always as a result of accurate understanding of its contents. These included Victor Pasmore, Kenneth Martin, Mary Martin, and Anthony Hill, all of whom entered into correspondence with the American.

Before settling in Red Wing, Biederman had been influenced by a number of artists and art movements of the Old World, most notably Mondrian and de Stijl, but structurism, and particularly its concern with the pure and natural character of colour(s), cut him adrift from all but his own admirers.

It seems a far cry from the days when Biederman was best known for the illustration of his button collage which appeared in Alfred Barr's *Cubism and Abstract Art*—a picture which at the time of publication looked as if it was the work of an unknown but interesting "newcomer," perhaps a fluke or perhaps a signal of even better things to come. But thereafter, outside the United States, his fame was severely curtailed. A few isolated works were exhibited in London (across the decades!), but it was not until the Arts Council exhibition at London's Hayward Gallery—when the artist was in his 60's—that Londoners had a proper opportunity to see Biederman structural reliefs. Enthusiasm was moderate. Perhaps structurism is an acquired taste, or even more likely, most of those who came to stand and stare were not prepared to read and absorb Biederman's intellectual arguments.

—Sheldon Williams

BILL, Max.

Swiss. Born in Winterthur, 22 December 1908. Trained as silversmith, Kunstgewerbeschule, Zurich, 1924–27; studied art, Staatliche Bauhaus, Dessau, Germany, 1927–29. Served in the Swiss Army, 1939–45. Married Bibia Spoerri in 1931; son: Johann. Independent architect, painter, sculptor and graphic artist, Zurich, since 1929, and industrial designer, since 1944. Lecturer on the Theory of Form, Kunstgewerbeschule, Zurich, 1944–45; Co-Founder and Rector, Hochschule für Gestaltung, Ulm, Germany, 1951–56; Professor of Environmental Design, State Institute of Fine Arts, Hamburg, 1967–74. Member of the Communal Council, City of Zurich, 1961; National Councillor, Swiss Parliament, 1967–74. Member of the Central Board, Schweizerische Werkbund, 1952–62; Member, Swiss Federal Art Commission, 1961–69; Member of the Board, Geschwisten-School Foundation, Ulm, 1964; Member of the Superior Council (Creation Esthetique Industrielle), French Ministry of Industrial and Scientific Development, 1971–73. Member: Abstraction-Creation group, Paris, 1932–36; Allianz, Zurich 1937; CIAM (Congrès Internationaux d'Architecture Moderne), 1938; UAM (Union des Artistes Modernes), Paris 1949; Deutscher Werkbund 1956. Recipient: Grand Prize, *Triennale di Milano,* Milan, 1936, 1951, 1954; Kandinsky Prize, 1949; First Prize for Sculpture, *Bienal,* Sao Paulo, 1951; Gold Medal, Verucchio, Italy, 1966; City of Zurich Art Prize, 1968. Honorary Fellow, American Institute of Architects, 1964; Extraordinary Member, Akademie der Künste, West Berlin, 1972; Honorary Member, Royal Flemish Academy of Sciences, Literature and Arts, 1973. Agent: Marlborough Fine Art, 6 Albemarle Street, London WIX 3HF, England. Address: Albulastrasse 39, 8048 Zurich, Switzerland.

Individual Exhibitions:

1928	Staatliche Bauhaus, Dessau, Germany (with Albert Braun)
1929	Atelier des Kunstlers, Zurich
1939	Kunstmuseum, Basle
1946	Galerie des Eaux-Vives, Zurich
1948	Herber Hermann Galerie, Stuttgart (with Josef Albers and Jean Arp)
1949	Galerie d'Art Moderne, Basle
	Kunsthaus, Zurich (with Antoine Pevsner and Georges Vantongerloo)
1950	Museu de Arte Moderna, Sao Paulo
1951	Kunstverein, Freiburg im Breisgau, West Germany (with Julius Bissier and Georges Vantongerloo)
1956	Ulmer Museum, Ulm, West Germany (toured Germany)
1957	Helmhaus, Zurich
1958	Galerie Suzanne Bollag, Zurich
1959	Galerie Gelbes Haus, St. Gallen, Switzerland
	Städtisches Museum, Leverkusen, West Germany
	Studio F., Ulm, West Germany
1960	Staatsgalerie, Stuttgart
	Kunstmuseum, Winterthur, Switzerland
	Galerie Suzanne Bollag, Zurich
	Galerie im Ronca-Haus, Lucerne
1961	Galerie du Perron, Geneva
	Galerie Anna Roepke, Wiesbaden, West Germany
1962	Galerie Hilt, Basle
1963	Galerie Suzanne Bollag, Zurich
	Gimpel & Hanover Galerie, Zurich
	Staempfli Gallery, New York
	Pace Gallery, Boston
	Studio F., Ulm, West Germany
1964	Galleria Cadario, Milan
	Galleria del Deposito, Genoa
	Galleria dell'Accademia, Rome
	Galleria Suzanne Bollag, Zurich
1965	Galerie Aktuell, Berne
	Op-Art Galerie, Esslingen, West Germany
	Galleria Flaviana, Locarno, Switzerland
	Galerie 58, Rapperswil, Switzerland
	Gemeindehaus, Uster, Switzerland
	Galerie Suzanne Bollag, Zurich
1966	Staempfli Gallery, New York
	Galerie Hilt, Basle
	Hanover Gallery, London
	Galerie Suzanne Bollag, Zurich
1967	Galerie im Erker, St. Gallen, Switzerland
1968	Kunsthalle, Berne
	Kestner-Gesellschaft, Hannover
	Kunstverein für die Rheinland und Westfalen, Dusseldorf
	Haags Gemeentemuseum, The Hague
	Musée des Beaux-Arts, La Chaux de Fonds, Switzerland
	Kunsthalle, Nuremberg, West Germany
	Kunsthaus, Zurich
	Galerie Suzanne Bollag, Zurich
1969	Arts Club of Chicago
	Galleria La Bertesca, Genoa
	Galleria La Polena, Genoa
	Galleria Vismara, Milan
	Galerie Godard Lefort, Montreal
	Staempfli Gallery, New York
	Galerie Denise Renè, Paris
	Galleria Martano/Due, Turin
	Galerie Bischofberger, Zurich
	Centre National d'Art Contemporain, Paris
	Musée de Peinture et de Sculpture, Grenoble, France
1970	Galerie Bischofberger, Zurich
	Galerie Loeb, Berne
	Galerie im Weissen Haus, Winterthur, Switzerland
	San Francisco Museum of Art
	Galerie Appel und Fertsch, Frankfurt
	Galleria del Cavallino, Venice
	White Gallery, Lutry, Switzerland
	Galleria Arte Studio, Macerata, Italy
	Galerie Design II, Hamburg
	Galleria d'Arte Peccolo, Livorno, Italy
	Galleria del Cortile, Rome
	Galerie Kludschule, Zurich
	Staempfli Gallery, New York
1971	Galerie Reckermann, Cologne
	Galerie Denise René, Paris
	Galerie Suzanne Bollag, Zurich
	Galerie im Erker, St. Gallen, Switzerland

1972   Musée Rath, Geneva
        Galleria Lorenzelli, Milan
        Marlborough Galerie, Zurich
        Kunstmuseum, Aarhus, Denmark
        Galerie Hausdewell, Baden-Baden, West Germany
        Marlborough-Godard Gallery, Toronto (travelled to
            the Marlborough Gallery, Montreal)
1973   Galerie 58, Rapperswil, Switzerland
        Galerie Ziegler, Geneva
1974   Marlborough Fine Art, London
        Galleria Lorenzelli, Bergamo, Italy
        Galerie Media, Neuchâtel, France
        Galleria Medea, Milan
        Marlborough Galerie, Zurich
        Watari Gallery, Tokyo
        Albright-Knox Art Gallery, Buffalo, New York
            (toured the United States)
1975   Comsky Gallery, Los Angeles
        Art Institute, San Francisco
        Marlborough Gallery, New York
        Galleria Effereridi, Bologna
1976   Museum für Kunst und Gewerbe, Hamburg (toured
            Germany)
        Akademie der Künste, West Berlin
        Galleria Lorenzelli, Milan
1977   Universita di Parma, Italy
1978   Moderne Galerie, Bottrop, West Germany
1979   Pinturas, Esculturas, Grafica, Museo de Bellas
            Artes, Caracas
        Galerie Bossin, West Berlin
        Gallery Watari, Tokyo
1980   Galerie Seestrasse, Rapperswil, Switzerland
        Galerie Bossin, West Berlin
        Artline, The Hague
1981   Galerie Buhler, Biel, Switzerland
        Gallery Watari, Tokyo
1982   Galerie Bossin, West Berlin
        Galerie Denise Rene, Paris
        Gimpel-Hanover-Andre Emmerich Galerie, Zurich
1983   Galleria Narciso, Turin
        Galerie Bertram, Burgdorf, Switzerland
        Gimpel-Hanover-Andre Emmerich Galerie, Zurich
1984   Galerie Henz, Munich
        Galleria Narciso, Turin
        Deutsche Bank, Hamburg
1985   Galerie Wolfgang Ketterer, Munich
        Galerie Teufel, Cologne
        Galleria Lorenzelli, Milan
        Galerie Edith Wahlandt, Stuttgart
1986   Mucsarnok Art Gallery, Budapest
1987   National Gallery, Belgrade
        Kunsthalle, Frankfurt

Selected Group Exhibitions:

1930   *Bill/Valloton/Probst/Steck/Von May*, Kunsthalle,
            Berne
1944   *Konkrete Kunst*, Kunsthalle, Basle
1951   *Bienal*, Sao Paulo
1952   *Monument to the Unknown Political Prisoner*, Insti-
            tute of Contemporary Arts, London
1958   *Biennale*, Venice
1960   *Concrete Art: 50 Years of Development*, Kunsthaus,
            Zurich
1971   *La Peinture Non-Objective 1924–1939*, Galerie Jean
            Chauvelin, Paris (travelled to Annely Juda Fine
            Art, London, and Galleria Milano, Milan)
1972   *Konstruktivismus*, Galerie Gmurzynska + Bargera,
            Cologne
1973   *Kunst in Deutschland 1898–1973*, Kunsthalle, Ham-
            burg (travelled to Städtisches Galerie im Lenbach-
            haus, Munich)
1982   *Acquisition Priorities: Postwar European Painting*,
            Guggenheim Museum, New York

Collections:

Kunsthaus, Zurich; Kunstmuseum, Winterthur, Switzerland;
Musée d'Art et d'Histoire, Geneva; Musées Royaux des
Beaux-Arts, Brussels; Centre Georges Pompidou, Paris;
Wilhelm-Lehmbrock Museum, Duisburg, West Germany;
Galleria Nazionale d'Arte Moderna, Rome; Art Institute of

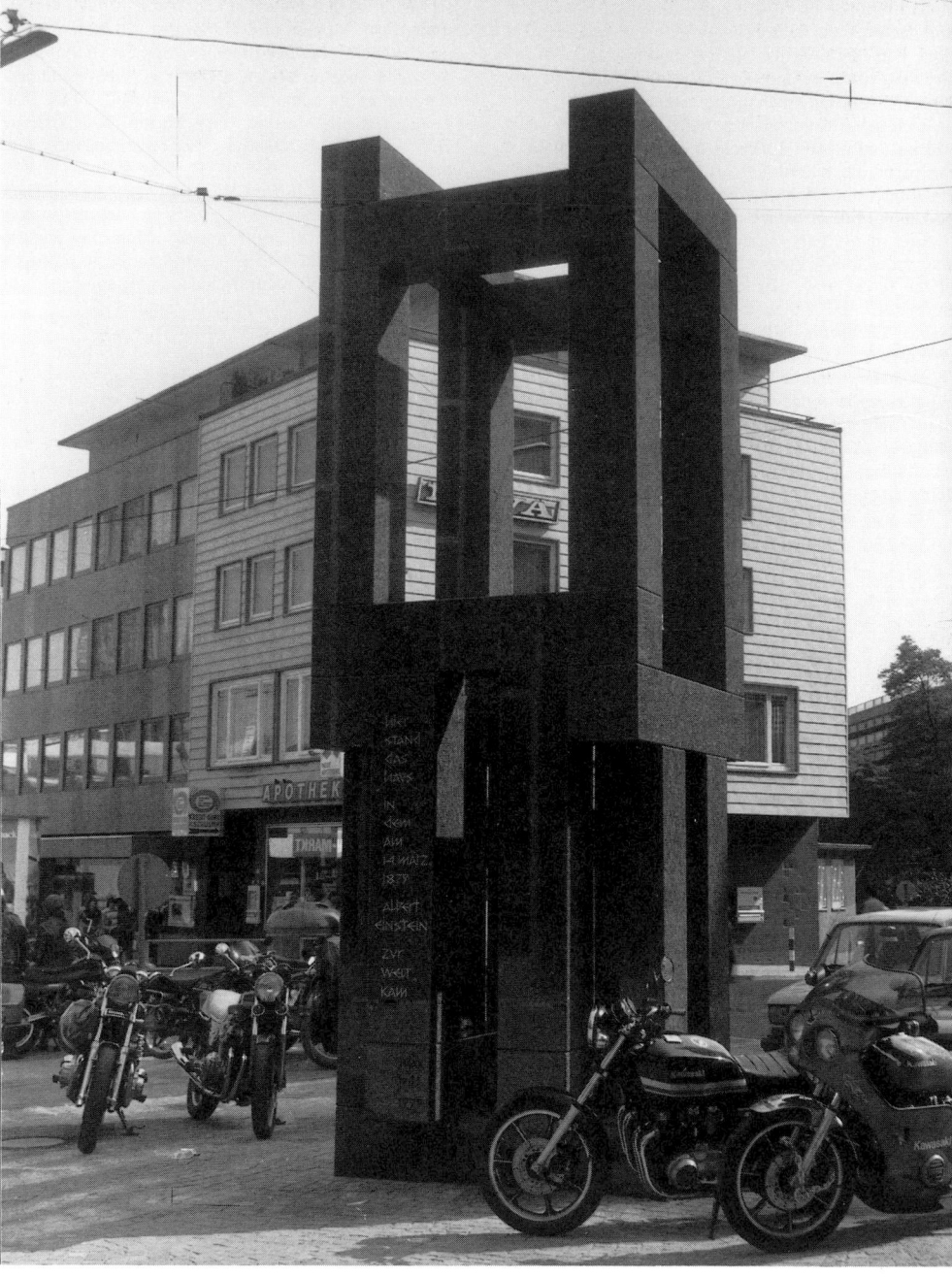

Max Bill: *Albert Einstein Memorial, Ulm*, 1982

Chicago; Albright-Knox Art Gallery, Buffalo, New York;
Hirshhorn Museum and Sculpture Garden, Washington, D.C.

Bill's architectural works, including his own house and studio
at Zumikon/Zurich, are extant throughout Europe in Aargau,
Ulm, Rhinfall, Leverkusen, Cologne, Tamins, Dusseldorf
and Esbly.

Publications:

By BILL: books—*Quinze Variations sur un meme Theme*,
Paris 1938; *Le Corbusier: Oeuvre Complete*, volume 3, editor, Zurich 1939, London 1964; *5 Konstruktionen + 5 Kom-
positionen*, Zurich 1941; *10 Original Lithos*, Zurich 1941;
X + X, Zurich 1942; *Leo Luppi: 10 Kompositionen*, Zurich
1943; *Konkrete Kunst*, exhibition catalogue, with others, Ba-
sle 1944; *Hans Arp: 11 Configurations*, with others, Zurich
1945; *Wiederaufbau*, Zurich 1945; *Wassily Kandinsky: 10
Farbige Reproduktionen*, Basle 1949; *Robert Maillart:
Brucken und Konstruktionen*, Zurich 1949, New York 1969;
Moderne Schweizer Architektur 1925–1945, Basle 1950;
Wassily Kandinsky, editor, Paris 1951; *Form: A Balance Sheet
of Mid-20th Century Trends in Design*, Basle 1952; *Uber des
Geistige in der Kunst*, editor, Berne 1952; *Mies van der
Rohe*, Milan 1955; *Essays über Kunst und Kunstler*, editor,
Stuttgart 1955, Berne 1963; *Die Gute Form*, Winterthur

1957; *Punkt und Linie zu Flache*, editor, Berne 1959; *Enzo
Mari*, with Bruno Munari, Milan 1959; *Konkrete Kunst: 50
Jahre Entwicklung*, exhibition catalogue, Zurich 1968, 1969;
11 x 4, Zurich 1970; *Jahresgabe 1972*, Berne 1972; *System
mit funf vierfarbigen Zentren*, St. Gallen Switzerland 1972;
8 = (2 x 4/4) = 8, Neuchâtel, Switzerland 1974; *16
Constellations*, Paris 1974; *7 Twins*, Neuchâtel, Switzerland
1977.

On BILL: books—*Max Bill*, Buenos Aires 1955; *Max Bill* by
Max Bense and others, Teufen, Switzerland 1958; *Max Bill*
by Margit Staber, St. Gallen, Switzerland 1971; *Max Bill* by
Eduard Huttinger, Zurich 1977, 1978; *Max Bill*, exhibition
catalogue, edited by Arturo Carlo Quintavalle, Parma 1977;
Max Bill: Pinturas, Esculturas, Grafica, exhibition catalogue, by Carlos Silva and Ricardo Axel Stein Nunex, Caracas 1979; *Contemporary Architects*, edited by Muriel
Emanuel, London and New York 1980.

One often speaks of the mathematics, the structure,
the systems in art. I also did so. Looking for a non-
individualistic approach to so-called art problems. I
did different kinds of research, and I wrote a few
statements which were publicized and interpreted
worldwide.

As life—and so ideas and art as one of the human activities—is in constant motion, and we hope permanent development, my ideas have also developed and become clearer. This because of more experience and an accumulation of knowledge.

When I wrote a quarter of a century ago about "the mathematical approach in contemporary art" this was a new way to see art which until then had been considered mostly as the more or less uncontrolled experience of an individual.

Today I know better that mathematics are only a part of the methods to be adapted for the regulation of so-called works of art. I know that a concept has to conform to its inner organization and its visual existence. This means that a concept and the finally executed work have to be a unity. This unit is the result of the logical approach to the solution of the problem and its realization.

I prefer today to describe this process as the logical approach to the problems of art. This means that every part of the creative process consciously follows step by step a logical analysis and feedback. This is the way I hope to best realize my vision.

—Max Bill

Among the painters of the 20th century Max Bill is one of the few who represents and puts into effect the Renaissance principle of the *uomo universale*. It is true that he is presented officially as an architect, but his painting and sculptural work is at least as important as his buildings. He is equally instigator and publicist, organizer, man of letters and teacher; he is versed in philosophy and involves himself in the cultural politics of his country. Judgment—the balance between rationalism and emotion—and order—the demonstration of law in the world—form the basis of his multiple activities. As an artist he became the most important representative of "concrete art" which he himself defined as follows: "We call those works of art concrete art which have arisen by virtue of their original means and laws—without external support from natural appearances or their transformation, therefore without abstraction . . . they are of that sharp, unequivocal and perfect nature as must be expected from works of the human intellect." The striving after perfection evident in the definition marks all Bill's creative work. In the realization of his buildings, sculptures and pictures, mathematics is, to him, not the only but the most important medium. A large part of his work could be understood as mathematics become visible, although not exhaustively. Bill himself speaks of an "application of logical thought processes in the organization of rhythms and relationships, of laws that have individual origins . . . ." In this emphasis on the individual is hidden the allusion to creative fantasy which Bill develops as much in purpose-free as in purposeful problems, perhaps in the design of a poster or a memorial.

His life's work presents itself as an explanation of the aesthetic principles he has himself defined. It possesses a chronology, yet hardly any development in the sense that no stylistic groups or periods are discernable in his work. A theme which preoccupies the artist can again be taken up by him after a number of years and varied with new methods of realization without any apparent breach.

Bill's work stands in a tradition which follows directly on Stijl and the Bauhaus. It continues this tradition in that it systematically and methodically pursues the experiments which had begun there. This aim was also served by the "Design School" in Ulm, which despite its short life after 1945 gained greater international influence than all other didactic art institutes of the last decades.

When in 1975/76 a comprehensive retrospective of Bill's pictures, sculpture, graphics and models was mounted in the USA and Germany, he himself spoke of certain modifications to his principles in the sense that he described the "design process as that of logical method" and made a clear differentiation between purposeful and purpose free activity: "while the problems of building, of the form of an object, of education or political decision must be solved in relation to their complex functions, the function of painting and sculpture is unequivocal: their usefulness rests on their intellectual/spiritual usefulness."

—Heinz Spielmann

BISHOP, Isabel.

American. Born in Cincinnati, Ohio, 3 March 1902. Studied illustration at the New York School of Applied Design for Women, 1918-20; painting, under Kenneth Hayes Miller and Guy Pène du Bois, at the Art Students League, New York, 1920-24; engraving, under Stanley William Hayter, at the New School for Social Research, New York, 1941. Married the neurologist Harold G. Wolff in 1934; son: Remsen. Established loft studio at 9 West 14th Street, New York, 1926; established and maintains studio in Union Square, New York, since 1934. Instructor, Art Students League, New York, 1936-37; Instructor, 1956-58, and Guest Lecturer, 1963, Skowhegan School of Painting and Sculpture, Maine; Visiting Artist, Yale University School of Fine Arts, New Haven, Connecticut, 1963. Recipient: Isaac N. Maynard Portrait Prize, 1936, Adolph and Clara Obrig Prize, 1942, Andrew Carnegie Prize, 1945, Benjamin Altman Prize, 1955, 1967, Joseph S. Isidor Medal, 1957, Samuel Finley Breeze Morse Medal, 1966, and Purchase Prize, 1973, National Academy of Design, New York; Newport Art Association Prize, Rhode Island, 1937, First Prize, 1940, and Noyes Memorial Prize, 1947, American Society of Etchers: Watercolor Prize, Butler Art Institute, Youngstown, Ohio, 1941; American Academy of Arts and Letters and National Institute of Arts and Letters Grant, 1943; William A. Clark Prize, *Corcoran Biennial Exhibition*, Washington, D.C., 1945; First Pennell Purchase Award, *Library of Congress National Exhibition of Prints*, Washington, D.C., 1946; Walter Lippincott Prize, *Pennsylvania Academy Annual*, Philadelphia, 1953; Gold Medal, 1968, and Best of Show Award, 1973, National Arts Club, New York; Purchase Prize, National Prints and Drawings Exhibition, Mount Holyoke College, Hadley, Massachusetts, 1974; Outstanding Achievement in the Arts Award, from President Carter, 1979. D.F.A.: Moore Institute of Art, Science and Industry, Philadelphia, 1954. Associate Member, 1940, and Academician, 1941, National Academy of Design; Member, 1944, and Vice-President, 1946, National Institute of Arts and Letters; Member, American Academy of Arts and Letters, 1944. Benjamin Franklin Fellow, Royal Society of Arts, London, 1964. Agent: The Midtown Galleries, 11 East 57th Street, New York, New York 10022. Addresses: (studio) 33 Union Square, New York, New York 10003; (home) 355 West 246th Street, New York, New York 10471, U.S.A.

Individual Exhibitions:

1932   *Paintings*, Midtown Galleries, New York
1935   *Drawings and Etchings*, Midtown Galleries, New York
1936   *Paintings, Drawings, and Etchings*, Midtown Galleries, New York.
1939   *Paintings and Drawings*, Midtown Galleries, New York
1940   Herbert Institute, Atlanta
1942   *Drawings*, Midtown Galleries, New York
1945   *Drawings*, Smithsonian Institution, Washington, D.C.
1948   American-British Art Center, New York (with Augustus John)
1949   *Paintings and Drawings*, Midtown Galleries, New York
1955   *Paintings and Drawings*, Midtown Galleries, New York

1957   Berkshire Museum, Pittsfield, Massachusetts
1960   *Paintings and Drawings*, Midtown Galleries, New York
     Judge the Jury: Perry T. Rathbone/Isabel Bishop/Richard Lippold, Virginia Museum of Fine Arts, Richmond
1967   *Paintings and Drawings*, Midtown Galleries, New York
1970   *Paintings, by Isabel Bishop/Sculptures by Dorothea Greenbaum*, New Jersey State Museum, Trenton
1971   *3 Figurative Painters*, Midtown Galleries, New York
1972   *Drawings and Prints*, Wood Art Gallery, Montpelier, Vermont
1974   *A Selection of Drawings and Prints*, Midtown Galleries, New York
     Isabel Bishop: The First Retrospective Exhibition Held in American Museums of Paintings, Drawings, Etchings, and Aquatints. University of Arizona Museum of Art, Tucson (travelled to the Wichita State University Art Museum, Kansas, and the Whitney Museum, New York, 1975)
1979   Midtown Galleries, New York
1980   *Prints*. Associated American Artists Gallery, Philadelphia (with Miller and Marsh)
1981   *Paintings and Drawings*, Midtown Galleries, New York
     Isabel Bishop: Etchings and Aquatints. Associated American Artists Gallery, New York (retrospective)

Selected Group Exhibitions:

1936   *Biennial Exhibition: Part I: Sculpture, Drawings, and Prints*, Whitney Museum, New York
1947   *American Printmaking 1913-1947*, Brooklyn Museum, New York.
1957   *Golden Years of American Drawings 1905-1956*, Brooklyn Museum, New York
1963   *Contemporary American Painting and Sculpture*, Krannert Art Museum, University of Illinois, Urbana (and 1967)
1966   *79 Original Drawings by 20th Century American Artists*, Storm King Art Center, Mountainville, New York
1971   *Boston Printmakers' Annual*, De Cordova Museum, Lincoln, Massachusetts
     Celebrate Ohio: 50th Anniversary Exhibition, Akron Art Institute, Ohio
1973   *Drawings U.S.A.*, Minnesota Museum of Art, St. Paul
1974   *National Prints and Drawings Exhibition*, Mount Holyoke College, South Hadley, Massachusetts

Collections:

Metropolitan Museum of Art, New York; Brooklyn Museum, New York, Museum of Fine Arts, Boston; Fogg Art Museum, Harvard University, Cambridge, Massachusetts; Pennsylvania Academy of Art, Philadelphia; Baltimore Museum of Art; Corcoran Gallery of Art, Washington, D.C.; Virginia Museum of Fine Arts, Richmond; British Museum, London.

Publications:

By BISHOP: books—*8 Etchings I, 1938-1959*, portfolio, New York 1978; *8 Etchings II, 1936-1959*, portfolio, New York 1981; articles—"Concerning Edges" in *Magazine of Art* (Washington, D.C.), May 1945; "Kenneth Hayes Miller" in *Magazine of Art* (Washington, D.C.) April 1953; "Isabel Bishop Discusses Genre Drawings" in *American Artist* (New York), Summer 1953; "Drawing the Nude" in *Art in America* (New York), December 1963; 2 essays in *Isabel Bishop: Prints and Drawings 1925-1964*, Brooklyn New York 1964.

On BISHOP: books—*Biennial Exhibition: Part I: Sculpture, Drawings, and Prints*, exhibition catalogue, New York 1936; *American Printmaking 1913-1947*, exhibition catalogue, with an introduction by Jean Charlot, Brooklyn, New York 1947; *Painting in America: The Story of 450 Years* by E. P. Richardson, New York 1956; *Golden Years of American Drawings 1905-1056*, exhibition catalogue, with text by Una E. Johnson, Brooklyn, New York 1957; *A History of American Art* by D. M. Mendelowitz, New York 1961; *Isabel*

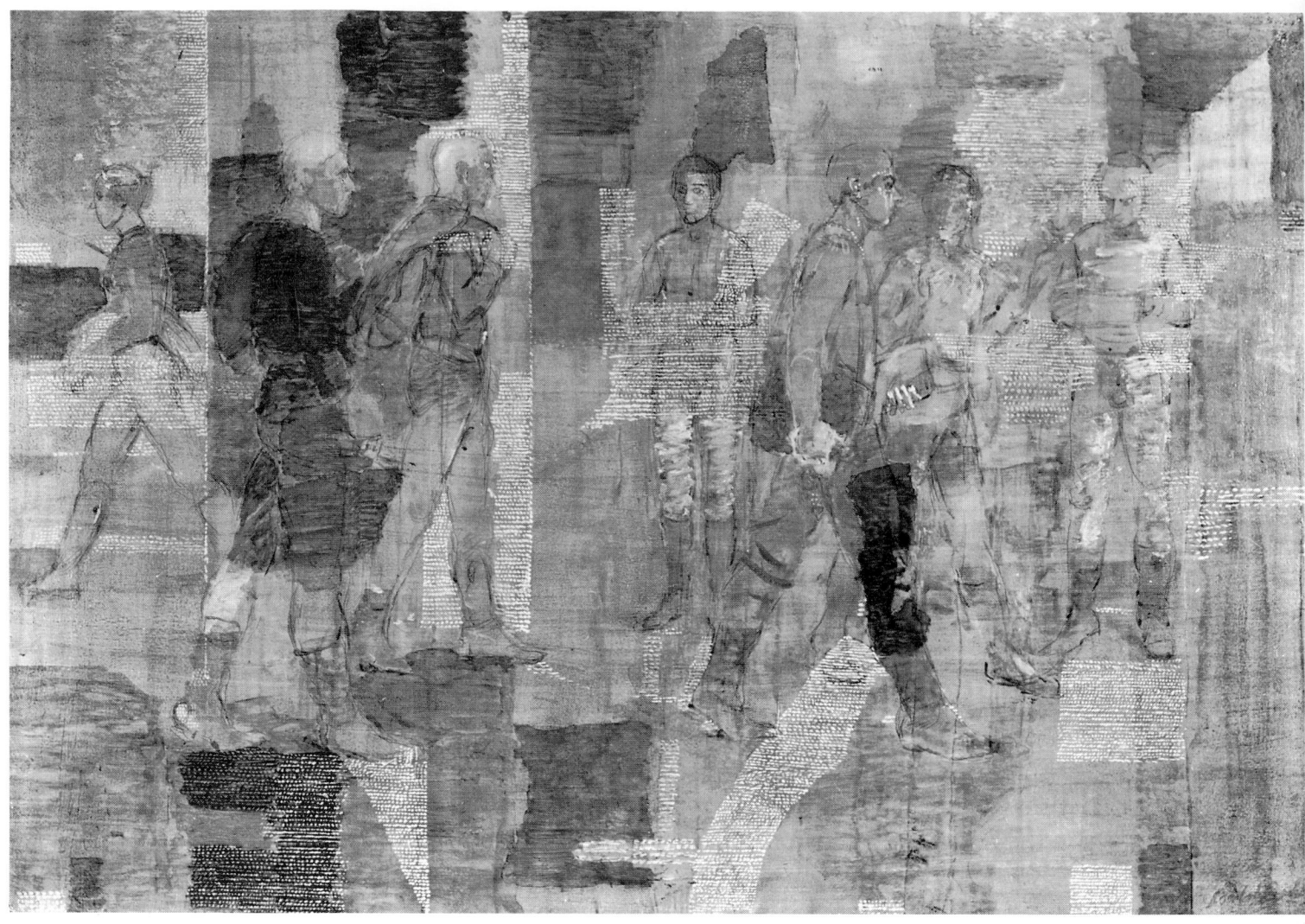

Isabel Bishop: *Variations on a Theme of Walking*, 1979

Bishop: Prints and Drawings 1925–1964, with text by Una E. Johnson, Brooklyn, New York 1964; *American Art since 1900: A Critical History* by Barbara Rose, New York 1967; *Paintings by Isabel Bishop/Sculpture by Dorothea Greenbaum*, exhibition catalogue, with an introduction by Suzanne Corlette, Trenton, New Jersey 1970; *Isabel Bishop*, exhibition catalogue, with a foreword by John I. H. Baur, introduction by Martin H. Bush, and text by Sheldon Reich, Tucson, Arizona 1974; *Isabel Bishop* by Karl Lunde, New York 1975; *Isabel Bishop: Etchings and Aquatints*, exhibition catalogue, compiled and edited by Susan Teller, New York 1981; articles—"Isabel Bishop" by Elaine de Kooning in *Artnews* (New York), May 1949; "Isabel Bishop" by Lawrence Campbell in *Artnews* (New York), November 1955; "Isabel Bishop" by George Dennison in *Arts Magazine* (New York), May 1960; "Light as the Beginning: The Art of Isabel Bishop" by Ernest Harms in *American Artist* (New York), February 1961; "Is There Discrimination Against Women Artists?" in *American Artist* (New York), May 1978; "American Realists of the 1930's: The 14th Street School" by M. S. Young in *Apollo* (London), March 1981.

For more than 40 years, from 1934 to 1978, Isabel Bishop occupied a painting studio which overlooked Union Square in New York City, Union Square is a busy area; below ground several subway lines converge in a labyrinthine station and above ground shoppers and shopkeepers walk to a multitude of discount stores of every description while street people conduct their own business in the Square. Isabel Bishop watched, drew, and painted the people of Union Square, and rode the subway with them morning and evening. Throughout her career, her paintings have contained metaphors about life above and below ground from "Dante and Virgil in Union Square," 1932, to the most recent, ethereal people rushing to the next chapter of their city lives. The presence of Dante and Virgil in such an unlikely setting immediately establishes a connection with hell and souls, and Bishop's use of architectonic space typical of the Renaissance increases the association with otherworldly, or at least religious, experience. In the recent paintings Bishop succeeds in putting figures on canvas without immobilizing them, and in so doing, fills them with strokes of light colored paint. She has expressed an interest in the mobility of figures, but what she appears to have captured is souls in transit.

Bishop, who studied with Kenneth Hayes Miller at the Art Students League in the 1920's, can be linked with other realist painters of city life—Guy Pène du Bois or Reginald Marsh—but it would be a great mistake to interpret Bishop's paintings as nothing more than city genre scenes. Even when her paintings contain only a few figures, Bishop conveys information about the masses in urban life. In an outdoor setting, a city square, even such details as clothing do not establish individuality; any park bench can be vacated and refilled within a few seconds. Since everyone in the square is a transient, the mobility of the figure is implied by the situation as well as suggested by Bishop's flitting brush style. City life in Bishop's paintings, even during the Depression, is not entirely a cement-bound, grimy affair but a multilayered existence of continuous motion.

Bishop also painted female nudes until the early 1970's, when, she has said, she felt no new impulse toward the subject. The nudes are often in the act of dressing or undressing, sometimes on a bed, and are among the least self-conscious nudes in art history. Perhaps they reflect Bishop's respect for comfortable relationships among women, evident in such paintings as "Two Girls," 1935 or "Lunch Hour," 1939. Non-competitive friendship between women is a rare subject in painting, yet Bishop has found and captured many relaxed acquaintanceships among her urban subjects. Although Bishop has cited Union Square as a long time source of artistic nourishment, clearly she has added many layers of meaning to 40 years of city life.

—Mary Stofflet

BISHOP, James.

American. Born in Neosho, Missouri, 7 October 1927. Educated at Syracuse University, New York, 1946–50, B.A. 1950; Washington University, St. Louis, Missouri, 1951–54; studied under Esteban Vicente, Black Mountain College, North Carolina, 1953; Columbia University, New York, 1955–56. Independent artist: lived and travelled in France, 1957–66; now lives and works in New York. Editorial Associate, *Artnews*, New York, 1969–70. Artist-in-Residence, Cooper Union, New York, 1969–70; University of California at Irvine, 1970; Carnegie-Mellon University, Pittsburgh, 1971; School of Visual Arts, New York, 1972. Recipient: Guggenheim Fellowship, 1970. Agent: Fourcade, Droll Inc. 36 East 75th Street, New York, New York 10021. Address: 5 Lispenard Street, New York, New York 10013, U.S.A.

Individual Exhibitions:

1963   Galerie Lucien Durand, Paris
         Galerie Smith, Brussels
1964   Galerie Lawrence, Paris

1966	Fischbach Gallery, New York
	Galerie Fournier, Paris
1968	Fischbach Gallery, New York
1970	Fischbach Gallery, New York
1971	Galerie Fournier, Paris
1972	Fischbach Gallery, New York
1973	Galerie Fournier, Paris
	The Clocktower, New York
1974	Rosa Esman Gallery, New York
1975	Galleria D'Alessandro-Ferranti, Rome
1976	Galerie Annemarie Verna, Zurich
	Galerie Fournier, Paris
1979	Droll/Kolbert Gallery, New York

Selected Group Exhibitions:

1965	*Promesses Tenues*, Musée Galliera, Paris
1967	*L'Art Vivant*, Fondation Maeght, St.-Paul-de-Vence, France
	Expo '67 Montreal
1968	*Preview '68*, Trinity College, Hartford, Connecticut
	Painting Annual, Whitney Museum, New York
1970	*One Man's Choice*, Dallas Museum of Fine Arts
	L'Art Américain, Foundation Maeght, St.-Paul-de-Vence, France
1971	*Award Invitational*, National Institute of Arts and Letters, New York
1972	*Zeichnungen Amerikanischer Künstler*, Galerie Annemarie Verna, Zurich
1973	*Options and Alternatives: Some Directions in Recent Art*, Yale University Art Museum New Haven, Connecticut

Collections:

San Francisco Museum of Modern Art; Centre Georges Pompidou, Paris

Publications:

On BISHOP: book—*Options and Alternatives: Some Directions in Recent Art*, exhibition catalogue, with texts by Anne Coffin Hanson, Klaus Kertess, and Annette Michelson, New Haven, Connecticut 1973; articles—"An Experiment in Reality: The Painting of James Bishop" by Marcelin Pleynet in *Art and Literature* (Paris), March 1964; "La Peinture et Son Sujet?" by Philippe Sollers in *Tel Quel* (Paris), Winter 1965; "Paris Letter" by Annette Michelson in *Art International* (Lugano, Switzerland), March 1965; "Post-Painterly Quattrocento" by John Ashbery in *Artnews* (New York), December 1966; "Symbol Lurking in the Wings" by Dore Ashton in *Studio International* (London), February 1967; "James Bishop: Reason and Impulse" by Robert Rosenblum in *Artforum* (New York), February 1967; "A Dying Style?" by Peter Schjeldahl in the *New York Times*, 3 May 1970; "New York Letter" by Carter Radcliff in *Art International* (Lugano, Switzerland), Summer 1970; "Pourquoi la Peinture?" by Marcelin Pleynet and "Peinture sur Peinture: James Bishop" by Philippe Sollers in *Peinture Cahiers Théoriques* (Paris), Winter 1972; "Le Couleur au Carré—Les Rides—Le Dessin" by Marcelin Pleynet in *Art International* (Lugano, Switzerland), 20 March 1972; "James Bishop" by Kenneth Baker in *Artforum* (New York), June 1972; "Once More, With Feeling" by Carter Radcliff in *Artnews* (New York), Summer 1972; "Towards A Theory and Practice of Painting: Abstract Expressionism and the Surrealist Discourse" by P. Rogers in *Artforum* (New York), March 1980; "Mostly Monochrome" by Carter Radcliff in *Art in America* (New York), April 1981.

Since the Second World War the character of art and artists has changed dramatically. Kandinsky's semi abstract and abstract work of the years 1911–14 provided a major impetus for the rediscovery of Abstract Expressionism in the 50s. This rediscovery also served as a response to the horrors made so familiar by the war: the destruction of cities and individuals, the barbarity of concentration camps and mass annihilation, found expression in paintings that spoke of violence and wounds. What started as an imperative art of protest developed into a style, or rather a whole range of styles unified by being more or less abstract

or expressionist in its free, almost vehement handling of paint and colour.

American James Bishop was among the first generation of post-war abstract expressionists who, though under the auspices of his group, is not without individual sensibility or the diversity of vision which affirms the vitality of contemporary art. Having studied at the famous Black Mountain College, Bishop was exposed to the leading figures in every domain of the avant-garde. He was also familiar with the latest artistic developments from first-hand experience in New York which were then labeled "Abstract Expressionism." During the late 50s in New York, he attempted to assimilate the important elements of Abstract Expressionism to modern art whilst avoiding the flamboyant splashes and dribbles of the de Kooning followers. As a result Bishop developed a pictorial organisation derived from the structure of the painting as a means of both controlling the flamboyance and to anchor his painting more firmly in the formal properties of its material. A contributing factor to his success is his strict insistence on using oil paint during a period when his contemporaries were relying on ubiquitous acrylics.

Bishop's method of painting is clearly his own. He first pours the oils onto a canvas placed flatly on the ground; then he tilts the stretcher so that the paint runs up to, and encroaches on, the painting's pictorial organisation, spilling over its delineations. After the paint has been applied in this manner, he reverts to a more traditional method of brushwork which allows him to control his surface, building up successive coats and paying meticulous attention to underpainting. The delicate tidal interaction between free-moving paint and the boundaries of pictorial organisation shows how Bishop plays off the gestural manner of abstract Expressionism against the more linear and structural approach of later painting.

Bishop distinguishes himself from his contemporaries by placing the crucial issue of "automatism" at the centre of his art. The notion of "psychic automatism," introduced by Breton from his reading of Freud, is the process of purging the unconscious, a preoccupation found in virtually all art, music and literature in the 20th century. Automatism plays a key role in Bishop's paintings because it answers for the mysterious disappearance in his subject matter, indeed in that of most modern art. Ironically, a close survey of his work reveals a new "subject" in the unravelled line of the classical figure.

The Surrealist provided Bishop with the necessary technique to unveil the new "subject." According to this method, the painter begins his picture with an automatic gesture in an effort to make contact with the world of his unconscious mind. First, his canvas is marked by the spontaneous impulse of the artist. Next, he uses this mark to prompt associations in his imagination so that the subject of the picture emerges in an embellishment of vivid imagery. Thus Bishop's subject seems to emanate from the interior of his painting.

In all of Bishop's paintings, his central preoccupation falls in his manipulation of rich and subtle tones of colour in a discreetly changed flow of liquid energy resulting in an intimate and withdrawn art. Collectively, these elements seem to hint at the perception of an underlying presence. The result, ironically, likens him to de Kooning, an artist primarily concerned with making and confronting an image. For Bishop, subject and image were one. Being an abstract expressionist in the 1950s meant working without apparent constraints whilst retaining something of a brand image that separated his work from another's. His art proved itself capable of remarkable refinement noting the marks made and the materials used.

—Carrie Barker

BLADEN, Ronald.

Canadian. Born in Vancouver, British Columbia, 13 July 1918. Studied at Vancouver School of Arts, and California School of Fine Arts, San Francisco. Sculptor: lives and works in New York. Awards: Rosenberg Fellowship from the San Francisco Art Association, California; National Arts Council Grant; Guggenheim Fellowship, 1970. Agent: Max Hutchinson Gallery, 138 Greene Street, New York, New York 10012. Address: 5 West 21st Street, New York, New York 10010, U.S.A.

Individual Exhibitions:

1953	Brata Gallery, New York
1955	University of British Columbia, Vancouver
1956	Six Gallery, San Francisco
1962	Green Gallery, New York
1967	Fischbach Gallery, New York
	Emily Lowe Gallery, Hofstra University, Hempstead, New York
1970	*Ronald Bladen/Robert Murray*, Vancouver Art Gallery
	Fischbach Gallery, New York
1971	Fischbach Gallery, New York
1972	Pasadena Art Museum, California
	Tyler School of Art, Philadelphia
	University of Wisconsin, Madison
	Fischbach Gallery, New York

Selected Group Exhibitions:

1963	*Paintings, Drawings and Prints Owned by Local Collectors*, The Wilmington Sociiety of the Fine Arts, Delaware Art Center
1965	*Concrete Epressionism*, Loeb Student Center, New York University
1966	*Sculpture Annual*, Whitney Museum, New York
	Primary Structures: Younger British and American Sculptors, Jewish Museum, New York
1967	*Scale as Content*, Corcoran Gallery of Art, Washington, D.C.
1968	*Minimal Art*, Gemeentemuseum, The Hague (travelled to the Akademie der Künste, Berlin; and Dusseldorf, 1968–69)
1970	*American Sculpture*, Sheldon Memorial Art Gallery, University of Nebraska Art Galleries, Lincoln
1973	*Art in Space*, Detroit Institute of Arts
1974	*Outdoor Sculpture 1974*, Merriwold West Gallery, New Jersey
1975	*Monumental Sculpture*, Janie C. Lee Gallery, Houston

Collections

Museum of Modern Art, New York; Los Angeles County Museum of Art; Albright-Knox Art Gallery, Buffalo, New York; La Jolla Museum of Art, California; South Albany Mall, New York; King Saud University, Riyadh, Saudi Arabia.

Publications:

On BLADEN: books—*Minimal Art* by Lucy Lippard and Enno Develing, Dusseldorf 1969; *Ronald Bladen/Robert Murray*, exhibition catalogue, Vancouver 1970; *Icons and Images of the 60's* by Nicolas and Elena Calas, New York 1971; articles—"Aspects of Art Called Minimal" in *Studio International* (London), April 1969, "The Artist Speaks" by Corinne Robins in *Art in America* (New York), September 1969, "Ronald Bladen/Robert Murray" by D. Cameron in *Arts-canada* (Toronto), June 1970; "Bladen and Murray: The Giants of Canadian Sculpture" by J. Lowndes in *Vie des Arts* (Montreal), Summer 1970; "New York Letter: Ronald Bladen" by G. Henry in *Art International* (Lugano, Switzerland), June 1971; "New York: Ronald Bladen" by K. Linville in *Artforum* (New York), June 1971; "Ronald Bladen" by K. Jürgen-Fischer in *Kunstwerk* (Baden-Baden, West Germany), March 1972; "Ronald Bladen" by K. Baker in *Artforum* (New York), April 1972.

Ronald Bladen has long been in the forefront of those artists seeking to realize the full potentials of abstract sculpture. Bladen was an established and exhibiting painter before he turned exclusively to sculpture in 1963. Before then he had evolved a thick, lush style of painting, influenced by Abstract Expressionism, first in San Francisco, where he lived and worked until 1957 and had maintained close connections with the city's burgeoning poetry movement of the 1950's, and then in New York City. In the last group of paintings, the "bas-reliefs", a growing concern with the physicality and object presence of these pictures that came off-the-wall is found. After some experimentation with three-dimensional paper collages. Bladen executed the first painted wood sculptures: "Untitled Construction" (1963–65) and "Untitled Construction No. 2" (1964). Like the later examples, they focused attention on the act and perception of construction. Each one offered a clear-cut presentation of the act of construction in the formation of a whole made from hard-edged geometric units like boxes, columns, and rectangular slabs joined together in an additive structure. Each one, also, focused attention on the perception of the different spaces, both the solid and void constructed by the sculptural structure. And even in these early examples is found a desire to activate the internal space of the sculpture, defined by the grid-oriented structure in "Untitled Constructivism" or the cantilevered structure in "Untitled Construction II."

Movement, whether real—in the case of the single kinetic piece "The Rockers" (1965)—or implied in the others is always a discrete matter of the precise and provocative integration of the placement, scale and contours. Bladen is able to impart strong dynamic sensations to massive and weighty forms by coordinating these factors. With "The X" (1967), these sensations invest this 23 foot high x-shaped sculpture with a tremendously forceful presence.

During the 1970's, Bladen became involved in public art, an activity that has necessitated the translation of the work, which he continues to build himself in wooden forms/models, into steel or aluminum. *Black Lightning* (1981), a black painted steel sculpture 24 foot long is based on a model executed in 1979. Its asymmetrical and sharply rhythmical forms and structures are representative of this period of the late 1970's and 1980's in his work.

An exciting recent development for Bladen is what he calls "private sculpture," a term used in acknowledgment of the speciific set of concerns distinguishing this body of work from the publiic commission pieces. Bladen has dedicated these aluminum and wood structures to the challenging task of illuminating space through the capturing of light.

The definitive way light is held its energy reflected on the shaped surfaces of the metal parts makes the sculptures like *Monarch* (1984) and *Moment* (1985) into genuinely moving experiences. Bladen here is using the objective face of the world of materials to get at the inner core of symbolic values animating the universe.

—Ronny H. Cohen

BLAKE, Peter (Thomas).

British. Born in Dartford, Kent, 25 June 1932. Studied at Gravesend Technical College, and Gravesend School of Art, Kent, 1946–51; and Royal College of Art, London, 1953–56. Served in the Royal Air Force, 1951–53. Married the artist Jann Haworth. Painter and graphic artist, London, since 1956. Recipient: Leverhulme Research Award, 1956; Guggenheim Painting Award, 1958; First Prize, *John Moores Exhibition,* Liverpool, 1961. Agent: Waddington Galleries, 2 Cork Street, London W1. Address: 8 Esmond Road, London W4, England.

Individual Exhibitions:

1962	Portal Gallery, London
1965	Robert Fraser Gallery, London
1967	*3 Painters: Peter Blake/Jim Dine/Richard Hamilton,* Midlands Arts Centre, Birmingham (travelled to Arts Council Gallery, Cambridge)
1969	Bristol City Art Gallery
	Portal Gallery, London
	Robert Fraser Gallery, London
	Leslie Waddington Prints, London
1970	Waddington Galleries, London
	Ashgate Gallery, Farnham, Surrey
1971	Peter M. David Gallery, Minneapolis
1972	Waddington Galleries, London
1973	Stedelijk Museum, Amsterdam (travelled to the Gemeentemuseum, The Hague, and the Gemeentemuseum, Arnhem, Netherlands)
	Kunstverein, Hamburg
	Palais des Beaux-Arts, Brussels
1974	Hayward Gallery, London
	Festival Gallery, Bath (with Jann Haworth)
1977	Waddington/Tooth Galleries, London
1979	Bohun Gallery, Henley-on-Thames, Oxfordshire
1980	Galleria Documenta, Turin
1983	Tate Gallery, London
	Kestner-Gesellschaft, Hannover
	Olympus Gallery, London
1984	Galerie Claude Bernard, Paris

Selected Group Exhibitions:

1954	*Summer Exhibition,* Royal Academy of Art, London
1958	*5 Painters,* Institute of Contemporary Arts, London
1964	*Carnegie International,* Carnegie Institute, Pittsburgh (and 1967)
1969	*Pop Art,* Hayward Gallery, London
1970	*Contemporary British Art,* National Museum of Modern Art, Tokyo
1976	*Arte Inglese Oggi 1960–76,* Palazzo Reale, Milan
1977	*British Painting 1952–1977,* Royal Academy of Art, London
1980	*Prints of the 70's by 6 British Artists,* National Art Gallery, Wellington (toured New Zealand)
1981	*The Brotherhood of Ruralists,* Arnolfini Gallery, Bristol (toured the U.K.)
1988	*The British Picture,* L.A. Louver Gallery, Venice, California

Collections:

Arts Council of Great Britain, London; British Council, London; Tate Gallery, London; Victoria and Albert Museum, London; Whitworth Art Gallery, Manchester; Bristol City Art Gallery; Museum Boymans-van Beuningen, Rotterdam; Wallraf-Richartz Museum, Cologne; Baltimore Museum of Art; Museum of Modern Art, New York.

Publications:

On BLAKE: books—*Peter Blake,* exhibition catalogue, with text by Robert Melville, London 1965; *3 Painters: Peter Black/Jim Dine/Richard Hamilton,* exhibition catalogue, with text by John English, Birmingham 1967; *Image as Language; Aspects of British Art 1950–1968* by Christopher Finch, London 1969; *Movements in Art since 1945* by Edward Lucie-Smith, London 1969; *Peter Blake,* exhibition catalogue, with text by Roger Coleman, Bristol 1969; *Pop Art Redefined* by John Russell and Suzi Gablik, London 1969; *Pop Art* by Michael Compton, London 1970 *English Pop Art: Figurative Art since 1945* by Robert Melville, London 1971; *Peter Blake,* exhibition catalogue, with text by Rainer Crone, Amsterdam 1973; *Peter Blake,* exhibition catalogue, with text by Uwe M. Schneede, Hamburg 1973; *Prints of the 70's by 6 British Artists,* exhibition catalogue, with text by Anne Kirker, Wellington 1980; *The Brotherhood of Ruralists* by Nicholas Usherwood, London 1981; *The British Picture,* exhibition catalogue with essays by Marina Vaizey, Catherine Lampert and William Feaver, Venice, California 1988.

The small panel surfaced with gold-leaf sheets never quite all in juxtaposition, the caparison-richness of

which is also occasionally disturbed by small abrasions betraying undercoating, is in no way typical, however early its creation stage, of the actual enduring character of the British painter Peter Blake and the essence of his works. "Painted" possibly as a Pop-art spoof, it was offered to a dealer in barter for a picture by a naïve fantasist that had caught Blake's fancy.

Yet in a way this anecdote unveils the dichotomy that invades the spirit (itself hydra-headed) of this artist's talent and personalised brilliance.

In his day Blake has given a tinpot (I was tempted to say tinsel) glitter to Pop Art at a time when it was reaching its English zenith. Not necessarily goldplated it is true, but none the less buoyant as he was neatly painting pop-realist images in carefully arresting colours on plaques of metal (seemingly tin, but probably copper) so as to meet art half-way between deliberate naivety and the echo of the old metal-based ads that used once to adorn sites where they were allowed to be nailed up (many decades before Blake was born), while at the same moment he was underlining the abiding simplicity that is the beguiling factor of so much "innocent" art.

One of the earliest of his paintings to catch the attention of the public had for subject a much-bemedalized self-portrait (again rendered in super-real honest exactitude), but this along with the sheets of metal in no fashion could place any limit on his inventiveness and the extent to which it could progress. If each of these avenues, taken together or apart, suggested an extraordinary marriage between Pop and Naïve—not Naïve in its true Art sense of course, because here was a highly sophisticated and fully-trained artist—such a quaint circumstance was to be still further expanded in near 3-dimensional set-ups with his *furniture* (Blake has always taken exceptional pleasure in the point-of-sale straight-forwardness of children's toys), and perhaps even more so with his decorated doors and their incorporated nooks and crannies alive with pin-ups, grafitti, scrappy press-cuttings even—all the pathetic short-lived enthusiast desiderata of the "with-it" poor.

In style and manner Blake had a culture breakthrough to population millions and was able to speak in visual terms in a voice that was at once direct, without art complications, and "popular."

Comes the interim . . . Since the heady days of *Swinging Britain* the artist has cooled down and, in doing so, he has joined the ranks of approved British Artists, acquiring all the rights, respect and relevance such acceptance implies. Career success assured, the quality of his works, the infusions of "reality" into them, the spontaneous innuendos (paradoxically subtle yet obvious) are untrammelled. Blake and his gifts have not been dislocated; it is the Times and the People who are out of joint.

—Sheldon Williams

BLUME, Bernhard-Johannes.

German. Born in Dortmund, in 1937. Trained as a decorative painter and graphic artist, Dortmund, 1956–60; liberal studies, under Joseph Fassbender, Kunstakademie, Dusseldorf, 1960–65; studied philosophy and art, Cologne, 1967–71. Independent painter and photo-artist, in Cologne, 1960–71, and in Bedburg, since 1971; collaborative photo-works with Anna Blume, since 1984. Agent: Galerie Philomene Magers, Handelstrasse 13, 5300 Bonn. Address: Gutenbergstrasse 10, 5000 Cologne 30, West Germany.

Individual Exhibitions:

1961	Galerie Hella Nebelung, Dusseldorf
1969	Kunstakademie, Dusseldorf
1970	Galerie Thelen/Jollenbeck, Cologne

1971 Galerie Thelen, Essen, West Germany (with Anna Blume)
1973 Galerie Thelen/Jollenbeck, Cologne
1974 Galerie Magers, Bonn
1975 Galerie Jollenbeck, Cologne
1976 Galerie Magers, Bonn (with Anna Blume)
Galerie Vor Ort, Hamburg
1977 Artothek der Stadtbucherei, Cologne
1978 Galerie Herta Klang, Cologne
Galerie AK, Frankfurt (with Maria Blume)
1979 Galerie Jollenbeck, Cologne
1980 Galerie Petersen, West Berlin (twice)
Galerie A, Amsterdam
Stedelijk Museum, Breda, Netherlands
Produzentengalerie, Hamburg
Galerie Klewan, Munich
Galerie Dany Keller, Munich
Galerie Magers, Bonn
1981 Kunstforum, Rottweil, West Germany
1982 Galerie Petersen, West Berlin
Galerie Magers, Bonn
Museum Folkwang, Essen, West Germany
Produzentengalerie, Hamburg
Galerie Krinzinger, Innsbruck, Austria
Galerie Dany Keller, Munich
1983 Galerie Peter Noser, Zurich
Kunstverein, Bonn
1984 Galerie Schurr, Stuttgart
Kunstlerhaus, Stuttgart (with Anna Blume)
Galerie Wilde, Cologne
Kunstfonds, Bonn (with Anna Blume)
Galerie AK, Frankfurt
1985 Galerie Dany Keller, Munich
1986 Galerie Magers, Bonn (with Anna Blume)
1987 Kunsthalle, Basle (with Anna Blume)
Galerie Klaus Littmann, Basle
Galerie Schiessel, Munich
1988 Portikus, Frankfurt (with Anna Blume; travelled to Cologne)
Landesmuseum, Bonn (retrospective)

Selected Group Exhibitions:

1964 *Fluxusaktionen*, Hochschule fur bildende Kunste, Dusseldorf
1969 *Anstrengungen zur Herbeibringung des Kreuzes*, Kunstakademie, Dusseldorf
1973 *Between*, Kunsthalle, Dusseldorf (travelled to London)
1976 *6 Kolner Kunstler*, Kunstverein, Cologne
1979 *Story Art*, Bonner Kunstverein, Bonn
1981 *Die Absage an das Einzelbild*, Museum Folkwang, Essen, West Germany
1982 *Mit Fotografie*, Museum Ludwig, Cologne
1984 *Kunstlandschaft Bundesrepublik*, Kunstverein, Wilhelmshaven, West Germany
1986 *Behind the Eyes: 8 German Artists*, San Francisco Museum of Modern Art
1987 *Een keuze/A choice*, Kunst RAI, Amsterdam

Publications:

By BLUME: books—*Anweisungen zum seligen Leben*, Cologne 1970; *Ideoplastie*, Cologne 1971; *Ich sehe die Gegenstande immer vor mir*, Cologne 1973; *Die vierte Dimension*, Dusseldorf 1974; *Schizo*, Cologne 1981; *Heilsgebilde*, Cologne 1983; *Naturlich, quasiphilosophisch-ideoplastischer Diavortrag*, Munich c. 1984; *Hellsehen als Schwarzsehen*, Munich 1986; *Heilig, heilig, heilig*, Munich 1986.

On BLUME: books—*Bernhard-Johannes Blume*, exhibition catalogue with texts by Gunther Schulte and Horst Walter, Bonn 1976; *Ideografien Bernhard Johannes Blumes*, exhibition catalogue with essay by Kurt Hamburger, Cologne 1977; *Polaroid Sofortbildfotografie*, exhibition catalogue with text by Johann Gerhardt Lischka, Berne 1977; *Von hier aus*, exhibition catalogue by Peter Weibel, Dusseldorf 1984; *Der vergessliche Engel* by Walter Grasskamp, Munich 1986; *Anna und Bernhard Blume: Fotos aus dem wirklichen Leben*, exhibition catalogue with introduction by Jean-Christophe Ammann, Basle 1987.

BLUME, Peter.

American. Born in Russia, 26 October 1906; emigrated to the United States, 1911: naturalized, 1919. Educated in Brooklyn public schools, and at the Educational Alliance School of Art, New York, until 1921; studied at the Art Students League, and the Beaux-Arts Academy, New York, 1921–24. Married Grace Douglas Craton in 1931. Worked briefly for a jewelry firm and a lithographic and engraving company, New York, 1920. Independent painter since 1924: established studio on 13th Street, New York, and subsequently in Patterson, New York, 1925; travelled in New England, 1926–27, and in Pennsylvania and South Carolina, 1930; established and maintains studio in Sherman, Connecticut, since 1930; travelled in Italy, France, and England, 1932; commissioned by United States Government to paint murals for Post Offices in Geneva, New York and Cannonsburg, Pennsylvania, and by local government to paint mural for the Court House in Rome, Georgia, 1941; travelled in Mexico, 1949, and in Italy and Sicily, 1952, 1956. Artist-in-Residence, American Academy, Rome, 1956, 1962, 1973. Recipient: Guggenheim Fellowship, 1932–1936; First Prize, *International Exhibition of Painting and Sculpture*, Carnegie Institute, Pittsburgh, 1934; Artists for Victory Prize, Museum of Modern Art, New York, 1942; National Institute of Arts and Letters Grant, 1947. Associate, National Academy of Design; Member, National Institute of Arts and Letters Grant, 1947. Associate, National Academy of Design; Member, National Institute of Arts and Letters. Agent: Terry Dintenfass Gallery, 50 West 57th Street, New York, New York 10019. Address: Route 1, Box 185, Sherman, Connecticut, 06784, U.S.A.

Individual Exhibitions:

1930 *Paintings*, Daniel Gallery, New York
1936 Julien Levy Galleries, New York
1941 The Downtown Gallery, New York
1947 The Downtown Gallery, New York
Durlacher Brothers Inc., New York
1949 Durlacher Brothers Inc., New York
1954 Durlacher Brothers Inc., New York
1958 Durlacher Brothers Inc., New York
1964 *Paintings and Drawings in Retrospect 1925–1964*, Currier Gallery of Art, Manchester, New Hampshire (travelled to the Wadsworth Atheneum, Hartford, Connecticut)
1968 Kennedy Galleries, New York
Recollections of the Flood and Related Works, Danenberg Gallery, New York
1970 Danenberg Gallery, New York
1975 *Bronzes about Venus*, Coe Kerr Gallery, New York
1976 *A Retrospective Exhibition*, Museum of Contemporary Art, Chicago
New Britain Museum, Connecticut (retrospective)
1980 *"From the Metamorphoses": Recent Paintings and Drawings*, Terry Dintenfass Gallery, New York

Selected Group Exhibitions

1933 *Century of Progress Exhibition I*, Art Institute of Chicago
1934 *Century of Progress Exhibition II*, Art Institute of Chicago
International Exhibition of Painting and Sculpture, Carnegie Institute, Pittsburgh
1938 *American Painting and Sculpture Annual*, Art Institute of Chicago

Collections:

Metropolitan Museum of Art, New York; Museum of Modern Art, New York; Whitney Museum, New York; Museum of Fine Arts, Boston; Williams College, Williamstown, Massachusetts; Fogg Art Museum, Harvard University, Cambridge, Massachusetts; Wadsworth Atheneum, Hartford, Connecticut; Newark Museum, New Jersey; Randolph-

Macon College, Lynchburg, Virginia; Gallery of Fine Arts, Columbus, Ohio.

Publications:

By BLUME: articles—statements in *Peter Blume: Recollections of the Flood and Related Works*, exhibition catalogue, New York 1970; statement in *Peter Blume: A Retrospective Exhibition*, catalogue, Chicago 1976; *Peter Blume: Paintings and Sculpture*, New York 1987.

On BLUME: books—*Painting in America: The Story of 450 Years* by E. P. Richardson, New York 1956; *Modern Art and the New Past* by James Thrall Soby, Norman, Oklahoma 1957; *From Realism to Reality in Recent American Painting* by Virgil Barker, Lincoln, Nebraska 1959; *Mainstreams of Modern Art* by John Canaday, New York 1959; *Paintings in the 20th Century* by Werner Haftman, 2 vols., New York 1960; *A History of American Art* by Daniel M. Mendelowitz, New York 1961; *Art: U.S.A.: Now*, edited by Lee Nordness, 2 vols., Lucerne 1962; *Peter Blume: Paintings and Drawings in Retrospect 1925-1964*, exhibition catalogue, with an introduction by Charles E. Buckley, Manchester, New Hampshire 1964; *American Art since 1900: A Critical History* by Barbara Rose, New York, 1967; *Peter Blume*, exhibition catalogue, with text by Frank Getlein, New York 1968; *Peter Blume: Recollections of the Flood and Related Works*, exhibition catalogue, New York 1970; *Peter Blume: Bronzes about Venus*, exhibition catalogue, with an introduction by Gordon Hendricks, New York 1974; *Peter Blume: A Retrospective Exhibition*, catalogue, with text by Dennis Adrian, Chicago 1976; *Peter Blume: "From the Metamorphoses": Recent Paintings and Drawings*, exhibition catalogue, with text by John Paul Driscoll, New York 1980.

During the 1930s Peter Blume produced four major paintings, and it is for these Magic Realist works that he is still best known. "Parade" (1930), "South of Scranton" (1931), "Light of the World" (1932) and "The Eternal City" (1934–37) invest contemporary scenes with a bizarre allegorical element of surreality. They are painted with a highly precise, meticulously detailed technique, using smooth contours and clear outlines, which is related with the illusionistic surrealism of Dali. Blume's earlier work had been closer to the American Precisionist vein, and his subsequent painting continued to be characterized by a detailed preparation and long term experimentation carried on with numerous sketches. Blume pursues complicated compositional schema and dramatically heightened imagery to portray humanity's struggles with a hostile world. The narrative element is unabashedly present in his works, and reality tends toward the horror/science fiction levels, especially those types of the genres which make the real into the animistic.

Most of Blume's paintings are on a rather generalized level, such as that in "Light of the World" (1932) which is a critical statement about the new technology as symbolized in the foreground and about the dark, church dominated past as depicted in the background. "The Eternal City" is Blume's most overtly political painting, directly portraying the ruthless menace of Fascism with an attitude of passionate hostility and very specific protest. In a wildly perverse and complicated setting which combines ancient Roman ruins with contemporary Roman ruins, the jack-in-the-box head of a green faced Mussolini with scowling red lips arises on his accordion-pleated "body". It is a purposefully dissonant visualization of the perversities of Italian Fascism, including two people looking toward the grotesque effigy of their leader as they come out of a primitive bomb shelter. Blume spent nearly four years exclusively developing this picture, whose combination of powerful human drama and highly skilled technique shows him at his best level of pictorial satire.

After "The Eternal City," Blume concentrated on more general human themes of struggle, always pursuing the long, slow route which produces fastidiously composed and executed paintings, in a relatively small number because each is the result of sustained periods of preparation. "The Rock" (1948) becomes the symbol of life and death, with man before it as if in judgment. "Man of Sorrows" (1951) communicates the sufferings of war.

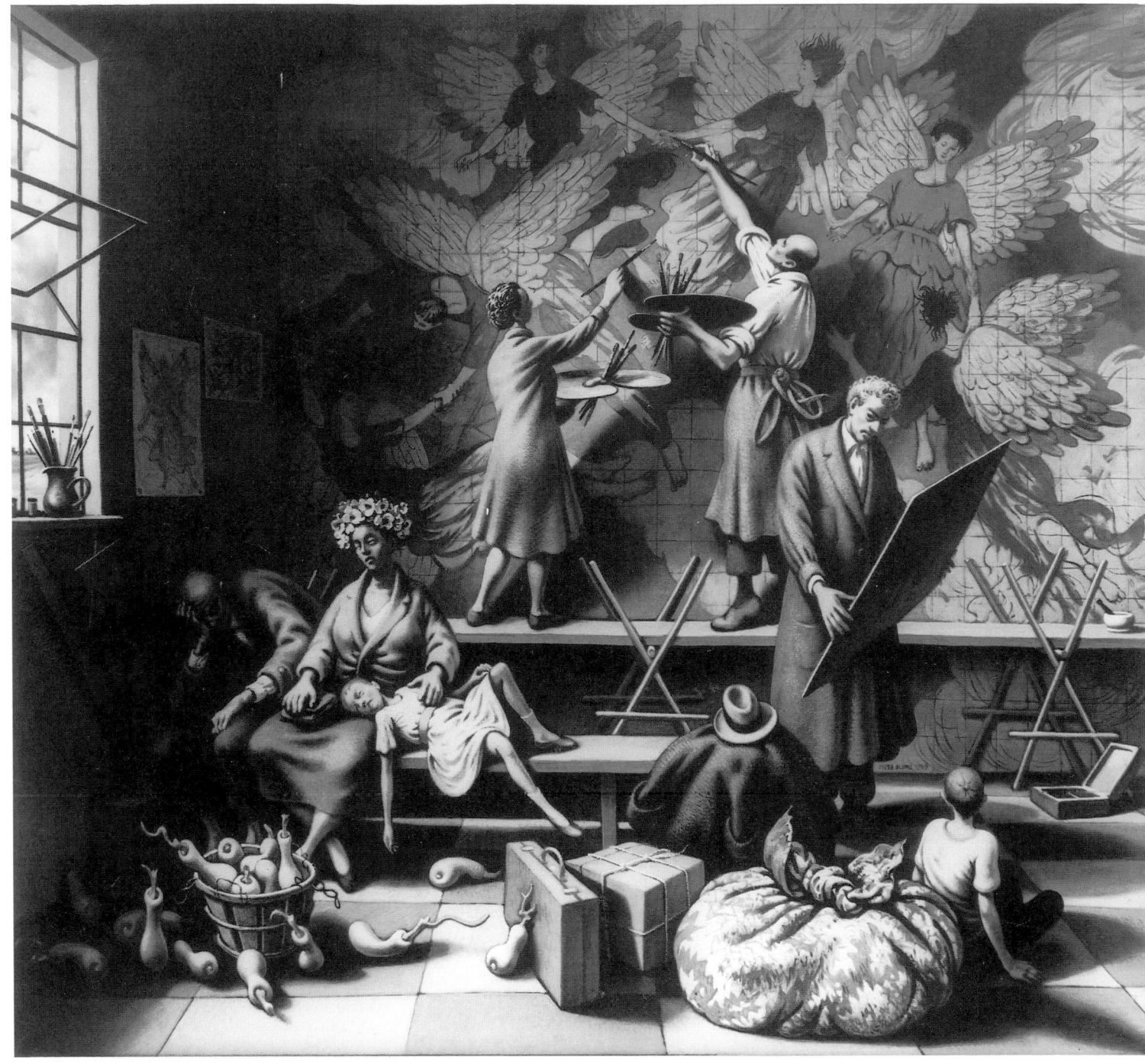

Peter Blume: *Recollection of the Flood*, 1969

Subsequent paintings portray Blume's more and more fervent involvement with Quattrocento techniques, and, in works such as "Hadrian's Villa" (1957), he lapses dangerously into dependence on the past, losing much of the potent satirical edge he had achieved earlier and remaining more in the realm of the mundane despite his always thoughtfully well-composed execution. This kind of prosaic pastorale quality continues to plague Blume's works, even in his most ambitious compositions such as "Recollection of the Flood" (1967) which, although it is skillfully composed in every detail, remains more sentimental than socially relevant, more an exercise in formal prowess than a conveyor of the human struggle. Perhaps there is a certain frustration underlying Blume's move to sculpture in the early 70's, but his series of "Bronzes About Venus" remain virtuoso displays of the classic Greek theme, refined and elegant, but beneath the level of Blume's achievements of earlier times.

—Barbara Cavaliere

BOCHNER, Mel.

American. Born in Pittsburgh, Pennsylvania, in 1940. Studied painting and philosophy at the Carnegie Institute of Technology, Pittsburgh, B.F.A. 1962. Now lives and works in New York. Instructor, School of Visual Arts, New York, since 1965. Agent: Sonnabend Gallery, 420 West Broadway, New York, New York 10012. Address: c/o School of Visual Arts, 209 East 23rd Street, New York, New York U.S.A.

Individual Exhibitions:

1966	Visual Arts Gallery, New York
1968	Galerie Konrad Fischer, Dusseldorf
	Bykert Gallery, New York
1969	Galerie Heiner Friedrich, Munich
	Ace Gallery, Los Angeles
	Yale University, New Haven, Connecticut
1970	Art and Project, Amsterdam
	Galleria Sperone, Turin
	Galleria Toselli, Milan
1971	112 Green Street Gallery, New York
	University of Rhode Island, Kingston
	Centro de Arte y Comunicacion, Buenos Aires
	Museum of Modern Art, New York
1972	Galerie Sonnabend, Paris
	Sonnabend Gallery, New York
	Lisson Gallery, London
	Hartford Art School, Connecticut
	Galerie MTL, Brussels
	Galleria Bonomo, Bari, Italy
	Galleria Toselli, Milan
1973	Galerie Sonnabend, Paris
	Sonnabend Gallery, New York
1974	Galerie Sonnabend, Paris
	Galleria Schema, Florence
	University of California Art Museum, Berkeley
1975	Sonnabend Gallery, New York
	Galerie Ricke, Cologne
1976	Sonnabend Gallery, New York
	Number and Shape, Baltimore Museum of Art

1977 Bernier Gallery, Athens
   Acconci/Bochner/LeVa, Sonnabend Gallery, New York
1978 Sonnabend Gallery, New York
   Daniel Weinberg Gallery, San Francisco
   Galleria Schema, Milan
   Galleria Schema, Florence
   Gallerie Sonnabend, Paris
1979 Galerie Art in Progress, Dusseldorf
1980 Sonnabend Gallery, New York
   Mel Bochner/Richard Serra, Massachusetts Institute of Technology, Cambridge
1981 Texas Gallery, Houston
   Daniel Weinberg Gallery, San Francisco
1982 Sonnabend Gallery, New York
   Centre de Creation Artistique, Abbaye de Senanque, Gordes, France
   Med a Mothi Galerie, Montpellier, France
1983 Sonnabend Gallery, New York
   Yarlow/Salzman Gallery, Toronto
   Daniel Weinberg Gallery, Los Angeles
   Pace Editions, New York
   Carol Taylor Gallery, Dallas, Texas
1984 Roger Ramsay Gallery, Chicago
1985 Sonnabend Gallery, New York
   Carnegie-Mellon University, Pittsburgh

Selected Group Exhibitions:

1970 *Information,* Museum of Modern Art, New York
1974 *Art and Image in Recent Art,* Art Institute of Chicago
1975 *Bochner/LeVa/Rockburne/Tuttle,* Contemporary Arts Center, Cincinnati, Ohio
1976 *Drawing Now,* Museum of Modern Art, New York
1977 *Whitney Biennale,* Whitney Museum, New York
1978 *Contemporary Drawing/New York,* University of California Museum, Santa Barbara
1979 *The Decade in Review,* Whitney Museum, New York
1981 *Murs,* Centre Georges Pompidou, Paris
1983 *Minimalism to Expressionism,* Whitney Museum, New York
1985 *New Abstraction,* Milwaukee Art Museum, Wisconsin

Collections:

Los Angeles County Museum of Art; Musée National d'Art Moderne, Paris.

Publications:

By BOCHNER: books—*Working Drawings and Other Visible Things on Paper,* New York 1966; *The Singer Notes,* New York 1968; *10 Misunderstandings (A Theory of Photography),* New York 1970; *Notes on Theory,* Kingston, Rhode Island 1971; *11 Excerpts,* Paris 1972; *Primer,* Milan 1973; *(Toward) Axiom of Indifference,* New York 1975; articles— "Less is Less (for Dan Flavin)" in *Art and Artists* (London), 1966; "Primary Structures" in *Art Magazine* (New York), June 1966; "Domain of the Great Bear (Hayden Planetarium)" in *Art Voices* (New York), Summer 1966; "Art in Process" in *Arts* (New York), October 1966; "The Beach Boys—100%" in *Arts Magazine* (New York), March 1967; "Serial Art (Systems. Solipsism)" in *Arts Magazine* (New York), Summer 1967, reprinted in *Minimal Art,* edited by Gregory Battcock, New York 1968; "The Serial Attitude" in *Artforum* (New York), December 1967; "Compilation for Robert Mangold" in *Art International* (Lugano), April 1968; "Alphaville, Godard's Apocalypse" in *Art International* (New York), May 1968; "7 Discrete Tiers" in *Aspen Magazine* (Colorado), June 1968; "Background Is Not the Margin" in *Art in Process* (New York), no. 4, 1969; "No Thought Exists . . . " in *Arts Magazine* (New York), April 1970; "Excerpts from Speculation" in *Artforum* (New York), May 1970; "3 Conditions" in *Art and Project Bulletin 27* (Amsterdam), September 1970; "10 Hypotheses de Travail" in *VH* (Paris), Fall 1970; "Bullshit" in *Artforum* (New York), October 1970; "Mental Exercise: No. 1 Counting" in *Data* (Milan), February 1972; "Concerning the Art of Dorothea Rockburne" in *Artforum* (New York), March 1972; "Parenthetical Reflections on 5 Earlier Statements" in *Flash Art* (Milan), May 1972 and in *Arts Magazine* (New York), Summer 1972; statement in *Some Recent American Art,* exhibi-

tion catalogue, by Jennifer Licht, New York 1973; "Interview", with L. Haller, in *Flash Art* (Milan), June 1973; "Book Review" in *Artforum* (New York), June 1973; "On Malevich", interview with John Coplans, in *Artforum* (New York), June 1974; "Statement on My Prints" in *Prints,* exhibition catalogue, Toronto 1975; films—*Walking a Straight Line Through Grand Central Station,* 1965; *NYC Windows,* 1965; *Dorothea in 15 Positions Stasis,* 1970.

On BOCHNER: books—*Mel Bochner,* exhibition catalogue, Milan 1971; *Mel Bochner,* exhibition catalogue, Buenos Aires 1972; *Line as Language: 6 Artists Draw,* exhibition catalogue, by Rosalind Krauss, Princeton, New Jersey 1974; *Mel Bochner/Barry LeVa/Dorothea Rockburne/Richard Tuttle,* exhibition catalogue, Cincinnati, Ohio 1975; *Drawing Now,* exhibition catalogue, by Berenice Rose, New York 1976; *Mel Bochner: Number and Shape,* exhibition catalogue, by Brenda Richardson, Baltimore 1976; *Mel Bochner 1973-1985,* exhibition catalogue, Pittsburgh 1985.

BOETTI, Alighiero E.
Italian. Born in Turin, 16 December 1940. Married Anne Marie Sauzeau; children: Matteo and Agata. Independent artist, Turin, 1965–72, and in Rome since 1972. Established the "One Hotel", Kabul, Afghanistan, 1971–73. Agent: Galleria Christian Stein, Via Lazzaretto 15, 20124 Milan. Address: Via del Pantheon 57, 00186 Rome, Italy.

Individual Exhibitions:

1967 Galleria Christian Stein, Turin
   Galleria La Bertesca, Turin
1968 Galleria De Nieuborg, Milan
   Galleria Sperone, Turin
   Galleria Christian Stein, Turin
1970 Galleria Toselli, Milan
   Galleria Acme, Brescia, Italy
   Aktionsraum I, Munich
1971 Galerie Konrad Fischer, Dusseldorf
   Galleria Sperone, Turin
1972 Galleria Toselli, Milan
1973 Galleria Marilena Bonomo, Bari, Italy
   John Weber Gallery, New York
   Galleria Sperone-Fischer, Rome
   Galerie MTL, Brussels
   Art and Project, Amsterdam
   Galleria Toselli, Milan
1974 Kunstmuseum, Lucerne
   Galleria Sperone, Turin
1975 John Weber Gallery, New York
   Galerie Annemarie Verna, Zurich
   Galleria Sperone, Rome
   Galleria Pascuala Trioprio, Naples
   Galleria Area, Florence
   Zwei Area Galerie, Munich
   Saman Gallery, Genoa
1976 Studio Marconi, Milan
   Galleria Lia Rumma, Naples
   Galleria d'Alessandro Ferranti, Rome
   Galleria Banco, Brescia, Italy
1977 Galleria Marlborough, Rome
   Galleria dell'Ariete, Milan
   Centre d'Art Contemporain, Geneva
   Galerie Annemarie Verna, Zurich
1978 Kunsthalle, Basle
   Galleria Christian Stein, Turin
   Galleria Mario Diacono, Bologna
   Galerie Paul Maenz, Cologne
   Galleria il Cortile, Rome
   Galleria Giuliana de Crescenzo, Rome
1979 Chiostro di Voltorre, Gavirate, Italy
1980 Salvatore Ala Gallery, New York
   Art Agency Gallery, Tokyo
   Galleria Banco, Brescia, Italy
1981 Galerie Chantal Crousel, Paris
   Galleria LP220, Turin (twice)
   Galleria Banco, Brescia, Italy

1982 Galleria Mario Diacono, Rome
   Galerie Annemarie Verna, Zurich
   Galleria Franco Toselli, Milan
1983 Galleria Mario Pieroni, Rome
   Galleria LP 220, Turin
   Galleria Giorgio Persano, Turin
   Galleria Enzo Cannaviello, Milan
1984 Faculty of Architecture, University of Rome
   Galerie Eric Franck, Geneva
   Galleria LP 220, Turin
   John Weber Gallery, New York
   Pinacoteca di Ravenna, Italy
1985 Galleria Il Cortile, Rome
   Galleria Marilena Bonomo, Bari, Italy
   Galleria Pero, Miozawo, Italy
   Galleria Chisel, Genova
1986 Le Nouveau Musée, Lyon, France
   Galerie Pietro Sparta, Chagny, France
   Michael Klein Inc., Amsterdam
   Galerie Susan Wyss, Zurich
   Van Abbemuseum, Eindhoven, Netherlands
   Villa Arson, Nice, France
1987 Galleria Lucio Amelio, Naples
   Galleria Christian Stein, Milan
   Galleria Sergio Casoli, Milan
   Galleria Alessandra Bonomo, Rome

Selected Group Exhibitions:

1967 *Arte Povera,* Galleria La Bertesca, Genoa (toured Italy)
1968 *Prospect 68,* Städtische Kunsthalle, Dusseldorf (and *Prospect 69*)
1969 *When Attitudes Become Form,* Kunsthalle, Berne (toured Europe)
1970 *Conceptual Art/Arte Povera/Land Art,* Galleria Civica d'Arte Moderna, Turin
1972 *Documenta 5,* Kassel, West Germany
1974 *8 Contemporary Artists,* Museum of Modern Art, New York
1978 *La Traccia del Racconto,* Villa Comunale Ormond, San Remo, Italy
1981 *Identité Italienne,* Centre Georges Pompidou, Paris
1984 *Il Modo Italiano,* California State University, Northridge
1987 *Arte Povera,* Galerie Durand Dessert, Paris

Collections:

Museo Sperimentale, Turin; Galleria Civica d'Arte Moderna, Turin; Stedelijk Museum, Amsterdam; Museum of Modern Art, New York.

Publications:

By BOETTI: books—*Insicuro Noncurante,* Genoa 1976; *Classifying the thousand longest rivers in the world,* with Anne Sauzeau Boetti, Rome 1977; *Alighiero Boetti,* exhibition catalogue, with Guido Fuaga, Rome 1977; *Alighiero & Boetti,* exhibition catalogue, Milan 1979; *Da uno a dieci,* edited by Rosellina Archinto, Milan 1980.

On BOETTI: books—*Alighiero Boetti,* exhibition catalogue, with texts by Henry Martin, Germano Celant and Tomasso Trini, Turin 1967; *Nuove Dimensioni della Scultura* by Udo Kultermann, Milan 1968; *7th Paris Biennale: Italy,* edited by Achille Bonito Oliva, Rome 1971; *Documenta 5: Befragung der Realität,* edited by Harald Szemann and others, Kassel, West Germany 1972; *Art Annual 73-74,* edited by Willem Sandberg, Cologne 1973; *6 Years: The Dematerialization of the Art Object* by Lucy R. Lippard, New York 1973; *8 Contemporary Artists,* exhibition catalogue, New York 1974; *Alighiero E. Boetti,* exhibition catalogue, with text by Jean-Christophe Ammann, Lucerne 1974; *Segni e disegni: Alighiero e Boetti 1976,* exhibition catalogue, Rome 1977; *Alighiero Boetti, La festa dell'immaginario visivo,* exhibition catalogue, edited by Tommaso Trini, Gavirate 1979; *Boetti,* exhibition catalogue, edited by Alberto Boatto, Ravenna 1984.

In 1969 Alighiero Boetti produced his "Little Traced Squares," a work which epitomizes his basic princi-

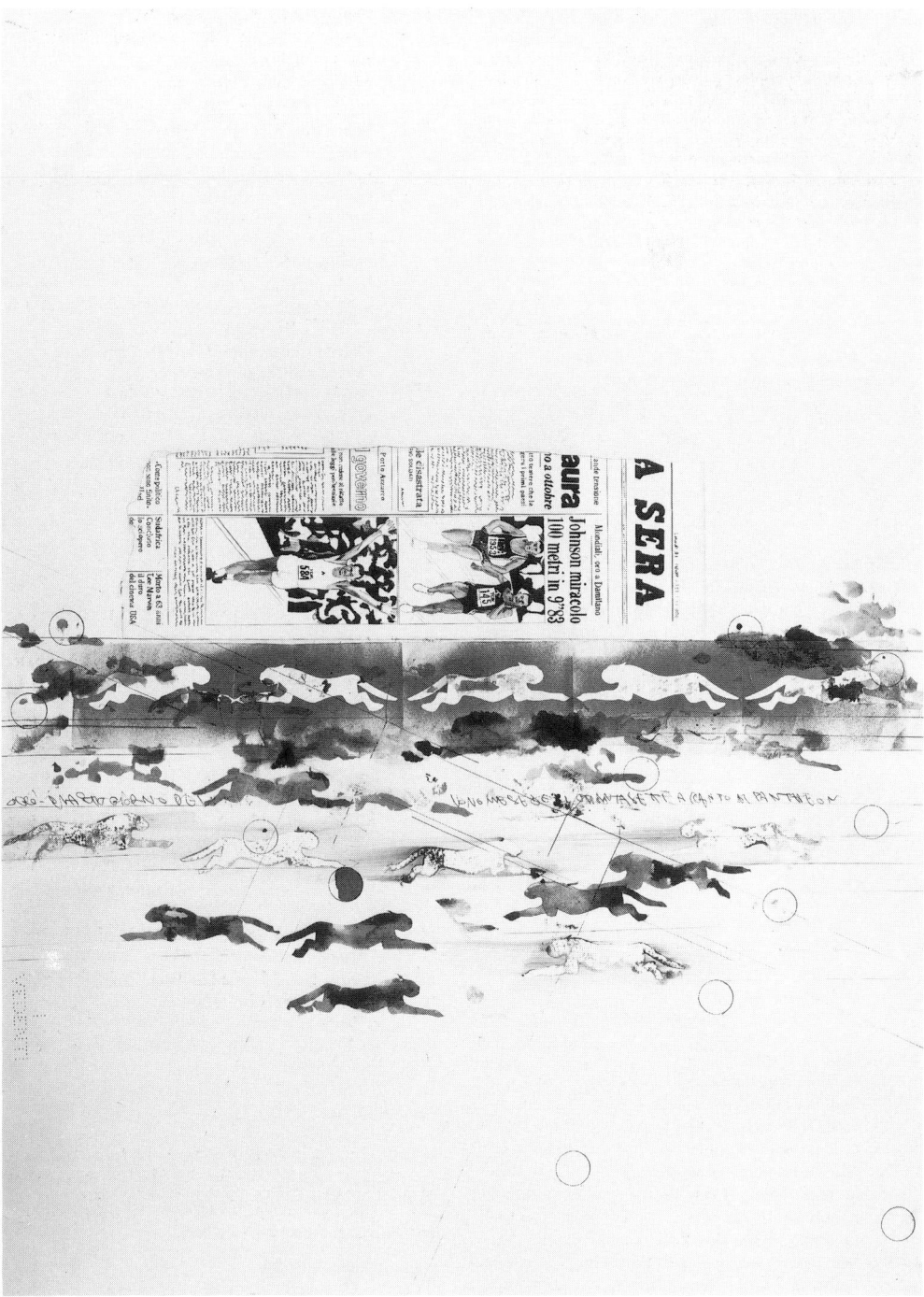

Alighiero Boetti: *Untitled*, 1985

BOEYEN, Mari.
Dutch. Born in Mook, Limbourg, 17 February 1951. Studied at Koninklijke Academie voor Kunst en Vormgevings, Hertogenbosch, 1968-71; Ateliers '63, Haarlem, 1971-73. Married Manny Kol in 1973 (divorced). Travelled in France and Germany, 1973, 1974 and 1975. Film Board Member, Ministry of Culture, The Hague, 1973. Address: Jacobijnestraat 21, Haarlem, Netherlands.

Individual Exhibitions:

1974   Groninger Museum voor Stad en Lande, Groningen, Netherlands
        Galerie het Venster, Rotterdam
        Galerie Yaki Kornblitt, Amsterdam
1975   Galerie Waalkens, Finsterwolde, Netherlands
1976   *Werken 1974-1976,* Van Abbemuseum, Eindhoven, Netherlands
        Hal Bromm Gallery, New York
1978   P.I.A.C., Amsterdam
1979   Galleria Peccolo, Livorno, Italy
        Museum Fodor, Amsterdam
1981   Galleria Peccolo, Livorno, Italy
1983   Haags Gemeentemuseum, The Hague
        Galerie Felison, Velzen, Netherlands (with R. de Vries)
1984   Frans Hals Museum, Haarlem (with S. Buisman and F. Benjamins)
        K.C.B. Gallery, Bergen, Norway
        Kruithuis, Den Bosch, Netherlands
1985   Galerie Suzanne Biederberg, Amsterdam

Selected Group Exhibitions:

1973   *Einde, Begin . . . ,* Noord Brabants Museum, Hertogenbosch, Netherlands
        8th Biennale de Paris, Musée d'Art Moderne, Paris
1974   *11 Dutch Artists,* Fruit Market, Edinburgh (travelled to the Aberdeen Museum, Scotland)
        Film als Beeldend Medium, Kunsthistorisch Instituut, Groningen, Netherlands
1975   *9th Biennale de Paris,* Musée d'Art Moderne, Paris
1976   *Photography as an Artwork,* Belgrade (toured Yugoslavia)
1978   *A Photo,* Studio Marconi, Milan (travelled to Rome and Antwerp)
        10 Jonge Nederlandse Kunstenaars, Stedelijk Museum, Amsterdam
1979   *Beelden van de eigen werkelijkheid,* Van Reekum Galerie, Apeldoorn, Netherlands
1980   *Camere Incantate,* Palazzo Reale, Milan
1983   *Ruimtelijk werk,* Gemeentemuseum/Akademie, Arnhem, Netherlands
1985   *Bienale van Noord Holland,* De Vaart, Hilversum, Netherlands

Collections:

Frans Hals Museum, Haarlem; Stedelijk Museum, Amsterdam.

Publications:

By BOEYEN: films—*Door I,* 1972; *Door II,* 1972; *Tripod,* 1972; *Sheet,* 1972; *Glasses,* 1973; *Turning Around,* 1973; *Self-Portrait Painting,* 1974; *The Expression of the Square,* 1974.

On BOEYEN: books—*Mari Boeyen,* exhibition catalogue, by Poul ter Hofstede, Groningen, Netherlands 1974; *11 Dutch Artists,* exhibition catalogue, by Caroline Tisdall, Edinburgh 1974; *Film als Geeldend Medium,* exhibition catalogue, by Lon de Vries-Robbe, Groningen, Netherlands 1974; *Mari Boeyen: Werken 1974-1976,* exhibition catalogue, introduction by R. H. Fuchs, Eindhoven, Netherlands 1976; *Europe—America: The Different Avant-Garde* by Achille Bonita Oliva, Milan 1976; *A Photo,* exhibition catalogue, Milan 1978; *10 Jonge Nederlandse Kunstenaars,* exhibition catalogue, Amsterdam 1978; *Beelden van de eigen werkelijkheid,* exhibition catalogue, Apeldoorn 1979; *Camere Incantate,* ex-

ples as an artist. Here he has taken a sheet of paper and traced on it, in pencil, a series of squares, thereby giving us an elemental situation which invites an endless series of interpretations, each with its own formal effect.

In all of his work Boetti uses this basic device of a minimalist whole with functional parts. Each work contains a secret, but a secret which is full of mysteries and possibilities. He has given us "Ping Pong," two signs placed close to each other which light up in turn and read, first "ping," then "pong." The spaces opened up by such works permit the perception of different units which are infinitely suggestive; and his works also set up elaborate cross-references among themselves which we are meant to recognize.

Different rhythms, gestures, repetitions, deliberate artifice—all of these are the basic elements of Boetti's experiments, and each work is designed to reflect a certain kind of mental operation or thought-process; for him art *is* really the manifestation of these processes.

In some instances the results are analytical and follow the pattern of elementary mathematical operations. This is the case, for example, with his "Alternating From 1 to 100" (1970) and "The Four Operations" (1980), in which the play of numbers and letters is reduced to a minimum: the end result is always the same, whether the process involved is addition, subtraction or multiplication. In other works—"Producing the World," for example, or "Other and Disorder"—he suggests an underlying creative, cosmic force. The basic elements remain the same but they now contain a much broader range of implications.

Recently Boetti has perfected a technique which synthesizes his earlier, more abstract concerns with a new regard for colour and subject matter. By incorporating bits of pre-existing objects (coins, stamps, and so forth) he has produced collages which give us a new, experessive symbolic language.

—Roberto G. Lambarelli

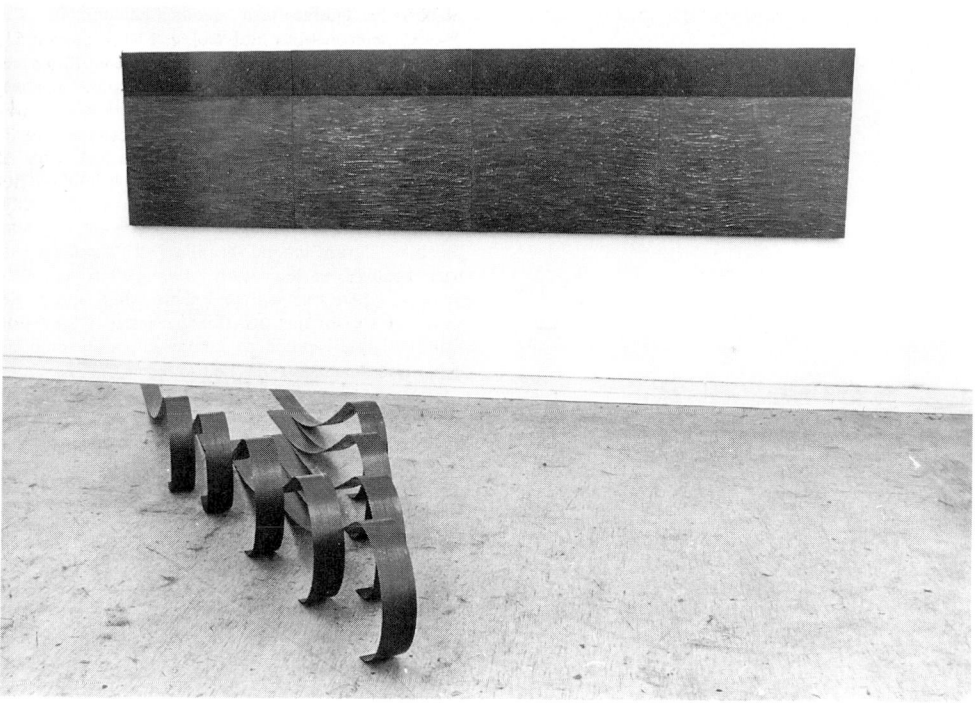

Mari Boeyen: *Ode I*, 1986

hibition catalogue, Milan 1980; *De eigen Ruimte* by P. Hefting, Amsterdam 1986; articles—"Intelligent spel me fotos" by Rudi Fuchs in *Niewe Rotterdamse Courant* (Rotterdam), July 1974; "Mari Boeyen" in *Flash Art* (Milan), February/March 1975.

The formula "art as reflection on art" covered both Conceptual and analytical painting. However (since every formula prefers definition to "nuance"), one basic fact was still left in the shade. While the reflection in Conceptual art was actuated only on the level of mental abstraction, putting forward for instance logical propositions on the general terms of art and regarding the importance of the material inscription of the work as superfluous, in the practice of analytical painting the reflection on the actual artistic operation was explained by means of investigation of the intrinsic potentialities of the material. Thus the material, the "basis" of the work of art, is not used with a view to the construction of definite "pictures" and a higher level of internal articulation; it does not "disappear in use"; on the contrary, it is made the object of an analysis that tests out its resistances and its possibilities.

Heir of the illustrious Dutch tradition of the period after the first World War, Mari Boeyen puts into his works the precision, the mental sharpness and the intrinsic rationality of a logical syllogism. When he made so many photographs of a pavement (this was in one of his old works) by setting them in rows, he cut and arranged them so that the connections between the tiles result in a form of detailed inscription. A demonstration, no more and no less, that it is possible to produce layers of codified meaning even starting from the phenomenal chaos of random everyday things. That it is possible therefore to prime the rational project not only by means of purely mental data but also by emphasizing the meaning by withdrawing it from the immediate living reality. "The material employed" could then take on the quality of Mari Boeyen's work.

The concreteness of the subject does not vanish; it is not volatilized by being concealed in a purely mental sphere, but is "displayed," "made clear" together with the psychological process which the artist has practised on it. It may be that the broad sector of artistic experimentation descended from rationalism, from a wholly European analytical process, does not respond today to the current pressures of a return to Significance and Metaphor. But its heredity is not dis-

regarded; it is not possible today, in the 1980s, for us to reconstruct a virginity—neither of feelings nor of intellect.

—Massimo Carboni

BOEZEM, Marinus.

Dutch. Born in Leerdam, 28 January 1934. Educated at the Akademie Artibus, Utrecht; Vrije Akademie, The Hague. Married Maria-Rosa Busato in 1966; daughter: Natasia. Discovered air as a plastic material, 1963; the shadow as suggestion of light, time and space, 1968; "artificial natureimpressions," 1968; Member, Council of Art of the Government of the Netherlands, 1976–80. Professor of Art, Architecture Section, Technical University of Delft, since 1979. Agent: Art and Project, 36 Willemsparkweg, Amsterdam 1007. Address: Bellinkstraat 25, 4331 gv Middelburg, Netherlands.

Individual Exhibitions:

1964	*Hommage à Marilyn Monroe*, Galerie Leiden, Netherlands
	Galerie Punt 31, Dordrecht, Netherlands (with Jan van Munster)
1965	Galerie 845, Amsterdam (with Jan van Munster)
	Dromedaris, Enkhuizen, Netherlands (with Jan van Munster)
1968	*Air Environment*, Galerie Swart, Amsterdam
	Boezem/Van Elk, Galleria Nuova Loggia, Bologna (with Ger Van Elk)
1969	*Korenveld*, Kunstkring, Rotterdam (with Ger Van Elk)
1970	Studium Generale, Economics High School, Rotterdam
	Modern Art Agency, Naples
	Art and Project, Amsterdam
	Boezem/Panamarenko, Stedelijk Van Abbemuseum, Eindhoven, Netherlands
1971	Yellow Now Gallery, Liège, Belgium
1975	Galerie Het Badhuis, Gorinchem, Netherlands

1976	Gemeentemuseum, The Hague
1978	Galerie Media, Neuchâtel, Switzerland
	Art Fair, Bologna
	Multi Art Points, Amsterdam
	Galleria Ferrari, Verona
1979	*Space Sculptures*, De Vleeshal, Middelburg, Netherlands
1980	Kunstcentrum Het Badhuis, Gorinchem, Netherlands
1981	Galerie Media, Neuchâtel, Switzerland
1982	Provinciaal Museum, Hasselt, Belgium
	De Vleeshal, Middelburg, Netherlands
	Musée Grenoble, France
1983	*Toren-Project*, at the *Festival De Stad*, Arnheim, Netherlands
	Galerie Media, Neuchatel, Switzerland
1984	Galerie Muller-Roth, Stuttgart
1985	Galerie Peter van Beveren, Rotterdam
	Anthony Reynolds Gallery, London
	Galerie Waalkens, Finsterwolde, Netherlands
1986	Galerie Muller-Roth, Stuttgart
1987	Wilhelm-Hack-Museum, Ludwigshafen, West Germany

Selected Group Exhibitions:

1968	*Les Structures Gonflables*, Musée d'Art Moderne de la Ville, Paris
1969	*Op Losse Schroeven*, Stedelijk Museum, Amsterdam
	When Attitudes Become Form, Kunsthalle, Berne
1970	*Between Man and Matter*, at the *Biennale*, Metropolitan Museum of Modern Art, Tokyo (travelled to the Kyoto Municipal Art Museum, and the Aichi Prefectural Art Gallery, Nagoya)
1979	*L'estetico e il selvaggio*, Galleria Civica, Modena
1981	*Contemporary Art from the Netherlands*, Museum of Contempory Art, Chicago (travelled to the Brooklyn Museum, New York; Little Rock Museum, Arkansas; La Jolla Museum, California; and the Art Gallery of Ontario, Toronto)
1983	*Ruimtelijk Werk*, Gemeentemuseum, Arnhem, Netherlands
1986	*Tu es Pierre*, Fonds Regional d'Art Contemporain, Limoges, France
1987	*Flags of 12 Artists*, Musée d'Art et d'Hisoire, Geneva

Collections:

Museum Boysmans van Beuningen, Rotterdam; Haags Gemeentemuseum, The Hague; Stedelijk Museum, Amsterdam; Van Abbemuseum, Eindhoven, Netherlands; Kunsthaus, Zurich; Musée Cantonal des Beaux Arts, Lausanne, Switzerland; Musée de Grenoble, France.

Publications:

By BOEZEM: books—*Boezem Airobjects*, 1966; *Paper-Events*, Antwerp 1970; *Anti-Art and Visual Education*, photo book, The Hague 1970; *Press-Art-Project*, Gorinchem, Netherlands 1974; *Podio del Mondo per l'Arte*, Middelburg, Netherlands 1975; films—*Sand-Fountain*, 1969; *Project Hoogland Church*, 1971; *A Little Breeze in May*, 1974.

On BOEZEM: books—*Boezem/Van Elk*, exhibition catalogue, with text by Renato Barilli, Bologna 1968; *Op Losse Schroeven*, exhibition cagalogue, text by W. Beeren, Amsterdam 1969; *Von Hodler zur Antiform* by Harold Szeeman, Berne 1970; *Boezem-Panamarenko*, exhibition catalogue, Eindhoven, Netherlands 1970; *Contemporary Art from the Netherlands*, exhibition catalogue, Chicago 1981; *Marinus Boezem*, exhibition catalogue, Grenoble, France 1982; *Marinus Boezem: La Lumière Cistercienne Clairvaux*, exhibition catalogue, Ludwigshafen 1987; articles—"Dall 'Olanda'" by Piero Gilardi in *Flash Art* (Milan), June 1968; "Primary Energy and the Micromotive Artists" by Piero Gilardi in *Artsmagazine* (New York), September/October 1968; "Imagination Takes Command" by Tommaso Trini in *Domus* (Milan), February 1969; "Dutch Artists on Television" by Carel Blotkamp in *Studio International* (London), June 1971; "Education and Art" by Frans Haks in *Museumjournaal* (Amsterdam), December 1974; "Narrative Art" by Liesbeth Brandt Corstius in *Museumjournaal* (Amsterdam), March 1975.

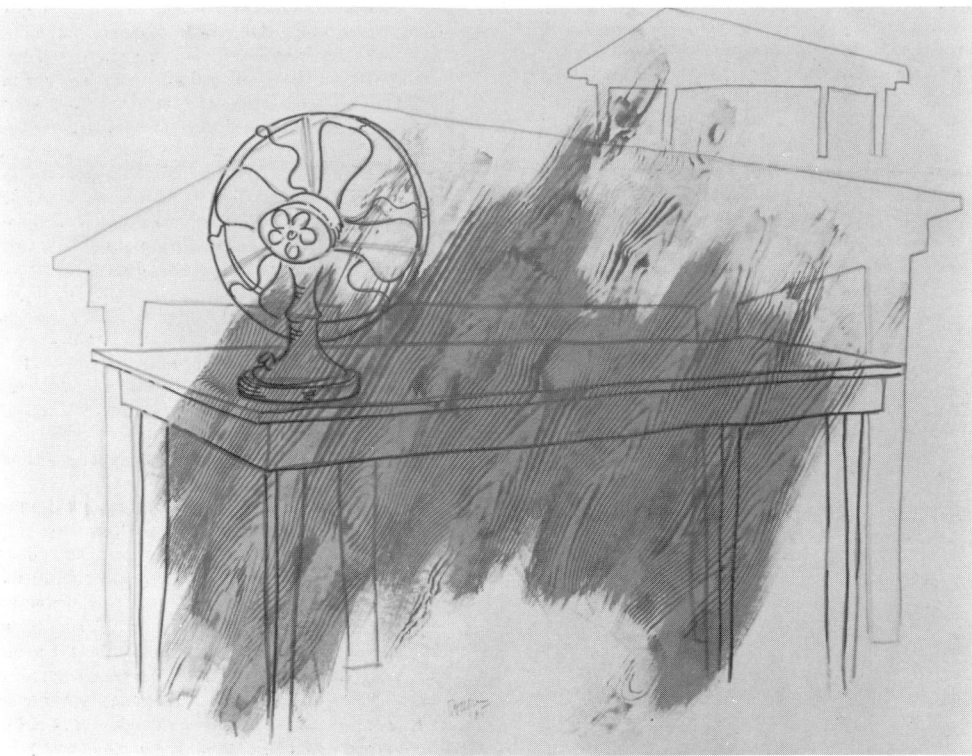

Marinus Boezem: *Untitled,* 1984

The world as the complement of the work of art.

In the course of years an image of my work has grown which cannot be described on formal grounds of conformity of form and/or material. The basic theme of these works is, over and over again, the search for a new concept in which art becomes art: the context of the work of art as its necessary complement.

The works all have much in common; they evoke a new "environment," interacting with the work. Both components thus form the work of art. The works do not refer to themselves. They endeavor to formulate a new context. As such, I do not make a "profile" of reality to reach a specialization of it, but place the spectator himself in the process of searching for that reality.

The works that originated in the 60's already point in this direction: both "Wind-Tables" (1968) and the photographic work "To Sign the Sky by an Aeroplane" (1968).

In the more recent works, this idea of interaction between the work and the spectator is materialized again, such as in the mirror-project "space-sculpture" (1978), in which two large mirrors are placed in the center of the exhibition room, the reflecting sides facing each other. Space and time are here expressed in themselves, not dependent on the surrounding architecture. This work, on the one hand, is a materially space-determining sculpture: dividing the physical space; on the other hand, it creates its own context as a concept.

The "wallpaper-project" (1970), later realized at the Gemeentemuseum in The Hague, also reacts to the physical quality of the museum room. For me, this means searching for expression and significance in the classical conception of sculpture as illustrated in a later work titled "Jump" (1981), in which I try to epitomize a classical socle.

This socle, placed in space with only my shoes on it, is in front of a wall which has a life-size photograph of myself, seen as background. Here, then, is a connection between plastic art and flat level. Hopefully, a dimension is created out of the shoes to the wall to sculpture.

In recent years, I was also engaged in studying gothic space, which apart from its specific form and rhythm, develops its own mythology as a metaphor. Such metaphors are used as a datum to suggest new spaces and to evoke new dimensions of them. The ground-plan as a given structure is used here to attain a new interpretation of sculpture.

My works try to illustrate a process of research in which the staging and interim results are shown by means of the works of art. That is why these works lack the stamp of a trademark. They attempt to approximate my own obsessions with relation to reality from a plural point of view, as if answers could be found.

—Marinus Boezem

From the very start, Marinus Boezem has made clear that his artistic activities were not to be hampered by the traditional painter's and sculptor's materials. In the year 1966, in a privately published booklet, he states that already in 1963 he discovered air 'as a purification, as a reality, as a conquest of space'. Boezem identifies air with freedom and he considers man himself 'as an object of art'.

In 1968 he shows his famous *Windtables,* covered with lightweight white cloth that is moved to wave by a ventilator. The atmosphere created by these Tables is poetically suggestive and, because of the empty cloth, brings some good painterly associations to the fore. During these years, around 1970, Boezem's work can be seen at international exhibitions like *Op Losse Schroeven* (Stedelijk Museum, Amsterdam, 1969). For this show he proposed to give a number of gigantic white sheets some airing by opening the huge first floor windows of the museum and let these hang over the window-sill out in the open.

Contrary to his colleagues Jan Dibbets and Ger van Elk, Boezem's work has retained a process-like character; he has not chosen a production of traditionally framed objects. Already in 1969 he demonstrated the expansive but at the same time substantially non-permanent status of an individual signature in a piece called *Sign the sky above the port of Amsterdam with an areoplane.* Another piece, dating from 1967 and realised in 1981, illustrates the possibility of combining a heavy, unmovable form with a never ending process. Boezem measures the outline of the shadow of a given tree, at a certain time of a certain day, and fills this with a black granite. As the tree in the course of time grows and changes, and correspondingly the shadow, the granite form becomes autonomous as a three-dimensional piece of sculpture.

From 1980 onwards Boezem has concentrated on a new project, the 'Etude Gothique'. At its starting point is the groundplan of a gothic cathedral, a continuously recurrent motif that functions as the vehicle for various images, including many self-portrayals. A recent manifestation is the planting of poplars literally following the lines of a cathedral plan. Within a number of years the trees will touch the sky and sheep will graze among its pillars. This project has been realised in the newly developed Ysselmeer-polders, where one will find some other large-scale works of art, for instance Robert Morris' Observatorium, originally proposed for the important outdoor exhibition *Sonsbeek buiten de Perken* in 1971.

Boezem works at the fringe of the artistic scene in Holland, in the quiet provincial town of Middelburg in Zealand. In this city, together with his wife Maria-Rosa, he yearly organizes a symposium where artists, critics and audience meet in a well motivated and concentrated atmosphere.

—A. F. Wagemans

BOLOTOWSKY, Ilya.

American. Born in Petrograd, Russia, 1 July 1907; emigrated to the United States 1923: naturalized, 1929. Educated at the College of St. Joseph, Istanbul, 1921–23, and the National Academy of Design, New York, 1924–30. Travelled in Europe, 1932; influenced by the Mondrians in the Gallatin Collection, and the Mirós at the Pierre Matisse Gallery, leading to first abstract work, 1933; Member of *The Ten* with Rothko, Gottlieb and others, in the mid-1930s; active member of the WPA Federal Arts Project Program, 1935–40; co-founder and charter member of American Abstract Artists, 1936; co-founder of Federation of Modern Painters and Sculptors, 1939; began collecting North West Coast Indian and Eskimo art 1942; emergence of Mondrian-influenced Neo-Plastic style, 1945. Acting Head of Department, Black Mountain College, North Carolina, 1946–48; Associate Professor of Art, University of Wyoming, Laramie, 1948–57; Adjunct Professor, Brooklyn College, New York, 1954–56; Professor of Art, State Teachers' College, New Paltz, New York, 1957–65; Adjunct Professor of Art, Hunter College, New York, 1963–64; Professor Art, University of Wisconsin at Whitewater, 1965–71; Visiting Professor of Art, University of New Mexico, Albuquerque, 1969; Lecturer, Graduate School of Fine Arts, Columbia University, New York, 1970; Adjunct Professor, graduate honors course, Queens College, New York, 1973; retired from teaching 1976; Artist-in-Residence, Fort Wayne Museum of Art, Indiana, 1978. Recipient: 1st Prize for Drawing, 1925, 1926, and Hallgarten Prize for Painting, National Academy of Design, New York, 1929–30; Scholarship, Tiffany Foundation, New York, 1929–30; Fellowship, Yaddo Foundation, Saratoga Springs, New York, 1933; Grant, Museum of Non-Objective Painting, New York, 1941; Grant for Experimental Film Work, University of Wyoming Graduate School, Laramie, 1953–54; First Prize for Painting, Sharon Creative Arts Foundation, Connecticut, 1959; First Prize for Metanoia, *Midwest Film Festival,* University of Chicago, 1963; Abstract Painting Prize, National Institute of Arts and Letters, 1971; Guggenheim Foundation Grant, 1973. Agent: Grace Borgenicht Gallery, 1018 Madison Avenue, New York, New York 10021. *Died (in New York City) 22 November 1981.*

Individual Exhibitions:

1930   G.R.D. Studios, New York
1946   New Art Circle, J. B. Neumann, New York

1947 The Pinacotheca, New York
1950 The Rose Fried Gallery (The Pinacotheca), New York
1952 New Art Circle, J. B. Neumann, New York
1954 Grace Borgenicht Gallery, New York
1956 Grace Borgenicht Gallery, New York
1958 Grace Borgenicht Gallery, New York
1959 Grace Borgenicht Gallery, New York
1959 Grace Borgenicht Gallery, New York
1960 State University College, New Paltz, New York
1961 Grace Borgenicht Gallery, New York
1963 Grace Borgenicht Gallery, New York
1964 Art Depot Gallery, La Grangeville, New York
1966 Grace Borgenicht Gallery, New York
     East Hampton Gallery, New York
1967 Gorham State College Art Gallery, Maine
1968 Grace Borgenicht Gallery, New York
     George Gershwin College, Stony Brook, New York
1970 Grace Borgenicht Gallery, New York
     Painting and Columns, University Art Museum, University of New Mexico, Albuquerque (toured the United States)
     Art Harris Gallery, Los Angeles
1971 London Arts Gallery
1972 Grace Borgenicht Gallery, New York
     David Barnett Gallery, Milwaukee
1973 Wichita Art Museum, Kansas
1974 Grace Borgenicht Gallery, New York
     Guggenheim Museum, New York (retrospective; travelled to The National Collection, Washington, D.C.)
1976 Grace Borgenicht Gallery, New York
1978 Grace Borgenicht Gallery, New York
     Fort Wayne Art Gallery, Indiana
1980 Grace Borgenicht Gallery, New York
1981 Salt Lake Art Center, Utah
1982 Yares Gallery, Scottsdale, Arizona
1983 *Bolotowsky and His Circle,* Grey Art Gallery, New York University
1984 Washburn Gallery, New York
     Il Punto Blu Gallery, Southampton, New York
     River Gallery, Irvington-on-Hudson, New York
     Pembroke Gallery, Houston, Texas
1987 Washburn Gallery, New York

Selected Group Exhibitions:

1942 *2nd Annual Federation of Modern Painters and Sculptors,* Wildenstein Galleries, New York (and annually in New York until 1971)
1946 *10th Annual Exhibition, American Abstract Artists,* American-British Center, New York until 1972)
1950 *Whitney Annual,* Whitney Museum, New York (and regularly until 1972)
1971 *The Non-Objective World,* Galerie Jean Chauvelin, Paris (toured Europe)
1972 *Geometric Abstraction—1930's,* Zabriskie Gallery, New York (toured the United States)
     Post-Mondrian Abstraction in America, Museum of Contemporary Art, Chicago
1978 *Painting and Sculpture Today,* Indianapolis Museum of Art
1979 *Recent Acquisitions,* Metropolitan Museum of Art, New York

Collections:

Metropolitan Museum of Art, New York; Museum of Modern Art, New York; Guggenheim Museum, New York; Whitney Museum, New York; Albright-Knox Art Gallery, Buffalo, New York; Art Institute of Chicago; Walker Art Center, Minneapolis; The Phillips Collection, Washington, D.C.; National Collection of Fine Arts, Washington, D.C.; Hirshhorn Museum and Sculpture Garden, Washington, D.C.

Publications:

By BOLOTOWSKY: book—*Russian/English Dictionary of Painting and Sculpture,* New York 1962; articles—in *Réalités Nouvelles* (Paris), no. 4, 1950; *Réalités Nouvelles* (Paris), no. 6, 1952; "Russian Constructivism: An Interview with Ilya Bolotowsky," with Ibram Lassaw, in *The World of Abstract Art,* New York 1957; "On Neoplasticism and My Own Work, A Memoir," in *Leonardo* (London), no. 2, 1969; "Concerning My Tondo Paintings" in *Art Now* (New York), vol. 2, no. 2, 1970; statement in *Bolotowsky,* exhibition catalogue, New York 1972; "Moholy Nagy, ed. Richard Kostelanetz" (book review) in *Leonardo* (London), vol. 6, no. 1, 1973; interview, with Louise A. Svendsen and Mimi Poser, in *Ilya Bolotowsky,* exhibition catalogue, New York 1974; statement in *Paintings and Columns,* exhibition catalogue, New York 1974; "Going Abstract in the 30's, "interview with Susan Carol Larsen, in *Art in America* (New York), September/October 1976; films—*Bolotowsky Shows* (various dates); early shorts; western shorts, 1953–57; *David Smith,* 1953; *Haunted House,* 1954; *Broadway,* 1955; *Constant,* 1955; *Dead End,* 1955; *Gabo,* 1955; *Highways,* 1955; *George L. K. Morris,* 1955; *The Museum of Modern Art,* 1955; *The National Gallery,* 1955; *The Philadelphia Museum,* 1955; *Zeeron,* 1955; *Ruth Asawa,* 1955; *Avery,* 1956; *Nell Blaine,* 1956; *Rhys Caparn,* 1956; *Wolf Kahn Paints a Picture,* 1956; *Nevelson,* 1956; *David Smith,* 1956; *Knute Stiles,* 1956; *Sand Creek,* 1956–57; *DeRivera,* 1958; *Subways,* 1958; *Andrew Winter,* 1958; *Narcissus in a Gothic Mood,* 1959–60; *Positive Negative* (Metanoia), 1961; *Metanoia,* 1961–62; *The Last Orpheus,* 1961; *Walking Dream,* 1967; *Afternoon of a Fawn,* 1968; *The Eye,* 1968; *The Ambassadors,* 1969; *Torreon,* 1969; *The Parnassian,* 1971; also, numerous plays and stories.

On BOLOTOWSKY: books—*Ilya Bolotowsky,* exhibition catalogue, New York 1947; *Ilya Bolotowsky,* exhibition catalogue, New York 1950; *Abstract Painting and Sculpture in America* by Andrew Carnduff Ritchie, New York 1951; *Ilya Bolotowsky,* exhibition catalogue, with text by George L. K. Morris, New York 1952; *Dictionary of Contemporary American Artists* by Paul Cummings, New York 1966 and subsequent editions; *Constructivism: Origins and Evolutions* by George Rickey, New York 1967; *American Art since 1900: A Critical History* by Barbara Rose, New York and Washington 1967; *Ilya Bolotowsky: Paintings and Columns,* exhibition catalogue, text by Robert M. Ellis, Albuquerque, New Mexico 1970; *Bolotowsky,* exhibition catalogue, New York 1972; *Geometric Abstraction 1926-1942,* exhibition catalogue, Dallas 1972; *The New York School: A Cultural Reckoning* by Dore Ashton, New York 1972; *Ilya Bolotowsky,* exhibition catalogue, New York 1974; *Paintings and Columns,* exhibition catalogue, with notes by J. D. Cohn, New York 1974; *Ilya Bolotowsky,* exhibition catalogue, by John Krushenick, Fort Wayne, Indiana 1978; *Ilya Bolotowsky—WPA Murals,* exhibition catalogue, New York 1980; articles—"Towards A Plastic Revolution" by Brie Taylor in *Art News* (New York), March 1964; "Ilya Bolotowsky" by Leif Sjoberg in *Konstrevy* (Stockholm), vol. 4, no. 2/3, 1964; "The Growing IInfluence of Mondrian" by Robert Welsh in *Canadian Art* (Toronto), January 1966; "Squaring the Circle and Vice-Versa" by Lawrence Campbell in *Art News* (New York), February 1970; "American Geometric Abstraction in The Late 30's" by John Elderfield in *Artforum* (New York), December 1972; "Noland" by Kenworth Moffett in *Art International* (Lugano), Summer 1973; "Mondrian's American Circle" by J. Burnham in *Arts Magazine* (New York), September 1973; review by Thomas B. Hess in *New York,* 22 April 1974; "Ilya Bolotowsky" by J. Tannenbaum in *Arts Magazine* (New York), October 1974; "Ilya Bolotowsky: Pure Precise Loveliness" by H. Herrera, in *Art News* (New York), November 1974.

Ilya Bolotowsky is best known for having developed a uniquely personal brand of expression influenced by the rigorous and purist Neo-Plastic approach of Mondrian. After acquiring a solid academic background, Bolotowsky began the difficult task for an American artist in the early 1930's of becoming a modernist. His investigative assimilation of the melange of European sources popular then—Picasso, Braque, Miró, Kandinsky, Mondrian—are evident in paintings of the 1930's. For example, both the analytical geometric structures of Cubism and the biomorphic forms of Surrealism can be found in the abstract mural he designed for the Williamsburg Housing Project in New York in 1936. Also, in 1936, he became a founding member of the American Abstract Artists, a group dedicated to the discussion and the pursuit of abstraction. Unlike others of his colleagues, Bolotowsky did not abstract from nature and aimed, instead, towards a pure pictorial expression.

The strong influence of Mondrian is detectable in his paintings executed after World War II. In such examples as *Upright in Gold and Violet* (1945) a new and confident orderliness is present in the color-planar composition that, also, featured the thick, scaffolded lines which were a signature in Mondrian's painting. By the late 1940's Bolotowsky had limited his forms to right angle relationships. Like Mondrian, he decided to banish the diagonal because this element disturbed the equilibrous spatial tension he aimed to achieve. At this time, also, Bolotowsky introduced the diamond shaped format in which he would do many of his most complex and challenging pictures. Some examples are *Configuration Within a Diamond* (1951), a wondrously rhythmical composition that features a complicated interplay of many, variously sized and shaped color bars; *Large Cobalt Diamond* (1957), a composition with fewer and larger color shapes where the angles of the picture's edges balance the linear movements of the image; *Deep Blue Diamond* (1973), an elegant composition in blue, black, red and white in which the various sections are made to work together by pulling against each other.

In 1961, his paintings which had already began to spill over the edges of the canvas, led him to develop three-dimensional, columnar sculptures. The painted imagery on the surface of the sculpture echoed the paintings. Other shaped formats that Bolotowsky mastered include the ellipse and tondo: *Light Yellow Tondo* (1981) and *Open Space Blue Tondo* (1981) are outstanding examples of the high degree of control he had in the late work. It allowed Bolotowsky to create what he called "ideal, balanced harmony" out of the dynamic interplay of the building blocks of art: line, color and plane.

In addition to painting, Bolotowsky made films and wrote plays in which he dealt with the kinds of subjective and emotional issues that he had consciously eliminated from his Neo-Plastic pictorial expression.

—Ronny Cohen

BOLTANSKI, Christian.
French. Born in Paris, 6 September 1944. Self-taught in art. Professional photographer and artist, Paris, since 1969. Agent: Sonnabend Gallery, 420 West Broadway, New York, New York 10012, U.S.A.; and Galerie Sonnabend, 12 Rue Mazarine, 75005 Paris. Address: 746 Boulevard Camelinat, 92240 Malakoff, France.

Individual Exhibitions:

1970 Galerie Templon, Paris (with Jean Le Gac)
     Musée d'Art Moderne, Paris
1971 Galerie Sonnabend, Paris
     Galerie M. E. Thelen, Cologne
1972 Galerie Folker Skulima, Berlin
     Studio Santandrea, Milan
1973 Galleria Lucio Amelio, Naples
     Kunsthalle, Baden-Baden, West Germany
     Sonnabend Gallery, New York
     Museum of Modern Art, Oxford
     Israel Museum Jerusalem
1974 *Saynette Comique,* Westfalischer Kunstverein, Münster, West Germany
     Louisiana Museum, Humlebaek, Denmark
     Centre National d'Art Contemporain, Paris (with Jacques Monory)
1975 Sonnabend Gallery, New York
     Kunsthalle, Kiel, West Germany
     Centre d'Art Contemporain, Geneva
     Württembergische Kunstverein, Stuttgart
     Galerie Seriaal, Amsterdam
1976 Musée d'Art Moderne, Paris
     Rheinisches Landesmuseum, Bonn
1977 Museum of Contemporary Art, La Jolla, California
     Galleria Bruno Soletti, Milan
     Galerie Sonnabend, Paris

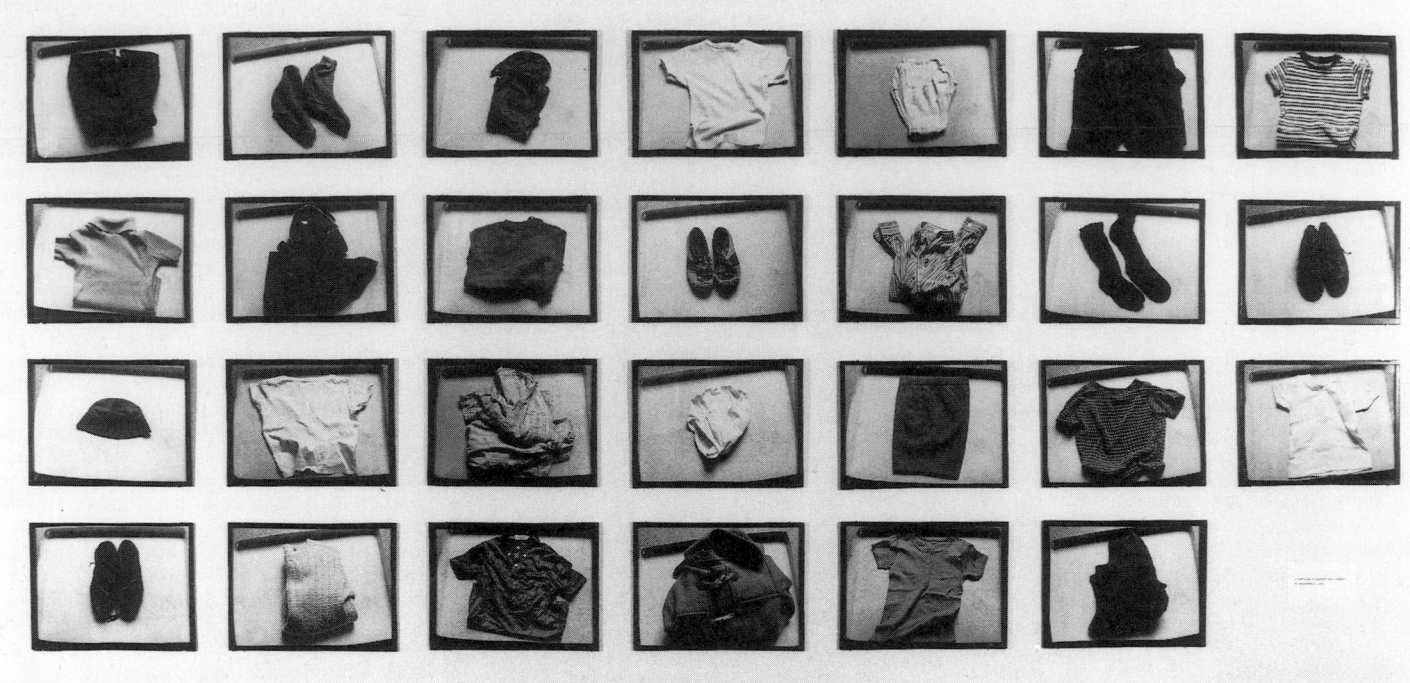

Christian Boltanski: *29 Apparels de François C.*, 1972

1978	Badischer Kunstverein, Karlsruhe, West Germany
	Galerie Jollenbeck, Cologne
	Galerie Malacorda, Geneva
	Galerie Foksal, Warsaw
1979	*Compositions,* Musée de Peinture, Calais
	Galerie Sonnabend, Paris
	Carpenter Art Center, Harvard University, Cambridge, Massachusetts
1981	Musée d'Art Moderne, Paris (retrospective)
1982	Sonnabend Gallery, New York
	Le Nouveau Musée, Lyon, France
1983	Aldrich Museum of Contemporary Art, Ridgefield, Connecticut
1984	Centre Georges Pompidou, Paris
	Kunsthaus, Zurich
	Staatliche Kunsthalle, Baden-Baden, West Germany
	Galerie 't Venster, Rotterdam
1985	Galerie Optica, Montreal
	Galerie Crousel-Hussenot, Paris
	Le Consortium Centre d'Art Contemporain, Dijon, France
1986	Galerie Elisabeth Kaufmann, Zurich
	Galerie Crousel Hussenot, Paris
	Galerie des Ponchettes, Nice, France
	Kunstverein, Munich

Selected Group Exhibitions:

1969	*Biennale de Paris,* Musée d'Art Moderne, Paris
1971	*Prospekt 71,* Kunsthalle, Dusseldorf
1972	*Documenta 5,* Museum Fridericianum, Kassel, West Germany (and *Documenta 6,* 1977)
1974	*Pour Memoire,* Centre d'Art Plastique Contemporain, Bordeaux, France (travelled to Paris)
1977	*Malerei und Photographie im Dialog,* Kunsthaus, Zurich
1979	*3rd Biennale of Sydney,* Art Gallery of New South Wales, Sydney
1980	*Artist and Camera,* Mappin Art Gallery, Sheffield, Yorkshire (travelled to Stoke, Durham and Bradford)
1983	*Kunst mit Photographie,* Nationalgalerie, West Berlin
1986	*Photography as Performance,* Photographers' Gallery, London

Collections

Musée d'Art Moderne, Paris; Musée d'Art, Dijon, France; Kunsthalle, Hamburg; Kunsthalle, Kiel, West Germany; Neue Galerie, Aachen, West Germany; Louisiana Museum, Humlebaek, Denmark; Boymans-van Beuningen Museum, Rotterdam; Museum of Fine Arts, Lodz, Poland; Israel Museum, Jerusalem; Art Institute of Chicago.

Publications:

By BOLTANSKI: books—*Tous ce que reste de mon enfance,* Paris 1969; *Reconstitutions des Gestes,* Paris 1971; *10 Portraits Photographiques,* Paris 1972; *Album Photographique,* Hamburg 1972; *Inventaire,* Münster, West Germany 1973; *Quelques Interpretations,* Paris 1974; *20 Regles et Technique,* Copenhagen 1975; *Les Morts pour Rire,* Antibes, France 1975; *Modellbilder,* with others, Bonn 1976; film—*La Vie Impossible de Christian Boltanski,* 1968.

On BOLTANSKI: books—*L'Art en France: Une Nouvelle Generation* by Jean Clair, Paris 1973; *Saynette Comique,* exhibition catalogue, by Klaus Honnef, Münster, West Germany 1974; *Reconstitution* by Andreas Franke, Paris 1978; *Les Modeles* by Paull-Hervé Würz, Paris 1979; *Spurensicherung* by Günter Metken, Cologne 1979. *Compositions,* exhibition catalogue, by Dominique Vieville, Calais 1980; *Christian Boltanski,* exhibition catalogue, Baden-Baden 1984; *Christian Boltanski: Lecon des Tenebres,* exhibition catalogue, Munich 1986.

BONTECOU, Lee.

American. Born in Providence, Rhode Island, 15 January 1931. Educated at the Arts Students League, New York, 1952–55; Skowhegan School of Art, Maine, 1954 (on scholarship); studied in Rome, 1956, 1958 (on Fulbright Scholarships). Independent sculptor and printmaker. Recipient: Lewis Comfort Tiffany Award, 1959; Competition Award, *Biennial Exhibition,* Corcoran Gallery of Art, Washington, D.C., 1963; First Prize, *Annual Invitational,* National Institute of Arts and Letters, 1966. Agent: Leo Castelli Gallery, 4 East 77th Street, New York, New York 10021. Address: Post Office Box 1290, East Hampton, New York 11937, U.S.A.

Individual Exhibitions:

1959	*Sculpture,* "G" Gallery, New York
1960	Leo Castelli Gallery, New York
1962	Leo Castelli Gallery, New York
1965	Galerie Ileana Sonnabend, Paris
1966	Leo Castelli Gallery, New York
1968	*Sculpturen, Tekeningen, Lithos,* Museum Boymans-van Beuningen, Rotterdam
	Städtisches Museum Schloss Morsbroich, Leverkusen, West Germany (travelled to Kunstverein, Haus am Waldsee, West Berlin)
1971	Leo Castelli Gallery, New York
1972	Museum of Contemporary Art, Chicago
1974	*Prints and Drawings,* Davison Art Center, Wesleyan University, Middletown, Connecticut

Selected Group Exhibitions:

1960	*New Media—New Forms I + II,* Martha Jackson Gallery, New York
1963	*Biennial,* Corcoran Gallery of Art, Washington, D.C.
1964	*Painting and Sculpture of a Decade 1954–1964,* Tate Gallery, London
1966	*Flint Invitational,* Flint Institute of Arts, Michigan
1967	*Sculpture: A Generation of Innovation,* Art Institute of Chicago
1970	*L'Art Vivant,* Fondation Maeght, St.-Paul-de-Vence, France
1971	*Works on Paper,* University of North Carolina at Chapel Hill
1973	*American Drawing 1970–1973,* Yale University, New Haven, Connecticut
1975	*Recent American Etching,* Davison Art Center, Wesleyan University, Middletown, Connecticut (travelled to the National Collection of Fine Arts, Smithsonian Iinstitution, Washington, D.C., 1977)

Collections:

Whitney Museum, New York; Museum of Modern Art, New York; Chase Manhattan Bank, New York; Corcoran Gallery of Art, Washington, D.C.; Washington Gallery of Modern Art, D.C.; Art Institute of Chicago; Museum of Fine Arts, Houston; Museum of Fine Arts, Dallas; Stedelijk Museum, Amsterdam.

Publications:

On BONTECOU: books—*Lee Bontecou,* exhibition catalogue, with texts by Gillo Dorfles, Gérald Gassiot-Talabot, and Annette Michelson, Paris 1965; *New Art Around the World: Painting and Sculpture,* edited by Sam Hunter, New York 1966; *Lee Bontecou: Sculpturen, Tekeningen, Lithós,* exhibition catalogue, with text by Dore Ashton, Rotterdam 1968; *Lee Bontecou,* exhibition catalogue, with texts by Rolf Günter Dienst, Rolf Wedewer, Wibke von Bonin, and Dore Ashton, Leverkusen, West Germany 1968; *Minimal Art: A Critical Anthology,* edited by Gregory Battcock, New York 1968; *Lee Bontecou,* exhibition catalogue, with text by Carter Ratcliff, Chicago 1972; *Lee Bontecou: Prints and Drawings,* exhibition catalogue, with text by Richard S. Field, Middletown, Connecticut 1974; *Recent American Etching,* exhibition catalogue, with text by Richard S. Field, Middletown, Connecticut 1975; *American Artists 76: A Celebration,* exhibition catalogue, with text by Alice C. Simkins, San Antonio, Texas 1976; articles—"Lee Bontecou's Aquatints" by R. S. Field in *Art International* (Lugano, Switzerland), November 1970; "Lee Bontecou" by Lil Picard in *Kunstwerk* (Baden-Baden, West Germany), Summer 1971; "A Diversity of Approaches in Contemporary Art: Rauschenberg, Bontecou, and Noland" by Lincoln Johnson in *Honolulu Academy of Arts Journal,* vol. 1, 1974.

The bulky constructions by Lee Bontecou loom out from the walls upon which they have been hooked and invite the eyes to go down into the mirky depth of a central orifice whose sexual connotations have been happily dwelt upon by a number of professional critics. But is the sense of a boiler-room sex the natural and immediate reaction of those who have never seen her works before? After initial surprise-coupled-with-consternation, they are far more likely to lay about them in the upper recesses of their minds looking for a visual twinship with something less emotional, something more matter-of-fact. The emotion, in any case, has been provided by the constructions themselves. Everyday eyes are less inclined to light upon the factor of sexuality, however implicit; they will equate the "hole" with the hollow shaft that once acted as the protuberance to hold an airplane propeller in the days before jets. The taut stretched canvas facets stitched to their wire framework enhance this image of early aircraft and the variations of grey and rusts which colour the entire construction do nothing to reduce this offbeat identification.

These comments are made because as well as being pertinent in the context of a first introduction to Lee

Lee Bontecou: *Untitled Sculpture,* 1961

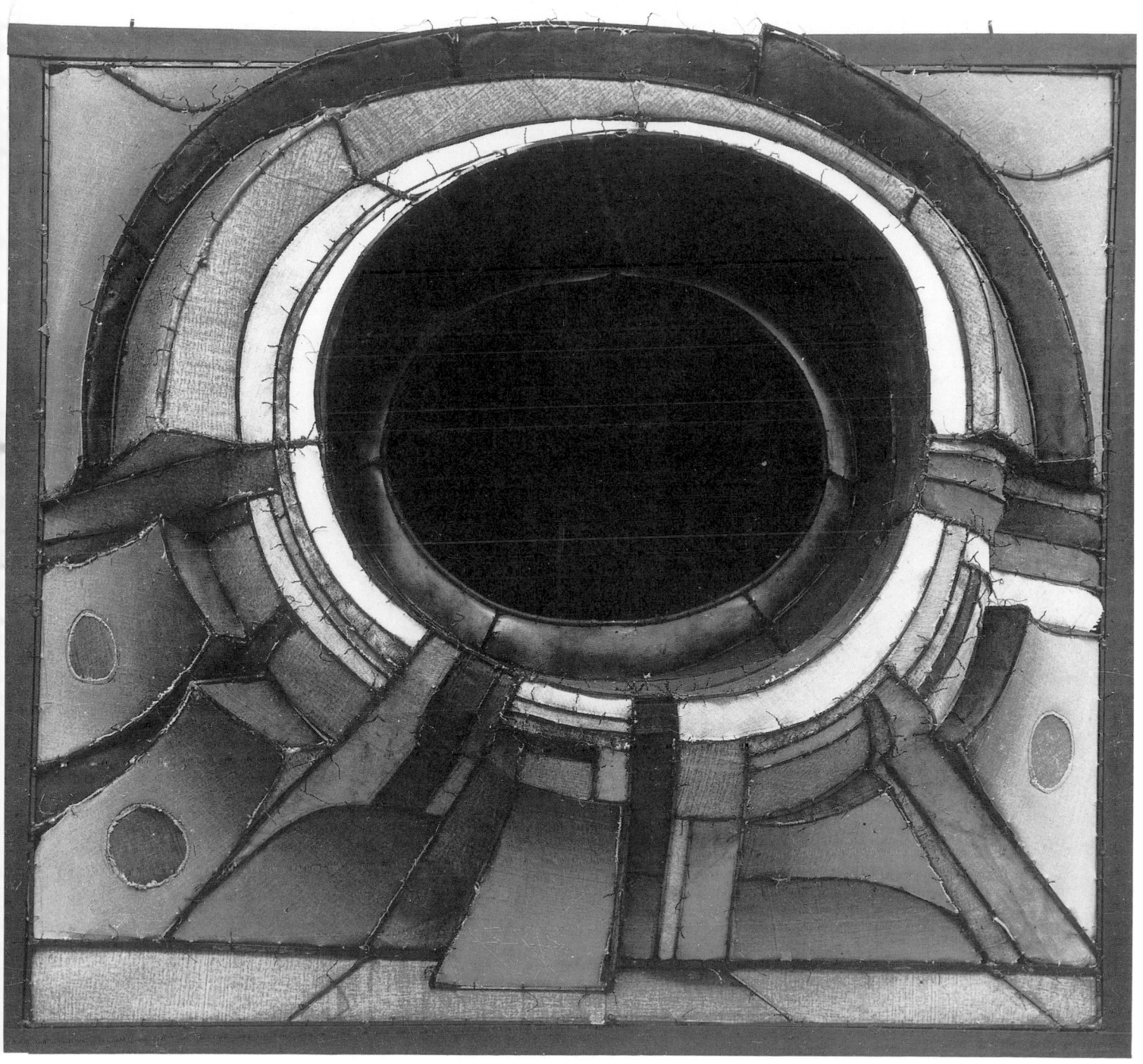

Bontecou's work, they also help to place it in its proper chronological setting which is somewhere between the mid-20th Century and now.

What is left? It needs asserting that this artist is telling a terrible story, oft repeated, that we live in self-destructive times and that they have somehow harnessed the power of the machine (or something very like it) to act, not with us, but virtually independently to proliferate a state of sado-masochism that is fundamentally corrupt. Not perhaps for sado-masochists, but clearly for everyone else. Grim warnings are maybe unappealing, but this in no way reduces their relevance.

On the credit side, Lee Bontecou's constructions and drawings are original, striking and possessed of a personal beauty that translates them, without psychological hang-ups, into the world of art where they belong.

—Sheldon Williams

BOOTH, Peter.

Australian. Born in Sheffield, England, in 1940; emigrated to Australia in 1958. Studied at the Sheffield College of Art, 1956-57, and National Gallery School, Melbourne, 1962-65. Painter: lives and works in Melbourne. Agent: Pinacotheca, Richmond. Address: c/o Pinacotheca, 10 Waltham Place, Richmond, Victoria 3121, Australia.

Individual Exhibitions:

1969	Pinacotheca, Melbourne
	Central Street Gallery, Sydney
1970	Pinacotheca, Melbourne
1972	Pinacotheca, Melbourne
1973	Chapman Powell Gallery, Melbourne
1974	Chapman Powell Gallery, Melbourne
1975	Pinacotheca, Melbourne
1976	Monash University Gallery, Melbourne
	Project 12: Peter Booth, Art Gallery of New South Wales, Sydney
	Pinacotheca, Melbourne
1977	Pinacotheca, Melbourne
1978	Pinacotheca, Melbourne
1979	Pinacotheca, Melbourne
1980	Pinacotheca, Melbourne
1981	Pinacotheca, Melbourne
1982	*Works by Peter Booth and Rosalie Gascoigne,* at the *Biennale,* Venice
1984	Museum of Modern Art, New York
	Guggenheim Museum, New York
1987	CDS Gallery, New York

Selected Group Exhibitions:

1968	*The Field,* National Gallery of Victoria, Melbourne (travelled to the Art Gallery of New South Wales, Sydney)
1973	*Recent American Art,* Art Gallery of New South Wales, Sydney
1976	*Minimal Art,* National Gallery of Victoria, Melbourne
	Drawing: Some Definitions, Ewing and George Paton Galleries, University of Melbourne
1979	*Third Biennale of Sydney: European Dialogue,* Art Gallery of New South Wales, Sydney
1981	*Australian Perspecta 1981: A Biennial Survey of Contemporary Australian Art,* Art Gallery of New South Wales, Sydney
1982	*Eureka! Artists from Australia,* Serpentine Gallery, London

Collections:

Australian National Gallery, Canberra; National Gallery of Victoria, Melbourne; Monash University Art Gallery, Melbourne; Geelong Art Gallery, Victoria; Ballarat Fine Art Gallery, Victoria; Bendigo Art Gallery, Victoria; Mornington Peninsula Art Gallery, Mornington, Victoria; Art Gallery of South Australia, Adelaide; Art Gallery of New South Wales, Sydney; Queen Victoria Museum and Art Gallery, Launceston, Tasmania.

Publications:

On BOOTH: books—*Project 12: Peter Booth,* catalogue broadsheets, with text by Frances Lindsay, Sydney 1976; *Australian Perspecta 1981,* exhibition catalogue, with text by Bernice Murphy, Sydney 1981; *Australia: Venice Biennale 1982: Works by Peter Booth and Rosalie Gascoigne,* exhibition catalogue, with an essay by Gary Catalano, Sydney 1982; *Eureka! Artists from Australia,* exhibition catalogue, with essays by Nancy D. H. Underhill, Ian Burn and Paul Taylor, London 1982; articles—"Peter Booth" by Frances Lindsay in *Art and Australia* (Sydney), vol. 16, no. 1, 1978; "Images of Tradition" by Gary Catalano in *The Australian Arts Today,* edited by John Colmer, London 1980.

I feel that my work has to speak for itself, and that the viewer should be free to make his/her own interpretations.

—Peter Booth

Like those of many Australian artists who began to exhibit in the late 1960's, Peter Booth's early works were decidedly minimal in appearance. Characteristically his paintings of the time often contained nothing more than a black rectangle bounded on its upper horizontal and two vertical sides by a thin strip of lighter-toned canvas. During the past 6 or 7 years the

Peter Booth: *Untitled,* 1982

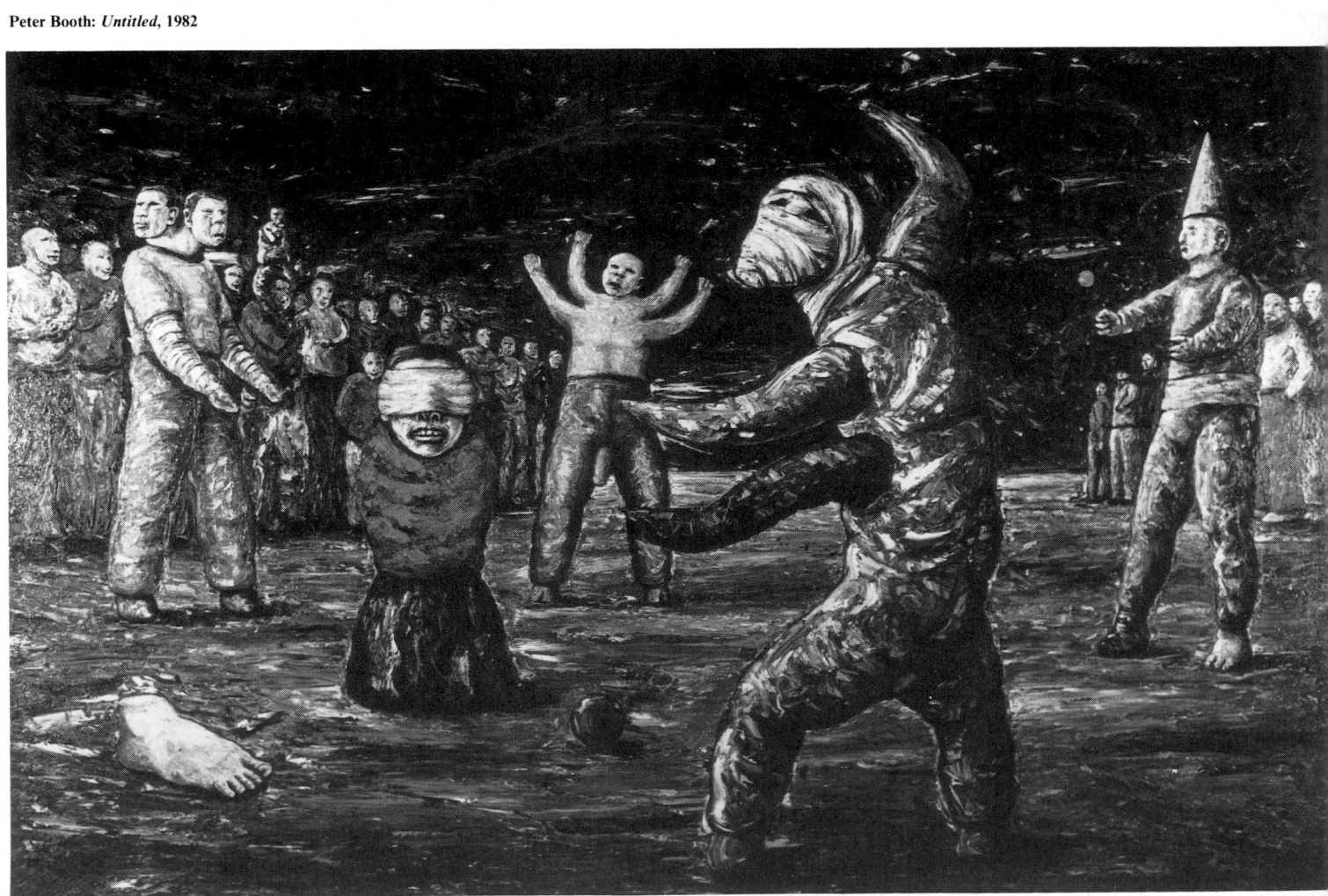

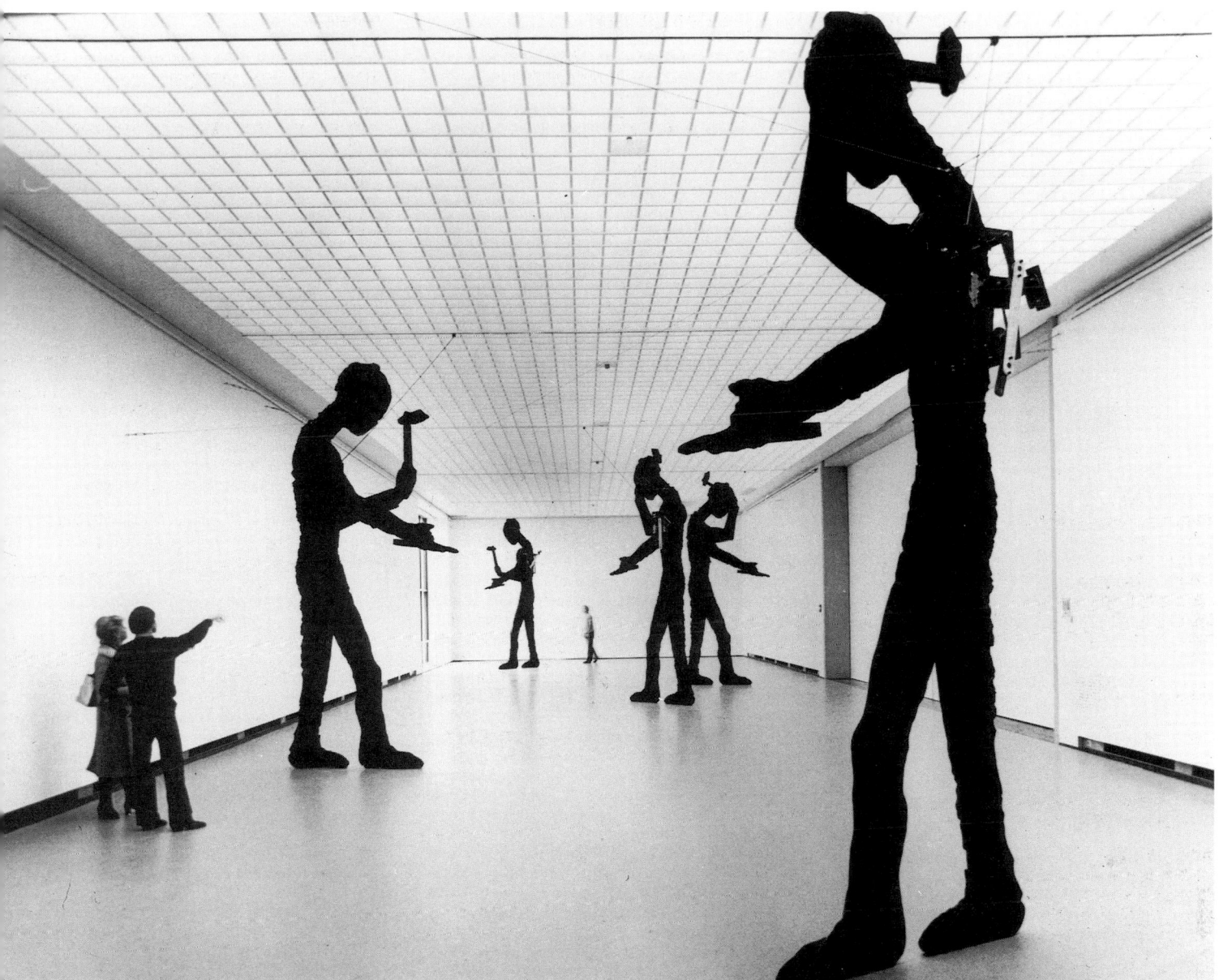

Jonathan Borofsky: Installation at the Museum Boymans-van Beuningen, Rotterdam, 1982

appearance of his work has greatly altered. Figurative images are now to the fore. Yet in one important sense Booth's concerns have not changed, for human society is still the major theme of his work. While the blank facades of his early paintings gave symbolic form to the alienating power of society, his more recent paintings present a more direct image of society's tensions and conflicts.

This change has certainly been facilitated by his obsessive graphic activity. Born in the English industrial city of Sheffield, Booth has continually sketched the industrial landscapes of his adopted Melbourne. Even an unpractised eye can see the similarities between the proportions of his early minimal paintings and those found in the facades of the factories and warehouses which he has sketched. A further influence on his work stems from his interest in certain romantic and symbolist writers of the 19th century. William Blake is of particular importance to him. The influence of Blake's graphic illustrations can be discerned in Booth's drawings of the mid-1970's. In these drawings Booth first unveiled many of the specific images to be found in his current paintings—the winding roads, the fire-engulfed monoliths, the totemic symbols.

For a number of years now Booth has recorded his dreams in pictorial form. His recent paintings can often be traced back to these dream images. By combining such material with scenes or incidents directly experienced, Booth attempts to show what it is like to be alive in our day and age. His is the ambition of most romantic artists: to be true to one's self, to be true to one's time.

—Gary Catalano

BOROFSKY, Jon(athan).

American. Born in Boston, Massachusetts, in 1942. Educated at Carnegie Mellon University, Pittsburgh, B.F.A. 1964; Ecole de Fontainebleau, France, Summer 1964; and Yale School of Art and Architecture, New Haven, Connecticut, M.F.A. 1966. Independent artist, New York, and now California, since 1966. Teacher, School of Visual Arts, New York, 1969–77, and California Institute of the Arts, Valencia, since 1977. Agent: Paula Cooper Gallery, New York. Address: c/o Paula Cooper Gallery, 155 Wooster Street, New York, New York 10012, U.S.A.

Individual Exhibitions:

1975   Paula Cooper Gallery, New York

1976   *Matrix 18,* Wadsworth Atheneum, Hartford, Connecticut
        Paul Cooper Gallery, New York
1977   University of California at Irvine
1978   Protetch-McIntosh Gallery, Washington, D.C.
        Thomas Lewallen Gallery, Los Angeles
        University of California Art Museum, Berkeley
        Corps de Garde, Groningen, Netherlands
        Projects Gallery, Museum of Modern Art, New York
1979   Paula Cooper Gallery, New York
        INK: Halle für Internationale Neue Kunst, Zurich
        Portland Center for the Visual Arts, Oregon
1980   Paula Cooper Gallery, New York
        Hayden Gallery, Massachusetts Institute of Technology, Cambridge
1981   Contemporary Arts Museum, Houston
        Galerie Rudolf Zwirner, Cologne
        Kunsthalle, Basel
        Institute of Contemporary Arts, London
1982   Museum Boymans-van Veuningen, Rotterdam
        Museum van Hedendaagse Kunst, Ghent, Belgium
        Paula Cooper Gallery, New York
        Gemini G.E.L., Los Angeles
        Friedrich Gallery, Berne
1983   Kunstmuseum, Basel
        Galleria dell'Ariete Grafica, Milan
        Akron Art Museum, Ohio
        Paula Cooper Gallery, New York
        Gemini G.E.L., Los Angeles

1984 University of Miami, Coral Gables
Louisiana Museum, Humlebaek, Denmark
Israel Museum, Jerusalem
Moderna Museet, Stockholm
Kunsthalle, Bielefeld, West Germany
Carl Solway Gallery, Cincinnati
Seattle Art Museum, Washington
Philadelphia Museum of Art, Pennsylvania
Gallery Watari, Tokyo
Galerie Susanna Kulli, St. Gallen, Switzerland
1985 Philadelphia Museum of Art, Pennsylvania (travelled
to New York; Berkeley, California; Minneapolis;
Washington, D.C.; Los Angeles, 1985–86)
Gemini G.E.L., Los Angeles
1986 St. Louis Art Museum, Missouri
Gemini G.E.L., Los Angeles
Harvard University Art Museum, Cambridge, Mas-
sachusetts
Paula Cooper Gallery, New York
Heath Gallery, Atlanta, Georgia
Milwaukee Art Museum, Wisconsin (travelled to
Des Moines Art Center, Iowa)
1987 Cathedral of St. John the Divine, New York
Metropolitan Museum of Art, Tokyo (travelled to
Shiga, Japan)
Galerie Yvon Lambert, Paris
Gallery Watari, Tokyo

Selected Group Exhibitions:

1974 *Drawing and Other Work,* Paula Cooper Gallery,
New York
1976 *Soho,* Akademie der Kunste, West Berlin (travelled
to the Louisiana Museum, Humleback, Denmark)
1977 *New York: The State of Art,* New York State Museum, Syracuse
Surrogates/Self-Portraits, Holly Solomon Gallery,
New York
1978 *Contemporary Drawing, New York,* University of
California Art Museum, Santa Barbara
1979 *Visionary Images,* Renaissance Society, University
of Chicago
10 Artists: Artists Space, Neuberger Museum, State
University of New York at Purchase
1983 *Back to the USA,* Rheinisches Landesmuseum, Bonn
(travelled to Lucerne and Stuttgart)
1985 *Modern Machines: Recent Kinetic Sculpture,* Whitney Museum, New York
1987 *Berlinart,* Museum of Modern Art, New York (travelled to San Francisco Museum of Modern Art)

Collections:

Whitney Museum, New York; Museum of Modern Art, New
York; BankAmerica Corporation, San Francisco; Philadelphia Museum of Art, Pennsylvania; Commodities Corporation, Princeton, New Jersey; Tate Gallery, London.

Publications:

On BOROFSKY: books—*6 Years: The Dematerialization of
the Art Object from 1966 to 1972* by Lucy Lippard, New
York 1973; *Jon Borofsky: Matrix 18,* exhibition catalogue,
with text by Mark Rosenthal, Hartford, Connecticut 1976;
Contemporary Drawing, New York, exhibition catalogue,
Santa Barbara, California 1978; *Drawings: A Contemporary
Approach* by Claudia Betti and Teel Sale, New York 1980;
Drawing: The Pluralist Decade, with an introduction by Janet
Kardon, Philadelphia 1980; *20 Artists: Yale School of Art
1950–1970,* exhibition catalogue, by Irving Sandler, New
Haven, Connecticut 1981; *Jonathan Borofsky: Dreams 1973–
81,* exhibition catalogue with essay by Joan Simon, London
and Basel 1981; *Jonathan Borofsky: Zeichnungen 1960–
1983,* exhibition catalogue with texts by C. Geelhaar and D.
Koepplin, Basel 1983; *Jonathan Borofsky,* exhibition catalogue with essays by Mark Rosenthal and Richard Marshall,
Philadelphia and New York 1984; *Jonathan Borofsky: New
Works,* exhibition catalogue with introduction by Peter Nis-
bet, Cambridge Massachusetts 1986; *Jonathan Borofsky:
Dreams,* Tokyo 1987; *Borofsky: Drawings, Printings and
Multiples,* exhibition catalogue with essay by Mark Rosenthal, Tokyo 1987; articles—"Jonathan Borofsky at
2,096,974" in *Artforum* (New York), November 1974; "Be-

fore the Reason of Images: The New Work of Jon Borofsky"
in *Arts* (New York), October 1976; "Jon Borofsky's Dream
Language" in *Artweek* (Oakland, California), 23 April 1977;
"Jon Borofsky" by Philip Smith in *Arts Magazine* (New
York), March 1978; "Energism: An Attitude" by Ronny H.
Cohen in *Artforum* (New York), September 1980; "Art:
Transformations of Jonathan Borofsky" by John Russell in
the *New York Times,* 24 October 1980; "Strike: A Project by
Jonathan Borofsky" in *Artforum* (New York), February 1981;
"A Walk Through Borofsky's Brain" by Nancy Grimes in
Artnews (New York), Summer 1985.

Jonathan Borofsky's installation at the L.A. County
Museum, 1981, included a large figure painted on
both wall and ceiling. The image had giant rabbit
ears, a haunted face, and eyes which were circled in a
deadened, exacerbated state. He presented a flying
man at Basel's Kunsthalle, and a running man in the
Hayden Gallery, M.I.T. At Paula Cooper Gallery he
painted legions of black-streaked humans which hur-
ried over the wall. Also installed was a ping-pong
table set in the middle of the space, along with assorted debris, a stopped black human form, large
scissors, and 80 to 100 other strewn objects attached
to the installation. Also at Basel: a 26 foot high, two-
dimensional planar sculpture, which is Borofsky's
hammering man, with a hand-held object, head-hung,
feet plodding, a techno-cave man, an emblematic cut-
out.

Borofsky's work is shadowy. At first one thinks the
work could be a mistake, since the painting is often
done on the gallery walls. Even in his sculptural
work, objects generally appear awry. Soon, though,
the relationship between the clear, interior lit gallery
space becomes apparent against the underlife of
Borofsky's mammoth figures. The images and the
people are private possessions of Borofsky's; therein
lies their unfocused dream-like reference. They are
exposed interior beings in which a particular imagination chooses as it wants, rather than as it dreams.

For years Borofsky worked with numbers, counting
incessantly. He literally wrote out numbers onto
pieces of paper, reaching over two million in several
years. He still occasionally counts and is now past
three million. This pile of sheets of numbers was exhibited in Borofsky's first New York show at Artists
Space. Later Borofsky learned to use numbers as numerical signification, as a "signature" next to his imagery. This impersonal quality of signature assisted in
placing his imagery within a larger opus, similar to
the type of posthumous textual studies usually written
and catalogued by scholars. In a sense Borofsky was
creating the categorization of his work, if not the
analysis, at an early stage.

Most of Borofsky's work belies bourgeois scale and
therefore "civilized" dwellings. The rooms and
buildings are appropriately the wrong size for the
work: either they are too small or misshaped for the
quantity of strewn objects exhibited. The work is not
hesitant, though obviously the sign of odd inward intelligence, a fulfilled combination of form turning
into crazed function. The rational mind explains itself
inside out in Borofsky's work. "Self-Portrait in
Closet at 2490197" was shown at the Morgan
Thomas Gallery in Los Angeles, painted over and
also inside of a closet, with the closet door ajar. The
blunt, dark markings picture Borofsky with a down-
cast gaze, a hat and its brim, closed and tight lips,
and the closet door which opens and closes through
the portrait, suggesting certain transparencies. The
portrait is softer in tone than the rest of the work.

—John Robinson

BORY, Jean-Francois.
French. Born in Paris, 2 May 1938. Studied animal
physiology at the Université de Paris, 1956–58.
Served as infantryman in the 54th Battalion of the
French Army, in Ouarsenis, Algeria, 1958–61.

Worked as a barman, Paris 1962, as re-writer, Association Francais du Presse, Paris 1963. Independent
artist, Paris since 1964. Agent: Galerie Lara Vincy,
41 rue de Seine, 75007 Paris. Address: 85 rue St.
Dominique, 75007 Paris, France.

Individual Exhibitions:

1970 Galleria Il Canale, Venice
Galleria Santandrea, Milan
Galleria Studio Brescia, Brescia, Italy
1972 Gallerie Les Mains Libres, Paris
Galerie Lara Vincy, Paris
1985 Galerie J. et J. Donguy, Paris
1986 Galerie J. et J. Donguy, Paris

Selected Group Exhibitions:

1967 *Biennale de Paris,* Musée d'Art Moderne, Paris (and
1969, 1971)
1972 *Biennale,* Venice
Concrete Poetry, Stedelijk Museum, Amsterdam
Contemporanea, Parcheggie Villa Borghese, Rome
1986 *Biennale,* Venice

Collections:

Centre Georges Pompidou, Paris; Stedelijk Museum, Amsterdam; Museo d'Arte Moderna, Bologna, Italy.

Publications:

By BORY: books—*Once Again,* New York 1967; *Post-
Scriptum,* Paris 1970; *Made in Machine,* Brescia, Italy 1970;
Logorinthe, Rome 1970; *Untitled,* Paris 1973; *Un Auteur
sous Influence,* Paris 1986; articles—"Proposition pour une
lecture de Jean-Francois Bory" in *Artitudes* (St. Jeannet),
July/September 1972; "La Poésie Visuelle dans le Monde"
in *Opus International* (Paris), January 1973; "Hommage à
Pavlov" in *Artitudes International* (St. Jeannet), February/
March 1973; "Le dechet du festa" in *Artitudes International*
(St. Jeannet), June/September 1975.

On BORY: book—*Bory, L'Anarchiste,* exhibition catalogue,
with text by Alain Borer, Paris 1986; articles—"Portrait of
Bory as a Young Bory" by Richard Kostelanetz in *Art International* (Lugano, Switzerland), August/September 1971;
"J. F. Bory: un classico" by G. Lista in *NAC* (Milan), February 1973; "Jean-Francois Bory" in *Chroniques de l'Art Vivant* (Paris), March 1973; "Jean-Francois Bory ou
l'Ubiquite" by P. Bourgeade in *Opus International* (Paris),
September 1973; "Jean-Francois Bory" by S. Dupey in *Art
Press* (Pariis), September 1973; "Logique de Jean-Francois
Bory" by P. Bourgeade in *Artitudes International* (St. Jeannet), December 1973/March 1974; "Jean-Francois Bory" in
Opus International (Paris), April 1975.

End of the book, end of the world, of the work, of the
world.

—Jean-Francois Bory

BOSHIER, Derek.
British. Born in Portsmouth, Hampshire, in 1937.
Studied at the Yeovil School of Art, Somerset, 1953–
57; Royal College of Art, London, 1959–62. Served
in the British Army, 1957–59. Lecturer, Central
School of Art and Design, and Hornsey College of
Art, London, since 1963. Visiting Lecturer, University of Victoria, 1975; and University of Houston,
1980–81. Recipient: Arts Council Young Contemporaries Award, 1961; Indian Government Scholarship,
1962; Peter Stuyvesant Foundation Travel Bursary to
the United States, 1964; British Government Cultural

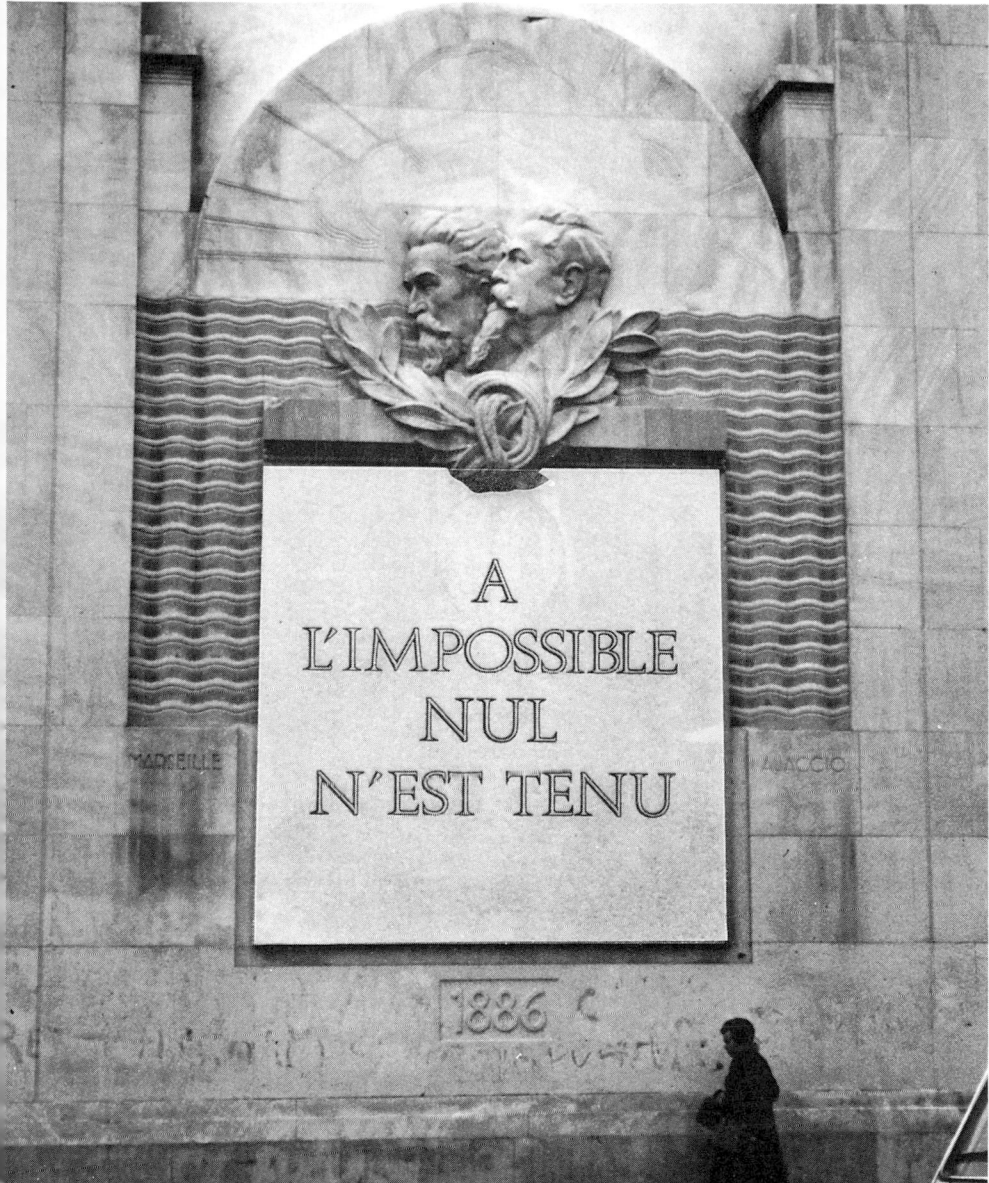

Jean-Francois Bory: *Opera*, 1986

Exchange Programme Grant, 1968; Minister of Affairs Prize, *7th Print Biennale,* Tokyo, 1970; Film Grant, Arts Council of Great Britain, 1970. Agents: Angela Flowers, London; Robin Cronin, Houston, Texas. Address: 25 Ladbroke Gardens, London W11, England.

Individual Exhibitions:

1962	*Image in Revolt,* Grabowski Gallery, London (with Frank Bowling)
1965	Robert Fraser Gallery, London
	Galerie Aujourd'hui, Brussels
1967	Galerie Bischofberger, Zurich
1968	Robert Fraser Gallery, London
1970	Edizioni O, Milan
	Nigel Greenwood Gallery, London
	Galerie Bucholtz, Munich
	Galerie Varenne, Paris
1971	Hayward Gallery, London
1972	Arnolfini Gallery, Bristol (toured the U.K., 1972–73)
1974	Angela Flowers Gallery, London
1975	Art Net, London
	Whitworth Art Gallery, Manchester
	Angela Flowers Gallery, London
1976	Angela Flowers Gallery, London
1977	Peterloo Gallery, Manchester
1979	Felicity Samuel Gallery, London
1980	Angela Flowers Gallery, London
1981	Angela Flowers Gallery, London
	Painting 1980–81, Contemporary Art Museum, Houston
	Muzeum Sztuki, Lodz, Poland
1982	Cronin Gallery, Houston, Texas
	Institute of Contemporary Arts, London
1983	Bluecoat Gallery, Liverpool, Merseyside
	Texas Gallery, Houston
1985	Edward Totah Gallery, London
	Texas Gallery, Houston
1986	Totah-Stelling Art, New York
1987	Edward Totah Gallery, London
	Texas Gallery, Houston

Selected Group Exhibitions:

1963	*3rd Biennale des Jeunes,* Paris
1964	*The New Generation,* Whitechapel Art Gallery, London
1967	*New Shapes of Color,* Stedelijk Museum, Amsterdam (toured the Netherlands)
1969	*12 British Artists,* Kunstlerhaus Galerie, Vienna
1973	*Henry Moore to Gilbert and George,* Victoria and Albert Museum, London
1977	*British Painting 1952–1977,* Royal Academy of Art, London
1979	*A Generation,* Scottish National Gallery of Modern Art, Edinburgh
1982	*The Human Figure,* Contemporary Arts Center, New Orleans
1984	*Content: A Contemporary Focus,* Hirshhorn Museum, Washington, D.C.
1987	*Still-Life: Theme and Variation,* Glassel School of Art, Houston, Texas

Collections:

Arts Council of Great Britain, London; Victoria and Albert Museum, London; City Art Gallery, Manchester, National Museum of Wales, Cardiff; Museum of Modern Art, New York.

Publications:

By BOSHIER: books—*16 Situations,* London 1971; *6 Cities* (series of postcards), London 1972; articles—"Derek Boshier on His Constructed Prints: A Suite of Three, in Conversation with Christopher Fox" in *Studio International* (London), December 1970; statement in *Studio International* (London), November 1973; films—*Link,* 1970; *Circle,* 1971; *Reel,* 1973; *Watch,* 1975.

On BOSHIER: books—*Derek Boshier,* exhibition catalogue, London 1973; *Boshier,* exhibition catalogue, Manchester 1975; *Lives: An Exhibition of Artists Whose Work Is Based on Other People's Lives,* selected by Boshier, exhibition catalogue, London 1979; *Derek Boshier: Painting 1980–81,* exhibition catalogue, by Cheryl Brutvan, Houston 1981; articles—"Derek Boshier: Hayward Gallery" by Eddie Wolfram in *Arts Review* (London), December 1970; "Derek Boshier Situations" in *Creative Camera* (London), June 1971; "The Impossibility of Sculpture" by Paul Overy in *The Times* (London), June 1973.

Of the class of 1962 at the Royal College of Art, taking his diploma with David Hockney and Peter Phillips, Derek Boshier was one of the successes of the Pop movement in England. With Frank Bowling he showed under the title *Image in Revolt* at the Grabowski Gallery, London, in the same year. In large canvases he expressed his personal rejection of the conventional format for pictures. Chiefly the motives were those of printed symbols, many of them from commercial packaging and cheap comics.

This employment of ready-made and widely known characters from the media aligned the work with the proletarian connection in Pop art, though this aspect was bent by Boshier to narrative content concerned with S.F. and a fanciful quasi-surrealist effect. Large-scale compositions emphasized the repetitive elements, mostly tiny figures representing mankind in situations of symbolic compulsive direction or motivation.

Fascinated by ambiguities, Boshier saw some of his earlier Pop paintings as embodying social comment based on autobiographical experience, though this was not always explicit. Strangely enough, after he had gone to India for a year on a scholarship, he completely rejected the figurative element in his painting. In *The New Generation* exhibition at the Whitechapel Gallery in 1964, Boshier's post-Indian paintings echoed more the eye-dazzling stripes and hard-edge patterns of Bridget Riley and Frank Stella than any assimilated visual data from the East. The use of shaped stretchers for surfaces that projected beyond the usual rectangular enclosure implied a possible allegorical meaning in the shape of the canvas. The colour bands, stepped and curbed, alternately straight and diagonal, embody a symbolism more subtle than any exercise in abstract Op organization. The Pop allusion (that of a giant table game akin to "Monopoly") is played down in a cool context, but the metaphors can be no less than intentional. Traffic signs, painted wall and street insignia and directions—these are all part of the universal eye-reaction vocabulary.

In common with several of his generation, Boshier is concerned less with a medium for its own character than for its capacity to carry the message he loads into it. Experiments in plastic constructions, though inconclusive, indicated his versatility and adaptability

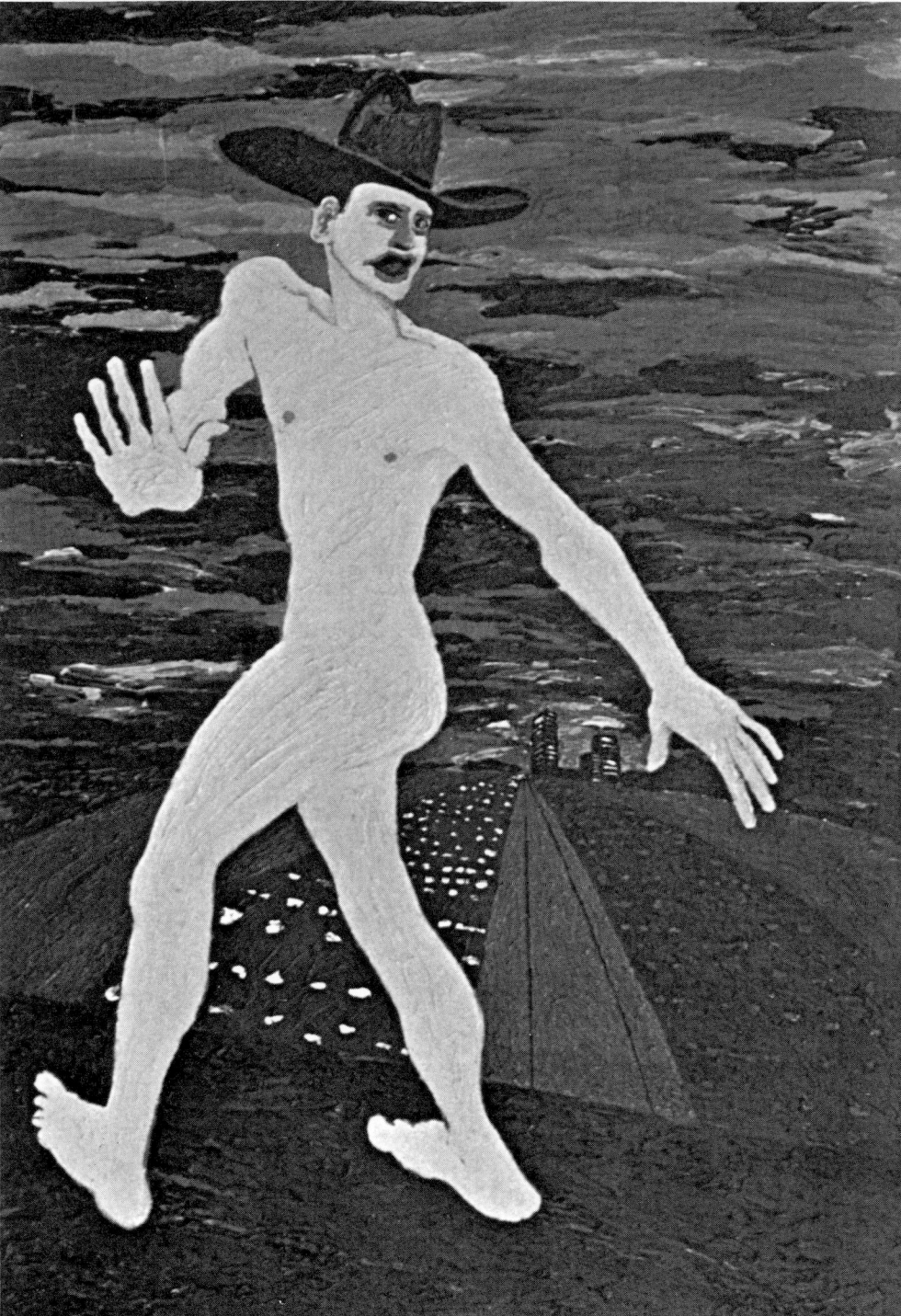

Derek Boshier: *Frightened Cowboy*, 1986

1952-53; spent summers in Paris, 1953-54; lived and established studio in Florence, and travelled throughout northern Italy to study fresco sites, 1953-54; influenced strongly by exhibition of the works of Piero della Francesca, Paolo Uccello, Andrea del Castagno, and Domenico Veneziano, Florence, 1954; returned to Bogota, 1955; lived in Mexico City, 1956-57; travelled to New York and Washington, D.C., 1957, 1958; lived in Bogota, 1957-60; commissioned by Banco Central Hipotecario to paint a fresco in its Medellin branch, 1960; lived in New York, 1961-73: rented a loft studio at MacDougal and Third Streets in Greenwich Village, 1961-64, moved to Tomkins Square on Lower East Side, 1963-71, built summer house and studio on Stephen's Hand Pass Road, Easthampton, Long Island, and established a studio at 214 West 14th Street, 1964-72, moved to 30 Fifth Avenue, 1971; rented an apartment in Paris, and established studio in Bogota, 1971; rented studio on rue Monsieur-le-Prince, Paris, and bought house in which to spend summers in Cajicá, north of Bogota, 1972; has lived in Paris since 1973; concentrated almost entirely on sculpture, 1976-77; established Sala Pedro Botero, with 16 of his works, at the Museo de Zea, Medellin, 1977; established and maintains studio on rue du Dragon in building formerly housing the Académie Julian, Paris, since 1978. Professor of Painting, Escuela de Bellas Artes, Universidad Nacional, Bogota, 1958-60. Recipient: First Prize for Painting, *Salon Anual de Artistas Colombianos*, Bogota, 1958; Colombian Section Award, *Guggenheim International Award Exhibition*, New York, 1960; Andrés Bello Award, President of Venezuela, 1975. Cruz de Boyacá for service to Colombia, Government of Antioquia, 1977. Agent: Marlborough Fine Art, New York. Address: c/o Marlborough Fine Art, 40 West 57th Street, New York, New York 10019, U.S.A.

Individual Exhibitions:

1951	Galerias de Arte Foto-Estudio Leo Matiz, Bogota
1952	Galerias de Arte de Leo Matiz, Bogota
1955	Biblioteca Nacional, Bogota (travelled to Club de Profesionales, Medellin, Colombia)
1957	Galeria Antonio Souza, Mexico City
	Fernando Botero of Colombia, Pan American Union, Washington, D.C.
1958	*Oleos*, Galeria Antonio Souza, Mexico City
	Recent Oils, Watercolors, Drawings, Gres Gallery, Washington, D.C.
1959	*Obras Recientes*, Biblioteca Nacional, Bogota
1960	Gres Gallery, Washington, D.C.
1961	Galeria de Arte El Callejón, Bogota
1962	Gres Gallery, Chicago
	The Contemporaries, New York
1964	*Obras Recientes*, Museo de Arte Moderno, Bogota
	Bosquejos Realidades, Galeria Arte Moderno, Bogota
1965	*Recent Works*, Zora Gallery, Los Angeles
1966	Staatliche Kunsthalle, Baden-Baden, West Germany (travelled to the Galerie Buchholz, Munich)
	Ölbilder und Zeichnungen, Galerie Brusberg, Hannover
	Recent Works, Milwaukee Art Center
1968	Galeria Juana Mordó, Madrid
	Paintings by Fernando Botero and Leopold Richter, Walter Engel Gallery, Toronto
	Galerie Buchholz, Munich
1969	Center for Inter-American Relations, New York
	Peintures, Pastels, Fusains, Galerie Claude Bernard, Paris
1970	*Bilder 1962-1969*, Staatliche Kunsthalle, Baden-Baden, West Germany (travelled to Haus am Waldsee, Berlin; Städtische Kunsthalle, Dusseldorf; Kunstverein, Hamburg; and Kunsthalle, Bielefeld)
	Botero/Coronel/Rodon, Museo de la Universidad de Puerto Rico
	Hanover Gallery, London
	Botero/Cuevas: Paintings, Drawings. Walter Engel Gallery, Toronto

in approach. He says: "Art is about ideas, and your medium is the medium that is best suited to your ideas." As a friend of poets and writers, he is interested in film-making and in writing for communication—e.g., fiction. He has written a novel, and—as he demonstrates—his approach to art is open-ended.

—G. S. Whittet

BOTERO, Fernando.

Colombian. Born Fernando Botero Angulo in Medellin, Antioquia, 19 April 1932. Educated at primary and secondary schools in Medellin, 1938-49; Liceo de la Universidad de Antioquia, Medellin, 1950, baccalaureate; studied at the Real Academia de Bellas Artes, San Ferdinando, Spain, and copied paintings of Goya, Veláquez, and others at the Museo del Prado, Madrid, 1952; studied fresco painting at the Accademia San Marco, and art history, under Roberto Longhi, at the Università degli Studi, Florence, 1953. Married Gloria Zea in 1955 (divorced, 1960); children: Fernando, Lina, and Juan Carlos; married Cedilia Zambrano in 1964 (divorced, 1975); son: Pedro (died in auto crash, 1974). Worked as an illustrator for the Sunday Literary Supplement of *El Colombiano*, Medellin, 1948- 51; worked briefly as a set designer for the Compania Lope de Vega touring Spanish theatre group, 1950. Independent artist since 1951: lived in Bogota, then moved to Tolú on the Gulf of Morrosquillo, also painting at Coveñas and the islands of San Bernardo, 1951; returned to Bogota, then travelled to Barcelona, and lived in Madrid,

1971   *Botero/Lindner/Wesselmann: Ausgewähte Bilder, Zeichnungen und Grafik.* Galerie Brusberg, Hannover

1972   Marlborough Gallery, New York
       Bleisiftzeichnungen, Sepiazeichnungen, Aquarelle, Galerie Buchholz, Munich
       Pastels, Fusains, Sanguines, Galerie Claude Bernard, Paris

1973   *Retrospectiva 1948–1972,* Colegio San Carlos, Bogota
       Marlborough Galleria d'Arte, Rome
       Botero/Akawie, Pyramid Galleries, Washington, D.C.

1974   *Aquarelle und Zeichnungen,* Galerie Brusberg, Hannover
       Sala de Arte, Biblioteca Publica Piloto, Medellin, Colombia
       Marlborough Galarie, Zurich

1975   Museum Boymans-van Beuningen, Rotterdam
       Galeria Adlec Castillo, Caracas
       Marlborough Gallery, New York (travelled to Marlborough Godard, Toronto; and Marlborough Godard, Montreal, 1976)

1976   *Aquarelles et Dessins,* Galerie Claude Bernard, Paris
       Museo de Arte Contemporaneo, Caracas
       Pyramid Galleries, Washington, D.C.
       Arte Independencia, La Galeria de Colombia, Bogota

1977   *Las Sala Pedro Botero,* Museo de Arte Medellin, Colombia
       Sculptures, at *FIAC,* Grand Palais, Paris

1978   *Das Plastische Werk,* Galerie Brusberg, Hannover (travelled to Skulpturenmuseum der Stadt Marl, West Germany)

1979   Galerie Isy Brachot, Knokkc, Belgium
       Musée d'Ixelles, Brussels (travelled to Konsthall, Lund, Sweden; and Sonja Henie-Neils Onstad Foundations, Oslo)
       Galerie Claude Bernard, Paris
       Galeric Brusberg, Hannover
       Hirshhorn Museum and Sculpture Garden, Smithsonian Institution, Washington, D.C. (travelled to the Art Museum of South Texas, Corpus Christi, 1980)

1980   *Aquarelles, Dessins, Sculptures,* Galerie Beyeler, Basle

1981   Marlborough Gallery, New York
       Betsy Rosenfield Gallery, Chicago

1982   *Sculpture and Drawings,* Hokin Gallery, Chicago

1983   Galerie Beyeler, Basle
       Thomas Segal Gallery, Boston

1984   Proctor Institute, Utica, New York
       Everhart Museum, Scranton, Pennsylvania
       Cornell University, Ithaca, New York
       Purdue University, Lafayette, Indiana
       Botero, at the *International Art Expo,* Chicago

1985   National Museum, Bogota, Colombia
       Museo de Ponce, Puerto Rico
       Marlborough Gallery, New York

1986   Museum of Contemporary Art, Caracas, Venezuela
       Kunsthalle der Hypo-Kulturstiftung, Munich
       Kunsthalle, Bremen, West Germany
       Tokyo Art Gallery, Tokyo
       Daimaru Museum, Osaka, Japan
       City Art Museum, Niigata, Japan

Selected Group Exhibitions:

1948   *Exposición de Pintores Antioqueños,* Instituto de Bellas Artes, Medellin, Colombia

1952   *Salón Anual de Artistas Colombianos,* Biblioteca Nacional, Bogota (and 1957, 1958, 1959)

1956   *Gulf-Caribbean Art Exhibition,* Museum of Fine Arts, Houston (toured the United States, 1956–57)

1958   *Guggenheim International Award,* Guggenheim Museum, New York (and 1960)

1959   *Botero/Grau/Obregón/Ramirez/Villegas,/Wiedemann,* Galeria de Arte Callejón, Bogota
       Arte de Colombia, Galleria Nazionale d'Arte Moderna, Rome (travelled to Liljevalchs Konsthall, Stockholm; Rautenstrauch-Joest-Museum, Cologne; Staatliche Kunsthalle, Baden-Baden; and the Sociedad Española de Amigos del Arte, Madrid)

1965   *The Emergent Decade: Latin American Painting,* Guggenheim Museum, New York (toured the United States and Canada, 1965–67)

1970   *Latin American Paintings and Drawings from the Collection of John and Barbara Duncan,* Center for Inter-American Relations, New York (toured the United States, 1970–72)

1971   *12 Artists from Latin America,* Ringling Museum of Art, Sarasota, Florida

1977   *Recent Latin American Drawings 1969–1976: Lines of Vision,* Center for Inter-American Relations, New York (toured the United States and Philippines, 1977–79)

Collections:

Museo de Zea, Medellin, Colombia; Museo de Arte Moderno, Bogota; Museo de Bellas Artes, Santiago; Museum of Modern Art, New York; Guggenheim Museum, New York; New York University; Baltimore Museum of Art; Neue Pinakothek, Munich; Museo d'Arte Moderno del Vaticano, Rome; Museo de Arte Contemporaneo, Madrid.

Publications:

By BOTERO: books—*Botero,* portfolio of 20 black-and-white reproductions, with an introduction by Walter Engel, Bogota 1952; articles—"Picasso y la Inconformidad en el Arte" in *El Colombiano* (Medellin), 17 July 1949; "Anatomia de Una Locura" in *El Colombiano* (Medellin), 7 August 1949; interview, with Wibke von Bonin, in *Fernando Botero,* exhibition catalogue, New York 1972; interview, with Titia Berlage, in *Fernando Botero,* exhibition catalogue, Rotterdam 1975.

On BOTERO: books—*Fernando Botero,* exhibition catalogue, Bogota 1951; *Botero,* exhibition catalogue, Bogota 1952; *Botero* by Walter Engel, Bogota 1952; *Gulf-Caribbean Art Exhibition,* catalogue, with foreword by Lee Malone and an introduction by José Gómez-Sicre, Houston 1956; *Fernando Botero of Colombia,* exhibition catalogue, Washington, D.C. 1957; *Fernando Botero: Recent Oils, Watercolors, Drawings,* exhibition catalogue, Washington, D.C. 1958; *Botero: Obras Recientes,* exhibition catalogue, Bogota, 1959; *Botero,* exhibition catalogue, Chicago 1962; *Botero: Recent Works,* exhibition catalogue, Los Angeles 1965; *Fernando Botero,* exhibition catalogue, with text by Daniel Robbins, Baden-Baden, West Germany 1966; *Fernando Botero: Recent Works,* exhibition catalogue, with a foreword by Tracy Atkinson, Milwaukee 1966; *The Emergent Decade: Latin American Painters and Painting in the 1960's,* Ithaca, New York 1966; *Paintings by Fernando Botero and Leopold Richter,* exhibition catalogue, Toronto 1968; *Fernando Botero,* exhibition catalogue, with foreword by Stanton Catlin, and essay by Klaus Gallwitz, New York 1969; *Botero: Peintures, Pastels, Fusains,* exhibition catalogue, with text by Fernando Arrabal, Paris 1969; *Botero* by Klaus Gallwitz, Munich 1970; *Botero: Pastels, Fusains, Sanguines,* exhibition catalogue, with an introduction by Jean paget, Paris 1972; *Fernando Botero: Retrospectiva 1948–1972,* exhibition catalogue, with text by Tracy Atkinson, Bogota 1973; *Botero* by Marta Trata, Mexico City 1973; *Fernando Botero* by German Arciniegas, Madrid 1973, translated by Gabriela Arciniegas, New York 1977; *Botero,* exhibition catalogue, by Antonio Hernandez Barrera, Medellin, Colombia 1974; *Fernando Botero,* exhibi-

Fernando Botero: *Man on Horseback*, 1982

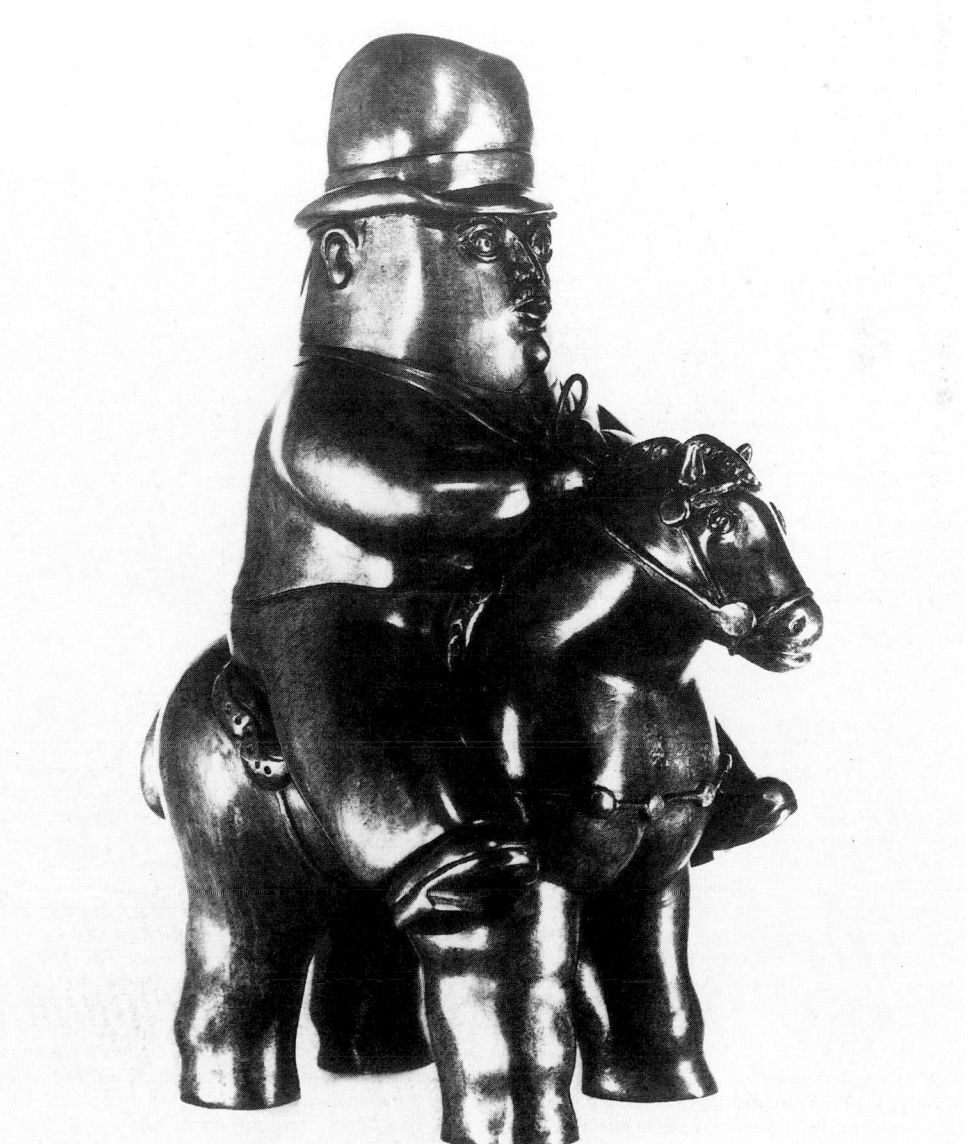

tion catalogue, with an introduction by R. Hammacher-van den Brande, Rotterdam 1975; *Fernando Botero,* exhibition catalogue, with an introduction by Sam Hunter, New York 1975; *Los Intocables: Botero, Grau, Negret, Obregón, Ramirez V.* by Fausto Panesso, Bogota 1975; *Botero: Aquarelles et Dessins,* exhibition catalogue, with an introduction by Severo Sarduy, Paris 1976; *Fernando Botero,* exhibition catalogue, with an introduction by Sofia Imber, Caracas, Venezuela 1976; *Botero,* exhibition catalogue, with text by Robert Pinzón, Bogota 1976; *Fernando Botero* by Klaus Gallwitz, New York, London, and Stuttgart 1976; *Modern Art* by Sam Hunter and John Jacobus, New York 1976; *La Sala Pedro Botero,* exhibition catalogue, with text by Belisario Betancur, Medellin, Colombia 1977; *Recent Latin American Drawings 1969–1979: Lines of Vision,* exhibition catalogue, with essays by Barbara Duncan and Damián Bayón, New York 1977; *Fernando Botero: Das Plastische Werk* by Ursula Bode, Hannover 1978; *Fernando Botero,* exhibition catalogue, with text by Marie-Françoise Carolus-Barré, Brussels 1979; *Fernando Botero,* exhibition catalogue, by Cynthia Jaffee McCabe, with foreword by Abram Lerner, Washington, D.C. 1979; *Fernando Botero: Malerier, Tegninger, Skulpturer,* exhibition catalogue, with texts by Marianne Nanne-Brahammar and Ole Henrik Moe, Oslo 1979; *Botero: Aquarelles, Dessins, Sculptures,* exhibition catalogue, with an introduction by Ernst Beyeler, Basle 1980; *Botero* by Carter Ratcliff, New York 1980.

Fernando Botero is one of those fortunate artists whose subject or style becomes immediately recognizable. His pneumatic nudes and overdressed, adipose children form a personal, fantasy world of undeniable conviction. The combination of obese, exaggerated, human forms, elaborately decorative costumes and the oversweet colours of South American peasant art results in images in which wit and sympathy are undermined by an aggressive irreverence.

It must be noted that the two major influences in Botero's art are Goya and Veláquez. Born in the industrial centre of Colombian life, Medellin, he moved to to Bogota, where he held his first exhibitons, and then entered the Academia in San Ferdinando, Spain. Here the work of the two great Spanish masters had their effect; from Goya he absorbed a critical view of the human comedy, whilst in the meticulously painted, realistic still-lifes, one recognizes the influence of Velázquez. In Europe Botero also studied fresco techniques in Florence, especially impressed by the famous series of wall paintings by Piero della Francesca in Arezzo. These disparate forces in his development were bound into an artistic whole by Botero's love for his native Colombia, whose daily life, religious myths and folk art, descended from the Indians, remain his basic subjects.

The resultant images are curiously enigmatic; he is neither as open a commentator as Goya, nor as willing a participant as Velázquez. On the other hand, nor is he merely a recording camera. Whilst the real world is Botero's point of departure, he feels at liberty to use anti-natural devices common to native art—or to the "primitive" painters of Christian Europe—his own depiction as a tiny figure, carrying palette and brushes, beside a full-length portrait, or his self-portrait on Communion Day, with two tiny devils whispering into his ear.

—Charles Spencer

BOTO, Martha.

Argentinian. Born in Buenos Aires, 27 December 1925. Studied drawing, Academy Prilidiano Pueyrredon, Buenos Aires, 1942–43; Ernesto de la Cracova Superior Academy of Fine Arts, Buenos Aires, 1944–46. Married to Gregorio Vardanega. Independent artist since 1946, producing kinetic sculptures and installations that alter light: has lived and worked in Paris since 1959. Founding Member, Groupe Artistes non-Figurative Argentins, 1956. Recipient: Painting Prize, Museo Quinquella Martin, Buenos Aires, 1947. Agent: Galerie Denise Rene, 196 Boulevard Saint-Germain, 75007 Paris. Address: Atelier 127, 21 rue de l'Admiral-Roussin, 75015 Paris, France.

Individual Exhibitions:

1951	Galerie van Riel et Krayd, Paris (and each year through 1955)
1957	Galeria Galatea Pizarro, Buenos Aires
1960	Galerie H. Buenos Aires
1969	Galerie Denise René, Paris
1970	Galerie Thelen, Essen
1972	La Belle Epine, Val de Marne, France
1976	Centre Culturel, Sceaux, France

Selected Group Exhibitions:

1962	*Trente Argentins de la nouvelle generation,* Galerie Creuze, Paris
1963	*L'Art Lationamericain,* Musée d'Art Moderne, Paris
1964	*Chromocinétisme,* Maison des Beaux-Arts, Paris
1968	*Art Cinétique,* Maison de la Culture, Greenoble, France
1970	*Denise René in London,* Hayward Gallery, London
1971	*Art Argentin,* Kunsthalle, Basel
1973	*Art Cinétique,* Bagneaux, France
1981	*Grands et Jeunes d'Aujourd'hui,* Grand Palais, Paris
1983	*Electra,* Musée d'Art Moderne de la Ville, Paris
1987	*Féerie Cinetique,* Monte Carlo, Monaco

Collections:

Centre Georges Pompidou, Paris; Prefecture of Paris; Museo Nacional de Bellas Artes, Buenos Aires; Torcuato di Tella, Buenos Aires; Recklinghausen Museum, West Germany; Tel-Aviv Museum, Israel.

Martha Boto: *Vallée,* 1982

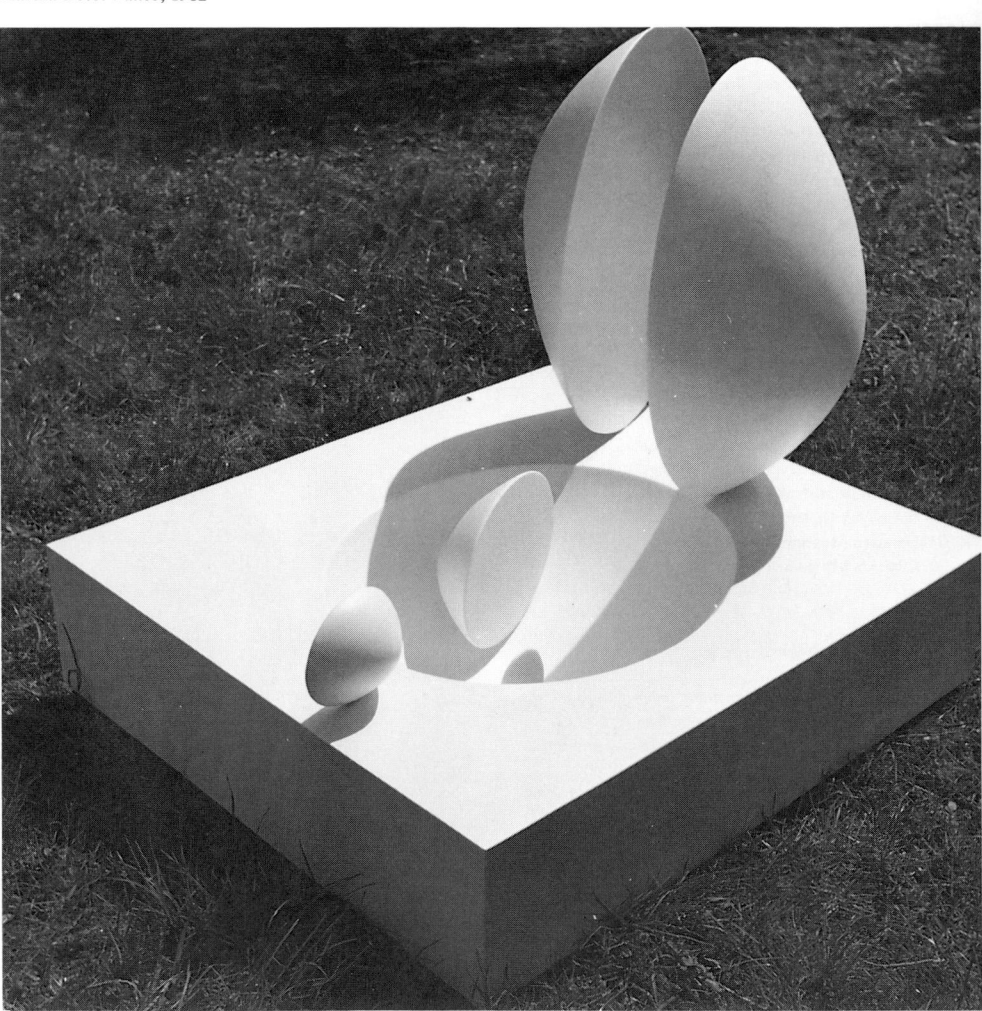

Publications:

On BOTO: books—*Artes y Letras Argentinas* by Cordova Iturburu, Buenos Aires 1961; *Naissance de l'Art cinétique* by Frank Popper, Paris 1966; *Art et Mouvement,* exhibition catalogue, by Denys Chevalier, Montreal 1967; *Martha Boto,* exhibition catalogue, by Michael Ragon, Paris 1969; *L'Art Actuel* by Tronche, Paris 1973; *L'Art Abstrait,* vol. 4, by Michel Ragon and Michel Seuphor, Paris 1975; articles—"L'Art de la lumiére artificielle" by Frank Popper in *L'Oeil* (Paris), December 1966; "Buenos Aires, nouvelle capitale artistique" by Michel Ragon in *Jardin des Arts* (Paris), April 1967; "Dalla Francia con amore" by Ettore Sottsas in *Domus* (Milan), July 1967; "Lumiére et mouvement" by Frank Popper in *Art Cinétique à Paris,* exhibition catalogue, Paris 1967.

Ever since we evolved into true human beings, we have been able to perceive or intuit the relationships which govern the cosmos, with its mysterious systems of energy and equilibrium. We are part of this evolving whole, and the interplay of permanence and change forms the very basis of our lives. The artist is the person who recognizes his place in this system and is able to reveal it to others.

From the very beginning, when I did my first impressionistic paintings of the natural world, I was fascinated by motion, color and light, and have always tried to reveal their sensuousness and evanescent rhythms. During my surrealist period, which was a natural reaction to my slavery to realism, I abandoned representation and sought to express the irrational and unconscious by means of symbolic figures. Thus by a more or less logical progression, I was drawn towards abstraction and a concern for spatial relationships.

I now became eager to escape from flat surfaces. I experimented with mobiles moving in space and with transparent construction which contained moving, colored water. The impulse to control light, color and motion, and to see natural movements in their relationship to space and time brought me to new aesthetic horizons. With my kinetic works I am now trying to create analogies to the underlying processes of cosmic motion.

I have tried to achieve this by two primary means. First, I have projected shifting forms on flat surfaces, thereby creating a sense of sudden changes, of appearances and disappearances, of transformations and luminous disclosures of changing rhythmic motions. Second, I have created various kinds of tubes, discs and mirrored surfaces—over which lights are programmed to play—in order to produce shimmering labyrinths and color and movement. A fixed structure is thus dissolved and diffused into a myriad of images, sometimes by means of mirrors placed on its sides or along its curved surfaces.

I have also experimented with translucent columns and mobiles, producing groups of reflections which once again express the relationships which exist between forms and space and between forms and time. I have sometimes used little steel balls which move through transparent structures at different rates of speed and with different kinds of natural rhythms. All of these attempts to integrate movement, light, color and space give my work a kind of instability which is sometimes hypnotic for viewers, sometimes pleasant—and sometimes disquieting. At the moment I am working with related groups of shapes, combining different volumes and white polygraphisms to suggest figures which have in themselves a principle of motion or seem to be moved by wind and water. What dominates my work is a sense of free forms, joyous, expressive, humanized; I have created my kinetic and illuminated structures to vitalize the urban spaces in which they are placed.

—Martha Boto

Martha Boto belongs to the tradition of South American Constructivism and has taken a prominent part in its conversion into kinetic art. Light and movement appear in all their purity and dynamism in her art, but there is always an underlying formal structure which can be seen or sensed.

Boto's works concentrate upon such features as rapid movement, circular forms and intense luminous effects. The light source itself is constantly moving in many of her works, and this results in a strong impression of contraction and expansion in the interplay of circles and planes, as well as a tendency for forms to appear and disappear, ranging from intensity to diffusion.

Martha Boto's investigation leads from the principle of repetition into the world of reflection and the progressive transformation of the image. In her "chromokinetic" works she has rarely used more than one colour, usually an ultramarine blue or a transparent rose. But the variations of the hues are many. They allow her to add an individual sense of completeness to the distinctive arrangements of movement through the manipulation of transparent light and enable the graphic properties inherent in the circle to emerge.

Boto's environment works realized since 1971 in and around Paris reflect all the accomplishments of the earlier research, yet in these works the sensuality of the rhythm, the hypnotizing variations of speeds, the subtle programmation of form transformation and the original treatment of colour and space take on a new dimension and most clearly demonstrate the interrelationship between the artist's technical/aesthetic achievements and her distinctive personality.

—Frank Popper

BOTSCHUYVER, Theo.

Dutch. Born in Rotterdam, 8 January 1943. Studied at the Academie voor Industriele Vormgeving, Eindhoven, 1960–65. Independent artist, Amsterdam, since 1967: Founder, with Jeffrey Shaw, Eventstructure Research Group (E.R.G.), Amsterdam 1967–82 (with the participation of Sean Wellesley-Miller 1967–69). Guest Lecturer, Department of Architecture, University of Eindhoven, 1970–71. Recipient: Grant from Arts Council, Amsterdam, 1967; Grants from Dutch Ministry of Culture, The Hague, 1970–75. Address: 126 Javastraat, Amsterdam 1094 HP, Netherlands.

Individual Exhibitions: (with E.R.G.)

1967	Sigma Projects, Amsterdam
	Sigma Projects, Rotterdam
	Casino Communal, Knokke, Belgium
1968	Museum of Modern Art, Oxford
	Open-Air display, at the *Brighton Festival*, Sussex
	Open-Air display, at the *City of London Festival*
1969	Institute of Contemporary Arts, London
	Six Events display, Amsterdam
	Six Events display, Rotterdam
	St. George's Art Center, Liverpool (with John Latham)
1970	Stedelijk Museum, Amsterdam
1972	National Gallery of Victoria, Melbourne
1973	Pinacotheca Gallery, Melbourne
	Tolarno Gallery, Melbourne
1974	Stedelijk Museum, Amsterdam
	De Lantaren, Rotterdam
	Drama Institute Theatre, Amsterdam
1975	National Bus Company, London (with Artist Placement Group)
1976	Genesis World Tour (with Genesis rock group)
1978	Stitching de Appel, Amsterdam
1979	Koopwaarders Plantsoen, Amsterdam Noord (permanent installation)
1980	De Hoogeberg, Velsen, Netherlands (permanent installation)
1981	Frascati Theatre, Amsterdam (permanent installation)
1982	Scholengemeenschap, Tilburg, Netherlands (permanent installation)

Selected Group Exhibitions:

1968	*Structure Gonfables*, Musée d'Art Moderne, Paris
	Contemporary Art from Holland, Kunsthalle, Berne
1969	*Kinetic Objects*, Frans Halsmuseum, Haarlem, Netherlands
1970	*Street Art Programme*, Hannover
1971	*Between 5*, Kunsthalle, Dusseldorf
1972	*British Avant-garde*, Gallery House, London
1974	*Tabarka Festival*, Tunisia
1975	*9th Biennale de Paris*, Musée d'Art Moderne de la Ville, Paris

Collections:

Dutch National Collection, The Hague; City Collection, Haarlem, Netherlands; City Collection, Amsterdam.

Publications:

By BOTSCHUYVER: books—*Evenstructures*, with E.R.G., Delft 1972; *Prospectus for the Strombeeld Foundation*, with E.R.G., Amsterdam 1980; articles—"Inflatable Structures and Participation," with E.R.G., in *Robho* (Paris), Spring 1968; "Concepts for an Operational Art," with E.R.G., in *Arts and Artists* (London), January 1969.

On BOTSCHUYVER: books—*Arthropods* by Jim Burns, New York 1971; *Kunst van Nu*, Amsterdam 1971; *Sonsbeek 71 Report*, Arnhem 1972; *9e Biennale de Paris*, exhibition catalogue, Paris 1975; articles—"Evenstructures" by Albrecht Kwast in *Pneutube*, exhibition catalogue, London 1969; "Eventstructure Research Group" by Ruud Englander in *Mickery Mouth* (Amsterdam), no. 11, 1971; "E.R.G. in Australia" by Terry Smith in *Studio International* (London), October 1972; "Diadrama" by Max Adrian in *Toneel Teatral* (Amsterdam), no. 1, 1974.

In 1980 the Museum Boymans-van Beuningen in Rotterdam published a catalogue with the very meaningful title: *Action, reality and fiction in the arts of the sixties in The Netherlands*. It is a detailed report, put together by students of the Institute of Arthistory, Groningen University. It is a well-documented overview of a roaring period that brought about a lot of good art.

Fluxus and Happening, as well as a typical Dutch phenomenon like the Provo-movement, short-lived collaborations between artists who later would occupy leading, individual positions in a more traditionally oriented artclimate, the whole repertory of artistic expressions that move out of the well-established boundaries, have been put in the correct chronological order. Theo Botschuyver's activities were closely related with this general atmosphere of cultural liberation that reigned during the sixties. They take place at the end of the period and they are, in a way, its closing end because of the organizational dimensions and applied technical facilities.

The first documented project (together with Jeffrey Shaw and Tjebbe van Tijen) was a hundred meter air-filled tube that meandered through a labyrinth-like space that formed the setting for a Happening-like party entitled *Hommage a Clovis Trouille* (1965). This project still had an improvised character, the next one demanded extensive preparation and organization. The title of the project was Corpocinema, executed in Rotterdam and Amsterdam in 1967. From a thirty meter distance slides and films were projected over a large polythene construction that was transparent and that moved, not only in form but in color as well. The audience had access to this moving form and formed part of its totality, overwhelmed. At the same time, for those remaining outside, one was a moving element in this continuously changing form. Five nights different pieces were performed with meaningful titles like *Smokespawn*, *Fluidomatics*, *Jellyquake*, *Foamswell*, *Splattersplode*. In the Amsterdam version a beatband performed a program inside entitled the *Dolly Pond Church of Cacophony*. Corpocinema has been one of the projects coordinated by the Sigma-centre, also responsible for the famous Continuous Drawing (1967) leading from London through Amsterdam to Rotterdam and the *Concerto for three grinding-organs* (1967) on Dam Square, Amsterdam. Together with Jeffrey Shaw, in 1969 Botschuyver initiated the Eventstructure Research Group that recapitulates some elements of the Corpocinema. Large air-filled objects are placed in the streets, as play-things, inviting the people to participate by crawling over them.

—A. F. Wagemans

BOURGEOIS, Louise.

American. Born in Paris, France, 25 December 1911; moved to New York, 1938. Educated at the Lycée Fenelon, Paris, 1932; Sorbonne, Paris, 1932–35; Ecole de Louvre, Paris, 1936–37; Académie des Beaux-Arts, Paris 1936–38; Atelier Bissière, Paris, 1936–37; Académie Julian, Paris, 1938; Atelier Fernand Léger, Paris, 1938; also studied with Marcel Duchamp in New York. Married Robert Goldwater in 1938; children: Michel, Jean-Louis and Alain. Independent artist, New York, since 1938. Taught at the Academie de la Grande Chaumière, Paris, 1937–38; Great Neck Public Schools, New York, 1960; Brooklyn College, New York, 1963, 1968; and Pratt Institute, New York, 1965–67. Professor of Sculpture, School of Visual Arts, New York; Lecturer, Lebanon College, New York University; Critic, New York Studio School. Recipient: National Endowment for the Arts Grant, 1973; Outstanding Visual Arts Achievement Award, Women's Caucus for Art, New York, 1980; Skowhegan Medal, Skowhegan School of Painting and Sculpture, Maine, 1984. Honorary doctorate: Yale University, New Haven, Connecticut,

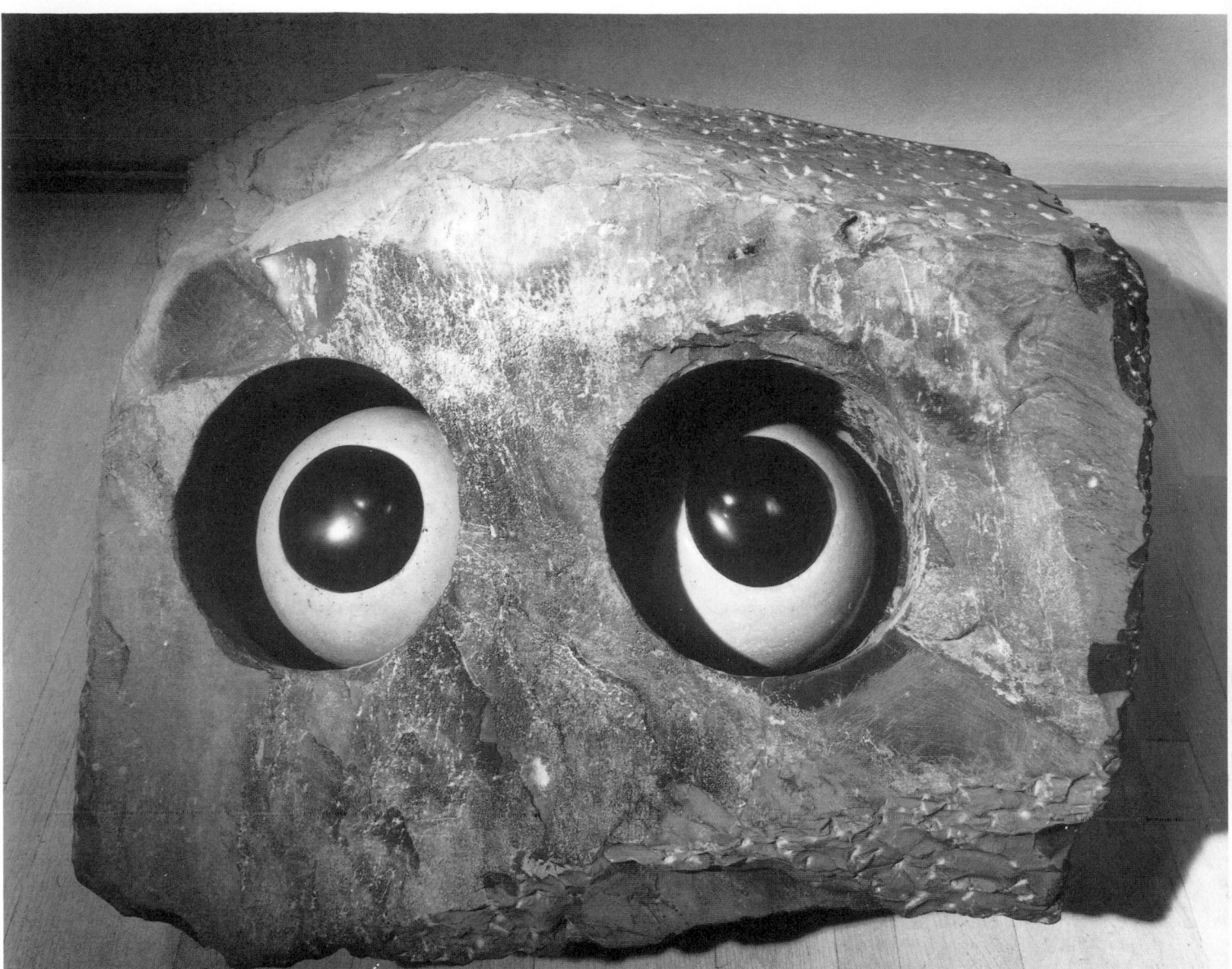

Louise Bourgeois: *Nature Study—Velvet Eyes*, 1984

1977; Bard College, Annandale-on-Hudson, New York, 1981; Massachusetts College of Art, Boston, 1983; Maryland Art Institute, Baltimore, 1984; The New School, New York, 1987. Agent: Xavier Fourcade Inc., New York; and Max Hutchinson Gallery, 138 Greene Street, New York, New York 10012. Address: c/o Xavier Fourcade Inc., 36 East 75th Street, New York, New York 10021, U.S.A.

Individual Exhibitions:

1945   Bertha Schaefer Gallery, New York
1947   Norlyst Gallery, New York
1949   Peridot Gallery, New York
1950   Peridot Gallery, New York
1953   Peridot Gallery, New York
        Allan Frumkin Gallery, Chicago
1959   Cornell University, Ithaca, New York
1964   The Stable Gallery, New York
        Rose Fried Gallery, New York
1974   112 Greene Street Gallery, New York
1975   Stable Gallery, New York
1978   *Structures*, Xavier Fourcade Inc., New York
        Confrontations, Hamilton Gallery, New York
1979   *Sculptures 1941–53*, Xavier Fourcade Inc., New York
        Art Museum, University of California, Berkeley

1980   *The Iconography of Louise Bourgeois*, Max Hutchinson Gallery, New York
        Sculpture: The Middle Years 1955–1970, Xavier Fourcade Inc., New York
1981   University of Chicago
1982   Robert Millery Gallery, New York
        Museum of Modern Art, New York (retrospective; travelled to Chicago and Akron, Ohio, 1983)
1984   Daniel Weinberg Gallery, Los Angeles
        Daniel Weinberg Gallery, San Francisco
        Robert Miller Gallery, New York
1985   Serpentine Gallery, London
        Galerie Maeght-Lelong, Zurich
        Galerie Maeght-Lelong, Paris (retrospective)
1986   Eyes Gallery, Doris Freedman Plaza, New York
        Texas Gallery, Dallas
1987   Robert Miller Gallery, New York
        Yares Gallery, Scottsdale, Arizona
        Taft Museum, Cincinnati (toured the United States, 1987–90)

Selected Group Exhibitions:

1945   *Whitney Annual*, Whitney Museum, New York (and regularly until 1973)
1969   *International Sculpture Biennale*, Carrara, Italy
1975   *200 Years of American Sculpture*, Whitney Museum of American Art, New York

1977   *Permanent Collection of American Art*, Whitney Museum, New York
1980   *The Originals: Women in Art*, Graham Gallery, New York
1981   *Decade of Transition 1940–50*, Whitney Museum, New York
1982   *Sculpture 1982: 20 American Artists*, San Francisco Museum of Modern Art
1983   *Portrait Sculpture*, State University of New York, Buffalo
1985   *Traces: Sculpture and Monuments*, Kunsthaus, Zurich
1987   *Von Chaos und Ordnung der Seele*, Universität Mainz, West Germany

Collections:

Museum of Modern Art, New York; Whitney Museum, New York; New York University; Storm King Arts Center, Mountainville, New York; Rhode Island School of Design, Providence; Detroit Institute of Arts; Musée d'Art Moderne, Paris; National Gallery of Australia, Canberra; Kunstmuseum, Lucerne, Switzerland.

Publications:

By BOURGEOIS: articles—"Louise Bourgeois: A Search for

Gravity," interview with Marcia Pels, in *Art International* (Lugano), October 1979.

On BOURGEOIS: books—*Nature in Abstraction* by John Baur, New York 1958; *American Art of Our Century*, exhibition catalogue, by Lloyd Goodrich and John Baur, New York 1961; *Form and Space; Sculpture in the 20th Century* by Eduard Trier, New York 1968; *The Iconography of Louise Bourgeois*, exhibition catalogue. New York 1980; *Louise Bourgeois* by Deborah Wye, New York 1982; articles— "Some Reflections Prompted by the Recent Work of Louis Bourgeois" by William S. Rubin in *Art International* (Lugano), April 1969, "Louise Bourgeois" by J. P. Marandel in *Art International* (Lugano), December 1971; "Louise Bourgeois from the Inside Out" By Lucy Lippard in *Artforum* (New York), March 1975; "Louise Bourgeois" by Carter Ratcliff in *Art International* (Lugano), November/December 1978; "The Discreet Charm of Louise Bourgeois" in *Art News* (New York), February 1980; "Louise Bourgeois" by Carter Ratcliff in *Vogue* (New York), October 1980.

A study of Louise Bourgeois' work from the late thirties to the present indicates that style and the evolution thereof are not fundamental to her character as an artist. Rather, it reveals the struggle of an individual actively attempting to define herself through her art. Bourgeois looks to herself for inspiration; consequently her work is personal and deeply autobiographical in content. Art functions for her as a psychological outlet, for making art is the process of giving tangible form to, and thus exorcising, the gripping, subconscious states of being that fill one with anxiety. Bourgeois' greatest achievement has been her ability to capture—and animate—the depth of the human psyche within a wide range of inventive and meaningful images.

Most of her prominent themes can be traced back to her years in France when a series of unresolved psychological conflicts governed her imagination. Her art belies the tension of her family life as created by the opposition of a clear-thinking, calm, and nurturing mother, and a powerful, volatile, and oppressive father. The polarity exacted anxiety, pain and anger, emotions that became the sources of Bourgeois's art. The psychological trauma of the war years, during which time her father was wounded, also had an impact on her work. After the war an English tutor caused the Bourgeois family additional problems because of her eventual liaison with Louise's father. The complications inherent in that triangle, the betrayals and primordial jealousies, seem to constitute a convincing origin for the violence in a significant part of her oeuvre.

Bourgeois' career began to take form in the mid-1940's after studying at several schools in France, including the Academic Ransom, the Academic Julian, the Academie de la Grande-Chaumiere, and the Ecole des Beaux-Arts, from 1934 to 1938. Stylistically, by the end of 1944 a grid scheme began to dominate the compositions of her paintings. She has related her use of this surface structure to her early family connections with tapestries and the delineation of their weave. During this period she developed an interest in balancing the formal issues of abstraction with the depiction of symbolic subject matter, a concern which she shared with the Abstract Expressionist tradition. As the decade progressed, Bourgeois' painting began to evolve toward a more personal, quasi-figurative imagery, with an underlying spirit of Surrealism. Her work moved toward the exploration of the reality of the subconscious. In effect, Surrealism encouraged her to tap the complex texture of her personal life as a source for her art.

Not to be overlooked in these early years is Bourgeois' involvement with feminism. The "Femme-Maison" paintings of 1947, portrayals of women with houses perched on their bodies in place of heads, are among her most powerful images. They are also symbols, moving in thematic directions that preoccupy the rest of her career. In them, a woman's sign of identity, her face, has been replaced by a house, implying that domesticity becomes the very definition of these women, since they have no other means by which to speak. Interestingly, the feminist dimension

of her early imagery was not recognised until 30 years later.

In 1949 Bourgeois abandoned painting as a medium and began to explore the possibilities of sculpture, with the greatest level of substantiality and physical impact afforded by its three-dimensional nature. By 1950 she had made over thirty sculptures and had achieved a surprising breadth of emotion through an increasingly formal sophistication. Her 1953 piece "Foret" embodied a new sculptural concept that would characterize her formal and thematic development of wood sculpture in the fifties. In this piece Bourgeois crowded a large assemblage of unusual elements together on a single base, suggesting a primordial group of plants. Due to the group's placement on the floor, it seems to be growing, as sprouting seeds or pods. Furthering the theme of growth, Bourgeois exhibited "One and Others" in 1955. With its colourful, separate spools, this piece appears as a garden or bouquet. Yet viewed from certain angles, it takes on the form of a single flower whose blooming petals crate an organic symbol of health and burgeoning fecundity. The title, however, brings the sculpture back to the human world, suggesting individuals of various shapes and sizes huddling in mutual support and interdependence. This technique of clustering and crowding elements on a base is one that Bourgeois has employed persistently as a visual counterpart or symbol for the interactions of groups.

After 1953, Bourgeois participated in no solo shows until 1964 in New York. The highly politicized atmosphere of the 60s may have contributed to the transition of her formal development, as she was actively involved with certain issues. Her work was still an investigation of psychological and symbolic meaning. Yet the entire decade represented a time of wide experimentation with plaster, cement, rubber, latex, plastics, marble, and bronze. She toyed with twisted arrangements, labyrinthine formations, and amorphous masses of plaster or cement. With these eccentric pieces she tried to animate such psychological states as fear, vulnerability, and loss of control. She revived her favourite themes of withdrawl, hiding, protection, sheltering and nurturing. "Lairs," cavernous plaster structures resembling cocoons, illustrate these themes. The 1967 "Landscape" series expanded the format of "Lair," yet they bear the suggestions of human contours which are the beginnings of the sexual works that follow.

During the 60s and 70s, when feminism was gathering strength, sexuality finally emerged explicitly in her work. Her previous definition of woman—that of being helpless, expendable, and utterly without identity—gradually gave way to a new conception tending toward a greater aggressiveness, sophistication, and elegance.

Her work in the 70s seemed to fill a distinct aesthetic need for personal content and meaning well beyond her earlier achievements. "The Destruction of the Father," 1974, a continuation of her earlier preoccupation with the hidden recesses of the plaster "Lairs," was the loudest personal statement of her career. This piece was the reincarnation of a childhood fantasy in which the members of her family dismembered and devoured its self-important, domineering father.

The wide interest in and new recognition of Bourgeois's work in the late 70s and early 80s were demonstrated by several distinguished awards and a series of four exhibitions that focused on earlier periods of her work. She received an honorary degree from Yale University in 1977; an outstanding achievement award from the Women's Caucus for Art in 1980; and a secondary honourary degree from Bard College in 1981. The exhibitions of her early wood figures, her early paintings, and her middle-period sculpture in 1980 allowed Bourgeois to further explore and interpret her former imagery and themes. In conjunction with this work, she continued making new sculpture.

Bourgeois's work is best understood when it is looked at as a significant, singular entity its distinctive features identified, and its essence revealed. This

approach defies the intellectual framework of contemporary art history, for it does not progress logically in the development of style. The independent course of Bourgeois's work, its variety of forms, limits the results of this traditional approach.

—Carrie Barker

BOYD, Arthur (Merrick Bloomfield).

Australian. Born in Murrumbeena, near Melbourne, Victoria, 24 July 1920. Educated at State School, Murrumbeena 1927–35; mainly self-taught in art from 1935, but influenced initially by the painter Jo Bergner, Melbourne, 1937–38. Served as cartographic field surveyor, Australian Army, in Melbourne and Bendigo, 1940–43. Married Yvonne Hartland Lennie in 1945; children: Polly, Jamie and Lucy. Worked in paint factory, Melbourne, 1934–36; as potter, Melbourne, 1943–48; independent artist, concentrating exclusively on painting, Melbourne 1948–55, in Beaumaris, Victoria 1955–59, in Nowra, New South Wales, and in London and Woodbridge, Suffolk, since 1959: first theatre decors, Edinburgh, 1963. Recipient: *Encyclopedia Britannica* Award, 1971; Fellowship in Creative Arts, Australian National University, Canberra, 1971–72. Officer, Order of the British Empire (O.B.E.), 1970; Officer, Order of Australia (A.O.), 1979. Agent: Fischer Fine Art, 30 King Street, St. James, London S.W.1. Address: c/o The Commercial Bank of Australia, 34 Piccadilly, London W 1, England; or Box 343, North Nowra, New South Wales 2540, Australia.

Individual Exhibitions:

1937	Westminster Gallery, Melbourne
1939	Royden White Library, University of Melbourne (with Jo Bergner)
1940	Athenaetum Gallery, Melbourne
1949	Kozminsky Galleries, Melbourne
1950	David Jones Gallery, Sydney (retrospective)
1951	Princes Gallery, Melbourne (retrospective, travelled to the Marodian Gallery, Brisbane)
	John Martin's Gallery, Adelaide
1952	Princes Gallery, Melbourne
	Peter Bray Galleries, Melbourne
	Macquarie Galleries, Sydney
1953	Peter Bray Galleries, Melbourne (retrospective)
	Johnstone Gallery, Brisbane
1954	Peter Bray Galleries, Melbourne
1958	Australian Galleries, Melbourne
	South Australian Society of Arts, Adelaide
	Terry Clune Gallery, Sydney
	David Jones Gallery, Sydney
1960	Zwemmer Gallery, London
1962	Whitechapel Art Gallery, London (retrospective)
1963	Australian Galleries, Melbourne
	Terry Clune Gallery, Sydney
	Ceramic Paintings by Arthur Boyd, Zwemmer Gallery, London
1964	National Gallery of South Australia, Adelaide (retrospective)
	Museum of Modern Art and Design, Melbourne (retrospective)
	Bear Lane Gallery, Oxford
1965	Skinner Gallery, Perth
	Australian Galleries, Melbourne
1966	Hungry Horse Art Gallery, Sydney
1969	*Retrospective Exhibition*, Richard Demarco Gallery, Edinburgh
	Arthur Tooth & Sons, London
	Hamet Gallery, London
	Maltzahn Gallery, London
1971	Australian National University, Canberra Skinner Gallery, Perth
1973	*Recent Paintings*, Fischer Fine Art, London
1977	Fischer Fine Art, London

1980 Folkstone Arts Centre, Kent
      Fischer Fine Art, London
1981 Britten-Pears School, Aldeburgh, Suffolk
1982 Queensland University, Brisbane
      Australian Galleries, Melbourne
1983 Fischer Fine Art, London
1984 Art Gallery of South Australia, Adelaide
1986 Fischer Fine Art, London

Selected Group Exhibitions:

1942 *Contemporary Art Society,* Athenaeum Gallery, Melbourne (and annually until 1946)
1953 *12 Australian Artists,* New Burlington Galleries, London (toured the U.K.)
1955 *Australian Contemporary Painting.* National Gallery of Victoria, Melbourne (toured Australia)
1958 *Biennale,* Venice
1963 *Australian Painting and Sculpture in Europe Today,* New Metropole Arts Centre, Folkstone, Kent (toured West Germany and the Netherlands)
1966 *Australian Painters 1964–66.* Corcoran Gallery, Washington, D.C.
1972 *Australian Prints,* Victoria and Albert Museum, London
1981 *Australian Drawings of the 30s and 40s,* Victoria and Albert Museum, London
1983 *The Boyd Family,* Arts Council Gallery, Canberra
1985 *Representations Abroad,* Hirshhorn Museum, Washington, D.C.

Collections:

Department of External Affairs, Canberra; Australian National University, Canberra; National Gallery of Victoria, Melbourne; Art Gallery of New South Wales, Sydney; National Gallery of Queensland, Brisbane; National Gallery of South Australia, Adelaide; Art Gallery of Western Australia, Perth; Museum and Art Gallery of Tasmania, Hobart; Contemporary Art Society, London; Rhodes House Trust, Oxford.

Publications:

By BOYD: books—*Saint Francis of Assisi,* with text by T. S. R. Boase, London 1968; *Nebuchadnezzar: 34 Paintings and 18 Drawings by Arthur Boyd,* with text by T. S. R. Boase, London 1972; *Jonah,* with poems by Porter, London 1973.

On BOYD: books—*Arthur Boyd,* exhibition catalogue, with text by Bryan Robertson, London 1960; *Australian Painting* by Bernard Smith, Melbourne 1962, rev. ed. as *Australian Painting 1788–1970,* Melbourne 1971; *Arthur Boyd,* exhibition catalogue, with text by Bryan Robertson, London 1962; *Ceramic Paintings by Arthur Boyd,* exhibition catalogue, with text by T. S. R. Boase, Oxford 1964; *Day of My Delight* by Martin Boyd, Melbourne 1965; *Arthur Boyd* by Franz Philipp, London 1967; *Encyclopaedia of Australian Art* edited by Alan MacCulloch, Melbourne 1968; *Arthur Boyd: Retrospective Exhibition* catalogue with texts by T. G. Rosenthal and Cordelia Oliver, Edinburgh, 1969; *Art in Britain 1969–1970* by Edward Lucie-Smith and Patricia White, London 1970; *Arthur Boyd: Etchings and Lithographs* by Imre von Maltzahn, London 1971; *Arthur Boyd: Drawings 1934–1970,* with a foreword by Laurie Thomas, London 1973; *Arthur Boyd: Recent Paintings,* exhibition catalogue, with text by Robert Melville, London 1973; *Outlines of Australian Art: The Joseph Brown Collection* by Daniel Thomas, Melbourne and Sydney 1973, London 1974; *Arthur Boyd,* exhibition catalogue, with an introduction by Robert Melville, Folkestone, Kent 1980; *The Art of Arthur Boyd* by Ursula Hoff, London 1986.

Arthur Boyd is a distinguished member of the remarkable generation of Australian artists who transferred to Britain in the post-war period and made a profound impact on European art. He also typifies the curious phenomenon (discernible in many other artists who move away physically from their origins) whereby aspects of native culture and subject-matter become more profoundly realised as a result of transplantation. Thus as with Sidney Nolan, Boyd remains

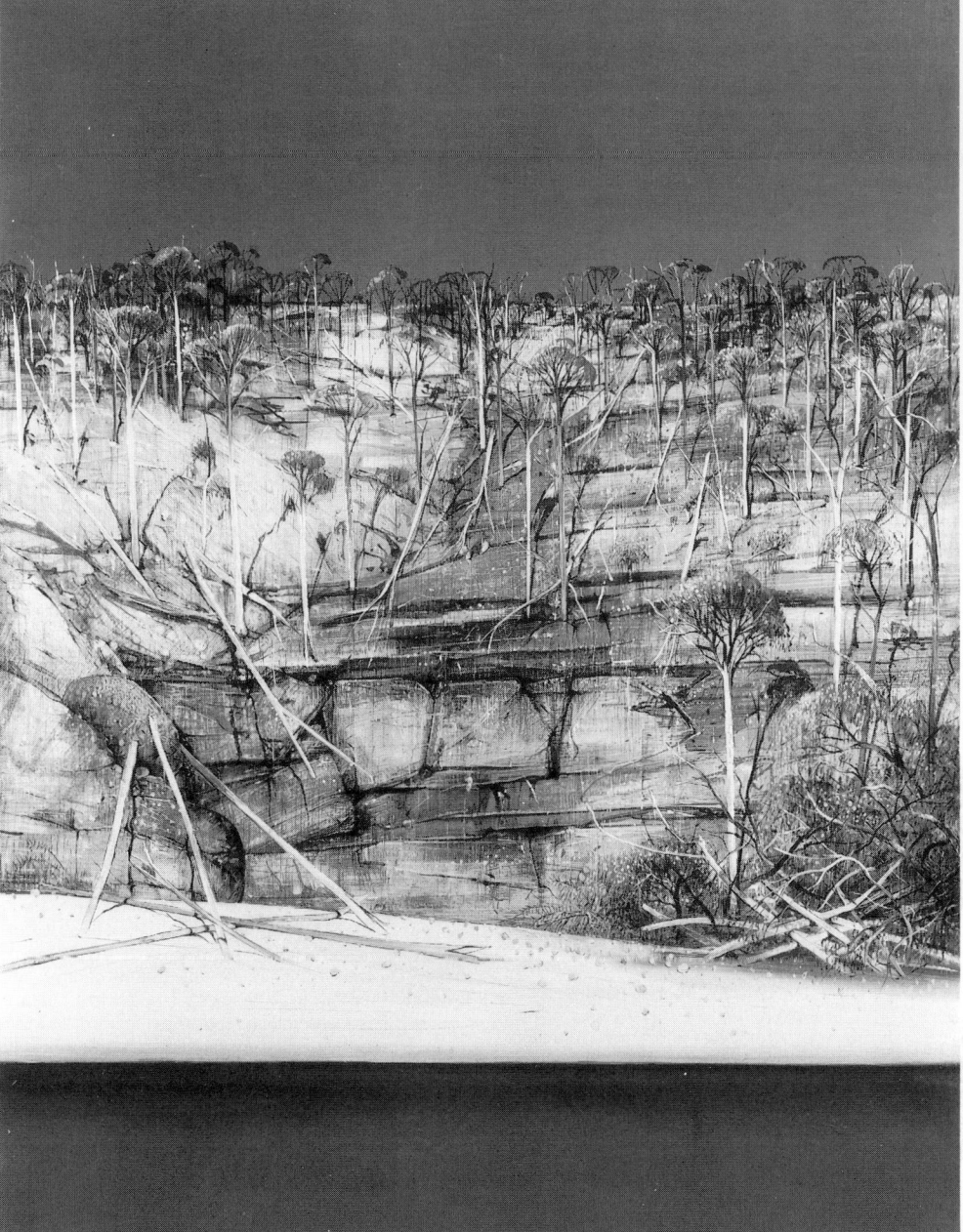

Arthur Boyd: *Australian Landscape with Pond,* 1976

deeply influenced by the richly diverse landscape of his native country and the equally strange mythology rooted in the original settlement of the country by criminals and other exotic characters.

Boyd comes from a long line of Australian artists; his parents and grandparents included popular painters, and various aunts and uncles are also represented in national collections. His brother David Boyd is a successful painter, also resident in England.

Arthur Boyd's first important paintings, in the immediate post-war period, depicted the charming Victorian architecture of Melbourne, but soon after, as a result of his admiration for the Flemish masters Breugel and Bosch, a series of religious paintings emerged, subjects such as "The Assumption" and "The Prodigal Son" being used in architectural murals, and also on a brilliant series of ceramic tiles. Pottery led to sculpture, still on religious themes, re-interpreting Flemish expressionism in the new medium. Picasso and Chagall influenced this period of Boyd's career, coinciding with his earliest absorption with the Australian folk hero, Ned Kelly.

The Chagallian strain then emerged to dominate Boyd's series of "Bride" paintings in which a small white-faced female figure accompanies her aboriginal husband. Whilst residence in England has heightened the painter's involvement in Australian themes, the urgency of the "Bride" series, with their anatomy of inter-racial problems, has never been repeated or surpassed.

Boyd's technical control remains impressive, and his versatility has extended to designing for theatre, lithography and etching.

—Charles Spencer

BOYLE, Mark
British. Born in Glasgow, Scotland, 11 May 1934. Studied law at the Glasgow University 1955–56;

mainly self-taught in art, from 1956. Served in the British Army, 1950–53. Has lived with the artist Joan Hills since 1958; children: Sebastian and Georgia. Worked as labourer, Stewarts and Lloyd steelyard, Parkhead, Glasgow, 1953–54; as park keeper, office clerk, barman and head-waiter, all London, 1955–58. Independent artist, London, since 1958; collaborated on light-environments for theatrical events, 1960–65; Co-Director, with Joan Hills, Sensual Laboratory, London, since 1966; light-shows for U.F.O. Club, London, 1967; light-environments for music groups Jimi Hendrix Experience and Soft Machine, U.S.A., 1968–69; has worked on Earth Pieces since 1964, and Journey to the Surface of the Earth since 1967. Instructor, Waterford School of Art, 1966–67. Recipient; Painting Prize, *5th Biennale de Paris*, 1967; Painting Prize, *15th Premio Lissone*, Italy, 1967; Painting Prize, *Zagreb International*, Yugoslavia 1968. Agent: A Notional Gallery, Greenwich, London. Address: c/o A Notional Gallery, Hillside House, Crooms Hill, Greenwich, London SE10, England.

Individual Exhibitions:

1963   Woodstock Gallery, London
      Traverse Gallery, Edinburgh
      Citizens' Gallery, Glasgow
1964   *Suddenly Last Supper*, South Kensington, London (event)
      Richard Demarco Gallery, Edinburgh
      Exit Music, Strand Electric Theatre, London (with Ken Dewey and Charles Marowitz)
      The Street, London (event)
1965   *O, What A Lovely Whore*, Institute of Contemporary Arts, London (event)
      Any Plan or No Play, Theatre Royal, Stratford East, London (event)
1966   Indica Gallery, London
      Dig, Shepherd's Bush, London (event)
      Son et Lumiére for Earth, Air, Fire and Water, Cochrane Theatre, London (event)
      Son et Lumiére for Insects, Reptiles and Water Creatures. Cochrane Theatre, London (event)
      Bodily Fluids and Functions, Roundhouse, London (event)
1967   Bluecoat Gallery, Liverpool

1969   Institute of Contemporary Arts, London
1970   Gemeentemuseum, The Hague
      Bela Centre, Copenhagen
      Institute of Contemporary Arts, London
1971   Henie-Onstad Kunstsenter, Oslo
      Requiem for an Unknown Citizen, Rotterdam (event)
      Galerie Paul Maenz, Cologne
1972   Henie-Onstad Kunstsenter, Oslo
      Galerie Paul Maenz, Cologne
1973   Kelvin Hall, Glasgow
      Galerie Müller, Stuttgart
      McRoberts Centre, Stirling, Scotland
1974   Galerie Paul Manez, Cologne
1975   Serpentine Gallery, London
1977   Felicity Samuel Gallery, London
1978   British Pavilion, at the *Biennale*, Venice
      Kunstmuseum, Lucerne
      Kulturhuset, Stockholm
      Seattle Museum of Art
      Henie—Onstad Kunstsenter, Oslo
1979   Louisiana Museum, Humlebaek, Denmark
      Museum am Ostwall, Dortmund, West Germany (with Joan Hills)
1980   Charles Cowles Gallery, New York
      Kunstmuseum, Lucerne
      Art Gallery of South Australia, Adelaide
      Richard Hines Gallery, Seattle, Washington
1981   Seattle Art Museum, Washington
      Newport Harbor Art Museum, Newport Beach, California
1982   Institute of Contemporary Art, Boston
      San Francisco Museum of Modern Art
1983   Nishimura Gallery, Tokyo
1985   Henic-Onstad Kunstsenter, Hovikodden, Norway
      A Notional Gallery, London
1986   Cornerhouse Arts Centre, Manchester, Lancashire
      Hayward Gallery, London
1987   City Art Gallery, Southampton, Hempshire
      Glasgow Art Gallery and Museum, Scotland
      Museum of Modern Art, Oxford
      Muzeum Sztuki, Lodz, Poland (travelled to Sopot)
      British Pavilion, *Bienal de Sao Paulo*, Brazil
      Gardner Centre, Brighton, Sussex
      Warwick Arts Centre, Warwickshire
      Turske und Turske Galerie, Zurich
      Turske and Whitney Gallery, Los Angeles
1988   Galerie Lelong, Paris
      Paco Imperial, Rio de Janeiro

Selected Group Exhibitions:

1967   *Biennale de Paris*, Musee d'Art Moderne de la Ville, Paris
1968   *International Exhibition*, Zagreb, Yugoslavia
1973   *Magic and Strong Medicine*, Walker Art Gallery, Liverpool
1976   *Arte Inglese Oggi 1960–76*, Palazzo Reale, Milan
1980   *British Art 1940–80*, Hayward Gallery, London
1981   *Approaches to Landscape*, Tate Gallery, London
1983   *Aspects of British Art*, Metropolitan Art Museum, Tokyo (toured Japan)
1985   *Exhibition Dialogue*, Fundaco Calouste Gulbenkian, Lisbon
1986   *Between Object and Image: British Contemporary Sculpture*, Palacio de Velazquez, Madrid (trevelled to Barcelona and Bilbao)
1987   *British Art in the Twentieth Century*, Royal Academy, London (travelled to Stuttgart)

Collections:

Tate Gallery, London; British Council, London; Ulster Museum, Belfast; Scottish National Gallery of Modern Art, Edinburgh; Städtisches Museum, Bochum, West Germany; Kaiser-Wilhelm Museum, Krefeld West Germany; Gemeensemuseum, The Hague; Sonja Henie-Nils Onstad Kunstsenter, Oslo; Australian National Gallery, Canberra; Seattle Museum of Art.

Publications:

By BOYLE. books—*Journey to the Surface of the Earth: Mark Boyle's Atlas and Manual*, with introduction by J. L. Locher, The Hague 1970; *Boyle Family Archives*, Oslo 1985; *Familia Boyle: 19a, Bienal de Sao Paulo*, Sao Paulo 1987.

On BOYLE: books—*Art in Britain 1969–70* by Edward Lucie-Smith and Patricia White, London 1970; *Art Without Boundaries 1950–1970* by G. Woods, P. Thompson and J. Williams, London 1972; *Magic and Strong Medicine*, exhibition catalogue, with text by Norbert Lynton, Liverpool 1973; *Projekt 74: Aspekte Internationaler Kunst am Anfang der 70er Jahre*, exhibition catalogue, with texts by Dieter Rönte, Evelyn Weiss, Marlis Gruterich and others, Cologne 1974; *Venice Biennale: Mark Boyle*, exhibition catalogue, with text by Michael Compton, London 1978; *Mark Boyle's und Joan Hills' Reise um die West 3: Schweizer Serie*, exhibition catalogue, with text by Martin Kunz, Lucerne 1980.

Mark Boyle: *Broken Path with Tiles (West London)*, 1983

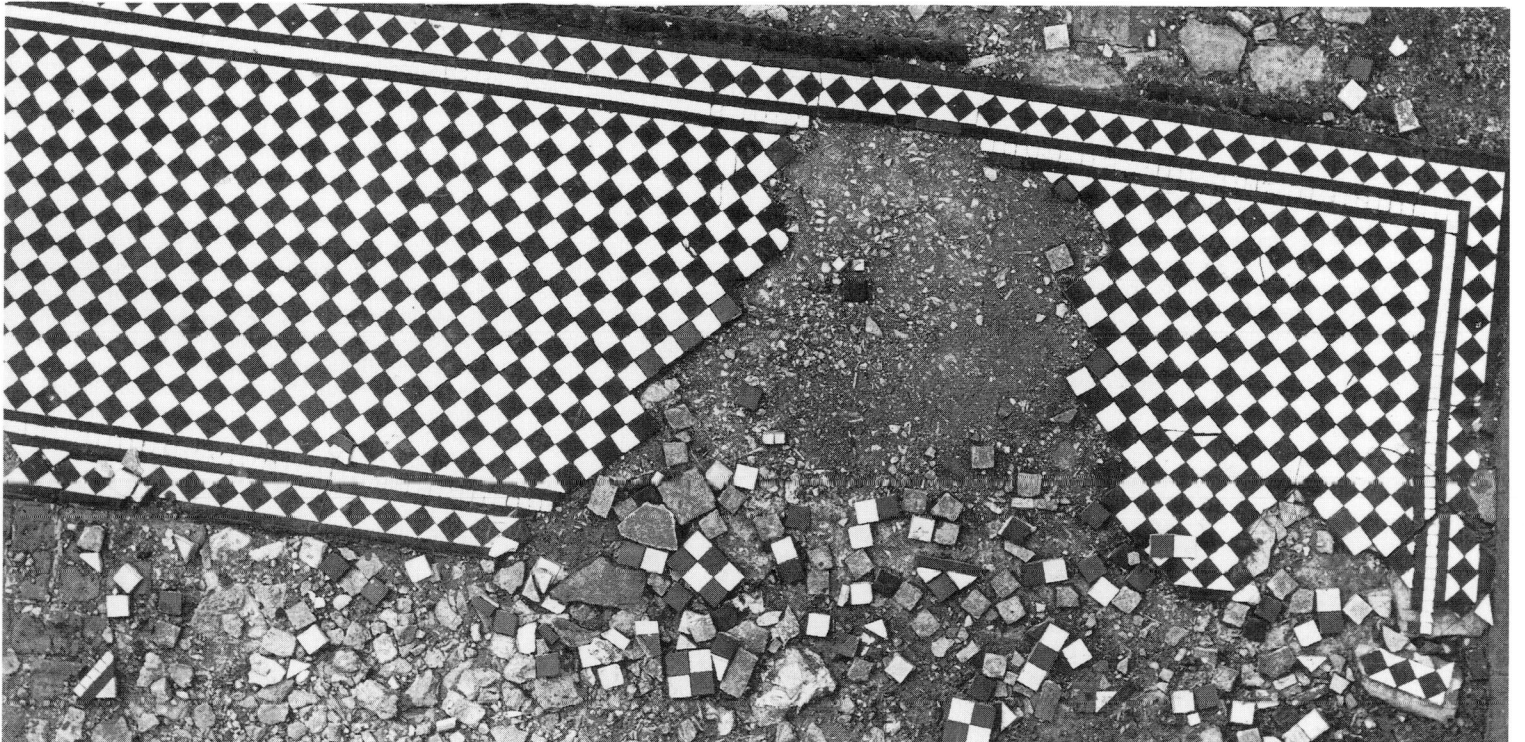

In a condition of adamant doubt you are asked for explanations when all you want is for someone to explain anything. And you are asked for purposes when you are learning to accept that a purpose is not going to emerge ever. And you are asked for a statement of intent when the head seethes with all your fluctuating statements of the past instantly and meticulously taken down and which you use constantly, with increasing derision, in evidence against yourself. And you remember years ago deciding that art, if the work had any meaning, should be waged like war and how, according to all the strategists, you had to locate the enemy and evaluate your own forces and assess the terrain and clarify your objectives and work out your strategy and your tactics and, whatever you do, do not forget your logistics, and how after months of thinking you succeeded with point one and it's not the dealers or the critics or the intellectuals or the government or the rich or the bourgeoisie or "them" and it's not even like Father Xmas your father all the time but the only enemy is yourself and maybe it doesn't matter too much whether you win or lose.

—Mark Boyle

Journey to the Surface of the Earth is the unwavering conceptual excursion of Mark Boyle and his collaborator/wife, Joan Hills. This "journey" is Boyle's ongoing series of "earthprobes," the literal mapping in every minute detail of 6-ft. square sections of the earth's surface.

In 1970 Boyle handed visitors to his studio a dart to throw at a large Mercator projection map of the world. Eventually a thousand sites were randomly selected for the Boyles to document. A closely guarded and painstaking procedure lifts topographical surface texture, extraneous natural or man-caused materials, and whatever surface deformations are present (shifting beach sands, tire tracks, railroad ties, ploughed fields, ablating rock formations, etc.), onto a molded fiberglass shell. Real and ersatz materials are added to achieve versimilitude. Full documentation includes the surface casting, a cast vertical sampling of the substrata, and photographic enlargements of microscopic details of plants and insects gathered on-site, hair, and fluid wastes from the artist's body, all revealed as crustaceous or crystalline molecular patterns of structure.

The meticulous factuality of these relief panels are presented in the rarified space of the gallery. They demand and invite scrutiny. The works are not intended as abstractions of nature, though formal relationships of texture, shape and compositional balance can be readily ascertained in the patterns of wave-tossed sand, tilled soil and geologic outcroppings. Rather, the viewer is re-sensitized by the direct immediacy of these panels, to look at nature in terms of Boyle's process, product and attitude. The moral and ethical imperative is to heighten and engage, in a non-militant yet forceful way, a greater sensitivity to ecological matters. The "grand scheme" of nature merges in the macro-and micro-cosmic units of reality: the flecks of stone, the crusty exoskeleton of a mite, the kaleidoscopic rainbow colors of crystals and molecules. The world beneath one's feet seems more real, more solid and palpable, after seeing the work of Mark Boyle.

—Ron Glowen

BRAUER, Erich or Arik.
Austrian. Born in Vienna, 4 January 1929. Educated in elementary schools in Vienna, 1935–42; studied art, under Robin Anderson and Albert Paris Gütersloh, Academy of Fine Arts, Vienna, 1945–51; also studied singing at the City Conservatory, Vienna, 1949–53. Married Naomi Dahabany in 1955; daughters: Timma, Talija and Ruth. Served in underground resistance, Vienna, 1942–45. Bicycled to Paris to work as folk singer; travelled to Algeria, stayed in Sahara Desert, 1950; travelled to France, Spain, Greece, Israel and Austria, earned living as folk-singer, 1951–58; settled in Paris, performed as folk-singer, with wife Naomi, 1958; former friendship, with Hundertwasser, Paris, 1958. Has painted full time in Vienna, since 1960, and in Ein Hod, Israel, since 1964; has also worked as a costume and set designer for operas, in Zurich, Vienna and Paris, since 1970. Agent: Joram Harel Management, Vienna. Address: c/o Joram Harel Management, Colloredogasse 32, 1180 Vienna, Austria.

Individual Exhibitions:

1956	Neue Gallerie, Vienna
1957	Artist's House, Jerusalem
1958	Galerie Ernst Fuchs, Vienna
	Galerie Wolfgang Gurlitt, Munich
1959	Galerie La Cour d'Ingres, Paris
	Artist's House, Jerusalem
1960	Galerie Delta, Basle
1961	Galerie Brochstedt, Hamburg
	Galerie Sydow, Frankfurt
	Galerie Raymond Cordier, Paris
1963	Galerie Karl Flinker, Paris
1964	Galerie Sydow, Frankfurt
	Galerie Karl Flinker, Paris
1965	Galerie Peithner-Lichtenfels, Vienna
	Felix Landau Gallery, Los Angeles
1966	Galerie Sydow Fine Art, Frankfurt
1967	Felix Landau Gallery, Los Angeles
	Landau Gallery, New York
1968	Galerie 3 + 2, Paris
	Kunstlerhaus Peithner, Vienna
	Galerie Sydow, Frankfurt
	Galerie Sydow, West Berlin
1969	Marlborough New London Gallery
	Galerie Haas, Vaduz, Lichtenstein
	Galerie Passepartout, Copenhagen
	Galerie 3 + 2, Paris
	Galleria La Vetrina, Rome
	Galerie Wolfgang Ketterer, Munich
1970	Galerie Wendtorf, Dusseldorf
	Buhler Graphics, Stuttgart
	Galerie Le Grenier d'Art, Geneva
	Galleria Vicotti, Turin
1971	Galerie des 20, Jahrhunderts, Vienna
	Galerie Peithner-Lichtenfels, Vienna
	Galerie d'Halluin, Dusseldorf
	Galerie Hartmann, Munich
	Oils, Goaches, Watercolors and Etchings, Marlborough-Gerson Gallery, New York
1973	Galerie Hartmann, Munich
	Galerie Wolfrum Vienna
	Galerie Lochte, Hamburg
	Marlborough Galerie, Zurich
1974	*Das Graphische Werk 1951–1974,* Die Graphische Sammlung Albertina, Vienna (toured Norway, Yugoslavia and Latin America 1977–78, Turkey, 1979, Germany 1980–81, and France, 1982)
1975	Museum for Culture and Fine Arts, University of Marburg, West Germany
1976	Kurpfalzisches Museum Heidelberg
	Kunst und Kulturverein, Esslingen, West Germany
	Museum Mazowiecki, Plock, Poland (toured Poland)
	Galerie Facchetti, Paris
	Städtische Galerie, Rosenheim, West Germany
	Osterreichische Galerie im Oberen Belvedere, Vienna
	Oberbach Fine Art, New York
1977	St. Mary's University Art Gallery, Halifax
	Galerie Facchetti, Paris
	Galerie in der Staatsoper, Vienna
1978	Goldmann Fine Art, Basle
	Beethovenhaus, Schwenningen, West Germany
	Kunstverein Hochrhein, Sackingen, West Germany
1979	*Austria Presents Brauer to the Continents,* The Jewish Museum, New York (and world tour, 1979–83)
1985	Jack Rutberg Gallery, Los Angeles

Selected Group Exhibitions:

1961	*Micro Salon,* Tokyo Gallery
	Der Gegenstand in Der Osterreichischen Malerei und Plastik Secession, Vienna
1962	*Surrealismus, Phantastiche Malerei der Gegenwart,* Kunslerhaus, Vienna
	Graphik aus Osterreich, Ljubljana, Yugoslavia
1963	*Grands et Jeunes d'Aujourd'hui,* Musée d'Art Moderne de la Ville, Paris
1964	*Salon de Mai,* Paris
1965	*Bienal,* Sao Paulo
1968	*Die Entwicklung der Wiener Schule,* Kunstlarhaus, Vienna
1972	*Die Wiener Schule des Phantastischen Realismus,* Museum des 20, Jahrhunderts, Vienna
1975	*22nd Biennale Premia Del Fiorina,* Palazzo Strozzi, Florence

Collections:

Albertina, Vienna; Historisches Museum der Stadt Wien, Vienna; Osterreichische Galerie des 19th and 20th, Jahrhunderts, Vienna; City of Vienna; Moderne Galerie und Graphische Sammiung Rupertinum, Salzburg; Des Moines Art Center, Iowa; The Jewish Museum, New York; Tel Aviv Museum, Israel

Publications:

By BRAUER: books—*Human Rights,* portfolio, New York, London and Paris 1975; *Die Zigeunerziege,* Munich 1976; *Das Runde Fliegt,* Munich 1983; *Monography,* Harenberg, West Germany 1984; records—*Arik Brauer,* Vienna 1971; *Alles was Flugel Hat Fliegt,* Vienna 1974; *Poesie mit Krallen,* Vienna 1984; television show—*Alles was Flugel Hat Fliegt,* Vienna 1973.

On BRAUER: books—*Brauer,* exhibition catalogue by Wieland Schmied, Frankfurt 1964; *Brauer: Malerei des Phantastischen Realismus,* Munich 1968; *Brauer,* exhibition catalogue, London 1969; *Art in Britain 1969–70* by Edward Lucie-Smith and Patricia White, London 1970; *Brauer: Oils Goaches, Watercolors and Etchings,* exhibition catalogue, by Wolfgang Fischer, New York 1971; *Brauer: Monographie mit Werkkatalog* by Wieland Schmied, Vienna 1972; *Erich Brauer: Morgenrot, Morgengrau,* Vienna 1972; *Brauer,* exhibition catalogue, by Gustav Rene Hocke, Zurich 1973; *Brauer Small Monography,* Salzburg 1973; *Malerei aus Bereichen des Unbewussten; Kunstler experimenteeren unter LSD* by Richard P. Hartmann, Cologne 1974; *Brauer: Das Graphische Werk 1951–1974* by Walter Koschatzky, Vienna 1974; *Die Wiener Schule des Phantastischen Realismus* by Johann Muschik, Vienna and Munich 1974; *Brauer's Bunte Mauer* by Erich Lessing, Munich 1975; *Brauer: New York,* Glarus, Switzerland 1975; *Brauer: Paris,* Glarus, Switzerland 1976; *Austria Presents Brauer to the Continents,* Glarus, Switzerland 1979; articles—"Erich Brauer" in *Mizue* (Tokyo), 1969; "Brauer" by Wieland Schmied in *Graphis* (Zurich), December 1973/January 1974.

I have been painting ever since I can remember, and I have done so from 7 to 8 hours a day over the past 30 years. Even though I painted more or less always the same, painting has never lost its fascination for me.

My first studio was the windowsill in my father's workshop. He was a bootmaker. The window was on the ground floor and I could thus sit astride, one leg inside the shop and the other dangling outside into the street. It gave me a grand feeling of commanding the crossroads of two worlds.

On the other side of the street lived a charcoal-dealer. His door was decorated with faggots and coalsacks. There were many cats around his place. I believe that those cats made me understand movement and sequences of motion. For years I drew the cats and admired their well-rounded grace. I even played at cats myself and prowled around on all fours between the bundles of leather. I slid down the big pile of solo-leather and mewed. I understood the cats. My father hummed yiddish songs and asked: "And what are you today?" He did not ask: "What do you paint today?" My movements and my painting had become as one.

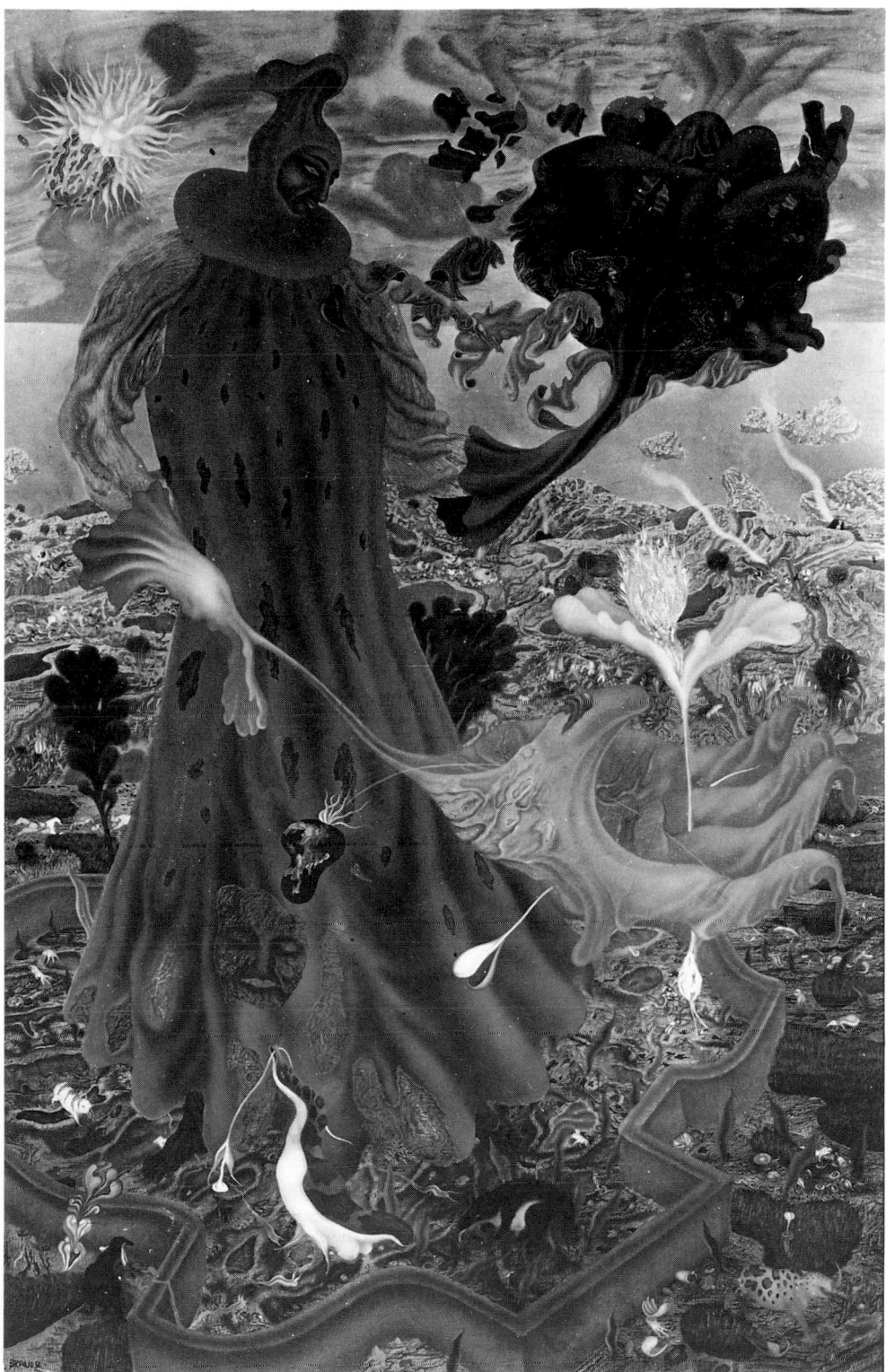

Erich Brauer: *Fehdehandschuh—Friedehandschuh*, 1971

topics of his paintings may therefore quite often grow out of these objects. When painting a given subject, the situation is reversed: the painter is confronted with the difficult but exciting task of fitting the literary content to his personal forms. If, for instance, a painter's style is particularly apt for the representation of plants, an interesting tension ensues if he tries to do buildings or machinery. I do not believe that the theme can enhance the quality of a painting, but I do believe that a subject can provide an added impetus and trigger the artist's best effort.

Among the many ways which lead towards painting, one passes through story-telling. Jewish history has almost never been painted. Those who should have created the images did not do so for religious reasons. Only the future will show whether I was big enough to fill that gap.

The history of oppression and persecution of a minority is the same for all nations. I have therefore quite often used the symbols and signs of other oppressed nations. I do not care whether the stories and contents of all the details and all the backdrops are seen my way. The subjects are unequivocal, but my paintings are resilient and open to interpretation. They ought to stimulate the imagination. Every spectator should continue to think them to their very conclusion.

Painting is influenced by so many unconscious, subconscious processes that it really cannot be learnt. It will always remain an exciting, risky endeavour, full of attraction for a lifetime. In painting there are no recognizeable, generally valid laws. One painter's quality is the other's weakness. The art of painting cannot be stolen. The purloined artistic gold turns to pitch in the hands of the thief. This holds equally true for the painter who steals from his own painting, that is who tries to repeat his own, old ideas over and over without inner need. It is impossible to fake an idea and even untrained spectators can tell an artist's living work from his empty, barren products. A visitor who approaches an exhibit with a total lack of understanding, even with disgust, will nevertheless arrive at a relatively correct judgement of the works of art. Painting is a veritable hour of truth, and one may lie with words but not with images.

The idea that strikes the artist is at the core of every work of art. The word "strike" suggests something which hits one from the outside, as if an artist could not do anything by himself but would have to wait until "art" comes to him. This is not so. I am convinced that nothing ever comes from waiting alone. I believe, on the contrary, that "being struck" is a spiritual act which a gifted person can bring about by concentration. These basic ideas, the very essence of a painting, of its forms and colours, are usually so simple that, once executed, they seem self-evident, almost two-dimensional eggs of Columbus.

Painting, unlike language, knows no frontiers in space and time. Looking at works of art created many thousand years ago, one can still re-live the artists' efforts and feelings. One can experience the same, deep understanding for the works of foreign cultures, for Chinese or African art. The fine arts seem to express something that is common to all mankind, something everybody can understand. Potentates and dictators of all kind react to painting with astounding irritability. The poetic world of forms and colours may be a closed book to them; but with the heightened senses of the wrongdoer they understand the psychological and, even more so, the political impact of painting. It is not the light-hearted art it might seem at first glance.

Painting must become a mass-activity, like speaking. Professional painters should stop feeling like miracle-workers whose magic is inaccessible to the average person. They should become examples and stimuli, almost like top-athletes in sport. The painting on houses and public institutions should not be forbidden, but should be promoted and rewarded. Industry ought to produce objects of daily use with a surface that lends itself to colouring. Children in particular should be encouraged to paint their schools inside and out.

Next to motion, my painting's second base is colour. I discovered my true colours rather late and quite suddenly, from one day to the next. I had finished my studies at the Academy in Vienna and was on my first visit to Israel. One evening I sat on the beach and looked at a small shell. In a flash I suddenly realized that a colour appears luminous when it is enhanced by a second colour: a reddish-brown leaf, for example, turns red at the edge, a yellow ball turns white around the middle.

To know and to realize are not the same in painting. My "realization" of this intensification of colour was certainly not new then and is known to every better commercial artist. But I alone can make use of it in my own way. The sudden realization found me ready, encountered a subjective inclination, which changed mere knowledge into creative understanding. There and then I went home and started painting. My head grew hot, and I understood what impact the little shell had had upon my life.

For the next twenty years, the cat's movements and the shimmering shell were my spiritual baggage. Sometimes, and out of mere curiosity, I tried different styles of painting, perhaps a plainer surface, or a harder contour, but all such attempts ended in crisis. I have now understood that one man can do one painting only, even if he seems to pass through different periods. Other paintings, other painters.

My own painting has always been figurative and literary. In my graphic work in particular, I have often illustrated stories or followed a theme. Every artist has certain objects and forms suited to his style. The

Painting is a mysterious and singular activity that cannot be replaced by anything else and may well have the power to solve problems of our time.

—Erich Brauer

There is a school in Vienna, a school with very few pupils. It is dedicated to the teaching of *misch-technik,* a kind of melding of the ancient painting craft (from the times before oils and canvases became the natural raw materials for aspiring artists) and its mysteries—some of them far from easy to comprehend and then be able to harness effectively—together with antique lore and alchemies. Ernst Fuchs could be regarded as a champion of this "other" art; but the misch-technik school is not the only source of painted magic in contemporary Vienna. It is quoted here because it is an important part of his magico-medieval cultural atmosphere in which so many exotic flowers bloom. Side by side with these unexpected outcrops of archaic imagination and learning there is the Vienna School of Phantastic Realism of whose artists perhaps the best known is Erich Brauer, painter and erstwhile lute-player, folk-singer and dancer.

The fluttering petals that invade so many of Brauer's pictures recall in imagery some of the details in paintings by Naumowski, except that the Yugoslav has none of the finesse of the Austrian, nor does he impart any of the same romantic strangeness.

Even though the majority of Brauer's paintings, watercolours and etchings tend to have titles that have an everyday ring about them like "Naomi on Friday Evening," this picture suggests a parallel unreality with "The Angel Tree" or "The Flying Saucers Weep." In all three can be found a kindred iridescence. The cuffs of Naomi's dress are like the flowers of "The Redheaded King." The Orpheus-figure in "Looking Back" is accompanied by a dog whose ears are like diaphanous wings. Every image sprouts vegetally, whether through its limbs or its garments or out of the landscape itself. A world of articulated Turkish delight, except that everything is more delicately rendered and the colours are not the pale evanescences of pastel, but the burnished hues expanded in an imaginative furnace.

These are narrative pictures. The stories they tell are in a visual language for the sensitive eye. They are beguiling, a natural mirror for children's dreams. Brauer treats luxury with respect.

—Sheldon Williams

BRAVO, Claudio.

Chilean. Born in Valparaiso, Chile, 8 November 1936. Studied with Miguel Venegas, 1947–48. Lived in Spain, 1961–72. Has lived in Tangier since 1972. Agents: Galeria Vandres, Don Ramon de la Cruz 26, Madrid 1, Spain; Marlborough Fine Art, 40 West 57th Street, New York, New York 10019, U.S.A. Address: 49 rue du Village. Marshan, Tangier, Morocco.

IIndividual Exhibitions:

1970	Gallery Staempfli, New York
1971	Galeria Egam, Madrid
1972	Gallery Staempfli, New York
	Galeria Vandres, Madrid
1980	F.I.A.C, Paris
1981	Marlborough Gallery, New York
1982	Marlborough Gallery, New York
	Museum of Monterrey, Mexico
1983	Marlborough Fine Art, London
1984	Marlborough Gallery, New York
	Galeria Quintana, Bogota, Colombia
1985	Marlborough Gallery, New York

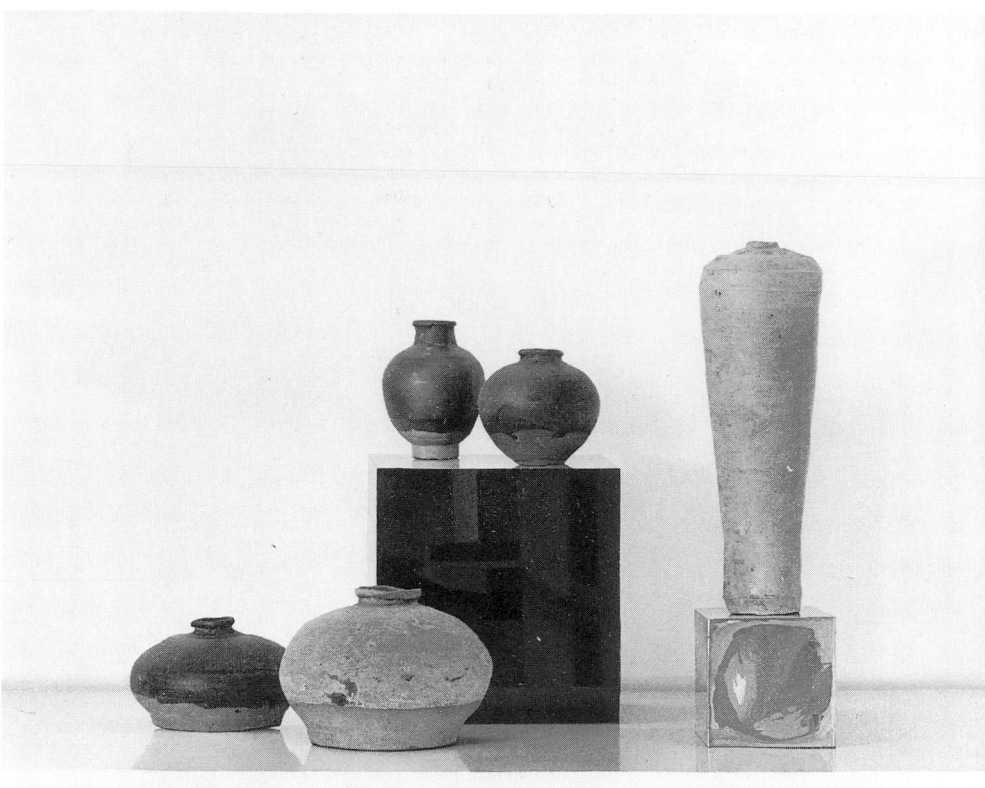

Claudio Bravo: *Still Life,* 1970

Selected Group Exhibitions:

1972	*Documenta 5,* Kassel, West Germany
	Relativerend Realisme Stedelijk Van Abbemuseum, Eindhoven, Metherlands
1973	*Artistes Hyper-realistes,* Galerie des Quatre Mouvements, Paris
1974	*Ars 74: Alternatives of Realism,* Fine Arts Academy of Finland, Helsinki
1976	*Modern Portraits: The Self and Others,* Wildenstein Galleries, New York
1981	*International Contemporary Art,* Museo Rufino Tamayo, Mexico City
1983	*48th Carnegie International,* Carnegie Institute, Pittsburgh
1984	*The Classic Tradition in Painting and Sculpture,* Aldrich Museum of Contemporary Art, Ridgefield, Connecticut
1985	*Contemporary Narrative Figure Painting,* Moravian College, Bethlehem, Pennsylvania

Collections:

University of Pennsylvania Art Museum, Philadelphia; Princeton University Art Museum, New Jersey; Ponce Art Museum, Puerto Rico; Museo de Arte Abstracto, Cuenca, Spain; Museum Boymans-van Beuningen, Rotterdam; Museum of Art, Helsinki.

Publications:

On BRAVO: books—*Documenta 5,* exhibition catalogue, Kassel, West Germany 1972; *Relativerend Realisme,* exhibition catalogue, Eindhoven, Netherlands 1972; articles—"Lettre de New York: Claudio Bravo, Staempfli Gallery" by J. P. Marandel in *Art International* (Lugano, Switzerland), January 1971; "Flashback su Kassel" in *Flash Art* (Milan), September/October 1972; "The New Spanish Realists" by W. Dyckes in *Art International* (Lugano, Switzerland), September 1973.

At present nothing interests me except the resurrection. I don't want movements or fashions. Art is something so subtle that these things do not last. They are poor flowers that test the brightness and quickly fade

One has to be forgotten, and work as an honest labourer, perhaps for some years, not to be mistaken as the follower of a trend. Neither Leonardo nor Vermeer knew anything about tendencies; they did what they had to do and what they believed in—alone, very alone and quietly.

One has to be forgotten, like the dead—to disappear.

I live beside a Moroccan cemetery that I see every morning when I open my window to let the sun into my place on the bed. My experiences each day are so long and serene that I don't have even a moment to think of the neurotic involvements of other artists in big cities. I am apart from time in my beautiful Arabian palace, quiet and white like a dove sitting next to a rose.

Hyperealism, realism, superrealism and other isms will pass; they fly far above my studio and only come to visit. I am shut in, painting, and don't open my windows to them: like Abel with the Angel I will fight to be alone.

One day will come the resurrection.

—Claudio Bravo

Claudio Bravo is a painter, draughtsman, sculptor and lithographer of exhaustive accurate realism. Although it is hard to believe that some of the subjects of his works could—in real life—exist with the same dust-free stillness, this in no way invalidates the effect of his achievement. Quite rightly he holds himself to be aloof from all art movements past and present. His work is carried out in a condition of seclusion that might well be compared with that of an anchorite, and perhaps like the more successful hermits, who found both lack of company and the failure of the world to impinge upon their solitude was conducive to practical meditation, perhaps like them Claudio Bravo has been able to create a distillation (of vision, in his case) that would be difficult for an actively involved member of human society to imitate.

The "artificiality" of Bravo's works might be said

to measure up to the improbability of a character without stain; the famous ointment has no fly in it.

And yet, with all this respectable attitude of withdrawal, Bravo slots neatly into place amongst contemporary artists. He might not like his exquisitely packed and strung parcels, marvels of painted observation, to be hung beside the packages of Christo and Manzoni, yet—for all their difference in construction—they would be fit companions. He would be appalled if his elegant drawings of boots shared exhibition with pop-art metal castings of the same subject, and yet both are part of the modern art scene.

Works by Bravo have been shown in the black museum at Cuenca, normally a venerated show-place for nonfigurative art, but such an action merely underlies the proof, if underlining were necessary, that the accomplished artist ought never to be hidebound by the dictates of contemporary taste. The unrecognisable can be the ineffable just as easily as can exact representation. Claudio Bravo might not agree with such a statement, but to substantiate it the whole history of mankind's creativity ought to be enough.

—Sheldon Williams

BRECHT, George

American. Born in New York City, 7 March 1926. Studied at the Philadelphia College of Pharmacy and Science, 1946-50, B.Sc. 1950; New School for Social Research, New York, 1958-59. Served in the United States Army, 1943-45. Married Marceline Allemand in 1951 (divorced); son: Eric. Worked as analytical chemist and quality control supervisor, Chas. Pfizer and Co., Brooklyn, New York; Quality control supervisor, research chemist, engineer and inventor, Johnson and Johnson, New Brunswick, New Jersey; research inventor, chemist and engineer, Mobil Chemicals, New Brunswick, New Jersey. Independent artist active in areas including performance, artists' writings and conceptual art; early associate of Fluxus group; founded *Sight Unseen* journal: has lived and worked in Cologne since 1972. Research Fellow, Leeds College of Art, England, 1968-69. Agent: Renate Fassbender, Pienzenauerstr. 98, 8000 Munich 81. Address: Wildenburgstrasse 9, 5 Cologne-Sulz, West Germany.

Individual Exhibitions:

1959	*Toward Events*, Rueben Gallery, New York
1965	*The Book of the Tumbler on Fire*, Fischbach Gallery, New York
1967	Galleria Schwarz, Milan
1969	Galleria Schwarz, Milan
1970	Galerie Michael Werner, Cologne
	Galerie Hansjörg Mayer, Stuttgart
	Los Angeles County Museum of Art
1973	Galerie Onnasch, New York
1978	*Beyond Events*, Kunsthalle, Bern

Selected Group Exhibitions:

1961	*The Art of Assemblage*, Museum of Modern Art, New York
1962	*Fluxus International Festival*, New York
1965	*11 From the Reuben Gallery*, Guggenheim Museum, New York
1967	*Poems to be Seen, Paintings to be Read*, Museum of Contemporary Art, Chicago
1968	*Chemistry of Music*, Moderna Museet, Stockholm
1969	*La Cedille Qui Sourit*, Städtisches Museum, Mönchengladbach, West Germany
1970	*Art in the Mind*, Allen Art Museum, Oberlin College, Ohio
1972	*Documenta 5*, Kassel, West Germany

1984	*Salvaged: Altered Everyday Objects*, Project Studios One, Long Island City, New York
1986	*Europa-Amerika*, Museum Ludwig, Cologne

Collections:

Museum of Modern Art, New York; Städtisches Museum, Mönchengladbach, West Germany; Archiv Sohm, Markgroningen, West Germany; Staatsgalerie, Berlin; Centre Georges Pompidou, Paris.

Publications:

By BRECHT: books—*Chance Imagery*, New York 1966; *Games at the Cedillas or the Cedilla Takes Off*, with Robert Filliou, New York 1967; *Vicious Circles and Infinity*, with Patrick Hughes, New York 1975; *Hsin-hsin-ming*, Cologne 1987; articles—"3 Dances" in *New Departures* (London), no 4, 1962; "Chance Imagery" in *Collage* (Palermo, Italy), December 1964; "Conversation sur Autre Chose," with Ben Vautier, in *Identities* (Nice, France), no. 11-12, 1965; "Dances, Events and Other Poems" in *Something* (New York), vol. 1, no. 2, 1965; "An Inteview," with Henry Martin in *Art International* (Lugano, Switzerland), November 1967; "From the Brecht/Lovell Motto Board" in *Big Venus* (London), no. 3, 1969; "George Brecht: An Interview" by Robin Page and others in *Art and Artists* (London), October 1972.

On BRECHT: books—*Postface* by Dick Higgins, New York 1964; *Assemblage, Environments and Happenings* by Allan Kaprow, New York 1966; *An Introduction to George Brecht's Book of the Tumbler on Fire* by Henry Martin, Milan 1978; articles—"Environments, Situations, Spaces at Martha Jackson Gallery" by J. Kroll in *Artnews* (New York), September 1961; "The Value of Didactic Art" by Barbara Rosc in *Artforum* (New York), August 1967; "Non-Games" by Jasia Reichardt in *Studio International* (London), March 1968; "An Art of Multiple Dimensions" by Jan van der Marck in *Art in America* (New York), July/August 1974.

To paraphrase Satie: "I was born unborn into a very young world."

—George Brecht

George Brecht is always mentioned as one of the original members of the Fluxus group, and like many of the others he had participated in the composition course that John Cage held at New York's New School for Social Research in 1958 and 1959. But

Brecht's own attitude to the movement (or "nonmovement") that claims him is, "I say, let it go. After all, FLUXUS is a Latin word Maciunas dug up. I never studied Latin. If it hadn't been for Maciunas nobody would ever have called it anything. We would all have gone our separate ways like the man crossing the street with his umbrella, and a woman walking a dog in another direction."

After an initial period of splashing liquid paint on canvases that he then folded up so as to allow the colors to blot and bleed, Brecht went on to begin to work with the idea of the "event." Some of his events are performance pieces, and some of them are not, and with some it is a little difficult to say. A 100 or so of these events were all printed on small squares of paper and published in 1962 in a box called "Water Yam." One card, for example, says "Three aqueous events: ice, water, steam." Another says "Table: on a white table, glasses, a puzzle, and (having to do with smoking)." Still another requires a performer to make a vertical pile of playing blocks on the strings of an open grand piano until one or more of the blocks fall off.

Many of these events were later to find a more physical and permanent form as assemblages, and as such they entered that continuing and ever-growing collection of experiences that's entitled *The Book of the Tumbler on Fire*. Though later dated retroactively to include certain works from as early as 1962, it was begun in 1964 and contains almost all the work that Brecht has done since. Its various chapters consist of series of assemblages of odds and ends in shallow cotton-filled specimen boxes (like the ones for presenting collections of butterflies), other assemblages in deeper boxes that allow the objects in them to move, various arrangements of chairs or tables with specific objects placed upon them (a glove, for example, or a pepper-mill, or a blind man's black-and-white cane and an orange) and sometimes associated as well with quotations from the *Guinness Book of Records*. One chapter consists of signs that say things like "No Smoking," or "Sans Issue," or "Silence" spelled out in cork letters on canvas; another is dedicated to an aerodynamic redesigning of the letters of the alphabet; another is a translation of a book by Robert Filliou. There's also a collection of paradoxes (the first in the history of philosophy) done in collaboration with Patrick Hughes and published by Doubleday and Company: this is Part III of Volume III of the *Book* . . . Part I is a work called "Donna dei Nodi": a full-sized reclining figure of a naked woman

George Brecht: *Void*, Munster, West Germany, 1987

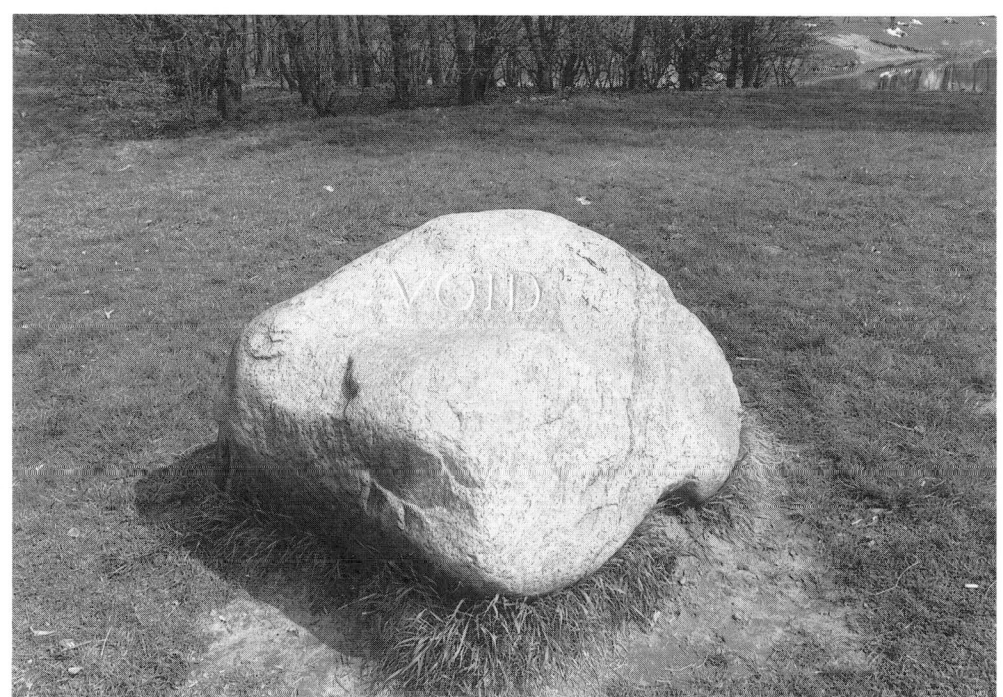

carved in marble by a tomb-stone sculptor and holding in her hand a large monkey's paw knot at the end of a rope the strands of which separate to end in a series of other knots at her side and feet. The artist has also made maps containing proposals for the displacement of various land-masses from one part of the earth to another. Other works are crystals grown in Petri dishes and housed in leather boxes that may also have a row of smaller lateral compartments for objects such as keys, dice, pieces of wood, and tiny spheres of marble. He has also done an English translation of the Chinese original of Seng-ts'an's *Hsing-Hsing Ming,* the first of the classical texts of Zen Buddhism. Some of Brecht's most recent works have been stones, large and small, inscribed with the word "Void."

The internal logic of George Brecht's work is entirely impossible to describe, since his problem as an artist is always and only to work towards an intuitive grasp of the problems of knowledge and awareness that are central to his own individual being in the universe. He has written, "Science tells us that the universe is what we conceive it to be, and chance enables us to determine what we conceive it to be (for the conception is only partly conscious). The receptacle of forms available to the artist thus becomes openended, and eventually embraces all of nature, for the recognition of significant form becomes limited only by the observer's self." His works, then, are simply things that he has *done* in the course of trying to clarify his relationship to the rest of existence, and they don't try to posit themselves as symbolic expressions with which the artist has established any simple kind of psychological identification. Brecht's works, like many of Marcel Duchamp's, seem marvellously arbitrary. They're about that experience of inner freedom that *allows* an individual to be arbitrary—arbitrary with respect to any and all previous conditioning. This is to say that Brecht stands behind his work much as we can stand in front of it: he, the work, and we are all a part of a larger arrangement in which both artist and spectator have the potential to realize a condition in which they're of entirely equal status. We can do with Brecht's works whatever we like: but to discover that they are beautiful is not to fall in line with an artist's revelation of a definition of beauty; it's rather to discover that the discovery of beauty is itself an entirely personal event of which all of us are individually capable.

—Henry Martin

BREER, Robert C.

American. Born in Detroit, Michigan, 30 September 1926. Educated at the Detroit University School, 1932–43; Stanford University, California, 1943–45, 1947–49, B.A. 1949. Served in the United States Army, 1945–47. Married Frances Foote in 1955; children: Julia, Emily, and Harriet. Lived in Paris, 1949–59, now resident in New York State. Adjunct to Carnegie Professor, Films and Kinetics, Cooper Union, New York City, since 1972. Member, Board of Directors, Filmmakers Cooperative, New York 1967–72; Co-Designer, Pepsi-Cola Pavilion, Expo '70, Osaka, Japan, 1970. Recipient: Annual Painting Award, Stanford University, 1949; Creative Film Foundation Award, 1957–61; Diplome Speciale, Bergamo, Italy, 1962; Max Ernst Award, Oberhausen, West Germany, 1968; Film Culture Award, New York, 1972; Guggenheim Fellowship, 1978. Agents: Cinegate Ltd., 70 Portobello Road, London W11, England; Projection Galerie Ursula Wevers, Am Rinkenpfulh 20–26, 5000 Cologne 1, West Germany; and Filmmakers Cooperative, 175 Lexington Avenue, New York, New York 10016. Address: 80 Sparkill Avenue, Tappan, New York 10983, U.S.A.

Individual Exhibitions:

1956   Palais des Beaux-Arts, Brussels
          American Students and Artists Center, Paris
1960   Gallery Mayer, New York
1961   Charles Cinema, New York (film retrospective)
1962   Bleecker Cinema, New York
1963   Dwan Gallery, Los Angeles (film retrospective)
1965   Galeria Bonino, New York
1966   Galeria Bonino, New York
1968   Galerie Ricke, Cologne
1969   Museum of Contemporary Art, Chicago
1970   Galeria Bonino, New York
          Museum of Modern Art, New York
1972   J. L. Hudson Gallery, Detroit
          Millenium Film Workshop, New York
1973   Hammarskjold Plaza, New York
1974   IBM Plaza, New York
          Michael Berger Gallery, Pittsburgh
1975   Film Forum, New York (film retrospective)
          Museum of Modern Art, New York (film retrospective)
          Whitney Museum, New York (film retrospective)
1977   Whitney Museum, New York
1979   St. Louis Art Museum
          Walker Art Center, Minneapolis
1980   Whitney Museum, New York (film retrospective)
          Albright Knox Art Gallery, Buffalo, New York
          Art Institute of Chicago
1981   Exterior Film Forum, New York (mural painting)

Selected Group Exhibitions:

1976   *Une Histoire du Cinema,* Centre Beaubourg, Paris
1977   *Paris-New York,* Centre Beaubourg, Paris
1978   *Filmex: American Independent Animation,* Hollywood, California
1979   *Contemporary Sculpture,* Museum of Modern Art, New York
          Film as Film, Arts Council of Great Britain, London
          Biennial Exhibition, Whitney Museum, New York
          Americans in Paris: The 50's, California State University at Northridge
1980   *The Pleasure Dome: American Experimental Film 1939–79,* Moderna Museet, Stockholm
1981   *Biennial Exhibition,* Whitney Museum, New York

Collections:

Museum of Modern Art, New York; New York Public Library; Anthology Film Archives, New York; Institute of Contemporary Art, London; Musée National d'Art Moderne, Paris; Austrian Film Archives, Vienna; Moderna Museet, Stockholm; National Film Archives, Canberra, Australia.

Publications:

By BREER: articles—"On 2 Films" in *Film Culture* (New York), Summer 1961; "What Happened" in *Film Culture* (New York), Fall 1962; "Interview with Robert Breer," with Guy Cote, in *Film Culture* (New York), Winter 1962; "A Statement" in *Film Culture* (New York), Summer 1963; films—*Form Phrases I,* 1952; *Form Phrases II,* 1953; *Form Phrases III,* 1953; *Form Phrases IV,* 1954; *Images by Images I,* 1954; *Un Miracle,* 1955; *Image by Images II,* 1955; *Image by Images III,* 1955; *Image by Images IV,* 1966; *Cats,* with Frances Breer, 1956; *Recreation I,* with spoken text by Noel Burch, 1956–57; *Recreation II,* 1956–57; *Jamestown Baloos,* 1957; *A Man and His Dog Out for Air,* 1957; *Par Avion,* 1958; *Eyewash,* 1958–59; *Homage to Jean Tinguely's Homage to New York',* 1960; *Blazes,* 1961; *Horse Over a Tea Kettle,* 1962; *Pat's Birthday,* 1962; *Breathing,* 1963; *Fistfight,* 1964; *66,* 1966; *69,* 1968; *OBL No. 2,* 1968; *70,* 1970; *Gulls and Buoys,* 1972; *Fuji,* 1974; *Rubber Cement,* 1975; *77,* 1977; *LMNO,* 1978; *TZ,* 1979.

On BREER: books—*Robert Breer* by Michel Seuphor, Paris 1956; *Hard Center* by Nicholas and Elena Calas, New York 1964; *Film: A Montage of Theories* by Richard Dyer, New York 1966; *Animation in the Cinema* by Ralph Stephenson, London 1967; *An Introduction to the American Underground Film* by Sheldon Renan, New York 1967; *The New American Cinema* by Gregory Battcock, New York 1967; *Art of Time*

by Michael Kirby, New York 1969, *The American Independent Film* by P. Adams Sitney, Boston 1971; *Experimental Cinema* by David Curtis, New York 1971; *Pavilion* by Nilo Lindgreen, Barbara Rose, and Calvin Tomkins, New York 1972; *Experimental Animation* by Robert Russett, New York 1976; *Robert Breer* by Sandra Moore, Minneapolis 1980; *Robert Breer: A Study of His Work in the Context of the Modernist Tradition* by Louis Mendelson, Ann Arbor, Michigan 1981; articles—"4 Artists as Film-Makers" by Adrienne Mancia and Willard Van Dyke in *Art in America* (New York), January 1967; "The Experience of Kinesis" by Michael Kirby in *Art News* (New York), February 1968; "Onward and Upward with the Arts," by Calvin Tomkins, in *The New Yorker,* October 1970; "Gulls and Buoys" by Scott Hammen in *Afterimage* (Rochester, New York), December 1974; notes by Lucy Fischer in *Museum of Modern Art Circulating Films,* exhibition catalogue, New York 1976; "The Other Cinema" by Noel Carroll in *Soho Weekly News* (New York), 25 January 1979; "Robert Breer's LMNO" by Elena Simons in *Millenium Film Journal* (New York), nos. 4 and 5, 1979; "On A Breer Day" by Amy Taubin in *Soho Weekly News* (New York), 28 May 1980; "Robert Breer's Animated World" by J. Hoberman in *American Film* (Washington, D.C.), September 1980; "Robert Breer, Whitney Museum" by Amy Taubin in *Artforum* (New York), September 1980.

. . . is my major contribution, these big things I call floats—other people call them creepies—these large dome-shaped objects. They're motorized underneath by batteries to move very, very slowly. We are talking about film, the way I got these floats, or at least the connection to film, is obviously one of motion. Ironically enough, these things move, the speed is so slow it's almost barely perceptible. When you're standing there one bumps into you, you don't really notice it, and, of course, with the films, they're ultra fast my films—so fast, there again, you almost don't realize that they're moving, it breaks up the motion so much. In looking back at what I've done, I guess, there is a connection there. I play with thresholds of perception very closely, I think, and in the case of the concrete object, here is something improbable, that it would move, looking at it, and lo and behold, it does. With cinema, it's the other way round.

—Robert Breer

The art of traditional animation—with very modest means—has been the medium in which Robert Breer has invented filmic language paralleling the evolution of recent attitudes towards form and content in the visual arts. His oft-quoted statement best approaches the long-evolved, and even anti-animation, effect of his films: "I'm interested in the domain between motion and still pictures . . . the single frame is the basic unit of film, just as bricks are the basic unit of brick houses." And thus his films have generally offered a sense of the sequence of separate images that compose the film rather than a continuous flow. His art has been described as an animated film variant comprising the Pop art use of everyday accessories, especially as in Dine and Oldenburg; the color fields and geometric hard edge of Ellsworth Kelly; pictorial collage and stream-of-consciousness flow as in Rauschenberg; and cubist-like line found in the paintings of Stuart Davis.

The son of an engineering prodigy then working in Detroit, Breer himself first studied engineering. In 1949 he went to Paris intending to be a painter, but soon became interested in documenting the process by which his final work was achieved. With his father's borrowed Bolex, he began to construct films as geometric abstraction paralleling and reviving the pre-World War II graphic cinema tradition of Richter and Eggeling—with which Breer was then only little acquainted. In 1954 he began a loop work *Image by Image,* which became a series where single framing became the structural and ideational base. In this manipulation, although unknown to one another at that time, Breer has been likened to the Viennese Peter Kubelka. With *Recreation I* (1956–57), Breer began his use of the collage of actual objects, and thus referred to the type of graphic cinema originated in Léger's *Le Ballet Mechanique;* and then a year after, Breer began to produce film based upon a combina-

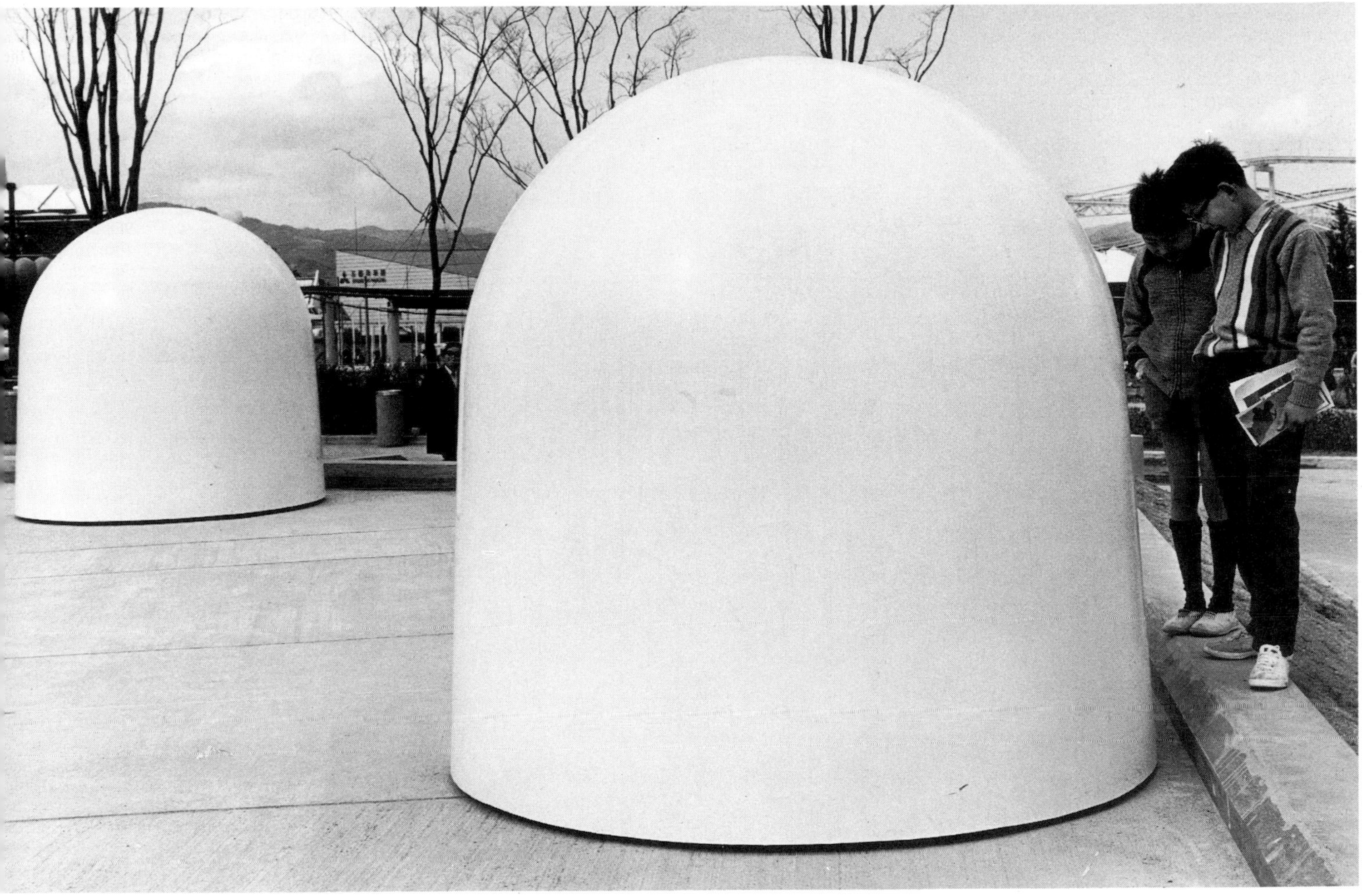

Robert Breer: Self-Propelled Sculptures in Osaka, 1970

tion of literal figure collage and abstract geometric patterns as in *Jamestown Baloos*. During the years 1957–64, he produced essentially animated cartoons in this manner, including *Man and His Dog Out for Air* (1957) which through long commercial run in New York spread his reputation beyond the avant-gardist film community. At that time, he also began to use 3 by 5 inch flip cards to construct his films, and has since offered mutoscopes—a device that permits the hand-cranking of these flip cards—in his public exhibitions, e.g.,his retrospectives at the Whitney Museum of American Art in 1977 and 1980.

Breer returned to the U.S. in 1959, and absorbed at first the open vulgarity of Pop—perhaps best felt in the autobiographical *Fist Fight* (1964); and then the abstract vigor of Minimalism. Under the influence of the latter, he reworked his earliest films *Form Phases* (1952-3), and then went on to create his finest abstract films, each setting itself specific problems of color, illusion, and image control, *66* (1966), *69* (1969), and *70* (1970). At this time, which coincided with a strong rise of interest in the United States in a Tech-art, Breer also became known as the maker of extremely slow-moving abstract geometric, motorized, sculptures; less well-known were the violently moving mylar sheet constructions. In the next decade Breer's films made more liberal use of literal content as he began the use of the rotoscope which permits a frame-by-frame tracing of live action footage. With it, he continued his exploration of the connections between figuration and abstraction through retarded movement and figure-dissolution. His most recent works, such as *LMNO* and *T.Z.* (1978 and 1980), continue his long-time synthesis of literal subject and geometric pattern.

—Joshua Kind

BREHMER, K. P.

German. Born in Berlin, 12 September 1938. Studied applied graphics at the Werkkunstschule, Krefeld, West Germany, 1959 60, and printmaking at the Staatliche Kunstakademie, Dusseldorf, 1961–63. Married Monika Aich in 1963; children: Sebastian and Jelle. Worked as photographic technician, Carl Lange Verlag publishers, Duisburg, West Germany, 1957–59. Independent graphic artist, Dusseldorf, 1963–71, Hamburg, 1971–74, and in West Berlin, since 1974; also filmmaker, since 1959. Professor, Hochschule für Bildende Künste, Hamburg, 1971–74. Lives in West Berlin, Hamburg and Vietze an der Elbe, West Germany. Agent: Galerie René Block, Schaperstrasse 11, 1000 Berlin 12. Addresses: Lerchenfeld 2, 2000 Hamburg 76, West Germany; Regensburgerstrasse 27, 1000 Berlin 30, West Germany.

Individual Exhibitions:

1964	Graphisches Kabinett der Freien Galerie, West Berlin
1965	Galerie René Block, West Berlin
1966	Galerie Patio, Frankfurt
1967	Galerie Rudolf Zwirner, Cologne
	Galerie René Block, West Berlin
1969	Galerie René Block, West Berlin
1970	Goethe-Institut, Athens
	Galerie Centro, Oldenburg, West Germany
	Deutsch Bibliothek, Rome
1971	*Produktion 1962-1971*, Kinstverein, Hamburg (retrospective)
1972	Galerie Bama, Paris
1973	Galerie René Block, West Berlin
	Galerie Magers, Bonn
	Galerie Inge Baecker, Bochum, West Germany
1975	René Block Gallery, New York
1976	René Block Gallery, New York

	Museum Wiesbaden, West Germany
1977	Galerie René Block, West Berlin
1985	DAAD-Galerie, West Berlin
1986	Stadtgalerie Saarbrucken, West Germany
	Buro Orange, Munich
1987	Galerie Vorsetzen, Hamburg

Selected Group Exhibitions:

1964	*Kapitalistischer Realismus*, Galerie René Block, West Berlin
1966	*Kritische Kunst*, Dum panu z kunstatu, Brno, Czechoslovakia
1968	*Ars Multiplicata*, Kunsthalle, Cologne
1970	*Information*, Museum of Modern Art, New York
1972	*Documenta 5*, Kassel, West Germany
1974	*Art into Society/Society into Art*, Institute of Contemporary Arts, London
1979	*Kunstler/Sozialarbeiter/Eremit/Forscher*, Kunstverein, Hamburg
1981	*Art Allemagne Aujourd'hui*, ARC/Musee d'Art Moderne, Paris
1984	*Der Mang zum Gesamtkunstwerk*, Akademie der Kunste, West Berlin
1987	*Berlinart*, Museum of Modern Art, New York (travelled to San Francisco Museum of Modern Art)

Collections:

Kaiser-Wilhelm Museum, Krefeld, West Germany; Museum of Modern Art, New York; DAAD-Buro, West Berlin.

Publications:

By BREHMER: films—*Madame Butterfly*, 1969; *Ideale Landschaft*, 19679; *Musikfilm—Stumm*, 1969; *Die ges-*

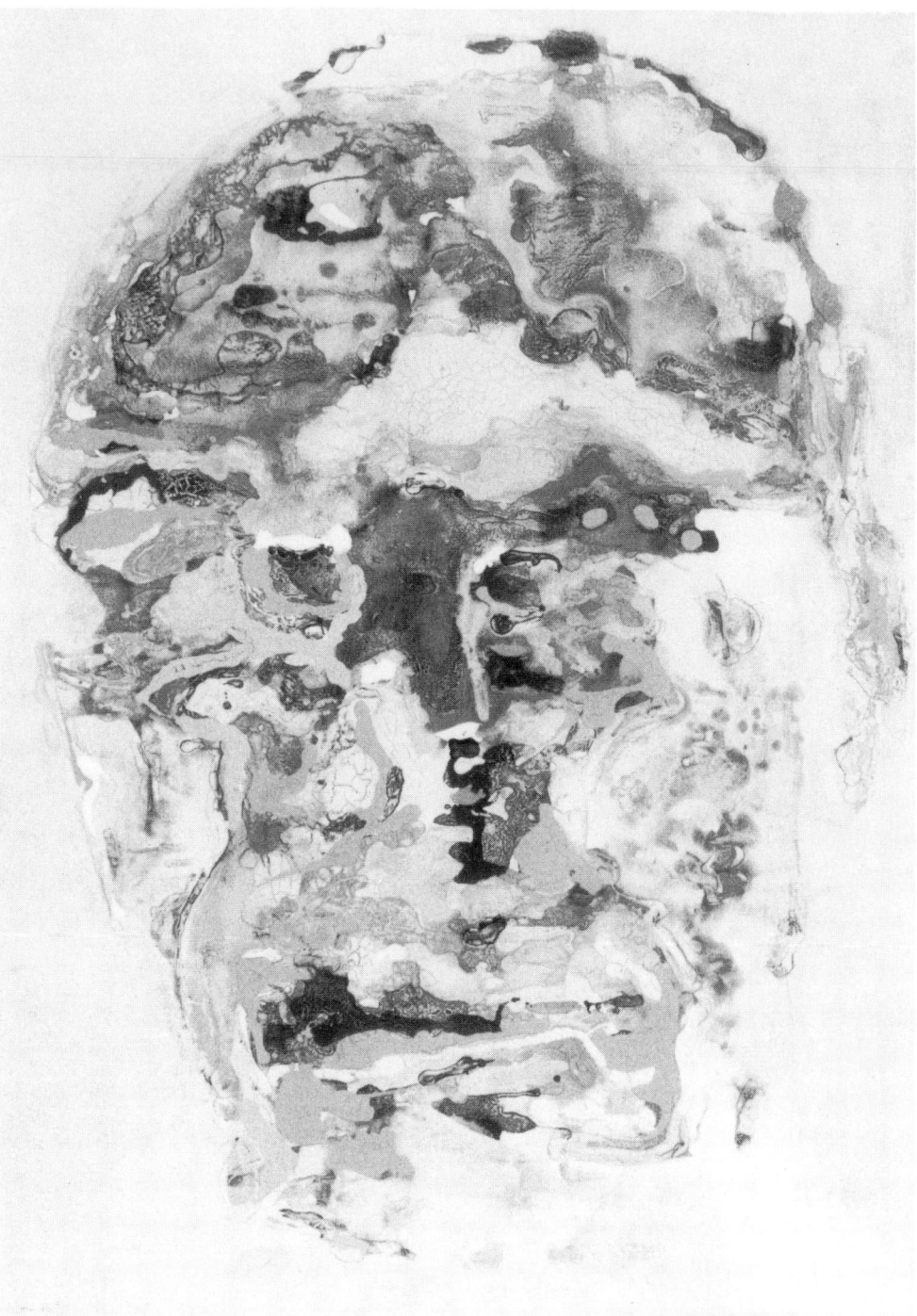

K. P. Brehmer: *Wie mich die Schlange sieht*, 1985

chiedene Frau, 1969; *Walkings*, 1969; *Nr. 1 (Sieg)*, 1969; *Nr. 2 (Mauer)*, 1969; *Nr. 3 (Stanley Brouwn)*, 1969; *Nr. 4 (Passer)*, 1969; *Nr. 5 (Parallel/Identitat)*, 1969; *Nr. 6 (Out/In—Imaginar)*,1969; *Die Welt im Kopf—Skala*, 1970; *Helmut von Florenz*, 1970; *MA MA*, 1970; *Fernsehoper*, 1970.

On BREHMER: books—*Ars Multiplicata*, exhibition catalogue, Cologne 1968; *K. P. Brehmer: Produktion 1962–1971*, exhibition catalogue, with an interview by Werner Rohde, Hamburg 1971; *Documenta 5: Befragung der Realitat*, exhibition catalogue, edited by Harald Szeemann and others, Kassel, West Germany 1972; *Kunst im Politischen Kampf*, exhibition catalogue, Hannover 1973; *Art into Society/Society into Art*, exhibition catalogue, London 1974; *Tampons d'Artistes*, edited by Herve Fischer, Paris 1974; *K. P. Brehmer: Wie mich die Schlange sieht*, exhibition catalogue, with text by Bernd Schulz, Munich 1986.

It is my view that the only progress achieved by art is that represented by the transference of its whole intensity from "I" to "we." Through ideological klep-tomania, so to speak, we must intervene in bourgeois culture, whereby the value of personal possessions, which is inherent in artistic creation, is reduced. This is possible by withholding "creativity" and substituting "imitation." This modification consists of the reduction of "artistic language" to apparent theft and adoption of collective symbols.

The transformation of art from the ideology of self to a social plane signifies stepping away from the private act of individual creation in favour of a collective and anonymous stance, in order to recognize reality through a frame of reference and to provide an orientation for oneself and the on-looker.

In this way the artist develops from a lone hero to an active participant.

—K. P. Brehmer

BRISLEY, Stuart.

British. Born in Haslemere, Surrey, in 1933. Studied at Guildford School of Art, Surrey, 1949–54; Royal College of Art, London, 1956–59; Akademie der Bildenden Künste, Munich, 1959–60; and Florida State University, Tallahassee, 1960–62. Independent artist, concentrating on performance and installation works, London since 1963: Artist in Residence, Imperial War Museum, London, 1987. Founder-Member, Arts Information Registry, London, 1967, and Artists' Union, London, 1972; Member, Artists Placement Group, London, 1967–71. Recipient: Bavarian State Stipendium, 1959–60; Fulbright Travel Award, to Florida, 1960–64; Deutscher Akademischer Austauschdienst (D.A.A.D.) Scholarship, West Berlin, 1973; British Council grant, 1976, 1977. Address: 28 Oakhill Road, London SW15, England.

Individual Exhibitions:

1960	Galerie Deutscher Bucherbund, Munich
1961	Studio F. Ulm, West Germany
1962	Cornell University, Ithica, New York
1963	Washington and Jefferson College, Washington, Pennsylvania
	Cornell University, Ithica, New York
1965	New Vision Centre, London
1966	McRoberts and Tunnard Gallery, London
1967	Museum of Modern Art, Oxford (with Bill Culbert)
	Herbert Art Gallery, Coventry (with Bill Culbert; travelled to Trinity College, Dublin, and the University of Bristol)
1968	*Bromsgrove Festival*, Worcestershire (with Bill Culbert)
	Tate Gallery, London (with Peter Sedgeley)
	Camden Arts Centre, London (with Bill Culbert)
	Madame Tussaud's Waxworks, London (with Bill Culbert)
1969	Camden Arts Centre, London
1970	*Guest of Honour*, New Arts Laboratory, London
	Sigi Krauss Gallery, London
1971	Centro de Arte y Communicacion, Buenos Aires
1972	*You Know It Makes Sense*, Ikon Gallery, Birmingham
	Zl656395C, Gallery House, London
	Artist as Whore, Gallery House, London
1973	*10 Days*, Paramedia Editions, West Berlin
1975	*12 Days*, Kunsforum, Rottweil, West Germany
	Moments of Decision/Indecision, Palac Kultury i Nauki, Warsaw
1976	Battersea Arts Centre, London
	Northern Arts Gallery, Newcastle upon Tyne
1981	Institute of Contemporary Arts, London (travelled to Ikon Gallery, Birmingham)
	Acme Gallery, London (with Iain Robertson)
1986	Orchard Gallery, Derry, Northern Ireland
1987	Imperial War Museum, London

Selected Group Exhibitions:

1953	*Young Contemporaries*, R.B.A. Galleries, London (and 1957, 1958, 1959)
1960	*Grosse Sommer Ausstellung Neue Gruppe*, Haus der Kunst, Munich
1965	*The London Group*, Art Federation Galleries, London
1968	*Artists for Czechoslovakia*, Camden Arts Centre, London
1970	*Come Together*, Royal Court Theatre, London
1972	*A Survey of the Avant-Garde in Britain*, Gallery House, London
1973	*Magic and Strong Medicine*, Walker Art Gallery, Liverpool
1976	*Arte Inglese Oggi 1960–76*, Palazzo Reale, Milan
1978	*Spring Show 2*, Serpentine Gallery, London
1982	*Group Exhibition*, Lewis Johnstone Gallery, London

Publications:

By BRISLEY: articles—"Wanted: A New Deal in Art Schools?" in *Penrose Annual*, London 1969; "Environments" in *Studio International* (London), June 1969; "Physical Situations," interview with Simon Field, in *Art and Artists* (London), August 1971; "No, It Is Not On" in *Studio International* (London), March 1972; "Anti-Performance Art" in *Arte Inglese Oggi 1960–76*, exhibition catalogue, Milan 1976; "Stuart Brisley," interview with John Roberts, in *Artlog* (London), April/May 1981.

On BRISLEY: books—*Play Orbit*, edited by Jasia Reichardt, with texts by several authors, London 1969; *Art Event and Happenings* by Udo Kultermann, London 1971; *A Survey of the Avant-Garde in Britain*, volume 1, with an introduction by Rosetta Brooks, London 1972; *Magic and Strong Medicine*, exhibition catalogue, with text by Norbert Lynton, Liverpool 1973; *Stuart Brisley*, exhibition catalogue, with texts by Paul Overy and John Roberts, London 1981.

The work of Stuart Brisley is concerned with pain.

In a period when art has upped stakes and moved from its position of lofty detachment to set up its own stall at the Vanity Fayre, when painters celebrate the latest fashions in automobiles, ladies' shoes or pop singers in a joyful and colourful discord, when sculptors rush to imitate the recent inventions of a mechanical age, when artists of all persuasions are glad to see their work sold to the highest bidder with all the television and champagne razzmatazz of the big gallery opening, Brisley has taken it upon himself to be the conscience of the art world, reminding it that art also contains a more somber tradition of horror and disgust, protest and pain.

Such a role is difficult to sustain; it could easily become strident or embarrassing, which is possibly why Brisley has always been meticulous about his techniques, about what is and what is not permissible, and is certainly why in his work the pain is transmitted to the audience via himself. To paint pictures of the ills of society could easily become mere preaching, but to use himself as the illustration safeguards the artist from such a tendency.

A typical Brisley piece, and one of his best, was his "Bath" performance at Gallery House in London. This, now sadly defunct, avant-guard gallery invited Brisley to take part in a survey of recent British art and followed its usual policy of allowing the artists to choose their own space. The gallery had once been a private house and Brisley choose the bathroom.

On the day the exhibition opened, visitors, drawn to the location by the gathering crowd, could see Brisley lying fully clothed in the bath with only his nose and mouth above water. He had put dye in the water which gave it a stagnant look and had not attempted to clean the room, which had been unused for sometime. On the floor were scattered pieces of raw meat.

The image was powerful, with overtones of police state torture or lonely suicide. It worked as well as a photograph of the real thing might do and clearly had a strong effect on the spectators. But Brisley was not yet finished: the exhibition ran for three weeks and every day he spent lying in the bath just able to breathe. After about three days the flies in the neighborhood woke up to the fact that a magnificent free meal was available to them in the form of the now rotting flesh; after 10 days the stench was unbearable, and Brisley's fellow artists had to ask him to terminate the performance.

The effect of such a work is shock, but because Brisley is careful to do work slowly and submit his own mind and body to far greater pressure than he inflicts on his audience, it avoids being mere shock and becomes instead archetypal and thought provoking.

Brisley's earliest performances took place in gridlike sculptural settings and featured large casts dressed in white medical-looking clothes and bandages. This phase of working with others reached its culmination in an exhibition in Edinburgh where the artist worked in a disused car saleroom on one of the main streets. In this grid was replaced by wrecked cars, some of which still were capable of movement, and Brisley spent the exhibition driving them headlong into each other until the whole area was littered with wreckage. He eventually had to stop this when

affected by carbon monoxide poisoning from the exhaust fumes.

Since that time Brisley has realized that he cannot ask others to take part in his art and has worked alone. In one recent piece he had himself locked for five days in a room containing just one chair and one lightbulb continuously burning; the floor was swimming in water. Visitors to the exhibition could see him through a small barred window.

There are other artists who are working in similar fields of self-inflicted pain and humiliation, but only Brisley brings to this highly questionable type of activity a dignity and an ability to relate the images he creates to the wider issues of society. Where others indulge in exhibitionistic masochism, Brisley by carefully removing his individuality from the situation and by using his own body as if it were inert sculpture, often achieves the difficult feat of enabling the spectator to overcome his feelings of shock and embarrassment and, in their place, to contemplate the creepy-crawlies that still lurk under the stone of our affluent and somewhat complacent society.

—Alastair Mackintosh

BROODTHAERS, Marcel.

Belgian. Born in Brussels, 28 January 1924. Studied chemistry briefly; mainly self-taught in art. Married Maria Bilessen; daughter: Marie-Puckc. Worked as a book dealer and guide in art museums, Brussels; as writer and poet; became artist in 1964; settled in London in the late 1960s. *Died* (in Cologne) *28 January 1976*.

Individual Exhibitions:

1964	Galerie Smith, Brussels
	Galerie St. Laurent, Brussels
1965	Palais des Beaux-Arts, Brussels
1966	Galerie J., Paris
	Wide White Space Gallery, Antwerp
1967	Palais des Beaux-Arts, Brussels
1968	Galerie 44, Brussels
	Wide White Space Gallery, Antwerp
	Librarie Saint Germain des Pres, Paris
1969	Wide White Space Gallery, Antwerp
	Galerie R. Roucke, Ghent
	Galerie Basenge-Katz, Berlin
1970	Galerie Michael Werner, Cologne
	Galerie MTL, Brussels
	Galerie Skulima, Berlin
1971	Wide White Space Gallery, Antwerp
	Galerie Michael Werner, Cologne
	Städtisches Museum, Mönchengladbach, West Germany
	Galerie Yvon Lambert, Paris
1972	Wide White Space Gallery, Antwerp
	Galerie Heiner Friedrich, Munich
	Modern Art Agency, Naples
	Städtische Kunsthalle, Dusseldorf
	Galerie Grafikmeyer, Karlsruhe
	Jack Wendler Gallery, London
1973	Galerie Michael Werner, Cologne
	Galerie Heiner Friedrich, Munich
	Galerie Francoise Lambert, Milan
	Cinema Arsenal, Berlin
	Galerie Loehr, Frankfurt
	Art and Project, Amsterdam
	Galerie Rudolf Zwirner, Cologne
	Galerie Yvon Lambert, Paris
1974	Palais des Beaux-Arts, Brussels
	Wide White Space Gallery, Antwerp
	Galerie MTL, Brussels
	Cinema Melville, Paris
	Kunstmuseum, Basle
	Galerie René Block, Berlin
	Petersberg Press, London

1975	Galerie Grafikmeyer, Karlsruhe
	Nationalgalerie, Berlin (travelled to Museum of Modern Art, Oxford, and the Centre Georges Pompidou, Paris)
	Kunsthalle, Dusseldorf
	Institute of Contemporary Arts, London
	Nigel Greenwood Gallery, London
1977	Nigel Greenwood Gallery, London
	Hester van Royen Gallery, London
	Tate Gallery, London
	New 57 Gallery, Edinburgh
1978	Galerie Heiner Friedrich, Munich
	Galerie Isy Brachot, Brussels
1980	Galerie Michael Werner, Cologne
	Tate Gallery, London
	Museum Ludwig, Cologne
1981	Museum Boymans-van Beuningen, Rotterdam
1982	Kunsthalle, Berne
	Moderna Museet, Stockholm
1983	Galerie Michael Werner, Cologne
1984	Mary Boone Gallery, New York

Selected Group Exhibitions:

1958	*Films Experimentaux*, Knokke-le-Zoute, Belgium
1964	*Jeune Sculpture Belge*, Palais des Beaux-Arts, Brussels
1965	*Pop Art, Nouveau Realisme, etc.*, Palais des Beaux-Arts, Brussels
1969	*Language 3*, Dwan Gallery, New York
1972	*Documenta 5*, Kassel, West Germany
1973	*Bilder: Objekte: Film: Konzepte*, Städtische Galerie Lenbachhaus, Munich
1975	*Functions of Drawing*, Rijksmuseum Kröller-Müller, Otterio, Netherlands
1976	*Biennale*, Venice
1980	*Printed Art: A View of Two Decades*, Museum of Modern Art, New York
1983	*Der Hang zum Gesamtkunstwerk*, Kunsthaus, Zurich

Collections:

Musée des Beaux-Arts, Brussels; Städtisches Museum, Mönchengladbach, West Germany; Sammlung Hahn, Cologne.

Publications:

By BROODTHAERS: books—*Mon Livre d'Ogre*, Ostend 1957; *Minuit*, Brussels 1960; *La Bete Noire*, Brussels 1962; *Pense-Bete*, Brussels 1963; *Phantomas*, Brussels 1966; *Le Corbeau et le Renard*, book and film, Antwerp 1968; *Un Coup de Des Jamais n'Abolira le Hasard*, Antwerp and Cologne 1969; *Vingt ans Après*, Brussels, Brussels 1969; *Plan Vert*, Cologne 1972; *Magie (Art et Politique)*, Paris 1973; *Je hais le Mouvement qui Deplace les Lignes*, Hamburg 1973; *Jeter due Poisson sur le Marche de Cologne*, Cologne 1973; *Un Jardin d'Hiver*, London 1974; *A Voyage on the North Sea*, London, Hamburg, and Cologne 1974; *Rascisme Vegetal*, Cologne 1974; *Pauvre Belgique*, Brussels 1974; *En lisant la Lorelei oder wie ich die Lorelei gelesen habe*, Paris and Munich 1975. films—*La Clef de l'Horloge (Kurt Schwitters)*, 1957; *Le Corbeau et le Renard*, 1967; *Section 29th Siècle (Musée d'Art Moderne, department des Aigles)*, 1968; *La Signature*, 1970; *La Pluie (Projet pour un Texte)*, 1970; *La Pipe (René Magritte)*, 1970; *Un Film de Ch. Baudelaire*, 1971; *Histoire d'Amour (Dr. Huysmans)*, 1971; *Le Poisson*, 1971; *Paris*, 1971; *Au dela de cette Limite*, 1972; *Chere petite soeur,*1972; *Voyage en mer du Nord*, 1973; *Ah, que la chasse soit le plaisir des rois*, 1972; *Un Jardin d'Hiver*, 1974; *Eau de Cologne*, 1974; *Berlin oder ein Traum mit Sahne*, 1974; *Jeremy Bentham*, 1974; *The Battle of Waterloo*, 1975–76.

On BROODTHAERS: books—*Marcel Broodthaers*, exhibition catalogue, Paris 1975; *Marcel Broodthaers* by Freddy de Vree, Antwerp 1979; *Marcel Broodthaers*, exhibition catalogue, London 1980; *Marcel Broodthaers*, exhibition catalogue, Cologne 1980 (with complete bibliography).

Broodthaers was raised in French speaking Belgium and was persuaded to study chemistry rather than art which he had wanted to study. He subsequently worked in a bank and then as a bookdealer. Before

1964 his interest in writers and in books as objects had led him to become a poet with excursions into photography and film-making.

Early on in his life Broodthaers had been fascinated by the work of Rene Magritte, Belgium's most famous twentieth century artist, and his major works, produced in the last ten years of his life, were to reflect similar preoccupations with puzzles, hidden messages and irony and the use of the written word as an element in visual art. His first film, *La Clef de l'Horloge,* produced in 1957, was a cinematographic poem in honor of Kurt Schwitters

In 1963 Broodthaers was introduced to the Pop Art of Jim Dine, Roy Lichtenstein and Claus Oldenberg, which prompted him to write an article on Magritte's influence on Dine. Broodthaers' link with Magritte was strongest in the use of literary and visual puns—a concept dear to the heart of 1930s Surrealism which sprang from poetry in the first instance.

Between 1967–75 Broodthaers produced films, books, works using words, photography, sound tapes and slides, and during this time established his position in the visual art world with *Musée d'Art moderne, Départment des Aigles.* This was a 'museum' with 'departments' of 'many sections' which Broodthaers erected in houses and galleries between 1968 and 1974. Behind it was the idea of the worker who takes over his workplace, and though it was a parody, it was not a parody of the museum, but a comment upon the sociology of the museum or the curator who usurps the role of the creator—the artist—a very elaborate piece of irony.

Though Broodthaers could be seen as a sort of latter day Dadaist or Surrealist, in his use of 'found' imagery, his aggregation of objects tended to reflect the 'good life'—European style, food, wine, literature, etc. Like the Surrealists who preceded him, Broodthaers' visual art rests heavily on a poetic base. This base, in Broodthaers' case, relies for its strucure on "metonymy," which is a term of rhetoric meaning, (according to the *Shorter Oxford English Dictionary),* "A figure in which the name of an attribute or adjunct is substituted for that of the thing meant, e.g., sceptre for authority."

Though he remained, in his time, very much on the fringes of the art world, (at a time of Pop Art he was almost a throwback to Surrealism), his work was acknowledged by the art world in the 1970s with the rise of interest in Conceptual and Performance Art.

—Victoria Keller

BROOKS, James.
American. Born in St. Louis, Missouri, in 1906. Studied at Southern Methodist University, Dallas, 1923–25; Art Students League, New York, under K. Nicolaides and Boardman Robinson, 1927–30. Served in the United States Army, as an Art Correspondent, in the Middle East, 1942–45. Married Mary MacDonald in 1938; married the artist Charlotte Park in 1947. Full-time artist, New York and East Hampton, New York. Taught at Columbia University, New York, 1946–48, and Pratt Institute, New York, 1948–55; Visiting Critic in Advanced Painting, Yale University, New Haven, Connecticut, 1955–60; Artist-in-Residence, American Academy, Rome, 1963; Visiting Critic, New College, Sarasota, Florida, 1965–67; Professor of Art, Queens College, New York, 1966–69; Visiting Critic, University of Pennsylvania, Philadelphia, 1972–75; Andrew Carnegie Visiting Professor of Art, Cooper Union, New York, 1975. Recipient: First Painting Prize and Logan Medal, 1957, and Normal Waite Harris Silver Medal and Prize, 1961, Art Institute of Chicago; Ford Foundation Purchase Award, Pennsylvania Academy of Fine Arts, 1962; Guggenheim Fellowship, 1969; National Endowment for the Arts Grant, 1973. Member, American Academy and Institute of Arts and Letters, 1973. Agent: Gruenebaum Gallery,

415 West Broadway, New York, New York 10012. Address: 128 Neck Path, The Springs, East Hampton, Long Island, New York 11937, U.S.A.

Individual Exhibitions:

1950	Peridot Gallery, New York
1951	Peridot Gallery, New York
1952	Miller-Pollard Gallery, Seattle
	Peridot Gallery, New York
1953	Peridot Gallery, New York
1954	Grace Borgenicht Gallery, New York
1957	Stable Gallery, New York
1959	Stable Gallery, New York
1961	Kootz Gallery, New York
1962	Kootz Gallery, New York
1963	Whitney Museum, New York (retrospective; toured the United States, 1963–64)
1965	Kootz Gallery, New York
1966	Philadelphia Art Alliance
1968	Martha Jackson Gallery, New York
	Southampton College, Southampton, Long Island, New York
1969	Berenson Gallery, Miami
1970	The Century Association, New York
1971	Martha Jackson Gallery, New York
1972	Museum of Fine Arts, Dallas (retrospective)
	Martha Jackson Gallery, New York
1975	Martha Jackson Gallery/Finch College Museum of Art, New York (retrospective of paintings and drawings; travelled to Guild Hall Museum, East Hampton, New York; Flint Institute of Arts, Michigan; Grand Rapids Art Museum, Michigan; Cranbrook Academy of Art, Bloomfield Hills, Michigan; and University of Connecticut, Storrs)
	Galleria Lorenzelli, Milan
	Works in Progress, Cooper Union, New York
1976	Summit Art Center, New Jersey (retrospective)
	Robinson Galleries, Houston
	Martha Jackson Gallery, New York
	Foire International d'Art Contemporain, Paris
1977	Carone Gallery, Fort Lauderdale, Florida
	Himelfarb Gallery, Watermill, New York
1978	Lerner-Heller Gallery, New York
	Himelfarb Gallery, Watermill, New York
1979	Montclair Museum, New Jersey
	Gruenebaum Gallery, New York (with Giorgio Cavalion)
1981	Gruenebaum Gallery, New York
	Himelfarb Gallery, Watermill, New York

Selected Group Exhibitions:

1958	*Jong Amerika Schildert,* Stedelijk Museum, Amsterdam
1960	*60 American Painters,* Walker Art Center, Minneapolis
1961	*American Abstract Expressionists and Imagists,* Guggenheim Museum, New York
1967	*200 Years of Watercolor Painting in America,* Metropolitan Museum of Art, New York
1969	*The New American Painting and Sculpture: The First Generation,* Museum of Modern Art, New York
1973	*Exhibition of Newly Elected Members,* American Academy and Institute of Arts and Letters, New York
	American Art Mid-Century Exhibition, National Gallery of Art, Washington, D.C.
1980	*Arte Americana Contemporanea,* Civic Museum, Udine, Italy
1981	*American Painting 1930–1980,* Haus der Kunst, Munich
1982	*5 Distinguished Alumni: The WPA Federal Art Project,* Hirshhorn Museum, Washington, D.C. (with DeKooning, Neel, Bolotowski and Lassaw)

Collections:

Guggenheim Museum, New York; Metropolitan Museum of Art, New York; Museum of Modern Art, New York; Whitney Museum, New York; Fogg Art Museum, Harvard University, Cambridge, Massachusetts; Hirshhorn Museum, Washington, D.C.; Detroit Institute of Art; Art Institute of Chicago; Museum of Fine Arts, Houston; Tate Gallery, London.

Publications:

On BROOKS: books—*The Story of Modern Art* by Sheldon Cheney, New York 1958; *Art Since 1945* by Sam Hunter, New York 1959; *American Painting in the 20th Century* by Henry Geldzahler, New York 1960; *The Unknown Shore* by Dore Ashton, Boston 1962; *James Brooks* by Sam Hunter, New York 1963; *History of Modern Art* by H. H. Arnason, New York 1969; *James Brooks,* exhibition catalogue, by Merrill Ruepple, Dallas 1972; *A History of American Art* by George M. Cohen, New York 1973; *James Brooks,* exhibition catalogue, by Elayne H. Varian, New York 1975; articles—"James Brooks and the Abstract Inscape" by Irving Sandler in *Artnews* (New York), February 1963; "James Brooks" by H. H. Arnason in *Art International* (Lugano, Switzerland), March 1963; "James Brooks: Stain into Image" by April Kingsley in *Artnews* (New York), December 1972; "James Brooks: The Man and His Art" by Barbara Delatiner in the *New York Times,* 29 June 1975; "James Brooks at Finch College and Martha Jackson Gallery" by Phyllis Derfner in *Art in America* (New York, July/August 1975; "The Paintings of James Brooks" by Carter Ratcliff in *Arts Magazine* (New York), September 1978.

I work under these assumptions. That a private symbolism is not possible; that my work will occupy others as it has me; that whether it does, and how soon, depends on things we can not know—the ultimate power of the painting and the need felt for it; that manipulation of form to assure an audience would destroy the reality of the work and debase the concept of communication; that good painting, as always, is a door opened to man's spirit; that it will not repel because of its obscurity, but may because of its directness.

—James Brooks

Like Guston, Frankenthaler, and his own long-time friend Bradley Walker Tomlin, Brooks stands with those New York School artists who, about the onset of the 1950s, took the overtly emotive and tactile-based improvisatory flow of Pollock and DeKooning, and made it a more meditative, slow-paced gesture, an even cherishing kind of painterly act. Before his military service in World War II, where he was a combat artist, Brooks had been a commercial artist, and had then, from 1936 until 1942, worked with the Federal Art Project, a subdivision of the Works Progress Administration (WPA). A major portion of his time was devoted to the creation of a 235 feet long mural *Flight* in the rotunda of the Marine Terminal at LaGuardia Airport in New York City. Admired as an important work at the time, and overpainted in the 1950s, the painting has recently been restored to revived acclaim. With his return to New York in 1946, Brooks met Guston and Pollock (with whom he would be in close contact in the last years of the 1940s), and found the push towards a new confidence and a new style in American art already well underway. Yet he remained a Cubist, who needed the painterly epiphany of an intimate personal confrontation with abstraction to move him unhesitatingly into that mode. It is said to have occurred only in 1948 when Brooks saw the glue seepage of a collage on the reverse canvas side. In a sense, he is still that artist, surprised by the elegance of chance and the softer dispersion of paint into the canvas surface. He has been claimed (A. Kingsley) as the first American artist to stain pigment directly into raw canvas: and thus the premier American to grasp the wider-ranging significance of Pollock's drip techniques. (T. Hess remarked, in 1951, that Brooks' forms "stayed in the weave of the canvas.")

The general aura of his work appears a genial disorder, with a lyricism based upon essentially organic terrain the guiding force since the 1950s' close. Before then, during his first decade of non-representational art, there may have been a more easily detected rhythm still infused with the pattern of

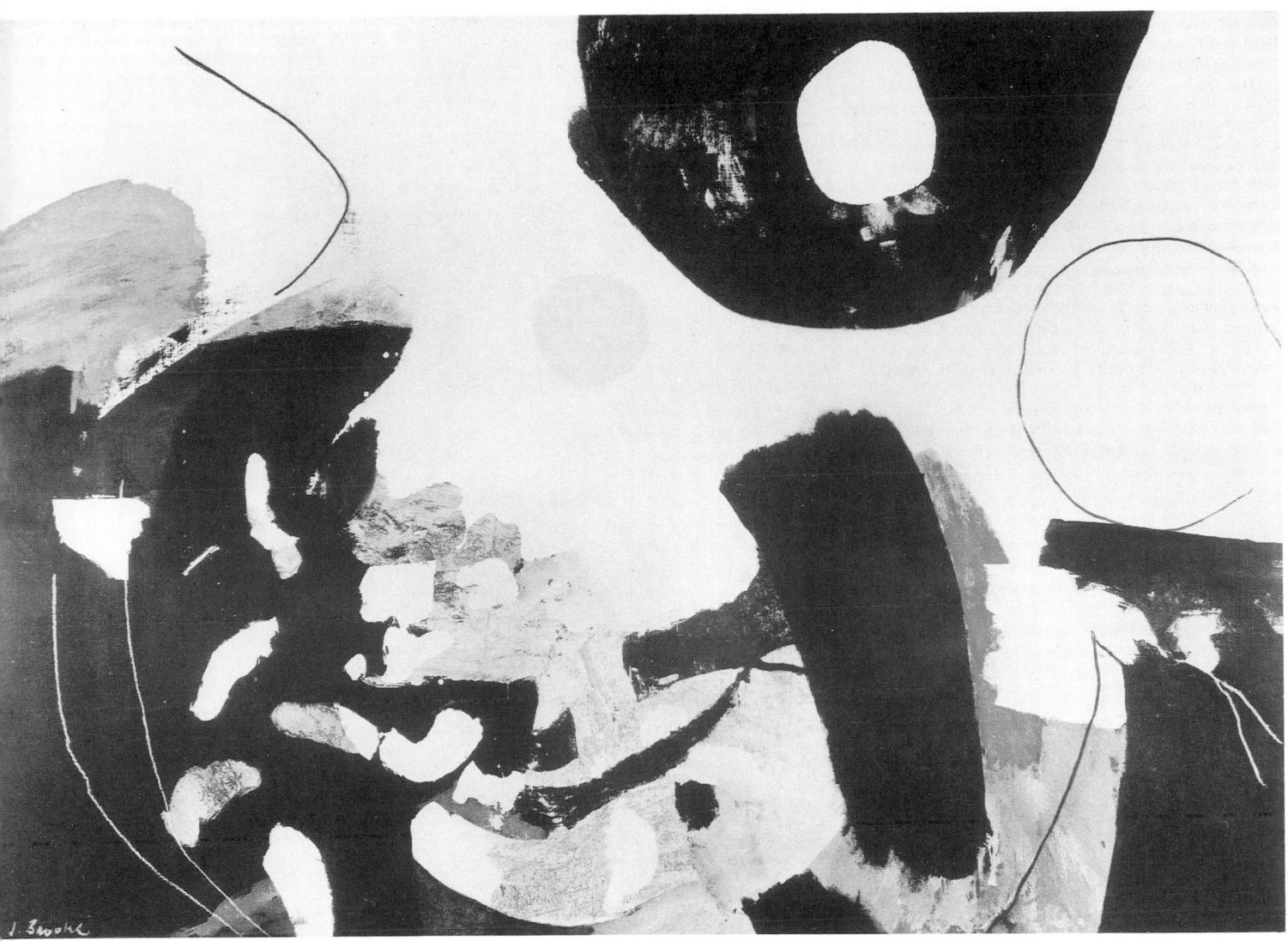

James Brooks: *Ealand*, 1973

Cubism. More and more, Brooks gave into the au-tomatist influence of Surrealism—although that mode has never been easily assignable to his art—to achieve a pulse quite his own with wire-like linearities and fluctuating biomorphic shapes. (A part of his ac-knowledged success is the only momentary sense of reference to Arp or Miro that surfaces in his many works.) His creative methods have always been canted towards improvisation, so that he will fre-quently turn the canvas while engaged in the painting process; just so, he has used blotting techniques and paint randomly dispersed in the effort to achieve a personally authentic significance. It is also known that he, quite self-consciously, will work on but one painting at a time, so as to avoid any carryover of form and pattern invention in a successive image. Still active at the onset of this penultimate decade of the modernist century, Brooks may well be hailed as "an old master of modernism" in his continual and enlivening manipulation of these once-radical pre-cepts. Such continual self-challenge has moved him as well into the position of "father of recent lyrical abstraction."

—Joshua B. Kind

BROUWN, Stanley.
Dutch. Born in Paramaribo, Surinam, in 1935. Edu-cated in Paramaribo; self-taught in art. Independent artist, Amsterdam, since 1960; first "This Way Brouwn" works, Amsterdam, 1960; associated with the Fluxus performance artists, Amsterdam, from 1962. Address: Willem de Zwygerlaan 60-1, Am-sterdam, Netherlands.

Individual Exhibitions:

1970   Stedelijk Museum, Schiedam, Netherlands
         Städtisches Museum, Mönchenglabach, West Ger-many
1971   Zentrum fur Aktuelle Kunst, Aachen, West Ger-many
1976   Van Abbemuseum, Eindhoven, Netherlands (trav-elled to the Kunsthalle, Berne)
1977   Whitechapel Art Gallery, London

Selected Group Exhibitions:

1970   *18 Paris iv 70*, Paris
1972   *Documenta*, Kassel, West Germany
1978   *Werke aus der Sammiung Crex*, Ink, Zurich (trav-elled to the Louisiana Museum, Humiehack, Den-mark, Städtische Galerie in Lenbachhaus, Munich, and the Van Abbemuseum, Eindhoven, Netherlands)
1979   *Mit Zeichnerischen Mittein gemacht*, Stadtschloss, Fulda, West Germany

Collections:

Van Abbemuseum, Eindhoven, Netherlands; Stedelijk Mu-seum, Amsterdam; Kunsthalle, Berne.

Publications:

By BROUWN: books—*This Way Brouwn*, Cologne and New York 1971; *Afghanistan/Zambia*, Aachen, West Germany 1971.

On BROUWN: books—*18 Paris iv 70*, edited by Michel Claura, Paris 1970; *Concept Art* by Klaus Honnef, Cologne 1971; *Documenta 5: Befragung der Realiat Bildwelten huete*, exhibition catalogue, edited by Harald Szeeman and others, Kassel, West Germany 1972; *Stanley Brouwn*, exhibition cat-alogue, edited by Coosje van Bruggen and Rudi H. Fuchs, Eindhoven, Netherlands 1976; *Werke aus der Sammlung Crex*, exhibition catalogue, by Cristel Sauer and Urs Rauss-muller, Zurich 1978; *Mit Zeichnerischen Mitteln gemacht*, exhibition catalogue, with text by Michael Lingner, Fulda, West Germany 1979; articles—"Dutch Artists on Television" by Carel Blotkamp in *Studio International* (London), June 1971; "Stanley Brouwn: Door Kosmischestralen Lopen" by J. Cladders in *Museumjournaal* (Amsterdam), July 1971; "Stanley Brouwn: Steps" in *Avalanche* (New York), Spring 1972.

BRUS, Günter.
Austrian. Born in Ardning, 27 September 1938. Edu-cated at Volkschule and Hauptschule, Mureck, 1944–50, and Hauptschule, Stainz, 1950–56; studied at the Kunstgewerbeschule, Graz, 1953–57; Akademie fur Angewandte Kunst, Vienna, 1957–60. Served in the Austrian Federal Army, 1961. Married Anni Steiner

in 1962; daughter: Diana. Independent artist; has lived and worked in Vienna, 1960–69, West Berlin, 1969–79, and in Graz, Austria, since 1979; produced first action works and self-painting works, Vienna, 1964; Founder Member, with Hermann Nitsch, Otto Muehl and Rudolf Schwarzkogler, Wiener Aktionismus group, Vienna, 1964; Founder, with Otto Muehl, Institut fur Direkte Kunst, Vienna, 1966; Founder, with Arnulf Meifert, *Deutsche Trivialeum*, West Berlin, 1974; Founder Editor, with Arnulf Meifert, *Die Schastrommel*, later *Die Drossel* newspaper of the Osterreichische Exilregierung, West Berlin, 1969–76. Recipient: Wurdignungspreis des Ministeriums fur Unterricht und Kunst, Vienna, 1981, 1982; Kunstpreis, City of Graz, 1986; Kunstpreis, City of Vienna, 1986. Agent: Galerie Heike Curtze, Citadellstrasse 11, 4000 Dusseldorf 1, and Seilerstatte 15/14, 1010 Vienna. Address: Einspinnergasse 3, 8010 Graz, Austria.

Individual Exhibitions:

1961   *Aktionsmalerei*, Galerie Junge Generation, Vienna (with Alfons Schilling)

1965   *Malerie-Selbstbemalung-Selbstverstümmelung*, Galerie Junge Generation, Vienna

1971   *Handzeichnungen*, Galerie Michael Werner, Cologne

1973   *Zeichnungen*, Galerie Grünangergasse 12, Vienna
       Fotos von Aktionen, Galleria Diagramma, Milan

1974   *Zeichnungen*, Galerie Krauthammer, Zurich
       Fotos von Aktionen, Studio Morra, Naples
       Der Vollschmerz, Galerie Springer, Berlin

1975   *Das Namenlos*, Galerie Wiener and Würthle, Berlin
       Der Vollschmerz und Arbeiten von 1973 und 1975, Galerie Van de Loo, Munich
       Nachtfreudenwalzer, Galerie Grünangergasse 12, Vienna

1976   *Nachtfreudenwalzer*, Galerie Stummer und Hubschmid, Zurich
       Auszüge aus dem Laufenden Werk, Galerie Gactan, Carouge, Geneva
       Zeichnungen, Galerie Klein, Bonn
       Das Aulicht, Rathaus, Mureck, Austria
       Brus: Werke, Galerie Kalb, Vienna
       Zeichnungen und Schriften, Kunsthalle, Berne

1977   *Zeichnungen, Bücher und Mappenwerke*, Galerie A. Amsterdam
       Bilder aus Gebenedeitanien, Galerie Springer, Berlin
       Die Gärten in der Exosphäre, Galerie Van de Loo, Munich
       Herzeigung, Galerie Jörg Stummet, Zurich (travelled to the Galeriei Gysin, Dübendorf, Switzerland)

1978   *Die Pracht der Hellsten Freude*, Goethe-Institut, Amsterdam
       Amorphophallus Titanum, Studio Morra, Naples

1979   *Franz Schreker: Die Gazeichneten*, Frankfurt Oper
       Reizfluten, Galerie Heike Curtze, Vienna
       Franz Schreker: Die Gezeichneten, Staatsoper, Vienna
       Bild-Dichtungen, Galerie Heike Curtze, Dusseldorf
       Das Knaben Wunderhorn, DAAD Galerie, Berlin
       Abendwerke und Nachtarbeiten, Galerie Jörg Stummer, Zurich

1980   *Bild-Dichtungen*, Whitechapel Art Gallery, London (travelled to the Kunstverein, Hamburg, and the Kunstmuseum, Lucerne)
       Schadelschrei-Romantik, Galerie Van de Loo, Munich
       Augenmusik, Galerie Heike Curtze, Dusseldorf
       Augenmusik: Trugschattengewächse, Galerie Bloch, Innsbruck

1981   *Bild-Dichtungen*, Kulturhaus, Graz, Austria
       Traumentiziehungskur, Galerie Heike Curtze, Vienna
       Weisser Wind, Gallerie Jörg Stummer, Zurich

1982   *Unruhe nach dem Sturm*, Galerie A, Amsterdam
       Blaues Herz im Nerveninfernal, Galerie Zell am See, Austria
       Zyankal-Zyklamen, Galerie Van de Loo, Munich

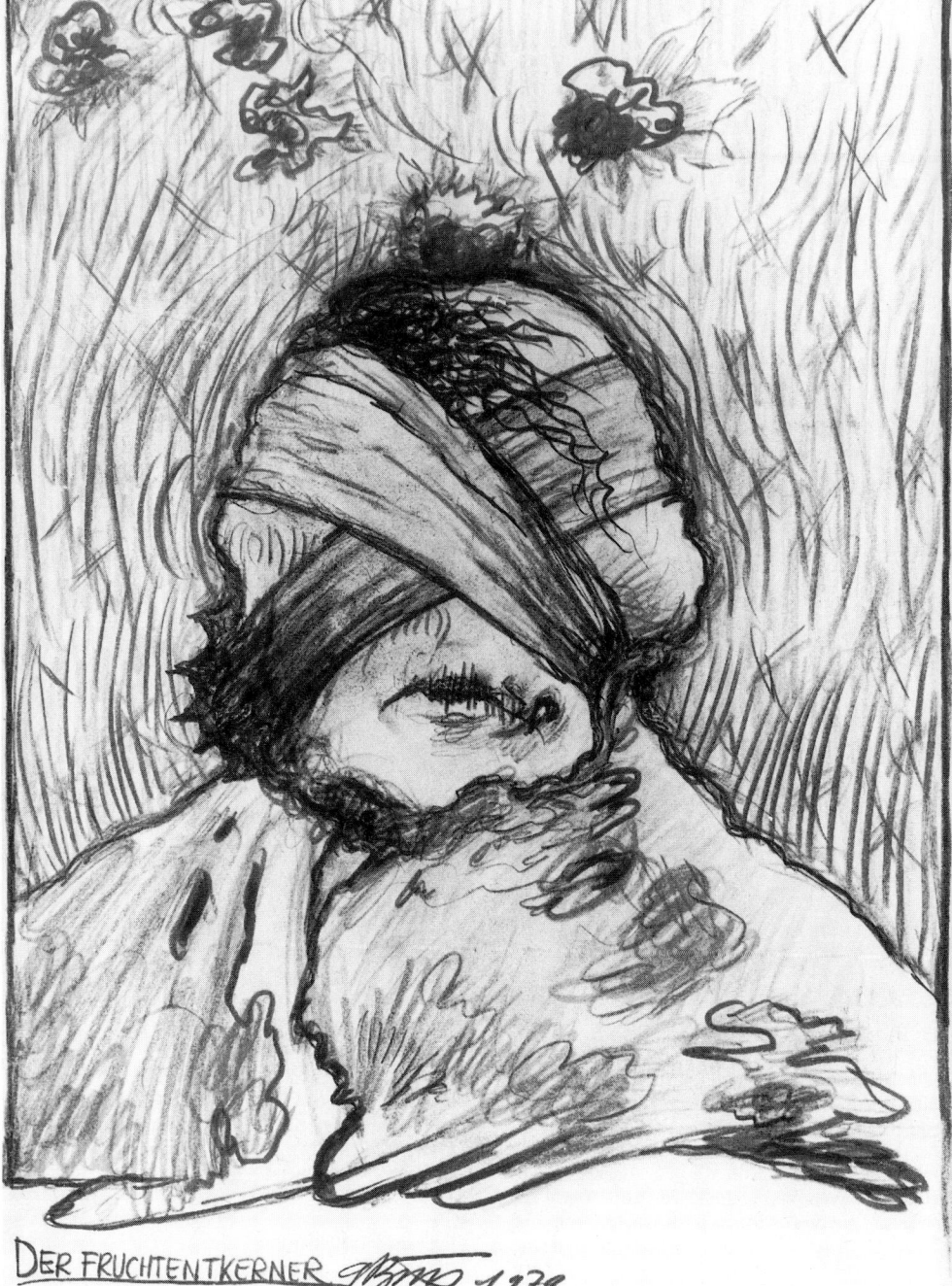

DER FRUCHTENTKERNER

Günter Brus: *Der Fruchtentkerner*, 1979

1983   *Rasende Geduld*, Maximilianverlag Sabine Knust, Munich
       Lichtsprache—Le Langage de la Lumière, Galerie Farideh Cadot, Paris
       Die Gärten in der Exosphäre und andere Bild-Dichtungen, Rupertinum, Salzburg
       Blindes Brot, Petersen Galerie, West Berlin
       Trunkene Triebe, Galerie Heike Curtze, Dusseldorf

1984   *Morchposten des Pulsschlags*, Galerie Jörg Stummer, Zurich
       Sonata Domestica, Galerie Bleich-Rossi, Graz, Austria
       Augensternstunden, Van Abbemuseum, Eindhoven, Netherlands
       Franz Schreker: Die Gezeichneten, Rupertinum, Salzburg
       La Croce del Veneto, Galerie Heike Curtze, Vienna
       Eisblut, blauer Frost, Edition Hundertmark, Cologne

1985   *Astres de la nuit—Nachtgestirne*, Galerie Maeght Lelong, Paris
       Eisblut, blauer Frost, Galerie A, Amsterdam
       Bühnebild-und Kostümentwürfe zu G. Roth, Kulturhaus, Graz, Austria

1986   *Der Ausblick*, Galerie Heike Curtze, Vienna (and Galerie Zell am See, Austria)
       Stichproben, Maximilianverlag Sabine Knust, Munich
       Stumme Gewitter, Galerie Jörg Stummer, Zurich

1987   *Ballungsträume*, Galerie Thaddaeus Ropac, Salzburg

Selected Group Exhibitions:

1966   *Ornament ist ein Verbrechen*, Galerie Dvorak, Vienna (with Otto Muehl, Loos-Villa and Wien-Hietzig)

1967   *Direct Art Festival*, Porrhaus, Vienna

1972   *Documenta 5*, Kassel, West Germany

1975   *Body Works*, Museum of Contemporary Art, Chicago

1978   *11 Artists Working in Berlin*, Whitechapel Art Gallery, London

1980   *Kunst der Siebziger Jahre*, at the *Biennale*, Venice

1981   *Westkunst*, Rheinhallen, Cologne

1983   *New Art* Tate Gallery, London

1985   *Rennweg*, Castello di Rivoli, Turin, Italy

1987 *Berlinart 1961-87*, Museum of Modern Art, New York (travelled to San Francisco Museum of Modern Art)

Collections:

Uno-City, Vienna; Tate Gallery, London; Museum of Modern Art, New York; Musee d'Art Moderne, Paris; Van Abbemuseum, Eindhoven, Netherlands; Kunsthalle, Hamburg; Kunstmuseum, Winterthur, Switzerland; Festspielhaus, Bregenz; Landessammlungen Rupertinum, Salzburg; Staatsgalerie, Stuttgart.

Publications:

By BRUS: books—*Malerei-Selbstemalung-Selbstverstrümmelung*, Vienna 1965; *b & m—direkte kunst*, with Otto Muehl, Vienna 1967; *Burs/Muehl: Direkte' Theatre*, Vienna 1967; *Patent Urinoir*, Vienna 1968; *Patent Merde*, Vienna 1968; *Unter dem Ladentisch*, Berlin 1969; *Die Schastrommel* no. 1–11, Berlin 1969-73; *Burs: Bausch-und-Bogen-Scheisse*, Cologne 1970; *Korperanalyse*, Berlin 1970; *Handzeichnungen*, Cologne/New York 1971; *Irrwisch* Frankfurt 1971; *Der Balkon Europas*, Berlin 1972; *Die Neue Dekadenz*, Berlin 1972; *Art des Giftes, Dauer der Vergiftung, Sitz der Schmerzer*, Berlin 1973; *Zereissprobe*, Berlin 1974; *Nacht freudewalzer*, Berlin 1975; *Das Namelos, Die Drossel, Nr. 14*, Berlin 1975; *Circannual, Die Drossel Nr. 16*, Berlin 1976; *Die Luchende Verwesung*, Berlin 1976; *Hohes Gebrechen*, Altona and Hohengebraching 1976; *Der Frackzwang*, Altona and Hohengebraching 1976; *Das Aulicht*, Stuttgart 1977; *Jeden jeden Mittwoch*, with D. Steiger, Berlin 1977; *Farbige Zeichnungen aus den Jahren 1970–77*, Altona and Hohengebraching 1977; *Phantom Palaste*, Berlin 1978; *Gestirn-Abzeichan*, Altona and Hohengebraching 1978; *Die Falter des Vorschlafs*, Altona and Hohengebraching 1978; *Die Gärten in der Exosphäre*, Altona and Hohengebraching 1979; *Das Rufwort*, Altona and Hohengebraching 1979; *Die Herbsttrompete*, Vienna and Munich 1981; *Zyankal-Zyklamen*, Munich 1982; *Rasende Geduld*, Munich 1983; *Stillstand der Sonnenuhr*, Vienna and Munich 1983; *Die Geheimnistrager*, Salzburg 1984; *Die Wundharmonika*, Eindhoven 1984; *Die Ruine*, Paris 1985; *Stumme Gewitter*, Zurich 1986; *Amor und Amok*, Salzburg 1986; *Gebrauchsmystik*, Vienna and Munich 1986; films—*Ana*, with Kurt Kren, 1964; *Selbstbemalung*, Vienna 1964; *Selbstverstümmelung*, with Wiener Spaziergang, Vienna 1965; *Transfusion*, Vienna 1965; *Gut and Gerne*, 1966; *10 Rounds*, with Otto Muehl and Kurt Kren, 1966; *20 September*, Vienna 1967; *Einatmen und Ausatem*, 1967; *Direct Art Festival*, Vienna 1967; *Aktion mit Diana*, Vienna 1967; *Mit Schwung ins Meue Jahr*, with Otto Muehl and Rudolf Schwartzkogler, 1967; *Kunst und Revolution*, Vienna 1968; *Satisfaction*, Vienna 1968; *Der Helle Wahnsinn*, Aachen, West Germany 1968; *Direkte Kunst*, Dusseldorf 1968; *Strangulation*, Vienna 1968; *Impudenz im Grunewald*, Berlin 1969; *Blummenstuck, nach einem Gedicht von G. Ruhm*, Berlin 1969; *Intelligenztest*, Berlin 1969; *Korperanalyse, Zerreissprobe*, Munich 1970; *Psycho-Dramolett*, Munich 1970.

On BRUS: books—*Günter Brus: Zeichnungen und Schriften*, exhibition catalogue, with text by Johannes Gachnang and Arnulf Meifert, Berne 1976; *Die Gärten in der Exosphäre*, exhibition catalogue, Munich 1977; *Die Pracht der hellsten Freude*, exhibition catalogue, Amsterdam 1978; *Amorphophallus Titanum*, exhibition catalogue, Naples 1978; *11 Artists Working in Berlin*, exhibition catalogue, London 1978; *Franz Schreker: Die Gezeichneten*, exhibition catalogue, Frankfurt 1979; *Reizfluten*, exhibition catalogue, Vienna 1979; *Des Knaben Wunderhorn*, exhibition catalogue, with text by Wieland Schmied and Arnulf Meifert, Berlin 1979; *Kunst der 70er Jahre*, exhibition catalogue, Venice 1980; *Günter Brus: Bild-Dichtungen*, exhibition catalogue, with text by Arnulf Meifert, London 1980; *Gunter Brus: Arbeiten auf Papier 1987*, exhibition catalogue, with introduction by Helga Kocher, Salzburg 1987.

It is perhaps no great surprise that the vehemence of Gunter Brus's art has generated a good deal of extreme commentary. On the one hand he has been called neurotic, obsessive; on the other, a hero, an artist of "titanic temperament." As an unashamed Romantic, Brus would no doubt claim that the former was in some way bound up with the latter.

Brus gave up live work in 1970 for the state of his own mental health after being hounded out of Austria by the police for offending public decency. Threats

were also made against his life. Exiled in West Berlin, he began to draw and paint and write poetry. The self-image of the outcast, which in the "Aktions" took the extreme form of public purging (the "Suffering Servant") today is reflected in work which is uncompromisingly conventional. In rejecting modernism Brus has turned to traditional forms of representation (the fairy tale) as a form of Aktionismus.

The tradition of the seer or visionary is very important to him. Blake, Munch, Bosch. It is Blake who has been the most direct influence. The unity of word and image. The mythic struggle between good and evil. The utopianism. Brus's first drawings, coming directly after the Aktions and his work with Nitsch, Muehl and Schwarzkogler, were very much retaliatory, Sadian fantasies of unremitting horror and degradation. "A successful drawing . . . shocks the sufferer back into life." In the fairytale drawings this Nietzchian combativeness (in a world without religion, it is the artist who must take on the ills of the world) takes on an obverse, festive side. If the earlier drawings showed the horror that prevents beauty, the new drawings, or "Soul Screens" as he calls them, celebrate the creation of new worlds—an idyllic vision of arbours and gardens, peopled by weird and wonderful creatures (pixies, homuncules) from his vivid imagination.

Brus's creation of a "world apart," like Blake's, is a moral stand. Nostalgia doesn't come into it. Whatever one thinks of Brus's millenarianism (in a sense it is only by accepting such extremes that Brus can create such an "extreme" art), he has created a formidable body of work

—John Roberts

BRZOZOWSKI, Tadeusz (Alexander).

Polish. Born in Lvov, now U.S.S.R., 1 November 1918. Studied at the Academy of Fine Arts, Krakow, 1936-39, and, under Fryderyk Pautsch, at the School of Decorative Arts, Cracow, 1940-42. Married Barbara Gawdzik in 1952; sons: Lawrence and Joachim. Painter, in Cracow, 1944-54, in Zakopane, 1954 until his death in 1987. Member, Tadeusz Kantor's underground theatre group, 1943-45; Association of Polish Artists, Cracow, since 1945; Grupa Krakowska artists' group, Cracow, 1954; "Phases" international artists' group, Zakopane, from 1957. Assistant Design Instructor, Faculty of Architecture, Technical University, Cracow, 1945-54; Design Instructor 1954-69, and Director 1959- 61, Kenar's School of Art Technics, Zakopane. Professor, Academy of Fine Arts, Poznan, 1962-87; Professor 1979-81, and Professor Emeritus 1981-87, Academy of Fine Arts, Krakow. Recipient: 5th International Hallmark Award, 1960; Francesco Nullo Award, Venice *Biennale*, 1962; Chivalric Cross 1969, and Commander's Cross 1980, Order of Polonia Restituta; Acquisition Prize, *2nd International Exhibition of Design*, Rijeka, 1969; Ministry of Culture and Arts Prizes, Warsaw, 1970, 1975, 1980; Gold Medal Association of Polish Artists, 1974. Agent: Desa Gallery, Jana 3, 31-017 Cracow. *Died* (in Zakopane) *in 1987*.

Individual Exhibitions:

1956   Desa Gallery, Warsaw
1960   Krzywe Kolo Gallery, Warsaw
        Galerie Lambert, Paris
1963   Mpik Gallery, Torun, Poland
        13 Muz Gallery, Szszecin, Poland
        National Museum, Poznan, Poland
1964   S.P.A.M. Gallery, Warsaw
1965   Od Nowa Gallery, Poznan, Poland
1966   Galerie Yvon Lambert, Paris
        Desa Gallery, Cracow
1968   Galerie Wspolczesna, Warsaw

1969   Azyl Club, Torun, Poland
1970   Galerie PSP-ZPAP, Katowice, Poland
        Desa Gallery, Cracow
        Galeria Em, Wroclaw, Poland
1974   National Museum, Poznan, Poland (retrospective)
1976   Museum of Wschowa, Poland
1978   Desa Gallery, Warsaw
1979   Museum of Rzeszow, Poland
1980   BWA Gallery, Bialystock, Poland
        Desa Gallery, Cracow
1981   *Tadeusz Brzozowski: His Friends, His Disciples*, BWA Gallery, Poznan, Poland

Selected Group Exhibitions:

1959   *5th Bienal*, Sao Paulo (and *13th Bienal*, 1975)
1961   *15 Polish Painters*, Museum of Modern Art, New York
1962   *Biennale*, Venice
1965   *Arte Actual de Polonia*, Museo de Arte Moderna, Buenos Aires (toured Uruguay, Mexico and Cuba)
1970   *1,000 Years of Art in Poland*, Royal Academy of Art, London
1976   *Contemporary Polish Painting*, Fundacao Gulbenkian, Lisbon (travelled to Madrid and Valencia)

Collections:

National Museum, Warsaw; National Museum, Cracow; National Museum, Wroclaw, Poland; National Museum, Poznan, Poland; Muzeum Sztuki, Lodz, Poland; Tatra Museum, Zakopane, Poland; Muzei na Sovremena Umetnost, Skopje, Yugoslavia; Stedelijk Museum, Amsterdam.

Publications:

On BRZOZOWSKI: books—*Artisti Polacchi d'Oggi* by Giuseppe Marchiori, Venice 1967; *Ricerche dopo Informale* by Enrico Crispolti, Rome 1968; *Tadeusz Brzozowski*, exhibition catalogue, Poznan, Poland 1974; articles—"5 Pittori Polacchi d'Oggi" by Giuseppe Marchiori in *Il Milione* (Milan), no. 25, 1958; "Polish Art: The Younger Figurative Painters" by Aleksander Wojciechowski in *The Studio* (London), no. 79, 1959; "Quatra Peintres Polonais d'Aujourd'hui" by Juliusz Starzynski in *Quandrum* (Brussels), no. 8, 1960; "La Face Inconnue de la Terra" by Eduard Jager in *Phases* (Paris), January 1960; "Romantik-Expression-Emotion" by Aleksander Wojciechowski in *Das Kunstwerk* (Baden-Baden, West Germany), no. 8, 1961; "The Younger Generation in Polish Painting" by Aleksander Wojciechowski in *Polish Art Review* (Warsaw), no. 1, 1971; films—*Interpretacje* by J. Brzozowski, 1964; *Tadeusz Brzozowski* by M. Szczepanski and Franci Slak, 1978; *Bruch* by A. Papuzinski, 1979; *Tadeusz Brzozowski* by Cz. Kruszelnicki, 1980.

I steal blood and sweat tar milk and salt and I paint pictures with them that is but a joke I just paint my pictures with . . . paints.

—Tadeusz Brzozowski (1983)

Tadeusz Brzozowski started as an artist in the mid-1930s, being at that time associated with the then radical "Cracow group," seeking to break down conventional ways of thinking in art. This attitude was adopted by a movement of young artists in Cracow, which developed clandestine activity during the Nazi occupation. Tadeusz Brzozowski also belonged to that circle. Among other things, he was an actor in the clandestine theatre of Tadeusz Kantor, where the expressive treatment of the motifs of reality and the use of "ready made" were combined with the surrealisticizing aspect. At the same time, the artist passionately studies painting technology—secrets of dyes, binders, primers, glazings and varnishes. He did it in a conviction that a picture transmits its message primarily through its being saturated with paint substance; that was how his private philosophy of a picture as a specific form of the existence of matter was born.

Immediately after the end of the war Tadeusz Brzo-

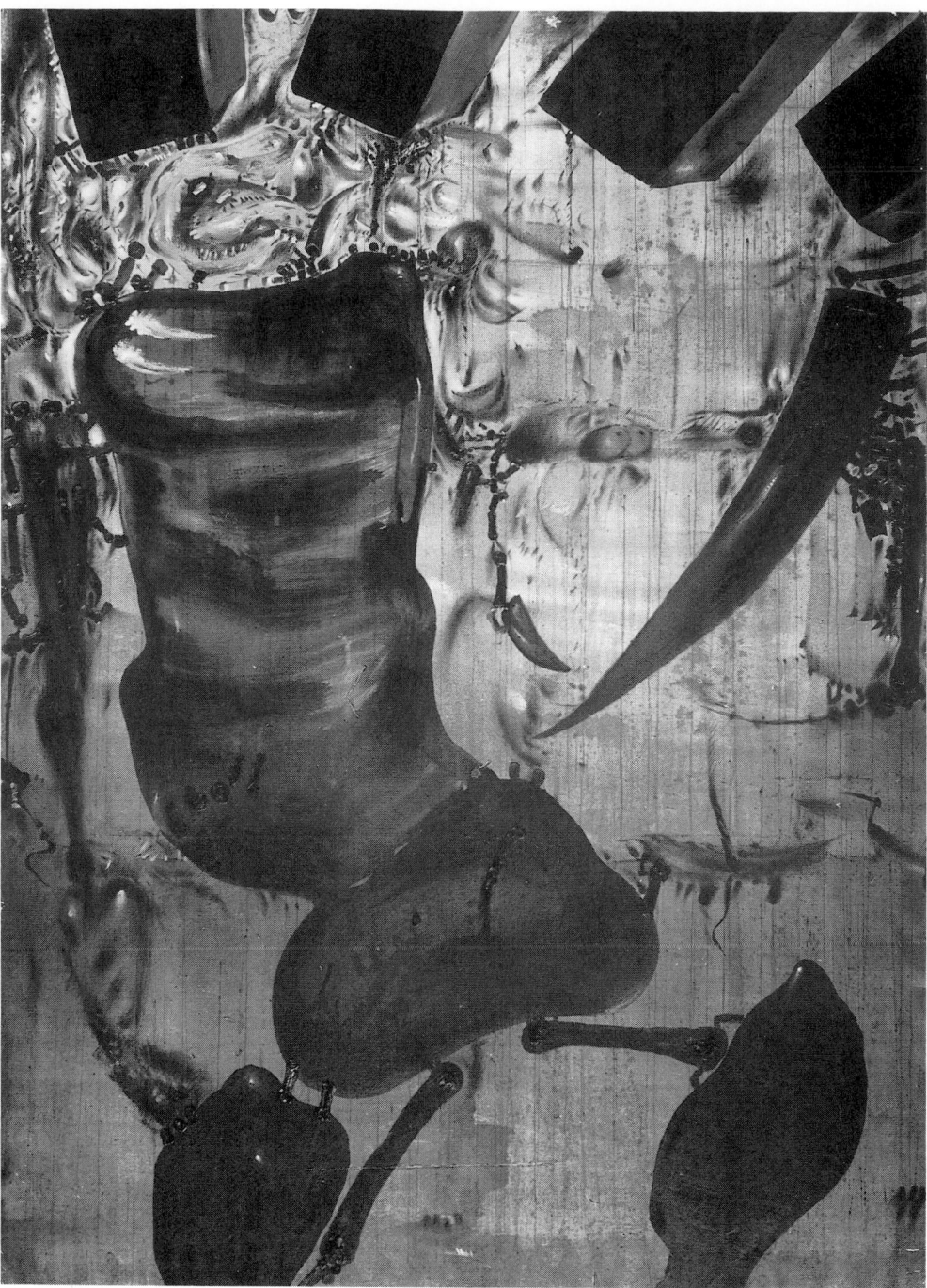

in his dialectical struggle with his own condition.

In the 1970s, the role of drawing, usually executed in pen and ink, increased (i.e., the series of Self-portraits). The lines become simpler, but lose nothing of their expression. They are still full of pen's "stag-gerings" and sudden turns. They move like in a gro-tesque revealing what is truly dramatic in a grotesque. In their essence, the drawings are pictures of a dialogue with one's own inner self, which throws outside its anxieties and whims. Through those acts of externalization the artist overcomes his solipsism and goes beyond his individual fate, showing how in-dividual drama is human drama in general.

At the time when Tadeusz Brzozowski's art was de-veloping, Poland, just like the whole of Europe, was swept with the waves of informel, painting of the mat-ter and many other currents. Brzozowski's art resists classification in any of them, although informel was probably the one which became close to the artist owing to its painting generosity. However, the tempta-tion of gestural freedom has never lured Brzozowski. Even using floating patches of paint he has always remained faithful to his "Flemish" precision and his own painting technique. His art remains personal, just like personal is one's creed.

Brzozowski used to say: "I am trying to be faithful to myself—although it's not too fashionable. That is why I am digging the same whole ever deeper, want-ing my art to be ever deeper, ever more perfect, al-though I don't know whether I do succeed in it. In this way I am seeking contact with other people, as I would like to tell them important things—truth about man, about human condition, its lameness—and that we are able to overcome this lameness. Of course, I do not tackle this problem, the most important one in my art, directly . . ."

—Alicja Kepinska

Tadeusz Brzozowski: *Misericordia,* 1982

zowski associated himself with a young "Modern group" in Cracow, one of the most dynamic groups in Polish art at that time. The group was dominated by the tone of surrealisticizing metaphor, which has also become a significant element of Brzozowski's art. The artist expresses himself in painting and in draw-ing, which has become for him an autonomous field, equally important as painting, sometimes even domi-nating. It is in the drawing technique that he executes characteristic figures with traits of vexing grotesque. Their soul-penetrating existence has accompanied the artist throughout his lifetime.

These figures are transposed into painting and with time change into semi-abstract creatures, torn with expressive, thorny drawing. The lines of black draw-ing sometimes painfully injures the substance of col-our patches, emphasizing its intensity and brightness.

Brzozowski's pictures are always given specific ti-tles, virtually impossible to be expressed in any other language but Polish. ("Dygi", "Kuszer", "Mecyje", "Kretes", etc.). These names draw on the colloquial language, popular sayings, parables, that is "genius loci". There are also universal names, such as

"Fraucymer", "Sakwojaz", "Antichambre", etc.; none of them directly explains the presented motif but supplement the climate of this art by spotting unex-pected images of the world. In any case, titles are here equally important as in the surrealist art.

Because of this integral melting of the element of metaphor with painting expression in the 1960s Brzo-zowski's art reaches the peak of its splendour. The matter of pictures thickens and shines, clashing with the neurons of drawing. Brightness and translucency of liquid colour patches reminds one of sensual quali-ties of old Flemish masters. It is an effect of constant improvement of technological alchemy. The artist uses resin, rubber and distemper binders, applies paints in several thin layers, freely applies glittering varnishes. This painting glamour, which clashes with perfidious titles, is accompanied by Brzozowski's statements disclosing actual intentions of this art: "I make colour maximally intensive, and then suddenly tone it down. It is just like our experiences fade away. Like contrasts of human fate are born. I always have in mind beautiful people stained with dirt". Thus, this painting is a constant metaphor of the fate of man

BUCKLEY, Stephen.

British. Born in Leicester, 5 April 1944. Educated at the University of Newcastle, 1962–67; University of Reading, 1967– 69. Married Stephanie Buckley in 1973; children: Scarlet, Matilda and Felix. Indepen-dent painter, London, since 1969. Part-time Lecturer, Canterbury College of Art, Kent, 1969–71; and Leeds College of Art, Yorkshire, 1969–71; Visiting Artist, Chelsea School of Art, London, 1971–80; Artist-in-Residence, King's College, Cambridge, 1972–74. Recipient: Painting Prize, *John Moores Ex-hibition,* Liverpool, 1974; Prize, Chichester National Art Exhibition, 1975; Painting Prize, Tolly-Cobbold Exhibition 1977; Agents: Brooke Alexander, 20 West 57th Street, New York, New York 10019; and Knoedler Gallery, London. Address: c/o Knoedler Gallery, 22 Cork Street, London W1X 1HB, En-gland.

Individual Exhibitions:

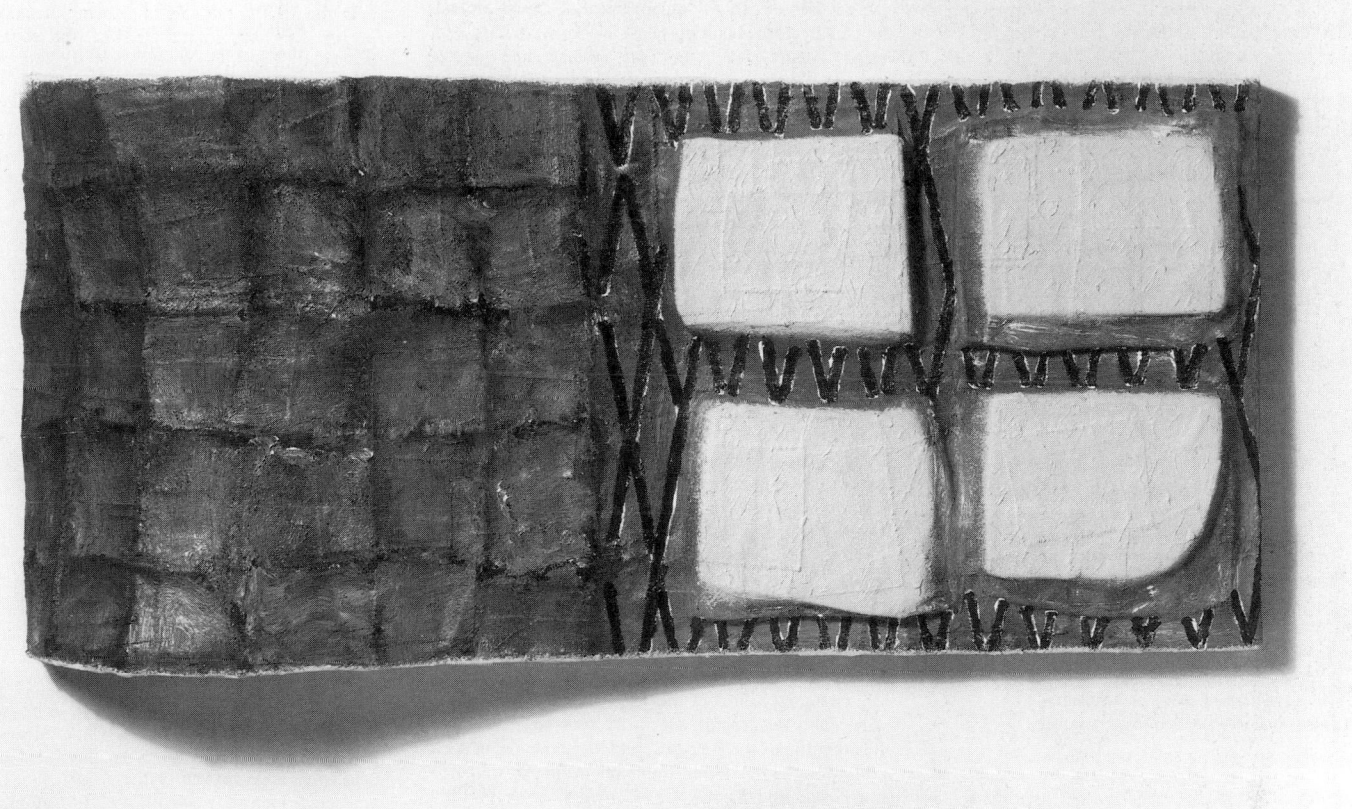

Stephen Buckley: *Dredger*, 1986

1980 Knoedler Gallery, London
Amano Gallery, Osaka, Japan
Bernard Jacobson Gallery, London
1981 Brooke Alexander Gallery, New York
Knoedler Gallery, London
1982 L. A. Louver Gallery, Los Angeles
Knoedler Gallery, London
1983 Brooke Alexander, New York
Knoedler Gallery, London
1984 Thorden-Wetterling Galleries, Goteborg, Sweden
1985 Museum of Modern Art, Oxford
Walker Art Gallery, Liverpool
Brooke Alexander, New York
Clock Tower, New York
Yale Center for British Art, New Haven, Connecticut

Selected Group Exhibitions:

1969 *6 at the Hayward*, Hayward Gallery, London
1972 *Objects and Documents*, Arts Council Gallery, London (toured the U.K.)
1973 *La Peinture Anglaise d'Aujourd'hui*, Musée National d'Art Moderne, Paris
1975 *3rd Triennale—India*, La Kit Kala Akademi Rabindra Bhavan, New Delhi
1976 *The Human Clay*, Hayward Gallery, London (toured the U.K.)
1977 *British Painting 1952–1977*, Royal Academy of Art, London
1979 *Un Certain Art Anglais*, Musée d'Art Moderne de la Ville, Paris
1981 *Baroques '81*, Musée d'Art Moderne de la Ville, Paris
1983 *Twentieth-Century Art from the Metropolitan Museum*, Queens Museum, Flushing, New York
1985 *14th John Moores Exhibition*, Walker Art Gallery, Liverpool, Merseyside

Collections:

Tate Gallery, London; Arts Council of Great Britain, London; Victoria and Albert Museum, London; Walker Art Gallery, Liverpool; Cambridge University; Aberdeen Art Gallery, Scotland; National Art Gallery of New Zealand, Wellington; Metropolitan Museum of Art, New York.

Publications:

On BUCKLEY: books—*Objects and Documents*, exhibition catalogue, London 1972; *La Peinture Anglaise Aujourd'hui*, exhibition catalogue, by Edward Lucie-Smith, Paris 1973; articles—"London Letter" by William Feaver in *Art International* (Lugano, Switzerland), January 1973; "Stephen Buckley" by L. Morris in *Art Press* (Paris), September 1973; "Profile of Stephen Buckley" by Peter Fuller in *Arts Review* (London), 3 May 1974; "Buckley in Midstream" by John McEwan in *The Spectator* (London), 11 October 1975; "Who Will Be Who in the 1980s" in *Sunday Times Magazine* (London), 2 April 1978; "Four British Painters" by John McEwan in *Artforum* (New York), December 1978; "Serenity and Restlessness" by Neal Menzies in *Artweek* (Oakland), 24 April 1982.

*   *   *

As an art student in the 1960's Stephen Buckley came under the influence of surrealism, pop art (through Richard Hamilton) and abstract expressionism. Today one sees traces of this background in the grand scale of much of his work, the willingness to let chance take a part in the creation of his objects and in the use of discarded "popular" items. There are also elements of the "L.A. Look" as seen in the work of, for example, Charles Christopher Hill, who weaves together found materials, then buries, washes or pounds them.

Drawing upon these influences but keeping strongly to his own view of his environment, Stephen Buckley selects raw materials autobiographically. Discarded stretchers from a friend's attic, his mother's curtains, paintings by himself or others, his own personal clothing are transformed and renewed in his hands.

Once selected, Buckley does not treat these things gently. They are torn, scorched, twisted or stretched to their limits, then woven or stitched together. The actual process of creation is important enough to Buckley for him to share it with us so the worked-upon materials are often partially turned over to show the back side of the work. The stretchers—whether found or made—are also revealed or even placed on the front of the painting. And it is important to remember that Buckley sees himself specifically as a painter. Having provided himself with sensuously textured surfaces, he works in warm, earthy colours. A conservationist's nightmare, he also may add plaster, floor polish, wax or even yoghurt to his oils, acrylics, watercolours and enamels.

Since 1977 Buckley has created several sets of etchings, building the finished image with several plates arranged for printing on one sheet—using the medium with a painter's rather than merely a printmaker's eye—a continuation of his exploration into colours, textures and materials.

—Marlee Robinson

BULLMORE, Edward (Aaron Alexander).

New Zealander. Born in Lumsden, Southland, 6 July 1933. Educated at Christchurch Boys High School, 1947–50 (open champion in boxing); School of Fine Arts, Canterbury University College, Christchurch, 1951–55 (Canterbury Rugby Football Union Representative, 1953–55); Auckland Teachers Training College, 1956. Married Jacqueline Anne La Roche in 1958. Painter; taught art at Tauranga Boys College, 1957–59; travelled to Italy, and studied in Florence, 1959; settled in London, 1960, and worked as a scene shifter at the Royal Court Theatre, London, for a number of years, also taught at various secondary schools and art schools, including Ravensbourne College of Art and Design, Epsom School of Art, and Brixton School of Building; elected member of the London Group, 1965; returned to New Zealand and settled in Rotorua, 1969, and taught full-time, then part-time at Rotorua Boys High School. *Died (in Rotorua) 15 November 1978.*

Individual Exhibitions:

1959 Williston Gallery, Wellington
Tauranga Art Society
1969 Tama Gallery, London
1971 *A Decade in London*, Barry Lett Galleries, Auckland
1972 Rotorua Art Society
1974 Wellington Settlement Gallery
1977 *Mamaku Bush and Farmland Exhibition*, Rotorua Art Society
1978 *Icons*, Barry Lett Galleries, Auckland
1979 *Edward Bullmore Memorial Exhibition*, Rotorua Art Gallery

Selected Group Exhibitions:

1964 *New Zealand Artists Exhibition*, Qantas Gallery, London
1965 *Biennale of Abstract Art*, Commonwealth Institute, London
1967 *Edinburgh Open 100*
The Enchanted Domain, Exeter City Gallery, Devon
1968 *From the Human Form*, Grosvenor Gallery, London
London Group, Royal Institute Galleries, London
1971 *Contemporary New Zealand Painting*, National Art Gallery, Wellington
1975 *New Zealand Society of Sculptors and Painters Exhibition*, Barry Lett Galleries, Auckland
1979 *Images of Women*, Rotorua Art Gallery
1981 *Drawing from Life*, Rotorua Art Gallery

Collections:

National Art Gallery, Wellington; Victoria University, Wellington; Dowse Gallery, Lower Hutt, New Zealand; Rotorua Art Gallery, New Zealand.

Publications:

On BULLMORE: books—*Edward Bullmore*, exhibition catalogue, with an introduction by Mario Amaya, London 1967; *New Zealand Drawing '76*, exhibition catalogue, Auckland 1976; *New Zealand Painting since 1960: A Study in Themes and Developments* by Peter Cape, Auckland 1979; articles— "Second Commonwealth Biennale Exhibition" in *Arts Review* (London), 13 November 1965; "London Group Exhibition" in *Arts Review* (London), 18 February 1967; "Edward Bullmore Exhibition" in *Art and Artists* (London), May 1967; "Edward Bullmore Exhibition" in *Studio International* (London), May 1967.

In retrospect Edward Bullmore's work falls rather neatly into two groups: work up to 1959, and work from 1960 until his death. Such a division makes for comparative ease in observing the great changes that occurred in his work and at the same time, in noting the characteristic qualities which remained as constant factors throughout his working life.

In the early New Zealand period his work was comparatively academic which can be seen in the impressive and dominant figure studies he produced. From c. 1957, however, it is clear that his artistic horizons were broadening and his painting reflected an awareness of contemporary Australian artists such as Dobell and Drysdale.

The desire to enrich and broaden his artistic life led to his travelling overseas, first to Florence where he stayed for six months. This was a period of assimilation and transition during which time he came to terms with the art of the Renaissance. In so doing he modified his painting considerably, with the result that he developed a type of painting which was nostalgic and romantic, with a touch of De Chirico thrown in for good measure.

Bullmore's arrival in London coincided with the emergence of a very fluid and affluent society, despite the pessimism engendered by the Cuba crisis. The intellectual stimulation he received provided the catalyst which projected Bullmore into what was to become his mature style of painting. He rapidly

discarded the literalness of his previous work and began a series of gloomy abstract works, based around the Cuban confrontation. These works were dark and relied greatly for effect on collage and objets trouvés—like leaves and scraps of cloth. This was but an interlude, however, and as he was supporting himself by working as a stage hand for the Royal Court Theatre he was permitted to use scraps of canvas from scenery and floor coverings which he incorporated into his own canvas. The torn fragments were repaired by neat stitching (a skill he had acquired as a farmer's son) and around this necessity he formed the genesis of his highly original form of expression. The first works in his new vein were a series of landscape inspired constructions (Hiku-rangi series) in which he developed a very sculptural fecund female form which could be interpreted as a writhing and convulsing landscape. The pieces of torn canvas, wooden chair frames, padded leather and painted sections were literally stitched together with coarse leather thongs with the result that the completed work was a disturbing, yet compelling, three-dimensional construction evoking memories of a certain region of New Zealand which in his words depicted "a sort of mythological idea about the sky and earth being male and female!"

This series prepared the way for the next, the Astroform series, shaped canvases in which female and erotic connotations are much more explicit. In retrospect it was, perhaps, Bullmore's reaction to the rapidly changing mores of the 1960's. As such, they are remarkably successful. His work now began to draw the attention of some critics, and his showings in such exhibitions as the *Young Commonwealth Artists, London Group* and *Biennale of Commonwealth Abstract Art* led to his most important invitation to participate in the Surrealist exhibition, *The Enchanted Domain*.

His return to New Zealand after the absence of 10 years meant a considerable change in style of life and subject matter, and at the time of his death he was again concerning himself with aspects of the landscape.

His vision was highly personal and his work was marked by a fastidious craftsmanship. These two factors stamped his work with a quality which, while overly erotic, was never prurient, and, as Kenneth Coutts-Smith observed, his work was far removed "from the sophisticated eroticism of . . . Bellmer, Jones or Wunderlich." His work had a primeval equality, an animal vigour which was disturbing. Yet beyond this, his creations are stamped with a sensitivity and awareness that have given him a unique place in New Zealand art.

—Melvin N. Day

BURDEN, Chris.

American. Born in Boston, Massachusetts, 11 April 1946. Educated at Pomona College, Claremont, California, B.F.A. 1969; University of California at Irvine, 1970-71, M.F.A. 1971. Conceptual artist and sculptor. Instructor in Avant-Garde Art, LaVerne College, California, 1973-74; Visiting Artist, Fresno State University, California, 1974. Recipient: New Talent Award, Los Angeles County Museum of Art, 1973; National Endowment for the Arts Grant, 1974. Agent: Ronald Feldman Fine Arts, New York. Address: c/o Ronald Feldman Fine Arts, 31-33 Mercer Street, New York, New York 10013, U.S.A.

Individual Exhibitions:

1971 *Five Day Locker Piece*, University of California at Irvine
Bicycle Piece, University of California at Irvine
1972 *Bed Piece*, Market Street, Venice, California
Match Piece, Pomona College, Claremont, California

Jaizu, Newport Harbor Art Museum, Newport Beach, California
Riko Mizuno Gallery, Los Angeles
1973 *Movie on the Way Down*, Oberlin College, Ohio
Through the Night Softly, Main Street, Los Angeles
1974 Riko Mizuno Gallery, Los Angeles
Ronald Feldman Fine Arts, New York
Hansen-Fuller Gallery, San Francisco
1975 Riko Mizuno Gallery, Los Angeles
Ronald Feldman Fine Arts, New York
1979 Ronald Feldman Fine Arts, New York
1983 Ronald Feldman Fine Arts, New York
1984 Rosamund Felsen Gallery, Los Angeles
Art Park, New York

Selected Group Exhibitions:

1985 *Modern Machines: Recent Kinetic Sculpture*, Whitney Museum, New York

Collections:

Museum of Modern Art, New York; Long Beach Arts Museum, California.

Publications:

On BURDEN: articles—"Church of Human Energy" by Sharp and Bear in *Avalanche*, Summer/Fall 1973; "Young Sadhu" in *Time Magazine* (New York), 24 February 1975; "Through the Night Softly" by Jan Butterfield in *Arts Magazine* (New York), March 1975.

Chris Burden did his first Performances in 1971 while still a graduate student in Southern California. It was one of those rare cases when an artist going through the art educational system arrived at an individualistic, perceptive grasp of his own direction. In "Five-Day Locker Piece," Burden interred himself in locker "number 5" for five days below five gallons of bottled water and above an empty five gallon bottle. It was the beginning of an artistic output which was to cause mixed feelings of consternation, attention, misinterpretation and praise over the next decade which brought more than 60 works from Burden's head.

Burden's performances and sculptures are about the fears and anxieties faced by the individual in the midst of the complex psychological and social context of the late 20th century. Many earlier works, such as his (overly) notorious "Shoot" (1971, in which he had a friend shoot him in the arm) and "220" (which involved real dangers of electrocution for the participants), were rather overtly "macho" in attitude, but the vast majority of Burden's pieces which suggest real danger are very much under the artist's control. "Transfixed" (1974), for example, in which Burden had himself "crucified" on the back end of a Volkswagen with nails driven through his hands, was well researched and caused little real physical pain, expressing, rather, the symbolic element behind our attachments to the objects of our industrial environment.

In a number of works, Burden has used his body as sculptural form to express the tensions we feel in trying to maintain our individuality as artists or as anybody else dealing with our already post-industrial age. In "Bed Piece" (1972) and in "White Light/White Heat" (1975), among other works, Burden placed himself in a state of isolation for long periods of time, assuming states of mental/physical deprivation with elements of withdrawal from contact and sight which both showed the benefits of introspective meditative states and caused anxious moments for viewers and friends in the process. Among his most seductively and frighteningly alluring works is "Through the Night Softly" (1973) in which Burden crawled through broken glass, incurring multiple small cuts on his almost naked body. Burden's quiet, controlled attitude, not unlike that of the Zen master, portrays more centrally the idea of risk sacrifice and atonement and the mental capacity to get through danger than it does a masochistic self-destruction.

Works since the mid-70's have tended to be less dramatic, though no less involved in using self as conveyor of anxious mental states. In many, Burden opens up elements of his private life to prolong/dispel the personal "myth" of the artist built up over the past years of work. In his second television "commercial" (1976), Burden adds his own name to the list of the five most well-known (from survey) artists, in a listing which reads "Leonardo da Vinci, Michaelangelo, Rembrandt, Van Gogh, Picasso, Chris Burden." Continuing in his continually dialectical fashion, Burden, in the same year, acted as unidentified "Garcon" throughout the duration of a gallery group show, and also charged admission for a tour of his studio in Venice, California.

Along with the issues of confinement, time, fear, threat and control, Burden has also concerned himself with the state of the individual in relationship to technology and to the threat of nuclear war. In "Art and Technology" (1975) and "Death Valley Run" (1976), he created vehicles of transportation for one person which were fuel efficient, lightweight and capable of practical transport through space and, suggestively through personalized technology, into the mind. "C.B.T.V." (1977) reconstructed the primitive television precursor of 1915 in an effort to show us the nature and origin of the medium which dominates us in the present.

Among Burden's recent works are those which are concerned with the weapons of war so imminently upon us. In an exposition of another prevalent anxiety, "The Reason for the Neutron Bomb" (1979) is a grid of 50,000 nickels, each with a match on top, emblematic of the number of tanks the Soviets have on the border between Eastern and Western Europe. It is a fascinating prediction of subsequently current events and a potent visual symbol as well. Burden's recent sculptural mini-environment, "A Tale of Two Cities," incorporates a variety of toys. Medieval castles, modern buildings, airplanes and weapons of varied vintage, warriors including knights, soldiers and futuristic robots interact to create a tiny panorama of the persistence of human war, which shows no sign of abating in the foreseeable future. Looking at it through the spyglasses provided by Burden, one is forced to see us as we really are and as science fiction predicts the future. As always, there is a sardonic wit and topical pertinence in Burden's continual portrayals of our personae in this post-industrial time, in which there is more trouble than ever in dealing with psychological and sociological basics.

—Barbara Cavaliere

BUREN, Daniel.

French. Born in Boulogne-Billancourt, 25 March 1938. Educated at Lycée Condorcet, Paris, 1946–56; studied at the Ecole Nationale Supérieure des Métiers d'Art, Paris, graduated 1960. Independent artist, Paris. Member, Buren, Mosset, Parmentier (Michel) and Toroni association, 1967. Address: 21 rue de Navarin, 75009 Paris, France.

Individual Exhibitions:

1967   *Buren o Toroni o Chichessia*, Galleria Flaviana, Lugano, Switzerland
1968   Musée d'Art Moderne de la Ville, Paris
       Galleria Apollinaire, Milan
1969   Wide White Space Gallery, Antwerp
       Interruption, Galerie Yvon Lambert, Paris
       Position/Proposition, Galerie Konrad Fischer, Dusseldorf
       Galerie Eva Buren, Stockholm

1970   Galleria Francoise Lambert, Milan
       Art and Project, Amsterdam
       Une pièce/peinture, Bradford College, Massachusetts
       Galerie MTL, Brussels
       Galerie Yvon Lambert, Paris
1971   Wide White Space Gallery, Antwerp
       Galerie Folker Skulima, Berlin
       Galerie Michael Werner, Cologne
       Städtisches Museum, Mönchengladbach, West Germany
1972   Modern Art Agency, Naples
       Jack Wendler Gallery, London
       Galleria Sperone, Turin
       Peinture Affichée/Pittura Affissa, Incontri Internazionali d'Arte, Rome
       Theatre de la Ville, Belgrade
       Wide White Space Gallery, Antwerp
1973   New Theatre, New York
       Sanction of the Museum, Museum of Modern Art, Oxford
       Fragment I, II and III, Mezzanine Gallery and Anna Leonowens Gallery, Halifax, Nova Scotia
       Part 2, John Weber Gallery, London
       California Institute of Art, Valencia
       3 Paintings, Galerie Konrad Fischer, Dusseldorf
       Within and Beyond the Frame, John Weber Gallery, New York
       Démultiple, Städtisches Museum, Monchengladbach, West Germany
1974   *Trasposizione*, Galleria Toselli, Milan
       Triptyque, Galerie Rolf Preisig, Basle
       Transparency, Art and Project, Antwerp
       3 Passages, Galerija Grada, Zagreb
       Wide White Space Gallery, Antwerp
       Transparency-Opacity, Max Protetch Gallery, Washington, D.C.
       Between and Through, Cusack Gallery, Houston
       On the Hang Up, 11501 West Rico, Los Angeles
       Passage Between Inside and Outside, Portland Center for Visual Arts, Oregon
1975   Kunstmuseum, Lucerne
       Akademie der Künste, Berlin
       Galerie Folker-Skulima, Berlin
       Städtisches Museum, Mönchengladbach, West Germany
1976   *Hier*, Stedelijk Museum, Amsterdam
       Rijksmuseum Kröller-Müller, Otterlo, Netherlands
       Ailleurs/Elders, Stedelijk van Abbemuseum, Eindhoven, Netherlands
       Institute of Contemporary Arts, London
1977   *3 Installationem*, Galerie Paul Maenz, Cologne
1978   Galerie Yvon Lambert, Paris
       John Weber Gallery, New York
1979   National Galerie of Victoria, Melbourne
1980   *Il Est Encore Une Fois—Toile, Toile/Voile*, Kunstmuseum, Lucerne
       Art Institute of Chicago
1981   Stedelijk van Abbemuseum, Eindhoven, Netherlands
1982   Krefeld Museum, West Germany
1984   Galerie Gewad, Ghent, Belgium
       Galeria Zona, Florence
       Galerie Arca, Marseille, France
       Galerie Arca, Paris

Selected Group Exhibitions:

1968   *Prospect '68*, Galerie Apollinaire, Dusseldorf
1970   *Conceptual Art and Conceptual Aspects*, New York Cultural Center
1971   *Situation Concepts*, Galerie Nächst St. Stephan, Vienna
1972   *Documenta 5*, Kassel, West Germany
1973   *Contemporanea*, Villa Borghese, Rome
       Bilder: Objekte: Filme: Konzepte, Städtische Galerie, Munich
1974   *Political Art*, Max Protetch Gallery, Washington, D.C.
       Projekt '74, Kunsthalle, Cologne
1975   *Corridor Passage*, Museum of Modern Art, New York
       12 x 1, Palais des Beaux-Arts, Brussels

Collections:

Centre Georges Pompidou, Paris; Van Abbemuseum, Eindhoven; Netherlands; Stedelijk Museum, Amsterdam; Kunstmuseum, Lucerne.

Publications:

By BUREN: books—*Daniel Buren: Legend, Vol. 1 and II*, London 1973; *5 Texts*, New York 1973; *Daniel Buren: Voile/Toile, Toile/Voile*, with Bernd Mahr and Horst Merten, Berlin 1975; articles—"Beware" in *Studio International* (London), March 1970; "Mise en Garde No. 3" in *Vh 101* (Paris), Spring 1970; "Extrait de Position-Proposition" in *VH 101* (Paris), Spring 1971; "Art Is Not Free" in *Studio International* (London), June 1973; "Daniel Buren: An Interview with Jean-Marc Poinsot" in *Art and Artists* (London), July 1973; "The Function of the Museum" in *Artforum* (New York), September 1973; "The Function of an Exhibition" in *Studio International* (London), December 1973; film—*Identification*, London 1973.

On BUREN: books—*Daniel Buren*, exhibition catalogue, by Jean-Christophe Ammann, Lucerne 1975; *Daniel Buren: Hier*, exhibition catalogue, with text by E. de Wilde, Michel Claura and Germano Celant, Amsterdam 1976; *Daniel Buren: 3 Installationen*, exhibition catalogue, Cologne 1977; *Daniel Buren: Il est Encore Une Fois—Voile/Toile, Toile/Voile*, exhibition catalogue, with text by Martin Kunz, Lucerne 1980; articles—"Paris Commentary: Buren at Prospect '68, Dusseldorf" by Michel Claura in *Studio International* (London), January 1969; "La Proposition de Buren" by G. Gassiot-Talabot in *Opus International* (Paris), June 1969; "Lettre de Paris: Daniel Buren" by M. Pleynet in *Art International* (Lugano, Switzerland), February 1971; "Daniel Buren" by Jean Clair in *Chroniques de l'Art Vivant* (Paris), April 1971; 1973; "On Daniel Buren" by R. Smith in *Artforum* (New York), September 1973; "Das Prinzip der Wiederholung" by Georg F. Schwarzbauer in *Magazin Kunst* (Mainz), no. 4, 1974; "Le Groupe BMPT" by Otto Hahn in *Art Press* (Paris), June 1974.

I have often been criticized for the almost absolute "reductionism" of my work. That was the criticism leveled at me when I began, and continues even now. The main reason of these criticisms, which is particularly revealing about those who express them, is that people are accustomed to looking at a painting or an object in an exhibit as the be all and end all. In other words, they look at the visual materials that I used as if they were a painting. I never have and never will respond to such absurd comments, for I have the impression that they are talking about something other than my work. Why should I have to defend something that is not being attacked? It is as though I were being criticized under the pretext that for the opening of every one of my shows, it rains . . .

Right from the start I have always tried to show as clearly as I could that indeed a thing never exists in itself, in a kind of *"en soi."* A fortiori, this is true of all my work. Nothing that I show—the materials I use, to begin with—exists unrelated to something else that is clearly refined. Anyone who experiences my work directly—provided he agrees to make the minimum of effort required, of course—perceives that the "reduction" is in fact the widening of one's field of vision. Widening of such dimension that—for the very first time—what is being challenged in fact is the entire field of painting itself—nothingless—as being a reducing factor in art. From this stems the whole debate on art (criticism and history), based on the autonomy of a work of art; a debate which has also perforce a reducing effect, being simplistic and too good to be true. To reconsider works and their contexts, in fact to realize that their autonomy in a table supported by an idealistic proportion, is not only to challenge the proposition itself but also, to a great extent, the works which it supports, that is, art in general.

The Marxist label, used by some who believe it offers a way to escape this debate, obviously does not change a thing. On the other hand, the concept of the non-autonomy of a work of art opens new doors to a field of study and work that is very vast and unexplored. Of course, this field has nothing to do with

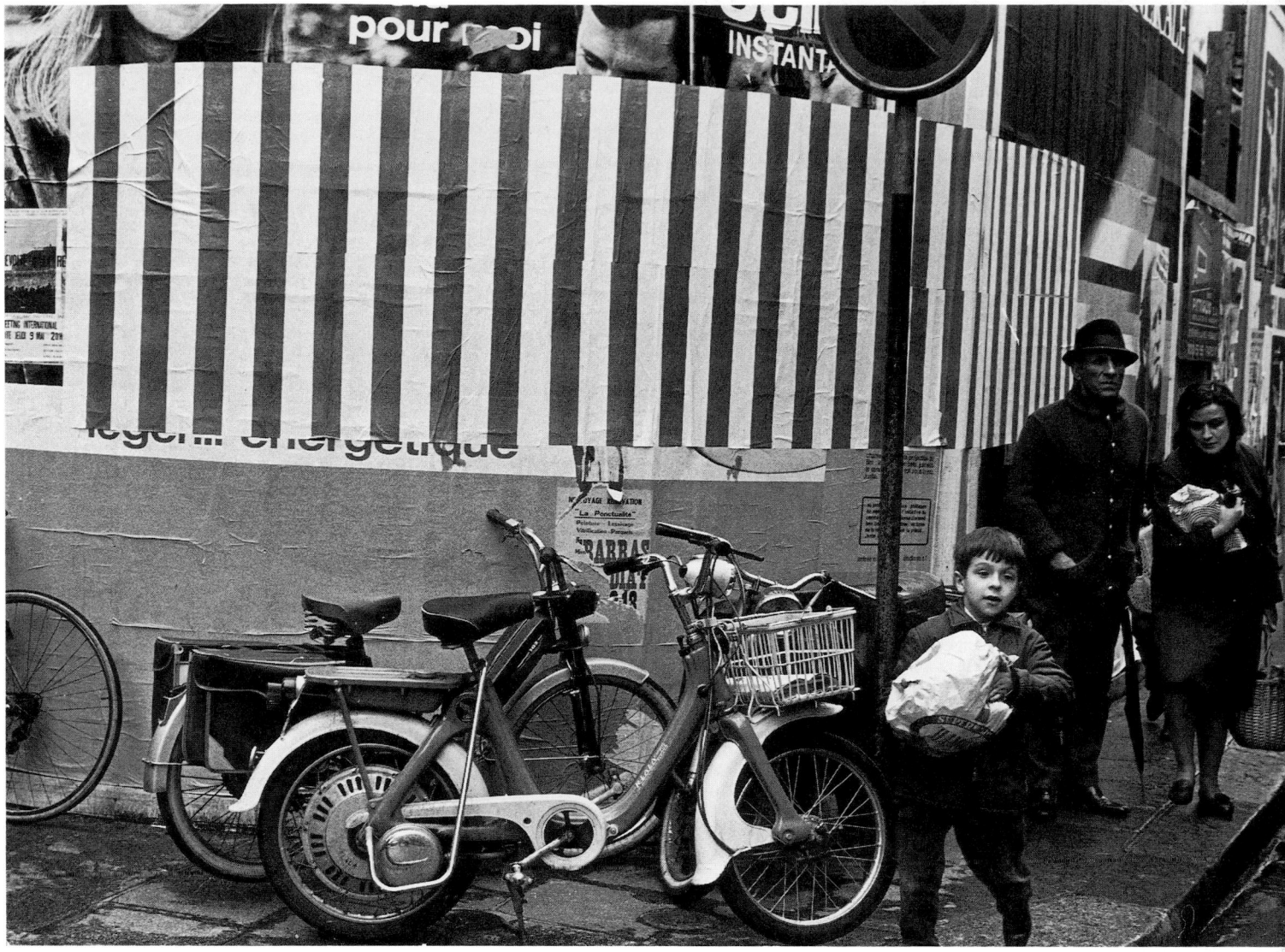

Daniel Buren: Work for the *Salon de Mai*, Paris, 1968

any sociological art nor a sociology of art. It is only with plastic means—to be completely overhauled—that it is possible to question and deal seriously with plastic problems and their implications.

—Daniel Buren

Daniel Buren is a painter, but since the 1960s he has become an environmental artist, and it is on his environmental art that his fame has rested ever since. He is a painter in that he paints his environments rather than, say, covering them, as Christo does.

To say that he is a geometrical abstract painter is somewhat of an understatement. For nearly two decades he has confined himself to painting parallel black and white or coloured and white stripes. They resemble some of the structures of Bridget Riley but, unlike hers and those of other optical artists, his stripes are broad and the optical effect is kept to a minimum, though it may operate at a distance.

Restricted, repetitious, and seemingly unpromising though this material may be, Buren manages to put it to an almost inexhaustible number of original uses. With these simple means he can produce all manner of visual effects.

In a gallery space or other interior he will adapt his stripes to the space and transform it. Sometimes this will mean exploiting the possibilities of an interesting and complex space, as, for instance, a succession of receding rooms opening on to one another. Here perspective plays a part, alters the stripes, and may even give an overall two-dimensional effect.

At other times he will take an uninteresting gallery

space and enhance it to the point of distorting its size and shape (as usually perceived).

These works he calls 'installations,' with the usual implication that they have to be installed and will later be taken away. In other words, they are ephemeral. This attitude to art—among others—he holds in common with Christo.

Like Christo, he is also concerned with the great outside. His contacts with it is various. One of his practices is to paint steps or friezes or plinths of columns or parts of solemn buildings with black and white stripes. Another is to fly striped flags on important buildings, such as the Louvre or that ancient emporium, La Samaritaine, or drape striped banners around them. The point of this, as with Christo's wrapped buildings, is to draw attention to the building, to make it conspicuous, to draw attention to aspects of it, to make us look at it anew and to transform it. He even invades the streets with sandwich-boards in black and white stripes (a change from 'Prepare To Meet Your Doom' but possibly no less disturbing).

Buren has made installations the world over: Chicago, 1977, 'Step by Step, Up and Down, In and Out'; Sydney, 1979, 'Upside Down' (!), and, the same year, in Los Angeles, 'Frost and Defrost', and so on till the present day.

Though most of these works are ephemeral, Buren, like Christo, carefully records them. He has done so since the 1960s with his 'photo/souvenirs'.

His most recent, most ambitious, most controversial and most prestigious work has just (1987) been installed—and permanently, not ephemerally (unless

certain elements of the public get their way)—in, of all places, the Cour d'Honneur of the Palais Royal, Paris. It is, by any standards, a spectacular work. Called 'Deux plateaux', which I take to mean 'two levels or plains', it consists of columns of various heights, partly above ground, partly below (but still visible through a grating) and, of course, with black and white stripes, forming the most elaborate patterns as one walks around the courtyard. It has outraged many Parisians who walk through it to the beautiful gardens beyond. There is certainly a note of incongruity. But with what? The Palais Royal was destroyed by the Commune in 1871; what we have now is a 19th century reconstruction. There the matter rests at present.

—D. C. Barrett

BURGIN, Victor.
British. Born in Sheffield, Yorkshire, 24 July 1941. Studied at the Royal College of Art, London, 1962–65, A.R.C.A. (1st class) 1965; Yale University, New Haven, Connecticut, 1965–67, M.F.A. 1967. Artist based in London, since 1967. Lecturer, Department of Fine Art, Trent Polytechnic, Nottingham, 1967–73. Senior Lecturer in the History and Theory of the

Visual Arts, School of Communication, Polytechnic of Central London, since 1973. Picker Professor of Fine Arts, Colgate University, Hamilton, New York, 1980. Recipient: U.S./U.K. Bicentennial Arts Exchange Fellowship, 1976–77; Deutscher Akademischer Austauschdienst (DAAD) Fellowship, Berlin, 1978–79. Agents: John Weber Gallery, 420 West Broadway, New York, New York 10012, U.S.A.; Liliane and Michel Durand-Dessert, 43 rue de Montmorency, 75003 Paris, France. Address: 25 St. Mary-le-Park Court, Albert Bridge Road, London SW11 4PJ, England.

Individual Exhibitions:

1970   Camden Arts Centre and Swiss Cottage Library, London (with Art and Language and Keith Arnatt)
1974   Galleria Banco, Brescia, Italy
1975   Musée d'Art et d'Industrie, St. Etienne, France (with Art and Language)
1976   Institute of Contempoary Arts, London
       Robert Self Gallery, London
1977   *Victor Burgin: Work,* Stedelijk van Abbemuseum, Eindhoven, Netherlands (travelled to the John Weber Gallery, New York)
1978   Museum of Modern Art, Oxford
1979   Deutscher Akademischer Austauschdienst, Berlin (travelled to the John Weber Gallery, New York; Liliane and Michel Durand-Dessert Gallery, Paris; and Max Hetzler Gallery, Stuttgart)
1980   *Victor Burgin: US 77/ZOO 78,* Picker Art Gallery, Colgate University, Hamilton, New York
1981   Zwigzek Polskich Artstow Fotografikow, Warsaw
       Musée de la Ville, Calais, France
1982   John Weber Gallery, New York
1983   National Gallery of Canada, Ottawa
1984   Galerie Durand-Dessert, Paris

Selected Group Exhibitions:

1969   *When Attitudes Become Form,* Institute of Contemporary Arts, London
1970   *Idea Structures,* Camden Arts Center, London
       Information, Museum of Modern Art, New York
1971   *6th Guggenheim International,* Guggenheim Museum, New York
1972   *Documenta,* Kassel, West Germany
       The New Art, Hayward Gallery, London
1976   *Arte Inglese Oggi,* Palazzo Reale, Milan
1977   *Aspects of European Art in the 70's,* Art Institute of Chicago (toured the United States, 1977–79)
1980   *Kunst im Sozialen Kontext,* Badischer Kunstverein, Karlsruhe, West Germany
1987   *Berlinart 1961–87,* Museum of Modern Art, New York (travelled to San Francisco)

Collections:

Tate Gallery, London; Victoria and Albert Museum, London; Arts Council of Great Britain, London; British Council, London; Walker Art Gallery, Liverpool; Graves Art Gallery, Sheffield; Museum of Modern Art, Oxford; Centre Georges Pompidou, Paris; Bibliothèque Nationale, Paris; Van Abbemuseum, Eindhoven, Netherlands.

Publications:

By BURGIN: books—*Work and Commentary,* London 1973; *Two Essays on Art, Photography, and Semiotics,* London 1976; *Family,* New York 1977; *Newcastle Writings,* with others, London 1977; *Thinking Photography: Essays in the Theory of Photographic Representation,* editor, London 1981; *Essays: Interview: Work,* Berlin 1981; articles—"Art Society Systems" in *Control* (London), no. 4, 1968; "Situational Aesthetics" in *Studio International* (London), October 1969; reprinted in *Conceptual Art,* edited by Ursula Meyer, New York 1972; "Thanks for the Memory" in *Architectural Design* (London), August 1970; "Rules of Thumb" in *Studio International* (London), May 1971; "Interview with Varsity" in *Varsity* (Cambridge), October 1971; "Margin Note" and "Interview" in *The New Art,* exhibition catalogue, edited by Anne Seymour, London 1972; "In Reply" in *Art-Language* (Leamington Spa, Warwickshire), Summer 1972; "Photographic Practice and Art Theory" in *Studio International* (London), July/August 1975; "Socialist Formalism" in *Studio International* (London), July/August 1975; "Socialist Formalism" in *Studio International* (London), March/April 1976; "Art, Common-Sense and Photography" in *Camerawork* (London), no. 3, 1976; "Modernism in the Work of Art" in *20th Century Studies* (Canterbury, Kent), no. 15/16, 1976; "Looking at Photographs" in *Screen Education* (London), Autumn 1977; "Images of People" in *Studio International* (London), no. 2, 1978; "Seeing Sense" in *Artforum* (New York), February 1980; "Photography, Fantasy, Function" in *Screen* (London), Spring 1980.

On BURGIN: book—*Victor Burgin: Work,* exhibition catalogue, Eindhoven, Netherlands 1977; articles—"Victor Burgin: La Representation par le Text" by A. Pacquement in *Art Press* (Paris), no. 5, 1973; "Victor Burgin" by E. Tynan in *Studio International* (London), September/October 1976; "Victor Burgin in Oxford" by D. Reed in *British Journal of Photography* (London), March 1978.

From the early photo-essay *Work and Commentary* (with its rather formalist foray into semiotics) to the recent captioned advertisement style documentary panels, Vic Burgin has been involved with photography as a *signifying* practice, with its inseparability—as with all visual images—from language. In the 1970's this was called conceptualism. Today it offers—for Burgin at least, who has never found the artworld conducive to his own needs—the possibility of a wholly new practice. "I feel I'm working across the fringe areas—for example . . . where "art," ad-

Victor Burgin: image from *US 77,* 1977

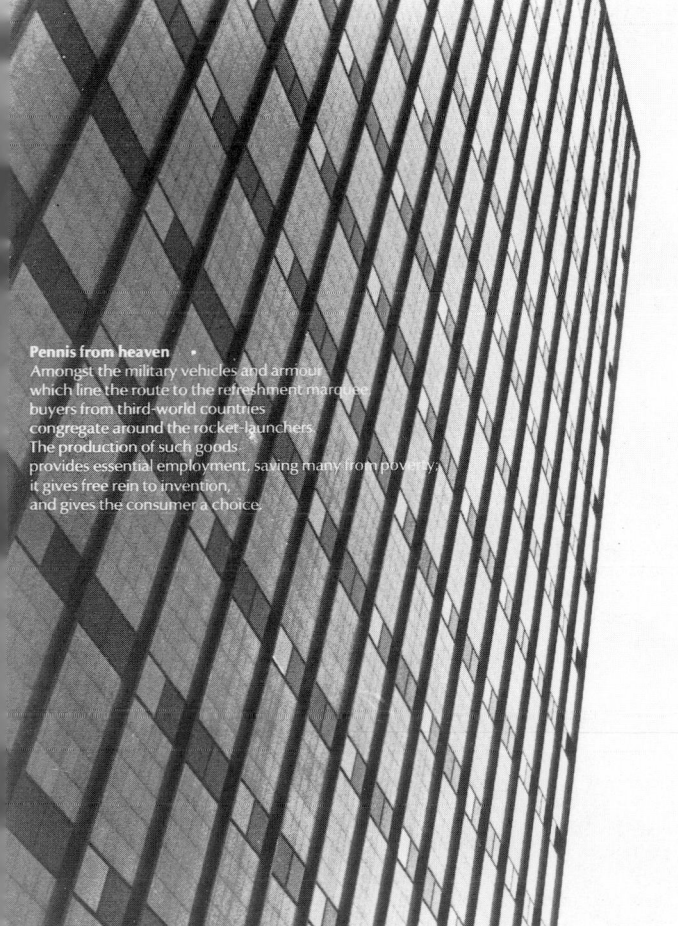

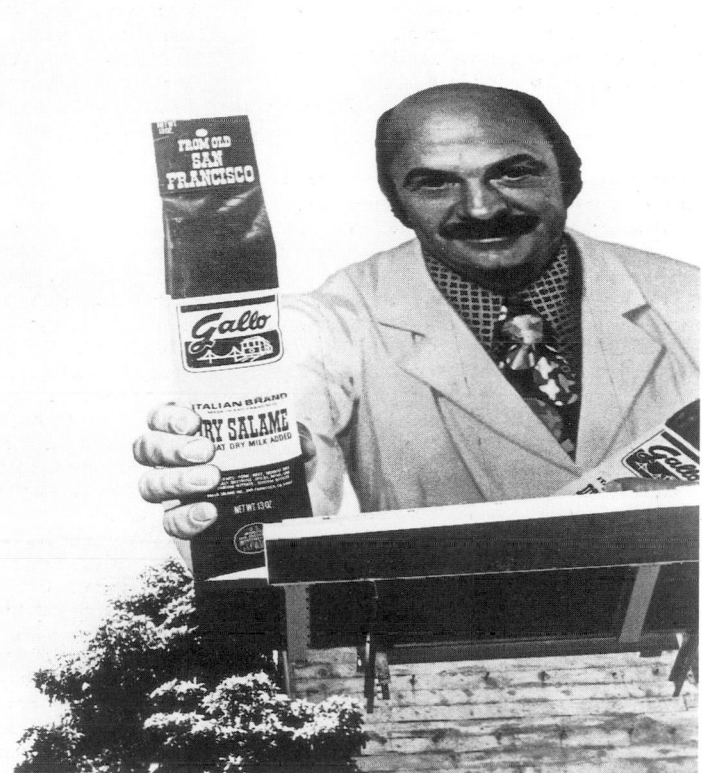

vertising, "documentary," "theory" etc. overlap." Burgin in fact makes no hierarchical distinction between his writing (which has been extensive) his activities as a teacher and lecturer and his photography; all are part of the same *political* education—Burgin's role as an artist is, in an old fashioned sense, pedagogic.

Burgin's involvement with photography as a language has been a critique of the notion of the "purely visual," which art-historically has come to mean Greenberg's modernism, but which in reality covers a whole range of what Burgin sees as academic prephotographic art teaching. Like many artists who questioned the primacy of painting (or rather the primacy of post-war American painting), Burgin has attempted to give back image-making certain cultural responsibilities, to "interfere," albeit peripherally, with dominant forms of representation. In the early 70's—when the Art and Society debates were at their height—Burgin attempted a populist approach, putting his images into circulation in the community itself. His poster campaign in Newcastle upon Tyne (the poster showed a young attractive couple embracing, underneath the slogan: 7% of the population own 84% of the wealth) came in for a good deal of criticism for its cosmeticism and somewhat condescending airs. It was not a success. Burgin's recent work though has been less tendentious. Series such as "US 77" and "Zoo" (shown at the *Hayward Annual* in 1979) show Burgin moving towards allegory; captions, almost poetic in their scansion, are superimposed over single shot photographs of predominantly urban scenes, some sparse and barren, some a welter of signs, symbols and narrative fragments.

Burgin's attempt to work on the margins of mainstream visual culture represents an important shift in thinking towards re-engagement with *culture as a whole*; the problem, though, still remains one of finding a broad audience for that engagement. Burgin's decision to work outside of what is notionally known a the "artworld" can only help to promote it.

—John Roberts

BURRA, Edward.

British. Born in London, 29 March 1905. Educated in London schools, 1910–18; studied at the Chelsea Polytechnic, London, 1921–23, and the Royal College of Art, London, 1923–24. Suffered poor health from rheumatic fever in childhood. Lived with his parents until 1967. Visited Paris with William Chappell, 1923, and with Paul Nash, 1930; Member, Unit One, group of architects, painters and sculptors, founded by Nash, London, 1933; visited Spain, 1935, and travelled in the United States, 1934, 1937, 1948, 1955; set and costume designs for the ballets, *Barbau*, 1938, and *Miracle in the Gorbals*, 1944, for the Sadlers Wells Ballet Company, London. C.B.E. (Commander, Order of the British Empire), 1971. Agent: Lefevre Gallery, 30 Bruton Street, London WIX8JD, England. *Died* (in Rye, Sussex) *22 October 1976*.

Individual Exhibitions:

1929	Leicester Galleries, London
1932	Leicester Galleries, London
1937	Springfield Museum of Fine Art, Massachusetts
1942	Redfern Gallery, London
1947	Leicester Galleries, London
1949	Leicester Galleries, London
1952	Lefevre Gallery, London
1955	Lefevre Gallery, London
	Swerzoff Gallery, Boston
1957	Lefevre Gallery, London
1959	Lefevre Gallery, London
	Whiteworth Art Gallery, Manchester (with Greaves and Dalwood)
1961	Lefevre Gallery, London
1963	Lefevre Gallery, London
1965	Lefevre Gallery, London
1967	Lefevre Gallery, London
1970	Hamet Gallery, London
1971	Hamet Gallery, London
	Nicholas Treadwell Gallery, London
	Lefevre Gallery, London
1972	Postan Gallery, London
1973	Tate Gallery, London
	Lefevre Gallery, London
1975	Lefevre Gallery, London
1976	Towner Art Gallery, Eastbourne, Sussex
1977	Lefevre Gallery, London
1979	Blond Fine Art, London
1980	Anthony D'Offay Gallery, London
	Lefevre Gallery, London

Selected Group Exhibitions:

1934	*Unit One*, Mayor Gallery, London
1936	*London Surrealist Exhibition*, Burlington Galleries, London
	Fantastic Art, Dada, Surrealism, Museum of Modern Art, New York
1939	*Exhibition of Contemporary British Art*, National Gallery of Canada, Ottawa
1942	*Contemporary British Art*, Toledo Museum of Art, Ohio
1948	*La Jeune Peinture en Grande Bretagne*, Galerie René Drouin, Paris
1951	*21 Modern British Painters*, Vancouver Art Gallery (toured Canada and western United States)
1963	*Mixed Modern Paintings*, Lefevre Gallery, London
1971	*Britain's Contribution to Surrealism of the 30's and 40's*, Hamet Gallery, London
1972	*John Banting and his Friends*, Rye Art Gallery, Sussex

Contributions:

National Gallery of Victoria, Melbourne; Art Gallery of New South Wales, Sydney; National Gallery of New Zealand, Wellington; Beaverbrook Gallery, New Brunswick, Canada; Museum of Modern Art, New York.

Edward Burra: *Snowdonia No. 2*, 1974

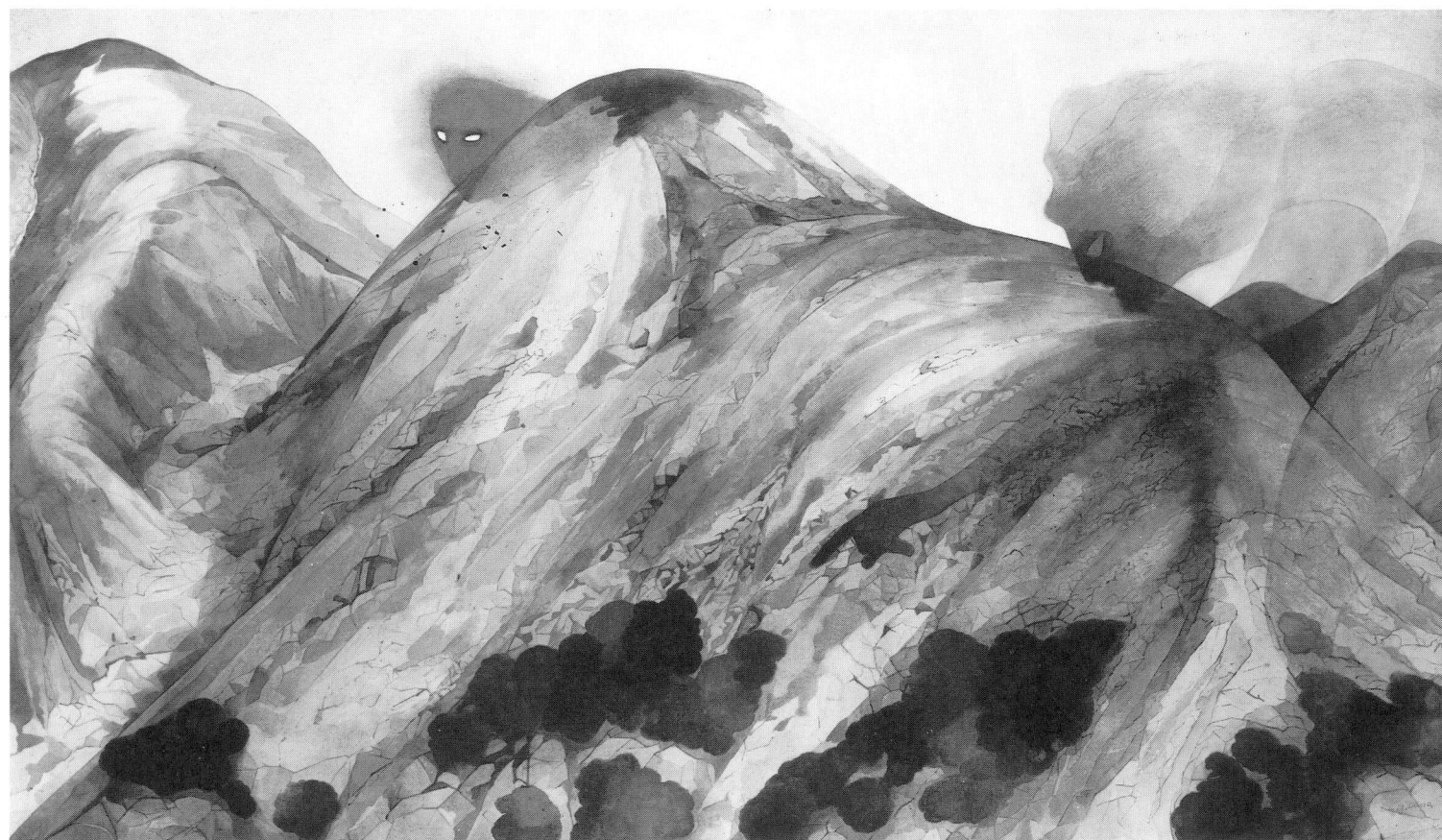

Publications:

By BURRA: articles—"Letters and Postcards" in *Edward Burra*, exhibition catalogue, by John Rothenstein, London, 1973.

On BURRA: books—*Edward Burra* by John Rothenstein, London 1945; *Edward Burra*, exhibition catalogue by John Rothenstein, London 1973; *Modern English Painters: Wood to Hockney* by John Rothenstein, London 1974; articles—"Edward Burra" by J. Burr in *Apollo* (London), October 1971; "Style and Ideology in British Art and Photography" by Ian Jeffrey and David Mellor in *Studio International* (London), July 1975; "Edward Burra," obituary, in *The Times* (London), October 1976.

*

"He had a wicked eye . . . ," we say, chuckling. This seems to express the essence of an artist who has yet to achieve the international recognition that his art deserves—not least as an "honorary American," whose recently-unearthed paintings of Boston bars and suchlike scenes in the 1930's and 1940's are a major contribution to "American Scene" painting.

Chronic ill health in early childhood left Edward Burra a semi-invalid, yet he overcame his perpetual near-exhaustion with an iron will, conserving his powers by social isolation, but travelling widely; and his magnificent facility for memorising every detail of a scene without any visual note-taking enabled him to re-create those cheap, vulgar, debased but vigorous scenes of low-life which he uncritically enjoyed, with a stimulating accuracy which is bracing, witty and humane. Believing, wrongly, that his painting in oils was not appreciated, he developed a technique of repeated overpainting of his huge, resonant watercolours so that they have all the stature of oils on the wall.

The first sight of a typical early Burra looks like something between the savage perceptions of George Grosz and the witty economics of a social cartoonist. Burra shares with Grosz and Bacon an eye for the demonic in the 20th century, but more from the standpoint of an uninvolved observer. From private works of indulgent—but highly talented—fantasy, Burra's work opened out to include elements of social realism and many aspects of landscape, one where surrealist creatures disturbingly invade the scene; and he extended, particularly in the latter part of his life, this view of the demonic into the vegetable world: his flower forms, his vegetation and his landscapes all partake of an indefinable menace. He might have been an ideal illustrator for Evelyn Waugh; in fact, he was a major stage-designer between 1932 and 1958—six ballets, one opera and a musical play.

The "amused eye" is a surface aspect of deep feelings in Burra's act, and its surrealism is the natural breakthrough of emotion and inner vision through outer form. Burra had strong feelings of affinity with Spain, Mexico and Spanish America, long before visiting (and his remarkable affinities with Rivera have yet to be studied), and his concern with these countries' troubles produced some intense religious scenes. He learned much, too, from acute observation of the visual forms in film. Burra's perceptions of the 20th century (little known in Britain until his retrospective of 1973) deserve a place on museum walls beside those of Grosz, Beckmann and Rivera.

—Michael Shepherd

BURRI, Alberto.

Italian. Born in Città di Castello, Umbria, 12 March 1915. Studied medicine in Perugia 1934–39; mainly self-taught in art, from 1944. Served as medical officer in the Italian Army, in North Africa, 1940–43; prisoner-of-war, Camp Hereford, Texas, 1943–45. Married Minsa Craig in 1945. Independent artist, Perugia, 1945–48, and in Rome, 1948–53; lived in the United States, 1953–69; returned to Rome, 1960; first abstract paintings, 1949; Member, with Colla, Capogrossi and Balloco, "Gruppo Origine," Rome 1951. Recipient: International Award, *Carnegie International*, Pittsburgh, 1958; Premio dell' Ariete, Milan 1959; Unesco Prize, *5th Biennal de Sao Paulo*, 1959; Critics' Prize, *Biennale*, Venice, 1960; Premio Marzotto, 1964; Grand Prix, *8th Bienal de Sao Paulo*, 1965; Feltrinelli Prize, Milan 1972. Agent: Galleria Marlborough, Rome. Address: c/o Galleria Marlborough, Via Gregoriana 5, 00187 Rome, Italy.

Individual Exhibitions:

1947	Galleria La Margherita, Rome
1948	Galleria dell'Angelo, Città di Castello, Italy
	Galleria Margherita, Rome
1949	Galleria dell'Angelo, Città di Castello, Italy
1952	Galleria dell'Obelisco, Rome
	Galleria d'Arte Contemporanea, Florence
1953	Fondazione Origine, Rome
	Allan Frumkin Gallery, Chicago
	Stable Gallery, New York
1954	Galleria dell'Obelisco, Rome
	Allan Frumkin Gallery, Chicago
1955	Stable Gallery, New York
	Colorado Springs Fine Arts Center
	Oakland Art Museum, California
1956	Seligmann Gallery, Seattle
	Galleria del Cavallino, Venice
	Galerie Rive Droite, Paris (with Cesar)
1957	Galleria Del Naviglio, Milan
	Galleria dell'Obelisco, Rome
	Galleria La Loggia, Bologna
	Galleria La Bussola, Turin
	Carnegie Institute, Pittsburgh
1958	Arts Club of Chicago
	Albright-Knox Art Gallery, Buffalo, New York
	San Francisco Museum of Art
	Galleria La Salita, Rome
	Galleria Blu, Milan
	Galleria Alberti, Brescia, Italy
1959	Galerie d'Art Moderne, Basle
	Palais des Beaux-Arts, Brussels
	Galleria La Loggia, Bologna
	Galleria La Tartaruga, Rome
	Museum Haus Lange, Krefeld, West Germany
	Galerie Beyeler, Basle
	Galerie Wiener Sezession, Vienna
	Museum am Ostwall, Dortmund, West Germany
1960	Martha Jackson Gallery, New York
	Hanover Gallery, London
	Museo Nacional de Bellas Artes, Buenos Aires
	Galerie Anne Abels, Cologne
1961	Galleria La Medusa, Rome
	Galerie de France, Paris
1962	Castello Cinquecentesco, L'Aquila, Italy
	Galleria Marlborough, Rome
1963	Marlborough New London Gallery
	Museum of Fine Arts, Houston
1964	Walker Art Center, Minneapolis
	Albright-Knox Art Gallery, Buffalo, New York
	Pasadena Art Museum, California
	Marlborough-Gerson Gallery, New York
1965	Galleria La Bussola, Turin
	Galleria Toninelli, Milan (with Marino Marini and Afro)
1966	Galleria Il Segno, Rome
1967	Kunsthalle, Darmstadt
	Museum Boymans-van Beuningen, Rotterdam
	Museum of Modern Art, New York (with Lucio Fontana)
	Galleria La Tartaruga, Rome
	Palazzo Vitelli, Città di Castello, Italy
1968	Galleria Blu, Milan
1969	Galleria Notizie, Turin
	Galleria Giussi, Turin (With Marini and Moreni)
	Galleria San Luca, Bologna
1970	Galleria La Tartaruga, Rome
	Galleria Acme, Brescia, Italy
	Qui Arte Contemporanea, Rome
	Transart, Milan
1971	Galleria Il Margutta, Rome
	Galleria Civic d'Arte Moderna, Turin
	Modern Art Agency, Naples
	Libreria Stampatori, Turin
	Libreria-Galleria Congrande, Verona
1972	Musée d'Art Moderne, Paris
1973	Galleria San Luca, Bologna
1974	Galerie Jacques Benador, Geneva
	Galleria Grafica Oggi, Milan
1975	Sacro Convento di San Francesco, Assisi, Italy
	Disegni, Tempere e Grafica, Galleria Il Segnapassi, Pesaro, Italy
1976	Galleria Nazionale d'Arte Moderna, Rome
1977	Fundacao Calouste Gulbenkian, Lisbon
	Santa Barbara Museum of Art, California (toured the United States)
1978	P & P Galerie, Zurich
	Marion Koogler McNay Institute, San Antonio, Texas
	Milwaukee Art Center
	Museo di Capodimonte, Naples
	Guggenheim Museum, New York
1979	Galleria Lorenzelli, Milan
	Studio Marconi, Milan
	J. Corcoran Gallery, Los Angeles
	Galleria D'Ascanio, Rome
	Essiccatoio del Tabacco, Città di Castello, Italy
1980	Rocco Paolina, Perugia, Italy (with Joseph Beuys)
	Staatsgalerie Moderner Kunst, Munich
	Instituto Italiano di Cultura, New York
	Instituto Italiano di Cultura, Madrid
	Orsanmichele, Florence
1981	Galleria L'Isola, Rome
1982	Desert Museum, Palm Springs, California
	Galleria San Luca, Bologna, Italy
	Brooklyn Museum, New York
	Columbus Museum of Art, Ohio
	San Francisco Museum of Modern Art
1983	Cantieri Navali alla Guidecca, Venice
	Galerie Sapone, Nice, France
	Galerie des Ponchettes, Nice, France

Selected Group Exhibitions:

1947	*Art Club of Rome*, Galleria Nazionale d'Arte Moderna, Rome
1951	*Gruppo Origine*, Fondazione Origine, Rome
1952	*Biennale*, Venice (and 1956, 1966, 1968, 1983)
1953	*Younger European Painters*, Guggenheim Museum, New York
1959	*Bienal*, Sao Paulo (and 1965)
1967	*Contemporary Italian Art*, Ulster Museum, Belfast (toured the U.K.)
1971	*New Italian Art: 1953-1971*, Walker Art Gallery, Liverpool
1980	*Arte Astratta Italiana 1909-1959*, Galleria Nazionale d'Arte Moderna, Rome
1982	*Documenta 7*, Museum Fridericianum, Kassel, West Germany
1985	*The European Iceberg*, Art Gallery of Ontario, Toronto

Collections:

Galleria Nazionale d'Arte Moderna, Rome; Nationalgalerie, West Berlin; Centre Georges Pompidou, Paris; Carnegie Institute, Pittsburgh.

Publications:

On BURRI: books *Burri* by James Johnson Sweeney, Rome 1955; *Burri* by Enrico Crispolti, Milan 1961; *I Ferri di Burri* by G. Marchiori and M. Drudi Gambillo, Rome 1961; *Ottocento e Novecento* by A. M. Brizio, Turin 1962; *Alberto Burri* by Cesare Brandi, Rome 1963; *Le Due Avantguardi*, 2 vols., by Maurizio Calvesi, Milan 1966, 1971; *New Italian Art 1953-1971*, exhibition catalogue, with text by Giovanni Carandente, Liverpool 1971; *Alberto Burri* by Maurizio Calvesi, Milan 1971; *Alberto Burri*, exhibition catalogue, with texts by Enrico Crispolti, Nello Poente, Giuseppe Marchiori and others, Rome 1971; *Art Without Boundaries 1950-1970*, edited by Gerald Woods, Philip Thompson and John

Williams, London 1972; *Alberto Burri*, exhibition catalogue, with texts by Jean Leymarie, Aldo Passoni and others, Paris 1972; *Burri* by Vittorio Rubiu, Turin 1975; *Burri: Disegni Tempere e Grafica*, exhibition catalogue, with text by Maurizio Calvesi, Pesaro 1975; *Burri*, exhibition catalogue, with text by Bruno Mantura, Lisborn 1977; *Alberto Burri: Prints 1959-1977* by Vittorio Rubin and others, Rome 1977; *Burri: La Forma e l'Informe* by Flavio Caroli, Milan 1979; *Alberto Burri: Il Viaggio*, with text by Nemo Sarteanesi and Erich Steingraber, Milan 1980; *Arte Astratta Italiana 1909-1959*, exhibition catalogue, with text by Giorgio de Marchis, Rome 1980; *Burri: Sestante*, edited by Vanni Bramanti, with introduction by Giulio Carlo Argan, Milan 1983.

The work of Alberto Burri—one of the greatest artists of this century—is an endless game with material. Sacks, wood, iron, plastics, Cellotex; he burns these materials, twists them, tears them, or else gently arranges them into amazing, calm 15th century compositions. And sometimes, dramatically, both these things are combined in a single design. With Burri the material is identified with space; it becomes pure presence, the affirmation of existence; first of all, it *is*. But (and this is a paradox to be found only in art) it is only when a human works it, forces it, building up an eminently, wholly erotic relationship with it, that it reaches the essential state. Memory, a great memory of impressionist and tonal painting, informs the whole of Burri's work, alive like no others to delicate shading (even when the material is most crushed and contaminated), to the spreading of tone within a particular colour—as in the "sacks," where the splits, the stitching, the holes, the patches that stretch the coarse stuff to its limits tell of nothing but the violence and pain of the material (and the material is the World), yet also of the chromatic chances by which everything creates colour: the shadows, the protrusions, the different tissues of the texture and the broken lines they follow.

In his different series of works there is always a strong tension between the defined space of the picture's surface and the irruptions on one side and another made by the "wounds" in these materials, natural or artificial, always poor but redeemed in the passage from quantity to quality. The "irons" of the later 1950's, for example, jammed hard together against each other so as to cover the whole rectangular frame given them, at once respect and transgress the surface of the pictorial design. They respect it because they are bent by main force to conform with it, ruled by the formal command to adhere to the design; they transgress it because, being forced in this way, they protrude in menacing spikes which encroach on the space and create a volume with the shadows they project on the others still held at the level of the surface. The burns on plastic—in which we may see a "baroque" in Burri—and on wood relate to the primordial power of fire, seat and symbol of life and so also of destruction, of biological poetry. From the subtle ambiguities between abstraction and *trompe-l'oeil*, between artifice and nature in the "cracks" (like coagulated streams of lava in which there are endless splits and fissures), to the clear, bright oblong shapes and patches of colour in the gerat impaginations of the series in Cellotex (a compound derived from the scission of cellulose). Burri's journey remains unique. And here, stupendously incarnate, breathes the absolute.

—Massimo Carboni

BURRI, Pol.

Belgian. Born in Haine-Saint-Pierre, 26 April 1922. Studied painting, drawing and decoration under Louis Buisseret and Louis Navez, Academie des Beaux-Arts, Mons, 1938-39. Served in the Belgian resistance movement, Brussels, 1943. Painter and sculptor, living and working in Belgium, La Louviére, 1939-61, in Fontenay-Aux-Roses, near Paris, 1961-65, in Saulx-les-Chartres, France, 1965-73, and in Perdreauville, Yvelines, France, since 1973: produced first abstract paintings, 1947; first mobile-kinetic sculptures, 1957. Founder-member, with Archille Chavée and André Lorent, Group Rupture, La Louviére, 1939-40; Young Belgian Painters group, Brussels, 1947; member, with Christian Dotremont and Pierre Alechinsky, COBRA (Copenhagen-Brussels-Amsterdam) group, Brussels, 1949-51; member, Art Abstrait group, Brussels, 1952; founder, with André Balthazar, Academie de Montbliart and Verlag de Montbliart publishing house, Brussels, 1953. Designed sets for ballet *Der Spiegel;* also involved in filmmaking, since 1970. Instructor in Sculpture, University of California, Berkeley, 1970; Minneapolis College of Art and Design, 1973; Professor of Monumental Sculpture, Ecole Nationale Supérieure des Beaux-Arts, Paris, 1983. Recipient: Marzotto Prize, 1964; Grand Prix National de Sculpture, Paris, 1985. Honorary Doctorate: Minneapolis College of Art and Design, 1973. Agent: Lefebre Gallery, 47 East 77th Street, New York, New York 10021. Addresses: Vallée de la Taupe-Perdreauville, 78200 Mantes-la-Jolie, France; 236 boulevard Raspail, 75014 Paris, France.

Individual Exhibitions:

1953	Galerie Apollo, Brussels
1955	Galerie Les Contemporains, Brussels
1957	Galerie du Verseau, Brussels
1959	Galerie St. Laurent, Brussels
1960	Galerie St. Laurent, Brussels
1961	A.P.I.A.W., Liège, Belgium
1962	Galerie Iris Clert, Paris
1963	Galerie Iris Clert, Paris
1964	Lefebre Gallery, New York
1965	Felix Landau Gallery, Los Angeles
1966	*Twice Pol Bury: Cinetizations, Moving Sculptures,* Lefebre Gallery, New York
	Galerie La Hune, Paris
1967	Kasmin Gallery, London
1968	Lefebre Gallery, New York
1969	Galerie Pierre, Stockholm
	Galerie Maeght, Paris
1970	University of California, Berkeley (toured the United States)
1971	*A Way Out,* Lefebre Gallery, New York
	Estudio Actual, Caracas
	Gallery Moos, Toronto
	Kestner-Gesellschaft, Hannover (travelled to the Nationalgalerie, West Berlin and the Kunsthalle, Dusseldorf)
1972	Palais des Beaux-Arts, Charleroi, Belgium (travelled to Centre National d'Art Contemporain, Paris)
	Kunsthalle, Dusseldorf
1973	Museum Boymans-van Beuningen, Rotterdam
	Louisiana Museum, Humlebaek, Denmark
1974	*25 Tonnes de Colonnes,* Foundation Maeght, St. Paul de Vence, France
1976	Musée d'Art Moderne, Brussels
	Woodprints, Lefebre Gallery, New York
1977	Museo de Arte Moderno, Mexico City
1978	F.S. Wright Art Galleries, University of California at Los Angeles
	University of Texas at Austin
	Portland Art Museum, Oregon
	University of Georgia, Athens
1979	Musée Saint-Georges, Liége, Belgium
	Oeuvres de 1963 à 1978, Cloitre Saint-Trophime, Arles, France
1980	Guggenheim Museum, New York
1981	Herning Museum, Denmark (with Pablo Palazuelo)
1982	Musée d'Art Moderne de la Ville, Paris (retrospective)

Selected Group Exhibitions:

1945	*Surrealisme,* Galerie des Editions La Boetie, Brussels
1955	*Le Mouvement,* Galerie Denise René, Paris
1959	*Breer, Bury, Klein, Mack, Munari, etc.,* Hussenhuis, Antwerp
1964	*Biennale,* Venice
	Documenta 3, Kassel West Germany
1967	*Dix Années de l'Art Vivant 1955-65,* Galerie Maeght, Paris
1972	*Douze Ans d'Art Contemporain en France,* Grand Palais, Paris
1973	*Hommage à Picasso,* Kestner-Gesellschaft, Hannover

Collections:

Neue Nationalgalerie, West Berlin; Kaiser Wilhelm Museum Krefeld, West Germany; Kunstmuseum, Dusseldorf; Stedelijk Museum, Amsterdam; Belgian State Collection, Brussels; Museum of Modern Art, New York; Guggenheim Museum, New York; Albright-Knox Art Gallery, Buffalo, New York; Menil Foundation, Houston.

Publications:

By BURY: books—illustrations for *L'Aventure devorante,* with COBRA group, Brussels 1950; illustrations for *La Main Heureuse,* Brussels 1950; *Dix Sérigraphies de Pol Bury,* with an introduction by R. V. Gindertael, La Louvière, Belgium 1955; *La Boule et le Trou,* Brussels 1961; *Le Petit Commencement,* La Louvière, Belgium 1965; *La Boule et le Cube,* Brussels 1967; *Milano, cinetizzazioni,* Venice 1967; *Derrière le Miroir,* Paris 1969; *Décalcomanies,* La Louvière, Belgium 1970; *L'Art à bicyclette et la Revolution à cheval,* Paris 1972; *Art is too serious to be left in the hands of artists . . . ,,* Minneapolis 1973; *Douze Ramollissements du Président Mao,* Paris 1973; *Ramollissements de 17 corps,* Paris 1973; *Les petits Moutons blancs qui sorten en rang du Lavoir,* Montpellier 1976; *Infracritique de l'Oeuvre plastique de Prof, Froeppel,* La Louvière, Belgium 1976; *Le Vélo de Joseph Staline et le Circuit idéologique,* La Louvière, Belgium 1976; *Les Sexes des Anges et celui des Géometres,* Paris 1976; *Léon III, l'Isaurien, dit l'Iconomaque, Essai d'Iconophobie,* Brussels 1976; *Les Horribles mouvements de l'immobilité* (collected writings), Paris 1977; *L'Art inopiné dans les Collections publiques,* La Louvière 1982, *Les Gaietés de l'Esthétique,* Paris 1984; article—"Tribune Libre" in *Chroniques de l'Art Vivant* (Paris), December 1970; films—*Tour Eiffel,* with Clovis Prevost , 1971; *8,500 Tonnes de Fer,* with Clovis Prevost, 1971; *Une Lecon de Geometrie plane,* with Clovis Prevost, 1972; *135 kilometres-heure,* with Clovis Prevost, 1972; *25 Tonnes de Colonnes,* with Clovis Prevost, 1973; *L'Art illustre,* 1975; *L'Oeuvre plastique du Professeur Froeppel,* with Claude Gaspari, 1976.

On BURY:—*Pol Bury,* exhibition catalogue, with texts by Roger Bordier and André Balthazar, New York 1964; *Twice Pol Bury: Cinetizations, Moving Sculptures,* exhibition catalogue, with text by Eugene Ionesco, New York 1966; *Pol Bury* by André Balthazar, Milan 1967; *Pol Bury,* exhibition catalogue, with interview by Peter Selz, introduction by Eugene Ionesco, essay by André Balthazar, Berkeley 1970; *Pol Bury* by Dore Ashton, Paris 1970; *Pol Bury,* exhibition catalogue, with text by Clara Diament de Sizo, Caracas 1971; *Pol Bury,* exhibition catalogue, edited by André Balthazar, Hannover 1971; *Icons and Images of the 60's* by Nicolas and Elena Calas, New York 1971; *Pol Bury,* exhibition catalogue, edited by Andr3 Balthazar, Paris 1972; *Douze Ans d'Art Contemporain en France,* exhibition catalogue, Hannover 1973; *Pol Bury: 25 Tonnes de Colonnes,* exhibition catalogue, with an interview by André Balthazar, St. Paul de Vence, France 1974; *Pol Bury: Oeuvres de 1963 à 1978,* exhibition catalogue, with texts by Michel Moutashar, Anne Tronche, Roger Bordier, Dore Ashton and others, Arles, France 1979; *Les Fontaines de Pol Bury* by Pierre Descargeus, La Louvière 1986.

Until 1953 when he gave up easel painting completely, Pol Bury was one of the most enterprising young Belgian painters. He studied at the Mons Academy of Art from 1938 to 1939, when he joined the experimental surrealist group formed locally by two poets. He was a member of the Jeune Peinture Belge group, and until 1951 was associated with the COBRA group. His first experiments with mobile constructions were exhibited at Galerie Apollo, Brussels, in 1953, a series of *plans mobiles,* flat planes of black and white that could be fitted together to pro-

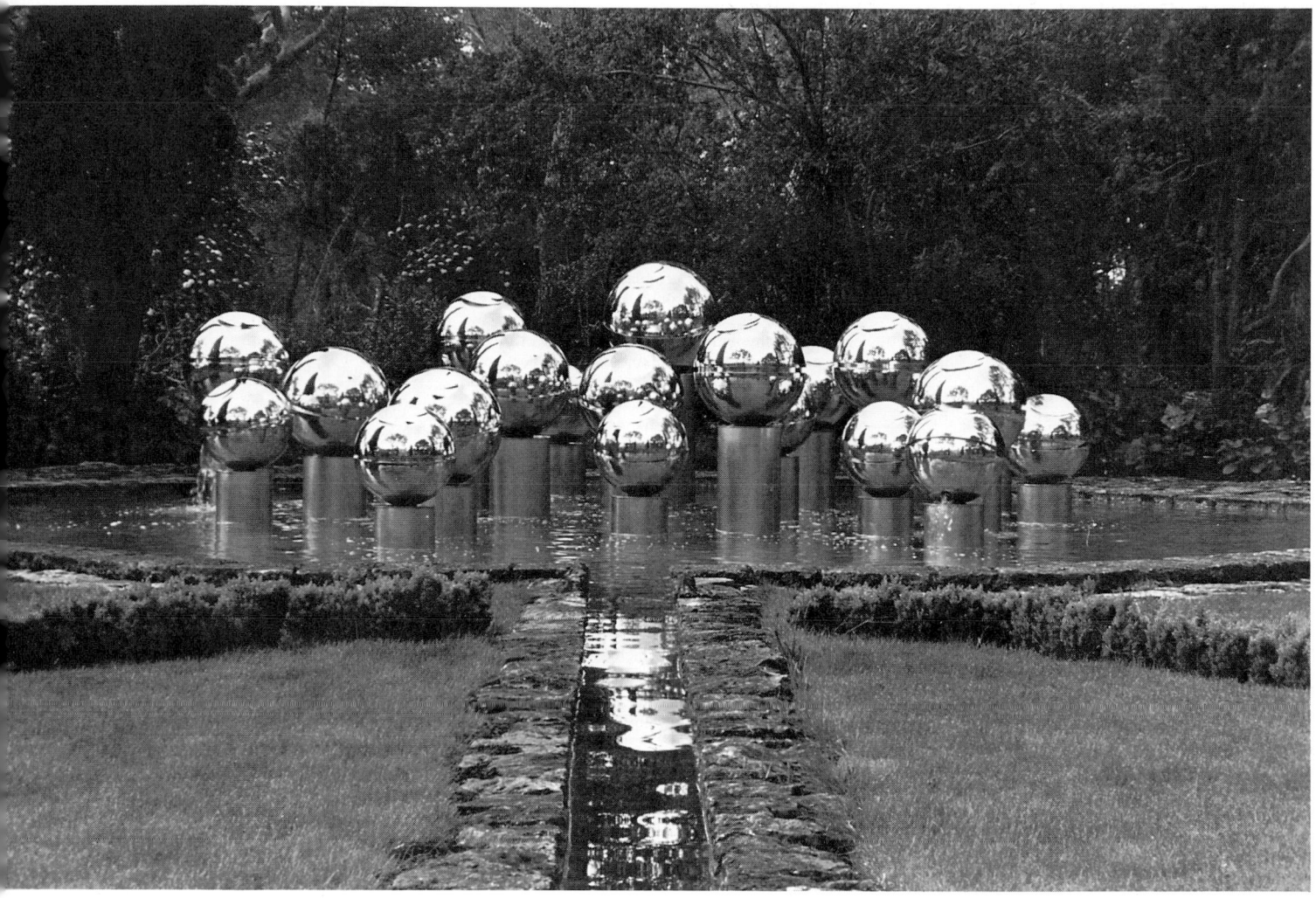

Pol Bury: *Stainless Steel Hydraulic Sculpture*, 1987

duce a variety of patterns. With Calder, Soto, Tinguely and Vasarely, Bury showed in the 1955 "Mouvements" exhibition at Galerie Denise René in Paris.

Electric motors were first used in Bury's works in 1957. *Multiplans*, flat rectangles set edge to edge, were painted with an overall abstract design that changed by minute degrees when moved by the power. These were succeeded in 1959 by his "Ponctuations" shown at the Galerie St. Laurent, Brussels, where perforated black and white discs performed constantly changing patterns and rigid and pliable stems rose and fell according to their phasing by the current. His show at Galerie Iris Clert showed a further development in "Entités erectiles" of 1963, where the spheres and globes appeared for the first time setting up subtle and almost imperceptible shudders. This contrast with rapid movement imposed its own intrinsic character in the work. Bury described it: "Speed limits space, slowness multiplies it." The sensuous associations suggested by the nudging of the globes are summarised by Bury: "Two slownesses gently grazing each other even go so far as to rub against each other. We dare henceforward speak of such activity no longer in terms of geometry but almost in the language of the boudoir."

From kinetics Bury progressed to constructions of finely carved and painted wooden objects comprising balls, cylinders and other cubes assembled in apparent disarray on flat ramps. Other works of hammered copper in freely curving arabesques fixed in panels carried hints of shock in their end tremors. Such is the reputation acquired by Bury's almost immobile mobiles that a structure of his designed for permanent static life can produce an hallucinatory effect on the onlooker, who easily imagines that it *does* move. As Bury insists, the difference is so slight.

Following representations at the Venice *Biennale* in 1964 and at exhibitions in the U.S.A. and Europe, Bury is to be seen in most major museums of the world. Swerving of bodies in space and the frailty of seemingly fixed galactic systems is further illustrated by analogy in Bury's "Cinematisations" where photographs and reproductions have circular details cut out and replaced in collages only slightly awry so that the Eiffel Tower or a Gothic cathedral seems ominously out of true, less obviously than the Tower of Pisa, but on that account all the more nerve-tingling.

—G. S. Whittet

BUSH, Jack.
Canadian. Born in Toronto, 20 March 1909. Educated in Montreal primary schools; studied evenings under Edmund Byonnet and Adam Sherriff Scott while an apprentice in the art department of Rapid Grid Company of Montreal, 1926–28; continued study of art in evening classes at the Ontario College of Art, Toronto, under Frederick Challender, John Alfsen and Charles Comfort, while working as a commercial artist for Rapid Grid in Toronto, 1928. Married Mabel Teackle in 1934; had 3 sons. Independent artist, Toronto. Co-Founder, with Bill Ronald, Hortense Gordon and others, Painters Eleven, 1953; travelled extensively in Europe, 1962; Member, Canadian Group of Painters, 1964. Visiting Artist, Michigan State University, East Lansing, 1965, and Cranbrook Academy of Art, Bloomfield Hills, Michigan, 1968. President, Canadian Society of Painters in Watercolor, 1964. Recipient: Ralph Clark Stone

Award, Ontario Society of Artists, 1946; Arts Directors Club of Toronto Medal, 1951, 1954; J. W. L. Forster Award, Ontario Society of Artists, 1953; First Prize, Canadian Sports Hall of Fame, 1957; Canada Council Senior Fellowship, 1962; Grand Award, *Montreal Museum of Fine Arts Spring Exhibition*, 1965; Albert H. Robinson Prize, Montreal Museum of Fine Arts, 1967; Guggenheim Fellowship, 1968. Associate, Royal Canadian Academy; Fellow, Ontario College of Art, 1976. O.C. (Officer, Order of Canada), 1976. *Died* (in Toronto) *24 January 1977.*

Individual Exhibitions:

1945	Hart House, Toronto (with William Winter)
1946	Trinity College, Toronto
1949	Gavin Henderson Galleries, Toronto
1952	Roberts Gallery, Toronto
1958	Park Gallery, Toronto
1959	Park Gallery, Toronto
1961	Park Gallery, Toronto
1962	Robert Elkon Gallery, New York
	Gallery Moos, Toronto
1963	Robert Elkon Gallery, New York
	Museum of Fine Arts, Montreal (with Francoise Sullivan Ewen)
1964	Norman Mackenzie Art Gallery, Regina, Saskatchewan
	Bennington College, Vermont
	Robert Elkon Gallery, New York
	Gallery Moos, Toronto
	Waddington Galleries, London
1966	André Emmerich Gallery, New York
	David Mirvish Gallery, Toronto
	Trinity College, Toronto (with Ina Meares and James Gordancer)

1967	Waddington Galleries, London
	André Emmerich Gallery, New York
	David Mirvish Gallery, Toronto
1968	David Mirvish Gallery, Toronto
1969	Galerie Godard-Lefot, Montreal
	Waddington Galleries, London
1970	Norman Mackenzie Art Gallery, Regina, Saskatchewan
	André Emmerich Gallery, New York
	Edmonton Art Gallery, Alberta
	Harcus Krakow Gallery, Boston
1971	Waddington Galleries, London
	Nicholas Wilder Gallery, Los Angeles
	Harcus Krakow Gallery, Boston
1972	Museum of Fine Arts, Boston
	André Emmerich Gallery, New York
	David Mirvish Gallery, Toronto
1973	André Emmerich Gallery, New York
	Edmonton Art Gallery, Alberta
1974	André Emmerich Gallery, Zurich
	André Emmerich Gallery, New York
	David Mirvish Gallery, Toronto
	Waddington Galleries, London
1975	David Mirvish Gallery, Toronto
	Jack Pollock Gallery, Toronto
	Prints on Prince Street, New York
1976	Waddingtton Galleries, London
	Theo Waddington Gallery, Montreal
	Jack Bush: A Retrospective, Art Gallery of Ontario, Toronto (toured Canada, 1976–77)
1978	Waddington Galleries, London
	Waddington Galleries, Toronto
1979	Theo Waddington Galleries, Montreal
	Waddington Galleries, Toronto
1980	Theo Waddington Gallery, Montreal
	André Emmerich Gallery, New York
	University of Edinburgh (travelled to the Serpentine Gallery, London, and the Ikon Gallery, Birmingham)

Selected Group Exhibitions:

1952	1st Canadian All Abstract Exhibition, Oshawa, Ontario
1954	Painters Eleven, Roberts Gallery, Toronto (travelled to Ottawa)
1956	20th Annual Exhibition of American Abstract Artists, with Painters Eleven of Canada, Riverside Museum, New York
1958	Painters Eleven, Ecole des Beaux-Arts, Montreal (toured Canada)
1963	5th Biennale of Canadian Painting, Tate Gallery, London
1967	Bienal, Sao Paulo
1968	Canada: Art d'Aujourd'hui, National Gallery of Canada, Ottawa (toured Europe)
1970	Color and Field, Albright-Knox Art Gallery, Buffalo, New York (toured the United States)
1974	The Great Decade of American Abstraction: Modernist Art 1960-1970, Museum of Fine Arts, Houston
1976	Changing Visions: The Canadian Landscape, Art Gallery of Ontario, Toronto (toured North America)

Publications:

By BUSH: articles—"Letter to the Editor" in *Artscanada* (Toronto), June 1969; "Some Thoughts on His Painting" and "Reminiscences of His Earlier Career" in *Jack Bush*, exhibition catalogue, London 1980.

On BUSH: books—*Contemporary Canadian Painting* by William Withrow, Toronto 1972; *Jack Bush: A Retrospective*, exhibition catalogue, by Terry Fenton, Toronto 1976; *Jack Bush*, exhibition catalogue, London 1980; articles—"In Terms of Color: Jack Bush" by Terry Fenton in *Artforum* (New York), May 1969; "Jack Bush" by Carter Ratcliff in *Artnews* (New York), December 1970; "A Balanced Judgment" by J. Burr in *Apollo* (London), October 1971; "A Garden for the Eye: The Paintings of Jack Bush" in *Artscanada* (Toronto), December 1980/January 1981; film—*Jack Bush* by Murray Battle, National Film Board of Canada, 1979.

Jack Bush is Canada's most important contemporary painter, not only because of the quality of his work in relation to his Canadian colleagues, but also because he is the only one of his generation to take his place, on merit alone, beside his international contemporaries. Nevertheless, Bush's position in the history of recent Canadian art is significant. In the '20s and '30s he was a young painter at a time when a nationalistic movement of landscape painters, the Group of Seven, set standards of approved Canadian modernism with their stylized views of untouched nature. Bush's early works echo the Group's example in many ways, but they remain resolutely unlike the paintings they attempt to emulate. In later years Bush said that he had been troubled, at the time, by this apparent failure, but eventually realized that it was part of his strength. In the 1940's he experimented with a personal brand of expressionism, populating his paintings with anguished, white robed figures, who eventually became more and more generalized, until they disappeared. By the early '50's, Bush had discovered American Abstract Expressionism, at first through reproductions and later through visits to New York. His rapid assimilation of the possibilities of gestural abstraction set him apart from the majority of his colleagues. He and ten like-minded painters, in fact, banded together to exhibit as Painters Eleven because their atypical commitment to abstraction set them apart from the rest of the art community in conservative Toronto.

Bush's paintings of the '50s are noteworthy for their energy and for gestures which anticipate his later drawing, but their layered construction and reliance on strong contrasts of dark and light often obscure his real gifts. Bush's economical, simplified watercolors of the period, however, serve as models of what was to come.

Bush's mature work begins in the late '50s. Following the suggestions of his watercolors, he gradually evolved a personal way of using the legacy of Matisse, painting with a remarkable range of thin, radiant colors, presented in clear, discrete shapes. Bush's expansive compositions, after about 1955, similarly owe a debt to Matisse, although it's apparent from works of the early '60's that he learned a great deal from Miró and Adolph Gottlieb as well. By this time he had established friendships with many of his American colleagues, such as Noland and Olitski, and these contacts proved stimulating.

The earliest well-developed series, the "Thrusts," set the pattern for the amalgamation of color and generous drawing which remains characteristic of Bush's best work. His imagery varies from stacks of colored bars, in the "Sashes" of the '60s and their variations, to the unconfined calligraphy of the "Garden" pictures of the early '70's, and the floating color strokes of the last two years of his life. Bush often spoke of his dependence upon his garden as a source of images and colors, but it is clear from clues provided in titles and notebooks that he was capable of finding stimulus in even the most banal aspects of his surroundings. Neckties, women's clothing, wallpaper, giftwrap, road signs and the like could all serve as visual triggers, and be translated into typical "Bush" configurations, wrenched from any literal meaning and transformed into his idiosyncratic, deliberately uningratiating handwriting.

These eccentric shapes are simply the carriers of Bush's remarkable color, and are improvised jazz-fashion from things seen. The analogy is an apt one, since Bush loved jazz and was an accomplished jazz pianist. There is even some indication that in his late works he attempted some kind of visual equivalence for sounds. In some instances, the scale, positioning and color of floating strokes seem to have been provoked by specific musical compositions.

Whatever their intention, however, it is evident that Bush's last paintings, those of 1975 and '76, are among his best. Their richly inflected, sponged-on grounds, fluttering shapes and dark, sonorous color assure Bush's pre-eminence in Canada and his position among his colleagues anywhere.

—Karen Wilkin

BUTHE, Michael.

German. Born in Sonthofen, Allgau, 1 August 1944. Studied at the Werkkunstschule, Kassel, 1962–64 under Arnold Bode, Hochschule fur bildende Kunste, Kassel, 1964–66. Independent painter and environmental artist, in Kassel, 1966–68, in Cologne since 1969, and in Marrakesh since 1970: adopted pseudonym Michel de la Sainte Beaute, 1971. Professor, Akademie der Kunste, Dusseldorf, 1982 (resigned, 1982). Recipient: Villa Romana Prize, Florence, 1976. Agents: Moderne Kunst Dietmar Werle, Spichernstrasse 44, 5000 Cologne 1; Galerie Bama, 40 rue Quincampoix, 75004 Paris; Galerie Toni Gerber, Gerechtigkeitsgasse 74, 3011 Berne. Address: Drb al Hammam 52, Marrakech-Mouazzin, Morocco.

Individual Exhibitions:

1968	Galerie Ricke, Kassel, West Germany
1969	Galerie Ricke, Cologne
	Von-der-Heydt-Museum, Wuppertal, West Germany
1970	Galerie Kuhn, Aachen, West Germany
	Kabinett für Aktuelle Kunst, Bremerhaven, West Germany
	Galerie Renée Ziegler, Zurich
	Galerie Ernst, Hannover
1971	Galerie Toni Gerber, Berne
	Galerie Renée Ziegler, Zurich
1972	Galerie Mollenhoff, Cologne
1973	Galerie Onze, Brussels
	Kunstverein, Cologne
	Kunstmuseum, Lucerne
	Galerie Pablo Stahli, Lucerne
	Galerie Oppenheim, Cologne
1974	Galerie Loeb, Berne
	Galeria Vandres, Madrid
	Galerie Oppenheim, Cologne
1975	Galerie Magers, Bonn
	Oppenheim-Studio, Cologne
1976	Atelier des Kunstlers, Cologne
1977	Galerie AK, Frankfurt
	Tarahumaras, Stadtisches Museum Schloss Morsbroich, Leverkusen, West Germany
	Kunstmuseum, Dusseldorf
1978	Galerie Gerhild Grolitsch, Munich
	Galerie Toni Gerber, Berne
	Stadtisches Galerie, Ravensburg, West Germany
1979	Galerie Bama, Paris
	Galerie 't Venster, Rotterdam
	Galerie Harlekin Art, Wiesbaden, West Germany
1980	Die endlose Reise der Bilder, Museum Folkwang, Essen
	Kunstverein, Kassel, West Germany
1981	Galerie Munro, Hamburg
	Galerie Bernier, Athens
	Galerie Bama, Paris
	Galerie Toni Gerber, Berne
	Galerie Nachst St. Stephan, Vienna
1982	Galerie Krinzinger, Innsbruck, Austria
	Galerie Art in Progress, Munich
	Galerie Baronian/Lambert, Ghent, Belgium
	Villa Romana, Florence
	Holly Solomon Gallery, New York
1983	Galerie Toni Gerber, Berne
1984	Galerie Munro, Hamburg
	Galerie Bama, Paris
	Museum Villa Stuck, Munich
1987	Moderne Kunst Dietmar Werle, Cologne

Selected Group Exhibitions:

1968	Programm I, Galerie Ricke, Kassel, West Germany
1969	When Attitudes Become Form, Kunsthalle, Berne (toured Europe)
1970	14 x 14, Staatliche Kunsthalle, Baden-Baden, West Germany
1972	Documenta 5, Museum Fridericianum, Kassel, West Germany (and Documenta 6, 1977; Documenta 7, 1982)
1973	Yes, Sir, That's My Baby(etween), Gallery House, London

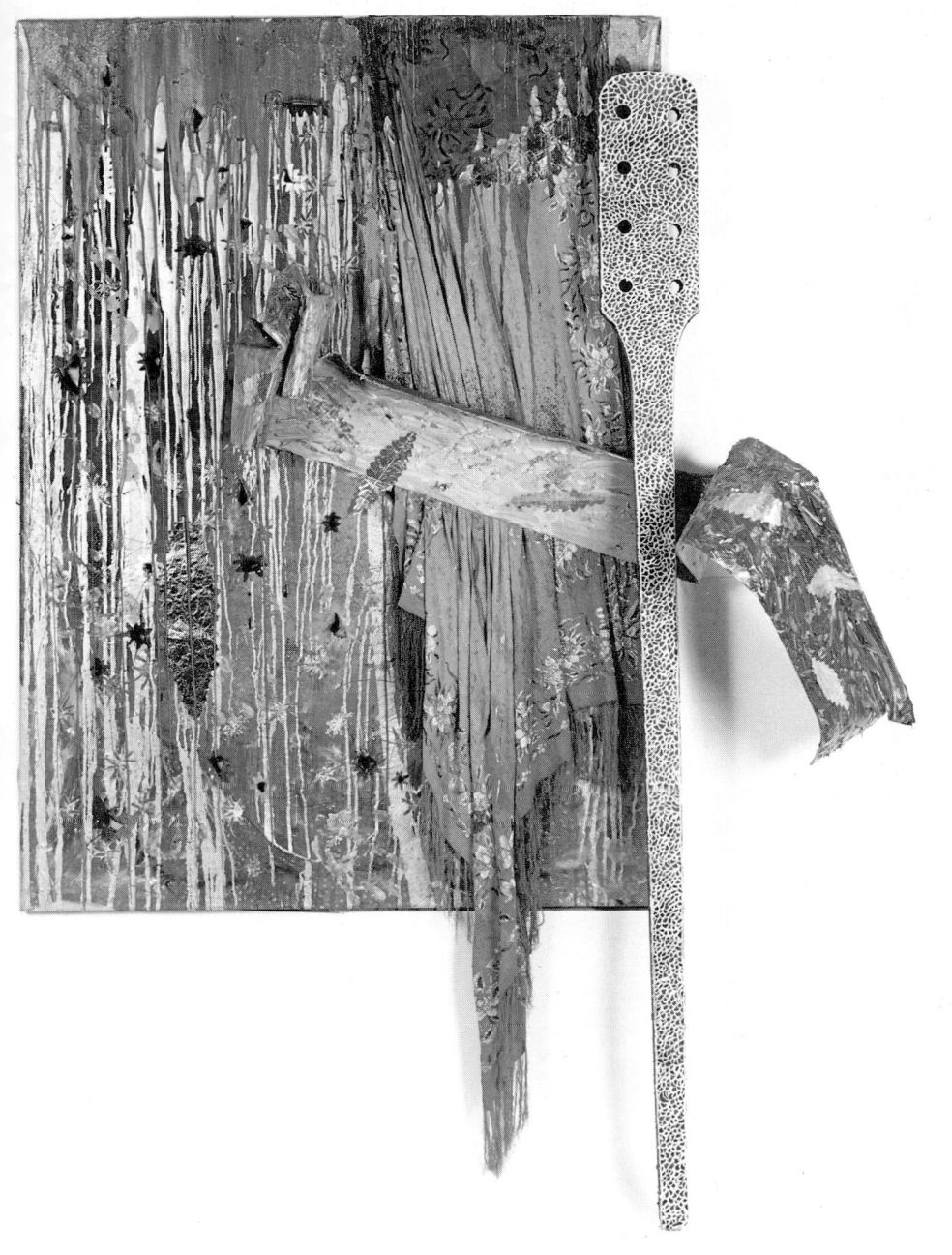

Michael Buthe: *Lucrezia Borgia*, 1981

Collections:

Kunstmuseum, Dusseldorf; Kunstmuseum, Lucerne; Centre Georges Pompidou, Paris; Museum des 20. Jahrhunderts, Vienna; Museum der Stadt, Linz; Museum Ludwig, Cologne; Von-der-Heydt-Museum, Wuppertal; Stadtisches Museum, Ulm; Kunsthalle, Kiel; Nationalgalerie, West Berlin.

Publications:

By BUTHE: books—*Freunde/Friends*, Dusseldorf 1971; *Lukretia bagann damals gerade von der Kuste weg zu ziehen*, Zurich 1971; *Die Wunderlose Reise des Saladin Ben Ismael*, Cologne 1977; *Der Vortrag uber die Schonheit des absoluten Positivismus: le dernier Empire*, Essen 1980.

On BUTHE: books—*Deutsche Kunst: eine neue Generation* by Rolf-Günter Dienst, Cologne 1970; *Bis Heute* by Karin Thomas, Cologne 1971; *Michael Buthe: Le Dieux de Babylon*, exhibition catalogue box with pamphlets, Cologne 1973; *Michael Buthe: Tarahumaras*, exhibition catalogue, with text by Rolf Wedewer, Leverkusen, West Germany 1977; *Weich und Plastische/Soft-Art*, exhibition catalogue edited by Erika Billeter, Zurich 1979; *Michael Buthe: Die endlose Reise der Bilder*, exhibition catalogue, with text by Zdenek Felix, Essen 1980.

*

Chronologically, one could say that Michael Buthe's work has covered three areas: space, stories, journeys. Thematically these areas overlap and flow transparently into each other. The drawings of 1967–69 are almost all imaginary ground plans for spatial projects or designs for torn fabrics; whatever is revealed as "autonomous" work, as immediate in the level of perception of the figurative drawing, is seen from its starting point, a localization of a relationship game in which are woven particular experiences, or "stories" as Buthe calls them. Line movement is direct emotion and afterthought, and is experienced as process and recollection; in the drawing, objects are a deliberate "disturbance" and intentional permanent peculiarities which, as ciphers, express the object experienced. While Michael Buthe lived in his studio, it also shaped his world, and the many people who came and went were its protagonists. The fabrics, torn with delicate aggression, later sewn together and coloured with dogged tenacity, are, in the physical and psychical sense, a journey within the material itself.

The first Moroccan journey of 1970 brought about the invasion of colour. With it the points are switched for a considerable alteration in the expresion of adventure contained in Buthe's work. Travel introduced spatial expansion, colour transforms the drawing, indeed, often, by maintaining an intense significance, takes its place.

Work carried out since 1970 stands now exclusively in relation to several periods spent in Africa (Benin) and Persia.

An erupting consciousness of form and color produces simultaneously impressions sensed under completely new circumstances.

"Journey" becomes journey via myth; "stories" are stories of demons, angels, gods, and witch doctors. Buthe remains close to them because for him they are beings whose realm of experience he wishes to make his own. It is significant that Buthe does not use myth as an example, as a catch-phrase as it were "for a better future." He experiences it through people and transforms it into reality; and this capacity for experience is also found in his work, as in the scenery of "The God of Babylon" and "Zarathustra." Materials are brought together to evoke a crocodile or a ship; they are not there with a representative function but are primarily particular sculptural forms which the function of crocodile or ship approaches. The canvas stretched over a massive circular frame, coated with beeswax and scattered with splashes of gold, is picture/object *and* "sun"; the vast red-coloured fabrics are painting *and* firmament, roof of heaven and home; the rectangular structure built from strong branches, covered with wax and rose leaves, is sculpture *and* bed. In other words, the significance of the objects ensues first from something produced by the artist not in any particular context, even though they apparently fix seamlessly into it.

It is a great temptation to join, in words and in imagination, in the "journeys" of Michael Buthe, but one runs the risk thereby of considering scenery, objects, and drawings—which on their own mark out a time in boundless groups—too much under the aspect of his overwhelming sense of fantasy, fantasy which even throws out of balance the related mythologies which move very freely among themselves.

Michael Buthe's work is primarily a convincing performance of creative intelligence, born from a commitment which today can in no way be presumed to be self-evident.

—Jean-Christophe Ammann

BUTLER, Reg(inald Cotterell).

British. Born in Buntingford, Hertfordshire, 28 April 1913. Studied architecture, 1937; self taught in art. Produced first sculptures, 1920; worked as architect and industrial technologist, 1937–50; blacksmith, during the war, Sussex, 1941–45; full-time sculptor from 1950. Studio Master, Architectural Association, London, 1937–39; Lecturer, Slade School of Fine Art, London 1950; Visiting Artist, University of Leeds (Gregory Fellow), 1950–53. Recipient: Grand Prize, International Competition for Monument to "The Unknown Political Prisoner," London, 1953. *Died 23 October 1981.*

Individual Exhibitions:

1949   Hanover Gallery, London

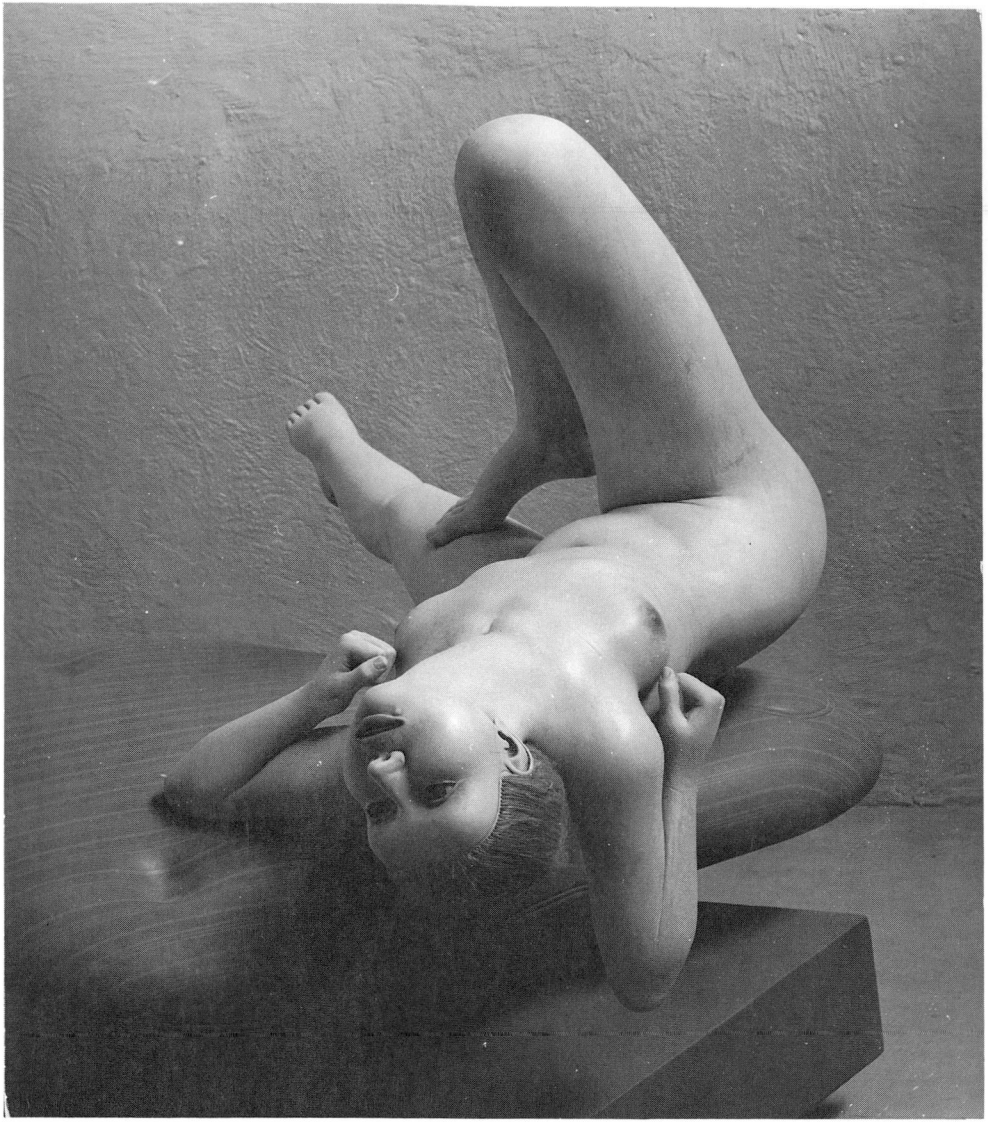

Reg Butler: *Nude*, 1977

1953	Curt Valentin Gallery, New York
1954	Hanover Gallery, London
1955	Curt Valentin Gallery, New York
1956	*Biennale*, Venice
1957	Hanover Gallery, London
	Kunstkring, Rotterdam
	Galerie Springer, Berlin
1958	Galerie Alex Vomel, Dusseldorf
1959	Pierre Matisse Gallery, New York
1960	Hanover Gallery, London
	Pierre Matisse Gallery, New York
	Kunstmuseum, Gothenburg, Sweden
	Gummessons Konstgalleri, Stockholm
1961	Galleria Obelisco, Rome
1962	Pierre Matisse Gallery, New York
1963	Hanover Gallery, London
	J. B. Speed Art Museum, Louisville, Kentucky
1964	New Metropole Arts Centre, Folkstone, Kent
	Queens Square Gallery, Leeds
1967	Welsh Arts Council Gallery, Cardiff
1973	Pierre Matisse Gallery, New York
1983	Galeria Freite, Caracas, Venezuela
1986	Tate Gallery, London

Selected Group Exhibitions:

1952	*Biennale*, Venice
1955	*Young British Sculptors*, Arts Club of Chicago (toured the United States and Canada)
1958	*Pittsburgh International*, Carnegie Institute, Pittsburgh
1961	*Biennale*, Middelheim, Antwerp
1964	*Contemporary British Sculpture*, Cannon Hill Park, Birmingham (toured the U.K.)
1974	*12 Views of Mankind*, MacRobert Centre Art Gallery, University of Stirling, Scotland
1977	*Greater London Parks Exhibition*, London

Collections:

Tate Gallery, London; Arts Council of Great Britain, London; City Art Gallery, Aberdeen, Scotland; City Art Gallery, Bristol; Konstmuseum, Gothenburg, Sweden; Galleria d'Arte Moderna, Venice; Museum of Modern Art, New York; Albright-Knox Art Gallery, Buffalo, New York; Museum of Fine Arts, Boston; City Art Museum, St. Louis, Missouri.

Publications:

By BUTLER: book—*Creative Development: 5 Lectures to Art Students*, London 1962.

On BUTLER: books—*The Hand and Eye of the Sculptor* by Paul Waldo Schwartz, London 1969; *Reg Butler*, exhibition catalogue, by John Russell, New York 1973; *12 Views of Mankind*, exhibition catalogue, by Douglas Hall, Stirling, Scotland 1974; articles—"Objectified Images" by E. Wolfram in *Art and Artists* (London), June 1974; "Obituary" in *The Times* (London), 24 October 1981.

Reg Butler came to public prominence as the winner of the International Sculpture Competition "The Un-

known Political Prisoner" in 1953, when, in fact, his model was destroyed by a protesting member of the public. His work at this time represented elongated, female figures, involved in strenuous energetic movements, sometimes in the process of dressing and undressing. There were similarities with the work of Giacometti, without any of that master's highly individual, stylised and disciplined view of mankind; there were also elements in common with the postwar English figurative school of sculptors, partly reacting to Moore and Hepworth's lyrical abstraction, in which the human form was used as the basis for emotional, nervous expression. Butler, however, was no tragedian, nor indeed a moralist. The early figure studies gave way to a more monumental, abstract style, ranging from the Calderesque wire constructions of the Unknown Prisoner maquette, to solid, heaving, cruciform bronze towers, which possibly reflected the influence of Henry Moore, whom Butler had assisted at one period.

In his *Concise History of Modern Sculpture*, Herbert Read linked Butler with what he termed the "vitalist tradition" (including Giacometti, Richier, Chadwick), which seeks images arising from the unconscious as the means of imposing order on chaos. It is a rather too generalised theme, since it could be said to apply to art of all periods and all styles. In the 60's Butler appeared in the forefront of British sculpture, having been presented at the Venice *Biennale* as early as 1952, which led to international attention. He also established a reputation as a teacher and theoretician, publishing *Creative Development: Five Lectures to Art Students* in 1962, in which he attempted to define the aims of modern art: "Recognition of the quality of things; their hardness and softness, heaviness and lightness, tautness and slackness, smoothness and roughness. Recognition of unities and similarities, rhythms and analogues, differences. The character of space, the definition of space, the penetration of things into space. The nature of illumination, its determination of what we see (as opposed to what we know otherwise than by vision from a static point in space). The news value of colour. The way our reading of experience is controlled by the means by which we perceive." This concern for the "essence" of things, the relationship between perception and creation, made Butler a remarkable teacher.

A common feature of British art history is the seeming impossibility of maintaining a public debate; the public, on the whole, is totally uninterested in aesthetic theories or social manifestos, and artists, even when in youth they show concern for group activities and theoretical debate, eventually revert to isolated individualism. The pattern, whether collectively or singly, is always the same. Similarly in English art is it rare to find the saintly or the disciplined, sacrifice for the sake of art and mystical experience; no Van Goghs, Maleviches, Mondrians, and the like. The English artist is usually a romantic poet, and at his worst a compromiser. In his last years Butler almost totally withdrew from the public art scene in England, rarely exhibiting, never publicly expressing his views. He abandoned abstract, didactic, public sculpture for the female nude, usually posed in strange positions, personal, erotic, even, some might say, self-indulgent.

—Charles Spencer

BUTTERFIELD, Deborah (Kay).
American. Born in San Diego, California, 7 May 1949. Educated at San Diego State College, 1966–68; University of California at Davis, 1969–73, B.A. 1972, M.F.A. 1973; studied at the Skowhegan School of Painting and Sculpture, Maine, 1972. Independent artist, concentrating on assemblages and sculpture, since 1973. Assistant Professor of Sculpture, University of Wisconsin at Madison, 1975–76, and at Montana State University, Bozeman, since 1979.

Recipient: Guggenheim Fellowship, 1980. Agents: Zolla/Lieberman Gallery, 368 West Huron Street, Chicago, Illinois 60610; O. K. Harris Gallery, 383 West Broadway, New York, New York 10012. Address: 11229 Cottonwood Road, Bozeman, Montana 59715, U.S.A.

Individual Exhibitions:

1969	Zolla/Lieberman Gallery, Chicago
1974	*2 Sculptors,* University of California, Berkeley
1976	Zolla-Lieberman Gallery, Chicago
1978	O. K. Harris Gallery, New York
1979	Hansen-Fuller-Goldeen Gallery, San Francisco
	Zolla/Lieberman Gallery, Chicago
1980	O. K. Harris Gallery, New York
	Open Gallery, Eugene, Oregon
	Hansen-Fuller-Goldeen Gallery, San Francisco
1981	*Jerusalem Horses,* Israel Museum, Jerusalem
	Arco Center for Visual Art, Los Angeles
1982	Mayor Gallery, London
	Dallas Museum of Fine Art, Texas
1983	Oakland Museum, California
1986	Contemporary Art Center, Honolulu

Selected Group Exhibitions:

1979	*Biennial,* Whitney Museum, New York
	The Decade in Review, Whitney Museum, New York
1980	*8 Sculptors,* Albright-Knox Gallery, Buffalo
	Painting and Sculpture Today, Indianapolis Museum of Art

Collections:

Whitney Museum, New York; Museum of Modern Art, New York; San Francisco Museum of Modern Art; Walker Art Center, Minneapolis; Hirshhorn Museum, Washington, D.C.; Metropolitan Museum of Art, New York; Israel Museum, Jerusalem.

Publications:

On BUTTERFIELD: books—*Painting and Sculpture Today,* exhibition catalogue, Indianapolis 1980; *Deborah Butterfield: Jerusalem Horses,* exhibition catalogue, Jerusalem 1981; articles—"Unique Balance of Realism, Art" by Thomas Albright in the *San Francisco Chronicle,* 15 June 1974; "Butterfield's Horses Surface Sensationally" by Alan G. Artner in the *Chicago Tribune,* 27 August 1976; "An Unusual Look at Nature" by Judith L. Dunham in *Artweek* (Oakland, California), 11 November 1978; "Sculptor Butterfield Plunges Deeper into a Substantial Body of Work" by Alan G. Artner in the *Chicago Tribune,* 18 May 1979; "Critic's Choice" by Franz Schulze in the *Chicago Sun-Times,* 17 June 1979; "Behold a Pale Horse (or Two)" by Kay Larsen in the *Village Voice* (New York), 28 November 1979; "Deborah Butterfield" in *Artnews* (New York), March 1980; "Explicit Horses" by J. Kelley in *Artweek* (Oakland, California), 19 December 1981.

*   *   *

The dominant theme in the work of Deborah Butterfield is the contemporary creative expression of the horse. She finds endless and new variations of this old motif using handmade steel, chicken-wire armature, and a variety of found materials which are all channelled to define the emotional qualities of individual horses. Even though the materials are rough, they, nevertheless, result in a most delicate definition of spatial gestures and underlying emotions of the individual horse with whom she identifies: "I first used the horse image as a metaphorical substitute for myself—it was a way of doing a self-portrait one step removed from the specificity of Deborah Butterfield."

Butterfield's horse sculptures are different from the classical image given to the horse in art. Hers constitute a completely new sculptural figuration which is a meaningful drawing in space with found materials. The theme carefully depicts specific animals in a specific moment with all the inherent individuality and vulnerability equal to that of a human being.

The artist's horses are expressions of a contemporary attitude toward life in general: "The horses in this exhibition are the most recent in a progression of work using found materials, all having their own 'history' and diverse visual qualities. These horses are no longer hollow shells but are built up from within and reveal the interior space. The gesture is continued and internalized while the posture is quiet and still. Action becomes anticipated rather than captured. Each horse represents a framework of presence which defines a specific energy at a precise moment."

Butterfield's horses have been interpreted as meditations on death, as symbols of suffering, and as signs of death and survival. These are fragmentary analogies of her work when considering the preciseness of an imagery which touches on human value and human endurance in terms of a gentle and delicate proposition of life in general.

Udo Kultermann

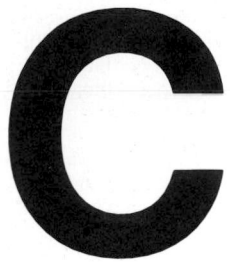

C

CADMUS, Paul.

American. Born in New York, 17 December 1904. Educated at Townsend Harris High School, New York, 1917-19; studied at the National Academy of Design, New York, with Charles Hawthorne, Charles Curran and William Auerbach-Levey, 1919-26; Art Students League, New York, with Joseph Pennell and Charles Locke, 1928. Worked for Blackman and Company advertising agency, New York, 1928-31; lived and worked with Jared French, who was an important influence, Majorca, and travelled in Europe, 1931-33; returned to the United States, and worked for the Public Works of Art Project, New York, 1933; designed costumes and set for the ballet *Filling Station,* New York, 1938. Vice-President, Arts Students League, New York, 1935. Recipient: Witkowsky prize, Art Institute of Chicago, 1945; National Institute of Arts and Letters grant, 1961. Member, National Institute of Arts and Letters, 1975; Associate Member, 1979, and Academician, 1980, National Academy of Design. Agent: Midtown Galleries, 11 East 57th Street, New York, New York 10022. Address: Post Office Box 1255, Weston, Connecticut 06883, U.S.A.

Individual Exhibitions:

1937   Midtown Galleries, New York
1942   *3 American Painters,* Baltimore Museum of Art
1945   Midtown Galleries, New York
1949   Midtown Galleries, New York
1956   Midtown Galleries, New York
1967   Palm Beach Galleries, Florida
1968   Midtown Galleries, New York (retrospective)
1976   Midtown Galleries, New York
1977   Midtown Galleries, New York
1979   *75th Birthday Exhibition,* Midtown Galleries, New York
1981   *Paul Cadmus: Yesterday and Today,* Miami University Art Museum, Oxford, Ohio (retrospective; travelled to the Ulrich Museum of Art, Wichita, Kansas; Gribbes Art Gallery, Charleston, South Carolina; and the William Benton Museum of Art, Storrs, Connecticut, 1981-82)
1983   Midtown Galleries, New York
1985   *Eightieth Birthday Celebration,* Midtown Galleries, New York
1986   Louis Newman Galleries, Beverly Hills, California

Selected Group Exhibitions:

1935   *Whitney Annual,* Whitney Museum, New York
1936   *Murals in Federal Art,* Corcoran Gallery, Washington, D.C.
1939   *Art in Our Time,* Museum of Modern Art, New York
1942   *20th Century American Portraits,* Museum of Modern Art, New York
1950   *American Symbolic Realism,* Institute of Contemporary Arts, London
1966   *Art of the United States 1670-1966,* New York Cultural Center
1972   *Collectors Anonymous,* New York Cultural Center
1975   *Work by Newly Elected Members,* National Institute of Arts and Letters, New York

1986   *Treasures from the National Museum of American Art,* Seattle Art Museum, Washington (travelled to Minneapolis, Fort Worth, Atlanta and Washington, D.C.)
1987   *Twentieth Century American Art,* Whitney Museum at the Equitable Center, New York

Collections:

Metropolitan Museum of Art, New York; Whitney Museum, New York; Museum of Modern Art, New York; Sara Roby Foundation Collection, New York; Fogg Art Museum, Harvard University, Cambridge, Massachusetts; National Museum of American Art, Smithsonian Institution, Washington, D.C.; Library of Congress, Washington, D.C.; J. B. Speed Art Museum, Louisville, Kentucky; Georgia Museum of Art, Atlanta; Los Angeles County Museum of Art.

Publications:

By CADMUS: book—*Ballet Alphabet: A Primer for Laymen,* with Lincoln Kirstein, New York 1939.

On CADMUS: books—*Art U.S.A. Now,* edited by Nordness, Lucerne 1962; *Paul Cadmus: Prints and Drawings* by Una E. Johnson, New York, 1968; *Paul Cadmus: Yesterday and Today,* exhibition catalogue, by Philip Eliasoph, Oxford, Ohio 1981; *Paul Cadmus* by Lincoln Kirstein, New York 1984; articles—"Paul Cadmus: Enfant Terrible" by Harvey Salpeter in *Esquire* (Chicago), July 1937; "Paul Cadmus: Etcher" by Childe Reece in *Magazine of Art* (New York), November 1937; "Paul Cadmus of Navy Fame Has His First Art Show" in *Life* (New York), March 1937; "Paul Cadmus Continues" by Ralph Pomeroy in *After Dark* (New York), December 1970; "The Figure Drawings of Paul Cadmus" by Diane Casella Hines in *American Artist* (New York), November 1972; "Profile on Paul Cadmus" by Raymond J. Steiner in *Art Times* (Woodstock, New York), May 1986; "Paul Cadmus" in *American Artist* (New York), February 1987; film—*Paul Cadmus: Enfant Terrible at 80* by David Sutherland, 1984.

*

A poet is not expected to give an exegesis of a poem. I don't think that a painter should do one of a painting. (*Aims* differ with each work.) I have made statements in the past, now I know better. Let art majors, art historians, etc. say their says.

In 1987 a continuing aim is clarity, a clarity that does not preclude mystery but does eschew mystification; also a technique that is delicate, precise and unobtrusive—no matter what the subject matter be.

—Paul Cadmus

*

Before he was 10 years old, Paul Cadmus had decided to become an artist. Although he produced a number of paintings in the 1930's and 40's, it is an interest in drawing which began as a teenager that Cadmus has sustained throughout his career. Working in a tightly rendered style, using masses of figures in motion and perspective schemes akin to those of the Italian Renaissance, Cadmus concentrated on contemporary social issues in his paintings, drawings, and etchings. The effects of densely populated city life on human behavior particularly interested the artist during the 1930's, and he chose to paint social interaction among the sexually promising.

A scandal arose in 1934 when a Cadmus painting, "The Fleet's In!," attracted negative attention from the U.S. Navy. Done as a Public Works of Art Project, "The Fleet's In!" depicted sailors smoking, drinking, and carousing with women who were behaving similarly. The Navy was outraged by Cadmus' satirical view and denounced the painting as "undignified, sordid, and depraved." Newspapers nationwide covered the incident. Cadmus, wise to the ways of Renaissance artists in pre-photography days, made an etching of the painting, pulled 50 prints, and thereby disseminated the image through his own devices, a fortunate move since the painting itself was "misplaced." Cadmus was not deterred from satire and social realism, however, and went on to paint "Hinkey-Dinkey Parlez-Vous" and "Sailors and Floosies," perhaps his best known work.

In keeping with his interest in artistic concerns of the Renaissance, Cadmus occasionally painted in egg tempera, and when he turned primarily to drawing in the mid 1950's he again used Renaissance methods—light colored strokes on toned paper. Cadmus takes his drawing seriously, regarding it as a fulfilling discipline rather than a casual study. His style and content have changed, however. "To the Lynching," 1935, for example, shows a swirling mass of horseflesh and humanity at its ugliest, while more recent drawings emphasize a single nude figure, carefully modeled. The interest in muscular tensions and dramatic foreshortening remains although the view of humanity has grown gentler.

—Mary Stofflet

CAGE, John.

American. Born in Los Angeles, California, 5 September 1912. Educated at primary schools and Los Angeles High School, until 1928 (class valedictorian); studied piano privately, 1920-28; studied at Pomona College, Claremont, California, 1928-30; studied architecture, and piano under Lazare Levy, Paris, 1930-31; studied composition, under pianist Richard Bühlig, Los Angeles, and under composers Adolph Weiss and Henry Cowell, New York, 1931-34; studied counterpoint and analysis, under Arnold Schönberg, at the University of Southern California, Los Angeles, and at the University of California at Los Angeles, 1934; studied philosophy and traditional music of India, under Gita Sarabhai, and attended lectures on Zen Buddhism by Daisetz T. Suzuki, Columbia University, New York, 1945-47. Married Xenia Andreyevna Kashevaroff in 1934 (separated, 1945). Independent composer, painter, printmaker, and writer, since 1931; travelled to Paris, Biskra, Majorca, Madrid and Berlin, painting and writing poetry, also began to compose music, 1930-31; composed chromatic music, and became increasingly interested in percussion music and rhythmic structure, 1935-36; Composer-Accompanist, dance

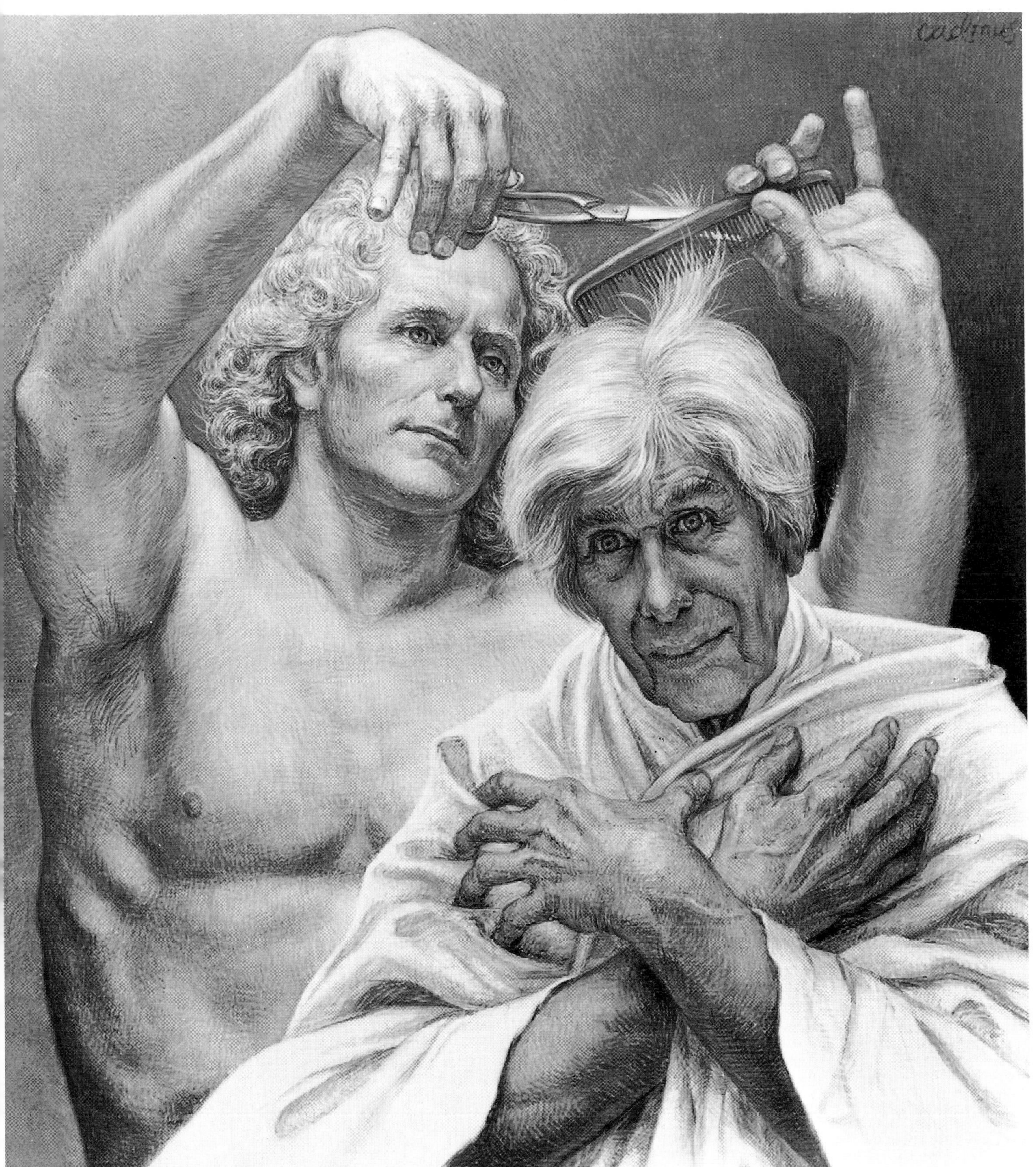

Paul Cadmus: *Haircut,* 1986

classes of Bonnie Bird, Cornish School, Seattle, where he met Merce Cunningham, then a student at the school, also composed and performed percussion music with groups and performed percussion music with groups that he organized, collecting various types of instruments, including "junk" objects, 1937–39; commissioned by CBS-Radio to create a score, *The City Wears a Slouch Hat*, with the poet Kenneth Patchen, Chicago, 1941; moved to New York and began a lifelong collaboration with Merce Cunningham, 1942; commissioned by the New York Ballet Society to score *The Seasons*, with choreography by Cunningham and sets by Isamu Noguchi, 1947; influenced by the thought of R. Buckminster Fuller, 1948; travelled to Europe, 1949; began collaboration with pianist David Tudor on many performances and projects, 1950; worked with Tudor, and composers Morton Feldman, Christian Wolff, and later, Earle Brown, to free sounds from memory, taste and fixed relationship to each other, making experiments and discoveries in the area of electronic music, 1950; influenced by Abstract Expressionist painters, 1950; introduced to the *I Ching* (Chinese *Book of Changes*), which became very important to the composition of his music and printmaking, 1951; moved with friends to a small cooperative community near Stony Brook, New York, where he became interested in nature, and concentrated on the study of mushrooms, 1954–72; made European concert tour with David Tudor, which influenced experimental music abroad, 1954; travelled to Europe with David Tudor, 1958; commissioned by the Montreal Festival Society to write major orchestral work, *Atlas Eclipticalis*, composed with astronomical charts, 1961; travelled to Japan on concert tour with David Tudor, 1962; travelled with Merce Cunningham on world tour, 1964; became interested in working with language: letters, syllables, words, and phrases free from syntax and meaning, 1969; became interested in lecture/performance for voice and tape, influenced by the writings of Mao Tse-Tung, 1971; moved back to New York, 1972; commissioned by Canadian Broadcasting Corporation to create a work related to the Bicentennial, *Lecture on the Weather*, 1975; commissioned by Seiji Ozawa and the Boston Symphony Orchestra to create a work for the Bicentennial, *Renga*, and *Apartment House 1776*, 1976; became intensely preoccupied with *Finnegans Wake*, 1976; invited by Kathan Brown to begin printmaking sessions at Crown Point Press, Oakland, California, 1978; devised way of "translating" any book into music, which he put to use on *Finnegans Wake*, 1979. Musical Director, Cunningham Dance Company, 1944–66, and President, Cunningham Dance Foundation, since 1965. Co-Founder, New York Mycological Society, 1962; Director, Foundation for Contemporary Performance Arts, since 1965. Visiting Instructor of Experimental Music, at invitation of László Moholoy-Nagy, Institute of Design, Chicago, 1941; Black Mountain College, North Carolina, 1948, 1952; New School for Social Research, New York, intermittently 1956–60; Darmstadt, West Germany, 1958; University of Hawaii, Honolulu, 1964; Fellow, 1960–61, 1970, and Associate, 1968–69, Center for Advanced Studies, Wesleyan University, Middletown, Connecticut; Composer-in-Residence, University of Cincinnati, 1967; Artist-in-Residence, University of California at Davis, 1969. Recipient: Guggenheim Fellowship, 1949; Award, American Academy of Arts and Letters and National Institute of Arts and Letters, 1949; Grand Honor, *International Biennial of Prints*, Tokyo, 1979. Member, American Academy of Arts and Sciences, 1979. Agent: Margarete Roeder Fine Arts, 545 Broadway, New York, New York 10012. Address: 101 West 18th Street, New York, New York 10011, U.S.A.

Individual Exhibitions:

1958 Stable Gallery, New York
1971 Galleria Schwarz, Milan
1977 *Renga*, Museum of Modern Art, New York (score)

1978 Museum Folkwang, Essen
      Städtisches Museum, Mönchengladback, West Germany
      Kunstverein, Cologne
1979 Kunstforum, Bonn
1982 *John Cage: Scores and Prints*, Whitney Museum, New York (travelled to the Albright-Knox Art Gallery, Buffalo, New York and the Philadelphia Museum of Art)

Performances:

1937 *The Future of Music: Credo*, Seattle (lecture)
1943 Museum of Modern Art, New York (concert of percussion music)
1944 Joint recital, Merce Cunningham Dance Company, New York
1950 *Lecture on Nothing*, Artist's Club, New York
1952 untitled "event," Black Mountain College, North Carolina (with Merce Cunningham, Robert Rauschenberg, David Tudor, and poets Charles Olson and Mary Caroline Richards)
1955 Joint recital, Clarktown High School, New York City (with Merce Cunningham)
1958 Concert for Piano and Orchestra, Town Hall, New York (retrospective)
      Lecture on Indeterminacy, at *World's Fair*, Brussels (30 "amusing" stories, read 1/minute)
      Water Walk, Milan (concert of theatre and music)
      Sounds of Venice, Milan (concert of theatre and music)
1963 *Vexations, With 840 Repetitions*, by Erik Satie, New York (director)
1967 *1st Musicircus*, University of Illinois, Urbana (simultaneous performances of as much unrelated music as possible)
1968 *Reunion*, Toronto (with others; game of chess on an amplified board in which moves activate sound systems created by various musicians)
1969 *HPSCHD*, Assembly Hall, University of Illinois, Urbana (multi-media audio-visual performance)
1970 *Musicircus*, at Paris Music Week
1972 *Mesostics* and *Mureau*, European tour (with David Tudor; latter is mix of writings of Thoreau, superimposed on electronic music of Tudor)
1974 *12 Haiku*, Stony Brook, New York
1975 *Lecture on the Weather*, Canadian Broadcasting Corporation studios, Toronto (chanted texts derived from Thoreau with film and recordings of breeze, rain, and thunder)
1976 *Renga* and *Apartment House 1776*, Boston (with Boston Symphony, conducted by Seiji Ozawa; incorporated live or recorded songs, calls, and hollers)
1978 *Roaratorio: An Irish Circus on Finnegans Wake*, IRCAM recording studios, Paris (uses several thousand sounds found in *Finnegans Wake*)
1981 *Empty Words*, National Public Radio, United States
      Compositions in Retrospect, at *Computer Music Conference*, Denton, Texas
      30 Pieces for 5 Orchestras, Pont-á-Mousson, France
1982 *Roarotorio*, Toronto
      several works, at *New Music America Festival*, Chicago

Selected Group Exhibitions:

1979 *International Biennial of Prints*, National Museum of Modern Art, Tokyo
1980 *Print Publishing in America*, Stedelijk Museum, Schiedam, Netherlands

Collections:

Metropolitan Museum of Art, New York; Museum of Modern Art, New York; Whitney Museum, New York; Museum of Fine Arts, Houston; San Francisco Museum of Modern Art; Stedelijk Museum, Amsterdam.

Compositions:

For piano—*Music for Xenia*, 1934; *2 Pieces*, 1935; *Metamorphosis*, 1938; *A Room*, 1943; *Experiences I*, 1945–48; *Ophelia*, 1946; *2 Pieces*, 1946; *Dream*, 1948; *In a Landscape*, 1948; *Suite for Toy Piano*, 1948; *Music of Changes*, 1951; *For M. C. and D. T.*, 1952; *Music for Piano I*, 1952; *7 Haiku*, 1952; *Waiting*, 1952; *Music for Piano 2*, 1953; *Music for Piano 3*, 1953; *Music for Piano 4-19*, 1953; *Music for Piano 20*, 1953; *Music for Piano 21-36, 37-52*, 1955; *Music for Piano 53-68*, 1956; *Music for Piano 69-84*, 1956; *For Paul Taylor and Anita Dencks*, 1957; *Winter Music*, 1957; *TV Koeln*, 1958; *Electronic Music for Piano*, 1964; *Cheap Imitation*, 1969; *Etudes Australes*, 1974–75; for prepared piano—*Bacchanale*, 1938; *Amores*, 1943; *Meditation*, 1943; *Totem Ancestor*, 1943; *A Book of Music*, 1944; *The Perilous Night*, 1944; *Prelude for Meditation*, 1944; *Root of an Unfocus*, 1944; *A Valentine out of Season*, 1944; *Daughters of the Lonesome Isle*, 1945; *Mysterious Adventure*, 1945; *3 Dances*, 1945; *Sonatas and Interludes*, 1946–48; *Music for Marcel Duchamp*, 1947; *2 Pastorales*, 1951; for voice—*20 Years After*, 1932; *Is It as It Was*, 1932; *At Eat and Ingredients*, 1932; *5 Songs for Contralto*, 1938; *Forever and Sunsmell*, 1942; *The Wonderful Widow of 18 Springs*, 1942; *Experiences II*, 1945–48; *A Flower*, 1950; *Aria*, 1958; *Solo for Voice 1*, 1958; *Solo for Voice 2*, 1960; *Song Books 1 & 2*, 1970; *Litany for the Whale*, 1980; *Empty Words*, 1981; for strings—*Nocturne for Violin and Piano*, 1947; *6 Melodies for Violin and Keyboard (Piano)*, 1950; *String Quartet in 4 Parts*, 1950; *Freeman Etudes*, 1977; for winds—*Sonata for Clarinet (Solo)*, 1933; *3 Pieces for Flute Duet*, 1935; *Music for Wind Instruments*, 1938; for harp—*In a Landscape*, 1948; for carillon—*Music for Carillon No. 1*, 1952; *Music for Carillon No. 2*, 1954; *Music for Carillon No. 3*, 1954; *Music for Carillon No. 4*, 1961; *Music for Carillon No. 5*, 1967; for various solos and ensembles—*6 Short Inventions*, 1933; *Solo with Obbligato Accompaniment of 2 Voices in Canon, and 6 Short Inventions on the Subject of the Solo*, 1933; *Sonata for 2 Voices*, 1933; *Composition for 3 Voices*, 1934; *3 Pieces for Flute Duet*, 1935; *She is Asleep*, 1943; *16 Dances*, 1951; *4'33"*, 1952; *59½ for a String Player*, 1953; *31'57.9864" for a Pianist*, 1954; *34'46.776" for a Pianist*, 1954; *26'1.499"for a String Player*, 1955; *27'10.554" for a Percussionist*, 1956; *Variations I*, 1958; *Variations II*, 1961; *0'00"*, 1962; *0'00" No. 2*, 1968; *Sound Anonymously Received*, 1969; *Score (40 Drawings by Thoreau) and 23 Parts*, 1974; *12 Haiku*, 1974; for orchestra and chamber orchestra—*The Seasons*, 1947; *Concerto for Prepared Piano and Chamber Orchestra*, 1951; *Concerto for Piano and Orchestra*, 1957–58; *Atlas Eclipticalis*, 1961–62; *30 Pieces for 5 Orchestras*, 1981; *Atlas Borealis (with chorus)*, 1982; for percussion (and electronic devices)—*Quartet*, 1935; *Trio*, 1936; *First Construction (in Metal)*, 1939; *Imaginary Landscape No. 1*, 1939; *Living Room Music*, 1940; *Second Construction*, 1940; *Double Music*, with Lou Harrison, 1941; *Third Construction*, 1941; *Credo in Us*, 1942; *March (Imaginary Landscape No. 2)*, 1942; *Imaginary Landscape No. 3*, 1942; *Imaginary Landscape No. 4 (March No. 2)*, 1951; *Imaginary Landscape No. 5*, 1952; *Speech*, 1955; *Radio Music*, 1956; *Cartridge Music*, 1960; *Music for Amplified Toy Pianos*, 1960; *Variations III*, 1963; *Variations IV*, 1964; *Variations VI*, 1967; *Variations VII*, 1967; *Variations VIII*, 1968; *Child of Tree*, 1975; *Branches*, 1976; *Renga*, 1976; *Apartment House 1776*, 1976; *A Dip in the Lake*, 1976; *Roaratorio, An Irish Circus on Finnegans Wake*, 1979; for magnetic tape—*Williams Mix*, 1952; *Fontana Mix*, 1958; *Music for "The Marrying Maiden,"* 1960; *WBAI*, 1960; *Rozart Mix*, 1965; for audio-visuals—*Water Music*, 1952; *Music Walk*, 1958; *Sounds of Venice*, 1959; *Water Walk*, 1959; *Theatre Piece*, 1960; *Variations V*, 1965; *Musicircus*, 1967; *Newport Mix*, 1967; *Reunion*, 1968; *HPSCHD*, with Lejaren Hiller, 1969; *Lecture on the Weather*, 1975. Many of these scores have been published by Henmar Press, New York; over 40 recordings of various works have been made since 1933.

Publications:

By CAGE: books—*Virgil Thomson*, with Kathleen Hoover, New York, 1959; *Silence*, Middletown, Connecticut 1961; *A Year from Monday*, Middletown, Connecticut, 1967; *Diary: How to Improve the World (You Will Only Make Matters Worse) Continued 1967*, pamphlet, New York 1967; *Diary: Part III*, New York 1967; *Diary: Part IV*, New York 1968; *Notations*, with Alison Knowles, New York 1969; *To Describe the Process of Composition Used in Not Wanting to Say Anything about Marcel*, Cincinnati 1969; *Mushroom Book*, with Lois Long at Alexander H. Smith, New York 1972; *Writings '67-'72*, Middletown, Connecticut 1973; *Writing Through Finnegans Wake*, New York 1978; *Empty Words: Writings '73-'78*, Middletown, Connecticut 1979; *Changes and Disappearances*, portfolio of prints, New York 1982; *On the Surface*, portfolio of prints, New York 1982;

The Mud Book, with Lois Long, New York 1982; articles—"Goal: New Music, New Dance" in *Dance Observer,* December 1939; "Chavez and the Chicago Drouth" in *Modern Music,* March/April 1942; "For More New Sounds" and "South Winds in Chicago" in *Modern Music* May/June 1942; "Grace and Clarity" in *Dance Observer,* November 1944; "Summer Music: The Parks" in *Modern Music* November/December 1944; "Dreams and Dedications of George Antheil" in *Modern Music,* January 1946; "East in the West" in *Modern Music* April 1946; "Forerunners of Modern Music" in *Tiger's Eye,* March 1949; "Contemporary Music Festivals Held in Italy" in *Musical America,* June 1949; "Satie Controversy" in *Musical America,* December 1950; "A Few Ideas about Music and Films" in *Film Music News,* January/February 1951; "Letters to the Editors: More Satie" in *Musical America,* 1 April 1951; "Manifesto on Music" in *Living Theatre Program* (New York), 1952; "Letter to Peter Yates" in *Arts and Architecture* (Los Angeles), November 1953; "Manifesto on Painting of Bob Rauschenberg" in the *New York Herald Tribune,* 27 December 1953; "Music Lover's Field Companion" in *United States Lines Parts Review,* 1954; "Experimental Music" in *The Score,* June 1955; "In This Day . . ." in *Dance Observer,* January 1957; "2 Pages, 122 Words on Music and the Dance" in *Dance Magazine,* November 1957; "To Describe the Process of Composition Used in 'Music for piano 21-52' " in *Die Reihe,* vol. 3, 1957; "Morris Graves," introduction to exhibition catalogue, Ogunquit, Maine 1957; "Erik Satie" in *Art News Annual,* New York, 1958; "Composition as Process: Interdeterminacy" in *Das Neue Forum,* vol. 8, nos. 4, 6, 8, 1958; "Composition as Process: Communication" in *The Village Voice* (New York), April 1958; "Roster on Varèse" in *Nutida Musik* (Stockholm), Fall 1958; "History of Experimental Music in the United States" in *Beiträge zur Neuen Musik* (Darmstadt), vol. 4, 1959; "Unbestimmtheit" in *Die Reihe,* vol. 5, 1959; "Lecture on Nothing" in *Incontri Musicali,* August 1959; "Lecture on Something" in *It Is,* 1959; "Form Is a Language" in *Artnews* (New York), April 1960; "On Robert Rauschenberg, Artist, and His Work" in *Metro* (Milan), May 1961, "Where Are We Going? and What Are We Doing?" in *Ring des Arts,* Summer 1961; "Where Do We Go from Here?" in *Dance Perspectives,* vol. 16, 1962; "26 Statements re Duchamp" in *Mizue* (Tokyo), September 1962; "Jasper Johns: Stories and Ideas" in *Jasper Johns* by Alan R. Solomon, New York 1964; "Nam June Paik: A Diary" in *Nam June Paik,* exhibition catalogue, Rio de Janeiro 1965; interview, with Michael Kirby and Richard Schechner in *Tulane Drama Review* (New Orleans), Winter 1965; interview, with Ilhan Mimaroglu in *Discoteca,* November 1965; "Diary: Emma Lake Music Workshop 1965" in *Canadian Art,* January 1966; "Letters to the Editor: Electronic Souls" in the *Village Voice* (New York), 20 January 1966; "Seriously Comma" in *Preuves* (Paris), March 1966; "Rhythm" in *Module, Proportion, Symmetry, Rhythm,* edited by Gyorgy Kepes, New York 1966; "Diary: How to Improve the World (You Will Only Make Matters Worse) 1965" in *Joglars,* vol. 1, no. 3, 1966; "A Lethal Measurement," interview, with Michael Zwerin, in the *Village Voice* (New York), 6 January 1966; "Diary: How to Improve the World (You Will Only Make Matters Worse) 1966" in *Paris Review,* Spring 1967; "Diary: Audience 1966" in *Arts: Planning for Change,* 1967; "Remarks about Merce Cunningham" in *Dance Perspectives,* Summer 1968; "John Cage," interview, with Richard Kostelanetz, in *The Theatre of Mixed Means,* New York 1968; "HPSCHD," interview, with Larry Austin, in *Source,* vol. 2, no. 2, 1968; "Soixante Résponses à Trente Questions," interview, with Daniel Charles, in *Revue d'Esthétique* (Paris), 1968; "How to Improve the World (You Will Only Make Matters Worse) 1968 (Revised 1969)" in *Tri-Quarterly* (Evanston, Illinois), no. 18, 1970; essay in *Sound on Paper: Music Notation in Japan,* exhibition catalogue, New York 1981.

On CAGE: books—*Zen and American Thought* by Van Meter Ames, Honolulu, Hawaii 1962; *Happenings,* edited by Jürgen Becker and Wolf Vostell, Hamburg 1965; *The Bride and the Bachelors: 5 Masters of the Avant-Garde (Duchamp, Tinguely, Cage, Rauschenberg, Cunningham)* by Calvin Tomkins, New York 1965; *The New Art,* edited by Gregory Battock, New York 1966; *Die Unvermeidliche Musik des John Cage* by Werner Bartsch and others, Kolb, Switzerland 1969; *The New Music,* edited by Gregory Battcock, New York 1970; *Print Publishing in America,* exhibition catalogue, Schiedam, Netherlands 1980; *John Cage: Scores and Prints,* exhibition pamphlet, New York 1982; articles—"Cage, Composer, Shows Calligraphy of Note" by Dore Ashton in the *New York Times,* 6 May 1959; "Figure in an Imaginary Landscape" by Calvin Tomkins in *The New Yorker,* 28 November 1964; "Poets and Kings" by Jill Johnston in the *Village Voice* (New York), 8 November 1967; "Social Concern" by Calvin Tomkins in the *New York Times Book Review,* 21 January 1968; "Cage—Wissenschaftlich Betrachlet" by Hans Rudolf Zeller in *Zur Theorie der Offenen Form,* edited by Konrad Boehmer, Frankfurt 1968; "The

American Avant-Garde, Part II: John Cage" by Richard Kostelanetz in *Stereo Review* (New York), May 1969; "John Cage: Some Random Remarks" by Richard Kostelanetz in *Denver Quarterly,* Winter 1969.

John Cage was born September 5, 1912, in Los Angeles. In his long career as composer he has encompassed many interests, delighted many people and enraged or antagonized a number of others. Best known as a guiding force of the avant-garde in America since the end of World War II, Cage's influence on composers, poets, dancers and painters has been as extensive as his work output has been prolific. Yet people at large are not so familiar with his music. His reputation for levity and eccentricity has served to obscure the seriousness of his inventions and perhaps limited the audience for his teachings.

Central to Cage's teaching is the view that art should imitate nature in its multiplicity and synchronous operations. He sees his music as a means of awakening people to the world around them; he has exhorted people to listen to the sounds, or noises of their everyday lives, as worthy of attention in themselves, not just as they might be structured in a composition, where they tend to lose their inherent self-sufficient value. One of Cage's most infamous pieces, called 4' 3", consisted of the performer or performers playing nothing—the sounds of the piece were the sounds of the audience and the environment. But Cage has deployed a number of methods in serving his phenomenological interests.

His earliest acclaimed invention was the "prepared piano"—a piano turned into a kind of percussion orchestra (played by one) by the placement of screws and other materials between the strings. By then, in the 40's, Cage's deviant concern for "noise" as proper material for music had been established. As a young man in California he had studied with Arnold Schoenberg whose traditional base for musical structure, dividing the whole into parts by means of tonality and harmony, provided a point of departure for the independent Cage. To include noises in his work Cage first devised rhythmic structures, which also resulted from his work with dancers. Since the early 50's Cage has worked closely with dancer/choreographer Merce Cunningham, as composer, mentor, friend and performer.

In the 40's Cage moved to New York, becoming interested in Zen Buddhism and Indian aesthetic theory. He studied with D. T. Suzuki at Columbia, an association that led him to his lifelong obsession with removing his ego (conscious taste and memory) from his work. His introduction to the *I Ching,* or *Chinese Book of Changes,* gave him the tool for implementing this removal of self, as he saw it, from composition. Since 1950 he has used the *I Ching* continuously, though not exclusively, to determine, by tossing coins, the sequence of events or specific order of sounds, and sometimes even materials, in his work. It is these "chance operations" that have impressed so many other artists in their own quests for the unfamiliar. Akin to them are the various methods of Indeterminacy by which Cage has left or instructed his performers to supply aspects of his compositions that he has not himself. Things left to the performer's discretion, however, are not to be confused with improvisation, which remains dependent on personal likes and dislikes, taste and memory, etc: rather they are determined by the performers in advance of performance, in the creation of the score.

During the 70's Cage united his chance methodology with his admiration for Henry Thoreau and James Joyce, creating literary Dada-like variations on the famous texts: *Walden* and *Finnegans Wake.*

He has also pioneered the use of tape and electronic music, and is known for producing the prototypical "happening"—at Black Mountain College in 1952.

—Jill Johnston

CALDER, Alexander.

American. Born in Philadelphia, Pennsylvania, 22 July 1898. Educated in primary school in Berkeley, California; studied mechanical engineering, Stevens Institute of Technology, Hoboken, New Jersey, 1915–18, M.E. 1918; studied drawing and painting at the Art Students League, New York, with Boardman Robinson, 1923–25, and at the Academie de la Grande Chaumière, Paris, 1926–27. Married Louisa James in 1931; children: Sandra and Mary. Served in the United States Navy, 1918. Worked as engineer, Rutherford, New Jersey, 1919; draftsman and engineer, West Coast logging camps, 1919–23; lived and worked in New York, 1923–30; contributed sketches to *National Police Gazette,* New York, 1925–26; joined cargo boat crew, travelled to England and Paris, 1926; worked on wood sculpture, produced miniature circus, Paris, 1927–28; first performance of *The Circus,* Paris, 1927; travelled in Europe and settled in Paris, 1930; member, *Abstraction-Creation* group, Paris, 1930–31; created first mobiles, Paris, 1931; purchased farm in Roxbury, Connecticut, 1933; house in Sache, near Tours, France, 1953, and spent much time there after 1960; added workshop, 1961. Set Designer, Martha Graham ballets, and *Socrate,* by Erik Satie, 1935; set designer, *Provocation,* by Pierre Halet, 1963; first performance of his ballet, *Work in Progress,* Rome Opera House, 1968; set designer, *Metaboles,* Odeon, Paris, 1969; *Eppur si muove,* opera, by Francis Miroglio, 1971. Recipient: First Prize, Plexiglass Sculpture Competition, Museum of Modern Art, New York, 1939; First Prize for Sculpture, *Biennale,* Venice, 1952; Outstanding Citizen Award, Philadelphia, 1955; First Prize, *Carnegie International,* Pittsburgh, 1958; Gold Medal, Architectural League of New York, 1960; Creative Arts Award, Brandeis University, Waltham, Massachusetts, 1962; Gold Medal, American Academy of Arts and Letters, 1971; Grand Prix, National des Arts et Lettres, Paris, 1974; Honors Award, 2nd Biennal Awards Program of the United States General Services Administration, 1975; United Nations Peace Medal, 1975. Honorary doctorates: Grand Valley State College, Allendale, Michigan, 1969; Stevens Institute of Technology, Hoboken, New Jersey, 1969; University of Hartford, Connecticut, 1973. Commandeur, Legion d'Honneur, 1968. *Died* (in New York) *11 November 1976.*

Individual Exhibitions:

1928	Weyhe Gallery, New York
	Salon des Indépendants, New York
1929	Galerie Billet, Paris
	Galerie Neumann and Nierendorf, Berlin
	Elizabeth Hawes Showroom, New York
	56th Street Gallery, New York
	Weyhe Gallery, New York
1930	Harvard University, Cambridge, Massachusetts
1931	Galerie Percier, Paris
1932	Galerie Vignon, Paris
	Madison Avenue Gallery, New York
	Julien Levy Gallery, New York
1933	Galerie Pierre Loeb, Paris
	Galerie Pierre Colle, Paris
1934	Pierre Matisse Gallery, New York
1935	University of Chicago Arts Club
	Pierre Matisse Gallery, New York
1936	Vassar College, Poughkeepsie, New York
	Pierre Matisse Gallery, New York
1937	Freddie Mayor Gallery, London
	Pierre Matisse Gallery, New York
1938	Pierre Matisse Gallery, New York
1939	Pierre Matisse Gallery, New York
1940	Pierre Matisse Gallery, New York
1941	Pierre Matisse Gallery, New York
	Wallace K. Harrison House, Huntington, Long Island, New York
	Marian Willard Gallery, New York
1942	Pierre Matisse Gallery, New York (with Yves Tanguy)
1943	Museum of Modern Art, New York

1944   Buchholz Gallery, New York
1945   Samuel Kootz Gallery, New York
        Buchholz Gallery, New York
1946   Galerie Louis Carre, Paris
1947   Portland Art Museum, Oregon
        Buchholz Gallery, New York
        Stedelijk Museum, Amsterdam (with Fernand
            Leger)
1948   Buchholz Gallery, New York
        Ministry of Education, Rio de Janiero (travelled to
            the Museo do Arte, Sao Paulo)
        Gallery of Contemporary Art, Washington, D.C.
1949   Buchholz Gallery, New York
        Margaret Brown Gallery, Boston
        Richmond Museum of Fine Arts, Virginia
1950   Galerie Blanche, Stockholm
        Massachusetts Institute of Technology, Cambridge
        Galerie Maeght, Paris
1952   Curt Valentin Gallery, New York
        Galerie Parnasse, Wuppertal
        Galerie der Spiegel, Cologne
        Galerie Otto Stangl, Munich (with Joan Miró)
1953   Frank Perls Gallery, Beverly Hills, California
        Wadsworth Atheneum, Hartford (with Naum Gabo)
        Galerie Christian Zervos, Aix-en-Provence, France
        Walker Art Center, Minneapolis
1954   Galerie Maeght, Paris
        Cahiers d'Art, Paris
1955   Curt Valentin Gallery, New York
        Kunsthalle, Basle
        Museo de Bellas Artes, Caracas
        Reid and Lefevre Gallery, London
1956   Frank Perls Gallery, New York
        Galleria dell'Obelisco, Rome
        Galerie Lucie Weill, Paris
        Musée Grimaldi, Antibes
1957   Kunsthalle, Basle
1958   Galerie Blanche, Stockholm (travelled to the Frank
            Perls Gallery, New York)
1959   Galerie Maeght, Paris
        Museo do Arte Moderno, Rio de Janeiro
        Stedelijk Museum, Amsterdam (toured Germany)
        Haus der Jugend, Wuppertal-Barmen, West Ger-
            many
        Kunstverein, Wuppertal, West Germany
        Kunstgewerbe Museum, Zurich
        Palais des Beaux-Arts, Brussels
1960   Frank Perls Gallery, New York
        Museo do Arte Moderno, Rio de Janeiro
1961   Museo de Bellas Artes, Caracas
        Frank Perls Gallery, New York
        Lincoln Gallery, London
        Stedelijk Museum, Amsterdam
        Moderna Museet, Stockholm
        Louisiana Museum, Humlebaek, Denmark
1962   Frank Perls Gallery, New York
        Tate Gallery, London
        Brook Street Gallery, London
        Galerie Blanche, Stockholm
        Galerie La Hune, Paris
        Musée de Rennes, France
1963   Galerie Maeght, Paris
        Frank Perls Gallery, New York
        Galerie Alex Vomel, Dusseldorf
1964   Frank Perls Gallery, New York
        Museum of Fine Arts, Houston
        Guggenheim Museum, New York (toured the United
            States)
1965   Musée National d'Art Modern, Paris
1966   Galerie Krugier et Cie, Geneva
        Galerie Maeght, Paris
        Frank Perls Gallery, New York
        Galerie Francoise Mayers, Brussels
        Institute of Contemporary Arts, London
1967   Frank Perls Gallery, New York
        Akademie der Künste, Berlin
        Middleheim Promoters, Antwerp
        Galleria Arco d'Alibert, Rome
1968   Frank Perls Gallery, New York
        Galerie Maeght, Paris
        Wittenborn Gallery, New York
        Dayton's Gallery 12, Minneapolis
        Maison de la Culture, Bourges, France (travelled to
            Musée des Augustins, Toulouse)

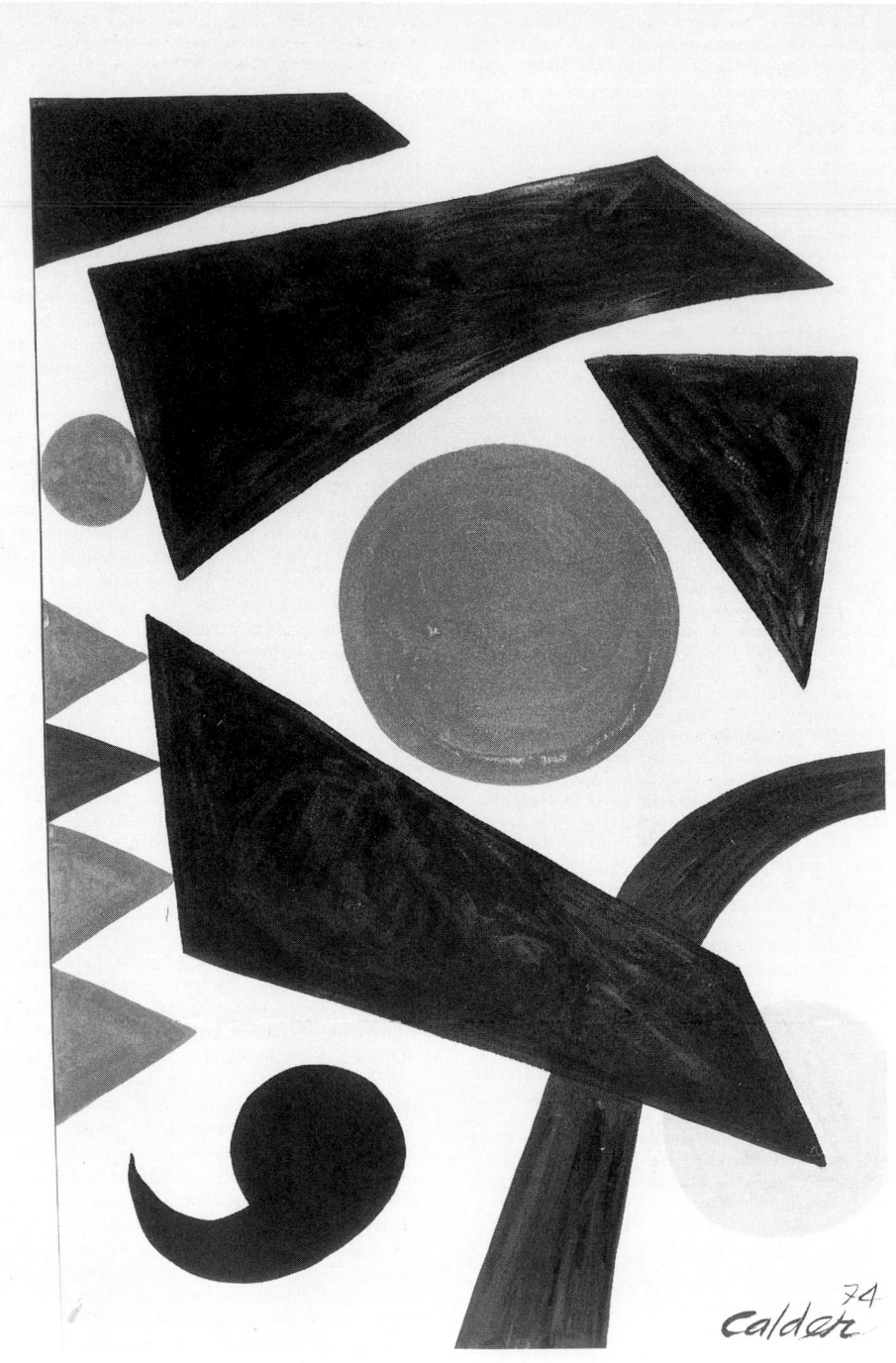

Alexander Calder: *The River—Chicago*, **1974** Courtesy Museum of Contemporary Art, Chicago

Art et Culture Festival, Noisy-le-Sec, France
1969   Frank Perls Gallery, New York
        Gimpel Fils Gallery, London
        Fundacion Eugenio Mendoza, Caracas
        Fondation Maeght, St. Paul de Vence, France (trav-
            elled to Louisiana Museum, Humlebaek, Den-
            mark)
        Grand Rapids Museum, Michigan
        Donald Morris Gallery, Detroit
        Grand Valley State College, Allendale, Michigan
        Museum of Modern Art, New York
1970   Long Beach Museum of Art, California (travelled to
            San Diego and Phoenix, Arizona)
        Frank Perls Gallery, New York
        Galerie Blanche, Stockholm
        Chateau de Ratilly, Treigny, France (with Jean Ba-
            zaine)
        Kovler Gallery, Chicago

1971   Frank Perls Gallery, New York
        Galleria dell'Obelisco, Rome
        Galerie Maeght, Paris
        American Academy of Arts and Letters, New York
        Whitney Museum, New York (toured the United
            States)
        Studio Marconi, Milan
        Musée Toulouse Lautrec, Albi, France (travelled to
            the Maison des Arts et Loisirs, Sochaux, France)
        Taft Museum, Cincinnati, Ohio
        Society of the 4 Arts, Palm Beach, Florida (with
            Louise Nevelson and David Smith)
        Brook Street Gallery, London
        Galerie d'Art Moderne, Basle
        John Berggruen Gallery, San Francisco
        Museo Nacional de Belas Artes, Buenos Aires
1972   Leonard Hutton Gallery, New York
        Frank Perls Gallery, New York

Galerie Veerière, Paris
Sala Pelaires, Palma de Majorca
Galerie Bollack, Strasbourg
Fuji Television Company Gallery, Tokyo (with Joan Miró; travelled to Galerie Beyeler, Basle)
1973   Frank Perls Gallery, New York
Galerie Maeght, Paris
Kunsthalle, Bielefeld, West Germany
Galerie T. Roussel, Perpignan, France
Palais des Beaux-Arts, Charleroi, Belgium
Detroit Institute of Arts
University of Hartford, Connecticut
Galleria Delta, Rome
Sala Gaspar, Barcelona
Guggenheim Museum, New York
Galerie Maeght, Zurich
Whitney Museum, New York (with Louise Nevelson and David Smith)
1974   Frank Perls Gallery, New York
Esther Robles Gallery, Los Angeles
Katonah Gallery, New York
Centre Culturel de St. Pierre des Corps, France
Galerie Jeanne Albeille, Toulouse
Musée Municipal, Cluny, France
Calder Festival, Chicago
Museum of Contemporary Art, Chicago
Galerie Cour St. Pierre, Geneva
Galerie Denise René-Hans Meyer, Dusseldorf
1975   Frank Perls Gallery, New York
Galerie Maeght, Paris
Pace Gallery, New York
Haus der Kunst, Munich (travelled to the Kunsthaus, Zurich)
Galerie Parallele, Geneva
Center for the Arts Gallery, Wesleyan University, Middletown, Connecticut (toured the United States)
Bhirasi Institute of Modern Art, Bangkok
Mitchell Sewall Gallery, New York
1976   Frank Perls Gallery, New York
Pennsylvania Academy of Fine Arts, Philadelphia
Calder Festival, Philadelphia
Makler Gallery, Philadelphia
Whitney Museum, New York (toured the United States)
1977   Margaret Fisher Gallery, London
1978   Centre Georges Pompidou, Paris
1980   Kettles Yard, Cambridge, England
1981   Manor Gallery and Waddington Galleries, London
Whitney Museum, New York
1984   Whitney Museum, New York

Selected Group Exhibitions:

1927   *Salon des Humoristes,* Paris
1929   *Salon des Indépendants,* Paris
1934   *Art in Our Time,* Museum of Modern Art, New York
1938   *Trois Siècles d'Art aux Etats-Unis,* Jeu de Paume, Paris
1952   *Biennale,* Venice
1958   *Carnegie International,* Carnegie Institute, Pittsburgh
1964   *Documenta 3,* Kassel, West Germany
1966   *Trois Siècles de Tapisseries,* Gobelins and Centre Municipal, Toulouse

Collections:

Metropolitan Museum of Art, New York; Museum of Modern Art, New York; Addison Gallery of American Art, Andover, Massachusetts; Philadelphia Museum of Art; Museum of Fine Arts, Dallas; Stedelijk Museum, Amsterdam; National Museum, Stockholm; Louisiana Museum, Humlebaek, Denmark; Musee National d'Art Moderne, Paris; Neue Nationalgalerie, Berlin.
Commissioned sculptures in public plazas and buildings in Europe and the United States.

Publications:

By CALDER: books—*Animal Sketching,* New York 1926, 1973; *Fables of Aesop,* Paris 1931, New York 1967; *Calder's Circus,* New York 1964; *An Autobiography with Pictures,* New York 1966; *Calder at the Zoo,* Washington, D.C. 1974; illustrated books—*3 Young Rats,* edited by James Johnson Sweeney, New York 1944; *The Rhyme of the Ancient Mariner* by Samuel Taylor Coleridge, New York 1946; *Jean de la Fontaine's Selected Fables,* New York 1948; *A Bestiary,* edited by Richard Wilbur, New York 1955; *Fêtes,* with Jacques Prévert, New York 1955, Paris 1971; *La Proue de la Tables* by Yves Elleouet, Paris 1967; *Santa Claus* by D. Jon Grossman, Paris 1974; article—"What Abstract Art Means to Me" in *Museum of Modern Art Bulletin* (New York), 1951; ballet—*Work in Progress,* 1968.

On CALDER: books—*Alexander Calder* by James Johnson Sweeney, New York 1951; *The Changing Forms of Art* by Patrick Heron, London 1955; *Essays in Aesthetics* by Jean Paul Sartre, New York 1963; *Alexander Calder,* exhibition catalogue, by Jean Cassou, Paris 1965; *Calder: A Study of the Works* by H. H. Arnason and Pedro E. Guerraro, Princeton, New Jersey 1966; *Calder: Mobiles and Stabiles* by Michel Ragon, New York and Paris 1967; *Calder* by Peter Bellow, Dusseldorf 1969; *Alexander Calder: A Pictorial Essay* by Bernice Winslow Mancewitz, Grand Rapids, Michigan 1969; *Calder* by James Johnson Sweeney, Paris 1971; *Calder's Circus,* edited by Jean Lipman and Nancy Foot, New York 1972; *Hommage to Alexander Calder,* edited by G. di San Lazzaro, special edition of *20th Siècle* (Paris), 1972; *Calder,* exhibition catalogue, New York 1984; *Alexander Calder and His Magic Mobiles* by Jean Lipman and Margaret Aspinall, London 1987; films—*Alexander Calder,* directed by Hans Aerlis, Berlin 1929; *Alexander Calder: Sculpture and Constructions* by Agnes Rindge Claflin, New York 1944; *Dreams That Money Can Buy* by Hans Richter, New York 1948; *Works of Calder* by Burgess Meredith, New York 1951; *Cirque Calder* by Carlos Vilardebo, Paris 1961; *Alexander Calder: From the Circus to the Moon* by Hans Richter, New York 1963; *Mobiles* by Carlos Vilardebo, Paris 1966; *The Great Sail* by Robert Gardner, New York 1966; *Alexander Calder: The Creation of a Stabile,* New York 1967; *Calder: un Portrait* by Charles Chaboud, Paris 1969; *Les Gouaches de Sandy* by Carlos Viladebo, Paris 1973.

*

There seems to be something peculiarly American about the combination in Alexander Calder of Yankee humor, pioneering inventiveness, down-to-earth tinkering, and pie-in-the-sky poetry. The playful, the practical, the dare-devil originality have deepened and broadened throughout his long career into a body of sculpture that stands high in the range of "delectable mountains" (e. e. cummings' phrase) thrown up by sculptors in our time.

The son of a distinguished academic sculptor, Calder caught the imagination of the *avant-garde* in Paris before the Second World War with his mad, funny, touching sinister, lyrical little circus—a hodge podge of wires, wheels, string, cloth with which he put on a show that revealed all his best qualities—or nearly all: his genius for capturing the individuality of things—a horse or clown or high wire performer—along with his fascination for the way things move.

Somewhere along the way his interest in movement lead to the creation of sculptures that move. Dubbed "mobiles," they have found their way into the mainstream of 20th century art. Usually painted in bold, basic colours—black, red and white is a favorite combination—they turn, bob and rotate to the whims of the slightest wind, natural or man-made. Some of them play tunes as well, either unexpectedly or by design: one work has a gong so arranged that it is the climax to the rotating "petals" as they wind or unwind.

These works are rather like trees with their "leaves" and "twigs," their extending "branches" and "limbs." Another series, the paradox-opposite one might say, are static as stone. Understandably called "stabiles," they resemble inanimate crabs or spiders, their large forms arching like claws or legs. These latter works have attained very large scale—as much as fifty feet or more in height—and have a grand, heroic effect. No wonder they have found their way into public squares and plazas.

No wonder either that Calder painted a series of actual airplanes—objects that move on a grand scale. It seems both logical and inevitable.

—Ralph Pomeroy

CALDERARA, Antonio.
Italian. Born in Abbiategrasso, 28 October 1903. Studied engineering at the Politecnico, Milan, 1921–24. Served as a corporal in the Infantry Battalion, Rome, 1924–25. Married Carmela Finnati in 1933. Full-time painter from 1926; first abstract works, 1959. Recipient: Gold Medal, Ente Provinciale del Turismo di Novata, 1974. *Died* (in Vacciago) *27 June 1978.*

Individual Exhibitions:

1923   Alberto Maulini, Vacciago, Italy
1933   Nuova Vita, Milan
1934   Galleria Bolaffio, Milan
1944   Galleria Como, Italy
1947   Galleria della Spiga, Milan
1948   Galleria Del Camino, Milan
1949   Galleria del Grattecielo, Legnano, Italy
1950   Instituto di Cultura Italiana, Lisbon
1953   Galleria Obelisco, Rome
1955   Schettini Galleries, New York
Galleria Spotorno, Milan
1956   Galleria Campana, Milan
1960   Studio F., Ulm-Doneau, West Germany
Galleria Gruppo Enne, Padua
1961   Galerie Charles Lienhard, Zurich
1962   Galleria Cadario, Milan
1963   Galleria Gavana, Trieste
Galleria Gritti, Venice
1964   Galleria Levi, Milan
Galleria La Polena, Genoa
1965   2000 Galleria d'Arte, Bologna
Centro Proposte, Florence
Museo d'Arte Moderna, Rio de Janeiro
Cenobio di Milano, Milan
Op Art Galerie, Esslingen, West Germany
Galerie 132, Krefeld, West Germany
Studio Und, Munich
1966   Galerie H., Hannover
Galerie Toni Gerber, Berne
Galleria Milano, Milan
1967   Studio Und, Munich
Galerie Toni Gerber, Berne
1968   Kestner Gesellschaft, Hannover
Kunst-Centrum t'Venster, Rotterdam
Stedelijk Museum, Schiedam, Netherlands
Documenta, Kassel, West Germany
Udstillingen Ved, Charlottenborg, Copenhagen
1969   Galleria La Polena, Genoa
Studio Und, Munich
Galleria Milano, Milan
Galerie Appelbaum, Karlsruhe
Ommagio a Calderara, Galleria Alberti, Omegna, Italy
Galerie Defet, Nuremberg
Galleria Barozzi, Venice
Kunstmuseum, Lucerne
Galerie Nachst St. Stephan, Vienna
Galerie Anne Marie Verna, Zurich
1970   Studio Berggemende, Frankfurt
Kozmopolitan Gallery, New York
Zimmergalerie, Detmold-Hiddesen, West Germany
Galerie Reckermann, Cologne
Galerie Berner, Stuttgart
Galerie M, Bochum, West Germany
Stadtische Galerie Die Fahre, Salgau, West Germany
1971   Galerie Nachst St. Stephan, Vienna
Galerie Anne Marie Verna, Zurich
Galerie Diogenes in Cubus, Berlin
Hofhauspresse Hans Moller, Hubbelrath, West Germany
Galerie Francoise Mayer, Brussels
Galerie im Taxispalais, Innsbruck
Aargauer Kunsthaus, Aarau, Switzerland
Galerie Denise René, Paris
1972   Galleria Milano, Milan
Galerie Anne Marie Verna, Zurich
Galerie M, Bochum, West Germany
Galerie Interior, Frankfurt
Galerie Ubu, Karlsruhe

Galerie Regio, Friburg Lorrach, West Germany
Galerie Drosche, Hamburg
Galerie Thomas Keller, Starnburg, West Germany
Galleria Peccolo, Livorno, Italy
Badische Kunstverein, Karlsruhe
Galerie Zodiaque, Geneva
Galerie Collection d'Art, Amsterdam
Kunstmuseum, Dusseldorf
Galerie Schottle, Munich
Studio Eyck, Heerlen, Netherlands
1973 Galleria Milano, Milan
Galerie Anne Marie Verna, Zurich
Galerie Thomas Keller, Starnburg, West Germany
Kunstmuseum, Dusseldorf
Galerie Schottle, Munich
Galerie Club 44, La Chaux de Fonds, Switzerland
Galleria Godel, Rome
Galerie Lens Fine Art, Antwerp
Galleria l'Incontro, Borgomanero, Italy
Salone Annunciata, Milan
Galleria Marlborough, Rome
Kunstmuseum, Solingen, West Germany
Galleria Schettini, Milan
1974 Galleria Schottle, Munich
Galleria Schubert, Milan
Studio V, Vigevano, Italy
Castello Svevo, Termoli, Italy
Museo de Arte Contemporaneo, Cuidad Bolivar, Venezuela
1975 Galleria La Polena, Genoa
Galleria Milano, Milan
Galerie Anne Marie Verna, Zurich
Arte Contacto, Caracas
Galleria Pellegrino, Bologna
Piura Edizioni, Milan
Galleria E., Bolzano, Italy
Galerie Nouvelle Images, The Hague
Galleria de Arte Centro El Bosque, Caracas
Palazzo dell'Arengario, Monza, Italy
Galleria Team Colore, Milan
Galleria Grazia Bosser, Turin
1976 Galerie Reckermann, Cologne
Galerie Thomas Keller, Starnburg, West Germany
Annely Juda Fine Art, London
Kunstverein, Freiburg, West Germany (travelled to the Kunstverein, Brunswick, West Germany)
Stadtische Galerie, Villengen-Schwenningen, West Germany
1977 Galerie Schottle, Munich
Salone Annunciata, Milan
Museum of Modern Art, Bottrop, West Germany
Stedelijk Museum, Amsterdam
Museum des 20. Jahrhunderts, Vienna
Kunstcentrum Badhuis, Gorinchem, Netherlands
1978 Stedelijk Museum, Schiedam, Netherlands
Studio La Città, Verona
Ohio State University Gallery of Fine Arts, Columbus
Galerie Dorothea Loehr, Frankfurt
Galleria Martano, Turin
Palazzo Municipale, Novara, Italy
1979 Galleria La Polena, Genoa
Galleria Vismara, Milan
Galerie Bossin, Berlin
1980 Galerie Schottle, Munich
Galerie 44 Kaarst, Dusseldorf
Galleria Spriano, Omegna, Italy
1981 Studio La Città, Verona
Padiglione d'Arte Contemporanea, Parco Mazzari, Ferrara, Italy
Galerie Christel, Stockholm
Parco Massari, Ferrara, Italy
Studio La Città, Verona, Italy
1982 Wilhelm-Hack-Museum, Ludwigshafen, West Germany

Selected Group Exhibitions:

1929 *Gallery Group*, Galleria del Naviglio, Milan
1934 *Biennale di Brera*, Milan
1936 *Mostra Nazionale della Promotrice*, Turin
1945 *Esposizione Fondo Natteotti*, Milan

1948 *Biennale*, Venice
1956 *Biennale*, Venice
1962 *Moderne Italiensk Malerei*, Kunstbiblioteket Nikolay Kiske, Copenhagen
1966 *International Exhibition of Engraving*, Museum of Modern Art, Tokyo
1967 *Art and Movement*, Museum of Contemporary Art, Montreal
1969 *Les Grandes et les Jeunes d'Aujourd'hui*, Musée d'Art Moderne de la Ville, Paris

Publications:

By CALDERARA: illustrated books—*Tempo Spazio Luce*, music score, by Bruno Canino, Milan 1963; *Misura di Luce*, edited by Umberto Eco, Milan 1964; *Il Numero Cromatico* by Andries van Onck, Milan 1965; *Frequenze Ortogonali* by Carlo Guilio Argan, Milan 1965; *Sequenzen* by Herbert August Haseke, Munich 1968.

On CALDERARA: books—*Antonio Calderara* by Rafaello Giolli, Milan 1946; *Antonio Calderara* by Giorgio Nicodemi, Milan 1947; *Antonio Calderara: Disegni* by Agnoldomenico Pica, Milan 1955; *Antonio Calderara e Gruppo I* by Guilio Carlo Argan, Milan 1966; *Omaggio a Calderara*, exhibition catalogue, by Reimer Jochims, Starnburg, West Germany 1972; *Gli Acquerelli di Antonio Calderara* by Carlo Belloli, Milan 1975; *Antonio Calderara: Acquerelli dal 1958 al 1975* by Tommaso Trini, Milan 1975; *Antonio Calderara*, exhibition catalogue, by Bernhard Holezzek, Freiburg, West Germany 1976; *Antonio Calderara 1903-1978* by Friedrich W. Heckmanns, Cologne 1982.

Though he held his first exhibition in 1923, it was not until 1959 that Antonio Calderara made his first abstract painting: he exhibited it in the following year. It is perhaps significant that in the intervening years the lists of his shows have lengthened with an almost equal division of venues between his native Italy and Germany and Switzerland. His popularity in the latter two countries is readily understandable in the light of his style and format.

In appearance these works bear a strong affinity to those of Josef Albers, the German-born painter whose apt phrase, "homage to the square," summarized his work. The selection of the colour field that set the mood of paintings and watercolours was for Calderara the dominant effect. His choice of body hue was usually on the warm side—quivering cadmium reds, strong yellows that by their proportions within square and rectangular boundaries set up equations of vibrating chords tuned to the scale of the areas covered and the distance separating them from the spectator.

Mostly small in format, the works took on their appropriate range of radiation when hung in juxtaposition on a gallery wall. In general, while the immediate response seemed to form a complete saturation from edge to edge, closer examination revealed the note of comparison, sometimes as a tiny square on the border deeper in tone than the even spread of the whole yet in its concentration echoing the dimensions of the larger ground. In other words, the suggestion of a paler halation of open rectangles overpainted by the general red gave more than a hint of Rothko's colour vibrations but within a rigid geometric base subtly subdued by the elimination of contrast. This marriage of emotional stimulation from colour fields of evocative hues and the classic ratio of height to width was consummated by the nicely judged relationships of size with the carrying power of the design.

Eminently rare for his capacity of self-generated warmth and balance in small formats, Calderara is a supreme miniaturist in the abstract idiom whose calculations are as precise in terms of visual engineering. Strictly speaking, nothing is left to chance, for all that was placed on the canvas or on paper was preceded by the artist's experimental testing of values—the vibratory sensation of pigment surface obscuring interior straight edges by the slightest change in weight. Delicate though the differences are, Calderara's works maintain something ineluctably

Italian in their certainty of execution, preserving historic vitality through a high chromatic key and a sense of architectural order expressed in small and two-dimensional limits. Yet, by their projection of their quivering shadows in a given section of the spectrum, Calderara's paintings operate most powerfully through the variable and magic third dimension that radiates between their surface and the eye of the beholder.

—G. S. Whittet

CALZOLARI, Pier Paolo.
Italian. Born in Bologna in 1943. Studied at the Accademia di Belle Arti, Urbino, 1967. Married; has one child. Independent artist, Bologna, since 1967. Agent: Sonnabend Gallery, 420 West Broadway, New York, New York 10012, U.S.A. Address: Via San Felice 13, 40122 Bologna, Italy.

Individual Exhibitions:

1965 Sala Studio Bentivoglio, Bologna
1967 Sala Studio Bentivoglio, Bologna
1969 Galleria Sperone, Turin
1970 Galerie Sonnabend, Paris
Galleria Sperone, Turin
1971 Sonnabend Gallery, New York
Galerie Sonnabend, Paris
Modern Art Agency, Naples
1973 Galerie Skulima, Berlin
1975 Galleria de Domizio, Pescara, Italy
1976 Galleria Toselli, Milan
1977 Galleria Tucci Russo, Turin
1978 Galleria San Ala, Milan
1979 Galerie Jean und Karen Bernier, Cologne
Galerie Tucci Russo, Cologne
1980 Stanze, Genazzano, Italy
LP 220, Turin
Galleria Paludetto, Turin
Cantieri Navali/Luigi De Ambrogi, Venice
Galleria di Capricorno, Naples
1981 Galerie Eric Fabre, Paris
Galerie Eric Schurr, Stuttgart
1982 Galerie Knoedler, Zurich
1983 Galleria Luigi De Ambrogi, Milan
1984 Galerie de France, Paris
Galerie Bernier, Athens
Galerie Pakesch, Vienna

Selected Group Exhibitions:

1968 *Teatro delle Mostra*, Galleria La Tartaruga, Rome
1969 *Square Pegs in Round Holes*, Stedelijk Museum, Amsterdam
When Attitudes Become Form, Kunsthalle, Berne
1970 *Conceptual Art/Arte Povera/Land Art*, Galleria Civica d'Arte Moderna, Turin
1971 *Biennale des Jeunes*, Paris
1974 *Projekt 74*, Cologne
1975 *Americans in Florence/Europeans in Florence*, Long Beach Museum of Art, California
1978 *Biennale*, Venice (and 1980)
1981 *A New Spirit in Painting*, Royal Academy of Art, London
1986 *Aspects of Italian Art 1960-85*, Kunstverein, Frankfurt

Publications:

On CALZOLARI: books—*Calzolari*, exhibition catalogue, by Alberto Boatta, Bologna 1967; *Teatro delle Mostra*, exhibition catalogue, by Maurizio Calvesi, Rome 1968; *Documenta 5*, exhibition catalogue, Kassel, West Germany 1974; *Pierpaolo Calzolari*, exhibition catalogue with essay by Dieter Ronte, Vienna 1984; *Pier Paolo Calzolari*, exhibition catalogue with text by Denys Zacharopoulos, Paris 1984; articles—"Nuovo al Fabeto per Corpo e Materia" by Tommaso Trini in *Domus* (Milan), no. 470, 1969, "Pier Paolo Calzolari" by Germano Celant in *Studio International* (London), July 1970; "Pier Paolo Calzolari" by Gregory Battcock in *Arts Magazine* (New York), February 1972; "Pier Paolo Calzolari" by Denys Ropp-Zacharopoulos in *Artistes* (Paris), October/November 1980.

After some work in the field of "poor art," in which he showed his main interest in ephemera and in fairy-tales (some significant works of the period were "The Filter," "Welcome to the Angel" and "Horoscope," 1967), Pier Paolo Calzolari moved on to painting. His first works in this field date from the 1970's. He did not abandon the object all at once; it is present as dramatic "comment" both in and outside the painting. He adds to the materiality of the painting, so that his all-embracing spatiality is also full of existential meanings. But what emerges most of all is the grandeur of the surface, abounding in grotesque multicoloured material. There is a sort of love-hate relationship between the object, essentially poor, and the positively opulent painting, as if the artist were struggling against the imaginativeness of his experience. For Pier Paolo Calzolari, art proceeds by metamorphoses; it faces destiny rather than the project, so that his work is always somewhat unfinished. His art is above all possessed of a violent gesturality, which unites differing significances; enigmatic symbols of a vitality that breaks down the whole surrounding reality, which is constantly changing and so seems unpredictable. Thus the artist is the one who meets reality in the space of an essay open to the shifting play of the elements between object and painting. If in his "poor art" he was exalting the contradiction of the ephemeral, in his recent painting he demonstrates the deflagration of the material of art. His fulfillment is achieved only in the gesture, through which he completes the picture's destiny.

Calzolari's painting distorts itself. A material in expansion and contraction dramatizes its striking quality, which takes in also the space outside the picture. The material of painting consists of paints—soft, mellow paints, responding to the light. It is their coagulation that is informal. The material colours are firmly obedient to the urgency of the gesture.

In his big pictures Calzolari's creative gesture has a primordial fury which breaks up the material, and with it any possible figuration. The abstraction is powerful, incontrovertible, hermetically closed/opened. It brings out obvious surprise effects in the wide surface of the picture. Calzolari thus comes near to a painting made by continual, striking attacks which break down the growth of the abstraction. It is only in appearance that this approaches the informal. But Calzolari is not a post-informal artist, and he possesses a creative density too firm to be channelled into the flow of the new painting. If anything he is looked on as the initiator of a "diverse" materiality of painting. In fact, his work, at once noble and terrifying, shows how painting can be liberated (especially from the material point of view). A movement prevails on the surface that spreads out in all directions (interrupted only by external elements—a dagger, for instance, thrust into the canvas). Calzolari is thus a "visionary" artist who materializes the secret magma contained in the creative gesture.

—Italo Mussa

CAMPUS, Peter.

American. Born in New York City, 19 May 1937. Educated at Ohio State University, Columbus, 1955-60, B.Sc. 1960. Served in the United States Army, 1960-62. Associated with artist Robert Grosvenor; began informal art studies, New York, 1960-62. Worked as production assistant and film editor, with William Shatner, on the television series *For The People*, Plantus Productions, New York; *Trials of O'Brien*, with Peter Falk, Filmways Inc., New York, 1962-70. Influenced by the work of Ian Wilson, Charles Ross, Robert Smithson, Nancy Holt, Yvonne Rainer and Joan Jonas, New York, 1962-70. First art works, New York, 1970. Video Consultant, Education Department, Metropolitan Museum of Art, New York, 1970-72. Instructor, Massachusetts Institute of Technology, Cambridge, 1976-80; Rhode Island School of Design, Providence, 1982-83. Recipient: Guggenheim Fellowship, 1975-76; Advanced Visual Studies Fellowship, Massachusetts Institute of Technology, Cambridge 1975-76; National Endowment for the Arts Grant, 1976. Agent: Paula Cooper Gallery, New York. Address: c/o Paula Cooper Gallery, 155 Wooster Street, New York, New York 10012, U.S.A.

Individual Exhibitions:

1972	Bykert Gallery, New York
1973	Bykert Gallery, New York
1974	*Closed Circuit Video*, Everson Museum of Art, Syracuse, New York
1975	Bykert Gallery, New York
1976	Leo Castelli Gallery, New York
	Hayden Gallery, Massachusetts Institute of Technology, Cambridge
	Projects Gallery, Museum of Modern Art, New York
1977	The Kitchen, New York
	Ohio State University, Columbus
1978	Whitney Museum, New York
	Sarah Lawrence College, Bronxville, New York
	Atlantic Gallery, Boston
1979	Akron Art Institute, Ohio
	Paula Cooper Gallery, New York
	Protetch-McIntosh Gallery, Washington, D.C.
	Kölnischer Kunstverein, Cologne
	Neuer Berliner Kunstverein, West Berlin
1980	Centre Pompidou, Paris
1981	Paula Cooper Gallery, New York
	McIntosh-Drysedale Gallery, New York
1982	Paula Cooper Gallery, New York
1983	Paula Cooper Gallery, New York
	Hayden Gallery, Massachusetts Institute of Technology, Cambridge (with David Deutsch)
1985	Paula Cooper Gallery, New York
1986	Paula Cooper Gallery, New York
1987	Albright College, Reading, Pennsylvania (travelled to the Institute of Contemporary Art, Philadelphia)

Selected Group Exhibitions:

1973	*Circuit: A Video Invitational*, Everson Museum of Art, Syracuse, New York (toured the United States and travelled to the Kunstverein, Cologne)
1975	*Bienal*, Sao Paulo
1976	*Autogeography*, Whitney Museum, New York
1977	*Documenta 6*, Kassel, West Germany
1978	*Biennale*, Venice
1979	*Art on Paper 1979*, Weatherspoon Art Gallery, University of North Carolina, Greensboro
1980	*Lynda Benglis/Jon Borofsky/Peter Campus/Michael Hurson*, Paula Cooper Gallery, New York
1982	*PostMinimalism*, Aldrich Museum of Contemporary Art, Ridgefield, Connecticut
1984	*Content: A Contemporary Focus 1974-84*, Hirshhorn Museum, Washington, D.C.
1987	*Photography and Art 1946-86*, Los Angeles County Museum of Art (travelled to Fort Lauderdale, Florida; Flushing, New York)

Publications:

By CAMPUS: articles—statement in *Peter Campus: Closed Circuit Video*, exhibition catalogue, Syracuse, New York 1974; in *Studio International* (London), May/June 1976; essay in *Peter Campus*, exhibition catalogue, Cologne 1979; in *Studio International* (London), no. 1008, 1985.

On CAMPUS: books—*Peter Campus: Closed Circuit Video*, exhibition catalogue, with an introduction by Jane Harithas, essay by David A. Ross, Syracuse, New York 1974; *Video Art*, exhibition catalogue, by Susan Delehanty, Philadelphia 1975; *Peter Campus*, exhibition catalogue, Cologne 1979; *5 Artists, 5 Technologies*, exhibition catalogue, Grand Rapids, Michigan 1979; *The Elusive Image*, exhibition catalogue, Minneapolis 1979; *Peter Campus Photographs/David Deutsch Paintings and Drawings*, exhibition catalogue, with essay by Kathy Halbreich and Katy Klein, Cambridge, Massachusetts 1983; articles—"Video Is Being Invented" by Bruce Kurtz in *Arts Magazine* (New York), December 1972; "Fields: Peter Campus" by Bruce Kurtz in *Arts Magazine* (New York), May 1973; "Video Art by Peter Campus" by John Perreault in the *Village Voice* (New York), 11 October 1973; "Inference and Actuality" by Robert Pincus-Witten in *Projected Images*, exhibition catalogue, Minneapolis 1974; "Beyond Flashing Lights" by Mike Steele in *Art News* (New York), December 1974; "Epistemological TV" by Joseph Lorber in *Art Journal* (New York), Winter 1974-75; "Video: The Aesthetics of Narcissism" by Rosalind Krauss in *October* (New York), Spring 1976; "The Ins and Outs of Video" by Jeff Perrone in *Artforum* (New York), June 1976; "About Faces: The New Work of Peter Campus" by Roberta Smith in *Art in America* (New York), March/April 1977; "Galleries: A Dark Seriesof Portraits" by Benjamin Forgey in the *Washington Star*, 28 March 1979; "Inside Out: Peter Campus" by Ingrid Sischy in *Artforum* (New York), March 1985; "Peter Campus" by Hearne Pardee in *Arts Magazine* (New York), May 1985.

I work in both closed circuit video installations and video tape. The closed circuit installations include viewer participation where his/her image is projected in front of him/her in some altered state. This work concerns itself with projections and confrontation of self, light, space and accumulations in time. My videotapes generally have me performing some activity that continuously alters the image. These tapes are more concerned with narrative, utilizing questions of figure-ground, surface, illusion, time and space.

—Peter Campus

Peter Campus is an artist who knows how to create psychologically charged visual fields. After working in commercial films and television, he decided in the late 1960's to change careers and become an artist. Video remained the dominant concern during the 1970's. He produced both videotapes and video environments in which a superbly precise and efficient mastery of this electronic technique was channeled to the creative investigations of the perceptual and emotional politics of seeing and knowing the self. In each medium time is an active and aggressive element.

Structured episodically, the videotapes, though of short duration, took the individual as the subject. Many of them featured a deep, dark spatially ambiguous background before which close-ups of faces, often in emotively laden split and repetitive structures, were highlighted. "Three Transitions" (1973) and "East Ended Tapes" (1976), both six minutes in length, are examples. In the video environments, time is a direct factor of the viewing, which, in turn, depends on the presence and participation of the audience. Usually composed of a basic set-up consisting of one or more video cameras and infrared lights, projectors and monitors in a darkened room, they are closed-circuit installations, "closed" or activated by the viewer's entry into the boundaries of the designated situation. Once in a camera view, the viewer, in essence, the viewer's image, is the piece. Each environment/installation is designed to reveal different aspects of the complex relationship involving the self and the image of the self. The image of the self is manipulated, for example, in "Interface" (1972) to offer a confrontation between the projected video image and a reflected mirror image, and in "Num," "lus" and "aen" (1976-77) the imagery consisted of enlarged, expressionistically shadowed and inverted pictures of the viewer's head.

In 1979, a projected slide-piece signalled a turning away from video towards photography. This development was a natural one dictated by the work in response to a lessening interest in time and a growing interest in what Campus has called "tangible image."

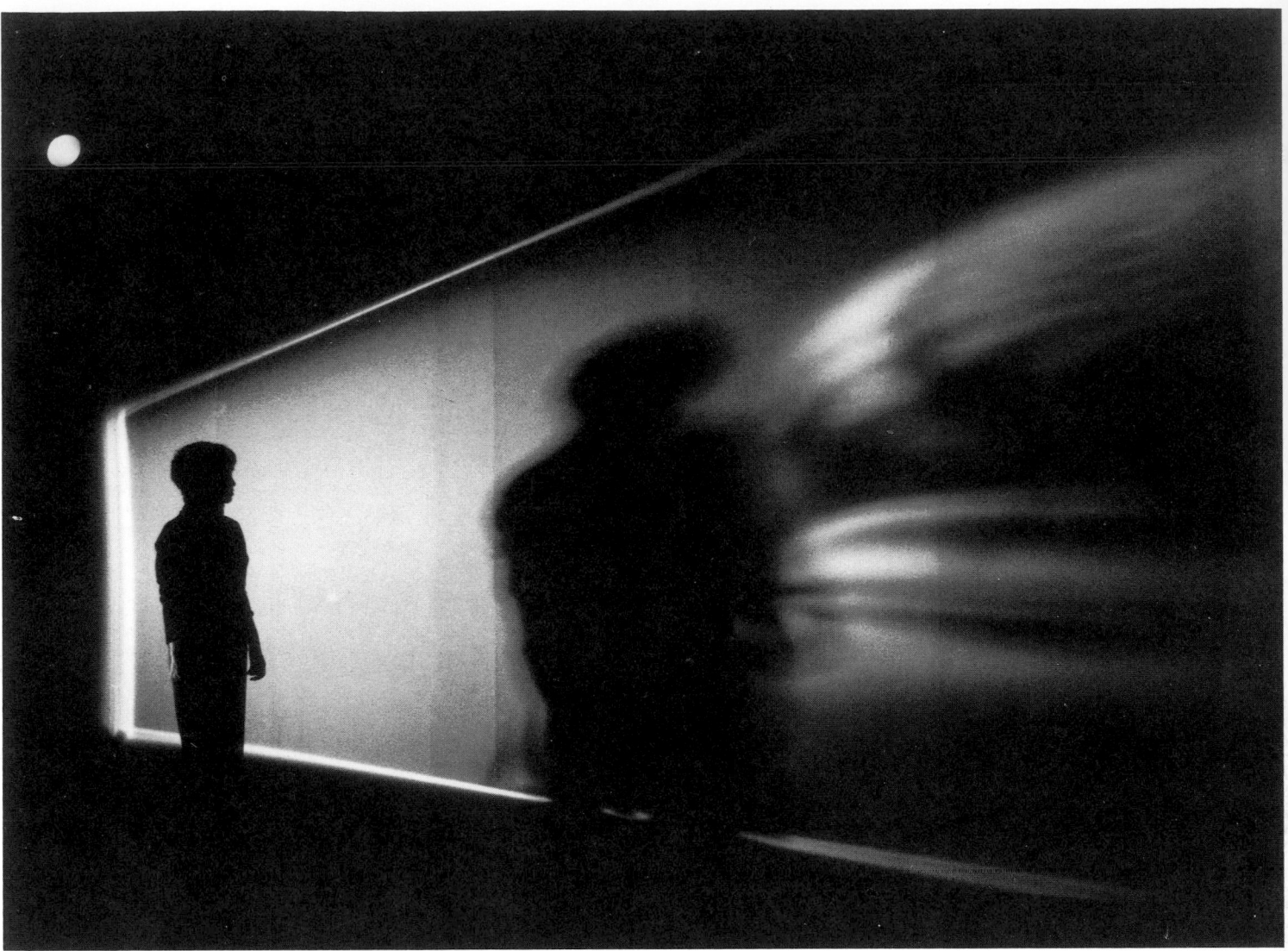

Peter Campus: *Mem* (closed circuit TV installation), 1974

Photography has been the central concern since 1980.

In the silverpoint photographs he has done of various landscape subjects, reality is being reconstituted in the concreteness of the illusion these images give. Campus' careful modulation of light and dark values allows him to create a composition that conveys the material essence of forms. In *Slow Tide* (1987), a close-up of a rock on a pebble-covered ground, the luminous intensity of the surface is suggestive of metaphorical concerns.

—Ronny Cohen

CANE, Louis.

French. Born in Beaulieu-sur-Mer, Alpes-Maritimes, 13 December 1943. Studied at the Ecole Nationale des Arts Décoratifs, Nice, 1961–64; Ecole Nationale Supérieure des Arts Décoratifs, Paris, 1964–68. Independent painter, Paris, since 1968. Co-Founder and Director of the review *Peinture*, Paris, from 1971. Agent: Galerie Daniel Templon, 30 rue Beaubourg, Paris 3. Address: 37 rue d'Enghein, 75010 Paris, France.

Individual Exhibitions:

1969 Galerie Givaudan, Paris

1970	Galerie Daniel Templon, Paris
1971	Galerie Yvon Lambert, Paris
	Galleria Francoise Lambert, Milan
1972	Galerie Yvon Lambert, Paris
1973	Galerie Daniel Templon, Paris
	Institute of Contemporary Arts, London
	Galleria Daniel Templon, Milan
	Galleria Lia Rumma, Naples
1974	Galerie Rudolf Zwirner, Cologne
	Galleria del Cortile, Rome
1975	Galerie D., Brussels
	Galerie Daniel Templon, Paris
	Galleria Daniel Templon, Milan
	Galerie Konrad Fischer, Dusseldorf
1976	Galerie Bischofberger, Zurich
	Louisiana Museum, Humlebaek, Denmark
	Musée d'Art Contemporain, Montreal
	Kunstverein, Frankfurt
1977	Galerie Daniel Templon, Paris
	Galleria Spagnoli, Florence
	Leo Castelli Gallery, New York
	Galerie Arnessen, Copenhagen
	Centre Georges Pompidou, Paris
1978	Galleria del Milione, Milan
	Galerie Daniel Templon, Paris
	Louis Cane 1968–1978: The First 10 Years of a Painter, Israel Museum, Jerusalem
	Art 9'78, Basle
	Kunsthalle, Bielefeld, West Germany
1979	Galerie Art in Progress, Dusseldorf
	Galerie Art Line, The Hague
	Galerie Charles Kriwin, Brussels
	Musée d'Art Moderne, Strasbourg
	Galleria Mantra, Turin
	Galerie Daniel Templon, Paris

1980	Galerie Art in Progress, Munich
	Galerie Artline, La Haye, Netherlands
1981	Galerie Daniel Templon, Paris
	Galerie Ressle, Stockholm
	Galerie Art in Progress, Dusseldorf
	F.I.A.C., Grand Palais, Paris
1982	Leo Castelli Gallery, New York
	Galerie Art in Progress, Munich
	Inoue Gallery, Tokyo
	Ecole National Superieure des Beaux-Arts, Paris
1983	Galerie J. Giraud, Toulouse, France
	Fondation Maeght, St. Paul de Vence, France
1986	Galerie Reckermann, Cologne

Selected Group Exhibitions:

1968	*Salle Rouge pour le Vietnam*, Musée d'Art Moderne de la Ville, Paris
1969	*ABC Production*, Maison de la Culture, Montpellier, France
1971	*Biennale*, Paris
1973	*Réalité-Réalité*, Musée de Saint Etienne, France
	Biennale, Paris
1975	*Fundamental Painting*, Stedelijk Museum, Amsterdam
	Europalia, Palais des Beaux-Arts, Brussels
1976	*Europa-America*, Bologna
1977	*Documenta 6*, Kassel, West Germany
1979	*Biennale*, Sydney

Collections:

Centre Georges Pompidou, Paris; Musée d'Art Moderne de

la Ville, Paris; Musée de Saint-Etienne, France; Musée de Grenoble, France; Louisiana Museum, Humlebaek, Denmark; Kunstmuseum, Basle; Ghent Museum; Musée d'Art Contemporain, Montreal; Museum of Modern Art, New York.

Publications:

By CANE: book—*Paroles sur l'Art Moderne,* exhibition catalogue with Camille Saint-Jacques, St. Paul de Vence 1983; articles—"Pour un programme théorique pictural," with Daniel Dezeuze, in *Peinture* (Paris), June 1971; "Le peintre sans modèle" and "Vivela Chine révolutionnaire" in *Peinture* (Paris), January 1972; "Louis Cane," interview with Catherine Millet, in *Art Press* (Paris), March/April 1973; "Sur le sol, pliée, avec lacouleur," introduction to a Don Judd interview with John Coplans, and "Sur la peinture d'Alain Kirili" in *Peinture* (Paris), April 1973; "La Mort de Germanicus" and "Sur James Bishop" in *Peinture* (Paris), February 1974; "Marc Devade, piongée dans la couleur" in *Art Press* (Paris), February 1974; "Robert Ryman, peinture à tempera" in *Art Press* (Paris), March/April 1975; "Peinture fondamentale, une exposition au Stedelijk Museum d'Amsterdam" in *Art Press* (Paris), July/August 1975; "Le métier de peintre" in *Peinture* (Paris), November 1975; "James Bishop: Savoir le près pour voir le loin" in *Art Press* (Paris), March/April 1976; "L'Hétérogènesous gène" in *Peinture* (Paris), March 1977; "A propos de Rubens" in *Art Press* (Paris), January 1978; "Philipe Sollers: Interview" in *Peinture* (Paris), May 1978; "Un peintre en analyse," interview with Catherine Millet, in *Art Press* (Paris), January 1979; "Ce qui ira" in *Skira Annuel,* Geneva 1980; "L'age mur de l'avant-garde," interview with Catherine Millet, in *Art Press* (Paris), January 1981; "Cy Twombly" in *Art Press* (Paris), March 1981; "L'Art Moderne" in *Spirali* (Milan), June 1982; "Yves Klein" in *art Press* (Paris), February 1983.

On CANE: articles—"Notes sur un peintre opérant dans de beaux draps" by Marc Devade and "Les toiles systématiquement temponnées de Louis Cane" by Daniel Dezeuze in *Louis Cane,* exhibition catalogue, Paris, 1971; "L'intervention picturale de Louis Cane" by Marcelin Pleynet in *Art Vivant* (Paris), April 1971; "Quelques problèmes de la peinture moderne: Louis Cane" by Marcelin Pleynet in *Louis Cane,* exhibition catalogue, Paris 1972; "Forme et couleur découpées de la peinture de Louis Cane" by Marcelin Pleynet in *Art Press* (Paris), March/April 1973; "Louis Cane" by Claire Stoulig in *Cimaise* (Paris), May-August 1974; *Louis Cane,* exhibition catalogue, with text by Marcelin Pleynet, Paris 1977; *Louis Cane 1968–1978: The First 10 Years of a Painter,* exhibition catalogue, with interview by Michael Pauseback, Jerusalem 1978; "La rupture de l'avant-garde"

by Catherine Millet in *Connaissance des Arts* (Paris), January 1981; "Louis Cane: la peinture et la loi" by Michel Brandeau in *Art Press* (Paris), no. 70, 1983.

To tell the truth, I think that for the most part the type of painting which can be seen in galleries today is deliberately deluding itself. Sunk in ignorance, it pretends there is nothing to know. It shows nothing because there is nothing to show. Simplicity turns out to be over-simplification.

It is a fact, and I think a true one, that drawing and lines result in composition: i.e., a set of forms well adjusted together and also adjusted into a kind of unitary relation with my desire to paint. Adjusted so that the desire I cast into it will correspond to the desire I expect from it. In this sense, composition can't be but a compromise: even unfinished paintings cannot invalidate this. As a "composer" I am a subject who is calling upon and summoning himself as Another to be identified in the lines of the drawing. And I call myself into it to thwart somehow, to undo what unconsciously forces me to be me and not, if only for a moment, possessing the other. Drawing which orders form is the first stage in a process of identification of this Other whom painting displays. More precisely, I think I have a certain conception of painting but finally "Painting" is nothing else than a certain conception I have of the "other." The "other" could be the recollection of something: I remember an old art teacher used to give me the following piece of advice: "Keep hold of forms with the lines and you'll have composition!"

The simple question today is to know whether our painter's means and ways, in a word our painter's craft, correspond to the end of naturalism or whether, in the making of abstract painting, there's not still a conception of painting which comes too close to the old naturalist school.

In his notes on painting, Shi Tao (1641–1717) says about receptivity and knowledge that receptivity comes first and knowledge follows. I think that Shi Tao is right. He is right not only because his statement has the truthfulness of practice but also because he seems to suggest that I give more attention to my own receptivity so that my knowledge be not limited to the knowledge of others. This is how, for me, time spent painting can become time spent learning.

—Louis Cane

The fundamental characteristic of every *avant-garde* movement has always been the trying out of new languages, of unfamiliar cultural situations, the production of subjects or ideas that, in their deepest significance, would violate the traditional orders to which the artistic experience of the time was subject. "A drive towards the new" is a phrase often used to describe this characteristic, with its significant Freudian references. For a painter like Louis Cane, the *avant-garde* coincided with the Support/Surface period, during which material features of painting were subjected to a rigorous critical-ideological analysis which tended to disclose things in them which had been kept quiet but which, for that very reason, were still operative. Later, the French artist—whose work as a painter has a strong background of theory—took up the history of art as a subject on which to set down his working reflections. This history became a really authoritative source, taking in all the multiple and contradictory interpretations of current artistic practice; the work was based essentially on an inextricable round of reading (of the sources) and writing (the production of a new authoritative text on painting). The architecture of Brunelleschi, 14th and 15th century Tuscan painting and the non-objective painting of the United States were the great reference points of these masterly paintings, evident in the pictorial quality and in the formal layout, always complex and thick with references.

More recently, making a decision which, for him, evidently cloaked a great, profound and "philosophical" significance, Louis Cane rediscovered the figure, the image, and there appeared his series of women in which we can see the influence of Picasso and Giacometti, of De Kooning and of primitive rock paintings. Here Man appears in his essential pristine nakedness—the anthropological body untouched by any cultural transformation belonging to the times. He appears as in Matisse (though the two men's methods and rhythms of composition are fundamentally different), isolated in a solitary expanse of colour which is neither background nor surroundings, and he assumes primitive, sometimes indecent, poses. But it is still the pictorial significance that is final and conclusive, arising as it does from the history of art which Louis Cane is still rewriting, taking on himself the responsibilities of the present time and its dramatic, neurotic conflicts.

—Massimo Carboni

Louis Cane: *Untitled Painting,* **1975**

CANOGAR, Rafael (Gomez).
Spanish. Born in Toledo, 17 May 1935. Educated at Madrid High School, 1945–50; studied with the painter Daniel Vazquez-Diaz, in Madrid, 1948–53, Married Ann Jane McKenzie in 1960; children Susana, Daniel, Diego and Robert. Independent painter, Madrid, since 1956. Founder-member, El Paso group, Madrid, 1957. Visiting Professor of Art, Mills College, Oakland, California, 1965–66; Guest artist, Tamarind Lithography Workshop, Los Angeles, 1969. Recipient: Third Prize, *2nd International Festival of Painting,* Gagnes-sur-Mer, France, 1970; Grand Prize, *Bienal,* Sao Paulo, 1971; D.A.A.D. Artist in Residence, Berlin, 1972 and 1974; Grand Prize, International Triennial of Painting, Sofia, 1982; National Prize for Plastic Arts, Madrid, 1982. Chevalier, Ordre des Arts et des Lettres, France, 1985. Address: Ronda de la Abubilla 31, Parque Conde de Orgaz, Madrid 28043, Spain.

Individual Exhibitions:

1954   Galeria Altamira, Madrid
1955   Galeria Fernando Fe, Madrid
1956   Galerie Arnaud, Paris
          Galleria Numero, Florence

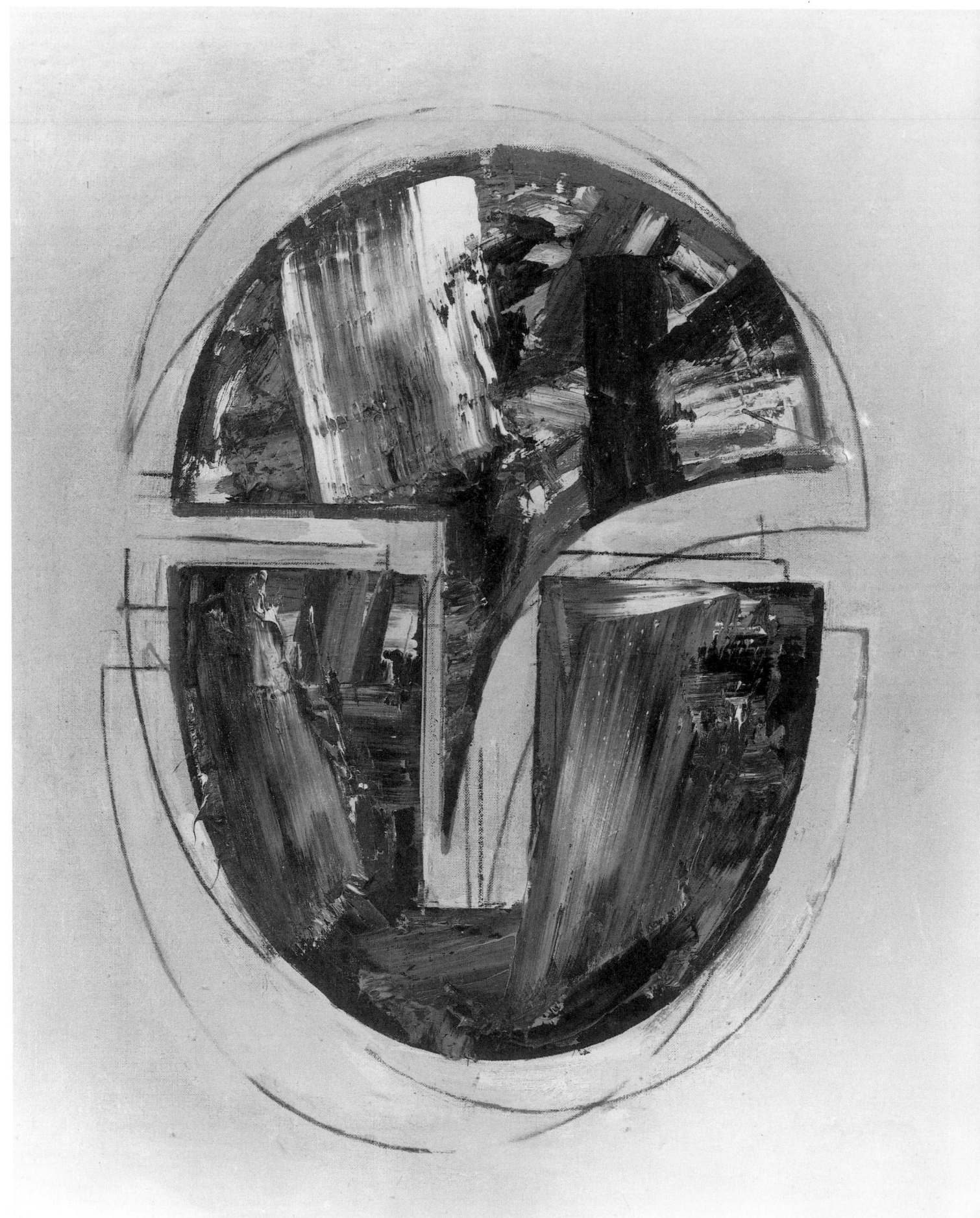

Rafael Canogar: *Cabeza*, 1987

1959	Galleria L'Attico, Rome
	Galleria Blu, Milan
1960	Galerie Aujourd'hui, Brussels
1961	Galleria L'Attico, Rome
	Galerie Rive Gauche, Paris
1962	Galerie Anne Abels, Cologne
	Galleria Naviglio, Milan
	Galleria Il Cancello, Bologna
1963	Galerie Rive Gauche, Paris
	Galeria Biosca, Madrid
1964	Galleria L'Attico, Rome
1965	Galeria Juana Mordo, Madrid
1966	Mills College Art Gallery, Oakland, California
	De Young Memorial Museum, San Francisco
	Salle Communali del Palazzo Constanzi, Trieste
	Galleria 3, Pescara, Italy
1967	Bertha Schaefer Gallery, New York
1968	Galeria Grises, Bilbao, Spain
	Galeria Juana Mordo, Madrid
1969	Silvan Simone Gallery, Los Angeles
	Deson-Zaks Gallery, Chicago
	Galleria Senior, Rome
	Galerie Withofs, Brussels
	Galleria Sanluca, Bologna
1970	Galerie Klang, Cologne
	Galerie Poll, Berlin
1971	Istituto di Storia dell'Arte, Parma
	Galeria Tolmo, Toledo
1972	Museo Espanol de Arte Contemporaneo, Madrid
	Galeria Rayuela, Madrid
	Silvan Simone Gallery, Los Angeles
	Galleria Naviglio, Milan
	Galerie Poll, Berlin
	Galeria Punto, Valencia
	Galeria Adria, Barcelona
	Galeria Luzaro, Bilbao
1973	Galeria Alcoiart, Altea, Spain
	Galeria Juana Mordo, Madrid
1974	Galeria Arte-Contacto, Caracas
	Galerie Poll, Berlin
	Galleria Bocchi, Milan
	Galleria Bocchi, Parma, Italy
	Galleria Brazia Bosser, Turin
1975	Silvan Simone Gallery, Los Angeles
	Musée d'Art Moderne de la Ville, Paris
	Sonia Henie Foundation, Oslo
	Kunsthalle, Lund, Sweden
	Galleria d'Art San Michele, Brescia, Italy
	Pirkanpohja-75, Nykytaidetta, Ah-Tarissa, Finland
1976	Galeria Juana Mordo, Madrid
	Galerie Christel, Stockholm
1977	Galerie Nordenhake, Malmo, Sweden
	Galerie Nordenhake Rykken, Oslo
	Galerie Benet Malmgram, Gothenburg, Sweden
1978	Galerie Nouvelles Images, The Hague
	Galeria Punto, Valencia
1979	Galleria Esse Arte, Rome
	Galeria San Diego, Bogota
1980	Galeria 3i5, Gerona, Spain
	Colegio Oficial de Arquitectos, Canary Islands
	Sala Luzan, Zaragoza, Spain
1981	Casa Municipal de Cultura, Aviles, Spain
1982	National Library of Spain, Madrid
	Galeria Punto, Valencia
	Caja de Ahorros, Alicante (travelled to Murcia)
1983	Casa de los Caballos, Caceres, Spain
	Galeria Cadaques, Gerona, Spain
1984	Contemporary Art Museum, Madrid
	Galeria Juana Mordo, at Art 15/84, Basel
1985	Galeria Bronda, Helsinki
	Galeria Sala Gaspar, Barcelona
	Galerie Poll, West Berlin
1986	Galeria Cadaques, at Arco 86, Madrid
	Municipal Cultural Centre, Alcoy, Valencia (retrospective)
1987	Paris Art Center, Paris (retrospective; travelled to Museum Bochum, West Germany)

Selected Group Exhibitions:

1955	*3rd Biennale Hispano-Americana*, Barcelona
1956	*Biennale*, Venice
1959	*13 Peintres Espagnois*, Musée Des Arts Décoratifs, Paris
1960	*Junge Spanische Kunst*, Kunsthalle, Berne (toured Europe)
1971	*Bienal*, Sao Paulo
1973	*Tra Rivolta e Rivoluzione*, Museo Civico, Bologna
1977	*Exposition International des Arts Plastiques*, Modern Art Museum, Belgrade
1980	*Printed Art: A View of Two Decades*, Museum of Modern Art, New York
1984	*Arte Espanol Contemporaneo*, Pinacoteca Nacional, Athens
1986	*Spagna: 75 anni di protagonisti nell'arte*, Villa Malpensata, Lugano, Switzerland

Collections:

Galleria Civica d'Arte Moderna, Turin; Galleria Civica d'Arte Moderna, Bologna; Museo de Arte Contemporaneo, Barcelona; Museo de Arte Contemporaneo, Seville; Contemporaneo de la Universidad, Sao Paulo; Staatliche Museum, Berlin; Haags Gemeentemuseum, The Hague; Carnegie Institute, Pittsburgh; Museum of Modern Art, New York; Art Institute of Chicago.

Publications:

On CANOGAR: books—*Rafael Canogar* by Enrico Crispolti, Madrid 1959; *Neue Kunst nach 1954* by U. Apollonio, Cologne 1959; *Canogar* by J. Dypreau, Cirlot and others, Rome 1962; *Canogar* by J. Castro Arines, Barcelona 1964; *Pintura Espanola: La Ultima Vanguardia* by J. Moreno Galvan, Madrid 1969; *Arte Dopo II 1945 "Spagna"* by U. Aguilera Cerni, Bologna 1970; *Canogar*, exhibition catalogue, Parma 1971; *Treinta Anos de Arte Espanol* by Carlos A. Arean, Madrid 1972; *Canogar* by A. Garcia-Tizon, Madrid 1973; *Rafael Canogar: Evolution dans la Synthese*, exhibition catalogue, with essay by J. M. Ballester, Paris 1975; *Rafael Canogar, pintor*, exhibition catalogue by Daniel Giralt-Miracle, Madrid 1976; *Rafael Canogar*, with texts by Ante Glibota, Peter Spielmann and Gerard Xuriguera, Paris 1987; articles—"Still und Entwicklung bei R. Canogar" by Juan Eduardo Cirlot in *Musee Labirinthe* (Aschaffenburg, Germany), no. 1, 1963; "Reality and Silence" by U. Aguilera Cerni in *Art International* (Lugano, Switzerland), January 1969; "Rafael Canogar" by D. W. Case in *Art and Artists* (London), February 1970; special Canogar issue of *Nueva Forma* (Madrid), December 1971; "La Aventura Plastica de Rafael Canogar" by F. Calvo Serraller in *El Pais* (Madrid), 25 September 1982; "Rafael Canogar: Beyond Modernism" by Keith Patrick in *Studio International* (London), no. 1007, 1984; "Rafael Canogar, Sala Gaspar" by Gloria Moure in *Artforum* (New York), September 1985.

*

My present position is above all eclectic, and at the same time a synthesis, a resume of many things from my earlier periods; an encounter between abstraction and figuration. I am not particularly interested in figurative images *per se*, but they do give the work its structure or framework, the spinal column to which the painting adheres. The images are totemic, mental, emblematic: large heads or masks, a flower, a bottle—like elements out of cubism. An excuse for painting and painting freely, as a means of communication and self-realization. Painting as the ultimate subject and the expressiveness of brush strokes, texture, color, all vital elements.

—Rafael Canogar

*

Before 1962 Rafael Canogar's paintings and graphics bore a strong resemblance to the passionate churned-up images of Saura, and the matière painting of the gifted, post-war Spanish school. He was then 27, and had developed from meticulous depictions of his native Toledo (following in the footsteps of El Greco), to Miro-like linear compositions. The powerful abstracts of the 60's, with their flashing, cutting, brush strokes, sombre colours, and sense of urgency, expressed a frustration with Spanish life. Saura, Millares and other compatriots were involved in similar imagery and similar situations.

By 1966 a return to figuration tentatively concerned itself with intimate, domestic matters, although there was already evidence in the gestural dominance of limbs, of the dramatic narrative manner of Canogar's now celebrated political paintings. In 1967 he began to use a mixture of media, both to encrust, so to speak, reality onto his canvas, and convey a sense of shock. Photography, often newspaper images of accidents or police confrontations, would be used, with isolated elements emerging from a solid black background, emphasized by collage, so that a pair of real trousers would be used with a drawn or painted figure.

Gradually the collage method developed into full-scale sculptural relief, so that the insistent gesture, present in all Canogar's work, became the movement of a simulated hand or leg. The protagonists were now openly political; demonstrating mobs versus uniformed members of the state; sometimes a group of raised hands symbolizing the demand for freedom and liberty; the titles "Protest," "Arrest," "Desolation," "Aggression," "The Escape," "Tumult," making no effort to disguise the inspiration or purpose of the impassioned images.

They are, of course, in the great tradition of Goya, sufficiently generalized to include all forms of state violence and denial, to be applicable to governmental systems and methods in many parts of the world. For this reason, perhaps, Canogar has been able to function and exhibit in his native Spain, as well as winning respect internationally.

—Charles Spencer

CAPOGROSSI, Giuseppe.

Italian. Born in Rome, 7 March 1900. Educated at the University of Rome, 1919-23; Instituto Massimiliano Massimo, Rome, 1915-17; studied painting privately with Felice Carena, Rome, 1926. Served as a Second Lieutenant in the Mountain Regiment, Adamello, Italy, 1918. Married Costanza Menney in 1956; daughters: Beatrice and Olga. Lived in Paris, 1927-33, then returned to Rome; Co-Founder, with Mario Ballocco, Alberto Burri and Ettore Colla, Gruppo Origine, Rome, 1951; Co-Signer, with Lucio Fontana, Emilio Scanavino, Roberto Crippa and others, *3rd Manifesto dello Spazialismo*, Milan, 1952. Lecturer in Painting, Liceo Artistico, Rome, 1946-55, and Academia di Belle Arti, Naples, 1965-70. Recipient: Premio Einaudi, 1954, and Grand Prize, 1962, *Biennale*, Venice; Etching Prize, *Graphics Biennale*, Venice, 1959; First Prize, *International Etching Exhibition*, Ljubljana, 1969; 20th Anniversary Prize, *Bienal*, Sao Paulo, 1971; Prix d'Honneur, *International Exhibition of Engraving*, Ljubljana, 1971; Cultural Merit Medal, Ministero di Pubblica Istruzione, Italy, 1971. *Died* (in Rome) *9 October 1972.*

Individual Exhibitions:

1946	Galleria San Marco, Rome
1950	Galleria del Secolo, Rome
	Galleria Il'Milione, Milan
	Galleria del Cavallino, Venice
1951	Galleria del Naviglio, Milan
	Galleria Numero, Florence
1952	Zimmergalerie Franck, Frankfurt
	Galleria del Cavallino, Venice
	Galleria del Naviglio, Milan (with Roberto Crippa and Gianni Dova)
1953	Galleria del Naviglio, Milan
	Circolo della Cultura e delle Arti, Trieste
1954	Galleria del Cavallino, Venice
1955	Galleria del Naviglio, Milan
1956	Galleria Selecta, Rome
	Galleria del Cavallino, Venice
	Galleria del Naviglio, Milan
	Galerie Rive Gauche, Paris

Università degli Studi di Milano, Gargnano sul
Garda, Italy
1957 Institute of Contemporary Arts, London
Galleria del Naviglio, Milan (with Giacomo Balla
and Robert Crippa)
1958 Galleria del Cavallino, Venice
Leo Castelli Gallery, New York
Galleria Casanuova, Trieste
1959 Palais des Beaux-Arts, Brussels
1960 Galerie 22, Dusseldorf
Galleria Tornabuoni, Florence
Galeria Sistina, Sao Paulo
1961 Galerie du 20th Siècle, Paris
Galleria Santacroce, Florence
1962 Galleria La Bussola, Turin
Assetto/Capogrossi/Scanavino, Joachim Gallery,
Chicago
Galleria L'Attico, Rome
1963 Galerie Handschin, Basel
Galleria del Naviglio, Milan
Galerie Schmela, Dusseldorf
Tokyo Gallery
Capogrossi/Sangregorio, Galerie Muller, Stuttgart
1964 Galleria del Cavallino, Venice
Galleria Rotta, Genoa
Galleria La Medusa, Rome
Capogrossi/Fontana, Gutai Pinacotheca, Osaka, Japan
1965 Galerie im Erker, St. Gallen, Switzerland
1966 Galleria 3, Pescara, Italy
Galleria Il Segno, Rome
1967 Staatliche Kunsthalle, Baden-Baden, West Germany
(travelled to the Kunsthalle, Nuremberg, and the
Europa Centre, Berlin)
Mala Galerija, Ljubljana, Yugoslavia
Kunstverein, Kassel, West Germany
1968 Galleria del Cavallino, Venice
Galleria del Naviglio, Milan
1969 Galleria Marlborough, Rome
Galleria d'Arte La Nuova Loggia, Bologna
Arte Studio, Macerata, Italy
1970 Galleria Martano, Turin
Erker-Presse, St. Gallen, Switzerland
Galerie George Moos, Geneva
1971 Galleria Il Centro, Naples
1972 Studio LD, Pescara, Italy
1973 Galleria Qui Arte Contemporanea, Rome
Galleria Bon a Tirer, Milan
1974 Galleria Nazionale d'Arte Moderna, Rome
1975 Galleria Santoro, Rome
Galleria Nazionale d'Arte, Rome (retrospective)
1976 Galleria dello Scudo, Verona, Italy
1977 Galleria Trimarchi, Bologna, Italy
Westend Galerie, Frankfurt
Galleria 72, Bergamo, Italy
1979 Galleria del Naviglio, at the *Arte Fiera,* Bologna,
Italy
Centro Iniziative Culturali, Pordenone, Italy
1980 Galleria Civica d'Arte Moderna, Ferrara, Italy
Galleria Images, Padua, Italy
1982 Galleria l'Isola, Rome

Selected Group Exhibitions:

1932 *Mostra del Sindacato Fascista Belle Arti,* Rome
1950 *Mostra Annuale dell'Art Club,* Galleria Nazionale
d'Arte Moderna, Rome
1953 *Younger European Painters,* Guggenheim Museum,
New York
1957 *Trends in Watercolors Today,* Brooklyn Museum,
New York
1960 *Contemporary Italian Art,* Illinois Institute of Technology, Chicago
1964 *Painting and Sculpture of a Decade 1954–64,* Tate
Gallery, London
1967 *Contemporary Italian Art,* Museum of Modern Art,
Tokyo (toured Poland, Germany and Sweden)
1969 *Contemporary Art: Dialogue Between East and
West,* Museum of Modern Art, Tokyo
1972 *5 Maestri,* Galleria La Medusa, Rome
1974 *L'Arte della Stampa,* Galleria d'Arte Moderna,
Rome

Collections:

Galleria Nazionale d'Arte Moderna, Rome; Galleria Comunale d'Arte Moderna, Rome; Museum of Fine Arts, Houston.

Publications:

By CAPOGROSSI: book—*Callo e Formiche: Pittori che
scrivono,* edited by L. Sinisgalli, Milan 1946; articles—statement in *Galleria San Marco* (Rome), January 1946;
statement in *The New Decade,* exhibition catalogue, New
York 1955.

On CAPOGROSSI: books—*Capogrossi* by Michel Seuphor,
Venice 1954; *Capogrossi* by M. Tapie, Venice 1962; *Capogrossi* by Giulio Carlo Argan, Rome 1967; *Giuseppe Capogrossi,* exhibition catalogue, by Palma Bucarelli, Rome 1974;
Giuseppe Capogrossi, exhibition catalogue edited by Galleria
L'Isola, Rome 1982; *Capogrossi fino al 1948* by Bruno Mantura, Spoleto 1986.

*

The case of Giuseppe Capogrossi is undoubtedly a
very unusual one in postwar Italian painting: an isolated artist who had neither master nor followers,
who took no part in "manifestos" and who was over
40 when he began his rapid ascent in the world of
contemporary painting with a renewed creative adolescence.

The Roman artist, who already had a long, busy
experience of painting behind him, begun with the
Roman expressionist group of Scipione, Mafai, Pirandello, found himself unexpectedly at the centre of interest and attention in the artistic world after he
adopted an expressive language that was quite new
and quite different from that of his earlier work. It
was in about 1950 that Capogrossi exhibited his new
abstract canvases for the first time, the result of some
two years' meditation and of assiduous efforts to free
himself from the naturalistic object and work out a
new pictorial grammar. It was in the first exhibition,
at the Galleria del Secolo in Rome, that there appeared in his paintings that unique, mysterious factor,
that emblematic sign which some people soon came
to describe as a "comb" or "fork", a sign that had in
it not only an undeniable plastic and compositional
effectiveness but also a mysterious, cryptic nature,
almost as if it had been drawn from the reappearance
of an ancient symbol taken from a Hermetic head or
an alchemist's formula.

We need not analyze Capogrossi's "sign" from a
semeiological point of view. What matters is that Capogrossi, making use almost exclusively of his personal graphico-pictorial alphabet, has succeeded in
building up an immensely complex and dense *oeuvre*
of undoubted expressive value. The artist, in fact,
once having taken over his "alphabet," has been able
to make surprising use of it, with no need for recourse to other modes of expression. If we look at the
vast amount of pictorial and graphic material he has
produced, we can see what a range of different "variations" can be obtained from a single "graphic"
theme. Sometimes the symbolical elements are minutely small, superimposed or set apart, but always
forming a unity of composition; sometimes they are
used rhythmically in widely spaced groups, leaving a
good deal of empty space; sometimes again they are
single elements of giant size that cover the whole canvas.

Capogrossi, once related from the refined atmospheric tonalism that characterized the Roman
school, no longer needed to return to the dubious support of chromatic tonalism, and always used essentially timbric colouring. That is why he was able from
the very first days of his new creative phase to start
firmly on a new line of "symbolic" (even if decidedly
"asemantic") art, in which a single ideogram—or,
better, "pictogram"—has enabled him to express
himself with a precision and certainty that make his
case one of the most remarkable events in the painting
of our times.

—Gillo Dorfles

CARO, Anthony (Alfred)

British. Born in London, 8 March 1924. Educated in
Hampshire and Surrey primary schools; apprenticed
to the sculptor Charles Wheeler during school vacations, 1937–42; studied engineering at Christ's College, Cambridge, 1942–44; attended Farnham School
of Art, 1944; studied sculpture, then drawing at the
Royal Academy Schools, London, under Charles
Wheeler, 1947–53. Served in the Fleet Air Arm,
1944–45. Married the artist Sheila Girling in 1949;
son: Tim. Worked as a part-time assistant to Henry
Moore, Much Hadham, Hertfordshire, 1951–53; settled in Hampstead, London, 1954; produced first abstract welded, bolted steel and aluminum works,
1959; visited Mexico and the United States, 1959;
and continued working visits to the U.S. from 1965;
worked in Kenneth Noland's studio, Shaftsbury, Vermont, 1970; worked with James Wolfe, Ripamonte
Factory, Verduggio, Italy, 1972–73; worked on York
Sculptures, York Steel Corporation, Ontario, Spring
and Summer 1974. Part-time Lecturer, St. Martin's
School of Art, London, 1952–53; Lecturer in Sculpture, Bennington College, Vermont, 1963–65; and St.
Martin's School of Art, London, 1964–72; Artist-in-Residence, Summer Workshop, University of Saskatchewan, Emma Lake, 1977; Lecturer, Slade
School of Fine Art, London, since 1982; Founder/
Lecturer, Triangle Summer Sculpture Workshops,
Pine Plains, New York, since 1982. Council Member,
Royal College of Art, London, 1981–83; Trustee,
Tate Gallery, London, since 1982; Recipient: Ford
Foundation Travel Grant, 1959; Prize for Sculpture,
Paris Biennale, 1959; David Bright Sculpture Prize,
Biennale, Venice, 1966; Prize for Sculpture, *Bienal,*
Sao Paulo, 1969. Honorary Fellow, Christ's College,
Cambridge, 1979; honorary doctorate: University of
East Anglia, 1979; University of York, 1979; Brandeis University, Waltham, Massachusetts, 1981;
Cambridge University, 1985; Honorary Fellow: Royal
College of Art, London, 1986; honorary degree: University of Surrey, Guildford, 1987. C.B.E. (Commander, Order of the British Empire), 1969; Knight
Bachelor, 1987. Address: 111 Frognal, London
NW3, England.

Individual Exhibitions:

1956 Galleria del Naviglio, Milan
1957 Gimpel Fils, London
1963 Whitechapel Art Gallery, London
1964 André Emmerich Gallery, New York
1965 Gallery of Modern Art, Washington, D.C.
Kasmin Gallery, London
1966 André Emmerich Gallery, New York
David Mirvish Gallery, Toronto
Galerie Bischofberger, Zurich
1967 Kasmin Gallery, London
David Mirvish Gallery, Toronto (with Kenneth Noland)
Rijksmuseum Kröller-Müller, Otterlo, Netherlands
1968 André Emmerich Gallery, New York
Metropolitan Museum of Art, New York (with Kenneth Noland and Morris Louis)
1969 Hayward Gallery, London
Dayton's Gallery 12, Minneapolis (with Kenneth
Noland and Frank Stella)
1970 André Emmerich Gallery, New York
1971 David Mirvish Gallery, Toronto
Kasmin Gallery, London
1972 André Emmerich Gallery, New York
Kasmin Gallery, London
1973 *Norfolk and Norwich Triennial Festival,* Norwich
André Emmerich Gallery, New York
1974 André Emmerich Gallery, New York
Kenwood House, London
David Mirvish Gallery, Toronto
Galleria dell'Ariete, Milan
1975 Museum of Modern Art, New York (toured the
United States)
Watson de Nagy Gallery, Houston
1976 Richard Gray Gallery, Chicago
Lefevre Gallery, London

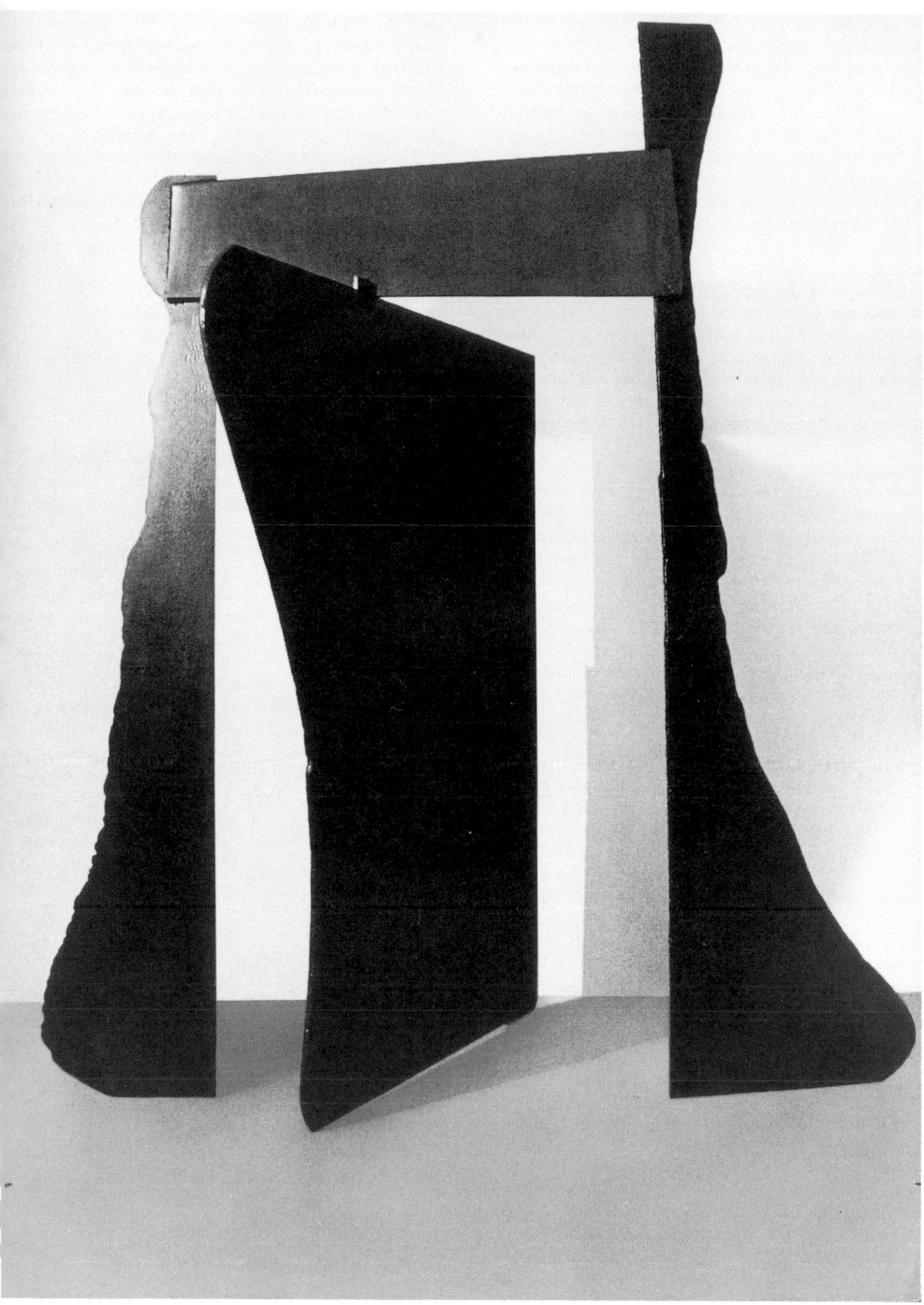

Anthony Caro: *Veduggio Sound*, 1973

Galerie Wentzel, Hamburg
Museum of Fine Arts, Boston
1977   Galerie Piltzer-Rheims, Paris
      Waddington and Tooth Galleries, London
      Tel Aviv Museum (toured New Zealand, Australia
      and travelled to Ottawa, 1977–79)
1978   Knoedier Gallery, London
      Galerie André Emmerich, Zurich (with Ben Nichol-
      son)
      Harcus-Krakow Gallery, Boston
      Richard Gray Gallery, Chicago
      Galerie Wentzel, Hamburg
      Ace Gallery, Venice, California
      Antwerp Gallery
1979   Kunstverein, Brunswick, West Germany
      Gallery Kasahara, Osaka, Japan
      Ace Gallery, Vancouver
      Stadt Galerie im Lenbachhaus, Munich
      Kunstverein, Frankfurt
      Kunsthalle, Mannheim
1980   *The York Sculptures*, Christian Science Center, Bos-
      ton

Aquavella Contemporary Art, New York
Galerie André, Berlin
1981   Kenwood House, London
1982   Hunterian Art Gallery, Glasgow (toured the U.K.,
      1982–83)
1983   Knoedler Gallery, London
      Waddington Galleries, London
      Galerie de France, Paris
1984   Knoedler Gallery, London
      Galerie Wentzel, Cologne
      Martin Gerard Gallery, Edmonton, Alberta
      Andre Emmerich Gallery, New York
      Acquavella Galleries, New York
      Serpentine Gallery, London
      Whitworth Art Gallery, Manchester
      Leeds City Art Gallery, Yorkshire
      Ordrupgaard Samlingen, Copenhagen
1985   Kunstmuseum, Dusseldorf
      Fondacion Joan Miro, Barcelona
      Galerie Wentzel, Cologne
      Galerie Andre Emmerich, Zurich
      Grimaldis Gallery, Baltimore, Maryland

      Gallery One, Toronto
      Galerie Blanche, Stockholm
      Galleri Lang, Malmo, Sweden
      Galerie Artek, Helsinki
      Harcus Gallery, Boston
      Galleria Stendhal, Milan
      Norrkopings Kunstmuseum, Sweden
1986   Richard Gray Gallery, Chicago
      Andre Emmerich Galery, New York
      Acquavella Galleries, New York
      Galeria Joan Prats, Barcelona
      Comune di Bogliasco, Genoa, Italy
      Knoedler Gallery, London
      Waddington Galleries, London
      Iglesia de San Esteban, Murcia, Spain
1987   La Lonja, Valencia, Spain
      Galeria Soledad Lorenzo, Madrid
      Grimaldis Gallery, Baltimore, Maryland

Selected Group Exhibitions:

1955   *New Sculptors and Painter-Sculptors*, Institute of
      Contemporary Arts, London
1958   *Pittsburgh International*, Carnegie Institute, Pitts-
      burgh
1959   *1st Biennale des Jeunes*, Musée d'Art Moderne,
      Paris
1954   *Painting and Sculpture of a Decade: 1954-1964*,
      .Tate Gallery, London
1968   *New British Sculpture and Painting*, University of
      California, Berkeley (toured the United States and
      Canada)
1970   *Contemporary British Art*, Museum of Modern Art,
      Tokyo
1974   *The Great Decade of American Abstract Art*, Mu-
      seum of Fine Arts, Houston
1980   *Hayward Annual*, Hayward Gallery, London
1983   *Aspects of British Art*, Guggenheim Musuem, New
      York
1987   *British Painting and Sculpture in the 1980s*, Mu-
      seum of Modern Art, Oxford (toured Hungary,
      Poland, Czechoslovakia)

Collections:

Tate Gallery, London: Arts Council of Great Britain, London; Kunsthaus, Zurich; Museum of Modern Art, New York;
National Gallery of Art, Washington, D.C.

Publications:

By CARO: articles—"The Master Sculptor" in *The Observer*
(London), 27 November 1960; "Conversation with Anthony
Caro, Ken Noland and Jules Olitski" by David Thompson in
Nonad (London), January 1964; statement in *Art Now* (New
York), September 1969; "Some Thoughts after Visiting Flor-
ence" in *Art International* (Lugano, Switzerland), May 1974;
"An Interview with Anthony Caro," with Phyllis Tuchman,
in *Anthony Caro* by Richard Whelan and others, London
1974; "Conversations with Anthony Caro" by Lutz Haufs-
chile in *Arts Magazine* (New York), June 1978; interview,
with Christopher Andreae, in the *Christian Science Monitor*
(Boston), August 1980; "A Conversation with Anthony
Caro," with Yorick Blumenfeld, in *Architectural Digest* (Los
Angeles), September 1981.

On CARO: books—*Anthony Caro*, exhibition catalogue, by
Michael Fried, London 1969; *Anthony Caro* by Richard
Whelan and others, London 1974; *Anthony Caro* by William
Rubin, New York and London 1975; *The York Sculptures*,
exhibition catalogue, Boston 1980; *Anthony Caro*, exhibition
catalogue, New York 1980; *The Sculpture of Anthony Caro:
Catalogue Raisonné*, 3 vols., edited by Dieter Blume, Cologne 1981-86; *Anthony Caro: Sculptures*, exhibition catalogue with text by Karen Wilkin, New York 1981; *Anthony
Caro* by Diane Waldman, Oxford and New York 1982 (includes bibliography); *Anthony Caro Sculpture 1969 84*, exhi
bition catalogue with foreword by Joanna Drew and Catherine
Lampert, London 1984; *Anthony Caro* by Terry Fenton, London and Barcelona 1986.

You cannot explain abstract art in ten minutes, and
you cannot expect yourself to like it on the very first

glance, any more than you'll like a piece of unfamiliar serious music on the first hearing. It takes a lot of listening and a lot of looking to get the rewards of difficult art, but it is worthwhile in the end.

—Anthony Caro

Anthony Caro's reputation was established by his superb welded steel pieces of the 1960's. He is rightly acclaimed as having pushed sculpture even further into abstraction, by eliminating any lingering figurative references and by freeing it completely from the constraints of the pedestal.

Caro's works of the '60's usually develop horizontally, appropriating the viewer's own space. They claim and animate that space simply by looking like nothing other than themselves. They are built of industrial materials—I-beams, stock angles, expanded metal mesh and the like—but in spite of the literal strength and weight of their components, they appear weightless, like disembodied drawings which hover above the floor rather than resting heavily upon it. This is partly due to the thinness of their members; they are sculptures of plane, edge, and line, not of mass. It results, too, from Caro's practice of painting these works in uniform, often rather light colors, which homogenizes the disparate components and makes the sculptures declare themselves as single, unified objects. More importantly, the apparent weightlessness of Caro's work depends on his habit of deliberately confusing supporting and pictorial elements. He often establishes elevated surrogate horizon planes, and disposes forms above and below them, so that these elements appear to float freely.

Caro's sculptures of the '60's expanded our notions of what sculpture could be, picking up, as they did, the implications of Picasso and Gonzalez's metal constructions as well as those of David Smith's work, and making them still more abstract and more optical. For once, the over-used term "drawing in space" seems apt. Caro's sculptures of the period were conceived as transparent three-dimensional objects. Their eloquent gestures and comfortable human scale made us aware of our own bodies' ability to move, yet at the same time, they were purely visual structures.

The small scale Table sculptures of more or less the same time were equally remarkable. In these, Caro at first established scale by incorporating real grips and handles (in ungraspable positions) to instantly give a sense of the hand. Later, perhaps to contradict this reference to ordinary objects on a table, which were distinguished because they *could* be picked up, Caro eliminated the handles. Instead, he established scale through positioning. The Table Pieces often spring over the edges of their supporting bases, appearing as weightless and animated as their larger counterparts, but perceived differently because of their small size. We tend to see each of their component parts as something of great importance, since we are so close to them.

If Caro had done nothing but the linear painted pieces and the Table Pieces, his place in the history of contemporary sculpture would still be secure, but in the '70's and early '80's, he has retained his pre-eminence with a body of inventive work which explores new territory and new materials. In the early '70's, Caro seemed to fall in love with the properties of his chosen material, with the surface inflections of steel, its weight and mass, after years of dissembling. A series of extremely painterly, relatively massive sculptures, made of rolled sheets, revelled in the particularities of magnificent pieces of metal. As if to emphasize his pleasure in the individual sheet, Caro often presented them vertically, for the viewer's inspection, rather than horizontally, as in earlier works. Works of this type began with the Verduggio series, made in Italy, and continued with the Durham series, after Caro found a British rolling mill which could provide him with the irregular sheets and folded slabs which come at the end of a run, or when the mill makes a mistake. They culminated in the York Pieces of 1974-75, Caro's first very large scale works. Pre-

viously, his improvisatory approach demanded that his sculptures be kept within a scale which he could manipulate himself, or with a minimum of assistance. Larger scale implied using maquettes or fabricators, intermediaries antithetical to his working methods. But in making the York Pieces, he had at his disposal, for the first time, men and equipment which allowed him to work on big sculptures without altering his approach. The York series, for all their size and the sheer weightness of their tilted, layered slabs, have all the immediacy of his early work, albeit with a new solemnity and dignity.

Similarly, Caro had not worked in bronze since abandoning figuration in the late '50's. Again, the medium seemed too indirect, to require too much preconception. In the early '70's, however, an invitation to make sculpture in clay at Syracuse University led Caro back to bronze without forcing him to give up his usual collage method. By having forms made in clay (or other equally manipulable material) which he could then alter and have cast in bronze, Caro assembled a lexicon of eccentric personal elements. He used these in combination with brass rods and sheets, to make bronzes as directly and spontaneously as he did works in steel, assembling and constructing unique works, rather than preparing maquettes for casting. The resulting sculptures have ranged from intimate Table Pieces which evoke Chinese temple bronzes as much as they do the tradition of modernism, to large scale "Screens" built of cascading planes which spring against vertical walls in the same way that the horizontal drawing of earlier works skimmed the floor.

Despite his interest in new formal concerns, such as verticality and mass, and new materials, such as lead, silver and bronze. Caro has continued to make expressive linear sculptures in steel. The Emma Lake pieces of 1977-78 are large scale, drawing-like works which recall earlier sculptures but are developed in the round in ways relatively new to Caro. It is as though their slender configurations had been informed by the density and substance of his painterly "slab" pieces of the early '70's. The Writing Pieces, small calligraphic works of 1978, and a recent series of larger, rather densely packed steel sculptures, both make free use of found objects from small tools to bollards. In the recent steel pieces, as well as the bronzes. Caro has begun to make use of color in new ways, varying tones and patinas to enhance structure and emphasize form, rather than applying a uniform and unifying skin of color.

Small calligraphic sculptures continued this linear vein well into the 1980s, while the most extreme examples of the persistence of this mode were a group of sculptures made at an international artists' workshop in Barcelona, in 1987, perhaps as a response to the omnipresent Catalan ironwork balconies and railings.

Yet mass and implied volume, along with an intense physical presence, have characterized much of Caro's sculpture since 1980. His steel constructions, whether polychromed or unpainted, are often very large, (within the context of his preference for human scale), massive accretions of thick members; some incorporate huge, sliced marine floats that, because of their size and hollowness, have inevitable associations with architecture and shelter. Caro acknowledges that he has been looking hard at medieval and Renaissance churches, in recent years, but as always, his best works declare themselves independently of literal allusions.

Most surprisingly, the man who long maintained that, for him, sculpture had to be abstract if was to be "real"—that is, to have the same intensity and authority as anything in the existing world—has been working from the model since the early '80s. His richly inflected cast bronze figures are a clear homage to Matisse, but they owe as much to Caro's own abstract sculpture as to any of the figurative sculptors whose work interests him; certainly they are articulated in ways that have little to do with Caro's thickest figures of the 1950s, made before he began to work abstractly in steel. The bronze figures seem to have,

in turn, influenced a recent series of abstract bronzes whose swelling, sensuous forms are abutted in a manner that is typical of Caro—whose work always depends upon placement—and at the same time, evokes classic Indian sculpture, which Caro admires greatly.

Knighted in 1987, at 63, in recognition of his past achievement, Caro continues to make challenging and original sculpture. Most impressive is his enduring ability to respond to new notions and to reexamine his conception of what sculpture can be.

—Karen Wilkin

CARR-HARRIS, Ian.

Canadian. Born in Victoria, British Columbia, 12 August 1941. Studied modern history, Queen's University, Kingston, Ontario, 1959-63; library science, University of Toronto, 1963-64; sculpture, Ontario College of Art, Toronto, 1967-71. Married in 1966 (divorced); daughter: Lisa Renee. Independent sculptor, Toronto, since 1971. Director of Library Services since 1972, and Instructor in Art Theory and Practice since 1975, Ontario College of Art, Toronto. Board Member, A Space Gallery, Toronto, 1970-71, 1982-83, and The Power Plant (formerly, The Art Gallery at Harbourfront), Toronto, 1983-87; Member of the Contemporary Acquisitions Committee, Art Gallery of Ontario, Toronto, 1987-88. Contributor to the periodicals *Parachute*, *Vanguard* and *C Magazine*, since 1975. Member, Royal Canadian Academy, 1976. Agent: Carmen Lamanna Gallery, 988 King Street West, Toronto, Ontario M5V 1N6. Address: 68 Broadview Avenue, 4th floor, Toronto, Ontario M4M 2E6, Canada.

Individual Exhibitions:

1971   A Space, Toronto
1972   Nova Scotia College of Art and Design, Halifax
1973   Carmen Lamanna Gallery, Toronto (and annually, since 1973)
1981   Yajima/Galerie, Montreal
1982   Dalhousie University, Halifax, Nova Scotia
        Scarborough College, Toronto
1983   49th Parallel Centre, New York
1987   London Regional Art Gallery, Ontario
1988   Art Gallery of Ontario, Toronto

Selected Group Exhibitions:

1970   *Concept '70*, Nightingale Gallery, Toronto
1974   *Investigations*, Mount Allison University, Sackville, New Brunswick
1977   *Another Dimension*, National Gallery of Canada, Ottawa
1978   *Kanadische Kunstler*, Kunsthalle, Basle
1979   *Confrontations*, Vancouver Art Gallery, British Columbia
1981   *Canada in Birmingham*, Ikon Gallery, Birmingham, England
1984   *41st Biennale*, Venice
1986   *Luminous Sites*, Western Front and Video Inn, Vancouver
1987   *Documenta 8*, Museum Fridericianum, Kassel, West Germany

Collections:

Art Gallery of Ontario, Toronto; Canada Council, Ottawa; National Gallery of Canada, Ottawa.

Publications:

By CARR-HARRIS: articles—"John Greer" in *Parachute*

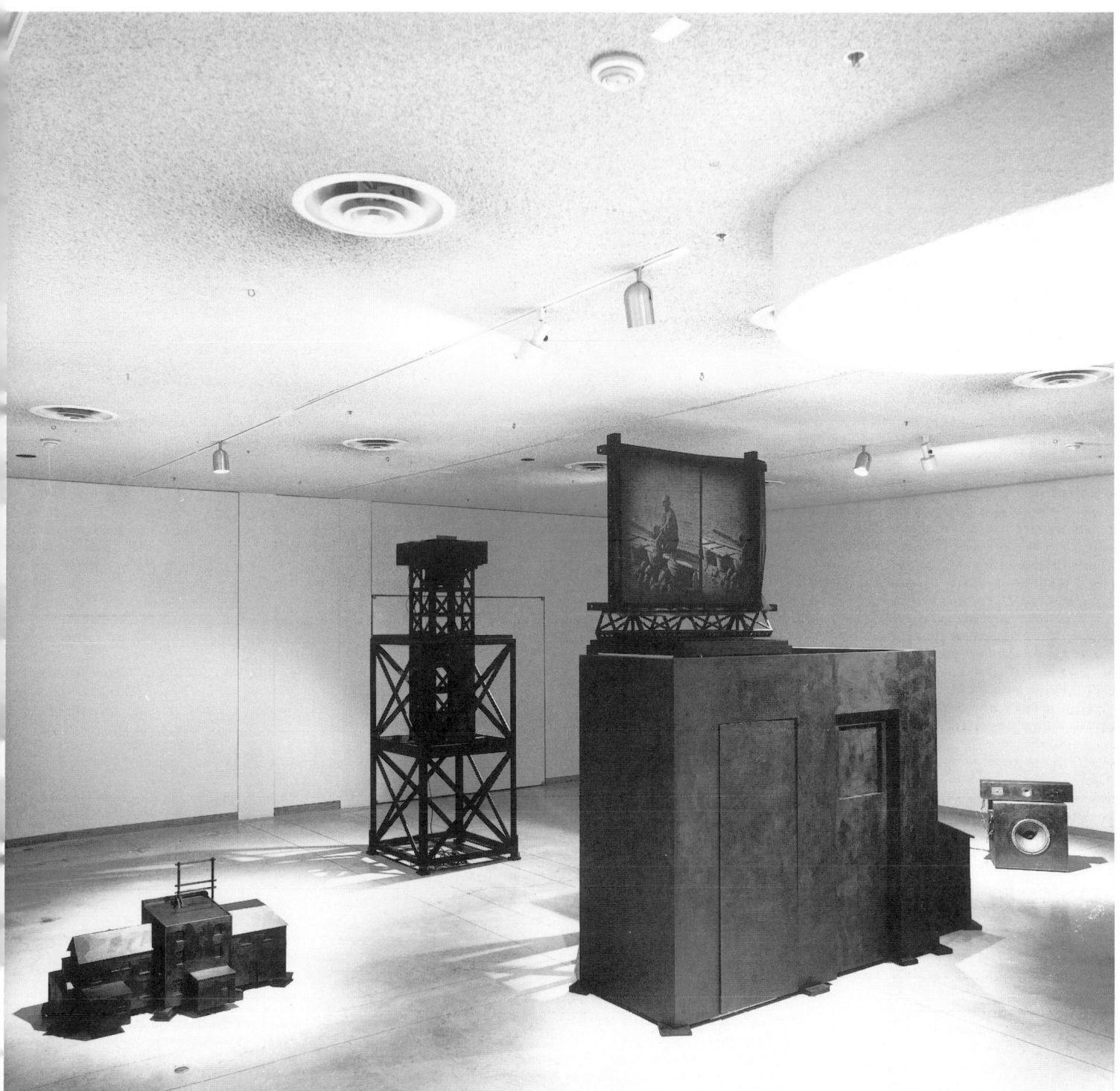

Ian Carr-Harris: *Reconstruction of the View From My Room,* 1987

(Montreal), December/February 1982–83; "Museums in the 80s", with Goldie Rans, in *Vanguard* (Vancouver), March 1983; "Philip Monk, Sentences on Art" and "Vincent Tangredi" in *Parachute* (Montreal), March/May 1983; "A. R. Penck" in *Parachute* (Montreal), June/August 1983; "From Here to Zero: Stephen Horne" in *C Magazine* (Toronto), no. 1, 1983; "Sex and Representation" in *Vanguard* (Vancouver), November 1984; "Women's Work" in *Vanguard* (Vancouver), December 1987.

On CARR-HARRIS: books—*Art in Boxes* by A. Mogelin and N. Laliberte, New York 1974; *Another Dimension,* exhibition catalogue with text by Mayo Graham, Ottawa 1977; *Confrontations,* with text by Ann Pollock, Vancouver 1979; *Ian Carr-Harris: Recent Work,* exhibition catalogue with text by Linda Milrod, Halifax 1982; *Visions: Contemporary Art in Canada* by Diana Nemiroff, Toronto 1983; *Ian Carr-Harris/Liz Magor: Canada, XLI Biennale di Venezia 1984,* exhibition catalogue with text by Jessica Bradley, Ottawa 1984; *Toronto: A Play of History,* exhibition catalogue with text by Louise Dompierre, Toronto 1987.

I have a number of concerns about what artworks can accomplish, and they fall roughly into two intersecting categories. These have to do on the one hand with their suggestiveness and the meanings they can construct dialectically in the imagination of the viewer by virtue of their permissiveness; and on the other hand with the intentions of the artist—who at least holds responsibility for the existence of the work—in directing meaning and presenting to the social consciousness of the viewer particular codes of value. When taken together—and all artworks exhibit both these categories—they act to define and to counter our own individual productions of meaning. They both produce and deny those productions: this is what artworks accomplish.

—Ian Carr-Harris

CARRINO, Nicola.

Italian. Born in Taranto, 15 February 1932. Educated in Taranto primary schools; self-taught in art. Served in the Italian Army, 1955–56. Married Angela Colacicco in 1960; children: Veneranda and Velentina. Concentrated on painting, 1952–62; has worked as a sculptor since 1962. Founder, with G. Biggi, N. Frasca, A. Pace, P. Santoro and G. Uncini, Gruppo I. Rome, 1962–67. Professor of Drawing, Istituto d'Arte, Grottagie, Italy, 1961; Professor of Figure-drawing, Liceo Artistico, Lecce, Italy, 1962–64, and Liceo Artistico, Rome, 1965–77; Professor in Visual Studies, ISIA, Rome, 1966–70 and 1975; Professor of Painting, Accademia delle Belle Arti, Bari, Italy, 1978; Professor of Sculpture, Accademia delle Belle Arti, Frosinone, Italy, 1979, 1983, 1986, Accademia di Belle Arti, Lecce, 1980–82, and Accademia di Belle Arti, Bari, 1984–85. Recipient: 2nd Prize, with Gruppo I, *Biennale di San Marino,* 1963; Premio Internacional, *11th Bienal de Sao Paulo*, 1971. Agent: Studio Carlo Grossetti, Via dei Piatti 9, 20123 Milan. Address: Via Ippolito Pindemonte 32, 00152 Rome, Italy.

Individual Exhibitions:

1960	Galleria Taras, Taranto, Italy
1961	Galleria Taras, Taranto, Italy
	Galleria Numero, Prato, Italy
1962	Galleria Numero, Milan
1966	Galleria Space and Time, Spoleto, Italy
1968	Galleria Qui Arte Contemporanea, Rome
1969	Galleria Christian Stein, Turin
	Galleria Il Segno, Rome
1970	Salone Annunciata, Milan
	Nicola Carrino, at the *Biennale*, Venice
1972	Street Sculpture, Milan
	Galerie Defet, Nuremberg
	Galleria Godel, Rome
1973	Salone Annunciata, Milan
	Forum Kunst, Rottweil, West Germany
	Galleria Primo Piano, Rome
	Studio 3Bi, Bolzano, Italy
	Nicola Carrino, at the *Biennale del Metallo*, Gubbio, Italy
1974	Galerie Arges, Brussels
	Galleria d'Arte di Porta Ticinese, Milan
	Circolo Italsider, Taranto, Italy
1975	Salone Annunciata, Milan
	Galleria Primo Piano, Rome
1976	Marlborough Galleria d'Arte, Rome
	Galeria M., Bochum, West Germany
	Salone Annunciata, Milan
1977	Galeria Denise René-Hans Mayer, Dusseldorf
	Gallerie Civica d'Arte Contemporanea, Suzzara, Italy
1979	Salone Annunciata, Milan
	Galeria Denise René, New York
1980	Galleria Comunale d'Arte Contemporanea, Taranto, Italy
	Galerie Walter Storms, Munich
	Galleria E Tre, Rome
1981	Studio Carriere, Martina Franca, Italy
	Galleria Il Centro, Naples
	Studio Carlo Grossetti, Milan
1982	Galerie Schissel, Munich
1983	Galleria Plurima, Udine, Italy
1984	Studio Carlo Grossetti, Milan
1985	Galleria Primo Piano, Rome
1986	*Nicola Carrino*, at the *Biennale*, Venice
	Galleria Comunale d'Arte Contemporanea, Arezzo
	Centro Culturale Dune, Molfetta, Italy
1987	Torre di Santa Caterina, Nardo, Italy

Selected Group Exhibitions:

1960	*Mostra Internazionale d'Arte Astratta*, Palazzo Pretoria, Prato, Italy
1966	*Biennale*, Venice
1969	*Zwolf Italienische Bildauer*, Kunstverein, Hamburg
1971	*Bienal*, Sao Paulo
1977	*Zestien Italiaanse Kunstenaars*, Museum Boymans-van Beuningen, Rotterdam
1978	*Metafisica del Quotidiano*, Galleria d'Arte Moderna, Bologna
1981	*Linea della Ricerca Artistica in Italia, 1960–1980*, Palazzo delle Esposizioni, Rome
1982	*Arte italiana 1960–82*, Hayward Gallery, London
1984	*Carte Blanche a Denise Rene*, Paris Art Center, Paris
1986	*Arte Astratta 1952–81*, Galleria Nazionale d'Arte Moderna, Rome

Collections:

Galleria Nazionale d'Arte Moderna, Rome; Museo Sperimentale d'Arte Contemporanea, Turin; Museum of Modern Art, Skopje, Yugoslavia; Museum of Modern Art, Haifa, Israel; Potsdam Art Galerie, Germany; Ruhr Universität Museum, Bochum, West Germany; Museum Art, Ciudad Bolivar, Venezuela.

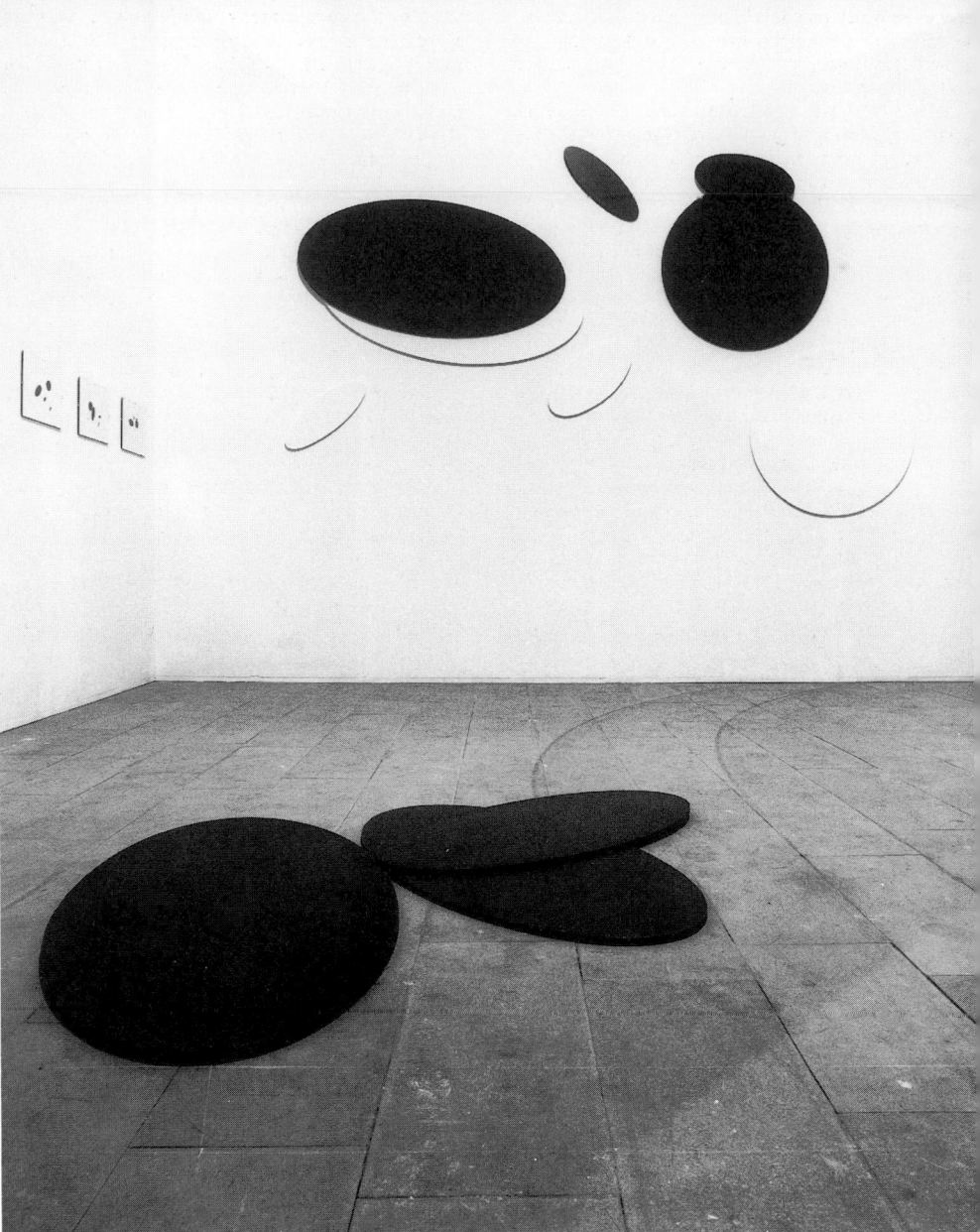

Nicola Carrino: Installation at the *XLII Biennale*, Venice, 1986

Publications:

By CARRINO: books—*Costruttivi Grasformabili 1969–70*, Rome 1970; *Costruttivi/Testo 4*, exhibition catalogue, Milan 1973; *Costruttivo 74 Module L*, with J. de Sanna, Milan 1974; *Costruttivi Trasformabili/Processi I-10 di Trasformazione*, exhibition catalogue, Rome, 1976; *Costruttivo Trasformabile I-10 T-77/Intervention*, exhibition catalogue, New York 1978; *Opere e Interventi 1959-1979*, exhibition catalogue, Taranto, Italy 1979; *Azione e Trasformazione 1957-1985*, exhibition catalogue, Arezzo, Italy 1986; *Costruttivi Trasformabili 1969-1975*, exhibition catalogue, Nardo, Italy 1987; articles—several texts in *Dall'Occhio al Cervello*, Gruppo I, edited by F. Sossi, Taranto, Italy 1963; "Nicola Carrino" in *Flash Art* (Milan), March/April 1970; "Costrutti/Testo 1 e 2" in *Progetto, Intervento e Verifica*, exhibition catalogue, Milan 1972; "Didattica come Conoscenza e Comportamento" in *Rassengna dell'Istruzione Artistica* (Urbino, Italy), vol. 7, nos. 3–4, 1972; "Costruttivi/Testo 3" in *Faites votre Jeu*, Venice 1974; "Costruttivi/Testo 5" in *Dal Progetto al Opera*, exhibition catalogue, Verona 1974; "Nicola Carrino" in *Flash Art* (Milan), no. 48–49, 1974; "Costruttivi/Testo 10" in *Art Essata: Approcci di Critica Analitica*, edited by F. Torriani, Turin 1974; "Costruttivi/Testo 8" in *La Ricerca Scientifica come Modello Estetico in Architettura*, edited by F. Facilla, Rome 1975; "Costruttivi/Testo 11" in *R2*, Rome 1975; "Unformbare Construtionselemente/Transformationen" in *Heute Kunst* (Milan), no. 14/15, 1976; "Die Konstruktivien" in *Magazine Kunst* (Mainz), no. 3, 1976; "La Creatività So-

ciale e Rivoluzione Continuà" in *Qui Arte Contemporanea* (Rome), no. 17, 1977; "Costruttivi Trasformabili/Trasformazione dello Spazio" in *L'Opera dei Celebranti*, exhibition catalogue, Ancona, Italy 1981; "Critica dell'Arte" in *La Critica dell'Arte*, exhibition catalogue, Ancona, Italy 1981; "L'Arte e il Pensiero dell'Arte" in *Taide* (Salerno, Italy), no. 1, 1981; "Forma e Luogo" in *Il Luogo della Forma*, exhibition catalogue, Verona 1981; "Trasformazione dello Spazio/Ellissi" in *G7 Studio* (Bologna), vol. 6, no. 3/4, 1981; "Nicola Carrino" in *Al Vivo*, edited by S. Lux, Rome 1981; "Auto-interview" in *Neue Kunst in Europa* (Munich), no. 8, 1985.

On CARRINO: book—*Calderara e Gruppo I* by Guilio Carlo Argan, Milan 1966; articles—"Carrino" by R. Sanesi in *Opus International* (Paris), no. 35, 1972; "Nicola Carrino" by J. de Sanna in *Opus International* (Paris), no. 59, 1976; "Nicola Carrino" by J. Tannenbaum in *Arts Magazine* (New York), June 1978; "Le Ricerche di Arte Ottico-Visiva nei Gruppi Romani" in *L'Arte in Italia nel Secondo Dopoguerra*, edited by R. Barilli, Bologna 1979; "The Italian Art Scene" by Henry Martin in *Art News* (New York, vol. 80, no. 3, 1981; "Nicola Carrino" by M. Vescovo in *XLII Biennale di Venezia*, exhibition catalogue, Venice 1986.

The idea of transformation is the base of my work. In the 'sixties, I used three-dimensional iron modules that I called "Costruttivi Trasformabili". With them made transformations of form and of environmental spaces in which they inhabited in a dynamic and dialectical time-continuous between built-up and destroyed form, project and randomness, personal and collective actions.

Since 1980, the "Construttivi Ellissi" are formal systems consisting of several sets of modules as ellipsis, ellipses-circle, ellipsis-serrated modules, ellipsis-circle-square and as did previously the "Costruttivi Transformabili" suggest the idea of transformation and combining in that they can be arranged together in different ways depending upon the environment and the method of analysis used. The "Costruttivi Ellissi" can be realized as sculptures, iron or painted-wood reliefs or as a wall-painting, but are defined by environmental space.

The perception of such systems should not be limited to the work itself but completely inhering in the environmental space that the work measures and defines. Thus the space of the gallery as well as the methods of analysis used to visualize it together with the sculpture are the basic elements of my artistic work. I am also convinced that sculpture should spring from the need of the space and identify itself with it. Therefore, environment and sculpture are an organic whole which I call environment-sculpture.

Geometry and project are only a means and not the end of the artistic work. Nothing that controls or that makes the formal systems stiffen but only means of analysis, of checking and controlling the possibilities of the project itself. I may affirm that geometry and project constitute the methodological rigour that justifies the essential arbitrariness of research. Geometric form represents itself. There is no image problem. Every form is figure and every figure, though geometrical, is image. Thus, the formal whole determined by "Costruttivo Ellissi" may also express a cosmic, galactic aspect. In this case I would affirm that the "Costruttivi", as finite systems, investigate situations of infinite order. In modern research a project like Ellissi, taken as a critical and dialectical concept, is a necessity to express creatively a freedom of imagination, a consciousness of reality. "Progetto Ellissi", then, is not only use of form according to the archetype, but behaviour of the form and the being, both free and conscious, expressed with projectual rigour and necessity of intervention.

Actually, my idea is that it should be possible to develop research in art directly in the social contexts in which the project is the media between the social demand and the individual proposal of the artist. I also believe that in such interventions it is possible to go through the aestetics of an artistic operation in order do determine more productive moments to the social aims of art.

Nicola Carrino

Artistic development in Italian art of the 'fifties followed a direct route. To begin with, the debate was predominantly between abstract and figurative, followed by (for some artists) the cubist deconstruction of the picture plane, and finally pure abstraction.

Nicola Carrino was born in 1932. In his twenties, he tried out a variety of styles. But between 1959 and 1962 he arrived at a form in which the picture plane became an arena for expressions of a geometric nature, but executed in modest materials such as wood or metal sheet. In this mode he produced, between 1959 and 1960, the series *Realta.* In the works which followed (until mid-1962) he mastered the canvas, arriving at a result similar to the tendencies then current in Europe and the United States and typified by the work of Gotz, Kline and Pollock.

In the second half of 1962 Carrino made a complete break from the pictorial to the constructive. The new works were constructed of geometric units, organized and mounted on a surface as in *Costruttivo Alta* (1963). In the same year he co-ordinated the group known as Gruppo 1, together with Biggi, Frasca, Pace, Santoro and Uncini. They disbanded in 1967. Concurrent with this period were the works *Struttura Plastica* (1964) and the series *Spaziostruttura* (1965-67). This work resulted from the modulation of geometric forms used not only for their formal potential but also for their capacity to influence surrounding space. The series *Costruttivi* moved in both these directions. *Costruttivo 1* (1963) belongs to the initial phase in which Carrino used geometric elements on a flat surface. *Costruttivo 3,* of the same year, employs elements of geometric form (in this case, concave rectangles) organized as a self-supporting structure in space.

But it is in 1969, after a number of advances in this direction, that Carrino crystallized the concept of *Costruttivo* into its final formulation. The *Costruttivo* then became based on a module and realized in iron and steel. The component modules, when combined with all the others, make up the complete artistic object. What is of interest to the artist is the constructive and deconstructive quality of the work contained within the limits of the work itself, rather than the final formal result. Through these works he conveys meanings which become on occasion performances, creative interventions demanding social participation.

Carrino wrote in 1974 of the *Costruttivi:* "It is the fruit of its message. The artist re-enters the arena with a plausible system that is not an end in itself, but an instrument for a liberal and creative intervention applicable both to the work of art and to reality."

Between 1978 and 1979 Carrino made a series of *Trasformazioni dello spazio,* that is, a harnessing of environment within colour fields of black. The use of varnish over these blacks fields emphasies the spatial quality. Amongst this group of eorks are *Ellissi* or *Costruttivi/Ellissi,* made of iron, canvas or wood which, among a variety of readings, determine a constructive rapport with space. This theme remains constant in all Carrino's recent work, from *Trasformazione dello spazio* to *Interventi nell'architettura.*

—Roberto Lambarelli

CASCELLA, Pietro.

Italian. Born in Pescara, Italy, 2 February 1921. Studied with his father Tommaso, and at the Accademia di Belle Arti, Rome. Married; children: Benedetta, Tommaso, Susanno and Jacopo. Sculptor. Recipient: First Prize, Monument to Auschwitz Competition, 1960; Prize Prize, *Biennale di Carrara,* 1967. Address: Castello della Verrucola, Fivizzano, Italy.

Individual Exhibitions:

1950	Galleria l'Obelisco, Rome (with Andrea Cascella)
1954	Galleria del Naviglio, Milan
1955	Galleria Cavallino, Venice
1957	Galleria Selecta, Rome
1960	Galleria del Milione, Milan
1962	Galleria l'Obelisco, Rome
1963	Galerie du Dragon, Paris
1965	Bonino Gallery, New York
	Galleria Milano, Milan
1966	*Biennale,* Venice
	Galleria Milano, Milan
1967	Galleria Milano, Milan
1968	Galerie du Dragon, Paris
	Galleria Milano, Milan
	Musée d'Ixelles, Brussels
1969	Galleria Arte Borgogna, Milan
	Galleria Nuova Pesa, Rome
1971	Palais des Beaux-Arts, Brussels
	Galleria Arte Borgogna, Milan
	Musée d'Art Moderne de la Ville, Paris
	Rotonda di via Besana, Milan
1972	*Biennale,* Venice
1973	Galleria Goethe, Bolzano, Italy
	Galleria Etrusculundens, Rome
1974	Galleria Forni, Bologna
	Galleria Giulia, Rome
1975	Galleria Forum, Trieste
1976	Galleria Nizzoli, Parma, Italy
	Kloster Camiore di San Lazzaro, Italy
	Galleria Salotto, Como, Italy
	Galleria Nove Colonne, Trento, Italy
1977	Galleria Stendhal, Milan
	Grafica Club, Milan
	Centro Arte Moderna, Pisa
	Centro Storico, Rimini, Italy
1979	Galerie Godula, Buchholz, West Germany
1980	Galleria del Naviglio, Milan
1983	Galleria Bergamini Diarte, Milan
1984	Galleria Gian Ferrari, Milan

Selected Group Exhibitions:

1948	*Biennale,* Venice
1950	*Consorso Internazionale,* Rome
1952	*Consorso per il Monumento di Albisola,* Italy
1960	*Auschwitz Monument Competition Exhibition,* Auschwitz, Poland
1964	*Pittsburgh International,* Carnegie Institute, Pittsburgh
1973	*Middelheim Sculpture Biennale,* Antwerp
1975	*Disegni di 34 Scultori,* Salone delle Conference, Milan
1977	*Arte in Italia 1960-77,* Galleria Civica d'Arte Moderna, Turin
1981	*Linee della Ricerca Artistiche in Italia 1960-80,* Palazzo delle Esposizioni, Rome
1983	*Memoria dell'Uomo: La Grande Metafora,* Villa Pacchiani, Santa Croce sull'Arno, Italy

Collections:

Museo d'Arte Moderna, Bologna; Middelheim Museum, Antwerp.

Commissions include: War Memorial, Albissola, Italy, 1956; Auschwitz Memorial, with Andrea Cascella and the architect Lafuente, Auschwitz, Poland 1960; Mazzini Monument, Piazza della Republica, Milan 1974.

Publications:

On CASCELLA: books—*Il Monumento di Auschwitz,* exhibition catalogue, by Mario de Michel, Milan 1960; *Pietro Cascella* by Cesare Vivaldi, Milan 1966; *Mostra dell Besana* by Guido Ballo, Milan 1971; *Pietro Cascella* by Guido Vegani, Milan 1974; *Maestri Contemporanei: Pietro Cascella* by Roberto Sanesi, Milan 1983; *Pietro Cascella* by Enrico Crispolti, Florence 1984.

From a distinguished family of sculptors, Pietro Cascella and his brother Andrea have emerged as two of the most gifted practitioners in contemporary Italian art. The two brothers are similar in their media preference and imagery, but Pietro can be identified principally for his choice of more monumental conceptions, in which scale, simplicity, and in particular rough unfinished marble are basic components.

Stone carvers are comparatively rare in modern art but for an Italian it is both a challenge and a reference to national history and the natural scene. Cascella has said that one cannot consider the process "in terms of the consumer society; the method of working, and the time required, belongs to a former age; it is an art of patience." He prefers to confront a huge block of marble (à la Michelangelo, perhaps).

Two distinct forms emerge in Pietro Cascella's work; rounded, feminine, sexual shapes, similar in a generalised way to the shapes found in Henry Moore's reclining females; but with Cascella there is no evocative comparison of the nude body to a gentle, rolling landscape. He is more involved in the complexities of the body, sexually curious, isolating and examining details, so that the emergent sculptures are enlarged combinations of rounded forms and orifices. They do not resemble landscape, or indeed nature in general, except that their organic nature evokes memories and references. Enormously enlarged, physically dominating, and abstracted beyond original inspiration, they manage to promote the idea of intimacy and inevitability.

His sculptures neither provoke nor disturb. More open to doubt is the development from these organic, intimate, sensual conceptions, to extended public monuments, some of which he has worked on with his brother Andrea. These include the "Auschwitz Monument," the "Gate of Peace" at Tel Aviv, the "National Congress Monument" at Strasbourg and the Mazzini commemoration in Milan. Once can see the reason for such commissions since it is difficult to think of other modern sculptors who can undertake such portentous requests. Individual characteristic works by sculptors are often commissioned as public monuments, and no doubt enhance the space they occupy; Cascella, in the great Mediterranean tradition, produces massive public celebrations, partly architecture, part landscape, partly sculpture. They inevitably lack the personal involvement of the more intimate works, combining with the intimate rounded forms, the more architectural details of flat pavements and geometrical intersections.

—Charles Spencer

CASTELLANI, Enrico.

Italian. Born in Castelmassa, Rovigo, Italy, 4 August 1930. Educated in Novara and Milan; studied painting and sculpture at the Académie Royale des Beaux-Arts, Brussels, 1952–56, and architecture at the Ecole Nationale Supèrieure de la Cambre, Belgium, 1956. Has lived and worked in Milan since 1956: Founder, with Piero Manzoni, *Azimuth* journal, Milan, 1959; associated with the Zero Group, Milan, 1962. Recipient: Painting Prize, Nagaoka Museum, Tokyo, 1967; Gold Medal, *Biennale di San Marino*, 1967. Agent: Galerie M, Haus Weitmar, Bochum, West Germany. Address: 01010 Cellere, Vitterbo, Italy.

Individual Exhibitions:

1959   Galerie Kasper, Lausanne, Switzerland
1960   Galleria Azimut, Milan
1961   New Vision Centre, London
       Galleria La Tartaruga, Rome
1962   Galerie Aujourd'hui, Brussels
1963   Galleria dell'Ariete, Milan
1964   Galleria La Polena, Genoa
       Galleria Notizie, Turin
       Galleria del Leone, Venice
       Galerie Wulfengasse, Klagenfurt, Austria
1965   Galleria La Tartaruga, Rome
       Galerie Lawrence, Paris
1966   Galleria Notizie, Turin
       Betty Parsons Gallery, New York
       Tokyo Gallery
1968   *Documenta*, Kassel, West Germany
1970   Galerie M. Bochum, West Germany
1971   Artestudio, Macerata, Italy
1972   Galleriaforma, Genoa

Selected Group Exhibitions:

1960   *Monochrome Malerei*, Städtisches Museum, Leverkusen, West Germany
1961   *Nove Tendencije I*, Zagreb
1962   *Zero*, Stedelijk Museum, Amsterdam
1964   *Guggenheim International*, Guggenheim Museum, New York
1965   *The Responsive Eye*, Museum of Modern Art, New York
1966   *Third Exhibition*, Nagaoka Museum, Tokyo
1968   *Many Italian Artists*, Jewish Museum, New York
1971   *11 Italiener Heute*, Museum am Ostwall, Dortmund, West Germany

1981   *Artee Critica*, Galleria Nazionale d'Arte Moderna, Rome
1986   *Aspects of Italian Art 1960–85*, Kunstverein, Frankfurt

Collections:

Galleria Nazionale d'Arte Moderna, Rome.

Publications:

On CASTELLANI: books—*Visites d'Atelier* by Giulia Veronesi, Lausanne, Switzerland 1959; *La Linea dell'Arte Italiana* by Guido Ballo, Milan 1964; *Testo del Libro Castellani Pittore* by Vincenzo Agnetti, Milan 1968; *Op Art* by Cyril Barrett, London 1970; articles—"La Peinture Objet dans l'Art Italien Contemporain" by Gillo Dorfles in *L'Oeil* (Paris), no. 121, 1965; "Il Purismo di Castellani" by M. F. dell Arco in *L'Avanti* (Milan), no. 6/8, 1966.

By 1956, when he and Piero Manzoni founded the review *Azimuth*, Enrico Castellani had already worked out the basic principles which have governed his artistic experiments ever since. The monochromatic surfaces which he now began to produce were essentially reactions against his earlier irrationalist exercises, with their explosive colors and violent imagery. Thus his later work is basically abstract in character: in intensity and aim he comes close to the conceptualism of an artist like Lucio Fontana.

In his monochromatic surfaces Castellani has explored new areas of painting, yet he also wishes to work within the tradition which leads back to the neoplastic origins of art, as Gestalt psychological theory defines them. These red, yellow, blue, white and silver canvases are hung over projecting nails of varying lengths, so that the surface is contoured. And over these surfaces lights play, half-lights corresponding to the convexities, shadows to the concavities. These chiaroscuro effects give his work some affinity with of the early Op-Art of the early 1960's, but the intensity of Castellani's work goes far beyond those cold experiments.

At the corner of his work lies the quintessentially modern concern with space and time. He expresses the problem by means of his contoured surfaces—"spatial modulators," as Dorfles calls them—which both contain and liberate space. Castellani wishes us to grasp the flexibility of space; and the lights which play over the surfaces at varying rates of speed are designed to express the continuity of time and the relationship which exists between time and space themselves. His experiments have opened up new vistas.

—Roberto G. Lambarelli

CASTELLI, Luciano.

Swiss. Born in Lucerne, 28 September 1951. Studied at the School of Art and Design, Lucerne, 1969. Lived and worked in Lucerne until 1977, Rome, 1977–78, and in Berlin since 1978. Recipient: Kiefer Hablitzel Stipendium, 1970–71; Bundes Stipendium, 1973–75. Agents: Galerie Stahli, 39 Gruezgasse, Zurich 8008, Switzerland; Galerie de Appel, 196 Brouwersgracht, Amsterdam, Netherlands. Address: Reckenbuhlstrasse 17, 6005 Lucerne, Switzerland.

Individual Exhibitions:

1971   Galerie Toni Gerber, Berne
1975   Galerie Stahli, Zurich
       Galerie de Appel, Amsterdam
       Galerie t'Venster, Rotterdam
       Salle Municipal Palino, Geneva

1978   Galerie Handschin, Basle
1979   Galerie Stahli, Zurich
1981   Centre d'art contemporain, Geneva
       Galerie Farideh Cadot, Paris
       Annina Nosei Gallery, New York
1983   CAPC/Musee d'Art Contemporain, Bordeaux France (with Fetting and Salome)
1984   Galerie Farideh Cadot, Paris

Selected Group Exhibitions:

1971   *Biennale des Jeunes*, Paris
1972   *Documenta 5*, Museum Fridericianum, Kassel, West Germany
1974   *Transformer-Aspekte der Travestie*, Kunstmuseum, Lucerne
1975   *Biennale des Jeunes*, Paris.
1980   *Biennale*, Venice
1981   *Schweizer Kunst '70–'80*. Kunstmuseum, Lucerne
       Im Westen nichts Neues, Kunstmuseum, Lucerne
       12 Kunstler aus Deutschland, Kunsthalle, Basle
1982   *A l'Ouest rien de Nouveau*, Centre d'Art Contemporain, Geneva
1987   *Berlinart 1961–87*, Museum of Modern Art, New York (travelled to San Francisco)

Collections:

Kunstmuseum, Basle, Kunstmuseum, Lucerne.

Publications:

By CASTELLI: articles—interview by Jean-Christophe Ammann in *Rapport der Innerschweiz*, exhibition catalogue, Zurich 1974; interview by Jean Christophe Amman in *Transformer-Aspekte der Travestie*, exhibition catalogue, Lucerne 1974; interview by Jacques Clayssen in *Identité Identifications*, exhibition catalogue, Paris 1976.

On CASTELLI: books—*Visualierte Denkprozesse*, exhibition catalogue, by Jean-Christophe Ammann, Lucerne 1971; *Giovanne Arte Svizzera*, exhibition catalogue, by W. Schonenberger and Theo Kneubuhler, Milan 1972; *Aspekte der Travestie*, exhibition catalogue, Lucerne 1974; *9th Biennale*, exhibition catalogue, Paris 1975; *Fundatie*, exhibition catalogue, Amsterdam 1979; *Schweizer Kunst '70–'80*, exhibition catalogue, Lucerne 1981; *12 Kunstler aus Deutschland*, exhibition catalogue, Basle 1982; *A l'Quest rien de Nouveau*, exhibition catalogue, with texts by Martin Kunz and Eberhard Roters, Geneva 1982.

—How is the link accomplished between objects and the work on the body?

My work is much too closely linked to my life for me to be able to disassociate objects, either from the sculptures or from the photographic works. Photography is the most direct means. Objects such as the handkerchief, the motorcycle helmet, are everyday objects but they have become pipes, which is to say personal objects. As the act of smoking was very important during this period, I reconstructed that importance around objects; I found it more interesting to occupy myself with objects which concerned me and which, as a result, taught me more about myself. The link is probably to be found in the treatment of the body in my work: I use it as an object.

—The perception of the body is [put at one remove] by the photo, but do you use a mirror to realize these photographs?

I use the mirror uniquely to control the appearance; the image of the mirror is not a partner.

—You don't seek the help of a photographer?

No, it's simply a question of independence. I can get up at two o'clock in the morning to work if I want to. I use an automatic release to give me greater freedom.

—Would the voyeurism of a photographer irritate you?

I work at certain moments in very precise conditions; any person not directly involved in my work would therefore be an irritation.

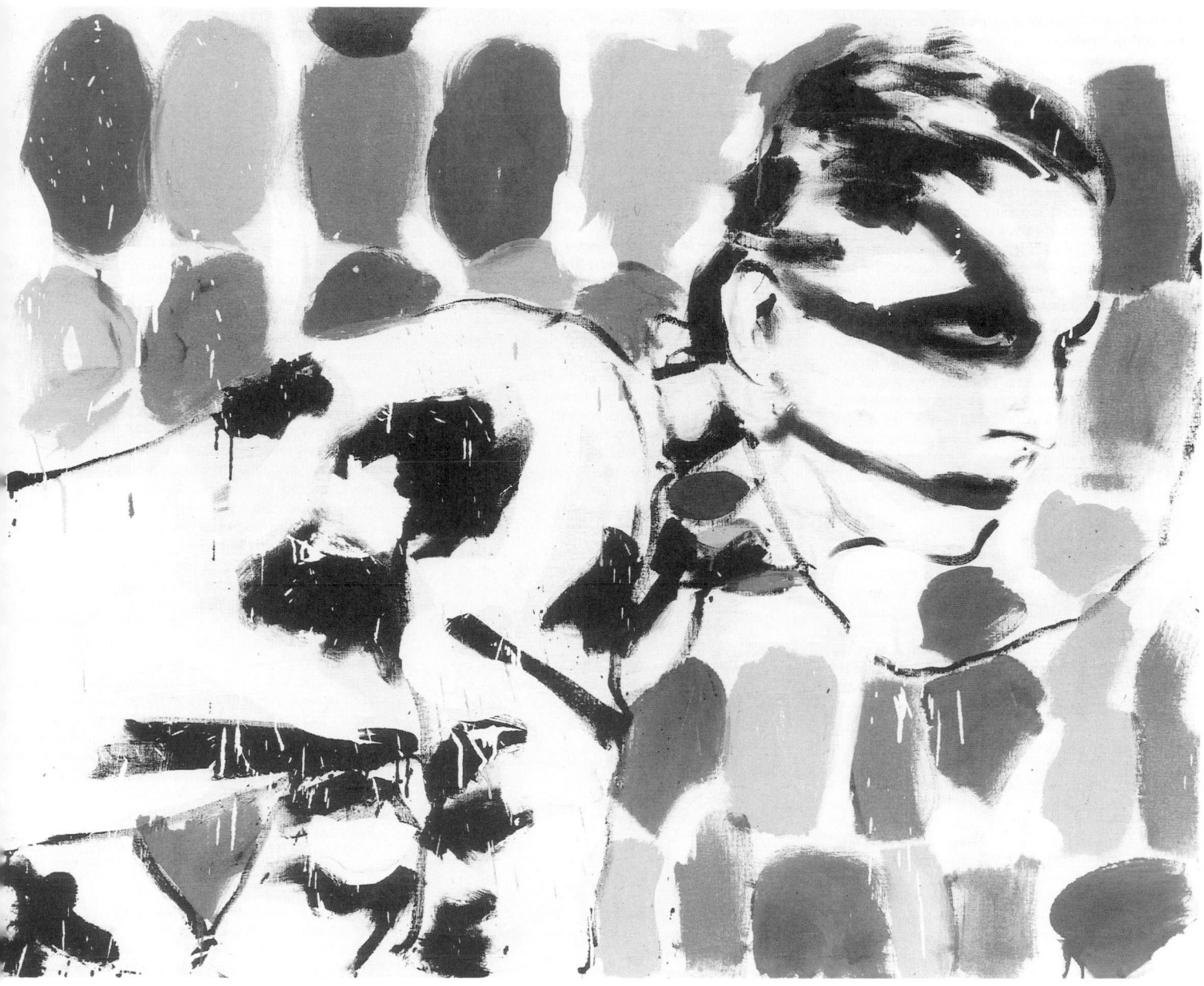

Luciano Castelli: *Hund I*, 1981

—What are the origins of what you represent in a sculpture such as the oyster with a body coiled in the shell?

I made the figure first. Then, while doing so, I thought of mother of pearl, and its sweetness preoccupied me. And in Roxy Music the phrase "mother of pearl" rose up so strongly that I made the oyster shell. I plan to continue along these lines with sculptures, water-colours, objects. I don't want to use photos any more.

—Transvestism is no longer a preoccupation?

It's not really preoccupation any more. Transvestism was the provocative form of an ambiguity which I have within me, between the masculine and the feminine, but the complementary feminine element always forms part of my work. I always dealt with this feminine element in my earlier objects, notably in my drawings. When I'd had very long hair, I had done a drawing after smoking some hashish and, suddenly, I had had the impression that my trousers were becoming a dress and that I was like a woman—an optical illusion.

—At a certain moment, in your photo's, you use some very unusual garments, animal skins . . . .

There's no special scheme in the use of this type of clothing. The arrangement came about fortuitously; luck and the concordance with the spirit in which I was working brought it about that I used them.

—In the most recent works, it is no longer a question of transvestism by garments, but the accent is put on poses, expressions. There are in fact no more garments?

No.

—It's the poses which denote a certain pattern of femininity?

I gave up transvestism by make-up and clothing to try to show one of its resultants, which is aggressivity, provocation transformed into a more animal characteristic. I have done several series on this theme.

—Animal in the pose?

Yes, but I consider that the term animal, of animal appearance, is as much masculine as feminine. The animal side is aggressivity and, perhaps, brutality. But the female side masks a little of this approach.

—The pose is lascivious?

Yes, it's the feline side that I feel in myself.

—The transvestism established itself in terms of provocation, of aggression against the exterior world, but on the artistic plane?

When I use make-up, I satisfy an interior necessity. There is make-up and there is make-up; on the one hand, a make-up which is banal and entirely superficial, on the other a more considered form which, at the moment when it is confronted with the exterior by the form adopted and the context in which one presents it, becomes provocation.

—Make-up is a discourse.

Yes, absolutely.

—Can one talk of auto-analysis?

I think that this continual working has taught me a lot about myself. I have learnt from my experiments insofar as they have allowed me to see, to visualize certain elements which I carry within myself. All these images come from me, but for myself, I don't know if I get from them anything but the pleasure of seeing them.

—Your work remains a method of artistic expression.

I expressed at a certain moment the masculine-feminine side in the field of art by insisting on that which touches me closely, and I think that in this type of work it's the masculine side which is emphasized. Art is the last link of a chain; my activity expresses itself as a work which shows the ambivalence and allows me to assume it as a strategy. It is not without problems that I have accepted this ambivalence in my work. But in itself transvestism is not a problem; one must differentiate between transvestite and transvestism.

—So one can say that you are not transvestite except during the transvestism?

Yes, one can put it that way. I consider this moment as the expression of the masculine-feminine bipolarity. My works are my life, my [region of the] imaginary.

—Luciano Castelli,
from an interview with Jacques Clayssen

Luciano Castelli's painting is painting for effect; it shows off its colours with unbridled eroticism and aestheticism. Between the rapid brush-strokes there appear fragments or details of an image, a "prisoner" of the swift play set in motion by the colour-shape itself. The result is a surface abstraction/figuration, with no spatial depth. It is the emotive effect of an instant projected towards a chance pleasure. The artist gives free rein to the gesture, to the sensual peacefulness of his becoming, to the eclecticism of his deviations. The artist has only love of himself; his "inner emotions" last only a moment and are therefore exploited to the full. It would be sheer hypocrisy to emerge from this perverted state of grace; he has rather to enter freely into it, to make clearer the duration of the gestural orgasm.

Castelli is an artist by vocation; his daily prayers are made to beauty and to exhausting pleasure. Hedonism is the unknown, to be violated, to be gratified. Hence the screaming density of the colour-shape, the fragments of image exposed in the grip of excitement. The surface, crowded in this way, looks like a film show which we attend as *voyeur*. The artist, moving within the transient multicoloured light, creates unexpected situations; his movements (posed or dancing), charged with exhibitionism, let that self-love shine through above all.

Castelli's painting (like that of Rainer Fetting, Helmut Middendorf and Salomè) is pervaded with auto-erotism. With or without the self-portrait, the artist always portrays a little of himself. Painting is thus a marvellous, exhilarating, freethinking, ambiguous medium to exalt or satisfy the call to be an artist. It does not aim at surprise effects; any that are produced are only apparent. It is actually the appearance, and the wonderful melancholy of it, that attract and seduce the artist. In the self-portrait he seems to see how deviation changes aspect, obedient to an implacable fate that inexorably deforms the reality. But the self-portrait is disconcerting to anyone who looks for the logic of the likeness in it. Instead, the artist thirsts for extravagance; he is filled with an urge to follow the irreverent, shocking path of his narcissism in order to hide the true, fleeting image. Luciano Castelli disguises himself in order to fling out something disturbing through the medium of a painting whose very facility makes it pungent and enigmatic. It may be that his painting reflects a tendency to déjà vu, and why ever should it represent the invisible? An enervating scepticism does not consort with the art of the self-portrait.

—Italo Mussa

CASTILLO, Jorge.

Spanish. Born in Pontevedra, Galicia, 16 July 1933. Educated in Argentina, until 1940; studied at the School of Fine Arts, Buenos Aires, 1941–45; influenced by artist Raquel Ferrer. Served in the Spanish Army, 1956–57. Married Maria-Helena Castillo (died, 1963); daughter: Ruth; married Marienza Castillo in 1966; son: Taggio. Independent artist, Buenos Aires, 1945–55, in Madrid and Barcelona, 1957–63, in Paris, Geneva and Barcelona, 1963–66, in Loano, Italy, 1966–69, in West Berlin, and Barcelona, 1970–74, in Barcelona, since 1975: first sculptures, 1965. Recipient: International Drawing Prize, Darmstadt 1964; D.A.A.D. Fellowship, West Berlin 1969–70. Agent: Galerie Calart, Geneva. Address: c/o Galerie Calart, 4 bis Rue Prevost-Martin, Place des Philosophes, 1205 Geneva, Switzerland.

Individual Exhibitions:

1959	Galeria Altamira, Madrid
1960	Galeria Abril, Madrid
	Galeria San Jorge, Madrid
1961	Bodley Gallery, New York
	Galeria Diario de Noticias, Lisbon
	Galeria Mediterraneo, Madrid
1962	Galeria Mediterraneo, Madrid
1963	Galerie Andrè Schoeller, Paris
	Galerie Raymond Cordier, Paris
1964	Kunstverein, Dusseldorf
1965	Galerie Andrè Schoeller, Paris
	Galleria Galatea, Turin
	Galeria Belarte, Barcelona
	Galerie Brusberg, Hannover
	Musée d'Art et d'Histoire, Fribourg, Switzerland
1966	Musée de l'Athenée, Geneva
	Paintings and Drawings, Richard Demarco Gallery, Edinburgh
1967	Loeb and Krugier, New York
	Gallery of Modern Art, Scottsdale, Arizona
1968	*Vers un Peinture Generative*, Galerie Krugier, Geneva
1969	Frankfurter Kunstkabinett, Frankfurt
1970	Galerie Contemporaine, Geneva
	Galeria Iolas-Velasco, Madrid
	Galeria Seiquer, Madrid
	Nationalgalerie, West Berlin
	Galerie Rudolf Springer, West Berlin
1971	Galerie Krugier, Geneva
	Galerie Ariadne, Cologne
	Galerie Ariadne, Vienna
	Traverse Art Gallery, Edinburgh
	Galerie Herbert Meyer-Ellinger, Frankfurt
	Musée d'Art et d'Histoire, Geneva
1972	Galeria Adria, Barcelona
	Gemalde/Aquarelle/Zeichnungen/Druckgraphik, Kunstverein, Darmstadt
	Galerie Pels-Leusden, West Berlin
	Galerie Richard P. Hartmann, Munich
1973	*Radierungen*, Kestner-Gesellschaft, Hannover
1974	Galerie Stephane Janssen, Brussels
	Galeria 42, Barcelona
	Werke 1973/74, Galerie Michael Hertz, Bremen, West Germany
1976	Galeria Joan Prats, Barcelona
1977	Lefebre Gallery, New York

Selected Group Exhibitions:

1959	*El Bodega Espanol*, Galeria Darro, Madrid
1960	*20th Century Drawings and Graphics*, Galeria Darro, Madrid
1961	*Bienal*, Sao Paulo
1962	*Grands et Jeunes d'Aujourd'hui*, Grand Palais, Paris
1963	*Salon de Mai*, Musée d'Art Moderne, Paris
1964	*Internationale der Zeichnung*, Darmstadt
1973	*Hommage à Picasso*, Kestner-Gesellschaft, Hannover
1987	*Arco 87*, Madrid

Collections:

Musée Cantonal des Beaux-Arts, Lausanne, Switzerland; Kunstmuseum, Essen; Kunstmuseum, Bochum, West Germany; Kunstverein, Darmstadt; Nationalgalerie, West Berlin; Museum am Ostwall, Dortmund, West Germany; Museum des 20, Jahrhunderts, Vienna.

Publications:

On CASTILLO: books—*Castillo*, exhibition catalogue, with text by Luigi Carluccio, Turin 1965; *Jorge Castillo: Paintings and Drawings*, exhibition catalogue, with text by Jean-Luc Daval, Edinburgh 1966; *Jorge Castillo: Vers un Peinture Generative*, exhibition catalogue, with text by Jean-Luc Daval, Geneva 1968; *Jorge Castillo*, exhibition catalogue, with text by Werner Haftmann, West Berlin 1970; *Jorge Castillo: Citations*, exhibition catalogue, Geneva 1971; *Jorge Castillo: Gemalde/Aquarelle/Zeichnungen/Druckgraphik*, exhibition catalogue, with texts by G. Hofmann and B. Krimmel, Darmstadt 1972; *Hommage à Picasso*, exhibition catalogue, with texts by Wieland Schmied, Werner Haftmann and Daniel Kahnweiler, Hannover 1973; *Jorge Castillo: Radierungen*, exhibition catalogue, with texts by Wieland Schmied and Werner Haftmann, Hannover 1973; *Castillo: Werke 1973/74*, exhibition catalogue, with text by Werner Haft-

mann, Bremen, West Germany 1974; *Jorge Castillo*, exhibition catalogue, with text by Werner Haftmann, New York 1977.

At the *Basel International Art Fair*, three dealers—a German, a Russian (out of Spain) and a Frenchman—were involved in a complicated multiway enterprise to try to exchange five of Dali's San Francisco coloured etchings for a painting by Jorge Castillo. After four days of maneuvering and intense plotting and counterplotting the Frenchman won the day, but he had to throw in still more ballast to clinch the bargain. No money changed hands, but equity on both sides was regarded as considerable. Reference is made to this small commercial episode to indicate that from 1970 onwards Castillo has come to be reckoned as viable art market currency.

He was born in 1933 which makes him a comparatively young man to have his works high-financed in such a sub-rosa fashion. And yet his reputation has somehow managed to outstrip cognizance of his work, all too little known to the art world at large, although German collectors, during the 1970's, became specially interested in his paintings and only slightly less in his graphics.

What are the qualities that have combined to give him a particular place and consideration in the crowded corridors of contemporary art?

Castillo is essentially a Latin painter; perhaps galloromantic would be a better description in view of his quirky illogicality and personalised invention. It is as if he had painlessly digested all the twists of 20th century figurative art and then found a contemporary accent with which to make the old new, and the new old in a manner never likely to prove disruptive to those aware of the way in which modern figurative art has developed.

His is the voice of Hispañola, not España. Nobility in his oeuvres is never allowed to blot out cleverness; and cleverness is never permitted to make his imagery over-literary. His colours do not shout. They murmur. But their quiet tones in no way reduce the validity of the messages they clothe.

The impression of a contained version of collage (or, in the case of the watercolours, drawings, aquatints and etchings, maybe the underlying expression of assemblage would be a more opposite implication) could be a clue to the subliminal reason of his mysterious appeal. In plain language, it means that Castillo "builds" his pictures. However perverse the imagery of a drawing like "La petite dormeuse" of 1970, the compositional architecture is there even if he takes liberties with it. The fauteuil is enormous and the little figure is half swathed in the shadow which has somehow crept across part of the back of the chair, slipped through into the seat beyond and engulfed the figure. This is a sort of "imaginary" collage of the kind of referred to above.

Nor is Castillo limited to traditional methods. He has made some interesting experiments with mischtechnik. "The Group of Figures" he made in Barcelona in 1965 shows what an astonishing range of tonality and perspective he can achieve with media-alchemy on a sheet of drawing paper.

So Castillo is a technician as well as an artist. That in itself is not a unique position to hold in the field of visual arts. What this combination adds to his stature is that it is wedded to an offbeat mind. "Our Lady of the Sorrows" (1973) sits against a background of two goalposts and a storm-tossed tree. "Flight from the Monster" (1960) is like a cross between a circus and a ballet. The foreground figure looks as if he is going to curve into a pirouette, and the monster is sulking anyway.

Castillo is a master of surprise. All his shocks have the immediacy of wit. Sometimes sardonic, sometimes closer to the belly laugh. All his non-shocks have a curious monumentalism made paradoxical because they so often appear to be momentary.

—Sheldon Williams

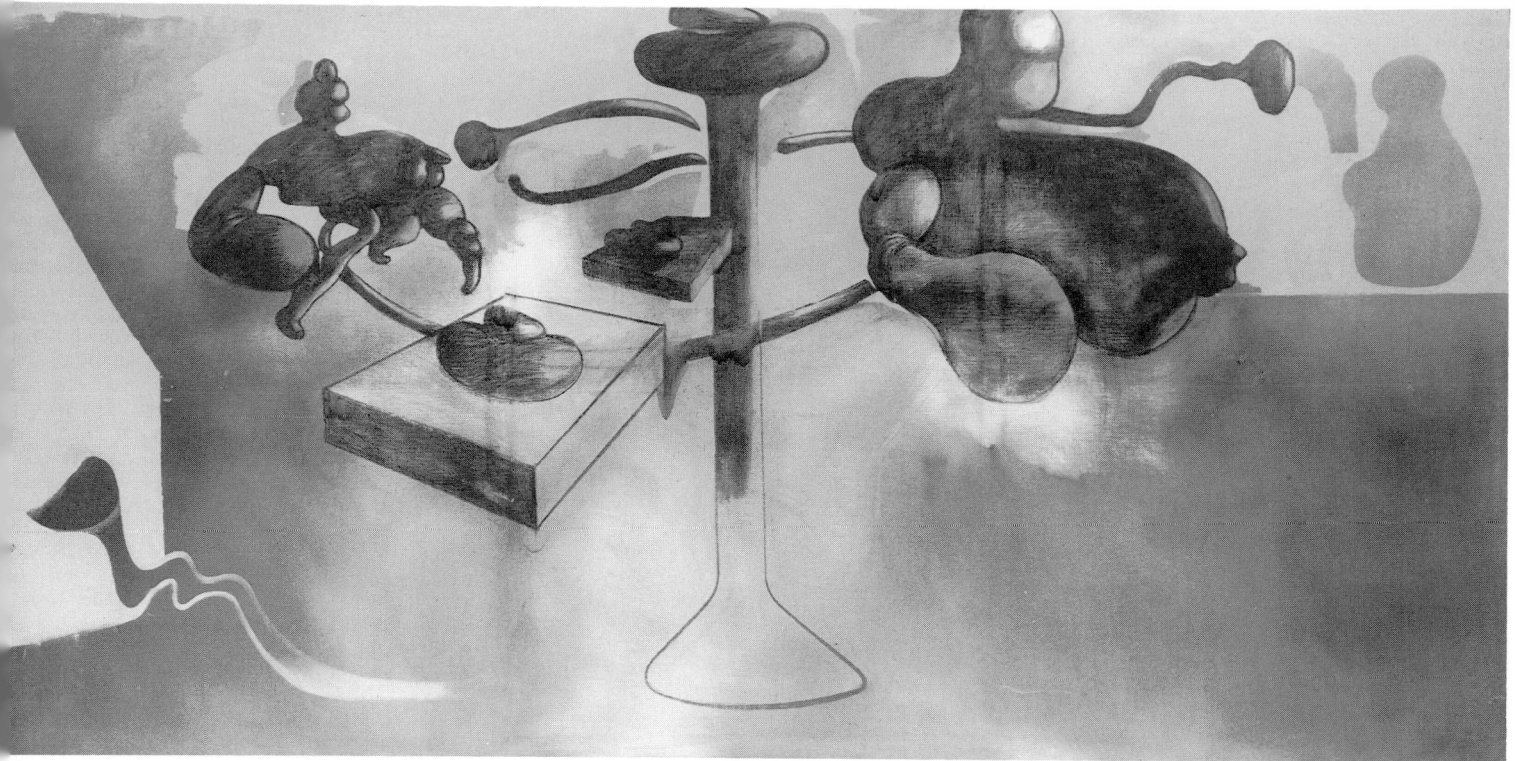

Jorge Castillo: *Jardin de Boissano*, 1970

CAULFIELD, Patrick.

British. Born in London in 1936. Studied at the Chelsea School of Art, London, under Jack Smith, 1956–60, and at the Royal College of Art, London, 1960–63. Painter and printmaker: lives and works in London. Lecturer, Chelsea School of Art, 1963–71. Recipient: Prix de Jeunes Artistes (graphics), 1965. Agent: Waddington Galleries, London. Address: c/o Waddington Galleries, 11 Cork Street, London W1, England.

Individual Exhibitions:

1965	Robert Fraser Gallery, London
	Galerie d'Aujourd'hui, Brussels (with Derek Boshier)
1966	Robert Elkon Gallery, New York
1967	Studio Marconi, Milan
	Robert Fraser Gallery, London
1968	Robert Elkon Gallery, New York
1969	Waddington Galleries, London
1971	D. M. Gallery, London
	Waddington Galleries, London
1972	Galerie Stadler, Paris (with Howard Hodgkin and Michael Moon)
	Sweeney Reed Galleries, Victoria, Australia
1973	Waddington Galleries, London
	Europalia, Brussels
1974	O. K. Harris Gallery, New York
	Kinsman Morrison Gallery, London
1975	Waddington Galleries, London
	Scottish Arts Council Gallery, Edinburgh
1976	Arnolfini Gallery, Bristol
1977	Tortue Gallery, Santa Monica, California
1978	Tate Gallery, London
1979	Waddington Galleries, London
1980	Hughes Gallery, Brisbane
	IAC, Basle
	Tolarno Galleries, Melbourne
	Gardner Centre for the Arts, University of Sussex, Brighton (travelled to the Oriel Gallery, Cardiff, and the Midland Group Gallery, Nottingham)
1981	Walker Art Gallery, Liverpool (travelled to the Tate Gallery, London, 1982)
	Waddington Galleries, London
1982	Nishimura Gallery, Tokyo
1983	Arnolfini Gallery, Bristol
1985	Waddington Galleries, London
	Bernardelli Gallery, Rio de Janeiro (toured South America, 1985–87)

Selected Group Exhibitions:

1964	*The New Generation*, Whitechapel Art Gallery, London
1965	*Biennale des Jeunes*, Musée National d'Art Moderne, Paris
1966	*Recent Still Life*, Rhode Island School of Design, Providence
1967	*Jeunes Peintres Anglais*, Palais des Beaux-Arts, Brussels
1969	*Marks on a Canvas*, Museum am Ostwall, Dortmund, West Germany
1971	*Junge Englander*, Kunststudio Westfalen, Bielefeld, West Germany
1974	*British Painting 74*, Hayward Gallery, London
1976	*Arte Inglese Oggi*, Palazzo Reale, Milan
1982	*Aspects of British: Art Today*, Metropolitan Art Museum, Tokyo (toured Japan)
1984	*British Artists' Books 1970–83*, Atlantis Gallery, London

Collections:

Arts Council of Great Britain, London: Tate Gallery, London; Walker Art Gallery, Liverpool; Whitworth Art Gallery, Manchester; Hirshhorn Museum and Sculpture Garden, Washington, D.C.: Virginia Museum of Fine Arts, Richmond; Art Gallery of Ontario, Toronto.

Publications:

By CAULFIELD: articles—"Why Do Artists Make Prints?" in *Studio International* (London), June 1967; "Questionnaire" in *London Magazine*, April/May 1979.

On CAULFIELD: books—*Paintings by Patrick Caulfield*, exhibition catalogue, London 1967; *Patrick Caulfield* by Christopher Finch, London 1971; *Patrick Caulfield*, exhibition catalogue, London 1975; *Patrick Caulfield: Paintings and Prints*, exhibition catalogue, by Norbert Lynton, Edinburgh 1975; *Patrick Caulfield Print Retrospective: Complete Works 1964–1976*, exhibition catalogue, Santa Monica, California 1977; *Patrick Caulfield: Paintings 1963–81*, exhibition catalogue by Marco Livingston, London 1981; *Patrick Caulfield*, exhibition catalogue edited by the Waddington Galleries, London 1985; *Patrick Caulfield* by John McEwan, London 1987; articles—"From Illusion to Allusion" by Christopher Finch in *Art and Artists* (London), April 1966; "Comic Strip Pop" by John Loring in *Arts Magazine* (New York), September 1974; "Patrick Caulfield" by William Feaver in *The Observer* (London), 30 November 1975; "A Talent in English Painting" by James Burr in *Apollo* (London), July 1979.

*

Patrick Caulfield is a deceptive artist. At first glance his work looks easy, unimaginative, almost childlike. When you examine it more closely, things look very different. The comparisons with Lichtenstein and other "Pop" artists are ridiculous. Caulfield is a profoundly European painter who never seeks to glamourise or depict American merchandise. Caulfield selects everyday objects and sometimes juxtaposes them with exotic ones. In "Still Life with Dagger" a dull jug stands next to an exotic turquoise dagger from the Victoria and Albert Museum. Banality is linked with sophistication such as in "Still Life on a Table." Highly decorative china is placed against a background of a parody of modern art. In "Pony" the horse has taken an imposing Stubbs pose but looks as though it had been painted by numbers. In "Still Life with Candle" the vanitas theme without the skull appears. The candle is burnt out, the bread is being eaten by a mouse and the glass has fallen over. In "View of the Rooftops" Caulfield has become romantic. The flame red background is reminiscent of the great fire in "Gone with the Wind." In the successful "Bend in the Road" the bend is executed in the corniest of ways by leading the viewers' eye into the canvas—similar to the children walking down the road into the sunset advertising Start Rite shoes. Sometimes Caulfield makes perverse subject choices such as the "Smokeless Coal Fire" or the room divider.

Humans are rarely present but their presence is felt. In "Window at Night" a window is open and a light is on. The contrast between the warm glow of the room and the blackness of the night is superbly portrayed. Caulfield makes little attempt at shading or modelling, but the familiar black lines create vitality. In the painting "Inner Office" there is again a contrast between the external and internal world. The

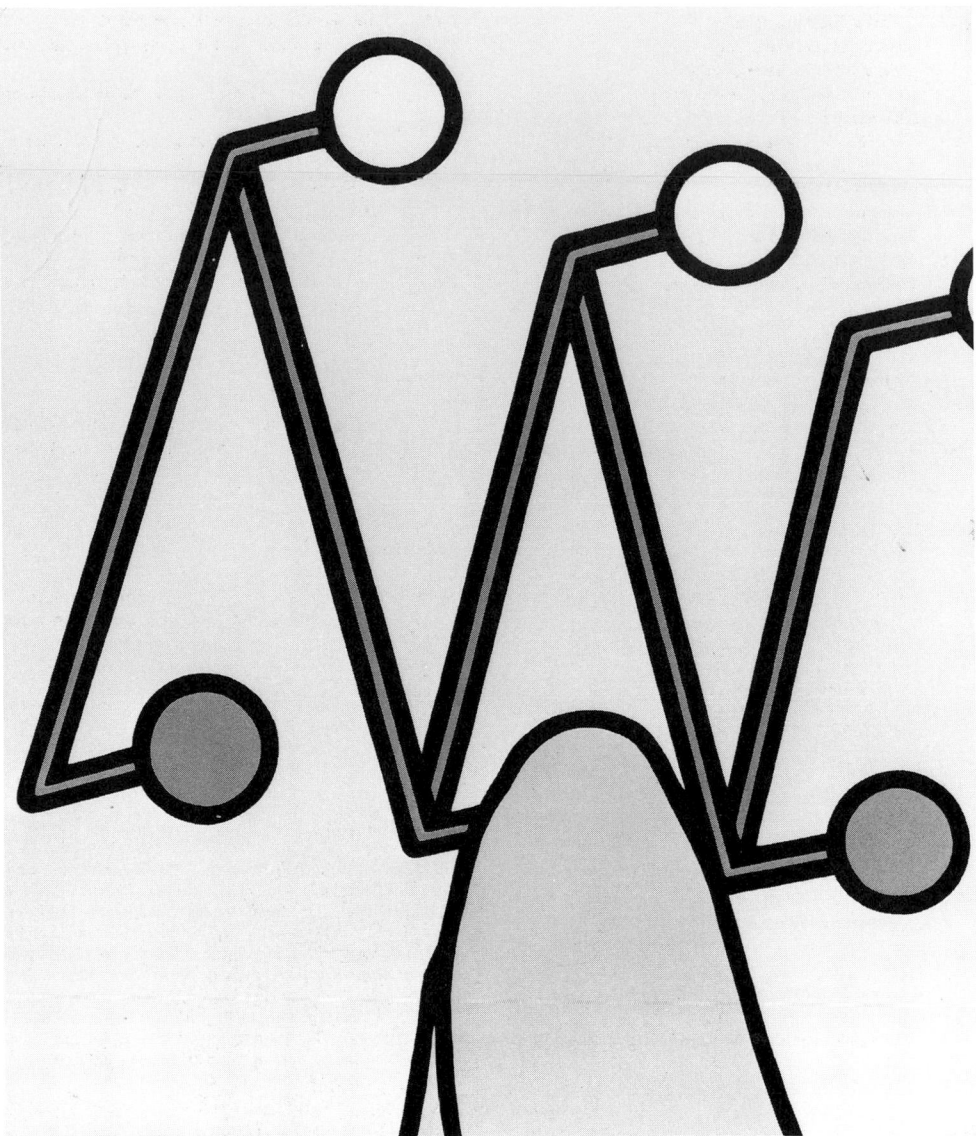

Patrick Caulfield: *Thus She Would Come, Escaped, Half Dead to My Door*, 1973

Collections:

Galleria Nazionale d'Arte Moderna, Rome; Gemeentemuseum, The Hague; Carnegie Institute, Pittsburgh.

Publications:

By CAVALIERE: article—"Notes for a Dialogue Beyond the Work" in *Alik Cavaliere: 3 Environments*, exhibition catalogue, Milan 1971.

On CAVALIERE: books—*Alik Cavaliere*, exhibition catalogue, by Enrico Crispolti, Milan 1967; *Alik Cavaliere*, by Guido Ballo, Turin/Milan, 1967; *New Italian Art 1953-1971*, exhibition catalogue, by Giovanni Carandente, Liverpool 1971; article—"Cavaliere" by Guido Ballo in *Art and Artists* (London), May 1971.

Alik Cavaliere thinks of sculpture as entertainment. Sculpture to him is an inversion of reality, a variant repetition that thumbs its nose at the world of experience. His aim is to reconstruct a habitat that fits the technique. Art remarks the world, and remakes it as a false construction, a nihilist deception.

Cavaliere does not want to erect monuments, to use form to celebrate events; his works are rather real life experiences, able to stage events. So his sculpture is no longer a restricted form, defined and complete, no longer a super-object to be gazed at; it has become a stage technique able to act its own plays and its own tricks.

For Cavaliere, the sculptor's work is not a formally enclosed territory, a formal event crystallized, but a mini-world made by the play of skilled hands; it is the space where the performance takes place.

The works comprised in the 1959/1962 series called "The Adventures of G. B." are all carried out on multiple levels of interpretation. They give life to little things, to a number of happenings, using scenery made up from simple elements, very small but still essential, as are the people that populate them. They look to us like little stage plays in which the producer—the sculptor, in this case—has amused himself by directing a theatre made up of random extracts, familiar happenings punctuated by continual surprises.

At the time he was producing these works Cavaliere occupied a studio in an area of ill repute at the heart of Milan—an area that has now disappeared. The room where he worked was like a maze, a network of doors and windows, dark areas and light areas; and it may be that this extraordinary place is to some extent reflected in his work, for that too is all played out in a space with a great many scenes.

Later that artist moved into a sort of oasis, still in Milan; his studio is completely surrounded by a huge, luxuriant garden in which nature seems to produce every known plant. Cavaliere's interest in nature, its theatricality and the manifold formal possibilities that it offers, dates from this time.

The tree and the forest became then, and still are, the dominant themes of all works. First he examined the roots (and it was a surprise to Cavaliere to discover how spectacular those hidden parts, the basis of

desk is silhouetted, and the objects lying on it are highly defined—the little bronze picture of the wife and so on. In "Paradise Bar" it looks as though one would never have to go outside. Plastic vines cascade from the ceiling, food and wine are plentiful, art is present in the form of a mural—nothing else is needed, except real life maybe. In "Office Party" the traces of life can certainly be seen. Empty Verdicchio bottles and wine glasses are placed against the background of Spoleto Cathedral. Against a background of such grandeur the objects would normally seem meaningless but Caulfield has turned the tables.

Caulfield has said that "nothing is stranger than life itself." In his brilliantly executed visions he certainly proves it.

—Carine Maurice

CAVALIERE, Alik.

Italian. Born in Rome, 5 August 1926. Studied at the University of Milan, and at the Accademia di Belle Arti, Milan, 1956. Sculptor: lives and works in Milan. Lecturer and assistant to Marino Marini, later Professor of Sculpture, Accademia di Belle Arti, Milan. Address: Via Foppa 49a, 20144 Milan, Italy.

his sculpture in some ways, can be), then the trunk, the leaves and the fruit.

Playing as they do on the artificiality of nature, these works, carried out in bronze like the earlier ones, do not try to take over the natural element; they do not want to play with the actual properties but to play a game of substitution and repetition.

Interest in theatrical invention is evident in these works too; falsehood is introduced, and with it purely theatrical mechanisms are activated. Nature becomes artifice, opening itself up to complex combinations, to endless games.

—Loredana Parmesani

CEROLI, Mario.

Italian. Born in Castelfrentano, Chieti, Italy, 17 May 1938. Worked in a studio with Leoncillo, Ettore Colla and Pericle Fazzini. Served in the Italian Army, 1961. Designed scenery for Pier Paolo Pasolini's *Orgia*, Teatro Stabile, Turin, and Giordano Bruno's *Candelaio*, Festival Theatre, Venice, 1962–64. Independent sculptor and performance artist, Rome since 1964. Recipient: Prize, *Mostra Nazionale di Termoli*, Italy, 1964; Third Prize, *Biennale d'Arte Metallo*, Gubbio, Italy, 1965; Gollin Prize, *Biennale*, Venice, 1966; Bolaffi Prize, Turin, 1972. Agent: Galleria Il Naviglio, via Manzoni 45, Milan. Address: Via della Pisana 1138, Rome, Italy.

Individual Exhibitions:

1964	Galleria La Tartaruga, Rome
1965	Galleria La Tartaruga, Rome
1966	Galleria del Naviglio, Milan
1967	Galleria del Naviglio, Milan
	Modern Art Agency, Naples
	Bonino Gallery, New York
	Galleria Sperone, Turin
	Galerie Thomas, Munich
	Galerie Schmela, Dusseldorf
	Galleria de Foscherari, Bologna
	Mana Art Market, Rome
1969	Galleria del Naviglio, Milan
	Modern Art Agency, Naples
	Kunstverein, Karlsruhe, West Germany
	Galerie René Block, Berlin
	Galerie Brusberg, Hannover
	Salone delle Scuderie, Parma, Italy
	Kunsthalle, Hannover
	Palais des Beaux-Arts, Brussels
	Palazzo Ducale, Pesaro, Italy
	Albright-Knox Art Gallery, Buffalo, New York (with Michelangelo Pistoletto)
1970	Galleria La Tartaruga, Rome
	Galleria de Foscherari, Bologna
	Galleria Ferrari, Verona
	Museum Folkwang, Essen
1971	Kunstverein, Frankfurt
	Museum am Ostwall, Dortmund, West Germany
	Galleria Colophon, Milan
	Galleria La Tartaruga, Rome
	Haus am Waldsee, Berlin
1972	Galleria Forma, Genoa
	Palazzo Ducale, Pesaro, Italy
1974	Betty Parsons Gallery, New York
	Studio Marconi, Milan
	Galleria Plurima I, Udine, Italy
1975	Galleria Graziussi, Venice
	Galleria de'Foscherari, Bologna
1976	Centro Colombo Americano, Bogota, Colombia
	Nova Arte Moderna, Prato, Italy
	Galleria La Tartaruga, Rome
	Galleria Marin, Turin
	Fundacion Eugenio Mendoza, Caracas, Venezuela
1977	Galeria Sandiego, Bogota, Colombia
1978	Galleria Plurima I, Udine, Italy

1979	Galleria Il Centro, Naples
	Galleria Aries, Bari, Italy
	Galleria de'Foscherari, Bologna
	Galleria San Soaze, Treviso, Italy
	Galleria Franca Mancini, Pesaro, Italy
1980	Galleria Mario Diacono, Rome
	Galleria Torbandena, Trieste, Italy
1981	Galleria Editalia, Rome
	Galleria La Chiocciola, Padua, Italy
	Galleria Meta, Florence
1982	Galleria La Tartaruga, Rome
	Galleria de'Foscherari, Bologna
	Studio Marconi, Milan
	Mario Ceroli, at the *Biennale*, Venice
1983	Banco di Santo Spirito, Rome
	Forte Belvedere, Florence
1984	*Mario Ceroli*, at the *Biennale*, Venice
1985	Galleria de'Foscherari, Bologna
1986	Palazzo degli Alessandri, Viterbo, Italy
	Galleria 2RC, Milan

Selected Group Exhibitions:

1960	*Quadriennale*, Galleria Nazionale d'Arte Moderna, Rome

Mario Ceroli: *Giove*, 1983

1965	*8 Italienischer Kunstler*, Kunsthaus, Zurich
1968	*Young Italians*, Institute of Contemporary Art, Boston
1971	*New Italian Art 1953–71*, Walker Art Gallery, Liverpool
1973	*Il Ritratto Oggi*, Villa Faraggiana, Albissola, Italy
1977	*XIV Bienal de Sao Paulo*, Brazil
1980	*One Hundred Years of Italian Art*, Museum of Modern Art, Tokyo
1982	*Arte Italiana 1960–82*, Hayward Gallery, London
1985	*Italia Oggi*, Villa Arson, Nice, France
1986	*Aspekte Italienischen Kunst 1950–85*, Kunstverein, Frankfurt

Collections:

Galleria Nazionale d'Arte Moderna, Rome; Kaiser-Wilhelm Museum, Krefeld, West Germany; Kunstmuseum, Dusseldorf.

Publications:

On CEROLI: books—*Ceroli*, exhibition catalogue with text by Gillo Dorfles, Milan 1966; *4 Artistes Italiens plus que*

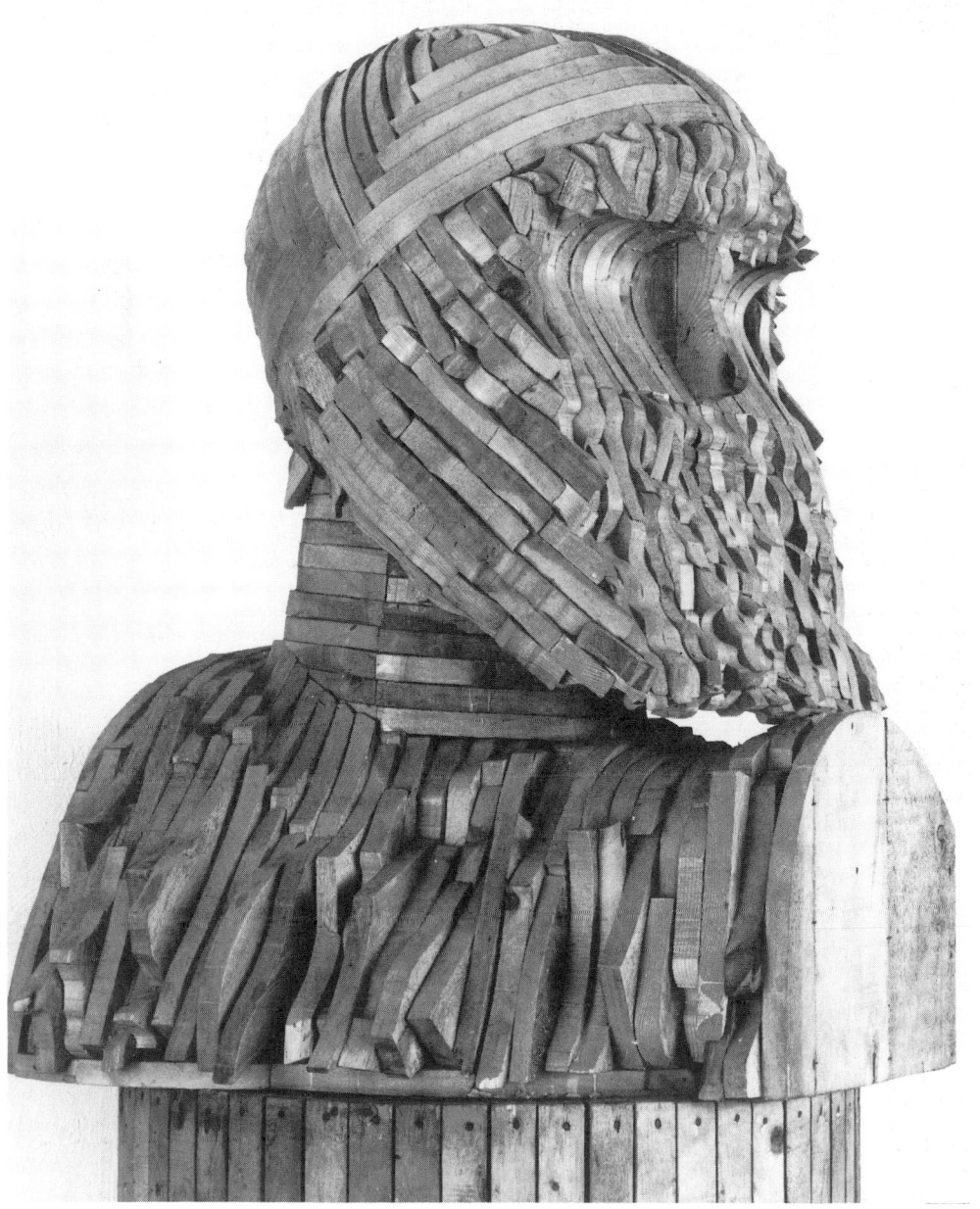

Nature, exhibition catalogue by Maurizio Calvesi, Paris 1969; *Ceroli*, exhibition catalogue with essay by Arturo Carlo Quintavalle, Parma 1969; *Mario Ceroli / Michelangelo Pistoletto*, exhibition catalogue with text by Robert M. Murdock, Buffalo, New York 1969; *New Italian Art 1953-1971*, exhibition catalogue by Giovanni Carandente, Liverpool 1971; *Le Due Avanguardie*, 2 vols., by Maurizio Calvesi, Bari 1971; *Kunst um 1970*, edited by Wolfgang Becker, Aachen 1972; articles—"Mario Ceroli" by G. Schoenenberg in *Art International* (Lugano), June 1968; "Ceroliade" by Tommaso Trini in *Domus* (Milan), April 1969; "Ceroli", special issue of *Flash Art* (Milan), January 1971; "Mario Ceroli a Pesaro" in *Data* (Milan), Summer 1972.

Following a brief period of works characteristic of the 'informal' movement after his military service, Mario Ceroli produced the first work marking his personal style. From this first period lasting little more than four years from 1956 to 1961 comes the sculpture *Legno con Chiodi* (1958), constructed out of a tree trunk pierced by large nails. This work in some respects anticipates Arte Povera, the movement with which Ceroli was briefly associated.

From 1962 comes the piece *Lettere*, whose title is decriptive of the row of letters roughly hewn out of wood: A.S.O.Z., a partial alphabet in which is anchored in a poetry opposed to the then ubiquitous informal. *Lettere* formulates the ideas soon to be seen in his best works. *Adam and Eve* and *Leonardo's Man* are explicitly based on classical themes or the artistic culture of the past. At the same time, Ceroli created works which refer to objects of daily use, as in *Clock* and *Telephone*. In these and successive works we see his poetry ripen as his techniques reach full maturity.

Maurizio Calvesi has written of *Adam and Eve* and the related works: "The plastic marquetry is complicated by the employment of empty spaces where shadows are modelled as if they were solid matter, and settle into a cunning play of relationships between empty and full areas; the first Cerolian silhouettes occur springing and taut, produced through a system of alternating projections of image or shadow." The works which follow attain a formal coherence. The rhythms of fullness and emptiness and of light and dark are intensified, as in *Casa di Dante* (1965), which, like subsequent pieces, reveals a new element. This element is a ladder which extends forward as an invitation to climb in and enter the sculpture. Not only does this element aspire to involve the spectator, as in *La Scala* (1965), but its three-dimensionality adds a new constituent to the work's expressive possibilities. In *Casa Sistina* (1966), the diverse tendencies of the preceding works are clarified. From the outside, the work looks like a huge packing case with two small doors located on opposite walls, inviting the spectator to enter the interior whose walls are covered with silhouettes and woodcut figures standing erect at balconies. This work, a prize-winner at the Venice Biennale, is indubitably one of Ceroli's most important creations to date. Here, contemporary and historical memories meet to become one with the space and the spectator.

This creative period is followed by another phase which takes on a conceptual accent. In a 1967 exhibition, *Lo Spazio dell'Immagine*, Ceroli exhibited the piece *Centoucelli*. Three cubes inserted into one another recall early works of abstraction and minimalism, a trend which was to continue into successive works, such as *Primavera di Daria* (1968), where the juxtaposition of an infinite number of wooden poles, each square in section, were built up to form a large, tightly-packed, parallelopiped structure. It was during this phase that Ceroli took part in the first Arte Povera exhibition, and in this climate is to be found his work produced for the cultural fair *Teatro delle mostre* promoted in 1968 by the Galleria La Tartaruga. This work, entitled *Dal caldo al freddo*, was conceived as the experience of travelling through a series of wooden doors until one arrived in front of a wall of ice.

Very soon, Ceroli was to turn to re-working and inventing themes with that originality that has always been his distinguishing mark. Additionally, his work as a scenographer, notably for Luca Ronconi's production of *Richard III* in 1968, has brought him recognition most importantly for his vocation as a sculptor.

—Roberto Lambarelli

CESAR (Baldaccini).

French. Born in Marseilles, 1 January 1921. Studied at Ecole des Beaux-Arts, Marseilles, 1935-43; Ecole des Beaux-Arts, Paris, 1943-50. Served in French Army 1939-40. Married Rosine Groult in 1960; daughter: Anna. Sculptor, Paris, since 1950: first "compressions", 1960; first polyester "expansions", 1967. Instructor in Sculpture, Ecole Nationale Supérieure des Beaux-Arts, Paris, 1968-86. Recipient: Prix des trois arts, Ecole des Beaux-Arts, Marseilles, 1954; Sculpture Prize, *Biennale of Carrara*, Italy 1957; Silver Medal, *Exposition Universal*, Brussels, 1958; Grand Prix National de Sculpture, France, 1980. Chevaliere de la Legion d'Honneur, 1976; Officier de l'Ordre National du Merite, France, 1982; Commandeur de l'Ordre des Arts et Lettres, France, 1984. Address: 10 bis, Rue Roger, 75014 Paris, France.

Individual Exhibitions:

1954	Galerie Lucien Durand, Paris
1955	Galerie Rive Droite, Paris
1957	Galerie Creuzevalt, Paris
	Hanover Gallery, London
1959	Galerie Claude Bernard, Paris
1960	*Recent Sculpture*, Hanover Gallery, London
1961	Saidenberg Gallery, New York
	Galleria Apollinaire, Milan
1966	Stedelijk Museum, Amsterdam (travelled to the Wilhelm-Lehmbruck-Museum, Duisburg, West Germany)
	Outdoor Expansions, Kunstmuseum, Munich (travelled to Sao Paulo, Rio de Janeiro, and Montevideo)
	Musée Cantini, Marseilles (retrospective)
	Galleria Il Fante di Spade, Rome
	Galleria Galatea, Turin
1968	Galleria Buren, Stockholm (travelled to the Konstmuseum, Gothenburg)
	Outdoor Expansions, Tate Gallery, London (and European tour)
1969	Musée des Arts Décoratifs, Paris
	Galerie Mathias Fels, Paris
1970	Centre National d'Art Contemporain, Paris
	Galerie Creuzevalt, Paris
	Galleria del Leone, Venice (travelled to Galleria Schwarz, Milan)
	Galleria del Naviglio, Milan
	Galleria Victor Emmanuel, Milan
	Galerie Rive Gauche, Brussels
	Galerie Argos, Nantes, France (with Pavlos and Miralda)
	Galerie Soisson, Nice (with Farhi and Arman)
1971	Palais des Beaux-Arts, Brussels
	Kunsthalle, Hamburg
	Galerie Semiha Huber, Zurich
	Galerie Rive Gauche, Brussels
	Eat-Art Gallerie, Dusseldorf
	Galerie Municipale A. M. Douet, Montreuil, France
	Galleria Il Centro, Naples
	Henie-Onstad Kunstsenter, Oslo
	Galerie Creuzevalt, Paris
	Maison de la Culture, Rennes, France
1972	Musee Cantini, Marseilles
	Galerie Mathias Fels, Paris
	Galerie Lucien Durand, Paris
	Cesar à Nice, Galerie des Ponchettes, Nice
	Galerie Fred Lanzenberg, Brussels
1973	*Tête á Tête*, Galerie Creuzevalt, Paris
	Cesar en Arles, Cloitre Saint Trophine, Arles, France
	Galerie Semiha Huber, Zurich
	Theatre Municipal, Angers, France
	Centre Culturel, Romainville, France
1974	Rotonda della Besana, Milan (travelled to the Galerie L'Expression, Strasbourg)
	Galleria Il Fauno Due, Turin
1975	Galerie Sapone, Nice
1976	*Retrospective des Sculptures*, Musee Rath, Geneva (travelled to the Musée des Beaux-Arts, Grenoble, France; Casino Communal, Knokke, Belgium; Museum Boymans-van Beuningen, Rotterdam; and the Musée d'Art Moderne de la Ville, Paris)
	Galerie Semiha Huber, Zurich
	Galerie Beaubourg, Paris
1977	Galerie Kriwin, Brussels
1978	Musee Picasso, Antibes, France
	Galerie Sapone, Nice
	Galerie Bornand, Marseilles
1979	Chateau de Jau, Perpignan, France (with Arman)
	Les Expansions, Galerie Daniel Templon, Paris
	Galerie Olga, Stockholm
1980	Galerie Beaubourg, Paris
	Galerie Kriwin, Brussels
1981	Fondation Veranneman, Kruishoutem, Belgium
	Musée de Cabriès-en-Provence, France (retrospective; travelled to Brest and Roubaix)
	Musée d'Art Moderne, Liège, Belgium
	Galerie Zanetacci, Geneva
1982	Espace nicois d'art et de culture, Nice, France (retrospective)
	Fondation Seibu, Tokyo (retrospective)
	Museum of Ohara, Japan (retrospective)
	Yoshibi Gallery, Tokyo
	Galerie Beaubourg, Paris
	Musée de Villetaneuse, France
	Galerie Asbaeck, Copenhagen
1983	Musée Picasso, Antibes, France
	Pavillon des Arts, Paris (retrospective)
	Christian Fayt Art Gallery, Knokke-le-Zoute, Belgium
	Galerie Verrière, Lyon, France
	Galerie Cupillard, Saint-Tropez, France
1984	Musée de la Poste, Paris
	Galleria Forni, Bologna, Italy
	Fondation Cartier, Jouy en Josas, France
	Palazzo Grassi, Venice
1985	Musée d'Art Contemporain, Dunkerque, France
	Galerie Artio, Athens
	Galerie Beaubourg, Paris
	Chateau de Brecey, France
1986	Art Centre, Hong Kong
	Fondation Cartier, Jouy en Josas, France
	Galerie Zanetacci, Geneva
1987	Musée d'Aix en Provence, France (retrospective)
	Musée de Montbélliard, France
	Cesar, at the *Salon d'Automne*, Brive, France
	Galerie Beaubourg, at FIAC 87, Paris
	Musée de Middelheim, Antwerp, Belgium

Selected Group Exhibitions:

1956	*Biennale*, Venice
1957	*Bienal*, Sao Paulo
1958	*Carnegie International*, Carnegie Institute, Pittsburgh
1959	*Documenta 2*, Kassel, West Germany
1961	*L'Objet*, Musée des Arts Décoratifs, Paris
1967	*Superlund*, Konsthall, Lund, Sweden
1974	*Jewelry as Sculpture as Jewelry*, Institute of Contemporary Art, Boston
1976	*L'Animal—de Lascaux à Picasso*, Musée d'Histoire Naturelle, Paris
1984	*Peinture en France*, Palazzo Sagredo, Venice
1986	*Les Nouveaux Realistes*, Musee d'Art Moderne, Paris

Collections:

Centre Georges Pompidou, Paris; Musée Cantini, Marseilles; Tate Gallery, London; Scottish National Gallery of Modern

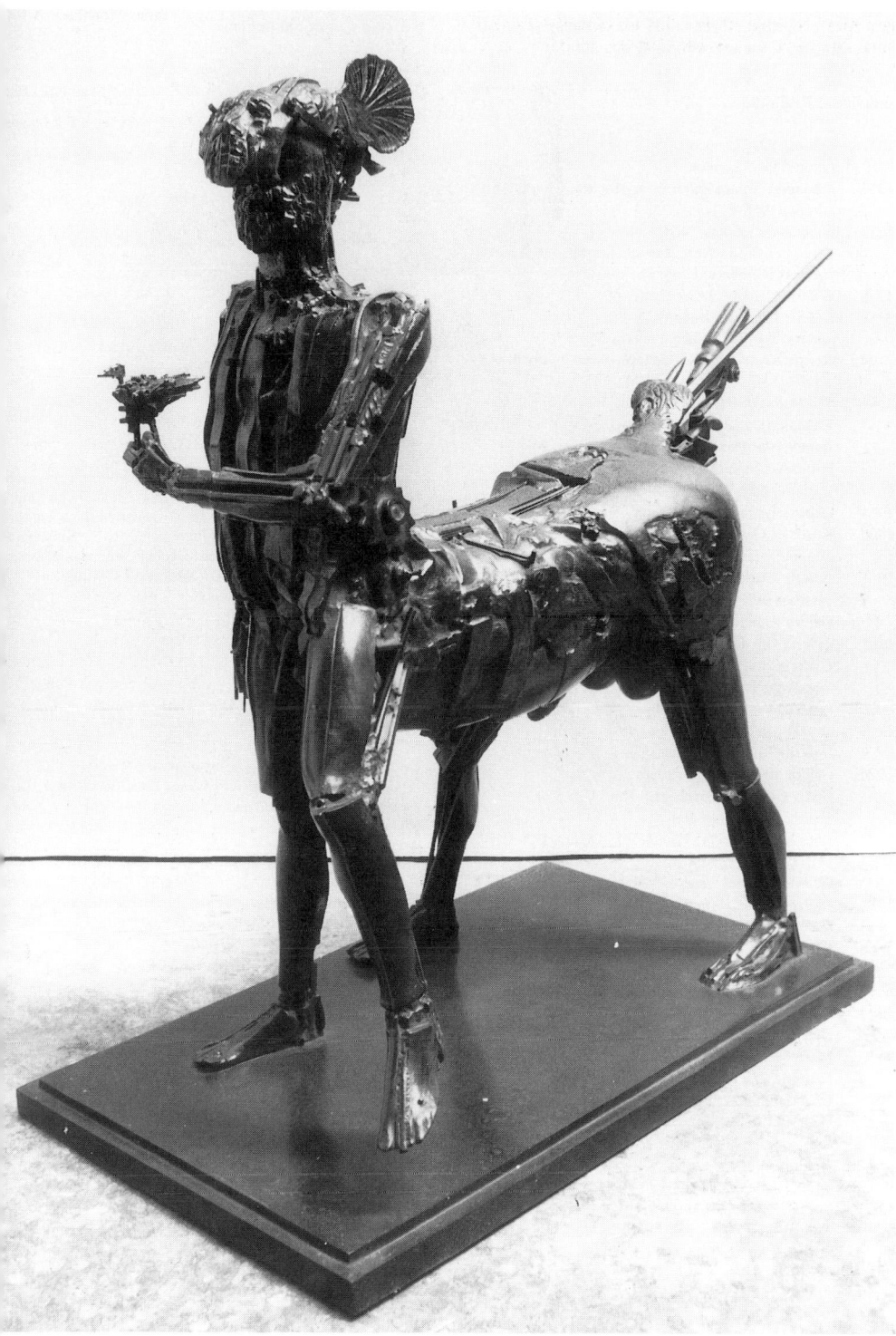

Cesar: *Centaure—Hommage à Picasso*, 1983

Expansions, exhibition catalogue, with text by Catherine Millet, Paris 1979; *Cesar,* exhibition catalogue, with text by Pierre Restany, Tokyo 1982; *Les Fers de Cesar,* exhibition catalogue, by Marie-Claude Beaud, Pierre Restany and Catherine Franchlin, Jouy en Josas, France 1984; *Cesar 1955–1985,* exhibition catalogue, Dunkerque 1985.

I would say that I am, above all, a man in love with art, and yet I can't explain what I do since one doesn't explain art. It's a question of feeling and sensibility. What I can explain are practical things: how to make a mould, what glue to use, different techniques. I am not an intellectual artist, but I create my own bit of culture. I have my own deep-rooted culture with respect to my experiences, to the life I have led, to the training I have undergone, to the work I have executed. People may identify me with "Compressions", but curiosity has led me to make other discoveries too, to use a whole variety of materials: leather, iron, steel, bronze, marble, crystal, polyurethane, gold . . . . But behind every material there's the same person at work. Each day one can start the same piece of work again and each day it can be different.

There's also the question of conviction: if you believe in it, you don't make a product, you're aiming at creating something. But what does create mean? Is one creative because one has a lot of imagination? Am I creative because I've compressed cars? People will tell me that I've got imagination, but sometimes it seems to me that I haven't got any at all. I think physically and I feel a physical need to sculpt. I'm not a person who can think abstractly, who can foresee or make plans. Circumstances, events, encounters with the material, 'accidents' sometimes make me look at my work differently. But then, nobody creates anything in fact! We simply receive the heritage of one person or another, of all those who were here before us. As far as I am concerned it's the work of, among others, Duchamp and Picasso which has enabled me to progress. I should add that sculpture today is a confused notion. Anything that occupies a place in space is called sculpture. But just because it's three-dimensional an object isn't necessarily a piece of statuary. I think of my compressions, for example, as objects and not as sculptures. I've simply quoted this example at random, but it brings us back to the sculptor/artist debate, for a sculptor isn't necessarily a creator of statuary and may in fact never reach that level. A sculptor may make a torso and if it reaches the level of statuary, that torso will be enough in itself, will need no explanation, no story. The work will exist like a piece of sculpture dug up in Greek soil. It may be a fragment of a human body, without head or legs. No one will ever know who made it or when, but it will have the evocative power of Greek sculpture. It will be useless to restore it or to attach a story to it. It exists and that is enough, whereas a section of my 'compressions', for example, cannot be elaborated on by being read about. My *Venus de Villetaneuse,* in contrast, even without a head lacks nothing, and nothing can be added to it. Even if my signature is removed, and even if it's mutilated by an earthquake, my *Centaure* will continue to exist. I disown nothing that I've done, I ask simply that my work be given several 'readings'.

—Cesar

Cesar is the sculptor's sculptor. After his long studies, like many of his fellows, he was forced into another activity in order to earn his living while continuing to pursue his art in his spare time as far as possible. Which was not very far, for materials were not only difficult to obtain, they were also expensive. His choice of ready-made scraps of metal that he welded together was forced on him by economic necessity, yet at the same time the method of construction had its provocative challenge. His early constructions of insects, animals and fish are rich in improvised invention and humorous in their juxtaposition of diverse parts. His unique combination of passionate and pawky styles developed from the consistent forming of elements into a work such as the

Art, Edinburgh; Rijksmuseum Kröller Müller, Otterlo, Netherlands; Musée Royal des Beaux-Arts, Brussels; Moderna Museet, Stockholm; Galleria Nazionale d'Arte Moderna, Rome; Museum of Modern Art, New York; Carnegie Institute, Pittsburgh.

Publications:

By CESAR: book—*Cesar par Cesar,* edited by Pierre Cabanne, Paris 1971.

On CESAR: books—*Cesar,* exhibition catalogue, with text by John Russell, London 1957; *Cesar: Recent Sculpture,* exhibition catalogue, with text by Pierre Restany, London 1960; *Cesar* by Douglas Cooper, St. Gallen, Switzerland 1960; *Cesar,* exhibition catalogue, with text by Gerhard Handler, Duisberg, West Germany 1966; *Cesar,* exhibition catalogue, with texts by Francois Mathey and Douglas Cooper, Marseilles 1966; *Cesar Balaccini,* exhibition catalogue, with text by Luigi Carluccio, Rome 1966, *Cesar,* exhibition catalogue, with texts by Luigi Carluccio, Turin 1966; *Cesar,* exhibition catalogue, with text by Francois Mathey, Amsterdam 1966; *Cesar: Compressions,* exhibition catalogue, with text by Pierre Restany, Paris 1969; *Cesar Expansions Controlées,* exhibition catalogue, with text by Pierre Restany, Gothenburg 1969; *Cesar: Plastiques,* exhibition catalogue, with texts by Francois Mathey and Pierre Restany, Paris 1970; *Cesar,* exhibition catalogue, with text by Pierre Restany, Milan 1970; *Cesar à Nice,* exhibition catalogue, with texts by Jacques Medecin and Daniele Giraudy, Nice 1972; *Cesar,* exhibition catalogue, with text by Daniele Giraudy, Marseilles 1972; *Cesar en Arles,* exhibition catalogue, with texts by Douglas Cooper, Arles, France 1973; *Tête à Tête,* exhibition catalogue, with text by Pierre Restany, Paris 1973; *Cesar: Compressions d'Or,* with text by J. Baldwin, Paris, 1973; *Cesar,* exhibition catalogue, with text by Janus, Turin 1974; *Cesar,* exhibition catalogue, with text by Pierre Restany, Milan 1974; *Cesar* by Pierre Restany, Munich and New York 1975; *Cesar: Retrospective des Sculptures,* exhibition catalogue, edited by Rainer Michael Mason, Geneva 1976; *Cesar: Les*

life size "Seated Nude" (1954) where the skeletal figure has a skin of emaciated iron strips.

By 1956 the sensitive modelling of the human prototype had made evident the underlying humanism of Cesar. It was humanism that not only showed itself of the tactile shaping of the torso, in the plastic tributes to birdman Leo Valentin, but also in the symbolic winged men and central figures against a background of facetted metal akin to the placing of a statue of a saint against a stained glass window in an old chapel. His use of screens lent mystic, almost religious, presence to universal imagery.

His temporary detour into the sphere of "compressions" when he enjoyed the new sensation of surface obtained by crushing cars in an hydraulic press was but one of his investigations into the possibilities available in the treatment of the ready-made. Its significance rested in this explosive moulding of the metal in an exciting exploratory system rather than arriving at an end product of sculptural finality; they represent milestones instead of wayside shrines built in celebration of life. The same could be said of his plastic works when the liquid hardens to its ultimate form in three minutes. Captivated by the accidental results possible, similar to Jackson Pollock's poured pigment, Cesar enjoyed the speed in which a form would arrive in brilliant colour. Plastic expansions like "The Thumb," as large as its creator, marked further steps in the continuous quest, though in retrospect some appear as self-indulgence. Cesar has defended their appearance as examples of automatic and subconscious gestalts.

For Cesar the 1960's were shadowed by personal setbacks, but his ebullient spirit was not to be subdued for long, and he returned to the fray with elan and resource. His reliefs of metal junk and scrap were full of quirky formal jokes like "Portrait of Patrick Waldberg" (1961). Some of the early welded figures were now translated in bronze casts that reflected in the sympathetic metal the rigidity and angularity of the movements of cocky chickens and poised insects. His self-identification and his commitment to material came through with characteristic vitality in the series of 30 masks in bright bronze he called "Tête à tête". Self-portraits: he shows himself in them as an actor of roles having their formal roots in art history from the Roman senatorial to the caricatural; by turns he is the clown, the tragic fate-doomed sufferer, yet each work has its thumbmark of mercurial, almost primitive, power. It is scarcely accidental that, of the race of Michelangelo and Donatello, Cesar also reflects in his sculpture much of the droll worldly humour of his birthplace: Marseilles.

—G. S. Whittet

CHADWICK, Lynn (Russell).

British. Born in London, 24 November 1914. Educated at schools in London; trained as an architectural draughtsman; mainly self-taught in art. Served as a pilot in the Fleet Air Arm, 1941–44. Married Charlotte Ann Secord in 1942: one son: Frances Mary Jamieson in 1959 (died, 1964): two daughters; Eva Reiner in 1965: one son. Sculptor since 1948: in private practice as architectural draughtsman, 1946; worked with the architect Rodney Thomas, 1947; settled in Upper Coberley, 1947; made first metal mobiles in the early 1950's; executed three works commissioned for the *Festival of Britain*, London, 1951; now lives and works in Gloucestershire. Recipient: Prize, International Competition for Unknown Political Prisoner, 1953; International Sculpture Prize, *Biennale*, Venice, 1956; First Prize, *Consorso Internazionale del Bronzetto*, Padua, 1959; Prize, *International Exhibition of Drawings and Engravings*, Lugano, Switzerland, 1960. C.B.E. (Commander, Order of the British Empire), 1964; Officier, Ordre des Arts et Lettres, France, 1986. Address: Lypiatt Park, Stroud, Gloucestershire, England.

Individual Exhibitions:

1950	Gimpel Fils, London
1952	Gimpel Fils, London
1956	*Biennale*, Venice (with Ivon Hitchens; toured Europe, 1956–57)
1957	Saidenberg Gallery, New York
	Palais des Beaux-Arts, Brussels (travelled to the Arts Council Gallery, London)
1958	Galerie Daniel Cordier, Paris
1959	Galerie Charles Lienhard, Zurich
	Galerie Daniel Cordier, Frankfurt
1960	Kestner-Gesellschaft, Hannover (with Kenneth Armitage)
1961	Marlborough Fine Art, London
	Knoedler Galleries, New York
	Bienal, Sao Paulo
1963	Forum Gallery, Bristol
	Carborundum Company, New York
1964	Galerie Wilhelm Grosshennig, Dusseldorf
1965	Knoedler Galleries, New York
	Sunsvall Museum, Hasten, Sweden
1966	Galerie Grosshennig, Dusseldorf
	Marlborough Fine Art Gallery, London
	Galerie Günther Franke, Munich
1968	Galerie Gerald Cramer, Geneva
	Galleria Blu, Milan
	Waddington Gallery, Montreal
	Galerie d'Eendt, Amsterdam
1969	Dorsky Gallery, New York
	Galerie Withofs, Brussels
1970	Galerie d'Eendt, Amsterdam
	Court Gallery, Copenhagen
	Galerie Blu, Stockholm
	Louisiana Museum, Humlebaek, Denmark
1971	Dorsky Gallery, New York
	Galerie Zodiac, Geneva
1972	Gallery Moos, Toronto
	Galerie Zodiac, Geneva
	Gloucester City Museum
	Galleria Blu, Milan
	Waddington Gallery, Montreal
1974	Marlborough Fine Art Gallery, London
	Galerie Farber, Brussels
	Marlborough Galerie, Zurich
	Marlborough Galleria d'Arte, Rome
1975	Galleria Toninelli, Milan
	Galleria Contacto, Caracas
	Marlborough-Godard Gallery, Toronto
	Hokin Gallery, Chicago
	Wolpe Gallery, Cape Town
	Goodman Gallery, Johannesburg
	Court Gallery, Copenhagen
	Galerie Carlssen, Gothenburg, Sweden
1976	Galerie d'Eendt, Amsterdam
	Galerie Farber, Brussels
	JPL Fine Arts, London
1978	Court Gallery, Copenhagen
	Marlborough Fine Art, London (travelled to the Marlborough Galerie, Zurich)
1979	Galerie 99, Bay Harbor Island, Florida
	Century Gallery, Henley-on-Thames, Oxfordshire
	The Keys Gallery, Londonderry, Northern Ireland
	Arts Council Gallery, Belfast
	Galerie D'Eendt, Amsterdam
1980	Galerie Regards, Paris
	Galerie Farber, Brussels
	Waddington/Shell Galleries, Toronto
	Fondation Veranneman, Kruishoutem, Belgium
1981	Galeria Freites, Caracas, Venezuela
	Theo Waddington Galleries, Montreal
1982	Christie's Contemporary Art, New York (with Victor Pasmore)
1983	Mercury Gallery, Edinburgh
	Gallery Ueda, Tokyo (with Victor Pasmore)
	Galerie Herbage, Cannes, France
	Artcurial, Paris
	Margaret Fisher Gallery, London
1984	Theo Waddington Galleries, Montreal
	Marlborough Fine Art, London

Selected Group Exhibitions:

1947	*Building Trades Exhibition*, London
1951	*International Open-Air Exhibition of Sculpture*, Battersea Park, London
1952	*Biennale*, Venice
1955	*The New Decade*, Museum of Modern Art, New York
1958	*10 Young British Sculptures*, Museo de Arte Moderno, Rio de Janeiro
1962	*British Art Today*, San Francisco Museum of Art
1964	*Painting and Sculpture of a Decade 1954–1964*, Tate Gallery, London
1967	*Expo '67*, Montreal
1982	*Chadwick/Cuevas/Manzu/Matta/Moore*, Tasende Gallery, La Jolla, California
1983	*International Art Exposition*, Navy Pier, Chicago

Collections:

Tate Gallery, London; Victoria and Albert Museum, London; Musée Royaux des Beaux-Arts, Brussels; Middelheim Sculpture Park, Antwerp; Rijksmuseum Kröller-Müller, Otterlo, Netherlands; Centre Georges Pompidou, Paris; Kunsthaus, Zurich; Louisiana Museum, Humlebaek, Denmark; Museum of Modern Art, New York; Art Institute of Chicago.

Publications:

By CHADWICK: articles—"A Sculptor and His Public" in *The Listener* (London), October 1954; statement in *The New Decade*, exhibition catalogue, New York 1955.

On CHADWICK: books—*Contemporary Sculpture: An Evolution in Volume and Space* by Carola Giedion-Welcker, London 1956; *Lynn Chadwick*, exhibition catalogue, by Robert Melville, Venice 1956; *Lynn Chadwick* by Herbert Read, Amriswill, Switzerland 1960; *Sculpture of This Century: Present-Day Sculpture in Great Britain* by Michel Seuphor, London 1960; *Lynn Chadwick* by J. P. Hodin, Amsterdam and London 1961; *Lynn Chadwick* by Alan Bowness, London 1962; *Chadwick*, exhibition catalogue edited by Marlborough Fine Art, London 1984.

Lynn Chadwick was one of the prominent group of young British sculptors who were enthusiastically acclaimed, internationally, following the discovery that in Henry Moore Britain had produced a major sculptor. Like many artists of this generation, his studies and activities were delayed by war-time service, so that he was 36 years old before he held a one-man exhibition at Gimpel Fils. With Moore winning the Venice *Biennale* Sculpture Prize in 1948, the British Council promoted the younger generation, and in the group exhibition at the 1952 *Biennale* launched a large group of new sculptors, including Armitage, Butler, Paolozzi, Turnbull, on to exciting international careers. Chadwick was in some senses the most successful of them all, returning to Venice in 1956 to win the International Sculpture Prize. His exhibition was then toured throughout Europe, with Chadwick showing his work in the leading museums in Vienna, Munich, Paris, Amsterdam, Brussels, as well as in London. There followed important international contracts, and for the next ten years Chadwick's work continued to excite wide-spread attention.

It is, however, significant that in recent years he has rarely exhibited in London. His work, in fact, has shown little development. Like a number of modern sculptors, Chadwick's roots lie in architecture, and there is also reason to assume that his experience as a war-time pilot influenced his sculpture. Movement in space, the example of Calder, inspired his earliest efforts, and his work in defining space took on menacing, animalistic forms with spiky legs and antennae. Eventually more recognisable, though still aggressive, bird-like creatures emerged, and the bleak desperation of their stance seemed to symbolise the experience of war and its aftermath. Gradually the dramatic, worrying aspects of these forms were weakened in the employment of smoother surfaces and less aggressive extensions, and by the evolution of human

or animal forms less in conflict with themselves, or
us.

Stylistic formulas of pyramid shapes or wingspans
have now been reduced to anecdotal, almost sentimental symbols; seated couples, walking figures, or
standing forms, reminiscent of the gentler imagery of
his contemporary, Kenneth Armitage.

—Charles Spencer

CHAGALL, Marc.

Russian. Born Moisei Segal in Vitebsk, Russia, 7
July 1887. Studied privately with the painter Jehuda
Pen, Vitebsk, 1906; studied at the Imperial School
for the Protection of Arts, St. Petersburg, 1907, and
privately with Saidenberg and Leon Bakst, St. Petersburg, 1908–09. Married Bella Rosenfeld in 1915
(died, 1944); daughter: Ida; married Vava Brodsky in
1957. Lived in St. Petersburg, 1907–10, returning
frequently to Vitebsk; lived in Paris, 1910–13, St.
Petersburg, 1915–17, and Vitebsk, 1918–29; Commissar for Art, Vitebsk, 1918; Founder Director, Vitebsk Academy, with El Lissitsky, Jean Pougny and
Kasimir Malevich as members of staff, 1919–20 (resigned following quarrel with Suprematists); settled
in Moscow, 1920, and created first stage designs for
the Kameray State Jewish Theatre; lived in Berlin,
1922, then settled in Paris, 1923 until the Occupation, when he moved to New York: associated with
Leger, Mondrian, Zadkine and other emigre artists in
New York; lived in Sag Harbor and High Falls, New
York, 1945–46; returned to France, 1948, and lived
in Oregeval, Saint-Germaine-en-Laye; lived in St.
Paul-de-Vence from 1950; visited Israel and worked
on first sculptures, 1951; worked with the glass
painter Charles Marq from 1957, and continued to
work on designs for opera and ballet, murals, tapestries, and stained glass windows. Visiting Lecturer,
University of Chicago, 1958. Recipient: Carnegie
Prize, Pittsburgh, 1939; Erasmus Prize, with Oskar
Kokoschka, Copenhagen, 1960. Honorary doctorate:
University of Glasgow, 1959; Brandeis University,
Waltham, Massachusetts, 1960; Notre Dame University, Indiana, 1965. Honorary Member, American
Academy of Arts and Letters, 1959. Honorary Citizen, St. Paul-de-Vence, 1962; City of Jerusalem,
1977. Grand Cross of the Legion of Honour, France,
1977. *Died* (in Saint-Paul-de-Vence) *28 March 1985.*

Individual Exhibitions:

1914	Galerie der Sturm, Berlin
1924	Galerie Barbazange-Hodebert, Paris
	Graphisches Kabinett, Munich (with Lyonel Feininger)
1926	Reinhart Galleries, New York
1928	Galerie Le Portique, Paris
1930	Galerie Bernheim-Jeune and Galerie Le Centaure, Paris
	Galerie Flechtheim, Berlin
1932	Stedelijk Museum, Amsterdam
1933	Kunsthaus, Basle
1934	Galerie Dra Feigla, Prague
1935	Leicester Galleries, London
1938	Palais des Beaux-Arts, Brussels
	Lilienfeld Galleries, New York
1940	Pierre Matisse Gallery, New York
1946	Museum of Modern Art, New York (travelled to the Art Institute of Chicago)
1947	Musée National d'Art Moderne, Paris
	Pierre Matisse Gallery, New York
	Stedelijk Museum, Amsterdam
1948	Tate Gallery, London
	Pierre Matisse Gallery, New York
1949	Galerie Rosengart, Lucerne
1950	Galerie Maeght, Paris
	Kunsthaus, Zurich
	Kunsthalle, Berne

	Galerie Samlaren, Stockholm
	Israel Museum, Jerusalem (toured Israel)
1952	Curt Valentin Gallery, New York
	Galerie des Ponchettes, Nice
	Galerie Maeght, Paris
	Galleria dell'Obelisco, Rome
1953	Museo Civico d'Arte Moderna, Turin
1954	Galerie Maeght, Paris
1955	Kestner Society, Hannover
1956	Kunsthalle, Basle
	Kunsthalle, Berne
	Stedelijk Museum, Amsterdam
1957	Palais des Beaux-Arts, Brussels
	Kunstmuseum, Basle
	Bibliothèque Nationale, Paris
	Galerie Welz, Salzburg
	Cercle Royal, Charleroi, Belgium (with Paul Delvaux)
	Art Club, Hamburg
1959	Haus der Kunst, Munich
	Musée des Arts Décoratifs, Paris
	Staedel Institute of Art, Frankfurt
1960	Musée des Beaux-Arts, Reims, France
	Grosvenor Gallery, London
1961	Casino Communal, Knokke-le-Zoute, Belgium
	Galerie Klipstein und Kornfeld, Berne
	O'Hana Gallery, London
	Musée des Arts Décoratifs, Paris
1962	Musée Massena, Nice
	Musée Rath, Geneva
	Galerie Madoura, Cannes
1963	Museum of Western Art, Tokyo (travelled to the Municipal Museum, Kyoto)
	Musée des Beaux-Arts, Rouen
1965	Israel Museum, Jerusalem
1967	Kunsthaus, Zurich
	Musée du Louvre, Paris
	Fondation Maeght, St. Paul-de-Vence, France
	Kunsthalle, Cologne
	Musée des Augustins, Toulouse
	Galerie Rosengart, Lucerne
1968	Pierre Matisse Gallery, New York
1969	*Hommage à Marc Chagall*, Grand Palais, Paris
1971	Galerie Maeght, Zurich
1972	Galerie Rosengart, Lucerne
1973	Los Angeles County Museum of Art
	Pierre Matisse Gallery, New York
1975	Guggenheim Museum, New York
	Pierre Matisse Gallery, New York
1976	National Museum of Modern Art, Tokyo (toured Japan)
1977	Musée du Louvre, Paris
	Pierre Matisse Gallery, New York
1978	Palazzo Pitti, Florence
	Museum of Modern Art, New York
	Haus der Kunst, Munich
1979	Pierre Matisse Gallery, New York
1980	Musée Rath, Geneva
	Redfern Gallery, London
	Galerie Matignon, Paris
	Galerie Maeght, Paris
	Galerie Maeght, Zurich
1982	Moderna Museet, Stockholm
	Galerie Patrick Cramer, Geneva
	Pierre Matisse Gallery, New York
1984	Fondation Maeght, St. Paul de Vence, France
	Centre Georges Pompidou, Paris
	Museo Capitolino, Rome
	Musee National Message Biblique Marc Chagall, Nice, France
1985	Royal Academy of Art, London
	Kestner-Gesellschaft, Hannover
	Philadelphia Museum of Art, Pennsylvania
1987	Jewish Museum, New York

Selected Group Exhibitions:

1912	*Salon des Independants*, Paris
1915	*Year 1915*, Salon d'Art de Michailova, Moscow
1916	*Knave of Diamonds*, Moscow
1917	*Exposition de Peintures et Sculptures d'Artistes Juifs*, Galerie Lemercier, Moscow
1948	*Biennale*, Venice
1958	*Pittsburgh International*, Carnegie Institute, Pittsburgh
1970	*Russian Art of the Revolution*, Andrew Dickson White Museum of Art, Cornell University, Ithaca, New York (travelled to the Brooklyn Museum, New York)
1971	*The Russian Avant-Garde*, Leonard Hutton Galleries, New York
1977	*40 Modern Masters*, Guggenheim Museum, New York
1982	*Guggenheim, Venezia/New York: 60 Opere 1900–1950*, Pinacoteca Capitolina in Campidoglio, Rome and the Guggenheim Museum, New York

Collections:

Centre Georges Pompidou, Paris; Musée de Peinture et
Sculpture, Grenoble, France; Kunstmuseum, Basle; Na-
tionalgalerie, Berlin; Wallraf-Richartz Museum, Cologne;
Russian Museum, Leningrad; Tel Aviv Museum, Israel; Gug-
genheim Museum, New York; Museum of Modern Art, New
York; Los Angeles County Museum of Art.

Principal commissions: stained glass windows, Metz Cathedral, France, 1960; synagogue of the Hadassah Medical
Centre, Jerusalem, 1962; ceiling, Paris Opera House, 1964;
murals/facade, Metropolitan Opera House, New York, 1965.

Publications: ·

By CHAGALL: books—*Marc Chagall: My Life*, Paris, 1957;
Chagall, edited by Charles Sorlier, London 1979; illustrated
books—*Dead Souls* by Gogol, 1925; *The Fables of La Fon-
taine*, 1931; *Arabian Nights*, 1948; *Daphnis and Chloe*,
1977, etc.; articles—"Reflections on Art" in *Witebskvi Listok*
(Vitebsk, Russia), January 1919; "The Revolution in Art" in
Revoluzionnoje Iskustwo (Vitebsk, Russia), no. 1, 1919;
"Reflections on the People's Fine Arts Academy, Vitebsk" in
Schkola Revoluzia (Vitebsk, Russia), August 1919; "Chez
Marc Chagall," interview, with Georges Charensol, in *Paris-
Journal*, May 1924; "Marc Chagall," interview, with Jacques
Guenne in *L'Art Vivant* (Paris), December 1927; "My Work
in the Jewish Theatre of Moscow" in *Di Idiscze Welt* (Vilna,
Poland), 1938; "Delacroix" in *L'Intransigeant* (Paris), June
1930; "Marc Chagall," interview, with Pierre Courthion, in
Les Nouvelles Litteraires, (Paris), April 1932; "Pouvez-vouz
dire quelle est la Rencontre Capitale de Votre Vie?" in *Mino-
taure* (Paris), nos. 3–4, 1933; "Sur l'Art Aujourd'hui" in
Cahiers d'Art (Paris), nos. 1–4, 1935; "Interview with Marc
Chagall," with Raymond Abel, in *The League* (New York),
April 1942; "In Honor of Jacques Maritain" in *Jewish Fron-
tier* (New York), February 1943; "Message aux Peintres
Francais" in *Le Spectateur des Arts* (Paris), December 1944;
"An Interview with Marc Chagall," with James Johnson
Sweeney, in *Partisan Review* (New York), Winter 1944;
"Quelques Impressions sur la Peinture Francais" in *Renais-
sance Revue Trimestrielle des Hautes Etudes de New York*,
vols. 2 and 3, 194–45; "L'Art de la Recitude et de la Clarte"
in *Naje Lehn* (New York), June 1945; preface to *Di Ershte
Bagegenish* by Bella Chagall, New York 1947; "Letter to S.
Rosengart" in *Chagall*, exhibition catalogue, Lucerne 1949;
"5 Poems" in *Di Goldene Keyt*, Tel Aviv 1951; "Visite á
Chagall," interview, with Gisele d'Assailly, in *Le Figaro Litteraire* (Paris), March 1952; "Hommage à Matisse" in the
Yale Library Magazine (New Haven, Connecticut), 1955.

On CHAGALL: books: *La Fontaine par Chagall*, exhibition
catalogue, by Ambroise Vollard, Paris, 1930; *Chagall et
l'Ame Juive*, Paris 1930; *Marc Chagall* by Raissa Maritain,
New York, 1943; *Marc Chagall* by Lionello Venturi, New
York 1945; *Chagall: Paintings* by Leon Degand and Paul
Eluard, London 1947; *Chagall; ou L'Orage Enchante*, Ge-
neva 1948; *Chagall* by Michael Ayrton, London 1950; *Marc
Chagall: His Life and Work* by J. Kloomok, New York 1951;
Marc Chagall by Jacques Lassaigne, Geneva 1952; *Chagall:
A Biographical and Critical Study* by Lionello Venturi, Ge-
neva 1956; *The Jerusalem Windows of Marc Chagall* by Jean
Laymarie, New York 1962; *Chagall* by Jean Cassou, London
1965; *The World of Chagall* by Izis and Roy McMullen, New
York 1968; *Hommage à Marc Chagall*, exhibition catalogue,
by Jean Leymarie, Paris 1969; *Marc Chagall*, 4 vols., Monte
Carlo and Boston 1969–74; *The Lithographs of Chagall
1962–68* by Fernand Moulot and Charles Sorlier, Boston
1969; *The Ceramics and Sculptures of Chagall* by André
Malraux and others, Monaco 1972; *Marc Chagall* by Werner
Haftmann, New York 1972; *Marc Chagall: Life and Work* by
Horst Keller, New York 1978; *Marc Chagall* by Ernest Ra-
boff, London 1980; *Marc Chagall: Arbeiten auf Papier*, exhibition catalogue edited by the Kestner-Gesellschaft, Hannover

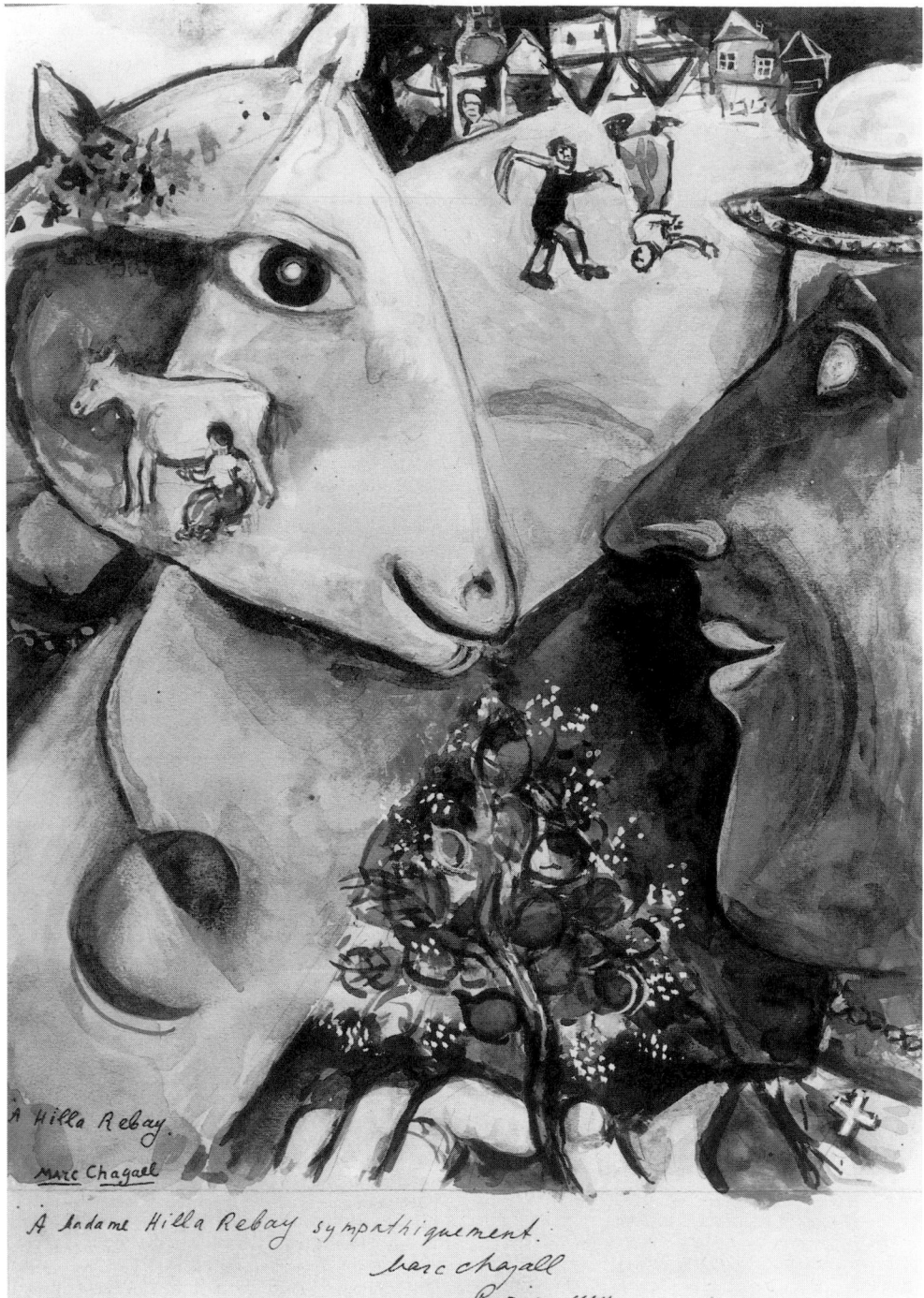

Marc Chagall: *I and the Village*, c. 1925 Courtesy Guggenheim Museum, New York

Mort," 1908). And since then there have been many eccentricities to be observed in the early self-portrait with so many fingers, the train proceeding along upside down past the Eiffel Tower in "Paris Through the Window," the cow that plays the violin and the man who *is* a violin . . . .

Bright colours enflame all these visions, especially the keepsake moments, pictures of Vitebsk, or of a Vitebsk that once was. The cluttered Jewish upbringing permeates so much of the imagery, although Chagall went on to add the New Testament to his original repertoire.

Gravity is just a scientific whim. Perspective may have returned in pictures like "Time Is a River Without Banks" (1930–39), but this does not prevent the fish equipped with a practical pair of wings from perching on a pendulum clock whose top and bottom are identical and whose pendulum, in any case, has its swinging circle attached at each end of the rod—the clock is in mid-air anyway.

Time is a River without Banks? Did Chagall find the riverside after 1940? Perhaps his lexicon of images was by then complete. The colours might get prettier. Instead of bright lights, candyfloss.

—Sheldon Williams

CHAMBERLAIN, John (Angus).
American. Born in Rochester, Indiana, 16 April 1927. Studied at the Art Institute of Chicago, 1950–52; University of Illinois; and Black Mountain College, North Carolina, 1955–56. Independent artist, New York and Florida. First works used crushed automobile motor and body parts, 1957–63; moved next to painting, urethane, galvanized metals and later plexiglass. Recipient: Guggenheim Fellowship, 1966, 1977; Art in Architecture Award, United States General Services Administration, 1978. Agent: Xavier Fourcade Inc., 36 East 75th Street, New York, New York 10021. Address: Ten Coconut Inc., 1315 Tenth Street, Sarasota, Florida 33577, U.S.A.

Individual Exhibitions:

1985; *Chagall* by Francois le Targat, Barcelona 1985, London 1987; *Marc Chagall: Druckgraphik,* Mainz 1986; *Chagall and the Bible* by Jean Bloch Rosensaft, New York 1987.

"I don't understand them at all," Chagall is claimed to have once said about his paintings; "they are not literature. They are only pictorial arrangements of images that obsess me . . . ."

He began making drawings when he was 13. It was an enthusiasm he was never to lose. What he tried to paint in Vitebsk before he left for his first visit to Paris was part the outcome of this love of making pictures, part the abortive results from attempts to become an art student in St. Petersburg. Yet those early paintings and those he made in the years following and leading up to the outbreak of the Second World War are the essence of the great Chagall, sometime cubist, pre-surrealist and restorer of the figurative image to a respected place in art appreciation between the two wars. All the elements of his best work came out of this period and, if they have been repeated since, the quality of those painted before 1940 has never been surpassed.

The big projects since the war—the Jerusalem windows or the redecoration of the Paris Opera House cannot compare with the great Chagalls like "Portrait of My Fiancee in Black Gloves" (1910), "The Poet" (1911), "I and the Village" (1911), "Paris Through the Window" (1913), the Rabbi paintings of 1914 (and 1933!), the 1917 "Promenade" still in the State Russian Museum in Leningrad, and "Lovers in the Flowers" (1931), to make only a random selection.

And during those 30 years Chagall's work was constantly developing. Quickly losing the hint of perspective he had had before leaving Vitebsk for the first time, he let the picture veer towards a kind of flatness which was not to be disturbed until he became involved with his own personal version of cubism. Altitude and distance had, in any case, never perturbed him very much. It was no chance that his fiddler sat on the roof in his earliest painting ("La

1977 Margo Leavin Gallery, Los Angeles
Dia Art Foundation Installation, Ward's Island, New York
Heiner Freidrich Gallery, New York
1979 Kunsthalle, Berne
Galerie Heiner Friedrich, Cologne
1980 Van Abbemuseum, Eindhoven, Netherlands
1982 Leo Castelli Gallery, New York
1983 Ringling Museum of Art, Sarasota, Florida
Butler Institute of American Art, Youngstown, Ohio
Robert L. Kidd Galleries, Birmingham, Michigan
Dia Art Foundation, New York
Multiples/Marian Goodman Gallery, New York
L.A. Louver Gallery, Los Angeles
1984 Palacio de Cristal, Madrid
Xavier Fourcade Inc., New York
Marian Goodman Gallery, New York
University of California, Santa Barbara (with Alan Saret)
1985 Margo Leavin Gallery, Los Angeles
1986 Galerie Fred Jahn, Munich (travelled to Cologne and New York)
Museum of Contemporary Art, Los Angeles
1987 Xavier Fourcade Inc., New York
Galerie 10, Munich
Fabian Carlsson Gallery, London
Fruit Market Gallery, Edinburgh
De Menil Foundation, Houston, Texas
Albright Knox Art Gallery, Buffalo, New York

Selected Group Exhibitions:

1959 *Recent Sculpture: USA*, Museum of Modern Art, New York
1964 *Painting and Sculpture of a Decade*, Tate Gallery, London
1969 *New Media: New Methods*, Museum of Modern Art, New York
1973 *Whitney Biennial: Painting and Sculpture*, Whitney Museum, New York
1975 *Painting, Drawing, and Sculpture of the 60's and 70's from the Collection of Dorothy and Herbert Vogel*, The Clocktower, New York (toured the United States)
1978 *Art About Art*, Whitney Museum, New York (toured the United States)
1980 *Sculpture on The Wall: Relief Sculpture of the 70's*. Fine Arts Center, University of Massachusetts, Amherst
1982 *Documenta 7*, Museum Fridericianum, Kassel, West Germany
1984 *Indiana Influence*, Fort Wayne Museum of Art, Indiana
1986 *American Renaissance*, Fort Lauderdale Museum of Art, Florida

Collections:

Museum of Modern Art, New York; Whitney Museum, New York; Guggenheim Museum, New York; Albright-Knox Art Gallery, Buffalo, New York; Hirshhorn Museum, Washington, D.C.; Dallas Museum of Fine Arts; Fort Worth Museum, Texas; Los Angeles County Museum; Pasadena Art Museum, California; Gallery of Modern Art, Rome; Moderna Museet, Stockholm.

Publications:

By CHAMBERLAIN: articles—"Conversation Between Elizabeth C. Baker, John Chamberlain, Donn Judd and Diane Waldman," (excerpts) in *John Chamberlain*, exhibition catalogue, New York 1971; "Interview with John Chamberlain," by Phyllis Tuchman, in *Artforum* (New York), January 1972; "An Interview with John Chamberlain", with Michael Auping, in *Art Papers* (Atlanta, Georgia), January/February 1983; films—*Wedding Night*, 1967; *The Secret Life of Hernando Cortez*, 1968; *Wide Point*, 1968; *Thumbsuck*, 1971.

On CHAMBERLAIN: books—*The New Art Scene* by Alan Solomon and Ugo Mulas, New York 1967; *A Report on the Art and Technology Program of the Los Angeles County Museum of Art 1967-1971* by Maurice Tuchmann, Los Angeles

1971; *John Chamberlain: A Retrospective Exhibition*, exhibition catalogue, by Diane Waldman, New York 1971; *John Chamberlain*, exhibition catalogue, by Johannes Gachnang and R. H. Fuchs, Berne 1979; *John Chamberlain: A Catalogue Raisonne of the Sculpture, 1954-1985* by Julie Sylvester, New York and Los Angeles 1986; *Structure to Resemblance* by Michael Auping, New York 1987; *Sculpture: John Chamberlain 1970s and 1980s* by Walter Hopps, Houston 1987; articles—"Chamberlain: Another View" by Brian O'Doherty and "How To Look at John Chamberlain's Sculpture" by Barbara Rose in *Art International* (Lugano), January 1964; "John Chamberlain" by Robert Creely in *Recent American Sculpture*, exhibition catalogue, New York 1964; "A New Medium for John Chamberlain" by Phillip Leider in *Artforum* (New York), February 1967; "The Secret Life of John Chamberlain" by Elizabeth C. Baker in *Art News* (New York), April 1969; "The Vicissitudes of Sculpture" by Peter Schjeldahl in the *New York Times*, February 1969; "Fashions in Living: John Chamberlain's Environments" in *Vogue* (New York), April 1970; "John Chamberlain's Sculptures" by John Canaday in the *New York Times*, April 1971; "The Chamberlain Crunch" by Elizabeth C. Baker in *Art News* (New York), February 1972; "An Important Sculpture by John Chamberlain" by E. B. Henning in *Bulletin of The Cleveland Museum of Art*, October 1973; "Die Schönheit liegt im Auge des Betrachters," by Jürg Federspeil in *Tages-Anzeiger Magazin* (Zurich), 20 May 1978; "Berichteiner Reise" by Johannes Gachnang in *Kunst-Bulletin* (Berne), April 1979; "In the Heart of the Tinman: an essay on John Chamberlain" by Duncan Smith in *Artforum* (New York), January 1984; "His Sculpture Transforms Scrap into Steel Poems" by John Russell in the *New York Times*, 17 August 1986.

Towards the end of the 1950's John Chamberlain exhibited sculptures fashioned largely from steel pipes and noticeably under the influence of David Smith. He next used bent and welded metal sheets from old discarded automobiles. In the 1960's he found his place within the ambit of the movement for which the critic Lawrence Alloway coined the term "Junk art." In order to avoid any suggestion of deliberate craftsmanship the artists in this movement drew their materials from demolition yards, junk piles and refuse tips of urban waste. In this they followed a trend which had its origins in the "hautes pâtes" of Dubuffet and was exemplified in the "combines" of Robert Rauschenberg. Within this aesthetic context Chamberlain, like the Italian artist César, made his specialty polychrome "sculptures" from crushed automobile bodies.

Analogies are often made between the techniques of "Junk" sculpture, those of Chamberlain in particular, and the free brushstrokes of Willem de Kooning. But there is a world of difference between the apparently random but controlled effects of Action Painting and the deliberate randomization of Richard Stankiewicz and Chamberlain.

Much has been written, too, about the social and philosophical implications of putting to aesthetic use the discarded materials and scrap of modern urban civilisation. But the interest of Chamberlain himself was usually in the formal qualities of his finished work rather than in any implicit social comment. Although the element of serendipity inevitably features largely in an art which relies on mechanical crushing, Chamberlain in most of his works allowed suggestions from the shapes of his metal sheets to guide the composition and structure of his work. This is evident in such pieces as "Sweet William" (1962). About the mid-1950s Chamberlain also began to use new and brightly painted pieces of automobiles brand new from the factory. Later he worked with such materials as urethane, transparent plastic and fibreglass, moving on to galvanized steel and aluminium. Examples in these techniques are "Héng" (1967, urethane) and "Tippecanoe" (1967, galvanized steel and aluminium).

—Harold Osborne

CHARLTON, Alan.
British. Born in Sheffield, Yorkshire, 26 February

1948. Studied at the Sheffield School of Art, 1965-66, Camberwell School of Art, London, 1966-69, and the Royal Academy Schools, London, 1969-72. Married in 1966. Painter: lives and works in London. Agent: Konrad Fischer, Dusseldorf. Address: c/o Konrad Fischer, Platanenstrasse 7, 4 Dusseldorf, West Germany.

Individual Exhibitions:

1972 Galerie Konrad Fischer, Dusseldorf
Nigel Greenwood Inc., London
Whitechapel Art Gallery, London
1973 Galerie Konrad Fischer, Dusseldorf
Nigel Greenwood Inc., London
1974 Galleria Gian Enzo Sperone, Turin
Sperone-Fischer Gallery, Rome
Art and Project, Amsterdam
1975 Galerie Konrad Fischer, Dusseldorf
Galerie Bischofberger, Zurich
Museum of Modern Art, Oxford (travelled to the Stedelijk van Abbemuseum, Eindhoven, Netherlands, 1976)
1976 Leo Castelli Gallery, New York
1981 Lisson Gallery, London
1982 Stedelijk van Abbemuseum, Eindhoven, Netherlands
1985 John Hansard Gallery, Southampton, Hampshire
1988 Victoria Miro Gallery, London

Selected Group Exhibitions:

1972 *Drawings*, Museum of Modern Art, Oxford
1973 *7 aus London*, Kunsthalle, Berne
Prospekt 73, Kunsthalle, Dusseldorf
Exposition de Peinture Reunissant Certains Peintres qui Mettraient la Peinture en Question, Place Vendome, Paris (toured Europe)
1974 *Painting Exhibition*, Scottish Arts Council Gallery, Edinburgh
1975 *Fundamental Paintings*, Stedelijk Museum Amsterdam
1977 *Group Exhibition*, Lisson Gallery, New York
1982 *Documenta*, Kassel, West Germany

Collections:

Arts Council of Great Britain, London; Stedelijk Museum, Amsterdam.

Publications:

On CHARLTON: book—*Alan Charlton*, exhibition catalogue, Eindhoven, Netherlands 1982; *Alan Charlton*, exhibition catalogue edited by the John Hansard Gallery, Southampton 1985; articles—"Alan Charlton" by Lynda Morris in *Art Press* (Paris), July/August 1973; "European Cool Paiting" by Germano Celant in *Domus* (Milan), October 1973; "Alan Charlton" by H. Einzig in *Arts Review* (London), July 1981.

Curiously, the uniform monochrome painting appeared in caricatures of modern art before the 1914 war, some years before it appeared in art itself with Rodchenko in 1918. However, the evolving traditions of art resurrected this form of the medium in the late 1950's with Klein and Manzoni, later, for quite different reasons, Ryman and Marden.

The problem of a painting which is to be abstract to the point of eliminating any illusion whatever is to put a second colour, layer, or texture on any part of the surface. The reductionist tendency of art must lead to this crux.

Alan Charlton's painting has been monochrome, but it is not reductive in this way. His works have consisted now for many years of canvases painted uniformly grey. The precise shade of grey varies from work to work and may relate to the scale and configuration of the work. Very often rectilinear slots appear in the canvas, lined with a separate stretcher corresponding in depth to the main stretcher, which is about two inches deep—that is, deep enough to give the canvas the air of being an object. It is also deep enough to produce a distinct shadow on the wall in normal conditions of lighting. Canvases may be adjoined, or arranged in such a way that they form an overall configuration which includes the wall space between them. In certain cases a slot may form a complete margin in a canvas so that an island canvas remains in the centre. In each case the treatment of the inner and outer returns of the canvas over the stretcher are the same, so that the enclosure of an inner space implies the exclusion of the outer wall space. I hope it will not appear a paradox if I assert that this has the effect of comprising the outer space in the definition of the work just as the sea around it is necessary to define an island.

This discrimination deals with the formal characteristics of Charlton's work, but his is not a purely formal art—it is not tautological, like that of Lewitt or Andre, for example. It seems rather to be an art of feeling—closer in spirit to that of Rothko.

Charlton's painting, like the art of several of his contemporaries, has been much more highly estimated in continental Europe and the United States than in Britain.

—Michael Compton

CHIA, Sandro.

Italian. Born in Florence, 20 April 1946. Studied at the Accademia di Belle Arti, Florence, 1965–69. Divorced: has 2 children. Independent painter, in Ronciglione, near Rome, 1970–85, in New York since 1980, and in Montalcino, near Siena since 1985; worked in Monchengladbach, West Germany, 1980–81. Agent: Galerie Daniel Templon, 30 rue Beaubourg, 75003 Paris, France. Addresses: Castello Romitorio, Montalcino, Siena, Italy; 521 West 23rd Street, 9th floor, New York, New York 10011, U.S.A.

Individual Exhibitions:

1971	Galleria La Salita, Rome (and 1972, 1973, 1975)
1975	Galleria Lucrezia de Domizio, Pescara, Italy
	Galleria L'Attico, Rome
1976	Galleria Paolo Marinucci / Tucci Russo, Turin
	Galleria La Salita, Rome (and 1977)
1977	Galleriaforma, Genoa, Italy
	Galleria Gian Enzo Sperone, Rome
1978	Galleria dell'Oca, Rome
	Galleria Guiliana de Crescenzo, Rome
	Studio Antonio Tucci Russo, Turin
	Framart Studio, Naples
	Galerie Paul Maenz, Cologne (and 1979)
1979	Galleria Mario Diacono, Bologna, Italy
	Galleria Gian Enzo Sperone, Rome
1980	Art and Project, Amsterdam
	Galerie Paul Maenz, Cologne
	Sperone Westwater Fischer, New York (and 1981)
1981	Galerie Bruno Bischofberger, Zurich
	Galleria Mario Diacono, Rome
	Anthony D'Offay / Gian Enzo Sperone, London
1982	James Corcoran Gallery, Los Angeles
	Sperone Westwater, New York
1983	Stedelijk Museum, Amsterdam
	Galleria Mario Diacono, Rome
	Leo Castelli Gallery, New York
	Palazzo Grassi, Venice
	Galerie Bruno Bischofberger, Zurich
	Fruitmarket Gallery, Edinburgh
	Galerie Daniel Templon, Paris
	Galerie Natalie Seroussi, Paris
	Galleri Five, Stockholm
	Galerie Silvia Menzel, West Berlin
	Stadtische Museum, Monchengladbach, West Germany

	Kestner-Gesellschaft, Hannover
1984	Staatliche Kunsthalle, West Berlin
	Musée d'Art Moderne de la Ville, Paris
	Mathildenhohe, Darmstadt, West Germany
	Kunstverein, Dusseldorf
	Akira Ikeda Gallery, Tokyo
	Metropolitan Museum of Art, New York
	Galerie Schellmann und Kluser, Munich
	Galerie Daniel Templon, Paris
	Galleria Sima, Venice
	Museum des 20. Jahrhunderts, Vienna
	Galerie Ascan Crone, Hamburg
	James Corcoran Gallery, Los Angeles
1985	Galerie Michael Haas, West Berlin
	Leo Castelli Gallery, New York
	Galerie Bruno Bischofberger, Zurich
	Galerie Thaddaus Ropac, Salzburg, Austria
1986	Staatsgalerie moderne Kunst, Munich
	Akira Ikeda Gallery, Tokyo
	Kunsthalle, Bielefeld, West Germany
1987	Akira Ikeda Gallery, Tokyo
	Sperone Westwater, New York
	Fischer Fine Art, London
1988	Galerie Daniel Templon, Paris
	Sperone Westwater, New York

Selected Group Exhibitions:

1977	10e. Biennale de Paris, Musée d'Art Moderne de la Ville, Paris
1979	XV Bienal de Sao Paulo, Brazil
1980	The Cut-Off Hand, Kunstverein, Bonn (travelled to Wolfsburg and Groningen)
1981	A New Spirit in Painting, Royal Academy of Arts, London
1982	Aspects of Italian Art Now, Guggenheim Museum, New York
1983	La Transavanguardia, Caja de Pensiones, Madrid
1984	Six in Bronze, Williams College, Williamstown, Massachusetts
1985	700 Eichen, Kunsthalle, Tubingen, West Germany (travelled to Bielefeld)
1986	40 Ans: Une Generation Mondiale, Palais de l'UNESCO, Paris

Collections:

Museum of Modern Art, New York; Guggenheim Museum, New York; Hirshhorn Museum, Washington, D.C.; Tate Gallery, London; National Gallery of Scotland, Edinburgh; Stadtisches Museum, Monchengladbach; Kunsthalle, Bielefeld; Stedelijk Museum, Amsterdam; Groninger Museum, Groningen; Musée d'Art Moderne / Centre Georges Pompidou, Paris.

Publications:

By CHIA: book—Monchengladbach Journal, with afterword by Johannes Cladders, Monchengladbach 1983.

On CHIA: books—La Transavantgarde Italienne by Achille Bonito Oliva, Milan 1980; The Draught of Dr. Jekyll: An Essay on the Work of Sandro Chia by Anne Seymour, London 1981; Sandro Chia / Enzo Cucchi: Scultura Andata / Scultura Storna, edited by Emilio Mazzoli, Modena 1982; Sandro Chia, exhibition catalogue with introduction by Carter Ratcliff, Edinburgh 1983; Sandro Chia, exhibition catalogue edited by Edy de Wilde and Alexander von Gravenstein, Amsterdam 1983; Sandro Chia: Bilder 1976-1983, exhibition catalogue with texts by Henry Geldzahler, Carl Haenlein and Anne Seymour, Hannover 1983; Sandro Chia: New Paintings, exhibition catalogue edited by Akira Ikeda Gallery, Tokyo 1984; Sandro Chia, exhibition catalogue with text by Heiner Bastian, Salzburg 1985.

Sometimes I ask myself which artists of the past have had an influence on my work and the answer that comes to mind is that any true artist would have to make his own the theoretical revolutionary statement from the beginning of this century: "It is necessary to burn the museums".

In fact the artist must not for anything in the world

lose his sense of this spirit of revolt and of freedom because it is the essence of art. Free of all restriction and submission the artist participates in the conquest of this lost universe. Since the time when a man's skin ceased to be his limit, the soul has never again been the prisoner of death nor has beauty of aesthetics.

Even though today the museums are asking for nothing but to be "burned", and the spreading of freedom constitutes a new order, without the realization of the great alchemical or artistic dream coming true, it is imperative that the artist consider in a more subtle and sophisticated manner the concept of ancestry, the concept of autonomy and the concept of rebellion if he wants to be something other than the ape of modernity. In these years of intensive work, of torment and of joy, I have learned the truth of some things in metaphysics and in physics which I could also call "the passion for art".

Every man has two kinds of memory: the exterior memory of the things of the world and the interior memory of the things of the spirit, but the spirit is not, and even less are the angels, capable of seeing the world with their own eyes. If one really wants to know the reason for those eyes in spiral form on the face of the sculpture, the answer is that if works of art are not the eyes of the spirit and of the angels, at least they are their eyeglasses! The angel, a free thinking artist, looks, remembers and learns through the spectacles of art, but art, which has never been an objective instrument, obsessively weaves itself into civil, moran and strategic thinking. It is the struggle between the eyes and the head: the eyes are the superior party for looking at this civilization of the head, which the more it advances the more it deteriorates. There is a given definition of rebellion against which the angel rebels. Let us listen to his song in peace and avoid the damnation of prejudice: the soul of the whole world will reap the profit.

I think about what kind of thing art really is, and time stands still and slowly turns backwards. Yesterday Joseph Beuys died. Twenty-five years ago I decided in the glory of one night to consecrate my life to painting and to art. Meanwhile the enigmatic faces of a hundred artists are emerging from the density of time. They are a group of men fleeing from conventional history in order to attempt another way, and however much the world strives to capture them, they are beacons, they are lights, they are something which can in no way be completely hidden. To be born and to die are the same thing, to merge and to separate are the same thing, but man was not made to bear the burden of being bound for a long time without suffering or losing heart. The passion for art is identical with the passion for separation, for difference and for divorce, and if necessary I am aware that I must also be ready to divorce myself from the conventions of this contemporary art.

We were made for the plough, for hunting, for music, and for God, and instead we find ourselves with a pile of photographs in our hands, and a mistaken idea of success insists on wanting to govern us. Conscious neither of having received from nature, nor of having subsequently acquired any superior quality, I have only the love of art, and on this absolute premise, I have believed it legitimate to negotiate my existence with my contemporaries, but I have never lied, nor have I ever sought to spare myself by choosing the easiest way.

Nevertheless, it is as if I had forgotten to do something important, like killing the pig which is inside me and which dictates to me certain actions, certain formal solutions. Experience alone will teach me if my complex testimony is anything other than the dominance of mind over matter or of matter over sensuality or of sensuality over logic. Anyway one thing is certain, art can probably do without the beautiful, but not without the sublime.

This coming April twentieth I will be forty years old and in pain I would be able to write a treatise on how to break up friendships, to offend those one holds dear and perhaps to be ruined. After all, what was to be expected from someone who educated himself by reading the life of Cellini. But that is not suffi-

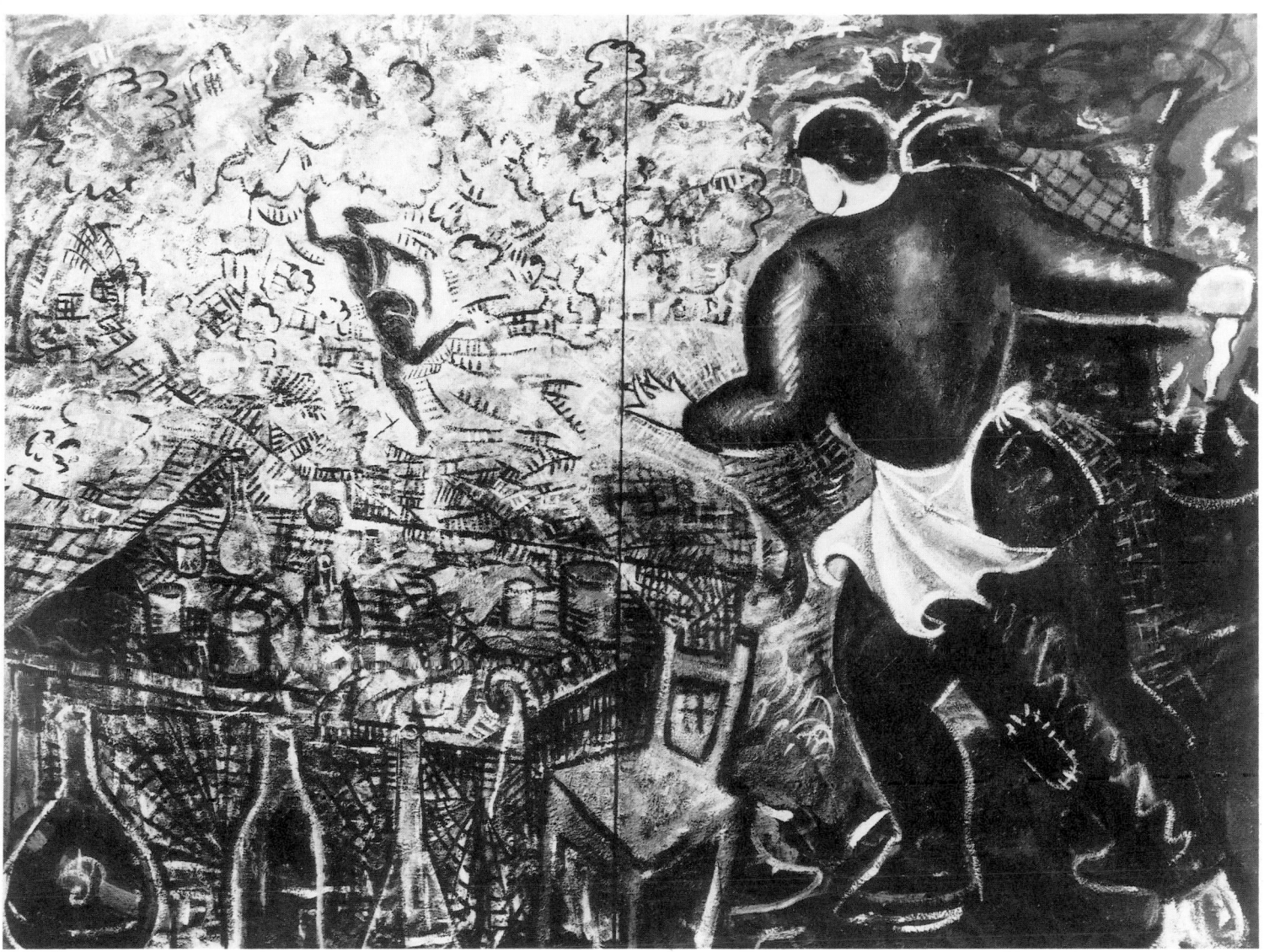

Sandro Chia: *The Pharmacist's Son*, 1981

cient, and does not explain for example this real pain provoked by something only a phantom.

It is clear that the voices which come from the world—be they those of censure or of praise—proceeding from either friendship or enmity, are phantoms. Sometimes these phantoms have the power to cause real suffering: An unbearable inhuman suffering, which lacerates the soul to its depths and devours the body with remorse. One decides then to change, but not even the will seems to have the power to break the stone of which we are made. If to understand, to repent, to suffer, to lose, is of absolutely no use and does not teach anything, so be it!

—Sandro Chia

In the first half of the 1980s, the Italian transavantgarde formed and imposed a style and taste on an entire epoch. It was the vital energy of this explosive pictorial figuration that was responsible for the outpouring of expressionism that rapidly spread and became an international style. Its success is based on the fact that the transavantgarde corresponds to a current need—the necessity to reconsider traditional ways of making art and to posit questions centred on disquiet.

Sandro Chia has taken radical steps within this movement. Arising from his experience related to concept and performance art and reminiscent of precedents set by Merz and Kounellis, around 1978 Chia turned to the pictorial, to design and sculpture of a rigorous figuration. His figuration, however, is not that of the Realists. Any conflict between realism and abstraction in his pictures dissolves. In no way does Chia share any ideological element forming the cor-

nerstone of that Realism whose role is to re-present the 'real'. Chia operates with an awareness that the picture is a system of self-referential signs which find their own truth in their own reality. He is particularly concerned to accentuate this character of *hortus conclusus* pertinent to the picture, while dismantling the idea of an external reality. The picture is the language of its history.

Chia's work adopts the role of "citationist": that is, the work is the fruit of a reflection on the pictures of the past. These he reads with a freely elective affinity and sentiment—an approach to the history of painting which is, of consequence, a purely ideological project. The explicit citation or quotation is evident only in rare cases—for example in *Bar Tintoretto* and *Natura Morta*, both of 1981. In the first picture, Chia reproduces not only the dominant chromatic green (precisely recording the Tintoretto original), the broken line and the fiery reds of the enflamed clouds which hang suspended above two mysterious figures in the foreground, but is also similar to certain features of Boccioni. In the distance, however, Chia has painted sketchy, agitated silhouettes which are inevitably associated with the dynamic dynamic figures of *Rissa in galleria*. In the second picture, quotation from Morandi is more openly declared, although the original lacks Chia's warm and enveloping light. In general, while Chia often retains a dynamic rhythm of broken and whirling Futurist marks, he does so without deconstructing the composition. Rather, Chia's marks form a foundation of tiny particles like a tissue of molecules, which is an irrestistible cosmic force going so far as to contaminate the image, thereby rendering it uncertain and difficult to recognize.

In Chia's iconography where the protagonist is the human figure, we also find that the ancestry is derived from something between the Metaphysical painters and those of the 1900s, between the coloration of Matisse and the structure of a Picasso. Carra, De Chirico, and—above all—Savinio appear to be the preferred sources of his inspiration. Chia shares with Savinio a certain ironic (when not completely satirical) character which, while shrouding the images with mystery, at the same time de-dramatizes them. If Savinio gave the heads of flamingoes to his noblewomen, Chia paints his people with a cartoonist's humour, though without diminishing their enigmatic nature.

The dominant literary and cultural references in Chia's work are expressed with a certain flavour of disenchantment. As Bonito Oliva has noted, Chia's thoughts are organically linked to the present. He doesn't forget that he lives in a world under continual bombardment by the mass-media and "images of the masses"; in this way he introduces into his work an omnivorous desire for signs that are iconic and heterogenous. The picture becomes a meeting-ground for images from high culture, stereotypes from pop culture and products of an industrial culture.

Chia in fact reveals the expression of the epoch's needs that he himself is answering to. Following the neo-avantgarde's break with tradition, and the dematerialization of the object as in conceptual art, art today measures up to the values of a subjectivity immersed in a high technology where sensuality is being reclaimed as a vehicle for a new and uninhibited sensibility.

—Giorgio Verzotti

CHIARI, Giuseppe.

Italian. Born in Florence, 26 September 1926. Studied mathematics and engineering at the University of Florence, 1946–51; also studied piano: concentrated on musical composition, 1950. Married Victoria Chiari in 1957; son: Mario. Artist and composer, Florence, since 1960. Founder, with Pietro Grossi, Vita Musicale Contemporanea Associazione, Florence, 1961; associated with New York Fluxus artists, 1962; worked with composer Sylvano Busotti, Florence, 1962; associated with Gruppo 70, Concrete Poets, Florence, 1964; visited Paris: worked with the Centre de Musique, 1965. Lecturer, Seminario di Musica d'Avanguardia, *Biennale,* Venice, 1969. Address: via Chiarugi 12, 50136 Florence, Italy.

Individual Exhibitions and Concert Performances:

1962	Galleria Blu, Milan
	Fluxus Festival, Centre de Musique, Paris
	Galleria Numero, Rome
	Fluxus Festival, Wiesbaden, West Germany
	Conservatorio Cherubini, Florence
	Teatro Verdi, Trieste
1963	Galleria La Salita, Rome
	Auditorium Società Aquilana dei Concerti, L'Aquilla, Italy
	Forte Belvedere, Florence
	Arte Viva, Trieste
	4th Settimana Internazionale Nuova Musica, Palermo
1964	Centre de Musique, Paris
	Neue Musik, München, Munich
	Avant-Garde Festival, Judson Hall, New York
	Forte Belvedere, Florence
	Ensemble Die Reihe, Vienna
	Institute of Contemporary Arts, London
	Galleria Blu, Milan
	Staatstheater, Oldenburg, West Germany
	Kölner Kurse für Neue Musik, Cologne
1965	Musica Nova, Reykjavik, Iceland
	Galerie René Block, Berlin
	Goethe Universität, Frankfurt
	Galleria Numero, Florence
	Philadelphia College of Art
	Festival de la Libre Expression, Paris
	Galerie Zwirner, Cologne
	Ford Foundation, Berlin
	Centre de Musique, Paris
	Roverto Vezzosi, Florence
	La Scaletta, Matera, Italy
	5th Settimana Internazionale Nuova Musica, Palermo
	Centre de Musique, Paris
	Creative and Performing Arts Center, Buffalo
	Teatro delle Arti, Rome
	Musikalskur Leikur, Reykjavik, Iceland
	Biennale, Zagreb, Yugoslavia
	Fluxus Festival, Washington Square Gallery, New York
	Museum des 20, Jahrhunderts, Vienna
	Galerie Parnass, Wuppertal, West Germany
1966	Casa della Cultura, Livorno
	Academia Filarmonica Romana, Rome
	University of Madrid
	Liberia Feltrinelli, Rome
	Avant-Garde Festival, New York
	Galerie Zwirner, Cologne
1967	*Vita Musicale Contemporanea,* Florence
	Galleria Feltrinelli, Rome
	Unione Culturale, Turin
	Teatro dei Satiri, Rome
	St. Paul's American Church, Rome
	Avant-Garde Festival, Central Park, New York
	Art Total, Lugano, Switzerland
1968	Institute of Contemporary Arts, London
	Film Studio, Rome
	Teatro Verdi, Trieste
	Film und Fernsehakademie, Berlin
	Teatro Politeama, Palermo
	Palazzo Strozzi, Florence
	Cafe Gebler, Berlin

	Premio Masaccio, San Giovanni Valderno, Italy
1969	Galleria Milano, Milan
	Galleria Il Centro, Naples
	Teatro Verdi, Trieste
	8th Biennale d'Arte, San Benedetto del Tronto, Italy
	Autunno Musicale, Como, Italy
	Unione Culturale, Turin
	Unione Goliardica, Mantua, Italy
1970	Warszawska Jesien, Warsaw
	Palazzo Grassi, Venice
	Centro Techne, Florence
	Film Studio, Rome
	University of Rome
	Filarmonica Landuna Messina, Sicily
	Sendesaal Rasio, Bremen, West Germany
	Teatro La Fede, Rome
1971	Rondo di Bacco, Florence
	Associazione Musicale Lucchese, Lucca, Italy
	Istituto Italiano di Cultura, Cologne
	Palazzo Strozzi, Florence
	Chalet I Tigli, Florence
	Autunno Musicale, Como, Italy
1972	Galleria Toselli, Milan
	LP 220, Turin
	Staatstheater, Kassel, West Germany
	Bitef, Belgrade
	Modern Art Agency, Naples
	Istituto Italiano di Cultura, Strasbourg
	Teatro Verdi, Pisa
	Istituto Italiano di Cultura, Budapest
	Arte Viva, Trieste
	Contemporanea, Rome
	Centro Lepetit, Milan
	Palazzo Pitti, Florence
1973	Galleria Il Cortile, Rome
	Kunstmuseum, Lucerne
	Galerie 11, Paris
	Kunstverein, Hannover
	Spot, Kiel, West Germany
	Quadriennale, Rome
	University of Florence
	Galerie René Block, Berlin
1974	Galerie Baecker, Bochum, West Germany
	Royal College of Art, London
	Lucrezia de Comizio, Pescara
	Galleria Martano, Turin
	Projekt 74, Cologne
1975	Art Tapes 22, Florence
	Galerie Stampa, Basle
	Galleria Schema, Florence
	Studio Carla Ortelli, Milan
	Maud Center, Varese, Italy
	Situation Gallery, London
1976	ARC, Paris
1977	Chantal Pontbriand, Montreal
	Instituto Italiano di Cultura, Tokyo
	Centre Art Contemporaine, Geneva
1978	*Biennale,* Venice
1979	Centre Georges Pompidou, Paris
1980	Musée St. Georges, Liége, Belgium
1981	Galerie René Block, Berlin
	Light-Concert, Antwerp, Belgium
	Fluxus Festival, Enschede, Netherlands
1982	*Fluxus 1962–82,* Wiesbaden, West Germany
	Kunstverein, Cologne
	Universidad de Bellas Artes, Madrid
	Kunstler Haus, West Berlin
1983	*Piano Concert,* Valencia, Spain
	Modern Art Galerie, Vienna
	Villa Romana, Florence
1984	Galleria N2, Bologna, Italy
	Galleria Dada, Florence
1985	Silbermann Gallery, Chicago
1986	Galleria Milano, Milan
	Galleria Vivita, Florence
	Piano Concert, Middelburg, Netherlands
1987	Galleria Chisel, Milan (with Ben Vautier)
	Piano Concert, Pratolino, Florence
	Carl Solway Gallery, Chicago

Collections:

Centro Di, Florence; Kunstmuseum, Lucerne.

Publications:

By CHIARI: books—*Giuseppe Chiari: Extra,* exhibition catalogue, Florence 1986; *Chiari: Aesthetik,* Frankfurt 1987; article—"Interview mit Giuseppe Chiari" with Giancarlo Politi, in *Heute Kunst* (Dusseldorf), July/August 1973; musical scores—*Intervalli; Studi su una Sola Frequenza: Gesti sul Piano; Per Arco; Teatrino; Il Silenzio; Play What You Like; Rompere; La Strada; Whisky; Don't Trade Here;* since 1960.

On CHIARI: books—*Il Territorio Magico* by Achille Bonito Oliva, Florence 1971; *Projekt 74,* exhibition catalogue, Cologne 1974; *Il Metodo per suonare di Giuseppe Chiari* by Gillo Dorfles, Turin 1976; *Aktions-kunst* by Jürgen Schilling, Frankfurt 1978; *Identité Italienne* by Germano Celant, Paris 1981; *Giuseppe Chiari: Music is Easy,* exhibition catalogue with text by Enrico Pedrini, Florence 1983; *Fluxus: An Anthology of Chance Operations* by Marco Meneguzzo, Genoa 1987; articles—"Giuseppe Chiari" by Gillo Dorfles in *Nuovi Miti, Nuovi Riti,* Turin 1969; "Chiari" by John Cage in *Notations,* New York 1970; "What's Music?" in *Data* (Milan), no. 2 1972; "Music and Teaching" by Tommaso Trini in *Data* (Milan), no. 13, 1973; "Fluxus" by Tommaso Trini in *Data* (Milan), no. 18, 1976.

*

Art is easy; music is easy.

—Giuseppe Chiari

The visual quality of Giuseppe Chiari's works results directly from their morphological-syntactical quality; it never comes from graphic tricks or arbitrary flourishes and arabesques. The "symbols" that Chiari has often used are spare and functional, never given any "picturesque" or graphic emphasis. What is it, then, that accounts for the remarkable interest that these works ("scores," one might perhaps call them) have aroused in the past ten years, particularly in the field of visual art rather than the musical field? I believe that their success—like that of Chiari's other activities (actions on the keyboard, "playing" different objects and so on)—is due mainly to their conceptual placing, to their starting from a precise formative idea applied to definite situations, to definite musical (and non-musical) processes, acoustic and gestural; in short, to the fact that Chiari has understood—ever since his "Teatrino" of 1965 and his "Gestures on the Piano," performed in 1962 at the *Fluxus Festival* in Paris—the importance of an analysis of the actions that were appropriate long before western art was overwhelmed by the powerful wave of Concept Art. That is probably why Chiari's works have been associated with those—very different in themselves and in their background—of some Concept artists who used words (Art and Language), gestures and the body itself (Body Art) to express themselves.

The revolt against the object in visual art corresponds closely with the re-utilization of the object itself, no longer as something ready-made but as something "to be played"; to be used, that is, for its form and its structural characteristics in the musical field.

The main task that Chiari set himself was that of disclosing the inner quality of the form of objects and of instruments so as to be able to "play" them by making use of all their morphological features. Even when Chiari speaks of "playing the chair" (1969), what he means is that he has studied the possibilities of handling the object, acoustically if not musically, for long months.

The case of the pianoforte is similar but more complex; here too it is not just a matter of producing certain sounds from the keyboard, but of studying the whole structure of the instrument, of weighing up the morphologically expressive possibilities it has in addition to the production of sounds, even through a symbiosis with the player's body.

It remains to add some observations on the artist's presentation of himself as the author of the performances. This aspect of his art came after the strictly musical and the "graphic" aspects; it is only since 1964 that the artist has taken to performing his own works and so inaugurated a new phase of his work.

Some of his performances inevitably remind us of Beuys, Ben or Palestine. In all those artists, as in

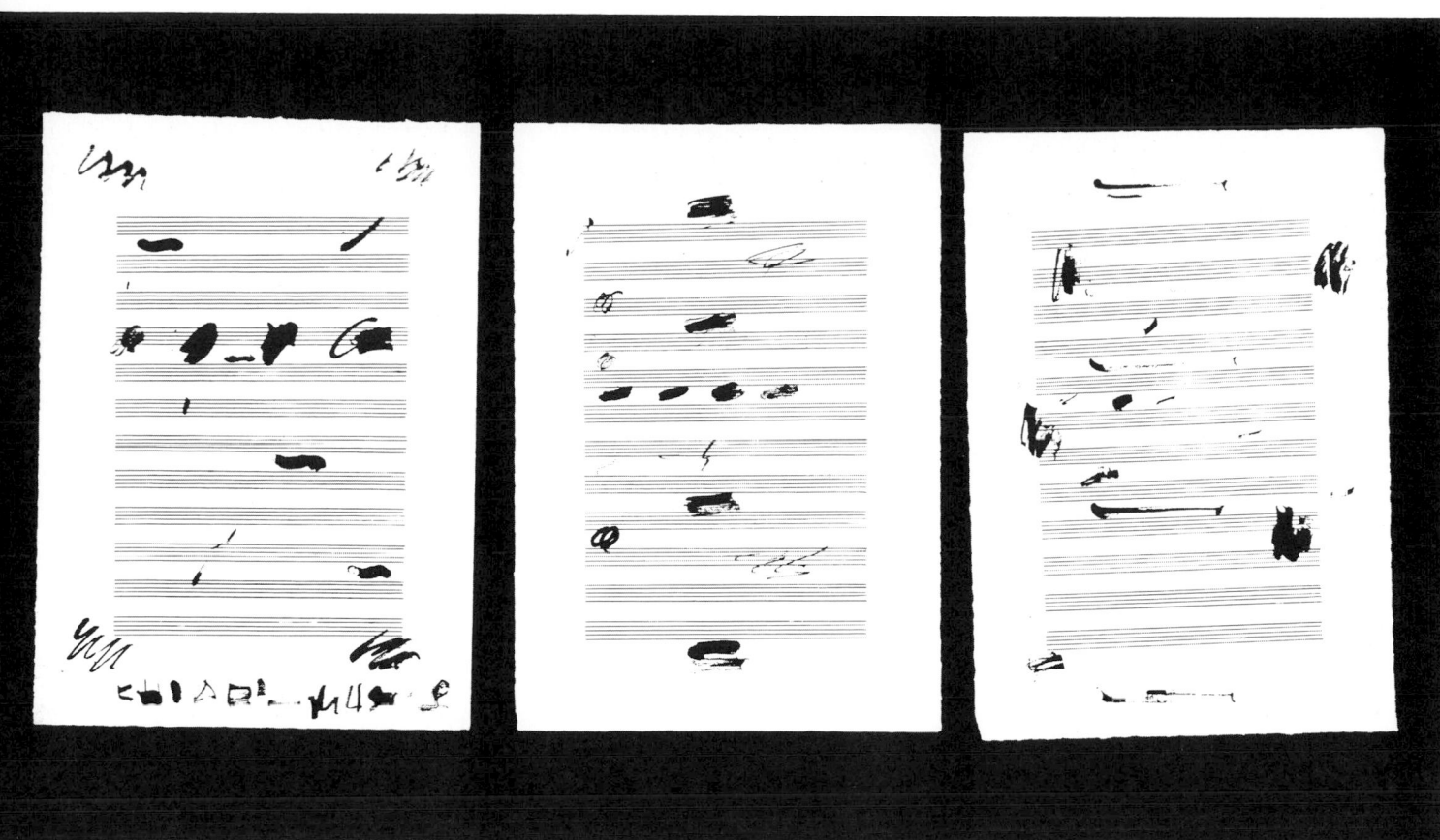

Giuseppe Chiari: *Music Is Easy*, 1982

Chiari, the element most specifically present is that of Body Art. But in Chiari the self-presentation, the narcissistic gestures, that mark the Body Art artists is always subordinated to a precise end: to bring out the "action" qualities of his musical compositions or of his actions through the objects handled, which are the medium through which he expresses himself. This puts him in the forefront of those who have identified the most authentic matrix of an aesthetic activity in the manipulation of the substance of their own bodies.

—Gillo Dorfles

CHICAGO, Judy.

American. Born Judy Cohen in Chicago, Illinois, 20 July 1939. Educated at the University of California at Los Angeles, 1960-64, B.A. 1962, M.F.A. 1964; influenced by the work of Emily Carr, Georgia O'Keeffe, Barbara Hepworth, and Louis Nevelson. Married Jerry Gerowitz in 1961 (died, 1963); married Lloyd Hamrol in 1969. Instructor, University of California Extension, Los Angeles, 1963-69; Painting Instructor, University of California Institute Extension, Irvine, 1966-69; Assistant Professor, California State University at Fresno (started first women's art program), 1969-71; Faculty Member and Co-Founder, Feminist Art Program, California Institute of Arts, Valencia, 1971-73; Artist-in-Residence, Western Washington State College, Bellingham, 1973. Co-Director, Womanhouse, Los Angeles, 1972; Co-Founder, Woman-Space Art Gallery, Los Angeles, 1972; Co-Founder and Instructor, Feminist Studio Workshop, Los Angeles, 1973-74; Co-Founder, Woman's Building, Los Angeles, 1974. Recipient: Woman of the Year Award, *Mademoiselle* magazine, New York, 1973; Individual Artist Grant, 1976, and Services to the Field Grant, 1977, National Endowment for the Arts. Agents: Kenmore Galleries, 122 South 18th Street, Philadelphia, Pennsylvania

19103; and JPL Fine Arts, 23 Grafton Street, London W1X 31D, England. Address: Post Office Box 834, Benicia, California 94510, U.S.A.

Individual Exhibitions:

1966	Rolf Nelson Gallery, Los Angeles
1969	Pasadena Art Museum, California
1970	Faculty Club, California State College, Fullerton
	Fresno State College, California
1972	Jack Glenn Gallery, Corona de Mar, California
1973	Grandview Gallery, Woman's Building, Los Angeles
1974	Kenmore Galleries, Philadelphia
	Artemisia Gallery, Chicago
	Coe College, Cedar Rapids, Iowa
	Judy Chicago and Lloyd Hamrol, Western Washington State College, Bellingham
1975	College of St. Catherine, St. Paul, Minnesota
	Fe/Vision, Los Angeles
	JPL Fine Arts, London
1976	Quay Ceramics, San Francisco
1977	Schaffner Gallery, Los Angeles
1979	Schaffner Gallery, Los Angeles
	Anhalt-Barnes Gallery, Los Angeles
	The Dinner Party, San Francisco Museum of Modern Art (toured the United States and Canada)
1980	Hadler-Rodriguez Gallery, Houston
	Parco Gallery, Tokyo
	Parco Gallery, Osaka

Selected Group Exhibitions:

1967	*Scuppture of the 60's*, Los Angeles County Museum of Art (Travelled to the Philadelphia Museum)
1972	*Color as Structure*, Whitney Museum, New York
1974	*16 Los Angeles Women Artists*, Cerritos College, Norwalk, California
1975	*Woman as Viewer*, Winnipeg Art Gallery
1976	*Painting and Sculpture in California: The Modern Era*, San Francisco Museum of Modern Art
1977	*Frauen machen Kunst*, Galerie Magers, West Germany

	Overglaze Imagery: Cone 019 to 016, California State University at Fullerton Art Gallery
1979	*Works on Paper*, Institute of Contemporary Art, Boston
	The 1970's: New American Painting, organized by the New Museum, New York (toured Eastern Europe)
	Creativity, A Human Resource, Academy of Sciences, San Francisco (toured the United States and Canada)

Collections:

Museum of Modern Art, New York.

Publications:

By CHICAGO: books—*Through the Flower: My Struggle as a Woman Artist*, New York 1975; *The Dinner Party: A Symbol of Our Heritage*, New York 1979; *Embroidering Our Heritage: The Dinner Party Needlework*, New York 1980; *The Birth Project*, New York 1985; articles—statement in *Everywoman Newspaper* (Los Angeles), 7 May 1971; statement and introduction, with Miriam Shapiro, in *Womanhouse*, exhibition catalogue, Los Angeles 1972; introduction to *Invisible/Visible*, exhibition catalogue, Long Beach, California 1972; "Let Sisterhood Be Powerful" in *Womanspace Journal* (Los Angeles), February/March 1973; "Female Imagery," with Miriam Shapiro, in *Womanspace Journal* (Los Angeles), Summer 1973; "Letter to A Young Woman Artist," with Arlene Raven, in *Anonymous Was A Woman*, Valencia, California 1974; "2 Artists Interview Each Other," with Lloyd Hamrol, in *Criteria* (Vancouver), 1974; "Interview with Judy Chicago," with Arlene Raven and Susan Rennie, in *Chrysalis* (Los Angeles), no. 4, 1977; films—*Judy Chicago and The California Girls*, with J. Dancoff, Los Angeles 1971; *Womanhouse*, with Johanna Demetrakis, Los Angeles 1972.

On CHICAGO: books—*Primary Structures*, exhibition catalogue, by Kynaston McShine, New York 1966; *Painting, Sculpture, Photographs of Judy Chicago*, by Dextra Frankel, Fullerton, California 1970; articles—"Thru The Feminist Loking Glass with Judy Chicago" by Susan Stocking in the *Los Angeles Times*, July 1972; "Woman's Art: A Theoretical

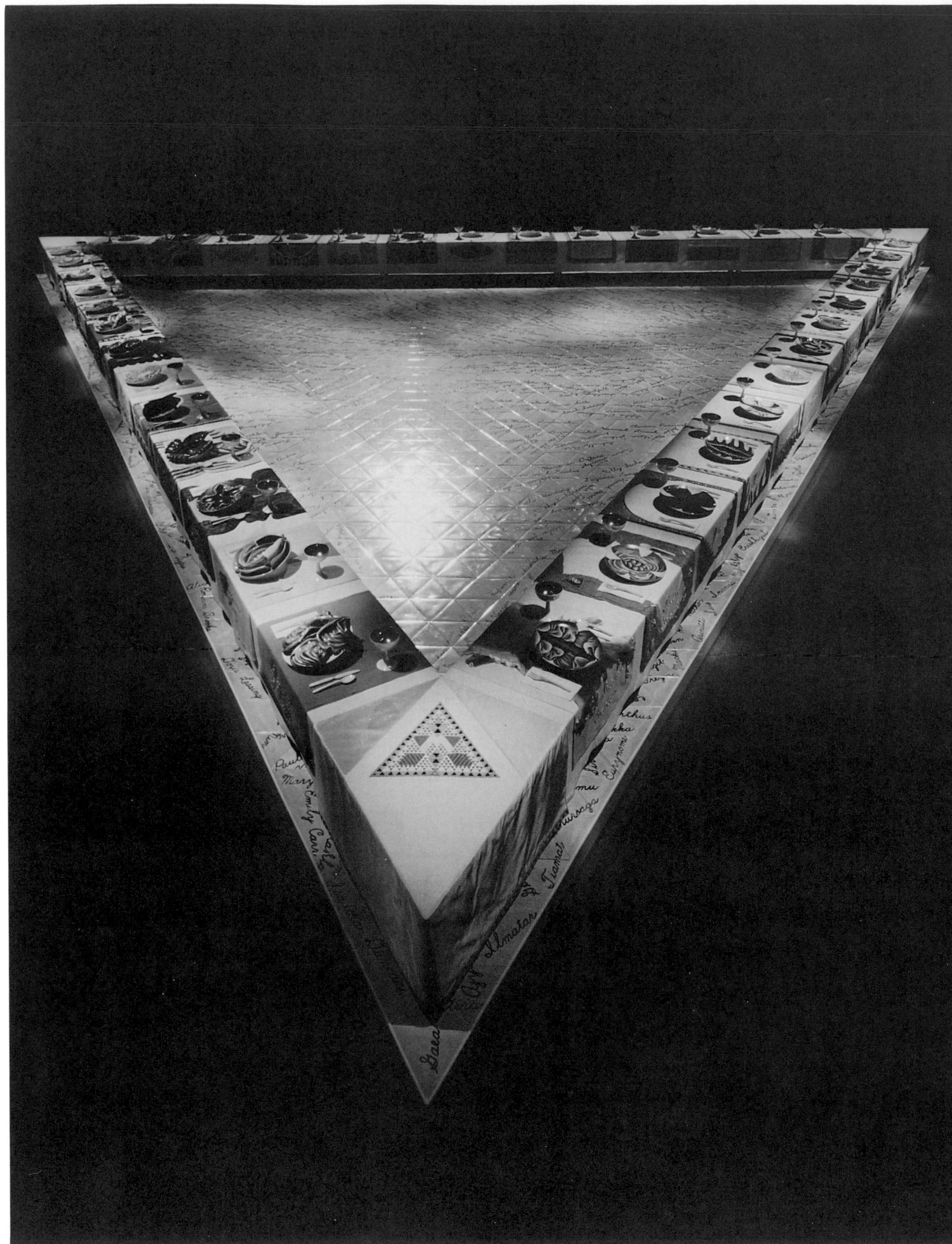

Judy Chicago: *The Dinner Party*, 1979

Perspective" by Arlene Raven in *Womanspace Journal* (Los Angeles), February/March 1973; "Judy Chicago at Kenmore" by Judy Stein in *Art in America* (New York), July/August 1974; "Judy Chicago Talking to Luch R. Lippard" in *Artform* (New York), September 1974; "Judy Chicago and Trials of 'Dinner Party' " by Grace Glueck in the *New York Times*, 30 April 1977; "Judy Chicago: World of China Painter" in *Ceramics Monthly* (Columbus, Ohio), May 1978.

I organized the first feminist art program in America in 1970 and have been instrumental in developing the Women's Building in Los Angeles, which is committed to a feminist perspective in art-related professions. I am a feminist artist, interested in making the female experience stand for an aspect of the human condition which has been shrouded in mythology and fantasy. I am committed to expanding the perspective of my world through breaking the historical silence of women. I believe in art that is connected to real human feeling, that extends itself beyond the limits of the art world to embrace all people who are striving for alternatives in an increasingly dehumanized world. I am trying to make art that relates to the deepest and most mythic concerns of human kind and I believe that, at this moment of history, feminism is humanism. I believe that art, if authentic, can reach across all gaps between people and create understanding.

—Judy Chicago

"I wanted to wed my skills to my real ideas and to aspire to the making of art that could clearly reveal my values and point of view as a woman . . . integrating my art and my feminism."

—Judy Chicago
from *Through the Flower*

Painter, sculptor, teacher, director, organizer, political activist, writer. Judy Chicago is all these.

She originally studied traditional painting and sculpture. Later—struggling for male acceptance—she learned spray painting in an auto body shop, taught herself carpentry, discovered how to use machinery in an industrial arts shop, studied pyrotechnology, made a lithograph—"toughing it out". Her autobiography, *Through the Flower*, is partly an attempt to escape that search for masculine approval and to resolve the conflict of how to be a woman *and* an artist.

Chicago's early work was often labelled "Judy's cunts," but she soon hid her aggressive female imagery in minimalism. In painting series whe explored "hard" and "soft" interactions through colour relationships. In sculpture three-domed shapes represented both her physical self and the family of mother/father/child.

Driven to share her experiences, Chicago initiated an art class for women in Fresno, California, then created "Womanhouse" with a group of working female artists. "Womanhouse" involved renovating a dilapidated house—so learning "male" skills and crafts—then transforming it into environmental statements. The women, working alone or in teams on individual rooms, emerged stretched emotionally mentally and artistically. Chicago grew and learned with them.

"Womanhouse" taught Chicago that a woman's art benefits from being shown with art of other women—in context, so to speak. It also stimulated her to "wave a red flag" at the bull of the male-dominated art community with renewed emphasis in her work on recognizable female imagery. "Red Flag" is the title of her first lithograph—an overt highly-coloured image of a used Tampax being withdrawn from a woman.

In 1973 Chicago began a major five-year project—"The Dinner Party." A "symbolic history of women's achievements and struggles," it is an evolutionary summation of Chicago's own achievements begun with the inspiration of a single hand-painted plate. Thirty-nine women are honoured with a full place at Chicago's triangular-shaped table. Each place setting is marked by an embroidered runner and a ceramic plate. The strong three-dimensional plate designs, reminiscent of Chicago's early specific imagery, fight to rise from their bases—trapped butterflies straining for freedom. The entire work stands on a porcelain floor of triangles painted in gold with names of 999 "supporting" women. A feminist statement is made using traditional female crafts and activities.

"The Dinner Party," which has been travelling since its completion, is both a celebration and a challenge—a celebration of accomplishments from the primordial goddess of ancient religions to Katherine Hepburn. It celebrates women's successes in art, politics, science and religion. "The Dinner Party" would, however, be a beautiful failure if it did not also challenge, demanding of men and women a better knowledge of and interest in contributions of women to every facet of life—and a demand that women continue to answer the challenge. That is the reason for "The Dinner Party"—and for the art and life of Judy Chicago.

—Marlee Robinson

CHILLIDA, Eduardo.

Spanish. Born in San Sebastian, 10 January 1924. Educated at Classical High School, San Sebastian, 1930–42; studied architecture at the University of Madrid, 1943–47, and painting at a private art school, Madrid, 1947. Married Pili de Belzunce in 1950; children: Guiomar, Pedro, Ignacio, Carmen and Suzanna. Independent artist, in Paris, 1948–49, in Villaines-sous-Bois, France, 1950, in Hernani, Spain, 1951–58, in San Sebastian, since 1959. Visiting Professor, Carpenter Center, Harvard University, Cambridge, Massachusetts 1971. Recipient: Diploma of Honour, *Triennale di Milano*, 1954; Sculpture Prize, Comune di Venezia, 1958; Graham Foundation Award, Chicago 1958; Kandinsky Prize, 1960; Carnegie Sculpture Prize, Pittsburgh, 1964; Nord-Rhein Prize, Dusseldorf, 1966; Wilhelm-Lehmbruck Sculpture Prize, Duisburg, West Germany, 1966; Rembrandt Prize, San Sebastian, 1975; Engraving Prize, Japanese Ministry of Culture, 1976; Peach Prize, Victor Seix Institute, 1978; Andrew W. Mellon Prize, with Willem de Kooning, Carnegie Institute, Pittsburgh, 1978; Gold Medal of Merit for Fine Arts, Madrid, 1981; European Plastic Arts Prize, Strasbourg, 1983; Grand Prix des Arts et des Lettres, Paris, 1984; Wolf Foundation Prize, Herzlia, Israel, 1985; Kaiserring Award, Goslar, West Germany, 1985; *Revista Euzkadi* Prize, Bilbao, Spain, 1986; Premio de Asturias, Madrid, 1987; Premio Lorenzo il Paris Magnifico, Florence, 1987; Order of Merit for Science and Art, Bonn, 1987. Agents: Sala Gaspar, Consejo de Ciento 323, Barcelona, and Galerie Maeght, 13 rue do Tehran, 75008 Paris, France. Address: Intzenea—Paseo del Faro 26, 20008 San Sebastian, Spain.

Individual Exhibitions:

1954	Galeria Clan, Madrid
1956	Galerie Maeght, Paris
1961	Galerie Maeght, Paris
1962	Kunsthalle, Basle
1964	McRoberts and Tunnard Gallery, London
1966	Galerie Maeght, Paris
	Wilhelm-Lehmbruck-Museum, Duisburg, West Germany
	Galerie Buchholz, Munich
	Museum of Fine Arts, Houston
1967	Munson-Williams-Proctor Institute, Utica, New York
	City Art Museum, St. Louis
	Alex Galerie, Dusseldorf
	Konstsalongen Samlaren, Stockholm
1968	Galerie Maeght, Paris
	Galerie Im Erker, St. Gallen, Switzerland
1969	Kunstmuseum, Basle
	Kunsthaus, Zurich
	Stedelijk Museum, Amsterdam
	Galerie-Verein München e.V, Munich
	Galerie Buchholz, Munich
	Galerie im Erker, St. Gallen, Switzerland
1970	Kunstkabinett, Frankfurt
	Galerie Maeght, Paris
	Librairie-Galerie La Hune, Paris
	Galerie Renée Ziegler, Zurich
1971	Sala Gaspar, Barcelona
1972	Galeria Iolas-Velasco, Madrid
	Konsthall, Lund, Sweden
	Ulmer Museum, Ulm, West Germany
1973	Galerie Maeght, Paris
	Caja de Ahorros, Pamplona, Spain
	Caja de Ahorros, Sorguesa, Spain
	Caja de Ahorros, Estella, Spain
	Galerie Wünsche, Hamburg
1974	Hastings Gallery/Spanish Institute, New York
	Galeria 42, Barcelona
	Galeria Juana de Aizpuru, Seville
	Galeria Turner, Madrid
	Chateau de Ratilly, France
	Galleria d'Art Serfontana, Morbio Inferiore, Italy
	Galerie d'Art Moderne, Basle
1975	Galerie Nouvelle Images, The Hague
	Galerie Numaga, Neuchâtel, Switzerland
	Galeria Internacional de Arte, Madrid
1976	Kulturhuset, Hellerup, Denmark
1977	Galeria Iolas-Velasco, Madrid
	Museo de Durango, Spain
	Caja de Ahorros, Pamplona, Spain
	FIAC 77, Grand Palais, Paris
	Carpenter Center, Harvard University Cambridge, Massachusetts
	Galerie Art in Progress, Munich
1978	Staatliche Kunsthalle, Baden-Baden, West Germany
	Galerie Maeght, Zurich
	Galerie Schmela, Dusseldorf
	Galerie Artek, Helsinki (with Luginbuhl and Tinguely)
1979	Landau-Alexander Gallery, Los Angeles
	National Gallery, Washington, D.C.
	Carnegie Institute, Pittsburgh
1980	Galerie Maeght, Paris
	Guggenheim Museum, New York (retrospective)
	Palacio de Valezquez, Madrid
	Esculturas/Obra Grafica, Galeria Maeght, Barcelona
	Galerie Maeght, Paris
1981	Museo de Bellas Artes, Bilbao
	Skulpturen, Kestner-Gesellschaft, Hannover
	Galerie Maeght, Zurich
	Frances Aronson Gallery, Atlanta, Georgia
	Galerie Marghescu, Hannover
	Galerie Hans Ostertad, Frankfurt
1982	Galerie Beyeler, Basle
	Galerie Maeght, Zurich
1983	Maison de Goya, Bordeaux, France
	Galeria Maese Nicolas, Leon, Spain
	Erker Galerie, St. Gallen, Switzerland
	Galerie Herbert Meyer-Ellinger, Frankfurt
1984	Sala Celini, Madrid
	Galerie Kaj Forsblom, Helsinki
	Galerie Grariart, Turku, Finland
	Galerie Brusberg, Hannover
	Galerie Adrien Maeght, Paris
	M. A. Martin Gallery, New York
	Tasende Gallery, La Jolla, California
1985	Caja Ahorros Municipal, Elgoibar, Spain
	Anne Berthoud Gallery, London
	Galerie Biedermann, Munich
	Caja Laboral Popular, Portugalete, Spain
	Caja Laboral Popular, Algorta, Spain
	Galerie Beaumont, Luxembourg
	Abadia Montmajour, Arles, Franch
	Musee d'Art Moderne, Brussels
	Galerie Maeght-Lelong, Zurich
1986	Fondacion Miro, Barcelona
	Caja Laboral Popular, Aretxabaleta, Spain (toured Spain)

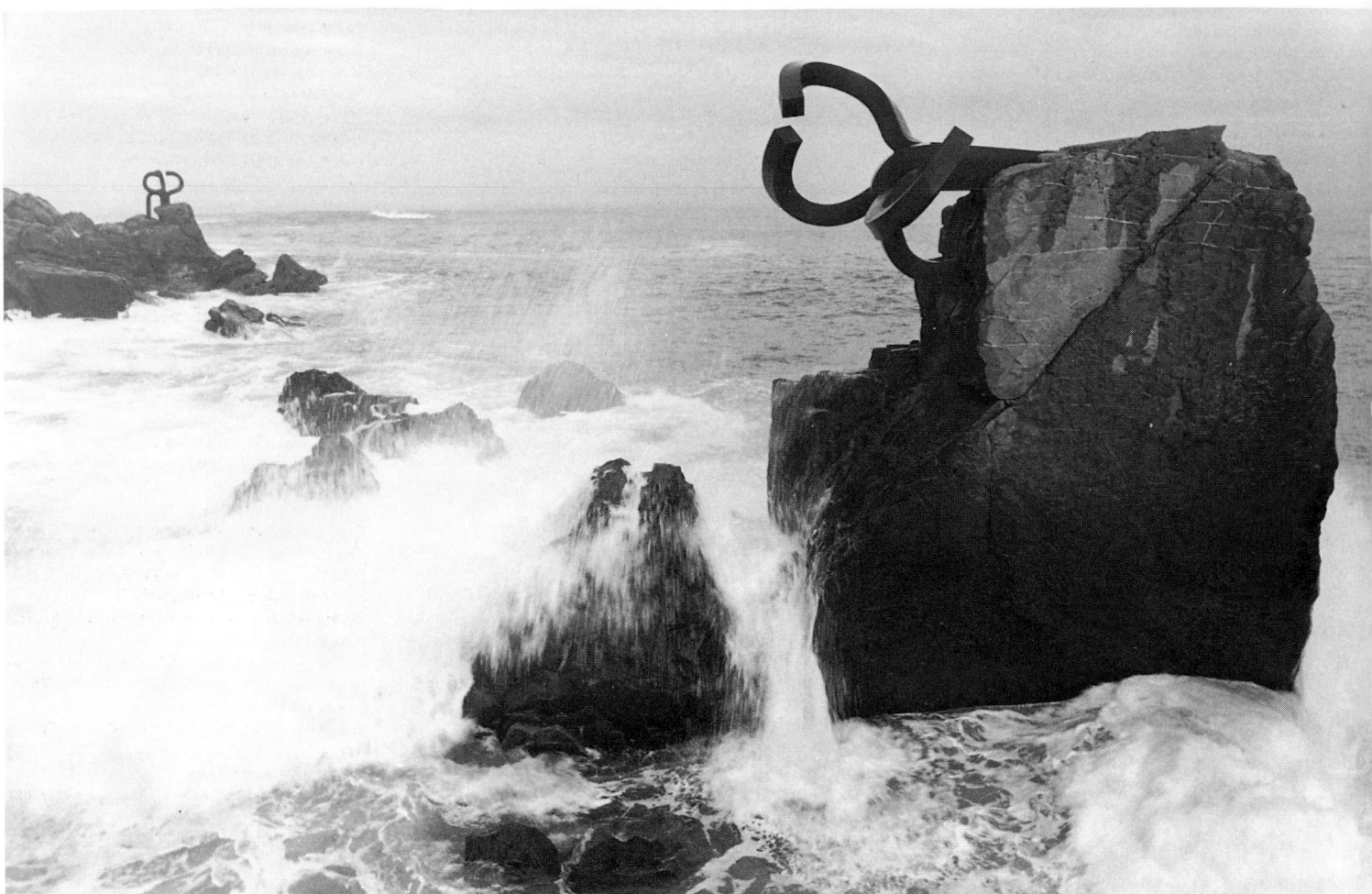

Eduardo Chillida: *Peine del Viento*, 1976

Centro de Arte Reina Sofia, Madrid
Neue Galerie der Stadt, Linz, West Germany
Galerie Meyer-Ellinger, Frankfurt
Dresdner Bank, Frankfurt
Museo de Bellas Artes, Bilbao, Spain
Tasende Gallery, La Jolla, California
Ospedale degli Innocente Florence
Fondacion Miro, Barcelona
1987 Galeria Joan Prats, Barcelona
Galerie Ulysses, Vienna
Galeria Ederti, Bilbao, Spain
Stadtmuseum, Pforzheim, West Germany

Selected Group Exhibitions:

1949 *5th Salon de Mai*, Musée d'Art Moderne, Paris
1954 *10th Triennale di Milano*
1958 *Biennale*, Venice
1964 *Documenta 3*, Kassel, West Germany (and *Documenta 4*, 1968; *Documenta 6*, 1977)
1967 *Guggenheim International*, Guggenheim Museum, New York
1974 *9th Biennale of Prints*, National Museum of Modern Art, Tokyo (travelled to the Museum of Modern Art, Kyoto)
1975 *Contemporary Spanish Painters*, Cultural Center, New York
1979 *L'Univers d'Aime Maeght*, Maison de la Culture, Rennes, France
1983 *Arte abstracto espanol*, Fundacion Juan March, Madrid
1987 *Monumenta*, Middelheim Museum, Antwerp, Belgium

Collections:

Wilhelm-Lehmbruck-Museum, Duisburg, West Germany;

Kunstmuseum, Basle; Kunsthaus, Zurich; Tate Gallery, London; Galleria, Nazionale d'Arte Moderna, Rome; Museo Civico, Turin; Museum of Modern Art, New York; Guggenheim Museum, New York; Art Institute of Chicago; Museum of Fine Arts, Houston.

Publications:

By CHILLIDA: books—*Hommage à Georges Braque*, Paris 1964; *Chillida*, portfolio, with foreword by Carola Giedion-Welcker, Paris 1964; *Chillida: Sculptures*, with foreword by Juan Daniel Fullaondo, Paris 1968; books illustrated—*Le Chemin des Devins/Menerges* by André Frenaud, Paris 1966; *Meditationen in Kastillien* by Max Holzer, St. Gallen, Switzerland 1968; *Die Kunst und der Raum* by Martin Heidegger, St. Gallen, Switzerland 1969; *Poetes-Peintres-Sculpteurs*, Paris 1960; *Mas alla* by Jorge Guillen, Paris 1973; *Die Penser* by Aeschylus, Madrid 1978.

On CHILLIDA: books—*Dictionary of Modern Sculpture* by Micel Seuphor, Neuchâtel, Switzerland 1959; *Contemporary Sculpture: An Evolution in Volume and Space* by Carola Giedion-Welcker, London 1961; *Chillida*, exhibition catalogue, with text by Franz Meyer, Basle 1962; *Eduardo Chillida*, exhibition catalogue, with text by James Johnson Sweeney, Houston 1966; *Chillida* by Pierre Volboudt, Paris 1967; *Form and Space* by Eduard Trier, London 1968; *Vingt-Cing Ans d'Art Vivant* by Michael Ragon, Paris 1968: *The Eye and the Hand of the Sculptor* by Paul Waldo Schwartz, London 1969; *Chillida* by Claude Esteban, Paris 1971; *Los Espacios de Chillida* by Gabriel Celaya, Barcelona 1974; *Hablando con Chillida,escultor vasco* by Marin de Ugalde, San Sebatian 1975; *Chillida* by Luis Figuerola-Ferretti, Madrid 1976; *Cuaderno Chillida*, edited by Revista de Occidente, Madrid 1976; *Eduardo Chillida: Akte-Hande-Formen* by Werner Schmalenbach, West Berlin 1977; *Chillida:Oeuvre Graphique* by Julien Clay, Paris 1978; *Chillida* by Octavio Paz, Paris 1979; *Chillida*, exhibition catalogue, with text by Octavio Paz, New York 1980; *Chillida: Esculturas/Obra Grafica*, exhibition catalogue, with text by Santigo Amon, Barcelona 1980; *Eduardo Chillida; Skulpturen*, exhibition catalogue, with text by Carl-Albrecht Haenlein, Hannover

1981; *Chillida*, exhibition catalogue, with text by Octavio Paz, Zurich 1981; *Eduardo Chillida: Graphic Works*, exhibition catalogue with text by R. Hohl, La Jolla, California 1984; *Eduardo Chillida*, exhibition catalogue by Michael Semff, Pforzheim, West Germany 1987.

Since the deaths of Gonzalez and Picasso, Eduardo Chillida is the most distinguished living Spanish sculptor. He is, however, a Basque, and does not share with those two great compatriots, and many other Spanish artists, a concern for surrealistic fantasy or narrative necessity. Cubism and the Constructivism seem to be part of his formal inheritance, but from his native background he also brings the influence of artianship, in the use of heavy metals and the making of positive, forged shapes. A slow, contemplative artist, Chillida has always preferred to live and work away from international centres.

It was not until the early 60's that Chillida established a positive style. Earlier work in wood and forged iron, elaborated from heavy, gestural, twisted forms, is reminiscent, at times of Gonzalez, but, in the eclectic change of manner, clearly searching for a final, personal form. Since then Chillida's sculptures have become more and more ascetic and controlled, the twisted, writhing, interlocking forms, carefully articulated into rhythmic definitions of space. This maturity is the result of a return, both physically and emotionally, to his native soil. His drawings, on paper, or the lead-inlaid marble calligraphy, as well as the attenuated sculptures, are deeply involved in the landscape of a mountainous country which plunges into a turbulent ocean. The division and meeting of these natural elements are vigorously delineated by Chillida, with a mixture of energy and elegance which brings to mind the stylised images of Japanese landscape painting. His sculptures further explore natural forces, through a medium which has roots in

Spanish artisanship. They are concerned with flow, not conflict; he avoids intersections which interfere with the monumental rhythms of his forms.

Chillida says his subject is the relationship between time and space, defined by three-dimensionality: ". . . the two elements of space, one which might be called negative, the other positive, are in a relationship which I call a dialogue." This dialogue is concerned with poetic values, not scientific definitions, and derives from the observation of nature.

—Charles Spencer

CHRISTO. (Christo Javacheff).

American. Born in Gabrovo, Bulgaria, 13 June 1935; emigrated to the United States, 1964: naturalized, 1973. Educated at Fine Arts Academy, Sofia, Bulgaria, 1952–56; Burian Theatre, Prague, 1956; Fine Arts Academy, Vienna, 1957. Married Jeanne-Claude de Guillebon in 1960; son: Cyril. Lived in Paris 1958–64; moved to New York, 1964; designed first packages and wrapped objects, 1958; first showcases, 1963; first storefronts, 1964, and first packaged public buildings, 1968. Recipient: Cassandra Award, Bill and Noma Copley Foundation, Chicago, 1966; Colorado Award for Engineering Excellence, 1973; Sonoma-Marin County Ranchers Award, California, 1976; Honarary Citizenship, City of New Orleans, 1977; Process and Environment Award, Skowhegan School of Painting and Sculpture, Maine, 1979; Royal Danish Academmy of Art Award, Copenhagen, 1979; Award of Excellence, Chelterham Art Center, Pennsylvania, 1980; Admiral's Award of the Fleet of Miami, Florida, 1986; Liberty Award, New York, 1986; Menotti Artist in Residence Award, College of Charleston, South Carolina, 1987; Kaiser Ring Award, Goslar, West Germany, 1987. DHL: College of Saint Rose, Albany, New York, 1986. Agent: Jeanne-Claude Christo, 48 Howard Street, New York, New York 10013. Adress: 48 Howard Street, New York, New York 10013, U.S.A.

Individual Exhibitions:

1961   Galeria Haro Lauhus, Cologne
1962   Galerie J. Paris
1963   Galerie Schmela, Dusseldorf
      Galleria Apollinaire, Milan
      Galleria de Leone, Venice
1964   Gallerie Schmela, Dusseldorf
      Galleria del Leone, Venice
      Galerie Ad Libitum, Antwerp
      Galleria G.E. Sperone, Turin
      Galleria La Salita, Rome
1966   Stedelijk van Abbemuseum, Eindhoven, Netherlands
      Leo Castelli Gallery, New York
1967   Wide White Space Gallery, Antwerp
      Galerie Der Spiegel, Cologne
1968   John Gibson Gallery, New York
      Museum of Modern Art, New York
      Galleria del Leone, Venice
1969   John Gibson Gallery, New York
      Lo Giudice Gallery, Chicago
      Wide White Space Gallery, Antwerp
      Central Street Gallery, Sydney
      National Gallery of Victoria, Melbourne
      Galerie der Spiegel, Cologne
1970   The New Gallery, Cleveland
      Galerie Francoise Lambert, Milan
      Galerie Rene Ziegler, Zurich
      Kaiser-Wilhelm Museum, Krefeld, West Germany
1971   Annely Juda Gallery, London
      Galerie Yvon Lamberg, Paris
      Haus Lange Museum, Krefeld, West Germany
      Museum of Fine Arts, Houston
      Kunstsammlungen-Stadt Nurnberg, Nuremberg

      Galerie Victor Loeb, Berne
      Kunsthaus, Hamburg
      Colophon Galleria, Milan
      Centro La Capella, Trieste
      Ars Studeo, Copenhagen
      Galerie Mikro, Berlin
      Centro de Arte y Comunicacion, Buenos Aires
1972   The New Gallery, Cleveland
      La Jolla Museum of Contemporary Art, California
      Santa Barbara Museum of Art, California
      The Friends of Contemporary Art, Denver
      Joslyn Art Museum, Omaha, Nebraska
      Contemporary Arts Center, Cincinnati, Ohio
      The Morgan Gallery, Kansas City
1973   Stedelijk Museum, Amsterdam
      Seriaal Galerie, Amsterdam
      Alan Frumkin Gallery, New York
      Miami Dade Junior College
      Ball State University, Muncie, Indiana
      University of Washington Art Museum, Seattle
      La Rotonda, Milan
      Galeria Francoise Lambert, Milan
      Galerie Charles Kriwin, Brussels
      Neue Pinakoteck, Munich
      Max Protetch Gallery, Washington, D.C.
      Museu La Tertulia, Cali, Columbia
      Kalamazoo Institute of Arts, Michigan
      Rosa Esman Gallery, New York
      Kunsthaus, Zurich
      Kunsthalle, Dusseldorf
      Kroller-Muller Museum, Otterlo, Netherlands
      Kansas State University, Manhattan
      Galleria d'Arte Vinciana, Milan
1974   *The Wall Wrapped,* Rome
      Ocean Front, Newport, Rhode Lsland
      Louisiana Museum, Humleback, Denmark
      Sonja Henie-Niels Onstad Foundation, Oslo
      Galerie W. Aronowitsch, Stockholm
      Millersville State College, Pennsylvania
      Anncly Juda Gallery, Ondon
      Hatton Gallery, University of Newcastle-upon-Tyne, England
      Musée de Peinture et de Sculpture, Grenoble, France
1975   Musée Rath, Geneva
      White Gallery, Lutry, Switzerland
      Galeria Conkreight, Caracas
      Galerie Gimpel Hanover, Zurich
      Princeton University Art Museum, New Jersey
      Galleria d'Alesandro-Ferranti, Rome
      Galerie J. Benador, Geneva
      La Jolla Museum of Contemporary Art, California
      Oakland Museum, California
      Institute of Contemporary Art, Boston
      Musée Jenisch, Vevey, Switzerland
      M. H. de Young Memorial Museum, San Francisco
      Alberta College of Art Gallery, Calgary
      Memorial Union Art Gallery, University of California at Davis
      Grinnell College, Iowa
      Galeria Ciento, Barcelona
      Fabian Fine Arts, Cape Town
      Harcus-Krakow-Rasoen-Sonnabend Gallery, Boston
      Galerie Der Spiegel, Cologne
      Galleria Buonaparte, Milan
1976   Foundation Veranneman, Kruishoutem, Belgium
      Museum des 20. Jahrhunderts, Vienna
      San Francisco Museum of Modern Art
      Museum of Contemporary Art, La Jolla, California
      Pasadena City College, California
      Fine Arts Center, University of Massachusetts, Amherst
      Broxton Gallery, Los Angeles
      Art Association, Newport, Rhode Island
1977   Colorado Springs Fine Arts Center
      Galeria Juan Prats, Barcelona
      Galeria Trece, Barcelona
      Israel Museum, Jerusalem
      Newcomb College Art Department, Tulane University, New Orleans
      Metropolitan Museum, Miami
      Museum Boymans-van-Beuuingen, Rotterdam
      Landische Museum, Bonn
      Kestner Gesellschaft, Hannover

      Minami Gallery, Tokyo
      Annely Juda Fine Arts, London
      American Center, Kyoto
1978   Louisiana Museum, Humlebaek, Denmark
      Sonja Henie-Niels Onstad Foundation, Oslo
      The American Foundation for the Arts, Miami
      Western Michigan University, Kalamazoo
      Murray State University, Kentucky
      Galerie Art in Progress, Munich
      Kunstgewerbe Museum, Zurich
      Palais des Beaux-Arts, Brussels
      Musée de Grenoble, France
      Atkins Museum, Nelson Gallery of Art, Kansas City, Missouri
      Wadsworth Atheneum, Hartford, Connecticut
      University of Arkansas, Little Rock
1979   Weiner Secession, Vienna
      Appalachian State University, Boone, North Carolina
      Greenville County Museum of Art, South Carolina
      Institute of Contemporary Arts, London
      Institute of Contemporary Art, Boston
      Kunstverein, Freiburg, West Germany
      Annely Juda Fine Arts, London
      Wright State University, Dayton, Ohio
      Hunter Museum of Art, Chattanooga, Tennessee
      Laguna Gloria Museum, Austin, Texas
      Corcoran Gallery, Washington, D.C.
      Appalachian State University, Boone, North Carolina
      Nash Gallery, University of Minnesota, Minneapolis
      Galerie Catherine Issert, Saint Paul de Vence, France
1980   Newport Harbor Museum, Newport Beach, California
      The New Gallery, Cleveland
      Swen Parson Gallery, Northern Illinois University, DeKalb
      Midwest Museum of American Art, Elkhart, Indiana
      Mississippi Museum of Art, Jackson
      Winnipeg Art Gallery
      Hatton Gallery, Colorado State University, Fort Collins
      French Cultural Center-Alliance Francaise, Abu Dhabi
      Artspace, Peterborough, Ontario
      Cabrillo College Gallery, Apros, California
      Sonoma Arts Council, Santa Rosa, California
1981   American Graffiti Gallery, Amsterdam
      Hokin Gallery, Miami, Florida
      Metropolitan Museum, Miami, Florida
      Tennessee Tech University, Cookeville
      Albuquerque Museum, New Mexico
      Musee d'Art Contemporain, Montreal
      Santa Monica City College, California
      Community College of Lancaster, Pennsylvania
      University of Texas, El Paso
      Museum Ludwig, Cologne
      Juda-Rowan Gallery, London
      Portland Center for the Visual Arts, Oregon
      La Jolla Museum of Contemporary Art, California
      Madison Art Center, Wisconsin
      Conejo Valley Art Museum, Thousand Oaks, California
1982   Nickle Arts Museum, University of Calgary, Alberta
      University of Maine, Orono
      Colby College Museum of Art, Waterville, Main
      Stadel Museum, Frankfurt
      Kunstlerhaus Bethanian, West Berlin
      Biuro Wystaw Artystycznych, Krakow, Poland
      Art Gallery of Hamilton, Ontario
      Miami-Dade Public Library, Florida
      Galerie Catherine Issert, St. Paul de Vence, France
      Elvehjem Museum of Art, University of Wisconsin, Madison
      Dumont-Landis Gallery, New Brunswick, New Jersey
      Hara Museum of Contemporary Art, Tokyo
1983   Snite Museum of Art, University of Notre Dame, Indiana
      Fukuoka Municipal Museum of Art, Japan
      National Museum of Osaka, Japan
      Contemporary Arts Center, Cincinnati, Ohio

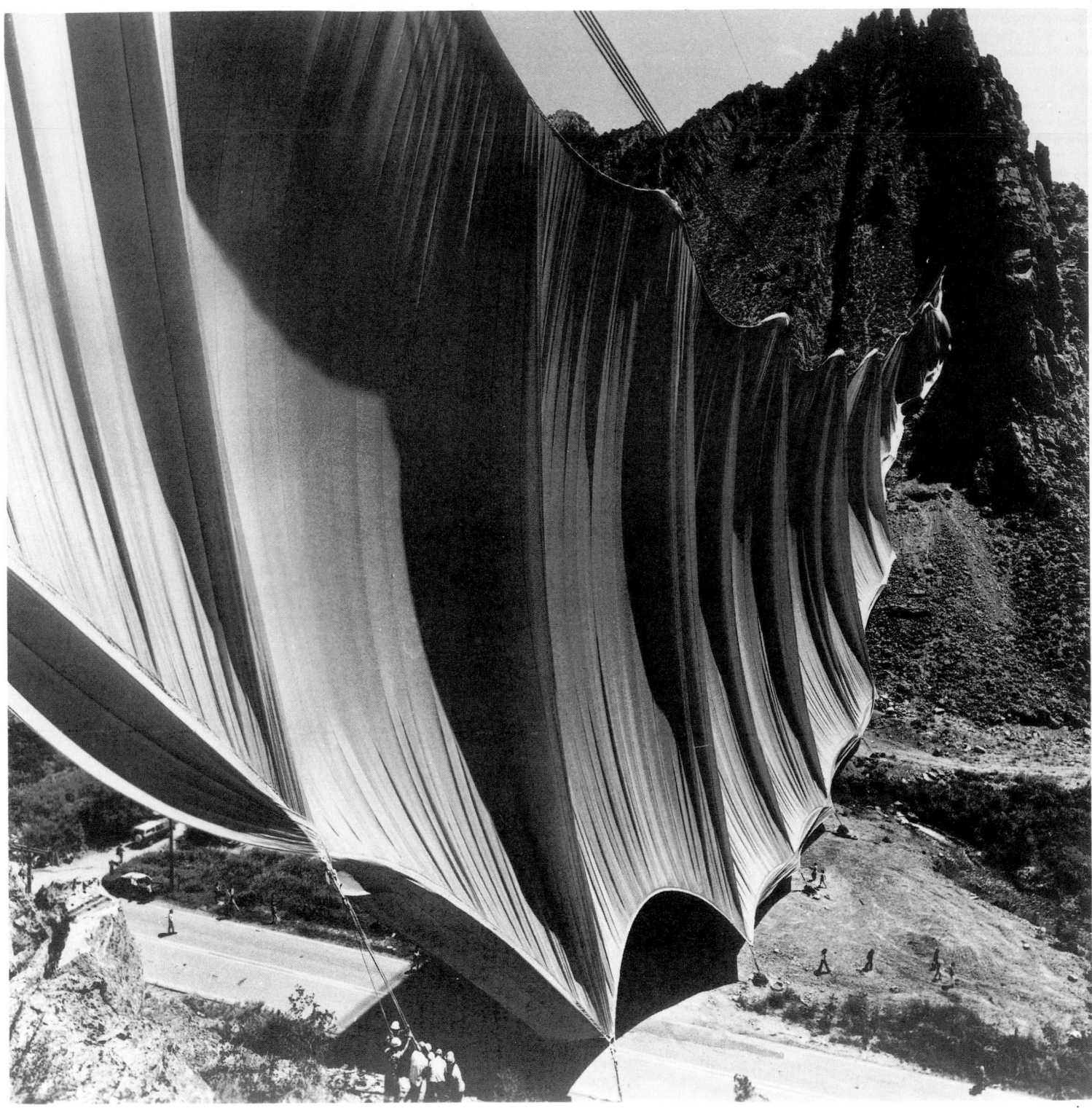

Christo: *Valley Curtain*, Rifle, Colorado, 1972

Art Museum of Santa Cruz County, Soquel, California
Delahunty Gallery, Dallas
Galleria Pero, Milan
1984 Hartnell College, Salinas, California
Luther Burbank Center for the Arts, Santa Rosa, California
Harron School of Art, Indiana University, Indianapolis
Satani Gallery, Tokyo
Nationalgalerie, West Berlin
Annely Juda Fine Art, London
Sun Valley Center for the Arts and Humanities, Idaho
Henie-Onstad Foundation, Oslo
Westport-Weston Arts Council, Connecticut

Boston Atheneum, Massachusetts
1985 University of West Florida, Pensacola
Kunsthalle, Hamburg
New Britain Museum of American Art, Connecticut
Fondation Maeght, St. Paul de Vence, France
Rijksmuseum Kroller-Muller, Otterlo, Netherlands
Carpenter + Hochman Gallery, Dallas
1986 Florida State University, Tallahassee
Fundacion Caja de Pensiones, Madrid
Galeria Joan Prats, Barcelona
Southern Illinois University, Carbondale
Bass Museum, Florida
Alternative Work Site, Omaha, Nebraska
Barrett Art Gallery, Utica College, New York
Satani Gallery, Tokyo
Real Art Ways, Connecticut

1987 Musee Cantonal des Beaux-Arts, Lausanne, Switzerland
Lehman College, Bronx, New York
Aldrich Museum of Contemporary Art, Ridgefield, Connecticut
Elizabeth Galasso Fine Art, Ossining, New York
Halsey Gallery, College of Charleston, South Carolina
Museum van Hedendaagse Kunst, Ghent, Belgium
Seibu Museum of Art, Takanawa, Japan
Museo de Arte Moderno, Bogota, Colombia
1988 Seibu Museum of Art, Tokyo
Schneider Museum, Southern Oregon State College, Ashland
Annely Juda Fine Art, London

Selected Realized Projects:

1961   *Stacked Oil Drums*, Cologne Harbour, West Germany
1962   *Iron Curtain*, Rue Visconti, Paris
       Stacked Oil Drums, Gentilly, Paris
       Wrapping a Girl, London
1966   *42,390 Cubic Feet Package*, Walker Art Center, Minneapolis
1968   *Packaged Fountain and Tower*, Spoleto, Italy
       1,240 Oil Drums/2 Tons of Stacked Hay, Philadelphia Institute of Contemporary Art
1969   *Packed Museum of Contemporary Art/Wrapped Floor*, Chicago
       Wrapped Coast, Little Bay, Australia
1971   *Valley Curtain*, Grand Hogback, Rifle, Colorado
1974   *The Wall Wrapped*, Rome
       Ocean Front, Newport, Rhode Island
1975   *Running Fence*, Sonoma-Marin County, California
1977   *Wrapped Walkways*, Kansas City, Missouri
1980   *Surrounded Islands*, Biscayne Bay, Florida
1985   *Pont Neuf Wrapped*, Paris
1986   *Wrapped Reichstag*, West Berlin

Collections:

Museum of Modern Art, New York; Whitney Museum, New York; Philadelphia Museum of Fine Arts, Pennsylvania; Stedelijk Museum, Amsterdam; Kunsthaus, Zurich; Moderna Museet, Stockholm; Rheinisches Landesmuseum, Bonn; Tate Gallery, London; Hara Museum of Contemporary Art, Tokyo; National Gallery of Art, Canberra.

Publications:

By CHRISTO: books—*Christo*, text by David Bourdon, Otto Hahn and Pierre Restany, Milan 1965; *Christo: 5600 Cubic Meter Package*, Munich 1968; *Christo*, text by Lawrence Alloway, New York 1969; *Christo: Wrapped Coast, One Million Square Feet*, Minneapolis 1969; *Christo*, text by David Bourdon, New York 1970; *Christo: Valley Curtain*, New York 1973; *Christo: Ocean Front*, texts by Sally Yard and Sam Hunter, Princeton, New Jersey 1975; *Christo: Running Fence*, text by Calvin Tomkins and David Bourdn, New York 1978; *Christo: Wrapped Walk Ways*, New York 1978; *Christo, Surrounded Islands, Biscayne Bay, Greater Miami, Florida, 1980-83*, with essay by Jonathan Fineberg, New York 1986.

On CHRISTO: books—*Christo*, exhibition catalogue, with text by Pierre Restany, Cologne 1961; *Christo*, exhibition catalogue, with text by Lawrence Alloway, Eindhoven, Netherlands 1966; *Christo*, exhibition catalogue with text by William Rubin, New York 1968; *Christo*, exhibition catalogue, with text by S. Prokopoff, Philadelphia 1968; *Christo*, exhibition catalogue, with text by Jan van Der Marck, Melbourne 1969; *Christo*, exhibition catalogue, with text by Paul Wember, Krefeld, West Germany 1971; *Christo*, exhibition catalogue, with text by John Matheson, Dusseldorf 1973; *Christo*, exhibition catalogue, with text by Maurice Besset, Grenoble, France 1974; *Christo*, exhibition catalogue, with text by Alexandre Cirici, Barcelona 1975; *Christo: The Running Fence* by Werner Spies, New York 1977; *Christo*, exhibition catalogue, with text by Yusuke Nakahara, Tokyo 1977; *Christo*, exhibition catalogue, with text by Wieland Schmied and Tilmann Buddensieg, London 1977; *Christo*, exhibition catalogue, with text by Carl Albrecht Haenlein, Munich 1978; *Christo*, exhibition catalogue, with an introduction by R. Oxenaar, text by Ellen Joosten, Otterio, Netherlands 1978; *Christo*, exhibition catalogue with an introduction by H. J. Painitz, text by Werner Spies, Vienna 1979; *Christo: Complete Editions 1964-82*, with introduction by Per Hovdenakk, Munich and New York 1982; *Christo: Works 1958-83*, with text by Yusuke Nakahara, Tokyo 1984; *Christo. Surrounded Islands, Biscayne Bay, Greater Miami, Florida, 1980-83*, with text by Werner Spies, Cologne 1984, New York 1985; *Christo—Der Reichstag*, compiled by Michael Cullen and Wolfgang Volz, Frankfurt 1984; *Christo*, with text by Dominique Laporte, Paris 1985, New York 1986; films—*Wrapped Coast*, Blackwood Productions 1969; *Christo's Valley Curtain*, Maysles Brothers and Ellen Giffard 1972; *Running Fence*, Maysles Brothers and Charlotte Zwerin 1977; *Wrapped Walk Ways*, Blackwood Productions 1978; *Islands*, Maysles Brothers and Charlotte Zwerin 1985; *The Pont Neuf*, Maysles Brothers 1986.

In all of his packages, Christo transforms familiar objects into ambivalent presences, sometimes rendering them unrecognizable and often raising doubts about their past, present, and future identity and function. In his more epic endeavors, he questions the relationship of art at both the urban and natural environments. In a materialistic age, his art is a profound comment on the chronic expectations and frustrations aroused by the increasing number of consumer products and services that are "enhanced" through packaging.

No other artist so fully illuminates the 20th century's preoccupation with packaging. By appropriating and wrapping familiar objects, buildings and sites, making them visible in a new way, he has created a wide range of disturbing and strangely beautiful art works that collectively call for a double take.

—David Bourdon

CHRYSSA.

American. Born in Athens, Greece, 31 December 1933. Educated at Académie de la Grande Chaumière, Paris, 1953-54; California School of Fine arts, San Fransciso, 1954-55. Has lived and worked in New York since 1955. Recipient: Guggenheim Fellowship, 1973. Address: c/o Albright-Knox Art Gallery, 1285 Elmwood Avenue, Buffalo, New York 14222, U.S.A.

Individual Exhibitions:

1961   Betty Parsons Gallery, New York
       Guggenheim Museum, New York
1962   Cordier and Ekstrom, New York
1963   Museum of Modern Art, New York
1965   Institute of Contemporary Arts, Philadelphia
1966   Pace Gallery, New York
1968   Pace Gallery, New York
       Harvard University, Cambridge, Massachusetts
       Walker Art Center, Minneapolis
       Galerie Rive Droite, Paris
1969   Galerie der Spiegel, Cologne
       Obelisk Gallery, Boston
1970   Graphics Gallery, San Francisco
       Galleria d'Arte Contemporenea, Turin
1973   Galerie Denise René, New York
       Galerie Denise René-Hans Mayer, Dusseldorf
1974   Galerie Denise René, Paris
       Musée d'Art Contemporain, Montreal
       Andre Emmerich Galerie, Zurich
1976   Galerie Denise René, Paris
1978   Galerie Denise René, New York
1979   *Oeuvres Récentes*, Musée d'Art Moderne de la Ville de Paris
1980   National Pinacotheque Museum Alexander Soutsos, Athens
1982   Albright-Knox Art Gallery, Buffalo, New York

Selected Group Exhibitions:

1966   *68th American Exhibition*, Art Institute of Chicago

1967   *Light-Motion-Space*, Walker Art Center, Minneapolis
       Art of the 60's, Los Angeles County Museum of Art (travelled to Philadelphia Museum of Art)
1968   *Documenta 4*, Kassel, West Germany
1969   *Bienal*, Sao Paulo
1970   *Annual Exhibition of Contemporary American Sculpture*, Whitney Museum, New York
1971   *Annual Exhibition of Contemporary American Sculpture*, Whitney Museum, New York
1972   *Biennale*, Venice

Collections:

Museum of Modern Art, New York; Guggenheim Museum, New York; Whitney Museum, New York; Albright-Knox Art Gallery, Buffalo, New York; Walker Art Center, Minneapolis; Corcoran Gallery of Art, Washington D.C.; Hirshhorn Museum and Sculpture Garden, Washington D.C.; Musée d'Art Contemporain, Montreal; Tate Gallery, London; Pinacotheque Nationale, Athens.

Publications:

By CHRYSSA: articles—statement in "The Artists Say—Chryssa" in *Art Voices* (New York), Fall 1965; interview with John Gruen in the *New York Herald Tribune*, 27 March 1968.

On CHRYSSA: books—*Pop Art* by Lucy Lippard, New York 1966; *Chryssa*, exhibition catalogue, New York 1966; *Chryssa*, exhibition catalogue, with text by Pierre Restany, Paris 1968; *Minimal Art: A Critical Anthology*, edited by Gregory Battcock, New York 1968; *Chryssa: Selected Works 1955-1957*, exhibition catalogue, New York 1968; *Icons and Images of the 60's* by Nicolas and Elena Calas, New York 1971; *Art Without Boundaries 1950-1970*, edited by Gerald Woods, Philip Thompson and John Williams, London 1972; *Chryssa*, exhibition catalogue, New York 1973; *Chryssa* by Sam Hunter, London and New York 1974; *Chryssa* by Pierre Restany, New York 1977; *Chryssa: Oeuvres Récentes*, exhibition catalogue, Paris 1979; articles—"The Role of the Inscription in Painting" by James Reaney in *Canadian Art* (Toronto), October 1966; "Chryssa" by Don Cyr in *School Arts* (Cherry Hill, New Jersey), March 1967; "Light Art" by Nan R. Piene in *Art in America* (New York), May/June 1967; "Torino: Chryssa" in *NAC* (Milan), February 1971; "New York Letter" by Carter Ratliff in *Art International* (Lugano), December 1972; "Chryssa" by Sam Hunter in *Art News* (New York), 3 May 1973; "Chryssa: Some Observations: by V. Campbell in *Art International* (Lugano), April 1973; "Chryssa Sculptures with Neon Tubes" by James Mellow in th *New York Times*, 21 April 1973; "Mysteries of Neon" by Robert Hughes in *Time* (New York), 4 June 1973.

Birthright and nationality are not necessarily built in to the thumbprint of an artist, Chryssa, for all her Hellenic origins, cannot claim—as she does, and as others have done for her—to have inherited a cultural legacy from Ancient Greece. This is sheer lunacy. If she wants a public to be impressed with the classical Greek accent of her "Cycladic Books" (sculpture which she made in the 1950s), then she could expect that public to trace the same influence in Brancusi's "Kiss". Of course the Greek civilization (and the Roman) left its mark on Europe, but it was a mark not a last-will-and-testament.

This will-point needs to be established because if Chryssa the artist is not *typically Greek*, neither can she claim to have become Americanized after naturalization. For all her New World methods and media, this sculptor/constructor/luminator retains a European character. After she abandoned her early experiments with lay-out moulds on newsprint scale or blown up even larger and began investigating the optentialities of the alphabetical confusion of shop signs, she was continuing the coutcome of the cubist papier-collé rather than exploring variants of Jasper Johns' interest in the same field. From the refuse dumps and demolition years, like many European artists before her, she was able to extract and reassemble material of more than objet-trouvé stature. Scrap of this kind can be on a large scale and at this time of her development her works often had a monumentality that derived their dimensions more from origins than from invention.

The change, in size as well as importance, came when she started examining the opportunities afforded by neon lighting. If at first this new medium came about as the result of chance encounter, it was soon to be a matter of far less casual concern. Chryssa studied the nature of neon and how it could be made subservient to her will. Today, a brilliant technician, she is capable of discussing the science of illuminated signs with people whose entire business lies in that field.

Her neon works she calls *luminates,* but she is not wholly concerned with light and colour. She parallels her views with those of a maker of mobiles. If an Alexander Calder mobile looks beautiful when it is still and in repose, why cannot a luminate claim just as fine an appearance when the lights have been extinguished as when it blazes with colour? This is an issue she takes up with anyone who complains about the limited longevity of neon tubing. Either have the tube replaced or live with your Chryssa in the dark.

—Sheldon Williams

CIESLEWICZ, Roman.

French. Born in Lvov, Poland, now U.S.S.R., 13 January 1930; emigrated to France, 1963; naturalized, 1971. Studied at the Academy of Fine Arts, Cracow, Independent graphic artist, working for several magazines and book publishers, Warsaw, 1955–62, in Paris since 1963; Art Director, *Elle* magazine 1964, 1966–69, *Vogue* magazine 1966, and M.A.F.I.A. publicity agency, 1969–72; Designer, *Opus International* magazine, 1967–69, *Kitsch* magazine, 1970–71, *Musique en Jeu* magazine, 1970–73, *CNAC-Archives* publications, 1971–74, *Kamikaze* magazine 1976, and *XX Siècle* magazine, 1976; Graphics Designer, *Festival d'Automne,* 1976–77. Instructor, Ecole Nationale Supérieure des Arts Graphiques, Paris, 1973–75; Ecole Supérieure des Arts Graphiques, Paris, from 1975. Recipient: Trepkowski Prize, Poland 1955; Grand Prix, Czech Cinema Posters Awards, 1964; Grand Prix, *4th Biennale of Posters,* Warsaw, 1972; Special Prize for Cinema Poster, Cannes, 1973; Grand Prix, *4th Biennale of Photomontage,* Poland, 1979; Grand Prix, *Affiche Francaise,* Paris, 1980. Address: c/o *Elle,* 100 rue Réaumur, 75002 Paris, France.

Individual Exhibitions:

1959   Salon d'Ecran, Warsaw
1960   Salon CBWA—ZPAP, Cracow
1961   Galerija Likovnih Umjetnosti, Rijeka, Yugoslavia
1963   Goethe-Institut, Frankfurt
        Librairie Mandragore, Paris
1964   Club Synergie, Paris
1965   Théâtre de la Cité, Villeurbanne, France
        Salon CBWA—ZPAP, Szczecin, Poland
        Galerie in der Biberstrasse, Vienna
1967   Salon CBWA—ZPAP, Warsaw
1968   Galerie Aurora, Geneva
1971   *Wystawa Foto-grafiki 1962–1971,* Muzeum Sztuki, Lodz, Poland
        Galerie Aurora, Geneva
1972   *Graphismes,* Musée des Arts Décoratifs, Paris
        Musée du Grenoble, France
1973   Stedelijk Museum, Amsterdam
        Hotel de Ville, Dieppe, France
        Galerija Suvremene Umjetnosti, Zabreg
        Razstavno Salon Ratzovz, Maribor, Yugoslavia
1974   Galerie l'Oeil de Boeuf, Paris
        Musée de l'Affiche, Vilanov, Poland
        Galerie Saluden, Quimper, France
1975   Salon G.V.N., Amsterdam
        Mala Galeria, Wroclaw, Poland
        Galerie Baumeister, Munich
        Galerie Aurora, Geneva
        Galerie 13/Theatre Municipal, Angers, France

1976   Centre Jean Prevost, Saint-Etienne-du-Rouviray, France
        Cantieri Navali, at the *Biennale,* Venice
1977   Galerie l'Oeil de Boeuf, Paris
        Martinischule am Rhein, Emmerich, West Germany
        French Institute, Stockholm
1978   Konsthall, Lund, Sweden
        Galeria Stu, Teatr Stu, Wroclaw, Poland
        Galeria Fotografii, Wroclaw, Poland
        B.W.A. Salon Krytykow, Lublin, Poland
        Palais Rihour, Lille, France
        Galerie Baumeister, Munich
        Stedelijk Museum, Amsterdam
1979   Maison de la Culture, Grenoble, France
        Librairie-Galerie La Hune, Paris
        Maison du Tourisme, Auxerre, France
1980   Centre Choreographique, Nancy, France
        House of Culture, Legnica, Poland
        Teatr Narodowy, Warsaw
        FNAC—Montparnasse, Paris
        Centre Dramatique, Nanterre, France
        Théâtre National Populaire, Villeurbanne, France
        Centre Dramatique, Nice
        FNAC, Toulouse
        Photomontages, Maison de la Culture, Grenoble, France
1981   *Photomontages,* Chelsea School of Art, London

Selected Group Exhibitions:

1962   *International Poster Exhibition,* Smithsonian Institution, Washington, D.C.
1963   *Bienal,* Sao Paulo
1964   *Documenta 3,* Kassel, West Germany
1965   *Internationale Buchkunstausstellung,* Messehaus, Leipzig
1967   *Affischer ur Tekniska Museet,* Fagersta Stadsbibliothek, Fagersta, Sweden
1968   *Experimental 4,* Casino, Knokke-le-Zoute, Belgium
1970   *4th Biennale of Graphic Arts,* Moravska Galerie, Brno, Czechoslovakia
1971   *Word and Image,* Museum of Modern Art, New York (toured the United States)
1972   *Biennale,* Venice
        International Graphic Exhibition Arkcenter, London

Collections:

Stedelijk Museum, Amsterdam, Moderna Museet, Stockholm, Umelecko-Proumyslove Muzeum, Prague; Musée des Arts Décoratifs, Paris; Museum Narodowe, Warsaw; Museum Narodowe, Poznan, Poland; Muzeum Sztuki, Lodz, Poland; Museo de Arte Moderna, Sao Paulo; Museum of Modern Art, New York; Library of Congress, Washington, D.C.

Publications:

On CIESLEWICZ: books—*Polnische Plakatkunst* by Jozek Mroszczak, Dusseldorf 1962; *Das Plakat* by Anton Sailer, Munich 1965; *Roman Cieslewicz* by Aleksander Wojciechowski, Warsaw 1966; *Roman Cieslewicz: Wystawa Fotografiki 1962–1971,* exhibition catalogue, with text by Ursula Czartoryska, Lodz, Poland 1971; *Les Chefs-d'Oeuvre du Kitsch* by Jacques Sternberg, Paris 1971; *Roman Cieslewicz: Graphismes,* exhibition catalogue, with text by Alain Jouffroy, Paris 1972; *Histoire Concise de l'Affiche* by John Barnicoat, Paris 1972; *Roman Cieslewicz,* exhibition catalogue, with text by Roland Topor, Amsterdam 1973; *Roman Cieslewicz: Photomôntages,* exhibition brochure, with text by Yann Pavie, Grenoble, France 1980; *Roman Cieslewicz: Photomontages,* exhibition brochure, with text by Nick Wadley, London 1981.

Roman Cieslewicz, the Polish graphic artist who has lived in Paris since 1963, operates on the "borderline" between two areas of artistic exploration—popular art addressed to the consumer of mass media and art with cognitive pretensions, that of creating images of modern man's spiritual experiences.

Since his debut in 1955 Cieslewicz has succeeded in appealing both to the man in the street and to an elitist audience. At the same time as his work appeared at the 1976 Venice *Biennale,* every passerby in Paris (and perhaps elsewhere) carried his shopping in a bag or paper decorated with a Cieslewicz collage. With the help of Cieslewicz and a few more artists of similar ilk, the graphics of mass media was ennobled into a tool—a tool that would spread the visions of today.

Cieslewicz had several revelations along his artistic path: they made a great impression on everything that lay within his sphere of capability. While still in Warsaw, he discovered the possibilities that collage offered to 20th century art, in particular expressionist and surrealist collages as understood by Max Ernst. As a result, he decided to part with all traditional graphical equipment—brushes, paint, pen and ink. Instead, he began to use scissors, glue, a rule, photographic paper and a darkroom. Under what came to be called photomechanical technique, his dramatic theatrical and operatic posters came to life. The collage, in fact, remains the basis of Cieslewicz's artistry, though it now appears in many forms.

Another result of the time spend in the darkroom was a series of experiments with photographic materials. "I am trying," he said, "to obtain something that has nothing to do with photographic technique—a screen, the network of thread that is . . . the polygon which opens all possibilities." By means of this work without a camera, the joint structures of photographics (the separation of the two words is important) were born. Rooted in photography, these structures laid the foundations for the pictures that were to appear. A few methods worthy of mention were: the separation of an image by the use of a screen with a varied gradation of points; the use of contrast with no half-shades; reflections and rotations; multiple images; plain colour (grounds) and other sallies by colour into black-and-white photography.

His next artistic adventure was the discovery of the originality of expression of a repeated image. These images were an offshoot of his photo-graphical work. Developed in an epoch of mass media, they revealed man's lack of defense against the aggression of his visual surroundings.

His last revelation came as a result of contact and identification with Pop Art as a universal style. "I not only thought, but was quite certain," he said in an interview, "that this would be a never-ending style. That it would register reality forever." This, course, was not to be. But—until it fizzled out—Pop, which added the whole of consumer life to art—mass production, fashion, sex, amusements, advertisements, the lights and shadows of the great metropolis, rape, kitsch and horror—all became Cieslewicz's sources of ideas and inspiration. He was infected by Pop's dynamism—as were most young people keen on rock and pop music. He acted as Artistic Director of *Elle* and *Vogue,* edited such exclusive periodicals as *Kitsch* and *Kamikaze* and *Opus International,* designed theatrical posters and programmes (for Arabal, among others), and founded a new kind of visual publication.

The second half of the 1970's saw a "change of climate" in Cieslewicz's work. This is the title that he gave to the cycle of photomontage exhibited at the Galerie l'Oeil de Boeuf in Paris. The critics pointed to the artist's spriitual evolution, his tendency toward contemplation and metaphysics. As shown in these colorful pictures reminiscent of the old masters, the world is full of peace and harmony. The artist no longer interferes with it as brutally as before but offers a modern interpretation, a new and possible way of reading the representational.

—Szymon Bojko

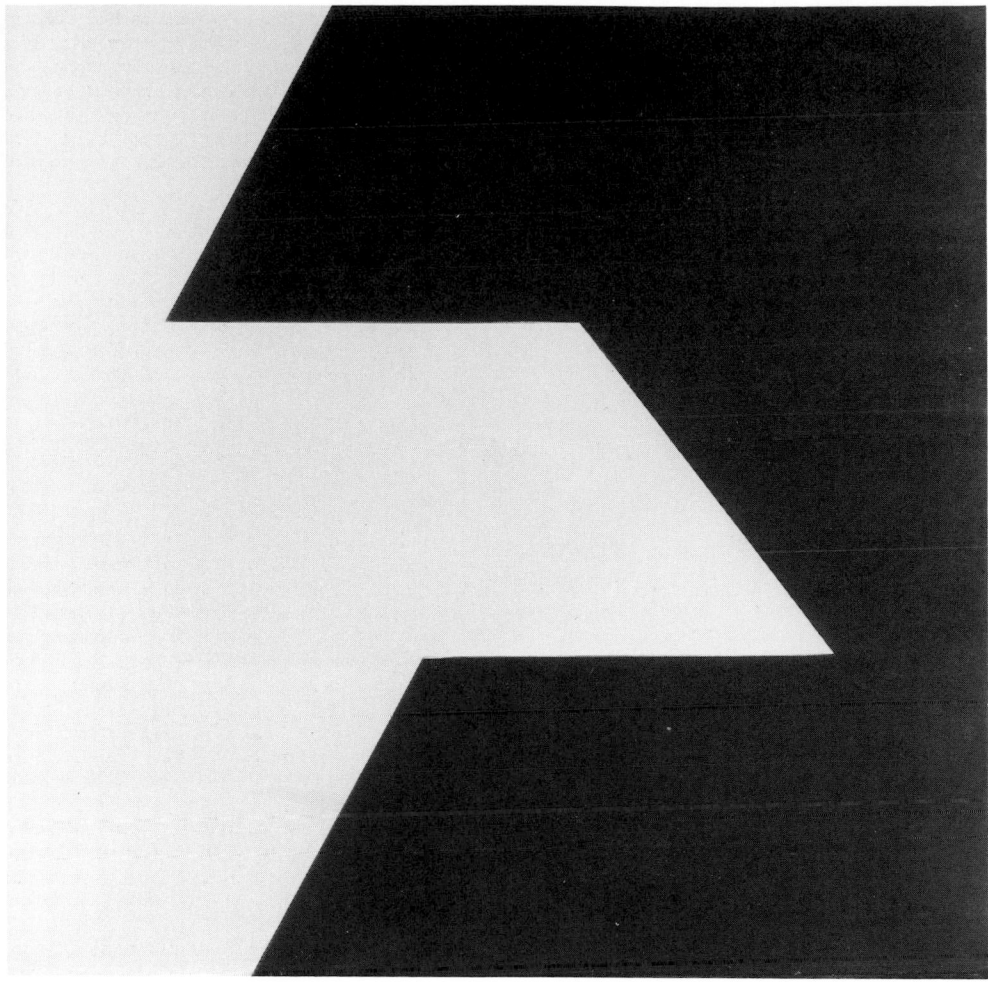

Lygia Clark: *Superficie Modulada,* 1965

CLARK, Lygia.

Brazilian. Born Lygia Pimentel Lins in Belo Horizonte, Minas Gerais, Brazil, 23 October 1920. Educated at Ecole Normale, Belo Horizonte, 1934–37, Teaching Certificate, 1937; studied art, under Roberto Burle-Marx, Rio de Janeiro, 1947; with Arpad Szenes and Dobrinsky, under Fernand Léger, Paris, 1948–50. Married Aloizio Clark in 1939 (died, 1968); children: Elisabeth, Alvaro, and Eduardo. Lived in Paris and Stuttgart, 1964, in Venice and Paris, 1968, in California, 1969, and in Paris since 1970. Instructor, Institute for the Deaf and Dumb, Rio de Janeiro, 1950–55. Professor of Nostalgy of the Body, Sorbonne, Paris, since 1972. Recipient: Frederico Schmidt Prize, Rio de Janeiro, 1952; Prize, *Bienal,* Sao Paulo, 1957, 1961; Revelation Artistique de l'Année, Rio de Janeiro, 1962; Grand Prize, *Bienal,* Bahia, Brazil, 1966. Addresses: 67 Boulevard Brune, 75014 Paris, France; 16 Hueuida Prado Junior, Apartment 801, 6 Jacebana, Rio de Janeiro, Brazil.

Individual Exhibitions:

1952	Galerie Institut End Plastique, Paris
	Ministere de L'Education et la Culture, Rio de Janeiro
1960	Galeria Bonino, Rio de Janeiro
1963	Luis Alexander Gallery, New York
	Museu de-Arte Moderna, Rio de Janeiro
1964	Technische Hochschule, Stuttgart
1965	Signals Gallery, London
1966	*Bienal,* Bahia, Brazil (retrospective)
1968	Museu de Arte Moderna, Rio de Janeiro
	Galerie M.E. Thelen, Essen
	Biennale, Venice (retrospective)
1970	Galerie Camargo, Sao Paulo

Selected Group Exhibitions:

1953	*Bienal,* Sao Paulo (and 1955, 1959)
1963	*Biennale,* Venice (and 1962)
1963	*Arte Neoconcrete,* Museu de Arte Moderna, Rio de Janeiro
1964	*Festival of Modern Art in Latin America,* Signals Gallery, London
1965	*Mouvement 2,* Galerie Denise René, Parie
	Art et Mouvement, Galerie Denise René, Paris (toured the U.K.)
1969	*Symposium of Survival Art,* at *International Tactile Sculpture Symposium,* California State University at Long Beach
1970	*Kunstmarkt,* Cologne

Collections:

Museu de Arte Moderna, Rio de Janeiro: Museu de Arte Moderna, Sao Paulo; Museo de Arte Moderno, La Paz, Bolivia; Museum of Modern Art, New York; Arts Council of Great Britain, London; Centre National d'Art Contemporain, Paris.

Publications

By CLARK: articles—several articles in *Signals* (London), April/May 1968; several articles in *Robho* (Paris), no.4, 1968; "Le Corps Est la Mai'sm" in *Robho* (Paris), nos. 5/6, 1971; "L'art c'Est le Corps" in *Preuves* (Paris), 1973; "Tote Kultur—Lebende Kultur," with Adviniula, in *Heute Kunst* (Dusseldorf), no. 9, 1975.

On CLARK: book—*Kinetic Art* by Guy Brett, London 1968; articles—"La IX Biennale de Sao Paulo" by Pierre Restany in *Domus* (Milan), no 457, 1967; "Lygia Clark and Spectator Participation" by C. Barrett in *Studio International* (London), no. 173, 1967; special issue of *Robho* (Paris), 1968;

"De Kunst ur Lygia Clark" by Frans Haks in *Vroumbiar Huis* (Hilversum, Netherlands), September 1969.

From the *Beasts* to the *Tramping* to the silent thought, the author climbs as a precursor the slope which leads from the manipulable object, which does not exist other than by participation, to pure gestural experience, untrammelled by any objective support, where the artist is no more than a catalyst, part creator, part group leader, part therapist.

My work has always consisted, at least since 1954, of a changing of the relationship artist/work/spectator, or rather of a displacement and a deconstruction of these concepts. Certainly, the radical overthrow of these classical notions (genius, frozen and predetermined object, passive contemplation) has come about in fits and starts, through successive crises, in proportion as I became aware of the implications of my experiments. But the key to my research is, from the origin, the *participation* of the public: the breaking of the barrier separating the spectator from the work and from its "creator". From it I also arrived 8 years ago, at collective experiences in which the object abolishes itself and where man, a cell in a biological architecture constituted by his own body, becomes the object of his own sensation. These propositions, sorts of elastic spider webs stretched by the participants whose every gesture is more or less determined by those of the others—and vice versa—or indeed sorts of plastic tunnels where man is the support and which the participants support and cross through by turns—these propositions have a tribal and initiatory character. It is in truth a matter of a *rite without the myth:* mythology, the metaphysics exterior to man, is abandoned so that man can replace it in assuming his own myth in these ritual gestures.

This outcome—for me essential because, leaving the field of "art", it issues forth upon life—has a very old origin: it is a matter of the *Beasts.* Since 1954 the problem of the frame, of the plan of the limits of the picture, has preoccupied me.

—Lygia Clark

The essence of Lygia Clark's art is spectator participation, for her kinetic works are not mechanically operated by motors but have to be touched and manipulated. Her works are in fact primitivistic rather than technological, luring the participants into play which has sensual and erotic implications, often needing two people in collaboration to join in, and giving them a heightened awareness of their bodies and their physical surroundings. Her art has constantly been directed to the rediscovery of the sensual and instinctive sides of life, which have been suppressed both by the social constraints of civilized life and by the ever-increasing dominance of the intellect, even in art.

And in evolving new and ever simpler means of getting people involved in sensual games she has moved further and further from the art object for its own sake. In 1959 she was a co-founder of the Brazilian neo-concrete group MAM, which was inspired by the discoveries of abstract artists, above all Mondrian. At that time she was making reliefs which were symmetrical and elementary in form and colour, with shallow changes of level. These "modulated surfaces" developed into her "counter-reliefs," consisting of two superimposed planes, the upper of which could be folded back like a shutter, thus allowing different compositions according to how far it was folded. It was from this idea of folding that she developed in 1960 the articulate aluminium sculptures she called *animals.* These have hinged planes, which enable the spectator to fold them into different shapes, and are often suspended, giving an additional range of movements. They were called *animals* because she stressed their *organic* aspect: each has his own, well-defined cluster of movements which react to the promptings of the spectator. He is not made of isolated static forms which can be manipulated at random as in a game; no, his parts are functionally related to each other, as if he were a living organism; and the movements of these parts are interlinked. The interlinking of the spectator's action and the "animal's" immediate answer is what forms this new relationship, made possible precisely because the "animal" moves—i.e., has a life of its own.

Thus the "animals" do enable the spectator to be not merely a passively receptive observer of works of art, but to become an active partner with forces which develop of their own accord. There is no longer a static work of art to be passively contemplated. This resembles the development in avantgarde music which leaves the performer free to interpret the work within a certain range of possibilities, and Lygia Clark herself sees the spectator's act in co-operating with the artist to move the work as a moment of self-awareness. Her aim is to make this a rewarding experience, an intensification of the faculties, and her later works are all further developments of the idea of sensual interplay between art object and spectator or participant. The works she calls *bichos* (a Portuguese word referring to animals without backbones, from worms to caterpillars, which have a generally wriggly motion) are ribbon forms cut out of completely flexible materials such as rubber, so that playing with them reveals their elasticity and marvellous freedom from constraint. These led on to her "dialogue of hands" with her fellow-Brazilian artist Helio Oiticaca, in which the "art object" as such is reduced to a band which links the two participants' hands while they explore each other in a sensual dialogue.

One of her unrealized projects is an *Architecture fantastique*, an articulated architecture capable of taking on an almost limitless number of shapes as people move about inside it. At the Venice *Biennale* in 1968 she did realize a labyrinth called "The House Is the Body," where participants went through a series of cells which were designed to give them the feeling of conception and birth, from the copulatory act of entering, through ovulation and fertilization to expulsion from the womb at the other end. Her TUNNELS are further developments of this idea that "art is the body," plastic tunnels which are brought to life by being crossed and held in position by the participants who move in and through them. She has used all sorts of other objects such as nets, sacks, air-filled plastic bags and pebbles, to evoke complex sensations of life, from breathing to sex, with very simple but concrete means. They often involve several participants working together, for instance with her large shaped sheets of transparent plastic where one person has to lie on the ground while another manipulates the sheets. In such works she aims at a tribal, initiatory quality which she describes as "a question of *ritual without myth:* mythology, which is a metaphysic external to man, is abandoned in order that man may take his place and perform his own myth in these ritual gestures."

Lygia Clark is a highly articulate artist whose writings on spectator participation and the metaphysical implications she sees in it are among the best things so far written on movement in time and space. Her own work has consistently aimed at the withering away of the venerated and valuable art object towards simple means of making the participant use his own energy to give a heightened awareness of himself, his body and his senses. Thus her art, which has been among the most successful of those aiming to encourage active and creative participation, is a contribution to making contemporary man more aware of that disastrous split between intellect and emotions which has been one of the main concerns of artists ever since the Romantic Movement rebelled against the shallow and superficial rationalization of life.

—Konstantin Bazorov

CLARKE, John Clem.
American. Born in Bend, Oregon, 6 June 1937. Studied at Oregon State University, Corvallis; Mexico

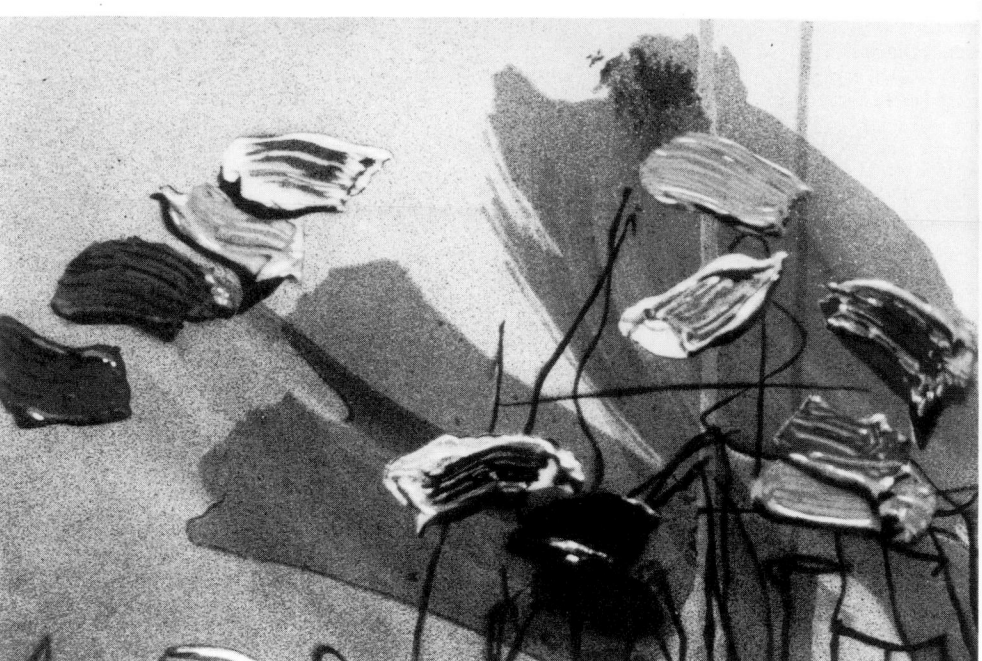

John Clem Clarke: *Abstract No. 5*, 1973

City College; University of Oregon, Eugene, B.F.A. 1960. Lives and works in New York. Agent: O.K. Harris Gallery, 383 West Broadway, New York, New York 10012, U.S.A.

Individual Exhibitions:

1968 Kornblee Gallery, New York
1969 Franklin Siden Gallery, Detroit
1970 O.K. Harris Gallery, New York
       Michael Walls Gallery, San Francisco
       Galerie M.E. Thelen, Essen
1971 Kornblee Gallery, New York
       Phyllis King Gallery, Chicago
       Pyramid Gallery, Washington, D.C.
       Galerie de Gestlo, Hamburg
1972 Jack Glenn Gallery, Corona del Mar, California
       O.K. Harris Gallery, New York
       Carl Solway Gallery Cincinnati, Ohio
1974 D.M. Gallery, London
1981 O.K. Harris Gallery, New York
       Morgan Gallery, New York

Selected Group Exhibitions:

1969 *New Aspects of Realism,* Milwaukee Art Center
       (toured the United States)
1970 *22 Realists,* Whitney Museum, New York
1971 *New Realism,* State University of New York at Potsdam
       Radical Realism, Museum of Contemporary Art, Chicago
1972 *Realism Now,* New York Cultural Center
1973 *New York Avant-Garde 74,* Saidye Bronfman Centre, Montreal
       Hyperrealisme, Galerie Lsy Brachot, Brussels
1974 *Biennale,* Tokyo
       Contemporary Painting from the Lewis Collection, Delaware Art Museum, Wilmington
       New Realism Revisited, State University of New York at Potsdam

Collections:

Museum of Modern Art, New York; Whitney Museum, New York; Metropolitan Museum of Art, New York; Hirshhorn Museum, Washington, D.C.; Flint Institute, Michigan; Milwaukee Arts Center; Nelson Museum of Art Kansas City; Museum of Fine Arts, Dallas; University of California,

Berkeley; Security Pacific National Bank Collection, Los Angeles.

Publications:

On CLARKE: books—*Neue Formen des Realismus* by Peter Sager, Cologne 1973; *Selection 3: Contemporary Graphics from the Museum's Collection,* catalogue, by D. L. Johnson, Providence, Rhode Island 1973; articles—"An Art of Transmission: John Clem Clarke at Kornblee" by Jeanne Siegel in *Arts Magazine* (New York), Summer 1969; "John Clem Clarke Transmits a Picture" by William S. Wilson in *Artnews* (New York), Summer 1969; "Oedipus and the Sphinx" in *Art Now: New York,* vol. 2, no. 5, 1970; "Bar Area Survey: John Clem Clarke, Michael Walls Gallery" by B. Richardson in *Arts Magazine* (New York), November 1970; "San Francisco: John Clem Clarke, Michael Walls Gallery" by J. Tarshis in *Artforum* (New York), December 1970; "New York Letter: John Clem Clarke, Kornblee Gallery" by Carter Ratcliff in *Art International* (Lugano, Switzerland). March 1971; "The Deductive Image" by J. P. Marendel in *Art International* (Lugano, Switzerland). September 1971; "Szene Rhein-Ruhr" by B. Kerber in *Art International* (Lugano, Switzerland). Summer 1972.

In a century which has focused on the question, what is real? John Clem Clarke is often classed with the Super Realists. His illusionary paintings of wood and wood grain, for example, the convoluted meshes of the transistor, are certainly kin to their concern with the photograph as a means of transmitting subjects, but Clarke's real subject is more the camera as a means of seeing than the subjects it transmits, more how did it get there? than what is it?

Anything, then, can serve Clarke as subject, including the paintings already painted by artists of the past. He has even exhibited numbered versions of replays of the same painting, their subtle differences derived from the subtle differences between one slide of the painting and the next. For the observer this seems subtle indeed, though, apparently, to the artist the differences are clear.

Apparent differences are what the story is, the emphasis being on this apparentness and not its primal subject. All of this recognizes that modern recognition, a formalist concern which goes back at least to Denis, that the painting in itself, since it is a 2-dimensional representation of what exists in 3, is an illusion. Clarke points out the illusion of painting through the medium of paint. If, then, the medium is the message, as by his example he appears to agree, he succeeds in presenting it through the sheer virtuos-

ity of his *trompe l'oeil* technique, dazzlingly illusionistic paintings about painting. He recreates, for
example, not only the grain of wood, but even the way
rough stroked lettering soaks into it, and can take on
the way other artists painted, from obscure Dutch
masters to Grant Wood. But in so doing, another element enters, in for, say, in his sly replicas of Bouge-
reau, Clarke not only offers a representation, he
criticizes it. There is irony in this. Irony is an attitude, and artists have always painted in the context of
the attitudes of the age, inevitably present in any
work. But this conscious painting of attitude, of perception, is a specifically twentieth century point of
view. Wittingly or otherwise, artists have always
quoted artists who have gone before, but before Kant
and then the phenomenologists art did not raise the
question how do we perceive? Now in the last years
of the century it has become a concern handled
through the medium of paint.

In painting modes of transmission, Clarke is dealing with a very old opposition as well, the opposition
of content versus form. Clarke says, through his art,
as do some others in the present, that content can be
anything. Yet in this decade, the heyday of formalism
having, for now, passed, there is a new interest in
content, and content is something transmitted by the
artist to the person who sees the work. This raises,
then, another question, for if Clarke's paintings come
off as paintings about painting, as pictured modes of
picturing, what does the person who sees the work
receive? Does the observer remain simply an observer or is he involved?

—Barbara Cortright

CLEMENTE, Francesco.

Italian. Born in Naples in 1952. Married to Alba Clemente; has two children. Independent painter, since
1973: lives and works in New York, Rome and Madras. Agents: Galerie Daniel Templon, 30 rue
Beaubourg, 75003 Paris, France; Anthony D'Offay
Gallery, 9 Dering Street, New Bond Street, London
W1, England; Sperone Westwater, 142 Greene Street,
New York, New York 10012, U.S.A. Address: Via
dei Riari 59, 00165 Rome, Italy.

Individual Exhibitions:

1974 Galleria Area, Florence
1975 Galleria Gian Enzo Sperone, Rome
     Galleria Gian Enzo Sperone, Turin
     Galleria Massimo Minini, Brescia, Italy
     Galleria Franco Toselli, Milan
1976 Galleria Gian Enzo Sperone, Rome
     Galleria Lucrezia de Domizio, Pescara, Italy
1977 Galleria Paolo Betti, Milan
1978 Centre d'Art Contemporain, Geneva
     Art and Project, Amsterdam
     Galerie Paul Maenz, Cologne
1979 Gian Enzo Sperone, Turin
     Art and Project, Amsterdam
     Galerie Paul Maenz, Cologne
     Lisson Gallery, London
     Galerie Annemarie Verna, Zurich (with Mimmo Pa-
        ladino and Nicola de Maria)
     Galleria Emilio Mazzoli, Modena, Italy
     Galleria Guiliana de Crescenzo, Rome
     Galleria Lucio Amolio, Naples
1980 Galleria Gian Enzo Sperone, Rome
     Art and Project, Amsterdam
     Galerie Paul Maenz, Cologne
     Sperone Westwater Fischer Gallery, New York
     Padiglione d'Arte Contemporanea, Milan
     Galleria Mario Diacono, Rome
1981 Vereniging voor het Museum van Hedendaagse
        Kunst, Ghent
     Anthony d'Offay Gallery, London
     Sperone Westwater Fischer Gallery, New York

Galerie Bruno Bischofberger, Zurich
University of California, Berkeley (travelled to Long
   Beach, California; Hartford, Connecticut)
1982 Galerie Daniel Templon, Paris
     Galerie Paul Maenz, Cologne
     Galleria Mario Diacono, Rome
     Galerie Bruno Bischofberger, Zurich
1983 Whitechapel Art Gallery, London (travelled to Gro-
        ningen, Karlsruhe, Stockholm and Nice)
     Anthony D'Offay / Gian Enzo Sperone, London
     Galerie Ascan Crone, Hamburg
     Galleria Mario Diacono, Rome
     A Space, Toronto
     Sperone Westwater / Mary Boone Gallery, New
        York
     Akira Ikeda Gallery, Tokyo and Nagoya, Japan
     Kunsthalle, Basle
     James Corcoran Gallery, Los Angeles
     Fruitmarket Gallery, Edinburgh
     Arts Council Gallery, Belfast
1984 Nationalgalerie, West Berlin (travelled to Essen,
        Amsterdam and Tubingen)
     Kestner-Gesellschaft, Hannover

Akira Ikeda Gallery, Tokyo
Riverside Studios, Hammersmith, London
1985 Sperone Westwater / Leo Castelli Gallery, New York
     Mary Boone / Michael Werner Gallery, New York
     Galerie Bruno Bischofberger, Zurich
     Metropolitan Museum of Art, New York
     Ringling Museum of Art, Sarasota, Florida (trav-
        elled to Minneapolis, Dallas, Berkeley, Buffalo
        and Los Angeles)
     Museum fur Gegenwartskunst, Basle
1986 Akira Ikeda Gallery, Tokyo
     Anthony D'Offay Gallery, London
     Sperone Westwater, New York
     Museum of Modern Art, New York
1987 Galerie Ascan Crone, Hamburg
     Museum fur Gegenwartskunst, Basle
     Galerie Bruno Bischofberger, Zurich (twice)
     Fundacion Caja de Pensiones, Madrid
     Art Institute of Chicago
     Galerie im Taxispalais, Salzburg, Austria
     Ulmer Museum, Ulm, West Germany
     Kunstmuseum, Basle (travelled to Groningen, Ulm,
        Cologne, Lausanne, Frankfurt and Nice)

Francesco Clemente: *Two Men*, 1981 Courtesy Anthony D'Offay Gallery, London

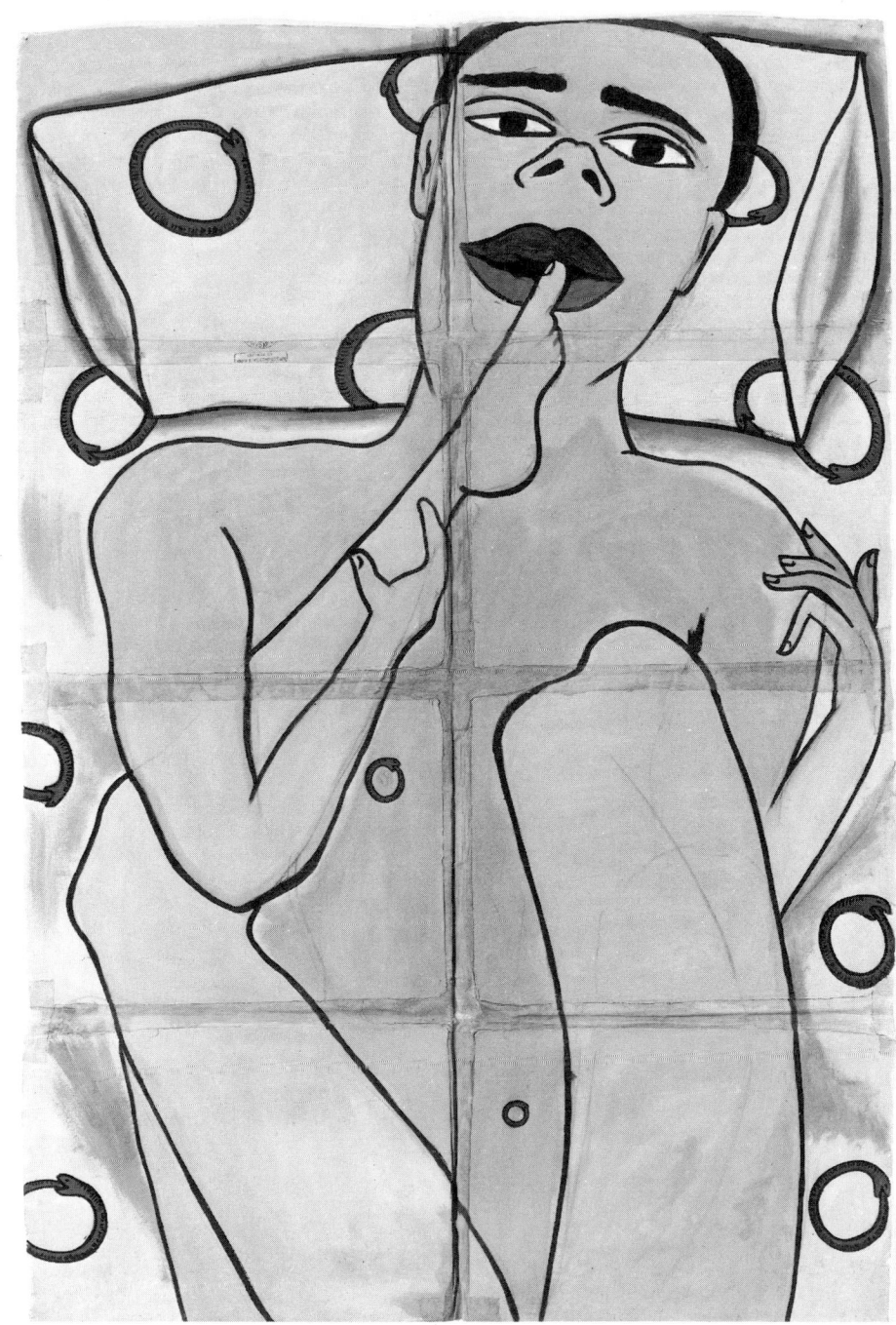

Selected Group Exhibitions:

1973   *Italy Two*, Civic Center Museum, Philadelphia
1975   *Bienal*, Sao Paulo
1977   *X Biennale de Paris*, Musée National d'Art Moderne, Paris
1979   *Europa '79*, Stuttgart
1980   *Die Enthauptete Hand: 100 Zeichnungen aus Italien*, Kunstverein, Bonn
1981   *Westkunst*, Cologne
1982   *Documenta 7*, Kassel, West Germany
1984   *Content: A Contemporary Focus 1974–84*, Hirshhorn Museum, Washington, D.C.
1985   *India and the Contemporary Artist*, Museum of Modern Art, New York
1987   *Avant-Garde in the Eighties*, Los Angeles County Museum of Art

Publications:

By CLEMENTE: books—*The Pondicherry Pastels*, London and Madras 1986; *India*, with John Wieners, Altadena, California 1987; articles—"An Interview with Francesco Clemente", with Achille Bonito Oliva, in *Flash Art* (Milan), Summer 1980; "Francesco Clemente at the Metropolitan", interview with Danny Berger, in *Print Collector's Newsletter* (New York), March / April 1982; "Francesco Clemente", interview with Edit deAk, in *Interview* (New York), April 1982; "Samtale me Francesco Clemente", interview with Heiner Bastian, in *Louisiana Revy* (Humlebaek), June 1983; "A Project for Artforum", in *Artforum* (New York), March 1987.

On CLEMENTE: books—*The Different Avantgarde: Europe / America*, by Achille Bonito Oliva, Milan 1976; *The Italian Trans Avantguarde* by Achille Bonito Oliva, Milan 1980; *Francesco Clemente: il viaggiatore napoletano*, exhibition catalogue with essay by Rainer Crone, Cologne 1982; *Francesco Clemente: The Fourteen Stations*, exhibition catalouge edited by Mark Francis, London 1983; *Currents: Francesco Clemente*, with text by Elisabeth Sussman, Boston 1984; *Francesco Clemente: Pastelle 1974–83*, with texts by Rainer Crone, Zdenek Felix and Lucius Grisebach, Munich 1984; *Francesco Clemente*, exhibition catalogue with texts by Mark Ormond and Marianna Adams, Sarasota 1985; *Francesco Clemente* by Michael Auping, New York 1985; *Francesco Clemente CVIII*, with text by Dieter Koepplin, Basle 1987.

Francesco Clemente has made an impression as one of the most significant personalities in the panorama of "new tendencies" characterized by the renewed interest in the image and in traditional painting techniques. The pre-eminence of the concept in art, with the consequent tendency to dematerialism, is being seriously re-examined in the work of the younger artists, those whose work began to take shape at the end of the 1970's. The optimistic, evolutionist theory of *avant-garde* ideology starts to decline; together with the revival of techniques hitherto regarded as obsolete, artists are trying out the end of ideologies as a theory of a new cultural orientation, pointing to a reinterpretation of the past and a revival of local cultures. There is an established international movement which no longer wants to model itself on a parallel "international style," but prefers to stimulate the differences between one culture and another in a free cross-fertilization of ideas.

Clemente has adopted the stylistic eclecticism that is the most significant outcome of these tendencies and the consequence of an aesthetic attitude that argues the case for the values of subjectivity. Like a number of others, the artist has moved on from photographic media and has abandoned them in favour of manual techniques (collages, oil painting, pastels, tempera, fresco, mosaic, drawing . . .) giving more immediate access to the objects of an ambiguously expressed expressiveness. Clemente's pictures are, as it were, intrinsically ambivalent; they allude to an explicit perverted erotic phantasmagoria, yet at the same time escape from recognizability, closed in the blazons of a private heraldry ("emblems" is the title of a series of works by Clemente). Clemente has often expressed a lively interest in esoteric ideas, in astrol-

ogy, the history of religion and Indian civilization, from whose symbolism he has drawn inspiration for his own pictorial language. In addition, his painting explicitly recalls the world of late Roman culture, an era of surprising cultural and stylistic eclecticism. This purpose can be recognized especially in Clemente's self-portraits, which have become a recurrent theme with him. A common enough theme in the pictorial tradition, here the self-portrait becomes an elaboration of the idea of self through a self-denigrating rhetoric with a literary flavour, near to the influence of an Egon Schiele, near in short to an "accursed" nature, strongly intellectualized.

The identity loses its familiar features and becomes an unreal, iridescent apparition, organically degenerate, connected with the world of impulses. The artist depicts himself as a convulsed body, an eroticized object ready for any metamorphosis. The image in Clemente springs from the encounter between the this body, this cheerful intensity, and objects and entities transformed by a similar tension into emblems, enigmatic fragments, already completely detached from the totality. The figures are flattened on to the surfaces, suspended in an irrationally defined spatiality. With no depth, a caricature of itself, the picture no longer tries to come to terms with reality, and the painting becomes an example of excess. The excess lies in the recourse to ambiguity. It even dictates the selection of forms: sometimes the drawing looks ugly, crude, like "anti-graceful" graffiti, deliberately elementary, but at other times its studied elegance and surprising fastidiousness are astonishing. The painting fluctuates between a "neo-savage," aggressively *brut* style, even in the choice of colours, and a style that is courtly and sumptuous, with backgrounds of delicately evanescent colour.

The painter's knowledge is there to see in his virtuoso skill, or else lies hidden in coprophilia; it becomes clear in the stylistic polymorphism of one who, in his painting, wishes not to find an identity but to lose himself. As Edit deAk has written, Clemente is a clever chamaleon cynically content with his own state of grace.

—Giorgio Verzotti

CLOSE, Chuck.

American. Born in Monroe, Washington, 5 July 1940. Educated at Everett Community College, Washington, 1958–60; University of Washington, Seattle, 1960–62, B.A. 1962; Yale Summer School of Art and Music, Norfolk, Connecticut, 1961; Yale University, New Haven, Connecticut, 1962–64, B.F.A. 1963, M.F.A. 1964; Akademie der Bildenden Künste, Vienna, 1964–65. Married Leslie Rose in 1967; daughters: Georgia Molly and Maggie Sarah. Independent artist, since 1966: has lived and worked in New York since 1967. Instructor, University of Massachusetts, Amherst, 1965–67; School of Visual Arts, New York, 1967–71; New York University, 1970–73; University of Washington, Seattle, Summer 1970; Yale Summer School of Art and Music, Norfolk, Connecticut, 1971, 1972. Recipient: Fulbright Grant, 1964; National Endowment for the Arts Grant, 1973. Agent: Pace Gallery, 32 East 57th Street, New York, New York 10022. Addresses: (studio) 75 Spring Street, New York, New York 10012; (home) 271 Central Park West, New York, New York 10024, U.S.A.

Individual Exhibitions:

1967   University of Massachusetts Art Gallery, Amherst
1970   Bykert Gallery, New York
     3 Young Americans: A Biennial, Allen Memorial Art Museum, Oberlin College, Ohio (with Ron Cooper and Neil Jenney)

1971   *Recent Work*, Los Angeles County Museum of Art
     Bykert Gallery, New York
1972   Museum of Contemporary Art, Chicago
1973   Museum of Modern Art, New York
     Akron Art Institute, Ohio
     Bykert Gallery, New York
1974   *3 Realists: Close, Estes, Raffael*, Worcester Art Museum, Massachusetts
1975   Edwin Ulrich Museum, Wichita State University, Kansas
     Mint Museum of Art, Charlotte, North Carolina
     Ball State University Art Museum, Muncie, Indiana
     Phoenix Art Museum, Arizona
     Laguna Gloria Art Museum, Austin, Texas
     Texas Gallery, Houston
     Art Museum of South Texas, Corpus Christi'
     Minneapolis Institute of Arts
     Center for Visual Arts, Portland, Oregon
     San Francisco Museum of Modern Art
     Bykert Gallery, New York
1976   Contemporary Art Center, Cincinnati, Ohio
     Baltimore Museum of Art
     Richard Artschwager/Chuck Close/Joe Zucker, David Weinberg Gallery, San Francisco (travelled to the La Jolla Museum of Art, California, and the University of California at Davis)
1977   *Matrix 35*, Wadsworth Atheneum, Hartford, Connecticut
     Recent Work, Pace Gallery, New York
1979   Kunstraum, Munich
     New Painting of Mark and Recent Drawings, Pace Gallery, New York
1980   *Close Portraits*, Walker Art Center, Minneapolis (retrospective 1968–80; travelled to the St. Louis Art Museum, Missouri; Museum of Contemporary Art, Chicago; and the Whitney Museum, New York, 1981)
1982   *Photographs*, California Museum of Photography, Riverside (travelled to Berkeley, California)
     Paperworks, Richard Gray Gallery, Chicago (travelled to Minneapolis; Jacksonville; St. Louis)
1983   *Recent Work*, Pace Gallery, New York
1984   *Paper Works*, Herbert Palmer Gallery, Los Angeles (travelled to Cheney, Washington; Milwaukee; DeKalb, Illinois: Columbia, South Carolina)
1985   *Works on Paper*, Contemporary Arts Museum, Houston
     Fuji Television Gallery, Tokyo
     Photographs, Pace/MacGill Gallery, New York
     Large Scale Photographs, Fraenkel Gallery, San Francisco
1986   *Maquettes*, Pace/MacGill Gallery, New York
     Recent Works, Pace Gallery, New York
1987   *Polaroids*, Aldrich Museum of Contemporary Art, Ridgefield, Connecticut

Selected Group Exhibitions:

1969   *Annual Exhibition*, Whitney Museum, New York
1970   *22 Realists*, Whitney Museum, New York
1971   *Prospect 71*, Städitische Kunsthalle, Dusseldorf
1972   *Documenta 5* Kassel, West Germany (and *Documenta 6*, 1977)
1974   *Hyperréalistes Américains/Réalistes Européens*, Centre National d'Art Contemporain, Paris (toured Europe)
1978   *American Painting of the 1970's*, Albright-Knox Art Gallery, Buffalo, New York
1980   *Printed Art: A View of 2 Decades*, Museum of Modern Art, New York
1982   *Great Big Drawings*, Massachusetts Institute of Technology, Cambridge
1984   *Drawings 1974–84*, Hirshhorn Museum, Washington, D.C.
1986   *Nude, Naked, Stripped*, Massachusetts Institute of Technology, Cambridge

Collections:

Museum of Modern Art, New York; Whitney Museum, New York; Allen Memorial Art Museum, Oberlin College, Ohio; Walker Art Center, Minneapolis; National Museum of Can-

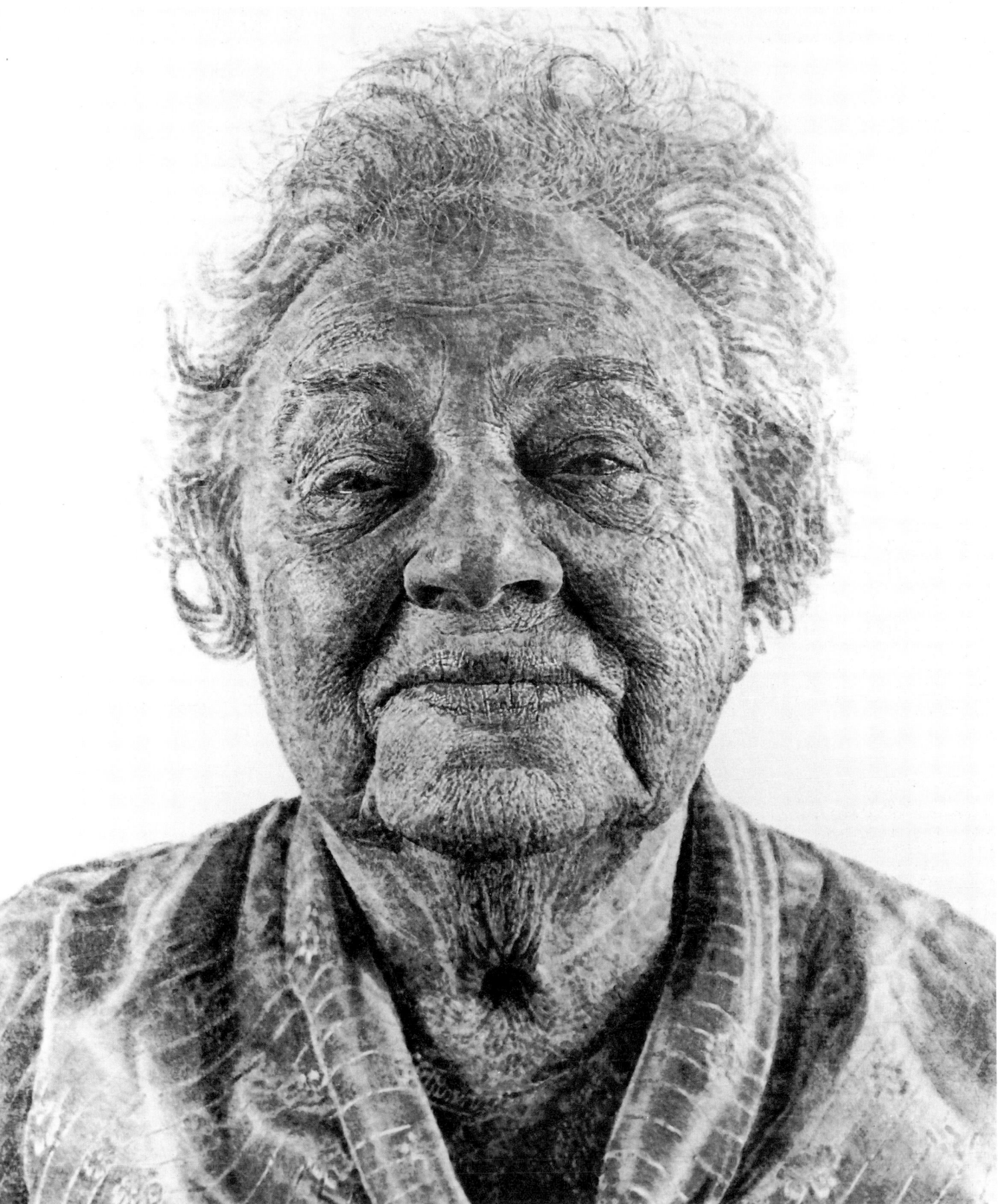

Chuck Close: *Fanny (fingerpainting)*, **1985**

ada, Ottawa; Art Gallery of Ontario, Toronto; Neue Gallery, Aachen, West Germany; Museum Boymans-van Beuningen, Rotterdam; Australian National Gallery, Canberra.

Publications:

By CLOSE: articles—"An Interview with Chuck Close," with Cindy Nemser, in *Artforum* (New York), January 1970; interview, in "Photo-Realists: 12 Interviews" by Linda Chase and Ted McBurnett in *Art in America* (New York), November/December 1972; statement in "The Artist and the Face: A Modern American Sampling: by Gerrit Henry in *Art in America* (New York), January 1975; statement in "The Art of Portraiture in the Words of 4 New York Artists" in the *New York Times*, 31 October 1976; interview in "The 20th Century Artists Most Admired by Other Artists" by Grace Glueck in *Artnews* (New York), November 1977; "An Interview with Chuck Close," with Barbara Harshman, in *Arts Magazine* (New York), June 1978; interview, with Barbaralee Diamonstein, in *Inside New York's Artworld*, New York 1979; "An Interview with Chuck Close", with Jane Cottingham, in *American Artist* (New York), May 1983; "New York in the Eighties: A Symposium" in *The New Criterion* (New York), Summer 1986.

On CLOSE: books—*22 Realists*, exhibition catalogue, with text by James Monte, New York 1970; *3 Young Americans: A Biennial*, exhibition catalogue, with text by Athena Spear, Oberlin, Ohio 1970; *Chuck Close: Recent Work*, exhibition catalogue, with text by Gail R. Scott, Los Angeles 1971; *The Painter and the Photography* by Van Deren Coke, Albuquerque, New Mexico 1972; *American Art since 1900* by Barbara Rose, New York 1972; *Neue Formen des Realismus* by Peter Sager, Cologne 1973; *Photo-Realism: The Ludwig Collection*, exhibition catalogue, London 1973; *3 Realists: Close, Estes, Raffael*, exhibition catalogue, Worcester Massachusetts 1974; *Super Realism: A Critical Anthology*, edited by Gregory Battcock, New York 1975; *History of Modern Art* by H. H. Arnason, New York 1977; *Chuck Close/Matrix 35*, exhibition catalogue, Hartford, Connecticut 1977; *Chuck Close: Recent Work*, exhibition catalogue, New York 1977; *Malerei und Photographie im Dialog* by Erika Billeter, Zurich 1977; *Super-Realism* by Edward Lucie-Smith, New York 1979; *What Is Art?* by John Canaday, New York 1980; *Printed Art: A View of 2 Decades*, exhibition catalogue, New York 1980; *Close Portraits*, exhibition catalogue, with texts by Lisa Lyons and Martin Friedman, Minneapolis 1980; *Contemporary American Realism Since 1960* by Frank H. Goodyear, Jr., New York 1981; *Realists at Work* by John Arthur, New York 1983; *Chuck Close*, exhibition catalogue with text by John Perreault, New York 1983; *The Revenge of the Philistines: Art and Culture 1972–1984* by Hilton Kramer, New York 1985; *Chuck Close: Recent Work*, exhibition catalogue with text by Arnold Glimcher, New York 1986; *50 New York Artists* by Richard Marshall and Robert Mapplethorpe, San Francisco 1986; *Chuck Close* by Lisa Lyons and Robert Storr, New York 1987.

Portraiture is very important to my work, but not for what would seem like the most obvious reasons. Everyone knows something about the way people look—we have certain ideas about what's right and what's wrong. If the complexion is too green, all of a sudden it's not acceptable—whereas, if I were painting a tree, and it were a little too green or too red, no one but a botanist would know or care. I wanted to paint something that people cared about—a face contains very specific information that people can sense is either right or wrong. That keeps me on my toes, keeps me from letting well enough alone, or saying, this is close enough—no pun intended.

Likeness is an important by-product of what I do, but only to the extent that if the photograph I paint from looks like the person, the painting will look like the photograph. But the photograph may not look like the person and if it doesn't, it can be bothersome. I suppose I'd like to make the image like the person, but I've always felt it necessary to maintain a certain distance from the subject. When I painted myself, I always referred to it as "him"—I somehow couldn't deal with the fact that it was me and whether I looked ugly or handsome or whatever.

I have a hard time dealing with my work in terms of the history of portraiture—I don't know how it fits. A lot of great paintings, when I think about it, happen to be portraits, but I have a hard time with it—when I think of something called portrait painting. I think of how all portraits by Rembrandt look like paintings by Rembrandt—that would seem to be a shortcoming of portraiture.

I'm not really interested in photograph, but one thing I like about photographs is the snapshot or mugshot quality of a California driver's license. It's got such an immediacy and a strong reason to exist in terms of mailing down what a certain driver looks like. It doesn't have anything to do with vanity, it doesn't have anything to do with the ego of the sitter or whatever. I've never done commissioned portraits because I never wanted to get involved with those ego problems. If somebody wants a nine-foot-high picture of their head, they must be involved with how they look. I'd hate to have the feeling that I needed to straighten teeth.

As to sitters, I just photograph my friends. Most of the people are relatively anonymous when I photograph them; sometimes they don't stay too anonymous, but I don't try and paint art stars or anything like that.

I never see someone and say, oh, you'd be great to paint. What I do is, get together a whole bunch of people and shoot them, and some of them turn out to be interesting photographs. I don't really think about interesting *people*. I scan a contact sheet and try to imagine what it would be like to paint from that photograph. Some of them seem better than others, not in terms of the overall iconography but in terms of what kind of painting experience they would be—how sharp and how blurry.

But I do care that they are people. I think sometimes it sounds like I don't care, or for that matter, that I don't think they're people. But if you're going to spend three to six months on a painting, you can't just worry about the image and say, gee, I just want this to be a picture of so-and-so. The workaday problems of making a painting tend to take over in my mind. Of course, for the last six or seven years, at least, I haven't really felt like painting anything else, so there must be something there.

—Chuck Close

A key to the work of Chuck Close lies in his statement: "I liked the fact that I wasn't thinking of the cheek in relation to the ear and trying to decide which was closer and which farther away . . . if a person were simply panning across or scanning the cheek and some informational change took place, he would realize that he was moving back and forth in space . . . ." It is such disattachment from his subject—through the huge scale that breaks free of the normal human facial confrontation; through his success at the challenge to keep the visage impersonal yet of course recognizable; through the tight-'sandwich' of clear focus that Close established when he blurred the nose tip in the frontally positioned heads which he himself photographs with a 190mm/. lens so that clarity reigns only in a zone ending at the back of the cheeks; through the melange of non-gestural marks that comprise all his works both the very large and small; through the grids left visible in the watercolors, pastels, and prints, but not present in the large paintings ("By breaking—the grid—down this way, I can make the act of painting exactly the same all the way through."); all such attitudes and processes have led to Close quite suitably being labelled a Minimalist and Conceptualist—his subject matter thus disregarded.

Close appeared at a time when a photographic style in painted art was ostensibly logical because of the triumph of Pop Art and photography's importance there. He had worked on Big Nude, a 20-feet long, black-and-white canvas based on his photograph, but found that he had to avoid 'hot subject matter.' And so as he worked, in the late 1960s, to develop an anthology of techniques to avoid any gestural pictorialism and subjective color, he worked with his spray painting, rag smearing, and razor markings. ("My invention is an invention of means, rather than an invention of shape and other things.") Close then was a pioneer Photo-Realist, used only his own features in these early large works, and remains one of the few Photo-Realists to use the figure. When be began to use color in the early 70s—on the basis of his pleasure with the previous monochromatic images where no color mixing was involved as the black was diluted on the white picture surface—Close wished to continue without palette. From his color photographs, as the image of the icon-like frontal head has remained unvaried, Close had three color separation prints made which he then matched in three painting campaigns (magenta, cyan, yellow) across the canvas from the top down. He thus avoided traditional paint-mixing necessities as he himself produced a handicrafted image based upon the chemical-mechanical photographic process. At this time as well, since he wished neither to change his image nor his a-subjective approaches, he changed the nature of his studio practice in order to maintain his interest in the experience of the technical process. He developed the use of a grid which allowed him to present the same kind of marking unit throughout the image: i.e., the title of the work gave the specific number of grid points, even when as in large works, *Robert 104,072*, 1973–74, 108 by 84 inches, they are not visible as a grid. With smaller works, where they might be but 2760 grid points and they were left clearly distinct as individual, unblended marks, there is a striking resemblance to computer-generated, so-called digital images. In yet another variant of such attempts at a relatively depersonalized creative process, Close more recently has used dyed paper pulp, cut into tiny curved-edged chips, glued onto the picture surface to produce the most tactile work of his mature career.

Perhaps Close is easily appreciated as a hybrid in his fusion of Pop Art and Mimimalism: his image, while by no means sentimental, does of course force the introduction of species-recognition and its concommitant instantaneous search for sentiment; and more cogently his subject choice of the human face (as seen by the camera), led the artist of necessity to invent a pictorial means to achieve both the image and his Minimalist, purist and anti-sentimental surface. He has then used the camera image to establish—in his larger works—a phenomenological reduction to the emblem of consciousness. In his smaller works, where a grid remains, Close may appear a skeptic who does not understand the contents of his consciousness and thus relies upon a photograph for the source of his attempt at "mimicry" of the non-imaginative and neuro-chemical constructive processes of appearance.

—Joshua B. Kind

COHEN, Bernard.

British. Born in London, 28 July 1933. Educated at schools in London; studied shorthand and typing at Clark's College, Leytonstone, London, 1947, and art at South West Essex Technical College and School of Art, 1949–50, St. Martin's School of Art, London, 1950–51, and Slade School of Fine Art, London 1951–54. Married Jean Britton in 1959. Painter: lives and works in London: lived in Paris and travelled in France, 1954–56, and spent several months in Rome, 1956; lived in Hertfordshire, 1959; returned to London, and shared house with William Turnbull, 1961–63, then settled in Putney, South London, 1963; worked on design for stage curtain, Theatre Royal, Stratford, East London, 1965; built studio in Kingston-on-Thames, Surrey, 1967. Part-Time Lecturer, Hammersmith School of Art, London, 1957–60; Lecturer, Ealing School of Art, London, 1961–64; Guest Lecturer, St. Martin's School of Art, London 1963–64; Lecturer, Chelsea School of Art, London, 1966–68, and Slade School of Fine Art, 1967–73 and since 1977. Visiting Professor, Department of Art, University of New Mexico, Albuquerque, 1969–70. Recipient: French Government Travel

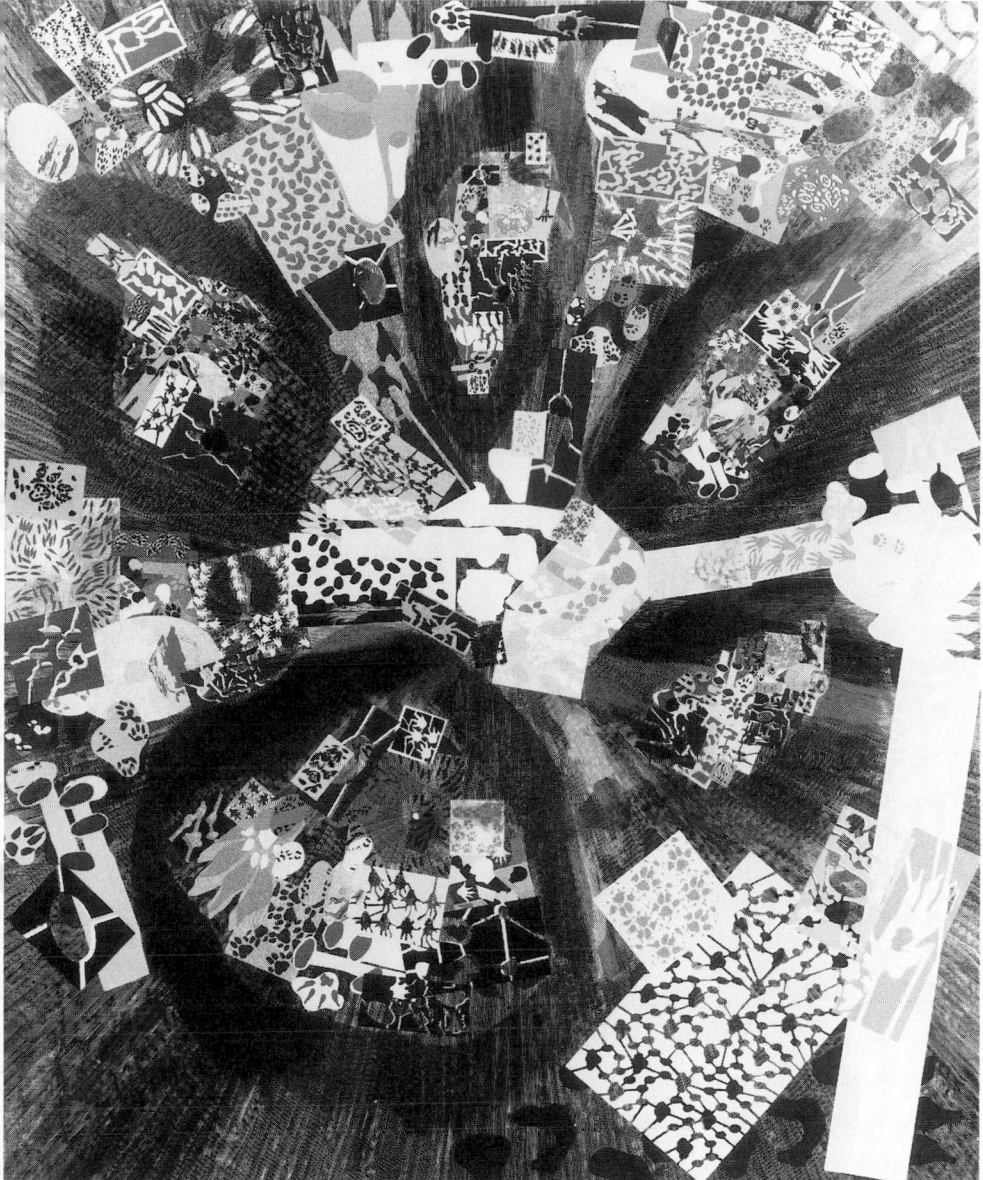

Bernard Cohen: *Home Territory*, 1979

Publications:

By COHEN: articles—"Gesture and Style" in *Gazette* (London), no. 2, 1961; "International Union of Architects Congress Buildings, South Bank, London" in *Architectural Design* (London), November 1961; "Observations about the Photograph of the Painting Generation" in *Cambridge Opinion*, January 1964; interview, with Denis Bower, in *Arts Review* (London), December 1964; "The Art That Launched a Thousand Ships" in the *Sunday Times Colour Magazine* (London), November 1965; statement in *Bernard Cohen*, exhibition catalogue, Bristol 1967; statement in *Recent British Painting* by Alan Bowness, London 1968; statement in *Arte Inglese Oggi*, exhibition catalogue, Milan 1976.

On COHEN: book—*Bernard Cohen: Paintings and Drawings 1959-71*, exhibition catalogue, by Richard Morphet, London 1972; articles—"Bernard Cohen and Harold Cohen: From Gesture to Symbol: in *London: The New Scene*, exhibition catalogue by Martin Friedmann, Minneapolis 1965; "Bernard Cohen" by David Thompson in *5 Young Painters*, exhibition catalogue, Vence, France 1966; "Bernard Cohen" by Andrew Forge in *The Listener* (London), April 1972; "The Work of Bernard Cohen" by B. Bernstein in *Studio International* (London), June/July 1972.

There has been a dramatic change in Bernard Cohen's paintings; in the 1960s they resembled highly coloured spaghetti, arranged on the canvas in a mixture of meticulous care and free association. One could see why he pointed to their narrative quality, since, in Klee's immortal phrase, they were rather like taking a line, or a tube, for a walk. The churned-up, intestinal association of the imagery also suggested intense, emotional elements, and there were indications that the paintings were, so to speak, graphs of both the process of painting and the physical experience before the canvas.

Cohen is a member of that English generation of artists whose greatest influences came from the United States; whilst he refers to his admiration for such artists as Fontana, Dubuffet, Miró and Dali—and one certainly notes the mixture of informality and surrealism in this early period—there can be little doubt that the most relevant example is Jackson Pollock. The American painter's famous drip paintings are precisely images which record the effort of creation, as well as being monuments to that creativity: they are facts and sequences of time. Cohen's narratives clearly sought to experience the same direct intensity of creation, and to record that experience on canvas. He also refers to his liking for *art nouveau*, which relates to the sinuous convolution of these painted linear graphs.

More recently he has pushed his way through the morass of neo-organic matter, into the fresh air, into uncluttered space; the result is a series of almost white canvases, arranged in a series of oblong areas, against acid-coloured backgrounds, in which pale, distantly burning, lunar symbols float in corners of space. Meticulously conceived and painted, this new phase is immediately more elegant and sophisticated, suggesting a search for idealistic physicality, for a meditative stance through which to reflect metaphysical notions of the physical world and human life. Most recently Cohen has returned to the undisturbed space of a single canvas, in which the clinically white surface is broken not by single sums, but galaxies of coloured spots, floating, drifting rhythmically through space. Perhaps they suggest the smallness of individual man, the non-uniqueness of the earth, the remote mystery of the universe.

—Charles Spencer

Scholarship, 1954; Boise Scholarship, University of London, 1955. Address: 17 Leyborne Park, Kew, Surrey, England.

Individual Exhibitions:

1958	Gimpel Fils, London (with James Tower)
	Midland Group Gallery, Nottingham
1960	Gimpel Fils, London
1962	Molton Gallery, London
1963	Kasmin Gallery, London
1964	Kasmin Gallery, London
1967	Kasmin Gallery, London
	Arnolfini Gallery, Bristol
	Betty Parsons Gallery, New York
	Lady Margaret Hall, Oxford
1972	Arnolfini Gallery, Bristol
	Hayward Gallery, London
	Waddington Galleries, London
	Studio LaCitta, Verona
	Hester van Royen Gallery, London
1973	Galleria Annunciata, Milan
	Waddington Galleries, London
1974	Waddington Galleries, London
1977	Waddington Galleries, London
1979	Waddington Galleries, London
1980	Amano Gallery, Osaka, Japan

Selected Group Exhibitions:

1958	*Abstract Impressionism*, Arts Council Gallery, London
1960	*Situation*, Federation of British Arts Galleries, London
1964	*Painting and Sculpture of a Decade*, Tate Gallery, London
1965	*London: The New Scene*, Walker Art Center, Minneapolis
1967	*Jeune Peintres Anglais*, Palais des Beaux-Arts, Brussels
1969	*Marks on Canvas*, Museum am Ostwall, Dortmund, West Germany
1970	*British Painting*, National Gallery, Washington, D.C.
1973	*New British Painting*, Musée National d'Art Moderne, Paris
1976	*Arte Inglese Oggi*, Palazzo Reale, Milan
1982	*Carnegie International*, Pittsburgh

Collections:

Tate Gallery, London; Arts Council of Great Britain, London; Whitworth Art Gallery, Manchester; Museum am Ostwall, Dortmund, West Germany; Museum of Modern Art, New York; Walker Art Center, Minneapolis; Museum of Modern Art, Caracas.

COLEING, Anthony.
Australian. Born in Warrnambool, Victoria, in 1942. Studied at the National Art School, Sydney, 1958–59. Recipient: First Prize, Kolotex Competition, 1968; Flotta Lauro Prize, 1971; Australian Visual Arts Board Grant, 1973, 1976, and Studio Grant in New

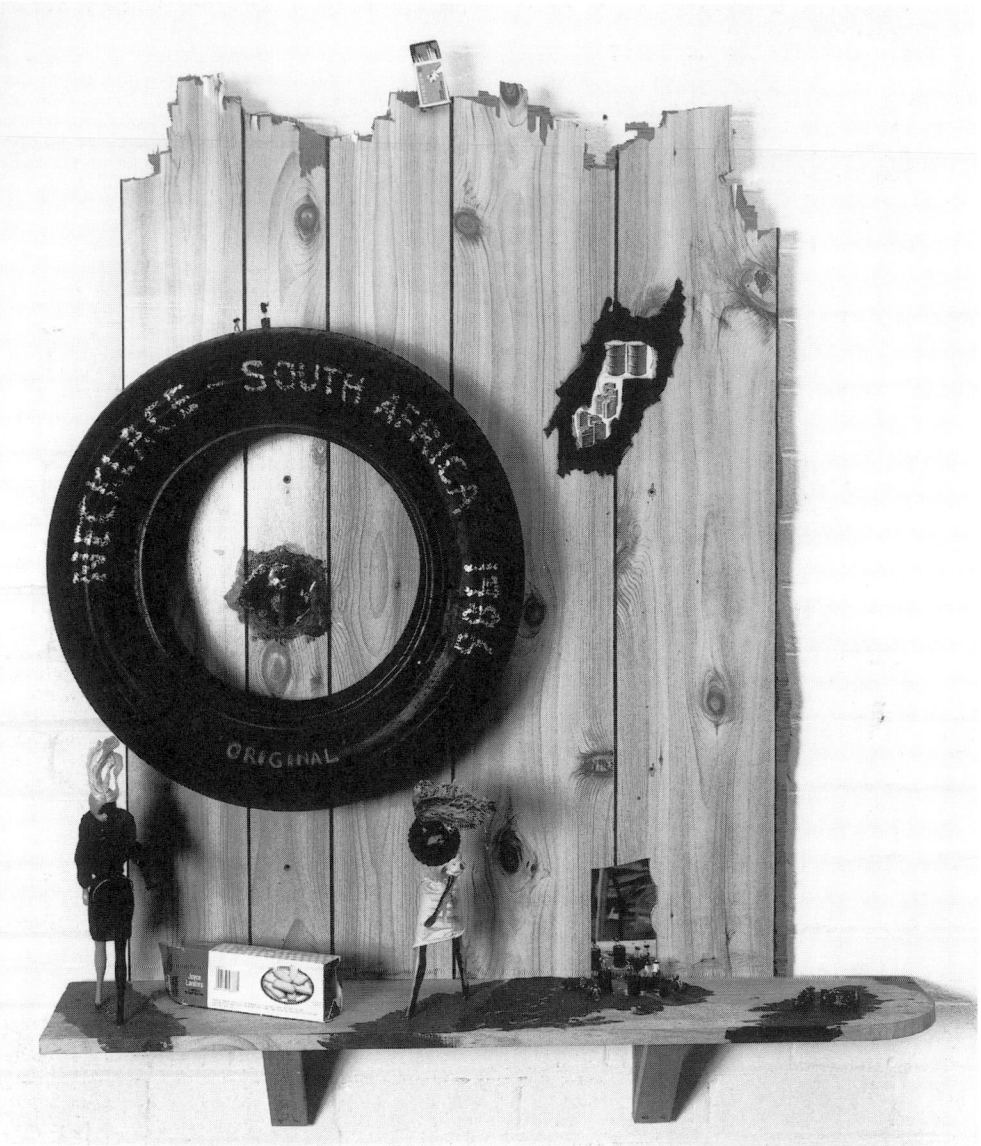

Tony Coleing: *If the Tyre Fits ...*, 1979

exhibition catalogue by Robin Wallace-Crabbe, Canberra 1980; *The Development of Australian Sculpture* by Graeme Sturgeon, Sydney 1983.

Tony Coleing is a mid-career artist with a pronounced collage sensibility which expresses itself in both two dimensional and three dimensional forms.

A major survey of Australian collage pursuits entitled 'The Age of Collage', held in Sydney during 1987, gave us some insight into Coleing's experiments with two dimensional works on paper since his schooldays. The pattern-making pursuits of a youngster were gradually replaced by photo-collages (many combined with other media) expressing an increasingly ironic view of man and the world.

Some would condemn Coleing as a pessimist; that is a man who lacks faith. I see him as a realist who can penetrate beneath the surface of things and perceive the truths of the human condition. Coleing delights in conveying those insights which can be achieved through the intelligent juxtaposition of unlikely images. From strange bedfellows revealing truths are born.

Much of his work is autobiographical, confronting issues dealing with sexuality, mortality and greed. Personal elements are reinforced by those of a more objective nature. Social concerns show a healthy disrespect for conventional party political philosophies and a cynical acknowledgement of the more ruthless aspects of human endeavour. There is little room for any form of idealism in Coleing's scenario, although his activities as an artist possess a sense of outrage which seems to propel him as a kind of 'noble' prophet and philosopher.

By shunning many of the 'niceties' of the art-making process and electing, instead, for a more brutally sparse approach, Coleing, is, in his own way, offering us a role-model for human survival. Who needs high technology, uranium and Star Wars? Not the likes of Coleing and those who reject the propaganda of political leaders, industrial magnates and newspaper and television moguls.

Coleing's art during the past two decades has embraced formats which have enabled him to extend his flair for juxtaposition in installation formats (as at the Venice Biennale in 1980) and in large canvases dealing with international military confrontations. A series of 'Pope Cards' mocked the hypocrisy of the Roman Catholic church.

A 1980 Venice Biennale installation analysed Australia's role as a producer of 'yellowcake' for the production of uranium and the ruthless exploitation by overseas interests of a uniquely isolated and extraordinary environment. In his catalogue notes for this Venice Biennale piece, Robin Wallace Crabbe observed that one of Coleing's major achievements was his "avoidance of the chic of radicalism. His art protests but offers no fringe luxuries, no 'my god that was worth doing but really . . . . waiter! another scotch on the rocks.' Instead the statement remains unavoidable in its simplicity, relentless, and with seedy comedy, tragically uncomic."

Much of Coleing's best work faces up to issues which are simultaneously regional and universal in significance. Some critics attacked an installation work of Coleing's at Venice 1980 as being too parochial, because it incorporated jars of an Australian bread and butter spread called Vegemite and two mounted Kangaroo heads. They missed the point. Does Australia actually *own* its own Vegemite, or yellowcake, or anything else for that matter? What price becoming a fully-fledged, paid-up member of the global community?

—Arthur McIntyre

York, 1987; Mussellbrook Art Prize, 1986; Patron Print Award, Print Council of Australia, 1987. Agent: Ray Hughes Gallery, Brisbane. Address: c/o Ray Hughes, 11 Enoggera Terrace, Red Hill, Brisbane, Queensland, Australia.

Individual Exhibitions:

1969	Gallery A, Melbourne (and Sydney)
1971	Gallery A, Sydney
1974	Watters Gallery, Sydney (and 1975)
1977	Ray Hughes Gallery, Brisbane (and 1978, 1980)
1980	Australian Pavilion, *39th Biennale*, Venice
1981	Institute of Modern Art, Brisbane
	123 Charlotte Street, Brisbane (with Kevin Mortensen)
1982	Roslyn Oxley 9 Gallery, Sydney
	Tony Coleing/Margaret Dodd, at the *Adelaide Festival*, South Australia
	123 Charlotte Street, Brisbane (with Adrian Hall)
1983	Ray Hughes Gallery, Brisbane
1984	Ray Hughes at Reconnaissance, Melbourne
1985	Ray Hughes Gallery, Brisbane
	Ray Hughes Gallery, Sydney

Selected Group Exhibitions:

1968	*Young Commonwealth Artists*, Whitechapel Art Gallery, London
1969	*Mildura Sculpture Triennial*, Mildura, Victoria
1973	*Object and Idea*, National Gallery of Victoria, Melbourne
1975	*Survival Kits*, Melbourne University, Victoria
1976	*Contemporary Australian Sculpture*, Art Gallery of South Australia, Adelaide
1980	*The Queensland Connection*, Contemporary Art Society, Adelaide
1982	*A Photographer's Choice*, Darling Downs Institute of Advanced Education, Toowoomba, Queensland (travelled to Brisbane)
1984	*International Survey of Painting and Sculpture*, Museum of Modern Art, New York
1986	*Biennale of Sydney*, Art Gallery of New South Wales, Sydney
1987	*Urban Anxieties*, Australian National Gallery, Canberra

Collections:

Australian National Gallery, Canberra; Art Gallery of New South Wales, Sydney; National Gallery of Victoria, Melbourne; Art Gallery of South Australia, Adelaide; Queen Victoria Museum and Art Gallery, Launceston, Tasmania; Mildura Arts Centre, Victoria; Ballarat Fine Art Gallery, Victoria; Museum of Contemporary Art, Brisbane; Darling Down Art Gallery, Queensland; National Gallery of New Zealand, Wellington.

Publications:

On COLEING: books—*Tony Coleing: Venice Biennale 1980*,

COLEMAN, James.
Irish. Born in Ballaghaderreen, County Roscommon,

July 1941. Studied at the Ecole des Beaux-Arts, Paris, 1960–61, Central School of Arts and Crafts, London, 1961–63, National College of Art and Design, Dublin, 1963–66, and Accademia di Belle Arti, Milan, 1966–71. Lives and works in Dublin and Milan. Recipient: Arts Council of Ireland grant, 1968, 1970; Irish-American Cultural Institute Award for the Arts, 1977; Irish Arts Council Award, 1979. Agents: Studio Marconi, via Tadino 15, 20124 Milan; David Hendricks, 119 St. Stephen's Green, Dublin, Ireland; and Nigel Greenwood Inc., 4 New Burlington Street, London W1, England. Address: 189 Emmet Road, Inchicore, Dublin 8, Ireland.

Individual Exhibitions:

1965   Molesworth Gallery, Dublin
1967   Design Studio, Amsterdam
1970   Studio Marconi, Milan
1972   *Projections*, Galleria Toselli, Milan
1973   *Habitual Object*, David Hendricks Gallery, Dublin
       Habitual Object, Studio Marconi, Milan
1974   Ulster Museum, Belfast
       Slide Piece, Studio Lia Rumma, Naples
       Installation Made for Location and Slide Piece, Galerie t'Venster, Rotterdam
       2 Seagulls; or, One Seagull Twice, Cork Arts Society, Ireland
1975   *Clara and Dario*, Studio Marconi, Milan
1978   *Strongbow*, Project Arts Centre, Dublin
1979   *Box*, Galleria Schema, Florence
       Box, Nigel Greenwood Inc., London (with Marc Chaimowicz)
1980   *Connemara Landscape*, University College Art Gallery, Galway, Ireland
       So Different . . . and Yet, Nigel Greenwood Inc., London
       Douglas Hyde Gallery, Dublin

1981   *Now and Then, So Different . . . and Yet*, Project Arts Centre, Dublin
       So Different . . . and Yet, Franklin Furnace, New York
1982   *Slide Piece*, John Hansard Gallery, Southampton, England
       Nigel Greenwood Inc., London
       Douglas Hyde Gallery, Trinity College, Dublin (travelled to the Arts Council of Northern Ireland Gallery, Belfast)
       Ignotum per Ignotius, Lantaren Theatre, Rotterdam (toured Netherlands)
1983   Whitechapel Art Gallery, London
       Orchard Gallery, Derry, Northern Ireland
       Teatro Estudio Citac, Coimbra, Portugal (travelled to Lisbon)
1984   Douglas Hyde Gallery, Dublin
       David Bellman Gallery/Art Metropole, Toronto
1985   Dungaire Castle, County Clare, Ireland
       Renaissance Society, Chicago (retrospective; travelled to Institute of Contemporary Arts, London)
1987   Galerie Rudiger Schottle, Munich
       Galeria Johnen und Schottle, Cologne

Selected Group Exhibitions:

1972   *Living Art*, Project Arts Centre, Dulbin
1973   *Biennale de Paris*, Musée d'Art Moderne de la Ville, Paris
1976   *Living Art*, National Gallery of Ireland, Dublin
1977   *ROCS '77*, Hugh Lane Municipal Gallery of Modern Art, Dublin
1978   *Milano '80*, Palazzo Reale, Milan
       Biennale, Venice
1980   *Without the Walls*, Institute of Contemporary Arts, London
1982   *Biennale*, Sydney
1986   *In De Maalstroom*, Palais des Beaux-Arts, Brussels

1987   *From the Europe of Old*, Stedelijk Museum, Amsterdam

Collections:

Ulster Museum, Belfast; Arts Council of Northern Ireland, Belfast; Municipal Gallery of Dublin.

Publications:

By COLEMAN: articles—statement in *VIII Biennale de Paris*, exhibition catalogue, Paris 1973; article in *Art Press* (Paris), September 1973; articles in *Prospect* (Milan), March/April 1973; "Essay from Coleman" in *Art in Ireland* (Dublin), vol. II, no. 3, 1974; article in *Data* (Milan), Summer 1974; "Flash Piece 1970 and Slide Piece 1972/73" in *Bolaffi Selected Artists*, Turin 1974; statement in *Rotterdam Art News*, September/October 1974.

On COLEMAN: books—*Installation Made for Location and Slide Piece*, exhibition catalogue, by Achille Bonito Oliva, Rotterdam 1974; *Europe-America: The Different Avant Gardes* by Achille Bonito Oliva, Milan 1976; *James Coleman*, exhibition catalogue, by Jean Fisher, Dublin 1982; *The Enigma of the Hero in the Work of James Coleman* by Jean Fisher, Londonderry 1983; *James Coleman: Selected Works*, exhibition catalogue with essays by Anne Rorimer and Michael Newman, Chicago and London 1985; articles—"James Coleman à la Tête de l'Avant-garde à la Biennale de Paris" by George Astalos in *Nouvelle Europe* (Paris), no. 6, 1973; "Causality and the Interpretation of Information" by Ricardo Luccio in *Data* (Milan), May/June 1976; "Review from Dublin" by Dorothy Walker in *Art Monthly* (London), November 1978; "Installations and Performances in Ireland" by Dorothy Walker in *Flash Art* (Milan), October/November 1979.

In the theatre the audience interpret what they see and hear to reconstruct the narrative and its meaning. James Coleman foregrounds this process of interpre-

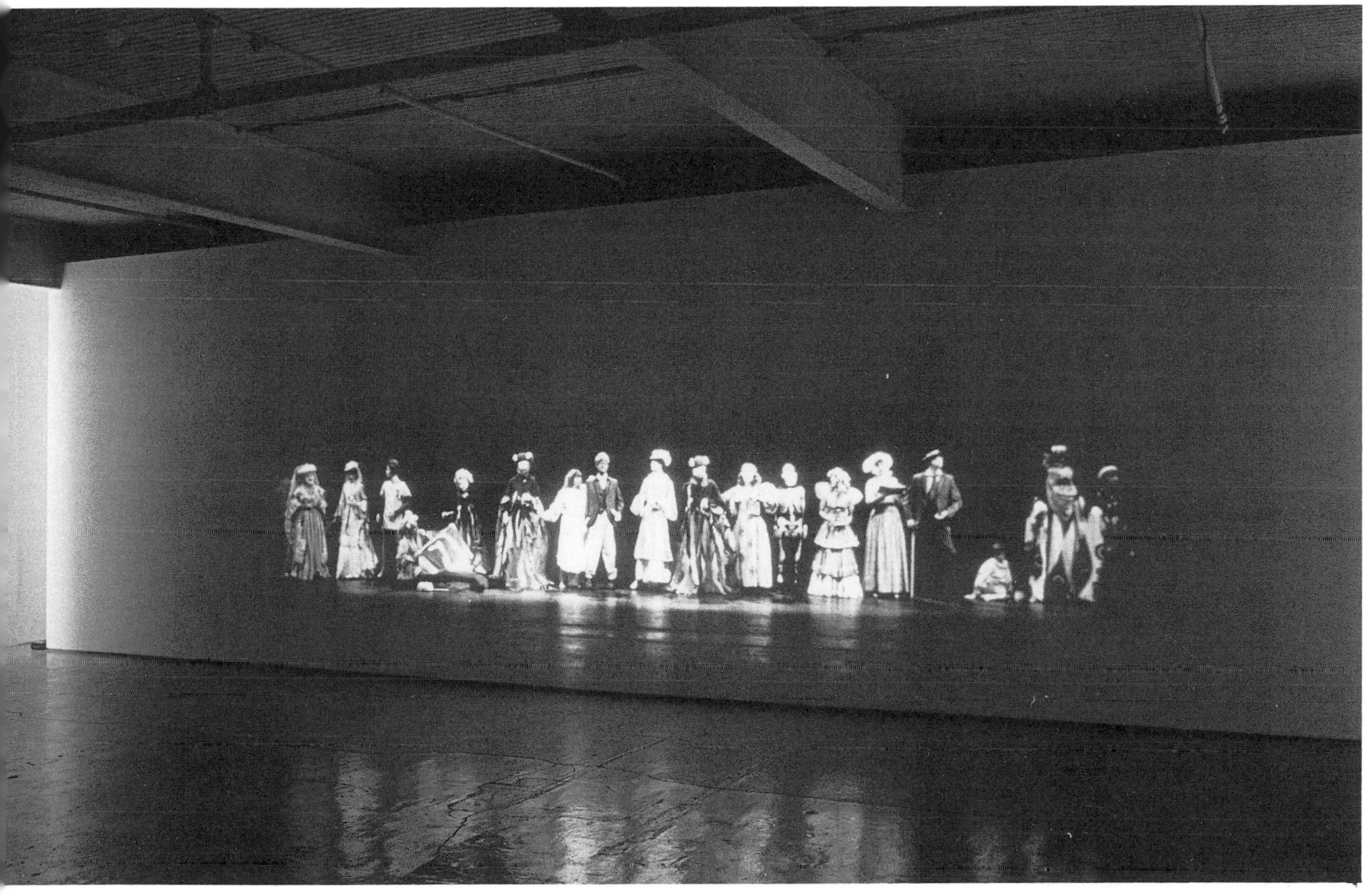

James Coleman: *Living and Presumed Dead*, tape/slide installation, Toronto, 1986

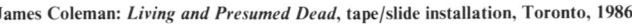

tation in his work which has taken a variety of forms since the early 1970s including slide projection, tape-slide, film, video, installation, and performance using actors. By constructing the work as an enigma, by fragmenting the narrative and making the relation of images to text not an obvious or illustrative one, Coleman draws attention to the way in which the viewer or audience is drawn into the work by the interpretative act. The way in which images and text intersect to constitute the position of the interpreter becomes a subject of the work. Through the process of interpretation the subject—the interpreter—is constituted within Language.

Coleman builds into his works allusions to different codes. The slide projection *Connemara Landscape* (1980) deconstructs the implications of romantic depictions of the Irish landscape by simultaneously providing clues for and frustrating interpretation. The video work *So Different . . . and Yet* (1980) could be interpreted according to the discourse of psychoanalytic theory: this would focus on the fetishistic pose of the woman, and the fetishism of the green dress and woman as an object of desire in the fragmented romantic-fiction narrative. For those familiar with the code of Irish national and literary history the green dress and the proper names of the characters take on additional symbolic functions. Yet another interpretation, this time according to the code of mythology, is hinted at by the horns on the head of the pianist in the video image—a possible reference to Cernunnos, the horned god of pre-Christian Irish myth—as well as the structural relationships within the narrative. Yet while the act of interpretation is continually provoked it is never allowed to be conclusive, to terminate in a "transcendental signified." The fragmentation of the linear chain of the narrative—where one thing would otherwise lead smoothly to another—opens the space for the "vertical" metaphorical substitutions of interpretation. Yet, like the needle of a record player which jumps to another track, these possible interpretations don't lead outside Language to the signified as thing-in-itself, whether artist's intention, viewer's experience, or enclosing context. One signifier only leads to another, and yet another. The title invites completion: "So Different, and yet—the same." But this "same" is suspended as absence, as an identity that cannot be provided, as the void or lack which instigates the desire which motivates the play of signifiers.

One of the features which contributes to the extraordinary richness of Coleman's work is that it involves a modern reworking of age-old themes. While he employs contemporary media and techniques of handling text and images, Coleman draws on such central texts of the Western tradition as Sophocles' *Oedipus the King* and the Irish epic the *Táin Bó Cuailnge.* Not only do his works thematize interpretation, they are also reinterpretations of tradition—interpretations in terms of the interpretative act itself. In this sense they are reflexive—analytical—allegories of the theatrical scent of interpretation with the interpreter—the viewer or member of the audience—as protagonist, both victim and murderer.

To see identity as something which is constituted in a process and involved with interpretation is to prise it away from what is often taken to be its natural relation to the fully rounded character. Coleman uses theatricality to deconstruct the identification of the actor with character as if he or she were a real person. Rather the figures in the narrative of *So Different . . . and Yet* and in the tableaux of *Living and Presumed Dead* (1983-85) serve as what V. Propp in *The Morphology of the Folktale* called "functions" in a narrative structure. Just as the figures in a dream are not real characters but elements in a structure which expresses, in a distorted form, a repressed unconscious wish, so the functions in *So Different . . . and Yet* and *Living and Presumed Dead* only become interpretable (in a way that is always problematic and reflexive) in terms of their interrelationship and, in this process of allegorical reading, construct a position for the interpreter.

In *Living and Presumed Dead* the narrative of identity is also a story of a secret discovered, of a search

for the father or the hero, of murder and of revenge. The murderer turns out to be an obscure figure without face who is unnamed in the action and listed only as "Mr." This designation functions linguistically as a shifter, like "I" or "you," a syntactical position filled by whoever performs the utterance or is designated by it. This is the point where the act of enunciation encounters the symbolic order, where the living speaker assumes a position within language, in a sense "dying" into representation. It could be said that the interpreter is both the murderer and the victim of the interpretation, in that he or she both constructs a symbolic order and takes a position within it, freezing being—the living flow of desire—into meaning.

—Michael Newman
(from *The Analytical Theatre,*
Independent Curators Inc., 1987)

COLLINS, James.

British. Born in Northampton, England, 1939; emigrated to United States, 1970. Studied at St. Martins School of Art, London, 1959-63; Hornsey School of Art, London, 1963-64. Independent artist: lives and works in both New York and London. Taught at London College of Printing, High Wycombe and Epsom Schools of Art, England, 1964-69; taught at New York University, 1970-75; taught at Hartford University, Connecticut, 1976-77. Recipient: Prix de Rome Scholarship (Painting), 1964; National Endowment for the Arts Fellowship, 1977. Address c/o Max Protetch Gallery, 37 West 57th Street, New York, New York 10019, U.S.A.

Individual Exhibitions:

1975	Galleria Françoise Lambert, Milan
	Galerie Gaetan, Geneva
	John Gibson Gallery, New York
	Patrick Verelst Gallery, Antwerp
1976	Galleria Il Capricorno, Venice
	York University Gallery, Toronto
	Galleria Renzo Spagnoli, Florence
	Galerie Folker Skulima, Berlin
	Galleria Piergiorgio Firinu, Turin
	Galleria Pasquale Trisorio, Naples
	Galerie Ingrid Oppenheim, Cologne
1977	Palomar College, San Marcos, California
	Galerie Isy Brachot, Brussels
	Galleria Pasquale Trisorio, Naples
	Galerie Tanit, Munich
	Akron University, Ohio
	Galerie Krinzinger, Innsbruck, Austria
	Galeria Stampa, Basel
	Western Front Gallery, Vancouver
	Galleria Cicconi, Macerata, Italy
	Galleria Ginevra Grigolo, Bologna
	A Space Gallery, Toronto
	Galleria Arte Verso, Turin
	University of California at Santa Barbara
1978	Arnolfini Gallery, Bristol
	Institute of Contemporary Arts, London
	University of Wisconsin, Menomonie
	Emily Carr College, Vancouver
1979	Washington Project for the Arts, Washington, D.C.
	University of South Florida, Tampa
	University of Iowa, Iowa City
	Max Protetch Gallery, New York
	Galleria Paolo Tonin, Truin
	Glen Hanson Gallery, Minneapolis
	University of Florida, Miami
	Galleria Arte Borgogna, Milan
1980	Pallazzo dei Diamanti, Ferrara, Italy
	Galerie Linssen, Bonn
	Galleria Arte Borgogna, Milan
	Galleria Pasquale Trisorio, Naples
	L'Incontro Galleria d'Arte, Imola, Italy
1981	Hans Redman Gallery, Berlin
	'123' Gallery, Antwerp
	Galleria Anna D'Ascanio, Rome
	Mississippi Museum of Art, Jackson
1982	Anne van Horenbeeck Gallery, Brussels
	Galleria Paolo Tonin, Turin
	Galleria Pasquale Trisorio, Naples

Selected Group Exhibitions:

1976	*Foto & Idea,* Comune di Parma, Italy
1977	*Documenta 6,* Kassel, West Germany
	Contemporary Figuration, Ohio State University, Columbus
1979	*AA on Paper,* University of North Carolina, Greensboro
	Concept, Narrative, Document, Museum of Contemporary Art, Chicago
1980	*Presences The Figure and Man-Made Environments,* Albright College, Reading, Pennsylvania
	Refigurations, Max Protetch Gallery, New York
1981	*Genius Loci,* Ferrara, Italy
1982	*Façons de Peindre,* Chalon-sur-Saône, France

Publications:

By COLLINS: book—*Narrative Art,* exhibition catalogue, Brussels, 1974; articles—"Things and Theories" in *Artforum* (New York), May 1973; "Pointing, Hybrids and Romanticism: John Baldessari" in *Artforum* (New York), October 1973; "Remarks on Romanticism" in *Flash Art* (Milan), June 1975; "The Importance of Not Being Earnest About Photography" in *Skira 76,* Geneva 1976; "The Rise of Europe" in *Flash Art* (Milan), October 1981.

On COLLINS: books—*6 years* by Lucy Lippard, New York 1973; *Europa/America* by Achille Bonita Oliva, Milan 1979; *James Collins,* edited by Giancarlo Politi and Helena Kontová, with an essay by Sarah Kent, Milan 1978; articles—"The Semantics of Concept Art" by Gopnik in *Artscanada* (Toronto), April 1970; review by David Bourdon in the *Village Voice* (New York), September 1975; review by Romano Giachetti in *L'Express* (Paris), October 1975; "The Boulevard of Soho Dreams" by Mona Da Vinci in the *Soho Weekly News* (New York), 18 September 1975; review by Walter Robinson in *Art in America* (New York), December 1975; "The Erotic and the Didactic" by Robert Pincus-Witten in *Art. Magazine* (New York), January 1976; "James Collins Voyeuredonista" by Angelo Calabrese in *Documentioggi* (Naples), March 1976; "Photography: A Specific Communication for Artistic Research" by Ilaria Bignamini in *Flash Art* (Milan), June 1976; "New Movements in Conceptual Art" by Margaret Sheffield in *Studio International* (London), November/December 1976; "James Collins" by Werner Lippert in *Kunstforum* (Mainz), June 1976; "James Collins Double Portraits" by Margaret Sheffield in *Artforum* (New York), April 1977; review by A. A. Bronson in *Artscanada* (Toronto), May 1977; review by Anne-Sargent Wooster in the *New York Arts Journal,* no. 15, 1979; review by John Russell in the *New York Times,* July 1979.

My 1973 essay, "Things and Theories" was really a corrective attack against the extremes of conceptual art and a defense of then beleagured "painting," and I say painting in inverted commas because at that time I was interested in the idea of promoting a very open kind of situation, and I've always looked at my photographs as just one kind of painting, but I must say recently I'm interested in painting in perhaps more traditional terms—some kind of mark.

When I started photographs in late 1968, it was an avant-garde activity—at least as a kind of painting. The history of people using photographs in fine arts was short, and photographs seemed a new area not explored. I didn't know the history of photography, and it was an interesting new way of working. Now the whole art world is full of people using photographs, and it no longer has those avant-garde ramifications. This is one complaint. My other complaint is the limited visual things you can do with photographs; it's a kind of "a priori" activity. You set the situation up, you photograph it, you can manipulate the photograph afterwards to some extent, but you can't manipulate it the same way you can manipulate

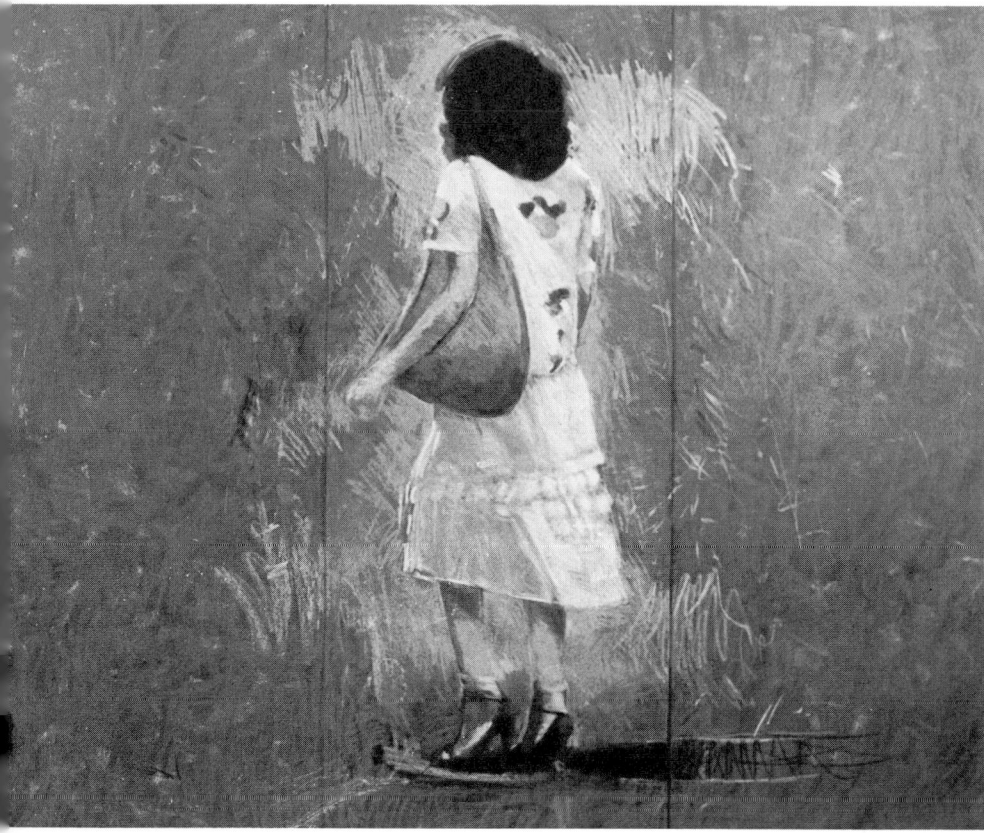

James Collins: *And There She Goes Just Walking Down the Street*, 1981

a drawing or an image. What I like about drawing particularly, for example, is that it's a kind of fiction where you can bring together very disparate elements, whereas in a photograph you have to actually get hold of the elements and then photograph them. It's a different kind of activity.

I started off as a painter, and I still consider myself a painter. And what's interesting about painting is its limitations: all you have is a surface and marks to move people with. That's it! What puts me off about so many other art areas is the apparatus. Never could I image myself being a film-maker just because of the Mickey Mouse organization stuff. You have to orchestrate the lives of 50 people for 6 months, raise money, etc., etc. Activities interesting perhaps sociologically—but they are not my main interests. I'm an image maker: my passion is making images to move people. Photography was merely a way to make those images quickly. Now I'm finding that photographs do move people, but they move them within certain limitations.

You run into big problems any time you make marks on canvas, however you make those marks. I'm interested in trying to find visual equivalent to the speed of photography—images almost like handwriting, having some reference to the world, having the speed of handwriting, but getting information across quickly. I wouldn't mind mixing the sensuousness of Morris Louis with the subjects of Richard Pryor.

—James Collins

James Collins's work is comprehensively characterized by the intermixed use of the media, from abstract and figurative painting to conceptual photography. Even if the changes of media are often caused by external events and by artistic fashions, there is a persisting continuity around which his work is built. He has in fact been concentrating for the past ten years on a single theme, "Watching Women," a sort of intellectual voyeurism which is presented in a number of variations: on the beach, on the grass, in bed or in the artist's studio, but always as observer. The only one who can observe the girl is in fact someone at the front, in front of the picture.

Voyeurism, which the artist says has been a lifetime obsession, has since 1973 become his basic poetry.

As early as 1969-1971 his "Introduction Pieces" were based on his introducing himself to unknown people whom he had met casually. All that was necessary was to change the situation from one of sexual indifference to one of eroticism to bring about the different result. His photography, which looked at first like something from the newspapers or the police records, turned into a photography directly executed by the artist, becoming much more evocative and esthetic.

Later works left simple photo-documentation even further behind and moved towards formal solutions, such as the segmentation of the panels, symmetry between objects and persons (i.e. the woman and the artist), the use of a monochromatic background, and painting. The situations photographed became increasingly artificial and composed until they formed a meticulous design.

The pastels of girls or of voyeuristic situations done in the last years are mostly based on photographic portraits collected from time to time during a journey, in the street or in an art gallery. Certain details in the figure, standing out against the monochrome field, are highly focused so as to emphasize the eroticism of the model. The extremely elegant and controlled painting, like that of Balthus or Klossowski, whom Collins greatly admires, with its startling contrasts of light and colour, succeeds in maintaining the tension of an aloof eroticism.

—Helena Kontova

COLOMBO, Gianni.

Italian. Born in Milan, 1 January 1937. Self-educated in art. Began artwork using various materials, 1954; produced first monochrome reliefs, 1958; first changeable objects, 1959. Co-Founder, with Giovanni Anceschi, Davide Boriani and others, Gruppo T, 1959. Organized Nouvelle Tendance, 1963. Lecturer, Faculty of Architecture, University of Berlin, 1982. Recipient: Gold Medal for Industrial design, *13th Triennale*, Milan, 1964; Gold Medal, *14th Covegno Internazionale Artisti*, Rimini, 1964; 1st Prize, *34th Biennale*, Venice, 1968; Giolli Prize, 1980; First Prize, *Kunst am Bau* competition, West Berlin, 1981. Address: Via Giacosa 52, 20127 Milan, Italy.

Individual Exhibitions:

1960	Galleria Pater, Milan
1965	Galleria Vismara, Milan
	Galleria La Salita, Rome
1966	Galerie Loehr, Frankfurt
1967	Galleria del Deposito, Genoa
	Galleria Flaviana, Locarno, Switzerland
1968	Galleria Schwarz, Milan
	Galleria L'Attico, Rome
	Galleria Guida, Naples
	Biennale, Venice
	Galerie Tony Gerber, Berne
	Studio di Informazione Estetica, Turin
1969	Galleria del Leone, Venice
1970	Studio Marconi, Milan
	Kunstlersiedlung Halfmannshof, Gelsenkirchen, West Germany
	Galerie Suzanne Bollag, Zurich
	Galleria La Città, Verona
1971	Galerija Suvermeni Umjetnosti, Zagreb
	Galleria La Polen, Genoa
	Neue Galerie am Landesmuseum, Graz, Austria
	Plus-Kern, Ghent (with Morellet and Stein)
1972	Galerie Thomas Keller, Munich
	Palazzo dei Diamanti, Ferrara, Italy
	Galerie M., Bochum, West Germany
	Galerie Suzanne Bollag, Zurich
1973	Sineron, Brescia, Italy
	Studio Marconi, Milan
	Studio Casati, Merate, Italy
1974	Galerie Swart, Amsterdam
	Galerie Lydia Megert, Berne
	Centro Serre Ratti, Como, Italy
1975	Studio V., Vigevano, Italy
	Galleria Giuli, Lecco, Italy
	Galerie Media, Neuchâtel, Switzerland
	Galleria Uxa, Novara, Italy
	Studio Marconi, Milan
	Galerie Muller-Roth, Stuttgart
	Städtisches Museum, Leverkusen, West Germany
1976	Kunsthalle, Baden-Baden, West Germany
	Kunsthalle, Kiel, West Germany
	Galleria G7, Bologna
	Galleria A, Parma, Italy
1977	Studio Marconi, Milan
	Galleria Solferino, Milan
1978	Arte Struktura, Milan
	Galleria 2000, Bologna
	Centro Culturale, Fara d'Adda, Italy
1981	Van Abbemuseum, Eindhoven, Netherlands
	Studio Grosetti, Milan
	Centro Serre Ratti, Como, Italy
1982	Nuovo Spazio Metropolitano, Milan
	Raad Galerie, West Berlin
1983	Galleria Civica d'Arte Contemporanea, Suzzara, Italy
1984	Padiglione d'Arte Contemporanea, Milan
	Italian Pavilion, *XLI Biennale*, Venice
1985	Galleria Pero, Milan
	Galerie Hoffman, Friedberg, West Germany
	Galerie Scholler, Dusseldorf

Selected Group Exhibitions:

1960	*Contemporary Italian Art*, Institute of Design, Chicago
1965	*Licht und Bewegung*, Kunsthalle, Berne (toured Europe)
1966	*Kunst-Licht-Kunst*, Stedelijk van Abbemuseum, Eindhoven, Netherlands
1970	*Kinetic Art*, Hayward Gallery, London
1974	*Fotomedia*, Museum am Ostwall, Dortmund, West Germany

1976	*Biennale*, Sydney
1978	*Metafisica del Quotidiano*, Galleria d'Arte Moderna, Bologna
1980	*Pier and Ocean*, Hayward Gallery, London (travelled to the Rijksmuseum Kröller-Müller, Otterlo, Netherlands)
1983	*Electra*, Musée d'Art Moderne de la Ville, Paris
1987	*Mathematik in der Kunst*, Wilhelm-Hack-Museum, Ludwigshafen, West Germany

Collections:

Galleria Nazionale d'Arte Moderna, Rome; Museo Sperimentale, Turin; Museum des 20, Jahrhunderts, Vienna; Städtisches Museum, Bochum, West Germany; Museum of Modern Art, New York; Columbia University, New York.

Publications:

By COLOMBO: books—*Miriorama 1*, Milan 1960; *After Structures*, exhibitions catalogue, Genoa 1967; *Lo Spazio dell'Immagine*, Foligno, Italy 1967; articles—"Im Elastichen Raum" in *Trigon*, exhibition catalogue, Graz 1967; "Spazioelastico-Ambiente" in *Studio V* (Vigevano, Italy), 1975; films—*Vobulazione e Bieloquenza Neg*, with Vicento Agnetti, Milan 1970; *Arte programmata*, Milan 1972.

On COLOMBO: books—*Nature and Art of Motion* by Gyorgy Kepes, New York 1965; *Gianni Colombo* by Gillo Dorfles, Rome 1965; *Rapporto 60* by Maurizio Fagiolio dell'Arco, Rome 1966; *L'Art Cinetic* by Frank Popper, Paris 1967; *Constructivism: Origins and Evolution* by George Rickey, New York 1967; *Gianni Colombo*, exhibition catalogue, by Guido Balla, Venice, 1968; *Gianni Colombo*, exhibition catalogue, by Rolf Wedewer, Gelsenkirchen, West Germany 1970; *Gianni Colombo*, exhibition catalogue, by Guilio Carlo Argan, Ferrara, Italy 1972; *Gianni Colombo*, exhibition catalogue, by Antije von Graevenitz, Eindhoven, Netherlands 1981; *Gianni Colombo*, exhibition catalogue, by Marco Meneguzzo, Suzzara, Italy 1983; *Gianni Colombo*, exhibition catalogue, by Jean Louis Scheffer, Milan 1984.

To construct is that particular dimension of a work (not only the work of art) that implies a coming into contact with the manifold inventory of materials. It is work carried out through a 'culture of materials' which technology continuously develops through time. It is the universe of technologies that consigns to us not only materials but also the ways to put them together in order to concretise 'the construction'.

Once we understand art as something to do with construction, materials, and technology as the 'working supervisor', does the presentation of such materials represent a 'technological universe'?

As far as the relationship with the technological is concerned, in may case it it is just a question of multiplying the usage of different techniques toward concentrating on the opposite ends of technology—i.e., the impact it has on man's behaviour. My art means placing the notion of behaviour within the operation of environmental planning, where 'environment' is understood as he visualization of the specific condition of planning itself.

—Gianni Colombo

Gianno Colombo's earliest works (1954) were non-figurative, 'multimaterial' (sort of collage) pieces. From these he went on to make monochrome pieces, reliefs composed of rectangles arranged vertically in rows. By 1959 these had become mobile. They were either moveable by the spectator or on their own account. In either case they moved rhythmically, the rectangular elements coming out and going in: *In and Out* or *Pulsating Structures*. This was the beginning of his interest in kinetic art. In that year he became a founder member of Gruppo T and four years later the group joined the Nouvelle Tendence.

The next year, 1960, he began to make 'Fluid Structures'. These consisted of moving, transparent plastic tapes that writhed within an enclosed space. In 1964, like many of the Nouvelle Tendence, he turned to optical-kinetic and environmental art. This began

with his 'Roto-optic' work which produced strange moving luminous forms, like X-rays of organs pulsating with life. Pulsation and rhythmic, organic movement means much to him and he finds various ways of displaying it.

But his most adventures light structures were his 'Elastic Spaces', begun in the mid-1960s. These consisted of cubes of elastic florescent cords, subdivided into regular sections and lit by ultra-violet light. The cords either distort themselves rhythmically or are distorted by the spectator walking through them.

In the 1970s Colombo turned from kinetic and light works to lopsided structures of various kinds, mostly interiors. These seem to have been inspired by a house built by Buster Keaton in the film *A Week* (1920). Everything about the house—roofs, windows the door—is askew, but it holds together; and Keaton stands back, saw in hand, looking at it admiringly. Colombo sometimes uses pillars arranged at odd angles and looking like the ruins of an ancient city that had been struck by earthquake. At other times he constructs interiors rather on the lines of the rooms constructed by the psychologist, Ames (*Ames room*) to illustrate illusions of space. The floor is tilted, possibly the ceiling also, in consequence the walls are inevitably out of kilter. He calls these works 'Topestesia' or 'Architettura Cacogonimetrica', which loosely translates as fruitfully bad architecture, but the words themselves are lopsided and strictly meaningless.

These are among the most original works to come from Colombo's fertile imagination. The source of inspiration he acknowledges, but he alone exploited it. Hitherto he had tended to swim with the tide that flowed: kinetic-optical-light art. But in these later works he has struck out on his own. Not that he was not original when swimming with the tide. He invariably was. Three things seem to obsess him: a striving for purity and clarity of expression, characteristic of the Nouvelle Tendence; a feeling for and love of the fluctuations and pulsations and the rhythms of living forms; and the oddness of our perception of the world around us.

—D. C. Barrett

COLVILLE, Alex.
Canadian. Born David Alexander Colville in Toronto, Ontario, 24 August 1920. Studied, under Stanley Royle, at Mount Allison University, Sackville, New Brunswick, 1938–42, B.F.A. 1942. Served in Canadian Infantry, 1942–46: Lieutenant, then Captain; War Artist, 1944–46. Married Rhoda Wright in 1942; children: Graham, John, Charles, and Ann. Independent painter, Nova Scotia, since 1963. Commissioned to Design Canadian Centennial Coinage, 1967. Assistant to Associate Professor, Mount Allison University, 1946–63. Visiting Artist, University of California at Santa Cruz, 1967–68; Künstler Program, West Berlin, 1971. Member, Canada Council, 1966–72. Recipient: Dunn International Award, 1963; Canada Council Award, 1975. Honorary degrees: Trent University, Peterborough, Ontario; Dalhousie University, Halifax, Nova Scotia; Simon Fraser University, Burnaby, British Columbia; University of Windsor, Ontario; Acadia University, Wolfville, Nova Scotia; Officer, 1967, and Companion, 1982, Order of Canada. Agents: Mira Godard Gallery, 22 Hazelton Avenue, Toronto, Ontario M5R 2E2; Galerie Claude Bernard, 9 Rue des Beaux-Arts, 75006 Paris, France. Address: Box 550, Wolfville, Nova Scotia, Canada.

Individual Exhibitions:

1951	New Brunswick Museum, St. John
1953	Hewitt Gallery, New York
1955	Hewitt Gallery, New York
1963	Banfer Gallery, New York

1966	Hart House, University of Toronto
1969	Kestner Gesellschaft, Hannover
1970	Marlborough Fine Art Gallery, London
1971	*Serigraphs*, University of Moncton, New Brunswick (toured Canada, 1971–73)
1976	Fischer Fine Art, London
	Norman Mackenzie Art Gallery, Regina, Saskatchewan
	Lynnwood Arts Center, Simcoe, Ontario
1977	*Bilder und Zeichnungen 1970–1977*, Kunsthalle Dusseldorf (travelled to Fischer Fine Art, London)
1978	Mira Godard Gallery, Toronto
1983	Art Gallery of Ontario, Toronto
	Staatliche Kunsthalle, West Berlin
	Museum Ludwig, Cologne
1984	Museum of Fine Arts, Montreal
	Dalhousie Art Gallery, Halifax, Nova Scotia
	Vancouver Art Gallery, British Columbia
	Exhibition Hall, Beijing, China
1985	University of Hong Kong
	Teien Art Museum, Tokyo
	Canada House, London

Selected Group Exhibitions:

1964	*Canadian Painting*, Tate Gallery, London
1967	*Statements: 18 Canadian Artists*, Norman Mackenzie Art Gallery, Regina, Saskatchewan
1973	*Kunst nach Wirklichkeit*, Kunstverein, Hannover (toured Europe)
	Ekstrem Realisme, Louisiana Museum, Humleback Denmark
1974	*Hyperréalists Américains/Réalistes Européens*, Centre National d'Art Contemporain, Paris (toured Europe)
1975	*Realismus und Realität*, Kunsthalle, Darmstadt
	Der Einzelne und die Masse, Städtische Kunsthalle Recklinghausen, West Germany
1976	*Aspects of Realism*, Rothman's of Pall Mall travelling exhibition, Stratford Art Gallery, Ontario (toured Canada, 1976–78)

Collections:

National Gallery of Canada, Ottawa; Art Gallery of Hamilton, Ontario; Art Gallery of London, Ontario; Montreal Museum of Fine Arts; New Brunswick Museum, St. John; Beaverbrook Museum, Fredericton, New Brunswick; Museum of Modern Art, New York; Kestner Gesellschaft, Hannover; Museum Boymans-van Beuningen, Rotterdam; Centre National d'Art Contemporain, Paris.

Publications:

On COLVILLE: books—*Statements: 18 Canadian Artists*, exhibition catalogue, Regina Saskatchewan 1967; *Neue Formen des Bildes* by Udo Kultermann, Tübingen, 1969; *The Art of Alex Colville* by Helen J. Dow, Toronto 1972; *Neue Formen des Realismus* by Peter Sager, Cologne 1973; *Der Neue Realismus in Amerika* by Linda Chase, Berlin 1973; *High Realism in Canada* by Paul Duval, Toronto 1974; *Hyperréalistes Américains/Réalistes Européens*, exhibition catalogue, Paris 1974; *Colville* by David Burnett, Toronto 1983; articles—"Realism, Surrealism and Celebration: The Paintings of Alex Colville in the National Gallery of Canada" by Patrick Hutchings in *National Gallery of Canada Bulletin* (Ottawa), vol. 4, no. 2, 1966; "For Real" by Robert Melville in *New Statesman* (London), January 1970; "Alex Colville" by Peter Kipphoff in *Die Zeit* (Hamburg), October 1970; "Alex Colville as Image Maker" by Helen J. Dow in *The British Journal of Aesthetics* (London), Summer 1972; "Alex Colville: La Perfection dans le Realisme" by Virgil G. Hammock in *Vie des Arts* (Montreal), Autumn 1976; "Modes of Representational Art" by Micheal Greenwood in *Artscanada* (Toronto), December 1976/January 1977.

Born in Toronto and brought up in the salty atmosphere of the Maritimes, Alex Colville studied at the Mount Allison University School of Fine Art until 1942, when he joined the Canadian Army. He served in Europe as a war artist, painting and drawing scenes

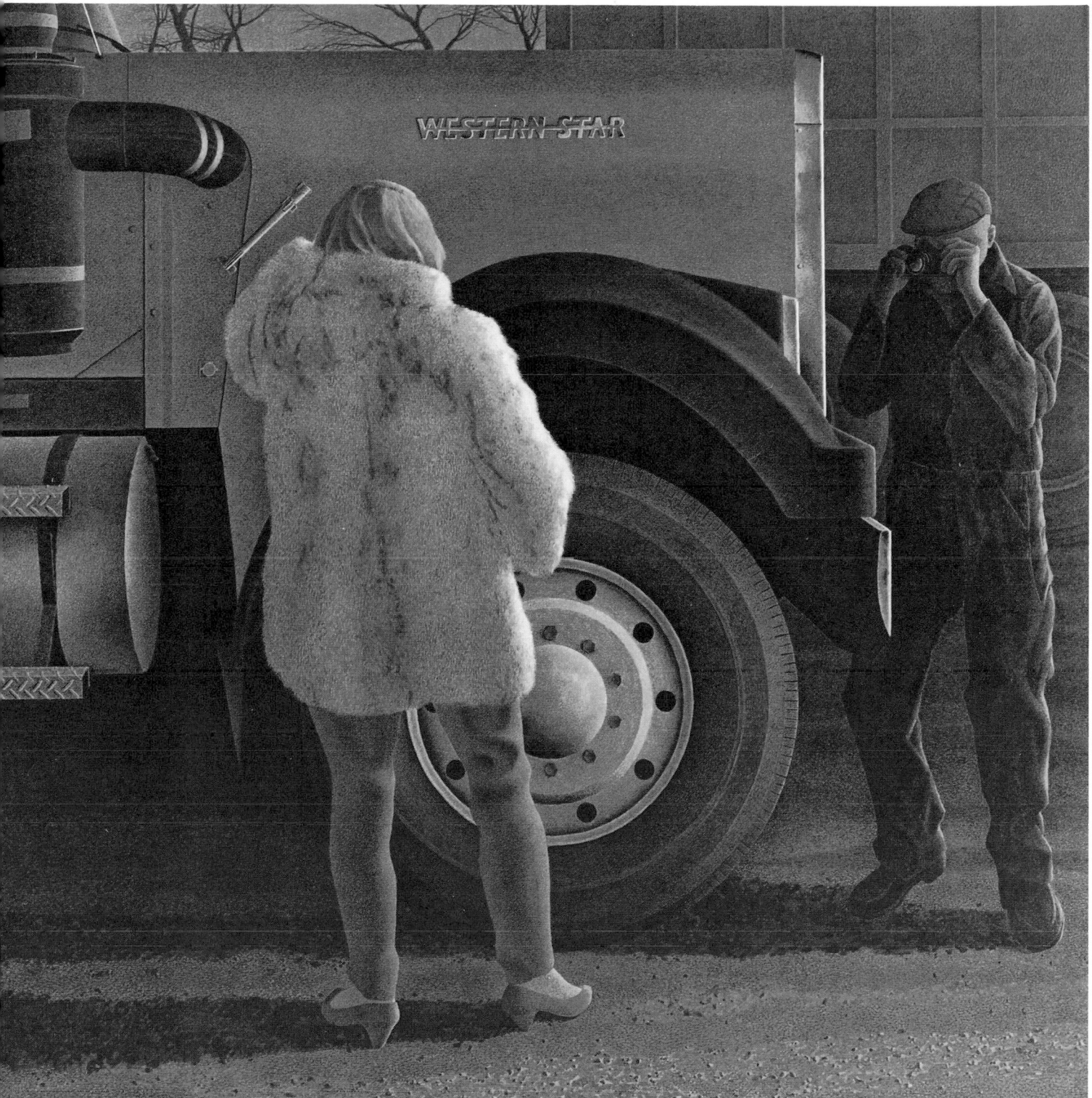

Alex Colville: *Western Star*, 1985

and action in Belgium, Holland and Germany. On de-mobilization, Colville returned to Mount Allison as professor of painting, though now he paints only pro-fessionally.

Colville is a realist painter who aims at epitomising Jung's definition by attempting a synthesis of total ex-perience. Details from life are observed and noted; then they are articulated within a setting composed for the purpose of making evident a sensation of fact.

"Magic Realism" is the term that covers Colville's approach, but though it verges on a noncommital lack of emphasis common to Photo-Realism, its precise definition and lighting, together with the purposeful focus on individuals and objects, create an irresistible atmosphere of significance. The square of canvas re-veals a segment of actuality, often of the most com-mon place aspect, and it paradoxically endows this

chosen viewpoint with a signal intensity. Unlike Im-pressionism, his intention is not to capture light in the division of the spectrum. Colville imposes a univer-sality of tone across the whole field of vision.

Often there is an implied aura of loneliness akin to some of Andrew Wyeth's works such as "Christina's World." "Hound in a Field" of 1958 shows Colville's grasp of drama in the selection of an incident or a moment of time, freezing it within the framework of the canvas. Sometimes the realism is as airless as a still life *trompe l'oeil,* but the scale again distorts its presence.

The freezing may take place on a large oil-on-masonite, such as "Elm Tree at Horton Landing" of 1965, representing its own environmental tragedy. This once handsome tree standing alone is now flawed and damaged, some of its branches stricken

and bleached. It nonetheless retains some original dignity in its upright stance. Viewed from ground level, it becomes more than a tree preserved for its lost beauty. It has the pathetic note of a graceful crea-tion singled out for accidental violation; whether by vandalism or act of God is unknown. The effect, how-ever, is endowed with Colville's unique paint touch, immaculate in strength and balance of tone.

Often the import is meteorological. The cold steril-ity of a winter day clarifies a landscape of snow in one even tone of whiteness, shadowed and pocked by changes of contour. The sky is a level blue, and the chill almost strikes our bones. In the human figures, the blood seems frozen too, as they stand immersed in suspended action. One aspect runs through Col-ville's painting; it is the stillness of the final scene. No words pass between his people, mute in the trivial commonplaces of the day, silent evidence of the unremarkable, miraculously immobilized in clinical antiseptic objectivity.

—G. S. Whittet

CONNER, Bruce.

American. Born in McPherson, Kansas, 18 November 1933. Educated at Kansas City Art Institute, Missouri, and Wichita State University, Kansas, 1951–52; University of Nebraska, Lincoln, 1952–56, B.F.A. 1956; Brooklyn Museum, with Reuben Tam, 1956–57; University of Colorado, Boulder, 1957. Married Jean Connor in 1957; son: Robert. Independent painter and filmmaker, since 1957. Taught 8mm film-making, California College of Arts and Crafts, Oakland, 1965; life drawing, 1966–67, and painting and sculpture, 1972, at the San Francisco Art Institute; taught "The Art of Assemblage" at UCLA Extension, 1973; beginning and advanced painting, San Jose State University, California, 1974; film-making, San Francisco State University, 1976. Recipient: Ann Bremer Award, San Francisco Art Association, 1958; Second Prize, Church Art Today, San Francisco Episcopal Diocese, 1960; First Prize, Art Competition of the National Council of Churches, 1960; Neallie Sullivan Award, San Francisco Art Association, 1963; Ford Foundation Fellowship, 1964; Tamarind Lithography Workshop Fellowship Grant, 1965; Copley Foundation Award 1965; Gold Medal, *Sesta Biennale D'Arte*, San Marino 1967; National Endowment for the Arts Grant 1973; American Film Institute Grant, 1974; Francis Scott Key Award, 1975; Guggenheim Fellowship, 1975; Citation in Film, Brandeis University Creative Awards, Waltham, Massachusetts, 1979. Agents: Fraenkel Gallery, 55 Grant Avenue, San Francisco, California 94108; and Smith-Andersen Gallery, 200 Homer Street, Palo Alto, California 94301. Address: 45 Sussex Street, San Francisco, California 94131, U.S.A.

Individual Exhibitions:

1956	Rienzi Gallery, New York
1958	East West Gallery, San Francisco
	Designers Gallery, San Francisco
1959	Spatsa Gallery, San Francisco
1960	Alan Gallery, New York
	Batman Gallery, San Francisco
1961	Alan Gallery, New York
1962	Batman Gallery, San Francisco
	Glantz Gallery, Mexico City
	Antonio Souza Gallery, Mexico City
1963	Neallie Sullivan Award Show, San Francisco
	Wichita Art Museum, Kansas
	Alan Gallery, New York
	Swetzoff Gallery, Boston
1964	Batman Gallery, San Francisco
	Alan Gallery, New York
	George Lester Galleria, Rome
	Robert Fraser Gallery, London

1965	University of British Columbia Art Gallery, Vancouver
	Rose Art Museum, Brandeis University, Waltham, Massachusetts
	Galerie "J", Paris
	Alan Gallery, New York
1966	Quay Gallery, San Francisco
1967	Institute of Contemporary Art, Philadelphia
	San Francisco Art Institute
1971	San Francisco Art Institute
	Molly Barnes Gallery, Los Angeles
	Reese Palley Gallery, San Francisco
1972	Reese Palley Gallery, San Francisco
	Martha Jackson Gallery, New York
	Willis Gallery, San Francisco
	Texas Gallery, Houston
	Nicholas Wilder Gallery, Los Angeles
1973	Texas Gallery, Houston
1974	Quay Gallery, San Francisco
	Tyler Art Museum, Texas
	Gallerie Smith-Anderson, Palo Alto, California
	DeYoung Museum, San Francisco (retrospective toured United States)
1980	North Point Gallery, San Francisco
1984	Smith-Andersen Gallery, Palo Alto, California
1986	Smith-Andersen Gallery, Palo Alto, California

Selected Group Exhibitions:

1967	*Funk Art*, University of California Art Museum, Berkeley
	Sculpture of the 60's, Los Angeles County Museum of Art

Bruce Conner: *Ink Blot*, 1975

1969 *Human Concern/Human Torment*, Whitney Museum, New York

1972 *Family Show of Work by Robert, Jean and Bruce Conner*, Quay Gallery, San Francisco

1973 *Family Show of Work by Robert, Jean and Bruce Conner*, Jacqueline Anhalt Gallery, Los Angeles

1975 *Poets of the Cities*, Museum of Fine Arts, Dallas (travelled to San Francisco Museum of Modern Art, and the Wadsworth Atheneum, Hartford, Connecticut)

1976 *The Modern Era: California Painting and Sculpture*, San Francisco Museum of Modern Art (travelled to National Collection of Fine Art, Washington, D.C.)

1979 *Biennial Exhibition*, Whitney Museum, New York

1981 *Remember It's Only Art*, Civic Arts Gallery, Walnut Creek, California

1986 *Seven Artists in Depth: The Creative Process*, San Francisco Museum of Modern Art

Collections:

Museum of Modern Art, New York; Whitney Museum, New York; Los Angeles County Museum of Art; San Francisco Museum of Modern Art; Oakland Art Museum, California; University Art Museum, University of California, Berkeley; Norton Simon Museum of Art, Pasadena, California; Rockhill Nelson Gallery, Kansas City, Missouri; Art Institute of Chicago; Centre Georges Pompidou, Paris.

Publications:

By CONNER: articles—"Bruce Conner Makes a Sandwich" in *Artforum* (New York), September 1967, "Bruce Conner: A Discussion at the 1968 Flaherty Film Seminar" in *Film Comment* (New York), No. 4, 1969; films—*A Movie*, 1958; *Cosmic Ray*, 1961; *Looking for Mushrooms*, 1961-67; *Report*, 1963-67; *Vivian*, 1964; *Breakaway*, 1966; *White Rose*, 1967; *Permian Strata*, 1969; *5 X Marilyn*, 1973; *Crossroads*, 1976; *5:10 to Dreamland*, 1976; *Valse Triste*, 1977; *Mongoloid*, 1978; *America Is Waiting*, 1981.

On CONNER: books—*Bruce Conner*, exhibition catalogue, New York 1960; *Bruce Conner*, exhibition catalogue, New York 1965; *Bruce Conner*, exhibition catalogue, with text by Thomas Garver, Waltham, Massachusetts 1965; *Bruce Conner*, exhibition catalogue, with text by Joan C. Siegfried and Stephen S. Prokopoff, Philadelphia 1967; *Assemblage in California: Works from the Late 50's and Early 60's*, exhibition catalogue, with texts by John Coplans, Walter Hopps, Philip Leider, and Hal Glicksman, Irvine, California 1968; *Bruce Conner: Drawings 1955-1975*, exhibition catalogue, San Francisco 1974; *Bruce Conner* by Anthony Reveaux, St. Paul, Minnesota 1981; articles—"Bruce Conner" by Cecile McCann in *Artweek* (Oakland, California), March 1974; "The Artist as Dactylographer" by Peter Selz in *Art in America* (New York), July/August 1974; "Bruce Conner's Cinematic Drawings" by A. Flanagan in *Artweek* (Oakland, California), November 1974; "Fallout: Some Notes on the Films of Bruce Conner" by W. Moritz and B. O'Neill in *Film Quarterly* (Berkeley, California), Summer 1978.

Bruce Conner has long been acknowledged as a seminal force behind the collage and assemblage movement of the early 1960's. Yet, he is probably one of the most misunderstood and underexposed artists of his generation. Although drawing has been his primary form of artistic expression since 1964, he is still recognized mainly for his collages and small sculptures and for the films that grew out of his collage sensibility. At times, even they are overlooked because of their iconoclastic content, or dismissed on the basis of their heterodoxy, when they could best be appreciated in stylistic terms—for example, "Last Supper," (1961), or "Couch," (1963), two sculptures whose mordantly satirical subject matter obscured their fundamental contribution to an expressionistic tradition that reaches back to Bosch, Bruegel, Goya, Daumier and, more recently, George Grosz.

In 1974-75, in recognition of Conner's skill with the medium, San Francisco's de Young Museum organized a traveling exhibition of his drawings, highlighting the various factors that influenced their development over a period of some 17 years. Unfortunately, by focusing entirely on the drawings instead of showing them in the context of his other works, and despite a comprehensive catalog essay stressing the connection, the exhibition isolated the drawings visually instead of emphasizing their relationship to other aspects of the artist's repertoire. Since then, he has been included in many museum group shows but, save for a limited retrospective at the North Point Gallery (San Francisco), the totality of his oeuvre has never been fully explored or documented. As a result, the significance of his contribution to the history of American art in the realm of mysticism has been greatly diluted. For, by taking a separative rather than combinative approach, curators have missed the opportunity to demonstrate both the correlation that exists between his handling of various media and the continuity of his style over a period of some 25 years.

That mysticism is at the core of Bruce Conner's vision is obvious from the entire body of his drawings and from the photograms and paintings of the 1970's. Drawn from such variant sources as religious symbolism, ethnic mythology, and private spiritual experience, their iconography often alludes to the cosmos—to distant stars and galaxies whose suggested forms seem to be undergoing visionary transmutations into geometrical and metaphysical shapes. The mystical implications of the collages and assemblages of the 60's are not as readily apprehensible. More intellectual than visual, their content is based upon philosophically esoteric notions that portend cataclysmic events and challenge our concepts of God, life, and death.

The seeds of an expressionist revival scattered in the late 70's throughout the art scene of Western Europe and the United States are currently being nurtured by the depressing financial condition of the world. Talented young artists anxious to ride the wave of avant-garde breakthroughs are, in increasing numbers, trading ultimate objectivity for emotionally-charged subjectivity. But it takes time and experience to become a master—someone who not only understands the lessons of the past, but who also has the ability to press those lessons into service of the present. Bruce Conner is such an artist. A veteran expressionist, he has demonstrated his ability to grow and change within the continuity of a highly mystical vocabulary. In his custody, the future of the medium is in good hands.

—Andrée Maréchal-Workman

CONSAGRA, Pietro.

Italian. Born in Mazara del Vallo, Sicily, in 1920. Studied at the Accademia di Belle Arti, Palermo, 1938-44. Sculptor: lives and works in Rome, since 1944; Founder, with Piero Dorazio, Achille Perilli, Giulio Turcato and others, Forma I, Rome, 1947. Recipient: Second Prize, *Biennale del Bronzetto*, Padua, 1955; Metallurgica Prize, *Bienal*, Sao Paulo, 1955; Premio Einaudi, *Biennale*, Venice, 1956; Belgium Critics Prize, 1958; First Prize for Sculpture, *Biennale*, Venice, 1960. Agent: Marlborough Galleria d'Arte, via Gregoriana 5, 00187 Rome. Address: Via Cassia 1162, 00189 Rome, Italy.

Individual Exhibitions:

1947 Galleria Mola, Rome
1948 Galleria Sandri, Venice
1949 Galleria del Secolo, Rome
1951 Galleria del Pincio, Rome
1953 Galleria del Naviglio, Milan
1956 *Biennale*, Venice
1958 Palais des Beaux-Arts, Brussels
Galleria Tartaruga, Rome
1959 Galerie de France, Paris
Bienal, Sao Paulo

1960 *Biennale*, Venice
1961 Galleria Blu, Milan
Mostra di Disegni di Pietro Consagra, Galleria Odyssia, Rome
Galerie Charles Lienhard, Zurich
1962 Staempfli Gallery, New York
Bonino Gallery, Buenos Aires
1963 Pace Gallery, Boston
1964 Odyssia Gallery, New York
1965 Galleria dell'Ariete, Milan
1966 Marlborough Galleria d'Arte, Rome
1967 Galleria dell'Ariete, Milan
Boymans van Beuningen Museum, Rotterdam
Marlborough-Gerson Gallery, New York
1969 Marlborough Galleria d'Arte, Rome
Galleria dell'Ariete, Milan
Galleria Rampa, Naples
Grafica Romera, Rome
1971 Galleria dell'Ariete, Milan
1972 Marlborough Galleria d'Arte, Rome
Galleria Peccolo, Livorno
1973 Galleria Editalia, Rome
Palazzo dei Normanni, Palermo
Qui Arte Contemporanea, Rome
Salone Annunciata, Milan
1974 Galleria del Bibliofili, Milan
Marlborough Galleria d'Arte, Rome
Galleria Ferrari, Treviglio, Italy
1975 Galleria Annunciata, Milan
1976 Marlborough Galleria d'Arte, Rome
1977 *Disegni 1945-1977*, Galleria Stendhal, Milan
Museo di Castelvecchio, Verona
Galleria Il Disegno, Rome
Studio L'Arco, Rome
1981 Galleria Editalia, Rome
Palazzo dell'Arengo, Rimini
Museo d'Arte Grafica, Gibellina, Italy
1984 Bottega dell'Incisione, Turin
1985 Qui Arte Contemporanea, Rome

Selected Group Exhibitions:

1946 *Group Exhibition*, Rome
1950 *Biennale*, Venice
1953 *Junge Italienische Kunst*, Kunsthaus, Zurich
1959 *European Art Today*, Minneapolis Museum of Art (toured the United States)
1964 *Decade 1954-1964*, Tate Gallery, London
1966 *Moderne Kunst aus Italien*, Museum am Ostwall, Dortmund, West Germany
1971 *New Italian Art 1953-71*, Walker Art Gallery, Liverpool
1977 *Disegni 1945-77*, Galleria Scheiwiller, Milan
1981 *Omaggio a Serpotta*, Galleria dell'Arco, Rome
1983 *Giornale di Manovra*, Galleria della Cometa, Rome

Collections:

Galleria Nazionale d'Arte Moderna, Rome: Tate Gallery, London; Musée Royaux des Beaux-Arts, Brussels; Centre Georges Pompidou, Paris; Middelheim Sculpture Park, Antwerp; Galerija Suvremene Umjetnosti, Zagreb; Museo d'Arte Moderna, Sao Paulo; Museum of Modern Art, New York; Guggenheim Museum, New York; Art Institute of Chicago.

Publications:

By CONSAGRA: books—*Necessita della Scultura*, Rome 1952; *L'Agguato c'e*, Rome 1960; *LaCitta Frontale*, exhibition catalogue, Rome, Milan and Bari, Italy 1969; *Poema Frontale*, Milan 1973; *Fotografia L'Arte*, Milan 1973; *Malumore*, Milan 1974; *Welcome to Italy*, Milan 1974; *La Ruota Quadrata*, Milan 1976; *Approssimativamente*, Milan 1977; *Vita Mia*, Milan 1980; articles—"Teorema dell Scultura" in *Forma I* (Rome), March 1947; "Disegno" in *Traits* (Paris), no. 6, 1947; "Mangeri" in *Noi Donne* (Rome), July 1951; "Scultura" in *Domus* (Milan), no. 2, 1951; "Plastico" in *Spazio* (Milan), December 1951; "In Difesa dell'Astratismo" in *Calendario del Popolo* (Milan), September 1951; "Design for Sculpture" in *Contemporary Drawings from 12 Countries*, exhibition catalogue, Chicato 1952; "Autoritratto" in *Arte Libera* (Naples), October 1952; "La

Fiamma Issidrica" in *Paese Sera* (Rome), March 1953; "Der Eiserne Arm" in *Junge Italienische Kunst*, exhibition catalogue, Zurich 1953; "Inchieste sull-Arte Contemporanea" in *Il Nuovo Corriere* (Florence), February 1954; "Colloqui" in *Paese* (Rome), January 1955; "Uno Scultore guidica l'Architettura" in *L'Architettura* (Rome), May 1956; "Intervista a Pietro Consagra," with Lonzi, in *Pietro Consagra*, exhibition catalogue, Milan and Rome 1967; "Una Lezione di Scultura" in *Civiltà delle Macchine* (Rome), vol. XVIII, 1970; "L'Ogetto" in *Consagra*, exhibition catalogue, Milan 1971; "Avere di me: in *Consagra*, exhibition catalogue, Rome 1972; statement in *Pietro Consagra*, exhibition catalogue, Rome 1974; "Io Consagra" in *Bolaffiarte* (Turin), October 1980.

On CONSAGRA: books—*Pietro Consagra* by Umbro Apolliono, Rome 1956; *Mostra di Disegne Pietro Consagra*, exhibition catalogue, by Marisa Volpi Orlandini, Rome 1961; *Pietro Consagra* by Giulio Carlo Argan, Neuchâtel, Switzerland 1962; *Consagra*, exhibition catalogue, by Giovanni Carandente and others, Palermo 1973; *Pietro Consagra* by Marisa Volpi Oraldini, Milan 1977; *Pietro Consagra: Disegni 1945–1977*, Milan 1977; *Pietro Consagra*, exhibition catalogue, by Guido Ballo, Rimini, Italy 1981; *Consagra*, exhibition catalogue with essay by Lorenza Trucchi, Rome 1985.

One of Pietro Consagra's distinctions is that unlike most Italian sculptors of his generation, he originates from Sicily, arriving in Rome at the age of 24; it is however interesting to note that the painter Guttuso, his senior by eight years, was also born in Sicily. In some senses the term sculptor does not quite fit Consagra; he is a maker of icons rather than an investigator of three-dimensional space, a manufacturer of screens rather than sculptural volumes. Whilst there may be some original preoccupation with Sicilian Baroque architecture, or the richly decorated mosaic walls of some of the island's famous chapels, Consagra's more obvious influence derives from Cubist definition of space.

Consagra belongs to the important post-war movement in Italian sculpture which sought a new language, a renewal in the face of the relaxed inheritance of classical forms which marked the older generation, Marini, Manzu, Greco, or the achievements of the Futurists. It is one of the fascinations of modern Italian art that in addition to brilliant craftsmanship, inventive form, striking intelligence and undeniable elegance and taste, many of the most gifted artists have felt the need to adopt mannerisms or styles which suggest violence or self-hatred. It is as though they distrust the very gifts which Italian civilization and taste have given them; hence the violation of space and form in Fontana, the torn and scratched techniques of Burri, the satire of Baj, the aggressive calligraphy of Capogrossi, Colla's spiky gestures, and the variations of bruised bronze surfaces or penetrated images found in Cavaliere, Arnaldo Pomodoro and Mastroianni.

Consagra is of this school. His standing screens, often brightly coloured, are images of aggression and destruction, giving the impression of torn fabric scarred wood, or disintegrated matter. The starting point is a simple square, manipulated out of all recognition. Consagra is a brilliant technician, working in every variety of material, bronze casting, welded steel, oxidizing, aluminium forms either cut into strange, oriental patterns, or elaborating a Calderesque hanging manner, each misshapen petal suspended by wire. Consagra is more organic than his fellow Italians, sometimes building up webbed or comb-like structures, patterned on some natural system of growth or development. His famous polemical manner—the author of numerous essays and manifestos on sculpture—is evident in the sculptures, and saves them from the more obviously over-designed decorativeness of some of his compatriots.

—Charles Spencer

COOPER, Ron(ald).

American. Born in Venice, California, 24 July 1943. Studied at the Chouinard Art Institute, Los Angeles, 1963-65. Environmental artist and photographer, Los Angeles, since 1965. Commissioned by Library of Congress to do *Floating Volume Atmosphere*, Washington, D.C., 1968; travelled in the United States and Europe, 1969-70; and in Central America, 1971. Director, Los Angeles Institute of Contemporary Art, since 1981. Board Director, Artist's Equity Association, 1980–81. Recipient: Purchase Award, Los Angeles County Museum of Art, 1968; National Endowment for the Arts Award, 1970; Theodoron Purchase Award, Guggenheim Museum, New York 1971. Agent: Galerie Alfred Schmela, Mutter-Ey-Strasse 3, 4000 Dusseldorf, West Germany. Address: 1310 Main Street, Venice, California 90291, U.S.A.

Individual Exhibitions:

1969   Ace Gallery, Los Angeles
1970   Michael Walls Gallery, San Francisco
       Pomona College Art Gallery, Claremont, California
       Galerie Schmela, Dusseldorf
       3 Young Americans: A Biennal, Allen Memorial Art Museum, Oberlin College, Ohio (with Chuck Close and Neil Jenney)
1972   Pasadena Art Museum, California
       Ace Gallery, Los Angeles
1973   Galerie Folker Skulima, West Berlin
1974   Galerie Alfred Schmela, Dusseldorf
1979   Rosamund Felsen Gallery, Los Angeles

Selected Group Exhibitions:

1967   *Arp to Artschwager*, Goldowsky Gallery, New York
1969   *Annual Exhibition*, Whitney Museum, New York
1970   *Prospect '69*, Städtische Kunsthalle, Dusseldorf
1970   *Permutations: Light and Color*, Museum of Contemporary Art, Chicago
1971   *10 Young Artists*, Guggenheim Museum, New York
       Theodoron Awards Invitational, Guggenheim Museum, New York
1972   *Art in Progress*, Kunsthaus, Zurich
       Documenta 5, Kassel, West Germany
1974   *Light*, Lang Art Gallery, Scripps College, Claremont, California
1979   *California Perceptions: Light and Space*, California State University at Fullerton

Collections:

Whitney Museum, New York; Guggenheim Museum, New York; Art Institute of Chicago; Los Angeles County Museum of Art; Kaiser Wilhelm Museum, Krefeld, West Germany; Stedelijk Museum, Amsterdam.

Publications:

On COOPER: books—*3 Young Americans: A Biennial*, exhibition catalogue, with text by Athena Spear, Oberlin, Ohio 1970; *California Perceptions: Light and Space*, exhibition catalogue, Fullerton, California 1979; articles—"Ronald Cooper" by Jane Livingston in *Artforum* (New York), Summer 1969; "Reflections of Close, Cooper and Jenny: 3 Young Americans at Oberlin" by Athena Spear in *Arts Magazine* (New York), May 1970; "Ronald Cooper" by Peter Plagens in *Artforum* (New York), April 1971; "Ronald Cooper" by M. Terbell in *Arts Magazine* (New York), April 1971; "Ronald Cooper" by M. Hartman in *Glass Art Magazine* (Oakland, California), October 1973.

Since the late 1960's the career of Ron Cooper has reflected two main tendencies, the first being the experimental research with and manipulation of light, the second being either an attempt to reproduce honestly the physical properties of the material or to exact the pictorial qualities of the characteristics of the process involved.

That his career began in the late 1960's is demonstrated by his early work: he began by painting transparent vertical bars, which was followed by his making large square fiberglass and polyester resin paintings which acted as light traps. Later, he eliminated the object altogether and simply dealt with volumes of light which he documented with a camera—and particularly since 1974 Cooper has totally devoted himself to exploring the possibilities of making art with the camera.

Like that of several of his peers from the Los Angeles school (Robert Irwin, Larry Bell, etc.), Cooper's art focuses on how we perceive things and illustrates the perennial theme of how deceptive is our appearance-reflecting world. His goal is to pose or propose a perceptual dilemma rather than make a beautiful object capturing the poetic discourse of the ever-changing sunlight. Cooper is, of course, like Irwin, concerned with the process of perception though he is not concerned like him—as it seems—with meditation and emptiness.

He has also become more and more interested in the problem-solving ability of the camera rather than in the technique of photography which he practices from a painter's "point of view." His most recent works are series of photographs entitled "What It Is" and "Torsos."

—Jean-Luc Bordeaux

COPLEY, William Nelson. (CPLY).

American. Born in New York City, 24 January 1919. Educated at Phillips Academy, Andover, Massachusetts, until 1938; Yale University, New Haven, Connecticut, 1938–42. Served in the United States Army, in Africa, Sicily, and Italy, 1942–46. Married Chuang-Hua. Began painting in 1946; Director, with John Ployardt, Copley Galleries, showing the work of Magritte, Cornell, Matta, Tanguy, Man Ray, and Ernst, Beverly Hills, California, 1946–48; lived in Paris, associating with Max Ernst, Man Ray, and Marcel Duchamp, 1951–64; returned to the United States and has lived in New York since 1964. Agent: Phyllis Kind Gallery, New York and Chicago. Address: c/o Phyllis Kind Gallery, 136 Greene Street, New York, New York 10012, U.S.A.

Individual Exhibitions:

1947   Royer's Bookstore, Los Angeles
1953   Galerie Nina Dausset, Paris
1954   Galerie Monte Napoleone, Milan
1956   *Peintures Récentes*, Galerie du Dragon, Paris
       Iolas Gallery, New York
1958   Iolas Gallery, New York
1959   Galerie Furstenberg, Paris
1960   Galleria Naviglio, Milan
       Galleria Cavallino, Venice
       Iolas Gallery, New York
1961   *Recent Paintings by CPLY*, Institute of Contemporary Arts, London
       Galleria Schwarz, Milan
       Galerie Iris Clert, Paris
1963   *Paintings*, Hanover Gallery, London
       Les Suffragettes Erotiques, Galerie Iris Clert, Paris
       Iolas Gallery, New York
1964   David Stuart Gallery, Los Angeles
1965   Louisiana Gallery, Houston
       Southwestern College, Chula Vista, California
       Allan Frumkin Gallery, Chicago
1966   *Projects for Monuments to the Unknown Whore*, Galerie Iolas, Paris (travelled to the Iolas Gallery, New York)
       Entertainment for Men, Stedelijk Museum, Amsterdam
1967   *Homage to Robert W. Service*, Iolas Gallery New York (travelled to the Galerie Iolas, Paris)
1968   Bodley Gallery, New York
1969   Merida Gallery, Louisville, Kentucky

1970 Galerie Neuendorf, Cologne
Project for a Dictionary of Platitudes, Galleria Iolas, Milan (travelled to Iolas Gallery, New York)
CPLY, Magritte and Brauner, Louisiana Gallery, Houston
1972 Galerie Springer, West Berlin
Galerie Aspects, Brussels
David Stuart Gallery, Los Angeles
Mail Order, Galleria Iolas, Milan (travelled to the Iolas Gallery, New York)
1973 CPLY, Galeria Anselimo, Turin
1974 *X—Rated*, New York Cultural Center
Western Songs, Onnasch Gallery, New York (retrospective; travelled to Moore College of Art, Philadelphia, and Galerie Onnasch, Cologne)
Galerie Iolas, Paris
Nounes, Galleria Iolas, Milan (travelled to the Iolas Gallery, New York)
1975 Erik Nord Gallery, Nantucket, Massachusetts
1976 Iolas Gallery, New York
1978 Iolas Gallery, New York
Galerie Fassbinder, Munich
Galerie Springer, West Berlin
Galerie Zwirner, Cologne
1979 Iolas Gallery, New York
Reflections on a Past Life, Institute for the Arts, Rice University, Houston
1980 Iolas Gallery, New York
Museum of Fine Arts, St. Petersburg, Florida
Kunsthalle, Berne (travelled to the Centre Georges Pompidou, Paris, and the Stedelijk Van Abbemuseum, Eindhoven, Netherlands)
1981 Iolas Gallery, New York
Sierra Nevada Museum of Art, Reno
Colorado Springs Fine Arts Center
1982 Phyllis Kind Gallery, Chicago
1983 Reinhard Onnasch Ausstellungen, West Berlin
1985 Galerie Susanna Kulli, St. Gallen, Switzerland

Selected Group Exhibitions:

1962 *Collage out of California*, Pasadena Art Museum, California
L'Antagonisme de l'Objet, Musée des Arts Décoratifs, Paris
1964 *New Directions in American Painting*, Brandeis University, Waltham, Massachusetts
Surrealism: Sources/History/Affinities, Galerie Charpentier, Paris
1966 *Surrealist Exhibition*, University of California at Santa Barbara
1972 *Humor in Art*, New School for Social Research, New York
1973 *Erotic Art*, New School for Social Research, New York
1975 *3 Generations of American Nudes*, New York Cultural Center
1977 *Artists' Rendering of Paintings*, Brera Museum, Milan (travelled to Le Louvre, Paris)

Collections:

Museum of Modern Art, New York; Whitney Museum, New York; New York Cultural Center; Philadelphia Museum of Art; Art Institute of Chicago; Los Angeles County Museum of Art; Tate Gallery, London; Centre Georges Pompidou, Paris; Stedelijk Museum, Amsterdam; Nagaoka City Museum, Japan.

Publications:

By COPLEY: books—*The Evil Story of My Life by CPLY*, New York 1965; *CPLY: Project for a Dictionary of Platitudes*, exhibition catalogue, Milan and New York 1970; *Notes on a Project for a Dictionary of Ridiculous Images*, Cologne and New York 1972; *Variations on a Theme by Francis Picabia*, New York 1979; articles—"Introducing the Paintings of Serge Charchoune" in *Artnews* (New York), March 1960; "Man Ray: The Dada of Us All: in *Portfolio* (New York), Winter 1963.

On COPLEY: books—*Copley: Peintures Récentes*, exhibition catalogue, with text by Patrick Waldberg, Paris 1956; *William Copley: 470, Mostra del Cavallino*, exhibition catalogue, with text by Roberto Rossellini, Venice 1960; *History of Surrealist Painting* by Marcel Jean, New York 1960; *Recent Paintings by CPLY*, exhibition catalogue, London 1961; *Bill Copley*, exhibition catalogue, with text by Roland Penrose, Milan 1962; *W.N. Copley: Paintings*, exhibition catalogue, with text by Robert Melville, London 1963; *Les Suffragettes Erotiques de Bill Copley*, exhibition catalogue, with texts by Marcel Duchamp and others, Paris 1963; *CPLY: Projects for Monuments to the Unknown Whore*, exhibition catalogue, with text by Julien Levy, Paris and New York 1966; *Copley: Entertainment for Men*, exhibition catalogue, with text by Roland Renrose, Amsterdam 1966; *CPLY:Homage to Robert W. Service*, exhibition catalogue, New York and Paris 1967; *Pop Art* by Lucy Lippard, New York 1967; *CPLY: Mail Order*, exhibition catalogue, Milan and New York 1972; *CPLY*, exhibition catalogue, with text by Janus, Turin 1973; *CPLY: Nounes*, exhibition catalogue, Milan and New York 1974; *CPLY: X-Rated*, exhibition catalogue, with an introduction by Sam Hunter, New York 1974; *CPLY: Western Songs*, exhibition catalogue, Cologne 1974; *CPLY: Reflections on a Past Life*, exhibition catalogue, Houston 1979; *William N. Copley*, exhibition catalogue, with texts by Johannes Gachnang and Marianne Schmidt, with an introduction by R. H. Fuchs, Berne 1980; *William N. Copley*, exhibition catalogue with essay by Ilona Lindenburg, West Berlin 1983.

Though born a full generation after the original Surrealists, William Copley—a.k.a. CPLY—calls himself a Surrealist, lives as a Surrealist, paints as a Surrealist, in fact, is a Surrealist. At first glance this may seem a retrogressive role for a post-World War II American artist. But the important paradox in Copley's career is that he saw and, without chauvinism, *admitted* the influence of classic European Surrealism on American art while simultaneously his own work anticipated some of the directions in which American art has grown from these historic roots.

As early as 1946 Copley (with a brother-in-law) was running a Surrealist gallery in Los Angeles. There, the first Surrealist they met was Man Ray, who said, "There's more Surrealism rampant in Hollywood than all the Surrealists could invent in a lifetime." Through Man Ray, Copley met Duchamp in New York, Max Ernst in Arizona, and gradually other surviving Dadaists, Surrealists, and modern masters. He bought their work—first for the gallery, then for himself, for pleasure and as sort of visual reference library. At the same time, he taught himself to paint innocently and playfully, absorbing the Surrealists' improvised, free-associative spirit and abandoning (as they did) aesthetic and moral prejudices.

Copley's theme was, is, and, presumably, always will be sex—sex in its most cheerful, anxiety-free form, dirty but not filthy, erotic but not pornographic. By the late 40's he developed an iconography of curvy, cartoon-like women who cavort through his paintings, often being chased, kissed, ogled, mounted, etc. by a small man in a derby who is not only closely related to Copley himself but to the Keystone Cops and other heroes of silent film, and to the bourgeois males in the work of Magritte. Authority, when it appears, is an equally playful and cartoon-like French cop (un flic). As Duchamp said, "Cops pullulate, Copley copulates." A painting like Copley's "Capella sextina" (1961) makes Delacroix' "Le bain turque" look spare and monogamous.

While raiding the zaniness of comic strips and Hollywood (Mae West, W. C. Fields, and the Marx Brothers are other Copley favorites), he also reinvented popular images from advertising (THINK), newspapers (the crossword puzzle), Robert Service's ballads (the Yukon bars and whorehouses), patriotic symbols (the flag, the Liberty Bell), slogans (BEAT YALE, Copley's university), etc. All of his very large production of drawings and paintings are flat, non-illusionistic, "American." As Julien Levy said, Copley was "a Pop of Pop in 1948." That's true, and so is the fact, which Copley is the first to acknowledge, that the grandparents of Pop (and Abstract Expressionism) were Dada and Surrealism. In recent years, Copley has shown regularly at the Phyllis Kind Gallery in New York City and Chicago, in addition to travelling shows in the United States and abroad.

—B. H. Friedman

CORNEILLE.
Dutch. Born Cornelis Guillaume Beverloo, in Liège, Belgium. 3 July 1922; emigrated to the Netherlands 1940; subsequently naturalized. Studied drawing at the Rijksakademie, Amsterdam, 1940–43, etching, under S. W. Hayter, at Atelier 17, Paris, 1953, and ceramics, with Mazzotti, at Albisola Mare, Italy, 1954–55. Independent painter and graphic artist, Amsterdam, 1943–53, and in Paris since 1950: Co-Founder, Dutch Experimental Group, Amsterdam 1948, and COBRA (Copenhagen-Brussels-Amsterdam) group, with Appel, Jorn, Constant, Alechinsky, Pedersen, etc., 1949–51; worked in Mallorca and Cadaques, Spain, 1961–66. Recipient: Guggenheim Netherlands Prize, 1956; Graphics Prize, Ibiza, 1972. Agent: Galerie Krikhaar, Spuistraat 330, 1012 VX Amsterdam, Netherlands. Address: 58 Rue Vieille du Temple, 75003 Paris, France.

Individual Exhibitions:

1946 Het Beerenhuis, Groningen, Netherlands
1947 Europai Iskola, Budapest
1950 Galleri Birch, Copenhagen
1951 Martinet en Michels, Amsterdam
Galerie t'Venster, Rotterdam
1953 Kunstkabinett Horemans, Antwerp
1954 Galerie Colette Allendy, Paris
1956 Galerie Craven, Paris
Palais des Beaux-Arts, Brussels
Stedelijk Museum, Amsterdam
Stedelijk Museum, Schiedam, Netherlands
1957 Museum of Curacao, Dutch Antilles
1959 Galerie Espace, Haarlem, Netherlands
Galerie Le Gendre, Paris
1960 *Tekening van Corneille*, Stedelijk Museum, Amsterdam
1961 Galerie Ariel, Paris
Haags Gemeentemuseum, The Hague
Stedelijk Van Abbemuseum, Eindhoven, Netherlands
Brook Street Gallery, London
K.B. Galleri, Oslo
1962 Lefebre Gallery, New York
Galerie Mathias Fels, Paris
1963 Galleria del Naviglio, Milan
Musée d'Antibes, France
Galleri Blanche, Stockholm
Galerie Le Point Cardinal, Paris
Galerie Creuzevalt, Paris
1964 Galeria Souza, Mexico city
Lefebre Gallery, New York
Galleria Schwarz, Milan, Italy
1965 Cultureel Centrum, Hilversum, Netherlands
Galerie Stangl, Munich
Lefebre Gallery, New York
1966 Stedelijk Museum, Amsterdam
Kunsthalle, Dusseldorf
Galeria Relevo, Rio de Janeiro
1967 Galerie Kaleidoskoop, Ghent
Lefebre Gallery, New York
1968 Galerie Espace, Amsterdam
Galerie Casse, Paris
1969 Galerie Stangl, Munich
Galeria Ivan Spence, Ibiza, Spain
1970 Galerie Ariel, Paris
Galerie La Pochade, Paris
Lebebre Gallery, New York
Galeria Ivan Spence, Ibiza, Spain
1971 Galerie Rive Gauche, Paris
Palais Walderdorf, Trier, West Germany
Galeria Ivan Spence, Ibiza, Spain
Galleria d'Arte, Trieste
Kunstverein, Salzburg
Lefebre Gallery, New York
1972 Galleria 70, Potenza, Italy
Schillerhof, Graz, Austria
1974 Galleria La Medusa, Rome
The Quartier Rose of Amsterdam, Lefebre Gallery, New York
Galerie Montjoie, Brussels
Palazzo Buonacorsi, Macerata, Italy
Palais des Beaux-Arts, Charleroi, Belgium

Retrospective Tentoonstelling: Corneille, Museum
voor Schone Kunsten, Ghent
Studio Erre, Rome
Galleria La Medusa, Rome
1975 Galleria del Cavallino, Rome
Petite Galerie, Rio de Janeiro
Galerie l'Oeil de Boeuf, Paris
Meseu de Arte Moderno, Sao Paulo
Galerie Espace, Amsterdam
Institut Neerlandais, Paris
Galleria Gian Ferrari, Milan
Galerie Krikhaar, Amsterdam
Galleria M. Arte, Milan
Galleria C.M., Rome
Carnegie Institute, Pittsburgh
Lefebre Gallery, New York
Galleria Gregory, Rome
1976 Galleri Documenta, Copenhagen
Centro d'Arte, Sarono, Italy
Galerie Riis, Trondheim, Norway
Galerie Fabien Boulakia, Paris
Galerie Moderne, Silkeborg, Denmark
Lefebre Gallery, New York
1977 Galerie Espace, Amsterdam
Galleri Documenta, Copenhagen
Maison Bernard, Caracas, Venezuela
1978 Galerie Orientale, Geneva
Galleri Kanda Malare, Jonkoping, Sweden
Galleria Bonaparte, Milan
1979 Galerie Fabien Boulakia, Paris
Galerie L'Oeil de Boeuf, Paris
New Gallery, Jabbeke, Belgium
Galerij Maeyaert, Ostend, Belgium
1980 Galerie Delta, Rotterdam
Galerie Michel Casse, Paris
Galerie Reflex, Amsterdam
1981 Galerie Fabien Boulakia, Paris
Galleri Hammerlunds, Osla
Galerie de Kuil, The Hague
Galerie Jas, Utrecht, Netherlands
1982 Galerie Krikhaar, Amsterdam

Selected Group Exhibitions:

1946 *Junge Schilders,* Stedelijk Museum, Amsterdam
1949 *COBRA,* Stedelijk Museum, Amsterdam
1951 *Salon de Mai,* Musée d'Art Moderne, Paris
1953 *Bienal,* Sao Paulo
1956 *Carnegie International,* Carnegie Institute, Pittsburgh
1959 *Documenta 2,* Kassel, West Germany (and *Documenta 3,* 1964)
1964 *Guggenheim International,* Guggenheim Museum, New York
1973 *Hommage à Picasso,* Kestner-Gesellschaft, Hannover
1978 *Cobra 1948–78,* Statens Museum for Konst, Copenhagen
1983 *Cobra 1948–51,* Musée d'Art Moderne, Paris

Collections:

Stedelijk Museum, Armsterdam; Stedelijk Museum, Schiedam, Netherlands; Stedelijk Van Abbemuseum, Eindhoven, Netherlands; Palais des Beaux-Arts, Brussels; Musée de Liège, Belgium; Collection de la Ville de Paris; Museum Charlottenborg, Copenhagen; Nasjonalgalleriet, Oslo; Brooklyn Museum, New York; Museum of Djakarta, Indonesia.

Publications:

By CORNEILLE: book—*Journal de la Tour,* Paris 1981.

On CORNEILLE: books—*Corneille,* exhibition catalogue, with text by Charles Estienne, Paris 1954; *Corneille,* exhibition catalogue, with text by Edouard Jaeger, Amsterdam 1956; *Tekening van Corneille,* exhibition catalogue, with text by Imre Pan, Amsterdam 1960; *Corneille,* exhibition catalogue, with texts by Lawrence Alloway and E. L. L. de Wilde, London 1961; *Corneille,* exhibition catalogue, with text by A. M. Hammacher, The Hague 1961; *Corneille,* ex-

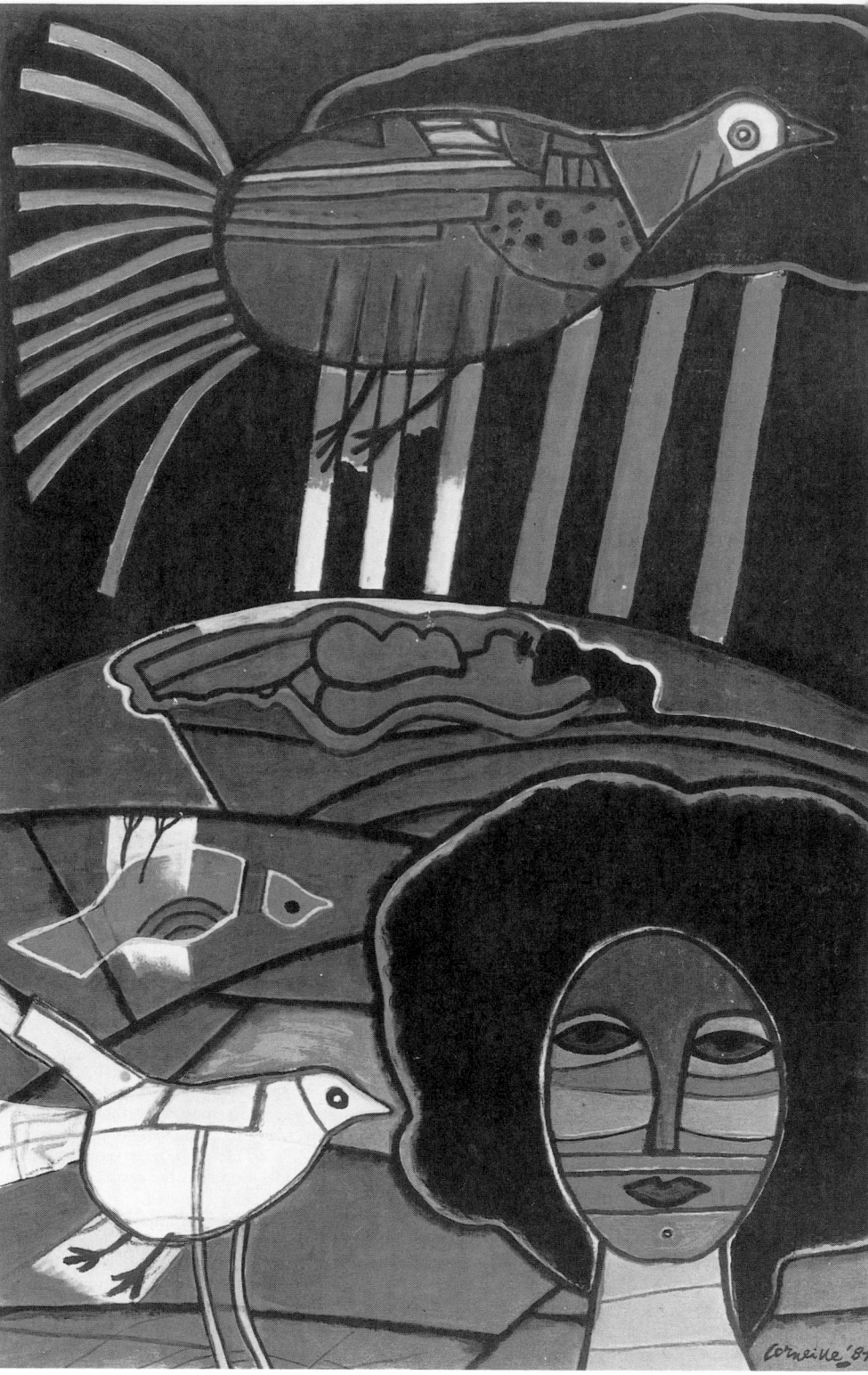

Corneille: *Le Grand Oiseau de l'Eté,* 1981

hibition catalogue, with text by Karl K. Ringstrom, Oslo 1961; *Corneille,* exhibition catalogue, with text by Lawrence Alloway, New York 1961; *Corneille,* exhibition catalogue, with text by Willem Sandburg, New York 1964; *Corneille,* exhibition catalogue, with text by Werner Haftmann, New York 1965; *Corneille,* exhibition catalogue, with text by Max Loreau, Amsterdam 1966; *Corneille,* exhibition catalogue, with an interview by Christian Bussy, New York 1967; *Ariel 17: Corneille,* exhibition catalogue, with texts by D. H. Lawrence, Octavio Paz and Malcolm Lowry, Paris 1970; *Corneille,* exhibition catalogue, with text by André Laude, New York 1970; *Corneille,* exhibition catalogue, with text by Gunnar Jespersen, New York 1971; *Hommage à Picasso,* exhibition catalogue, with texts by Wieland Schmied, Werner Haftmann and Daniel H. Kahnweiler, Hannover 1973; *Corneille Le Roi—Image* by André Laude, Paris 1973; *Corneille et la Vie* by Elvirio Maurizi, Macerata, Italy 1974; *Corneille:*

The Quartier Rose of Amsterdam, exhibition catalogue, New York 1974; *Corneille,* exhibition catalogue, with text by Elvirio Maurizi, Rome 1974; *Retrospective Tentoonstelling: Corneille,* exhibition catalogue, Ghent 1974; *Corneille Aujourd'hui* by Andre Laude, Stockholm 1978; *Corneille* by Daniel Marchesseau, Paris 1980.

COBRA was a nest of poets as well as artists. Corneille, a co-founder of the group, even if he is now wholly concerned with painting, injects into all his work the haunting suggestion of halfheard verse.

In his way he is a cyclic artist. Starting, as so many COBRA painters did, with what Lawrence Alloway has described as a "hectic display of birds and moonheads in free-fall," he later departed from this style of imagery and concentrated on a series of compacted landscapes, pictures in which every tiny facet of colour was bounded by a rugged edge of paint in contrasting tone. All these areas of colour came together in a crowded amalgam like a delicious many-hued fruit of random shape. These paintings were veritable banquets.

Yet about 15 years ago he came back to his figures and figuration, albeit retaining the painted outline of every fragment of the picture. Colour areas increased in size. The sheer glutinous gravity of the landscapes was replaced by puckish humour. Mankind and the other creatures met once again, and they would be seen to be in a world which, if not real in the orthodox recognizable way, was still a world sprouting grass and trees and flowers under the canopy of a sky (however quirkily populated).

With or without COBRA affiliations, he stands out as an important artist of Northern Europe. His rejection of latin geometry and equal disinterest in a classical devotion to composition and style, has left him free to let the gamut of emotion in figures—or landscapes—run riot.

—Sheldon Williams

CORNELL, Joseph.

American. Born in Nyack, New York, 24 December 1903. Educated at Phillips Academy, Andover, Massachusetts, 1917–21; self-taught in art. Worked for the Whitman Textile Company, summer vacations, as salesman for woolen goods, New York, 1921–30; lived and worked in Flushing, New York, 1929 until his death, 1972; began painting and making assemblages, 1932, films, 1939; associated with the New York Surrealists, 1939–45. Recipient: Copley Foundation grant, 1954; Ada S. Garsh Prize, Art Institute of Chicago, 1959; Merit Award, American Academy of Arts and Letters, 1968. *Died* (in Flushing) *29 December 1972.*

Individual Exhibitions:

1932	Julien Levy Gallery, New York
1939	Julien Levy Gallery, New York
1940	Julien Levy Gallery, New York
1942	*Objects by Joseph Cornell/Box-Valise by Marcel Duchamp/Bottles by Lawrence Vail,* Art of This Century, New York
	Ayer Galleries, Philadelphia
	Wakefield Gallery, New York
1946	Park Lane Hotel, New York
	Arthur A. Everts, Dallas
	Hugo Gallery, New York
1948	Julien Levy Gallery, New York (with Marcel Duchamp and Yves Tanguy)
	Copley Galleries, Beverly Hills, California
1949	Egan Gallery, New York
1950	Egan Gallery, New York
	New York Public Library
1953	Egan Gallery, New York
	Allan Frumkin Gallery, Chicago
	Walker Art Center, Minneapolis
1955	Stable Gallery, New York
1956	Wittenborn and Company, New York
1957	Stable Gallery, New York
1959	New Gallery, Bennington College, Vermont
1962	Ferus Gallery, Los Angeles
1963	Loeb Student Center, New York University
1965	J. L. Hudson Gallery, Detroit
1966	Robert Schoelkopf Gallery, New York
	Cleveland Museum of Art
	Alan Stone Gallery, New York
	Pasadena Art Museum, California
1967	Guggenheim Museum, New York
	Walker Art Center, Minneapolis
1968	Rose Art Museum, Brandeis University, Waltham, Massachusetts
	Queens College, Flushing, New York
1970	Cosmopolitan Club, New York
	Metropolitan Museum, New York
1971	Galleria Galatea, Turin
1972	Gimpel and Hanover Galerie, Zurich
	Cooper Union, New York
	Alan Stone Gallery, New York
	Albright-Knox Art Gallery, Buffalo, New York
	Kestner-Gesellschaft, Hannover
1973	Queens County Art and Cultural Center, New York
	Hopkins Center and Galleries, Dartmouth College, Hanover, New Hampshire
	National Collection of Fine Arts, Smithsonian Institution, Washington, D.C.
1974	Museum of Contemporary Art, Chicago
1975	Pyramid Galleries, Washington, D.C.
	ACA Galleries, New York
	College of Creative Studies, University of California at Santa Barbara
1976	James Corcoran Gallery, Los Angeles
	Leo Castelli Gallery, New York
	Rice Museum, Houston
	John Berggruen Gallery, San Francisco
1977	James Corcoran Gallery, Los Angeles
	Edward Hopper House, Nyack, New York
	L'Attico, Rome
	Akron Art Institute, Ohio
1978	James Corcoran Gallery, Los Angeles
	Gatodo Gallery, Tokyo
1979	Institute of Contemporary Arts, Boston
	University of California Art Museum, Berkeley
1980	Baudoin Lebon, Paris (travelled to Musée de Toulon, France)
	Castelli/Feigen/Corcoran Galleries, New York
	Sierra Nevada Museum, Reno
	Ulrich Museum of Art, Wichita State University, Kansas
	Museum of Modern Art, New York (travelled to Whitechapel Art Gallery, London)
1986	Pace Gallery, New York
1987	Waddington Galleries, London

Selected Group Exhibitions:

1932	*Surrealist Group Exhibition,* Julien Levy Gallery, New York
1936	*Fantastic Art, Dada and Surrealism,* Museum of Modern Art, New York
1938	*Exposition International du Surrealisme,* Galerie Beaux-Arts, Paris
1944	*Abstract and Surrealist Art in the United States,* Denver Art Museum (toured the United States)
1958	*The Disquieting Muse: Surrealism,* Contemporary Art Museum, Houston
1961	*The Art of Assemblage,* Museum of Modern Art, New York (travelled to Museum for Contemporary Arts, Dallas, and the Museum of Art, San Francisco)
1964	*Painting and Sculpture of a Decade 1954–1964,* Tate Gallery, London
1970	*New York Painters and Sculptors,* Metropolitan Museum of Art, New York
1985	*Transformations in Sculpture,* Guggenheim Museum, New York
1986	*Seven Artists in Depth: The Creative Process,* San Francisco Museum of Modern Art

Collections:

Museum of Modern Art, New York; Whitney Museum, New York; Museum of Fine Arts, Boston; Walters Art Gallery, Baltimore, Hirshhorn Museum, Washington, D.C.; Norton Simon Museum of Art, Pasadena, California; Tate Gallery, London; Musée National d'Art Moderne, Paris; Kaiser Wilhelm Museum, Krefeld, West Germany.

Publications:

By CORNELL: articles—"M. Phot," scenario, in *Surrealism,* edited by Julien Levy, New York 1936; "Enchanged Wanderer" in *View* (New York), December 1941; "Recorded Conversations with Belle Krasne" in *Design Quarterly* (Minneapolis), no. 30, 1954, films—*Rose Hobart,* with Stan Brakhage, 1939; *Gnir Rednow,* with Stan Brakhage, 1955; *Centuries of June,* with Stan Brakhage, 1955; *Aviary,* with Rudy Burckhardt, 1955; *What Mozart Saw on Mulberry Street,* with Rudy Burckhardt, 1956; *A Fable for Fountains,* with Rudy Burckhardt, 1957; *Angel,* with Rudy Burckhardt, 1957; *Nymphlight,* 1959; *Cotillion,* with Larry Jordan, 1969; *The Children's Party,* with Larry Jordan, 1969; *The Midnight Party,* with Larry Jordan, 1969.

On CORNELL: books—*The History of Surrealist Painting* by Marcel Jean, New York 1960; *Joseph Cornell,* exhibition catalogue, by Diane Waldman, New York 1967; *Joseph Cornell,* exhibition catalogue, Pasadena, 1967; *Art Works and Packages* by Harold Rosenberg, London 1969; *A Joseph Cornell Album* by Dore Ashton, New York 1974; *Joseph Cornell Portfolio,* edited by Sandra Leonard Starr, New York 1976; *Joseph Cornell* by Diane Waldman, New York 1977; *Joseph Cornell,* exhibition catalogue, by Kynaston McShine, New York 1980; *Joseph Cornell: Art and Metaphysics* by Sandra Leonard Starr, New York 1982; *Joseph Cornell,* exhibition catalogue with text by Brian O'Doherty, New York 1986.

Joseph Cornell: *Cassiopeia No. 3,* c. 1954

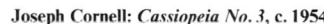

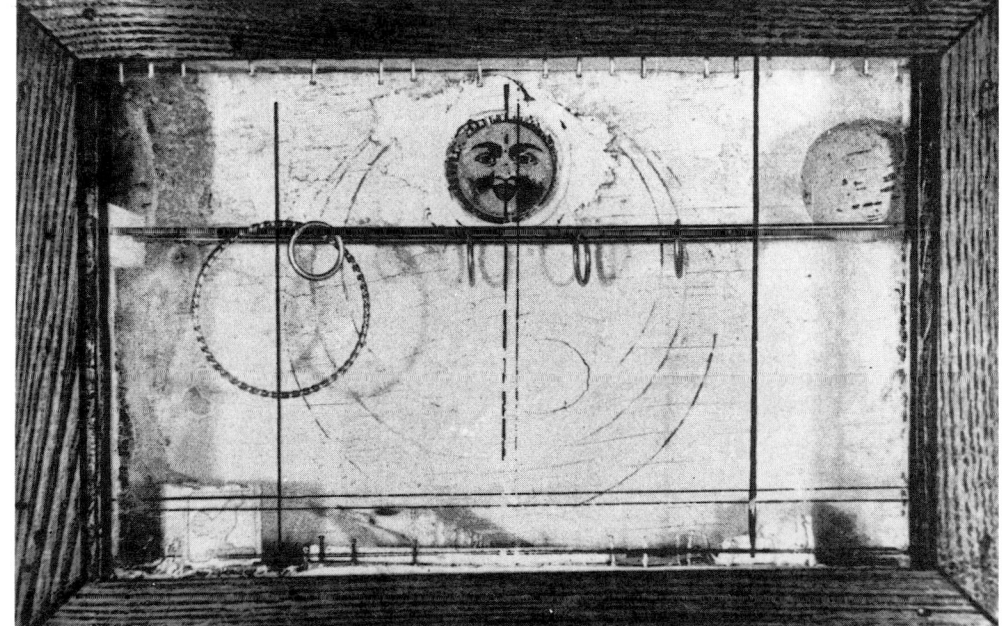

During the 1930's Joseph Cornell began arranging found objects in glass and wooden boxes, creating three-dimensional collage constructions which are the immediate forerunners of Assemblage, an art form highly popularized in America during the 1950's and 1960's. Over a span of about 40 years, Cornell fashioned a magical miniature world by arranging the trivia and memorabilia he retrieved from antique and secondhand shops, on beaches and in backyards.

Maps, balls, butterflies, figurines, springs, printed cards and papers, jars, glass, glasses, photo-engravings and reproductions of famous people and art from the historical past, compasses, feathers, marbles, toys, pipes, dried flowers, counters— Cornell juggled so much so tenaciously, to convey his message of time, mortality and the infinite. He was early in using mirrors, movement and sound, and he was also early in using series. He often used astronomical maps and astrological charts, alluding to our fateful destiny in the hands of the sun, moon and planets. He often used images out of the past, making the Medici or dancers, for example, participants in his obsession to create a historical present which sees through the cultural past. Alongside the gentleness there is an element of warning, seducing with no nostalgic sentimentality but always with a sense of intelligent intimacy with the accumulated treasures he collected from nature, from culture and from the industrial world.

Cornell questioned what's real and what's artificial, what's precious and what's mundane. Sometimes apothecary jars are arranged in grid-cabinets, filled with a variety of things, like some inexplicable medicine, like spices and equally like some inexplicable warning of impending encapsulation. Cornell's dioramas convey the wonderment in all aspects of life, using juxtaposition to heighten consciousness of the interconnectedness of so many things and of the past and the present. And always the magic is informed by a highly refined formal prowess, both when the compositions are filled and when they are more spare, as in the later years.

Cornell's transformation of the ordinary into the extraordinary is related to the methods of the Surrealists, and he did find inspiration from the likes of Max Ernst, Miró and Duchamp. He was, however, concerned with seduction rather than with surrealist shock, and he chose his repertoire as treasures in a spirit vastly differing from the more tough and junky castaways preferred by Kurt Schwitters. Cornell does not fit comfortably into any "ism" and is best understood as one of the independents in art history who, like Redon, Ryder, Poe and Klee, is basically a hermetic spell caster, small in scale but monumental in magic, and is endowed with an ingenuous imagination capable of reshaping the modest into the wondrous symbol as mysterious as life itself.

—Barbara Cavaliere

COSTA, Claudio.

Italian. Born in Tirana, Albania, 22 June 1942; moved with his family to Italy, 1944. Studied architecture at the Polytechnico, Milan, 1963–65; studied engraving, Atelier Hayter, Paris, 1965–67. Married Anita Zeiro in 1967; daughter: Marisol. Independent artist, Genoa, since 1967. Agents: Galleria Massimo Valsecchi, Via S. Marta II, Milan; Galleria Unimedia, Vico dei Garibaldi I, Genoa. Address: Vico dei Garibaldi 1, 16123 Genoa, Italy.

Individual Exhibitions:

1969	Galleria La Bertesca, Genoa
1970	Galleria Modulo, Milan
1971	*Il Cervello sul Muro*, Modern Art Agency, Naples
	Galleria Barozzi, Venice
	Produzenten Galerie, Berlin
	Tele Acide: Tele Acidate, Galleria Ferrari, Verona
1972	Galleria Duemila, Bologna
	Galleria del Leone, Venice
1973	Galleria La Bertesca, Genoa
1974	*In the Company of the Human Brain and Prehistoric Man*, Neue Galerie, Aachen, West Germany
	Galerie Klang, Cologne
	Galleria Nuovi Strumenti, Brescia, Italy
1975	Galleria Massimo Valsecchi, Milan
	Foundation of the Museum of Anthropology, Monteghirfo, Genoa
1976	Galleria Arteverso, Genoa
	Galleria Civica, Moderna, Italy
1977	Galleriaforma, Genoa
	Studio di Via Crugoni, Genoa
	Studio Torelli, Ferrara, Italy
1978	Galleria Arte Moderna, Portofino, Italy
	Fabjbasaglia Galleria, Bologna
	Galleria Arte Moderna, Alessandria, Italy
	Galleria Nuova 13, Alessandria, Italy
1979	Galleria Nuovi Strumenti, Brescia, Italy
	Galleria R. Rotta, Genoa
	Galleria Unimedia, Genoa
	Galleria Arco d'Alibert, Rome
	Galleria Il Luogo di Gauss, Milan
1980	Galleria De Amicis, Florence
	Galleria Il Gabbiano, La Spezia, Italy
	Studio Cesare Manzo, Pescara, Italy
	Salone Villa Romana, Florence
1981	Galleria Massimo Valsecchi, Milan
	Galeria Andata-Ritorno, Geneva
1982	Galleria R. Rotta, Genoa
	Galleria del Cavallino, Venice
	Galleria Unimedia, Genoa

Selected Group Exhibitions:

1969	*Rassegna Biennale*, Galleria di Tendenza, Modena, Italy
1973	*8th Biennale*, Paris
1974	*Spruensicheerung: Archaeologie und Erinnerung*, Hamburg and Munich
1976	*Identité: Identification*, CAP, Bordeaux
1978	*Arte e Cinema negli Anni 70*, Pinacoteca Civica, Ravenna, Italy
1979	*Metafisica del Quotidiano*, Galleria d'Arte Moderna, Bologna
1980	*Work in Progress*, Galleria Arte Moderna, Genoa
1981	*Mythos and Ritual*, Kunsthaus, Zurich
1982	*Deserto*, Comune di Bergamo, Italy

Collections:

Neue Galerie, Aachen, West Germany

Publications:

By COSTA: books—*Interpretazione Intera*, Genoa 1970; *Sintomi di un Lavoro*, Naples 1971; *Evolution: Involution*, Berlin and Genoa 1971; *Due Esercizi di Antropologia*, Brescia, Italy 1974; *Materiale e Metaforico*, Genoa 1979; *Sublimato Potabile*, Milan 1981.

On COSTA: books—*Il Cervello sul Muro*, exhibition catalogue, by Corrado Maltese, Naples 1971; *Tele Acide: Tele Acidate*, exhibition catalogue, by Renato Barilli, Verona 1971; *In the Company of the Human Brain and Prehistoric Man*, exhibition catalogue, by Wolfgang Becker, Aachen, West Germany 1974; *Maori's Eyes Reflect the Latent Colours of the Forest* by Lorenza Trucchi, Rome 1974; articles— "Metodologia del fare" by Edda Gazzerro in *Due Esercizi di Antropoliga*, Brescia, Italy 1974; "Noi i Primitivi" by Franco Torriani in *Gala* (Milan), February 1975.

After a period of quite general activity, I turned to experimentation in the most difficult means of expression: I slowly acquired the use of the "substance" as a means referring to itself and to its history. At that time I worked particularly on acid and acidified canvas.

In the meantime I had acquired a consciousness of a precise interest in man. I then ideally reconstructed the brain and the brain-pan, assimilating it to the polar skull-cap: this interest produced a big file of engravings and of other works.

My intention was the definition of an "absolute" geographical place as an ambiguous sign of existence. At that time I began to make use of chalk and afterwards of raw clay.

And I also worked, at that time, on research into man's memory. Works such as "portraits by heart" are of this category.

To be more exact, the work about man's evolution began in 1971. The book *Evolution: Involution* is of this period too. In it I also tried to present the idea, which I consider as fundamental, of recovering the past in a critical perspective: I started the work as research into the "possibilities of space and of time" which man has altered and lost during his evolution.

I studied pre-historic man, and I extracted and reproduced his peculiar traits. The casts of living persons, reconstructed according to the different periods of evolution, belong to this period. Then I studied primitive cultures that have preserved their original way of life and original tools. I have also been interested in man's "habitat," and some of my works have to be considered as studies of its changes.

Afterwards I recognized in the objects used by man signs of his way of life: the object reveals the relationship it has with man. The reconstructions on which I work or the appropriation of certain objects, inserted into the works, have precisely this purpose: they are a sign of reality; they propose it again as directly as possible.

In the work of reconstruction of the "Active Museum of Monteghirfo" it was my intention to collect and preserve in their original setting these objects of use—signs of a culture crushed by our consumer civilization.

Through this work I have identified things, persons, places, nuclei of families, the human aggregate and the environment—an exact and fated living mosaic. A certain number of document-works have been the result of this interest. In these works the materials used are photographic enlargements of environments or of objects and the objects themselves, which I have covered with clay.

I make use of anthropology as a means of knowing, but in my work it is only a tool aiding my intuition and emotion, which more decidedly are the means to urge me to operate and perform.

I believe that man, as all the things on earth, must be perceived in himself, in what he is in his totality beyond and outside scientific knowledge, which ends by concealing, by darkening our lives and the existence of things.

—Claudio Costa

In the making of a work, Claudio Costa behaves according to a methodology of "doing," which is typical of that kind of contemporary conceptual art of which he is certainly a prominent practitioner. His work consists of perfectly identifiable images or objects, and they can "placed" historically: they are documents (both real and faithfully reconstructed) of periods prior to contemporary life. Annotations explaining the cultural references are inserted into the works. Thus, the construction has form and functions as a channel for communication in a typically contemporary particularization of inquiry and expression.

However, this description is not sufficient to convey the fundamental characteristics of his art. Costa's work is not complete within itself or within the conceptual/rational reference in which it places itself as praxis (which is, more or less, the characteristic of the art-concept), for it is his intention to establish a relationship of knowledge as from the objects as facts. A relationship of this kind, as realized by Costa, does not exhaust itself in mere rational fact; it aims to go further, to become a kind of feedback on man facing his history—in a process analogous in its psychic mechanism to that of the emotional, nonformal genesis of classic expressionism.

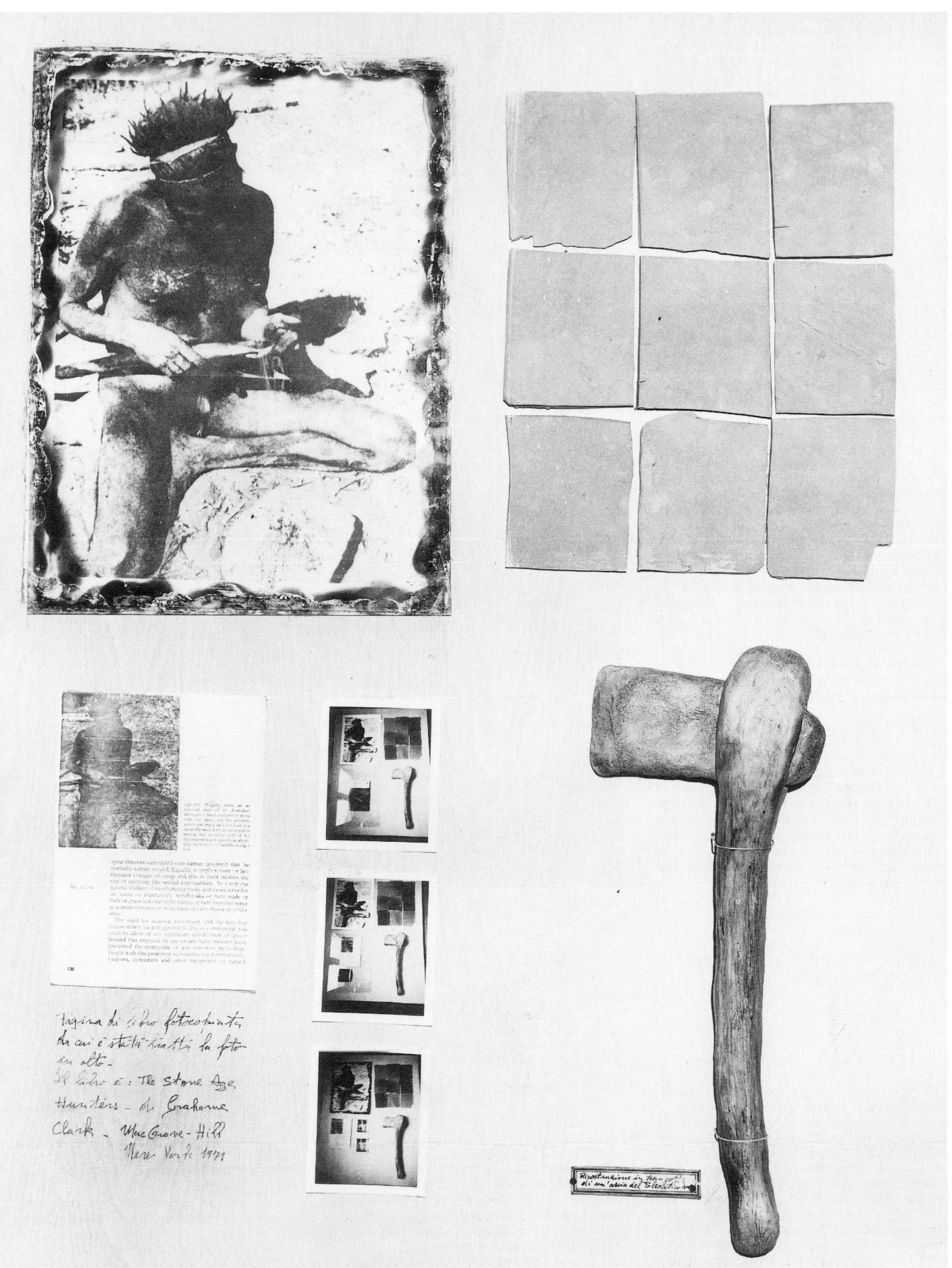

Claudio Costa: *Old Making of Man*, 1975

As for the composition of the work: the chosen object—identified, indicated—is not used for the image it offers of itself, nor as an indication, a reference, of external reality to be analyzed for ethical or social values. Claudio Costa's "object" is, as it were, a laboratory finding, a cognitive moment in itself, to be regarded as such. In this sense the artist is a kind of anthropologist—not only in his interests but also in his methods. He reports his findings without loading them with symbols or myths; he does not report according to some basic cultural perspective.

His form of analysis is a propaedeutic methodology, and therefore neutral. And his work should be regarded in its entirety, so as to differentiate it from that of those contemporaries who also use historical, archaeological or anthropological findings in their works. For Costa such findings do not involve an occasional fact or a chance discovery of an unusual source of images and objects. Rather, they are the result of a constant "observation" of man and his natural habitat.

In the past Costa has edited the memory of man; he has proposed a relation with Cromus; he has analyzed "lived" space in relation to "possible" space. He has investigated the materiality, the availability, the modifications of habitat. From the relationship between man and space-time, as well as habitat, he has extracted the "object"—an object which, however, does not report on itself but on something other than itself.

If for most artists one can speak of the object-as-code or the sign-as-code, for Costa one must speak perhaps of some primary, preliminary code in the sense that the significant means are external to the object and to its meaning. These "means" rest between object and observer, and they are constituted not as conventional signs but as evocations of a relationship. It is a code composed of object/man means, in which the sign is not the object nor the man but the action occurring between the two and modified (i.e., further codified) by the remote, philogenetic, and consequently, present experience. Costa uses this relationship as an art object, an intuitive means of knowledge, and, paradoxically, his work is characterized by the absence of real time: what he proposes is proposed always in the present, without temporal references.

Costa's analysis proceeds synchronically (that is, descriptively); the sign juxtapositions of another type which he also uses do not actuate a diachronism (that is, comparison with different systems) but are notes in a thought progress within the work, which thus are taken for single cognitive moments: he proceeds by simple elements to which he juxtaposes in a differentiated and conscious manner more complex cultural indications, which are, however, always placed *a posteriori* as regards the single cognitive moment. Thus Costa injects himself, by a route of his own, into the context of contemporary thought, which recognizes man's sources of knowledge as contingent and contained within himself as well as within his biologically delimited being. Through his work Costa creates a cognitive, intuitive/emotional, biologically recognizable moment.

—Edda Gazzerro

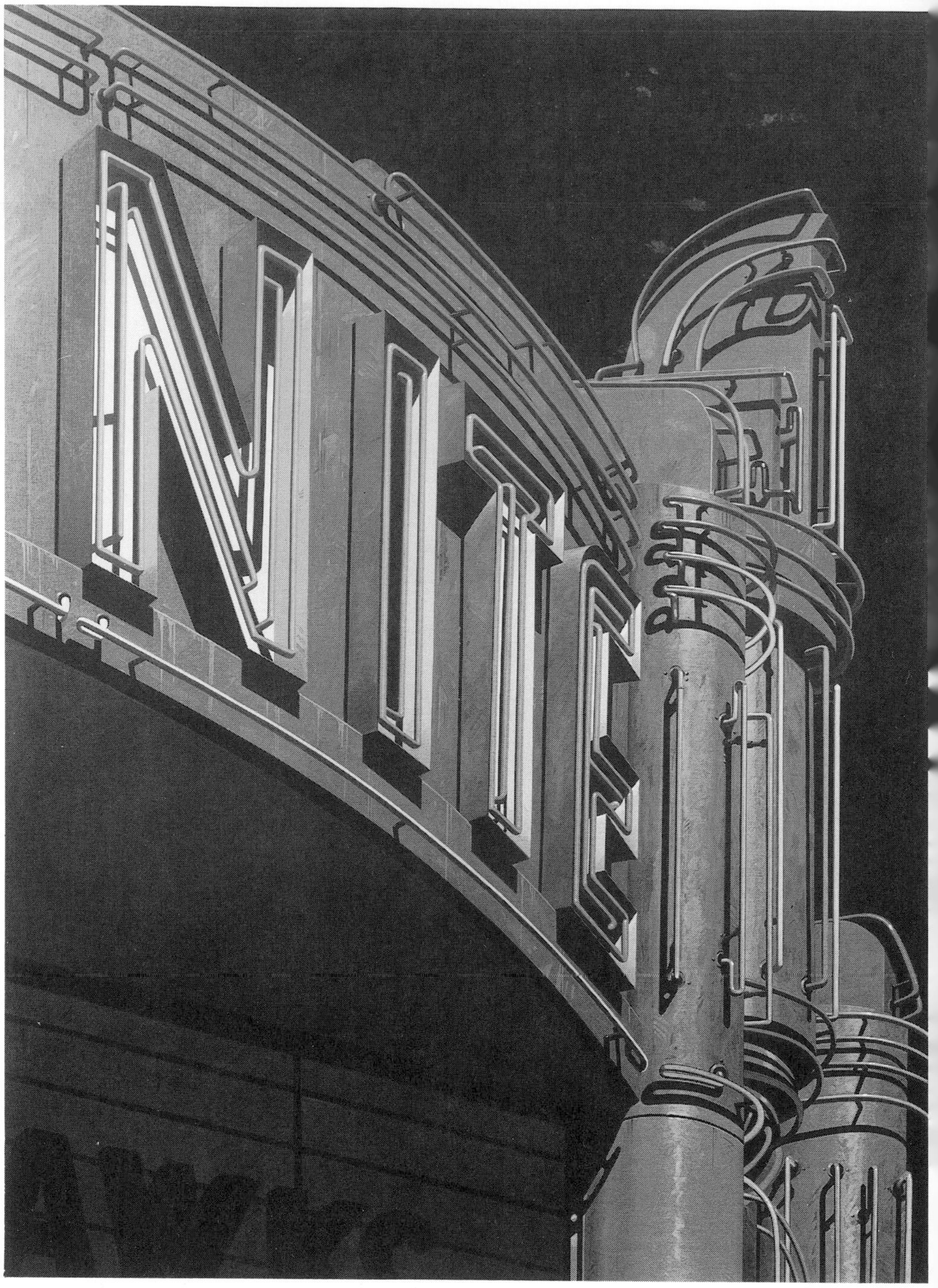

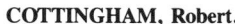

Robert Cottingham: *Nite*, 1986

COTTINGHAM, Robert.

American. Born in Brooklyn, New York, 26 September 1935. Studied at the Pratt Institute, Brooklyn, 1959–64, Associate Degree in Advertising Art 1962. Served in the United States Army, in Com-Z Unit, Orleans, France, 1955–58: Specialist 3rd Class. Married Jane Marie Weismann in 1967; daughters: Reid Ann, Molly Jane and Kyle Annie Bliss. Art Director, Young and Rubicam Advertising Inc., New York, 1959–64, and Los Angeles, 1964–68. Independent painter, since 1968. Instructor, Art Center College of Design, Los Angeles, 1969–70. Recipient: National Endowment for the Arts Grant, 1974; Artist of the Year Award, Fairfield Chamber of Commerce, Connecticut, 1988. Agents: Gimpel and Weitzenhoffer, 724 Fifth Avenue, New York, New York 10019; Fendrick Gallery, 3059 M Street NW, Washington, D.C. 20007; Roger Ramsay Gallery, 212 West Superior Street, Chicago, Illinois 60610. Address: P.O. Box 604, Blackman Road, Newton, Connecticut 06470, U.S.A.

Individual Exhibitions:

1968	Molly Barnes Gallery, Los Angeles
1969	Molly Barnes Gallery, Los Angeles
1970	Molly Barnes Gallery, Los Angeles
1971	O.K. Harris Gallery, New York
1974	O.K. Harris Gallery, New York
1975	D.M. Gallery, London
	Galerie de Gestlo, Hamburg
1976	O.K. Harris Gallery, New York
	John Berggruen Gallery, San Francisco
1977	Landfall Press Gallery, Chicago
1978	Morgan Gallery, Kansas City, Missouri
	Bethel Art Gallery, Connecticut
	O.K. Harris Gallery, New York
1979	Aldrich Museum, Ridgefield, Connecticut
	Beaver College, Glenside, Pennsylvania
	Landfall Press Gallery, Chicago
	Galerie de Gestlo, Cologne
	Delta Gallery, Rotterdam
	Getler-Pall Gallery, New York
	Dean Junior College, Franklyn, Massachusetts
1980	University of Bridgeport, Connecticut
	Thomas Segal Gallery, Boston
	Ball State University, Muncie, Indiana
	Madison Art Center, Wisconsin
1981	Fendrick Gallery, Washington, D.C.
	Mattatuck Museum, Waterbury, Connecticut
	Swain School of Design, New Bedford, Massachusetts
1982	Coe Kerr Gallery, New York
1983	Signet Arts, St. Louis, Missouri
	Modernism Gallery, San Francisco
	Wichita Art Museum, Kansas

1984	Coe Kerr Gallery, New York
	Fendrick Gallery, Washington, D.C.
	Springfield Art Museum, Missouri
	Palace Theatre, New Haven, Connecticut
1985	The Art Guild, Farmington, Connecticut
	Abilene Christian University, Texas
	Roger Ramsay Gallery, Chicago
	Reynolda House Museum of American Art, Winston-Salem, North Carolina
	Arkansas Arts Center, Little Rock (travelled to Washington, D.C.; St. Louis, Missouri; Odessa, Texas)
1986	Signet Arts, St. Louis, Missouri
	Museum of Art, Science and Industry, Bridgeport, Connecticut
	Gallery Karl Oskar, Westwood Hills, Kansas
	Brenda Kroos Gallery, Columbus, Ohio
	Springfield Art Museum, Missouri (travelled to Chattanooga, Tennessee; Kansas City, Missouri; Joplin, Missouri; Norman, Oklahoma; Cedar Rapids, Iowa)

Selected Group Exhibitions:

1970	*The Highway,* Institute of Contemporary Art, University of Pennsylvania, Philadelphia (travelled to the Institute for the Arts, Rice University, Houston, and the Akron Art Institute, Ohio.)
1971	*Radical Realism,* Museum of Contemporary Art, Chicago
1972	*Documenta 5,* Kassel, West Germany
1973	*Photo-Realism: The Ludwig Collection,* Serpentine Gallery, London
1974	*Hyperréalistes Américains/Réalistes Européens,* Centre National d'Art Contemporain, Paris (toured Europe)
1978	*Art about Art,* Whitney Museum, New York (travelled to the North Carolina Museum of Art, Raleigh; Frederick S. Wright Art Gallery, University of California at Los Angeles; and the Portland Museum, Oregon)
1981	*Contemporary American Realism since 1960,* Pennsylvania Academy of Fine Arts, Philadelphia
1983	*Painting New York,* Museum of the City of New York
1985	*American Realism: The Precise Image,* Isetan Museum, Tokyo (travelled to Osaka and Yokohama, Japan)
1986	*Hollywood: Legend and Reality,* Smithsonian Institution, Washington, D.C. (toured the United States)

Collections:

Whitney Museum, New York; Syracuse University, New York; Hirshhorn Museum and Sculpture Garden, Smithsonian Institution, Washington, D.C.; Indianapolis Museum of Art; Honolulu Academy of Art; Museum of Modern Art, New York; Art Institute of Chicago; Arts Council of Great Britain, London; Boymans-van Beuningen Museum, Rotterdam.

Publications:

By COTTINGHAM: article—interview in "Photo-Realists: 12 Interviews" by Linda Chase and Ted McBurnett in *Art in America* (New York), November/December 1972.

On COTTINGHAM: books—*New Realism* by Udo Kultermann, Tübingen, West Germany 1972; *Photo-Realism: The Ludwig Collection,* exhibition catalogue, London 1973; *Hyperréalistes Américains/Réalistes Européens,* exhibition catalogue, Paris 1974; *Realists at Work* by John Arthur, New York 1983; *Robert Cottingham—A Print Retrospective 1972–86,* edited by John Arthur, Springfield, Missouri 1986; articles—"Too Easy to Be Art" by Peter Schjeldahl in the *New York Times,* May 1974; "Robert Cunningham: The Capers of the Signscape" by Toni del Renzio in *Art and Artists* (London), February 1975; "Cottingham's Air: Letter Perfect" in *New Art Examiner* (Chicago), December 1985.

*   *   *

For more than twenty years now I have been painting and drawing a uniquely American subject—the neon signs, shop fronts and movie marquees of our cities and downtown neighborhoods.

My interest in these cultural icons seems to derive from my Brooklyn upbringing, my fascination with letter forms as symbols and my interest in society's use of language as a means of persuasion.

During the four year period from 1983 through 1986, I became particularly intrigued by a row of shop fronts that included such diverse commercial establishments as a barber shop, a hotel, a bar, a newsstand, a liquor store, and a Mexican restaurant named Barrera-Rosa's. This panorama of facades and messages struck me as an image rich with aesthetic possibilities, not only as a singular, unified vision, but as a network of separate and overlapping compositional fragments. I began an extensive exploration of this image, dissecting and analysing its parts, in an attempt to reveal its abstract underpinnings. This pictorial foray resulted in an output of 45 individual works executed in a multitude of media, including watercolor, acrylic, gouache, ink, graphite, woodcut, linoleum cut, etching, lithography and oil.

The three prints in the *Barrera-Rosa* portfolio played an important part in this exploration. Each deals with a specific means of visual expression: line(dry-point etching), mass(linoleum cut), and color(lithograph). Each print, while a finished graphic work in its own right, contributes significantly to the overall investigation of the image's substructure; its abstract patterns, the formal relationships of interlocking shapes, the nuances of line, value and color—in short, the fundamental components of composition.

And beyond these formal issues there is, of course, the subject matter itself. I like to think of these prints and my work in general as a celebration of the signs and urban iconography that have given American cities their peculiar energy. Monumental, poignant, absurd, and surreal, these structures stand as vivid testimony to the vitality and variety of contemporary American life.

—Robert Cottingham

*   *   *

Robert Cottingham ascribes to Pop Art the essential permissiveness that allowed him to paint images of mundane urban reference, with an emphasis upon a display of letter types in commercial signs, and clearly based upon the photograph. Although Cottingham has always used photographs—which he himself takes in carefully planned forays to various American cities—he has likewise always handpainted his images without the use of compressed air spray techniques. He thus joins Richard Estes and others among prominent "Photo-Realists" who ironically enough combine the traditional liking for the handicraft and brushed facture of easel painting with the apparently antithetical feel of the mechanically-produced photographic print. His etchings and lithographs are also handwork, and not photo-transcriptions of painted works.

After an earlier career in advertising and a move from the East Coast to California, Cottingham's first exhibition in Los Angeles, in 1968, already presented the themes and compositional orderings which have remained constant throughout his career.

These early works, of city landmarks from the pre-World War II era, such as "Ralph's Market" and the "Pan Pacifica Auditorium" (the latter still one of his largest works at 10 feet in width), presented a passerby's view of the building's upper parts; while lettering was already a clear intent in these works, the structures were seen broadly against the sky. At the onset of the next decade, Cottingham had painted one of his most often reproduced works, "Art," 1971: a closely-cropped—the photo terminology clearly appropriate—view of a theatre marquee which goes on beyond the picture frame. Although the light bulbs are missing and have been replaced by neon light strips and the letter character is clearly inter-war, nostalgia and good-humored wordplay are only infrequently the clear goal of the artist. More pointedly, these paintings are intended as brilliantly hued, abstracted plays of line and movement.

Cottingham himself has affirmed that it is not the social character of the letters as much as their visual interest that led him initially to those parts of American cities (sections which he has found often changed in his subsequent returns). In interviews he has spoken of his calculated use of three lenses on the cameras with which he gathers materials for his studio production. And his paintings have easily reflected this photographic practice—the use of telephoto lenses with their close-up, "zoom" focus. Although Cottingham's best-known works have been signage seen at sharp angles from below, he has also produced more relaxed, less camera-referential and more personal, perceptual. The omnipresence of the photographic image in our culture has neither diminished his productivity nor style qualities. His mid-decade work is still based upon the "fading" urban neighborhood. There may now more often appear a dazzling, even mannered, interplay of a multitude of elements, but perhaps more often presented both more parallel and more perpendicular to the picture plane. A touch of the long American love for *trompe l'oeil* has been added to another Populist tradition—the neighborhood realism of the Ash Can School of the early twentieth century—and modernist abstraction is likewise touched with pre-modern attitudes. Cottingham has said of his particular poignant formalism: "I'm not primarily interested in documentation, although I think there is a certain documentary aspect to my work. It's unavoidable because of the degree of realistic depiction involved and by the nature of the subject matter. It's a vision exclusive to the century and is fading fast."

—Joshua Kind

CRAGG, Tony.

British. Born in Liverpool, Merseyside, in 1949. Studied art, Gloucestershire College of Arts and Technology, Cheltenham, 1968–70; painting, Wimbledon School of Art, London, 1970–73; sculpture, Royal College of Art, London, 1973–77, MA 1977. Married Ute Uberste-Lehn in 1977; sons: Daniel and Thomas. Worked as a laboratory technician, Natural Rubber Producers Association, Liverpool, 1966–68. Independent sculptor, in Wuppertal, West Germany, since 1977. Instructor in sculpture, Ecole des Beaux-Arts, Metz, France, 1976; instructor, Kunstakademie, Dusseldorf, since 1979. Agents: Galerie Crousel-Robelin, 40 rue Quincampoix, 75004 Paris, France; and Lisson Gallery, London. Address: c/o Lisson Gallery, 67 Lisson Street, London NW1, England.

Individual Exhibitions:

1979	Lisson Gallery, London (and 1980)
	Lutzowstrasse Situation, West Berlin
	Kunstlerhaus Weidenallee, Hamburg
1980	Arnolfini Gallery, Bristol
	Galerie Konrad Fischer, Dusseldorf
	Galerie Chantal Crousel, Paris
	Lutzowstrasse Situation, Buro Berlin
	Galleria Lucio Amelio, Naples
	Galleria Franco Toselli, Milan
	Saman Galleria, Genoa, Italy
1981	Galerie Schellmann und Kluser, Munich
	Musee d'Art et d'industrie, St. Etienne, France
	Whitechapel Art Gallery, London
	Front Room, London
	Nouveau Musee, Lyon, France (and 1982)
	Von der Heydt Museum, Wuppertal, West Germany
	Galerie Vacuum, Dusseldorf
1982	Badischer Kunstverein, Karlsruhe, West Germany
	Kanransha Gallery, Tokyo
	Nisshin Gallery, Tokyo
	Marian Goodman Gallery, New York (and 1983)

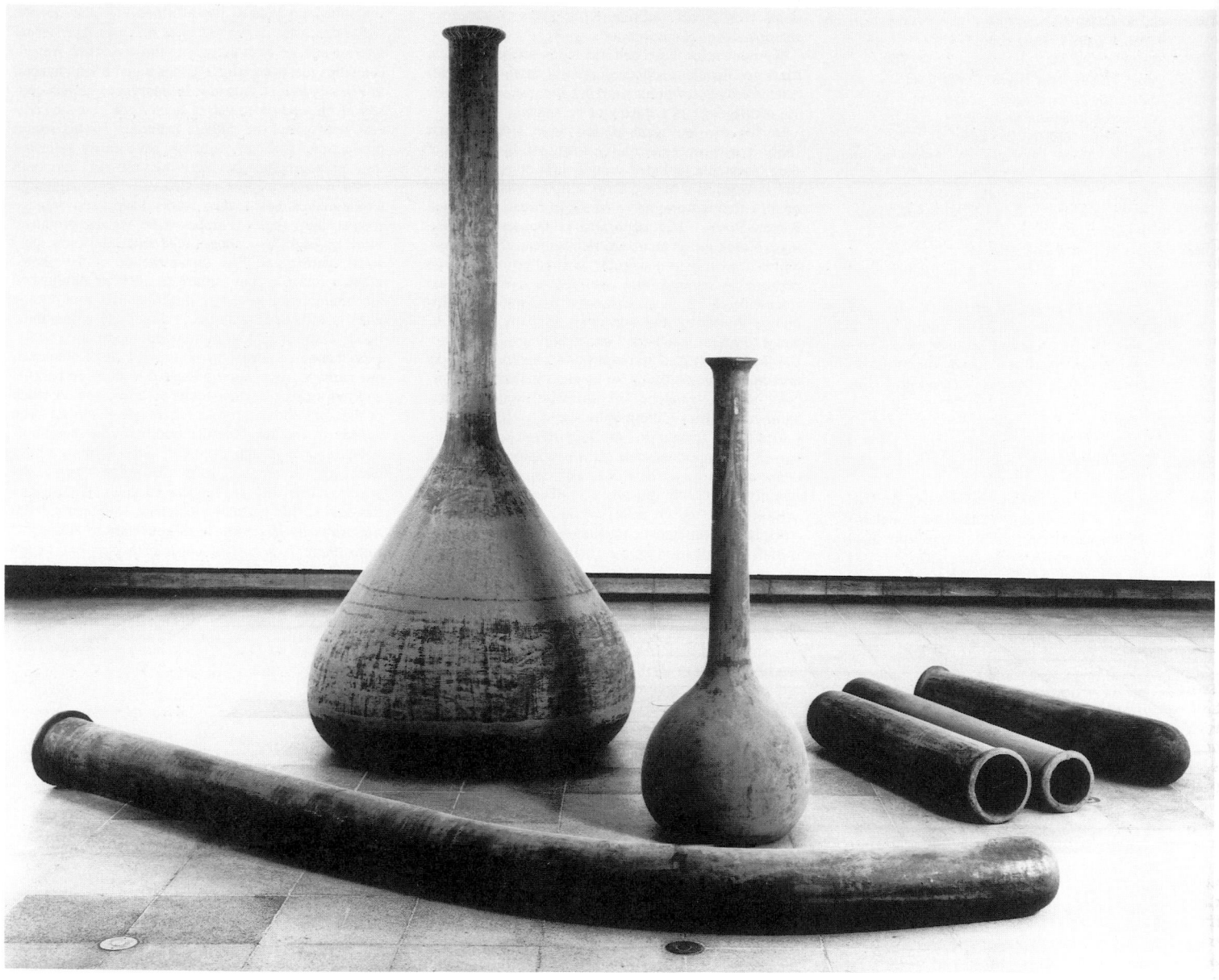

Tony Cragg: *Instinctive Reactions*, 1987 Courtesy Lisson Gallery, London

Galerie Chantal Crousel, Paris
Buro Berlin
Lisson Gallery, London
Galerie Konrad Fischer, Dusseldorf
Museum Kroller-Muller, Otterlo, Netherlands
Galerie Schellmann und Kluser, Munich
1983 Galleria Lucio Amelio, Naples
Kunsthalle, Berne
Art and Project, Amsterdam
Galeria Thomas Cohn, Rio de Janeiro
Galleria Franco Toselli, Milan
Galerie Buchmann, St. Gallen, Switzerland
1984 Yarlow and Salzmann, Toronto
De Vleeshal, Middelburg, Netherlands
Louisiana Museum, Humlebaek, Denmark
Galerie Schellmann und Kluser, Munich
Marian Goodman Gallery, New York
Kanransha Gallery, Tokyo
Galerie Crousel-Hussenot, Paris
Kunstverein, Cologne
Galleria Tucci Russo, Turin
1985 Kunsthalle Waghaus, Winterthur, Switzerland
Staatsgalerie Moderner Kunst, Munich
Donald Young Gallery, Chicago
Lisson Gallery, London
Art and Project, Amsterdam
Palais des Beaux-Arts, Brussels
ARC/Musee d'Art Moderne de la Ville, Paris
1986 Kestner-Gesellschaft, Hannover
Galerie Bernd Kluser, Munich

Galerie Joost Declercq, Ghent, Belgium
Brooklyn Museum of Art, New York
Galerie Pierre Huber, Geneva
University of California, Berkeley
1987 Hayward Gallery, London
Galleria Tucci Russo, Turin
Marian Goodman Gallery, New York
1988 Galeria Marga Paz, Madrid
Galerie Buchmann, Basle
Galerie Crousel-Robelin, Paris

Selected Group Exhibitions:

1977 *RCA Degree Show*, Royal College of Art, London
1980 *Kunst in Europa na '68*, Museum van Hedendaagse Kunst, Ghent, Belgium
1981 *British Sculpture in the 20th Century*, Whitechapel Art Gallery, London
1982 *Kunst wird Material*, Nationalgalerie, West Berlin
1983 *Edges and Shadows: Sculpture in Britain*, Hayward Gallery, London (and Serpentine Gallery, London)
1984 *The British Art Show*, City Art Gallery, Birmingham (and Ikon Gallery, Birmingham; travelled to Edinburgh, Sheffield and Southamption)
1985 *Mobel—Objekte und Installationen*, Von der Heydt Museum, Wuppertal, West Germany
1986 *Beuys zu Ehren*, Stadtische Galerie in Lenbachhaus, Munich

1987 *A Quiet Revolution: British Sculpture since 1965*, San Francisco Museum of Modern Art (travelled to Newport Beach; Washington, D.C.; Buffalo)
1988 *Brittanica: Vingt-cinq ans de sculpture*, Musee des Beaux Arts, Le Havre, France (travelled to Evreux, Rouen and Antwerp, 1988-89)

Collections:

Tate Gallery, London; British Council, London; Arts Council of Great Britain, London; Museum of Modern Art, New York; Fonds Regional d'Art Contemporain Rhone-Alpes, France.

Publications:

By CRAGG: books—*Tony Cragg: Skulpturen*, exhibition catalogue, with others, Hannover 1985; *Tony Cragg*, exhibition catalogue, with Lynne Cooke, London 1987.

On CRAGG: books—*Tony Cragg*, exhibition catalogue with foreword by Bernard Ceysson, St. Etienne 1981; *Tony Cragg*, exhibition catalogue with text by Ursula Peters, Wuppertal 1981; *Tony Cragg: Skulpturen*, exhibition catalogue with essay by Michael Newman, Karlsruhe 1982; *Tony Cragg*, exhibition catalogue with text by Nobuo Nakamura, Tokyo 1982; *Tony Cragg*, exhibition catalogue with texts by Jean-Hubert Martin and Germano Celant, Berne 1983; *Tony Cragg: Zwei Landschaften*, exhibition catalogue with text by Armin

Wildermuth, St. Gallen 1984; *Tony Cragg*, exhibition catalogue with essay by Armin Wildermuth, Cologne 1984; *Tony Cragg*, exhibition catalogue with texts by Anneliese Pohlen and Demosthenes Davvetos, Brussels and Paris 1985.

Tony Cragg is a part of that generation of artists who, following Philip King, Richard Long and Barry Flanagan, have renewed the scope of English sculpture by insisting on a critical rereading and one sensitive to the value of the object in the contemporary plastic arts. Though close to the trends of the seventies, Cragg's work nevertheless departs from the rigorous formulas and strictly 'objectual' criteria of minimal art in order to address itself to the crisis of our modern consumer society.

Cragg, who has lived in West Germany since 1979, trained as a biologist and then worked in a research laboratory, which taught him to consider "art as an extension of science" (T. C.) From the time of his first artistic creations, while he was still a student at London's Royal College of Art, it was as an 'archaeologist' of the technological era that he discovered and utilised the formal, emotional and narrative potential of the industrial object.

All the products-throwouts of consumption, used and discarded, those reject materials which clutter our daily world, are retrieved by the artist near his place of work, then 'staged' in the exhibition area. The materials are displayed without modifications according to a system of accumulation which demonstrates the complex interactions that take place between man and his creations, the object being the projection and the receptacle of socio-economic interests and of individual pretensions. "I think that objects have the capability to carry valuable information for us, to be important to us, but the fact is that most objects are made in ways which are irresponsible and manipulative. Irresponsible because people—the makers of this or that—don't really consider in any metaphysical way the meanings of the objects that they are making: and manipulative because things are made for a variety of commercial and power based reasons" (T. C.). In his work Tony Cragg ignores the functional side of objects; the plastic unity of his assemblages is subjectively determined by the preliminary choice of a form (one of his first pieces, *Stapel*, 1977, is made up of planks, stones and diverse other materials which together build up a perfect cube) or of a colour (for *Spectrum*, 1984, the materials have been put together in series of blues, reds, yellows and greens). For his first compositions Cragg primarily used plastic objects that had been worn out by time or use, and bits and pieces of artificially coloured synthetic materials, placing them one beside the other so that they filled out the human figures which he had outlined on walls or ground. A veritable critical cartography of society and of the object's vocabulary, these assemblages represent life-size human silhouettes (self-portraits, groups, *Britain seen from the north*, 1981, *Polizist*, 1981, *Riot*, 1987 . . .) which have the quality of historical and metaphysical symbols. Some of the figures take on the magnified shape of one of the objects of the composition (*Green bottle*, 1980) or of a natural element (*Red skin*, 1979), or of an object-type in the artistic (*Palette*, 1982) or poetic vocabulary (*Blue moon*, 1980).

From 1982 Cragg's working methods became more diversified. By covering objects with a uniform layer of white or speckled paint and thereby obscuring the qualities themselves of the material, he accorded particular importance to the form and to the equilibrium of the work as a whole (*Lens*, 1985, *No place for a rabbit*, 1985, *Aquaduct*, 1986).

From 1982 Cragg also developed an interest in organic objects and in hand-crafted objects, in a pretechnological mode of production where manual work plays a direct part in the transformation of the material. *Axe*, for example, in which an axe figures as part of the overall image, brings into contact with one another certain wooden objects of varying volume and complexity which, in view of the means of their production, carry within themselves this very axe.

The tool, symbol of man's creative capacities and of his control over matter, became the object of a number of Cragg's sculptures. Chosen for the purity of their volumes, various tools were magnified and worked in wood, glass or steel in works which underline the interaction between form and function (*Mortar and pestle*, 1986, *Eye bath*, 1986).

With the series entitled *Landscape* (1982, 1983) Cragg distances himself once again from industrial society in order to linger over the organisation of natural elements, in the face of which man abandons rationalism and returns to his ancient role as creator of images and inventor of myths. The austere compositions of *Landscape* seem to be insisting still on the arbitrary forms and structures of stones, the result of fractures to the original block from which they have split. Certain compositions in which crude materials are assembled are then exploded by the introduction of a geometric shape symbolising the intrusion of architecture into the landscape (*Installation in Cadillac*, 1985, *Jurassic landscape*, 1986). With *Echo*, 1984, a piece which is made up of large geometric volumes uniformly covered with repetitive and depersonalising graffiti, the artist analyses urban architecture. The degradation and dehumanisation of the natural or city environment occupy a prominent place in Cragg's work as a whole.

In some of his latest works (*The Worm Returns*, 1986, *DNA-Molecule*, *Bacchus Drops*, 1985, *Inverted Sugar Crop*, 1987 . . .) Cragg demonstrates his interest in science, alluding to chemical processes upon which the manufacture of certain food products like sugar and wine is based. From a preoccupation with the manufacturing techniques of various objects, via an interest in the modifications directly imposed on the molecular structure of natural elements and the material changes resulting therefrom, Cragg was naturally led to reconsider the creative function (in both artistic and scientific terms) in its primary alchemical acceptation as a transforming power.

Besides the diversity of its scientific, social and historical associations and the constant reappraisal of its plastic solutions, the work of Tony Cragg should be regarded above all as a sensitive and frequently philosophical approach to the human situation, as testified by the following extract from an interview with Cragg: "In a sense, it's obvious that in terms of the physical world scientists make the more fundamental statements, but artists and philosophers don't have a less important job. They humanize, they find out what the significance of science is for human beings . . . . I think you have to make images of objects which are like thinking models to help you get through the world."

—Dominique Liquois

CRAIG-MARTIN, Michael.

British. Born in Dublin in 1941; moved with his family to the United States, 1946; returned to Britain, 1966. Educated at Yale University, New Haven, Connecticut, 1961-63; studied at the Yale School of Art and Architecture, 1964-66. Divorced; has one daughter. Settled in Corsham, Wiltshire, 1966-68; lived in London, 1968-70, and since 1972. Lecturer, Bath Academy of Art and Canterbury College of Art, 1970-72; Principal Lecturer, Goldsmiths' College, London, 1973. Agent: Waddington Galleries, London. Address: c/o Waddington Galleries, 2 Cork Street, London WIX 1PA, England

Individual Exhibitions:

1969	Rowan Gallery, London
1970	Rowan Gallery, London
1971	Arnolfini Gallery, Bristol
	Richard Demarco Gallery, Edinburgh
1972	Rowan Gallery, London
1973	Rowan Gallery, London
1974	Rowan Gallery, London
	Galerie December, Münster, West Germany
1975	Rowan Gallery, London
1976	Rowan Gallery, London
	Selected Works 1966-1975, Turnpike Gallery, Leigh, Lancashire (toured the U.K.)
1977	Third Eye Centre, Glasgow
	Oliver Dowling Gallery, Dublin
1978	Galerie December, Dusseldorf
	Institute of Modern Art, Brisbane (toured Australia)
	Rowan Gallery, London
1979	Galerie Foksal, Warsaw
	Galerie Akmulatory, Poznan, Poland
	Oliver Dowling Gallery, Dublin
1980	Rowan Gallery, London
	Galerie BaMa, Paris
1981	Galerija Suvremene Umjetnosti, Zagreb
1982	Waddington Galleries, London
1983	Waddington and Shiell Galleries, Toronto
1985	Waddington Galleries, London
1988	Waddington Galleries, London

Selected Group Exhibitions:

1966	*First II*, Jewish Community Center, New Haven, Connecticut
1970	*Critics' Choice*, Tooths Gallery, London
1972	*The New Art*, Hayward Gallery, London
1973	*Henry Moore to Gilbert and George*, Palais des Beaux-Arts, Brussels
1974	*Idea and Image in Recent Art*, Art Institute of Chicago
1975	*Bienal*, Sao Paulo
1976	*Sydney Biennale*, Art Gallery of New South Wales, Sydney
1979	*Un Certain Art Anglais*, Musée d'Art Moderne de la Ville, Paris
1980	*ROSC*, University College Gallery, Dublin (travelled to the Crawford Gallery, Cork)
1982	*Aspects of British Art Today*, Metropolitan Art Museum, Tokyo (toured Japan)
1984	*When Attitudes Became Form 1965-72*, Kettle's Yard Gallery, Cambridge (travelled to Edinburgh)
1986	*Esculturas sobre la Pared*, Galerie Juana de Aizpuru, Madrid

Collections:

Tate Gallery, London; Arts Council of Great Britain, London; Victoria and Albert Museum, London; Fitzwilliam Museum, Cambridge; Australian National Gallery, Canberra; Baltimore Museum of Art; City Art Gallery, Southhampton, Hampshire; Allen Art Museum, Oberlin College, Ohio; Swindon Art Gallery, Wiltshire.

Publications:

By CRAIG-MARTIN: articles—"Acquisitions" in *The Tate Gallery Biennial Report 1968-70*, London 1970; "A Procedural Proposition: Selection, Repetition, Extension, Exchange" in *Studio International* (London), September 1971; "An Interview with Simon Field" in *Art and Artists* (London), May 1972; "Acquisitions" in *The Tate Gallery Biennial Report 1970-71*, London 1972; interview with Anne Seymour in *The New Art*, exhibition catalogue, London 1972; "Acquisitions" in *The Tate Gallery Biennial Report 1972-74*, London 1974; statement in *Michael Craig-Martin*, exhibition catalogue, Zagreb 1981.

On CRAIG-MARTIN: books—*Michael Craig-Martin: Selected Works 1966 75*, exhibition catalogue, by Anne Seymour, Leigh, Lancashire 1976; *Michael Craig-Martin*, exhibition catalogue with text by Richard Stone, London 1985; articles—"Michael Craig-Martin" by Merete Bates in *The Guardian* (London), March 1976; "Best of British" by Marina Vaizey in the *Sunday Times* (London), 31 July 1977; "Sculptor's Visit Is Bound to Have an Impact" by Gertrude Langer in *Courier Mail* (Brisbane), 17 February 1978; "The State of British Art: It's a Bewilderment" by William Feaver in *Art News* (London), January 1980.

I have a thought, not clearly formulated, but a sense of the possibility of a particular meaning.

I am focusing my attention, seeking the words to express this thought, to give it form. I am using words I know. (My vocabulary is not static, new words enter it, others fall from use.)

These words are in common usage. They have immediacy and flexibility. Each word carries great associative resonance.

I am employing the grammar I know, putting the words together to make phrases and sentences, simple and complex.

I am stating facts, expressing opinions, making allusions, drawing comparisons, revealing values.

I have used these words many times, but this is the first time I have used them to express this thought in this way.

This is how I do my drawings.

—Michael Craig-Martin

Like a number of other "post-object" artists (to use the then-fashionable phrase) who took part in the *New Art* show at the Hayward Gallery in 1972, Michael Craig-Martin has been preoccupied with how we see and judge the veracity of a picture. What constitutes a picture? In what ways do words anchor or interfere with images? During the 1970's, of course, these concerns were for the most part the basis for reflections on photography. Craig-Martin's work, though, has had little to do—in any formal sense—with photography.

Trained as a sculptor, Craig-Martin's investigations into "ways of seeing" have been based—until recently—on the manipulation of objects and words. In an early installation work he involved the spectator in a simple experiment on the limits of our field of perception (what we take in, what we lose). Using numerous mirrors, Craig-Martin re-presented a composite view of the spectator. Craig-Martin has been called an illusionist. These powers are perhaps no better illustrated than by a piece he did in 1973. A glass of water was exhibited on a shelf as an oak tree. Here our partial or subjective perception of things is troubled by an obvious conflict between the sign and the signifier. But besides acting as a kind of visual example of Sausserian linguistics, the work achieved something else. In the most simple of ways it tapped the transforming powers that artists claim as magic (or rather the institutions from within which artists operate, label magic). It is charming work and takes its place alongside other object-pieces of the same period which test the limits of the real.

In the recent work (post-78) this gap between a present and an absent object, or rather the gap between picture and pictured, has shifted away from objects to images—isometric drawings of domestic objects projected onto the gallery wall. These large scale objects are superimposed over each other, creating a dense jungle of projecting lines. Ambiguity here is based on a static simultaneity of objects. In the mirror piece, simultaneity was the result of the break-up of a single image; the mirrors acted very much like a camera, panning around the object. In these drawings, the play between absence and presence becomes a kind of half-way house. Objects hover in and out of view. The eye can only take in one object at a time. Although visible, the other objects remain half-hidden, submerged. This has a lot to do with the scale of the objects. All the objects are uniform in size. We are therefore unable to read off objects according to their normal scale.

Picturing for Craig-Martin has nothing to do with interpretation, but rather with establishing a framework for inquiry. Each set of works adopts (adapts) a perceptual model which decentres the single and unitary vantage point of the viewer. In principle, Craig-Martin's work could be said to be structuralist in origin. It works on the interstices between things, between names, pictures and signs.

—John Roberts

CREMONINI, Leonardo.

Italian. Born in Bologna, 26 November 1925. Studied at the Accademia delle Belle Arti, Bologna, under the painters Alfred Protti and Giuglielmo Pizzirani and sculptor Luciano Minguzzi, 1932–36; attended art classes, Paris, 1951. Moved to Milan, 1945; settled in Paris, 1951, but worked often in Forio d'Ischia, until 1955; spent time in Douarnenez, Finistere, 1956; lived in Panarea, Eolian Islands, 1958–59. Professor, Ecole des Beaux-Arts, Paris, Lives in Florence and Paris. Agent: Galerie Claude Bernard, 7 rue des Beaux-Arts, 75006 Paris. Address: 11 rue de Buci, 75006 Paris, France.

Individual Exhibitions:

1951	Centre d'Art Italien, Paris
1952	Catherine Viviano Gallery, New York
1954	Galleria dell'Obelisco, Rome
	Frank Perls Gallery, Beverly Hills, California
	Catherine Viviano Gallery, New York
1955	Hanover Gallery, London
1957	Catherine Viviano Gallery, New York
1960	Galleria del Milione, Milan
	Galleria Galatea, Turin
	Galerie du Dragon, Paris
	Galerie Lacloche, Paris
1962	Catherine Viviano Gallery, New York
	Galerie du Dragon, Paris
1963	Galleria Galatea, Turin
1964	Galerie du Dragon, Paris
	Biennale, Venice
1966	Galerie du Dragon, Paris
1967	Galleria Il Fante di Spade, Rome
1969	Palais des Beaux-Arts, Brussels
	National Gallery, Prague
	Kunsthalle, Basle
	Konsthall, Lund, Sweden
	Museo Civico, Bologna (retrospective)
	Galleria Il Bisonte, Florence
	Musée d'Art Moderne de la Ville, Paris
1970	Kunsthalle, Darmstadt
1971	Galleria Giulia, Rome (toured Italy, Brussels, Paris)
1972	Galerie du Dragon, Paris
	Galleria dei Lanzi, Milan
	Galleria Il Gabbiano, Rome
1973	Galerie du Dragon, Paris
	Maison des Arts et Loisirs, Montbeliard, France
	Maison de la Culture, Rennes
	Musée d'Art Moderne, Strasbourg
1974	Galerie du Dragon, Paris
	Galleria Il Portico, Cesena, Italy
	Maison de la Culture, Grenoble
	Galleria Eidos, Milan
	Maison de la Culture, Amiens, France
1975	Galerie Jan Krugier, Geneva
1976	Galerie Forni, Amsterdam
	Maison de la Culture, Gretil, France
	Maison de la Culture, Corbeil, France
1977	Galleria Il Gabbiano, Rome
	Galleria Forni, Bologna
	Galleria Santacroce, Florence
	Galleria Adelphi, Padua
1978	Galleria Santacroce, Florence
	Galleria Communale, Prato, Italy
	Galleria Communale, San Gimignano, Italy
1979	Galerie Claude Bernard, Paris
1980	Galleria Forni, Bologna
	Seibu Museum, Tokyo
	Galerie La Hune, Paris
	Musée Dechelette, Roanne, France
1982	Centre Culturel Le Parvis, Tarbes, France
	La Chartreuse, Villeneuve-les-Avignon, France
1983	Galerie Claude Bernard, Paris
	Musée de Grenoble, France
	Tours Narbonnais, Carcassonne, France
	Galerie Jean Claude David, Grenoble, France
1984	Palazzo Racani-Arroni, Spoleto, Italy
1985	Palazzo Pubblico, Siena, Italy
1986	Galleria Tentadue, Milan
	Institut Culturel Francais, Athens
	Spedale di Santa Maria della Scala, Siena, Italy
	Castello Aragonese, Ischia, Italy
1987	Galerie Claude Bernard, at *FIAC 87*, Grand Palais, Paris

Selected Group Exhibitions:

1952	*Pittsburgh International*, Carnegie Institute, Pittsburgh
1956	*Modern Italian Art*, Tate Gallery, London
1961	*Italian Contemporary Art*, Museum of Kamakura, Japan
1967	*Le Monde en Question*, Musée National d'Art Moderne, Paris
1971	*Aspetti della Nuova Figurazione*, Palazzo Reale, Naples
1977	*Arte in Italia 1960–1977*, Galleria d'Arte Moderna, Turin
1978	*Biennale*, Venice
1981	*Il Materiale delle Arte*, Castello Sforzesco, Milan
1984	*L'Immagine e il suop Doppio*, Palazzo Bagatti Valsecchi, Milan (travelled to Galleria Rondanini, Rome)
1986	*Il Viaggio del Dialogo*, Villa Medici, Rome

Collections:

Museum of Modern Art, New York; Albright-Knox Art Gallery, Buffalo, New York; Carnegie Institute, Pittsburgh; Hirshhorn Museum and Sculpture Garden, Smithsonian Institution, Washington D.C.; Princeton University, New Jersey; Israel Museum, Jerusalem; Galleria d'Arte Moderna, Bologna; Galleria d'Arte Moderna, Milan; Centre Georges Pompidou, Paris; Musée d'Art Moderne de la Ville, Paris.

Publications:

By CREMONINI: articles—"Artisanat Populaire et Artisanat Colonise" in *Revolution* (Paris), no. 3, 1963; "Picasso? 13 Peintres Réspondent" in *Le Jardin des Arts* (Paris), October 1970; "Dialogue avec Michel Troche" in *La Nouvelle Critique* (Paris), December 1970; "Nature bien ordonnee," with Marc le Bot, in *Traverses* (Paris), October 1976; "Art et Machine: Entretien à propos du Multiple avec Cremoni et Cueco" in *ATAC Informations* (Paris), April 1978; "La Commande Sociale dans les Arts Plastiques Seminaire du Creusot" in *Cracap Informations* (Le Creusot), May 1978; "Biennale '78: Il Pluralism o la Cattava Coscienza dell' Avanguardia" in *La Loggia dei Mercanti* (Milan), May 1978; "La Pudeur n'est pas Parole: L'Image Autobiographique" in *Skira Annuel*, Geneva 1978; "Modeles de l'Histoire" in *Skira Annuel*, Geneva 1979.

On CREMONINI: books—*Cremonini* by Marco Valsecchi, Milan 1962; *Cremonini* by Franco Solmi, Michel Butor and Louis Althusser, Bologna 1969; *Cremonini: 80 Dessigni* by Giuliano Briganti, Florence 1970; *Leonardo Cremonini* by Jacques Brosse and others, Bologna and Paris 1979 (includes bibliography); *Das kritische Engagement in Leonardo Cremoninis Malerei 1965-1980*, thesis by Petra Spatazza, Ruprecht Karl University, Heidelberg 1981; *Approche des peintures et dessins (1953-1978) de Leonardo Cremonini et des discours du peintre*, thesis by Jean Louis Fauthoux, University of Toulouse Le Mirail 1981; *Om relationemmellan rummet, objekten och Manniskan i Leonardo Cremoninis Maleri*, thesis by Carina Heden, University of Goteborg 1981; *Leonardo Cremonini*, with texts by William Rubin, Italo Galvino, Alain Jouffroy and others, Geneva 1987; films—*Grand Portrait: Leonardo Cremonini ou les jeux sans regle* by Jean Louis Roy, 1973; *Peintre de notre temps: Cremonini* by Georges Paumier, 1977.

Leonardo Cremonini is one of the group of Italian artists who were influenced and inspired by Picasso's "Guernica" to develop a dramatic, realistic style, enabling them to translate a concern for everyday life and human tragedy into a stylized, illustrative manner. It is no wonder, therefore, that in 1951, in his mid-30's, Cremonini transferred himself to Paris, where he has remained ever since, though he maintains regular contact with Italy; in 1969 he was honoured with a major retrospective at the Museo Civico in his native Bologna.

His work, apart from the example of Picasso, reveals the profound influence of such Renaissance art-

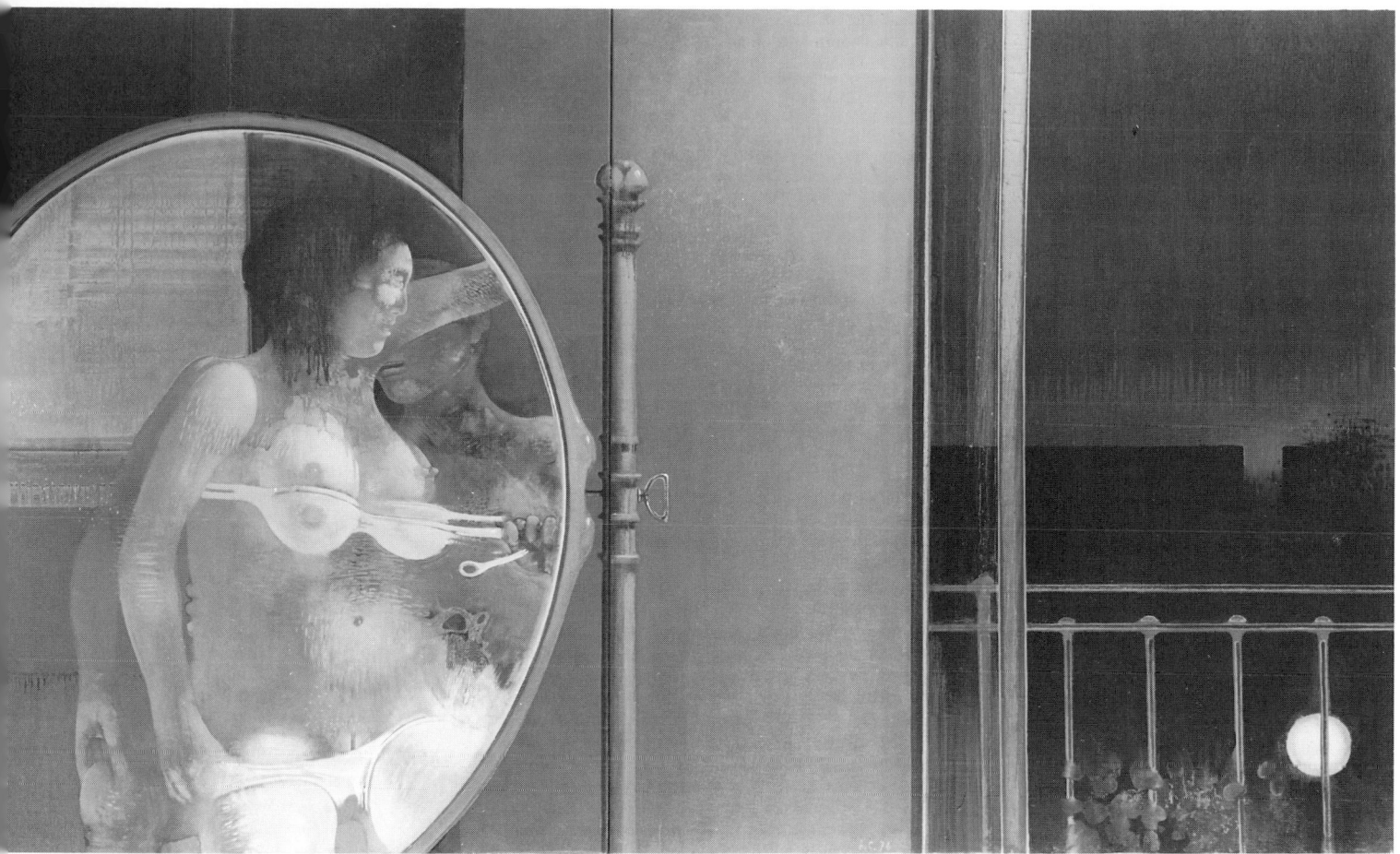

Leonardo Cremonini: *Le Silence du Désir*, 1976

ists as Giotto, Masaccio and Piero della Francesca, especially in the balance that he has struck between rounded, almost sculptural human depiction, and an anti-natural, linear, geometrical form of composition. His preoccupations, however, have always been more dramatic and tense than these masters, almost theatrical in the investigation of torture, accidents, and the like, at the same time investing even the most innocent setting (figures in the interiors of autobuses, children at play, lovers in a park, or the wall furniture of a bathroom) with strange, nervous overtones. Cremonini is a brilliant draughtsman, and there are aspects of his figures, in their doll-like rounded stylization, which are reminiscent of such fellow Italians as Campigli and Manzu. His stated subject is "l'homme social," or man in existentialist relationship to the world. Certainly there is usually present a sense of uncertainty, as though one were waiting for the catastrophe to occur.

In his earlier work, often landscapes, isolating vegetation as huge, fleshy forms, he used paint in deep impasto with bright, brash colour. Gradually, as he adopted the idea of the figure in landscape, albeit urban landscape, he refined both his draughtsmanship and thinned down his palette. The early 1960's saw violent subjects, tortures, road accidents, often involving children (reminiscent of the Yugoslav painter Velickovic). Although the superficial drama of these subjects was eventually abandoned, precisely the same sense of unease is contained in the interior views of buses, with the bulbous heads barely in view, or in the beach-scenes and domestic interiors. There is something cinematic in Cremonini's visual definitions, as if he were seeking to place his figures at odd angles to their architectural settings. Throwing them, and us, so to speak, off balance.

—Charles Spencer

CRIPPA, Roberto.

Italian. Born in Monza in 1921. Studied at the Accademia di Brera, Milan, under Carpi, Funi and Carra. First Italian artist to practice action painting, 1947–52; signed, with Lucio Fontana, Emilio Scanavino, Gianni Dova and Giuseppe Capogrossi, *3rd Manifesto dello Spazialismo*, Milan, 1952. Also internationally renowned acrobatic pilot; represented Italy at the world championship air acrobatics, Hullavington, Wiltshire, England. Recipient: Premio Leonardo da Vinci, 1947; Premio Sipra, 1947; Premio Giani, 1952; Premio Graziano, 1956; Premio di Scultura, Città di Carrara,1957; Premio Viterbo, 1958; Premio Giovane Pittura Europea, Menton, 1960; Gran Premio, *Triennale di Milano*, 1963; Premio Nazionale Umberto Biacamana, 1970; Premio Einaudi, 1970. *Died* (in flying accident, near Milan) *in 1972*.

Individual Exhibitions:

1947	Galleria Bergamini, Milan
1948	Galleria di Pittura,Milan
1949	Galleria San Fedele, Milan
1950	Galleria San Fedele, Milan
1951	Alexander Iolas Gallery, New York
1952	Alexander Iolas Gallery, New York
	Galleria del Cavallino, Venice
	Stable Gallery, New York
	Galleria del Naviglio, Milan
	Galleria d'Arte Contemporanea, Florence
	Galleria del Cavallino, Venice (with Gianni Dova)
1953	Alexander Iolas Gallery, New York
	Hugo Gallery, New York
	Galerie d'Arte Latine, Stockholm
	Galleria del Naviglio, Milan (with Gianni Dova and Giuseppe Capogrossi)
1954	Galleria del Cavallino, Venice
	Galleria del Naviglio, Milan
1955	Galleria del Cavallino, Venice
	Galleria del Naviglio, Milan

	Obelisk Gallery, Washington, D.C.
1956	Galleria del Naviglio, Milan
	Galerie du Dragon, Paris
	Galleria Selecta, Rome
1957	Alexander Iolas Gallery, New York
	Galleria del Naviglio, Milan (with Giuseppe Capogrossi and Giacomo Balla)
	Galeria du Dragon, Paris
1958	Alexander Iolas Gallery, New York
	Galleria del Cavallino, Venice
	Galleria del Naviglio, Milan
	Galerie Bernard, Arrau
1959	Galleria del Naviglio, Milan
	Arts Council Gallery, Edinburgh (with Lucio Fontana and Gianni Dova)
	Palais des Beaux-Arts, Brussels (travelled to Concertgebouw, Bruges, and the Palais des Beaux-Arts, Charleroi, Belgium)
	Galerie Bernard, Grenchen, Switzerland
1960	Alexander Iolas Gallery, New York
	Städtisches Museum, Leverkusen, West Germany
	Stone Gallery, Newcastle upon Tyne
	Galerie d'Art Moderne, Basle
	Galerie Smith, Brussels
1961	Galleria del Naviglio, Milan
	Galleria del Cavallino, Venice
	Tokyo Gallery
1962	Alexander Iolas Gallery, New York
	Gallery One, London
	Galleria Schwarz, Milan
	Galleria Toninelli, Milan
1963	Alexander Iolas Gallery, New York
	Galerie Alice Pauli, Lausanne
	Museum Haus Lange, Krefeld, West Germany
1964	Galleria Schwarz, Milan
	Palazzo Reale, Milan
	Galleria S. Rocco, Scregno, Italy
	Biennale, Venice
1965	Museum am Ostwall, Dortmund, West Germany
	Kunsthalle, Mannheim
	Galerie Argos, Nantes, France

Galleria Carlevaro, Genoa

1966   Alexander Iolas Gallery, New York
Galleria del Naviglio, Milan
Galerie Alice Pauli, Lausanne
Daytons, Minneapolis
Galleria Blu, Milan

1967   Galerie Alexandre Iolas, Paris
Galleria La Bussola, Turin
Galleria Il Salotto, Como, Italy
Aspects, Chexbres, Switzerland
Galerie Alexandre Iolas, Geneva
Galleria Blu, Milan (with Gianni Dova)
Galleria Iolas Galatea, Rome

1968   Galleria Il Cosmo, Bergamo, Italy
Galleria Lo Zodiaco, Genoa
Galleria Tassoni, Modena, Italy
Palais des Beaux-Arts, Brussels
Galleria Lo Scudo, Verona
Galeria Iolas Velasco, Madrid
Galleria Cortina, Milan
Galleria Giraldi, Livorno

1969   Palais des Beaux-Arts, Brussels
Galleria Cortina, Milan
Galleria Stefanoni, Lecco, Italy
Galleria Schreiber, Brescia, Italy
Galleria Sylvia, Rome

1970   Galleria Cortina, Milan
Galleria Giraldi, Ivorno
Galleria Schettini, Milan
Galleria Gissi, Turin
Galleria Torbandena, Trieste
Galleria Cecchini, Perugia, Italy
Palazzo delle Prigioni, Venice
Galleria Il Centro, Naples

1971   Galerie Alexandre Iolas, Paris
Galleria Cortina, Milan
Alexander Iolas Gallery, New York
Galleria Iolas, Milan
Palazzo Reale, Milan

Selected Group Exhibitions:

1948   *Biennale*, Venice
1951   *Arte Astratta e Concretea in Italia*, Galleria Nazionale d'Arte Moderna, Rome
1955   *Pittura Italiana Contemporeanea*, Palacio de la Vierreina, Barcelona
1958   *Pittsburgh International*, Carnegie Institute, Pittsburgh
1960   *Sculpture Italienne Contemporaine*, Musée Rodin, Paris
1961   *The Art of Assemblage*, Museum of Modern Art, New York (travelled to Museum for Contemporary Arts, Dallas, and the Museum of Art, San Francisco)
1966   *L'Art dans l'Usine*, Musée du Louvre, Paris
1968   *7th Biennale dell'Incisione Italiana Contemporanea*, Venice
1970   *Biennale de Menton*, Palais de la Mediterranée, Menton

Collections:

Moderna Museet, Stockholm; Galleria d'Arte Moderna, Rome; Museum am Ostwall, Dortmund, West Germany; Museum Haus Lange, Krefeld, West Germany; Palais des Beaux-Arts, Brussels; Tate Gallery, London; Centre Georges Pompidou, Paris; Museum of Modern Art, New York.

Publications:

By CRIPPA: articles—"Lo Spazio Ovunque" in *Corriere d'Informazione* (Milan), December 1968; "Dippinge le Sue Poesie" in *Corriere d'Informazione* (Milan), May 1969; "Ricordando Victor Brauner, Alchimista Vittorioso" in *Corriere d'Informazione* (Milan), June 1969; "Il Teorema di Rubini" in *Corriere d'Informazione* (Milan), June 1969; "Tony Dallara in una Mostra alla 'Cortina'" in *Il Miliardo* (Carrara-Avenza), June 1969; "Affamato di Cielo" in *Corriere d'Informazione* (Milan), July 1969; "Principessa Rispondi . . ." in *Corriere d'Informazione* (Milan), July 1969; "Vede il sole durante e la Terra che gli Gira Attorno" in *Bolaffiarte* (Turin), February 1972.

On CRIPPA: books—*Lo Spazialismo* by G. Giani, MIlan 1955; *Manifesto per Crippa* by Alain Jouffroy, Milan 1962; *Crippa*, exhibition catalogue by Robert Lebel and Franco Russoli, Rome 1967; *Roberto Crippa*, exhibition catalogue, Perugia, Italy 1970; articles—"Crippa sui Valori della Rhodesia" by Ugo Longho in *Tempo* (Milan), May 1967; "Personale di Roberto Crippa" in *Le Arti* (Milan), February 1969; "Roberto Crippa" by Guido Ballo in *D'Ars Agency* (Milan), November 1969/April 1970; "Visita alla studio di Crippa" by Enzo Fabiana in *Notizie d'Arte* (Milan), 1970; "La Morte di Roberto Crippa" in *Bolaffiarte* (Turin), April 1972.

*

That Roberto Crippa came to regard himself as a Spatialist, along with his friend Fontana, is at first hard to digest. How could the man who brought his own version of action painting (his spiral vortexes) to Italy have anything in common with the maker of anonymous ceramic urns and slashed canvases? But this is to overlook the stern nature of the development which so much of his work was subsequently to take, and it is to fail to understand the urgency of his non-figurative assemblages, bereft of messages but not of meaning.

Crippa's art changed at the time of the Hungarian revolution when Imre Nagy was deposed and a European bloodbath took place. For him, art is close to life, not close to the career-conscious pirouetting of quasi-successful artists. It is significant that he renamed the Venice *Biennale*, the "Banale." So it is not surprising to find his dedicating his cork and wood bark offerings to "Man of Hiroshima" and Caryl Chessman ("I died innocent").

All his work was the outcome of an interior *coup de force*. He did not regard his pictures as opportunities to demonstrate his undeniable dexterity with mixed media. He had the same passion for the renaissance of scraps and tatters that Kurt Schwitters lavished upon his *merz*.

Roberto Crippa was not concerned with *making pictures:* for him his works were doorways which will yield to the touch of a true friend.

Always so sober? No. In his last years he was able to indulge himself a little by making large-scale collages in flippant colours, but it is the great assemblages of the early 1960s that stay in the mind's eye.

—Sheldon Williams

CRUZ-DIEZ, Carlos.

Venezuelan. Born in Caracas, 17 August 1923. Studied at the School of Plastic and Applied Arts, Caracas, 1940–45, Diplomas in Artistic Education and Manual Arts, 1945; studied advanced techniques of art and publicity, New York, 1947. Publications Designer, Creole Petroleum Corporation, 1944–45; Art Director McCann-Erickson Advertising Agency, Venezuelan Subsidiary, 1946–51; Illustrator, *El Nacional*, Caracas, 1953–55; travelled to Barcelona, and to Paris to study physical qualities of color, 1955–56; Designer of Publications, Ministry of Education, and Designer, *El Disco Anaranjado*, Caracas, from 1957; lived in Paris, 1960–80, before returning to Caracas. Teacher, 1953–55, Professor and Assistant Director, School of Arts, Caracas, 1958–60; Professor, School of Journalism, Central University of Venezuela, Caracas, 1959–60; Professor, 1972–73, and Juror, 1973–80, Ecole Supérieur des Beaux-Arts, Paris. Recipient: First Prize, Alphabetization Poster Contest, Caracas, 1946; José Loreto Arismendi Prize, 1950, Artistides Rojas Prize, 1952, and Enrique Otero Vizcarrando Prize, 1953, *Official Exhibition of Venezuelan Art*; Emilio Boggio Prize, *Ateneo de Valencia Exhibition*, Venezuela, 1950; First Prize, *Bienal*, Cordoba, Argentina, 1966; Subsecretaria de la Cultura Award, Cordóba, 1966; International Painting Prize, *Bienal*, Sao Paulo, 1967; First Prize, *Nacional de Artes Plasticas*, Venezuela, 1971; Premio de Intervención del Arte en la Arquitectura, *Bienal de Arquitectura*, Venezuela, 1976. Agents: Galerie Denise René, 124 rue de la Boetie, 75008 Paris, France; Galeria Adler Castillo, Edificio Galipan Avenida Francisco de Miranda, Caracas 106. Address: Qta. Romali, Avenida Berlin La California Norte, Caracas, Venezuela.

Individual Exhibitions:

1947   Instituto Venezolana Americano, Caracas
1955   Museum of Fine Arts, Caracas
1956   Galeria Buchholz, Madrid
1960   Faculty of Architecture, Central University of Venezuela
      Museum of Fine Arts, Caracas
1965   Galleria La Polena, Genoa
      Galleria Il Punto, Turin
      Signals Gallery, London
      Physichromies de Cruz-Diez: Oeuvres do 1954 à 1965, Galerie Kerchache, Paris
1966   Galerie M.E. Thelen, Essen
      Galeria Fundacion Mendoza, Caracas
1967   Galeria Corkright, Caracas
1968   Galerie Art Intermedia, Cologne
      Galerie Accent, Brussels
      Gallerie K.B., Oslo
      Museum am Ostwall, Dortmund, West Germany
1969   *Cruz-Diez et les 3 Etapes la Couleur Moderne*, Galerie Denise René, Paris (Rive Droite and Rive Gauche)
      Galeria Corkright, Caracas
1970   Galerie Ursula Lichter, Frankfurt
      Artestudio Macerata, Macerata, Italy
1971   *Physichromies, Couleur Additive, Induction Chromatique, Chromointerferences*, Galerie Denise René, New York
      Galeria Corkright, Caracas
1972   Galerie Buchholz, Munich
      Galerie Formes et Muraux, Lyons
1973   Galleria Falchi, Milan
      Galerie Denise René, Paris
      Galleria Christian Stein, Turin
      Galeria Cadafe, Caracas
1974   Galleria Trinita, Rome
      Génesis, Eclosión y Absoluto del Color, Galeria Corkright, Caracas
1975   Galeria Aele, Madrid
      Galerie Denise René, Paris
      Museo de Arte Contemporáneo, Bogota
      Galeria Barbie, Barcelona
      Museo La Tertulia, Cali, Colombia
      Artiste et Ville, Caracas
1976   Galeria de Arte Mikeldi, Bilbao, Spain
      Museo de Arte Moderno, Mexico City
      Pabellón de Arte de la Ciudadela, Pamplona, Spain
      Galerie Denise René, New York
      Musée de la Chaux des Fonds, Switzerland
1977   Galerie Latzer, Kreuzlingen, Switzerland
      Allianza Francesa, Caracas
      Galerie Venezuela, New York
      Galerie Noroit, Arras, France
      Art in the Street, Imperial College, London
1978   *Art in the Street*, University of Reading
      Ausbildungszentrum USB, Wolfsberg, Switzerland
      Pavillon Werd, Zurich
      Umjetnik i Grad, Galerija Suvremene, Zagreb
      Ibero-Amerikansiches Institut, West Berlin
1979   Arte Contacto, Caracas
      Galerija Zgraf, Sarajevo, Yugoslavia
1980   Universidad Simon Bolivar, Caracas
      Art in the Street, University of Liverpool
      Casa de las Americas, Havana
1981   *Didactica y Diálectica del Color*, at *Triennale*, Caens (travelled to the Museo de Bellas Artes, Pordenone, Italy; and Museo de Arte Contemporáneo, Caracas)

Selected Group Exhibitions:

1950   *Official Exhibition of Venezuelan Art*, Caracas (and 1952, 1953)
1953   *Bienal*, Sao Paulo (and 1963, 1967, 1979)

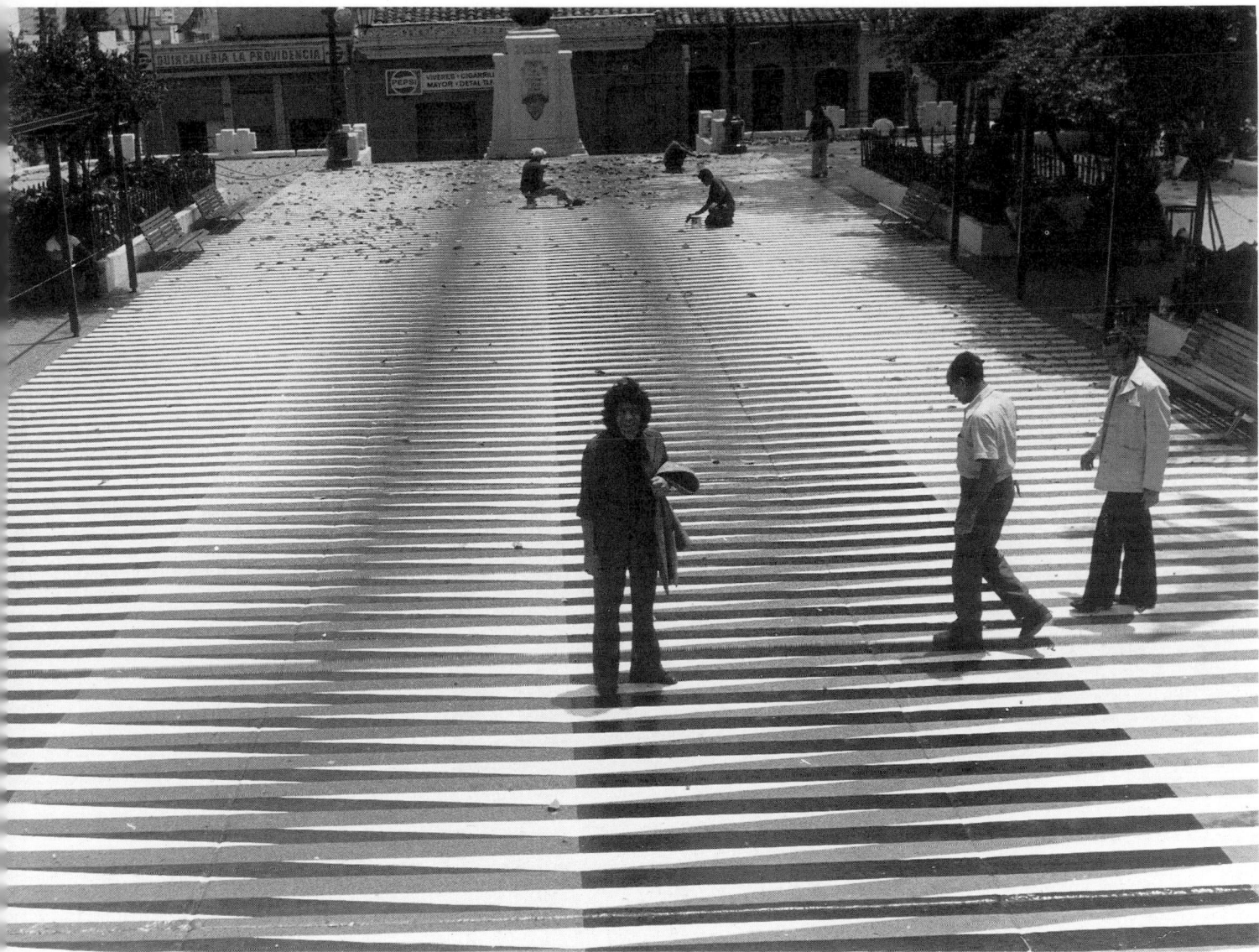

Carlos Cruz-Diez: *Induction Chromatique*, Plaza de la Pastora, Caracas, 1981

1962   *Biennale, Venice*
1964   *Mouvement II*, Galerie Denise René, Paris
1965   *Anthology of Kinetic Sculpture and Perceptual Art*, Signals Gallery, London
1966   *Licht und Bewegung*, Kunstverein, Dusseldorf
1968   *Art Vivant*, Foundation Maeght, St.-Paul-de-Vence, France
1972   *12 Ans d'Art Contemporain en France*, Grand Palais, Paris
1977   *3 Villes, 3 Collections*, Centre Georges Pompidou, Paris
1979   *Modern Latin American Art*, Lowe Art Museum, University of Miami

Collections:

Museo de Bellas Artes, Caracas; Casa de la Cultura, Havana; Museum of Modern Art, New York; Museum of Contemporary Art, Chicago; Musée d'Art Contemporain, Montreal; Victoria and Albert Museum, London; Städtisches Museum, Leverkusen, West Germany; Museum des 20. Jahrhunderts, Vienna; Centre National d'Art Contemporain, Paris, Musée d'Art Moderne de la Ville, Paris.

Publications:

On CRUZ-DIEZ: books—*Physichromies de Cruz-Diez: Oeuvres de 1954 à 1965*, exhibition catalogue, with text by Frank Popper, Paris 1965; *Carlos Cruz-Diez*, exhibition catalogue, with text by Carlos Dorante, Caracas 1967; *Cruz-Diez et les 3 Etapes de la Couleur Moderne*, exhibition catalogue, with text by Jean Clay, Paris 1969; *Relief and 3-Dimensional Structures* by Cyril Barrett, London 1970; *An Introduction to Opitcal Art* by Cyril Barrett, London 1971; *The Techiques of Kinetic Art* by John Tobey, New York 1971; *12 Ans d'Art Contemporain en France*, exhibition catalogue, with text by Jean-Luc Allerant, Paris 1972; *Carlos Cruz-Diez: Génesis, Eclosión y Absoluto del Color*, exhibition catalogue, with text by Roberto Guevara, Caracas 1974; *Cruz-Diez* by Alfredo Boulton, Caracas 1975; *Cruz-Diez: Didactia y Dialectica del Color*, exhibition catalogue, with text by Umbro Apollonio, Caracas 1981.

Cruz-Diez's main preoccupation is to set up "situations" of various kinds which in their turn give rise to certain sequences of events whose interest lies in an intense experience of colour. These "chromatic events" are obtained by transforming "concepts" into sensory phenomena and in this way colour, which is traditionally subordinate to subject or form, acquires an existence of its own and pursues its own evolution in space and time.

All of Cruz-Diez's chromatic propositions—*Physichromies, Chromointerferences, Chromosaturations, Transchromies*— are based on this particular theoretical position, but the artist expresses a different aspect of the problem in each type of work.

The *Physichromies* are changing structures which project colour from a surface into space. They set up an atmosphere of coloured light which varies with the intensity and the position of the light source and with the position and the distance of the spectator. These statements combine three modalities of colour: addition, reflection and subtraction. The *Chromointer-* *ferences* are formal networks which bring into the foreground the phenomenon of chromatic waves produced by interference. While these works are based in general on a plane surface, the *Chromosaturations*, on the contrary, are conceived in terms of the appropriation of three-dimensional space for the purpose of bringing the experience of pure colour into the foreground. The *Transchromies* differ from the other colour experiments by Cruz-Diez through the use of effects which derive from the superimposition of various different chromatic scales and the accent is placed specifically on transparency, on optical mixture and the instability of the chromatic vision.

All of these researches by Carlos Cruz-Diez have given rise to large-scale architectural and environmental applications in-and outside private dwellings, industrial plants, administrative buildings and town squares in his native Venezuela and in Europe.

The artist has also undertaken a number of chromatic "actions" in public places involving the spectator both physically and psychologically in the creative process. In fact, in all his statements involving space and taking place in time, Cruz-Diez aims through the intermediacy of the public, to achieve perpetual transformation of both event and colour.

—Frank Popper

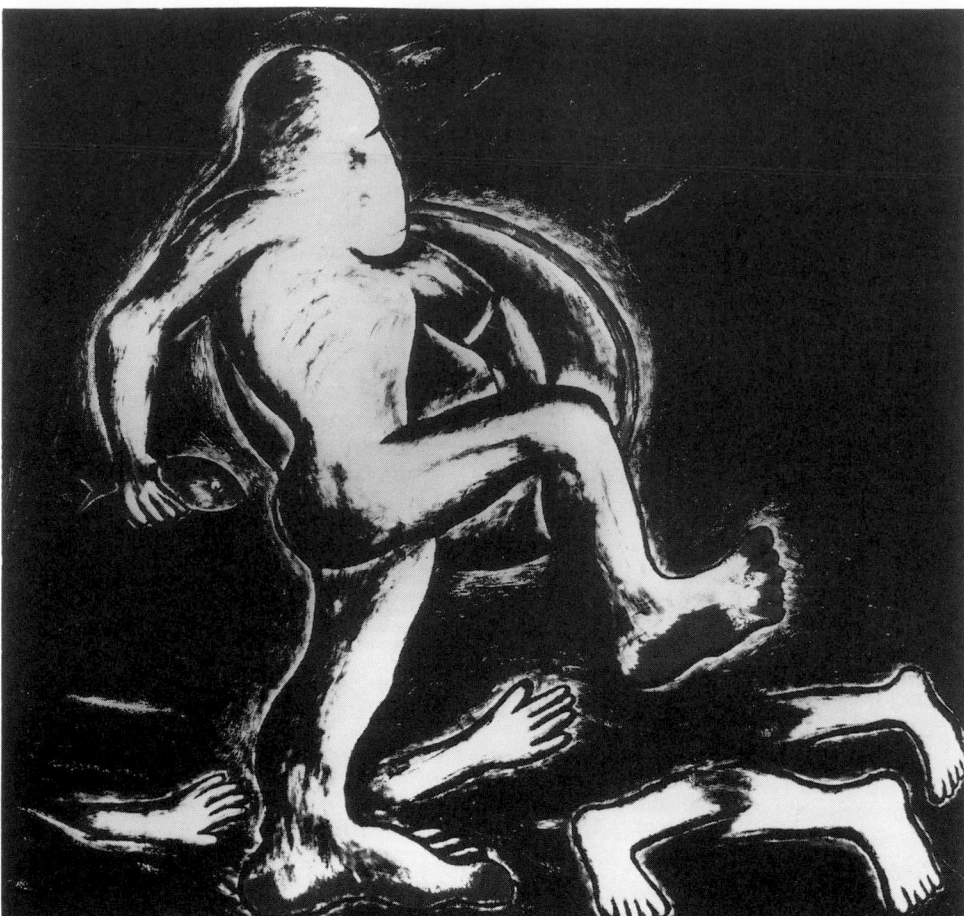

Enzo Cucchi: *Under the Wind*, 1982

CUCCHI, Enzo.

Italian. Born in Morra d'Alba, near Ancona, in 1950. Married to Brunella Cucchi. Independent painter, living and working in Ancona. Agents: Anthony D'Offay Gallery, 9 Dering Street, London W1; Galerie Paul Maenz, Bismarckstrasse 50, 5000 Cologne 1; and Galleria Lucio Amelio, Naples. Address: c/o Galleria Lucio Amelio, Piazza dei Martiri 58, 80121 Naples, Italy.

Individual Exhibitions:

1977	Incontri Internazionali d'Arte, Rome
1978	Galleria de Crescenzo, Rome
1979	Galleria Mario Diacono, Bologna
	Galleria Tucci Russo, Turin
	Galleria Mozzoli, Modena, Italy
1980	Galerie Paul Maenz, Cologne
1981	Gallery Sperone/Westwater/Fischer, New York
	Galleria Sperone, Rome
	Galerie Bruno Bischofberger, Zurich
	Galleria Mario Diacono, Rome
	Galerie Paul Maenz, Cologne (travelled to Art and Project, Amsterdam, 1982)
1982	Galerie Beyeler, Basle
	Kunsthaus, Zurich (travelled to the Groningen Museum, Netherlands)
1983	Museum Folkwang, Essen, West Germany
	Galerie Schellmann und Kluser, Munich
	Sperone-Westwater, New York
1984	Akira Ikeda Gallery, Tokyo
	Anthony D'Offay Gallery, London
	Sperone-Westwater, New York
	Kunsthalle, Basle
1985	Galerie Daniel Templon, Paris
	Galerie Bernd Kluser, Munch
	Kunstmuseum, Dusseldorf
	Louisiana Museum, Humlebaek, Denmark
1986	CAPC/Musee d'Art Contemporain, Bordeaux, France
	Guggenheim Museum, New York
	Centre Georges Pompidou, Paris
1987	Galerie Beyeler, Basle

Selected Group Exhibitions:

1979	*Alternativa del Nuovo*, Palazzo delle Esposizioni, Rome
1980	*Die Enthauptete Hand: 100 Zeichnungen aus Italien*, Kunstverein, Bonn (travelled to the Städtische Galerie, Wolfsberg, West Germany, and the Groningen Museum, Netherlands)
1981	*Westkunst: Zeitgenossiche Kunst seit 1939*, Rheinhallen, Cologne
1982	*'60-'80: Attitudes, Concepts, Images*, Stedelijk Museum, Amsterdam
1983	*New Art*, Tate Gallery, London
1984	*International Survey of Recent Painting and Sculpture*, Museum of Modern Art, New York
1985	*The European Iceberg*, Art Gallery of Ontario, Toronto
1987	*Avant-Garde in the Eighties*, Los Angeles County Museum of Art

Publications:

By CUCCHI: books—*Treo Quattro Artisti Secchi*, exhibition catalogue, Modena, Italy 1979; *Canzone*, Modena, Italy 1979; *Enzo Cucchi*, exhibition catalogue, Basle 1984; *Enzo Cucchi: Italia*, London 1984; articles—"Designo Finto" in *Enzo Cucci*, exhibition catalogue, Rome 1978; "Die Hauser fullen sich alle bis auf halbe Höne" in *Sieben Junge Kunstler aus Italien*, exhibition catalogue, Basle 1980; "Di Certo Communque ce che l'Immagine" in *Enzo Cucchi*, exhibition catalogue, Cologne 1981.

On CUCCHI: books—*Enzo Cucchi*, exhibition catalogue, Rome 1978; *Enzo Cucchi*, exhibition catalogue, Cologne 1981; *Die Enthaupieie Hand: 100 Zeichnungen aus Italien*, exhibition catalogue, with W. M. Faust, Bonn 1980; *The Italian Trans-Avantgarde* by Achille Bonito Oliva, Milan 1980; *Seiben Junge Kunstler aus Italien*, exhibition catalogue, by Jean-Christophe Ammann, Basle 1980; *Mythe/Drame. Tragedie*, exhibition catalogue, by Achille Bonito Oliva and others, Saint-Etienne, France 1982; *Enzo Cucchi: Zeichnungen*, exhibition catalogue with texts by Ursula Perucch and Frans Haks, Zurich 1982; *Baldessari/Borofsky/Chia. Clemente/Cucchi/Disler/Penck/Winnewisser*, with foreword by Frans Haks, introduction by Steven Kolsteren, New York and Groningen 1982; *Enzo Cucchi*, exhibition catalogue with essay by Diane Waldman, New York 1986.

Towards the end of the 1970's there were a number of Italian painters who were looking for new foundations for their work, new horizons, and new ways of dealing with the artistic problems of the recent past. By using some of their experiments Enzo Cucchi was able to realize a poetic style of his own, although his debt to these artists is apparent in those first works of his which clearly reveal a kind of tension between form and content. These are works which bear his own personal signature and yet still reflect a general preoccupation with the problematic relationship between a work of art and the space it occupies. More precisely, Cucchi is interested in the conflicts which characterize such relationships.

Two of his exhibitions are particularly relevant here. In the first of these, *Alla lontana alla francese* (January, 1979), Cucchi gave us a canvas, loosely hung from the wall, which depicted an ordered series of houses in silhouette. In the foreground is a large cane, curved at the top, and a white-enamel ceramic form. And further away is another canvas, bearing the artist's signature, which depicts a series of repeated animal forms. In the second exhibition, *Lacavalla, Azzura* (February, 1979), there is an unbleached canvas, thickly overlaid with earthy, red-orange pigment, one corner of which has been curled up to reveal a large terracotta ladle, resting on two easels below. The aim here is to establish a rapport among the canvas, the paint, and the objects themselves.

After these two exhibitions, Cucchi turned his attention to the pictorial image, which until now had played a secondary role in his work. There is a kind of transitional period, in which he moves from his earlier concern for relationships to works in which the images themselves carry the full burden of his meaning. Here we have paintings in which the object to be represented is tied to the canvas or placed nearby. And now, in his recent work, the depicted object becomes the primary vehicle of his sensibility—a sensibility nourished by the mountains and valleys and forests of rural Italy and its villages and the traditions behind them.

—Robert G. Lambarelli

CUEVAS, José Luis.

Mexican. Born in Mexico City, 26 February 1934. Studied at the School of Painting and Sculpture, La Esmeralda, Mexico City, 1944–47; studied engraving with Lola Cueto, Mexico City, 1948. Married Bertha Lilian in 1961; children: Mariana, Zimena and Marie-Jose. Independent painter and graphic artist, Mexico City and New York, Professor of Drawing, Latin American University, Mexico City, 1956–57; Artist-in-Residence, Philadelphia Museum School of Art, 1957–58, San Jose State College, California, 1970, and Fullerton College, Los Angeles, 1975. Recipient: First International Drawing Award, *Bienal*, Sao Paulo, 1959; First Prize, *Mostra Internazionale di Bianco e Nero*, Lugano, Switzerland, 1962; "Madeco" Prize, *Bienal de Santiago*, Chile, 1965; First International Award, *Triennale*, New Delhi, 1968; First Prize, *Bienal de Grabado Latinoamericano*, San Juan, Puerto Rico, 1977; National Fine Arts Award,

Mexico, 1981. Agents: Galeria de Arte Mexicano, Milan 18, Mexico City; Marisa Del Re Gallery, 41 East 57th Street, New York, New York 10019; Tasende Gallery, 820 Prospect Street, La Jolla, California 92037. Address: Galeana 109, San Angel, Mexico City 20, Mexico; and 14 West 17th Street, New York, New York 10011, U.S.A.

Individual Exhibitions:

1953   Galeria Prisse, Mexico City
1954   Pan American Union, Washington, D.C.
1955   Galerie Edouard Loeb, Paris
1956   Galeria Proteo, Mexico City
       Palacio de Bellas Artes, Havana
1957   Aenille Gallery, New York
1958   Instituto de Arte Contemporáneo, Lima, Peru
       Galeria de Arte Contemporáneo, Caracas
1959   Galeria Bonino, Buenos Aires
1960   David Herbert Gallery, New York
       Silvan Simone Gallery, Los Angeles
       Fort Worth Art Center, Texas (retrospective)
1961   Galleria L'Obelisco, Rome
       University of Texas at Austin
       Santa Barbara Museum of Art, California
1962   Galleria Sixtina, Milan
       Jerrold Morris Gallery, Toronto
       Occidental College, Toronto
1963   Pan American Union, Washington, D.C. (graphic works retrospective, 1947-62)
       Andrew Morris Gallery, New York
       228 Gallery, St. Louis
       Galeria Antonio Souza, Mexico City
1964   Galleria Profili, Milan
       Silvan Simone Gallery, Los Angeles
       Biblioteca Luis Angel Arango, Bogota
1965   Grace Borgenicht Gallery, New York
       Munson-Williams-Proctor Institute, Utica, New York
       Cuevas antes de Cuevas, Galeria Mer-Kup, Mexico City
1966   Galeria Misrachi, Mexico City
       Silvan Simone Gallery, Los Angeles
1967   Walter Engel Gallery, Toronto
1969   Glade Gallery, New Orleans
1970   Galeria Misrachi, Mexico City
       San Francisco Museum of Art
       University Museum, Ciudad Universitaria, Mexico City
1971   Grace Borgenicht Gallery, New York
       La Sala Nacional de Exposiciones, San Salvador
       Galeria El Morro, San Juan, Puerto Rico
       Museo de Bellas Artes, Toluca, Mexico
1972   Michael Wyman Gallery, Chicago
       Museo de Arte Moderno, Mexico City
1973   Rothman Galleries, Toronto
       Museo de Arte Moderno, Bogota
       Galeria Aele, Madrid
       Galeria Pecanins, Barcelona
1974   Palais de Beaux Arts, Brussels
       Galeria Multipla, Sao Paulo
       Museo de Arte Contemporáneo, Caracas
1975   San Diego Museum of Fine Arts, California
       Phoenix Art Museum, Arizona
       Palace of the Legion of Honor, San Francisco
       Fullerton College, Los Angeles
       Bienal, Sao Paulo
       Museum of Modern Art, Gothenburg, Sweden
1976   Museo de Arte Moderno, Mexico City
       Musée d'Art Moderne, Paris (retrospective)
1977   Galeria Estudio Actual, Caracas
       Musée des Beaux-Arts, Chartres, France
       Galeria Misrachi, Mexico City
       Galerie de Seine, Paris
1978   Grace Borgenicht Gallery, New York
1979   Museo de Arte Moderno, Mexico City
       Tasende Gallery, San Diego, California
1980   Museo de Monterrey, Mexico (retrospective)
1981   Meeting Point Gallery, Miami
       Galeria Joan Prats, Barcelonia
       Museo de Ponce, San Juan, Puerto Rico
1982   Marisa del Re Gallery, New York

Selected Group Exhibitions:

1957   Quatre maitres de la ligne: José Luis Cuevas, Alexander Calder, Stuart Davis and Morris Graves, Napoule Museum, Napoule, France
1967   Rosc 67, Dublin
1970   Collection of José Gómez Sicre, College Art Gallery, State University of New York at New Paltz
1972   Biennale, Venice
1978   Documenta, Kassel, West Germany

Collections:

Museum of Modern Art, New York; Hirshhorn Museum, Smithsonian Institution, Washington, D.C.; Pan American Union art Collection, Washington, D.C.; Munson Williams-Proctor Institute, Utica, New York; Fine Arts Gallery of San Diego, California, Art Gallery of Ontario, Canada; Museo de Arte Moderno, Mexico City; Museo de Bellas Artes, Caracas; Museo de Arte Moderno, Bogota; Museum of Art, Tel Aviv.

Publications:

By CUEVAS: books—Cuevas por Cuevas, Mexico City 1965; Cuevario, Mexico City 1973; books illustrated—The World of Kafka and Cuevas, Philadelphia 1959; Recollections of Childhood, Los Angeles, 1962; Cuevas-Charenton, Los Angeles 1966; Crime by Cuevas, New York 1968; Homage to Quevedo, San Francisco 1969; Cuevas Comedies, San Francisco 1972; La Rue des Mauvais Garcons, Paris 1972; Cuaderno de Paris, Mexico City 1977; Zarathustra, Milan 1979; Les obsesions noires de J.-L. Cuevas, Paris 1982; Letters to Tasende, San Diego 1982.

On CUEVAS: books—José Luis Cuevas by Jean Cassou, Philippe Soupault, and Flores Sanchez, Paris 1955; José Luis Cuevas by Carlos Valdes, Mexico City 1967; El Mundo de José Luis Cuevas by Carlos Fuentes, Mexico City 1969; Confesiones de José Luis Cuevas by Alaide Foppa, Mexico City 1975; Revelando a José Luis Cuevas by Daisy Ascher, Mexico City 1979; Cuevas: Ipotesi per una lettura by Roberto Sanesi, Milan 1979; Cartas para una exposicion, Mexico City 1981; José Luis Cuevas by José Gomez Sicre, Barcelona 1982.

I hate accident, improvisation, play with materials for their own sake. I believe in "originality" only when it comes from the very essence of tradition. I believe an artist is original only when he shows his own accent or his full voice through materials given by his predecessors.

Today my main interest is the work of the great artist of the past: Van Eyck, Hals, Velazquez, Zurbaran, etc., and above all the great Chinese draftsmen of the 16th and 17th centuries.

—José Luis Cuevas

Jose Luis Cuevas is one of this century's most expressive draftsmen. His expressive power stems from a tension between the monstrous crudeness of the people he portrays, deformed, distorted, seamed and ridged, and an extreme delicacy of touch and technical skill. Like Leonardo, he sets down the line very swiftly, and, should the stroke in a slightly different place seem better to him, leaves the first and adds the second, to produce an impression of the artist's hand, sure and immediate. His line, most often done with the pen, combines with a system of washes in greys and blacks, or a spectrum of watered down hues, pale, evoking faded things like dried flowers under glass, lavender in keepsakes, whatever has no juice. The vital elixir is drained. By choosing to work in the dessicated colors of the funeral wreath, the artist calls up sensations of mortality, a modern day memento mori, which fixes the moment before transition to another stage.

The presence of death has been constant with Cuevas since, at the age of 9, he was bedridden for a year with rheumatic fever. During that time he read intensely in European literature, which gave him a background in that culture and an understanding of its

history coupled with respect, and he drew. His images have, ever since, reflected that background and the hallucinatory quality of the fevered sickbed.

They reflect as well his familiarity with the life of the miserable poor. Born himself in a poor quarter of Mexico City, living in rooms above his grandfather's pencil factory, he came to know intimately the lives of people society has trained us not to see: the old and sick, the cripple, the prostitute, the criminal. Through the remarkable compelling quality of his art he brings the observer to a headon confrontation with these subjects, at once marvelous and grotesque.

The frequency of the autoretrato in his oeuvre makes it clear that it was the artist himself who was first forced to this confrontation and to this fascination, in the end. As with the image of death, which he has often, through continuing ill health, been forced to contemplate, his contemplation ends in an erotic embrace: "When the last heartbeat stops pounding, my good lady will bend down and give me a kiss." Death the Sweet Sister.

This attitude is very much in tune with the Mexican obsession with death, evident in the ritual festivities in the cemetery, the sweet candy skulls of the Day of the Dead, the cult of mutilation and sacrifice in the ancient religions of Mexico. Indeed, the bulbous heads in his drawings hark back to Olmec ancestors, yet Cuevas is no Mexican nationalist in his art. He abhors "the Cactus Curtain" and insists that art must build on the European tradition which has gone before, feeling a special affinity to many of the European masters, especially Rembrandt and Velasquez. This affinity has much to do with the international staus which has always been accorded him, and much of his art has to do with European cities as well as his own.

But neither the European past nor echoes from ancient Mexico really determine his choice of subject, but rather the present day reality of the streets, the jails, cafes, brothels, where the struggle from day to day is all too real. It is this continual, brooding concern with the tragedy of life in this century, the conviction that life is not only absurd but a waste, a conviction born of experience, which makes his art ring true.

—Barbara Cortright

CURNOE, Greg.
Canadian. Born in London, Ontario, 19 November 1936. Educated at Wortley Road Public School, London, 1940-50; South Collegiate Institute, London, 1950-54; studied art at H.B. Beal Technical School, London, 1954-56; Doon School of Art, Ontario, 1956; Ontario College of Art, Toronto, 1957-60. Married Sheila Curnoe in 1965; children: Owen, Galen, and Zoe. Worked with Survey Crew, City of London, 1957-60; worked as a trucker for Coca Cola Company, London, 1961. Independent artist in London since 1960: established studio on Richmond Street, 1960-63, on King Street, 1963-68, and on Weston Street, since 1968. Founder-Member, Garrett Gallery artists' cooperative, Toronto, 1957-59; Region Gallery, London, 1961-63; 20/20 Gallery, London, 1966-70; and Forest City Art Gallery, London, since 1973. Founder-Editor, Region magazine, London, 1961-78; Contributing Editor, 20 Cents Magazine, London, 1967-70. Member, Société pour l'Etude du Mouvement Dada, London, 1954; President, Nihilist Party of Canada, since 1961; kazoo manufacturer, and member, Nihilist Spasm Band, since 1966; member, and former Racing Secretary, London Centennial Wheelers Club, since 1971; Founder-Member, Association for the Documentation of Neglected Aspects of Culture in Canada popular culture group, since 1972; Spokesman, Canadian Artists Representation, Ontario, 1974-75. Artist-in-Residence, University of Western Ontario, London, 1975-76. Agents: Isaacs Gallery, 832 Yonge Street,

Toronto 5, Ontario; Forest City Art Gallery, 432 Richmond Street, London, Ontario. Address: 38 Weston Street, London, Ontario, Canada.

Individual Exhibitions:

1964 *Exhibition of Things,* Richard E. Crouch Branch Library, London, Ontario
Isaacs Gallery, Toronto
McIntosh Memorial Art Gallery, London, Ontario
Region Gallery, London, Ontario

1962 *Greg Curnoe/Larry Russell,* Region Gallery, London, Ontario
McIntosh Memorial Art Gallery, London, Ontario

1963 McIntosh Memorial Art Gallery, London, Ontario
Greg Curnoe/Brian Dibb, Region Gallery, London

1964 *Imports and Local Works: Curnoe/Urquhart,* McIntosh Memorial Art Gallery, London, Ontario
David Mirvish Gallery, Toronto
Norman MacKenzie Art Gallery, Regina, Saskatchewan

1965 David Mirvish Gallery, Toronto

1966 *Paintings by Greg Curnoe,* Vancouver Art Gallery (travelled to Edmonton Art Gallery)
New York from Sowesto Greg Curnoe, Isaacs Gallery, Toronto
Recent Collages, New Design Gallery, Vancouver

1967 *Series,* 20/20 Gallery, London, Ontario
Time Series, Isaacs Gallery, Toronto
Chambers/Curnoe, McIntosh Memorial Art Gallery, London, Ontario

1969 *Bienal,* Sao Paulo

1970 *Drawings,* McIntosh Memorial Art Gallery, London, Ontario
Collages 1961-70, Isaacs Gallery, Toronto
Views of Victoria Hospital and Wings over the Atlantic, Isaacs Gallery, Montreal

1971 Waddington Galleries, Montreal

1972 *Display of Water Colours, Measurements and Clockings,* London House, Ontario

1973 Isaacs Gallery, Toronto
Watercolours and Drawings, Polyglot Gallery, London, Ontario

1974 *The Great Canadian Sonnet,* Drawings, National Gallery, Ottawa (toured Canada)
Watercolours, Forest City Art Gallery, London, Ontario

1975 *Recent Watercolours,* Isaacs Gallery, Toronto
Some Lettered Works 1961-69, London Art Gallery, Ontario

1976 *Biennale,* Venice

Selected Group Exhibitions:

1967 *Statements: 18 Canadian Artists,* Norman Mackenzie Art Gallery, Regina, Saskatchewan

1969 *Canada: Art d'Aujourdhui,* Centre Georges Pompidou, Paris (toured Europe)
The Heart of London, National Gallery of Canada, Ottawa (toured Canada, 1968–69)
Canada 101, at the Edinburgh Festival

1973 *Realism: Emulsion and Omission,* Kingston, Ontario

1974 *Bienal Americana de Arts Graphics,* at Colombia Art Mart, Kitchener-Waterloo Art Gallery, Ontario

Collections:

University of Western Ontario, London; London Public Library and Art Gallery, Ontario; The Canada Council, Ottawa; National Gallery of Canada, Ottawa; Art Gallery of Ontario, Toronto; Art Institute of Ontario, Toronto; Museum of Fine Arts, Montreal; Vancouver Art Gallery; City Trust, Vancouver, Norman MacKenzie Art Gallery, Regina Saskatchewan.

Publications:

On CURNOE: books—*Paintings by Greg Curnoe,* exhibition catalogue, Vancouver 1966; *Chambers and Curnoe,* exhibition catalogue, London, Ontario 1967; *Statements: 18 Cana-*

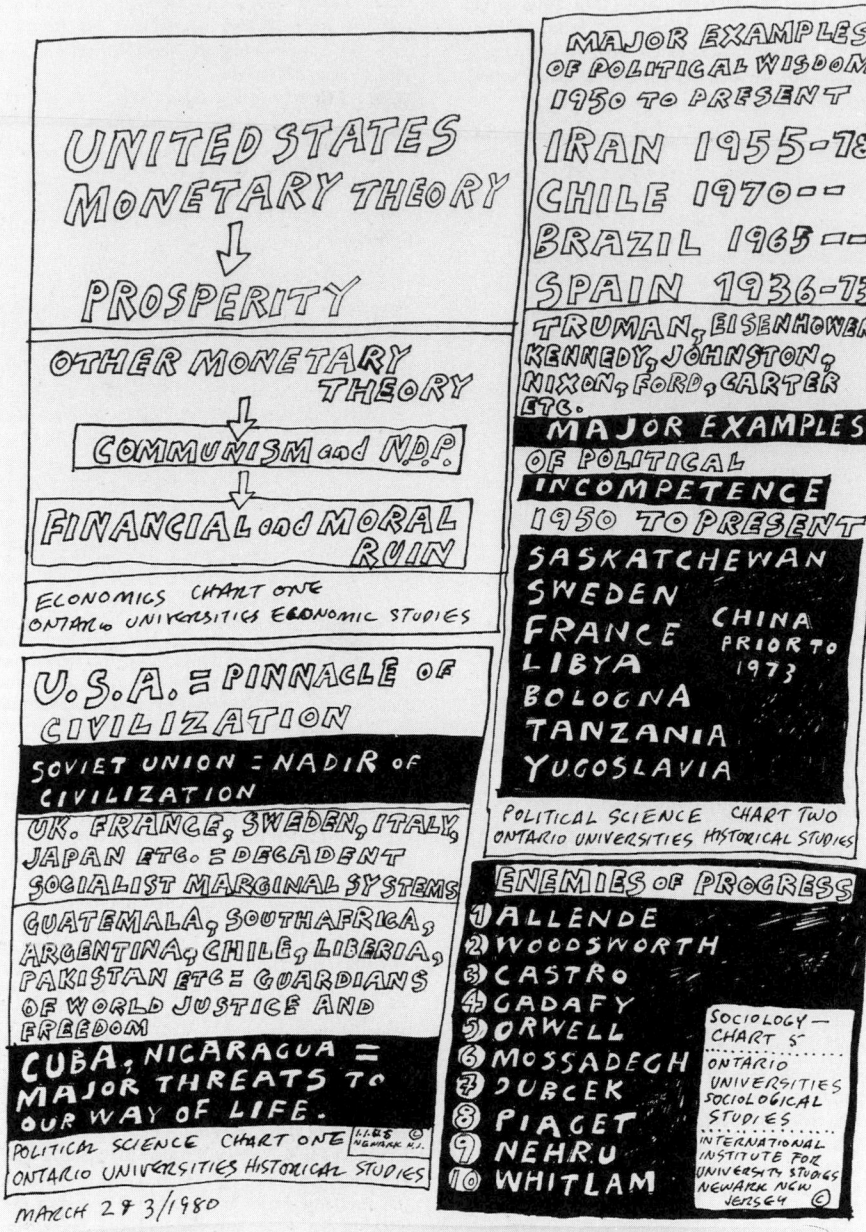

Greg Curnoe: *The Way It Is,* 1980

dian Artists, exhibition catalogue, Regina, Saskatchewan 1967; *Canada; Art d'Aujourdhui,* exhibition catlogue, Paris 1968; *The Heart of London,* exhibition catalogue, Ottawa 1968; *Greg Curnoe: Canada,* exhibition catalogue, Sao Paulo 1969; *Canadian Art Today* by William Townsend, London 1970; *Realism: Emulsion and Omission,* exhibition catalogue, with text by M. Kluyver-Cluysenaer, Kingston, Ontario 1973; *Greg Curnoe,* exhibition catalogue, Venice 1976; articles—"More Words on Curnoe's Worldly World" by John Chandler in *Artscanada* (Toronto), April 1969; "The Language of the Eyes: Windows and Mirror" by Ross Mendes in *Artscanada* (Toronto), October 1969; "Painting from Life: Greg Curnoe at the Isaacs Gallery" by J. N. Chandler in *Artscanada* (Toronto), June 1971; "Knowing: The Surface" by V. Coleman in *Artscanada* (Toronto), February 1972; "Sources, Resources: Greg Curnoe" by J. N. Chandler in *Artscanada* (Toronto), February 1973.

I frequently work in series, but what I do does not come from any general concept or framework of ideas. I work with people, places and things. Any ideas that I have and conclusions that I make come from the people, places and things I know.

I assemble all kinds of material. Assembling, sorting, listing and collecting has been the basis of most of my work.

I have strong feelings: about where I was born, about living in a relatively small city slightly over 200km away from a large one, about living in a sparsely populated large country beside a heavily populated large one. I live in an extended family and that makes me think a lot about the shared culture in my community contrasted with other cultural activities that only a small number of people are aware of. My work operates in both of these contexts. I also think a lot about eroticism and pornography and about how they relate to community and individual tastes.

My work is about resisting as much as possible the tendency of American culture to overwhelm other cultures. I also resist, as much as possible, any attempt to elevate what I do to the level of high art.

—Greg Curnoe

"The world is your own backyard," says Greg Curnoe. More important, he might add, your own background is your world. For Curnoe, a sense of Regionalism is the key to authentic work. His is based on London, Ontario (he was born there in 1936), more humid in summer and colder in winter than other parts of southern Ontario. It's a place with its own confident, dynamic creative milieu, to some extent associated with the University of Western Ontario. It's a breeding-ground for artists, most of whom, like Curnoe, receive a firm foundation at H. B. Beal Technical School where he studied from 1954 to 1956.

Curnoe first came into contact with Dada through his teachers at Beal in 1954. In 1961, he participated with Michael Snow and Joyce Wieland in a Neo-Dada exhibition. His work is remarkable for its bold design sense, bright primary flat colours, clean outlines, a complete rejection of modelling. His work is spare and deft.

From 1964, Curnoe has expressed his concerns in works like "Springs on the Ridgeway," using words to describe the real world around the edge, and in the picture space, a real curtain, metal rod and yoyo. Combined with these "real" objects are a cut-out of a radio and a lushly painted and flat nude seen from the back. In later works, like his masterpiece, the mammoth "View of Victoria Hospital, Second Series," 1969-1971, Curnoe adds wires and electric lights. Here, his fine, harmonious colour is modelled on Robert Delaunay and county town carnivals, strident oranges and greens or rainbow tints.

In works expanded from his journals, wordscapes, he records what he sees in lettered words that seem almost compulsive. At times, the results are bland and overly earnest, but they are personal documents too, perhaps even the most personal, recording the pattern of his life, his trips, his thoughts, his conversations.

Curnoe is an original. Today, he may paint his wife Sheila, Toronto's C. N. Tower, or his Maraposa or Doc Morton bikes—he's an amateur competitive cyclist. But his kind of painting always has the feel of the real, "Made in Canada." "I am afraid of art," he once said. "It could still kill me."

—Joan Murray

CUTFORTH, Roger.

British. Born in Sleaford, Lincolnshire, 29 October 1944. Studied at the Nottingham College of Art, 1962-63; and the Ravensbourne College of Art, England, 1963-66. Independent conceptual artist and photographer, since 1966: moved to New York City in 1968, concentrated on making films of women in landscapes, 1973-75; now lives and works in Texas. Recipient: National Endowment for the Arts Photography Fellowship, Washington, D.C., 1984. Agent: Hal Bromm Gallery, 170 Avenue A at Eleventh, New York, New York 10009. Address: Box 375, Terlingua, Texas 79852, U.S.A.

Individual Exhibitions:

1969	Pinacotheca Gallery, Melbourne
1971	Lisson Gallery, London
	Nova Scotia College of Art, Halifax
1972	Pinacotheca Gallery, Melbourne
1974	John Gibson Gallery, New York
	Galerie Kornblit, Amsterdam
	Studio Cannaviello, Rome
1975	Galerie Kornblit, Amsterdam
1976	Galerie Gaetan, Geneva
	John Gibson Gallery, New York
	Studio Cannaviello, Rome
1977	Galleria II Diaframma, Milan
	Studio 46, Turin
1978	John Gibson Gallery, New York
	Studio Cannaviello, Milan
1979	Unimedia, Genoa
	Studio Cannaviello, Milan
1981	Hal Bromm Gallery, New York
1983	Hal Bromm Gallery, New York
1986	Dos Amigos Gallery, Terlingua, Texas
	Hal Bromm Gallery, New York
1987	University of Texas, El Paso
	AIR Gallery, Austin, Texas

Selected Group Exhibitions:

1970	*Art in the Mind*, Allen, Memorial Art Museum, Oberlin College, Ohio
	Information, Museum of Modern Art, New York
1971	*Prospect 71*, Studtische Kunsthalle, Dusseldorf
1972	*Artists Using Photographs*, Inhibodress, Sydney
1975	*Artists' Bookworks*, British Council travelling exhibition, London (toured West Germany)
1976	*Photo as Art*, Contemporary Art Museum, Zagreb, Yugoslavia
1977	*Artists Super 8 Film Exposition*, Artists Space, York
1979	*New Acquisitions*, Wallraf-Richartz Museum, Cologne
1980	*Printed Art*, Museum of Modern Art, New York
1981	*Biennale*, Sydney
1987	*This is Not A Photograph*, Ringling Museum, Sarasota, Florida

Collections:

Museum of Modern Art, New York; Metropolitan Museum of Art, New York; Wallraf-Richartz Museum, Cologne; Stadtisches Museum Abteiberg, Monchengladbach.

Publications:

By CUTFORTH: books—*The Empire State Building: A Reference Work*, New York 1969; *The Visual Book*, New York 1970; *Cleopatra's Needle/Eiffel Tower/Empire State Building*, London 1971.

On CUTFORTH: books—*Situation de l'Art Conceptual* by Catherine Millet, Paris 1970; *Conceptual Art* by Ursula Meyer, New York 1971; *6 Years: The Dematerialization of the Art Object* by Lucy Lippard, New York 1973; *La Linea Analitica de Arte Moderna* by Menna Filiberto, Turin 1975; *Skira Annuel*, Geneva 1977; *Skira Annuel*, Geneva 1980; *The Gallery of World Photography: New Directions*, edited by Weston Naef, New York 1984; *Thought Objects*, edited by Barbara Ess and Glenn Branca, New York 1987; articles—"Personal Spaces" by James Collins in *Artforum* (New York), September 1973; "Roger Cutforth" by Valentin Tatransky in *Arts Magazine* (New York). September 1978; article by Loredana Parmesani in *Segno* (Pescara, Italy), no. 13, 1979, "Roger Cutforth" by Jean Fisher in *Aspects* (Newcastle upon Tyne), no. 13, 1981.

My portrait work began as a group of experimental photographic works in 1984. They grew out of a feeling of frustration with conventional photography, i.e., the single image lying behind a glasslike surface in which any presence of the artist is excluded. For me, photography was always a sequence of images connected either in time, or in the consciousness of the person who had taken them. What follows is an outline of some of the problems I saw in photography. The notes begin by referring to painting. I was, and still am, a painter, though I've worked mainly in photography for the last fifteen years.

In painting it is not so much an issue about how things look as about how things feel. Photography is almost exclusively about how things look. I'm cutting up photographs and sticking them together so that I can get details from different frames all into one picture. The photographs are portraits of people I know. One thing can be said in favor of photography in this respect: it is revealing. Most of us have lots of trouble with photographs of ourselves. I search all the frames of the films for details that really interest me. These details of various images become a key for me as to

Roger Cutforth: *Portrait of Kim Gordon*, 1983

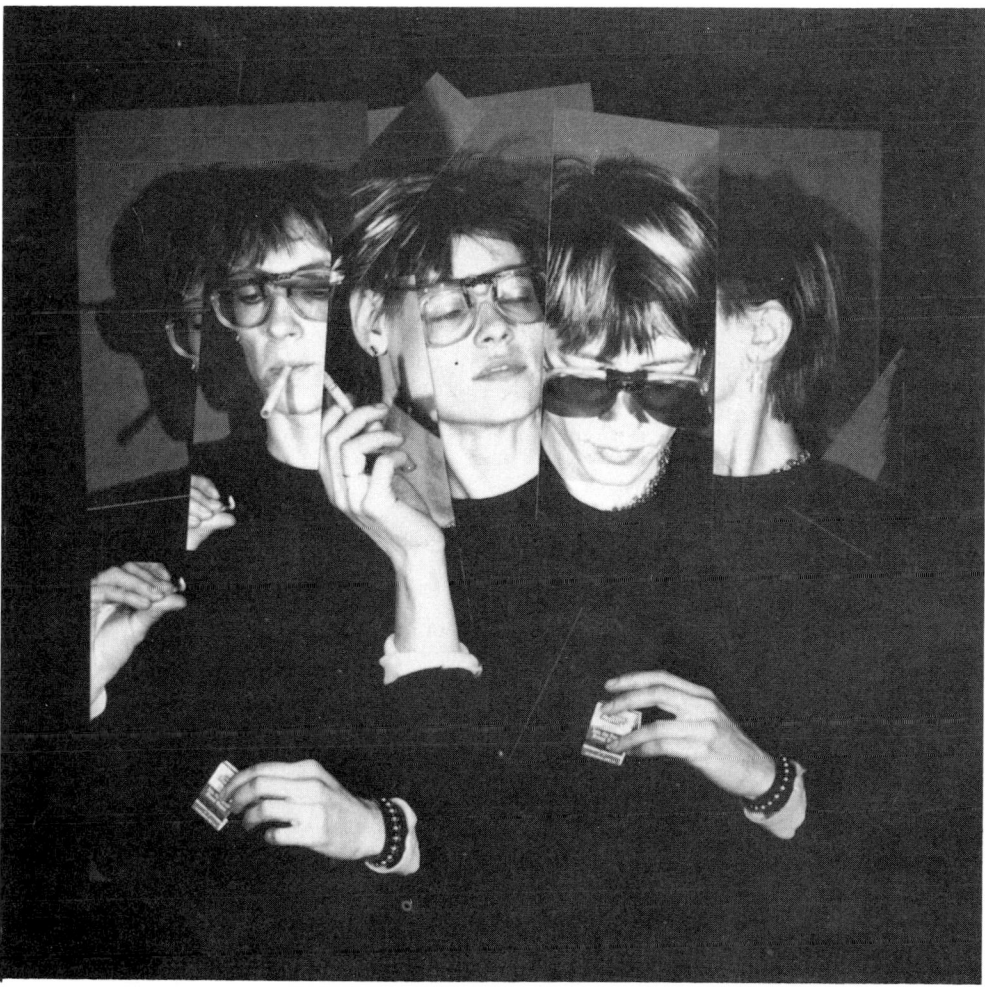

what is interesting about this medium. Thoughts on the portrait of Kim Gordon work fast so that ideas stay ahead of the medium. By this I mean, what interests me in the images should stay ahead of any consideration of them as photographs. Think about the irrational. Is it possible to subvert the rational construction of the world, that the camera constantly hands to us? One of the things wrong with conventional photography is that the medium speaks for itself and tells us next to nothing. Yet, another picture of the world (the direct photography of the nineteenth century, where the world was seen freshly through photographs) only exists for us today in the family snap-shot album. I think it was Carl Andre who once said, "Photographs are like rumors" (i.e. unverified information of uncertain origin). What I want from photography is the possibility of working creatively with the medium after the pictures have been taken. I want the process by which a picture is constructed to show in the end result. Photography, as a mechanical means of reproduction, naturally avoids this issue. This, plus the fact that there's no visible presence of the artist, is the reason photography has such a shaky footing as an artform.

I want the work to reveal something that was not previously known. The psychology of the photographer or artist must come forward and play a role in the finished work. "Sometimes you can hide behind a photograph but you can't hide behind a line."

(Paulette Nenner)

Man Ray set us a good example but we have regressed.

What the world doesn't need is another pretty picture.

Some friends are rephotographing photographs. I see this not only as a comment on our media-based culture, but also as a reflection of the fact that everything has been photographed a hundred times over. Photographs no longer bear any relationship to anything other than an endless, ongoing series of visual statements. The issue of photography is a false track. The medium is invisible, forget it. Lift from the film whatever interests you and follow your intuition; it's the only route to whatever power there is left in the process in its relation to life. I tell Dan Graham I know what I'm trying to do with photography. I want to show a certain kind of truth about it that's contained in what I consider the dross of my existence, test strips. The strips, made of the most interesting part of the image, accumulate in piles on my floor. I catch myself thinking that they probably contain a more interesting picture than the finished print on the wall. Bethany Jacobson asks me why I don't use the test strips? Because I think I may hate what the work made up of them looks like. I think I may hate what really interests me. I constantly have to tell myself to go ahead and make a mess, to subvert the idealized perfection of the photographic image. "Photographs are always presented as if the photographer doesn't exist. You are reinstating the photographer in the picture." (Jean Fisher) The portrait work is becoming even more unpredictable, the result of a performance between the person photographed, myself, and the camera. I want the finished work to reflect these aspects. It's odd that we think portraits can reveal something hidden about the person portrayed, yet do not see that they speak just as much of the person who made the portrait. It's impossible for me not to see the portraits as mirroring my own desire, of being equally that which I want to see, as well as that which is shown to me. Photographing women the camera obviously becomes a phallic extension through which I am intimate with them and take what I wish. But what about the men? The portrait with Jean Fisher makes me realize that the missing element in the construction of these works is myself. Jean plays me off against myself. Before the camera she displays an embarrassed prostituted image of femininity, then turning the camera on me, forces me into beng a parody of my own expectations of her. This work is hard for me to take. I feel I am naked in it both physically and symbolically.

From this work I realize I can no longer handle the images I collect without being aware that they are also references to an unconscious meaning that is demanding to be brought out.

—Roger Cutforth

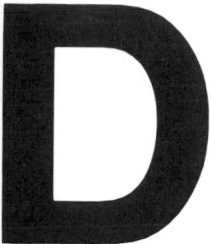

DADO.

Yugoslav. Born Miodrag Djuric in Cetinjie, Montenegro, 4 October 1933. Studied at School of Fine Art, Hercognovi, Montenegro, 1947-52; Academy of Fine Arts, Belgrade, 1952-56. Worked as a lithographic printer, Paris, 1956-58. Independent painter, draughtsman and printmaker, Paris and Courcelles, France, since 1958. Agent: Galerie Jeanne Bucher, Paris. Address: c/o Galerie Jeanne Bucher, 53 rue de Seine, 75006 Paris, France.

Individual Exhibitions:

1958	Galerie Daniel Cordier, Paris
1960	Galerie Daniel Cordier, Frankfurt
1962	Galerie Daniel Cordier, Paris
1964	Galerie Daniel Cordier, Paris (2 shows)
1965	Cordier and Ekstrom Gallery, New York
1967	Galerie d'Aujourd'hui, Brussels
1970	Byron Gallery, New York
	Centre National d'Art Contemporain, Paris (retrospective)
1971	Galerie Jeanne Bucher, Paris
	Galerie Therese Roussel, Perpignan, France
1973	Galerie Jeanne Bucher, Paris
1974	Museum Boymans-van Beuningen, Rotterdam (retrospective)
	Aberbach Fine Art, New York
	Galerie Jeanne Bucher, Paris
1975	Galerie Isy Brachot, Brussels
	Galerie Jeanne Bucher, Paris
1976	Aberbach Fine Art, New York
1978	*Dessins*, Galerie Isy Brachot, Paris
	Malningar teckningar grafik, Konsthall, Lund, Sweden
1979	Galerie Isy Brachot, Knokke, Belgium
	Galerie Isy Brachot, at *Art 10, '79*, Basle
1979	Fondation Veranneman, Kruishoutem, Belgium
	Aberbach Fine Art, New York
	Galerie Isy Brachot, Paris
1981	Galerie André-Francois Petit, Paris
1982	Centre Georges Pompidou, Paris

Selected Group Exhibitions:

1960	*Antagonismes*, Musée des Arts Décoratifs, Paris
1963	*Carnegie International*, Carnegie Institute, Pittsburgh (and 1967)
1964	*Documenta 3, Kassel*, West Germany
1965	*European Drawings*, Guggenheim Museum, New York
1968	*The Obsessive Image*, Institute of Contemporary Arts, London
1969	*Malerei des Surrealismums*, Kunstverein, Hamburg
1972	*Creation Artistique en France 1960-72*, Grand Palais, Paris
1976	*Les Espaces Insolites*, Palais des Congress. Strasbourg
	Contemporains IV, Musée d'Art Moderne, Paris
1978	*FIAC 78*, Grand Palais, Paris

Collections:

Centre Georges Pompidou, Paris; Centre National d'Art Contemporain, Paris; Stedelijk Museum, Amsterdam; Museum Boymans-van Beuningen, Rotterdam; Guggenheim Museum, New York; Art Institute of Chicago.

Publications:

On DADO: books—*Dado*, exhibition catalogue, with text by Georges Limbour, Frankfurt 1960; *Dado*, exhibition catalogue, with text by Patrick Waldberg, Paris 1967; *Dado*, exhibition catalogue, with text by Daniel Cordier, Paris 1970; *Dado*, exhibition catalogue, with text by Gaeton Picon, Paris 1971; *Dado*, exhibition catalogue, with text by Richard E. Friedman, New York 1974; *Dado*, exhibition catalogue, with an introduction by R. Hammacher-van den Brande, text by Francois Mathey, Rotterdam 1974; *Dado*, exhibition catalogue, with text by Michael Peppiatt, Paris 1975; *Dado: Dessins*, exhibition catalogue, with text by Bernard Noel, and an interview by Michael Peppiatt, Paris 1978; *Dado: Malningar teckninger grafik*, exhibition catalogue, with texts by Marianne Nanne-Brahammer and Jacques Adelin Brutaru, Lund, Sweden 1978; *Dado; L'Exasperation du Trait*, exhibition catalogue, with texts by Christian Derouet and others, Paris 1981.

Dado cannot be classified, neither in his times and its isms of art, nor in a country, nor in a culture. He cites Martin Schongauer, Konrad Witz and Dürer as his great ideals and loves the Renaissance painting of the North. From the richly historical Montenegrin alpine landscape of his native country the artist has withdrawn—with occasional excursions to the pygmies in Africa and to New York—to a Norman watermill in France, as far away as possible from the Parisian art world; he prefers to maintain contact with his surroundings through his children.

Dado came at an early stage to his own style—in the manner of the old masters—which achieved its perfect expression in the graphic works. To him, drawings are always of specific value; they are never sketches or designs for paintings whose themes they in any case share. The impetus to Dado's creative activity starts from obsessions which are so intense that only extreme precision in their portrayal is able to liberate the artist from them momentarily. In 1973/74 Dado destroyed a large number of earlier drawings in order to form the pieces into an assemblage showing in one picture the total horror of his vision. Since 1973 his frightening images have grown ever larger. In correlation to the consequent slow down in the production of paintings, there is a simultaneous intensification of graphic activity. From 1976, as the paintings were undergoing a stylistic change, the most remarkable feature of which is in a new distribution of light, the drawings also show larger free zones in front of which on various planes and in detail passing images unite to form an exciting style.

The fascinating effect of Dado's style lies in the juxtaposition of detailed realistic images and indefinable fantastic scenes. The viewer is attracted by a seemingly hazy painting which often seems bathed in luminous rosy colours—and is deceived by the changing play on perception, appearance and reality. Behind the delicate haze graphic elements appear in various places, and on closer inspection one sees them condense to form gruesome images. Yet the details cannot be identified precisely. If one thinks that one sees pictures of the atrocities of concentration camps or Hiroshima, after longer inspection one finds that the scenery blurs to a vision of unutterable horror which as yet has no name in contemporary art and which perhaps as a vision of the future constitutes the originality of Dado's work. There one discovers children "in limbo" to whom no life is allotted and an "ancestral gallery" of old people who have outlived themselves, drawn by one who "above all sees in nature not life but death" and who dreads one day the loss of the seeing eye. Idyllically painted children are disfigured with repulsive hydrocephalus, animals with bodies torn open turn into hideous legendary creatures, plants are destructively rampant, and poisonous mushrooms develop dangerous explosive matter. Walls and buildings crumble away beneath the spectator's gaze and fall in ruins. In the midst of putrefaction arise monstrosities, terrifying mutants are born of dislocated and mutilated beings. The Book of Job, the interpretation of which Dado has pursued since the 1950's, always with a fresh technical approach, gains in his hands an added contemporary dimension. Mankind's frightful primeval visions couple with contemporary anxieties about organ transplants in living bodies, the fear of cancer and the bomb—without any hope of salvation.

Dado produces pictures of anxiety, superbly crafted with the precision of an old master, on which the eye cannot rest but in confusion wanders from one scene to another. It is only at first sight that one thinks to have discovered the work of a modern Brueghel (he has, after all, an acquaintance with Hans Bellmer, Max Ernst, Magritte and Dali). Yet Dado does not see the world with the same eyes as the old masters in the Christian Occident; he also does not view it with the profound psychologically acute vision of a contemporary adult, who perhaps delights in cruelties; he looks with the wide open eyes of a terrified child who sometimes (with the help of diluted ink) artificially "ages" his drawings so that he is relieved of his visions, a child who refuses to learn to suppress the dread of being devoured or turned to stone, who regards the old and the sick with dread and mortal terror, who stares with horror at deformity, a child who perhaps frightens others with terrifying spiders but does not himself tear off the legs of insects.

—Dagmar Sinz

DAHMEN, K(arl) F(red).

German. Born in Stolberg, 4 November 1917. Studied at the Kunstschule, Aachen, West Germany, 1931-33. Served in the Light Anti-Aircraft Artillery Division 84, German Army, in France, the Balkans and Russia, 1939-45. Married Ursula Hesse in 1940; son: Volker. Associated with Raoul Ubac and Serge Poliakoff, 1950-54; travelled regularly in Spain, 1960-67, in the United States, 1974. Guest Professor,

Kunstschule, Bremen, 1963–64; Professor, Akademie der Bildenden Künste, Munich, from 1967. Recipient: Swiss International Art Prize, Lausanne, 1959; Karl-Ernst-Osthaus Prize, Hagen, 1966; Graphics Prize, Ibiza, Spain, 1972. Agents: Galerie Gunther Franke, Maximilianstrasse 22, 8000 Munich 22; Galerie Muller-Wintersberger, Lindenstrasse 20, 5000 Cologne; Galerie Rothe, Werderplatz 17, 6900 Heidelberg; and Galerie Albert Verbeke, 7 Place Furstenberg, Paris. *Died* (in Preinderdorf, West Germany) *12 January 1981.*

Individual Exhibitions:

1946	Suermondt Museum, Aachen, West Germany
1948	Suermondt Museum, Aachen, West Germany
	Galerie Leithauser, Wuppertal, West Germany
1949	Suermondt Museum, Aachen, West Germany
1951	Galerie Kasper, Ascona, Switzerland
1955	Galerie Arnaud, Paris
1956	Galerie La Roue, Paris
1957	*Olbilder—Wachsmalerei*, Galerie Vertico, Bonn
	Zimmergalerie Franck, Frankfurt
	Galerie Arnaud, Paris
	Galerie CCC, Schiedam, Netherlands
1958	Leopold-Hoesch Museum, Düren, West Germany
	Galerie 22, Dusseldorf
	Galerie La Roue, Paris
	Galerie Behr, Stuttgart
1959	Galerie Aujourd'hui, Brussels
	Kunsthalle, Mannheim
	Galerie Parnass, Wuppertal, West Germany
1960	Galerie Hella Nebelung, Dusseldorf
	Insel Galerie, Hamburg
	Kabinett Grisebach, Heidelberg
	Galerie d'art Moderne, Stuttgart
	Studio F, Ulm, West Germany

	Galerie Boukes, Wiesbaden, West Germany
1961	Galerie Anne Abels, Cologne
	Galleria Pater, Milan
	Galerie Baier, Milan
	Galerie La Roue, Paris
1962	Galerie Günther Franke, Munich
	Städtisches Museum, Ulm, West Germany
1963	Galerie Rothe, Heidelberg
	Galeria Ivan Spence, Ibiza, Spain
	Lefebre Gallery, New York
	Galerie Haaken, Oslo
	Galerie Delta, Rotterdam
	Von-der-Heydt Museum, Wuppertal, West Germany
1964	Galerie Widman, Bremen, West Germany
	Galerie Prestel, Frankfurt
	Galerie Günther Franke, Munich
1965	Suermondt Museum, Aachen, West Germany
	Kleine Grafik Galerie, Bremen, West Germany
	Landolinshof, Esslingen, West Germany
	Galerie Brechbühl, Grenchen, Switzerland
	Kölnischer Kunstverein, Cologne
	Galleria Flaviana, Locarno, Switzerland
	Museum, Mönchengladbach, West Germany
	Galerie Hammerlund, Oslo
	Galerie La Roue, Paris
1966	Galerie Les Trois Feuilles d'Or, Beirut
	Galeria Ivan Spence, Ibiza, Spain
	Galerie Raeber, Lucerne
	Galerie Lauter, Mannheim
	Galerie Numaga, Neuchâtel-Auvernier, Switzerland
1967	Galerie Regio, Lörrach, West Germany
1969	Kunstverein, Augsburg, West Germany
	Galerie 66, Hofheim, West Germany
	Galeria Ivan Spence, Ibiza, Spain
	Galerie Regio, Lörrach, West Germany
	Galerie Lauter, Mannheim
	Galerie Günther Franke, Munich
1970	Kunstverein, Kassel, West Germany

	Kunstverein, Freiburg, West Germany
	Galerie Raeber, Lucerne
	Kunstverein, Ravensburg, West Germany
1971	Galerie Hardenstein, Bremen, West Germany
	Forum Kunst, Rottweil, West Germany
	Städtisches Museum, Ulm, West Germany
1972	Kleine Galerie, Bremen, West Germany
	Galerie Lauter, Mannheim
	Galerie 66, Hofheim, West Germany
	Galerie Schneider, Karlsruhe
	Galerie Kessler, Bad Godesberg, West Germany
	Galerie 2, Stuttgart
	Galerie Merian, Krefeld, West Germany
	Kunstverein, Munich
1973	Galerie Schottenring, Vienna
	Kunstverein, Aachen, West Germany
	Galerie Kuhn, Aachen, West Germany
	Galerie Regio, Kunstmesse Basle, Switzerland
	Galerie Schlieper und Busch, Hagen, West Germany
	Galerie Dr. Vogel, Augsburg, West Germany
	Kulturkreis, Berg-Neustadt, West Germany
	Galerie Kuhn, Dusseldorf
	Galerie Rothe, Heidelberg
1974	BMW Galerie, Munich
	Galerie Jaeschke, Braunschweig, West Germany
	Galerie Vonderbank, Frankfurt
	Galerie Lometsch, Kassel, West Germany
	Studio Kausch, Kassel, West Germany
	Galerie Riis, Trondheim, Norway
	Galerie im Zilemp, Olten, Switzerland
	Kunstverein, Darmstadt
1975	Galerie Hennermann, Bonn
	Galerie Nothelfer, Berlin
	Galerie Limited, Munich
	Galerie Hermanns, Fürstenfeldbruk, West Germany
	Galerie Rothenstein, Bremen, West Germany
	Galerie Moderne, Silkeborg, Denmark
	Galerie Hennemann, Dusseldorf
	Galerie Loehrle, Schiefbahn bei Dusseldorf
	Galerie Günther Franke, Munich
	Junior Galerie, Dusseldorf
	Galerie Rothe, Heidelberg
	Junior Galerie, Cologne
1976	Neue Galerie der Stadt, Linz, Austria
	Junior Galerie, Zurich
	Kunstverein, Salzburg
	Galerie Verbeke, Paris
	Galerie Golong, St. Paul de Vence, France
	Junior Galerie, Copenhagen
	Galerie BLA, Oslo
	Museum Duren, West Germany
	Galerie Rohklan, Augsburg, West Germany

Selected Group Exhibitions:

1948	*Neue Aachener Gruppe*, Suermondt Museum, Aachen, West Germany
1955	*Beteiligung an den Manifestationen bei den Ausstellungen "Divergence" 3, 4, and 5*, Galerie Arnaud, Paris
1963	*German Artists* touring exhibition (toured United States)
1966	*13 Aspekte deutscher* touring exhibition (toured West Germany)
1967	*Deutsch Kunst im 20 Jahrhundert*, Suermondt Museum, Aachen, West Germany
1970	*Internationale Kunstmesse*, Basle
1972	*1st International Graphic Biennale*, Fredrikstad, Norway
1973	*Sammlung Dobermann*, Landesmuseum, Münster, West Germany
1974	*25 Jahre Kunst in der Bundesrepublik Deutschland*, Kunstmuseum, Bonn
1976	*Salon des Réalités Nouvelles*, Paris

Collections:

Suermondt Museum, Aachen, West Germany; Sammlung Ludwig, Aachen, West Germany; Städtisches Museum, Bonn; Kunsthalle, Bremen, West Germany; Staatsgalerie, Stuttgart; Kunsthalle, Hamburg; Städtisches Museum, Mönchengladbach, West Germany; Städtisches Museum, Wup-

Karl Fred Dahmen: *Reduktion einer Landschaft*, 1975

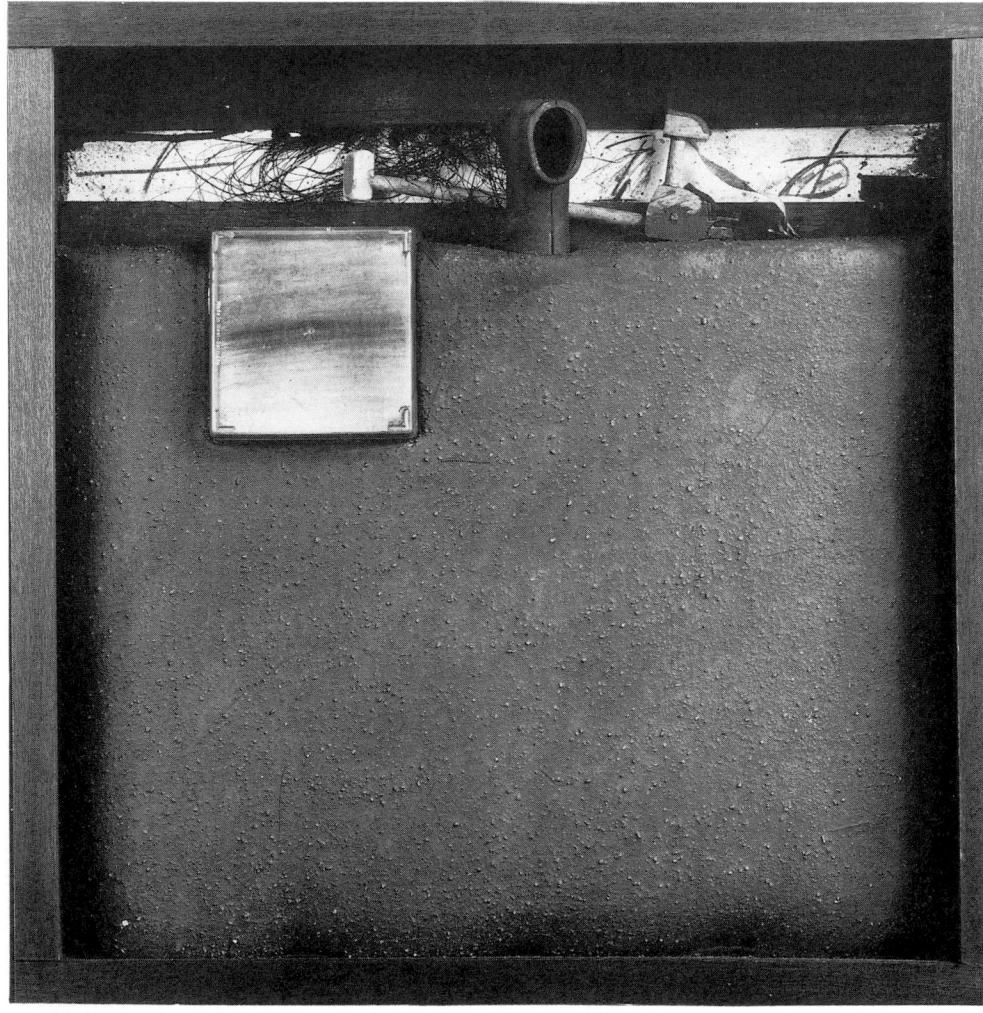

pertal, West Germany; Nationalgalerie, Oslo; Museo de Arte Moderna, Caracas.

Publications:

By DAHMEN: books—*Tradition und Gegenwart*, exhibition catalogue, Leverkusen, West Germany 1966; *Depot Schloss Morsbroich*, Leverkusen, West Germany 1969.

On DAHMEN: books—*K. F. Dahmen: Olbilder—Wachsmalerei*, exhibition catalogue, Bonn 1957; *K. F. Dahmen*, exhibition catalogue, with texts by Rolf Wedewer, Carl Linfert, Jacques Lassaigne and others, Cologne 1965; *Geschichte der modernes Kunst* by H. Harvard Arnason, Bremen, West Germany 1971; *K. F. Dahmen: Das malerische Werk 1950–72*, Munich 1972; articles—"K. F. Dahmen" by Roger von Gindertael in *Cimaise* (Paris), no. 5, 1955; "K. F. Dahmen" by Karl-Heinz Goerres in *Das Kunstwerk* (Baden-Baden, West Germany), no. 5, 1956–57; "Der Maler K. F. Dahmen" by Karl-Heinz Goerres in *Quadrum* (Brussels), no. 5, 1958; "K. F. Dahmen" by Günther Ladstetter in *Deutsche Zeitung* (Stuttgart), April 1959; "Present Day German Painting" by Stefan Munsing in *Art News and Review* (London), vol. II, no. 4, 1959; "Bilder und Collagen von K. F. Dahmen" by J. A. Thwaites in *Deutsche Zeitung* (Stuttgart), November 1960; "K. F. Dahmen" by Marco Valsecchi in *Il Giorno Milano*, May 1961; "K. F. Dahmen" by Charlotte Weidler in *Arts Magazine* (New York), November 1963; "The Informal and the Surreal in New German Art" by Hanns Th. Flemming in *Studio International* (London), June 1964; "K. F. Dahmen" by Jacques Michel in *Le Monde* (Paris), March 1965; "K. F. Dahmen" by Hanns Th. Flemming in *Studio International* (London), August 1965; "Neue Material montegan von West Germany" by Kramer-Badoni in *Die Welt* (Bonn), no. 106, 1969; film—*K. F. Dahmen* by Rolf Wiesselmann, 1958.

By one of those strange combinations of impulses that are as likely to occur in art as in other forms of self-expression, it was in the 1950's that Tapies, Burri, Dubuffet and others began the styles of object making that became known as Tachisme and Informal Art. In Germany the chief exponent was Karl Fred Dahmen, and the works he made are among the most powerful in the category, having force and cathartic shock capable of penetrating the inertia of the casual onlooker to cause a definite reaction.

1950 was for Dahmen the point of departure in an abstract style. Landscapes and townscapes gradually became submerged in masses owing some of their structure to Cubism. Space-plan pictures evolved in which the motive became sublimated within the material. Free play of creative means was given its head so that in the end his earth-crust pictures are truly described; the coruscating colour and the irregular surface take on a volcanic rocky contour. This extreme indentation and irregularity of the surface raised in relief carries in it a history of mural and vegetable deterioration and organic change: dilapidated walls gleam in a strange patina of damp and fungus, rotting bark, petrified lava and the porosity of pumice stone. Beyond this engrossment in the texture and skins of the canvas's camouflage, the marking of the graffiti and the linear design is man-formed in hieroglyph and pictograph, suggesting evidence of ancient civilization brought now to life by archaeological discovery. The surprise of historic recall is alternated by traces of a new Pompeii in a collage of a newspaper partially obliterated and scrawled with some runic note.

For Dahmen chance was not a prerequisite of composition. His choice was wide and the random sources were selected with care for nuances of colour and texture in each picture. He had a painterly concern for effect, though the pure pigment and its ordered synthesis in colour design had no attraction to compare with the object itself, the ready-made that took its place in works of intense presence and direct attack. This unconventional vocabulary would be vapid without the existence of the catalysing talent. Dahmen belonged to the rare band of artists who, despising the demands for pedantic purity, reap from the bountiful crop of improvisation, and the unexpected, exotic fruit to adorn his creations. Unlike Ar-

chimboldo's proficient transmutations by paint worked in figurative idiom, Dahmen produced a severe organic tremor by surrealist juxtaposition. History-laden materials from many places combine to exude, under the artist's hands, a palpable spirit of primitive and magic complexity.

—G. S. Whittet

DAHN, Walter.

German. Born in St. Tonis bei Krefeld, 8 October 1954. Studied art, under Joseph Beuys, Kunstakademie, Dusseldorf, 1971–77. Painter, in Cologne, since 1976. Agent: Galerie Paul Maenz, Bismarckstrasse 50, 5000 Cologne 1. Address: Klapperhof 33, 5000 Cologne 1, West Germany.

Individual Exhibitions:

1982 Galerie Paul Maenz, Cologne (and 1983)
 Galerie Helen van der Meij, Amsterdam
 Galerie 't Venster, Rotterdam (with Georg Dokoupil)
 Galerie Hetzler, Stuttgart
1983 Galerie Chantal Crousel, Paris
 Produzentengalerie, Hamburg (with Georg Dokoupil)
 Galerie Six Friedrich, Munich (with Georg Dokoupil)
 Mary Boone Gallery, New York
1984 Galerie Six Friedrich, Munich (and 1985)
 Groninger Museum, Groningen, Netherlands (with Georg Dokoupil)

Galerie Paul Maenz, Cologne (and 1985)
 Marian Goodman Gallery, New York
 Galerie Crousel-Hussenot, Paris (and 1985)
1985 Galerie Barbara Jandrig, Krefeld, West Germany
 Galerie Paul Maenz, Cologne (with Georg Dokoupil)
 Galerie Vera Munro, Hamburg (with Georg Dokoupil)
 Gallery Paule Anglim, San Francisco
 Asher/Faure, Los Angeles
 Rheinisches Landesmuseum, Bonn
 Groninger Museum, Groningen, Netherlands
1986 Museum fur Gegenwartskunst, Basle
 Kaiser Wilhelm Museum, Krefeld, West Germany
 Kunsthalle, Basle
 Museum Folkwang, Essen, West Germany
 Galerie Paul Maenz, Cologne
 Galerie Six Friedrich, Munich
1987 Van Abbemuseum, Eindhoven, Netherlands
 Galerie Roger Pailhac, Marseille, France
 Neuer Aachener Kunstverein, Aachen, West Germany
 Galerie Luis Campana, Stuttgart
1988 Galerie Paul Maenz, Cologne
 Galerie F. C. Gundlach, Hamburg
 Galerie Six Friedrich, Munich

Selected Group Exhibitions:

1980 *Auch wenn das Perlhuhn leise weint*, Hahnentorburg, Cologne
1981 *Phoenix*, Alte Oper, Frankfurt
1982 *La Giovane Pittura in Germania*, Galleria d'Arte Moderna, Bologna
1983 *Expressionisten—Neue Wilde*, Museum am Ostwall, Dortmund, West Germany
1984 *International Survey of Recent Painting and Sculpture*, Museum of Modern Art, New York

Walter Dahn: *Mann am baum*, 1982 Courtesy Museum of Contemporary Art, Chicago

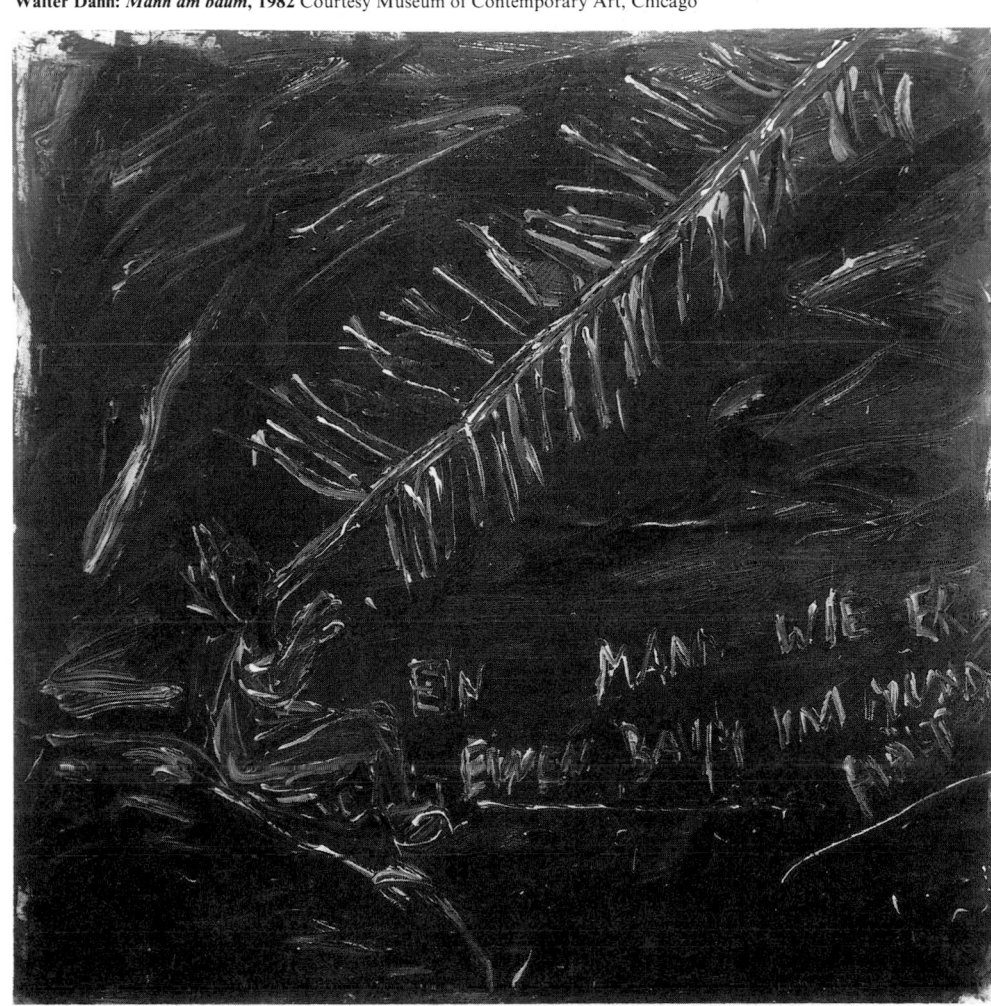

1985   *Koln-Kunst*, Kunsthalle, Cologne
1987   *Avant-Garde in the Eighties*, Los Angeles County Museum of Art

Collections:

Museum Folkwang, Essen; Hessisches Museum, Darmstadt; Bonnefantenmuseum, Maastricht; Groninger Museum, Groningen; Van Abbemuseum, Eindhoven; Staatsgalerie, Stuttgart; Kaiser Wilhelm Museum, Krefeld; Museum fur Gegenwartskunst, Basle; Museum am Ostwall, Dortmund.

Publications:

On DAHN: books—*10 Junge Kunstler aus Deutschland*, exhibition catalogue with text by Zdenek Felix, Essen 1982; *Walter Dahn*, exhibition catalogue with text by Patrick Frey, Cologne 1982; *Dahn und Dokoupil: Die Afrika-Bilder*, exhibition catalogue with text by Wilfried Dickhoff, Groningen 1984; *Walter Dahn: Zeichnungen, 12 Skulpturen*, exhibition catalogue with text by Dieter Koepplin, Basle 1986; *Walter Dahn: Gemalde 1981–1985*, exhibition catalogue edited by Wilfried Dickhoff, Basle 1986.

The first unequivocal manifestation of Walter Dahn's independent position was his painting, in 1981, *Maler ohne Idee* (Painter without Idea), undoubtedly a self-portraiture. This title is a paradox that, for those who do not recognize it as such, seemed to confirm the common presumption that Dahn, as well as his former Mullheimer Freiheit colleagues (Adamski, Bommels, Dokoupil, Kever, Naschberger) were merely a bunch of naive 'wild painters'. It is important to realize that these Cologne-based artists were very keen to distinguish themselves from the group of Berlin expressionists that included among others Fetting and Salome.

After the dissolution of Mullheimer Freiheit, Dahn went his own way, although he regularly worked together with Georg Dokoupil. In 1982–83 both did the series of Ricki-paintings, based on the motif of a shower splashing water over various objects such as an oven, a transistor radio, a pair of gloves, an armchair. These paintings might be considered as playful ironies of Fetting's expressionist Dusche-Bilder. However, the following collaboration project is of a different character. These Afrika–paintings from the end of 1983 show a sincere respect towards the visual qualities of primitive painting.

Like Dokoupil, Dahn produces in considerable quantity, although in less chameleontic fashion. While Dokoupil, above all, seems to be involved with continuous comment and irony concerning the artworld's codes and conventions, Dahn, on the other hand, concentrates on his own personal impulse in relation to the relics of other cultures. He tries to balance direct emotional response with the reproduction techniques through which we learn about the existence of these relics. For him there exists a correlation between his own imagery and the things from the past, not in terms of subconscious mythology but in those of potential subject–matter to be painterly reproduced.

From 1985 onwards he has put a lock to his spontaneous way of painting by complicating his procedure. This resulted in a series of monotype silkscreens on cloth, where there is no relief in the paint at all, a technique also employed by the American artist Robin Winters in his Bonaparte's Party series (1984).

From 1986–87 dates a group of large paintings, among these a painting that shows the figure of an Australian native. On a monochrome ground there is a multitude visible of massive black forms, blow-ups of photographic mass-reproduction. This painting demonstrates two complementary ways of seeing and enjoying. Nearby the expression is a painterly one. It is only at a distance that the image appears. The subject-matter is not anecdotal and, by its archaism, brings the viewer in a state that conflicts with his sheer esthetic pleasure.

Dahn has also done a group of small bronzes with subject-matter that includes a large number of self-portrayals. He also shows photopieces taking his friends, street life and shop windows for subjects. Altogether Dahn seems to grow as a painter, as an artist who does not depend on the circumstantial evidence of the current art world.

—A. F. Wagemans

DALI, Salvador.
Spanish. Born Salvador Felipe Jacinto Dali y Domenech, in Figueras, Gerona, 11 May 1904. Educated at Marist Friars School, Figueras, 1914–18; studied at San Fernando Academy of Fine Arts, Madrid, 1921–25. Married Gala Eluard in 1930. Worked as book and magazine illustrator, Figueras, 1919–21; independent artist, in Sitges, 1925–30, Paris, 1930–40, Pebble Beach, California, 1940–48, and in Port-Lligat, Spain, since 1948; worked on films with Luis Bunuel, 1929; member, André Breton's Surrealist Group of artists and writers, Paris, 1930–34; first theatre decors, 1939; first classical and religious paintings, 1948; first 3-dimensional works, 1964; established Dali Museum, Figueras, 1973. Editor, *L'Amic des Arts* magazine, Sitges, 1926–29, and *Manifest Groc*, with S. Gasch and L. Montanya, Sitges, 1928. Agent: Knoedler and Co., 21 East 70 Street, New York, New York 10021, U.S.A. Address: Port-Lligat, Cadaques, Spain.

Individual Exhibitions:

1925   Galeria Dalmau, Barcelona
1927   Galeria Dalmau, Barcelona
1929   Galerie Goemans, Paris
1931   Galerie Pierre Colle, Paris
1932   Julien Levy Gallery, New York
        Galerie Pierre Colle, Paris
1933   Galeria d'Art Catalunya, Barcelona
        Julien Levy Gallery, New York
        Galerie Pierre Colle, Paris
1934   Julien Levy Gallery, New York
        Galeria d'Art Catalunya, Barcelona
        Zwemmer Gallery, London
        Galerie Quatre Chemins, Paris
        Galerie Jacques Bonjean, Paris
1936   Alex Reid and Lefevre Gallery, London
        Julien Levy Gallery, New York
1939   Dali Studio, Paris
        Julien Levy Gallery, New York
1941   Museum of Modern Art, New York
        Julien Levy Gallery, New York
        Julien Levy Gallery, Hollywood, California
1942   Museum of Modern Art, New York
1943   M. Knoedler and Co., New York
1945   Bignon Gallery, New York
1946   M.Knoedler and Co., New York
1947   Cleveland Museum of Art
        Bignon Gallery, New York
1948   Bignon Gallery, New York
1950   Carstairs Gallery, New York
1951   Galerie David Weill, Paris
        Alemany and Ertman, New York
        Lefevre Gallery, London
1952   Carstairs Gallery, New York
        Alemany and Ertman, New York
1953   Santa Barbara Museum of Art, California
1954   Palazzo Pallaricini-Rospigliosi, Rome
        Carstairs Gallery, New York
1955   Philadelphia Museum of Art
        Denver Art Museum
1956   Casino Communal, Knokke, Belgium
        Carstairs Gallery, New York
1958   M. Knoedler and Co., New York
        Carstairs Gallery, New York
1959   French and Co., New York
1960   Musée Galliera, Paris
        Finch Gallery, New York
        Carstairs Gallery, New York

1963   M. Knoedler and Co., New York
1964   Prince Hotel Gallery, Tokyo (travelled to Prefectural Museum of Art, Nagoya and the Municipal Art Gallery, Kyoto)
        Los Angeles Municipal Art Gallery
1965   M. Knoedler and Co., New York
        Phyllis Lucas Gallery, New York
1966   Gallery of Modern Art, New York
1967   Hotel Meurice, Paris
        Galerie D, Prague
        Staempfli Gallery, New York
1968   Palais des Beaux-Arts, Charleroi, Belgium
        London Graphic Art Gallery
        Phyllis Lucas Gallery, New York
1969   Galerie Les Heures Claires, Paris
        Hiram College, Ohio
        Galerie Knoedler, Paris
        Zachary Walker Gallery, Los Angeles
1970   Museum Boymans-van Beuningen, Rotterdam (retrospective)
        M. Knoedler and Co., New York
        Galleria Guissi, Turin
        Musée de l'Athenée, Geneva
        Galerie Andre-Francois Petit, Paris
        M. Knoedler and Co., New York
        Karl-Ernst-Osthaus Museum Hagen, West Germany
1971   *Gemalde, Zeichnungen, Objekte Schmuck*, Staatliche Kunsthalle, Baden-Baden, West Germany
        Art-in-Jewels Exhibition, Whitechapel Art Gallery, London
        Museum Boymans-van Beuningen, Rotterdam
1972   *Holograms Conceived by Dali*, M. Knoedler and Co., New York
        Museum Boymans-van Beuningen, Rotterdam
        Galerie Isy Brachot, Brussels
1974   Städtisches Galerie/Stadelsches Kunstinsitut, Frankfurt
1977   *Bilder, Gouachen, Zeichnungen, Skulpturen*, Sammlung Levy, Hamburg
1979   *Retrospective 1920–1980*, Centre Georges Pompidou, Paris
1980   Tate Gallery, London
1982   *Obra Grafica*, Caja de Ahorros, Madrid
1984   Galeria Surrealista, Barcelona
1987   Galerie 1900–2000, Paris

Selected Group Exhibitions:

1921   *Group Exhibition*, Galeria Dalmau, Barcelona
1933   *Exposition Surrealiste*, Galerie Pierre Colle, Paris
1936   *Fantastic Art, Dada & Surrealism*, Museum of Modern Art, New York
1940   *Exposicion Internacional del Surrealismo*, Galeria de Arte Mexicano, Mexico City
1951   *Surrealisme en Abstractie*, Stedelijk Museum, Amsterdam
1959   *Exposition Internationale du Surrealisme*, Musée d'Art Moderne, Paris
1965   *Bienal*, Sao Paulo
1968   *Dada, Surrealism and Their Heritage*, Museum of Modern Art, New York
1970   *Surrealism*, Moderna Musset, Stockholm
1982   *A Century of Modern Drawing*, British Museum, London (travelled to the Boston Museum of Fine Arts, and the Cleveland Museum of Art)

Collections:

Salvador Dali Museum, Figueras, Spain; Centre Georges Pompidou, Paris; Nationalgalerie, West Berlin; Stedelijk Museum, Amsterdam; Museum Boymans-van Beuningen, Rotterdam; Kunsthaus, Zurich; Tate Gallery, London; Museum of Modern Art, New York; Guggenheim Museum, New York; Cleveland Museum of Art (A guide to Dali's work in public museums is published by Cleveland Museum of Art, 1974)

Publications:

By DALI: books and pamphlets—*La Femme Visible*, Paris 1930; *L'Amour et al Memoire*, Paris 1931; *Conquest of the*

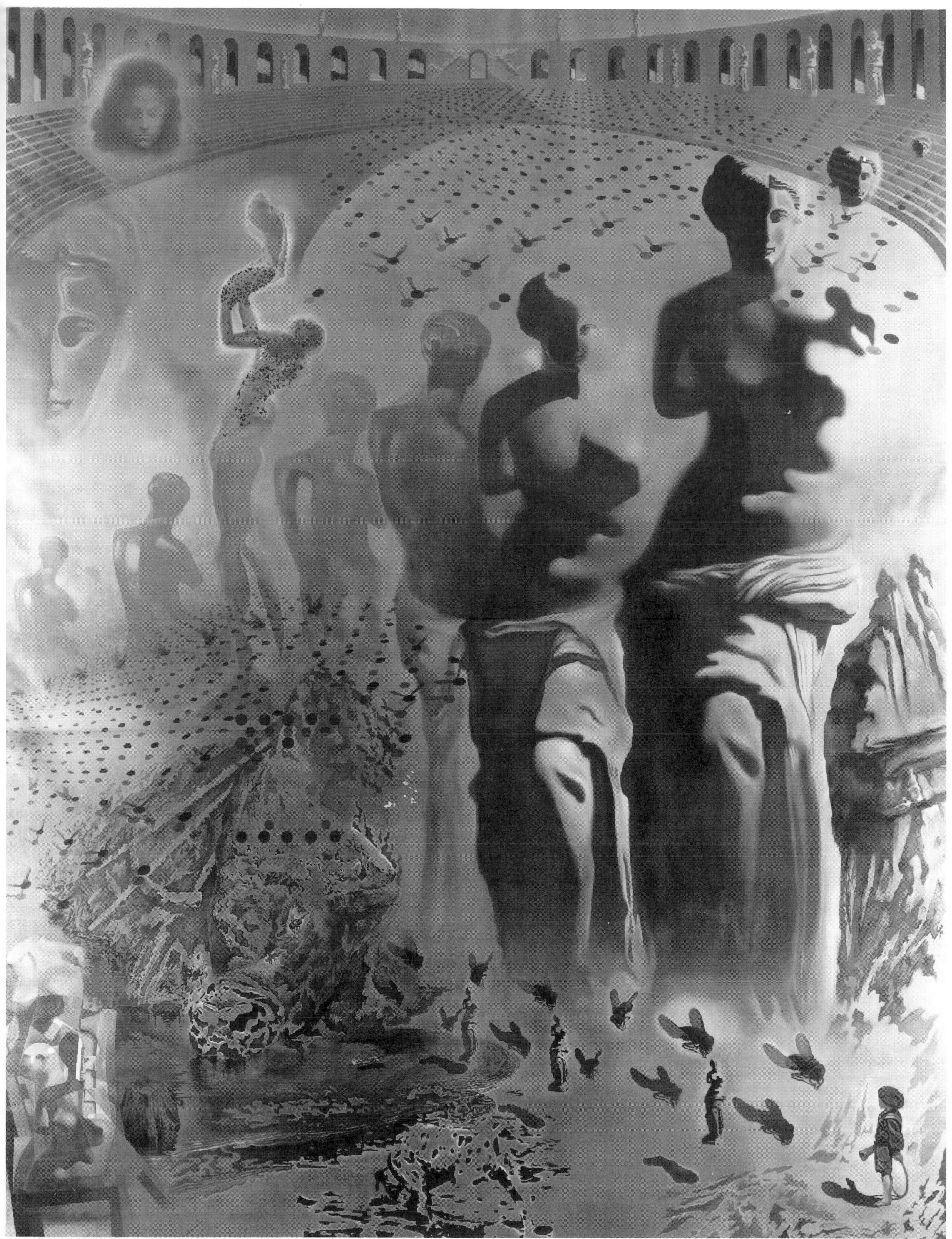

Salvador Dali: *The Hallucinogenic Toreador,* **1970** Courtesy Salvador Dali Museum, St. Petersburg, Florida

Irrational, Paris 1935; *The Metamorphosis of Narcissus,* 1937; *Declaration of the Independence of the Imagination and the Rights to His Own Madness,* 1938; *Hidden Faces,* New York 1944; *The Secret Life of Salvador Dali,* London 1948; *Mystical Manifesto,* 1951; *Dali's Moustache,* 1954; *The Cuckolds of Old Modern Art,* 1956; *The Tragic Myth of Millet's Angelus,* 1963; *Diary of a Genius,* 1964; *Dali de Draeger,* Paris 1968; *Dali by Dali,* New York 1970; *Les Diners de Gala,* New York 1963; *The Unspeakable Confessions of Salvador Dali,* New York 1976; films—*Un Chien Andalou,* with Luis Bunuel, 1929; *L'Age d'Or,* with Luis Bunuel, 1930; *The Prodigious History of the Laceworker and the Rhinoceros,* with Robert Descharnes, 1954.

On DALI: books—*Dickens, Dali and Others: Studies in Popular Culture* by George Orwell, New York 1946; *Salvador Dali* by James Thrall Soby, New York 1946; *Catalogue of Works by Salvador Dali* by A. Reynolds Morse, Cleveland 1956; *Dali* by Michel Tapie, Paris 1957; *Dali,* edited by Linda Livingstone, Greenwich, Connecticut 1959; *The Case of Salvador Dali* by Fleur Cowles, London 1959; *A New Introduction to Salvador Dali* by A. Reynolds Morse, Cleveland 1960; *The Salvador Dali Museum* by A. Reynolds Morse, Cleveland 1962; *Dali Exhibition-Japan 1964,* exhibition catalogue, edited by Shuzo Takiguchi, Yoshiaki Tono and Shin Ohoka, Tokyo 1964; *Salvador Dali 1910–1965,* exhibition catalogue, with an introduction by Carl J. Weinhardt Jr., New York 1965; *Dali: Miró* by Paul Walton, New York 1967; *Dali,* edited by Max Gerard, New York 1968; *In Quest of Dali* by C. Lake, New York 1969; *Dada and Surrealist Art* by William S. Rubin, London 1970; *Dali,* exhibition catalogue, with texts by Patrick Waldberg, Robert Descharnes and Gerrit Komrij, Rotterdam 1970; *Dali: Paintings and Drawings 1965–1979,* exhibition catalogue, with text by Thomas B. Hess, New York 170; *A Short Survey of Surrealism* by David Gascoyne, London 1970; *Deli: The Masterworks* by A. Reynolds Morse, Cleveland 1971; *Dali: Gemalde, Zeichnungen, Objekte, Schmuck,* exhibition catalogue, with a foreword by Klaus Gallwitz, texts by Patrick Waldberg, Gerrit Komrij and others, Baden-Baden, West Germany 1971; *Dali: Art-in-Jewels Exhibition,* exhibition catalogue, London 1971; *The Surrealists* by William Gaunt, London 1972; *Antologie Grafica del Surrealismo* by Maurice Henry, Milan 1972; *Holograms Conceived by Dali,* exhibitoin catalogue, with an introduction by Dennis Gabor, New York 1972; *Salvador Dali: Catalogue of a Collection—93 oils 1917–1970,* edited by A. Reynolds Morse, Cleveland 1972; *The World of Salvador Dali* by Robert Descharnes, London 1972; *The History of Surrealism* by Maurice Nadeu, London 1973; *Salvador Dali/ Pablo Picasso* by A. Reynolds Morse, Cleveland 1973; *Surrealisme et Sexualité* by Xaviere Gauthier, Paris 1971; *Dictionnaire de la Peinture Surrealiste* by Sarane Alexandrian, Paris 1973; *Malerei des Surrealismus* by Uwe M. Schneede, Cologne 1973; *A Dali Primer* by A. Reynolds Morse, Cleveland 1970; *The Draftsmanship of Dali,* with an introduction by A. Reynolds Morse, Cleveland 1970; *Dali,* edited by David Larkin, with an introduction by J. G. Ballard, London 1974; *Dali: A Guide to His Works in Public Museums* by A. Reynolds Morse, Cleveland 1974; *Salvador Dali,* exhibition catalogue, with a foreword by Klaus Gallwitz, texts by several authors, Frankfurt 1974; *Salvador Dali: Bilder, Gouachen, Zeichnungen, Skulpturen* exhibition catalogue, Hamburg 1977; *Salvador Dali: Retrospective 1920–1980,* exhibition catalogue, with texts by Daniel Abadie and others, Paris 1979; *Salvador Dali,* exhibition catalogue, with text by Simon Wilson, London 1980; *Dali: Obra Grafica,* exhibition catalogue, with texts by Javier Tusell, Ramon Gomez de la Serna and others, Madrid 1982; *Salvador Dali,* exhibition catalogue with essay by Robert Descharnes, Paris 1987.

After faltering Impressionist and then Cubist beginnings, Salvador Dali settled rapidly on a world and language of his own and on a style of painting not unlike that of the old masters. At the age of 25, in 1929, he was in full control of his art. It is for that reason that he went through the entire Surrealist era an absolute master. Furthermore, the theory he had just developed, labeled "paranoiac critical method," made it possible for him to present all his erotic, libidinous and scabrous obsessions in a fairy-tale-like context, thus transcribing visually everything Freud had expressed in words. André Breton wrote that in this method, Dali had provided the Movement with "an instrument of the utmost importance." Dali was to apply it with equal care and success to painting, to poetry, to film-making *(Un Chien Andalou, L'Age d'Or,* made with Luis Bunuel), to the construction of the familiar surrealist objects (the telephone with receiver in the shape of a lobster, the Venus of the drawers, the sofa in the shape of Mae West's lips), to fashion (he designed for Elsa Schiapparelli) and to any sort of exegesis (for instance, his theories on the emperor Trajan and Romania). Later on, Dali maintained that the greatest of his discoveries was doubtless still the paranoiac critical method. He doesn't know exactly what the term means, but he's sure it has brought him millions and millions of dollars.

All joking aside, it is the Surrealist period which clearly dominates his works, and which gives us a master of the art of painting: "The Great Masturbator" (1929), "The Enigma of Desire" (1929), "The Persistence of Memory: Limp Watches" (1933); watches can be anything, even limp, provided they show the correct time, says the artist. The power of words (reinforcing as they do the pictorial image, while the image sends us back to the title) nearly take us outside the limits of painting: the artist becomes a medium. This period is also that of Dali's historical intuitions represented by such magnificent canvases as The "Enigma of William Tell" (1933), showing a figure with tentacle-like legs and a raw chop on one knee, and the *shapka* (Russian hat) picture, held up by a crutch, showing a Lenin who had already sacrificed the children of his Revolution. There are also works foretelling the Spanish Civil War: "Prémonition de la Guerre Civile" (1936).

The 1950's marked the gradual disappearance of this emotion-filled, profoundly upsetting a content, so full of eccentricities, sadism, solitude, and those complexes necessarily a part of Dali's erotically-based universe. The images of Christ, where Dali is trying to leave the spectator breathless through his panoramic, plunging views, are the reflection of a different world.

As everybody knows, Dali did more than anyone else to make himself an object of discussion, giving a tragic example to the new generations. "I want people to talk about me, even if they say nice things" he declared in that period of his youth when he was already formulating the following principle: "Painter, if you wish to take your place in society, you must at a very tender age launch a terrific kick at its left leg." Such violence began as instinctive and was later refined; Dali was, doubtless, the first to evaluate to the status of doctrine a notion which was to become one of the signs of our times. Increasingly "different," increasingly eccentric, forever doing the opposite of what others did in order to set himself apart, and forever calling into question his position as madman or genius, Dali left a lifeless and declining bourgeoisie increasingly astounded; and he made them pay the outrageous price for his psychological maneuverings.

The story of his eccentricities is a long one, and has been brilliantly told by Dali himself in his books. The most important of them is a literary masterpiece, as well as one of the most entertaining pieces one could hope to encounter: *The Secret Life of Salvador Dali* by Salvador Dali. Its first chapter is cleverly entitled "Am I a genius?", a question which he answers repeatedly throughout the book, and which is treated again in a sequel. Of course he's a genius. The title of the second volume, by the way, is highly revelatory: *Diary of a Genius* by Salvador Dali. What can we learn from these books concerning the most celebrated of living artists? At six years of age, he wanted to be a cook, and at seven, Napoleon. Since then, he assures us, his ambition has never ceased to grow; nor his megalomania.

Dali has gone about building his universal kingdom and temple of "genius" in a number of different ways. He has been doing so in his mind since his birth on May 11, 1904, or perhaps even before if one takes into account the intrauterine memories he has continued to describe in minute detail right up to present day. Along more concrete lines he has built, ten years ago, a theater-museum in his birthplace, Figueras, for the self-glorification of his genius.

The persistent nature of Dali's torment has led to a curious identification with the ultimate incarnations of power, be they Lenin, Stalin, Hitler, Mao, Franco, King Juan Carlos; money (the Dollar) or Science. But, the same Dali who tried to assimilate all new discoveries, all forms of power, and who never hesitated to use extravagant forms of provocation to establish his position as "genius," has at the same time, as a rule, been obsessively strict when it came to painting. In painting he is against "freedom" and for restraint. He favors form. "Classicism stood for integration, synthesis, cosmogony, instead of break-up, experimentation on scepticism" wrote this enemy of the "old modern art."

The specter of Picasso constantly confronts Dali. It is undeniable that just as the former revolutionized painting, the latter revolutionized the behavior of the painter. Seeing the two juxtaposed in this way, we can notice how very different their work has been. "Picasso," says Dali, "pushed ugliness to its furthest extreme." Breaking up the shape of reality and yet continually clashing with objects, Picasso remained a prisoner to his perceptions. Having broken up the universe, with his tireless worker's hands, he put it back together, using the smashed pieces. Dali did just the opposite. The two geniuses are mutally exclusive in their fundamental approach. Interested rather in beauty and in the hidden harmony of things, Dali stands as the great manipulator of myths in our time—of myths and not simply of media. That is perhaps the most interesting thing about him, and certainly the most important as well, at a period in history when people are satisfied with myths which have been debased or made caricatures, which are useless in helping us to live.

In person, Dali is touching, serious, well-informed. He is infinitely charming. The persona he has created for himself, on the other hand, demonstrates an egotistical inflation without parallel, and is devouring, cruel, extravagant and provocative. Now if this persona has been able to endure and to continue to be identified with the notion of *genius* for more than 50 years, it is because Dali has simultaneously cultivated a second art—that of *galateo,* the art of laughing at oneself invented in 16th century Tuscany, of finding one's weaknesses, of publicly identifying them and of blowing them up to such proportions that we are forced to regard him with tenderness and humor rather than with what might have been hatred. For we will have recognized something of ourselves in this hero who up till then had seemed sublime and without weakness.

The concept of *genius,* peculiar to the 19th century, was applied above all to the *artist*—that person who could not prove his place in society and who was subject to both divine grace and disgrace. He was chosen by the gods and damned by society, whence the helpless rebellion expressed his Alfred de Vigny in *Moise:*"—Why me?" However, no one has done as much as Dali to amass unto himself the advantages of being *chosen.*

The notion of *genius* has suffered a loss of favor since 1930, but has remained in use from Napoleon right up through Dali. (Remember that he wanted to be Napoleon as a child.) We have learned from Zielsel and Isac Kapuano that the concept of *genius* cannot exist without that of flaw or Achilles heel. Dali seems to have sensed this instinctively in his perpetual effort to call attention to his own weaknesses ("How cowardly I am," "At any rate, I'm completely impotent," "I used to read Kant and understand nothing"). One might also conclude that *genius* is necessarily eccentric, that is *ex-centric.* But it remains to be known whether genius can coexist in the same person as the initiate who, by definition, is supposed to be *the center.*

—Radu Varia

DANBY, Ken.

Canadian. Born in Sault Sainte Marie, Ontario, 6 March 1940. Studied under Jock MacDonald, Ontario College of Art, Toronto, 1957–60. Married Judith E. Harcourt in 1965; sons: Sean, Ryan, Noah. Worked in mining tower construction, Wawa, Canada, 1958; Set Designer, CJIC-TV, Toronto, 1960;

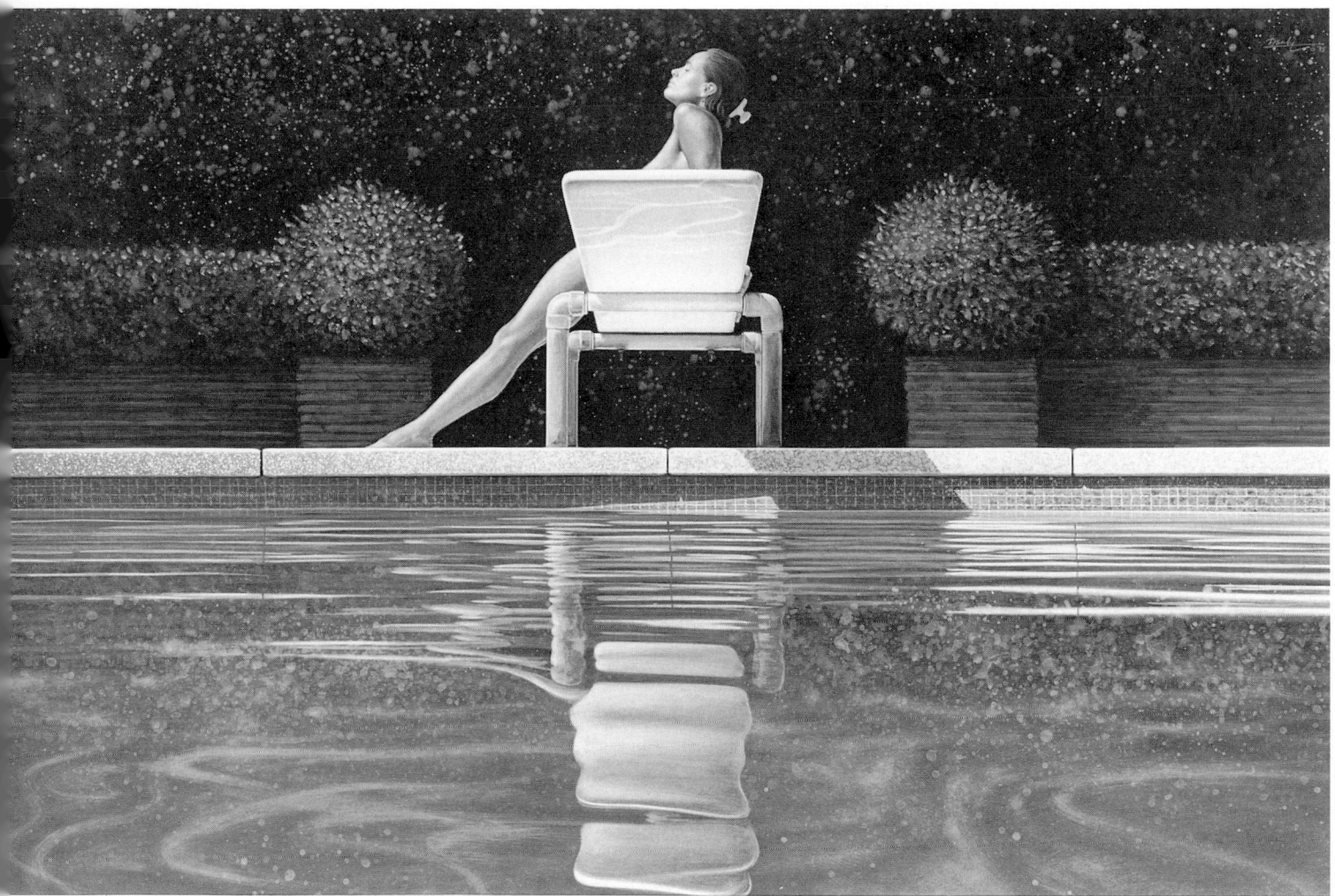

Ken Danby: *Acapulco*, 1985

Promotions Designer, *The Telegram* newspaper, Toronto, 1960–62. Independent artist: influenced by
Andrew Wyeth exhibition, New York, 1962; moved to
Speed River, Guelph, Ontario, 1967; commissioned
to design Series III Olympic Coinage, 1976. Mem-
ber, Canada Council, 1985. Recipient: Purchase
Award, *Four Seasons Exhibition,* Toronto, 1962; Jes-
sie Dow Best Painting Award, Museum of Fine Arts,
Montreal, 1964; Drawing Award, *Hadassah Exhibi-
tion,* Toronto, 1965; R. Tait McKenzie Chair for
Sport Award, National Sport and Recreation Centre
and Labatt Breweries, Ottawa; Ontario Arts Council
Award, 1976; Queen's Canadian Silver Jubilee
Medal, 1977. Member, Royal Canadian Academy of
Arts, 1976. Agent: Gallery Moos Ltd., 136 Yorkville
Avenue, Toronto, Ontario M5R 1C2. Address: R.R.
4, Guelph, Ontario N1H 5J1, Canada.

Individual Exhibitions:

1964   Gallery Moos, Toronto
1965   Gallery Moos, Toronto
1966   Gallery Moos, Toronto
         Galerie Agnes Lefort, Montreal
1967   Gallery Moos, Toronto
1968   Gallery Moos, Toronto
1969   *Kunstmarkt,* Cologne
         Gallery Moos, Toronto
1970   Gallery Moos, Toronto
1971   Gallery Moos, Toronto
1972   William Zierler Gallery, New York
         Gallery Moos, Toronto
         Images Gallery, Toledo, Ohio
1973   Galerie Allen, Vancouver
         Fleet Gallery, Winnipeg
         Continental Art Agencies, Vancouver
         William Zierler Gallery, New York

1974   *Brown/Danby/Forrestall,* Canadian Consulate, New
         York
         Gallery Moos, Toronto
         Wallack Gallery, Ottawa
         Galerie Moos, Montreal
         Kitchener-Waterloo Gallery, London, Ontario (retro-
         spective; toured Southern Ontario)
1975   *Algoma Arts Festival,* Sault Ste. Marie, Ontario
         Galerie Allen, Vancouver
         Gallery Moos, Toronto
1976   Gallery Moos, Toronto
1977   Canadian Consulate, New York
         Arras Gallery, New York
         de Vooght Galleries, Vancouver
         Gallery Moos, Toronto
1978   Gallery Moos, Toronto
1979   Gallery Moos, Toronto
1980   *Ken Danby: The Graphic Work: Lithographs and
         Serigraphs,* Art Gallery of Hamilton, Ontario
         (toured Canada, 1980–82)
         De Vooght Galleries, Vancouver
1982   Gallery Moos, Toronto
1983   Galerie Mihalis, Montreal
         Americas Cup Gallery, Newport, Rhode Island
1985   Gallery Moos, Toronto
         Kenneth G. Heffel Fine Art, Vancouver

Selected Group Exhibitions:

1964   *Drawings and Watercolours,* National Gallery of
         Canada, Ottawa
1966   *Magic Realism in Canadian Art,* London Art Gal-
         lery, Ontario
1970   *Survey 70: Realisms,* Art Gallery of Ontario, To-
         ronto (travelled to the Museum of Fine Arts, Mon-
         treal)
1971   *Biennale,* Paris

1972   *Silk Screen: History of a Medium,* Philadelphia Mu-
         seum of Art
1974   *Canadian Realists,* Canadian Cultural Centre, Paris
         (toured Europe)
1976   *Aspects of Realism,* Rothman's of Pall Mall travel-
         ling exhibition, Stratford Art Gallery, Ontario
         (toured Canada, 1976–78)
1980   *Canadian high Realism,* Bayard Gallery, New York
1981   *Champions of American Sports,* National Portrait
         Gallery, Washington, D.C. (travelled to Los Ange-
         les, Chicago, New York)
1985   *A Celebration of Amateur Sport,* Queen's Park, To-
         ronto

Collections:

National Gallery of Canada, Ottawa; Visual Arts Bank, Canada Council, Ottawa; Museum of Fine Arts, Montreal; Art
Gallery of Vancouver; Mendel Art Gallery, Saskatoon, Saskatchewan; Museum of Modern Art, New York; Museum of
Fine Arts, Indianapolis; Art Institute of Chicago; University
of California, Berkeley; Bradford City Art Gallery and Museum, England.

Publications:

By DANBY: article—interview, with Andrew J. Oka, in *Ken
Danby: The Graphic Work: Lithographs and Serigraphs,* exhibition catalogue, Hamilton, Ontario 1980.

On DANBY: books—*Ken Danby,* exhibition catalogue, with
texts by Russell J. Harper and Paul Duval, Toronto 1967; *Ken
Danby,* exhibition pamphlet, by Mario Amaya, New York
1972; *4 Decades* by Paul Duval, Toronto 1972; *High Realism
in Canadian Art* by Paul Duval, Toronto 1974; *Neue Formen
des Realismus* by Peter Sagel, Cologne 1974; *Ken Danby* by
Paul Duval, Toronto, deluxe edition 1974, trade edition 1976;
Danby Images of Sport by Hubert de Santana, Toronto 1978;

Super Realism by Edward Lucie-Smith, London 1979; *Siebdruck: Technik, Praxis, Geschichte* by Wolfgang Hainke, Cologne 1979; *Ken Danby: The Graphic Work: Lithographs and Serigraphs*, exhibition catalogue, with a foreword by Glen E. Cumming, Hamilton, Ontario 1980; *Contemporary Canadian Art*, by David Burnett and Marilyn Schiff, Toronto 1983; *Ken Danby: The New Decade* by Paul Duval, Toronto 1984; film—*Ken Danby*, produced by Rex Bromfield, Toronto 1971.

Throughout the history of art, we have witnessed a great metamorphosis taking place, which continues to alter and expand our appreciation of art. A constant exploration, into the various elements of the visual world, together with individual interpretation, has always been at the core of fine art.

As important discoveries and insights have been offered, the posture of the "art community" has been unsettled and then adjusted over a period of time, according to the degree of accommodation necessary. For example, for centuries, a great effort was made to resolve the applications of simple perspective, in drawing and painting. Equally so, was the attempt to create form and dimension through the use of strong light and shade; chiaroscuro.

While acknowledging that continued experimentation is essential, I also feel that it is time to integrate that which we have learned; in a cohesive and constructive manner, as well as in an experimental one. The individual entities of art; colour, shape, light, dimension, texture, etc., are but the pieces of the whole. Rather than continue the procedure of assessing these elements separately, I prefer to utilize their particular assets collectively, in creating a complete statement—a total integration of all I have learned and am learning. Only in this way, can I hope to communicate successfully, and be satisfied with the results.

—Ken Danby

Born in Sault Ste. Marie, Ontario, Ken Danby studied at the Ontario College of Art in Toronto from 1958 to 1960 with the well-known abstractionist, J. W. G. (Jock) MacDonald, and began his own career as an abstract painter, but soon returned to his first love, realism. The palette of his early abstractions with their colours of coral, grey and brown set the tone for later work. Nor did he forget the techniques he'd learned as an abstract artist—he used them later. But in the meantime, the subjects of his paintings changed to carefully posed, snapshot like views, often of rural Ontario. In 1962 a visit to an Andrew Wyeth exhibition at Buffalo, N. Y., confirmed for Danby that a realist artist could be respected. In his maturity as an artist Danby enjoyed painting personal friends and family, and anonymous sports figures. In his *At the Crease* (1972), the masked ice-hockey goalie recalls knights of an earlier day. For many in Canada that painting has become something of a national symbol.

In its mix of abstraction and realism, Danby's work recalls that of Christopher Pratt, but Danby's atmosphere is not so rarefied and cerebral. He did not hesitate to deal with almost Caravaggesque low-life, as in *Motel* (1971) which recounts the cigarettes, coffee, and crumpled pillow of the lonely motel room. Over the last decade, he has increasingly sought poetic, simple, effects; the almost invisible division between water and land in *The Sculler* (1976); the way the water in *Acapulco* (1985) is abstractly treated while the woman seated on the diving board, and the setting, are realistic. "The symmetrical design was challenging, as was the need to create a sensuous and luminous light," said Danby of *Acapulco*. "I was intrigued by the fact that the work combines both a confrontational thrust with a peaceful calm."

—Joan Murray

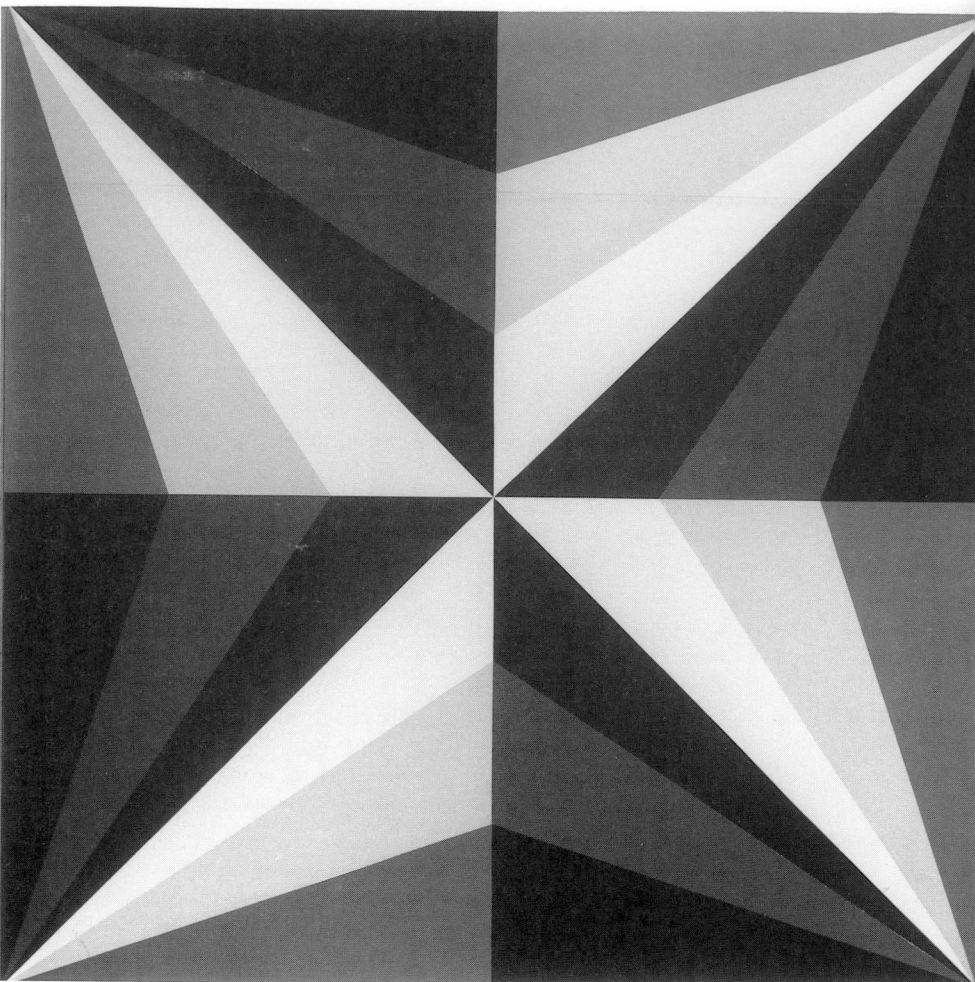

Nassos Daphnis: *101–71*, 1971

DAPHNIS, Nassos.

American. Born a United States citizen, in Krokeai-Sparta, Greece, 23 July 1914; settled in the United States, 1930. Studied at the Art Students League, New York 1946–49; Académie Frochot, Paris, 1950–51; Institute Statale d'Arte, Florence, 1951–52. Served in the United States Army, 1942–45. Married Helen Avlonitis in 1956; children: Artemis, Demetrios. Independent artist, New York, since 1938. Member, American Abstract Artists, New York, since 1957. Member of the Board, City Walls Incorporated, New York, since 1969. Recipient: Ford Foundation Award, 1962; Purchase Award, Whitney Museum, New York, 1962; National Foundation of Art and Humanities Award, 1966; National Endowment of the Arts grant, 1971; Prize, *New England 350th Celebration Exhibition,* 1972; A. P. Saunders Medal 1973; Tree Peony Award 1973; Guggenheim Fellowship, New York, 1977; Francis J. Greenburger Foundation Award, New York, 1987; Pollock/Krasner Foundation grant, New York, 1987. Agent: Leo Castelli Gallery, 4 East 77th Street, New York, New York 10021. Address: 362 West Broadway, New York, New York 10013, U.S.A.

Individual Exhibitions:

1938	Contemporary Arts Gallery, New York
1947	Contemporary Arts Gallery, New York
1949	Contemporary Arts Gallery, New York
1950	Colette Allendy Galerie, Paris
1959	Leo Castelli Gallery, New York
1960	Leo Castelli Gallery, New York
1961	Leo Castelli Gallery, New York
	Toninelli Arte Moderna, Milan
1962	Galerie Iris Clert, Paris
1963	Leo Castelli Gallery, New York
1965	Leo Castelli Gallery, New York
1967	Franklin Siden Gallery, Detroit
1968	Leo Castelli Gallery, New York
1969	Albright-Knox Museum, Buffalo, New York (retrospective)
	Everson Museum, Syracuse, New York
1970	Brockton Art Center, Massachusetts
1971	Leo Castelli Gallery, New York
1973	Leo Castelli Gallery, New York
1974	Ande Zarre Gallery, New York
1975	Leo Castelli Gallery, New York
1980	*Paintings of the 50's.* Leo Castelli Gallery, New York
	Phillips Gallery, Salt Lake City
	Eaton-Shoen Gallery, San Francisco
1983	Leo Castelli Gallery, New York
	Andre Zarre Gallery, New York
1985	Kouros Gallery, New York
	Leo Castelli Gallery, New York
	Eaton-Shoen Gallery, San Francisco
	Andre Zarre Gallery, New York
1986	Leo Castelli Gallery, New York

Selected Group Exhibitions:

1960	*International Art of a New Era*, Museum of Fine Arts, Osaka, Japan
	American Abstract Expressionists and Imagists Guggenheim Museum new York
1963	*Formalists*, Washington Gallery of Modern Art Washington, D.C.
1965	*White on White*, DeCordova Museum, Lincoln Massachusetts
1967	*10 Years*, Leo Castelli Gallery, New York
1969	*Color in Control*, Museum of Fine Arts, St. Petersburg, Florida
1972	*Monoprints.* Trica Karlis Gallery, Provincetown Massachusetts

1974 *Drawings.* Leo Castelli Gallery Downtown, New York

1987 *Leo Castelli y sus Artistas,* Centro Cultural Arte Contemporaneo, Mexico City

Collections:

Whitney Museum, New York Museum of Modern Art, New York; Guggenheim Museum, New York; Albright-Knox Gallery, Buffalo, New York; Everson Museum, Syracuse, New York; Baltimore Museum of Art; Museum of Art, Pittsburgh; Akron Art Institute, Ohio; Utah Art Museum Salt Lake City; Tel Aviv Museum, Israel.

Publications:

On DAPHNIS: books—*Nassos Daphnis: Paintings of the 50's,* exhibition catalogue, by April Kingsley, New York 1980; *Nassos Daphnis: Biomorphic Paintings 1947-48,* exhibition catalogue with essay by John Gruen, New York 1985; articles—"Nassos Daphnis: A Perennial Order" by James R. Mellow in *Art International* (Lugano, Switzerland) March 1969; "Nassos Daphnis" by A. Brunelle in *Art News* New York). April 1973; "Nassos Daphnis: Wall Painting at 620 West 47th Street, New York" in *Art Now: New York* (New York), 1973; review in *Artforum* (New York), June 1973; "New York" by April Kingsley in *Art International* (Lugano, Switzerland), Summer 1973; *Nassos Daphnis at Leo Castelli*" by Elizabeth Frank in *Art in America* (New York), Summer 1980; "Nassos Daphnis" by Mary Anne Staniszewski in *Art News* (New York). Summer 1980; *Organic Geometry*" by Blair T. Birmelin in *Art in America* (New York), October 1985.

For the past few years, I have been searching for images which convey the energies that permeate the universe. I try to portray the forces of energy itself, its wavelengths, its movement through space and its interaction with other waves as their paths intersect. While the visual patterns of color which I use are free of content, my intention is to express creative, life-giving forces, although, from time to time, more violent, ambiguous forces come into play.

Since 1952, I have used geometric forms to express my ideas. I have concentrated on pure color, using only the primaries—blue, red, yellow, white and black. By so doing, I can achieve the most vibrant qualities inherent in each color. It is also extremely important for me to try to liberate color from form. In my paintings, color is an element in and of itself, eloquent and independent in its presentation.

In 1957, I developed my own color theory, according to which each color exists relative to the planal space which it occupies. I order colors according to their characteristic spatial depth. This permits me to create visual space without using perspective or modelling, and contributes simultaneously to the complex interactions of forces in conjunction or tension with each other.

—Nassos Daphnis

When Nassos Daphnis began hybridizing exotic tree peonies, crossing rare Chinese species with hardy native varieties, he had to outsmart the nearly insurmountable sterility of the hybrid to reestablish the line of offspring that may extend into the future. This need to circumvent dead ends, to predate dogmatic trends, has characterized Daphnis' work since the beginning of his career. Paying homage to the pure and simple during the freewheeling period of expressionism in the 50s, he precociously hybridizes a blunt forthrightness to create a strain of geometric abstraction that has borne fruit ever since.

More than a painter, Daphnis is a pioneer. His work has been a succession of experiments, surviving complex alterations to achieve the degree of simplification encompassed in his recent paintings. Yet through each phase, his attention to purity of colour and image has remained consistent. In 1938 Daphnis began painting landscapes that made direct, legible statements in bold, intense colours neatly bound within hard edges. In 1947 critics noticed a change in style when he exhibited quasi-surrealistic representations of charred trees in barren landscapes. His work in camouflage and relief maps during the war years may have been responsible for the new forms and textures in his paintings. His 1950 travels to Greece, where the light "flattened everything," slanted his perspective towards abstraction. The effect eliminated texture and surface incident, prompting Daphnis to research optical properties of colour and the activities of planes.

His commitment to "pure" colour resulted in a colour theory which has sustained the basic structure of his subsequent work. Visualizing an arbitrary scale of 1 to 100, he gave each colour a value: black, the most intense colour, occupies planes 0–10; blue from 10–70 followed by red, yellow and finally white, being "without substance but an expanding essence" from 90–100. The colour planes extend back to infinity behind the picture plane. A colour becomes a tonal value and loses the energy of pure colour whenever it goes beyond its limit.

Around 1955 his painting became highly complex in design in efforts to overcome the strict limitations of "pure" art. The adherence to his colour theory nevertheless remained tenacious. Yet the seeming arbitrary change from one approach to the next suggests a consistent trend which moves cyclically—and cathartically—from complex design to simplified, reductive purity. In 1958 he discovered acrylic paints. First by applying the paint consistently with rollers, then by masking and spraying his canvases, Daphnis achieved effects of uniformity and geometric precision while maintaining pure bands of colour. He increased his scale, creating nearly wall-sized surfaces, and engendered a feeling of absorption into the paintings by choosing red for its intensity and strength. The viewing experience bore obvious comparisons to that of Abstract Expressionist work, though Daphnis himself is reluctant to acknowledge any analogy to the gestural approach of this school.

Daphnis added another variable to his work with the introduction of wood reliefs, physical planes which compliment and augment the painted ones. Plastics, which succeeded this phase in 1962, included the elements of translucency and transparency to the now three-dimensional bands. The interaction between actual and painted elements produced colour vibrations and spatial constituencies stronger than those in earlier paintings. This relief method allowed Daphnis to incorporate colour into sculpture. His red and black column is best known in this series. Large in scale, it commands space and absorbs light. The core of the piece is clear plastic which calls attention away from its mass creating spatial ambiguity and intensifying colour contrasts. It suggests change, and is an architectural statement of structure and continuation.

In pursuit of pure abstraction, his ingenuity captured critical attention around 1960 with his invention of a large, compass-like instrument used to delineate arcs with perfect precision. The arcs appear to continue on their great trajectories out of the picture space on either side indefinitely with the same exactitude. Yet the unsettling behavior of the arc's position on the canvas within the soothing geometric order creates the vital energy of his paintings.

Having earned a place in recent history, Daphnis is also likely to receive exposure as an important artist of the future. His devotion to purity predicted '60s Minimalism, his systematic approach predated systematic painting. Now, another phase of his work completed, he is ever exploring new possibilities. His art resists stagnation, for it is still developing, still anticipating new experiments.

—Carrie Barker

DARBOVEN, Hanne.

German. Born in Munich, 29 April 1941. Studied art at the Hochschule für Bildende Kunst, Hamburg. Independent artist, working with number-concepts, Hamburg and New York, since 1966. Agent: Leo Castelli Gallery, 420 West Broadway, New York, New York 10012. Address: Am Burgberg 20, 2000 Hamburg 90, West Germany.

Individual Exhibitions:

1967 Galerie Konrad Fischer, Dusseldorf

1968 Galerie Konrad Fischer, Dusseldorf

1969 Städtisches Museum, Mönchengladbach, West Germany
Galerie Heiner Friedrich, Munch

1970 Galerie Michael Werner, Cologne
Galerie Konrad Fischer, Dusseldorf
Art & Project, Amsterdam
Galleria Sperone, Turin

1971 Westfälischer Kunstverein, Münster, West Germany
Galerie Konrad Fischer, Dusseldorf

1972 Galerie Heiner Friedrich, Cologne
Galerie M. T. L. Brussels
Galleria Toselli, Milan
Galleria Marilena Bonomo, Bari, Italy
Studio Lia Rumma, Naples
Kabinett für Aktuelle Kunst, Bremerhaven, West Germany
Museum für Kunst und Gewerbe, Hamburg

1973 Galerie Yvon Lambert, Paris
Leo Castelli Gallery, New York

1974 Art & Project/M. T. L., Antwerp (travelled to Amsterdam and Brussels)
Palais des Beaux-Arts, Brussels
Museum of Modern Art, Oxford
Kabinett für Aktuelle Kunst, Bremerhaven, West Germany
Leo Castelli Gallery, New York
Ein Monat, ein Jahr, ein Jahrhundert: Arbeiten von 1968 bis 1974, Kunstmuseum, Basle
Sonnabend Gallery, New York

1975 *Een Maand, een Jaar, een Eeuw: Werken van 1968 tot en met 1974,* Stedelijk Museum, Amsterdam
Leo Castelli Gallery, New York
Leo Castelli Gallery, New York
Kunstmuseum, Lucerne

1976 *For Jean-Paul Sartre,* Leo Castelli Gallery, New York

1978 Leo Castelli/Sperone-Westwater-Fischer, New York

1988 Kunstraum Munchen, Munich

Selected Group Exhibitions:

1967 *Normal Art,* Lannis Museum of Normal Art, New York

1968 *Language II,* Dwan Gallery, New York

1969 *When Attitudes Become Form,* Kunsthalle, Berne (toured Europe)

1970 *Conceptual Art/Arte Povera/Land Art,* Galleria Civica, Turin

1971 *7th Biennale de Paris,* Musée d'Art Moderne de la Ville, Paris
Guggenheim International, Guggenheim Museum, New York

1972 *Documenta 5,* Kassel, West Germany (and *Documenta 7,* 1982)

1973 *Bienal,* Sao Paulo

1974 *Projekt 74,* Kunsthalle, Cologne

1985 *The European Iceberg,* Art Gallery of Ontario, Toronto

Collections:

Stedelijk Museum, Amsterdam; Kaiser-Wilhelm-Museum, Krefeld, West Germany

Publications:

By DARBOVEN: book—*Ein Jahrhundert.* Amsterdam 1971; articles "6 Manuskripte '69" with others, in *Kunstzeitung* (Dusseldorf), no. 3, 1969, "Words" in *Avalanche* (New York), Spring 1972; film—*6 books, 68–6,* 1971.

On DARBOVEN: books—*Arte Povera* by Germano Celant, Milan, Tübingen and New York 1970; *Hanne Darboven* by Ingrid Krupka, Cologne 1972; *Hanne Darboven*, exhibition catalogue with texts by Klaus Honnef and Johannes Cladders, Münster, West Germany 1971; *Guggenheim International Exhibition 1971*, catalogue with texts by Thomas M. Messer, Diane Waldman and Edward F. Fry, New York 1971; *Was Die Schonheit sei, das Weiss ich Nicht, Kunstler, Theorie, Werk*, Nuremberg 1971; *Documenia 5: Befragung der Realiät*, exhibition catalogue, edited by Harald Szeemann and others, Kassel, West Germany 1972; *Six Years: The Dematerialization of the Art Object* by Lucy R. Lippard, London and New York 1973; *Bilder, Objekie, Filme, Konzepte*, exhibition catalogue, with texts by J. Herbig, M. Petzet and A. Sweite, Munich 1973; *Projekt 74: Aspekte internationaler Kunst am Anfang der 70er Jahe*, exhibition catalogue, with texts by Dieter Ronte, Evelyn Weiss, Marlis Gruterich and others, Cologne 1974; *Hanne Darboven: ein Monat, ein Jahr, ein Jahrhundert: Arbeiten von 1968 bis 1974*, exhibition catalogue, with text by Franz Meyer, Basle 1974; *Hanne Darboven: Een Maand, een Jaar, een Eeuw: werken van 1968 tot en met 1974*, exhibition catalogue, with text by Franz Meyer, Amsterdam 1975; *Hanne Darboven: For Jean-Paul Satre*, exhibition folder, New York 1976; *Hanne Darboven*, exhibition folder, New York 1978.

Whatever the function in which numbers crop up, they are at all times subordinated to definite ends. Economic ends, political, practical and sometimes even mystical ends. Because of this, in a bourgeois society such as ours, which is conditioned to accept the use value of any-and everything, the idea of a completely purpose-free, so to say frivolous, operation with numbers must seem decidedly nonsensical, if not indeed shocking and dangerous.

All this is relevant to Hanne Darboven, an artist who, in common with Joseph Beuys, the other great mythologue of the younger art world in Germany, impresses herself on the general consciousness ever more commandingly as one of the really challenging figures of the contemporary art world. Hanne Darboven takes the numeral at its word, as it were. She takes numbers as pure numbers, concretely: letters. She writes texts with numbers, and those texts have no more, and no other, content than numbers signify in a type-face. In her texts numbers do not represent—they present. They present themselves.

Herein lies the provocativeness of her work. Numbers are stripped bare in an orderly manner. They are relieved of the task of serving as a symbol for something exterior. In Hanne Darboven's artistic programme they retain also none of the almost mystical qualities which appear involuntarily when one is confronted by the vertiginous totalling up of numbers.

Their poetic qualities are equally little played-with. As for example the letter in the clutches of "concrete poetry". Gertrude Stein's pretty manifestation: "A rose is a rose is a rose" is not allowed in Hanne Darboven's work to be twisted back into a number is a number is a number and nothing more than a number. That would be concrete poetry. An analogous formation might rather read: "1 is 1 is 1" or "One is one is one" or even "One plus one is two ones". This hardly evokes associations.

Speech and the object of speech are identical. Hanne Darboven does not describe—she scribes.

Hanne Darboven came to numbers by way of geometrical drawing. In the mid 1960's she began to occupy herself with geometric constructions. These constructions were placed on millimetre graph paper. The finely-graven squares of the millimetre paper made a good reference structure for the graphic projections. Drawn construction and the structure of the paper always stand in a reciprocal relationship to each other.

Later on Hanne Darboven did without the diagrammatic exposition. Instead of this she created constructions from pure accumulations of numbers. For years she came to terms with the problems of the calendar in a sheer endless series. She produced a century calendar, in which every conceivable date is recorded. The date of birth of so-and-so, as well as the date of his death. The date of death of the actual user crops up side by side with the date of Shakespeare's death. Hanne Darboven transposed her calendar-sequences into drawings which were regulated according to a definite system. This system consisted of a code, which prevented the numerical quantities from developing towards infinity. At the same time the code was so chosen that the drawings should not forfeit their clarity. The solution offered a mathematical method which was founded on the insight that only the numbers from one to nine are pure numbers. Consequently several digits ranked one behind the other are not looked at as a homologous number, but as isolated quantities. In the mathematical process of cross-addition the single digits are added. Hence 71 produces 7 plus one which gives 8.

Because Hanne Darboven sets forth series of dates in her calendar drawings, instead of isolated individual dates, she succeeds in representing visually the course of time. Time is seen as a continual and inexorable advance. On account of this, it is striking that the passing of time is accomplished by virtue of the systematising of the series of dates as a circular movement.

Hanne Darboven, moreover, in an intelligent and illuminating way overcomes the old artists' problem of "Representation" and "Articulation." Art has settled this problem at least since the statement of Theo van Doesburg that nothing is more concrete than a line or a right angle. Hanne Darboven's drawings are concrete, because they concretise an abstract material—which is what numbers really are. "Representation" and "Articulation," that which is "depicted" via artistic articulation, just as speech itself is articulated, are no longer separated in her works.

The same is true of Hanne Darboven's recent drawings. These are handwritten translations of literary texts. She has translated Sartre's novel *Les Mots*. Through the exact transcription of a "text," a report composed of and expressed in words, she lends it a new perceptual dimension, behind which its original content dwindles into insignificance.

Hanne Darboven does not seek to illustrate; she tries to aim at a visualization of the essence of the text by graphical means. In this Hanne Darboven is a significant artist. She makes strange what is familiar, opens our eyes to its hidden strictures, or allows it to appear in a new light. And at the same time she incorporates her objects into her original universe, which, mystical though it may seem, is the universe of all men.

—Klaus Honnef

D'ARCANGELO, Allan.

American. Born in Buffalo, New York, 16 June 1930. Studied history and government, University of Buffalo, New York, 1948-53. B.A. 1953; also studied at City College of New York and New School for Social Research, New York, 1953-54; privately with Boris Lurie, New York, 1955-56; and at Mexico City College, under John Golding and Fernando Belain, 1957-59. Painter: lives and works in New York. Instructor, School of Visual Arts, New York 1963-68; Professor of Art, Cornell University, Ithaca, New York, 1968. Professor of Art, Brooklyn College, New York, since 1973; Graduate Instructor, School of Visual Arts, New York, since 1983. Artist-in-Residence, Aspen Institute, Colorado, 1965, 1967; Visiting Artist, Yale University, New Haven, Connecticut, 1969; University of Syracuse, New York, 1971; University of Alabama 1972; St. Cloud State University, Minnesota, 1972; University of Wisconsin 1972; Skowhegan School of Art, Maine, 1974; Memphis Academy of Art, 1975; Minneapolis College of Art and Design, 1977. Recipient: First Purchase Prize, University of Omaha, 1966; First Prize, First Annual Exhibition, Hofstra University, Hempstead, New York, 1967. Address: P.O. Box 33, Kenoza Lake, New York 12750, U.S.A.

Individual Exhibitions:

1961	Long Island University, New York
1963	Thibaud Gallery, New York
	Fischbach Gallery, New York
1964	Fischbach Gallery, New York
1965	Fischbach Gallery, New York
	Galerie Ileana Sonnabend, Paris
	Galerie Zwirner, Cologne
	Galerie Neuendorf, Hamburg
	Galerie Muller, Stuttgart
1966	Dwan Gallery, Los Angeles
1967	Fischbach Gallery, New York
	Württembergischer Kunstverein, Stuttgart
	Galerie Rolf Ricke, Kassel, West Germany
	The Highway Painter, Minami Gallery, Tokyo
1968	Franklin Siden Gallery, Detroit
	Lambert Galerie, Paris
1969	Fischbach Gallery, New york
1971	*Paintings 1963-70*, Institute of Contemporary Art, Philadelphia
	Paintings 1963-70, Albright-Knox Art Gallery, Buffalo, New York
1972	Marlborough Gallery, New York
1974	Schact Fine Art Center, Russell Sage College, Troy, New York
	Patricia Moore Gallery, Aspen, Colorado
	Hokin Gallery, Chicago
1975	Marlborough Gallery, New York
	Gallery Kingpitcher, Pittsburgh
1977	Contemporary Art Forms, Encino, California
	Fiterman Gallery, Minneapolis
1978	Neuberger Museum, State University of New York at Purchase
1979	Virginia Museum of Fine Arts, Richmond
	Art Package, Highland Park, Illinois

Selected Group Exhibitions:

1964	*American Landscape Painting*, Museum of Modern Art, New York (travelled to the *Spoleto Festival*, Italy)
1965	*The New American Realism*, Worcester Art Museum, Massachusetts
1966	*Sculpture and Painting Today*, Museum of Fine Arts, Boston
	2 Decades of American Painting, Museum of Modern Art, New York (toured Japan, Australia and India)
1967	*New Forms*, Stedelijk Museum, Amsterdam
	Environment USA: 1957-1967, at the *Bienal*, Sao Paulo
	Premio International, Instituto Torquato dei Tella, Buenos Aires
1976	*In Priase of Space: The Landscape in American Art*, Corcoran Gallery of Art, Washington, D.C.
	American Art Since 1945, Museum of Modern Art, New York
1977	*Private Images: Photograph by Painters*, Los Angeles County Museum of Art

Collections:

Museum of Modern Art, New York; Guggenheim Museum, New York; Whitney Museum, New York; New York University Art Collection; Albright-Knox Art Gallery, Buffalo, New York; Wadsworth Atheneum, Hartford, Connecticut; Hirshhorn Museum, Smithsonian Institution, Washington, D.C.; Wallraf-Richartz Museum, Cologne; Museum of Contemporary Art, Nagaoka, Japan.

Publications:

By D'ARCANGELO: articles—"Landscape" in *Art Now: New York* (New York), February 1969; interview in *Allan D'Arcangelo: Paintings 1963-1970*, Buffalo, New York 1971.

On D'ARCANGELO: books—*D'Arcangelo*, exhibition catalogue, with an essay by Nicolas Calas, Paris 1965; *The Highway Painter*, exhibition catalogue, with an introduction by Yoshiaki Tono, Tokyo 1967; *Art and the Age of Risk*, by Niolas Calas, New York 1968; *Icons and Images of the 60's* by Nicolas Calas, New York 1971; *Allan D'Arcangelo: Paintings 1963-1970,* exhibition catalogue, Philadelphia 1971; *Allan D'Arcangelo,* exhibition catalogue, New York 1975; *Topics in American Art since 1945* by Lawrence Alloway, New York 1975; articles—"D'Arcangelo and the New Landscape" by David Antin in *Art and Literature* (Lausanne), Summer 1966; "Highway Culture: Man at the Wheel" by Lawrence Alloway in *Arts Magazine* (New York), February 1967; "The Subject at His Own Uneasiness" by Peter Schjeldahl in the *New York Times.* 4 November 1971; "Highway Cultures" by Gregory Battcock in *Art and Artists* (London), January 1972, "The Terror of a Wooden Match" by John Perreault in the *Village Voice* (New York), January 1972; review by Mona DaVinci in *Soho News* (New York), 23 January 1975; "Allan D'Arcangelo" by Jane Bell in *Arts Magazine* (New York) March 1975; "In Search of America" by Ralph Grier in the *Christian Science Monitor* (Boston), June 1976.

During the early 1960s, Allan D'Arcangelo was linked with Pop Art, and naturally so, considering pictures such as "Marilyn" (1962) and "Madonna and Child" (1963). "Marilyn" depicts an illustrative head and shoulders on which the facial features are marked by lettered slits to be "fitted" with the eyebrows, eyes, nose and mouth which appear off to the right in the composition. In "Madonna and Child," the featureless faces of Jackie Kennedy and Caroline are ringed with haloes, enough, for the period, to make their status as contemporary icons perfectly clear.

D'Arcangelo is better known for his pictures of highways and roadblocks made during the 1960's. The first of these pictured deep perspectival vistas in a simplified, flat plane, the view as seen from the driver's seat as one zooms along the seemingly never-ending American highway in most any state. Next came a series called "Barriers," in which cropped, abstracted imagery of road barriers were superimposed over the one-point perspectival highway vistas. These were a move further toward concern with abstract, two-dimensionality without negating the element culled from seen aspects of the American landscape. The series called "Constellations" (there are 120 in all) further abstracted the view of road barriers into perspectival, jutting patterns thrusting across the canvas against a white ground. The element of the seen is never obliterated and always primary in D'Arcangelo's dialectic, as amply evidenced in his return to highway imagery more directly in the 1970's.

For several years during that decade, D'Arcangelo slowed down his formerly prolific output. In the Spring of 1982, he had his first one-man exhibition in New York in five years. The new pictures are rather scenic landscape vistas, simplified and showing his ongoing concern with jutting perspectival space, now inhabited by flatly painted images of highway overpasses, a jet wing, grain field, electric lines. Indications of the American industrial scene seem more related to the hand-painted, pristine look of Charles Sheeler than to the Pop of, say, Roy Lichtenstein. In form, there is also a reminiscence of field painting in the simplicity and emblematic quality of these new works. Now, as before, the main element in D'Arcangelo's pictures is the post-abstraction search for, as he has put it, "icons that matter," monumental archetypes of the contemporary American expansive landscape highway.

—Barbara Cavaliere

d'ARMAGNAC, Ben.

Dutch. Born Bernard Jean Jacques d'Armagnac, in Antwerp, Belgium, 28 March 1940; later settled in the Netherlands. Studied painting at the Kunstnijverheidsschool, Amsterdam, 1960-63, and with the artist Anton Heyboer, Den Ilp, Netherlands, 1965. Married Joke Lingmont in 1967. Independent artist, working mostly with Gerrit Dekker, in Amsterdam, 1966-67, in Lewedorp, Zeeland, 1967-73, in Zuid-Limburg, 1973-77, and again in Amsterdam, 1977-78: first environmental works, 1972; first performance work, 1973. *Died* (in Amsterdam) *28 September 1978.*

Individual Exhibitions:

1966	Galerie de Sfinx, Amsterdam (with Gerrit Dekker)
1967	Galerie J34, Terneuzen, Netherlands (with Gerrit Dekker)
	Zeeuws Museum, Middelburg, Netherlands (with Anton Heyboer and Gerrit Dekker)
1968	Municipal Gardens, Terneuzen, Netherlands (with Gerrit Dekker)
	Galerie J34, Terneuzen, Netherlands (with Gerrit Dekker)
1969	Wide White Space, Antwerp (with Gerrit Dekker)
	Galerie Mickery, Loenersloot, Netherlands (with Gerrit Dekker)
	Galerie Mickery, Loenersloot, Netherlands
	Stedelijk Museum, Schiedam, Netherlands (with Gerrit Dekker)
	Galerie Mickery, Loenersloot, Netherlands (with Gerrit Dekker)
1970	Galerie Mickery, Loenersloot, Netherlands
1971	Galerie Mickery, Loenersloot, Netherlands
	Opbouwhuis Bickerseiland, Amsterdam
1974	Bonnefantenmuseum, Maastricht, Netherlands
	Galerie Seriaal, Amsterdam (with Gerrit Dekker)
	Galerie De Appel, Amsterdam (with Gerrit Dekker)
1975	Galerie de Mangelgang, Groningen, Netherlands (with Gerrit Dekker)
	Galerie de Mangelgang, Groningen, Netherlands
	Galerie De Appel, Amsterdam
	Gemeentemuseum, Roermond, Netherlands
1976	Jan Van Eyck Academie, Maastricht, Netherlands
	Stedelijk Museum, Amsterdam
	Universiteit van Maastricht, Netherlands
1977	Bonnefantenmuseum, Maastricht, Netherlands
	Ontmoetin scentrum Schaapoord, Knokke, Belgium
1978	112 Greene Street, New York
1981	Stedelijk Museum, Amsterdam (retrospective; travelled to the Kunsthalle, Wilhelmshaven, Gemeentelijke van Reekumsgalerijk, Apeldoorn, and De Vleeshal, Middelburg, Netherlands)

Selected Group Exhibitions:

1968	*Jonge Zeeuws Talent,* Zeeuws Museum, Middelburg, Netherlands
1969	*Op losse schroeven,* Stedelijk Museum, Amsterdam
	Prospekt '69, Städtische Kunsthalle, Dusseldorf
1970	*Binnen en Buiten het Kadar,* Stedelijk Museum, Amsterdam
1971	*Sonsbeek Buitende Perken,* Sonsbeek Park, Arnheim Netherlands (travelled to the Kunstkring de Waag, Almelo)
1974	*II Dutch Artists,* Fruit Market Gallery, Edinburgh
1975	*Biennale de Paris,* Musée d'Art Moderne de la Ville, Paris
1977	*K45: International Art Fair,* Kunstlerhaus, Vienna
	Documenta, Kassel, West Germany
1978	*European Performance,* Brooklyn Museum, New York

Publications:

By d'ARMAGNAC: books—*Negen Dagboekbladen,* Deventer, Netherlands 1970; *d' Armagnac/Dekker 1968-1973,* with Gerrit Dekker, Amsterdam and Zurich 1973; *Twee Bladen,* Amsterdam 1974; *Een Blad,* Amsterdam 1975.

On d'ARMAGNAC: books—*Biennale de Paris,* exhibition catalogue, with texts by Georges Boudaille, Günter Metken, Lucy Lippard and Douglas Davis, Paris 1975; *Documenta 6, Band I: Malerei, Plastik, Performance,* exhibition catalogue, with texts by Arnold Bode, Günter Metken, Klaus Honnef and others, Kassel, West Germany 1977; *Ben d'Armagnac,* exhibition catalogue, with a foreword by Edy de Wilde, compiled by Jan Brand, Gerrit Dekker, Alexander van Grevenstein, Louwrien Wetjers and Erna Donker, Amsterdam 1981; articles—"Houtstapels van Ben d'Armagnac en Gerrit Dekker" by Piet van Daalen in *Gazet van Antwerpen,* 28 February 1969; "d'Armagnac en Dekker" by Louwrien Weijers in *Museumjournaal* (Amsterdam), August 1969; "Weer Beeldende Kunst in Mickery: Dramatisch Project van Ben d'Armagnac" by Tom Frenken in *Eindhovens Dagblad,* 2 December 1970; "Mentaliastraum I: Kunstler in Holland; by Johannes Gachnang in *Kunst Bulletin* (Zurich), May 1974; "d'Armagnac en Dekker" by Liesbeth Brand Corstius in *Museumjournaal* (Amsterdam), October 1974; "Ben d'Armagnac" by Antje van Graeveintz in *Dutch Art + Architecture Today* (Amsterdam), November 1978; "Ben d'Armagnac: Eentekstcollage" by Antje van Graevenitz in *Museumjournaal* (Amsterdam), December 1978.

In his short life, the performance–artist Ben d'Armagnac has made an intense and lasting impression on those people who have witnessed his work. The photographic documentation and videoregistrations that remain of his performances only give an idea of the dramatic, extremely personal but at the same time, strangely enough, objective expressiveness. The audience present felt as if in a mentally unavoidable grip. Retrospectively seen in the light of his sudden and unexpected death—he drowned—his last performance seems of an almost cruel character. During a full hour d'Armagnac lay on his back on the ground, outside of the Brooklyn Museum, with a powerful beam of cold water aimed at his heart.

Most of his performances consisted of a combination of physical and mental exhaustion that brought the artist in a sumblime and tranquil state. D'Armagnac has been one of those rare performers who, despite long and monotonous repetitive movements, imposed himself visually, whose concentrated determination radiated from his sober, white–clad figure.

Around 1965 his first teacher was the artist Anton Heyboer, an artist who proclaimed the unity of art and life. From this period dates a series of monumental etchings on paper on zinc on wood, with titles like *Making Connections, Equilibrium, The Protection of Joke.* At the present moment these impressive works are in the Bonnefantenmuseum, Maastricht.

Between 1967 and 1969 d'Armagnac lived in the quiet province of Zealand, away from artistic centres, together with his friend Gerrit Dekker and both their wives. With Dekker he built huge pieces of sculpture out of material that belonged to the local ambiance, like 'Chincilla Cages' and 'Oystersieves' used by breeders and cultivators from the villages. These improvised sculptures were not to live long.

In 1969 both artists developed for Ritsaert ten Cate's Galerie Mickery (Loenersloot) the *Project for a bathroom, bedroom, kitchen, diningroom, toilet and some non-specified spaces.* From 1973 to 1977 d'Armagnac lives and works in Maastricht, in the southern part of The Netherlands, a city that during these years has been a centre for media-oriented activities and performances, largely due to the Agora-studio and Jan van Eyck-academy. In his last years d'Armagnac was closely associated with the program of the Amsterdam-based Foundation De Appel.

—A. F. Wagemans

DAVIE, Alan.

British. Born in Grangemouth, Scotland, in 1920. Studied at the Edinburgh College of Art, 1937-40. Married Janet Gaul in 1947; daughter: Jane. Served in the Royal Artillery, 1941-46. Worked as a jazz musician, 1947; travelled extensively in Europe, 1947-49; worked as a jeweller, 1949-53; visited New York, 1956; Gregory Fellow, University of Leeds, 1956-59; Lecturer, Central School of Arts and Crafts, London, 1959-60; performed at public recital, Gimpel Fils Gallery and Tate Gallery, London:

first record issued, 1971; Member, Tony Oxley group: gave concerts and broadcasts, 1973–75; travelled in the West Indies, 1976; now lives in Hertfordshire and in St. Lucia, West Indies. Recipient: Guthrie Award, Royal Scottish Academy, Edinburgh, 1942; Prize, *Bienal,* Sao Paulo, 1953; Critics' Choice Award, London, 1956, 1958, 1960; Prix Guggenheim, Musée d' Art Moderne, Paris, 1956; First Prize, *International Graphics Exhibition,* Cracow, 1966; Saltine Award, Edinburgh, 1976. Honorary Royal Scottish Academician, 1976. C. B. E. (Commander, Order of the British Empire), 1972. Agent: Gimpel Fils, London. Address: Camels Studio, Rush Green, Hertford, Hertfordshire, England.

Individual Exhibitions:

1946   Grant's Bookshop, Edinburgh
1948   *Art and Inspiration,* Galleria Michelangelo, Florence
       The Forest, Galleria Sandri, Venice
1950   Gimpel Fils, London
1951   Gimpel Fils, London
1952   Gimpel Fils, London
1954   Gimpel Fils, London
1955   Gimpel Fils, London
1956   Catherine Viviano Gallery, New York
1957   Catherine Viviano Gallery, New York
1958   Wakefield City Art Gallery, Yorkshire (travelled to Whitechapel Art Gallery, London, and the Walker Art Gallery, Liverpool)
       University of Nottingham
1960   Gimpel Fils, London
       Galerie Charles Lienhard, Zurich
1961   Gimpel Fils, London
       Galleria del Naviglio, Milan
       Galerie Rive Droite, Paris
       Martha Jackson Gallery, New York
       Carnegie Institute, Pittsburgh
       Esther Robles Gallery, Los Angeles
1962   FBA Gallery, London (travelled to the Stedelijk Museum, Amsterdam)
       Carnegie Institute, Pittsburgh
       Esther Robles Gallery, Los Angeles
       Kunstnernes Hus, Oslo
1963   Galleria La Medusa, Rome
       Gimpel Fils, London
       Commercial Centre of the Brazilian Embassy, London
       Kunsthalle, Berne
       Kunsthalle, Baden-Baden, West Germany
1964   Gimpel and Hanover Galerie, Zurich
       Crestline Galerie, Edinburgh
1965   Gimpel Fils, London
       Martha Jackson Gallery, New York
       Galerie Rudolf Zwirner, Cologne
       Graves Art Gallery, Sheffield (toured the U.K.)
       Court Gallery, Copenhagen
       Galerie d'Aujourd'hu, Brussels
1966   Gimpel Fils, London
       Commonwealth Institute Gallery, Edinburgh
       Castle Museum, Norwich
       Kunstkring, Rotterdam
       Usher Gallery, Lincoln
       Queen Square Gallery, Leeds
1967   Gimpel Fils, London
       Gimpel and Hanover, Zurich
       Galerie de France, Paris
       Arts Club of Chicago (travelled to University of Minnesota, Minneapolis)
       Kestner-Gesellschaft, Hannover
1968   Kunstverein, Dusseldorf
       Galerie Overbeck-Gesellschaft, Lübeck
       Richard Demarco Gallery, Edinburgh
       Hudson Gallery, Detroit
1969   Gimpel Fils, London
       Kunstmuseum, Basle
       Galleria La Medusa, Rome
       Gimpel Fils, New York
1970   Gimpel Fils, London
       Galleria La Medusa, Rome
       Galerie Stangl, Munich

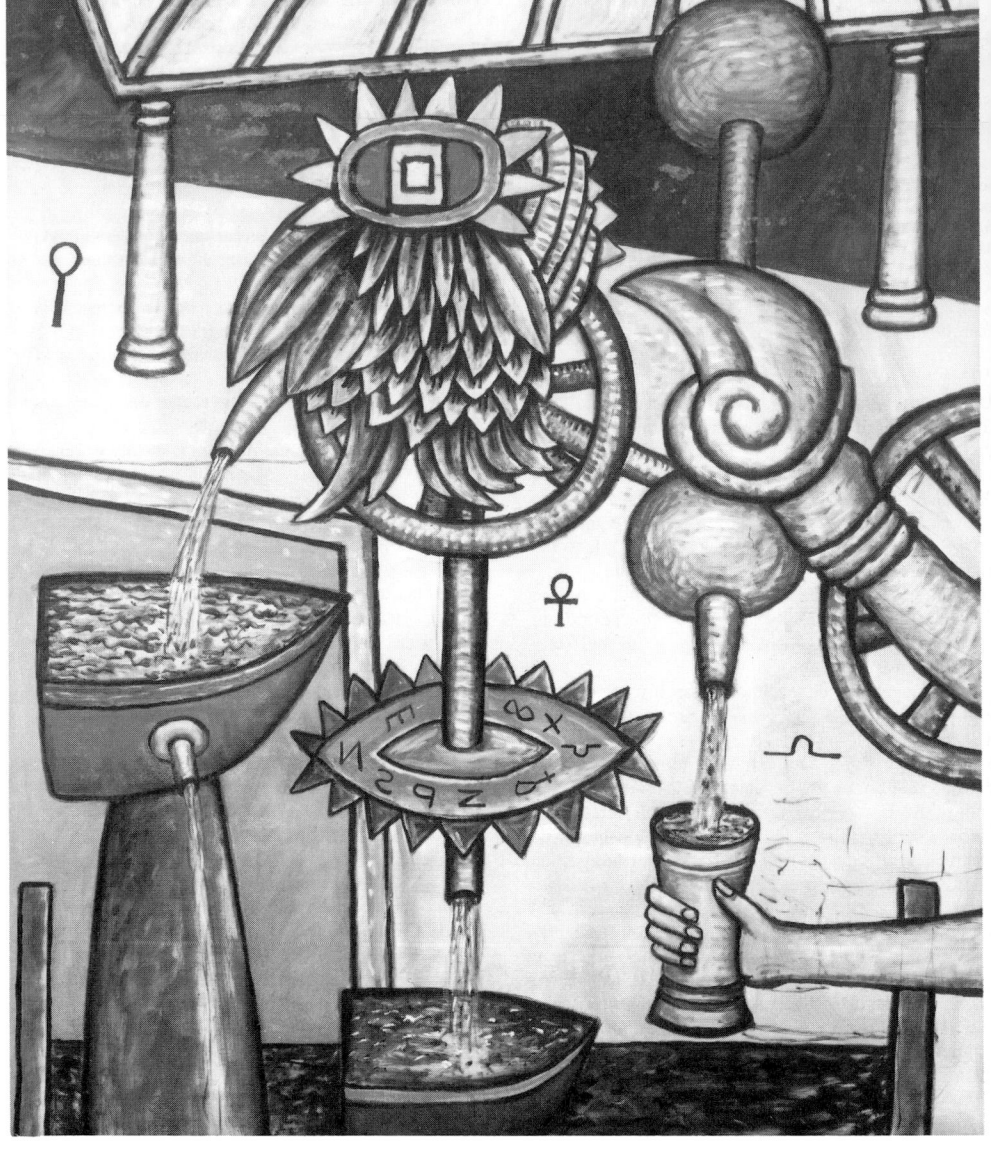

Alan Davie: *Magic Fountain No. 7,* **1987** Courtesy Gimpel Fils, London

1971   Gimpel Fils, London
       Galerie Lambert Monet, Geneva
       Gimpel and Hanover Galerie, Zurich
1972   Gimpel Gallery, New York
       Gimpel and Weitzenhoffer Gallery, New York
       Royal Scottish Academy Edinburgh (travelled to the Kunstverein, Brunswick, and the Bädischer Kunstverein, Karlsruhe, West Germany)
1973   Gimpel Fils, London
       Galleria d'Arte Rotta, Genoa
1974   Gimpel Fils, London (travelled to Gimpel and Hanover Galerie, Zurich)
       Gimpel and Weitzenhoffer Gallery, New York
       Playhouse Gallery, Harlow, Essex
1975   Gimpel Fils, London
       Galleria d'Arte Rotta, Milan
       Galerie de France, Paris
       Arte '75, Basle
       Comskey Gallery, Los Angeles
1976   Galleria La Medusa Rome
       Chateau de Lucens, Switzerland
       Allan Rubiner Gallery, Royal Oak, Michigan
       Hokin Gallery, Chicago
1977   Gimpel Fils, London
       Zoumbarakis Galleria, Athens
       Caronne Gallery, Fort Lauderdale, Florida
       Le Demeure, Paris
       Art Galerie and Museum, Aberdeen, Scotland
1978   Kunsthandel Brinkman, Amsterdam

       Gimpel and Hanover Galerie, Zurich (travelled to the Galerie am Palmengarten, Frankfurt, and Gimpel Fils, London)
       Maercklin Galerie, Stuttgart
       Galerie Cour St. Pierre, Geneva
       Lister Gallery, Perth. Western Australia (travelled to the Art of Man Gallery, Sydney, and the Ray Hughes Gallery, Brisbane)
1979   Aitken Dott, The Scottish Gallery, Edinburgh
       Gimpel Fils, London
       Galerie Ado, Bonheiden, Belgium
1980   Gimpel and Weitzenhoffer, New York
       Gimpel and Hanover, Zurich
       Lister Gallery, Perth, Western Australia
1981   Gimpel Fils, London
       Galerie van Loe, Frankfurt
1982   Rosenberg Fine Art, Toronto
       The Scottish Gallery, Edinburgh
       Arcade Gallery, Harrogate, Yorkshire
       Arts Centre, Hong Kong
       Galerie de Raam, Breda, Netherlands
       Gimpel Fils, at *FIAC 82,* Grand Palais, Paris
1983   Galerie de'Eendt, Amsterdam
       Gimpel Fils, London
1984   Festival Gallery, Bath, Avon
       Community Arts Centre, Windsor, Berkshire
       Galerie Van Loe, Frankfurt
       Bede Gallery, Jarrow, Durham
       Loft Gallery, Ware, Hertfordshire

1985 Galerie Apicella, Bonn
Gimpel Fils, London
Yares Gallery, Scottsdale, Arizona
1986 Gimpel and Weitzenhoffer, New York
1987 Gimpel Fils, London
Moray House Gallery, Edinburgh
Galerie Louis Carre, Paris
Gimpel Fils, at *FIAC 86*, Grand Palais, Paris

Selected Group Exhibitions:

1950 *Aspects of British Art*, Institute of Contemporary Arts, London
1958 *50 Ans d'Art Moderne*, Palais des Beaux-Arts, Brussels
1960 *British Painting 1720–1960*, Pushkin Museum, Moscow (travelled to The Hermitage, Leningrad)
1961 *Pittsburgh International*, Carnegie Institute, Pittsburgh
1966 *International Graphics Exhibition*, Cracow
1970 *British Painting and Sculpture 1960–1970*, National Gallery of Art, Washington, D.C.
1973 *Hommage à Picasso*, Kestner Gesellschaft, Hannover
1977 *British Painting 1952–1977*, Royal Academy of Art, London
1985 *Recalling the Fifties*, Serpentine Gallery, London
1987 *British Art in the 20th Century*, Royal Academy, London

Collections:

Tate Gallery, London; Victoria and Albert Museum, London; Stedelijk Museum, Amsterdam; Museum des 20. Jahrhunderts, Vienna; Museum of Modern Art, Tel Aviv; Museum of Modern Art, New York; Albright-Knox Art Gallery, Buffalo, New York; Carnegie Institute, Pittsburgh; Museum of Fine Arts, Boston.

Publications:

By DAVIE: book—*Alan Davie: Major Works of the Fifties*, exhibition catalogue, London 1987; articles—statement in *Art and Inspiration*, exhibition catalogue, Florence 1948; statement in *The Forest*, exhibition catalogue, Venice 1948; statement in *Statements: British Abstract Art in 1956*, London 1957; statement in *Notes by the Artists*, exhibition catalogue, London 1958; "Notes on Teaching" in *The Developing Process*, exhibition catalogue, London 1959; "Towards a New Definition of Art: Some Notes on Now Painting" in *New Departures* (London), April 1960; "Personal Thoughts" in *Times Educational Supplement* (London), June 1960; "I Confess" in *Visone Colore*, exhibition catalogue, Venice 1963.

On DAVIE: books—*Contemporary British Art* by Herbert Read, London 1951: *Space in Colour*, exhibition catalogue, by Patrick Heron, London 1953; *Private View* by Bryan Robertson, John Russell and Lord Snowdon, London 1965; *Alan Davie* by Alan Bowness, London 1967; *The Art Scene* by Barrie Stuart-Penrose, London 1967; *Alan DAvies*, exhibition catalogue, by Alan Bowness, London 1972; *Alan Davie*, catalogue with text by Dore Ashton, London 1984; *Alan Davie*, exhibition catalogue with essay by Jacques Roche-Villiers, Paris 1987.

Writing about Alan Davie's painting makes you feel like Sisyphus pushing that huge boulder up the mountain. Just when you think you have attained a certain understanding, something else catches your eye, and you are thrown off balance yet again. This is what is so fascinating and at the same time frustrating about Davie's art. In many ways his work is reminiscent of a jam session by the saxophonist John Surman: constant improvisation, then settling down on one particular theme, then suddenly changing tracks.

Davie has made up his own world of signs and symbols. Each viewer is bound to have varying interpretations. Various images remain firmly embedded in the mind—such as the highly defined scarab which represents resurrection, the ankh which symbolises life or royal authority; dragons, serpents and birds are also always present. The influence of early Christian art can clearly be seen, and Davie's admiration for Bosch, Brueghel and Uccello is also very clear.

Davie's style is wild, exuberant, free. He paints just as if he were gliding—swooping here and there and finally reaching destination. Life is seen amid a flurry of colours: reds, mauves, pinks, greens and yellows go hand in hand in "Feathers for a Serpent" of 1963. In "Phantom in the Room" a wonderful vibrant red, pink and green room is set alight; the chessboard and hand of Fatima symbolise fate and the game of life.

Davie paints almost as if he were guided by some mysterious force. Some of his paintings give the impression that they were painted in a trance: images cascaded into his mind and he could not get them down quickly enough. In fact, Davie has said, "We must confront a painting empty and open-hearted"—but not completely empty, as when a Japanese monk enquired of his Zen master, "What would you advise if a man came to you with nothing." The master immediately replied: "Throw it away." Davie has also said that he practises art for enlightenment and that a picture "must happen in spite of me rather than because of me."

After long and meticulous preparation Davie puts on his painting boots and sets off into the canvas. He is not one of the self satisfied group who sits back and thinks that is another canvas finished. One senses that he worries endlessly and returns to past works—for him they are alive, still part of him, and it is this concern that gives the paintings their vitality. For Arp art was "a fruit grown on the tree of man." For Davie the fruit never stops growing.

There is no doubt that much of Davie's imagination and vision springs from his Celtic heritage. As one wanders about Scotland, one sees many of Davie's images, but they are usually seen against a dour grey backcloth. Davie has surrounded them with brilliant colour, which remain in the mind. "Like a bird I shall take up my colour and my brush, and I shall paint as the bird sings"—and so he does.

—Carrie Maurice

DAVIES, John.

British. Born in Cheshire, 14 July 1966. Studied painting at Hull and Manchester Colleges of Art, 1963–67; studied sculpture, Slade School of Fine Art, London, 1967–69; Gloucestershire College of Art and Design, Cheltenham (Sculpture Fellowship), 1969–70. Sculptor, London and Kent, since 1970, Recipient: Sainsbury Award, 1970. Agent: Marlborough Fine Art Ltd., London. Address: c/o Marlborough Fine Art (London) Ltd., 6 Albemarle Street, London WLX 4BY, England.

Individual Exhibitions:

1972 Whitechapel Art Gallery, London
1975 Whitechapel Art Gallery, London
1980 *Recent Sculpture and Drawings*. Marlborough Fine Art, London
1981 Kunstverein, Hamburg (travelled to the Wilhelm Lehmbruck Museum, Duisburg, and the Kunstverein, Karlsruhe, 1981–82)
1982 Ferens Art Gallery, Hull, Yorkshire
1984 Marlborough Fine Art, London
1985 Sainsbury Centre, University of East Anglia, Norwich, Norfolk

Selected Group Exhibitions:

1973 *Biennale des Jeunes*, Musée National d'Art Moderne, Paris
1974 *12 Views of Mankind*, MacRobert Centre, University of Stirling, Scotland
1976 *Biennale*, Venice
1977 *Documenta*, Kassel, West Germany
1979 *Europaische Realistische Plastik*, Kunsthalle, Bremen, West Germany
1981 *British Sculpture since 1900: Part II, 1950–1980*, Whitechapel Art Gallery, London
1982 *Aspects of British Art Today*, Metropolitan Museum of Art, Tokyo (toured Japan)
1984 *The British Art Show*, Museum and Art Gallery, Birmingham (and Ikon Gallery, Birmingham; toured Britain)

Collections:

Tate Gallery, London; Arts Council of Great Britain, London; Contemporary Arts Society, London; Sainsbury Centre for the Visual Arts, Norwich; Wigan Art Gallery, Lancashire; Ulster Museum, Belfast; Wilhelm Lehmbruck Museum, Duisburg; McCrory Corporation, New York; Queensland Museum, Brisbane, Australia.

Publications:

By DAVIES: article—discussion with Nicholas Wadley in *John Davies: Recent Sculpture and Drawings*, exhibition catalogue, London 1980.

On DAVIES: books—*John Davies: Recent Sculpture and Drawings*, exhibition catalogue, London 1980; articles—"A Show to be Seen" by Edward Lucie-Smith in the *Sunday Times* (London), 25 June 1972; "The Human Condition" by Robert Melville in *Architectural Review* (London), September 1972; "The Sculpture of John Davies" by Nicholas Wadley in *Art International* (Lugano, Switzerland), February 1980; "The Bald Facts" by Michael Shepherd in the *Sunday Telegraph* (London), 23 November 1980.

In his search to create 'something very real' John Davies soon found that mimeticism was not the answer: something, and often something drastic, had to be done to the figures in order to wrench them from the realm of art, from looking too much like sculpture and too little like human beings:

"I used to think that there was no limit to what I'd have to make the figures do to get something out of them, anything that extraordinary or novel, which—however strange it might have seemed—created something very real: making sense."

In an effort to secure this quality he placed 'devices', nose-bags or other kinds of masks or wire-mesh cones over his carefully modelled or life-cast heads. The attention required to by-pass the mask in order to 'read' the head better brings the face into sharper focus, making it more vivid than otherwise. This approach is closer to Francis Bacon's distorting of the sitter's features in an attempt to capture the truth than it is to a surrealist delight in the bizarre or shocking.

Since Davies found that the gaze was a key ingredient in eliciting the sense of animation and presence he desired, he sought to establish contact with the viewer by displaying these life-size heads on thin poles, at eye-level.

Recently he has eliminated the devices without losing the intense vitality. The heads have become tiny, often not more than a couple of inches high and the coloring less naturalistic, yet they are more potent. Given their size, the scrutiny normally accorded art objects does not reveal an excess of detail, like that found in a photograph: what is revealed is all that is given in just looking—the content of any ordinary glance.

In those works which contain life-size figures engaged in activities ranging from the extreme to the ordinary, Davies has sought a similar kind of reality:

"There is always a conflict for me between the qualities of made sculpture and what one might see on the street, but I strive to make the figures display the qualities of a human being rather than those of sculpture."

Yet the means by which this is achieved clearly belong to the realm of art. For example, the figures

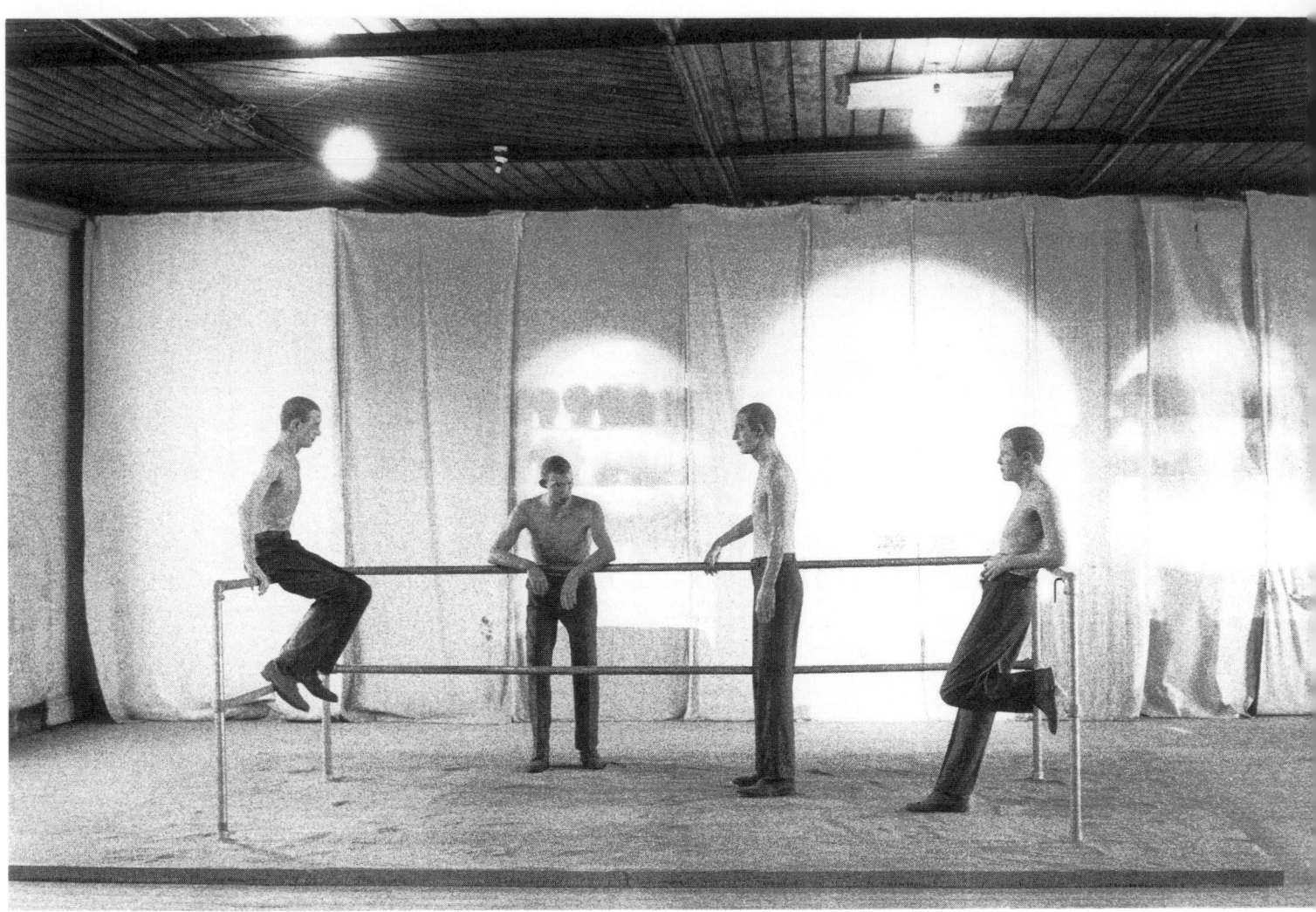

John Davies: *Figures and Railings*, 1981

often have a frozen quality, but this is very different from that found in snap-shots. They seem much closer to Egyptian sculpture where movement is conveyed through stasis. As one concentrates on these figures the props and other devices which accompany them gradually dissolve and the figures take on the immediacy and immutability of ancient sculpture. They are never merely genre or anecdotal works.

—Lynne Cooke

DAVIS, Douglas (Matthew).

American. Born in Washington, D.C., 11 April 1933. Studied at the Abbott Art School, Washington, D.C., 1948–50; American University, Washington, D.C., 1952–56, B.A. 1956; Rutgers University, New Brunswick, New Jersey, 1956–58, M.A. 1958. Married Mary Virginia Miller (divorced, 1967); Children: Laura and Mary; married the art critic Jane Bell in 1970. Painter until 1969; since then has concentrated on video-performance work. Teaching Fellow in English, Douglass College, 1957–60; freelance editor and writer, 1961–67; Art Critic, *National Observer*, Silver Spring, Maryland, 1965–69; Contributing Editor, *Art in America*, New York, 1968–70; Art Critic, *Newsweek*, New York, 1970–76 (now Senior Writer), Visiting Artist in Video, Corcoran Gallery, Washington, D.C., 1970–71; Artist-in-Residence, Television Laboratory, WNET-TV, New York, 1972; Visiting Artist, Northwood Experimental Art Institute, Dallas, 1972. Artistic Director, International Network for the Arts. Recipient: New York State Council on the Arts grant, 1970; National Endowment for the Arts grant, 1971, 1975; DAAD Exchange Fellowship, Berlin, 1977; National Endowment for the Arts grant, Washington, D.C., 1981. Agents: Galleria Forma, Largo San Giuseppe 18, 16121 Genoa, Italy; Ronald Feldman Fine Arts, 33 East 74th Street, New York, New York 109012; and Electronic Arts Intermix, 100 Fifth Avenue, New York, New York 10011. Address: 80 Wooster Street, New York, New York 10012, U.S.A.

Individual Exhibitions:

1970 Reese Palley Gallery, New York
1972 *Events, Drawings, Objects, Videotapes 1967–72*, Everson Museum of Art Syracuse, New York
1973 DeSaisset Museum, University of Santa Clara, California
1975 *Videotapes*, San Francisco Museum of Modern Art
1976 *3 Silent and Secret Acts*, The Kitchen Center for Video and Music, New York
1977 *4 Places, 2 Figures, 1 Ghost*, Whitney Museum, New York
1978 *Arbeiten 1970–77*, Neue Berliner Kunstverein and Kunstlerhaus Bethanien, Berlin (travelled to Basel and Essen)
1979 *Drawings, Objects and Soundboxes*, PS 1, New York
1980 *Double Entendre*, Whitney Museum, New York (objects and drawings, accompanied by satellite telecast between the Whitney and the Centre Georges Pompidou, Paris, broadcast on WNYC-TV and via satellite to National Public Radio Stations in the United States)
1981 *The Wizard of Malta and The Moving Obscura* (3-screen film and room-sized installation), Ronald Feldman Fine Arts, New York
1982 *Video, Objects, Graphics*, Museum Sztuki, Lodz, Poland (retrospective)
1986 Guggenheim Museum, New York

Selected Group Exhibitions:

1971 *10 Videotape Performances*, Finch College Museum of Contemporary Art, New York
1974 *L'Art Video*, Musée de l'Art Moderne de la Ville de Paris
1975 *Video Art*, Institute of Contemporary Art, Philadelphia
       Projected Video, Whitney Museum, New York
       Questions: Moscow-NY-NY-Moscow, San Francisco Museum of Modern Art
       Bodyworks, Museum of Contemporary Art, Chicago
1976 *Biennale*, Venice
1977 *Documenta*, Kassel, West Germany (installation and satellite telecast, "The Last 9 Minutes," with Nam June Paik and Joseph Beuys, broadcast to 25 countries)
1982 *Counterparts: Form and Emotion in Photography*, Metropolitan Museum of Art, New York

Collections:

Metropolitan Museum of Art, New York; Everson Museum of Art, Syracuse, New York; DeSaisset Museum, University of Santa Clara, California; Museo de Arte Contemporaneo, Caracas; Wallraf-Richartz Museum, Cologne; Museum Sztuki, Lodz, Poland; Centre Georges Pompidou, Paris

Publications:

By DAVIS: books—*Art and the Future*, New York and London 1973, Cologne 1975; *Fragments for a New Art of the 70's,* with Robert Stefanotty, Los Angeles 1975; *Artculture: Essays on the Post-Modern,* New York 1977; *Photography as Fine Art,* New York 1983; articles—numerous critical essays in the *National Observer, Art in America,* and particularly *Newsweek* (since 1970), and "For a New Esthetic" in *American Scholar* (Washington, D.C.), March/April 1966; "Media Art Media" in *Arts Magazine* (New York), April 1972; "A Conversation with Douglas Davis," with Marc Sapporta, in *Information and Documents* (Paris), May 1973; "Filmgoing/ Videogoing: Making Distinctions" in *American Film Institute Journal* (Washington, D.C.), May 1973; "What Is content? Notes Toward an Answer" in *Artforum* (New York), October 1973; "Time! Time! Time! The Context of Immediacy" in the *Museum of Modern Art Newsletter* (New York), January 1974; "Interview with Douglas Davis," with David Ross, in *Flash Art* (Milan), May 1975; "Artpolitics: Thoughts Against the Prevailing Fantasies" in the *New York Arts Journal,* May 1975; "Video in the Mid-70's: Prelude to an End/ Future" in *Video Art,* edited by Beryl Korot and Ira Schneider, New York 1976; "The Idea of a 21st Century Museum" in *Art Journal of the College Art Association* (New York), January 1976; "The Size of Non-Size" in *Art-forum* (New York), December 1976; "The End of Video: Black Death/White Vapor" in *Video End,* edited by Horst Gerhard Haberl, Graz, Austria 1976; "Die Euro American Generation" in *Favored-Forever?,* edited by Werner Hofer, Dusseldorf 1976; "Post-Modern Form: Stories Real and Imagined/Toward a Theory" in the *New York Arts Journal,* January/February 1978; "The Post-Modernist Dilemma," dialogue with Suzi Gablik, in the *Village Voice* (New York), 27 March 1978, 3 April 1978 and 10 April 1978; "How to Make Love to Your Television Set" in the *New York Arts Journal,* May/June 1979; "Post Post-Art Where Do We Go from Here?" in the *Village Voice* (New York), 25 June 1979; "Post Post-Art II: Symbolismo, Come Home" in the *Village Voice* (New York), 13 August 1979; "Post Post-Art III: Symbolismo Meets the Faerie Queen" in the *Village Voice* (New York), 17 December 1979; "Dialogue with David Schapiro" in the *New York Arts Journal,* February 1980; "Post-Everything" in *Art in America* (New York), February 1980; "After Photography" in the *Village Voice* (New York), February 1981; "Post-Performance ISM" in *Artforum* (New York), October 1981.

On DAVIS: books—*Douglas Davis: Events, Drawings, Objects, Videotapes 1967-72,* exhibition catalogue, by James Harithes, Nam June Paik and David Rose, Syracuse, New York 1972; *The Videotapes of Douglas Davis* by John Hanhardt, New York 1977; *Video Art,* edited by Beryl Korot and Ira Schneider, New York 1977; *Douglas Davis: Arbeiten 1970-77,* exhibition catalogue, with essays by Wulf Herzogenrath, Wieland Schmied and Ann Sargent-Wooster, Berlin 1978; *Douglas Davis: Video, Objects, Graphics,* with essays by Ryszard Stanislawski, Ursula Czartoryska, Irving Sandler, and John G. Hanhardt, Lodz, Poland 1982; articles—"Explorations in Video" by Gregory Battcock in *Art and Artists* (London), February 1973; "The Davis tapes" by Alfred Frankenstein in the *San Francisco Chronicle,* 6 October 1973; "Douglas Davis: Video Against Video" by David Ross in *Arts Magazine* (New York), January 1974; "Douglas Davis" by Walter Robinson in *Art-Rite* (New York), Autumn 1974; "Fragments for a New Art of the 70's" by Pierre Restany in *Domus* (Milan), December 1975; "Douglas Davis" by Cynthia Nadelman in *Artnews* (New York), May 1980; "Douglas Davis" by Jean-Paul Fargier in *Art Press* (Paris), July 1981.

The medium (video) is at once of no importance and of the greatest importance. It is simply the latest tool to be adopted by contemporary art, which has been since Duchamp reaching for new means of expression. Video is thus like film, light, sound, movement, linguistics. But it is far more profound in its implication than these tools because it can communicate instantly, everywhere. And it is related to the social-power complex, very directly. Art in a gallery or a museum, or even in a film theatre, is confined. Art on television is loose, free, and dangerous.

I think that the central problems that are attached to my work are two: 1) how to communicate on a very intense, private and personal level through a public medium (videotape is public whether broadcast or seen in a gallery); and 2) how to engage in a two-way dialogue with the eye and the mind of the viewer that goes beyond Duchamp—who simply said first that art needs the viewer to complete itself.

From these two points, it is clear that the overall direction in my work is "against video" in the sense that I am assaulting what the medium *is* and *has been*

(that is, bland, stupid, silly, and stiff). Video is simply the latest step in a process that is destroying the spectator ritual in art—the going-out to the temple to see it—but by no means the last. The next step is to get rid of the intervening structure, the cameras, the monitors, and telecasting circuitry.

My first thought about the television set was to activate it, as a link in a live sending as well as receiving link. We are almost blind to the two-way nature of television. Bertold Brecht wrote an astounding essay, "Theory of Radio," in 1929. He correctly pointed out that the decision to manufacture radio sets as receivers only was a political decision, not an economic one. The same is true of television. It is a conscious (and subconscious) decision that renders it one way. My attempt was and is to inject two-way metaphors— via live telecasts—into our thinking process. All my early two-way telecasts were structural invasions, then, very different from work I am doing now, though I hope that the two kinds of investigation will finally merge.

I don't even think of video as a medium anymore, but as an extension of myself, like drawing or speaking. The ideas expressed in my prints, drawings, performances and writings are all present in my work in television—and vice-versa.

Unless you use the camera as you use your hand, or a pencil—poking it wherever you want it to poke—the work will never come out like a drawing can, that is, close to your primal self. Art is a two-way process for me, whether it is printmaking, performance, drawing or video—knowing that I am involved in the evolution of a deeper, more diversified system of communication, between myself and the world and back.

—Douglas Davis

Television is the most influential mass medium of the modern world and a major icon of our culture. It has also managed to isolate and pacify a great majority of its target markets as a direct result of its de facto one-way nature. On the other hand, television has motivated a number of American, Asian and European visual artists, poets and writers towards the redevelopment of the video form and the re-structuring of the world information network. Douglas Davis is one of these contemporary artists whose refined ideas and philosophy has changed the face of mass communications.

Important to the understanding of Davis' work is the artistic and social climate out of which he developed. He was born and raised in Washington, D.C., a

city whose informational system involves global communication. His videotaping began in 1970 after he moved to New York City where media-orientation is thoroughly insular. These tapes emerged from the City's increasingly open-minded techniques. His first tape, "Look Out" (1970), documented exchanges with large numbers of people he met on the streets for 24 hours. In 1971 he produced "Electronic Hokkadim," in which thousands of viewers participated in a telephone to television direct access experiment, and "Talk-Out!" an open input dialogue allowing the artist both to send and receive messages from the viewing public.

Davis regarded the television as an archetypal form projecting light radiation in such a way as to reach primary levels of communication. At the same time what interested him about the screen is that it constitutes a barrier between him and the viewer, between his image in the television space and the viewer sitting in front of the screen. Consequently we see the theme "Breaking the Barrier" recurring in his work whether it be the television screen, the Iron Curtain, or Outer Space. Sometimes the barrier is the difficulty of communication itself. In making these videotapes, Davis' goal has been to relate, interpenetrate, juxtapose, and oppose different spaces at different times in a different media.

His performances explore the illusionistic properties of video space and time both by recording actions in different locations and by manipulating stored (taped) and real (live) time. Further, they offer the process of broadcast and reception as a tactile, visual and aural experience that the viewer completes before his own television set in the perception of the work. The television becomes the viewer's medium of self-awareness. For instance, in the "Austrian Tapes" (1974) Davis asks each viewer: "Please come to the television set in front of you. Place your hands against my hands. Think about our touching each other." The viewer is then asked to touch cheeks, lips, and so on, bringing him or her to the screen. In another work Davis succeeds in arranging a conversation between his own "live" person and his own "pre-recorded" person (a ghost).

Again in 1981 he treated the public perception of broadcast and reception by exploiting the ambiguities and myths of live transmission when he carried out a "long-distance" dialogue with a female performer speaking from the Centre Pompidou in France. The work entitled "Double Entendre: Two Sites Two Times (for Roland Barthes)" incorporated live and taped audio and video linked by satellite. The dia-

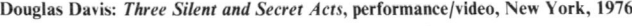

Douglas Davis: *Three Silent and Secret Acts,* performance/video, New York, 1976

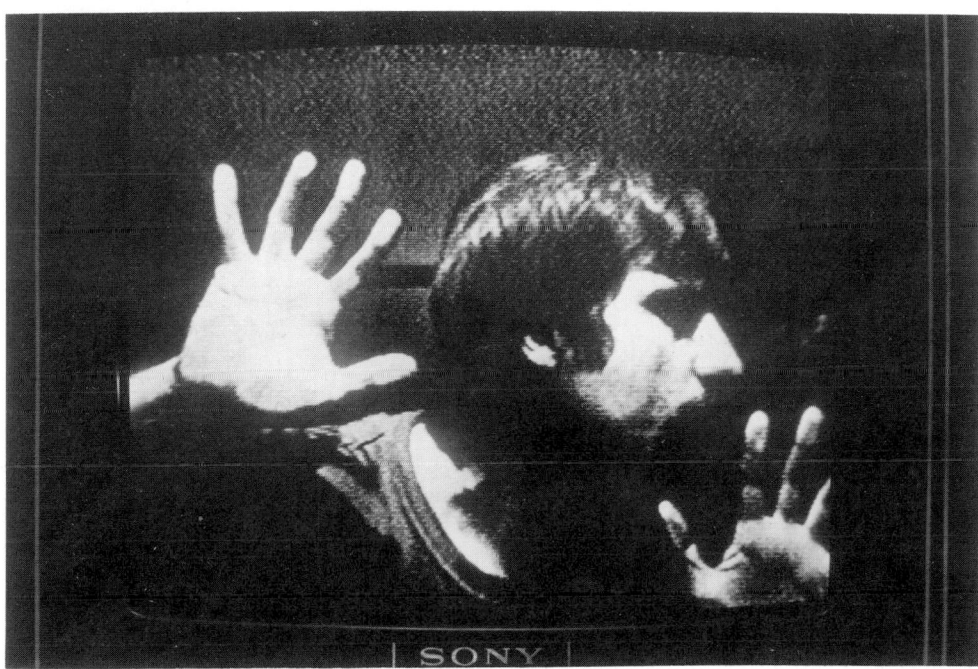

logue plied with the duality of the sexes and sites, with the difference in language, with radio and television, and with living persons. Both the paradoxes and the ultimate achieving of unity in spite of the distance constitutes the strength of the performance. The point at which the two merge summarizes Davis' concern and vision for re-shaping the television medium, as they declare in their own and each other's language: "Male and female, left and right, New York and Paris seem to become one figure, one line." By actively engaging the viewer in the work, by utilizing the ambiguity and complexity of real-time transmission, and lastly, by layering images and sound tracks, Davis' work becomes a multiple discourse, an unfolding narrative in which the self of the artist is expanded in the collective presence of the viewers.

—Carrie Barker

DAVIS, Gene.
American. Born in Washington, D.C., 22 August 1920. Educated at the University of Maryland, College Park, 1938-40; Wilson Teacher's College, Washington, D.C., 1941. Married Florence Coulson in 1960. White House correspondent, Transradio Press, Washington, D.C., 1942-52; worked as copy boy for the *New York Times,* reporter for United Press International, Jacksonville, Florida, Congressional correspondent for Newhouse Newspapers, and as a sports writer for the *Washington Daily News,* 1952-66. Assistant Professor, Corcoran Gallery School of Art, Washington, D.C., 1967-68, 1970-85; Instructor in Painting, American University, Washington, D.C., 1968-70; Artist-in-Residence, Skidmore College, Saratoga Springs, New York, Summer 1969; Artist-in-Residence, University of Virginia, Charlottesville, 1972. Recipient: Bronze Medal, *Biennial Exhibition of American Painting,* Corcoran Gallery of Art, Washington, D.C., 1965; National Endowment for the Arts grant, 1967; Guggenheim Fellowship, 1974-

75. Agent: Charles Cowles Gallery, 420 West Broadway, New York, New York 10012. *Died* (in Washington, D.C.) *6 April 1985.*

Individual Exhibitions:

1952	Dupont Theatre Gallery, Washington, D.C.
1953	Catholic University, Washington, D.C.
1955	American University, Washington, D.C.
1956	Jefferson Place Gallery, Washington, D.C.
1961	Jefferson Place Gallery, Washington, D.C.
1963	Jefferson Place Gallery, Washington, D.C.
	Poindexter Gallery, New York
1964	Corcoran Gallery of Art, Washington, D.C.
1965	Poindexter Gallery, New York
1966	Poindexter Gallery, New York
	Hofstra University, Hempstead, New York
1967	Poindexter Gallery, New York
	Jefferson Place Gallery, Washington, D.C.
	Massachusetts Institute of Technology, Cambridge
	Galerie Ricke, Cologne
	Art Center, Des Moines, Iowa
	Fischbach Gallery, New York (and yearly until 1975)
1968	Corcoran Gallery of Art, Washington, D.C.
	Museum of Art, San Francisco
	Washington Gallery of Modern Art, Washington, D.C.
	Jewish Museum, New York
	Henri Gallery, Washington, D.C.
	Kunstmarkt 68, Cologne
1969	Atelier Chapman Kelley, Dallas
	Henri Gallery, Washington, D.C.
	Axiom Gallery, London
	Boymans Museum, Rotterdam
	Yale University, New Haven, Connecticut
1970	Early Paintings 1950-60, Corcoran Gallery, Washington, D.C.
	Fendrick Gallery, Washington, D.C.
	Nova Scotia College of Art, Halifax
1970	Annamaria Verna Galerie, Zurich
	Dunkelman Gallery, Toronto
1972	Dunkelman Gallery, Toronto
	J. L. Hudson Gallery, Detroit

	Museum of Fine Arts, University of Utah, Logan
	Friends of Contemporary Art, Denver
	Joslyn Art Museum, Omaha, Nebraska
	Max Protetch Gallery, Washington, D.C.
1973	Michael Berger Gallery, Pittsburgh
	Quay Gallery, San Francisco
1974	New Gallery, Cleveland
	Tibor de Nagy Gallery, Houston
1975	Reed College, Portland, Oregon
1976	Harcus-Krakow Gallery, Boston
1977	Corcoran Gallery of Art, Washington, D.C.
	Fischbach Gallery, New York
	Max Protetch Gallery, Washington, D.C.
	Paris Art Fair
1978	Corcoran Gallery of Art, Washington, D.C.
	Fischbach Gallery, New York
	Walker Art Center, Minneapolis
	Dayton Art Institute, Ohio
	Protetch-McIntosh Gallery, Washington, D.C.
1979	Droll-Kolbert Gallery, New York
1980	Droll-Kolbert Gallery, New York
	Protetch-McIntosh Gallery, Washington, D.C.
	Arts Gallery, Baltimore, Maryland
1981	Frank Kolbert Gallery, New York
	Feldman Galleries, Sarasota, Florida
	McIntosh/Drysdale Gallery, Washington, D.C.
1982	Charles Cowles Gallery, New York
	Brooklyn Museum, New York
1983	Middendorf/Lane Gallery, Washington, D.C.
	Delaware Art Museum, Wilmington
	Washington Project for the Arts, Washington, D.C.
1984	Charles Cowles Gallery, New York
	U.M.K.C. Gallery of Art, Kansas City, Missouri
	Middendorf Gallery, Washington, D.C.
	Charles Cowles Gallery, New York
1986	Charles Cowles Gallery, New York
1987	National Museum of American Art, Washington, D.C. (memorial exhibition)

Selected Group Exhibitions:

1967	*The 60's,* Museum of Modern Art, New York
1971	*The Structure of Color,* Whitney Museum, New York

Gene Davis: *Dr. Peppercorn,* 1967

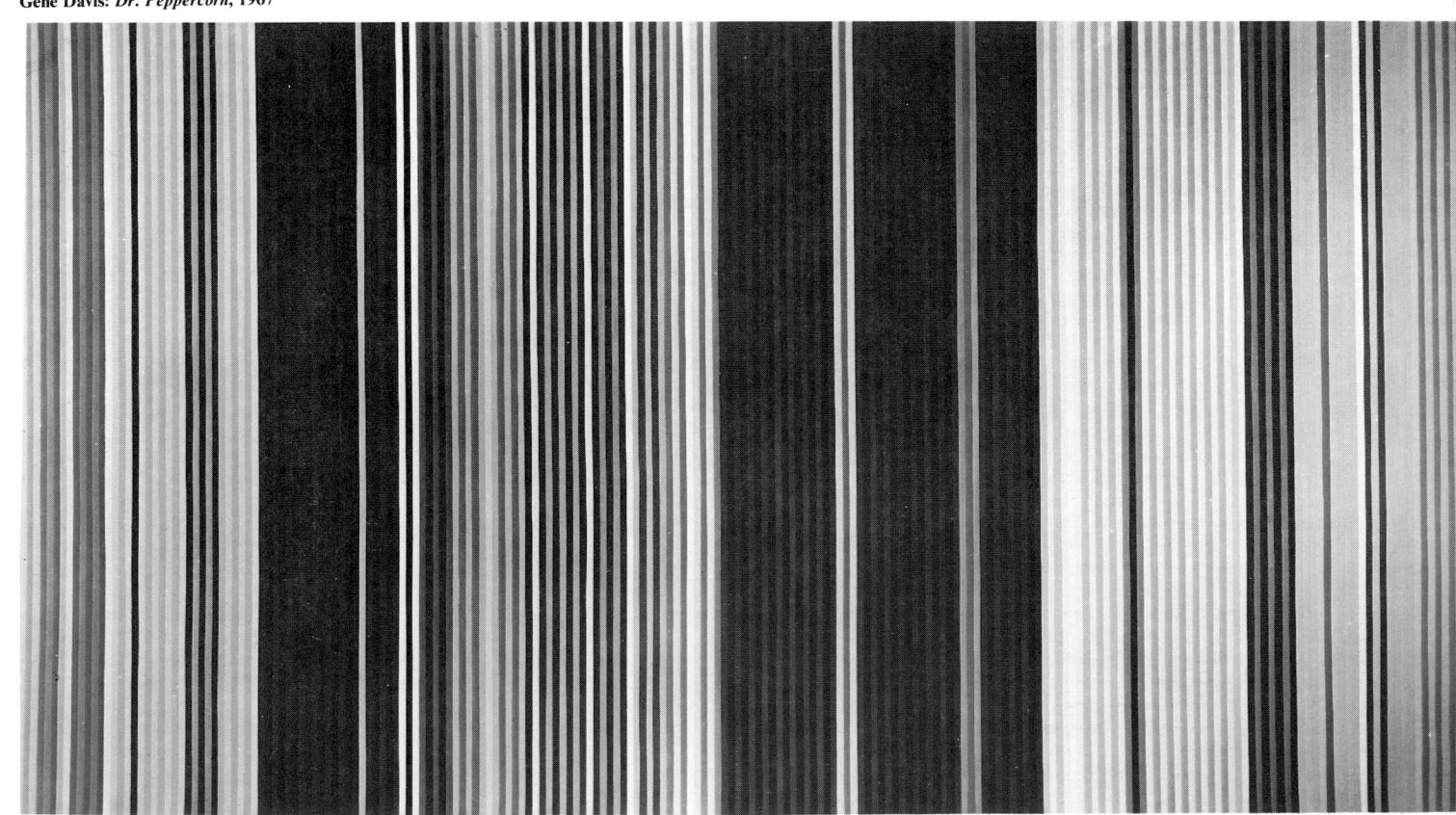

1974 *Within the Decade*, Guggenheim Museum, New York

1975 *34th Biennial of American Painting*, Corcoran Gallery of Art, Washington, D.C.

1977 *Summer Exhibition of the Permanent Collection*, Guggenheim Museum, New York

1979 *Selections from the Permanent Collection*, Museum of Modern Art, New York

1980 *American Art 1900-1980*, Guggenheim Museum, New York

1982 *Thirty Painters: Given and Promised*, Metropolitan Museum of Art, New York

1984 *Generations of the Washington Color School*, George Washington University, Washington, D.C.

1986 *The Window in Twentieth Century Art*, Neuberger Museum, State University of New York, Purchase

Collections:

Museum of Modern Art, New York; Whitney Museum, New York; Metropolitan Museum of Art, New York; Guggenheim Museum, New York; Albright-Knox Art Gallery, Buffalo, New York; National Gallery of Art, Washington, D.C.; Hirshhorn Museum, Washington, D.C., Corcoran Gallery, Washington, D.C.; Art Institute of Chicago; Walker Art Center, Minneapolis; Tate Gallery, London.

Publications:

By DAVIS: articles—"Preoccupation with Colour: Conversations with Gene Davis and Albert Stadler" by Gene Baro in *Studio International* (London), November 1967; "Statement by the Artist" in *Art Now* (New York), February 1970; "A Conversation with Gene Davis" by Barbara Rose in *Artforum* (New York), March 1971; "Random Thoughts on Art" in *Art International* (Lugano, Switzerland), November 1971; "Gene Davis on Gene Davis," in collaboration with Donald Wall, in *Art in America* (New York), May 1973; "Gene Davis and the Stripe as Subject Matter," interview with Walter Hopps, in *Art News* (New York), February 1975; "Painter's Reply" in *Artforum* (New York), September 1975; "Gorky Taught Me That—A Remembrance of Arshile Gorky" in *Art Magazine* (New York), March 1976; "Starting Out in the 50's" in *Art in America* (New York), July/August 1978; interview, with David Tannous, in *Art in America* (New York), July/August 1978; "Of Stripes on Canvas: A Conversation with Gene Davis" by Jean Lawlor Cohen in the *Washington Star* (Washington, D.C.), 17 December 1978; "An Interview with Gene Davis" by Mary Swift in *Washington Review* (Washington, D.C.), December/January 1979/80; interview, with Percy North, in *Abstractions from the Phillips Collection*, exhibition catalogue, Fairfax, Virginia 1983.

On DAVIS: books—*Gene Davis: New Paintings and Drawings*, exhibition catalogue with essay by Tom Haulik, Baltimore 1980; *Gene Davis Drawings* by Gene Baro, New York 1982; *Gene Davis* by Steven W. Naifeh, New York 1982; *Gene Davis: The Random and the Ordered*, exhibition catalogue, with essay by Pinky Kase, Kansas City 1984; *Gene Davis*, exhibition catalogue with essay by Jacquelyn Days Serwer, Washington, D.C. 1987; articles—"Gene Davis" by Ralph Pomeroy in *Arts Magazine* (New York), March 1970; "Gene Davis: New paintings" by Donald Wall in *Arts Magazine* New York), "Gene Davis: The Drawn Image" by Gene Baro in *Arts Magazine* (New York), September/October 1976; "Gene Davis at the Corcoran and the Protetch" by Davis Tannous in *Art in America* (New York), May/June 1977; "Gene Davis: A Review" by Norman Turner in *Arts Magazine* (New York), September 1977; "Art: New Drawings by Gene Davis" by Hilton Kramer in the *New York Times*, 9 March 1979; "Classical Shoppers" by William Zimmer in *The Soho Weekly News* (New York), 15 March 1979; "Out of Left Field" by John Ashbery in *New York Magazine*, 2 April 1979; "Single-Idea Art, Singularly Filmed" by Benjamin Forgey in *Washington Star News* (Washington, D.C.), 6 January 1980.

As an artist renowned for his majestic paintings of stripes, Gene Davis has left an impressive legacy of works, including early abstract expressionist oils, collages, gestural drawings, and prints. In the early 1960's, Davis emerged as a prominent member of the Washington Color School, whose artists explored painting's basic elements and the technique of straining raw canvas with thin washes of color. Like many painters of his generation, Davis fathomed the essential properties of color and space as the subject, form, and content of his work.

In creating his broad repertoire of stripe paintings, Davis likened himself to a jazz musician, "playing by eye". He felt the music of the stripes and painted them intuitively. Davis' complex and expansive investigation of the stripe format yielded numerous series, among which are hard-edge, free-hand or "bleed" stripes and broad, narrow, or pin-striped bands. Intrigued by the impact of scale, Davis challenged established perceptions of architectural space by creating minuscule "micro" paintings in 1967, countered by two monumental "street" paintings, one in front of the Philadelphia Museum in 1977 and the other at New York's Artpark in 1979. He also designed a pattern of colored tubes of water for a solar wall at the College of William and Mary's Muscarelle Museum in Williamsburg, Virginia. In the early 1980's, Davis exhibited a provocative series of large black silhouette self-portrait heads (in conjunction with "micro" replicas of the same) and offered a new investigation of interval in contrast with his brilliant stripe palette.

Davis' remarkable versatility is highlighted by a vast number of works on paper (ink, collage, colored pencil, pastel, and crayon), which were produced as drawings in themselves rather than painting studies. Among his late works are a collaborative project in 1983 which juxtaposes a series of his drawings with those of children, and a number of drawings which combine his pattern of stripes with pictographs, symbols, and collage, bringing together all the components of his artistic expression.

—Percy North

DAVIS, John.

Australian. Born in Ballarat, Victoria, in 1936. Educated at Melbourne State College, Caulfield Institute of Technology, Melbourne University, and Royal Melbourne Institute of Technology, 1955-57; studied sculpture, under Lenton Parr and Vincent Jomantis, R. M. I. T., 1963-66. Married Shirley Heberle in 1961; children: Penelope and Martin. Lives and works in Victoria. Instructor in Art, Queenscliff High School, 1958; instructor in Woodcraft, Numurkah High School, 1959-60; instructor in Art, Mildura High School, 1961-62; instructor, Highett High School, 1963-66; Lecturer in 3D Design and Sculpture, Caulfield Institute of Technology, 1967-71; Tutor in Sculpture, Summer School, Monash University, 1969-70; Lecturer in Charge of Sculpture and 3D Design, Prahan College of Advanced Education, 1973-80; Senior lecturer in charge of sculpture, 1975-80, and Co-ordinator of Post-graduate Studies, Victorian College of the Arts, 1981. Recipient: Comalco Invitation Award, Melbourne, 1970. Agents: Art Projects, 566 Lonsdale Street, Melbourne; Watters Gallery, 109 Riley Street, East Sydney. Address: 41 Crisp Street, Hampton, Victoria 3188, Australia.

Individual Exhibitions:

1969 Strines Gallery, Melbourne
1971 Watters Gallery, Sydney
1972 Gallery One Eleven, Melbourne
1974 Pinacotheca Gallery, Melbourne
C. A. S. Gallery, Adelaide
1977 Watters Gallery, Sydney
1978 National Gallery of Victoria, Melbourne
Art Gallery of New South Wales, Sydney
1979 Art Projects, Melbourne
Watters Gallery, Sydney
1980 Institute of Modern Art, Brisbane
Wollongong City Gallery, New South Wales
Q Space Annex, Brisbane

1981 Art Projects, Melbourne
Watters Gallery, Sydney
1984 Cettenball Gallery, Wolverhampton, Staffordshire

Selected Group Exhibitions:

1970 *Comalco Invitation Sculpture Competition*, Melbourne
1973 *Recent Australian Art*, Art Gallery of New South Wales, Sydney
1976 *Biennale of Sydney*
1978 *4th Indian Triennial*, New Delhi
Biennale, Venice
1981 *Landscape Art: Two-way reaction*, Australian National Gallery, Canberra
1st Australian Sculpture Triennial, Latrobe University, Melbourne
Perspecta '81, Art Gallery of New south Wales, Sydney
Relics and Rituals, National Gallery of Victoria, Melbourne
Patrick White's Choice, Art Gallery of New South Wales, Sydney

Collections:

Australian National Gallery, Canberra; Art Gallery of New South Wales, Sydney; Shepparton City Art Gallery, Victoria; Geelong City Art Gallery, Victoria; Mildura City Art Gallery, Victoria; National Gallery of Victoria, Melbourne; Hobart Art Gallery, Tasmania; Brisbane Art Gallery; Art Gallery of Western Australia, Perth; Wollongong City Art Gallery, New South Wales.

Publications:

On DAVIS: books—*Place*, exhibition catalogue, by Noel Hutchison, Melbourne 1975; *Skira Annual Special Issue 1970-1980*, Geneva 1980; articles—article by Elwyn Lynn in *Art International* (Lugano, Switzerland), July 1977; "Quadrant" in the *Venice Biennale*, exhibition catalogue, Venice 1978; "The Venice Biennale" by Henry Martin in *Art International* (Lugano, Switzerland), October 1978; article by Elwyn Lynn in *Art International* (Lugano, Switzerland), vol. XXLL/5-6, 1978; "Report from Australia" by Suzi Gablik in *Art in America* (New York), "Mildura Rides Again" by Graeme Sturgeon in *Art and Australia* (Sydney), Summer 1981; "Report from Australia, part 1, by Suzi Gablik in *Art and Australia* (Sydney), Autumn 1981; "In" in *Exchange of Contemporary Art* (Tokyo), December 1981.

A Sense of Place

In 1976 I rediscovered an informal education in the Australian Bush denied to me through urbanization and formal education. It is as relevant to my understanding of what it is to be an Australian in 1982 as is my interpretation of European and Aboriginal histories. In other words, I have attempted to establish within myself a sense of place and of time, eventually transferring this into the work.

And like all people, I am bound to carry certain aspects of history about with me. In my response to the impulse to make art, I refer to this consciously and subconsciously so that whatever evolves in the "work space" is somehow an amalgamation of that which is ancient and that which is a new experience.

The beginning is in the tying of two twigs. Then it takes its own direction, full of inconsistencies, contradictions, ambiguities and alliances, moving as nature does; or how Australia country towns eventuate; or how themes in music or poetry evolve into metaphor. Each piece is part of a larger on-going work, a specific and at the same time general occurrence, a mass of detail demanding close scrutiny because of its close approximation and juxtaposing; it demands that the viewer step back to encompass 'the view'.

Like all things in nature, it is fragile and subject to easy destruction; each part is dependent on another for its identity and difference, eventually indicating its position in another place, moving into or retreating from the location where it finds itself.

—John Davis

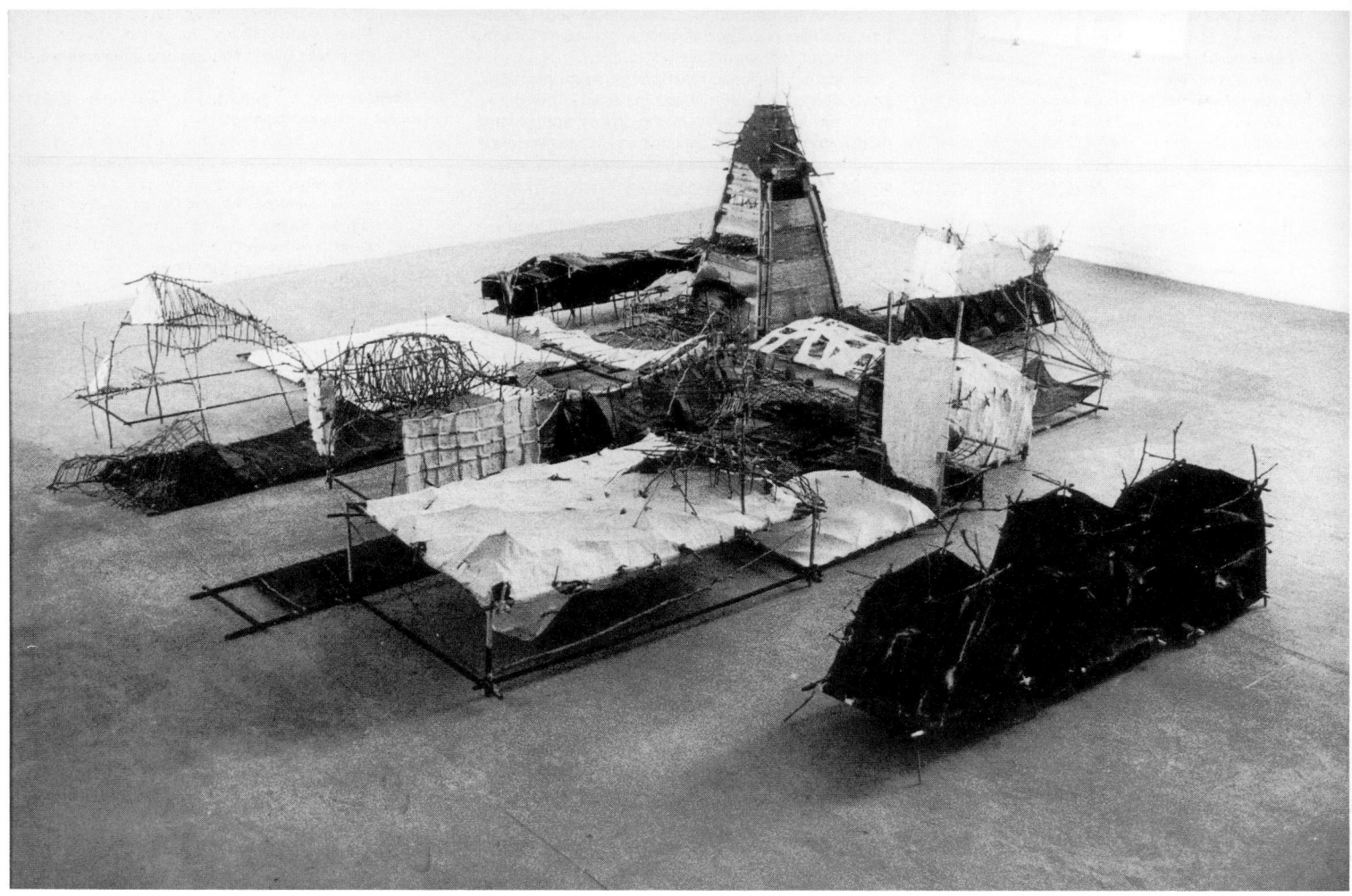

John Davis: *Region*, 1981

John Davis is an Australian. He inhabits, with the majority of his fellow Australians, the small crescent of coastal land in the south-eastern corner of a massive continent. He lives in a pleasant house in a residential suburb of Melbourne. He is married, with children. He is a convivial man, who loves the bush and the sea and believes in the sanctity of Saturdays. John Davis is in many ways a very typical Australian.

In other respects, John Davis belongs to a wider community. He is idealistic, humanist, passionate, socialist and, in the very best sense of the word, nationalistic. Most atypical of all, he chooses to make manifest his beliefs, his hopes and, often, his fears in sculptures that are at one and the same time delicate and monolithic. The fragile bindings of twigs and paper, into brooding towers and mountains or spaced marks on an endless plain, echo the fragility of the environment. The spatial relationships which characterise Davis's sculptures reflect his awareness of and empathy with landscape on a monumental scale. Davis's sculptures may not be physically large, but emotionally and conceptually they embrace the dimensions of a continent.

Davis's sculptures grow, like living organisms. In this sense too, Davis is concerned with nature. But this concern is devoid of romantic notions. Australia is a difficult and complex land from a Western standpoint. The Australian Aborigines learned, in the Dreamtime, that the means by which man might live in this contradictory land was by accepting and accommodating nature rather than trying to improve upon it. Many of the political conflicts that exist in contemporary Australia are conflicts between ecologically conservative forces and those which would seek to perpetuate the exploitative philosophies of the Industrial Revolution. Davis believes in the possibilities of a harmony (of sorts) between these two attitudes.

The Melbourne critic, Robert Rooney, coined the deathless phrase "twiggery folkery" in response to the work of John Davis and other artists who employ natural materials in their art. In so doing, Rooney was revealing a commonly held fear of a sentimental response to the Australian landscape, and a parochial sense of identity, rather than making serious criticism. The fear is that a cloying romanticism towards the landscape (perhaps a hangover from the champagne days of Tom Roberts et al) will reveal Australians as intellectually barren land-lovers. The gum-tree school of painting is an embarrassment: we often seek to legitimise our artistic status by adopting a preference for international modes in art and in rejecting that which smacks of the "pretty" or of sources closely identified with heroic concepts of landscape art. "Nature," in Australian art terms, can often appear to be a euphemism for cliché and corn. Yet the "natural" pattern of Australia is a violent one—fire is needed for the germination of some plant seeds, drought and floods re-occur, often within one season. Balance does exist, but often between extremes. John Davis's sculptures are a lucid and loving attempt to recreate not only the balances and relationships that exist in this most unorthodox of climes, but also, through his own experience, the balances and relationships of those who live in the environment and who choose to be affected by it.

In so doing Davis transcends his "Australianness" and offers concepts and statements that can be recognized and understood on an international level. By embracing an accessible specific, Davis speculates on the universal.

—Alison Fraser

DAVIS, Ronald (Wendel).
American. Born in Santa Monica, California, 29 June 1937. Studied engineering, University of Wyoming, Laramie, 1955–56; art, San Francisco Art Institute, 1960–64, under Philip Guston, Yale University Summer School of Music and Art, Norfolk, Connecticut, 1962. Worked as a sheet metal machinist, Cheyenne, Wyoming, 1956–58; and as a radio announcer, Cheyenne, 1958. Independent painter since 1959; has lived in Greeley, Colorado, 1959–65, in Pasadena, then Los Angeles, 1965–73, and in Malibu, California, since 1973. Instructor, University of California at Irvine, 1966. Recipient: National Endowment for the Arts Grant, 1968, 1972. Agent: Nicholas Wilder Gallery, 8225 ½ Santa Monica Boulevard, Los Angeles, California 99046. Address: 29715 Cuthbert Road, Malibu, California 90265, U.S.A.

Individual Exhibitions:

1965   Nicholas Wilder Gallery, Los Angeles
1966   Tibor de Nagy Gallery, New York
1967   Nicholas Wilder Gallery, Los Angeles
1968   Leo Castelli Gallery, New York
           Vancouver Art Gallery
           Kasmin Gallery, London
1969   University of Saskatchewan, Saskatoon
           Nicholas Wilder Gallery, Los Angeles
           Leo Castelli Gallery, New York
1970   Albright-Knox Art Gallery, Buffalo, New York
           Leo Castelli Gallery, New York
           Paintings Never Before Exhibited, David Mirvish Gallery, Toronto
           Joseph Helman Gallery, St. Louis
           Kasmin Gallery, London
           Gemini Gallery, Los Angeles

Pasdena Museum of Art, California
1972 Walker Art Center, Minneapolis
Galleria dell'Ariete, Milan
Joseph Helman Gallery, St. Louis
1973 Nicholas Wilder Gallery, Los Angeles
John Berggruen Gallery, San Francisco
1974 Gemini Gallery, Los Angeles
Western Galleries, Cheyenne, Wyoming
Leo Castelli Gallery, New York
1975 Mirvish Gallery, Toronto
John Berggruen Gallery, San Francisco
Boise State University, Idaho
Greenberg Gallery, St. Louis
Leo Castelli Gallery, New York
Ronald Davis/Tom Holland: Works from the Collection of Mr. and Mrs. Robert A. Rowan, Los Angeles Municipal Art Gallery, Barnsdall Park
1976 Aspen Gallery of Art, Colorado
Seder-Creigh Gallery, Coronado, Colorado
Paintings 1962–1976, Oakland Museum, California
1977 Church Fine Arts Gallery, University of Nevada, Reno
1979 Blum-Helman Gallery, New York

Selected Group Exhibitions:

1968 *Documenta 4*, Kassel, West Germany
1969 *Corcoran Biennal*, Washington, D.C. (and 1973)
1970 *Annual American Exhibition*, Art Institute of Chicago
1971 *6 Painters*, Fine Arts Academy, Buffalo, New York
1972 *Biennale*, Venice
1973 *25 Years of American Painting*, Des Moines Art Center, Iowa
1975 *Current Concerts Part 1*, Institute of Contemporary Art, Los Angeles
1976 *Painting and Sculpture in California*, San Francisco Museum of Modern Art (travelled to Washington, D.C.)
1978 *4 Contemporary Painters: Arakawa/Bruce Boice/ Ronald Davis/Agnes Martin*, Cleveland Museum of Art
1979 *Reality of Illusion*, University of Southern California, Los Angeles (travelled to the Honolulu Academy of arts; Oakland Museum, California; and the University of Texas at Austin, 1980)
1984 *Olympian Gestures*, Los Angeles County Museum of Art

Collections:

Museum of Modern Art, New York, Albright-Knox Art Gallery, Buffalo, New York; Baltimore Museum of Art; Los Angeles County Museum of Art; San Francisco Museum of Modern Art; Tate Gallery, London; National Gallery of Victoria, Melbourne.

Publications:

On DAVIS: books—*Ron Davis*, exhibition catalogue, with text by Charles Kessler, Los Angeles 1970; *Ron Davis*, exhibition catalogue, with text by Barbara Rose, Milan 1973; *Ronald Davis/Tom Holland: Works from the Collection of Mr. and Mrs. Robert A. Owen*, exhibition catalogue, Los Angeles 1975; *Ronald Davis: Paintings 1962 1976*, exhibition catalogue, with text by Charles Kessler, Oakland, California 1976; *Ronald Davis*, exhibition catalogue, with text by John McCracken, Reno, Nevada 1977; *4 Contemporary Painters: Arakawa/Bruce Boice/Ronald Davis/Agnes Martin*, exhibition catalogue, with an introduction by Tom E. Hinson, Cleveland 1978; articles—"Ronald Davis: Surface and Illusion" by Michael Fried in *Artforum* (New York), April 1967; "Ron Davis" by J. Livingston in *Artforum* (New York), January 1968; "New Paintings by Ron Davis" by John Eiderfield in *Artforum* (New York), March 1971; "Imagine a Space, a Form, a World: The paintings of Ron Davis" by S. C. Larsen in *Artnews* (New York), January 1980.

The most commonly asked question about my plastic paintings has been, "How do you make them?" My reply usually has been, "The same way one makes a fiberglass boat or car body." In case you have never built a boat in your backyard, here is my attempt at a more technical explanation.

In 1966 I began to substitute polyester resin plus pigments and dyes for traditional painting media. Fiberglass cloth and mat replaced canvas as reinforcement and support for the colored resin (paint). These plastic paintings were painted with a brush face down, on a flat, waxed Formica mold. The mold itself was table height, and the preliminary drawings I had made for these paintings were cartooned up to scale on the mold. The illusionary plane *nearest* the viewer was masked out with tape and painted *first;* the planes further away from the viewer were painted last. The rapid chemical heatcuring properties of resin (about thirty minutes) allowed me to apply layer behind layer of colored resin until the painting was completed. Layers of fiberglass impregnated with resin were then laminated to the back of the painting, giving it a support, and a wood stretcher bar the shape of the image was attached to the painting. The completed painting was peeled from the waxed mold and polished. It was then that I viewed the painting for the first time.

On later plastic paintings, i.e. "Eleven Colors," 1967, the wood was eliminated and instead the sides were molded onto the painting as one piece, and a backing sheet of resin and fiberglass was added for structural support. In 1970 I began to use a flexible type resin, i.e. "Single Sawtooth," 1971, eliminated the sides entirely, and attached the painting directly to the wall with Velcrotape.

For health and aesthetic reasons I discontinued the use of resin and fiberglass in 1972.

—Ronald Davis

Ron Davis emerged on the art scene in the turbulent 60's winning critical acclaim afforded few west coast artists of the era. Though his first exhibition in New York City was coolly received, it was not long before formalist art critic Michael Fried heralded his paintings in *Artforum* as being ". . . among the most significant produced anywhere during the last few years . . ." which propelled Davis on to the honor roll of American art. Clearly, he proposed a new alternative to the growing notion of sculpture as painting or vice-versa.

An admirer of the perspectival illusionism of Renaissance painters, most notably Uccello, Davis resurrected the long discarded principles of two-point perspective. By slicing the illusion free from a rectangular format, the images (geometric donut shapes, squares within squares, etc.) hovered independently and illogically on gallery walls. Illogically, because not only was their uncanny sense of depth disarming, but also, although one viewed them at eye level, they depicted objects as would be seen perspectively from above. This seductive contradiction, coupled with Davis's use of polyester resins and fiberglass, lent a real sense of freshness to the work and to an art world drenched with minimalism.

Though they satisfied many of the more traditional requirements of painting, using resins freed Davis to manipulate the thin skin of his plastic paintings in a new way. Juxtaposing translucent resins with opaque pigment, which was often laced with pearlessence and buffed until glossy, somehow liberated the surface, making it appear to teasingly float apart from the imagery. Davis is undeniably a painter, but was and continues to be fed by an emphatically sculptural aesthetic.

For various reasons, not the least of which was health, Davis discontinued his use of resins in 1972. He began a series of small-scale canvases which seemed almost to deify varying arrangements of sundry geometric shapes. Like tiny two-dimensional Stonehenges, each grouping of shapes was bathed in dramatic light and shadow and saturated with rich, jewel-like color.

Towards the late 70's Davis's scale and his application of paint once again both changed drastically. The new paintings were so large that they easily overwhelmed entire walls or even rooms. These acrylic paintings defined a fictitious environment distorted by dramatically foreshortened spatial planes. The objects, often sitting on checkerboard surfaces or sim-

Ron Davis: *Diamond in a Box*, 1975

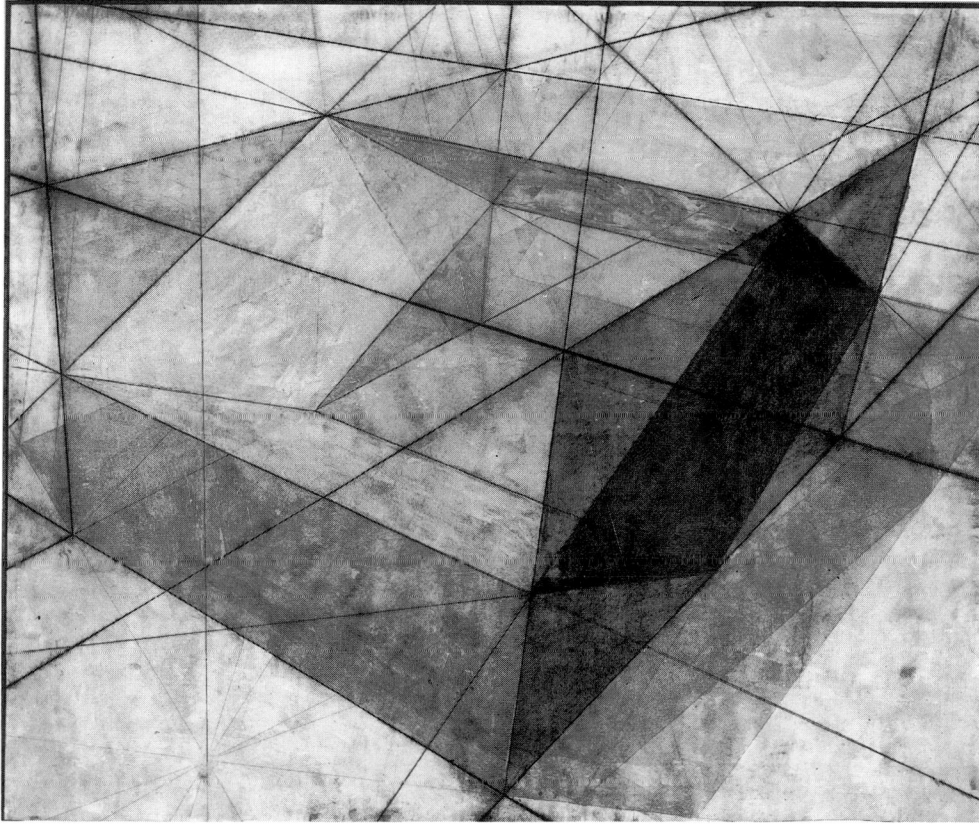

ply dangling in space, changed too. Now they were more tent-like, their form fully described by a complex network of perspectival chalk snap-lines which elucidated the infra-structure of each structural component. Splashy, rhoplex laden paint lent an element of expressioniam to the pieces which had been only hinted at in earlier pieces.

Davis continues to paint irregular geometric shapes in space today. He also pursues, on a less professional level, a keen interest in musical composition.

—Janet Goleas

DEACON, Richard.

British. Born in Bangor, Caernarvonshire, Wales, in 1949. Studied at Somerset College of Art, Taunton, 1968–69; Saint Martin's School of Art, London, 1969–72; Royal College of Art, London, 1974–77; part-time, Chelsea School of Art, London, 1977–78. Independent sculptor, London, since 1978. Instructor, Central School of Art, London, 1978. Recipient: Turner Prize, Tate Gallery, London, 1987. Agent: Lisson Gallery, London. Address: c/o Lisson Gallery, 67 Lisson Street, London NW1 5DA, England.

Individual Exhibitions:

1975	Royal College of Art, London
1976	Royal College of Art, London
1978	Acre Lane Studio, Brixton, London
1980	Acre Lane Studio, Brixton, London
1981	City Polytechnic, Sheffield
1983	Lisson Gallery, London
	Orchard Gallery, Londonderry, Northern Ireland
1984	Riverside Studios, Hammersmith, London
	Chapter Gallery, Cardiff, Wales
	Fruitmarket Gallery, Edinburgh
	Le Nouveau Musee, Lyon-Villeurbanne, France
1985	Donald Young Gallery, Chicago (with Tony Cragg)
	Israel Museum, Jerusalem (with Julian Opie and Richard Wentworth)
	Tate Gallery, London
	Centre International du Verre, Aix-en-Provence, France
	Margarete Roeder Fine Arts, New York (with Jackie Winsor)
	Serpentine Gallery, London (with Richard Rogers and John Tchalenko)
1986	Marian Goodman Gallery, New York
	Interim Art, London
	Galerie Artlogos, Nantes, France
	Aberystwyth Arts Centre, Wales (toured Britain)
1987	Lisson Gallery, London
	Bonnefanten Museum, Maastricht, Netherlands (travelled to Lucerne, Madrid, Antwerp)
1988	Lisson Gallery, London
	Ecole des Beaux Arts, Macon, France
	Marian Goodman Gallery, New York

Selected Group Exhibitions:

1978	*Staff Sculpture*, Central School of Art, London
1980	*Lambeth Summer Festival*, Winchester School of Art, Hampshire
1981	*Objects and Sculpture*, Institute of Contemporary Arts, London (travelled to Bristol)
1982	*Englische Plastik Heute*, Kunstmuseum, Lucerne
1983	*The Sculpture Show*, Hayward Gallery/Serpentine Gallery, London
1984	*The British Art Show*, City Museum/Ikon Gallery, Birmingham (travelled to Edinburgh; Sheffield; Southampton)
1985	*Transformations in Sculpture*, Guggenheim Museum, New York
1986	*Skulptur: 9 Kunstnere fra Storbrittanien*, Louisiana Museum, Humlebaek, Denmark
1987	*A Quiet Revolution: British Sculpture Since 1968*, Museum of Contemporary Art, Chicago (travelled to San Francisco; Newport Beach, California; Washington, D.C.; Buffalo, New York)
1988	*All That Matters*, Art Gallery of Windsor, Ontario (travelled to Saskatoon and Montreal)

Richard Deacon: *Blind, Deaf and Dumb A*, **1985** Courtesy Lisson Gallery, London

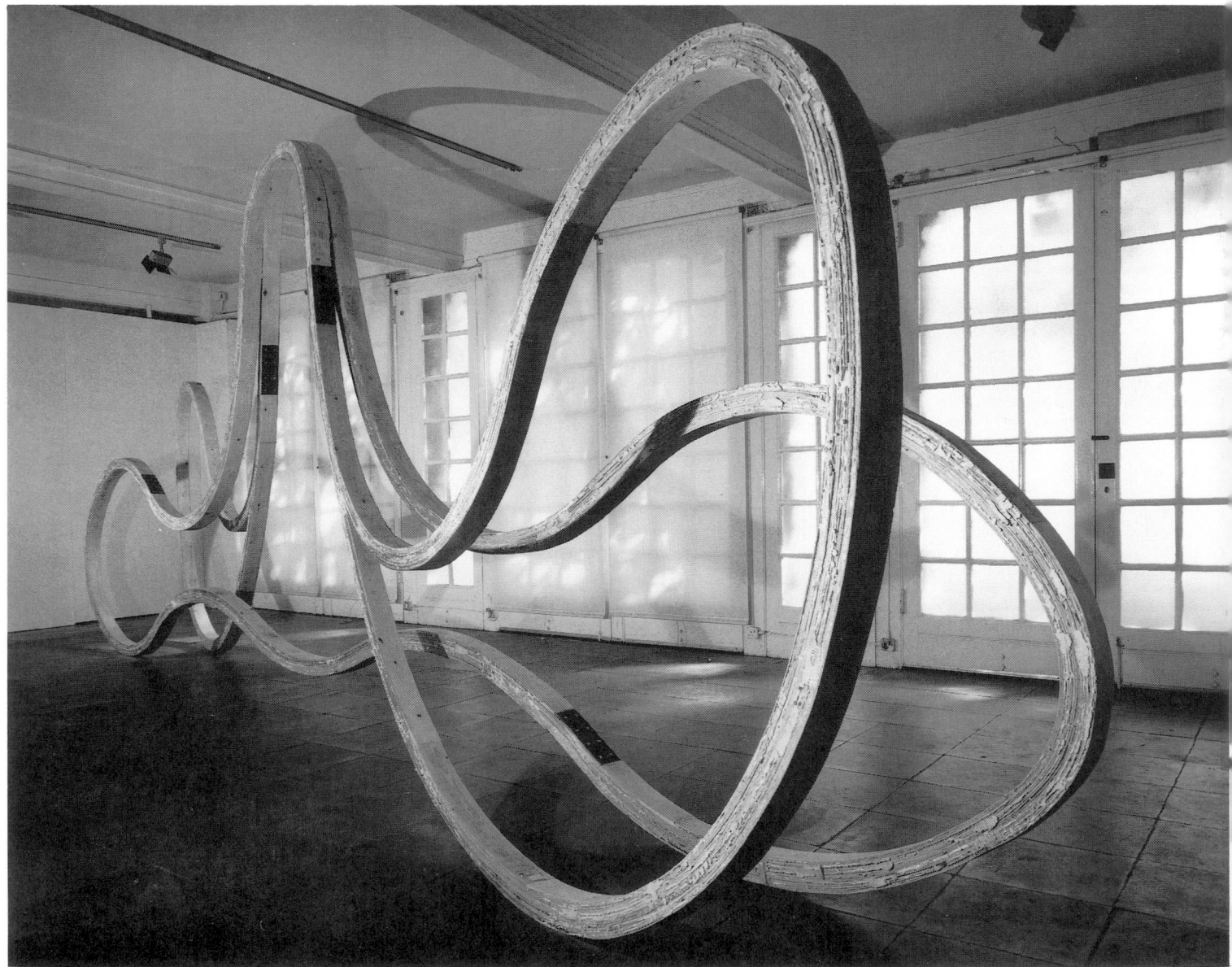

Collections:

Tate Gallery, London; British Council, London; Arts Council of Great Britain, London; Fonds Regional d'Art Contemporain des Pays de la Loire, France; Fonds Regional d'Art Contemporain Rhone-Alpes, France; Le Nouveau Musee, Lyon-Villeurbanne; Museum of Modern Art, New York.

Publications:

By DEACON: books—*Stuff Box Object*, London 1972, Cardiff 1984; *Jacqui Poncelet: New Ceramics*, exhibition catalogue, London 1981; *Carol McNicoll*, exhibition catalogue, London 1985; *For Those Who Have Ears No. 2*, London 1985; *For Those Who Have Eyes*, exhibition catalogue, Aberystwyth 1986.

On DEACON: books—*Objects and Sculpture*, exhibition catalogue with texts by Iwona Blaszcwyk, Lewis Biggs and Sandy Nairne, London 1980; *Englische Plastik Heute*, exhibition catalogue with texts by Martin Kunz and Michael Newman, Lucerne 1982; *Richard Deacon: Sculpture*, exhibition catalogue with text by Lynne Cooke, Londonderry 1983; *Making Sculpture: Richard Deacon*, broadsheet edited by the Tate Gallery, London 1983; *Richard Deacon: The Face of Things*, exhibition catalogue with text by Michael Newman, Edinburgh 1984; *Richard Deacon*, exhibition folder with text by Richard Francis, London 1985; *Richard Deacon: Recent Sculpture*, exhibition catalogue with text by Charles Harrison, Maastricht 1987; *Richard Deacon*, exhibition catalogue with text by Peter Schjeldahl, New York 1988.

Richard Deacon is one of the younger generation of British sculptors who have won international acclaim in the last few years. He himself prefers the term 'fabricator' as a more accurate description of what he does as he is neither a modeller nor a carver. The materials he works with, such as laminated wood, linoleum or galvanised steel or aluminium, are chosen primarily for their structural potential rather for any intrinsic value or sensual properties.

As an undergraduate at St. Martin's School of Art in the 'seventies he was much involved in Performance Art, but even then he was not using his own body as the basic material as had his immediate predecessors, Bruce McLean or Gilbert and George. In Deacon's performances he used materials which underwent a transformation or were resolved into a final object, so though he was accepted for the experimental post-graduate course at the Royal College of Art on the basis of his performance art, process became of much less importance than the object in mind. The works he made about this time were strong, architectonic shapes with emphasis on integration of surface and structure. There is no hidden armature in these works, no distraction of surface detail from the spare, angular shapes. Already the young artist seems to be pondering on the centuries-old pre-occupations of sculptors—the relationships of skin and structure, inner and outer surfaces, mass and volume and edge conditions, and this exploration continued when he went to the United States in 1978 /9. After his return from America his ideas start to cohere in a series of confident and mature constructions. Some of Deacon's work is reminiscent of the moving parts of machinery—of mills and steam engines and others are evocative of propellors and conic sections. There is often the suggestion of potential movement. There are forms which remind one of navigation aids in pre-radar days—those spherical, open basket shapes on top of high poles at harbour mouths. (Interestingly, for Deacon has never mentioned them as source material, one of these round open basket forms is entitled *For Those Who Have Eyes*). Other works indicate that Deacon enjoyed and was inspired by the geometry of conic sections—the ellipse, the circle, the parabola and the hyperbola—but he then became increasingly interested in organic and biomorphic forms and the expressive content of his work deepened accordingly.

Whilst he was in the States he had made a series of drawings entitled *Orpheus When There's Singing* which were inspired by *Sonnets to Orpheus* by Rainer Maria Rilke. Deacon says that these drawings started with a geometric figure with parts linked by a spiral. "A series of arcs and curves build up a network or ground against which specific shapes are allowed to emerge." That is an accurate description of the series *For Those Who Have Ears*. The Orpheus myth is about music, both the making of music and the hearing of music. In *For Those Who Have Ears No. 2 1983*, which is made of curving loops of laminated wood, the shapes can suggest both ears and also lyres—the ears to hear and the lyres to make music. The forms in this work are open, generous and flowing; the luxuriant curves are sensuous and suggest sexual imagery. It is a large sculpture, $9 \times 13 \times 13$ feet, but Deacon can handle large scale works which never become monumental. It sits lightly on the ground and is particularly pleasing in its balance and poise and its subtle delineation of shifting forms expressed in a linear context. The process of the making is indicated by the glue which oozed out when the strips of wood were pressed together.

His later work seems to have certain basic themes which deal with growth processes and with a continuing concern with orifices where the sexual imagery and the penetration of the forms becomes more evident. Works which appear initially to have a limpid simplicity develop a haunting and mysterious presence. The titles with their references to poetry and literature remind us of the artist's recurrent dilemma of the balance between form and content and the need to synthesise abstraction and nature.

Interestingly, Richard Deacon has recently collaborated with a Dance Company, designing and making objects which can be moved about the stage by the dancers, demonstrating once again the wide variety of arenas in which the 20th century artist is not only mixing his media but also moving freely in other modes of artistic expression.

—Mary Ellis

DE ANDREA, John (Louis).

American. Born in Denver, Colorado, 24 November 1941. Educated at the University of Colorado, Boulder, 1961-65, B.F.A. 1965; University of New Mexico, Albuquerque, 1966-68 (on art assistantship). Sculptor: lives and works in Denver. Agent: O.K. Harris Gallery, 465 West Broadway, New York, New York 10013. Address: 4646 Grove Street, Denver, Colorado 80211, U.S.A.

Individual Exhibitions:

1970	O. K. Harris Gallery, New York
1971	O. K. Harris Gallery, New York
1972	Wilmaro Gallery, Denver
1973	O. K. Harris Gallery, New York
1976	O. K. Harris Gallery, New York
1981	Tortue Gallery, Santa Monica, California
1982	Aspen Center for the Visual Arts, Colorado

Selected Group Exhibitions:

1970	*Annual Exhibition*, Whitney Museum, New York
1971	*Biennale*, Paris
1972	*Documenta 5*, Kassel, West Germany
1973	*Amerikansk Realism*, Lunds Konsthall, Sweden
1974	*Hyperréalistes Américains/Réalistes Européens*, Centre National d'Art Contemporain, Paris (toured Europe)
1976	*Aspects of Realism*, Rothman's of Pall Mall travelling exhibition, Stratford Art Gallery, Ontario (toured Canada, 1976-78)
1977	*The Nude: Avery and the European Masters*, Borgenicht Gallery, New York
1979	*7 on the Figurine*, Pennsylvania Academy of Fine Arts, Philadelphia
1981	*Contemporary American Realism Since 1960*, Pennsylvania Academy of Fine Arts, Philadelphia
1982	*Real, Really Real, Super Real*, San Antonio Museum of Art, Texas (travelled to Indianapolis, Tucson and Pittsburgh)
1988	*Figure It Out: Visual Body Language*, Helander Gallery, Palm Beach, Florida

Collections:

Everson Museum, Syracuse, New York; Neue Galerie, Aachen, West Germany.

Publications:

By DE ANDREA: article—"The Verist Sculptors: 2 Interviews: Duane Hanson and John De Andrea," with J. Masheck, in *Art in America* (New York), November/December 1972.

On DE ANDREA: books—*Hyperréalistes Américans/Realistes Européens*, exhibition catalogue, Paris 1974; *Aspects of Realism*, exhibition catalogue. Stratford, Ontario 1976; *Neue Formen des Realismus* by Peter Sager, Cologne 1974; *John De Andrea: Sculptures 1978-81*, exhibition catalogue with essay by Philip Yenaivine, Aspen, Colorado 1982; articles—"A New Realism in Sculpture" by Grace Glueck in *Art in America* (New York), November/December 1971; "Downtown Uptown, Not 10th Street" by John Perreault in the *Village Voice* (New York), December 1971; "Art in the Artist" by Emily Genauer in the *New York Post*, December 1971; "Neutral Style" by Edward Lucie-Smith in *Art and Artists* (London), August 1975; "Hyper-Realistic Dreiklang" in *Du* (Zurich), July 1979.

John De Andrea casts his figures straight from life, and equivalent of Photo Realism in 3-D. Still, however much his painted polyvinyl seems at first like living flesh, one would never take them for the people in the street. The people in the street are not young, untarnished, gracefully formed nudes. They have, besides, a beauty of gesture; they present a dynamic, rhythmic, harmonious composition of torso and limb as they leave or enter an embrace, play ball, lie easily asleep. It is this carefully caught grace of body and motion which has led to the classification of De Andrea's nudes as classic and ideal, in spite of his disclaimer: "How can you idealize from casts?"

It is true that he practices total honesty. Every fold of skin, every pore, every broken capillary, shows, yet in the models that he chooses there are few of these. By opposing the present, transitory beauty of the model's flesh to the imagined beauty of the classic past, the work comes off as emphasizing a transcendent loveliness in the here and now. The idealization lies in selection, of gesture and of model, just as with Pheidias the ideal form, the ideal act, was the one portrayed.

Seemingly unposed, these figures appear as studiedly dispassionate, objectified. They never address the observer directly through the gaze of their real-seeming eyes, and by this means a distance is created which sets off the work as art, not life, even more effectually than a frame would do. They are not nature caught as if by the camera, with all the attendant out-of-jointedness which accident, while freezing motion, can create, but something based on life, distilled and offered as apart from it.

As his work has developed in recent years, De Andrea has widened it to include, beside the recreation of single figures, the figure in dialog with another, sometimes as becoming itself, as for example in the artist—De Andrea complete with spattered jeans and beard—painting the sculpted model, Pygmalion catching himself in the act. There are also quotations from other works, like the *Déjeuner sur l'herbe*, into which the artist enters, a tableau in which the author joins.

By this means De Andrea has allied himself with the twentieth century tradition of offering the work of

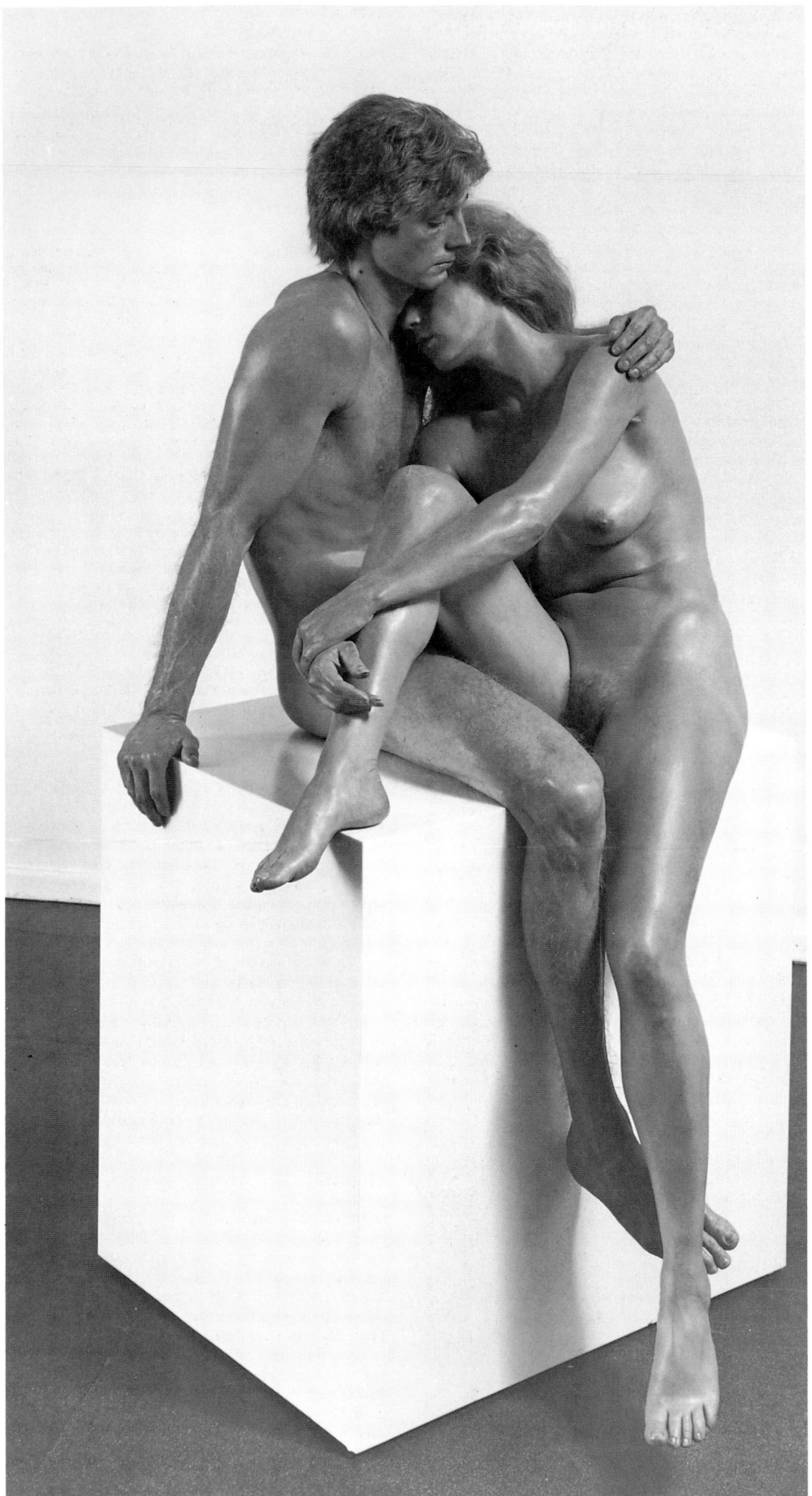

John De Andrea: *Seated Man and Woman,* 1981

art as comment on art, as in, say, Duchamp, but the difference seems to be that De Andrea still believes in and affirms the beauty of the human form.

—Barbara Cortright

de CAMARGO, Sergio.

Brazilian. Born in Rio de Janeiro, Brazil, 8 April 1930. Educated at Santo Inacio-Rio Champagnat, Buenos Aires, 1935–47; Faculty of Law, Buenos Aires, 1947–48; Faculté de Lettres, Paris, 1948–51; studied sociology and art, under Pierre Francastel, Ecole Pratique de Haute Etudes, Paris, 1961–64. Married Marie-Louise Berthodin in 1950; children: Cristovao, Carlos, and Maria; married Aspasia Brasiliero Alcantra in 1970. Recipient: Hors Concours, *Salón Nacional de Arte Moderna,* Rio de Janeiro, 1954; Acquisition Prize, *Salao Paulista de Arte Moderna,* Sao Paulo, 1954; International Sculpture Prize, *Biennale,* Paris, 1963; Gold Medal, Bienal, Sao Paulo, 1965; Stern Prize, Rio de Janeiro, 1965. Agents: Galeria Luis Buarque de Hollanda and Paulo Bittencourt, Rio de Janeiro; Gimpel Fils, 50 Davies Street, London W1, England; Gimpel and Hanover Galerie, Claridenstrasse 35, Zurich, Switzerland; Gimpel and Weitzenhoffer, 1040 Madison Avenue, New York, New York 10020, U.S.A. Address: c/o Galerie Luis Buarque de Hollanda and Paulo Bittencourt, 19 rua das Palmerias, Rio de Janeiro, Brazil.

Individual Exhibitions:

1958	Galerie GEA, Rio de Janeiro
	Galeria de Arte das Folhas, Sao Paulo
1964	Signals Gallery, London
1965	Museu de Arte Moderna, Rio de Janeiro
1966	*Biennale,* Venice
1967	Galleria del Naviglio, Milan
	Galleria del Obelisco, Rome
	Galleria La Polena, Genoa
1968	Gimpel Fils Gallery, London
	Galleria Notizie, Turin
	Galerie Buchholz, Munich
1969	Gimpel and Weitzenhoffer Gallery, New York
1970	Gimpel Fils Gallery, London
	Artestudio, Macerata, Italy
	Artestudio, Brescia, Italy
	Gallerie Grumholt, Oslo
	Galerie Buchholz, Munch
	Galerie M. Bochum, West Germany
1972	Estudio Actual, Caracas
	Galeria Collectio, Sao Paulo
	Petite Galeria, Rio de Janeiro
1974	Gimpel Fils Gallery, London
	Gallerie Gromholt, Oslo
	Museo de Arte Moderno, Mexico City
1975	Museu de Arte Moderna, Rio de Janeiro
	Galeria Luis Buarque de Hollanda and Paulo Bittencourt, Rio de Janeiro
	Galerie de Arte Global, Sao Paulo
1982	Gimpel Fils Galery, London

Selected Group Exhibitions:

1955	*Bienal,* Sao Paulo (and 1957, 1965)
1957	*Arte, Moderno Brasileo,* Buenos Aires (toured South America)
1963	*Biennale,* Paris
1965	*Mouvement II,* Gallerie Denise René, Paris
1966	*White Structures,* Kunsthalle, Bern
1967	*Structures et Mouvement,* Galerie Denise René, Paris
	Lumière et Mouvement, Musé d'Art Moderne, Paris
1968	*Documenta 4,* Kassel, West Germany
1969	*Vision 24,* Instituto Italo Americano, Rome
1974	*Basically White,* Institute of Contemporary Arts, London

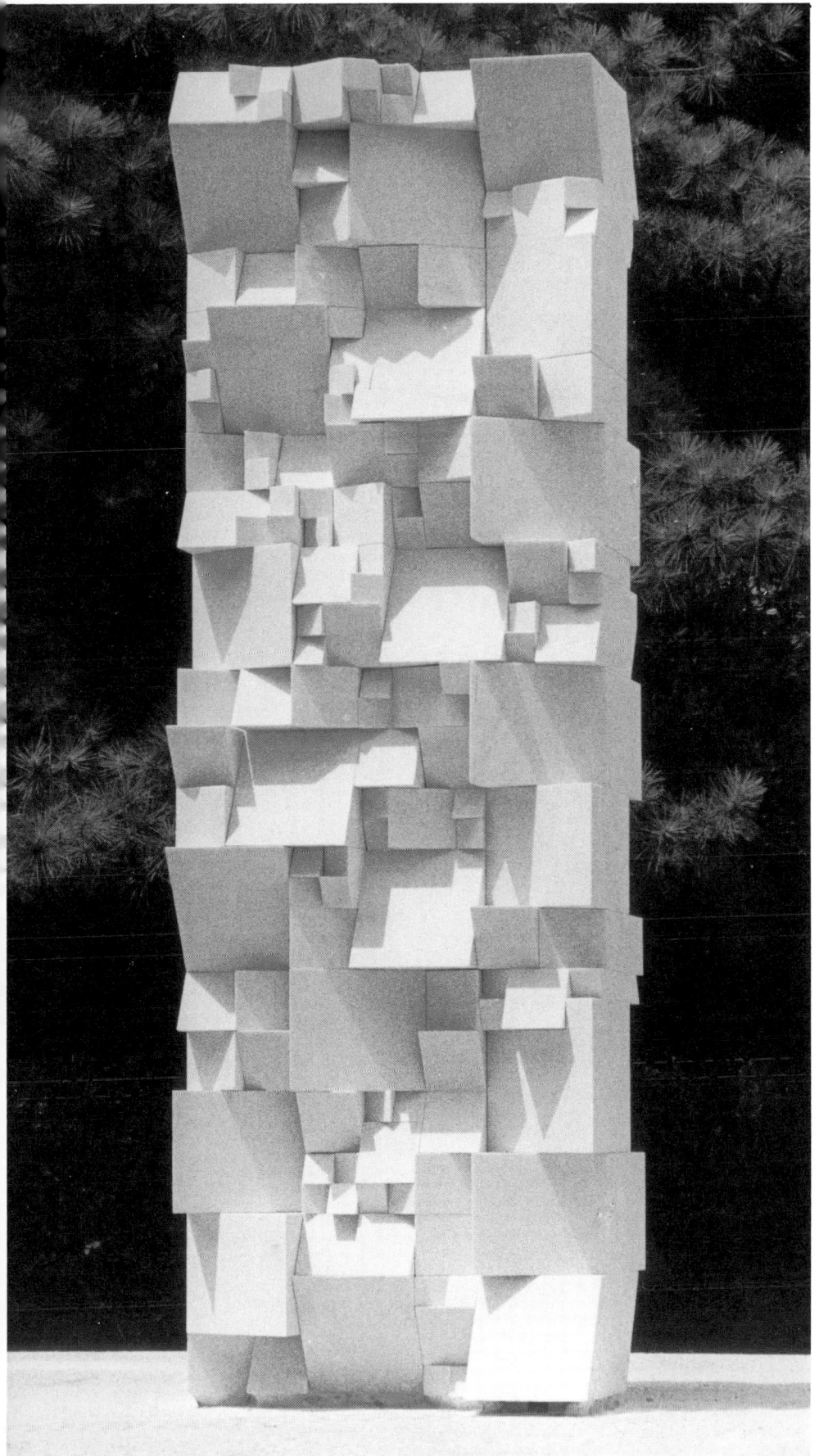

Sergio de Camargo: *Carrara Marble Piece*, **1972** Courtesy Gimpel Fils, London

Collections:

Museu Nacional de Belas Artes, Rio de Janeiro: Pinacoteca do Estadio, Sao Paulo; Museu de Arte Moderna, Sao Paulo; Museu de Arte Moderno, Mexico City; Albright-Knox Art Gallery, Buffalo, New York; Contemporary Art Society, London; Tate Gallery, London; Ulster Museum, Belfast; Galleria Nazionale d'Arte Moderna, Rome; Rijksmuseum Kröller-Müller, Otterlo Netherlands

Publications:

On de CAMARGO: books—*Camargo,* exhibition catalogue, by Jean Clay, London 1967; *Naissance de l'Art Cinetique* by Frank Popper, Paris 1967; *Optical and Kinetic Art* by Michael Compton, London 1967; *New Brazilian Art* by Pietro Maria Bardi, London 1970; *Sergio de Camargo,* exhibition catalogue with essay by Ronaldo Brito, London 1982; articles—"Sept Brasiliens de l'Ecole" by Georges Boudaille in *XX Siécle* (Paris), no. 22, 19634; "Camargo" by Denys Chevalier in *Aujourd-nui* (Paris) no 46, 1964; "Sergio de Camargo" by Stuart Penrose in *Arts Review* (London), no 28, 1965; "Camargo: Unica Gestaldo"; by Jaimé Mauricio in *Correio de la Manha* (Rio de Janeiro), November 1972; "Camargo" by Jasia Reichardt in *Architectural Design* (London), no. 3. 1974; "Camargo: Juegos Luminicos . . ." by Juan Acha in *Plural* (Mexico City), July 1975.

DE DOMINICIS, Gino.

Italian. Born in Ancona, Italy, in 1947. Settled in Rome, 1965. Address: c/o Galleria L'Attico, via del Babuino 114, 00187 Rome, Italy.

Individual Exhibitions:

1969	Galleria L'Attico, Rome
1970	Galleria Toselli, Milan
	Galleria L'Attico, Rome
1971	Galleria L'Attico, Rome
1979	Galleria Mario Pieroni, Rome (with Jannis Kounellis and Ettore Spalletti)

Selected Group Exhibitions:

1970	*Biennale d'Arte Contemporanea,* Bologna
	Group Exhibition, Galleria L'Attico, Rome
1971	*Comportamento e cose di 13 Uomini che invecchiano e muoiano,* Munich
1978	*Biennale,* Venice
1982	*Documenta,* Kassel, West Germany

Collections:

Stedelijk Museum, Amsterdam.

Publications:

On DE DOMINICIS: book—*L'Arte Moderna* by Renato Barilli, Milan 1975.

As one critic has observed, by 1970 Gino De Dominicis had become the most important "find" of the Galleria L'Attico where a year before he had held his one-man exhibition of "invisible" objects. "Invisible Pyramid" may serve as an example: here we have the square base of a pyramid drawn on the floor, while nearby there is a placard which gives the title of the work and the date. In 1970, at the same gallery, he exhibited "The Zodiac," a large work which demonstrates his own particular imaginative powers: here he has provided a very literal and concrete version of the zodiac in which a lion stands for Leo, a young woman for Virgo, and so forth. And in the same year De-

Dominicis participated in two group shows and made a statement which sums up his aesthetic: "To have true existence, things must be eternal and immortal. "Invisibility" and "ubiquity" are also key concepts rendered in mythic terms: it is immortality which is the greatest attribute of the gods, and as was the case with "The Zodiac," artistic representation involves a kind of anthropomorphism. He asserted his position once again in the Venice *Biennale* of 1972 and caused a scandal by placing a mongoloid on display as the symbol of a particular attitude towards death. This goes to the center of De Dominicis' work: the victory over death which proves man's genuine existence. His basic assumption is that without immortality there is no true life. Thus the mongoloid became a symbol of the triumph of life over death: he is indifferent to fate or change or death: he simply exists.

The boundaries of De Dominicis' art are the cosmic and the mythic. He uses archetypal images to provoke esoteric sensations and emphasizes once again the ability to overcome the laws of nature. To this end he also uses the discoveries of technology and the efforts of science to conquer death. In "Greeting Card" (1971) he seems to be wishing immortality of the body for everyone. For him immortality means the capacity to overcome nature, in terms drawn from myth and evolutionary struggle. "Attempt at Flight," for example, is a video-tape produced by Gerry Schum in 1970 in which the artist makes repeated attempts to fly. Once more De Dominicis is struggling to overcome the natural order and limits of things: the laws of nature are what bind man to one place and time, and force him to grow old. To transcend even one of these limitations would be to prove the possibility of attaining the great goal of immortality.

—Roberto G. Lambarelli

DEEM, George.

American. Born in Vincennes, Indiana, 18 August 1932. Studied, under Paul Wieghardt and Boris Margo, at the School of the Art Institute of Chicago, 1950–51, 1953–57, B.F.A. 1957; under Willi Baumeister, Stuttgart. 1951–52. Served in the United States Army. 1951–53. Restoration Assistant, Metropolitan Museum of Art, New York, 1958–60; Assistant to Josef Albers, School of Fine Arts, Yale University, New Haven, Connecticut, 1960–61. Independent artist since 1960; lives and works in New York; spent 1970 living and working in Cortana and Arezzo, Italy. Painting Instructor, College of Art and Technology, Leicester, England, 1966–67, and University of Pennsylvania, Philadelphia. 1968–69; Visiting Artist, Illinois State University, Normal, 1982. Agents: Nancy Hoffman Gallery, 429 West Broadway, New York, New York 10012; Merida Gallery, 2007 Frankfort Avenue, Louisville, Kentucky 40206. Address: 10 West 18th Street, New York, New York 10011, U.S.A.

Individual Exhibitions:

1962	Allan Stone Gallery, New York
1963	Allan Stone Gallery, New York
1964	Allan Stone Gallery, New York
	Merida Gallery, Louisville, Kentucky
1965	Goodman Gallery, Buffalo, New York
	Allan Stone Gallery, New York
1966	Allan Stone Gallery, New York
1968	Allan Stone Gallery, New York
	Merida Gallery, Louisville, Kentucky
1969	Ferrier Gallery, Houston
	Allan Stone Gallery, New York
1974	*Paintings and Drawings,* Indianapolis Museum of Art (travelled to the Witte Memorial Museum, San Antonio, Texas)

1975	Allan Stone Gallery, New York
1979	*The Making of a Masterpiece: Recent Paintings.* Evansville Museum of Arts and Sciences, Indiana

Selected Group Exhibitions:

1964	*Nieuwe Realisten,* Gemeentemuseum, The Hague (toured the Netherlands and West Germany)
	4 American Painters, Yale University, New Haven, Connecticut
1968	*New Realism,* Walker Art Center, Minneapolis
1969	*Painting and Sculpture Today,* Indianapolis Museum of Art
1972	*Recent Accessions 1966–1972,* Indianapolis Museum of Art
1974	*Contemporary American Painting and Sculpture 1974,* University of Illinois, Urbana
1978	*Artists Look at Art,* Spencer Museum of Art, University of Kansas, Lawrence
	Art about Art, Whitney Museum, New York
1981	*Contemporary American Realism since 1960,* Pennsylvania Academy of Fine Arts, Philadelphia

Collections:

Memorial Art Museum, Rochester, New York; Albright-Knox Art Gallery, Buffalo, New York; Hirshhorn Museum and Sculpture Garden, Washington, D.C.; J. B. Speed Museum, Louisville, Kentucky; Oberlin College, Ohio; Indianapolis Museum of Art; Museum of Art, Houston; San Francisco Museum of Modern Art; Neue Galerie, Aachen, West Germany.

Publications:

By DEEM: books—*Bruna Seviri, Sun and Moon,* with Ronald Vance, 1978; *Aanababcac, Sun and Moon,* 1979; *Mona Lisa Washington, Zone,* 1980; *Extra Genre, White Walls,* 1981.

On DEEM: books—*The New Realism* by Udo Kultermann, New York 1972; *Recent Accessions 1966–1972,* exhibition catalogue, Indianapolis 1972; *Deem: An Exhibition of Paintings and Drawings,* exhibition catalogue, Indianapolis, 1974; *The New Painting* by Udo Kultermann, Tübingen, West Germany 1975; articles—"Painting Lists" by Ronald Vance in *Art and Artists* (London), February 1968; "George Deem" by Edgar Buenaquiro in *Arts Magazine* (New York), November 1977; "Vermeer and Contemporary American Painting" by Udo Kultermann in *American Art Review* (Los Angeles), November 1978.

Back home in Indiana, some of the women back home in Indiana give remnants of fabric that could be useful for making quilts to their friends, and the women are made very happy who receive the scraps of cloth and who give them. Reproductions of my paintings are satisfying. My paintings are paintings of reproductions, and when my paintings in turn become reproductions a circuit is completed. It is now Thursday. Two people have come to my loft this week and between them bought three drawings and what up until now was a lost week of too many things to do and of too many people is not a lost week after all but just a week wearing a different face from the weeks when all I do is paint. Tomorrow I am going to Philadelphia to visit the art museum and a friend. Other friends I have been seeing now it is summer are come to dinner and meet new people friends, and I go to dinners and I meet new people and the cooking is usually good and the vodka and tonic everybody offers this year and going to Fire Island every few weeks for a few days and coming home to my loft where everything is as usual and I realize again that all the play world I have been visiting in is like a Saturday afternoon movie when I was a boy that I thought of all the next week on the farm and I could never really get to to the movie again not even when I went back and saw it again. One has always a style and an attitude to work with or against. Archaic: A time when everything that had been taken as given breaks up. Some artists

George Deem: *Still Life with Rug*, 1970

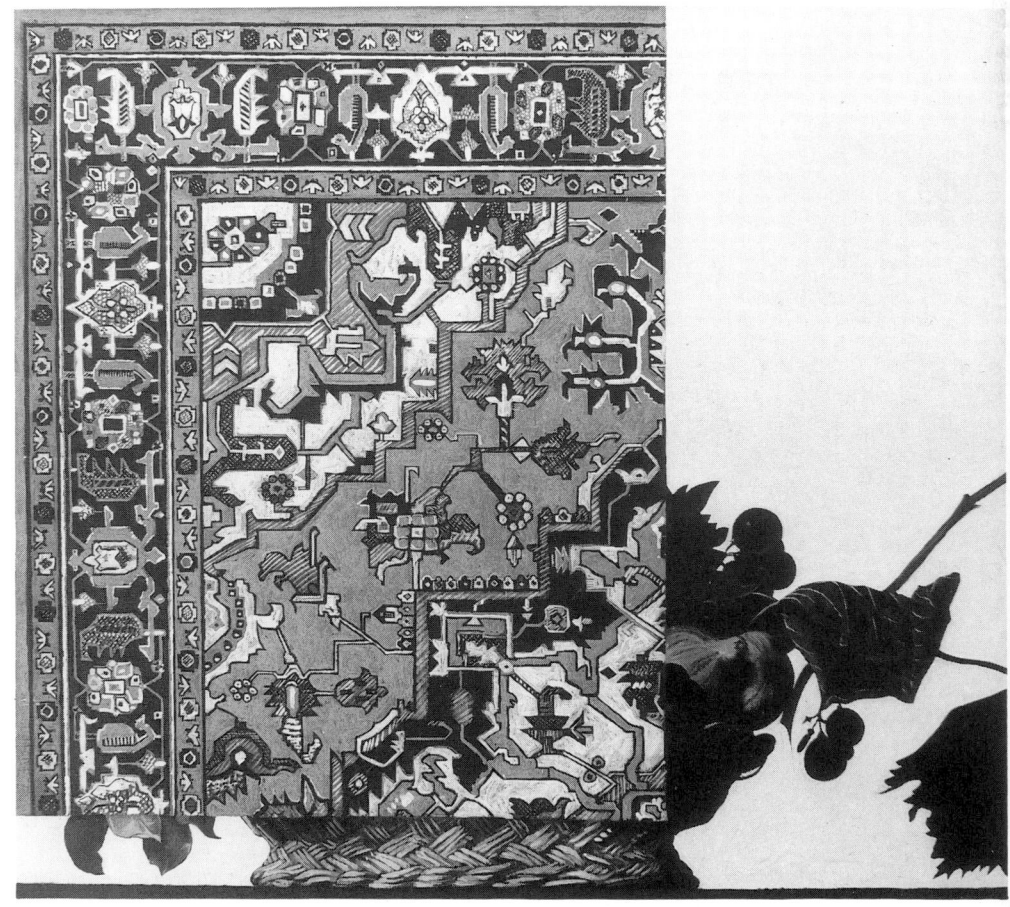

continue by trying to pour new wine into broken bottles. Archaic. There may be several pockets of space but the one we are in is the one we know. When Marcel Duchamp went to look out of the window he used to bump his forehead against the pane. Every work of art calls upon the spectator to continue it. Most of the time it is this way: I have worked harder on paintings that are merely inevitable than on paintings that are miraculously unforeseeably themselves; and if one is ever to paint any unforeseen paintings it does seem one has to work hard to complete a very large number of merely inevitable paintings until one comes at last no longer to think about any such thing at all.

—George Deem

The paintings of George Deem are devoted to the exploration and rediscovery of prefigurated themes of art from the past. He uses images of paintings by artists such as Vermeer, Caravaggio, Rubens and Rogier van der Weyden as subject matter to express a contemporary sensibility revitalizing and translating the themes of the old masters. It is, therefore, necessary for the viewer to have a pre-knowledge of the original work in order to fully appreciate the fresh adaptation. The re-cycling and complexity of dealing with the source is a serious form of contemporary painting and reflects the historic dimension in contemporary art.

One of the major thematic sources for Deem is the work of Vermeer van Delft, whose paintings are often used by Deem as a point of departure from which new and exciting results are achieved. Vermeer's images are transformed to a contemporary level which finds an equivalent in Deem's masterly painting technique. In several of his works Deem identifies with the artist from the past by translating past centuries into the 20th century. Through this identification new aspects of the content are introduced, thereby constituting the earlier work into a more complex one in which old and new are combined.

In other paintings by Deem new aspects of serial art have emerged. Following the pioneering examples by Jasper Johns and Andy Warhol, Deem added a new variation to the theme in paintings such as "Eight Women" (1967). Another innovative aspect of his work can be seen in a complex combination of historic images. One such example is "Mona Lisa Washington" of 1972, which is a combination of two images from different sources painted into one new complex form inaugurating an interpersonal figuration. The dimension of this complex image has yet to be fully appreciated.

The work of George Deem between 1960 and 1982 is of consistent character in its exploration of thematic prefigurations which relate art of our time to art of the past. His work transcends the concept of the avantgarde and is one of the many parallels in the spectrum of contemporary art.

—Udo Kultermann

DE FOREST, Roy (Dean).

American. Born in North Platte, Nebraska, 11 February 1930. Educated at Yakima Junior College, Washington, 1948-50, A.A. 1950; studied painting, drawing, astrology and meteorology, California School of Fine Arts, San Francisco, with Edward Corbett, Hassel Smith, Elmer Bischoff, James Budd Dixon and David Park, 1950-52; San Francisco State College, with Alexander Nepote, Seymour Locks, Dr. May Byrce, 1952-53, 1956-58, B.A. 1953, M.A. 1958. Served as a Specialist 3rd Class, 3rd Engineering Regiment, United States Army, Fort Lewis, Washington, 1953-55. Married Gloria Scott in 1974; daughter: Oriana. Children's Painting Instructor and Gallery Assistant, San Francisco Museum of Art, 1955-58; Instructor, and Director of the Larson Gallery, Yakima Junior College, Washington, 1958-60; Art Instructor, Contra Costa Junior College, San Pablo, California, 1960-61; Painting Instructor, San Francisco State College, 1961-62; Art Instructor, Junior Center of Arts and Sciences, Oakland, California 1963, and San Quentin Prison, California 1964; Painting Instructor, California College of Arts and Crafts, Oakland 1964-65. Lecturer and Associate Professor, University of California at Davis, since 1965. Chairman, Artists Council, San Francisco Art Association, 1964. Recipient: San Francisco Art Association Award, 1954; Purchase Prize, Bay Printmakers' Society, Oakland Art Museum, California, 1956; Nealie Sullivan Award, San Francisco Art Institute, 1962; Purchase Prize, La Jolla Museum of Art, California, 1965; National Endowment for the Arts Fellowship, 1972. Agents: Allan Frumkin Gallery Inc., 50 West 57th Street, New York, New York 10019; Hansen Fuller Gallery, 228 Grant Avenue, San Francisco, California 94569, U.S.A. Address: P.O. Box 47, Porta Costa, California 94569, U.S.A.

Individual Exhibitions:

1955	East and West Gallery, San Francisco
1958	East and West Gallery, San Francisco
1959	Stone Court Gallery, Yakima, Washington
1960	Stone Court Gallery, Yakima, Washington
	Dilexi Gallery, San Francisco
1962	Dilexi Gallery, Los Angeles
	San Francisco Art Association
1963	Dilexi Gallery, San Francisco
1966	Allan Frumkin Gallery, New York
	Peninsula Gallery, Menlo Park, California
	Dilexi Gallery, San Francisco
1967	Dilexi Gallery, San Francisco
	City College of Sacramento
1968	Candy Store Gallery, Folsom, California
1969	San Francisco Art Institute
	Cowell College, University of California at Santa Cruz
1971	Gallery Marc, Washington, D.C.
	The Fantasy Watercolors of Roy De Forest/The Sculpture World of David Gihooly, Leadville Galleries, Sun Valley, Idaho
	Candy Store Gallery, Folsom, California
	Manolides Gallery, Seattle
	California Palace of the Legion of Honor, San Francisco
	Hansen Fuller, Gallery, San Francisco
1972	Manolides Gallery, Seattle
	Allan Frumkin Gallery, New York
1973	Hansen Fuller Gallery, San Francisco
	Allan Frumkin Gallery, Chicago
1974	San Francisco Museum of Modern Art (retrospective; travelled to Fort Worth Art Center Museum, Texas; Utah Museum of Fine Art, Salt Lake City; and Whitney Museum, New York)
	Galerie Darthea Speyer, Paris
	Glenbow-Alberta Gallery, Calgary
1975	Hansen-Fuller Gallery, San Francisco
	Allan Frumkin Gallery, New York
1976	Hansen Fuller Gallery, San Francisco
	Fendrick Gallery, Washington, D.C.
1977	Galerie Darthea Speyer, Paris
	Allan Frumkin Gallery, New York
	Clark-Benton Gallery, Sante Fe, New Mexico
	Institute of Contemporary Arts, Boston (with Robert Hudson)
1978	Hansen Fuller Gallery, San Francisco
1979	Fresno City College Art Space Gallery, California
1980	Crocker Art Museum, Sacramento, California

Selected Group Exhibitions:

1968	*West Coast Now*, Portland Art Museum, Oregon
1971	*California Works on Paper 1950-1971*, University of California Art Museum, Berkeley
1973	*Extraordinary Realities*, Whitney Museum, New York
1975	*Painting and Sculpture in California: The Modern Era*, San Francisco Museum of Modern Art
1976	*3 from California*, Dalhousie Art Gallery, Halifax
1977	*New in the 70's*, University of Texas Art Museum, Austin
	Recent Works on Paper, Madison Art Center, Wisconsin
1978	*West Coast Artists*, New Gallery of Contemporary Art, Cleveland
	Late 20th Century Art, Virginia Commonwealth University, Richmond
1984	*The Human Condition*, San Francisco Museum of Modern Art

Collections:

California College of Arts and Craft, Oakland; Oakland Art Museum; University of California Art Museum, Berkeley; San Francisco Museum of Modern Art; Crocker Art Gallery, Sacramento, California; Stanford University Museum of Art, California; Arizona State University, Tempe; Art Institute of Chicago; Weatherspoon Gallery, University of North Carolina; Philadelphia Museum of Art.

Publications:

On DE FOREST: books—*Roy De Forest*, exhibition catalogue, San Francisco 1963; *Roy De Forest: Retrospective*, exhibition catalogue, San Francisco 1974; *Roy De Forest: Retrospective*, exhibition catalogue, by John Humphrey, New York 1975; *Roy De Forest*, exhibition catalogue with essay by Roger D. Clisby, Sacramento, 1980; articles—"San Francisco" by David Zack in *Art News* (New York), September 1969; "Stepped-up Pitch, Color in Roy De Forest Art" in *San Francisco Chronicle*, 21, November 1969; "Another Part of De Forest" by Charles Johnson in the *Sacramento Bee* (Sacramento, California), 21 March 1971; "De Forest Is De Forest Is De Forest" by Juris Prudence in *Artweek* (Oakland, California), 27 November 1971; "Art" by Hilton Kramer in the *New York Times*, 22 January 1972; "A Master of Fantasy" by Alfred Frankenstein in the *San Francisco Chronicle*, 8 March 1973; "The National Scene: San Francisco" by Jerome Tarshish in *Art News* (New York), May 1973; "Smutty Jokes by Sophisticated Yokels" by Hilton Kramer in the *New York Times*, October 1973; "De Forest Amuses with His Fantasy Art" by Hilton Kramer in the *New York Times*, 29 March 1975; review by Da Vinci in *Soho Weekly New* (New York), 10 April 1975.

One day while talking to an obscure poet, I expressed my belief in the artificer as an eccentric individual creating fantasy art with the amazing intention of totally building a miniature cosmos into which the artful alchemist could retire with all his friends, animals and paraphernalia.

And so said we, "The work of peculiar and eccentric, fastidious being can truly be described as the mechanic and conductor of the convoluted, rambling, roundabout vehicle of journey to central Tibet in the company of a French Count and his constant companion, a mangy sheepdog of Lombardy. The mechanical artificer travels in a phantasmagoric micro-world, small and infinitely compact, as the light of a dwarf star imploding inward as it collapses paradise and hell to one vanishing whole, while we are forever with our joys, sorrows and unrequited love. A black hole in the reconstructed night is mysterious and hermetic in the darkness, slyly cunning and opulent in the firelight."

"Furthermore," wrote an obscene hyena, "Maniacal art is a squirrel in the forest of visual delights." "Scenic nature art constitutes a scarlet robot striding forward immune to the light of distant street lamps," announced the horse of a different color. "Tinted canvas beckons the dogmatic fellow to antisocial aristocracy," shouted Rover, a domesticated but still recalcitrant Dingo. "I give a howl to the phantasmagoric artist," barked Samuel Johnson, distinguished short-haired poet of the Terriers. He growled, "Oh how I abhor the fond lap dogs, the surly spaniels—those clever thieves of current taste. And what is current taste but old desires made palatable by present boredom."

All of us, obscure poet, myself (obscure visual

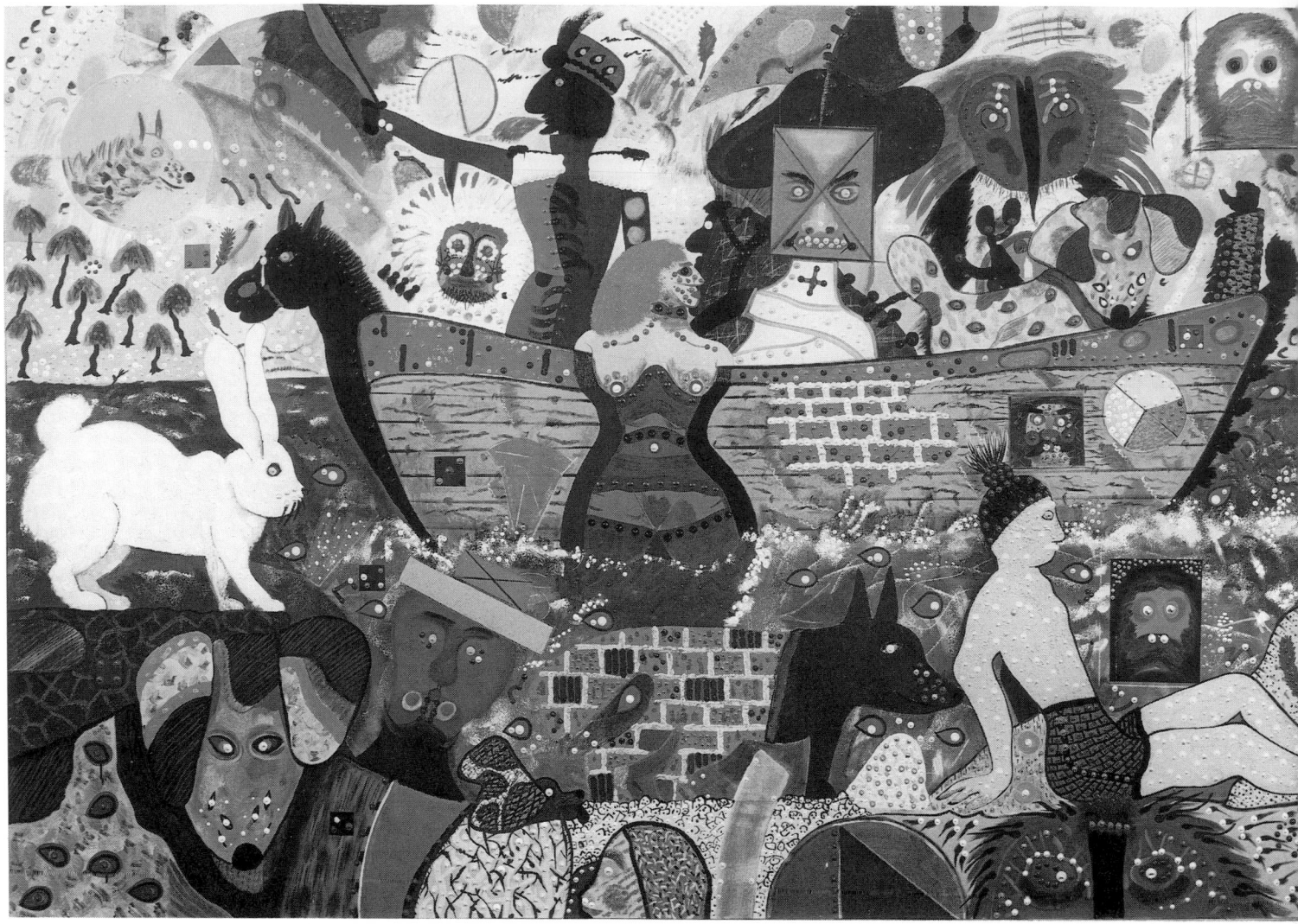

Roy De Forest: *On the Sea Wall,* 1976

constructor of mechanical delights), a travelling French Count and his mangy sheepdog, a black mongrel of the night, an obscene hyena, Samuel Johnson (distinguished Terrier), and Rover (domesticated Dingo) shouted, barked and howled, "Picturesque art is now and forever the hope of the future as well as the dream of the past."

"All too true," lisped the horse of a different color as he stood marking the earth with his translucent hooves. Would that I could have read the significance of those abstract channels chiselled in the moist earth.
—Roy De Forest

"See Through Jane," 1970, has a vacant-looking woman, with animals placed in a television set occupying her mind. Dabs of paint are placed on the edges of the frame, remaining stiffened and upright. These characteristic dabs of Roy De Forest are like circus lights framing our arrival at the carnival. All of De Forest's paintings are circus-colored and candy-treated. De Forest's animals serve as testament to a double-edged appreciation. They both haunt and please.

These worlds of De Forest, peculiar to themselves, having few people we know who inhibit them, directly treat our imaginative life and our sense of how we travel in the internal world. A number of recent color drawings have no titles, yet are easily distinguishable from each other because of certain standoffish figures. A woman with a pink face appears to be spitting. A man with a red and yellow face, with musical hieroglyphic notes on his face, appears to have x-ray vision. Other untitled drawings include a population of spitters, cylindrical robot-like men, tall-hatted men, and rabbits, horses and coyotes. All

the animals look out at the viewer through the window of the canvas. As in one drawing, there is an attenuated excursion through the desert mountains with a friend and dog.

De Forest has worked in the color art land of the University of California at Davis, where, with his, the careers of Thiebaud, Nauman and Arneson were also developing. Strangely enough, color appears masked in the real countryside of Davis, and all the animals appear hidden to general, immediate observation. Always, delightful miscalculations of crisscrossed people and animals, party hats, over-sized glasses, long shoes.

—John Robinson

DE KEYSER, Raoul.

Belgian. Born in Deinze, 29 August 1930. Studied art at the Academie of Deinze, 1963. Served as adjunct in the welfare section, Belgian Army, in West Germany, 1950–51. Married Dina Baudoneq in 1952; children: Luc, Piet and Jan. Independent painter, Deinze, since 1963. Non-teaching Adjunct Advisor, University of Ghent, since 1970. Recipient: Jeune Peinture Belge Prize, Brussels, 1967. Address: Kouterlosstraat 118, 9800 Deinze, Belgium.

Individual Exhibitions:

1965   Galerie Drieghe, Wetteren, Belgium

        Kaleidoskoop, Ghent
1966   Galerie Les Contemporains, Brussels
        3 Vlaamse Schilders, Groninger Museum, Groningen, Netherlands (with Elias and Raveel)
1967   Celbeton, Dendermonde, Belgium
        M.A.S., Deinze, Belgium
1968   Galerie Contour, Brussels
        Galerie Kaleidoskoop, Ghent
1969   Galerie Les Contemporains, Brussels
1970   Galerie Denise-Emmanual, Brussels
        Korrekelder, Bruges
        Galerie Richard Foncke, Ghent
        Museum, Antwerp
        Groninger Museum, Groningen, Netherlands
        Museum, Haarlem, Netherlands
        Museum, 'sHertogenbosch, Netherlands
1971   Galerie de Vaart, Hilversum, Netherlands
        Galerie Plus-Kern, Ghent
1972   Galerie Ado, Bonheiden, Belgium
        Galerie Grafiek 50, Wakken, Belgium
        Galerie Plus-Kern, Ghent
1973   Galerie Aksent, Waregem, Belgium
        Provinciaal Begijnhof, Hasselt, Belgium
1974   Van Abbemuseum, Eindhoven, Netherlands (with Amedée Cortier)
        Galerie de Mangelgang, Groningen, Netherlands
1975   Galerie Aksent, Waregem, Belgium
        E v H Loringhoven Galerie, Ghent
        Neue Galerie, Aachen, West Germany (with Norbert Heyers)
1976   Galerie de Mangelgang, Groningen, Netherlands
        Galerie Grafiek 50, Wakken, Belgium
1977   Galerie Drieghe, Wetteren, Belgium
        Wittepoppetoren, Hasselt, Belgium (with Hugo Duchâteau)
1978   Galerie Jeanne Buytaert, Antwerp

Galerie Jean Leroy, Paris
Museum van Hedendaagse Kunst, Ghent
1979 Galerie Waalkens, Finsterwolde, Netherlands
Bilder 1976–1978, Belgisches Haus, Cologne
1980 Galerie Declercq, Knokke, Belgium
Galerie Jeanne Buytaert, Antwerp
International Cultureel Centrum, Antwerp
1982 Kunsthandel Lambert Tegenbosch, Heusden aan de
Maas, Netherlands
Galerie Richard Foncke, Ghent, Belgium
1983 Vereniging Aktuele Kunst Gewad, Ghent, Belgium
1984 Villa des Roses, Ghent, Belgium
1985 Dam 43, Middelburg, Netherlands
Galerie Drieghe, Wetteren, Belgium
Ado, Bonheiden, Belgium
1986 Museum Mw. J. Dhondt-Dhaenens, Deurle, Bel-
gium
Paleis voor Schone Kunsten, Brussels
1987 Vereniging voor het Museum van Hedendaagse
Kunst, Ghent, Belgium
Villa des Roses, Ghent, Belgium

Selected Group Exhibitions:

1967 *Premio Lissone,* Milan
1968 *Alternative Attuali 3,* L'Aquila, Italy

Raoul De Keyser: *Knauw,* 1984

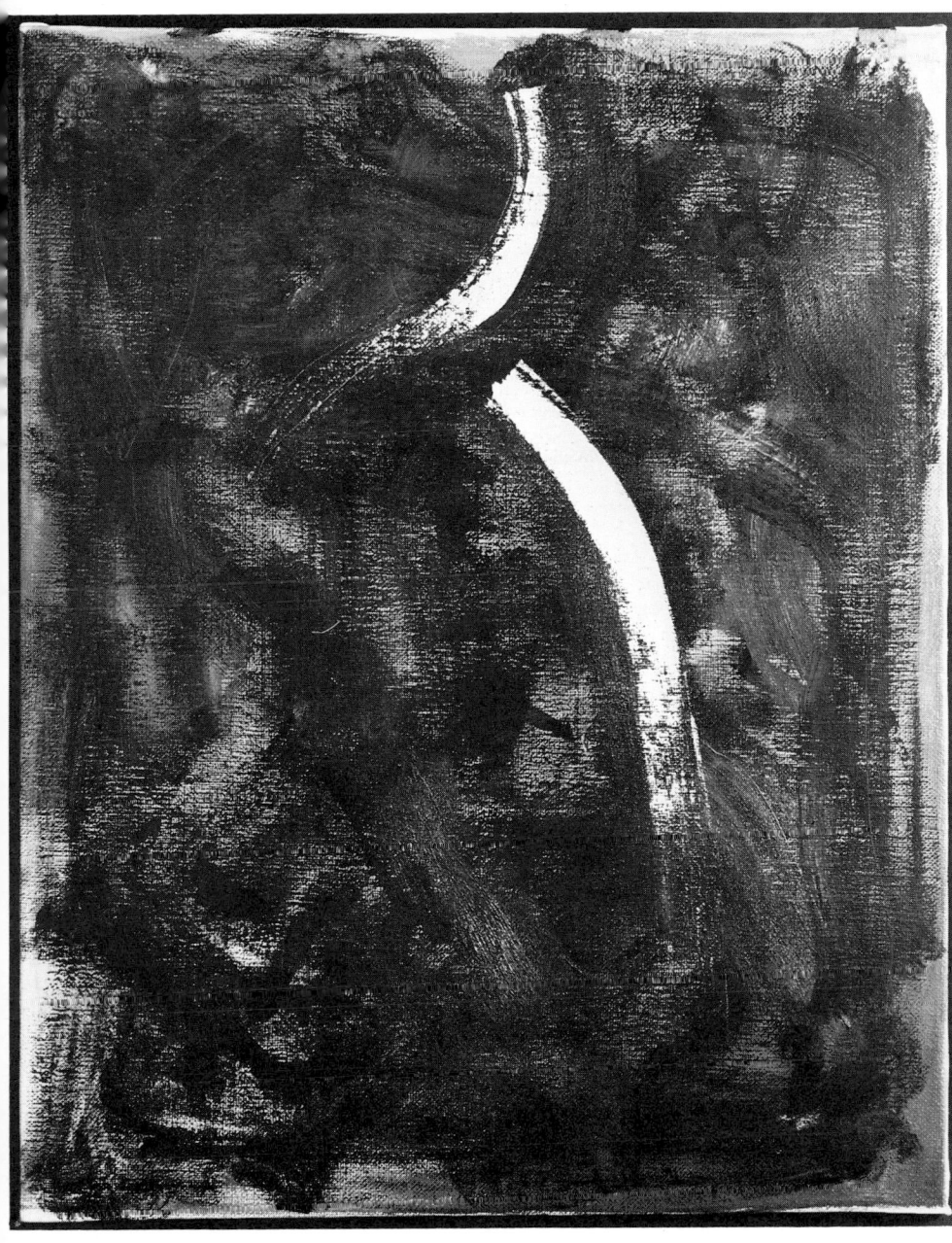

1971 *D'Aprés,* Museo Civico, Lugano, Switzerland
Bienal, Sao Paul
1973 *Fortunately There Is Still Some Grass,* Camden Arts
Centre, London
1974 *3rd Triennale,* Bruges
1975 *Concerning Painting,* Museum van Bommel—Van
Dam, Venlo, Netherlands (toured the Netherlands)
1980 *Beervelde 1966—nu,* De Vleeshal, Middelburg,
Netherlands
Belgie–Nederland: Kunst na '45, Palais des Beaux-
Arts, Brussels (travelled to the Museum Boymans-
van Beuningen, Rotterdam)
1986 *Een keuze/un choix,* KunstRAI, Amsterdam

Collections:

Museum van Hedendaages Kunst, Ghent; Groeninge Museum, Bruges; Museum voor Schone Kunsten, Courtrai, Belgium; Provinciaal Museum, De Lakenhalle, Ypres, Belgium;
Gemeentekrediet van Belgie, Brussels; Museum, Dienze,
Belgium; Groninger Museum, Groningen, Netherlands; Museum voor Moderne Kunst, Brussels.

Publications:

By DE KEYSER: book—*More Is Less,* with Roland Jooris,
Deinze, 1972.

On DE KEYSER: books—*Raoul De Keyser,* exhibition cata-
logue, with text by Roland Jooris and Paul Vries, Groningen,
Netherlands 1970; *Raoul De Keyser: Het samengaan van ge-
geven en schilderij* by Roland Jooris, Wakken, Belgium 1972;
Raoul De Keyser: Nota najaar 73, by Roland Jooris, Deinze,
Belgium 1973; *Amedée Cortier and Raoul De Keyser,* exhibition catalogue, with text by Yves De Smet and Roland Jooris,
Eindhoven, Netherlands 1974; *Raoul De Keyser* with text by
Roland Jooris, Antwerp 1978; *Raoul De Keyser,* exhibition
catalogue, with texts by Jan Hoet, Marc Callewaert and Ro-
land Jooris, Ghent 1978; *Raoul De Keyser: Bilder 1976–
1978,* exhibition catalogue, with text by Roland Jooris,
Cologne 1979; *Raoul De Keyser,* exhibition catalogue, with
text by Roland Jooris, Heusden, Netherlands, 1982; *Raoul
De Keyser,* exhibition catalgoue with text by Bart De Baere,
Deurle 1986; *Raoul De Keyser,* exhibition catalogue with text
by Olivier Hamerlynck, Ghent 1987.

DEKKERS, Ad(rian).
Dutch. Born in Nieuwpoort, Netherlands, 21 March
1938. Studied at the Art Academy, Rotterdam, 1954–
58. Married; had one child. Independent full-time
painter and sculptor, Gorcum, from 1960. *Died (in
Gorcum, Netherlands) 27 February 1974.*

Individual Exhibitions:

1961 Galerie t'Venster, Rotterdam (with van Munster)
1962 Galerie de Drie Hendricken, Amsterdam (with van
Munster)
1964 De Bijenkorf, Rotterdam
Galerie de Nieuwe Doelen, Gorinchem, Netherlands
(with Joost Balijeu)
Kunststichtung de Lijnbaan, Rotterdam
1965 Galerie Walenkmap, Leiden
Galerie Swart, Amsterdam
1966 Galerie Reflex, Hilversum, The Netherlands
Galerie Swart, Amsterdam
Stedelijk Museum, Schiedam, The Netherlands
(with Koetsier)
1967 Stedelijk Museum, Amsterdam
Technical College, Delft, Netherlands
Galerie Orez, The Hague
1968 Museum voor Stad en Lande, Groningen, The Neth-
erlands
Galerie Walenkmap, Leiden
Stedelijk Museum, Amsterdam
Galerie Orez, The Netherlands
Galerie der Spiegel, Cologne
Galerie ad Libitum, Antwerp
1969 Galerie Dorothea Loehr, Frankfurt
1970 Stedelijk van Abbemuseum, Eindhoven, Netherlands
Plus Kern, Ghent
1971 Galerie Swart, Amsterdam
Galerie M, Bochum, West Germany
1972 Gemeentemuseum, The Hague
1973 Lucy Milton Gallery, London
1974 Stedelijk van Abbemuseum, Eindhoven, Netherlands
Rosa Esman Gallery, New York
Kunsthalle, Dusseldorf
1977 Rijksmuseum Kröller-Müller, Otterlo, Netherlands
1982 Staatliche Kunsthalle, Baden-Baden, West Germany

Selected Group Exhibitions:

1964 *Stichting Liga Nieuwe Beelden,* Stedelijk Museum,
Amsterdam
1965 *4th Biennal des Jeunes Artistes,* Musée d'Art Moderne de la Ville, Paris
1966 *Weiss auf Weiss,* Kunsthalle, Berne
1967 *Dutch Contemporary Art,* at the *Expo '67,* Montreal
1968 *Kleur Object,* Middelheim Open Air Museum, Antwerp
1968 *10 Dutch Artists,* Midland Group Gallery, Nottingham (toured the U.K.)
1970 *Sammlung Etzold,* Kunstverein, Cologne, West Germany

1971	*Tendances Constructivistes dans l'Art Hollandais après 1945*, Musée des Beaux-Arts, Liége, Belgium
1972	*Amsterdam/Paris/Dusseldorf*, Guggenheim Museum, New York
1973	*Lof der Tekenkunst*, Stedelijk van Abbemuseum, Eindhoven, Netherlands

Collections:

Stedelijk Museum, Amsterdam; Stedelijk van Abbe Museum, Eindhoven, Netherlands; Rijksmuseum Kröller-Müller, Otterlo, Netherlands; Museum voor Stad en Lande, Groningen, Netherlands; Gemeentemuseum, The Hague; Museum Boymans van Beuningen, Rotterdam; Stedelijk Museum, Schiedam, Netherlands; Tate Gallery, London; McCrory Corporation, New York.

Publications:

By DEKKERS: articles—"Statement on My Work" in *Structure* (Amsterdam), no. 6, 1964; *Inleiding*, exhibition catalogue, Utrecht 1969; "Over de Lijn" in *Museumsjournaal* (Amsterdam), December 1971.

On DEKKERS: books—*Dekkers* by Jean Leering, Frankfurt 1973; *Ad Dekkers*, exhibition catalogue with texts by Siegmar Holtzen and Katharina Schjmidt. Baden-Baden 1982; articles—"Modern Dutch Art" by Enno Develing in *Art and Artists* (London), October 1969; "Dutch Commentary Drawings in Holland" by Carol Blotkamp in *Studio International* (London), December 1970; "Shifted Squares and Quartering by a Left to Right Sawn Groove" by M. Vos in *Studio International* (London), May 1973; "Ad Dekkers," obituary, by Liesbeth Brandt Corstius in *Studio International* (London), May 1974.

The early death of Dekkers robbed the world and Holland in particular of one of the most successful sculptors in the constructivist vein. In terms of association it has been suggested that he is a natural descendant aesthetically of the de Stijl experimentalist Van Doesburg (not in the early distortions of figuration—like Van Doesburg's famous canvases of the cow, starting with semi-realism and winding up in subtle sotto-voce abstract symbols—but rather in that artist's excursions into unreal architectural design); and, in the late fifties and early sixties a degree of style-contact in Dekkers' work of that time can also be discerned which shows a kinship with methods employed by the Swiss artists Lohse and Max Bill. Development leading to his final stage of uncomplicated and absolutist reliefs went through a gradual refinement over the years.

First serious art works from Dekkers had taken the form of exact realism. But when this ceased to satisfy his artistic intentions, he allowed these images to become modulated and eventually to go increasingly geometric in concept. Internationally, it is the ultimate parting from any form of realistic imagery that this artist took which made his final style most familiar to the global framework of contemporary modern art.

There had come a time in the progress of his creativity when he abandoned painting 'pictures' altogether, settling instead for flat reliefs and other low-level reliefs where the only variant would be a straightline incision (carved into the wood at a rising or falling level). Literally his output had become confined to rectangles, squares, triangles and circles. (towards the end of his life Dekkers switched from 'working drawings' to graphic work which could stand on its own rather than act as a guide to creation of a new relief. Sometimes as plain in character as the reliefs themselves, on occasions he did also investigate the promises extended by straightline shading, maybe dividing the square with a diagonal line, but shading the resultant triangles in different straightline intensities and in so doing evoking a visual attraction, magnetic and magic in its compulsion).

Reliefs—and drawings—were the constructed fulfilment to his demanding ambition: total clarity. Perhaps this clarity was still further emphasised after

1968 by the same principles being extended to free-standing sculptures, not in tandem with but also not disassociated from the purity of the reliefs.

The largest, and probably most formidable, of his major works in the field of construction, completed only a few years before his death, was the commission he undertook for the Kröller-Müller Museum in Otterlo. Working from his designs, he built a pair of reliefs for the two walls chosen for the Museum's new extension wing. The logical advance of refined economy that is observed here in a 14-year-long art career, beginning with true and careful recording of visible reality and ending with spatial construction of tireless precision editing, does not give the background out of which this artist's mastery proceeded. His gradual shredding of realism and the vicissitudes through which it passed were seemingly out of context with the prevailing taste for Dutch artistic modernism at the time, veering as it did towards forms of romantic and undisciplined non-figuration and abstraction, distinctly at odds with the clean geometric elements in the pictures painted by Dekkers. True, he had the stern unyielding hard geometry practised by the de Stijl artists running parallel with his other kind of Abstract painting, but Mondrian and his colleagues were not at that period at the centre of modern Dutch Art, interest in their theories and conclusions was far more prominent outside Holland and, whilst admiring Piet Mondrian for much of what he was achieving, Dekkers found his rejection of the triangle and the circle incompatible just because triangle and circle in the conception of the de Stijl ran contrary to total pictorial harmony.

In consequence, to find agreeable encouragement for the way in which Dekkers wanted to pursue his own artistic intentions, he had to find consolation from abroad in the quiet seclusion of Dutch museums of which the Kröller-Müller was a prime example; places where he could see examples of works by Ben Nicholson and Hans Arp. He was also aware in this way of oeuvres of Biederman, Baljeu, Judd, LeWitt and Morris. It was the performance of artists like these, carried out in complete contrast to the indifference to his careful approach to geometric nonfiguration which he had experienced from the teachers when he was attending Rotterdam Art Academy effectively making him a loner during his student days, which helped provide comfort to him in cultural isolation, gladdened his heart and steeled his patience while he pressed on for ultimate recognition.

—Sheldon Williams

DEKKERS, Ger(rit Hendrik).
Dutch. Born in Borne, 21 August 1929. Educated at secondary school in Hangelo, 1942-46; studied graphics at the Academie voor Kunst en Industrie, Enschede, 1950-54. Served in the Dutch Army, in Indonesia, 1948-50. Married Hilda Hartsuiker in 1954; children: Henriette and Jose. Freelance artist and photographer, Enschede, 154-73, and in Giethoorn, since 1973. Member, Photo Section, Gebonden Kunstenfederatie (GKf), since 1969. Recipient: Dutch Ministry of Culture Grant, 1970, 1971, 1975, 1976; City of Amsterdam Stipendium, 1976. Agents: Galerie M., Haus Weitmar, 463 Bochum-Weitmar, West Germany; and Galerie Nouvelles Images, Westeinde 22, The Hague, Netherlands. Address: Dwarsgracht 31, 8355 CV Giethoorn, Netherlands.

Individual Exhibitions:

1972	*Landscape Perception*, Rijksmuseum Kröller-Müller, Otterlo, Netherlands.
1973	*Landscape Perception*, Museum Bochum-Kunstsammlung, Bochum, West Germany.
	Landscape Perception, Neue Galerie-Kunstsammlung Ludwig, Aachen, West Germany
1974	*Landscape Perception*, Stedelijk Museum, Amsterdam

	Landscape Perception 1968-1975, Gemeentemuseum, The Hague
1975	*Landscape Perception*, Palais des Beaux-Arts, Brussels
	Landscape Perception, Galleria del Cavallino, Venice
1976	*Landscape Perception*, Kunstmuseum, Aarhus, Denmark
	Landscape Perception, Print Gallery Peiter Brattinga, Amsterdam
	Landscape Perception, Galerie M. Bocum, West Germany
1977	*Planned Landscapes*, Rijksmuseum Kröller-Müller, Otterlo, Netherlands
	Plastic, Museum Boymans van Beuningen, Rotterdam
1978	*Plastic*, Gemeentemuseum, Arnhem, Netherlands
	Planned Landscapes, De Vishal, Haarlem, Netherlands
1979	*New Dutch Landscape*, Hayden Gallery, Massachusetts Institute of Technology, Cambridge
	Planned Landscapes, Print Gallery Pieter Brattinga, Amsterdam
	Planned Landscapes, Provincial Begijnhof, Hasselt, Belgium
1980	*Planned Landscapes*, Kunstcentrum Markt 17, Enschede, Netherlands
	Planned Landscapes, Rijksplanologische Dienst, The Hague
1981	*Planned Landscapes*, Stadium Generale, Wageningen, Netherlands
	Planned Landscapes, Städtische Galerie, Nordhorn, West Germany

Selected Group Exhibitions:

1969	*Atelier 6*, Stedelijk Museum, Amsterdam
1971	*Sonsbeek 71*, Central Station, Amsterdam
1974	*Projekt 74*, Kunsthalle, Cologne
1977	*Sequenzen*, Kunstverein, Hamburg
	Documenta 6, Kassel, West Germany
	Museum of Drawers, Kunsthaus, Zurich (now permanent installation)
1978	*Fotografie in Nederland 1940-75*, Stedelijk Museum, Amsterdam
	Fotografie als Kunst/Kunst als Fotografie 2, Fotoforum der Gesamthochschule, Kasel, West Germany (toured Germany, Poland, Portugal, Spain and the United States)
1979	*To Do With Nature*, travelling exhibition (toured the Netherlands, Sweden, Belgium, West Germany, Denmark, and Portugal)
	Kunst als Fotografie 1949-79, Tiroler Landesmuseum Ferdinandeum, Innsbruck (travelled to the Neue Galerie am Wolfgang Gurlitt Museum, Linz, Austria; Neue Galerie am Landesmuseum Joanneum, Graz, Austria; and the Museum des 20. Jahrhunderts, Vienna)

Collections:

Rijksmuseum Kröller-Müller, Otterlo, Netherlands; Stedelijk Museum, Amsterdam; Frans Halsmuseum, Haarlem, Netherlands; Museum Boymans van Beuningen, Rotterdam; Gemeentemuseum, The Hauge; Gemeentemuseum, Arnhem, Netherlands; Ministry of Culture, The Hague; Sammlung Ludwig, Cologne; Kunsthalle, Hamburg; Museum Bochum-Kunstsammlung, Bochum, West Germany.

Publications:

By DEKKERS: book—*Planned Landscapes: 25 Horizons*, with an introduction by R. W. D. Oxenaar, Amsterdam 1977; *Graven en begrave in Overijssel*, editor, with H. Schelhaas and B. Molenaar, Zwolle 1980.

On DEKKERS: books—*Ger Dekkers: Landscape Perceptions*, exhibition catalogue, with text by R. W. D. Oxenaar, Otterlo, Netherlands 1972; *Ger Dekkers: Landscape Perceptions*, exhibition catalogue, with text by Peter Spielmann, Bochum, West Germany 1973; *Ger Dekkers: Landscape Perceptions*, exhibition catalogue, with text by Wolfgang Becker, Aachen, West Germany 1973; *Ger Dekkers: Landscape Perceptions 1968-1975*, exhibition catalogue, with text by J. L. Locher and Manfred Schneckenburger, The Hague 1974; *Fotografie in Nederland 1940-1975*, exhibition catalogue, with text by Els Barents, Ingeborg Leyerzapf and others, The Hague 1978; *New Dutch Landscape*, exhibition catalogue, by Marc S. Gerstein, Cambridge, Massachusetts 1979; *The Artist as Photographer* by Marina Vaizey, London 1982; articles—"Ger Dekkers" in *Flash Art* (Milan), December 1974/January 1975; "Ger Dekkers" by A. Van Berswordt-Wallrabe in *M-Bochum* (Bochum, West Germany), no. 3, 1976, "Ger Dekkers" by Betty van Garrel in *Volker Post* (Rotterdam), no. 4, 1978; "Ger Dekkers" by Dolf Welling in the *Holland Herald* (Amsterdam), July 1979; "Ger Dekkers" by Fred Hazelhoff in *Foto* (Hilversum, Netherlands), September 1980; "Ger Dekkers" by Herman v. Buuren in *Bijvoorbeeld* (Amsterdam), no. 2. 1981.

My actual subject is the effect that our culture has on landscape. The Dutch landscape with its polders provides an excellent example.

I am aware that my work is a personal expression, in which my personality is one factor. My principal action—to record a situation that I encounter—I experience myself as an intruder.

My concern with the subject and its surroundings does not go further than emotionally choosing the angle of the camera and focussing it, and later on making a selection and carefully completing the process.

The horizon acts as a middle line in the square pictures: this gives a continuous line that runs throughout the series and thus the whole project.

The medium I use is another factor.

I find only a limited number of phototechnical possibilities important. It is not the gimmicks of photography that mean most to me but its very irrevocability, its inevitability. From these factors, but mainly, I hope, from its essence, my work derives its validity.

—Ger Dekkers

In his works Ger Dekkers makes visible the way in which the Dutch landscape reveals itself to the observer as a continuous series of organized data—although a simple disclosure itself is not necessarily an ordered achievement. Thus it is no accident that around 1972 the color photographs of Ger Dekkers were at the center of a debate about the differences between photography as a means of recording reality and as a plastic art.

Dekkers' large exhibition at the Rijksmuseum Kröller-Müller gave the distinguished critic Rudi Fuchs an occasion to consider the nature of photography. For Fuchs, the most important elements of photography are the possibilities afforded by direct manipulation, especially by the deliberate placing of objects and the process of excision. But he goes on to accuse Dekkers of using the medium in an unnatural way, of denying the history of photography and structuring his work according to the aesthetic of a particular trend of the moment, in this case Minimal Art. He accuses Dekkers of going beyond the bounds of his medium, of borrowing from the plastic arts without giving anything in return: Dekkers does not even bother to acknowledge that the boundaries are problematic. On another occasion Fuchs defended those works by Jan Dibbets in which there is a living relationship between an impersonal medium and the artist's individuality. But in general Dekkers is an artist because he *makes,* and Dibbets, because he merely *registers,* is not.

The importance of Ger Dekkers work is that its quality is apparent whether it is a photograph, a slide or a book. For example, in cooperation with the Art Animation in Groningen (since 1977 the Corps de Garde) he produced a series of carefully planned catalogues. These are particularly relevant to the question raised by Conceptual Art: is plastic art necessarily confined to particular forms and occasions? No doubt the particular qualities of the Dutch landscape are especially suited to the point of view of constructivism and minimalism. That Dekkers has been influenced by them is itself unimportant: what matters is what he has done with dikes, the forests and fields of grain

and playgrounds. The special realms of the gallery and museum are not for him. Much more appropriate, in fact, are busy public buildings—the Netherlands railway stations, for example, where some of his photographs now appear.

—A. F. Wagemans

de KOONING, Willem.

American. Born in Rotterdam, Netherlands, 24 April 1904; emigrated to the United States as stowaway on a ship, 1927. Studied at the Akademie voor Beeldende Kunsten en Technischen Wetenschappen, Rotterdam, 1916-24, 1926-27. Married Elaine Marie Catherine Fried in 1943; daughter: Lisa. Apprentice to the commercial artists Jan and Jaap Gidding, Rotterdam 1916; assistant to Bernard Romein, art director of a Rotterdam department store, 1920-23; worked as house painter, Hoboken, New Jersey 1927; moved to New York and held various commercial art jobs, 1927-28; met John Graham, Arshile Gorky and Stuart Davis, New York, 1928-29; full time painter from 1935; shared studio with Arshile Gorky, New York 1937; designed and painted murals, Federal Arts Project, New York, 1935-39. Instructor, Black Mountain College, Beria, North Carolina, 1948, and Yale University, New Haven, Connecticut, 1950-51, 1959-60. Recipient: Logan Medal and Purchase Prize, Art Institute of Chicago, 1951; President's Freedom Award Medal, 1964; Talens Prize International, Amsterdam 1968; Gold Medal, American Academy of Arts and Letters, New York, 1975; Artist of the Year Award, Fairfield Arts Festival, Connecticut, 1978; Mellon Prize (with Eduardo Chillida), Carnegie Institute, Pittsburgh, 1979; Max Beckman Prize, Frankfurt, 1984; Kaiser Ring Award, Goslar, 1984; National Medal of Arts, Washington, D.C., 1986; Mayor's Liberty Medal, New York, 1986.

Member, National Institute of Arts and Letters, 1960; Member, Royal Academy of Fine Arts, Stockholm, 1986. Agent: Xavier Fourcade Inc., New York. Address: c/o Xavier Fourcade Inc., 36 East 75th Street, New York, New York 10021, U.S.A.

Individual Exhibitions:

1948	Charles Egan Gallery, New York
1951	Charles Egan Gallery, New York
	De Kooning/Pollock/Shahn, Arts Club of Chicago
1943	Sidney Janis Gallery, New York
	Boston Museum Art School (retrospective; travelled to the Workshop Art Center, Washington, D.C.)
1955	Martha Jackson Gallery, New York
1956	Sidney Janis Gallery, New York
1959	Sidney Janis Gallery, New York
1961	Paul Kantor Gallery, Beverly Hills, California
1962	*Barnett Newman and Willem de Kooning,* Allan Stone Gallery, New York
1964	Allan Stone Gallery, New York
	'Woman' Drawings by Willem de Kooning, James Goodman Gallery, Buffalo, New York
1965	Paul Kantor Gallery, Beverly Hills, California
	Smith College Museum of Art, Northampton, Massachusetts (retrospective; travelled to the Massachusetts Institute of Technology, Cambridge)
1966	*De Kooning's Women,* Allan Stone Gallery, New York
1967	M. Knoedler and Company, New York
	Allan Stone Gallery, New York
1968	*Peintures Récentes,* M. Knoedler et Cie, Paris
	Stedelijk Museum, Amsterdam (retrospective; travelled to the Tate Gallery, London)
1969	Museum of Modern Art, New York (retrospective)
	M. Knoedler and Company, New York
1971	M. Knoedler and Company, New York
	Allan Stone Gallery, New York
1972	Allan Stone Gallery, New York
	Baltimore Museum of Art
	Sidney Janis Gallery, New York
1974	University of Alabama, University (toured the United States)

Willem De Kooning: *Untitled VI,* 1985

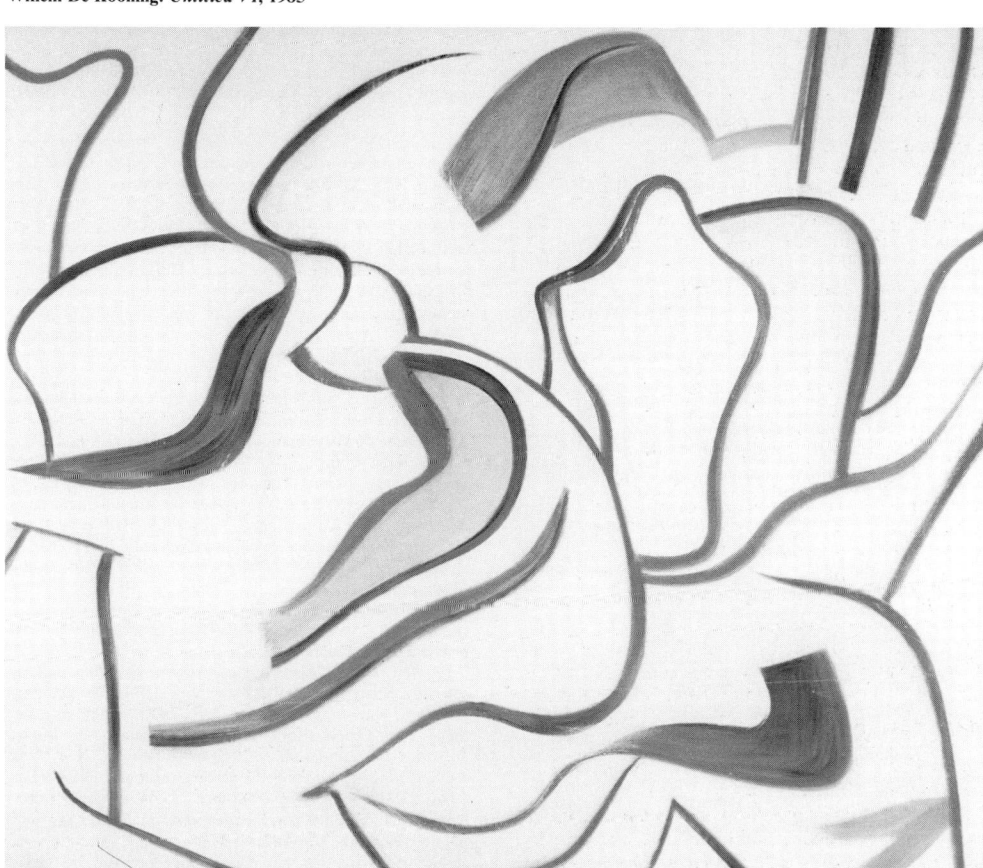

Walker Art Center, Minneapolis (toured the United States and Canada)
Richard Gray Gallery, Chicago
1975 *New Works: Paintings and Sculpture*, Xavier Fourcade Inc., New York
Paintings, Drawings, Sculpture 1967-75, Norton Gallery of Art, Palm Beach, Florida
1976 Seattle Art Museum
Stedelijk Museum, Amsterdam
Collection d'Art, Amsterdam
Gimpel Fils, London
Gimpel Fils, Zurich
New Paintings 1976, Xavier Fourcade Inc., New York
Blaffer Gallery, University of Houston
1977 Collection d'Art, Amsterdam
Xavier Fourcade Inc., New York
Wilheim Lembruck Museum, Duisburg, West Germany
Musée de Grenoble, France
The Sculpture of de Kooning with Related Paintings, Drawings and Lithographs, Arts Council of Great Britain, London
Galerie Templon, Paris
Museum of Modern Art, Belgrade
Museum of Modern Art, Ljubljana, Yugoslavia
1978 *Willem de Kooning in East Hampton*, Guggenheim Museum, New York
Museum of Art, Science and Industry, Bridgeport, Connecticut
Romanian National Museum of Art, Bucharest
Branch Post, Cracow
Helsinki National Museum of Art
America House, East Berlin
University of California Art Museum, Berkeley
De Kooning 1969-1978, University of Northern Iowa, Cedar Falls
1979 St. Louis Art Museum
Contemporary Arts Center, Cincinnati, Ohio
Akron Art Institute, Ohio
March Foundation, Alicante, Spain
Fundación Juan March, Madrid
Norwegian National Gallery of Art, Oslo
Dordrechts Museum, The Netherlands
Pittsburgh International Series, Museum of Art, Pittsburgh
1980 Richard Hines Gallery, Seattle
Richard Gray Gallery, Chicago
Galerie Hans Strelow, Dusseldorf
1981 Janie C. Lee Gallery, Houston
Guild Hall, East Hampton, New York
1982 C. Grimaldis Gallery, Baltimore
Xavier Fourcade Inc., New York
1983 *The North Atlantic Light 1960-63*, Stedelijk Museum, Amsterdam (travelled to Denmark and Sweden)
Xavier Fourcade Inc., New York
De Kooning Drawings, Whitney Museum, New York (travelled to West Berlin and Paris)
Retrospective Exhibition, Whitney Museum, New York (travelled to West Berlin and Paris)
De Kooning Sculpture, Josef-Haubrich-Kunsthalle, Cologne
Sculpture Court, Philip Morris, New York
Galerie Maeght LeLong, New York
1984 Colorado State University, Fort Collins
Intimate Gallery, Lincoln Center, Fort Collins, Colorado
Stadelsches Kunstinstitut, Frankfurt
Xavier Fourcade Inc., New York
Das Moenchehaus Museum, Goslar, West Germany
Galerie Daniel Templon, Paris
Galerie Hans Strelow, Dusseldorf
Anthony D'Offay Gallery, London
1985 Studio Marconi, Milan
Xavier Fourcade Inc., New York
Margo Leavin Gallery, Los Angeles
1986 Fabian Carlsson Gallery, London
Anthony D'Offay Gallery, London
1987 Margo Leavin Gallery, Los Angeles
C. Grimaldis Gallery, Baltimore
Richard Gray Gallery, Chicago

Selected Group Exhibitions:

1945 *Group Show*, Charles Egan Gallery, New York
1950 *Biennale*, Venice
1951 *60th Annual of American Painting and Sculpture*, Art Institute of Chicago
1954 *Biennale*, Venice
1969 *Festival of 2 Worlds*, Spoleto, Italy
1978 *Sculpture and Works on Paper from the 1930's and 1940's*, Washburn Gallery, New York
1981 *A New Spirit in Painting*, Royal Academy, London
1982 *New York School: Four Decades*, Guggenheim Museum, New York
1985 *Flying Tigers: Painting and Sculpture in New York 1939-46*, Brown University, Providence, Rhode Island (travelled to Worcester, Massachusetts; Southampton, New York)
1987 *L'Epoque, la mode, la morale, la passion*, Centre Georges Pompidou, Paris

Collections:

Museum of Modern Art, New York; Metropolitan Museum of Art, New York; Guggenheim Museum, New York; Whitney Museum, New York; Art Institute of Chicago; Carnegie Institute, Pittsburgh; National Gallery, Washington, D.C., Centre Georges Pompidou, Paris; Tate Gallery, London; Stedelijk Museum, Amsterdam; Bayerische Staatsgemaldesammlung, Munich

Publications:

By de KOONING: articles—letter to the editor, on Arshile Gorky in *Art News* (New York), January 1949; interview, with Martha Boudrez, in *The Knickerbocker* (New York) May 1950; "Artists' Sessions at studio 35 (1950)" in *Modern Artists in America*, edited by Robert Motherwell and Ad Reinhardt, New York 1951; "The Renaissance and Order" in *Transformation* (New York), vol. 1, no. 2, 1951; "What Abstract Art Means to Me" in *Museum of Modern Art Bulletin* (New York), Spring 1951; interview in *Conversations with Artists* by Selden Rodman, New York 1957; "Is Today's Artist with or Against the Past?", interview, with Thomas B. Hess, in *Artnews* (New York), June 1958; film-script in *Sketchbook No. 1:3 Americans*, (New York), 1960; "Content is a Glimpse . . ." interview, with David Sylvester, in *Location* (Easthampton, New York), 1963; interview, with James T. Valliere, in *Partisan Review* (New York), Fall 1957; interview in *Vrij Nederland* (Amsterdam), 5 October 1968; "A Desperate View" in *Willem de Kooning* by Thomas B. Hess, New York 1969; "Interview with Willem de Kooning," with Harold Rosenberg, in *Artnews* (New York), September 1972.

On de KOONING: books—*De Kooning Retrospective*, exhibition catalogue, with a foreword by Clement Greenberg, Boston 1953; *De Kooning*, exhibition catalogue, New York 1955; *Willem de Kooning* by Thomas B. Hess, New York 1959; *De Kooning* by Harriet Janis and Rudi Blish, New York and London 1960; *Willem de Kooning*, exhibition catalogue, with text by Clifford Odets, Beverly Hills, California 1961; *Willem de Kooning*, 3 volume unpublished collections of photographs, critical commentaries and annotations, compiled by William C. Agee, New York 1962; *De Kooning-Newman*, exhibition catalogue, with comments by Allan Stone, New York 1962; *'Woman' Drawings by Willem de Kooning*, exhibition catalogue, with a preface by Merle Goodman, Buffalo, New York 1964; *Willem de Kooning*, exhibition catalogue , with preface by William Inge, Beverly Hills, California 1965; *De Kooning's Women*, exhibition catalogue, New York 1966; *De Kooning: Recent Paintings*, exhibition catalogue, by Thomas B. Hess, New York 1967; *De Kooning: Peintures Récentes*, exhibition catalogue, Paris 1968; *Willem de Kooning*, exhibition catalogue, with an introduction by Thomas B. Hess, Amsterdam 1968; *De Kooning: January 1968—March 1969*, exhibition catalogue by Thomas B. Hess, New York 1969; *Drawings of Willem de Kooning* by Thomas B. Hess, Greenwich, Connecticut 1972; *Willem de Kooning* by Gabriella Drudi, Milan 1972; *De Kooning* by Harold Rosenberg, New york 1974; *American Masters: The Voice and the Myth* by Brian O'Doherty, New York 1974; *De Kooning: Paintings, Drawings, Sculpture 1967-1975*, exhibition catalogue, Palm Beach, Florida 1975; *De Kooning: New Works, Paintings and Sculpture*, exhibition catalogue, New York 1975; *Willem de Kooning*, exhibition catalogue, Amsterdam 1976; *De Kooning: New Paintings, 1976*, exhibition catalogue, New York 1976; *The Sculpture of de Kooning with Related Paintings, Drawings and Lithographs*, exhibition catalogue, with text by Andrew Forge, foreword by David

Sylvester, London, 1977; *American Art at Mid-Century: The Subjects of the Artist* by E. A. Carnean, Jr. and Eliza R. Rathbone, Washington, D.C. 1978; *Willem de Kooning in East Hampton*, exhibition catalogue, by Diane Waldman, New York 1978; *De Kooning 1969-1978*, exhibition catalogue, edited by Sanford Shman, with text by Jack Coward, Cedar Falls, Iowa 1978; *Willem de Kooning: Pittsburgh International Series*, exhibition catalogue, Pittsburgh 1979; *Willem de Kooning: The North Atlantic Light 1960-83*, exhibition catalogue, Amsterdam 1983; *Willem de Kooning: Skulpturen*, exhibition catalogue, Cologne 1983; *Willem de Kooning: Drawings, Paintings, Sculpture*, exhibiiton catalogue, New York 1983; *Willem de Kooning: Retrospective*, exhibition catalogue, West Berlin and Paris 1984.

The de Kooning style of work has spread itself across a variety of influences, not all of them comfortable bedfellows.

His successful childhood apprenticeship with the commercial artists' company run by the decorators Jan and Jaap Gidding in Holland prompted Jaap to arrange for him to enter the Rotterdam Academy of Fine Arts and Techniques where he remained a student for eight years absorbing the breadth of a wide curriculum which was nevertheless strict in its determination to give every aspirant a stern academic training in the arts and a mastercraftsman's proficiency in craft techniques. During this time he also became aware of what the de Stijl group of Mondrian and van Doesburg believed creative art should achieve.

Later on when, after several vain attempts, he left Holland behind and entered the United States, he was able to bring with him the balance of a training that gave him an aptitude for both painting and making things. He was practical as well as accomplished.

When he started to paint seriously—as an artist—his first development was in the direction taken by Arshile Gorky (in his early portraits), but these de Kooning paintings of the 1930s were in double-harness with untitled, non-figurative works which may have owed something to de Stijl (but had none of the hard-edge of the Dutch School) and something also to the later and more fantastic Gorky. At all events, in both categories there lurked a strong flavour of the United States.

In the mid-1940s the character of his paintings took on two other aspects. A number of them (generally based on figures and usually those of women) seemed to transmute at least a part of what Jackson Pollock had discovered. Rarely with Pollock's random attack (most of them, but by no means all, were very carefully strung together in professionally correct composition), they still inspired the same effect of splintered or sprawling confusion—an emotional confusion rather than a visual one. For all their frequent and decorous attention to expert tailoring, these pictures—full of pastel tints and black outlines or dark areas edged with white—were moving proof that here was an artist who combines taste with passion.

Side by side with them, and with increasing frequency, appeared the figure studies. No hint of early Gorky this time. These paintings are a fascinating mixture of picassoid distortions with Cobra School vehemence and vibrant colouring (a curious, if long delayed legacy from the Netherlands where he was born). The Spaniard's part in all this alchemy at the hands of a contemporary art apothecary has been gradually phased out, but the Cobra element remains and has since entered the near-abstract landscapes and pictures of atmosphere like "Rosy-Fingered Dawn at Louse Point."

Without question Willem de Kooning is a well-organised modern artist. He works steadily and never totally rejects what he has been able to glean from experience. His newest development has been to try his hand—with some success—at sculpture. He can make things.

—Sheldon Williams

DEL PEZZO, Lucio.

Italian. Born in Naples in 1933. Studied land surveying at the Accademia di Belle Arti, Naples, 1954–58; mainly self-taught. First paintings, 1954; full-time artist, Milan, 1958–64, and in Paris, since 1965; Founder, with Alberto Biasi, Mario Persico, Sergio Fergola and others, Gruppo 58, Naples, 1958; regular contributor to the avant-garde periodical *Documento Sud*, Naples and Milan, 1958-59. Agent: Studio Marcomi, Milan. Address: c/o Studio Marconi, Via Tadino 15, 20124 Milan, Italy.

Individual Exhibitions:

1960	Galerie Senatore, Stuttgart
1961	Galleria Schwarz, Milan
1962	Knapik Gallery, New York
1963	Gallerie Schwarz, Milan
	Alexandre Iolas Gallery, New York
	Galerie J., Paris
1964	Galleria Il Cavallino, Venice
1965	Galleria L'Arco d'Alibert, Rome
	Rijksmuseum Kröller-Müller, Otterlo, Netherlands
	Stadtische Museum Schloss Morsbroich, Leverkusen, West Germany
	Galleria Odyssia, Rome
1966	Galleria Il Centro, Naples
	Il Costruttore di Quadri Moderni, Studio Marconi, Milan
	Italian Pavilion, at the *Biennale,* Venice
	Galleria del Deposito, Genoa
1967	Studio Marconi, Milan
1968	Galerie Blumenthal-Mommaton, Paris
	Galleria de Foscherari, Bologna
	Galleria del Minotauro, Brescia, Italy
1969	Galleria La Chiocciola, Padua
	Studio Marconi, Milan
1970	Galerie Germain, Paris
	Galerie Brusberg, Hannover
	Galerie Foncke, Ghent
	Palais des Beaux-Arts, Brussels
	La Pilotta, Istituto di Storia dell'Arte, University of Parma
1971	Marlborough Galleria d'Arte, Rome
	Studio Marconi, Milan
1972	Galerie Ostermaim, Stockholm
1973	Galerie Lucien Durand, Paris
	Galerie Visat, Paris
1974	Studio Marconi, Milan
	Rotonda de Via Besana, Milan

Selected Group Exhibitions:

1962	*Kunst von 1960 bis Heute,* Museum des 20. Jahrhunderts, Vienna
1963	*Biennale de Paris,* Musée National d'Arte Moderne, Paris
1964	*Biennale,* Venice
1966	*Dada 1906-1966,* Museo d'Arte Moderna, Milan
1968	*International Exhibition of Drawings,* University of Puerto Rico
1970	*Salon de Mai,* Paris
1971	*Biennale,* Tokyo
	Art et Anti-Art 1910-1979, Palais des Beaux-Arts, Brussels
1973	*Kunst Markt,* Cologne
1982	*Arte Italiana 1960-82,* Hayward Gallery, London

Collections:

Galleria Nazionale d'Arte Moderna, Rome; Centre Georges Pompidou, Paris; Centre National d'Art Contemporain, Paris; Stedelijk Museum, Amsterdam; Victoria and Albert Museum, London; Museum of Modern Art, New York; Guggenheim Museum, New York; Carnegie Institute, Pittsburgh; Museum of Fine Art, Montreal; Art Gallery of Ontario, Toronto.

Publications:

On DEL PEZZO: books—*Del Pezzo,* exhibition catalogue, with text by Giorgio Kaisserlain, Milan 1961; *Lucio Del Pezzo,* exhibition catalogue, Milan 1963; *Lucio Del Pezzo: Techiche Miste su Cartone,* exhibition catalogue, with text by Cesare Vivaldi, Rome 1965; *Lucio Del Pezzo,* exhibition catalogue, with text by Roberto Sanesi, Genoa 1966; *Lucio Del Pezzo: Il Costruttore di Quadri Moderni,* exhibition catalogue, with texts by Enrico Baj, Gillo Dorfles and Alain Jouffroy, Milan 1966; *Del Pezzo,* exhibition catalogue, with text by Gillo Dorfles, Brescia, Italy 1968; *Lucio Del Pezzo,* exhibition catalogue, with text by Tommaso Trini, Rome 1971; *Lucio Del Pezzo,* exhibition catalogue, with text by Guido Ballo, Milan 1974.

DELVAUX, Paul.

Belgian. Born in Antheit, near Huys, 23 September 1897. Educated in Brussels; studied architecture, 1916–17, then painting under Constant Montald and Jean Delville, 1919–21, Academie des Beaux-Arts, Brussels. Served in the Belgian Army, Brussels, 1920–21. Married Anne-Marie (Tam) DeMartelaere in 1952. Painter from 1921; established studio in Brussels, 1924; visited Paris, 1926; travelled in Italy, 1938, 1939; worked in seclusion during the German occupation, 1940–44; worked on designs for *Adame Mirroir,* ballet by Jean Genet, Theatre Marigny, Paris, 1948; lived in Choisel, France, 1949. Professor of Painting, Ecole Nationale Supérieure d'Art et d'Architecture, Brussels, 1950–62. President, Académie Royale des Beaux-Arts, Brussels, 1965. Recipient: Prix de l'Académie Picard, Brussels, 1938; Prix de Reggio Emilio, 1955; Grand Prize for Painting, Province of Liège, 1961; Rembrandt Prize, Amsterdam, 1969; Prix Septemnnal, Province of Liège, 1987. Honorary Doctorate: Free University of Brussels, 1979. Member, Institut de France, 1977; Honorary Citizen, Town of Furnes, 1978. Foundation Paul Delvaux established, 1980; Musée Paul Delvaux, Saint-Idesbald, established, 1982. Address: Foundation Paul Delvaux, 42 Kabouterweg, 8460 Saint-Idesbald, Belgium.

Individual Exhibitions:

1925	Galerie Breckpot, Brussels (with Robert Giron)
1926	Galerie Manteau, Brussels
1927	Galerie Manteau, Brussels
1928	Galerie Manteau, Brussels (with Robert Giron)
	Palais des Beaux-Arts, Brussels
1929	Galerie Manteau, Brussels
1939	Palais des Beaux-Arts, Brussels
1933	Atelier de la Grosse-Tour, Brussels
1934	Palais des Beaux-Arts, Brussels
1936	Palais des Beaux-Arts, Brussels (with Rene Magritte)
1937	Palais des Beaux-Arts, Brussels
	Galerie Esher Surrey, The Hague
1938	Palais des Beaux-Arts, Brussels
	London Gallery
1940	Palais des Beaux-Arts, Brussels
1943	Galerie Lou Cosyn, Brussels
1944	Palais des Beaux-Arts, Brussels
1946	Julien Levy Gallery, New York
	Redfern Gallery, London
1948	Julien Levy Gallery, New York
	APIAW, Liège, Belgium
	Galerie René Drouin, Paris
	Sidney Janis Gallery, New York
1949	Palais des Beaux-Arts, Brussels
	Société Royale des Beaux Arts, Verviers, Belgium
1952	Casino Communal, Knokke-le-Zoute, Belgium (with Rene Magritte)
1955	Atelier Veranneman, Courtrai, Belgium
	Het Atelier, Deurne, Antwerp
1956	Atelier Veranneman, Courtrai, Belgium
1957	Maison Haute, Boitsfort, Belgium
	Cercle Royal, Charleroi, Belgium (with Marc Chagall)
1959	Staempfli Gallery, New York
1962	APIAW, Liège, Belgium
	Musée des Beaux-Arts, Ostende, Belgium
	Renée Lachowsky and Lou Cosyn, Brussels
1963	Staempfli Gallery, New York
1964	Galerie Helikon, Hasselt, Belgium
	Staempfli Gallery, New York
1965	Musée des Beaux-Arts, Mons, Belgium
	Galerie Luttece, Paris
1966	Galleria del Naviglio, Milan
	Gallerie del Naviglio, Turin
	Gallerie Krugier, Geneva
	Palais des Beaux-Arts, Lille, France
1967	Galerie Bateau-Lavoir, Paris
	New Smith Galerie, Brussels
	Musée d'Ixelles, Brussels
1968	Société Royale des Beaux Arts, Verviers, Belgium
	Belgisches Haus, Cologne
1969	Staempfli Gallery, New York
	Musée des Arts Décoratifs, Paris
1970	Musée de Peinture et de Sculpture, Grenoble, France
1971	Staempfli Gallery, New York
1972	Atelier Veranneman, Courtrai, Belgium
1973	Casino Knokke-Heist, Belgium
	Museum Boymans-van-Beuningen, Rotterdam
1974	Art Salon Ginza Nova, Tokyo
	Museo de Arte Moderno, Mexico City (with James Ensor and Rene Magritte)
	Cultural Center, New York
	Galerie Isy Brachot, Brussels (with Domenico Gnoli and Rene Magritte)
1975	Museum of Modern Art, Tokyo (travelled to the Museum of Modern Art, Kyoto)
	Galerie Isy Brachot, Brussels
	Palais des Beaux-Arts, Brussels (with James Ensor)
1976	Palais de l'Europe, Menton, France
1977	Galerie Isy Brachot, Brussels
	Galerie Isy Brachot, Basle
	Ilot St. Georges, Liège, Belgium
	Musée Royaux des Beaux-Arts, Brussels
1978	Galerie Isy Brachot, Paris
1980	Centre Cultural de la Communaute Francaise de Belgique, Paris
	San Francisco Museum of Modern Art
	Museum of Fine Art, Montreal
1981	Museum of Art, Newport Beach, California
	La Chataigneraie, Flemalle, Liège, Belgium
	Bienal, Sao Paulo
1982	Museum of Modern Art, Rio de Janeiro
	Museum of Modern Art, Caracas

Selected Group Exhibitions:

1924	*Le Sillon,* Brussels
1935	*Exposition Internationale d'Art Moderne,* Brussels
1938	*Exposition Internationale du Surrealisme,* Galerie des Beaux-Arts, Paris
1942	*Surrealist Exhibition,* 451 Madison Avenue, New York
1948	*Biennale,* Venice
1952	*Contemporary Belgian Art,* Mitsikoshi Department Store, Tokyo
1961	*Midwestern Exhibition of Belgian Painters,* Arts Club of Chicago (toured the Midwestern states)
1968	*Dada, Surrealism and Their Heritage,* Museum of Modern Art, New York
1972	*Peintures de l'Imaginaire: Symbolistes et Surrealists Belge,* Grand Palais, Paris
1982	*A Century of Modern Drawing,* British Museum, London

Collections:

Delvaux Museum, St. Idesbald, Belgium; Musee Royaux des Beaux-Arts, Brussels; Musee Royaux des Beaux-Arts, Antwerp; Musee d'Art Moderne, Brussels; Musee des Beaux-Arts, Charleroi, Belgium; Gemeentemuseum, The Hague; Tate Gallery, London; Centre Georges Pompidou, Paris; Museum of Modern Art, New York; Art Institute of Chicago.

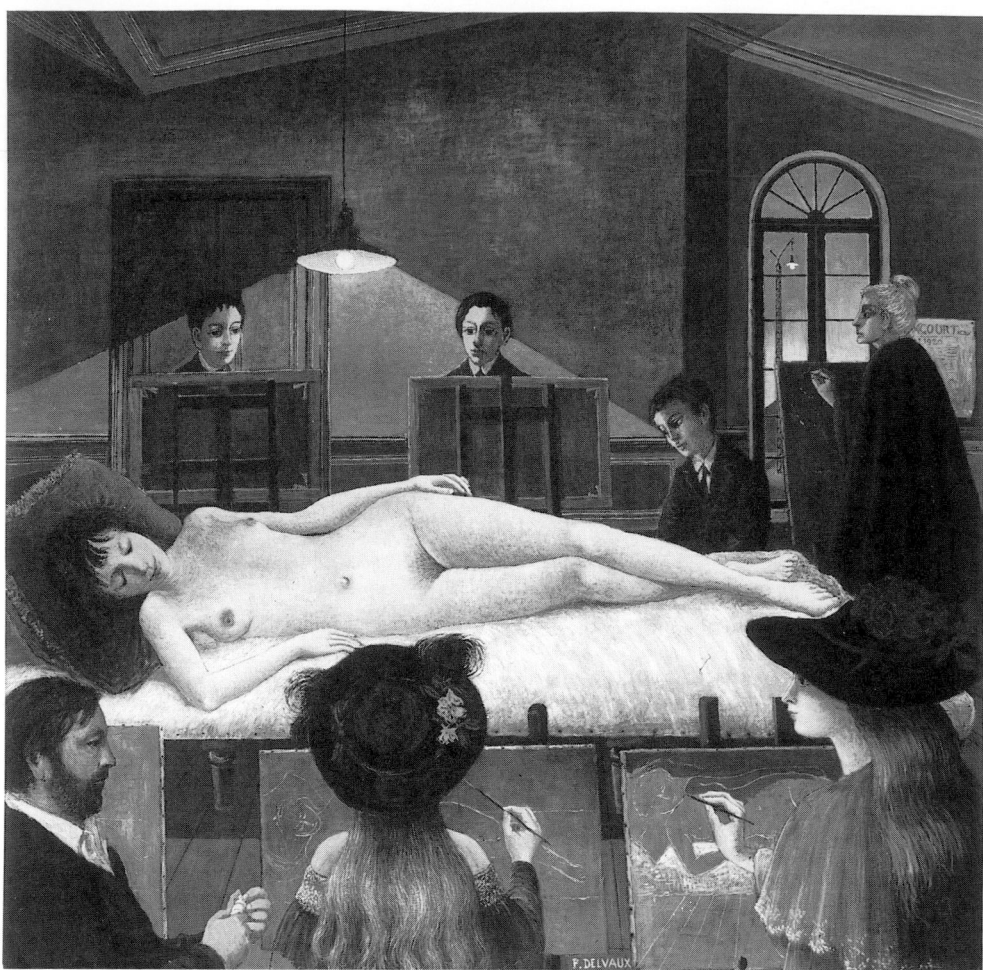

Paul Delvaux: *La Pose*, 1979

many cases, however, it simply represents the armature of the body and as such acquires a purely architectural significance. Beginning in 1939 the artist introduced a character taken from Jules Verne's *Journey to the Center of the Earth*, the heroic scientist Prof. Otto Liedenbrock (Prof. von Hardwigg in the English translations). In painting after painting, including "The Phases of the Moon" (1939), we see the good professor intent on examining a mineral specimen, totally oblivious to the bevy of nude beauties surrounding him. This is a frequent theme in his work: the impossibility of significant connection between the sexes. Certainly it reflects the artist's own ambivalence toward women, springing from a childhood shaped by a domineering mother. This explains why all the women in his paintings look the same—they are all equally seductive, all equally threatening. Part of the fascination of a Delvaux painting resides in its violation of the taboo against public nudity. Typically he places his nude-or semi-nude female protagonists in a public setting where they remain totally unaffected by the experience, distracted, even aloof. Undeniably attractive, they seem impervious to our stares. In the last analysis Delvaux specializes in tantalizing his audience—and himself—with unattainable dreams. Above all, he is the master of frigid eroticism.

—Willard Bohn

Publications:

By DELVAUX: book—*Sept Dialogues avec Paul Delvaux, Accompagnes de Sept Lettres Imaginaires*, with Jacques Meuris, Paris 1971; articles—"Notice sur James Ensor" and "Notice sur Alfred Bastien" in *Annuaire de l'Académie Royale de Belgique*, Brussels 1963; "A propos d'un Voyage en Grece" in *Bulletin de l'Academie Royale de Belgique*, Brussels 1965.

On DELVAUX: books—*Paul Delvaux ou les Rêves Eveillés* by René Gaffe, Brussels 1945; *Paul Delvaux* by Claude Spaak, Antwerp 1948; *Paul Delvaux: Der Mensch, her Maler* by Paul Aloise de Bock, Hamburg 1965, as *Paul Delvaux: L'Homme. Le Peintre: Psychologie d'Un Art*, Brussels 1967; *Cahiers Paul Delvaux I: Premières Lithographies*, Paris 1969; *Paul Delvaux II: L'Oeuvre Grave 1966–69*, Paris 1969; *Paul Delvaux* by Antoine Terrasse, Paris 1972; *Paul Delvaux: Catalogue Raisonne* by Michel Butor and Jean Clair, Brussels 1974; *Paul Delvaux: Catalogue de l'Oeuvre Peint* by Michel Butor, Jean Clair and Suzanne Houbart-Wilken, Brussels 1975; *Paul Delvaux, Graphic Work* by Mira Jacob, Paris 1976; *Delvaux* by P. Emerson, Antwerp 1985.

Paul Delvaux' earliest paintings belong to the Post Impressionist mode. "Holy Cross Square" (1923) is a typical cityscape in the style of Utrillo, while "Promenade on the Isle of Huy" (1926) derives from Cézanne's landscape studies. In the late 1920's Delvaux adopted a primitive style reminiscent of Henri Rousseau. Depicting stylized nude figures in sylvan settings, "Figures in the Forest" (1928) and "Pink and White" (1929) achieve a remarkable serenity through simplicity of line and color. Over the next few years this style became increasingly expressionistic, focusing on crowd scenes in urban settings and culminating in "Sleeping Venus" (1932) and "The Spitzner Museum" (1933). In both works a supine female nude is juxtaposed with clothed figures in a museum environment of skeletons and display cases. As the artist later explained, their source was a bizarre exhibit he had encountered at the *Brussels Fair*. "I was struck by an extraordinary display by the Spitzner Museum," he noted, "with red velvet draperies at the window, two skeletons and a mechanical sleeping Venus . . . which was very sad and strange amid the hubbub of the merry-go-rounds and the frantic fun-seeking characteristic of such large carnivals." That this display deeply affected him is evidenced by the many skeletons and sleeping Venuses in his later work.

Toward 1934, fortified by his experience at the Museum, Delvaux discovered Giorgio de Chirico—an encounter that was to leave a lasting impression on his work. Among other things, it precipitated his conversion to Surrealism which was to occupy him for the rest of his life. To some extent his preexisting iconography was superimposed on de Chirico's. His sleeping Venuses resemble the latter's reclining Ariadnes, while his skeletons correspond to various de Chirico statues and mannequins. In general he borrows freely from the Italian master, appropriating his vast, deserted public squares, his architectural settings, his claustrophobic interiors ("The Mirror," 1936), and his old-fashioned trains. Like the latter, and pursuant to Surrealist doctrine, he devotes himself to the "marvelous"—revelatory experience springing from the unconscious. Whence the supreme importance of mystery and enigma.

Drawing on this background and on his own experience, Delvaux creates paintings that are profoundly original, exerting a strange hypnotic power on the viewer. His scenes, which often take place at twilight, are essentially dramas of the mind in which figures, objects, and settings are juxtaposed according to the processes of dream. In this context his aesthetics revolve around inconguity and contradiction. Delvaux' characters are also uniquely his own. To some extent the skeleton illustrates the traditional mortality theme, especially in the late 1940's and 1950's when it appears in a series devoted to Christian subjects. In

DEMARCO, Hugo.

Argentinian. Born in Buenos Aires, 13 July 1932. Married Amalia Aguirre in 1959; Children: Marcello, Paula and Valerie. Painter. Professor of Painting, Drawing and Engraving, National School of Fine Art, Buenos Aires. Recipient: French Government Grant, to work in Paris, 1960. Address. 24 rue de Pressoir, Paris 20, France.

Individual Exhibitions:

1967   Op-Art Galerie, Esslingen, West Germany
1968   Galerie Denise René, Paris
        Galerie Grises, Bilbao, Spain
        Galerie Denise René/Hans Meyer, Dusseldorf
1969   Galerie Rubbers, Buenos Aires
1970   Estudio Actual, Caracas
        Hayward Gallery, London
1972   Galeria Antonona, Carcas
        Galleria del Naviglio, Milan
1973   Galleria La Polena, Geneva
        Galleria Sincron, Brescia, Italy
1974   Galleria Proposte, Cuneo, Italy
        Galleria A. Parma, Italy
        Galleria Zen, Milan

Selected Group Exhibitions:

1963   *Latin American Art*, Musée d'Art Moderne, Paris
1965   *The Responsive Eye*, Museum of Modern Art, New York
        Lumiére Mouvement et Optique, Palais des Beaux-Arts, Brussels
1967   *Biennale*, Paris
        Lumière Mouvement et Optique, Palais des Beaux-Musée d'Art Moderne, Paris
1968   *Documenta*, Kassel, West Germany
1971   *Art Argentin Contemporain*, Kunsthalle, Basle
1972   *Biennale*, Venice
1974   *Latin American Painters*, at the *Festival Royan*, Royan, France

Collections:

Museo Nacional de Bellas Artes, Buenos Aires; Collection di

Tella, Buenos Aires; Museo Bellas Artes, Caracas; Museo de Arte Contemporaneo, Caracas; Museo Soto, Ciudad Bolivar, Venezuela; Centre Georges Pompidou, Paris; Peter Stuyvesant Collection, Amsterdam; Kunsthalle, Recklinghausen, West Germany; Tel Aviv Museum.

Publications:

By DEMARCO: book—*La Prisionière,* with Crouzot, Paris 1967.

On DEMARCO: books—*Art cinetique* by Frank Popper, Paris 1967; *Kinetic Art* by Cyril Barrett, London 1968; *Encyclopedia Universalis,* Paris 1970; articles—Kineticists Working in Paris" in *Studio International* (London), October 1970; "Lettera da Milano" in D'Ars (Milan), March/April 1973.

Hugo Demarco is one of the Kinetic artists who has developed his research meticulously and surely from basic plastic problems such as colour in its most essential form to environmental integrations with their spatial, temporal, luminous and chromatic components.

In his "Dynamisations," "Superpositions spatiales" and "Réflexions changeantes" he has first reduced colour to pure vibration and set it off in a series of different planes. By introducing metal surfaces in space ans sometimes adding a transparent plane of perspex with a certain number of geometrical forms marked in translucent colours, he obtains transformations of structure and new intensities of light and colour. From the basis of this experience, real movement is integrated with the elements or reflecting bodies which are provided as a mechanical basis, and possibilities of combinations of movement, interrelations of speeds and directions emerge. In this way Demarco has managed to transpose harmonically

problems connected with "optical art" into lumino-kinetic areas which he enriches by a series of works utilizing "black" or ultraviolet light in view of creating strong vibratory effects and in order to intensify the relationship between form, space, and motion.

More recently Demarco has turned again to his research into "space dynamisations" which follow the intuitions of the earliest Kinetic artists like Gabo (wtih his "Virtual Kinetic Volume" of 1920) by carrying them into the environmental sphere. In these constructions, which he calls "Relations," Demarco studies the spatial relationships between the movement and the relexions of metal rods and structures in such a way as to bring into focus the dematerialisation of the art object while at the same time creating a climate in which the spectator becomes aware of the basic qualities and the aesthetic implications not only of space but also of light, form and colour.

In fact all of Demarco's endeavours are directed towards the intensification and the diversification of the image, the dynamisation of the perceptive field of the spectator and the creation of plastic forms demonstrating the properties of time and, above all, its immaterialness.

—Frank Popper

DE MARIA, Nicola.

Italian. Born in Foglianise, near Benevento, Italy, 6 December 1954. Lives and works in Turin. Address: Corso G. Agnelli 46/12, 10137 Turin, Italy.

Individual Exhibitions:

1975	Galleriaforma, Genoa
1976	Galleria Amelio, Naples
1977	Galleria Toselli, Milan
1978	Galleria Toselli, Milan
	Galerie Maenz, Cologne
	Galleria Persano, Turin
1979	Galleria Mario Diacono, Bologna
	Galerie Annemarie Verna, Zurich (with Francesco Clemente and Mimmo Paladino)
1980	Galleria Toselli, Milan
	Galerie Maenz, Cologne
	Galleria Persano, Turin
	Galerie Annemarie Verna, Zurich
1983	Kunsthalle, Basle

Selected Group Exhibitions:

1980	*Arte e Critica 1980,* Galleria Nazionale d'Arte Moderna, Rome (and 1981)
1981	*Identité Italienne,* Centre Georges Pompidou, Paris
1985	*The European Iceberg,* Art Gallery of Ontario, Toronto
1986	*Aspects of Italian Art 1960–85,* Kunstverein, Frankfurt

Publications:

On DE MARIA: book—*The Italian Trans-Avantgarde* by Achille Bonito Oliva, Milan 1980; *Nicola De Maria,* exhibition catalogue with text by Jean-Christophe Ammann, Basle 1983; articles—"Nicola de Maria" by M. Bandini in *Data* (Milan), October/November 1976; "Espansivo Eccessivo: Osservazioni sulla Giovane ARte Italiana" by Jean-Christophe Ammann in *Domus* (Milan), April 1979; "Il Primo Catalogo degli Artisti Nuovi" by F. Alinovi, R. Barilli and R. Daolio in *Bolaffiarte* (Turin), March 1980.

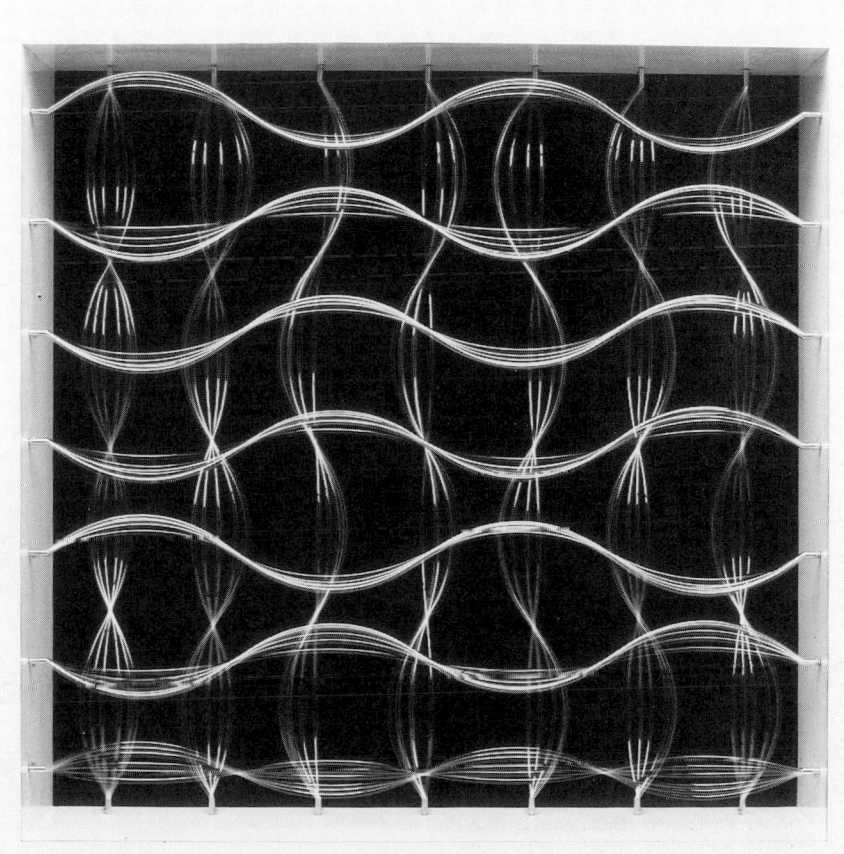

Hugo Demarco: *Relations H. g. V.,* 1973

Among the artists of the *Transavantgarde,* Nicola De Maria certainly has the least recourse to "quotation." His pictorial lyricism is extravagant, devoid of figuration and abstraction and relative designs. Nearly always conceived in relation to the surroundings (and so beyond the borders of the picture), his painting, always annotated in a symbolic writing, is wholly manifested in a space that seems as far distant as the heavenly vault. The space of his painting, a vision of the void, is crowded with moments of colour, very thin forms and evanescent shapes freely interwoven and generating rich "contaminations." In this respect Nicola De Maria comes close to the compositional balances of Paul Klee, particularly to those that alternate the visible and the invisible.

As early as 1978, in a work with the significant title of "Philosophy of Magic and of Works of Art," De Maria had stressed his rapport with the liberation of painting. The form and colour indicated a vision made of distances, of chromatic improvisations. Their spatiality was something enigmatic and impalpable.

Ut pictura poesis might be De Maria's motto. Painting as a poetry of silence, of something constantly changing in the infinity of light, animates his noble work through beauty of design and colour. The artist paints as if he was digging in the transcendental splendour of an eternal sunset. But the sunset—not the decline—of art presages a new dawn. Its own shadow or reflection, De Maria's changeful painting is the most complete manifestion of that. He concentrates regard on it until it is lost, for the changing of the colours is at once visible and hidden.

De Maria loves the unaccustomed and the exotic: indeed, one of his works is called "I Am African, I Am Asian" (1980).

In another work, "Quore" (1982), he portrays an environment that might be called a (provisional) exposition of the work of art, a study of the rich path taken by responses between the single parts of a work and the spatiality of the work as a whole. The single elements of which it is composed (a big painted card, a handbag also painted, and a series of little squares) have a clear meaning in themselves and, of course, in the context in which they are found. In "Quore" the spatiality of the colours expands their specificity, setting the real significant symbols of the painting at an almost unattainable distance. The inimitable visual evolution seems to take place somewhere else, somehow outside the visual range of the eye. It is a magical moment, coloured by painting that continually changes even when it displays subtle material thicknesses and spontaneous writing. The ensemble is in unstable equilibrium, which extends the moment in contemplative rapture. Invisible at the centre of the work, there dominates the fantasy of the artist (or the heart of art); the shifts of his imagination recognizable in the colours and the writing can be vaguely seen. The effect of the writing, the handmaid of the work, leads to the heart of art, to the rediscovery of an unsullied grace of colour and symbol. But it is the existential abyss that gives them their beauty; to paraphrase Ungaretti, when Nicola De Maria finds a colour or a symbol it is as if it was discovered in the abyss of the starry heavens. Thus his work, an esoteric work, is a sort of maze, not walled at all but open to the far distance of an interior light, visible only to the veiled eye of poetry.

—Italo Mussa

DE MARIA, Walter (Joseph).
American. Born in Albany, California, 1 October 1935. Studied at the University of California, Berkeley, 1953–59, B.A. in history 1957, M.A. in art 1959. Organized "happenings" at the University of California and at the California School of Art, San Francisco, 1959–60; drummer with the group Velvet Underground, 1965. Now lives and works in New York. Recipient: Guggenheim fellowship, 1969; Mathew Sculpture Prize, Art Institute of Chicago, 1976. Agent: Xavier Fourcade Inc., New York. Address: c/o Xavier Fourcade Inc., 26 East 57th Street, New York, New York 10021, U.S.A.

Individual Exhibitions:

1963	9 Great Jones Street, New York
1965	Paula Cooper Gallery, New York
1966	Cordier Ekstrom Gallery, New York
1968	Nicholas Wilder Gallery, Los Angeles
	Galerie Heiner Friedrich, Munich
1969	Dwan Gallery, New York
1972	Kunstmuseum, Basel
1974	Heinrich Friedrich Inc., New York
	Hessisches Landesmuseum, Darmstadt
1977	*The New York Earth Room/The Equal Area Series,* Heiner Friedrich Gallery, New York
1979	*The Broken Kilometer,* Heiner Friedrich Gallery, New York
1981	*360° I Ching/64 Sculptures,* Centre Georges Pompidou, Paris
1982	Centre Georges Pompidou, Paris
1986	Xavier Fourcade Inc., New York

Selected Group Exhibitions:

1968	*Directions 1: Options,* Milwaukee Art Center
1969	*When Attitudes Become Form,* Kunsthalle, Berne (toured Europe)
1970	*Information,* Museum of Modern Art, New York
1971	*Guggenheim International,* Guggenheim Museum, New York
1972	*Diagrams and Drawings,* Kunstverein, Stuttgart (toured Switzerland and the Netherlands)
1973	*Medium Fotografie,* Stadisches Museum, Leverkusen, West Germany
1975	*Masterworks in Wood: The 20th Century,* Portland Art Museum, Oregon
1976	*Rooms,* P.S. 1: Institute for Art and Urban Resources, New York
1977	*Biennale,* Venice

Walter De Maria: *Lightning Field,* 1977

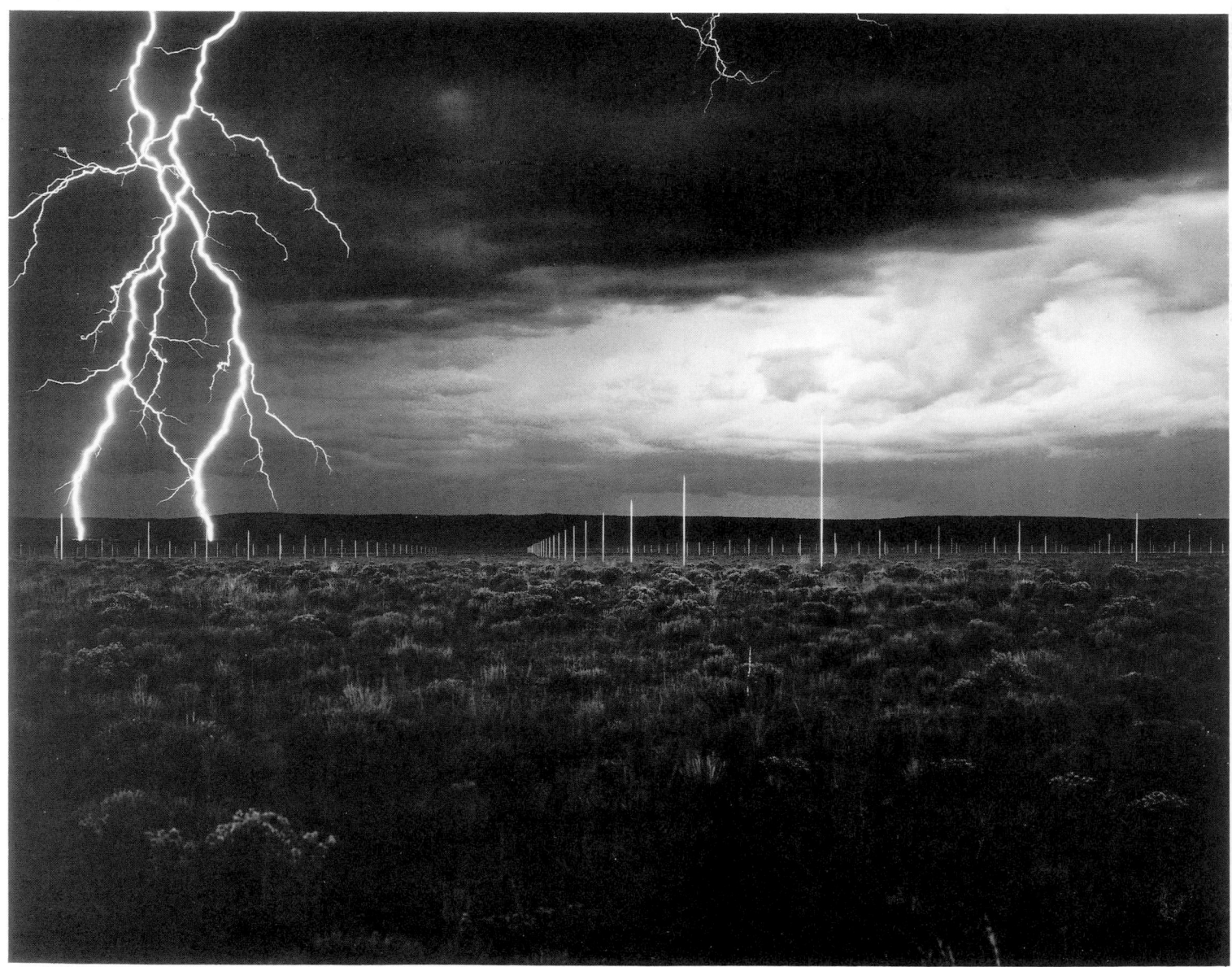

Collections:

Museum of Modern Art, New York; Whitney Museum, New York; Dia Art Foundation, New York; Kunstmuseum, Basel.

Publications:

By DE MARIA: articles—text in *The New Avant-Garde*, New York and London 1972; "Project for Munich" in *Domus* (Milan), Aguust 1973; "The Lightning Field" in *Artforum* (New York), April 1980.

On DE MARIA: books—*Changing: Essays in Art Criticism* by Lucy Lippard, New York 1971; *The New Avant-Garde* by Gregoire Muller, New York and London 1972; *6 Years: The Dematerialization of the Art Object* by Lucy Lippard, New York and London 1973; *Walter De Maria*, exhibition catalogue, with text by H. H. Schmidt, Darmstadt 1974; *Walter De Maria*, exhibition catalogue edited by Xavier Fourcade, New York 1986; articles—"Walter DeMaria" by Jill Johnston in *Artnews* (New York), February 1963; "Walter De Maria: Word and Thing" by Dennis Adrian in *Artforum* (New York), January 1967; "A Sedimentation of the Mind: Earth Projects" by Robert Smithson in *Artforum* (New York, September 1968; "Walter De Maria: The Singular Experience" by David Bourdon in *Art International* (Lugano, Switzerland), December 1968; "Walter De Maria" by Germano Celant in *Casabella* (Milan), March 1969; "Drawing Lines in the Desert" by Eric Cameron in *Studio International* (London), October 1970; "Artworks on the Land" by Elizabeth C. Baker in *Art in America* (New York), January 1976; "De Maria: Elements" by Roberta Smith in *Art in America* (New York), May 1978; "Walter De Maria's 'The Broken Kilometer' " by Brian Wallis in *Arts Magazine* (New York), February 1980; "Walter De Maria: Les Danger de l'Art" by Jean-Marc Poinsot in *Art Press* (Paris), May 1981; "Exerzitien in der Wüste: Eine Reise zu Walter De Maria's 'Biltzfeld' nach Neu-Mexiko" by Günter Metken in *Die Zeit* (Hamburg), 9 April 1982.

I feel proud to have started minimal art and land art.

—Walter De Maria

DENES, Agnes (Cecilia).

American. Born in Budapest, Hungary, 31 May 1938; left Hungary with parents to live in Stockholm, 1948; moved to the United States, 1954. Studied at the New School for Social Research, New York, 1959–63; City College of New York, 1961–62; Columbia University, New York (M. L. Robinson Scholar), 1964–66. Lives and works in New York. Lecturer, School of Visual Arts, New York, 1971–79; Skowhegan School of Painting and Sculpture, Maine, 1979; University of Genoa, Italy, 1986. Recipient: Creative Artists Public Service Grant, New York, 1972, 1974; National Invitational Purchase Award, Albion College, Michigan, 1973; National Endowment for the Arts Fellowship, 1974, 1975, 1981; National Invitational Purchase Award, Rutgers University, New Brunswick, New Jersey, 1975; DAAD Fellowship, West Berlin, 1978; Berthe Von Moschzisker Prize, 1980, and McPhail Award, 1982, Print Club of Philadelphia; Sponsored Grant, New York State Council of the Arts, 1984; Purchase Award, American Academy and Institute of Arts and Letters, New York, 1985. Agent: Associated American Artists, 663 Fifth Avenue, New York, New York. Address: 595 Broadway, New York, New York 10012, U.S.A.

Individual Exhibitions:

1965	Columbia University, New York
1966	Granite Gallery, New York
1967	New Masters Gallery, New York
1968	Ruth White Gallery, New York
1972	A.I.R. Gallery, New York
1974	Ohio State University, Columbus

	Perspectives, Corcoran Gallery, Washington, D.C. (toured the United States)
1975	Stefanotty Gallery, New York
	Galleria Forma, Genoa
	Sawyer Gallery, San Francisco
	University of California Art Museum, Berkeley
	Long Beach Art Museum, California
1976	Douglass College, Rutgers University, New Brunswick, New Jersey
	University of Akron, Ohio
1977	Tyler School of Art, Temple University, Philadelphia
	112 Greene Street Gallery, New York
	Rice/Tree/Burial, Artpark, Lewiston, New York (installation)
1978	Amerika Haus, West Berlin
	Ikon Gallery, Birmingham, England
	Franklin Furnace, New York
	Centre Culturel Americain, Paris
1979	Institute of Contemporary Arts, London
	Studio d'Arte Cannaviello, Milan
	Time Capsule I, Artpark, Lewiston, New York (installation)
	Great Ideas, Container Corporation of America, Chicago (installation)
1980	Hayden Gallery, Massachusetts Institute of Technology, Cambridge
	Lund Galleriet, Sweden
	Galerie Aronowitsch, Stockholm
	Elise Meyer Gallery, New York
1981	Elise Meyer Gallery, New York (print retrospective)
1982	Kunsthalle, Nuremberg, West Germany
	Wheatfield—A Confrontation, Downtown Manhattan, New York (installation)
1985	University of Hawaii, Honolulu
	Northern Illinois University, Evanston
1986	Ricardo Barreto Arte Contemporaneo, Guadalajara, Mexico
	Stelae, Department of Cultural Affairs, Genoa, Italy (installation)
1987	*Hypersphere*, Equitable Tower, New York (installation)
	Flying Pyramids for the Twenty-Second Century, Tamiami Airport, Florida (installation)

Selected Group Exhibitions:

1970	*Software*, Jewish Museum, New York
1971	*New Acquisitions*, Whitney Museum, New York
	Art Systems, Museum of Modern Art, Beunos Aires (toured South America)
1972	*American Women Artists*, Kunsthaus, Hamburg
1973	*American Drawings 1963-1973*, Whitney Museum, New York
1974	*Painting and Sculpture Today*, Indianapolis Museum of Art (toured the United States)
1977	*Documenta*, Kassel, West Germany
1980	*From Reinhardt to Christo*, Allen Memorial Art Gallery, Oberlin College, Ohio
1986	*V Bienal Americana de Artes Graficas*, Museo de Arte Moderno, Cali, Colombia
1988	*Making Their Mark*, Cincinnati Art Museum, Ohio (toured the United States)

Collections:

Museum of Modern Art, New York; Whitney Museum, New York; Neuberger Museum, State University of New York at Purchase; University of Massachusetts, Amherst; National Collection of Fine Arts, Washington, D.C.; National Air and Space Museum, Washington, D.C.; Corcoran Gallery, Washington, D.C.; Allen Memorial Art Museum, Oberlin College, Ohio; Albion College, Michigan; Israel Museum, Jerusalem.

Publications:

By DENES: books—*Sculptures of the Mind*, Akron, Ohio 1976; *Paradox and Essence*, Rome 1977; *Isometric Systems in Isotropic Space*, Rochester, New York 1979; *Book of Dust: The Beginning and the End of Time, and Thereafter*, Rochester, New York 1988; articles—statement in *Software*, exhibition catalogue, New York 1970; "Psychographic" in *Duration Piece No. 8* by Douglas Huebler, New York and Turin 1973; "Study of Distortions" in *Flash Art* (Milan), July/August 1977; "Wheatfield—A Confrontation" in *Reaktion* (Alsbach), no. 7, 1983.

On DENES: books—*6 Years: The Dematerialization of the Art Object* by Lucy Lippard, New York 1973; *Agnes Denes: Perspectives*, exhibition catalogue, with texts by Roy Slade, Lawrence Alloway, and Susan Collins, Washington, D.C. 1974; *Agnes Denes: Sculptures of the Mind*, exhibition catalogue, with an introduction by Thomas Deecke, West Berlin 1978; *Agnes Denes: Drawings, Objects, Graphics, Photos*, exhibition catalogue, Lund, Sweden 1980; *Agnes Denes 1968-1980*, exhibition catalogue with text by Garry Garrels, Cambridge, Massachusetts 1980; *Art in a Turbulent Era* by Peter Selz, Ann Arbor, Michigan 1985; articles—"Agnes Denes" by Barbara Reise in *Studio International* (London), December 1974; "A Visual Presentation of Meaning: The Work of Agnes Denes" by Peter Selz in *Art in America* (New York), March 1975; "Agnes Denes: The Ironies of Comprehension" by D. B. Kuspit in *Arts Magazine* (New York), December 1981; "Agnes Denes: The Triumph of the Will" by Ronny Cohen in *Print Collectors Newsletter* (New York), November 1982.

All my work up to now seems to culminate in my environmental art. From the early poetry to the philosophical drawings, from the abandonment of painting to working without color for eleven years (a self-imposed discipline that allowed concepts to dictate the mode of presentation), this complex body of work I have created; the art put out into the world is the most fully realized.

My work that always reached beyond the boundaries of the art area (to bring about a flow of communication among alien disciplines) now addresses controversial global issues questioning the status quo and the endless contradictions we seem to accept into our lives. It touches on ecological, territorial, social and cultural issues, celebrating our achievements, calling attention to our misconceptions and the most endearing of all human traits—our follies.

It's important to put art out into the world where it loses its preciousness but not its beauty, so it can touch all levels; it can elevate, communicate, be mysterious, provocative, ask disturbing questions and have a conscience. And it can be realized on a monumental scale when necessary. The art is freed to be true to itself. Before, I allowed it to dictate the mode of presentation; now I let it breathe and touch people's lives. Whether permanent or temporary, these are fully realized works that live and evolve in the environment.

—Agnes Denes

Although her work bears no likeness to Moholy-Nagy's. Agnes Denes shares his awareness that science and philosophy can be used in the service of art for the purpose of sensitizing the individual and society. Like the brilliant earlier modernist, Denes does not fit into any art movement or school. Although she has been described as a Conceptual artist by some critics, and although like certain Conceptualists she deals with a variety of intellectual problems, she gives palpable form and specific aesthetic beauty resulting from the visual clarification of complexity to her scientific and/or philosophic probes. Her work brings new thoughts and insights into the art arena, stretching its boundaries, toward a new breadth of thought and vision.

Increasingly, as many artists have rejected formalist aesthetics, they have absorbed and appropriated material from other disciplines for art (or non-art) purposes and Denes has turned to philosophy and science. But this is where we may easily misunderstand her. Denes is not interested in providing new scientific information. What she does rather is use the latest stages of scientific knowledge for the enrichment of artistic possibilities. She extends art, which traditionally had dealt with life and nature, into the realms of science; she is drawn to the enormous significance and creative energy in scientific thought.

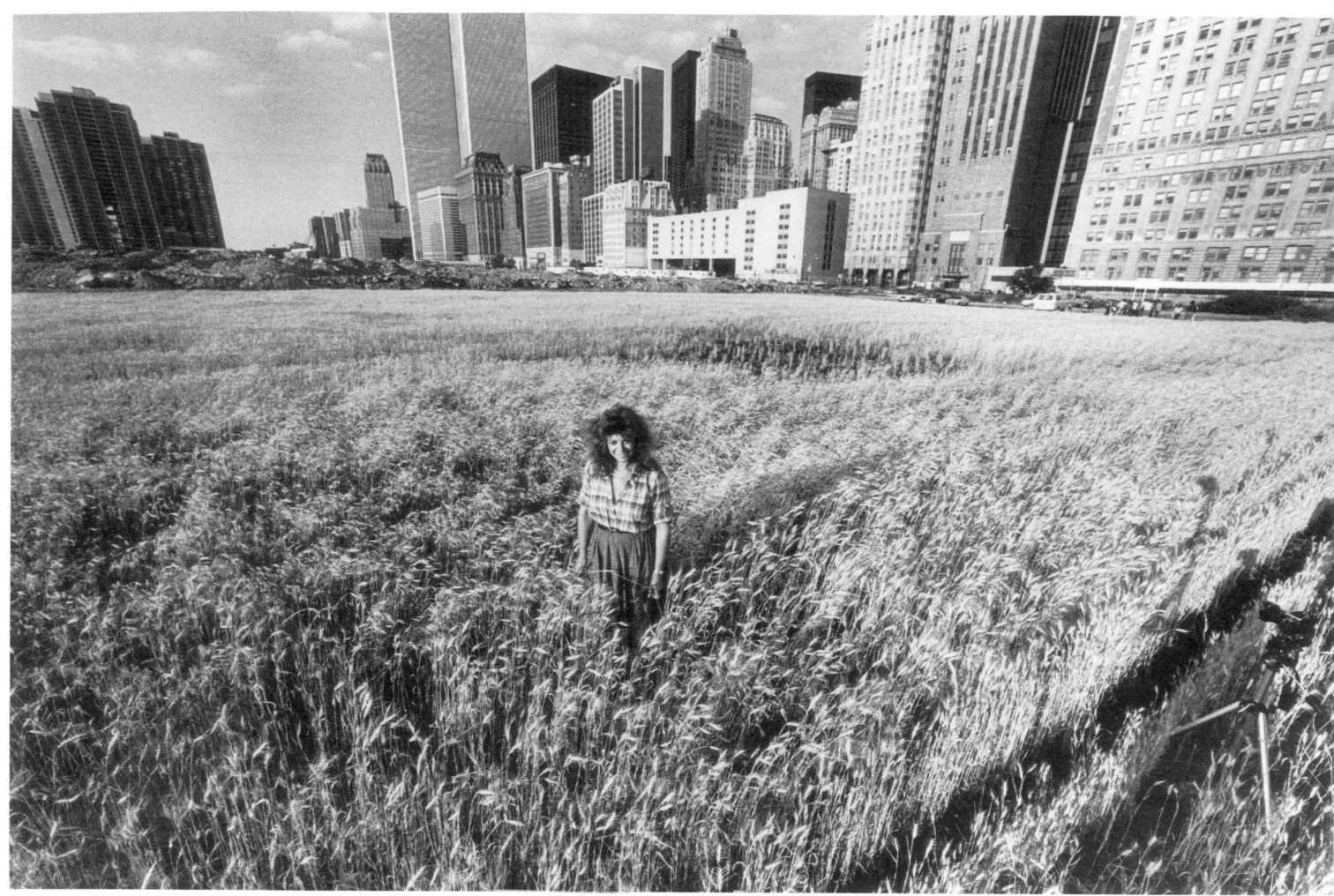

Agnes Denes: *Wheatfield—A Confrontation*, Downtown Manhattan, 1982

She also sees parallels between the structure of science and the structure of art.

At first encounter with Denes' work, one wonders about the relationship between X-ray photographs of the underlayers of famous paintings, diagrammatic studies of time and truth, the visualization of Pascal's triangle, concern with dust and bones, a visual presentation of human evolution, the exploration of organic cells through extreme magnification, a psychograph of artists' "Profiles" based on questionnaires, various "abstract" studies of the meaning of language and communications, and many other such analytical works. Yet a certain unity of concept and form slowly emerges.

In all her forays, Denes is attracted to the most basic of questions—the structure of matter and idea, the void, the meaning of life, the place of humanity in the world, the mysteries of human existence. It may be useful to point out that while her subject matter is essentially a unified one when viewed in terms of her broadest concerns, it is expressed in several different ways. Like much new and innovative art, some of it may be difficult to grasp. We are not accustomed to art which is presented in a philosophical/mathematical form. Her physical investigations (X-rays of paintings, magnifications of cell tissue, etc) or those which use anthropological and psychological material are, of course, more immediately accessible.

In 1968–69 Denes created her first major environmental project when she planted rice seeds to represent life and growth, chained trees to indicate interference with life and imply death, and buried her own Haiku poetry to symbolize the dialectical synthesis: human intellectual power. Since that time she has continued with important outdoor projects, outstanding among which was *Wheatfield—A Confrontation* (1982): the planting of a two-acre wheatfield at Battery Park in Lower Manhattan and the harvesting of

1,000 pounds of wheat. In 1987 she embarked on a commission for the Tamiami Airport in Florida of three large fields of green shrubs, wild flowers and poured concrete in the shape of *Flying Pyramids*. Also in 1987 she completed *Hypersphere—The Earth in the Shape of the Universe,* a lobby environment in New York's Equitable Tower of 144 panels of carved, frosted glass to form the ceiling which represents one of her earlier map projections.

Denes brings new philosophic insight into the abundance of available information, dealing with man's "importance or insignificance in the universe". Her work is analytic in the Kantian sense. Her singular contribution is in the fact that her symbols remain visual, her attitude romantic, her approach intuitive. Denes' unique position in today's art is at the place where systematic and intuitive knowledge intersect.

—Peter Selz

de RIVERA, José.

American. Born in West Baton Rouge, Louisiana, 18 September 1904. Studied drawing with John W. Norton, Chicago, 1926; mainly self-taught in sculpture. Served as an armorer with the United States Army, 1942–43, and as a designer of training aids for the United States Navy, 1943–46. Married Rose Covelli in 1926 (divorced); son: Joseph; married Lita Jeronimo in 1955. Worked as a draftsman, designer, etc. in foundries and the machine tool industry, Chicago, 1924–32; independent sculptor, living in New York, 1930 until his death in 1985: worked on the

WPA Federal Art Project, New York, 1937–38. Instructor in Sculpture, Brooklyn College, New York, 1953; Critic in Sculpture, Yale University, New Haven, Connecticut, 1953–55; Instructor in Sculpture, School of Design, North Carolina State College, Raleigh, 1957–60. Recipient: Watson F. Blair Prize, Art Institute of Chicago, 1957; National Institute of Arts and Letters grant, 1959; Creative Arts Medal, Brandeis University, Waltham, Massachusetts, 1969. D.F.A.: Washington University, St. Louis, 1974. Agent: Grace Borgenicht Gallery, 724 Fifth Avenue, New York, New York 10019. *Died* (in New York) 18 March 1985.

Individual Exhibitions:

1946	Mortimer Levitt Gallery, New York
1952	Grace Borgenicht Gallery, New York
1955	Grace Borgenicht Gallery, New York
1957	Walker Art Center, Minneapolis (retrospective)
	Grace Borgenicht Gallery, New York
1959	Grace Borgenicht Gallery, New York
1960	Grace Borgenicht Gallery, New York
1961	Whitney Museum, New York (retrospective; toured the United States)
1969	Grace Borgenicht Gallery, New York
1972	Whitney Museum, New York (retrospective)
	Isaac Delgado Museum, New Orleans
	Retrospective Exhibition 1930–1971, La Jolla Museum of Contemporary Art, California
	Grace Borgenicht Gallery, New York (retrospective)
1975	Grace Borgenicht Gallery, New York
1978	Grace Borgenicht Gallery, New York
1980	Grace Borgenicht Gallery, New York
1983	Grace Borgenicht Gallery, New York
1985	Grace Borgenicht Gallery, New York (memorial exhibition)

Selected Group Exhibitions:

1930 *Annual Exhibition*, Art Institute of Chicago (and 1931)

1934 *Whitney Annual*, Whitney Museum, New York (and regularly until 1968)

1939 *Worlds Fair*, New York

1946 *Contemporary Sculpture, Objects, Constructions*, Yale University, New Haven, Connecticut

1951 *American Sculpture*, Metropolitan Museum of Art, New York

1956 *Abstract Sculpture*, Galerie Denise René, Paris

1959 *Contemporary Sculpture*, Museum of Modern Art, New York (toured the United States)

1960 *Konkrete Kunst*, Kunsthaus, Zurich

1963 *Sculpture of Our Time*, Gallery of Modern Art, Washington, D.C.

1967 *Sculpture of the 60's*, Los Angeles County Museum of Art (travelled to the Philadelphia Museum of Art)

Collections:

Museum of Modern Art, New York; Whitney Museum, New York; Metropolitan Museum of Art, New York; Memorial Art Gallery, Rochester, New York; Newark Museum Association, New Jersey; Hirshhorn Museum and Sculpture Garden, Smithsonian Institution, Washington, D.C.; Museum of Fine Arts, Richmond, Virginia; Art Institute of Chicago; Tate Gallery, London.

Publications:

On de RIVERA: books—*José de Rivera*, exhibition catalogue, with text by John Gordon, New York 1961; *José de Rivera: Retrospective Exhibition 1930-1971*, exhibition catalogue, with text by Thomas S. Tibbs, La Jolla, California 1972; *The Non-Objective World*, exhibition catalogue, with text by George Rickey, London, 1972; *The Age of the Avant-Garde: An Art Chronicle of 1956-1972* by Hilton Kramer, New York and London 1974; *José de Rivera: Constructions* by Dore Ashton and Joan M. Marter, Madrid 1980.

*

Art for me is a creative process of individual plastic production without immediate goal of finality. The prime function is the total experience of production. The social function: the communication of that experience. In the attempt to find plastic harmony in my work, I am conscious always of the necessary for a prime, visual, plastic experience. The content, beauty and source of excitement is inherent in the interdependence and relationships of the space, material and light, and is the structure.

—José de Rivera (1983)

*

Each piece of work by José de Rivera reflects the impeccable craftsmanship of an individual who achieves a fluid balance of opposite tensions by using four elements; light, space, time, and material. The result—heavy, sensuous, flawlessly smooth metal sculptures, in which time and space go hand in hand. Whether one moves around the sculpture or stands in place as it slowly revolves, the line continues unbroken by the slightest hesitancy. The skillfully refined curvilinear forms dissolve into tracings of light or liquid, while the voids within become the forms themselves, swelling and diminishing with such ease as to belie the complex geometry of their being.

De Rivera's strength as a sculptor rests not only in his ability to produce a body of work as endlessly subtle in variation and nuance as time and space suggest, but also in his use of light. Each sculpture is polished through many gradations of abrasion to a brilliant, gleaming surface. Final polishing is achieved with jeweler's rouge and wood felt buffer.

Whereas in traditional sculpture light causes shadows to fall on the piece, in de Rivera's case the material used—be it aluminium, copper, bronze or stainless steel—is transformed into light by reflections from the surface of the piece. When set in rotation, beams of light are cast out into the distance with the points of cross-over constantly changing. This produces the optical effect of sudden deflections of light, a process eloquently illustrated by de Rivera's 1955 "Construction I: Homage to the world of Minkowski", a piece dedicated to the Russian mathematician and physicist Herman Minkowski, whose philosophy of an inseparable time and space inspired de Rivera's career.

Born in 1904 in Louisiana, USA, the son of a sugar mill engineer, de Rivera acquired skills at an early age which provided a base for a future sculptor. He was an adept blacksmith and capable of repairing machinery. After graduating from high school in 1922, he moved to Chicago where his knowledge of pipe-fitting and the making of tools and dies secured him employment in machine shops almost immediately. Between 1928 and 1931 de Rivera studied drawing under the painter John W. Norton at the studio school in Chicago. During these years he was influenced by Mondrian, Brancusi, and Georges Vantongerloo, a Belgian artist and theorist. Finally, after a year of travelling through Europe visiting galleries and museums in 1932, de Rivera re-affirmed his decision to be a sculptor.

He released his first pieces in 1930, "Owl", "Form Synthesis", and "Bust", three works of highly polished metal, gleaming with purity and simplicity. From 1938 to 1940 he worked on a cavalry monument for El Paso, Texas. Finding this type of commission too restricting, he devoted himself to the type of work which allowed him the freedom he required. In 1938 he constructed the aluminium "Flight" for the Newark Airport, a work which became the highlight of the Federal Art Project Sculp-

José De Rivera: *Construction No. 199*, 1983

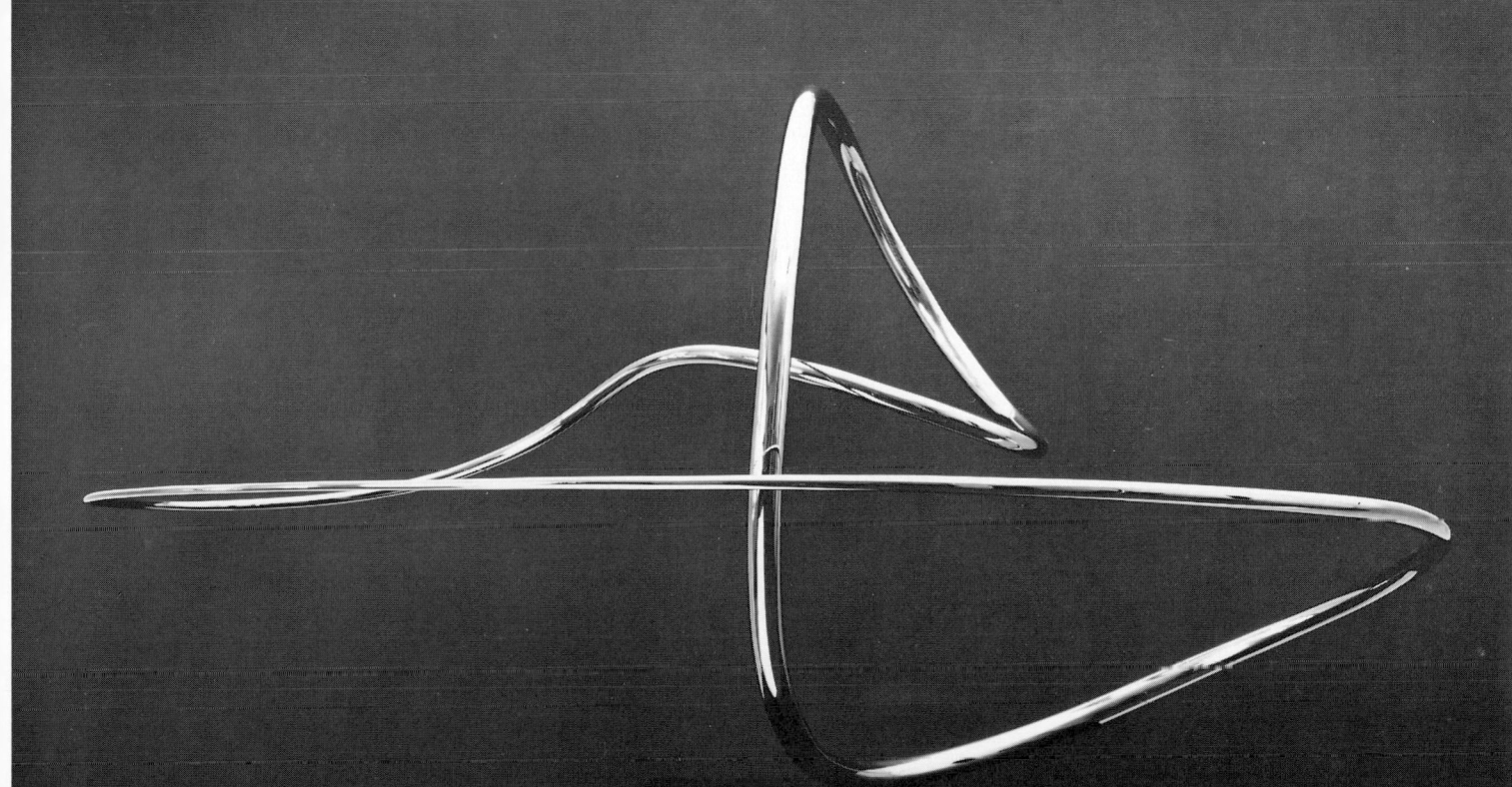

ture Division Show in New York that year. Simple, human in scale, it was a beautiful symbol of aviation.

That year proved to be an important one for his development as a sculptor. His construction "Black and Red, Double Element" began an abstract analysis of space, form and material with the addition of colour. It consisted of two shaped and painted aluminium sheets mounted in opposing positions and attached to the same base. The desired shape was then cut out of a flat sheet of metal, the surface filed and rubbed with abrasives, and was then painted with primary colours. De Rivera's reputation as an internationally acclaimed sculptor was enhanced yet again the following year in 1939 when his designs for stainless steel reliefs for the Soviet Pavilion were exhibited at the New York World's Fair.

Working in collaboration with architect William Lescaze and builder William Kaufman in 1955, de Rivera produced the relief "Continuum" for the stainless steel lobby wall 711 Third Avenue in New York City. Following that success he was commissioned by the Hotel Statler-Hilton in Dallas to construct a flashing steel and cadmium yellow piece which revolved once every six minutes in an open courtyard. The late 50's and 60's marked the highlight of his career; his major works were exhibited at the Brussel World Fair in 1958, he was featured at the New York World Fair in 1964, and the spectacular piece "Infinity" of 1966, which was installed in front of the Smithsonian Institution in Washington D.C., earned him further critical attention.

Throughout his career José de Rivera has engaged himself in an analytical and unrelenting search for elemental values. The fruits of his labours have been borne out by his wide acclaim as a contemporary sculptor, whose works are sublimely endowed with perfect fluid gestures, gently ebbing and flowing in timeless revolution.

—Carrie Barker

DEVADE, Marc.

French. Born in Paris, 5 November 1943. Painter: lives and works in Paris. Founder-Member, with Daniel Dezeuze, Vincent Bioules, Patrick Saytour, Louis Cane, Claude Viallat and Andre Valensi, Supports-Surfaces group, Paris. Editor of *Peinture: Cahiers Théoriques*, Paris. Address: 10 rue Toullier, 75005 Paris, France.

Individual Exhibitions:

1970	Galerie Le Haut Pavé, Paris
1972	Galerie Daniel Templon, Paris
1973	Galleria Daniel Templon, Milan
	Institute of Contemporary Arts, London
1974	Galerie Daniel Templon, Paris
	Maison de la Culture, Rennes, France
1975	Galleria Daniel Templon, Milan
	Galleria Lia Rumma, Naples
	Galerie D, Brussels
	Galerie Le Flux, Perpignan, France
	Galerie Piltzer, Paris
1976	Galleria Lia Rumma, Rome
	Galleria Daniel Templon, Milan
	Galerie Quadrum, Lisbon
1977	Galerie Piltzer, Paris
	Galleria La Bertesca, Genoa
	Galleria Mantra, Turin
	Galerie C. M., Saint-Etienne, France
	Galerie La Bertesca, Dusseldorf
	Galerie Arnesen, Copenhagen
	Centre International de Création Artistique de Sénanque, France
	Galerie Lavunn, Ghent
	Galerie N. R. A., Paris
1978	Galerie Le Dépot, Bourges, France

	Galerie Gerald Piltzer, Paris
	Musée d'Art Moderne de la Villa, Paris
1979	Galerie Lavuun, Ghent
	Galerie Quadrum, Lisbon
1981	*Peintures 1979–1981*, Galerie Blancs-Monteaux Espace Expositions, Paris

Selected Groups Exhibitions:

1970	*Support-Surface*, Musée d'Art Moderne de la Ville, Paris
1971	*Peinture, cahiers théoriques*, Galerie Yvon Lambert, Paris
1974	*L'art au present*, Galerie Daniel Templon, Paris
1975	*Analitische Malerei*, Galerie La Bertesca, Dusseldorf
1976	*I colori della pittura*, Galleria del Milione, Milan
	Tendenser I Europaeisk Kunst, Galerie Arnesen, Copenhagen
1977	*Biennale*, Paris
1978	*Biennale*, Venice
1979	*Tendances de l'art en France 68–78*, Musée de la Ville, Paris
1981	*Tel Quel*, Galerie La Hune, Paris

Publications:

By DEVADE: articles—"Poème" in *Tel Quel* (Paris), no. 18, 1964; "Réponse à un questionnaire sur l'art abstrait" in *Lettres Francaises* (Paris), no. 41, 1970; "Note pour la théorie materialiste de la pratique picturale" in *Support-Surface*, exhibition catalogue, Paris 1970; "Notes sur une peinture operant dans de beaux draps" in *Louis Cane*, exhibition catalogue, Paris 1971; "Pourquoi une revue" in *V. H. 101* (Paris), 1971; "Comment voir la Chine en peinture" in *Peinture: Cahiers Théoriques* (Paris), no. 2-3, 1972; "On va partir de Cézanne," interview, with Francois Pluchart in *Artitudes* (St. Jeannet, France), no. 6, 1972; "La peinture et son double" in *Peinture: Cahiers Théoriques* (Paris), no. 4-5, 1972, partially reprinted in *Tracks* (New York), April 1976; "Dates, repères, références et commentaires" in *Peinture: Cahiers Théoriques* (Paris), no. 6-7, 1973; "Comment me vient la peinture" in *Promesse* (Paris), no. 34-35, 1973; "La peinture vue d'en-bas" in *Peinture: Cahiers Théoriques* (Paris), no. 8-9, 1974; "Note sur la Chine et la modernité" in *Peinture: Cahiers Théoriques* (Paris), no. 8-9, 1974; "La situation ideologique et politique en peinture" in *Peinture: Cahiers Théoriques* (Paris), no. 8-9, 1974; *Passages, programme théorique et graphique*, exhibition catalogue, Paris 1974, partially reprinted in *Data* (Milan), no. 16-17, 1975; interview with Catherine Millet, in *Art Press* (Paris), no. 9, 1974 and *Flash Art* (Milan), no. 54-55, 1975; article in *Les uns-postures ou quand la sculpture se colore*, exhibition catalogue, Paris 1975; "La matière du sujet de la peinture" in *Peinture: Cahiers Théoriques* (Paris), no. 10-11, 1975; "Théorie ou les figures de la peinture" in *Peinture: Cahiers Théoriques* (Paris), no. 12, 1977; responses to a questionnaire in *Bilder öhne Bilder*, exhibition catalogue, Bonn 1977; "May 1968, May 1978—Peinture, l'impossible quotidien" in *Art Press International* (Paris), 1978; "Picasso nous regarde" in *Documents sur* (Paris), October 1978; "L'après coup de pinceau," interview, with Klaus Honnef in *Peintures: Cahiers Théoriques* (Paris), May 1979; "La peinture au plus près" in *Peinture: Cahiers Théoriques* (Paris), no. 14-15, 1979; "Une architectonique de plaques" in *Tony Long*, exhibition catalogue, Paris 1979; "Dix ans, encore, toujours", interview, with Catherine Millet, in *Art Press International* (Paris), October 1979; "La peinture en excès" in *Peinture: Cahiers Théoriques* (Paris), no. 1, 1980; "Une peinture en personne," interview, with Marcelin Pleynet, in *Peinture: Cahiers Théoriques* (Paris), no. 16, 1981; interview with Catherine Millet and Jacques Henrie in *Art Press* (Paris), June 1981.

On DEVADE: books—*Quelques Problèmes de la Peinture Moderne* by Marcelin Pleynet, Paris 1972; *Art en France* by Jean Clair, Paris 1974; *L'art actuel en France* by Anne Tronche and Hervé Gloaguen, Paris 1974; *Marc Devade: Peintures 1979–1981*, exhibition catalogue, with a preface by Philippe Sollers, and an interview by Marcellin Pleynet, Paris 1981; articles—"Des idées, des critiques, de la peintures et des galeries . . . Marc Devade" by Marcelin Pleynet in *Art International* (Lugano, Switzerland), Summer 1971; "Vio-

Marc Devade: *Peinture*, 1973

lence Feutrée et Attention Flouttant" by Bernard Lamarche-Vadel in *Art Press* (Paris), no. 18, 1975; "Effet Devade" by Bernard Lamarch-Vadel in *Cimaise* (Paris), no. 125–126, 1976; "Waiting for Gloire" by Nancy Marmer in *Artforum* (New York), February 1977; "Le risque du geste et celui du regard" by Catherine Millet in *Art Press International* (Paris), October 1977; "Matière, geste et hasard" by Marc Le Bot in *XXe Siècle* (Paris), no. 49, 1977; "La nuova pittura" by Filiberto Menna in *L'arte Moderna* (Milan), no. 110, 1978; "Contemporary Painting in France" by Paul Rodgers in *Artscribe* (London) August 1978; "Toward a Theory/Practice of Painting in France" by Paul Rodgers in *Artforum* (New York), April 1979; "Le Parti du parti pris" by Geneviève Breerette in *Le Monde* (Paris), 22 September 1979.

Marc Devade has been a member of the French group 'Supports/Surface', and it is within this context that he has worked as a painter. Members of the group included such artists as Dezeuze, Cane, Viallat, Dolla and Saytour. The group's primary aim was to state the problems of art—or, more specifically, painting—at a structuralist level, following Althusser's Marxist interpretation and some Freudian theories enriched by the ideas of Lacan. It was therefore a kind of practice which constantly matched itself to theory. From its formation in 1971, the group expressed its views in the journal *Peinture-Cahiers Theoriques* which represented an up-to-date analysis of the painting of the 'seventies. Far from being dogmatic (and particularly far from any kind of Marxist dogmatism), the group—and Devade in particular—employed a dialectical method of analysis. Devade wrote, "To act and think stand in a dialectical relationships, within which the one term works as a reference point for the other, in a never-ending movement. The unity of theory and praxis is neither a compromise nor an appeal for order; it is rather the safest means to induce transformation in either field".

Furthermore, Devade made use of psychoanalytic theory to establish an enquiry into the pictorial event, not merely limited to the analysis of its media, constituent elements or pertinence, but extending beyond these areas to stress the problem of the place of the Subject vis-a-vis Language. What displaces the positivist position of the subject is the element of sexuality which is expressed as rhythm in the painting prior to becoming formalised and institutionalised. Devade applies himself to the problems of colour, to the extent that it 'produces' the painting as it drives the needs of the subject engaged in the act of painting.

Devade is inspired by American experiences such as Kenneth Noland's, by a kind of practice that locates painting in its own physical field and self-referentiality. Devade's analysis, however, was not limited to this. His analysis also succeeded in grasping and expressing the movement between the poles of geometry and colour—a rhetoric of impulses. His structure of painting-within-the-painting during 1968–69 (of the square frame within which the painting is enclosed) became a code within which the moment a construction made possible a rational reading of the work it also posited itself as one of the dialectical poles.

The other critical element was colour, with its quasi-evocative values—a kind of colour that imposed on the painting autonomous values of the chromatic surface. In later works (1972), the artist eliminated the geometrical linear grid that delimited the organization of the colour; at the same time, he substituted inks for acrylic colours, as the fluidity of ink allows the artist to deal with the surface as a field of events quite independent of his own will. In this way, he obtains layered effects, more or less saturated areas and haloes of colour. For the earlier preconceived structure, he substituted a fragile and aleatory system, sometimes splitting the canvas in two to form a diptych. In certain cases, Devade applied strips of wood as enclosures to delimit particular areas of the canvas. These areas would be free of colour, creating more or less rectangular white spaces. At times, such areas would appear to the viewer as the mnemonic relics of a geometric universe which by then had disintegrated.

By thus interrupting the surface, Devade actually acted upon the structural, signifying a differentiation between design and colour. At this stage, colour is no longer a complement to line, mark or form; on the contrary, it comes to indicate form as an absence, meaning that the formal hypothesis appeared within the visual field of the work as a pointer to the beyond and to the void.

—Giorgio Verzotti

de VREE, Paul.

Belgian. Born in Antwerp, 13 November 1909. Educated at l'Ecole Normale, Antwerp, 1924–28, and at the University of Ghent, 1934–38. Served as a Reserve Lieutenant, Belgian Army, 1929–47; mobilized, 1939–40. Married Charlotte Marie Versterren, 1932; son: Frits. Visual poet; lives and works in Antwerp. Primary School Teacher, Antwerp, 1932–41; Professor of Secondary Instruction, Antwerp, 1941–44, and at the Athenaeum, Lier, Belgium, 1951–69. Editor, *De Brug* magazine, Antwerp, 1944–51. Recipient: Poetry Prize, Province of Antwerp, 1935; Order of Knighthood, Brussels, 1974; Prize for complete works, Province of Antwerp, 1981. Agent: Studio Brescia, Italy. Address: 46 Camille Huysmanslaan, 2020 Antwerp, Belgium.

Paul De Vree: *Lady Chatterley*, **1972**

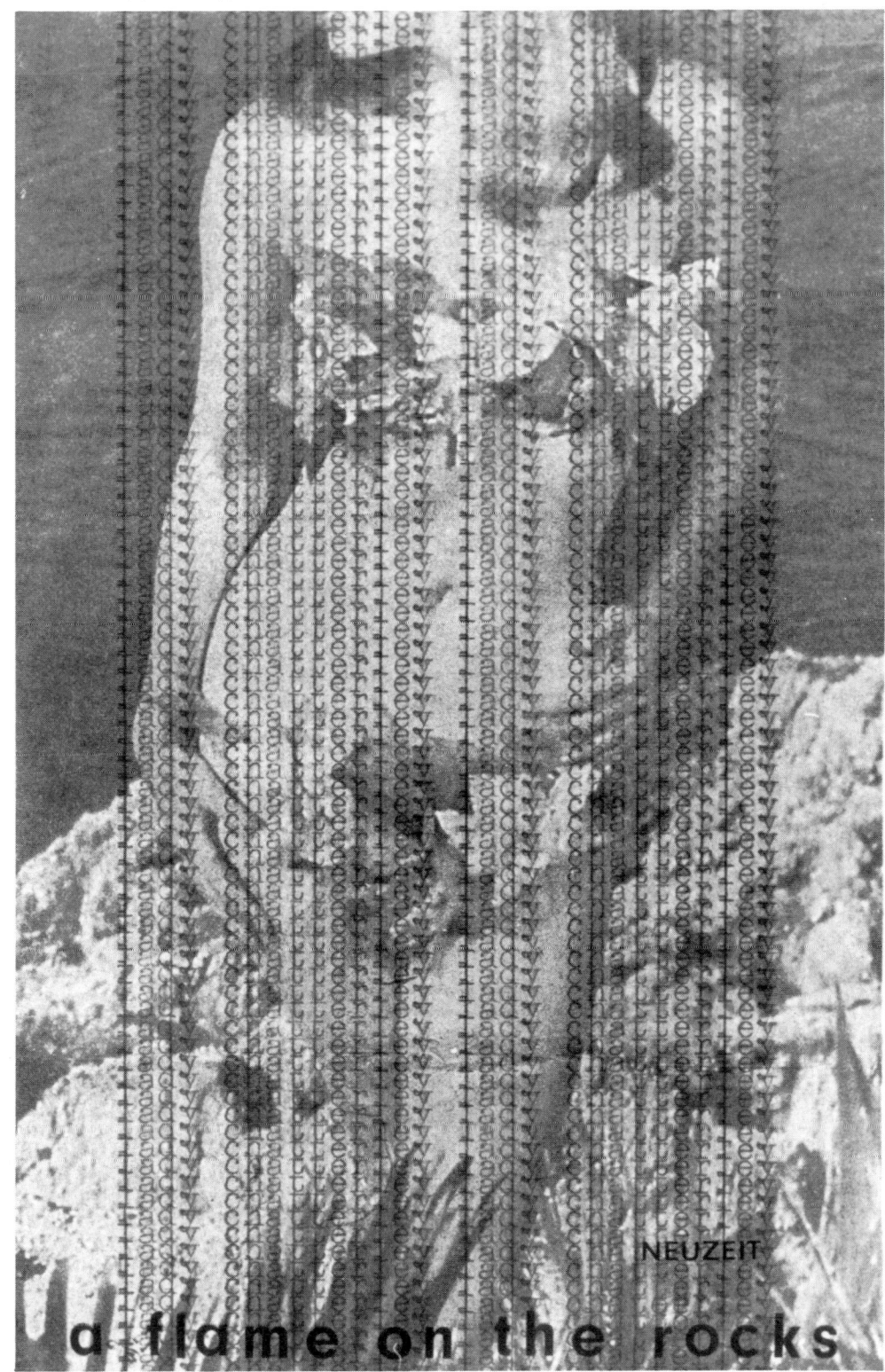

Individual Exhibitions:

1971	Galleria S. Chiara, Brescia, Italy
	DeVaart Galerie, Hilversum, Netherlands
1972	Museum Van Vlaamse Letterkunde, Antwerp
	Studio Santandrea, Milan
1973	Studio Brescia, Brescia, Italy
1974	Galleria Il Canale, Venice
	Museum Van Schone Kunsten, Antwerp
1975	Galerie Au Quai, Liège, Belgium
	Galleria Santelmo, Salo, Italy
1976	Galerie Richard Foncke, Ghent
1977	Galerie Artel, Antwerp
	Galerie Drieghe, Wetteren, Belgium
1979	Galerie Candid, Ghent
	Galerie Buytaert, Antwerp
1981	Provinciaal Begijnhof, Hasselt, Belgium
	Galerie De Brakke Grond, Amsterdam

Selected Group Exhibitions:

1971	*Konkrete Poezie*, Stedelijk Museum, Amsterdam (travelled to the International Cultureel Centrum, Antwerp)
1972	*Poesia Visiva*, travelling exhibition (toured Italy, Germany and Gellgium, until 1974)

Collections:

Museum of Fine Arts, Antwerp; Museum of Modern Arts, Ieper, Belgium; Ministry of Culture, Brussels.

Publications:

By de VREE: books—*Posia Visiva*, Rome 1975; *Verzamelde Gedichten*, Bruges 1978; *De Brandwonden*, Verona 1979; *The Street Tells the Truth*, Verona 1979; *Naar het einde*, Hilversum, Netherlands 1979; articles—"Zimprovisaties" in *De Tafelronde* (Antwerp), 1968; "Poezie in Fusie" in *De Balden Voor de Poezie* (Lier), 1968; article in *Konkrete Poezie*, exhibition catalogue, Amsterdam 1970; "Verbaal Gelaat" in *De Tafelronde* (Antwerp), 1970; "Poezien" in *Amodula* (Brescia, Italy), 1971; "Maskers" in *De Tafelronde* (Antwerp), 1973; article in *Jozef Peeters*, exhibition catalogue, Antwerp 1973; "De Visule Poezie in Belgie en Nederland" in *De Tafelronde* (Antwerp), no. 4, 1973.

On de VREE: books—*10 huize van . . . 13* by Joos Florquin, Louvain 1977; *Monographie Paul De Vree* by Henri Floris Jespers, Antwerp 1977; *Paul de Vree*, exhibition catalogue, Hasselt, Belgium 1981; articles—"Poesia Visiva-Visuelle Poezie" by Urs Graf in *Werk* (Berne), LIX 1972; "Paul de Vree" by Erik Salgter in *Litareir Lustrum* (Amsterdam), no. 2, 1973; "Monography Paul de Vree" by Sarenco in *Lotto Poetica* (Brescia, Italy), no. 37–38, 1974.

The texture and structure of my poetry have, as a whole, evolved from the audio-visual phase to that of visual poetry, pure synglossy: the indivisible unity of the work and image. The spirit of this poetry is not born from the desire to amuse myself with letters, nor from the need to employ graphics, mechanical means and collage to attain aesthetic effects. The new methods, by which since Mallarmé, the futurists and the dadaists have restored to poetry its freshness and its striking power, these methods I have applied, above all since the revolutionary days of May 1968, to find with several spiritual companions a poetry which fitted the demands which communication poses in relation to the recoil that consciousness undergoes when information is manipulated by the authorities.

—Paul de Vree

DE VRIES, Herman.

Dutch. Born in Alkmaar, 11 July 1931. Studied at the Ecole des Beaux-Arts, Montpellier, France, 1949–52. Married in 1956 (divorced 1968); children: Mirgam, Marc, Dirk, Merik and Herman Vincent. Worked in the plant protection service, at the Institute for Applied Biological Research in Nature, Alkmaar, 1952–68. First art activities, Alkmaar, 1953; first mobile works, 1954; first monochrome paintings and collages, 1956; participated in Zero group exhibitions, 1961–63; researched random systems, 1962–75; experimental language and poetry, 1965; chance and change processes, 1970. Published *NUL=Zero* magazine, Amsterdam, 1961–64; *Revue Integration*, Amsterdam, 1965–72; and Eschenau Summer Press (temporary travelling press), since 1974. Agents: Antoinette Hilgemann, Havendijk 40, Gorinchem, Netherlands; Galerie Muller-Roth, Blumentstrasse 15, Stuttgart; and Galerie Lydia Megert, Munstergasse 6, Berne, Switzerland. Address: 8729 Eschenau nr. 8, Knetzgau bei Hassfurt/Main, West Germany.

Individual Exhibitions:

1959	Galerie 31, Dordrecht, Netherlands
1960	Mensa, Delft
1963	Galerie Wulfengasse 14, Klagenfurt, Austria
	Metz and Company, Amsterdam
1964	Galerie D., Frankfurt
1965	Galerie Knoll, Basle
	Galerie Akruell, Berne
	Galerie Loehr, Frankfurt (with Colombo)
1967	'tVenster, Rotterdam
	't Ouwe Tientje, Arnhem
	Galerie Julicher, Mönchengladbach, West Germany
	Galerie Hansjorg Mayer, Stuttgart
1968	Gemeentemuseum, The Hague
	Nederlandse Kunststichting, Zeist, Netherlands
	Felison, Ijmuiden, Netherlands
1969	Art Academy, Copenhagen
1970	Galerie Swart, Amsterdam
	Galerie Swart, Amsterdam (with Frieder Nake)
	Kunsthistorisch Instituut, Amsterdam
	Galerie M., Bochum, West Germany
1971	Utrechtse Kring, Utrecht
	Galerie Swart, Amsterdam
	Galerie Lichter, Frankfurt
	I.K.I., Dusseldorf
1972	Galerie Teufel, Koblenz
	Aktionsgalerie, Berne (with Sarenco)
	I.K.I./Modern Art Galerie, Dusseldorf
1973	Galerie Swart, Amsterdam
1974	Lucy Milton Gallery, London
	Galerie Swart, Amsterdam
	Galerie Lydia Megert, Berne
	Galerie am Wochenende, Feldkirchen, West Germany
1975	Galerie Hermanns, Furstenfeldbruck, West Germany
	Stedelijk Museum, Amsterdam
1976	*At Random*, Kunstcentrum Badhuis, Gorinchem, Netherlands
	Galerie Swart, Amsterdam
1977	Galerie Lydia Megert, Berne
	Galerie Muller-Roth, Stuttgart
	Galerie Magazijn, Groningen, Netherlands
1978	Lieftinghsbroek Nature Reserve, Groningen, Netherlands
1979	De Vleeshal, Middelburg, Netherlands
	Galerie Lydia Megert, Berne
	Galerie Muller-Roth, Stuttgart
1980	*Werken 1954–1980*, Groninger Museum, Groningen, Netherlands
	Galerie Swart, Amsterdam
	Galerie Magazijn, Groningen, Netherlands
	Kunsthistorisch Instituut, Groningen University, Netherlands
1981	Van Reckum Museum, Apeldoorn, Netherlands
	Het Apollonius, Eindhoven, Netherlands
1982	Gemeentemusuem, The Hague
	Gomera, Canary Islands

Selected Group Exhibitions:

1957	*Natuur en Kunst*, Stedelijk Museum, Amsterdam
1962	*Nul*, Stedelijk Museum, Amsterdam
1965	*Licht und Bewegung*, Kunsthalle, Berne
1970	*Konkrete Poesie*, Stedelijk Museum, Amsterdam
1974	*Basically White*, Institute of Contemporary Arts, London
1975	*Poesia Concreta 1952–1967*, Biblioteca Nazionale, Florence
1976	*System + Program*, Patac Kulturyi Nanki, Warsaw
1979	*Zero*, Kunsthaus, Zurich
1980	*Pier + Ocean*, Hayward Gallery, London
1981	*Lapidar*, Galerie Muller-Roth, Stuttgart

Collections:

Sammlung Albertina, Vienna; Haggs Gremeentemuseum, The Hague; Stedelijk Museum, Amsterdam; Van Abbemuseum, Eindhoven, Netherlands; Kröller-Müller Museum, Otterlo, Netherlands; Kunstmuseum, Dusseldorf; Staatsgalerie, Stuttgart; Kunsthaus, Zurich; Museum Sztuki, Lodz, Poland; Museum of Modern Art, New York.

Publications:

By DE VRIES: books—*Wit is overdaad*, Amsterdam 1960; *Manifest van de gecastreerde werkelijkheid*, Amsterdam 1960; *Wit*, with introduction by J. C. Van Schagen, Amsterdam 1962; *Permutierbard Text*, Stuttgart 1967; *Wit/Weiss*, Stuttgart 1967; *Change*, Amsterdam 1970; *Ramdom Objectivations*, Brescia, Italy 1972; *Chance-fields/Chancefelder: An Essay on the Topology of Randomness*, Dinkelscherben 1973; *The Wittgenstein Paper, I and II*, Berne 1974; *To Be All Ways to Be*, Katmandu 1974; *Vijf Manifesten over Taal—en een Gedicht*, Berne 1975; *Asiatische und Eschenauer Texte*, portfolio, Berne 1975; *October, February, June*, Eschenau 1977; *The Dust of Some Roads and Leaf from a Tree*, Eschenau 1977; *Some Early Change Projects/Einige fruhe anderungs Projekte 1963–1967*, portfolio with tape cassette, Berne 1977; *16 dm2, an Essay*, Berne 1979; *Concept*, Eschenau 1981; *Documents of a Stream*, Eindhoven, Netherlands 1981; *From Here*, Gorinchem, Netherlands 1982; articles—"Nul=0" in *Nul=0* (Amsterdam), vol 1, no. 10, 1962; "Random Objectivations" in *Nul=0* (Amsterdam), vol. 2, no. 34–35, 1963; "Objektivitat und Wirklichkeit" in *Nul=0* (Amsterdam), vol. 4, no. 83–85; "Visuel Informatie/Visual Information/Visuelle Information/Information Visuelle" in *Revue Integration* (Amsterdam), vol. 1, 1965; "Wit/White/Blanc" in *Revue Integration* (Amsterdam), vol 9, 1967; "Fragmentarische Argumenten: in *Felison—Kahier* (Ijmuiden), no. 10, 1968; "Notes for a Random Reader" in *Panel 13 Information* (Copenhagen), no. 1, 1968; "The Lines of Life and Love" in *Bulletin Festival 200* (Copenhagen), no. 1, 1969; "Chance and Change" in *Prospectus Galerie Swart*, exhibition catalogue, Amsterdam 1974; "The Wittgenstein Papers—framentarische argumenten" in *Taal Beeld Taal* (Brummen), no. 1, 1975; "A Line" in *Museumjournaal* (Amsterdam), no. 6, 1976; films—*Look Out of any Window*, 1972; *100 Ansichten von grossen Knetzberg*, 1972; *Chance and Change*, 1973; *A Letter from James*, 1977; *The Flower-Sutra*, 1979; *Film-Notes*, 1979; *Water Pictures*, 1980; sound-recordings—*Natura Artis Magistra*, tape-cassette, 1967; *Humanae Vitae*, tape-cassette, 1967; *Natura Artis Magistra and Humanae Vitae*, tape-cassette with drawing, 1971; *Water—The Music of Sound*, 1977.

On DE VRIES: books—*Herman De Vries* by Walter Aue, Cologne 1966; *Constructivism: Orgins and Evolution* by George Rickey, New York 1967; *Herman De Vries*, exhibition catalogue, with text by Herbert V. Franke, Bochum, West Germany, 1970; *Konkret Dichtung* by Siegfried J. Schmidt, Munich 1972; *Asthetik als Informationsverarbeitung* by Frieder Nake, Vienna and New York 1974; *Programmi Sistematici* by Jean Leering, Milan 1975; *Herman De Vries: At Random*, exhibition catalogue, with an introduction by Antoinette Hilgemann-de Stiger, Gorinchem, Netherlands 1976; *Konstruktive Konzepte* by Willy Rotzler, Zurich 1977; *Nederlandse Kunstenarsboeken* by Flip Bool and G. J. de Rook, The Hague 1978; *Herman De Vries: Werken 1954–1980*, exhibition catalogue, with an introduction by Frans Haks, and essays by Urs and Ros Graf, Groningen, Netherlands 1980.

Around 1960, my grey-white informal paintings changed slowly to empty white canvases under the influence of the Buddhist thought of emptiness.

Some years later, I was looking for structure without giving up the objectivity, the emptiness of limited

Herman De Vries: *Das grosse Rasenstuck*, 1979

and limiting meaning I had gained in the white paintings with homogenous surfaces.

In my biological work I used randomness as a means for leaving out the influence of the researcher in the research series, and discovered that this system was very useful to come to form again and not to have to say anything. In the following 14 years I was mainly occupied with "random objectivations"—researching visual relationships in random programs. During this work, I became interested in the nature of randomness and chance: the existing definitions were not satisfying nor did they coincide with the results of my work. By following definitions of randomness and of art and always having to change them again and again, I realized that there are limits to the intellect. In this period, I also found that the patterns of *chance* were connected to *change:* they were all around in everyday reality. I tried to document them, first in photo-series at the beginning of the 70's, and later in the facts of reality itself—works which I now call "actuality as a document of itself."

Last year I crossed the border between art and non-art, between art and actuality, so becoming free of an important contradiction. My parallel ongoing preoccupations with philosophy and poetry all became integrated.

A final statement is not possible to give. When I say "all," I include the negation "not all"; so I prefer to leave it open.

—Herman de Vries

From 1949 to 1952 Herman de Vries was a student at the Montpellier Ecole des Beaux-Arts. Even that was for him a period when he was intensely caught up with the patterning wrought by geometric fragments hanging together as mobiles, but subsequently conjured into monochrome oil paintings which proved a short step to collages of the same character.

In 1965 he made his first experiments with *con-*

crete poetry and by 1968 had become an active contributor to the Edition Hansjörg Mayer's great anthology exhibition at the Hague's Gemeentemuseum with a number of exhibits which (besides unnumbered blank or patterned pages) included a wild conglomeration of interwoven linear triangles with title: "empty space for an empty space prepared for you by herman de vries this one is for him".

Ten years after found him at work upon pocket-multiples (white squares each with ten black spots, dots would be a more accurate description of them, in quasi-casual disarray on their surfaces) and—rather larger—1 decimeter^2 in dimension and when fully assembled stretching 16 decimeters in extent. These were not only bigger than the pocket-multiples, the black images set central on each part of the full assembly of squares were non-fugurative, of course, but more complicated than those of the pocket-multiples and were richly different, each from each.

Herman de Vries, in his casual economy of means, with a predominant desire to establish what imagery he does employ in implied boundless space, has somehow translated the freedom of the mobile onto a two-dimensional surface. In doing so he has endowed his works with an enduring character of liberty.

—Sheldon Williams

DEWASNE, Jean.

French. Born in Lille, 21 May 1921. Studied music, the classics and architecture, at the Ecole des Beaux-Arts, Paris. Produced first abstract paintings, Paris, 1943; Member, Abstract art group, with Hartung, Schneider, de Staël, Poliakoff and Deyrolle, Paris, 1945; Founder-Member, with Jean Arp, Antoine Pevsner, Sonia Delaunay and others, Salon des Réalités Nouvelles, Paris, 1945; painted first large mural commission, Paris, 1948; Founder-Director, Studio of Abstract Art, Paris, 1950–53. Has travelled and lectured extensively in Europe and America, since 1951. Recipient: Kandinsky Award, Paris, 1945. Address: 18 rue du Bourg-Tibourg, 75004 Paris, France.

Individual Exhibitions:

1949	Arne Bruun-Rasmussen Galerie, Copenhagen
1955	Palais des Beaux-Arts, Brussels
	Arne Bruun-Rasmussen Galerie, Copenhagen
1956	Galerie Cordier, Paris
1959	Palais des Beaux-Arts, Brussels
1961	Galleria Lorenzelli, Milan
1962	Carrefour Galerie, Brussels
1963	Galerie Cordier, Paris
	Galerie Hybler, Copenhagen
	Esbjerg Museum, Denmark
1965	Cordier-Ekstrom Gallery, New York
1966	Kunsthalle, Berne (retrospective)
1967	Galleria Lorenzelli, Bergamo, Italy
1969	Musée d'Art Moderne, Paris
	Palais des Beaux-Arts, Brussels
1971	Galerie Creuzevalt, Paris
1972	Lefebre Gallery, New York
	Galerie Janssen, Brussels
1973	Galerie Francoise Tournier, Paris
	Galerie Artel, Geneva
	Soto Museum, Ciudad Bolivar, Venezuela
1974	Louisiana Museum, Humlebaek, Denmark
	Nordyllands Kunstmuseum, Aalborg, Denmark
	Orly Airport, Paris
1975	Galerie Mark, Zurich
	Centre d'Art et Loisirs, Privas, France

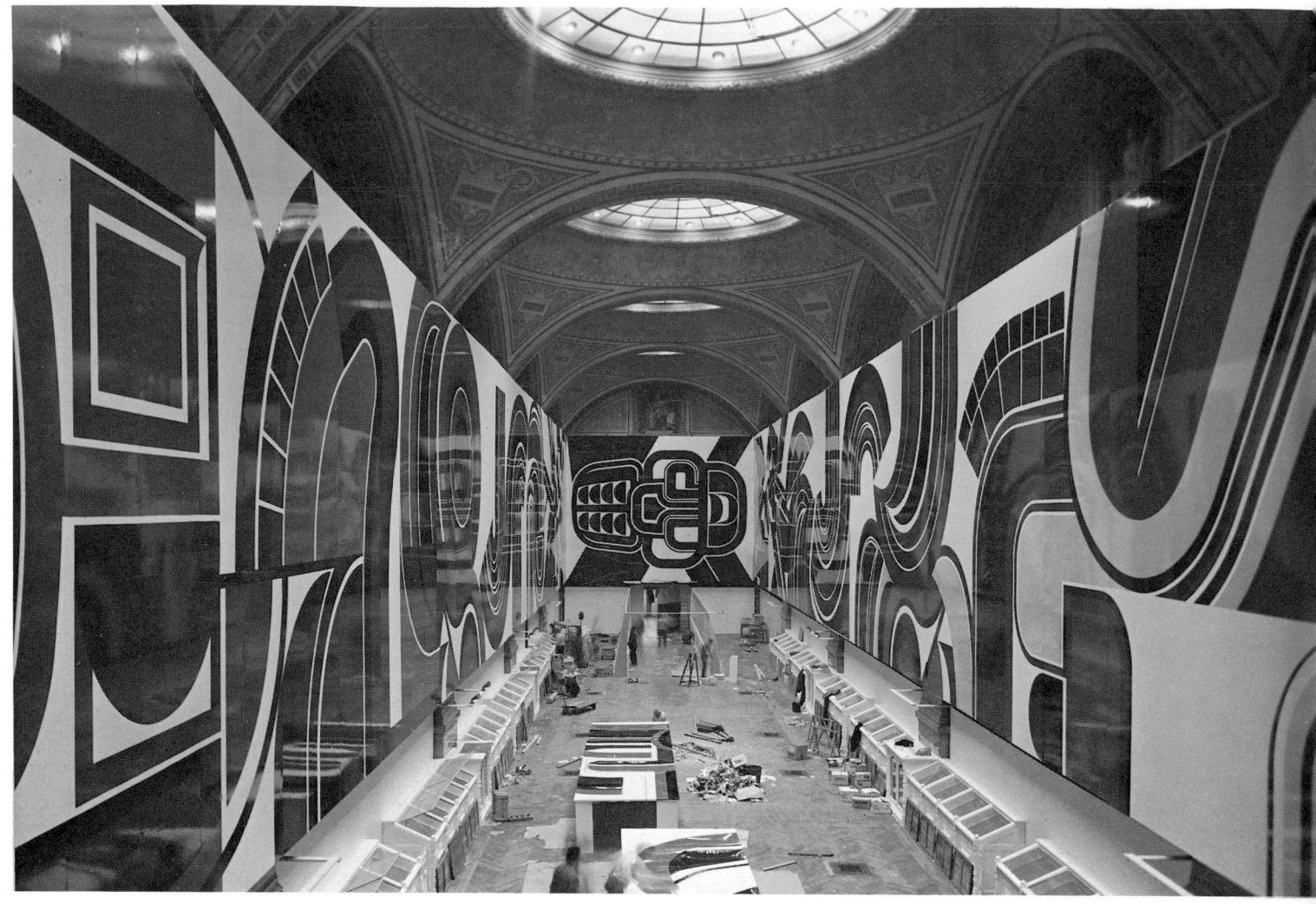

Jean Dewasne: Mural at the Musée de Grenoble, France, 1970

Maison des Arts et Loisirs, Sochaux, France (toured
France)
Musée d'Art Moderne de la Ville, Paris
Carnegie Institute, Pittsburgh (toured the United
States)
Musée d'Art Moderne, Paris
Galerie Remarque, Trans en Provence, France
Esbjerg Kunstforening, Denmark (toured Denmark)
Idées Contemporaines, Pontaven, France
Galerie Attali, Paris
Jean Dewasne, Muraliste, Kunstverein, Hannover
Centre Culturel Pablo Neruda, Corbeil, France
Centre Action Culturel, Macon, France
1976 Centre d'Art et Communication, Vaduz, Liechten-
stein
Galeria d'Arte Contacto, Caracas
1977 *Gouches et Dessins,* Galerie Asbaek, Copenhagen
Galerie Groninger, Groningen, Netherlands
Antisculptures et Gouaches, Nordjyllands Kunstmu-
seum, Aalborg
1978 *Antisculptures, Maxi-Peintures, Gouaches,* Henie
Onstad Museum, Oslo
Conceptions, Institut Francais, Stockholm
1979 Galerie Sapone, Nice
Museum of Modern Art, Caracas
1980 Grand Palais, Paris
1981 *La Longue Marche,* Centre Georges Pompidou,
Paris

Selected Group Exhibitions:

1945 *Salon des Réalités Nouvelles,* Paris
1968 *Biennale,* Venice
1972 *The Non-Objective World 1939–1955,* Annely Juda
Fine Art, London (toured Europe)

Douze Ans d'Art Contemporain en France, Grand
Palais, Paris
1975 *Kunstmesse Art 6/75,* Basle
Art Fair, Cologne
1976 *Artists from France,* Covent Garden, London
1981 *Paris—Paris 1937–1957,* Centre Georges Pompidou, Paris

Collections:

Nordyllands Kunstmuseum, Aalborg, Denmark; Louisiana
Museum, Humlebaek, Denmark; Boymans van Beuningen
Museum, Rotterdam; Musée des Beaux-Arts, Brussels; Cen-
tre Georges Pompidou, Paris; Musée de Grenoble, France,
Carnegie Institute, Pittsburgh; Guggenheim Museum, New
York; Museum of Modern Art, New York.

Publications:

By DEWASNE: books—illustrations for *Preface to a Future
Book* by Lautreamont, Copenhagen 1949; *Robert Jacobsen,*
Copenhagen 1950; *Vasarely,* Paris 1952: *Traité de la peinture*
(written in 1949), Paris 1972; articles—"Mathematical Space
and Abstract Art" in *20th Siècle* (Paris) no. 2, 1952; "The
Paintings of the Cuzco School" in *Lettres Francaises* (Paris),
September/October 1952; "Visit to the Secret City of
Macchu-Picchu" in *Lettres Francaises* (Paris), March 1956;
"Romanesque Paintings and Gothic Painting in Denmark" in
Lettres Francaises (Paris), October 1956; "Andrea del Castagno" and "The Gods of Saint Augustine" in *Letters Francaises* (Paris), August 1957; "What Is Avant-Garde in 1958"
in *Lettres Francaises* (Paris), June 1958; "Reflections on Abstract Art in *Quadrum* (Brussels), no. 7, 1959; "Abstract Art
and Objectivity" in *Nouvelle Critique* (Paris), September
1968; "The Problem of the Wall" in *L'Oeil* (Paris),
September/October 1971; "De la Théorie au Concept" with

E. Mavrommatis, in *Opus* (Paris), no. 37, 1972; "Dedie au
spectateur" in *Galerie des Arts* (Paris), March 1977; "Une
création mathématisée" in *Gazette des Beaux-Arts* (Paris),
September 1977.

On DEWASNE: books—*Jean Dewasne* by Pierre Descargues, Paris 1952; *Jean Dewasne,* exhibition catalogue, with
texts by several authors, Milan 1961; *Dewasne,* exhibtion catalogue, with text by Daniel Cordier, New York 1965; *Dewasne,* exhibition catalogue, with text by Daniel Cordier,
New York 1972; *The Mondial Art 1960–1975,* edited by Germain Viatte, Geneva 1975; *From Thorvaldsen to the Atomic
Age,* edited by Sigurd Schultz, Copenhagen 1975; *Art Actuel:
Skira Annuel 75,* Geneva 1975.

Here is a general theory of aesthetic creation:
The artist begins by formulating dynamic currents
in order to express the drama of plastic happenings.
Because of this, the assemblies cannot be isolated
from their liaisons. The rhythm of these liaisons gives
the work its main meanings. The dynamic currents
and the filiations impose the sittings and the positions.
The positions, within the currents, give rise to
other plastic assemblies which momentarily hold the
spectator's attention. This period of contemplation
and analysis permits the spectator to experience mental speculations which can ensure and multiply his
pleasure. They prepare him to then throw himself into
the torrent of the current; this, in its turn, can be
considered as a significant assembly, one that can be
analysed, a detectable one. The relative positions, the
situations, the combinations triumph over the form-
colour elements that were visible at first. The structures of association will liberate from the

constellations and, indirectly, as a result, from the configurations of the fabric of the messages.

The adagios, the lentos intermingle with the baroque "fortes," taking support in invisible outlines that are very complex in themselves, submitting to the topological laws of the situation.

In the course of the formulation of the work, the artist knowingly runs the maximum of possible dangers: many errors are voluntarily touched upon many losses envisaged. In the choices constantly incited by the creation, the artist opts for risk. His strategy of decision always leads him towards the uncomfortable, the unknown. When the evolution of the happenings of the creation at its various levels seems too sober, he voluntarily provokes skidding. If the position shows itself to be unmaintainable, the creator has the opportunity to advance towards some interesting result.

The work of art does not have to search for a maximum probability. It would quickly become banal and boring. It must deliberately opt for the most unforeseen probability. When a fairly improbable plastic thought provokes a new solution, it immediately acquires the most powerful affective charge. Here, logic does not control creation; it is at its service: it does not close, it opens.

The overall effects of the creation do not at all depend on the overall initial conditions, but on the interactions, the correlations, the feed-back effects, rebounds and ricochets of the creative action.

It is to be wished that the phenomena intensify from the beginning to the end of the plastic happening. The total work incites a cumulative phenomenon.

—Jean Dewasne

After training as a sculptor Jean Dewasne turned to painting in the hard-edged geometrical styles associated with Vasarely and Herbin. From easel paintings he has enlarged his formats to long and continuously evolving patterns in which channels of colours follow their progressive rhythms in interchanging directions to arrive at their starting point, repeating in two-dimensional equivalents the perimeter of a building or the track of a stadium.

In 1949 Dewasne wrote *Traité de la peinture,* reflections on the creative process of painting which he expresses thus: "The work results from contact between two facts acting according to their own laws and which coincide in one: the material and the artist—the work says more than its creator." His development has stressed the mural potential in painting beyond the rectangular format of traditional character and more towards the architectural domination of the environment by dynamically placed areas of strong colour. These murals such as that for the ice stadium at Grenoble which is 3 metres high and 60 metres wide and the "Longue marche" that measures 2 metres high and 100 metres long become by themselves backgrounds and curtain walls whose space exercises optical control over everything before it assumes the proportions of natural phenomena such as a cliff or ski run.

While Optical art has generated the climate of acceptance of Dewasne's massive compositions he has achieved a unique synthesis of the formal motives embodied in his paintings and their progressive unfolding of the basic knots of formal design in a formal unity, suggestive of landscape gardening and the mosaics of Moresque architecture. Something of modern technological plotting is inherent in the boldly hued strips running parallel and crossing and interchanging in their progressive journey, yet their inevitable structure implies a movement time has arrested. Curved, triangular and stepped conjunctions move to and fro in balanced harmonies of weight and contrast. The eye is not dazzled as in a Bridget Riley painting; the continuity of strips in associations of width and space achieve an empathy with the spectator leaving a neutral reaction in terms of individual shapes, but their linking produces a feeling of satisfaction in regard to evolution in time.

Eminently expressive of the artist's theories relating to spatial control of an environment no matter how limited, Dewasne's work is capable of great expansion in its role in dictating the mood and planar atmosphere of buildings or boundary surfaces. His "Antisculptures," in which he took parts of automobile bodies and errected them as freestanding objects that he proceeded to paint in patterns breaking up their outlines in the fashion of wartime comouflage, were somewhat equivocal in their results in as much as their effects were to some extent controlled by their backgrounds and angles of viewing—less successful than his mural colour tracks where painting becomes its own background and thus dominates the casual objects that come before it.

—G. S. Whittet

DEZEUZE, Daniel.

French. Born in Ales-Gard, 1 February 1942. Educated at the Ecole des Beaux-Arts, Montpellier, 1959–62; studied Spanish literature at the Faculté des Lettres, University of Montpellier, 1959–62 (Licence-és-Lettres, 1962, Diplome d'Etudes Supérieures, 1965); also studied at the School of Architecture, Mexico University, 1964–65, and at the Sorbonne, Paris, 1967–70 (Doctorat 1970). Married Karen Nesbitt in 1974. Served as assistant in charge of cultural affairs, French Consulate, Toronto, 1965–66. Instructor, Alliance Francaise, Avila, Spain, 1962–63; Lecturer, French Department, University of Toronto, 1966–67, and French Summer School, McGill University, Montreal, Summers 1969–1970; Instructor, Ecole des Arts Décoratifs, Nice, 1973–74, and Ecole Nationale des Beaux-Arts, Bourges, 1974–75; Professor, Ecole des Beaux-Arts, Montpellier, since 1982. Agents: Yvon Lambert, 5 rue Grenier Saint Lazare, 75005 Paris, France; Albert Baronian, 67 Boulevard St. Michel, 1040 Brussels, Belgium. Address: Villa Lucia, Chemin de Saint Clair, impasse 27/4, 34200 Sete, France.

Individual Exhibitions:

1971	Galerie Yvon Lambert, Paris
1973	Galerie Yvon Lambert, Paris
1974	Galerie Albert Baronian, Brussels
1975	Galerie Yvon Lambert, Paris
1976	Galerie Maillard, St. Paul de Vence, France
	Galerie D'Allessandro-Ferranti, Rome
	Maison de la Culture, Bourges, France
1977	Julian Pretto Gallery, Fine Arts Building, New York
	Galerie ADDA, Marseilles
	Galerie Depot, Bourges, France
	Galerie Yvon Lambert, Paris
1978	Galleria Artra Studio, Milan
	Galerie Rudolf Zwirner, Cologne
	Foundation M.L. Jeanneret, Boissano, Italy
	Galerie Albert Baronian, Brussels
1979	Galerie Meda-Mothi, Montpellier, France
	Musée du Parc de la Boverie, Liège, Belgium
1980	Galerie Artline, The Hague
	Musée d'Art et d'Industrie, Saint-Etienne, France
	Musée de l'Abbaye Sainte-Croix, Les Sables d'O-lonne, France
1981	Galerie Yvon Lambert, Paris
1982	Artra Studio, Milan
1983	Galerie Yvon Lambert, Paris
	Galerie L'Hermite, Coutances, France
1984	Galerie l'Ollave, Lyon, France
1985	Galerie Yvon Lambert, Paris
	Galerie L'Hermite, Coutances, France
1986	Galerie des Arènes, Nîmes, France
	Galerie Archétype, Nice, France
1987	Galerie Yvon Lambert, Paris
	Gemeentemuseum, The Hague

Selected Group Exhibitions:

1969	*Biennale,* Paris
1970	*Supports/Surfaces,* Musée d'Art Moderne de la Ville, Paris
1972	*Bioules/Cane/Dezeuze/Devade,* Galleria Francoise Lambert, Milan
1975	*Europalia 12 x 1,* Palais des Beaux-Arts, Brussels
1978	*Aspects de l'Art en France,* Kunstmesse, Basle
1979	*Tendances de l'Art en France 1968–1979,* Musée d'Art Moderne de la Ville, Paris
1981	*The Subject of Painting,* Museum of Modern Art, Oxford (travelled to the Arnolfini Gallery, Bristol)
1984	*Ecritures dans la Peinture,* Villa Arson, Nice, France
1986	*Pictura Loquens,* Villa Arson, Nice, France (travelled to Palazzo Reale, Milan)

Collections:

Musée d'Art et d'industrie, Saint Etienne, France; Musée Cantini, Marseille, France; Musée Sainte Croix, Les Sables d'Olonne, France; Musée Fabre, Montpellier, France; Musée Picasso, Antibes, France; Musée National d'Art Moderne, Paris; Australian National Gallery, Canberra.

Publications:

By DEZEUZE: books—*Les toiles systématiquement tamponnées de Louis Cane,* Paris 1971; *Note sur le système euclidien et le dessin,* Paris 1971; *Brève relation d'un lointain voyage,* Melun, France 1983; *S-Clavo,* Paris 1986; articles—essay in *Support/Surfaces,* exhibition catalogue, Paris 1970; "Notes sur le Systeme Euclidien et le Dessin" in *Dezeuze,* exhibition catalogue, Paris 1971; "Les Toiles Systematiquement Tamponnées de Louis Cane" in *Louis Cane,* exhibition catalogue, Paris 1971; "Situation et Travail du Groupe Supports/Surfaces" in *VH 101* (Paris), Spring 1971; "Pour un Programme Théorique Pictural," with Louis Cane, and "Note Complementaire" in *Peinture: Cahiers Théoriques* (Montpellier) no. 1, June 1971; "Sans Titre" in *Actualité d'un Bilan,* exhibition catalogue, Paris 1972; "Lecture d'un Texte de Thomas Herbert" in *Peinture: Cahiers Théoriques* (Paris), no 2–3, January 1972; "La notion de non-representation chez Tchouang Tseu" in *Spirali* (Milan), no. 1, 1978; "Daniel Dezeuze: entretien", with E. Grazioli, in *Flash Art* (Milan), April 1987.

On DEZEUZE: books—*Le Nouveau Grand Espace* by Marcelin Pleynet, Paris 1971; *Art en France, Une Nouvelle Generation* by Jean Clair, Paris 1972; *L'Art Actuel en France* by Anne Tronche and Hervé Gloaguen, Paris 1973; *Daniel Dezeuze* by E. Grazioli, Milan 1978; *Daniel Dezeuze,* exhibition catalogue, with text by Bernard Ceysson, interview by Jacques Beauffet, Saint-Etienne, France 1980; *Comme la Peinture/Like Painting (Daniel Dezeuze)* by Christian Prigent, Paris 1983; *Support/Surface* by J. Poinsot, Paris 1983; *Daniel Dezeuze,* exhibition catalogue with text by P. Javault, The Hague 1987; articles—"Daniel Dezeuze, La Peinture et son Espace" by Christian Prigent in *Art Press* (Paris), March/April 1975; "Du Differe d'un Discours" by Marcelin Pleynet in *Europalia,* exhibition catalogue, Brussels 1975; "D'un Trait" by Alain Coulange in *Gamme* (Paris), no. 6, 1977; "Daniel Dezeuze" by B. Ceysson in *Catalogue Blickfelder 81,* exhibition catalogue, Bielefeld 1981.

What's happened to the empty space that was so central to your previous work?

It's true that emptiness was an important feature in the sense that it recurred as part of a geometrical repetition; it was rhythmical, exposed by repetition and by a geometrical infrastructure. Here, it's true, there are far fewer empty spaces, particularly with regard to the wooden assemblages which are on the contrary extremely compact and heavily grounded. But I wasn't in any sense trying to do the opposite of what I'd done before; that's not it at all. I think that when I was working with masses I concentrated on the cut of the outline in the way that I'd done to a large extent with gauzes, but, obviously, I abandoned the notion of emptiness in order to create something very concentrated, something which wasn't about to disappear or disperse into thin air, but which was on the contrary extremely dense and closed in on itself.

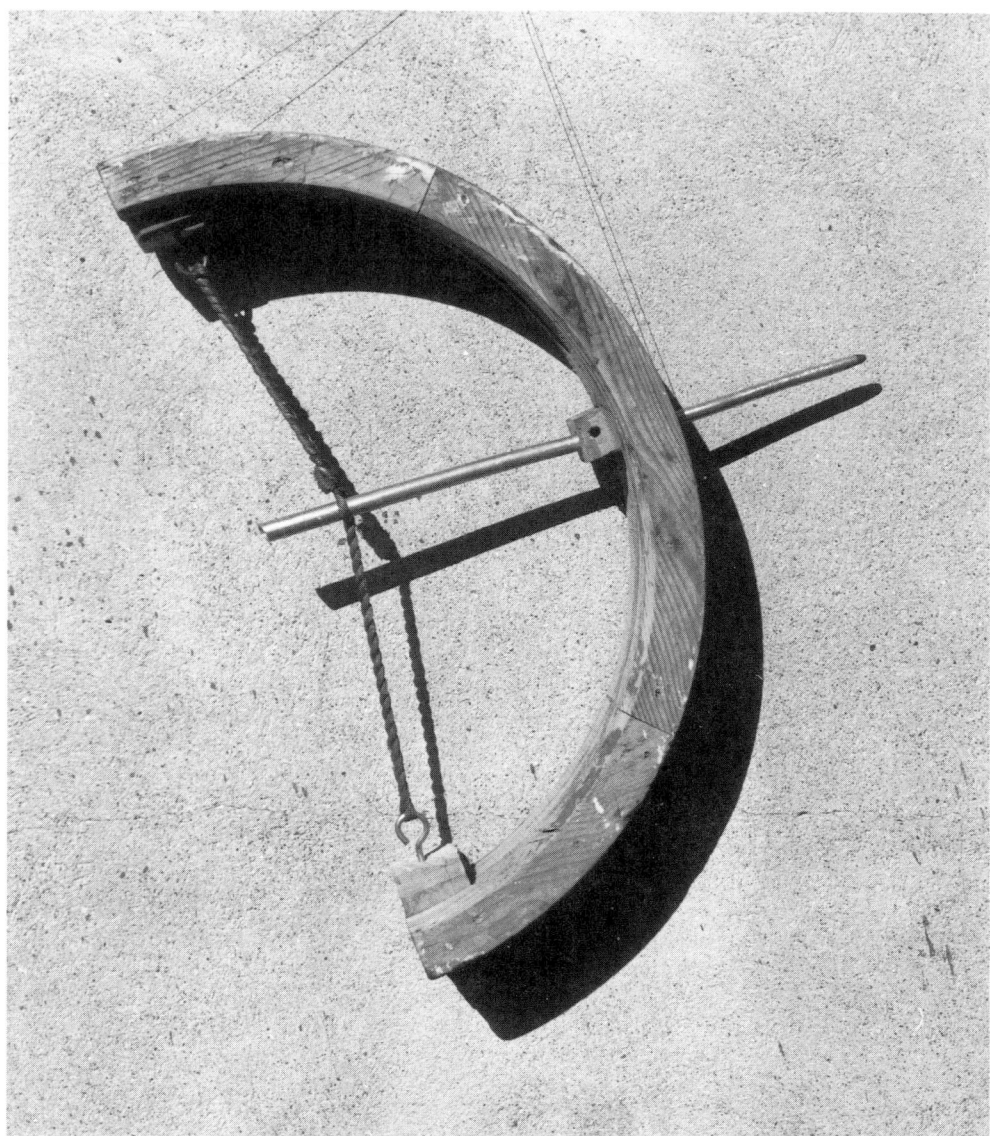

Daniel Dezeuze: *Petit Arc*, 1985

A weapon is an object which very often takes up very little space and has at the same time the maximum potency; that's often its secret and in that sense it's an exemplary object—only in that sense, of course!
—Daniel Dezeuze (from an interview, 1987)

DIAS, Antonio.

Brazilian. Born in Campina Grande, Paraiba, 22 February 1944. Married Iole de Freitas. Painter: lives and works in Milan. Recipient: Acquisition Prize, *Salao de Arte Moderna*, Belo Horizonte, Brazil, 1962; First Prize for Drawing, *Salao do Parana*, Brazil, 1963; "Hors Concours," *Salao Nacional de Arte Moderna*, Rio de Janeiro, 1964; International Painting Prize, *Biennale*, Paris, 1965; Drawing Prize, *Young National Drawing Exhibition*, Sao Paulo, 1965; Critics Prize, *Resumo*, Rio de Janeiro, 1965; Acquisition Prize, *Salao de Abril*, Rio de Janeiro, 1966; Critics Prize, *Resumo JB*, Rio de Janeiro, 1968; P. Favro Prize, San Fedele Award, Milan, 1968; Guggenheim Fellowship, 1971; Drawing Prize, *International Exhibition*, Rijeka, Yugoslavia, 1972. Address: Foro-Buonaparte 74, 20121 Milan, Italy.

Individual Exhibitions:

1962	Galeria Sobradinho, Rio de Janeiro
1964	Galeria Relèvo, Rio de Janeiro
1965	Galerie Houston-Brown, Paris
1966	Galeria Guignard, Belo Horizonte, Brazil
1967	Galerie Delta, Rotterdam
	Galeria Relèvo, Rio de Janeiro
1969	Galleria Acme, Brescia, Italy
	Studio Marconi Grafica, Milan
	Studio Marconi, Milan
	Galleria La Chiocciola, Padua
1970	Galerie Richard Foncke, Ghent
1971	Galleria Breton, Milan
	Studio Marconi, Milan
1972	Galerie Stampa, Basel
	Galleria Toselli, Milan
1973	Galeria Ralph Camargo, Sao Paulo
	Galeria Delta, Brussels
	Bolsa de Arte, Rio de Janeiro
	Centro de Arte y Communicacion, Buenos Aires
	Galerie Stampa, Basel
1974	Galerie Nächst St. Stephan, Vienna
	Galleria Nuovi Strumenti, Brescia, Italy
	Museu de Arte Moderna, Rio de Janeiro
1976	Galerie Albert Baronian, Brussels
	Galleria Lucio Amelio, Naples
	Galleria Nuovi Strumenti, Brescia, Italy
	Galerie Eric Fabre, Paris
	Palais des Beaux-Arts, Brussels
1978	Arte Global, Sao Paulo
	Coleman/Dias/Nespolo, Palazzo Reale, Milan
	Gravura Brasileira, Rio de Janeiro

	Galeria Luisa Strina, Sao Paulo
1979	Nucleo de Arte Contemporanea, Joao Pessoa, Brazil
	Galeria Saramenha, Rio de Janeiro
1980	Galerie Walter Storms, Munich
	Galleria Nuova Strumenti, Brescia, Italy
	Biennale, Venice
1982	Gravura Brasileira, Rio de Janeiro
	Galerie Walter Storms, Munich
1983	Galerie Albert Baronian, Brussels
	Thomas Cohn Arte Contemporanea, Rio de Janeiro
	Galerie Beatrix Wilhelm, Leonberg, West Germany
1984	Stadtische Galerie im Lenbachhaus, Munich
1985	Taipei Fine Arts Museum, Taiwan
1986	Galleria Piero Cavellini, Milan

Selected Group Exhibitions:

1965	*Biennale*, Paris
1969	*Dialogue Between East and West*, National Museum of Modern Art, Tokyo
1971	*International Exhibition*, Guggenheim Museum, New York
1973	*Record as Artwork*, Galleria Forma, Genoa (travelled to the Galleria Francoise Lambert, Milan, and the Royal College of Art, London)
1974	*Projekt '74*, Wallraf-Richartz Museum, Cologne
	Video Art, Institute of Contemporary Art, Philadelphia (travelled to the Museum of Contemporary Art, Chicago)
1977	*Art and Cinema*, Centro Internazionale di Brera, Milan (travelled to the *Biennale*, Venice, 1978)
1981	*Kunstlerbucher*, Kunstverein, Frankfurt
1984	*International Survey of Recent Painting and Sculpture* Museum of Modern Art, New York
1985	*Italian Contemporary Art*, Porin Taidemuseo, Pori, Finland

Collections:

Museu de Arte Contemporanea, Sao Paulo; Museu de Arte Moderna, Rio de Janeiro; Museu de Arte, Campina Grande, Brazil; Museu de Arte, Belo Horizonte, Brazil; Museum of Modern Art, New York; Wallraf-Richartz Museum, Cologne; Power Gallery, Sydney.

Publications:

By DIAS: books—*The Illustration of Art: Art*, Buenos Aires, 1972; *Some Artists Do, Some Don't*, Milan 1974; *The Illustration of Art: The Meaning of Production Models*, with text by Paulo Sergio, Milan 1974; *The Illustration of Art: A Public Portrait*, Milan 1974; *The Art of Transference*, Milan 1974; *The Illustration of Art: Economy (Model)*, Cologne 1974; *Untitled*, Rio de Janeiro 1974; article—"The Illustration of Art" in *Kunst Nachrichten* (Lucerne), April 1973; recording—*The Space Between*, Milan 1971; films and videotapes—*The Illustration of Art No. 1*, Milan 1971; *The Illustration of Art No. 2*, Milan 1971; *The Illustration of Art No. 3*, Milan 1971; *The New York Information System*, New York 1972; *The Illustration of Art: GIMMICK*, Milan 1972; *The Illustration of Art: Working Class Hero/Eating/Washing*, Milan 1972; *The Illustration of Art: Conversation Piece*, Milan 1973.

On DIAS: books—*Antonio Dias*, exhibition catalogue, with an essay by Pierre Restany, Rio de Janeiro 1964; *Antonio Dias*, exhibition catalogue, with an essay by Helio Oiticica, Rio de Janeiro 1967; *Record as Artwork*, exhibition catalogue, with an essay by Germano Celent, London 1973; *Antonio Dias*, exhibition catalogue, with an essay by Ronaldo Brito, Rio de Janeiro 1974; *Antonio Dias*, exhibition catalogue, with text by Sérgio Duarte, Venice 1980; *Antonio Dias: The Invented Land*, exhibition catalogue with essay by Helmut Friedel, Munich 1984.

A Brazilian artist living in Italy, Antonio Dias has become, since the end of the 1960s, distinguished in the field of Conceptual Art. Among his early works were the series of *Trame* (1968), woodcuts of essentially linear graphic outlines, abandoned at an elementary stage. These pieces (*Evergreen Monument to Agriculture/Grass Covered Pyramid*) had the appearance of projects that remained unrealizable because of he paucity of available data. In these and other works, the predicative function of the arts that constituted the input—i.e., the intention of the work—was underlined by the anonymity of its making, and by the constant supportive function which Dias assigned to the work's subtitle.

Dias considers art as a system (ideological and economical), and his study of it revolves around those aspects of art most compromised by ideology (*The Illustration of Art*, 1970–74). He then broadens his field of investigation to take into account the most widespread channels of mass-communication. He deals with newspapers as if they were 'tazebao' (handwritten mural papers of the Chinese Cultural Revolution), whereas magazine illustrations are treated as material for the study of their signifying functions. He then continues to analyse the relationship, however recondite, between the macrosystem of cultural industries and the microsystem of contemporary art. The object of his analysis is the specific iconic quality of language, investigated by means of long, painstaking work on handmade paper onto which he organizes a series of dots to form a constellation. In addition, he has investigated the legitimizing codes that art has produced for itself in order to become an autonomous discipline.

In the cycle *The Illustration of Art/Model Society* (1974), Dias gives us an ensemble of black squares, each marked by a smaller white square in the upper right corner. The inscription of one figure within another is to be found in several examples of Dias' work. Besides being a metonymic representation of art (as a system that produces ideas), the work opens up a specific relationship with space. The white rectangle determines an ambiguous perception inasmuch as it may be perceived by the viewer as part of the whiteness of the wall behind—and so become a sign open to the continuity of the space; at the same time Dias uses the white rectangle in a structure that can represent a map of the gallery in which it is exhibited. The viewer is here offered the opportunity to reflect on the complexity of a particular system, signified by the different meanings he can attribute to the concept of space. Space, in this case, can be understood either as proper painted space, or as wall-space, both in their physical, not symbolic, functions. Alternatively, such space may be understood as that sociological space defined according to its function, or as symbolic space in which communicative exchange takes place, touching on such matters as sociability and the commodity value of signs.

This elaboration of the picture as agent of semantic displacements is present in Dias' most recent work, too. Handmade paper has now become his preferred material, chosen after a long journey to Nepal, where the artist worked with the local craftsmen. Since the paper is entirely handmade, from the very beginning it is already speckled with impurities—minimal materic 'events'. The colours subsequently used by the artist are entirely of vegetable origin, so that nature becomes the first and foremost ambience of the picture, the primordial space that the picture carries inscribed within itself.

The signs drawn on the paper, all the more conforming to allusive symbols, at times repeat the structure of the rectangle inscribed within the square, or else suggest it—in a negative sense—as empty space. The visual repertoire is now open to an array of symbols from a variety of sources (the dollar, a bone, a flag, or some other abstract form). These often allude to the differences between Western cultures (from which a number of symbolic stereotypes are derived) and Eastern cultures, understood as the 'primary' sources from which archetypal symbols are quoted.

Thus, meanings are displaced and interchanged, or at least made relative. At times, they are even totally transformed. The images, uprooted from their original context and rendered as heraldic figures on the fragmented surfaces of the paper, are at the same time both ironically treated and ennobled by the sumptuousness of the artefact.

—Giorgio Verzotti

DIBBETS, Jan.

Dutch. Born Gerardus Johannes Marie Dibbets, in Weert, 9 May 1941. Studied at Bisschoppelijk College, Weert, 1953–59; art education, Academie voor Beeldende en Bouwende Kunsten, Tilburg, 1959–63; private painting studies under Jan Gregoor, Eindhoven, 1961–63; Saint Martin's School of Art, London, 1967. Married Bianka Francisca de Poorter in 1967; daughter: Hiske Karool. Independent artist, in Antwerp 1964, in Enschede 1964–67, in Amsterdam since 1968; abstract paintings 1964–68; photographic works, since 1967. Co-Founder, with Reinier Lucassen and Ger Van Elk, International Institute for the Re-education of Artists, Amsterdam 1968. Art instructor, Enschede, 1964–67; and Ateliers 63, Haarlem, since 1968; Visiting Artist, Nova Scotia College of Art and Design, Halifax, 1971; Professor, Staatliche Kunstakademie, Dusseldorf, since 1983. Recipient: British Council Scholarship, 1967; Heineken Prize, The Hague 1969; Cassandra Foundation Award, 1971; Rembrandt Prize, Goethe-Stiftung, Basle, 1979. Agents: Waddington Galleries, 11 Cork Street, London W1X 1PD, England; Galerie Konrad Fischer, Platanenstrasse 7, 4000 Dusseldorf, West Germany. Address: Boerhaaveplein 6, 1091 Amsterdam, Netherlands.

Individual Exhibitions:

1965	Galerie 845, Amsterdam
	Galerie Swart, Amsterdam
1966	Galerie Swart, Amsterdam
1967	*Demontable Multiples*, Galerie Swart, Amsterdam
1968	Galerie Konrad Fischer, Duseldorf
1969	Seth Siegelaub Gallery, New York
	Videogalerie Gerry Schum, Dusseldorf
	Art and Project, Amsterdam
	Museum Haus Lange, Krefeld, West Germany
1970	Galerie Yvon Lambert, Paris
	Galleria Francoise Lambert, Milan
	Zentrum für Aktuelle Kunst, Aachen, West Germany
	Aktionstraum 1, Munich
1971	Galleria Sperone, Turin
	Galerie Konrad Fischer, Dusseldorf
	Art and Project, Amsterdam
	Stedelijk Van Abbemuseum, Eindhoven, Netherlands
1972	Galerie MTL, Brussels
	Galerie Yvon Lambert, Paris
	Jack Wendler Gallery, London
	Galleria Toselli, Milan
	Bezalel National Museum, Jerusalem
	Dutch Pavilion at the *Biennale*, Venice
	Stedelijk Museum, Amsterdam
1973	Leo Castelli Gallery, New York
	Jack Wendler Gallery, London
	Galleria Sperone-Fischer, Rome
	Galerie Konrad Fischer, Dusseldorf
	Art and Project, Amsterdam
	Kabinett für Aktuelle Kunst, Bremerhaven, West Germany
1974	Galleria Sperone, Turin
	Galerie Konrad Fischer, Dusseldorf
	Galerie Rolf Preisig, Basle
	Galerie Yvon Lambert, Paris
1975	Galerie MTL, Brussels
	Galleria Marilena Bonomo, Bari, Italy
	Art and Project, Amsterdam
	Autumn Melody, Kunstmuseum, Lucerne
	Cusack Gallery, Houston
	Claire Copley Gallery, Los Angeles
	Leo Castelli Gallery, New York
1976	Scottish Arts Council Gallery, Edinburgh (travelled to the Arnolfini Gallery, Bristol; Chapter Arts Centre, Cardiff; and the Museum of Modern Art, Oxford)
	Galerie Konrad Fischer, Dusseldorf
1978	Leo Castelli Gallery, New York
	Galerie Charles Kriwin, Brussels
1979	INK, Zurich, Switzerland
1980	Stedelijk Van Abbemuseum, Eindhoven, Netherlands (travelled to the Musée d'Art Moderne de la Ville, Paris; and the Kunsthalle, Berne)
	Galerie Yvon Lambert, Paris
1981	Galerie Konrad Fischer, Dusseldorf
	Galleria Christian Stein, Turin
1982	Museum Fodor, Amsterdam
	Anthony d'Offay Gallery, London
	Centre International de Création Artistique, Paris
	Kamakura Gallery, Tokyo
	Galerie Karen and Jean Bernier, Athens
	Leo Castelli Gallery, New York
1984	Galerie Dam 43, Middelburg, Netherlands
	Waddington Galleries, London
1985	Galerie Maeght Lelong, Paris
	Van Abbemuseum, Eindhoven, Netherlands
	Muzej Savremene Umetnosti, Belgrade (travelled to Galerija Suvremene Umjetnosti, Zagreb)
1987	Galerie Konrad Fischer, Dusseldorf
	Guggenheim Museum, New York (travelled to Minneapolis, Detroit, West Palm Beach, and Eindhoven, Netherlands)

Selected Group Exhibitions:

1967	*Serielle Formationen*, Universität Frankfurt, Frankfurt
1970	*10th International Biennale of Art*, Tokyo
1971	*Guggenheim International*, Guggenheim Museum, New York
1972	*Konzept-Kunst*, Kunstmuseum, Basle
1974	*Contemporanea*, Parcheggio Villa Borghese, Rome
1977	*Europe In the 70's*, Art Institute of Chicago
1979	*European Dialogue*, at the *3rd Biennale of Sydney*, Art Gallery of New South Wales, Sydney
1982	*Documenta*, Kassel, West Germany
1984	*La Grande Parade*, Stedelijk Museum, Amsterdam
1987	*Photography and Art 1946–86*, Los Angeles County Museum of Art

Collections:

Stedelijk Museum, Amsterdam; Stedelijk Van Abbemuseum, Eindhoven, Netherlands; Museum Boymans-van Beuningen, Rotterdam; Tate Gallery, London; Centre Georges Pompidou, Paris; Louisiana Museum, Humlebaek, Denmark; Kunstmuseum, Basle; Museum Ludwig, Cologne; Museum of Modern Art, New York; Walker Art Center, Minneapolis.

Publications:

By DIBBETS: book—*Robin Redbreast's Territory: sculpture 1969, April–June*, Cologne and New York 1970; films & video—*Land Art*, edited by Gerry Schum, 1968; *Fire/Feuer/Feu/Vuur*, 1968; *12 Hours Ride/Objects with Correction of Perspective*, 1969; *Painting 1*, 1970; *Painting 2*, 1970; *Vertical-Horizontal-Diagonal-Square*, 1970; *Horizon I–Sea*, 1970; *Venetian Blinds*, 1971; *Horizon II–Sea*, 1971; *Horizon III–Sea*, 1971; *Vibrating Horizon*, 1971; *Video—2 Diagonals*, 1971; *Video—3 Diagonals*, 1971.

On DIBBETS: books—*Jan Dibbets: Demontable Multiples*, exhibition folder, with text by Marcel Vos, Amsterdam 1967; *Jan Dibbets*, exhibition catalogue, with text by Paul Wember, Krefeld, West Germany 1969; *Jan Dibbets*, exhibition catalogue, with text by Klaus Honnef, Aachen, West Germany 1970; *Jan Dibbets*, exhibition catalogue, with text by Rudi H. Fuchs, Eindhoven, Netherlands 1971; *Jan Dibbets*, exhibition catalogue, with texts by E. de Wilde, Rini Dippel and Marcel Vos, Amsterdam 1972; *Jan Dibbets: Autumn Melody*, exhibition catalogue, with text by Jean-Christophe Ammann, Lucerne 1975; *Jan Dibbets*, exhibition catalogue with texts by Barbara Reise and M. M. Vos, Edinburgh and Cardiff 1976; *Jan Dibbets*, exhibition catalogue, with text by Rudi H. Fuchs, Eindhoven, Netherlands 1980; *Jan Dibbets*, exhibition catalogue, with texts by Suzanne Page, M. M. Vos and Carole Naggar, Paris 1980; *Jan Dibbets*, exhibition catalogue, with texts by Martin Friedman, M. M. Vos and Rudi Fuchs, New York, Minneapolis and Amsterdam 1987.

Jan Dibbets' art grows out of the relationship which exists between our sight, the eye of the camera, and nature. Here, nature is a landscape that is the person-

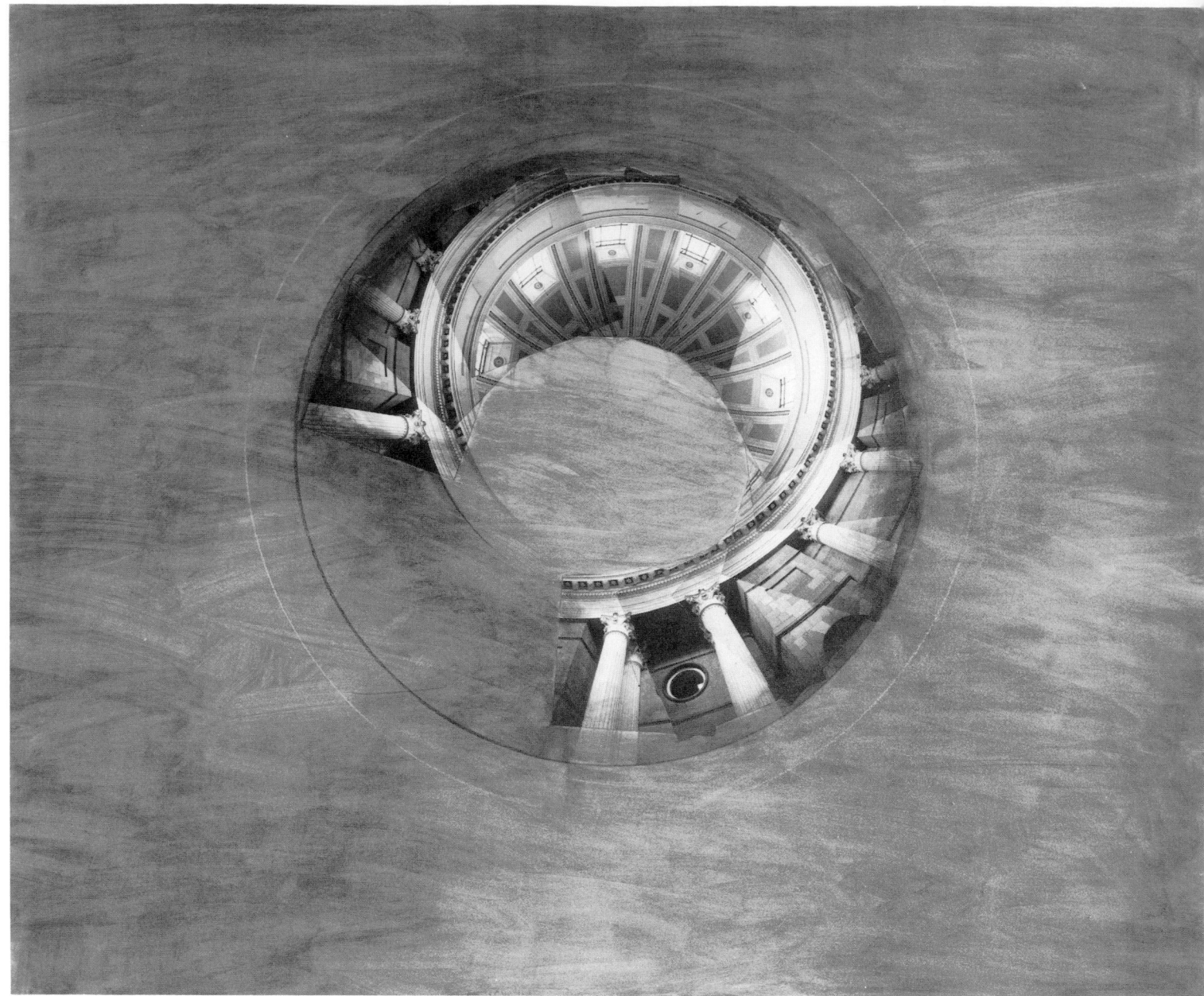

Jan Dibbets: *Four Courts, Dublin*, 1984

ification of the flatness of the Dutch landscape; flat land, sea, horizon. Working on these levels since 1968, Dibbets began to achieve "corrections of perspective," introducing geometric forms into the landscape, drawing them, for example, by means of a lawn-mower. This form, when seen by the eye of the camera from a particular chosen point, seems to take on a different shape. For example, an ellipse appears to be a circle that has been "knocked out of" equilibrium by gravity. The reality of a photograph—which is a prerequisite for such a situation—collides with the reality of seeing with the naked eye. Both systems of sight correct each other. A tension arises between them, placing us in a state of uncertainty—which is true of reality: the trapezoid drawn on the flat ground or wall, or the same shape shown from the point of view of the camera as a square.

Both ways of looking are, however, facts: we are dealing with two realities which do not cohere but which modify one another instead. The play between the reality (as it were) of illusion and the reality of "reality" is clearly shown by "Fireplace," 1968, where two kinds of fact appear: film about a fire that burnt a TV screen and the physical fire burning the screen on which this event is being shown. Reality appears as illusion repeated. The fact of the incident and the fact of its registration are treated as equals—a tension, "conversation," is created where these two

perspectives meet.

The fact that the camera is always ready to register allows one to make yet another kind of "adjustment." The camera can show the progressive transformation of a place with respect to time (e.g., "The Shadows in My Studio Photographed Every Ten Minutes"). Photography is used in such a way that it shows that which seeing would catch naturally—only at random. For example, the path a ray of sunlight makes when it comes in through a window and the slow mutations it makes of that particular piece of reality.

The camera's movement, as employed by Dibbets, allows a new reality to come into being, as in the series "Dutch Mountains," which was constructed from polder photographs. In the "Horizon" video films, the camera's movement in a vertical direction causes the horizon to appear at different levels when particular pieces of the landscape are shown. In the film *Horizon I—Sea*, 1970, the rising and falling horizon is referred to the frame of the screen so that the sky and the land lose their material character. The effect, however, is immediately negated by the "naturalness" of the pounding waves of the sea.

Movement of the camera is also used to tilt the horizon at a specified angle. The whole principle of horizontality is undermined: we feel that we have lost our bearings when we see the horizon at a slant.

Dibbets' actions disturb our conventional trust in

photographs. At times, we believe that the conversation that has been used (especially in the case of "correction of perspective") is justified; at other times—e.g., "the slanting of the horizon"—we recognize manipulation. the artist deceives us by appealing to the objectivity of the camera and of geometry; he shows the ambiguity of a point of view; he reveals the changes that our sight undergoes when the area is limited (the use of frames). He invokes situations that disagree with rational speculation and arrest expectations. This also happens when he builds an integral continuity by systematically breaking it up ("Komety").

Dibbets creates a natural reality and a registered reality as occurrences of equal ontological status. Both exist as facts. Equalizing these facts does not, however, devalue natural reality. On the contrary, one feels it more strongly when it has undergone these "corrections" and "slants." The infringement of customary norms of seeing intensifies sight itself. It also makes one experience more intensely that whose shape one doubts. We get what might be called a new pair of eyes from the artist. It happens that the world, so frequently identified by us (as it was very carefully by 17th century Dutch landscape painters), can be reinterpreted.

—Alicja Kepinska

DIEBENKORN, Richard (Clifford Jr.)

American. Born in Portland, Oregon, 22 April 1922. Educated at Stanford University, California, 1940–43, B.A. 1949; University of California, Berkeley, 1943–44; California School of Fine Arts, San Francisco, 1946–47; University of New Mexico, Albuquerque, 1950–52, M.A. 1952. Served in the United States Marines, 1943–45. Married Phyllis Gilman 1943; children: Gretchen and Christopher. Independent artist, California, since 1952. Taught at California School of Fine Arts, San Francisco, 1947–50; University of Illinois, Urbana, 1952–53; California College of Arts and Crafts, Oakland, 1955–60; and San Francisco Art Institute, 1961–66; Artist-in-Residence, Stanford University, 1963–64; Professor of Art, University of California at Los Angeles, 1966–73. Member, National Council on the Arts, Washington, D.C., 1966–69. Recipient: Rosenberg Travelling Fellowship 1959; National Institute of Arts and Letters Award, 1962; Tamarind Fellowship, 1962; Cultural Exchange Grant, to Europe and U.S.S.R., United States Department of State, 1964; Beck Gold Medal, Pennsylvania Academy of Fine Arts, Philadelphia, 1968; Edward MacDowell Medal, MacDowell Colony, Peterborough, New Hampshire, 1978; Skowhegan Medal for Painting, Skowhegan School of Art, Maine, 1979. Member, National Council on the Arts, Washington, D.C.; Member, National Institute of Arts and Letters, 1967; Member, American Academy of Arts and Letters, 1985. Agent: M. Knoedler and Company Inc., 19 East 70th Street, New York, New York 10021. Address: 334 Amalfi Drive, Santa Monica, California 90402, U.S.A.

Individual Exhibitions:

1948	California Palace of the Legion of Honor, San Francisco
1951	University of New Mexico, Albuquerque
1952	Paul Kantor Gallery, Los Angeles
1954	Paul Kantor Gallery, Los Angeles
	San Francisco Museum of Art
	Allan Frumkin Gallery, Chicago
1955	University of California, Berkeley
1956	Poindexter Gallery, New York
	Oakland Art Museum, California
1957	Swetzoff Gallery, Boston
1958	Poindexter Gallery, New York
1960	*Recent Paintings by Richard Diebenkorn*, California Palace of the Legion of Honor, San Francisco
	Pasadena Art Museum, California (retrospective)
1961	Phillips Collection, Washington, D.C.
	Poindexter Gallery, New York
1962	National Institute of Arts and Letters, New York
1963	M. H. de Young Memorial Museum, San Francisco
	Poindexter Gallery, New York
1964	Washington Gallery of Modern Art, Washington, D.C. (retrospective)
	Stanford University Art Gallery, California
1965	Jewish Museum, New York
	Pavilion Art Gallery, Newport Beach, California
	Waddington Galleries, London
	Paul Kantor Gallery, Los Angeles
	Poindexter Gallery, New York
1967	Waddington Galleries, London
	National Institute of Arts and Letters, New York
	Stanford University Art Gallery, California
	Peale House, Pennsylvania Academy of Fine Arts, Philadelphia
1968	Peale House, Pennsylvania Academy of Fine Arts, Philadelphia
	Nelson-Atkins Art Gallery, Kansas City, Missouri
	Richmond Art Center, California
	Poindexter Gallery, New York
1969	*The Ocean Park Series*, Poindexter Gallery, New York
	New Paintings of Richard Diebenkorn, Los Angeles County Museum of Art
1971	Irving Blum Gallery, Los Angeles
	Poindexter Gallery, New York

	The Ocean Park Series: Recent Work, Marlborough Gallery, New York
	Galerie Smith-Andersen, Palo Alto, California
1972	*Paintings from the Ocean Park Series*, San Francisco Museum of Art
	Lithographs, Gerald John Hayes Gallery, Los Angeles
	Herbert Mondavi Gallery, Oakville, California
	The Ocean Park Series: Recent Work, Marlborough Fine Art, London
	Marlborough Galerie, Zurich
1974	*Drawings 1944–1973*, Mary Porter Sesnon Gallery, University of California at Santa Cruz
1975	*Early Abstract Works 1948–1955*, James Corcoran Gallery, Los Angeles
	John Berggruen Gallery, San Francisco
	Marlborough Gallery, New York
1976	*Monotypes*, Wight Art Gallery, University of California at Los Angeles
	Albright-Knox Art Gallery, Buffalo, New York (toured the United States)
	Museum of Contemporary Art, Chicago
1977	M. Knoedler and Company, New York
1979	M. Knoedler and Company, New York
1980	M. Knoedler and Company, New York
1981	*Matrix/Berkeley 40*, University of California, Berkeley
	Etchings and Drypoints 1949–80, Minneapolis Institute of Arts, Minnesota (toured the United States, 1981–83)
	Marlborough Gallery, New York
1982	M. Knoedler and Company, New York
	Crown Point Gallery, Oakland, California
	Intaglio 1961–80, Brooklyn Museum, New York

1983	*Works on Paper*, John Berggruen Gallery, San Francisco
	Paintings 1948–83, San Francisco Museum of Modern Art
1984	M. Knoedler and Company, New York
	Etchings and Drypoints 1965, L.A. Louver Gallery, Venice, California
1985	Sheldon Memorial Art Gallery, University of Nebraska, Lincoln (travelled to Brooklyn Museum, New York)
	Etchings and Drypoints, Patricia Heesy Gallery, New York
	M. Knoedler and Company, New York
1986	Crown Point Press, New York

Selected Group Exhibitions:

1964	*Painting and Sculpture of a Decade 1954–1964*, Tate Gallery, London
1966	*Art of the United States 1670–1966*, Whitney Museum, New York
1968	*Biennale*, Venice
1969	*Annual Exhibition*, Whitney Museum, New York
	Kompass, Stedelijk van Abbemuseum, Eindhoven, Netherlands
1972	*70th American Exhibition*, Art Institute of Chicago
1973	*Biennial of Contemporary American Painting*, Corcoran Gallery of Art, Washington, D.C.
1978	*Biennale*, Venice
	American Paintings of the 1970's, Albright-Knox Art Gallery, Buffalo (toured the United States, 1978–79)
1979	*Works on Paper*, Knoedler Gallery, London

Richard Diebenkorn: *Ocean Park*, 1981

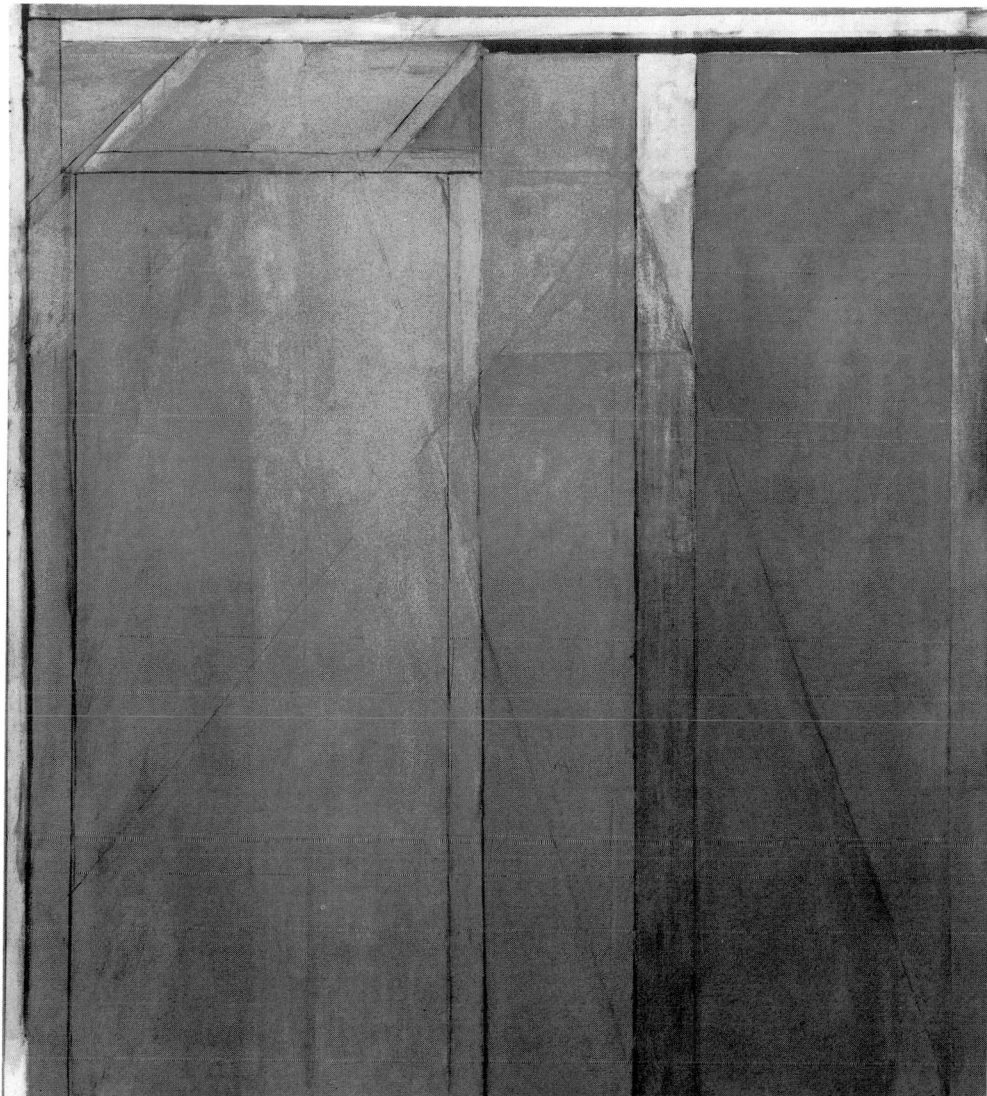

1980 *American Drawing in Black and White,* Brooklyn Museum, New York
1984 *The Figurative Mode: Bay Area Paintings 1956-66,* Grey Art Gallery, New York University (travelled to Newport Harbor Art Museum, California)
1986 *After Matisse,* Queens Museum, Flusing, New York (toured the United States, 1986-88)

Collections:

California Palace of the Legion of Honor, San Francisco; Los Angeles County Museum of Art; Albright-Knox Art Gallery, Buffalo, New York; Metropolitan Museum of Art, New York; Whitney Museum, New York; Museum of Modern Art, New York; Guggenheim Museum, New York; Corcoran Gallery, Washington, D.C.; Hirshhorn Museum, Smithsonian Institution, Washington, D.C., Art Institute of Chicago.

Publications:

By DIEBENKORN: books—*Drawings,* edited by Lorenz Eitner, Stanford, California 1965; *41 Etchings, Drypoints,* Berkeley, California 1965.

On DIEBENKORN: books—*Recent Paintings by Richard Diebenkorn,* exhibition catalogue, introduction by Howard Ross Smith, San Francisco 1960; *Richard Diebenkorn,* exhibition catalogue with an introduction by Thomas B. Leavitt, Pasadena, California 1960; *Richard Diebenkorn,* exhibition catalogue, with an essay by Gifford Phillips, Washington, D.C. 1961; *The Collector in America,* edited by Jean Lipman and others, New York 1961; *A Short History of Painting in America* by E. P. Richardson, New York 1963; *Richard Diebenkorn,* exhibition catalogue, London 1965; *50 Years of Modern Art 1916-1966,* by Edward P. Henning, Cleveland 1966; *American Art since 1960* by Barbara Rose, New York 1967; *History of Modern Art: Painting, Sculpture, Architecture* by H. H. Arnason, New York 1968; *Richard Diebenkorn,* exhibition catalogue, Richmond, California 1968; *New York Painting and Sculpture 1940-1970* by Henry Geldzahler, New York 1969; *New Paintings of Richard Diebenkorn,* exhibition catalogue, with an essay by Gail Scott, Los Angeles 1969; *The Ocean Park Series,* exhibition catalogue, New York 1969; *A History of American Art* by Daniel M. Mandelowitz, New York 1970; *The Ocean Park Series: Recent Work,* exhibition catalogue, with an essay by Gerald Nordland, New York 1971; *Richard Diebenkorn: Lithographs,* exhibition catalogue, Los Angeles 1972; *Contemporary Art 1942-72: Collection of the Albright—Knox Art Gallery,* New York 1972; *Richard Diebenkorn: Paintings from the Ocean Park Series,* exhibition catalogue, essay by Gerald Nordland, San Francisco 1972; *The Genius of American Painting,* edited by John Wilmerding, London 1973; *Richard Diebenkorn, The Ocean Park Series: Recent Work,* exhibition catalogue, essay by John Russell, London 1973; *American Impressionism* by Richard J. Boyle, Boston 1974; *Richard Diebenkorn: Drawings 1944-1973,* exhibition catalogue, with an essay by Philip Brookman and Walker Melion, Santa Cruz, California 1974; *Early Abstract Works 1948-1955,* exhibition catalogue, Los Angeles 1975; *Richard Diebenkorn: Monotypes,* exhibition catalogue, essay by Gerald Nordland, Los Angeles 1976; *Richard Diebenkorn,* exhibition catalogue, New York, 1979; *Richard Diebenkorn: Paintings and Drawings 1943-80,* New York 1980; *Richard Diebenkorn: Etchings and Drypoints 1949-80,* Houston 1981; *Richard Diebenkorn: Works on Paper,* edited by Richard Newlin, Houston 1987.

*

Since he began painting during the 1940's, California painter Richard Diebenkorn has evolved through three distinct phases, moving from early work in an abstract vein related to Abstract Expressionism of the de Kooning, Clyfford Still variety, to a period of gestural figuration, arriving finally at his Ocean Park Series of abstracted, painterly landscapes.

During the period covering the years between 1943 and 1955, Diebenkorn developed his basic concern, to abstract from his perceptions of things seen: painterly, atmospheric, lightfilled distillations of the Western American landscape. From the beginning, the work was rooted in visual impressions of his environment which he translates in terms of painterly areas of colored light accompanied by geometrical framing. Diebenkorn's central concerns are formal, and he uses his considerable skills to develop a vocabulary which is not autobiographical in the sense of stressing private associational meanings but is rather more broadly evocative of outer and inner realms.

In 1954 Diebenkorn began working directly from the model, along with his teacher, David Park, and another painter, Elmer Bischoff, in San Francisco. In a 1957 exhibition, national recognition came for this group of figurative, gestural painters whose work is characterized by slapdash brushstrokes, sensuous color and a generally rough and lush atmosphere. Diebenkorn's figuration of the late 1950's and early 60's is exemplified by "Girl On A Terrace" (1956). The expressionistic figure is part of a setting combining indoors and outdoors; her bodily form acts as part of an implied window frame which both separates and links the overall atmosphere. She is more a formal element in the composition than a suggestion of particular subject matter. Her presence is used as an element to complete the structural tensions and it also enhances the pervasive mood of sober contemplation.

In pictures such as "Cityscape I" and "Landscape I" (both 1963), the figure disappears. Housetops, terraced hillsides, lots are undergoing a process of schematization, becoming geometrical patternings, defining spaces inhabited only by atmospheric colors awash with a kind of energetic quietude. In 1966 Diebenkorn moved to Santa Monica, California, and in 1967 he made the first of his Ocean Park Series pictures, named for a section of that area which borders on the ocean. It was a series he would develop throughout the 70's finding multiple variations in a schema which consists of a highly formalized conjunction of geometry and painterly field, enlivened by the misty light which emanates from the areas of soft off-colors. These areas are variously sized, shaped and activated by subtle remnants of the painting process to achieve the feeling of what Diebenkorn called the "tension beneath calm." Colored borders act both to divide and conjoin the translucent spaces, adding additional tension to the illusion that there is an active presence hidden within the emotively empty fields. Sometimes the viewpoint is that of looking upward, and often it suggests aerial sitings from a great distance below. Always there is the tense balance of inside/outside, and always there is the sense of ultimate origination from things perceived analytically and at a remove which borders in between alienation and intimacy.

The Ocean Park Series is the outgrowth of Diebenkorn's persistence over many years to refine his painter's skills. The pictures are informed by a quality of color as light which is highly personal and grows out of studious perception. Diebenkorn is by no means a revolutionary painter. His are steps out of earlier masters, Matisse, Mondrian, Monet and Abstract Expressionism, and present in his pictures are the souvenirs gathered from these precursors. Yet, by sticking to his own experience, so particularly Western American, he has managed to distill things from each of them and translate them into a visualization which is quite his own.

—Barbara Cavaliere

DIEHL, Hans-Jürgen.

German. Born in Hanau/Main, 22 May 1940. Studied art at Staatliche Zeichenakademie, Hanau, 1956-59; Akademie für Bildenden Künste, Munich, 1959-62; Ecole National Supérieur des Beaux-Arts, Paris, 1962-63; and under Hann Trier, at the Hochschule für Bildende Künste, West Berlin, 1963-66; M.A. 1966. Married Margrit Wiebe in 1966; son: Hannes. Painter, West Berlin, since 1966: Founder-Member, Grossgorchen 35, West Berlin 1964; Member, Co-operative 10/9, Munich, since 1972. Guest Professor of Painting, 1973-76, and Professor since 1977, Hochschule für Bildende Künste, West Berlin. Member, Deutscher Kunstlerbund, Bonn, 1972. Agent: Galerie Poll, Lutzowplatz 7, 1000 Berlin 30. Addresses: 47 Clinton Street, New York, New York 10002, U.S.A.; and Halberstadterstrasse 7, 1000 Berlin 31 (West), Germany.

Individual Exhibition:

1964 Galerie Grossgorchen 35, West Berlin
1965 Galerie zu Fasan, Konstanz, West Germany
1966 Galerie Groosgorchen 35, West Berlin
1967 Galerie Junge Generation, Hamburg
1968 Galerie Schmucking, Braunschweig, West Germany
Galerie Ostentor, Dortmund
Volkshochschule, Bremen, West Germany
1969 Galerie Niepel, Dusseldorf
1970 *Diehl/Petrick/Sorge: Malerei, Graphik, Material,* Haus am Waldsee, West Berlin (travelled to Bädischer Kunstverein, Karlsruhe)
Galerie Brusberg, Hannover
Galerie Kerlikowsky und Kneiding, Munich
1971 Kunstverein, Dusseldorf
Kunstmuseum, Ludwigshafen, West Germany (with Wolfgang Petrick)
Galerie 2000, West Berlin
1972 Institut fur Moderne Kunst, Nuremberg, West Germany
1973 Karl-Ernst-Osthaus Museum, Hagen, West Germany (with Wolfgang Petrick)
Zimmergalerie Hesse, Augsburg, West Germany
Galerie Wolfgang Ketterer, Munich
1974 Galerie 2000, West Berlin
1976 Galerie Poll, West Berlin
1977 Ulmer Museum, Ulm, West Germany (travelled to the Kunstverein, Hannover)
1980 Galerie Poll, West Berlin
1981 Galerie Lucklum, West Germany
1984 Galerie Friedrich, Cologne
1985 Staatliche Kunsthalle, West Berlin

Selected Group Exhibitions:

1964 *Kunstpreis Junger Westen,* Kunsthalle, Recklinghausen, West Germany (and 1965)
1966 *Junge Berliner Kunstler,* Kunsthalle, Basle
1967 *Neuer Realismus,* Haus am Waldsee, West Berlin (toured Germany)
1970 *Berliner Realisten,* Bädischer Kunstverein, Karlsruhe, West Germany
1972 *Prinzip Realismus,* Deutsche Akademischer Austauschdienst, West Berlin (toured Germany, Sweden, Norway, Italy, and Greece, 1972-74)
1975 *Deutsche Grafik,* Lawrence Gallery, Kansas City, Missouri
1976 *Deutsche Grafik im 20. Jahrhundert,* Kestner-Gesellschaft, Hannover
1977 *Berlin Now,* New School for Social Research, New York
1978 *Ugly Realism,* Institute of Contemporary Arts, London
1985 *Fifteen Berlin Artists in Brazil,* toured Brazil

Collections:

Nationalgalerie, West Berlin; Kupferstichkabinett, West Berlin; Landesmuseum, Hannover; Kestner-Gesellschaft, Hannover; Karl-Ernst-Osthaus Museum, Hagen, West Germany; City Art Museum, Helsinki.

Publications:

On DIEHL: books—*Pop und die Folgen* by Heinz Ohff, Dusseldorf 1968; *Kunstjahrbuch I,* edited by Jurgen Harten and others, Hannover 1970; *Diehl, Petrick, Sorge: Malerei, Graphik, Material* exhibition catalogue, West Berlin 1970; *Kritischer Realismus,* exhibition catalogue, with text by Heinz Ohff, West Berlin 1971; *Deutsche Kunst der 60er Jahre: Malerei, Collage, Op-Art, Graphik,* edited by Juliane Roh, Munich 1971; *Kunst ist Utopie* by Heinz Ohff, West Berlin 1974; *Hans-Jurgen Diehl: Bilder und Zeichnungen 1963-1977* exhibition catalogue with texts by Johann Karl Schmidt and Eberhard Roters, Ulm, West Germany 1977; *Diehl,* exhibition catalogue, with text by Dore Ashton and J. K. Schmidt, West Berlin 1985.

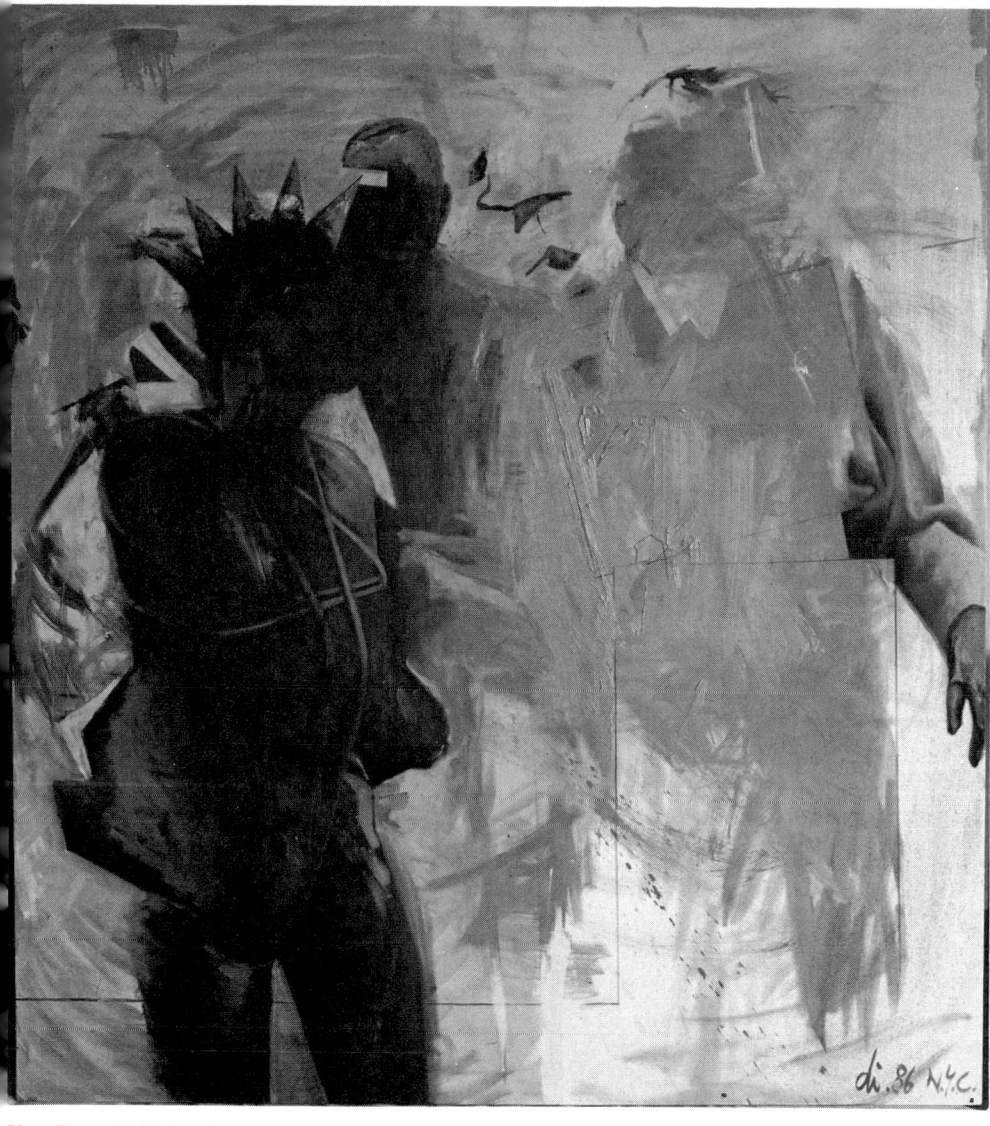

Hans-Jürgen Diehl: *Das Zeichen*, 1986

Rendering reality visible does not, for me, mean portraying reality as optically perceived; it means objectivising the situation to the extent that the different planes of reality are transformed via the medium of painting. The socio-psychological and the optically observable planes of reality, and the plane of one's own personal base (ideology) determine form and content which are linked in a dialetical relationship.

A picture which claims to be "Art" is not to my mind something which illustrates an idea. My work is directed towards the society of which I am a part. I believe that by engaging in a critical dialogue with my surroundings, positive and negative emotions arise which can be reflected during the work process and which are transposed into the paintings as result and object of sense-perception. For the viewer, the subjective intention becomes objectivised, and the statements are associable within a predetermined range.

—Hans-Jürgen Diehl

If Hans-Jürgen Diehl were a novelist, he would be Joyce. His natural instinct is to work in the time-honoured approach of free association, which allows for compendious abstractions adding up to reality. The results are demonic, almost apocalyptic paintings: a sudden flash of insight revealing the implications of a culture estranged from the world and so utterly without a unifying identity since the Thirty Years' War.

Diehl had several reasons to feel alienated as a modern German artist. First, being a painter, he had to deal with art history— a history that in Germany, with its special historic circumstances, is riddled with significant ruptures and turbulent debates. He chose to live in Berlin during a period when Berlin painters were accused of being unimaginative realists. Diehl rejected this prosaic, realist tradition. Second, during the post-war years when the Americans began rebuilding the country, they brought with them a culture that was anything but German. Subsequently Diehl's preoccupation with his own heritage was tinctured with considerations of foreign traits. His traditon and state of mind being splintered, the "fragment" emerged as the central leitmotif of his work.

Since the mid-60s, Diehl's paintings have been a response to this uprooted, mechanized, fragmented and manipulated existence which epitomized Berlin. His work is generated on an impulse of beauty, always present in Diehl, in spite of everything, and a need to speak of this wound. The human figures in his early paintings are truncated, mutilated, damned: puppets impaled on a wall, mounds of bodies on a grid. He lovingly models his figure, recording the details of unkempt pleats and folds, cracks in damp leather jackets in photographic precision. However he omits their life-imbuing qualities, leaving them helplessly without heads or faces, imprisoned by their cruel surroundings. The figures appear embryonic; it is as if by trying to climb out of the canvas, they'll find their missing parts and achieve wholeness. So unresolved are the paintings that they often resemble a photograph taken out of the developer when only bits and pieces have begun to appear.

In 1966, under the impact of the Wirtschaftswunder and all its ugly implications, Diehl abandoned the sensuous, allusive approach and harnessed an idiom that carries unmistakable references to the recent past. The careful attention to detail interrupted by deliberate fragmentation was a technique employed during the Weimar period. He favoured urban settings until the mid-70s whose undertone of shame and scandal became a kind of exorcism. During the 70s Diehl moved to New York where, living in a slum of the Lower East Side, he experienced loneliness, disorientation, and, above all, chaos. Capturing both German and American urban ambiance, these subtle feelings of alienation enter in his New York paintings.

This fermenting chaos, this monstrous mutant of social organism that New York is, severing, killing, biting off its own limbs, unhesitantly sprouting new shoots out of the cadaver, spills onto Diehl's canvases. It is these new shoots that deliver a secondary theme: evolvement. Diehl subtly reminds us of the latencies, possibilities and repressed realities embodied in his figures. Often the fragmented, truncated bodies never realize their potential because of other bodies crowding, imposing, occupying their space on the canvas. Diehl relies on an even more effective technique to convey this message: completely developed figures stand behind crossbars, as behind prison bars, looking out at other bodies still undeveloped, still in a state of latency on the other plane of the picture. The sharp polarity of each distinct reality is forced to coincide. Like Kafka, Diehl records the particulars of both sides with ghastly precision, yet put together, they lack coherence and unity, a metaphor for a society thoroughly rationalized and administered in its single segments but perfectly irrational as a whole.

Upon his return to Berlin in 1983 he completed the diptych, The Bath, a painting which became one of his key works. The painting, on first glance, is a harmonious, vernal scene. Yet it is riddled with hidden meaning and bears definite historical resonances. Diehl's returns to the lake country of Berlin, as did early 20th century German painters, for his setting. Merging two images, he first conjures a past: on the left, the bather, absorbed by nature into the shadows. The scene with its rustic hues, recalls early 19th century German landscape painters, notably Karl Rottmann. Then to break the continuity, he strategically places a car of another era in the triangular axis in the center of the painting. The triangular crux highlights the gloom of nature implying both the inaccessibility of his ambiguous paradisical vision and the distancing that history demands.

During the 80s Diehl diffused the intensity of his earlier paintings. His colours, once harsh and dissonant, take on more earthy and natural tones. More than ever he uses light to unfold space. Even the figures, previously estranged from the often layered backgrounds, are a more integral part of the now textured and animated environment. Diehl has opened dialogue between them by capturing gestures in motion rather than locking the figures in fixed, rigid positions. The resulting dialogue is a more open-ended narration than a revelation. As in the past the figures remain mere adumbrations of bodies. Yet the missing parts are deemphasized: rather they seem to have slipped back into the canvas and fused themselves into their surroundsings. Consequently, Diehl's use of space has become obfuscated by its expansion and various "layers" within the picture.

Diehl's return to Berlin seems only befitting to polish the themes of his career. The paintings which so aptly express alienation—both individual and cultural, artistic and political, historical and current—must be contained in Berlin. It is a city of exile—physical exile from a German nation, psychological exile, reinforced by the formal occupation of other nations. Diehl has found means to express this mood of inner exile, for his paintings re-possess history, confronting the ruins that lie in memory if not in the city itself.

—Carrie Barker

DIETMANN, Erik.

Swedish. Born in Malmo in 1937. Has lived and worked in Paris since 1960. Agent: Galerie Bama, Paris. Address: c/o Galerie Bama, 40 rue Quincampoix, 75004 Paris, France.

Individual Exhibitions:

1964	Galleria Sperone, Turin
1966	Galerie Mathias Fels, Paris
	Galleria L'Elefante, Venice
	Galerie 20, Amsterdam
1967	Galleri Hedenius, Stockholm
1968	Galerie 20, Amsterdam
	Galleria Apollinaire, Milan
	Galleria Christian Stein, Turin
1969	Galerie Mathias Fels, Paris
1970	Galerie Mathias Fels, Paris
1971	Galleri Buren, Stockholm
	Jysk Kunstgalleri, Copenhagen
1972	Eat-Art Galerie, Dusseldorf
1973	Galerie Bama, Paris
1974	Galleria Massimo Valsecchi, Milan
	Galerie Bama, Paris
1975	Hotel d'Angleterre, Copenhagen
	Musée d'Art Moderne de la Ville, Paris (retrospective)
1976	Galerie Bama, Paris
	Galerie Tanit, Munich
	Galerie Valois, Paris
	Galleria Massimo Valsecchi, Milan
	Academie Royale, Copenhagen
	Moderna Museet, Stockholm
1977	Galleria Arte Verso, Genoa, Italy
	Galerie Bon Valois, Paris
1978	Galerie Lucien Durand, Paris
1979	Galerie Herta Klang, Cologne
	Nordjyllands Kunstmuseum, Aalborg, Denmark
1980	Galleri Ahlner, Stockholm
	Galerie Leger, Malmo, Sweden
1981	Galerie Gerzli Konstsalong, Goteborg, Sweden

	Galerie Forum, Stockholm
	Galerie Arnesen, Copenhagen
1982	Jonkoping Museum, Sweden
	Galerie Sonia Zannettacci, Geneva
1983	Lunds Galleriet, Lund, Sweden
1984	Galerie Aronowitsch, Stockholm
	Galerie Bama, Paris
1985	Fundacao Gulbenkian, Lisbon
	Lilla Galleriet, Helsinki
	Galerie Asbaek, Copenhagen
	Anthony Reynolds Gallery, London
1987	Moderna Museet, Stockholm

Selected Group Exhibitions:

1967	*Superlund*, Konsthall, Lund, Sweden
1980	*Malmo*, Malmo Konsthall, Sweden
1981	*Autoportraits Photographiques*, Centre Georges Pompidou, Paris
1982	*Transes l'a Van Garde*, Galerie Bama, Paris
1983	*Sculptures*, Galerie Camomille, Brussels
1984	*Ceramiques*, Galerie Camomille, Brussels
1985	*Sculpture*, Fondation Cartier, Jouy-en-Josas, France

Collections:

Moderna Museet, Stockholm; Centre Georges Pompidou, Paris; Louisiana Museum, Humlebaek, Denmark.

Publications:

On DIETMANN: books—*Hommage à Dietmann* by F. T. Bidlake, Olle Granath and Outil O'Toole, Paris 1975; *Erik Dietmann*, exhibition catalogue with essay by Roland Topor, London 1985; *Erik Dietmann*, exhibition catalogue with essay by Olle Granath, Stockholm 1987.

*

When Erik Dietmann wishes to refer to other artists, in order to illuminate his work, he will choose authors like the Swedish poet Gunnar Ekelöf, or Raymond Roussel and James Joyce, rather than other figurative artists. In his capacity as a multilingual maker of objects he feels more at home in Paris, where he has lived since 1960, than in Sweden. Language is for him an unlimited theatrical wardrobe, which allows practically any disguise. He lets his personality break through the language, or rather languages, as through a prism. The word-play and the multiplicity of meaning transform his literary objects into picture-puzzles, the solution of which turns out to be an absurdity. Art in his case does not answer any questions; it is rather a temporary arrangement, which constitutes a fragile support in daily life. He has, loosely based on Dali, described it as a crutch of a "BUT," which in French means an aim or a support, while in English it becomes an objection.

Vulnerability is a theme in Dietmann's art. The absurd and the meaningless do not arouse his aggression, but rather his tenderness. This emotion was already present in his early objects, which were all carefully coated with plaster. Far removed from all large gestures, he is a gentleman who stands with clumsy awkwardness in the entrance-hall, dressed in a bowler and tie, with a tulip in his hand—all scrupulously covered in plaster. He has described the situation like this: "Your qualities surpass your charms." Even though he addresses the spectators with this statement, it still contains a description of himself. Through all he does there also runs a warm stream of light and diverting humour, somewhat like peeing one's name in the snow, an action which he also recorded in one of his objects.

His attitude contains a disassociation from the ratrace, which enables him to let others take in the making of a work of art. Art is finally an attempt to fill a vacuum with a dialogue. In the considerably older poet and connoisseur of life, Fabian Tommyrot Bidlake, who in many cases has contributed ideas and texts to the works, Dietmann has found a kindred spirit. Their collaboration has nourished both of them.

Dietmann's gestures and sometimes breakneck wordgames, have from the beginning helped to establish "guarded crossings" (in French *Passage Cloutée*) between the real events on the one hand, and artlanguage on the other. As a pacifist in exile, he was in 1962 employed building a sea-side restaurant in Sainte Maxime, when he committed a symbolic act: he swallowed a couple of metres of gauze bandage, as a complement to that gauze bandage required for the external injuries of the inexperienced buildingworker. He was well aware that the aims of pacifism should never be limited to avoiding the external injuries to man and his surroundings. The root of the evil lies in the already inflicted internal injuries, in a language which is so tattered and torn, that acts of violence replace communication.

Dietmann made, for Pierre Restany's exhibition *Superlund* in Lund's Konsthall in Sweden 1967, a "guarded crossing", which was a "demonstration dependent on you, just like the future." In front of the entrance to the gallery was a small wooden hut with a plexi-glass box, through which one could put nickel balls. They rolled down through a labyrinth which made up the word VOLVO (I roll). In order to pass from the hut into the exhibition one had to walk through another labyrinth, which made one write the word WALK with one's body. That is how a guarded crossing looks, as does a picture of a dream: the action and the language as one invisible unit.

—Olle Granath

Erik Dietmann: *Livre Sterling* (detail), 1976

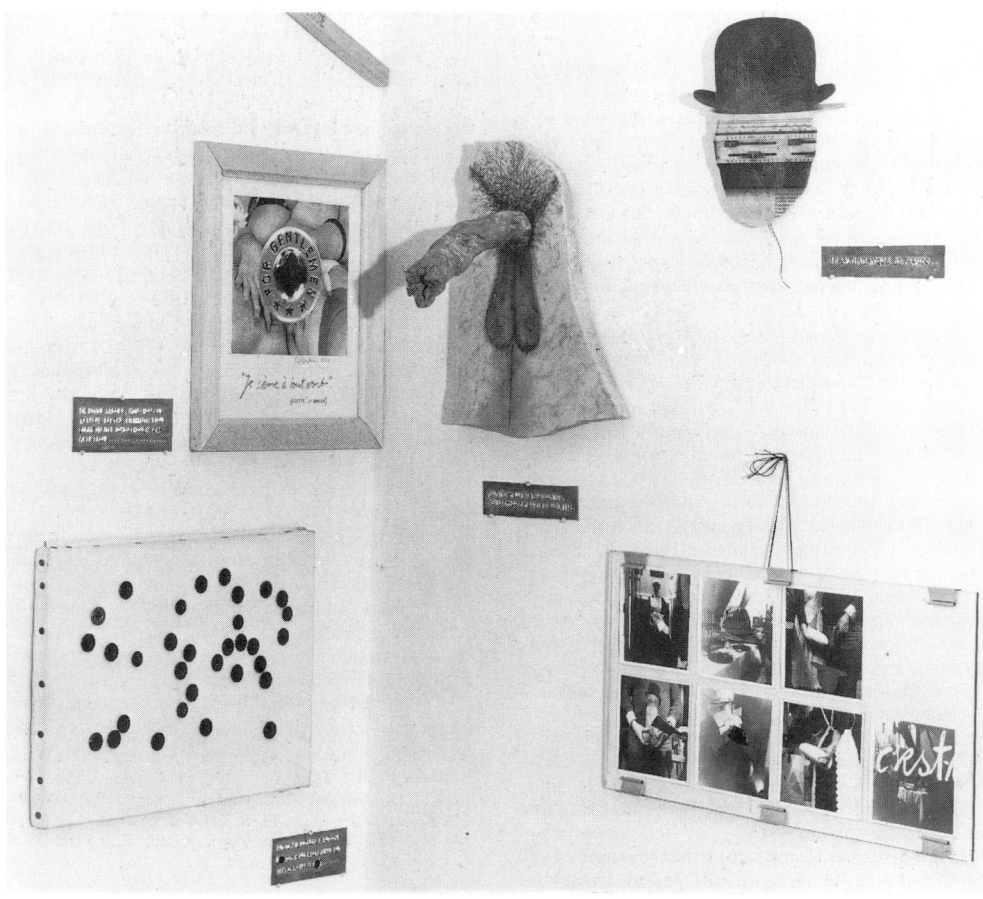

DIMITRIJEVIC, Braco.

Yugoslav. Born in Sarajevo, 18 June 1948. Educated at Gymnasium, Sarajevo, 1962–66; studied at the Academy of Fine Arts, Zagreb, 1968–71, and St.

Martin's School of Art, London, 1971-73. Married Nena Bal in 1969. Independent artist, in Zagreb 1968-71, in London since 1971. Recipient: 300th Anniversary Painting Prize, University of Zagreb, 1969; Skoj Fine Arts Award, Zagreb, 1975; D.A.A.D. Fellowship, West Berlin, 1975; Arts Council Award, London, 1978; Prix Jean Dominique Ingrès, Paris, 1979. Address: 25 Somers Road, London SW2, England.

Individual Exhibitions:

1968	Radnicki Univerziter, Sarajevo
1969	Galeria Studio Centre, Zagreb
1970	Veza Frankopanska 2a, Zagreb
	Galeria 212, Belgrade
	Salon Tribine Mladih, Novi Sad, Yugoslavia
	Aktionsraum 1, Munich
1971	Galeria Suvremene Umjetnosti, Zagreb
	Modern Art Agency, Naples
1972	Situation Gallery, London
	Galerie Konrad Fischer, Dusseldorf
	Galeria Jabuka, Zagreb
1973	Museum of Contemporary Art, Zagreb
	Situation Gallery, London
1974	Galleria Sperone, Turin
	Museum of Temporary Art, Lauterbach, West Germany
	Galleria Francoise Lambert, Milan
1975	Palais des Beaux-Arts, Brussels
	Museo del Arte Temporanea, Albioli, Italy
	Städtisches Museum, Mönchengladbach, West Germany
	Sperone Gallery, New York
	Galeria Nova, Zagreb
	P.M.J. Self Gallery, London
1976	Galleria Sperone, Turin
	Galerie René Block, West Berlin
	Kabinett für Aktuelle Kunst, Bremerhaven, West Germany
1977	Galleria Civica d'Arte Moderna, Modena, Italy
	Nuovi Strumenti, Brescia, Italy
	Hetzler + Keller, Stuttgart
	Robert Self Gallery, Newcastle upon Tyne
1978	Centre d'Art Contemporain, Geneva
	Galerie Ecart, Geneva
	MTL Gallery, Brussels
1979	Museum & Garden Charlottenburg, West Berlin
	Arbeiten/Works 1968-1978, Badischer Kunstverein, Karlsruhe, West Germany
	Stedelijk Van Abbemuseum, Eindhoven, Netherlands
	Underground Train Stations, London
	Kunsthalle, Tübingen, West Germany
	Institute of Contemporary Arts, London
1980	Peter Velebit Factory, Belgrade
1981	*New Culturescapes,* Waddington Galleries, London
1982	Galerija Roman Petrovic, Sarajevo
	Deweer Art Gallery, Otegem, Belgium
1983	Zoological Garden, Sarajevo
1984	Museum Ludwig, Cologne
	Kunsthalle, Berne
	Galerie Ingrid Dacic, Tubingen, West Germany
	Galerie Marika Malacorda, Geneva
1985	Tate Gallery, London
	Galerie Philomene Magers, Bonn
1986	Galerie Ingrid Dacic, Tubingen, West Germany
1987	Galerie de Paris, Paris
	Le Consortium Centre d'Art Contemporain, Dijon
	Hillman Holland Fine Arts, Atlanta, Georgia
	Wilhelm-Hack-Museum, Ludwigshafen, West Germany

Selected Group Exhibitions:

1970	*Bitef 4,* Galeria 212, Belgrade
1971	*7th Biennale de Paris,* Musée d'Art Moderne de la Ville, Paris
1972	*Documenta 5,* Museum Fridericianum, Kassel, West Germany (and *Documenta 6,* 1977)
1976	*Biennale,* Venice (and 1982)

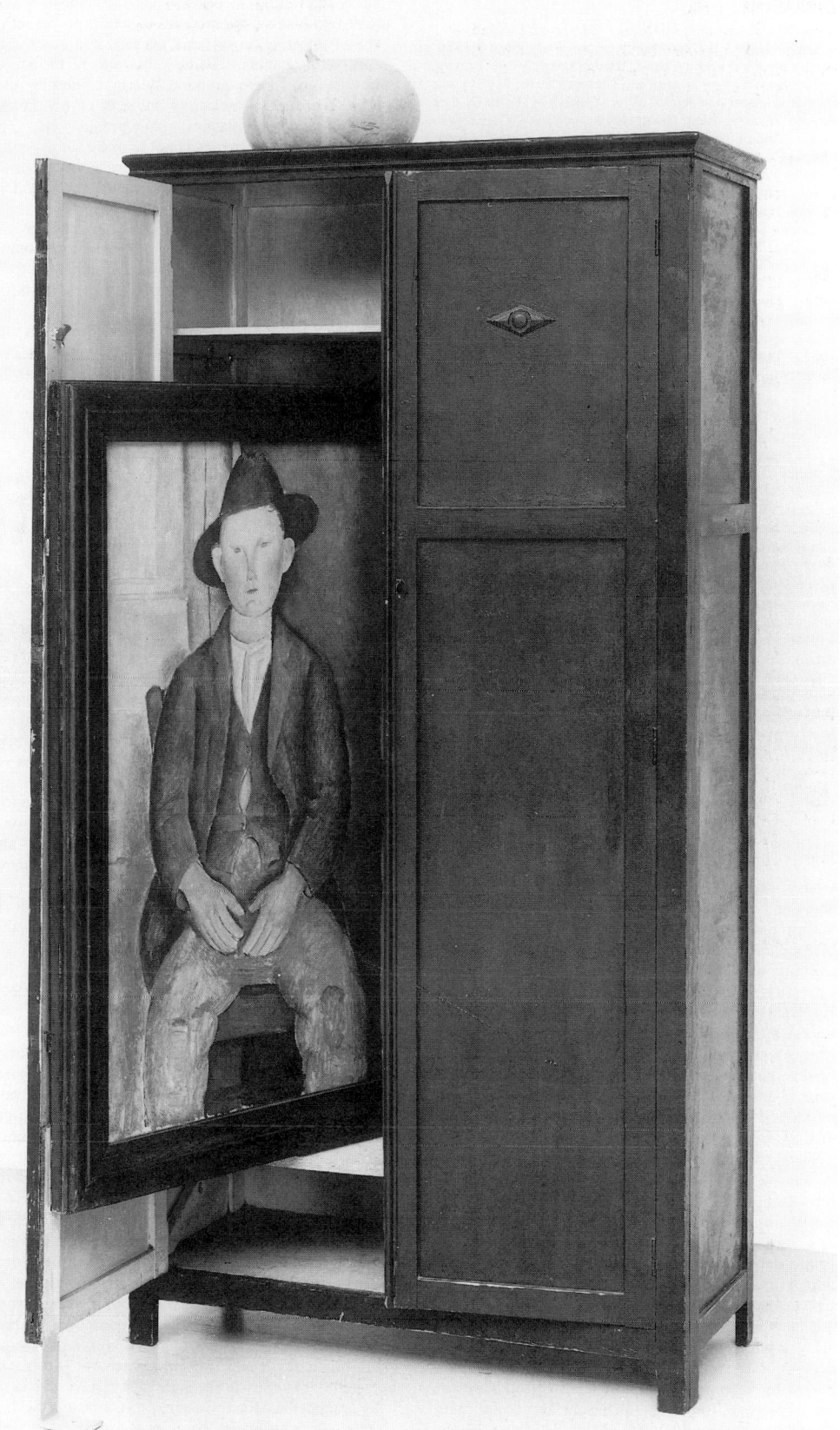

Braco Dimitrijevic: *Triptychos Post Historicus,* 1978-85

1978	*The Record as Artwork,* Museum of Contemporary Art, Chicago
1979	*Biennale of Sydney,* Art Gallery of New South Wales, Sydney (and 1986)
1980	*British Art 1940-80,* Hayward Gallery, London
1982	*Aspects of British Art Today,* Metropolitan Museum, Tokyo (toured Japan)
1985	*Promenades,* Centre d'Art Contemporain, Geneva
1987	*Vis a Vis,* Musee Saint-Denis, Rheims, France

Collections:

Museum of Contemporary Art, Zagreb; Museum of Modern Art, Belgrade; Arts Council of Great Britain, London; Centre Georges Pompidou, Paris; City of Cologne, West Germany; Museum and Garden Charlottenburg, West Berlin; Städtisches Museum, Mönchengladbach, West Germany; Museum van Hedendaagse Kunst, Ghent; Cincinnati Museum of Art, Ohio.

Publications:

By DIMITRIJEVIC: books—*Interview Book*, Zagreb 1974; *Tale of an Artist and a Castle*, Bremerhaven, West Germany 1976; *Tractatus post Historicus*, Tübingen 1976; *Self Portrait After Rembrandt and Miguel Perez*, Geneva 1978; *An Obelisk Beyond History*, West Berlin 1979; articles—"Grupa penzioner Tihomir" in *Novine GSC* (Zagreb), no. 2, 1969; "Some Changes" in *Aktionsraum 1* catalogue, Munich 1970; "Just as Piano Is Not Music, Painting Is Not Art", in *Dimitrijevic* exhibition catalogue, Zagreb 1973; "Why I Paint Like Pollock" in *Tendencije 5* exhibition catalogue, Zagreb 1973; "Towards a New Way of Behavior" in *Studio International* (London), February 1974; "My Mind is Between Sociology and Sculpture" in *Flash Art* (Milan), no. 46–47, 1974; "All'Inizio dell'Alfabeto dell'Arte" in *Data* (Milan), October 1974; "Three Museum Exhibitions of Braco Dimitrijevic" in *Dimitrijevic* exhibition catalogue, Zagreb 1975; "Status Historicus—Status Post Historicus", in +-(Brussels), no. 18, 1977; "Three Museum Exhibitions," in *Studio International* (London), no. 990, 1980; record—*His Pencil's Voice*, 1973.

On DIMITRIJEVIC: books—*7e Biennale de Paris*, exhibition catalogue, with texts by Jesa Denegri and others, Paris 1971; *Braco Dimitrijevic*, exhibition catalogue, with text by Caroline Tisdall, Zagreb 1973; *6 Years: The Dematerialization of the Art Object* by Lucy R. Lippard, New York and London 1973; *Happenings and Environments* by Adrian Henri, London 1973; *Braco Dimitrijevic*, exhibition catalogue, with text by Johannes Cladders, Mönchengladbach, West Germany 1975; *Off Media* by Germano Celant, West Berlin 1977; *The Record as Artwork: From Futurism to Conceptual Art*, exhibition catalogue, with text by Germano Celant, Chicago 1978; *Braco Dimitrijevic*, exhibition catalogue, with text by Sarah Kent, London 1979; *Braco Dimitrijevic*, exhibition catalogue, with text by Clara Weyergraf, Tübingen 1979; *Braco Dimitrijevic: Arbeiten/Works 1968–1978*, exhibition catalogue, with texts by Michael Schwarz and Manfred Schmalriede, Karlsruhe, West Germany 1979; *Braco Dimitrijevic: New Culturescapes*, exhibition catalogue, with text by David Brown, London 1981; *Braco Dimitrijevic*, exhibition catalogue with text by David Brown, London 1985; *Braco Dimitrijevic*, exhibition catalogue with essays by Bernhard Holeczek, Richard Gassan and Lida von Mengden, Ludwigshafen 1987.

I have attempted to change our customary relationships and reactions in our encounters with everyday reality. Since it would be impossible to consider this relationship in its entirety, it is necessary to restrict attention to certain fragments of the whole: my interest is in specific, rather than in general, information. By "specific information" I mean information transmitted by contemporary mass media as well as by "historical" media: monuments, memorial plaques, books, pictures, photographs, etc. On the other hand, general information is usually understood to consist of a wealth of data which the environment offers in its totality.

The first intention of my work is to establish a new qualitative relationship between man and specific information, then, secondly, between man and his exterior reality. It is important to change that with which, as a result of acquired and inherited experience, we have a definite and established *a priori* relationship. I refer primarily to our automatic acceptance of particular forms of information dispersal (while disregarding its real content) and to the passive and negative attitude which is passed through education from one generation to the next. We accept the messages transmitted through these channels automatically and unconsciously as important historical and social facts. As we discover new content within old forms of presentation, it is possible that in the future we may doubt the exclusiveness of one-way information. This may also result in the creation of a new system of associations well outside the established forms. Realizing that the faces and names on the posters and memorial plaques were selected at random and presented for the sole purpose of making an artistic statement, it is possible that we might also question that data received earlier through similar channels. The moment we begin to doubt the *a priori value* of information offered to us, we necessarily create a criterion for accepting it. In a wider sense, this new criterion makes for a new relationship with our environment and results in a different sort of behavior and activity.

It is interesting to observe the mechanism which creates art history, the methods of selection, the influence of information systems, on the creation of concepts and names. Using the same forms of presentation, I have deliberately emphasized the element of chance in selecting subjects of my monuments, memorial plaques, photographs, etc. The purpose of these activities is not to make some people famous, but rather to point out the relativity of criteria for promoting some individuals/ideas instead of others.

The aesthetic and visual characteristics of the means I employ to realize this programme are unimportant. The work can be presented through any form of communication, and its idealistic intensity is increased through repetition.

In 1976 I started working in several European museums on a series of works entitled "Triptychos Post Historicus." These are triadic compositions consisting of an original master painting, an object of everyday use, and a product of nature. All three are presented on a plinth which at the same time promotes and questions all the elements involved. One Triptychos was described by John del Bosna as a "universe in small, represented with three objects only."

—Braco Dimitrijevic

Throughout his career as an artist Braco Dimitrijević has concerned himself with change; with fame and notoriety. "Why" he seems to ask "in our mayfly existence on the surface of the earth, why should this man, this day, this event be of any more significance than any other?" Casting a cynical eye over the proliferation of memorial sculptures, plaques, and equestrain statues which abound in our towns and cities he has responded by giving instant 'fame' to persons selected at random by installing large scale photographs of them in public spaces. On one occasion he made a marble bust of another 'unknown' and placed it on a plinth with the sitter's name carved and gilded and installed it for several weeks in the centre of a famous London Square. He has endeavoured to subvert conventional, hierarchical values and also, perhaps, to suggest the potential for greatness and creativity that may exist in masses of unknown people.

In a work called 'Louvre', for instance, he has made eight busts; four are of Leonardo da Vinci, Dürer, Rembrandt and Turner—the other four, equally impressive in appearance, are of four 'unknowns'. The expectations of viewers are of a series of the famous and their reactions are bewilderment which may be blended with amusement as they grasp his point or in other cases downright exasperation! Working in the 20th century Duchampian tradition Dimitrijević's work jolts pre-conceived ideas and overturns the accepted values of the art world and the conditioned responses of the gallery goer.

In his series, Triptychos Post Historicus which he started in 1976, the title refers to "the time which escapes the 'objectivity' of traditional history; time when, it is realised, different qualities co-exist on an equal basis." (David Brown, *Triptychos Post Historicus*. Tate Gallery. 1985). They are composed of three part still life arrangements of a well known painting, a man-made object and fruit or vegetables. Viewers react with incredulity at the sight of a garden rake casually propped against Cezanne's 'Gardener' with a scatter of fruits at its base or a Modigliani 'Little Peasant' negligently placed half in and half out of a shabby wardrobe with a pumpkin on the top shelf. Usually the viewer assumes that the painting must be a reproduction and then incredulity in many cases turns to irritation and anxiety when it is realised that the picture is 'the real thing'! Dimitrijević's arrangements are so deceptively casual that they always imply a certain 'risk factor' to the treasured, cult, high art object. It is at this point that the viewer may break through to a new awareness of the content of the painting by the established master as he realises the new associations and readings made possible by the anti-hierarchical trinity.

—Mary Ellis

DINE, Jim.

American. Born in Cincinnati, Ohio, 16 June 1935. Educated at University of Cincinnati, Ohio; Boston Museum School; and Ohio University, Athens 1953–57, B.F.A. 1957. Married Nancy Minto in 1957; has 3 sons. Settled in New York, 1958; now lives and works in New York and Putney, Vermont. Visiting lecturer, Yale University, New Haven, Connecticut, 1965; Artist-in-Residence, Oberlin College, Ohio, 1965; Visiting Critic, Cornell University, Ithaca, New York, 1967. Recipient: Norman Harris Silver Medal, Art Institute of Chicago, 1964. Agent: Pace Gallery, New York. Address: Pace Gallery, 32 East 57th Street, New York, New York, 10022, U.S.A.

Individual Exhibitions:

1959	*The Smiling Workman*, Judson Gallery, New York
1960	*Car Crash*, Reuben Gallery, New York
	Jim Dine's Vaudeville, Reuben Gallery, New York
1962	Galleria dell Ariete, Milan
	Martha Jackson Gallery, New York
1963	Galerie Zwirner, Cologne
	Galerie Sonnabend, Paris
	Palais des Beaux Arts, Brussels
	Sidney Janis Gallery, New York
1964	Sidney Janis Gallery, New York
1965	Galleria Gian Enzo Sperone, Turin
	Natural History (The Dreams), First New York Theatre
	Allen Memorial Art Museum, Oberlin College, Ohio
	Robert Fraser Gallery, London
1966	Robert Fraser Gallery, London
1967	Galerie Ricke, Kassel, West Germany
	Galerie Zwirner, Cologne
	Gallery Upstairs, Buffalo, New York
	Harcus-Krakow Gallery, Boston
	Museum of Modern Art, New York
	Sidney Janis Gallery, New York
	Stedelijk Museum, Amsterdam
	White Museum of Art, Cornell University, Ithaca, New York
1969	Galerie Sonnabend, Paris
	Kunstverein, Munich
	Kunsthalle, Nuremberg
	Robert Fraser Gallery, London
1970	Whitney Museum, New York
	Kestner-Gesellschaft, Hannover
	Galerie Mikro, Berlin
	Galerie van der Loo, Munich
	Sonnabend Gallery, New York
	Dunkelman Gallery, Toronto
	Palais des Beaux-Arts, Brussels
	Museo Civico Galleria d'Arte Moderno, Turin
	Neue Galerie der Stadt, Linz, Austria
	Wolfgang Gurlitt Museum, Linz, Austria
1971	Museum Boymans-van-Beuningen, Rotterdam
	Nationalgalerie, Berlin
	Staatliche Kunsthalle, Dusseldorf
	Staatliche Kunsthalle, Baden-Baden, West Germany
	Galerie Sonnabend, Paris
	Sonnabend Downtown Gallery, New York
	D.M. Gallery, London
	Kunsthalle, Berne
	Contract Graphics, Houston
1972	Galerie Sonnabend, Paris
	Sonnabend Downtown Gallery, New York
	Gimpel and Hanover Galerie, Zurich
	Aronson Gallery, Atlanta
	Jack Glenn Gallery, Newport Beach, California
1973	John Berggreun Gallery, San Francisco
	Galerie Gerald Cramer, Geneva
	Gimpel Fils, London
	D.M. Gallery, London
	Dine/Kitaj, Cincinnati Museum of Art, Ohio
	Felicity Samuel Gallery, London
	Sonnabend Gallery, New York
1974	Sonnabend Gallery, New York
	Knoedler Prints Gallery, New York
	Institute of Contemporary Arts, London
	Museum of Contemporary Art, La Jolla, California

Galerie Ileana Sonnabend, Geneva
Hopkins Center Art Galleries, Dartmouth College, Hanover, New Hampshire
1975 Sonnabend Gallery, New York
Galerie Sonnabend, Paris
Centre Culturel Americain, Paris
Centre d'Arts Plastiques Contemporains, Bordeaux
1976 Neue Galerie, Graz, Austria
1977 *Paintings, Drawings, Etchings 1976*, Pace Gallery, New York
Jime Dine Works on Paper 1975-1976, Waddington and Tooth Galleries, London
Galleria Civica d'Arte Moderna, Ferrara, Italy
Prints 1970-1977, Williams College Museum of Art, Williamstown, Massachusetts
1978 *New Painting*, Pace Gallery, New York
Makler Gallery, Philadelphia
Pace Gallery, Columbus, Ohio
Jim Dine's Etchings, Museum of Modern Art, New York
1979 *Jim Dine: The Animate Objects*, Katonah Gallery, Katonah, New York
Jim Dine, Oeuvres sur Papier 1978-79, Galerie Cluade Bernard, Paris
Jim Dine: Figure Drawings 1975-1979, California State University at Long Beach (toured the United States)
1980 Pace Gallery, New York
Galerie Alice Pauli, Lausanne
Janie C. Lee Gallery, Houston
Harcus Krakow Gallery, Boston
1981 *Jim Dine: An Exhibition of Recent Figure Drawings 1978-1980*, Richard Gray Gallery, Chicago
1982 Waddington Galleries, London
1983 Richard Gray Gallery, Chicago
Los Angeles County Museum of Art
1984 Walker Art Center, Minneapolis
John Berggruen Gallery, San Francisco
Barbara Krakow Gallery, Boston
Fay Gold Gallery, Atlanta, Georgia
Cantor Leinberg Gallery, Detroit
Thorden Wetterling Galleries, Goteborg, Sweden
1985 Toni Birkhead Gallery, Cincinnati, Ohio
Akron Art Institute, Ohio
Albright-Knox Art Gallery, Buffalo, New York
Hirshhorn Museum, Washington, D.C.
Pace Gallery, New York
1986 University of Texas, Austin
Los Angeles County Museum of Art
Toledo Museum of Art, Ohio
Des Moines Art Center, Iowa
Williams College of Art, Williamstown, Massachusetts
Pace Gallery, New York
Galerie Baudoin Lebon, Paris
Fuji Television Gallery, Tokyo
Galerie Alice Pauli, Lausanne

Selected Group Exhibitions:

1969 *International Exhibition*, Carnegie Institute, Pittsburgh
1973 *Annual Exhibition*, Whitney Museum of American Art, New York
Modern Art in Prints, Museum of Modern Art, New York
1974 *Poets of the Cities: New York and San Francisco 1950-1965*, Museum of Fine Arts, Dallas
1976 *The Human Clay*, Hayward Gallery, London
1977 *Documenta 6*, Kassel, West Germany
Drawings of the 70's, Art Institute of Chicago
1979 *Drawings About Drawing: New Directions 1968 1978*, Ackland Memorial Art Center, Chapel Hill, North Carolina
Emergence and Progression: 6 Contemporary Artists, Milwaukee Art Center
1984 *Olympian Gestures*, Los Angeles County Museum of Art

Collections:

Museum of Modern Art, New York; Metropolitan Museum

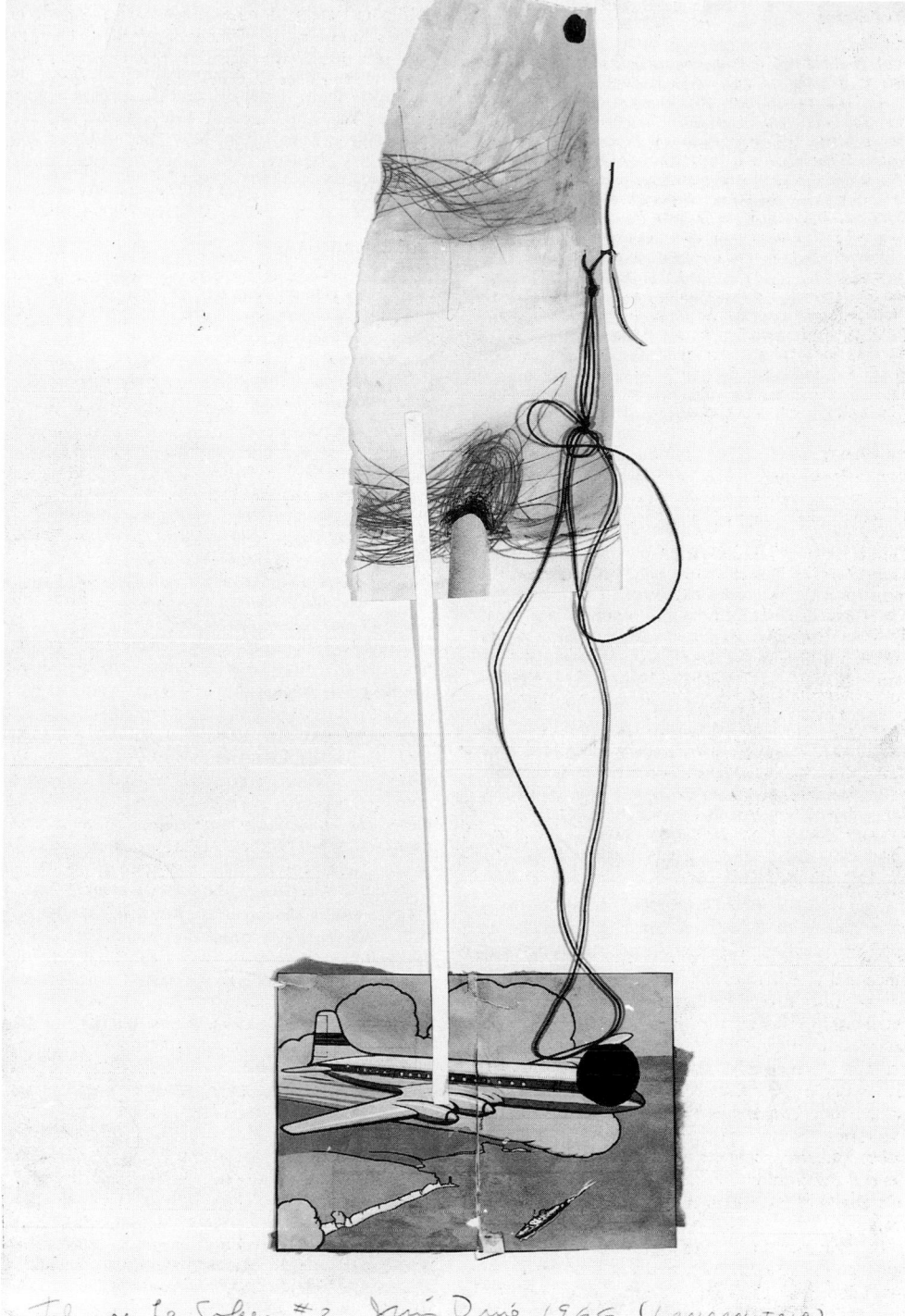

Jim Dine: *Thorpe-le-Soken No. 2*, 1966

of Art, New York; Guggenheim Museum, New York; Whitney Museum, New York; Williams College Museum of Art, Williamstown, Massachusetts; Hirshhorn Museum and Sculpture Garden, Smithsonian Institution, Washington, D.C.; Art Institute of Chicago; Museum of Contemporary Art, Chicago; Carnegie Institute, Pittsburgh; Museum of Fine Arts, Dallas.

Publications:

By DINE: books—*Jim Dine Designs for A Midsummer Night's Dream*, New York 1968; *Picture of Dorian Gray*, stage script after Oscar Wilde, London 1968; *Work from the Same House* with Lee Friedlander, London 1969; *Welcome Home Lovebird*, London 1969; *Adventures of Mr. and Mr. Jim and Ron*, with Ron Padgett, London 1970; *Letters to Nancy*, New York 1970; articles—"What Is Pop Art," interview, with G. R. Swenson, in *Artnews* (New York), November 1963; statement in *American Drawings*, exhibition catalogue, New York 1964; "Eye to I," interview with Charlotte Willard, in *Art in America* (New York) March/April 1966; "Dining with Jim" interview, with Robert Fraser, in *Art and Artists* (London), September 1966; answers to "Test in Art," prepared by Kenneth Koch, in *Artnews* (New York), October 1966; statement in "Jim Dine's Red Mural for the United States Pavilion" by William C. Lipke in *Artscanada* (Toronto), October 1976; "Lithographs and Original Prints: Two Artists Discuss their Recent Work" in *Studio International* (London), June 1968; interview, with Thomas Krens, in *Jim Dine Prints 1970-1977*, by Riva Castleman, New York 1977.

On DINE: books—*6 Painters and the Object*, exhibition catalogue, by Lawrence Alloway, New York, 1963; *The Popular Image Exhibition*, exhibition catalogue, with an essay by Alan R. Solomon, Washington, D.C. 1963; *The New American Realism*, with an introduction by Martin Carey, preface by Daniel Catton Rich, Worcester, Massachusetts 1965; *Pop Art and the American Tradition*, exhibition catalogue, by Tracy Atkinson, Milwaukee 1965; *Prints by 5 New Artists*, exhibition catalogue, New York 1969; *Jim Dine*, exhibition catalogue, New York 1970; *Jim Dine. Complete Graphics* by John Russell and others, London 1970; *Dine/Kitaj*, exhibition catalogue, by R. F. Boyle and R. B. Kitaj, Cincinnati 1973; *Jim Dine*, exhibition catalogue, Bordeaux 1975; *The Human Clay*, exhibition catalogue, by R. B. Kitaj, London 1976; *Drawing Now*, exhibition catalogue, by Bernice Rose, New York 1976; *Jim Dine*, exhibition catalogue, by Paola Serra Zanett, Ferrara, Italy 1977; *Jim Dine Works on Paper 1975–1976*, exhibition catalogue, by R. B. Kitaj, London 1977; *Jim Dine: Paintings, Drawings, Etchings 1976*, exhibition catalogue, New York 1977; *Jim Dine Prints 1970–1977* by Riva Castleman, New York 1977; *Jim Dine: Prints 1970–1971*, exhibition catalogue, Williamstown, Massachusetts 1977; *Jim Dine's Etchings* by Riva Castleman, New York 1978; *Jim Dine: New Painting*, exhibition catalogue, New York 1978; *Jim Dine: Figure Drawings 1975–1979* by Constance W. Glenn, New York 1979; *Jim Dine*, exhibition catalogue, text by James R. Mellow, New York 1980; *Jim Dine: An Exhibition of Recent Figure Drawings 1978–1980*, exhibition catalogue, with text by David Shapiro, Chicago 1981; *Jim Dine Prints 1977–1985*, exhibition catalogue with texts by Ellen G. D'Oench and Jean E. Feinberg, Los Angeles 1986; *Jim Dine: Une Exposition pour Paris*, exhibition catalogue with essay by Anne Dagbert, Paris 1986.

Though Jim Dine has been loosely associated by some critics with Pop art, the essential thing about his work is that like Oldenburg's it first developed in the atmosphere of environments and happenings which was one of the responses to Abstract Expressionism. And Dine has developed the idea of the collage event in various directions, exploring audience participation and total theatre in his own happenings, and making paintings which are essentially combines or assemblages, fastening all sorts of ready-made objects such as clothes or tools to the canvas. Dine owed much to the climate created by Rauschenberg and Johns. Like Rauschenberg he tackles the problem of combining objects and painting into a single entity, and he is concerned to continually extend the boundaries of what is permissible aesthetically in a work of art, while like Johns he conducts a dialogue between painting and the real object.

Right from the start of his career Dine was active as an organizer of Happenings (four of them during 1959–60, such as "The Car Crash") sometimes in collaboration with Oldenburg, who was close to his own spirit. At the same time he was producing collage-paintings that incorporate actual objects as part of the design, such as his "Green Suit" (1959). Clothing and simple household objects bulk large among his subjects, so that his paintings have included bathrobes, ties, household appliances such as a toaster, bathroom cabinets, tools. Some of these works are large, so that they become environments, like his bathrooms. But these objects are often displaced and dissociated from their everyday contexts by Dine's use of painting, since he combines them with freely painted surfaces in the Abstract Expressionist manner to which he has remained loyal.

His paintings of paint-boxes, palettes and colour charts are reminiscent of Jasper Johns, and like Johns he sometimes combines painted areas with words, as if to study the relationship between painting and other methods of specification. Dine's interest in tools and the mechanical is a very American as well as a very personal one, especially when he combines a down-to-earth fourfoot Clamp with a "Walking Dream" in the shape of lots of shapely girls's legs. In his "Tool Box" suite of screen prints he similarly juxtaposes the mechanical and the organic, for instance by placing a pair of lips alongside a row of hammers. Some of his works are overtly aggressive, with an axe plunged into a plank, or a saw bisecting a blue field of paint. Others seem overtly sexual, like his canticles to the penis, made during a visit to London in 1966, and seized by the police later that year from the Robert Fraser gallery for allegedly being indecent! But Dine's drawing and painting are too exquisite, despite the robustness of his graphic images, to be attacked in such crude terms. The juxtapositions in his works often make their initial impact as visual puns, and Max Kozloff has well-described the unique quality of this elusive artist by talking about his "entertainment psychology."

—Lavinia Learmont

DI SUVERO, Mark.

American. Born in Shanghai, China, 18 September 1933. Studied at San Francisco College; University of California, Berkeley. Sculptor: lives and works in New York. Built "Tower of Peace" as protest against Vietnam War, Los Angeles, 1966. Agent: Oil and Steel Gallery, Long Island, New York. Address: c/o Oil and Steel Gallery, 3030 Vernon Boulevard, Long Island, New York 11102, U.S.A.

Individual Exhibitions:

1960	Green Gallery, New York
1965	Dwan Gallery, Los Angeles
1966	Park Place Gallery, New York
1968	Lo Guidice Gallery, Chicago
1972	Van Abbemuseum, Eindhoven Netherlands
	Wilhelm-Lembruck Museum, Duisburg, West Germany
	La Ville de Chalon-sur-Saone, France
1975	Jardin des Tuileries, Paris
	Whitney Museum, New York (retrospective)
1978	*New Sculpture*, Janie C. Lee Gallery, Houston
1980	*Inner Search*, Northwestern Operations Center, Minneapolis (permanent installation)
1981	Governors State University, Park Forest, Chicago
	Ace Gallery, Venice, California
1982	Gemini Gallery, Los Angeles

Selected Group Exhibitions:

1962	*Continuity and Change*, Wadsworth Atheneum, Hartford, Connecticut
1964	*Recent American Sculpture*, Jewish Museum, New York
1968	*Documenta*, Kassel, West Germany
1969	*Sculpture of the 60's*, Los Angeles County Museum of Art
	New York Painting and Sculpture 1940–70, Metropolitan Museum of Art, New York
1970	*Monumental Art*, Contemporary Art Center, Cincinnati, Ohio
1971	*Works for New Spaces*, Walker Art Center, Minneapolis
1974	*Public Sculpture/Urban Environment*, Oakland Museum, California
1975	*Biennale*, Venice
1980	*Sculpture in California 1975–1980*, San Diego Museum of Art, California

Collections:

New York University; Whitney Museum, New York; Wadsworth Atheneum, Hartford, Connecticut; Rhode Island School of Design, Providence; Massachusetts Institute of Technology, Cambridge; Art Institute of Chicago; St. Louis Art Museum; University of Iowa, Iowa City.

Publications:

By DI SUVERO: article—"Mark di Suvero à Chalon-sur-Saone," interview, in *Art Press* (Paris), December/January 1974.

On DI SUVERO: books—*Mark di Suvero*, exhibition catalogue, by James K. Monte, New York 1975; *Mark di Suvero: New Sculpture*, exhibition catalogue, with text by Barbara Rose, Houston 1978; *Sculpture in California 1975–1980*, exhibition catalogue, San Diego, California 1980; *Mark di Suvero*, exhibition catalogue, Los Angeles 1982; articles—"Mark di Suvero" by Jill Johnston in *Recent American Sculpture*, exhibition catalogue, New York 1964; "Di Suvero: The Pressures of Reality" by H. Rothenstein in *Artnews* (New York), February 1967; "Mark di Suvero" by Max Kozloff in *Artforum* (New York), Summer 1967; "Mark di Suvero" by Carter Ratcliff in *Artforum* (New York), November 1972; "Mark di Suvero's Burgundian Season" by E. C. Baker in *Art in America* (New York), May/June 1974; "Mark di Suvero: An Epic Reach" by Donald Goddard in *Artnews* (New York), January 1976; "Idealism Realized: Two Public Commissions by Mark di Suvero" by J. Klein in *Arts Magazine* (New York), December 1981.

It is difficult for any art historian to avoid the dialectic of Hegelism. From a distance the confusion of art movements and isms can be seen to settle into patterns of thesis, antithesis, and synthesis, a slow (and nowadays, not so slow) swing of the pendulum backwards and forwards. Every new development that occurs can be seen as a historical necessity, and the new artists are not original thinkers but players carrying out the dictates of the role that history has assigned them.

Such a view leads to a scepticism where originality among artists is concerned. A development that seemed revolutionary at the time it first became manifest, now takes its place as a small variation in the continuous rhythm of action and reaction. Artists are no longer seen as free agents, breaking new ground with every advance, but as manifestations of the process, needed by history to carry out a particular role.

Hence the critical acclaim lavished on any particular artist is absurd; one might as well praise winter for coming after autumn. This publication contains hundreds of examples of meaningless acclamation, claims made on the behalf of artists which have no validity, which are, in the end, ridiculous.

I make these remarks because I am not going to say that Mark Di Suvero is the greatest sculptor since Michaelangelo, or that his work has "seminal" influence, or that it is the best or the biggest or the most important around. Personally I like what I have seen, but that in itself is insignificant; my liking something means nothing.

What one can do, however, is explain where Suvero fits into the dialectical pattern of recent American art, what is the historical necessity of his work, because his sculpture inhabits a turning point, a corner in the process, where one idea became another one.

Suvero inherited a dilemma. Fifties art concerned itself with the emotional level of the human being. It tended to do so more successfully in painting than in sculpture, probably because sculpture is a slow process and much 50's art depended on the instant release of emotion on to the canvas. There is no real school of Abstract Expressionist sculptors.

In the 60's through the influence of David Smith, a native style of sculpture emerged. It began as essentially constructivist, and then, through the discovery of symmetry, became monumental. Artists such as Bryden, Tony Smith, Judd and Morris established a massive style, based upon straight lines used in a balanced and symmetrical way.

The problem was that sculpture began to look more and more like office blocks. The associations of the new style were certainly not human but mechanical and artificial. The sculpture contained no accidents, no reference to the random nature of life and of human emotion. They were too controlled.

Suvero was among those who tried to solve the problem, and his solution remains the best to date. He retained the concept of "presence," which is found among the monumental school. His work is usually on a large scale and forces itself upon the viewers' attention. He also retained the constructivist element; his work has "parts" which have been put together, but in a manner that is much more fluid than one would expect from the minimalists.

The most significant change is in choice of materials. Here he seems to have learnt from the 50's fashion for "objets trouvé." Instead of using the polished and enamelled steel so beloved of minimal sculptors, he employs bits of rusty chain, old wooden beams, punctured tyres. The style is a rhetoric of the vernacular, a synthesis of the 50's and 60's.

An inevitable and necessary development perhaps; but one may be glad that it has been done so well.

—Alastair Mackintosh

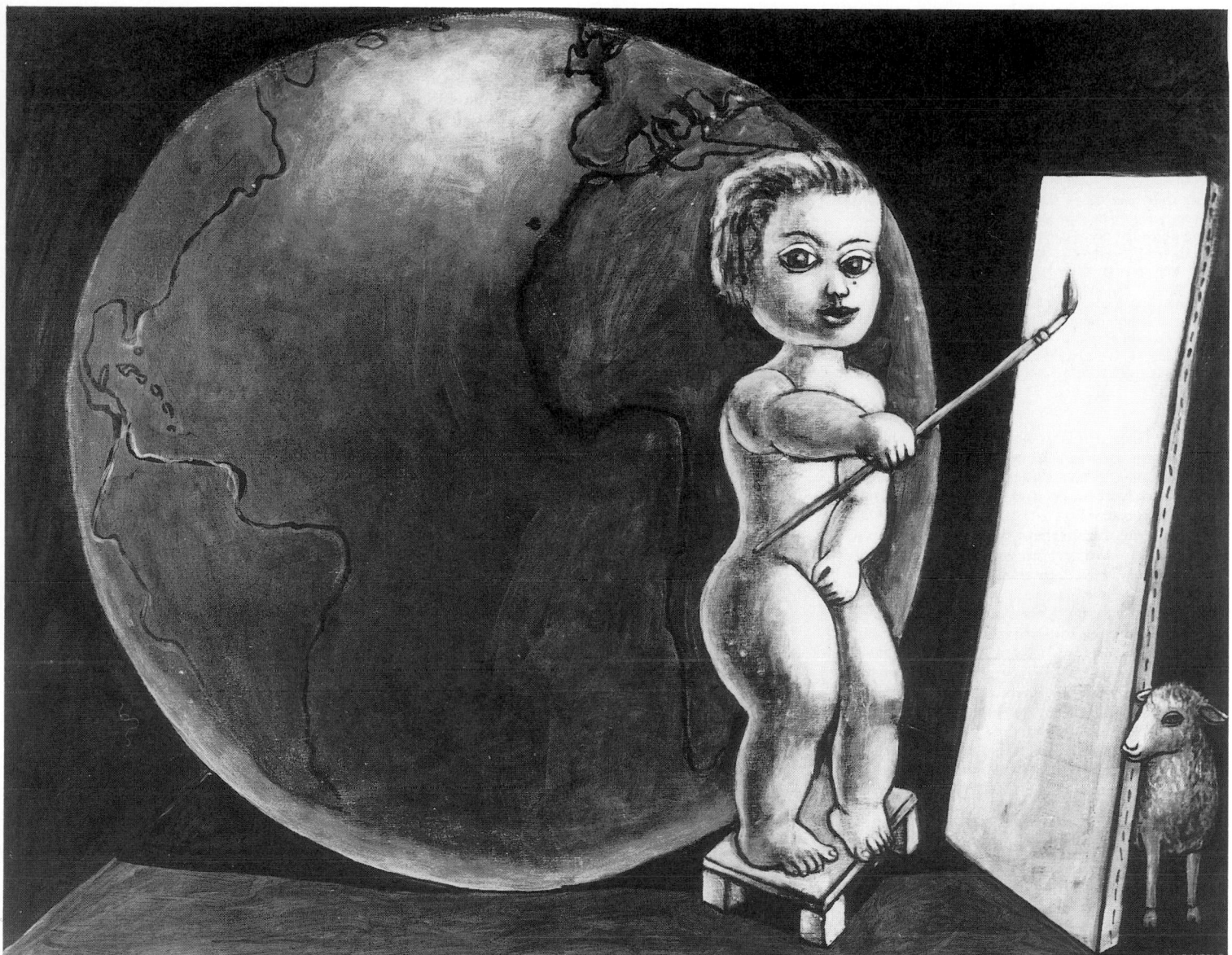

Jiri Georg Dokoupil: *Das Atelier*, 1984

DOKOUPIL, Jiri Georg.

Stateless. Born in Krnov, Czechoslovakia, 3 June 1954; emigrated to West Germany, 1968. Studied fine arts in Cologne and Frankfurt, and under Hans Haacke at the Cooper Union, New York, 1976–78. Independent painter and sculptor, Cologne, from 1978: currently lives in Cologne and Santa Cruz de Tenerife, Canary Islands. Instructor, Staatliche Kunstakademie, Dusseldorf, 1983–84. Agent: Galerie Paul Maenz, Bismarckstrasse 50, 5000 Cologne 1. Address: Aachener Strasse 21, 5000 Cologne 1, West Germany.

Individual Exhibitions:

1982 Galerie Paul Maenz, Cologne
Galerie 't Venster, Rotterdam (with Walter Dahn)
Galerie Magers, Bonn (with Walter Dahn)
Galerie Chantal Crousel, Paris
Galerie Helen van der Meij, Amsterdam
1983 Galerie Paul Maenz, Cologne
Galerie Six Friedrich, Munich
Produzentgalerie, Hamburg (with Walter Dahn)
Galerie Six Friedrich, Munich (with Walter Dahn)
Galerie Paul Maenz, Cologne (with Walter Dahn)
Mary Boone Gallery, New York
Galerie Chantal Crousel, Paris
1984 Galerie Schurr, Stuttgart

Groninger Museum, Groningen, Netherlands (with Walter Dahn)
Galerie Paul Maenz, Cologne
Museum Folkwang, Essen, West Germany
1985 Kunstmuseum, Lucerne, Switzerland
Galerie Crousel-Hussenot, Paris
Galerie Leyendecker, Santa Cruz de Tenerife
Galerie Paul Maenz, Cologne (with Walter Dahn)
Groninger Museum, Groningen, Netherlands
Galerie Paul Maenz, Cologne
Espace Lyonnais d'Art Contemporain, Lyon, France
Galerie Vera Munro, Hamburg
Paule Anglim Gallery, San Francisco
Asher/Faure Gallery, Los Angeles
Heinrich Erhardt Galerie, Frankfurt
Leo Castelli Gallery, New York
1986 Galerie 121, Antwerp
Galleria Marilena Bonomo, Bari, Italy
Sonnabend Gallery, New York
1987 Galerie Paul Maenz, Cologne
Galeria Leyendecker, Santa Cruz de Tenerife
Galerie Six Friedrich, Munich
Galerie Swart, Amsterdam
Galerie Dacic, Tubingen, West Germany
Studio Marconi, Milan
Galerie Bischofberger, Zurich
1988 Galleria Marilena Bonomo, Bari, Italy
Galeria Juana de Aizpuru, Madrid

Selected Group Exhibitions:

1980 *Auch wenn das Perlhuhn leise weint*, Hahnentorburg, Cologne
1981 *Die Seefahrt und der Tod: Mulheimer Freiheit*, Kunsthalle, Wilhelmshaven, West Germany (travelled to Wolfsburg)
1982 *Documenta 7*, Museum Fridericianum, Kassel, West Germany
1983 *Expressionisten—Neue Wilde*, Museum am Ostwall, Dortmund, West Germany
1984 *International Survey of Recent Painting and Sculpture*, Museum of Modern Art, New York
1985 *Kunst in der Bundesrepublik 1945–85*, Nationalgalerie, West Berlin
1986 *Wild, Visionary, Spectral: New German Art*, Art Gallery of South Australia, Adelaide
1987 *Avant-Garde in the Eighties*, Los Angeles County Museum of Art

Collections:

Van Abeemuseum, Eindhoven; Neue Galerie/Sammlung Ludwig, Aachen; Groninger Museum, Groningen; Staatsgalerie, Stuttgart; Museum Boymans-van Beuningen, Rotterdam; Kunsthaus, Zurich; Museum Folkwang, Essen; Nationalgalerie, West Berlin; Museum am Ostwall, Dortmund; Emanuel Hoffman Stiftung, Basle.

Publications:

By DOKOUPIL: books—*Neue Kolner Schule*, exhibition catalogue, Cologne 1982.

On DOKOUPIL: books—*Das Bilderbuch*, edited by Karl Pfefferle, Munich 1981; *Junger nach Bildern: Deutsche Malerei der Gegenwart* by Wolfgang Max Faust and Gerd de Vries, Cologne 1982; *10 junge Kunstler aus Deutschland*, exhibition catalogue with text by Zdenek Felix, Essen 1982; *Walter Dahn und Georg Dokoupil*, photographs by Roman Soukup, foreword by Paul Maenz, Cologne 1982; *Die Sammlung FER—The FER Collection* by Christel Sauer, Cologne 1983; *Die Afrika-Bilder: Dahn/Dokoupil*, exhibition catalogue with texts by Frans Haks and Wilfried W. Dickhoff, Groningen 1984; *Dokoupil: Arbeiten 1981–84*, exhibition catalogue with texts by Zdenek Felix, Frans Haks, Martin Kunz and Thierry Raspail, Cologne 1984; *Jiri Georg Dokoupil: Corporations and Products—The Sculptures*, edited by Paul Maenz, Cologne 1985; *Jiri Georg Dokoupil*, exhibition catalogue with texts by Ernst A. Busche and Paul Maenz, Cologne 1987.

The artist Georg Jiri Dokoupil has manifested himself as a versatile and chameleontic painter, as one gifted with the talent to take a central position in the art-debate of the day while at the same time he forfeits current expectations.

Already for six years now he plays the game successfully. It is virtually impossible to circumscribe his already enormous oeuvre in a few lines, just as it does not make much sense to deal with some of the paintings individually. As his self-designed catalogue (Folkwang Museum, Essen; Groninger Museum, Groningen and others, 1984), shows, he works in groups of paintings, very often done for particular gallery-exhibitions. His production scheme seemed especially fit to match any number and size of exhibitions. By continuously changing his themes and by applying a wide range of painting-techniques he is able to make each show look different. In this respect Dokoupil gives one the impression of being the artist par excellence for a commercial market system, precisely because his method allows for marketable surprise. To him the commercial system has never been a bondage; on the contrary, it is a stimulus. Critical doubt about superficiality or lack of seriousness, the traditional claim that a painting should show a certain struggling with its materials and its subject matter does not hold here. His way of painting allows for no doubts and hesitations, in its mechanical character it reminds one of many of Picasso's achievements. Despite his great success Dokoupil has retained something of an anarchistic and combative spirit.

Around 1980 Dokoupil was part of the Cologne-based artist-group 'Mullheimer Freiheit' (with Adamski, Bommels, Dahn, Kever, Naschberger). From 1982/83 onwards, from the moment that the young German painters generation rapidly became successful, in Germany as well as abroad, Dokoupil has made clear that the art from Cologne should not be confused with the expressionist 'wild painting' from Berlin (Fetting, Salome) or even Hamburg (Oehlenbrothers, Büttner).

Possibly, one of Dokoupil's reasons to collaborate intensively with Walter Dahn (1982/83) has been the need to demonstrate the relativity of an individual, 'expressive' signature. For him the year 1982 was a very productive one, witness the *'Amsterdam-Bilder'* that deal with schizophrenic painting as well as the gigantic *'History of the Universe'* that seems to be a monumental and public translation of microscopic-cosmic fertilization.

Remarkable as well is the series of *'Frottee-Bilder'* from 1983/84, framed sweat-cloth supplied with buttons and zippers, workshop-products that associate themselves with Fontana's spatial, eroticizing cuts. A group of ceramics called 'Corporations and products' (Paul Maenz Gallery, Cologne, 1985) offers all the potentials of a well-organized firm. The gallery-show consisted of a large amount of baked logos of international firms, all reduced to one (Dokoupil) vocabulary. Recently Dokoupil started a new collaboration, with the young Dutch artist Rob Scholte.
—A. F. Wagemans

DOLLA, Noël.

French. Born in Nice, 5 May 1945. Educated at Ecole Nationale d'Art Décoratif, Nice, 1962–66. Served in the French Army, 1968. Independent painter, Nice, since 1966. Professor, Ecole Nationale d'Art Décoratif, Nice, since 1974. Agents: Galerie Sapone, 25BD Dubouchage, Nice, France; Galerie Van Horenbeeck, 183 Chaussée de Charleroi, Brussels, Belgium; Galerie Fagergren, Rosengarden 9, 1174 Copenhagen, Denmark. Address: 6 rue Fodéré, 06300 Nice, France.

Individual Exhibitions:

1969   *Restructuration N. 2*, Cime de l'Authion, Alpes Maritimes, France
1970   *Restructuration N. 3*, Cime de l'Authion, Alpes Martimes, France.

Noel Dolla: *Leurre*, **1987**

1972   *Restructuration N. 4*, Galerie de la Salle, St. Paul de Vence, France
1973   Galerie Chez Malabar et Cunégonde, Nice
         Dolla/Isnard/Viallat, Galleria La Bertesca, Milan
         Galleria La Bertesca, Genoa
         Galleria La Bertesca, Milan
         Galerie Albert Baronian, Brussels
1975   Galerie Paul Maenz, Cologne
         Galerie Gérald Piltzer, Paris
         Galleria Spagnoli, Florence
         Galerie La Bertesca, Dusseldorf
1976   Galerie Chez Malabar et Cunégonde, Nice
         Galerie Gérald Piltzer, Paris
1977   Galerie La Bertesca, Dusseldorf
1980   *Restructuration Spatiale No. 5*, Galerie d'Art Contemporain des Musées de Nice
         Galerie Sapone, Nice
         Galerie Anne Van Horenbeeck, Brussels
         Galerie Nothelfer, Berlin

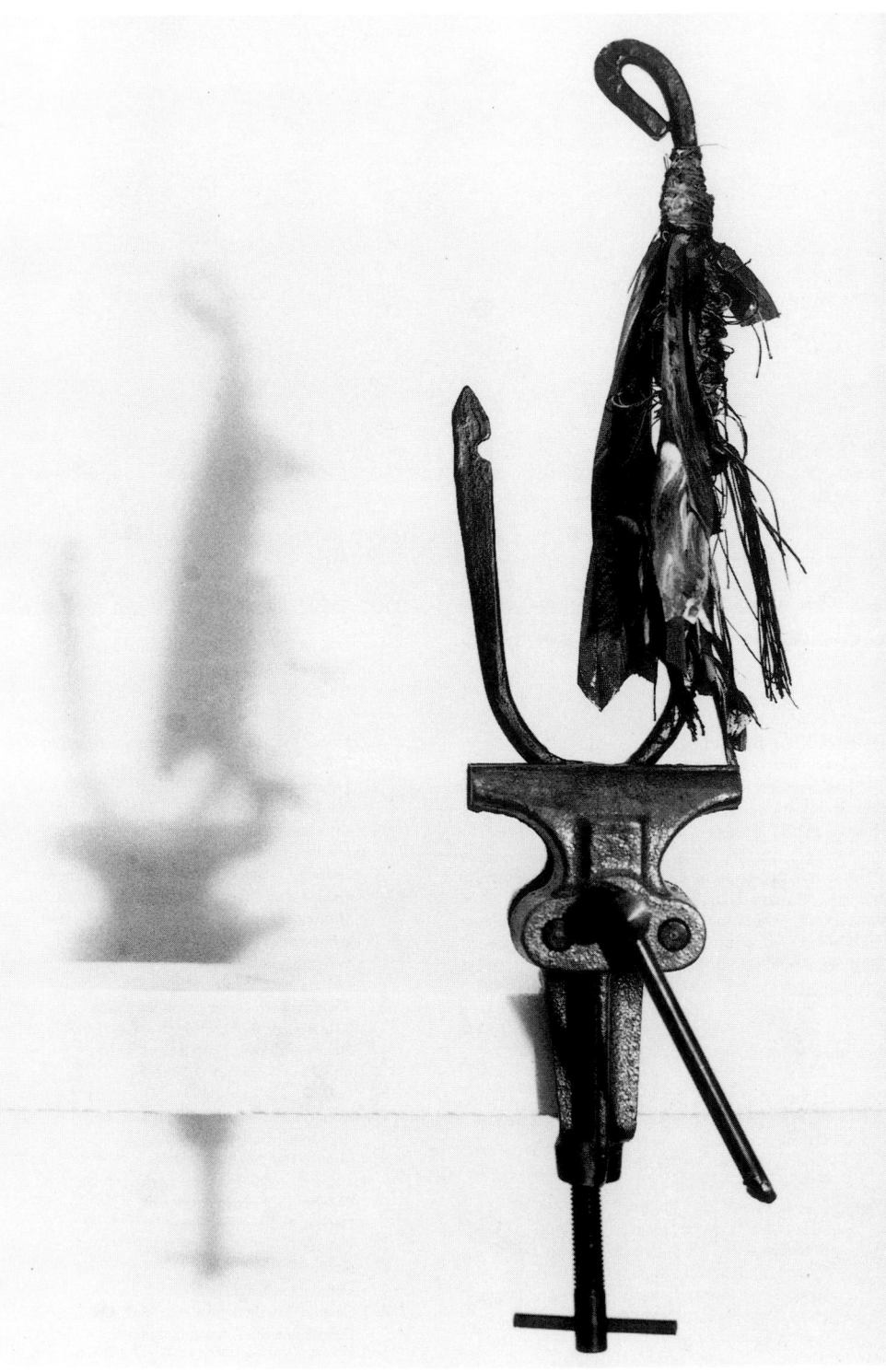

Musée de St. Paul de Vence, France
1981 Galerie Errata, Montpellier, France
1982 Galerie Fagergren, Copenhagen
1983 Arène de Cimiez, Nice
1984 Galerie Sapone, Nice
1985 *Performance Photographique*, Cologne, West Germany
Arène de Cimiez, Nice
1986 Palais de Congrés, Nice
Galerie Archétypes, Nice
Galleria Chisel, Genoa, Italy
1987 Galleria Cooperativa Comunale, Bologna, Italy
Galerie Ferrero, Nice
Galerie Le Chantjour, Nice

Selected Group Exhibitions:

1974 *Nouvelle Peinture en France*, Musée d'Art et d'Industrie, St. Etienne, France
1975 *Analytische Malerei*, Galerie La Bertesca, Dusseldorf
Biennale, Paris
3 Artistes de la Biennale de Paris, Galerie La Bertesca, Dusseldorf
1976 *A proposito della pittura*, Van Bommel-Van Dam Museum Venlo, Netherlands
1977 *Canvas Without Stretchers*, Galerie Gimpel Fils, London
Ecole de Nice, dix ans, Galerie de la Salle, St. Paul de Vence, France
1979 *Le Tondo de Monet à nos jours*, Musée de l'Abbaye Sainte-Croix, Les Sables d'Olonnes, France
1980 *Nice à Berlin*, DAAD Galerie, Berlin
1981 *Futur Corps Passes*, Musée Fabre, Montpellier, France

Collections:

Centre Georges Pompidou, Paris; Musée de Nice; Musée de Toulon, France; Musée Fabre, Montpellier, France; Musée Cantini, Marseille, France; Fonds Régional d'Art Contemporain, Lorraine, France.

Publications:

By DOLLA: books—*Cent artistes dans la ville*, exhibition catalogue, Montpellier, France 1970; article—interview, with Anne Helaine, in *1968-1978-1988*, exhibition catalogue, Nice 1978.

On DOLLA: books—*Origine Nice*, exhibition catalogue, by Raphael Monticelli, Tours 1969; *Douze Ans d'Art Contemporain en France*, exhibition catalogue, by Michel Vachey, Paris 1972; *Art en France: Une Nouvelle Generation* by Jean Clair, Paris 1972; *Noël Dolla*, exhibition catalogue, by Raphael Monticelli, Nice 1973; *Dolla/Isnard/Viallat*, exhibition catalogue, by Jacques LePage and Raphael Monticelli, Milan 1974; *Noël Dolla*, exhibition catalogue, by Raphael Monticelli, Milan 1974; *Nouvelle peinture en France*, exhibition catalogue, by Mathieu Benezet, St. Etienne, France 1974; *Noël Dolla*, exhibition catalogue, by Bernard Lamarche Vadel, Florence 1975; *Noël Dolla*, exhibition catalogue, Nice 1980; articles—"Dolla" by Michel Vachey in *Art Vivant* (Paris), January 1972; "Noël Dolla" by Bernard Lamarche Vadel in *Art Press* (Paris), February 1975; "Les tarlatanes de Noël Dolla" by Bernard Lamarche Vadel in *Opus* (Paris) January 1977; "L'Ecole de Nice" by Claude Fournet in *Connaissance des Arts* (Paris), June 1978.

From induction to deduction, painting consists in making sure that PAINTING won't anymore be thought of with the conceptual tools the critics have been using since the Renaissance in order to decide the CANVAS's fate.

Between sterile shamming and a return to a simplistic figurative painting of the MATISSE/POP/EXPRESSIONIST type, I work, sticking to an evolutionary principle based upon the continuous shifting of formal work, in order to bring to the fore what has been, for a century, the only revolution in painting: THE SPIRIT OF ABSTRACTION.

—Noël Dolla

DOMELA, César.

Dutch. Born César Domela Nieuwenhuis in Amsterdam, 15 January 1900. Educated at gymnasium in Hilversum, Netherlands, 1913–18. Married Ruth Deremberg in 1928; children: Lie and Anne. Visited Henri Laurens' Paris atelier, 1914; began drawing, 1918; moved to Ascona, 1920, to Berlin, 1923; met Piet Mondrian and Theo van Doesburg; joined De Stijl group, 1925; moved to Amsterdam, 1925; returned to Berlin, 1927; advertising photographer, with own commercial studio, Berlin-Wilmersdorf, 1928–33; joined Ring Neue Werbegestalter group, founded by Schwitters, 1929; lecturer, Berlin, Munich and Stuttgart typography companies, 1931; burned personal anarchist literature, and returned to Paris, 1933; opened silkscreen studio, with Frederick Kann; member, Cercle et Carré/Abstraction-Création groups, Paris, 1934; founded *Plastique* magazine, with Jean Arp and Sophie Täuber-Arp, 1937; worked with jewelry, 1941; currently lives and works in Paris. Visiting instructor, Skowhegan School of Painting, Maine, 1977. Agent: Galerie de Seine, 18 rue de Seine, 75006 Paris. Address: 65 Boulevard Arago, 75013 Paris, France.

Individual Exhibitions:

1924 Galerie d'Audretsch, The Hague
1934 Galerie Pierre, Paris
1936 Museum of Living Art, New York
1939 Galerie Pierre, Paris
1947 Galerie Denise René, Paris
1948 Galerie Apollinaire, London
1949 Galerie Allendy, Paris
1950 Galerie Huinck en Scherjon, Amsterdam
1951 Galerie Allendy, Paris
1952 Galerie de Babylone, Paris
1953 Galerie Cahiers d'Art, Paris
1954 Museu de Arte Moderna, Rio de Janeiro (retrospective; travelled to the Museu de Arte Moderna, Sao Paulo)
1955 Stedelijk Museum, Amsterdam
1956 Galerie 93, Paris
1959 Galerie Simone Heller, Paris
1960 Gemeentemuseum, The Hague
1961 Chalette Gallery, New York
1962 Galerie Simone Heller, Paris
1964 Galerie d'Eendt, Amsterdam
Galerie Cahiers d'Art, Paris
1965 Institut Neerlandais, Paris
1967 Galerie Cahiers d'Art, Paris
1968 Galerie Klihm, Munich
1969 *Retrospective 1922–1969*, Galerie Verrière, Lyons
Galerie Simone Heller, Paris
1970 Maison de la Culture, St. Etienne, France (retrospective)
1971 Galerie de Seine, Paris
1972 *Werke 1922–1972*, Kunsthalle, Dusseldorf (retrospective)
Institut Goethe, Paris
1973 Galerie Weiler, Paris
Galerie Klihm, Munich
Collection d'Art, Amsterdam
Retrospective, Annely Juda Fine Art, London
1974 Maison de la Culture, Bourges, France
1978 Galerie Dobbelhoff, Antwerp
1979 Birla Museum, Calcutta
1980 Galerie de Seine, Paris
Schilderijen, Reliefs, Beelden, Grafiek, Typografie, Fotos, Gemeentemuseum, The Hague
1981 Galerie Carmen Martines, Grand Palais, Paris
Galerie Martini and Ronchetti, Geneva
1984 Modern Museum, Dordrecht, Netherlands
Modern Museum, Apeldoorn, Netherlands
Galerie Tanit, Munich
1985 Galerie Susanna Kulli, St. Gallen, Switzerland
1986 Galerie Spiess, Paris
1987 Musée d'Art Moderne de la Ville, Paris
Musée de Grenoble, France

Selected Group Exhibitions:

1931 *Fotomontage*, Staatliche Kunstbibliothek, Berlin
1932 *Exposition Internationale de la Photographie*, Palais des Beaux-Arts, Brussels (travelled to Lakenhal, Leiden)
1936 *Cubism and Abstract Art*, Museum of Modern Art, New York
1938 *Abstrakte Kunst*, Stedelijk Museum, Amsterdam
1954 *Contour Beeldende Kunst*, Museum Prinsenhof, Delft, Netherlands
1955 *Artistes Etrangers en France*, Petit Palais, Paris
1957 *Art Abstrait Premières Generations 1910–39*, Musée d'Art et d'Industrie, St. Etienne, France
1970 *Léger and Purist Paris*, Tate Gallery, London
1976 *Art 7, 76*, Kunstmuseum, Basle
1979 *Fotografie in Nederland 1920–40*, Gemeentemuseum, The Hague
1980 *Abstraction 1910–40*, Annely Juda Fine Art, London

Collections:

Staatsgalerie. Stuttgart: Bayerische Staatlichen Sammlungen, Munich; Stedelijk Museum, Amsterdam; Gemeentemuseum, The Hague; Centre Georges Pompidou, Paris; Museum of Modern Art, Jerusalem; Museu de Arte Moderna, Rio de Janeiro; Guggenheim Museum, New York; Philadelphia Museum of Art; Hirshhorn Museum, Washington, D.C.

Publications:

By DOMELA: articles—"Entretien avec César Domela," with Roger van Gindertael, in *Cimaise* (Paris), November/December 1970; "Quelques Apercus et Conceptions sur l'Art Moderne" in *Domela*, exhibition catalogue, Paris 1971; "Entretien avec César Domela," with Henry Galy-Carles, in *Les Lettres Francaises* (Paris), December 1971.

On DOMELA: books—*Domela* by Wassily Kandinsky, Paris 1943; *Presentation de l'Oeuvre de Domela* by Roger van Gindertael, Paris 1951; *Domela* by Marcel Brion, Paris 1961; *Domela* by Marcel Pobe, Hilversum, Netherlands 1965; *Domela* by Christian Zervos, Amsterdam 1965; *Functional Graphic Design in the 20's* by Eckhard Neumann, New York 1967; *Domela: Retrospective 1922-1969*, exhibition catalogue, with text by Marcel Brion and others, Lyons 1969; *Domela*, exhibition catalogue, Paris 1971; *César Domela: Werke 1922-1972*, exhibition catalogue, with foreword by Karl-Heinz Hering, text by Jean Laude, Dusseldorf 1972; *Cesar Domela: Retrospective*, exhibition catalogue, with introduction by Gerhard Weber, London 1979; *Domela: Catalogue Raisonnée de l'Oeuvre*, edited by Alain Clairet, Paris 1978; *Fotografie in Nederland 1920-1940*, exhibition catalogue, by Flip Bool and Kees Broos, The Hague 1979; *Domela: Schilderijen, Reliefs, Beelden, Grafiek, Typografie, Fotos*, exhibition catalogue, with text by Kees Broos, Flip Bool and and Mathilde Visser, The Hague 1980; *Domela* by H. C. L. Jaffe, Paris 1980; *Cesar Domela: Fotografie, Fotomontaggi, Disegni* by G. B. Martini and A. Ronchetti, Genoa 1981; *Domela: 65 Ans d'Abstraction*, exhibition catalogue, Grenoble 1987.

I, for my part, should like my reliefs to be structurally the exact and absolute expression of the inner reality which gives rise to them. The message I should like them to convey is one of the repose, and I should like to think of them as the concrete representation of a certitude of a knowledge that fills the soul and is the reflection of a strict order.

This strict order, without which the meditation behind a work of art is impossible, makes it necessary for me to have a method enabling me to put into a work the maximum of intensity. When I set out to work on a relief, I try to find my gravitational field, then the laws governing come into play, lines are given a direction, colors are brought in, a rhythmic pattern orders the dynamic units of the composition and takes command of the nascent work.

—César Domela

The full name of this Dutch-born artist is Domela Nieuwenhuis. He left Holland in 1919, for Switzer-

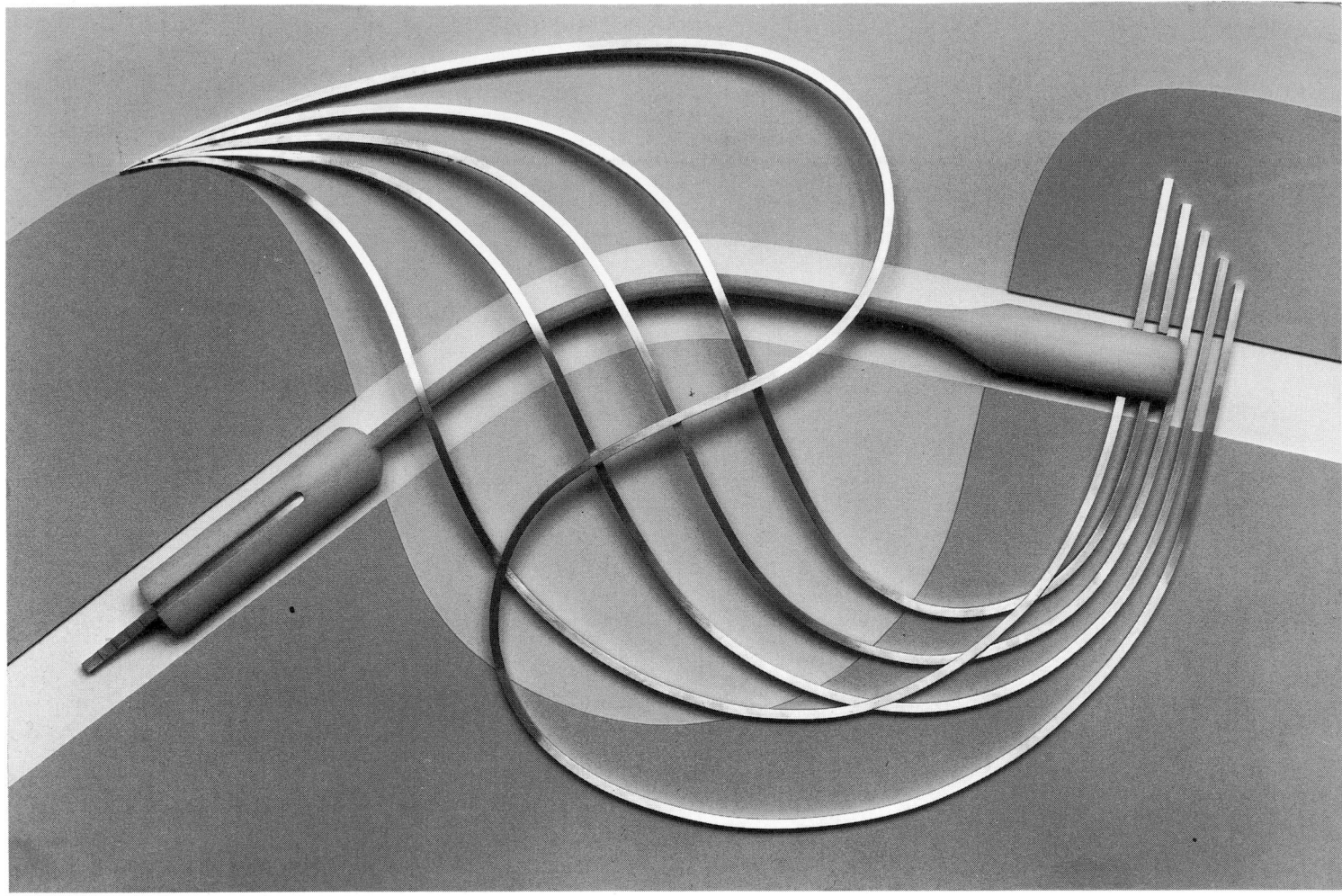

César Domela: *Clairet No.176*, **1964**

land, and in his early years was a landscape painter. In the 1920's he became interested in Russian Constructivist ideas and made his first attempts at abstraction. Contact with Mondrian and Van Doesburg in Paris brought him back to Dutch activities, leading to an exhibition in The Hague and membership of the de Stijl group in 1925. The close connections between de Stijl and the Bauhaus were reinforced by his long stay in Berlin, 1927 to 1933, during which he turned from flat painting to the construction of reliefs, searching for subtle forms. In Paris, where he worked after the rise of Hitler, he began experiments in multi-coloured reliefs, exploiting the contrasting effects of different materials.

Domela, whilst enormously influenced by Mondrian and Van Doesburg, can only be regarded as a peripheral member of de Stijl. His earlier work reveals considerable originality in applying to the rigid, balanced confrontation of simple geometrical shape and primary colours, a new sense of space and decoration. In particular he produced a three-dimensional basis, developing the basic elementarism into new forms of neo-plasticism, largely by the superimposed layers of different materials. This was clearly at variance with strict de Stijl principles, even though Domela's reliefs have much in common with the movement's functional designs and architecture. But in his case the moral and social basis of de Stijl is somewhat undermined by the tendency to picture-making for its own sake, rather than as philosophical or social statements. Domela, incidentally, was also a typographer of considerable achievements.

It is little wonder that in about 1930 Domela's association with de Stijl became tenuous and that in time he left the movement. His later reliefs are increasingly multi-coloured, bordering on the decorative, introducing curved linear elements into his compositions, which reveal the influence of Jean Arp. It must, however, be said that, as a survivor of the de Stijl generation, Domela, with Vordemberg-Gildewart and Herbin, has kept alive the great achievements of the Dutch group and their contribution, no matter how diluted, to the abstract movement. In fact it was only Mondrian who remained devoted to the ascetic, original principles of de Stijl. Domela's long, active career has recently been rewarded by renewed interest in his work, part of the re-investigation of the purposes and achievements of the great experimental movements early in the century, and their striving for a new relationship between art and society.

—Charles Spencer

DORAZIO, Piero.
Italian. Born in Rome, 29 June 1927. Studied architecture at the University of Rome, 1945; attended lectures by Lionello Venturi on Cézanne, Impressionism and Medieval Art, Rome, 1945–46; studied painting at the Ecole Supérieure, Paris, 1947–48. Married Virginia Dortch in 1953; has two daughters. Member, Gruppo Arte Sociale, and Co-Editor, with Carlo Accardi, Pietro Consagra, Giulio Turcato and others, *Manifesto del Formalismo: Forma I,* Rome, 1945–47; first abstract paintings, Rome, 1946; lived in Paris, 1947–48; Founder, with Guerini and Achille Perilli, Age d'Or, cooperative galleries, Rome and Florence, 1950; Founder, with Alberto Burri, Ettore Colla and others, Fondazione Origine, and edited the magazine *Arti Visive,* Rome, 1952; lived in the United States, 1953; first sculptures in wood, plexiglass and metal, 1955; founded experimental ceramic workshop, with

Perilli, 1956; settled in Todi, Umbria, 1974; worked on designs for sets and costumes for *Rideau Reversible,* ballet by Stravinsky/Petrassi, for the *Maggio Musicale Fiorentino,* Florence, 1980; received commission for 4 glass sculptures, 1981; Founder, with Perilli, Santomaso and Alfieri, *Retina* magazine, Rome, 1981. Participant, Summer International Seminar, Harvard University, Cambridge, Massachusetts, 1953; Lecturer, Positano Art Workshop, Italy, 1956; Organizing Director of the School of Fine Art, 1960, Lecturer, 1961, Chairman of the Department, 1961, and Professor, 1967, University of Pennsylvania, Philadelphia. Recipient: Prize, *Biennale,* Venice, 1960; Prize, *Biennale,* Paris, 1960; Kandinsky Prize, 1960; Premio Lissone, 1965; Medaglia d'Oro, *Mostra Internazionale Grafica Contemporanea,* Bologna, 1968; Medaglia d'Oro del Vive Commissario del Boverno, *Biennale,* Bolzano, 1969; Prix International, Cracow, Poland, 1970. Agent: Marlborough Galleria d'Arte, Rome. Address: Canonica, 06100 Todi, Italy.

Individual Exhibitions:

1953 Wittenborn One-Wall Gallery, New York
1954 Rose Fried Gallery, New York
1955 Galleria Apollinaire, Milan
 Galleria del Cavallino, Venice
1956 Galleria La Strozzina, Palazzo Strozzi, Florence
1957 Wittenborn One-Wall Gallery, New York
 Galleria La Tartaruga, Rome
1959 Galerie Springer, Berlin
 Wittenborn Gallery, New York
 Galerie Seide, Hannover
 Galerie Gells Nebelung, Dusseldorf
1960 *Biennale,* Venice
1961 Howard Wise Gallery, Cleveland
 Galerie Nächt St. Stephan, Vienna

Kunstverein, Dusseldorf
Galerie ad Libitum, Antwerp
1962 Galerie Fried, Ulm, West Germany
Galerie Muller, Stuttgart
Galleria Quadrante, Florence
Galleria dell'Ariete, Milan
Galerie Suzanne Bollag, Zurich
Galerie Rottloff, Karlsruhe, West Germany
1963 Galeria Bognici, Rio de Janeiro
Bienal, Sao Paulo (travelled to the Galerie Relevo, Rio de Janeiro)
1964 Galleria Il Segno, Rome
Marlborough Galleria d'Arte, Rome
Kleine Galerie, Schwenningen am Neckar, West Germany
1965 Marlborough-Gerson Gallery, New York
Museum of Art, Cleveland
Galleria dell'Ariete, Milan
Galleria Il Punto, Turin
1966 Marlborough Fine Art, London
Galerie im Erker, St. Gallen, Switzerland
Biennale, Venice
Galerie Heseler, Munich
Kunstverein, Stuttgart
Galleria Ferrari, Verona
Galerie Bonnier, Lausanne, Switzerland
1967 Galleria dell'Ariete, Milan
Kleine Galerie Schwenningen am Neckar, West Germany
Galleria Arte Oggi, Pescara, Italy
Galleria del Deposito, Genoa
Musée des Beaux-Arts, La Chaud de Fonds, Switzerland
Galleria Zen, Brescia, Italy
Gallery Mackler, Philadelphia
Svensk-Franska Konstgalleriet, Stockholm
1968 Galerie Suzanne Bollag, Zurich
Galleria del Deposito, Genoa
Galleria Lorenzelli, Bergamo, Italy
Galleria Barozzi, Venice
Galleria Fiori, Florence
Galerie Springer, Berlin
Westend Galerie, Frankfurt
Deutsch-Italienische Vereinigung, Frankfurt
1969 Bennington College, Vermont
Haus am Waldsee, Berlin
Marlborough-Gerson Gallery, New York
Palais des Beaux-Arts, Brussels
Galleria dell'Ariete, Milan
Galleria Boni + Schubert, Lugano, Switzerland
Galleria La Bussola, Bari, Italy
Kunststudio Westfalen-Blatt, Bielefeld, West Germany
Kunstverein, Freiburg, West Germany
Galleria Arte Studio, Macerata, Italy
1970 Muzej Savremene Unmentnosti, Belgrade
Bilder 1967–1970, Galerie Im Erker, St. Gallen, Switzerland
Galleria Martano, Turin
Grafico Romero, Rome
Galleria Alfieri, Venice
Gallerie Il Centro, Naples
Stadtische Kunstsammlung, Ludwigshafen, West Germany
Galleria Il Segnapassi, Pesaro, Italy
1971 Galerie d'Art Moderne, Basle
Galleria Quattro Venti, Palermo, Sicily
Studio La Citta, Galleria d'Ariete, Verona
Centro di Cultura Antonio Rosmini, Trento, Italy
Galleria Peccolo, Livorno, Italy
Galerie Suzanne Feigel, Basle
1972 Deutsch-Italienische Vereinigung, Frankfurt
Westend Galerie, Frankfurt
Marlborough Galleria d'Arte, Rome
Nuova Citta Galleria d'Arte, Brescia, Italy
Galleria Il Salotto, Genoa
1973 Marlborough Fine Art, London
Marlborough Galleria d'Art, Rome
Galleria Bodel, Rome
Galleria San Gallo, Florence
Studio 3b, Bolzano, Italy
Marlborough Godard Gallery, Toronto
Galerie Margret Biedermann, Munich
1974 Studio Marconi, Milan

Ariete Grafica, Milan
Gallery Patricia Moore, Aspen, Colorado
Galleria Marlborough, Rome
Studio E, Bolzano, Italy
1975 Palazzo del Popolo, Todi, Italy
Mantra Galleria d'Arte, Turin
Galleria del Milione, Milan
Galleria dell'Ariete, Milan
Galleria Beniamino, San Remo, Italy
1976 André Emmerich Gallery, New York
Parametro Galleria d'Arte, Rome
Galleria Bluart, Varese
Galleria d'Arte Il Solo, Bolzano, Italy
Galerie im Erker, St. Gallen, Switzerland
1977 Galleria La Piramide, Florence
Studio La Torre, Pistoia, Italy
André Emmerich Gallery, New York
Studio Effe, Aosta, Italy
Galerie Springer, Berlin
Galleria Lorenzelli, Bergamo, Italy
Galleria Wirz, Milan
Galerie Biedermann, Munich
Galleria Lorenzelli, Milan
Galleria Piero della Francesca, Arezzo, Italy
Galleria Sanluca, Bologna
Westend-Galerie, Frankfurt

Kunststudio, Westfalen-Blatt, Bielefeld, West Germany
Galleria Editalia, Rome
Galerie Kornfeld, Zurich
1979 Grafica Romero, Rome
Kunst Galerie 63, Klosters, Switzerland
André Emmerich Gallery, New York
Musée d'Art Moderne de la Ville, Paris
FIAC, Paris
Galliata Arte Contemporanea, Alassio, Italy
Galleria Paulo Guili, Lecco, Italy
Albright-Knox Art Gallery, Buffalo, New York
Galleria Il Sagittario, Perugia, Italy
1980 Sale Comunale d'Arte Contemporanea, Bra/Cuneo, Italy
Galleria L'Angolo, Arte Contemporanea, Bra/Cuneo, Italy
Galerie Margret Biedermann, Munich
Galleria Lorenzelli, Milan
Galleria Il Chiodo Arte Contemporanea, Mantua, Italy
Galleria Sagittario, Perugia, Italy
Galleria Planetario, Trieste
Dartmouth College Museum and Galleries, Hanover, New Hampshire
Museum of Art, Fort Lauderdale, Florida

Piero Dorazio: *Rara,* 1982

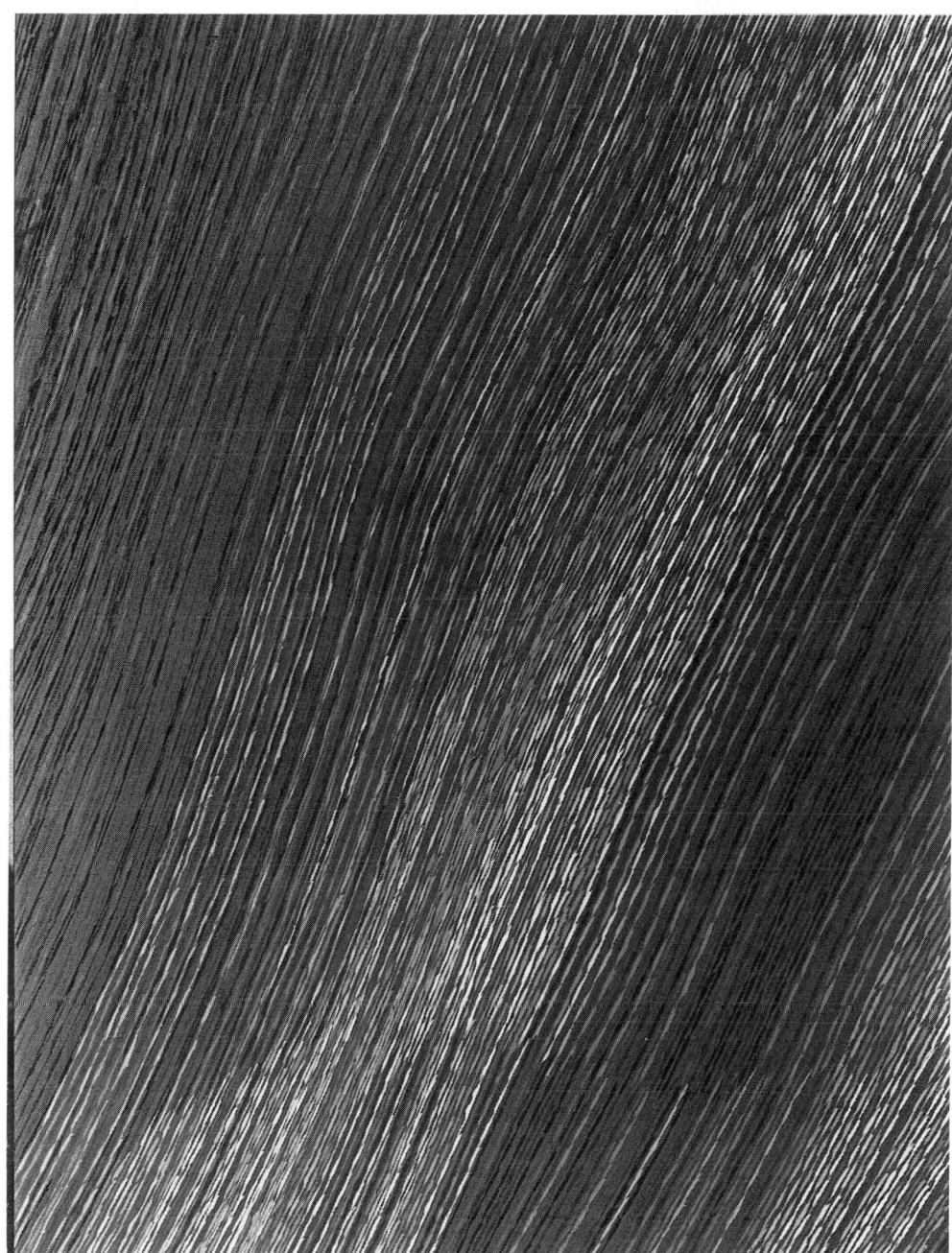

Chrysler Museum, Norfolk, Virginia
Dayton Art Institute, Ohio
Krannert Art Museum, University of Illinois, Urbana

1981 *Fiera Internazionale d'Arte Contemporanea*, Bari, Italy
Galleria L'Angelo, Bra, Italy
André Emmerich Gallery, New York
Galerie im Erker, St. Gallen, Switzerland
Myra Godard Gallery, Toronto
Museo Civico di Castelvecchio, Verona, Italy
Wilhelm-Hack-Museum, Ludwigshafen, West Germany
Bayersichen Staatsgemaldesammlungen, Munich
Museo Palasso Casali Cortona, Italy
Commune di Trissino, Vicenza, Italy
FIAC, Paris

1982 Studio d'Arte Contemporanea, Dabbeni, Lugano, Switzerland
Galerie von Braunbehrens, Munich
Lorenzelli Arte, Milan
Galleria Il Ponte, Rome
Galleria Duchamp, Cagliari, Italy
Galleria Plurima, Udine, Italy
Galleria La Citta, Verona
Galleria Il Sole, Bolzano, Italy
Galerie Edition E, Munich
Galleria La Torre, Postoia, Italy
Galleria Stamparte, Bologna
Galleria Expo Arte VII, Bari, Italy
Galleria L'Angelo, Bra, Italy
Galerie im Erker, St. Gallen, Switzerland

1983 Galerie Edith Wahlandt, Schwabisch Gmund, West Germany
Galerie Luise Krohn, Badenweiler, West Germany
Galleria Il Ponte, Vicenza, Italy
Westend Galerie, Frankfurt
Forum Kunst, Rottweil, West Germany
Galleria Vinciana, Milan

1984 Galleria Nazionale d'Arte Moderna, Rome

1986 Galleria d'Arte Moderna Internazionale, Florence

Selected Group Exhibitions:

1948 *Arte Astratta in Italia*, Galleria di Roma
1951 *Tic-Tac di Spazio*, Fondazione Origine, Rome
1952 *Biennale*, Venice
1955 *Arte e Technica*, Galleria Nazionale d'Arte Moderna, Rome
1959 *Documenta*, Kassel, West Germany
1965 *The Responsive Eye*, Museum of Modern Art, New York
1969 *Plus by Minus*, Albright-Knox Art Gallery, Buffalo, New York
1979 *Zero*, Kunsthaus, Zurich
1981 *Italian Art: Four Different Directions*, Fort Lauderdale Museum of Art, Florida
1983 *Registrazione di Frequenze*, Galleria d'Arte Moderna, Bologna
1988 Galerie Biedermann, Munich

Collections:

Galleria Nazionale d'Arte Moderna, Rome; Museo Civico, Turin; Peggy Guggenheim Collection, Venice; Stedelijk Museum, Amsterdam; Nationalgalerie, Berlin; Städtisches Museum, Leverkusen, West Germany; Kunstmuseum, Dusseldorf; Haus der Kunst, Munich; Kunstmuseum, Berne; Musée des Beaux-Arts, La Chaud de Fonds, Switzerland.

Publications:

By DORAZIO: book: *La Fantasia dell Arte nella Vita Moderna*, Rome 1954; illustrated books—*Croazia Segreta* by Giuseppe Ungaretti, Croation translation by Drago Ivanisevie, Rome 1969; *Cinque Poesie* by Vinicius de Moraes, Rome 1969; *La Luce* by Guiseppe Ungaretti, St. Gallen, Switzerland 1971; *Erke-Treffem I*, with others, St. Gallen, Switzerland 1972; *La Nave* by Rafael Alberti and Pablo Neruda, Milan 1973; *Erker-Treffen 2*, with others, St. Gallen, Switzerland 1974; *Unbewohnbar die Trauer* by Peter Huchel, St. Gallen, Switzerland 1976; *Poesie di Leopold*

Senghor, Rome 1977; *New Jersey* by Ruggero Orlando, Locarno, Switzerland 1979; *Jean Cassou: Vingt-deux Poèmes*, with others, St. Gallen, Switzerland 1979.

On DORAZIO: books—*Piero Dorazio: Bilder 1967-1970*, exhibition catalogue, St. Gallen, Switzerland 1970; *New Italian Art 1953-1971*, exhibition catalogue, Liverpool 1971; *Dorazio* by Guiseppe Ungaretti, St. Gallen, Switzerland 1975; *Dorazio*, Milan 1977; *Dorazio* by Eugene Ionesco, St. Gallen, Switzerland 1980; *Piero Dorazio: Opere su Carta* by Flaminio Gualdoni, Rome 1982; *Piero Dorazio*, exhibition catalogue with essay by Vanni Bramanti, Florence 1986.

*

Piero Dorazio is one of the most lively and energetic members of the post-war Italian art scene, the catalyst of many of its domestic and international manifestations.

In imagery and formal manner, although not at all in technique, there is a striking similarity between Dorazio's paintings in oils and his contemporary Rotella's decollage pictures based on torn posters. Both arrive at ragged, geographical elements, built up into powerful, energetic, rhythmic formulae which suggest the inspiration of landscape. At the same time the imprecise, rhythmic definitions of Italian futurism have also contributed non-static qualities to this imagery. Dorazio seems to wish to envelop the viewer in a chromatic and dynamic condition, both by the scale of his work and the almost mesmeric effect of strong colour and winding, climbing, web-like movement. This verticality in Dorazio's work provides a sense of drama, or of idealism, reminiscent of growth in nature, especially of greatly slowed-down photographic records on plant-life. The works concerned with horizontality are equally suggestive of nature, landscape depicted with a serialization that almost suggests the record, in one limited space, of a long, evolving journey. One must also take into account the fact that Dorazio was trained as an architect, that he played a major role in the revival of Futurist and Abstract traditions, and that he has lived and worked in the United States. Various possible influences have emerged from formal, Mondrianesque cubist colour balance: the flow of form and colour, at times resembling stained-glass windows. Dorazio is a master technician with the intellectual power to analyze and, even more important, to retain highly complex, living, growing compositions throughout lengthy, detailed, painstaking periods of work.

Perhaps, in the end, Dorazio is almost too rational. This kind of aesthetic balance—compounded of instinctive elegance and the gift for perfect design—is one of the pitfalls that Italian artists have to face. His work reflects the warmth and liveliness of his personality, a spontaneous delight in light and movement, a clear, positive optimism. There is less evidence of the intense personal experience of a Morandi or a Fontana, of the sense of the inexplicable mystery of life that infuses the best of de Chirico.

—Charles Spencer

DRYSDALE, (George) Russell.
Australian. Born in Bognor Regis, Sussex, England, 7 February 1912; settled, with family, in Queensland, Australia, 1923. Educated at the Grange School, Sussex, and Geelong Grammar School, Victoria; education interrupted by serious eye trouble, 1929, culminating in loss of one eye, 1935; trained in the sugar industry in North Queensland, 1930; visited England, 1931; met George Bell, Head of the School of Modern Painting, Melbourne, 1932, and after further two years on the land decided to study painting seriously: studied at the School of Modern Painting, under Bell and Arnold Shore, 1935-38, at the Grosvenor School of Art, London, 1938, and at La Grande Chaumiere, Paris, 1939. Married Elizabeth Stephen in 1935 (died, 1963); children: Lynne and

Timothy; married Maisie Joyce Purves-Smith in 1965. Met Peter Purves-Smith and other artists, Melbourne, 1938; moved to London with Purves-Smith, 1938, and shared studio with him in Paris, 1939; returned to Melbourne and worked with George Bell, 1939; settled in Sydney, 1940, and worked there until his death, 1981; visited London, 1950, 1957; accompanied zoological expedition to Kimberley and Central Desert of Western Australia, 1958. Australian Delegate, Congress of International Association of Plastic Arts, Dubrovnik, 1957; Member, Commonwealth Art Advisory Board, 1962-73; Trustee, Art Gallery of New South Wales, Sydney, from 1963. Director, Pioneer Sugar Mills Ltd. Recipient: Wynne Prize for Landscape, Sydney, 1947; Melrose Prize for Figure Composition, Adelaide, 1949; *Encyclopaedia Britannica* Australian Award, 1965. Knighted, 1969; Companion, Order of Australia, 1980. *Died* (in Hardy's Bay, New South Wales) *28 June 1981*.

Individual Exhibitions

1938 Riddells Galleries, Melbourne
1942 Macquarie Galleries, Sydney
1943 Macquarie Galleries, Sydney
1945 Macquarie Galleries, Sydney
1949 Macquarie Galleries, Sydney
1950 Leicester Galleries, London
      Macquarie Galleries, Sydney
1953 Macquarie Galleries, Sydney
1958 Leicester Galleries, London
1960 Art Gallery of New South Wales, Sydney (retrospective)
1961 Queensland Art Gallery, Brisbane (retrospective)
1964 John Martin Gallery, Adelaide
1965 Leicester Galleries, London
1967 Johnstone Gallery, Brisbane
1972 Leicester Galleries, London
1973 Joseph Brown Gallery, Melbourne
1975 Sale Regional Arts Centre, Victoria
1980 Art Gallery of New South Wales, Sydney (travelled to the Brisbane Civic Art Gallery, and the Art Gallery of South Australia, Adelaide)
1981 Joseph Brown Gallery, Melbourne

Selected Group Exhibitions:

1946 *Exposition Nationale d'Arte Moderne*, Musée National d'Art Moderne, Paris
1948 *Contemporary Australian Art*, City Art Gallery, Auckland
1950 *110 Years of Australian Art*, Blaxland Galleries, Sydney
1953 *A Retrospective Exhibition of Australian Painting*, Art Gallery of New South Wales, Sydney
     12 Australian Artists, New Burlington Gallery, London (toured the U.K.)
1954 *Biennale*, Venice
1956 *Contemporary Australian Painting*, Art Gallery of New South Wales, Sydney (toured Australia, New Zealand and the United States)
1957 *Contemporary Painting*, City Art Gallery, Auckland
1960 *Contemporary Australian Art*, City Art Gallery, Auckland

Collections:

National Gallery of Australia, Canberra; National Gallery of South Australia, Adelaide; Queensland Art Gallery, Brisbane; National Gallery of Victoria, Melbourne; Art Gallery of New South Wales, Sydney; Aberdeen Art Gallery, Scotland; National Gallery, London; Tate Gallery, London; Metropolitan Museum of Art, New York; Museum of Modern Art, New York.

Publications:

By DRYSDALE: books—*Impressions of a Painter in Europe Today*, Sydney 1959; *Journey among Men*, with Jack Marshall, London 1962; articles—"Art and the People" in *Soci-*

ety of Artists Book, Sydney 1942; "Notes on Peter Purves-Smith, William Dobell, Donald Friend and Elaine Haxton" in Australian Present Day Art, Sydney 1943; "What Is Modern Art" in the Daily Telegraph (Sydney), 27 January 1953; "Capricornia" in Russell Drysdale, exhibition catalogue, London 1958; introduction to Form: Colour: Grandeur by Allen David, Melbourne 1962; "Journey to Gallery Hill" in Art and Australia (Sydney), May 1963; "Colonial Letters" in Duets for Dulcimer and Dance, edited by Paul Haefliger, Sydney 1979.

On DRYSDALE: books—The Paintings of Russell Drysdale by Joseph Burke, Sydney 1951; Russell Drysdale: A Retrospective, exhibition catalogue, with an introduction by Paul Haefliger, Sydney 1960; Australian Painting 1788–1970 by Bernard Smite, Melbourne 1962; Australian Painters: 40 Profiles by John Hetherington, Melbourne 1963; Russell Drysdale, by Geoffrey Dutton, London 1964; Exhibition of Paintings and Drawings by Russell Drysdale, exhibition catalogue, with a preface by Alan Ross, London 1965; Masterpieces of Drysdale by Charles Osborne, London 1975; Russell Drysdale, exhibition catalogue, with a foreword by Lou Klepac, Sydney 1980; Russell Drysdale, exhibition catalogue with texts by Patrick McCaughey and Joseph Brown, Melbourne 1981.

*

Russell Drysdale arrived in Australia from England at the age of eleven. He spent most of his youth in country areas preparing for a career as a sheep-farmer prior to beginning art studies at George Bell's influential private school in Melbourne in the latter half of the 1930's. An impressionable child newly arrived from the other side of the globe, Drysdale made firsthand contact with country folk and the Australian bush, which provided him with a continuing source of inspiration for much of the subject matter of his best-known and most highly acclaimed work as a professional artist.

His student work under the guidance and inspiration of George Bell was typically European in flavour, reflecting his tutor's preoccupations with ideas related to classical composition combined with romantic expressionism. Nude studies dating from 1938 are reminiscent of the French Fauves and German Expressionists.

"Moody's Pub," painted in 1941, marked the beginning of a new vision of the Australian landscape and man's relationship to it. It was a clumsily painted work emphasising truth to spirit rather than appearances. The figures of the local Australians were distorted for expressive purposes. Dramatic elongation conveyed a "lean and hungry" look, a characteristic of Drysdale's handling of his bush people in numerous paintings to follow. By 1943 a variety of inconsistencies which had tended to mar Drysdale's paintings had been removed and his "Albury Station" was a notable achievement with its melancholy mood and emphasis on the essential isolation of the human condition. The eerie mood of "Albury Station" was, undoubtedly, partly the result of war-time mentality. A stage-like setting with exaggerated perspective related convincingly to the lonely, distorted figures placed in the foreground.

During the 1940's, Drysdale absorbed influences from several sources, including Graham Sutherland and Henry Moore, especially in his handling of organic forms and in the fluid graphic approach of his drawings of soldiers. Elements of European Surrealism manifested themselves in paintings such as "Bush Fire" (1944) and "Deserted Out-Station" (1945) with their unexpected juxtapositions of devastated pieces of human dwellings eroded by time and natural calamities. "The Rabbiters," painted in 1947, was Drysdale's first real analysis of the organic forms of outback rocks and decaying tree trunks. Once again the figures were overwhelmed by the vastness of their environment. A strong feeling for the inherent sculptural qualities of the natural phenomena made the figures appear fleeting, while the landscape forms remained fixed, even eternal.

Drysdale drew and painted the Australian Aboriginal many times. His fascination with the original inhabitants of "the timeless land" probably stemmed from a respect for the Aboriginal's harmony with his natural environment which mostly alienated the white

man. While Drysdale was obviously sympathetic to the Aboriginal, he remained culturally and intellectually removed, invariably leaving their faces bland and devoid of meaningful expression. In "Station Blacks, Cape York" (1953) he grouped his subjects in the manner of a self-conscious staged photograph. More successful were the paintings from the late 1950's and early 1960's inspired by the Puckamanni Aboriginals. Despite the recurrence of frontal, staged posing of figures, there was less superficial theatricality because of the merging of the Aboriginal subjects with their surroundings, mostly tribal totems, which brilliantly echoed the human forms.

Drysdale's drawings invariably display a raw, nervous energy— skeletal simplicity and purity of line. His paintings are quite different. He was always a slow, indirect painter who laboured hard and long over the application of oil paint in the manner of the old masters. Drysdale's approach to painting was the antithesis of that of Sidney Nolan. The reason that two painters with such widely divergent approaches to their craft should have met with enormous approval in London during the post-war period is probably simple. Most English critics felt that both Drysdale and Nolan had a legitimate subject in their choice of the great Australian wilderness and its lonely occupants. Life in the far-flung colonial outpost could hardly have been depicted otherwise 30 years ago.

—Arthur McIntyre

DUBUFFET, Jean.

French. Born in Le Havre, 31 July 1901. Educated in Le Havre, 1908–18; studied at the Académie Julian, Paris, 1918. Married Paulette Bret in 1927 (divorced, 1936); daughter: Isalmina; married Emilie Carlu in 1937. Served in the Compagnie Météorologique, L'Armée de l'Air, Paris and Fort St. Cyr, Paris and Rochefort, France, 1939–40. Painter: associated with Valadon, Dufy, Jacob, Cingria and Léger, Paris 1918; stopped painting, 1924–32: worked as central heating designer, Buenos Aires, 1924–25; returned to Le Havre, and worked in family wine business, 1925; founded own wine business, Bercy, France, 1930; again concentrated on painting, Paris 1933–37; returned to wine business, Bercy, 1937–39, 1940–42; began painting again, Paris, 1942: first significant exhibition, Paris, 1944; travelled in El Golea, Hoggar, Beni-Abbes and Timinoun, Algeria, 1947–49; founded Société dè l'Art Brut, Paris, in Vence, France, 1955–61; produced first experimental music works, with Asger Jorn, Paris, 1960; lived alternately, in Paris and Vence, 1961–62; built home and lived occasionally in Touquet, France, 1962–69; produced first architectural environments, Paris, 1967; began work on studio complex, Perigny, 1969; designed first theatre sets, Perigny, 1971. Agents: Pace Gallery, 32 East 57th Street, New York, New York 10022, U.S.A.; Galerie Beyeler, Baumleingasse 9, 4001 Basle, Switzerland. Estate: Fondation Jean Dubuffet, 137 Rue de Sèvres, 75006 Paris, France. Died (in Paris) 12 May 1985.

Individual Exhibitions:

1944	Galerie René Drouin, Paris
1946	Galerie René Drouin, Paris
1947	Galerie René Drouin, Paris
	Pierre Matisse Gallery, New York
	Galerie André, Paris
1948	Pierre Matisse Gallery, New York
1949	Pierre Matisse Gallery, New York
	Galerie Geert van Bruaene, Brussels
1950	Galerie Nina Dausset, Paris
	Pierre Matisse Gallery, New York
1951	Galerie Rive Gauche, Paris
	Arts Club of Chicago
1952	Pierre Matisse Gallery, New York

1953	Libraire La Hune, Paris
1954	Cercle Volnay, Paris (retrospective)
1955	Institute of Contemporary Arts, London
1957	Städtische Museum, Leverkusen, West Germany (retrospective)
1958	Arthur Tooth and Sons, London (retrospective)
1959	Galerie Daniel Cordier, Paris
	Pierre Matisse Gallery, New York
1960	Arthur Tooth and Sons, London
	Kunsthaus, Zurich
	Galleria Blu, Milan
	Van Abbemuseum, Eindhoven, Netherlands
	Stedelijk Museum, Amsterdam
	Kestner Gesellschaft, Hannover
1961	Galerie Daniel Cordier, Frankfurt
	Galleria del Naviglio, Milan
	Musée des Arts Décoratifs, Paris (retrospective)
	Silkeborg Museum, Denmark
1962	Museum of Modern Art, New York (retrospective; toured the United States)
	Galerie Daniel Cordier, Paris
1964	Palazzo Grassi, Venice
	Stedelijk Museum, Amsterdam
	Museum of Art, Philadelphia
	Galerie Claude Bernard, Paris
1965	Instituto Torcuato di Tella, Buenos Aires
1966	Dallas Museum of Fine Arts (retrospective)
	Institute of Contemporary Arts, London
	Robert Fraser Gallery, London
	Tate Gallery, London (retrospective)
	Stedelijk Museum, Amsterdam (retrospective)
	Guggenheim Museum, New York (retrospective)
1967	Galerie Jeanne Bucher, Paris
	Stedelijk Museum, Amsterdam
	Musée des Arts Décoratifs, Paris
1968	Galerie Beyeler, Basle
	Pace Gallery, New York
	Museum of Modern Art, New York
1969	Musée des Beaux-Arts, Montreal (retrospective)
	Feigen Gallery, New York
1970	Centre National d'Art Contemporain, Paris
	Kunstmuseum, Basle
	Svensk-Franska Konsgalleriet, Stockholm
	Kunstmuseum, Basle
	Art Institute of Chicago
1971	Galerie Jeanne Bucher, Paris
1972	Musée d'Art Moderne de la Ville, Paris
	Waddington Galleries, London
	Museum of Modern Art, New York
1973	Pace Gallery, New York
	Guggenheim Museum, New York (retrospective)
	Grand Palais, Paris
	Walker Art Center, Minneapolis
1974	Delaware Art Museum, Wilmington
	Städtische Kunsthalle, Dusseldorf
	Museum Kröller-Müller, Otterlo, Netherlands
	Galerie Kriwin, Brussels
	Galeria Ynguanzo, Madrid
	Galerie Schreiber, Basle
1975	Passages Castillans, Sites Tri-colors, Centre National d'Art Contemporain, Paris
	Galerie Beyeler, Basle
	Pace Gallery, New York
	Waddington Galleries, London
1976	Fundación Juan March, Madrid
	William Pall Gallery, New York
	Musée des Arts Décoratifs, Paris
	Galerie Claudine Planque, Lausanne, Switzerland
	B. C. Holland, Chicago
	Pace Gallery, Columbus, Ohio
	Galerie Beyeler, Basle
1977	Hokin Gallery, Palm Beach, Florida
	Musée des Beaux-Arts André Malraux, Le Havre, France (retrospective)
	Bibliothèque Municipale, Le Havre, France
	Bundner Kunstmuseum, Chur, Switzerland
	Badischer Kunstverein, Karlsruhe, West Germany
	Makler Gallery, Philadelphia
	Théatres de Mémoire: Recent Work 1974–76, Pace Gallery, New York
	Albert White Gallery, Toronto
	Théatres de Mémoire: Assemblages 1976–1977, Galerie Rudolf Zwirner, Cologne
	Galerie Daniel Gervis, Paris

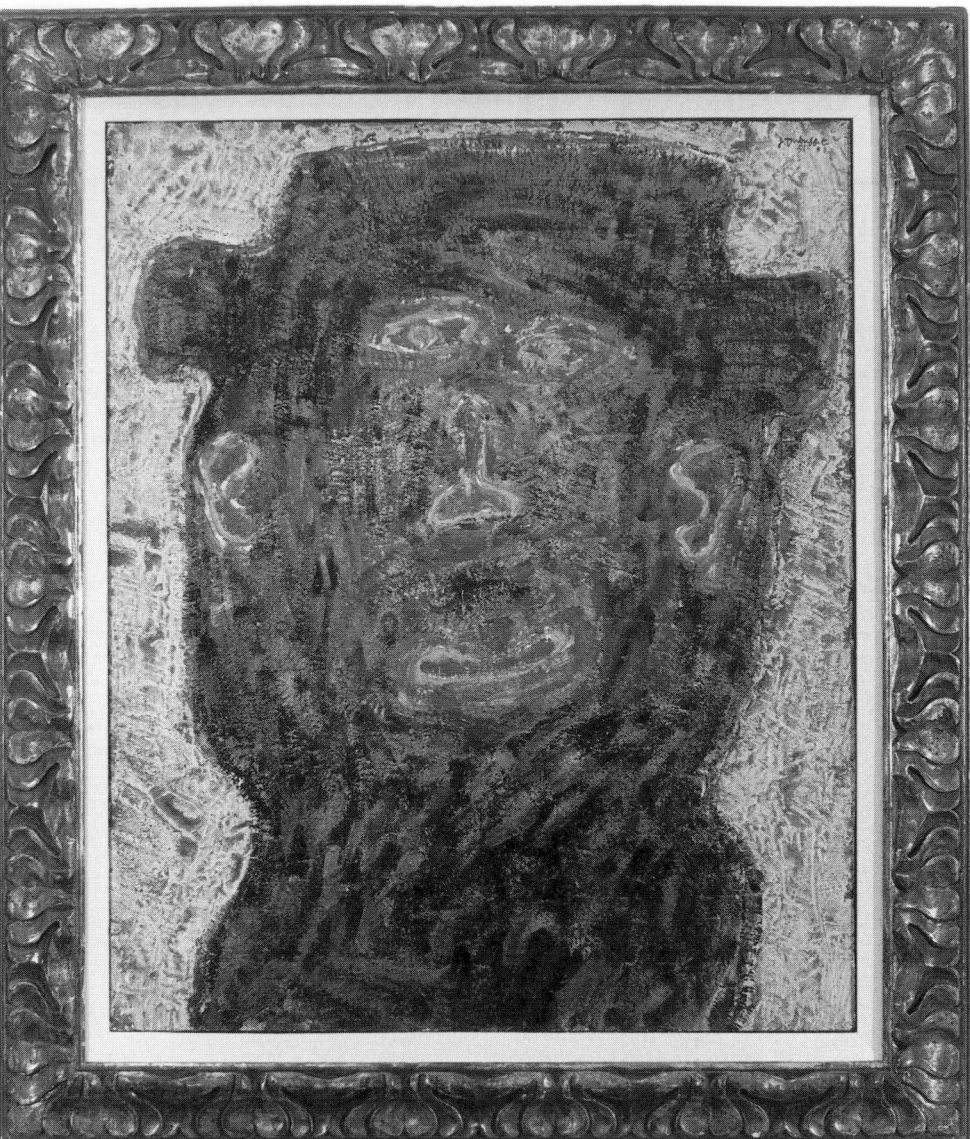

Jean Dubuffet: *La Verrue Sous le Nez,* 1951 Courtesy Museum of Contemporary Art, Chicago

Selected Group Exhibitions:

Collections:

Stedelijk Museum, Amsterdam, Museum Kröller-Müller, Otterlo, Netherlands; Kunstmuseum, Basle; Kunstmuseum, Dusseldorf; Musée des Arts Décoratifs, Paris; Centre Georges Pompidou, Paris; Museum of Modern Art, New York; Guggenheim Museum, New York; Albright-Knox Art Gallery, Buffalo, New York; Art Institute of Chicago.

Publications:

On DUBUFFET: books—*Prospectus aux Amateurs de Tout Genre,* Paris 1946; illustrations for *La Metromanie* by Jean Paulhan, Paris 1950; *Jean Dubuffet, Prospectus et Tous Ecrits Suivants,* edited by Gallimard, Paris 1967; *Asphyxiante Culture,* Paris 1968; *Jean Dubuffet, l'Homme du Commun à l'Ouvrage,* Paris 1973; musical recordings—*Experiences Musicales,* 6 discs, with Asger Jorn, Venice 1960; *La Fieur de Barbe,* Rome 1965; *Compositions Musicales,* New York 1973.

On DUBUFFET: books—*Tableau bon levain à vous de cuir la pate* by Georges Limbour, Paris 1953; *Jean Dubuffet: Brave Introduction à son oeuvre* by James Fitzsimmons, Brussels 1958; *Les Assemblages de Jean Dubuffet* by Pierre Volboudt, Paris 1958; *Les Dessins de Jean Dubuffet* by Daniel Cordier, Paris 1960; *Jean Dubuffet* by Lorenza Trucchi, Rome 1965; *Dubuffet et le Voyage au Centre de la Perception* by Max Loreau, Paris 1966; *Jean Dubuffet, Délits Déportements, Lieux de Haut Jeu* by Max Loreau, Geneva 1971; *Jean Dubuffet,* exhibition catalogue, by Gaeton Picon, London 1972; *Jean Dubuffet aux Sources de la Figuration Humaine* by Francois Gagnon, Montreal 1972; *Jean Dubuffet: A Retrospective,* exhibition catalogue, by M. Rowell and T. M. Messer, New York 1973; *Cahier de l'Herne cousaire à Dubuffet* by Jacques Berne, Paris 1973; *Le Travail de Jean Dubuffet* by Gaeton Picon, Geneva 1973; *Jean Dubuffet: Strategies de la Création* by Max Loreau, Paris 1973; *Jean Dubuffet* by Andreas Franzke, Basle 1975; *Jean Dubuffet: Passages Castillans, Sites Tricolors,* exhibition catalogue, with an introduction by K. G. Pontus Hulten, Paris 1975; *Jean Dubuffet, Object et Projet, le Cycle de l'Hourloupe* by Renato Barilli, Turin and Paris 1977; *FIAT Presenta Jean Dubuffet,* exhibition catalogue, edited by Ezio Gribaudo, Turin 1978; *Dubuffet Zeichnungen* by Andres Franzke, Munich 1980; *Jean Dubuffet,* exhibition catalogue, with texts by Karl Ruhrberg and Christoph Brockhaus, Cologne 1980; *Dubuffet Retrospektive,* exhibition catalogue, with text by Jorn Merkert, West Berlin 1980; *Brefs Exercices d'Ecole Journalière,* exhibition catalogue, with text by Peter Schjeldahl, New York 1980; *Dubuffet* by Andreas Franzke, Munich 1980, New York 1981; *Jean Dubuffet: Sites aux Figurines et Psycho-Sites,* exhibition catalogue, with text by Dominique Bozo and Daniel Abadie, Paris 1981; *Jean Dubuffet: Lavori Recenti,* exhibition catalogue with text by Renato Barilli, Milan 1982; *Jean Dubuffet,* exhibition catalogue with text by Andreas Franzke, West Berlin 1987.

A series of catalogues of Dubuffet's work from 1942 (32 volumes by 1982) is published by Editions de Minuit, Paris.

In his *Masters of Modern Art* (1954) A. H. Barr, Jr. wrote: "Possibly the most original painter to have emerged in Paris since the war is not abstract in his art. A man of exceptional intelligence and maturity, Jean Dubuffet combines a childlike style with bold innovations in surface handling and a grotesque sense of humour." In the exhibition with which he shocked the art world of Paris in 1946 Dubuffet took over and developed the technique of "haut pâte" which had already been used by Fritz Winter, Baumeister and more recently by Fautrier. An unusually thick mélange made up of plaster and putty, asphalt, concrete and glue, in which were embedded pebbles, sherds and rubbish of all kinds, was worked with a palette knife in order to bring out the expressive value of the material. Into this magma were scratched and scribbled graphic signs reminiscent of the childlike figures of Paul Klee and the graffiti on old and crumbling walls. Of these works Werner Haftmann wrote as follows: "The paintings disclosed a remarkable combination of magical tricks and disarming naiveté. The surface had been treated with a plastic mixture of glue, sand, and asphalt. The *'haute pâte'* was obviously taken from Fautrier, but Dubuffet used it for other purposes. It gave his surfaces a highly unusual character. With their modelled forms, their haphazard scratches and blemishes, their spots of colour seemingly applied without aim or purpose, they gave the impression of those aged weather-beaten walls into whose cracks and discolorations our fancy likes to read images. Here it is the *material* of the surface that releases images. Under its spell the painter began to scribble on the wall. Heads, masks, figurines, droll landscapes with droll inhabitants emerged from the mould and mud, little scribbled men roamed over the wall, or picture ground, transforming it into a smiling land of childhood."

In these works Dubuffet was the precursor of a widely disseminated movement to abandon the traditional materials of fine art and in their place to work with worthless materials, rubbish and waste, exploiting these for their expressive impact. The movement had its echoes in the "arte povera" of Italy, the "junk art" of America, the work of Antoni Tápies in Spain, the Greek Vlassis Caniaris, the Italian Alberto Burri, and similar movements in Japan to make artistic use of discarded war material. In the 1950's in his "Sols et Terrains" and his "Terres Radieuses" series Dubuffet gave a more concrete significance to his "hautes pâtes," modelling his thick impasto to suggest the vestiges of telluric happenings and geological structures with the signs of fossils and the imprint of organic weathering, etc. During the 1950's he also exhibited small figures composed from discarded newspaper, foil, clinker and other waste materials and produced "assemblages" in the manner of Kurt Schwitters composed from pieces cut from painted canvases, bits of tin foil, old paper, dried flowers, leaves, butterfly wings, etc.

Under the name of "art brut" Dubuffet also continued his enthusiasm for the productions of children, the mentally handicapped and the insane, collecting and studying these and modelling his own work more closely upon them. In this regard his production had close affinities with the "anti-art" movements stemming from Dada.

Critics were and have remained divided as to the value of Dubuffet's contribution. He has created no masterpieces but he has been exceptionally fertile of ideas which have had important reverberations over more than two decades. His main themes have been the expressive potentialities of discarded materials stamped with the impress of "experience" and the use of the "faux naif" as a cloak for intelligence and skill. G. H. Hamilton has summed him up as follows: "Dubuffet made all aspects of our environment, without exception, available to the artist. By denying any possibility of distinguishing between beautiful and ugly objects he, as much as anyone else, created the aesthetic conditions for the "junk culture" and "Pop art" of the 1960's."

—Harold Osborne

DUCHAMP, (Henri-Robert) Marcel.

French. Born in Blainville, Normandy, 28 July 1887; brother of the artists Jacques Villon, Raymond Duchamp Villon, and Suzanne Duchamp. Studied at the Ecole Bossuet, Rouen, 1898-1904; Academie Julian, Paris, 1904-05. Served in the French National Infantry, 1905-06. Married Lydie Sarazine-Levassor in 1927 (divorced, 1928); married Alexina (Teeny) Sattler in 1954; children (Sattler-Matisse children): Paul, Jacqueline, and Peter. Painter from 1902; worked for a printer and engraver, Rouen, 1905; drew cartoons for *Le Courrier Francais* and *Le Rire*, Paris, 1905-10; moved to Paris, 1906; lived in Neuilly-sur-Seine, 1908-13; associated with an artists group in Puteau, France, including his brothers and Gleizes, Fresnaye, Metzinger, Léger, Ribemont-Dessaignes, Apollinaire and Picabia, 1910; painted "Nude Descending a Staircase," and made first drawings for "Bride Stripped Bare by her Bachelors," 1912; worked as a Librarian, Bibliothèque Saint-Geneviève, Paris, 1913; lived in New York, 1915-27; worked as a Librarian at the French Institute, New York, 1915; Founder Member, Society of Independent Artists, New York, 1916-17; Founder, with Roche, Arensberg and Beatrice Wood, *The Blind Man* and *Rong-Wrong* reviews, New York, 1917; Captain's Secretary, French Mission for the War, New York, 1917-18; associated with the surrealists Aragon, Breton, Eluard, Ribemont-Dessaignes, Rigaut, Soupault, and Tzara, Paris, 1919; occasionally used pseudonym "Rrose Selavy," from 1920; Founder Member, with Man Ray and Katherine Dreier, Société Anonyme, New York, 1920-39; returned to New York, and associated with exiled surrealists Breton, Ernst, Lam, Masson, Matta and Tanguy, 1942; Editorial Adviser, with Breton and Ernst, David Hare's *VVV* magazine, New York, 1942; completed first sketches for last major work, "Etant Donnes," New York, 1944; Guest Director, Florine Stettheimer exhibition, Museum of Modern Art, New York, 1946; assisted André Breton with surrealist exhibitions in Paris and New York, 1946-60. Also, Chess Champion for Haute Normandie, 1924; Winner, Paris Chess Tournament, 1932; Member and Delegate, Committee of the French Chess Federation, 1931-37; French Team Captain, First International Chess by Correspondence Olympiad, 1935. Member, National Institute of Arts and Letters, 1960. Honorary doctorate: Wayne State University, Detroit, 1961. Agent: Xavier Fourcade Inc., 36 East 75th Street, New York, New York 10021, U.S.A. *Died* (in Neuilly-sur-Seine) *2 October 1968.*

Individual Exhibitions

1937   Arts Club of Chicago
1942   Art of This Century, New York (with Joseph Cornell and Lawrence Vail)
1945   Yale University, New Haven, Connecticut (with Jacques Villon and Suzanne Duchamp)
1948   Julien Levy Gallery, New York (with Joseph Cornell and Yves Tanguy)
1952   Rose Fried Gallery, New York (with Jacques and Raymond Villon and Suzanne Duchamp)
1953   Rose Fried Gallery, New York (with Francis Picabia)
1957   Guggenheim Museum, New York (with Jacques and Raymond Villon)
1959   *Sur Marcel Duchamp*, Sidney Janis Gallery, New York
       Institute of Contemporary Arts, London
       Galerie La Hune, Paris
1960   *Dokumentation über Marcel Duchamp*, Kunstgewerbemuseum, Zurich
1963   Galerie Buren, Stockholm
       Alan Gallery, New York (with Francis Picabia and Kurt Schwitters)
       By or of Marcel Duchamp or Rrose Selavy, Pasadena Art Museum, California
1964   *Omaggio a Marcel Duchamp*, Galleria Schwarz, Milan (toured Europe)
1965   *Not Seen and/or Less Seen of/by Marcel Duchamp/ Rrose Selavy*, Cordier and Ekstrom Gallery, New York
       Kestner Gesellschaft, Hannover
       Stedelijk van Abbemuseum, Eindhoven, Netherlands (travelled to the Gemeentemuseum, The Hague)
1966   *The Almost Complete Works of Marcel Duchamp*, Tate Gallery, London
       The Bride Stripped Bare by Her Bachelors, Even Again, University of Newcastle upon Tyne, England
1967   Musée des Beaux-Arts, Rouen (with Jacques and Raymond Villon and Suzanne Duchamp)
       Musée National d'Arte Moderne, Paris (with Raymond Villon)
       Galerie Givaudon, Paris
1969   Galerie Spala, Prague
1971   *Marcel Duchamp: Grafica e Ready-Made*, Galleria Schwarz, Milan
       Palazzo dei Diamanti, Ferrara, Italy
1972   Galleria Il Fauno, Turin
       M. Knoedler and Company, New York
       Drawings, Etchings for the Large Glass, Readymades, Israel Museum, Jerusalem
       Marcel Duchamp: 66 Creative Years, Galleria Schwarz, Milan
1973   Palazzo Reale, Naples
       Philadelphia Museum of Art (travelled to the Museum of Modern Art, New York, and the Art Institute of Chicago)
       Galerie im Lenbachhaus, Munich (with Man Ray and Francis Picabia)
1974   Galerie Charles Kriwin, Brussels
1975   Galerie Marin, Turin
       Framart Studio, Naples
1977   Centre Georges Pompidou, Paris
       Holly Solomon Gallery, New York
1978   National Gallery of Canada, Ottawa
       Readymades, Vancouver Art Gallery
       Moderna Galerija, Sarajevo, Yugoslavia
1982   Central Museum and Art Gallery, Dudley, Worcestershire (toured the U.K.)
1984   Museum der Stadt, Cologne
       Museo de Arte, Barcelona
       Tokyo Gallery, Tokyo
1985   Galerie Bonnier, Geneva
1987   Luhring Augustine and Hodes Gallery, New York
       Kunstmuseum, Winterthur, Switzerland

Selected Group Exhibitions:

1913   *International Exhibition of Modern Art* ("Armory Show"), 69th Regiment Armory, New York (travelled to the Art Institute of Chicago and Copley Hall, Boston)
1926   *International Exhibition*, Brooklyn Museum, New York
1936   *Fantastic Art, Dada, Surrealism*, Museum of Modern Art, New York
1938   *Exposition Internationale du Surrealisme*, Galerie des Beaux-Arts, Paris
1943   *Art in Progress*, Museum of Modern Art, New York
1959   *Exposition Internationale de Surrealisme*, Galerie Daniel Cordier, Paris
1961   *Art in Motion*, Stedelijk Museum, Amsterdam (travelled to the Moderna Museet, Stockholm)
       Art of Assemblage, Museum of Modern Art, New York
1966   *Dada Ausstellung*, Kunsthaus, Zurich (travelled to the Musée d'Art Moderne, Paris)
1968   *Dada, Surrealism and Their Heritage*, Museum of Modern Art, New York

Collections:

Centre Georges Pompidou, Paris; Musée de Rouen; Guggenheim Collection, Venice; Museum of Modern Art, New York; Guggenheim Museum, New York; Yale University, New Haven, Connecticut; Annenberg Collection, Philadelphia Museum of Art; Art Institute of Chicago; National Gallery of Canada, Ottawa; Australian National Gallery, Canberra.

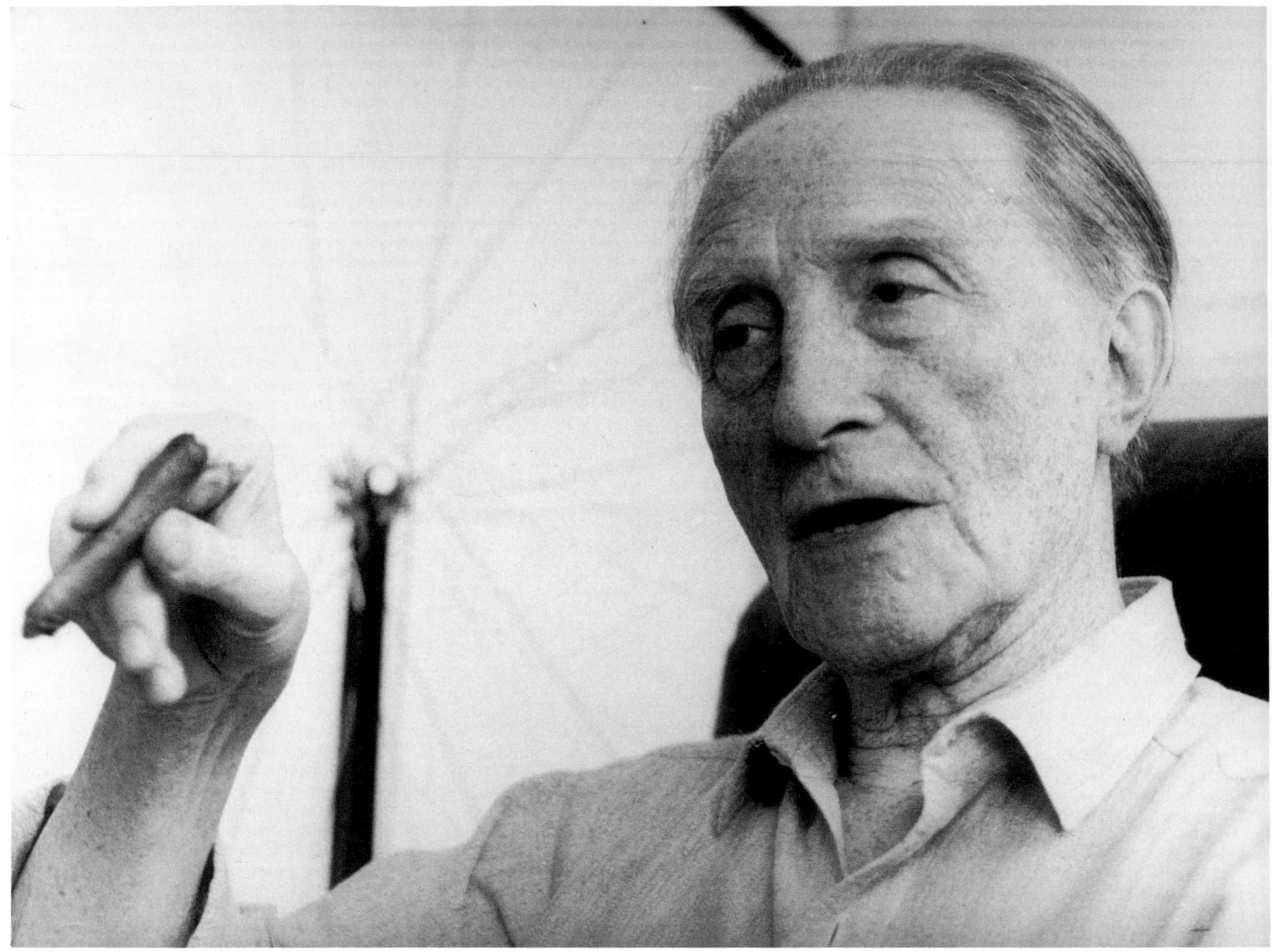

Marcel Duchamp photo by Manuel Bidermanas

Publications:

By DUCHAMP: books—*L'Opposition et les Cases conjugées sont reconciliées*, text on chess, with V. Halberstadt, Paris and Brussels 1932; *La Mariée mise à nu par ses célibataires, meme*, Paris 1934; *Rrose Selavy*, Paris 1939; *Box in a Valise*, New York 1941; *Marchand du Sel: Ecrits de Marcel Duchamp*, edited by Michel Sanouillet, Paris 1958, as *The Essential Writings of Marcel Duchamp*, edited by Michel Sanouillet and Elmer Peterson, New York 1973, London 1975; *A L'Infinitif: Notes of 1912–20*, New York 1966; *Entretiens avec Marcel Duchamp*, edited by Pierre Cabanne, Paris 1967, as *Dialogues with Marcel Duchamp*, New York 1971; *Notes and Projects for the Large Glass*, edited by Arturo Schwarz, New York 1969; articles—"A Complete Reversal of Art Opinions by Marcel Duchamp," interview, in *Arts and Decoration* (New York), September 1915; "Can a Photograph Have the Significance of Art?" in *Manuscripts* (New York), December 1922; "L'Homme qui a perdu son Squelette," with Hans Arp, Paul Eluard and others, in *Plastique* (Paris and New York), no. 4–5, 1939; interview in "11 Europeans in America," with James Johnson Sweeney, in *Museum of Modern Art Bulletin* (New York), no. 4–5, 1946; statement in *Collection of the Société Anonyme*, New Haven, Connecticut 1950; "Dans l'Atelier de Marcel Duchamp," interview, with Michel Sanouillet, in *Les Nouvelles Litteraires* (Paris), 16 December 1954; "Une Lettre de Marcel Duchamp" in *Medium* (Paris), January 1955; "The Creative Act" in *Artnews* (New York), Summer 1957; "Dada," interview, with Robert Cowan, in *Evidence* (Toronto), Autumn 1961; "Marcel Duchamp," interview, with Katharine Kuh, in *The Artist's Voice: Talks with 17 Artists*, New York 1962; "Duchamp: 50 Years Later," interview, with Francis Steegmuller, in *Show* (New York), February 1963; "What Happened to Art," interview, with C. Seitz, in *Vogue* (New York), February 1963; interview, with Alain Jouffroy, in *Une révolution du regard*, Paris, 1964; "An Interview with Marcel Duchamp," with Dore Ashton, in *Studio International* (London), June 1966; "Passport No. G255300," interview, with Otto Hons, in *Art and Artists* (London), July 1966; "Apropos of Readymades" in *Art and Artists* (London), July 1966; film—*Anemic Cinema*, with Man Ray and Marc Allegret, 1925.

On DUCHAMP: books—*Duchamp's Glass* by Katherine Dreier and Matta Echaurren, New York 1944; *Sur Marcel Duchamp* by Robert Lebel, Paris 1959; *Marcel Duchamp: Readymades, etc.* by Walter Hopps, Ulf Linde and Arturo Schwarz, Paris 1964; *The World of Marcel Duchamp* by Calvin Tomkins and the Time-Life Editors, New York 1966; *The Complete Works of Marcel Duchamp* by Arturo Schwarz, New York 1969; *Marcel Duchamp; or, The Castle of Purity* by Octavio Paz, London 1970; *Duchamp: The Bride Stripped Bare by Her Bachelors* by John Golding, London 1972; *Marcel Duchamp*, edited by Anne d'Harnoncourt and Kynaston McShine, Greenwich, Connecticut 1973; *Marcel Duchamp*, exhibition catalogue, Brussels 1974; *Miroir de la mariée* by Jean Suquet, Paris 1974; *Marcel Duchamp in Perspective*, edited by Joseph Masheck, Englewood Cliffs, New Jersey 1975; *Marcel Duchamp ou le grand Fietif* by Jean Clair, Paris 1975; *Duchamp invisible: la construzione del simbolo* by Maurizio Calvesi, Rome 1975; *Marcel Duchamp* by Arturo Schwarz, New York 1975; *Les Freres Duchamp* by Pierre Cabanne, Neuchatel, Switzerland 1975; *Marcel Duchamp* by Sarane Alexandrian, New York 1977; *Marcel Duchamp* by Yoshiaki Tono, Tokyo 1977; *Duchamp Readymades*, exhibition catalogue, Vancouver 1978; *Marcel Duchamp: Appearances Stripped Bare* by Octavio Paz, New York 1978; *Marcel Duchamp als Zeitmaschine* by Wouter Kotte, Cologne 1987.

Having as great an influence on modern art by his attitudes in general as by his own individual works, Marcel Duchamp was a brother of artists Jacques Villon and Raymond Duchamp-Villon. He was first a librarian in Paris, then he worked as a draughtsman and illustrator for *Courrier Francais*. Between 1908 and 1910 his first experiments in painting were made deliberately in the style of the Impressionists to acquaint himself with their techniques. Then in 1910 he joined the Section d'Or Group, and the following year showed with them his notorious "Nude Descending a Staircase."

Included in the historic 1913 Armory Show in New York, it aroused immediate controversy for its depiction of five human figures partially superimposed as they climbed down a spiral staircase. It was palpably linked with the breakdown of form initiated by analytical Cubism and the inspired aims of the Futurists towards a representation of time and simultaneous movement in a work of art.

In New York, giving French lessons for a livelihood, he met Picabia. He did not produce many pictures; he never did—but between 1915 and 1923 he created his major work "The Bride Stripped Bare by her Bachelors, Even." More than nine feet high, it showed the bride connected by wires to nine uniformed swains. Constructed of cut-out metal on transparent glass the work was uniquely reflective of the decade's *zeitgeist* when Dada and Surrealism spread their propaganda from Zurich and Paris to New York, Berlin and London. Duchamp also created scandals of deliberately multiplying effect with his exhibited ready-mades, such as a bottle dryer, a urinal and reproduction of the Mona Lisa on which he added a moustache and the joke title "L.H.O.O.Q."

Duchamp was an articulate writer and critic, and by 1917 he was editing two magazines, *The Blind Man* and *Rong-Wrong*. In 1920 he was making experimental films. Deeply involved in Surrealism, he invented the ceiling of coal sacks for the 1938 *International Surrealist Exhibition* in Paris. He also helped organize the *New York Surrealist Exhibition* in 1941, and its post-war equivalent in Paris in 1947.

His 20 canvases and glass panels, sold to friends during his lifetime, found their way by bequest as he wished to the Philadelphia Museum, where is concentrated the greatest collection of his works. It comprises the material evidence of a genius who, more than any other, recognized the self-contained capacity of mundane objects to be exploited for publicity purposes, and for altering outworn interpretations of art in a context of changing social and philosophical standards.

New York was his chosen home for most of his life. American artists' iconoclastic feelings towards the decadent art of the European museums were attuned to his own. To those feelings, Duchamp created something revealing and lasting by his cocksnooking at tradition and at supporters of redundant conventions in pictorial ideas—especially necrophiliac official connoisseurs.

—G. S. Whittet

DUMITRESCO, Natalia.

French. Born in Bucharest, Rumania, 20 December 1915; emigrated to France, 1947; naturalized, 1965. Studied at the Académie des Beaux-Arts, Bucharest, 1934–39, and at the Académie André Lhote, Paris, 1947–48. Married the painter Alexandre Istrati in 1939. Settled in Paris, 1947; formed friendship with sculptor Constantin Brancusi, and worked in Brancusi's Paris studio, 1947 until his death, 1957. Recipient: Prix du Groupe Espace, Paris, 1952; Prix Kandinsky, Paris, 1955; Prix des Amateurs et Collectionneurs d'Art, Paris, 1957; Carnegie Prize, Pittsburgh, 1959; Prix *Salon International de la Femme,* Paris, 1969. Agent: Artcurial, 9 Avenue Matignon, 75008 Paris. Address: 9 rue Jean Zay, 75014 Paris, France.

Individual Exhibitions

1950	Galerie Breteau, Paris
1951	Galerie Huit, Paris
1952	Galerie Arnaud, Paris
1954	Galerie Arnaud, Paris
1956	Galerie Arnaud, Paris
	Galerie Aujourd'hui, Brussels
	Palais des Beaux-Arts, Brussels
1957	Galerie Arnaud, Paris
1959	Saidenberg Gallery, New York
	Galerie La Roue, Paris
1960	Kunstverein, Cologne
	Galleria del Naviglio, Milan
	Galerie de la revue XXeme Siècle, Paris
1961	Galerie Hybler, Copenhagen
	Hanover Gallery, London (with Alexandre Istrati)
1962	Galerie Cavalero, Cannes
	Galerie Leonhart, Munich
	Galerie Argos, Nantes, France
1963	Städtische Kunsthalle, Mannheim
1964	Galerie Hilt, Basle
1965	Galerie Cavalero, Cannes
	Galerie Lauter, Mannheim
	Galerie Beno d'Incelli, Paris
1966	Galerie Beno d'Incelli, Zurich
1967	Galerie de l'A.P.I.A.W., Liège, Belgium
1968	Galerie Raeber, Lucerne
1969	Galerie Daniel Gervis, Paris
	Centre H.E.C., Jouy en Josas, France
1970	Galerie Cavalero, Cannes
1971	Galerie Lauter, Mannheim
1972	Galerie Alliance et Hostebro, Copenhagen
	Kunstmuseum, Copenhagen
1974	Galerie Raymond Cazenave, Paris
1975	Galerie Cavalero, Cannes
1976	Artcurial, Paris (with Alexandre Istrati)
1977	Musée Despiau-Wlerik Mont De Marsan, France (with Alexandre Istrati)
1978	Galerie Cavalero, Cannes
1981	Galerie Tokoro, Tokyo (with Alexandre Istrati)
1986	Galerie Praestegarden, Denmark (with Alexandre Istrati)
1987	Musée des Arts Décoratifs, Paris (with Alexandre Istrati)

Selected Group Exhibitions:

1955	*Biennale de Menton,* Musée Palais d'Europe, Menton, France
1957	*Biennale 1957,* Musée des Arts Décoratifs, Paris
1958	*Leven met Beelden,* Stedelijk Museum, Amsterdam
1959	*Carnegie International,* Pittsburgh
1962	*Ecole de Paris,* Galerie Charpentier, Paris
1963	*Exposition National et International d'Art Contemporain,* Luxembourg Institut Francais, Munich
1974	*Dix Ans de Galerie Sélection du Salon d'Automne à Téhéran,* Galerie Raber, Lucerne
1981	*Paris, Paris,* Centre Georges Pompidou, Paris
1984	*Un art autre/un autre art,* Artcurial, Paris
1986	*Sculptures Polychromes,* Mairie d'Eymoutiers, France

Collections:

Kunstmuseum, Basle; Städtische Kunsthalle, Mannheim; Centre Georges Pompidou, Paris; Musée d'Art Moderne de la Ville, Paris; Musée de Nantes, France; Musée de St. Etienne, France; Tel Aviv Museum; Guggenheim Museum, New York; Walker Art Center, Minneapolis; City Art Museum, St. Louis.

Publications:

By DUMITRESCO: books—illustrations for *Histoire de Brigands* by Constantin Brancusi, Paris 1969; *Brancusi,* with Pontus Hulten and Alexandre Istrati, Paris 1986; articles—"Neuf Annees aupres de Brancusi" in *Brancusi,* exhibition catalogue, Duisburg 1976; "Brancusi photographie ses oeuvres" in *Constantin Brancusi Photographies,* exhibition catalogue, Tokyo 1978; "Brancusi grosser Hahn" in *Artis* (Konstanz, West Germany), no. 6, 1980.

On DUMITRESCO: books—*Dictionnaire de la Peinture Abstraite* by Michel Seuphor, Paris 1957; *La Jeune Ecole de Paris* by André Rolland de Reneville, Paris 1958; *Ecole de Paris* by R. Nacenta, Paris 1960; *Natalia Dumitresco,* exhibition catalogue, with text by André Rolland de Renneville, Paris 1960; *Dumitresco/Istrati,* exhibition catalogue, with introduction by Eugene Ionesco, London 1961; *La Peinture Abstraite,* Paris 1964; *Catalogo Bolaffi d'Art Moderne,* Turin 1966; *Histoire de l'Art Abstrait* by Michel Seuphor and Michel Ragon, Paris 1974; *Natalia Dumitresco,* exhibition catalogue, Paris 1976; *Dumitresco-Istrati,* exhibition catalogue, Paris 1976; *Dumitresco-Istrati,* exhibition catalogue by Pontus Hulten, Tokyo 1981; *Dumitresco et le Regiments des Puces,* with text by Claude Bouyeure, Paris 1981; *Dumitresco,* exhibition catalogue with text by Dominique Le Buhan, Paris 1985; *Istrati-Dumitresco,* exhibition catalogue with preface by Pontus Hulten, Paris 1987.

DYE, David.

British. Born in Ryde, Isle of Wight, 23 October 1945. Studied sculpture at St. Martin's School of Art, London, 1967–71; Goldsmith's College, London, 1984–86, MA 1986. Artist, working with film and photography, London, since 1971. Lecturer, Brighton Polytechnic, 1972–76. Part-time Lecturer, Newcastle Polytechnic, since 1979. Artist-in-Residence, Univer-

Natalia Dumitresco: *Points Bleus,* 1986

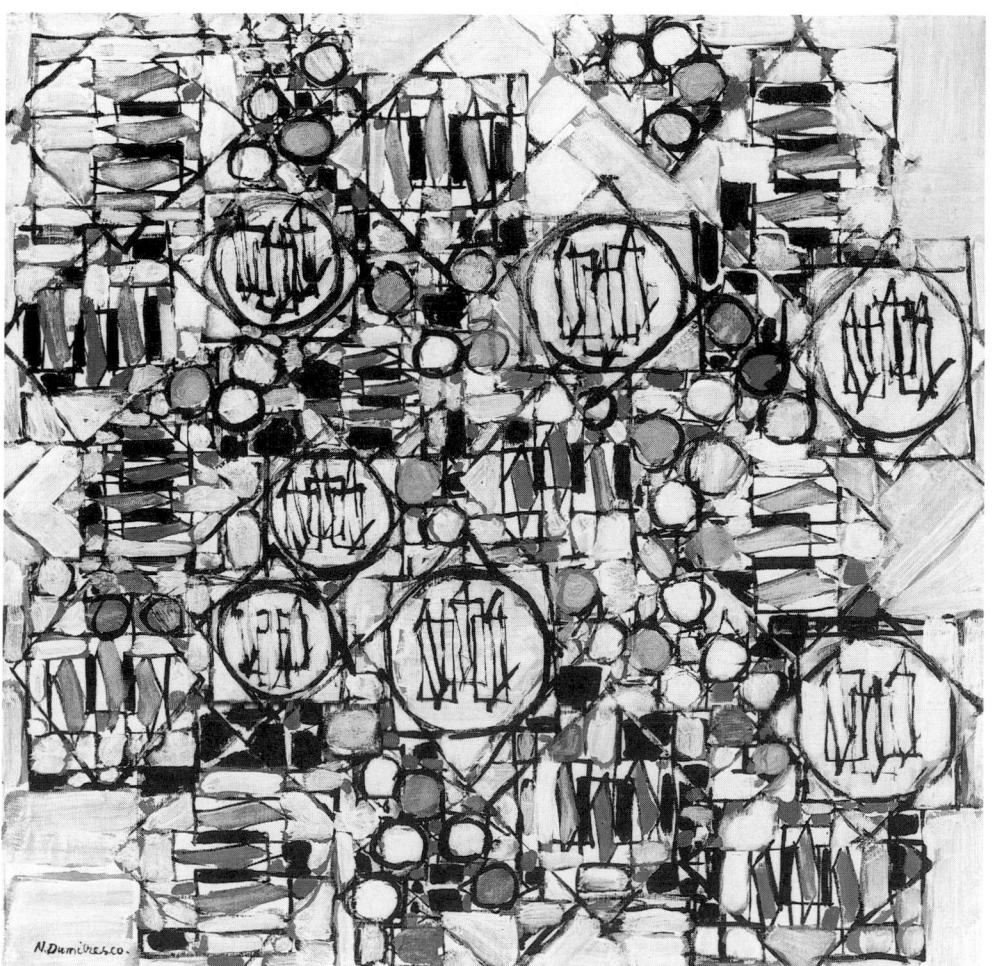

sity of Reading, 1982. Recipient: Arts Council of Great Britain Film Grant, 1973, and Arts Council Award, 1976. Addresses: (studio) 6A Peacock Yard, Iliffe Street, London SE17, 3LH; (home) 76 Burton Road, Myatts Fields, London SW9 6TQ, England.

Individual Exhibitions:

1972   Institute of Contemporary Arts, London
1975   Lisson Gallery, London
1976   Robert Self Gallery, London
1977   Arnolfini Gallery, Bristol

Selected Group Exhibitions:

1971   *The English Avant-Garde*, Cultural Center, New York
1972   *The New Art*, Hayward Gallery, London
1974   *Beyond Painting and Sculpture*, Leeds City Art Gallery (toured the U.K.)
1975   *Biennale de Paris*, Musee National d'Art Moderne, Paris
1976   *Arte Inglese Oggi*, Palazzo Reale, Milan
1977   *Time, Words and the Camera*, Kunstlerhaus, Graz, Austria (toured Austria and West Germany)
1978   *Scale for Sculpture*, Serpentine Gallery, London (toured the U.K., 1978–79)
1981   *Extended Photography*, Vienna Secession
1984   *When Attitudes Became Form*, Kettle's Yard, Cambridge (travelled to Fruitmarket Gallery, Edinburgh)
1987   *Under the Sign of Saturn*, Nigel Greenwood Gallery, London

Collections:

Arts Council of Great Britain, London; Victoria and Albert Museum, London

Publications:

By DYE: articles—"Interview with David Dye," with Simon Field, in *Art and Artists* (London), December 1972; interview, with Anne Seymour, in *The New Art*, exhibition catalogue, London 1972; films—*Mirror*, 1971; *Two Cameras*, 1971; *Cross Reference*, 1972; *Projection/Introjection*, 1972; *Window*, 1972; *Unsigning 1*, 1972; *Hand Piece*, 1972; *Unsigning 2*, 1972; *Unsigning 3*, 1972; *Unsigning for Eight Projectors*, 1972; *Overlap*, 1973; *Open/Close*, 1973; *Western Reversal*, 1973; *4 Slide Projector Piece*, 1973; *Static, Contracted, Vertical/Moving, Stretched, Horizontal*, 1973; *Western Reversal*, 1974; *4 Slide Projector Piece*, 1975; *Edges Guess*, 1975; *Throw*, 1975; *Light Interruptions*, 1975; *Commercial Break*, 1975; *Scan*, 1976; *Letter to Rita*, 1978; *Man in Space*, 1979; *3-D* (installation), 1979–80.

On DYE: articles—"Artists Seeking the Potential of Film" by Richard Cork in the *Evening News* (London), 4 May 1972; "Artist as Film-Maker" by Annabel Nicolson in *Art and Artists* (London), December 1972; "David Dye, Artist/Film-Maker?" by Alan Sheridan in *Studio International* (London), November/December 1975; "David Dye" by Hugh Adams in *Studio International* (London), September/October 1977; "David Dye: 3-D" in *Aspects* (London), Spring 1980.

For many years I have been using film and photography as a medium. I'm not interested in making "film" into "art," an idea which I feel is closely aligned to the "consumer" "novelty" culture, but I use film and photography because perhaps they are more transparent and less individuated than painting or sculpture. No, my concern has not been about the medium itself as such; although some of my works seem "self-referential," it is because they reject conventional notions of film as exemplified in the commercial cinema, and can only be understood in terms of that rejection.

My work has always been ambiguous, dualistic, paradoxical, or any other words that signify a contradiction or ambivalence of stance or intention.

Ambivalence, because I am aware of the way art is

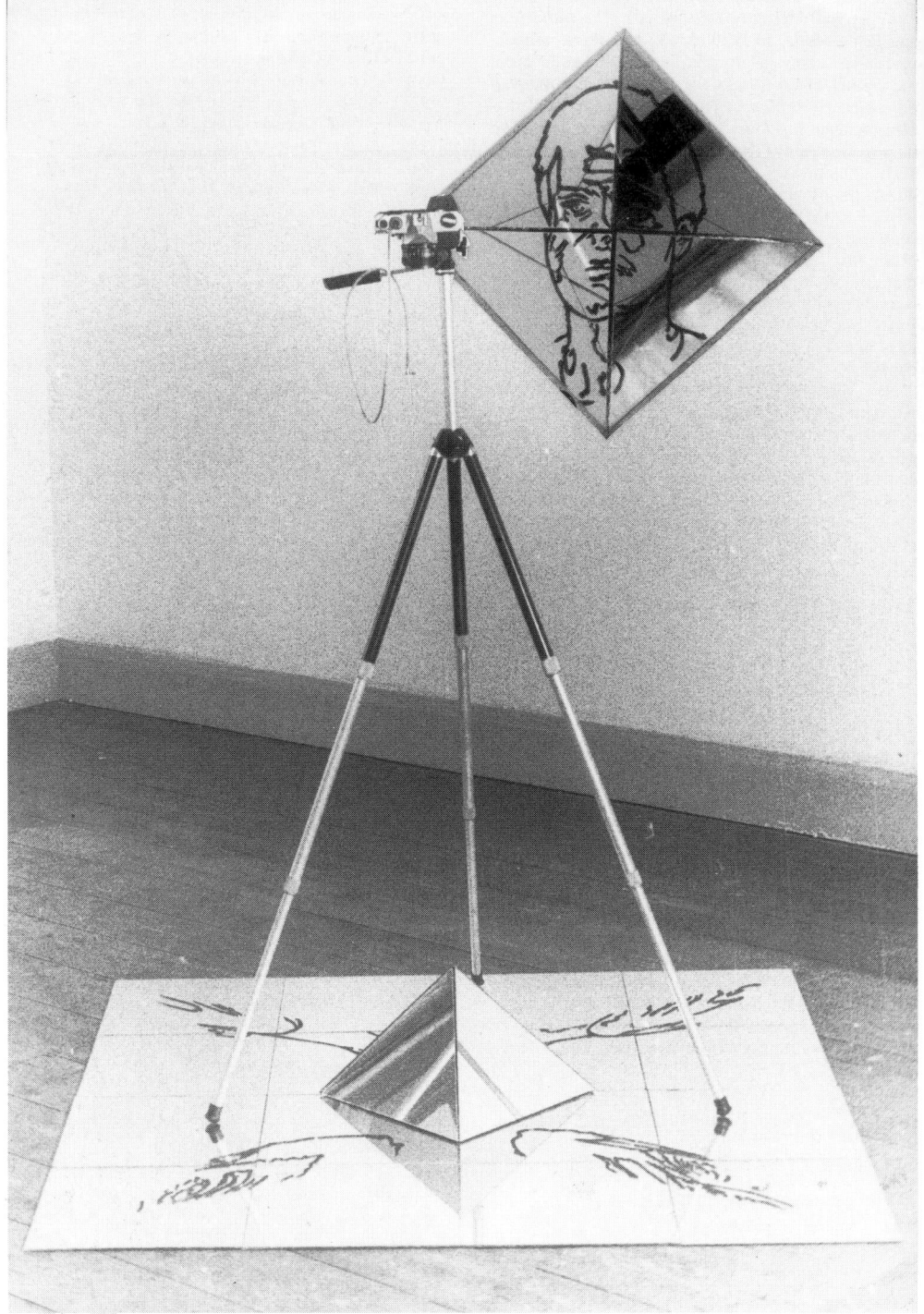

David Dye: *Mirror Portrait for Camera*, 1981

relative to a particular culture at a particular time. We are, in a sense, locked into our time. I am also aware that our culture has created the myth of subjectivity, self-expression, and individualism.

This myth of the romantic outsider could be seen to relate directly to the status-quo; if you see art as art only, isolated pure, ideal, then that naturally blinkers you to the institutions and economics that uphold it. The ideology of "art for art's sake" is a conservative viewpoint that eschews relations and upholds territoriality.

This "pedestal" viewpoint links up to the myth of the artist as "knower," "seer," "God," an internalization of paternalism. I believe that the interpersonal and conventional systems which traverse the individual make him a space in which forces and events meet rather than individuated essence.

All my work has been done in relationship to the "art" situation I find myself in—most of it ironic and

self-deprecatory. I try to embody contradictions which I feel exist in myself, and by definition, our Western culture.

—David Dye

DZUBAS, Friedel.

American. Born in Berlin, Germany, 20 April 1915; emigrated to the United States in 1939, and subsequently naturalized. Educated at Berlin Gymnasium until 1931; studied at the Prussian Academy of Fine Art and Kunstgewerbeschule, 1931–33; studied with Paul Klee in Dusseldorf, 1933–36. Married Mary

forms what comes to hand: one piece of sheet metal becomes a "Moon Sail," another the "Boar Mask," iron prongs bend into "Fairy-tale Princes," pieces of wood and bronze form an "Overflowing Bodice," etc., totally inexhaustible, restless, never standing still, the perpetuum mobile of continual creativity. Admittedly one easily forgets the artistic skill necessary to make from plexiglass, stone and zinc for example a convincing showpiece like "Fine Friend Small Mask."

In order to work like Eggenschwiler, one must have certain prerequisites: an unusually sensitive awareness, an openness to visual and tactile qualities which, as it were, lie waiting to be noticed; and this constant preparedness for perception, if it is to be artistically productive, must be allied with a strong capacity for association, an imaginative ability of extraordinary energy and flexibility, which, by the favour of fortune, the favourable moment, becomes active and takes action, recognizes aesthetic possibilities and immediately accomplishes the presentation in outline; then, a thorough knowledge of materials and pronounced manual skills are needed, an acquaintance with different materials, indispensable in order to combine into a whole in an aesthetic, charming and confident manner, to work and unwork pieces of different materials or to produce block prints of extraordinary diversity; finally, in the execution of the artistic activity, a sharp intellect must come into operation which fastidiously and without favour prunes the possibilities and reduces chance to a proportion which gives to the resulting combination of forms the appearance of the bare essentials: in this way and no other it can and must be! And last but not least, there must be a taste of irony, perplexing and irritating, the suggestion of strangeness which shoots through the whole and stops the feeling that anything may really be entirely certain: nothing is entirely certain, and art repeatedly breaks open the taboo of various certainties, along with judgments and prejudices, beliefs and ideologies, condensed to so-called good taste.

It was all already there once, it was already once made, already made use of and used, it already lay on the pathway, it is the old story of the déjà vu: discovered, rediscovered—but now the found object, the *objet trouvé*, in deliberate combination, artistically considered and coolly arrived at, the found complex from thing, object and particular experience in the auratic sphere of the exponent: now look here, you can see it here! What then? The work of Art? The found object? The combination of materials? The veining of the wood? The layers of colour print? Yes, all that, if one wants to; but in all, over all and through all, still more: the dissolution of object and work in the execution. Keep your eyes open! the draughtsman, painter and sculptor Franz Eggenschwiler reminds us: look what is happening in the world, what is to be discovered, what can be perceived, and pay attention to the fact that the division of the world into outside object and the subjective within us does not exist; our power of imagination, aesthetically productive, shows how both connect; we live neither without nor within; we live in the transcendent: creative as we are, we are aesthetic transcendents.

—Gerolf Fritsch

ENGELS, Pieter.
Dutch. Born in Rosmalen, 3 December 1938. Studied painting, drawing and material research at the Koninklijke Academie, The Hague, 1955–58, and painting, sculpture, drawing, architecture and art history, Rijksacademie, Amsterdam, 1958–62. Married Liesbeth Vandergraaf in 1961; children: Manuela and Wladimir. Independent artist, Amsterdam, since 1962: Founder, Engels Products Organization (E.P.O.), Amsterdam, 1964–69; Engels New Interment Organization (E.N.I.O.), Amsterdam, 1968–69; Engels Third Institute for Research in Subcultural Brainbuilding (E.T.I.F.R.I.S.B.B.), Amsterdam, 1969–74; and Engels Genesis Foundation, Amsterdam, 1974. Recipient: Koninklijke Subsidy, 1959; Dutch Government grants, 1967, 1969, 1970, 1971, 1974; Cassandra Foundation Award, Philadelphia, 1971. Agent: Galerie Yaki Kornblit, Willemsparkweg 69, Amsterdam. Address: Willem Nuijenstraat 26, Amsterdam; or Grote Wittenburgstraat 37, Amsterdam, Netherlands.

Individual Exhibitions:

1963   Galerie Orez, The Hague
       Galerie t'Venster, Rotterdam
       De Krabbedans, Eindhoven, Netherlands
1965   Galerie 845, Amsterdam
       Galerie A. Arnhem, Netherlands
       Galerie Arti Schunck, Maastricht, Netherlands
1966   Galerie Swart, Amsterdam
       Koninklijke Academie, The Hague
       Gemeentemuseum, The Hague
       Galerie 20, Amsterdam
       Galerie 845, Amsterdam

Pieter Engels: *Before the Hierarchy of Painting*, 1975

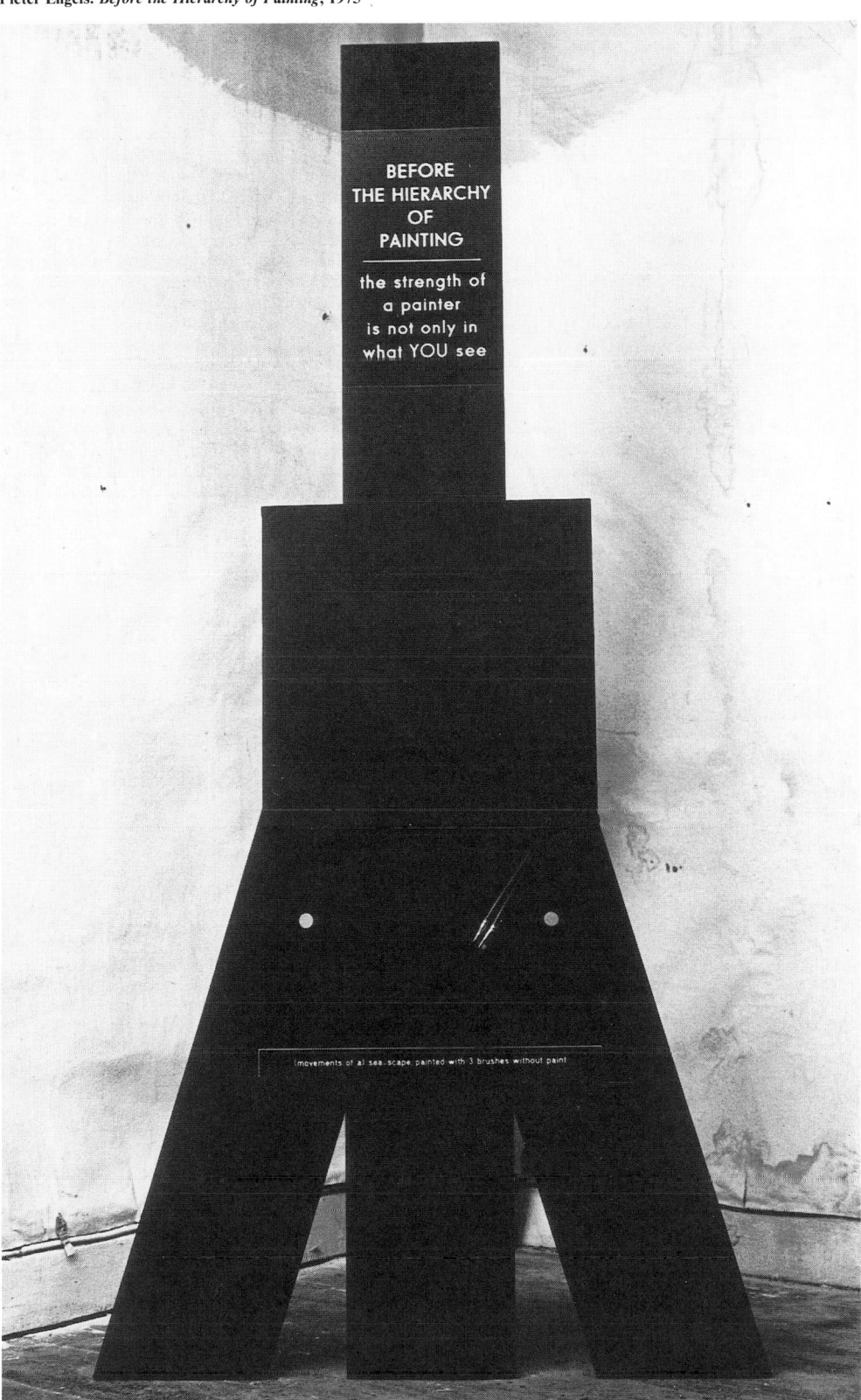

Selected Group Exhibitions:

Collections:

Stedelijk Museum, Amsterdam; Stedelijk Van Abbemuseum, Eindhoven, Netherlands; Gemeentemuseum, The Hague; Museum Boymans-van Beuningen, Rotterdam; Centraal Museum, Utrecht; International Cultureel Centrum, Antwerp; Bank Lambert, Brussels; McCrory Corporation, New York.

Publications:

By ENGELS: books—*Engels New Interment Organization,* with Simon Es, Amsterdam 1968; *Resurrection of Art,* Amsterdam 1974; articles—"Engels: Image of an Image," with Simon Es, in *Museumjournaal* (Amsterdam), no. 1, 1967; "Engels: (pre) Hume Ghost Writer of a Non-Existent Vanguard," with Simon Es, in *Engels: Self-Portrait of This Century* exhibition catalogue, Amsterdam 1972; films— *Paramarche,* television film, 1972; *Oral Signature,* 1972; *Self Portrait,* 1972; records— *Oral Signature,* Rotterdam 1972.

On ENGELS: books—*Engels: Self-Portrait of This Century,* exhibition catalogue, Amsterdam 1969; *De Eksplosie van het Intellekt* by Jan Donia, Hilversum, Netherlands 1968; *Metamorfose van het Objekt,* exhibition catalogue, with text by Jean Dypreau, Brussels 1971; *Pieter Engels,* exhibition catalogue, with text by Carel Blotkamp, Amsterdam 1972; *11 Dutch Artists,* exhibition catalogue, with text by Caroline Tisdall, Edinburgh 1974; *Engels: Self-Portrait of This Century,* exhibition catalogue, with an introduction by R. Hammacher-van den Brande, Rotterdam 1975; *Pieter Engels: Recent Work 1979-1980,* exhibition folder, with texts by Tijmen van Grootheest and Dirk Pietørs, Amsterdam 1981.

For more than 20 years now Pieter Engels has been producing a steady stream of works in a variety of media which define his own particular gifts as an artist and also make a comment on the position of the artist in society. As a person he seemed to retreat, at first, behind the facade of EPO (the Engels Product Organization, founded in 1964), whose skillful sales manager was Simon Es. By this time Engels had also

produced some of his *materieachtig* work ("Dirty Picture," for example, from 1961).

In 1964 EPO created a stir with an exhibition held in Galerie A in Arnhem. Included here were "Restored Furnishings," groupings of functionless pieces of furniture which seemed to be conversing with each other. And in 1966 there was "Girl's Coat-Piece," a rain-slicker stretched on a canvas which was also a kind of comment on the work of the American artist Jim Dine.

In 1968 Engels founded ENIO: Engels' New Interment Organization (New Methods for the Interment Field). Here the aim was to dispel any notion that a funeral had to be a sad occasion. In its brochure ENIO offers cheerful alternatives and concludes with the enticing invitation to "Think it over—have a good ending for your life . . . . We will prepare you. Our funerals are gorgeous and luxurious—and so are our prices."

In 1969 and 1970 Engels exhibited aural works in Galerie 20 in Amsterdam (in one of these works you can hear street noises recorded simultaneously from each of the four floors of the building). In 1972 he produced an important photographic work which can be regarded as his first venture into the field of painting. The "Painting Piece for Four Hands" consists of three photographs, the last of which has a caption which explains helpfully "painting of Engels' left hand painted blue by Engels' blue-painted right hand." In this same year Engels also made a brief statement which sums up his intentions as an artist: "The artist is a cat among the pigeons."

There is a series of particularly concentrated works from 1974, including portraits and still-lifes, which Engels painted in the dark or while blindfolded. He also founded the Engels Genesis Foundation in 1974, the mission of which was to construct a monumental work (completed in 1977) in de Bijlmer, a suburb of Amsterdam. Underground there are boxes which contain tape recordings and collections of objects over which cement has been poured. Above ground are images of the objects buried below. Here according to Engels is a cross section of the urban life of the three cities of the "Randstad"—Amsterdam, Utrecht and Rotterdam.

Despite the continually changing nature of his work, Engels has succeeded in coming to a prominent place in the Dutch art world of the 1980's. Since 1970 his work has won a place in private collections and museums as well, reaching a kind of highpoint in the *Self-Portrait of the Century* exhibition at the Boymans-van Beuningen Museum in Rotterdam in 1975.

—A. F. Wagemans

ERNST, M(aximilian).

French. Born in Brühl, Rhineland, Germany, 2 April 1891; emigrated to the United States, 1941: naturalized, 1948; emigrated to France, 1953: naturalized, 1958. Educated in Brühl primary schools; studied philosophy and art history at the University of Bonn, under Wilhelm Worringer, 1909–12. Served as an Artillery Engineer, in France and Poland, 1914–17. Married the art historian Louise Strauss in 1918 (divorced, 1921); son: Ulrich (Jimmy); married Marie Berthe Aurenche in 1927 (divorced, 1936); married the collector Peggy Guggenheim in 1941 (divorced, 1941); married the painter Dorothea Tanning in 1946. Member, Young Rhineland Circle, 1911; lifelong friendship with Hans Arp, from 1914; lived in Cologne, 1918–22; Co-Founder, with J. T. Baargeld (later joined by Arp), Dada Zentrale w/3 Supidia, Cologne, 1919; Co-Editor, with Baargeld, *Der Ventilator,* Cologne, 1919–20; co-signed *Dada Manifesto,* with Tristan Tzara and Hans Arp, 1921; lifelong friendship with Paul Eluard, from 1921; settled illegally in France, with Paul Eluard, in Eaubonne, 1922; worked on murals for the Eluard home, 1923;

worked in factory, producing cheap jewelry, Paris, 1922–24; travelled with Eluard in the Far East, 1924; involved with Surrealists, Paris, 1924–38; rented studio in Paris, 1925; worked with Juan Miro on decor for Diaghilev ballet *Romeo and Juliet,* Paris, 1926; settled in Meudon, 1927; participated in Luis Bunuel's film, *L'Age d'Or,* 1930; Set Designer, for Alfred Jarry's *Ubu Enchaine,* Comedie des Champs-Elysees, Paris, 1937; lived with Leonora Carrington in St. Martin d'Ardeche, France, 1938–39; interned by Gestapo, in 1939; fled to the United States, with the help of Peggy Guggenheim, 1941, and settled in Provincetown, Massachusetts; Member with André Breton, Editorial Board, *VVV,* New York, 1941; worked with Dorothea Tanning, in Arizona and Long Island, 1943–44; acted in Hans Richter's film, *Dreams That Money Can Buy,* 1946; returned to Europe and lived in Paris, 1953–55, Huismes, near Chinon, 1955–64, and Seillans, in Southern France, from 1964; collaborated on films, *Die Widerrechtliche Ausuburg der Astromie,* with Peter Schamoni, 1966; *Selbsportrat,* with Werner Spies, 1966; set designer, *La Turangalila* ballet, by Oliver Messiaen, at the Paris Opera, 1968. Visiting Lecturer, University of Hawaii, Honolulu, 1952. Recipient: First Prize for Painting, *Biennale,* Venice, 1954; Grand Prix, *Nordhein-Westfalen Art Exhibition,* Dusseldorf 1957; Grand Prix National des Arts ets Lettres, Paris, 1959; Stephen Lochner Medal, Cologne, 1961. Honorary Professor, Nordrhein-Westfalen, 1964; D.Phil. University of Bonn, 1972. Officier, Légion d'Honneur, 1965. *Died* (in Paris) *1 April 1976.*

Individual Exhibitions:

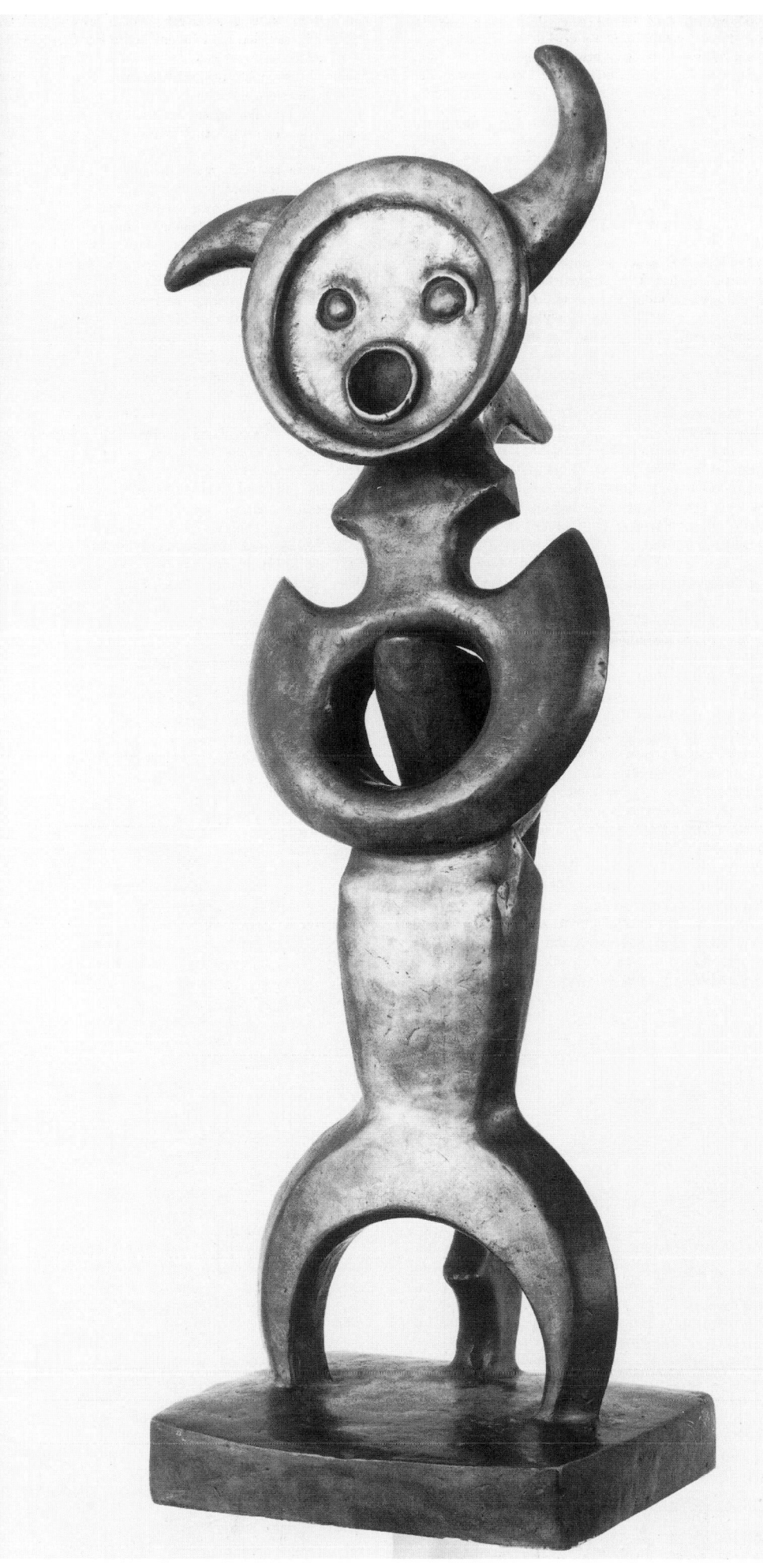

Max Ernst: *Moonmad*, 1944

1960 Bodley Gallery, New York (with Yves Tanguy)
      Galerie der Spiegel, Cologne (with Hans Arp)
1961 Galerie Andre-Francois Petit, Paris (with Yves Tanguy)
      Bodley Gallery, New York
      Museum of Modern Art, New York (travelled to Art Institute of Chicago, and the Tate Gallery, London)
      Galerie au Pont des Arts, Paris
      Galerie Le Point Cardinal, Paris
1962 Alexander Iolas Gallery, New York
      Wallraf-Richartz Museum, Cologne
      Roland Browse and Delbanco, London
1963 Alexandre Iolas Galerie, Geneva
      Kunsthaus, Zurich
      Ecrits et Oeuvre Grave, Bibliothèque Municipale, Tours (travelled to the Galerie Le Point Cardinal, Paris)
1964 Galerie der Spiegel, Cologne
      Galerie au Point des Arts, Paris
      Musée Grimaldi, Antibes, France
1965 Alexandre Iolas Galerie, Paris
      Hanover Gallery, London
1966 Jewish Gallery, New York
      Galerie Alphonse Chave, Venice
      Palazzo Grassi, Venice
1967 Alexander Iolas Gallery, New York
      Galerie Fronta, Prague (travelled to the Kunsthalle, Hamburg)
1968 Galeria René Metras, Barcelona
      Galerie Alphonse Chave, Venice
1969 Galerie André-Francois Petit, Paris
      Moderna Museet, Stockholm
      Städtisches Museum ot Mulheim an der Ruhr, West Germany
      Alexandre Iolas Gallery, New York
      Galerie au Pont des Arts, Paris
      Alexandre Iolas Galerie, Paris
1970 Württembergischer Kunstverein, Stuttgart
      Stedelijk Museum, Amsterdam
      Rice University, Houston (toured the United States and Europe)
      Musée d'Art et d'Histoire, Geneva
      Städtische Kunsthalle, Dusseldorf
      Galleria Il Fauno, Turin
      Kunsthalle, Hamburg (toured West Germany)
1971 Galerie Alphonse Chave, Venice
      Orangerie des Tuileries, Paris
1972 Kunstverein, Krefeld, West Germany
1973 Mary Atkins Museum of Fine Arts, Kansas City
      Müller Galerie, Stuttgart
      Alexandre Iolas Galerie, Paris
      Mayor Gallery, London
1974 Galerie Beyeler, Basle
      Alexandre Iolas Galerie, Paris
      Fogg Art Museum, Cambridge, Massachusetts
      Galerie Jan Krugier, Geneva
1975 Bibliothèque National, Geneva
      Scottish Arts Council Gallery, Edinburgh (toured the U.K.)
      Guggenheim Museum, New York
      Grand Palais, Paris
1976 Foundation Veranneman, Kruishoutem, Belgium
      Galerie Baukunst, Cologne
1977 Seibu Museum of Art, Tokyo (travelled to the Museum of Modern Art, Kobe)
      Musée National d'Art Moderne, Paris
      Galerie Isy Brachot, Brussels
1978 Kunsthaus, Zurich (travelled to the Kunstinstitut, Frankfurt, and the Städtische Galerie im Lenbachhaus, Munich)
1979 Goethe Institut, London
      Kunstsammlung Nordrhein-Westfalen, Dusseldorf
      Galerie Suzanne Bollag, Zurich
      Haus der Kunst, Munich (travelled to the Nationalgalerie, Berlin)
      Glenbow Museum, Calgary, Alberta
1980 Bundeskanzleramt, Bonn
1981 Fondation Maeght, St. Paul de Vence, France
1982 Acquavella Galleries, New York
      Billingham Art Gallery, Durham, England (toured Britain)
1983 Foundation Maeght, St. Paul de Vence, France
1986 Fundacion Joan Miro, Barcelona

Fundacion Juan March, Madrid
Graphisches Kabinett Wolfgang Werner, Bremen, West Germany
1987 Cavaliero Fine Arts, New York

Selected Group Exhibitions:

1913 *Erster Deutscher Herbstsalon*, Galerie der Sturm, Berlin
1919 *Dada Ausstellung*, Kunstverein, Cologne
1923 *Salon des Indépendants*, Paris
1936 *International Surrealist Exhibition*, New Burlington Galleries, London
1940 *Esposicion Internacional del Surrealismo*, Galerie de Arte Mexicano, Mexico City
1944 *Abstract and Surrealist Art in the United States*, Museum of Art, San Francisco (toured the United States)
1958 *Dada: Dokumente einer Bewegung*, Städtische Kunsthalle, Dusseldorf (travelled to the Stedelijk Museum, Amsterdam)
1966 *Dada Ausstellung zum 50. Jahrigen Jubilaum*, Kunsthálle, Zurich (travelled to the Musée National d'Art Moderne, Paris)
1973 *Futurism: A Modern Focus*, Guggenheim Museum, New York
1983 *Modern Art in the West*, Metropolitan Museum, Tokyo

Collections:

Nationalgalerie, Berlin; Kunstmuseum, Dusseldorf; Stadt Museum, Brühl, West Germany; Museum des 20. Jahrhunderts, Vienna; Centre Georges Pompidou, Paris; Peggy Guggenheim Collection, Venice; Tate Gallery, London; Museum of Modern Art, New York; Guggenheim Museum, New York; Philadelphia Museum of Art.

Publications:

By ERNST: books—*Les Malheurs des Immortels*, with Paul Eluard, Paris 1922; *La Femme 100 Tetes*, Paris 1929; *Reve d'un Petite Fille qui Voulut entrer au Carmel*, Paris 1930; *Une Semaine de Bonte, ou Les Sept Elements Capitaux*, Paris 1934; *At Eye Level: Poems and Comments, Paramyths: New Poems and Collages*, with writings by Breton, Calas, Crevel, Desnos, Eluard, Mondraian and others, Beverly Hills, California 1949; *Sept Microbes, Vus á Travers un Temperament*, Paris 1953; *Histoire Naturelle; dessins inedits*, Paris 1959; *Jean Arp/Max Ernst*, with poems by Arp, Cologne 1960; *Die Nacktheit der Frau ist wieser als die Lehre der Pilosophen*, Cologen 1962; *Maximiliana ou l'Exercise Illegal de l'Astronomie*, Paris 1964; *22 Mikroben*, with texts by Arp and Fabri, Cologne 1965; *Paramythes*, Paris 1967; articles—preface to *Was ist Surrealismus?*, exhibition catalogue, Zurich 1934; numerous writings and contributions to Dada and Surrealist periodicals, Berlin, Cologne and Paris, 1917-38; illustrated books—*Logique sans Peine* by Lewis Carroll, 1966; *Dent Prompte* by René Char, 1969.

On ERNST: books—*My Life with Max Ernst: End of My Life with Max Ernst* by Peggy Guggenheim, New York 1946; *Max Ernst* by Joe Bousquet and Michel Tapie, Paris 1950; *Max Ernst* by Patrick Waldberg, Paris 1958; *Max Ernst* by Eduard Trier, Recklinghausen, West Germany, 1959; *Max Ernst* by Georges Bataille, and others, Paris 1960; *Confessions of an Art Addict* by Peggy Guggenheim, New York 1960; *Hommages à Max Ernst* by Hans Arp, René Magritte, Paul Eluard, and others, Cologne 1960; *Max Ernst: Ecrits et Oeuvre Grave*, exhibition catalogue, by Hughes and Poupard-Lieussen, Tours 1963; *Max Ernst: Life and Work* by John Russell, New York 1967; *Max Ernst: Frottages* by Werner Spies, New York 1969; *Max Ernst* by Giuseppe Gatt, London and New York 1970; *Max Ernst* by Sarane Alexandrian, Paris 1971; *Max Ernst's Celebes* by Roland Penrose, Newcastle upon Tyne 1972; *The Essential Max Ernst* by Uwe Schneede, London and New York 1972; *Max Ernst 24 Frottagen* by Jean Tardieu, Zurich 1973; *Max Ernst: Maximiliana* by Peter Schamoni, Munich 1974; *Max Ernst 1950-1970* by Werner Spies, Cologne 1974; *Max Ernst: Collagen, Inventar und Widerspruch* by Werner Spies, Cologne 1974; *Max Ernst*, exhibition catalogue, by Sabine Rewald, New York 1975; *Max Ernst*, edited by David Larkin, New York 1975; *Max Ernst: Oeuvre Katalogue—Volume I: Das Graphische Werk* by Helmut R. Leppien; *Volume II: Werke 1906-25* by Werner Spies, Sigrid and Günther Metken; *Volume III: Werke 1926-* 1929 by Werner Spies, Sigrid and Günther Metken; and *Volume IV:Werke, 1929-1938* by Werner Spies, Sigrid and Günther Metken, Houston and Cologne 1975-1978; *Max Ernst* by Edward Quinn, London 1977; *Max Ernst* by Ian Turpin, Oxford 1979; *Leaves Never Grow on Trees: Max Ernst's Histoire Naturelle*, exhibition catalogue with introduction by Roland Penrose, London 1982; *Max Ernst*, exhibition catalogue with text by Jean-Louis Prat, St. Paul 1983; *Max Ernst: Livros e Obra Grafica*, exhibition catalogue with essay by Werner Spies, Madrid 1986; *Max Ernst*, exhibition catalogue with introduction by John Cavaliero, New York 1987.

The plastic bird-cages gummed onto the canvases of the 1950's and 1960's followed the dense forest that somehow came to an unexpected conclusion in Max Ernst's version of The Temptation of St. Anthony that he made for MGM. Before that there had been so many Max Ernsts. The *frottages*, made like brass rubbings, the palette-knife swirls like exotic flowers and the marbling of paint to compose skyscapes and seascapes and *earth*-scapes, the ultimate in narrative collages epitomised in the "100 Têtes". And the landmark pictures: "The Airplane Traps," "The Bride of the Wind" and "Loplop"—so many undreamt of magic visions. There are even paintings, the dates of which the artist himself could not recall which spliced together the imagery of Chagall and Campendonk. And of course there were the sculptures, bronzes which, unlike those of Magritte, were original inventions and not culled from imagery in his own pictures.

Ernst was always a creator, but not one content to use the raw materials of existence and left-overs of tradition. His position in the surrealist hierarchy is secure because if what he made is not out of dreams, then no other source could be readily described. From his mind and hands flowed a proliferation of unidentifiable imagery, which for all its strangeness is privately recognizable in some way by those who have eyes to see. Whatever visual conjuring with pigment (and all manner of other media) the artist may have indulged in, there is a reality—superreality—about his work which, while it may disturb the eye, never perplexes it to the point of non-realization.

In bronze, paint, collages and mixed media, Max Ernst was equally at ease and splendidly efficient. His imagination and craftsmanship carried him from one epoch of his crowded career to another. One never shows signs of overwhelming the rest, and it should be remembered that he was a valuable contributor to the Surrealist film *Dreams That Money Can Buy*.

—Sheldon Williams

ERRÒ, (Gudmundur Gudmundsson).

Icelandic. Born in Olafsvik, 19 July 1932. Studied at the Academy of Art, Reykjavik, 1949-51 (Art Professor's Diploma, 1951); painted frescoes, Academy of Art, Oslo, 1952-54; studied fresco painting, Academy of Art, Florence, 1954. Married Myriam Bat-Yosef in 1956 (divorced, 1964); married Vilai Permchit in 1972. Worked on frescoes and mosaics, Reykjavik, 1955-58; moved to Paris, 1958; produced first Catastrophe Happenings, with Jean Jacques Lebel, Paris, 1962; travelled in the United States, performing happenings, 1963; lived and worked in New York, 1964; lived in New York and Paris, 1966-71; in Thailand and the Far East, 1972-85. Agents: Galerie Le Dessin, 27 rue Guenegaud, 75006 Paris; and Galleria Borgogna, Via Borgogna 7, 20121 Milan. Address: 39 rue Fondary, 75015 Paris, France.

Individual Exhibitions:

1955 Galerie Saint Trinity, Florence
1956 Galerie Montenapoleone, Milan
Galerie Schneider, Rome

1957 Maison des Artistes, Reykjavik
1958 Bezalel National Museum, Jerusalem
Museum of Modern Art, Tel Aviv
Museum of Modern Art, Haifa
1960 Galerie Chirvan, Paris
Maison des Artistes, Reykjavik
1961 Galleria del Cavallino, Venice
Galleria del Naviglio, Milan
1962 Galerie J. Dols, Liège, Belgium
1963 Galerie Sydow, Frankfurt
Galerie St. Germain-des-Pres, Paris
1964 Galerie Gertrude Stein, New York
Galleria Edouard Smith, Milan
Galleria Schwarz, Milan
1965 Galerie L'Attico, Rome
Maison des Artistes, Reykjavik
Galerie St. Germain, Paris
1966 Galerie Kaleidoscope, Ghent
1967 Galleria Schwarz, Milan
Galerie Krikhaar, Amsterdam
1968 Galerie Givaudan, Paris
Galerie Mendoza, Caracas
1969 Musée d'Art Moderne, Paris
Galerie Heland, Stockholm
Galerie Givaudan, Paris
Galerie M. E. Thelen, Essen
1971 Galerie André, Berlin
Galerie 3 Laplace, Paris
Kerlikowsky Galerie, Munich
1972 Galerie Boulakia, Paris
1973 Galerie Buchholz, Munich
Galleria d'Arte Borgogna, Milan
Galerie Benador, Geneva
Kunstmarkt, Cologne
Galerie Buchholz, Munich
1974 D. K. Bookhouse, Bangkok
1975 Musée des Beaux-Arts, Brest, France
Palais des Papes, Avignon, France
Sigma, Bordeaux
Tableaus Chinois, Kunstmuseum, Lucerne
Galerie Buchholz, Munich
Galerie Fred Lanzenberg, Brussels
Galleria d'Arte Borgogna, Milan
Neue Galerie, Aachen, West Germany
1976 Musée Despiau et Wlerick, Mont-de-Marsan, France
Kunstichting Lijnbaancentrum, Rotterdam
Galerie Beaubourg, Paris
O. K. Harris Gallery, New York
Maison de la Culture, Amiens, France
Musée d'Ethnographie, Bastia, Corsica
1977 Beaux-Arts Angoulème, Centre d'Art, Flaine, France
Centre d'Art Contemporain, Chelles, France
Galerie Fred Lanzenberg, Ibiza, Spain
Galerie Beaubourg, Paris
Reykjavik Art Festival
1978 Galerie Sven Hanssen, Copenhagen
Galerie Buchholz, Munich
1979 Galerie Beaubourg, Paris
Galerie Claude Givaudan, Geneva
Galleria d'Arte Borgogna, Milan
Galerie Fred Lanzenberg, Brussels
1980 Galerie Impact, Vannes, France
1981 Galerie Maeght, Zurich
Lunds Konsthall, Lund Sweden (travelled to the Kunstforeningen, Bergen; Nordisk Konstcentrum, Sveaborg; Pohjoismainen taidekeskus, Helsingfors; and the Kunstforeningen, Copenhagen)
1982 Galerie Jan Six, Paris
Maison de la Culture, Chalon-sur-Saône, France
Salle Demangel, Montpellier, France
Musée Rigaud, Perpignan, France
Musée des Beaux-Arts, Nîmes, France
Tour Narbonnaise, Carcassonne, France
Musée Fabrégal, Béziers, France
Galerie le Dessin, at *FIAC 82*, Grand Palais, Paris
Art Front Gallery, Tokyo
Museum voor Hedendaagse Kunst, Utrecht, Netherlands
1983 Miroir d'Encre, Brussels
Galerie Jaqueline Storms, Lille, France
Galerie Municipale, Gennevilliers, France
Galerie Fernand Leger, Ivry-sur-Seine, France

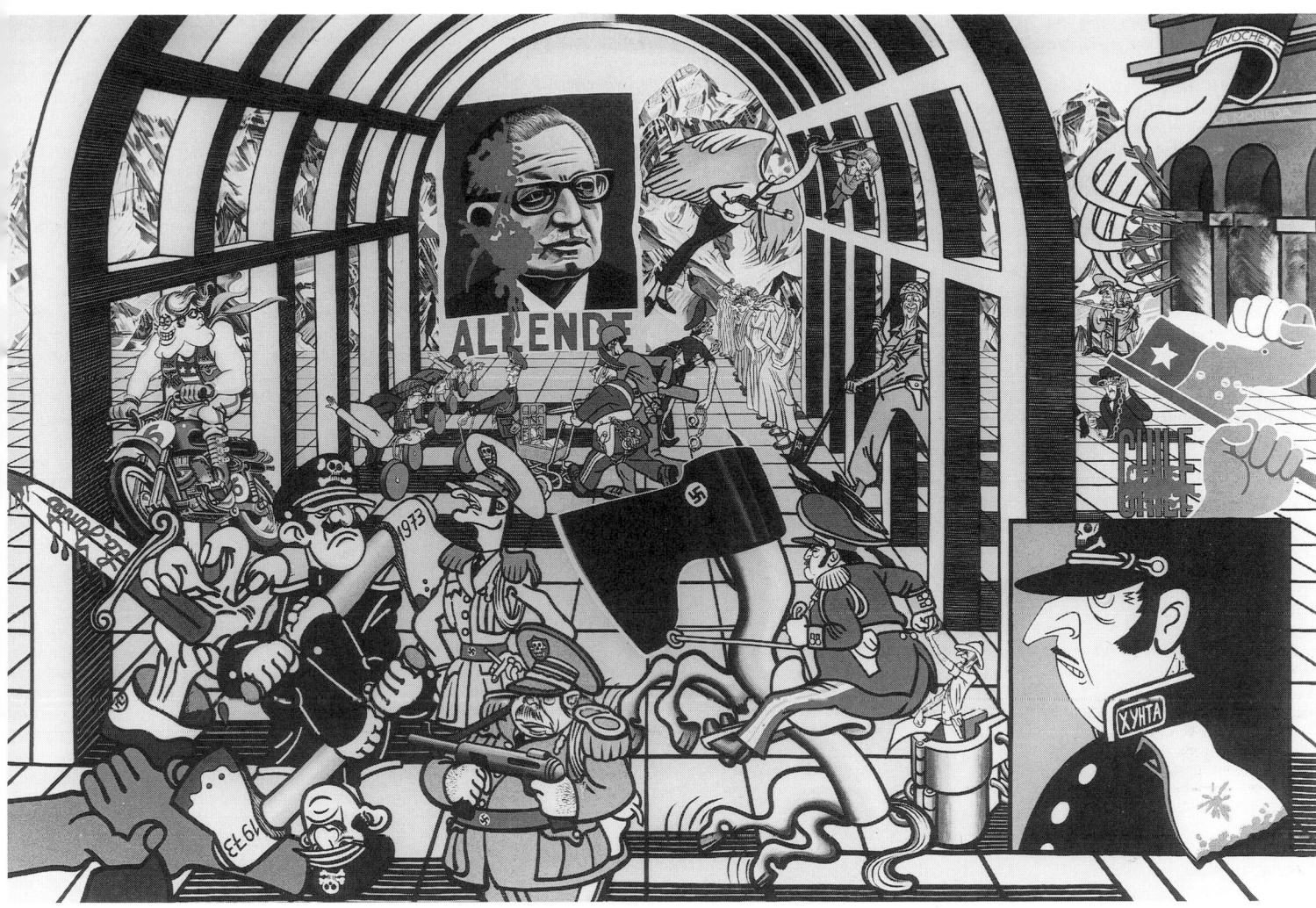

Errò: *Allende*, 1975

Piscine Municipale, Le Pré Saint-Gervais, France
Galerie Electrochoc 2, Caen, France
1984 Centre Culturel Gérard Philippe, Brétigny-sur-Orge,
    France
    Galerie Zannettaci, Geneva
    Centre Culturel Pablo Neruda, Corbeil-Essonnes,
    France
    Espace des Cordeliers, Châteauroux, France
    Galerie d'Art Contemporain, Tours, France
    Galerie Poll, West Berlin (with Arroyo and Monory)
    Miroir d'Encre, Brussels
1985 Galerie Loft, Paris
    Galerie Gilbert Brownstone, Paris
    ARC/Musée d'Art Moderne de la Ville, Paris
    Musée du Dôle, France
    Centre d'Art Contemporain, Montbeliard, France
    Stadtmuseum, Rattingen, West Germany
    Centre d'Art Contemporain, Annecy, France
1986 Norreina Husid, Reykjavik
    Maison de la Culture, Le Havre, France
    Maison de la Culture, Bourges, France
    Galerie Municipale, Saint-Priest, France
    Château de Belfort, France
    Abbaye de Montmajour, Arles, France

Selected Group Exhibitions:

1963 *Biennale*, Musée d'Art Moderne, Paris
1964 *Biennale*, Museum of Modern Art, Tokyo
1966 *L'Art Fantastique Contemporain*, Musée d'Antibes,
    France
1967 *Le Monde en Question*, Musée d'Art Moderne, Paris
1968 *Surrealismus in Europa*, Galerie Baukunst, Cologne
1969 *Kunst und Politik*, Kunstverein, Karlsruhe
1975 *Biennale*, Venice
1980 *Science au Futur*, Palais Rameau, Lille, France

1982 *Printed Art Since 1965*, Museum of Modern Art,
    New York
1985 *Figuration Narrative 1960–80*, Galerie des Arènes,
    Nîmes, France

Collections:

Moderna Museet, Stockholm; National Museum, Jerusalem;
Temperas Museum, Tel Aviv; Museum de la Révolution, Al-
giers; National Museum, Reykjavik; Nationalgalerie, West
Berlin; Musée National d'Art Moderne/Centre Georges Pom-
pidou, Paris; Hara Museum, Tokyo; National Air and Space
Museum, Washington, D.C.; Museum of Modern Art, New
York.

Publications:

By ERRÒ: books—*Mecanifest*, Venice 1962; *Macanfest 2*,
Venice 1963; films—*Mecamorphoses*, with Eric Duvivier,
1962; *Grimaces*, 1964; *Stars*, 1966.

On ERRÒ: books—*Errò* by Gilbert Brownstone, Paris 1972;
Errò, exhibition catalogue, with text by Udo Kultermann,
Munich 1973; *Errò: Tableaux Chinois*, exhibition catalogue,
with text by Jean-Christophe Ammann, Lucerne 1975; *Errò.
Catalogue General*, Milan and Paris 1976; *Errò* by Pierre
Tilman, Paris 1976; *Errò* by B. Asgeirsson and M. Johannes-
son, Reykjavik 1978; *Errò* by Philippe Sergent, Paris 1979;
Errò by Jehiro Hairu, Tokyo 1979; *Errò*, exhibition cata-
logue, with text by Jean-Christophe Ammann, Zurich; *Errò*,
exhibition catalogue, by Marianne Nanne-Brahammar and
Jacques Adelin Brutaru, Lund, Sweden 1981; *Errò* by Xavier
Moreau, New York and Paris 1983; *Errò, 1974–1986: Cata-
logue General II*, Paris 1986.

Working material can be anything from any place. A

good combine happens often by materials from far-
away distances. Like the combine for the "American
Interieurs" was found partly in Havana and the other
part in New York, three years later. The material is
classified after subjects, like rivers, hands, bodies,
comics. There are about 80 different subjects. While
working, composing and looking for a special subject
I often fall on a completely different image which has
more meaning and stronger contrast or the contrary.
Nothing is too difficult to paint, and I never avoid a
subject because it is too much work or hard to paint.
                                  —Errò

Errò paints with a demoniacal frenzy and intensity, as
if the world were being held in suspense. His output
comprises several thousand pictures and collages
mostly in large format. "Holding the world in suspense" is no chance metaphor. In the process of producing and reproducing societies of all degrees of
latitude through picture worlds, in the rhythm of the
productive imagination of his own pictures, his work
has the significance of a crucible.

Like no other painter Errò has traversed the "World
of Painting" within an incomparable campaign of
conquest, seemingly effortlessly, because he assigns
to these picture worlds of his no deeper significance.
They form a closed system, regenerate and fertilize
themselves according to an intrinsic dynamic, and
what they contain by way of allusions to reality stands
in an inverse relationship to what they express. To put
it even more strongly, Errò must have clearly recognized that the statements of a code of painting inherent in mass culture primarily state nothing but
themselves, and are formulated only on the plane of
the portrayal of specific objects, whilst reference to
reality is of general banal character.

So it is not surprising that the most capricious things come together in a purely associative undertaking. Errò does not explain things. And yet he unmasks stereotyped *Leitbilder* with stalwart pleasure; but not according to a "didactic" method, rather through the spontaneous blending of insignificant features which demonstrate all the more the characteristic nature of the image and of its effect.

Thus at first sight one is often inclined to consider Errò's paintings to be as stupid as the material upon which they are based. Often it is not easy to separate oneself from the individual factors of the content and look at them in their connection as standpoint and painting of Errò's. Already the circumstance that Errò makes a point of maintaining neutrality towards his material, that he manipulates it in accordance with is own laws, and reduces it ad absurdum, makes his pictures lose sight of their original aim. For the criterion of kind of picture and the way it is painted is not decisive. Errò paints just as well as the copy—always a collage—demands; with highest precision and differentiated tonalities or just summarily with coarse textures, Errò's art lies in the intuitive grasp of the possibilities lying dormant in the material itself, possibilities of a contentual, formal or syntactic nature; he makes the most of it, and places it without protection, utilizes it constantly at the same time to tell its own story (and this impetus knows no bounds). Not that he sets it up vicariously; he trains his protagonists, whether human or animal, for a game of life and death, fetches out of the reserve bank whatever he needs and finally drives the whole pack into the cockpit when he has finished a picture-series.

—Jean-Christophe Ammann

ESTES, Richard.

American. Born in Keewane, Illinois in 1932. Studied at the Art Institute of Chicago, 1952–56. Lived in Evanston, Illinois, and worked as illustrator for publishing and advertising layout work; moved to New York, 1959; lived and painted in Spain, 1962; full-time painter from 1966; now lives and works in New York and Maine. Recipient: National Council of the Arts Fellowship 1971. Agent: Allan Stone Gallery, 48 East 86th Street, New York, New York 10028. Address: 300 Central Park West, New York, New York 10028, U.S.A.

Individual Exhibitions:

1968	Allan Stone Gallery, New York
	Hudson River Museum, Yonkers, New York
1969	Allan Stone Gallery, New York
1970	Allan Stone Gallery, New York
1972	Allan Stone Gallery, New York
1974	Allan Stone Gallery, New York
	3 Realists: Close, Estes, Rafael, Worcester Art Museum, Massachussets
	Museum of Contemporary Art, Chicago
1978	Museum of Fine Arts, Boston
	Museum of Contemporary Art, Chicago
1978	Museum of Fine Arts, Boston
	Museum of Art, Toledo, Ohio
	Nelson Gallery-Atkins Museum, Kansas City, Missouri
1979	Hirshhorn Museum, Smithsonian Institution, Washington, D.C.
1983	Museum of Fine Arts, Boston
	Allan Stone Gallery, New York

Selected Group Exhibitions:

1973	*Stuart M. Speiser Collection of Photo Realism*, Meisel Gallery, New York (toured the United States)
1975	*Trends in Contemporary American Realist Painting*, Museum of Fine Arts, Boston
1976	*America 1976*, Corcoran Gallery, Washington, D.C. (toured the United States)
	America as Art, National Collection of Fine Arts, Smithsonian Institution, Washington, D.C.
	A Selection of American Art: The Skowhegan School 1946–1979, Institute of Contemporary Art, Boston (travelled to Colby College Museum, Waterville, Maine)
	Alumni Exhibition, School or the Art Institute of Chicago
	American Master Drawings and Watercolors, Whitney Museum, New York
	New Acquisitions Exhibitions, Museum of Modern Art, New York
1977	*Biennial*, Whitney Museum, New York

Collections:

Metropolitan Museum of Art, New York; Whitney Museum, New York; Museum of Modern Art, New York; Hirshhorn Museum and Sculpture Garden, Smithsonian Institution, Washington, D.C.; Art Institute of Chicago; Des Moines Art Center, Iowa; William Rockhill Nelson Gallery of Art-Atkins Museum of Fine Art, Kansas City, Missouri; Toledo Museum of Art, Ohio; Centre Georges Pompidou, Paris; Kaiser Wilhelm Museum, Krefeld, West Germany.

Publications:

By ESTES: book—*Urban Landscape*, portfolio, New York 1971; articles—interview in "The Photo-Realists: 12 Interviews" in *Art in America* (New York), November/December 1972; "The Real Estes," interview, with Herbert Raymond, in *Art and Artists* (London), August 1974.

On ESTES: articles—"Rent is the Only Reality: or, the Hotel Instead of the Hymns" by Ivan Karp in *Arts Magazine* (New York), December 1971/January 1972; "The Real Thing" by Gerrit Henry in *Art International* (Lugano, Switzerland) Summer 1972; "A Critic's Valedictory: The Americanization of Modern Art and Other Upheavals" by John Canady in the *New York Times*, 8 August 1972; "Pop-Art Inspired Objective Realism" by Mary Lou Kelley in *Christian Science Monitor* (Boston), 1 April 1974; "An Unnatural Silence" by John Russell in the *New York Times*, 25 May 1974; "Treacle and Trash" by Barbara Rose in *New York Magazine*, 27 May 1974; "Estes" by Chris Hemphill in *Andy Warhol's Interview* (New York), October 1974; "The Neutral Style" by Edward Lucie-Smith in *Art and Artists* (London), August 1975; "Photo-Realism: Post Modernist Illusionism" by Linda Chase in *Art International* (Lugano Switzerland), March/April 1976; "Realism Rules: O.K.?" by Edward Lucie-Smith in *Art and Artists* (London), September 1976.

Superficially Richard Estes is seen as one of the new American hyper-or photo-realists and, indeed, his imagery does parallel that of members of that movement. But, as is true for one or two other new realists, his is a far more painterly approach than that of the majority of artists so labelled. (The danger of just such labels is once again made evident). One has only to look closely at a work by Estes to see how richly painted it is. The pigment is applied with considerable painterly elan, with virtuoso handling of the brush here and there—as seductive as touches in a Guardi or Vermeer. Just because Estes refers to photographs for pictorial information doesn't preclude his profound interest in composition, drawing, color and form.

This interest in picture-making has caused him to edit a great deal. In no way is he a slave to the images captured by his camera. He applies geometry to his compositions. And balances out his complex subjects through careful counterpointing of forms, color, tonality and line. He does a nice bit of spatial footwork as well—in and out, up and down—on the canvas plane. The movement is so overall that the pictures appear harmonious, even quiet, without remaining static or in any way inert. Estes deals with perspective, but plays around with it. Like one of Cézanne's typical tables with the edge starting at one place and coming out from behind a vase or pile of fruit at another, a street is shifted as it recedes making the viewer aware of space beyond whatever it is that comes between it and his perception of it. Estes' use

Richard Estes: *Cafeteria*, 1970

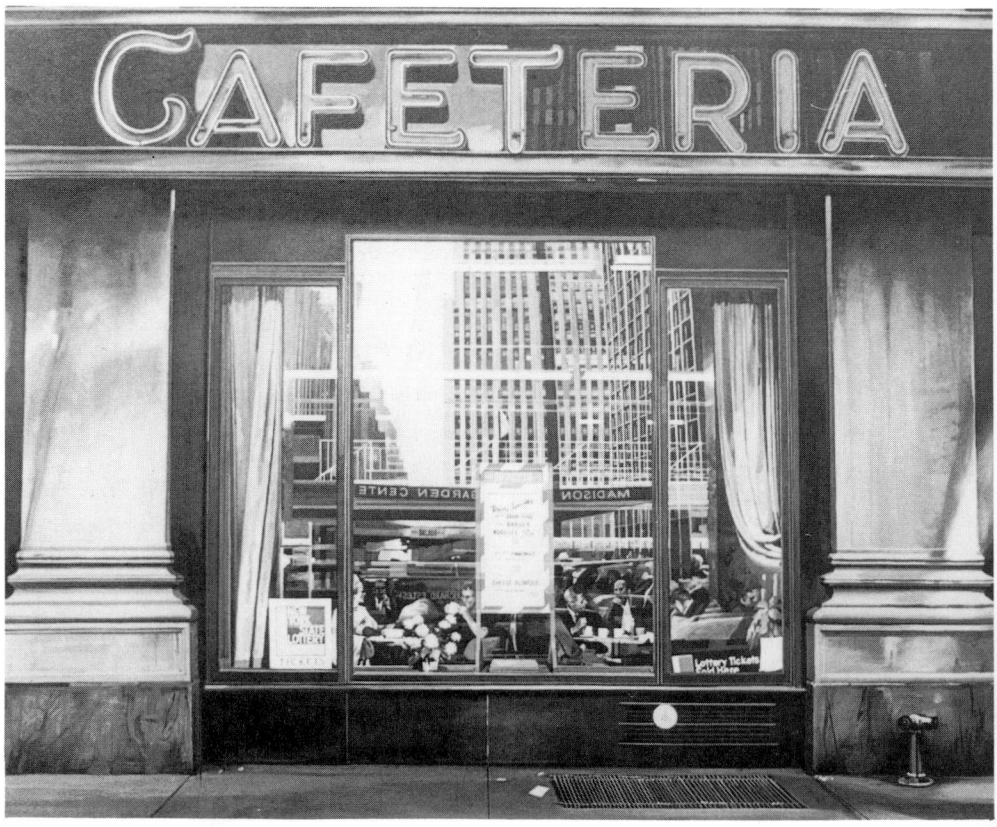

of reflections accomplishes much the same thing: in one of his front-on store windows we become aware of what is *behind* us, outside of the painting altogether, through the multiple imagery recorded in the glass. In a painting where the store window is viewed from the side, we are given visual information about what's on the other side of the street. In a way it is all like three-dimensional tic-tac-toe.

Estes' interest in and use of buildings is akin to that of Sheeler and O'Keeffe in the 30's. Buildings are, after all, already abstract in their forms as are many man-made objects. Thus does a "new realist" redefine our ideas about the process of abstracting.

—Ralph Pomeroy

ESTÈVE, Maurice.

French. Born in Culan, Chor, 2 May 1904. Educated in Paris, 1913–22; mainly self-taught in art, but attended free classes at Académie Colarossi, Paris, 1924. Served in the French Army, 1939–40. Worked as fabric designer in a textile factory in Barcelona, 1923; independent painter, Paris, from 1924. Address: c/o Louis Carré, 10 avenue de Messine, 75008 Paris, France.

Individual Exhibitions:

1942	Galerie Berri-Raspail, Paris
1945	Galerie Louis Carré, Paris (with Jean Bazaine and Charles Lapique)
1946	Stedelijk Museum, Amsterdam
1947	Statens Museum for Konst, Copenhagen
	Foreningen for Nutida Konst, Stockholm
1948	Galerie Louis Carré, Paris
1954	Galerie Dupont, Lille, France
1955	Galerie Villand-Galanis, Paris
1956	Galerie Villand-Galanis, Paris
	Statens Museum for Konst, Copenhagen (retrospective)
	Svensk-Franska Konstgalleriet, Stockholm
1957	Galerie Dupont, Lille, France
	Galerie Benador, Geneva
1958	*Aquarelles Récentes*, Galerie Villand-Galanis, Paris
1960	Galerie Villand-Galanis, Paris
	Galerie Benador, Geneva
1961	*Peintures Récentes*, Galerie Villand-Galanis, Paris
	Kunsthalle, Basle (travelled to the Kunstverein, Dusseldorf; Statens Museum for Konst, Copenhagen and the Kunstnernes Hus, Oslo)
1963	*Aquarelles*, Galerie Villand-Galanis, Paris
	Dom Galerie, Cologne
1965	Galerie Louis Carré, Paris
1969	Neue Galerie, Zurich
1973	*Aquarelles*, Neue Galerie Dr. Peter Nathan, Zurich
	Galerie Claude Bernard, Paris
1974	Galerie Claude Bernard, Paris
1977	*Peintures Récentes*, Galerie Claude Bernard, Paris
1982	Galerie Nathan, Zurich
1984	Fundacion Joan Miro, Barcelona

Selected Group Exhibitions:

1930	*Salon des Surindépendants*, Paris (and annually, to 1938)
1942	*Desnoyer/Esteve/Latapie/Touault/Villon*, Galerie St. Germain-des-Près, Paris
1943	*5 Peintres d'Aujourd hui*, Galerie de France, Paris
1952	*Tendances Actuelles de l'Ecole de Paris*, Kunsthalle, Berne
1953	*11 Painters from Paris in Holland*, Stedelijk Museum, Amsterdam
1954	*Biennale*, Venice
1959	*French Painting from Gauguin to the Present*, Narodni Galerie, Warsaw
1962	*Henie-Onstad Collection*, Tate Gallery, London

1965	*Peinture Francaise Contemporaine*, Museo de Arte Moderno, Rio de Janeiro (travelled to Museo Nacional de Bellas Artes, Buenos Aires; Museo Nacional de Bellas Artes Montevideo; and the Museo de Arte, Lima)
1974	*Eroffnungsausstellung*, Galerie Nathan, Zurich

Collections:

Centre Georges Pompidou, Paris; Kunsthalle, Basle.

Publications:

On ESTÈVE: books—*Estève: Aquarelles Récentes*, exhibition catalogue, with poem by André Frénaud, Paris 1958; *Estève: Peintures Récentes*, exhibition catalogue, with text by Jean-Paul Raus, Paris 1961; *Maurice Estève*, exhibition catalogue, with text by Alf-Jorgen Aas and Reidar Revold, Oslo 1961; *Maurice Estève*, exhibition catalogue, with text by Arnold Rudlinger and Joseph-Emile Müller, Basle 1961; *Estève: Aquarelles*, exhibition catalogue, with text by Georges Borgeaud, Paris 1963; *Estèves: Aquarelle*, exhibition catalogue, with an introduction by Dora Vallier, Zurich 1973; *Estève: Collages 1965–1973* by Jean Leymarie, Paris 1974; *Estève: Collagen*, with text by Pierre Francastel, Zurich 1969; *Estève: Peintures Récentes*, exhibition catalogue, with text by Pierre Volboudt, Paris 1977; *Estève*, exhibition catalogue, with foreword by Jean Leymarie, Zurich 1982; *Maurice Estève*, exhibition catalogue with text by Jacques Queralt, Barcelona 1984.

Like Lapique, Le Moal and Lanskoy, Maurice Estève started from a mode of poetic Naturalism which strove to expand the tradition of Cubism by enriching the harmony of colour and intensifying the expressive power of form. The figure compositions, interiors and still-lifes which were his principal subjects during the 1930's laid the essential foundations for the Tachist abstractions of his later years. "La Partie de Cartes" and "Canapé blue," both painted in 1935, reveal his interest in the formal innovations of Cézanne, while his "Cantate de Bach," painted three years later, shows his preoccupation with the post-Cubist work of Picasso and Braque in its affinity particularly with Braque's "Duo" painted in 1937. The work done in collaboration with Robert Delaunay on decorations for the Air and Railway pavilions at the *Exposition Universelle* of 1937 is particularly important as manifesting the vivid decorative talent which never abandoned his work. His colour was always bold and vital without lacking in subtlety. These various trends matured into a richly personal style, somewhat akin to that of Edouard Pignon, which anticipated his transition into abstraction. An excellent example of this style is the painting "Jeune Fille au Pichet" of 1942.

In his abstract work Estève belonged to the group of artists who, following the precepts of Roger Bissière, took their inspiration from the visual world but, like Jean Bazaine, attempted to render the expressive and structural qualities of their subjects without having recourse to natural appearances. His Tachist paintings are remarkable for the breadth and boldness of their contoured lines and for their play of vividly contrasting colours, as in the painting "Haut-Berry," 1953. The vitality of movement and vigour of contrast in the subtle disposition of his interlaced semi-geometrical forms may be seen to advantage in "Intérieur de Juillet" 1950 and "Danseuse du Far West," 1951.

—Harold Osborne

EVERGOOD, Philip.

American. Born in New York, 26 October 1901; moved with his mother to England, 1909. Educated at primary schools in New York and at various English boarding schools, including Eton; studied piano from an early age; studied French and mathematics in Belgium; student at Trinity Hall, Cambridge, for one year; studied drawing, under Henry Tonks, and sculpture, under Harvard Thomas, Slade School of Fine Art, London, 1921–23; studied drawing, under William von Schlegell and George Lukas, Art Students League, New York, 1923; attended evening sketching classes at the Education Alliance School, New York, 1923; studied etching, with Philip Reisman and Harry Sternberg, New York, 1923; also studied briefly with Jean-Paul Laurens at the Académie Julian and with André Lhote, Paris, 1924, and spent six months at the British Academy, Rome, 1925; studied engraving with Stanley William Hayter, 1930. Married the painter Julia Cross in 1931. Returned to the United States and settled in New York, 1926; worked with his wife at the Amelia White Gallery of American Indian Art, New York, 1931; worked for the Federal Art Project of the Works Progress Administration, 1935–38, in the Mural Section, 1936, and as Managing Supervisor of the Easel Division, 1938; Member, Midtown Gallery Group, New York, 1935; moved to Woodside, New York, 1936; spent four months in hospital after cancer diagnosed, 1941; appointed an official artist to make pictorial record of the war; worked at the Midtown Frame Shop, New York, 1943; settled in Patchogue, New York, 1946; moved to Southbург, Connecticut, 1952, then to Bridgwater, Connecticut, 1963. Lecturer, American Artists School, New York, 1936–37; Resident Artist, Kalamazoo College, Michigan, 1940–42; Part-time Lecturer, Muhlenberg College, Allentown, Pennsylvania, 1942–43; Lecturer, Contemporary School of Art, Brooklyn, New York, and Jefferson School, New York, 1946. President, Artists Union and United American Artists; Founder Member, Artists Equity Association. Recipient: M. V. Kohnstamm Prize, Art Institute of Chicago, 1935; Carnegie Corporation Grant, 1941; William H. Tuthill Prize, Art Institute of Chicago, 1946; Alexander Shilling Purchase Award, 1946; American Prize, Hallmark Art Awards, 1949; Carol H. Beck Gold Medal, Pennsylvania Academy of Fine Arts, 1949; Baltimore Museum of Art Prize, 1955; Painting Grant, American Academy of Arts and Letters, 1956; Benjamin Altman Prize, National Academy of Design, 1971, Member, National Institute of Arts and Letters, *Died* (in Bridgwater, Connecticut) *11 March 1973*.

Individual Exhibitions:

1927	Dudensing Gallery, New York
1929	Montross Gallery, New York
1932	Balzac Galleries, New York
1933	Montross Gallery, New York
1935	Hollins College, Virginia
	Montross Gallery, New York
1936	Denver Art Museum
1937	Atheneum Gallery, Melbourne (with his father Miles Evergood)
1938	ACA Gallery, New York
1940	ACA Gallery, New York
	Kalamazoo Institute of Arts, Michigan
1941	McDonald Gallery, New York
1942	ACA Gallery, New York
1943	Lehigh University, Pennsylvania
1944	ACA Gallery, New York
1946	ACA Gallery, New York
1948	ACA Gallery, New York
	Norlyst Gallery, New York
1951	ACA Gallery, New York
1953	ACA Gallery, New York
	Kansas State Teachers College, Kansas City
	University of Louisville, Kentucky
	Garelick's Gallery, Detroit
1955	ACA Gallery, New York
	Garelick's Gallery, Detroit
	University of Minnesota, Duluth
1957	Newcomb Art School Galleries, Tulane University, New Orleans

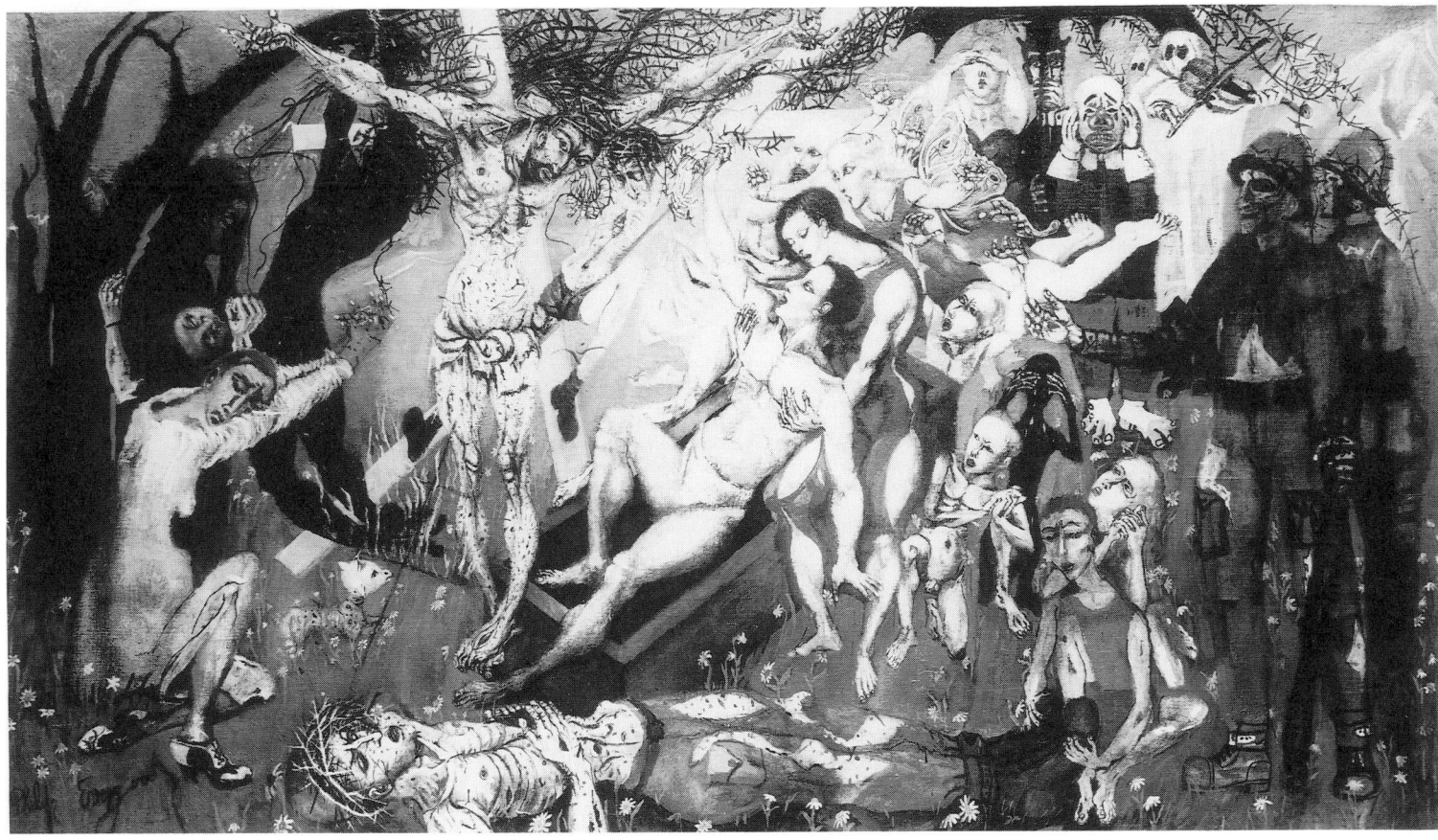

Philip Evergood: *The New Lazarus,* **1927–54** Courtesy Whitney Museum, New York

1960 ACA Gallery, New York
     Wadsworth Atheneum, Hartford, Connecticut (with
       Doris Caesar)
     Whitney Museum, New York
1961 ACA Gallery, New York
     Terry Dintenfass Gallery, New York
1962 ACA Gallery, New York
     Terry Dintenfass Gallery, New York
     Ross Talalay Gallery, New Haven, Connecticut
1963 Galleria 63, Rome
1964 Gallery 63, New York
1967 Hammer Galleries, New York
1969 Gallery of Modern Art, New York
1971 Kennedy Galleries, New York
1978 Hirshhorn Museum, Washington, D.C.

Selected Group Exhibitions:

1925 *Salon d'Automne,* Paris
1943 *Biennale,* Whitney Museum, New York
1951 *Revolution and Tradition,* Brooklyn Museum, New
     York
1974 *American Master Prints,* Associated American Art-
     ists Galleries, New York

Collections:

Metropolitan Museum of Art, New York; Whitney Museum,
New York; Museum of Modern Art, New York; National
Gallery of Victoria, Melbourne.

Publications:

By EVERGOOD: articles—foreword to *Remo Farruggio,* exhibition catalogue, New York 1935; reply to a questionnaire
sent to artists of the Mural Section of the Federal Art Project,
reprinted in *Art Front* (New York), February 1937; "Building
a New Art School" in *Art Front* (New York), April 1937;
response to editorial comments by Peyton Boswell in *Art Digest* (New york), March 1938; foreword to *Gillen/Kallen/
Neuwirth/Shulman,* exhibition catalogue, New York 1938;

"Should the Nation Support Its Art?" in *Direction* (New
York), April 1938; "Sure, I'm a Social Painter" in *Magazine
of Art* (New York), November 1943; "William Gropper" in
New Masses (New York), February 1944; "My Vote—and
Why!" in *New Masses* (New York), October 1944; "Social
Art: Its Background" in *American Contemporary Art,* New
York 1944; "Social Surrealism" in *New Masses* (New York),
February 1945; "The Albrights" in *New Masses* (New York),
November 1945; statement in *20 Years: Evergood* by Oliver
Larkin, New York 1946; "Evergood in Defense of Ever-
good" in *Art Digest* (New York), January 1950; "The Artist
and the Museum" in *Report of the Third Woodstock Art Con-
ference,* New York 1951; "Art in Our Time" in *The Educa-
tional Leader* (Kansas City), July 1954; statement in *Philip
Evergood,* exhibition catalogue, New York 1962; "Realism
or Representationalism Will Never Be Outmoded" and "The
Finished Product Should be Invigorating" in *Painters on
Painting,* edited by Eric Protter, New York 1963.

On EVERGOOD: books—*20 Years: Evergood* by Oliver
Larkin, New York 1946; *Revolution and Tradition in Modern
American Art* by John I. H. Baur, Cambridge, Massachusetts
1951; *Art and Life in America* by Oliver Larkin, New York
1960; *Philip Evergood* by John I. H. Baur, New York 1960,
1975; *American Art of Our Century* by Lloyd Goodrich and
John I. H. Baur, New York 1961; *The Graphic Work of Philip
Evergood* by Lucy Lippard, New York 1966; *Philip Evergood*
by Alfredo Valente, New York 1969; *The Indignant Eye* by
Ralph E. Shikes, Boston 1969; *Philip Evergood,* exhibition
catalogue with text by Kendall Taylor, Washington, D.C.
1978.

There is a strange, pungent, sometimes even diaboli-
cal, satirical wit which pervades in Philip Evergood's
pictures, beginning during the late 1920's and continuing until his death in 1973. Evergood always starts
with his personal experiences of people and events
which are quite everyday on the surface, and twists
them into fantastic visions which portray the physical
and psychological conditions of his subjects on a level
which is more symbolic than simply typical. In his
combination of the ordinary and the fantastic, Evergood is allied with the American Magic Realists of
the 1930's. Unlike those among the group who
painted in a vein connected with the slick preci-

sionism of illusionistic surrealism, however, Evergood's work is more closely related to that of the
expressionists and social realists of central Europe
whose sinuous line and skillfully awkward distortions
and exaggerations describes his preferred means.

During the decade of the 1930's, in the years of the
Great Depression, Evergood created many of his
most potent commentaries on the social conditions of
the oppressed poor, on the artist's role (too often separated from the realities around him), and on the regular individual's psycho-social states. Although
Evergood always painted each of these three types of
themes rather simultaneously throughout his career,
the social and personal violence and perversity which
dominated during the depression and war years inspired his most memorable compositions of that period. In the small, intimate composition called
"Don't Cry Mother" (1938–44), Evergood creates a
sense of heightened drama by his use of simple triangular elements and distortion of both figure and
starkly empty environment. Among his more elaborate and crowded scenes is "American Tragedy"
(1937), which uses complexity of composition to convey the more outwardly social violence of this theme
which depicts a group of workers attacked by police.
In the foreground is a horizontal pile-up of humanity
engaged in bloody turmoil, while the background is
rather schematized cityscape. This combination of
closely-packed, shallow space and distanced, generalized setting lends a symbolic aspect to the work that
lifts it out of the realm of the merely specific incident. Whether they are simple portrayals of an individual figure or complicated compositions of large
groupings, all of Evergood's pictures are informed by
a firm knowledge of structure and form, well learned
in his early rigorous training. Perhaps it is in his pictures of a more intimate nature that Evergood shows
his greatest abilities to convey a weird blend of humor
and grotesqueness that is both tough and delicate, and
certainly a painting such as "Lily and the Sparrows"
(1939) shows him doing just this at his best. The facial expression on the little girl who is reaching out a
window to feed some sparrows is a fusion of youthful

innocence, adult debauchery and ancient widsom. To find this expression, Evergood painted about 50 layers, subsequently scraping off many of them to reveal such a striking result.

Children take on strangely fantastic characters in all of Evergood's oeuvre. In one of his many portrayals of myth made contemporary, "Flight of Fancy" (1947), Evergood places a pitifully skinny little child on the back of a flamingo whose abnormally expansive wingspread helps him carry the child over a dreamy scape of generalized castles and cathedral/oil rig towers, in a scene which hints both at the Arabian Nights and The American Dream.

Evergood was particularly insightful in his coverage of women who span characteristics of the most vulgar to the most loving qualities. The plights and the vagaries of mothers from various social levels are recurrent themes, as are also the voluptuously full-figured nudes who are the artist's models and odalisques in compositions such as "The Jester" (1950) and "Portrait of an Artist As a Young Man" (1936, 48, 51) which portray the sometimes self-centered positions of the artist who is too much in his studio and too little sees the outside world.

Whether he was painting the most intimate views or the more socially oriented complexities of his expereiences, Evergood always used his considerable painter's skills with line, color and structure to transform particulars into visions of a much broader scope. Perhaps that is why so many of his pictures, even those from almost fifty years ago, still speak to us with sustained vigor and effect.

—Barbara Cavaliere

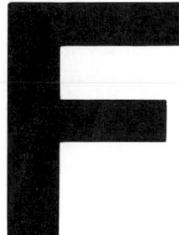

FABRO, Luciano.
Italian. Born in Turin, 20 November 1936. Lives and works in Milan. Dealer: Arte Borgogna, via Borgogna 7, Milan. Address: via della Pila 5, 20122 Milan, Italy.

Individual Exhibitions:

1965	Vismara Arte Contemporanea, Milan
1967	Galleria Notizie, Turin
	Teatro Stabile, Turin
1968	Qui Arte Contemporanea, Rome (with Jannis Kounellis and Giulio Paolini)
1969	Galleria Notizie, Turin
	Galleria La Salita, Rome
	Galleria Toselli, Milan
	Galleria de Nieubourg, Milan
1970	Aktionstraum I, Munich
1971	Galleria Il Leone, Venice
	Arte Borgogna, Milan
	Galleria Notizie, Turin
1973	Arte Borgogna, Milan
	Galleria Sperone Fischer, Rome
	Modern Art Agency, Lucio Amelio, Naples
	Salle Patino, Geneva
1974	Galleria Notizie, Turin
1975	Galleria Christian Stein, Turin
	Galleria Pieroni, Pescara, Italy
	Galleria Area, Florence
1976	Galleria del Cortile, Rome
1977	Framart Studio, Naples
1978	Galleria Il Collezionista, Rome
	Galerie Paul Maenz, Cologne
1979	Galleria Mario Pieroni, Rome
1980	Galleria Christian Stein, Turin
	Padiglione d'Art Contemporanea, Milan
	Salvatore Ala Gallery, New York
1981	Museum Folkwang, Essen West Germany (travelled to the Museum Boymans-van-Beuningen, Rotterdam)
	Galleria Mario Pieroni, Rome
1986	Galleria Christian Stein, Milan
1988	Galleria Christian Stein, Turin

Selected Group Exhibitions:

1965	*Group Exhibition*, Galleria Montenapoleane, Milan
1967	*Italian Contemporary Art*, Museum of Modern Art, Tokyo
1968	*Cento Opere d'Arte Italiana del Futurismo ad Ogge*, Galleria Nazionale d'Arte Moderna, Rome
1971	*New Italian Art 1953-1971*, Walker Art Gallery, Liverpool
1972	*Documenta*, Kassel, West Germany
1975	*Bienal*, Sao Paulo
1979	*100 Anni d'Arte Italiana*, Museum of Art, Osaka, Japan
1980	*Kunst in Europa na '68*, Centrum voor Kunst en Cultuur, Ghent
1981	*Art Italien 1960-1980*, Centre Georges Pompidou, Paris
1985	*The European Iceberg*, Art Gallery of Ontario, Toronto

Collections:

Galleria Nazionale d'Arte Moderna, Rome; Galleria d'Arte Moderna, Turin.

Publications:

By FABRO: books—*Letture Parallele*, Milan 1973; *Letture Parallele II*, Geneva 1974; *Attaccapanni*, edited by A. Izzo, Naples 1977; *Attaccapanni*, Turin 1978; *Regole d'Arte*, Milan 1980: articles—"Vorrei far rilevare" in *Lucio Fabro*, exhibition catalogue, Milan 1965; "Sto trattendo contemporaneamente" in *Documenta 5*, exhibition catalogue, Kassel, West Germany 1972; "Miracolo a Milano" with I. Nagasawa, F. Torrello and A. A. Trotta, in *Data* (Milan), Spring 1975; "Testi," with S. Vertone and J. de Sanna, in *Flash Art* (Milan), no. 72 / 73, 1977; "Lucio Fabro ad Antoine Laurent Lavoisier" in *La Citta di Riga II*, Pollenza, Italy 1977; "Intervista con Lucio Fabro" by L. L. Ponti in *Domus* (Milan), June 1977; "Tempo tendenze paura dell Arte: Intervista con Lucio Fabro" in *Domus* (Milan), no. 604, 1980.

On FABRO: books—*Il Problema della Nascita delle Idee* by S. Ceccato, Milan 1965; *Arte Povera* by Germano Celant, Milan 1969; *Precronistoria 1966-69* by Germano Celant, Florence 1976; *Lucio Fabro* by B. Risso, Turin 1980; *Lucio Fabro*, exhibition catalogue, Essen, West Germany 1981.

The first we heard of Luciano Fabro was in May 1965, when the artist showed his *"elaborati"* for the first time in Milan, accompanied by a poetry recital. The working climate of those days was in line with the teaching of Piero Manzoni or Yves Klein; the aim was to define the work of the artist as a purely imaginative process, leaving to the materials the ordinary role of tangible residue of the process itself. This radical attitude, the shifting of interest from the object to the subject of the operation, was continued through Manzoni's and Klein's different development of Concept Art.

Fabro is more a follower of Lucio Fontana, through that artist's determination to abstract nothing from the recognizable values that can be inferred from the physical shape, the material and the logical relation with the environment. Fabro works with things; all his work aims to establish a relationship between thought and that irreducible element that the thing, with its "encumbrances," opposes to it, according to a view opposite to that of, say, Malevich. The objects used by the artist are not the natural elements, his work does not shed light on the existential demand: nor does his interest in the object mean the reappearance of the ready-made, or a return to representative art. Fabro constructs object-emblems which he offers as logical propositions relating to the dynamic investigation of the environment, using a factual technique that visualizes the structure of the object itself ("Hole," "Round and Square," "Wheel"). The work constitutes the topos from which the logos originates (to use the artist's own terms), finding its proof in the effect made at the other pole, on the viewer.

Luciano Fabro: *L'Italia delle Regioni*, 1970

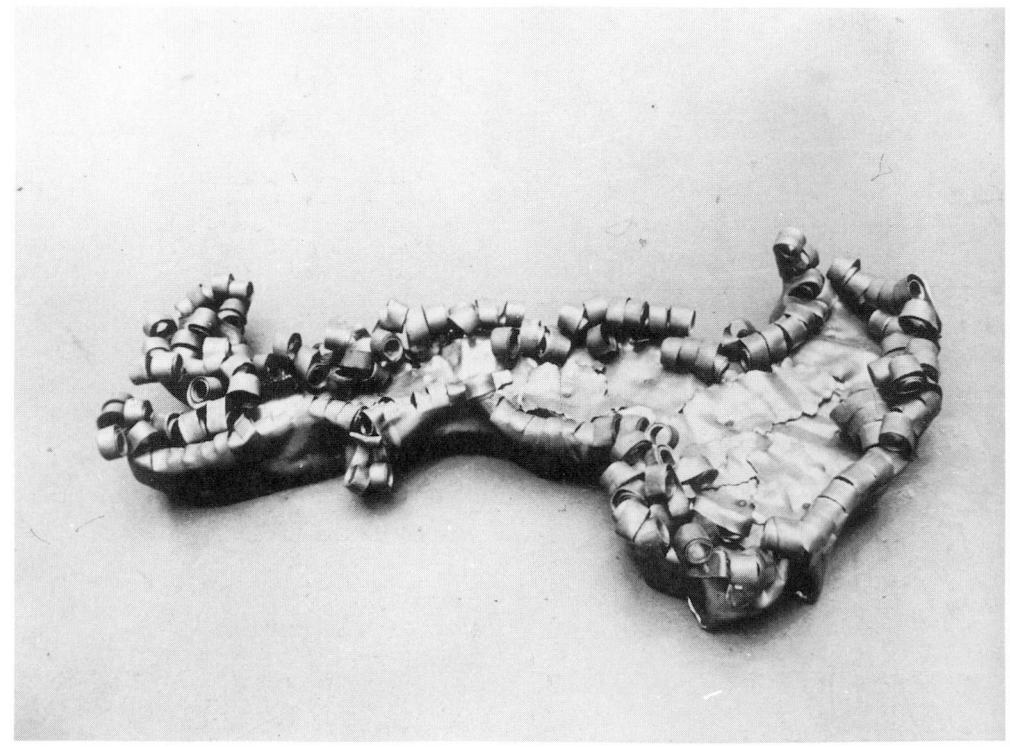

Fabro is a against ideologies; he is ready to criticize any component element in the organized teaching of art. The viewer is physically involved in bewildered sensory adventures (in "Cube," "Theatrical Production," 1966-1967) while the work emphasizes its inability to be reduced to "interpretation." The *tautologies* are outside the dialectic, propositions approaching the irony of paradox, inhibitions of the creative act, neutralized, ambiguous events generated by a thought that aims to induce criticism of the conventions. ("Contact," 1967; "Object with Device to Reduce Its Weight," "Sky," 1968 . . .).

A similar "debunking" intention animates the works that Fabro carried out after the tautologies. The opposite of the conventions of "elevated" culture are the banal ideas of familiar shapes, the non-scientific value of common sense elements that Fabro makes use of by "tripping them up," as he put it himself (see *Attacapanni*, Turin 1978). The discarding of logic is emphasized by a formal elaboration of the materials that sometimes approaches the limits of sumptuousness. Some of these works are intended as iconographic themes on which the artist insists by treating them as visual modules (the "Italies," 1968-1975) or which he works out starting from recognition of their symbolic functions ("Feet," 1971, "Iconographies," 1975). These works are devised in the light of a memory of the classics and the myths, of what can perhaps be defined as the ontological dimension of the artist's research.

In such works, be they single or serial pieces, the image recalls subtle and profound notions that form the base layers of the collective imagination. The materials employed often underline, through combination and form, the metaphorical function conferred on the work, as in *Io* and *Tu* (1978), *Il Guidizio di Paride* (1979), or *Cristo-Buddha-Zaratustra* (1981). Matter is analysed for its autonomous, signifying potential, and is therefore exhibited in its raw state; at the same time, it is dealt with as a matrix of form through which the image emerges as the sign of a harmonic order forged from primordial or natural chaos—as in *La Dialettica* (1985), *Efeso* (1986), or in the numerous *Italia* pieces.

In recent years, Fabro has produced installations which physically involve the spectator, as in the case of *Baldacchino* (1980), *Enfasi* (1982 and 1983), right up to the enigmatic *Proteo* (1986).

—Giorgio Verzotti

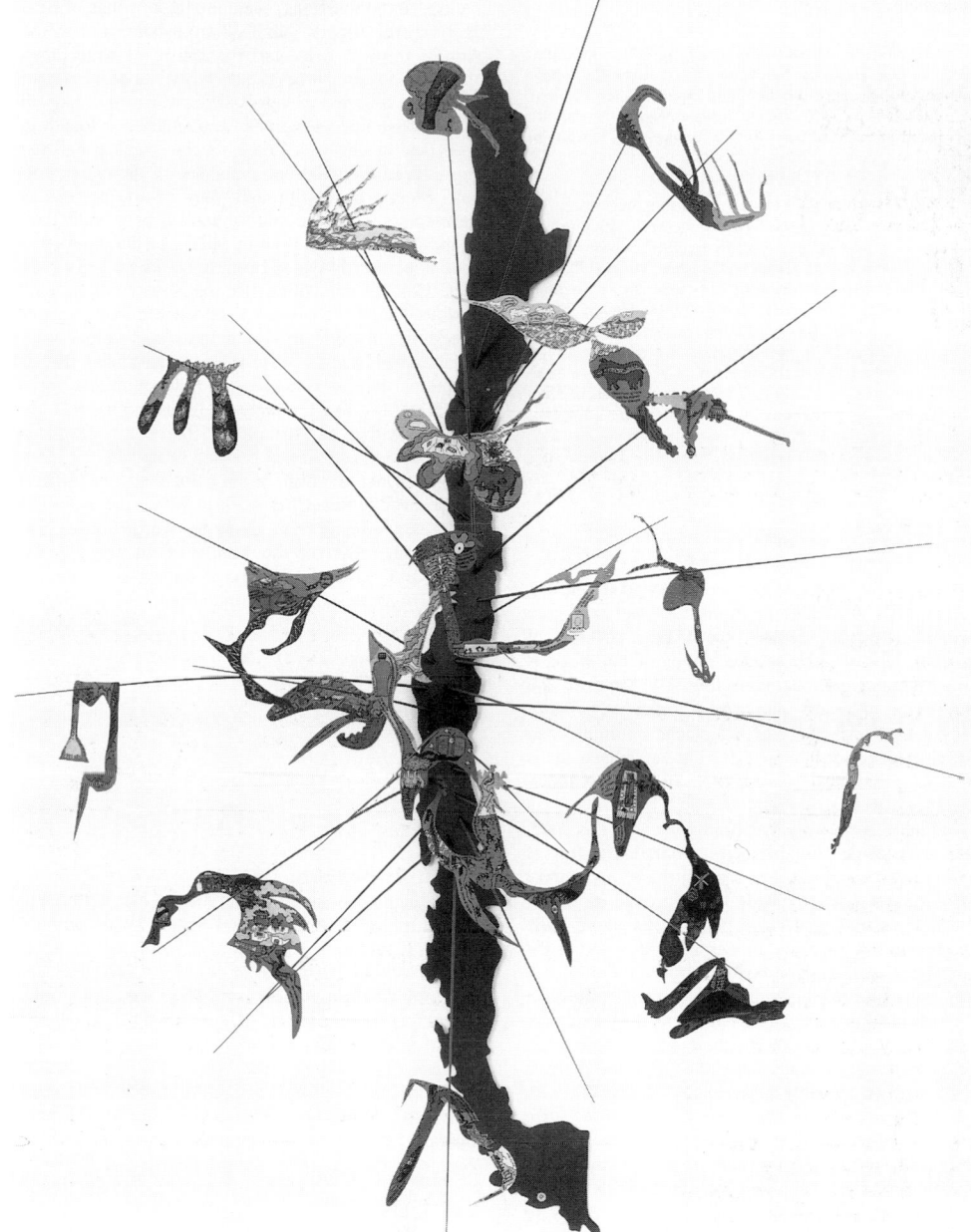

Oyvind Fahlstrom: *Chile II*, 1974

FAHLSTROM, Oyvind (Axel Christian).

Swedish. Born in Sao Paulo, Brazil, 28 December 1928; family returned to Sweden, 1939. Educated at the University of Stockholm, 1949-52; self taught in art. Married Birgitta Tamm in 1952 (divorced, 1958); married the artist Barbro Ostlihn in 1960 (divorced, 1976); married Sharon Avery in 1976. Theatre critic and journalist, Stockholm, 1950-55. Painter from 1954; spent time each year in Rome and Paris, 1952-60; co-signed *Concrete Poetry Manifesto*, Stockholm, 1953. Settled in New York; spent summers in Sweden and Italy, from 1961; first happenings and sound events, Stockholm and New York, 1962-66; first documentary films, 1966-69. Recipient: Painting Prize, *Bienal*, Sao Paulo, 1959; Western Art Prize, *Print Biennale*, Tokyo, 1974. *Died* (in New York) 8 November 1976.

Individual Exhibitions:

1952	Galleria Numero, Florence
1955	Galerie Aesthetica, Stockholm
1958	Galerie Daniel Cordier, Paris
1959	Galerie Blanche, Stockholm
1962	Galerie Daniel Cordier, Paris
1964	Cordier and Ekstrom Gallery, New York
	Moderna Museet, Stockholm
1966	*Biennale*, Venice
	26th Street Gallery, New York
1967	Sidney Janis Gallery, New York
1969	Sidney Janis Gallery, New York
	Galerie Zwirner, Cologne
1971	Sidney Janis Gallery, New York
1972	*Biennale*, Venice
1973	Sidney Janis Gallery, New York
	Moore College of Art, Philadelphia
	Foster Gallery, Eau Claire, Wisconsin
1974	Galerie Buchholz, Munich
	Galleria Multhipla, Milan
1975	*Le Belcanto de Fahlstrom*, Galerie Alexander Iolas, Paris
1976	Galleri Ahlner, Stockholm
	Sidney Janis Gallery, New York
	Moderna Museet, Stockholm (travelled to the Centre Georges Pompidou, Paris)
1982	Sidney Janis Gallery, New York
	Guggenheim Museum, New York

Selected Group Exhibitions:

1959	*Bienal*, Sao Paulo
1960	*Pittsburgh International*, Carnegie Institute, Pittsburgh
1952	*New Realists*, Sidney Janis Gallery, New York
1954	*Biennale*, Venice
1957	*Towards a Cold Poetic Image*, Galleria Schwarz, Milan
1968	*Documenta 4*, Kassel, West Germany
1969	*Pop Art Redefined*, Hayward Gallery, London
1972	*Swedish Art: contemporary Themes*, National Museum of Modern Art, Tokyo (travelled to Kyoto, Japan)
1973	*New York Collection for Stockholm*, Moderna Museet, Stockholm
1976	*Drawing Now*, Museum of Modern Art, New York (toured Europe)

Collections:

Moderna Museet, Stockholm; Wallraf-Richartz Museum, Cologne; Städtisches Museum, Stuttgart; Centre Georges Pompidou, Paris; Museum Moderner Kunst, Vienna.

Publications:

By FAHLSTROM: Books—*Poetry 1952-53*, Stockholm 1964; *Om Livskonst o.a.*, Stockholm 1971; film—*Du Gamla Du Fria*, Stockholm 1969; tape and tape collage—*Faglar i Sverige*, Stockholm 1962; *Helige Torsten Nilsson*, Stockholm 1966; word-game—*Checklist for Dr. Schweitzer*, Stockholm 1964.

On FAHLSTROM: books—*Oyvind Fahlstrom*, exhibition catalogue, Venice 1966; *Oyvind Fahlstrom* by T. Ekbom, R. Rauschenberg, and others, Stockholm 1967; *Oyvind Fahlstrom* by Achille Bonita Oliva and others, Milan 1975; *Le Belcanto de Fahlstrom*, exhibition catalogue, by Alain Jouffroy, Paris 1975; *Oyvind Fahlstrom* by Pontus Hulten, Milan 1976; *Oyvind Fahlstrom*, exhibition catalogue, by Pontus Hulten, Stockholm 1979, Paris 1980 (includes bibliography); articles—"Oyvind Fahlstrom" by Suzi Gablik in *Art News* (New York), June 1966; "Oyvind Fahlstrom: Models of Shattered Reality" by T. Ekbom in *Art International* (Lugano, Switzerland), Summer 1966; "Oyvind Fahlstrom" by Jane Livingston in *Art and Technology*, exhibition catalogue, Los Angeles 1971.

Oyvind Fahlstrom's relatively brief career has a structure so fine that one almost wants to avoid discussing it. His early works are a jumble of personal and mass-media mythology and an exorcism, perhaps, of personal neurosis; the second phase of his work is rife with radical political consciousness; the third and final period of his art is imbued with an overwhelming sadness in the face of *all* of the countless and crippling modes of human suffering—a sadness that's no longer "political" but lyrical and almost metaphysical.

And there are reasons to be unhappy with this statement even aside from the emotional discomfort of finding oneself in the act of turning the artist's career into a kind of poetic prelude to his premature death. It's also unsatisfying from a purely intellectual point of view since it's mainly concerned with some of the "externals" of Fahlstrom's work: the level of "content" with Fahlstrom is almost excessively retrievable since most of his paintings are to be read as well as to be looked at. Reading them, then, ought to be taken for granted and is simply not enough since there is much more to them than what they "say." But with Fahlstrom, one simply has to start somewhere, since he is always telling us that art is an extremely complex affair, and he has no facile way of summing up these complexities; he is very very humble in the face of them and never pretends that he knows how to create a work of art that can go beyond simply presenting them. He never invites us to think that their inter-relationships can become suddenly and permanently clear. One of the *forms* that Fahlstrom most frequently employed was the form of the puzzle, and the whole of his work is a puzzle that remains unsolved. That's a part of what makes it so constantly intriguing.

In addition to dealing with the "verbal" part of Fahlstrom's work (which also includes the "semiverbal" level of an extremely open iconography that includes easily decipherable symbols such as rats and bombs and scenes of torture as well as clearly recognizable caricatures of political figures like Nixon, Kissinger, Mao-Tse-Tung, Angela Davis and Malcolm X), one also has to come to grips with any of a number of levels of "style"—both in the style of the over-all presentation and the style of the individual elements of the work; it's usual in Fahlstrom's work, moreover, for various elements of style to be strikingly opposed to one another.

All the little individual figures that populate Fahlstrom's paintings tend to be unspeakably grotesque. His model was the Krazy Kat, Beetle, and Orphan Annie kind of cartoon image that the American Pop Artists had no use for (since they were primarily involved with stereotypes of beauty, courage, virility and success), and he often made use of these figures as movable magnetized images to be freely arranged on metal game boards. In the final phase of his work, these figures were grouped into fragments of narrative and painted onto metal forms that Fahlstrom called "improvisations"—automatic drawings of Surreal organic shapes that Fahlstrom compared to the fins of tropical fish—and the board on which they moved was simply a much larger improvisational shape. In a series of works dedicated to the coup in Chile, these improvisations were attached to long thin rods that fit into holes on a narrow metal panel that reproduced the geographical shape of the country itself. Most probably, though, they have to be seen as developments of the tightly interlocking individual shapes that the artist used in certain earlier works that look like crazy quilts or brightly colored jig-saw puzzles. Color is something else that's extremely important in Fahlstrom's work. He worked with a very precise color code in which individual colors were consistently used as correlatives to particular fact or emotions, but he also knew that the expressive force of his colors wasn't in any way limited to the referential values that he attributed to them. In one of his texts, he suggests in fact that the beauty in the "endlessly varying labyrinth of the color fields" is the part of the experience of his work to which the eye of an attentive viewer is most likely to want to return. But still another part of the beauty of his work is the moral and existential beauty of staying afloat among so many contrasts and contradictions.

—Henry Martin

FANGOR, Wojciech.

American. Born in Warsaw, Poland, 15 November 1922; emigrated to the United States, 1966; naturalized, 1971. Studied at Warsaw Academy of Fine Arts, 1945-46. Diploma in painting 1946. Painter. Taught at Warsaw Academy of Fine Arts, 1954-61; Instructor, Bath Academy of Art, Corsham, England, 1965-66. Professor, Fairleigh Dickinson University, Madison, New Jersey, since 1966. Visiting Critic in Architecture, Graduate School of Design, Harvard University, Cambridge, Massachusetts, 1967-68. Recipient: Institute of Contemporary Arts fellowship, Washington, D.C. 1962; Ford Foundation Grant to Berlin 1964-65. Address: Box 155, Summit, New York 12175, U.S.A.

Individual Exhibitions:

1949	Teatr Zydowski, Warsaw
1958	Teatr Zydowski, Warsaw
1962	ICA, Washington D.C.
1964	Galerie Lambert, Paris
	Museum Schloss Morsbroich, Leverkusen, West Germany
1965	Galerie Springer, Berlin
1966	Grabowski Gallery, London
1967	Galerie Chalette, New York
1969	Galerie Chalette, New York
1970	Guggenheim Museum, New York
	Galerie Chalette, New York
1971	Fort Worth Museum, Texas
	University of California Art Museum, Berkeley
1973	Chalette International, New York

Selected Group Shows:

1959	*Polish Painting Now*, Stedelujk Museum, Amsterdam
1964	*Guggenheim International*, Guggenheim Museum, New York
1965	*The Responsive Eye*, Museum of Modern Art, New York
1967	*Pittsburgh International*, Carnegie Museum of Art, Pittsburgh, Pennsylvania
1968	*Biennale*, Venice

Collections:

Guggenheim Museum, New York; Museum of Modern Art, New York; Rose Art Museum, Waltham, Massachusetts; Museum of Art, Trenton, New Jersey; Aldrich Museum, Ridgefield, Connecticut; Museum of Art, Lodz, Poland; Stedelijk Museum, Amsterdam; Museum Schloss Morsbroich, Leverkusen, West Germany; Museum of Modern Art, Munich; Power Gallery of Art, Sydney.

Publications:

By FANGOR: statement in *Art Now* (New York) August 1970.

On FANGOR: book—*Fangor*, exhibition catalogue, by Margit Rowell, New York 1970; articles—notes by R. C. Kenedy in *Art International* (Lugano, Switzerland) April 1966; "Fangor's Romantic Op" by John Canaday in the *New York Times*, February 1970.

YOU CAN'T WRITE A PAINTING
YOU CAN'T PAINT A NOVEL

THE CONTENT OF A PAINTING
IS ILLITERATE AND DEAF-MUTE
IT OFFERS ONLY ITS OUTER SKIN
TO THE GOSSIP AND THE CAMERA

IT OPENS TO THE OPEN EYES

—Wojciech Fangor

Like a number of non-figurative artists, Wojciech Fangor has been much concerned, and over a considerable period, with the circle. For many, he is best known for his luminous circles with their multinimbus collar.

But it would be unfair to write him off as a painter of circles; his non-hard-edge simple geometric symbols have the power of controlled inspiration. The blurred circle, nearly lost in a field of monochrome dots whose loosely strewn fish-grey changes from dark to pale as they cover the misty ring in the canvas' centre combine to have the same kind of cosmic impact as some of the skyborne images of Gottlieb and Rothko, except that in Fangor's case the colour character makes his pictures look closer to laboratory prints and astronomy photochromes than could have been said of those by the two Americans.

Outside his magic circles, and in much of his earlier work, Fangor had already proved his ability to give the impression of science with a soft edge. Take for instance the gently elliptical shape (double) that stretches from one side of the picture to the other, passing through a series of carefully painted red vertical lines suggesting the casually roughcast thickest bars of an undercoated cage. This too could be the fugitive illustration of some aspect of clinical research.

Nearly all Fangor's canvases are foursquare, rarely exceeding 1¼ feet in height and width.

Effectively he left Poland at the beginning of the 1960's. He has been a teacher in Warsaw, the United States and Britain. From 1953 until 1961 he collaborated with the Polish architects Soltan, Zamecnik and Hansen.

—Sheldon Williams

FAVRO, Murray.

Canadian. Born in Huntsville, Ontario, 24 December 1940. Educated at Beal Technical School, London, Ontario, 1958-64. Independent artist. Agent: Carmen Lamanna Gallery, Toronto. Address: c/o Carmen Lamanna Gallery, 840 Yonge Street, Toronto, Ontario, Canada M4W 2H1.

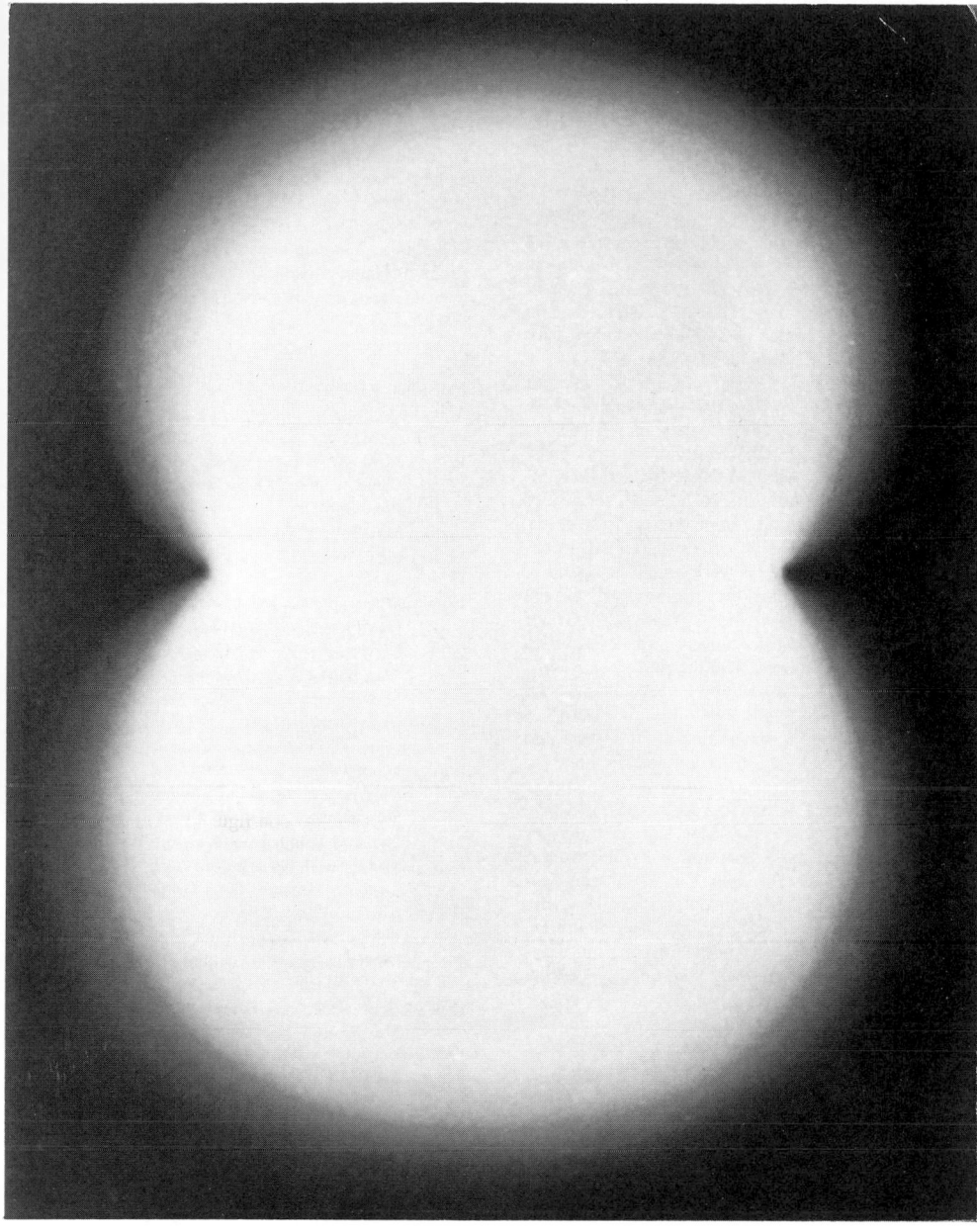

Wojciech Fangor: *Number 2*, 1963

Individual Exhibitions:

1968   20/20 Gallery, London, Ontario
      Carmen Lamanna Gallery, Toronto
1971   Carmen Lamanna Gallery, Toronto
1972   *Country Road*, Carmen Lamanna Gallery, Toronto
1973   *Synthetic Lake*, Carmen Lamanna Gallery, Toronto
      Forest City Gallery, London, Ontario
1974   London Public Gallery, Ontario
1975   *News*, Forest City Gallery, London, Ontario
1976   *Inventions*, Carmen Lamanna Gallery, Toronto
1977   *The Flying Flea*, Carmen Lamanna Gallery, Toronto
1978   Carmen Lamanna Gallery, Toronto
1980   Carmen Lamanna Gallery, Toronto
1981   Forest City Gallery, London, Ontario
1982   *18 Preparation Drawings to Construct a 55% Scaled Sabre Jet*, Whitewater Gallery, North Bay, Ontario
1983   Art Gallery of Ontario, Toronto (retrospective; toured Canada)

Selected Group Exhibitions:

1968   *Heart of London*, National Gallery of Canada, Ottawa (toured Canada)
1971   *Canadian National Exhibition*, Toronto
1973   *Canada Trajectories 73*, Musée d'Art Moderne, Paris

      Boucherville, Montreal, Toronto, London, National Gallery of Art, Ottawa
1974   *Projekt '74*, Wallraf-Richartz Museum, Cologne
1975   *Carmen Lamanna Gallery at the Owens Art Gallery*, Mount Allison University, Sackville, New Brunswick
      A Response to the Environment, Rutgers University Art Gallery, New Brunswick, New Jersey
1976   *Changing Visions: The Canadian Landscape*, Art Gallery of Ontario, Toronto
1977   *Another Dimension I & II*, National Gallery of Canada, Ottawa
1980   *10 Canadian Artists in the 1970s*, Art Gallery of Ontario, Toronto (toured Europe)

Collections:

National Gallery of Canada, Ottawa; Canada Council Art Bank, Ottawa; Art Gallery of Ontario, Toronto; McIntosh Gallery, University of Western Ontario, London, Ontario; London Regional Art Gallery, Ontario.

Publications:

By FAVRO: articles—"Notes" in *Region* (London, Ontario), Summer 1966; "Ron Martin's Conclusions and Transfers at 20/20 Gallery" in *20 Cents* (London, Ontario), September 1967; text in *Heart of London*, exhibition catalogue, Ottawa 1968; "Murray Favro's Journal" in *20 Cents* (London, Ontario), December 1969.

On FAVRO: books—*Realism: Emulsion and Omission*, exhibition catalogue, by M. Kluyver-Cluysenaer, Kingston, Ontario 1972; *Canada Trajectories 73*, exhibition catalogue, Paris 1973; *Boucherville, Montreal, Toronto, London*, exhibition catalogue, Ottawa 1973; *Projekt '74*, exhibition catalogue, Cologne 1974; *Murray Favro: Retrospective Exhibition*, catalogue with texts by Marie Fleming, Michael Snow and Greg Curnoe, Toronto 1983; articles—"Exhibit by 2 London Artists Draws Praise" by Leonore Crawford in *London Free Press* (Ontario), December 1966; "A New Regionalism" by Ross Woodman in *Artscanada* (Toronto), August 1967; "The Heart of London" by G. James in *Vie des Arts* (Montreal), Winter 1968; "Murray Favro, Carmen Lamanna Gallery" by Gary Dault in *Artscanada* (Toronto), February 1969; "Form-image Replicas: Murray Favro" by K. Dewdney in *Artscanada* (Toronto), December 1973.

Murray Favro's stance as guileless model-maker and inventor appears too playful to contain heroic ambitions. But appearances are only partial, and in truth Favro's wryly mock-primitive mechanistic investigations of natural phenomena or man-made things are a subtle strategy for posing profound questions about the nature of our contact with the world.

Favro traces the way he works to the influence of his brother, an innovative and versatile Mr. Fix-it, and to watching his "Uncle Walter (full-time inventor) trying to perfect his power-developing machine (which never worked)." From the latter, Favro recalls he "learned to value the activity of an inventor regardless of whether his inventions were useful or worked properly."

"Van Gogh's Room" is one of a group of "Projected Reconstructions" which Favro began to make in 1970. These are made up of a slide or film loop projected on an uncoloured three-dimensional mock-up of the subject matter of the slide or film, and thus constitute synthetic reconstructions of the physical world from its component sensory and material parts. Favro's first successful projected reconstruction was "Still-Life (The Table)," 1970, which consisted of a slide of a number of objects—books, boxes, a battery lying on a table top—projected onto a duplicate table top, its contents made of wood covered with canvas and painted white. The slide projector was angled from the same position as the camera which took the slide. Unexpectedly, the projected image and its reconstructed counterpart were not congruent, and in subsequent works Favro learned to rebuild the objects to incorporate the distortions which arose from projecting onto three-dimensional objects. An especially elaborate "projected reconstruction" recreated an expansive external view looking down a country road with a parked car, a tree stump, plants and a cliff.

"Van Gogh's Room" in at least three interrelated ways compounds the problem of the preceding works. It is a reconstruction, not of the real world, but of the work of art. It is a three-dimensional reconstruction of what was originally a flat image (which before that was based on physical reality). The slide image itself already incorporates distortions, so that a three-dimensional reconstruction of space and objects must be devised which will coincide with a projection of a "subjective" space rendered on a flat surface, further, if objectively, distorted in the projection itself because it is projected through various depths of space.

"Synthetic Lake," 1973, attempted to reconstruct actual natural motion by projecting a film of waves breaking on a beach onto an elaborate mechanical "wave machine" made from a hinged and roped wooden lattice-work construction whose slats rise and fall underneath a length of eight-foot-wide canvas moving to the even rhythm of a motor-driven, spiral fiberglass rotating shaft running the length of the machine.

Favro, of course, never achieves perfection in his constructions—and would not. The illusion always remains partial, and does so critically, so as to lay open the absurdity of this particular way of taking the world apart and putting it back together again. But if there are here metaphors at play which ultimately point to the entire gamut of disjunctions between experience and systematic knowledge, there is also an immediate inquisitiveness and fascination with things themselves and how they work or how they could work, provided the questions are cunning enough.

—Roald Nasgaard

FERNHOUT, Edgar (Richard Johannes).

Dutch. Born in Bergen, 17 August 1912; grandson of the painter Jan Toorop, and son of the painter Charley Toorop. Self-taught in art. Spent childhood in Bergen, Amsterdam and Paris; lived and worked in Amsterdam, 1931–35, and in Riva, Italy, 1936–39; during the Occupation lived in Bergen and Baarn, Netherlands, 1939–45; returned to Amsterdam, 1945; settled in Bergen, 1956. *Died* (in Bergen) *4 November 1974.*

Individual Exhibitions:

1932	Kunsthandel van Lier, Amsterdam
1933	Kunsthandel d'Andretsch, The Hague
1935	Kunsthandel d'Andretsch, The Hague
1937	Kunsthandel van Lier, Amsterdam
	Kunsthandel G. J. Nieuwenhuizen Segaar, The Hague (with Charley and Jan Toorop)
1938	Kunsthandel d'Andretsch, The Hague
1940	Kunsthandel van Lier, Amsterdam
1946	Kunsthandel van Lier, Amsterdam
1947	Kunsthandel Nieuwenhuizen Segaar, The Hague
1949	Kunsthandel Huinck and Scherjon, Amsterdam
1951	Kunsthandel Huinck and Scherjon, Amsterdam
1954	Stedelijk van Abbemuseum, Eindhoven, Netherlands
1955	De Waag, Nijmegen, Netherlands
1957	Galerie Magdalene Sothmann, Amsterdam
1959	Galerie Magdalene Sothmann, Amsterdam
1961	Galerie Magdalene Sothmann, Amsterdam
1963	Stedelijk van Abbemuseum, Eindhoven, Netherlands (travelled to the Stedelijk Museum, Amsterdam)
1965	Galerie Magdalene Sothmann, Amsterdam
1967	Galerie Magdalene Sothmann, Amsterdam
1968	Galerie Nouvelles Images, The Hague
1969	Galerie Magdalene Sothmann, Amsterdam
1970	Galerie Nouvelles Images, The Hague
1971	De Lakenhal, Leiden (with Charley and Jan Toorop; travelled to Dordrechts Museum and the Groninger Museum, Netherlands)
	Galerie Magdalene Sothmann, Amsterdam
1973	Galerie Magdalene Sothmann, Amsterdam
1976	Stedelijk van Abbemuseum, Eindhoven, Netherlands

Selected Group Exhibitions:

1933	*Het Stilleven,* Kunsthandel Goudstikkar, Amsterdam
1946	*Modern Dutch Art,* Helsinki
1958	*Het Stilleven in de Nederlandse Schilderkunst,* Gemeentemuseum, Apeldorn, Netherlands
1960	*Keerpunten in de Nederlandse Schilderkunst,* Stedelijk van Abbemuseum, Eindhoven, Netherlands
1963	*150 Jaar Nederlandse Kunst,* Stedelijk Museum, Amsterdam

Collections:

Stedelijk Museum, Amsterdam; Groningen Museum, Groningen, Netherlands; Rijksmuseum Kröller-Müller, Otterlo, Netherlands; Curacaosch Museum, Willemstad, Curacao.

Publications:

On FERNHOUT: books—*Movements and Personalities: 50 Years of Painting in the Netherlands* by A. M. Hammacher, Amsterdam 1955; *Edgar Fernhout,* exhibition catalogue, by L. Gans, Amsterdam 1963; *Edgar Fernhout* by G. L. P. Cammelbeeck, Amsterdam 1969; *Edgar Fernhout,* exhibition catalogue, by R. H. Fuchs, H. L. C. Jaffé, Marcel Vos and others, Eindhoven, Netherlands 1976; article—"Holland: Mondrian's Successors" by M. Vos in *Studio International* (London), September 1975.

In a short memorial notice published in the catalogue of the exhibition of Edgar Fernhout's work held in the Van Abbemuseum two years after that artist's death, the Dutch painter Jan Dibbets observed that "Fernhout, once regarded as a child wonder, was really a late bloomer! During the last years of his life he served as the artistic conscience of a much younger generation." The members of that generation include Dibbets himself, as well as artists like Van Elk, Struycken, Lucassen, Ad Dekkers and the critic Fuchs. All of these men have acknowledged how important Fernhout was to them, particularly because of the way in which he worked to protect art from extraneous pressures and false expectations. This is probably his real significance: his work served as a kind of moral bridge connecting the pre-war art of the Netherlands—especially the great work of Mondrian—and the work of new artists eager to maintain their connections with the past.

Edgar Fernhout was the scion of what was clearly a family of artists. His grandfather was Jan Toorop, a painter who had some recognition around 1900 and who was a friend of Odilon Redon and members of the Vienna Secession. Fernhout was the son of Toorop's daughter, Charley Toorop, herself an active figurative painter whose still-lifes and portraits are well-represented in the Rijksmuseum Kröller Müller in Otterlo and in the Boymans-Van Beuningen museum in Rotterdam. She maintained close ties with Mondrian, Rietveld and Van der Leck, among others, as well as with artists such as Pyke Koch, Jan Sluyters and John Rädecker, who were still working within the realist tradition.

It is obvious, then, that Fernhout grew up surrounded by a distinguished but also very diverse group of artists. He held his first exhibition when he was only 20, and during the 1930's produced a series of realistic paintings in which his main interest seemed to be the transitory nature of life (for example, his "Autumn Fields" and "Death Heads"). But what separates his work from the pessimism of such "magic realists" as Willink and Hijnckes is his intense concern for natural light and color. "Open Windows" (1933), for example, is a painstaking rendering of the way in which light coming in from the outside can determine the atmosphere of a room.

These paintings are realistic, but they also have an abstract, constructivist quality about them. In the self-portraits which Fernhout painted in 1944 and 1948 we can begin to see the new characteristics which led to the abstract paintings he did from 1960 until his death in 1974. Color is now engaged in a kind of dialogue with the artist's brush, which is no longer a subservient tool. In the 1948 self-portrait, for example, Fernhout is not merely looking at himself; he is also busy discovering his true nature as an artist who is interested in creating autonomous pictorial realities. Around 1955 he passed through a phase which can be compared to the luminism of Mondrian early in this century (in the 1909 "Seascape," for example). Fernhout's "Dune" (1958) and "The Beach" (1959) are still rooted in his observation of the Dutch landscape and seascapes and the play of light over those scenes. In the 1960's, however, he produced paintings with very generalized titles, such as "Autumn," "Winter" and "Thaw". Here he was seeking not exact representations or visual equivalents of reality, but rather looking for analogies between what he saw and the act of painting. In these intense, concentrated works from the last years of his life he reached a point where all the tangible traces of air and earth have disappeared, even for the most discerning eye.

—A. F. Wagemans

FERRARA, Jackie.

American. Born in Detroit, Michigan, in 1929. Independent sculptor and eviornmental design artist, New York, since 1970. Member of the policy, funding and planning panels for the National Endowment for the Arts, New York State Council on the Arts, The Bush Foundation, Ohio Arts Council, etc., since 1977. Recipient: New York State Council on the Arts grant, 1971, 1975; National Endowment for the Arts Grant, Washington, D.C., 1973, 1977, 1987; Guggenheim Foundation Grant, New York, 1976. Agent: Max Protetch Gallery, New York. Address: c/o Max Protetch Gallery, 560 Broadway, New York, New York 10012, U.S.A.

Individual Exhibitions:

1973	A. M. Sachs Gallery, New York
1974	A. M. Sachs Gallery, New York
1975	Daniel Weinberg Gallery, San Francisco
	Protetch-McIntosh Gallery, Washington, D.C.
	Max Protetch Gallery, New York
1976	Max Protetch Gallery, New York
1977	Ohio State University, Columbus
1978	Minneapolis College of Art and Design
	Max Protetch Gallery, New York
1979	University of Rhode Island, Kingston
	Glen Hanson Gallery, Minneapolis
	Max Protetch Gallery, New York
1980	Okun-Thomas Gallery, St. Louis
	University of Massachusetts, Amherst
1981	Max Protetch Gallery, New York
	University of Southern California, Los Angeles
	Marianne Deson Gallery, Chicago
	Laumeier International Sculpture Park, St. Louis
1982	Max Protetch Gallery, New York
	Lowe Art Museum, Coral Gables, Florida
1983	Lunds Galleriet, Sweden
	Janus Gallery, Los Angeles
	University of North Carolina, Chapel Hill
	Max Protetch Gallery, New York
1984	Susan Montezinos Gallery, Philadelphia
	Max Protetch Gallery, New York
1987	San Antonio Art Institute, Texas
	Moore College of Art, Philadelphia

Selected Group Exhibitions:

1972	*GEDOK American Woman Artist Show,* Kunsthaus, Hamburg
1973	*Biennial Exhibition,* Whitney Museum, New York
1974	*7 Sculptors,* Institute of Contemporary Art, Boston
1976	*New York-Downtown Manhattan: Soho,* Akademie der Kunst, Berlin
1979	*Biennial Exhibition,* Whitney Museum, New York
1980	*Drawings: The Pluralist Decade,* at the *Biennale,* Venice
1982	*Postminimalism,* Aldrich Museum of Contemporary Art, Ridgefield, Connecticut
1984	*Drawings by Sculptors,* Seagram Collection, New York (toured the United States)
1985	*Artists & Architects,* Cleveland Center for Contemporary Art, Ohio
1986	*Sculpture of the Eighties,* Queens Museum, Flushing, New York

Collections:

Museum of Modern Art, New York; Guggenheim Museum, New York; Whitney Museum, New York; Carnegie Institute, Pittsburgh; Cincinnati Art Museum, Ohio; High Museum of Art, Atlanta, Georgia; St. Louis Art Museum, Missouri; Louisiana Museum, Humlebaek, Denmark.

Publications:

By FERRARA: book—*Jackie Ferrara: Drawings, June and July 1977,* New York 1977.

On FERRARA: books—*Jackie Ferrara,* exhibition catalogue

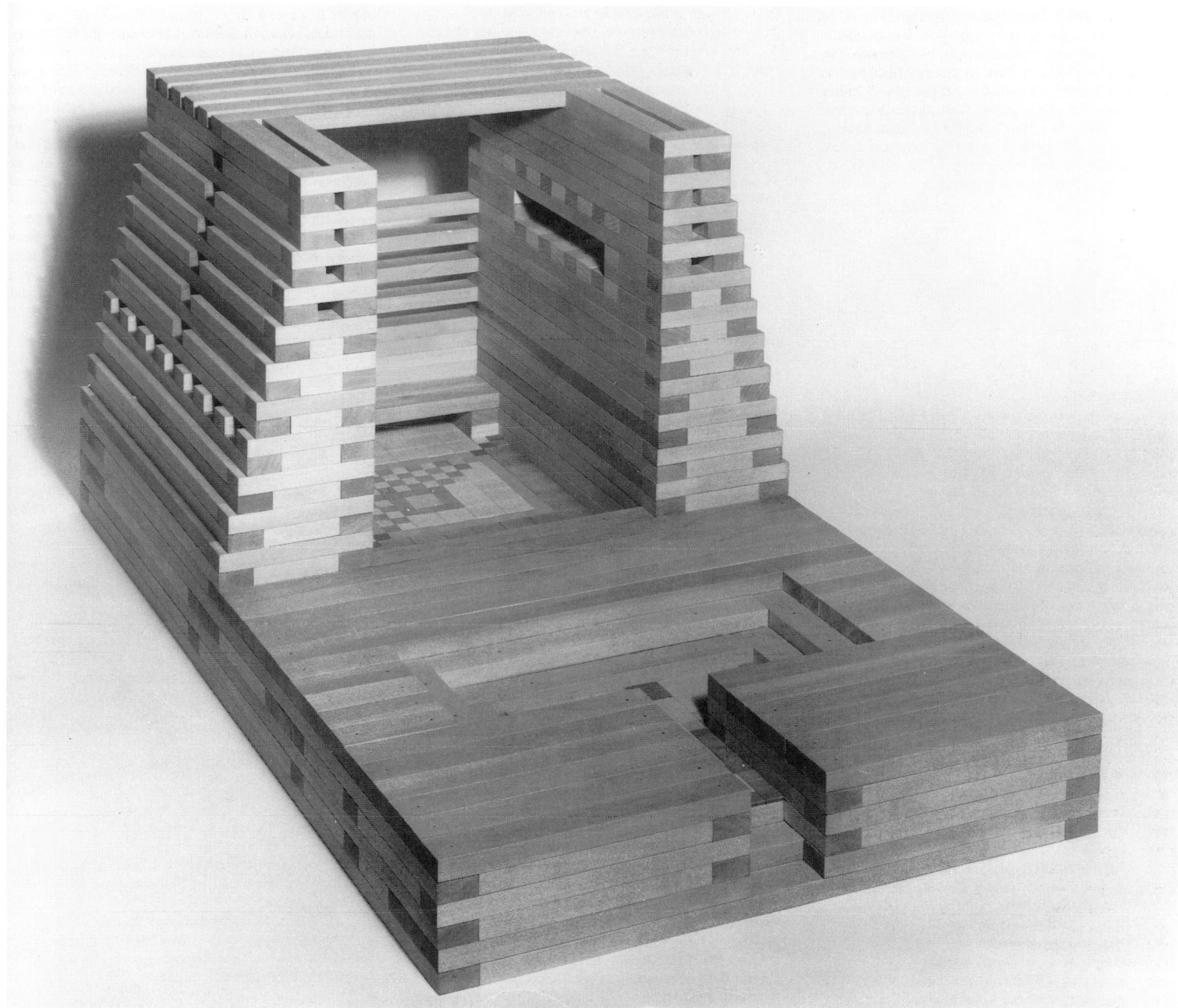

Jackie Ferrara: *Gray Ark*, 1986

with text by Michael Klein, Amherst, Massachusetts 1980; *Jackie Ferrara: Benches, Thrones, and a Table,* exhibition catalogue with text by Elsa Weiner Longhauser, Philadelphia 1987; articles—review by Laurie Anderson in *Artforum* (New York) January 1974; review by Edit DeAk in *Art in America* (New York) March/April 1975; "Jackie Ferrara: On the Cutting Edge of a New Sensibility" by David Bourdon in *Arts Magazine* (New York) January 1976; review by Nancy Foote in *Artforum* (New York) January 1976; "Jackie Ferrara: The Feathery Elevator" by Robert Pincus-Witten in *Arts Magazine* (New York) November 1976; review by Jeff Perrone in *Artforum* (New York) January 1977; review by Robert Berlind in *Art in America* (New York) March/April 1979; "Jackie Ferrara's Il-lusions" by Kate Linker in *Artforum* (New York) November 1979; "Jackie Ferrara" by Grace Glueck in the *New York Times* November 30, 1979; review by Richard Whelan in *Artnews* (New York) February 1980.

My work is about: the process of building form; the space within and surrounding the form; responding to site and situation; a quality of timelessness, so there is no historical certainty.

— Jackie Ferrara

Jackie Ferrara is known for her "Post-Minimalist" wood pyramidal structures composed of variously stacked, horizontally layered "steps." She has used this vocabulary and system of construction since the early 1970's to find multiple variations in a sequence of sculptures which admit quirky irregularities into a basically geometric and architectural pattern.

During the 1950's, Ferrara made ceramics and pottery in a primitivizing, crafty vein. By 1961 she was making small, Max Ernst-like works, and by the late 1960's she was creating fetishistic sculptures made from the type of hairy, raw flax which is used as packing material. These either hung from the ceiling or came up from the floor. What at first looked like weird heads became what she has described as "tails" and then turned into more abstracted but equally eccentric and metaphoric rope pieces. On the surface, there seems to be little connection between these earlier works and Ferrara's neater and cooler constructs of the 70's. There is, however, a connection in the continual development of an idiosyncratic personalized factor and a finely honed craft sensibility which persist in her mature works. These tendencies enter into Ferrara's concerns with the building process and with meticulous care for craft and fastidious attention for precise detail. They also relate with Ferrara's choices of specific configurations that are a bit off from the geometrically precise.

Ferrara's works are consciously pre-planned, worked out in detail in gridded drawings, precisely showing the shape of the structure and sometimes also indicating the quality of the surface down to the texture and direction of the wood grain. On one hand, the pyramidal stacks are extremely neat, clean, clear and simple, and on the other hand, they are informed by a individualized intellect, sensitized toward the hermetic and the ritualistic. The works show connections with a long-range cultural tradition, with the architecture of Egypt and Meso-America, and they are also strangely warped to change into something more irregularly hand made. The combined occurrences of slats and openings imply psychological implications involving inner and outer realms.

All of these elements add up to much more than the minimalist's concentration on literal presence and alll-at-onceness. Along with others who matured around 1970, Ferrara refused the hard-nosed formalism of 60's Minimalism and used systems to build a morphology which suggests extra-art connections.

Until a few years ago, her work remained within the scale of sculpture despite its relationships with architectural antecedents. In 1979, Ferrara built "Tower and Bridge for Castle Clinton," a more architecturally scaled piece with site-specified qualities.

Composed of two rectangular structures made by stacking cedar two by fours, the work was placed in the court of the almost circular early American fortress located in Battery Park in Lower Manhattan. It bears resemblances both to log cabins and to Indian teepees, constructs particularly harmonious in their setting. Access into "Tower and Bridge" adds another interior space to the site, and such physical access also adds another dimension to Ferrara's multiply layered configurations of the past decade.

—Barbara Cavaliere

FERRER, Rafael.

American. Born in Santurce, Puerto Rico, 1933. Educated at Staunton Military Academy, Virginia, 1948–51; Syracuse University, New York, 1951–52; University of Puerto Rico, Mayaquez, under E. Grannell, 1952–54. Married Irene Alvarez in 1962; children: Theresa, Diego. Worked as a drummer in a Latin band, Syracuse, 1951–52; visited Europe; associated with Surrealist group, Paris 1953; worked as a drummer in Spanish Harlem, New York, 1957; fulltime painter from 1959; moved to Philadelphia, 1965; visited Germany, 1969, Amsterdam, Barcelona and Cologne, 1970; first Body Art exhibitions, Amsterdam, 1970. Instructor, Philadelphia College of Art, 1967, and School of Visual Arts, New York, 1977–79. Agent: Nancy Hoffman Gallery, New York. Address: c/o Nancy Hoffman Gallery, 429 West Broadway, New York, New York 10012, U.S.A.

Individual Exhibitions:

1964	University of Puerto Rico Museum, Mayaquez
1966	Pan American Union, Washington, D.C.
1968	Leo Castelli Gallery, New York
1969	Galerie M. E. Thelen, Essen
	Eastern Connecticut State College, Hartford
1970	Leo Castelli Gallery, New York
	Galerie Mickery, Amsterdam
	Philadelphia Museum of Art
	Galerie M. E. Thelen, Cologne
	University of Hartford, Connecticut
1971	University of Rhode Island Fine Art Center, Kingston
	University of Pennsylvania, Philadelphia
	Whitney Museum, New York
1972	Pasadena Museum of Art, California
1973	Contemporary Art Center, Cincinnati, Ohio
1974	Nancy Hoffman Gallery, New York
	Museum of Modern Art, New York
1975	Nancy Hoffman Gallery, New York
1977	Albright-Knox Art Gallery, Buffalo, New York
	Marianne Deson Gallery, Chicago
	Galerie Dorothea Speyer, Paris
	Fort Worth Art Museum, Texas
1978	Nancy Hoffman Gallery, New York
	The New Gallery, Cleveland
1980	Hamilton Gallery of Contemporary Art, New York
	Frumkin Struve Gallery, Chicago
1982	Nancy Hoffman Gallery, New York

Selected Group Exhibitions:

1970	*Whitney Annual,* Whitney Museum, New York
1971	*Depth and Presence,* Corcoran Gallery, Washington, D.C.
1973	*Whitney Biennial,* Whitney Museum, New York
1977	*Drawings of the 70's,* Art Institute of Chicago
	Narrative Arts, Contemporary Art Museum, Houston
	A View of a Decade, Museum of Contemporary Art, Chicago

1978	*Private Myths,* Queens Museum, New York
	Masks, Tents, Vessels, Talismans, Institute of Contemporary Art, Philadelphia
1980	*The Pluralist Decade: Venice Biennale,* Institute of Contemporary Art, Philadelphia

Collections:

Metropolitan Museum of Art, New York; Whitney Museum, New York; Museum of Modern Art, New York; Albright-Knox Art Gallery, Buffalo, New York; Philadelphia Museum of Art; Museum of Contemporary Art, Chicago; Lehmbruck Museum, Duisburg, West Germany.

Publications:

By FERRER: book—*Deseo: An Autobiography,* Cincinnati, Ohio 1973; article—"Rafael Ferrer: An Interview," with Stephen Prokopoff, in *Art and Artists* (London), April 1972.

On FERRER: articles—"New York: Rafael Ferrer, Leo Castelli Gallery" by B. Vinklers in *Art International* (Lugano, Switzerland), March 1970; "A Different Drummer" by K. Levin in *Artnews* (New York), December 1971; "New York: Rafael Ferrer, Whitney Museum" by Kenneth Baker in *Artforum* (New York), March 1972; "Rafael Ferrer" by J. L. Dunham in *Artweek* (Oakland, California), November 1974; "Ferrer's Sun and Shade" by Carter Ratcliff in *Art in America* (New York), March 1980.

Rafael Ferrer's art has been a continuing attempt both to resolve his inherent sense of visual expression away from the Hispanic-American modernist tradition—surreal-expressionism—and incorporate more North American style. As well, Ferrer's entire career can be taken as a concerted effort to see how far the vein of primitivizing modernism might be stretched. In order to accomplish these ostensible aims, Ferrer—who is essentially self-taught after an earlier career as a professional musician—has formed, from the fragments of the abstract and anti-form traditions of the 1960's, his own humane and often poignant art.

He first came to prominence during the heady years and culmination of the protean inventiveness of the late 1960's. As an acquaintance of Morris, Serra, Italo Scanga, and others of similar inclination, Ferrer naturally participated in the free-form, "Process art" orientation of that moment. And thus he manipulated in free and non-referential patterns, such materials as grease, hay, ice, corrugated metal, and wooden poles, in transient installations. Perhaps his decisive insight was his understanding of the oddly clear Romantic possibilities inherent in the interaction of these natural industrial products, should a more clearly thematic element be introduced into the installations. Ferrer accomplished this within an archeo-anthropological frame—in this akin to artists of quite distinct stylistic bent, such as Jud Fine and Charles Simonds. And so specific geographic place names became the titles of his environmental groupings—Celebes; Patagonia; Sudan. The poignance of such names, often given as neon signs in darkened interiors, was supported by the intensity of the ensemble which typically included kayak-like boats, explorers' equipment and furniture—all assembled raggedly by Ferrer; exotic groupings of animal skins and overpainted printed maps, and the well-known masks of human heads drawn on brown paper bags; and the equally well-known sewn-canvas, hanging tent-like structures. Whatever calligraphic marking or drawing occurred on these surfaces was rendered with high naivete.

Since 1978, Ferrer has produced no installations, and instead has turned exclusively to easel painting. Nonetheless, the heroic adventurer aura which overlaid those earlier works can still be felt even though Ferrer's subject matter is predominantly contemporary life in Puerto Rico. Sexuality has been pervasive, with many images featuring a naked woman, at times mysteriously tangential to the other action. (One of Ferrer's ongoing fantasies centers upon the interaction of two unclothed women observed by others.) He

seems to present an elemental "Paradisical" world, and it has been observed that his paintings apparently challenge Puritanical tradition.

Unlike his work of the previous decade, Ferrer has evolved his representational style beyond mere naivete in a figurative and spatially coherent art. He has used a variety of photographic source material as an access to posture and psychology in figures and scenic views, often collaging together the cut-outs as working supports for the larger paintings. Recent work of the mid-decade has moved toward direct observation in an attempt to achieve a more fluid poetic atmosphere and perhaps to create his distinctive sensuality through a study of the literal effects of light, color and texture.

—Joshua Kind

FETTING, Rainer.

German. Born in Wilhelmshaven, West Germany, in 1949. Educated in Wilhelmshaven, 1959–66; apprentice journeyman carpenter, working in theatres, 1968–72; studied painting at the State Academy of Art, West Berlin 1972–76. Painter, West Berlin, since 1976; also filmmaker, since 1975: Founder, with Helmut Middendorf, Salomé and Bernd Zimmer, Galerie am Moritzplatz artists' co-op, West Berlin, 1977. Recipient: D.A.A.D. Scholarship, Berlin, to New York, 1978–79. Lives in Berlin-Kreuzberg. Agents: Galerie Silvia Menzel, Kurfurstendamm 195, 1000 Berlin 15 (West); Galerie Raab, Potsdamer Strasse 58, 1000 Berlin 30 (West), Germany.

Individual Exhibitions:

1977	Galerie am Moritzplatz, West Berlin
1978	Galerie am Moritzplatz, West Berlin
1979	Interni Galerie, West Berlin (with Bernd Zimmer and Helmut Middendorf)
1981	Anthony D'Offay Gallery, London
	Mary Boone Gallery, New York (with Helmut Middendorf)
	Galerie Bruno Bischofberger, Zurich
	Mary Boone Gallery, New York
1982	Anthony D'Offay Gallery, London
1983	Studio Cannaviello, Milan
	Galerie Yvon Lambert, Paris
	Galerie Silvia Menzel, West Berlin
	Galerie Raab, West Berlin
	Galerie Helen van der Meij, Amsterdam
	Galerie 5, Stockholm
	Galerie Maier-Hahn, Dusseldorf
	CAPC/Musee d'Art Contemporain, Bordeaux, France (with Salome and Castelli)
1984	Marlborough Gallery, New York
	Galerie Raab, West Berlin
1985	Galerie Daniel Templon, Paris
	Galerie Raab, West Berlin
	Galerie Thomas, Munich
1986	Museum Folkwang, Essen, West Germany
	Kunsthalle, West Berlin
	Studio Cannaviello, Milan
	Gallery Paule Anglim, San Francisco
	Marlborough Gallery, New York
	Kunsthalle, Basle

Selected Group Exhibitions:

1977	*Die zwanziger Jahre,* Hochschule der Künste, West Berlin
1978	*Photographien,* Galerie am Moritzplatz, West Berlin
1980	*Heftige Malerei,* Haus am Waldsee, West Berlin
1981	*Après le Classicisme,* Musée d'Art et d'Industrie, St.-Etienne, France
	A New Spirit in Painting, Royal Academy of Arts, London

1982 *10 Junge Kunstler aus Deutschland*, Museum Folkwang, Essen

1984 *The European Attack*, Galerie Barbara Farber, Amsterdam

1985 *Moritzplatz*, Kunstverein, Bonn

1987 *Berlinart 1961–87*, Museum of Modern Art, New York (travelled to San Francisco)

Publications:

By FETTING: films—several short films, 1975–79; *Geburstag 76*, 1976; *R. und S. in B.*, 1977; *Brooklyn 11238*, 1978–79.

On FETTING: books—*Im Westen nicht Neues*, exhibition catalogue, with text by Martin Kunz, Lucerne 1981; *10 Junge Kunstler aus Deutschland*, exhibition catalogue, with text by Zdenek Felix, Essen 1982; *12 Kunstler aus Deutschland*, exhibition catalogue, with text by Jean-Christophe Ammann, Basle 1982; *Rainer Fetting*, exhibition catalogue, by Anne Seymour, London 1982; *Rainer Fetting*, exhibition catalogue with text by Norman Rosenthal, New York 1986; *Rainer Fetting*, exhibition catalogue with texts by Jean-Christophe Ammann, Zdenek Felix and others, Basle 1986.

Characteristic of Rainer Fetting's painting is the swiftness with which the pictures are carried out, relying on emotiveness to present a subjectivity made up of memory, personal experience and everyday life. The colours are violent, the whole work played out in violent contrasts. The images are produced like vomit, a pulling out of what has been inside for some time to consummate it in the very act of creating it. The obliteration or abandonment of flowing colour is linked with the speed of the mind, with rapid intuition. The references to German expressionism or to Action Painting are a declaration of expressive freedom that denies the idea of style as linguistic coherence; the picture is a great screen on which images of actual existence are projected.

Nightmare pictures, portraits of friends, punk musicians, nocturnal violence and troubles, the Berlin of the wall. To paint is a way of relating painting to actual existence, of bringing subjectivity to life. Fetting's painting, like that of his *heftige Malerei* friends (Salomé, Bernd Zimmer, Helmut Middendorf and Luciano Castelli), expresses the violence of a motor accident: a game, a chance, of probabilism, frenzied vision, shouts and silence. In a single instant everything is burnt up; the individual self-liberations last only a few seconds. It is a sort of realism of catastrophe: Berlin lives through one of its perennial evils, a wall that divides the city in two, a wall that is a naked man waiting for you armed with an axe, a mirror that reflects its own image. The agonies warn of the burden of the existential condition of those who do not believe in the future, who have cast aside hopes and ideologies. If there is any ideology, it is rock music—noisy rhythm that can consume the mind.

—Demetrio Paparoni

FILLIOU, Robert.

French. Born in Sauve, Garde, 17 January 1926. Educated at the Lycee d'Ales, Gard, 1938–44; studied economics and science, University of California, Los Angeles, 1948–51, M.A. 1951; self-taught in art from 1950. Served in the French Resistance, 1944–45. Married Marianne Staffeldt in 1967; children: Bruce and Marcelle. Worked for the United Nations Korean Reconstruction Agency, Seoul, 1952–54; independent playwright, in Cairo, Barcelona, Copenhagen, London and Paris, 1954–60. Independent artist since 1960: action-poetry performances, from 1960; 'Galerie Legitime' events, from 1962; associated with Fluxus artists, from 1962; worked with Emmett Williams, 1962–65; La Cedille qui Sourit and Eternal Network projects, with George Brecht, from 1965; Poupoidrome works, with Joachim Pfeufer, 1963 and 1975–78; Genial Republic works, 1971–73. Artist-in-Residence, Akademie fur bildenden Kunste, Hamburg, 1982–83. Recipient: DAAD Fellowship, West Berlin, 1974; Arts Council of Canada grants, 1977, 1979, 1980. Agent Galerie Bama, 40 rue Quincampoix, 75004 Paris. Address: Pouillac, Peyzac le Moustier, 24620 Les Eyzies, France.

Individual Exhibitions:

1960 *Performance Piece*, several locations, Paris (with Peter Cohen)

1961 *Poi-Poi*, Galerie Koepcke, Copenhagen
A 53 Kilos Poem, Lille Kirkestrade no. 1, Copenhagen

1962 *Galerie Legitime*, street event, in Paris, Frankfurt and London
Pere Lachaise no. 2, Librairie-Galerie Le Fleuve, Paris
13 Ways to Use Emmett Williams' Skull, street event, Paris (with Emmett Williams)

1963 *Poeme Collectif*, Musee de la Ville, Arras, France (with Emmett Williams)
Le Poipoidrome, Liege, Belgium (with Joachim Pfeufer)
Au Comptoir, Galerie Raymond Cordier, Paris (with Emmett Williams)
Whispered Art History for a Jukebox, Kunstbiblioteket, Copenhagen

1964 *Soumission au Possible*, Cafe Theatre de la Vieille Grille, Paris
Platitudes en Relief, Galerie J., Paris (with Daniel Spoerri; travelled to Galerie Rudolf Zwirner, Cologne)

1965 *Streetfighting Singing Sade*, East End Theater, New York
Key Event, East End Theater and Penn Station, New York
La Cedille qui Sourit, Villefranche-sur-Mer, France (with George Brecht)
Cafe au Go-Go, New York

1966 *Exposition Intuitive*, Galerie Jacqueline Ranson, Paris
Galerie Renee Ziegler, Zurich, Switzerland
Librairie-Galerie La Hune, Paris
Galerie Aktuell, Berne, Switzerland

1967 *The Key to Art*, Tiffany's shop windows, New York (with photographer Scott Hyde)
The Poetic Science, Moderna Museet, Stockholm (with George Brecht)

1968 Galerie Hansjorg Mayer, Stuttgart, West Germany
Streetfighting, Kunstbiblioteket, Copenhagen

1969 *Leeds a new card game*, Royal College of Art, Leeds, England
The Eternal Network, Stadtisches Museum, Monchengladbach, West Germany (with George Brecht)
Galerie Handschin, Basle, Switzerland
The Principle of Equivalence, Galerie Alfred Schmela, Dusseldorf, West Germany

1970 *Commemor*, Neue Galerie, Aachen, West Germany
Galerie Michael Werner, Cologne, West Germany
Galerie Alfred Schmela, Dusseldorf, West Germany
Kabinett fur Aktuelle Kunst, Bremerhaven, West Germany

1971 Eat-Art Gallery, Dusseldorf, West Germany
Galerie Muller, Dusseldorf, West Germany
Galerie Michael Werner, Cologne, West Germany
Joint Works with . . . ., Galerie Rene Block, West Berlin
15 Works for the 3rd Eye, Wide White Space Gallery, Antwerp, Belgium
Artiste d'Avril, Galerie BDDT, Nice, France
Research at the Stedelijk, Stedelijk Museum, Amsterdam

1972 *9 Weeks Research: The Genial Republic*, Wide White Space Gallery, Antwerp, Belgium
Galerie Alfred Schmela, Dusseldorf, West Germany
Gallery House, London

3 Samples of the Work of Robert Filliou, Galerie Magers, Bonn, West Germany

1973 *The Genial Republic: 9 Weeks of Futurology*, Galerie Alfred Schmela, Dusseldorf, West Germany
Galerie Roberto Medici, Solothurn, Switzerland
Recherche en Pre-Biologie, Galleria Multipla, Milan, Italy
Studio Ferrero, Nice, France
Galerie Buchholz, Munich, West Germany
Neue Berliner Kunstverein, West Berlin
Der 1000010 Geburstag der Kunst, Neue Galerie, Aachen, West Germany

1974 *Recherche sur le pas fait*, Galerie Bama, Paris
Erforschung des Ursprungs, Stadtische Kunsthalle, Dusseldorf, West Germany
The Act of God Act, Museum of Modern Legislation, Copenhagen

1975 *Recherche sur l'Origine*, Kunstmuseum, Lucerne, Switzerland

1976 *Pantogrammes*, Galerie Handschin, Basle, Switzerland (with Andre Thomkins)
Telepathic Music, John Gibson Gallery, New York
Le Poipoidrome, Maison des Jeunes Artists, Budapest (with Joachim Pfeufer)
The Eternal Network, Galerie Bama, Paris

1977 *Le Poipoidrome*, Ecole d'Art, Nantes, France (with Joachim Pfeufer)
La Boutique Aberrante, Centre Georges Pompidou, Paris
Anton's, Calgary, Alberta
Western Front Society, Vancouver, British Columbia

1978 *Le Poipoidrome*, Reykjavik Art School, Iceland (with Joachim Pfeufer)
The Eternal Network, Partecipazione Arte Contemporanea, Genoa, Italy
La Fondation Poipoi, Centre Georges Pompidou, Paris (with Joachim Pfeufer)
Galerie Bama, Paris

1979 *Dessins sans Desseins*, Galerie Bama, Paris
Galerie Marika Malacorda, at *Art 10 '79*, Basle, Switzerland

1980 Musee d'Art Contemporain, Montreal, Quebec (with Ben Vautier and Dick Higgins)

1981 *Seeing on all sides*, Galerie Catherine Issert, St. Paul de Vence, France
Galerie Bama, Paris

1982 Galleria Mercato del Sale, Milan, Italy
Galerie Marika Malacorda, Geneva, Switzerland

1983 Galerie Bama, Paris

1984 Sprengel-Museum, Hannover
Musee d'Art Moderne de la Ville, Paris

1985 Kunsthalle, Berne

Selected Group Exhibitions:

1960 *Festival d'Art d'Avant-garde*, Palais des Expositions, Porte de Versailles, Paris

1962 *Festival of Misfits*, Gallery One, London

1965 *First World Congress: Happenings*, St. Mary's of the Harbor, New York

1970 *Happening and Fluxus*, Kolnischer Kunstverein, Cologne

1972 *Documenta 5*, Museum Fridericianum, Kassel, West Germany

1973 *Artists' Books*, Moore College of Art, Philadelphia

1977 *Bookworks*, Museum of Modern Art, New York

1979 *Fluxus and Chaos*, Espace Lyonnais d'Art Contemporain, Lyon, France

1982 *Fluxus 1962–1982*, Nassauischer Kunstverein, Wiesbaden, West Germany

1987 *Berlinart 1961–87*, Museum of Modern Art, New York (travelled to San Francisco)

Collections:

Kaiser-Wilhelm Museum, Krefeld; Stadtisches Museum, Monchengladbach; Westfalischer Landasmuseum, Munster; Neue Galerie/Sammlung Ludwig, Aachen; Museum am Ostwall, Dortmund; Museum Moderner Kunst, Vienna; Centre Georges Pompidou/Musee National d'Art Moderne, Paris; Musee de la Ville de Toulon; Musee de la Ville de Calais.

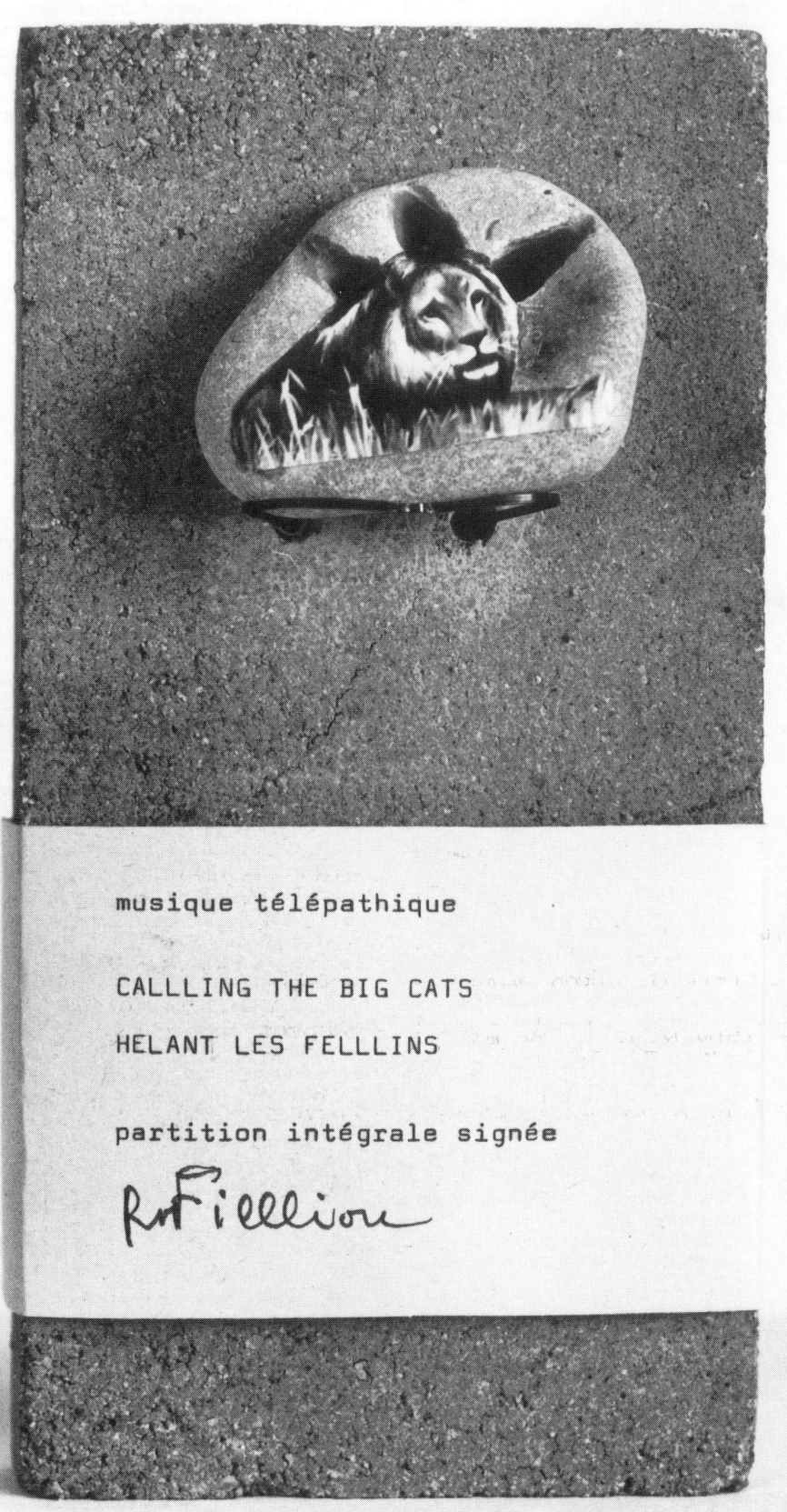

musique télépathique

CALLLING THE BIG CATS

HELANT LES FELLLINS

partition intégrale signée

Robert Filliou: *Calling the Big Cats*, 1982

Publications:

By FILLIOU: books—*A Five Year Plan for the Reconstruction and Development of South Korea*, with Robert Nathan, New York 1953; *Ample Food for Stupid Thought*, New York 1965; *Je Disais a Marianne*, Basle 1965; *L'Immortelle Mort du Monde*, New York 1967; *A Filliou Sampler*, New York 1967; *14 Songs and One Riddle*, Stuttgart 1968; *Teaching and Learning as Performance Arts*, with contributions by John Cage, Allan Kaprow, George Brecht and others, Cologne 1970; *A Thousand Japanese Poems*, Cologne 1970; *Le Siege des Idees*, with Edwige Regenwetter, Brussels 1977; *La Boite Futile*, Malmo 1978; *Je Meurs Trop*, Brussels 1979; *Musical Economy no. 1*, Florence 1980; *A New Way to Blow Out Matches*, Malmo 1980; *Le Livre Etalon*, Reykjavik 1981.

On FILLIOU: books—*Happenings, Fluxus, Pop Art, Nouveau Realisme*, edited by J. Becker and Wolf Vostell, Hamburg 1965; *Notations* by John Cage, New York 1969; *Happening and Fluxus*, exhibition catalogue compiled by Hanna Sohm, Cologne 1970; *Mail Art: Communication a Distance, Concept* by Jean-Marc Poinsot, Paris 1971; *Fluxshoe*, exhibition catalogue edited by David Mayor, Cullompton 1972; *Le Geste a la Parole* by Jacques Donguy, Paris 1981; *Fluxus 1962–1982*, exhibition catalogue with texts by George Brecht, Ludwig Gosewitz, Geoffrey Hendricks and others, Wiesbaden 1982; *Robert Filliou*, exhibition catalogue, Hannover 1984.

The majority of contemporary artists in the West, while rejecting the traditional forms of art, have accepted the traditional *role* of the artist. That is to say they see their products as being part of a continuous and historically legitimate process with its own internal logic and development. The artist will justify his work in terms of its relationship to work in the immediate past and his role, seen from this point of view, is to develop "Art."

As "Art," in this sense, is a somewhat limited activity, with little or no interest to anyone outside the art world, contemporary Western art is prone to academicism and the art-for-art's-sake fallacy. It tends to lose contact with the other half of the creativity equation—life—and concentrate rather on essentially sterile problems of style.

Artists who have become aware of this have invented various strategies to overcome the huge gap that now separates art from life. One can catalogue these strategies as Marxist, participatory, popular, anti-art and so on, although none of these has yet succeeded in evolving a convincing solution, as they all tend to rely upon the idea of bringing Art, as it is currently understood, to the people.

A more interesting and fertile approach can be found among those artists who, while retaining the idea that art is a metaphorical description of reality, have attacked the traditional role of the artists. Instead of trying to dilute contemporary art to a point where everybody can understand it, they defend the right to be "difficult" and self-indulgent, without claiming that anything they do has any relevance to contemporary art structures. Robert Filliou is one such artist.

Filliou's success has been based on failure. He has almost invariably failed to carry out any of the strategies he has invented to overcome what he considers to be the impossible position of the artist today. Faced with the problem of how to sell work and making a living without being absorbed in the system of values, market prices and critical reputations, he invented ideas which could not possibly work; an art gallery in his hat, a shop that was never open, books which were too expensive to buy or in editions too small to make any impact. As a result he has retained an enigmatic position which has allowed him freedom to experiment in any direction he chooses without being pinned down by the art public's expectations (of course, though, it hasn't solved the problem of income).

Strategies such as the above are clearly "absurd" and reflect the principal influence upon his art: Zen. The Zen koan of the "what is the sound of one hand clapping" variety, or the ridiculous answers given by Zen patriarchs to the earnest questions of their pupils are designed to explode the accepted categories of language and meaning, thus clearing the mind for the entrance of intuitively understood truth. The absurdity is not the absurdity of despair, in the existentialist mode, but a destructive technique which is seen as a necessary preliminary to reconstruction.

In the Zen tradition, Filliou's work is not only absurd; it also contains its positive elements based upon an optimism about the potential creativity of all people (his piece in the Edinburgh/Dusseldorf show was actually created by visitors, Filliou providing the framework only in the form of a game without rules). But for everybody to be creative, we must first destroy the idea that only a small proportion of people, artists in fact, have the right to creation. Filliou argues that this elitist attitude is not due to the artists themselves but the structures that surround them, thus the absurd attacks upon the ideas of galleries and marketing.

Filliou has also taken from Zen the idea of delicacy. Where most artists with a social or political point to make galumph into the arena like elephants who think they have discovered the Secret of Life, he works silently, stating as little as possible. There is a sense of poetry in his work, the idea that concepts are better illustrated than described. For instance, he takes a sheet of those red spots that galleries use to indicate a sale and writes across the top, "each morning wear a new brain in the centre of the forehead" and signs it Robert Filliou, gaga-yogi, taoist de gauche. The idea came to him, he records, when he saw his wife slip into a pair of paper panties.

Possibly his best known images are the words "innocence" and "imagination," often made in neon tubing and attached to objects or environments that one would not normally consider as having anything to do with Art: a tool box, for instance, or a garden shed. The results of such juxtapositions are mysterious and poetical, seeming to contain meaning yet resisting classification by the mind, just far enough within the boundaries of contemporary art to be recognized as such, but containing implications of a much more interesting territory beyond.

Because of his aesthetic of failure, Filliou will probably never achieve wide recognition in the orthodox art world. As most of his art is fragile and transitory in nature, it will not be found in the major art collections. I doubt if he would wish it otherwise, as this very elusiveness gives him a potency that would soon be lost in the glare of critical acclaim. He is one of those underground artists, the secret moulders of the future, and when the history of 20th century art can be seen clearly, unaffected by market values, Filliou will emerge as one of the more important and honest artists of our time.

—Alastair Mackintosh

FINLAY, Ian Hamilton.

British. Born in Nassau, Bahamas, of Scottish parents, 28 October 1925. Studied at Mackintosh's School of Art, Glasgow. Married Susan Finlay; children: Eck and Ailie. First short stories published, Edinburgh, 1958. Founder, with Sue Finlay, Wild Hawthorn Press, Edinburgh, 1961–66, Easter Ross, 1966–69 and Dunsyre, since 1969. First concrete poems, 1963; first graphic images, 1967. Founder, Society for the Protection of the Arts against the Arts Council, 1974, and Free Arts Society, 1978. Recipient: Scottish Arts Council bursary, 1966, 1967 and 1968; Atlantic-Richfield Award, Boston, 1968. Address: Little Sparta, Stonypath, Dunsyre, Lanarkshire, Scotland.

Individual Exhibitions:

1963   Ledlanet House, Fife, Scotland
1968   Axiom Gallery, London
1969   Pittencrieff House and Park, Dunfermline, Scotland
1970   Coelfriths Bookshop Gallery, Sunderland, County Durham
1971   Winchester College of Art, Hampshire
1972   Scottish National Gallery of Art, Edinburgh (travelled to the MacRobert Centre, University of Stirling, and Laing Art Gallery, Newcastle upon Tyne)
1974   National Maritime Museum, London
1975   Hamilton Technical College, Lanarkshire, Scotland
1976   Coracle Press, London
        Graeme Murray Gallery, Edinburgh
        Art Gallery, Civic Centre, Southampton, Hampshire
1977   Serpentine Gallery, London
        Kettles Yard, Cambridge
1980   Graeme Murray Gallery, Edinburgh
        Collins Exhibition Hall, University of Strathclyde, Scotland
1981   Graeme Murray Gallery, Edinburgh
1986   Aberdeen Art Gallery, Scotland
1987   Victoria Miro Gallery, London

Selected Group Exhibitions:

1964   *Cambridge International Exhibition of Concrete Poetry*
1976   *Inscape: Works by Contemporary Scottish Artists*, Fruit Market Gallery, Edinburgh
1978   *Exhibition of Concrete Poetry*, Battersea Art Centre, London
1982   *Inner Worlds*, E. M. Flint Gallery, Walsall, Staffordshire (toured the U.K., 1982–83)
1984   *The British Art Show*, City Art Gallery, Birmingham (and Ikon Gallery, Birmingham; travelled to Edinburgh, Sheffield and Southampton)
1985   *Promenades*, Parc Lullin, Genthod, Geneva

Collections:

Tate Gallery, London; Towner Art Gallery, Eastbourne, Sussex; Gallery of Modern Art, Lodz, Poland.

Publications:

By FINLAY: numerous cards and folding cards, poem/prints, published by Wild Hawthorn Press, Edinburgh/Easter Ross/Dunsyre, Scotland, since 1963, and numerous books and booklets, including *The Sea-Bed and Other Stories*, 1958; *The Weed Boat Masters Ticket, Preliminary Text, Part Two*, 1971; *Poems to Hear and See*, 1971; *Sail/Sundial*, 1972; *Jibs*, 1972; *Honey by the Water*, 1972; *Butterflies*, 1973; *A Family*, 1973; *Exercise X*, 1974; *Heroic Emblems*, 1977; *The Boy's Alphabet Book*, 1977; *Woods and Seas*, 1979; *Romances, Emblems, Enigmas*, 1981; *3 Developments*, 1982.

On FINLAY: books—*Ian Hamilton Finlay*, exhibition catalogue, by Stephen Bann, Edinburgh 1972; *Ian Hamilton Finlay*, exhibition catalogue, by Stephen Scobie, Southampton, Hampshire 1976; *Ian Hamilton Finlay*, exhibition catalogue, by Stephen Bann, London 1977 (includes bibliography); *Ian Hamilton Finlay* by Francis Edeline, Paris 1978; *Coincidence in the Work of Ian Hamilton Finlay*, exhibition publication by Christopher McIntosh, Edinburgh 1980; *Ian Hamilton Finlay: A Visual Primer* by Yves Abrioux, Edinburgh 1985, New York 1986; *Homage to Ian Hamilton Finlay*, exhibition catalogue with essay by Yves Abrioux, London 1987.

*

The Scottish poet Ian Hamilton Finlay has established himself as the major exponent of concrete poetry in the British Isles, producing work which has influenced many younger poets in the United States and Canada as well as Britain. But more recently he has moved on to produce his own unique and distinctive form of environmental art.

Concrete Poetry explores the common ground between poetry and painting by using words or letters as a graphic medium. It thus becomes a visual as well as a verbal art, because it is poetry in which the writer tries to give greater meaning to the words by forming them into a particular shape, either on the printed page or, in Finlay's case, often by laying them out on the ground, in for instance a garden, on large scale.

Such ideas are far from being new, going back through Lewis Carroll's pictorial typography for the mouse's tale in the shape of a mouse's tail, to the egg-shaped poem written by the Greek poet Simmias around 300 B.C. But the modern rise of concrete poetry has its roots in the experiments of the Futurists and Dadaists.

Finlay's poems include all sorts of visual experiments. He too has in fact written a pear-shaped poem, made up of repetitions of the phrase "au pair girl"—a sort of visual pun. In "Acrobats" the letters of this word arranged repeatedly in a rectangular shape becomes a sort of Op Art poem, with the word springing out across the various diagonals, like actual acrobats in a circus. The "XM poem" is rather like Lewis Carroll's mouse tail, a Scottish stream swaying down the page, with different kinds of type suggesting the altering nature of the water as it flows. "Pleure—pleut" is a poem which by repetitions gives the effect of rain splashing down a window, so much so that it ends with a para-pluie to provide the reader with an umbrella. A collage made up of the poetic names of actual trawlers suggests, and almost becomes, a traditional sea lyric:

Green Waters
Blue Spray
Grayfish etc.

The poem "wave/rock," originally executed on glass, combines a picture of sea and rocks with the repeated letters of the word "wave," which seem to move from left to right, where they come up against the massed letters of the word "rock," thus successfully combining visual verbal symbols. He has also made a series of standing poems as well as large poem-constructions in glass and concrete. And he also makes effective use of colour to add another dimension or to emphasize an analogy, as in a poem made up of such simple elements as "fish," "nets," "stars," "night," where the actual words glow in yellow ink while the enclosing elements reach around them coloured in deep blue.

His more recent work has been a progressive elaboration of the environment around his own Lanarkshire farm, by inscriptions on carved stones, constructions such as sundials and weathercocks, or other alterations which show the interaction of the poet with the landscape, so that in place of individual works this becomes a continuous form of permanent artistic activity in which the poet progressively creates his own environment.

In 1960 Finlay founded the Wild Hawthorn Press, producing his own highly individual prints and cards; and he also edits the magazine *P.O.T.H., Poor Old Tired Horse*. Such publication of his own and many other experimental poet's work has made him an indispensable agent in the spreading and promotion of concrete poetry.

—Lavinia Learmont

FISCHL, Eric.

American. Born in New York City, 9 March 1948. Studied at California Institute of Arts, Valencia, BFA 1972. Independent painter, in California, 1972–74, in Nova Scotia, 1974–78, and in New York, since 1978. Assistant Professor, Nova Scotia College of Art and Design, Halifax, 1974–78. Agent: Mary Boone Gallery, 417 West Broadway, New York, New York 10012. Address (studio): 735 East 9th Street, New York, New York 10009, U.S.A.

Individual Exhibitions:

1975   Dalhousie Art Gallery, Halifax, Nova Scotia
1976   Galerie B, Montreal
        The Studio, Halifax, Nova Scotia
1978   Galerie B, Montreal

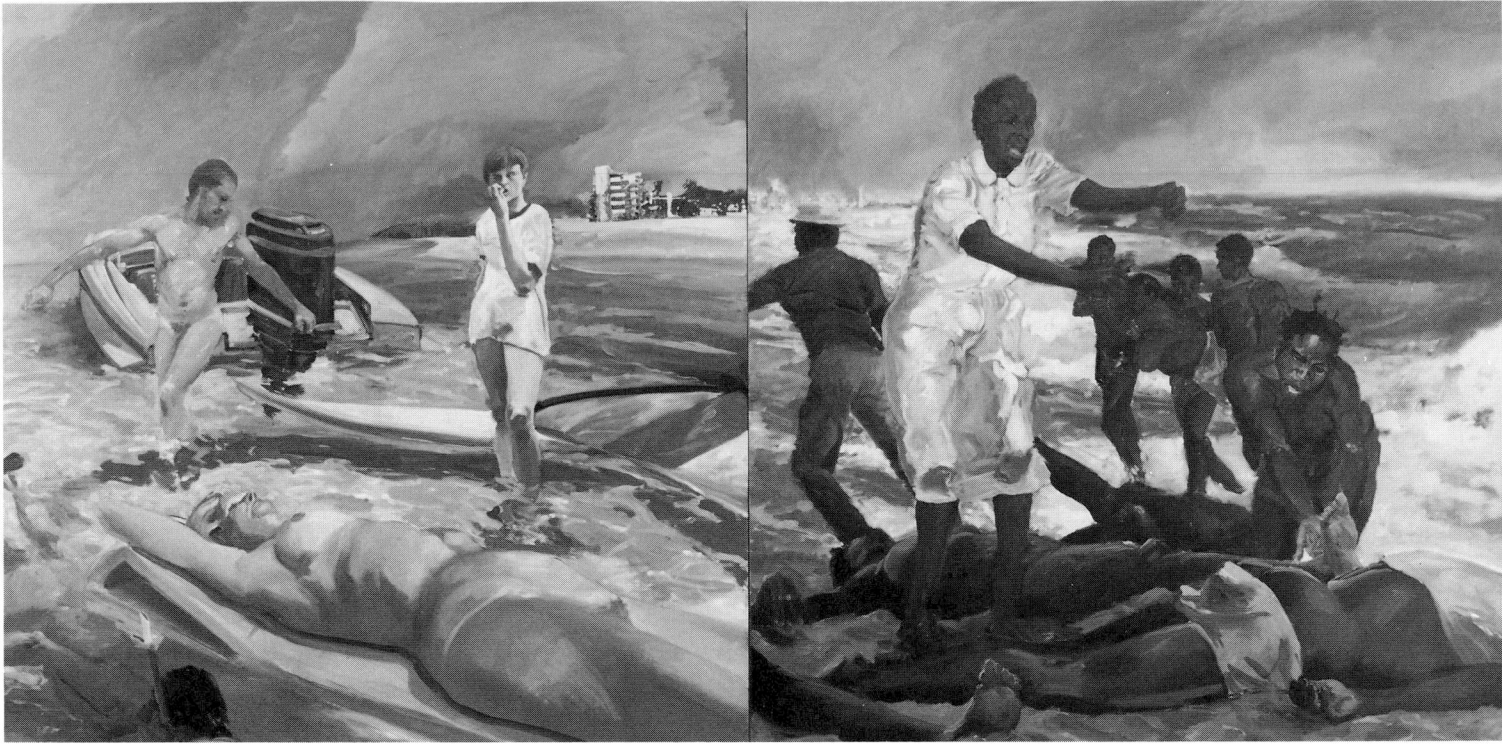

Eric Fischl: *A Visit To/A Visit From/The Island*, **1983** Courtesy Whitney Museum, New York

1980	Edward Thorp Gallery, New York
	University of Akron, Ohio
1981	Edward Thorp Gallery, New York
	Sable-Castelli Gallery, Toronto
1982	Edward Thorp Gallery, New York
	Sable-Castelli Gallery, Toronto
	University of Colorado, Boulder
1983	Larry Gagosian Gallery, Los Angeles
	Galleria Mario Diacono, Rome
	Multiples/Marian Goodman Gallery, New York
	Nigel Greenwood Gallery, London
	Saidye Bronfman Centre, Montreal
	Concordia University, Montreal
1984	Mary Boone Gallery, New York
1985	Mendel Art Gallery, Saskatoon, Saskatchewan (travelled to Eindhoven, Basle, London, Toronto, Chicago and New York, 1985–86)
1986	California State University, Long Beach (travelled to Berkeley, Honolulu, Baltimore and St. Louis, 1986–87)
1987	Walker Art Center, Minneapolis (with Vernon Fisher and Laurie Simmons)

Selected Group Exhibitions:

1975	*The Canadian Canvas*, Time Canada Ltd., Toronto
1976	*17 Artists: A Protean View*, Vancouver Art Gallery, British Columbia
1978	*Neun Kanadische Kunstler*, Kunsthalle, Basle
1979	*The Great Big Drawing Show*, Project Studio One, Queens, New York
1981	*The Reality of Perception*, Rutgers University, Newark, New Jersey
1982	*Focus on the Figure: Twenty Years*, Whitney Museum, New York
1984	*Paradise Lost, Paradise Regained*, at the *Biennale*, Venice
1985	*The Allegorical Image in Recent Canadian Painting*, Agnes Etherington Art Centre, Kingston, Ontario
1987	*Avant Garde in the Eighties*, Los Angeles County Museum of Art
1988	*Contemporary American Art*, Sara Hilden Art Museum, Tampere, Finland (travelled to Oslo)

Collections:

Museum of Modern Art, New York; Metropolitan Museum of Art, New York; Art Institute of Chicago; Museum of Contemporary Art, Los Angeles; Whitney Museum, New York; Des Moines Art Center, Iowa; De Menil Foundation, Houston; California State University, Long Beach; National Gallery of Canada, Ottawa.

Publications:

By FISCHL: books—*Eric Fischl: Bridge, Shield, Shelter*, exhibition catalogue, Halifax 1975; *Sketchbook with Voices*, with Jerry Saltz, New York 1986; articles—"Eric Fischl" in *Neun Kanadische Kunstler*, exhibition catalogue, Basle 1978; "Picasso: A Symposium" in *Art in America* (New York), December 1980; "Eric Fischl" in *Impressions* (New York), Winter 1982; "Figures and Fiction" in *Aperture* (Millerton, New York), Winter 1985; "The Man Who Exposes Himself to Women" in *Normal* (Illinois), Summer 1987.

On FISCHL: books—*Eric Fischl: Dessins*, exhibition catalogue with text by Bruce W. Ferguson, Montreal 1983; *Eric Fischl: Birthday Boy* by Mario Diacono, Rome 1983; *Eric Fischl: Paintings*, exhibition catalogue with text by Sandra Paikowsky and Bruce W. Ferguson, Montreal 1983; *Eric Fischl: Paintings*, exhibition catalogue with texts by J. C. Ammann, D. Kuspit and B. Ferguson, Saskatoon 1985; *Eric Fischl: Scenes Before the Eyes*, exhibition catalogue by Constance W. Glenn and Lucinda Barnes, Long Beach 1986; *Fischl* by Donald B. Kuspit, New York 1987.

Eric Fischl's painting is highly symptomatic of the processes taking place in the American culture of the 1980s. His huge, figurative pictures depict the most popular motifs of the suburban "leisure" civilization, that is swimming pools, picnics, family outings, homosexual couples, as well as lonely people. Actually, all those figures, painted with a kind of unpleasant severity, are lonely. This manner of painting makes the American dream show its inside lining. Fischl himself says that today the best art in the United States derives from the crisis of American identity, that America is no longer a country from an advertisement: "Things smell, things have edges, people can get hurt."

In fact, people in Fischl's pictures look as if something painfully hurt both their physicality and mental disposition. They are neither good looking nor happy, defying what they are doing. Paralyzed with a mildew of sadness they participate in the rituals of "leisure" probably out of habit and attachment to the convention. But they feel, and the viewer feels it, that the rituals and symbolism of this participation are devoid of contents. These people are stuck in the nostalgia of fulfilment which has not been positively appraised by them. Therefore, we deal here with the crisis of values, universally felt though not universally realized. Fischl's art recognizes it and shows the reality.

Fischl's painting is apparently of a narrative character. Apparently—since the promise of narration is announced each time and never fulfilled. There is enough of it in each picture for the viewer to grasp the thread; after a while he realizes, however, that the thread is torn, that there are only fragments of plots and that "passages" between them are not sufficient to continue the story.

The viewer does not really know what is happening here, but at the same time he is prompted to read individual plots. He is drawn into them by the great visual persuasiveness of these pictures, their outspoken figurativeness and the scale, which does not allow the eyes to skip them. Critics have already noticed that these pictures are discussed and evaluated primarily as regards their contents rather than from the point of view of formal means used; they are received like a film, in which we want to follow the plot and to learn who killed whom.

But in fact it is the form, painting qualities elaborated by Fischl that decide about such a discussion and reception of his art. Fischl decided to practice "wrong" painting and with this risky step he prepared his success. The artist behaves as if he lacked artistic talent and technical skills; with this he again puts the viewer at the edge of uncertainty. He creates his own esthetics, incoherent and inconsistent. He leads the brush on a canvas in an unorganized manner, without any method. He brings to life large, flat patches, deprived of artistic intensity, blunt and "displeasing" the eye. Colours are at the same time bright and toned down, like on a dust-covered poster. There are errors in the outline of figures, disguised like disability happens to be hidden; in such a form they persist in their stationary existence. Also the composition of scenes is affected with dislocations, due to which the rhythm of the picture thickens or thins in an irrational way. Every while we sense a fallacy and this is distressful to us because at the same time we feel that this is the way to revealing the truth.

Fischl improvises his great figural scenes directly

on a canvas, without previous sketches, and the viewer can sense it. Perceptible is also the presence of a pictorial background: there are universally known stereotypes behind Fischl's representations—pictures from advertising magazines, snapshots, etc. But at the same time the artist uses a live model. This dual option, simultaneous reference to medial image and to nature additionally enhances the viewer's ambivalence of feelings. However, whatever his reactions would be he has to yield to the rejuvenating force of this painting, for it is a surprise in the artistic panorama of the 1980s.

It is also something more—a revelation of a certain state of consciousness, which starts to penetrate public imagination in the United States. In this imagination, for such a long time fed with stereotypes of happiness and easiness of entering their frameworks, painful spots begin to appear. The stereotype starts to hurt with its sharp edges; instead protecting an individual by ensuring him a place in culture it alienates him.

Eric Fishcl's painting is a great, stopped panoramic movie telling about the nostalgia of the world which has already exhausted its ethos but is still not able to part with it. That is why the people existing in it are exposed to invisible blows which deform the entirety of their lives and leave them helpless in the face of pain which they did not expect.

—Alicja Kepinska

FISHER, Joel.

American. Born in Salem, Ohio, 6 June 1947. Studied at Kenyon College, Gambier, Ohio, 1965-69. Started painting, Salem, Ohio, 1956; first paintings purchased by Butler Institute, Youngstown, Ohio, 1965; moved to New York and began paper works 1969; occasional work as bartender, furniture remover, jobbing painter, in New York, 1969-71; lived in Berlin 1974-75. Recipient: Thomas J. Watson Travelling Fellowship, 1969; Berliner Kunstlerprogram (D.A.A.D.), 1974. Agent: Max Protetch Gallery, New York. Address: c/o Max Protetch Gallery, 37 West 57th Street, New York, New York 10019, U.S.A.

Individual Exhibitions:

1970   Mansfield Fine Arts Center, Ohio
        Whitney Art Resource Center, New York
1971   Victoria and Albert Museum, London
        Nigel Greenwood Inc., London
1972   Galerie Ileana Sonnabend, Paris
        Gallcria Marilena Bonomo, Bari, Italy
1973   New Gallery, Cleveland
        Galerie Stampa, Basle
1974   Galerie Folker Skulima, Berlin
        Neue Galerie, Aachen, West Germany
        Galerie Ileana Sonnabend, Paris
1975   Max Protetch Gallery, Washington, D.C.
        Ila Greene Street, New York
        Galerie Ernst, Hannover
        Stadt Museum, Monchengladbach, West Germany
1976   Nigel Greenwood Inc., London
1977   Max Protetch Gallery, New York
        Palais des Beaux Arts, Brussels
        Museum of Modern Art, Oxford
1978   Stedelijk Museum, Amsterdam
        Galeria Foksal PSP, Warsaw
        Salvatore Ala, Milan
1981   Marianne Deson Gallery, Chicago
1984   Matt's Gallery, London
1986   Nigel Greenwood Gallery, London
1987   Galerie Susanna Kulli, St. Gallen, Switzerland

Selected Group Exhibitions:

1972   *Documenta*, Kassel, Germany
        12 Artists for Documenta, Sonnabend Gallery, New York
        120 West Broadway at the *Spoleto Festival*, Italy
        Small Series, Paula Cooper Gallery, New York
1973   *Seven*, Museum of Modern Art Penthouse Gallery, New York
        Xerox Corporation Exhibition, Rochester, New York
        Drawings, Sonnabend Gallery, New York
        Aspects de l'Art Actuel (Festival d'Automne), Museé Galliera, Paris
1974   *Seraphon*, Amerika Haus, Berlin
1986   *Esculturas sobre la Pared*, Galeria Juana de Aizpuru, Madrid

Collections:

Butler Art Institute, Youngstown, Ohio; Virginia Museum of Fine Arts, Richmond; Victoria and Albert Museum, London.

Publications:

By FISHER: books—*An Image in Blankness,* Oxford 1977; *The Second Furlong,* London 1984; articles—"On Paper," interview by Simon Field, in *Art and Artists* (London), January 1972; "Joel Fisher," interview, with Lisa Bear, in *Avalanche* (New York), December 1974.

In the beginning the idea of paper was the idea of ground. Over and over again I watched the paper rise from the water. The materials I used were simple: 1. a tub of water in which the paper pulp floated in dispension; 2. a wooden frame with a filter mesh stretched over it; and 3. some squares of felt to which the wet and fragile paper could be transferred until it was strong enough to be picked up.

The filter screen is drawn through the water. Water falls back, and the tiny cellulose fibers interlock, fiber upon fiber, each holding in place and in turn being held by others. There is no glue, for it is unnecessary; it is a self-structuring surface maintaining itself.

For me papermaking is not only an activity but also an event. The paper forms at that instant when its constituent fibers are pulled from the water and enter the air. The surface of the water is a plane which creates a plane. A tension is established; the substance is differentiated. In its creation each sheet is separated from the materials which is itself. It remains a subsidiary only of itself; a surface connecting by identity to its base. The paper is not an idea itself but contains an idea—almost as a cognate to thought. Always and throughout, what is meant is equal to what is not meant. Within the sheet of paper there is great structural homogeneity; back, front, inside, and outside are all equal. Although paper is not a *carte blanche* (contrary to my original expectations), it still remains a balanced and adequate ground for experience.

A sheet of paper can be repaired by returning it to its liquid state and making it anew (much as the mudpies of children can be repaired and reformed eternally by adding water). The form and structure of the material is perceived as beyond all barriers of separate objects with beginnings and ends. It is a fugitive with a history of other manifestations. As one of the most polymorphous of materials, paper goes back and forth between its structured and unstructured states with relative ease. One senses an inherent potential in this general fluidity. Conscious of the nature of a pulp which constantly allows itself to renew and define, I concern myself only with those acts which establish a simple, fugitive, structuring relationship.

On spun lines: Several years ago I went to Scotland in order to learn to spin. A strange old lady taught me using a stone she picked up from the beach and a thick clump of wool which was clinging to a low shrub. As a shepherdess, years ago, she would save the wool which clung to fences and shrubs by spin-

ning it in this manner—one stone for white wool, one for the black—the process is simply this: after the wool is gathered it is picked apart, allowing any small particles of dirt to fall out. This increases the volume but not the weight. Usually the next step is to "card" the wool using wire brushes. This aligns the fibers in roughly parallel lines. The carded fibers are then rolled along one's thigh into long rolls called "rolags." From these rolags a thread is spun pulling out a few fibers at a time. This is called "drawing" or "drafting" and the resultant line is really a thread; the tension between the fibers which was destroyed by pulling the fibers apart is now re-established. The fibers spin around each other in a linear spiral—holding themselves together—drawing a line. When shorter fibers have been twisted together into a long strand, this strand becomes stronger than the cumulative strength of the untwisted fibers. The spinning operation combines two separate movements: a twisting and longitudinal movement away from the drafting or drawing zone. These two forces—the twisting and the pulling—must always be kept in balance.

—Joel Fisher

Joel Fisher's creative activity is strongly involved with the processes of vital functions: it is tied to experiencing the kind of work that one decides to carry out alone, from the start, with one's own hands. The artist produces his own paper (occasionally from scraps of his own clothes), which then becomes the basis for his thought processes and for their formulations.

On receiving a clean piece of paper, the artist stands simultaneously in the presence of both a void and its disturber. The paper is full of irregularities: the edges of the sheets are uneven. One can also notice the fibers that remain after the sheet has been dried—on a layer of felt. Sometimes, the artist pays attention to one of these fibers, which then takes on a meaning and stands out as a form. This fiber may then be enlarged, drawn onto paper and become a sign ("Apographs"). It can also lose its background and be transferred onto a wall as a pattern, newly created from repetition of the original.

The moment that the artist notices and chooses the fiber, and the attention paid to the unevenness of the sheet edges, don't, however, form a clear boundary from whence the creative act begins. This includes the whole work, beginning with the decision to produce one's own paper. Thus is paper not a "background" to the expression, but itself takes part in its construction. That is why that all that the clean sheet offers becomes so important. Equally as important is the actual birth of the paper's surface, at the moment it emerges from water—this is where the idea of a "return" to the watery womb comes from. It becomes identified with a retrieval of the original moment in the process of creation (in a Happening in the Mönchengladbach Museum, the artist dissolved his previous works in water). "By making paper, I take part in the potential of the world," says Fisher.

The artist therefore attaches importance to the most basic ontological issues, those at the heart of human philosophy: he wishes to touch the original state of the material and to be at the heart of the first impulse, setting into motion thoughts and things. In this way, he wishes to take part in the "whole," in the actual core of the world. The philosophical attitude is contained in the artistic attitude and is expressed by means of art.

Paper treated in this way becomes the carrier of many reflections. Above all, by being ordinary and mundane, it seems to become invisible; it is "everywhere." The sheet of paper becomes a free space; "it absorbs and demarcates ends of the world." A reflection, on that place and its existence in time, then follows. It appears to us as a clean area, still unmarked, as the beginning of the day. It also fortells the end of the day's promise, of the advent of "evening," of darkness. The clean sheet that is "everywhere" thus begins to succumb to the action of linear time. We cannot free ourselves from a feeling for history: an empty place is its announcement, the promise of its fulfilment. An empty place is also the promise of the unknown—it gives us no certainty, not even the knowledge that it will still exist when we look at it again. This uncertainty becomes for the artist sui generis a guarantee of creativity, since certainty does not engage us at all; it is uncreative.

Clean paper also holds out the possibility of uninhibited expansion. It is true that the edges of the sheet make us aware of the limits of possibility, but they also identify the area that they enclose. That is why the edges become important: the artist sees them as lines that have a control over the actual interior of the paper. He thus draws into the paper the shape of these uneven edges; he repeats these lines in the direction of the centre of the sheet; he fills the inside with them so that he reaches the limits of possibility—going from emptiness to fullness. The paper loses its area, ceases to accept anything, "speaks but does not listen." It becomes filled just as the world becomes filled with things, our thoughts and fancies. The movement from the edge to the centre of the paper suddenly makes the boundaries appear elsewhere: they move aside from the edges, they carry their uncrossability to the centre. Now the centre becomes a threshold that must be crossed.

Crossed in order to recover the empty space. This is a very difficult step since even pointing out an empty space spoils its excellence, fills it with our intentional acts. That is why the artist suggests obtaining a distance by ignoring the spots and flaws. By setting up a certain threshold below which we will not notice visual material, one calls to mind the experience of seeing the earth at a great distance, when it appears to be uninhabited. The capacity to achieve an empty space is very important, just as one needs to recover the "beginning"; it becomes a condition of working, forcing one's will onto the material world.

Joel Fisher's art comes from the simplest of acts—and facts so obvious that they are almost "invisible." The artist notices possibilities of sublimation in them and turns them into such excellent ideas in the flesh that the beginning and end of the process become as one: the covered piece of paper regains its innocence, the day—the promise of a new beginning; the regained "empty place" makes the continued process of creation possible.

—Alicja Kepinska

FLANAGAN, Barry.

British. Born in Prestatyn, North Wales, 11 January 1941. Educated in Sussex; studied at the Birmingham College of Art, 1957-58, then briefly at various art schools, 1958-63; studied advanced sculpture, under Anthony Caro, Phillip King and William Tucker, at St. Martin's School of Art, London, 1964-66. Married Susan Lewis in 1963; children: Samantha and Tara. First stone carvings, Birmingham, 1958; spent several months in Devon and London, visited Montreal, then settled in Bristol; first structures using sand, with canvas and other fibres, 1966; first etchings made at St. Martin's School of Art, 1970, and later in his own studio; travelled in the United States, 1970; returned to stone carvings, in Italy, 1973. Lecturer, Central School of Art and Design, London, 1967-71, St. Martin's School of Art, 1967-71, and Omaha Municipal University, Nebraska, 1971-75. Recipient: Dover Street Materials Award, Institute of Contemporary Arts, London, 1965; Gulbenkian Foundation grant, 1972; Arts Council Award, 1975. Agent: Waddington Galleries, 2 Cork Street, London W1X 1PA. Address: Acton Farm, Aston-le-Walls, Daventry, Northamptonshire, England.

Individual Exhibitions:

1966   Rowan Gallery, London

1968   Rowan Gallery, London
        Galerie Ricke, Kassel, West Germany
        Galleria dell'Ariete, Milan
1969   Museum Haus Lange, Krefeld, West Germany
        Fischbach Gallery, New York
1970   Rowan Gallery, London
1971   Rowan Gallery, London
        Galleria del Leone, Venice
1972   Rowan Gallery, London
1973   Rowan Gallery, London
1974   Rowan Gallery, London
        Museum of Modern Art, New York
        Bluecoat Gallery, Liverpool
        Museum of Modern Art, Oxford
1975   Hogarth Galleries, Sydney
        Art and Project, Amsterdam
1976   Hester van Royen Gallery, London
1977   Art and Project, Amsterdam
        Appledorn Museum, Netherlands
        Stedelijk van Abbemuseum, Eindhoven, Netherlands
        Arnolfini Gallery, Bristol
1978   Serpentine Gallery, London
1980   Waddington Galleries, London
        New 57 Gallery, Edinburgh
1981   Waddington Galleries, London

        60's and 70's Prints and Drawings by Barry Flanagan, Mostyn Art Gallery, Llandudno, Wales (toured Wales and England)
1982   *Stone and Bronze Sculptures,* at the *Biennale,* Venice (travelled to the Whitechapel Gallery, London)

Selected Group Exhibitions:

1967   *British Drawings,* Museum of Modern Art, New York (toured the United States)
1969   *When Attitudes Become Form,* Kunsthalle, Berne
1971   *The British Avant Garde,* New York Cultural Center
1972   *The New Art,* Hayward Gallery, London
1975   *Biennale,* Musée National d'Art Moderne, Paris
1978   *Made by Sculptors,* Stedelijk Museum, Amsterdam
1980   *Pier + Ocean,* Hayward Gallery, London (travelled to the Rijksmuseum Kröller-Müller, Otterlo, Netherlands)
1982   *Aspects of British Art Today,* Metropolitan Art Museum, Tokyo (toured Japan)
1984   *The British Art Show,* City Art Gallery, Birmingham (and Ikon Gallery, Birmingham; travelled to Edinburgh; Sheffield; Southampton)

Barry Flanagan: *The Boxing Ones*, 1981

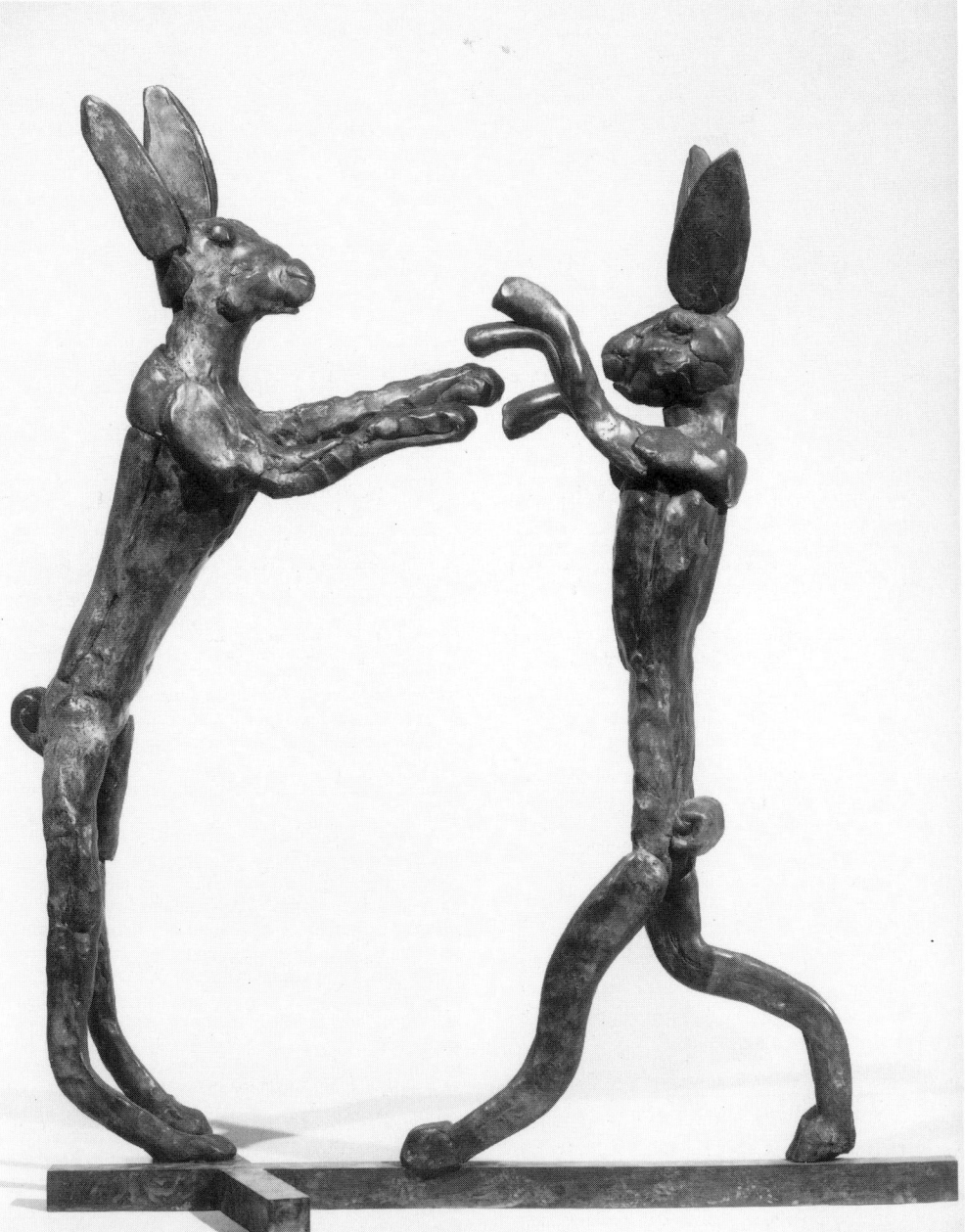

1987 *A Quiet Revolution: British Sculpture Since 1965,* San Francisco Museum of Modern Art (travelled to Newport Beach, California; Washington, D.C.; Buffalo, New York)

Collections:

Tate Gallery, London; Arts Council of Great Britain, London; Victoria and Albert Museum, London; Walker Art Gallery, Liverpool; Museum of Modern Art, New York; National Gallery of Canada, Ottawa.

Publications:

By FLANAGAN: article—"Sculpture Made Visible," discussion with Gene Baro, in *Studio International* (London), October 1969; films—*Hole in the Sea,* videotape, 1969; *The Works I,* 1970; *Atlantic Flight,* 1970; *Bus Ride,* 1970; *The Phantom Sculptor,* 1971; *The Lesson,* 1971; *Sand Girl,* 1971; *Line on Holywell Beach,* 1971.

On FLANAGAN: books—*Barry Flanagan,* exhibition catalogue, by Catherine Lampert, London 1980; *Barry Flanagan,* exhibition catalogue, by David Brown, Edinburgh 1980; *60's and 70's Prints and Drawings by Barry Flanagan,* exhibition catalogue, by Catherine Lampert, Llandudno, North Wales 1981; *Barry Flanagan: Stone and Bronze Sculptures,* exhibition catalogue, by Michael Compton and Tim Hilton, Venice and London 1982; articles—"British Sculpture: The Developing Scene" by Gene Baro in *Studio International* (London), October 1966; "British Sculpture Today" by Christopher Finch in *Art and Artists* (London), May 1967; "Doubts, Dilemmas, Eyelines: Some Leaves from Barry Flanagan's Notebook" by Anthony Fawcett in *Art and Artists* (London), April 1968; "Barry Flanagan's Sculpture" by Charles Harrison in *Studio International* (London), May 1968; "Barry Flanagan" by Catherine Lampert in *Studio International* (London), December 1974.

Barry Flanagan's oeuvre is marked by its diversity of appearance. Yet the absence of family likeness (a signature style) signifies neither loss of directions nor a rampant eclecticism, for Flanagan's approach to sculpture has been informed by a singleness of vision, one which is perhaps best summarized in his statement: "within the sculpture there are carried its own solutions; we invest it with problems, ideas and excitements. One merely causes the things to reveal themselves to the sculptural awareness. It is the awareness that develops, not the agents of the sculptural phenomena."

Trained, in part, at St. Martin's School of Art during the heyday of its sculptural activity, Flanagan gained the habit of questioning all dogmas and preconceptions: from the beginning his work has been made against the grain. "aaing j gni aa," for example, in which brightly colored Miróesque turds have been clumped insouciantly together, struck a dada note at odds with the prevailing climate of more solemn inquiry. Others, like "Heap," "Pile," "Stack," and "Bundle," examined the nature of those concepts, their titles named through such unorthodox materials as dyed hessian filled with paper, foam or sand. Later works, including "Untitled '70," resemble nomadic tents, and like such transitory phenomena seem to stake a minimum claim to space and permanence.

In the 70's Flanagan turned increasingly to traditional materials—stone and bronze—and conventional techniques—casting and carving—but, typically, he diverted them to new ends. In pieces like "a nose in repose," the nose appears to be a found form, its contours given, not shaped, by the artist; the carving element consists of a line etched into the surface of this stone, a line which appears to have little in common with the form in which it is imbedded. Flanagan's characteristic wit took a new turn in a series of recent stone works, like "Carving no. 13," 1981, which were executed by assistants enlarging small clay maquettes whose forms had been arrived at by Flanagan simply squeezing a lump of clay in his hand. In the process of transforming the model into the large stone version, the original forms had to be re-interpreted into a different material, one for whom such squashy,

spongy shapes are far from natural. Yet the irony deepens; the final image has taken on an organic naturalness, but it is a different kind of naturalness from that of the maquette, not at all reminiscent of its gestural beginnings.

Such witty yet profound questioning underlies most of Flanagan's work. In recent bronzes based on the image of a hare he has once again reinvigorated traditional concerns, for he has managed to introduce an anthropomorphic content in such a way that sculpture can at last return to tragic themes without heroics or self-consciousness.

—Lynne Cooke

FLAVIN, Dan.

American. Born in New York, 1 April 1933. Educated at Cathedral College of the Immaculate Conception, Douglastown, New York, 1947–52; United States Air Force Meteorological Technicians' Training School, 1953; University of Maryland Extension Program, Korea, 1954–55; New School for Social Research, New York, 1956; and Columbia University, New York, 1957–59; self-taught in art. Lecturer, Graduate Faculty, University of North Carolina, Greensboro, 1967; Albert Dorne Visiting Professor, University of Bridgeport, Connecticut, 1973. Recipient: William and Noma Copley Foundation Grant, 1964; Skowhegan Medal for Sculpture, Maine, 1976. Agent: Leo Castelli Gallery, New York. Address: c/o Leo Castelli Gallery, 420 West Broadway, New York, New York 10010, U.S.A.

Individual Exhibitions:

1961 Judson Gallery, New York
1964 Kaymar Gallery, New York
 Green Gallery, New York
1965 Ohio State University, Columbus
1966 Galerie Rudolf Zwirner, Cologne
 Nicholas Wilder Gallery, Los Angeles
1967 Kornblee Gallery, New York
 Galleria Sperone, Milan
 Museum of Contemporary Art, Chicago
1968 Galleria Sperone, Turin
 Galerie Heiner Friedrich, Munich
 Pennsylvania State University, University Park
 Dwan Gallery, New York
1969 Galerie Konrad Fischer, Dusseldorf
 Irving Blum Gallery, Los Angeles
 Galerie Bruno Bischofberger, Zurich
 Fluorescent Light, etc., National Gallery of Canada, Ottawa
 Vancouver Art Gallery
1970 The Jewish Museum, New York
 Dwan Gallery, New York
 Leo Castelli Gallery, New York
 Los Angeles County Museum of Art
 Galerie Heiner Friedrich, Munich
1971 Leo Castelli Gallery, New York
 Galerie Heiner Friedrich, Munich
 John Weber Gallery, New York
 Janie C. Lee Gallery, Dallas
 Galerie Heiner Friedrich, Cologne
1972 Leo Castelli Gallery, New York
 Rice University, Houston
 Albright-Knox Art Gallery, Buffalo, New York
1973 John Weber Gallery, New York
 Leo Castelli Gallery, New York
 City Art Museum, St. Louis
 3 Installations in Fluorescent Lights Galerie Heiner Friedrich, Cologne
 University of Bridgeport, Connecticut
 Locksley Shea Gallery, Minneapolis
 Lisson Gallery, London
1974 Leo Castelli Gallery, New York
 The Greenberg Gallery, St. Louis

 Jared Sable Gallery, Toronto
 Galleria Pasquale Trisorio, Naples
 Daniel Weinberg Gallery, San Francisco
1975 Leo Castelli Gallery, New York
 Museum Boymans-Van Beuningen, Rotterdam
 Fort Worth Art Museum, Texas
 Funf Installationen in Fluoreszierendem Licht van Dan Flavin, Kunstmuseum, Basel
1976 Leo Castelli Gallery, New York
 Fort Worth Art Museum, Texas
 Charlotte Square Gallery, Edinburgh
 Scottish National Gallery of Modern Art, Edinburgh
 Portland Center for the Visual Arts, Oregon
 Heiner Friedrich Gallery, New York
1977 Heiner Friedrich Gallery, New York
 Otis Art Gallery, Los Angeles
 Ace Gallery, Los Angeles
 Art Institute of Chicago
 Ace Canada, Vancouver
 Contemporary Arts Center, Cincinnati, Ohio (with Michael Venezia)
1978 Heiner Friedrich Gallery, New York (twice)
 University of California Art Museum, Berkeley
 Leo Castelli Gallery, New York
 Parrish Art Museum, Southhampton, New York
 Galerie Heiner Friedrich, Cologne
1979 Leo Castelli Gallery, New York
 Hudson River Museum, Yonkers, New York (travelled to the Laguna Gloria Art Museum, Austin, Texas)
 National Gallery of Canada, Ottawa
1981 Leo Castelli Gallery, New York
1985 CAPC Musée d'Art Contemporain, Bordeaux, France
 Rijksmuseum Kroller-Muller, Otterlo, Netherlands

Selected Group Exhibitions:

1957 *Roslyn Air Force Station Art Exhibit,* North Shore Community Center, Roslyn, New York
1964 *Black, White and Grey,* Wadsworth Atheneum, Hartford, Connecticut
1966 *Primary Structures,* Jewish Museum, New York
1971 *Art and Technology,* Los Angeles County Museum of Art
1975 *Sculpture: American Directions 1945–1975,* National Collection of Fine Arts, Smithsonian Institution, Washington, D.C.
1976 *Drawing Now,* Museum of Modern Art, New York
1977 *Early Work: André/Flavin/Judd/LeWitt,* Sperone, Westwater, Fischer Inc., New York
1979 *The Reductive Object: A Survey of the Minimalist Aesthetic in the 1960's,* Institute of Contemporary Art, Boston
1980 *91st Exposition Société des Artistes Indépendants,* Grand Palais, Paris
1984 *Reflections: Contemporary Art Since 1964,* National Gallery of Canada, Ottawa

Collections:

Museum of Modern Art, New York; Metropolitan Museum of Art, New York; Guggenheim Museum, New York; Whitney Museum, New York; Philadelphia Art Museum; La Jolla Museum of Contemporary Art, California; Pasadena Art Museum, California; National Gallery of Canada, Ottawa; Stedelijk Museum, Amsterdam.

Publications:

By FLAVIN: articles—letter to the editor in *Artnews* (New York) April 1963; ". . . In Daylight or Cool White: An Autobiographical Sketch" in *Artforum* (New York), December 1965; "Flavin Speech" in *Blockprint* (Providence, Rhode Island), 21 March 1966; statements in *Artforum* (New York), December 1966; letter to the editor in *Arts Magazine* (New York), February 1967; "Some Other Comments . . ." in *Artforum* (New York), December 1967; statements in *Don Judd,* exhibition catalogue, New York 1968; letters to the editor in *Artforum* (New York), March 1968, April 1968, October 1968; letter to the editor in *Artnews* (New York), Summer 1968; ". . . In Daylight or Cool White" in *Fluorescent Light,*

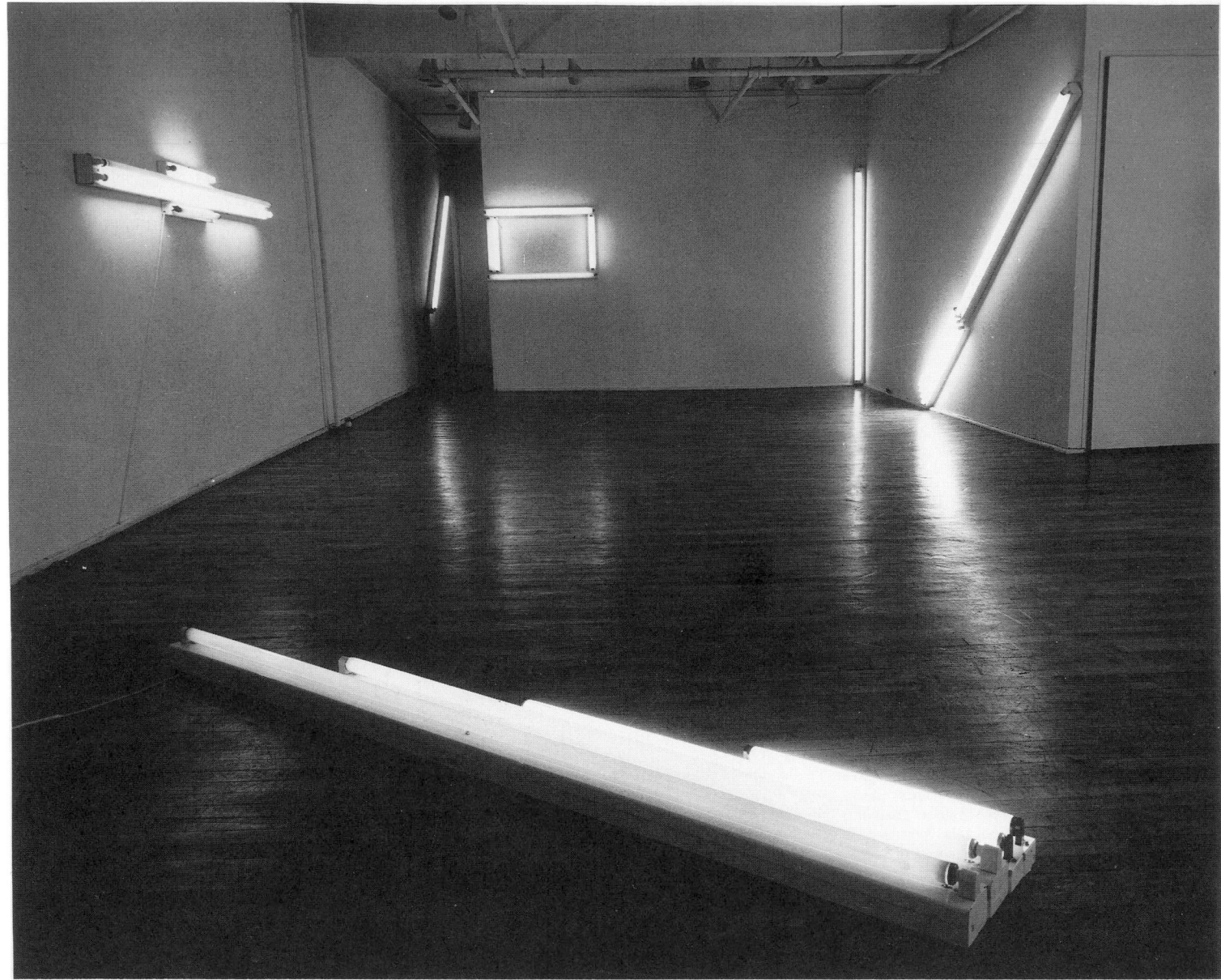

Dan Flavin: Fluorescent installation at the Green Gallery, New York, 1964

etc., exhibition catalogue, Ottawa 1969; "Dan Flavin" in *Art Now: New York,* March 1969; statement in *Studio International* (London), April 1969; "Fluorescent Light, etc. from Dan Flavin: A Supplement," with Brydon Smith, in *Arts-canada* (Toronto), October 1969; "Untitled, To Dear Durable Sol from Stephen, Sonja and Dan" in *Sol LeWitt,* exhibition catalogue, The Hague 1970; "Correspondence: The Guggenheim Affair" in *Studio International* (London) July/August 1971; letter in *Artforum* (New York), October 1971; statement in "Around Barnett Newman" by Jeanne Siegel in *Artnews* (New York), October 1971; "Comment by the Artist" in *Studio International* (London), December 1972; "Address Delivered by Dan Flavin at the National Gallery of Canada for Don Judd's Retrospective Exhibition" in *Studio International* (London), September 1975.

On FLAVIN: books—*Dan Flavin,* exhibition catalogue, Turin 1968; *Late Modern: The Visual Arts since 1945* by Edward Lucie-Smith, New York 1969; *Dan Flavin, Fluorescent Light, etc.,* exhibition catalogue, by Brydon Smith, Ottawa 1969; *Modern Painting: The Movement, the Artists and Their Work* by Burton Wasserman, New York 1970; *Art and Technology,* Los Angeles 1971; *Icons and Images of the 60's* by Nicolas and Elena Calas, New York 1971; *The New Avant Garde: Issues for the Art of the 70's* by Gregoire Muller, New York 1972; *Dan Flavin: 3 Installations in Fluorescent Lights,* exhibition catalogue, Colgone 1973; *Funf Installationen in Fluoreszierendem Licht van Dan Flavin,* exhibition catalogue, Basel 1975; *Dan Flavin,* exhibition catalogue, Otterlo 1985.

When Dan Flavin began exhibiting his rhythmic arrangements of fluorescent tubes of light in the early 60's, the New York art world shuddered with delight. Though minimal painting and sculpture were well on their way to solving every art-making problem (or so it seemed), Flavin's sculptures opened up Pandora's box of new considerations. Not that the art establishment wasn't ripe for this kind of intrusion. After all, Flavin wasn't the only one making waves. But he was one of very few making waves with light waves. The sculptures were hard to pin down. Though they satisfied all the requirements of minimalism, they were more contradictory, more vulnerable, less static than their close cousin of the era. The fact that they were store bought, ready-made items which were arranged in only one geometrical composition out of the infinite possibilities from which a particular arrangement could be made was central to Flavin's concept. It was therefore unnecessary for one to pay heed to the eerie light which they shed. But one could hardly help noticing the light by which they were engulfed upon entering these subtly manipulated spaces. In this way, the pieces were more intuitive, less self-referential than Judd's or Lewitt's or Andre's.

Flavin used the tubes as neutral lines of light much in the same way, he proposed, that a painter used line. Predetermining their configurations, Flavin pointed and watched while each construction was installed by electricians. They were parallel, adjacent groupings flush against walls, stretching across corners, tunneling through hallways or pointing away from walls at varying angles. Though Flavin made no attempt to compose these tubes with any respect to a particular environment, they filled any room from wall to wall, sometimes negating the room entirely with their eerie illumination, isolating their own essence from the walls, ceilings and floors. Though they shared with other minimal art of the era a radical independence of the artist's touch, this quality of illumination made them ironically dependent upon the variables inherent in any gallery with natural light. Thus, they necessarily developed a partnership with their environment, even though they did not help to define or enhance it. Also, the idea of their need for an electrical outlet brought inevitable questions of how these disparate concepts (light and form) were interrelated. Where did the art stop and start, and, indeed, what exactly was the art?

Flavin's work has not changed much in the last 20 years. Much of his older work, like icons or a rich tradition from the past, is exhibited around the world.

—Janet Goleas

FONTANA, Lucio.

Italian. Born in Rosario di Santa Fe, Argentina, 19 February 1899. Educated in Milan primary schools; Istituto Tecnico Carlo Cattaneo, Milan, 1914–15; privately, with his sculptor father, Buenos Aires, 1922–28; studied sculpture, Accademia di Brera, Milan, under Adolfo Wildt, 1928–30. Member, Abstraction-Creation, Paris, 1934; co-signed with Melotti, Ghiringelli, and others, *Manifesto of Italian Abstract Art,* Milan, 1935; worked on ceramics, Sèvres, France, 1937; lived in Buenos Aires, 1940–47, then returned to Italy; collaborated on publication of *Manifesto Spazialismo,* Milan, 1948, revised annually, until 1952; developed "Ambienti Spaziali," 1948, "Concetti Spaziali," 1952, and perforated pastel watercolor canvases, in 1954. Recipient: Grand Prix, *Biennale,* Venice, 1966. *Died* (in Comabbio, Varese, Italy) *7 September 1968.*

Individual Exhibitions:

1930	Galleria del Milione, Milan
1931	Galleria del Milione, Milan
1932	Galleria del Milione, Milan
1935	Galleria del Milione, Milan
1937	Galerie Jeanne Bucher, Paris
	Galleria del Milione, Milan
1938	Galerie Zach, Paris
	Galleria del Milione, Milan
1939	Galleria del Milione, Milan
1948	Galleria Il Camino, Milan
1949	Salto Bookshop, Milan
1950	Galleria del Milione, Milan
1952	Galleria del Naviglio, Milan
1953	Galleria del Naviglio, Milan
1955	Galleria S. Fidele, Milan
	Galleria del Zodiaco, Rome
1957	Galleria del Naviglio, Milan
	Galleria d'Arte Selecta, Rome
	Galleria Il Prisma, Turin
	Galleria del Cavallino, Venice
1958	*Biennale,* Venice
	Galleria Gruppo, Bergamo, Italy (with Enrico Baj and Piero Manzoni)
1959	Galleria del Naviglio, Milan
	Galerie Stadler, Paris
	Pozzetto Chiuso, Albisola Mare, Italy
	Galleria L'Attico, Rome
	Galleria di Notizie, Turin
	Arts Council Gallery, Edinburgh (with Guiseppe Capogrossi)
1960	Galerie Alfred Schmela, Dusseldorf
	Galleria del Designo, Milan
	McRoberts and Tunnard Gallery, London
1961	Galleria del Grattacioelo, Milan
	Galerie Senatore, Stuttgart
	Galerie Iris Clert, Paris
	Galerie Rive Droite, Paris
	Galleria del Triangolo, Rome
	Martha Jackson Gallery, New York
1962	McRoberts and Tunnard Gallery, London
	Galleria Pater, Milan
	International Centre of Aesthetic Research, Turin
	Galerie Zodiaque, Brussels
	Galleria Apollinaire, Milan
	Städtisches Museum, Leverkusen, West Germany
1963	Galleria Il Centro, Naples
	Galleria dell'Ariete, Milan
	Galerie Gimpel-Hannover, Zurich
	Kunstverein, Cologne
1964	Galerie Iris Clert, Paris
	Galleria Blu, Milan
	Galleria Marlborough, Rome
	Galleria La Polena, Genoa
	Gutai Pinacotheca, Osaka, Japan (with Capogrossi and Dova)
	Galerie Pierre, Stockholm
1965	Galleria di Notizie, Turin
	Galleria Apollinaire, Milan
	Galerie Anne Abels, Cologne
	Galerie XXe Siècle, Paris
	Galerie Bonnier, Lausanne, Switzerland

1966	Galleria La Polena, Genoa
	Galleria di Notizie, Turin
	Galleria Apollinaire, Milan
	Biennale, Venice
	Museo Castagnino, Rosario de Sante Fe, Argentina
	Galleria Il Punto, Turin
	Walker Art Gallery, Minneapolis (travelled to the University of Texas, Austin)
	Marlborough Gerson Gallery, New York (travelled to Instituto Torcuato di Tella, Buenos Aires)
	Galerie Alexandre Iolas, Paris
	Galleria del Leone, Venice
	Galleria Flaviana, Locarno, Switzerland
	Studio Bellini, Milan
1967	Il Bilico, Rome
	Galleria Goethe, Bolzano, Italy
	Museum of Modern Art, New York
	Louisiana Museum, Humlebaek, Denmark
	Galleria Ferrari, Verona
	Galleria La Busola, Turin
	Stedelijk Museum, Amsterdam (travelled to the Stedelijk van Abbemuseum, Eindhoven, Netherlands)
	Moderna Muséet, Stockholm
1968	Marlborough Gallery, New York
	Galleria Borgogna, Milan
	Kestner-Gesellschaft, Hannover

1969	Istituto Italo-Latino Americano, Rome
	Galerie Couturier, Paris
	Galerie Mathias Fels, Paris
	Galleria Martano, Turin
	Galerie Benador, Geneva
	Kunstmuseum, Wuppertal, West Germany
1970	Martha Jackson Gallery, New York
	Musée d'Art Moderne de la Ville, Paris
	Galleria del Leone, Venice
	Galerie Bonnier, Lausanne, Switzerland
	Galerie Couturier, Paris
	Galleria d'Arte Moderna, Turin
	Vismara Arte Contemporanea, Milan
	Galleria Milano, Milan
	Galleria Fonci, Bologna
	Galerie Benno d'Incelli, Paris
	Studio Condotti 85, Rome
	Galleria San Luca, Bologna
	Neue Galerie, Baden-Baden, West Germany
	Alexander Iolas Gallery, New York
	Quatro Venti Proposte d'Arte Contemporanea, Palermo
1971	Galleria di Notizie, Turin
	Galleria Il Centro, Naples
	Galleria Morone, Milan
	Galleria Contini, Rome

Lucio Fontana: *La Fine di Dio,* 1964

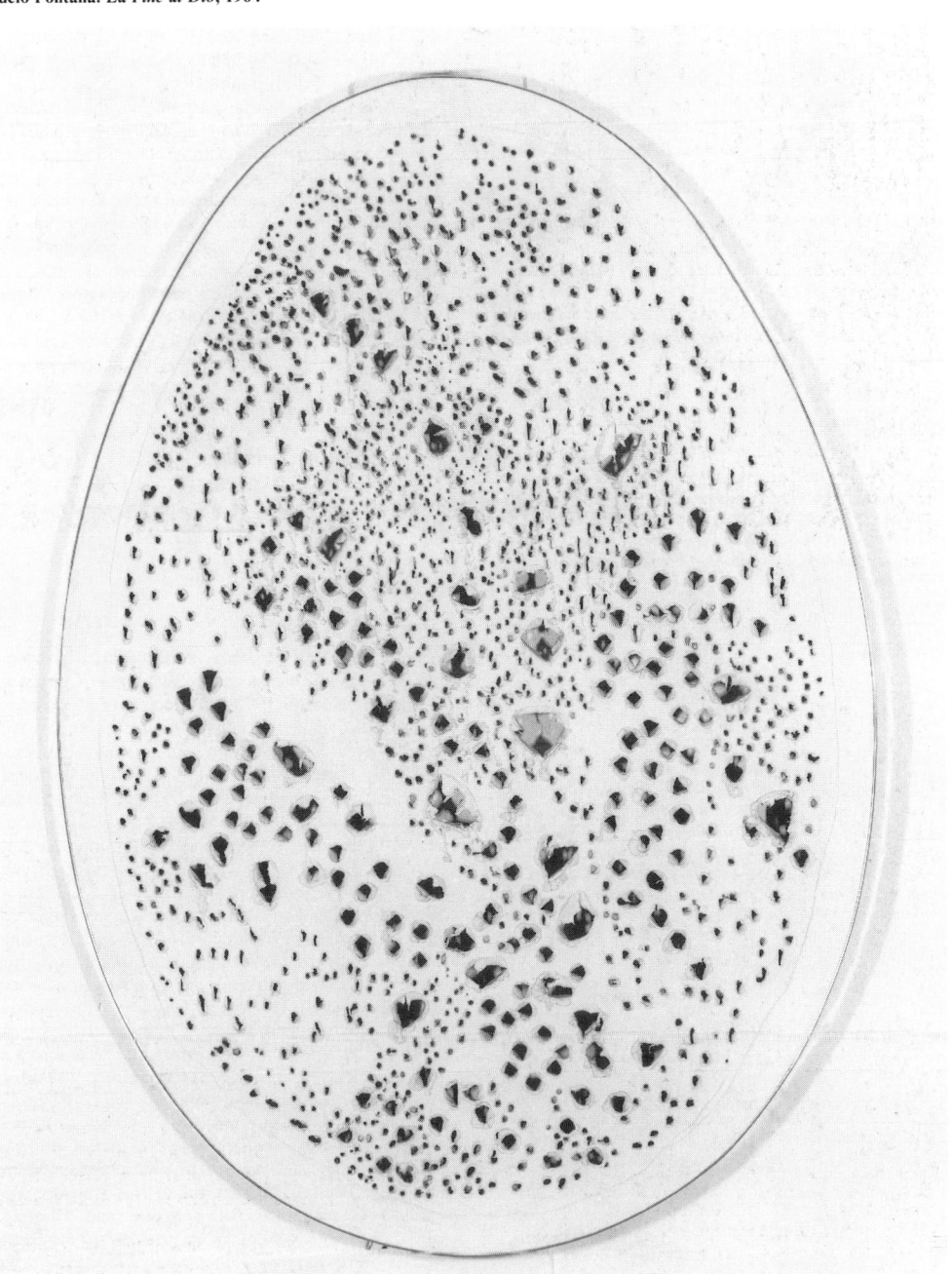

Galleria Flori, Florence
Galleria Levi, Milan
1972 Istituto Italo-Latino Americano, Rome
Palazzo Reale, Milan (travelled to the Palais des Beaux-Arts, Brussels)
Galleria 32, Milan (with Sassu)
1974 Museo de Arte Contemporaneo, Caracas
Studio 3 Bi, Bolzano, Italy
1976 Kunsthaus, Zurich
1977 Castello Sforzesco, Milan
Guggenheim Museum, New York
1979 Palazzo Reale, Milan
1980 Palazzo Pitti, Florence
1982 Palacio de Velazquez, Madrid
Salon Comunale d'Arte Contemporanea, Rimini, Italy
1984 Staatsgalerie Moderne Kunst, Munich
Mathildenhohe, Darmstadt, West Germany
1986 Museum of Modern Art, Tokyo
Seibu Museum of Modern Art, Takanawa, Japan
Seibu Museum of Art, Tokyo
Seibu Tsukashin Hall, Amagasaki, Japan
Castello di Rivoli, Turin
Marisa del Re Gallery, New York
1987 Galerie Neuendorf, Hamburg

Selected Group Exhibitions:

1930 *Biennale*, Venice
1934 *Abstraction-Creation*, Paris
1949 *Ambienti Spaziali*, Galleria del Naviglio, Milan
1950 *Biennale*, Venice
1951 *Bienal*, Sao Paulo
1955 *Exposicion de Arte Italiano Contemporaneo*, Madrid
1957 *Italian Art from 1910 to the Present*, Haus der Kunst, Munich
1960 *New Sculpture: Form, Structure and Meaning*, Städtische Galerie, Munich
1961 *Italian Contemporary Sculpture*, Takashumaya Gallery, Tokyo
1967 *Contemporary Italian Art*, Ulster Museum and Art Gallery, Belfast (travelled to the Richard Demarco Gallery, Edinburgh)

Collections:

Stedelijk Museum, Amsterdam; Stedelijk van Abbe Museum, Eindhoven, Netherlands; Rijksmuseum Kröller-Müller, Otterlo, Netherlands; Kunsthaus, Zurich; Kunstmuseum, Dusseldorf; Kaiser Wilhelm-Museum, Krefeld, West Germany; Louisiana Museum, Humlebaek, Denmark; National Gallery of Victoria, Melbourne.

Publications:

By FONTANA: book—*Italian Abstract Art*, exhibition catalogue, with others, Turin 1935.

On FONTANA: books—*Lucio Fontana* by Eduardo Persico, Milan 1936; *Su alconi Giovani . . . Fontana* by G. C. Argan, Florence 1936; *Lucio Fontana: Ceramiche* by H. Baumbach, Milan 1937; *Lucio Fontana* by J. Zocchi, Buenos Aires 1946; *Concetti Spaziali di Lucio Fontana* by G. Joppolo, Milan 1951; *Fontana* by G. P. Giani, Venice 1958; *Devenir de Fontana* by Michel Tapie, Turin 1965; *Lucio Fontana* by J. E. Girlot, Barcelona 1966; *Lucio Fontana* by Gillo Dorfles, New York 1966; *Fontana: Idea per um Ritratto* by Guido Ballo, Turin 1970; *Omaggio a Fontana* by Enrico Crispolti, Rome 1971; *Lucio Fontana: Catalogue Raisonne des Peintures, Sculptures et Environnements Spatiaux*, 2 vols., edited by Enrico Crispolti and Jan van der Marck, Brussels 1974; *L'Ironia Teologica de Fontana* by Giorgio Manganelli, Milan 1978; *Lucio Fontana* by Roberto Sanesi, Milan 1980; *Lucio Fontana*, exhibition catalogue with essay by Franco Russoli, Tokyo 1986; *Lucio Fontana*, exhibition catalogue with texts by Rudi Fuchs, Johannes Gachnang, Cristina Mundici and others, Turin 1986; *Lucio Fontana 1938-66*, exhibition catalogue with essay by Katharina Hegewisch, Hamburg 1987.

To slash the canvas, to pierce it with a sharp instrument. What is there to admire in such audacity? For many these acts of aggression are the essence of Lucio Fontana, and if that was all his contribution to contemporary art there would be little left to say.

But his claims to be a *Spatialist,* however intellectually unacceptable with all its gaudy bravura, are far more telling than would at first seem probable.

In the 1930's (and sometimes subsequently) Fontana made large ceramic amphorae, glazed in dull browns intermingled with a modicum of grey. They were not jars in the true sense of the word because they had no practical mouths, although this did not mean that incisions were not made in some of them. They were sometimes scored with grafitti (another form of creative activity with which he was involved at that time). Having no base, they would lie on their sides like free agents only slightly in the context of physical gravity.

Was this *spatialism?*

Fontana would probably have replied in the affirmative.

But all his development as an artist in the succeeding forty years was with the picture, generally, but not always, in the orthodox quadrilateral frame. The Spatialism had grown in two directions; that of sumptuous baroque (some of the pictures even encrusted with glittering coloured glass fragments), and that of total abstraction whose naked monochrome canvases have been slashed and punctured. A single colour determines the "mood" of the painting. Black, gold, red or blue make the wounds he inflicted become features of a reality deliberately projected into outer space and rendered timeless.

This is not to say that Fontana did not experience the siren call of surrealism, and indeed in a later series of manifestations he drew close to the pop art image when he carved simple symbols of landscape or consumer goods and allowed these in careful flat colouring to join up with the edges of the by now incorporated frame of the picture or, in some cases, slop over the frame's straightline geometric rim.

Contemporary art has seen many innovators. Some, like Malevich, have described themselves as *liberators.* Fontana, in attacking the canvas with knives or clotting its surface with junk jewel fragments or with carved symbols, has plainly a right to be reckoned amongst the liberators.

—Sheldon Williams

FOULKES, Llyn.

American. Born in Yakima, Washington, 17 November 1934. Studied at Central Washington College of Education, Seattle, 1953-54; University of Washington, Seattle, 1954; Chouinard Art Institute, Los Angeles, with Don Graham and Richard Rubeun, 1957-59. Served as Private First Class, 547th Medical Clearing Company, United States Army, Darmstadt and Frankfurt, 1954-56. Married Kelly Kimball in 1960 (divorced, 1970); child: Laurey; married Kati Breckenridge in 1971; children: Jenny and Breck. Painter: lives and works in Southern California. Worked as Road Crewman, Yakima County Engineering Department, Washington, 1952-53; part-time Loader, Bullocks Department Store warehouse, Los Angeles, 1957-59; taxi driver, Los Angeles Yellow Cab Company, 1960-61; Head of Production, Artcraft Picture and Frame Company, Hollywood, 1961-62. Professor of Art, University of California at Los Angeles, 1965-71; Resident Painter/Instructor, Art Center School, Los Angeles, 1971, 1975-76; Professor of Art, University of California at Irvine, 1981-82; Distinguished Professor of Art, California State University at Long Beach, 1982. Founder Member, Llyn Foulkes' Rubber Band, Los Angeles. Recipient: First Award for Drawing and Painting, Chouinard Art Institute, 1959; First Award for Painting, *San Francisco Museum Annual*, 1963; First Prize for Painting, *Biennale*, Paris, 1967. Agents: David Stuart Gallery, 807 North La Cienega Boulevard, Los Angeles, California; Willard Gallery, 29 East 72nd Street, New York, New York; and Galerie Darthea Speyer, 6 rue Jacques Callot, 75006 Paris, France. Address: 2002 Tuna Canyon Road, Topanga, California 90290, U.S.A.

Individual Exhibitions:

1961 Ferus Gallery, Los Angeles
1962 Pasadena Art Museum, California
1963 Rolf Nelson Gallery, Los Angeles
1964 Oakland Museum of Art, California
Rolf Nelson Gallery, Los Angeles
1969 David Stuart Gallery, Los Angeles
1970 Galerie Darthea Speyer, Paris
1974 Newport Harbor Art Museum, Newport Beach, California (retrospective)
David Stuart Gallery, Los Angeles
1975 Willard Gallery, New York
Galerie Darthea Speyer, Paris
1977 Grunebaum Gallery, New York
1978 Museum of Contemporary Art, Chicago (retrospective)
1983 Asher Faure Gallery, Los Angeles
1984 Los Angeles Institute of Contemporary Art
Zolla Lieberman Gallery, Chicago
1985 Gallery Paule Anglim, San Francisco
1986 Santa Barbara Contemporary Arts Forum, California
1987 Kent Fine Arts, New York

Selected Group Exhibitions:

1959 *Invitational Exhibition*, Ferus Gallery, Los Angeles
1964 *4 California Artists*, Allan Frumkin Gallery, Chicago
1965 *5 Los Angeles Artists*, Los Angeles County Museum of Art
1971 *American Art of Our Century*, Whitney Museum New York
1975 *4 Los Angeles Artists*, Visual Arts Museum, New York (travelled to the Corcoran Gallery, Washington, D.C., and the Wadsworth Atheneum, Hartford, Connecticut)
1977 *Painting and Sculpture in Southern California*, National Collection of Fine Arts, Washington, D.C.
1981 *California Landscapes*, Santa Barbara Museum of Art, California
1983 *Paintings of the 70s*, Los Angeles County Museum of Art
1985 *Black and White Drawings*, Newport Harbor Art Museum, Newport Beach, California
1987 *California Masters*, Herbert Palmer Gallery, Los Angeles

Collections:

Guggenheim Museum, New York; Museum of Modern Art, New York; Whitney Museum, New York; Art Institute of Chicago; Los Angeles County Museum of Art; Oakland Museum of Art, California; San Francisco Museum of Modern Art; Centre Georges Pompidou, Paris; Museum des 20. Jahrhunderts, Vienna; Museum Boymans van Beuningen, Rotterdam.

Publications:

On FOULKES: books—*9th Biennal*, exhibition catalogue, with an essay by William Seitz, Sao Paulo 1967; *The New Painting* by Udo Kultermann, St. Louis 1969; *Modern American Painting* by Jan Kriz, Prague 1970; *Pop Art* by Michael Compton, London 1970; *Llyn Foulkes*, exhibition catalogue with essay by Peter Selz, New York 1987; articles—"Llyn Foulkes' Portraits" by Martha All in *Artweek* (Oakland, California), May 1974; "Llyn Foulkes Retrospective" by Melinda Wortz in *Artweek* (Oakland, California), October 1974; "Llyn Foulkes: Commentary and Interview" by Sandy Ballatore in *Journal* (Los Angeles), December 1974; "Art about Imagination" by Kristine McKenna in *Artweek* (Oakland, California), May 1976; "Llyn Foulkes in Santa Barbara" by Peter Clothier in *Artforum* (New York), no. 25, 1986.

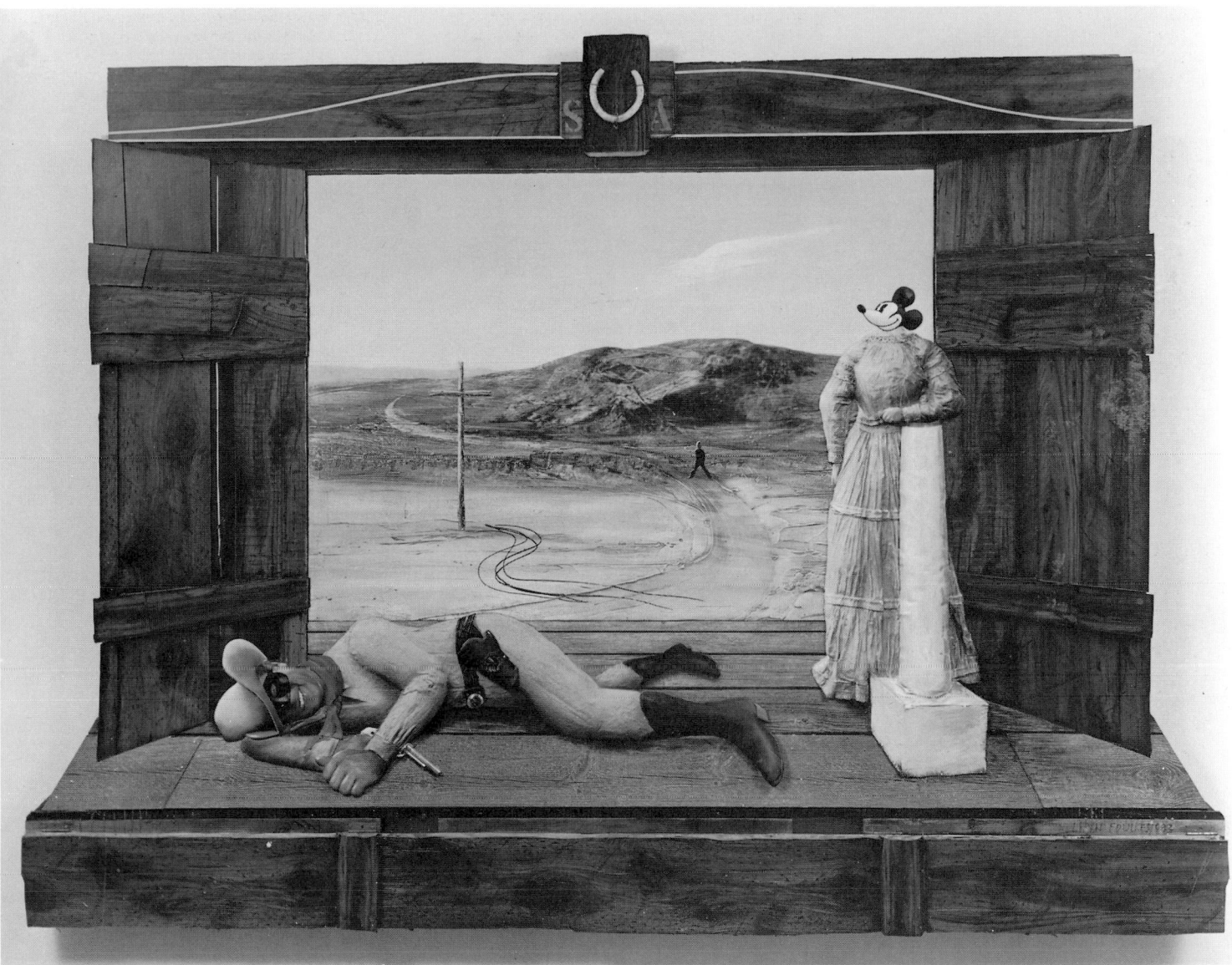

Llyn Foulkes: *The Last Outpost*, 1983

I believe that art is becoming (or perhaps has always been) a historical game for critics and collectors. The people don't much give a damn for it, and, frankly, neither do I. The role of the artist must change. He or she must communicate more broadly. When there was no photography, motion pictures or television, the painter was the communicator. The masters painted for kings; now the leaders of the world watch television.

People who have enough money to buy what a well-known artist produces use it as "money in the bank" (ready to sell it when the next line comes in). I believe that very few people buy paintings for love; besides, who *needs* it at that price. I have seen many good creators destroyed by the game, left as products incapable of taking a chance.

I believe that I am still ahead of the game. I refuse and will always refuse to become a product for the sake of ART. I am still challenging my securities to find if they are real and my mistakes to find if they are mistakes. I believe in the most direct approach to art. If it is going to live, it must take from everything (including itself). It must find a valid reason for existing in an overstimulated world.

—Llyn Foulkes

Out of the tradition of Dada/Surrealism, Llyn Foulkes has forged his own personal, quirky/zany variant.

Since his early work of 1959–60, Foulkes has continued to pursue his characteristically "bad boy" tactics, designed to break stylistic rules by inventing sardonic/comedic combinations which scramble landscape painting, graphic overlay, portraiture, assemblage, collage, with a kind of California Popishness and knowing disregard for high art seriousness.

Foulkes' major themes of the 1960's were "rocks", "post cards" and "animals". In a work such as "Geography Lesson" (1960), Foulkes mixes painting and collage in a Jasper Johnsian composition that substitutes rocks for body parts. It is the element of visual correspondence between a particular rock (in Eagle Rock, California) and a cow's skull which propelled Foulkes into a whole series of works in which landscape takes on animal/human presence. In many works from the early 60's Foulkes adds scribbles, scrawls and/or compulsively hand-written messages, while also creating frames which take on a presence all their own which is quite capable of equal attention with the picture itself. Such purposefully flamboyant contrivances aim attention toward the deviousness of art as precious object which soothes the viewer and carries us away from the messiness and jumble of life. The frame as primary element is further developed in Foulkes' series of "portraits" beginning during the early 1970's. In these mixed media emblems of the horrible and the hilarious, Foulkes is at his best, having located a method and vocabulary well suited for

his devilishly underhanded personality and intentions.

Building each image through accumulation, layer on top of layer, Foulkes comes up with preposterously contrived "altered states," in which the explicit portrait turns into a Magritte-like persona, its identifiable features disguised and generalized by a variety of ambiguously significative items. These masking elements are sometimes geometrically outlined and populated by diverse scraps of found objects, and are other times oozing, amoeba-like overgrowths which seem to be taking over the monsterized subject. Compositions tend toward the symmetrical and simple, and images are accompanied by inscriptions or dedications in many instances. The frames are wildly intent and differ considerably according to the particular work. They act as compulsive structural schema, surrounding the small-scaled image forcefully and often almost swallowing it up and taking over completely. Always there is a tension between the playful and the grotesque, a spirit linking Foulkes with older European artists of the fantastic such as Paul Klee and Max Ernst.

Foulkes is not an artist who sets precedents for the future art, nor is he one who breaks ground in the art historical vein. His is a persistently perverse rearranging from Dada/Surreal precursors, enlivened by that personal spark inherent in those whose art unnerves with a twinkle and twinkles with nerve.

—Barbara Cavaliere

FOX, Terry (Alan).

American. Born in Seattle, Washington, 10 May 1943. Studied at Cornish School of Allied Arts, Seattle, while working for Boeing Aircraft Corp.; studied at Accademia di Belle Arti, Rome 1962, then settled in San Francisco. Second European visit 1968-70. Now lives and works in Florence, Italy. Recipient: Adaline Kent Annual Award for Californian Artists, 1977; DAAD Artists Fellowship, West Berlin, 1982. Agent: Ronald Feldman Fine Arts, 31 Mercer Street, New York, New York 10013. Address: Via dell'Albero 13, 50123 Florence, Italy.

Individual Exhibitions:

1970	Reese Palley Gallery, San Francisco
	Museum of Conceptual Art, San Francisco
	Richmond Art Center, California
1971	Reese Palley Gallery, New York
	Reese Palley Gallery, San Francisco
1972	Galerie Ileana Sonnabend, Paris
	Reese Palley Gallery, San Francisco
	Modern Art Agency Lucio Amelio, Naples
1973	University of California, Berkeley
1974	Everson Museum of Art, Syracuse, New York
1975	Galleria Schema, Florence
	Long Beach Museum of Art, California
	And/Or Gallery, Seattle, Washington
1976	The Kitchen, New York
1977	Site, San Francisco
	The Kitchen, New York
	Galerie De Appel, Amsterdam
	Galerie Krinzinger, Innsbruck, Austria
1978	Podio del Mondo per l'Arte, Middelburg, Netherlands
	San Francisco Art Institute
1979	Galerie Nachst St. Stephen, Vienna
	Galerie Dany Keller, Munich
1980	Museum of Modern Art, New York
1982	Kunstmuseum, Lucerne, Switzerland
	Galleria Fernando Pellegrino, Bologna, Italy
	Museum Folkwang, Essen, West Germany
	Daad-Galerie, West Berlin
1983	Galerie Grita Insam, Vienna
1984	Ronald Feldman Fine Arts, New York
1985	Kunstraum Munchen, Munich
	Galleria del Cavallino, Venice

Selected Group Exhibitions:

1969	*The Return of Abstract Expressionism*, Richmond Art Center, California
1970	*The 80's*, University of California Art Museum, Berkeley
1971	*Project: Pier 18*, Museum of Modern Art, New York
1972	*Documenta 5*, Museum Fridericianum, Kassel, West Germany (and *Documenta 6*, 1977)
1978	*Adaline Kent Awards*, San Francisco Art Institute
1980	*Space, Time, Sound*, San Francisco Museum of Modern Art
1983	*Site Strategies*, Oakland Museum, California
1984	*Content: A Contemporary Focus 1974-84*, Hirshhorn Museum, Washington, D.C.
1986	*California Sculpture 1959-80*, San Francisco Museum of Modern Art
1987	*Berlinart 1961-87*, Museum of Modern Art, New York (travelled to San Francisco)

Collections:

University of California Art Museum, Berkeley; San Francisco Museum of Modern Art; Museum Folkwang, Essen; Museum Moderner Kunst, Vienna; Kunstmuseum, Lucerne.

Publications:

By FOX: book—*Catch Phrases and Hobo Signs*, Munich 1985; films—*If Marcia Ever Gets Back with the Butane, This Film Will Be a Gas*, with Willoughby Sharp, 1969; *Rain*, 1970; *Sweat*, 1970; *3-Minute Film*, 1970; video tapes— *Tonguing*, 1970; *The Rake's Progress: In the Service of Art*, 1971; *Turgenscent Sex*, 1971; *Clutch*, 1971.

On FOX: books—*Terry Fox*, exhibition catalogue, Essen 1982; *Terry Fox*, exhibition catalogue with essay by Christine Tacke, Munich 1985.

FRANCIS, Sam.

American. Born in San Mateo, California, 25 June 1923. Studied medical sciences at the University of California, Berkeley, 1941-43; began painting while a tuberculosis patient at hospitals in Denver and San Francisco, studying privately with David Park, 1944-47, and during convalescence at the Artists' Colony, Carmel, California, 1947; returned to the University of California as an art student, 1948-50, B.A. 1949, M.A. 1950, then studied at the Académie Fernand Léger, Paris, 1950. Served in the United States Army Air Corps, 1943-44. Married Mako Ioemitsu; son: Osamu; married Margaret Smith in 1986. Full-time artist since 1950; worked in Paris, with travel to Mexico, Tokyo and throughout Europe, 1950-58; moved to New York, 1959; lived in Berne, 1960-61; moved to Santa Monica, California, 1962; lived in Tokyo, 1973-74; collaborated with the group "Single Wing Turquoise Bird," 1968; established studio in San Leandro, California, 1981-83; founded Lapis Press, Santa Monica, California, 1984. Recipient: *International Biennial Exhibition of Prints* Award, Tokyo, 1962; Dunn International Prize, 1963; Tamarind Fellowship, 1963. Honorary Ph.D.: University of California, Berkeley, 1969. Agent: Smith-Andersen Gallery, 200 Homer Street, Palo Alto, California 94301. Address: 345 West Channel Drive, Santa Monica Canyon, Los Angeles, California 90402, U.S.A.

Individual Exhibitions:

1952	Galerie Nina Dausset, Paris
	Galerie du Dragon, Paris
1955	Galerie Rive Droite, Paris
1956	Galerie Rive Droite, Paris
	Martha Jackson Gallery, New York
1957	Martha Jackson Gallery, New York
	Gimpel Fils Ltd., London
	Kornfeld und Klipstein, Berne
1958	Kornfeld und Klipstein, Berne
	Galerie Olaf Hudtwalcher, Frankfurt
	Martha Jackson Gallery, New York
	Zoe Dusanne Gallery, Seattle
	Kunstverein, Dusseldorf
1959	Pasadena Art Museum, California (travelled to the San Francisco Museum of Art and the Seattle Art Museum)
1960	Kunsthalle, Berne (travelled to the Modern Museet, Stockholm)
	David Anderson Gallery, New York
	Galleria La Notizie, Turin
1961	David Anderson Gallery, New York
	Galerie de Seine, Paris
	Kornfeld und Klipstein, Berne
	Grabowski Gallery, London
	Galleria Il Segno, Rome
	Galerie Jacques Dubourg, Paris
	Minami Gallery, Tokyo
	Galerie Alfred Schmela, Dusseldorf
	Galerie St. Stephan, Vienna
1962	Galerie Benador, Geneva
	Galerie Edwin Engelberts, Geneva
	Esther Bear Gallery, Santa Barbara, California
	Galerie Olaf Hudtwalcher, Frankfurt
	Galerie Pauli, Lausanne
	Galerie Brusberg, Hannover
1963	Kornfeld und Klipstein, Berne
	Kestner-Gesellschaft, Hannover
	Galerie Anderson-Mayer, Paris
	Martha Jackson Gallery, New York
1964	Martha Jackson Gallery, New York
	Galerie Ernst Hauswedell, Baden-Baden
	Minami Gallery, Tokyo
	Pasadena Art Museum, California
1965	Kornfeld und Klipstein, Berne
	Auslander Gallery, New York
	Württembergischer Kunstverein, Stuttgart
	Arthur Tooth and Sons Ltd., London
	Galerie Ricke, Kassel, West Germany
1966	Kornfeld und Klipstein, Berne
	California State College at Fullerton
	Minami Gallery, Tokyo
	Galerie Edwin Engelberts, Geneva
	Pasadena Art Museum, California
1967	Dom Galerie, Cologne
	Pierre Matisse Gallery, New York
	Museum of Fine Arts, Houston (travelled to the University of California Art Museum, Berkeley, and the San Francisco Museum of Art)
	University of California at Los Angeles
	Dickson Art Center, Los Angeles
	Skupina Ceskoslovenskych Umelcu Orajiku-Hollar, Prague
1968	Martha Jackson Gallery, New York
	Kunsthalle, Berne
	Kornfeld und Klipstein, Berne
	Minami Gallery, Tokyo
	Badischer Kunstverein, Karlsruhe
	Stedelijk Museum, Amsterdam
	Tokyo Central Gallery
	Centre National d'Art Contemporain, Paris
	Galerie du Bac, Paris
1969	University of Minnesota, Minneapolis
	Andre Emmerich Gallery, New York
	Felix Landau Gallery, Los Angeles
1970	Los Angeles County Museum of Art
	Martha Jackson Gallery, New York
	Minami Gallery, Tokyo
	Nicholas Wilder Gallery, Los Angeles
1971	Andre Emmerich Gallery, New York
1972	Stanford University, California
	Albright-Knox Art Gallery, Buffalo, New York (retrospective; travelled to the Corcoran Gallery, Washington, D.C., Whitney Museum, New York; Museum of Fine Arts, Dallas; and the Oakland Museum of Art, California)
1973	Kornfeld und Klipstein, Berne
1974	Gimpels Fils, London
	Minami Gallery, Tokyo
1975	Nicholas Wilder Gallery, Los Angeles
	Galerie Jean Fournier, Paris
	Andre Emmerich Gallery, New York
	Richard Gray Gallery, Chicago
	Kornfeld und Klipstein, Berne
	Smith-Andersen Gallery, Palo Alto, California
1978	Nicholas Wilder Gallery, Los Angeles
1979	Galerie Jean Fournier, Paris
	Andre Emmerich Gallery, New York
	Brooke Alexander Inc., New York
1980	Riko Mizuno Gallery, Los Angeles
	James Corcoran Gallery, Los Angeles
	Smith-Andersen Gallery, Palo Alto, California
1981	Andre Emmerich Gallery, New York
	Ace Gallery, Melrose, Los Angeles
	Ruth Schaffner Gallery, Santa Barbara, California
	Faith and Charity in Hope Gallery, Idaho
1982	Andre Emmerich Gallery, New York
	Nantenshi Gallery, Tokyo
	Richard Gray Gallery, Chicago
1983	Andre Emmerich Gallery, New York
	Galerie Kornfeld, Berne
	Smith-Andersen Gallery, Palo Alto, California
	Fondation Maeght, St. Paul de Vence, France
	Studio Marconi, Milan
	Colorado State University, Fort Collins
	Galerie Jean Fournier, Paris
	Art Attack Gallery, Idaho
	John Berggruen Gallery, San Francisco
	Nantenshi Gallery, Tokyo
	Art Museum Association, New York (toured the United States)

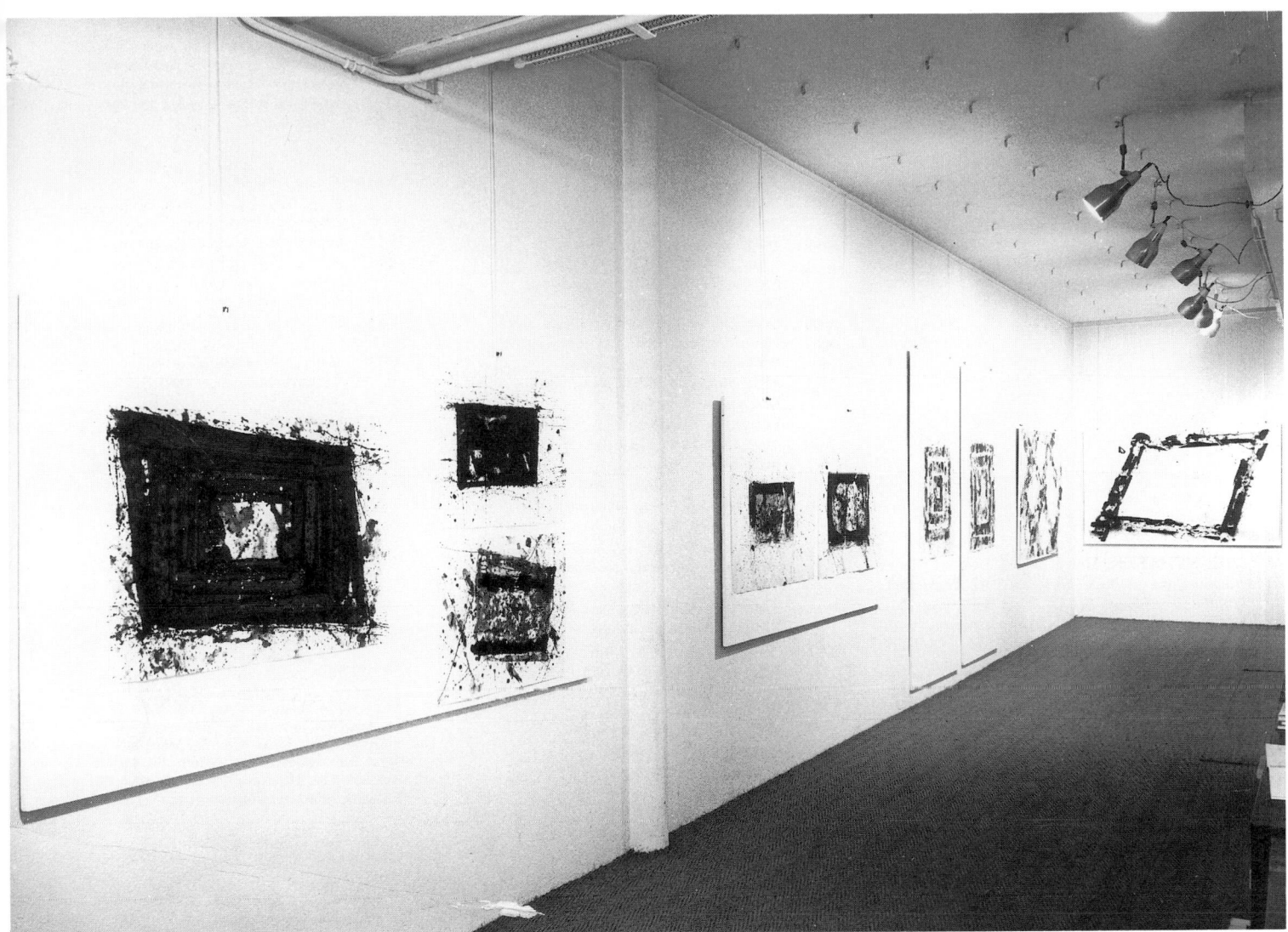

Sam Francis: Installation at the Galerie Jean Fournier, Paris, 1976

1984   Andre Emmerich Gallery, New York
        Pamela Auchincloss Gallery, Santa Barbara, California
        Brooke Alexander Inc., New York
        Cantor/Lamberg Gallery, Michigan
        Robert Elkon Gallery, New York
1985   Galerie Kornfeld, Berne
        Galerie Jean Fournier, Paris
        Nantenshi Gallery, Tokyo
        Richard Gray Gallery, Chicago
        Smith-Andersen Gallery, Palo Alto, California
1986   Andre Emmerich Gallery, New York
        Galerie Jean Fournier, Paris
        Nantenshi Gallery, Tokyo
        Angles Gallery, Santa Monica, California
1987   Knoedler Gallery, London
        Andre Emmerich Gallery, New York
        Pamela Auchincloss Gallery, Santa Barbara, California
        Heland Thorden Wetterling Galleries, Stockholm

Selected Group Exhibitions:

1950   *Salon de Mai*, Musée National d'Art Moderne, Paris
1955   *Tendances Actuelles*, Kunsthalle, Berne
1956   *12 Americans*, Museum of Modern Art, New York
        (toured the United States)
1958   *50 Ans d'Art Moderne*, Palais des Beaux-Arts, Brussels
1964   *Biennale*, Venice
1968   *British International Print Biennial*, City Art Gallery, Bradford, Yorkshire
1972   *Amerikanische Graphik seit 1960*, Bunder Kunsthaus, Chur, Switzerland (toured Switzerland)

1973   *25 Years of American Painting*, Des Moines Art Center, Iowa
1974   *Variations of Abstractions*, Andre Emmerich Gallery, New York
1977   *Art In Progress*, Louisiana Museum, Humlebaek, Denmark (travelled to the Centre Pompidou, Paris, Liijevalchs Konsthall, Stockholm, and the Israel Museum, Jerusalem, 1977-79)
1987   *American Painting: Abstract Expressionism and After*, San Francisco Museum of Modern Art

Collections:

Museum of Modern Art, New York; Whitney Museum, New York; Albright-Knox Art Gallery, Buffalo, New York; National Gallery, Washington, D.C.; Los Angeles County Museum of Art; Tate Gallery, London; Musée National d'Art Moderne, Paris; Nationalgalerie, Berlin; Stedelijk Museum, Amsterdam; Idemitsu Museum, Tokyo.

Murals: for the Sogetsu School of the sculptor and flower arranger, Sofu Teshigahara, Tokyo, 1957; Chase Manhattan Bank, New York, 1959; Kunsthalle, Berne, 1960; Weinstock's Department Store, Sacramento, California, 1980; General Services Administration Building, Anchorage, Alaska, 1980.

Publications:

On FRANCIS: book—*Sam Francis*, exhibition catalogue, by James Johnson Sweeney, Houston 1967; articles—"Summer Events: Paris: Sam Francis" by Pierre Schneider in *Art News* (New York), Summer 1955; "Sam Francis" by Berto Moruccio in *Aujourd'hui* (Paris), May 1963; "Sam Francis" by

C. H. in *Werk* (Winterthur, Switzerland), June 1968; "New York Letter" by Carter Ratcliff in *Art International* (Lugano), January 1970; "Sam Francis: From Field to Arabesque" by Lawrence Alloway in *Artforum* (New York), February 1973; "New Editions" in *Art News* (New York), November 1974.

Francis studied medicine and psychology at the University of California at Berkeley from 1941-43. After the war he studied painting with David Park at the California School of Fine Art in San Francisco (1948-50), and received his B.A. (1949), and M.A. (1950) from the University of California. In 1950 he went to Paris where he became friendly with the Canadian abstract painter Jean-Paul Riopelle and had his first solo show in 1952. From 1950-58 he worked in Paris, with travels to other European countries and, further afield, to Mexico and Japan. Dubbed by Barbara Rose in *American Art Since 1900* a second generation Abstract Expressionist, his work at this time was characterized by a cool palette and the compression of elements into segments of the canvas. The pigment was kept thin, which allowed for delicate dripping. By the late 1950s his paintings were composed of masses of brilliant colour floating on expanses of unpainted canvas.

His career has been well punctuated with inclusion in major international exhibitions and retrospectives, (Sao Paulo Bienal and Kassel Dokumenta in 1959; The Museum of Fine Arts, Houston and the University of California, Berkeley in 1967; Los Angeles County Museum of Art in 1970; Albright Knox in Buffalo in 1972).

Francis lived and exhibited in Tokyo from 1973-74 which strengthened his interest in Oriental simplicity.

By the late 1970s Francis's paintings had become more obviously structured, with large multicoloured grids dominating the picture surface. The surface was then covered with splashes and drips, all thinly laid on and 'blooming' out of each other. Also at this time came an interest in the monotype, with a major exhibition of these at the Los Angeles County Museum of Art in 1980. The monotypes used, often all at the same time, watercolour, gouache, dry pigment, inks, acrylic and oil, laid on a copper plate and put through a press. Since the early 1980s Francis has been producing both large monotypes and paintings characterized by their glowing colours. He has said of his attitude to colour: "Color is light on fire. Each color is the result of 'burning', for each substance burns with a particular color."

—Victoria Keller

FRANKENTHALER, Helen.

American. Born in New York City, 12 December 1928. Studied at Dalton School, New York, with Rufino Tamayo; Bennington College, Vermont, with Paul Feeley, 1945–49, B.A. 1949; Art Students League, New York, with Vaclav Vytlacil, 1946; privately with Wallace Harrison, New York, 1948; privately with Hans Hofmann, New York, 1950. Married Robert Motherwell, *q.v.*, in 1958. Independent painter, since 1950: lives and works in New York. Instructor, New York University, 1958–59; Painting Instructor, Yale University, New Haven, Connecticut, 1962; Princeton University, New Jersey, Hunter College, New York, 1970; University of Rochester, New York 1971; Bennington College, 1972; Brooklyn Museum Art School, New York, 1973; Swarthmore College, Pennsylvania, 1974; Drew University, Madison, New Jersey, 1975; Bard College, Annandale-on-Hudson, New York, 1977; University of Arizona, Tucson, 1978; Art Institute of Chicago, 1983; Skowhegan School of Painting and Sculpture, Maine, 1986; etc. Trustee, Bennington College, Vermont, 1967–82; Fellow of Calhoun College, Yale University, since 1968; Member, Corporation of Yaddo, Saratoga Springs, New York, 1974–78; Member, National Council on the Arts, Washington, D.C., 1985. Recipient: First Prize, *Biennale,* Paris, 1959; Gold Medal, *International Graphics Biennale,* Catania, Italy, 1972; Garrett Award, Art Institute of Chicago, 1972; National Conference of Christians and Jews Award, 1978; Bennington College Alumni Award, 1979; Mayor's Award of Honor, New York 1986. DHL: Skidmore College, 1969; DFA: Smith College, 1973; Moore College of Art, 1974; Bard College, 1976; Radcliffe College, 1978; Amherst College, 1979; New York University, 1979; Harvard University, 1980; Philadelphia College of Art, 1980; Williams College, 1980; Yale University, 1981; Brandeis University, 1982; University of Hartford, 1983; Syracuse University, 1985. Member, National Institute of Arts and Letters, 1974. Agent: André Emmerich, 41 East 57th Street, New York, New York 10022. Address: 173 East 94th Street, New York, New York 10028, U.S.A.

Individual Exhibitions:

1951	Tibor de Nagy Gallery, New York
1952	Tibor de Nagy Gallery, New York
1953	Tibor de Nagy Gallery, New York
1954	Tibor de Nagy Gallery, New York
1956	Tibor de Nagy Gallery, New York
1957	Tibor de Nagy Gallery, New York
1958	Tibor de Nagy Gallery, New York
1959	André Emmerich Gallery, New York
1960	Jewish Museum, New York
1961	André Emmerich Gallery, New York
	Everett Ellin Gallery, Los Angeles
	Galerie Lawrence, Paris
	Neufville Galerie, Paris
1962	Galleria dell'Ariete, Milan
	André Emmerich Gallery, New York
	Bennington College, Vermont
1964	Kasmin Gallery, London
1965	David Mirvish Gallery, Toronto
	André Emmerich Gallery, New York
1966	Windham College, Putney, Vermont
	André Emmerich Gallery, New York
1967	Nicholas Wilder Gallery, Los Angeles
	Gertrude Kasle Gallery, Detroit
1968	André Emmerich Gallery, New York
1969	Whitney Museum, New York (retrospective)
	Whitechapel Art Gallery, London
	André Emmerich Gallery, New York
	Kongress-Halle, Berlin
	Kunstverein, Hannover
1970	André Emmerich Gallery, New York
1971	Heath Gallery, Atlanta
	André Emmerich Gallery, New York
	Galerie Godard Lefort, Montreal
	David Mirvish Gallery, Toronto
1972	Fendrick Gallery, Washington, D.C.
	John Berggruen Gallery, San Francisco (print retrospective)
	André Emmerich Gallery, New York
	Portland Art Museum, Oregon
1973	David Mirvish Gallery, Toronto
	André Emmerich Gallery, New York
	Waddington Gallery, London
	Janie C. Lee Gallery, Dallas
	Metropolitan Museum of Art, New York
1974	Galerie Emmerich, Zurich
1975	André Emmerich Gallery, New York
	Waddington Gallery, London
	Corcoran Gallery, Washington, D.C. (retrospective)
	David Mirvish Gallery, Toronto
	Guggenheim Museum, New York
	ACE Gallery, Vancouver
	Rosa Esman Gallery, New York
1976	Diane Gilson Gallery, Seattle
	Janie C. Lee Gallery, Houston
1977	Greenberg Gallery, St. Louis
	André Emmerich Gallery, New York
	Jacksonville Art Museum, Florida
	Galerie Wentzel, Hamburg
1978	Knoedler Gallery, London
	International Communications Agency, World Tour (retrospective)
	Bennington College, Vermont
	Nelson Gallery of Art, Kansas City
	Janie C. Lee Gallery, Houston
1979	André Emmerich Gallery, New York
	John Berggruen Gallery, San Francisco
	Fendrick Gallery, Washington, D.C.
1980	*Helen Frankenthaler: Works of the 70s,* Saginaw Art Museum, Michigan (travelled to Grand Rapids Art Museum and Kalamazoo Institute of Arts, Michigan)
	Phillips Collection, Washington, D.C.
	Janie C. Lee Gallery, Houston
1981	André Emmerich Gallery, New York
	Knoedler Gallery, London
	Thomas Segal Gallery, Boston
	Toledo Museum of Art, Ohio
1982	Janie C. Lee Gallery, Houston
	Andre Emmerich Gallery, New York
	John Berggruen Gallery, San Francisco
	Getler/Pall Gallery, New York
1983	Rosa Esman Gallery, New York
	Gallery One, Toronto
	Knoedler Gallery, London
	Dana Reich Gallery, San Francisco
1984	Andre Emmerich Gallery, New York
	Katonah Gallery, New York
1985	Guggenheim Museum, New York (travelled to Edmonton, Alberta; Toronto; Milwaukee; Baltimore; San Francisco; Houston; and Cambridge, Massachusetts, 1985–86)
	Knoedler Gallery, London
1986	John Berggruen Gallery, San Francisco
	Andre Emmerich Gallery, New York
1987	John Berggruen Gallery, San Francisco
1989	Museum of Modern Art, New York (retrospective; travelled to Los Angeles; and Fort Worth, Texas, 1989–90)

Selected Group Exhibitions:

1950	*Fifteen Unknowns,* Kootz Gallery, New York
1955	*Carnegie International,* Pittsburgh
1961	*Abstract Expressionists and Imagists,* Guggenheim Museum, New York
1970	*American Artists of the 1960's,* Boston University
1971	*The Structure of Color,* Whitney Museum, New York
1974	*Abbott/Frankenthaler/Grossman/Nevelson,* Smith College Museum of Art, Northampton, Massachusetts
1978	*Two Decades of American Abstraction,* University of Tampa, Florida
1980	*Woman: Artist and Image,* Columbus Museum of Art, Ohio
1983	*The American Artist as Printmaker,* Brooklyn Museum, New York
1986	*After Matisse,* Queens Museum, Flushing, New York (travelled to Norfolk, Virginia; Miami Beach, Florida; Washington, D.C.; Dayton, Ohio; and Worcester, Massachusetts, 1986–88)

Collections:

Metropolitan Museum of Art, New York; Museum of Modern Art, New York; Whitney Museum, New York; Brooklyn Museum, New York; Everson Museum, Syracuse, New York; Bennington College, Vermont; Cleveland Museum of Art; Baltimore Museum of Art; Art Institute of Chicago; San Francisco Museum of Modern Art.

Publications:

By FRANKENTHALER: articles—"New Talent in the U.S." in *Art in America* (New York), March 1957; "Discussion: Is There a New Academy?" in *Artnews* (New York), June 1959; "An Interview with Helen Frankenthaler," with Henry Geldzahler, in *Artforum* (New York), October 1965; "A Conversation with Helen Frankenthaler," with Donald J. Cyr, in *School Arts* (Worcester, Massachusetts), April 1968.

On FRANKENTHALER: books—*Helen Frankenthaler,* exhibition catalogue, by Frank O'Hara, New York 1960; *Helen Frankenthaler* by Eugene C. Goossen, New York 1969; *Helen Frankenthaler* by Barbara Rose, New York 1971, 1975; *Frankenthaler: The 1950s* by Carl Belz, Waltham, Massachusetts 1981; *Frankenthaler: Works on Paper 1949–1984* by Karen Wilkin, New York 1984; *Helen Frankenthaler* by John Elderfield, New York 1987; articles—"The Art Galleries" by Robert M. Coates in *The New Yorker,* November 1951; "Helen Frankenthaler" by E. C. Goossen in *Art International* (Zurich), October 1961; "Poet of the Surface" by William Berkson in *Arts Magazine* (New York), May/June 1965; "The Achievement of Helen Frankenthaler" by Gene Baro in *Art International* (Lugano, Switzerland), September 1967; "Painting Within the Tradition: The Career of Helen Frankenthaler" by Barbara Rose in *Artforum* (New York), April 1969; "Frankenthaler" by J. Goldman in *Artnews* (New York), November 1974; "Helen Frankenthaler: The Moment and Distance" in *Arts Magazine* (New York), April 1975; "Helen Frankenthaler at the Guggenheim" by Phyllis Tuchman in *Art in America* (New York), September/October 1975; "Helen Frankenthaler's Art in the 50's" by Hilton Kramer in the *New York Times,* 7 June 1981; film—*Frankenthaler: Toward a New Climate,* produced and directed by Perry Miller Adato, 1978.

Helen Frankenthaler's first mature pictures were produced, astonishingly, when she was in her 20's. This is rare for an abstract artist, since most don't hit their stride until their 40's, but it's clear that Frankenthaler's early paintings are marked not only by audacity and ambition (in the best sense) but also by pure ability. We see her taking on the artists she admired, not by imitating their manner, but by examining the substance of their work. If, for example, we are some-

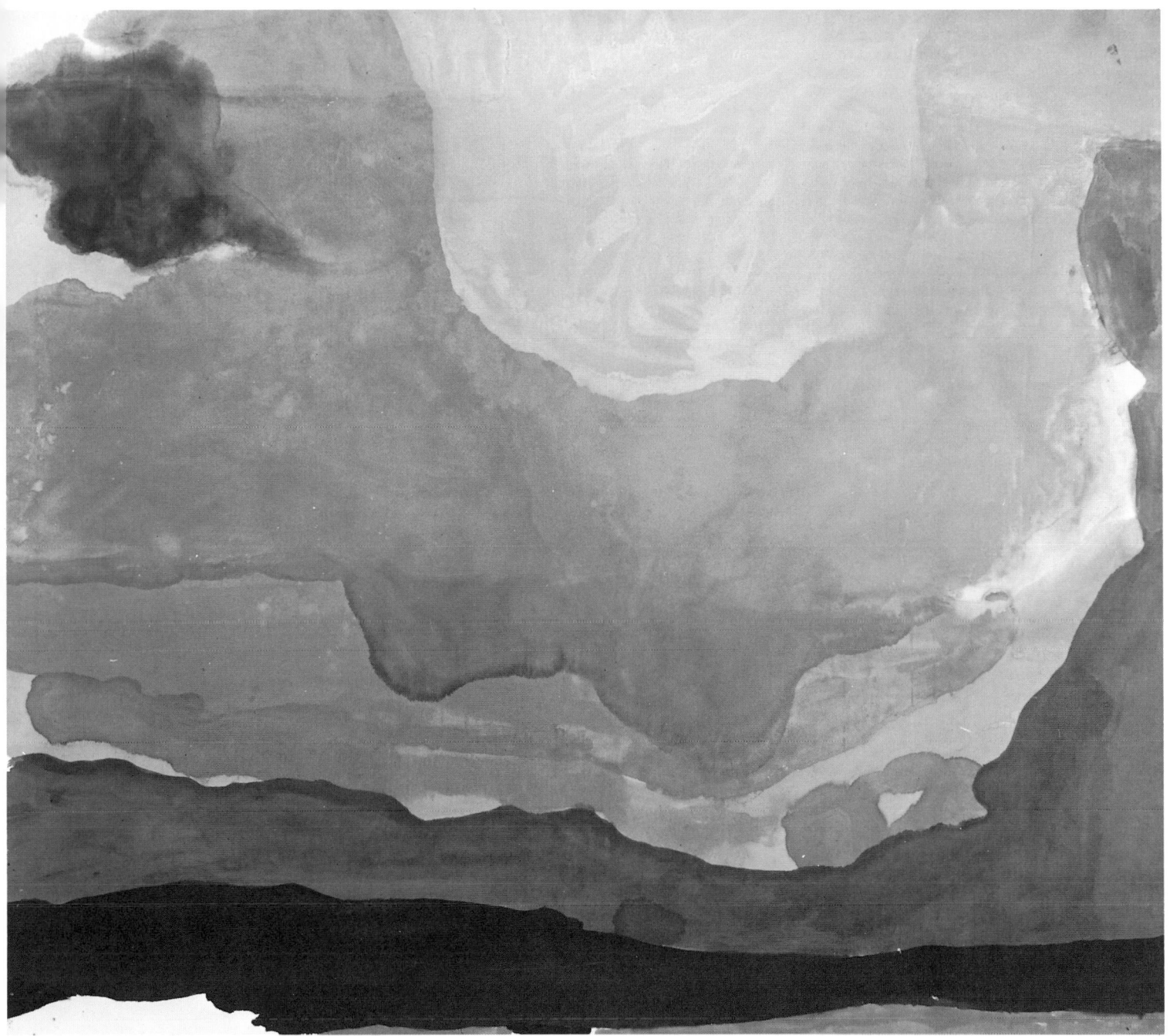

Helen Frankenthaler: *Flood,* **1967** Courtesy Whitney Museum, New York

times reminded of Pollock or Miró, it is because of the fluidity of Frankenthaler's gesture or the multiplicity of her evocative images; it is not because the paintings evoke existing Pollocks or Mirós.

From Pollock, she took the notion of fusing drawing and painting, translating this idea into her own suggestive, mysterious calligraphy. There is a now-famous litany which accompanies these early works: Frankenthaler stained paint directly into unprimed canvas, and achieved, on a large scale, the immediacy and transparency of watercolor. The white of the canvas set off her expansive drawing and led to greater openness, more disembodied color and more purely optical painting. The litany continues with the legendary visit of Kenneth Noland and Morris Louis to Frankenthaler's studio, which spurred their own investigations into the possibilities of staining with close-valued color, and changed the course of American abstraction.

Frankenthaler's early work has been the subject of a good deal of recent re-interpretation, which links its symbolic allusive qualities to an earlier generation of Abstract Expressionists, rather than stressing its evident connections with later-blooming members of Frankenthaler's own generation, such as Noland, Louis and Jules Olitski. Veiled references to personal experience and observation certainly pervade the early works, but like the artists she stimulated, Frankenthaler, too, gradually abandoned overt allusion for a no less moving, but more painterly and less specific kind of radiant color painting. Her pictures of the '60s and early '70s are distinguished by pools and flows of transparent color which paradoxically seem both to have their own shape and to have been manipulated by a very specific individual. It is impossible to separate color and drawing in these works; the floods of color seem self-determined because subtle adjustments of density and hue combine to make the result seem inevitable, but at the same time the shapes formed by these pools appear personal and expressive, never accidental or arbitrary. The continuous expanses of the areas of stained color are stiffened by drawn lines and drawing created by the edges of the color areas.

Since the mid-70's Frankenthaler's paintings have become denser and even lusher. The drama of color is intensified by the drama of surfaces. She reveals her debt to Hans Hofmann in a range of paint applications which vary from thick encrustations to transparent washes, but the imagery and drawing are unmistakeably her own. She still insists on our awareness of paint as a fluid, spreading liquid, but her paintings of the past five years or so no longer depend upon staining. Instead, we are given layers of transparent color, floating "clumps" of paint, and sensuous puddles. Small incidents of painting, set against broad sweeps of layered color, become as important as the allusive images of earlier works. These evocative palimpsests of paint have considerable spatial complexity; at the same time they are clearly about matter on a surface, and considerable emotional complexity as well.

Frankenthaler's work since about 1985 has been characterized by a new daring and a new emphasis on drawing. While she is still capable of lush layerings and transparencies, her recent work has relied on broad, relatively uninterrupted expanses of color against which she plays large scale drawn strokes and patches of varied textures and contrasting hues. The paintings have a startling clarity and immediacy.

Frankenthaler has explored many media in the 1980s. She has continued her investigation of printmaking techniques, producing monotypes, acqua-tints, and working with a master woodblock maker in Japan. She has done sets and costumes for the ballet, renewed her interest in making sculpture, and produced a large body of works on paper, some as rich and complex as her canvases.

There is high risk of failure in Frankenthaler's mature work. There is the danger that the superimposed layers of her paintings of the early '80s can become opaque and clotted, or that the bold sheets of color in her more recent work can appear too inert and uninflected; units of drawing and thick paint can look too artful, too placed, rather than spontaneously achieved. But at their best, Frankenthaler's canvases are simultaneously lyrical, intensely romantic and uncompromisingly tough. At the risk of overstatement, they invite comparison with the tradition of Delacroix and Turner, perhaps of Beethoven. Like that of her distinguished predecessors, Frankenthaler's recent works achieve extraordinary resonance through richness of color and density of texture. Most impressive however, in a career that spans more than 35 years (although she will not be 60 until the end of 1988) Frankenthaler has continued to evolve, to take new risks and to respond to new challenges.

—Karen Wilkin

FRASER, Donald Hamilton.
British. Born in London, 30 July 1929. Studied at St. Martin's School of Art, London, 1949–52, and in Paris, 1952–54. Served in the Royal Air Force, 1947–49. Married the illustrator Judith Wentworth-Shields in 1954; daughter: Catherine Jane. Tutor in Painting, Royal College of Art, London, 1958–84. Honorary Secretary, 1975–81, and Chairman, 1981–87, Artists General Benevolent Institution, London; Member of the Royal Fine Arts Commission, London, since 1986. Associate, 1975, and Royal Academician, 1986, Royal Academy of Art, London. Fellow of the Royal College of Art, London, 1981. Address: Bramham Cottage, Remenham Lane, Henley-on-Thames, Oxon. RG9 2LR, England.

Individual Exhibitions:

1953	Gimpel Fils, London
1957	Gimpel Fils, London
	Galerie Craven, Paris
1958	Paul Rosenberg, New York
1959	Gimpel Fils, London
1960	Paul Rosenberg, New York
1961	Gimpel Fils, London
1963	Gimpel Fils, London
	Paul Rosenberg, New York
1964	Paul Rosenberg, New York
1965	Gimpel Fils, London
1966	Paul Rosenberg, New York
1967	Gimpel-Hanover, Zurich
1968	Gimpel Fils, London
	Paul Rosenberg, New York
1969	Gimpel Fils, London
1970	Paul Rosenberg, New York
1971	Gimpel Fils, London
1973	Paul Rosenberg, New York
1975	Paul Rosenberg, New York
1976	Paul Rosenberg, New York
1977	Bohun Gallery, Henley-on-Thames, Oxfordshire
1978	Paul Rosenberg, New York
1979	Bohun Gallery, Henley-on-Thames, Oxfordshire
1980	Gallery Ten, London
1981	Scottish Gallery, Edinburgh
	Bohun Gallery, Henley-on-Thames, Oxfordshire
1982	Gallery Ten, London
1983	Bohun Gallery, Henley-on-Thames, Oxfordshire
1984	Gallery Ten, London
1985	Christies' Contemporary Art, London

Christies' Contemporary Art, New York (travelled to Tulsa, Oklahoma; Oklahoma City; Kansas City, Missouri; and Carmel, California, 1985–86)
1987   CCA Galleries, London

Selected Group Exhibitions:

1953	*British Romantic Painting in the 20th Century,* National Museum of Wales, Cardiff (toured Wales)
1954	*British Painting,* Whitechapel Art Gallery, London
1956	*6 Young British Painters,* Ashmolean Museum, Oxford
1957	*6 British Painters,* Art Club of Chicago (travelled to the Albright-Knox Art Gallery, Buffalo, New York and National Gallery of Canada, Ottawa, 1957–58)
1963	*British Art Today,* Dallas Museum of Art
1964	*Englische Kunst der Gegenwart,* Städtische Kunstgalerie, Bochum, West Germany

1967	*Pittsburgh International,* Carnegie Institute, Pittsburgh
1973	*Earth Images,* Scottish Gallery of Modern Art, Edinburgh
1977	*British Painting 1952–77,* Royal Academy of Arts, London
1980	*Israel Observed: 10 British Painters,* Israel Museum, Jerusalem

Collections:

Arts Council of Great Britain, London; Hirshhorn Museum and Sculpture Garden, Washington, D.C.; Museum of Fine Arts, Boston; Albright-Knox Art Gallery, Buffalo, New York; Carnegie Institute, Pittsburgh; Yale University, New Haven, Connecticut; National Gallery of Canada, Ottawa; National Gallery of Victoria, Melbourne.

Donald Hamilton Fraser: *Dance Study,* 1987

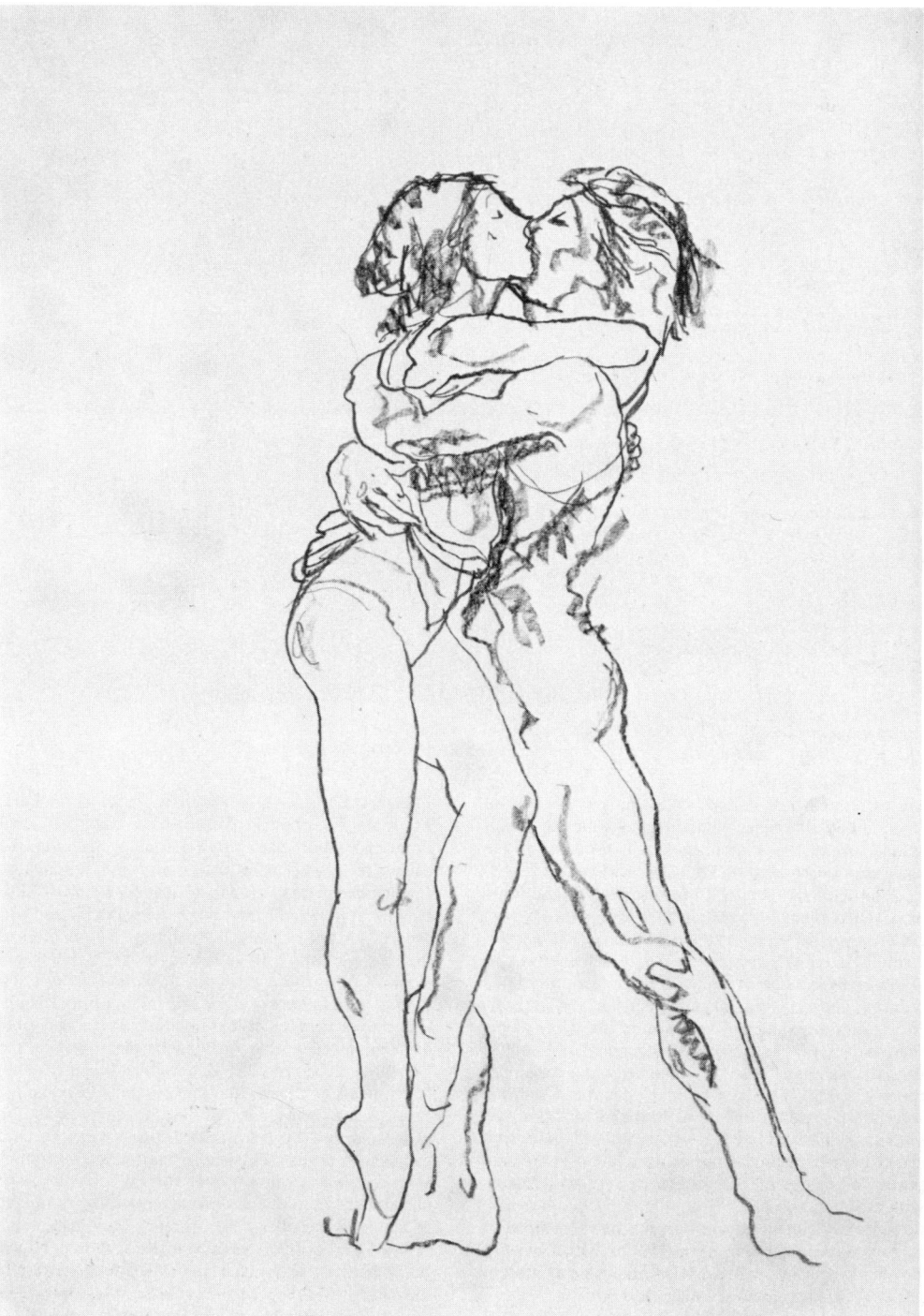

Publications:

By FRASER: book—*Gauguin's "Vision after the Sermon"*, London, 1969; article—"Interview" in *Studio* (London), June 1958.

On FRASER: book—*Conversations with Artists*, by Neal Barber, London 1964; *Private View*, by Lord Snowdon, John Russell and Bryan Robertson, London, 1968; article—"Donald Hamilton Fraser" by Oswell Blakeston, in *Arts Review* (London), January 1971; "Donald Hamilton Fraser's Dance Drawings" by Nicholas Usherwood in *R.A. Magazine* (London), September 1987.

There has always been a sort of painting that resists the written word. It is drawn simply from the eye and the heart, and is about the experience of the present moment. I suppose my own work is of that kind.

—Donald Hamilton Fraser

Donald Hamilton Fraser lies in a direct line of image response to de Stael. Physical reality is intensified by the transference of an original visual experience, through the mind, in intervening layers of time and reflection, to the point where emotionally the painting acquires an identity as of itself alone. The affinity is heightened by the choice of scenes in the Mediterranean littoral de Stael loved. Fraser, however, makes his own decision in regard to elaboration of the picture plane, both by linear perspective, and a subtle and sensitive manipulation of paint in both colour and texture.

In the late 1950's the paintings were of a liquescent spread, so that still-life subjects confined on the two opposing planes of table top and background wall became enlivened in a suggestion of space fired in varied strengths of hue, reflecting and contrasting with each other in aerial vibrations. Later work thickened in pigment, with accents placed more firmly in context, though the over-painting and adjustment of tone, together with a glow of halation on outlines, preserve the depth and shadow of the mass.

Something of the classic formula of planar division of the perspective gives Fraser's work a link with tradition, but, though he denies chance as a factor in conception he rejects also the possibility of self-analysis. It is true that recreation of a visual experience is implicit in his art. He has said: "A stretch of seashore, a pot of flowers in the sun, a patch of hillside, almost anything may suddenly seem to become almost inconceivably significant." This significance belongs to Fraser's make-up where painting and poetry are insoluble ingredients conditioning his outlook. It may be dismissed as of little experimental or progressive importance, yet in itself it constitutes a personal refinement of shared artistic climates with Paris having a powerful sway.

Transparency from solid medium, space from physical enclosure, light from shadow-casting substance—the triumph over those contradictory imponderables are Fraser's constant preoccupation with an emotional rather than a rational basis for his figurative intention is summed up by him as having the basic impulse 'to create a recognizable image in terms of paint.'

In the French lineage of "la belle facture" his painting is none the less its own contemporary animus. It could scarcely be otherwise, considering the exposure of the artist to new work in London and on the Continent, work that has taken its place for assessment and effect in the attitudes of a consistent number of the middle post-war generation of British artists, coming to maturity through operative as opposed to conceptual activity. Material involvement with oils, and occasionally acrylic, and his appreciation of its depth of capacity in the historic process leads one to believe that Fraser will surprise only by his own maturing in a purity of achievement disregarding any accusation of anachronism.

—G. S. Whittet

FREUD, Lucian.

British. Born in Berlin, 8 December 1922; son of the architect Ernst Freud, and grandson of Sigmund Freud; emigrated to England in 1932; naturalized, 1939. Studied at the Central School of Arts and Crafts, London, 1942; studied drawing, part-time, at Goldsmiths College, London, 1942–43. Served in the Merchant Marine, 1941. Married Kitty Epstein in 1947. Painter: spent time in Wales, associating with Stephen Spender and David Kentish, 1939; has lived and worked in London since 1941; close friendship with the painter Francis Bacon, from 1945. Recipient: Arts Council Prize, 1951. Agent: Anthony d'Offay Gallery, 9 Dering Street, London W1. Address: 227 Gloucester Terrace, London W2, England.

Individual Exhibitions:

1944	Lefevre Gallery, London (with Julian Trevelyan and Felix Kelly)
1947	London Gallery, (with John Craxton)
1950	Hanover Gallery, London (with Roger Vieillard)
1951	London Gallery
1952	Hanover Gallery, London (with Martin Gray)
1954	Hanover Gallery, London
	Biennale, Venice
1956	Hanover Gallery, London
1958	Marlborough Fine Art, London
1963	Marlborough Fine Art, London
1968	Marlborough Fine Art, London
1972	Gray Art Gallery, Hartlepool, County Durham
	Anthony d'Offay Gallery, London
1974	Hayward Gallery, London (toured the U.K.)
	Anthony d'Offay Gallery, London
1977	Tate Gallery, London (with Francis Bacon)
1978	Anthony d'Offay Gallery, London
1982	Anthony D'Offay Gallery, London
1988	Hayward Gallery, London

Selected Group Exhibitions:

1946	*Recent Paintings*, Lefevre Gallery, London
1948	*La Jeune en Grand Bretagne*, Galerie René Drouin, Paris
1951	*21 Modern British Painters*, Vancouver Art Gallery
1977	*British Painting 1952–1977*, Royal Academy of Arts, London
1981	*8 Figurative Painters*, Yale Center for British Art, New Haven, Connecticut
1982	*Aspects of British Art Today*, Metropolitan Art Museum, Tokyo (toured Japan)
1987	*A School of London*, Louisiana Museum, Humlebaek, Denmark (travelled to Venice and Dusseldorf)
1988	*The British Picture*, L. A. Louver Gallery, Venice, California

Collections:

Tate Gallery, London; Arts Council of Great Britain, London; Walker Art Gallery, Liverpool; Museum of Modern Art, New York; Beaverbrook Foundation, Fredericton, New Brunswick, Canada.

Publications:

On FREUD: books—*Lucian Freud*, exhibitions catalogue by John Russell, London 1974; *Lucian Freud* by Lawrence Gowing, London 1982; *Lucian Freud: Six Etchings 1984–85*, edited by James Kirkman and Brooke Alexander, London and New York 1986; articles—"Lucian Freud: Clairvoyeur" by John Russell in *Art in America* (New York), January/February 1971; "Lucian Freud" by William Feaver in the *Sunday Times Magazine* (London), February 1974.

Lucian Freud's father Ernest Freud, Architect, was the younger son of the famous Sigmund Freud. With his family, Lucian Freud came to England when he was nine. He had a precocious commitment to be an artist. Drawing was his earliest love, and a full frontal treatment of the human face was even then inescapable from his images. In his pictures of around 1940 to 1942 there is a stylised distortion in the figure with a barbed comment akin to that of Grosz. By the early 50's he had acquired an assurance in the delineation of physiognomy, instilling a factual presence from paint unequivocal and demanding in its essence. More frequently the models were nameless, but their identity is never in doubt. In the named portraits of his friends John Minton and Francis Bacon of 1952, physical characteristics are projected with an emphasis almost embarrassing in close-up. An early success was the prize-winning "Interior at Paddington," a major painting surprise of the 1951 *Festival of Britain* competition, suggesting the trapped defiance of ordinary people in ordinary circumstances.

Often mistaken for surrealist juxtapositions, household objects in his paintings assume significance by implication rather than intention. Broadly speaking, Freud is a realist of uncompromising devotion to what he sees. This sense of truth to object retreated in the 60's from stress on the linear elements to reliance on texture and modelling that resulted from greater involvement with paint. Pigment, however, was never allowed to obtrude more than was necessary, and tone remains the constant of his value-treatment, particularly in the paintings of factories and waste ground amidst Paddington slums in the early 1970s.

Colour is restrained to the extent that a monochrome reproduction of a Lucian Freud painting loses a minimum amount as compared with, say, an Ivon Hitchens. This total basis exudes a coldness of attitude, not from lack of feeling, but from the implied avoidance of sentiment as an influence in responding to purely visual stimulus. Thus his unclothed models are never titled as nudes, but as "naked girl" or "naked child," because the nude calls into consideration a relationship with all other known paintings of the subject. For Freud, the only parameter is the model herself and the painting she induces. Nakedness is thus the key to what Freud is about.

His series of small portraits of his mother 1971/3 varies only in expression and slightly in posing. Their unsmiling truth to appearance is never in doubt. They are paintings of an individual as impersonal as it is possible to be without tipping the delicate balance to a caricature. They are not portraits. Freud is no more capable of portraiture in the convention than was Cézanne.

He has, he says, a horror of the idyllic and, by inference, of art itself. To transpose the appearance and the nature of people whom he knows becomes a continuous nagging dialogue between his brush and the canvas. His mind, to a worrying degree, is a distracting factor as well as a filter and reactor. It is not accidental that pictures of people will always outnumber those of still life or townscape. The latter do not stare at the spectator, though the leaves and the curtains may conceal the peering face of "someone else."

—G. S. Whittet

FRINK, Elisabeth.

British. Born in Thurlow, Suffolk, 14 November 1930. Studied at the Guildford School of Art, Surrey, 1947–49, and The Chelsea School of Art, London 1949–53. Married Michel Jammet in 1956 (divorced, 1963), and Edward Pool in 1970 (divorced, 1972); married Alexander Csaky in 1974. Sculptor: lived in France, 1969–73; now lives and works in Dorset. Lecturer in Sculpture, Chelsea School of Art, 1951–61, and St. Martin's School of Art, London, 1954–62; Visiting Lecturer, Royal College of Art, London, 1965–67. Member, Royal Fine Art Commission, 1977. Trustee of the British Museum, London, since 1975. Associate, 1972, and Royal Academician, 1977, Royal Academy of Arts; Honorary Fellow, St. Hilda's College, Oxford, 1986. D.B.E. (Dame Com-

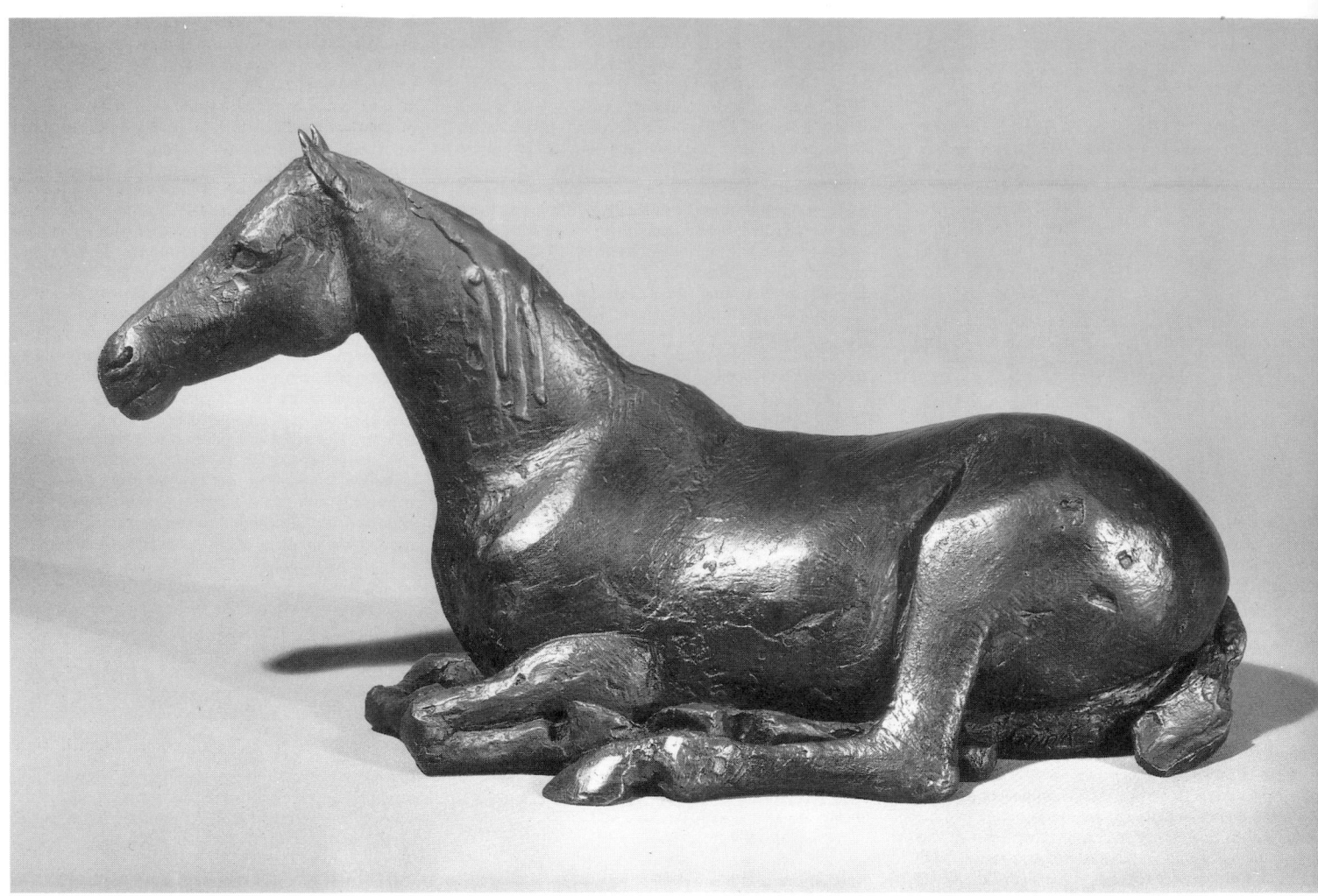

Elisabeth Frink: *Horse Lying Down*, 1975

mander, Order of the British Empire), 1982. Agent: Waddington Galleries, 2 Cork Street, London W1, England.

Individual Exhibitions:

1955   St. Georges Gallery, London
1959   Waddington Galleries, London
       Bertha Schaefer Gallery, New York
1961   Felix Landau Gallery, Los Angeles
       Waddington Galleries, London
       Bertha Schaefer Gallery, New York
1963   Waddington Galleries, London
1967   Waddington Galleries, London
1968   Waddington Galleries, London
1969   Waddington Galleries, London
1971   Waddington Galleries, London
1972   Waddington Galleries, London
1974   Maltzahn Gallery, London
1976   Waddington Galleries, London
1977   Waddington Fine Arts, Montreal
       Galerie D'Eendt, Amsterdam
1979   Terry Dintenfass Gallery, New York
1981   Winchester Great Hall, Hampshire
1982   Dorset County Museum, Dorchester
       Beaux-Arts Gallery, Bath, Avon
1983   Bohun Gallery, Henley-on-Thames, Oxfordshire
       Yorkshire Sculpture Park, Bretton Hall
       Terry Dintenfass Gallery, New York
1984   University of Surrey, Guildford
       St. Margaret's Church, King's Lynn, Norfolk
1985   Royal Academy of Art, London
       Fitzwilliam Museum, Cambridge

Selected Group Exhibitions:

1951   *London Group*, Beaux-Arts Gallery, London

1952   *Biennale*, Venice
1954   *Holland Park Open Air Exhibition*, London
1956   *Aldeburgh Festival*, Suffolk
1957   *Open Air Exhibition*, Sonsbeek, Netherlands
1959   *Biennale*, Middelheim, Antwerp
1971   *Summer Exhibition*, Royal Academy of Arts, London
1977   *Jubilee Exhibition*, Waddington and Tooth Galleries, London
1982   *Hayward Annual 1982: British Drawing*, Hayward Gallery, London
1984   *Man and Horse*, Metropolitan Museum of Art, New York

Collections:

Tate Gallery, London; National Gallery of Victoria, Melbourne; Museum of Modern Art, New York; Hirshhorn Museum, Washington, D.C.; British Museum, London; Walker Art Gallery, Liverpool; Fitzwilliam Museum, Cambridge; Brisbane Art Gallery, Queensland; South African National Gallery, Cape Town.

Publications:

By FRINK: illustrated books—*Aesops Fables*, London 1968; *Canterbury Tales*, London 1972; *The Iliad and The Odyssey*, London 1975; article—"Elisabeth Frink: A Conversation with Dulan Barber" in *Transatlantic Review* (London), Summer 1973.

On FRINK: books—*The Art of Elisabeth Frink* by Edwin Mullins, London 1972; *Elisabeth Frink*, exhibition catalogue with text by Sarah Kent, Dorchester 1982; *Elisabeth Frink*, exhibition catalogue with essay by Sarah Kent, London 1985; articles—"Goggle-Eyed Obsession" by Paul Savage in the *Daily Telegraph Magazine* (London), January 1970; "Elisabeth Frink: Sculpture and Drawings" by Hilton Kramer and Sarah Kent in the *Massachusetts Review* (Boston), Spring 1980.

*   *   *

Heavy, but without being grotesquely monumental, the sculpture of Elisabeth Frink started by swinging to and fro between the lepidoptera imagery of Germaine Richier and the sort of forceful presentation that was later to be associated with Ipousteguy. To which point of the compass did she eventually turn?

Perhaps to neither. A very sincere feeling for nature, horses (not the Marino Marini kind), birds and beasts in general cut across her other subjects like archaic figures and astronauts in goggles. This nature period was also given extra emphasis because of the subject matter she found, and created, in her graphics.

Elisabeth Frink today has settled for a reality that marries comfortably with her contemporary style. The roughness of 1954 (a seated man betraying no emotion), the warrior of 1957 (in which the war-weary head has become one with the helm), or the spinning man of 1960 (more a baby than a man, and perhaps that is a telling fact), or even the Dead King of the early 1960's; progress has been steady and logical. There will be those who miss the grating edge and the mute drama of these early pieces, but they were a part of her development and the impression reached now is that Elisabeth Frink has found her true nature as a sculptor and, more important, the way in which she would mould it.

Frink herself looks like a sculptor, someone capable of wrestling from irascible materials shapes and imagery that will teeter on the brink of the archaic or of unmelodramatic science fiction with nature somewhere in the middleground acting as referee.

—Sheldon Williams

FROST, Terry.

British. Born in Leamington Spa, Warwickshire, 13 October 1915. Educated in Leamington Spa until 1929; attended evening classes at Birmingham Art College, 1945; studied at the St. Ives School of Painting, Cornwall, under Richmond and Harry Rowntree and John Park, 1945–47, at Camberwell School of Art, London, under Victor Pasmore, William Coldstream and Lawrence Gowing, 1947–50, and at Penzance School of Art, Cornwall, 1950–51. Served in the British Army, 1939–45, in France and Palestine, and with the Commandos in Sudan, Abyssinia, Egypt and Crete, 1941; prisoner-of-war in Salonika, Poland and Germany, 1941–45. Married Kathleen Clarke in 1945; 5 sons and 1 daughter. Took up painting while a prisoner-of-war; after the war worked for electrical wholesalers, 1945, then became ill and settled in St. Ives; worked with his wife as domestic servants, 1947; returned to London, 1947; first abstract paintings, 1949, and low-relief constructions in the early 1950's; worked as an assistant to Barbara Hepworth on *Festival of Britain* sculptures, St. Ives, 1951; lived in Leeds, 1955–57; began to paint full-time in St. Ives, 1957; with Peter Lanyon opened art school, St. Peters Loft, St. Ives, 1957–60; visited the United States and met the American abstractionists, 1960; lived in Banbury, Oxfordshire, 1963–67, then settled in Newlyn, Cornwall. Lecturer in Life Drawing, Bath Academy, 1952–54; Part-time Lecturer in Painting and Anatomy, Willesden, London, 1953–54; Lecturer in Basic Design, Leeds School of Art, 1956–57; Part-time Lecturer, Coventry Art College, 1963; Lecturer, San Jose University, California, Summer 1965; Lecturer, Voss Summer School, Norway, 1967, and Banff Summer School, Alberta, 1975. Part-time Lecturer in Painting, 1964, Full-time Lecturer, 1965–70, Reader in Painting, 1970–77, Professor, 1977–81, and Professor Emeritus since 1981, University of Reading. Recipient: Gregory Fellowship in Painting, University of Leeds, 1954; Fellowship in Fine Art, University of Newcastle upon Tyne, 1964; Painting Prize, *John Moores Exhibition*, Liverpool, 1965; Painting Prize, *Open Painting Exhibition*, Ulster Museum Belfast, 1966. LLD: Council for National Academic Awards, 1977. Agents: Angela Flowers Gallery, 11 Tottenham Mews, London W1; Gillian Jason Art Gallery, 42 Inverness Street, London NW1. Address: Gernickfield Studio, Tredavoe Lane, Newlyn, Penzance, Cornwall TR18 5DL, England.

Individual Exhibitions:

1944	Leamington Spa Public Library, Warwickshire
1947	G. R. Downing's Bookshop, St. Ives, Cornwall
1952	Leicester Galleries, London
1956	Leicester Galleries, London
1958	Leicester Galleries, London
1960	Bertha Schaefer Gallery, New York
1961	Waddington Galleries, London
1962	Bertha Schaefer Gallery, New York
1963	Galerie Charles Lienhard, Zurich
	Gallery 5, Reading, Berkshire
1964	Laing Art Gallery, Newcastle upon Tyne (toured the U.K. and United States)
1966	Waddington Galleries, London
1967	Queen Square Gallery, Leeds
	Lincolnshire Association Centre, Lincoln
1968	Bear Lane Gallery, Oxford
1969	Museum of Modern Art, Oxford
	Waddington Galleries, London
	Gallery Caballa, Harrogate, Yorkshire
1970	City Art Gallery, Plymouth, Devon
	Bear Lane Gallery, Oxford
1971	Waddington Galleries, London
	Dartington Hall, Totnes, Devon
	Peterloo Gallery, Manchester
	Institute of Contemporary Arts, London
1972	Arnolfini Gallery, Bristol
1973	Leeds Playhouse Gallery
	Waddington Galleries, London
1974	Oxford Gallery (with Denis Mitchell and Ronald Searle)
1976	Plymouth City Museum and Art Gallery, Devon (toured the U.K., 1976–77)
1978	Compass Gallery, Glasgow
	Oxford Gallery
1980	New Art Centre, London
	Franz Wynan Art Core, Vancouver
1981	Rufford Craft Centre, Ollerton, Nottinghamshire
	London Regional Art Gallery, Ontario
1983	New Art Centre, London
1986	University of Reading, Berkshire
	Angela Flowers Gallery, London

Selected Group Exhibitions:

1944	*Exhibition of Arts and Crafts of Prisoners of War*, Daily Telegraph Newspaper Offices, London
1955	*Pittsburgh International*, Carnegie Institute, Pittsburgh
1964	*Contemporary British Painting and Sculpture*, Albright-Knox Art Gallery, Buffalo, New York
1967	*Recent British Painting*, Tate Gallery, London
1970	*British Paintings 1960–1970*, National Gallery of Art, Washington, D.C.
1974	*British Painting*, Hayward Gallery, London
1977	*British Painting 1952–1977*, Royal Academy of Arts, London
1980	*Art in the Making*, King Street Gallery, Bristol (travelled to Bath, Avon)
1985	*St. Ives 1939–64*, Tate Gallery, London

Collections:

Tate Gallery, London; Victoria and Albert Museum, London; Arts Council of Great Britain, London; Vancouver Art Gallery; National Gallery of Canada, Ottawa; Tel-Aviv Museum; Christchurch Art Gallery, New Zealand; Art Gallery of South Australia, Adelaide; West Australian Art Gallery, Perth; Art Gallery of New South Wales, Sydney.

Publications:

By FROST: articles—statement in *9 Abstract Artists: Their Work and Theory* by Lawrence Alloway, London 1954; "Writings of Terry Frost" in *Terry Frost: Paintings, Drawings and Collages*, exhibition catalogue, London 1976; introduction to *Terry Frost*, exhibition catalogue, Ollerton, Nottinghamshire 1982.

On FROST: books—*9 Abstract Artists: Their Work and Theory* by Lawrence Alloway, London 1954; *Terry Frost: Paintings, Drawings and Collages*, exhibition catalogue, by David Brown, London 1976; *Terry Frost: Painting in the 1980's*, exhibition catalogue with texts by Dennis Farr and Adrian Heath, Reading, Berkshire 1986.

*

St. Ives, the charming Cornish fishing village, where Ben Nicholson lived for some time, and near which Barbara Hepworth set up her famous studio, is the centre of the only regional movement in modern British art. In the past, particularly related to the 18th and 19th century landscape tradition, different areas of Britain, such as Norfolk, produced important and distinctive provincial styles. St. Ives was never the centre of locally-born painters, concerned with a traditional way of life, or identifying with a particular landscape; the painters who came to live in the area—including Heron, Hilton, Lanyon, Bell, Bryan Wynter—did so not out of aesthetic or philosophic unity, but either for purely practical reasons, or because they enjoyed the quasi-romantic isolation but, at the same time, because they did, in fact, find something of common interest locally. They certainly shared a very British involvement in landscape, as a means of identification, as the source of their work. They also shared a form of abstraction which inclined towards expressionism, in larger, more gestural shapes, more overblown colour, than, say you would find in Nicholson, or for that matter Pasmore.

Terry Frost's work reveals an effort to impose formality and severity on this kind of temperamental abstraction; the earlier works, whose titles referred to their colour harmonies, often high-pitched Yellows or Oranges, were loose arrangements of linear forms, dialogues between stiff, almost puritanical elements, and more sensuous curves, with, beneath these arrangements, a positive sense of land and sea. He gradually imposed firmer, overall formality, in quasi-geometrical shapes, spheres, verticals, V-shaped wedges, still maintaining the sense of dialogue, perhaps now of conflict.

Most recently he has reconciled these opposed forces into kinetic arrangement of oval shapes, cunningly arranged to suggest uniformity, whilst in fact very different in weight and substance. The intense, emotional colours of the past have been put aside for the simplicity of blue and black on white. This may be the result of a less passionate middle-age, or the refinement of the artist's relationship to his subject-matter.

—Charles Spencer

FRUHTRUNK, Günter.

German. Born in Munich, May 1923. Educated at Technische Hochscule, Munich, 1940–41; with William Straube, at the Überlingen-Leutkirch, Bodensee, 1945–50; under Fernand Léger, Paris, 1952. Married Hilda Steffens in 1968; children: Ulrike Dehne and Wolf-Arnim. Served in the German Army, in Poland, 1941; in Finland, at Murmansk front 1942–45. Full-time artist, France and Germany, since 1950. Professor, Akademie der Bildenden Künste, Munich, since 1967. Recipient: scholarships from Baden-Württemberg, West Germany, and from the French Government, 1954; Jean Arp Prize, Cultural Section of the German Industrial Association, Cologne, 1961; Prix d'Europe Silver Medal, Ostend, 1966; Burda Prize for Painting, *Gross Kunstausstellung*, Munich, 1967. Agents: Galerie Denise René, 124 rue la Boetie, 75008 Paris, France; Galleria Lorenzelli, Via Sant'Andrea 19, 20121 Milan, Italy; and Galerie der Spiegel, Richartz-strasse 10, Cologne, Germany. Address: 22 Rue de Trevise, 75009 Paris, France.

Individual Exhibitions:

1947	Galerie der Kunstspiegel, Freiburg
1948	Französisches Institute, Überlingen, West Germany
1949	Kunstverein, Konstanz, West Germany
1960	Galerie Denise René, Paris
1962	Galleria Pagani del Grattacielo, Milan
1963	Galerie Charles Garibaldi, Marseilles
	Museum am Ostwall, Dortmund
	Wilhelm-Morgner-Haus, Soest, West Germany
1964	Galerie Gunar, Dusseldorf
	Kunstkabinett Klihm, Munich
	Galleria Pagani del Grattacielo, Milan
1964	Galerie Charles Garibaldi, Marseilles
	Galerie der Spiegel, Cologne
1966	Studio UND, Munich
1967	Galerie Heseler, Munich
1968	Galerie nächst St. Stephan, Vienna
	Taxis-Palais, Innsbruck
	Galerie Appel und Fertsch, Frankfurt
	Galerie Appel und Fertsch, at the *Kunstmarkt*, Cologne
1969	Galerie Furneisen, Hamburg
	Kunsthalle, Mannheim
1970	Musée d'Art Moderne de la Ville, Paris
	Galerie Denise René-Hans Meyer, Krefeld, West Germany
	Galerie St. Johann, Saarbrucken
	Galleria Barozzi, Venice
	Galerie de Vries, Rotterdam
	Galerie 58, Rapperswil, Switzerland
1971	Galleria Lorenzelli, Bergamo
	Galerie Stangl, Munich
1972	Galerie Müller, Stuttgart
	Galleria Lorenzelli, Milan

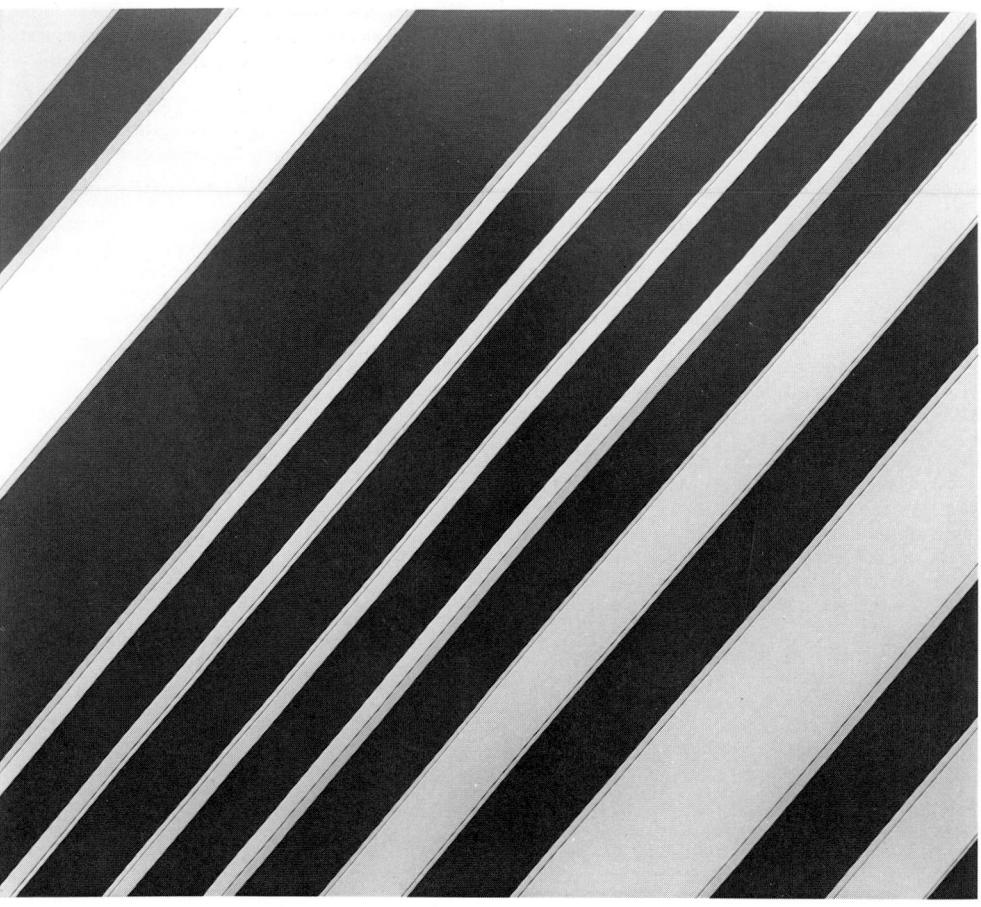

Günther Fruhtrunk: *Schwarz Roter Spuren*, 1974

1973	Städtische Galerie im Lenbachhaus, Munich (travelled to Badischer Kunstverein, Karlsruhe, and the Museum Bochum, West Germany)
	Galleria Lorenzelli, Milan
1974	Galleria Denise René, Paris
	Galleria Lorenzelli, Milan
1975	Galerie Lorenzelli, Milan
1976	Galerie Bossin, Berlin
	Galerie der Spiegel, Cologne
	Galerie Defet, Nuremberg
1977	Galerie Bossin, Berlin
	Europalia, Brussels
	Museum Quadrat, Bottrop, West Germany
	Galerie Appel und Fertsch, Frankfurt
1978	Galerie Dany Keller, Starnberg, Munich
	Galerie Defet, Nuremberg
1979	Galleria Lorenzelli, Milan
	Bayerische Staatsgemäldesammlungen, Munich
1980	Galerie Defet, Nuremberg
	Bilder 1956–1970, Galerie Bossin, Berlin
	Galerie Schoeller, Dusseldorf
1981	Galerie Oben, Hagen, West Germany
	Galerie Schottle, Munich
1982	Galerie Schottle, Munich
1983	Galerie Defet, Nuremberg
1984	Kunstverein, Braunschweig, West Germany

Selected Group Exhibitions:

1958	*Jeune Art Constructif Allemand*, Galerie Denise René, Paris
1962	*Antagonisme II: l'Objet*, Musée des Arts Décoratifs, Paris
1965	*The Responsive Eye*, Museum of Modern Art, New York
1966	*Junge Generation*, Akademie der Bildenden Künste, Berlin
1967	*Deutsche Kunst der Gegenwart*, Museum Hodinin, Prague
1968	*Grands et Jeunes d'Aujourd'hui*, Musée d'Art Moderne de la Ville, Paris
1970	*International Biennal Exhibition of Prints*, Tokyo
1974	*Kunst 1949–74*, Kunstmuseum, Bonn
1981	*Forme, Lumière, Mouvement*, Musée de Marseille, France
1984	*Neue Malerei in Deutschland*, Nationalgalerie, West Berlin (travelled to Munich and Dusseldorf)

Collections:

Neue Staatsgalerie, Berlin; Bayerische Staatsgemäldesammlungen, Munich; Staatsgalerie, Kassel, West Germany; Städtische Museum and Museum der Universität, Bochum, West Germany; Wallraf-Richartz Museum, Cologne; Museum für Kunst und Gewerbe, Hamburg; Centre Georges Pompidou, Paris; Albright-Knox Art Gallery, Buffalo, New York.

Publications:

By FRUHTRUNK: articles—"Nicht Formeisprache sondern Verdichtung" in *Fruhtrunk*, exhibition catalogue, Munich 1973; "Orientierung" in *Fruhtrunk*, exhibition catalogue, Berlin 1976; *Ethische Begrundung für Quiet Room*, New York 1978.

On FRUHTRUNK: books—*Fruhtrunk*, exhibition catalogue, with a preface by Clara Wullf, Überingen 1948; *Fruhtrunk*, exhibition catalogue, by Alberto Sartoris, Milan 1962; *Fruhtrunk*, exhibition catalogue, by Carlo Belloli and Francois Mathey, Dortmund 1963; *Fruhtrunk*, exhibition catalogue, by Frank Elgar, Marseilles 1963; *Les Contemporains* by Albert Sartoris, Paris 1966; *Fruhtrunk Siebdrucken Portfolio*, with a preface by Umbro Apollonio, Cologne 1967; *Fruhtrunk*, exhibition catalogue, by Jürgen Wissmann, Munich 1967; *Fruhtrunk*, exhibition catalogue, by Maurice Besset, Paris and Krefeld, West Germany 1970; *Fruhtrunk*, exhibition catalogue, by John Anthonyy Thwaites, Saarbrucken 1970; *Kunst der 60er Jahre in Deutschland* by Juliane Roh, Munich 1971; *Fruhtrunk*, exhibition catalogue, by Jürgen Wissman, Paris 1974; *Fruhtrunk Horizons* by Max Imdahl, Paris 1974; *Fruhtrunk*, by Dieter Honisch, Cologne 1976; *Fruhtrunk*, exhibition catalogue, Berlin 1977; *Fruhtrunk*, by Eugen Gomringer, Max Imdahl and Gabriele

Sterner, Starnberg, West Germany 1978; *Gunther Fruhtrunk*, exhibition catalogue with essay by Max Imdahl, Braunschweig 1984.

The word "abstract" went out of fashion—and to some extent went out of serious usage—when artists firmly declared that they were no longer "abstracting" from world imagery, either by distortion or by latching onto symbols nearer or further from the appearance of the "absent" model: for these artists, subject matter belonged to the past. Whether they sought to make their stand on the platform of suprematism, non-objectivity, prounism, neo-plasticism, constructivism, or under the wide-spread umbrella of the "non-figurative"—in those early days they wanted to give the lie once and for all to Ozenfant's dictum that just as every straight line was male and every curved line was female, so no artist could entirely escape figuration however hard he tried. Günter Fruhtrunk, now just 65, may not go that far back in the history of contemporary art, but he has, nevertheless, been one of the most ardent champions of the theory of utterly nonfigurative art.

Fruhtrunk's ambition has been to paint works that defy any attempt to relate them with any *thing*. Nothing he paints, he vows, has anything to do with either nature or man's reorganizations of nature. Further, he has been at pains to dredge out from his work any traces of accepted geometry, of mathematics itself, and of scientific formulae. Even these, for him, must act as adulterants to pure nonfigurative art.

Fruhtrunk would describe his artworks as "concrete," meaning by that assertion that not only are they free from all the scars of abstraction and the automatic planned realization of mathematical or scientific truths, but also they are purged of any personal characteristics they might have picked up from their creator (in this case, Fruhtrunk the anonyme). To this extent, but hardly in any other sense, his paintings might be said to squeeze into the same vein of creation as automatic writing. The difference—and it is plain to see—is that everything that Fruhtrunk does is so deft, neat and well-constructed. If there were an iota-subscript to this factor, it would be that no Fruhtrunk "picture" really has a beginning or an end. In this context, the edge of the canvas or wall is no more than an accident of nature or a practical device having, either way, no connection with the activities of the artist. Fruhtrunk art is fluid and continuous.

—Sheldon Williams

FUCHS, Ernst.

Austrian. Born in Vienna, 13 February 1940. Studied painting privately with Emmy Steinbeck, Vienna; also studied at Frohlich's Painting School, St. Anna, Vienna, 1943–45, Academy of Fine Arts, Vienna, 1945, and with Albert Gutersloh, Paris, 1946–50. Painter and graphic artist, in Paris, 1950–60, in Vienna since 1960: associated with the "school of fantastic realism": Anton Lehmden, Erich Brauer, Rudolf Hausner, Wolfgang Hutter and others, Vienna. Recipient: Painting Prize, *Bienal*, Sao Paulo, 1969; Art Prize, City of Vienna, 1972. Address: Huttelbergstrasse 24, 1140 Vienna, Austria.

Individual Exhibitions:

1946	Galerie Halm und Goldmann, Vienna
1949	Galerie du Siècle, Paris
1950	Galleria La Bussola, Turin
	Galerie Wolfgang Gurlitt, Munich
1951	Neue Galerie, Linz, Austria
1952	Galeria Buchholz, Madrid
	Galerie 55, Paris
1954	Galerie Allard, Paris

957 Fuchs' House, Jerusalem
     Galerie St. Stephan, Vienna
958 Galerie Wolfgang Gurlitt, Munich
     St. George's Gallery, London
     Galerie St. Stephan, Vienna
960 Galerie Raymond Cordier, Paris
961 Galerie Ernst Fuchs, Vienna
962 Galerie Die Insel, Worpswede, West Germany
963 Banfer Gallery, New York
964 Galerie Willy Verkauf, Vienna
965 Aoki Gallery, Tokyo
966 Galerija Kolektiva, Belgrade
     Sphinx, Galerie Snow, Frankfurt
967 Galleria El Carpino, Rome
     Kiko Gallery, Houston
     Galerie Wolfgang Ketterer, Munich
     Galerie Sydow, Frankfurt
     Galerie Peithner-Lichtenfels, Vienna
968 Pintorarium Harmann, Munich
     Galerie Toni Brechbuhl, Berne
     Rathaus Tempelhof, West Berlin
     Karntner Landesgalerie, Klagenfurt, Austria
     Aoki Gallery, Tokyo
     Galerie 6, Vienna
     Galerie Koch, Hannover
     Galerie Haas, Vaduz, Lichtenstein
     Felix Landau Gallery, Los Angeles
     Graphische Sammlung Albertina, Vienna
1969 Galerie Gmurzynska, Cologne
     Galerie Wentdorf, Dusseldorf
1970 Galerie von der Holm, Hamburg
     Galleria Viotti, Turin
     Galerie Ariadne, Vienna
     Galerie d'Halluin, Dusseldorf (toured Germany and
       Austria)
     Zeichnungen und Druckgraphik, Galerie Welz, Salz-
       burg
     Paintings and Drawings, Felix Landau Gallery, Los
       Angeles
     Aoki Gallery, Tokyo
     Galerie Buhler, Stuttgart
1971 Kunstverein, Heidelberg
     Goethe-Institut, Marseilles
     Galerie Commeter, Hamburg
     Galerie Romanum, Vienna
     Galerie Heismann, Essen
     Galleria Don Chisciotte, Rome
     Galerie Moser, Graz, Austria
1972 Die Galerie, Mannheim
     Galerie Hippolyt, St. Polten, Austria
     Neufeld-Galerie, Lustenau, Austria
     Galerie Herzmansky, Vienna
     Odaky Department Store, Tokyo
     Museum of Modern Art, Hyogo, Japan
     Museum of Modern Art, Aichi, Japan
     Museum des 20. Jahrhunderts, Vienna
1973 Baukunst, Cologne
1974 Aberbach Fine Art, New York
1975 *Oeuvre Grave*, Musée d'Art et d'Histoire, Fribourg,
       Switzerland
     Galleria Don Chisciotte, Rome
     Palazzo Costanzi, Trieste
     Kuperion, Murano, Italy
1976 Galleria del Naviglio, Milan
1977 Galleria Forni, Bologna
     Galleria Viotti, Turin
     Stamperia della Bezuga, Florence
1979 Galleria La Medusa, Rome
1981 Kulturgeschichtliches Museum, Osnabruck, West
       Germany

Selected Group Exhibitions:

1969 *Bienal*, Sao Paulo
1972 *Phantastischer Realismus*, Tiroler Landesmuseum
       Ferdinandeum, Innsbruck
1974 *19. und 20. Jahrhunders*, Galerie Wolfgang Ket-
       terer, Munich

Publications:

On FUCHS: books—*Ernst Fuchs: Sphinx*, exhibition cata-

logue, with an introduction by Heinrich von Sydow-Zirkwitz, Frankfurt 1966; *Ernst Fuchs: Paintings and Drawings*, exhibition catalogue, with an introduction by Johann Muschik, Los Angeles 1970; *Ernst Fuchs: Zeichnungen und Druckgraphik*, exhibition catalogue, with text by Johann Muschik, Salzburg 1970; *Phantastischer Realismus: Malerei und Graphik aus dem Besitz der Stadt Wien*, exhibition catalogue, with text by Robert Waissenberg, Innsbruck 1972; *Le Réalisme Fantastique* by J. C. Guilbert, Paris 1973; *Ernst Fuchs*, exhibition catalogue, with text by Gustav René Hocke, Cologne, 1973; *Ernst Fuchs: Oeuvre Grave*, exhibition catalogue, with text by Michel Terrapon, Fribourg, Switzerland 1975; *Ernst Fuchs*, exhibition catalogue, Osnabruck 1981.

Ernst Fuchs in Vienna, and in many other places as well, stands for a kind of imagery that is a mixture of sex, medievalism, mysticism and modernism that is hard to parallel in the work of any other artist. Perhaps in the recent past his closest cousin, in feeling and story if not in appearance, is Odilon Redon.

A master of the *mischtechnick*, he is also a brilliant graphics artist utterly capable as investigator into litho techniques with all the contemporary variants plus some that he has invented for himself; an etcher, a dry-pointer, aquatinter, mezzotinter, prolific graphics producer apparently untroubled by any challenge to his skills.

What does Fuchs choose as imagery? The basilisk in all his complications, the carnal sphynx, the Venus/Aphrodite/Hecate, young love, idolatry, and all the esoteric and occult mysteries of centuries past.

Nor is this all. Fuchs not only has the ability to make whatever he likes out of his subject matter, he also has a seemingly boundless range in feeling, able to evoke the refrigerated majesty of ancient days with the same puissance as he can convey the hot passion of erotic loveplay.

And the methods he uses . . . equally comfortable before the easel or at the drawing board, this Viennese not only extracts the best possible out of the traditions of the past, he also has few difficulties when it comes to expanding the means of graphic presentation.

Colour. Fuchs has a natural taste for exotic tinting, frequently of a twilight kind, but he is as variable with his colours as he is with his choice of subjects—sometimes proposing a near monochrome subtlety of tints, at others, in another mood, allowing violent clashes.

Where does Fuchs fit into the world of contemporary artists. His work and his styles find a warm response not only from those interested in art, but also from a great number which has looked for so long in vain for a master craftsman who could revivify the world of magic and ancient lore and do this in such a way that it would avoid becoming a pale copy of the past. Ernst Fuchs has supplied this want and, by so doing, has opened up a new area of art appreciation.

—Sheldon Williams

FULTON, Hamish.

British. Born in London in 1946. Studied at Hammersmith School of Art, London, 1964–65; St. Martin's School of Art, London, 1966–68; Royal College of Art, London, 1968–69. Professional artist since 1970. Lives in Canterbury, Kent. Address: c/o Waddington Galleries, 2 Cork Street, London W1, England.

Individual Exhibitions:

1969 Galerie Konrad Fischer, Dusseldorf
1970 Galleria Sperone, Turin
1971 Galerie Konrad Fischer, Dusseldorf
     Situation, London

     Richard Demarco Gallery, Edinburgh
1972 Galleria Sperone, Turin
     Art and Project, Amsterdam
     Galleria Toselli, Milan
     Galerie Konrad Fischer, Dusseldorf
     Museum of Modern Art, Oxford
     Galerie Yvon Lambert, Paris
1973 Kabinett für Aktuelle Kunst, Bremerhaven, West
       Germany
     Stedelijk Museum, Amsterdam
     Galleria Sperone-Fischer, Rome
     Situation, London
     Galerie Yvon Lambert, Paris
     Art and Project-M.T.L., Antwerp
1974 Galleria Marilena Bonomo, Bari, Italy
     Museum of Modern Art, Oxford
     Galleria Sperone, Turin
     Galerie Konrad Fischer, Dusseldorf
1975 Art and Project, Amsterdam
     Galerie Rolf Preisig, Basle
     P.M.J. Self Gallery, London
     Kunstmuseum, Basle
1976 Sperone-Westwater-Fischer Gallery, New York
     Cusack Gallery, Houston
     Institute of Contemporary Arts, London
     Hester van Royen Gallery, London
     Robert Self Gallery, London
     Claire Copley Gallery, Los Angeles
1977 Galerie Rolf Preisig, Basle
     City Museum, Canterbury, Kent
     Stedelijk Van Abbemuseum, Eindhoven, Nether-
       lands
     Robert Self Gallery, London
     Sonnabend Gallery, New York
1978 Galerie Konrad Fischer, Dusseldorf
     Galerie Nancy Gillespie/Eliszabeth de Laage, Paris
     Museum of Modern Art, New York (project exhibi-
       tion)
     Centre d'Art Contemporain, Geneva
     Galerie Tanit, Munich
1979 Whitechapel Art Gallery, London
     Galerie Rolf Preisig, Basle
     Art and Project, Amsterdam
1980 Galerie Gillespie de Laage, Paris
     Thackrey and Robertson Gallery, San Francisco
     Sperone-Westwater-Fischer Gallery, New York
     Graeme Murray Gallery, Edinburgh
     Kanransha Gallery, Tokyo
     Waddington Galleries, London
1981 Galleria Massimo Valsecchi, Milan
     Centre Georges Pompidou, Paris
1982 Waddington Galleries, London
     Orchard Gallery, Londonderry, Northern Ireland
1983 Galerie Gillespie-de Laage-Salomon, Paris
     Kanransha Gallery, Tokyo
     Galleria Massimo Valsecchi, Milan
     John Weber Gallery, New York
     Coracle Gallery, London
1984 Waddington Galleries, London
     Centre d'Art Contemporain, Geneva
1985 Van Abbemuseum, Eindhoven, Netherlands (trav-
       elled to Le Nouveau Musee, Lyon; Fruit Market
       Gallery, Edinburgh; Mendel Art Gallery, Saska-
       toon; Castello di Rivoli, Turin)
     Coracle Gallery, London
1986 Galerie Tanit, Munich
     Galerie Dietmar Werle, Cologne
     Kanransha Gallery, Tokyo
     Galerie Gillespie-de Laage-Salomon, Paris
1987 Victoria Miro Gallery, London

Selected Group Exhibitions:

1969 *Konzeption/Conception*, Städtisches Museum,
       Leverkusen, West Germany
1970 *Information*, Museum of Modern Art, New York
1972 *Documenta 5*, Kassel, West Germany
1973 *Medium Fotografie*, Städtisches Museum, Leverku-
       sen, West Germany
1974 *Project 74*, Kunsthalle, Cologne
1975 *Artists over Land*, Arnolfini Gallery, Bristol
1978 *Art as Photography, Photography as Art*, Institute of
       Contemporary Arts, London

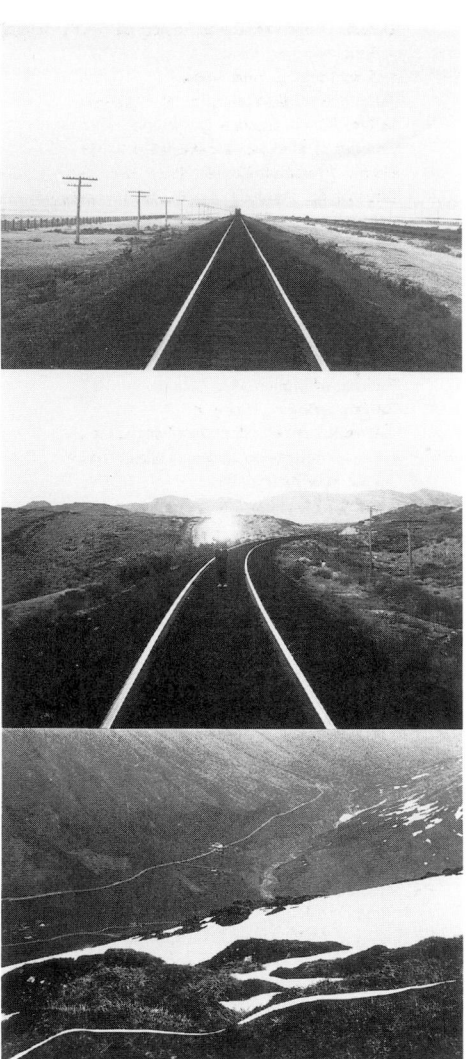

Hamish Fulton: *Untitled,* 1969

1980 *The British Art Show,* Mappin Art Gallery, Sheffield (toured the U.K.)
1982 *Approaches to Landscape,* Tate Gallery, London
1984 *Photographs in Contemporary Art,* National Museum of Modern Art, Tokyo

Collections:

Tate Gallery, London; Arts Council of Great Britain, London; British Council, London; Stedelijk Museum, Amsterdam; Kunstmuseum, Basle, Musée d'Art Moderne, Paris; Art Gallery of South Australia, Adelaide; Museum of Modern Art, New York; Metropolitan Museum of Art, New York; National Gallery of Canada, Ottawa.

Publications:

By FULTON: books—*Hollow Lane,* London 1971; *The Sweet Grass Hills of Montana,* Turin 1971; *10 Views of Brockmans Mount,* Amsterdam 1973; *Hamish Fulton,* Milan 1974; *Skyline Ridge,* London 1977; *Nepal 1975,* Eindhoven, Netherlands 1977; *Nine Works, 1969–1973,* London 1977; *Roads and Paths,* Munich 1978; *Wild Flowers,* Paris 1981; *Song of the Skylark,* London 1982; *Horizon to Horizon,* Londonderry 1983; *Twilight Horizons,* Bordeaux 1983; *Camp Fire,* Eindhoven 1985; *Coast to Coast Walks,* London 1985; *Cloud River,* 1985.

On FULTON: books—*Photography as Art* by Volker Kahmen, Tubingen 1973, London 1974; *Concept/Narrative/Document* by Judith Tannenbaum, Chicago 1979; *The Artist as Photographer* by Marina Vaizey, London 1982; *Earthworks and Beyond,* New York 1984; articles—"Hamish Fulton" by Hal Foster in *Artforum* (New York), February 1978; "Richard Long and Hamish Fulton" by Allan Davies in *Art Monthly* (London), April 1979; "Moral Landscapes" by Mi-

chael Auping in *Art in America* (New York), February 1983; "Hamish Fulton" by Charles Fagan in *Artforum* (New York), January 1984.

My work is about the experience of walking. The framed artwork is about a state of mind—it cannot convey the experience of the walk. A walk has a life of its own; it does not need to be made into art. I am an artist and choose to make my artworks from real life experiences. All the walks I make are easy. I prefer to go out into the world and be influenced and changed by events rather than work from my imagination in one fixed place.

—Hamish Fulton

Hamish Fulton's gallery works consist of a photograph or photographs together with a caption and brief explanatory text. The essential point to register in looking at these works is that they come from a 'walking' experience. The starting point of all of Fulton's work is just that—the walk. It is a walk that may last for a few hours or go on for days. It may be over the smooth Downs of southern England, the hills and crags of Scotland or further afield in the lonely vastnesses of places such as Iceland. It may be only a few hours scrambling up a hillside or a long steady trek over a flat countryside. The scenery around him may be full of historical associations or an untouched wilderness, but whatever it may be, on his walk he seems able to absorb its particular resonances and encapsulate them in the photograph, the artwork which is the final result. The walking, that most natural of human rhythms, provides the gestation period for his response. His cool, black and white photographs with their laconic accompanying text have a quiet, but nevertheless emotional impact.

Walking—looking-photographing. During these walks Fulton takes photographs of what lies before him, sometimes a bare handful of shots but on other occasion he may take hundreds. The one which seems particularly appropriate to his feelings is usually one which selects itself on the walk and rarely from later viewing of all that he has taken. He does not process his own shots nor does he often choose to touch up or make many changes in the prints. Should using the camera on a blustery day result in a blurred and grainy print then that is accepted if that is the view which best represents what he has experienced.

The texts which accompany his photographs are of equal importance and though they may appear at first to be only straightforward, factual captions, when read in conjunction with the picture they can provide a rich stimulus to the imagination. In FRANCE ON THE HORIZON (1975) Fulton adds the following information:-21 MILES ACROSS THE CHANNEL/ A ONE DAY 50 MILE WALK BY WAY OF THE WHITE CLIFFS OF DOVER/ ENGLAND SUMMER 1975. The photograph itself, which was taken about 5.0 a.m. shows the coast line of France, barely visible in the far distance, a white fringed diagonal line or waves breaking on the English beach which lies far beneath a rough patch of grass at the cliff top. The artist says that as he stood there he was reminded of the historic associations of that nearest point between the two countries, the Second World War song, 'The White Cliffs of Dover' and the evacuation from Dunkirk.

In a print entitled NO DARKNESS which resulted from a week long trek through Iceland the title can be taken to refer to the white nights of the Icelandic summer. Below that SOFT GROUND probably refers to the thawing out of the icebound earth while TRACKS OF AN ARCTIC FOX and LATE SPRING convey their own meaning. The mysterious DRIFTWOOD FROM SIBERIA, the artist has revealed, refers to driftwood washed up on the Icelandic coast that summer and the Russian lettering on some of the wood proved what great distances it had travelled.

Asked if he had studied landscape painting of past centuries Fulton replied that he was not interested in Western landscape painting but that he did study Oriental landscape painting and this influence may be

seen in the spareness and elegance of his compositions.

—Mary Ellis

FURNIVAL, John.
British. Born in London, 29 May 1933. Educated at schools in London; studied at Wimbledon College of Art, London, 1952–56, and Royal College of Art, London, 1958–60. Served in the Royal Fusiliers, London, 1955; studied Russian at the Joint Services School for Languages; worked as an Intelligence Officer in the War Office, London, 1956–57. Married Astrid Hennig in 1960; children: Eve, Jack and Harry. Independent artist, Gloucestershire, since 1960. Editor, with Dom Sylvester Houedard and Edward Wright, Openings Press, since 1964. Lecturer in Painting, Gloucestershire College of Art and Gloucester City College, 1960–66; Lecturer in Graphic Design, Bath Academy of Art, 1966–86. Founder, Dorothy's Umbrellas environmental group, Woodchester, Gloucestershire, 1972 (now Dorothy's Umbrellas Dining Society), and Saties Faction, group perpetuating the works of Erik Satie, 1975. Recipient: First Prize, Arnolfini Gallery Open Competition, Bristol, 1962; Prize, *Bradford Print Biennale,* Yorkshire, 1972. Agent: Thumb Gallery, 20–21 D'Arblay Street, London W1. Address: Rooksmoor House, Woodchester, Gloucestershire, England.

Individual Exhibitions:

1964 Arnolfini Gallery, Bristol
Piccadilly Gallery, London
1966 Arnolfini Gallery, Bristol (with Dom Sylvester Houedard and Ken Cox)
Midland Group Gallery, Nottingham (with Dom Sylvester Houedard)
1967 Galerie Riquelme, Paris
1968 Ikon Gallery, Birmingham
1971 Laing Art Gallery, Newcastle upon Tyne
1972 Arnolfini Gallery, Bristol
1974 Thumb Gallery, London
1979 Thumb Gallery, London (with Tom Phillips)
1987 Galerie Hoss, Stuttgart

Selected Group Exhibitions:

1965 *Between Poetry and Painting,* Institute of Contemporary Arts, London
1966 *Concrete/Spatial Poetry,* Midland Group Gallery, Nottingham
1967 *Aktual Art International,* San Francisco Museum of Art
1969 *Multiples Unlimited,* Ikon Gallery, Birmingham
1970 *The World as Image,* Jewish Museum, New York
Concrete Poetry, Stedelijk Museum, Amsterdam (toured Europe)
1979 *The Open and Closed Book,* Victoria and Albert Museum, London
1980 *Mazes,* Rochdale Art Gallery, Lancashire (travelled to the Ferens Art Gallery, Hull, Yorkshire)
1982 *Le Livre-Objet,* Centre Georges Pompidou, Paris
1986 *The Bordeaux Collection,* Thumb Gallery, London

Collections:

Arnolfini Trust, Bristol; McAlpine Collection, London; Sammlung Cremer, Stuttgart; Pinakothek, Munich; Arts Council of Great Britain, London; Staatsgalerie, Stuttgart; Roswell Museum, New Mexico; British Council, London.

Publications:

By FURNIVAL: books—numerous publications in small editions by Openings Press, Woodchester, Gloucestershire, since 1965, also *Teapoth,* Dunsyre, Lanarkshire 1967; *The Bang Book,* with Rom Meyer, Highlands, North Carolina 1971; *Erik Satie,* with Stuart Hodges and Gary Birch, Corsham, Wiltshire 1976; illustrated books—*Sports and Divertissements* by Ronald Johnson, Dunsyre, Lanarkshire 1965; *Ten and the Ox Eye Daisy* by Ronald Johnson, Dunsyre, Lanarkshire 1965; *The Lucidities* by Jonathan Williams, London 1967; also, contributions to *Concrete Poetry,* edited by Stephen Bann, London 1967; *Anthology of Concrete Poetry,* edited by Emmett Williams, New York 1967; *Anthology of Concretism,* Chicago 1967; *Concrete Poetry: A World View,* edited by Mary Ellen Solt, Terre Haute, Indiana 1968; *Group and Woup,* edited by Bob Cobbing, Gillingham, Kent 1974; *The Deck of Card,* London 1979; *Blind Date,* with Thomas Meyer, London 1980; *Letters to the Great Dead,* with Jonathan Williams, Woodchester, Gloucestershire 1984; *The Bordeaux Collections,* suite of 4 etchings, Nailsworth, Gloucestershire 1986.

On FURNIVAL: books—*Experimentalni Poezie,* Prague 1967; *Once Again,* edited by Jean Francois Bory, Paris 1968; *Der Kunstliche Baum* by Ernst Jandl, Berlin 1969; *Svetova Literatura '68,* Prague 1968; *The World as Image,* edited by Berjouhi Bowler, London 1970; *Imaged Words and Worded Images* by Richard Kostelanetz, New York 1970; *Signal 2-3* by Miroljub Todorovic, Belgrade 1971; *John Furnival: Ceolfrith 14,* Sunderland, County Durham 1971; article—"John Furnival" by K. Power and J. Williams in *Arts Review* (London), October 1978.

I continue to work in the same manner—developing, I hope. I spent a year in Roswell, New Mexico, between 1983 and 1984, and this gave me a welcome break from teaching, upon which I rely for my basic income. That year, apart from anything else, enabled me to earn enough money to extend my studio facilities in England, including the setting up of a proper etching studio. I seem to be able to just about exist without being too much involved with the regular art establishment, which suits me perfectly. Most of my sales are to the United States, although I have recently been making incursions into Germany; and the establishment of Wine Arts in 1986 has widened my catchment area considerably.

Until 1986 I taught at the Bath Academy of Art, Corsham—which has since been moved into Bath proper, and is now euphemistically entitled "Bath College of Higher Education"—BCHE for short!

—John Furnival

Although they have worked together, John Furnival's concrete poetry is, in its imagery, far removed from that of Dom Sylvester Houedard, co-editor with him of Openings Press. Furnival's actual use of words, whether printed or cursive, is also much more congested than that of the monk's, and the scale upon which he works is frequently far larger. Nevertheless, both believe in the efficiency of the "obvious" (*obvious,* as Furnival puts it, in the sense that Vincent van Gogh's sunflowers are *obvious*). There is a kind of classical control running through his work that is not always evident in the "poetry" of his contemporary Henri Chopin for instance, yet this is not the sort of scholarly discipline that infuses the output of the concrete poets of Munich—not sources upon which to draw if the spirit moves him: he has a classical background of Latin and Greek, very clearly a wide knowledge of English literature and has also managed—as a paradoxical bonus—to pick up Russian. An unfulfilled ambition of his—possibly not serious—is to acquire fluency in Chinese at one time or another. And this is easily perceptible in his work for those who are prepared to take on the intellectual challenge of assessing the textual meanings in the poems, although he himself is on record as saying that his "tower" pictures are for looking at, not for reading.

Furnival loots trash rather in the same way as Kurt Schwitters kept a wary eye open for valuable *Merz* material. There the resemblance between the performances of the two artists ends. Whatever he may say, Furnival is on the look-out for lyrical impact, whereas Schwitters, if he often produced works in poetic vein, did so more by a series of *happy inci-*

dents because he had an eccentric genius for emancipating rubbish from the threat of the ecological incinerator.

Furnival declares that the term "artist" is an archaism born out of the Renaissance and overdue for retirement. Not without practical verity, he asserts that he wants to pull alongside the dustman and keep the postman busy. For one so productive, insofar as print and poetry are concerned, the rising cost of any volume of mail must have a baleful ring about it. After all, "Mail Art," as Jean-Marc Poinsot points out in his book of that title—which illustrates Furnival's "Watch Warranty" and "From your soldier boy"—this particular corner of contemporary art is expanding rapidly. It would be sad if this development were killed by cost.

—Sheldon Williams

FUSSMANN, Klaus.

German. Born in Velbert, Rhineland, 24 March 1938. Studied drawing, under Karl Klode, Essen, 1950-53; Folkwang-Schule, Essen, 1957-61; art, under Professor Lortz, Hochschule fur bildende Kunste, West Berlin, 1962-66. Married Barbara Gordon in 1971. Independent painter, in West Berlin, since 1966. Professor, Hochschule der Kunste, West Berlin, since 1974. Lives in West Berlin and in Gelting. Recipient: Villa-Romana-Prize, Florence, 1971; Bottcherstrasse Prize, Bremen, 1972; Kunstpreis, City of Darmstadt, 1979. Agents: Galerie Timm Gierig, Braubachstrasse 26, 6000 Frankfurt 1; Galerie Schuler, Kurfurstendamm 51, 1000 Berlin 15 (West); Galerie Zwang, Paulinenallee 28, 2000 Hamburg 19; and Achim Moeller Fine Arts, 52 East 76th Street, New York, New York 10021. Address: Grainauer Strasse 19, 1000 Berlin 30 (West), Germany.

Individual Exhibitions:

1968	Galerie 6, West Berlin
1969	Galerie Schuler, West Berlin
1970	Baukunst-Galerie, Cologne
1971	Paula-Becker-Modersohn-Haus, Bremen, West Germany
	Nationalgalerie, West Berlin (with Hoffmann and Waldenburg)
1972	Villa Hammerschmidt, Bonn
	Galerie Gunzenhauser, Munich
	Galerie Schuler, West Berlin
1973	Kunsthalle, Darmstadt (and the Kunstverein and Magistrat, Darmstadt)
	Galerie am Steinernen Tor, Frankfurt
1974	Galerie Kornfeld, Zurich
	Galerie Lietzow, West Berlin
1975	Galerie Schuler, West Berlin
	Galerie Kammer, Hamburg
	Baukunst-Galerie, Cologne
1976	Galerie Gunzenhauser, Munich
	Lefebre Gallery, New York
	Galerie Nickel-Zadow, Nuremberg, West Germany
1977	Overbeck-Gesellschaft, Lubeck, West Germany
	Galerie Schuler, West Berlin
	Baukunst-Galerie, Cologne
	Galerie Walther, Dusseldorf
1978	Lefebre Gallery, New York
	Galerie im Kirschgarten, Mainz, West Germany
	Achim Moeller Gallery, London
	Galerie Schuler, West Berlin
	Kunsthandel Lambert Tegenbosch, Netherlands
	Galerie Haus II, Karlsruhe, West Germany
	Galerie im Winter, Bremen, West Germany (with Albert Held)
1979	Galerie Pudelko, Bonn
	Galerie Gierig, Frankfurt
	Lefebre Gallery, New York
	Galerie Internie, West Berlin
	Galerie Nickel-Zadow, Nuremberg, West Germany
1980	Suermondt-Ludwig-Museum, Aachen, West Germany
	Galerie Roedel, Mannheim, West Germany

	Galerie Landesgirokasse, Stuttgart (with Albert Held)
1981	Lefebre Gallery, New York
	Galerie Haus II, Karlsruhe, West Germany
	Galerie Thomas, Munich
	Galerie Hartwig und Bethke, West Berlin
	Galerie Peerlings, Krefeld, West Germany
1982	Kunsthandel Lambert Tegenbosch, Netherlands
	Galerie Schuler, West Berlin
	Mathildenhohe, Darmstadt, West Germany
	Galerie Thomas, Munich
1983	Lefebre Gallery, New York
	Baukunst-Galerie, Cologne
1984	Lefebre Gallery, New York
1985	Galerie Timm Gierig, Frankfurt
	Lefebre Gallery, New York
1986	Baukunst Gallery, Cologne
	Galerie Steinrotter, Munster, West Germany
1987	Schleswig-Holsteinisches Landesmuseum, Schleswig, West Germany
	Galerie Zwang, Hamburg
	Galerie Schuler, West Berlin
	Achim Moeller Fine Arts, New York
1988	ZDF-Galerie, Mainz-Lerchenberg, West Germany
	Henri Nannenmuseum, Emden, West Germany

Selected Group Exhibitions:

1985   *Representations Abroad,* Hirshhorn Museum, Washington, D.C.

Collections:

Albertina, Vienna; Kupferstichkabinett, West Berlin; Nationalgalerie, West Berlin; Rheinisches Landesmuseum, Bonn; Kunsthalle, Bremen; Stadtische Sammlung, Darmstadt; Neue Pinakothek, Munich; Wurttembergischer Staatsgalerie, Stuttgart; Metropolitan Museum of Art, New York.

Publications:

By FUSSMANN: books and portfolios—*Zwergnase,* portfolio of 5 lithographs, West Berlin 1964; *Spuren,* portfolio of 7 lithographs, with text by Peter O. Chotjewicz, West Berlin, Frankfurt and Vienna 1974; illustrations to *Die Gegenstande der Gedankenstille* by Peter O. Chotjewicz, Dusseldorf 1976; *Tage, 7 Gedichte,* 7 lithographs with text by Wittich Rohleder, Karlsruhe 1977; *Grossere Versuche uber den Schmutz,* 7 lithographs with text by Christian Enzensberger, West Berlin 1980; *Die verschwundene Malerei,* West Berlin 1985.

On FUSSMANN: books—*Klaus Fussmann: Gemalde und Gouachen,* exhibition catalogue with text by Bernd Krimmel, Darmstadt 1973; *Klaus Fussmann* by Werner Haftmann, West Berlin, Frankfurt and Vienna 1976; *Klaus Fussmann: Gemalde, Gouachen, Aquarelle, Zeichnungen,* exhibition catalogue with essays by Joachim Fest, Bernd Krimmel and Elisabeth Krimmel, Darmstadt 1982; *Klaus Fussmann: Self-Portraits and Landscapes,* exhibition catalogue with introduction by Kenneth Baker, New York 1985.

Art is almost as great an illusion as religion, has as much to do with sophistry as philosophy has, and remains mysteriously bound up with both. Art has its own metaphysics, and with this sign language can penetrate that particular darkness where words can no longer follow. But that is necessarily problematic and quickly leads, as we have seen in the late modern period, to misunderstandings and to interpretations that no longer make sense. And yet, despite so many imponderables, art remains the medium whereby man in all his complexity can express himself. In and through art man mirrors his being and the world, and he keeps creating this mirror of art for himself anew—in the hope of finally discovering something about what determines his being. And now and then a transfiguration is thus effected, showing man in harmony with nature. Such a situation—however shortlived—brings such new-found meaning and is so inspiring in its effects that it repays every effort.

—Klaus Fussmann

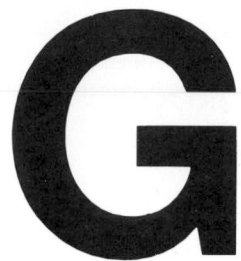

GASTINI, Marco.

Italian. Born in Turin in 1938. Studied at the Accademia Albertina di Belle Arti, Turin. Independent painter, Turin, since 1964. Agents: Galleria Martano, Via Cesare Battisti 3, 10123 Turin; Carlo Grossetti, Salone Annunciata, via Manzoni, 20121 Milan. Address: Strada del Nobile 37/3i, 10131 Turin, Italy.

Individual Exhibitions:

1964	Galleria del Falo, Alba, Italy
1967	Galleria della Steccata, Parma, Italy
	Galleria il Girasole, Rome
1968	Galleria Pozzi, Novara, Italy
	Galleria Il Punto, Turin
1969	Salone Annunciata, Milan
1970	Galleria Gap, Rome
1971	Galleria LP 220, Turin
	Salone Annunciata, Milan
	Galleria Wspolczesna, Warsaw
	Galerie Arges, Brussels
1972	Galleria Flori, Florence (with Giorgio Griffa)
	Galleria Benjamino, San Remo, Italy
	Les Halles, Bruges, Belgium
	Salone Annunciata, Milan
1973	Galleria Primo Piano, Rome
	Galerie Arges, Brussels
	Galerie Annemarie Verna, Zurich
1974	Galleria Banco, Brescia, Italy
	Galerie M. Bochum, West Germany
	Galleria Il Sole, Bolzano, Italy
	Galerie D + C/Müller-Roth, Stuttgart
	Galerie Swart, Amsterdam
	Galleria Perrari, Verona
	Galleria Claudio Bottello, Turin
	Nova Arte Moderna, Prato, Italy
1975	Salone Annunciata, Milan
	Cirrus Gallery, Los Angeles
	Galleria Peccolo, Livorno
1976	Galleria Sperone, Rome
	Salone Annunciata, Milan (with Giuseppe Spagnulo)
	Galleria Primo Piano, Rome
	Galerie Baronian, Brussels
	Galerie Annemarie Verna, Zurich
	Biennale, Venice
1977	Galleria Christian Stein, Turin
	Galerie Müller-Roth, Stuttgart
	Galleria Forma, Genoa
	John Weber Gallery, New York
	Galleria Spagnoli, Florence
1978	Galerie Walter Storms, Munich
	Studio Grossetti, Milan
1979	*Marks and/on Spaces*, John Weber Gallery, New York
	Galerie Baronian, Brussels
	Studio G7, Bologna
1980	Galerie Walter Storms, Villingen, West Germany
	Galerie Annemarie Verna, Zurich
	Centre d'Art Contemporain, Geneva
1981	Galleria Taide, Salerno, Italy
	Galleria Martano, Turin
	Galerie Appel und Fertsch, Frankfurt
	Karmeliter-Kloster, Frankfurt
	Villa Romana, Florence
	Galleria Vigato, Alessandria, Italy
1982	Galleria d'Arte Moderna, Bologna, Italy
	Studio G.7, Bologna, Italy
	Stadtische Galerie, Munich
	John Weber Gallery, New York
	Galleria Meta, Bolzano, Italy
1983	Olsson Gallery, Stockholm
	Galleria l'Isola, Rome
	Galleria Civica, Modena, Italy
	Galleria Plurima, Udine, Italy (with Mario Nigro)
	Ariete Grafica, Milan
	Galerie Muller-Roth, Stuttgart
1984	Galerie Susanna Kulli, St. Gallen, Switzerland
	Padiglione d'Arte Contemporanea, Milan
	Galleria Plurima, Udine, Italy
	Studio Dossi, Bergamo, Italy
	Galerie Krohn, Badenweiler, West Germany
	Studio Grossetti, Milan
1985	Olsson Gallery, Stockholm
	Galleria Martano, Turin
	Gallery Nordenhake, Malmo, Sweden
1986	Galerie Appel and Fertsch, Frankfurt
	Krista Miola Gallery, Helsinki
	John Weber Gallery, New York
	Galerie Edition E, Munich
	Galerie Walter Storms, Munich
1987	Galerie Susanna Kulli, St. Gallen, Switzerland
	Galleria Martano, Forum, Zurich
	Studio Grossetti, Milan
	Arte ed Altro, Milan
	Galleria Rossanaferri, Modena, Italy

Selected Group Exhibitions:

1968	*Alternative attuali 3*, Castello Spagnolo, L'Aquila, Italy
1970	*Arte e Critica '70*, Galleria Civica, Modena, Italy
1972	*Vers le Blanc* at the *Festival International du Livre*, Nice
1974	*Italy Two: Art Around '70*, Civic Center, Philadelphia
1977	*Apparent Contrast: 16 Italian Artists*, Museum Boymans van Beuningen, Rotterdam
1980	*Arte e Critica '80*, Galleria Nazionale d'Arte Moderna, Rome
1982	*Arte Italiana 1960–1982*, Hayward Gallery, London
1984	*Confronto per opera*, Galleria d'Arte Moderna, Bologna, Italy
1986	*Aspekte italienischer Kunst 1960–85*, Kunstverein, Frankfurt
1987	*La struttura del gesto*, Sala 1, Rome

Collections:

Galleria Nazionale d'Arte Moderna, Rome; Museo d'Arte Moderno, Milan; Galleria Civica d'Arte Moderna, Turin; Museo Civico, Bologna; Museum of Modern Art, New York; Museum Boymans-van Beuningen, Rotterdam; Moderna Museet, Stockholm; Konsthall, Malmo.

Publications:

By GASTINI: Books—*(in) Spazio*, Turin 1971; *Progetto*, Turin 1971; *Progetto*, Milan 1974; *New York project/ten possibilities*, New York 1977; *Parete*, New York 1977; *Pantomina*, Turin 1978; *21/29, 7=71/100=435/640=paesaggio*, Munich 1979, Bologna 1980; *La parete e l'angolo*, Lugo 1982.

On GASTINI: books-*Ricerche dopo l'Informale* by Enrico Crispolti, Rome 1969; *Ultime Tendenze dell'Arte d'Oggi* by Gillo Dorfles, Milan 1973; *Marco Gastini* by Paolo Fossati, Turin 1976; *Europe/America: The Different Avant-Gardes* by Achille Bonito Oliva, Milan 1976; *Il Divenire della Critica* by Gillo Dorfles, Turin 1976; *Marco Gastini: Marks and/on Spaces*, exhibition catalogue, New York 1979; *Marco Gastini*, exhibition catalogue, by Peter Weiermair and Pier Giovanni Castagnoli, Frankfurt 1981; *Marco Gastini: Come di un Respiro che preme nei Polmoni* by Tommaso Trini, Turin and Munich 1981; *Marco Gastini*, exhibition catalogue, by Paolo Fossati and Flaminio Gualdoni, Bologna 1982; *Marco Gastini*, exhibition catalogue with text by Flamino Gualdoni, Modena 1983; *Marco Gastini: Milano 1984*, exhibition catalogue with texts by Paolo Fossati and Flaminio Gualdoni, Milan 1984.

*   *   *

I have always painted very large pictures, so large that I couldn't see them properly even by standing back in the far recesses of my studio. I felt a compulsion to paint this way because I wanted to call into play the space in which I move. It was a kind of 'being inside it', a total immersion in that space, as if living through the entire complex of different realities that surround me and constitute the world of my work. In short, I aimed at fixing onto the canvas the continuity between the act of painting and the painting itself.

I talk about painting as 'becoming immersed'. One cannot isolate just one part of it: as soon as one begins, suddenly painting is everything—very much like a fever. But whilst one sees everything, one simultaneously perceives each fragment of that everything: like vertigo.

Spaces are many: the moment you focus on a landscape and attain a definition of one specific field of vision, then the tensions between you and space, of 'you' and of 'outside yourself', generate other spaces infinitely. It is not a matter of dimension, but of immersion. You feel as if your want to be part of an all-and-sundry space. Time does not flow with its own inexorable logic: it simply does not exist. The very slowest or fastest speed of the marks you are drawing have the duration and viscosity of total immersion, as if your were stretching yourself inside it. Duration of working becomes one with space—a space constrained only by one's own dimensions. It is the space that you are using: you meet it, and it comes forward to you. It is a kind of space/time that entirely embraces you, an objective, tangible reality. Such is the the picture, *the work*: what I call 'the work' is what I produce and exhibit.

A number of other realities come into play, though I don't know whether they really belong to the work; they are just things seen or merely thought. But they all enter that space. The picture takes on the form of an autonomous entity, even though it is born out of oneself. I would like the work to always be in motion, moving off of its own accord. It is necessary for the picture to contradict the basic formal structure and stability I have conferred on during the act of painting. I want it to be transient in regard to that aspect of formalization. Everything strives to reach its own potential, either by reaching outward or pressing back

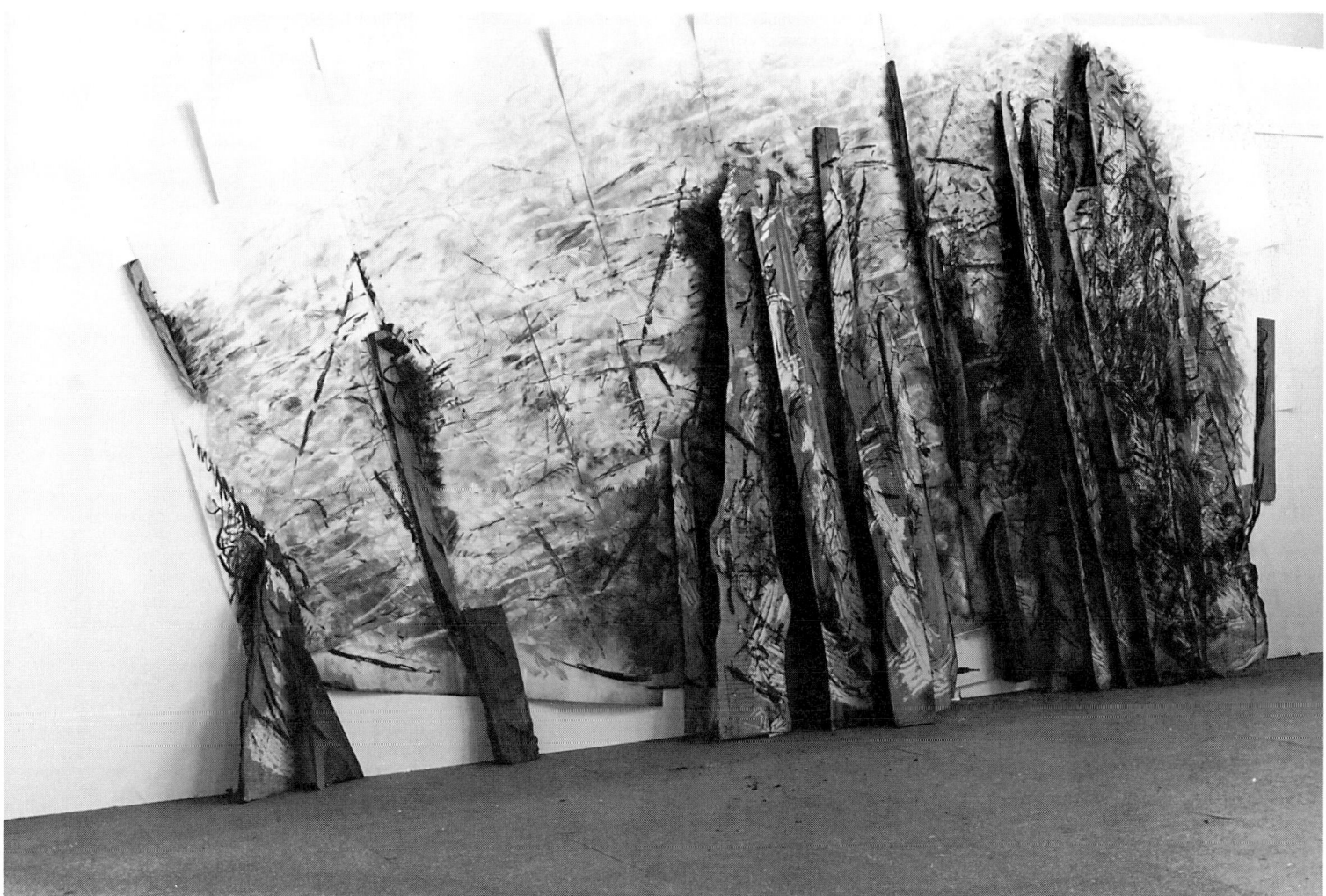

Marco Gastini: *Lo Specchio del Paesaggio,* 1986

into its own constraints. It has to unbalance and compromise the intentionality, that moves the picture toward a specific, predetermined direction. I believe that my painting must be precisely that.

Is any of this attainable? Is it possible to make visible both the immersion and the tension? I wish it were, and with sensitivity.

—Marco Gastini

Painting is carried out, it take shape, in space. Other fields, other dimensions may—and should—be born from it, but it is still in space that it occurs. The work of Marco Gastini reminds us all the time of this simple, irrefutable, Kantian reality. He actually speaks of "infinite spaces," which interact, reflecting and reacting on each other. In the complex, technically skilful pattern of streaks and blots, signs and spots, a dynamic is created and developed, generated by progressive additions which involve the conventional space of the canvas (which is also "worked" in Gastini, analysed, decomposed and recomposed) with the physical nature of the environment, of life in osmosis with art. The perceptive intuition—itself intimately dynamic—does not therefore stop at the discovery of what happens within the frame of the canvas, but expands to absorb the environmental development and to draw attention to it.

It is an illusion to try to define and specify the "discipline" (painting, sculpture) in which Gastini's work is carried out; there is an air of totality all round the whole work, involving every aspect of it. Interactions: for Gastini (who here echoes a train of thought that may or may not be contemporary) being is purely a matter of relationships. A thing—a gesture, a spot, a material, a brush-stroke—is related to other things not only in the spatial field but also in the conceptual. It is only in this way that a thing—a being—passes

from mere existence to being, to action in the world, and it is only thus that it becomes an object to be perceived.

The more fields there are, then, the more languages: that is what the antimony, the lead, tin, carbon, parchment and mother-of-pearl are that are used in his work. Materials, of course; but each has a specific language of its own, which can be made clear to the extent to which it is interwoven with the language of the other material, and united with that to form that totality in variety that seems to be one of the essential keys to Gastini's work—work that also takes in organic, vitalistic components (a tree trunk, for instance), all then reconnected in the single dimension of the painting but all still agents of emotive, physical tensions. And at the end of the journey (but there is no real end), perceived instinctively at the heart of the work, sealing all the material, gestural and spatial—and also, mental—stratifications, there is energy in the pure state, which, when fully unfurled, reveals the intimate, essential nature of the work.

—Massimo Carboni

GAUCHER, Yves.

Canadian. Born in Montreal, Quebec, in 1934. Studied at the Ecole des Beaux-Arts, Montreal, 1954–56. Married Germaine Chausse in 1965; sons: Benoit and Denis. Painter and printmaker: lives and works in Montreal (first intaglio printing, 1960; concentrated exclusively on printmaking, 1964–65). Assistant Professor of Fine Arts, 1966–69, and since 1970 Associate Professor, Sir George Williams University, Montreal. Recipient: Graphics Award, *Salon de la Jeune Peinture,* Montreal, 1959; First Graphics Prize, Province of Quebec Competition, 1961, 1963; Second Prize, National Print Competition, Vancouver, 1961; First Prize, National Print Competition, Burnaby, British Columbia, 1961; Purchase Prize, *Winnipeg Biennial,* 1962; Canada Council Grant, 1962, 1967, 1972; Purchase Prize, *Montreal Spring Exhibition,* 1963; *Thomas More Institute Exhibition* Prize, 1963; *Hadassah Exhibition* Prize, Montreal, 1964; Second Prize *International Triennale of Coloured Prints,* Grenchen, Switzerland, 1964; Grand Prize, *Sandage '68,* Montreal Museum of Fine Arts, 1968. Agent: Mira Godard Gallery, 22 Hazelton Avenue, Toronto M5R 2E2. Address: 3498 Wilson Avenue, Montreal, Quebec H4A 2T5, Canada.

Individual Exhibitions:

1973	Marlborough Godard Gallery, Montreal
1975	Marlborough Godard Gallery, Toronto
	New York Cultural Center
1976	Musée d'Art Contemporain, Le Havre, France
1979	Art Gallery of Ontario, Toronto (retrospective)
1984	Canada House Gallery, London

Selected Group Exhibitions:

1961	*Biennale*, Paris
	Exposition Internationale de Gravures, Ljubljana, Yugoslavia (and 1962, 1963)
1963	*American Biennial of Prints*, Santiago, Chile
1964	*Contemporary Painters as Printmakers*, Museum of Modern Art, New York
1966	*Biennale*, Venice
1967	*Canadian '67*, Institute of Contemporary Art, Boston
1968	*Canada: Art d'Aujourd'hui*, Palais des Beaux-Arts, Brussels
1970	*Expo '70*, Osaka, Japan
1974	*Aspects of Canadian Art*, Albright-Knox Art Gallery, Buffalo, New York
	13 Artists from Marlborough Godard, Marlborough Gallery, New York

Collections:

Musée d'Art Contemporain, Montreal; Museum of Fine Arts, Montreal; Sir George Williams University, Montreal; National Gallery of Canada, Ottawa; Art Gallery of Ontario, Toronto; Vancouver Art Gallery; Museum of Modern Art, New York; Library of Congress, Washington, D.C., Art Institute of Chicago; Tate Gallery, London.

Publications:

On GAUCHER: books—*Yves Gaucher: Paintings and Graphics*, exhibition catalogue, by Doris Shadbolt, Vancouver 1969; *Canadian Art Today* by William Townsend, London 1970; *Contemporary Canadian Painting* by William Withrow, Toronto 1972; articles—"Eminence Grise at Edinburgh" by Bryan Robertson in the *Spectator* (London), August 1968; "A Canadian Scene" by David Thompson in *Studio International* (London), October/November 1968; "A Kind of Silence" by Nigel Gosling in *The Observer* (London), October 1969; "Seeing Is Believing: Yves Gaucher's New Paintings" by M. and I. Gopnik in *Artscanada* (Toronto), October/November 1971; "Reverie de l'Absolu" by Michel Ragon in *Vie des Arts* (Montreal), Spring 1973; "Canadian Art in Review" by Dore Ashton in *Artscanada* (Toronto), December 1974.

*

Yves Gaucher's art matured in the 1960's when in North America the modernist imperative was requiring an uncompromising purification of painting's means of expression. Though his work, like post-painterly abstraction in the United States, turned on the activation of colour planes, Gaucher, working in Montreal, made formal choices which countered not so much the dictums as the taste of dominant American criticism. Where, for example, stain painting kept its preference for the personal and lyrical touch, Gaucher's practice of working with sprayed or rolled-on surfaces obliterated personal touch, signs of process and evidence of surface support. His impersonal art seemed to embrace too much of the idealist tradition of geometric abstraction, and was suspected of being European, which then meant regressive.

The general preconditions for Gaucher's work were, however, entirely North American. Gaucher has remarked on his realization, during his first visit to Paris in 1962 (his first purely abstract work appeared in 1963), that he was not French, but a French-speaking North American, with affinities not with current European abstraction but with contemporary New York painters such as Jasper Johns and Morris Louis. The reference to Barnett Newman in the "Jericho" paintings of 1977 is also a reassertion of Gaucher's partiality for an art which, though rooted in the European abstract tradition, above all in Mondrian, was, in North America, to expand its theatre of action into a monumental arena for personal struggle and moral and existential affirmation.

Gaucher's way of composing has been called "algebraic" because of its requirements that successive moves be made, and that these moves in turn be successively compensated for. This is in the tradition of Mondrian and of relational painting such as Newman claimed to overthrow; though as Gaucher agrees, Newman did not abandon relational painting, he merely changed the terms by reducing the components so that the remaining elements could function in a more complex manner. It is a kind of painting, which even within its strict formal limit requires the full play of intuition and judgment. Gaucher has consequently never deferred decision making in his work to predetermined givens. He would quarrel with those of his contemporaries who have adopted standards and repeatable compositions in order to focus on other problems or with Albers' admonition not to worry about colour because what it does happens without you. "What happens in my colours," insists Gaucher, "happens because I put it there." In the various phases of his work Gaucher has consequently never proceeded towards reduction or simplification but towards increased complexity. In practice this has meant that in all the stages of his career over the last two decades he has moved from relative symmetry to increasing asymmetry. A handwritten text signed and dated 29/1/79 hanging on Gaucher's studio wall reads: "l'asymétrie est l'affirmation d'un esprit indépendent".

To understand a Gaucher painting requires seeing it, almost simultaneously from several perspectives, each of which, of course, is incomplete. If, for example, looking at one of the large "Jericho" paintings, we take the lead of the upward and lateral thrusts of the truncated triangle in order to attempt to complete its gestalt, the leftover white "ground" begins to fall away. If, on the contrary, we scan the canvas laterally it divides down the vertical white band and the outward pressures of the coloured wedges threaten to split the painting asunder. At the same time, however, we discover that the white "ground" shapes which were so reticent before now assert themselves as precisely measured surface shapes calculated to resist the outward forces of the coloured shapes, which we discover, as well, are gripped together across the centre by their subservience to the gestalt of the original triangle. Finally, because both colour and structure are perfectly turned, equilibrium prevails and each thrust, however complex and multi directional, is checked by another, and the surface of the painting attains a breathtaking tautness right to its very edges. It is this visual holding together in face of imminent discord and break that keeps our attention and speaks of spiritual victory over disruptive forces.

—Roald Nasgaard

GAUL, Winfred.

German. Born in Düsseldorf, 9 July 1928. Educated at Cologne University, 1949–50; studied at the Kunstakademie, with Baumeister, Stuttgart, 1950–53. Married Barbara Jeckstadt in 1969. Independent painter, since 1955: lives and works in Düsseldorf; lived in New York, 1962; worked in Antwerp, 1967–68; in Genoa, 1968–69. Guest Lecturer, Staatliche Kunstschule, Bremen, 1965; Visiting Lecturer, Bath Academy, England, 1965; Visiting Lecturer, Regional College, Hull, England, 1966. Recipient: Confederation of German Industrialists' Painting Prize (B.D.I.), 1958; Villa Romana Painting Prize, Florence, 1964. Agents: Roberto Peccolo, Piazza della Republica 12, Livorno, Italy; Galerie Carla Stützer, Kamekestrasse 21, 5000 Cologne; Galerie Hennemann, Poppelsdorfer Allee 17, 5300 Bonn. Address: An St. Swidbert 56, Düsseldorf-Kaiserwerth, West Germany.

Individual Exhibitions:

1956	Galerie NRZ, Duisburg, West Germany
	Contra-Kreis, Bonn
	Galerie Gurlitt, Munich
1957	Galerie 22, Dusseldorf
	Galerie Nohl, Siegen, West Germany
	Galerie 33, Berne
	Galerie Schüler, Berlin (with O. H. Hajek)
	Galeria Apollinaire, Milan
1958	Galerie St. Laurent, Brussels
	Galerie Inge Ahlers, Mannheim
1959	Galerie Aujourd'hui, Palais des Beaux-Arts, Brussels (with K. F. Dahmen)
1960	Galerie Anne Abels, Cologne
	Galerie St. Stephan, Vienna
1961	Kunstkring, Rotterdam
	Galleria Blu, Milan
1963	Galerie Müller, Stuttgart
1964	Galerie J. Dumay, Paris
	Galerie Niepel, Dusseldorf
	Städtische Museum, Wiesbaden, West Germany
1965	Galerie René Block, Berlin
	Galleria del Deposito, Genoa
1966	Institute of Contemporary Arts, London
	Städtische Kunsthalle, Mannheim
1967	Karl-Ernst-Osthaus Museum, Hagen, West Germany
	Galerie Swart, Amsterdam
	Galerie Orez International, The Hague
	Galerie Brechbühl, Grenchen, Switzerland
	Galerie Räber, Lucerne
	Galerie Tobiès and Silex, Cologne
	Galerie Springhornhof-Falazīk, Neuenkirchen, West Germany
	Palais des Beaux-Arts, Brussels
1968	Galerie Niepel, Dusseldorf
	Galerie Nickel, Bad Godesberg, West Germany
	Galerie Rewolle, Bremen, West Germany
	Galerie Foncke, Ghent
	Zentrum für aktuelle Kunst, Aachen, West Germany
1969	Galleria il Segnapassi, Pesaro, Italy
	Studio 2B, Bergamo, Italy
	Galleria Arco d'Alibert, Rome
	Galleria La Polena, Genoa
	Galerie Fürneisen, Hamburg
	Galerie Mutzenbach, Dortmund, West Germany
1970	Overbeck-Gesellschaft, Lübeck, West Germany (with K. L. Schmaltz and H. Sundhaussen)
	Galleria del Cavallino, Venice
1971	Galerie Wilbrand, Cologne
	Galleria Sincron, Brescia, Italy
	Kunstverein, Münster, West Germany
	Kunstverein, Wiedenbruck, West Germany
	Kunststudio, Bielefeld, West Germany
	Galerie Apfelbaum, Karlsruhe
1972	Galleria Il Segnapassi, Pesaro, Italy
	Studio Kausch, Kassel, West Germany
	Galleria Peccolo, Livorno, Italy
1973	*Retrospektive 1953–1973*, Westfälischer Kunstverein, Münster, West Germany (travelled to Ludwigshafen, Ulm, and Bielefeld, 1973–74)
1974	Galleria Peccolo, Livorno, Italy
	Galleria La Polena, Genoa
	Stufidre Arte Contemporanea, Turin
	Galerie Karsten Greve, Cologne
1975	Galleria Il Milione, Milan
	Malerei 1959–1961, 1974–1975, Wilhelm-Lehmbruck Museum, Duisburg, West Germany
	Galleria Seconda Scala, Rome
1977	Galerie Peccolo, Cologne
	Galerie Wintersberger, Cologne
	Zeichen + Malen, Karl-Ernst-Osthaus Museum, Hagen, West Germany
	Paula-Becker-Modersohn-Haus, Bremen, West Germany
1978	Galleria La Polena, Genoa
	Werkverzeichnis der Druckgraphik und Objekte, Kunsthalle, Kiel, West Germany
1979	Kunstverein, Heidelberg
	Galerie Schönbrunn, Frankfurt
	Galerie Wintersberger, Cologne
	Arbeiten 1953–1961, Galerie Hennemann, Bonn
	Galerie Karsten Greve, Cologne
1981	Galleria Sincron, Brescia, Italy

1982 Dibbert Galerie, Berlin
Lavori Su Carta 1956-1981, Pinacoteca di Macerata, Italy (retrospective of drawings)
Galerie Hennemann, Bonn
Galerie 44, Kaarst, West Germany

1983 Galerie Wintersberger, Cologne
Galleria Morone 6, Milan

1984 Galleria Martano, Turin
Galleria Peccolo, Livorno, Italy
Galerie Lupke, Frankfurt
Stadtische Galerie, Quakenbruck, West Germany

1985 Galerie im Winter, Bremen, West Germany
Galerie Gruppe Grun, Bremen, West Germany
Galerie Hennemann, Bonn
Galerie Beck, Erlangen, West Germany

1986 Galerie Schuppenhauer, Essen, West Germany
Hans-Thoma-Gesellschaft, Reutlingen, West Germany

1987 Kunstverein, Freiburg, West Germany
Kunstverein, Emmerich, West Germany

1988 *Works on Paper 1955-87*, toured West Germany 1988-89

Selected Group Exhibitions:

1959 *Carnegie International*, Pittsburgh
1960 *Antagonismes*, Musée des Arts Décoratifs, Paris
1963 *Schrift und Bild*, Stedelijk Museum, Amsterdam (travelled to the Staatliche Kunsthalle, Baden-Baden, West Germany)
1965 *Pop Art, Nouveau Realisme, etc.*, Palais des Beaux-Arts, Brussels

1970 *Klischee und Anti-klischee*, Neue Galerie, Aachen, West Germany
1974 *Geplante Malerei*, Kunstverein, Munster, West Germany (travelled to the Galleria Milione, Milan)
1979 *5 x 30: Düsseldorfer Kunstszene aus 5 Generationen*, Kunstverein and Kunsthalle, Dusseldorf
1983 *Kunst nach '45*, Kunstverein, Frankfurt
1985 *1945-85: Kunst in der Bundesrepublik*, Nationalgalerie, West Berlin
1987 *Analytische Malerei—ein Ruckblick*, Galerie Schuppenhauer, Cologne

Collections:

Städtisches Kunstmuseum, Bonn; Städtisches Kunstmuseum, Bochum, West Germany; Wilhelm-Lehmbruck Museum, Duisburg, West Germany; Städtisches Kunstmuseum, Dusseldorf; Landesgalerie, Hannover; Städtische Kunsthalle, Mannheim; Westfälischer Landesmuseum, Münster; Museum voor Schone Kunsten, Ghent; Museum of Modern Art, New York; Carnegie Institute, Pittsburgh.

Publications:

By GAUL: books—*First Quibb-Manifesto*, with H. P. Alvermann, Dusseldorf 1962; *Opinioni Eretiche di un Produttore d'Arte*, Florence 1972; articles—statement in *Das Kunstwerk* (Baden-Baden, West Germany), no. 11, 1962; "Die Welt der Slogans und der Phrasen" n *Die Welt* (Hamburg), January 1963; "Amerika has du es besser" in *Das Kunstwerk* (Baden-Baden, West Germany), no. 9, 1963; "Segni e Segnali Stradali" in *Marcatre* (Milan), no. 11-13, 1965; "Picasso und die Beatles" in *Frankfurter Allgemeine* December 1966; "Traffic Signs and Signals" in *ICA Bulletin* (London), January 1966; "Gutes Deutsch auf der Strasse" in *Tragesspiegel* (Berlin), February 1968; "Verkehrszeichen als Totem" in *Frankfurter Allgemeine*, January 1969; "Traffic Signs and Signals" in *Gebrauchsgraphik* (Munich), no. 11, 1970; statement in *Seit 45* (Brussels), vol. 1, 1970; "Due Esempi della mia Pittura" in *Data* (Milan), no. 4, 1974; "Sulla Pittura" in *Paint 1*, Milan 1974, reprinted in *Winfred Gaul*, exhibition catalogue, Livorno 1974, *Winfred Gaul*, exhibition catalogue, Turin 1974, *Winfred Gaul*, exhibition catalogue, Genoa 1974, and *Winfred Gaul*, exhibition catalogue, Milan 1974; "Uber Malerei" in *Winfred Gaul*, exhibition catalogue, Duisburg, West Germany, 1975; "Uber Malerei" in *Magazine Kunst* (Mainz, West Germany), no. 4, 1975; statement in *Catalogue Documenta 6*, exhibition catalogue, Kassel, West Germany 1977; "Ein verfuhrerischer Traum, zur gesellschaftlichen Integration des Kunstlers" in *Mitteilungen des Institut für Moderne Kunst* (Nuremberg), August 1981; "Disegnare e Dipingere" in *Winfred Gaul: Lavor Su Carta 1956-1981*, exhibition catalogue, Macerata, Italy 1982.

On GAUL: books—*Geschichte der Deutschen Kunst von 1900 biz zur Gegenwart*, by Franz Roh, Munich 1958; *Lyrisme et Abstraction* by Pierre Restany, Milan 1960; *Deutsche Malerei von 1900, bis heute* by Franz Roh, Munich 1962; *Abstract Painting: 50 Years of Accomplishment from Kandinsky to the Present* by Michel Seuphor, New York 1961; *Happenings, Pop Art, Nouveau Realisme etc.*, by Hans Joachim Dietrich, Dusseldorf 1965; *Winfred Gaul*, exhibition catalogue, with text by Heinz Fuchs, Mannheim 1966; *Deutsche Kunst—eine Neue Generation* by Rolf Günter Dienst, Cologne 1970; *Deutsche Kunst der sechziger Jahre* by Juliane Roh, Munich 1971; *Kunst Praxis Heute* by Karin Thomas, Cologne 1972; *Verkehrskultur* by Klaus Honnef, Recklinghausen, West Germany 1972; *Geschichte der Deuts-*

Winfred Gaul: *To Thelonious Monk*, 1985

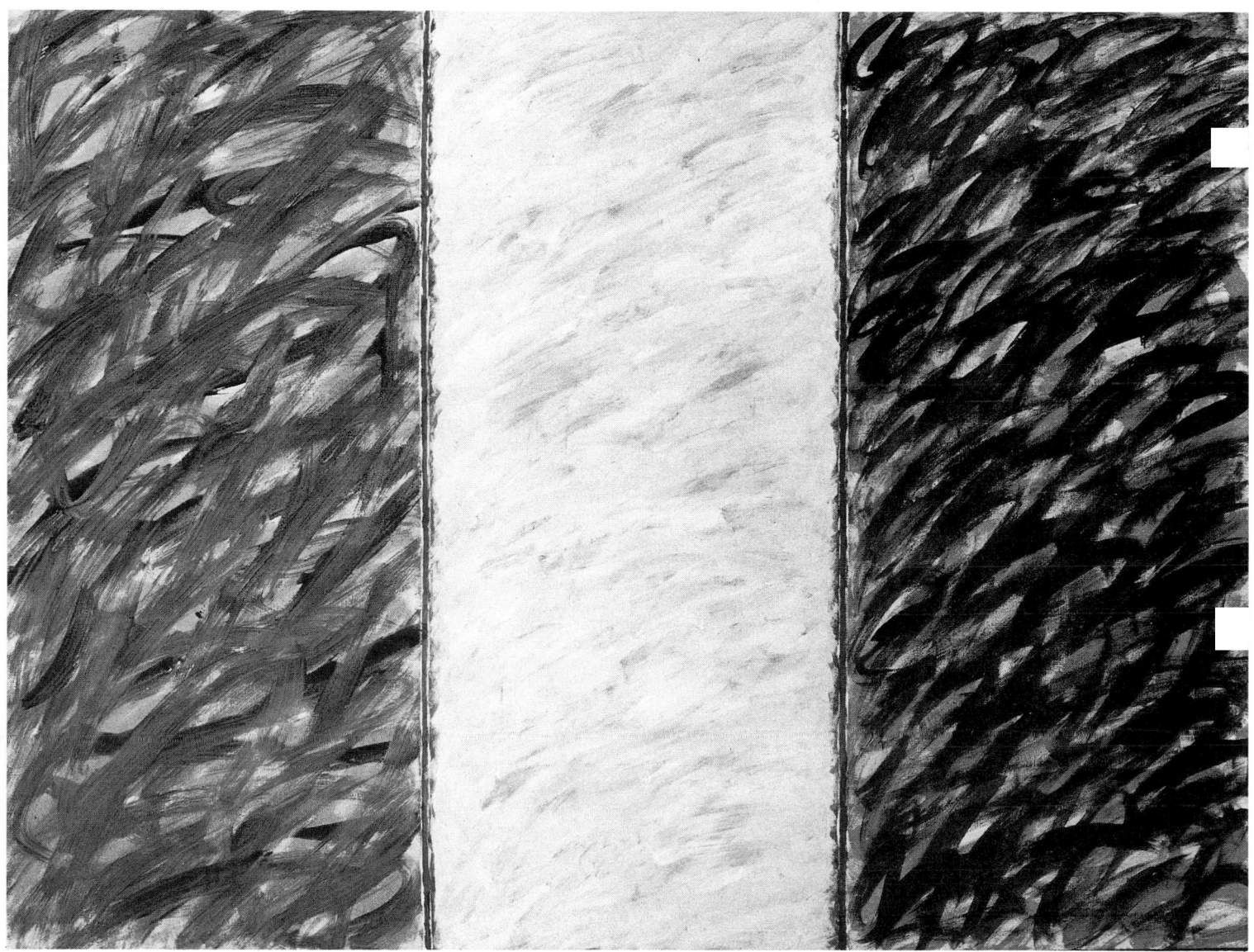

chen Malerei im 20. Jahrhundert by Paul Vogt, Cologne 1972; Art Without Boundaries 1950-70 by Gerald Woods, London 1972; Winfred Gaul—20 Jahre Malerei, exhibition catalogue, by Klaus Honnef, Bielefeld, West Germany 1973; Winfred Gaul: Retrospektive 1953-1973, exhibition catalogue, with text by Klaus Honnef and others, Münster 1973; Deutsche Druckgraphik seit 1960 by Juliane Roh, Munich 1974; Geschichte der deutschen Malerei im 20. Jahrhundert by Paul Vogt, Cologne 1974; Winfred Gaul: Malerei 1959 1961, 1974-1975, exhibition catalogue, with texts by Manfred de la Motte and Karlheinz Nowald, interview by Klaus Honnef, Duisburg, West Germany 1975; Winfred Gaul: Zeichen + Malen, exhibition catalogue, with text by Johann H. Müller, Hagen, West Germany 1977; Winfred Gaul: Werkverzeichnis der Druckgraphik und Objekte, with texts by Jens C. Jensen and Eberhard Freitag, Kiel, West Germany 1978; Winfred Gaul: Arbeiten 1953-1961, with texts by Manfred de la Motte, Pierre Restany, Will Grohmann and others, Bonn 1979; Winfred Gaul: Arbeiten auf Papier aus der Serie Recycling, exhibition catalogue with introduction by Jurgen Weichardt, Bremen 1985; Winfred Gaul: Arbeiten des Informel, exhibition catalogue with text by Diethelm Rohnisch, Emmerich 1987.

When I was twenty, I wanted to be a sculptor. I worked with wood, plaster and ceramics, but also tried to paint in a semi-abstract way influenced by reproductions I had seen in catalogues.

It was only in 1953 when I decided that painting was the right thing for me. I've stuck to it ever since, and I'm still curious to find out what painting is all about.

Compared with other media which have become so attractive to other artists recently, painting might seem to be rather old fashioned, restricted in its means and loaded with the burden of tradition. It is, but it does not make painting less attractive to me.

I think a painter who dedicates himself seriously to his medium sooner or later will find himself a part of that big "stream" called tradition and will learn to appreciate it.

As far as I'm concerned, I accept the conditions of painting as any chess player accepts the rules of the game, knowing that within the rules there are infinite chances to win or lose.

For me as a painter it is even more exciting since I cannot rely on the same rules twice. If there are rules in painting they are valid only for a given series of works. After a series is finished, these rules are replaced by new ones which will fit into a new series.

What I mean is: I do not want to restrict my painting to one particular style or formal device, but to keep it open to all ends, to make use of the full range of possibilities offered by the medium and my own capacities.

Right from the start, my main interest was the materials of painting. Instead of artist's colours, I preferred to work with non-artistic or "poor" materials such as printing ink, industrial varnish or house paint. I replaced the brush with sponge, roller or rags soaked into paint. I used knives and razor blades, children's crayons, blackboard chalk or my fingers and hands. I still like to change the tools, the colours, the scale as well as the concept. When I have worked for a certain period, with the full range of spectrum, I have always felt a need to work exclusively with black and white and vice versa. The variety of materials used and their application to the process of painting determines the variety of the linguistic means.

—Winfred Gaul

An artist who conceives of the purpose of art as "an incessantly-renewed aesthetic subversion" is difficult to describe. His works do not in the long term admit of being squeezed into the narrow confines of preconceived judgments; they slip out just when they seem to have been stored in one of thought's many filing drawers. Such an artist is Winfred Gaul. For nearly 25 years he has been producing paintings that are characterized on the one hand by what appear to rapid radical shifts of style, on the other by an immense consistency, especially when one considers them from the perspective of his central themes.

Gaul's field of artistic operations was from the beginning painting. He has never limited himself to a partial treatment, but has always attempted to explore manifold expressive possibilities of painting, at the same time confirming their essential theoretical and practical postulates. It is not surprising, therefore, that his artistic work has always been accompanied by constant reflection, which he has set out in numerous essays. Even less surprising is Gaul's gradual turning toward the analysis of the most elementary procedures and relationships of the medium of painting, after he had dedicated himself years before to his diverse images and stylistic changes. Gaul has in recent years become a leading exponent of "analytical painting." This form of painting leads those artictic efforts, from Claude Monet's water-lily picture via Matisse's collages to Fontana's radical gestures and Ryman's artistic refusals, which determine modern painting, back to the fundamental essence.

For the analytical painter, painting is, to quote Gaul, "one specific method, among other specific methods, of making art." It plumbs the depths, as it were, of the linguistic dimensions of the medium of painting, and in doing so it forcibly restricts this enquiry to taking as its object the medium of painting. An artistic process is facilitated thereby which has no need of reference to extra-medial categories. The object and the means of examination are identical.

In the exhibition Planned Painting in Milan, 1974, Gaul exhibited a triptych. In this picture one can not only distinguish the separate stages of his productive process, but also discern the goals of Analytic Painting as a whole.

The first decisions which the artist took concerned the materials. The materials consist of the canvas, the paint, and the tools with which the colour is applied to the canvas.

Gaul selected as a base brown, coarsely textured canvas. This he stretched on wedge-shaped frames. As a carrier of artistic operations other backgrounds are also conceivable, for example walls.

After the question of background had been disposed of, Gaul produced an artistic programme. This programme is always so widely laid out that it permits various possible methods of realization. Of course the expressive possibilities are already decisively preconditioned by the choice of background.

A further limitation occurs through the choice of kind of colour. Gaul decided to use a synthetic resin solution, thinned with water, to which, from one part of the picture to the other, he from time to time added a small percentage of black colour. Through the various kinds of colour application, the individual parts of the picture experienced differentiated coloration. The colouration can result from various instruments.

In the case in question Gaul used sheepskin paintrollers, such as home decorators use. He used several layers of colour one over another, so that there occurred an inter-penetration of the individual layers of colours.

The colorization is nevertheless only one component of the picture. To this is added a second: the hatching. The hatching develops a dialectical relationship with the colour. Gaul makes use of hatching as horizontal, or vertical, sometimes also diagonal lines, in a stage therefore where it has not yet constructed itself into a sign-figure. In the triptych the signs manifest themselves as a black perpendicular dividing line with thoroughly differentiated perception content. In the blackest part of the picture the line almost wholly disappears.

"Analytic Painting," as another of its exponents, Gianfranco Zappettini sums it up, is "a question of looking afresh at the data of painting from a more radical perspective; it concerns the problem of painting in that it explores the fundamental linguistic uniformities in their relation one to another." The result of analytic painting is therefore not limited to the enumeration of structural elements, but broadens itself out over the structural relationships of these elements. The object of inquiry is the structuring process. It is this which Gaul brings to the fore.

—Klaus Honnef

GECCELLI, Johannes.

German. Born in Königsberg, 14 October 1925. Studied at the Kunstakademie, Dusseldorf, 1947–51, Dip. Art Teaching 1953; Universität Koln, 1952. Served as signals operator, German Army, in Poland, Czechoslovakia and Yugoslavia, 1943–45; prisoner-of-war, Austria and Britain, 1945–47. Married Audrey Morris in 1953 (died, 1972); children: Markus, Nina, Martina and James; married Regina Hendel in 1974. Independent artist, Dusseldorf, 1952–65, West Berlin, since 1965. Worked as teacher in Gymnasium, Dusseldorf and in Mulheim-Ruhr, 1952–65; Guest Professor, Hochschule für Bildende Kunst, Hamburg, 1964; Professor, Hochschule für Bildende Künste, West Berlin, 1965; Visiting Professor, Hunter College, New York, 1980. Recipient: Forderpreis, North Rhine/Westphalia, 1958; Villa Romana Prize, Florence, 1960; Ruhr-preis, Mulheim-Ruhr, 1963. Agents: Galerie Appel und Fertsch, Taunuslange 21, 6000 Frankfurt; Galerie Niepel, Grabenstrasse 11, 4000 Dusseldorf. Address: Bayerischer Platz 4, 1000 Berlin 30, West Germany.

Individual Exhibitions:

1957	Abendatelier Pieng, Dusseldorf
1959	Galerie Niepel, Dusseldorf
1960	Galerie Parnass, Wuppertal, West Germany (retrospective)
1961	Galerie Springer, West Berlin
1962	Galerie Muller, Stuttgart
1963	Von-der-Heydt Museum, Wuppertal, West Germany
	Galerie Niepel, Dusseldorf
1964	Galerie Springer, West Berlin
	Kunstverein, Oldenburg, West Germany
1965	Galerie Brusberg, Hannover
	Staatliche Kunsthalle, Mannheim (retrospective)
	Galerie Niepel, Dusseldorf
1967	Galerie Brusberg, Hannover
1968	Galerie Klang, Cologne
	Galerie Rothe, Heidelberg
1970	Galerie Defet, Nuremberg
1971	Galerie Appel und Fertsch, Frankfurt
	Kunstverein, Kassel, West Germany (retrospective)
1973	Museum, Mulheim-Ruhr, West Germany (retrospective)
	Kunstverein, Heidelberg (retrospective)
1974	Galerie Niepel, Dusseldorf
1975	Galerie Appel und Fertsch, Frankfurt
1977	Galerie Niepel, Dusseldorf
1978	Neuer Berliner Kunstverein, West Berlin
	Kunsthalle, Kiel, West Germany
1979	Galerie Appel und Fertsch, Frankfurt
	Galerie Bossin, West Berlin
1980	Galerie Suzanne Fischer, Baden-Baden, West Germany
1981	Bilder 1978–81, Westfälischer Kunstverein, Münster, West Germany
1982	Galerie Braunbehrens, Munich
1983	Galerie Schoeller, Dusseldorf
1984	Galerie Bossin, West Berlin
1985	Galerie Dobele, Stuttgart
	Onnasch Galerie, West Berlin

Selected Group Exhibitions:

1960	Monochrome Malerei, Städtisches Museum, Leverkusen, West Germany
1964	Carnegie International, Carnegie Institute, Pittsburgh
1966	Junge Generation, Akademie der Künste, West Berlin
1968	Menschenbild, Kunsthalle, Darmstadt
1977	Rationale Konzepte 77, Städtische Kunstsammlungen, Gelsenkirchen, West Germany
1978	Konkrete Konzepte, Galerie Bossin, West Berlin
1979	20 Jahre Ausstellung, Galerie Appel und Fertsch, Frankfurt
1982	Hommage a Barnett Newman, Nationalgalerie, West Berlin
1985	Kunst in der Bundesrepublik 1945-85, Nationalgalerie, West Berlin

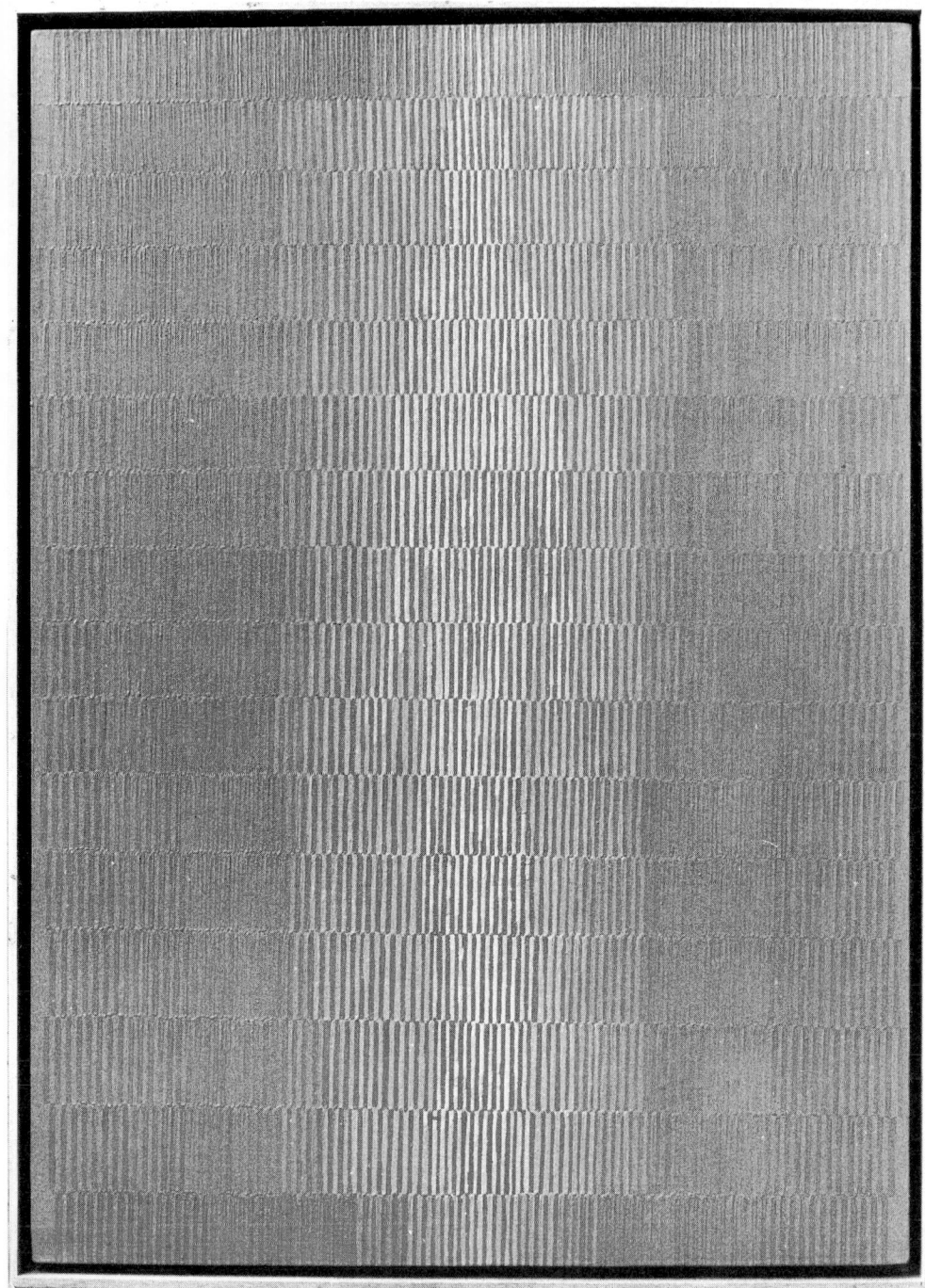

Johannes Geccelli: *Kaum Projekt*, 1975

The impossibility of abandoning the objective brings the form into the picture. It derives from the action of the "free" colour. This contradiction remains.

A shadow under the hem of a coat, a faint difference in colour from the surroundings, slight shifts of angle, a few structures definable by their contents, suffice to recognize the human form.

Even the slightest change in surface texture—of skin or fabric—which attract the attention of the senses, set in motion a practised recognition-mechanism. Only a few contrasts are necessary in order to recognize the human form: the rest is taken care of by accumulated knowledge: the picture that we already have of it.

I am always at the mercy of this picture. It is true that I need it in everyday life, to stay on my feet. I know it well. It was drummed into me. I could draw its outline. But I must insist that it isn't true, that I can't identify with it. Painters have chosen not to reproduce the old picture, rather than be untruthful.

"Natural" perception wants contrasts. I don't give them where they are wanted. They predominate on the edge of the picture. Complimentary contrasts. Stable colour-relations. Well suited, in fact, for distinguishing the figure from the background. RED—GREEN. Towards the centre, where it is least expected, they both flow together. Red will no longer be the same red that it was at the edges, because the green has imperceptibly changed at the same time. It's turning into blue. The eye perceives that the red is losing its unequivocalness because of the gradual changes taking place in its vicinity. It has to be redefined according to circumstances. Where stability should be, there is ambiguity. The colour is taking itself to the centre, to an area where, close together, it scarcely moves on from one contrast to another. The colour is in motion. What it reveals is not yet determined; it struggles against the outline. A constellation in the colour continuum: the figure.

The painter's centuries-long relations with pigments, tints, pastels, hinders our understanding of colour. It still prevents the necessary thinking-through of the phenomenon. But the knowledge that colours are "the acts and creatures of light" should have altered the artistic process. The mixing and application of pigments is an intermediary activity of light.

It is misleading to talk about colour as if it were a thing. It is not an object for a subject. You can't talk about it without considering the perceiver. It is neither external to the seer, nor wholly internal. (Dualistic thinking must dissolve in the experience of colour.???)

Colour is the experience of a dialectical occurrence. It is not wholly given, but always mediated. The experience of colour is the reflection of a mediation which is constantly taking place. It is the process, the continuum, in which we are united with all visible things. Colour is the outward sign of an undeniable mediation between man and the whole of creation.

—Johannes Geccelli

Collections:

Neuer Berliner Kunstverein, West Berlin; Kunsthalle, Mannheim; Kunsthalle, Recklinghausen, West Germany; Stadtmuseum, Ludwigshafen, West Germany; Städtisches Museum, Mulheim-Ruhr, West Germany; Landesmuseum, Oldenburg, West Germany; Städtisches Museum, Witten-Ruhr, West Germany; Städtisches Kunstsammlungen, Augsburg, West Germany; Guggenheim Museum, New York.

Publications:

On GECCELLI: books—*Malerei und Plastik* by Alfons Hoffmann and others, Essen 1960; *Junge Kunstler 1962/63* by John Anthony Thwaites, Cologne 1963; *Johannes Geccelli,* exhibition catalogue, with text by Heinz Fuchs, Mannheim 1965; *Deutsche Kunst: eine neue generation* by Rolf-Günter Dienst, Cologne 1970; *Deutsche Kunst der 60er Jahre: Malerei, Collage, Op-Art, Graphik* by Juliane Roh, Munich 1971; *Bis Heute* by Karin Thomas, Cologne, 1971; *Johannes Geccelli,* exhibition catalogue, with text by Helmut Heissenbuttel, Mulheim-Ruhr, West Germany 1973; *Malerei nach 1945* by Wieland Schmied, West Berlin 1976; *Johannes Geccelli: Bilder 1978–81,* exhibition catalogue, with texts by Thomas Deecke and Gottfried Boehm, Münster, West Germany 1981; *Johannes Geccelli,* exhibition catalogue with essay by Bernd Growe, West Berlin 1985.

Among the diffuse, visual supply of colours and structures, man seeks the shape of his own kind. He has an evolutionary need to recognize friend or foe in his surroundings. The preservation of the species, among other things, depended on this reaction. So his perception requires only a few clues in order to make out a human form.

With the emancipation of painting from all extra-artistic requirements, man's way of seeing was also gradually liberated from those earlier constraints. As painting developed towards the abstract and concrete every blurred factor, every objective association, had to be eliminated, in order to develop the liberated colour as a function of light. If the free colour in its pure interactions was brought into the picture, the structure determining it must arouse no memory of the objective.

GENERAL IDEA.
Canadian Group. Formed in 1968 by AA Bronson, Felix Partz and Jorge Zontal. AA Bronson: also known as Michael Tims—born in Vancouver, British Columbia in 1946; attended University of Manitoba School of Architecture, 1964–67. Felix Partz: also known as Ron Gabe—born in Winnipeg, Manitoba in 1945; attended the University of Manitoba School of Art, 1963–67. Jorge Zontal: also known as Jorge Saia—born in Parma, Italy in 1944; studied at Dalhousie University, Halifax, Nova Scotia, B.A. in architecture 1968. The group works collectively in print, video, performance and installations.

Individual Exhibitions:

1971 *The 1971 Miss General Idea Pageant Entries*, Art Gallery of Ontario, Toronto
1972 *Light-On*, Carmen Lamanna Gallery, Toronto
1973 *Manipulating the Self*, Galerie B, Montreal
1974 *Luxon B.V.*, Carmen Lamanna Gallery, Toronto
1976 *Search for the Spirit*, Galerie Gaetan, Geneva
1977 *Artists and Models*, Carmen Lamanna Gallery, Toronto
   Sex and Responsibility, Nova Gallery, Vancouver
1978 *Reconstructing Futures*, Carmen Lamanna Gallery, Toronto (travelled to Canada House, London, England, and the Canadian Cultural Centre, Paris)
   Menage à Trois, Lucio Amelio Gallery, Naples
1979 *Playing the Triangle*, Samangallery, Genoa
   Colour Bar Lounge, Stedelijk Museum, Amsterdam
1980 *Consenting Adults*, Carmen Lamanna Gallery, Toronto
1981 *Miss General Idea Boutique*, Carmen Lamanna Gallery, Toronto
   The Honeymoon Is Over, Stampa Gallery, Basel
   Representations Confusés, Carmen Lamanna Gallery, Toronto (travelled to the 49th Parallel Gallery, New York)
1982 *Ziqqurat Paintings 68-69*, Carmen Lamanna Gallery, Toronto
   A Space, Toronto
   Centre for Art Tapes, Halifax, Nova Scotia
1983 *P is For Poodle*, Music Gallery, Toronto
   Carmen Lamanna Gallery, in Vienna
   Mondo Cane, Galleria Stampa, Basle
1984 *Baby Makes Three*, Carmen Lamanna Gallery, Toronto
   Miss General Idea Pavilion, Kunsthalle, Basle
   Vancouver Art Gallery, British Columbia
1985 Art Gallery of Ontario, Toronto
   Musée d'Art Contemporain, Montreal
1988 Galleria Stampa, Basle

Selected Group Exhibitions:

1973 *Canada Trajectoires '73*, Musée d'Art Moderne de ls Ville, Paris
1976 *Forum '76*, Musée des Beaux-Arts, Montreal
1977 *Biennale des Jeunes*, Paris
1978 *Kanadischer Kunstler*, Kunsthalle, Basel
1979 *Perspective '79*, at the *Basel Art Fair*
1980 *Biennale*, Venice
   Pluralities, National Gallery of Canada, Ottawa
1981 *Terminal Building*, A Space, Toronto
1982 *Documenta*, Kassel, West Germany
1984 *International Survey of Recent Painting and Sculpture*, Museum of Modern Art, New York

Collections:

Art Gallery of Ontario, Toronto; Art Gallery of Hamilton, Ontario; National Gallery of Canada, Ottawa; Loyola University, Quebec; Vancouver Art Gallery; Centre d'Art Contemporain, Geneva; Stedelijk Museum, Amsterdam.

Publications:

On GENERAL IDEA: books—*General Idea 1968-1984*, exhibition catalogue, Basle 1984.

Since its formation in 1968, General Idea has been known for its irony, its clever arrogance, typified perhaps by the often-quoted excerpt from *Glamour*, and extended photo/text piece published in *FILE* Magazine, autumn 1975 and used subsequently in their videotape *Pilot*, 1977:

This is the story of General Idea and the story of what we wanted. We wanted to be famous. We wanted to be glamorous. We wanted to be rich.

That is to say we wanted to be artists, and we knew that if we were famous, if we were glamorous, we could say "WE ARE ARTISTS" and we would be.

We never felt we had to produce great art to be great artists.

We knew great art did not bring Glamour and fame.

We knew we had to keep a foot in the door of art.

We were conscious of the importance of berets and paint brushes.

We made public appearances in painters' smocks.

We knew that if we were famous, if we were glamorous, we could say "WE ARE ARTISTS" and we would be.

We did and we are.

We are famous, glamorous artists.

General Idea continues to work collaboratively in a variety of media: print, video, performance, photography, sculpture and intermedia formats. They have published *FILE* Magazine regularly since 1972—a noteworthy attempt to use the magazine format as an art work in itself—which remains a barometer of their interests and concerns: from its early days as an intervention in mail-art, fluxus and neo-dada activity, with lists, commentaries, photoworks and profiles of "outrageous" friends, *FILE* has evolved into an informed and opinionated showcasing of individuals and trends relevant to the international avant-garde.

General Idea's early performance works (especially the *1971 Miss General Idea Pageant* at the Art Gallery of Ontario, Toronto) were elaborate productions of "contemporary rituals" modelled on the lines of the beauty pageant and various awards ceremonies, but in recent years the performance formats have changed. The recent *The Honeymoon is Over*, for example, and the *XXX* presentations at the Sydney *Biennale* (1982) and "Okanada" in Berlin (January 1983) have more the character of outdoor installations with sculptural elements, sound, film, and implied narrative; the works are site-specific but seem more private, more thoughtful, and are revealed more slowly. By 1980 the tone of the print, video and performance works in general had modified, the spectacular waiting-for-the-future mythification replaced by a future-past tense. Their 1982 exhibition at the Carmen Lamanna Gallery, in Toronto, for example, showed "Fragments From the Pavillion" in a ruined, archaeological mode, installed on the walls as if in reconstruction. Pompeii had replaced Metropolis as the model, and the sensibility has a scholarly, didactic quality, for all its humour and continuing irony. Videotapes from 1982, *Cornucopia* and *Loco*, utilise the same archaeological metaphor, discussing "the room of the unknown function" and presenting "recently discovered" early film fragments, respectively. Where 1970's works anticipated the construction of The 1984 Miss General Idea Pavilion, by the beginning of the 1980's General Idea was presenting documentation of the Pavillion's ruins. As the fateful date (*1984* is the title of George Orwell's apocalyptic novel about the inevitable future loss of individual privacy and identity in favour of the totalitarian state . . .) approached in actuality, General Idea turned to achieving its history and ideas, considering its past in preparation for retrospect, reconsidering neglected portions of their work and ordering their thoughts and images into a form of history.

General Idea operates with a kind of active semiotics, and continues their investigation of languages: systems of cultural signs and meanings, the languages of implication and explication. Their first works investigated glamour, myth and art-world codes through plays on mass-media issues and formats; they usurped roles and claimed themselves parasites, rejecting the art-world's preference for "individual genius" and "unique personality". Cultural norms rather than a hierarchy of object and status were their concern. As General Idea approaches the end of its second decade of work together, these aims and perceptions remain in place, honed through experience and through shifts in avant-garde developments themselves. Their wit and precision continue to evolve.

—Peggy Gale

GENOVES, Juan.
Spanish. Born in Valencia in 1930. Studied art at the Escuela Superior de Bellas Artes San Carlo, Valencia, and in Madrid. Painter and graphic artist, Valencia, since 1950: Member, Gruppo Parpallo, and Gruppo Hondo; Founder-Member, *Exposición de Primavera*, Madrid, 1953. Recipient: National S.E.U. Prize, Spain 1950; First Prize, *15th Salon del Circulo de Bellas Artes*, Madrid, 1955; Gold Medal, *6th Biennale di San Marino*, 1967; Premio Marzotto, Italy, 1968. Agent: Marlborough Fine Art, 6 Albemarle Street, London W1, England. Address: Arandilla 17, Aravaca, Madrid-23, Spain.

Individual Exhibitions:

1956 Galeria Alfil, Madrid
1957 Museo de Arte Moderno, Havana
   Galerie Dintel, Santander, Spain
1958 Ateno, San Juan, Puerto Rico
1960 Ateneo, Madrid
1962 Galeria Diario de Noticia, Lisbon
   Galeria El Corsario, Ibiza, Spain
1965 Sala de Bellas Artes Moderno, Madrid
   Galerie Relevo, Rio de Janeiro
1966 Sal de San Eloy, Salamanca, Spain
   Museo de Arte Moderno, Bilbao, Spain
1967 Marlborough-Gerson Gallery, New York
   Marlborough Fine Art, London
1969 Tokyo Gallery
   Marlborough Galleria d'Arte, Rome
   Galleria La Bussola, Turin
1971 Kunstverein, Frankfurt
   Haus am Waldsee, West Berlin
1972 Württembergischer Kunstverein, Stuttgart
   Städtisches Kunsthalle, Recklinghausen, West Germany
   Fundacio Eugenio de Mendoza, Caracas
   Museo d'Arte Moderno, Bogota
   Museum Boymans-van Beuningen, Rotterdam
1973 Galeria Val i 30, Valencia, Spain
   Galeria Vandres, Madrid
   Galerie Marlborough-Godard, Montreal
   Marlborough Gallery, New York
1974 *Mostra Retrospectiva*, Galeria Alcoiarts, Alicante, Spain
1976 Marlborough Galerie, Zurich

Selected Group Exhibitions:

1954 *Bienal Hispano-Americana*, Casa de las Americas, Havana
1964 *World's Fair*, New York
1965 *Bienal*, Sao Paulo
1966 *Biennale*, Venice
1967 *Carnegie International*, Carnegie Institute, Pittsburgh
1970 *Kunst und Politik*, Badischer Kunstverein, Karlsruhe, West Germany
1972 *Kunst um 1970*, Neue Galerie, Aachen, West Germany
1974 *Contemporary Spanish Art*, Marlborough Fine Art, London (toured Europe)
1975 *Realismus und Realität*, Kunsthalle, Darmstadt

Collections:

Museo Nacional de Arte Contemporaneo, Madrid; Galleria Nazionale d'Arte Moderna, Rome; Museum Boymans-Van-Beuningen, Rotterdam; Kulturministerium Baden-Württemberg, Stuttgart; Centre National d'Art Contemporain, Paris; Musée Royal des Beaux-Arts, Brussels; Museo de Arte Moderno, Rio de Janeiro; Museum of Modern Art, New York; Guggenheim Museum, New York; South African National Gallery, Cape Town.

Publications:

On GENOVES: books—*Genoves*, exhibition catalogue, with text by José M. Moreno, Lisbon 1962; *Kunst und Politik*, exhibition catalogue, with texts by Robert Kudielka, Gérald Gassiot-Talabot, Herbert Marcuse and others, Karlsruhe, West Germany 1979; *Juan Genovés,* exhibition catalogue, with texts by Alfonso Sastre and G. Bussmann, Frankfurt 1971; *Juan Genovés,* exhibition catalogue, with text by J. van der Wolk, Rotterdam 1972; *Art Without Boundaries 1950– 1970* by Gerald Woods, Philip Thompson and John Williams, London 1972; *Kunst um 1970/Art Around 1970,* exhibition catalogue, with text by Wolfgang Becker, Aachen, West Germany 1972; *Juan Genovés,* exhibition catalogue, New York 1973; *Juan Genovés: mostra retrospectiva,* exhibition catalogue, Alicante, Spain 1974.

Juan Genovés once described himself as a "pictorial journalist," by which I imagine he regards himself as someone providing the public with facts and images as reportage on current events. Perhaps Goya would have similarly described himself. Genovés, like his Spanish contemporary Canogar, is part of the second wave of post-war Spanish artists, who were prepared to express themselves in realistic terms, rather than define opposition to the state through passionate abstract images.

After his impressive exhibition at the 1966 Venice *Biennale,* Genovés was launched on an international career by the Marlborough Galleries, preceding the photo-realistic school. Photographic images have been used by artists for a hundred years, and, in particular, Muybridge's pioneering records of human and animal movement have inspired numerous artists, notably Francis Bacon. Genovés was influenced by the films of Eisenstein. His paintings are based on photographic records of crowd scenes, or remembered images. They look like enlarged photographs of frightened, fleeing crowds, strangely anonymous, without reference to place or purpose, to attitude or objective. In that sense they have a Kafkaesque atmosphere, and whilst one assumes they relate to Spain, they could equally, even more relevantly, apply to many other countries and many other conflicts. Genovés, in fact, is far more motivated by visual ideas than by social comment; the critic Robert Melville commented, after his 1967 London exhibition, "His interest in crowds may well be more philosophical than political." In 1966 Genovés saw the films of Eisenstein, *Potemkin* and *October,* at a film club in Madrid, and then recalled having seen them before, in Valencia, as a boy. It would appear that the impact of those disturbing, often horrific, scenes of threatened, hysterical crowds remained in his memory.

Born in Valencia, he studied in Madrid, and started to paint the crowd scenes in 1964, seven years after his first one-man show. Earlier, in complete contrast, he worked in collage, usually on single figures, concerned, he says "with the problems of solitude," sometimes depicting men in prison. He passionately believes that the artist must be involved in the human situation, and in adapting film techniques to image making he regards "the cinema as the art form of our times. I wanted to adopt the language of films, of television, and photography, in order to reach more people." To do so, he had to invent a complex technique of exactly articulated tiny forms in narrative sequences, incorporating the art of cutting and montage, as well as a highly skillful use of draughtsmanship and paint.

—Charles Spencer

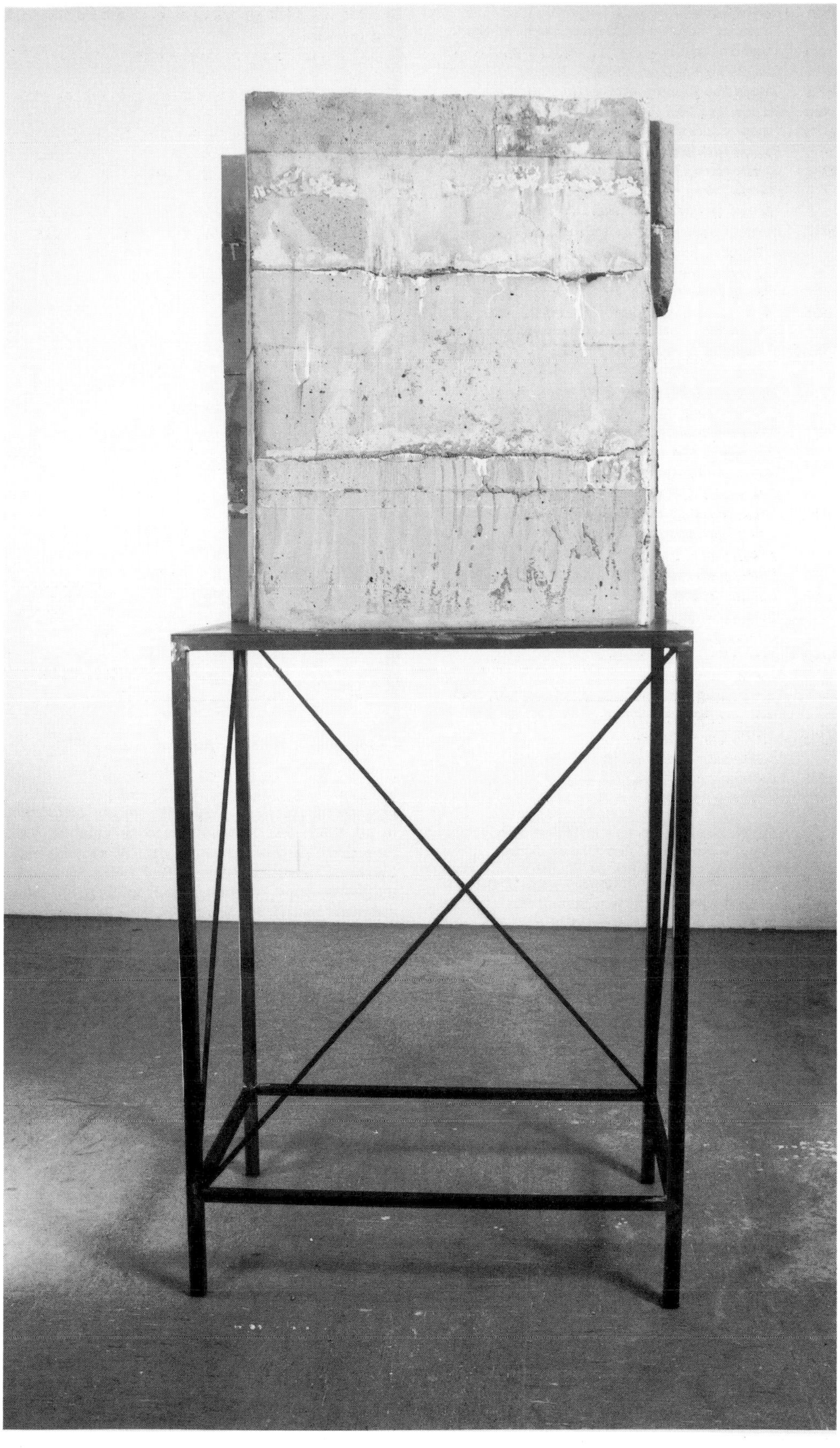

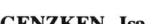

Isa Genzken: *Mies,* 1987

GENZKEN, Isa.

German. Born in Bad Oldesloe, 27 November 1948. Studied painting, under Alvir Mavignier, Hochschule fur bildende Kunste, Hamburg, 1969–71; photography and graphics, Hochschule fur bildende Kunste, West Berlin, 1971–73; painting, under Gerhard Richter, Staatliche Kunstakademie, Dusseldorf, 1973–77. Married the artist Gerhard Richter in 1982. Independent painter, sculptor and photographer, Dusseldorf, 1977–82, and in Cologne since 1983. Instructor in sculpture, Staatliche Kunstakademie, Dusseldorf, 1977–78; instructor in design, Fachhochschule Niederrhein, Krefeld, 1978–79. Recipient: Karl-Schmidt-Rottluff Scholarship, West Berlin, 1978; Kunstpreis, West Berlin, 1980. Agent: Galerie Konrad Fischer, Platanenstrasse 7, 4000 Dusseldorf. Address: Bismarckstrasse 50, 5000 Cologne 1, West Germany.

Individual Exhibitions:

1976   Galerie Konrad Fischer, Dusseldorf
1978   Kabinett fur aktuelle Kunst, Bremerhaven, West Germany
1979   Museum Haus Lange, Krefeld, West Germany (with H. Schuler)
1980   Galerie Max Hetzler, Stuttgart
       Galerie Van Krimpen, Amsterdam

1981   Galerie Konrad Fischer, Dusseldorf
1982   Kolnischer Kunstverein, Cologne (with W. Nestler
        and H. Schuler)
1983   Galleria Pieroni, Rome (with G. Richter)
1985   Galerie Van Krimpen, Amsterdam
1986   Galerie Fred Jahn, Munich
        Galerie Konrad Fischer, Dusseldorf
        Galerie Jean Bernier, Athens
1987   Galerie Harald Behm, Hamburg
        Galerie Daniel Bucholz, Cologne
        Galleria Pieroni, Rome (with G. Richter)
1988   Galerie Ghislaine Hussenot, Paris

Selected Group Exhibitions:

1979   *Schlaglichter*, Rheinisches Landesmuseum, Bonn
1981   *Art Allemagne Aujourd'hui*, Musee d'Art Moderne
        de la Ville, Paris
1982   *Documenta 7*, Museum Fridericianum, Kassel, West
        Germany
1983   *Standort Dusseldorf*, Kunsthalle, Dusseldorf
1984   *Ein anderes Klima*, Kunsthalle, Dusseldorf
1985   *Schwarz-Weiss*, Galerie Holtmann, Cologne
1986   *Bodenskulptur*, Kunsthalle, Bremen, West Germany
1987   *Juxtapositions: Recent Sculpture from England and
        Germany*, Institute for Art and Urban Resources,
        New York
1988   *Biennale of Sydney*, Art Gallery of New South
        Wales, Sydney

Collections:

Nationalgalerie, West Berlin; Staatsgalerie, Stuttgart; Stedelijk Van Abbemuseum, Eindhoven; Rijksmuseum Kroller-
Muller, Otterlo.

Publications:

By GENZKEN: articles—interview in *Schlaglichter*, exhibition catalogue, Bonn 1979; "Die Objekte liegen . . ." in
Kunstforum International (Mainz), no. 36, 1979; "Ein Preis
oder ein Arbeitsstipendium . . ." in *Junge Kunst in Deutschland*, edited by Dieter Honisch, West Berlin 1982.

On GENZKEN: books—*Isa Genzken/Horst Schuler*, exhibition catalogue with texts by Birgit Pelzer and Marianne
Stockebrand, Krefeld 1979; *5 Deutsche*, exhibition catalogue
with text by Paul Groot, Amsterdam 1981; *Art Allemagne
Aujourd'hui*, exhibition catalogue with text by Bernhard Kerber, Paris 1981; *Isa Genzken/Horst Schuler/Wolfgang Nestler*, exhibition catalogue with text by Bernhard Kerber,
Cologne 1982; *Isa Genzken/Gerhard Richter*, exhibition catalogue with text by Rudi H. Fuchs, Rome 1983; *Isa Genzken*,
exhibition catalogue with text by Paul Groot, Munich 1986;
Juxtapositions: Recent Sculpture from England and Germany,
exhibition catalogue with text by Joshua Decter, New York
1987.

Concrete is forced nature. When I visit a museum and
enter a room full of bad pictures but then suddenly
find a picture I can linger in front of for a while, I
forget the others. Public sculpture is today located in
the area of tension between a modern house and a
traditional monument. I find the rough brickwork
construction of new buildings more interesting than
the routine concealment of facades with pseudo-
precious materials, since with the former the engineer's rational thinking is more closely concerned
with truth.

—Isa Genzken

GERSTNER, Karl.

Swiss. Born in Basle, 2 July 1930. Educated at primary school and gymnasium in Basle, 1937–44; studied graphic design and typography at the Allgemeine

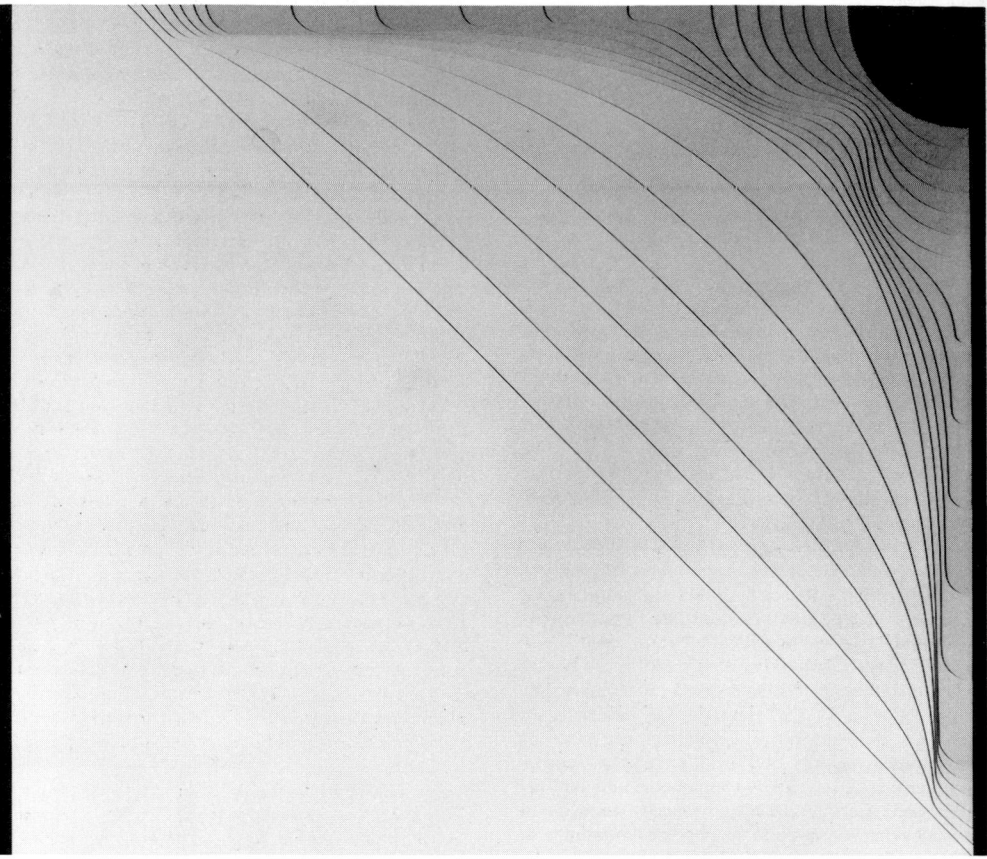

Karl Gerstner: *Color Form: Blue Conversion*, 1977

Gewerbeschule, Basle, 1945–46; mainly self-taught
in art from 1947, but influenced by Georges Vantongerloo, Marcel Duchamp, Josef Albers, Max Bill,
Camille Graeser and Richard Paul Lohse. Served in
the Swiss Army. Married Inge Hoechberg in 1958;
daughter: Muriel. Painter, Basle, from 1947: first interchangeable paintings 1952, first programmed
paintings 1953; also worked as a typographer,
graphic designer and photographer, Basle, 1947–60;
Founder-Director, with Markus Kutter and Paul Gre-
dinger, GGK Advertising Agency, Basle, 1959–70;
full-time painter, Basle, Paris and Hippoltskirch, Alsace, since 1970. Visiting Lecturer, Royal College of
Art, London; Massachusetts Institute of Technology,
Cambridge; University of California, Berkeley; University of Hawaii, Honolulu; and other institutions,
from 1970. Agents: Galerie Denise René, 196 Boulevard Saint-Germain, 75007 Paris; Galerie Hans
Mayer, Grabbeplatz 2, 4000 Dusseldorf; and
Staempfli Gallery, 47 East 77th Street, New York,
New York 10021. Address: Leonhardsgraben 52,
4051 Basle, Switzerland.

Individual Exhibitions:

1957   Club Bel Etage, Zurich
1961   Galerie Suzanne Bollag, Zurich
1962   Galerie Denise René, Paris
1963   Galerie Der Spiegel, Cologne
        Haus am Lutzowplatz, West Berlin
1965   Staempfli Gallery, New York
1966   Op-Art-Galerie Hans Mayer, Esslingen, West Ger-
        many
        Tokyo Gallery
        Galerie Der Spiegel, Cologne
1967   Galerie Denise René, Paris
        Staempfli Gallery, New York
1969   *D'ou vous est venue cette idée?*, Galerie Denise
        René, Paris
        Programmierte Bilder, Karl-Ernst-Osthaus Museum,
        Hagen, West Germany
        Galerie Denise René/Hans Mayer, Dusseldorf
1970   Galerie Swart, Amsterdam

        Haus am Lutzowplatz, West Berlin
1971   Galerie Denise René/Hans Mayer, Dusseldorf
1973   Museum of Modern Art, New York
        Galerie Liatowitsch, Basle
        Denise René Gallery, New York
1974   Kunstmuseum, Dusseldorf
        Galerie Denise René, Paris
1975   Galeria Arte/Contacto, Caracas
        Galerie Jasa, Munich
        Galerie Liatowitsch, Basle
        Color Sounds, Denise René Gallery, New York
1977   Galerie 58, Rapperswil, Switzerland
1978   Galerie Denise René/Hans Mayer, Dusseldorf
        Quadrat-Bottrop Moderne Galerie, Bottrop, West
        Germany
        Kunstmuseum, Solothurn, Switzerland
1979   *Bericht über den Versuch: Karl Gerstner anzugehen*,
        Galerie Brigitte Lopes, Zurich
1981   *Color Forms*, Galerie Denise René/Hans Mayer,
        Dusseldorf
        Studio Bombelli, Cadaques, Spain
1982   Galerie Denise René, Paris
1984   Galerie Der Spiegel, Cologne
1985   Staempfli Gallery, New York
1986   Galerie Denise René, Paris
        Galerie Appel und Fertsch, Frankfurt

Selected Group Exhibitions:

1960   *Konkrete Kunst*, Helmhaus, Zurich
1965   *The Responsive Eye*, Museum of Modern Art, New
        York
1968   *Documenta 4*, Kassel, West Germany
1969   *Freund, Freunde, Friends*, Kunsthalle, Dusseldorf
1971   *Dusseldorf Art Scene*, at the *Edinburgh Festival*
1974   *Aspekte der Düsseldorfer Kunstszene*, Neue Galerie
        am Wolfgang Gurlitt Museum, Linz, Austria
1977   *Kunst, was ist das?*, Kunsthalle, Hamburg
1980   *Schweizerische Plastik-Ausstellung*, Biel, Switzer-
        land
1982   *Vor 150 Jahren: Goethe . . .*, Kunstverein, Hanno-
        ver
1986   *Biennale*, Venice

Collections:

Kunstmuseum, Solothurn, Switzerland; Kunstmuseum, Dusseldorf; Leopold-Hoesch-Museum, Duren, West Germany; Kunsthalle, Nuremberg, West Germany; Staatsgalerie, Stuttgart; Museum des 20. Jahrhunderts, Vienna; Museum of Modern Art, New York; Albright-Knox Art Gallery, Buffalo, New York; Arco Center, Los Angeles; Tate Gallery, London.

Publications:

By GERSTNER: books—*Kalte Kunst?*, Teufen, Switzerland 1957; *Programme entwerfen/Designing Programs*, Teufen, New York, Tokyo and Barcelona 1963; *Mit dem Computer Kunst produzieren*, Zagreb 1968; *Do-it-yourself Kunst*, Cologne 1970; *Kompendium für Alphabeten/Compendium for Literates*, Teufen 1970, Cambridge, Massachusetts 1972; *Typographisches Memorandum*, St. Gallen, Switzerland 1972; *Think Program*, New York 1973; *André Thomkins: Inspiration und Methode*, Hannover 1974; *15 Variationen über einen Satz von Max Bill*, Ulm, West Germany 1978; *Gute Kunst, schlechte Kunst*, Hamburg 1981; *Der Wert der Kunst*, Basle 1982; *Kunst in der Demokratie—eine Utopie*, Frankfurt 1981; *Der Kunstler und die Mehrheit*, Frankfurt 1986; *The Forms of Color*, Cambridge, Massachusetts 1986.

On GERSTNER: books—*Karl Gerstner: d'ou vous est venue cette idée?*, exhibition catalogue, Paris 1969; *Karl Gerstner: Programmierte Bilder*, exhibition catalogue, Hagen, West Germany 1969; *Prinzip seriell*, exhibition catalogue, by Friedrich W. Heckmanns, Dusseldorf 1974; *Karl Gerstner: Color Sounds*, exhibition catalogue, with interview by Wibke von Bonin, New York 1975; *Bericht über den Versuch: Karl Gerstner anzugehen*, exhibition catalogue, Zurich 1979; *Karl Gerstner: Color Forms*, exhibition catalogue, with text by Grace Glueck, Dusseldorf 1981; *Der Geist der Farbe: Die Kunst von Karl Gerstner/L'Esprit des Couleurs: L'Art de Karl Gerstner/The Spirit of Color: The Art of Karl Gerstner*, edited by Henri Stierlin, Stuttgart, Geneva, Paris and Cambridge, Massachusetts 1981; *Karl Gerstner's Private Pinakothek*, Solothurn, Switzerland 1983; *Herr über tausend Farben* by Dieter Bachmann, Hamburg 1983; *Science + Art* by Ans von Berkum and Tom Blekkenhorst, Utrecht 1985; *Gerstners Muhle*, Hamburg 1985.

*

Kandinsky was concerned with the correlation between geometric forms and primary colors. This being granted, his correlations can also be reproduced. But is it correct to proceed from given primary colors or basic forms?

With regard to color it has not yet been possible to fix a norm. And even in the case of the undisputed primary colors yellow/red/blue it remains undecided which yellow, which red and which blue satisfy the quality of the primary color.

And with regard to forms the case is anything but unequivocal. True, there are the platonic figures which are defined by the same length of side. The triangle is quite definitely a basic form with sides of the same length and equal angles. The same goes for the square. And the pentagon. But what about polygons having 17, 18, 19 and so on sides? Is there any dividing line between polygons which are basic forms and those which are basic forms no longer? Or do polygons with an increasing number of sides diminish in quality as a basic form? Right up to the preeminent case of the circle, which has an infinite number of corners, that is to say none at all.

I am concerned in my speculations neither with physically defined primary colors nor with basic geometric forms—even if there were norms for them. I am interested solely in colors and forms which are elementary in respect of the sensation they evoke.

My intention: to design a model in which the correspondence between the elementary colors and elementary forms (elementary as just defined) contains the sum of all that I could learn and have myself experienced: the color form continuum. It is not a fixed construction but a variable (computer generated) structure. This structure is conclusive, transforms (and/or transcolors) colors and forms in continuous steps.

—Karl Gerstner

*

Karl Gerstner advanced from advertisement art to that form of Constructivism to which the name Cold Art (*Kalte Kunst*) was given. Like Kenneth Martin and his associates later in England, Max Bill, the founder of Concrete Art in Switzerland, had maintained that works of art can be constructed in accordance with mathematical formulae, claiming that mathematical thought is one kind of rational thought and that "it is by rational thought that we are able to arrange the sensorial values in such a way as to produce a work of art." Following in Max Bill's footsteps, Karl Gerstner, together with Richard Lohse, applied his principles to the realm of colour, advocating the use of sequential systems to generate colour patterns. From an initial formula he derived whole series and sequences of hues and tones. Consistently with these principles, he quite logically advocated Multiple or Programmatic art, since any number of identical art works can obviously be generated from one and the same mathematical programme. Nothing was lost by mechanical reproduction. Allied to all this he lent his support and encouragement to the idea of Modular or Generative art of the kind in which art works are composed of identical units put together in a variety of ways like a child's building blocks. Finally, he has been an enthusiastic advocate of spectator participation, and at an exhibition of the Nouvelle Tendance in 1964 he declared: "Our aim is to make you a partner . . . our art depends on your active participation. What we are trying to achieve is your joy before the work of art, that it may be no longer that of an admirer but of a partner." Whether this squares with the recondite mathematical basis of his *Kalte Kunst* is not clear.

In his writings on *Kalte Kunst* Gerstner has made few concessions to traditional aesthetic ideas of composition, balance, harmony, etc. This is not what he was aiming at. When his own works are exhibited and seen in bulk they give the impression of some obscure scientific demonstration or advertisement display. They do not invite visual enjoyment. Appreciation and enjoyment must be intellectual, based upon understanding of the mathematics involved, and for this reason the mathematical systems are exhibited along with the works derived from them. How far if at all this comes within the scope of what is commonly understood by "art" is an open question.

—Harold Osborne

GERTSCH, Franz.

Swiss. Born in Moerigen, Berne, 8 March 1930. Educated at the Sekundarschule, Berne, 1940–47; studied painting at the Malschule Max von Muehlenen, Berne, 1947–50. Married Maria Meer in 1963; has five children. Painter, since 1947. Recipient: DAAD Fellowship, Berlin, 1974. Agent: M. Knoedler Zurich AG, Kirchgasse 24, 8001 Zurich. Address: Huslistatt, 3154 Ruschegg-Heubach, Switzerland.

Individual Exhibitions:

1968	Galerie Martin Krebs, Berne
1969	Galerie Riehentor, Basle
1970	Galerie Toni Gerber, Berne
	Galerie Stampa, Basle
1971	Galerie Verna, Zurich
1972	Kunstmuseum, Lucerne
	Galerie Mikro, Berlin
1973	Nancy Hoffman Gallery, New York
1975	Akademie der Künste, Berlin (travelled to the Kunstverein, Braunschweig, West Germany; Kunsthalle Dusseldorf; and the Palais des Beaux-Arts, Brussels)
	Kunsthalle, Basel
	Galerie Turske, Cologne
1976	Galerie Turske, Cologne
1977	Galerie Turske, Cologne
1979	Galerie Turske, Cologne
1980	Kunsthaus, Zurich
	Kunstmuseum, Hannover
1981	Louis K. Meisel Gallery, New York
1982	M. Knoedler Zurich AG, Zurich
1986	Kunsthalle, Basle

Selected Group Exhibitions:

1972	*Documenta 5*, Museum Fridericianum, Kassel, West Germany
1973	*Prospect*, Kunsthalle, Dusseldorf
	The Super-Realist Vision, De Cordova Museum, Lincoln, Massachusetts
1974	*Hyperrealistes Americains-Realistes Europeens*, Centre National d'Art Contemporain, Paris
1976	*Aspects of Realism*, The Gallery, Stratford, Ontario (toured Canada)
1977	*Malerei und Photographie im Dialog*, Kunsthaus, Zurich
1978	*Dalla Natura all'Arte, dall'Arte alla Natura*, at the *Biennale*, Venice
1979	*Bilder einer Ausstellung*, Kunsthalle, Berne
1980	*Printed Art*, Museum of Modern Art, New York
1981	*Art 12, '81 (Turske Fine Art)*, Kunstmesse, Basle

Collections:

Museum Moderner Kunst, Vienna; Museum Ludwig, Cologne; Bayerische Staatsgemaldesammlung, Munich; Kunsthalle, Kiel; Nationalgalerie, Berlin; Kunstmuseum, Hannover; Kunstmuseum, Berne; Kunstmuseum, Lucerne; Kunsthaus, Zurich; National Gallery of Australia, Canberra.

Publications:

By GERTSCH: articles—"Interview mit Franz Gertsch," with P. Killer, in *Abendezeitung* (Zurich), February 1971; "Entretien entre Franz Gertsch et Urs Graf" in *L'Art Vivant* (Paris), March 1973; "Ein Statement" in *Projekt '74*, exhibition catalogue, Cologne 1974; "Meine Strategie des Malens" in *Franz Gertsch*, exhibition catalogue, Berlin 1975; interview, with Jürgen Glaesemer, in *Franz Gertsch*, exhibition catalogue, Zurich 1980.

On GERTSCH: books—*Neue Formen des Bildes* by Udo Kultermann, Tübingen 1969, 1975; *Franz Gertsch*, exhibition catalogue, with texts by Jean-Christophe Ammann, Timothy Leary, Harald Szeemann and others. Lucerne 1972; *Neue Formen des Realismus* by Peter Sager, Cologne 1973; *Super-Realism: A Critical Anthology*, edited by Gregory Battcock, New York 1975; *Franz Gertsch*, exhibition catalogue, with texts by Karl Ruhrberg, Harald Szeeman, Jean-Christophe Ammann and others, Berlin 1975; *Franz Gertsch*, exhibition catalogue, with texts by Jean-Christophe Ammann, Erika Billeter, Joachim Buchner and others, Zurich 1980; articles—"Franz Gertsch" by Jean-Christophe Ammann in *Art International* (Lugano, Switzerland), vol. 12, no. 10, 1968; "Franz Gertsch" by Leonardo Bezzola in *Werk* (Basle), February 1972; "Franz Gertsch at Nancy Hoffmann" in the *Village Voice* (New York), 20 September 1973; "Bilder von Bildern von Bildern" by Francois Grundbacher in *Berner Zeitung* (Berne), 11 August 1979; "Wozu die virtuose Fleissarbeit des Franz Gertsch: Art pour art?" by Hans Jurg Kupper in *Basler Zeitung* (Basle), 10 May 1980; "A Newer Objectivity: Franz Gertsch's Photo-Realist Paintings" by Agnes von Borch in *Arts Magazine* (New York), December 1981.

*

Swiss born painter Franz Gertsch is the best known European exponent of the Photo-Realist approach. Gertsch has been making portraits since he was a child and has always been attracted to the representational in painting. In 1952 he was already painting from photographs and working to reach an element of "objectivity" and "stylelessness" in his pictures. It wasn't until 1969, however, that he reached his characteristic method and started painting from projected slides.

During the past ca. 12 years, Gertsch has produced about 37 canvases. His working method is almost excruciating meticulous and painstakingly slow, especially considering that he works with small, extra fine brushes rather than with the air brush employed by many of the American Photo-Realists. Gertsch begins

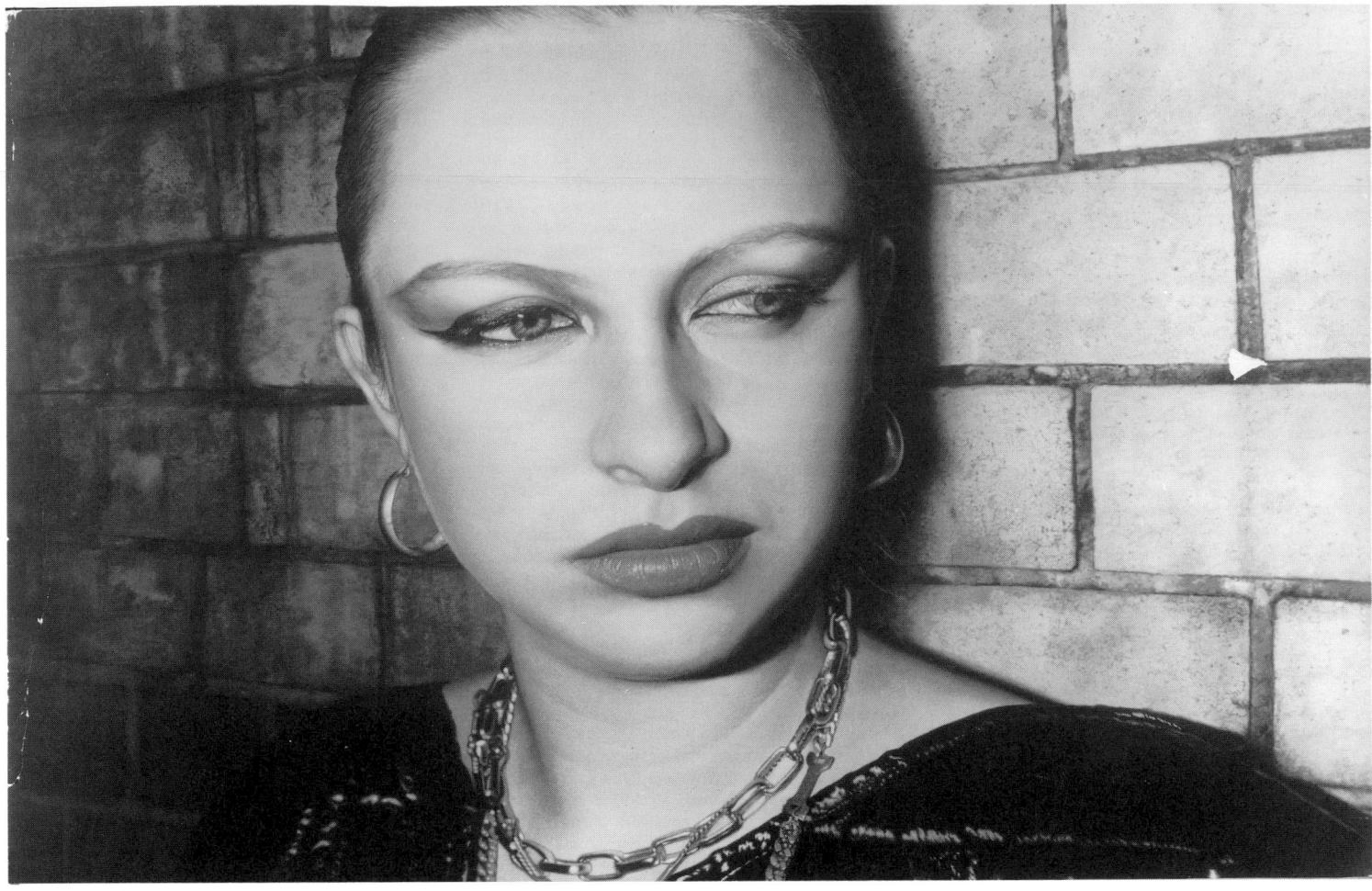

Franz Gertsch: *Tabea*, 1981

with photographs which he takes himself, and he chooses his models for the paintings from among a large number taken of each subject. His subjects are mainly either himself or family and friends, people he is highly familiar with and who usually reflect a lifestyle which is a bit off-center from the regular and ordinary work-a-day populace. His compositions seem to lie somewhere between the candid spontaneous and the posed, as if they were the result of pointing the camera, saying "smile" and rapidly snapping. Probably because the subjects are people he knows relatively well, he captures characteristic personality traits recognizably individualistic and yet relatable as types. It is a combination of intimacy and remove which gives life to his works as a whole, with little need for detailed surrounding environment. Consider, for example, the portrait of "Franz and Luciano" (1973) which, with very little extra paraphernalia surrounding the subjects, amply communicates their connections with painting and rather "hip" way of life by the inclusion of portions of paintings behind them and by their style of hair and dress, almost but not quite rock star in appearance. A later and more developed example is Gertsch's large (100 x 154″) painting of "Irene" (1980), which reveals a lot about her character within the limiting context of the head and shoulder view. Her aggressive, almost scowling expression, heavy makeup, large sword earrings and campily natural, severe hairdo are enough to portray a type of "New Wavey," *Cabaret* character who, by the way, is also the sustained subject for a number of penetrating watercolor studies.

It is such persistently tough and individualistic subjects which Gertsch seems to prefer, perhaps because they display a literal quality equal to his own pertinacious approach to the canvas. His apt blending of the ruggedly literal and the straightforwardly emotive is amplified by one of the most striking features of his painting. It is the way the images break up on closer scrutiny, revealing the painterly brushstroke quality of the handmade. It's a quality which gives the work a physicality as paint on a level beyond that of the literal Photo-Real, bringing visual satisfaction too often missing in the genre and suggesting that Gertsch's slow methodology is somehow worth it.

—Barbara Cavaliere

GERZ, Jochen.

German. Born in Berlin, 4 April 1940. Educated at Gymnasium, Dusseldorf, 1951–58; studied American and German literature and Sinology, University of Cologne, 1959–60; English language, St. Mary College, London, 1961–62; German literature and prehistory, University of Basle, 1963–64. Married Veronika von Buren in 1963; daughter: Francis Jan. Worked as news agency volunteer, Dusseldorf, 1956–59; newspaper car driver, *Evening Standard,* London, 1962; graphist and public relations for Gerstner and Kutter, Basle, 1963–67; correspondent for a news agency, Paris, 1968–73. Interested in poetry since 1959; has produced visual texts since 1966, and photo texts since 1969; has worked in video, performance and installations since 1971; collaborations with Esther Shalev-Gerz, from 1984: lives and works in Paris. Agent: Galerie Bama, 40 rue Quincampoix, 75004 Paris. Address: 4 rue René Villermé, 75011 Paris, France.

Individual Exhibitions:

1968   Galleria Rinascita, Modena, Italy (with Jean-Francois Bory)
1969   Galerie Groh, Oldenburg, West Germany (with K. H. Krull)
    Aktionstraum I, Munich
1970   Galleria la Communes, Brescia, Italy
    Galerie Ben Doute de Tout, Nice
    Galerie Yellow, Liège, Belgium
    Galerie Mediacontact, Dusseldorf
1971   Galleria Tool, Milan
    Galerie NW 8, Beindersheim, West Germany
1972   Galerie Bama, Paris
    Danert Galeriet, Copenhagen
    Galerie Stampa, Basle
1973   German Institute, Amsterdam
    German Institute, Bordeaux
    Centro Diffusione Grafica, Florence
    Galerie Delta, Brussels
1974   Studio Gap, Rome
    Kunsthalle, Kiel, West Germany
    Galerie Stampa, Basle
    Galerie S. Press, Hattingen, West Germany
    Kunstmuseum, Bochum, West Germany
    Galerie Entre, Paris
    Galerie Klein, Bonn
    Galerie Bama, Paris
1975   Kunstverein, Karlsruhe
    Musée d'Art Moderne de la Ville, Paris
    Musée d'Art et d'Industrie, St. Etienne, France
    Galerie Nächst St. Stephan, Vienna
    Wilhelm-Lehmbruck Museum, Duisburg, West Germany
1976   Tranegarden Kunstbibliothek, Hellerup, Denmark (with Paul-Armand Gette)
    Foto/Texte und Stucke, Kunstverein, Braunschweig, West Germany
    Galerie Art in Progress, Dusseldorf

German Pavilion, at the *Biennale*, Venice (with Joseph Beuys and Reiner Ruthenbeck)
Kunstraum V, Munich
1977 Studio d'Arte Cannaviello, Rome
Painting Box, Zurich
Association pour Musée d'Art Actuel, Ghent
Galerie Stampa, Basle
Galerie André, Berlin
Video-Studio Mike Stein, Berlin
Galerie Bama, Paris
Galerie Art in Progress, Munich
Stätische Galerie in Lenbachhaus, Munich
1978 Bundner Kunstmuseum, Chur, Switzerland
Der Stein will zuruck zur Schleuder, Landesmuseum Joanneum, Graz, Austria
Galerie Klein, Bonn
Foto/Texte 1975–1978, Kestner-Gesellschaft, Hannover
Kulchur Pieces 1, 2, 3, Westfälischer Kunstverein, Münster, West Germany
Centro de Arte Contemporaneo, Oporto, Portugal (travelled to the Fundaco Calouste Gulbenkian, Lisbon
1979 *The Depot: Kulchur Piece No. 4*, Ikon Gallery, Birmingham, England
1980 *5 Installations*, Frankfurter Kunsterverein, Frankfurt
Galerie Stampa, Basle
Galerie Bama, Paris
Jochen Gerz, Nachtbilder, Kasseler Kunstverein, Kassel, West Germany
1981 *Mit 1 Publikum (Performances 1968–80)*, Kunsthalle, Bielefeld, West Germany
The Flat, Copenhagen
1982 *Le Grand Amour*, Kunstverein, Freiburg, West Germany
Fotografien und Texte 1980–81, Galerie Dany Keller, Munich
Galerie AK, Frankfurt
Galerie A, Amsterdam
Galerie Bama, Paris
Galerie Stampa, Basle
1983 Maison de la Culture, Chalon-sur-Saone, France
Galerie Stampa, Basle
1984 Galerie Holtmann, Cologne
Banff Arts Centre, Alberta
Yuill/Crowley Gallery, Sydney (travelled to the Australian Centre for Contemporary Art, Melbourne)
Wilhelm-Hack-Museum, Ludwigshafen, West Germany
Kunstverein, Heidelberg, West Germany
1985 Galerie Bama, Paris
Museum fur Photographie, Braunschweig, West Germany
Neuer Berliner Kunstverein, West Berlin
Stadtglaerie, Saarbrucken, West Germany
Or Gallery, Vancouver
1986 Kunstraum, Munich
Passages Centre d'Art Contemporain, Troyes, France
Musee des Beaux-Arts, Calais, France
Galerie de l'ancienne Poste, Calais, France
Musee des Beaux-Arts, Chartres, France
Galerie Cora Holzl, Dusseldorf
Espace Lyonnais d'Art Contemporain, Lyon, France
Coburg Gallery, Vancouver
1987 La Criee, Rennes, France
Galerie Optica, Montreal
Yuill/Crowley Gallery, Sydney
Galerie Kicken/Pauseback, Cologne

Performances: *Rufen bis zur Erschopfung*, Paris, *Der Saal, die Wiedergabe*, Paris, and *Schreiben mit der Hand*, Frankfurt, 1972; *Das was sich beschreiben last*, Rome, and *Thomas Jefferson*, Florence, 1973; *Leben*, Kunstmuseum, Bochum, West Germany, and *Das Vergehen von Horen und Sehen*, Kunstmuseum, Bochum, West Germany, 1974; *Das Auto-Portrait*, Galerie Nachst St. Stephen, Vienna, *Ich bin gleich zuruch (Eurydike)*, Kunstverein, Karlsruhe, *Prometheus*, Lembruck Museum, Duisburg, West Germany, and *Nacht, lass den Jager schlafen*, Kunstverein, Braunschweig, West Germany, 1975; *Marsyas*, Kunstmarket, Basle, and *Snake Hoods and Dragon's Dreams*, Videogalerie Steiner, Berlin, 1977; *Marsyas*, Stadtpark Forum, Graz, Austria, *Marsyas*, Kunstmarket, Cologne, *Raum mit Grabrelief und*

Jager, at the *Bremen Performance Festival*, 1978; *Purple Cross for Absent Now*, Centre d'Art Contemporain, Geneva, *Nice to Meet You*, and the *Lyons Performance Festival*, *ABC of Reading*, Centre Georges Pompidou, Paris, and *Letter to Jane*, Palazzo Grassi, Venice, 1979; *Welcome Home*, Basle, and *We Are Coming*, Centre Georges Pompidou, Paris, 1980; *Die Reise*, Kunstverein, Heidelberg, 1981; *Pionniers!*, Off Off Centre, Calgary, Alberta, 1982; *Chinook*, Stadtsches Museum, Monchengladbach, 1985; *Purple Cross for Absent Now no. 2*, at Documenta 8, Kassel, West Germany, 1987.

Selected Group Exhibitions:

1969 *Visuelle Poesie*, Westfälischer Kunstverein, Münster, West Germany
1970 *3 Towards Infinity: Multiples*, Whitechapel Art Gallery, London
1972 *Biennale*, Venice
1973 *L'Estample Contemporaine*, Bibliothéque Nationale, Paris
1974 *Demonstrative Fotografie*, Kunsthalle, Heidelberg
Video Art, Musée des Arts Décoratifs, Lausanne, Switzerland
1977 *Malerei und Photographie im Dialog*, Kunsthaus, Zurich
1978 *Artwords—Bookworks*, Los Angeles Institute of Contemporary Art
1986 *Kunst in der Bundesrepublik 1945–85*, Nationalgalerie, West Berlin
1987 *Les Annees 70*, Abbaye Saint-Andre, Meymac, France

Collections:

Kunsthalle, Kiel, West Germany; Kunstmuseum, Dusseldorf; Städtisches Museum, Bonn; Centre Georges Pompidou, Paris; Bibliothéque Nationale, Paris; Kunsthaus, Zurich; Kunstmuseum, Lucerne; Museum for Contemporary Art, Livorno; Australian National Gallery, Canberra.

Publications:

By GERZ: books—*Footing*, Paris 1968; *Replay*, Paris 1969; *Resurrection*, Brescia, Italy 1970; *Recto Verso*, Florence 1971; *Annoncenteil*, Berlin 1971; *Die Beschreibung des Papiers*, Darmstadt 1973; *Contacts*, Toronto 1974; *Die Schwierigkeit des Zentaurs beim vom Pferd Steigen*, Munich 1976; *A Danish Exorcism*, Ringkobing 1976; *Das zweite Buch (Die Zeit der Beschreibung)*. Lichtenberg 1976; *Exit/Das Cachau-Projekt*, Frankfurt 1978; *The Fuji-Yama-Series*, Saarbrucken 1981; *Le Grand Amour*, Saarbruki 1982; *Das vierte Buch (Die Zeit der Beschreibung)*, Spenge 1983; *Von der Kunst/De l'art*, Dudweiler 1985; *Texte*, Bielefeld 1985; articles—"The Arts in the Museum of Illiteracy" in *Klepht*, Swansea, Wales 1970; "Pour un Langage du Faire" in *Opus International* (Paris), no. 40–41, 1972; "Kritik an der Gesellschaftlichen Produktion auf dem Gebiet der Kultur" in *Kunst Praxis Heute*, Cologne 1972; "Bedingungen der Visuellen Poesie" in *Nachrichten des Instituts für Moderne Kunst* (Nuremberg), no. 4, 1972; "La difficulte du centaure a descendre du cheval" in *Monsieur Bloom* (Paris), no. 3, 1979; "Le Voyage" in *Travereses* (Paris), no. 33/34, 1985; "Objects are withdrawing from me more and more" in *Acts* (San Francisco), no. 5, 1986.

On GERZ: books—*Neue Bucher* by Helmut Heissenbuttel, Hamburg 1971; *Jochen Gerz*, exhibition catalogue, Rome 1974; *Jochen Gerz*, exhibition catalogue, Kiel, West Germany 1974; *Jochen Gerz*, exhibition catalogue, St. Etienne, France 1975; *Jochen Gerz: Foto/Texte und Stucke*, exhibition catalogue, Braunschweig 1976; *Jochen Gerz: Biennale Venedig 76*, Venice 1976; *Jochen Gerz*, exhibition catalogue, Chur, Switzerland 1978; *Jochen Gerz: Der Stein will zuruck zur Schleuder*, exhibition catalogue, Graz, Austria 1978; *Jochen Gerz: Foto/Texte 1975–1978*, exhibition catalogue, edited by Carl-Albrecht Haenlein, Hannover 1978; *Jochen Gerz*, exhibition catalogue, Lisbon 1978; *Jochen Gerz: Kulchur Pieces 1, 2, 3*, exhibition catalogue with texts by Fernando Pernes, Carl-Albrecht Haenlein and Thomas Deecke, Münster 1978; *The Depot: Kulchur Piece No. 4*, exhibition catalogue, with text by R. C. Kenedy, Birmingham 1979; *Jochen Gerz: 5 Installations*, exhibition catalogue, Frankfurt 1980; *Jochen Gerz, Nachtbilder*, exhibition catalogue, Kassel, West Germany 1980; *Jochen Gerz: Mit 1 Publikum (Performances 1968–80)*, exhibition catalogue, Bielefeld, West Germany 1981; *Jochen Gerz: Le Grand Amour*, exhibition

catalogue, Freiburg 1982; *Jochen Gerz: La Chasse/The Strip*, exhibition catalogue with text by Christine Tacke, Munich 1986.

What does art represent for you today?

It's something fragile. If I think of art, I don't think of any particular time or place or rectangular thing. I don't even think about *making* something. Sooner or later, I think about being. So art stays in touch with its origin, being, for me. In that sense, it's fragile. It's also the most radical manifestation of the unsaid you can produce, if not actually be—and the most opposite to us. Perhaps you make what you cannot be. It's emotionally disturbing that man is capable of making art. Criticizing this possibility is the same as criticizing oneself. No detour or consolation seems possible, or even necessary.

Do you think that works of art should have some sort of usefulness in our society?

And what if they weren't *for* anything . . . ? I like things that are useful, but isn't being *for nothing* already being good for something? Today, every single thing seems conceived and conceivable only in function of its finality. Everything is useful, profitable, explainable. In a useful world, art is a spoon. It's through misunderstanding or ignorance that it's good *for nothing*, rather than out of some elaborate strategy of refusal. More out of indifference. Every strategy has its season. Afterwards, it has no object and becomes a kind of decoration . . .

Art shows or hides, maybe, above all, the social consensus about the gratuitous, useless games, solitude, intensity   it does that more than all the *ritual places*: movies, casinos, churches, stadiums. Isn't this consensus based on the fact that we were all kids once?

The gratuitous aspect of love, of all of life, right to the end—what else would make these things relevant? This gratuitous thing is a real provocation in a civilization that is separated into users and tools.
—Jochen Gerz (from an interview with Patrick Le Nouéne)

Suppression of pictures is one of Jochen Gerz's main categories of creation. In addition, there is also suppression of writing. Pictures, as they emerge, are concealed, painted over with brown paint remover, brushed over or produced in such an indistinct and washed-out manner that they necessarily remain irrecognizable. He writes with the left hand or in mirror cript so that the text is illegible, or rather it is composed in such a way that the words with which something is described merely revolve round the subject or the event, approach it cautiously as if it were about to disappear or were only a vague memory. Whether in pictures or in words, Jochen Gerz manages to hold fast to nothing, to establish nothing, which in any case and by definition would not be a reality, a life lived, but a recapitulation of it.

To imprison, photograph or manufacture pictures is like a hunt for life which kills life. In his opinion all art is reproduction, duplication, a tombstone, the beginning of disintegration; unless, and that seems to Gerz to be the only way out, its means of expression were fundamentally to contradict its original function. The best texts are therefore those that neutralize themselves through the indifference of their language, the best pictures those that suppress themselves, as Gerz made clear in an exhibition in Saint-Etienne in 1975. He showed canvases without pictures, with the paradoxical challenge to the spectator: "Don't look at me," "Don't remember me." As in this case, Jochen Gerz uses an essential part of his work to expose a genuine negative dialectic of art. Pictures appear as seducers which do not lead to reality, but turn away from it until we are incapable of recognizing it at all.

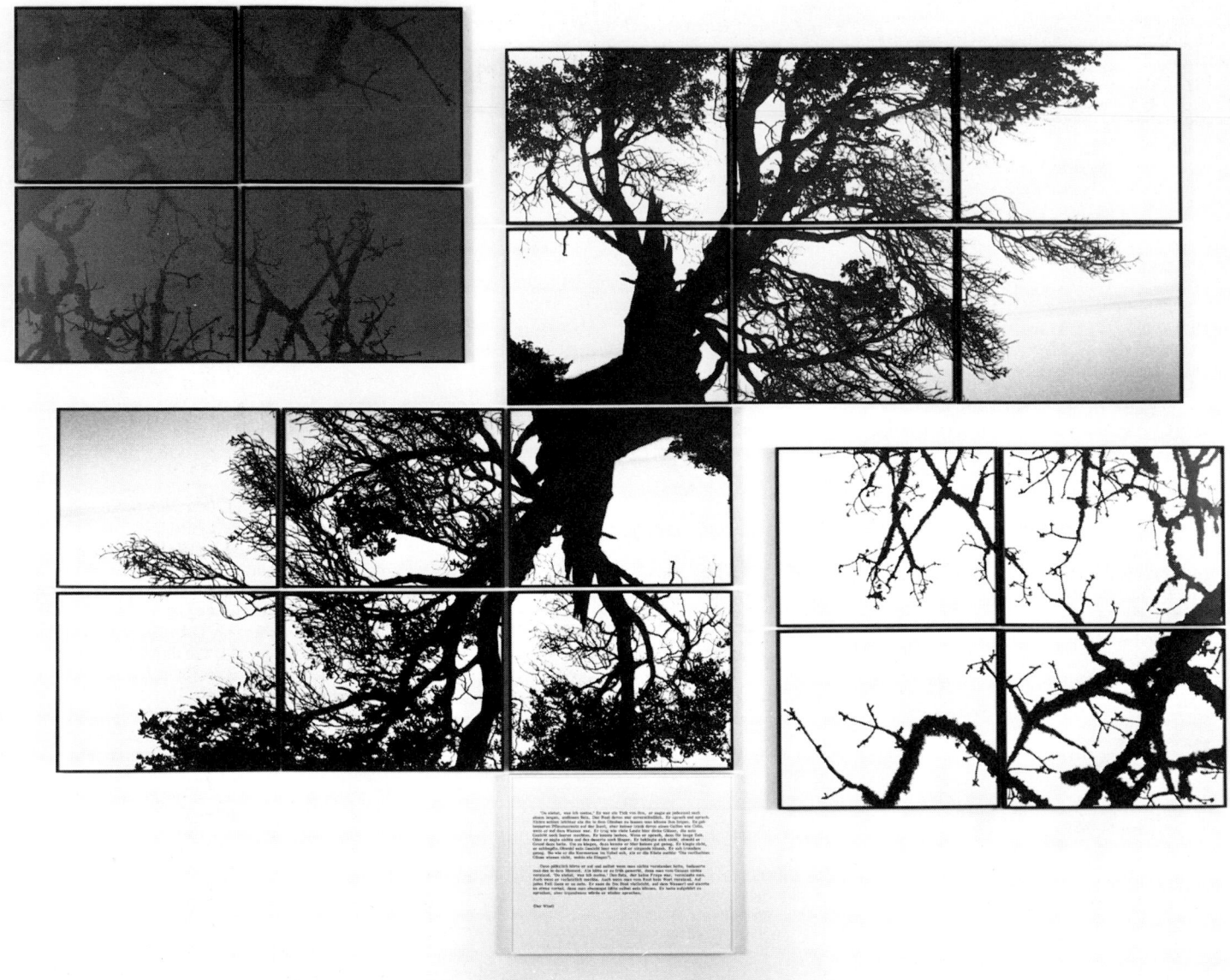

Jochen Gerz: *The Wind*, 1986

Instead of this, art should serve to refer the viewer to himself and his times, to the here and now of his life. Pictures as well as words have this effect of course only when they deny themselves. The main point is rather to discover fresh possibilities, to avoid altogether the conventional forms of expression and to uncover new artistic languages, which Gerz has attempted by performance, by the use of video and by his installations. An art which does not want to betray life should take place in a zone between reality and reproduction, in a fluctuating zone which functions beyond all permanently fixed forms. Languages have to be discovered which would not or could not be adopted by the culture industry and which will be used outside of the mass media. All communication today seems perverted into a mere barter system for contemporary myths and phantasms, and, in order to escape this system, Gerz invents languages which will not be spoken in it. He prefers to use his body and his gestures, and the space which surrounds him, his voice, physical exertion, even pain and exhaustion.

By all these means he tries to turn the viewer away from the beautiful illusion, from the aura of the work of art, and to bring him to himself. Whenever Gerz gathers the themes of his actions from Greek myths or even from the new myths which are closer to us and more dreadful in memory, as perhaps the "Concentration Camp," he does so to strike at the fundamental conditionality of art. In all these actions and installations it becomes clear: art exists only on condition that it bows to its own negation. In this way Gerz follows the tradition of language criticism which was characterized in Germany by Wittgenstein and Karl Kraus, but which, after the Second World War, Theodor Adorno enhanced and enlarged into a new universal examination of the present culture industry.

Initially there is in Jochen Gerz a declaration of mistrust in relation to the use of language and pictures which is equally complaisant to all political and ideological aims, the suspicion of ideas and signs which had served Fascism and continued to be used without reflection. What he, who is likewise obliged to use pictures and signs, is able to propose in opposition is either negation or destruction or artful evasion. Gerz has made use of all possibilities in his works. He has decomposed and disowned pictures and texts, has himself renounced and replaced them. In renouncing a picture and in its place making actions, spaces, art with the body and the public, it can result that something of the present time prior to suffocation and something of the world prior to the final violence will be preserved through culture.

—Marie Luise Syring

GIACOMETTI, Alberto.

Swiss. Born in Bogonova, near Stampa, Grisons, Switzerland, 10 October 1901. Educated in Grisons public schools; studied painting with his father, the artist Giovanni Giacometti, 1919, and briefly, under David Estoppey, Ecole des Beaux-Arts, Geneva, 1919; studied sculpture, under Maurice Sarkissoff, Ecole des Arts et Metiers, Geneva, 1919; spent nine months in Rome sketching old masters and antiquities, 1921; studied drawing and sculpture in Bourdelle's class at the Académie de la Grande Chaumière, Paris, 1922–24. Married Annette Arm in 1949. Sculptor: lived and worked in Paris; shared studio with brother, Diego, Paris, from 1925; associated with Surrealists: participated in their activities, 1930–35; designed furniture, vases, chandeliers, home furnishings, executed by Diego, for the interior decorator Jean-Michel Franck, 1929; spent time in hospital, with serious foot injury, after automobile accident, 1938; lived in Geneva during the occupation; returned to Paris, 1945; designed set for *Waiting for Godot* by Samuel Beckett, Paris, 1953; worked on Chase Manhattan Plaza project (not realized), 1959–60. Recipient: Sculpture Prize, *Pittsburgh International*, 1961; Sculpture Prize, *Biennale*, Venice, 1962; Guggenheim International Award, 1964; Grand Prize in Art of the City of Paris, 1965. Honorary doctorate: University of Berne, 1965. *Died* (in Chur, Switzerland) *11 January 1966.*

Individual Exhibitions:

1925	Galerie Aktuaryas, Zurich (with Giovanni Giacometti)
1930	Galerie Pierre, Paris (with Hans Arp and Joan Mirò)
1932	Galerie Pierre Colle, Paris
1934	Julien Levy Gallery, New York
1945	Art of This Century, New York
1946	Galerie Pierre Loeb, Paris
1947	Galerie Arts, Paris
1948	Pierre Matisse Gallery, New York
1950	Pierre Matisse Gallery, New York
	Kunsthalle, Basle (with André Masson)
1951	Galerie Maeght, Paris
1952	Wittenborn Gallery, New York
1953	Arts Club of Chicago
1954	Galerie Maeght, Paris
1955	Pierre Matisse Gallery, New York
	Arts Council Gallery, London
	Guggenheim Museum, New York
	Kaiser Wilhelm Museum, Krefeld, West Germany (toured West Germany)
1956	Kunsthalle, Berne
	Biennale, Venice
1957	Galerie Maeght, Paris
1958	Pierre Matisse Gallery, New York
1959	Galerie Kipstein und Kornfeld, Berne
1960	World House Galleries, New York
	Galerie Beyeler, Basle
1961	Pierre Matisse Gallery, New York
	Hanover Gallery, London
	Pittsburgh International
	Galleria Galatea, Turin
	Galerie Maeght, Paris
1962	*Biennale,* Venice
	Kunsthaus, Zurich
1963	Galerie Beyeler, Basle
	Phillips Collection, Washington, D.C.
	Galerie Krugier, Geneva
	Libreria Einaudi, Rome
1964	Pierre Matisse Gallery, New York
	Fondation Maeght, St. Paul de Vence, France
	Galerie Stiftung, Zurich
1965	Tate Gallery, London
	Museum of Modern Art, New York (toured the United States)
	Louisiana Museum, Humlebaek, Denmark
	Kunstkabinett, Berlin-Weissensee
1966	Galerie Krugier, Geneva
	Sidney Janis Gallery, New York (with Jean Dubuffet)
	Kunsthalle, Basle
	Kestner-Gesellschaft, Hannover
	Loeb and Krugier Gallery, New York
1967	Galerie Engelberts, Geneva
	Brook Street Gallery, London
1968	Galerie Claude Bernard, Paris
	Sidney Janis Gallery, New York
1967	L'Orangerie des Tuileries, Paris
1970	Rhode Island School of Design, Providence
	Milwaukee Art Center (toured the United States)
	Frank Perls Gallery, Beverly Hills, California
	Académie de France, Villa Medici, Rome
	Galerie Engelberts, Geneva
1971	Musée Jenisch, Vevey, Switzerland
1972	Kunstmuseum, Olten, Switzerland
	Galerie Gerald Cramer, Geneva
	Galerie Scheidegger und Maurer, Zurich
1973	Museo Civico di Belle Arti, Lugano, Switzerland
	Galerie Seibu, Tokyo (travelled to Museum of Modern Art, Kobe, and the Art Museum, Ishikawa, Japan)
1974	Guggenheim Museum, New York (toured the United States and Canada)
1975	Fondación Juan March, Madrid
	Louisiana Museum, Humlebaek, Denmark
	Amos Anderson Museum, Helsinki
1977	Wilhelm-Lehmbruck Museum, Duisburg, West Germany
	Fondation Sonja Henie-Niels Onstad, Oslo
	Moderna Museet, Stockholm
	Thomas Gibson Fine Art, London
1978	Sidney Janis Gallery, New York
	Fondation Maeght, St. Paul de Vence, France

	Bundner Kunstmuseum, Chur, Switzerland
	Galerie Kornfeld, Zurich
	American Federation of Arts, New York
1979	Scottish National Gallery of Art, Edinburgh
1980	Galerie Maeght, Zurich
	Bletchley Leisure Centre, Milton Keynes, Buckinghamshire (toured the U.K.)
1981	Whitworth Art Gallery, Manchester (travelled to Museum and Art Gallery, Bristol, and the Serpentine Gallery, London)
	Musée d'Arte d'Industrie, St. Etienne, France
	Galeria Maeght, Barcelona
1982	Printmakers' Workshop, Edinburgh
1984	Sainsbury Centre for the Visual Arts, University of East Anglia, Norwich
1985	Galerie Claude Bernard, Paris
1986	Musee Rath, Geneva
	Haags Gemeentemuseum, The Hague
1987	Centre Georges Pompidou, Paris
1988	Hirshhorn Museum, Washington, D.C. (travelled to San Francisco)

Selected Group Exhibitions:

1925	*Salon des Tuileries,* Salle des Cubistes, Paris (yearly until 1928)
1928	*Artisti Italiani di Parigi,* Salon de l'Escalier, Paris
1929	*Exposition Internationale de la Sculpture,* Galerie Georges Bernhcim, Paris
1933	*Salon des Surindépendants,* Paris
1935	*These-Antithese-Synthese,* Kunstmuseum, Lucerne
1937	*Fantastic Art, Dada and Surrealism,* Museum of Modern Art, New York
1940	*Exposición Internaciónal de Surrealismo,* Galeria d'Art Mexicano, Mexico City
1951	*L'Ecole de Paris, 1900–1950,* Royal Academy of Art, London
1974	*The Human Form in Sculpture,* University of Stirling, Scotland
1985	*Painterly Visions 1940–85,* Guggenheim Museum, New York

Collections:

Giacometti Foundation, Zurich; Kunstmuseum, Zurich; Centre Georges Pompidou, Paris; Fondation Maeght, St. Paul-de-Vence, France; Tate Gallery, London; Museum of Modern Art, New York; Carnegie Institute, Pittsburgh; Detroit Institute of Arts.

Publications:

By GIACOMETTI: articles—"Objet Mobiles et Muets" in *Le Surréalisme au Service de la Révolution* (Paris), December 1931; "Poem," "Le Rideau brun," "Charbon d'Herbe" and "Hier, sables mouvants" in *Le Surréalisme au Service de la Révolution* (Paris), May 1933; "Palais de 4 Heures" in *Minotaure* (Paris), December 1933; "Le Dialogue en 1934," with André Breton, in *Documents* (Brussels), June 1934; "Un Sculpteur vu par un Sculpteur" in *Labyrinthe* (Geneva), January 1945; "A propos de Jacques Cellot" in *Labyrinthe* (Geneva), April 1945; "Le Reve, le Sphinx et la Mort de T" in *Labyrinthe* (Geneva), December 1946; "Letter to Pierre Matisse" in *Alberto Giacometti,* exhibition catalogue, New York 1948; "Un Aveugle avance la main dans la Nuit" in *XXe Siècle* (Paris), January 1952; interview with Gualtiere di San Lazzaro in *XXe Siècle* (Paris), 1952; interview with Yvonne Taillander in *Konstrevy 28,* Stockholm 1952; "Gris, Brun, Noir . . ." in *Derrière le Miroir* (Paris), June 1952; "Mai 1920" in *Verve* (Paris), January 1953; interview with Alexander Liberman in *Vogue* (New York), January 1955; interview with Alain Joulfroy in *Arts, Lettres, Spectacles* (Paris), December 1955; "Derain" in *Derrière le Miroir* (Paris), February 1957; "Ma Réalité" in *XXe Siècle* (Paris), June 1957; letter to Peter F. Atthaus in *Du* (Zurich), March 1958; "My Artistic Intentions" and "Concerning the Human Image" in *New Images of Man,* exhibition catalogue, New York 1959; interview with Alexander Watt in *Art in America* (New York), no. 4, 1960; interview with Pierre Schneider in *L'Express* (Paris), 8 June 1961; interview with André Parinaud in *Arts, Lettres, Spectacles* (Paris), 13 June 1962; interview with Pierre Schneider in *Preuves* (Paris), September 1962; interview with Grazia Livi in *Epoca* (Milan), January 1963; interview with Pierre Dumaret in *Le Nouveau Candide* (Paris), June 1963; interview with Jean-Luc Duval in *Journal de*

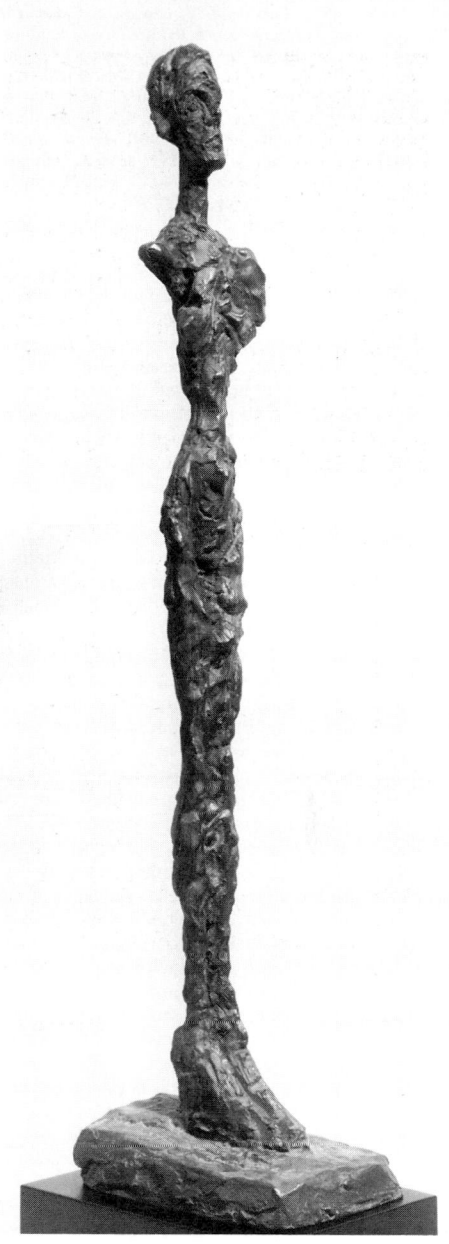

Alberto Giacometti: *Bronze Figure,* 1961 Courtesy Pierre Matisse Gallery, New York

Geneve, 8 June 1963; interview with Jean Clay in *Réalités* (Paris), December 1963; interview with Marianne Adelmann in *The Studio* (London), January 1964; interview with J. P. Hodin in *XXe Siècle* (Paris), December 1964; "31 Aout 1963" in *Derrière le Mirror* (Paris), no. 144–146, 1964; interview with Carlton Lake in the *Atlantic Monthly* (Boston), September 1965; "La Mort du Professor Tedlicka" in *Neue Zürcher Zeitung* (Zurich), 21 November 1965; interview with Gotthard Jedlicka in *Neue Zürcher Zeltung* (Zurich), 16 January 1966; interview with Raoul-Jean Moulin in *Les Lettres Francais* (Paris), January 1966; "Notes sur les Copies" and "Tout cela n'est pas grand-chose" in *L'Ephemere* (Paris), no. 1, 1967; interview with Jean Clay in *Realités* (Paris), October 1969.

On GIACOMETTI: books—*L'Atelier d'Alberto Giacometti* by Jean Genet 1958; *Alberto Giacometti* by Isaku Yanaibara, Tokyo 1958; *Alberto Giacometti,* exhibition catalogue, Berne 1959; *Alberto Giacometti* by Jacques Dupin, Paris 1962; *Giacometti* by Palma Bucarelli, Rome 1962; *Alberto Giacometti,* exhibition catalogue, Basle 1963; *Alberto Giacometti,* exhibition catalogue, by Peter Selz, New York 1965; *Alberto Giacometti,* exhibition catalogue, by David Sylvester, London 1965; *Il mio Giacometti* by Giorgio Soavi, Milan 1966; *Alberto Giacometti* by David Sylvester, London 1967; *Alberto Giacometti* by Douglas Hall, London 1967; *Alberto Giacometti: Dessins 1914–1965* by André du Bouchet, Paris 1969; *Giacometti: The Complete Graphics* by Herbert C. Lust, New York 1970; *Alberto Giacometti* by Willy Rotzler and Marianne Adelman, Berne 1970; *Alberto Giacometti: Drawings* by James Lord, Greenwich, Connecticut 1971; *Al-*

berto Giacometti: Sculpture, Painting, Drawing by Reinhold Hohl, Stuttgart 1971, London 1972; Disegni di Giacometti by Giorgio Soavi, Milan and Rome 1973; Giacometti: Katalog des Graphischen Werkes 1888–1963 by Norb R. du Carrois, Zurich 1977; Alberto Giacometti's Woman with Her Throat Cut, 1932 by Douglas Hall, Edinburgh 1980; Alberto Giacometti: Zeichnungen und Druckgraphik by Reinhold Hohl and Donald Koepplin, Stuttgart 1981; Alberto Giacometti, exhibition catalogue with text by Jean-Paul Sartre, Norwich 1984; Alberto Giacometti: Retour a la Figuration 1933–1947, exhibition catalogue, Paris 1986.

Alberto Giacometti is the most significant of all the artists from the Swiss mountain canton of Graubünden. Indeed the genius loci is itself embodied in his work: individual, obstinate, sensitive and reserved, meditative and tenacious, arrogant and profound, introverted, both dark and bright eyed, violent, destructive and constructive. All the years in the metropolis of Paris, the decades of international celebrity, did not erase or even in essentials retouch Giacometti's mountain origins. He always remained the mountain man from the southern valley of Graubünden, a valley surrounded by lofty peaks where one speaks Italian and thinks and feels puritanically, where, on high—even in high summer—the bare rock shimmers among ice and snow and lower down at the exit from the valley the sweet chestnut ripens in vast forests.

His surrealist works of the 1920's and 30's were accordingly only episodes: competent to be sure, rich in invention, as striking and impressive as from any of the great surrealists. But Giacometti was no surrealist; just as little or just as much as he was an expressionist, a realist or impressionist, he was Alberto Giacometti who had decided to get to the bottom of appearances whether of mountains, people or things. His work concept grew out of this: first construct and then demolish, and demolish further, until the essence emerges from the phenomena, the heart of the matter, the thing in itself, in people the inner "characteristic form which in living develops" (Goethe). Pursuing this principle, which includes a method of seeing and is at the same time a principle of aesthetic perception, he skeletonised phenomena: for where else other than within would he grasp that which they actually are, their soul, their character, their innermost being, their building law, their developing structural form and expression? That is the paradox of Giacometti's artistic activity: as an artist he had to strive for intuition, be concerned about perception and representation in space, but in fact he was looking for that which is not visible: laws, principles of form, the operative force behind appearances, the mystery behind the veils of this life—the power of the eye, not its beauty, the attractiveness of the view; he searched for that which philosophers search: ultimate perception, the final meaning.

Giacometti is an aesthetic reductionist; out of this contradiction grows the extraordinary sharpness, severity, formal consistency and at the same time almost incorporeal elegance which disconcerts the viewer of his works, particularly his plastic figures but also his drawings, graphics and paintings. Here is someone at work for whom work is indeed not a blessing but a curse: austere, vigorous, indefatigable and incessant, obsessed, possessed, not only in the sweat of his brow but also with bleeding hands, suicidal, purposeless, disappointed and dissatisfied towards a goal that does not exist—the plastic cladding of the character of being, the heart of perception, of the pulse beat of living time after the flight from appearances, the decay, the disintegration of things. Driven from paradise like every man, he strives through hard work to return to that revelation through which knowledge is gained, the true essence of things. So he has to go back along the path through the flesh which we have taken since the expulsion from the state of innocence. In the disturbing logic of his formulations is betrayed the conflict between material nature and spirit, substance and idea, the Christian-Platonic ideal and the pleasures of the world, the pleasure that our senses find in it.

This attitude of mind has been called existential. There is no doubt that one may use that term. But it does not explain much; different interpretations are always possible, always admissible and artistically acceptable, in so far as it is diversity through which artistic creation proves its existence. In order to describe and understand the style and effect of Giacometti's work, it seems to me to be more productive to consider the genetic perspective which puts origin, development, creation of structures in several concentric circles, in rings which are not to be forced open but are to be extended and by reciprocal interlacing are to be drawn apart: the valley, the rocks towering above, the distant view, the landscape a vast, thin scaffolding; the mother, love, Eros divided; the wife, the mistress, the eternal feminine that one deforms and destroys; things, fruit, still life: nature morte—in itself the signs of death. Precisely that: death is the master in the scene; he is the immortal around whom appearance, form, substance creep and constantly decay. He is the heart of the matter. There is something of the passionate fanatical mystic in Giacometti as he meditates on such problems, as he tries to find the trail of such mysteries and sets up memorials to them: tall, slender, on high socles; and something of the myth of Sisyphus, modified in the scenery of the Bregaglia valley: the mountain peasant, haggard, longboned, stubborn, who shifts a gigantic load of hay, certainly not down towards the valley but constantly upwards towards the peaks, the inaccessible peaks . . . .

—Gerolf Fritsch

GIJZEN, Wim.

Dutch. Born Willem Fredrik Gijzen in Rotterdam, 9 October 1941. Studied painting and graphic arts at the Vrije Academie, The Hague, 1962–63. Married Jeanette C. van Os in 1966; sons: Marc and Casper. Independent artist, Rotterdam, since 1964. Artist-Instructor, Academie van Beeldende Kunsten, Rotterdam, since 1980. Recipient: Dutch Ministry of Culture Grant, 1971, 1972. Agent: Galerie Helen van der Meij, Prinzengracht 116, 1015 EA Amsterdam. Address: Gravendijkwal 163B, 3021 EM Rotterdam, Netherlands.

Wim Gijzen: *Untitled,* 1981

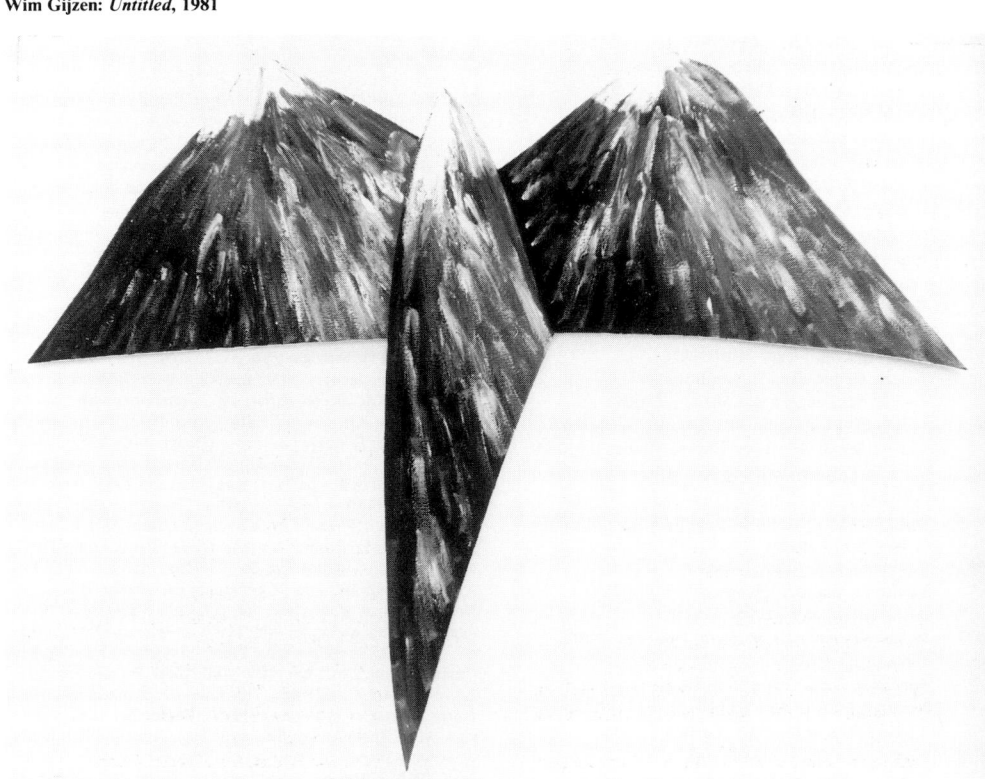

Individual Exhibitions:

1966   Galerie Delta, Rotterdam
1967   Galerie Margaretha de Boeve, Assenede, Belgium
1968   Galerie Mickery, Loenersloot, Netherlands
1969   Galerie Mickery, Loenersloot, Netherlands
1970   De Doelen, Rotterdam
1971   Galerie Design, Rotterdam
1973   A Visit to All 864 Municipalities of the Netherlands, Museum Boymans-van Beuningen, Rotterdam
        Lijnbaancentrum, Rotterdam
1974   Projects, Gemeentemuseum, The Hague
1975   Galerie Yaki Kornblitt, Amsterdam
1976   De Doelen, Rotterdam
        Hal Bromm Gallery, New York
1978   Galerie Helen van der Meij, Amsterdam
1979   Galerie Helen van der Meij, Amsterdam
1982   Galerie Helen van der Meij, Amsterdam

Selected Group Exhibitions:

1968   3 Blind Mice, Van Abbemuseum, Eindhoven, Netherlands (travelled to St. Pieters Abdij, Ghent)
1969   Nederlandse Beeldhouwkunst 1964–69, Centraal Museum, Utrecht
1970   Pop Art/Nouveau Realisme, Casino, Knokke-le-Zoute, Belgium
1971   Biennale of Middelheim, Antwerp
1973   Nyatt fra Nederland, Henie-Onstad Kunstsenter, Oslo
        Mail Art, Kunsthistorisch Instituut, Amsterdam
1974   11 Dutch Artists, Fruit Market Gallery, Edinburgh (travelled to the Art Gallery and Museum, Aberdeen)
1975   Biennale de Paris, Musée d'Art Moderne de la Ville, Paris
1978   Fotografie in Nederland 1940–75, Stedelijk Museum, Amsterdam

Collections:

Stedelijk Museum, Schiedam, Netherlands; Museum Boymans-van Beuningen, Rotterdam; Gemeentemuseum, The Hague.

Publications:

By GIJZEN: books—*Streets: Rotterdam/Amsterdam*, map, Rotterdam 1971.

On GIJZEN: books—*A Visit to All 864 Municipalities of the Netherlands*, exhibition catalogue, Rotterdam 1973; *Wim Gijzen: Projects*, exhibition catalogue, with introduction by Kees Broos, The Hague 1974; *Fotografie in Nederland 1940–1975*, exhibition catalogue, edited by Els Barents, Amsterdam 1978; articles—"Wim Gijzen" in *Rotterdam Art News*, no. 1, 1972; "The Constant in the Work" by Jan Donia in *Museumjournaal* (Amsterdam), February 1973.

The artist Wim Gijzen, who lives and works in Rotterdam, attracted a good deal of attention with his 1973 project "A Visit to the Netherlands." This project, sponsored by the Netherlands Art Foundation, stipulated—among other things—that Gijzen visit all of the Dutch municipalities, have himself photographed next to a sign indicating the name of the place, and then send out picture-postcards for which he provided the postmark. The whole undertaking is reminiscent of On Kawara's "I Got Up," although Gijzen's work is much more anecdotal than Kawara's. The scope of Gijzen's undertaking was limited, of course, by the number of municipalities to be visited: thus the project is constructed of 864 independent frames, but carried out on an epic scale with many colorful, interconnecting details.

Gijzen's compulsion to inventory the peculiarities of what he has seen is clearly visible in "Projection No. 2" from 1972. Here he has assembled photographs of 293 street-names from Amsterdam and Rotterdam and contrasted them within one framework. In this same period Gijzen also put his signature on the contours of the countries of Europe. Thanks to his imagination, his rendering of their outlines takes on independent life in our own imaginations. Gijzen's work during these years is attractive and spirited.

—A. F. Wagemans

GILBERT and GEORGE.

British. Gilbert: born in the Dolomites, Italy, in 1943; studied at the Wolkenstein School of Art, and Hallein School of Art, Austria, and the Akademie der Kunst, Munich. George: born in Totnes, Devon, England, in 1942; studied at the Dartington Adult Education Centre, Devon; Dartington Hall College of Art; and Oxford School of Art. Met while they were students at the St. Martin's School of Art, London, and have lived and worked together in London since 1968. Recipients: Turner Prize, Tate Gallery, London, 1986. Agents: Anthony d'Offay, London; Sonnabend Gallery, New York; Art and Project, Amsterdam; and Konrad Fischer Galerie, Dusseldorf. Address: Art for All, 12 Fournier Street, London E1, England.

Individual Exhibitions:

1968 Frank's Sandwich Bar, London
St. Martin's School of Art, London
Allied Services Bacon Factory, London
Robert Fraser Gallery, London
1969 Frank's Sandwich Bar, London
Geffrye Museum, London
Royal College of Art, London
Camberwell School of Art, London
Slade School of Fine Art, London
Royal College of Art, London (with Bruce McLean)
St. Martin's School of Art, London (with Bruce McLean)
Hannover Grand Preview Theatre, London (with Bruce McLean)

Ripley, Bromley, Kent (with David Hockney)
Studio International Office, London
Marquee Club, London
The Lyceum, London
National Jazz and Blues Festival, Plumpton, Sussex
Institute of Contemporary Arts, London
Cable Street, London
Stedelijk Museum, Amsterdam
Robert Fraser Gallery, London
St. Martin's School of Art, London
1970 Fournier Street, London
Art and Project, Amsterdam
Konrad Fischer Galerie, Dusseldorf
Francoise Lambert Galleria, Milan
Folker Skulima Galerie, Berlin
Heiner Friedrich Galerie, Cologne
Nigel Greenwood Gallery, London
BBC Studios, Bristol
Museum of Modern Art, Oxford
Leeds Polytechnic
Kunsthalle, Dusseldorf
Kunstverein, Hannover
Block Gallery Forum Theatre, Berlin
Art and Project, Amsterdam
Konrad Fischer Galerie, Dusseldorf
Kunstverein, Recklinghausen, West Germany
Heiner Friedrich Galerie, Munich
Württembergischer Kunstverein, Stuttgart
Museo d'Arte Moderna, Turin
Sonja Henie/Niels Onstad Foundation, Oslo
Stadsbiblioteket Lyngby, Copenhagen
Folker Skulima Galerie, Berlin
Gegenverkehr, Aachen, West Germany
Heiner Friedrich Galerie, Cologne
Kunstverein, Krefeld, West Germany
Nigel Greewood Gallery, London
1971 Galleria Sperone, Turin
Sonnabend Gallery, New York
Nigel Greenwood Gallery, London
Art and Project, Amsterdam
Louise Department Store, Brussels
Whitechapel Art Gallery, London
Stedelijk Museum, Amsterdam
Kunstverein, Dusseldorf
1972 Museum voor Schone Kunsten, Antwerp
Oh the Grand Old Duke of York, Kunstmuseum, Lucerne
Galleria L'Attico, Rome
Konrad Fischer Galerie, Dusseldorf
Gerry Schum Video Galerie, Dusseldorf
Anthony d'Offay Gallery, London
Nigel Greenwood Gallery, London
Situation Gallery, London
Galleria Sperone, Rome
1973 Sonnabend Galerie, Paris
Galleria Sperone, Turin
Nigel Greenwood Gallery, London
Sonnabend Gallery, New York
National Gallery of New South Wales, Sydney (travelled to the National Gallery of Victoria, Melbourne)
1974 Konrad Fischer Galerie, Dusseldorf
Art and Project/MTL Galerie, Antwerp
Nigel Greenwood Gallery, London
Galleria Sperone, Rome
1975 Sonnabend Galerie, Paris
Sonnabend Galerie, Geneva
Lucio Amelio Galleria, Naples
Collegiate Theatre, London
Sperone Westwater, New York
Art Agency, Tokyo
1976 Sonnabend Gallery, New York
Albright Knox Art Gallery, Buffalo, New York
Konrad Fischer Galerie, Dusseldorf
Lucio Amelio Galleria, Naples
Robert Self Gallery, London
Robert Self Gallery, Newcastle upon Tyne
1977 Art and Project, Amsterdam
Konrad Fischer Galerie, Dusseldorf
Galleria Sperone, Rome
Art Fair, Sperone/Fischer, Basle
MTL Galerie, Brussels
Museum van Hedendaagse Kunst, Ghent
Stedelijk Museum, Amsterdam

1978 Dartington Hall Gallery, Devon
Sonnabend Gallery, New York
Art Agency, Tokyo
1980 Art and Project, Amsterdam
Konrad Fischer Galerie, Dusseldorf
Karen and Jean Bernier Gallery, Athens
Sonnabend Gallery, New York
Anthony d'Offay Gallery, London
Gilbert and George 1968–1980, Stedelijk van Abbemuseum, Eindhoven, Netherlands (travelled to the Kunsthalle, Dusseldorf; Kunsthalle, Berne; Centre Georges Pompidou, Paris; and the Whitechapel Gallery, London, 1980–81)
1981 Galerie Chantal Crousel, Paris
1982 Anthony D'Offay Gallery, London
Galerie Gewad, Ghent, Belgium
1983 Sonnabend Gallery, New York
David Bellman Gallery, Toronto
Crousel-Hussenot Galerie, Paris
1984 Baltimore Museum of Art, Maryland
Contemporary Arts Museum, Houston
Norton Gallery of Art, West Palm Beach, Florida
Anthony D'Offay Gallery, London
Galerie Schellmann und Kluser, Munich
Galleria Pieroni, Rome
1985 Milwaukee Art Museum, Wisconsin
Guggenheim Museum, New York
Sonnabend Gallery, New York
1986 CAPC Musee d'Art Contemporain, Bordeaux, France
Fruit Market Gallery, Edinburgh
Kunsthalle, Basle
1987 Palais des Beaux-Arts, Brussels
Palacio Velazquez, Madrid
Stadtisches Museum im Lenbachhaus, Munich
Hayward Gallery, London
Anthony D'Offay Gallery, London
Sonnabend Gallery, New York

Selected Group Exhibitions:

1969 *Conception*, Stadtisches Museum, Leverkusen, West Germany
1970 *Information*, Museum of Modern Art, New York
1972 *The New Art*, Hayward Gallery, London
1973 *From Henry Moore to Gilbert and George*, Palais des Beaux-Arts, Brussels
1976 *Arte Inglese Oggi*, Palazzo Reale, Milan
1979 *Un Certain Art Anglais*, Musée d'Art Moderne de la Ville, Paris
1981 *British Sculpture in the Twentieth Century*, Whitechapel Art Gallery, London
1983 *Photography in Contemporary Art*, National Museum of Modern Art, Tokyo
1985 *Biennale de Paris*, Grande Halle de La Villette, Paris
1987 *British Art in the Twentieth Century*, Royal Academy of Art, London

Collections:

Stedelijk Museum, Amsterdam; Arts Council of Great Britain, London; Kunstmuseum, Lucerne; Guggenheim Museum, New York.

Publications:

By GILBERT and GEORGE: books—*Side by Side*, London 1971; *The Paintings (with Us in Nature) of Gilbert and George: The Human Sculptors*, Amsterdam 1971; *Dark Shadow*, London 1974; articles—"A Magazine Sculpture" in *Studio International* (London), May 1970; "Underneath the Arches" in *Interfunktionen* (Cologne), no. 4, 1970; "A Day in the Life of Gilbert and George" in *Flash Art* (Milan), May 1972; "Gilbert and George," interview, with Anne Seymour, in *The New Art*, exhibition catalogue, London 1972.

On GILBERT and GEORGE: books—*Oh the Grand Old Duke of York*, exhibition catalogue, by Jean-Christophe Ammann, Lucerne 1972; *Gilbert and George 1968–1980*, exhibition catalogue, by Carter Ratcliff, Eindhoven, Netherlands 1980; *Gilbert and George*, exhibition catalogue with essay by Brenda Richardson, Baltimore 1984; *Gilbert and George:*

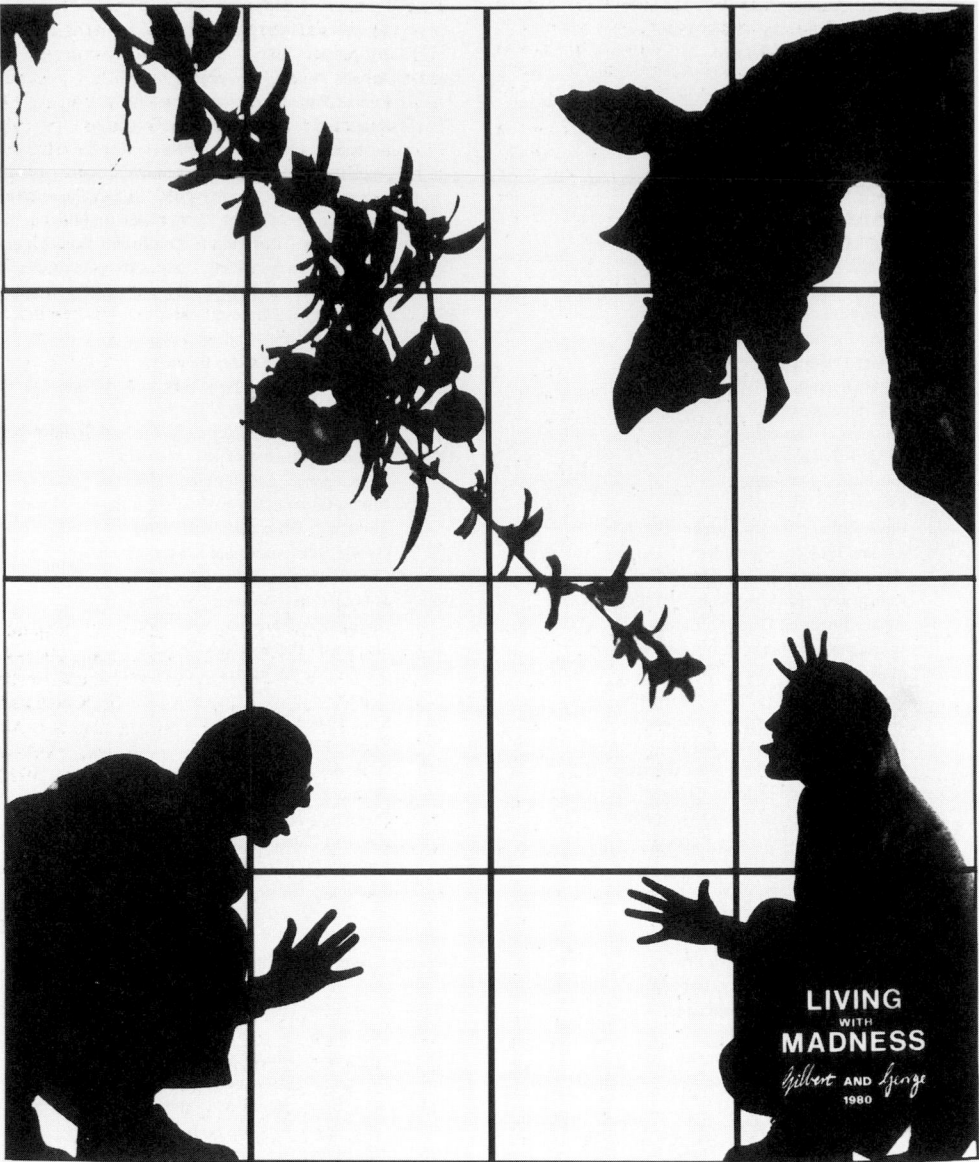

Gilbert and George: *Living with Madness*, 1980

The Charcoal on Paper Sculptures, exhibition catalogue with introduction by Demosthenes Davvetas, Bordeaux 1986; *Gilbert and George: The Paintings 1971*, with text by Wolf Jahn, Edinburgh 1986; *Gilbert and George: The Complete Pictures 1971–85*, with text by Carter Ratcliff, London 1986.

We are:
   Unhealthy, middle-aged, dirty-minded, depressed, cynical, empty, tired-brained, seedy, rotten, dreaming, badly behaved, ill-mannered, arrogant, intellectual, self-pitying, honest, successful, hard-working, thoughtful, artistic, religious, fascistic, blood-thirsty, teasing, destructive, ambitious, colourful, damned, stubborn, perverted and good. We are artists.
                    —Gilbert and George

The wholly original artform of which Gilbert and George themselves form a vital part is unique. As they push their art to borderlines of bad taste and pornography, however, these artists have increasingly attracted controversy and censure.

   Meeting as sculpture students at London's Saint Martins School of Art in 1967, alongside contemporaries Bruce McLean, Richard Long and Victor Burgin, their collaboration began in an era when Conceptual Art was the dominant vogue. The rejection of the art-for-art's sake aesthetic that gained currency in the late 1960s took the form of a rigorous investigation into the nature of the art-object itself, and a movement in favour of content and figuration rooted in social reality: a revolt against elitism.

Gilbert and George amalgamated both forms. Taking the conceptualist argument to its logical conclusion, they designated themselves 'living sculptures', utilizing both their public and private lives as part of their work.

   "To be with art is all we ask", they declared. The aim was to become artists of their era: "We are modern times artists. We have to devise a vocàbulary which reflects this age. We don't want to hide our weaknesses, our sexual behaviour, our thinking, our suffering, and all that belongs to mankind." They moved into the working class neighborhood of Spitalfields, from where they took much of their art's material, labelled their Fournier Street home "Art for All", and daily wore identical bland, grey suits, "the responsibility suits of our art." Early works included the 'Singing Sculpture' *Underneath the Arches*, a non-music hall version of the Flanagan and Allen number performed for several hours until the song itself was rendered numbingly meaningless and the viewer became strongly aware of the 'sculpture' (Gilbert and George, in their grey suits, with hands and faces painted silver) alone.

   Such 'performance' pieces were drastically reduced over subsequent years, and by 1977 their prolific output encompassed a wide range of media: books, videotapes, photographs, drawings, as well as just *being* sculptural objects. The first black and white photo pieces appeared in 1971, beginning as individual photographs placed together on the wall to form loose assemblages. In 1974, red colouring was introduced to heighten the expressive quality of work,

and later photo pieces became combinations that formed a grid-like autonomous whole. The series of 1976 and 1977, *Mental, Dirty Words* and *Red Morning*, were the most overtly political and included some of Gilbert and George's best work to date, operating both as moral comment and as neutral reportage. The images dealt with physical dereliction, power and oppression, religion, graffiti, and other manifestations of the culture of urban decay.

   By 1981–82, vivid hues were being employed in the photo works in the service of a cartoon-style narrative along explicitly sexual themes. Personal fears and concerns appeared to be replacing any broader social issues. Forms of human excretion were relentlessly examined under such titles as *Sperm Eaters* and *Hard Cocks*, until such titles held more force than the images they related to. These works developed into long friezes featuring somewhat overworked images of the artists alongside young men, the familiar icons now bearing cliche-titles like *Life Without End.*

   The award of the 1986 Turner Prize was followed by a major exhibition of Gilbert and George's work at the Hayward Gallery. Critical opinion reacted with doubts about the award and a certain jaded quality permeating much of the exhibition. The use of glamourized violence from slick porno movies for an immediate, and ultimately personal, sensation made the work seem too superficial—but the most controversial aspect of Gilbert and George's imagery had always been the naked young males. Vulnerable or menacing, the youths were finally as vacuous as the traditional female pin-up they here supplanted. Gilbert and George's lavatorial and homosexual iconography had left critics floundering on the hurdle moral concern. Cheap personal thrills or works of great aesthetic and ideological power?

                    —Sharon Lancer

GILLIAM, Sam.

American. Born in Tupelo, Mississippi, in 1933. Educated at Madison Junior High School, Louisville, Kentucky; studied at the University of Louisville, 1952–56, 1958–61, B.A. 1955, M.A. 1961. Served in the United States Army, 1956–58. Married Dorothy Buller in 1962; has 3 daughters. Painter: lives and works in Washington, D.C. Recipient: National Endowment for the Arts Individual Artist Grant, 1967, 1973, 1974; Artist's Fellowship, Washington Gallery of Modern Art, 1968; Norman B. Harris Prize, Art Institute of Chicago, 1969; Longview Foundation Award, 1970; Guggenheim Fellowship, 1971; Activities Grant, National Endowment for the Arts, 1973–75. Agent: Middendorf/Lane Gallery, Washington, D.C. Address: c/o Middendorf/Lane Gallery, 2009 Columbia Road N.W., Washington, D.C. 20010, U.S.A.

Individual Exhibitions:

1956	Univsersity of Louisville, Kentucky
1963	Frame House Gallery, Louisville, Kentucky
	Adam Morgan Gallery, Washington, D.C.
1964	Adam Morgan Gallery, Washington, D.C.
1965	Jefferson Place Gallery, Washington, D.C.
1966	Jefferson Place Gallery, Washington, D.C.
1967	Jefferson Place Gallery, Washington, D.C.
	Phillips Gallery, Washington, D.C.
1968	Jefferson Place Gallery, Washington, D.C.
	Byron Gallery, New York
1969	*Gilliam/Krebs/McGowin*, Gorcoran Gallery, Washington, D.C.
1970	Jefferson Place Gallery, Washington, D.C.
	Galerie Darthea Speyer, Paris
1971	Museum of Modern Art, New York
1972	Jefferson Place Gallery, Washington, D.C.

Selected Group Exhibitions:

Collections:

Museum of Modern Art, New York; Baltimore Museum of Art; Corcoran Gallery, Washington, D.C.; Phillips Gallery, Washington, D.C.; Smithsonian Institution, Washington, D.C.; Art Istitute of Chicago; Walker Art Center, Minneapolis; Boymans van Beuningen Museum, Rotterdam; Tate Gallery, London; Centre Georges Pompidou, Paris.

Publications:

By GILLIAM: article—statement in *Gilliam/Edwards/ Williams: Extensions,* exhibition catalogue, Hartford, Connecticut 1974.

On GILLIAM: books—*Art in Washington* by Leslie Judd Ahlander, Washington, D.C. 1968; *Art and Ideas* by William Fleming, New York 1973; *The Great American Salt Works* by Jack Burnham, New York 1974; *Sam Gilliam,* exhibition cat-

alogue, Louisville, Kentucky 1976; *Modern Painters at the Corcoran: Sam Gilliam* by John Beardsley, Washington, D.C. 1983; articles—"Meet the Artist: Sam Gilliam: by Cornelia Noland in *The Washingtonian,* October 1965; "A Gallery Without Walls" by Barbara Rose in *Art in America* (New York), March/April 1968; "Painting Is Alive and Well: by Barbara Rose in *Vogue* (New York), November 1969; "3 Washington Artists" by Walter Hopps and Nina Felshin Osnos in *Art International* (Lugano, Switzerland), May 1970; "Energy Is the Catalyst in Sam Gilliam's Formula" in the *Washington Star,* 19 October 1975; "Sam Gilliam: Recent Black Paintings" by Jay Kloner in *Arts Magazine* (New York), February 1978; "Skin Deep" by Kay Larson in *New York Magazine,* 23 March 1981; "Amplifications" by Marjorie Welish in *Art in America* (New York), November 1981.

Gilliam is best known for—if not indeed forever to be identified with his variant of color field paints; loosely spattered, almost automatist stained canvas, unstretched, and then freely manipulated through folding, draping, or hanging. As if in reaction to the limitation of post-painterly abstraction, he began to work with these arranged displays in the late 1960s, and worked so exclusively for about a decade, with the technique then remaining occasionally active in his repertoire. Gilliam, who came to Washington, D.C. in 1962, had been influenced by and himself became representative of the lyrical abstract art fostered by the stain painting of Louis, Noland, and Downing. And so the typical look of his first mature style was a canvas stained by soaking, spattering, and folding to achieve a depth of translucent hues. Such surfaces then became but a background for his presentation, since Gilliam would then take the canvas and manipulate it to produce sculptural effects as the material fell from vertical, overhead, and floor-based supports. It is felt that Gilliam thinks in terms of landscape imagery, and so his work has been likened to the heroic American landscape tradition. His sense of the impermanent positioning of the canvas may have been inspired by the process and anti-form attitudes of that time; in fact, his works have been labelled "a painterly form of process art." His critics have faulted him for a too-great dependence upon these three-dimensional effects, and have remarked on the lack of invention in the paint markings themselves. The style reached its apex quickly so that *Autumn Surf* (1974) was not at all unusual in its 75 feel length. It appears that the poly-phony of such work in the interplay of structure and improvisation was to be a matured creative motif felt throughout his career.

In 1977, he gave up his long usage of stain technique, and unstretched works, to work with a thick acrylic surface with various painterly approaches, in-

cluding graining. He also began to produce, as in a series of circular paintings in 1976, images collaged with wedges cut from others of his pictures. Such juxtaposition of clearly-edged and differing surface treatments, in fairly rapid sequence, remains a Gilliam signature to the present. Like his use, in 1980, of irregular rectangular formats on rigid beveled supports, Gilliam seems to wish—as in his draped works—to break up the planarity and evoke a three-dimensional variety and movement. During the present decade, Gilliam has produced several very large public works in major American cities. The style of these planar painted constructions, in traditional stabilizing compositional modes is reminscent of Frank Stella's 70s works; and yet, despite Gilliam's constant search for means to energize his essentially quietist vision, his imagery remains elegantly modernist.

—Joshua Kind

GIRONCOLI, Bruno.

Austrian. Born in Villach, Carinthia, 27 September 1936. Educated at Villach primary school, 1942–46, and high school, 1946–51; apprentice metal-worker, Innsbruck, 1953–58; studied art at the Kunstakademie, Vienna, 1958; painting, under E. Baumer, Akademie dür Angewandte Kunst, Vienna, 1960–62. Married Christl Melichar in 1961 (divorced, 1970); Edith Matuskovics in 1970 (divorced, 1974); Indrig Kedren in 1974 (divorced, 1975); daughter: Ina. Independent artist, Vienna, since 1962. Agent: Kurt Kalb, Vienna. Address: c/o Kurt Kalb, Grunangergasse 12, 1010 Vienna, Austria.

Individual Exhibitions:

Bruno Gironcoli: Untitled Object, 1980

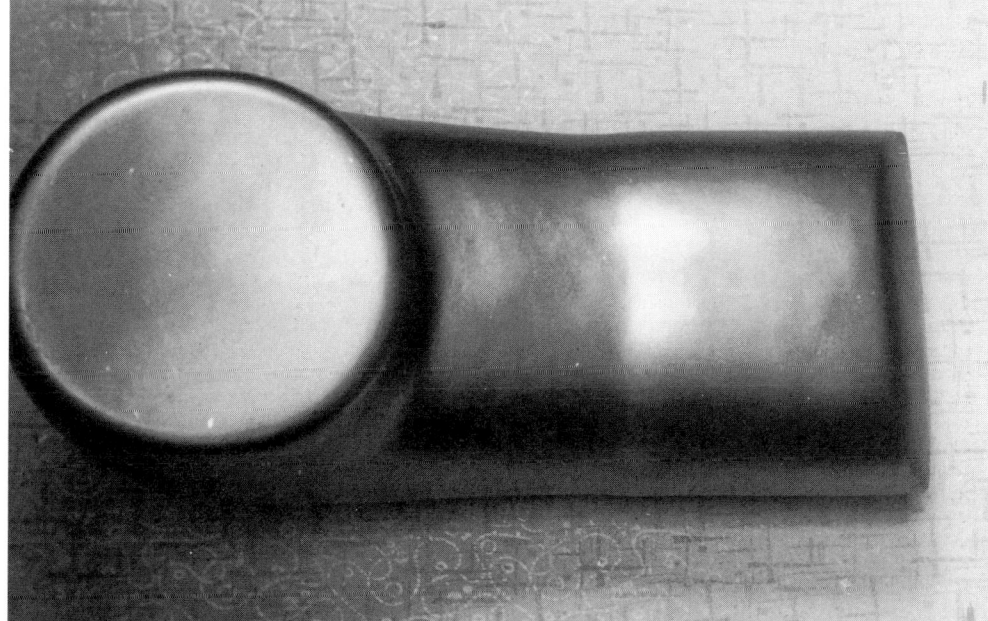

1972 Galerie Krinzinger, Bergenz, Austria
Galerie Krinzinger, Innsbruck
1973 Galerie Franzius, Munich
1974 Galerie Dorothea Leonhardt, Munich
Galerie Kalb, Vienna
Karntzer Landesgalerie, Klagenfurt, Autria (with F. X. Olzant)
Kulturhaus, Graz, Autria (with F. X. Olzant)
1975 Scholoss Porcia, Spittal/Drau, Austria
Galerie Grunangergasse, Vienna
1976 Galerie Schapira und Beck, Vienna
1977 Museum des 20. Jahrhunderts, Vienna (travelled to Städtische Galerie im Lenbachhaus, Munich; Galerie im Taxispalais, Innsbruck; Kunstverein, Salzburg; and Kulturhaus, Graz)
Galerie Schapira und Beck, Vienna
1978 Galerie Krinzinger, Innsbruck

Selected Group Exhibitions:

1966 *Konfrontation 66*, Galerie Heide Hildebrand, Klagenfurt, Austria
1968 *Profile 8: Osterreichische Kunst heute*, Städtisches Museum, Bochum, West Germany
1970 *14 x 14*, Kunstverein, Baden-Baden, West Germany
1973 *The Austrian Exhibition*, Richard Demarco Gallery, Edinburgh (travelled to the Institute of Contemporary Arts, London)
1974 *Zeichnungen der Osterreichischen Avantgarde*, Innsbruck (travelled to Leverkusen, Basle and Geneva)
1975 *Plastik in Schloss Eggenburg*, Graz, Austria
1976 *Attersee/Gironcoli/Pichler/Rainer/Steiger*, Galerie Schapira und Beck, Vienna
Parallelaktion: neue kunst aus Osterreich, Von-der-Heydt Museum, Wuppertal, West Germany
1984 *Arte Austriacca 1960–84*, Galleria d'Arte Moderna, Bologna, Italy

Collections:

Museum des 20. Jahrhunderts, Vienna

Publications:

On GIRONCOLI: books—*Gironcoli*, exhibition catalogue, with text by Alfred Schmeller, Vienna 1970; *Austria: Bruno Gironcoli-II Bienal de Sao Paulo*, exhibition catalogue, with text by Hermann Schurrer, Vienna 1971; *Osterreichische Kunst von heute*, edited by Oswad Oberhuber and Kurt Sotriffer, Vienna and Munich 1971; *Bruno Gironcoli*, exhibition catalogue, with text by Peter Weiermair and Armin Zweite, Vienna 1977; articles—"Bruno Gironcoli" by Otto Mauer in *Alte und Moderner Kunst* (Vienna), May-June 1969; "New Tendencies in Austrian Art" by Peter Weiermair in *Studio International* (London) May 1972; "Uber Bruno Gironcoli" by Jürgen Morschel in *Das Kunstwerk* (Baden-Baden, West Germany), May 1974.

GLARNER, Fritz.

Swiss. Born in Zurich. 20 July 1899. Educated in primary schools in Italy and France; studied painting in Milan and Rome, and at the Istituto di Belle Arte, Naples, 1913–23. Married Louise Powell in 1928. Painter: lived in Paris, 1923–35; spent time in United States, 1930–31, in Switzerland, 1935; settled in New York, 1936; Member, Abstraction-Creation, New York, 1931–36; Founder-Member, Allianz group, Zurich, 1935; Member, American Abstract Artists, New York, 1938–44; moved to Huntington, Long Island, 1957; decorated Nelson Rockefeller apartment, New York, 1963–64; worked in the studio of the sculptor Remo Rossi, Locarno, Switzerland, Winter 1965–66; settled in Locarno, 1971. Recipient: Prize, Corcoran Gallery, Washington, D.C., 1957. *Died (in Locarno) 18 September 1972.*

Individual Exhibitions:

1926 Galerie D'Art Contemporain, Paris
1928 Galerie Povlosky, Paris
1930 Galerie Povlosky, Paris
1931 Civic Club, New York
1945 Kootz Gallery, New York
1949 Rose Fried Gallery, New York
1951 Rose Fried Gallery, New York
1952 Galerie Louis Carre, Paris
1954 Rose Fried Gallery, New York (with Georges Vantongerloo)
1955 Galerie Louis Carre, Paris
1956 Kunsthaus, Zurich (with Josef Albers and Friedrich Vordemberge-Gildewart)
1966 Galerie Louis Carre, Paris
1968 *Biennale*, Venice (with Hans Aesbacher)
1970 *Fritz Glarner's Geometry: A Personal Language*, Museum of Art, San Francisco (travelled to Institute of Contemporary Art, University of Pennsylvania, Philadelphia, and the University of Iowa, Iowa City)
1972 Kunsthalle, Berne
Gimpel Fils, London (travelled to Gimpel und Hanover Galerie, Zurich)
1976 Gimpel und Hanover Galerie, Zurich
1978 Modern Galerie, Quadrat Bottrop, West Germany
1979 *Dressins, Peintures*, Musée d'Art et d'Histoire, Geneva
Musée de l'Abbaye Sante-Croix, Les Sables d'Olonne, France

Selected Group Exhibitions:

1938 *American Abstract Artists*, Whitney Museum, New York
1947 *American Abstract and Surrealist Art*, Art Institute of Chicago
1949 *Contemporary Painting*, Art Gallery of Ontario, Toronto
1951 *Abstract Painting and Sculpture in America*, Museum of Modern Art, New York
1954 *Younger American Painters*, Guggenheim Museum, New York
1957 *25th Biennial Exhibition*, Corcoran Gallery, Washington, D.C.
1962 *A Survey of Geometric Abstraction in America*, Whitney Museum, New York
1963 *The Formalists*, Gallery of Modern Art, Washington, D.C.
1966 *Schweizer Malerei 1945–65*, Pforzheim, West Germany (toured West Germany)
1971 *The Swiss Avant Garde*, Cultural Center, New York

Collections:

Kunstmuseum, Basle; Kunstmuseum, Berne; Kunstmuseum, Winterthur, Switzerland; Kunsthaus, Zurich; Museum of Modern Art, New York; Whitney Museum, New York; Albright-Knox Art Gallery, Buffalo, New York; Baltimore Museum of Art; National Gallery, Washington, D.C.; Philadelphia Museum of Art.

Publications:

By GLARNER: article—"What Abstract Art Means to Me" in *Museum of Modern Art Bulletin* (New York), vol. 13, No. 3, 1951.

On GLARNER: books—*Abstract Painting and Sculpture in America*, exhibition catalogue, New York 1951; *Revolution and Tradition in American Art* by John I. H. Baur, Cambridge, Massachussetts 1951; *American Art of Our Century* by Lloyd Goodrich and John I. H. Baur, New York 1961; *New Art in America* by Dorothy Miller, New York 1967; *Fritz Glarner's Geometry: A Personal Language*, exhibition catalogue, by Natalie Edgar, San Francisco 1970; *Fritz Glarner*, exhibition catalogue, by Margit Staber London 1972; *Fritz Glarner: Dessins, Peintures*, exhibition catalogue, by Daniel Abadie, Geneva 1979.

In 1938, a few years after he had emigrated to Amer-

ica, Fritz Glarner joined the American Abstract Artists. He had begun developing his version of geometric abstract painting during the mid-1920's, when he encountered European practitioners such as Van Doesburg and Mondrian in Paris. Like other painters from this rather heterogeneous group, such as Burgoyne Diller, Harry Holtzman, Ilya Bolotowsky and Charmion von Wiegand, Glarner remained in a geometrically abstract vein developed out of Constructivism, de Stijl and especially Mondrian during the decades following the 1930's. Also like these other artists, Glarner was a great admirer of Mondrian, and he spent many hours discussing pictures with Mondrian during the early 1940's when Mondrian was living in New York and greatly supporting the American abstractionists.

It was out of Mondrian's paintings of 1942–44 such as "Broadway Boogie Woogie" that Glarner found the basics for his own future direction. Inspired by the flickering rhythms and energy of Mondrian's late overall patterns of rectangular reds, yellows and blues, Glarner began, in 1944, to create active surfaces filled with irregularly situated small rectangles. Within the context of those who sought a personal variant out of the route invented by Neo-Plasticism, Glarner was among the most successful in finding fertile territory for exploration.

Beginning in 1945 Glarner called his pictures "relational paintings," and he continually pursued variations relating rectangular and circular shapes with color in ways which make shape and ground alternate to produce what he called "pumping planes" of considerable energy and liminism. Glarner made use of tilting, warping planes which produce a disorientation in their sliding diagonal thrust that is very different from Mondrian's more stable balancing of pure horizontality and verticality. As Jack Burnham noted, it is almost like a deliberate dissolution of Neo-Plastic ideas. Glarner also gave the color gray an active quality of alternately shape/ground missing in earlier geometric abstraction. In place of the grid structure, Glarner developed a system of interlocking rectangles and wedges in a tight mosaic patterning which admitted off-angle motions and colors outside of the usual Neo-Plastic limitations. The wedges, both linear and planar, and the accompanying rectangles within the framing rectangle, agitate with a forward/backward and almost eccentrically warped rhythm, "pumping" in a forceful syncopation which suggests a tense state that is based more on subjective than on objective intentions. In his "Relational Paintings, Tondos," Glarner adds another non-Neo-Plastic dimension to his sets of interrelationships. In some of these circular compositions, linear wedges spin outward from the center, creating a centrifugal forcefulness which find vibrating balance in concert with the rectangular areas that share the space.

Glarner created several murals, including ones for the Time-Life Building in New York (1958–60) and for Dag Hammarskjold Library at the United Nations (1961), both of which show Glarner's ability to sustain a measure of monumentality within the framework of "Relational Painting" format. It is a concept of de Stijl that painting should strive to change architectural spaces and move closer to architectural ideas, and Glarner's murals certainly help illustrate this possibility.

Glarner developed his art in the long shadows cast by still-living inventors and masters of geometric abstraction. He was so deeply affected by their accomplishment that he willingly chose to work for a personalized statement out of their vocabulary. By continued dedication to this intention so difficult for an artist of his time and context, Glarner managed to locate some rather admirably inventive elements.

—Barbara Cavaliere

GNOLI, Domenico.

Italian. Born in Rome, 3 May 1933. Educated in Rome primary schools; privately at Carlo Alberto Retucci School, Rome, 1946–49. Full-time artist from 1950: visited London, 1953, and Paris, 1953–54, 1956 and 1958; spent several months in New York, 1955; worked on theatre designs for the *Summer Festival*, Zurich, from 1953, and the Old Vic Theatre, London, 1956; lived partly in Rome and Majorca, 1963–65; visited Seville, 1964; Warsaw and London, 1967; contributed illustrations to numerous periodicals including *Harper's Bazaar, Esquire, Time*, during 1960's. *Died* (of cancer, in New York) *17 April 1970*.

Individual Exhibitions:

1950	Galleria La Cassapanca, Rome
1954	Arthur Jeffress Gallery, London
1955	Sagittarius Gallery, New York
1957	Arthur Jeffress Gallery, London
1958	Bianchini Gallery, New York
1960	Arthur Jeffress Gallery, London
1961	Philadelphia Print Club
	Calhoun Gallery, Dallas
1962	Bianchini Gallery, New York
	Hazlitt Gallery, New York
1964	Galerie André Schoeller, Paris
1965	Kovler Gallery, Chicago
1966	Galleria La Galatea, Turin
1967	Galleria Il Centro, Naples
	Galleria de'Foscherari, Bologna
	Galeria Odyssia, Rome
1968	Palais des Beaux-Arts, Brussels
	Kestner-Gesellschaft, Hannover
1969	Sidney Janis Gallery, New York
	Janis und Schmela Galerie, Dusseldorf
1970	Galerie Schmela, Dusseldorf
	Galerie Krugier, Geneva
1973	Kunsthalle Darmstadt
	Museum Boymans-van-Beuningen, Rotterdam
	Centre National d'Art Contemporain, Paris
1974	Galeria Arts Contacts, Paris
	Galerie Isy Brachot, Brussels (with Paul Delvaux and James Ensor)
	Galerie Herbert Meyer-Erlinger, Frankfurt
1978	Galerie Isy Brachot, Paris
	Biennale, Venice
1981	Kunsthalle, Bremen, West Germany
1982	Galleria d'Arte Moderna, Verona, Italy
1983	Galerie Levy, Hamburg
	Musee Cantonal des Beaux-Arts, Lausanne
1985	Palazzo Racani-Arroni, Spoleto, Italy
	Padiglione d'Arte Contemporanea, Milan
1986	Galerie Isy Brachot, Paris
1987	Galleria Nazionale d'Arte Moderna, Rome
	Galerie Isy Brachot, Brussels
	Fondation Maeght, St. Paul de Vence, France

Selected Group Exhibitions:

1953	*Mostra Arte Figurative*, Spoleto
1956	*Italian Graphics*, San Francisco Museum of Art
1967	*Le Portrait*, Galerie Claude Bernard, Paris
1968	*Documenta 4*, Kassel, West Germany
1970	*Art 70*, Basle
1974	*Hyperrealisme*, Galerie Isy Brachot, Brussels
1976	*Aspekte zum Menschenbild*, Kunsthalle, Nuremberg, West Germany
1981	*Linee della Ricerca Artistica in Italia 1960–80*, Palazzo delle Esposizioni, Rome
1983	*Pop Art in Italia*, Castello Viscontio, Pavia, Italy
1985	*Dinge des Menschen*, Kunsthalle, Recklinghausen, West Germany

Collections:

Kaiser Wilhelm Museum, Krefeld, West Germany; Neue Galerie, Aachen, West Germany; Städtisches Suermondt Museum, Aachen, West Germany; Wallraf-Richartz Museum, Cologne; Stedelijk Museum, Amsterdam; Gemeente-museum, The Hague; Sonia Heni-Mils Onstad Foundation Oslo; Victoria and Albert Museum, London; Museum of Modern Art, New York; Baltimore Museum of Art.

Publications:

By GNOLI: book—*Orestes or the Art of Smiling*, New York 1962; illustrated books—*Alberic the Wise and Other Journeys* by Norton Juster, New York 1962; *A Journal of Plague Year* by Daniel Defoe, New York 1965.

On GNOLI: books—*Metaphysical Painting* by Werner Helwid, Frankfurt 1965; *Domenico Cnoli*, exhibition catalogue, Geneva 1970; *Domenico Gnoli*, exhibition catalogue, by Bernard Krimmel, Darmstadt 1973; *Domenico Gnoli*, exhibition catalogue, by Max Pohl Fouchet, Parit 1974; *Domenico Gnoli* by Luigi Carluccio, Woodstock, New York 1975; *L'Opera Grafica di Domenico Gnoli: catalogo ragionato*, edited by Annie de Garrou Gnoli and Vittorio Sgarbi, Milan 1986; *Domenico Gnoli*, exhibition catalogue with essay by Bruno Mantura, Rome 1987.

*

Domenico Gnoli has had the rather curious fate of being much better known abroad than in Italy, and that's a real irony when one considers that the spirit of his work is in fact much more local than international. Even though he was grouped among the Pop Artists and the New Realists, his vision of the ordinary had very little to do with the flash and speed of Marshall McLuhan's 1960ish vision of a neon global village, and his work makes absolutely perfect sense in an entirely Italian tradition that finds its best previous articulations in Campigli, Carrá, and Morandi.

Gnoli's fame is quite solidly based on his close-up vision of chair-backs, button holes, shoes and hair stylings—works that date from 1965 to the artist's death in 1970—but his scrutiny of the common-place was always a part of a search for absolute elegance and always imbued with a very great sense of classical repose. Some of his perfectly geometrical paintings of beds seem almost a reminiscence of Carpaccio's "Dream of St. Ursula." One has the feeling that Gnoli's eye discarded a great deal more than it accepted and that his sense of the world was entirely unruffled; what's most remarkable in his capacity for repetitive detail in both line and color is that it never seems tainted with either obsession or anxiety.

Just how radical Gnoli's decisions were in working his way toward a mature and self-assured style can be seen in the work that dates from the periods previous to his having achieved it. His earlier paintings were done with a mixture of sand and gouache that allowed him to work up usually dark-toned images of simple objects in low relief, but capturing the magic of the sheer physical presence of his subjects—a group of wicker laundry baskets or an old rustic cupboard, for example—went hand in hand for a while with a vague fairy-land air of Mediterranean expressionism. Gnoli also had to come to terms with his prodigious talents as an illustrator with a manner not entirely dissimilar to what one expects from Saul Steinberg, and sometimes even with an echo of Ben Shahn. In addition to the stage and costume designs that he did for the Shakespearean productions at the Zurich Spielhaus and the Old Vic in London, his sketches also move through a range that goes from mythical fantasies of monster to curious conundrums like his drawing of a horse in a sinking barrel-like boat, to apparently hasty scribblings of work gangs at the CBS New York studios or of crowds of agitated spectators seated in rows in Harlem theaters.

Whereas Gnoli's earlier paintings reveal a romantic tendency to humanize the world of objects, his drawings show an equally romantic fascination with the fantastic and grotesque and these are precisely the impulses that were so perfectly excluded from all of his later paintings. What's curious is that the exorcism could have been so complete. Gnoli's exquisitely rendered particulars tell us remarkably little about the world from which he abstracted them, and his achievement seems to lie in his having established a personal and aristocratic right to a style of vision that was entirely a matter of choice, entirely a question of what his eye most arbitrarily wanted to look at.

—Henry Martin

GOERITZ, Mathias.

German. Born in Danzig, 4 April 1915; moved to Mexico, 1949. Educated at the Kaiserin-Augusta-Gymnasium, Charlottenburg, Berlin, 1924–34; Friedrich-Wilhelms-Universität, Berlin, 1934–40, Ph.D. 1940; Kunstgewerbeschule, Charlottenburg, Berlin, 1937–39. Married Marianne Gast in 1942 (died, 1958); Ida Rodriguez Prampolini in 1960; son: Daniel. Professor, Centro de Estudios Marroquies, Tetuan, Spanish Morocco, 1940–44; painter in Granada, Spain, 1945–47, and Madrid, 1947–49; Professor of Visual Education and Design, Escuela de Arquitectura, Universidad de Guadalajara, Jalisco, Mexico, 1949–54. From 1953, painter, sculptor and architect in Mexico City, and Founder/Professor, Department of Basic Design, Universidad Nacional Autónoma de Mexico, Mexico City. Founder/Director, Escuela de Artes Plasticas y Escuela de Diseño Industrial, Universidad Iboamericana, Mexico City, 1957–60; Artist-in-Residence, Aspen Institute for Humanistic Studies, Aspen, Colorado, 1970–72. Editor, Art Section, *Arquitectura Mexico*, Mexico City, from 1958. Founder, la Escuela de Altamira movement, Santillana del Mar, Santander, Spain, 1948, and Los Hartos movement, with José Luis Cuevas, Pedro Freideberg, Jesus Reyes Ferreira, and others, Mexico City, 1961. Member of GIAP (Group International d'Architecture Prospective), from 1965. Recipient: Zeev Rechter Prize for Architecture, Israel, 1987. Member, Akademie der Künste, Berlin, 1973; Honorary Fellow, Royal Academy of The Hague, 1976; Honorary Academician, Academia Nacional de Arquitectura, Mexico, 1984; Academia Mexican de Diseno, 1985; Academia de Artes, Mexico, 1986. Chevalier, Ordre des Arts et des Lettres, France, 1984. Agent: Caleria Mer-Kup, Moliere 328-C, Col. Polanco, Mexico D.F.-5. Address: Apartado 20–390, Mexico (20), D.F., 01000 Mexico.

Individual Exhibitions:

1946	Sala Clan, Madrid
1948	Salon Alerta, Santander, Spain
1949	Galeria Palma, Madrid
1950	Galeria Camarauz, Guadalajara, Mexico
	Galeria Clardecor, Mexico City
1952	Galeria Sapi, Palma de Majorca
	Galeria Jardin, Barcelona
	Galeria de Arte Mexicano, Mexico City
1953	El Eco Museo Experimental, Mexico City
1955	Galeria Proteo, Mexico City
1956	Carstairs Gallery, New York
1959	Galeria de Arte Mexicano, Mexico City (retrospective)
1960	Carstairs Gallery, New York
	Galerie Iris Clert, Paris
	Galeria de Antonio Souza, Mexico City
1961	Galeria de Arte Mexicano, Mexico City
1962	Carstairs Gallery, New York
1980	Israel Museum, Jerusalem
1984	Museo de Arte Moderno, Mexico City

Selected Group Exhibitions:

1960	*New Media/New Forms*, Martha Jackson Gallery, New York
	Aspects de la Sculpture Americaine, Galerie Calude Bernard, Paris
	New Europeans, Contemporary Arts Museum, Houston
1961	*Art of Assemblage*, Museum of Moder Art, New York
1962	*Carnegie International*, Pittsburgh

From 1962 Goeritz ceased active participation in many of the one-man and group exhibitions of his work.

Collections:

Museo de Arte Moderno, Mexico City; Museum of Modern Art, New York; Israel Museum, Jerusalem; Kunsthalle, Hamburg.

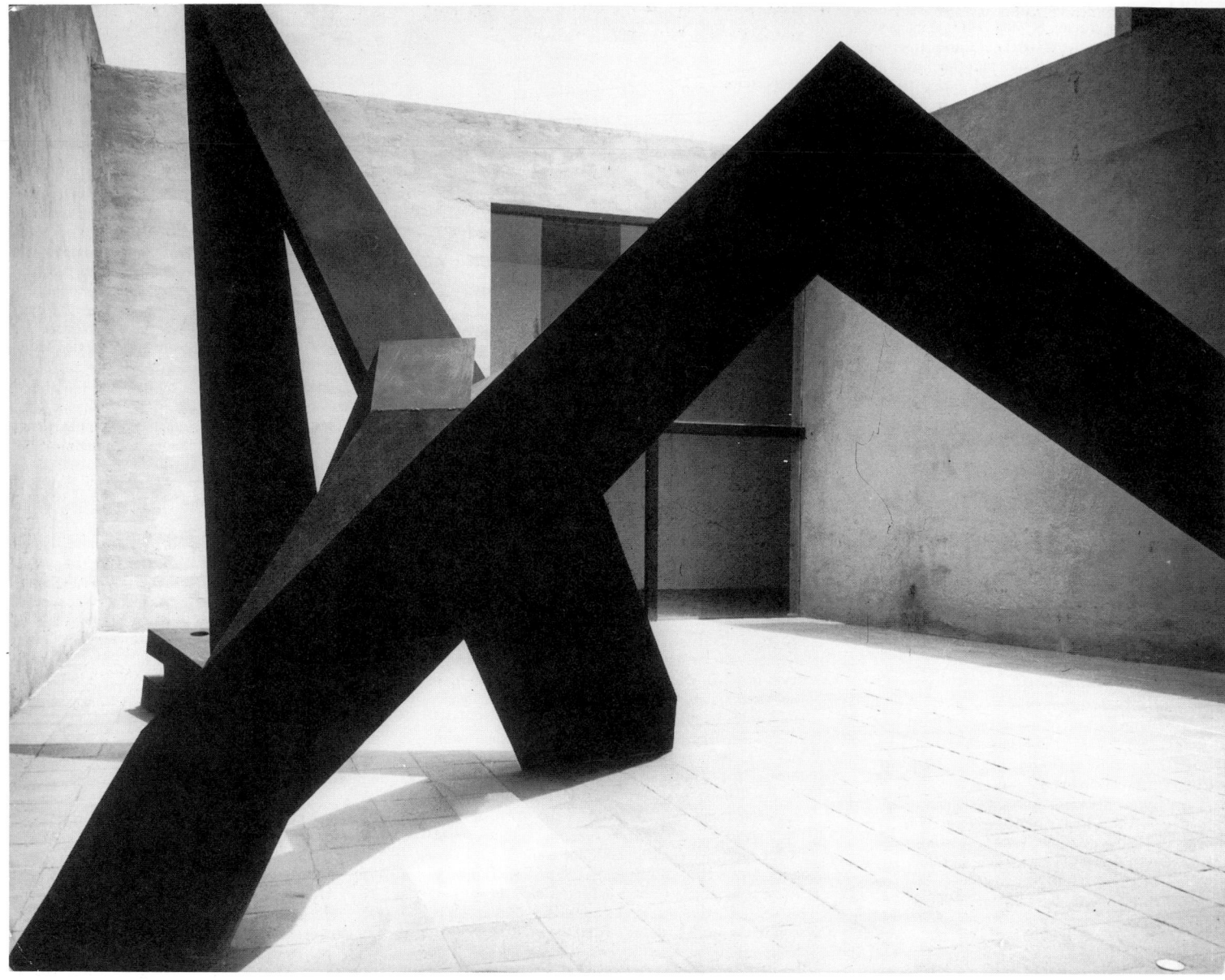

Mathias Goeritz: *La Serpiente del Eco*, 1952

Publications:

By GOERITZ: books—*Manifesto of the School of Altamira*, Santander, Spain 1948; *Manifesto: Estoy Harto*, Mexico City 1960; *Manifesto: Estamos Hartos*, Mexico City 1961; articles—"Manifesto: arquitectura Emocional" in *Cuadernos de Arquitectura* (Guadalajara), no. 1, 1954; "Statement" in the catalog for his one-man show, Carstairs Gallery, New York 1962; statement in *Contemporary Architects*, edited by Muriel Emmanuel, London and New York 1980.

On GOERITZ: books—*Encyclopédie de l'Architecture Nouvelle* by Alberto Sartoris, Milan 1954; *Encyclopaedia of Modern Architecture* by Max Cetto, London 1963; *Art in Latin American Architecture* by Paul F. Damaz, New York 1964; *Mathias Goeritz* by Oliva Zuniga, Mexico City and New York, 1963, 1964; *Arquitectura Contemporanea Mexicana* by Israel Katzman, Mexico City 1964; *Bouwmeesters van morgen* by J. J. Beljon, Amsterdam 1964; *El Arte Contemporaneo* by Ida Rodriguez Prampolini, Mexico City 1964; *Les Cités de l'Avenir* by Michel Ragon, Paris 1966; *Builders in the Sun* by Clive B. Smith, New York 1967; *The Aesthetic of Contemporary Architecture* by Michel Ragon, Neuchatel 1968; *A History of Latin American Art and Architecture* by Leopoldo Castedo, New York 1969; *Histoire Mondiale de l'Architecture et de l'Urganisme Modernes* by Michel Ragon, Paris 1972; *Mathias Goeritz* by Frederico Morais, Mexico City 1982; *Mathias Goeritz* by Lily Kassner, Mexico City 1984; *Arquitectura Emocional* by Rita Eder, Mexico City 1984; articles—"El Eco: Ein Experimental-Museum in Mexico" in *Baukunst und Werkform* (franfurt), no. 4 1954; "Architektur in Mexiko" by Helmuth Borcherdt in *Baumeister* (Munich), November 1959; "Mathias Goeritz" by Michel Ragon in *Cimaise* (Paris), no. 106, 1972.

Aesthetics without a secure ethical background may produce interesting, even beautiful results, but not art. Art is a service. As long as art has no spiritual function, all our efforts are condemned to lead to nothing but a kind of egocentric folk art, done by intellectuals for intellectuals. The over-emphasis on individual expression has, in the end, destroyed its importance. The artist, instead of concentrating on his independent and nonconformist genius, should admit that his works are actually nothing but isolated, temporary designs or expressive spots on the wall, and that all the rest is vanity, propaganda or business.

When people asked me to define my own work, I used to say that I considered it an experiment of poetry in space, the truth is that it is a rather desperate attempt to find the right language for a prayer.

—Mathias Goeritz

Following his studies of philosophy in Berlin Goeritz became involved in the history of art and after his travels in Europe he gradually became engaged in its practice. He frequented the circle of the German Expressionists and took some of the experimental spirit of modern sculptors such as Arp.

He spent the war years in Morocco before settling in Spain where he founded the School of Altamira, a group that influenced the younger artists emerging with interests expressed in the abstract idiom.

In 1949 he was invited to teach at the University of Guadalajara in Mexico. His sculptures and mural decorations aroused opposition from the native artists including Rivera and Siqueiros. His best known works are the Five Towers in the Square of that name built at the entrance to a satellite town in Mexico in 1957–58. This group of giant monoliths ranging in height from 120 to 185 feet combines five units three in white, one in yellow and the other in orange.

This daring concept with its affinity to modern architecture of skyscrapers and to the grouping of ancient menhirs created its own mystique of pure form and mysteriously poised relationship with space and the surrounding environment. In the various fields of education, writing, poetry, architecture and sculpture Goeritz always maintained a philosophical attitude to the visual forms of art seeking to express something of the physical presence to convey spiritual messages. Biblical subjects became refined from Expressionist and emotional figures to a simpler abstract iconography where unconventional materials were used to form assemblages. His series called "Clouages" are large panels on which cut-out-shapes of tin, plastic and other metals are nailed in patterns of symbolic intent. One such work "Message XI" (1958) measuring 63 by 71 inches and based on a text from the Book of Job "I shall be condemned: why do I then labour in vain?", has its unique impact in its severe and secret metaphor of the written words.

Through the language of free form Goeritz maintained a link with the conventionally recorded stories of the Old Testament and in such series as "Realisations" and "Commentaries" he substituted his own epigrammatic rhymes of nail-heads and shape outlines in monumental "tablets" striking lyrical responses from the imagination. His sensitive recycling of ready-made materials into reliefs of compulsive power was achieved by concentration on spacing and texture of the various elements arriving at formal conclusions seemingly pre-ordained. They present the ultimate in significant parables of the spirit expressed in dramatic non-allusive terms of materials whose properties are transmuted by the strength of the artist's numinous purpose.

—G. S. Whittet

GOINGS, Ralph (Ladell).

American. Born in Corning, California, 9 May 1928. Studied at the California College of Arts and Crafts, Oakland, 1950–53, B.F.A. 1953; California State University, Sacramento, 1965–66, M.A. 1966. Served as Corporal in the United States Army, 1946–48. Married Shanna Leslyn in 1951; children: Mark, Cameron, Drew and Kevin. Independent artist known for photo-realist paintings. Instructor, Del Norte High School, Crescent City, California, 1955–59; Chairman of Art Department, La Sierra High School, Carmichael, California, 1959–70; Instructor, California State University, Sacramento, 1971; Instructor, University of California at Davis, 1972. Lives in Charlotteville, New York. Agent: O. K. Harris, New York.

Address: c/o O. K. Harris Works of Art, 383 West Broadway, New York, New York 10012, U.S.A.

Individual Exhibitions:

1960	Artists Cooperative Gallery, Sacramento, California
1962	Artists Cooperative Gallery, Sacramento, California
1968	Artists Cooperative Gallery, Sacramento, California
1970	O. K. Harris Works of Art, New York
1973	O. K. Harris Works of Art, New York
1977	O. K. Harris Works of Art, New York
1980	O. K. Harris Works of Art, New York
1983	O. K. Harris Works of Art, New York
1985	O. K. Harris Works of Art, New York
1987	Tampa Museum of Art, Florida (with Chuck Close)

Selected Group Exhibitions:

1969	*Directions 2: Aspects of a New Realism,* Milwaukee Art Center
1970	*The Highway,* University of Pennsylvania, Philadelphia (toured the United States)
1971	*Radical Realism,* Museum of Contemporary Art, Chicago
1972	*Documenta V,* Kassel, West Germany
1974	*Tokyo Biennale 74*
1976	*American Master Drawings and Watercolors,* Whitney Museum, New York
1977	*Representations of America,* Metropolitan Museum, New York (travelled to Moscow, Leningrad and Minsk)
1981	*Contemporary American Realism Since 1960,* Pennsylvania Academy of Fine Arts, Philadelphia
1984	*Automobile and Culture,* Museum of Contemporary Art, Los Angeles (travelled to Detroit)
1986	*Boston Collects,* Museum of Fine Arts, Boston

Collections:

Museum of Modern Art, New York; Guggenheim Museum, New York; Neue Galerie, Aachen, West Germany; Whitney Museum, New York; Museum of Contemporary Art, Chicago; Tampa Museum of Art, Florida; Portland Museum of Art, Oregon; Sheldon Memorial Art Museum, University of Nebraska, Lincoln.

Publications:

By GOINGS: article—"The Photo Realists: 12 Interviews" by Brian O'Doherty in *Art in America* (New York), November/December 1972.

On GOINGS: books—*Directions 3: 8 Artists,* exhibition catalogue, by John Taylor, Milwaukee 1971; *New Realism* by Udo Kultermann, Tübingen, West Germany 1972; *Man Made Nature Vol. 5* by Yusuke Nakahara, Tokyo 1972; *Topics in Modern Art* by Lawrence Alloway, New York 1975; *Super Realism* by Edward Lucie-Smith, New York 1979; *Late Modern: The Visual Arts since 1945* by Edward Lucie-Smith, New York 1980; *Surrealist Painting and Sculpture* by Christine Lindey, New York 1980; *Art in the 70s* by Edward Lucie-Smith, New York 1980; *Photorealism* by Louis Meisel, New York 1980; *Realist at Work* by John Arthus, New York 1983; *Ralph Goings* by Linda Chase, New York 1988; articles—"Ralph Goings" by Jean-Louis Bourgeois in *Artforum* (new York), November 1970; "The Real and the Artificial" by William Seitz in *Art in America* (New York), November/December 1972; "New York" by Peter Schjeldahl in *Art in*

Ralph Goings: *The Waitresses—Afternoon Break,* 1986

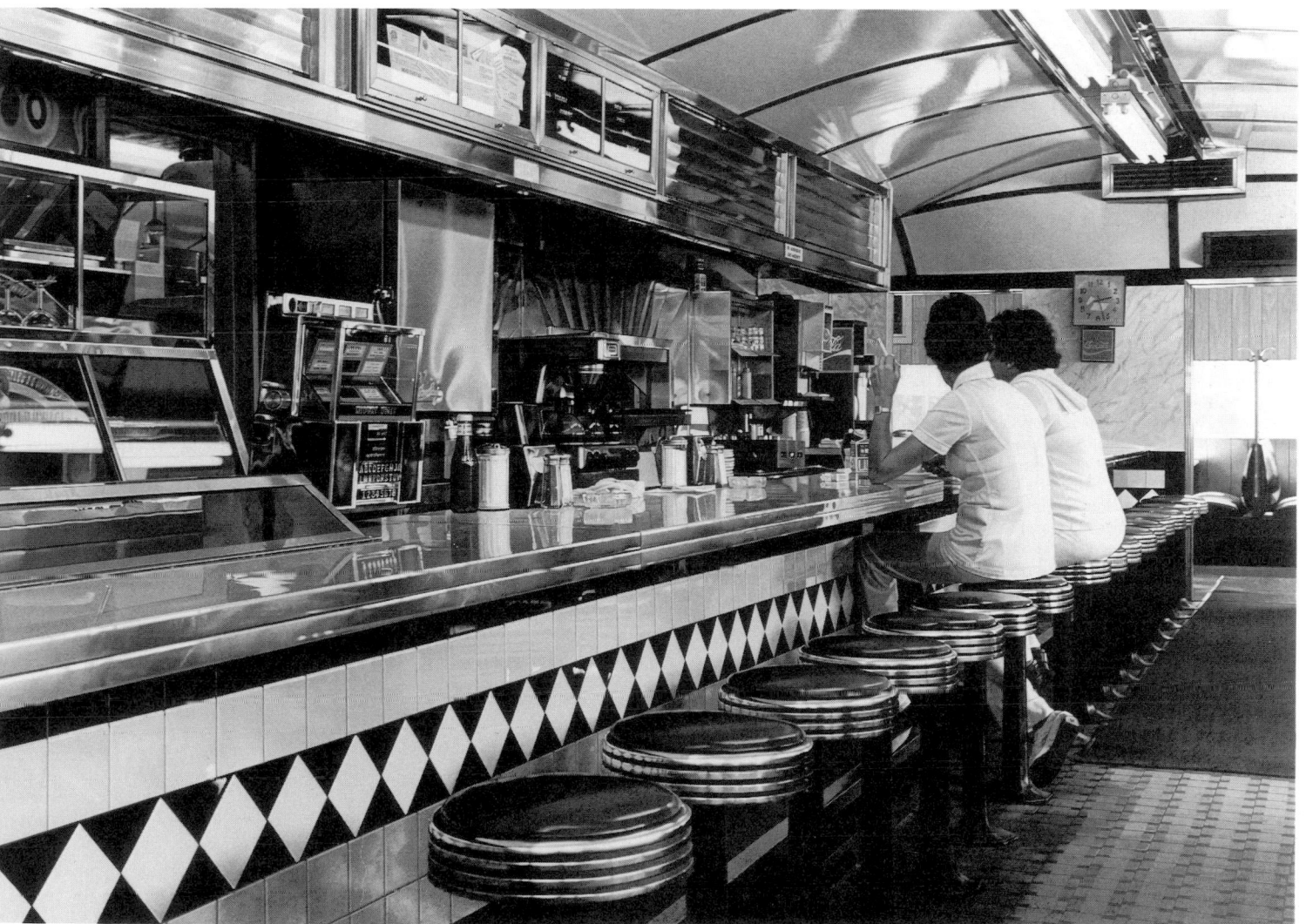

America (New York), September/October 1973; "The Connotation of Denotation" by Linda Chase in *Arts Magazine* (New York), February 1974; "Ralph Goings at O. K. Harris" by Pepe Karmel in *Art in America* (New York), May 1980; "Les hyper-duettistes" by H. F. Debailleux in *Liberation* (Paris), 20 June 1984.

Ralph Goings is one of the many Photo-Realist painters who came into prominence at the beginning of the 1970's. His pictures are characteristically clearcut, illusionistically precise transpositions from 35mm slides. His favored subject matter is the synthetic American scene, and he chooses things such as pickup trucks, franchised hamburger stands, California banks and deserted airports, all cool, and obviously artificial and timebound views, located in "Anywhere U.S.A."

Like Richard Estes, Robert Cottingham and a few others, Goings is aggressively anti-expressionist and emphasizes the glossiness of mass-produced industrial objects in non-hieratic compositions stressing painstaking craftsmanship and description of visual fact. Out of the artificiality of the industrial location, come pictures emanating with static, undisturbed order and anonymity. Goings' attitude is anti-style; his aim, to suppress individuality and limit interpretation in terms of stylistic analysis and emotive content. How can one read these meticulously handmade reduplications of the photographic becomes an open-ended question. All this suppression and consciously accurate stress on visual elements of texture, light and reflection sets Goings in a new category of "realism," one which connects with mass culture and the industrial environment but not with Nature, with what's new now and not relatable with past art. There are elements of Hopper and William Harnett, but with a large difference. The closest connections are with Pop Art, but the subject matter is not rearranged as it is with 1960's Pop, and the deadpan is achieved by Goings through faithfulness to the photographically seen as counterfeited by arduous craftsmanship.

Goings' pictures are matter-of-fact, deductive, frontal depictions of visual fact. But when one views paintings such as "Rose Bowl Parade," "Bank of America" or "Dick's Union General," feelings of irony, lament or celebration creep in. What is depicted is glossy, so inhuman, so populist neat and available. But what is depicted is also quick to get old, becoming yesterday's signs of industrialized, mass-produced vigor. Goings' trucks and his franchised fast food stands are "period pieces," even now turning America's hopes for fastly achieved equal opportunity into reminders of their temporary status and boring sameness. The slow, laborious process of painting these scenes, already rendered doubly artificial, brings heightened consciousness of painting's relationship with the new Nature that surrounds us in our present environment. Once you get over the initial awe of Goings' technical abilities at reduplication, you're left with his choice of subject matter with a definitely individualistic eye and mind. Consider, for instance, that in Goings' "Burger Chef Interior" the traditionally mystical dodecahedron is a hanging light, illuminating formica booths and dispensing machines and co-habiting equally with the latest model bus and Wonder Bread truck. All will soon become outdated in favor of next year's mass-made models.

—Barbara Cavaliere

GOLUB, Leon (Albert).

American. Born in Chicago, Illinois, 23 January 1922. Studied at the University of Chicago, 1940–42, B.A. in art history 1942; School of the Art Institute of Chicago, under Paul Wieghardt, Kathleen Blackshear, Robert Lifuendahl, 1946–50, B.F.A. 1949, M.F.A. 1950. Served as Sergeant in the 942nd Engineers, Aviation Typographic Battalion, in Europe, 1943–46. Married the artist Nancy Spero, *q.v.*, in 1951; sons: Stephen, Philip, and Paul. Independent artist, since 1950. Art Instructor, Wright Junior College, Chicago, 1950–55, and Illinois Institute of Technology, Chicago, 1955–56; travelled in Europe, and lived in Italy, 1956–57; Assistant Professor of Art, Indiana University, Bloomington, 1957–59; lived in Paris, 1959–64; Lecturer, Tyler School of Art, Temple University, Philadelphia, 1965–66; Instructor, School of Visual Arts, New York, 1966–69; Assistant Professor of Art, Fairleigh Dickinson University, Rutherford, New Jersey, 1969. Professor, 1970–84, and John C. Van Dyck Professor of Visual Art since 1984, Mason Gross School of the Arts, Rutgers University, New Brunswick, New Jersey. Recipient: Florsheim Memorial Prize, *61st American Exhibition*, Art Institute of Chicago, 1954; Ford Foundation grant, 1960; Watson F. Blair Purchase Prize, *65th American Exhibition*, Art Institute of Chicago, 1962; Tamarind Lithography Grant, 1965; Cassandra Foundation grant, 1967; Guggenheim grant, 1968; National Institute of Arts and Letters Award, 1973; Rutgers University Research Council Faculty Fellowship, 1975–76; Bartels-Cahn-Campana Award, Art Institute of Chicago, 1986. Agents: Barbara Gladstone Gallery, 99 Greene Street, New York, New York 10012; Rhona Hoffman Gallery, 215 West Superior Street, Chicago, Illinois 60610; Galerie Hans Neuendorf, Beethovenstrasse 71, 6000 Frankfurt-am-Main 1, West Germany; Galerie Darthea Speyer, 6 rue Jacques Callot, 75006 Paris, France. Address: 530 La Guardia Place, New York, New York 10012, U.S.A.

Individual Exhibitions:

1950	Contemporary Gallery, Chicago
1951	Purdue University, West Lafayette, Indiana
1952	Wittenborn and Company Gallery, New York
1954	Artists Gallery, New York
	Wittenborn and Company Gallery, New York
1955	Feigl Gallery, New York
	Allan Frumkin Gallery, Chicago
1956	Feigl Gallery, New York
	Allan Frumkin Gallery, Chicago
	Pomona College, California
	Pasadena Museum of Art, California
1957	Allan Frumkin Gallery, Chicago
	Institute of Contemporary Arts, London
1958	Allan Frumkin Gallery, Chicago
	Indiana University, Bloomington
1959	Allan Frumkin Gallery, Chicago
1960	Allan Frumkin Gallery, Chicago
	Centre Culturel Americain, Paris
1961	Allan Frumkin Gallery, Chicago
1962	Allan Frumkin Gallery, Chicago
	Galerie Iris Clert, Paris
	Hanover Gallery, London
1963	Allan Frumkin Gallery, Chicago
	Gallery A. Melbourne
1964	Allan Frumkin Gallery, Chicago
	Tyler School of Art, Temple University, Philadelphia (retrospective)
	Galerie Iris Clert and Galerie Europe. Paris (joint exhibition)
1966	Cliffdwellers Gallery, Chicago
	University of Chicago (retrospective)
1968	10 Downtown, New York (studio exhibition)
1970	LoGiudice Gallery, Chicago
	Hayden Gallery, Massachusetts Institute of Technology, Cambridge
	National Gallery of Victoria, Melbourne
1971	Galerie Darthea Speyer, Paris
1972	Herbert Lehman College, New York
	Bienville Gallery, New Orleans
1973	Musée de l'Abbaye Sainte Croix, Sable d'Olonne, France
1974	*Leon Golub: The Development of His Art*, Museum of Contemporary Art, Chicago (retrospective)
1975	State University of New York at Stony Brook
	New Jersey State Museum, Trenton
1976	Haverford College, Pennsylvania
	San Francisco Art Institute
1977	Bienville Gallery, New Orleans
	Olympia Galleries, Philadelphia
	Walter Kelly Gallery, Chicago
1978	State University of New York at Stony Brook
	Portraits of Power, Colgate University, Hamilton, New York
1979	Visual Arts Museum, School of Visual Arts, New York
1980	Protetch-McIntosh Gallery, Washington, D.C.
1981	*Leon Golub/Nancy Spero*, Swarthmore College, Pennsylvania
1982	Susan Caldwell Inc., New York
	Vietnam War, Tweed Arts Group, Plainfield, New Jersey (with Nancy Spero)
	Kipnis Works of Art, Atlanta
	Young Hoffman Gallery, Chicago
	Institute of Contemporary Arts, London
1983	University of California, Berkeley
	University of New Mexico, Albuquerque (with Nancy Spero)
	Honolulu Academy of Arts, Hawaii
	Mercenaries, Interrogations and Other Works, University of Houston, Texas (travelled to Portland, Oregon; Tucson, Arizona; Oxford, Ohio; Storrs, Connecticut; Syracuse, New York)
	College of Art and Design, Detroit (with Nancy Spero)
1984	Installation Gallery, San Diego, California
	Susan Caldwell Inc., New York
	Gallery Paule Anglim, San Francisco
	New Museum of Contemporary Art, new York (retrospective; travelled to La Jolla, California; Chicago; Montreal; Washington, D.C.; and Boston, 1985)
	Galerie Darthea Speyer, Paris
1985	Institute of Contemporary Art, Boston
	Rhona Hoffman Gallery, Chicago
	Printworks, Chicago
	Donald Young Gallery, Chicago
	Stanford University, California
1986	Barbara Gladstone Gallery, New York
	Greenville County Museum of Art, South Carolina
	Appalachian State University, Boone, North Carolina
1987	Kunstmuseum, Lucerne
	Kunstverein, Hamburg
	Orchard Gallery, Derry, Northern Ireland

Selected Group Exhibitions:

1948	*Exhibition Momentum*, Roosevelt University, Chicago
1954	*Young American Painters*, Guggenheim Museum, New York (toured the United States)
1959	*Images of Man*, Museum of Modern Art, New York
1968	*The Obsessive Image 1960–68*, Institute of Contemporary Arts, London
1972	*Chicago Imagist Art*, Museum of Contemporary Art, Chicago
1977	*Paris-New York*, Centre Georges Pompidou, Paris
1984	*ROSC '84*, Dublin, Ireland
1985	*Nouvelle Biennale de Paris*, La Villette, Paris
1986	*75th American Exhibition*, Art Institute of Chicago
1987	*Documenta 8*, Museum Fridericianum, Kassel, West Germany

Collections:

Museum of Modern Art, New York; Smithsonian Institution, Washington, D.C.; Hirshhorn Museum, Washington, D.C.; Corcoran Gallery, Washington, D.C.; Art Institute of Chicago; Museum of Contemporary Art, Chicago; Los Angeles County Museum of Art; National Gallery of Victoria, Melbourne; Seattle Art Museum, Washington; Musee des Beaux-Arts, Montreal.

Publications:

By GOLUB: articles—"A Critique of Abstract Expressionism" in *College Art Journal* (Bloomington, Indiana), Winter 1955; "The Artist as an Angry Artist" in *Arts Magazine* (New York), April 1967; "Bombs and Helicopters: The Art

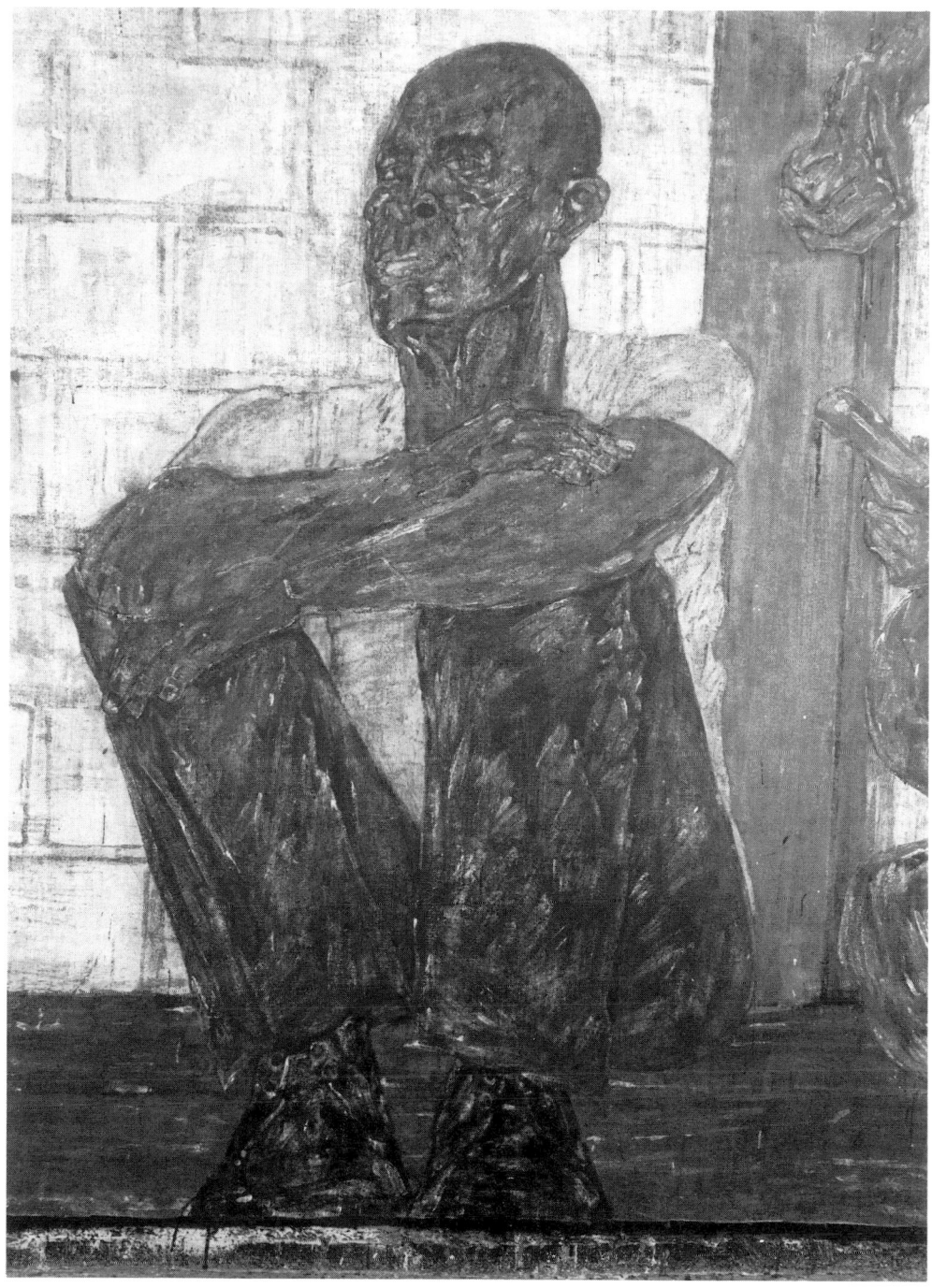

Leon Golub: *Three Seated Black Men*, 1986

of Nancy Spero" in *Caterpillar I* (New York), 1967; "An Interview with Leon Golub," with Irving Sandler, in *Arts Magazine* (New York), February 1970; "Regarding the Lehman and Rockefeller Gifts to the Metropolitan Museum" in *Artforum* (New York), November 1970; "Utopia/Anti-Utopia" in *Artforum* (New York), May 1972; "2D/3D" in *Artforum* (New York), March 1973; "16 Whitney Museum Annuals of American Painting: Percentages 1950–1972" in *Artforum* (New York), March 1973; "Art Politics and Ethics: Interview with Leon Golub and Nancy Spero," with Derek Guthrie, in *New Art Examiner* (Chicago), April 1977; "The Mercenaries' " An Interview with Leon Golub," with Matthew Baigell, in *Arts Magazine* (New York), May 1981; "On Being Taken for Granted" in *New Art Examiner* (Chicago), October 1981; "Leon Golub", interview with Suzanne Davies, in *Art-Network* (Sydney), Autumn 1985.

On GOLUB: books—*Leon Golub*, exhibition catalogue, by Lawrence Alloway, Chicago 1957; *Leon Golub*, exhibition catalogue, by Robert Melville, London 1957; *New Images of Man* by Peter Selz, New York 1959; *Art: USA: Now* by Allan Weller, Lucerne 1962; *Leon Golub: Retrospective Catalogue* by A. James Speyer, Philadelphia 1964; *The Arts and the Public* by James E. Miller and Paul Herring, Chicago 1967; *Leon Golub*, exhibition catalogue, by Barbara Klein, Cambridge, Massachusetts 1970; *Leon Golub*, exhibition catalogue, by Corinne Robbins, Melbourne 1970; *Fantastic Images: Chicago Art since 1945* by Franz Schulze, Chicago 1972; *Leon Golub: The Development of His Art*, exhibition catalogue, by Lawrence Alloway, Chicago 1974; *Leon Golub*, exhibition catalogue, by Dennis Adrian, Trenton, New Jersey 1975; *Portraits of Power*, exhibition catalogue, by Edward Bryant, Hamilton, New York 1978; *The New York School* by Irving Sandler, New York 1978; *Golub*, exhibition catalogue by Lynn Gumpert and Ned Rifkin, New York 1984; *Leon Golub: Existential/Activist Painter* by Donald Kuspit, New Brunswick 1985; *Leon Golub 1986*, exhibition catalogue by Peter Schjeldahl, New York 1986; *Leon Golub: Selected Paintings 1967–1986*, exhibition catalogue, Derry 1986; *Leon Golub*, exhibition catalogue by Donald Kuspit, Lucerne and Hamburg 1987; articles—"A New Imagery in American Painting" by Peter Selz in *College Art Journal* (Bloomington, Indiana), Summer 1956; "Leon Golub" by Robert Pincus-Witten in *Art International* (Lugano, Switzerland), February 1962; "Chicago Letter" by Franz Schulze in *Art International* (Lugano, Switzerland), 20 January 1967; "Styles of Radical Will" by Susan Sontag in *Caterpillar* (New York), October 1969; "Golub: Mythes a l'heure du Napalm" by G. Gassiot Talabot in *Opus International* (Paris), March 1971; "Leon Golub: Art and Politics" by Lawrence Alloway in *Artforum* (New York), October 1974; "Majestic Existentialism" by Franz Schulze in *Artnews* (New York), October 1974; "Golub's Assassins: An Anatomy of Violence" by Donald Kuspit in *Art in America* (New York), May/June 1975; "Aesthetics of Mutilation" by Harold Rosenbert in *The New Yorker*, 12 May 1975; "Leon Golub: The Faces of Power" by Corinne Robbins in *Arts Magazine* (New York), February 1977; "Leon Golub" by Peter Fuller in *Beyond the Crisis in Art*, London 1980; "Leon Golub's Gigantomachies: Pergamon Revisited" by Joseph Dreiss in *Arts Magazine* (New YOrk), May 1981; "Leon Golub's Murals of Mercenaries" by Donald Kuspit in *Artforum* (New York), May 1981; "Leon Golub" by Joseph Dreiss in *Arts Magazine* (New York), January 1982; "Leon Golub's Mean Streets" by Gerald Marzorati in *Art News* (New York), February 1985.

The "Mercenaries" (1979-), the "Interrogations" (1980-), "White Squads" (1982-), and "Blacks" (1985-) occur on a public scale; the figures are approximately twice life size. (The paintings range from 10 feet in height to 12 to 16 feet in length.) Despite the enormous scale, the figures are intended to be viewed directly, confrontationally, intimately. The mercs and police agents intervene (move into) our space, and we are *inserted* into their space, their actions. This "intimacy" pinpoints our direct awareness of the possibilities and consequences of such actions and events, part of the history of these times. The black individuals are seen as alerted to or resistant to the viewer, our presence in their space.

"Irregular" actions occur at the peripheries of public or government control. Power is control, and governmental agencies or political groups will use extra-legal means when it suits their purposes, that is, when they can get away with it. This occurs to varying and changing degrees in all societies.

The mercs or interrogators are observed directly. We publicly acknowledge and voyeuristically observe them. They are raunchy, irritable, mocking, imply racial hostility and/or sexual ambivalence. Violence and implied violence are immediate and instantaneous, and the mercs and interrogators indicate no compunction in their actions. They are casually self-conscious and eye us, alerted to our observation and interest in their actions. The "Black" paintings continue this point of view but from the context of blacks in contact or tension with whites, a seared presence.

—Leon Golub

Leon Golub, a Chicagoan, aroused some hostility and irritation when he attacked Abstract Expressionism at a time when Franz Kline, Willem de Kooning and the Action Painters had achieved a total break-through to a punch-drunk public. His belief, which he made plain at the time (1955), was that "abstract expressionism had discarded the individualist of the Renaissance," and he stressed this not only as a fellow painter but also as an Arts History BA and a Fine Arts MA.

His way of painting, except for a short period at an early age when he experimented with nonfiguration, was to bulk together patches of turgid pigment, scarcely relieved by touches of white and by almost hidden candy colours, so as to present the figure of MAN.

Not Man the Master of the Universe, but Man at odds with his developed civilization. Of "Thwarted Man" Peter Selz wrote that this 1953 painting showed a creature of Herculean strength who "lacks the instruments by which (he) assumes control over his environment . . . no neck to turn and view, no arms . . . an image of tragic frustration." The Golub colouration is like turkish delight submerged in old cement, a thick stew with fragments of pastel-coloured candied peel lodged in it here and there.

In the early figurative work could be found traces of Pre-Columbian influences added to symbolism drawn from legends, but as the MAN became more and more identifiable as a human being so the tilt of his vision drew closer to that of late Roman sculpture (and there is still a strong sculptural effect in Golub's massy pigment and its clay like character.)

After Man comes the sphinx, a creature upon

whom Golub bestows a head, fore and aft. "Birth" too is another of his chosen subjects in which he preaches the old story of man born in pain, but somehow triumphant.

—Sheldon Williams

GOODE, Joe.

American. Born in Oklahoma City, Oklahoma, 23 March 1937. Studied at the Chouinard Art Institute, Los Angeles. Married Judy Goode in 1960 (divorced 1962); daughter: Stephanie; married Natalie Bieser. Sculptor and painter, also known as Jose Bueno. Recipient: American Federation of Arts Award, 1966; Copley Foundation Award, 1967. Agent: Charles Cowles Gallery, New York. Address: c/o Charles Cowles Gallery, 420 West Broadway, new York, New York 10012, U.S.A.

Individual Exhibitions:

1962	Dilexi Gallery, Los Angeles
1963	Rolf Nelson Gallery, Los Angeles
1966	Nicholas Wilder Gallery, Los Angeles
1967	Rowan Gallery, London
1968	Kornblee Gallery, New York
	Joe Goode/Ed Ruscha, Newport Art Museum, California
1969	Nicholas Wilder Gallery, Los Angeles
1970	Galerie Neuendorf, Hamburg
1971	*West Wall Reliefs*, Pomona College Art Gallery, Claremont, California
	Galleria Milano, Milan
	La Jolla Museum of Art, California
	Mueller Gallery, Dusseldorf
1972	Contract Graphics, Houston
	Margo Levin Gallery, Los Angeles
	Corcoran Gallery, Miami
	Minneapolis Institute of Art
	Felicity Samuel Gallery, London
	Galerie Neuendorf, Cologne
	Nicholas Wilder Gallery, Los Angeles
1973	Felicity Samuel Gallery, London
	Galerie Neuendorf, Hamburg
	Margo Levin Gallery, Los Angeles
	Work Until Now, Fort Worth Art Museum, Texas
	Houston Contemporary Art Museum
	Contract Graphics, Houston
1974	Nicholas Wilder Gallery, Los Angeles
1975	Felicity Samuel Gallery, London
	Nicholas Wilder Gallery, Los Angeles
	Galerie Neuendorf, Hamburg
	Seder-Creigh Gallery, Coronado, California
1976.	James Corcoran Gallery, Los Angeles
	Recent Work, Washington University, St. Louis
1977	Mount St. Mary's College, Los Angeles
1978	Nicholas Wilder Gallery, Los Angeles
1979	Nicholas Wilder Gallery, Los Angeles
	Texas Gallery, Houston
1980	Charles Cowles Gallery, New York

Selected Group Exhibitions:

1969	*Pop Art*, Hayward Gallery London
	West Coast 1945-1969, Pasadena Art Museum, California
1970	*9 Portfolios*, Museum of Modern Art, New York
1971	*32nd Biennial*, Corcoran Gallery of Art, Washington, D.C.
	Oversize Prints, Whitney Museum, New York
1974	*8 from California*, Smithsonian Institution, Washington, D.C.
1975	*4 Lost Angeles Artists*, School of Visual Arts, New York (travelled to Corcoran Gallery of Art, Washington, D.C., and the Wadsworth Atheneum, Hartford, Connecticut)

1976	*California Painting and Sculpture: The Modern Era*, San Francisco Museum of Art
1978	*American Painting in the 70's*, Albright-Knox Art Gallery, Buffalo, New York
	Aspects of Abstract, Crocker Art Museum, Sacramento

Collections:

Museum of Modern Art, New York; Oklahoma Art Center, Oklahoma City; Fort Worth Art Center, Texas; Pasadena Art Museum, California; Los Angeles County Museum of Art; San Francisco Museum of Modern Art.

Publications:

By GOODE: article—"Bengston, Grieger, Goode: 3 Interviews" in *Art in America* (New York), March 1973.

On GOODE: books—*Pop Art* by Lucy Lippard, New York 1966; *Joe Goode/Ed Ruscha*, exhibition catalogue by Henry Hopkins, Balboa, California 1968; *West Wall Reliefs*, exhibition catalogue, with an introduction by Helene Winer, Claremont, California 1971; *Sunshine Muse* by Peter Plagens, New York 1972; *Joe Goode: Lithographs 1962-1972*, exhibition catalogue, Los Angeles 1972; *Joe Goode: Work Until Now*, exhibition catalogue, by Henry Hopkins, Fort Worth, Texas 1973; *Joe Goode: Recent Work*, exhibition catalogue, by Graham W. J. Beal, St. Louis 1976; articles—"Form Follows Function" by Andrew Rubeneck in *Design Quarterly* (Minneapolis), no. 73, 1968; "4 Defectors to Los Angeles" by William Wilson in *Art in America* (New York), vol 56, 1968; "Joe Goode Drawings" by C. Lampert in *Studio International* (London), October 1973; "On the Nature of Pop" by C. R. Baldwain in *Artforum* (New York), June 1974; "Painting under Contract" by A. Schoenfeld in *Artweek* (Oakland, California), 19 May 1979.

GOODNOUGH, Robert (Arthur).

American. Born in Cortland, New York, 23 October 1917. Studied at Syracuse University, New York, 1938-40 (Hiram Gee Fellowship, 1940), B.A. 1940; New School for Social Research, New York, 1949; New York University, 1949-50, M.A. 1950; Ozenfant School of Art, New York, 1950-51; and Hans Hofmann School of Art, New York, 1951. Served in the United States Army, 1941-45. Painter: Critic for *Artnews*, New York, 1950-57; Secretary, *Documents of Modern Art*, New York, 1951. Art Instructor, New York University, 1953, Fieldston School, Riverdale, New York, 1953-60, and Cornell University, Ithaca, New York, 1960. Recipient: Ada S. Garrett Prize, Art Institute of Chicago, 1961; Ford Foundation Prize, 1963. Agent André Emmerich Gallery, 41 East 57th Street, New York, New York 10022. Address: 55 Christopher Avenue, New York, New York 10014, U.S.A.

Individual Exhibitions:

1952	Tibor de Nagy Gallery, Los Angeles (and regularly until 1962)
1959	Dwan Gallery, Los Angeles
1960	Dwan Gallery, Los Angeles
	Ellison Gallery, Fort Worth, Texas
	Jefferson Place Gallery, Washington, D.C.
	Art Institute of Chicago
1961	Nova Gallery, Boston
	Art Institute of Chicago
	Dwan Gallery, Los Angeles
1962	Dwan Gallery, Los Angeles
1964	University of Minnesota, Minneapolis
	University of Notre Dame, Indiana
	New Vision Centre Gallery, London
	Arts Club of Chicago
1965	Tibor de Nagy Gallery, New York
1967	University of Notre Dame, Indiana

1969	Axiom Gallery, London
1972	André Emmerich Gallery, New York
1975	Waddington Gallery, London
	André Emmerich Gallery, New York
	Tooth Galleries II, London
	Galerie André Emmerich, Zurich
1977	Knoedler and Company, New York
1978	Hokin Gallery, Chicago
	Nina Freudenheim Gallery, Buffalo, New York
	Wichita State University, Kansas
1979	Klondaridis Inc., Toronto
	Watson/de Nagy, Houston
1981	Harcus Krakow Gallery, Boston
	Klonaridis Inc., Toronto
1982	André Emmerich Gallery, New York
1985	Tibor de Nagy Gallery, New York

Selected Group Exhibitions:

1950	*New Talent*, Kootz Gallery, New York
1956	*4 Younger Americans*, Sidney Janis Gallery, New York
1964	*Annual Exhibition*, Whitney Museum, New York
1969	*New American Painting and Sculpture*, Museum of Modern Art, New York
1970	*Biennale*, Venice

Collections:

Whitney Museum, New York; Guggenheim Museum, New York; Museum of Modern Art, New York; New York University; Albright-Knox Art Gallery, Buffalo, New York; Wadsworth Atheneum, Hartford, Connecticut; Baltimore Museum of Art; North Carolina Museum of Art, Raleigh; Art Institute of Chicago; Los Angeles County Museum of Art.

Publications:

By GOODNOUGH: article—interview, with Martin H. Bush, in *Arts Magazine* (New York), February 1979.

On GOODNOUGH: book—*Goodnough* by Martin H. Bush and Kenworth Moffett, Wichita, Kansas 1973; articles—"Robert Goodnough" in *Art Now: New York*, April 1969; "Notes on Goodnough's Recent Work" by K. Moffett in *Art International* (Lugano, Switzerland), October 1970; "Studying Hofmann" in *Art in America* (New York), May 1973; "Goodnough" by M. H. Bush in *Art International* (Lugano, Switzerland), March 1974; "Glow of Authority" by Charlotte Moser in the *Houston Chronicle*, 21 January 1979.

The American art world looks upon Robert Goodnough as a freak of culture. He is the American painter who does not fit into comfortable categories. Not only has he examined and reconditioned for his own purposes lessons to be learnt from the early Mondrian, before or just during the time when he was deserting figuration, Goodnough has also learnt some private truths from cubism at its wildest. Although he has been painting for a long time, he really only became a serious artist after serving as an enlisted man (during which period he painted many pictures—portraits for the officers; murals for the men) when he entered the contemporary art arena under the tutelage of Amedée Ozenfant and Hans Hofmann, from both of whom he plainly drew some interesting sustenance.

Goodnough probably started his "art" when he was in the first grade at school. He did a drawing called "Skunk in Trap" of which his father said the only way you could tell what it was meant to be was by its title. In the artist's own words, "It must have been pretty abstract."

Perhaps, in spirit at any rate, he has hardly changed. If some of his pictures are "pretty abstract," others are like the "Skunk in Trap"—it is easy enough to know what the picture is if you know the title. This is an artist who is not only difficult to place, he is also able to work in two or three styles at the same time—a pragmatist who seizes upon any factor that will help the picture to finalize itself. This is not generally a kind of artistic behaviour that the public appreciates. Nevertheless, Goodnough's pictures are well liked and as an artist he attracts respect in the United States.

—Sheldon Williams

GORCHOV, Ron.

American. Born in Chicago, Illinois, 5 April 1930. Educated at the University of Mississippi, 1947–48; Art Institute of Chicago, 1948–50; University of Illinois, 1950–51, B.F.A. 1951. Painter: lives and works in New York. Assistant Professor of Art, Hunter College, New York, since 1962. Recipient: Ingram Merrill Foundation Grant, 1959; Honorable Mention, National Arts Club Annual, New York 1959. Agent: Marlborough Gallery, 40 West 57th Street, New York, New York 10019. Address: c/o Department of Art, Hunter College, 6951 Park Avenue, New York, New York 10021, U.S.A.

Individual Exhibitions:

1960 Tibor de Nagy Gallery, New York
1963 Tibor de Nagy Gallery, New York
1966 Tibor de Nagy Gallery, New York
1972 Everson Museum of Art, Syracuse, New York
1975 Fischbach Gallery, New York
1976 Texas Gallery, Houston
1977 Suzanne Hilberry Gallery, Birmingham, Michigan
1978 Galerie M. Bochum, West Germany
       Matrix Program, University of California Art Museum, Berkeley
1979 *Pittura Ambiente*, Palazzo Reale, Milan
       Entrance, P.S.1, Long Island City, New York
       Young Hoffman Gallery, Chicago
       Hamilton Gallery, New York
       Lynda Benglis and Ron Gorchov, Suzanne Hilberry Gallery, Birmingham, Michigan
       Palazzo Reale, Milan
       P.S.1, Long Island City, New York

Selected Group Exhibitions:

1960 *Young America: Painters Under 36*, Whitney Museum, New York
1962 *Pittsburgh International*, Carnegie Institue, Pittsburgh
1974 *Cologne Art Fair*
1976 *New York-Downtown Manhattan: Soho*, Akademie der Kunst, Berlin
1977 *Biennial Exhibition*, Whitney Museum, New York
1979 *Born in Chicago*, Young-Hoffman Gallery, Chicago (with Eve Sonneman and Laurie Anderson)
       The Decade in Review, Whitney Museum, New York
       The 1970's: New American Painting, New Museum, New York
1980 *Painting and Sculpture Today*, Indianapolis Museum of Art, Indiana

Collections:

Metropolitan Museum of Art, New York; Whitney Museum, New York; Guggenheim Museum, New York; Everson Museum of Art, Syracuse, New York; Wadsworth Atheneum, Hartford, Connecticut; Detroit Institute of Arts.

Publications:

On GORCHOV: books—*Name Book 1: Statements on Art*, edited by Nancy Davidson and Donald Sultan, Chicago 1977; *1977 Whitney Biennial*, exhibition catalogue, New York 1977; articles—review by Lawrence Campbell in *Artnews* (New York), June 1963; review by Scott Burton in *Artnews* (New York), May 1966; "New Talent U.S.A.: Painting," edited by Dorothy Miller, in *Art In America* (New York), Spring 1969; reviews by Roberta Smith and by Noel Frackman in *Artforum* (New York), May 1975; "Ron Gorchov at Fischbach Gallery" by Edit DeAk in *Art in America* (New York) September/October 1975; "Shape and Form in Ron Gorchov's Painting" by Morris Kearse in *Artforum* (New York), May 1977; "Noticing Ron Gorchov" by Betsey Hansell in *Detroit Artists Monthly*, June 1977.

The continuing satisfactions found within the spiritual potentialities of abstract painting—beyond its purely visual statement—may be at the heart of Ron Gorchov's career. For him, it is ease and fulfilment in the studio, and for his viewers, a hovering sense of primordial energy within the well-understood tradition of abstract painting. Since 1969, he has worked almost exclusively upon a shaped canvas that is curved-corner and saddle-shaped; and just as focusedly, Gorchov has projected a freely-brushed monochromatic field broken only by two vertical shapes aligned on either side of the implied center of the canvas. These marks, hook-shaped and knife-blade-like, and usually organic, have been disposed in many differing ways both to support and deemphasize the symmetry. And in combination with the apparently widely-felt "shield-like" character of Gorchov's convex-concave form, most of his primitive and yet sophisticated works are rendered mysterious as though they were cult emblems. Most likely his art is akin to that of other highly reductive American artists—some with austere poetical stance verging on the mystic—such as John McLaughlin, Barnett Newman, Myron Stout, and Burgoyne Diller; but just so Minimalism's reductive symmetry and object-search is also within his debt. As well, Gorchov's peculiar shaped canvas and its dual marks may both be due to a visual abnormality of which he was unaware in earlier life. Apparently his eyes do not focus together, so that roundness as well as singularity are difficult to achieve: it is then as if his two most distinctive qualities as form designer have had to do with an unconscious understanding of his need to compensate for them.

As a protege of John Graham, Gorchov's earlier works offer little surprise if they are read as an alchemical yearning translated into an American abstract-expressionist idiom: skeins of totemic-like crusted paint and shimmering surreal effects. But by the mid-60's, he had already reduced this love of the exotic to flat surface embellished by single shapes such as a falling curve and treble-clef-like forms. Since then, he has retained the centralized two-mark format, varying it even by such extreme means as stapling and gluing the canvas on to his curved stretchers. Gorchov has also produced cast paper editions of his painting type; requiring no support, these small pictorial sculptures, in their slightly roughened edge and surface, self-supporting and thus in need of no stretcher, have proven an ideal accompaniment to his painting production.

Perhaps the artist is best understood in his synthesis of old and new world modernist attitudes. His art appears in its gruff good nature as an American pragmatism, yet one combined with a yearning for an ideal state. But Gorchov's aloofness and pretension, if European then, is tempered by that very pragmatism to be accepted as a sensual, immediate and object art—which is not Gorchov's intention. His further evolution into the mid-80s is still projected onto the saddle-shaped canvas, and still produces that strain of duality. However, the rigorous insistence upon austere symmetry and heraldic distance is gone, and more clearly readable organic forms often resembling body parts appear; and so the shaped concave surface seems obviated—no longer necessary to convey the still amorphous, yet more typically Symbolist content.

—Joshua Kind

GORDY, Robert.

American. Born in Jefferson Island, Louisiana, 14 October 1933. Studied at Louisiana State University, Baton Rouge, 1951–55, B.A. 1955, M.A. 195; studied with Hans Hofmann at Yale University, New Haven, Connecticut (Yale-Norfolk Fellowship), 1953; did graduate work at State University of Iowa, Iowa City, 1955. Independent artist, New Orleans, producing pattern-like figurative images with comic and ironic overtones, 1955 until his death in 1985. Artist-in-Residence, Tamarind Workshop, Albuquerque, New Mexico, 1971. Recipient: Purchase Prize, Museum of Art, New Orleans, 1958, 1967, 1971, 1973; National Endowment for the Arts grant, 1967, 1978; Purchase Prize, Fine Arts Center, Oklahoma City, 1969; Purchase Prize, Museum of Fine Arts, Dallas, 1969. Agents: Galerie Simonne Stern, 2727 Prytania Street, New Orleans, Louisiana 90130; Delahunty Gallery, 2611 Cedar Springs Road, Dallas, Texas 75201; Phyllis Kind Gallery, 139 Spring Street, New York, New York 10012 and 226 E. Ontario Street, Chicago, Illinois 60611. *Died* (in New Orleans, Louisiana) *in 1985.*

Individual Exhibitions:

1965 Lowe Gallery, New Orleans
1967 Glade Gallery, New Orleans
1968 Glade Gallery, New Orleans
1969 Galerie Simonne Stern, New Orleans
       Recent Paintings and Drawings, Tampa Bay Art Center, Tampa, Florida
       Hank Baum Gallery, San Francisco
1971 Cranfill Gallery, Dallas
1972 *Drawings and Prints*, Glasgow College of Arts
       Galerie Simonne Stern, New Orleans
1973 Mills College, Oakland, California
       Galerie Simonne Stern, New Orleans
1974 New Orleans Museum of Art
1975 Long Beach Museum of Art, California (drawings)
1979 Phyllis Kind Gallery, New York
1980 *Image into Pattern*, P.S.1, New York
1981 *Robert Gordy: Paintings and Drawings 1960–1980*, New Orleans
       Museum of Art (toured the United States)

Selected Group Exhibitions:

1967 *Invitational*, Whitney Museum, New York
1969 *The Spirit of the Comics*, Institute of Contemporary Art, Philadelphia
1973 *Divergent Representation: 5 Contemporary Artists*, Smithsonian Institution, National Collection of Fine Arts, Washington, D.C.
       Extraordinary Realities, Whitney Museum, New York
1975 *Art USA: The South*, International Communications Agency (toured Central and South America)
1978 *21st National Print Exhibition*, Brooklyn Museum, New York
1979 *The 1970's: New American Painting*, International Communications Agency (toured Eastern European capitals)
1980 *The Figurative Tradition*, Whitney Museum, New York
       American Figure Painting 1950–1980, Chrysler Museum, Norfolk, Viriginia
       American Drawings in Black and White 1970–1980, Brooklyn Museum, New York

Collections:

Whitney Museum, New York; Brooklyn Museum, New York; National Collection of Fine Arts, Washington, D.C.; Corcoran Gallery, Washington, D.C.; New Orleans Museum of Art; Museum of Contemporary Art, Chicago; Museum of Fine Arts, Dallas; Fort Worth Art Center, Texas.

Publications:

By GORDY: articles—"Interview with Robert Gordy," with

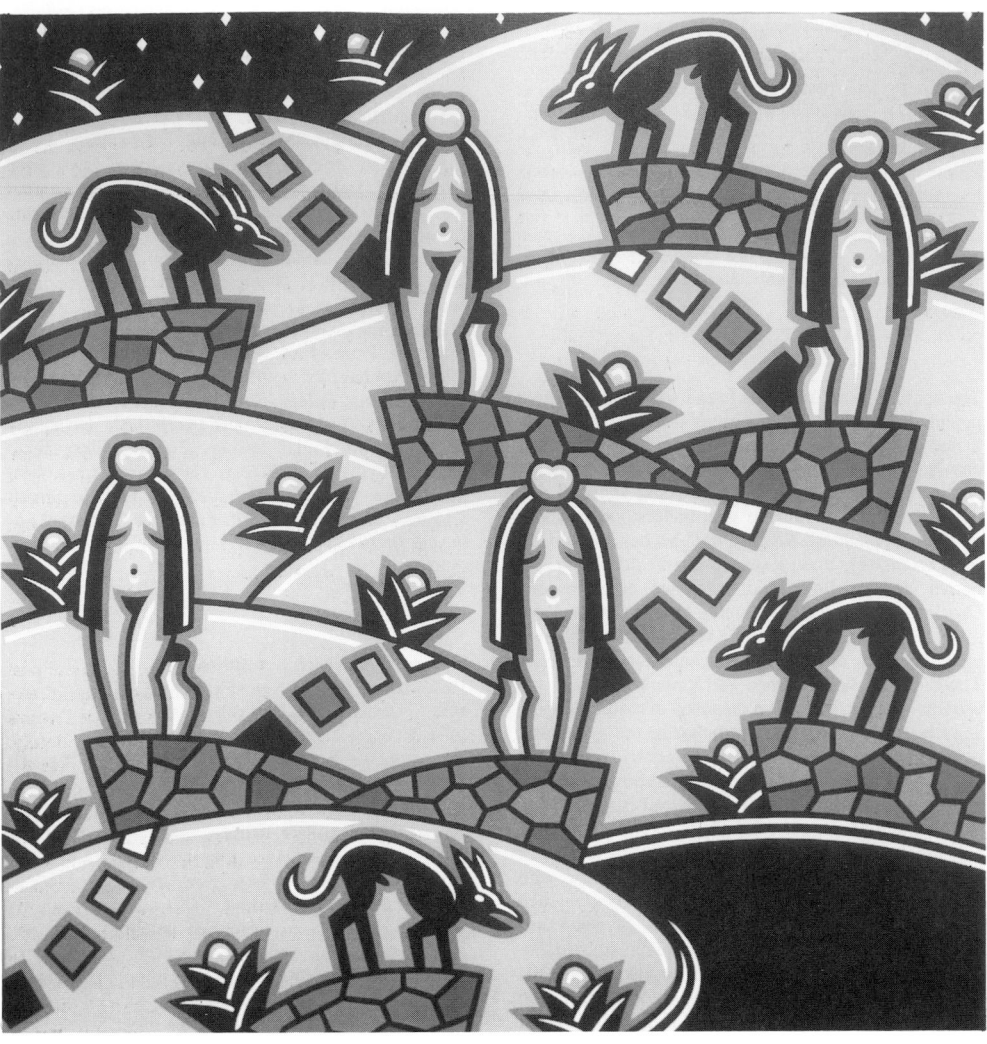

Robert Gordy: *Dog Worship No. 3*, 1974

Joseph Mashek, in *Studio International* (London), December 1969; interview, with William Fagaly, in "On Location, 4 Interviews, 6 Artists" in *Art in America* (New York), July/August 1976.

On GORDY: books—*Robert Gordy: Recent Paintings and Drawings*, exhibition catalogue, Tampa, Florida 1969; *The Spirit of the Comics*, exhibition catalogue, Philadelphia, 1969; *21st National Print Exhibition* catalogue, Brooklyn, New York 1978; *The 1970's: New American Painting* by Alan Schwartzman, Kathleen Thomas and Marcia Tucker, exhibition catalogue, new York 1979; *Robert Gordy: Paintings and Drawings 1960-1980*, exhibition catalogue, by Gene Baro, New Orleans 1981; articles—article by Ted Calas in *The Art Gallery* (Ivoryton, Connecticut), February 1968; "Native Son" by Ted Calas in *The Art Gallery* (Ivoryton, Connecticut), May 1972; "Southern Exposure" by Elizabeth Baker in *Art in America* (New York), July/August 1976; "Robert Gordy's Decorative Illusionism" by Mark Thistlewaite in *Artweek* (Oakland, California), December 1979; "Images, Patterns and the Mainstream" by Hilton Kramer in the *New York Times* (New York), 9 May 1980; "Image into Pattern at P.S.1" by Donald Kuspit in *Art in America* (New York), January 1981.

*

I intend my work to have a sense of pictorial irony. It is a little like trying to track down the abominable snowman.

—Robert Gordy (1982)

*

After extensive travel, culminating in a two-year residency in New York City, Gordy at 33 returned to his home state and settled in New Orleans in 1964. For the next two decades, he came to a limited public attention with witty, quasi-naive pattern paintings. The general form type that the artist adopted—an abstracted, good-humored linear simplification easily reminscent of 20s Art Deco stylization from Cubism—was distinct from the prevailing Pop mode in another way. Gordy's use of a repetitive, all-over flattened pattern in many of his fully resolved larger works produced a disarming decorative ease by further denying the "fine art" qualities of easel painting: From the realms of naive art and the utilitarian "crafts," pattern had not functioned as a total organizational device in earlier modernism. In this regard, Gordy's art may be taken as pioneering Pattern and Decoration, as that movement came to be known in 1975.

Although he held exhibitions in major east coast cities, Gordy was not mainstream P and D, as his idiosyncratic, perhaps Southern "regional accent" made his work appear quaint in a non-dogmatic pleasure in subtle eroticism and folk-like story-telling. And so the critical press usually stayed away. From 1982 on, Gordy produced only monotype prints of the human head alone, with a fervid intensity and search for inner meaning like Jawlensky's long series of heads begun before World War I. Less abstracted than his earlier pattern pictures, these prints were often more than 3 feet in height and at times acheived a classicizing three-dimensionality as Gordy called into play modelling skills which he had rarely before used. Through grimace and distortion, their overall expressionist message called out a grace under suffering.

—Joshua Kind

GOSEWITZ, Ludwig.
German. Born in Naumburg/Saale, 20 January 1936. Studied music at the Akademie für Tonkunst, Darmstadt, 1956–57; studied German literature, linguistics, history and philosophy at the Johann-Wolfgang-Goethe Universität, Frankfurt and Philipps Universität, Marburg/Lahn, 1957–65; studied glassblowing at the Glasfachschule, Zwiesel, Bavaria, 1972. Married Uta Lippert in 1958 (divorced, 1969); children: Aino and Valentin. Independent artist, Berlin, since 1965. Public relations manager, Springer Verlag publishers, Berlin, 1967–68; worked as a glass-blower, Berlin-Kreuzberg, 1973–78, and in various glass studios in the United States, Austria, Sweden and Britain, since 1977. Guest Instructor/Artist-in-Residence, Hochschule für Bildende Künste, Hamburg, 1981. Recipient: Will-Grohmann Prize, Akademie der Bildenden Künste, Berlin, 1974; Forderpreis, Heitland Foundation, 1981. Agents: Rene Block, c/o DAAD, Berlin (West); Edition Hundertmark, Brusseler Strasse 29, 5000 Cologne 1; Galerie Marlene Frei, P.O. Box 72, 8042 Zurich, Switzerland. Address: Helmstedter Strasse 5, 1000 Berlin 31 (West), Germany.

Individual Exhibitions:

1971   Galerie Michael Werner, Cologne
       Museum of Modern Art, Copenhagen
1972   Galerie René Block, Berlin
       Galerie Michael Werner, Cologne
1973   Galerie Cornels, Baden-Baden, West Germany
       Galerie Klein, Bonn
       Galerie Michael Werner, Cologne
1975   Galerie Stampa, Basle
1976   Galerie Nächst St. Stephan, Vienna
       Galerie A, Amsterdam
       Galerie Loa, Haarlem, Netherlands
       Galerie am Mehringdamm, Berlin
1980   Galerie Michael Werner, Cologne
       Gessamelte Werke 1960–1980 und Neues Glas, DAAD-Galerie, Berlin
1983   Galerie Petersen, West Berlin
       Galerie Fred Jahn, Munich
1985   Edition Hundertmark, Cologne
       Galerie Fred Jahn, Munich
       Galerie A, Amsterdam
1986   Galerie Marlene Frei, Zurich
       Galerie Petersen, West Berlin

Selected Group Exhibitions:

1963   *Schrift en Beeld*, Stedelijk Museum, Amsterdam
1964   *Festival der Neuen Kunst* Technische Hochschule, Aachen, West Germany
1970   *Visuelle Poesie*, Stedelijk Museum, Amsterdam
1972   *Fluxshoe*, Falmouth Art School, England (toured the U.K.)
1975   *8 from Berlin*, Fruit Market Gallery, Edinburgh
1978   *11 Artists Working in Berlin*, Whitechapel Art Gallery, London
1981   *Art Allemagne Aujourd'hui*, ARC/Musée d'Art Moderne de la Ville, Paris
1982   *Documenta 7*, Museum Fredericianum, Kassel, West Germany
1985   *Kunst in der Bundesrepublik 1945–85*, Nationalgalerie, West Berlin
1987   *Berlinart 1961–87*, Museum of Modern Art, New York (travelled to San Francisco Museum of Modern Art)

Collections:

Berlinische Galerie, West Berlin; Stadtisches Kunstmuseum, Bonn.

Publications:

By GOSEWITZ: books—*Typogramme I*, Frauenfeld, Switzerland 1962; *Von Phall zu Phall*, with Tomas and Maruta

Schmit, Berlin 1966, Cologne and New York 1971; *Anthology of Concrete Poetry*, edited by Emmett Williams, New York 1967; *Knud Pedersen: Der Kampf Gegen die Burgermusik*, Cologne 1973; *Teutonic Schmuck*, edited by David Mayor and Felipe Ehrenberg, Cullompton, Devon 1975; *Objets en Verre*, Berlin 1976; *Ludwig Gosewitz: Gesammelte Werke 1960-1980 und Neues Glas*, exhibition catalogue, with Helga Retzer, Berlin 1980; *Von Phall zu Phall*, Cologne 1982; *Continue! Variations on op. 57*, Cologne 1985; *Konstellatiionen und astrologische Diagramme*, Zurich 1986; *Die Konstruktion der Rose (fur Joseph Beuys)*, Heidelberg 1986; articles—"3 Typograms" in *Experimentalni Poezie* , Prague 1967; "Something Written" in *Fluxshoe*, exhibition catalogue, edited by David Mayor, Cullompton, Devon 1972; "Ludwig Gosewitz" in *Heute Kunst* (Dusseldorf), no. 6, 1974; "12 Zirkelkonstruktionen" in *8 from Berlin*, exhibition catalogue, Edinburgh 1975; "Stammbaum oder die Plantanenlehre" in *16 Os—und Westdeutsche Kunstler*, East Berlin 1976; "Illustration zum I Ging" and "Sonne, Mond und Sterne" in *Ausgabenr. 3* (Berlin), 1978; "7 Multiplications" in *11 Artists Working in Berlin*, exhibition catalogue, London 1978; "In der Fremde Afrika?" in *Zweitschrift* (Hannover), no. 4-5, 1979; "Die Erinnerungen" in *Zehn Jahre Edition Hundertmark*, exhibition catalogue, Berlin 1980; "15 unterschidlich verhaltnisse" in *Ludwig Gosewitz in Art Allemagne Aujourd'hui*, exhibition catalogue, Paris 1981; "From my notebook" in *Ausgabe* (Cologne), no. 7, 1982/83; "Ing K. erzahlte . . ." in *Vom Zeichen*, exhibition catalogue, Frankfurt 1985.

On GOSEWITZ: book—*Konstellationen und astrologische Diagramme*, exhibition catalogue with text by Dieter Schwarz, Zurich 1986; articles—"Sonne, Monde und Sterne" by Heinz Ohff in *Der Tagesspeigel* (Berlin), September 1972; "Die Zeichen der Erinnerung" by Dieter Buchholtz in *Generalzeiger* (Bonn), March 1973; "Philosophie mit Glas, Farnen und Bleistift" by Rosemarie Frank in *Bonner Rundschau* (Bonn), March 1973; "Asthetik, Meditatives, Zeitkritisches" in *Wiener Zeitung* (Vienna), January 1976; "Ludwig Gosewitz in der Galerie Nächst St. Stephan" in *Kurier* (Vienna), January 1976; "Ein Mystiker mit Witz" by Heinz Ohff in *Der Tagesspiegel* (Berlin), November 1980; "20 Jahre Gosewitz" by Barbara Schnierle in *Tip* (Berlin), November 1980; "Irisierende Augenweide" in *Kolner Stadtanzeiger* (Cologne), February 1985.

Why in the world aren't we interested first and foremost in what we see? Why in the world don't we start recording the truth with our sense-brain, our eyes? There is no such thing as an optical illusion. The drawings that go by that name are the first harbingers of our wonderful world. Let's start taking them seriously and start basing the way we conceptualize the world on what our eyes tell us! It all began with careful drawings of objects, simple outline drawings, some of which I filled in with color later. I can't remember ever having felt so happy as in September 1968 when I transferred the shapes of a gas cigarette lighter, an ashtray, and two pears onto paper. I made use of that particularly human freedom to take an object, a thing, with identifiable characteristics, and add something completely new to it—its image. That is happiness.

At about this time I saw a drawing by Tomas Schmit which he had made using the so-called "inversion of the circle" formula. The figure enclosed in the circle is projected outside it by the square of the circle's diameter. Where the curved lines of the figure turn a corner, the straight lines of the "squared" figure outside form an angle. The transcendence of the infinite circle is transformed by means of the finite square. An image is formed that seems to give a human dimension to the mathematical constant Pi. A new and previously hidden meaning becomes visible. A human figure reveals its relationship to that of a butterfly; the body of a boy is held up physically by the emblem sewn onto his windbreaker.

What I am trying to do—is to "detranscendentalize" the transcendence of the concept Pi, which has had an absolute hegemony in saying something meaningful about the sphere up to now, but does not actually do so in a manner that is useful or understandable in human terms—in other words, my goal is to explain the infinity of the sphere in terms of the finity of the cube. These and similar thoughts moved me to project the spatial relationships of a face and a hand onto paper. I saw points in space as the points where two spheres (on paper, two circles) intersect. (This must have been the method—passed on to initiates for generations—used by the first icon painters to project round masses onto a plane.) There is a very special quality about the points at which two systems intersect. In one drawing using this method, a shape like the wing of a butterfly may appear (the butterfly—the space animal!); in another, the positions of the planets in the solar system, usually given in terms of a unicentered system, become visible with incredible plasticity. A new geometry of the eye! The old image of the isolated living being, set out by chance on a planetary body somewhere in the trackless void of space, is confronted with a new image—that of man learning to grasp his unique home in space as the incarnation of meaning itself.

—Ludwig Gosewitz

The work of Ludwig Gosewitz, which spans almost thirty years now, includes literary texts, essays, drawings, *objets d'art* and glassware. These various means of expression bespeak, if looked at more closely, great powers of concentration, which linger over the particular rather than straining towards the monumental. Using inconspicuous materials and limiting himself to small formats and even miniatures, Gosewitz sets out from a variety of different starting points but aims repeatedly at the same goal: a correct representation of phenomena with the means at our disposal.

But which phenomena? What is meant 'correct'? And what means are there at our disposal? As an accomplished Germanist, Gosewitz does not disown his learned background. He always bears in mind the function and clarity of his designs and ignores the standards of conventional aesthetic art. His glassware is based on objects of everyday utility, as his horoscope drawings are based on experimental diagrams, and his geometric constructions on the investigation of hidden laws. This leads him to discoveries which infinitely extend the original function of his creations. During his studies of literature and philology, one branch of the latter had particularly interested Gosewitz: phonetics, which is concerned not with complex forms of speech, but with its simplest elements—sounds. Thanks to phonetics, we have methods for describing speech as abstract differentiated sounds or, conversely, for synthesising phonetic notation as speech utterances. The 'phenomena' in this area are the physically perceptible acoustic speech utterances which can be taken up, dissected and represented in a formalised fashion by the speaker himself—a cycle in which the researched remains constantly bound to the object being researched.

With regard to Gosewitz's drawings, the 'phenomena' are located, in conformity with the medium, in the visible rather than the audible, and if speech sounds always come from the speaker, the thing seen always derives from the world that confronts the eyes. Everything visible is also capable of representation—we need not speak of what is invisible—or, in Gosewitz's words, "Optical illusions do not exist." But in the same way that sounds cannot be transcribed but only analysed, so can a view not be copied but only reconstructed on paper. In drawing, Gosewitz's aim was that of art in general around 1960: to replace realistic representation with the realism of the object itself, a directly presented fragment of reality. So when Gosewitz draws something he sees, he treats the representation not as a reduction of three-dimensions to a single plane; rather, he takes into account the stereoscopic qualities of seeing with two eyes and the curvature and area of the paper surface. A body appearing before one's eyes is transmuted into another body—on paper. Out of seeing comes a new conception, not in the sense of a mere positivistic

Ludwig Gosewitz: *Radix for Mr. Gurdjieff*, 1982

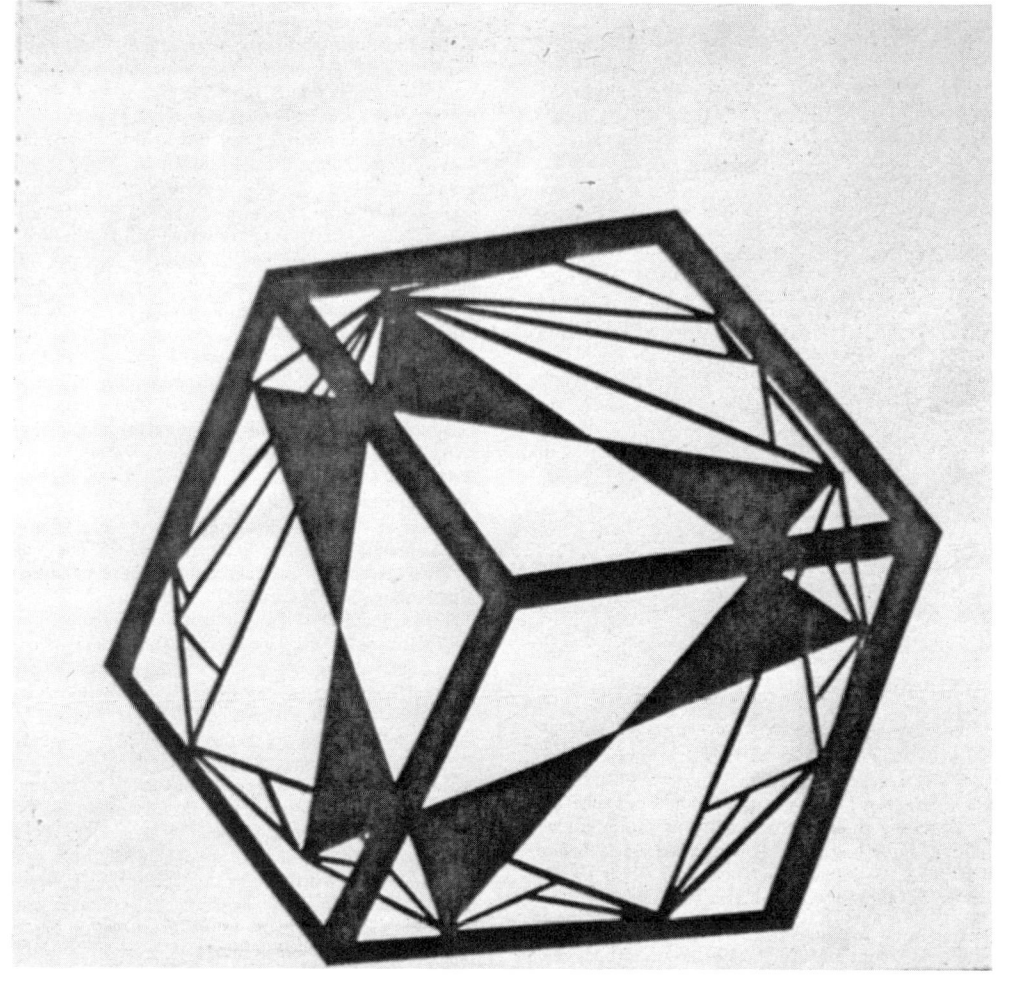

recording of facts, but in the construction of concepts such as infinity or transcendence within the finite.

In the astrological drawings, the position of the planets at the time of birth of a given individual are represented by brightly coloured segments of spheres. This design in then thrown outwards over the edges of a square which has been placed around the circle; a new design is created which—though rigidly constructed—bears a surprising relationship to the sphere segment on which it is based. In this way the transformation of one body into another is demonstrated in the drawing as a model. The constellation of planets, instead of being submitted to a narrative interpretation, becomes a picture of crystal clarity. A vision of the stars, seeing in a metaphorical sense, is represented here in a way that neither explains nor transforms. This representation holds up for us to see and compare whatever Ludwig Gosewitz, on his journey of universal reportage, deems worthy of mention.

—Dieter Schwarz

GOTTLIEB, Adolph.

American. Born in New York, 14 March 1903. Educated in the Art Students League, New York, under Robert Henri and John Sloan, 1919–21 and 1923–24; attended art classes, Académie de la Grande Chaumiére, Paris, 1921; studied at Parsons School of Design, New York, 1923; Cooper Union, New York, 1924; Educational Alliance Art School, New York, 1927–29. Married Esther Dick in 1932. Taught arts and crafts in settlement houses, New York, 1924–31; established close friendship and vacationed with Mark Rothko and Milton Avery; Co-Founder, with Rothko, Ilya Bolotowsky, Louis Harris and others, The Ten, abstract-expressionist group, New York, 1935–40; worked in the Easel Division, Works Progress Administration Federal Art Project, New York, 1936; lived in the desert, near Tucson, Arizona, 1937–39; signed statement, with Mark Rothko, Milton Avery, William Baziotes, Joseph Stella, and others, withdrawing from American Artists' Congress, and founded Federation of Modern Painters and Sculptors, New York, 1940: President, 1944–45; first pictographs, New York, 1944; settled in Easthampton, Long Island, 1960. Lecturer, Pratt Institute, Brooklyn, New York, and University of California at Los Angeles, 1958; Lecturer and Jury Member, Arizona State University, Tempe, 1973. Member, Art Commission, New York, 1967–74. Recipient: Joint Prize, Dudensing International Competition, New York, 1929; Mural Commission Award, United States Treasury, 1939; Purchase Prize, University of Illinois, Urbana, 1951; Third Prize, *Pittsburgh International,* 1961; Grand Prize, *Bienal,* Sao Paulo, 1963; American Academy of Achievement Award, Dallas, 1965. Honorary Member, National Institute of Arts and Letters, 1972. *Died* (in Easthampton, Long Island, New York) *4 March 1974.*

Individual Exhibitions:

1930	Dudensing Galleries, New York (with Konrad Cramer)
1934	Uptown Gallery, New York
	Theodore A. Kohn and Son, New York
1940	Artists Gallery, New York
1942	Artists Gallery, New York
1944	Wakefield Gallery, New York
1945	Gallery 67, New York
	Nierendorf Galleries, New York
1947	Kootz Gallery, New York
1949	Jacques Seligmann Gallery, New York
1950	Kootz Gallery, New York
1951	Kootz Gallery, New York
1952	Kootz Gallery, New York
1953	Kootz Gallery, New York
	Area Arts Gallery, San Francisco
1954	Kootz Gallery, New York
	Bennington College, Vermont (travelled to Williams College, Williamstown, Massachusetts)
1957	Martha Jackson Gallery, New York
	Jewish Museum, New York
	HCE Gallery, Provincetown, Massachusetts
1958	André Emmerich Gallery, New York
1959	André Emmerich Gallery, New York
	Galerie Rive Droit, Paris
	Institute of Contemporary Arts, London
	Paul Kantor Gallery, Beverly Hills, California
1960	Sidney Janis Gallery, New York
	Galerie Neufville, Paris
	French and Company, New York
1961	Galleria dell'Ariete, Milan
	Galerie Handschin, Basle
1962	Sidney Janis Gallery, New York
1963	Walker Art Center, Minneapolis (travelled to the *Bienal,* Sao Paulo)
1964	Marlborough Gerson Gallery, New York
1966	Marlborough Gerson Gallery, New York
	Massachusetts Institute of Technology, Cambridge
1967	Arts Club of Chicago
1968	Whitney Museum, New York/Guggenheim Museum, New York (simultaneously; travelled to the Corcoran Gallery, Washington, D.C., and Rose Art Museum, Brandeis University, Waltham, Massachusetts)
1969	Gertrude Kasle Gallery, Detroit
1970	Gertrude Kasle Gallery, Detroit
	Galleria Lorenzelli, Bergamo, Italy
	Marlborough Gallery, New York
	Marlborough Galleria d'Arte, Rome
	University of Maryland, College Park
1971	Norman MacKenzie Art Gallery, Regina, Saskatchewan
	Marlborough Fine Art, London (travelled to the Marlborough Galerie AG, Zurich, 1972)
1973	Marlborough-Godard Gallery, Toronto
	Gertrude Kasle Gallery, Detroit
1975	National Institue of Arts and Letters, New York
1977	André Emmerich Gallery, New York
	Pictographs, Edmonton Art Gallery, Alberta (toured Canada)
1979	André Emmerich Gallery, New York
1981	Corcoran Gallery of Art, Washington, D.C.
	Tampa Museum, Florida
	Toledo Museum of Art, Ohio
1982	University of Texas, Austin
	Flint Institute of Art, Michigan
	Indianapolis Museum of Art, Indiana
	Los Angeles County Museum of Art
	Albright-Knox Art Gallery, Buffalo, New York
1984	Galerie Wentzel, Cologne
1985	M. Knoedler and Company, New York
1986	Knoedler Gallery, London

Selected Group Exhibitions:

1935	*The 10,* Montross Gallery, New York
1939	*Mural Designs,* Corcoran Gallery, Washington, D.C. (travelled to the Whitney Museum, New York)
1946	*American Painting from the 18th Century to the Present Day,* Tate Gallery, London
1950	*Contemporary American Painting,* Whitney Museum, New York
1955	*International Exhibition,* Museum of Modern Art, Tokyo
1958	*Pittsburgh International,* Carnegie Institute, Pittsburgh
1963	*Bienal,* Sao Paulo
1970	*New York Painting and Sculpture 1940–70,* Metropolitan Museum, New York
1974	*The Great Decade,* Museum of Fine Arts, Houston

Collections:

Guggenheim Museum, New York; Jewish Museum, New York; Metropolitan Museum of Art, New York; Museum of Modern Art, New York; Art Institute of Chicago; Los Angeles County Museum of Art; Victoria and Albert Museum, London; Tate Gallery, London; Bezalel Museum, Jerusalem; Tel Aviv Museum.

Publications:

By GOTTLIEB: articles—letter, with Mark Rothko, in the *New York Times,* 13 June 1943; letter in the *New York Times,* 22 July 1945; "The Attitudes of 10 Artists on Their Art and Contemporaneousness" in *Tiger's Eye* (New York), December 1947; "Graphic Artists Write" in *Tiger's Eye* (New York), June 1949; "My Painting" in *Arts and Architecture* (Los Angeles) Apring 1951; "The Artist and the Public" in *Art in America* (New York), December 1954; interview, with David Sylvester, in *Living Arts* (New York), June 1963; "A New York Interview with Adolph Gottlieb," with Gordon Brown, in *Art Voices* (New York), February 1964; "Jackson Pollock: An Artists' Symposium" in *Art News* (New York), April 1967; radio program—"The Portrait and the Modern Artist," with Mark Rothko, *Art in New York,* WNYC Radio program, New York, October 1943.

On GOTTLIEB: books—*Adoph Gottlieb,* exhibition catalogue, by Martin Friedman, Minneapolis 1963; *Adolph Gottlieb* by Diane Waldman and Robert Doty, New York 1968; *Adolph Gottlieb,* exhibition catalogue, Rome 1970; *Adolph Gottlieb,* exhibition catalogue, by Harold Rosenberg, London/Zurich 1971; *Adolph Gottlieb: Pictographs,* exhibition catalogue, by Karen Wilkin, Edmonton, Alberta 1977 (with Bibliography); *Adolph Gottlieb: A Retrospective,* with texts by Lawrence Alloway and Mary Davis MacNaughton, New York 1981; *Adolph Gottlieb,* exhibition catalogue with texts by Lawrence Alloway and Clement Greenberg, Cologne 1984.

Myth does not deny things . . . simply it purifies them, it makes them innocent, it gives them a natural and eternal justification.

Roland Barthes, *Mythologies*

Adolph Gottlieb's Burst paintings, in their projection of simple polarities, have generally been seen as presenting a distinct break with the artist's Pictographs, a series of totemic images based on the format of the grid. But, in fact, a sense of continuity exists in the stylistic and conceptual evolution of Gottlieb's work. Rather than proclaiming the beginning of a new style, the Burst paintings would seem to mark the culmination of a process that began 15 years earlier.

From 1941 to 1952, Gottlieb, relying on the subject of ancient myth as his principal iconographic source, explored the formal possibilities of the Pictograph. Although Gottlieb had painted "American scenes" during the 1930's, he came to reject the provincial or political tone of established American painting—Regionalism and its urban counterpart Social Realism. The artist innately understood myth's potential for transcendence, its ability to liberate the artist from social realist concerns: "we assert that the subject is crucial," he wrote with Mark Rothko in reference to myth, "and only that subject matter is valid which is tragic and timeless." The preoccupation of the American avant-garde with the human conflicts inherent in myth (an interest rooted in the writings of Jung and seen as an answer to the Surrealist fascination with the dream) was undoubtedly a function of American pessimism during the Second World War, a pessimism intensified by the bombing of Pearl Harbor and the subsequent nuclear holocaust at Hiroshima and Nagasaki.

In fact, the early Pictographs were decidedly about the imagery of myth. Gottlieb's "Oedipus" (1941), a representative example of an early Pictograph, offers a simplistic, self-conscious projection of mythic icons on a flat, "primitive" surface. However, the artist's interest in myth waned in the late 1940's. His later Pictographs, at times untitled and thus uncharged with a verbal index from myth, lost much of the self-consciousness of the earlier works. By 1950, the interest in mythology disappeared altogether; from arrangements of mythic icons, the Pictograph had evolved into an art that was dominated by the structure of the grid. The "emergence" of the grid reached its pictorial extreme in "Construction Number 1" (1953) in which intersecting slats of wood

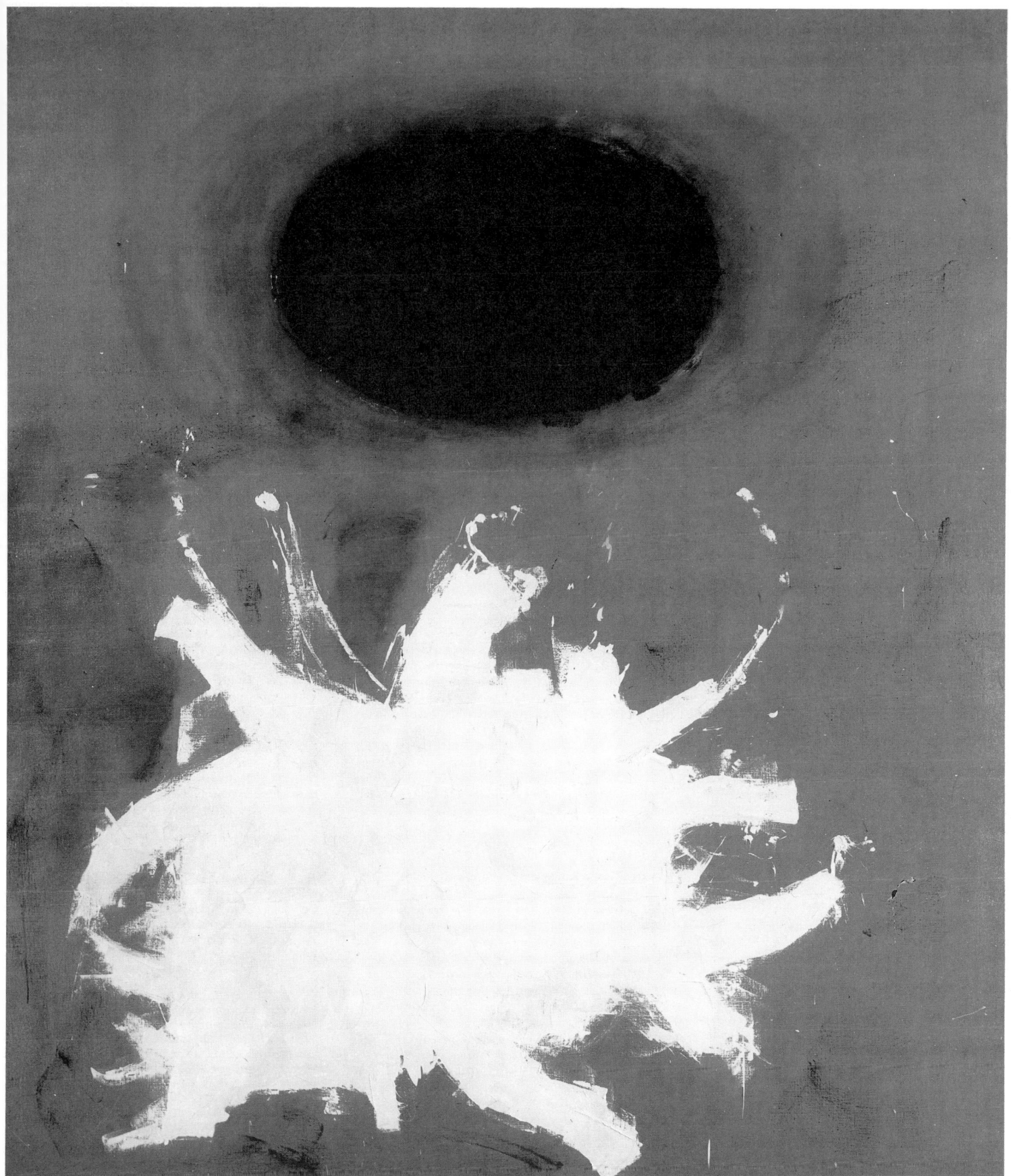

Adolph Gottlieb: *Crest*, 1959

were actually applied to the Pictograph's surface. While the grid was always essential to the composition of the Pictograph, it was at first subtle and subservient to the iconography. As the series progressed, the grid became more and more overt, ultimately supplanting all other visual considerations.

From these observations, it is clear that Gottlieb intuitively understood the ability of the grid to act as myth in its capacity to suspend conflict within its structure. The flat, non-hierarchical matrix could give him the anti-illusionism, the *truth,* that he sought. So too, the allusion to the cross, implied in the structure of the grid, would support notions of the "tragic," the "timeless," and the "spiritual" (as it had, for example, in the works of Mondrian and Malevich). In short, the grid symbolized the "neurosis" of which Gottlieb spoke; it became the force which could contain the inherent modernist conflict between truth and belief—a belief shaken by the explosive reality of the Second World War.

The development of Gottlieb's painting style in the period between the last Pictographs and the beginning of the Burst series not only strengthens the idea that the totemic paintings were about the containment of conflict, but reinforces the notion of continuity between Pictograph and Burst. As early as 1948, the grid began to disintegrate in Gottlieb's work, an effect clearly noted in "Nocturnal Beams" of 1954. In the early 1950s, in Gottlieb's Imaginary Landscapes, the canvas surface had actually polarized into two distinct horizontal zones. From these later developments Gottlieb arrived at the Burst format, a pictorial formula that would preoccupy him until his death in 1974. The simple placement of red disc over black rectangle in "Burst" of 1957 presents a dramatic polarity that alludes to a number of opposing forces; the artist's subconscious, pictographic labyrinths, had evolved into searing, explosive landscapes.

—Maurice Berger

GRAHAM, Dan.

American. Born Daniel Harry Graham in Urbana, Illinois, 31 March 1942. Independent film, video, installation and performance artist. Lectured at University of California, San Diego, 1969–70; lectured at Nova Scotia College of Art and Design, Halifax, 1970–71. Recipient: New York State Creative Artists Public Service Program Multi-Media Grant, 1973–74. Agent: Lisson Gallery, 67 Lisson Street, London NW1, England. Address: 84 Eldridge Street, New York, New York 10002, U.S.A.

Individual Exhibitions:

1969	John Daniels Gallery, New York
1970	Anna Leonowens Gallery, Nova Scotia College of Art and Design, Halifax
1972	Fourth Floor Gallery, Halifax, Nova Scotia
	Lisson Gallery, London
	Protetch-Rivkin Gallery, Washing, D.C.
	Galleria Toselli, Milan
	Project, Inc., Cambridge, Massachusetts
1973	Galerie MTL, Brussels
	Galerie Zwirner, Cologne
	Galeria Schema, Florence
	Gallery A 402, California Institue of the Arts, Valencia
1974	Galleria Marilena Bonomo, Bari, Italy
	Galerie 17, Paris
	Royal College of Art, London
	Lisson Gallery, London
1975	Modern Art Agency, Naples
	Galerie MTL, Brussels
	John Gibson Gallery, New York
	Palais des Beaux-Arts, Brussels

International Cultural Centrum, Antwerp
Otis Art Institute Gallery, Los Angeles
Griffiths Art Center, St. Lawrence University, Canton, New York

1976	Sperone Westwater Fischer, New York
	Salle Patino, Geneva
	Samangallery, Genoa
	Galerie Vega, Liège, Belgium
	Institute of Contemporary Arts, London
	Galerie Anne-Marie Verna, Zurich
	Galleria Banco, Brescia, Italy
	Kunsthalle, Basel
1977	Leeds Polytechnic Gallery, England
	René Block Galerie, Berlin
	Van Abbemuseum, Eindhoven, Netherlands
	Studio Terelli, Ferrara, Italy
	Museum van Hedendaagse Kunst, Ghent
1978	Corps de Gard, Groningen, Netherlands
	Museum of Modern Art, Oxford
1979	Franklin Furnace, New York
	Galerie Rüdiger Schöttle, Munich
	Galleria Paola Betti, Milan
	Center for Art Tapes, Halifax, Nova Scotia
	Locus Solus, Genoa
1980	Rüdiger Schöttle, Munich
	Museum of Modern Art, New York
	City of Los Angeles Central Library
	Museum of Contemporary Art, Lisbon
	Institute for Art and Urban Resources at P.S.1, New York
1981	Renaissance Society at the University of Chicago
	Center for the Arts, Muhlenberg College, Allentown, Pennsylvania
	Video at 30th Street Station, Institute of Contemporary Art, Philadelphia
	LIsson Gallery, London
	Galerie Durand-Dessert, Paris
1982	Hotel Wolfers, Brussels
1983	Kunsthalle, Berne

Selected Performances: *Lax/Relax,* Nova Scotia College of Art and Design, Halifax, 1969; *Video Camera/Monitor Performance,* Loeb Student Center, New York University, 1970; *Two Consciousness Projection(s)* and *Past Future Split Attention,* 98 Green Street Loft, New York, 1972; *Intention Intentionality Sequence I,* Lisson Gallery, London, 1972; *#7 and Nude,* Nova Scotia College of Art and Design, Halifax, 1975; *Performance/Audience Sequence,* Hallwalls, Buffalo, New York, 1975; *Performer/Audience/Mirror,* "de appel," Amsterdam, 1977; *Eventworks,* Massachusetts College of Art, Boston, 1980; *New Wave and Feminism,* Institue of Contemporary Arts, London, 1980.

Selected Group Exhibitions:

1967	*Focus on Light,* New Jersey State Museum, Trenton
1969	*Konzeption/Conception,* Stadtisches Museum, Leverkusen, West Germany
1970	*Information,* Museum of Modern Art, New York
1971	*Sonsbeek 71,* Arnhem, Netherlands
1972	*Documenta,* Kassel, West Germany
1974	*Kunst Bleibl Kunst: Projek: 74,* Kunstverein, Cologne
1974	*Video Art,* Institute of Contemporary Art, Philadelphia (travelled to the Museum of Contemporary Arts Center, Cincinnati, Ohio; Museum of Contemporary Art, Chicago; and the Wadsworth Atheneum, Hartford, Connecticut)
1976	*Ambiente Arte,* at the *Biennale,* Venice
1979	*73rd American Exhibition,* Art Institue of Chicago
1981	*Construction in Process,* Lodz, Poland

Collections:

Allen Memorial Art Museu, Oberlin, Ohio; Museum of Fine Arts, Dalls; Tate Gallery, London; Van Abbemuseum, Eindhoven, Netherlands; Centre Georges Pompidou, Paris.

Publications:

By GRAHAM: books—*Selected Works, 1965–72,* New York 1972; *Textes,* Paris 1974; *For Publication,* Los Angeles 1975; *Films,* Geneva 1977; *Articles,* edited by R. H. Fuchs, Eindhoven, Netherlands 1978; *Video-Architecture-Television: Writings on Video and Video Works 1970–1978,* Halifax, Nova Scotia and New York, 1979; *Dan Graham/Static at Riverside Studios,* Audio Arts tape edition, London 1980; *Buildings and Signs,* Chicago 1981; articles—"Homes for America" in *Arts Magazine* (New York), December/January 1966/67; "Muybridge Moments" in *Arts Magazine* (New York), February 1967; "The Book as Object" in *Arts Magazine* (New York), May 1967; "Schema" in *Aspen* (New York), no. 5–6, 1967; introductory text to *Dan Flavin,* exhibition catalogue, Chicago 1967; "Two Parallel Essays" in *Artists and Photographs,* New York 1969; editorial note and contribution, *Aspen* (New York), no. 9, 1970; "Pieces" in *Interfunktionen* (Cologne), no. 5 1970; "Thoughts on Two Structures," in *Sol LeWitt,* exhibition catalogue, The Hague 1970; "Eleven Sugar Cubes" in *Art in America* (New York), May/June 1970; "Performance as a Perceptual Process" in *Interfunktionen* (Cologne), no. 7 1971; "Film Pieces: Visual Field" in *Interfunktionen* (Cologne), no. 8 1972; "Eight Pieces by Dan Graham" in *Studio International* (london), May 1972; "TV Camera/Monito Performance: in *TDR*(New York), June 1972; "Intention Intentionality Sequence" in *Arts Magazine* (New York), April 1973; "Dan Graham I/ Eve", with Tommaso Trini, in *Domus* (Milan), February 1973; "Two Consciousness Projection(s)" in *Arts Magazine* (New York), December 1974; "The Book as Object" and "Notes on Income (Outflow) Piece" in *Interfunktionen* (Cologne), no. 11, 1974; "#7, Pefomance/Audience Sequence, Notes on 'Income Piece' " in *Control Magazine,* no. 9 1975; "The Glass Divider, Light and Social Division, Video Feedback, '+ 0' " in *Revue d'art contemporain* (Paris), September 1976; "Interior Space/Exterior Space" in *Video Art,* edited by I. Schneider and B. Korot, New York 1976; "Elements of Video/Elements of Architecture" in *Video by Artists,* edited by P. Gale, Toronto 1976; "Public space/Two Audiences" in *Art Actuel,* Skira Annual, Geneva 1977; essay in *Time,* exhibition catalogue, Philadelphia 1977; "Art in Relation to Architecture/Architecture in Relation to Art" in *Artforum* (New York), February 1979; " 'Punk': Political 'Pop' " in *Journal* (Los Angeles), March/April 1979; "Dan Graham a Linao" in *Domus* (Milan), no. 594, 1979; "Dan Graham" in *New Art* (Frisa, Italy), autumn 1980; "L'Espace de la Communication" in *Skira Annual '80,* Geneva 1980; "Signs" in *Artforum* (New York), April 1981; "New Wave Rock en het Feminiene" in *Museumiournaal* (Amsterdam), 1981; "Not Post-Modernism" in *Artforum* (New York), November 1981.

On GRAHAM: books—*Minimal Art,* edited by Gregory Battcock, New York 1968; *Conceptual Art* by Ursula Meyer, New York 1972; *6 Years: The Dematerialization of the Art Object2R* by Lucy Lippard, New York 1972; *Performance Art* by Rose Lee Goldberg, London 1980; *Dan Graham,* exhibition catalogue, Berne 1983; articles—"Quasi-Infinites and the Waning of Space" by Robert Smithson in *Arts Magazine* (New York), November 1966; "Serial Art" by Mel Bochner in *Artforum* (New York), November 1967; "Some Other Remarks" by Dan Flavin in *Artforum* (New York), December 1967; "Introduction" by Terry Atkinson in *Art and Language* (London), vol. 1, no. 1, 1968; "A Museum of Language in the Vicinity of Art" by Robert Smithson in *Art International* (Lugano, Switzerland), March 1968; "Dan Graham" by David Antin in *Studio International* (London), July 1970; "Body Art" by Cindy Nemser in *Arts Magazine* (New York), September 1971; "Pier 18" by Robert Pincus-Witten in *Artforum* (New York), September 1971; "Artist as Filmmaker" by Annabel Nicholson in *Art and Artists* (London), December 1972; "Video" by Wulf Herzogenrath and Marlis Grüterich in *Kunst Magazine* (Mainz), no. 4, 1974; "A Space, A Thousand Words" by Rose Lee Goldberg in *Architectural Design* (New York), May 1976; "Pygmalion Reversed" by Max Kozloff in *Artforum* (New York), November 1975; "Past/ Present" by Rosemary Mayer in *Art in America* (New York), November-December 1975; "Performance" by Marc Chaimowicz in *Studio International* (London), January/ February 1976; "Dan Graham: Appearing in Public" by Eric Cameron in *Artforum* (New York), November 1976; "Dingen gebeuren binnen het gezichtsveld" by Antje von Graevenitz in *Museumjournaal* (Amsterdam), no. 2, 1977; "Moments of History in the Work of Dan Graham" by B. H. D. Buchloh in *Articles,* Erindhoven, Netherlands 1978; introduction by Judity Tannenbaum to *Concept/Narrative/Docment,* exhibition catalogue, Chicago 1979; "A Contemplative Chicago Show" by John Russell in the *New York Times,* 29 July 1979; "Dan Graham, Paola Beti/Milano" by Louisa Somaini in *Flash Art* (Milan), June/July 1979; "Dan Graham at the Mudd Club" by Amy Taubin in *SoHo Weekly News* (New York), 14 June 1979; "Conceptual Art and the Continuing Quest for a New Social Context" by Robert Morgan in *Journal* (Los Angeles), June/July 1979; "Dan Graham" in *Saman* (Genoa), March/April 1979.

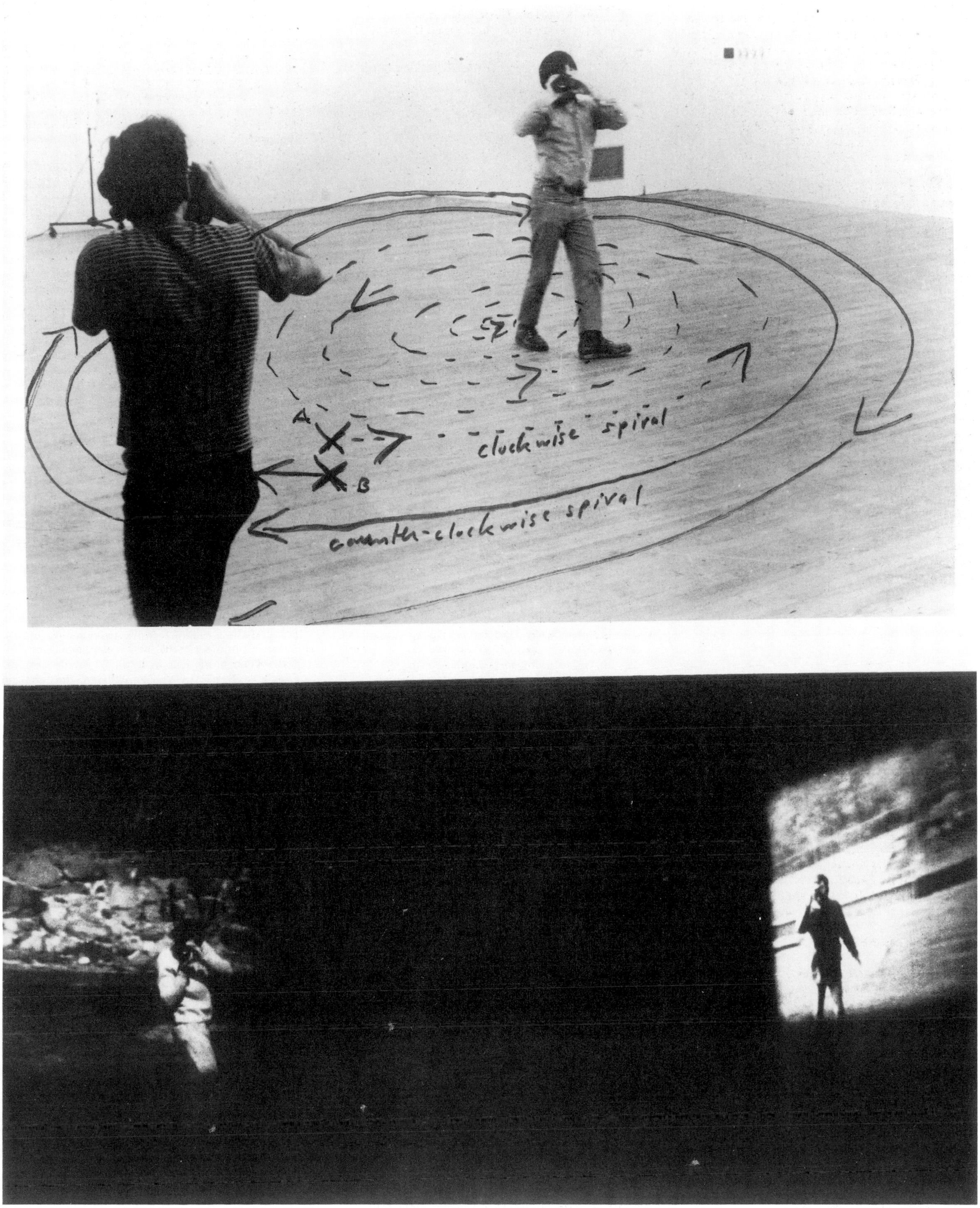

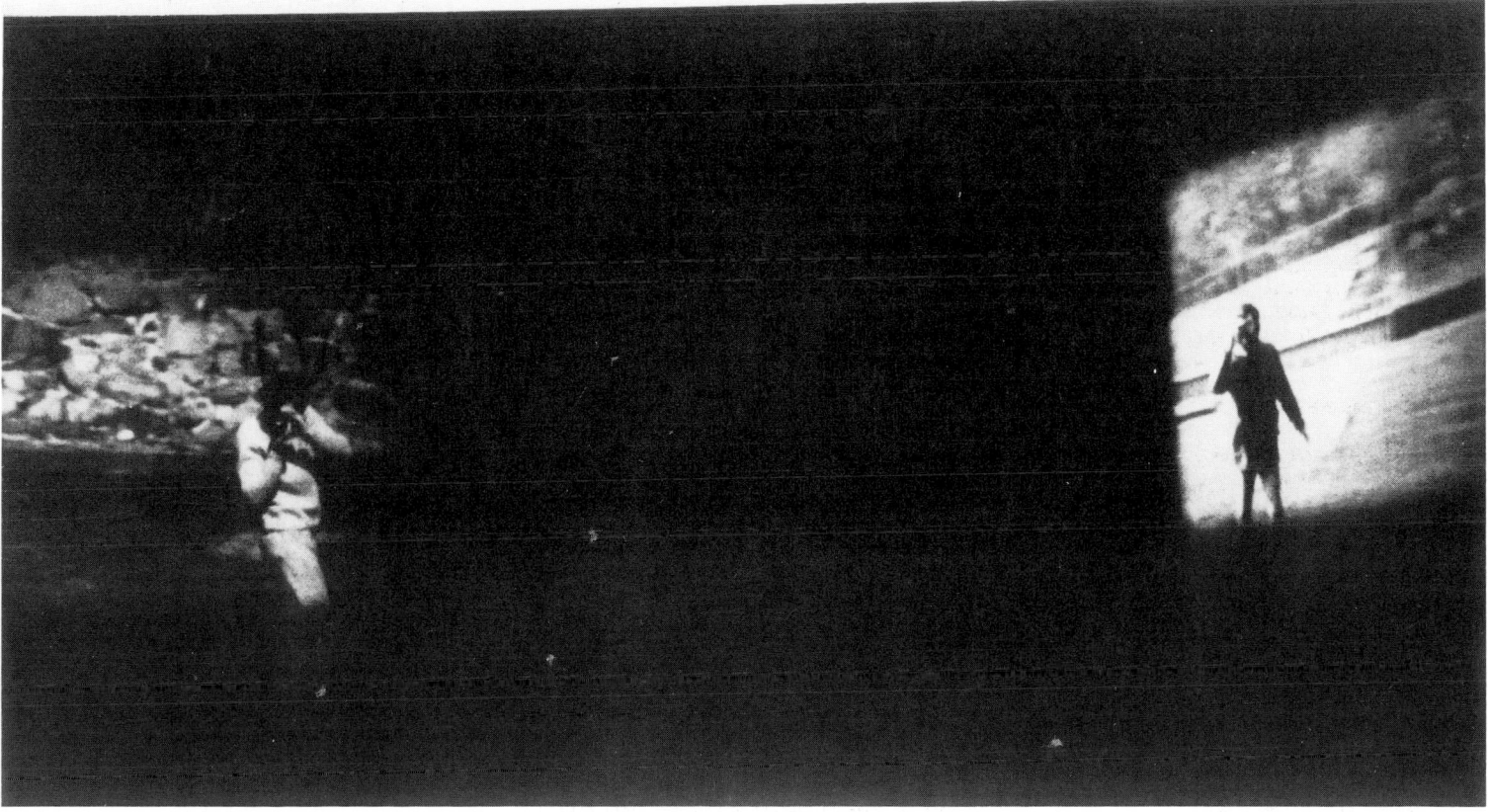

Dan Graham: *Two Correlated Rotations*, 1969

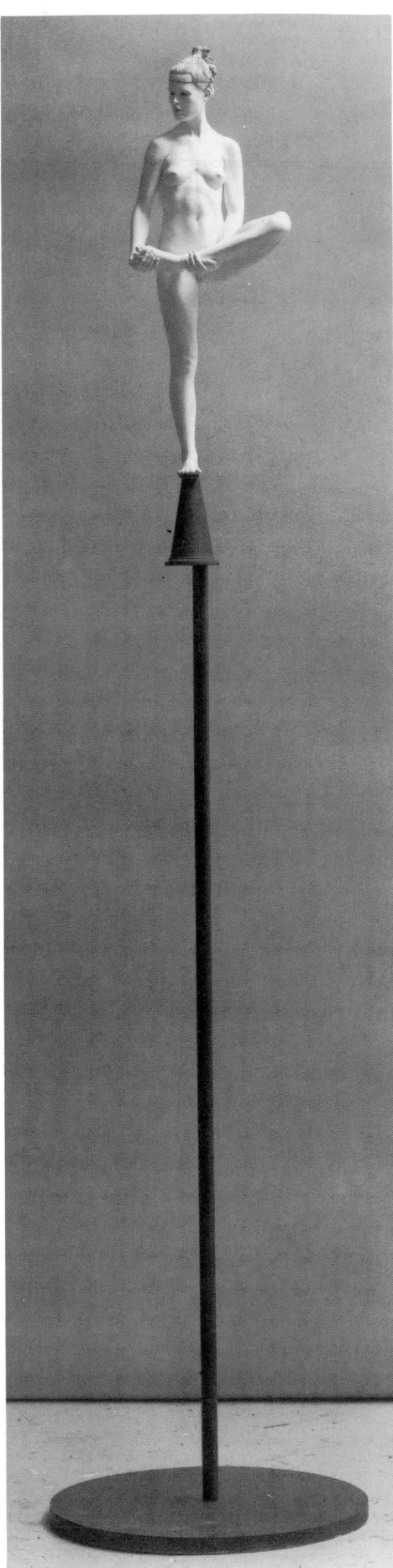

Robert Graham: *Lise—Dance Figure I*, 1979

GRAHAM, Robert.

American. Born in Mexico City, Mexico, 19 August 1938. Educated at San Jose State College, California, 1961–63; San Francisco Art Institute, 1963–64. Lived in Los Angeles and began making small art figures, 1964–69; lived and worked in London, 1969–70, then returned to Venice, California. Address: 69 Windward Avenue, Venice, California 90291 U.S.A.

Individual Exhibitions:

1964 Lanyon Gallery, Palo Alto, California
1966 Nicholas Wilder Gallery, Los Angeles
1967 Nicholas Wilder Gallery, Los Angeles
      Galerie Thelen, Essen
1968 Kornblee Gallery, New York
      Galerie Neuendorf, Hamburg
      Galerie Zwirner, Cologne
      Galerie Neuendorf, Cologne
1969 Kornblee Gallery, New York
      Nicholas Wilder Gallery, Los Angeles
1970 Galerie Neuendorf, Hamburg
      Galerie Neuendorf, Cologne
      Galerie Mollenhoff, Cologne
      Galerie Rene Block, Berlin
      Whitechapel Art Gallery, London
1971 Sonnabend Gallery, New York
      Kunstverein, Hamburg
1972 Galerie Herbert Meyer-Ellinger, Frankfurt
      Museum of Fine Arts, Dallas
      Courtney Sale Gallery, Dallas
1974 Nicholas Wilder Gallery, Los Angeles
      Galerie Neuendorf, Hamburg
      Galerie Zwirner, Cologne
      Felicity Samuel Gallery, London
      Galerie Neuendorf, Cologne
      Gimpel and Hanover Galerie, Zurich
      Texas Gallery, Houston
1975 Felicity Samuel Gallery, London
      Gimpel and Hanover Galerie, Zurich
      Texas Gallery, Houston
      Dorothy Rosenthal Gallery, Chicago
      Gimpel and Hanover Gallery, at the *Basel Art Fair*
      Nicholas Wilder Gallery, Los Angeles
1976 Greenberg Gallery, St. Louis
      Galerie Neuendorf, Hamburg
      Galerie Neuendorf, Cologne
      Gimpel Fils, London
1977 Nicholas Wilder Gallery, Los Angeles
      John Stoller Gallery, Minneapolis
1978 Robert Miller Gallery, New York
      Dorothy Rosenthal Gallery, Chicago
      Los Angeles County Museum of Art
1979 Robert Miller Gallery, New York
      Galerie Neuendorf, Hamburg
      Dag Hammarskjold Plaza, New York
1980 Dorothy Rosenthal Gallery, Chicago
1981 Los Angeles County Museum of Art
      Walker Art Center, Minneapolis
1982 Norton Gallery, West Palm Beach, Florida
1983 Des Moines Art Center, Iowa
      San Francisco Museum of Modern Art
      Joslyn Art Museum, Omaha

Selected Group Exhibitions:

1966 *Whitney Biennial*, Whitney Museum, New York (and 1969, 1971)
1971 *3 Americans*, Victoria and Albert Museum, London
1972 *West Coast U.S.A.*, Kunstverein, Hamburg (toured Germany)
1974 *Biennial*, Art Instiue of Chicago
1975 *Sculpture: American Directions 1945-1975*, National Collection of Fine Arts, Smithsonian Institution, Washington, D.C.
1976 *L.A. 8: Painting and Sculpture 76*, Los Angeles County Museum of Art
      Painting and Sculpture in California: The Modern Era, San Francisco Museum of Modern Art

1978 *Contemporary Artists Series, Number 1*, Rutgers University Art Gallery, New Brunswick, New Jersey
1980 *Aspects of the 70's: Directions in Realism*, Danforth Museum, Farmington, Massachusetts
1986 *California Sculpture 1959-80*, San Francisco Museum of Modern Art

Collections:

Museum of Modern Art, New York; Whitney Museum, New York; Hirshhorn Museum and Sculpture Garden, Washington, D.C.; Los Angeles County Museum of Art; Oakland Museum of Art, California; San Francisco Museum of Modern Art; Hamburg Kunst Museum; Kunst Museum, Cologne; Museum Ludwig, Aachen, West Germany.

Publications:

On GRAHAM: books—*Robert Graham 1963-1969*, exhibition catalogue, Cologne 1970; *Robert Graham: Statues* by Graham W. J. Beal and George W. Neubert, Minneapolis 1981; articles—"Through Western Eyes" by Leo Rubinfien in *Art in America* (New York), September/October 1978; "Robert Graham: Ignoring the Lessons of Modern Art" by Barbara Isenberg in *Art News* (New York), January 1979; "The Collectors: Contemporary Elan" by Peter Carlsen in *Architectural Digest* (New York), March 1979; "ART: American Figurative Sculpture" by David Bourdon in *Architectural Digest* (New York), November 1979; "Critic's Choice" by Grace Glueck in the *New York Times*, 23 November 1979; "Robert Graham" by Jon R. Friedman in *Arts Magazine* (New York), January 1980; "Robert Graham" by Tomas Lawson in *Flash Art* (Milan), January/February 1980; "'Local' Art Hits the Big Time" by Michael Tennesen and Richard B. Marks in *Los Angeles Magazine*, February 1980; "Wheels and Deals Keep California Venice Spinning" by Charles Lockwood in the *Smithsonian* (Washington, D.C.), March 1980.

The strength of Robert Graham's compelling bronzes derives from a series of subtle, overlapping oppositions. Though life-like in detail if not in size, the women he depicts are imbued with a distinct element of the hallucinatory. The effect holds the viewer at a psychological distance, who, as a matter of recourse, sees them as types rather than as individuals. With increasing accuracy Graham transposes his studio model into permanent form, maintaining that the sculptures serve not only as reproduction but also as "a metaphor for the human spirit."

Nearly all of Graham's career has been devoted to the human figure. During his early narrative stage in the sixties, when his medium was wax, the psychological tensions began to emerge from his work. Graham's wax miniature sybarites were applauded for their equisite detail, yet covered by their plexiglass domes they remained remote and permanently separated from the viewer's world. They were kept in a vacuum, sealed from touch, off-setting the onlooker's sense of scale, forcing him into the role of voyeur. With the actual distance between sculpture and viewer indeterminate, the tiny personages were both approachable and distant.

Around 1970 Graham diverted his attention from narrative sculpture to experimenting with simultaneous views of the same figure. For the first time he employed a camera and a casting mold, two devices he found crucial for his subsequent work. Graham's first series of bronze pieces recalled the 19th Century Eadweard Muybridge photographs of figures in action. Engaged in simple movements—walking, bending, arising—Graham strove to make every gesture a simple and as immediate as possible, thereby eliminating the ambiguity of the earlier works. Graham's deepening interest in fusing motion into his composition resolved into a lengthy series of reference photographs. After photographing different models, each one executing basic actions in different ways, he derived a master figure from which the mold of subsequent figures was made.

Graham's wax figures progressed into bronze in 1971. With this came the departure of the plexiglass covers and the descriptive colouring he applied to the wax. The ambiguities returned however. In his 1973 "Single Head", Graham defiantly executes a "bust" whose portrayal of face and shoulders is sensitive and veristic, yet lacking in two important animating features—the head is hairless and the eyes have no pupils.

His 1973 "Eight Heads", a piece in which each head bears a distinct facial expression, assumes classical overtones. With both hair and pupils still absent, the piece seems, paradoxically, complete within itself and, as one critic described, "from another world". The plexiglass that once separated onlookers physically has been replaced by a psychological barrier. Again the spectator is forced to become a voyeur.

Graham abandoned his eerie, science-fiction personages in the following years in pursuit of depicting specific individuals. This shift in focus necessitated a dramatic increase in scale. As his attention to detail heightened, the sense of real flesh and bone, of contours and dimples, intensified the reality of the bronze. Ironically the soothing order is disrupted by the abrupt, almost brutal truncation of the figure. The viewer is thus trapped between the astonishing realism and the drastic editing.

In 1977 Graham returned to a convention he still favours: a figure approximately three feet tall on a minimal geometric base. He introduced the anatomically precise 'Lise' series whose poses range from the passivity of 'Lise I' to the near swagger of 'Lise II,' to the defiance of 'Lise III.' For the first time the figures seem to be observing the viewer as he observes them. In this series, Graham delicately shifts the literal interpretations of the statues to meaphorical: by reducing the scale he has distilled the figure to its essence.

Graham uses oil paint to colour his statues. Flesh colour becomes less important to him as he moves to using his own black and white photos for research. His concern, instead, rests with tonal values and thus he opts for a narrow range of purples, grays and greens. The bloodless hues created by these colours disturb the realistic modeling of the nudes, further contributing to the emotional gap between viewer and figure.

—Carrie Barker

GRAUBNER, Gotthard.

German. Born in Erlbach, Vogtland, 13 June 1920. Studied at the Hochschule für Bildende Künste, Berlin, 1947–48; Kunstakademie, Dresden, 1948–49,1951; Staatliche Kunstakademie, Dusseldorf, 1954–59. Independent painter, Dusseldorf, since 1959. Art Instructor, Lessing-Gymnasium, Dusseldorf, 1964–65; Instructor, 1965–69, and since 1969 Professor, Kunstakademie, Hamburg; Professor , Staatliche Kunstakademie, Dusseldorf, since 1976. Agent: Galerie M Bochum. Haus Weitmar, 4630 Bochum, West Germany. Address: Lohengrinstrasse 7, 4000 Dusseldorf-Oberkassel, West Germany.

Individual Exhibitions:

1960 Galerie Schmela, Dusseldorf
1964 Galerie D. Frankfurt
1965 Op Art Galerie, Esslingen, West Germany
Galerie H., Hannover
1966 Galerie Schmela, Dusseldorf
Modern Art Muscum, Munich
1967 Wide White Space Gallery, Antwerp
1969 Galerie Thomas, Munich
Kestner-Gesellschaft, Hannover
Stadtisches Museum, Leverkusen, West Germany
Kunsthalle, Dusseldorf
Kunstakademie, Braunschweig, West Germany
Galerie Ernst, Hannover
1970 Kunstverein für die Rheinlande und Westfalen, Dusseldorf
Kunsthalle, Cologne
1972 Galerie Schmela, Dusseldorf
Galerie Hans Meyer-Denise René, Dusseldorf
Galerie Elke Droscher, Hamburg
1974 André Emmerich Gallery, New York
1975 Galerie M, The Hague
Kunsthalle, Hamburg
Galerie Schellmann und Kluser, Munich
Galerie Elke Droscher, Hamburg
1976 Galerie André Emmerich, Zurich
Galerie René Ziegler, Zurich
Galerie Art in Progress, Munich
1977 Galerie M. Bochum, West Germany
Stadtische Kunsthalle, Dusseldorf
1978 Frankfurter Kunstverein, Frankfurt
Galerie Folker Skulima, Berlin
1979 Galerie Defet, Nuremberg
1980 Kunsthalle, Tübingen
Galerie Art in Progress, Munich
Kunsthalle, Baden-Baden, West Germany
1982 Stadtisches Museum, Monchengladbach, West Germany
1983 Kunstmuseum, Dusseldorf
Konsthall, Malmo, Sweden
1985 Galerie M, Bochum, West Germany
Kirche Sankt Markus-Nied, Frankfurt
Galerie Defet, Nuremberg, West Germany
Galerie Nordenhake, Malmo, Sweden
Raum fur Malerei, Cologne
1986 Stadtisches Munstmuseum, Bonn
1987 Kunstsammlung Nordrhein-Westfalen, Dusseldorf
Galerie Schmela, Dusseldorf

Selected Group Exhibitios:

1957 *Das Rote Bild*, Abendausstellung, Dusseldorf
1962 *Neue Tendenzen*, Galerie Orez, The Hague
1965 *Group Zero*, Washington Gallery of Modern Art, Washington, D.C.
1970 *Strategy: Get Arts*, Richard Demarco Gallery, Edinburgh
1971 *Bienal*, Sao Paulo
1974 *Geplante Malerei*, Westfalischer Kunstverein, Munster, West Germany
1977 *Documenta 6*, Museum Fridericianum, Kassel, West Germany
1979 *Soft-Art*, Kunsthaus, Zurich
1982 *Biennale*, Venice
1985 *Zeichner in Dusseldorf 1955–85*, Kunstmuseum, Dusseldorf
1987 *Der unverbrauchte Blick*, Martin-Gropius-Bau, West Berlin

Collections:

Nationalgalerie, Berlin; Wallraf-Richartz Museum and Museum Ludwig, Cologne; Städtische Kunstmuseum, Dusseldorf; Staatsgaiene, Stuttpart; Neue Pinakothek, Munich; Kaiser-Wilhelm Museum, Krefeld, West Germany; Kunsthalle, Hamburg; Westfalisches Landesmuseum, Münster, West Germany; Rheinisches Landesmuseum, Bonn; Museum of Contemporary Art, Rio de Janeiro.

Publications:

By GRAUBNER: articles—in *Europaische Avantgarde*, Frankfurt 1963; in *Zauber des Lichts*, Recklinghausen, West Germany 1967.

On GRAUBNER: books—*Kunst Heute* by Jürgen Claus, Hamburg 1965; *Kunst unsere Zrit* by Will Grohmann, Cologne 1966; *Gedicht für Gotthard Graubner* by Franz Mon, Dusseldorf 1969; *Gotthard Graubner,* exhibition catalogue, with texts by Wieland Schmied and Volker Kahmen, Hannover 1969; *Noch Kunst* by Rolf-Günter Dienst, Dusseldorf 1970; *Deutsche Kunst* by Rolf-Günter Dienst, Cologne 1970; *Erotik in der Kunst* by Volker Kahmen, Tübingen 1971; *Kunst Heute* by Karin Thomas, Cologne 1971; *Gotthard Graubner* by Dietrich Helms, Recklinghausen, West Germany 1974; *Malerei nach 1945* by Wieland Schmied, Berlin 1975; *Sammlung Nordrhein-Westfalen* by Werner Schmalenbach, Dusseldorf 1975; *Gotthard Graubner,* exhibition catalogue, with text by Werner Hofmann and others, Hamburg 1975; *Gotthard Graubner: Malerei und Arbeit auf Papier 1958-1975,* exhibition catalogue, with text by Margit Staber, Zurich 1976; *Gotthard Graubner,* exhibition catalogue, with texts by H. A. Peters, K. Schmidt, M. Imdahl and V. Kahmen, Baden-Baden, West Germany 1980; *Gotthard Graubner,* exhibition catalogue with texts by Max Imdahl and Volker Kahmen, Malmo 1983; *Gotthard Graubner,* exhibition catalogue with essays by Max Imdahl and Joern Merkert, Dusseldorf 1986.

*

My paintings wax and wane depending on the light; beginning and ending are interchangeable. They describe no condition; they are a transition.

The action of the paint is crucial. At times, only one realm of color is necessary. The relationship between cold and warm values calls for tension and exchange. The paint spreads over the surface as if of its own volition. Its consistency dictates its movement, the way in which it runs its unconscious race. It arrives at dams; the color moves in the train of accumulations of pigment. The surface breathes.

The painter is responsible for this creation. He controls the execution of the painting's incidents and is thereby exalted to a process of meditation.

—Gotthard Graubner

GRAU-GARRIGA, Josep.

Spanish. Born in San Cugat del Valles, near Barcelona, 18 February 1929. Studied at the Escuela de Artes y Officios, Barcelona, 1943–47; Escuela Superior de Bellas Artes, Barcelona, 1947–51. Served in 1st Mountain Regiment, Spanish Army, Valle de Aran, 1952; soldier 2nd class. Married Aurea Quintana Baules in 1960 (separated, 1969); chidren: Esther and Jordi. Worked in interior design studio, Barcelona, 1943–45, and in graphic design studio, Barcelona, 1945–47; in Jean Lurcat's tapestry studio, Paris, 1958. Painter and tapestry artist, Barcelona, since 1953. Director, Catalan School of Tapestry, San Cugat del Valles, Barcelona, from 1958; Drawing Instructor, Montserrat Monastery, Barcelona, 1958–62, and Eina School of Design, Barcelona, 1965–66; Tapestry Instructor, Esculade de Artes y Officios, Barcelona, 1968; University of Art and Architecture, Marseille-Luminy 1972; Rochester Institute of Technology, New York, 1974, and Workshop in Fiber Expression, Costa Mesa, California, 1974. Agent: Arras Gallery, 24 West 57th Street, New York, New York 10019, U.S.A. Address: 373 Travessera de las Corts, Barcelon-29, Spain.

Individual Exhibitions:

1953 Monastery, San Cugat del Valles, Barcelona
1964 Sal Gaspar, Barcelona
1967 Sala Mainel, Burgos, Spain
Casa del Siglo 15, Segovia, Spain
Amics de les Arts, Manresa, Spain
Monastery, San Cugat del Valles, Barcelona
Museo de Arte Contemporaneo, Madrid
1968 Galerie La Demeure, Paris
Sala Domingo, Sao Paulo, Brazil
Sala Santa Catalina del Ateneo, Madrid
1969 Amics de l' Art, Terrassa, Spain
Galeria Galdeano, Zaragoza
Galerie La Demeure, Paris
1970 De Cordova Museum, Lincoln, Massachusetts
Galerie La Demeure, Paris
1971 *Retrospective Exhibit 1960-70*, Museum of Fine Arts, Houston
Arras Gallery, New York
Institute of International Education, New York
Birmingham Museum of Fine Arts, Alabama
1972 Galeria Antanona, Caracas
University of Marseille-Luminy, France

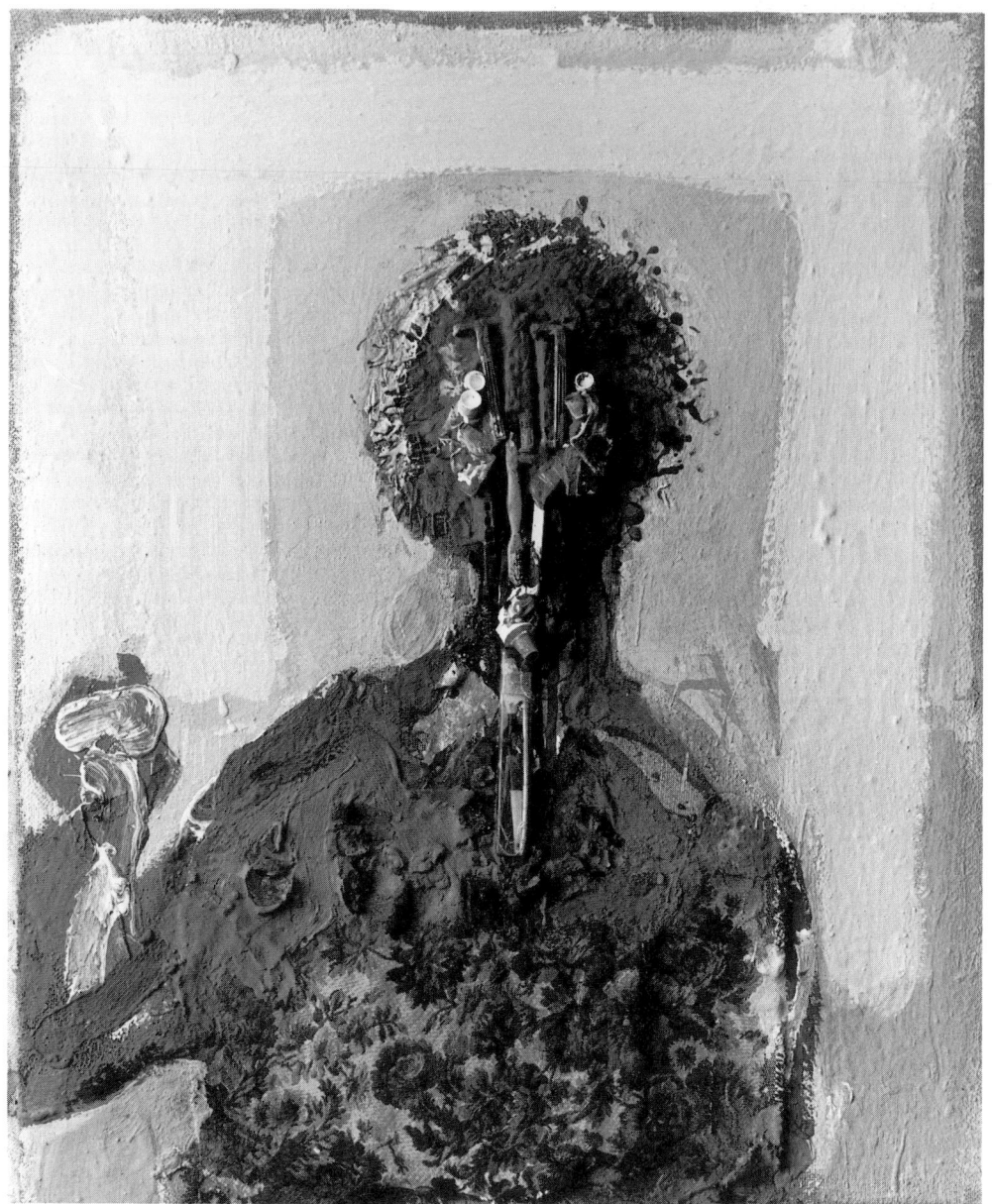

Josep Grau-Carriga: *Trabestit*, 1986

Museo Oviedo, Spain
Casa Municipal de Cultura, Aviles, Spain
Galeria Parc, Andorra
Maison de la Culture Le Parvis, Tarbes, France
Palacio de los Cordovas, Granada, Spain
Institut Francais, Barcelona
Musee Hyacinthe Rigaud, Perpignan, France
Casa Pairal Le Castillet, Perpignan, France
Musee Puig-Cdacc, Perpignan, France
Musee de la Chartreuse, Douai, France
Centre Cultural Manuel de Falla, Granada

1985 Musee de Montbeliard, France
Cloitre du Monastere de Sant Cugat del Valles, Barcelona
Aula de Cultura, Alacant, Spain
Chateau de Benedormiens, Castell d'Aro, Spain

1986 Galerie Expo-Art, Girona, Spain
Maison de la Cultura, Alcoi, Spain
Musee de Granollers, Barcelona
Abbaye des Cordeliers, Chateauroux, France

Selected Group Exhibitions:

1961 *Tapissos Contemporanis*, Galeria Biosca, Madrid
1965 *2nd Biennale de la Tapisserie*, Lausanne, Switzerland
1968 *Contemporary Tapestries*, IBM Gallery, New York
1971 *Filet Fer*, Musée de la Tapisserie, Aix-en-Provence, France
1972 *Fiber Structures*, Denver Art Museum
1976 *Contemporary European Tapestries*, Museum of Contemporary Art, Tokyo (travelled to Museum of Contemporary Art, Kyoto)
1978 *L'Art Moderne dans les Musées de Province*, Grand Palais, Paris
1983 *Aspectes de la pintura contemporania a Europa 1945–83*, Conselleria de Cultura, Andorra
1986 *La Tapisserie en France*, Musee Departemental de la Tapisserie, Aubusson, France

Collections:

Museo de Arte Contemporaneo, Madrid; Museo de Arte Contemporaneo, Seville; Museo Provincial Textil, Terrassa, Barcelona; Musée d'Art Moderne de la Ville, Paris; Musée Cantini, Marseilles; Musée Reattu, Arles, France; Metropolitan Museum of Art, New York; Museum of Fine Arts, Houston; Denver Art Museum; Museo Rufino Tamayo, Mexico City.

Publications:

On GRAU-GARRIGA: books—*Grau-Garriga: Retrospective Exhibit 1960–70*, exhibition catalogue, with texts by Georges Boudaille, Alexandre Cirici-Pellicer and Philippe de Montebello, Houston 1971; *La Nouvelle Tapisserie* by A. Kuenzi, Geneva 1972; *Grau-Garriga: Pintures, Tapissos*, exhibition catalogue, with texts by J. Corredor Mattheos and Alain Ohnenwald, Andorra 1972; *Cumella/Grau-Garriga*, exhibition catalogue/book by André Barey, Paris 1974; *Josep Grau-Garriga*, exhibition catalogue, with an introduction by George F. Kuebler, Oklahoma City 1975; *La Palabra del Arte* by Baltasar Porcel, Madrid 1976; *Textile Sculptures* by Irene Waller, London 1977; *Grau-Garriga* by Arnau Puig, Barcelona 1977; *Grau-Garriga en el Todo* by Baltasar Porcel, Barcelona 1978; *Grau-Garriga: Dibuixos del 1957 al 1978*, exhibition catalogue, with an introduction by José Maria Valverde, Barcelona 1979; *J. Grau-Garriga*, exhibition catalogue, with text by Alain Ohnenwald, Toulouse 1981; *Grau-Garriga* by Alain Ohnenwald, Paris 1982; *Josep Grau-Garriga*, exhibition catalogue, with texts by Bernadette Contensou and Alain Ohnenwald, Carcassonne, France 1982; *Grau-Garriga* by Arnau Puig, Barcelona 1985; *Grau-Garriga* by Enrique Llobregat, Gandia 1985; *Grau-Garriga a Chateauroux*, exhibition catalogue with texts by Arnau Puig, Lucien Cruzi and others, Chateauroux 1986.

Pintures, Tapissos, Sala del Consell General de les Valls, Andorra
Maison de la Culture, Rennes, France

1973 Galeria Rene Metras, Barcelona
Hospital de la Santa Creu, Barcelona
Arras Gallery, New York
Museu Provincial Textil, Terrassa, Spain (retrospective)

1974 Banco de Granada, Spain
Los Angeles County Museum of Art (retrospective)
Arras Gallery, New York
Maison de Culture, Rennes, France (with Antoni Cumella; toured France)

1975 Galerie La Demeure, Paris
Oklahoma Art Center, Oklahoma City (retrospective)
Birmingham Museum of Fine Arts, Alabama
Ohio State University, Columbus
Centre Culturel de Marais, Paris

1976 Palacio de la Lonja, Zaragoza
Prisma Galeria, Zaragoza
Université d'Angerts, France
Arras Gallery, New York
Monastery of Montmajour, Angers, France
Chateau de Nascoil, France (with Olga de Amaral)
University of Wisconsin at Eau Claire
Sanctuari de Meritxell, Andorra

1977 Arras Gallery, New York
Galeria Atenas, Zaragoza

1978 The Gallery at 24, Miami
Galeria Febo, San Gugat del Valles, Barcelona
Ecole des Beaux-Arts, Lyons

1979 Galeria Ficares, Almagro, Ciudad Real, Spain
Gra-Garriga: Dibuixos del 1957 al 1978, Monastery, San cugat del Valles, Barcelona
Galerie de l'Orangerie, Dieppe, France
Montgomery College, Washington, D.C.
Placa Sant Jaume, Barcelona

1980 Grau-Garriga-Sutido Concept, Harmelen, Netherlands
Arras Gallery, New York
Galeria Brossoli, Barcelona
Hyatt Hotel, Dubai, United Arab Emirates (permanent installation)

1981 Galerie les Couteliers, Toulouse

1982 Les Tours Narbonnaises, Carcassonne, France
Crocker Art Museum, Sacramento, California
Palais de Congres et Culture, Le Mans, France
Salle d'Expositions Permanentes, Andorra

1983 Maison de la Culture, Nantes, France
Maison de la Culture Le Parvis, Tarbes, France
Musee Goya, Castres, France
Musee Cambous, Montpellier, France
Galerie Margall, Montpellier, France
Caixa de Pensions, Valencia
Arras Gallery, New York

1984 Museo Gijon, Spain
Galeria Pinole, Gijon, Spain

In my work, I make use of the object (specially in painting), that has personal connotations. It seems to me more valid and authentic to use simple forms than beautiful ones. I am much more interested in reality itself than its representation. In tapestry I use materials that are tied to my memories and the image of my land. I try to reaffirm their value so that they speak for themselves. I only want to make evident what is already there. I am very much in love with life, and it may be because of that I am frequently touched by its sarcastic dramatism.

To me the work of art should be the author's own reflexion. After it achieves liberty, it has to denounce injustice, to introduce new forms, to meet and to express itself as an absolute lover of beauty in all senses.

I believe that the most important thing that I can say about my work is that it is more than an intent of approach of my sensations to other people, that these intimate sensations are strengthened and motivated by the exterior world for which I feel a total love. Every factor of life affects me, especially when it is a problem. By natural inclination, I take sides for two persecuted minorities and for the revindications that I believe in. I cannot stay indifferent, and therefore take a partisan position. Therefore, in my work what I try to tell is more important than the way I tell it. I believe that the content in the work of art is what communicates the artist's feelings to people and so is everlasting. I am interested in formal problems, for they are useful to express myself in my own way, but I see very clearly the esthetic problems.

—Josep Grau-Garriga

Joseph Grau-Garriga is a painter and tapestry designer, who should be described as a sculptor of soft forms. From his native Barcelona he came to Paris to work in the studio of Jean Lurcat, the basis of his understanding of the technique and future activities. Back in Catalonia he became a successful teacher of design and undertook a series of murals and stained glass windows in local buildings.

Appointment to the directorship of the Catalan School of Tapestry was followed by a series of teaching visits to the United States, Canada and Mexico. Grau-Garriga continues as a painter, and a print maker in lithography and lino-cuts, but his main creative technique is in tapestry hangings, or woollen murals. His approach is that of a painter, organizing powerful colours and contrasting textures, to build up complex counterbalances of form. Whilst wool remains the basic material, he often incorporates thick ropes, hemp, threads of metallic materials, to enhance the drama and decorative potential of his compositions.

Stylistically Grau-Garriga derives much of his style from Catalonian baroque. The weaving of the tapestries, at the Catalan School of Tapestry, has always enabled him to control the execution and to experiment with the traditional processes. Thus he has been able to incorporate knotted stitches, as in the manufacture of carpets, which result in tufts of wool, which can be modelled by hand. This relief technique results in a plastic density, a new dynamic contribution to the tapestry form. Compositionally, Grau-Garriga favours a central element around which he expands and builds up areas of colour or textural structure.

Recently he has experimented with plastics and the creation of free-standing woven structures. The incorporation of tiny plastic tubes in the woollen forms added elements of transparency and the conducting of light to otherwise solid images. In turn this suggested that flat, hanging "reliefs" limited the potential of additive possibilities, and the artist moved away from panels, or the flat picture image, to huge sculptures, exploring space both in an upright, vertical sense, as well as extending along the ground. In these works Grau-Garriga can be said to have enlarged the potential of his chosen medium.

—Charles Spencer

GRAVES, Morris (Cole).

American. Born in Fox Valley, Oregon, 28 August 1910; family moved to Seattle, 1920. Self-taught in art. Served in the United States Army, 1942–43. Travelled as seaman in the Far East, 1928–31; visited Texas, 1931, and California, 1933; Easel Painter, Federal Art Project, 1936–37; met and became close friends with John Cage, 1937; built country house in San Juan Islands, 1938–39; Instructor, Seattle Art Museum, 1940–42; visited Hawaii on Guggenheim Fellowship; studied at Honolulu Academy of Art, painting Oriental bronzes, 1946–47; travelled in France, 1948–49, Mexico, 1950, Japan, 1954, and Ireland, 1954– 56; returned to Seattle, 1956; visited Europe on Windsor Award, 1957, then lived in Ireland; travelled in India and Japan, 1961– 64; returned to United States, and settled in Loleta, California; travelled in Asia 1971, Africa and South America, 1972, and the Far East, 1973. Recipient: Purchase Prize, Seattle Art Museum, 1933; Guggenheim Fellowship, 1946; Harris Medal, 1947, and Blair Prize, 1948, Art Institute of Chicago; Purchase Prize, University of Illinois, Urbana 1955; National Institute of Arts and Letters Grant, 1956; Duke and Duchess of Windsor Award, 1957. Honorary Member, American Watercolor Society, 1968. Agent: Willard Gallery, New York. Address: c/o Willard Gallery, 29 East 72nd Street, New York, New York 10021, U.S.A.

Individual Exhibitions:

1936	Seattle Art Museum
1942	Willard Gallery, New York
1943	Willard Gallery, New York
	University of Minnesota, Minneapolis (retrospective)
	Arts Club, Chicago
	Detroit Institute of Arts
	Phillips Gallery, Washington, D.C.
1944	Willard Gallery, New York
1945	Willard Gallery, New York
1946	Philadelphia Art Alliance
1948	Santa Barbara Museum of Art, California
	California Palace of the Legion of Honor, San Francisco (retrospective)
	Art Institute of Chicago
	Los Angeles County Museum of Art
	Willard Gallery, New York
1950	Margaret Brown Gallery, Boston
1951	Manchester Pierce Studio Gallery, Bellevue, Washington
1952	Beaumont Art Museum, Texas
1953	Willard Gallery, New York
1954	Willard Gallery, New York
	Phillips Gallery, Washington, D.C.
1955	Kunstforening, Oslo
	Willard Gallery, New York
1956	Seattle Art Museum
	Museum of Fine Arts, Boston (toured the United States)
1957	Bridgestone Museum of Art, Tokyo
	La Jolla Art Museum, California
1959	Willard Gallery, New York
1960	Phoenix Art Museum, Arizona
1961	Roswell Museum and Art Center, New Mexico
	Kalamazoo Institute of Arts, Michigan
1963	Pavilion Gallery, Balboa, California (retrospective)
1966	University of Oregon, Eugene (retrospective)
1969	Richard White Gallery, Seattle
1971	Willard Gallery, New York
1973	Willard Gallery, New York
1975	American Federation of Arts, New York (circulating exhibition)
1976	Willard Gallery, New York
1978	Willard Gallery, New York
1979	Charles Campbell Gallery, San Francisco
1981	Willard Gallery, New York
1982	University of Oregon, Eugene
1983	Philips Collection, Washington, D.C.
	Greenville County Museum of Art, South Carolina
	Whitney Museum, New York
1984	Oakland Museum, California

Seattle Art Museum, Washington
San Diego Museum of Art, California

Selected Group Exhibitions:

1963	*American Painting*, Tate Gallery, London
1966	*Birds in Contemporary Art*, Phillips Collection, Washington, D.C.
	The Object Transformed, Museum of Modern Art, New York
1967	*Works on Paper*, Waddington Galleries, London
1963	*Painting and Sculpture Today*, Herron Museum of Art, Indianapolis
1969	*Art in America: Paintings, Drawings, Prints and Sculpture from the Museum's Collection*, Worcester Art Museum, Massachusetts
1971	*Drawings U.S.A. 71*, Minnesota Museum of Art, St. Paul
1973	*Drawing America 1973*, Albrecht Gallery, Museum of Art, St. Joseph, Missouri
1978	*Northwest Traditions*, Seattle Art Museum, Washington
1981	*Northwest Visionaries*, Institute of Contemporary Art, Boston

Collections:

National Institute of Arts and Letters, New York; Whitney Museum, New York; Metropolitan Museum of Art, New York; Museum of Modern Art, New York; Worcester Art Museum, Massachusetts; Phillips Collection, Washington, D.C.; Art Institute of Chicago, Seattle Art Museum; Portland Art Museum, Oregon; Tate Gallery, London.

Publications:

By GRAVES: articles—"Mystic Painters of the Northwest" in *Life* (New York), 28 September 1953; "3 Kinds of Space" in *Morris Graves: A Restrospective*, exhibition catalogue, Eugene, Oregon 1966; comments in *The Drawings of Morris Graves* by Ida E. Rubin, Boston 1974.

On GRAVES: books—*Morris Graves*, exhibition catalogue, by Frederick S. Wight, Berkeley and Los Angeles 1956; *Conversations with Artists* by Sheldon Rodman, New York 1957; *Morris Graves: A Retrospective*, exhibition catalogue, foreward by Wallace S. Baldinger, Eugene, Oregon 1966; *The Drawings of Morris Graves* by Ida E. Rubin, Boston 1974; *Morris Graves: Vision of the Inner Eye* by Ray Kass, New York 1983.

*   *   *

Morris Graves is a gentle visual poet of Oriental consciousness in a mechanical and secular world. Deeply influenced by Mark Tobey, Zen Buddhism and religious mysticism, Graves' delicate paintings aspire to the moment of awakening and enlightenment, the rasping of consciousness, by means of an animistic symbology.

Graves credits Tobey for inspiring his "Bird" paintings, and adapted Tobey's "white writing" and gouache washes on rice or mulberry paper as his medium. His iconography consists of invented representational forms with overt religious symbolism: chalices, birds, snakes, fishes, moon, and "ritual bronze" vessels. The fetishistic birds, for which Graves is best known, are the tokens of his transcendentalism. His inner vision conforms to Ananda Coomaraswamy's esthetic concepts of "phenomenal space" (the world outside the body), "mental space" (imagination and dreams), and the "space of consciousness" (symbolic, religious and spiritual thought). Lightly traced in calligraphic brush lines and filled with subtle washings, forms appear to assemble themselves out of the void. The "space of consciousness" is made manifest. A broader brushstroke reminiscent of *sumi* painting is sometimes used to outline form, lending an air of Oriental scrollwork. Concurrent with the animal paintings are unadorned still-lifes with simple vases, cups and flowers ceremoniously arranged.

For nearly his entire adult life, Graves has lived in seclusion in the coastal wilds of the northwestern

United States and, briefly, in Ireland during the late 1950's. The simple, unaffected and accidental occurrences of nature encountered there nourish his soul; the intrusions of man and technology are his anathema.

There is something almost painfully frail and awkward about his work, as if it might (spiritually) disintegrate under scrutiny. He seemed aware of this when he wrote in 1950, "Secular and scientific 'art' is concerned with evolution . . . Religious art is concerned with involution." Graves demands an inwardness of experience. Within this deep devotion resides the implications of a transcendent universal expression of the inner self.

—Ron Glowen

GRAVES, Nancy.

American. Born in Pittsfield, Massachusetts, 23 December 1940. Educated at Vassar College, Poughkeepsie, New York, 1958-61, B.A. 1961; School of Arts and Architecture, Yale University, New Haven, Connecticut, 1961-1964, B.F.A. and M.F.A. 1964. Independent artist, since 1966. Lived and worked in Florence, 1966; began making films, 1969. Resident, American Academy in Rome, 1979; currently lives and works in New York. Recipient: Fulbright-Hayes Grant in Painting, Paris 1965; Vassar College Fellowship, 1971; Paris *Biennale* Grant, 1971; National Endowment for the Arts Grant, 1972; Creative Artists' Program Service Grant, New York, 1974; Skowhegan Medal for Drawing/Graphics, Maine, 1980; Yale Arts Award, New Haven, Connecticut, 1985; Distinguished Visitor Award, Vassar College, Poughkeepsie, New York, 1986. Agent: M. Knoedler and Company, New York. Address: c/o M. Knoedler and Company Inc., 19 East 70th Street, New York, New York 10021, U.S.A.

Individual Exhibitions:

1968	Graham Gallery, New York
1969	Whitney Museum, New York
1970	National Gallery of Canada, Ottawa
1971	Gallery Reese Palley, New York
	Gallery Reese Palley, San Francisco
	National Gallery of Canada, Ottawa (and films)
	Sculpture, Drawings, Films 1969-71, Neue Galerie der Stadt, Aachen, West Germany
	Vassar College, Poughkeepsie, New York
	Museum of Modern Art, New York (and films)
	Wallraf-Richartz Museum, Cologne (and films)
	University of California Art Museum, Berkeley (and films)
	Walker Art Center, Minneapolis (and films)
	Yale University School of Art and Architecture, New Haven, Connecticut
	Pratt Institute, new York (and films)
1972	New Gallery of Contemporary Art, Cleveland
	Janie C. Lee Gallery, Dallas
	Institute of Contemporary Art, University of Pennsylvania, Philadelphia (and films)
	Contemporary Arts Center, Cincinnati, Ohio (and films)
	Whitney Museum, New York (and films)
1973	National Gallery of Canada, Ottawa
	The Berkshire Museum, Pittsfield, Massachusetts
	La Jolla Museum of Art, California
	Janie C. Lee Gallery, Dallas
	Art Museum of South Texas, Corpus Christi
1974	André Emmerich Gallery, New York
	Albright-Knox Art Gallery, Buffalo, New York
	Janie C. Lee Gallery, Houston
	Museum of Modern Art, New York (and films)
1975	Janie C. Lee Gallery, Houston
1977	André Emmerich Gallery, New York
	Janie C. Lee Gallery, Houston

	Galerie André Emmerich, Zurich
	Galerie im Schloss, Munich
1978	Hammarskjold Plaza, New York
	M. Knoedler and Company Inc., New York
	Gallery Diane Gilson, Seattle
	Janie C. Lee Gallery, Houston
1979	M. Knoedler and Company, Inc., New York
1980	M. Knoedler and Company, Inc., New York
	Albright-Knox Art Gallery, Buffalo, New York (toured the United States)
1981	M. Knoedler and Company Inc., New York
	Richard Gray Gallery, Chicago
1982	M. Knoedler and Company Inc., New York
	M. Knoedler AG, Zurich
1983	Santa Barbara Museum of Art, California
	Gloria Luria Gallery, Bay Harbor Islands, Florida
	Janie C. Lee Gallery, Houston
1984	M. Knoedler and Company Inc., New York
	Janie C. Lee Gallery, Houston
1985	Greenberg Gallery, St. Louis, Missouri
	M. Knoedler and Company Inc., New York
1986	Vassar College, Poughkeepsie, New York (travelled to Pittsfield, Massachusetts; Providence, Rhode Island)
	Richard Gray Gallery, Chicago
	M. Knoedler and Company Inc., New York
1987	Hirshhorn Museum, Washington, D.C. (retrospective; travelled to Fort Worth, Texas; Santa Barbara, California; Brooklyn, New York, 1987-88)
	Knoedler Gallery, London

Selected Group Exhibitions:

1970	*Information*, Museum of Modern Art, New York
1975	*American Drawings*, Leverkusen Museum, West Germany
1976	*American Bi-Centennial Exhibition*, Corcoran Gallery of Art, Washington, D.C. (toured the United States)
1977	*Documenta 6*, Kassel
1978	*American Painting of the 1970's*, Albright-Knox Art Gallery, Buffalo (toured the United States)
1979	*Supershow*, Hudson River Museum, Yonkers, New York (toured the United States)
1980	*Drawings: The Pluralist Decade*, United States Pavillion, *Biennale*, Venice
1982	*A Private Vision*, Museum of Fine Arts, Boston
1984	*Primitivism in 20th Century Art*, Museum of Modern Art, New York
1987	*Structure to Resemblance: 8 American Sculptors*, Albright-Knox Art Gallery, Buffalo, New York

Collections:

Whitney Museum, New York; Museum of Modern Art, New York; Metropolitan Museum of Art, New York; Albright-Knox Art Gallery, Buffalo, New York; Art Institute of Chicago; Des Moines Art Center, Iowa; Museum of Fine Arts, Houston; National Gallery of Canada, Ottawa; Wallraf-Richartz Museum, Cologne; Neue Galerie im Alten Kurhaus, Aachen, West Germany.

Publications:

By GRAVES: articles—"A Conversation with Nancy Graves," with Emily Wasserman in *Artforum* (New York), October 1970; "Remarks on Their Medium by 4 Painters: Pat Adams, Nancy Graves, Budd Hopkins and Irving Petlin," with Max Kozloff, in *Artforum* (New York), September 1975; statement in *American Painting: The 80's—A Critical Interpretation*, exhibition catalogue, by Barbara Rose, New York 1979.

On GRAVES: books—*Nancy Graves: Sculpture, Drawings, Films 1969-71*, exhibition catalogue, with an introduction by Phyllis Tuchman, Aachen, West Germany 1971; *Neue Galerie Der Stadt Aachen Der Bestant 71: Kunst Um 1970—Sammlung Ludwig in Aachen*, exhibition catalogue, Aachen 1972; *Nancy Graves*, exhibition catalogue, with an introduction by Martin Cassidy, Philadelphia 1972; *Bildwerke und Objekte* by Rainer Budde and Evelyn Weiss, Cologne 1973; *Nancy Graves*, exhbition catalogue, La Jolla, California 1973; *Strata*, exhibition catalogue, text by Lucy R. Lippard,

Vancouver 1977; *Masks, Tents, Vessels, Talismans*, exhibition catalogue, by Janet Kardon, Philadelphia 1979; *Nancy Graves: A Survey 1969-1980*, exhibition catalogue by Linda Cathcart, Buffalo, New York 1980; *Nancy Graves: Painting, Sculpture, Drawing, 1980-1985*, exhibition catalogue by Debra Bricker Balken, Poughkeepsie, New York 1986; *The Sculpture of Nancy Graves: A Catalogue Raisonne*, with texts by F. A. Carmean, Linda Cathcart, Robert Hughes and others, New York 1987; articles—"The Moving Eye . . . Nancy Graves' Sculpture, Film and Painting" by Robert Arn in *Artscanada* (Toronto), Spring 1974; "Distancing: The Films of Nancy Graves" by Lucy R. Lippard in *Art in America* (New York), November/December 1975; "Out in Front: American Women Artists—Dorothea Rockburne and Nancy Graves" by Barbara Rose in *Vogue* (New York), June 1977; "Art: Nancy Graves" by John Russell in the *New York Times*, 23 February 1979; "Nancy Graves" by Jeff Perrone in *Artforum* (New York), May 1979; "Nancy Graves" by Hilton Kramer in the *New York Times*, 21 March 1980; "Nancy Graves at Knoedler" by Elizabeth Frank in *Art in America* (New York), May 1980; "Nancy Graves" by Barbara Rose in *Vogue* (new York), June 1980; "Nancy Graves: A Survey 1969-1980" by Carolyn Kinder Carr in *Dialogue* (Akron, Ohio), July/August 1980; "Nancy Graves" by Cynthia Nadelman in *Artnews* (New York), September 1980; "Nature into Sculpture" by Michael Edward Shapiro in *Arts Magazine* (New York), November 1984; "Nancy Graves' New Age of Bronze" by Avis Berman in *Artnews* (New York), February 1986; "The Sculpture of Nancy Graves" by John Yau in *Sculpture* (New York), September/October 1987.

*

Without the aid of drawings I conceive a sculpture by selecting from an inventory of hundreds of directly cast organic forms. These are laid out on the floor and relationships are varied until the unexpected occurs. As parts are welded together changes in structure, balance, three dimensional relationships come into play. What originally appeared to be a vertical element could become a base. Whereas the casting may take months, the assembly takes a few hours. Historical expectations for this most traditional sculpture material are subverted by working against logic and without premeditation. In building I try to subvert what is logical—what the eye would expect—by assembling without premeditation the directly cast objects.

—Nancy Graves

*

It is no exaggeration to say that the career of Nancy Graves took off on the back of a camel. With the first sensational exhibitions of the large, life-size, enigmatic camel constructions in the late 1960's, Graves was placed at the forefront of the artists then involved in redefining sculpture. Made of polyurethane, burlap and paint, covered with animal skins and supported on wooden armature, the three-dimensional figures of the camels at rest or in grazing positions appeared at once in the galleries and museums wherever they were displayed shockingly real and strangely abstract. And like the sculptures which immediately followed, in most cases made of camel bones or hard forms— i.e. combinations of steel, latex, gauze, oil, marble dust, acrylic—fashioned to suggest bones, the camels were but part of Graves' on-going investigations of perceptual issues. These issues concerned the relationship of illusionism, reality and motion. Then, there is the notion of art as magical object. And the introduction of new materials, previously used in industrial contexts, as well as the presentation to consider in the appreciation of the sculptures. These various concerns come together in "Shaman" (1970) one of the most suggestive ritualistic pieces; made of steel, latex, gauze, oil, marble dust and acrylic, the large-scale, multiple format hanging work is a confrontational presence.

Graves also made films about camels during the early 1970s; *Goulimine* (1970) and *Izy Boukir* (1971) are among the best known examples. After working on drawings in 1970-71 related to the shapes and patterns in the films, she stopped the sculpture and returned to painting in 1972. Patterns, also, dominate the "Camouflage" series paintings which followed. Based on sea animals that naturally camouflage themselves by blending into their surroundings, the paintings challenged the viewers to discern the creatures

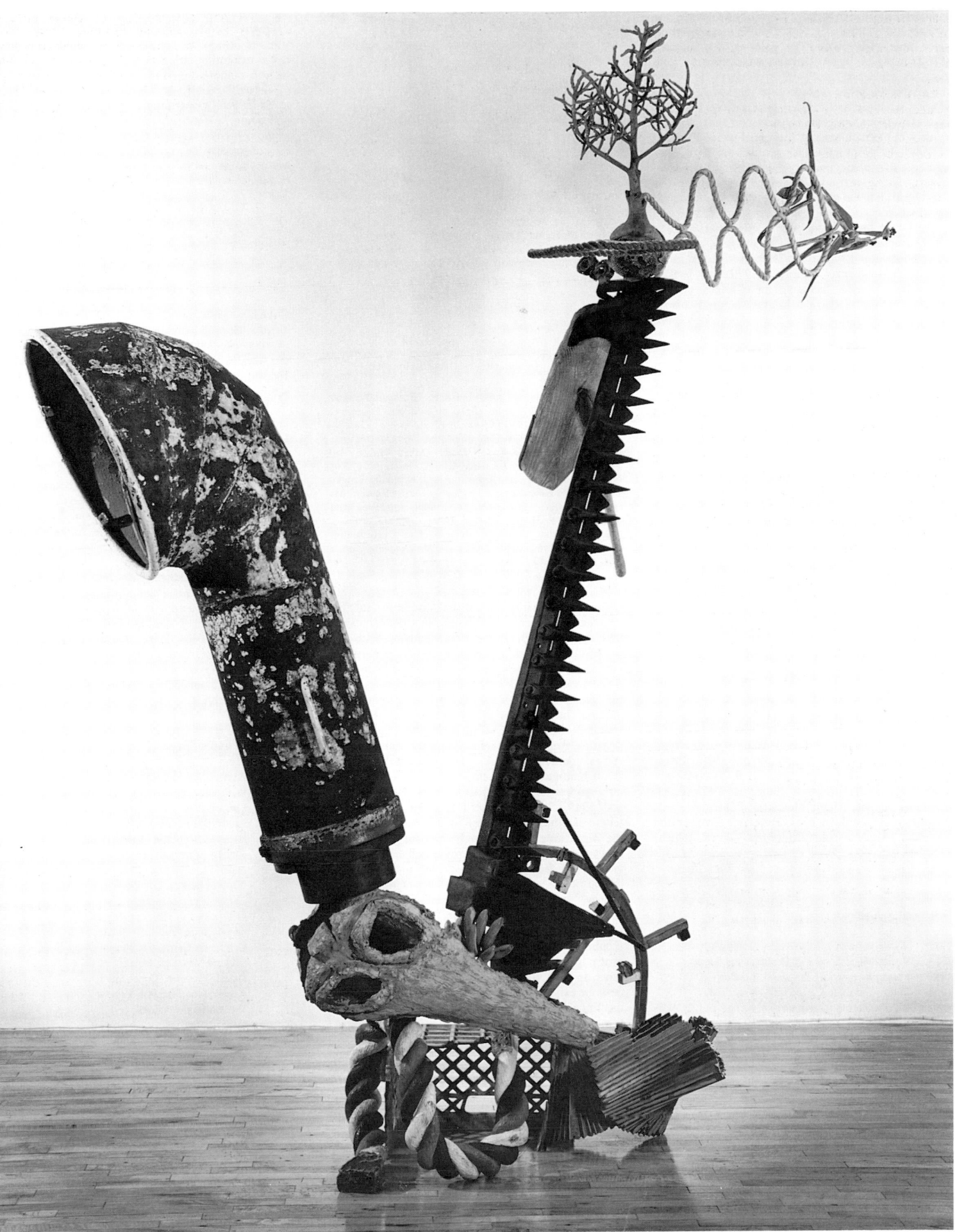

Nancy Graves: *Syclical,* **1987**

hiding within the colorful calligraphy of curves and straight lines. Another group of works executed at the same time used maps. The painting "Antarctica" (1972) in which pattern, again, was a primary concern, is an example. Satellite photographs of the moon and the other planets were the sources of the shaped, multiple and divided panels from 1973–74. And map-like information on place and atmosphere is evident in the monumental five panel work "Painting U.S.A." (1975). A group of pastels from 1976, containing calligraphic imagery based on the kinds of tracking and tracing notations found in maps, serve as the transition to the autonomous spirited work she has executed since 1977.

She began to make sculptures again in 1976. The recent works, though abstract in imagery, are energetic, vibrant and suggestive structures. Some forms such as the sculpture "Column" (1979) hark back to the earlier examples based on camel bones. Others, such as "Trace" (1980), a brightly colored bronze, steel and oil standing piece, make more open-ended associations involving interplays of nature, art and archeology. A growing concern with the pictorial aspects is a strong direction in her recent work.

In the mid 1980s the more flamboyant appearance of the cast metal sculptures made stronger the associations with nature. "Looping" (1985), with its dynamic structure, brings to mind some fantastically exotic plan that has sprung to life in mysterious fashion.

Nature continues to be a major source of inspiration for the paintings as well. In a series of paintings from 1983–84, both the manifold perceptual aspects and the psychological implications of the shadow, one of nature's most fascinating of fleeting phenomena, are investigated.

—Ronny Cohen

GRECO, Emilio.

Italian. Born in Catania, 11 October 1913. Sculptor and graphic artist: lives and works in Rome. Professor of Sculpture, Accademia di Belle Arti, Carrara, 1952. Recipient: St. Vincent Prize, 1948; Prize, *Quadriennale,* Rome, 1952; Premio al Concorso Nazionale per il Monumento a Pinocchio, 1953; Prize, *Biennale,* Venice, 1956; Medaglia d'Oro del Presidente della Repubblica, 1961. Honorary Member and Professor, Akademie der Bildenden Kunst, Munich; Member, Académie Royal de Belgique, Brussels. Address: Viale Cortina d'Ampezzo 132, Rome, Italy.

Individual Exhibitions:

1952	Roland Browse and Delbanco, London
1954	Rhode Island School of Design, Providence
1955	Roland Browse and Delbanco, London
1958	Centro Culturale Canavesano, Ivrea, Italy
	Palazzo Barberini, Rome
1959	Roland Browse and Delbanco, London
	Kunsthalle, Bremen, West Germany
	Städtische Galerie, Munich
	Zwerge Garten, Salzburg
1960	Kunstlerhaus, Vienna
1961	Musée Rodin, Paris
	Shirokiya Foundation, Tokyo
1963	Gulbenkian Foundation, Lisbon
1964	Istituto di Storia dell'Arte, Pisa
1965	Istituto di Storia dell'Arte, Catania, Italy
1966	Albert Hall, Canberra
	National Gallery of South Australia, Adelaide
	National Gallery of Victoria, Melbourne
1969	Galleria Pananti, Florence
1970	Galleria Civica d'Arte Moderna, Ferrara, Italy
1971	Modern Fine Arts Museum, Kobe, Japan
	Prefectural Museum, Yamaguchi, Japan
	Art Gallery, Hiroshima

1973	*Bronzes And Drawings* Roland Browse and Delbanco, London
1980	Municipal Gallery, Orvieto, Italy

Selected Group Exhibitions:

1971	*Scultori Italiani,* Palazzo Reale, Milan

Collections:

Galleria d'Arte Moderna, Milan; Galleria Nazionale d'Arte Moderna, Rome; Centre Georges Pompidou, Paris; Musee Municipal de Sculpture en Plein Air, Antwerp; Wallraf-Richartz Museum, Cologne; Tate Gallery, London; South African National Gallery, Cape Town; National Gallery of South Australia, Adelaide; City Art Gallery, Auckland, New Zealand.

Publications:

By GRECO: book—*Memoria dell'Estate,* Bologna 1980; ilustrated book—*Ars Amatoria* by Ovid, Berlin 1969.

On GRECO: books—*Emilio Greco* by Fortunato Bellonzi, Rome 1949, 1962; *Emilio Greco* by Bernhard Degenhart, Berlin and Mainz 1960;*Disegni di Emilio Greco: Catalogo dell'Opera Grafica* by I. Corbellini, Pisa 1964; *Mostra Antologica dell Opera Grafica di Emilio Greco,* Pistoia, Italy 1968; *Emilio Greco* by Leonardo Sciascia, Rome 1971; *Emilio Greco: Sculpture and Drawings* by J. P. Hodin, London 1971; *Emilio Greco: Opera Grafica* by Carlo Pirovano, Milan 1972; *Greco: Bronzes and Drawings,* exhibition catalogue, by J. P. Hodin, London 1973; *Omaggio a Emilio Greco,* exhibition catalogue edited by Pier Carlo Santini, Montecatini Terme 1974; *Emilio Greco: disegni e grafica,* with text by Carlo L. Ragghianti, Florence 1977.

L'Omino, the first important sculpture in Emilio Greco's artistic career, was produced in 1939 and exhibited at the fourth Rome Quadriennale. With this work, Greco began a period of tireless research focussed on a kind of archaic plasticism and accompanied by the subtle elegance of his own personal mark that was to remain constant throughout his entire production. In his series of *Omini* and *Teste Virili,* he revealed himself as a sensitive sculptor, prepared to progress from the realistic vein with which he had started, and to find his own personal language through an increasingly emphatic confrontation of his own work with that of past masters. Between 1939 and 1949, Greco produced a series of sculptures where careful plastic modelling emphasized light. At the same time he unfailingly propounded a strong message of human dignity, pride and hope. In two versions of *Il Lottatore* (dated 1947 and 1948), the drama of the whole figure explodes with a solemn energy, while the face expresses wisdom and strength. Another important work of this period is *Il Cavallo Morente* (1949), a small terracotta whose monumental aspirations are indicated by the drama of protruding bones, bloated stomach and twisted features. In such works, Greco reveals a peculiar awareness for existential pathos. Not only is he attentive to the linguistic achievements of the past and present, but constantly seeks to create a stunning impact through the work's emotional 'charge'.

At the beginning of the 1950s, a new phase began. Greco's research was now based on a single theme—woman. It was an attempt to crystallize a canon of beauty in the graceful movement of the female form. Thus were created important works such as *Il Grande Nudo* (1950) or *Figura Accoccolata* (1956), the latter being a most original sculpture of this period. In it, the figure is folded in on itself as though frozen in space in a quasi-architectural concept. With such works, Greco achieved widespread acclaim. In 1956 he was awarded the sculpture prize of the 18th Venice Biennale for his work *La Grande Bagnante,* a figure of a woman standing with legs spread, hands at her side and torso twisted in the manner of a column. The turning volumes are reminiscent, as Carlo Ragghianti noted, of a "melancholic Hellenism, an Ovidian Sensuality, exquisite and solemn, a cerebral passion".

Further offical approval followed in subsequent years to bring Greco numerous invitations to international exhibitions from as far away as Japan. In 1964 he was commissioned to create the door bosses for Orvieto cathedral. His monument to Pope John XXII in Saint Peter's was produced in 1965–67. But time and again he returned to his favourite themes—ice-skaters, bathers, female figures—in which, although the echoes of a long tradition are always evident, they are accompanied by a constant search for originality of form.

—Roberto Lambarelli

GREEN, Alan.

British. Born in London, 22 December 1932. Studied at the Beckenham School of Art, Kent, 1949–53, and the Royal College of Art, London, 1955–58. Married June Barnes in 1958: daughters: Paula and Julia. served as a corporal in the Royal Army Signal Corps, in Korea and Japan, 1953–55. Visiting Lecturer, Hornsey College of Art, London, 1959–61; Senior Lecturer in Fine Arts, Leeds College of Art, 1961–66; Senior Lecturer in Painting, Ravensbourne College of Art and Design, Kent, 1966–74. Recipient: Intaglio Print Prize 1974, and Giles Bequest Prize, 1976, *British International Print Biennale,* Bradford, Yorkshire, 1974; Third Prize, *Internationale de la Gravure,* Cracow, 1976; "Writer's Award," *Listowel Graphic Art Open Exhibition,* Ireland, 1978; Grand Prix, *Norwegian International Print Biennale,* Fredrikstad, 1978; National Museum of Art at Osaka Prize, *International Print Biennale,* Tokyo, 1979; Museum of Modern Art of Rijeka Prize, *International Biennale of Graphic Art,* Ljubljana, Yugoslavia, 1981; First Prize, *Graphica Creativa '81,* Luova Grafikka Alvar Aalto Museu, Jyvaskyla, Finland, 1981. Agent: Annely Juda Fine Art, 11 Tottenham Mews, London W1. Address: 291 Kent House Road, Beckenham, Kent BR31JQ, England.

Individual Exhibitions:

1963	A1A Gallery, London
1964	Wakefield City Art Gallery, Yorkshire
1967	London Press Exchange
1970	Annely Juda Fine Art, London
1972	Greenwich Theatre Gallery, London
1973	Annely Juda Fine Art, London
	Galerie Liatowitsch, Basle
	Editions Alecto, London
1974	Galerie Hervé Alexandre, Brussels
	Galerie Art in Progress, Munich
1975	Annely Juda Fine Art, London
	Galerie de Gestlo, Hamburg
	Galleria Vinciana, Milan
	Galerie Arnesen, Copenhagen
1976	Annely Juda Fine Art, London
	Tate Gallery, London
	Galerie Klaus Lupke, Frankfurt
	Oliver Dowling Gallery, Dublin
	Painting Box Galerie, Zurich
1977	Galerie Art in Progress, Dusseldorf
	Mappin Art Gallery, Sheffield (travelled to the University of Newcastle upon Tyne)
1978	Annely Juda Fine Art, London
	Oliver Dowling Gallery, Dublin
	Nina Freudenheim Gallery, Buffalo, New York
	Clark Gallery, Boston
	Susan Caldwell Inc., New York
	Roundhouse Gallery, London
	Galerie Palluel, Paris
1979	Artline, The Hague
	Galerie Loyse Oppenheim, Nyon, Switzerland
	Paintings 1969–1979, Kunsthalle, Bielefeld, West Germany
	Peterloo Gallery, Manchseter (with Nigel Hall)

Alan Green: *Four Irregular Blacks*, 1979

range from silk, paper laminates, cotton duck, linen, jute to board. I find it useful to think of paint primarily as a substance, then as a colour, This broadens the range of what can be included and of its function. (There can be no visible substance that does not have colour).

From this standpoint, it becomes a little more possible to actually move across a surface without recourse to gesture, calligraphy or any other devices. In the sequence in which one event determines another, parallels can exist between the on-going situation of a painting based on these premises and the interrelated and interdependent factors governing events in the external world. The neutrality of these premises allows a space for the natural inclusion of the human factor. Time spent, boredom, fatigue, excitement, impatience, can all be made visible. Again, the relation to the individual and the external world is evident. Thus a painting may be able to exist as a record of time lived. It is a form of action that has dispensed with heroics. Today, the most that can be reasonably hoped for is just to make an art statement.

—Alan Green

Alan Green's paintings require and deserve to have a great deal of time spent on them. At first walking into a room surrounded by seemingly sombre abstract paintings one feels bewildered—but when one stops and examines each work meticulously, one's feeling gradually change from distress to understanding and appreciation. Sometimes Art which has to be worked hard at to appreciate is the most rewarding.

In Green's 1982 exhibition there were 10 paintings and 5 etchings. "Three Rectangles/Square" is similar to a piece of music—it begins with a bang in the left hand corner. A panel full of gauges and scratches becomes a smooth grey plane tinged with burgundy, as if the blood/excitement were still seeping through, and finally progresses to soft cloud-like formations, the calm after the storm. In "2 Violets" the highly textured and meticulous surface is almost obsessively created. "Blue" is more expansive, relaxed. Specks of red and black appear with occasional dots—they take you by surprise. Each time you look, new forms appear.

Most of Green's paintings are made up of various panels which interact. In "Four Crimsons" rigid lines become more fluid but never vanish totally. The artist seems to be playing hide and seek with shapes. The less successful paintings lack texture and movement. The preparatory drawings are also extremely disappointing. They prove that Green's vision needs large expanses to create a sense of grandeur and vitality. These elements are also missing in "Blue Diagonal"; the use of colour is superb, but there is a total lack of thought. "One to Four 3 Parts" is almost completely uncoordinated although "One" is excellent—red glistens with mystery, peeping through the grey and blue. Green's etchings are not really resolved either. Texture is such an essential part of his work that without it the image cannot survive. Hence the etchings lack subtlety, mystery and surprise.

To look at Green's paintings is rather like looking at an Alain Resnais film. Something is constantly taking place from one panel to another. The mood is obsessive and melancholy and provokes an inexplicable affinity, especially when the blush of red seeps through.

—Carine Maurice

Selected Group Exhibitions:

Collections:

Tate Gallery, London; Victoria and Albert Museum, London; Kunstmuseum, Dusseldorf; Kunstmuseum, Zurich; Power Gallery of Contemporary Art, Sydney; Louisiana Museum of Modern Art, Humlebaek, Denmark; Musée d'Ixelles, Brussels; National Museum of Art, Osaka; Museum of Modern Art, New York; Guggenheim Museum, New York.

Publications:

By GREEN: articles—"Alan Green on His Paintings" in *Studio International* (London), October 1973; "Every Artist is a Con-man," a discussion with Roger Hilton, in *Studio International* (London), March 1974; "Alan Green: A Dialogue," with Bernard Denvir, in *Art International* (Lugano, Switzerland), November 1974; statement in *Colour in Painting,* exhibition catalogue, Rome 1976; interview, with Peter Rippon, in *Artscribe* (London), February 1977; interview, with Gerard Weber, in *Art Press,* (Paris), December 1978; statement in *Skira Annual,* Geneva 1979.

On GREEN: books—*Alan Green: Paintings 1969-1979,* exhibition catalogue, by Michael Pausenback and Martine Lignon, Bielefeld, West Germany, 1979; *Alan Green,* exhibition catalogue, by Waldemar Januszczak, Osaka 1981; *Alan Green,* exhibition catalogue with text by Seiji Oshima, Osaka 1986.

I find it necessary to be very specific about the carrying out of quite minor activities connected with my work—starting from the beginning and taking nothing for granted,

Every event in the making of a work has its part to play in determining the final outcome. Initially, the nature of the support has to be considered. If stretchers are to be used, I make my own. This allows for a more physical awareness of the area and leaves more options open. For example, the number and precise width of the stretcher and cross-bar edges that actually come into contact with the canvas surface sets up a dialogue between the surface and the hidden structure of the stretchers. The nature of the support itself is another basic in determining the work. It may

GREENBERG, Gloria.

American. Born in New York City, 4 March 1932. Educated at the High School of Music and Art, New York, 1946–52; studied at the Brooklyn Museum Art School, New York, 1952–53; influenced by instructors Nicholas Marsicano, Gabor Peterdi, John Ferren and Henrietta Schutz. Married Martin Bressler in

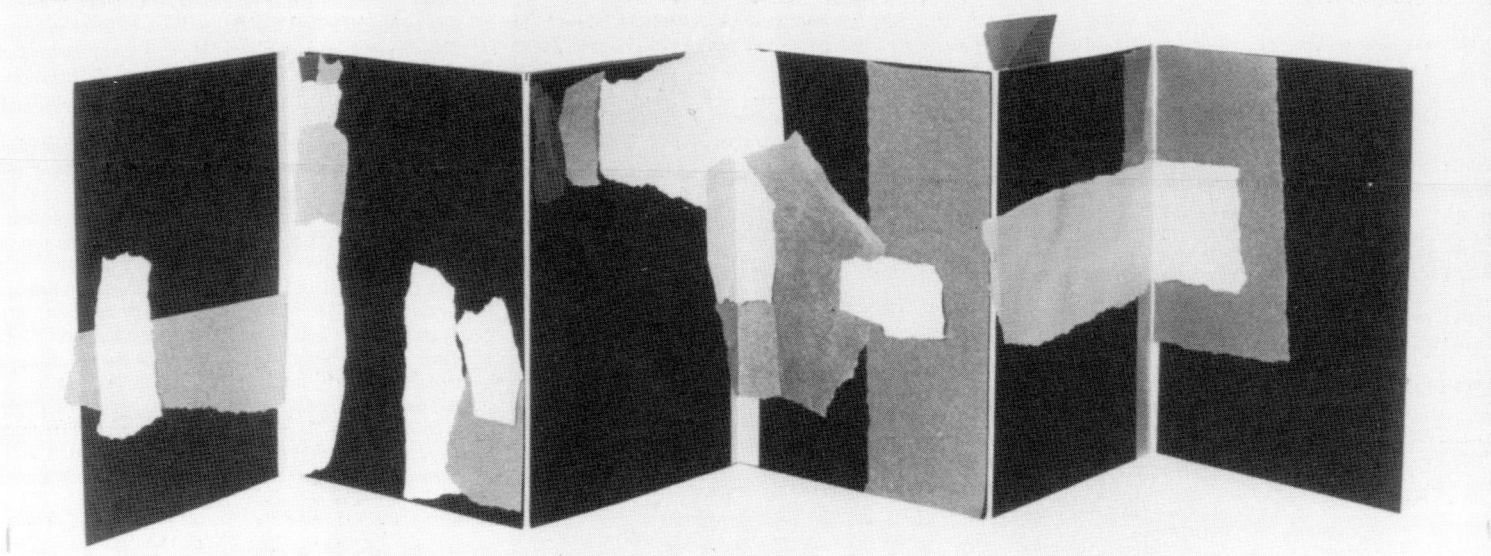

Gloria Greenberg: *Screens: The Other Side of the Picture*, 1982

1953; children: Rachel and Jonathan. Worked as a clerk in the Subscription Department, *Esquire* magazine, Boulder, Colorado, 1953; now a full-time artist, based in New York; lived in La Rochelle, France, 1957–60; Book Designer and Art Consultant, Harper and Row publishers, New York, 1965–74. Instructor of Drawing and Design, The Craft Students League, New York, 1965–66. Recipient: Yale-Norfolk Summer Art Fellowship, 1952; MacDowell Colony Fellowship, 1965, 1973. Agent: 55 Mercer Gallery, 55 Mercer Street, New York, New York 11013. Address: 118 East 17th Street, New York, New York 10003, U.S.A.

Individual Exhibitions:

1965   Columbia University, New York
1970   55 Mercer Gallery, New York
1971   55 Mercer Gallery, New York
1972   55 Mercer Gallery, New York
1973   55 Mercer Gallery, New York
1974   55 Mercer Gallery, New York
1975   55 Mercer Gallery, New York
1976   55 Mercer Gallery, New York
1977   55 Mercer Gallery, New York
1978   55 Mercer Gallery, New York
1979   *Looking Back/Looking Forwrd: The 60's and 70's,* Marist College, Poughkeepsie, New York (restrospective)
1980   55 Mercer Gallery, New York
1981   55 Mercer Gallery, New York
1982   55 Mercer Gallery, New York

Selected Group Exhibitions:

1953   *Regional Show, Denver Art Museum*
1964   *Waverly Gallery Group Show,* Waverly Gallery, New York
1967   *The Landscape,* Visual Arts Gallery, New York
1974   *New Drawings,* Women's Interart Center, New York
       Group Show: 55 Mercer, 55 Mercer Gallery, New York (toured the United States)

Collections:

International Arrivals Building, Kennedy International Airport, New York; Bankers Trust, Los Angeles.

Publications:

By GREENBERG: books—*Strange Plants and Animals,* New York 1963; *Away We Go,* New York 1964.

On GREENBERG: articles—by Jim Bishop in *Artnews* (New York), April 1971; by Jane Gollin in *Artnews,* (New York), April 1972; by Ellen Lubell in *Arts Magazine* (New York), May 1976.

The pieces are part of a larger piece.
The larger piece, in turn, is part of the wall.
The wall is part of a space.
The space makes the work.
The work makes the space.
The work grows *from* something,
Into something.
When it has been realized,
It is real.

               —Gloria Greenberg

GREENE, Balcomb.

American. Born in Niagara Falls, New York, 22 May 1904; lived in Iowa and in Colorado, 1905–20. Studied at Syracuse University, New York, 1922–26, B.A. in philosophy 1926; studied psychology in Paris and at University of Vienna under Freud, 1926; did graduate work in English literature, Columbia University, New York, 1927; studied art history, New York University 1940–43, M.A. Married the artist and sculptor Gertrude Glass in 1926 (died 1956). Painter: lives and works in New York. Taught English at Darmouth College, Hanover, New Hampshire, 1928–31, and began to write fiction; painted at Académie de la Grande Cahumiére, Paris (self-taught), 1931–32; returned to paint and write in New York City, 1933; Editor, *Art Front* magazine, New York, 1935–36; during Depression worked on Federal Arts Project of the W.P.A.—executed stained glass for a Bronx school and abstract murals for a Williamsburg, Brooklyn housing project and for the Federal Hall of Medcine at the 1939 Worlds Fair; fire in New York studio destroyed paintings and manuscripts, 1941; taught history of the arts at Carnegie Institute of Technology, Pittsburgh, 1942–59; built house and studio at Montauk Point, Long Island; worked in Paris for six months 1959–60. First Chairman, American Abstract Artists 1936–37, re-elected 1938–39, 1940–41. Awards: *Artnews* Critic's Choice, New York, 1950, 1953, 1955, 1956; Carol H. Beck Gold Medal, Pennsylvania Academy of the Fine Arts, 1961; Benjamin Altman Prize for Figure Painting,

National Academy of Design, New York. Agents: A.C.A. Galleries, 21 East 67th Street, New York, New York 10021; Harmon-Meek Gallery, 1258 South Third Street, Naples, Florida 33940. Address: 345 East 52nd Street, New York, New York 10022, U.S.A.

Individual Exhibitions:

1947   J. B. Neumann's New Art Circle, New York
1950   Bertha Schaefer Gallery, New York
1952   Bertha Schaefer Gallery, New York
1953   Bertha Schaefer Gallery, New York
       Arts and Crafts Center, Pittsburgh
1954   Bertha Schaefer Gallery, New York
1955   Bertha Schaefer Gallery, New York
1956   Bertha Schaefer Gallery, New York
1957   American University, Washington, D.C.
1958   Bertha Schaefer Gallery, New York
1959   Bertha Schaefer Gallery, New York
       Brookhanve National Laboratory, Long Island, New York
1960   American Cultural Center, Paris
1961   Whitney Museum, New York (retrospective)
1962   Saidenberg Gallery, New York
1963   Feingarten Gallery, Los Angeles
       Saidenberg Gallery, New York
1964   Feingarten Gallery, Los Angeles
1965   University of Florida, Gainesville
       Tampa Art Institute, Florida
       James David Gallery, Miami
       Saidenberg Gallery, New York
1966   Arts and Crafts Center, Pittsburgh
       James David Gallery, Miami
       Main Street Gallery, Chicago
       Santa Barbara Museum of Art, California
1967   Occidental College, Los Angeles
1968   Makler Gallery, Philadelphia
1970   Forum Gallery, New York
1972   Fairweather-Hardin Gallery, Chicago
1973   Fairweather-Hardin Gallery, Chicago
       Forum Gallery, New York
1974   Forum Gallery, New York
       Harmon Gallery, Naples, Florida
1975   Forum Gallery, New York
       Harmon Gallery, Naples, Florida
1976   Harmon Gallery, Naples, Florida
       International Oceanographic Institute, Key Biscayne, Florida
1977   Harmon Gallery, Naples, Florida
       A.C.A. Gallery, New York (retrospective)
1978   Guild Hall, East Hampton, New York (retrospective)
1981   A.C.A. Gallery, New York
1983   A.C.A. Gallery, New York

Selected Group Exhibitions:

1948 *Biennale*, Venice
1959 *New Images of Man*, Museum of Modern Art, New York

Collections:

Brooklyn Museum, New York; Guggenheim Museum, New York; Metropolitan Museum of Art, New York; Museum of Modern Art, New York; Whitney Museum, New York; Guild Hall, East Hampton, New York; Carnegie Institute, Pittsburgh; Walker Art Center, Minneapolis; Joslyn Art Museum, Omaha, Nebraska; Art Institute of Chicago.

Publications:

By GREENE: articles—"The Artist's Reluctance to Communicate" in *Artnews* (New York), January 1957; "The Fourth Illusion: or, Hunger for Genius" in *Artnews* (New York), September 1957.

On GREENE: book—*The Art of Balcomb Greene* by Robert Beverly Hale, New York 1977.

During the years between 1935 and 1942 Balcomb Greene was actively participating in the organization of artists who were struggling for recognition in New York. From 1936 until 1941, Greene was chairman of the American Abstract Artists, and his works of this period were extensions of the de Stijl and constructivist traditions, austerely geometrical and concerned with architectonic organization. After a period in the mid to late 30's when the work was composed of diagonal planes which denied the horizon, Greene began to restrict himself to a pattern consisting of one vertical and one horizontal asymmetrically placed and evoking the balancing of oppositions primary in Mondrian's paintings. In 1941, Greene was still within the boundaries of geometric abstraction, but a picture such as "Blue Space" (1941) shows a growing concern with the horizon and with shapes that seem to derive ultimately from the recognizable.

Fron 1942, Greene's works became more involved with the horizon as the most basic division betwen earth/sea and sky. He had begun to feel that the possibilities for strictly non-representational painting in the geometric vein had been worn thin after the accomplishments of Mondrian, and he had pulled away from personal and artistic involvements in that area. Over the decade of the 40's Greene's work became more visionary and internally based. He had continually done figure studies over the years, and Greene now began to combine figure and landscape, as well as continuing his studies of the horizon, particularly on the sea.

During the 1930's Greene had been a leading figure in the revolt against indigenous American Realism, and in 1939 he had written that abstract art was the "first international language of the brush." The admission of recognizable imagery into his subsequent paintings does not deny these earlier concerns, but rather allows Greene to develop a highly personal statement in which he uses a highly controlled underlying structure to produce crystalline energies which merge figure and ground in a flickering atmosphere of light and shadow. His images are blurred, made baseless by the light which annihilates the physicality of the surface with energetic brush-strokes. By combining his concerns with formal elements of structure and light with his desire to convey an intimately felt vision of the anxious, ineffective state of humanity in contemporary existence, Greene created a pictorial repertoire that communicates on a more universal level. Whether he is painting seascapes or figures in city settings, Greene portrays each element in merging/fracturing motions, evoking the spectral ambiguities of psychologically felt states directly through the visual interactions of subject and space, light and color.

Greene has remained firmly against the doctrinaire attitudes of his time and context, whether they be those of the purist abstractionist or the social realist. By merging an intellectually based attitude toward the painter's grasp of formal elements and an intuitively based involvement with capturing the spirit of figure and landscape, Greene has arrived at an individualistic painterly vision which is both sensuously felt and informed with a timeless, egoless humanism. The images are neither ugly nor sentimentally beautiful, but rather become heroic through their very fragility, emphasizing, as Greene has stated, "him who, without self-destruction, must feel it." Greene's pictures neither break radically from traditions nor rest comfortably on them. They are a deeply personal expression of humanity's struggles on the physical and psychological edge, finding a possibility for fresh visualization out of the most basic images of the history of painting, the figure and the landscape.

—Barbara Cavaliere

GRIFFA, Giorgio.

Italian. Born in Turin, 19 March 1936. Studied law, Turin, 1954–58; studied painting in the atelier of Filippo Scroppo, Turin, 1960–63. Married in 1970: one child. Independent artist, Turin, since 1963. Agent: Galleria Martano, Via C. Battisti 3, 10123 Turin. Address: Via Avogadro 19, 10121 Turin, Italy.

Individual Exhibitions:

1968   Galleria Martano, Turin
1969   Galleria Sperone, Turin
1970   Sonnabend Gallery, New York
        Galerie Ileana Sonnabend, Paris
1971   Galerie Ricke, Cologne
        Galleria Multipli, Turin
        Galleria Toselli, Milan
1972   Galleria Sperone, Turin
        Galleria Godel, Rome
1973   Galerie Annemarie Verna, Zurich
        Galleria dell'Ariete, Milan
        Galerie Daniel Templon, Paris
        Studio 3/Bi, Bolzano, Italy
        Galleria Flori, Florence (with Marco Gastini)
1974   Galleria Daniel Templon, Milan
        Galleria La Bertesca, Genoa, Italy
        Galleria Banco, Brescia, Italy
        Galerie Mikro, West Berlin
        Studio Lia Rumma, Naples
        Galerie Daniel Templon, Paris
1975   Galerie D, Brussels
        Galleria Sperone, Rome
        Galleria Primo Piano, Rome
        Galleria Claudio Bottello, Turin
        Galleria Nova, Prato, Italy
        Galerie Annemarie Verna, Zurich
        Kunstraum, Munich
1976   Galleria Banco, Brescia, Italy
        Galerie Art in Progress, Munich
        Galleria Daniel Templon, Milan
        Galerie Art in Progress, Dusseldorf
        Galleria Il Sole, Bolzano, Italy
1977   Galleria del Milione, Milan
        Samangallery, Genoa, Italy
        Galleria Marlborough, Rome
        Galleria La Piramide, Florence
1978   Galerie Annemarie Verna, Zurich
        Galleria Lorenzelli, Milan
        Stadtische Kunsthalle, Dusseldorf
        Galleria E. Tre, Rome
1979   Galerie Mantra-N.R.A., Paris
        Expo Arte, Bari, Italy
        Galleria Incontri, Taranto, Italy
        Galerie Artline, The Hague
1980   Galleria Martano, Turin
        Samangallery, Genoa, Italy
        Kunstverein, Braunschweig, West Germany
        Galerie Walter Storms, Villingen, West Germany
        Gallerie E. Tre, Rome
1981   Galleria Il Centro, Naples
        Galleria Il Sole, Bolzano, Italy
        Lorenzelli Arte, Milan
        Studio G7, Bologna, Italy
        Galerie Luise Krohn, Badenweiler, West Germany
        Galleria Sagittario, Perugia, Italy
        Galleria Taide, Salerno, Italy
        Galerie Annemarie Verna, Zurich
        Galerie Walter Storms, Munich
        Galleria Primo Piano, Rome
1982   Galerie Artline, The Hague
        Galleria Martano, Turin

Selected Group Exhibitions:

1969   *Prospect 69*, Stadtische Kunsthalle, Dusseldorf (and *Prospect 73*, 1973)
1971   *L'Azione Concreta*, Villa Olmo, Como, Italy
1973   *Contemporanea*, Parcheggio Villa Borghese, Rome
1975   *Concerning Painting*, Museum Venlo, Netherlands (travelled to Schiedam and Utrecht)
1977   *Art in Italia 1960–77*, Galleria Civica d'Arte Moderna, Turin
1980   *34th Biennale*, Venice
1982   *Kunst uber Kunst*, Museums-Paedagogisches Zentrum, Munich
1986   *Aspects of Italian Art 1960–85*, Kunstverein, Frankfurt

Publications:

By GRIFFA: books—*Giorgio Griffa*, exhibition catalogue, Turin 1980; *Cani schiolti antichisti*, Turin and Genoa 1980; *Drugstore Parnassus*, Turin and Aachen 1981; article—"Lettera a Politi" in *Flash Art* (Milan), May 1971.

On GRIFFA: books—*Giorgio Griffa*, exhibition catalogue with texts by Paolo Fossati and Albino Galvano, Turin 1968; *L'Azione Concreta*, exhibition catalogue with essay by Paolo Fossati, Como 1971; *Giorgio Griffa*, exhibition catalogue with text by Maurizio Fagiolo, Rome 1972; *Italian Painting Today*, edited by Giancarlo Politi, Milan 1975; *Giorgio Griffa*, exhibition catalogue with text by Hermann Kern, Munich 1975; *Giorgio Griffa*, exhibition catalogue with texts by Maurizio Fagiolo, Tommaso Trini and others, Dusseldorf 1978; *Alfano, Chiari, Griffa, Nannucci*, exhibition catalogue with text by Jurgen Schilling, Braunschweig 1980; *Giorgio Griffa*, exhibition catalogue with essay by Flaminio Gualdoni, Turin 1982.

Following an early phase of decorative work consisting of a series of flowers and insects painted on canvas, Giorgio Griffa held his first one-man show in his home town of Turin in 1968. This exhibition demonstrated that Griffa had already developed a personal poetic. The paintings, which were reduced to a series of signs painted onto raw, unprepared canvas, suggested a reflective concern with the idea of the 'gestural' in painting. *Quasi Tre*, a work from that year, consists of three juxtaposed squares: the first two are monochromatic and black, arranged in a parallel sequence; the third, only half painted, is rotated by 45 degrees to emphasize its incomplete quality. The artist himself recalls: "In 1969 I had completed a series of five works following the same hypothesis (of seven oblique lines of the same colour on canvas), and that operation had opened my eyes to the endless potential of those lines".

Around 1970, a definite trend toward analytical research in his painting began to emerge, and Griffa became a significant representative in this field. It is all the more significant, bearing in mind that the neo-dada development of the 1960s had brought about a wholesale rejection of traditional art-making methods in favour of the employment of heterogeneous materials—on the one hand, cast-off objects and detritus; on the other, new technological products (plexiglass, etc.). During those years Griffa systematically pursued his aim. In 1973, he wrote: "I have to choose only one idea as my point of departure, an idea that must be the most elementary and readily available". The principle motivating this work is the reiteration of slight differences occuring by chance between similar paintings, or between different parts of the same painting. Griffa was to conclude his 1973 paper with the peremptory statement: "I have chosen horizontal lines".

At the beginning of 1969, he had begun the series of *Linee Orizzontali* by drawing on unprepared canvas a number of long, parallel lines spanning the upper part of the picture from one side to the other.

In 1975 Griffa produced, with the publishing house Martano, a book entitled *There is no Rose without Thorns*. It consists of 27 quotes from various artists and writers, beginning with the title-quotation from Joyce's *Ulysses*. The core of the idea proposed a renunciation of one's own writing in favour of a type of thought based on re-editing what has already been written by others. Each proposition, borrowed as it is, remains a basic element to be interpreted at the level of expressive value carried solely within the quotation itself. Similarly, in Griffa's paintings the sign (a broken line) is to be interpreted as the minimum denominator of a new painting.

To this type of reiteration is added another fundamental element on which Griffa's work is based—the preference for the anonymity of the work, insofar as the artist gives priority to an analytical approach as opposed to the creative thrust of the romantic artist. Griffa's work remains basically contained within these two lines of research.

The pale, diluted colours used on raw canvas or paper laid on the floor of his studio penetrate to the contours of any supporting frame or stretcher, so that the very structure of object is revealed. The aim of Griffa's research is to investigate both artistic language and the very act of 'making art' as the formative aspect of art itself.

—Roberto Lambarelli

GRIPPO, Victor.

Argentinian. Born in Junin, Buenos Aires Province, 10 May 1936. Studied chemistry at the National University, La Plata, 1955–57, and National College of Junin, 1957–59; studied at the School of Fine Arts, National University, La Plata, 1961–62, 1966–67. Served in First Regiment, Argentine Army. Married Ruth B. Klinger in 1967. Painter. Private Art Tutor, 1955–72; Staff Member, Biological Institute, Buenos Aires, 1965–68; Adviser in Arts to Sub-secretary of Culture, Buenos Aires, 1968–71. Free-lance designer, Buenos Aires, since 1968. Recipient: First Painting Prize, National College, Junin, 1953; Graphics Prize, *Salon de Tandil*, Argentina, 1957; Summer Scholarship, Central University of Quito, Ecuador, 1959; First Visual Experiment Prize, *Arts Festival*, Tandil, 1970; Second Paolini Acrylics Prize, Museum of Modern Art, Buenos Aires, 1972; First Prize, U.N.O. 30, Unesco, Yugoslavia 1975; Gran Premio Itamaraty, *Bienal* Sao Paul, 1977. Agent: Jorge Glusberg, Centro de Arte y Comunicacion, Elpidio Gonzales 4070, Buenos Aires. Address: Juncal 2170, Box 3, Buenos Aires, Argentina.

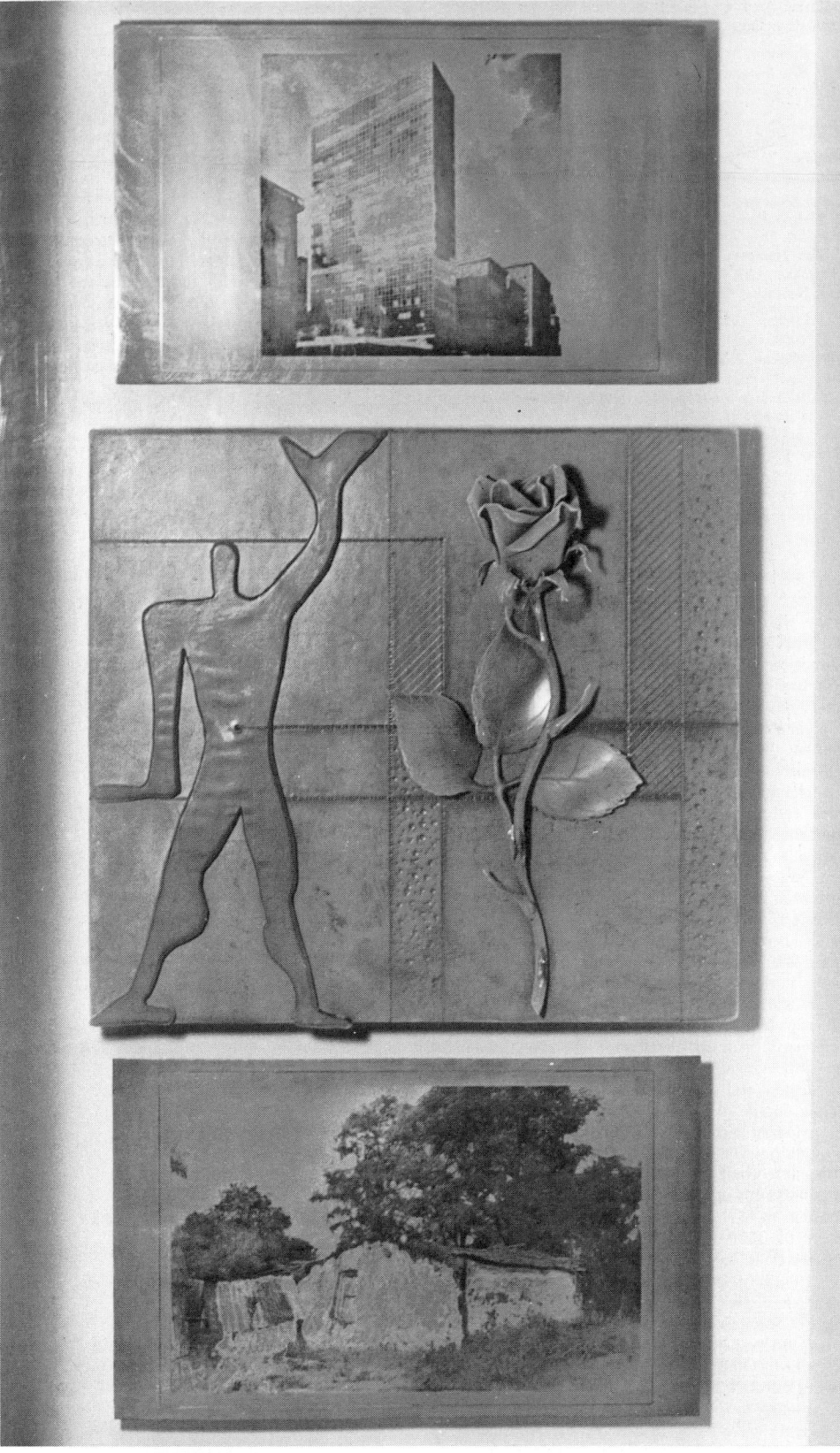

Victor Grippo: *Little Suitcase for Le Corbusier*, 1977

Individual Exhibitions:

1954	Museo Municipal Bellas Artes de Junin, Buenos Aires
1958	Salón Nueve Era, Tandil, Argentina
1959	Salón de Berisso, Buenos Aires
1966	Galeria Lirolay, Buenos Aires
1968	Galeria Lirolay, Buenos Aires

Selected Group Exhibitions:

1969   *Biennale,* Musée d'Art Moderne, Paris

1970   *Festival de las Artes,* Museo Provincial, Tandil, Argentina

1971   *Fotografia Tridimensional,* Centro de Arte y Comunicacion, Buenos Aires

1972   *Bienal de Arte Coltejer,* Medellin, Colombia
       Encuentro Internacional de Arte, Pamplona, Spain

1973   *Hacia un Perfil del Arte Latinoamericano,* Centro di Arte y Comunicacion, Buenos Aires (toured Europe and the United States)
       Homenaje a Salvador Allende, Museo de Bellas Artes, Santiago

1974   *Arte de Sistemas en Latinoamerica,* International Cultureel Centrum, Antwerp (toured Europe)
       Tendencias Actuales de la Pintura Argentina, Centre Artistique de Rencontres Internationales, Nice

1975   *El Arte y la Cultura de los Paises del Tercer Mundo,* Espace Pierre Cardin, Paris

Collections:

Museo de Bellas Artes, Tandil, Buenos Aires Province; Museo de Bellas Artes, La Plata, Buenos Aires Province; Museo Nacional de Bellas Artes, Buenos Aires.

Publications:

By GRIPPO: article—"Complementaridad de los pares opuestos," with others, in *Artinf 15* (Buenos Aires) November 1972.

On GRIPPO: articles—"Carta de Valeno Ferreyra al pintor Victor Grippo" by Valerio Ferreyra in *Diario Nueva Era* (Tandil), April 1958; "Por las Galerias" by Cordoba Iturburu in *Diario El Mundo* (Buenos Aires), August 1966; "Aspectos del Premio Ver y Estimar Modeladores del la Realidad" by Carlos Claiman in *Diario La Nacion* (Buenos Aires), April 1967; "A Noble Medium: Acrylics" by Kenneth Kemble in *Buenos Aires Herald*, August 1972; "Las perfecciones acrilicas" by Horacio Safons in *Revista Primera Plana* (Buenos Aires), August 1972; "Vanguardias Artisticas y Cultura Popular" by Nestor Garcia Canclini in *Transformaciones No. 90* (Buenos Aires) 1973; "Avantegarde et Fers de Lance" by Hugo Verlomme in *Quotidien de Paris*, February 1975; "Arte Popular y Sociedad en America Latina: Teorias esteticas y ensayos de transformacion" by Nestor Garcia Canclini in *Nueva Vision* (Buenos Aires) 1976.

At present the artist has the possibility of playing a role which transcends the importance of his own work. Situated as he is between the social force that nurtures him and the social force that he can derive from his creative imagination, the artist will be obliged to take as a point of departure, an ethical and genuinely progressive intention, transforming himself into the integrator of varied experiences. (Being in opposition to the continued fragmentation that oppresses our society.) In this way he can contribute to the conception of a more complete man.

My proposition is that of weakening the contradiction between art and science, through an aesthetic anchored in a complete chemical reaction between the logical-objective and the subjective-analogical, between the analytic and the synthetic. The imagination (not fantasy) is an instrument of creative knowledge no less rigorous than the one supplied by contemporary science.

Since 1970 I have completed a series of works, taking food (of Latin American origin) as the basic material. Through certain scientific approximations it was capable of provoking a reaction in the spectator's mind.

—Victor Grippo

Victor Grippo's most important concern consists of establishing a correlation between scientific production and the production of artistic events.

This correlation appeared spontaneously in some of the most important artists: Eddington, an astrophysicist, was a most excellent organist; Einstein played the violin; Heisemberg played the piano. Many of them have theorized about the relations between art and science. The Frenchman Gastón Bachelard, in particular, correlated conceptually both fields: his epistemological works and his "Poetica" are the expression of his totalizing thinking. Grippo is an artist as well as a scientist: draughtsman, painter and chemist, he makes this relation explicit through his artistic work.

The artificial production in the binary pair culturenature is characterized by the intentionality and the activity conditioned by a conscious objective. The different steps of the process of creation in the scientific production emerges from three basic elements: the previous history of the set of problems referred to the object of study (every hypothesis is based upon a previous one); the socio-cultural conditions of the social formation to which the investigators belong; and, lastly, the scientist's own capacity. The convergence of these three causes determines the issue of a scientific theory.

The analogy that exists between the production of a scientific theory and the artistic discourse arises clearly from Grippo's works. The convergence above mentioned is identical in the case of the process of the

artistic event: the historical, social, and individual factors not only determine a work of art, but also, in a certain characteristic way, they become apparent, they are present in it.

His work from the last 15 years seeks to show these analogies.

According to the historian Hyat Verrill, among the Incas "the cranial trephining determined in each case a new variety of potatoes. The curious fact is that in no other place were there so many varieties of potatoes as in Peru, nor so many trephined skulls."

Grippo is concerned about the relations between the tuber, which had a Latin American origin, and the human consciousness, because the potato, which first appeared in the Andes and was later known all over the world, contains forces and meanings that man has not been able even to suspect. Thus, in the same way, the human consciousness has an enormous untapped potential, especially in Latin America.

For him, the extension of the basic function of the potatoes (that is the feeding) would be the production of energy. As to consciousness, its extension would be: "obtain consciousness from energy."

Grippo once again dealt with the problems derived from the potato when he presented, in 1975, the opposition between the tuber in its natural form (vegetable) and its reproduction in transparent acrylic. We could say that his fundamental concern is the difference that exists between nature and culture or, in other words, between natural creation and artifical creation.

Within the cultural field, what Grippo is interested in, is the desciption of productive processes and instruments of production.

That is the leit-motiv of his exhibition *Crafts,* which consisted of a set of tools. The universe of social facts is represented by shovels, spoons, hammers, pliers, which the investigator-artist shows like forms of organization, reflecting the processes of production of the human group to which they belong.

For that reason, the reading of his works, provided that the spectator plays a real part in it, allows him to follow a clue leading to a whole set of economic, historical and cultural facts which are happening now.

"There is no work of art," Grippos says, "there exists the artist, with his incomplete manifestation, and the spectator, who, at present, completes and transforms it."

—Jorge Glusberg

GROOMS, Red.

American. Born in Nashville, Tennessee, 1 June 1937. Educated at Peabody College, Nashville, Tennessee; Art Institute of Chicago; New School for Social Research, New York; Hans Hofmann School, Provincetown, Massachusetts. Married Mimi Gross in 1964; child: Saskia. Settled in New York, 1957; first happenings and theatre events, New York, 1957; performed "The Burning Building" happening, New York, 1959; founded the multi-media environmental and performance company, Ruckus Productions, New York, 1963. Member, Board of Directors, Filmmakers Co-Op, New York. Recipient: Ingram Merrill Foundation Grant, 1968, 1974; American Academy of Arts and Letters Grant, 1969; Achievement in Art Award, *Who's Who in America*, 1970; Creative Artists' Program Service Grant in Filmmaking, New York, 1970. Agent: Marlborough Gallery Inc., 40 West 57th Street, New York, New York 10019. Address: 161 Mulberry Street, New York, New York 10013, U.S.A.

Individual Exhibitons:

1958   Sun Gallery, Provincetown, Massachusetts
        City Gallery, New York
1959   City Gallery, New York

1960   Reuben Gallery, New York
1962   Nashville Artists' Guild ·
1963   Tibor de Nagy Gallery, New York
1965   Tibor de Nagy Gallery, New York
1966   Tibor de Nagy Gallery, New York
1967   Tibor de Nagy Gallery, New York
        Allan Frumkin Gallery, Chicago
1968   Allan Frumkin Gallery, Chicago
1969   *Red and Mimi Hit the Road,* Tibor de Nagy Gallery, New York
1970   Tibor de Nagy Gallery, New York
1971   John Bernard Myers Gallery, New York
        Institute of Contemporary Art, Boston
        Harry N. Abrams Gallery, New York
1972   John Bernard Myers Gallery, New York
        Allan Frumkin Gallery, Chicago
        Barbara Fendick Gallery, Washington, D.C.
        Cheekwood Museum of Art, Nashville
        Graphics 1 and Graphics 2, Boston
1973   John Bernard Myers Gallery, New York
        The Ruckus World of Red Grooms, Rutgers University Gallery of Art, New Brunswick, New Jersey (travelled to New York Cultural Center, and to the Museo de Arte Contemporaneo, Caracas, 1973–74)
1975   Brooke Alexander Gallery, New York
        88 Pine Stret, New York
1976   *Red Grooms and the Ruckus Construction Company Present Ruckus Manhattan,* Marlborough Gallery, New York
1977   Galerie Roger d'Amecourt, Paris
        New Gallery of Contemporary Art, Cleveland
1978   Galerie Roger d'Amecourt, Paris
        Martin Wiley Gallery, Nashville
        State University of New York at Purchase
1979   Hudson River Museum, Yonkers, New York
1980   Lowe Art Museum, University of Miami
        Camp Gallery-Signet Fine Prints, St. Louis
        Colorado State University, Fort Collins
1981   Aspen Center for the Visual Arts, Colorado
        Montgomery Bell Academy, Nashville, Tennessee
        Burlington House, New York
1982   Institute of Contemporary Art, Philadelphia
        Benjamin Mangel Gallery, Philadelphia
        New Gallery of Contemporary Art, Cleveland, Ohio
1983   Unicorn Gallery, Aspen, Colorado
        Anderson Ranch, Aspen, Colorado
        North Carolina Museum of Art, Raleigh
1984   Marlborough Gallery, New York
1985   Marlborough Fine Art, London
        Hokin/Kaufman Gallery, Chicago
        Benjamin Mangel Gallery, Philadelphia
        Museum of Contemporary Art, Los Angeles
        Tennessee State Museum, Nashville
1986   Cumberland Gallery, Nashville, Tennessee
        Marlborough Gallery, New York
        Marlborough Fine Art, Tokyo
1987   Carpenter Center for the Visual Arts, Harvard University, Cambridge, Massachusetts
        Marlborough Gallery, New York

Selected Group Exhibitions:

1960   *New Media/New Forms,* Martha Jackson Gallery, New York
1966   *Still Life,* Museum of Modern Art, New York (toured the United States)
1974   *Poets of the Cities: New York and San Francisco 1950–1965,* Museum of Fine Arts and Southern Methodist University, Dallas (travelled to the San Francisco Museum of Art, and the Wadsworth Atheneum, Hartford, Connecticut)
1975   *Realismus und Realität,* Kunsthalle, Darmstadt
1976   *The Great American Rodeo,* Fort Worth Art Museum (travelled to Witte Memorial Museum, San Antonio, and Colorado Springs Fine Art Center, 1976–77)
1978   *Art About Art,* Whitney Museum, New York
1982   *Homo Sapiens: The Many Images,* Aldrich Museum of Contemporary Art, Ridgefield, Connecticut
1984   *Metamanhattan,* Whitney Museum, New York
1986   *Hollywood: Legend and Reality,* Smithsonian Institution, Washington, D.C. (toured the United States)

1987   *Contemporary Coutouts*, Whitney Museum, New York

Collections:

Museum of Modern Art, New York; New School Art Center, New York; Brooklyn Museum of Art, New York; Hudson River Museum, Yonkers, New York; Hirshhorn Museum and Sculpture Garden, Washington, D.C.; Art Institute of Chicago; Denver Art Museum; Fort Worth Art Center, Texas; Northern Kentucky University, Highland Heights; Museo de Arte Contemporaneo, Caracas; Moderna Museet, Stockholm.

PUblications:

By GROOMS: book—*Drawings*, with Mimi Grooms, Florence 1961; article—statement in *Art Now: New York*, July 1970; films—*The Unwelcome Guests*, 1961; *Shoot the Moon*, with Rudy Burckhardt, 1962; *Ruckus Shorts*, 1963–66; *Fat Feet*, with Yvonne Andersen, 1966; *Tappy Toes*, 1969–70; *Hippodrome Hardware*, 1972–73; *The Conquest of Libya by Italia 1912–1913*, 1972–73; *Ruckus Manhattan*, 1975–76; *Little Red Riding Hood*, 1978; *Small Fry Gangster*, 1985.

On GROOMS: books-*Happenings*, edited by Michael Kirby, New York 1965; *Assemblage, Environments and Happenings* by Allan Kaprow, New York 1966; *The Ruckus World of Red Grooms*, exhibition catalogue, by Dennis Cate, New Brunswick, New Jersey 1973; *Red Grooms*, exhibition catalogue, Caracas 1974; *Ruckus Manhattan*, exhibition catalogue, New York 1975; *Red Grooms and the Ruckus Construction Company Present Ruckus Manhattan*, exhibition catalogue, New York 1976; *Red Grooms and Ruckus Manhattan* by Judd Tully, New York 1977; *Red Grooms: retrospective 1956-1984*, exhibition catalogue with essays by Judith Stein, John Ashbery and Janet K. Cutler, Philadelphia 1985.

For months the piece is your real life, and then you're suddenly separated from it—it becomes an object.

There's a proletarian feeling about my work. That type of evergy and subject matter excites me a lot. And I've always felt a kinship to commercial people.

It irritates me that people associate themselves with my sculpture, that they receive it so warmly. Maybe they perceive it too quickly, they don't make an effort.

— Red Grooms

For more than 20 years, Red Grooms has been chronicling the disparate surrealisms of urban America with humor, ingenuity, passion and anything else that's available. Closely allied with Happenings in their earliest stages, his own vision has not changed nearly as much as the context into which it fits. His city-scapes, though they retain their crazy meanderings, their stage presence and certainly an uncanny cross-breeding of diverse materials, now occupy a category all their own. Grooms is the Walt Disney of the art world, a title to which he happily concedes.

In the 1950's and 60's environmental sculpture or sculptural painting was loaded with references to the avant-garde. Grooms, whose background indicates that his interests in the Ringling Brothers were at least as acute as those in fine art, was ripe for animating his paintings on stage. He found, after producing and performing "The Burning Building" in 1959, that he so enjoyed enveloping his audience that even in the 80's he continues to construct multi-media, all encompassing three-dimensional environments. You enter Grooms' sculptures, you don't simply view the caricatures of legendary figures, historical facts and morsels of contemporary city life. With Grooms' keen eye for detail, no matter how minute, everyone and everything is the butt of his witty tales.

But Grooms is not only entertainment. On closer examination, he strikes an edgy balance between simple documentation and an acerbic wit which encapsulates the ironies and inequities of his New York City. His perceptions of the Big Apple, evidently fed by a rabid sense of devotion, shed light on life's harsher realities such as rats, prices, congestion, pollution, graft.

In the mid-70's Grooms, his wife and the Ruckus Construction Company (a consortium of some 30 local artists, students and various other enthusiasts) embarked on a monumental project to recreate all of Manhattan on his own scale and in his own vernacular. He called it "Ruckus Manhattan: A Sculptural Novel." One would be hard-pressed to find a more suitable title, for this work really is novelistic in its rambling satires of this and that. Using every available material from wood to paint to cardboard, Grooms distorted, "kitsched-up" and poked fun at much of New York City. The spontaneous theatrics of his sprawling parodies delight huge audiences who knowingly laugh at the newspaper stands, the bums and themselves.

In celebration of its 300th birthday, Grooms' "Philadelphia Cornucopia" was spotlighted in *Life* magazine, which may indicate the depth of his popularity. This is art for the people . . . small "a", big "P".

—Janet Goleas

GROSSMAN, Nancy.

American. Born in New York City, 28 April 1940. Educated at the Pratt Institute, New York, 1958–62 (Haskell Scholarship for Foreign Travel, 1962), B.F.A. 1962; artwork influenced by Richard Lindner and David Smith. Independent artist since 1961: lives and works in New York. Member, Sculpture Jury, CAPS Fellowship, New York State Council on the Arts, 1973; Member, Sculpture Jury, Prix de Rome Fellowships, American Academy in Rome, 1974. Recipient: Guggenheim Fellowship for Painting, 1965; Inaugural Contemporary Achievement Award, Pratt Institute, 1966; American Academy of Arts and Letters National Institute of Arts and Letters Award, 1974; Sculpture Fellowship, National Endowment for the Arts, 1984. Agent: Heath Gallery, 416 East Paces Ferry Road, Atlanta, Georgia 30305. Address: 105 Eldridge Street, New York, New York 10002, U.S.A.

Individual Exhibitions:

1964   Oscar Krasner Gallery Inc., New York
1965   Oscar Krasner Gallery Inc., New York (twice)
1967   Oscar Krasner Gallery Inc., New York
1969   Cordier and Ekstrom Inc., New York
1971   Cordier and Ekstrom Inc., New York
1973   Cordier and Ekstrom Inc., New York
1975   *Collage Paintings*, Cordier and Ekstrom Inc., New York
1976   Cordier and Ekstrom Inc., New York
1978   Church Fine Arts Gallery, University of Nevada, Reno
1980   Barbara Gladstone Gallery, New York
1981   Heath Gallery, Atlanta, Georgia
1982   Barbara Gladstone Gallery, New York
1984   Terry Dintenfass Gallery, New York
1986   Heath Gallery, Atlanta, Georgia

Selected Group Exhibitions:

1961   *Forty Painters*, City Center Gallery, New York
1969   *Contemporary American Sculpture*, Whitney Museum, New York
1972   *Recent Figure Sculpture*, Fogg Art Museum, Harvard University, Cambridge, Massachusetts
1976   *Drawing Now: 10 Artists*, Soho Center for Visual Arts, New York
1977   *Contemporary Women: Consciousness Content*, Brooklyn Museum, New York
1978   *Women from Nostalgia to Now*, Alex J. Rosenberg Gallery, New York
1980   *American Sculpture: Gifts of Howard and Jean Lipman*, Whitney Museum, New York
1982   *The Americans: The Collage*, Contemporary Arts Museum, Houston

1984   *Dreams and Nightmares*, Hirshhorn Museum, Washington, D.C.
1987   *Modern American Realism*, National Museum of American Art, Washington, D.C.

Collections:

Whitney Museum, New York; Baltimore Museum of Art; Princeton University Art Museum, New Jersey; Museum of Fine Arts, Dallas; University of California Art Museum, Berkeley; Boymans Van Beuningen Museum, Rotterdam; National Museum of American Art/Smithsonian Institution, Washington, D.C.; Phoenix Art Museum, Arizona; Rice Museum, Houston; Virginia Museum of Fine Arts, Richmond.

Publications:

On GROSSMAN: books—*Open Secrets* by B. Diamonstein, New York 1972; *Recent Figure Sculpture*, exhibition catalogue, with an introduction by J. L. Wasserman, Cambridge, Massachusetts 1972; *Nancy Grossman*, exhibition catalogue, New York 1973; *Nancy Grossman: Collage Paintings*, exhibition catalogue, New York 1975; *Nancy Grossman: Collages and Pastels*, exhibition catalogue, New York 1976; *Art Talk*, conversations with 12 women artists, by Cindy Nemser, New York 1975; *Nancy Grossman*, exhibition catalogue, by Vals Osborne, Reno 1978; *Dreams and Nightmares*, exhibition catalogue with essay by Valerie J. Fletcher, Washington, D.C. 1983; *Modern American Realism*, exhibition catalogue with essays by Virginia M. Mecklenburg and William Kloss, Washington, D.C. 1987; articles—"Art Surprise from Nancy Grossman" by John Canaday in the *New York Times*, May 1970; "The Least Cruel Artist Alive" by John Canaday in the *New York Times*, November 1971; "Nancy Grossman Ledermonstren" by T. von Schroder and G. Mangold in *Twen* (Munich), May 1971; "Art and the Artist: Nancy Grossman" by Emily Genauer in the *New York Post*, December 1971; "New Realism in Sculpture: Look Alive!" by R. Constable in *Saturday Review* (New York), April 1972; "Art: Nancy Grossman" by John Canaday in the *New York Times*, October 1973; "Art and the Artist" by Emily Genauer in the *New York Post*, December 1973; "Man Is Anonymous: The Art of Nancy Grossman" by Corinne Robins in *Art Spectrum* (Lugano, Switzerland), February 1975; "Nancy Grossman" by Douglas Blau in *Arts Magazine* (New York), February 1981; review by Stephen Westfall in *Arts Magazine* (New York), February 1981; "Nancy Grossman" by Donald Kuspit in *Artforum* (New York), December 1984; "Not a Pretty Picture: Can Violent Art Heal?" by Arlene Raven in *Village Voice* (New York), 17 June 1986.

My work addresses both the philosophical and the physical. It is the Skeleton and structure of my attempt to find my own meanings.

The Hebrew command not to make graven images reverberates, but to create art that did not exist in the physical world before is more compelling.

I have made things whole which were not whole. I have taken possession of, and mystified, the most common pedestrian objects of everyday life—a book of matches, a walnut, a pebble. By looking/looking/looking at the object—looking so carefully at the thing itself that nothing can remain beneath attention. Then there is no boredom.

My work is the only diary of my life. It is the physical revelation of my inner life and intellectual concerns of the moment.

Making art is magical in its imaging the non-verbal, in its conjuring the non-visible into existence.

—Nancy Grossman

At the outset of her first wide reknown, Nancy Grossman said of her work: "It's the idea of making something and then hiding it again." And in a real sense, her entire mature career has been devoted to just that concept—both literally in the materiality of her work and, as well, metaphorically in the nature of her subject matter. Grossman, earlier in the mid-60's, had already used leather and metal (from her vast collection of objects) in planar and abstract collages with feminist subjects—Women Landscapes—and in paintings and prints had also surveyed sexual themes. Scarpitta's works, from earlier that decade, may have

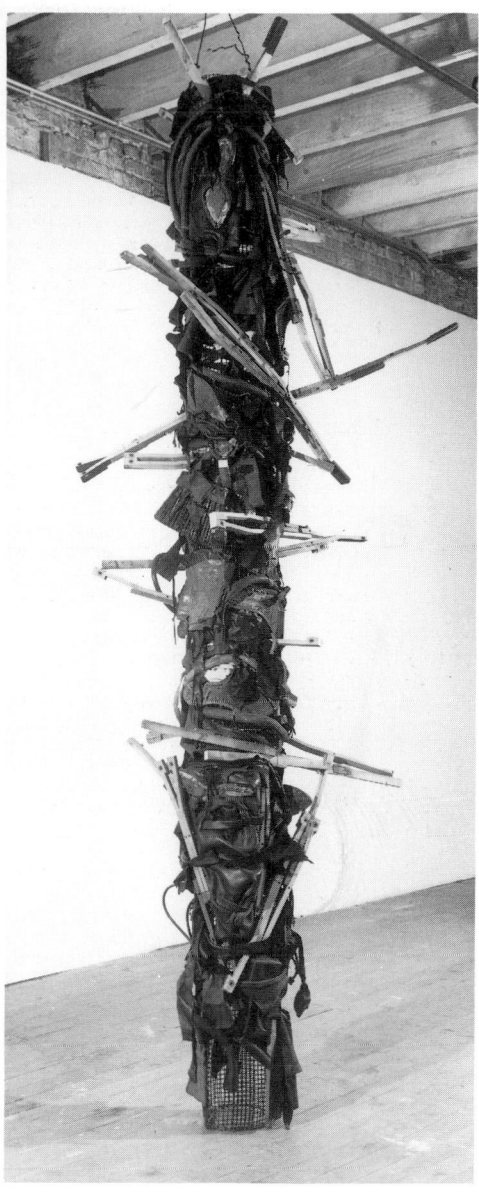

Nancy Grossman: *Succot*, 1983

been an influence. Since the start of the 70's, her signature image has been three-dimensional, life-size heads which became clearly male after 1972—some few torsos—covered over by meticulously crafted leather.

The carved wooden head forms within are apparently equally worked, and the airless fit of the at-first eyeless heads produced an exotic emblem of violence and a deviant sexuality. Yet with the focus, entirely upon the head in the great majority of her work (a well-received exhibition in 1974 offered drawn and painted, collaged bodies), an oddly poignant and a-sexual mood of repression and struggle is also felt. The whole group of these works, to the present moment, is redolent of a 19th century Maldoror-like, abstracted, evil; moreover, the frozen eroticism of classicism may be suggested by her technical perfection and aloofness. Perhaps her firmest success has been to bring the erotic emblem in high art up-to-date with her generalized Satanic and barbaric innuendo, so far removed from the urban and individualized decadence of Grosz, Lindner, and Bacon. This non-European quality—if that was her intention—was more clearly defined when Grossman added distinctly Negroid features to the nose and mouth parts of her sculptures; as well, large horns and other appendages have been added to the head form.

After a perhaps telling three-year hiatus from exhibition activity (1977-80), Grossman returned with work that seemingly has not extended either the com-

pass or the focus of her by-now carefully cultivated image. Although the artist has always naturally disallowed any personal involvement in the innuendo of her subject matter, one might argue, considering its persistence, for the depth of its meaning for her. On the other hand, the obsessive craft-force of all these works may be her real focus—and the overtly scandalous subjects persist since they allow her continued access to her craft love. Until this recent exhibition Grossman usually had kept the entire head covered by leather, eyeless with nose and mouth alone visible. Now zippers, shells, buttons have begun to serve as eye and mouth form indicators and their bizarre aspect further increased by fine-filed gold and silver spikes. If these now manifold accessories were an expansion of her craft interests, it was not to continue into the later 1980s. As if bidding an end to her long-held object-fascination, Grossman constructed *Succot*, a large columnar and totem-like collage tied with wire and labelled "phallo-centric." Since 1983, the larger body of her work has been two-dimensional images which nonetheless continue with Grossman's signature rage and violence, albeit no longer implicit as in the earliest sculptures. These drawing and paintings, with allusions to Da Vinci and Mannerism, show dogs, men, women in hysterical confrontation—the women usually calm—with no narrative causation suggested. With the shift of medium there has been no easing of the grip of sexual unease upon her art.

—Joshua Kind

GROSVENOR, Robert (Strawbridge).

American. Born in New York City, 31 March 1937. Studied at the Ecole des Beaux-Arts, Dijon, France, 1956; Ecole Supérieure des Arts Décoratifs, Paris, 1957–58; University of Perugia, Italy, 1958. Married Jacqueline Gardner in 1966; children: Kali, Marina and Jeremy. Sculptor: lives and works in New York. Formerly, Instructor, School of Visual Arts, New York. Recipient: National Council of the Arts Award, 1969; Guggenheim Fellowship, 1969; National Endowment for the Arts and Humanities Grant, 1970; American Academy of Arts and Letters Award, 1972. Agent: Paula Cooper Gallery, New York. Address: c/o Paula Cooper Gallery, 155 Wooster Street, New York, New York 10012, U.S.A.

Individual Exhibitions:

1965	Park Place Gallery, New York
1966	Dwan Gallery, Los Angeles
1967	Park Place Gallery, New York
1970	Galerie Ricke, Cologne
	Fischbach Gallery, New York
	Paula Cooper Gallery, New York
1971	Paula Cooper Gallery, New York
	La Jolla Museum of Contemporary Art, California
1974	Paul Cooper Gallery, New York
	Galleria Francoise Lambert, Milan
1975	Galerie Stampa, Basel
	Paul Cooper Gallery, New York
	Galerie Eric Fabre, Paris
	Pasquale Tridorio, Naples
1976	Institute for Art and Urban Resources, The Clocktower, New York
1977	Galerie Eric Fabre, Paris
1978	Paul Cooper Gallery, New York
1979	Paula Cooper Gallery, New York
1980	Paula Cooper Gallery, New York
1981	Paula Cooper Gallery, New York
1984	P.S.1/Institute for Art and Urban Resources, New York
1986	Paula Cooper Gallery, New York

Selected Group Exhibitions:

1966	*Primary Structures*, Jewish Museum, New York
1968	*Minimal Art*, Gemeentemuseum, The Hague (toured Europe)
1975	*Zeichnungen 3* Städtisches Museum, Leverkusen, West Germany
1977	*Documenta 6*, Kaseel, West Germany
1978	*Drawings for Outdoor Sculpture 1946–1977*, Amherst College, Massachusetts (travelled to the University of California at Santa Barbara, and the Massachusetts Institute of Technology, Cambridge)
1979	*The Minimal Tradition*, Aldrich Museum of Contemporary Art, Ridgefield, Connecticut
1981	*Amerikanische Zeichnungen der Siebziger Jahre*, Louisiana Museum, Humlebaek, Denmark (travelled to Basle, Munich and Ludwigshafen)
1983	*Objects, Structures, Artifice*, University of South Florida, Tampa
1985	*The Maximal Implications of the Minimal Line*, Bard College, Annandale-on-Hudson, New York
1987	*The Success of Failure*, Laumeier Sculpture Park and Gallery, St. Louis

Collections:

Museum of Modern Art, New York; Whitney Museum, New York; New York University; Storm King Art Center, Mountainville, New York; Aldridge Museum of Art, Ridgefield, Connecticut; Massachusetts Institute of Technology, Cambridge; Hirshhorn Museum and Sculpture Garden, Washington, D.C.; Walker Art Center, Minneapolis.

Publications:

On GROSVENOR: books—*Constructivism* by George Rickey, New York 1967; *Minimal Art*, exhibition catalogue with texts by Enno Develing, Lucy Lippard and Renata Sharp, Dusseldorf 1969; *Objects, Structures, Artifice: American Sculpture 1970–1983*, exhibition catalogue by Michael Klein, Tampa 1983; articles—"E=MC² a GoGo" by David Bourdon in *Art News* (New York), January 1966; "Indoor-Outdoor: Space and Materials, 6 Sculptors" by R. Mathias in *Arts Magazine* (New York), Summer 1972; "Robert Grosvenor's Sculpture" by Bruce Kurtz in *Arts Magazine* (New York), October 1975; "Robert Grosvenor: Specific Clarity" by Jeremy Gilbert-Rolfe in *Arts in America* (New York), March/April 1976; review by John Russell in the *New York Times* (New York), 21 April 1978; review by Deborah Perlberg in *Artforum* (New York), Summer 1978; "Robert Grosvenor" by Tiffany Bell in *Arts Magazine* (New York), January 1980; "Robert Grosvenor" by Donald Kuspit in *Artforum* (New York), Summer 1984; "Robert Grosvenor" by Ellen Hand in *Arts* (New York), Summer 1986.

Robert Grosvenor's career, at least outwardly, has encompassed a distinct turnabout from his earlier sense of sculpture. He came to public prominence in the mid-60's with work both minimalist and aggressively techno-romantic in its clear engineering and drama; yet since the onset of the 70's, he has consistently used large, dressed, wooden beams as his prime material. He rejected both fabrication and industrial finish to achieve an heroic and mute primitivism.

His well-known work of the previous period depended upon both their hollowed and faceted columnar forms, and a quality of forceful movement, given to them at times by cantilevering. The engineering of the latter type, which could not be discovered from their exterior, consisted of wiring systems and bolting to either ceiling (his still most well-known work "Transoxiana," 1965), or to the floor ("Tapanga," 1965—this work often likened to the Kitt Peak Solar Telescope housing in Arizona). This same effect of involvement with the architecture was visible in a work of this same time at the Loeb Center at NYU in New York; there two sections of the sculpture on the roof of the building appear to be extensions and thus continuations of the sculpture penetrated to the roof from the gallery area below.

A life-long interest in sailing and several years spent as a student of nautical engineering might be

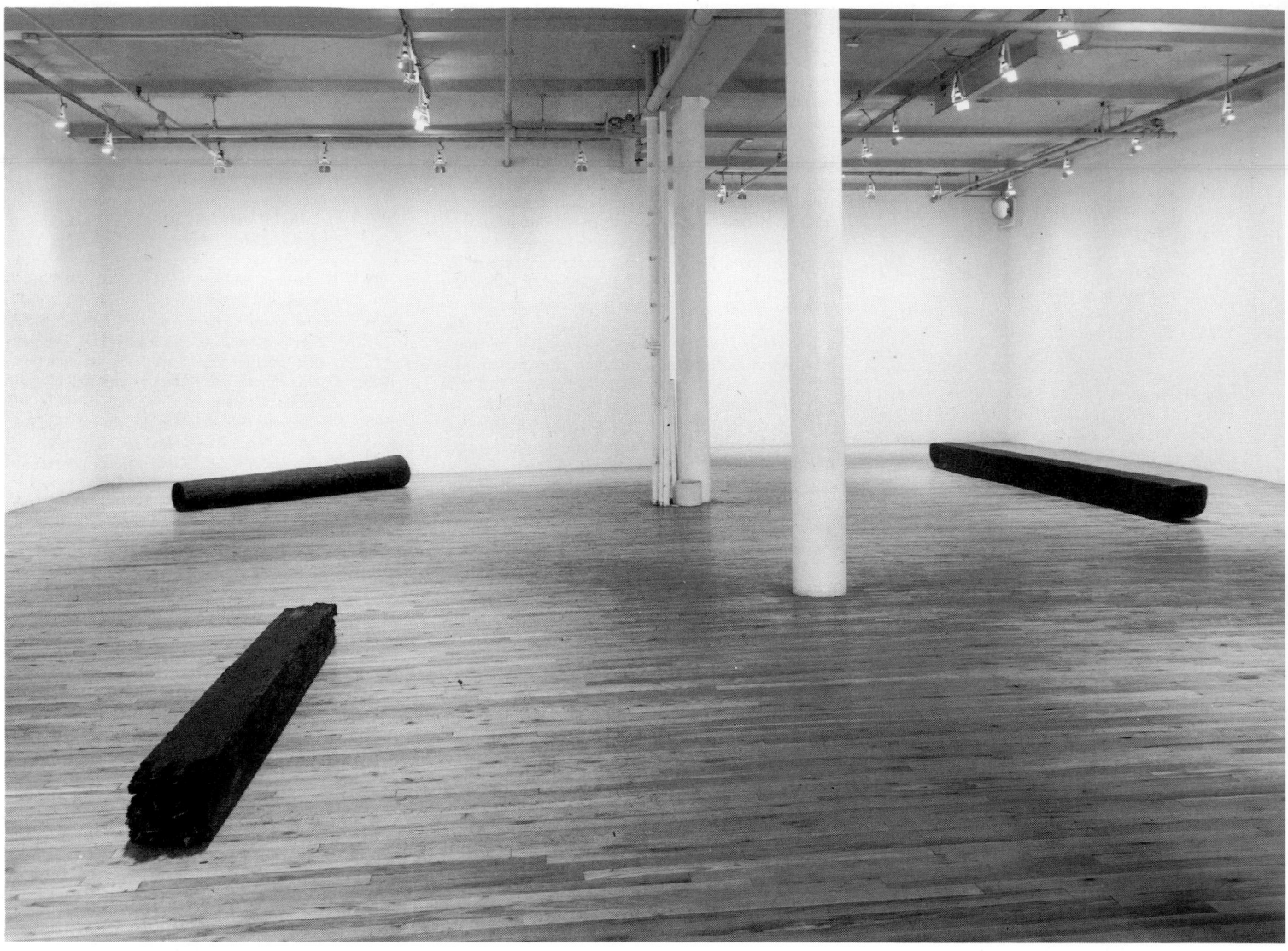

Robert Grosvenor: Installation at the Paula Cooper Gallery, New York, 1975

offered as some reference for these effects—Grosvenor himself denies it. His art was always expressionist, and so his shift of material and attitude at the start of the 70's may find precedent in his previous Constructivist work; and the works of the 70's—baffling to many critics—may the more be truly Minimalist in their reductive form and manipulation. Many of these recent timber sculptures—the lumber as large as 12 inches square and telephone pole (which have also been used) in length—were subjected to great pressure which cracked them in either one or several places. (In this aspect, Grosvenor's works retain a "technological" aura, as we imagine the enormity of the pressure necessary to have fractured these beams.) The cracks were often carefully mended, or left partially visible—and these sculptures were usually displayed singly, and on the floor itself.

In only the later 70's has Grosvenor returned to construction as a basis for his art. But his structures have remained as simple as their still beam-like parts and are composed of stacked beams, creosoted and dark; the obvious reference is the sea-coastal milieu. Perhaps these works might be understood as an eclectic blend of minimalism, the assemblage of abstract-expressionist sculpture, and earth art; or ironically, as sculpture really monumental and outdoor, yet seen only in traditional interior art gallery spaces. Their metaphorical poignance—their Promethean submission—may be but a guise for their more pointed reference to the currect artist's dilemma, akin perhaps to the anguish felt by the abstract-expressionist generation during the 1960s.

In a mid-80s piece, nest-like and metallic, an eclectic hovering of older motifs remain: large scale—the

older giganticism is gone—industrial and blackened, yet carefully assembled and seemingly repaired. As his first public work in several years, the private pace (i.e., non-professional in its infrequency) of his art's appearance now is as if a reflection of its muteness and enigma.

—Joshua Kind

GRÜTZKE, Johannes.

German. Born in Berlin, 30 September 1937. Studied under Peter Janssen, Hochschule für Bildende Künste, Berlin, 1957–64; under Oskar Kokoschka, Summer Academy, Salzburg, Austria, 1962. Married Roswitha Steinke in 1964 (divorced, 1971); son: Julius; lives with the costume designer Barbara Naujok since 1979; son: Gustav. Worked as a stagehand, Volksbühne Theatre, Theatre des Westens, and Renaissance Theatre, Berlin, 1958–64. Independent artist since 1964. Founder-member, Die Erlebnisgeiger music and performance group, Berlin, 1965 (from 1980, re-named Erlebnisgeigern und Klavier und Gesang); founder, with painters Manfred Bluth, Mattias Koeppel and Karlheinz Ziegler, Schule der Neuen Prächtigkeit artists' group, Berlin, 1973; founder with Barbara Naujok, *Die Schaukel* revue at the Metropol, Berlin, 1979; stage designer for director Peter Zadek and others, in Berlin, Stuttgart and Hamburg, from 1980; artistic adviser and designer, Deutsche Schauspielhaus, Hamburg, since 1985. Guest instructor, Hochschule für Bildende Künste, Hamburg, 1976–77; instructor in painting, Summer Academy, Salzburg, 1987. Agents: Ladengalerie Karoline Müller, Kurfürstendamm 64, 1000 Berlin 15 (West); Galerie Gunzenhauser, Maximilienstrasse 10, 8000 Munich 22. Addresses: Güntzelstrasse 53, 1000 Berlin 31 (West); Hegestrasse 40, 2000 Hamburg 13, West Germany.

Individual Exhibitions:

1964 Galerie "Pro", Bad Godesberg, West Germany
1965 Galerie Schütze. Bad Godesberg, West Germany
        Artibus, Berlin (with Otmar Alt)
1967 Kleine Weltlaterne, Berlin (with Gonschorr and Romolla)
1968 Galerie Schütze, Bad Godesberg, West Germany
1969 Neue Münchner Galerie, Munich
        Galleria La Bertesca, Genoa
1970 Galerie Tobies and Silex, Cologne
1971 Galerie Mikro, Berlin
        Galerie Grafikmeyer, Karlsruhe
1972 Nurnberger Oper, Nuremberg
1973 Galerie Holeczek, Freiburg
        Galerie Brusberg, Hannover
        Galerie Kleber, Berlin
1974 Schloss Charlottenburg, West Berlin (retrospective; travelled to the Kunsthalle, Nuremberg; Kunstverein, Freiburg; and the Kunstverein, Mannheim)
1975 Galerie Kleber, Berlin
        University Museum, Marburg, West Germany
        Galerie "k", Darmstadt

1976 Galerie an der Farbmühle, Wuppertal, West Germany
Galerie Schnecke, Hamburg
Galerie von Bartha, Basle
Galerie Buchholz, Munich
Galerie Heike Curtze, Vienna
1977 Galerie Heike Curtze, Dusseldorf
Galerie Kleber, Berlin
Gemälde 1964–1977, Kunstverein, Braunschweig, West Germany (retrospective)
Sydow Fine Art, Frankfurt
1978 Kunstverein, Wolfsburg, West Germany
Galerie Buchholz, Munich
Galerie Apex, Göttingen, West Germany
Editions le Cadre, Olten, Switzerland
1979 Kunstverein, Darmstadt
1980 Galerie Kunze, Berlin
Galerie Buchholz, Munich
1981 Galerie Etienne de Causan, Paris
Kunstverein, Unna, West Germany
Galerie Bäumler, Regensburg, West Germany
1982 Kunstverein, Neustadt/Weinstrasze, West Germany
Galerie Public Press, Dusseldorf
Lüner Galerie, Lüneburg, West Germany
Galerie Kunze, West Berlin
1983 Galerie Brockstedt, Hamburg
Galerie Etienne de Causans, Paris
Kunstverein, Gifhorn, West Germany
Galerie Merlin Verlag, Gifkendorf bei Luneburg, West Germany
Staatstheater, Stuttgart
1984 Galerie Gunzenhauser, Munich
Ladengalerie, at *Art 84*, Basle
Kunstverein, Luneburg, West Germany
Galerie am Rathaus, Frankfurt
Galerie Mora, West Berlin
Kunstverein Artig, Velen, West Germany
Nationalgalerie, West Berlin
1985 Ladengalerie, at *Art 85*, Basle
Ladengalerie, at the *Kunstmesse*, Cologne
Galerie Mora, West Berlin
1986 Deutsches Schauspielhaus, Hamburg
Heitland Foundation, Schloss Celle, West Germany
Galerie Hilger, Vienna
Kramp und Graff, Hamburg
Asperger and Bischoff Gallery, Chicago
1987 Galerie in der Mühle, Oldenburg, West Germany
Galerie Schloss Rimsingen, Breisach-Oberrimsingen, West Germany
Galerie Niepel, Dusseldorf
Ladengalerie, at *Art 87*, Basle
Galerie Burgdorf, Hannover
Galerie Gunzenhauser, Munich
Hypotheken-Bank, Salzburg, Austria
Mittelrhein-Museum, Koblenz, West Germany
Ladengalerie, West Berlin

Selected Group Exhibitions:

1968 *Documenta 4*, Museum Fridericianum, Kassel, West Germany
1970 *Kunst und Politik*, Kunstverein, Karlsruhe (toured West Germany)
1972 *The Berlin Scene*, Gallery House, London (toured West Germany)
1974 *Schule der neuen Prächtigkeit*, Kunstverein, West Berlin (toured West Germany)
1976 *Méfiez-vous de l'art*, Kunstmuseum, Olten, Switzerland
1978 *13°E: 11 Artists Working in Berlin*, Whitechapel Art Gallery, London
1980 *Liebe—Dokumente aus unserer Zeit*, Kunsthalle, Darmstadt, West Germany (travelled to Hannover)
1982 *Spiegelbilder*, Kunstverein, Hannover (travelled to Duisburg and West Berlin)
1984 *Realisten in Berlin*, Berlinische Galerie, West Berlin
1986 *Die Maler und das Theater im 20. Jahrhundert*, Schirn Kunsthalle, Frankfurt

Collections:

Kunstmuseum, Basle; Kunsthalle, Hamburg; Kunsthalle, Kiel; Kunsthalle, Nuremberg; Staatsgalerie, Stuttgart; Kupferstichkabinett, Dresden; Museum Oberhausen, West Germany; Berlinische Galerie; Centre Georges Pompidou, Paris; Sprengel Museum, Hannover.

Publications:

By GRÜTZKE: books—*Im Watt*, Hamburg 1978; *Pantalon Ouvert*, with Arno Waldschmidt and Jan Peter Tripp, Hamburg 1978; *Misch Du Dich nicht auch noch ein*, Frankfurt 1979; *Paarungen, Verwüstungen*, with Tilmann Lehnert, West Berlin 1983; *Aus den Leben Richard Wagners*, Gifkendorf 1983; *Der Kunstfreund, der Künstler und die Kunst*, West Berlin 1984; *Kunzes Freunde*, 14 colour drawings, Gifkendorf 1985; *Kolophon*, with Tilmann Lehnert, West Berlin 1987; *Die Manuskripte von Belo Horizonte*, Hamburg 1987.

On GRÜTZKE: books—*Johannes Grützke*, exhibition catalogue Cologne 1970; *Zu Johannes Grützke*, exhibition catalogue, by Lucy Schaner, Hannover 1973; *Johannes Grützke*, exhibition catalogue by Tilman Lehnert, Berlin 1974; *Kunst nach 45* by Wieland Schmied, Berlin 1974; *Schule der Neuen Prächtigkeit*, exhibition catalogue, with text by M. Bluth, M. Koeppel and K. Zeigler, Berlin 1974; *Johannes Grützke: Gemälde 1964–1977*, exhibition catalogue, with texts by Ekkehard Schenk zu Schweinsberg, Tilmann Lehnert and Bernhard Holeczek, Braunschweig, West Germany 1977; *Grützke*, exhibition catalogue, Paris 1981; *Johannes Grützke: Unser Fortschritt ist unaufhörlich*, exhibition catalogue with text by Lucius Griesebach, West Berlin 1984; *Johannes Grützke—Klassisch, übertrieben*, exhibition catalogue with text by Walter Schurian, Vienna 1986; *Johannes Grützke: Gedrucktes, Gemaltes, Gesagtes, Geschriebenes, Gespieltes* by Michael Perschke, West Berlin 1987; film—*Johannes Grützke*, directed by Peter West, Contemporary Artists series, BBC Television, 1979.

Johannes Grützke was born in Berlin in 1937 and lived there until 1984. He belongs to the pioneers of a new realism which arose in the early 1960's in parallel with pop-art in a reaction to the informalism and abstraction. In 1973, together with Manfred Bluth, Mathias Koeppel and Karlheinz Zeigler, he founded "The School of the New Magnificence," which he ironically celebrated several times in the following years with portraits of the members. The large format paintings have the effect of ordinary snapshots and show, in near life-size images, the trivial ritual of male group behavior as representations of alienated existence. Yet they are not really images of reality but rather arranged scenes in which the autonomous picture represses the image—actualized signs of a high degree of abstraction and level of artificiality.

Basically Grützke takes no position on realism as

Johannes Grützke: *Mannerprofil mit offnem Mund*, 1985

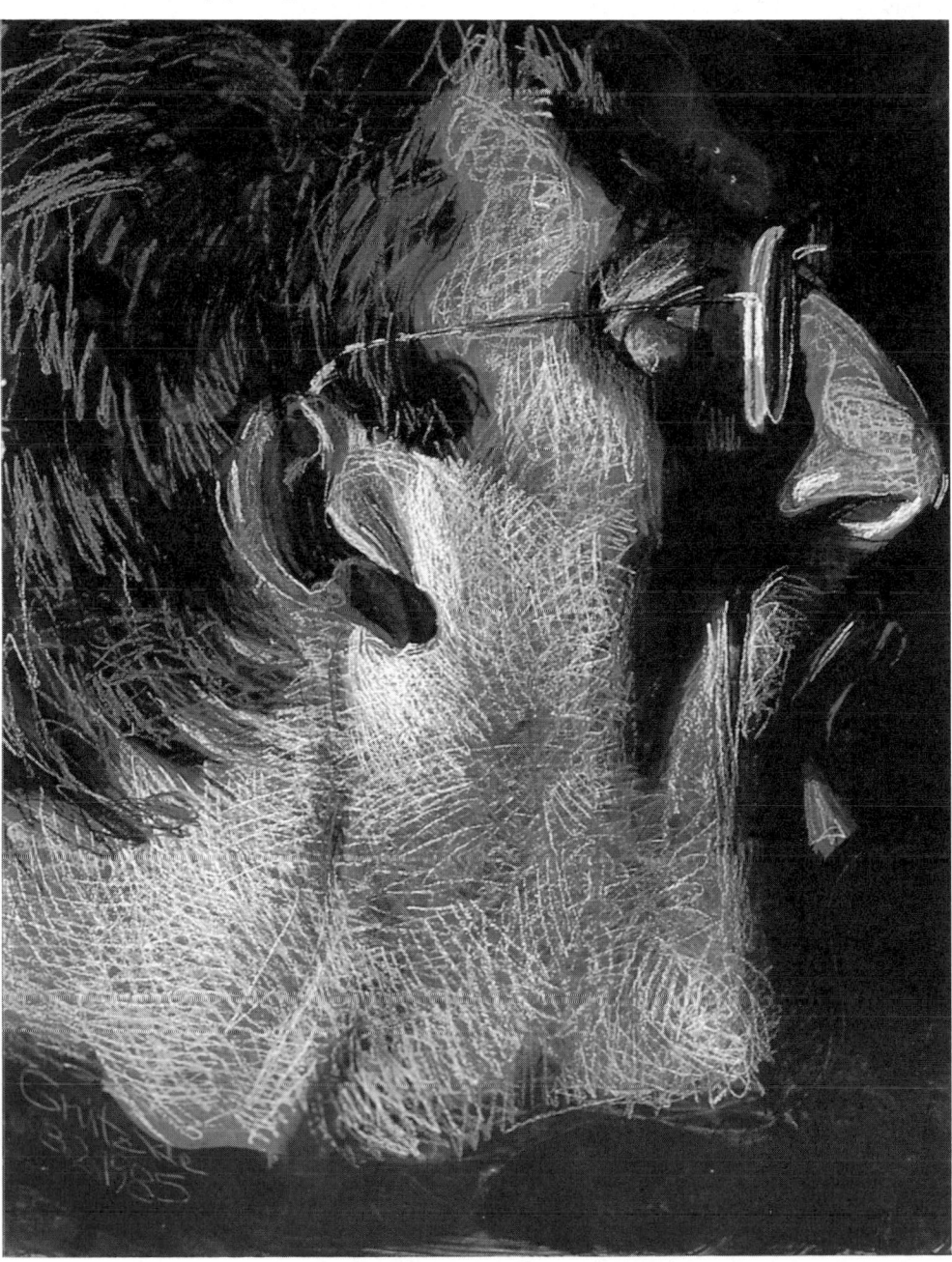

an artistic style but turns rather to reality which he spears both critically and satirically: "I don't copy what I see at all; I make visible what I think and that as if it were everyday reality." His pictures appear photorealistic at first sight but quickly prove to be a skillful staging of quotations from reality. This also makes possible the playfully anachronistic inclusion of historical personages from other epochs in the ordinary context of today, so that they appear as contemporaries of the viewer. Typical examples of this are "Sigmund Freud, Karl Marx, Herbert Marcuse and Julius Grützke" (the small son of the painter), "Bach Disturbed by His Children" or "Death of Socrates." Most frequently, however, Grützke quotes himself on the canvas—for example, even among "The Composers of the 1972/73 Nuremberg Opera Season," together with Monteverdi, Johann Strauss and Bartok. Grützke appears in his pictures simply as the contemporary who normally stares at the viewer with the ironic smile and forced merriment comparable to the agitated attitudes in advertising photographs.

This looking out from the picture in the traditional romantic style of "window pictures" is significant in Grützke's works. Many of the pictures seem to invite the viewer into the picture by abolishing the boundaries between picture space and real space. Perspective extends into the viewer's plane of reality and thereby reverses itself, for the pictures themselves are painted peculiarly flat, without depth and without any relation of the people to their ground. They tend, in their technical precision of a quality equal to the old masters, towards baroque painting and are not always free from mannerist features.

Grützke's graphics, in which political expression is more strongly emphasized, although the painter categorically denies the political potential of art, are of a consistently individual quality.

From the beginning of the 1980s Grützke devoted himself increasingly to the theatre. In collaboration with the director Peter Zadek, he designed numerous stage sets often vast perspectives in the style of his pictures in the background of more or less empty playhouses. When Zadek took up the post as director of the Deutsche Schauspielhaus in Hamburg, Grützke followed him. In Hamburg Grützke not only designed stage decors but also took on acting roles.

—Werner Schulze-Reimpell

GUSTON, Philip.

American. Born in Montreal, Quebec, Canada, 27 June 1913; moved to the United States, 1916. Studied at the Otis Art Institute, Los Angeles. Married Musa McKim in 1937; daughter: Musa Jane. Taught at the New York Studio School (Federal Art Program), 1935–40; Professor, State University of Iowa, 1941–45; Artist-in-Residence, Washington University, St. Louis, 1945–47; taught at the University of Minnesota, Minneapolis, 1950; Adjunct Professor, New York University, Washington Square College, 1951–58; also taught at the Pratt Institute, New York, 1953–57; Guest Critic, Yale Summer School, New Haven, Connecticut, 1961, 1963, 1970–71, 1973–74; Artist-in-Residence, Brandeis University, Waltham, Massachusetts, Spring 1966; Guest Critic, Columbia University Graduate School, New York, 1969, 1970, 1972; Artist-in-Residence, American Academy in Rome, 1970–71; University Professor, 1973–75, and Professor Emeritus, 1978–80, Boston University. Member, Board of Trustees, American Academy in Rome, 1970–80. Recipient: First Prize, Carnegie Institute, Pittsburgh, 1945; Guggenheim Fellowship, 1947, 1948; Altman Prize, National Academy of Design, 1947; Prix de Rome, 1948; Ford Foundation grant, 1959; Distinguished Teaching Award, College Art Association of America, 1975; Creative Arts Medal of Achievement in Painting, Brandeis University, 1980. D.F.A.: Boston University, 1980. Member, National Institute of Arts and Letters, and American Academy of Arts and Sciences. Agent: David McKee Inc., 41 East 57th Street, New York, New York 10022, U.S.A. Died (in Woodstock, New York) 7 June 1980.

Individual Exhibitions:

1945 Midtown Galleries, New York
1947 School of the Museum of Fine Arts, Boston
   Munson-Williams-Proctor Institute, Utica, New York
1952 Peridot Gallery, New York
1953 Egan Gallery, New York
1956 Sidney Janis Gallery, New York
1959 Bienal, Sao Paulo (retrospective)
1960 Biennale, Venice (retrospective)
   Sidney Janis Gallery, New York
1962 Guggenheim Museum, New York (retrospective; toured Europe and travelled to the Los Angeles County Museum of Art)
1966 Santa Barbara Museum of Art, California
   Recent Paintings and Drawings, Jewish Museum, New York
   Rose Art Museum, Brandeis University, Waltham, Massachusetts (retrospective)
1969 Gertrude Kasle Gallery, Detroit
1970 Marlborough Gallery, New York
   Boston University
1971 La Jolla Museum of Modern Art, California
1973 Gertrude Kasle Gallery, Detroit
   Metropolitan Museum of Art, New York
1974 Gertrude Kasle Gallery, Detroit
   New Paintings, Boston University
   David McKee Gallery, New York
1975 Makler Gallery, Philadelphia
   Gallery Paul Anglim, San Francisco
   David McKee Gallery, New York
1976 David McKee Gallery, New York
1977 Achim Moeller Ltd., London
   David McKee Gallery, New York
1978 Allan Frumkin Gallery, Chicago
   David McKee Gallery, New York
   San Francisco Museum of Modern Art
   Asher-Faure Gallery, Los Angeles (with Franz Kline)
1979 David McKee Gallery, New York
1980 San Francisco Museum of Modern Art (retrospective; travelled to the Corcoran Gallery, Washington, D.C.; Museum of Contemporary Art, Chicago; Denver Art Museum; and the Whitney Museum, New York)
   David McKee Gallery, New York
1981 The Last Works, Phillips Collection, Washington, D.C. (travelled to the Cleveland Museum of Art, and the Carnegie Museum of Art, Pittsburgh)
1982 Whitechapel Art Gallery, London
1983 Stedelijk Museum, Amsterdam
   Kunsthalle, Basle
1987 David McKee Gallery, New York

Selected Group Exhibitions:

1946 Twelve Americans, Institute of Modern Art, Boston
1951 Abstract Painting and Sculpture in America, Museum of Modern Art, New York
1964 Painting and Sculpture of a Decade 1954–64, Tate Gallery, London
1970 Art Vivant Americain, Fondation Maeght, St. Paul de Vence, France
1975 Drawings by 5 Abstract Expressionist Painters, Hayden Gallery, Massachusetts Institute of Technology, Cambridge (with Gorky, De Kooning, Pollock and Kline)
1978 American Painting of the 70's, Albright-Knox Art Gallery, Buffalo, New York (toured the United States)
1979 New Painting-New York, Hayward Gallery, London
1981 A New Spirit in Painting, Royal Academy of Arts, London
1984 The Human Condition, San Francisco Museum of Modern Art
1986 Seven Artists in Depth: The Creative Process, San Francisco Museum of Modern Art

Collections:

Whitney Museum, New York; Guggenheim Museum, New York; Metropolitan Museum of Art, New York; Museum of Modern Art, New York; Albright-Knox Art Gallery, Buffalo, New York; National Collection of Fine Arts, Smithsonian Institution, Washington, D.C.; Phillips Collection, Washington, D.C.; Art Institute of Chicago; San Francisco Museum of Modern Art; Tate Gallery, London.

Publications:

By GUSTON: articles—interview in Philip Guston, exhibition catalogue, by H. H. Arnason, New York 1962; "Piero della Francesca: The Impossibility of Painting" in Art News (New York), May 1965; "Dialogue with Philip Guston," with Bill Berkson, in Art and Literature (Lausanne), Winter 1965; interview with Harold Rosenberg, in Recent Paintings and Drawings, exhibition catalogue, New York 1966; interview, with Harold Rosenberg, in Boston University Journal, Fall 1974; "A Talk with Philip Guston," with Mark Stevens, in The New Republic (Washington, D.C.), 15 March 1980; film—Philip Guston, New York 1971, expanded version 1981.

On GUSTON: books—Philip Guston by Dore Ashton, New York 1959; Philip Guston, exhibition catalogue, by H. H. Arnason, New York 1962; The Unknown Shore by Dore Ashton, Boston 1962; Philip Guston: Recent Paintings and Drawings, exhibition catalogue, with an introduction by Sam Hunter, New York 1966; The Triumph of American Painting: A History of Abstract Expressionism by Irving Sandler, New York 1970; A Reading of Modern Art by Dore Ashton, New York 1971; The De-Definition of Art by Harold Rosenberg, New York 1972; The American Abstract Tradition by Frank O'Hara, New York 1974; Philip Guston: New Paintings, with an introduction by Dore Ashton, Boston 1974; Yes, But . . . A Critical Study of Philip Guston by Dore Ashton, New York 1976; Philip Guston, retrospective catalogue, with an essay by Ross Feld, New York 1980; Philip Guston: The Last Works, exhibition catalogue, with an essay by Ross Feld, New York 1980; Philip Guston: The Last Works, exhibition catalogue, with an essay by Morton Feldman, Washington, D.C. 1980; Philip Guston, exhibition catalogue with essay by Norbert Lynton, London 1983; Philip Guston 1930–80, exhibition catalogue with texts by Norbert Lynton and Nicholas Serota, Basle 1983.

Philip Guston is best known as a leading member of the New York School of Abstract Expressionism, but a considerable proportion of his work falls into other categories.

He was in his mid-30's and already a mature and accomplished artist before he began to move towards abstraction about 1947. This early period is characterized by traditional figurative paintings of which the subject matter was of clearly defined monumental and sculptural forms, usually in an urban setting. He organized these figure compositions in a manner which testified both to his fascination with the work of the Renaissance Masters Uccello and Piero della Francesca and to his perceptive study of the postcubist freedoms of Picasso and Max Beckmann. Caught up with the excitement of the new American painters in 1947 but not at first carried away by it, he was to spend the next three years in an exploration, at first somewhat tentative, producing a series of semi-abstract urban and landscape scenes.

By 1950 he was painting freely textural compositions made up of small, urgent, vertical and horizontal brushstrokes, the colour brighter and the brushstrokes more crowded in the centre of the canvas and spreading outwards against a pale background. The effect of these fragile colour structures was to give an effect of shimmering reflections. Because of the delicate, lyrical nature of these works he was sometimes referred to as an Abstract Impressionist. His work changed in the 50's, and the paintings became darker, the brushstrokes larger, and with these large brushstrokes he created more solid forms.

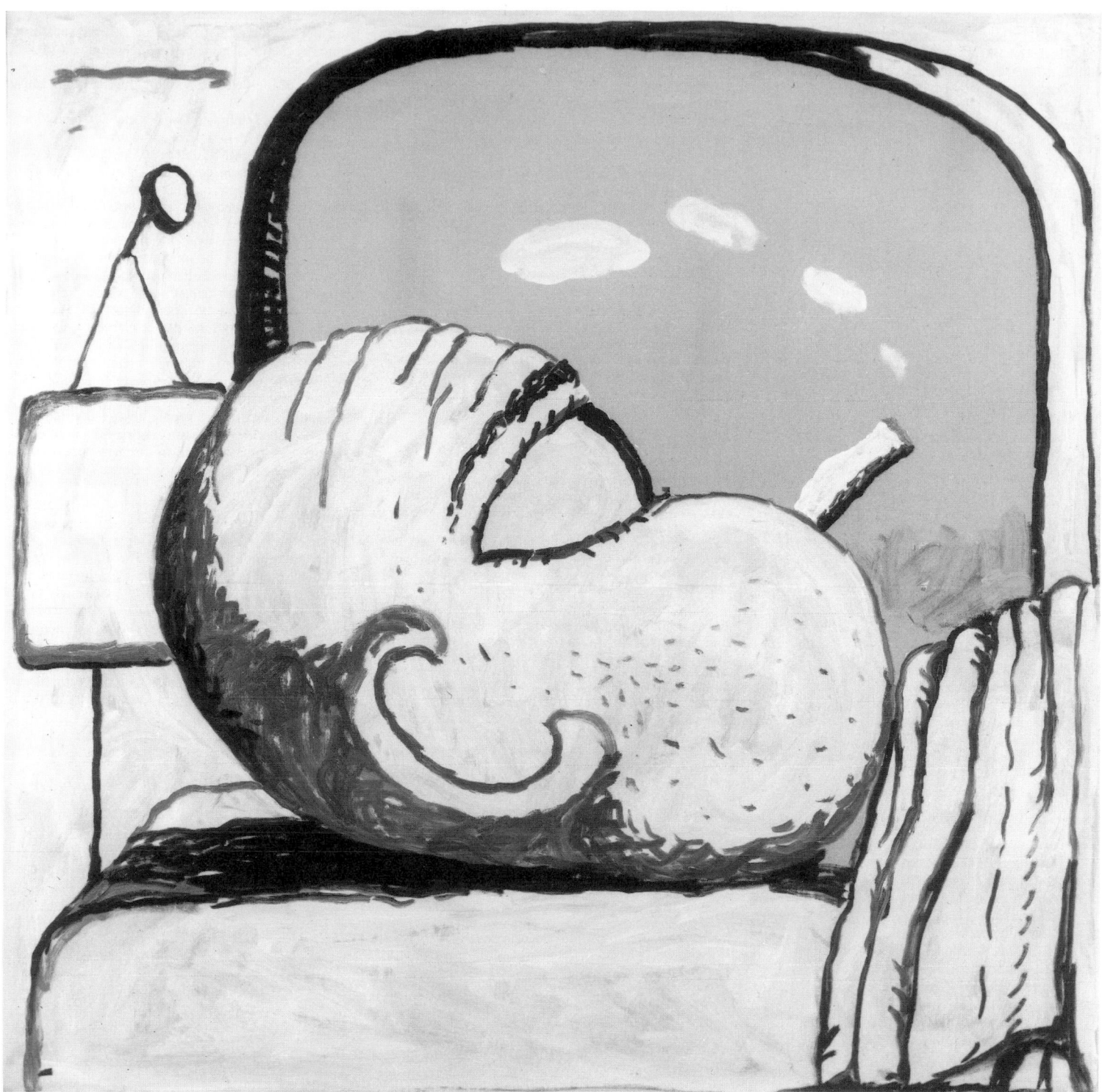

Philip Guston: *Smoking I*, 1973

At first these forms may appear completely abstract, but then the viewer becomes aware of very large figurative images, presences which are more than life size. Once the key to the scale has been identified, the images stabilize, and the forms are sustained right across the canvas. He gives clues to the reading of his images in the very deliberate emphasis on the brushstroke, its scale and its direction. Guston's use of the half-tone creates a dreamy atmosphere and enables him to present multiple images, primary and secondary, by setting the imagination to work. The peripheral areas are usually pale with a build-up towards strong and contrasting tones in the centre of the canvas. The use of light blues and greys suffused with pink in the background is characteristic of this period. The soft greys and blues drift across the picture surface so that the forms are seen as through a mist, now revealed and now obscured. This very finely wrought surface and the use of tonal modulation to suggest depth and recession differentiates his work from those artists of the New York School who were, about this time, obsessed with flatness and the maintenance of "the integrity of the picture plane."

Guston's art continued to change slowly from the 50's onwards, becoming ever darker, denser and more sombre in mood. The forms no longer appeared to float but were heavy and seemed to be engaged in violent struggles. It was a transitional period which seemed to reflect some deep inner anxiety and doubt. By 1968 he had worked his way through to a form of surrealistic juxtaposition of schematic images which appeared to derive from Kafka, de Chirico and Goya. In a spare, plain style, he assembled clocks, shoes, hands, hoods, and eyes in a way that mingled both the grotesque and the commonplace, into pictures which are full of a bleak disillusionment.

—Mary Ellis

GUTTUSO, Renato.

Italian. Born in Bagheria, Palermo, Sicily, 2 January 1912. Educated in Palermo; studied law in Palermo, and at the School of Rome, 1933; self-taught in art. Served in the Italian Army, 1935. Married to Mimise Guttuso (died, 1986). Began painting in 1931; settled in Rome, 1932; worked as a picture restorer for Galleria Perugia and Galleria Borghese, Rome, 1932; lived in Milan, 1935–37; Founder, with Ernesto Traccani, Renato Birolli, Enzio Morlotti and others, Corrente Group, opposing Fascist cultural policy, 1940–42; Member, Communist Party, 1942; joined the Partisans, 1943–45; travelled frequently to France from 1945; Founder, with Birolli, Morlotti, Pericle Fazzini and others, Fronte Nuovo delle Arti, Rome, 1947; independent social realist and expressionist painter, working in Rome and in Velate (Varese), 1947 until his death in 1987. Town Councillor of Palermo, 1975; Senator of the Italian Republic, 1976.

Professor of Painting, Academia delle Belle Arti, Rome, 1961; Guest Professor, Kunstschule, Hamburg, 1968. Recipient: Second Prize, Bergamo Competition, 1942; Marzotto Painting Prize, Rome, 1960; Lenin Peace Prize, Moscow, 1972. Honorary doctorate: University of Parma, 1971. Agent: Galleria del Milione, via Bigli 21, 20121 Milan. *Died* (in Rome) *17 January 1987.*

Individual Exhibitions:

1934	Galleria del Milione, Milan
1938	Galleria La Cometa, Rome
1941	Galleria Barbaroux, Milan (with Orfeo Tamburi)
1943	Galleria Zodiaco, Rome
1946	Galleria Margherita, Rome
1947	Studio Palma, Rome
1950	Hanover Gallery, London
1955	Leicester Galleries, London
1957	Galleria d'Arte Selecta, Rome
	Galleria Odyssia, Rome
1958	ACA Gallery, New York
	Heller Gallery, New York
	Vetrina di Chiurazzi, Rome
1959	Galleria del Milione, Milan
	Galleria Il Fiore, Florence
1961	Galleria La Nuova Pesa, Rome (with Giacomo Manzu)
	Vetrina di Chiurazzi, Rome
	Galleria Minima, Milan
	Pushkin Museum, Moscow (travelled to the Hermitage Museum, Leningrad)
	Galerie Welz, Salzburg
1962	Stedelijk Museum, Amsterdam
	Galleria La Nuova Pesa, Rome
	Bagheria, Sicily
1963	Palazzo della Pilotta, Parma
	Galleria del Milione, Milan
	Palais des Beaux-Arts, Charleroi, Belgium
1966	Galleria del Milione, Milan
1967	Nationalgalerie, West Berlin
	Kunsthalle, Recklinghausen, West Germany
	Kunsthalle, Darmstadt (toured Europe)
	Musée National d'Art Moderne, Paris
	Palazzo dei Normanni, Palermo
	Deutsche Akademie der Kunst, Berlin
1968	Galleria Toninelli, Rome
	Galleria La Medusa, Rome
	Galleria del Milione, Milan
	Galleria l'Annunciata, Milan
	Galleria Gissi, Turin
1969	Galleria Il Gabbiano, Rome
1970	Galerie Michael Hertz, Bremen, West Germany
1971	Musée d'Art Moderne de la Ville, Paris
	Galerie Wolfgang Ketterer, Munich
1972	Galleria la Medusa, Rome
	Neue Gesellschaft für Bildende Kunst, Berlin
	Galleria Schwarz, Milan
1973	Galerie Michael Hertz, Bremen, West Germany
1974	Galleria di Palazzo d'Accursio, Bologna
	Studio Mures, Molin di Falcade, Italy
1975	Il Collezionista d'Arte Contemporanea, Rome
	Kunstverein, Frankfurt
1976	Palazzo del Podolo, Todi, Italy
1977	Kunsthalle, Cologne
1978	Moderna Museet, Stockholm
	Museo della Basilica di San Francesco, Assisi
1979	Narodni Galerie, Prague
	Muzej Savremene Umetnosti, Belgrade (toured Eastern Europe)
	Marlborough Fine Art, London
	Palazzo del Turismo, San Marino
1980	Galleria del Milione, Milan
	Gastaldelli Arte Contemporanea, Milan
	Marlborough Fine Art, London
1981	Galleria d'Arte Moderna, Bologna
	Galleria Rondanini, Rome
1982	Opere dal 1931-1981, Centro di Cultura, Palazzo Grassi, Venice
1984	Gastaldelli Arte Contemporanea, Milan
1985	Villa Croce, Geneva
	Palazzo Reale, Milan
1986	Cittadella dei Musei, Cagliari, Italy

Selected Group Exhibitions:

1931	*Quadriennale*, Rome
1937	*Cinque Artisti Siciliani*, Galleria Mediterranea, Palermo
1950	*Biennale*, Venice
1962	*Italianische Meister des 20. Jahrhunderts*, Vienna
1963	*Dunn International*, Tate Gallery, London
1966	*Salon de Mai*, Paris
1970	*Kunst und Politik*, Badischer Kunstverein, Karlsruhe, West Germany
1972	*Kunst um 1970*, Neue Galerie, Aachen, West Germany

Collections:

Galleria Nazionale d'Arte Moderna, Rome; Galleria d'Arte Moderna, Palermo; Tate Gallery, London; Kunstakedemie, Berlin; Hermitage Museum, Leningrad; National Museum, Prague; National Museum, Warsaw; Museum of Modern Art, New York; Museu do Arte Moderna, Sao Paulo; Gallery of New South Wales, Sydney.

Publications:

By GUTTUSO: books—*Contadini di Sicilia*, Rome 1951; *Mestiere di Pittore: Scritti sull Arte e la Societa*, Bari Italy. 1972; articles—"Paura della Pittura" and "Avvertenza" in *Prospective* (Rome) 1942; "Del Realismo del Presente e Altro" in *Paragone* (Florence), 1957; "The Artist Writes" in *Guttuso: In the Manner of . . .*, exhibition catalogue, London 1980; essay in *Renato Guttuso*, exhibition catalogue, Milan 1985.

On GUTTUSO: books—*Prefazione a Renato Guttuso* by Gino Severini, Rome 1942; *Disegni di Guttuso* by Morosini, Milan 1941; *Renato Guttuso*, exhibition catalogue, by Douglas Cooper, London 1950; *Poema a Renato Guttuso Pittore Realista* by Pablo Neruda, Rome 1951; *Renato Guttuso* by Guiseppe Marchiori, Milan 1951; *La Spaiggia di Renato Guttuso* by John Berger, Dresden 1957; *Renato Guttuso* by Morosini, Rome 1960; *Storia di Renato Guttuso* by Elio Vittorini, Milan 1960; *Renato Guttuso*, exhibition catalogue, Moscow 1961; *Renato Guttuso* by Alberto Moravia, Palermo 1961; *Disegni di Guttuso* by Pier Paolo Pasolini, Rome 1962; *Guttuso, l'Occupazione delle Terre* by Mario de Michele, Milan 1970; *La Crocifissione di Renato Guttuso* by Enrico Crispolti, Rome 1970; *Catalogo della Mostra Antologica dell'Opera di Renato Guttuso* by Franco Grasso and others, Palermo 1971; *Renato Guttuso* by Werner Haftmann, Rome 1971; *Renato Guttuso: Disegni 1940-72* by Leonardo Sciascia, Naples 1972; *Renato Guttuso: I Disegni dell'Amore* by Antonio del Guercio, Milan 1974; *Guttuso: Opere dal 1931-1981*, exhibition catalogue, by Maurizio Calvesi and others, Venice 1982; *Renato Guttuso*, exhibition catalogue with introduction by Alberto T. Galimberti, Milan 1984; *Renato Guttuso: Il Bosco d'Amore*, Rome 1985; *Renato Guttuso*, exhibition catalogue with essays by Vittorio Rubin and Cesare Brandi, Cagliari 1986.

*   *   *

The critics have long debated whether Renato Guttuso's realism may be equated with socialist realism. Whether his expressionism is determined by German prototypes, whether his rediscovered Cubism in the Picasso manner and whether his abundant quotations in his later work from the great painters of the past are evidence of decadence or of a highly personal style. At the great retrospective of his work from 1931 to 1981 which Venice gave Guttuso for his 70th birthday, it became clear that his art has as little to do with flat, Eastern realism as with American hyperrealism which embalms reality.

Guttuso filters reality through intelligence and softens its harshness through compassion. Even the programmatic pictures of the convinced Communist, who sits in Parliament as senator of his party, have an artistic format—as in the bold concept of "Togliatti's Burial," a large format black and white drawing with many portrait heads among the mourners. A forest of red flags, colourful flowers around the bier and a glowing sunset provide a few touches of colour.

The Venice exhibition also made clear that Guttuso's quotations from past styles and works are not copies but milestones in his artistic development:

His first still-lifes and the self-portrait of 1936 are already early masterpieces and announce his strength and his weakness: a passion for colours and forms which sometimes goes beyond the frontiers of aesthetics. He gave to each of his pictures the flowing richness of life together with the tragedy of his native Sicily.

His most celebrated work, the "Crucifixion," brought him in 1941 a prize and a great deal of indignation. The naked Magdalene before the cross led the *Osservatore Romano* to threaten the "Pictor diabolicus" with the Index. This commissioned picture about which Guttuso recorded in his diary, "I want to paint the death of Christ as a scene of our time, as a symbol for everyone who, for their ideas, has to suffer agonies, prison and death," remained one of the key works of modern Italian painting. With the "Crucifixion" began the Cubist phase which Guttuso adhered to unswervingly when almost all his fellow artists were turning towards abstraction. One should find a new name for the still-lifes of this period because they vibrate with such completely sensuous brilliancy of colour as if they were filled with their own particular life.

Guttuso's pictures of people always have the same models: fishermen, peasantry, workers: a rural civilization, long since crushed to death by the industrial state, which the "reactionary" Guttuso tried to preserve in his paintings.

In the third phase, the "allegories" of the 1970's, he portrays as everyday figures famous figures from the paintings of Leonardo and Michaelangelo, Dürer and Caravaggio up to Picasso. These are mysterious and disturbing puzzle pictures in black and white.

Guttuso's late works are full of melancholy, as in the handsome portrait of Moravia of 1982. The colours shine out aggressively, as always, the line is of masterly clarity. But people and still-lifes have now become timeless symbols for life and death, are as if benumbed in pensive melancholy at life's brief span.

—Monika von Zitzewitz

GYSIN, Brion.

American. Born in Taplow, Buckinghamshire, England, 19 January 1916. Studied at Downside College, England, 1932-34; studied and researched slavery at the University of Bordeaux, 1949-52, and at University of Seville's Archivos de India, Spain, 1950-52. Served in U.S. and Canadian Armies studying Japanese and calligraphy, 1943-45. Lived in Paris from 1934 and studied at Sorbonne; met Surrealist Group and associated with Max Ernst, Meret Oppenheim, Yves Tanguy, Salvador and Gala Dali, Picasso, Soutine, Matta, Paalen, Kurt Seligmann, Léger, in Paris, 1935; first visited Algerian Sahara, 1938; settled in New York, 1940; Assistant to Irene Sharaff on 7 Broadway musicals, 1940-43; Produced Caribbean "decalcomania" serial landscape series, 1940-43; travelled with Paul Bowles to Tangiers and established residence there, 1950-73; began studies in Arab calligraphy, association with the Master Musicians of Joujouka, and restaurant "The Thousand and One Nights of Tangiers," Morocco, from 1953; collaborated with William S. Burroughs and Ian Sommerville in the Beat Hotel, inventing cutups, Permutation Poems and the Dreamachine, mostly in Paris, 1958-65; lived in New York preparing *The Third Mind* with William S. Burroughs, 1965. Independent painter and writer, living in Paris, 1965 until his death in 1986. Recipient: Fulbright Research Scholarship, 1949-52. Agent: Galerie zem Specht, Basel, Switzerland. *Died* (in Paris) *in July 1986.*

Individual Exhibitions:

1939	Galerie Quatre Chemins, Paris
1953	*Carnet de Voyage au Sahara*, Hotel Rembrandt, Tangiers

Museo de Bellas Artes, Las Palmas, Canary Islands
Museo de Bellas Artes, Tenerife, Canary Islands
1957 Sagittarius Gallery, New York
Dunbar Gallery, Chicago
Sagittarius-Obelisco Galleria, Rome
1958 Arthur Jeffress Gallery, London
1960 Heretics Club, Cambridge, England (Lecture/ Happening)
Institute for Contemporary Arts, London (Lecture/ Happening with WIlliam Burroughs and Ian Sommerville)
Verbal Theatre, La Boheme, Paris
1962 Galleria Trastevere, Rome
1964 Hotel Rembrandt, Tangiers
1965 *Permutated Poems*, Metro, New York
Permutated Poems, American Theatre for Poets Inc., New York (with William Burroughs)
1973 Galerie Weiller, Paris
1975 Galerie Germain, Paris
1976 Mollet-Vieville, Paris

Selected Group Exhibitions:

1935 *Surrealist Drawings*, Galerie Quatre Chemins, Paris
1960 *Salon des Réalités Nouvelles*, Paris
1962 *L'Objet*, Musée des Arts Décoratifs, Paris
1963 *La Lettre et le Signe*, Galerie Valery Schmidt, Paris
The Mysterious Sign, Institute of Contemporary Arts, London
1965 *Between Poetry and Painting*, Institute of Contemporary Arts, London
Biennale, Paris
1967 *Hepta*, Palais Galleria, Paris
1968 *Poesie Graphie, Poesie Action*, University of Rouen, France
1973 *Lettre-Signe*, Swedish Cultural Centre, Paris
Contemporanea, Villa Borghese, Rome

Collections:

Museum of Modern Art, New York; Museum of Fine Arts, Boston; Museum of Modern Art, Phoenix, Arizona; Centre Georges Pompidou, Paris.

Publications:

By GYSIN: books—*To Master A Long Goodnight*, New York 1946; *The History of Slavery In Canada*, New York 1946; *Minutes To Go*, with William S. Burroughs, Gregory Corso and Sinclair Beiles, Paris 1960; *The Exterminator*, with William S. Burroughs, San Francisco 1960; contributions to *The Ticket That Exploded* by William S. Burroughs, New York 1961; *Permutation*, Paris 1964; *The Process*, New York 1968; *Brion Gysin Let The Mice In*, New York 1973; illustrations for *The William Burroughs Catalogue*, London 1973; illustrations for *Revolution Electronique* by William S. Burroughs, Paris 1973; *The Third Man*, New York 1976; *The Third Mind*, with William S. Burroughs, New York 1978; *The Last Museum*, London 1986; articles—interview with William S. Burroughs, in *Permutations*, exhibition catalogue, Paris 1973; interview in *Actuel* (Paris), June/July 1974.

On GYSIN: article—"The Life of Brion" by David Darby in *Time Out* (London), 23 July 1986.

It is to be remembered that all art is magical in origin—music sculpture writing painting—and by magical I mean intended to produce very definite results. Paintings were originally formulae to make what is painted happen. Art is not an end in itself, any more than Einstein's matter-into-energy formula is an end in itself. Like all formulae, art was originally *functional*, intended to make things happen, the way an atom bomb happens from Einstein's formula.

Take a porcelain stove and disconnect it and put it in your living room with ivy growing over it . . . it may be a good-looking corpse but it isn't *functional* anymore. Or take a voodoo doll full of pins—authentic West African, $500 on 57th Street—and hang it on the wall of your duplex loft. It isn't killing enemies anymore, and the same goes for a $5000 shrunkdown head, which a fashionable shrink bought for his consultation room. Writing and painting were one in cave paintings, which were formulae to ensure good hunting. If the modern artist no longer expects to produce such direct effects in the so-called real world, he still intends to make something happen in the mind of the viewer.

The painting of Brion Gysin deals directly with the magical roots of art. His paintings are formulae designed to produce in the viewer the timeless everchanging world of magic caught in the painter's brush—bits of vivid and vanishing detail. His paintings may be called space art. Time is seen spatially, that is, as a series of images or fragments of images past present and future. I quote from *The Eternal Man* by Louis Pauwels and Jacques Bergier, referring to sculptures and bas-reliefs found on the plateau of Marcahuasi: "Sometimes the desired effect is achieved when sunlight falls on them; at others, only when it is twilight or when seen from a specific angle." Here is a Gysin scene from Marrakesh—moving figures, phantom bicycles, cars . . . this is a literal representation of what actually happens in the human nervous system: a street reminds you of a car that went by yesterday, or a boy on a bicycle years ago, in fact everything that you have experienced on that street and other streets associated with it. The pictures constantly change because you are drawn into time travel on a network of associations. Brion Gysin painted from the viewpoint of timeless space.

—William S. Burroughs

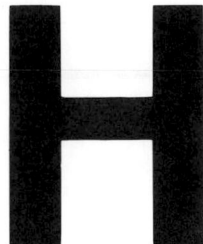

HAACKE, Hans.

German. Born in Cologne, 12 August 1936. Educated at Pädagogium Otto Kühne, Bonn-Bad Godesberg, 1948–52; Nicolaus-Cusanus-Gymnasium, Bonn-Bad Godesberg, 1952–56; Staatliche Hochschule für Bildende Künste, Kassel, 1956–60, M.F.A. 1960; Atelier 17, Paris, 1960–61; Tyler School of Art, Philadelphia, 1961–62. Married Linda Snyder in 1965; sons: Carl and Paul. Exhibited with the Zero Group, including Mack, Piene, Uecker, in Europe 1960–65. Assistant teacher, Pädagogische Hochschule, Kettwig, West Germany, 1963–64; Instructor, Modeschule, Dusseldorf, 1964–65; Visiting Lecturer, University of Washington, Seattle, 1965; Lecturer, Philadelphia College of Art, 1966–67; Adjunct Instructor, 1967–70, Visiting Professor, 1970–71, Assistant Professor, 1971–75, Associate Professor, 1975–79 and since 1979 Professor, Cooper Union, New York. Guest Professor, Hochschule für Bildende Künste, Hamburg, 1973; Guest Professor, Gesamthochschule, Essen, 1979. Recipient: Duetscher Akademischer Austauschdienst (D.A.A.D.), Paris, 1960–61; Fulbright Fellowship, Philadelphia, 1961–62; Guggenheim Fellowship, 1973–74; National Endowment for the Arts grant, 1978. Agent: John Weber Gallery, 142 Greene Street, New York, New York 10012. Address 463 West Street, New York, New York 10014, U.S.A.

Individual Exhibitions:

1965   Galerie Schmela, Dusseldorf
1966   Howard Wise Gallery, New York
1967   Hayden Gallery, Massachusetts Institute of Technology, Cambridge
1968   Howard Wise Gallery, New York
1969   Howard Wise Gallery, New York
1971   Paul Maenz Galerie, Cologne
1972   Galerie Francoise Lambert, Milan
        Museum Haus Lange, Krefeld, West Germany
        Galerie X-One, Antwerp
1973   John Weber Gallery, New York
        Paul Maenz Galerie, Brussels
1974   Paul Maenz Galerie, Cologne
1975   John Weber Gallery, New York
1976   Lisson Gallery, London
        Max Protetch Gallery, Washington, D.C.
        Kunstverein, Frankfurt
        Galerie Francoise Lambert, Milan
1977   Galerie Durand-Dessert, Paris
        John Weber Gallery, New York
        Amherst College, Massachusetts
        Badischer Kunstverein, Karlsruhe
        Wadsworth Atheneum, Hartford, Connecticut
        University of California at Santa Cruz
1978   Galerie Durand-Dessert, Paris
        California Institute of Technology, Pasadena
        Museum of Modern Art, Oxford
1979   Stedelijk van Abbemuseum, Eindhoven, Netherlands
        Recent Work, Renaissance Society, University of Chicago
        Catholic University, Tilburg, Netherlands
        Municipal Gallery, Middelburg, Netherlands
        John Weber Gallery, New York

1980   Museum of Contemporary Art, Zagreb
        Saman Galerie, Geneva
1981   John Weber Gallery, New York
        Paul Maenz Galerie, Cologne
        And/Or Gallery, Seattle, Washington
        Banff Centre, Alberta
1982   Bread and Roses Gallery, District 1199 Cultural Center, New York
        University of Alberta, Edmonton
1983   Galerie France Morin, Montreal
        John Weber Gallery, New York
1984   Tate Gallery, London
        Neue Gesellschaft fur Bildende Kunst, West Berlin
1985   Kunsthalle, Berne
        John Weber Gallery, New York
        Raum für Kunst, Hamburg
1986   Le Consortium, Dijon, France
        New Museum of Contemporary Art, New York
        (travelled to Saskatoon, Saskatchewan; La Jolla, California; Coral Gables, Florida; Charlotte, North Carolina)

Selected Group Exhibitions:

1962   *NUL*, Stedelijk Museum, Amsterdam (and 1965)
1968   *The Machine as Seen at the End of the Mechanical Age*, Museum of Modern Art, New York (toured the United States)
1969   *When Attitudes Become Form*, Kunsthalle, Berne (toured Europe)
1972   *Documenta 5*, Kassel, West Germany
1974   *Art into Society—Society into Art*, Institute of Contemporary Arts, London
1978   *Biennale*, Venice
1981   *Art Allemagne Aujourd'hui*, ARC/Musée d'Art Moderne de la Ville, Paris
1983   *Museums by Artists*, Art Gallery of Ontario, Toronto (travelled to Montreal and Calgary)
1986   *An American Renaissance*, Museum of Art, Fort Lauderdale, Florida
1987   *Avantgarde in the Eighties*, Los Angeles County Museum of Art

Collections:

Museum of Modern Art, New York; Neuberger Museum, Purchase, New York; Milwaukee Art Center; National Art Gallery of Canada, Ottawa; Art Gallery of Ontario, Toronto; Museum Haus Lange, Krefeld, West Germany; Museum of Contemporary Art, Zagreb; Moderna Museet, Stockholm; Stedelijk van Abbemuseum, Eindhoven, Netherlands; Museum van Hedendaagse Kunst, Ghent, Belgium.

Publications:

By HAACKE: books—*Hans Haacke—Werkmonographie*, with introduction by Edward Fry, Cologne 1972; *Art into Society—Society into Art*, exhibition catalogue text, London 1974; *Framing and Being Framed: 7 Works 1970–75*, Halifax and New York 1975; *Seurat's "Les Poseuses" 1888–1975*, small version, New York and Paris 1975; *A Breed Apart*, Oxford 1978; *Hans Haacke: 4 Works 1978–79*, New York 1979; *Der Pralinenmeister/The Chocolate Master*, Toronto 1982; articles—"Questions to Hans Haacke," interview with

Jack Burnham, in *Tri-Quarterly Supplement* (Evanston, Illinois), Spring 1967; "An Interview with Hans Haacke," with Jeanne Siegel, in *Arts Magazine* (New York), May 1971; "Editorial: Artists vs. Museums, Continued" in *Artnews* (New York), September 1971; interview with Karin Thomas, in *Kunst-Praxis Heute: Eine Dokumentation der aktuellen Ästhetik*, Cologne 1972; interview with John Anthony Thwaites in *Art and Artists* (London), November 1972; "Shapolsky et al Manhattan Immobilienbesita, ein gesellschaftliches Realzeitsystem, Stand 1.3.1972" in *Interfunktionen* (Cologne), no. 9, 1972; "Profil de l'habitat des visiteurs de la galerie" in *Art Press* (Paris), December/January 1973; "The Role of the Artist in Today's Society: A Symposium at Oberlin" in *Supplement to Allen Memorial Art Museum Bulletin* (Oberlin, Ohio), vol. 30, no. 3, 1973; transcript of talk in *Selbstdarstellung: Kunstler über Sich*, edited by Wulf Herzogenrath, Dusseldorf 1973; "Manet-Projekt '74" in *EXTRA* (Cologne), July 1974; interview in *Art Journal* (New York), Summer 1975; "Solomon R. Guggenheim Museum Board of Trustees" in *Tri-Quarterly* (Evanston, Illinois), Winter 1975; "Hans Haacke," interview with Margaret Sheffield, in *Studio International* (London), March/April 1976; "The Good Will Umbrella" in *Vision* (Oakland, California), no. 3, 1976; "The Constituency" in *Tracks* (New York), vol. 3, no. 3, 1977; "The Agent/Der Agent" in *What Do You Expect . . .* by Paul Maenz, Cologne 1977; "Hans Haacke Interviewed by Michele Patterson" in *Journal of Fine Arts* (Chapel Hill, North Carolina), Spring/Summer 1980; "Radical Attitudes to the Gallery" in *Studio International* (London), vol. 195, no. 990, 1980; "On Social Grease" in *Art Journal* (New York), Summer 1982; "Broadness and Diversity of the Ludwig Brigade", in *October* (New York), Fall 1984; "Entretien avec Hans Haacke", with Daniel Soutif, in *Cardinaus* (Paris), Spring 1987.

On HAACKE: books—*NUL*, exhibition catalogue, Amsterdam 1962; *Collage* by Harriet Janis and Rudi Blesh, Philadelphia 1967; *Origins and Development of Kinetic Art* by Frank Popper, London 1966; *Beyond Modern Sculpture* by Jack Burnham, New York 1968; *The Machine as Seen at the End of the Mechanical Age*, exhibition catalog, New York 1968; *Arte e Azione Povera* by Germano Celant, Milan, London, New York and Tübingen, 1969; *When Attitudes Become Form*, exhibition catalogue, Berne 1969; *The Structure of Art* by Jack Burnham, New York 1970; *Deutsche Kunst: Eine neue Generation* by Rolf-Gunter Dienst, Cologne 1970; *The Sculptural Idea* by James J. Kelly, Minneapolis 1970; *Conceptual Art* by Germano Celant, Turin 1970; *Tokyo Biennale*, exhibition catalogue, Tokyo 1970; *Information*, exhibition catalogue, New York 1970; *P.C.A.-Projekte, Concepte and Actionen* by Walter Aue, Cologne 1971; *A and T: A Report on the Art and Technology Program of the Los Angeles County Museum of Art 1967–1971* by Maurice Tuchman, Los Angeles 1971; *Concept Art* by Klaus Honnef, Cologne 1972; *Kunst-Praxis heute: Eine Dokumentation der aktuellen Asthetik* by Karin Thomas, Cologne 1972; *Conceptual Art* by Ursula Meyer, New York 1972; *Science and Technology in Art Today* by Jonathan Benthall, London and New York 1972; *Art as Action and Concept* by Ichiro Haryu, Tokyo 1972; *American Art of the 20th Century* by Sam Hunter, New York 1972; *Hans Haacke*, exhibition catalogue, with text by Paul Wember, Krefeld, West Germany 1972; *Documenta 5*, exhibition catalogue, Kassel, West Germany 1972; *Od Pop-Artu do Sziuki Konceptualnej* by Urszula Czartoryska, Warsaw 1973; *Contemporanea*, exhibition catalogue, Rome 1973; *Environments and Happenings*, by Adrian Henri, London 1974; *Beyond Modern Art* by Carla Gottlieb, New York 1976; *Hans Haacke*, exhibition catalogue with text by Georg Bussman, Frankfurt 1976; *Hans Haacke* exhibition catalogue, with text by Nan Rosenthal, Santa Cruz, California 1977; *Matrix 31: Hans Haacke*, exhibition catalogue, with text by Andrea M. Keller, Hartford, Connecticut 1977; *Hans Haacke*, exhibition catalogue, with text by Nan Rosenthal, Pasadena, California

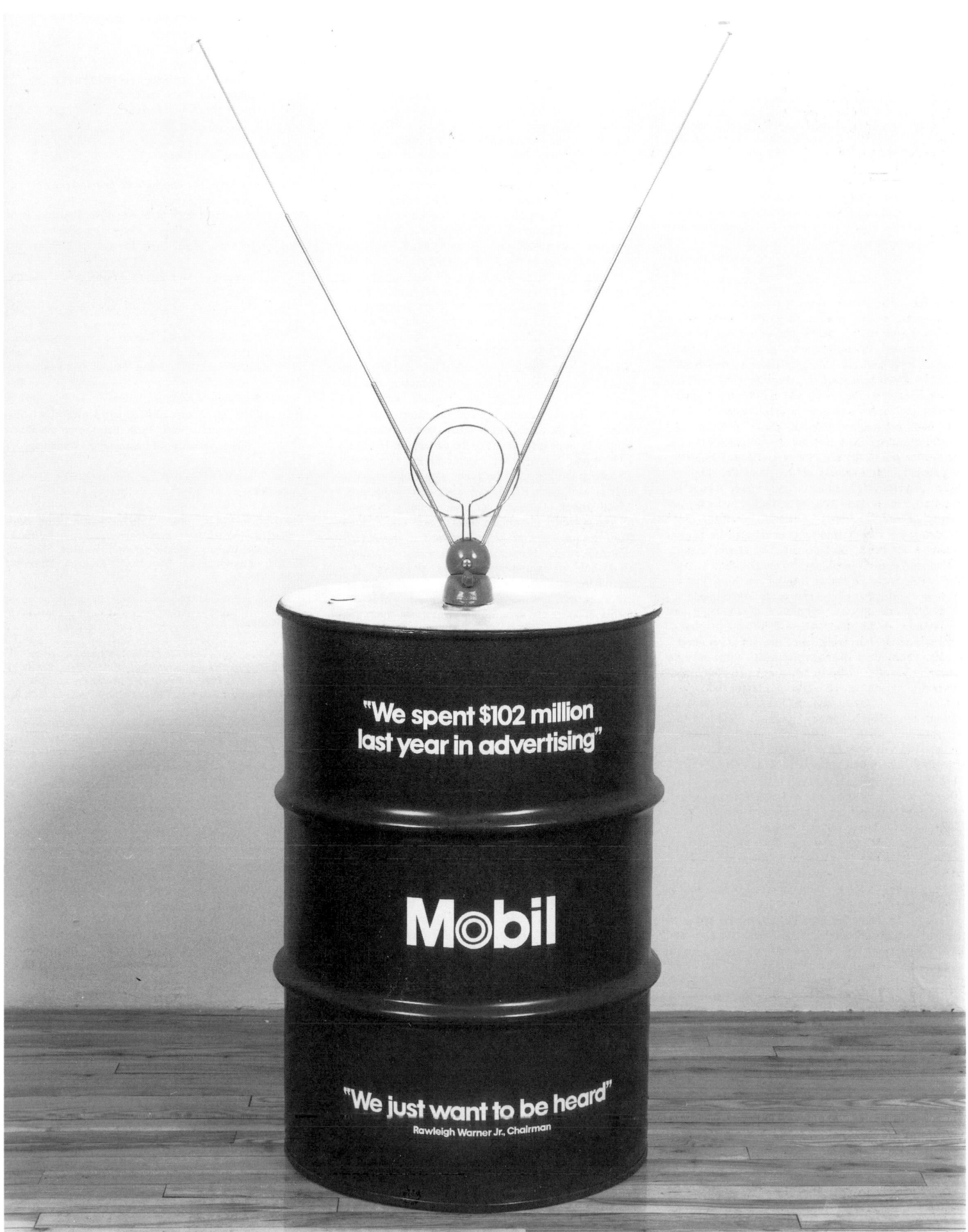

Hans Haacke: *Creating Consent*, 1981

1978; *Hans Haacke,* exhibition catalogue, Oxford and Eindhoven, Netherlands 1978; *Hans Haacke: Recent Work,* exhibition catalogue, with text by Jack Burnham, Chicago 1979; *Hans Haacke,* exhibition catalogue, with an introduction by Davor Maticevic, Zagreb 1980; *Hans Haacke: Volume II, Works 1978–1983,* exhibition catalogue with texts by Tony Brown and Walter Grasskamp, London 1984; *Hans Haacke: Nach allen Regeln der Kunst,* exhibition catalogue with texts by Ulrich Giersch, Jean-Hubert Martin and others, West Berlin 1984; *Hans Haacke: Unfinished Business,* exhibition catalogue edited by Brian Wallis, New York 1986.

If art contributes to, among other things, the way we view the world and shape social relations, then it does matter whose image of the world it promotes and whose interests it serves.

—Hans Haacke

Since the early 1960's, Hans Haacke has been making objects, events, prints and written works which use the forms, words and styles of various systems outside art to communicate the often hidden interdependencies and equivalencies between the various systems which surround us, from the physical and environmental to the social and political. By appropriating the means prevalent in these systems, selecting and organizing out of these sources and recontextualizing them into the art environment of the gallery or museum, Haacke offers possibilities for heightened consciousness of the ideas and implications underlying phenomena and events which we usually accept at face value as ordinary, everyday occurrences.

During the 1960's Haacke concentrated on natural systems. In 1963, in Germany, he began making "weather boxes," including "Condensation Cubes" with water enclosed within transparent walls, the water either condensing or evaporating on the inside according to the specific conditions of air, light and temperature in the space where they were displayed. Characterizing his work as "real time systems," Haacke continued his involvement with changes through time as effected by environmental conditions, producing a series of ice works and larger indoor and outdoor works about natural phenomena such as "Wind In Water (Mist)" (1968) and "Moss Transparent—Maintained in Artificial Microclimate." He also did a number of works about actual biological growth in plants and animals such as "Grass Cube" (1967), "Chickens Hatching" (1969) and "Grass Grows" (1970, for the *Earth Art* exhibition at Cornell University). In the last one, Haacke constructed a cone-shaped mound of topsoil and peat moss and planted fast-growing rye seeds which grew and died, completing its life cycle during the course of the show. The role of animals in natural cycle was explored in works such as "Goat Feeding in the Woods, Thus Changing It" (1970).

The 1970's launched Haacke into a new phase of systems art concerning socio-political systems and their connections with the art system. From 1969 to 1972 he did a series of "Visitors' Profiles," in which "20 questions" questionnaires posed 10 demographic and 10 opinion (on current socio-political issues) queries to the audience/participants. Resulting information gathered by Haacke was correlated in various ways including bar graphs and charts and accompanied by comparisons, for instance, with other surveys or other Haacke questionnaire polls, casting new light on who and what are the people who view new art and even choose to be a part of making it. It was one of Haacke's "Visitors' Profiles" which became part of the 1971 controversy which resulted in The Guggenheim Museum's cancellation of a proposed Haacke exhibition and the firing of Edward Fry, the curator who fought for the artist's rights to show his work without censoring. Also at issue were Haacke's "Real Estate" works which consist of a series of photographs of the facades of Manhattan real estate holdings, some tenements, others commercial properties, accompanied by captions which contain business information about ownership, acquisition and money values which Haacke had gathered from the public

records of the County Clerk's office. These works were determined to be too controversial (possibly making the museum legally libel) for The Guggenheim Museum, whose Director, Thomas Messer, cancelled the exhibition. Ironically, the flurry of publicity and the events of the cancellation became part of Haacke's work, demonstrating the powers inherent in work which succeeds in being socially relevant and outside art-as-art-alone formalism.

In recent years, Haacke has produced a number of series of prints which deal with large corporations' uses of culture and social commitment as a major thrust in their advertising and public relations campaigns. In a series of 4-color silkscreens titled "The Good Will Umbrella" (1976), Haacke reproduces facsimile pages from an address to the Eastern Annual Conference of the American Association of Advertising Agencies. The texts discuss in glowing terms the various ways in which the corporation is building up its public image, by doing public television, holding contests, commissioning art and underwriting art exhibitions, for example. In each work, the familiar emblem "MOBIL" is printed in heavy lettering and followed by a subheading which encapsulated the two pages of textual information that appears below. The simple, direct use of advertising format and the concise choice of material directly convey the message which takes on new meanings simply by appearing as art in the gallery. In Haacke's 1979 work, "Alcoa: We can't wait for tomorrow," Haacke's ability to hit the point with elegant directness is well exemplified. The work is a simple horizontal stretch of squared aluminum tubing on which mirror-polished aluminum letters spell out a quote from the president of Alcoa's address to the American Advertising Federation which reads: "Business could hold art exhibitions to tell its own story." It is one of the many works Haacke has made which appropriate exactly the most appropriate words and forms of extra-art systems and transform them into pertinent and eloquent statements of art's ability to communicate significant ideas and meanings about the interrelated realities in all areas of the world at large.

—Barbara Cavaliere

HAINS, Raymond.

French. Born in Saint-Brieuc, 9 November 1926. Studied at the Académie des Beaux-Arts, Rennes, 1945; associated with Jacques de la Villeglé, 1946. Worked as photographer, *France Illustration* magazine, Paris 1947. Independent artist, working with photography, multiple objects, mirror-games and "lettres eclatées", Paris, since 1947. Agent: Galerie Lara Vincy, 47 rue de Seine, 75006 Paris. Address: 20 rue Marbeau, 75016 Paris, France.

Individual Exhibitions:

1948	Galerie Colette Allendy, Paris
1949	Librairie des Nourritures Terrestres, Rennes, France
1950	Falconnerie de Tytgat, Knokke-le-Zoute, Belgium
1957	Galerie Colette Allendy, Paris (with Jacques de la Villeglé)
1961	Galerie J, Paris
1962	Galerie Handschin, Basle
	Palais des Beaux-Arts, Brussels
	Galerie du Cercle, Paris
1963	Galerie Henriette Legendre, Paris
1964	Galleria del Leone, Venice
1965	Galerie Iris Clert, Paris
	Galleria Apollinaire, Milan
1966	Galleria del Leone, Venice
1968	Galleria Il Elefante, Venice
1970	Galleria Sant'Andrea, Milan
1973	Galleria della Trinita, Rome

1976	Centre National d'Art Contemporain, Paris
	Galerie Verbeke, Paris
	Galerie Lara Vincy, Paris
1983	Galerie Eric Fabre, Paris
1986	Fondation Cartier, Jouy-en-Josas, France
	Galerie Lara Vincy, Paris
1987	Galerie Lara Vincy, Paris

Selected Group Exhibitions:

1952	*Exposition Internationale de la Photographie,* Lucerne, Switzerland
1959	*1st Biennale de Paris,* Musée d'Art Moderne, Paris
1960	*Les Nouveaux Réalistes,* Galleria Apollinaire, Milan
1961	*The Art of Assemblage,* Museum of Modern Art, New York
1968	*Documenta IV,* Museum Fridericianum, Kassel, West Germany
1970	*Nouveau Réalisme 1960–70,* Rotonda della Besana, Milan
1971	*Plakatabrisse aus der Sammlung Cremer,* Staatsgalerie, Stuttgart
1978	*Les Nouveaux Réalistes,* Musée des Ponchettes, Nice
1982	*Westkunst,* Messehallen, Cologne
1986	*1960: Les Nouveaux Réalistes,* Musée d'Art Moderne de la Ville, Paris (travelled to the Kunsthalle, Mannheim; Kunstmuseum, Winterthur)

Collections:

Musée National d'Art Moderne, Paris; Kunstmuseum, Winterthur; Stadtisches Museum, Monchengladbach; Westfalisches Landesmuseum, Munster; Kaiser Wilhelm Museum, Krefeld; Kunstmuseum, Dusseldorf; Museum Moderner Kunst, Vienna.

Publications:

By HAINS: book—*Hepérile Eclaté,* with Jacques de la Villegle, poem by Camille Bryen, Paris 1953; films—*Loi du 29 Juillet 1881,* 1949; *Saint-Germain-des-Pres-Colombien,* 1949; *Etude aux Allures,* 1950.

On HAINS: books—*Lyrisme et Abstraction* by Pierre Restany, Milan 1960; *Le Revolution du Régard* by Alain Jouffroy, Paris 1965; *Nouveau Réalisme 1960-1970,* exhibition catalogue with text by Pierre Restany, Milan 1970; *Raymond Hains,* exhibition catalogue, Paris 1976; article—"Kurzer Abriss der Geschichte der Affichistes" by Dieter Schwarz in *1960: Les Nouveaux Réalistes,* exhibition catalogue, Mannheim and Winterthur 1986.

Raymond Hains was trained as a photographer and his first artistic works were photos, which he produced by means of special lenses in an attempt to develop his own style of abstract photography.

Hains and Villeglé took a special interest in the work of Camille Bryen, including his phonetic poems, since they saw in him the representative of an older generation with whom they felt a close affinity. In 1953 they used an optical screen of fluted glass to distort Bryen's text *Hepérile,* which had appeared three years earlier; a new work was thus created: *Hepérile éclaté.* The *ultra-lettres,* which were created out of conventional letters by this optical method, differ from the contemporaneous letter constructions of the Lettristes in one important respect: they are not subjective deformations but distortions acquired through a technical process. The mechanics of the camera intervenes between the authors of the *éclatements* and its object, and this distance is also a determining factor in the creation of the poster abstract. Hains' and Villeglé's work is not therefore simply an attack on art but, in the tradition of Futurism and Constructivism, an attack on artistic craft.

The real history of the poster abstract began in Paris in December 1949 when Hains produced his first abstract after photographing a number of other posters. The pre-history goes back, however, to the nineteenth century when the poster established itself

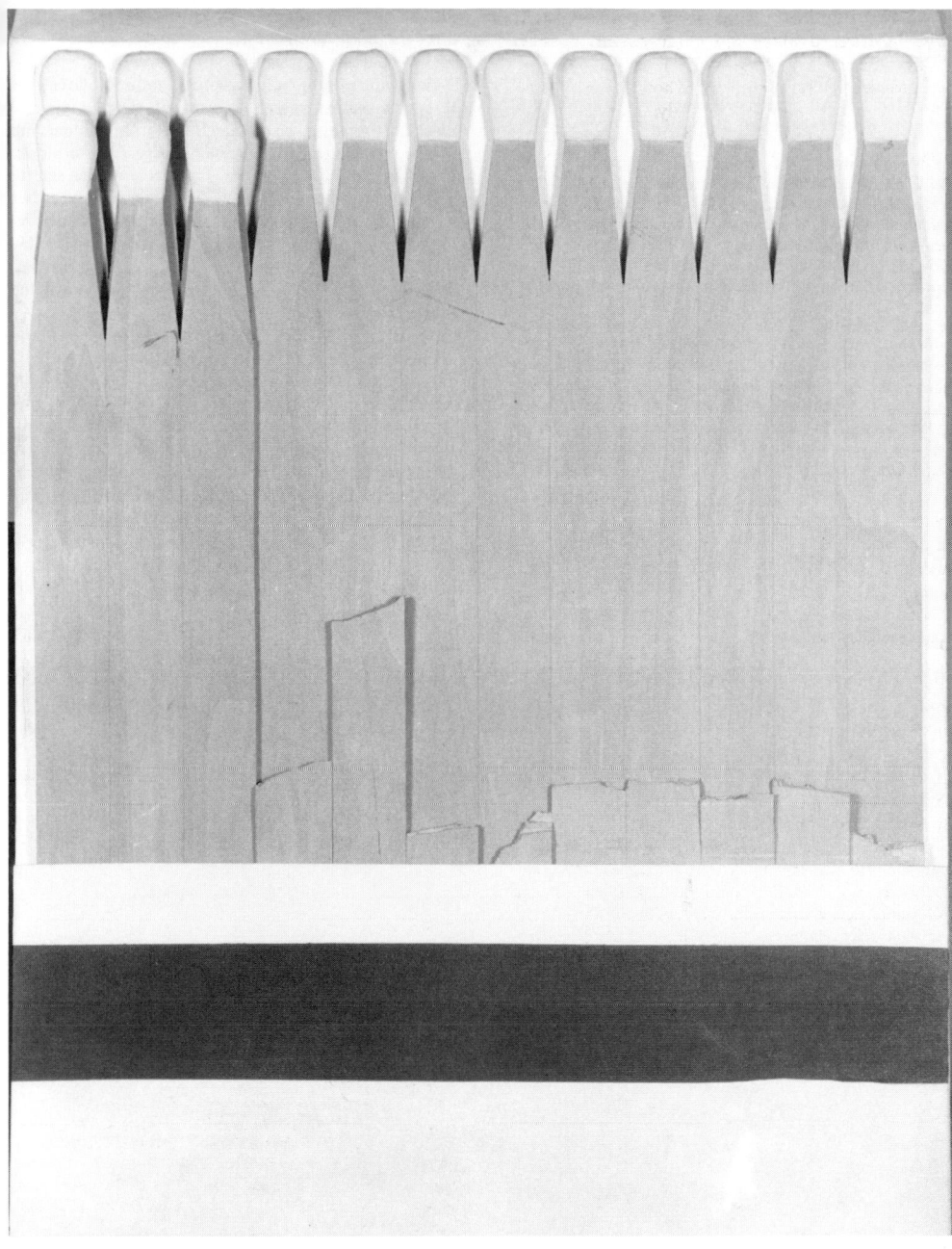

Raymond Hains: *Allumettes Seita*, 1964

compte sur vous, aidez-le, etc. Unlike the autonomous work of modernism, these abstracts do not represent objects closed in upon themselves, but remain closely linked with a particular historical environment, that of France and more precisely that of Paris in the 'fifties and 'sixties.

Hains avoided the danger of self-repetition by weaving a sort of fictional web around his activity as a poster artist. From the *palissade,* he progressed to *lapalissade,* named after the Village La Palice which lies halfway between Nice and Paris and which, according to Hains, constitutes the turning point between the *Ecole de Nice* (Arman, Klein, Raysse) and the Parisian *Nouveaux Réalistes;* and then to a 'sweet dish', the *entremets de la palissade,* which was the subject of an encyclopaedic exhibition at the Salon Comparaisons in 1960. Hains meanwhile became the ironic critic of his own work. "Le regardeur devient regardé", he said, calling himself—as the producer of *tôles—tôlard,* that is a prisoner of his own style.

In recent years Hains has turned his hand once more to photography. These latest photographs are not abstract works but arrangements of objects which playfully reflect the history of *Nouveau Réalisme.* In them, Hains demonstrates his theory of *abstractions personnifiées,* that is to say he discovers the trademarks of the artists of his generation in the things of everyday life.

—Dieter Schwarz

HAJDU, Etienne.
French. Born in Turda, Rumania, of Hungarian parents, 12 August 1907; emigrated to France, 1927: naturalized, 1930. Educated at Ecole Technique d'Art Décoratif, Budapest, 1923; Kunstgewerbeschule, Vienna, 1926; Académie de la Grande Chaumière, under Antoine Bourdelle, Paris, 1927; Ecole des Arts Décoratifs, under Niclausse, Paris, 1928; Ecole Nationale des Beaux-Arts, under Boucher, Paris, 1928. Served in French Army, 1931–32, 1939–40. Worked as stone-mason in marble works, Bagneres de Bigorre, 1940–44; produced first marble sculptures and small reliefs, 1944. Recipient: Sculpture Prize, Nordrhein-Westfalen, Germany 1965; Gold Medal, *International Exhibition of Ceramics,* Istanbul, 1967; Grand Prix National de Sculpture, Paris 1969. Officier de la Lègion d'Honneur, France, 1985. Agent: Artcurial, 9 Avenue Matignon, 75008 Paris. Address: 24 rue Bertie-Albrecht, 92220 Bagneux, France.

Individual Exhibitions:

alongside the newspaper as an industrially produced bearer of news to an anonymous city public. These media provide the basis for the invention of collage, photomontage and *décollage.* Like the reworking on Bryen's texts, the poster abstract is also a secondary artform which mirrors and comments upon primary artistic expressions. Hains selected numerous poster abstracts because their effect resembled the works of Abstract Expressionist paintings, without necessarily sharing the same aims. The technique of sticking loose poster sections on a board is still vaguely reminiscent of the art of collage. Hains appears to have been conscious of this problem from early on, for around 1950 he filmed his first *palissades,* or palings, which served the eager bill stickers as a welcome support. This conceptual extension of the art of the poster abstract clearly sufficed him, for it was not until 1959, under pressure from Dufrêne, that Hains exhibited at the first Biennale of Paris some twenty-seven lath frames entitled *Palissade des emplacements réservés.* In 1960 Hains introduced *tôles,* or sheet zinc, into his work as an equally useful surface on which posters could be mounted.

There is the closest association in these works between the picture and its support, which is exposed to view, not concealed like an adjustable frame, particularly when only a few sections of poster are left over so that the base is clearly in evidence. By this radical formulation, the poster abstract ironically succeeds in overcoming the division, with which monochrome painters such as Yves Klein were concerned at the time, between background and application of colour.

On closer observation, poster abstracts are seen to be composed of scraps of paper whose industrial origins are indicated by fragments of text and image still visible on them. In this way they are reminiscent of Schwitters' Merz collages; though, in using a variety of everyday objects, Schwitters did in fact subordinate them to the formal laws of his composition. The poster abstracts do not render up their narrative content; on the contrary: certain statements on the posters are angrily denied by anonymous interventions and gain more weight thereby. Hains' 1961 oneman exhibition at Galerie J, entitled *La France déchirée,* showed abstracts whose principal theme was the Algerian war, and which as a result were unsaleable. Their titles read like a resume of internal conflicts in France, a socio-historical reportage: *Paix en Algérie, L'Humanité est la vérité, Cet homme est dangereux* (Poujade), *C'est ça le renouveau?, OAS—fusillez les plastiqueurs, La cinquième fait naufrage, De Gaulle veut un bain de sang: il l'aura, De Gaulle*

1967	Centre Culturel, Bagneux, France
	Centre Culturel, Thonon-les-Baines, France
1968	*Sculptures Récentes*, Galerie Knoedler, Paris
1969	Nouveau Musée, Le Havre
	Recent Sculptures, M. Knoedler and Company, New York
1970	Centre Culturel, Toulouse
1971	*Sculptures: Encres de Chine*, Galerie Regence, Brussels
	Knoedler Galleries, New York
1972	*Werke der Sechziger Jahre 1964–1972*, Museum am Ostwall, Dortmund
	Centre Rizzoli, Milan
1973	Musée National d'Art Moderne, Paris
	Sculpteur, Estampilles, Dessins, Musée des Beaux-Arts, Nancy
1974	Galerie Regence, Brussels
	Fundacao Calouste Gulbenkian, Lisbon (retrospective)
1975	Musée des Ursulines, Mason
1977	Galerie La Cité, Luxembourg
1978	Musée des Beaux-Arts, Dijon (retrospective; toured France)
	Mucsarnok Museum, Budapest (retrospective)
	Musée des Beaux-Arts, Calais
	Musée des Beaux-Arts, Dunkirk
	Musée Galerie des Beaux-Arts, Bordeaux
1979	Musée des Beaux-Arts, Cannes
	Musée Municipal, Limoges
	Maison des Arts et des Loisirs, Montbeliard
	Muzuel de Arta, Bucharest
	Musée des Beaux-Arts, Cluj, Rumania
	Oeuvres sur Papier, Centre Georges Pompidou, Paris
	Terre Cuite et Porcelaine, Musée des Arts Décoratifs, Bordeaux
	Muzeul de Arta, Bucharest (retrospective; toured Rumania)
1980	Galerie Irtissen, Tunis
	Galerie La Cité, Luxembourg
1981	Galerie "M", Hannover
	Palais des Arts et de la Culture, Brest
1982	Salle des Ecuries de St. Hugues, Cluny, France
	Galerie Carré et Cie, Paris
1983	Galerie La Cité, Luxembourg
	Musée St. Denis, Reims, France
1985	Galerie La Cité, Luxembourg
1987	Artcurial, Paris
	Centre Artistique de Poudeous, France
	Galerie de Cluny, France

Selected Group Exhibitions:

1947	*Salon de Mai*, Paris
1951	*Biennale d'Anvers*, Antwerp
1958	*La Sculpture Contemporaine*, Musée Rodin, Paris
1968	*Bianca e Nero*, Lugano, Switzerland
1972	*100 Gravures Contemporaines*, Musée des Beaux-Arts, Calais
1976	*Un Siècle de Dessins des Sculpteurs*, Musée des Beaux-Arts, Lyon
1981	*Paris-Paris 1937–1957*, Centre Georges Pompidou, Paris
1983	*Sèvres de 1850 a nos jours*, Le Louvre des antiquaries, Paris
1985	*Fonds Régional d'Art Contemporain*, Musée du Luxembourg, Paris
1987	*Porcelaines de Sèvres au XXeme Siècle*, Musée National de Céramiques, Sèvres, France

Collections:

Centre Georges Pompidou, Paris; Musée des Beaux-Arts, Dijon, France; Lehmbruck Museum, Duisburg, West Germany; Museum of Modern Art, New York; Guggenheim Museum, New York; Hirshhorn Museum and Sculpture Garden, Smithsonian Institution, Washington, D.C.; Arts Club of Chicago; Museum of Fine Arts, Montreal.

Publications:

By HAJDU: articles—interview in *Chronique des Arts* (Paris), June 1973; text in *Christian Science Monitor* (Boston), 30 October 1977; "La cellule et son espace" in *Artcurial Journal* (Paris), May/June 1987.

On HAJDU: books—*Hajdu*, exhibition catalogue, with text by Michel Seuphor, New York 1958; *Etienne Hajdu*, exhibition catalogue, with text by Werner Schmalenbach, Leverkusen, West Germany 1961; *Hajdu*, exhibition catalogue, with text by Dora Vallier, Paris 1961; *Hajdu: Sculptures, Encres de Chine*, exhibition catalogue, Paris 1965; *Hajdu: Recent Sculptures*, exhibition catalogue, with text by Dora Vallier, New York 1969; *Etienne Hajdu: Werke der Sechziger Jahre, 1964–1972*, exhibition catalogue, with text by Eugene Thiemann, Dortmund 1972; *Etienne Hajdu* by Jonel Jianou, Paris 1972; *Etienne Hajdu*, exhibition catalogue, with texts by Jean Leymarie, Dominique Bozo, Nicole Barbier and Dora Vallier, Paris 1973; *Etienne Hajdu* by Mircea Deac, Bucharest 1976; *Hajdu: Oeuvres sur Papier*, exhibition catalogue, with text by Pierre Georgel, Paris 1979; *Etienne Hajdu: Terre Cuite et Porcelaine*, exhibition catalogue, with text by Jacqueline du Pasquier, Bordeaux 1979; *Hajdu* by Alexandre Cebus, Bucharest 1984; *Etienne Hajdu: Dessins* by Pierre Descargues, Paris 1987.

As an adolescent I carved with a tool that has not changed its form since antiquity. In the mountains around me everyday objects—the cradle, the furniture, the door, even the facades of the houses—were carved: the art was everywhere.

The rare photographic reproductions of Greek or Egyptian statues which I received were statues of marble or granite, so at that time in my life carving meant releasing a preconceived image from a block, giving organic life to matter. Later when I was sent to a technical school in the town I learned the other method of producing sculpture, the art of modelling clay, a shapeless, soft and obedient material. I threw myself into this new experience with great pleasure: day after day I modelled flowers, fruit, animals, the bust of my parents . . .

Then in Paris life around me was different: machines were invading all the professions, cars and aircraft were changing customs, the new vision of the world was dawning, and the pulsations of the machines enticed the poets away towards a new sensibility. In the plastic arts, lines, colours, forms were adopting strange, geometric and breathtaking rhythms and combinations. One glorified the Machine which would give man liberty and unite the world.

If marble is fitting for the slow and sensitive passage of light and shadows, the new vision demanded a

Etienne Hajdu: *Anise*, 1974

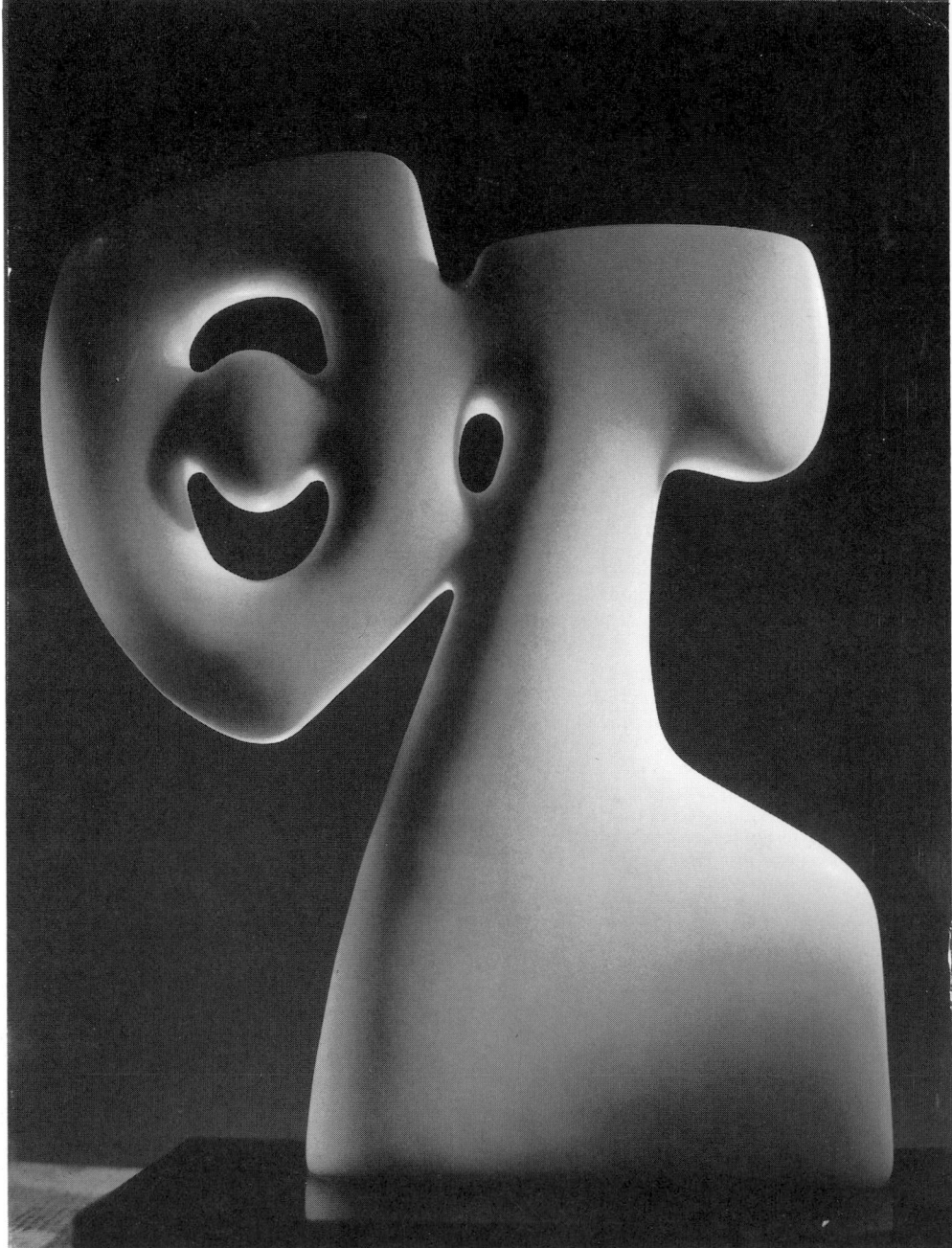

new medium. New sculpture could only be in metal.

In art, the medium and the tool are often determinant. Iron, aluminium, copper sheet or rod with multiple possibilities of machining, of assembly, of riveting and above all of welding. Little electric machines have given each of us personal possibilities, our hands have been multiplied by motors for shaping, milling, drilling, filing or polishing. Technology has profoundly changed our sensibility, our conception of space.

In 1945 I undertook the modelling of some large bas-reliefs; I orchestrated simple elements like the alphabet of a new language, a kind of totalisation of that which is living. I worked for eight years in clay, an intermediate material, and cast my reliefs in plaster; during that time I produced "The Aircraft Combat," "The Field of Force," "Homage to Béla Bartok," "Poem of Fire," and numerous other works which are in various museums and collections. When my plastic language seemed to me conceivable, I carried them out in a durable and definitive material; for that purpose I learnt to hammer large sheets of lead, copper and aluminium. In order to emboss copper one has to heat it. The fire gives to the metal an extraordinary coloration, the colour has a direct relationship with the depth of the forms, and is therefore organic to the expression. Aluminium can become silky, sensitive, luminous. Each material has its own personality; one has to understand, feel and respect this powerful alchemy charged with tellurial strength. The subtlety in the slow curves of forms brings to the density of the metal a suppleness, a sensuality, and unexpected tenderness; in addition the polish brings an incorporeal translucency: in this way common aluminium which in its lowliness was just good enough for kitchen utensils or industrial parts can become an astonishing medium. That is the series "Experiments with Metal."

Encouraged by the results, I multiplied forms in space, and on the undulating surface there are several high-reliefs and carvings. My elementary polished forms, shimmering and intersecting, create luminous echoes of unusual volumes. By just manipulating the planes, one can achieve an expansion of volume, an accumulation which grows and diminishes according to the movement of our perception.

I draw a lot. On paper I do not feel the resistance of the material, and the ink allows me boldness of form and liberty of imagination. My engravings are white on white or black on black—like the reliefs, they exist only because of the light.

—Etienne Hajdu

Looking at the cool, exquisite, near-oriental gentleness of finish in the works of Etienne Hajdu, it is hard to believe that this sculptor born to Hungarian parents in Rumania once served an apprenticeship in the studio of the brawny Bourdelle. This only goes to prove that the best students learn something but simultaneously preserve their own artistic personalities. One has only to check the list of the painters who passed through Léger's hands and survived his influence or, in the world of sculpture, those who were at one time or another students of or assistants to Henry Moore.

Hajdu's sculpture has featured in important museum exhibitions throughout the world. It is not that his imagery is out of step with contemporary styles so much as that the manner of presentation does not relate either to the passionate sturm-und-drang of much of modern sculpture or to the cold, often icy, anaemia of total non-figuration. In character, but not in appearance, his works have the same inbetween flavour of the sculptures of Hans Arp, though there is no evidence of Arp's fat humour in them and certainly nothing of Arp's dadaistic disruption of visual platitudes.

Hajdu's pieces preserve hints of figuration but clothe them in his own kind of oriental sublimity. It seems to matter little whether he is carving marble or working in metal bas-relief (beaten sheets of aluminium or copper); the same impact of cultured peace is maintained. Even at war Hajdu is at peace. This paradox is beautifully emphasized in his sheet copper relief "Soldiers in Armour" in the Museum of Modern Art in New York.

—Sheldon Williams

HALL, Nigel.

British. Born in Bristol, 30 August 1943. Studied at the West of England College of Art, Bristol, 1960–64; at Royal College of Art, London, 1964–67. Married Elizabeth Claire in 1965 (divorced, 1972); married Lyn Plenderleith in 1976 (divorced, 1977). Sculptor: lives and works in London. Lecturer, Royal College of Art, London, 1972–74; Principal Lecturer, Chelsea College of Art, London, 1974–81. Recipient: Harkness Travel Fellowship, 1967; Alecto Commission Prize, *Bradford Print Biennale,* 1974. Agent: Annely Juda Gallery, 11 Tottenham Mews, London W1. Address: 11 Kensington Park Gardens, London W11 3HD, England.

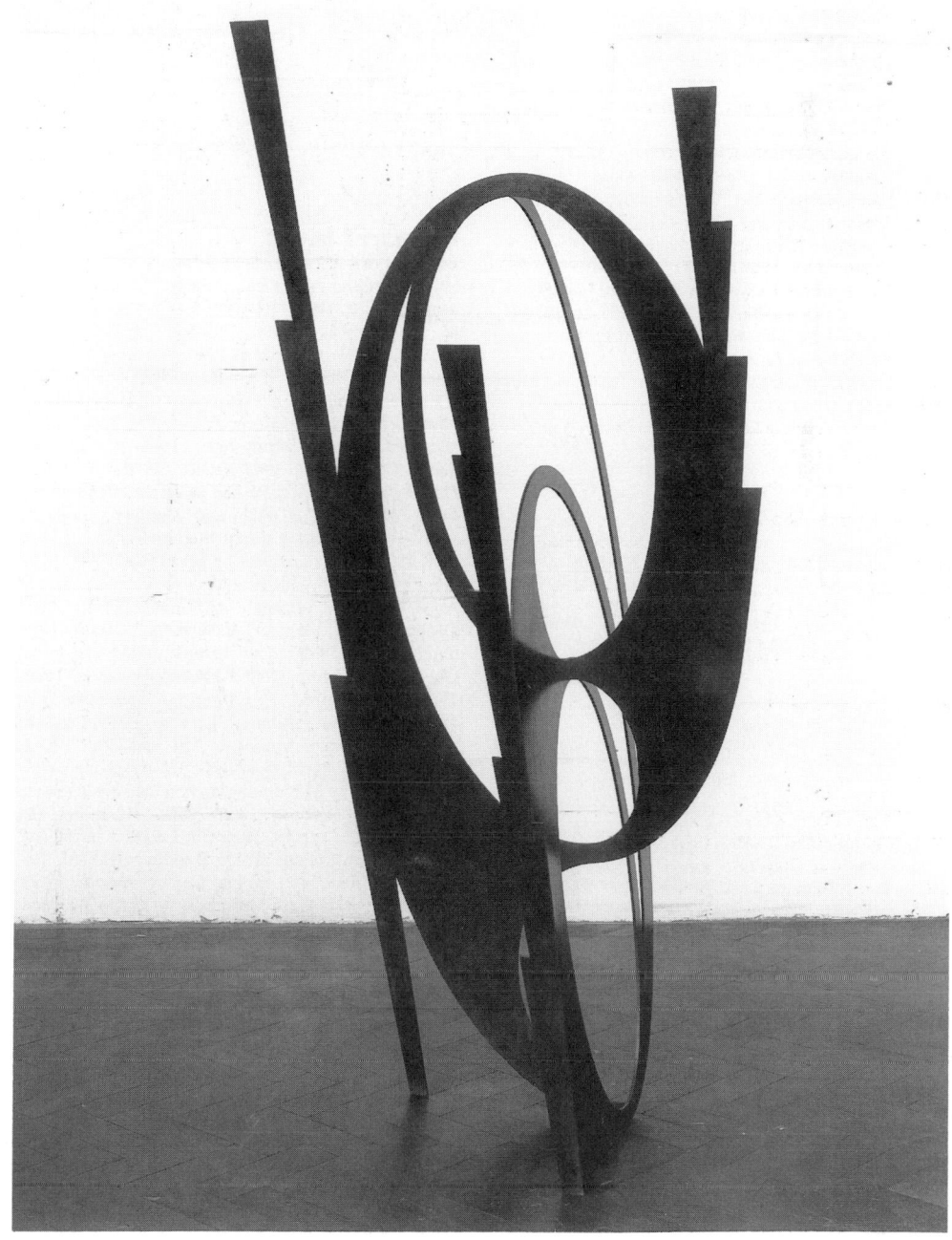

Nigel Hall: *Harsh and Soft Landscape,* 1986

Primo Piano Galleria, Rome
University of Southampton
Galerie Reckermann, Cologne
Peterloo Gallery, Manchester (with Alan Green)
1980 Warwick Gallery, London
Ceolfrith Gallery, Sunderland, County Durham
Nishimura Gallery, Tokyo
1981 Juda Rowan Gallery, London
Galerie Maeght, Paris
1982 Staatliche Kunsthalle, Baden-Baden, West Germany
Galerie Maeght, Zurich
Galerij 565, Aalst, Belgium
Kasahara Gallery, Osaka, Japan
1983 Robert Elkon Gallery, New York
Galerie Maeght-Lelong, Paris
Yuill/Crowley Gallery, Sydney
1984 Galerie Reckermann, Cologne
Nishimura Gallery, Tokyo
Galerie Lupke, Frankfurt
1985 Juda Rowan Gallery, London
Galerij 565, Aalst, Belgium
1986 Galerie Ziegler, Zurich
1987 Fondation Veranneman, Kruishoutem, Belgium
Garry Anderson Gallery, Sydney
Annely Juda Gallery, London

Selected Group Exhibitions:

1967 *New British Painting and Sculpture,* University of California at Los Angeles (toured the United States and Canada)
1972 *British Sculpture 72,* Royal Academy of Arts, London
1973 *Young English Artists,* Gothenburg Art Museum, Sweden
1975 *9th Paris Biennale*
1976 *Arte Inglese Oggi,* Palazzo Reale, Milan
1977 *Documenta 6,* Kassel, West Germany
1979 *Contructivism and the Geometric Tradition,* Albright-Knox Art Gallery, Buffalo, New York (toured the United States)
1980 *Reliefs: Formprobleme Zwischen Malerei und Skulptur im 20. Jahrhundert,* Westfälisches Landesmuseum, Münster, West Germany (travelled to the Kunsthaus, Zurich)
1982 *Aspects of British Art Today,* Metropolitan Art Museum, Tokyo (toured Japan)
1983 *The Sculpture Show '83,* Hayward Gallery, London

Collections:

Tate Gallery, London; Kunsthaus, Zurich, Louisiana Museum, Humlebaek, Denmark; National Museum of Art, Osaka, Japan; Australian National Gallery, Canberra; Museum of Modern Art, New York; Art Institute of Chicago; Nationalgalerie, West Berlin; Musée National d'Art Moderne, Paris; Metropolitan Museum of Art, Tokyo.

Publications:

By HALL: article—"Introduction: Conversation with Bryan Robertson" in *Nigel Hall,* exhibition catalogue, London 1980.

On HALL: books—*Arte Inglese Oggi,* exhibition catalogue, by Norbert Lynton, Milan 1976; *Aspects of British Art Today,* exhibition catalogue, by David Brown, Tokyo 1982; *Nigel Hall: Skulpturen und Zeichnungen,* exhibition catalogue, Baden-Baden 1982; *Nigel Hall: Recent Sculpture and Drawings,* exhibition catalogue, London 1985; *Nigel Hall: New Work,* exhibition catalogue, London 1987; articles—"Nigel Hall's Sculpture" by Jane Livingston in *Art and Artists* (London), December 1970; "London Letter" by Bernard Denvir in *Art International* (Lugano, Switzerland), February 1974; "Nigel Hall" by R. C. Kenedy in *Art International* (Lugano, Switzerland), March/April 1976; "Nigel Hall" by Bryan Robertson in *Art and Australia* (Sydney), Autumn 1985.

*   *   *

Nigel Hall is one of the most accomplished sculptors to emerge in England during the 70's. His sculptures are distinguished by the perfection of their finish and the degree of completion they reach in the technical sense. Aesthetically, they relate to Russian contructivism and have about them the quality of drawings suspended in space. This effect is due to several factors. The forms are made up of rods connected into geometric shapes like asymmetrical kites which are then cantilevered out from a supporting wall. Both the junctures where the rods meet and the sculpture attaches to the wall are superbly crafted so that we don't quite see how it is done. This sets up a mystery about technique which is not intrusive but thrilling. It is like the perfectionism of a jeweller taken to a larger scale. The big arcs and long lines move out from and double back to the anchoring wall and the viewer can see the structures from many angles simply by changing position. Depending on the lighting, there is the further element of the linear shadows cast by the rods onto the walls and floor. This, together with the fact that the rods may be painted different, close-valued colors—greys, dark greens, etc.—adds to the work's ambiguity. Colour not only acts as a weight control, in the sense of how heavy or light any part looks, but plays havoc with our reading of light and shadow and perspective.

Hall's work has immense elegance while remaining strong, even bold. The scale is perfectly judged to achieve this blending. What we see is a daring balancing act, a kind of series of high-wire maneuvers, translated into sculptural terms and fashioned in such a way that we can zero-in on the details to find the mechanics of the "performance" cunningly hidden, The combination is pretty irrestible.

—Ralph Pomeroy

HAMILTON, Richard.

British. Born in London, 24 February 1922. Studied at Westminister Technical College, London, under Mark Gertler, 1936; attended evening classes at St. Martin's School of Art, London, under Bernard Meninsky, 1936; studied at Royal Academy Schools, London 1938–40 and 1945–46; studied etching at the Slade School of Fine Art, London, under John Buckland Wright, 1948–51. Served in the Royal Engineers, Aldershot, Hampshire, 1946–47. Married Terry O'Reilly in 1947 (died, 1962); children: Dominy and Roderic. Worked as office boy in advertising department, Drake and Gouham, London, 1936–37; as display assistant, Reimann Studios, London, 1937–38; as engineering draftsman, EMI, London, 1941–45; organizer and designer, *Growth and Form* exhibition, Institute of Contemporary Arts, London, 1951; Member, Independent Group, London, 1952–53; worked on reconstruction of Marcel Duchamp's "Large Glass," Newcastle upon Tyne, 1965–66; organized, *The Almost Complete Works of Marcel Duchamp* exhibition, London, 1966. Lecturer in Design, Central School of Arts and Crafts, London, 1952–53; Lecturer in Basic Design, King's College, University of Durham, and created basic course "Developing Process," with Victor Pasmore, Ian Stephenson and others, 1956–58; Lecturer in Interior Design, Royal College of Art, London, 1957–61. Recipient: William and Noma Copley Award, 1960; First Prize, with Mary Martin, *John Moore's Exhibition,* Liverpool 1969; Talens Prize, Amsterdam, 1970. Agent: Waddington Graphics, 4 Cork Street, London, W1. Address: c/o Tate Gallery, London, S.W.1, England.

Individual Exhibitions:

1950 Gimpel Fils, London
1955 Hanover, Gallery, London
1957 Hatton Gallery, Newcastle upon Tyne (with Victor Pasmore)
1958 Hatton Gallery, Newcastle upon Tyne (with Victor Pasmore)

1964 Hanover Gallery, London
1966 Robert Fraser Gallery, London
1967 Robert Fraser Gallery, London
Galerie Ricke, Kassel, West Germany
Alexandre Iolas Gallery, New York
1968 Studio Marconi, Milan
1969 Studio Marconi, Milan
Robert Fraser Gallery, London
Galerie Neuendorf, Hamburg
1970 Galerie René Block, Berlin
Onnasch Galerie, Berlin
Tate Gallery, London (toured Europe)
National Gallery of Canada, Ottawa (toured Canada)
1971 Galerie René Block, Berlin
Studio Marconi, Milan
Stedelijk Museum, Amsterdam
Elvehjem Art Center, Madison, Wisconsin
Castelli Graphics, New York
1972 Studio Marconi, Milan
Whitworth Art Gallery, Manchester
Institute of Contemporary Arts, London
1973 Galerie René Block, Berlin
Neue Berliner Kunstverein, Berlin (with Dieter Roth and K. P. Brehmer)
Guggenheim Museum, New York (toured the United States and West Germany, 1973–74)
1974 Galerie Cadaques, Gerona, Spain
Studio Marconi, Milan
Scottish Arts Council Gallery, Edinburgh (toured Scotland and Wales)
1975 Serpentine Gallery, London
Kaiser Wilhelm Museum, Krefeld, West Germany
1976 Stedelijk Museum, Amsterdam (travelled to Bonnenfantemuseum, Maastricht, and the Gemeentemuseum, Arnhem)
1977 Le Musée, Grenoble, France (travelled to Musée des Beaux-Arts, Chambery, France)
Institute of Contemporary Arts, London (with Dieter Roth; toured the U.K. and Europe)
1978 *Studies 1937–1977,* Kunsthalle, Bielefeld, West Germany (travelled to the Kunsthalle, Göttingen and Kunsthalle, Tübingen)
Vancouver Art Gallery, British Columbia
1979 Stedelijk Museum, Amsterdam
1980 Anthony D'Offay Gallery, London
Waddington Graphics, London
Galerie Schellman + Kluser, Munich
Charles Cowles Gallery, New York
Severina Teucher AG, Zurich
1981 Galerie Maeght, Paris
1982 Provinciaal Museum, Hasselt, Belgium
Waddington Graphics, London
1983 Nishimura Gallery, Tokyo
Galerie Schellman + Kluser, Munich
Galeria Z, Zaragoza, Spain
Brooke Alexander Inc., New York
Tate Gallery, London
1984 Henie-Onstad Museum, Oslo
Nationalmuseum, Stockholm
Galeria Cadaques, Spain
Thorden and Wetterling, Stockholm
Wilhelm-Hack-Museum, Ludwigshefen, West Germany
Waddington Graphics, London
1985 Fundacio Joan Miro, Barcelona
Norton Gallery and School of Art, West Palm Beach, Florida
Fundacio Caja de Pensiones, Madrid
DAAD-Galerie, West Berlin
Nishimura Gallery, Tokyo
Yale University Art Gallery, New Haven, Connecticut
1986 National Gallery of Canada, Ottawa
Nishimura Gallery, Tokyo
Philadelphia Museum of Art, Pennsylvania
Galeria Cadaques, Spain
Los Angeles County Museum of Art
Walker Art Center, Minneapolis
1988 Fruitmarket Gallery, Edinburgh

Selected Group Exhibitions:

1956 *This Is Tomorrow,* Whitechapel Art Gallery, London

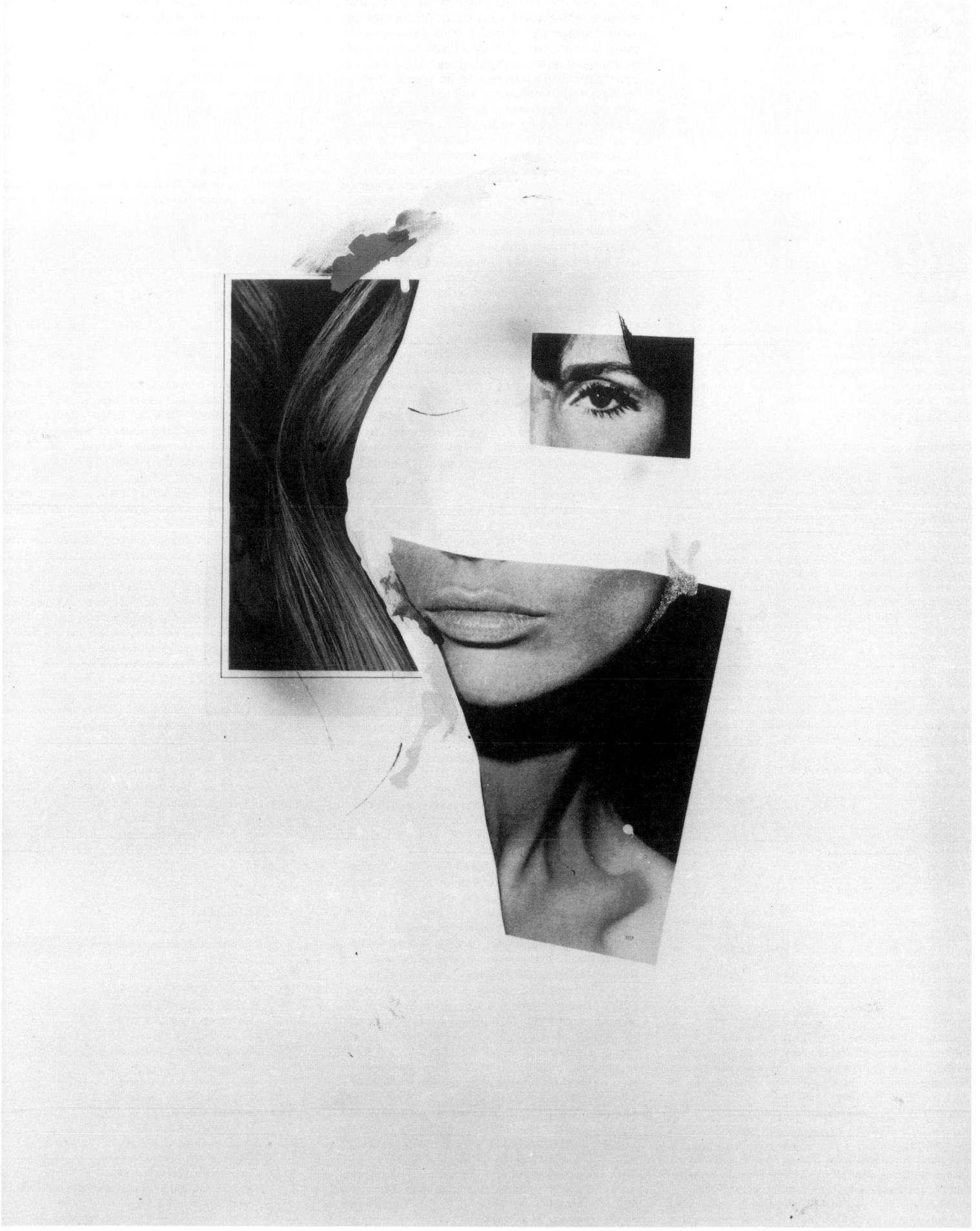

Richard Hamilton: *Fashion Plate Study*, 1969

1964   *Neuwe Realisten*, Gemeentemuseum, The Hague
1966   *European Drawings*, Guggenheim Museum, New York
1969   *Information*, Kunsthalle, Basle
1970   *Contemporary British Art*, Museum of Modern Art, Tokyo
1971   *Metamorphose de l'Objet*, Palais des Beaux-Arts, Brussels
1976   *Pop Art in England*, Kunstverein, Hamburg (travelled to the York Art Gallery, England)
1982   *Aspects of British Art Today*, Metropolitan Museum, Tokyo
1983   *Aspects of Postwar Painting in Europe*, Guggenheim Museum, New York
1987   *Berlinart 1961–87*, Museum of Modern Art, New York (travelled to San Francisco Museum of Modern Art)

Collections:

Tate Gallery, London; Guggenheim Museum, New York; Museum of Modern Art, New York; Nationalgalerie, West Berlin; Kunsthalle, Tubingen; Museum Ludwig, Cologne; Louisiana Museum, Copenhagen; Australian National Gallery, Canberra; Victoria and Albert Museum, London; National Gallery of Scotland, Edinburgh.

Publications:

By HAMILTON: books—*The Bride Stripped Bare by Her Bachelors Even*, London 1960; *The Bride Stripped Bare by Her Bachelors Even Again*, Newcastle upon Tyne 1966; *Polaroid Portraits Vol. 2*, Stuttgart 1978; *Interiors 1964–79*, London 1980; *Polaroid Portraits Vol. 3*, Stuttgart 1982; *In Horne's House*, London 1982; *Collected Words*, Stuttgart 1982; *Prints 1939–83*, London 1984; *The Transmogrifications of Bloom*, London 1986; articles—"Hommage á Chrysler Corp" in *Architectural Design* (London), March 1958; "Diagrammer" in *The Developing Process*, Newcastle upon Tyne, 1959; "Persuading Image" in *Design* (London), February 1960; "An Exposition of She" in *Architectural Design* (London), November 1961; "Duchamp" in *Art International* (Lugano, Switzerland), January 1964; "Son of the Bride Stripped Bare," with Mario Amaya, in *Art and Artists* (London), July 1966; "Roy Lichtenstein" in *Studio International* (London), March 1969; "Motion: Perspective" in *Richard Hamilton: Studies 1937–1977*, exhibition catalogue, Bielefeld, West Germany, 1978; "Recollections of Joseph Beuys" in *Art Monthly* (London), March 1986.

On HAMILTON: books—*Pop Art* by Lucy Lippard, London 1966; *Richard Hamilton*, exhibition catalogue, London 1970; *Richard Hamilton*, exhibition catalogue, New York 1973; *Richard Hamilton: Studies 1937–1977*, exhibition catalogue, Bielefeld, West Germany 1978; *Die Entwicklung der Pop Art in England*, thesis by Peter Lang, Frankfurt 1986; articles—"Pop Art and After" by Jasia Reichardt in *Art International* (Lugano, Switzerland), February 1963; "Hamilton's Guggenheim" by Gene Baro in *Art and Artists* (London), November 1966; "Popular Culture and Pop Art" by Lawrence Alloway in *Studio International* (London), July/August 1969; "Father of Pop Art" by Edwin Mullins in the *Daily Telegraph Magazine* (London), March 1970; "Richard Hamilton: Towards a New Definitive Statement?" by Gor Blok in *Museumjournaal* (Amsterdam), September 1970; "Image and History in the Art of Richard Hamilton" by R. Martin in *Arts Magazine* (New York), October 1985.

Although some of my pre-Pop pictures may seem to the casual observer to be 'abstract', I believe it is true to say that I have never made a painting which does not show an intense awareness of the human figure. In the case of earlier work it was the human configuration (two eyes situated at a certain distance from two mobile feet) confronting the picture that determined its composition.

Assumptions about the human figure were fundamental to the location of elements within the painting and the painting's relationship to the viewer was prescribed. That is to say, one justification for the picture was its value as a contribution to the total perspective of the spectator: a candid demonstration of the platitudinous concept that a work of art does not exist without its audience.

Later pictures of mine have absorbed into this external concern a recognition of the potency that representation of the human figure adds to this dialogue between image and witness. A fellow creature in the viewer's environment, either artificial (a semblance) or real, must be the strongest, most emotive factor in it; he will command attention for no other reason than his figurative identification with the ego. The force with which this *dramatis persona* can provoke displeasure is no less great than its capacity to provide companionship or to alter the construct of our lives. It, another self, real or semblance, revealed or implied, will always be a major factor in my art.

—Richard Hamilton

It should not be surprising that Richard Hamilton already was a mature artist at the time of *This Is Tomorrow*, the important exhibition held at the Whitechapel Art Gallery in London in August and September 1956, which launched him as a leading exponent of the Pop art movement it inaugurated. Hamilton's pre-Pop works included illustrations for James Joyce's *Ulysses* (1949), executed in various styles from realist to schematic, all intended as pictorial equivalents to the language of the scene from the book being interpreted; abstract drawings for paintings based on systemic notations of spirals and other linear markings (1950–51); and drawings and paintings that investigated different pictorial descriptions of movement: after the repetitive superimpositions of Muybridge, the Futurist emphasis on "subject motion" rendered by the devices of lines of force and centrifugal/centripetal planar structures, and the Cubist focus on "spectator movement" that involved the simultaneous rendering of an object or a scene from different perspectives (1952–54). His interests in such issues as the relationship of verbal and visual systems, the depiction of physical and perceptual sensations—i.e. weight and movement—found in the early art works are also developed in the didactic exhibition he designed and organized before *This is Tomorrow, Man, Machine & Motion* in 1955.

In *This is Tomorrow* the section that Hamilton designed offered sophisticated perceptual play with images borrowed from the popular, mass advertising culture. This is evident in his famous collage made specially for the exhibition, "Just What Is It That Makes Today's Homes So Different, So Appealing?" (1956). In it, he brought together in one interior an amalgam of images representative of popular commercial products and cosmetic fantasies—TV, vacuum cleaner, pin-up girl, muscle man, and anticipated the major formal and thematic issues that would occupy the Pop art movements in Europe and America during the late 1950's and through the 1960's.

Hamilton's Pop subjects have ranged from cars and toasters to Marilyn Monroe, John F. Kennedy and the Beatles. He has made paintings and reliefs, drawings and prints, and has used all sorts of popular, photographically-based imagery as sources for his own creations. The impact, however, of his intellectual and ironical treatments depend on the right and precise rendering of the pictorial relationships involving scale, color, and elisions of forms. For example, in the painting "Hers Is a Lush Situation" (1958) a real automobile is metamorphosed into a schematic image that not only suggests speed and power but the flashy, lustrous and sexual qualities of the vehicle which are its main selling points. The sexual aspect is even more strongly evoked by the introduction of a woman rider. Sex is also at issue in "She" (1958–61), a humorous depiction of woman's intimate relationships with her kitchen appliances, and in "Pin-Up" (1961), a relief work that exaggerates the most popular parts of the female anatomy.

Interiors have been a major theme in his recent works. Using a mix of graphic techniques that mirror the high degree of sharp specificity of image that the public has come to expect from the media, Hamilton imbues the renderings of domestic, public and pictorial interiors with sensual and emotive qualities. These aspects are evident in his paraphrases of "Picasso's meninas" and Jan van Eyck's "Arnolfini Wedding Portrait." In "Putting On De Stijl" (1979) the juxtaposition of two chairs by Gerrit Rietveld impresses as an ironic Pop statement.

Hamilton has done as well actual interiors for exhibition installations. A recent example is the one he designed for *Rooms* (1984), the Arts Council touring exhibition. It was inspired, he said, by "the bleak, disinterested, seedily clinical style of the establishment institution." In it, the impersonal and disquieting qualities of such spaces as a dentist's waiting room and a prison cell are chillingly captured.

Richard Hamilton is that rare artist who dares the audience to see and think about the perceptual and psychological implications of a forthright face-off between art and appearances.

—Ronny Cohen

HANSON, Duane.
American. Born in Alexandria, Minnesota, 17 January 1925. Educated at Parkers High School, Parkers Prairie, Minnesota 1943–44; Luther College, Decorah, Iowa, 1943–44; University of Washington, Seattle, 1944–45; Macalester College, St. Paul, Minnesota, 1945–46, B.A. 1946; Cranbrook Academy of Art, Bloomfield Hills, Michigan, 1950–51, B.F.A. 1951. Married Welsa Host in 1968; children: Maja and Duane Jr. Art Instructor, Twin Falls High School, Idaho, 1946–47; worked as a travelling salesman for Webb Publishing Company, St. Paul, serving western Minnesota and eastern South Dakota, 1949; Art Instructor, Decorah High School, Iowa, 1949–50; United States Army High School, Munich, 1953–57; United States Army High School, Bremerhaven, West Germany, 1957–60; United States Army High School, Atlanta, 1960–62; Oglethorpe University, Atlanta, 1962–65; and Miami-Dade Junior College, Florida, 1965–69; Part-time Art Instructor, New York University, 1971–72. Full-time artist, since 1969; has lived and worked in Davie, Florida, since 1974. Recipient: Grant for Sculpture, Ella Lyman Cabot Trust, 1963; Sculpture Award, *Florida State Fair Arts Exhibition*, 1968; Blair Award, Art Institute of Chicago, 1974; D.A.A.D. grant to work in Berlin, 1974; Moetti Award, Fort Lauderdale, Florida, 1984; *New York Times* Florida Artist Award, 1985. DHL: Nova University, Fort Lauderdale, Florida, 1979. Agent: Ivan Karp, O.K. Harris Works of Art, 383 West Broadway, New York, New York 10013. Address: 6109 South West 55th Court, Davie, Florida 33314, U.S.A.

Individual Exhibitions:

1951   Museum of Art, Cranbrook Academy, Bloomfield Hills, Michigan
1952   Wilton Gallery, Wilton, Connecticut
1958   Galerie Netzel, Bremen, West Germany
1970   O.K. Harris Gallery, New York
1972   O.K. Harris Gallery, New York
         Galerie Onnasch, Cologne
1974   Museum of Contemporary Art, Chicago
         O.K. Harris Gallery, New York
         Galerie de Gestlo, Hamburg
         Württembergischer Kunstverein, Stuttgart (retrospective)
         Neue Galerie, Aachen
1975   Louisiana Museum, Humlebaek, Denmark
         Akademie der Künste, Berlin
1976   O.K. Harris Gallery, New York
         Edwin A. Ulrich Museum of Art, Wichita State University, Kansas
         Sheldon Art Gallery, University of Nebraska, Lincoln
1977   Des Moines Art Center, Iowa
         University of California Art Museum, Berkeley
         Portland Art Museum, Oregon

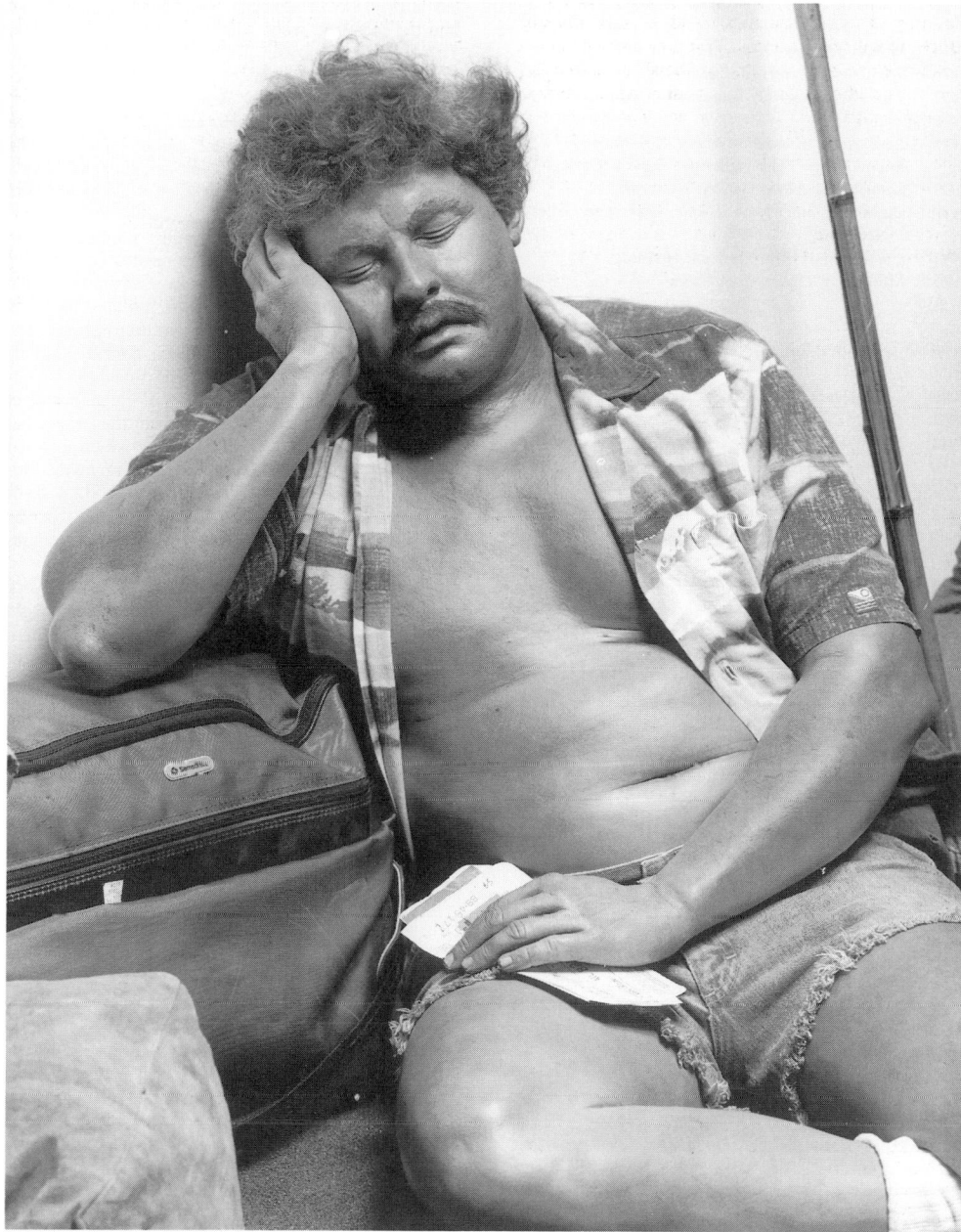

Duane Hanson: *Camper—Variation 3,* 1987

William Rockhill Nelson and Atkins Museum of Fine Arts, Kansas City, Missouri
Colorado Springs Fine Arts Center
Virginia Museum of Fine Arts, Richmond
Corcoran Gallery, Washington, D.C.
1978 Whitney Museum, New York
1980 O.K. Harris Gallery, New York
Jacksonville Art Museum, Florida
1981 Lowe Art Museum, University of Miami
Norton Art Gallery, Palm Beach, Florida
Loch Haven Art Museum, Orlando, Florida
Jacksonville Art Museum, Florida (travelled to Coral Gables, Florida; Orlando, Florida; West Palm Beach, Florida)
1984 O.K. Harris Gallery, New York
Wichita State University, Kansas (travelled to Tokyo, Osaka and Nagoya, Japan)
1985 Cranbrook Academy of Art, Bloomfield Hills, Michigan
1986 Carl Milles Gärden, Lindingö, Sweden
1987 Rune Stone Museum, Alexandria, Minnesota
Swedish American Institute, Minneapolis

Selected Group Exhibitions:

1968 *Human Concern/Personal Torment,* Whitney Museum, New York

1970 *Sculpture Annual,* Whitney Museum, New York (and 1973, 1978)
1972 *Documenta,* Kassel, West Germany
1974 *7 Realists,* Yale University Art Gallery, New Haven, Connecticut
1975 *Super Realism,* Baltimore Museum of Art
1979 *Reality of Illusion,* Denver Art Museum, Colorado (toured the United States)
1981 *Contemporary American Realism Since 1960,* Pennsylvania Academy of Fine Arts, Philadelphia (toured the United States)
1983 *Contemporary Trompe l'Oeil Painting and Sculpture,* Boise Gallery of Art, Idaho (toured the United States)
1985 *Pop Art 1955–70,* Art Gallery of New South Wales, Sydney (toured Australia)
1987 *Independence Sites,* Independence Mall, Philadelphia

Collections:

Whitney Museum, New York; Wadsworth Atheneum, Hartford, Connecticut; Richmond Museum, Virginia; Milwaukee Art Museum; William Rockhill Nelson Art Gallery and Atkins Museum of Fine Arts, Kansas City, Missouri; Neue Galerie, Aachen; Wallraf-Richartz Museum, Cologne; Wilhelm Lehmbruck Museum, Duisburg; National Museum, Utrecht; Museum of South Australia, Adelaide.

Publications:

By HANSON: articles—"Presenting Duane Hanson" in *Art in America* (New York), September/October 1970; "Martin Bush Interviews Duane Hanson" in *Art International* (Lugano, Switzerland), September 1977; "Duane Hanson Confounded by Ivan Karp" in *Interview* (New York), March 1978.

On HANSON: books—*Radikaler Realismus* by Udo Kultermann, Tübingen, West Germany 1972; *Duane Hanson,* exhibition catalogue, Cologne 1972; *The New Realism* by Udo Kultermann, New York 1972; *The Pop Image of Man* by Sam Hunter, New York 1972; *Neue Formen Des Realismus* by Peter Sager, Cologne 1973; *Duane Hanson* by Tilman Osterwold, Stuttgart 1974; *The New Humanism* by Barry Schwartz, New York and Washington, D.C. 1974; *American Art since 1900* by Barbara Rose, New York and Washington, D.C. 1975; *Duane Hanson,* exhibition catalogue, by Martin Bush, Wichita, Kansas 1976; *Duane Hanson* by Kirk Varnedoe, New York 1985.

In my sculpture, I attempt to detach myself from subject. Although my earlier works were rather expressionistic with outbursts against war, crime, and violence in general, I now find my most successful pieces are less topical and ideographic. They are naturalistic or illusionistic which results in an element of shock, surprise or psychological impact for the viewer. The subject matter that I like best deals with the familiar lower and middle class American types of today. To me, the resignation, emptiness and loneliness of their existence captures the true reality of life for these people. Consequently, as a realist I'm interested in the human form and especially faces and bodies which have suffered like some weather worn landscape the erosion of time. In portraying this aspect of life I want to achieve a certain tough realism which speaks of the fascinating idiosyncrasies of our time.

Ultimately, making a successful sculpture is my major task, which involves manipulating forms to make them look convincing. I want my sculptures to convey a certain sense of stylelessness which will capture the contemporary feeling of reality.

—Duane Hanson

Duane Hanson has been making life-size, super-real, polyester, sculpted people since 1967 after he had decided to turn back (at 40-plus years old) on his previous abstract work which had always dissatisfied him anyway.

Hanson's earliest works in the realist mode were tableaux of topical situations loaded with issues of the social significance of violence. Groupings such as "War," "Race Riot" and "Gangland Victim" capture a frozen moment of tense emotional/physical brutality and are more concerned with depicting the horror and waste within our contemporary society than with illusionism as such. Around 1970, with works such as "Supermarket Shopper" and "Woman Eating," waste is seen on another plane, that of the ordinary classes of Americans who, steeped in overabundance, become careless in habits and appearances, lumpy, sloppy and filling themselves with junk to excess. Perhaps his most sardonically sarcastic work from this period is "Tourists" (1970) in which a 5-foot 2-inch little elderly man and his 5-foot 4-inch out-of-shape wife look up in the typical stance of the tourist who, from the look of their outfits of plaid and Hawaiian pattern and their carry-along equipment including camera and accessories and bag-full of stuff, can only be in Miami from New York, as most any American will easily notice. A more soulfully humane attitude appears in Hanson's work from these and following years, beginning with his marvelously expressive "Hardhat" (1970) who is seated in a more introspective mood in his well-used workclothes and hat flashing the American flag proudly. He is weary, resting from a hard day's work with beer can in hand, evoking a far more sympathetic response than Hanson's tourist types. Perhaps it is the relationship with the artist/worker which evoked such empathy from Hanson, a factor reinforced by his "Seated Artist"

(1971) and "Artist with Ladder" (1972). Works since the early 70's tend to pare down on the accesories and build up the more contemplative approach as reaction to the regular, nextdoor types closer to home and heart.

Although it is this human, communicative quality somewhere between alienation and repose which Hanson stresses, there is no escape from the element of deception which pops up on first view of his people who, life cast and dressed in real clothes, appear very near flesh-and-blood real. The illusionism of these works is carried as far as is seemingly possible with the aid of the newest plastic materials (fiberglass reinforced polyester resin), which are skillfully manipulated for the most intricate details from body hairs to boils to wrinkles and bulges. Such verissimilitude as this is strikingly effective at conveying tense feelings of ambiguity about the realness of artificiality and the artificiality of reality in our everyday world of small businessmen on vacation, repairmen, housewives, and even artists.

Could Hanson's art be somehow "radical" in the avant garde intellectualism which has been his context? This is entirely possible, expecially if you consider the wide communicative effectiveness in evidence on observing the interactions between his people and the real folks who confront them in their gallery or museum settings with a mixture of amazement and disbelief that is both disarmingly humorous and a bit frightening to behold.

—Barbara Cavaliere

HARE, David.
American. Born in New York City, 10 March 1917. Educated in schools in New York, Colorado, and California, studying biology and chemistry, 1923–39. Full-time artist since 1940. Collaborated with Dr. Clark Whistler of Museum of Natural History on portfolio of color photographs on the American Indian, 1940; Editor, *VVV* surrealist magazine, in collaboration with Marcel Duchamp. André Breton, and Max Ernst, 1942–44; edited issue of *Temps Moderne* devoted to American writers, 1950. Artist-in-Residence, Delgado Museum, New Orleans, 1964; Visiting Sculptor-Instructor, Philadelphia College of Art, 1964–65; Visiting Artist, University of Oregon, Eugene, 1966; Resident in Lithography, Tamarind Institute, University of New Mexico, Albuquerque, 1972. Honorary doctorate: Maryland Institute of Art, 1969. Agent: Hamilton Gallery, 20 West 57th Street, New York, New York 10019. Address: 151 Spring Street, New York, New York 10012, U.S.A.

Individual Exhibitions:

1941	E. Weyhe Gallery, New York
1944	Peggy Guggenheim Gallery, New York
1946	Julien Levy Gallery, New York
	Peggy Guggenheim Gallery, New York
	Sam Kootz Gallery, New York
1947	San Francisco Museum of Art
1948	Maeght Gallery, Paris
1949	Sam Kootz Gallery, New York
	Julien Levy Gallery, New York
1952	Kootz Gallery, New York
1955	Kootz Gallery, New York
1956	Kootz Gallery, New York
1958	Kootz Gallery, New York
1959	Kootz Gallery, New York
1960	Saidenberg Gallery, New York
	Staempfli Gallery, New York
1961	Saidenberg Gallery, New York
1962	Saidenberg Gallery, New York
1963	Saidenberg Gallery, New York
1965	Philadelphia Museum College of Art
	Delgado Museum of Art, New Orleans

1969	Staempfli Gallery, New York
	Portland Museum of Art, Maine (retrospective)
1974	Watson/de Nagy Gallery, Houston
1976	*The Cronus Series*, Alessandra Gallery, New York
1977	*The Cronus Series*, Guggenheim Museum, New York
1978	*Landscapes*, Hamilton Gallery, New York
	Major Works, Zolla Lieberman Gallery, Chicago
1979	*Drawings* Hamilton Gallery, New York
1980	*Elephants and Flying Heads*, Hamilton Gallery, New York
1981	Contemporary Arts Museum, Houston
1982	Museum of Fine Arts, Houston

Selected Group Exhibitions:

1946	*14 Americans*, Museum of Modern Art, New York
1951	*Bienal*, Sao Paulo
1954	*The New Decade*, Whitney Museum, New York
1956	*International Exhibition of Contemporary Sculpture*, Musée Rodin, Paris
1958	*World's Fair Exhibition*, Brussels
1962	*Contemporary Sculpture and Drawings*, Whitney Museum, New York
1968	*Dada, Surrealism and their Heritage*, Museum of Modern Art, New York
1969	*New American Painting and Sculpture: The First Generation*, Museum of Modern Art, New York
1976	*200 Years of American Sculpture*, Whitney Museum, New York
1978	*American Painting of the 1970's*, Albright-Knox Art Gallery, Buffalo, New York (travelled to 5 other museums)

Collections:

Metropolitan Museum, New York; Museum of Modern Art, New York; Guggenheim Museum, New York; Whitney Museum, New York; Wadsworth Atheneum, Hartford, Connecticut; Yale University Art Gallery, New Haven, Connecticut; Albright-Knox Art Gallery, Buffalo, New York; Museum of Art, Carnegie Institute, Pittsburgh; Washington University Gallery of Art, St. Louis; San Francisco Museum of Modern Art.

Publications:

By HARE: articles—statement in *14 Americans*, exhibition catalogue, New York 1946; "The Work of the Artist" in *Trojan Horse* (Ithaca, New York), December 1961; "The Myth of Originality in Contemporary Art" in *Art Journal* (New York), Winter 1964/65; "On Robert Goldwater" in *Art Journal* (New York), Fall 1973.

On HARE: books—*14 Americans*, exhibition catalogue, New York 1946; *Sculpture of the 20th Century*, exhibition catalogue, New York 1952; *Dada, Surrealism and Their Heritage*, exhibition catalogue, New York 1968; articles—"L'Exceptionnel David Hare" by Alain Jouffroy in *Opus International* (Paris), December 1971; "Philosopher or Dog?" by Dore Ashton in *Arts Magazine* (New York), May 1976; "David Hare: A Painter of the Human Psyche" in the *New York Times*, 30 September 1977; "David Hare: American Surrealist" by Katharine Kuh in *Saturday Review* (New York), 1 October 1977; "An American Surrealist" by Harold Rosenberg in *The New Yorker*, 24 October 1977; "David Hare's Cronus Series" by Deborah Perlberg in *Artforum* (New York), December 1977.

Photographer, editor (of surrealist Magazine *VVV* in the 1940's), painter, and sculptor, Hare is probably best known for surrealist-inclined, welded steel sculpture of the 1950's and for a prolonged series of works in several media based on the myth of Cronus which he did in the 1960's. Hare occupies an unusual position among American sculptors, for although many artists were influenced to some degree by the post war presence of Max Ernst, André Breton, and Marcel Duchamp, only Hare, and in a different direction Joseph Cornell, display a fully surrealist sensibility. As a sculptor Hare has experimented with many materials but prefers welded steel because the metal is flexible and easy to manipulate. The metal also gives

the impression of strength, even when stretched out into the lace-fine webs which characterize his work. The attempt to render the workings of the subconscious in welded steel is clearly a hazardous undertaking, one which may be better suited to painting or tiny box assemblages, but Hare plunges right in, often starting directly with the metal, and by employing the constructivist convention of interior space, conveys a sense of ethereal figure, open mind, watcher and watched, and form in nature.

Following the period of surrealist sculpture, Hare immersed himself in one of the central concerns of abstract expressionism without ever assimilating the style. In the "Cronus" series, Hare has used the myth of the Titan who devours all his children (except one, Zeus, who escapes and murders his father) in an effort to maintain his power over the world. In its entirety, the tale of Cronus is a tale of creation and of the emergence of gods and man from the primordial ooze, a primary question of existence which inspired many abstract expressionists to refer to myths, totems, and rituals. Like the surrealists, Hare finds ideas through free associations, and like Picasso he carefully constructs composite images, always retaining a clearly defined sense of natural form.

It is not the intention of David Hare to create work with obscure, inaccessible meanings. A self-taught artist, Hare is also an articulate philosopher and theorist of art. His images often come from personal associations but unlike many surrealists and abstract expressionists he creates visual translations available to the careful viewer. "In 'the water where the artist swims,' the spectator shall at least wade, and so be made to shiver with some of 'the chills and fever which stimulate the imagination.' "

—Mary Stofflet

HARRISON, Helen (Mayer).
American. Born in New York City, 1 July 1929. Studied psychology at Cornell University, Ithaca, New York; studied at Queens College, Flushing, New York, BA in English Literature 1948; Studied at New York University, MA in philosophy of education 1953; did graduate and doctoral studies in philosophy of education at New York University, in psychology and human behaviour at United States International University, San Diego, and in anthropology, literature and psychology at New School for Social Research in New York, University of Pennsylvania in Philadelphia, and at University of New Mexico in Albuquerque. married Newton Harrison, *q.v.*, in 1953; children: Steven, Joshua, Gabriel and Joy. Independent artist since 1972: now lives and works in California. Recipient: DAAD Grant, to work in West Berlin, 1988. Agents: Ronald Feldman Fine Arts Inc., 31 Mercer Street, New York, New York 10013; The Wenger Gallery, 828 N. La Brea Avenue, Los Angeles, California 90038. Address: P.O. Box 446, Del Mar, California 92014, U.S.A.

Individual Exhibitions:

1974	Grandview Gallery, Los Angeles
	Ronald Feldman Fine Arts, New York (with Newton Harrison)
1975	Ronald Feldman Fine Arts, New York (with Newton Harrison)
1976	Detroit Institute of Fine Arts, New York (with Newton Harrison)
1977	San Francisco Art Institute (with Newton Harrison)
	San Francisco Museum of Modern Art (with Newton Harrison)
	Floating Museum, San Francisco (with Newton Harrison)
1978	Portland Center for the Visual Arts, Oregon (with Newton Harrison)

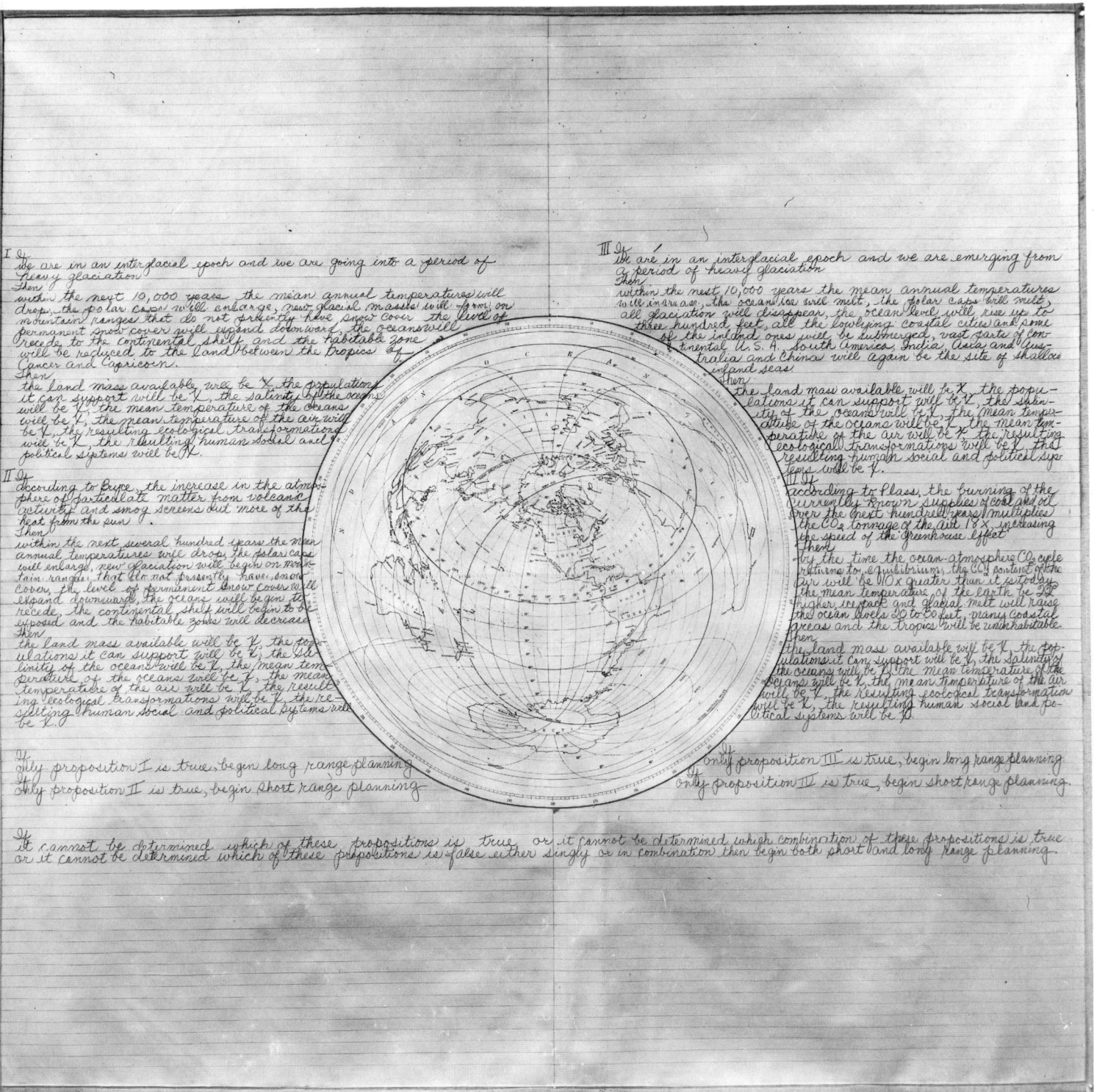

Newton and Helen Harrison: *If This Then That* (The First Four), 1974

Readings/Performances and Events: Solo—*Portable Fish*

Feast: Survival Piece 3, Hayward Gallery, London 1971; *Giveaway*, La Jolla Museum of Contemporary Art, California, 1971; *Catfish Feast*, Atelier Chapman Kelley, Dallas, 1972; *Citrus Feast*, California State University at Fullerton, 1972; *Fish Feast*, Palais des Beaux Arts, Brussels, 1972; *Making Strawberry Jam*, California State University at Fullerton, 1973, and at Grandview Gallery Women's Building, Los Angeles, 1974; *Visual Distortion: With My Glasses/Without My Glasses*, Grandview Gallery, Women's Building, Los Angeles, 1975; *From the Lagoon Cycle* (and lecture), Center for Music Experimentation, University of California at San Diego, La Jolla, 1978; with Newton Harrison—*From the Centers of the World*, P.S. 1, New York, 1976; *From the Meditations*, Center for Music Experiment, University of California at San Diego, La Jolla, 1977; *From the Meditations* (and lecture), Center for 20th Century Studies, University of Wisconsin, Milwaukee, also San Francisco Art Institute, and United Artists Coalition of San Diego, 1977; *On the Lagoon Cycle*, Museum of Contemporary Art, Chicago, 1977; also Claremont Graduate School, California, 1978; *Street Graffiti*, San Francisco Art Institute, also streets of San Francisco, 1977; *San Diego as the Center of the World*, University of Wisconsin, Milwaukee, 1977; *From the Great Lakes Meditations* (and lecture), Center for 20th Century Studies, University of Wisconsin, Milwaukee, 1978; *From the Lagoon Cycle* and *From the Meditations*, Portland Center for Visual Arts, Oregon, and University of California at San Diego, La Jolla, 1978; *Readings*, Franklin Furnace, New York, 1979; *The Watershed Series*, Franklin Furnace, New York, 1979; *Talking Water*, Ronald Feldman Fine Arts, New York, 1980; *Reading and Rapping*, 424 F. Street, San Diego, 1980; *Baltimore Promenade*, Washington Project for the Arts, Washington, D.C., 1982; *Fortress Atlanta*, Emory University, Atlanta, 1983; *San Jose*, San Jose Museum of Art, California, 1983; *Three Urban Pieces*, San Jose State University, California, 1983.

Selected Group Exhibitions:

1972   *Vesuvio*, Henry Gallery, University of Wisconsin, Seattle
1973   *In a Bottle: Strawberry Jam*, California State University at Fullerton
1975   *A Response to the Environment*, Rutgers University, New Brunswick, New Jersey
1976   *Art in Landscape*, University of Montana, Missoula
1977   *A View of a Decade*, Museum of Contemporary Art, Chicago
1978   *Artists Investigate the Environment*, Barnsdall Park Municipal Gallery, Los Angeles
1980   *Drawing: The Pluralist Decade*, at the *Biennale*, Venice
1982   *Common Ground: Five Artists in the Florida Landscape*, Ringling Museum, Sarasota, Florida
1984   *Disarming Images*, Contemporary Arts Center, Cincinnati, Ohio
1987   *Documenta 8*, Museum Fridericianum, Kassel, West Germany

Collections:

Brooklyn Museum, New York; Museum of Contemporary Art, Chicago; La Jolla Museum of Contemporary Art, California; Power Gallery of Contemporary Art, Sydney; Los Angeles County Museum of Art; Museum of Modern Art, New York; Georgia Museum of Art, Athens; Tel Aviv Museum, Israel.

Publications:

By HARRISON, with Newton HARRISON: books—*The Book of the Crab*, 1980; *The Lagoon Cycle*, exhibition catalogue, Ithaca, New York 1985; articles—"Sea Grant and Related Projects" in *Studio International* (London), May 1974; "San Diego as the Center of the World" in *Los Angeles Institute of Contemporary Art Journal*, February 1975; "Notes on a Recent Project" in *Los Angeles Institute of Contemporary Art Journal*, November 1977; "Nobody Told Us When To Stop Thinking", interview, in *Grey Matters* (New York), Autumn 1987.

On HARRISON: books—*Common Ground: Five Artists in the Florida Landscape*, exhibition catalogue, Sarasota, Flor-

ida 1982; *The Art of Performance: A Critical Anthology*, edited by Gregory Battcock and Robert Nickas, New York 1984; articles—"Art and Technology" by Maurice Tuchman in *Art in America* (New York), March/April 1970; "Corporate Art" by Jack Burham in *Artforum* (New York), October 1971; "Off Shellfish Farms and Other Works of Art" by David Bourdon in the *Village Voice* (New York), 16 December 1974; review by Paul Stinson in *Art in America* (New York), March/April 1976; "Newton and Helen Harrison: Art as Ecology" in *Artweek* (Oakland, California), 5 February 1977; "Helen and Newton Harrison: New Grounds for Art" by Kim Levin in *Arts Magazine* (New York), February 1978; "The Earth as Their Palette" by Grace Glueck in the *New York Times*, 4 April 1980; "Helen Mayer Harrison and Newton Harrison" by Ann Schoenfeld in *Arts Magazine* (New York), June 1980; "Helen Mayer Harrison and Newton Harrison" by Stephen Eiseman in *Arts* (New York), February 1983; "Helen and Newton Harrison's Book of the Seven Lagoons" by Kim Levin in *Village Voice* (New York), 16 December 1986.

See HARRISON, Newton.

HARRISON, Newton.

American. Born in Brooklyn, New York, 20 October 1932. Apprentice to sculptor Michael Lantz, New York, 1947–50; studied at Antioch College, Yellow Springs, Ohio, 1950–52; Pennsylvania Academy of Fine Arts, Philadelphia, 1952–53, 1955–57; Academia di Belle Arti, Florence, 1958; Yale University School of Art and Architecture, New Haven, Connecticut, 1963–65, B.F.A. 1964, M.F.A. 1965. Served in the United States Army, 1953–55. Married Helen Mayer (i.e., Helen Harrison, *q.v.*) in 1953: children: Steven, Joshua, Gabriel, Joy. Independent artist, since 1957: now lives and works in California. Lived in Florence, 1957–60; taught at Settlement House, New York, 1960–63; Assistant Professor, University of New Mexico, Albuquerque, 1965–67; Assistant Professor, 1967–70, Associate Professor, 1970–73, and Professor and Chairman from 1973, Department of Visual Arts, University of California at San Diego. Recipient: Research Grant, University of California at San Diego, 1969, 1972, 1973; Outstanding Educators of America Award, 1970; Ford Foundation Grant, 1974; Sea Grant, U.S. Department of Commerce, 1974; DAAD Grant, to work in West Berlin, 1988. Agents: Ronald Feldman Fine Arts Inc., 31 Mercer Street, New York, New York 10013; The Wenger Gallery, 828 N. La Brea Avenue, Los Angeles, California 90038. Addresses: Department of Visual Arts B-027, University of California at San Diego, La Jolla, California 92093; P.O. Box 446, Del Mar, California 92014, U.S.A.

Individual Exhibitions:

1961   10/4 Group Gallery, New York
1963   Stryke Gallery, New York
         Hudson River Museum, Yonkers, New York
1966   University of New Mexico, Albuquerque
1968   La Jolla Museum of Contemporary Art, California
1969   Washington State University, Pullman
         University of Idaho, Moscow
1972   California State College at Fullerton
         Atelier Chapman Kelley, Dallas
1974   Ronald Feldman Fine Arts, New York (with Helen Harrison)
1975   Ronald Feldman Fine Arts, New York (with Helen Harrison)
1976   Detroit Institute of Arts, Michigan (with Helen Harrison)
         National Academy of Sciences, Washington, D.C. (with Helen Harrison)
1977   San Francisco Art Institute (with Helen Harrison)
         The Floating Museum, San Francisco (with Helen Harrison)
1978   Portland Center for Visual Arts, Oregon (with Helen Harrison)

         Claremont Graduate School, California (with Helen Harrison)
         Ronald Feldman Fine Arts, New York (with Helen Harrison)
1979   University of Idaho, Moscow (with Helen Harrison)
         Williams College Museum of Art, Williamstown, Massachusetts (with Helen Harrison)
         Brown University, Providence, Rhode Island (with Helen Harrison)
1980   Ronald Feldman Fine Arts, New York (with Helen Harrison)
         Museum of Contemporary Art, Chicago (with Helen Harrison)
1981   Maryland Institute College of Art, Baltimore (with Helen Harrison)
1982   Washington Project for the Arts, Washington, D.C. (with Helen Harrison)
         Ronald Feldman Fine Arts, New York (with Helen Harrison)
1983   Emory University, Atlanta, Georgia (with Helen Harrison)
         San Jose Museum of Art, California (with Helen Harrison)
         San Jose State University, California (with Helen Harrison)
         Wenger Gallery, San Diego, California (with Helen Harrison)
1985   California Institute of Technology, Pasadena (with Helen Harrison)
         University of California, Irvine (with Helen Harrison)
         Cornell University, Ithaca, New York (with Helen Harrison)
         Tortue Gallery, Santa Monica, California (with Helen Harrison)
         Ronald Feldman Fine Arts, New York (with Helen Harrison)
         Wenger Gallery, San Diego, California (with Helen Harrison)
1986   Palomar College, California (with Helen Harrison)
         Culman Gouro, Los Angeles (with Helen Harrison)
1987   Grey Gallery, New York University (with Helen Harrison)
         Pasadena College of Art and Design, California (with Helen Harrison)
         Los Angeles County Museum of Art (with Helen Harrison)
         Wenger Gallery, San Diego, California (with Helen Harrison)
1988   Tel Aviv Museum, Israel

Readings/Performances and Events: with Helen Harrison—*From the Centers of the World*, P.S. 1, New York, 1976; *From the Meditations*, Center for Music Experiment, University of California at San Diego, La Jolla, 1977; *From the Meditations* (and lecture), Center for 20th Century Studies, University of Wisconsin, Milwaukee, also San Francisco Art Institute, and the United Artists Coalition of San Diego, 1977; *On the Lagoon Cycle*, Museum of Contemporary Art, Chicago, 1977, also Claremont Graduate School, California, 1978; *Street Graffiti*, San Francisco Art Institute, also streets of San Francisco, 1977; *San Diego as the Center of the World*, University of Wisconsin, Milwaukee, 1977; *From the Great Lakes Meditations*, 1978; *From the Lagoon Cycle* and *From the Meditations*, Portland Center for Visual Arts, Oregon, and University of California at San Diego, La Jolla, 1978; *Readings*, Franklin Furnace, New York, 1979; *The Watershed Series*, Franklin Furnace, New York, 1979; *Talking Water*, Ronald Feldman Fine Arts, New York, 1980; *Reading and Rapping*, 424 F. Street, San Diego, 1980; *Baltimore Promenade*, Washington Project for the Arts, Washington, D.C., 1982; *Fortress Atlanta*, Emory University, Atlanta, 1983; *San Jose*, San Jose Museum of Art, California, 1983; *Three Urban Pieces*, San Jose State University, California, 1983.

Selected Group Exhibitions:

1971   *Earth, Air, Fire Water: Elements of Art*, Museum of Fine Arts, Boston
1972   *"10"*, Museum of Contemporary Arts, Houston
1974   *Project 74*, Kunsthalle, Cologne

1975   *A Response to the Environment*, Rutgers University Art Gallery, New Brunswick, New Jersey (with Helen Harrison)
1976   *Art-World*, Whitney Museum, New York
1977   *A View of a Decade*, Museum of Contemporary Art, Chicago
1980   *Drawing: The Pluralist Decade*, at the *Biennale*, Venice
1982   *Common Ground: Five Artists in the Florida Landscape*, Ringling Museum, Sarasota, Florida
1984   *Disarming Images*, Contemporary Arts Center, Cincinnati, Ohio (toured the United States)
1987   *Documenta 8*, Museum Fridericianum, Kassel, West Germany

Collections:

Everson Museum, Syracuse, New York; Museum of Contemporary Arts, Houston; Palais des Beaux-Arts, Brussels; Power Gallery of Contemporary Art, Sydney; Los Angeles County Museum of Art; Museum of Modern Art, New York; Brooklyn Museum, New York; Georgia Museum of Art, Athens; La Jolla Museum of Art, California; Tel Aviv Museum, Israel.

Publications:

By HARRISON: books—*The Book of the Crab*, with Helen Harrison, 1980; *The Lagoon Cycle*, exhibition catalogue, Ithaca, New York 1985; articles—statement in *11 Los Angeles Artists*, exhibition catalogue, London 1971; statement in *10*, exhibition catalogue, Houston 1972; "Sea Grant and Related Projects" with Helen Harrison, in *Studio International* (London), May 1974; "San Diego as the Center of the World," with Helen Harrison, in *Los Angeles Institute of Contemporary Art Journal*, February 1975; "Forum: Should the Art School Curriculum Include Professional Job Training?", with Judith Brodsky, in *American Artists* (New York), October 1977; "Notes on a Recent Project," with Helen Harrison, in *Los Angeles Institute of Contemporary Art Journal*, November 1977; "Nobody Told Us When To Stop Thinking", interview, in *Grey Matters* (New York), Autumn 1987.

On HARRISON: books—*Art and the Future* by Douglas Davis, New York and London 1973; *Art and Technology in the Future* by Jonathan Benthall, New York 1973; *Great Western Salt Works: Essays on the Meaning of Post-Formalist Art* by Jack Burnham, New York 1974; *Sunshine Muse* by Peter Plagens, New York 1974; *The Art of Performance: A Critical Anthology*, edited by Gregory Battcock and Robert Nickas, New York 1984; articles—"Newton Harrison: Big Fish, Small Pool" by Jonathan Benthall in *Studio International* (London), December 1971; "The Education of the Un-Artist-III" by Allan Kaprow in *Art in America* (New York), January/February 1974; "Newton Harrison's Fourth Lagoon: Strategy Against Entropy" by José Barrio-Gray in *Arts Magazine* (New York), November 1974; "Newton and Helen Harrison: Art as Ecology" in *Artweek* (Oakland, California), 5 February 1977; "Helen and Newton Harrison: New Grounds for Art" by Kim Levin in *Arts Magazine* (New York), February 1978; "The Earth as Their Palette" by Grace Glueck in the *New York Times*, 4 April 1980; "Helen Mayer Harrison and Newton Harrison" by Ann Schoenfeld in *Arts Magazine* (New York), June 1980; "Helen and Newton Harrison's Book of the Seven Lagoons" by Kim Levin in *Village Voice* (New York), 16 December 1986; "Helen Mayer Harrison and Newton Harrison" by Patricia C. Phillips in *Artforum* (New York), September 1987.

Our work begins when we perceive an anomaly in the environment that is the result of opposing beliefs or contradictory metaphors. It is the moment when reality no longer appears seamless and the cost of belief has become outrageous that offers opportunity to create new spaces, first for the mind and thereafter in everyday.

The works that we are doing now are narratives or stories of projects that we have been engaged in or are currently involved with. The locales are cities, such as Baltimore, Maryland; San Jose, Pasadena, Santa Barbara and San Diego, California. In these places, we developed promenades, argued for grand canals, or proposed, for example, to cover channelized rivers and turn the concrete areas into park lands or to make plant and animal refuges along their banks and under flight paths and freeways or to reclaim spoils-piles

and dumps. We always compose with left-over spaces and invisible places. And there are many. We have worked in collaboration with ourselves, although lately, we have started to include other artists, ecologists, landscape architects, engineers, and alike in our dialogues.

—Helen and Newton Harrison

The Harrisons are working in a taboo area where art is dependent not on its own reflection but on the world at large. In their work art is given an aspect of both social comment and urgency, while social science is given a requisite amount of aesthetics, as well as the public relations which are necessary for any new system of observation. Here we have a case where the two disciplines assist each other, rather than vying, discipline-wise, for individual shares of "Progress." The projects they undertake have a sense of their own recognition, the type of cognizance cultures usually describe as some form of commonly-agreed upon knowledge, though usually remaining hidden as cultural visual activity. Because of the "real" nature of their work, the Harrisons are often subject to criticism from those who are more concerned with strictly visual advancement.

Helen Harrison's background was, specifically, the social sciences, while Newton Harrison has worked in both sculpture and painting, and with technological art. As they began collaborating, the disciplines began to mix, and the inadequacies and short sightedness of the contemporary specialized fields became more apparent. An early work, "Brine Shrimp Farm," at the Los Angeles County Museum of Art, consisted of several ponds, each 10 feet by 20 feet. The salt ponds, consisting of an ecological habitat of shrimp, algae, and water, netted a large number of shrimp. The ponds also had a look of painterly coloration from one pool to the next, as the salinity content changed in each habitat. "Brine Shrimp Farm" indicative, though, of the Harrisons' true interest in the earth as both material and medium, rather than as a purely aesthetic form, which many other earth artists were exploring at the time.

"The Lagoon Cycle" is a large work which has taken nearly 10 years to date, and which consists of meditations on the nature of human, animal and geologic ecology. For their exhibitions and presentations, the Harrisons used taped and live mantric-like readings, colored and detailed maps, and aerial and site photographs to examine several site-specific and terrain-specific problems. A recent work was titled "Thinking about the Mangrove and the Pine." The piece utilized an area in the Florida landscape for ecological observation. The text, which accompanied descriptive illustration, reads: "The pines colonize behind the mangroves/then gain the edge/and lose ground thereby." Much of the Harrisons' work emphasizes the problem of understanding the natural world through acute and simple perception. Certainly both the social sciences and the arts have defined themselves historically, in different periods, as being concerned with such perception. The Harrisons have realized the appropriateness of such vision, while living side-by-side with the specificity and grandiose nature of the technological vision. They see the importance of continuing personal observation in an era of machine-guided human vision.

—John Robinson

HARTIGAN, Grace.
American. Born in Newark, New Jersey, 28 March 1922. Educated in Milburn, New Jersey schools, 1929 40; studied privately with Isaac Lane Muse, New York, 1942–46. Married Robert Jachens in 1941 (divorced, 1947); son: Jeffrey; married Winston H.

Price in 1960. Worked as mechanical draftsman, in defense factory, 1943. Independent artist, since 1946: travelled in Europe; lived in San Miguel de Allende, Mexico, 1949; moved to Baltimore, 1960; Artist-in-Residence, Hoffberger Graduate School of Painting, Maryland Institute, Baltimore, 1967–68. Recipient: *Mademoiselle* magazine Merit Award for Art, 1957; Childe Hassam Purchase Award, National Institute of Arts and Letters, 1974. D.F.A.: Orre Institute of Art, Science and Industry, Philadelphia, 1969; Towson University, Maryland. Agent: Hamilton Gallery, 20 West 57th Street, New York, New York 10019. Address 17011/2 Eastern Avenue, Baltimore, Maryland 21231, U.S.A.

Individual Exhibitions:

1951   Tibor de Nagy Gallery, New York
1952   Tibor de Nagy Gallery, New York
1953   Tibor de Nagy Gallery, New York
1954   Tibor de Nagy Gallery, New York
       Vassar College Art Gallery, Poughkeepsie, New York
1955   Tibor de Nagy Gallery, New York
1957   Tibor de Nagy Gallery, New York
       Robert Keene Gallery, Southampton, Long Island, New York
1959   Tibor de Nagy Gallery, New York
1960   Gres Gallery, Washington, D.C.
1962   Martha Jackson Gallery, New York
1963   University of Minnesota, Minneapolis
1964   Martha Jackson Gallery, New York
       Franklin Siden Gallery, Detroit
1967   Martha Jackson Gallery, New York
       Maryland Institute College of Art, Baltimore
       University of Chicago
1970   Gertrude Kasle Gallery, Detroit
       Martha Jackson Gallery, New York
1972   Gertrude Kasle Gallery, Detroit
1974   Gertrude Kasle Gallery, Detroit
1975   William Zierler Gallery, New York
       American University, Washington, D.C.
1976   Gertrude Kasle Gallery, Detroit
1978   Genesis Gallery, New York
1979   University of Maryland, College Park
       Grimaldis Gallery, Baltimore
1980   State University of New York, Plattsburg
1981   Hamilton Gallery, New York
       Fort Wayne Museum, Indiana
       Grimaldis Gallery, Baltimore
1982   Grimaldis Gallery, Baltimore
1983   Lafayette College, Easton, Pennsylvania
1984   Gruenebaum Gallery, New York
       Grimaldis Gallery, Baltimore
1986   Gruenebaum Gallery, New York
       Grimaldis Gallery, Baltimore
1987   American University, Washington, D.C.
       Grimaldis Gallery, Baltimore
1988   Gruenebaum Gallery, New York

Selected Group Exhibitions:

1964   *Figuration and Defiguration*, Art Musuem, Ghent
1968   *Selections from Albright-Knox*, National Gallery, Washington, D.C.
1973   *Art in Embassies*, American Embassy, San Jose, Costa Rica
1974   *1961*, Allan Frumkin Gallery, New York
1975   *Biennial*, Corcoran Gallery of Art, Washington, D.C.
1976   *Poets and Painters*, National Collection of Fine Arts, Washington, D.C.
1977   *Critic's Choice*, Lowe Art Gallery, Syracuse, New York
1980   *Art of the 50's*, Hirshhorn Museum, Washington, D.C.
1982   *Hartigan/Louis/Still/Truitt*, Baltimore Museum of Art, Maryland
1984   *Action-Precision: The New Direction in New York 1955–60*, Newport Harbor Art Museum, Newport Beach, California (travelled to New York; Worcester, Massachusetts; Buffalo, New York)

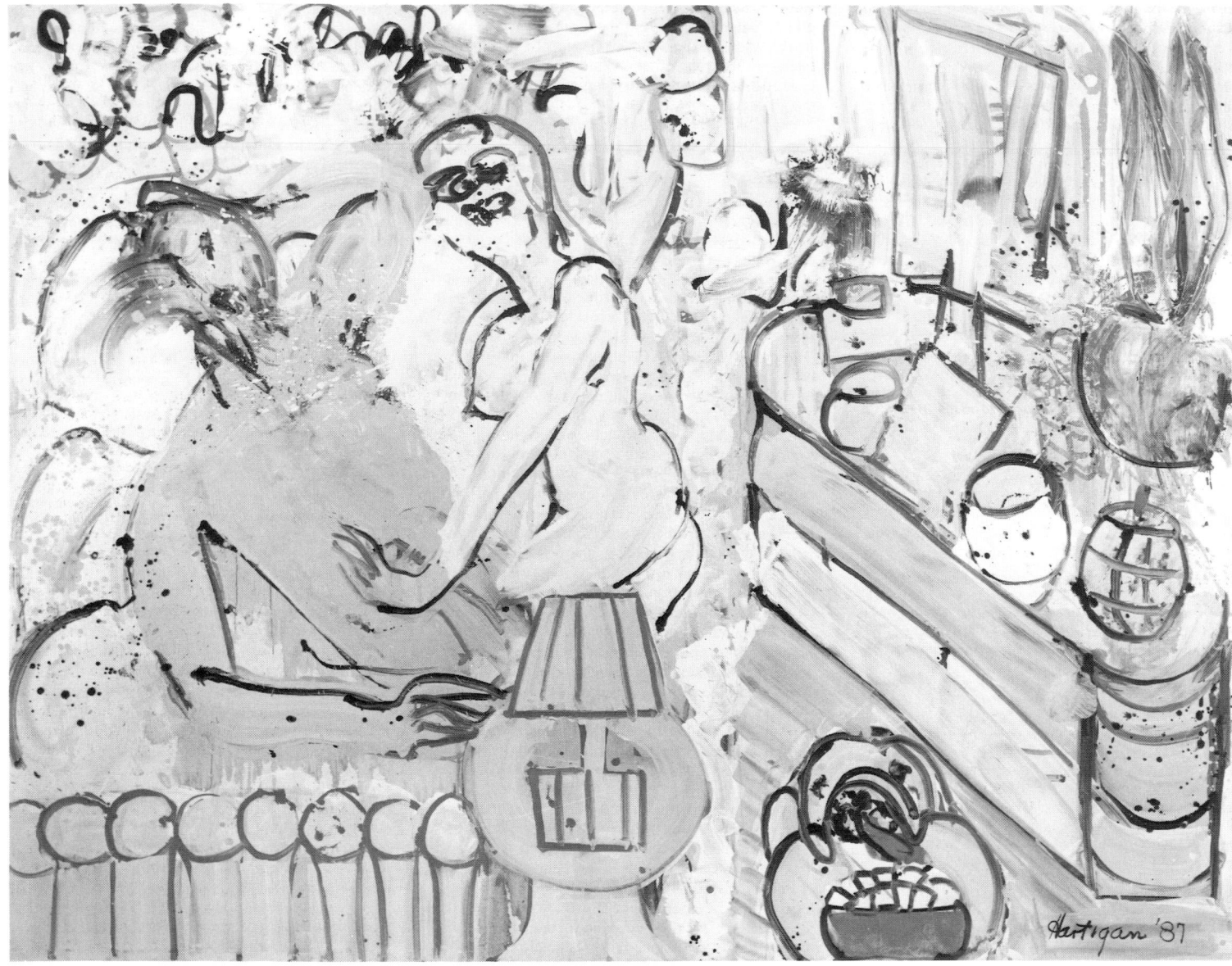

Grace Hartigan: *L.A. Boudoir*, 1987

Collections:

Whitney Museum, New York; Museum of Modern Art, New York; Metropolitan Museum of Art, New York; Albright-Knox Gallery, Buffalo, New York; Wadsworth Atheneum, Hartford, Connecticut; Baltimore Museum of Art; National Collection of Fine Arts, Washington, D.C.; Carnegie Institute Museum of Art, Pittsburgh; Art Institute of Chicago; Walker Art Center, Minneapolis.

Publications:

By HARTIGAN: article—"An Artist Speaks" in *The Arrow* (Pittsburgh), December 1960.

On HARTIGAN: books—*Modern American Painting and Sculpture* by Sam Hunter, New York 1959; *Art Since 1945,* by Sam Hunter, New York 1959; *Art Autre* by Michel Tapie, Paris 1960; *Morphologie Autre* by Michel Tapie, Turin 1961; *The New York School* by Irving Sandler, New York 1978; *Action/Precision: The New Direction in New York 1955-60,* exhibition catalogue by Paul Schimmel, B. H. Friedman and others, Newport Beach, California 1984; articles—"Grace Hartigan" by Emily Dennis in *School of New York: Some Younger Artists,* edited by B. H. Friedman, New York 1959; "Grace Hartigan" in *Arts Magazine* (New York), May 1959; "Miss Hartigan and Her Canvas" in *Newsweek* (New York), May 1959; "The Rawness and the Vast" in *Newsweek* (New York), May 1959; articles by Klaus Jürgen-Fischer in *Das Kunstwerk* (Baden-Baden), August 1959; "Woman in American Art" in *Life* (New York), September 1960; articles by Barbara Gold in *Baltimore Morning Sun,* 12 February 1967;

"Women Artists" by Michael and Arlene Batterberry in *Harper's Bazaar* (New York), July 1971; "Hartigan" by Allen Barber in *Arts Magazine* (New York), June 1974; "Grace Hartigan at Gruenebaum" by Gerrit Henry in *Art in America* (New York), May 1984; "Grace Hartigan: Painting Her Own History" by Robert Mattison in *Arts* (New York), January 1985.

I feel that we are living a very fragmented life; the whole world—you too. So I perceive the world in fragments. It is somewhat like being on a very fast train and getting glimpses of things in strange scales as you pass by. A person can be very, very tiny. And a billboard can make a person very large. You see the corner of a house or you see a bird fly by, and it's all fragmented.

Somehow, in painting I try to make some logic out of the world that has been given to me in chaos. I have a very pretentious idea that I want to make life, I want to make sense out of it. The fact that I am doomed to failure—that doesn't deter me in the least.

—Grace Hartigan

Grace Hartigan was perhaps the only woman painter to come to the fore in the early 1950's in New York as a disciple of the Action Painters. De Kooning and Pollock had their influence particularly, and in 1950 Clement Greenberg selected her work for inclusion in a New York show. Until 1953 she signed her paintings as "George Hartigan," but having made her point that there is sexual equality in the art, she subsequently dropped the forename.

Hartigan has expressed her viewpoint that she wishes her art to be resistant to entry, as a window in space, and her subject matter distilled until it evolves as its own essence. By the mid-1950's she had denied outright abstraction in favour of king-sized canvases on themes the contents of which could be recognized and bore relation to the given titles.

"Essex Market" (1956) has the strong and evocative attack of expressionist handling, fruit and the busy atmosphere of the setting presenting their various equivalents in swiftly brushed areas of mixed and pure colour, in which the drawing of forms dictate their plastic urgency. "City Life," another work of the same year, reflects the pace and the rhythms of street scenes in which the broad masses are hatched in a lateral diagonal progression. Life, one feels, is not frozen at a given moment of time but taken on the run—an impression that retains something of the movement inspiring it. The colour key tends to be aggressive and importunate, and the separation of the different masses is often defined by outline shadow as much as by differing colour contrasts.

Her commitment to the vulgarity and vitality of modern American life most usually in its urban environment gives a vivid monumentality to her canvases even when the physical references become fussed and ambiguously noted in the scheme of the composition. "Interior 'The Creeks' " (1957) is a large canvas that teeters on the verge of the illusionistic yet relies on its abstract dynamic of freely written motives to set up the tensile push-pull of their arrangement in space. "Shinnecock Canal" (1957) is a large broadly handled reflection of reality paraphrased in plangent banners of colour. Celebrations of swatches of existence where people live in community: the chords are musically strong, distinguished by movements in which the brass and the woodwind predominate over the strings in moods recalling New Orleans saloon jazz more than tasteful Carnegie Hall concertos.

G. S. Whittet

HARTUNG, Hans.

German. Born Heinrich Ernst Hartung in Dresden, 21 September 1904. Educated at the Humanistisches Gymnasium, Dresden, 1915–24; studied philosophy at the University of Leipzig, 1924–25, and art at the Akademie der Schonen Künste, Leipzig, 1924–26, and at the Kunstakademie, Munich, 1928. Served in the French Foreign Legion, under U.S. Forces, 1944; wounded in action, 1944. Married Anna-Eva Bergman in 1929 (divorced, 1938); married Roberta Gonzalez in 1939. Painter, in Germany, 1929–39, in Lot, France, 1940–41, in Figueras and Gerona, Spain, 1942–44, and in Paris, since 1945. Recipient: Guggenheim Award, 1956; Rubens Prize, The Hague, 1958; Grand Prize, *Biennale*, Venice, 1960; Grand Prize, *7th International Graphics Exhibition*, Ljubljana, 1967; Grand Prix des Beaux-Arts, Paris 1970. Honorary Member, Akademie der Künste, West Berlin, 1956, and Bayerische Akademie der Schonen Künste, Munich, 1958. Chevalier, Légion d'Honeur; Officier, Ordre des Arts et Lettres, Paris, 1960; Member, Order of Merit, Wissenschaft und Künste, Bonn, 1977; Member of the Institute, Académie dex Beaux-Arts, Paris, 1977. Agent: Lefebre Gallery, 47 East 77th Street, New York, New York 10021, U.S.A. Address: 5 rue Gauget, 75014 Paris, France.

Individual Exhibitions:

1931	Galerie Heinrich Kuhl, Dresden
1932	Galleri Blomqvist, Osla (with Anna-Eva Bergman)
1939	Galerie Henriette, Paris
1947	Galerie Lydia Conti, Paris
1948	Galerie Lydia Conti, Paris
1949	Galerie Stangl, Munich
	Hanover Gallery, London
1952	Galerie Rudolf Probs, Mannheim
	Kunsthalle, Basle
1953	Lefebre Gallery, London
	Galerie Marbach, Berne
1954	Palais des Beaux-Arts, Brussels
1956	Galerie de France, Paris
	Galerie Craven, Paris
1957	Kestner-Gesellschaft, Hannover (retrospective; toured Germany)
	Kleeman Gallery, New York
1958	Galleria Il Segno, Rome
	Gallerie Otto Stangl, Munich
1959	Musée Grimaldi, Antibes, France
	Kleeman Gallery, New York
1961	Galleria Lorenzelli, Milan
	Librería-Galleria Einaudi, Rome
	Museo del Ateneo, Madrid
	Contemporary Art Centre, Beirut
1962	Galerie de France, Paris
1963	Kunsthaus, Zurich (retrospective; toured Europe)
1965	Galleri Holst Halvorsen, Oslo
1966	Museo Civico, Turin
	André Emmerich Gallery, New York
1967	Galleria la Polena, Genoa
	Galleria d'Arte Narciso, Turin
1968	City Art Gallery and Museum, Birmingham, England

1969	Museum of Fine Arts, Houston (retrospective; toured Canada)
	Musée d'Art Moderne, Paris
1971	Lefebre Gallery, New York
	Galerie de France, Paris
	Fondation Maeght, St. Paul-de-Vence, France
	Galeria René Metras, Barcelona
1972	Gimpel Fils, London
	Galleria Ravagnan, Venice
	Galeria Egam, Madrid
1973	Galerie Maeght, Zurich
	Galerie Benador, Geneva
	Galerie Charles Kriwin, Brussels
1974	Galerie de France, Paris
	Galleria d'Arte Moderna, Turin
	Werke aus funf Jahrzehnten, Wallraf-Richartz-Museum, Cologne (travelled to the Nationalgalerie, West Berlin and the Städtische Galerie, Munich)
1975	Galerie Arnaud, Paris
	Galerie Govaerts-Hilton, Brussels
	Lefebre Gallery, New York
	Galerie Stangl, Munich
	American Artists Associations, New York
	Metropolitan Museum of Art, New York
1977	Galerie de France, Paris
1978	Fondation Veranneman, Kruishoutem, Belgium
	Musée de l'Abbaye Sainte-Croix, Les Sables-d'Olonne, France (retrospective)
1979	Musée Picasso, Antibes, France
	Centre Georges Pompidou, Paris
1980	Musée de la Poste, Paris (with Anna-Eva Bergman)
	Musée d'Art Moderne de la Ville, Paris
1981	*A Vision into Abstraction*, Fischer Finc Art, London (travelled to the Galerie Pels-Leusden, West Berlin)
1982	Centre Georges Pompidou, Paris
1983	Kupferstichkabinett, Dresden, East Germany
1984	Kunsthaus, Zurich
	Galeric du Luxembourg, Luxembourg
	Museum der bildenden Kunste, Leipzig, East Germany
	Galerie Wolfgang Ketterer, Munich
1985	Musee Picasso, Antibes, France
	Chapelle du Grand Couvent, Cavaillon, France
	Grand Palais, Paris
1986	Musee d'Evreux, France
	Galerie Carinthia, Klagenfurt, Austria
	Galerie Daniel Gervis, Paris
1987	Institut Francais, London
	Maison de la Culture, Metz, France
	Galerie Daniel Gervis, Paris

Selected Group Exhibitions:

1932	*Junge Kunstler*, Galerie Flechtheim, Berlin
1938	*20th Century German Arts*, Burlington Galleries, London
1946	*Salon des Réalités Nouvelles*, Musée d'Art Moderne, Paris (and annually to 1950)
1951	*Advancing French Art*, Louis Carré Gallery, New York
1954	*Biennale*, Venice (and *Biennale*, 1960)
1961	*Paris: Carrefour de la Peinture*, Stedelijk Museum, Amsterdam
1965	*Painting Without a Brush*, Boston Institute of Contemporary Art
1968	*Painting in France 1900–67*, National Gallery, Washington, D.C.
1969	*8 Mednarodna Graficna Razstava 1969*, Moderna Galerija, Ljubljana, Yugoslavia
1973	*Kunst in Deutschland 1898–1973*, Kunsthalle, Hamburg (travelled to the Städtische Galerie im Lenbachhaus, Munich)

Collections:

Centre Georges Pompidou, Paris; Nationgalerie, West Berlin; Tate Gallery, London; Museum des 20. Jahrhunderts, Vienna; Stedelijk Museum, Amsterdam, Musée Royal des Beaux-Arts, Brussels; Museo Civico d'Arte Moderna, Turin, Kunstmuseum, Basle; Museum of Modern Art, New York; Guggenheim Museum, New York.

Publications:

By HARTUNG: books—*Farandole: poème de Jean Proal, lithographies de Hans Hartung*, Barcelona 1971; *Hans Hartung: Album de Cinq Gravures*, Barcelona 1971; *Hans Hartung: Un Monde Ignore*, with poems by Jean Tardieu, Geneva 1974; *La Foudere Pilote l'Univers*, with text by Heraclitus, Paris 1977.

On HARTUNG: books—*Hans Hartung: Aquarelle 1922* by Will Grohmann, Paris 1922; *Hans Hartung* by Madeleine Rosseau and Ottomar Domnick, Stuttgart 1949; *Hans Hartung* by René de Solier, Paris 1956; *Hans Hartung* by Michel Ragon, Paris 1960; *Hans Hartung* by R. V. Gindertael, Paris and New York 1961; *Hartung* by Dominique Aubier, Paris 1961; *Hans Hartung* by Umbro Apollonio, Paris 1967; *Hans Hartung* by Jiri Siblik, Prague 1967; *Hans Hartung*, exhibition catalogue, with text by Bernard Dorival, Houston 1969; *Visages de l'Art Moderne* by Jean Clay, Paris 1969; *8 Mednarodan Graficna Rezstava 1969*, exhibition catalogue, with texts by Zoran Krzisnik, Raymond Cogniat, Werner Hofmann and others, Ljubljana 1969; *Hartung: Katalog der Druckgraphik*, compiled by Heidi Burklin, St. Gallen, Switzerland 1974; *Hartung*, exhibition catalogue, with text by Francois Le Targat, Paris 1974; *Salute to Hans Hartung*, exhibition catalogue, with text by Henry Geldzahler, New York 1975; *Hans Hartung* by Pierre Descargues, Barcelona 1977; *Hans Hartung: A Vision into Abstraction*, exhibition catalogue, London 1981; *Hans Hartung*, exhibition catalogue with essay by Jorn Merkert, Munich 1984; *Hartung*, exhibition catalogue with text by Pierre Daix, London 1987.

The lost drawings that Hans Hartung made as a child to ward off the threats of thunder and lightning were, by all accounts, precursors of the astonishing linear experiments he came to in his mature years. Hearsay has it that those childhood attempts to exorcise the menace of storms were never two alike. Not for the first time it needs to be emphasized that protagonists of the visual arts from time to time have absolutely natural talents in their make-up which should never be exposed to and certainly not hindered by attending art schools and experiencing the onus of training, no matter how valuable these orthodox preludes might be for others. Hartung's time studying Philosophy and History of Art at the University of Leipzig and simultaneously attending the Fine Arts Academy of Leipzig were a waste of time and robbed him of years that could have been rich and formative for the man who later joined Fautrier and Wols to launch the School of "Art Informel."

And Hartung had a bad war as an anti-Nazi, robbed of his passport, what little money he had purloined by the Third Reich, and escaping south of the border from Occupied France only to be imprisoned in a Spanish concentration camp. When he finally broke out and joined the Foreign Legion under the Americans, he was badly wounded in the battle for Belfort and had to have a leg amputated. The War, the Nazis, imprisonment and the loss of his leg all added up to another terrible time of artistic inactivity, but at least during the 1930's he had been able to start his true career and to make friendships with artists like Julio Gonzalez who had helped to spread interest in his work (an example of which was even reproduced in the British abstract art magazine of the period *Axis*).

But it was really not until the cessation of hostilities that Hartung was able to attend to his painting unharrassed by financial crises, health difficulties, politics, statelessness and War itself. Since that time he has been appreciated as an artist of considerable stature. Because of the nature of some of his work, he has been paired by some with Pierre Soulages, but this is a sterile comparison because Hartung is essentially expressionist, a gothic artist out of Germany, whereas Soulages (unlike his counterpart, more concerned with form than colour) is classical and latin.

Hans Hartung has made some useful discoveries while experimenting with various media. The way in which he can apply his linear style to vinyl over colour preparation by scratching his perfect skeins is as rewarding as it is individual (whether to make some abstract comet or to deluge the canvas in a massive fall of hair).

—Sheldon Williams

HAUSER, Erich.

German. Born in Rietheim, Tuttlingen, 15 December 1930. Educated at the Volksschule, Rietheim, 1936–40, and the Oberschule, Spaichingen, 1940–45; studied steel-engraving, Tuttlingen, and drawing, under Father Ansgar, Kloster Beuron, 1945–48; sculpture, Freien Kunstschule, Stuttgart 1949–51. Married Gretl Kauwaletz in 1955; children: Andrea and Markus. Sculptor and graphic artist, in Schramberg, 1952–58, in Rottweil, since 1959; first architectural sculpture commissions, 1959. Guest Instructor, Hochschule für Bildende Künste, Hamburg, 1964–65; Guest Professor, Hochschule für bildende Künste, West Berlin, 1984–85. Recipient: Kunstpreis der Jugend, Stuttgart, 1953, 1958; Kunstpreis Junger Westen, Recklinghausen, 1963; Kunstpreis der Stadt Wolfsburg, 1965; Sculpture Prize, *Bienal*, Sao Paulo, 1969; Verdienstkreuz, Bonn, 1972; Sculpture Prize, *Budapest Biennale*, 1975; Verdienstkreuz 1st class, Bonn, 1979. Address: 721 Rottweil-Alstadt, Saline, West Germany.

Individual Exhibitions:

1961 Galerie 62, Freiburg, West Germany
      Studio F, Ulm, West Germany
1962 Kunstverein, Freiburg, West Germany
1963 Galerie Müller, Stuttgart
      Galerie Nächst St. Stephan, Vienna
      Galerie Brusberg, Hannover
1964 Museum der Stadt, Ulm, West Germany
      Galerie Müller, Stuttgart
1965 Galerie Charles Lienhardt, Zurich
1966 Ausstellungsraum der Stadt, Hannover
      Kunsthalle, Mannheim
      Stadt Wolfsburg, West Germany
1967 Galerie Defet, Nuremberg
1968 Galerie der Stadt, Stuttgart
1969 Galerie Brusberg, Hannover
1970 *Werkverzeichnis Plastik 1962 bis 1969*, Galerie Defet, Nuremberg
      Kunstverein, Stuttgart
      Kunstverein, Mannheim
1971 Gimpel Hanover Galerie, Zurich
      Gimpel Fils, London
1972 Studio F, Ulm, West Germany
      Galerie KA, Mainz, West Germany
      Kunsthaus, Aargau, Switzerland
1973 Kunsthalle, Kiel, West Germany
1974 Kunstverein, Braunschweig, West Germany
1976 Galerie Hennemann, Bonn
      Galerie Müller, Stuttgart
1977 Städtische Galerie, Nordhorn, West Germany
1978 Forum Kunst, Rottweil, West Germany
      Galerie der Spiegel, Cologne
      Galerie St. Johann, Saarbrucken
      Städtische Galerie Altes Theater, Ravensburg, West Germany
1980 Galerie Lauter, Mannheim
1981 Germanisches Nationalmuseum, Nuremberg, West Germany
1982 Forum Kunst, Rottweil, West Germany
1983 Galerie Domberger, at *Art 83*, Basle
      Galerie Kunst und Design, Schloss Heutingsheim, Freiberg, West Germany
1984 Galerie Suzanne Fischer, Baden-Baden, West Germany
1985 Galerie am Winterberg, Vlotho, West Germany
1986 Landesgirokasse, Stuttgart
1987 Schlosshofgalerie Ewald Schrade, Schloss Mochental, West Germany

Selected Group Exhibitions:

1959 *Deutscher Kunstpreis der Jugend*, Kunsthalle, Baden-Baden, West Germany
1964 *Documenta 3*, Kassel, West Germany (and *Documenta 4*, 1968; *Documenta 6*, 1977)
1969 *Bienal*, Sao Paulo
1973 *12th Biennale für Plastik*, Middelheim Park, Antwerp
1976 *Kunst in Stuttgart*, Haus Baden-Württemberg, Bonn

1979 *Im Namen des Volkes*, Wilhelm-Lehmbruck Museum, Duisburg, West Germany
1981 *Phoenix*, Alte Oper, Frankfurt
1983 *Deutsche Bildhauer der Gegenwart*, Kunstverein, Augsburg, West Germany
1985 *Kunst in der Bundesrepublik 1945–85*, Nationalgalerie, West Berlin
1987 *Mathematik in der Kunst der letzten 30 Jahre*, Wilhelm Hack Museum, Ludwigshafen, West Germany

Collections:

Museum der Stadt, Ulm, West Germany; City of Hannover; Kunsthalle, Mannheim; Württembergischer Kunstverein, Stuttgart.

Publications:

On HAUSER: books—*Erich Hauser*, exhibition catalogue, with text by Otto Mauer, Stuttgart 1963; *Erich Hauser*, exhibition catalogue, with text by Heinz Fuchs, Mannheim 1966; *Erich Hauser: Werkverzeichnis Plastic 1962 bis 1969*, exhibition catalogue, with text by Gerhard Bott, Nuremberg 1970; *Erich Hauser*, exhibition catalogue, with introduction by Robert Kudielka, Zurich 1971; *Deutsche Kunst der 60er Jahre: Plastik, Objekte, Aktionen* by Jürgen Morschel, Munich 1972; *Erich Hauser*, exhibition catalogue, with text by Rolf Lauter, Mannheim 1980; *Erich Hauser: Werkverzeichnis 1970–1980*, Zirndorf 1980; *Erich Hauser*, exhibition catalogue with texts by Gerhard Bott, Manfred de la Motte and Jorn Merkert, Nuremberg 1981.

HAYTER, Stanley William.

British. Born in London, 27 December 1901. Educated in Croydon, Surrey; studied chemistry and geology at King's College, University of London, 1917–21, B.Sc.Hons. 1921; studied copper engraving with Joseph Hecht, Paris, 1926. Married Edith Fletcher in 1926 (divorced, 1929); married the sculptor Helen Phillips in 1940 (divorced, 1971); sons: William and Julian. Etcher, engraver and painter: worked as a researcher for Mond Nickel Company, 1917, and worked for Anglo-Iranian Oil Company, Persia, 1922–25; made first prints, 1921; lived in Paris, 1926–39; Founder Member and Director, Atelier 17, Paris, 1927; close friendship with Paul Eluard from 1933; returned to London, 1939, then lived in New York, 1940–46; founded Atelier 17, New York, 1941; returned to Paris: re-opened Atelier 17, 1950. Lecturer, California School of Fine Arts, San Francisco, 1940, 1948, 1960; Lecturer in Gravure, Brooklyn College, New York, 1949. Recipient: Annual Prize, Philadelphia Print Club, 1943; Liturgic Prize, *Biennale*, Venice, 1958; First Prize, *International Exhibition of Prints*, Tokyo, 1960; Grand Prix des Arts de la Ville de Paris, 1972. Honorary Doctorates: Hamline University, St. Paul, Minnesota, 1983; New School for Social Research, New York, 1983. Chevalier, Legion d'Honneur, 1951; Chevalier, 1968, and Commandeur, 1986, Ordre des Arts et Letters; Honorary Royal Academician, London, 1982. C.B.E. (Commander, Order of the British Empire), 1967. *Died* (in Paris) *4 May 1988.*

Individual Exhibitions:

1927 Sacre du Printemps, Brussels
1929 Claridge Gallery, London
      Palais des Beaux-Arts, Brussels
1932 Galerie Vignon, Paris
1938 Mayor Gallery, London
1940 San Francisco Museum of Fine Arts
1945 Mortimer Brandt Gallery, New York
1947 Durand-Ruel Gallery, New York
      Esther Robles Gallery, Los Angeles

      University of California at Los Angeles
1948 Gumps Gallery, San Francisco
1950 Perspectives, New York
1951 Galerie Louis Carré, Paris
1954 Kunsthalle, Berne
1955 Galerie Denise René, Paris
      Galerie Otto Stangl, Munich
      Galerie Betty Thommen, Basle
      St. George's Gallery Prints, London
1957 Whitechapel Art Gallery, London (retrospective)
      Museu de Arte Moderna, Rio de Janeiro
1959 Wallraf-Richartz Museum, Cologne (with William Scott and Kenneth Armitage)
1960 Esther Robles Gallery, Los Angeles
1961 Howard Wise Gallery, New York
      Museum of Contemporary Art, Dallas
1966 Kunstnernes Kunsthandel Gallery, Copenhagen
      Musée Rath, Geneva (toured Italy and the U.K.)
1967 City Art Gallery and Museum, Bradford, England (travelled to the University of Southampton, and Brighton College of Art, Sussex)
      Victoria and Albert Museum, London
      Grosvenor Gallery, London
      Esther Robles Gallery, Los Angeles
      University of Oregon Art Museum, Eugene
      University of Texas Art Museum, Austin
      Galerie Degée, Brussels
      Galerie Madeleine Sothmann, Amsterdam
1968 Kunsthaus, Bielefeld, West Germany
      Château-Musée, Dieppe, France
1969 Union Centrale des Arts Décoratifs, Paris
      Musée du Louvre, Paris
1970 La Tortue Gallery, Santa Monica, California
1972 Musée d'Art Moderne de la Ville, Paris
1973 Christopher Drake Ltd., London
      La Tortue Gallery, Santa Monica, California
1974 Galerie Madeleine Sothmann, Amsterdam
1976 Galerie de Seine, Paris
1977 University of Wisconsin, Madison (toured the United States, 1977–78)
1978 Kunsternes Hus, Oslo
      Michael Parkin Gallery, London
1979 La Tortue Gallery, Santa Monica, California
1980 Galerie Madeleine Sothmann, Amsterdam
1981 Oxford Gallery (with former pupils)
      Pier Arts Centre, Stromness, Scotland
      Chichester District Museum, Sussex (toured the U.K., 1981–82)
1982 District Museum, Chichester, Sussex
1985 Gallery Santiza, Kobe, Japan
1986 Galerie J. C. Riedel, Paris
1987 Robert Douwma Gallery, London

Selected Group Exhibitions:

1926 *Salon d'Automne*, Paris
1929 *Salon des Surindependants*, Paris
1934 *Atelier 17*, Galerie Pierre, Paris
1936 *Fantastic Art, Dada, Surrealism*, Museum of Modern Art, New York
1944 *Atelier 17*, Museum of Modern Art, New York
1947 *Salon de Mai*, Paris
1958 *Biennale*, Venice
1960 *International Exhibition of Prints*, Tokyo
1965 *Group Exhibition*, Howard Wise Gallery, New York

Collections:

Victoria and Albert Museum, London; Bibliothèque Nationale, Paris; Bibiothèque Royale, Brussels; Museum of Modern Art, New York; National Gallery, Washington, D.C.; National Gallery of Canada, Ottawa; National Gallery of Victoria, Melbourne.

Publications:

By HAYTER: books—*New Ways of Gravure*, New York 1949, London 1966; *About Prints*, Oxford 1962; articles—"The Development of Automatism" in *Possibilities* (New York), 1943; "The Lautrec Bite" in *Artnews* (New York), November 1955; "Execution d'un Tableau" in *S. W. Hayter*, exhibition catalogue, Paris 1976.

On HAYTER: books—*S. W. Hayter*, exhibition catalogue, by Bryan Robertson, London 1957; *Stanley Hayter* by G. Limbour, Paris 1962; *The Engravings of S. W. Hayter* by Graham Reynolds, London 1867; *Modern English Painters* by John Rothenstein, London 1974; *S. W. Hayter*, exhibition catalogue, by Alexander Dunbar, Stromness, Scotland 1981; *For Stanley Hayter on His 80th Birthday*, Oxford 1981; *S. W. Hayter*, exhibition catalogue with essay by Tokuhiro Nakajima, Kobe 1985; *Stanley William Hayter*, exhibition catalogue with text by John Russell, Paris 1986.

From a family of artists—one of his ancestors was a miniaturist who published a treatise on perspective—Stanley William Hayter studied chemistry and geology and took a degree with honours at King's College, London. Until then he had played around with paints in his father's studio and made his first prints in his graduation year—1921. For three years he worked with an oil company on the Persian Gulf, then on completion of his contract he decided to exchange his scientific career for an artistic one. He went to Paris and took painting classes at the Académie Julian. He made friends with artists, among them Calder, Balthus and Joseph Hecht, who taught him how to use the burin. The last was the decisive step for Hayter.

In 1927 Hayter set up Atelier 17 (from the number of the street where he worked). It was to be a printmaking centre where masters and pupils would learn from each other. Since the 1930s the Academy has spread its repute across the world. During the 1939–1945 war, he was forced to move it to New York and re-established it in Paris in 1950.

While Hayter had for a long time a great reputation as an etcher and engraver (also as a teacher and educator having written a great deal on his subjects of printmaking) it was not until his large retrospective at the Whitechapel Gallery in 1957 that the public were made aware of his gifts as a painter. Yet in both media there are parallel histories of working that differ primarily only on questions of scale.

His early interest in Surrealism since 1929 brought him partly into the organization of the *International Surrealist Exhibition* in London in 1936, and he exhibited in it. His imagery was conditioned not so much by invention of new juxtapositions of objects from the world of reality as from a partial reliance on the unconscious in developing motives primarily abstract in nature. This automatism had its connection with the experiments of Miró and Masson in practising a drip technique, and in applying paint with string developed further by Jackson Pollock in later years. Hayter would perform an arabesque on the canvas over a ground of one pure colour, then elaborate in consecutive action, arriving at a complexity of pattern in the total of gestural signs.

Movement always preoccupied Hayter strongly in the work he performed, whether in paint or as prints. Movement in water, particularly, exerted a powerful pull born from firsthand experience, as he was an enthusiastic sailor. He has said: "The trajectory of movement is more clearly defined in water. I can follow the laws of space better in the substance of water which is dense and at the same time fluid." The concentric circles of ripples from a fallen stone, the curvilinear rhythms of waves and the contrasting colour and tone of convexities and concavities of the moving surface inspired Hayter in both paintings and prints to unique contemporary statements of abstract forms in tension and repose.

—G. S. Whittet

HEAD, Tim.

British. Born in London in 1946. Studied fine art at the University of Newcastle, under Richard Hamilton, 1965–69, and sculpture at St. Martin's School of Art, London, 1969–70. Lives and works in London. Worked on exhibition layout at Stedelijk Museum, Amsterdam, Summer 1967; assistant to Claes Oldenburg, New York, 1968, and to Robert Morris, Tate Gallery, London, 1971. Lecturer, Goldsmiths College, London, 1971–79. Since 1976, Lecturer at the Slade School of Fine Art, London. Recipient: Gulbenkian Visual Arts Award, 1976. Fellow, Clare Hall, Cambridge, 1977–78. Agent: Anthony Reynolds Gallery, London. Address: c/o Anthony Reynolds Gallery, 37 Cowper Street, London EC2, England.

Individual Exhibitions:

1972 Museum of Modern Art, Oxford
1973 Gallery House, London
     Studio Show, London
1974 Whitechapel Art Gallery, London
     Garage Gallery, London
1975 Rowan Gallery, London
     Arnolfini Gallery, Bristol
1976 Rowan Gallery, London
1977 Anthony Stokes Gallery, London
1978 *Recent Work*, Kettle's Yard, Cambridge
     Henie-Onstad Kunstcenter, Oslo
     Rowan Gallery, London
1979 Institute of Modern Art, Philadelphia
     Galleria Paola Betti, Milan
     Serpentine Gallery, London (travelled to the Third Eye Centre, Glasgow, 1980)

Tim Head: *Still Life*, 1978

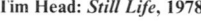

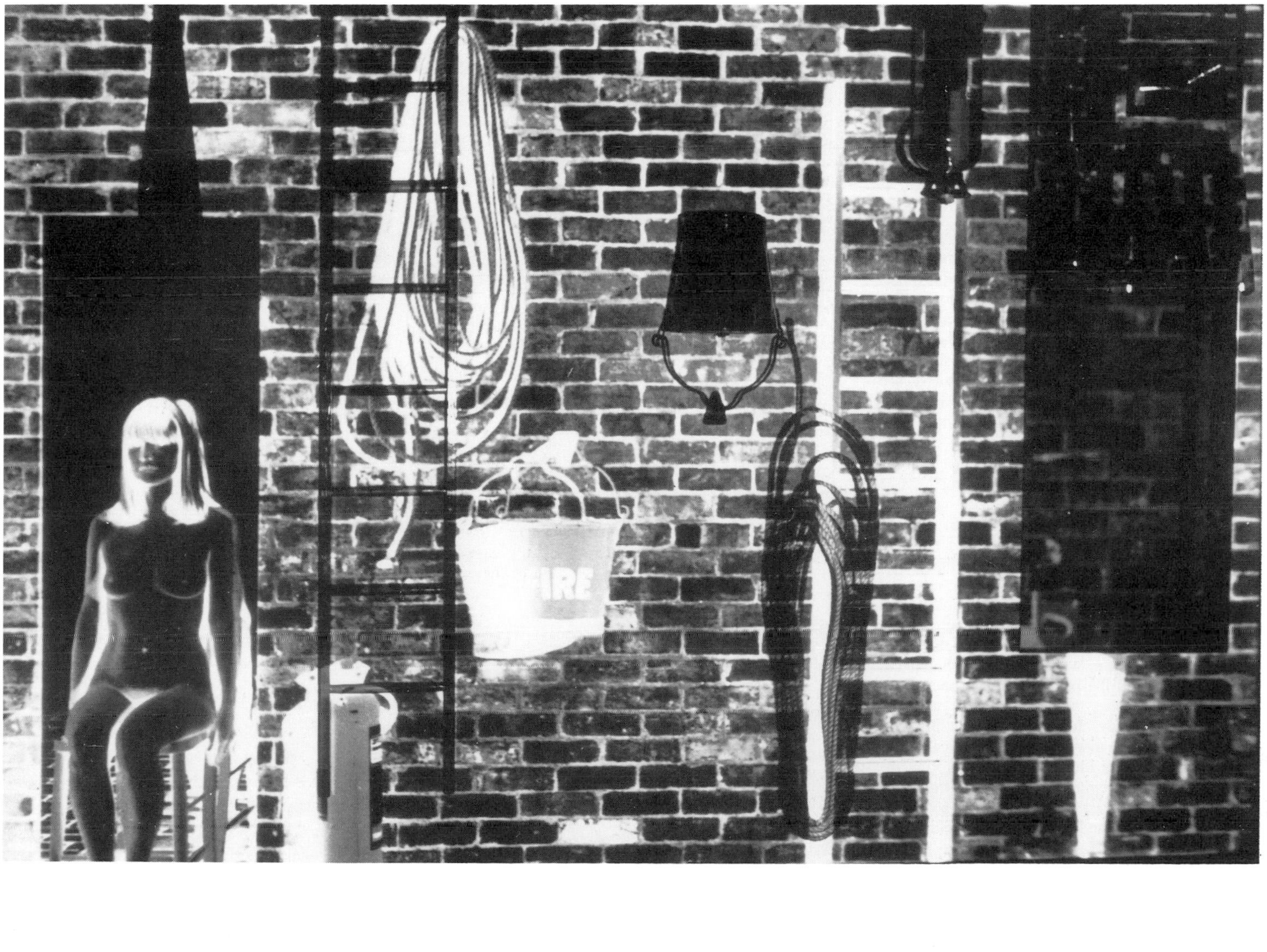

1980	*Biennale*, Venice
	Galerie Bama, Paris
1981	Vanilla Rehearsal Studios, London
1982	Tate Gallery, London
1983	Provinciaal Museum, Hasselt, Belgium
1985	Institute of Contemporary Arts, London
1988	Anthony Reynolds Gallery, London
	Marlene Eleini Gallery, London

Selected Group Exhibitions:

1970	*New Sculpture*, Hayward Gallery, London (toured the U.K.)
1971	*Art Spectrum*, Alexandra Palace, London
1972	*Open Air Sculpture Exhibition*, Holland Park, London
1973	*Biennale*, Paris
1976	*Arte Inglese Oggi 1960–76*, Palazzo Reale, Milan
1977	*Documenta*, Kassel, West Germany
1979	*Un Certain Art Anglais*, Centre Georges Pompidou, Paris
1980	*British Art Now: A Modern Perspective*, Guggenheim Museum, New York
	Beyond Surfaces, International Cultureel Centrum, Antwerp
1988	*The British Picture*, L.A. Louver Gallery, Venice, California

Publications:

By HEAD: book—*Reconstruction*, London 1973; articles— "Glossary: A Prelimination Sketch" in *Flash Art* (Milan), October/November 1974; "In Camera: A Projected Interview," with John Tagg, in *Studio International* (London), July/August 1975; statement in *Tim Head*, exhibition catalogue, London 1981.

On HEAD: books—*Arte Inglese Oggi 1960-1976*, exhibition catalogue, Milan 1976; *Tim Head: Recent Work*, exhibition catalogue by Fenella Crichton, Cambridge 1978; *Tim Head*, exhibition catalogue, by Norbert Lynton, Venice 1980; *Tim Head*, exhibition catalogue with essay by Jean Fisher, Hasselt 1983; *The British Picture*, exhibition catalogue with essays by Marina Vaizey, Catherine Lampert and William Feaver, Venice, California 1988; articles—"Artist's Artist" by Paul Overy in *The Times* (London), January 1975; "Displacements" by Caroline Tisdall in *The Guardian* (London), January 1975; "The New Image of Culture" in *Skira Annuel*, Geneva 1978; "The Venice Biennale: The British Representatives" by J. Bustard in *Art Monthly* (London), no. 38, 1980.

Tim Head is concerned, above all, with questions of illusion and reality as they manifest themselves in space, and thus he generally makes installation works expressly for the sites in which they are shown. But as titles such as "Displacement," "Dislocations" and "Present" indicate, these are as much mental spaces as physical ones. Photographs, mirrors and slide projectors, which are normally verificatory devices, are used to demonstrate that the reality we perceive is far more complicated than we usually acknowledge. Outward appearances are not unassailable, and our perceptions of any space are transformed by numerous factors, not least illusion and allusion (imaginative engagement).

In "Displacement" (Tate Gallery 1975-6), for example, photographs were taken of part of a room in which certain mundane objects of the kind that might conceivably be present, like chairs, a ladder, a bucket and a cloak, had been placed. These photographs were then projected back into the same context though slightly moved aside from the originals. Since the spectator was free to wander through the space, he inevitably crossed the path of at least one of the four projectors, causing the image on the opposite wall to be momentarily blocked out and/or his own silhouette to be thrown there. Given that the carousels were the only source of illumination in the room, interrupting their paths emphasized the fact that light may simultaneously reveal both illusion and actuality; turn the projectors off and not only the illusions disappear but also the actual contents of the space.

Moreover, the viewer's silhouette thrown onto the wall reveals him to himself as mere shadow, without substance; he *knows* that he occupies the space physically yet the only means he has of verifying this is through illusion—an image in a mirror, a shape on a wall.

Such issues constantly inform Head's works, yet this is conceptual art only in the broadest sense of the term, for his installations must always be actively occupied in order to be completed. Head makes no attempt to disguise the mechanics of his *mise-en-scène*, for our recognition of what is going on is crucial to his challenging of our perceptions of the world we think we know. In a darkened space the objects in a colored photograph projected onto a wall can seem more convincing, and thus more authentic, than the dimly perceived objects actually present. Head does not want to fool the eye, for it is the ordinary world, not a fantasy one, which is the subject of his art. As he demonstrates, this world can be as elusive or mysteriously complicated as any we might invent.

—Lynne Cooke

HEERICH, Erwin.

German. Born in Kassel, 29 November 1922. Studied under Ewald Matare, Staatliche Kunstakademie, Dusseldorf, 1945–50. Served in German Navy Artillery, in the North Sea, Atlantic and Adriatic, 1941–45; Lieutenant. Married Hildegard Muller in 1950; children: Thomas, Stefan, Martin and Andrea. Sculptor and graphic artist, Dusseldorf, since 1950. Lecturer, Seminar für Werktatige Erziehung. Dusseldorf, 1961–69. Professor, Staatliche Kunstakademie, Dusseldorf, since 1969. Honorary Member, Akademie der Künste, West Berlin, 1974. Agent: Galerie Alfred Schmela, Mutter-Ey-Strasse 3,4000 Dusseldorf. Addresses: Schubertstrasse 6, 4005 Meerbusch 2, West Germany; and c/o Staatliche Kunstakademie, Eiskellerstrasse 1,4000 Dusseldorf, West Germany.

Individual Exhibitions:

1964	Haus Grinten, Kranenburg, West Germany
1966	Galerie Alfred Schmela, Dusseldorf
1967	Galerie Müller, Stuttgart
	Städtisches Museum, Mönchengladbach, West Germany
1968	Stedelijk Van Abbemuseum, Eindhoven, Netherlands
	Cardboard Sculptures 1956-1968. Dwan Gallery, New York
1969	Galerie Alfred Schmela, Dusseldorf
	Galerie Borgmann, Cologne
1970	Galerie Appel und Fertsch, Frankfurt
	Galerie Renée Ziegler, Zurich
	Galerie Borgmann, Cologne
1971	Galerie Droscher, Hamburg
	Neue Galerie, Baden-Baden, West Germany
	Galerie Tangente, Heidelberg
1972	Kunstverein, Dusseldorf
	Galerie Klein, Bonn
	Galerie Szepan, Gelsenkirchen, West Germany
	Galerie René Block, West Berlin
1973	Landesmuseum, Darmstadt
1974	Landesmuseum, Bonn
	Griffelkunst, Hamburg
	Galerie Lauter, Mannheim
	Galerie Hetzler und Keller, Stuttgart
1979	Städtische Kunsthalle, Dusseldorf

Erwin Heerich: *O.T.*, 1977

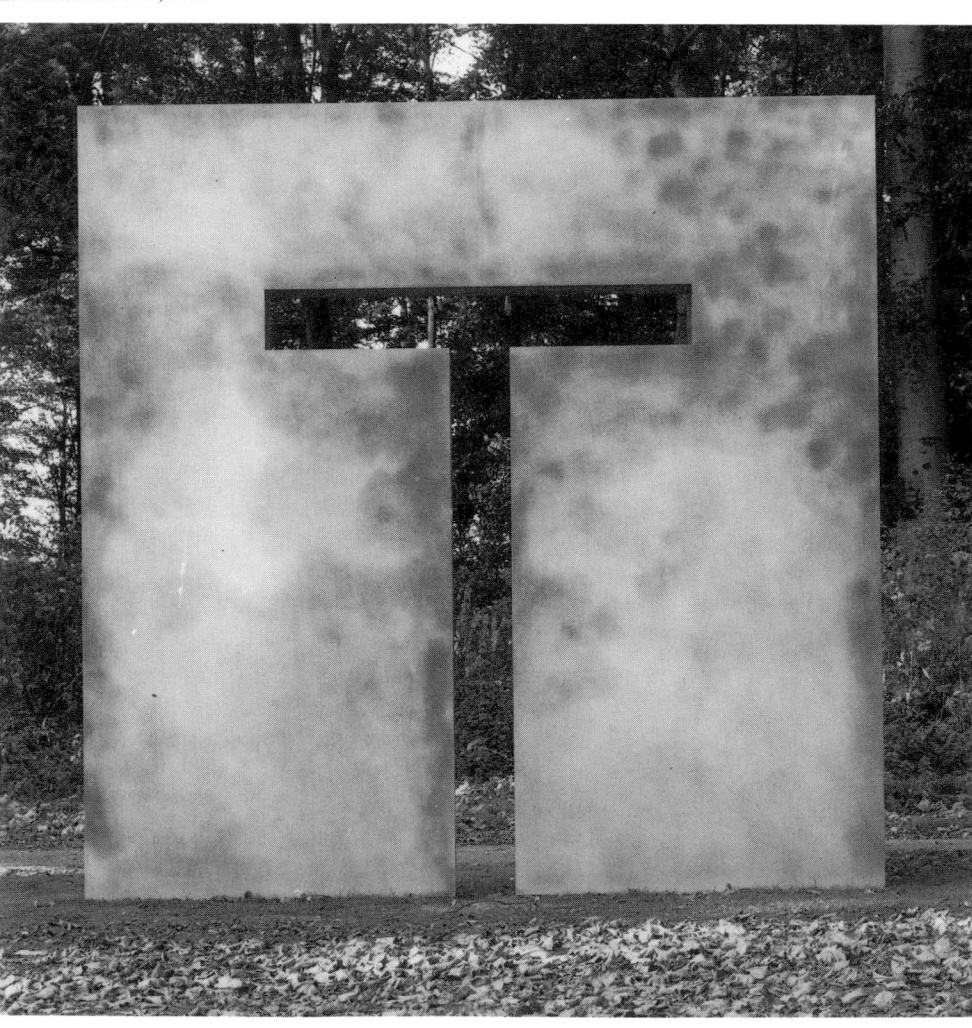

1982 *Raumliche und flachige Diagramme*, Museum Haus Esters, Krefeld, West Germany
1975 Galerie Schmela, Dusseldorf
1976 Kunstverein, Freiburg
Galerie Schmela, Dusseldorf
1979 Stadtische Kunsthalle, Dusseldorf
1980 Stadtisches Museum Schloss Morsbroich, Leverkusen
1981 Kunstverein, Mannheim
1982 Museum Haus Esters, Krefeld, West Germany

Selected Group Exhibitions:

1968 *Documenta 4*, Kassel, West Germany
1970 *Jetzt: Kunst in Deutschland*, Kunsthalle, Cologne
Strategy: Get Arts, Richard Demarco Gallery, Edinburg
1971 *Contemporary German Art*, National Museum of Modern Art, Tokyo
1972 *Szene Rhein-Ruhr*, Museum Folkwang, Essen
1973 *Bienal*, Sao Paulo
1974 *Projekt 74*, Kunstverein, Cologne
1979 *Matare und seine Schuler*, Akademie der Künste, West Berlin
1982 *Drawings for Sculpture Since 1945*, Kunstverein, Braunschweig

Collections:

Kunstmuseum, Dusseldorf; Städtisches Museum, Mönchengladbach, West Germany; Wilhelm-Lehmbruck Museum, Duisburg, West Germany; Stedelijk Van Abbemuseum, Eindhoven, Netherlands; Rheinisches Landesmuseum, Bonn; Museum Folkwang, Essen; Städtisches Museum, Hamburg; Kunstmuseum, Basle.

Publications:

On HEERICH: books—*Heerich* by Franz van der Grinten, Kranenburg, West Germany 1964; *Erwin Heerich: Cardboard Sculptures 1956–1968*, exhibition catalogue, New York 1968; *Heerich*, exhibition catalogue, with text by Johannes Cladders, Eindhoven, Netherlands 1968; *Deutsche Kunst: Eine neue Generation* by Rolf-Günter Dienst, Cologne 1970; *Deutsche Kunst der 60er Jahre* by Jürgen Morschel, Munich 1971; *Kunstjahrbuch 2*, edited by Jürgen Harten, Horst Richter, Karl Ruhrberg and Wieland Schmied, Hannover 1972; *Projekt 74: Aspekte internationaler Kunst am Anfang der 70er Jahre*, exhibition catalogue, with texts by Dieter Ronte, Evelyn Weiss, Manfred Schneckenburger and others, Cologne 1974; *Erwin Heerich*, exhibition catalogue, with text by Walter Jürgen Hofmann, Dusseldorf 1979; *Erwin Heerich: Oeuvre-Catalogue*, 4 vols., by Hans van der Grinten, Gerhard Storck and Johannes Cladders, Dusseldorf 1980–83; *Erwin Heerich: Raumliche und flachige Diagramme*, exhibition catalogue, with text by Julian Heynen, Krefeld, West Germany 1982.

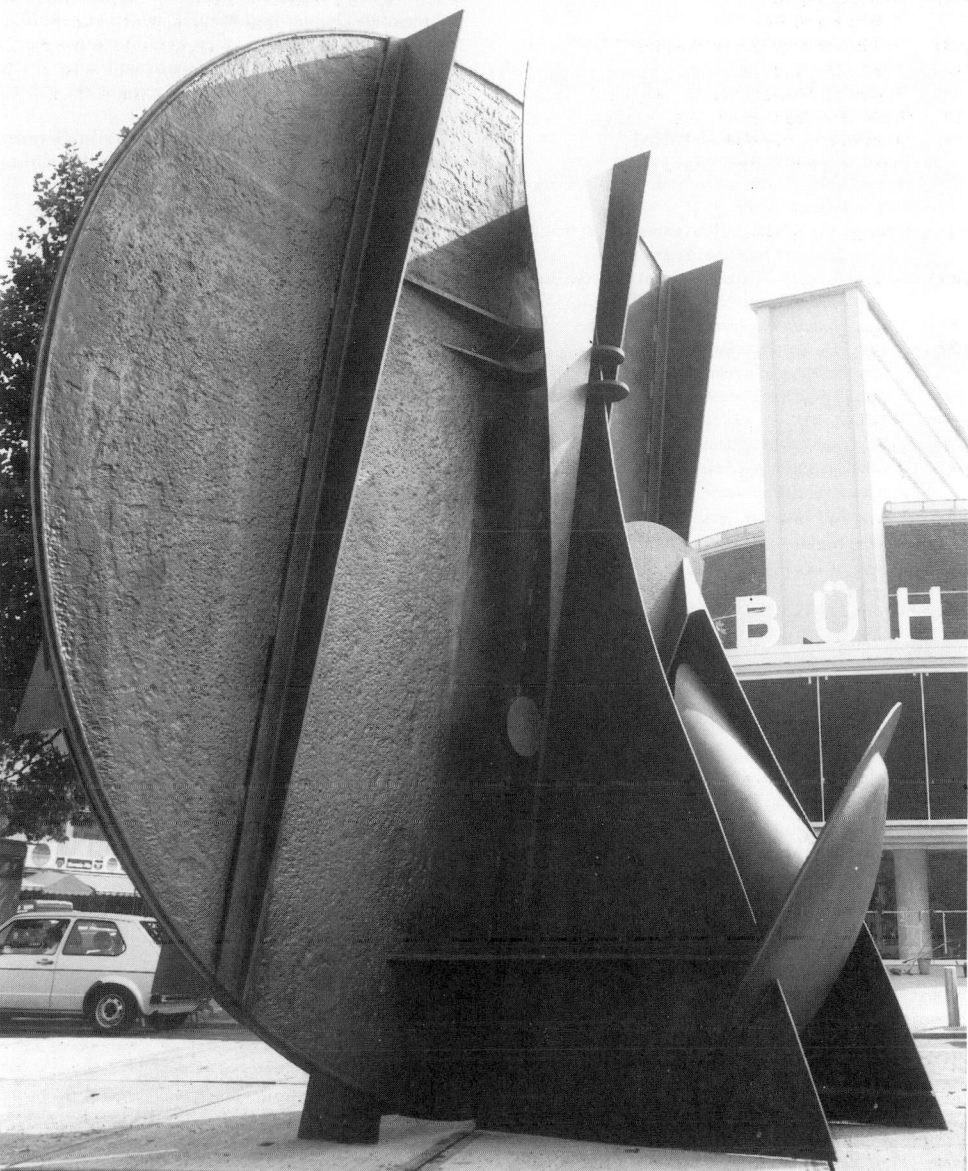

Bernhard Heiliger: *Auge der Nemesis*, 1980

HEILIGER, Bernhard.

German. Born in Stettin, 11 November 1915. Educated at the Kunstgeweberschule, Stettin, 1935–37; Hochschule für Bildende Künste, Berlin, 1938–41. Served in the German Army, 1941–45; prisoner of war, 1945. Travelled to Paris, 1939; introduced to the modern art of Maillio, Despiau and Brancusi; began career as sculptor, Berlin, 1945; first portrait sculpture, 1951. Instructor, Hochschule für Angewandt Kunst, Berlin-Weissensee, 1947–49, and Hochschule für Bildende Kunst, Berlin, since 1950. Set Designer, *Faust II*, Schiller Theatre, Berlin, 1966. Recipient: First Prize, Max Planck Competition, Berlin, 1949; Kunstpreis der Stadt Berlin, 1950; Kunstpreis der Stadt Köln, 1952; International Prize, Unknown Political Prisoner Competition, Institute of Contemporary Arts, London, 1953; Grosser des Landes, Nordrhein-Westfalen, Dusseldorf, 1956; First Prize, Sculpture Competition, Max Planck Institute für Physik und Astrophysik, Munich, 1959; Burda Prize for Sculpture, 1965; Lovis Corinth Prize, West Germany, 1975. Honorary Member, Accademia Fiorentina, Florence, 1978. Agent: Staempfli Gallery, 47 East 77th Street, New York, New York 10021, U.S.A. Address: Kauzchensteig 12, 1000 Berlin 33, West Germany.

Individual Exhibitions:

1946 Galerie Buchholz, Berlin
Bernhard Heiliger/Mac Zimmerman, Galerie Rosen, Berlin
1948 Galerie Bremer, Berlin
1950 Haus am Waldsee, Berlin
1951 Museum am Ostwall, Dortmund (toured West Germany)
Galerie Bremer, Berlin
1954 Graphisches Kabinett Dr. Hanna Grisebach, Heidelberg
1955 Freiburger Kunstverein, Freiburg
Städtisches Karl-Ernst-Osthaus Museum, Hagen, West Germany
Overbeck-Gesellschaft, Lübeck
Westfälischer Kunstverein, Münster

1956 *Kopfe*, Haus am Waldsee, Berlin (toured West Germany)
Kunstverein, Brunswick, West Germany
Kunsthalle, Bremen
Museum Folkwang, Essen
Kunstverein, Kassel, West Germany
Kunstverein, Cologne
Städtisches Museum, Mulheim an der Ruhr, West Germany
Plastik, Zeichnungen, Haus am Waldsee, Berlin
1958 Roland, Browse and Delbanco Gallery, London
Berhard Heiliger/Alexander Camaro, Lindolinshof, Esslingen, West Germany
1959 Galerie Hella Nebelung, Dusseldorf
Stadthalle, Wolfsburg, West Germany (travelled to Kongresshalle, Berlin, the Städtischen Kunsthalle, Mannheim, and the Kunstmuseum, Lucerne, 1959–60)
1960 Galerie Guenther Franke, Munich
1961 Staempfli Gallery, New York
1962 Galerie der Edition Rothe, Heidelberg
1963 German Embassy, Paris
1964 Galerie Springer, Berlin
Galerie im Erker, St. Gallen, Switzerland
Galleria Il Canale, Venice
1965 Galerie Emmy Widmann, Bremen
Galerie der Edition Rothe, Heidelberg
Galerie Guenther Franke, Munich

1966 Staempfli Gallery, New York
1970 Galleria Il Canale, Venice
     19 Neue Sculpturen, Galerie Guenther Franke, Munich
     Staempfli Gallery, New York
1971 Galerie Wuensche, Bonn
     Galerie Hella Nebelung, Dusseldorf
     Galerie Commeter, Hamburg
1972 Kunstkabinett Hanna Bekker vom Rath, Dusseldorf
1973 Galerie Bremer, Berlin
1975 akademie der Künste, Berlin (retrospective; travelled to the Saarland Museum, Saarbrucken)
1980 Erker-Galerie, St. Gallen, Switzerland (travelled to Grossplastic für der Noorwede, Hamburg)
1981 *8 Neue Sculpturen*, Galerie Dibbent, Berlin
1982 Galerie Pels-Leusden, Berlin
1984 Galerie Roswitha Haftmann, Zurich
1985 Wilhelm-Lehmbruck-Museum, Dusiburg, West Germany
     Galerie Muhlenbusch, Dusseldorf
1986 Middelheim Open-Air Museum, Antwerp
     Sculpture Park, Heilbronn, West Germany
1987 Galerie Pels-Leusden, West Berlin
     Galerie Winkelmann, Dusseldorf

Selected Group Exhibitions:

1953 *Bienal*, Sao Paulo
1954 *Living Art in Germany*, National College of Art, Dublin
1956 *Biennale*, Venice
1958 *Pittsburgh International Exhibition*, Carnegie Institute
1959 *Berliner Festwoche*, Kongresshalle, Berlin
1960 *Arte Alema desde 1945*, Museo de Arte Moderna, Rio de Janeiro
1964 *Sculpture Allemande du 20e. Siècle*, Musée Rodin, Paris
1967 *German Art in Berlin*, Musée des Beaux-Arts, Montreal

Collections:

Musée Royal des Beaux-Arts, Antwerp; Kunstmuseum, Winterthur, Switzerland; Nationalgalerie, Berlin; Museum am Ostwall, Dortmund; Kunsthalle, Hamburg; Palais Schaumburg, Bonn; Israel Museum, Jerusalem; Museo de Arte Moderna, Sao Paulo; Museum of Modern Art, New York; Guggenheim Museum, New York.

Publications:

By HEILIGER: books—text in *Bernhard Heiliger*, exhibition catalogue, Wolfsburg 1959; reprinted in *Bernhard Heiliger*, exhibition catalogue, Lucerne 1960; text in *Heiliger*, exhibition catalogue, St. Gallen, Switzerland 1964.

On HEILIGER: books—*Heiliger*, exhibition catalogue, by Will Grohmann, Berlin 1950; *Heiliger*, exhibition catalogue, by Will Grohmann, Dortmund 1951; *Bernhard Heiliger: Kopfe*, exhibition catalogue, with text by K. L. Skutsch, Berlin 1956; *Bernhard Heiliger: Plastik, Zeichnungen*, exhibition catalogue, with text by K. L. Skutsch, Berlin 1957; *Bernhard Heiliger*, exhibition catalogue, with texts by Hanns Theodor Flemming and Will Grohmann, London 1958; *Heiliger*, exhibition catalogue, by Joachim Tiburitus, Kurt Martin, and Umbro Apollonio, Wolfsburg 1959, reprinted as *Heiliger*, exhibition catalogue, Lucerne 1960; *Bernhard Heiliger*, exhibition catalogue, with introduction by Kurt Martin, New York 1961; *Bernhard Heiliger* by Hanns Theodor Flemming, Berlin 1962; *Heiliger*, exhibition catalogue, by George Schmidt and Martin Heidegger, St. Gallen, Switzerland 1964; *Bernhard Heiliger*, exhibition catalogue, with text by Piero Dorazio, Venice 1970; *Bernhard Heiliger: 19 Neue Sculpturen*, exhibition catalogue, Munich 1970; *Bernhard Heiliger*, exhibition catalogue, by Wieland Schmied and Hanns Theodor Flemming, Berlin 1975; *Bernhard Heiliger* by A. M. Hammacher, St. Gallen, Switzerland 1978; *Bernhard Heiliger*, exhibition catalogue with essay by Siegfried Salzmann, West Berlin 1987.

After his studies at the Stettin School of Arts and at the Berlin Academy, Bernhard Heiliger visited Paris at a time when it was still possible to come under the influence of Despiau and Maillol, whom he met. For a young artist in his 20's, they were formative years, though the results were not seen until after 1946 when he began to work towards recognition and to teach.

He ranks as the most important figure in German sculpture reaching maturity in the 1960's. His direction could be classified as towards the symbolic in plastic terms, verging from the stylized figurative to the abstract in shape and concept. "Recorded vitality" is the phrase Heiliger has used to describe his work, and this is apparent through a considerable body of sculptures. It can be seen in 1950 with his "Seraph I" that harks back to the winged torso of the Parthenon, while at the same time reflecting something of Brancusi's electric vigour.

Tension and movement in a sculpture having no allusive properties are inherent factors in much of his monumental oeuvre. His entry for the Memorial to the Unknown Political Prisoner competition in 1953, despite its hackneyed motive—a caged-in figure—had elements such as the riven torso that wrought sculptural drama from the rupture of his material.

Vegetable growth possessed by the human form in a kind of Daphne paraphrase also took its place in his imagery about 1955, and this symbolization of regeneration occurs in much subsequent work accompanied by the broken and wounded aspects of man's vulnerability. The bronzes "Sebastian" and "Vogeltod" of 1961 are elegiac in treatment, yet retain in their diagonal emphasis a hint of man rising from his earthbound discomfiture.

Heiliger's individual capacity for giving plastic form to unmaterial idea is best known in "Die Flamme" (The Flame), standing more than six metres high in the Ernst Reuter Platz, Berlin, a bronze of colour and animation that is a remarkable example of public sculpture in the non-figurative canon.

Architecture as the setting for sculpture has interested Heiliger, but primarily as a contrasting environment where the image preserves its own identity. His figure groups in the open, though stylized in pared and bone-like silhouettes, preserve the upright dignity of Hellenic prototypes. This spare reduction of form is carried into the sphere of portraiture without compromise of artistic truth. The heads of Ernst Schroder and Comte Philippe d'Arscot might suggest a slightness of content were it not for the tautness and nervous energy they transmit.

In smaller-scale pieces, Heiliger invests his figures with the classic primitivism of Cycladic alabasters. This fusion of the present with the past is a significant contribution from Heiliger, marking his sculpture by its catalytic force.

—G. S. Whittet

HEIZER, Michael.

American. Born in Berkeley, California, 4 November 1944. Studied at San Francisco Art Institute, 1963–64. Lives and works in New York and Nevada. Began excavation projects, Nevada 1967–68; major earthworks, Central Eastern Nevada, 1969–71, 1972–76. Agent: Xavier Fourcade Inc., New York. Address: c/o Xavier Fourcade Inc. 36 East 75th Street, New York, New York 10031, U.S.A.

Individual Exhibitions:

1969 Heiner Friedrich Galerie, Munich
1970 Dwan Gallery, New York
1971 Detroit Institute of Arts
1974 Ace Gallery, Los Angeles
     Fourcade Droll Inc., New York
1976 Xavier Fourcade Inc., New York
1977 Ace Gallery, Los Angeles
     Xavier Fourcade Inc., New York
     Ace Gallery, Venice, California
     Galerie am Promenadeplatz, Munich
1979 Folkwang Museum, Essen (travelled to the Kröller-Müller Museum, Otterlo, Netherlands)
     Richard Hines Gallery, Seattle
1980 St. Louis Art Museum
     Xavier Fourcade Inc., New York
1984 Museum of Contemporary Art, Los Angeles
1985 Rice University, Houston, Texas

Selected Group Exhibitions:

1968 *Sculpture Annual*, Whitney Museum, New York
1970 *When Attitude Becomes Form*, Kunsthalle, Berne (toured Europe)
1971 *Guggenheim International*, Guggenheim Museum, New York
1976 *200 Years of American Sculpture*, Whitney Museum, New York
1977 *Documenta*, Kassel, West Germany
     Probing the Earth: Contemporary Land Projects, Hirshhorn Museum, Washington D.C. (toured the United States)
1978 *Painting and Sculpture Today: 1978*, Indianapolis Museum of Art
1980 *L'Amerique aux Independants*, Grand Palais, Paris
1982 *Twenty American Artists: Sculpture 82*, San Francisco Museum of Modern Art
1984 *Geometric Extraction*, Whitney Museum, New York

Collections:

Metropolitan Museum of Art, New York: Fogg Art Museum, Harvard University, Cambridge, Massachusetts; Kröller-Müller Museum, Otterlo, Netherlands; Kunstmuseum, Basel; Bayerische Staatsgemaldesammlungen, Munich; Museum Ludwig, Cologne.

Publications:

By HEIZER: article—"The Art of Michael Heizer" in *Artforum* (New York), December 1969.

On HEIZER: books—*The New Avant-Garde: Issues for the Art of the 70's* by Gregoire Muller, New York 1972; *Michael Heizer*, exhibition catalogue, by Zdenek Felix and Ellen Joosten, Essen, Germany and Otterlo, Netherlands 1979; *Michael Heizer: Sculpture in Reverse*, exhibition catalogue edited by Julia Brown, Los Angeles 1984; *Michael Heizer*, exhibition catalogue with essay by William Camfield, Houston 1985; articles—"Holes Without History" by Diane Waldman in *Art News* (New York), May 1971; "The Earth Mover" by Douglas Davis in *Newsweek* (New York), 18 November 1974; "Michael Heizer: Complex One" in *Domus* (Milan), February 1975; "Artworks on the Land" by Elizabeth C. Baker in *Art in America* (New York), January/February 1976; "Earthshaking News from the Art World: Sculpturing the Land" by Earl Gottschalk, Jr. in the *Wall Street Journal* (New York), 10 September 1976; "Site Inspection" by Lawrence Alloway in *Artforum* (New York), October 1976; "New Landscapes in Art" by Kay Larson in the *New York Times Magazine*, 13 May 1979; "Sculpture on the Streets" by Hilton Kramer in the *New York Times*, 15 July 1979; "Sculpture in Public Places" in *Horizon* (New York), October 1979; "A New Stonehenge in Nevada" by Jed Horne in *Quest/80* (New York), September 1980.

HELD, Al.

American. Born in Brooklyn, New York, 12 October 1928. Educated in New York City public schools, 1933–45; Art Students League, New York, under Harry Sternberg, 1948–49; Grande Chaumière, Paris, under Zadkine, 1950–52. Served in the United States Navy, 1945–47. Married Sylvia Stone. Associated with American painters Frank Lobdell, Bill Rivers, Ellsworth Kelly, Jack Youngerman, Sam Francis, Milton Resnick, George Sugarman, Jules Olitski,

Shirley Jaffe, Ken Noland, Paris, 1950–52; returned to New York, 1953; worked as carpenter, truck-driver, and on road construction, San Francisco, 1954–55; started removal business, New York, 1955–60; Founder, with others, Brata Gallery, New York, 1956; first black and white paintings, New York, 1967. Associate Professor of Art, then Professor, Yale University, New Haven, Connecticut, since 1962. Recipient: Logan Medal, Art Institute of Chicago, 1964; Guggenheim Fellowship, 1966. Agent: André Emmerich Gallery, New York. Address: c/o André Emmerich Gallery, 41 East 57th Street, New York, New York 10022, U.S.A.

Individual Exhibitions:

1951	Galerie 8, Paris
1958	Poindexter Gallery, New York
1969	Poindexter Gallery, New York
1961	Poindexter Gallery, New York
	Bonino Gallery, Buenos Aires
1962	Poindexter Gallery, New York
1964	Galerie René Ziegler, Zurich
	Galerie Gunar, Dusseldorf
1965	André Emmerich Gallery, New York
1966	Stedelijk Museum, Amsterdam
	Galerie Muller, Stuttgart
1967	André Emmerich Gallery, New York
1968	André Emmerich Gallery, New York
	Museum of Art, San Francisco
	Corcoran Gallery, Washington, D.C.
	Recent Paintsings, Institute of Contemporary Art, Philadelphia (travelled to the Contemporary Arts Association, Houston)
1970	Galerie René Ziegler, Zurich
	André Emmerich Gallery, New York
1971	Donald Morris Gallery, Detroit
1972	*New Paintings,* André Emmerich Gallery, New York
1973	André Emmerich Gallery, New York
1974	Galerie André Emmerich, Zurich
	Donald Morris Gallery, Detroit
	Whitney Museum, New York (retrospective)
	Galerie Muller, Cologne
1975	André Emmerich Gallery, New York
	Jared Sable Gallery, Toronto
	Adler Castillo Gallery, Caracas
1976	André Emmerich Gallery, New York
1977	Galerie Roger d'Amecourt, Paris
	Galerie Marguerite Lamy, Paris
	Galerie Renée Ziegler, Zurich
	Annely Juda Fine Art, London
	Donald Morris Gallery, Birmingham, Michigan
1978	*New Paintings,* André Emmerich Gallery, New York
	Paintings and Drawings 1973–78, Institute of Contemporary Arts, Boston
	Janus Gallery, Venice, California
	Marianne Friedland Gallery, Toronto
1979	André Emmerich Gallery, New York
1980	*Al Held 1959–61,* Robert Miller Gallery, New York
	Gimpel-Hanover, Zurich
	Galerie André Emmerich, Zurich
	Quadrat Bottrop-Modern Galerie, Zurich
1982	Robert Miller Gallery, New York
1984	André Emmerich Gallery, New York
1985	Robert Miller Gallery, New York
	André Emmerich Gallery, New York
1987	André Emmerich Gallery, New York
	Robert Miller Gallery, New York

Selected Group Exhibitions:

1959	*Neue Amerikanische Malerie,* Kunstmuseum, St. Gallen, Switzerland
1964	*Post Painterly Abstraction,* Los Angeles County Museum of Art (toured the United States)
1967	*Documenta 4,* Museum Fridericianum, Kassel, West Germany
1970	*Contemporary American Painting and Sculpture from New York Galleries,* Wilmington Society of Fine Arts, Delaware Art Center
1973	*Whitney Biennial Exhibition,* Whitney Museum, New York

1976	*Drawing Today in New York,* Tulane University, New Orleans (toured the United States 1976–77)
1977	*A View of a Decade,* Museum of Contemporary Art, Chicago
1979	*Art Inc.: American Paintings from Corporate Collections,* Museum of Fine Arts, Montgomery, Alabama (toured the United States)
1982	*A Private Vision,* Museum of Fine Art, Boston
1986	*Action Precision,* Newport Harbor Art Museum, Newport Beach, California

Collections:

Museum of Modern Art, New York; Whitney Museum, New York; Metropolitan Museum of Art, New York; Yale University Art Gallery, New Haven, Connecticut; Fogg Art Museum, Harvard University, Cambridge, Massachusetts; Delaware Art Museum, Wilmington; Hirshhorn Museum and Sculpture Garden, Washington, D.C.; San Francisco Museum of Modern Art; Staatsgalerie, Stuttgart; Kunsthaus, Zurich.

Publications:

By HELD: articles—statement in *It Is* (New York), Autumn 1958; "Jackson Pollock: An Artist's Symposium, Part 1" in *Art News* (New York), April 1967; "On Art and Architecture" in *Perspecta: The Yale Architectural Journal* (New Haven, Connecticut), No. 11, 1967; interview with James Faure Walker, in *Artscribe* (London), July 1977.

On HELD: books—*Al Held,* exhibition catalogue, Amsterdam 1966; *Al Held,* exhibition catalogue, San Francisco 1968; *Al Held: Recent Paintings,* exhibition catalogue, Philadelphia and Houston, 1969; *Late Modern* by Edward Lucie-Smith, New York 1969; *Al Held,* exhibition catalogue, Zurich 1970; *La Pittura Americana del Dopoguerra* by Sam Hunter, Milan 1970; *Modern American Painting* by Dore Ashton, New York 1970; *The Visual Dialogue* by Nathan Knobler, New York 1971; *Icons and Images of the 60's* by Nicholas and Elena Calas, New York 1971; *Al Held: New Paintings,* exhibition catalogue, New York 1972; *Al Held,* exhibition catalogue, by Marcia Tucker, New York 1974; *Al Held: New Paintings,* exhibition catalogue, text by Andrew Forge, New York 1978; *Al Held: Paintings and Drawings 1973–78,* exhibition catalogue, Boston 1978; *The New School: The Painters and Sculptors of the 50's* by Irving Sandler, New York 1978; *Dictionary of American Art* by Matthew Baigell, New York 1979; *Al Held 1959–1961,* exhibition catalogue, with an essay by Irving Sandler, New York 1980; *Al Held,* exhibition catalogue, with an introduction by Willy Rotzler, Zurich 1980; *Al Held,* exhibition catalogue with essay by Irving Sandler, New York 1982; *Al Held,* exhibition catalogue with essay by Donald Kuspit, New York 1987; *Al Held* by Irving Sandler, London 1987.

One wants to shout in Al Held's case, "Boldness is all!" Not in a negative sense but by way of recognition. For there is an exhilarating ambition in Held's work. A kind of manic confidence that compels our attention. When it doesn't work we get bombast or rhetoric or hysteria. But it works a good deal of the time. Which is all one can expect from any artist.

Held likes to work to enormous scale—either literally on huge expanses of canvas or in *intention* within more modest dimensions. Either way the work is always expansive, big-voiced, almost Whitmanesque. By grasping only part of forms he shows us hugeness. Often his paintings are like fragments of some giant's world. The suggestion that there is much more of some form *off* the canvas is overwhelming, but the paintings don't fall apart. Strongly composed, strongly colored, they are held in by tensions within their asserted space that are the balancing act of a highly accomplished painter.

Essentially hard-edged, fairly minimal, Held's pictures play with space. There are suggestions of abstract-expressionism in the sense of gestural images in them as though, say, Kline had become neat. Diagonals thrust and cross, criss-cross in fact, setting up considerable activity. But this is not always true. There are also works with serene flat shapes that appear only skin deep except where the color reads as a field. And besides, even the thrust-and-parry works are checked by references to classical perspective so

that our knowledge of "where things should go" serves to stabilize the rocketting, fast forms. Held's talent for depicting relationships enables him to go for the grandiose without ending up with the merely inflated.

—Ralph Pomeroy

HÉLION, Jean.

French. Born in Couterne, Normandy, 21 April 1904. Educated at the Ecole Auguste Janvier, Amiens, 1912–18; studied chemistry, Institut Industriel du Nord, Lille, 1920–21; architecture, Ecole des Arts Décoratifs, Paris. 1922; painting, Académie Adler, Paris, 1925–26. Married Jacqueline Ventadour in 1963; children: Jean Jacques, Louis, Fabrice, David and Nicolas. Served in the French Army, 1927; mobilized, 1940; prisoner-of-war, Pomerania, 1940–42; escaped, 1942. Worked as pharmacist's assistant, Bagnoles-de-l'Orne, 1918–19; assistant, in architect's offices, Paris, 1921–24; private mathematics teacher, Paris, 1924–25. Produced first paintings, Paris, 1922; full-time painter, Paris, 1925–40, Rockbridge Baths, Virginia, and New York, 1942–46, Paris, 1946–73, and in Bigeonnette, near Chartes, 1973 until his death in 1987. Founder-member, with Theo Van Doesburg, Otto Carlsund and Leo Tutundjian, Art Concret group, (renamed Abstraction-Creation group, 1930), Paris, 1929–34; contributor, *Pyrenees Review,* 1929, *L'Art Concret Review,* 1930, and *Abstraction-Creation,* review, 1932–34. Designed the sets and costumes for *King Lear,* French television production, Paris, 1964. Recipient: Grand Prix de la Ville de Paris, 1979; Grand Prix National des Arts, France, 1983. Honorary Member, American Academy and Institute of Arts and Letters, 1979; Chevalier de la Légion d'Honneur, France, 1984; Commandeur, Ordre des Arts et Lettres, France, 1985. Agent: Art of This Century, 3 rue Visconti, 75006 Paris. *Died* (in Paris) *28 October 1987.*

Individual Exhibitions:

1932	Galerie Pierre, Paris
	Gallery John Becker, New York
1933	Gallery John Becker, New York
1936	Galerie Cahiers d'Art, Paris
	Valentine Gallery, New York
	Putzel Gallery, Hollywood, California
1937	San Francisco Museum of Art
1938	Arts Club of Chicago
	Galerie Pierre, Paris
	Grand Rapids Museum, Michigan
1939	Arts Club of Lynchburg, Virginia
	The Whyte Gallery, Washington
1940	Georgette Passedoit Gallery, New York
1942	Virginia Museum of Fine Arts, Richmond
1943	San Francisco Museum of Art
	Arts Club of Chicago
	Art of This Century, New York
	Bennington College, Vermont
	Stendahl Gallery, Los Angeles
1944	Paul Rosenberg Gallery, New York
	Hollins College, Virginia
1945	Museum of Fine Arts, Baltimore
	Caresse Crosby Gallery, Washington
	Paul Rosenberg Gallery, New York
1947	Galerie Renou et Colle, Paris
1951	Hanover Gallery, London
	Sala digli Specchi, Venice
	Galleria del Milione, Milan
	Feigl Gallery, New York
	Galleria San Marco, Rome
1953	Chez Mayo, Paris
1956	Galerie Cahiers d'Art, Paris
1958	Galerie Cahiers d'Art, Paris
1961	Galerie Cahiers d'Art, Paris

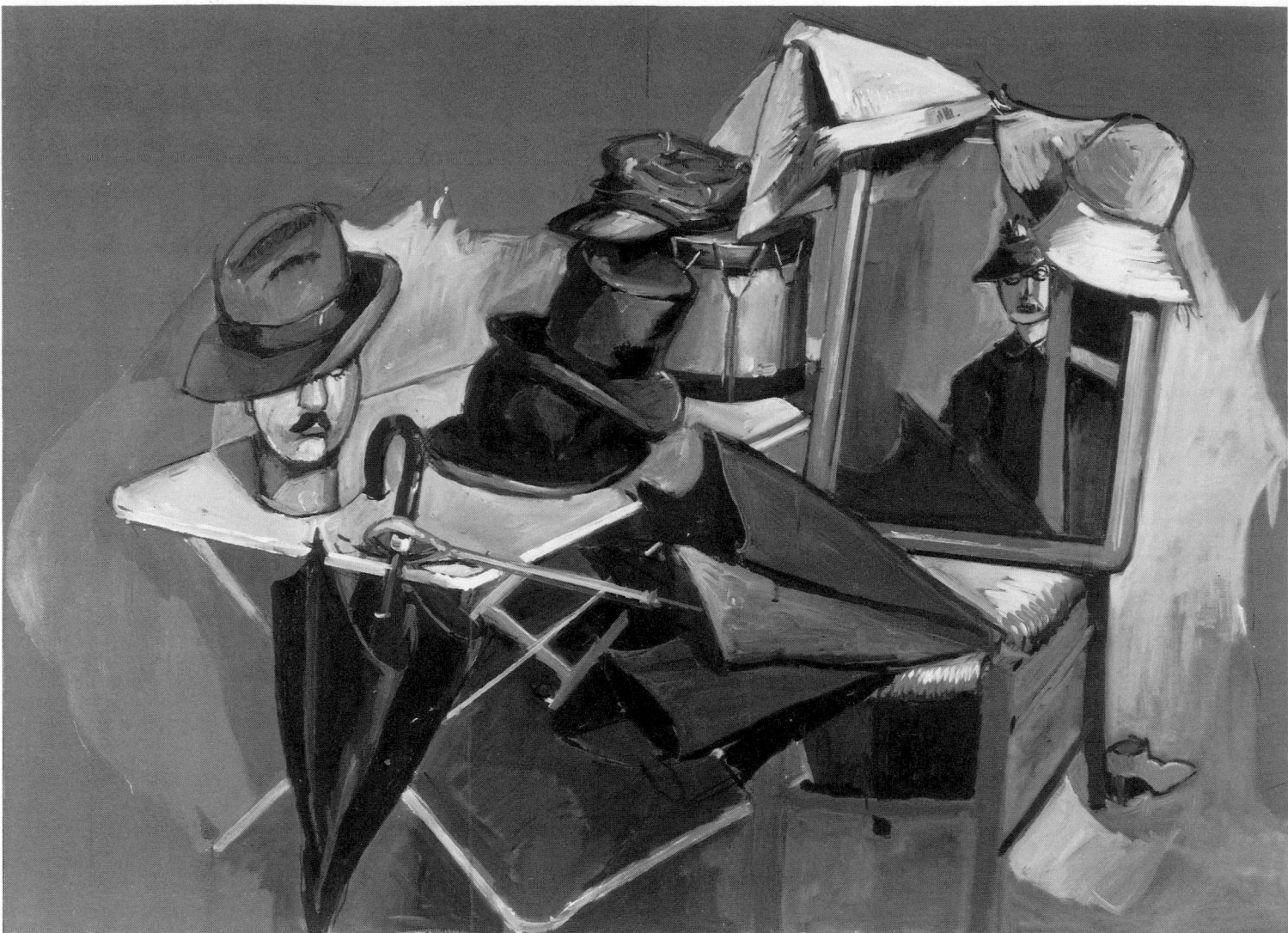

Jean Hélion: *Un Borsalino pour Emile*, 1981

1962	*Peintures 1929–1939*, Galerie Louis Carré, Paris
1964	*Paintings by Jean Hélion 1928–1964*, Gallery of Modern Art, New York
	Galerie Yvon Lambert, Paris
1965	Leicester Galeries, London
	Galerie René Andrieu, Toulouse
1966	Galerie du Dragon, Paris
1967	Willard Gallery, New York
	Galerie Arcanes, Brussels
1968	Galleria Mutina, Modena
	Galleria Il Fante di Spade, Rome
1969	Galerie Verriere, Lyon
	Galleria Eunomia, Milan
1970	*Cent Tableaux 1928–1970*, Cantre National d'Art Contemporain, Paris (toured France)
	Maison des Jeunes et de la Culture, Paris
1971	Galerie Weiller, Paris
	Galerie Henriette Gomes, Paris
1972	Galerie René Andrieu, Toulouse
1973	*Oeuvres Récentes*, Galerie Saint-Germain, Paris
1974	Musée Tavet, Pontoise, France
	Galerie Chauvelin, Paris
1975	Galerie St. Germain, Paris
	Galerie Flinker, Paris
	Maison de la Culture, Saint-Etienne, France
	Galerie der Spiegel, Cologne
1976	Spencer Samuels Gallery, New York
1977	Musée de l'Abbaye Sainte-Croix, Les Sables d'Olonne, France
	Galerie du Centre, Paris
	Musée d'Art Moderne de la Ville, Paris
1978	Galerie Karl Flinker, Paris
	Galerie Sapone, Nice
	Musée Ingres, Montaban, France

1979	*Bilder und Zeichnungen*, Galerie Thomas Borgmann, Cologne
	Galerie Michael Hasenclever, Munich
	Athens Gallery, Athens
	Peintures et Dessins 1929–1979, Musée d'Art et d'Industrie, Saint-Etienne, France
	Musée d'Art Moderne, Strasbourg
1980	Centre Georges Pompidou, Paris (toured France)
	Bilder und Zeichnungen 1929–1980, Galerie Poll, West Berlin
	Les Années 50, Galerie Karl Flinker, Paris
	Museum of Art, Peking (travelled to Shanghai and Nanchang)
	Musée des Beaux-Arts, Rennes
1981	Galleria Fonte d'Abisso, Modena
	Paintings and Drawings from the Years 1939–60, Robert Miller Gallery, New York
	Musée de Caen, France
	Musée de la Bouére, Liège, Belgium
	Kunstverein, Wolfsburg, West Germany
	Galerie Academia, Salzburg, Austria
	Galerie Karl Flinker, Paris
	Galerie Bronda, Helsinki
1982	Musée d'Etat, Luxembourg
1983	Galerie Karl Flinker, Paris
1984	Galerie Karl Flinker, Paris
	Galerie Poll, West Berlin
	Städtische Galerie im Lenbachhaus, Munich (retrospective; travelled to Musée d'Art Moderne de la Ville, Paris)
1985	Rachel Adler Gallery, New York
1986	Peggy Guggenheim Collection, Venice
1987	Louis Carré et Cie, Paris
	Aarhus Kunstmuseum, Denmark
	Albemarle Gallery, London

Selected Group Exhibitions:

1971	*Mercedes-Benz Show*, Paris
1975	*European Painting in the 70's*, Los Angeles County Museum of Art (toured the United States)
1976	*Biennale*, Venice
	Peinture Aujourd-hui, Maison de la Culture, Fontenay-sous-Bois, France
1980	*20th Century Art*, Centre Georges Pompidou, Paris (toured Japan)
1981	*A New Spirit in Painting*, Royal Academy of Arts, London
1982	*Panorama de l'Art Francais 1960–1980*, Vienna
1984	*Painting in France*, at the *Biennale*, Venice
1985	*Colour Since Matisse*, at the *Edinburgh Festival*, Scotland

Collections:

Centre Georges Pompidou, Paris; Musée d'Art Moderne de la Ville de Paris; Musée d'Art et d'Industrie, Saint-Etienne, France; Pinacothek, Munich; Tate Gallery, London; Museum of Modern Art, New York; Guggenheim Museum, New York; Museum of Fine Arts, Philadelphia; Museum of Fine Arts, Boston; Art Institute of Chicago.

Publications:

By HÉLION: books—*Book Upon Capitivity and Escape: They Shall Not Have Me*, New York 1943; *Kaleidoscope*, Paris, 1975; *Journal d'un Peintre: Carnets 1929–1984*, Marseilles 1984.

On HÉLION: books—*Arp, Calder, Hélion, Miró, Seligman*

by Anatole Jakovski, 1933; *Jean Hélion: A Coat of Many Colours*, edited by Herbert Read, London 1952; *Jean Hélion: Peintures 1929-1939*, exhibition catalogue, with text by Raymond Queneau, Paris 1962; *Paintings by Jean Hélion 1938-1964*, exhibition catalogue, with texts by Forrest Selvig, Pierre Bruguière and Christian Zervos, New York 1964; *Jean Hélion*, exhibition catalogue, with texts by Stephen Spender and Pierre Bruguière, London 1965; *Jean Hélion*, exhibition catalogue, with texts by Jean Pierre Burgant and others, Paris 1966; *Jean Hélion*, exhibition catalogue, with text by Katharine Kuh, New York 1967; *Jean Hélion*, exhibition catalogue, with text by René Micha, Rome 1968; *Hélion: Cent Tableaux 1928-1970*, exhibition catalogue, with texts by Francois Ponge, Roger Caillois, Daniel Abadie, Anatole Jakovsky, Pierre Mabille, Christian Zervos and Raymond Queneau, Paris 1970; *Hélion* by Pierre Bruguière, Paris, 1970; *Hélion: Oeuvres Récentes*, exhibition catalogue, with text by Daniel Abadie, Paris 1973; *Hélion*, exhibition catalogue, with text by Pierre G. Bruguière, Pontoise, France 1974; *Jean Hélion* by René Micha, Paris 1979; *Hélion: Peintures et Dessins 1929-1979*, exhibition catalogue, Cologne 1979; *Hélion: Les Années 50*, exhibition catalogue, with texts by Karl Flinker and Francois Ponge, Paris 1980; *Jean Hélion: Paintings and Drawings from the Years 1939-60*, exhibition catalogue, with text by Lawrence Alloway, New York 1981; *Jean Hélion: Abstraktion und Mythen des Alltags*, exhibition catalogue with texts by Armin Zweite, Merle Schipper and Pierre Bruguière, Munich 1984; *Hélion: Peintures et Dessins 1925- 1983*, exhibition catalogue with texts by Anne Moeglin-Délcroix and Pierre Bruguière, Paris 1984; *Hélion: Peintures de 1929 a 1983*, exhibition catalogue by Luc Lang, Paris 1987.

For ten years (1929-1939), I devoted myself entirely to abstract painting, until I found that it had transformed my vision of the world: the unknown world, so well hidden behind practical notions and conventions.

Then I could not resist trying to decode reality with renewed rhythms, sequences and qualities.

At the intersection of painting, experience and imagination, I wander and wonder.

—Jean Hélion (1983)

It is as if Jean Hélion had severed his roots and gone to another planet. For most people, if that happens, a period of reorientation must ensue. (Even a temporary visit to the moon is psychologically disturbing.) A new life, fresh vistas, different friends (although a few old faithfuls will still correspond and perhaps make occasional visits); but for some the break is crucial, the starting place for another existence.

Jean Hélion was/is a big name in the history of French modern art. His careful comments on bourgeois ambience, hard-edged and often like a dalliance with automata, helped launch him onto the Paris art scene, because such paintings, some of them of deft inventive charm, were exactly in tune with the tenor of art in the French capital of 1930. Nor did Hélion stay still. His chosen course and his increasing expertise won him natural admiration as the imagery became less and less figurative; matters reached a climax by 1934, by which time his canvases, some of them of commanding size, were completely non-figurative.

"Oh Hélion! Oh Headlights!" exclaimed one critic of the day, and his comment was duly repeated in *Axis*, the abstract magazine produced by John Piper and Myfanwy Evans. Indeed, the colour areas in these new paintings were like great luminous lenses. They clubbed together on canvas to form compositions whose nearest visual complements were the bulky make-up of the fat upholstery of easy chairs and sofas. From some early flirting with abstract conceptions Hélion had gone on to really find himself and alert the world to an important newcomer—a different *peintre non-figuratif!* This was perhaps the particularly exceptional quality that he brought to the range of abstract in the 1930's, that his paintings were not only beautifully wrought (hard-edge in the original abstract painting manner, but not hard on the eye) but also intensely individual, independent and different, seeming to be subject to no outside influence other than the prevailing drift towards non-figurative art.

Then everything changed. Not immediately. The switch was not as sudden as that, but it was rapid. Hélion went back to naturalism. Many who had acclaimed his abstract work shrank away, but probably an equal proportion of his admirers stayed faithful to him.

And besides abandoning the non-figurative style, he also changed his approach to the canvas. Hardedge, whether incorporated in his earlier style or carrying through into his style of the mid-1930's, disappeared to be replaced by rugged paint vigorously applied, a direct reflection of the countless drawings and water colours he was pouring out either through sheer enthusiasm, or as *croquis*, or as study sketches for some subsequent paintings. Only one element was constant: the keen appreciation he had always shown for logical composition remained intact.

Admittedly there were echoes of the subject matter from his earliest work which found their place in the paintings by the new Hélion—street scenes, shopping, bourgeois interiors, but to these were added ships and shipping and astonishing roofscapes. The new colours were wholly unrelated to what had gone before. Now there were plenty of cuprous pinks and cerulean blues, tints that had been scarcely ever evident previously.

The prevailing alteration in the pictures (qua pictures) was the atmosphere of crowded paint (and often crowded people—especially in butcher's shops). No more housefront compositions with perhaps a cast of one boy and one girl. No more cafe bars with one *serveuse* and maybe a couple of customers.

From the mid-1980s Hélion suffered from an increasing loss of sight. Until his death in 1987 he exercised his creative energy in writing—by dictation of course—lecture material and his theories on the realities of Art for the painter. He spent much of his time on a sort of memoir-journey based on notes kept about his entire artistic career. One of these notebooks was published in 1984. Rather more extraordinary was his dictation of instructions for imaginary pictorial compositions that he could, of course, never paint himself.

But before this loss of sight began to make itself felt, and particularly in the late 1970s and early 1980s, his pictures experienced a veritable Indian Summer. Compositions, especially those featuring a nude with the painter himself (as a young man) appeared on large canvases in glowing colours. The nude, mauve, natural or green, casually invaded the scene at ease or in painter's pose while the artist, soberly dressed in dark jacket, Breton-red trousers and open shirt, worked at a picture or lay back resting. In one such painting, a very large canvas, three men on a visit are entertaining the painter with music from a trombone, to enhance the peace of the moment. This swansong is truly moving.

—Sheldon Williams

HENDRICKS, Geoffrey.

American. Born in Littleton, New Hampshire, 30 July 1931. Educated at Amherst College, Massachusetts, 1949-53, B.A. 1953; studied sculpture at Smith College, Northampton, Massachusetts, under Peter Grippe, 1951-52, Cooper Union Art School New York, 1953-56, and Columbia University, New York, under Meyer Shapiro and Rudolf Wittkower, 1957-62, M.A. 1962. Married Beatrice (Bici) Forbes in 1961 (divorced, 1974); children: Tyche and Bracken. Lives and works in New York: Member, Fluxus artist group, since 1967; organized George Maciunas' *FluxMass/Olympiad*, Douglass College, Rutgers University, New Brunswick, New Jersey, 1970; Organizer, Flux Festschrift Banquet for George Maciunas, New York 1976. Co-Founder, Black Thumb Press, New York, 1965-72; Founder, with Brian Buczak, Money for Food Press, 1977. Member, Printed Editions, since 1977. Teacher, St. Barnabas Hospital for Chronic Diseases, Bronx, New York, 1953-56; Assistant Instructor, 1956-58, Art Instructor, 1958-61, Assistant Professor, 1961-67, and Associate Professor, 1967-80, Art Department, Douglass College, Rutgers University; Art Instructor, Windham College, Putney, Vermont, Summer 1957. Professor of Art since 1980, and Graduate Director for Visual Arts since 1981, Mason Gross School of the Arts, Rutgers University. Recipient: Research Fellowship, MacDowell Colony, Peterborough, New Hampshire, 1955; National Endowment for the Arts Grant, 1976; DAAD Berlin Artists Program Fellowship, 1980. Agent: Galerie Inge Baecker, Bergstrasse 54, D-4630 Bochum, West Germany. Address: 486 Greenwich Street, New York, New York 10013, U.S.A.

Individual Exhibitions:

1950　Carpenter Art Gallery, Dartmouth College, Hanover, New Hampshire

1953　Meade Art Building, Amherst College, Massachusetts

1956　Putney School, Vermont

1957　Douglass College Art Gallery, Rutgers University, New Jersey

1958　Douglass College Art Gallery, Rutgers University, New Jersey

1962　Douglass College Art Gallery, Rutgers University, New Jersey

1965　Cafe au GoGo, New York (with Bici Forbes)
　　　Cafe au GoGo, New York
　　　Judson Memorial Church, New York

1966　Judson Memorial Church, New York (3 times)
　　　Bianchini Gallery, New York
　　　New York Public Library

1967　Judson Memorial Church, New York
　　　Judson Gallery, New York
　　　Trude Heller's Trik, New York (with Lawrence Kornfield, Bici Forbes)
　　　Time-Life Auditorium, New York (with Flux Masters of the Rear Garde)
　　　Fluxhouse, New York

1968　Barnard College, New York
　　　Tokyo Gallery (twice)

1969　Fluxhouse, New York
　　　Voorhees Chapel, Douglass College, Rutgers University, New Jersey
　　　Loeb Center, New York University

1970　Loeb Center, New York University
　　　Algol Theatre, Brussels

1971　Apple Gallery, New York (with Billy Apple, Jerry Vis)
　　　Higgins Hall, Pratt Institute, New York
　　　California Institute of Arts, Burbank
　　　Apple Gallery, New York (3 times)
　　　331 West 20th Street, New York (with Bici Forbes, George Maciunas)
　　　Apple Gallery, New York (with Billy Apple, Jerry Vis)
　　　Apple Gallery, New York (with Stephen Varble)
　　　Super Nova, New York (with Stephen Varble)
　　　Global Village, London (with Stephen Varble)
　　　Neue Galerie der Stadt, Aachen, West Germany (with Dick Higgins, Stephen Varble)
　　　80 Wooster Street, New York
　　　Galerie Baecker, Bochum, West Germany

1973　Art Center, Summit, New Jersey
　　　La Mama Experimental Theatre Club, New York

1974　Byrkjefjellet, Kvamsskogen, Norway
　　　Galerie Baecker, Bochum, West Germany
　　　The Clocktower, New York

1975　Kunstverein, Munich
　　　Incontri Internazionali d'Arte, Rome
　　　Galleria Multhipla, Milan
　　　Pari and Dispari Stand, *Art Fair*, Basel

1976　Studio Morra, Naples
　　　Fine Arts Building, New York
　　　113 Green Street, New York
　　　The Clocktower, New York
　　　Pari and Dispari Stand, *Art Fair*, Bologna

1977　Galleria d'Arte Moderna, Bologna (with Brian Buczak)

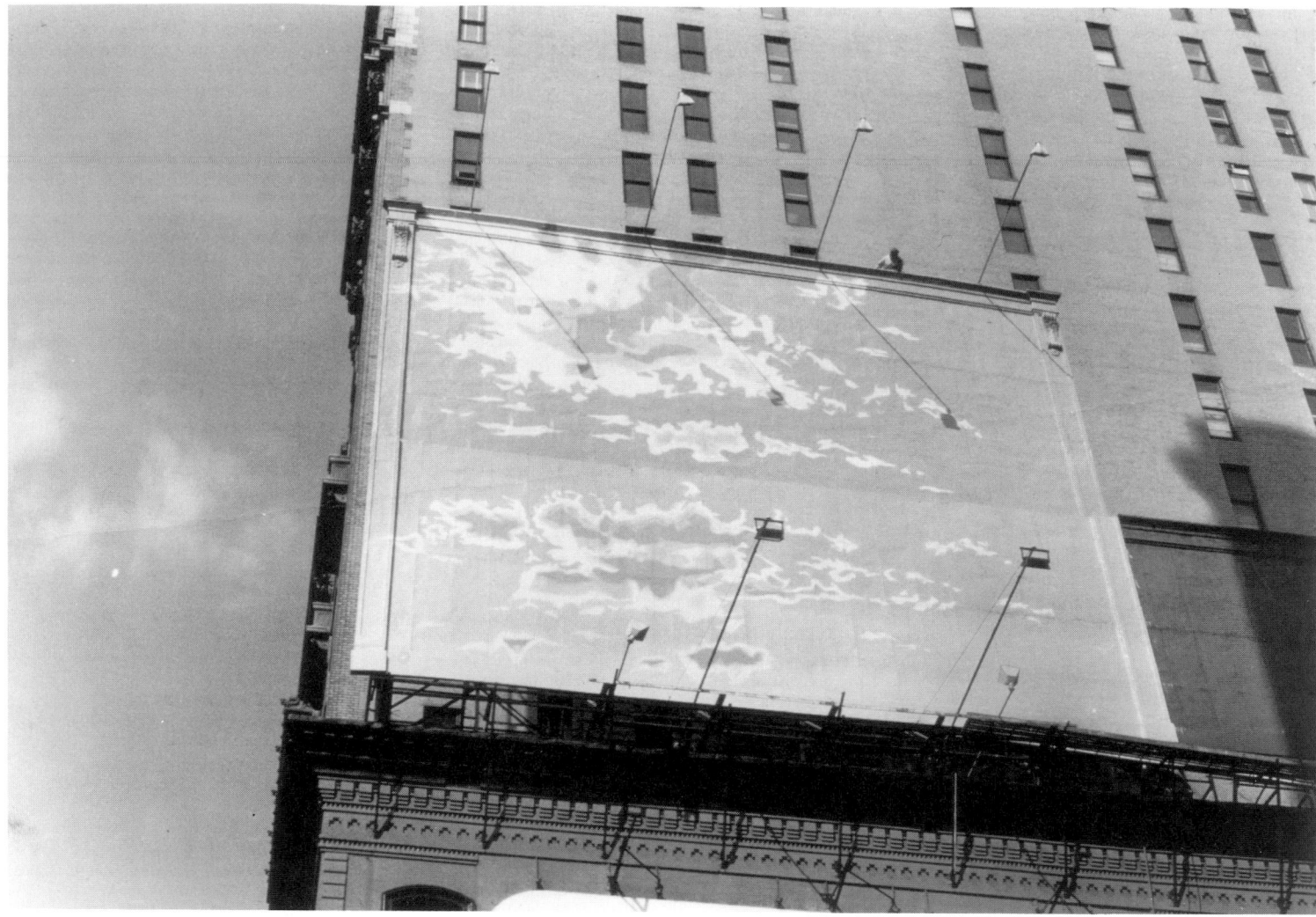

Geoffrey Hendricks: *Sky Billboard, Fifth Avenue, New York*, 1966

René Block Gallery, New York
1978 Aral Haus, Bochum, West Germany
Galerie Baecker, Bochum, West Germany
1979 *Ruhr Park Art Festival*, Bochum, West Germany
P.S. 1, New York (2 times)
1980 Studio Morra, Naples
1981 Studio Morra, Naples
1983 DAAD-Galerie, West Berlin
Galerie Donguy, Paris
Galerie Inge Baecker, Cologne
1984 Neue Galerie, Aachen, West Germany
Kunsthalle, Wilhelmshaven, West Germany
Badischer Kunstverein, Karlsruhe, West Germany
1986 Galerie Baecker, Cologne

Selected Group Exhibitions:

1958 *Work by New Jersey Artists*, Newark Museum, New
Jersey (and 1961, 1964, 1965, 1968)
1970 *Happening and Fluxus*, Kunstverein, Cologne
1973 *Combattimento per Un 'Immagine, Fotografie e Pittori*, Museo Civico de Torino Galleria d'Arte Moderna, Turin
1974 *Multiples, Ein Versuch die Entwicklung des Aufla-
genobjektes darzustellen*, Neuer Berliner Kunstverein, Berlin
1975 *The First New York City Post Card Show*, Contemporary Arts Gallery, Loeb Student Center, New York
University
1976 *Personal Mythologies*, Fine Arts Building, New
York
1978 *Hermetic Images in Contemporary Art*, P.S. 1, New
York
1982 *Fluxus 1962-82*, Museum Wiesbäden, West Germany (and at Nassauischer Kunstverein, and
Harlekin Art, Wiesbäden)

1983 *Fluxus etc.*, Neuberger Museum, Purchase, New
York
1987 *Aspects of Conceptualism*, Avenue B Gallery, New
York

Collections:

Metropolitan Museum of Art, New York; Museum of Mod-
ern Art, New York; Franklin Furnace Archive, New York;
New Jersey State Museum, Trenton; Springfield Art Mu-
seum, Massachusetts; Rose Art Museum, Waltham, Massa-
chusetts; Hopkins Art Center, Dartmouth College, Hanover,
New Hampshire; Witherspoon Gallery, University of North
Carolina, Chapel Hill; Lehmbruck Museum, Duisburg, West
Germany; Museum des 20. Jahrhunderts, Vienna.

Publications:

By HENDRICKS: books—*Ring Piece*, Barton, Vermont
1973; *Between 2 Points/Fra Due Poli*, Reggio Emilia, Italy
1974; *A Sheep's Skeleton and Rocks/Uno Scheletro di Pecaro
e Sassi*, New York and Asolo, Italy 1977; *Flux Wedding:
George and Billie*, with Brian Buczak, New York 1978; *The
Wisdom of the Money for Food Lady*, with Brian Buczak,
New York 1978; *100 Ways to Make Money*, with Brian Buczak, New York 1978; *Saved*, with Brian Buczak, New York
1979; *Le Capra*, New York and Naples, 1979; *5 Found Photos*, New York 1979; *A V TRE EXTRA*, New York 1979;
Vesuvius, Vesuvius in Eruption, New York 1981; *A Short History of Fluxus*, New York 1981; *Sky Anatomy*, New York
1981; *100 Skies*, with text by Henry Martin, Worpswede,
West Germany 1987; articles—a question, a letter to George
Brecht, a statement in *10 From Rutgers*, exhibition catalogue,
New York 1965; data in *Film Culture—Expanded Arts Special Issue* (New York), Winter 1966; "Sky/Why?" in *Renewal* (Chicago) June 1967; "Sky/Change" documentation in
Manipulations, New York 1968; "Notations and Statement"
in *Notations* edited by John Cage, New York 1969; "Flux-

relics" in *Flux-Reliquary* New York 1970; "101 Words" in
Notebook, edited by Dana Atchley, Victoria, British Columbia 1970; "Skutterudite" in *Space Atlas*, edited by Dana Atchley, Victoria, British Columbia 1971; "When You Are
Through . . ." in *Arts and Artists Fluxus Issue* (London),
October 1972; "For Jackson" in *Vort* (Silver Springs, Maryland), no. 2, 1975.

On HENDRICKS: books—*Experience Book* by Vlasta
Cihakova-Noshiro, Tokyo 1978; *Fluxus: The Most Radical
and Experimental Art Movement of the 60's* by Harry Ruhe,
Amsterdam 1979; *Alternatives in Retrospect: An Historical
Overview 1969-1975* by Jacki Apple, New York 1981; *Geoff
Hendricks*, exhibition catalogue with texts by Peter Frank and
Lawrence Alloway, Aachen 1984; articles—"Light Sculpture
and a Sky" by Michael Benedikt in *Art International* (Lu-
gano, Switzerland), September 1966; "The Art of Trompe-
L'Oeil: Hendricks and Gilardi" by Katsuo Nobuyki in
Bijutsu-Techo (Tokyo), April 1968; "Wolken und Gitarren"
by Gerd Winkler in *Kunstforum International* (Mainz), February 1974; "Artists as Writers, Part II" by Lawrence Alloway in *Artforum* (New York), April 1974; "Geoffrey
Hendricks" in *Flash Art* (Milan), February 1976; "New York
Fluxus" by Peter Frank in *Soho Downtown Manhattan*, Berlin 1976; "American Performance" by Szymon Bojko in *Projekt* (Warsaw), February 1981.

*   *   *

Following a recent performance, a woman came up to
me and said that she was perplexed by what I had
done. Would I explain my work to her? I instinctively
felt that to try to put into words what I had been
silently doing in activity for the previous hour would
be wrong. Instead, I began to ask her questions.

She had found the work too much like nature . . . the randomness of nature. She could not
connect it to her concepts of "art." I liked her puzzle-
ment and told her so. I spoke of how sometimes work
which became most important for me on first encounter left me with a gnawing bewilderment. I suggested

that she hold on to her feelings about my piece and that perhaps some answers would come to her. I felt the images she had experienced would be staying with her for some time.

One element in my performance was a chair with two brass plates on the back—French and German translations of the inscriptions: "Sit carefully in this chair until you remember one important event from your past. Following this moment of recall get up immediately." I asked her if she had read what was on the chair. She said "No." I proposed that she do so, and we parted.

From a distance I noticed that she spent some time looking at the chair, and finally sat in it for an extended period. When she got up she had a different expression on her face.

—Geoffrey Hendricks

Geoffrey Hendricks has been referred to as a "cloudsmith," but the text in which we find this thumb-nail sketch (a text written in 1973 by Dick Higgins as a note for a small book by Hendricks, entitled *Ring Piece*, published by The Something Else Press) continues with a list of fourteen other activities (lettered from "a" to "l") in which Hendricks is likely to be discovered "when not forming clouds." Higgins' duplex sense of symmetry seems quite right: painting clouds is only a fraction of Geoffrey Hendricks' creative activities, but it can also look like a unitary Ying that balances against and completes a Yang that scatters into manifold ritual expressions of itself.

Ever since the early 1960s, Geoffrey Hendricks has been one of the artists associated with the term "Fluxus," and what he shares with most of these artists is an enormous lack of prejudice and preconception about what art can be, and where one does best to look for it. He has written: "What is relevant for me in Art isn't objects, but what hovers in a metaphysical space between the artist and the object he is grappling with. I find art where I least expect it. What I see in galleries and museums often comes across to me as being about art, trying to be art, but isn't . . . . Art is about getting deep into your personal self, working, struggling (but all of this is not art), and then suddenly you have left yourself for something universal." (In *Between Two Points*, Edizioni Pari & Dispari, Reggio Emilia, 1975). One might then suggest a slight emendation of this statement that has been made by Lawrence Alloway: "Hendricks' development, as writers on art like myself like to call it, goes like this: from objects in the early 60s to the Sky paintings, 1965–68, to the present period [of performances] in which his concern is the experience and definition of self." (New York, 1973). Even aside from how Hendricks' paintings and performance have subsequently come to present themselves as parallel or even intertwining activities, one might insist that "the experience and definition of self" is the central, exclusive concern of all of Geoffrey Hendricks' work. Making paintings and watercolors of the sky is as ritualistic as the rest of his activity. Self-exploration, moreover, can take any number of forms, and Hendricks' striving is less for the kind of self-knowledge emphasized by psychoanalysis than rather for those moments of purifying intuition that grasp the certainty that the human mind, the human body, and the human artifacts through which they relate to one another are all continuous with nature, or rooted in nature, or motivated and energized by the very same forces that stand in control of nature. In pieces that are based on physically performed ritual (either in isolation or before an audience) Hendricks will bathe naked in frigid streams fed by mountain snows, pound rocks into colored pigments with which he covers his body, tie twigs and branches of flowering shrubs to his arms and legs and chest, cut off locks of his hair and weave it into locks of hair cut from goats, build cairns of stones or mounds of sea weed, cut chairs and ladders down the middle and lash the pieces back to back, perhaps decorating them with bones or flowers. Or at the opening of an exhibition he may put a bed in an art gallery and stay in it for two days, between blue sheets, making

notes on thoughts and dreams in a journal, the floor around him scattered with leaves and twigs and pieces of rope. Or he will dig up soil from a hill in Canada and bury it many months later into a hill in Norway or Italy. Hendricks seeks out a direct, bodily interaction with nature, but he is also concerned with the ways in which our senses carry us out beyond our bodies. He makes paintings of the sky because it is the part of nature that he cannot touch.

These images of the sky, moreover, have had an evolution all their own. At first they were highly stylized, deliberately stereotypical, much as Magritte often rendered the sky, and they were painted on various real objects: over the entirety of an automobile, or an old pair of boots, or on pillow-cases, socks, pants, underwear and T-shirt, hung out on a clothes line as though to dry. We have an *idea* of the sky, superimposed upon things that are more local and terrestrial, and we feel free to complete these works with little poetic fantasies of our own: it can be rather as though the sky had suddenly appeared on your very own laundry in your very own backyard, most probably just as you had finished hanging it out and turned your back to re-enter the house. Or one might say that they have the presence of a visionary dream from which you run the risk of suddenly and sadly waking up. The more recent sky paintings are a much more direct and sensual engagement with the heavens, and a real attempt to catch momentary images of the sky as it constantly changes. They are acts of contemplation, if not of meditation, and they belong to a process of awareness that posits itself as a continuum. Grounded into the earth, it looks as well towards the sky, both implying and suspending our questions as to whether the mind might possibly reach out still further.

—Henry Martin

HENRY, Maurice.

French. Born in Cambrai, 29 December 1907. Studied law at the Faculté de Droit, Université de Paris, 1927–28. Served in the French Army, 1939–40. Married Elda Zanetti in 1979. Independent artist, in Paris, from 1927, and in Milan, from 1968: Member, Le Grand Jeu group of artists, Paris, 1926–32; André Breton's surrealist group of artists and writers, Paris, 1932–51; graphic humour drawings, 1932–68; film writer and director, 1939–54; photographer, theatre director, cabaret writer, television and ballet designer, from 1949; also worked as freelance journalist for several periodicals, Paris, 1928–69. Recipient: Popular Photography Award, New York, 1955; First Prize, *Cartoonale Mondiale*, Heist Duinbergen, Belgium 1969; Grand Prix Granville de l'Humour Noir, Paris, 1975; First Prize, *Torre d'Anspetto*, Milan, 1978. Agents: Galleria Bonaparte, Via Moskova 58, Milan; and Galerie Marion Meyer, 15 rue Guenegaud, Paris. *Died* (in Milan) *23 October 1984*.

Individual Exhibitions:

1941	Galerie La Peau de Chagrin, Paris
1946	Galerie des Deux Iles, Paris
1960	Galerie du Pont-Royal, Paris
1961	Galerie Iris Clert, Paris
1962	Graphisches Kabinett, Heidelberg
1963	Galerie de Marignan, Paris
1964	Kunsthalle Netzel, Bremen, West Germany
1968	Galerie J. H. Perrin, Paris
	Galerie Jacqueline Ranson, Paris
	Galerie Valerie Schmidt, Paris
	Galerie Heide Hildebrand, Klagenfurt, Austria
	Galleria Solario, Milan
1970	Maison de la Culture, St. Etienne, France
	Galerie 3 + 3, Paris
	Galerie Hachette, London
	Galleria Ciak, Rome
	Galleria Solario, Milan
1971	Galleria Ghelfi, Verona
	Galleria Pianella, Cantu, Italy
	Galleria Borgonuovo, Milan (retrospective)
	Galerie Armand Zerbib, Paris
1972	Galleria Il Segnapassi, Pesaro, Italy
	Galleria Il Fauno, Turin
	Galleria Ciak, Rome
1973	Galleria La Bussola, Cosenza, Italy
	Palazzo dei Musei, Modena (retrospective)
	Ridotti del Teatro, Carpi, Italy
	Studio Marconi, Milan
	Galleria Il Traghetto, Venice
	Galleria Parquet, Saronno, Italy
	Galleria La Mela Verde, Turin
1974	Galeria Il Salotto, Genoa
	Galleria Il Salotto, Como, Italy
	Galleria A e A, Taranto, Italy
	Studio Arti Visive, Matera, Italy
	Centro Annunciata, Milan
1975	Galleria Eros, Milan
	Galleria La Colonna, Ancona, Italy
	Galleria Rizzardi, Milan
1976	Mood Gallery, Milan
	Galleria Interarte, Genoa
	Galleria Viotti, Turin
	Galleria Naviglio Grande, Milan
	Mood Gallery, Toronto
	Palais des Beaux-Arts, Brussels
	Studio d'Ars, Milan
1977	New Gallery, Catania, Italy
	Galerie Rivolta, Lausanne, Switzerland
	Galleria Il Salotto, Como, Italy
	Galerie Grafica Annunciata, Milan
	Galleria Al'Castello, Milan
	Centro Annunciata, Milan
	Galerie Heide Hildebrand, Klagenfurt, Austria
	Galleria Il Castello, Feltre, Italy
	Galleria Nucleo, Bologna
	Galleria La Tela, Palermo, Sicily
1978	Mood Gallery, Milan
1979	Galerie Prints, Paris
	Galleria Bonaparte, Milan
1980	Jardin de la Paresse, Paris
1981	Bastion Saint-Andre, Antibes, Frances
	Galleria Il Salotto, Como, Italy
	Galleria Viotti, Turin
1982	Galleria Asinelli, Bologna
	Galerie Marion Meyer, Paris
	Galleria Bonaparte, Milan

Selected Group Exhibitions:

1929	*Le Grand Jeu*, Galerie Bonaparte, Paris
1933	*Exposition Surrealiste*, Galerie Pierre Colle, Paris
1947	*Exposition Internationale du Surrealisme*, Galerie Maeght, Paris
1964	*Gag Festival*, Haus am Lutzowplatz, West Berlin
1972	*Humour et Contestation*, Musée d'Art Moderne, Paris
1973	*Maestri del Surrealismo*, Centro Annunciata, Milan
1976	*La Boite*, Musée d'Art Moderne de la Ville, Paris
1977	*Le Surrealisme*, Galleria Le Difference, Milan
1980	*Un Incertain Sourire*, Musée des Arts Décoratifs, Lausanne, Switzerland
1981	*Paris-Paris*, Centre Georges Pompidou, Paris

Collections:

Centre Georges Pompidou, Paris; Musée d'Art Moderne de la Ville, Paris; Museum of Modern Art, Skopje, Yugoslavia; Graphische Sammlung Albertina, Vienna; Palazzo dei Musei, Modena, Italy; Peggy Guggenheim Museum Collection, Venice.

Publications:

By HENRY: books—*Les Abattoirs du Sommeil*, Paris 1937; *Les Mystères de l'Olympe*, Paris 1945; *Les Paupieres de Verre*, Paris 1945; *Les Metamorphoses de Vide*, Paris 1955; *Maurice Henrys Kopfkissenbuch*, Zurich 1955; *Maurice*

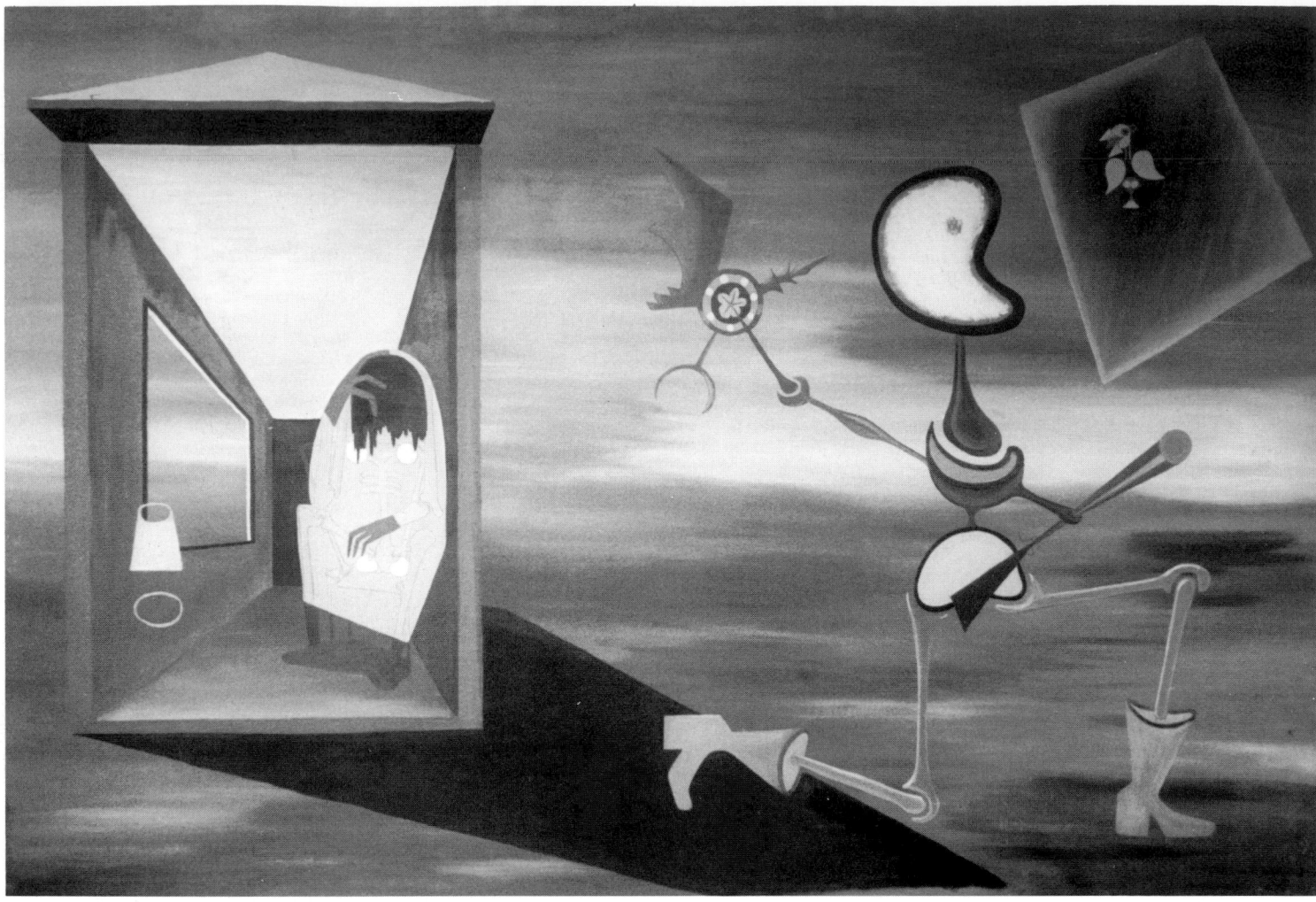

Maurice Henry: *Le Chasseur*, 1951

Henry 1930-1960, Paris 1961; *Les 32 Positions de L'Andro-gyne*, Paris 1961; *Le Moulage de l'Absence*, La Louviére, Belgium 1967; *Points de Repere*, Milan 1968; *Maurice Henry*, Prague 1968; *Hors Mesures*, Paris 1969; *Miniantho-logie*, Paris 1969; *Antologia Grafica del Surrealismo*, Milan 1971; *40 Années de Dessins*, Paris 1973; *Gags*, Paris 1979; *Voyages du Reveur*, Paris 1980; *L'Adorable Cauchemar*, La Louviére 1983; articles—"La Révolte" in *Le Grand Jeu*, Paris 1928; "A Perpetuité" in *Bifur* (Paris), 1930.

On HENRY: books—*Histoire de la Peinture Surrealiste* by Marcel Jean, Paris 1959; *Histoires du Surréalisme et Docu-ments Surréalistes* by Maurice Nadeau, Paris 1964; *Surreal-ism* by Patrick Waldberg, London 1966; *L'Arte Moderna: Il Surrealismo* by Robert Lebel, Milan 1967; *Histoire de Pein-ture Surréaliste* by René Passeron, Paris 1968; *Maurice Henry*, exhibition folder, with text by Renzo Margonari, Mi-lan 1968; *Die Collage* by Herta Wescher, Cologne 1969; *Dada and Surrealist Art* by William S. Rubin, London 1969; *Maurice Henry*, exhibition catalogue, with text by Janus, Turin 1972; *Le Surrealisme* by José Pierre, Paris 1973; *Pièce pour Maurice Henry* by Roberto Sanesi, Pollenza, Italy 1979; *Anthologie du Surréalisme*, Paris 1980; *Dictionnaire General du Surréalisme*, Paris 1982.

I am a surrealist.

—Maurice Henry (1983)

HEPWORTH, (Jocelyn) Barbara.
British. Born in Wakefield, Yorkshire, 10 January 1903. Educated in Wakefield primary schools; stud-ied at the Leeds School of Art, 1919-20, Royal Col-lege of Art, London (sculpture scholarship),

1920-23, and at the British School, Rome, 1924-26: studied carving under Ardini. Married the sculptor John Skeaping in 1925 (divorced, 1931); son: Paul (died, 1953); married Ben Nicholson, *q.v.*, in 1932 (divorced, 1951); children: (triplets) Simon, Rachel and Sarah. Settled in London, 1926, and lived in Hampstead, 1929-39, where Naum Gabo, Henry Moore, Walter Gropius, Piet Mondrian, László Moholy-Nagy, Marcel Breuer and Alexander Calder were neighbours; spent summers in Norfolk with Ben Nicholson, Henry Moore and his wife, and Ivon Hit-chens; Member, 7 x 5 Society, London, 1930-36; Abstraction-Creation group, Paris, and Unit One, London, 1933; lived in St. Ives, Cornwall, 1939 until her death, 1975: owned and operated nursery school and market garden, St. Ives, 1939-45; Co-Founder, with Naum Gabo, Bernard Leach and others, Penwith Society of Arts, St. Ives, 1949. Set and costume de-signer for *Electra*, Old Vic Theatre, London, 1951, and *Midsummer Night's Dream* by Michael Tippet, Royal Opera House, London, 1954. Recipient: Gold Medal, Hoffman Wood Trust, Leeds, 1951; Second Prize, Unknown Political Prisoner Competition, Lon-don, 1953; Grand Prize, *Bienal*, Sao Paulo, 1959; Grand Prix, Prefecture des Alpes-Maritimes, Nice, 1960; Foreign Minister's Award, *Tokyo Biennal*, 1963. Honorary degrees: University of Birmingham, 1960; University of Leeds, 1961; University of Exe-ter, 1966; Oxford University, 1968; London Univer-sity, 1970; and University of Manchester, 1971; Honorary Fellow, St. Anne's College, Oxford, 1968: Senior Fellow, Royal College of Art, London, 1970. Honorary Member, American Academy of Arts and Letters, 1973. C.B.E. (Commander, Order of the British Empire), 1958; D.B.E. (Dame Commander, Order of the British Empire), 1965. *Died* (in St. Ives) *20 May 1975.*

Individual Exhibitions:

1928	Beaux Arts Gallery, London (with John Skeaping and William Norman)
1930	Tooths Gallery, London (with John Skeaping)
1932	Tooths Gallery, London (with Ben Nicholson)
1933	Reid and Lefevre Gallery, London (with Ben Nichol-son)
1937	Reid and Lefevre Gallery, London
1943	Temple Newsam, Leeds (with Paul Nash)
1944	Wakefield City Art Gallery, Yorkshire (travelled to the Bankfield Museum, Halifax)
1946	Reid and Lefevre Gallery, London
1948	Reid and Lefevre Gallery, London
1949	Durlacher Brothers, New York
1950	*Biennale*, Venice
	Reid and Lefevre Gallery, London
	Penwith Society of Arts, St. Ives (with Ben Nichol-son and Victor Pasmore)
1951	Wakefield City Art Gallery, Yorkshire (travelled to the Manchester City Art Gallery)
1952	Reid and Lefevre Gallery, London
1954	Whitechapel Art Gallery, London
	Martha Jackson Gallery, New York
1955	Walker Art Center, Minneapolis (toured the United States and Canada, 1955-56)
1956	Gimpel Fils, London
1958	Gimpel Fils, London
	Leeds City Art Gallery
1959	*Bienal*, Sao Paulo (toured South America)
	Galerie Chalette, New York
1960	Galerie Charles Lienhard, Zurich
1961	Gimpel Fils, London
1962	Whitechapel Art Gallery, London
1963	Gimpel-Hanover Galerie, Zurich
1964	Moderna Museet, Stockholm (toured Scandinavia, 1964-65)

Guidehall, Library and Parish Church, St. Ives
    Cornwall (with Bernard Leach)
1965 Galleria Civica d'Arte Moderna, Turin
    Rijksmuseum Kröller-Müller, Otterlo, Netherlands
        (toured Europe)
1966 Gimpel Fils, London
    Marlborough Gerson Gallery, New York
1968 Tate Gallery, London
1969 Curwen Gallery, London
    Gimpel and Weitzenhoffer, New York
1970 Marlborough Fine Art, London
    Hakone Open-Air Museum, Kyoto
    Abbotsholme, Uttoxeter, Staffordshire (toured the
        U.K.)
1971 Gimpel Gallery, New York
    University of Texas Art Museum, Austin
    Curwen Gallery, London
    Gimpel and Wietzenhoffer, New York
1972 Gimpel Fils, London
    Marlborough Fine Art, London
1973 Marlborough-Godard Gallery, Toronto
    University of Exeter
1974 Marlborough Gallery, New York
1975 Gimpel Fils, London
    William Darby, London
    Marlborough Gallery, Zurich
1976 Royal Botanic Gardens, Edinburgh
1977 Burleighfield International Arts Centre, High Wy-
        combe, Buckinghamshire
    Gimpel and Weitzenhoffer, New York
1978 Scottish College of Textiles, Galashiels (toured Scot-
        land)
1979 Marlborough Gallery, New York
    Marlborough Gallery, London
1980 Yorkshire Sculptural Park, Bretton Hall, near Wake-
        field
1982 Marlborough Fine Art, London
1985 Elizabethan Exhibition Gallery, Wakefield, York-
        shire

Selected Group Exhibitions:

1931 *7 x 5 Society,* London (regularly until 1936)
1934 *Abstraction-Creation: Art Non-figuratif,* Paris
1936 *Abstract and Concrete,* 44 St. Giles, Oxford
1942 *New Movements in Art,* London Museum
1948 *1st International Open-Air Sculpture Exhibition,*
        Battersea Park, London
1953 *Unknown Political Prisoner International Sculpture
        Exhibition,* Tate Gallery, London
1956 *International Sculpture Exhibition,* Musée Rodin,
        Paris
1961 *Recent British Sculpture,* National Gallery of Can-
        ada (toured Canada, Australia and New Zealand,
        1961–63)
1973 *Edinburgh Festival*
1988 *The Non-Objective World Revisited,* Annely Juda
        Fine Art, London

Collections:

Barbara Hepworth Museum, St. Ives, Cornwall; Tate Gallery,
London; Victoria and Albert Museum, London; City Art
Gallery, Birmingham; City Art Gallery, Leeds; Museum and
Art Gallery, Leicester, Manchester City Art Gallery; Scottish
National Gallery of Modern Art, Edinburgh; Art Gallery and
Regional Museum, Aberdeen; Ulster Museum, Belfast.

Publications:

By HEPWORTH: book—*Barbara Hepworth: A Pictorial Autobiography,* Bath 1970; articles—"The Sculptor Carves Because He Must" in *The Studio* (London), December 1932;
statement in *Unit One,* edited by Herbert Read, London
1934; "Approach to Sculpture" in *The Studio* (London), October 1946; illustrated book—*Stone and Flower Poems 1935–
43* by Kathleen Raine, London 1943.

On HEPWORTH: books—*Barbara Hepworth* by William
Gibson, London 1946; *Barbara Hepworth: Carvings and
Drawings* by Alan Bowness, London 1952; *Barbara Hep-
worth* by A. M. Hammacher, London 1958; *Barbara Hep-*

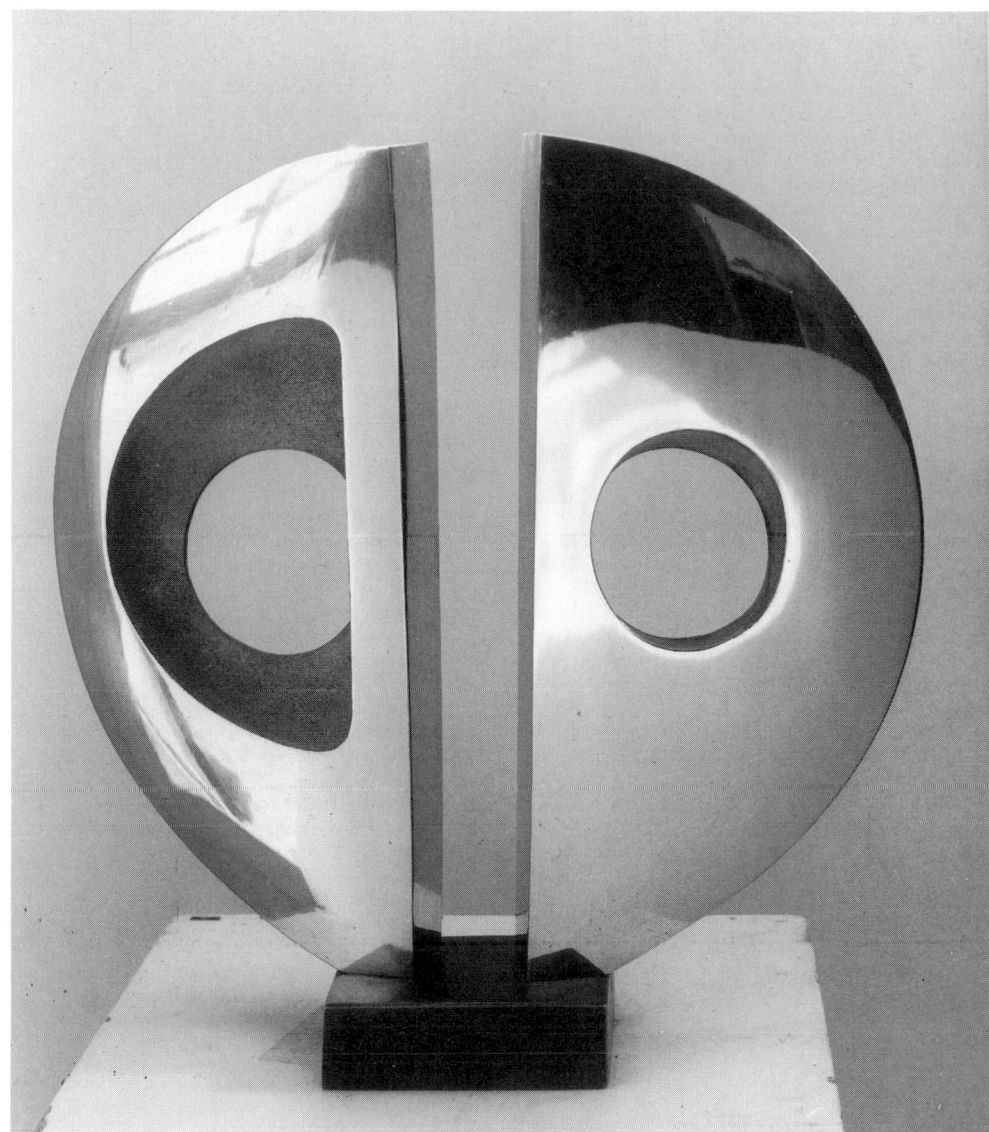

Barbara Hepworth: *Maquette for Divided Circle,* 1969 Courtesy Gimpel Fils, London

worth: Life and Work by J. P. Hodin, London 1961; *Barbara
Hepworth* by Michael Shepherd, London 1963; *Barbara
Hepworth: Drawings from a Sculptor's Landscape,* London
1966; *Barbara Hepworth* by A. M. Hammacher, London
1968; *Barbara Hepworth* by Alan Bowness, London 1971;
Barbara Hepworth, exhibition catalogue with foreword by
Gillian Spencer, Wakefield 1985; films—*Figure in Landscape*
by Dudley Shaw Ashton, British Film Institute, 1953; *Bar-
bara Hepworth* by John Reed, BBC Television, 1961; *This
Week in Britain: Barbara Hepworth* by Warren Forma, television, Central Office of Information, London 1964; *Barbara
Hepworth,* produced by John Reed, London, 1970.

Barbara Hepworth attended the Leeds School of Art
at the same time as Henry Moore and went on to the
Royal College of Art, after which their paths diverged. They were both involved in the new currents
from the Continent. Hepworth went to Italy in 1924,
where she became most interested in Romanesque
and early Renaissance sculpture. Though there was a
dearth of teachers, direct carving attracted her, and
she had the luck to study the techniques of marble
with Ardini in Rome. She began to develop, and in
her works of the 1920's there is a spare economy of
outline in the simplified treatment of stone and hardwood figures. Visits to France, where she met Picasso, Braque and other leading artists, had a
profound effect, and later she paid tribute to the impact that Brancusi and his work in progress made
upon her. She joined the Abstraction-Creation group
in Paris in 1933.

Then, though a reference to the human body might

be inserted in her forms, they were totally non-
objective in shape. Relationships of an abstract character with delicate differences in weight became
frequent in two-piece concepts. Her command of subtle perfecting of surface and form gave a premonition
of her future maturing. When leading abstractionists
Mondrian, Moholy-Nagy and Gabo came to live near
her in England, she found the intellectual contacts
stimulating and encouraging.

After moving to Cornwall in 1939, she neglected
sculpture for a few years. On her return to carving
she evolved a more geometrical system based on
crystalline structure. Precise shapes were hollowed
from the interior of the mass, and the several planes
were coloured in shades complementary to the light
following the contours. Her consciousness was pervaded by the landscape around St. Ives, so that in
many of the works enclosures of space and light in
arcs reflect her identification with the distinctive environment. This diffusion of the light is indicated by
the wood sculptures, usually of monolithic upright-
ness, deeply valleyed and penetrated with cavities like
the erosion of tide-washed caves. The natural tensions
and rhythmic curvature of growing trees are echoed in
the subtly shadowed depths of the carvings.

Allusive suggestions of people appear in "Group I
(Concourse)" (1951), recalling a first visit to Venice.
A visit to Greece in 1954 gave her a tremendous up-
lift, evident in her wood carvings, and within two
years she had began to work in metal with increasing
virtuosity. Modelling first in plastic and also casting
from earlier carvings created a successful range to

her bronzes, some, like the massive "Four-Square Walk-Through" of 1962, creating an architectonic enclosure of space.

Primarily Barbara Hepworth was a carver, and in her last decade she produced works of delicate tactile appeal, several of them abstract in meaningful juxtapositions and of sensuous impact in their chiselling of surface and angled voids. She sought continuously in sculpture to create equivalents for humanity. Formalized and abstract, they are evident to a superlative degree in some of her later carvings and in the upright shapes titled "Mehir."

—G. S. Whittet

HERON, Patrick.

British. Born in Leeds, Yorkshire, 30 January 1920. Educated in St. Ives, Cornwall; studied part-time at the Slade School of Fine Art, London, 1937–38. Conscientious objector during World War II. Married Delia Reiss in 1945 (died, 1979); children: Katherine and Susanna. Painter: designer for Cresta Silks, London, 1935–39, 1944–50; assistant to the potter Bernard Leach, St. Ives, 1944–45; Art Critic for the *New Statesman* and *New English Weekly,* London, 1945–50; London Correspondent for *Arts Magazine,* New York, 1955–58; settled in St. Ives, 1956. Lecturer in Painting, Central School of Arts and Crafts, London, 1953–56; Doty Lecturer, College of Fine Arts, University of Texas at Austin, 1978. Trustee, Tate Gallery, London, since 1980. Recipient: Grand Prize, *John Moores Exhibition,* Liverpool, 1959; Silver Medal, *Bienal,* Sao Paulo, 1965. C.B.E. (Commander, Order of the British Empire), 1977. Agent: Waddington Galleries, 2 Cork Street, London X1X 1PA. Address: Eagles Nest, Zennor, St. Ives, Cornwall, England.

Individual Exhibitions:

1947	Redfern Gallery, London
	Downing's Bookshop, St. Ives, Cornwall
1948	Redfern Gallery, London
1950	Bristol City Art Gallery
	Redfern Gallery, London
1952	Wakefield City Gallery, Yorkshire (toured the U.K.)
1953	*Bienal,* Sao Paulo (toured South America)
	Lady Margaret Hall, Oxford
1954	Redfern Gallery, London
1955	Simon Quinn Gallery, Huddersfield, Yorkshire
1956	Redfern Gallery, London
1958	Redfern Gallery, London
1959	Waddington Galleries, London
1960	Bertha Schaefer Gallery, New York
	Waddington Galleries, London
1960	Bertha Schaefer Gallery, New York
	Waddington Galleries, London
1962	Grinnell College, Iowa
	Bertha Schaefer Gallery, New York
1963	Galerie Charles Lienhard, Zurich
	Waddington Galleries, London
1964	Waddington Galleries, London
1965	Hume Tower, Edinburgh (with Bryan Wynter)
	Waddington Galleries, London (with Bryan Wynter and Roger Hilton)
	Bertha Schaefer Gallery, New York
	Bienal, Sao Paulo
1967	Dawson Gallery, Dublin
	Waddington Galleries, London
	Richard Demarco Gallery, Edinburgh
	Kunstnernes Hus, Oslo
1968	Waddington Galleries, London
	Museum of Modern Art, Oxford
	Bear Lane Gallery, Oxford
	Park Square Gallery, Leeds, Yorkshire
1970	Waddington Galleries, London
	Waddington Fine Arts, Montreal
	Rudy Komon Gallery, Sydney (toured Australia)
	Mazelow Gallery, Toronto
	Harrogate Festival of the Arts and Sciences, Yorkshire
1972	Whitechapel Art Gallery, London
1973	Waddington Galleries, London
	Midland Art Centre, Birmingham
	Hester van Royen Gallery, London
	Bonython Gallery, Paddington, New South Wales
	Compendium Galleries, Birmingham
1974	Skinner Galleries, Perth, Western Australia
	Prints on Prince Street, New York
1975	Waddington Galleries II, London
	Rutland Gallery, London
	Festival of Bath
1977	Waddington Galleries, II, London
	Galerie Le Balcon des Arts, Paris
1978	*Paintings by Patrick Heron,* University of Texas at Austin
1979	Waddinton Galleries II, London
	Oriel Gallery, Cardiff
1981	Riverside Studios, London
1983	Wassington Galleries, London
1984	Abbot Hall Gallery, Kendal, Cumberland
1985	Arcade Gallery, Harrogate, Yorkshire
	Art Gallery, Newlyn, Cornwall
	Barbican Art Gallery, London

Slected Group Exhibitions:

1949	*Salon de Mai,* Paris
1950	*Aspects of British Art,* Institute of Contemporary Arts, London
1959	*11 British Painters,* Jefferson Place Gallery, Washington, D.C.
1961	*Pittsburgh International,* Carnegie Institute, Pittsburgh
1962	*British Art Today,* San Fransicso Museum of Art (toured the United States)
1967	*Recent British Painting,* Tate Gallery, London
1970	*British Painting and Sculpture 1960–1970,* National Gallery, Washington, D.C.
1973	*Henry Moore to Gilbert and George,* Palais des Beaux-Arts, Brussels
1977	*British Painting 1952–77,* Royal Academy of Art, London

Collections:

Tate Gallery, London; Victoria and Albert Museum, London; British Museum, London; Boymans van Beuningen Museum, Rotterdam; Brooklyn Museum, New York; Albright-Knox Art Gallery, Buffalo, New York; Museum of Fine Arts, Montreal; Vancouver Art Gallery; National Gallery of Western Australia, Perth; National Gallery of Queensland, Brisbane.

Publications:

By HERON: books—*Vlaminck: Paintings 1900–1945,* London 1947; *Ivon Hitchens,* London 1953; *The Changing Forms of Art,* London and New York 1958; *Braque,* London 1958; *The Shape of Colour,* London 1973; *The Colour of Colour,*

Patrick Heron: *Emerald in Dark Red with Violet and Blue,* 1972

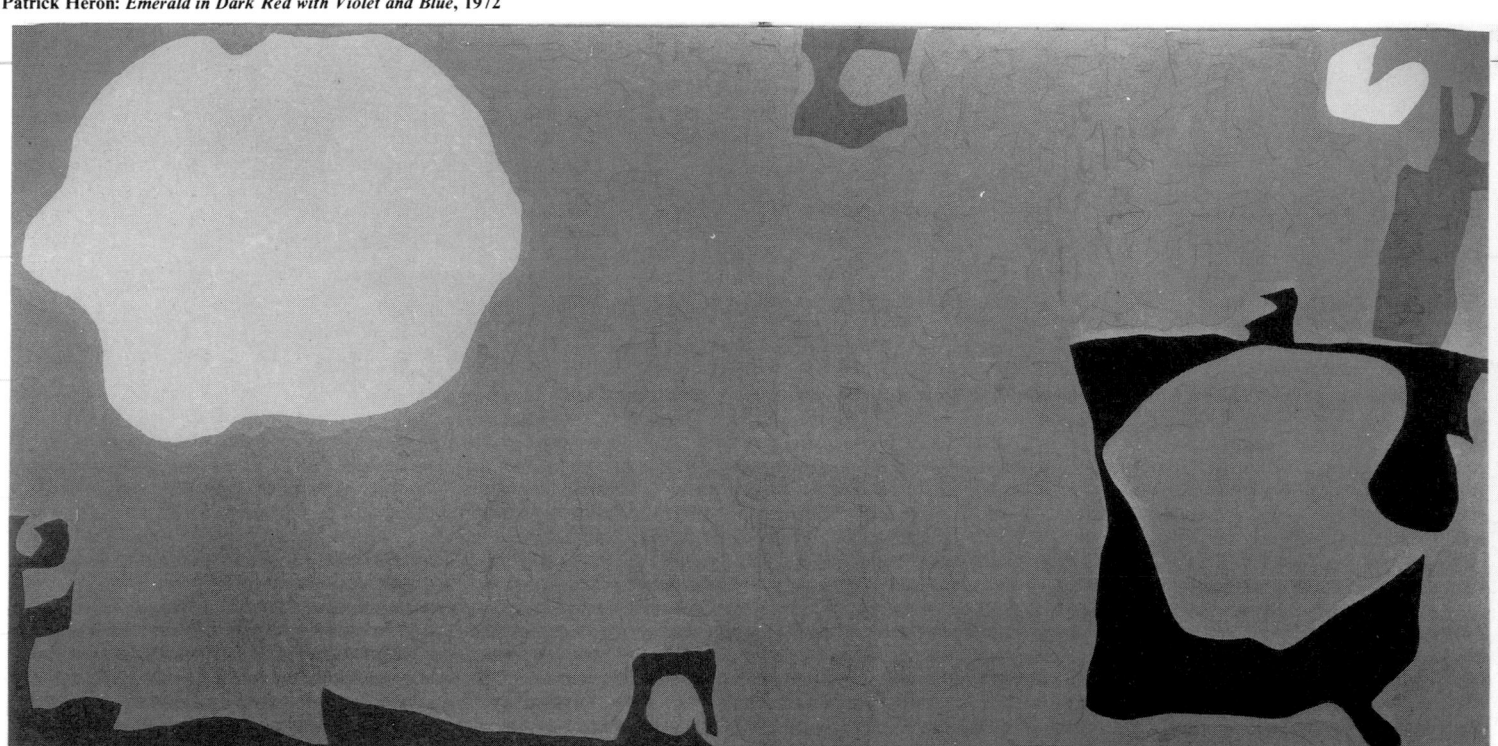

1978; articles—introduction to *Space in Colour*, exhibition catalogue, London 1953; "Americans at the Tate" in *Arts Magazine* (New York), March 1956; "5 Americans" in *Arts Magazine* (New York), May 1958; "A Quote on My Painting: 1962" in *Patrick Heron*, exhibition catalogue, Zurich 1963; "Bonnard in 1966" in *Bonnard*, exhibition catalogue, London 1966; "The Ascendancy of London in the 60's" in *Studio International* (London), December 1966; "A Kind of Cultural Imperialism" in *Studio International* (London), February 1968; "Colour in My Painting: 1969" in *Studio International* (London), December 1969; "Two Cultures" in *Studio International* (London), December 1970; "Murder of the Art Schools" in *The Guardian* (London), 12 October 1971; "Colour and Abstraction in the Drawings of Bonnard" in *Bonnard: Drawings from 1893-1946*, exhibition catalogue, New York 1972; "Notes on My Painting: 1953-1972" in *Perception: The Shape of Colour II*, exhibition catalogue, London 1972, Birmingham 1973; "The Shape of Colour" in *Studio International* (London), February 1974, reprinted in *Concerning Contemporary Art: The Power Lectures 1968-1973*, edited by Bernard Smith, Oxford 1975; "Art in Danger" in *The Observer* (London), May 1974; "The British Influence in New York" in *The Guardian* (London), 10, 11 and 12 October 1974; interview, with James Faure Walker and Brandon Taylor, in *Artscribe* (London), no. 2, 1976; "Notes on My Painting 1953-1973" and "Writings on Other Painters" in *Paintings by Patrick Heron*, exhibition catalogue, Austin, Texas 1978.

On HERON: books—*Paintings by Patrick Heron*, exhibition catalogue, by R. C. Kenedy, Alan Bowness and others, Austin, Texas 1978 (includes bibliography); *Patrick Heron*, exhibition catalogue with foreword by John Hoole, London 1985; article—"Patrick Heron" by Marina Vaizey in *Arts Review* (London), July 1972.

HESSE, Eva.

American. Born in Hamburg, Germany, 11 January 1936; emigrated with family to the United States in 1939; later became naturalized. Studied at the Pratt Institute, New York, 1952-53; Art Students' League, New York 1953; Cooper Union, New York, 1954-57; Yale University, New Haven, Connecticut, under Josef Albers, 1959. Married Tom Doyle in 1962 (separated, 1966). Lived in Kettwig, West Germany, 1964-65; returned to New York, 1965; travelled to Mexico, 1969. Lecturer, School of Visual Arts, New York, 1968-70. Recipient: Yale Norfolk Fellowship, 1957. *Died (in New York) 29 May 1970.*

Individual Exhibitions:

1963   Allan Stone Gallery, New York
1965   Kunstverein für die Rhein und Westfalen, Dusseldorf
1968   Fischbach Gallery, New York
1970   Fischbach Gallery, New York
1971   School of Visual Arts, New York
1972   Detroit Institute of Arts
        Guggenheim Museum, New York (toured the United States)
1974   Mayor Gallery, London
1977   Droll Kolbert Gallery, New York
1979   Whitechapel Arts Gallery, London (travelled to Rijksmuseum Kröller-Müller, Otterlo, Netherlands, and the Kestner Gesellschaft, Hannover, West Germany)

Selected Group Exhibitions:

1961   *International Watercolor Biennial*, Brooklyn Museum
1963   *Gallery Group*, Amel Gallery, New York
1964   *Winterausstellung*, Kunstverein, Dusseldorf
1966   *Abstract Inflationists and Stuffed Expressionists*, Graham Gallery, New York
1968   *Directions 1: Options*, Art Institute, Milwaukee (travelled to Museum of Contemporary Art, Chicago)

1969   *Anti-illusion: Procedures, Materials*, Whitney Museum, New York
        When Attitudes become Form, Kunsthalle, Berne (toured Europe)
1970   *New Media: New Methods*, Museum of Modern Art, New York
1985   *Transformations in Sculpture*, Guggenheim Museum, New York

Collections:

Guggenheim Museum, New York; Museum of Modern Art, New York; Whitney Museum, New York; Art Institute, Milwaukee; Aldrich Museum, Ridgefield, Connecticut; Allen Memorial Museum, Oberlin College, Ohio; National Gallery of Australia, Canberra; Tate Gallery, London.

Publications:

By HESSE: articles—letter in *Artnews* (New York), November 1963; statement in *Art in Process 4*, exhibition catalogue, New York 1969; letter in *Sol LeWitt*, exhibition catalogue. The Hague 1970; "An Interview with Eva Hesse," with Cindy Nemser, in *Artforum* (New York), May 1970; "Eva Hesse: Last Words" in *Artforum* (New York), November 1972; "Excerpts from Her Notebooks" in *Eva Hesse*, exhibition catalogue, London 1979.

On HESSE: books—*Eva Hesse*, exhibition catalogue, New York 1972; *Eva Hesse* by Lucy Lippard, New York 1976 (includes bibliography); *Eva Hesse*, exhibition catalogue, by Nicholas Serota, London 1979; articles—"Eccentric Abstraction" by Lucy Lippard in *Art International* (Lugano, Switzerland), November 1966; "Paragraphs in Conceptual Art" by Sol LeWitt in *Artforum* (New York), Summer 1967; "Eros Presumptive" by Lucy Lippard in *Minimal Art: A Critical Anthology*, edited by Gregory Battcock, New York 1968; "Eva Hesse: The Circle" by Lucy Lippard in *Art in America* (New York), May/June 1971; "Eva Hesse: Post Minimalism into Sublime" by Robert Pincus-Witten in *Artforum* (New York), November 1971.

*

Eva Hesse's untimely death in 1970 cut short an enormously promising career. Within only five years she had established herself as one of the most innovative sculptors of her generation. The strength of her work (which has been a source of strength for many women artists) lay in her courage not to do what was expected of her given the conventions she was working with, particularly when those conventions had no time for "personal" values in sculpture, let alone female values. Working out of minimalist discourse she subjected its codes (serial order, modular repetition, anonymity) to a personal, if publicly undisclosed, feminism. Hesse in a sense gave minimalism the benefit of those areas of experience (memory, sexuality) which minimalism had foreclosed by its idealism, its desire to be non-illusionistic, to create, or rather produce, real and verifiable objects-in-themselves. The openness of her work (a cliché now, perhaps, but then a real challenge to the technocratic bias of sculpture) gave primary value to areas of women's experience; here was a woman sculptor making sculpture about those very things which the women's movement had revalued: self-awareness, intuition, those things that today make up the overworked slogan the "personal is political." Hesse's work has had a profound influence on the development of sculpture during the 1970's. The view that modernist discourse was transgender, was shaped above such considerations as sexual difference, so strong in sculpture with its prizing of traditional male values—grandeur, monumentality—has in no small part been broken down by Hesse's influence.

Hesse's mature work can be divided into three periods: the objects made in 1965-66, with their overtly bodily references (testicular, penile, ovular); the matrixes of the following two years; and the large scale installations (the hanging rope piece "Untitled" and the fibreglass floor piece "Untitled") of 1970. As Rosalind Krauss has said, our awareness of the gravitational field of the work (the gravitational field which separates painting from sculpture) is always

shifting. Pieces stretch from the ceiling to the floor, are suspended from wall to wall; objects are given armatures, propped against walls (in the then current style). Much of minimalist thinking was concerned with breaking down the boundaries between the "painted object" and sculpture. Hesse's own concern with breaking down this distinction was in no sense an intellectual stand (as it was for McCracken and Morris) but a directly emotional one, a call to association. Hesse's sculptures are dream-objects, a collocation of personal and cultural effects: the memory of her "lost" German nationality, the childhood memories of strange objects found in attics, box-rooms and sheds, domestic work (cooking, tidying up), the "secrets" of nature (cobwebs)—in many ways a revisitation of childhood itself.

These qualities of course rest on her then unorthodox use of materials. Hesse's importance is in many ways attributable to her introduction and imaginative use of "new" processes and materials into sculptural language. Her innovatory use of latex to build up forms layer by layer and as a way of covering found objects are now well established studio processes. Up till then latex had been used primarily as a substance for mould making. (Ironically—as has been widely reported—her materials have unfortunately been less successful against the passage of time: many of the works are now crumbling.)

Hesse's work represented a decisive shift away from the modernist view that the artist should stick to a signature style. She constantly fought against the safeguards of a "method." As she said in an interview in *Artforum* shortly before her death. "There isn't a rule, I don't want to keep any rules. That's why my art might be so good, because I have no fear."

—John Roberts

HICKS, Sheila.

American. Born in Hastings, Nebraska, 24 July 1934. Studied at Yale University, New Haven, Connecticut, under Josef Albers, 1954-59, B.F.A. 1957, M.F.A. 1959. Married Henrik Schlubach in 1959 (divorced); married Enrique Zanartu in 1965; children: Itaka and Cristobal. Creator of tapestries; has lived and worked in Paris since 1963. Instructor, University of Santiago, Chile, 1968, and University of Mexico, Mexico City, 1962; Lecturer on Thread Exploration, Bath Academy of Art, England, 1964; established Taller-Huaquen Studio, Huaquen, Chile, 1968; worked on wall rugs with M. Nejjai, Rabat, Morocco, 1970; Founder, with Luis Barragan, Taller-Los Bravos, Valle de Bravo, Mexico, 1972; Chief Editor, *American Fabrics and Fashion* magazine, New York, 1980-83. Recipient: Fulbright Scholarship, 1957; Fribourg Grant, 1959; Gold Medal, American Institute of Architects, 1974; Silver Medal, Academie d'Architecture, Paris, 1986. Fellow, American Crafts Council, 1983. Agents: Carmen Martinez Gallery, 12 rue Roi de Sicile, 75001 Paris; Galerie Cora de Vries, Keizersgracht 516, 1017 Amsterdam. Address: 3 bis Coeur de Rohan, 75006 Paris, France.

Individual Exhibitions:

1958   Museum of Fine Arts, Santiago, Chile
1959   Galeria Galiera, Buenos Aires
1961   Galeria Antonio Souza, Mexico City
1963   Art Institute of Chicago
        Knoll Associates, Chicago
1964   Kunstgewerbemuseum, Stuttgart
        Knoll International, Hamburg (toured Germany and Switzerland)
1965   Interiors International, London
1966   Artek Gallery, Helsinki
        N.K. Inredning, Stockholm
        Interiors International, Stuttgart

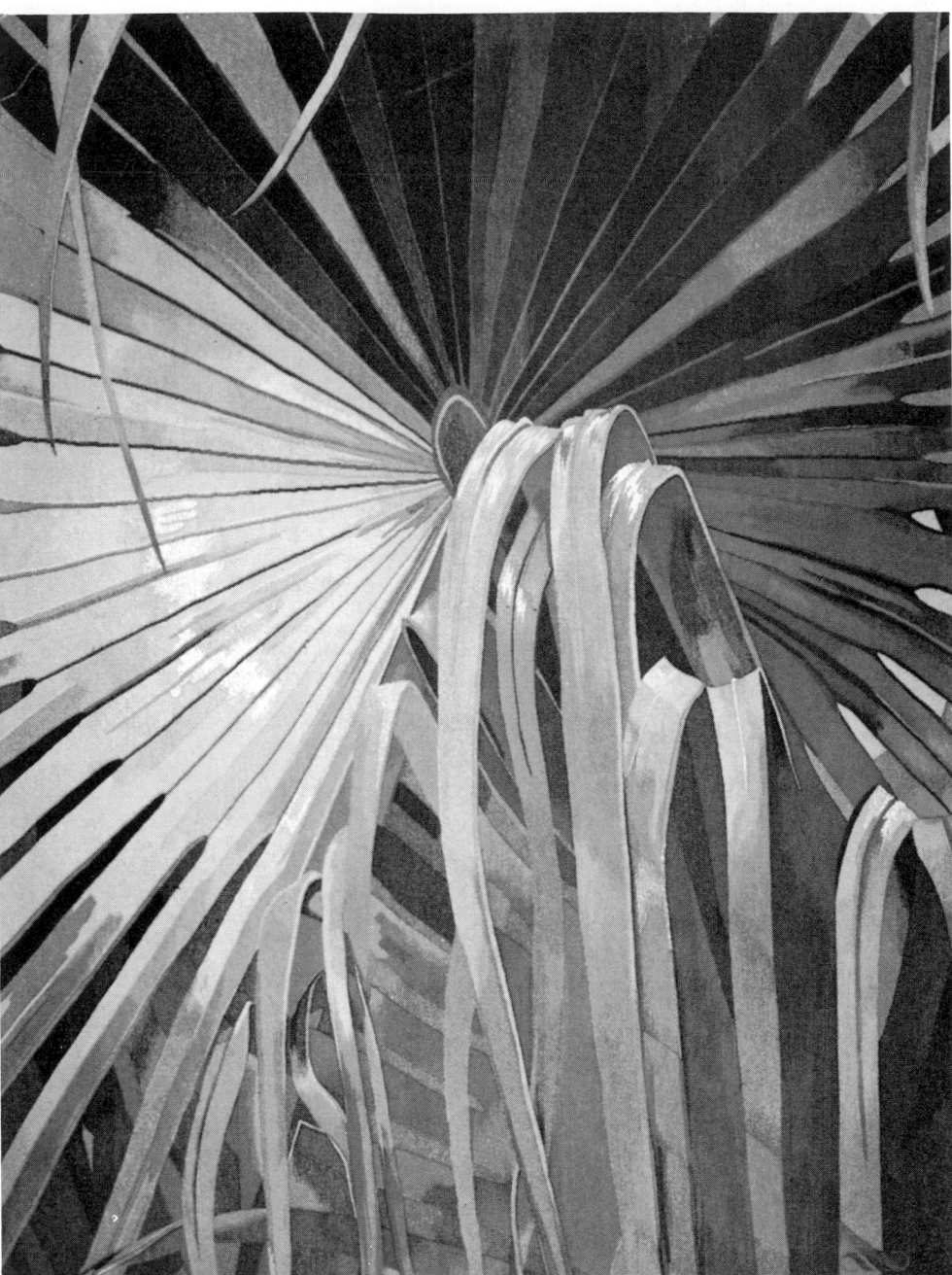

Sheila Hicks: *Le Palmier*, 1985

quarters, New York; Georg Jensen Center for Advanced Design, New York; Museum of Contemporary Crafts, New York; Art Institute of Chicago; Musée des Arts Décoratifs, Paris; Landesmuseum, Oldenburg, West Germany; Kunstgewerbemuseum, Zurich; Kunstgewerbemuseum, Stuttgart; Museo de Bellas Artes, Santiago.

Publications:

By HICKS: book—*Tecnicas Textiles Andinas*, exhibition catalogue, Santiago, Chile 1958; article—essay in *Claire Zeisler: A Retrospective*, exhibition catalogue, Chicago, 1980.

On HICKS: books—*The American Tapestry* by Ruth Kaufmann, New York 1968; *La Nouvelle Tapisserie*, by André Kuenzi, Geneva 1973; *Beyond Craft: The Art Fabric* by Mildred Constantine and J. L. Larsen, New York 1973; *Sheila Hicks* by Monique Levi-Strauss, London 1974; *Handmade in America* by Barbaralee Diamonstein, New York 1983.

Taken up during the 1950's with what Albers calls "the lack of connection between physical facts and psychic effects," I painted, and I even wove. At that period, I undertook to study pre-Inca textiles in South America, to go back to the sources of American tapestry. A long stay in Mexico increased the interest in architecture I already had.

When I was settling in Paris in 1963, my ideas became more clearly defined, because I was able to compare them to those which inspired the Gobelin school. Going over all my experiments, I concluded that if a painter does paintings, an artist working in thread creates directly from the thread. A sketch, a drawing or a collage may be starting points; but nothing replaces the close relation of the artist with his chosen material. Today my judgement would be less categorical—but I still believe that most discoveries arise during work. A certain lack of authenticity is inherent in a reproduced or second-hand work—hence my preference for original work.

I like to work on a small scale—that of my miniatures, which require neither cumbersome tools nor costly immobilisation. They allow me to elaborate a mode of writing which is at once personal and legible.

I am often tempted to take part in an exhibition, a "ritual," using only works to create an environment or a free space. This necessitates work on a larger scale and implies expenses and difficulties which may be considerable. These ephemeral manifestations arouse in me a sentiment of frustration, for which I try to compensate by making bas-reliefs of tapestry or voluminous hangings designed to intergrate into contemporary architecture with some chance of lasting.

—Sheila Hicks

1968	Art Museum, Jinrichove Hradec, Czechoslovakia
	American Cultural Center, Paris
1969	Benson Gallery, Bridgehampton, Long Island, New York
	Galerie Art Mural, Paris
	Crafts Alliance Gallery, St. Louis
1970	American Library, Brussels
	Galerie Suzy Langlois, Paris
	Franco-American Institute, Rennes, France
1971	Bab Rouah National Gallery, Rabat, Morocco
	Museum of Fine Arts, Brest, France
	Benson Gallery, Bridgehampton, Long Island, New York
1972	Mobilier International, Lyons
	Art Center, Wichita, Kansas
	Krannert Art Museum, University of Illinois, Urbana
	American Cultural Center, Dakar
	National Theatre, Abidjan, Dar es Salam
1974	Stedelijk Museum, Amsterdam (retrospective)
1977	Modern Master Tapestries, Inc., New York
1978	Galerie M. T. Douet, Montreuil, France
1980	Israel Museum, Jerusalem
1986	Konsthall, Lund, Sweden
	Milwaukee Art Museum, Wisconsin
	American Craft Museum, New York

Selected Group Exhibitions:

1963	*Woven Forms*, Museum of Contemporary Crafts, New York
1964	*Gewebte Formen*, Kunstgewerbemuseum, Zurich
1967	*New Acquisitions Design*, Museum of Modern Art, New York
1969	*Perspectief in Textiel*, Stedelijk Museum, Amsterdam
1970	*Formen in Faden*, Galerie Buchholz, Munich
1971	*Contemporary Weaving*, Iowa State University Design Center, Ames
	Experimental Textiles, Camden Arts Centre, London
	Deliberate Entanglements, University of California Galleries, Los Angeles (toured the United States and Canada)
1972	*Objects USA*, Musée d'Art Moderne de la Ville, Paris
1973	*Biennale Internationale de la Tapisserie*, Musée Cantonal des Beaux-Arts, Lausanne, Switzerland (and 1975, 1977)

Collections:

Museum of Modern Art, New York; Ford Foundation Head-

Sheila Hicks, since the early 1960's, has continued to explore the expressive potential in fiber forms. A strong fine arts background—she studied with Joseph Albers and Rico Lebrun at Yale University—has accounted no doubt for the emphasis on conceptual concerns and pictorial qualities in her work. Her studies of ancient Peruvian textiles and traditional Mexican weaving techniques were already evident in the first major series of artworks: the miniature woven pieces from the early 1960's. Made on a small weaving frame with heddles of her own design, they contained a wide variety of patterns and slits. "White Letter" (1962), a one color, single yard piece is revealing of her belief in the equivalents of threading/writing, fiber/culturally encoded communications.

By the middle 1960's, the scale of the works increased, and she began to experiment with industrial textile techniques. In Germany, she researched a special electric gun that allowed her to embroider dramatically sculptural wall hangings with heavily tufted sections in high relief. "Red Prayer Rug" (1964) is an example. In 1966 the experience of working in India as a consultant to a textile manufacturer led her to create a new kind of heavy woven fabric in which, using indigenous plain weave techniques, she embedded cotton inside the weaving to add sculptural mass and density. In 1967, working with interior designer Warren Platner and architect Kevin Roche, she executed a major commission for the Ford Foundation Building; a large-scale linen and silk wall piece in natural gray and gold featuring a series of round medallions in plied silks. By the late 1960's, her mastery of the techniques of wrapping is evident in the long cords in the hanging/suspended work "Principal Wife" (1969) and in the floor pieces.

Always sensitive to and even inspired by traditional textile techniques, she produced a striking group of rugs in 1970-71, based on her stay in Morocco, in which the colors as well as the imagery make references to Islamic architecture. Most of her recent work has been taken up with the execution of major public commissions. Stressing relief, bright colors, warmth and light, her fiber forms, whether shaped into a series of vertical cords, disks or horizontal tubes present a sensual visual experience.

"Free Fall", a collaborative project done in 1980 in conjunction with various elements of the Israeli textile community for the Israel Museum in Jerusalem attests to the deep-seated concerns she has for the many cultural implications that can be carried by contemporary fiber forms. In other exhibitions for which she has wrapped objects and even people, Sheila Hicks whilst taking textile art into the provocative arena between sculpture and performance is finding new expressive ground.

—Ronny H. Cohen

HIGGINS, Dick.

American. Born Richard Carter Higgins in Cambridge, England, 15 March 1938. Educated at St. Paul's School, Concord, New Hampshire, 1950-55; Yale University, New Haven, Connecticut, 1955-57; studied music at the New School for Social Research, New York, under John Cage, George Brecht, and Al Hansen, 1957-59; studied English and music, School of General Studies, Columbia University, New York, 1958-60; studied at Manhattan School of Printing, New York, 1960-61; studied English at New York University, 1975-79, M.A. Married Alison Knowles, q.v., in 1960 (divorced, 1970; remarried, 1984); daughters: Hannah and Jessica. Founder, Something Else Press, Vermont, 1964-74; developed "Intermedia" concept, 1965; Founder, Something Else Gallery, New York, 1966-68; taught at California Institute of the Arts, Burbank, 1970-71; moved to West Glover, Vermont, 1971; Founder, with Nelleke Rosenthal, Unpublished Editions, 1972-85 (became Printed Editions, 1978); Fellow, Center for 20th Century Studies, University of Wisconsin at Milwaukee, 1977. Member, Literature Panel, New York State Council on the Arts, 1979-81; moved to Barrytown, New York, 1981; Visiting Clark Professor in Art, Williams College, Williamstown, Massachusetts, 1987. Recipient: New York State Council on the Arts grant, 1968; D.A.A.D. Fellowship, Berlin, 1975, 1981-82; Research Support Grants, Purchase College Foundation, 1984-86. Address: Station Hill Road, Post Office Box 27, Barrytown, New York 12507, U.S.A.

Individual Exhibitions:

1973 Galerie René Block, Berlin
1974 Centro de Arte y Comunicacion, Buenos Aires
      Galerie S: T Petri, Lund, Sweden
      Véhicule Art, Montreal
1976 Museu de Arte Contemprânca, São Paulo
      Galerie Ecart, Geneva
1977 Galerie Ecart, Geneva
      La Mamelle, San Francisco
      Studio Morra, Naples
1978 Galerie Inge Baecker, Bochum, West Germany
      Micro Gallery, Sacramento, California

1979 Franklin Furnace, New York
      C Space, New York
      Galleri Sudurgata, Reykjavik, Iceland
1982 Galerie Inge Baecker, Bochum, West Germany
      Galerie Ars Viva,Berlin
      Gallery A, Amsterdam
1986 Emily Harvey Artworks, New York

Selected Group Exhibitions:

1961 *Hall of Issues*, Judson Gallery, New York
1969 *Telephone*, Museum of Contemporary Art, Chicago
1970 *Happening und Fluxus*, Kölnischer Kunstverein, Cologne
1972 *Data*, Museum of Modern Art, Copenhagen
      Fluxshoe, School of Art, Falmouth (toured U.K.)
1977 *Bookworks*, Museum of Modern Art, New York
1981 *Écouter par les yeux*, Musée d'Art Moderne, Paris
1982 *1962—Weisbaden Fluxus—1982*, Museum Weisbaden
1985 *Kunst in der Bundesrepublik 1945-85*, Nationalgalerie, West Berlin
1987 *Zauber der Medusa*, Kunstlerhaus Wien, Vienna

Collections:

Museu de Arte Contemporanea, Sao Paulo; Collection Hanns Sohm, Markgroningen, West Germany; University Library, University of Exeter, England; Berlinische Galerie, West Berlin; Gallery of Modern Art, Vienna; Sonja Henie-Nils Onstad Foundation, Oslo; Museum of Modern Art, Copenhagen; Staatsgalerie, Stuttgart; Museo Vostell, Estremadura, Spain.

Publications:

By HIGGINS: books—*What Are Legends*, New York 1960; *Jefferson's Birthday/Postface*, New York 1964; *A Book about Love and War and Death, Canto One*, New York 1965; *Towards the 1970's*, Dunkirk, New York, 1969; *FOEW&OMBWHNW*, New York 1969; *A Book about Love and War and Death, Cantos Two and Three*, San Francisco 1969; *Pop Architektur*, with Wolf Vostell, Dusseldorf 1969; *Die Fabelhafte Getrāme von Taifun-Willi*, Somerville, Massachusetts 1970; *Computers for the Arts*, Somerville, Massachusetts 1970; *Fantastic Architecture*, with Wolf Vostell, Millerton, New York 1971; *Eine Zweite Heutliche Deutliche Sprache*, Dusseldorf 1972; *Selected Early Works*, Berlin 1982; *1959/60*, Verona 1982; *Horizons: The Poetics and Theory of the Intermedia*, Carbondale, Illinois 1983; *Intermedia*, Warsaw 1985; *Fourteen Telephone Translations for Steve McCaffery*, edited by Piotr Rypson, Klodzko, Poland 1987; *Pattern Poems: Guide to an Unknown Literature*, Albany, New York 1987; *Five Hear-Plays*, Berkeley 1988; articles—"Two Constellations" in *An Anthology*, edited by Jackson Maclow and La Monte Young, New York 1961; text in *Happenings*, edited by Wolf Vostell and Jürgen Becker, Rheinbeck, West Germany 1966; "3-Day Curry" in *Anekdoten zu Einer Topographie des Zufalls von Daniel Spoerri mit Emmett Williams*, edited by Dieter Rot, Neuwied, West Germany 1969; "Teacher" in *Report to the President and Congress by the Commission on Instructional Technology*, Washington, D.C. 1970; text in *John Cage*, edited by Richard Kostelanetz, New York 1970; "Something Else about Fluxus" in *Art and Artists* (London), October 1972; films—*A tiny movie*, 1959; *The flight of the Florence bird*, 1960; *The flaming star*, 1962; *Invocation of canyons and boulders for Stan Brakhage*, 1962, *Plunk*, 1964; *For the dead*, 1965; *Scenario*, 1968; *Hank and Mary without apologies*, 1969; *Mysteries*, 1969; *Men and women and bells*, 1970.

On HIGGINS: books—*Kampen mod Borgermusikken* by Knud Pedersen, Copenhagen 1973; *Experimental Music: Cage and Beyond* by Michael Nyman, London 1974; *Metamorphosis in the Arts* by Richard Kostelanetz, New York 1980; *Something Else Press* by Peter Frank, London 1983; articles—"Dick Higgins: Jefferson's Birthday and Postface" by Juliet Arning Siragusa in *Collage* (Palermo, Sicily), September 1964; "Dick Higgins: Neo Dadaist" by Hugh Fox in *Studies in the 20th Century*, Troy, New York 1970; "An Analytical Checklist of Books from Something Else Press" by Hugh Fox in *Small Press Review* (Paradise, California), March 1974; "Dick Higgins and the Something Else Press" by Hugh Fox in *Arts in Society* (Madison,Wisconsin), vol. 11, no. 1, 1974; "Dick Higgins" by Richard Kostelanetz in *Twenties in the Sixties*, New York 1979.

I began as a composer, took to composing with words, and found that I had to involve myself with visual design—which involved visual art becoming a large part of what I do. For the last 25 years I have been interested in the interfacing of sounds, words and visual elements—and in the philosophical and social implications of this. For this reason what seems like a very heterogenous involvement is actually far more unified than it appears.

—Dick Higgins

Though Dick Higgin's work may be conventionally categorized as "writing," "theatre," "music," "film" and "book publishing," it is best to regard him as not a specialized practitioner of one or another of these arts, but as a true polyartist—a master of several arts, a specialist in none. Indeed, he is as various as Moholy-Nagy or van Doesburg—to cite two exemplary precursors; and some of his works contribute to two arts at once. In less than 25 years, he has produced a wealth of materials, both large and small, permanent and ephemeral, resonant and trivial. All this diversity notwithstanding, Higgins reveals five fundamental ways of dealing with the materials of each art he explores. These procedures are collage, representation, permutation, aleatory, and expressionism. In nearly all works, one or another procedure (or two) is dominant. Collage, briefly, is the accurate portrayal of extrinsic reality; permutation is the systematic manipulation of limited materials; aleatory is chance; and expressionism reflects personality or personal experience.

It might help to describe a few of his pieces. "7.7.73" (1973) is a series of 899 unique prints of various visual imagery, both abstract and representational, mostly on paper (but also on other materials), with forms repeated from one print to the next; its organizing principles are collage and aleatory. *Amigo* (1972) is a book-length poetic memoir of Higgins' love for a young man. "Danger Music No. 13 (May 1962)" reads in its entirety: "Scream! Scream! Scream! Scream! Scream! Scream!" *Postface* (1962) is a percipient and prophetic critical essay about advanced arts in the early 60's. *St. Joan at Beaurevoir* (1959) is a complicated long scenario that includes such incongruities as Dr. Johnson and St. Joan appearing on the same stage. *Men & Women & Bells* (1959) is a film that incorporated footage made by both his father and his grandfather. I remember it as the best of his films. *FOEW&OMBWHNW* (1969) is a book with four vertical columns across every two-page horizontal spread—one column continuously reprinting critical essays, a second column with poetry, a third with theatrical scenarios (including *St. Joan at Beaurevoir*), a fourth with drawings. Though the experience of reading *FOEW* is that of collage, the book as a whole is, of course, a representation of a multifaceted man.

—Richard Kostelanetz

HILL, Anthony.

British. Born in London, 23 April 1930. Studied at St. Martin's School of Art, London, 1947-49; at Central School of Art, London, 1949-51. Worked on constructional reliefs, 1954; abandoned painting in 1956; organized *Construction: England, 1950-60* exhibition at Drian Galleries, London, 1960; worked on construction screen, commissioned for International Union of Architects Congress, 1961. Lecturer, Regent Street Polytechnic, London, 1955-63. Honorary Research Associate, 1971-72, and since 1972 Visiting Research Associate, Department of Mathematics, University College, London. Recipient: Leverhulme Fellowship, 1971. Address: 24 Charlotte Street, London W1, England

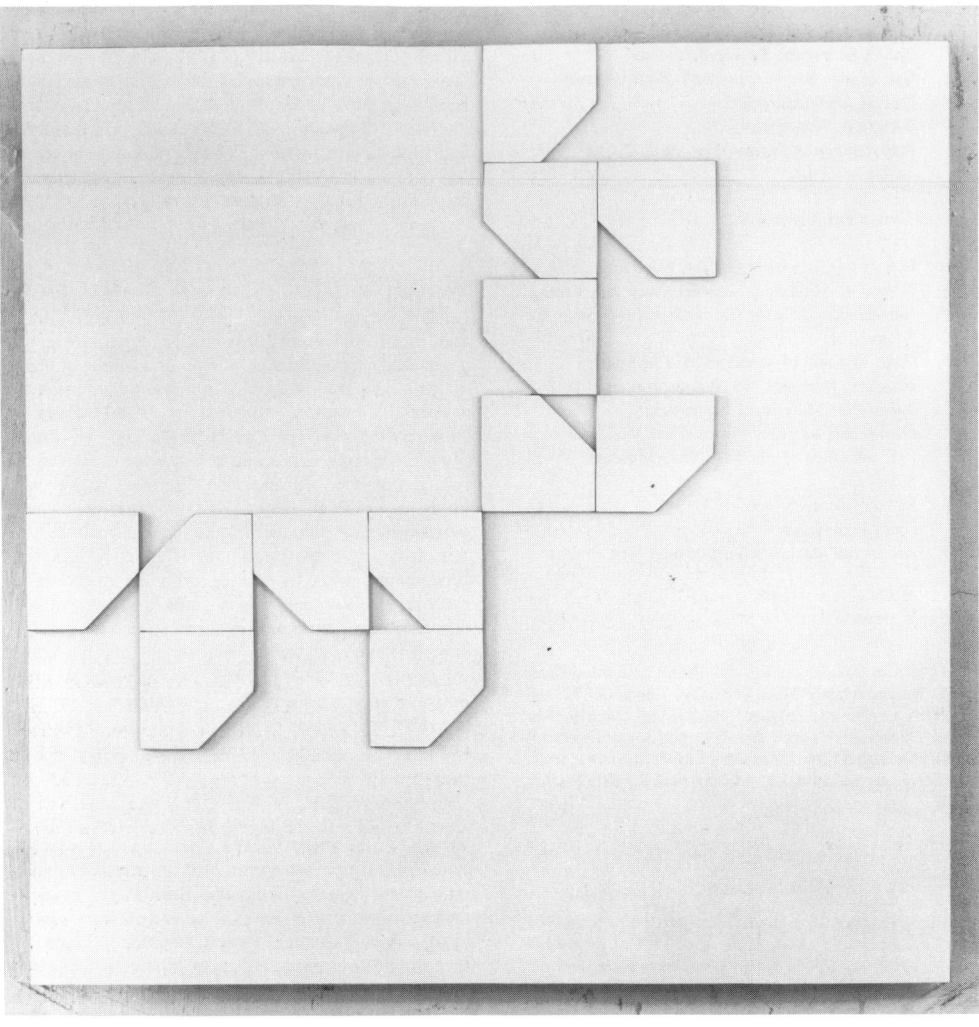

Anthony Hill: *Ingine 7*, 1979

Individual Exhibitions:

1958   Institute of Contemporary Arts, London
1963   Institute of Contemporary Arts, London
1966   Kasmin Gallery, London
1969   Kasmin Gallery, London
1980   Kasmin Gallery, London
1983   Hayward Gallery, London (retrospective)

Selected Group Exhibitions:

1950   *Aspects of British Art,* Institute of Contemporary Arts, London
1956   *This is Tomorrow,* Whitechapel Art Gallery, London
1962   *Experiment in Construction,* Stedelijk Museum, Amsterdam
1968   *Relief: Construction: Relief,* Museum of Contemporary Art, Chicago
1974   *British Art from the Tate Gallery,* Palais des Beaux-Arts, Brussels
1977   *Constructive Concepts,* Musée National d'Art Moderne, Paris
1980   *Pier and Ocean,* Hayward Gallery, London (travelled to the Rijksmuseum Kröller-Müller, Otterlo, Netherlands
1981   *British Sculpture in the 20th century: Part II, 1950-1980,* Whitechapel Art Gallery, London
1984   *English Art 1950-1960,* Serpentine Gallery, London
1986   *Konstruktivisme,* Louisiana Museum, Humlebaek, Denmark

Collections:

Tate Gallery, London; Victoria and Albert Museum, London; Arts Council of Great Britain, London; Whitworth Museum of Art, Manchester; Southampton Art Gallery, Hampshire; University of East Anglia, Norwich; Scottish Gallery of Modern Art, Edinburgh; Louisiana Museum, Humlebaek, Denmark; Tel Aviv Museum, Israel; Musée de Grenoble, France.

Publications:

By HILL: articles—"The Structural Syndrome" in *Module: Proportion: Symmetry: Rhythm,* edited by Gyorgy Kepes, New York 1966; "Constructivism: The European Phenomena" in *Studio International* (London), April 1966; "Structure: Program: Paragram" in *Data: Directions in Art Theory and Aesthetics,* London 1968; "Art and Mathesis: Mondrian's Structures" in *Leonardo* (Oxford), vol. 4, no. 3, 1968; "The Climate of Beiderman" in *Studio International* (London), September 1969; "On Construction, Nature and Structure" in *Structure* (Amsterdam), 2nd series, no. 1, 1969, reprinted in *The Tradition of Constructivism* by Stephen Bann, New York 1974; "The Spectacle of Duchamp" in *Studio International* (London), January/February 1975.

On HILL: books—*9 Abstract Artists: Their Work and Theory* by Lawrence Alloway, London 1954; *The Tradition of Constructivism* by George Rickey, London 1968; *Art Abstrait* by Michel Seuphor and Michel Ragon, Paris 1973; *The Tradition of Constructivism* by Stephen Bann, New York 1974; articles—"Anthony Hill" by Kenneth Frampton in *Studio International* (London), September 1969; "Anthony Hill" by R. C. Kenedy in *Art International* (Lugano, Switzerland), October 1976.

*

An art which uses none of the expected elements—depiction, illusion and "expression"—is in sharp contrast to all other forms of modern art which use the expected but in unexpected ways.

For artists working in this area there are extreme positions, but as yet not more so than in the heroic period, and, although there are marked differences, it is not clear if they are to be taken as advances or mutations in the evolution of a new tradition. The innovators tended to mount radical programs which sought to cover all the issues in propagating a new art, the rhetoric often pitched as if the main goal were an aesthetic revolution to be achieved on a world scale.

Reconvening the extreme innovations at a personal, rather than a collective, level has lead to a new polarising, viz, the over-projective (as in the capitalizing "megalomania" of minimalism) and attempts to find an alternate way, not for working, but for self-evaluation and object evaluation.

This, in turn, will involve the balance between the artist's innate subjectivity and the epistemic bias in a structure orientated art.

—Anthony Hill

*

Victor Pasmore's "conversion" to abstract art shortly after the end of the war is always quoted as signifying the emergence of a new movement of British abstract art. Anthony Hill was 20 in 1950, the year when he first came into contact not only with Pasmore but also with Kenneth and Mary Martin. The Martins and Hill have now for some time been recognized as the chief exponents of British Constructivism—a term which is widely disputed, as the aims and methods of all these artists have variously developed away from those of the great Russian pioneers.

But at the outset of his career Hill could not have been described as a Constructivist even in the loosest sense. At the time of his first exhibition, a group-show at the I.C.A., he was a painter of abstract shapes, often delightfully wayward and dynamic. It was not until 1954 that he turned away from painting and began making constructions. From that moment, with the exception of a two-dimensional work made especially for the Hayward *British Painting 74,* he has worked exclusively in three dimensions. The experience which precipitated his development into an artist of exceptional formal rigour was Charles Biedermann's *The Evolution of Visual Knowledge.* Biedermann expanded an analysis of past art into the proposition that the relief was the only viable form of modern art, thereby implying that both painting and sculpture had become obsolete. Although Hill disagreed with Biedermann on certain significant points, most notably in that he did not accept that the structural process level of reality is the only starting point for non-mimetic art, Biedermann's ideas nevertheless exercised a profound and far-reaching effect on his work. He began to make reliefs, using planes which were either parallel or set at right angles to the wall. For a period Hill restricted himself entirely to orthogonals, but in 1962 he began using angles which were set on the diagonal in plan. As a result his work became more complex, making it imperative for the spectator to view each work laterally as well as frontally.

It was at about this time that Hill first became aware of the problem of symmetry, considered as a mathematical proposition. Since then he has become actively involved in mathematics and has contributed several important papers to international conferences. Meanwhile his art has developed parallel to but quite separate from his work as a mathematician. Perhaps the most striking example of the complexity of Hill's attitude towards life and art is his adoption of an alter-ego, whom he calls Rem Oxford, a contraction of Rembrandt's Dogdhsfoodt. This alter-ego first manifested itself in the *Studio International* issue devoted to Duchamp (Jan/Feb 75). This indulgence in a post-Dadaist fancy, coupled with his work as a graph theorist, illustrate the range of contradictions which make up Hill the artist.

Hill has become known as one of the most stringent and austere practitioners of British formal abstract art. This recognition is on an international level; Hill first visited Paris in the early 50's, where he met Kupka, Picabia, and Vantongerloo, with whom he remained in contact up until the time of his death. But while Hill's reputation is fully deserved, he is also capable of making works which destroy the notion that pure Constructivism is devoid of wit. Although they are always constructed according to the most stringent principles, he possesses an aesthetic sense which ensures that they transcend the limitations implied by a mathematical basis. His most recent work is of such quality that it would seem that its value can only be increasingly recognized in the years to come.

—Fenella Crichton

HILLIARD, John.

British. Born Lancaster, 29 March 1945. Studied at Lancaster College of Art, 1962–64; St. Martin's School of Art, London, 1964–67, Dip. A. D. 1967. Artist and photographer since 1967. Part-time Instructor, Somerset College of Art, Taunton, 1968–71. Part-time Lecturer, Brighton Polytechnic, 1969–76, and since 1979; Associate Senior Lecturer in Painting, Camberwell School of Art, London; Visiting Lecturer in Painting, Slade School of Fine Art, London. Recipient: Visual Arts Fellowship, Northern Arts Association, 1976-78; David Octavius Hill Medal, Gesellschaft Deutscher Lichtbildner, 1986. Agents: Lisson Gallery, 56 Whitfield Street, London W1, England; John Gibson Gallery 392 West Broadway, New York, New York 10012, U.S.A.; and Galerie Durand-Dessert, 43 rue de Montmorency, 75003 Paris, France. Address: 97 Balfour Street, London SE17, England.

Individual Exhibitions:

1969 Camden Arts Centre, London
1970 Lisson Gallery, London
1971 Lisson Gallery, London
1972 Nova Scotia College of Art and Design, Halifax
1973 Lisson Gallery, London
1974 Museum of Modern Art, Oxford
Galleria Toselli, Milan
1975 Lisson Gallery, London
Galleria Banco, Brescia, Italy
1976 Galerie Hetzler + Keller, Stuttgart
Galerie Durand-Dessert, Paris
Robert Self Gallery, Newcastle upon Tyne
1977 Badischer Kunstverein, Karlsruhe
Galerie Durand-Dessert, Paris
Paul Maenz Gallery, Cologne
1978 Galerie Akumulatory 2, Poznan, Poland
Galleria Banco, Brescia, Italy
Studio Paola Betti, Milan
John Gibson Gallery, New York
Lisson Gallery, London
Laing Art Gallery, Newcastle upon Tyne
1979 Ikon Gallery, Birmingham
Galerie Foksal, Warsaw
Galerie Durand-Dessert, Paris
1980 Galerie Max Hetzler, Stuttgart
Lisson Gallery, London
1981 Galerie Durand-Dessert, Paris
Orchard Gallery, Londonderry
1982 Amano Gallery, Osaka, Japan
Ryo Gallery, Kyoto, Japan
1983 Galerie Durand-Dessert, Paris
Kunstverein, Cologne
Kunsthalle, Bremen, West Germany
1984 Kunstverein, Frankfurt
Kettle's Yard Gallery, Cambridge
Institute of Contemporary Arts, London
Galerie Media, Neuchatel, Switzerland
1985 Galerie Grita Insam, Vienna
1986 Provinciaal Museum, Hasselt, Belgium
1987 Sprengel Museum, Hannover
Galerie Durand-Dessert, Paris

Selected Group Exhibitions:

1971 *New English Enquiry,* at the *Bienal Sao Paulo Prospect '71,* Kunsthalle, Dusseldorf
1972 *The New Art,* Hayward Gallery, London
1976 *Arte Inglese Oggi,* Palazzo Reale, Milan
The Artist and the Photograph, Israel Museum, Jerusalem
1977 *Malerei und Photographie im Dialog,* Kunsthaus, Zurich
1979 *Photographie als Kunst 1879–1979,* Tiroler Landesmuseum Ferdinandeum, Innsbruck, Austria (travelled to Neue Galerie am Wolfgang Gurlitt Museum, Linz, Austria; Neue Galerie am Landesmuseum Joanneum, Graz, Austria; and Museum des 20. Jahrhunderts, Vienna)
1981 *Façons de Peindre,* Maison de la Culture, Chalon sur Saone, France
1983 *Kunst mit Photographie,* Nationalgalerie, West Berlin
1985 *Alles Und Noch Viel Mehr,* Kunstmuseum, Berne
1987 *The Other Body,* University of Boston

Collections:

Tate Gallery, London; Victoria and Albert Museum, London; Leeds City Art Gallery; Centre Georges Pompidou, Paris; Musée d'Art Moderne, Grenoble; Musée d'Art Moderne, Toulon; Kunsthalle, Hamburg; Kunsthaus, Zurich; Museum of Fine Arts, Lodz, Poland; Art Gallery of South Australia, Adelaide.

Publications:

By HILLIARD: books—*Elemental Conditioning,* Oxford 1974; *Black Depths, White Expanse,* London 1976; *From the Northern Counties,* London 1978; *Borderland,* Londonderry 1981; articles—"Unpopulated Rural Black and White Exteriors, Populated Urban Colored Interiors" in *Aspects* (London), Winter 1977; "John Hilliard," interview, with Ian Kirkwood, in *Art Log* (London), Summer 1978; "John Hilliard," interview, with Colin Painter, in *Aspects* (London), Autumn 1978; "Drawings (in anticipation) of Photographs" in *Aspects* (Newcastle-on-Tyne), no. 16, 1981; "Inverse Correspondences" in *Furor* (Geneva), no.10, 1983; "Four Works by John Hilliard" in *ZG* (New York), Summer 1984; "John Hilliard", interview with Marlen Schnele Schneyder, in *European Photography* (Gottingen), July 1986.

On HILLIARD: books—*The New Art,* exhibition catalogue, by Anne Seymour, London 1972; *Arte Inglese Oggi,* exhibition catalogue, by Luca Venturi and others, Milan 1976; *Analytical Photography* by Manfred Schmalreide, Karlsruhe 1977; *Fotografie als Kunst/Kunst als Fotografie* by Floris Neusüss, Cologne 1979; *Kunst als Photographie* by Peter Weiermair, Innsbruck 1979; *John Hilliard,* exhibition catalogue with text by Paul Bonaventura, Hasselt 1986; articles—"3 Pieces by John Hilliard" in *Studio International* (London), April 1972; "Artist as Filmmaker" by Annabel Nicolson in *Art and Artists* (London), December 1972; "From Sculpture to Photography: John Hilliard and the Issue of Self-Awareness in Medium Use" by Richard Cork in *Studio International* (London), July/August 1975; "John Hilliard—Scènes Gelées par des Temps Différents" by Regis Durand in *Art Press* (Paris), March 1984; "Schiebung mit offenen Karten" by Jörg-Uwe Albig in *Art* (Hamburg), no. 9, 1986.

HILTON, Roger.

British. Born Roger Hildesheim, in Northwood, Middlesex, 23 March 1911. Family name changed to Hilton, 1916. Educated at Bishop's Stortford College, Hertfordshire; studied under Henry Tonks, Slade School of Fine Art, London, 1929–31, 1935–36; Slade Scholarship, 1931; under Roger Bissière, Académie Ranson, Paris, 1936-39. Served as a commando in the British Army, 1939–45: prisoner-of-war, 1942–45. Married Ruth Catherine David in 1947 (divorced, 1964); one son and one daughter; married the painter Rose Julia Phipps in 1965; sons: Fergus and Bo. Painter, from 1930: lived and worked in London until 1965; settled in St. Just, Cornwall, 1965

John Hilliard: *Sixty Nine,* 1986

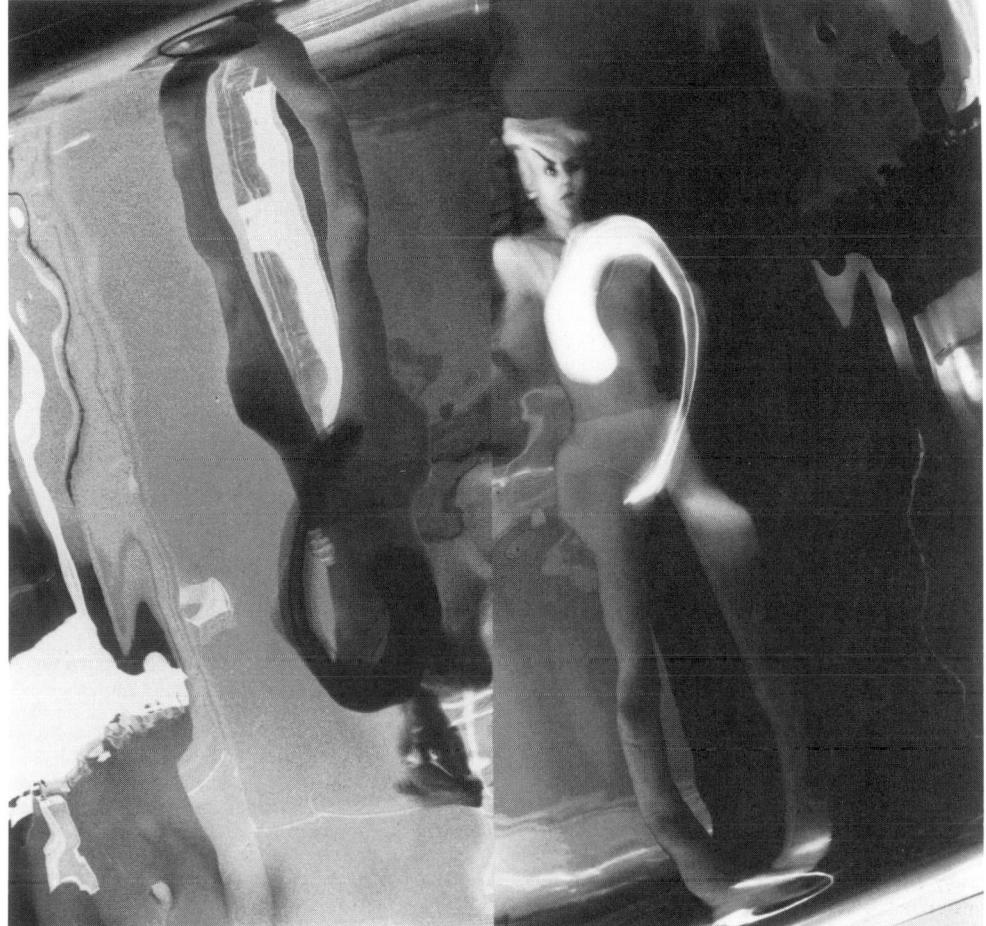

until his death in 1975; due to illness, abandoned oil painting and worked only in gouache, 1972-75. Lecturer in Art, Port Regis Preparatory School and Bryanston School, 1946-47; Lecturer in Drawing and Painting, Central School of Arts and Crafts, London, 1954-56. Recipient: Prize, *John Moore's Exhibition*, Liverpool, 1959, 1963; Unesco Prize, *Biennale*, Venice, 1964. C.B.E. (Commander, Order of the British Empire), 1968. *Died* (in St. Just, Cornwall) *23 February 1975.*

Individual Exhibitions:

1936	Bloomsbury Gallery, London
1951	Gimpel Fils, London
1954	Gimpel Fils, London
1955	Simon Quinn Gallery, Huddersfield, Yorkshire
1956	Gimpel Fils, London
1958	Institute of Contemporary Arts, London
1960	Waddington Galleries, London
1961	Galerie Charles Lienhard, Zurich
1962	Waddington Galleries, London
1963	Waddington Galleries, London
1964	Waddington Galleries, London
1966	Waddington Galleries, London
1967	New Art Centre, London
1968	Arnolfini Gallery, Bristol
1971	Waddington Galleries, London
1972	Park Square Gallery, Leeds, Yorkshire
1973	Compass Gallery, Glasgow
1974	Serpentine Gallery, London
	Waddington Galleries, London
	Scottish Arts Council Gallery, Edinburgh
1976	Wills Lane Gallery, St. Ives, Cornwall (with Denis Mitchell)
	Gruenebaum Gallery, New York
1980	Graves Art Gallery, Sheffield, Yorkshire
1982	Mendel Art Gallery, Saskatoon, Saskatchewan
1983	Waddington Galleries, London

Selected Group Exhibitions:

1937	*Agnew's Coronation Exhibition*, Agnew's Gallery, London
1951	*British Abstract Art*, Gimpel Fils, London
1959	*Recent Paintings by 6 British Artists*, Palacio de Bellas Artes, Mexico City
1960	*British Painting 1720-1960*, Pushkin Gallery, Moscow
1962	*Kompas 2: Contemporary Painting in London*, Stedelijk van Abbemuseum, Eindhoven, Netherlands
1964	*Biennale*, Venice
1967	*Recent British Painting*, Tate Gallery, London

Collections:

Arts Council of Great Britain, London; Tate Gallery, London; Victoria and Albert Museum, London; Ulster Museum, Belfast; Fitzwilliam Museum, Cambridge; Scottish National Gallery of Modern Art, Edinburgh; Walker Art Gallery, Liverpool; Stedelijk Museum, Amsterdam; Museum des 20 Jahrhunderts, Vienna; National Gallery of Canada, Ottawa.

Publications:

By HILTON: articles—statement in *Roger Hilton*, exhibition catalogue, London 1958; "Roger Hilton on Painting" in *Roger Hilton*, exhibition catalogue, London 1974.

On HILTON: books—*Roger Hilton: Paintings and Drawings 1931-1973*, exhibition catalogue, by Norbert Lynton, London 1974; *Night Letters and Selected Drawings* by Rosemary Hilton, London 1980; *Roger Hilton*, exhibition catalogue with essay by George Moppett, Saskatoon 1982; *Roger Hilton*, exhibition catalogue with introduction by David Brown, London 1983.

Roger Hilton is one of the most interesting and enigmatic figures in post-war British art, with closer connections with Paris than most artists of his generation. The influence of the painter Bissière, under whom he studied just prior to the war, remained a permanent feature of his artistic personality; after a tragic period as a prisoner of war, Hilton frequently returned to Paris. Ill health and the effects of drink seriously affected his working life, in which he gained a notoriety for belligerence, yet his remarkably vital spirit, his rich, untrammelled imagination, and the energetic, nervous style of his painting, remained completely unimpaired.

Hilton is frequently bracketed with the St. Ives school of landscape painters, including Lanyon, Heron, Bryan Wynter, who experience and transmit nature into broad abstract themes, in which inventive hieroglyphics represent a personal language of communication. Hilton, however, always displayed characteristics which lifted him beyond this extremely English romantic-mysticism, with its basically simplicist view of nature and art. He was saved, so to speak, by a certain lack of sophistication, so that his art does not rely on thematic generalizations, sensitive colour harmonies, or undisturbed decorations.

Hilton's work contains elements which were often disturbing, and certainly eccentric, a playful childishness in the narrative manner, the unrealistic juxtaposition of the objects and forms, a deeper, more aggressive, more expressionistic quality to the colour. It is not going too far to suggest an element of tragedy, or unbalance, in his work, as a further means of distinguishing it from the predominantly rational philosophy of typical English landscape painting in the modern abstract manner. Furthermore, the drama which Hilton suggested in his work was not a lyrical or narrative drama based on atmospherics, à la Turner or Constable, or its modern equivalent in the sculpture of Moore, Hepworth, and the "lyrical nature" school. Whatever drama was expressed by Hilton came from within and was able to find vivid, communicable expression without recourse to imitating nature.

The complexity of his art was further compounded by an impish wit, with its surprising and daring interbalance between formalism and playfulness. Energy, temperament, nervousness, and perhaps deeper, more intractable, personal qualities, all contributed to an art form which might be described as a mixture of Bissière's sophisticated taste, Klee's inventive wit with its overtones of deep seriousness, plus that strange English quality of surrealistic fantasy. Hilton, indeed, is probably the only English artist who was close in manner and spirit to the American Abstract-Expressionists without actually being influenced or allied with them. He is a figure who will undoubtedly require serious re-evaluation.

—Charles Spencer

HOCKNEY, David.

British. Born in Bradford, Yorkshire, 9 July 1937. Studied at Bradford College of Art, 1953-57, and the Royal College of Art, London, 1959-62. Independent painter, graphic artist and photographer, from 1962, and stage designer, from 1966: worked in London, from 1962, in Paris, 1973-75 and 1979-80, and in Los Angeles, 1964, 1973, and since 1977. Instructor, Maidstone College of Art, Kent, 1962: University of Iowa, Ames, 1963-64; University of Colorado, Boulder, 1965; University of California, Los Angeles, 1966-67; Slade Professor of Fine Art, Cambridge University, England, 1990. Recipient: Guinness Award, London, 1961; Painting Prize, *John Moores Exhibition*, Liverpool, 1961 and 1967; Gold Medal, Royal College of Art, London, 1962; Graphics Prize, *Biennale de Paris*, 1963; First Prize, *8th International Drawings and Engravings Biennale*, Lugano, Switzerland, 1964; Print Prize, *7th International Graphics Exhibition*, Liubliana, Yugoslavia, 1965; Graphics Prize, *First International Print Biennale*, Krakow, Poland, 1966; Gold Medal, *6th Norwegian International Print Biennale*, Oslo, 1982; Award of Excellence, Federal Republic of Germany, 1983; Skowhegan Graphics Award, Maine, 1983; Kodak Photography Book Award, Stuttgart, 1984; First Prize, International Center of Photography, New York, 1985. LL.D.: University of Bradford, Yorkshire, 1983; D.F.A.: San Francisco Art Institute, 1985; D.F.A.: Otis Parsons Institute, Los Angeles, 1985. Associate, Royal Academy of Art, London, 1985. Agent: Cavan Butler, the Pantechnicon, 2 Heathfield Terrace, London W.4., England. Address: 7506 Santa Monica Boulevard, Los Angeles, California 90046, U.S.A.

Individual Exhibitions:

1963	*Paintings with People in*, Kasmin Gallery, London
	The Rake's Progress and Other Etchings, The Print Centre/Editions Alecto, London
	City Art Gallery, Bradford, Yorkshire
1964	Alan Gallery, New York
	The Rake's Progress, Museum of Modern Art, New York
1965	*Pictures with Frames and Still Lifes*, Kasmin Gallery, London
1966	Stedelijk Museum, Amsterdam
	Drawings for Ubu Roi and Cavafy Etchings, Kasmin Gallery, London
	Palais des Beaux-Arts, Brussels
	Studio Marconi, Milan
	Galleria dell'Ariete, Milan
1967	Landau-Alan Gallery, New York
1968	Kasmin Gallery, London
	Galerie Mikro, West Berlin
	Museum of Modern Art, New York
1969	*Paintings and Prints*, Whitworth Art Gallery, Manchester, England
	Andre Emmerich Gallery, New York
	Recent Etchings, Kasmin Gallery, London
1970	Lane Gallery, Bradford, Yorkshire
	Paintings, Prints, Drawings 1960-70, Whitechapel Art Gallery, London (travelled to Hannover, Rotterdam and Belgrade)
	Kasmin Gallery, London
	Andre Emmerich Gallery, New York
	Galerie Springer, West Berlin
	Kestner-Gesellschaft, Hannover, West Germany
1971	*Zeichnungen, Grafik, Gemalde*, Kunsthalle, Bielefeld, West Germany
1972	Victoria & Albert Museum, London
	Kasmin Gallery, London
	Andre Emmerich Gallery, New York
1973	Holburne Museum, Bath, Avon,
	Andre Emmerich Downtown Gallery, New York
	Knoedler Gallery, New York
1974	Kinsman Morrison Gallery, London
	Garage Art, London
	Musée des Arts Décoratifs, Paris
	Dayton's Gallery 12, Minneapolis, Minnesota
	Michael Walls Gallery, New York
	Knoedler Contemporary Prints, New York
	La Medusa Graphica, Rome
1975	Dorothy Rosenthal Gallery, Chicago
	Galerie Claude Bernard, Paris
	European Gallery, San Francisco
	City Art Gallery, Bristol, Gloucestershire
	City Art Gallery, Manchester, England
	Nishimura Gallery, Tokyo
1976	Nicholas Wilder Gallery, Los Angeles
	Sonnabend Gallery, New York
	Laing Art Gallery, Newcastle-upon-Tyne
	Robert Self Gallery, London
	Jordan Gallery, London
	Festival Gallery, Bath, Avon
	National Gallery of Victoria, Melbourne (toured Australia)
	Henie-Onstad Kunstsenter, Oslo (travelled to the Kunstmuseum, Goteborg, Sweden)
	Waddington Galleries, London
	Galeria Juana Mordo, Madrid
1977	Andre Emmerich Gallery, New York

Dorothy Rosenthal Gallery, Chicago
Paintings and Drawings 1961–75, Galerie Neuendorf, Hamburg, West Germany
City Art Gallery, Wolverhampton, Staffordshire
1978 Gallery at 24, Miami, Florida
Drawings and Prints, Waddington Galleries, Toronto (travelled to the Albertina, Vienna; Tiroler Landesmuseum Ferdinandeum, Innsbruck; Galerie Bloch, Innsbruck; Kulturhaus, Graz; Kunstlerhaus, Salzburg; L. A. Louver Gallery, Venice, California
Travels with Pen, Pencil and Ink, Yale Center for British Art, New Haven, Connecticut (travelled to Minneapolis Institute of Arts, Minnesota; Cranbrook Academy of Art, Bloomfield Hills, Michigan; Nelson Gallery and Atkins Museum, Kansas City, Missouri; Hirshhorn Museum, Washington, D.C.; Art Gallery of Ontario, Toronto; Toledo Museum of Art, Ohio; Fine Arts Museum, San Francisco; Denver Art Museum, Colorado; Grey Art Gallery, New York University)
Sudley Art Gallery, Liverpool, Merseyside
1979 Museum of Modern Art, New York
M. H. de Young Memorial Museum, San Francisco
Frances Aronson Gallery, Atlanta, Georgia
Bradford Art Gallery, Yorkshire
Gimpel & Hanover/Andre Emmerich Galleries, Zurich
Britten-Pears School, Aldeburgh, Suffolk
Warehouse Gallery, London
Knoedler Gallery, London
1980 Graves Art Gallery, Sheffield, Yorkshire
Ashmolean Museum, Oxford, England
Laguna Beach Museum of Art, California
Andre Emmerich Gallery, New York
Getler/Pall Gallery, New York
Petersburg Press, New York
Albert White Gallery, Toronto
Knoedler/Kasmin Gallery, London
Tate Gallery, London
Arun Art Centre, Arundel, Sussex
Art and Furniture, Manchester, England
Tyler Graphics, Bedford, New York
1981 Andre Emmerich Gallery, New York
Castelli Graphics, New York
Riverside Studios, London
Galerie Claude Bernard, Paris
Knoedler/Kasmin Gallery, London
Gallery at 24, Miami, Florida
Gallery at 24, Palm Beach, Florida
Galerie Meyer-Ellinger, Frankfurt, West Germany
Ashmolean Museum, Oxford, England
1982 Andre Emmerich Gallery, New York
Christie's Contemporary Art, New York
L. A. Louver Gallery, Venice, California
Photographies 1962–82, Centre Georges Pompidou, Paris
Knoedler/Kasmin Gallery, London
Rex Irwin Gallery, Sydney, New South Wales
Susan Gersh Gallery, Los Angeles
New York Public Library, New York
1983 Andre Emmerich Gallery, New York
Knoedler/Emmerich Gallery, Zurich
Richard Gray Gallery, Chicago
L. A. Louver Gallery, Venice, California
Knoedler/Kasmin Gallery, London
Nishimura Gallery, Tokyo
Bjorn Bengtsson Gallery, Stockholm
Hockney Paints the Stage, Walker Art Center, Minneapolis (travelled to Museo Tamayo, Mexico City; Art Gallery of Ontario, Toronto; Museum of Contemporary Art, Chicago; Fort Worth Art Museum, Texas; San Francisco Museum of Modern Art)
Thomas Babeor Gallery, La Jolla, California
William Beadleston Fine Art, New York
Fotografien 1962–82, Kunsthalle, Basle
Hockney's Photographs, Hayward Gallery, London (toured Britain)
1984 Milwaukee Art Museum, Wisconsin
Prints, Art and Sport Gallery, Brussels
Prints and Drawings, Bjorn Wetterling Gallery, Stockholm
Selected Prints, Knoedler Gallery, Zurich

New Paintings and Drawings, Andre Emmerich Gallery, New York
Photographic Collages, Fraenkel Gallery, San Francisco
Photographic Collages, Greenberg Gallery, St. Louis, Missouri
New Drawings, Richard Gray Gallery, Chicago
Prints and Photographic Collages, Galerie Esperanze, Montreal, Quebec
Photographic Collages, Carpenter/Hochman Gallery, Dallas, Texas
Works on Paper, Patricia Heesy Gallery, New York (with Jim Dine)
1985 *Hockney Paints the Stage,* Hayward Gallery, London
Prints and Photocollages, Greg Kucera Gallery, Seattle, Washington
Photocollages, Andre Emmerich Gallery, New York
Lithos, paintings and collages, Knoedler Gallery, London
Paintings from the 1960's, Andre Emmerich Gallery, New York
Photocollages, State University of New York, New Paltz
New Lithographs and Paintings, Andre Emmerich Gallery, New York
New Lithographs, Nishimura Gallery, Tokyo
New Lithographs, Richard Gray Gallery, Chicago
New Lithographs, L. A. Louver Gallery, Venice, California
New Lithos, Photocollages, Drawings and Paintings, Galerie Claude Bernard, Paris
Photocollages, State University of New York, Albany
Photocollages, College of Santa Fe, New Mexico
Photocollages, Elaine Horwitch Galleries, Scottsdale, Arizona (with Roland Reiss)
1986 *Theatre Sets, Models, Drawings and Etchings,* Contemporary Art Center, Honolulu, Hawaii
Photocollages, Paintings, Drawings, Honolulu Academy of Art, Hawaii
Photocollages, Cibachromes, Polaroids and Prints, Pasadena Art Center, California
Tyler Prints, Harvard University, Cambridge, Massachusetts
Tyler Prints, Tate Gallery, London
Photocollages and Theatre Drawings, Gallery One, Toronto
Photographs by David Hockney, Boca Raton Museum of Arts, Florida (travelled to Davenport Art Gallery, Iowa; Spencer Museum of Art, Lawrence, Kansas; Elvehjem Museum of Art, Madison, Wisconsin; Santa Barbara Museum of Art, California; Toledo Museum of Art, Ohio; Ringling Museum of Art, Sarasota, Florida; Akron Art Museum, Ohio; Snite Museum of Art, Notre Dame, Illinois; Philbrook Art Center, Tulsa, Oklahoma)
Paintings and Photographic Collages, University of California, Berkeley
New Lithos and Mexican Hotel Painting, Andre Emmerich Gallery, Zurich
Self-Portraits, Blum Helman Gallery, New York (with Ellsworth Kelly and Francesco Clemente)
1987 Los Angeles County Museum of Art (travelled to the Metropolitan Museum of Art, New York; Tate Gallery, London, 1988)
Faces 1966–84, Loyola Marymount University, New York
1988 *Photocollages,* Santa Monica Community College, California

Selected Group Exhibitions:

1960 *London Group,* RBA Galleries, London
1963 *British Painting of the 60's,* Whitechapel Art Gallery, London
1965 *London: The New Scene,* Walker Art Center, Minneapolis
1969 *Pop Art Redefined,* Hayward Gallery, London
1975 *European Painting in the 70's,* Los Angeles County Museum of Art
1977 *British Artists of the 60's,* Tate Gallery, London
1981 *Instant Fotografie,* Stedelijk Museum, Amsterdam

1983 *Painter as Photographer,* Camden Arts Centre, London (travelled to Windsor, Berkshire; Bradford, Yorkshire
1984 *Olympian Gestures,* Los Angeles County Museum of Art
1987 *Berlinart 1961–87,* Museum of Modern Art, New York (travelled to San Francisco)

Collections:

Art Institute of Chicago; Arts Council of Great Britain, London; Centre Georges Pompidou, Paris; Los Angeles County Museum of Art; Museum of Modern Art, New York; National Gallery of Victoria, Melbourne; New York Public Library; Stedelijk Museum, Amsterdam; Tate Gallery, London; Victoria & Albert Museum, London.

Publications:

By HOCKNEY: books—*72 Drawings by David Hockney,* New York and London 1971; *David Hockney by David Hockney,* edited by Nikos Stangos, London 1976; *Twenty Photographic Pictures,* portfolio, edited by Sonnabend Gallery, New York and Paris 1976; *Paper Pools,* edited by Nikos Stangos, New York 1980; *David Hockney: Photographs,* New York, London and Paris 1982; *Cameraworks,* with text by Lawrence Weschler, New York and London 1984; *David Hockney on Photography,* New York 1984, Bradford, Yorkshire 1985; *Martha's Vineyard and Other Places,* London 1985; articles—"An Interview with David Hockney", with Peter Fuller, in *Art Monthly* (London), December 1978/January 1979; "A Conversation with David Hockney", with Mario Amaya, in *Architectural Digest* (Los Angeles), September 1980; "Paper Pools" in *Eastern Airlines Review* (New York), September 1980; "The Art World: True to Life", interview, with Lawrence Weschler, in the *New Yorker,* 9 July 1984; "Vogue par David Hockney" in *Vogue* (Paris), December 1985.

On HOCKNEY: book—*David Hockney: Paintings, Prints and Drawings 1960–70,* exhibition catalogue, with text by Mark Glazebrook, London 1970; *David Hockney: Zeichnungen, Grafik, Gemalde,* exhibition catalogue, with text by Gunther Gercken, Bielefeld, West Germany 1971; *David Hockney,* with an introduction by Henry Geldzahler, London 1976; *David Hockney: Prints and Drawings,* exhibition catalogue, with an introduction by Gene Baro, Washington, D.C. 1978; *David Hockney: Travels with Pen, Pencil and Ink,* with an introduction by Edmund Pillsbury, New York 1978; *David Hockney: Drawings and Prints,* exhibition catalogue, by Peter Weiermair, Vienna 1978; *Pictures by David Hockney* by Nikos Stangos, London 1979; *David Hockney* by Marco Livingston, New York and London 1981; *David Hockney: Paintings and Drawings for 'Parade',* exhibition catalogue, with text by Mark Glazebrook, London 1981; *Hockney Paints the Stage* by Martin Friedman and others, Minneapolis and New York 1983, London 1985; *Hockney's Photographs,* exhibition catalogue, with an introduction by Mark Haworth-Booth, London 1983; *David Hockney: Fotografien 1962–1982,* exhibition catalogue, with text by Alain Sayag, Basle and Paris 1983; *David Hockney: Paintings of the Early 1960s,* exhibition catalogue, with an introduction by Nicholas Wilder, New York 1985; *David Hockney: Faces 1966–1984,* exhibition catalogue with essay by Marco Livingstone, New York 1987; films—*David Hockney's Diaries* by Michael and Christian Blackwood, 1971; *A Bigger Splash* by Jack Hazan, 1974; *Hockney at Work,* BBC television film, by Peter Adam, 1980; *South Bank Show: David Hockney,* London Weekend Television Film, by Don Featherstone, 1983.

David Hockney, born in England, has found a home in California. The work he paints is of his new home, as if the paintings were a way of creating that home. Hockney's imagination of Los Angeles has given a special quality to his paintings, most of which are lit with daylight.

The architecture and the people Hockney chooses to portray have a dry, controlled, slowly motive, though largely at rest, quality about them. As with the painting "My Parents," emotions are subjected to inter-related contexts. There is no need for extraneous emotion, though there is a need for factual representation. This factualness, separating Hockney from both representational and abstract painters, describes an imagined and constructed world, of which Los Angeles is an example.

The key to seeing Hockney's work is ignoring, as

he does, the most obvious Hollywood movie symbolism of the area, and instead plunging into a newsworthiness, a *facility* of the image. The paintings therefore function as a form of reification of the L. A. imagination. Hockney is particularly a painter of a city, and a time in a city, so that we like his paintings as we observe L. A. The two are interchangeable. New York and San Francisco and Chicago and Des Moines and Washington, D.C. can see what they like of Los Angeles: the pools, art, boys, glass windows, low desert houses, irrigated and transported sprinkler and shower water.

The boys and men he paints contain the factuality, as discussed, which makes them both at home and, even while involved in appearances of homosexual relations, very approachable. So Hockney's paintings fight the Hollywood course of assumed romantic events. Life then appears before us before it passes. His "Model With Unfinished Self-Portrait" depicts an urban family life, Hockney and lover, as Hockney works throughout the night drawing. Flowers sit still, and only an approach of paint passes through the picture.

Hockney has worked with pulp paper of deep-hued watercolors. Recently he has worked on etchings, colored stage sets and now photographic arrangements of a three-dimensional nature. He went to art school in Bradford. His father was a pacifist, and he was a conscientious objector. In "My Parents and Myself" Hockney emerges as the artist in a mirror which is set in the room, a dressed young man, a mother looking out, the father quietly posed. "A Bigger Splash," of a pool with only the splash observed, the body submerged, leaves the viewer to observe the house, the palm trees, an empty chair.

—John Robinson

HODGKIN, Howard.

British. Born in London, 6 August 1932. Educated in primary schools in London, New York and Wales; studied at Camberwell School of Art, London, under Victor Pasmore, William Coldstream and Claude Rogers, 1949–50; at the Bath Academy of Art, Corsham, under Clifford Ellis, 1950–54. Married Julia Lane in 1955; sons: Louis and Sam. Painter: has visited India frequently since 1967; spent time at the Retreat in Ahmedabad, where he worked on a series of paintings, 1978. Lecturer, Charterhouse School, 1954–56, Bath Academy of Art, Corsham, 1956–66, and Chelsea School of Art, London, 1966–72; Artist-in-Residence, Brasenose College, Oxford, 1976–77. Trustee, Tate Gallery, London, 1973, and National Gallery, London, 1980. Recipient: Turner Prize, Tate Gallery, London, 1985. D. Litt: London University, 1985. C.B.E. (Commander, Order of the British Empire), 1977. Agent: M. Knoedler Gallery, 19 East 70th Street, New York, New York 10021, U.S.A. Address: 32 Coptic Street, London WC1A, England.

Individual Exhibitions:

1962	Arthur Tooth and Sons, London
1964	Arthur Tooth and Sons, London
1967	Arthur Tooth and Sons, London
1969	Kasmin Gallery, London
1970	Arnolfini Gallery, Bristol
	Dartington Hall, Devon
1971	Kasmin Gallery, London
	Galerie Muller, Cologne
1972	Arnolfini Gallery, Bristol
	Galerie Staedler, Paris (with Patrick Caulfield and Michael Moon)
1973	Kornblee Gallery, New York
1976	Tate Gallery, London
	Serpentine Gallery, London (toured the U. K.)
	Museum of Modern Art, Oxford
	Waddington Galleries II, London
1977	André Emmerich Gallery, Zurich (with David Hockney)
	André Emmerich Gallery, New York
1980	Waddington Galleries II, London
	Bernard Jacobson Gallery, New York
1981	M. Knoedler Gallery, New York
	Bernard Jacobson Gallery, New York
	Bernard Jacobson Gallery, Los Angeles
1982	Tate Gallery, London
	Knoedler Gallery, New York

Howard Hodgkin: *Menswear*, 1985

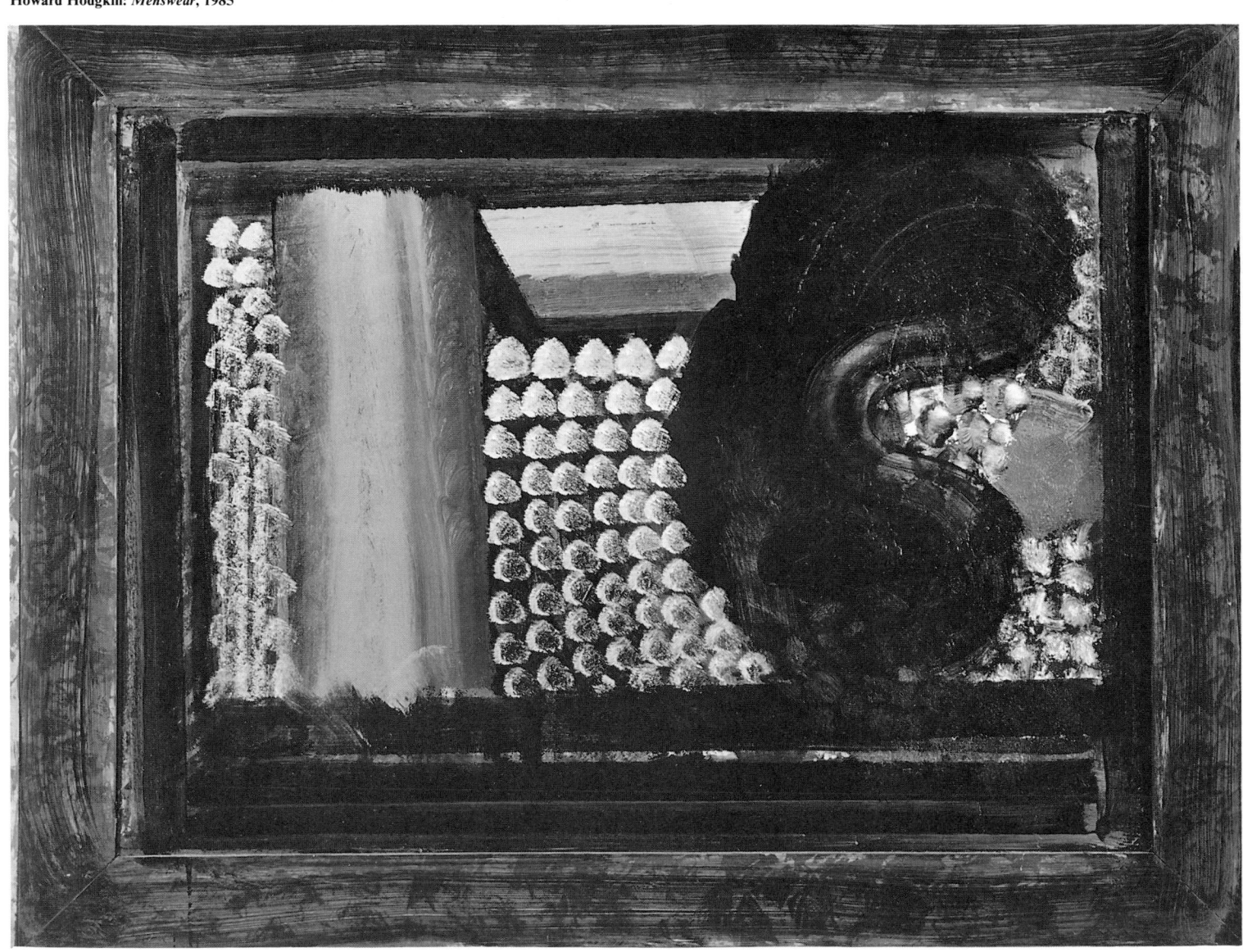

1984 Knoedler Gallery, New York
British Pavilion, *XLI Biennale,* Venice
Phillips Collection, Washington, D.C.
1985 Yale Center for British Art, New Haven, Connecticut
Kestner-Gesellschaft, Hannover
Whitechapel Art Gallery, London
1986 Knoedler Gallery, New York

Selected Group Exhibitions:

1959 *London Group,* RBA Galleries, London
1964 *British Malerei der Gegenwart,* Kunsthalle, Dusseldorf (toured West Germany)
1970 *Contemporary British Art,* Museum of Modern Art, Tokyo
1973 *Le Peinture Anglaise d'Aujourd'hui,* Musée d'Art Moderne de la Ville, Paris
1977 *British Painting 1952-1977,* Royal Academy of Arts, London
1981 *A New Spirit in Painting,* Royal Academy of Art, London
1982 *Aspects of British Art Today,* Metropolitan Art Museum, Tokyo (toured Japan)
1984 *Hard Won Image,* Tate Gallery, London
1987 *British Art in the 20th Century,* Royal Academy of Art, London

Collections:

Arts Council of Great Britain, London; Tate Gallery, London; British Museum, London; Victoria and Albert Museum, London; Louisiana Museum, Humlebaek, Denmark; Sao Paulo Museum; National Gallery of South Australia, Adelaide; Walker Art Center, Minneapolis; Museum of Modern Art, New York; Fogg Art Museum, Harvard University, Cambridge, Massachusetts.

Publications:

By HODGKIN: book—*Indian Drawing,* exhibition catalogue, London 1983; articles—"The Relevance of Matisse", discussion with Andrew Forge and Phillip King, in *Studio International* (London), July/August 1968; "An artist in residence" in *Oxford Art Journal,* October 1978; "Howard Hodgkin", interview with Timothy Hyman, in *Artscribe* (London), December 1978; "How to be an Artist" in *Burlington Magazine* (London), 1982.

On HODGKIN: books—*Howard Hodgkin,* exhibition catalogue, edited by Edward Lucie Smith, London 1962; *Howard Hodgkin: Forty Five Paintings 1949-75,* exhibition catalogue by Richard Morphet, London 1976; *Howard Hodgkin* by Lawrence Gowing, New York 1981; *Howard Hodgkin's Indian Leaves,* exhibition catalogue by Michael Compton, London 1982; *Howard Hodgkin: Forty Paintings 1973-84,* exhibition catalogue with introduction by John McEwen, London 1984; *Howard Hodgkin Prints 1977 to 1983,* exhibition catalogue by Richard Morphet, London 1985.

My pictures are finished when the subject comes back. I start out with the subject and naturally I have to remember first of all what it looked like, but it would also perhaps contain a great deal of feeling and sentiment. All of that has got to be somehow transmuted, transformed or made into a physical object and when that happens, when that's finally been done, when the last physical marks have been put on and the subject comes back—which, after all, is usually the moment when the painting is at long last a coherent physical object—well, then the picture's finished and there is no question of doing anything more to it. My pictures really finish themselves.
—Howard Hodgkin

A possible clue to Howard Hodgkin's strangely individual paintings is his love for Indian miniatures. His paintings are mixtures of reality, memory and abstracted shapes, making up elaborate assymetrical patterns, in strong, decorative colours.

He is a far less sophisticated painter than Hockney

or Allen Jones, the two English artists he most closely resembles. There are an easy, assured, satisfying flow of forms in their work and a knowing, worldly wit in the ironical, wry comments they make about modern life. Hodgkin, on the other hand, seems to be battling with the components of his pictures, wedging the shapes together, whilst the actual imagery and technique have a heavy, if not exactly naive, ponderousness.

He has explained that whilst he always paints from memory, his paintings have to relate to people and their relationships. It is only when working from a given theme that the free associations are able to function, and when completed he becomes aware that they concern intense, subjective recollections. This intensity is well conveyed in the solid, almost monumental, weightiness of the architectural divisions of the picture plane, and in the features of painstaking, enlarged pointillism. Strange stylistic juxtapositions relate to remembered details—wallpaper patterns, items of clothing, a particular colour, and especially the light or space connected with a given person.

He refuses to work self-consciously; it is rather on the basis of a stream of consciousness that he allows psychological and aesthetic preoccupations to intermingle and dictate the substance and style of his work. He never paints a "scene," as does Hockney, a known landscape, an arranged still-life, a living being; nor, like Jones, will he bring known or recalled elements together in order to make a social painting, a genuine Expressionist, unfashionably concerned with the surface quality of paint, battling between the introverted nature of his imagination and the need to examine and display it in these ponderous, genuine statements. Although linked to a flow of memory, there is always a positive formality to Hodgkin's work, either based on a central, elementary, sexual feature, or space dramatically divided into lozenges of colour and ambiguous forms. Most recently, his work appears to be more relaxed and closer to landscapes with figures, similar to Keith Vaughan, or the lush rural scenery of Hitchens.

—Charles Spencer

HOFLEHNER, Rudolf.

Austrian. Born in Linz, 8 August 1916. Educated at Staatsgewerbeschule für Maschinenbau, Linz, 1932-36; studied architecture at the Technische Hochscule, Graz, Austria, 1936-38; studied art at the Akademie der Bildenden Künste, Vienna, 1938-40. Married Luise Schaffer in 1939; daughter: Hanna. Served in the German Army, 1940-45. Painter and sculptor, in Linz, 1945-51, Vienna, 1951-62 (in Fritz Wotruba's studio, 1951-54), Stuttgart, 1962-81, and in Sudstadt, Austria, since 1981. Professor, Kunstgewerbeschule, Linz, 1945-51, and Akademie der Bildenden Künste, Stuttgart, 1962-81. Recipient: Kulturpreis des Landes Oberosterreich, 1949; Unknown Political Prisoner Prize, London, 1953; Unesco study-travel grant, to Greece, 1954; Preis der Stadt Wien, 1958; Adalbert Stifter-Preise des Landes Oberosterreich, 1967; Preis der Stadt Berlin, 1967; Grosser Österreichischer Staatspreis, 1969; Jerg-Ratgebpreis, 1977; Kulturpreis des Landes Oberösterrich, 1986. Member, Akademie der Künste, West Berlin, 1968; Bayrischen Akademie der Schonen Kunst, 1970. Address: Ottensteinstrasse 62, 2344 Sudstadt, Austria.

Individual Exhibitions:

1951 Galerie der Stadt, Linz, Austria
Galerie d'Art Moderne, Basle
1952 Galerie Wurthle, Vienna
1963 Museum des 20. Jahrhunderts, Vienna
Kunsthalle, Basle
Museum Folkwang, Essen
Städtisches Museum, Wuppertal, West Germany

Württembergischer Kunstverein, Stuttgart
1964 Kunstverein, Hamburg
Stedelijk Museum, Amsterdam
1965 Odyssia Gallery, New York
1966 Galerie Valentien, Stuttgart
Galerie Schmucking, Braunschweig, West Germany
1967 *Skulpturen 1959-1966, Handzeichnungen, Druckgraphik,* Haus am Waldsee, West Berlin
Städtisches Museum Schloss Morsbroich, Leverkusen, West Germany
1968 Städtische Galerie, Stuttgart
Manus Presse, Stuttgart
1969 Galerie Marz, Linz
1970 Galerie Wurthle, Vienna
1971 Galerie Mayer-Ellingen, Frankfurt
Galerie Die Treppe, Lahr, West Germany
1972 Graphische Sammlung Albertina, Vienna
Museum des 20. Jahrhunderts, Vienna
Neue Galerie der Stadt, Linz, Austria
1975 Galerie Michael Hertz, Bremen, West Germany
1976 Austrian Pavilion, at the *Biennale,* Venice
1982 *Gemalde und Zeichnungen,* Württembergischer Kunstverein, Stuttgart
1983 Neue Galerie, Vienna
1987 Bawag Foundation, Vienna

Selected Group Exhibitions:

1953 *Bienal,* Sao Paulo
1954 *Biennale,* Venice
1961 *2nd Exposition de la Sculpture Contemporaine,* Musée Rodin, Paris (and world tour)
1974 *20th Century German Graphics,* New School for Social Research, New York
1976 *5th International Exhibition of Drawings,* Rijeka, Yugoslavia
1977 *1st New York Drawing Biennal,* Bronx Museum of Art
1980 *Liebe-Dokumente unserer Zeit,* Kunsthalle, Darmstadt (travelled to the Kunstverein, Hannover)
1982 *Die Handzeichnung der Gegenwart,* Staatsgalerie, Stuttgart
1984 *Plastik seit 1945,* Museum Rupertinum, Salzburg
1987 *Neue Sezession,* Kunsthalle, Darmstadt, West Germany

Collections:

Museum des 20 Jahrhunderts, Vienna; Graphische Sammlung Albertina, Vienna; Nationalgalerie, West Berlin; Staatsgalerie, Stuttgart; Kunsthalle, Hamburg; Kunsthalle, Mannheim; Von der Heydt Museum, Wuppertal, West Germany; Niedersachsisches Landesmuseum, Hannover; Tate Gallery, London; Museum of Modern Art, New York.

Publications:

By HOFLEHNER: book—*Krieauer Kreaturen,* with Werner Spies, Vienna 1971.

On HOFLEHNER: books—*Plastik des 20. Jahrhunderts* by Werner Hofmann, Frankfurt 1958; *Contemporary Sculpture: An Evolution in Volume and Space* by Carola Giedion-Welcker, New York 1960; *Hoflehner,* exhibition catalogue, with text by Werner Hofmann, Vienna 1963; *Malerei und Plastik in Osterreich* by Kristian Sotriffer, Vienna 1963; *Rudolf Hoflehner,* exhibition catalogue, with text by Werner Hofmann, Hamburg 1964; *A Concise History of Modern Sculpture,* by Herbert Read, London 1964; *Rudolf Hoflehner,* exhibition catalogue, with text by Werner Hofmann, Amsterdam 1964; *Der nackle Mensch in der Kunst* by Frederich Bayl, Cologne 1964; *Rudolf Hoflehner* by Werner Hofmann, Stuttgart 1966; *Osterreichische Plastik seit 1945* by Johann Muschik, Baden bei Wien, Austria 1966; *Rudolf Hoflehner: Skulpturen 1959-1966, Handzeichnungen, Druckgraphik,* exhibition catalogue, with text by Kristian Sotriffer, West Berlin 1967; *A Concise History of Western Art* by Michael Levey, London 1970; *Hoflehner: Bilder und Skizzen 1967-71,* exhibition catalogue, with texts by Alfred Schmeller and Walter Koschatzky, Vienna 1972; *Der Fall Rudolf Hoflehner* by Wieland Schmied, Bremen, West Germany 1976; *Rudolf Hoflehner: Gemalde und Zeichnungen,* exhibition catalogue, with texts by Tilman Osterwold, Andreas Vowinckel and Magdalena M. Moeller, Stuttgart 1982.

Representation of mankind is the geometric place, the intersection point, of my decisions:

In sculpture in its existence as a plastic steely mass, impenetrable and capable of resistance. In painting as a rebellious and vulnerable, organic-sentient phenomenon.

The limit of my work is man, and the objective is form. Man is neither architecture nor machine. Man is a human being. But indifferent to architecture or flesh: art is artificial; that is the trouble.

Yet, in any event, art is an interpretation of the world.

—Rudolf Hoflehner

One of the features of post-war European sculpture (and to some extent painting) is the re-occurring symbols suggestive of human tragedy and suffering, of aggression, violence, destruction. In some cases, notably the sculpture of Germaine Richier, this takes the form of a complacent humanity, accepting, often with dignity, the woes which the gods have cast down. The Job-like stance also bears traces of the Greek sense of nemesis, in which man is both tested and made to reap his own human harvest.

Rudolf Hoflehner can be numbered among these humanist artists, who retain a basic interest in the human form and the human dilemma, but more than most others he has arrived at a symbolic style which enables him to express formal and emotional involvement with some degree of originality. Stylistically there is much in common with his compatriot, Wotruba, who also uses figures as reclining forms or tower-like totems, abstracted into featureless symbols. Wotruba, however, is much less complex than Hoflehner, building his forms in cubic blocks, or oblong volumes, arriving at a post-cubist formula. Hoflehner is altogether more passionate and aggressive, the violent forms and gestures increasing in intensity throughout his career. It was a visit to Greece, on a six-month Unesco scholarship, which helped him to consolidate his view of art. The great archaic figures of Greek sculpture, with the de-humanised realism, their dignified, formal manner, their ponderous symbolism, inspired Hoflehner to develop on similar lines. The early sculptures are altogether more heavy and solid, and the concentration on legs

and feet, on the thrust of limbs, eventually resulted in the virtual elimination of body and head, their substitution being effected by limited symbols, often similar to hammer-heads. The figures have a curious sense of purpose, or even doom, as though striding blindly to their fate. Here one arrives at the post-war idiom of dignified suffering and tragedy.

The titles of these iron pieces range from "Archaic Figure," concerned with frontality, "The Strider," "Split Figure," "Doric Figure." The splitting of the form was Hoflehner's next development, literally cutting the figure in half, from head to feet, possibly a substitute token of the cruciform symbolism of the previous period. By the end of the 1950's a new curvilinear motif was introduced, not, as in some artists, to suggest a softness to the rigid uprights, but emphasising their aggressive nature; these new head-like additions ended in huge pincers, rather like lobster limbs, or dangerous-looking rotary blades. The figures began to assume a science-fiction surrealism, followed by a more delicate period of dehumanised structures, seemingly standing on one leg, like slim dancers or oriental boxers, energetically forcing their second limb into wide-arched violence. It comes as no surprise to find them entitled "Aggressive Object". The most recent figures have become more and more monumental, more and more dehumanised, into strange, fantasy structures, part human, part animal, part machine, attacking with their open nut-cracker limbs, or resembling mobile guns and tanks. Thrusting energy, defiance, defence, challenge, these are the strident features of Hoflehner's work, but not without an undeniable sense of proud dignity.

—Charles Spencer

HOLLAND, Tom.

American. Born in Seattle, Washington, 15 June 1936. Educated at University of California, Santa Barbara and Berkeley, 1954–56; Williamette University, Salem, Oregon, 1956–58; Fulbright Fellow, Chile, 1959–60. Married Judith Lyon in 1958; children: Randolph, Brendon, and Joel. Independent artist, since 1960. Instructor, San Francisco Art Institute, 1963–68, 1971–75; Assistant Professor, University of California at Los Angeles, 1968–70. Recipient: Fulbright Grant, 1975; National Endowment for the Arts Sculpture Grant, 1975–76; Guggenheim Fellowship, 1980–81. Agents: Charles Cowles Gallery, 420 West Broadway, New York, New York 10012; James Corcoran Gallery, Firth Street, Santa Monica, California 90402; John Berggruen Gallery, 228 Grant Avenue, San Francisco, California 94108. Address: 28 Roble Road, Berkeley, California 94705, U.S.A.

Individual Exhibitions:

Rudolf Hoflehner: *Matrena*, 1985

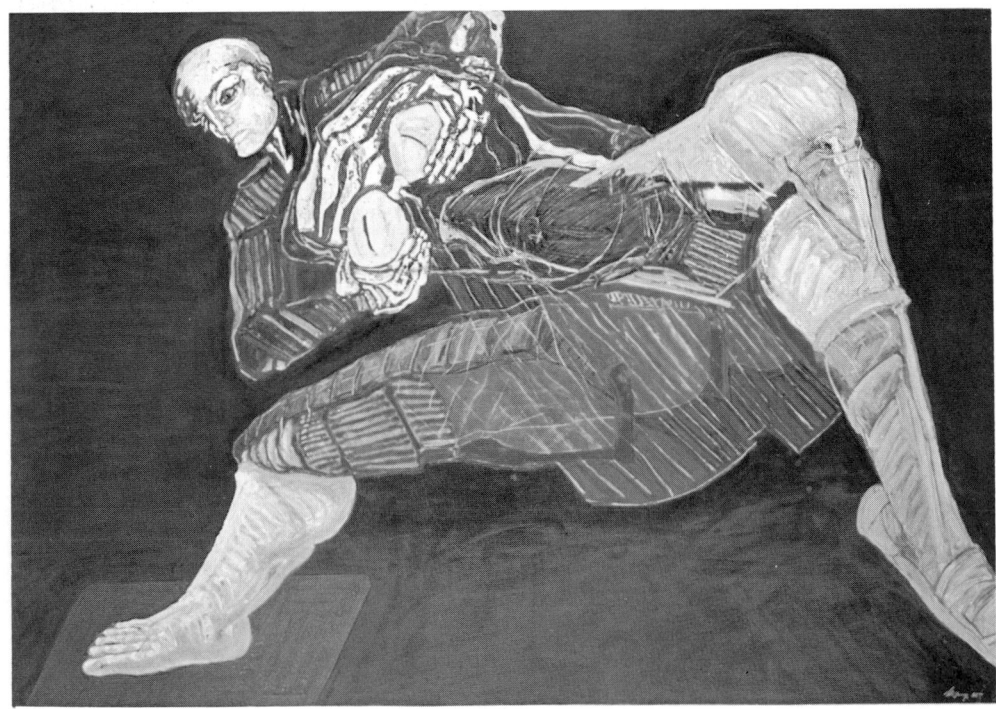

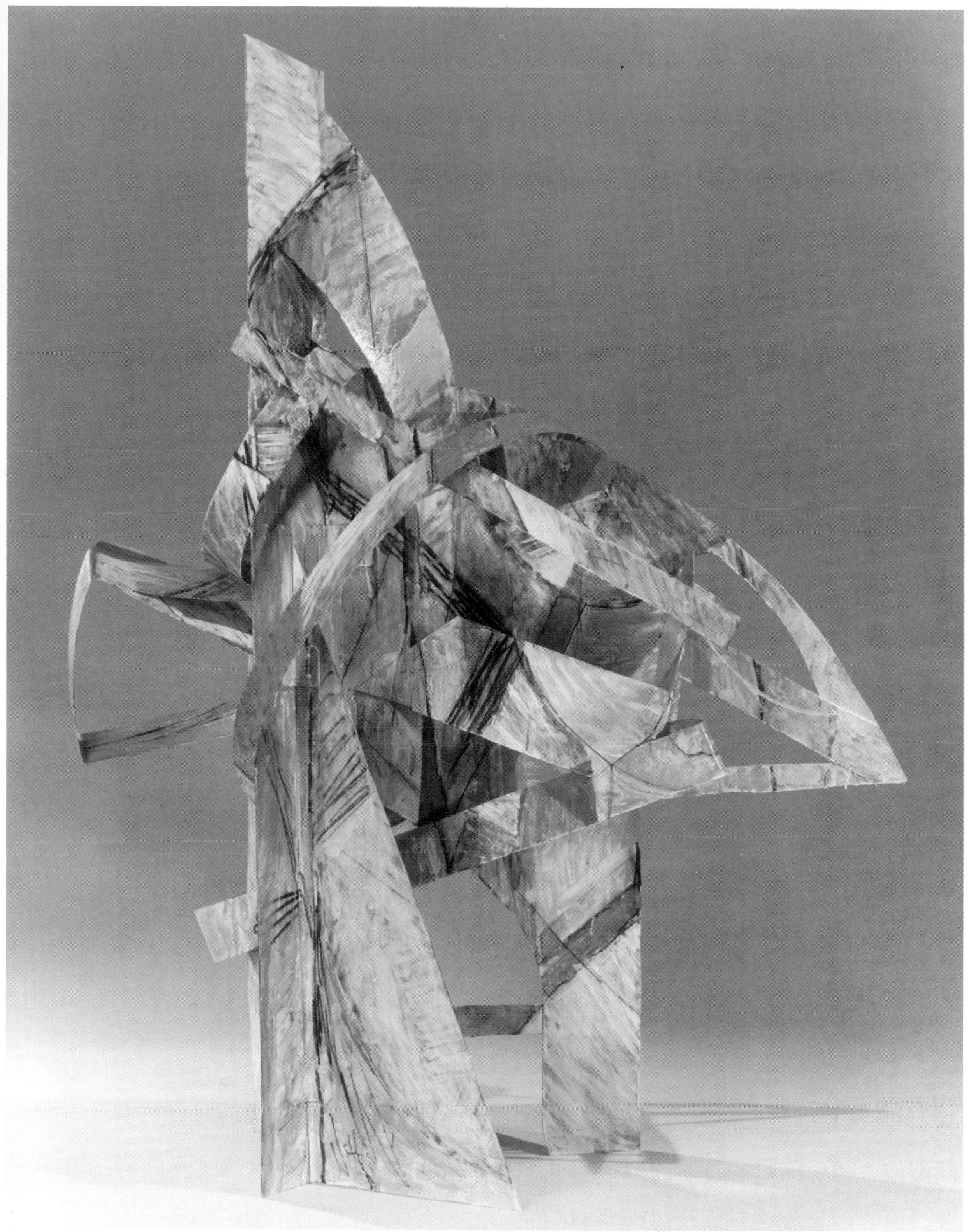

Tom Holland: *Caber*, 1982

1985	James Corcoran Gallery, Los Angeles
	Charles Cowles Gallery, New York
	John Berggruen Gallery, San Francisco
	Arts Club, Chicago
1986	Linda Farris Gallery, Seattle, Washington
	Charles Cowles Gallery, New York
	John Berggruen Gallery, San Francisco

Selected Group Exhibitions:

1964	*Bay Area Artists,* San Francisco Museum of Modern Art
1967	*Grotesque Images,* San Francisco Art Institute
1972	*New Options in Painting,* Walker Art Center, Minneapolis
1976	*California Painting and Sculpture: The Modern Era,* San Francisco Museum of Modern Art (travelled to the National Collection of Fine Arts, Washington, D.C.)
1979	*Artists Born Between 1935–1945: 20 Painters,* Nancy Caldwell Gallery, New York
1981	*New Work on Paper,* Museum of Modern Art, New York
1983	*On and Off the Wall: Shaped and Colored,* Oakland Museum, California (travelled to Boise, Idaho; Salt Lake City; Miami, Florida; Jacksonville, Florida; Palm Springs, Florida; Laguna Beach, California)
1985	*Abstract Painting Redefined,* Louis K. Meisel Gallery, New York
1987	*Not So Plain Geometry,* Crown Point Press, New York

Collections:

Guggenheim Museum, New York; Museum of Modern Art, New York; Whitney Museum, New York; Brooklyn Museum, New York; Hirshhorn Museum, Washington, D.C.; Art Institute of Chicago; Walker Art Center, Minneapolis; Museum of Contemporary Art, Seattle; Oakland Museum, California; San Francisco Museum of Modern Art.

Publications:

On HOLLAND: books—*14 Big Prints,* edited by Bernard Jacobsen, London 1972; *Tom Holland,* exhibition catalogue, San Francisco 1972; *Yngre Amerikans Kunst,* exhibition catalogue, by S. Laursen and P. Aproxine, Aarhus, Denmark 1973; articles—"Tom Holland" by Fidel Danieli in *Art International* (Lugano, Switzerland), January 1970; "Tom Holland: Elkon Gallery" by Robert Pincus-Witten in *Artforum* (New York), June 1970; "New York: Tom Holland, Elkon Gallery" by Carter Ratcliff in *Art International* (Lugano, Switzerland), Summer 1970; "Peter Gutkin, Paul Harris, Tom Holland" by J. Tarshis in *Artforum* (New York), October 1972; "Tom Holland: 10 Years of Work" by R. Losch in *Artweek* (Oakland, California), February 1974.

The Bay Area of California has cultivated a curious assortment of trends and traditions. The Beat generation had its heyday, funk art, what Hilton Kramer coined "dude ranch" Dada, a strong ceramics movement—and most of this was drenched with obscure humor and puns, eccentricity and individuality. But perhaps the most durable of all these movements, and one which still blankets much of the art being made there today, was expressionism. San Francisco developed its own brand of expressionism by interjecting figure and landscape into the bold, gestural canvases of post-war America.

Many would credit Clyfford Still with imparting his own sense of vehement individualism to the vicinity while living there and teaching in what is now the San Francisco Art Institute. Still may have laid the groundwork, but painters such as Elmer Bischoff, Richard Diebenkorn and David Park (to name only a few) are responsible for the sumptuous paintings which dominate this potent tradition of raw action painting. Though the northern California art scene has certainly transmutated in diverse paths since the 50's, second generation expressionists such as Tom Holland, Manuel Neri and Peter Voulkos continue

their use of gushing gestures and strident slashes, splashes, and strokes.

Tom Holland rakes over his three-dimensional paintings with unabashed vehemence. He constructs some free-standing, some wall-hung assemblages made of aluminum sheets, fiberglass or paper which are drenched with vibrant epoxy paints. Though he insists that he is a painter, he really has developed a hybrid of both painting and sculpture. In the free-standing pieces, shards of aluminum or some such material writhe about and stab at larger forms all of which ooze glutinous drips of lusty color. Each splash or cascade of dribbles reveals the action and process of this painter, as they glide down sharp corners or around the protruding bolts by which the fragments are joined.

Holland has another side as well, one that is more mellowed, and introspective. Some of the wall pieces are laced with splashes of pale blues, ochres and whites which drip and roll over undulating strips floating on top or woven through sheets of paper or fiberglass. These paintings carry a similarly all-encompassing power, with a softer, more seductive vitality.

Though one can read each composition in structural terms, in all the paintings the overwhelming sense is an emotional one. Oddly figurative, the free-standing pieces seem almost to wander about their gallery rooms. One notices their "gait," and inevitable comparisons to human scale arise, though many of Holland's pieces tower over one. Perhaps these impressions are unavoidable in any work which so underscores the rites of passion.

—Janet Goleas

HOLT, Nancy.

American. Born in Worcester, Massachusetts, 5 April 1938. Educated at Jackson College, Tufts University, Medford, Massachusetts, 1956–60, B.S. 1960. Married the artist Robert Smithson, *q.v.,* in 1963. Independent artist working in sculpture, film and video, and producing large-scale environmental and installation projects: has lived and worked in New York since 1960. Recipient: New York Creative Artists Public Service Grant (sculpture) 1975, (video) 1978; National Endowment for the Arts Fellowship, 1975, 1978, 1983, 1985; WNET-Channel 13 Artist-in-Residence Grant, 1977; Beard's Fund Grant, 1977; Guggenheim Fellowship, 1978; Design Honor Award, American Society of Landscape Architects, New Jersey Chapter, 1986. Agent: John Weber Gallery, 142 Greene Street, New York, New York 10012. Address: 166 Bank Street, Apt. 5D, New York, New York 10014, U.S.A.

Individual Exhibitions:

1972	University of Montana Art Gallery, Missoula
	University of Rhode Island Art Center, Kingston
1973	Lo Guidice Gallery, New York
1974	Bykert Gallery, New York
	Walter Kelly Gallery, Chicago
1977	Franklin Furnace, New York
1979	John Weber Gallery, New York
	Miami University Art Museum, Oxford, Ohio
1981	Saginaw Art Museum, Michigan
1982	John Weber Gallery, New York
	David Bellman Gallery, Toronto
1984	John Weber Gallery, New York
1985	Flow Ace Gallery, Los Angeles
1986	John Weber Gallery, New York
1987	Lakeside Gallery, Richland College, Dallas

"Works in the Land": *Buried Poems,* Florida, New Jersey, 1969, and Utah, 1971; *Views Through a Sand Dune,* Narragansett Beach, Rhode Island, 1972; *Missoula Ranch Locators,* near Missoula, Montana, 1972; *Hydra's Head,* along

the Niagara River, Lewiston, New York, 1972; *Sun Tunnels,* northwestern Utah desert, near Lucin, Utah, 1973–76; *Stone Enclosure: Rock Rings,* Bellingham, Washington, 1977–78; *Polar Circle,* Miami University, Oxford, Ohio, 1979; *Star Crossed,* Miami University, Oxford, Ohio, 1979–80; *30 Below,* Lake Placid, New York, 1979; *Wild Spot,* Wellesley College, Massachusetts, 1979–80; *Dark Star Park,* Rosslyn, Arlington, Virginia, 1979–84; *Annual Ring,* Saginaw, Michigan, 1980–81; *Time Span,* Laguna Gloria Museum, Austin, Texas, 1981; *Catch Basin,* St. James Park, Toronto, 1982; *Sole Source,* Marlay Park, Dublin, 1983; *Waterwork,* Gallaudel College, Washington, D.C., 1983–84; *Astral Grating,* IRT Subway Station, Fulton Street, New York, 1983–88; *End of the Line/West Rock,* Southern Connecticut State University, New Haven, 1984–88; *Rain Drains,* Islip Museum of Art, Long Island, New York, 1985; *Pipeline,* Visual Arts Center of Alaska, Anchorage, 1986; *Starfire,* Island in Sheepcreek River, Anchorage, 1986; *Franklin Crossing,* Philadelphia 1987.

Audio Works: *Studio Tour,* 799 Greenwich Street, New York, 1971; *Tour of the John Weber Gallery,* New York 1972; *Visual Sound Zones,* University of Rhode Island, Kingston, 1972; Franklin Furnace, New York, 1977, and a wash room, P.S. 1, New York, 1979; *U.S. 80 Solo* (radiowork for broadcast), A Space, Toronto, 1979.

Selected Group Exhibitions:

1969	*Language III,* Dwan Gallery, New York
1974	*Interventions in the Landscape,* Hayden Gallery, Massachusetts Institute of Technology, Cambridge
1977	*Probing the Earth: Contemporary Land Projects,* Hirshhorn Museum, Smithsonian Institution, Washington, D.C.
1980	*Architectural Sculpture,* Los Angeles Institute of Contemporary Art
1981	*Construction in Process in the Art of the 70's,* Archives of Contemporary Thought, Lodz, Poland (toured Poland)
1982	*PostMinimalism,* Aldrich Museum of Contemporary Art, Ridgefield, Connecticut
1984	*Content: A Contemporary Focus 1974–84,* Hirshhorn Museum, Washington, D.C.
1986	*Imagining Antarctica,* Museum der Stadt Linz, Austria
1987	*Women's Autobiographical Artists' Books,* University of Wisconsin, Milwaukee

Collections:

Museum of Modern Art, New York; Hartwick College, Oneonta, New York; University of Massachusetts, Amherst; Wellesley College, Massachusetts; Miami University, Oxford, Ohio; Western Washington University, Bellingham, Washington; Vancouver Art Gallery.

Publications:

By HOLT: books—*Ransacked,* New York 1980; *Time Outs,* Rochester, New York 1985; articles—"Hydra's Head" in *Arts Magazine* (New York), January 1975; "Views through a Sand Dune, Holes of Light" in *TriQuarterly* (Evanston, Illinois), Winter 1975; article in *Artpack Catalogue,* Lewiston, New York 1975; "Some Notes on Video Works" in *Video Art,* edited by Ira Schneider and Beryl Korot, New York 1976; "Sun Tunnels" in *Artforum* (New York), April 1977; "The Time Being (For Robert Smithson)" in *Arts Magazine* (New York), May 1978; "Massachusetts" in *Born in Boston,* exhibition catalogue, Lincoln, Massachusetts 1979; "Stone Enclosure: Rock Rings" in *Arts Magazine* (New York), June 1979; "Situation Esthetics: Impermanent Art and the 70's Audience" in *Artforum* (New York), January 1980; "Notes on a Few Coincidences of Art and Life" in *Chelsea* (New York), no. 39, 1981; videotapes—*East Coast—West Coast,* with Robert Smithson, 1969; *Locating #1 and #2,* 1972; *Zeroing in,* 1973; *Going Around in Circles,* 1973; *Points of View,* 1974; *Underscan,* 1974; *Revolve,* 1977; *Art in the Public Eye: The Making of Dark Star Park,* 1987; films—*Swamp,* 1971; *Pine Barrens,* 1975; *Sun Tunnels,* 1978.

On HOLT: books—*Probing the Earth: Contemporary Land Projects,* exhibition catalogue, by John Beardsley, Washington, D.C. 1977; *New Artists Video* by Gregory Battcock,

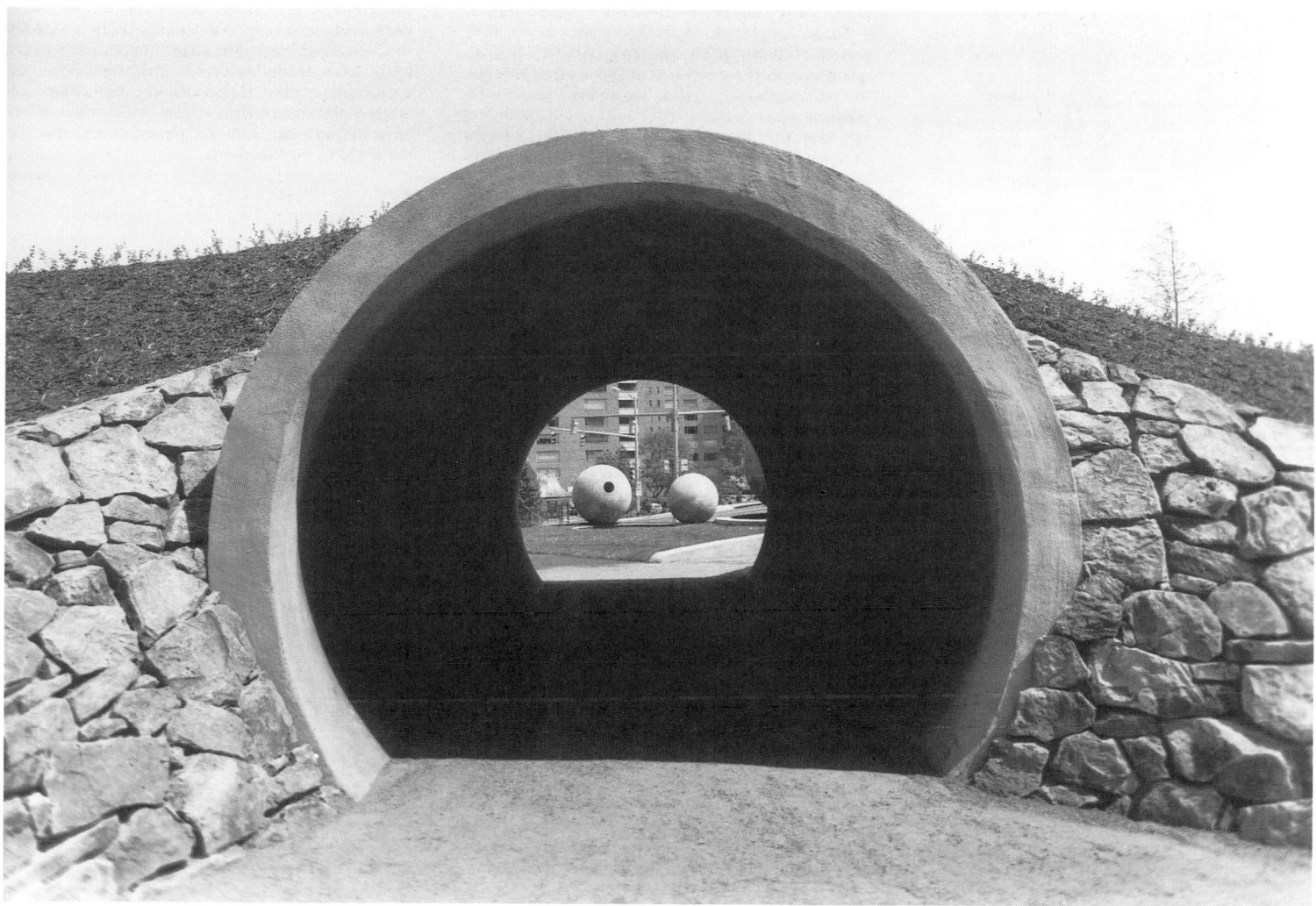

Nancy Holt: Dark Star Park, Rosslyn, Virginia, 1984

New York 1978; *Originals: American Women Artists* by Eleanor Munro, New York 1979; *Nature/Sculpture,* exhibition catalogue, by Andress Vowinckel, Stuttgart 1981; *Art in the Land,* edited by Alan Sonfist, New York 1983; *The Desert is no Lady: Southwestern Landscapes in Women's Writing and Art* by Vera Horwood and Janice Monk, New Haven, Connecticut 1987; articles—"The Earth Is a Cruel Master" by Robert Smithson and Gregoire Muller in *Arts Magazine* (New York), November 1971; "Video Is Being Invented" by Bruce Kurtz in *Arts Magazine,* (New York), December 1972/January 1973; "Camouflage: Films by Holt and Horn" by Lucy Lippard in *Art Rite* (New York), Fall 1975; "Art Outdoors: In and Out of the Public Domain" by Lucy Lippard in *Studio International* (London), no. 2, 1977; "6 Women at Work in the Landscape" by April Kingsley in *Arts Magazine* (New York), April 1978; "Complexes: Architectural Sculpture in Nature" by Lucy Lippard in *Art In America* (New York), January/February 1979; "The Expulsion from the Garden: Environmental Sculpture at the Winter Olympics" by Kay Larson in *Artforum* (New York), April 1980; "Holt's Volts" by John Perreault in the *Soho News* (New York), 2 February 1982; "Nancy Holt, Siteseer" by Ted Castle in *Art in America* (New York), March 1982; "Dark Star Park" by John Yau in *Artforum* (New York), April 1985; "Earthwork Odyssey" by Eleanor Munro in *Christian Science Monitor* (Boston), 25 March 1987.

All of my work is involved with site, time, inside vs. outside space, orientation in space (often in some way astronomically designated), and aspects of perception—light, space, framing, focus.

Since 1969 my primary concern has been in making sculpture in the landscape or in open urban spaces using stone, concrete, brick and steel. Although sometimes indoor spaces—entire rooms—are used as sites, the sites, both in and outdoors, are an integral part of the sculptures—the ideas for the works developing out of my involvement with the sites.

The sculptures of concrete, brick, stonemasonry, earth and steel evolve out of their sites and are concerned with, among other things, perception and space—changes in scale at various distances, perceptual disorientation between inside and outside space, and seeing in depth through layered openings and tunnels. Each work draws the viewer within its structure, creating a sense of transition from outside to inside, and often from light to dark. The works surround and enclose but at the same time frame and extend out to the horizon in the distance.

Natural elements—sunlight, stars, water, plants, earth, are part of the substance of the works. Patterns of sun and moonlight, astronomical alignments, and/or water reflections often bring the sky to earth, turning the landscape upside down, while astrally fixing each work in its site.

Some recent sculptures are functional, using systems of basic technology such as plumbing, electricity, drainage and heating to make often complex labyrinthian sculptures which can be walked through and turned on and off by the viewer.

The films, videotapes, and book, also conceived of in a perceptual framework, are usually evocations of landscapes or displacements of places. Indications of space (through tracking, pans, aerial, and walking shots) and aspects of nature—sunlight patterns, billowing dust, water reflections—are caught visually and transported elsewhere via film through time, while the psychology of the place is disclosed through the local voices, sounds, and/or music in the sound tracks or accompanying text.

—Nancy Holt

HOLZER, Jenny.
American. Born in Gallipolis, Ohio, 29 July 1950. Studied at Ohio University, Athens, 1971–72, BFA 1972; Rhode Island School of Design, Providence, 1975–77, MFA 1977; independent study program fellowship, Whitney Museum, New York, 1977. Married to Michael Glier. Independent artist, New York, since 1977. Recipient: Blair Award, 79th Americans Show, Art Institute of Chicago, 1982. Agents: Galerie Crousel-Robelin Bama, 40 rue Quincampoix, 75004 Paris, France; and Barbara Gladstone Gallery, New York. Address: c/o Barbara Gladstone Gallery, 99 Greene Street, New York, New York 10012, U. S. A.

Individual Exhibitions:

1978	Project Studio One, New York
	Franklin Furnace Window, New York
1979	Fashion Moda Window, Bronx, New York
	Printed Matter Window, New York
1980	Galerie Rudiger Schottle, Munich
	Onze Rue Clavel, Paris
1981	Le Nouveau Musée, Lyon, France
	Museum fur (Sub)Kultur, West Berlin
1982	Barbara Gladstone Gallery, New York
	Galerie Chantel Crousel, Paris
	American Graffiti Gallery, Amsterdam
	Artists Space, New York
	A Space, Toronto
1983	Barbara Gladstone Gallery, New York
	Lisson Gallery, London
	Institute of Contemporary Arts, London
	Institute of Contemporary Art, Philadelphia
1984	*Sign on a Truck,* Grand Army Plaza/Bowling Green Plaza, New York

Dallas Museum of Art, Texas
University of Massachusetts, Amherst
Le Nouveau Musée, Lyon, France
Kunsthalle, Basle
Galerie 't Venster, Rotterdam
Cranbrook Museum, Bloomfield Hills, Michigan
State University of New York, Old Westbury
Seattle Art Museum, Washington
1985 Barbara Gladstone Gallery, New York
Galerie Monika Spruth, Cologne
Galerie Crousel-Hussenot, Paris
Contemporary Arts Center, Cincinnati (with Cindy Sherman)
Am Hof, Vienna (with Keith Haring)
Israel Museum, Jerusalem (with Barbara Kruger)
1986 Des Moines Art Center, Iowa (toured the United States, 1986–88)
1987 Rhona Hoffman Gallery, Chicago

Selected Group Exhibitions:

1978 *Artwords and Bookworks*, Los Angeles Institute of Contemporary Art
1980 *Issue*, Institute of Contemporary Arts, London
1981 *Westkunst*, Messehallen, Cologne
1982 *Documenta 7*, Museum Fridericianum, Kassel, West Germany (and *Documenta 8*, 1987)
1983 *Art and Social Change*, Allen Memorial Museum, Oberlin, Ohio
1984 *Biennale of Sydney*, Art Gallery of New South Wales, Sydney
1985 *Kunst mit Eigen-Sinn*, Museum moderner Kunst, Vienna
1986 *In Other Words*, Corcoran Gallery of Art, Washington, D.C.
1987 *Avant-Garde in the Eighties*, Los Angeles County Museum of Art
1988 *Committed to Print*, Museum of Modern Art, New York

Collections:

Museum of Modern Art, New York; Whitney Museum, New York; Centro Cultural Arte Contemporaneo, Polanco, Mexico City; Tate Gallery, London; Musée d'Art Moderne/Centre Georges Pompidou, Paris; Kunsthalle, Berne; Kunsthaus, Zurich; Museum of Contemporary Art, Chicago; Stedelijk Van Abbemuseum, Eindhoven; National Gallery of Canada, Ottawa.

Publications:

By HOLZER: books—*A Little Knowledge*, New York 1978; *Black Book*, New York 1979; *Hotel*, with Peter Nadin, New York 1980; *Living*, with Peter Nadin, New York 1980; *Eating Through Living*, with Peter Nadin, New York 1981; *Eating Friends*, with Peter Nadin, New York 1981; *Abuse of Power Comes As No Surprise: Truisms and Essays*, Halifax, Nova Scotia 1983.

On HOLZER: books—*Jenny Holzer*, exhibition catalogue, Basle and Lyon 1984; *New Art*, edited by Phyllis Freenan, Eric Himmel, Edith Pavese and Anne Yarowsky, New York 1984; *Jenny Holzer/Keith Haring: Protect Me From What I Want*, exhibition catalogue with texts by Hubert Klocker and Peter Pakesch, Vienna 1986; *Jenny Holzer/Cindy Sherman*, exhibition catalogue with essay by Dennis Barrie, Cincinnati 1986; *Jenny Holzer: Signs*, exhibition catalogue, Des Moines 1986.

* * *

Since the end of the 'seventies Jenny Holzer has distanced herself from those currents of contemporary New York art which place the highest premium on plasticity. Abandoning traditional techniques, she has elected to use language as her principal means of expression, so that we are obliged to locate her work in a no-man's-land between writing and the visual arts where the artist is, by her own definition, a communications specialist in the sense of a social mediator: "It's strange; I don't even basically think of myself as an artist. Perhaps I'm half artist, half one of those odd individuals who stick up notices all over the place. Or perhaps just a universal voice" (J. Holzer).

The words of Jenny Holzer's language do not form part of a conceptual discourse or of a semiological interpretation of the work of art, as they may do for Joseph Kosuth for example, nor do they concretise a political debate, as with Hans Haacke, but, presented in a mediatory form accessible to the public at large, they are, like the graffiti in the underground, above all subversive and interventionary, destabilising the imagery and depersonalised vocabulary of the various information sectors.

Printed in capitals on plain paper, Holzer's first texts appeared in 1978 on the facades of public buildings in various quarters of New York, at the entrance to a bank, or a shop, or on already crowded hoardings. Taking possession of a collective space already saturated with symbols, the artist's placards, by their multiplication of messages, the studied neutrality of their format and the shock quality of their content, can "at the very least, suggest or demand a response, a stand on the part of the spectator" (J. Holzer).

The first two series, *Truisms* (1978) and *Inflammatory Essays* (1979–1982), are made up of short phrases—presented in alphabetical order in *Truisms*-which are written as affirmatives or imperatives and sound like judgments or convey declarations, personal points of view with regard to the basic facts of daily life (sleep, food, money) or relate, in a more general way, to events and social situations which are sometimes cruel and violent, sometimes falsely trivial (PRIVATE PROPERTY CREATED CRIME/YOU MUST REMEMBER YOU HAVE FREEDOM OF CHOICE/INHERITANCE MUST BE ABOLISHED, etc.). The artist does not intervene as critic, arbiter or denunciator, but takes a back seat behind a reality which is its own self-contradiction. Jenny Holzer's sentences pose as fragments of conversations or personal thoughts gleaned from a whole variety of sociocultural milieus, from racial minorities, from men and from women, and whose sum total is no more than a web of contradictions denying supposed truths and revealing instead the fragmentation of society, its taboos and its crimes.

In a third series entitled *Living* (1981–1982) the texts are punctuated with paintings by the American artist Peter Nadin representing portraits of men and women, hands, an eye, faces and bodies trivialised by the simplicity of the lines and by the fact that they are attached to metal supports reminiscent of traffic signals. The discourse reflects on topics such as the family, work, religion and the relationships based on hate, fear, pain and power which they imply, taking on a more personal and incisive quality which is intensified in the work that followed in 1983, *Survival Series*. From there the artist went on to develop other frameworks capable of increasing the visual impact of her works: illuminated signs, particularly well-suited to conveying information in the New York environment, and self-adhesive notices placed at strategic points (telephone kiosks, fountains, traffic lights. . .). Holzer's works have also been on exhibition in a similar fashion in art galleries and museums, where they form "lecture tours" studied in terms of a fixed visual unity.

Recently Holzer exhibited an architectural construction in the form of a set of granite blocks engraved with various texts in gold lettering (*Under a Rock*, 1986). These austere pieces, which inevitably make one think of funeral monuments, seem to be balancing the over-solemn immortality of the writing with the precariousness of human life.

Jenny Holzer's texts have also been made into books and video films. For one of these films, projected on to a giant screen outside the Centre Pompidou in Paris (1987), the artist presented an interrupted succession of anonymous faces, each seen close up and each spouting a sentence previously selected from *Truisms*. The spectator's preference for a certain type of message and his or her rejection of another points to one of the most fundamental aspects of this artist's work, the aim of which is to provoke reactions, thereby leading to an active participation on the part of the public.

The spectacular displays orchestrated by Jenny Holzer (huge illuminated signs) and her long-term work as writer and poster designer create a visually coherent ensemble and an utterly personal alternative to the excessive influence which the media exercise over contemporary society. Holzer has created an original precedent for integrating the formal sobriety of writing and the testimonial powers of language into the world of the visual arts.

—Dominique Liquois

* * *

HONEGGER, Gottfried.

Swiss. Born in Zurich, 12 June 1917. Studied art at the Kunstgewerbeschule, Zurich, 1932; apprentice window-dresser, Zurich, 1933–36; studied graphic design, under Warja Lavater, Zurich, 1937–39. Served in the Swiss Army, 1939–45: corporal. Married Warja Lavater in 1940; daughters: Bettina and Cordelia. Independent painter, sculptor and graphic artist, in Zurich from 1939, in New York 1957–60, and in Paris from 1961. Instructor, Kunstgewerbeschule, Zurich, 1937–39; Visiting Instructor, University of Dallas, 1969–70. Member, Swiss Werkbund, Zurich, 1944–45, and Association Internationale des Graphistes, 1952–56; Secretary, Swiss Graphic Artists Union, 1953–56. Recipient: Guggenheim Award, 1964; Bovard Purchase Prize, *Carnegie International*, Pittsburgh, 1967. Agents: Gimpel-Hanover + Andre Emmerich Galerien, Todistrasse 40, 8002 Zurich; Galerie Muller-Roth, Blumenstrasse 25, 7000 Stuttgart 1; Galerie Liliane et Michel Durand-Dessert, 3 rue des Haudriettes, 75003 Paris; and Annely Juda Fine Art, 11 Tottenham Mews, London W1. Addresses: 4 rue de Thorigny, 75003 Paris, France; Limmatstrasse 107, 8005 Zurich, Switzerland.

Individual Exhibitions:

1950 Galerie Chichio Haller, Zurich
1951 George Wittenborn Gallery, New York
1952 Galerie 16, Zurich
1958 Galerie Laubli, Zurich
1960 Martha Jackson Gallery, New York
1961 Galerie Fillon, Paris
1962 Galerie Lawrence, Paris
1963 *Tableaux-Reliefs, Sculpture*, Gimpel und Hanover Galerie, Zurich
1964 Martha Jackson Gallery, New York
Gimpel Fils, London
1965 Galerie M. E. Thelen, Essen
Gimpel und Hanover Galerie, Zurich
1966 Württembergischer Kunstverein, Stuttgart
Gimpel und Hanover Galerie, Zurich
1967 Kunsthaus, Zurich
1968 Gimpel Fils, London
Museum am Ostwall, Dortmund, West Germany
Galerie Heseler, Munich
1969 Valley House Gallery, Dallas
1970 Galerie M. E. Thelen, Cologne
1971 Gimpel und Hanover Galerie, Zurich
Galerie Quader, Chur, Switzerland
1972 Valley House Gallery, Dallas
Galerie Swart, Amsterdam
Bilder, Plastiken, Graphik, Badischer Kunstverein, Karlsruhe, West Germany
Galerie Teufel, Cologne
White Gallery, Lutry-Lausanne, Switzerland
1974 *Tableaux-Reliefs 1971–1973*, Gimpel und Hanover Galerie, Zurich, Switzerland
Galerie d'Art Moderne, Basle
Galerie Denise René, Paris
1975 Galerie Muller, Stuttgart
Galerie Denise René, Paris
French Pavilion at the *Bienal*, Sao Paulo
1976 Gimpel und Hanover Galerie, Zurich

1977 Galerie Seestrasse, Rapperswil, Switzerland
Acht Rote Bilder/Acht blaue Bilder, Gimpel und Hanover Galerie, Zurich
1978 Musée d'Art Moderne de la Ville, Paris
Abbaye de Senanque, Gordes, France
Galerie Nouvelles Images, The Hague
1979 Trudelhaus Foundation, Baden, Switzerland
Annely Juda Fine Art, London
Gimpel und Hanover/André Emmerich Galleries, Zurich
1980 Galerie Muller-Roth, Stuttgart
Ulmer Museum, Ulm, West Germany
1981 Atelier Lafranca, Lugano, Switzerland
Le Coin du Miroir, Dijon, France
1982 Galerie Muller-Roth, Stuttgart
1983 Gimpel-Hanover-Emmerich Galerien, Zurich
Galerie Durand-Dessert, Paris
Juda/Rowan Gallery, London
Galerie Nouvelles Images, The Hague
1984 Galerie Konstruktiv Tendens, Stockholm
Galerie Convergence, Nantes, France
Kunsthaus, Zug, Switzerland
Sculpture Park, Lille, France
1985 Galeries de la Vieille-Charite, Marseille, France
Galerie Lupke, Frankfurt

Selected Group Exhibitions:

1958 *Kunst und Naturform,* Kunsthalle, Basle
1961 *Avant-Gard '61,* Städtisches Museum, Trier, West Germany
1962 *Carnegie International,* Carnegie Institute, Pittsburgh
1965 *Salon des Réalités Nouvelles,* Musée d'Art Moderne, Paris (and 1966, 1968)
1971 *The Swiss Avant-Garde,* New York Cultural Center
1972 *12 Ans d'Art Contemporain en France,* Grand Palais, Paris
1975 *Bienal,* Sao Paulo
1976 *Mouvement Peint, Mouvement Agi,* Abbaye de Beaulieu-en-Rouerge, France
1980 *Art in Switzerland,* at the *Kunstmesse,* Basle
1988 *The Non-Objective World Revisited,* Annely Juda Fine Art, London

Collections:

Kunsthaus, Zurich, Switzerland; Centre National d'Art Contemporain, Paris; Musée Cantini, Marseilles; Marie-Louise and Gunnar Didrichsen Art Foundation, Helsinki; Israel Museum, Jerusalem; Carnegie Institute, Pittsburgh; Dallas Museum of Fine Arts; Hirshhorn Museum, Washington, D.C.; Museum of Modern Art, New York; Princeton University Art Museum, New Jersey.

Publications:

By HONEGGER: book—*Hommage à Cercle et Carre,* with Michel Seuphor, Zurich 1964; *Memoria,* with Jean-Yves Mock, Frankfurt 1985.

On HONEGGER: books—*Gottfried Honegger,* exhibition catalogue, with text by Aleksis Rannit, New York 1960; *Honegger,* exhibition catalogue, with text by Herbert Read, Paris 1962; *Gottfried Honegger: Tableaux-Reliefs, Sculpture,* exhibition catalogue, with text by Herbert Read, Zurich 1963; *Gottfried Honegger,* exhibition catalogue, with text by Udo Kultermann, Essen 1965; *La Vocation des Mots* by Michel Seuphor, Lausanne 1966; *Gottfried Honegger,* exhibition catalogue, with texts by René Wehrli, Michel Seuphor, Udo Kultermann and others, Zurich 1967; *Neue Dimensionen der Plastik* by Udo Kultermann, Tübingen 1967; *The New Sculpture* by Udo Kultermann, London 1968; *Gottfried Honegger: Bilder, Plastiken, Graphik,* exhibition catalogue, with texts by Jorg Walter Koch, Willy Rotzler and Michel Seuphor, Karlsruhe, West Germany, 1972; *12 Ans d'Art Contemporain en France,* exhibition catalogue, with texts by Francois Mathey, Daniel Cordier, Jean Clair and others, Paris 1972; *Gottfried Honegger: Works from 1939 to 1971* by Kurt W. Forster, Herbert Read, Willy Rotzler and others, Teufen, Switzerland, 1972; *Gottfried Honegger: Tableaux Reliefs 1971-1973,* exhibition catalogue, with text by Max Fritsch, Zurich 1974; *Gottfried Honegger: Acht rote Bilder/Act blaue Bilder,* exhibition catalogue, with texts by

Willy Rotzler and Helmut Heissenbuttel, Zurich 1977; *Gottfried Honegger,* exhibition folder, with text by Max Fritsch, Zurich 1979; *Peintres Suisses* by Marcel Joray, Zurich 1982; *Gottfried Honegger: Tableaux/Relief/Skulpturen, 1971–83,* Zurich and Paris 1983.

If my work up to the year 1970 was based upon a definite programme, I have since been using—while still keeping up the idea of the programme—a calculation of probabilities; I submit myself to the aleatory game.

"Chance and necessity" have become the terrain of my researches. This method gives me greater liberty and a link with the scientific thought of today. All my pictures and my sculptures, whether symmetrical or asymmetrical, are the result of this new conception.

The colour is monochrome, the treatment of the surface is subjective and completes the objectivity of forms. The sensual skin, the material of graphite and of colour are sustained by a geometry as simple as a spinal column. The relief of the pictures is obtained by a collage on canvas. Light, catching it, introduces the game of chance.

Fifteen years ago, I would have willingly explained the meaning of my work, its function, its goal. I knew exactly what I was doing and why.

Brought up in the spirit of the Bauhaus, I thought that art should improve the quality of life, of furnished and unfurnished rooms. I saw art as a means for reforming society.

Today, I have turned my back on the idealism which dominated part of my life. I produce a visual reality whose image is revealed in relation to the cultural landscape in which I am inscribed.

The meaning comes as much from what I show as from what I reject. Art can not be the maidservant of a morality without questioning the research into the unknown.

Gottfried Honegger: *Volume II,* 1967

The mute and materialist language of my painting is above all an electrocardiogram of my existence.
—Gottfried Honegger

In all of his canvases Gottfried Honegger links a very simple geometric structure to a semi-monochrome—similar to "color-field" painting. Thus he links the constructivist thinking which is more common in Europe than America with the absolute predominance of color as in the paintings of Barnett Newman or Mark Rothko. Honegger spent three years in New York from 1957 to 1960. His first-hand experience of American art could explain the link in his work between the two artistic languages of opposite character.

Influenced by a first taste of modern painting at Picasso's exhibition in Zurich in 1933, Honegger has tended to make the shapes that inhabit his canvases strictly geometric. He discovered the problem of dialectic, that is to say the tension that arises in painting comprised of contradictions. His paintings of the 1950's and 60's are characterized by a dichotomy between structured and non-structured planes or by the opposition of irregular, open surfaces and those which are hidden, closed. When he created his first sculptures at the beginning of the 1960's, he created a synthesis of the rough and smooth, of the worked and unworked form. In 1963 he began to limit his formal language to elementary geometric forms: the circle, the square the triangle. It is a language that seems to him to be rigorous, objective and anonymous. It also possesses a certain vulnerability. He always adheres to a very restrained structure, without metaphor or symbolic meaning, regular to the point of monotony, but expressive of our desire for sensuality. He shows that pictorial material is not only to be "thought" but also to be "felt."

If geometry corresponds to the mathematical and

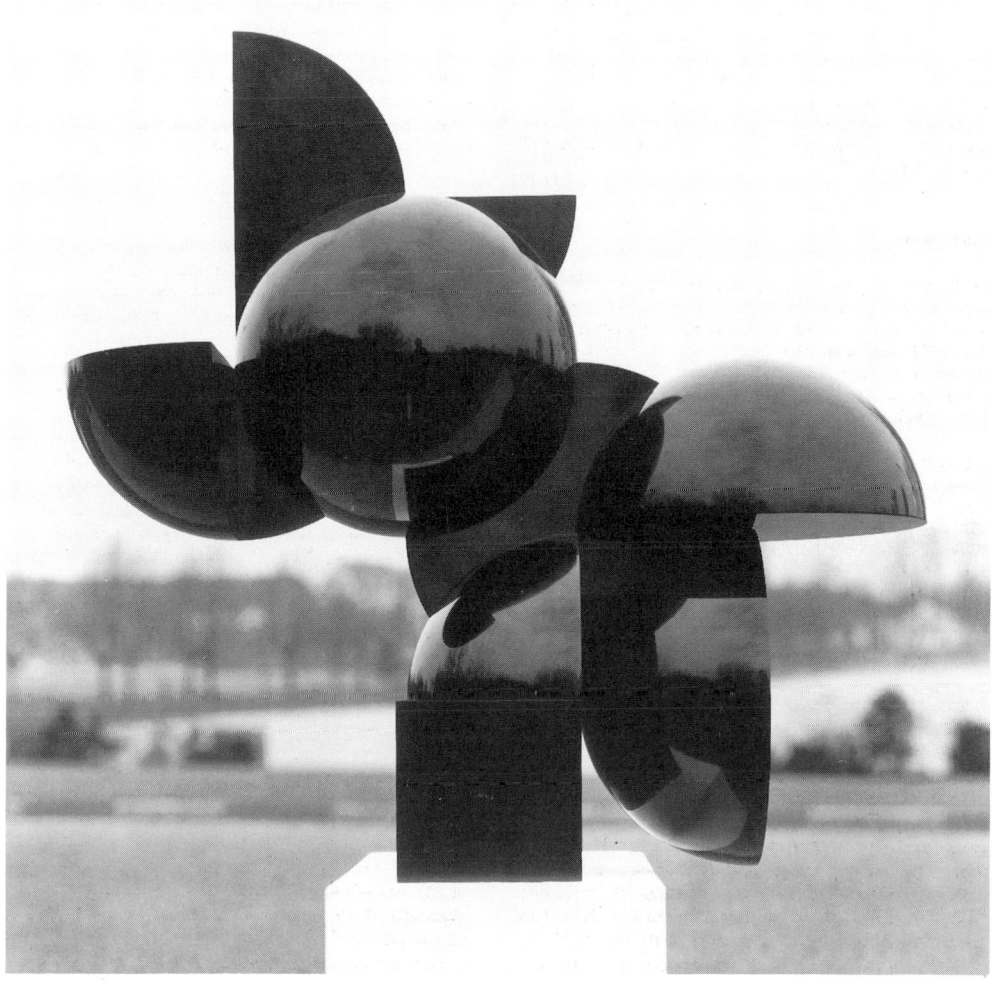

scientific character of the modern world, then the emphasis of the manual intervention of the artist must satisfy our wish for a subjective and individual space for desire. He does not translate this wish through images or hallucinations but through his method of treating material. "Concept" and "material" are the two essential elements of Honegger's work; its "theme" is their confrontaion. The concept is defined through geometry in all of its solidity: its character is transparent and intelligible. Then the unforeseen element appears through the introduction of a calculated risk or the movement of the paint. Hence, the geometric forms run the risk of being disturbed or destroyed, and the perfection of the conceptual grid is smashed as if living had triumphed over the ideal.

In Honegger's work, contingency has many functions: it creates disorder within the world posited by science, an enclosed world subject to natural law; it represents the creative and innovative principle necessary for the evolution of life; it acts as the artist's advocate for the subjective, however disguised; finally, it has the task of confusing all meanings that might be imposed through geometry. Weary of the mass of images and messages that constitute our world, Honegger would like our art to be one in which contradictions destroy all assertions, an art that has nothing more to say other than through its materiality, beauty, form and substance. Behind this apparently brusque and anti-social attitude lies that ancient Platonic ideal, which influenced Bauhaus thinking and which therefore has strongly influenced Honegger, the conviction that beauty, goodness and usefulness are of necessity identical.

—Marie Luise Syring

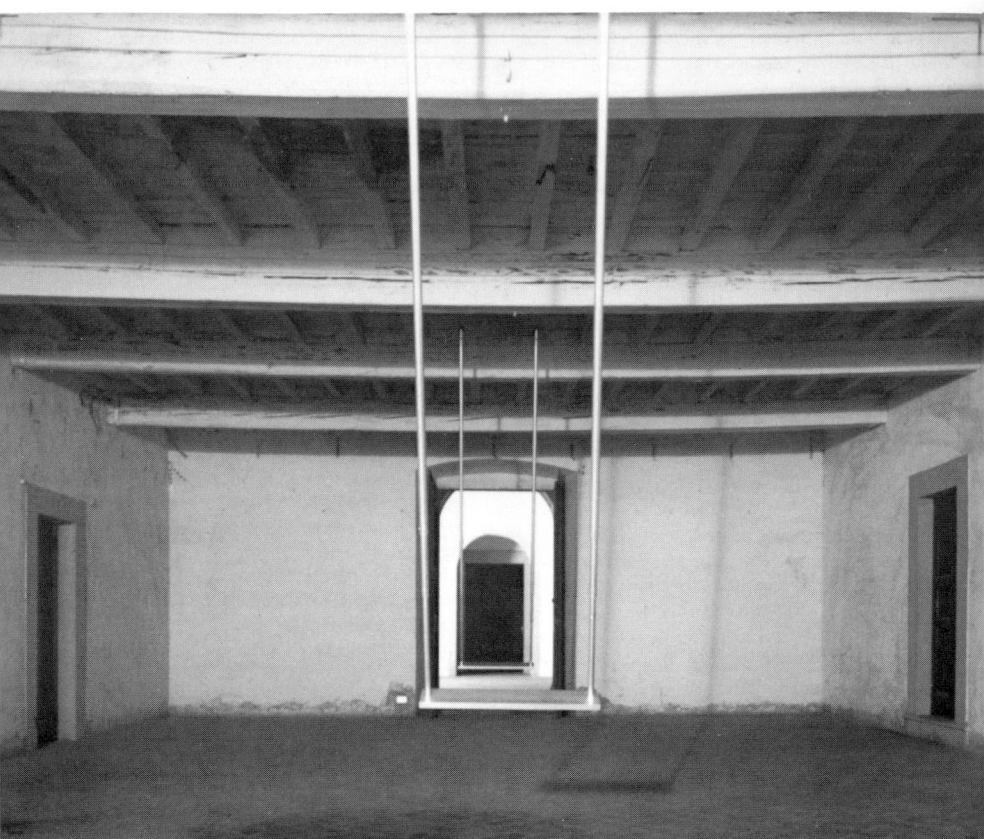

Rebecca Horn: *Dialogue of the Swings*, 1980

HORN, Rebecca.

German. Born in Michelstadt, 24 March 1944. Studied at the Hochschule für Bildende Künste, Hamburg, 1964–70. Independent artist in film, video and performance, Hamburg, 1968–71, London, 1971–72, in West Berlin, 1973–75, New York and West Berlin, 1976–80, and Bad Konig-Zell, since 1981. Guest Lecturer, California Art Institute, Los Angeles, and University of California at San Diego, 1974. Recipient: Deutsche Akademische Austendienst (D.A.A.D.), Fellowship to London and West Berlin, 1971–72; Verlieh Kritikerpreis, West Berlin, 1975; Arnold Bode Prize, *Documenta 8*, Kassel, 1986. Address: Im Neuroth 29, 6123 Bad Konig-Zell, West Germany.

Individual Exhibitions:

1973 Galerie René Block, West Berlin
1975 Galleria Saman, Genoa
1976 René Block Gallery, New York
 Galleria Saman, Genoa
 Galerie H, Graz, Austria
1977 *Zeichnungen, Objekte, Fotos, Video, Filme*, Kölnischer Kunstverein, Cologne (travelled to the Haus am Waldsee, West Berlin)
 Galleria Ala, Milan
1978 *Der Eintanzer*, Kestner-Gesellschaft, Hannover
 Galleria Saman, Genoa
1978 Van Abbemuseum, Eindhoven, Netherlands
 Kunstverein, Münster, West Germany
 Gallery Ala, New York
1982 *La Ferdinanda: Sonate für eine Medici-Villa*, Staatliche Kunsthalle, Baden-Baden, West Germany
 Stedelijk Museum, Amsterdam
 Galleria Saman, Genoa
1982 Galerie Gewad, Ghent, Belgium
1983 Galerie Eric Franck, Geneva
 Centre d'Art Contemporain, Geneva
 Kunsthaus, Zurich
 Serpentine Gallery, London
 John Hansard Gallery, Southampton, Hampshire

1984 Serpentine Gallery, London
 Museum of Contemporary Art, Chicago
1985 Galerie Eric Franck, Geneva
1986 Marian Goodman Gallery, New York
 Project Studio One, New York
 ARC/Musee d'Art Moderne, Paris
 Museum of Contemporary Art, Los Angeles
1987 Galerie Konrad Fischer, Dusseldorf
 Galerie Elisabeth Kaufmann, Zurich
 Marian Goodman Gallery, New York

Selected Group Exhibitions:

1972 *Documenta 5*, Kassel, West Germany
1974 *Projekt '74*, Kunsthalle, Cologne
 Video Artists, Museum of Modern Art, New York (travelled to the Institute of Contemporary Art, Philadelphia)
1975 *9th Biennale de Paris*, Musée d'Art Moderne de la Ville, Paris
1977 *Documenta 6*, Kassel, West Germany
1979 *Biennale of Drawing*, Nuremburg
1982 *Documenta 7*, Kassel, West Germany
1983 *Sculpture from Germany*, San Francisco Museum of Modern Art (toured the United States)
1985 *The European Iceberg*, Art Gallery of Ontario, Toronto
1987 *Wien Fluss*, Theater am Steinhof, Vienna

Collections:

Kunsthalle, Hamburg, Kestner-Gesellschaft, Hannover; Kölnischer Kunstverein, Cologne; Staatliche Kunsthalle, Baden-Baden, West Germany; Van Abbemuseum, Eindhoven, Netherlands; Stedelijk Museum, Amsterdam; Museum of Modern Art, New York; Anthology Film Archives, New York.

Publications:

By HORN: books—*Dialogo della Vedova Paradisiaca*, Genoa 1976; *Die chinesische Verlobte*, exhibition catalogue, Baden-Baden 1977; films—*Der Eintanzer*, New York, 1978; *Die Chinesische Verlobte*, New York, 1978; *La Ferdinanda, Artemino*, 1981; video—numerous productions, including *Conversation I*, New York, 1972; *Transformation*, New York, 1972–73; *Exercises*, New York, 1973; *Bleistiftmaske*, Hamburg, 1973; *Performances, Hamburg*, 1973; *Mit beiden Handen gleichzeitig die Wande beruhren Blinzeln*, 1975; *Zwischen den Feuchten Zungenblattern*, 1974–75; *Mit zwei Scheren gleichzeitig Haare schreiden*, 1974–75; *Berlin— Unbungen in neun Stucken*, 1974–75; *Paradieswitwe 1/ Paradieswitwe 2*, installation piece, 1975; *Die Chinesische Verlobte*, New York, 1975; *Ubung zu: Der Eintanzer*, New York, 1976.

On HORN: books—*Il Carpo come Linguaggio* by Lea Vergine, Milan 1974; *Rebecca Book I* by Timothy Brann, West Berlin 1975; *Rebecca Horn*, exhibition catalogue, with text by Horst Gerhard Haberl, Graz, Austria 1976; *Rebecca Horn: Zeichnungen, Objekte, Fotos, Video, Filme*, exhibition catalogue, with texts by Wulf Herzogenrath, Marlis Gruterich, Timothy Baum, Lucy R. Lippard and Zdenek Felix, Cologne 1977; *Rebecca Horn: Der Eintanzer*, exhibition catalogue, edited by Carl-Albrecht Haenlein, texts by Marlis Gruterich and Roland H. Wiegenstein, Hannover 1978; *Rebecca Horn: La Ferdinanda: Sonate für eine Medici-Villa*, exhibition catalogue, with texts by Katharine Schmidt and Germano Celant, Baden-Baden, West Germany 1981; *Documenta 7 Katalog/Band 2*, with texts by R. H. Fuchs, Gerhard Storck, Germano Celant and Coosje van Bruggen, Kassel, West Germany 1982.

Entering this room for the very first moment—a room as a completely remote and isolated world of itself; enclosed in its own continuity, formed by the memory of those who have lived here before . . . .

The walls, mirrors, and windows—all living their own singular life and experience—breathing and changing continuously in harmony with the intensity of the ever-changing light.

You feel all of these pasts alive in the objects which surround you, simultaneously evoking new associations and sensations— creating new and unoccupied space for your own fantasies. If you actually decide to inhabit this room, your daydreams will enlarge and become more intense; independence will re-arise as you become increasingly alive.

The only fact that will be unsure: Whether that story has already taken place or is now beginning to develop as an extension of the room itself . . . .

Until the new skin of events mingles so completely with the rest of the room that it finally becomes identical with the old skin.

—Rebecca Horn

In her work Rebecca Horn has inaugurated a new medium, which in its intensity and fascination explores dimensions of art previously unknown. By means of poetical imagination, mostly manifested in actions or processes, the artist has created a sensibility of great significance. In the center of all of her actions is the human being, specifically the body of woman, which is related to objects or instruments. The goal of Rebecca Horn is a ritual of initiation, which can not be achieved by means of rational argumentation; but which in its complexity provokes changes in the perceiving viewer or participant.

Born in 1944 the artist studied in Hamburg and in London and has taught in different countries. Through her actions in Italy, the Netherlands, Austria and the USA she has become one of the most important protagonists of international performance art. Her actions date back to 1968 when she began using the human body as a vehicle to communicate an experience which transcends the former borderlines of painting, sculpture, dance and pantomime. Since 1970 most of her works have been documented in films and since 1972 in video.

Rebecca Horn's early works, such as *Arm-Extensions (Arm Extensionen)* of 1968, *Cornucopia-Séance for Two Breasts (Cornucopia-Séance fuer zwei Brueste)* of 1970 and *Unicorn (Einhorn)* of 1971 use extensions of the body through which emotional and social forms of behavior are made transparent. The action *Pencil Mask (Bleistiftmaske)* of 1973 resembles magic ethnological rituals. In her work *Finger-Gloves (Handschuhfinger)* of 1972 fingers are extended through the use of light sticks of wood with which the artist touches certain objects but at the same time remains in a prescribed distance from them. In *Cockfeather Mask (Hahnfedermaske)* of 1973 this principle is further extended into an interpersonal contact. In *Berlin Exercises in Nine Pieces (Berlin—uebungen in neun Stuecken)* of 1974/1975 these tendencies are fully explored and details of the human body by means of extension and magnets are manipulated into an orchestrated vocabulary. *Measure Box (Messkasten)* of 1975 brings the human body in contact with a container, the human form and the mechanical apparatus relate to each other in a newly imaginative manner.

One of the culminations of the work of Rebecca Horn is *Paradise Widow (Paradieswitwe)* of 1975, an installation which was documented on video and had a highly suggestive significance. In this work an imaginative manifestation of unconscious processes and projections is realized in a precise and carefully planned form. In the years since 1975 Rebecca Horn's vocabulary has extended into a wide range of thematic areas: *The Chinese Fiancee (Die Chinesische Verlobte)* of 1976 and especially *The Dancing Cavalier (Der Eintaenzer)* of 1978 explore new possibilities, the latter work for the first time as a film with actors and a continuous script. Earlier elements of Horn's art are here incorporated into a more comprehensive ensemble of human body, objects and processes. The sensibility of woman remains in the center, and dimensions of an art experience which in previous times was unexplored are made possible.

Later works by Rebecca Horn also incorporate space and musical forms. *Dialogue Between Two Swings (Der Dialog der Zwillingsschaukeln)* of 1979 is with a musical composition by Hans Werner Henze. In *La Ferdinanda—Sonata for a Medici Villa (La Ferdinanda—Sonate fuer eine Medici Villa)* of 1981 several earlier tendencies are synchronized, and container, objects, feathers and human beings are elements of a larger ensemble which brings out mysterious and irrational realities. Works of recent years, such as *The Box of the Phoenix* of 1983, include alchemistic themes in a further extension of her earlier thematics and the theme of couples, such as *The En-*

gaged Couple (Die Verlobten) and *The Hybrid (Der Zwitter)*, both of 1987. The essence of all her works are, as the artist in 1972 articulated it, attempts at "creating new models of interaction rituals", a creative exploration of processes between human beings, their isolation and physical communication, their emotional and physical interrelatedness.

—Udo Kultermann

HOUEDARD, Dom (Pierre) Sylvester.

British. Born in Guernsey, Channel Islands, 16 February 1924. Studied history at Jesus College, Oxford, 1942–44, 1947–49; studied philosophy at the Benedictine University of Sant'Anselmo, Rome, 1955–55; ordained as a priest, 1959. Served in British Army Intelligence, in the Far East, 1944–47. Benedictine monk, Prinknash Abbey, Gloucester, since 1949: worked as a librarian at Farnborough Abbey, Hampshire, 1959–61; Literary Editor for the New Testament and Sub-Editor for the Old Testament, *Jerusalem Bible*, 1961. Member, International Liturgical Commission, 1966, and International Committee for the Liturgy in English, 1966; Vice-President, Poetry Society, London, 1974. Member and Vice-President, Association of Little Presses, London, since 1965. Address: Prinknash Abbey, Gloucester GL4 8EX, England.

Individual Exhibitions:

1964	St. Catherine's College, Oxford
	Galerie Riquelme, Paris
1965	Galerie Bressy, Lyons
	Galerie Denise-Davy, Paris
	Kornblee Gallery, New York
	Institute of Contemporary Arts, London
	Signals Gallery, London
1966	Tyler School of Art, Philadelphia
	Peacetower, Los Angeles
	Midland Gallery, Nottingham
	Galeria Universitaria Aristod, Mexico City
	Galeria Juana Mordo, Madrid
	Gallery 10, London
	Kunstcentrum 'tvenster, Rotterdam
	Arnolfini Gallery, Bristol
	Galeria Barandiaran, San Sebastian, Spain
	Castello del Valentino, Turin
	Subscription Rooms, Stroud, Gloucestershire
1967	*Brighton Festival*, Sussex
	Lisson Gallery, London
	New Metropole Arts Centre, Folkestone, Kent
	French Institute, London
	Festival de Fort Boyard, Rochefort-sur-Mer, France
	Studio 2B, Bergamo, Italy
1968	Absalon, Bath
	Galerie Nächst St. Stephan, Vienna
	Totem-1 Gallery, Salford, Lancashire
1969	Westfälischer Kunstverein, Münster, West Germany
	Fine Arts Gallery, Vancouver
	Axis, Bristol
1970	Ceolfrith Gallery, Sunderland, County Durham
	Stedelijk Museum, Amsterdam
	Victoria and Albert Museum, London (toured the U.K.)
1971	Avelles Gallery, Vancouver
	Bear Lane Gallery, Oxford
	Art Centre, Bristol
	Laing Art Gallery, Newcastle upon Tyne
1972	Laing Art Gallery, Newcastle upon Tyne
1974	Oval House, London
	LYC Museum, Brampton, Cumberland

Selected Group Exhibitions:

1965	*Between Poetry and Painting*, Institute of Contemporary Arts, London

Publications:

By HOUEDARD: books—*Yes-No*, Daneway, Gloucester 1963; *Thalamus-Sol*, Maidstone, Kent 1964; *Rock Sand Tide*, Woodchester, Gloucestershire 1964; *A Snow Mouse*, Bristol 1964; *Frog-Pond-Plop*, Woodchester, Gloucestershire 1965; *Atom*, Woodchester, Gloucestershire 1965; *Kinkon*, London 1965; *Worm-Wood, Womb-Word*, Daneway, Gloucestershire 1966; *A Book of Chakras: 8 Tantrics: Studies Towards Mechanical Fingers by dsh for Inner Moon Painting*, Watford, Hertfordshire 1966; *To Catch a Whiteman by His Manifesto*, Corsham, Wiltshire 1967; *Tantric Poems, Perhaps*, London 1967; *Book of 12 Mudras*, Corsham, Wiltshire 1967; *Book of Mazes and Troytowns*, Corsham, Wiltshire 1967; *Easter Frog Toy for Pesach-Skipover*, Corsham, Wiltshire 1967; *Eros A-Grape*, London 1967; *Semaine Euclidienne*, Sherborne, Dorset 1968; *Poster for the Breakdown of Nations Fourth World Conference*, London 1968; *Deus-Snap*, Corsham, Wiltshire 1968; *Miniposters*, Sherborne, Dorset 1968; *The Sun-Cheese Wheel-Ode: A Double-Rolling-Gloster Memorial for Ken Cox*, Sherborne, Dorset 1969; *En Trance*, Bristol 1969; *12 Nahuatl Dancepoems from the Cosmic Typewriter*, Sherborne, Dorset 1969; *Texts*, edited by John Sharkey, London 1969; *Streets Go Both Crazy Ways at Once*, Sherborne, Dorset 1969; *Book of Battledores*, Sherborne, Dorset 1969; *Book of Onomastikons*, Sherborne, Dorset 1969; *Splendid Weeping*, Corsham, Wiltshire 1969; *Successful Cube Tranceplant in Honor of Chairman Mao*, Corsham, Wiltshire 1970; *Ode to the Colonels*, Corsham, Wiltshire, 1970; *Grove Sings: Reflecting Poem for ihf*, Sunderland, County Durham 1970; *Auto-de-Chakra-Struction*, Oxford 1971; *Main Calm Line*, London 1972; *Like Contemplation*, London 1972; *Poems*, edited by Charles Verey, Sunderland, County Durham 1972; *Begin Again: A Book of Reflections and Reversals*, Brampton, Cumbria 1975.

On HOUEDARD: articles—in *Poems*, edited by Charles Verey, 1972 (includes bibliography).

HOYLAND, John.

British. Born in Sheffield, Yorkshire, 12 October 1934. Studied at Sheffield College of Art, Yorkshire, 1951–56; Royal Academy Schools, London, 1956–60. Independent painter, in Kingston-upon-Thames, Surrey, 1963–68, in Market Lavington, Wiltshire, 1968–73, and in London since 1970: visited New York, 1964, and associated with Helen Frankenthaler, Barnett Newmann, Robert Motherwell and other American painters, and subsequently spent long periods living and working in New York, 1967–79, and in Los Angeles, 1982. Lecturer, Croydon College of Art, Surrey, 1962; Lecturer, 1962, and Principal Lecturer, 1965, Chelsea School of Art, London; Charles A. Dana Professor of Fine Arts, Colgate University, Hamilton, New York, Spring/1972; Visiting Teacher, St. Martin's School of Art, Royal Academy Schools, and Slade School of Fine Art, all London, 1974–77; Artist-in-Residence, Studio School, New York, 1978, and Melbourne University, Australia, 1979; Teacher, Slade School of Fine Art, London, 1980, 1983. Recipient: Gulbenkian Foundation Purchase Award, 1963; Peter Stuyvesant Bursary, 1964; International Young Artists Award, Tokyo, 1964; Prize, *John Moores Exhibition*, Liverpool, 1965; Prize, *Open Painting Exhibition*, Belfast, 1966; First Prize (with Robyn Denny), *Edinburgh Open 100* exhibition, 1969; First Prize, Chichester National Art Exhibition, 1975; First Prize, *John Moores Exhibition*, Liverpool, 1983; First Prize, Athena Art Awards, London, 1987. Agent: Waddington Galleries, 2 Cork Street, London W1. Address: 41 Charterhouse Square, London EC1, England.

Individual Exhibitions:

1964	Marlborough New London Gallery
1965	Chelsea School of Art, London
1967	Whitechapel Art Gallery, London
	Waddington Galleries, London
	Galerie Heiner Friedrich, Munich

Robert Elkon Gallery, New York
Nicholas Wilder Gallery, Los Angeles
Waddington Fine Art, Montreal
1968 Waddington Fine Art, Montreal
1969 Robert Elkon Gallery, New York
Waddington Galleries, London
Leslie Waddington Prints, London
Bienal, Sao Paulo (with Anthony Caro)
1970 Waddington Galleries, London
André Emmerich Gallery, New York
Galleria dell'Ariete, Milan
1971 Waddington Galleries, London
André Emmerich Gallery, New York
Waddington Fine Art, Montreal
1972 Leslie Waddington Prints, London
André Emmerich Gallery, New York
Harcus-Krakow Gallery, Boston
Picker Gallery, Colgate University, Hamilton, New York
1973 Waddington Galleries, London
Galleria l'Approdo, Turin
1974 Nicholas Wilder Gallery, Los Angeles
Waddington Galleries, London
Studio La Città, Verona
1975 Waddington Fine Art, Montreal
Galleria E, Bolzano, Italy
Waddington Galleries, London
1976 Galleria La Bertesca, Milan
Galerie Modulo, Porto Modula, Lisbon
Waddington Galleries, London
Studio La Città, Verona
1978 Waddington Fine Art, Montreal
Waddington Galleries, London
1979 André Emmerich Gallery, New York
Bernard Jacobson Ltd., New York
Waddington Fine Art, Toronto
Serpentine Gallery, London (travelled to the Birmingham City Art Gallery, and Mappin Art Gallery, Sheffield, Yorkshire)
Art Contact, Coconut Grove, Florida
1980 University of Melbourne
Galerie von Braunbehrens, Munich
Kammer Galerie, Hamburg
1981 Waddington Galleries, London
Gumps Gallery, San Francisco
1982 Jacobson/Hochman Gallery, New York
Bernard Jacobson Gallery, Los Angeles
Compass Gallery, Glasgow
1983 Waddington Galleries, London
Hokin/Kaufman Gallery, Chicago
1984 Castlefield Gallery, Manchester, Lancashire
1985 Waddington Galleries, London
1986 Waddington and Shiell, Toronto
1987 Waddington Galleries, London
Oxford Gallery, Oxford
Lever/Myerson Gallery, New York

Selected Group Exhibitions:

1959 *Young Contemporaries,* RI Galleries, London
1964 *The New Generation,* Whitechapel Art Gallery, London (toured the U.K.)
1965 *Biennale des Jeunes,* Musée d'Art Moderne de la Ville, Paris
1968 *New British Painting and Sculpture,* University of California at Los Angeles (toured the United States)
1973 *La Peinture Anglaise aujourd'hui,* Musée d'Art Moderne de la Ville, Paris
1976 *Arte Inglese Oggi,* Palazzo Reale, Milan
1978 *Critics' Choice,* Institute of Contemporary Arts, London
1982 *Aspects of British Art Today,* Metropolitan Art Museum, Tokyo (toured Japan)
1984 *English Expressionism,* Warwick Arts Trust, London
1987 *British Art in the 20th Century: The Modern Movement,* Royal Academy, London (travelled to the Staatsgalerie, Stuttgart)

Collections:

Royal Academy of Arts, London; Tate Gallery, London; Vic-toria and Albert Museum, London; National Museum, Helsinki; Albright-Knox Art Gallery, Buffalo, New York; Colgate University, Hamilton, New York; Phoenix Museum, Arizona; Art Gallery of South Australia, Adelaide; University of Sydney.

Publications:

By HOYLAND: articles—"John Hoyland Talking to Colin Painter", interview, in *Aspects* (Newcastle on Tyne), Autumn 1981; "Hoyland at Home", interview with Mike van Joel, in *Art Line* (London), February 1983; "Painting is the head, hand and the heart", interview with Liz Finch, in *Ritz* (London), June 1984; "On Colour", interview with Sally-Ann Schilling, in *The Artist* (London), September 1986.

On HOYLAND: books—*The New Generation,* exhibition catalogue, by David Thompson, London 1964; *John Hoyland: Paintings 1960-67,* exhibition catalogue, by Bryan Robertson, London 1967; *Late Modern,* by Edward Lucie Smith, New York 1969; *Anthony Caro/John Hoyland,* exhibition catalogue, Sao Paulo 1969; *John Hoyland,* exhibition catalogue, by Bryan Robertson and others, London 1979; *John Hoyland,* exhibition catalogue by John McEwen, London 1987.

John Hoyland's painting is rich and subtle. It has evolved continually since 1960 from a linear, often symmetrical, abstraction to a free, painterly and complex arrangement of fields of intensely coloured paint. His work may be considered as a celebration of the qualities of paint as an independent medium. His pictures are generally occupied by distinct shapes or forms, but the characteristic silhouettes and the relationships between these have changed over the years.

The pictures of 1963 contained forms that were isolated from the flatly painted background but adhered together in the illusory space by touching or intertwining with one another. A group in the mid-60's comprise roughly rectilinear forms, architecturally assembled on a ground that is stained so as to appear veil-like or transparent. Some of these are built up from the edges and so appear to lie in the plane of the canvas; others are not so strictly located. However, any certainty may be contradicted by the intrusion of diagonals and is more subtly subverted by the spatial effects of the combinations of colours chosen and of the varying densities of the paint. In some cases these forms completely fill the field and may suggest an extension into the real space around the painting.

The scale of these paintings was often very large, one might say architectural.

The occasional runs or drips of liquid paint that occur in these pictures became increasingly dominant in works of the late 60's and 70's in which Hoyland's own development had led him close to the concept of painting taught and exercised by Hans Hofmann. As before, the composition was dominated by a single colour or pair of colours and a specific division of the canvas. His paint became thicker as well as more vivid and often unexpected in hue. The painterly "objects" within the picture were organized and related to one another by a skilfully deployed range of devices harmonically related to the dominant division. Among them were conspicuous superimposition of forms, discontinuous surfaces which allow lower strata to show through, reinforced or frayed out edges, parallels and angular divergences, and juxtaposition of similar or of contrasting hues and shades.

One is always very much aware of the artist having worked on and built on the surface. In general the characteristics of the works of the early and mid 70's was rectilinearity, diagonals forming the necessary exception.

The most recent paintings, that is those since about 1977-78, have been increasingly dominated by the diagonal. At first, this figured as a structural division of the canvas. In the last two or three years the paint has become less luxuriant, pictures have often been smaller in scale, and the objects in them formed of diagonals, that is they are lozenges, like the diamonds of a pack of cards, which have broken free and float in the picture of space.

Hoyland shows no sign of repeating himself or abandoning his basic approach to painting, which has a vitality and range comparable to that of any artist who has more directly looked for refreshment to nature itself.

—Michael Compton

HRDLICKA, Alfred.

Austrian. Born in Vienna, 27 February 1928. Studied art, under Albert Paris Gutersloh and Josef Dobrowsky, Vienna, 1946-53, and painting, under Fritz Wotruba, Vienna, 1953-57. Painter, sculptor and graphic artist, Vienna, since 1958. Head of painting classes, Summer Academy, Salzburg; Instructor, Akademie der Bildende Künste, Stuttgart, 1971-75, and Hochschule für Künste, Hamburg, 1973. Recipient: Ehrenpreis, Vienna, 1961; First Prize, *Graphics Biennale,* Ljubljana 1963; Bianco e Nero Prize, Lugano, Switzerland 1964; First Prize, *Biella Internazionale,* Italy, 1965; Graphics Prize, *5th Print Biennale,* Tokyo 1966; Graphics Prize, *7th International Exhibition of Gravure,* Ljubljana, 1967. Honorary Corresponding Member, Akademie der Kunst der DDR, East Berlin, 1978. Agent: Galerie Rothe, Werderplatz 17, Heidelberg, West Germany. Address: Kirchengasse 48, 1010 Vienna, Austria.

Individual Exhibitions:

1960 Zedlitzhalle, Vienna
1962 Kunstlerhaus, Vienna
Wiener Sezession, Vienna
1963 *Druckgraphik und Steinskulpturen,* Galerie Welz, Salzburg
Tiroler Kunstpavilion, Innsbruck
1965 Galleria Penelope, Rome
Neue Münchner Galerie, Munich
Württembergischer Kunstverein, Stuttgart
1966 Galleria Torre, Turin
Badischer Kunstverein, Karlsruhe, West Germany
Galerie Peithner-Lichtenfels, Vienna
1967 Osterreichisches Konsulat, Baden-Baden, West Germany
1968 Marlborough Fine Art, London
Galerie Valentien, Stuttgart
Galerie André, West Berlin
Galerie Siemenshaus, Hamburg
1969 Osterreich-Haus, West Berlin
Randolectil, Graphische Sammlung Albertina, Vienna
Galerie im Taxispalais, Innsbruck
Graphik, Galerie Valentien, Stuttgart
Galerie Welz, Salzburg
1970 Galerie d'Eendt, Amsterdam
1971 *Skulpturen, Zeichnungen, Radierungen,* Galerie Rothe, Heidelberg
Galleria Il Fante di Spade, Rome
Galerie Hartmann, Munich
1972 Suermondt-Museum, Aachen, West Germany
1974 Kestner-Gesellschaft, Hannover
Konstakademie, Stockholm
1975 Nationalgalerie, West Berlin
Kunstverein, Hamburg
Wallraf-Richartz-Museum, Cologne
Skulpturen und Zeichnungen, Galerie Valentien, Stuttgart
1976 Kunsthochschule, West Berlin
1978 *Wie ein Totentanz,* Kupferstichkabinette, Dresden
1981 Galerie Orangerie, Vienna
1982 Galerie Lietzow, West Berlin
1987 Galerie Hilger, Frankfurt
Galerie Hodl, Zurich

Selected Group Exhibitions:

1961 *The Object in Austrian Painting and Sculpture,* Wiener Sezession, Vienna

1964 *Biennale*, Venice
1966 *5th Biennale of Tokyo*, National Museum of Modern Art, Tokyo
1967 *Bienal*, Sao Paulo
1969 *6th Biennale Internazionale della Scultura*, Carrara, Italy
1973 *Biennale of Sculpture*, Middelheim Park, Antwerp

Collections:

Staatsgalerie, Stuttgart; Staatliche Kunstsammlung, Dresden.

Publications:

By HRDLICKA: book—*Alfred Hrdlicka*, edited by Heinz Moos, Munich 1969.

On HRDLICKA: books—*Alfred Hrdlicka: Druckgraphik und Steinskulpturen*, exhibition catalogue, with text by Ernst Koller, Johann Muschik and Josef Donnenberg, Salzburg 1963; *Alfred Hrdlicka*, exhibition catalogue, with text by Wolfgang Fischer, London 1968; *Alfred Hrdlicka: Randolectil*, with text by Kristian Sotriffer, Vienna 1969; *Alfred Hrdlicka, Alfred Hrdlicka*, by H. G. Dehr, G. Eisler and J. Muschik, Vienna 1969; *Alfred Hrdlicka: Drei Zyklen*, with text by Johann Muschik, Vienna 1969; *Alfred Hrdlicka*, exhibition catalogue, with text by Ina Stegen, Salzburg 1969; *Alfred Hrdlicka: Graphik*, exhibition catalogue, with text by Karl Diemer, Stuttgart 1969; *Alfred Hrdlicka: Skulpturen, Zeichnungen, Radierungen*, exhibition folder, with text by Wolfgang Rothe, Heidelberg 1971; *Alfred Hrdlicka*, exhibition folder, with text by Ernst Fischer, Rome 1971; *Alfred Hrdlicka*, exhibition catalogue, with texts by Wieland Schmied, Elias Canetti and Karl Diemer, Hannover 1974; *Malerei aus Bereichen des unbewussten* by R. P. Hartmann, Cologne 1974; *Alfred Hrdlicka: Skulpturen und Zeichnungen*, exhibition catalogue, with texts by Ernst Fischer, Wieland Schmied and Karl Diemer, Stuttgart 1975; *Alfred Hrdlicka: Wie ein Totentanz*, exhibition catalogue with text by Werner Schmidt, Dresden 1978; *Alfred Hrdlicka*, exhibition catalogue with essay by Gerhard Habarta, Vienna 1981.

To be a young boy in Vienna at the time of the Anschluss was a cathartic experience for anyone later to become an artist. Alfred Hrdlicka must early in his life have been cleansed of all the haunting doubts surrounding good and evil that run helter-skelter through the immature mind. As soon as he could think, he must have been aware of truth and lies and most of the gradations between the two. For him, truth spelt the ability to tell terrible stories that arose from a pervading atmosphere of cruelty, persecution, torture and blackmail. All these dark areas of existence are repeatedly present in both his graphic works and his sculpture. He allows himself a freedom of expression in manner and imagery that most times frightens the innocent or touches the passions and secret thoughts of the guilty.

Working in Wotruba's studio or casting wry looks at the paintings of Mondrian have done nothing to dull the spirit and inspiration of the uncensored commentator. The needle of his etchings is sharp with an acid hardly paralleled in the work of other graphic artists. However complex and tangled the ultimate print may appear, the storyline is lucid and devastating. As a painter he produced canvases that had all the venom of paintings by George Grosz but which, despite care and attention to detail, were bolder and more explicit than those of the German.

Hrdlicka's "social comments," his horrifying anecdotes of life under the Nazis, the regurgitations of biblical classics like the story of Samson and Delilah, and the smut are all there in the graphics. Major opera.

But the monumental Hrdlicka is very different. Often using the most unyielding stone, he carves masculine figures whose nakedness—generally at odds with the social system, bound like slaves, caught in the central situation of a drama, even swinging head downwards with the feet lashed together—is over life-size, if not always in fact, forever in the memory.

Hrdlicka is something of a titan. His mind, like his works, takes up grand themes. Yet this is the same man who plays games with the syndrome of the comic strip, fashioning its scenes and participants in his own fearless way, sometimes with an element of black humour, sometimes evoking a truer than life Grand-Guignol.

As Robert Graves pointed out, the White Goddess has many faces from the unspoilt countenance of a little girl to the raddled mask of a witch—and she has multiple personalities to match. Hrdlicka would say the same about SEX. In a series of outrageous photographs he shows a girl fondling the penis of one of his sculptures with the caption "Why can't the sexually unfulfilled claim an art-orgasm?" and goes on to title other photos "Hrdlicka knows what women want," "Women want Hrdlicka."

—Sheldon Williams

HUEBLER, Douglas.

American. Born in Ann Arbor, Michigan, 27 October 1924. Studied at the University of Michigan, Ann Arbor, 1946–53, MFA 1953; Academie Julian, Paris, 1947–48; and Cleveland School of Art, Ohio, 1952. Served in the United States Marine Corps, Air Combat Intelligence, South West Pacific, 1943–46. Independent artist, since 1953. Instructor, Harvard University, Cambridge, Massachusetts; California Institute of the Arts, Valencia. Agent: Leo Castelli Gallery, 420 West Broadway, New York, New York 10013.

Individual Exhibitions:

1953 Phillips Gallery, Detroit
1967 Obelisk Gallery, Boston
1968 Windham College, Putney, Vermont
     Seth Siegelaub, New York
1969 Eugenia Butler Gallery, Los Angeles
1970 Galerie Konrad Fischer, Dusseldorf
     Addison Gallery, Andover, Massachusetts
     Galleria Sperone, Turin
     Galerie Yvon Lambert, Paris
     Art and Project, Amsterdam
1971 Leo Castelli Gallery, New York
     Art and Project, Amsterdam
1972 California Institute of Arts, Valencia
     Galerie Yvon Lambert, Paris
     Galleria Toselli, Milan
     Jack Wendler Gallery, London
     Galerie Konrad Fischer, Dusseldorf
     Leo Castelli Gallery, New York
     Museum of Fine Arts, Boston
     Westfälischer Kunstverein, Münster, West Germany
1973 Von der Heydt Museum, Wuppertal, West Germany
     Städtische Kunsthalle, Kiel
     Leo Castelli Gallery, New York
     Galleria Fischer-Sperone, Rome
     Museum of Modern Art, Oxford
     Israel Museum, Tel-Aviv
1974 M.T.L. Gallery, Brussels
     Galleria Lia Rumma, Naples
     Galleria Sperone, Turin
     Galerie Yvon Lambert, Paris
     Galerie Konrad Fischer, Dusseldorf
     Galerie Rolf Preisig, Basel
1975 Galerie Francoise Lambert, Milan
     Cusack Gallery, Houston
1976 Galeria Akumulatory II, Poznan, Poland
     Sperone Westwater Fischer, New York
     Leo Castelli Gallery, New York
1977 Thomas Lewallen Gallery, Santa Monica, California
1978 Leo Castelli Gallery, New York
1979 Van Abbemuseum, Eindhoven, Netherlands
1981 Leo Castelli Gallery, New York
1983 Leo Castelli Gallery, New York
1984 Los Angeles Center for Photographic Studies (retrospective)
     Museum of Contemporary Art, Los Angeles
1985 Albright-Knox Art Gallery, Buffalo, New York
     Kuhlenschmidt/Simon Gallery, Los Angeles
1986 Leo Castelli Gallery, New York
1988 La Jolla Museum of Art, California

Selected Group Exhibitions:

1966 *Primary Structures*, Jewish Museum, New York
1969 *When Attitudes Become Form*, Kunsthalle, Berne (toured Europe)
1970 *Software*, Jewish Museum, New York
1972 *Documenta*, Kassel, West Germany
1973 *Contemporanea*, Parcheggio Villa Borghese, Rome
1976 *72nd Annual Exhibition*, Art Institute of Chicago
1980 *Reasoned Space*, Center for Creative Photography, University of Arizona, Tucson
1984 *Content: A Contemporary Focus 1974–84*, Hirshhorn Museum, Washington D.C.
1987 *Avant Garde in the Eighties*, Los Angeles County Museum of Art

Collections:

Museum of Modern Art, New York; Los Angeles County Museum of Art; Stedelijk Museum, Amsterdam; Boston Museum of Fine Art; Addison Gallery of American Art, Andover, Massachusetts; Tate Gallery, London; Israel Museum, Jerusalem; National Gallery of Canada, Ottawa; Australian National Gallery, Canberra; Van Abbemuseum, Eindhoven, Netherlands.

Publications:

By HUEBLER: books—*Untitled (Xerox-Book)*, New York 1968; *Durata/Duration*, Turin 1970; *Selected Drawings 1968–1973*, Hong Kong 1975; *Contemporary Portraits*, St. Lucia, Queensland 1975; *Douglas Huebler*, exhibition catalogue, Eindhoven 1979; *Crocodile Tears*, New York 1985, Los Angeles 1986; articles—"Letter to the Editor" in *Artnews* (New York), September 1966; "Statements + Location Pieces 1, 2" in *VH 101/3* (Paris), 1970; "Trois Travaux" in *VH101/6* (Paris), 1972; "Concept vs. Art Object: A Conversation Between Douglas Huebler and Budd Hopkins" in *Arts Magazine*, (New York), April 1972; "Talking with Douglas Huebler", interview with Michael Auping, in *LAICA Journal* (Los Angeles), July/August 1977; "Sabotage or Trophy? Advance or Retreat?" in *Artforum* (New York), May 1982.

On HUEBLER: books—*The Structure of Art* by Jack Burnham, New York 1971; *Concept Art* by Klaus Honnef, Cologne 1972; *Beyond Modern Art* by Carla Gottlieb, New York 1976; *Art Today, NYC* by Edward Lucie Smith, London 1977; *More Than You See* by Frederick Horowitz, New York 1985; articles—"Huebler: Une Perception Nouvelle" by Bernard Bourgeaud in *Pariscope* (Paris), March 1970; "Douglas Huebler, Leo Castelli" by W. Domingo in *Arts Magazine* (New York), September/October 1971; "Douglas Huebler" by April Kingsley in *Artforum* (New York), May 1972; "Douglas Huebler: Everything about Everything" by Lucy Lippard in *Artnews* (New York), December 1972; "Douglas Huebler" by Klaus Honnef in *Art and Artists* (London), January 1973; "Douglas Huebler" by Lynda Morris in *Studio International* (London), February 1973; "Douglas Huebler" by I. Lebeer in *Chroniques de l'Art Vivant* (Paris), April 1973; "Douglas Huebler: Two Recent Works" in *Studio International* (London), December 1974; "Douglas Huebler's Strategies" by James Welling in *Artweek* (Oakland, California), 3 December 1977; "Fictional Escapades: Douglas Huebler" by Paul Stimson in *Art in America* (New York), February 1982; "The Crocodile Tears of Douglas Huebler" by Hunter Drohojowska in *L.A. Weekly* (Los Angeles), 29 June 1984; "Douglas Huebler" by Colin Gardner in *Artforum* (New York), March 1986.

HUNDERTWASSER, Friedensreich.

Austrian. Born Friedrich Stowasser in Vienna, 15 December 1928; adopted the name Hundertwasser, 1949. Educated at the Montessori-School, Vienna, 1936–37; studied painting at the Academy of Fine Arts, Vienna, 1948. Married Herta Leitner in 1958 (divorced, 1960); married Yuko Ikewada in 1960 (divorced, 1966). Travelled in Tuscany with the painter René Brô, 1949; painted two murals with Brô at Saint Mandé, 1950; independent painter and graphic artist, Vienna, 1949–51, and in North Africa, France and Italy, 1951–68; has lived on his ship, *Regentag*, and travelled around the world, since 1968: concentrated on metal embossed graphics, Rome and Venice, 1967; worked with Peter Schamoni on the film *Hundertwasser's Rainy Day*, 1970–72; worked on architectural-ecological projects, 1972; collaborated with Japanese woodcutters for eleven years and produced first woodcut portfolio, *Nana Hiaku Mizu*, 1973; designed postage stamp, "Spiraltree," for Austria, 1974; designed peace flag for the Middle East, 1978, environmental poster, "Arche Noah 2000," 1980, anti-nuclear poster, "Plant Trees, Avert Nuclear Peril," for Ralph Nader's Critical Mass Energy Project, Washington, D.C., 1980; worked on architectural projects at the Rosenthal Factory, Selb, West Germany, 1982. Guest Lecturer, Kunsthochschule, Hamburg, 1959. Lecturer, Master School, Academy of Fine Arts, Vienna, since 1981. Recipient: Prix du Syndicat d'Initiative, *Biennale*, Bordeaux, 1957; Sanbra Prize, *Bienal*, Sao Paulo, 1959; Mainichi Prize, *International Art Exhibition*, Tokyo, 1961; Grosser Österreichisches Staatspreis für Kunst, Vienna, 1980; Austrian Naturschutzpreis, 1981; Environment Prize, Goslar, Germany, 1984; Gold Medal, Geneva, 1984. Agent: Joram Harel Management, Vienna. Address: c/o Joram Harel Management, Post Office Box 145, A–1013 Vienna, Austria.

Individual Exhibitions:

1952	Art Club, Vienna
1954	Studio Paul Facchetti, Paris
1955	Galleria del Naviglio, Milan
1956	Studio Paul Facchetti, Paris
1960	Galerie Raymond Cordier, Paris
1961	Tokyo Gallery
1962	Austrian Pavilion, *Biennale*, Venice
1963	*Hundertwasser Ist ein Geschenk für Deutschland*, Galerie Anne Abels, Cologne
1964	Kestner-Gesellschaft, Hannover (toured Europe)
	Stedelijk Museum, Amsterdam
	Kunsthalle, Berne
1965	Moderna Museet, Stockholm
	Museum des 20. Jahrhunderts, Vienna
	Galerie Paul Facchetti, Paris
	Hammerlunds Kunsthandel, Oslo
1967	Galerie Karl Flinker, Paris
	Galerie Krugier/Galerie Georges Moos, Geneva
	Galleria La Medusa, Rome
	Galerie Welz, Salzburg
	Hanover Gallery, London
1968	University of California, Berkeley (toured the United States)
1971	*Hundertwasser: Das Grafische Gesamtwerke Originale*, Galerie Hans Hoeppner, Hamburg
	M. Fisher Gallery, London
1973	Auckland City Art Gallery (toured New Zealand and Australia)
	Aberbach Fine Art, New York
1974	*Stowasser 1943—Hundertwasser 1974*, Graphische Sammlung Albertina, Vienna (and world tour from 1974)
	Galerie Paul Facchetti, Paris
1975	Haus der Kunst, Munich (retrospective)
	Austria Presents Hundertwasser, Musee d'Art Moderne de la Ville, Paris (and world tour from 1975)
1979	*Hundertwasser Is Painting*, Aberbach Fine Art, New York (and world tour)
1982	Artcurial, Paris

Selected Group Exhibitions:

1952	*Annual Exhibition*, Art Club, Vienna
1954	*Biennale*, Venice
1957	*1st Bienale de Bordeaux*, Musée des Beaux-Arts, Bordeaux
1959	*Biennal*, Sao Paulo
1961	*6th International Art Exhibition*, National Museum of Modern Art, Tokyo
	Documenta, Kassel, West Germany
1969	*Salon de Mai*, Musée d'Art Moderne, Paris (annually until 1976)
1972	*After Surrealism*, Ringling Museum of Art, Sarasota, Florida
1973	*Triennale*, Milan

Collections:

Kunsthalle, Hamburg; Kunsthalle, Mannheim; Bundesministerium, Vienna; Albertina Museum, Vienna; Stedelijk Museum, Amsterdam; Peggy Guggenheim Collection, Venice; Guggenheim Museum, New York; Museum of Modern Art, New York; St. Louis University.

Publications:

By HUNDERTWASSER: books—*Der Transautomatismus: Eine allgemeine Mobilmachung des Auges*, Rome/Paris 1956; *Verschimmelungs Manifest gegen den Rätionalismus in der Architektur*, Seckau, Austria 1958; *Architektur, Boykott Manifest*, Vienna 1968; *Scheisse-Manifest*, Munich 1975.

On HUNDERTWASSER: books—*Hundertwasser ist ein Gesh cent für Deutschland*, exhibition catalogue, Cologne 1963; *Hundertwasser*, exhibition catalogue, with text by Wieland Schmied, Amsterdam 1964; *Hundertwasser*, exhibition catalogue, with text by Wieland Schmied, Berne 1964; *Hundertwasser*, exhibition catalogue, edited by K. G. Hulten and Karin Bergquist Lindegren, Stockholm 1965; *Hundertwasser*, exhibition catalogue, with text by Wieland Schmied, Vienna 1965; *Hundertwasser*, exhibition catalogue, with text by Leif Ostby, Oslo 1965; *Hundertwasser*, by Chipp Herschel Richardson, New York 1968; *Hundertwasser: Das Grafische Gesamtwerke Originale*, exhibition catalogue, with text by Wieland Schmied, Hamburg 1971; *Hundertwasser 1973, New York*, with text by Joachim Jean Aberbach, Glarus, Switzerland 1973; *Zweihundert jahre Phantastische Malerei* by Wieland Schmied, Berlin 1973; *Hundertwasser*, with text by F. Welz, S. Poppe and W. Koscharzky, Glarus, Switzerland 1975; *Hundertwasser 1975–1980: USA*, with text by Walter Koschatzky, Joachim Jean Aberbach and Wieland Schmied, Glarus, Switzerland 1975; *Hundertwasser 1981: Austria*, with texts by Bruno Kreisky, Leopold S. Seuphor and Helmut Zilk, Glarus, Switzerland 1980; *Hundertwasser: peintures*, exhibition catalogue with texts by Andre Pieyre de Mandiargues and Alain Jouffroy, Paris 1982; articles—"Hundertwasser" by Annette Kuhn in *Artsmagazine* (New York), April 1969; "A Hundertwasser Retrospective" by B. A. Richardson in *Art Journal* (New York), September 1969; "Friedrich Hundertwasser" in *Mizue* (Tokyo), 1969.

The faery world of Friedensreich Hundertwasser is brightly coloured and is often constructed like an onion, one skin within another within another. The figuration is not always immediately apparent, but it is there nonetheless, sometimes with actual figures woven into the pattern, at others in magical architecture, all coloured bricks and stained-glass windows.

Friedensreich Hundertwasser: *Rain Castle*, 1975

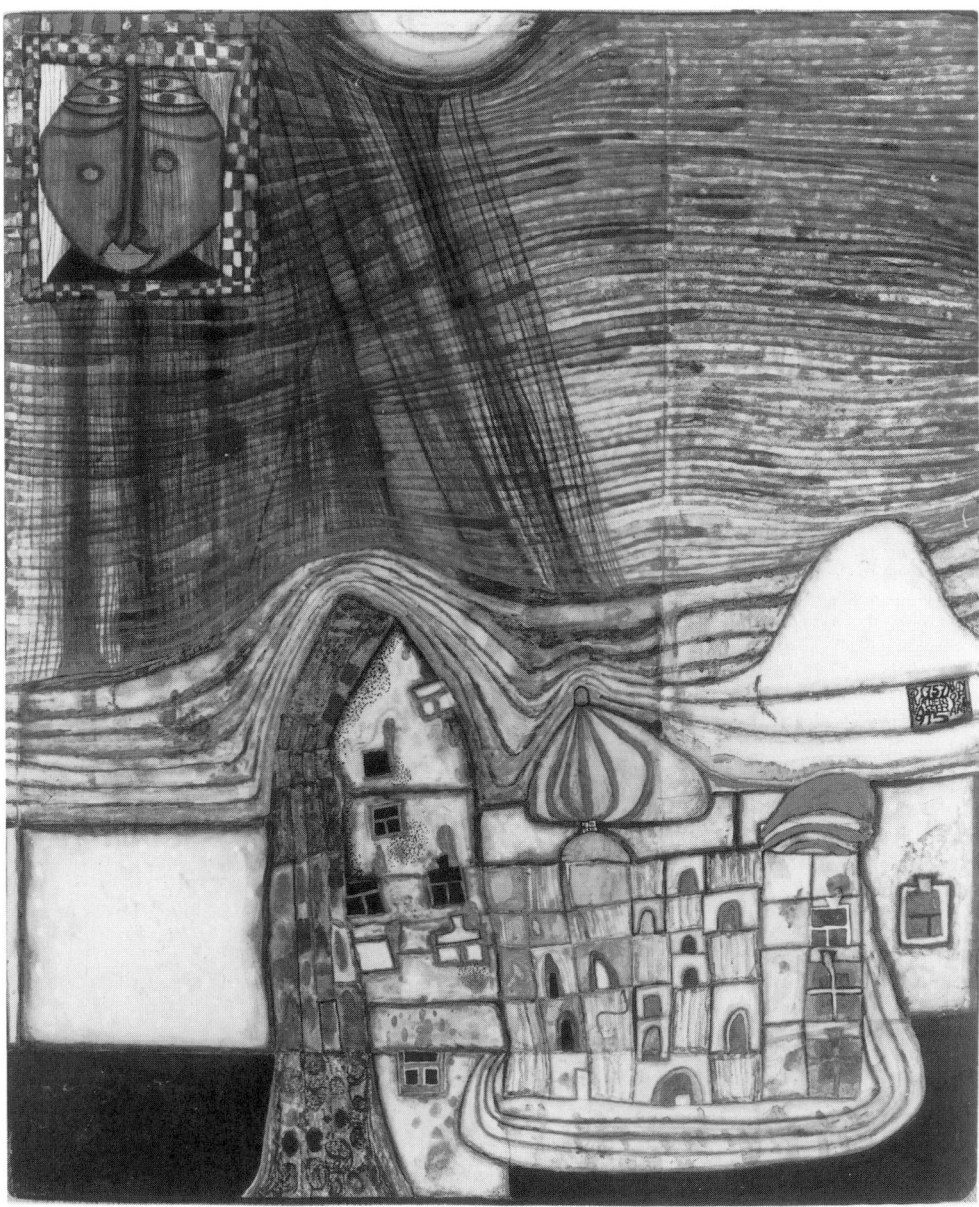

Although the artist has travelled extensively across southern Europe, Morocco and Tunisia and was working in Japan during 1961, he has never shrugged off the Central European character of his style. If today he commutes between Normandy, Giudecca and Waldviertel (Austria), he never really strays far from the atmosphere of his native Vienna, the Imperial Vienna of bright lights and Hapsburg gaiety—no matter how plebean.

Hundertwasser is indifferent to reality or, if this is not so, he has a reality that has little to do with that of anyone else. The colour is for children, the images are for adults who have never truly grown up. It is the combination of the two that makes Hundertwasser really stand out. The danger, and it can be too close at times, is not that this Viennese will slop over into sentiment or sweetness but that he will allow his decorative talents too much free rein.

Too much silver, too much gold can be embarrassing even in a Hundertwasser painting, even worse in his graphics (which include: "Regenstag," the phosphorescent "gouache" series, using metal-leaf techniques and requiring no less than four stencils for each image.)

At his best, his strange vision lies somewhere between Marc Chagall and Ernst Fuchs. Chagall because of the colours and the *Märchen,* Fuchs because of the deft fashion in which Hundertwasser can build the framework of his pictures. Like both of them he has found a firm place in the public's favour.

—Sheldon Williams

HUNT, Bryan.

American. Born in Terre Haute, Indiana, in 1947. Studied at the University of South Florida, Tampa, 1966–68; Otis Art Institute, Los Angeles, 1969–71, B.F.A. 1971; Member, Independent Study Program, Whitney Museum of American Art, New York, 1972. Independent sculptor, since 1973. Agent: Blum Helman Gallery, 20 West 57th Street, New York, New York 10019. Address: 9 White Street, New York, New York 10013, U.S.A.

Individual Exhibitions:

1974	Institute for Art and Urban Resources, at The Clocktower, New York
1975	Palais des Beaux-Arts, Brussels
1976	Daniel Weinberg Gallery, San Francisco
1977	Blum Helman Gallery, New York
1978	Blum Helman Gallery, New York
	Daniel Weinberg Gallery, San Francisco
	Greenberg Gallery, St. Louis
1979	Blum Helman Gallery, New York
	Bernard Jacobson Gallery, London
	Blum Helman Gallery, New York
	Galerie Bruno Bishofberger, Zurich
1980	Margo Leavin Gallery, Los Angeles
1981	Akron Art Institute, Ohio
	Blum Helman Gallery, New York
	Galerie Hans Strelow, Dusseldorf
1982	Daniel Weinberg Gallery, San Francisco
	Bernier Gallery, Athens
1983	Blum Helman Gallery, New York
	Margo Leavin Gallery, Los Angeles
	Los Angeles County Museum of Art
	Amerika Haus, West Berlin
	California State University, Long Beach
1984	John C. Stoller and Company, Minneapolis
1985	Galerie Knoedler, Zurich
	Blum Helman Gallery, New York
1986	Gillespie-Laage-Salomon, Paris
	Akira Ikeda Gallery, Tokyo
1987	Barbara Mathes Gallery, New York
	Blum Helman Warehouse, New York
1988	Wilhelm-Lehmbruck-Museum, Duisburg, West Germany

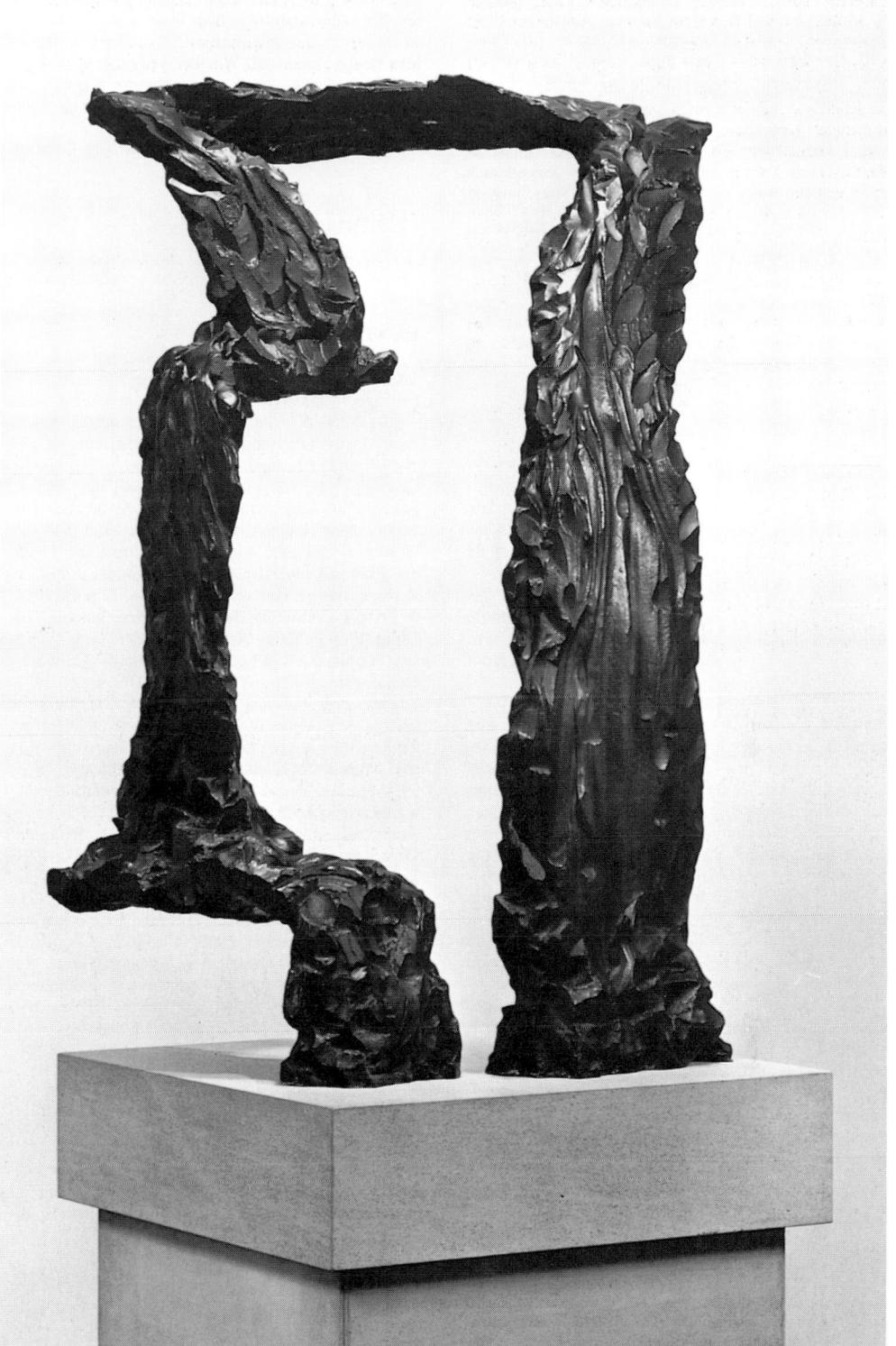

Bryan Hunt: *Caryatid,* 1981

Selected Group Exhibitions:

1978	*Young American Artists,* Guggenheim Museum, New York
	Made by Sculptors, Stedelijk Museum, Amsterdam
1979	*Biennial Exhibition,* Whitney Museum, New York
	Selections from the Collection: Contemporary Sculpture, Museum of Modern Art, New York
1980	*Biennale,* Venice
1982	*74th American Exhibition,* Art Institute of Chicago
1984	*Works in Bronze: A Modern Survey,* Sonoma State University, California (toured the United States)
1985	*Correspondences: New York Art Now,* Laforet Museum, Tokyo (travelled to Utsunomiya, Japan)
1987	*Cast in Bronze,* Kansas City Gallery of Art, Missouri

Collections:

Whitney Museum, New York; Guggenheim Museum, New York; Museum of Modern Art, New York; Albright-Knox Art Gallery, Buffalo, New York; Museum of Fine Art, Dallas; Museum of Fine Arts, Houston; San Francisco Museum of Modern Art; Stedelijk Museum, Amsterdam; Louisiana Museum, Humlebaek, Denmark; Lehmbruck Museum, Duisburg, West Germany.

Publications:

By HUNT: book—*Conversations with Nature,* New York 1982; article—"Bryan Hunt," with Robert Becker, in *Interview* (New York), January 1982.

On HUNT: books—*Made by Sculptors,* exhibition catalogue by Rini Dippel and Geert van Beijeren, Amsterdam 1978; *Bryan Hunt,* exhibition catalogue, with text by Carter Ratcliff, New York 1983; *Bryan Hunt: A Decade of Drawings,* exhibition catalogue by Constance W. Glenn and Jane K. Bledsoe, Long Beach 1983; *Bryan Hunt,* exhibition catalogue by Barbara Haskell, West Berlin 1983; *Bryan Hunt: Skulpturen und Zeichnungen,* exhibition catalogue by Barbara Haskell, Zurich 1985; articles—"A Pail of Water Without the Pail" by James Poett in the *Village Voice* (New York), March 1977; "Bryan Hunt: Blum Helman" by Peter Frank in *Artnews* (New York), October 1978; "Bryan Hunt: Blum Helman Gallery" by Carrie Rickey in *Artforum* (New York), May 1979; "Bryan Hunt: Blum Helman" by Ellen Schwartz in *Artnews* (New York), Summer 1979; "Art Boom" by Calvin Tomkins in *The New Yorker,* 22 December 1980; "Sculptors Who Triumph in Bronze" by Hilton Kramer in the *New York Times,* 24 May 1981; "Reviews from New York, Las Vegas, Los Angeles, San Francisco, Cologne and Rome" by Hal Foster in *Artforum* (New York), September 1981; "Bryan Hunt" by Dupuy Warrick Reed in *Flash Art* (Milan), October/November 1981.

*

To me what sculpture is is creating, constructing, carving, modeling, pouring—a process or a conceptualization of mass. When you think in and translate mass, there is gravity to deal with. You want to release mass, and give it a life and a definition of its own, which I think good sculpture can do.

Motion is part of the equation of it, not that it has to seem like it's in motion, but that it has potential motion or that it has the potential of a life of its own.

—Bryan Hunt

*

Abstract sculptor Bryan Hunt made his first "Airship" in 1973, and since then he has produced a series of "Airships" along with "Lakes" and "Waterfalls." In all three of these series Hunt shows his predilection for intimate scale, handmade surface tactility and summary form ultimately derived from either the natural landscape (water preferred) or the technology of the airship. Hunt's sculpture has become increasingly abstract, a prime concern being pinpointing the definition of pure form in its essence, but the hint of his ultimate relationship with seen sources persists as a positive element in the work's vocabulary of references.

The "Airships" are long, lean, sharp, sleek shapes which jut out horizontally from the wall, piercing it slightly as if about to penetrate the solid surface or perhaps as if just having emerged from the "other side". Over wooden frames, Hunt places silk and silk paper, metal leaf, or copper treated with acid, producing a handmade look, soft and luminous with painterly evanescence. Works are small in scale and are hung high on the wall, making the viewer's perspective that of looking upward, as if at some silent spaceship in the distant skies. The closest art historical connections are with the sleek verticals of Brancusi, but Hunt is obviously after a more scientific and late 20th century correspondence.

The "Lakes" are low-lying, horizontal, irregular ovoid shapes which rest on the floor to provoke sensations of aerial perspective as if seen from an Airship, perhaps. They are bronzes made through the lost wax process, and their tactile surfaces are indented in various patterns, linear configurations suggesting the rippling actions on water's surfaces caught in frozen suspension. Edges vary from sharp to fine to thick to dull, adding to the suggestion that Hunt's visual sources are in his studies of topographical maps and charts which show the different patterns which occur in various real bodies of water. The choice of either polished bronze or darker patinas for the surfaces of the "Lakes" evokes associations with various times of day or night. As in the "Lakes", Hunt's "Waterfalls", also reveal the more nature-oriented, even pantheistic, side of his personality which seems to regard water as a potent symbol of romantic ebb and flow.

Hunt himself credits such predecessors as Robert Smithson, Richard Serra, and Joel Shapiro, and the connections are surely in evidence in his development so far. Also involved is the Postminimalist combination of painting and sculpture in abstract forms which tend toward the idiosyncratic. Hunt's sculptures are less formally ambitious than these sources, and his work seems less involved with the grand or the art historically important. Whether you look up or down at Hunt's works, you get the feeling of a poetic, romanticizing humanist who sees both nature and technology with equally sympathetic eyes.

—Barbara Cavaliere

*   *   *

HUNT, Richard (Howard).

American. Born in Chicago, Illinois, 12 September 1935. Studied at the School of the Art Institute of Chicago, 1953–57, B.A.E. Served in United States Army, 1958–60. Sculptor: lives and works in Chicago. Instructor, School of the Art Institute of Chicago, 1960–61, and at University of Illinois at Chicago, 1960–62; Visiting Professor, Chouinard Art School, Los Angeles, 1964; Visiting Artist, Yale University, New Haven, Connecticut, 1964 and at Purdue University, Indiana, 1965; Visiting Professor, Northern Illinois University, De Kalb, summer 1968, and at Northwestern University, Evanston, Illinois, 1968–69; Artist Consultant, Hobart Welding School, Troy, Ohio, 1969; Visiting Artist, Wisconsin State University, Oshkosh, 1969, Southern Illinois University, Carbondale, 1969, and Washington University, 1977–78. Member: National Council on the Arts, 1968–74; Illinois Arts Council, 1970–75; Board of Directors, College Art Association, 1972–76; Board of Trustees, Museum of Contemporary Art, Chicago, 1975–79. Member, Board of Directors, American Council for the Arts, since 1974; Member, Board of Trustees, American Academy in Rome, 1980–82. Recipient: Logan Prize 1956, 1961, 1962, Palmer Prize 1957, James Nelson Raymond Travel Fellowship 1957, and Campana Prize 1962, Art Institute of Chicago; Guggenheim Fellowship, 1962; Tamarind Fellowship Artist, Ford Foundation, 1965; Cassandra Foundation Fellowship, 1970; Outstanding Chicagoan in the Arts Award, Chicago Junior Chamber of Commerce, 1971. Agent: Terry Dintenfass Gallery, 50 West 57th Street, New York, New York 10019. Address: 1017 West Lill Avenue, Chicago, Illinois 60614, U.S.A.

Individual Exhibitions:

1958	Alan Gallery, New York
1959	Stewart Rickard Gallery, San Antonio, Texas
1960	Alan Gallery, New York
1962	Alan Gallery, New York
1963	B. C. Holland Gallery, Chicago
	Alan Gallery, New York
1964	Wesleyan College, Macon, Georgia
	University of Tulsa, Oklahoma
1965	Felix Landau Gallery, Los Angeles
	Occidental College, Los Angeles
1966	University of Notre Dame, Indiana
	B. C. Holland Gallery, Chicago
	Ohio State University, Columbus
1967	Cleveland Museum of Art
	Milwaukee Art Center (retrospective)
1968	B. C. Holland Gallery, Chicago
	Dorsky Gallery, New York
	Fisk University, Nashville, Tennessee
1969	David Strawn Art Gallery, Jacksonville, Illinois
	Dorsky Gallery, New York
	Kendall College, Evanston, Illinois
	Wisconsin State University, Oshkosh
1970	Southern Illinois University, Carbondale
	Dorsky Gallery, New York
	Living Art Center, Dayton, Ohio
	Southern Illinois University, Carbondale
	Macalester College, St. Paul, Minnesota
	B. C. Holland Gallery, Chicago
	Carleton College, Northfield, Minnesota
	St. Olaf College, Northfield, Minnesota
1971	Museum of Modern Art, New York (retrospective)
	Dorsky Gallery, New York
	Art Institute of Chicago (retrospective)
1973	Dorsky Gallery, New York
1975	Dorsky Gallery, New York
	University of Iowa
1976	Dorsky Gallery, New York
	Sears Bank & Trust Co., Chicago
1977	Dorsky Gallery, New York
1979	Dorsky Gallery, New York
1980	*Prints by a Sculptor: Richard Hunt,* Baltimore Museum of Art
1981	Dorsky Gallery, New York
	St. Joseph Art Association, Michigan
	Springfield Art Museum, Missouri
	Columbia University, New York
	Westbeth Art Gallery, New York
	Fordham University, New York
1982	Brooklyn Artists Cultural Association, New York
1983	Terry Dintenfass Gallery, New York
1984	Terry Dintenfass Gallery, New York
1985	Martin Gallery, Washington, D.C.
1986	Terry Dintenfass Gallery, New York

Selected Group Exhibitions:

1962	*World's Fair,* Seattle
1966	*World Festival of Negro Art,* Dakar, Senegal
1979	*100 Artists, 100 Years: Alumni of the School of the Art Institute of Chicago,* Art Institute of Chicago

Collections:

Metropolitan Museum of Art, New York; Museum of Modern Art, New York; Whitney Museum, New York; Albright-Knox Art Gallery, Buffalo, New York; Hirshhorn Museum and Sculpture Garden, Washington, D.C.; Cleveland Museum of Art; Art Institute of Chicago; Milwaukee Art Center; William Nelson Rockhill Gallery of Art, Kansas City, Missouri; National Museum of Israel, Jerusalem.

Publications:

On HUNT: book—*The Sculpture of Richard Hunt* by Lieberman, New York 1971.

*

Richard Hunt has been described as a man both extremely reflective and as one unwilling to share his thoughts and feelings. Throughout his accomplished career since the 1950's, Hunt's work has been a response to his own introverted nature. His sculptures, charged with emotion yet without specific representational references, tend towards the sublime. As an abstract artist his statements are seldom direct, with the notable exception that he has always made explicit reference to the human figure. This technique of describing a clearly recognisable human form with abstraction illustrates Hunt's concern for understanding—and defining—the complex mechanisms of the human psyche.

In 1953 Hunt saw the work of the Spaniard Julio Gonzalez, who most influenced his development as a sculptor. Within two years of seeing Gonzalez's work, the young American had taught himself to be a master welder. Yet unlike the Spaniard, who forged and hammered the disparate metal parts which comprised his constructions, Hunt utilized the torch to maintain control over his medium.

More importantly than just being a member of the generation of "junk" sculptors, however, Hunt received critical acceptance as a result of a mid-century trend which valued the aesthetics of assemblage, a development which derived from Picasso and his innovative use of new materials. Hunt does not model or carve, and has consistently preferred to use metal, as opposed to plaster, stone, and wood. His favoured materials were discarded and broken machine parts, his scouring ground the metal junkyards of an industrial age. Not only were they an inexpensive source of material but the pre-fabricated shapes he found offered him immediate, direct, and conceptually clean

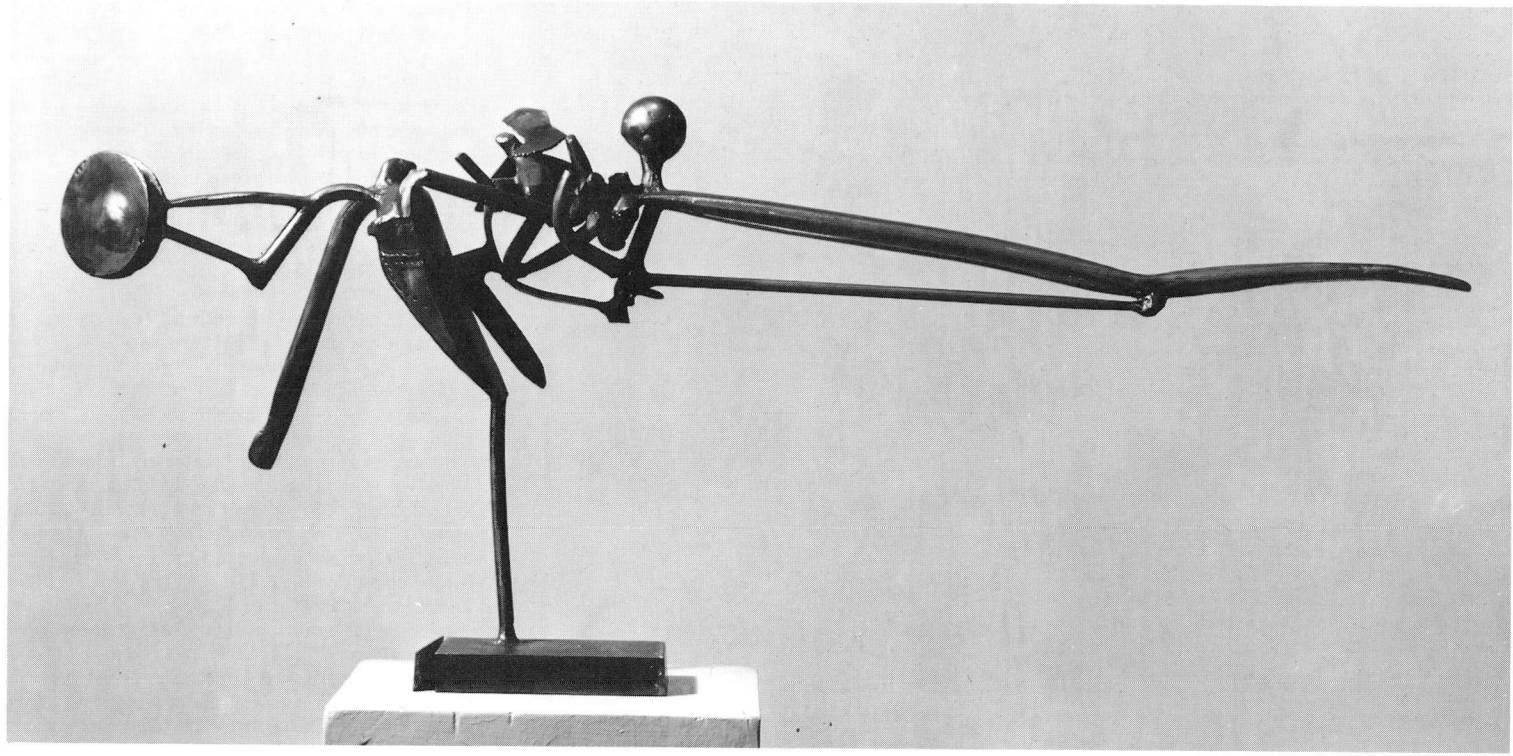

Richard Hunt: *Extending Horizontal Form*, 1958 Courtesy Whitney Museum, New York

forms which he could manipulate in space. He constructed and welded his first sculptures in copper and iron in the 1950's and gradually turned toward aluminum and steel in the subsequent decades.

In the 1960's Hunt constructed sculptures based on classical themes. In their conception and with their suggestion of velocity and energy, however, his works do credit more to the sculptures of Umberto Boccioni than to any Hellenistic examples. From classical experimentations he began a series somewhat more open and fused in space, out of which came his "hybrid figures", which eloquently synthesised elements of the human trunk and limbs with botanical and organic references.

During the 1960's Hunt began to work less and less in a calligraphic way; his forms became monolithic and enclosed, more solid and dense, providing new weight for linear elements. Later on the physical scale of his sculptures increased dramatically, the size, height, and spacial positioning of each piece controlling the emotional representation.

Hunt's sculptures are much less spontaneously conceived than they initially appear. They are, however, examples of total contemplation. In the same vein, first impressions leave the viewer feeling somewhat disillusioned by what might be regarded as the leftovers of 1950's "junk" sculpture. Yet Richard Hunt's well-established ability to endow his work with the deepest levels of introspection is what ranks him as one of America's foremost living sculptors.

—Carrie Barker

HUXLEY, Paul.

British. Born in London, 12 May 1938. Studied at the Harrow College of Art, London, 1949-51, Harrow School of Art, London, 1951-53, and Royal Academy Schools, London, 1956-60. Married Margaret Doris Perryman in 1957 (divorced, 1972); sons: Mark and Nelson. Independent painter, London, since 1960, and in New York, 1965-67. Member, Fine Arts Panel (NCDAD), London, 1972-74; Arts Council of Great Britain Arts Panel, London, since 1972; Committee Member, New Contemporaries Association, London, 1973-76. Lecturer, Oxford School of Art, 1960-61, Sidcup School of Art, Kent, 1960-64, Luton College of Art, Bedfordshire, 1961-62, Maidstone College of Art, Kent, 1963-65, Ravensbourne College of Art and Design, Kent, 1965, Central School of Art and Design, London, 1968-75; Professor, Cooper Union, New York, 1974. Since 1970, Lecturer at the Camberwell School of Arts and Crafts, London. Trustee, Tate Gallery, London, since 1975. Recipient: Peter Stuyvesant Travel Award, London, 1964; Harkness Fellowship, to the United States, 1965; Bours de Sejour, *Biennale de Paris*, 1965; Linbury Trust Award, London, 1977; Athena Arts Prize, London, 1985. Agent: Mayor Rowan Gallery, 31a Bruton Place, London W1. Address: 29 St. Albans Avenue, London W4, England.

Individual Exhibitions:

1963	Rowan Gallery, London
1965	Rowan Gallery, London
1967	Kornblee Gallery, New York
1968	Rowan Gallery, London
1969	Rowan Gallery, London
1970	Kornblee Gallery, New York
1971	Rowan Gallery, London
1974	Galeria da Emenda, Lisbon
	Rowan Gallery, London
1975	Forum Kunst, Rottweil, West Germany
1978	Rowan Gallery, London
1980	Rowan Gallery, London
1982	Juda Rowan Gallery, London

Selected Group Exhibitions:

1959	*Young Contemporaries*, RBA Galleries, London
1964	*The New Generation*, Whitechapel Art Gallery, London
1965	*British Painting*, Swedish Arts Council, Stockholm (toured Sweden)
1967	*Pittsburgh International*, Carnegie Institute, Pittsburgh
1968	*British Artists: 6 Painters/6 Sculptors*, Museum of Modern Art, New York (toured the United States)
1969	*Marks on Canvas*, Museum am Ostwall, Dortmund, West Germany (toured West Germany and Austria)
1974	*British Painting '74*, Hayward Gallery, London
1976	*Arte Inglese Oggi 1960-1976*, Palazzo Reale, Milan
1977	*British Painting 1952-1977*, Royal Academy of Arts, London
1980	*British Art 1940-80*, Hayward Gallery, London

Collections:

Tate Gallery, London: Victoria and Albert Museum, London; Walker Art Gallery, Liverpool; Museum of Modern Art, New York; Albright-Knox Art Gallery, Buffalo, New York; Art Gallery of New South Wales, Sydney; Art Gallery of South Australia, Adelaide.

Publications:

On HUXLEY: books—*The New Generation*, exhibition catalogue, by David Thompson, London 1964; *Private View* by Bryan Robertson, John Russell and Lord Snowdon, London 1965; *Marks on Canvas*, exhibition catalogue, by Anne Seymour, Dortmund, West Germany 1969; *Arte Inglese Oggi*, exhibition catalogue, by Norbert Lynton and others, Milan 1976.

*   *   *

The chief characteristic that distinguishes Paul Huxley's work is its self-imposed limitations. He was at art school during the 1950's when the influence of the New York Abstract Expressionists was making itself felt in England in an increasingly powerful way and when Lawrence Alloway's *Situations* exhibitions at the Institute of Contemporary Arts were reflective of the direction new painting was taking. More than at any other time the independent arena of the picture plane was establishing itself, and Huxley was one of those who accepted its challenge and its none the less rigorous conventions. For it is one thing to banish all illusionistic references from a picture but quite another to invent acceptable terms in which to present authentic and autographic prototypes. By 1963 when he had his first one-man exhibition he had made choices that to some extent remain valid up to the present time.

One of them was a square format for the support

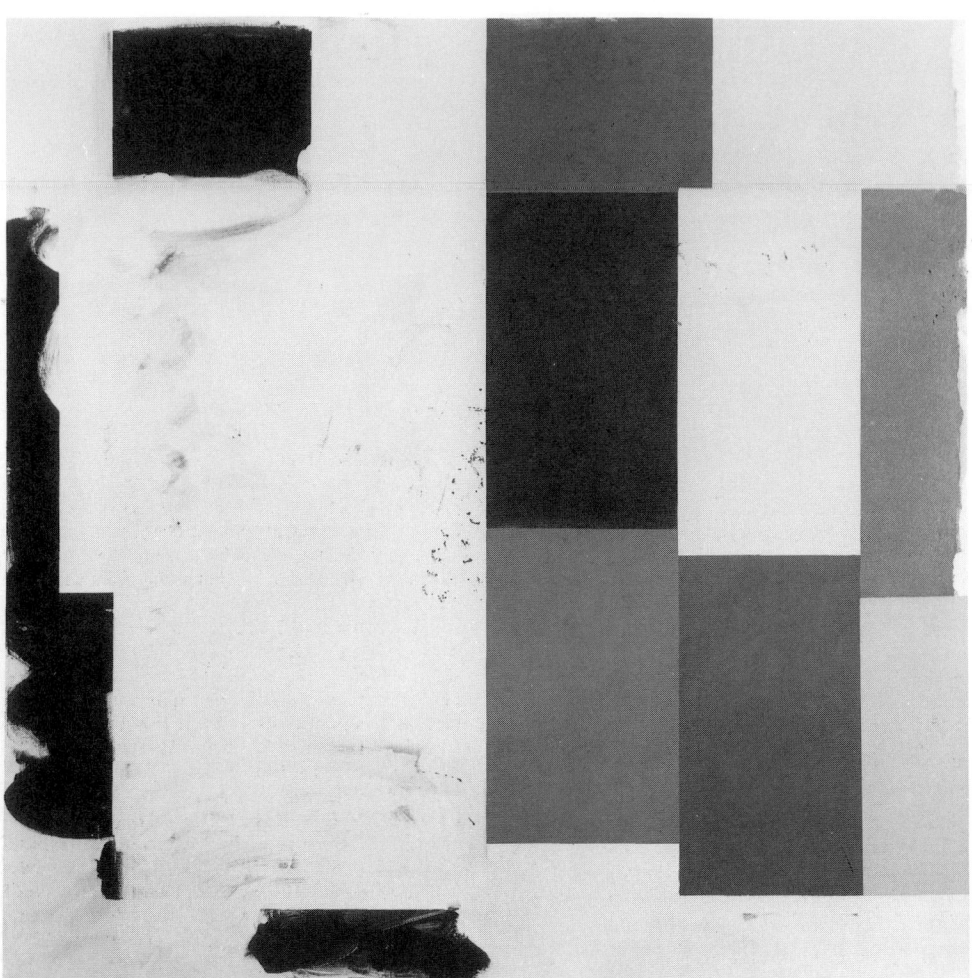

Paul Huxley: *Untitled No. 150*, **1974**

generally in sizes verging on six foot across. The ground was a pale tone on which one or two elements operated in a diagonal polarity. In one such work "Untitled No. 33" (1964) the activating paint form begins at the left top side of the canvas as if a double pool were cut off by the edge then almost centrally descends in a straight stem that bends and then loops in wider knots to what seems a larger pool, almost but not quite touching the lower right edge of the canvas. In effect it assumes the appearance of a stream of paint as it seems when dripped on a flat surface and having its course manipulated by tilting and folding. This allusion whether deliberately or accidentally induced does not detract from the autonomy of the painting which by its articulated path presents its powerful statement of gravitational flow.

In a work of a year later the single though continuous motive is replaced by two predominant shapes strongly coloured and in tonal contrast to the otherwise empty ground. Both are loosely defined, one roughly a pear shape, the other again cut off by the top left hand corner of the plane as a rhomboid. The name of the game now is relationships—of shape, weight, colour and balance against not only the other but the empty space on which they are placed and the four sides that enclose it.

Over the years this sense of opposition and complement has been refined but essentially on the basis that the ground will be the larger area of the picture, though the smaller elements are now more numerous and in some cases superimposed, raising secondary considerations regarding their special relationships as well as to the total. This assembly of squares and rectangles are relieved of a geometric rigidity by the occasional loose brushing of a side of the motive, a nonconformist gesture of somewhat illogical surprise. Scale continues to provide the necessary emphasis to formal arrangements that have their ineradicable affinities with Malevich's Suprematist originals.

—G. S. Whittet

IANNONE, Dorothy.

American. Born in Boston, Massachusetts, 9 August 1933. Studied at Boston University, 1953–57 (Phi Beta Kappa), B.A. 1957; graduate studies in English, Brandeis University, Waltham, Massachusetts, 1958. Employed as a Transportation Agent, Boston Army Base, 1951–52. Married James Phineas Upham in 1959 (divorced, 1967); lived with the artist Dieter Roth, 1967–74. Independent artist, since 1960: travelled extensively in Europe and the Far East, 1961–67; has lived in Europe since 1967, and in West Berlin since 1976; began study of Tibetan Buddhism, 1984. Instructor in open workshops, College of Arts, West Berlin, 1977, 1979; Guest Artist, Jan Van Eyck Academie, Maastricht, 1982, 1983, and Rijksacademie, Amsterdam, 1982, 1984. Recipient: DAAD Grant, West Berlin, 1976; Senate for Science and Art Award, West Berlin, 1980, 1982, 1984. Agent: Petersen Galerie, Goethestrasse 73, 1000 Berlin 12. Address: Leonhardtstrasse 2, 1000 Berlin 19 (West), Germany.

Individual Exhibitions:

1967	Stryke Gallery, New York
	Dieter Roth/Dorothy Iannone, Zwirner Galerie, Cologne
	Galerie Hansjorg Mayer, Stuttgart
1969	Handschin Galerie, Basel
1971	Wilbrand Galerie, Cologne
	Eat Art Galerie, Dusseldorf
	Galerie Jule Hammer, Berlin
1973	Galerie Steinmetz, Bonn
	Galerie Wahlandt, Schwabisch-Gmund, West Germany
1974	Gum Galerie, Reykjavik
1975	Galerie 38, Copenhagen
1976	Galerie Bama, Paris
1977	Studio Galerie, Berlin
	Wiener und Würthle Galerie, Berlin
	Other Books and So, Amsterdam
1978	Haus am Lutzowplatz, West Berlin
1979	Studio Galerie, at *Art 79*, Basle
1980	Neue Galerie, Aachen, West Germany
1981	Galleri Wallner, Malmo, Sweden
1982	Galerie Nikolaj, Copenhagen
	Galerie Ars Viva, West Berlin
1984	Galerie Rosenberg, Zurich
1986	Boekie Woekie, Amsterdam

Selected Group Exhibitions:

1966	*La Cedille qui Sourit*, Villefranche-sur-Mer, France
1969	*Erotic Art Show: Collections of Drs. Phyllis and Ebergard Kronhausen*, Kunsthalle, Stockholm (toured Europe)
1970	*Edinburgh Festival of Arts*
1975	*Biennale*, Venice
1976	*Daily Bul Exposition*, Fondation Maeght, St. Paul-de-Fence, France (toured Europe)
1980	*Ecouter par les yeux*, Musee d'Art Moderne, Paris
1985	*Livres d'Artistes*, Centre Georges Pompidou, Paris
1987	*Essen und Trinken*, Kunstverein, Wuppertal, West Germany

Collections:

Kunstverein, West Berlin; Kunstverein, Dusseldorf; Kunstverein, Braunschweig, West Germany; Neue Galerie, Aachen, West Germany; Bibliotheque Nationale, Paris; Musee Minicipale, Toulouse, France; Kunstmuseum, Basle; International Museum of Erotic Art, San Francisco.

Publications:

By IANNONE: books—*Lists IV*, Cologne 1968; *Story of Bern*, Dusseldorf 1970; *Extase*, with Robert Filliou, Stuttgart 1970; *75 Uncomplimentary Cards*, and *75 Complimentary Cards*, Dusseldorf 1971; *Danger in Dusseldorf*, Stuttgart 1973; *Speaking to Each Other*, with Mary Harding, West Berlin 1977; *Follow Me*, West Berlin 1978; *The Berlin Beauties*, West Berlin 1978; *Dorothy Iannone and Her Mother Sarah Pucci*, Aachen 1980; *The Whip*, West Berlin 1980; *Censorship and the Irrepressible Drive Toward Love and Divinity*, West Berlin 1982.

On IANNONE: book—*Dorothy Iannone*, exhibition catalogue with text by Wolfgang Becker, Aachen 1980; articles—by Ed Sommer in *Kunstforum International* (Mainz), Spring 1973; by Francois Pluchart in *Artitudes* (St. Jeannet), January 1976; by Dieter Schwarz in *Sondern* (Zurich), no. 3, 1978; by Wolfgang Richter in *Aachener Volkszeitung* (Aachen), 25 April 1980; by Heinz Ohff in *Der Tagespiegel* (West Berlin), 6 July 1982; by Liesbeth Brandt Corstius in *Ruimte* (Amsterdam), February 1986.

COMPLIMENTARY CARD (1975)
I love you because from the outset you caught on to characteristics of the men I control.

UNCOMPLIMENTARY CARD (1975)
How revolting to torture me when I am tied to you.

All the 150 cards were exhibited at the MAGNA—FEMININITY: ART & CREATIVITY Exhibition at the Galerie Nachst St. Stephan in Vienna, March/April 1975. Together with her pictures they offer some clues to the strange personality of this American-born artist.

Of all the Woman's Liberation artists Dorothy Iannone is the most heterosexual in her approach to the visual interpretation of carnal knowledge and desires, and in order to make her messages abundantly clear she usually spells out her thoughts in capital letters upon her pictures. Cries like "Alas I still cherish Slavery," "What does it mean when we do it this way?", "I admit sometimes I revel in you as a father" and so on. Words are for her as magical as images.

All the pictures are linear, decorative and brightly coloured. Were it not for their style they might be compared with Egyptian hieroglyphic works at their most figurative—particularly those which are made up like comic strips.

Sound also plays its part. This is emitted from boxes whose every side presents opportunities for more pictures. Once in a while, the women in these paintings sport an elaborate head-dress, but for the most part they and their male paramours are naked save for jewellery.

—Sheldon Williams

IIMURA, Taka(hiko).

Japanese. Born in Tokyo, 20 February 1937. Educated at Keio High School, Hiyoshi, Kanagawa, graduated 1956; studied political science at Keio University, Tokyo, 1956–59, B.A. 1959. Married Akiko Oguchi in 1966. Independent artist and filmmaker, since 1960: worked as a film director for Nichei Eiga Shin Sha, Iwanami Eiga Sha, TBS, etc., in Tokyo, 1960–66; formed Japan Film Independents, Tokyo, 1962. Has lived in New York, 1966–69, 1971–72, and since 1975. Visiting Instructor, Department of Studio Arts, University of Minnesota, Minneapolis, 1975–76; Visiting Assistant Professor, School of Art, Kent State University, Ohio, 1976–77; Assistant Professor, Department of Cinema, State University of New York, at Binghamton, 1978. Recipient: Special Prize, *International Experimental Film Festival*, Knokke, Belgium, 1963; Asia Foundation Fellowship, Harvard University International Seminar, Cambridge, Massachusetts, 1966; Cultural Exchange Visitor's Grant, Japan Society, New York, 1966; D.A.A.D. Artist-in-Residence Grant, Berlin, 1973–74; Creative Artists Public Service Grant, New York, 1975; Canada Council Travel Grant, 1977; National Endowment for the Arts Fellowship, 1980; Canada Council Fellowship, 1981; Australia-Japan Foundation Fellowship, Melbourne, 1984; New York Foundation for the Arts Fellowship, 1986; First Prize, Thomas Edison Film and Video Festival, 1986. Agents: Filmmakers' Cooperative, 175 Lexington Avenue, New York, New York 10016; Stefanotty Gallery, 50 West 57th Street, New York, New York 10016; PAP Film Galerie, Fihrenstrasse 112, 8031 Grobenzell, West Germany. Address: Box 431, Cooper Station, New York, New York 10276, U.S.A.

Individual Exhibitions (mainly films with performance):

1963	Naiqua Gallery, Tokyo (music by Yasunao Tone)
1966	Filmmakers' Cinematheque, New York
1968	Canyon Cinematheque, San Francisco
1969	Institute of Contemporary Arts, London
	Royal Film Archives, Brussels
1970	Scopio Theatre, Tokyo
1972	Millennium, New York
	Kitchen, New York
1973	Galerie Baecker, Bochum, West Germany
	Stadtische Galerie Lenbachhaus, Munich
1974	Galerie Projection, Cologne
	Cinematheque Francaise, Paris
	Galerie 23, Paris
1975	Museum of Modern Art, New York
1976	University of California Art Museum, Berkeley
	Anthology Film Archives, New York
1977	Millennium, New York
	International Cultureel Centrum, Antwerp
	Stedelijk Museum, Amsterdam
1978	Art Gallery of Ontario, Toronto
	Carnegie Institute, Pittsburgh
1979	*New Video: Taka Iimura and Shigeko Kubota*, Whitney Museum, New York
	State University of New York at Buffalo
	Centre Pompidou, Paris
	Volksbank Museum, Essen

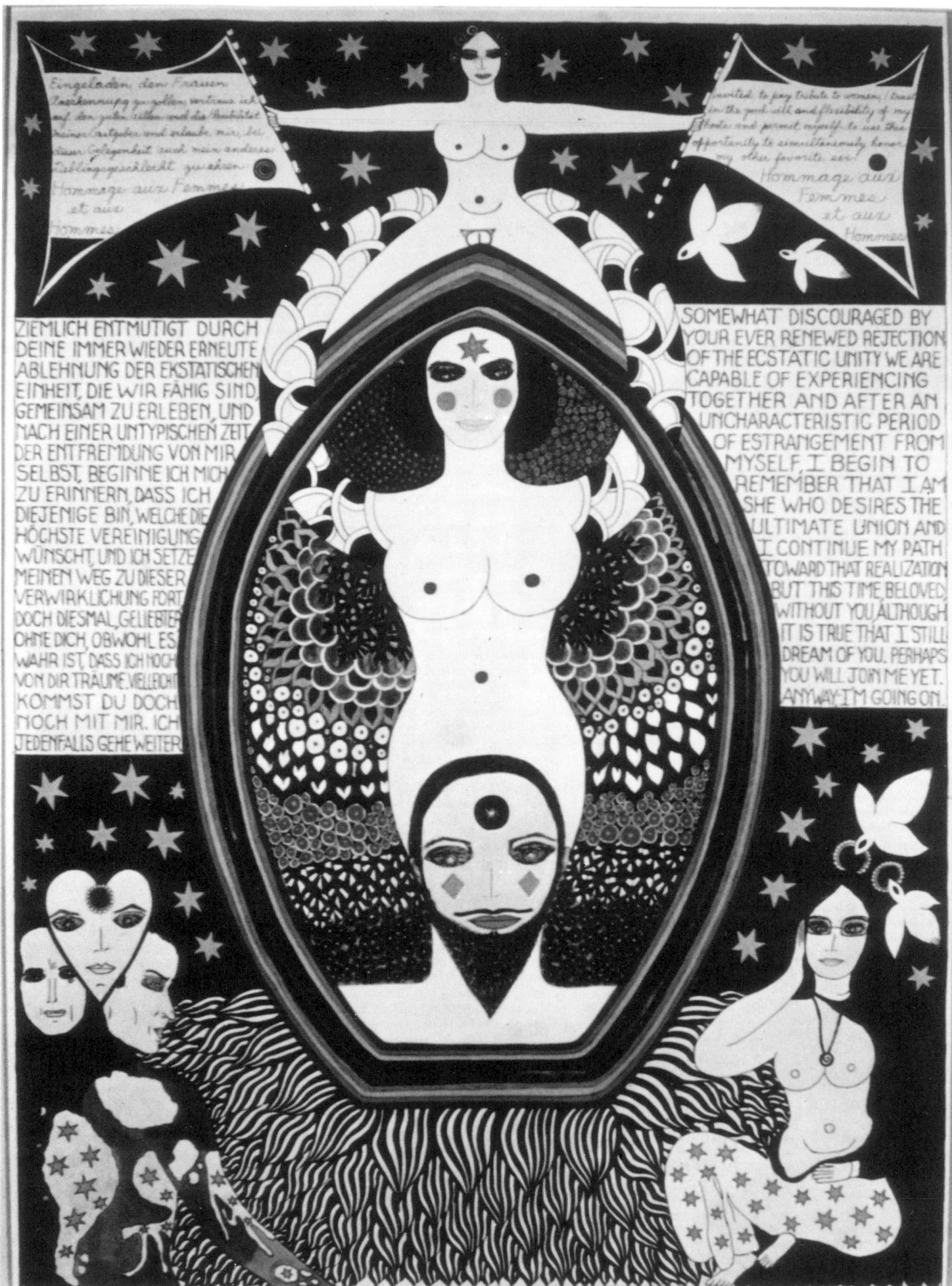

Dorothy Iannone: *Hommage aux Femmes et aux Hommes,* 1984

1980   Palais dex Beaux-Arts, Brussels
         Galerie Malina Dinkler, Berlin
         Seibu Museum, Tokyo
1981   Musée d'Art Contemporain, Montreal
         Museum of Modern Art, New York
1982   Hara Museum of Contemporary Art, Tokyo
         Contemporary Art Center, Osaka, Japan
1983   Seibu Museum of Art, Tokyo
1984   Glass House Theatre, Melbourne
1985   Multi-Media Centre, Zagreb, Yugoslavia
1986   Museum Square, Osaka, Japan
1987   Ted Greenwald Gallery, New York

Selected Group Exhibitions:

1963   *International Experimental Film Festival*, Knokke, Belgium
1966   *Japanese Experimental Film*, Museum of Modern Art, New York
1971   *Tokyo Biennale*, Metropolitan Museum, Tokyo
1973   *Neue Medien/Neue Methoden*, Palais Thurn und Taxis, Bregenz, Austria
1974   *Projekt '74*, Kunsthalle, Cologne
1976   *Video Art*, Institute of Contemporary Art, Philadelphia
1978   *Recent Japanese Avantgarde Film*, Museum of Modern Art, New York
1983   *History of Video Art*, Museum of Modern Art, New York
1985   *Japan: Avantgarde of the Future*, City Hall, Genoa, Italy
1987   *Video From Japan*, San Francisco Museum of Modern Art

Collections:

Anthology Film Archives, New York; Centre Pompidou, Paris; Neue Galerie Ludwig, Aachen, West Germany; Neue Berliner Kunstverein, Berlin; Royal Film Archives, Brussels; Metropolitan Museum, Tokyo; Hara Museum of Contemporary Art, Tokyo.

Publications:

By IIMURA: books—*Geijutsu to Hi-Geijutsu no Aida* (Between Art and Non-Art)*, essays, Tokyo 1970; *Paper Film-Love and Flowers' Orgy*, photos, Tokyo 1971; *Paris-Tokyo Cinema Journal*, Tokyo 1984; *Yoko Ono: Her Art and Life*, Tokyo 1985; *Eizo-Jikken no Tameni* (For Image Experimentation)*, Tokyo 1986; *Post Modern no Gensho* (New York Art Diary)*, Tokyo 1987; articles—"Cinema Experimental Japonaise" in *L'Art Vivant* (Paris), February 1975; "I Am (Not) Taka Iimura, I Am (Not) Akiko Iimura" in *The New Television*, Cambridge, Massachusetts 1977; "Cinéma Reflete" in *Cinéma Différent* (Paris), 1977; "Semiotics of Video" in *Art, Artist and the Media*, Graz, Austria 1977; "On Film Installation" in *Millennium Film Journal* (New York), 1978; "24 Frames Per Second" in *Ear Magazine* (New York), November 1978; "Visuality in the Structure of Japanese Art" in *Art and Cinema* (New York), December 1978; films—*Junk*, 1962; *Iro*, 1962; *AI/Love*, 1962–63; *Onan*, 1963; *A Dance Party in the Kingdom of Lilliput*, no. 1, 1964, no. 2, 1966; *I Saw the Shadow*, 1966; *White Calligraphy*, 1967; *Face*, 1968–69; *Film Strips I*, 1966–70; *Film Strips II*, 1966–70; *Filmmakers*, 1966–70; *Buddha Again*, 1969–70, later retitled *Cosmic Buddha: In the River*, 1969–70; *Shutter*, 1971; *Models* (2 reels), 1972; *Plus and Minus*, 1973; *1 to 60 Seconds*, 1973; *Parallel*, 1974; *24 Frames per Second*, 1975, revised 1978; *Sync Sound*, 1975, revised 1977; *Ma* (Intervals), 1975–77; *One Frame Duration*, 1977; *Repeated/Reversed Time*, 1980; *Talking in New York*, 1981; *Talking Picture*, 1981; film installations—*Projection Piece #1*, 1968–72; *Projection Piece #2*, 1972; *A Loop Seen as a Line*, 1972; *Timing #1, #2, #3*, 1972; *Minute and Second*, 1973; *A Loop Seen as a Line* (Mobius), 1973; *1 Sec. And-*, 1975; *Identity Piece*, 1976; video tapes—*A Chair*, 1970; *Blinking*, 1970; *Time, Time Trilogy 1*, 1971; *Moon Timed, Time Trilogy 2*, 1971; *Time Tunnel, Time Trilogy 3*, 1971; *Self Identity Series 1–5*, 1972–74; *Project Yourself*, Berlin tape 1973, Cologne tape 1974; *Register Yourself*, 1973; *Shifting*, 1974, revised 1975; *Field Works 1–3*, 1974; *Video Field 1–2*, 1975; *Observer/Observed*, 1975; *Observer/Observed/Observer*, 1976; *Camera, Monitor, Frame*, 1976; *Visual Logic (and Illogic)*, 1977; *Talking to Myself: Phenomenological Operation*, 1978; *Double Identities (on Turning the Double Negative to the Positive)*, 1979; *Self Introduction*, 1982; *Hit Your Own Back*, 1982; *Video Talking: Back to Back* (2 tapes), 1982; *Video Gesture* (2 tapes), 1982; *Video Self: I=You=He/She* (2 tapes), 1982; *A:I:U:E:O:N* (2 tapes), 1982; *Eight Aspects of a Face* (8 tapes), 1982; *This Is A Camera Which Shoots This*, 1983; *A Conversation with Video*, 1983; *Robina Rese and Me*, 1983; *Talking to Myself at P.S.1*, 1984; *New York Hotspring*, 1984; *Ayers Rock*, 1985; *Moments at the Rock*, 1985; *John Cage Portrait*, 1985; *Nightsongs*, 1986; *Arakawa: Atmospheric Resemblance (A Life of Blank)*, 1986; video installations—*Project Yourself*, 1972; *Register Yourself*, 1973; *Front and Back*, 1974; *Face/Ings*, 1974; *I=You=He/She*, 1974–79; *Face to Face*, 1977; *Interviewer/Interviewed*, 1980.

On IIMURA: books—*Film and Videotapes of Taka Iimura*, Berlin 1972; *Taka Iimura: Videotapes 1970–73*, Berlin 1973; *Neue Medien/Neue Methoden*, exhibition catalogue, by Peter Weiermair, Bregenz, Austria 1973; *Aktionen der Avantgarde*, exhibition catalogue, Berlin 1973; *Avantgardistischer Film 1951–71* by Gottfried Schlemmer, Munich 1973; *Taka Iimura: Video Plans*, Aalst, Belgium, 1974; *Taka Iimura: Film e Video*, Rome 1975; *Video Art*, exhibition catalogue, Philadelphia, 1976; *Cinema Underground Oggi*, edited by Sergio Luginbuhl, Padua 1972; *Kunst als Lebens Ritual*, edited by Horst Gerhard Habel, Graz, Austria 1974; articles—"Japanese Experimental Films" by Robert Steele in *Film Comment* (New York), Fall 1967; "On Taka Iimura" by Koichiro Ishizaki in *Bijutsu Techo* (Tokyo), June 1970; untitled article by Peter Gidal in *Ark* (London), October 1970; "Movie Journal" by Jonas Mekas in the *Village Voice* (New York), July 1972; "3X Avantgarde" by Gottfried Weimann in *Kino* (Berlin), no. 4, 1973; "Reflected Light" by Tony Rayns in *Sight and Sound* (London), Winter 1973; "Zeitablaufe, im Takt skandiert" by Wolfgang Kahlcke in *Die Welt* (Berlin), October 1973; "Vision" by Malcolm LeGrice in *Studio International* (London), November 1973; "Personal Cinema" by Paul Poggiali in the *Soho Weekly News* (New York), May 1974; "Taka Iimura" by Dominique Nogues in *Art Vivant* (Paris), February 1975; article by Malcolm Le Grice in *Time Out* (London), April 1975; article by Scott Macdonald in *Afterimage* (Rochester, New York), April 1978; "Electronic Linguistics" by Dan Collins in *Artweek* (Oakland, California), 6 December 1980.

During the past few years I have studied the structural relationships of language and video, using English in this case. Video is a unique system for applying this study which is capable of recording image and sound simultaneously. In the closed circuit system, which is self-referential, a camera (observer) is fed back by the monitor (observed), so that the image not only refers to the object which is shot, but also refers back to the subject, who is shooting. This constitutes a sentence-like structure. In language, too, what I am concerned with is not the word as object, but the sentence and its structure.

What I have tried to do in video in the relation of image to language is to include the observer "I" (as the subject) as an integral part of system and sentence. It is the structure of "seeing" involved in both the observer and the observed which is set up by the closed circuit system of video. Unlike film, in closed circuit video one can see the observer and observed at the same time—a feedback in time/space. The relation of the observer and observed is taken at language level as "I" and "You," as a sentence "I see you." The very sentence is transferred to a closed circuit system in which a camera and a monitor are mediated between "I" and "You," and the one with the camera is not only "I" who observes but also "You" who is observed. This means that an image functions as the observer in relation to speech: these are double functions, and speech is equal in importance to the image, either working separately (de-synchronized) from, or identically (synchronized) with, the image. The words "I" and "You" switch roles between what is one and off the screen (monitor), and then assume each other's position.

For instance, if the picture says "I," the off-screen voice says "You," or the picture says "You" and the off-screen voice says "I," then the role of the observer and observed shift accordingly. It is the direction of observation that is affected: from subject to object and object to subject in an interrelated manner. Consequently, an identical image has different implications according to the description of the words, and, conversely, identical speech is also able to indicate different images. All of these are taped using feedback control of a closed circuit system which permits manipulation of image and sound simultaneously at different levels. The relation of the observer and observed, therefore, has the structure of a round trip. And the feedback in the system is used neither for technical nor for aesthetic aims but used for and within the conceptual framework.

The "Observer/Observed" series (1975–76) was developed out of the basic pattern of "I see you" with variations and more complicated sentences such as "I see you (who is) shooting me" and "I see myself (who is) shooting you." These compound sentences are set up by two facing cameras and monitors which are fed back to each other, so that exact transfer of the sentence is possible, and are made switchable according to the image: who is shooting whom. The media employed in the tapes are three: image, voiced (and

Taka Iimura: Still from the video *I Love You*, 1973–87

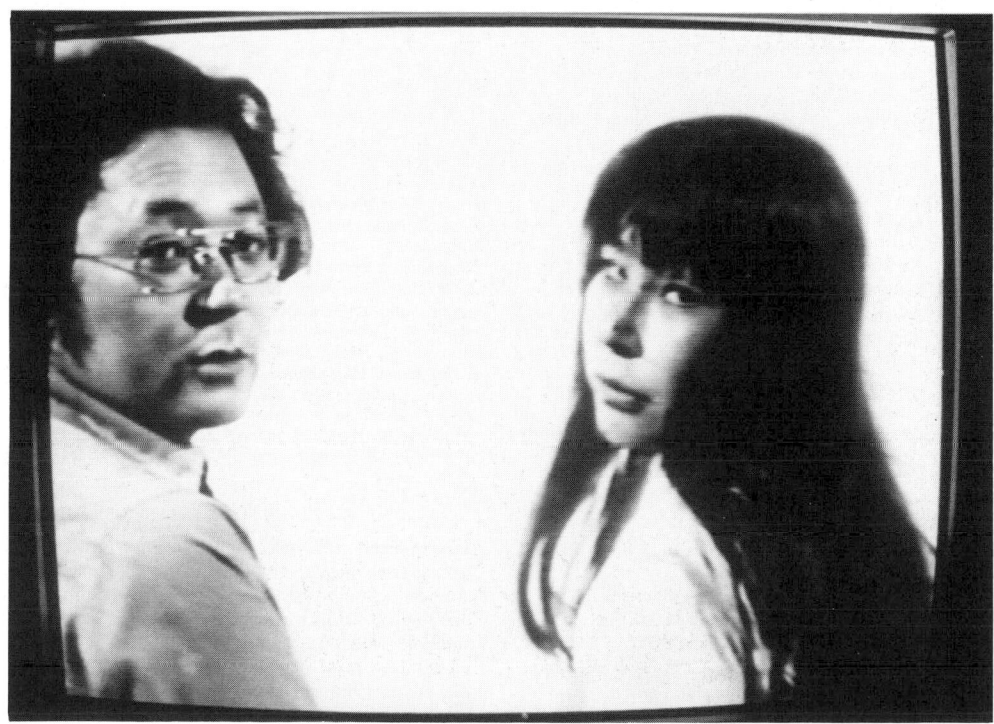

voiced over) sentence; and symbolic letters (superimposed). Each medium works independently, defining the others. The works are composed in advanced with diagrammed texts, and then taped.

—Taka Iimura

IMMENDORFF, Jorg.

German. Born in Bleckede bei Luneberg, 14 June 1945. Educated at a Volkschule and Gymnasium, Luneberg, until 1963; studied stage design, under Teo Otto, 1963–64, and art, under Joseph Beuys, 1964–66, Kunstakademie, Dusseldorf. Independent artist, Dusseldorf, since 1966: performed first art actions at the Kunstakademie, Dusseldorf, 1965–66; organized "Lidl" activities in Dusseldorf and other locations, 1968–69; made joint painterly activities and exhibitions with the artist A. R. Penck (Ralf Winkler), 1977–78; first "Cafe Deutschland" works, Dusseldorf, 1978; opened Cafe La Paloma, Hamburg, 1984. Guest Professor, Konsthogskolan, Stockholm, 1981; Guest instructor, Hamburg Kunstakademie and Trondheim Kunstakademie, 1982–83; Head of course at the Werkschule, Cologne, 1984. Member of the Green Movement, West Germany, 1979. Agents: Galerie Michael Werner, Gertrudenstrasse 24-28, 500 Cologne 1; Galerie Daniel Templon, 30 rue Beaubourg, 75003 Paris. Address: Gustav Poesgentstrasse 29, 4000 Dusseldorf-Oberlik, West Germany.

Individual Exhibitions:

1961	New Orleans-Club, Bonn
1966	Galerie Schmela, Dusseldorf
	Galerie Fulda, Fulda, West Germany
	Galerie Aachen, Aachen, West Germany
1967	Galerie Art Intermedia, Cologne
1968	Galerie Patio, Frankfurt
1969	Galerie Lichter, Frankfurt
	Galerie Michael Werner, Cologne (and 1971, 1972, 1973)
1973	Westfalischer Kunstverein, Munster, West Germany
	Galerie Loehr, Frankfurt
	Galerie Cornels, Baden-Baden, West Germany
1974	Daner Galleriet, Copenhagen
	Galerie Michael Werner, Cologne (and 1975)
1975	Galerie am Savignyplatz, West Berlin
	Galerie Nachst St. Stephan, Vienna
1976	Galerie Seriaal/Helen van der Meij, Amsterdam
	Galerie Michael Werner, Cologne
1977	Museum van Hedendaagse Kunst, Utrecht, Netherlands
	Galerie Michael Werner, Cologne (with A. R. Penck)
1978	Galerie Maier-Hahn, Dusseldorf
	Galerie Michael Werner, Cologne
1979	Kunstmuseum, Basel
	Galerie Helen van der Meij, Amsterdam
	Galerie Michael Werner, Cologne
1980	Kunsthalle, Berne
1981	Van Abbemuseum, Eindhoven, Netherlands
	Galerie Neuendorf, Hamburg
	Galeria Heinrich Ehrhardt, Madrid
	Van Abbemuseum, Eindhoven, Netherlands (with Jannis Kounellis)
1982	Galerie Michael Werner, Cologne
	Galerie Fred Jahn, Munich
	Kunsthalle, Dusseldorf
	Galerie Strelow, Dusseldorf
	Galerie Daniel Templon, Paris
	Vereiniging Aktuele Kunst vzw Ghent, Belgium
	Galerie Rudolf Springer, West Berlin
	Sonnabend Gallery, New York
	Edition Sabine Knust, Munich (with A. R. Penck)
1983	Kastrupgardsamlingen, Kastrup, Denmark
	Galerie Rudolf Springer, West Berlin
	Van Abbemuseum, Eindhoven, Netherlands
	Kunsthalle, Dusseldorf
	Ratinger Hof, Dusseldorf
	Galleria Cannaviello, Milan
	Edition Sabine Knust, Munich
	New 57 Gallery, Edinburgh
	Kunsthaus, Zurich
1984	Museum of Modern Art, Oxford
	Galerie Ascan Crone, Hamburg
	Michael Werner/Mary Boone Gallery, New York
	Museo de Bellas Artes, Bilbao, Spain
	Galerie Schurr, Stuttgart
	Galerie Michael Werner, Cologne
	Galerie Gillespie-Laage-Salomon, Paris
1985	Maison de la Culture, St. Etienne, France
	Galerie Sabine Knust, Munich
1986	Nigel Greenwood Gallery, London

Selected Group Exhibitions:

1967	*Hommage a Lidice,* Galerie René Block, West Berlin
1972	*Documenta 5,* Museum Fridericianum, Kassel, West Germany
1973	*Medium Fotografie,* Stadtisches Museum, Leverkusen, West Germany
1976	*Attualita Internazionale,* at the *XXXVII Biennale,* Venice
1979	*Malerei auf Papier,* Badischer Kunstverein, Karlsruhe, West Germany
1981	*Art Allemagne Aujourd'hui,* Musée d'Art Moderne de la Ville, Paris
1983	*New Figuration,* University of California, Los Angeles
1985	*The European Iceberg,* Art Gallery of Ontario, Toronto
1987	*Avant-Garde in the Eighties,* Los Angeles County Museum of Art

Collections:

Kupferstichkabinett, Basel; Neue Galerie, Aachen; Museum voor Hedendaagse Kunst, Utrecht; Museum Boymans-van Beuningen, Rotterdam; Van Abbemuseum, Eindhoven.

Publications:

By IMMENDORFF: books and leaflets—*Lidlstadt,* Dusseldorf 1968; *Den Eisbaren mal reinhalten,* Dusseldorf 1968; *Hier und jetzt: Das tun, was zu tun ist,* Cologne and New York 1973; *Deutschland mal Deutschland,* with A. R. Penck, Munich 1979; *Der Hund stosst im Laufe der Woche zu mir,* exhibition catalogue, with Siegfried Gohr, Stockholm 1981; *LIDL 1966–1970,* Eindhoven, Netherlands 1981; *Grusse von der Nordfront,* with poem by A. R. Penck, Munich 1982; *Kein Licht fur wen?,* Cologne 1982; *Brandenburger Tor,* with poems by A. R. Penck, New York 1982; *Cafe Deutschland-Gut,* Cologne 1983.

On IMMENDORFF: books—*Gedanken zu Jorg Immendorffs Babies und Aktionen,* leaflet by Chris Reinicke, Dusseldorf 1968; *Jorg Immendorff,* exhibition catalogue, with text by Wouter Kotte and Jurgen Kramer, Utrecht 1977; *Cafe Deutschland von Jorg Immendorff,* with text by Johannes Gachnang, Siegfried Gohr and Rudi H. Fuchs, Cologne 1978; *Jorg Immendorff: Cafe Deutschland,* exhibition catalogue, with text by Dieter Koepplin, Basel 1979; *Jorg Immendorff: Malermut rundum,* exhibition catalogue by Johannes Gachnang, Berne 1981; *Jorg Immendorff: Cafe Deutschland/Adlerhalfte,* exhibition catalogue by Jurgen Harten and Ulrich Kempel, Dusseldorf 1982; *Jorg Immendorff: Cafe Deutschland and Related Works,* exhibition catalogue with text by David Elliott and Harald Szeemann, Oxford 1984; *Jorg Immendorff,* exhibition catalogue by E. Daragon, St. Etienne 1985.

Jorg Immendorff is one of those German artists who, having been pupils of Joseph Beuys in Dusseldorf, later on established themselves along a very different line to that of their teacher. Instead of exploring novel solutions to the problem of the relationship between thought and matter, Immendorff has always preferred the more traditional means of artistic expression—those of painting, sculpting and drawing.

From his teacher, though, Immendorff inherited a profound involvement with art at the level of ideas, which, in his case, is put into practice as political involvement. Immendorff studied stage design, and thus became involved with theatre and painting 'on the road', which illustrates social issues by means of 'agit prop' and the styles of popular culture (Ho Chi Min, 1974).

Immendorff's political engagement, however, does not merely identify itself with an ideology for the sake of opposition. His critical stance prevents him from identifying unconditionally with the policy of a traditional and institutionalized Marxist Left, that is to say, with 'socialist realism'.

The most renowned of Immendorff's works, the cycle *Cafe Deutschland,* was conceived after seeing Renato Guttuso's *Cafe Creco.* At the 1976 Venice Biennale, this work of the Italian artist was hung next to that of Immendorff. It was a chance for Immendorff to strengthen his attempts at deconstructing the language of realism—a realism that depended on imposing idealistic pretensions onto painting in order to re-present a reality, even in its 'revolutionary' expression. To Immendorff, the 'real' itself cannot be represented except by recurring as an excessive, overblown language. Instead of a Roman cafe (a meeting place for artists so minutely described in Guttuso's work in its realistic 'truth'), in Immendorff we find a symbolic place, a locus of the mind bearing the marks of physical and spiritual degradation. *Cafe Deutschland* is a kind of bar-discotheque, crammed with mysterious and dark apparitions, full of private as well as collective symbols, all equally livid and unnerving. The atmosphere is vaguely anguished. The artist's intention, through the use of these symbolic images, is to make the viewer aware of the need to subvert political order.

Immendorff's concern with the political actualities of the two Germanies has been constantly at the core of his work, and just as deep is his determination to expose the recent past and its tragic implications for a contemporary Europe. Many of Immendorff's characters belong to German history: from Brecht to Schmidt and Honecker. Others represent the concept of despotic authority: the policeman, soldier or—as an allegory—the German Eagle or the Swastika. He includes portraits of himself, and of his friend and colleague Penck: their presence amounts to a declaration of the imperative need for the contemporary artist to be involved in social and political agitation.

Many of Immendorff's works are in fact the restatement of recurrent images with which he underlines this imperative. In his work, the Brandenburg Gate, a universal image of war and division, is often buttressed by Immendorff with extravagant totems of architectural detail or with common items of household furniture, so presenting it as an absurd and chaotic structure, deriding it as a mere piece of tinsel. Even more grotesquely rendered is the German Eagle, or particular scenes of the urban landscape to be found in several of his drawings. In his drawings, Immendorff seems to reject the flat referentiality of realism as a parody or caricature of itself. He in fact adopts a degraded language, a kind of sketchiness borrowed, not so much from popular culture of an immediate readable quality, as from expressionism, especially from the contemporary 'language' of juvenile urban culture.

It is not by chance that portraits of Punks appear often in Immendorff's paintings. From such a metropolitan culture or subculture, so rich in connotations as to render them near redundant, Immendorff adopts the degraded, derisive aspects, the expressive violence, and that anarchist spirit so difficult to label as 'right' or 'left'. In no instance, though, does the parody of visual vocabulary and violence become the vehicle for an indifferent discourse in his work.

In some recent statements, Immendorff has affirmed that his painting transcends manifest meanings—in regard to German history—inasmuch as it touches only upon the question of the Subject's position in the World. The concept of 'two Germanies', the clash between power and subversion, is to be understood as a metaphor for the universal principles of

Good and Evil, either of which the Subject has to choose. His aim is to give historical identity to these two principles. Through the paintings, he demonstrates that the choice is unavoidable. In this sense, over and above any ideological certainty, Immendorff's art today represents one of the finest attempts to actualize the concept of Tragic Art.

—Giorgio Verzotti

INDIANA, Robert.

American. Born Robert Clark in New Castle, Indiana, U.S.A., 13 September 1928. Studied at John Herron School of Art, Indianapolis, 1946; Munson-Williams-Proctor Institute, Utica, New York, 1947–48; School of the Art Institute of Chicago, 1949–53, B.F.A. 1953; University of Edinburgh and Edinburgh College of Art, 1953–54. Served in the United States Army, 1947–49. Painter: has lived and worked in New York since 1954. Artist-in-Residence, Center of Contemporary Art, Aspen, Colorado, summer 1968. Designed 8¢ U.S. postage stamp (400 million printed), 1973. Recipient: George Brown Travelling Fellowship, 1953; Summer Scholarship, Skowhegan School of Painting and Sculpture, Maine, 1953; Indiana Arts Commission Award, 1973. D.F.A.: University of Indiana, Bloomington, 1977. Agent: Marian Goodman Gallery, 38 East 57th Street, New York, New York 10022. Address: c/o Star of Hope, Vinalhaven, Maine 04863, U.S.A.

Individual Exhibitions:

1962	Stable Gallery, New York
1963	Walker Art Center, Minneapolis
	Institute of Contemporary Art, Boston
1964	Stable Gallery, New York
1965	Rolf Nelson Gallery, Los Angeles
	Dayton's Gallery 12, Minneapolis
1966	Stable Gallery, New York
	Galerie Alfred Schmela, Dusseldorf
	Stedelijk van Abbemuseum, Eindhoven, Netherlands
	Museum Haus Lange, Krefeld, West Germany
	Württembergischer Kunstverein, Stuttgart
1968	Institute of Contemporary Art, University of Pennsylvania, Philadelphia
	Toledo Museum of Art, Ohio
	Hunter Gallery, Aspen, Colorado
1969	Creighton University, Omaha, Nebraska
	Graphics, St. Mary's College, Notre Dame, Indiana
	Colby College Art Museum, Waterville, Maine
1970	Currier Gallery of Art, Manchester, New Hampshire
	Bowdoin College Museum of Art, Brunswick, Maine
	Brandeis University, Waltham, Massachusetts
1971	Galerie im Haus Behr, Hindenburgbau, Stuttgart
	Galerie de Gestlo, Bremen, West Germany
	Overbeck Gesellschaft, Lübeck
	Galerie Christoph Durr, Munich
	Galerie Droscher-Furneisen, Hamburg
	Badischer Kunstverein, Karlsruhe
	Amerika Haus, Berlin
1972	Denise René Gallery, New York
	Louisiana Museum, Humlebaek, Denmark
	Didrichsens Konstmuseum, Helsinki
1973	Summit Art Center, New Jersey
1975	Galerie Denisé René, New York
1976	Galerie Denisé Rene, New York
1977	University of Texas, Austin
	Chrysler Museum, Norfolk, Virginia
1978	State University of New York at Purchase
	South Bend Art Center, Indiana
1982	William A. Farnsworth Art Museum, Rockland, Maine
	Colby College, Waterville, Maine
1983	Miami University, Oxford, Ohio
1984	National Museum of American Art, Washington, D.C.

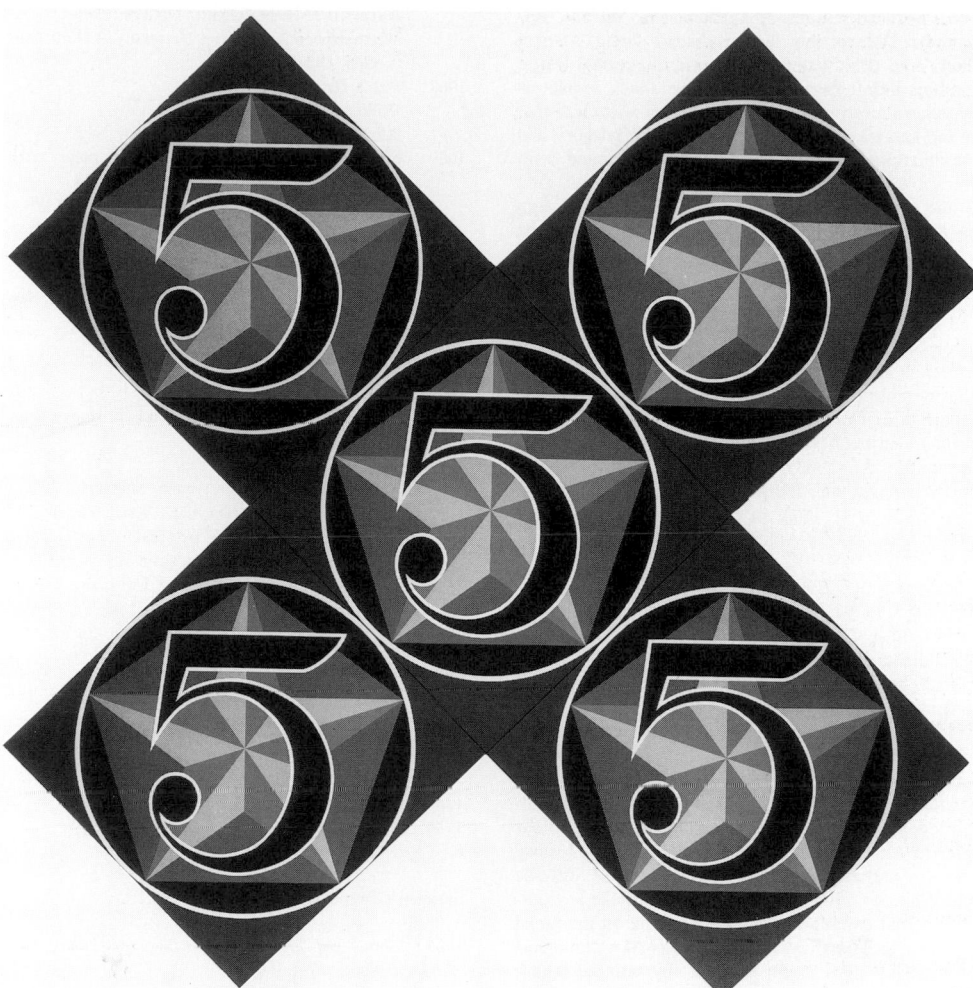

Robert Indiana: *The X–5,* 1963 Courtesy Whitney Museum, New York

Selected Group Exhibitions:

1968	*Documenta,* Kassel, West Germany
1969	*Pop Art Redefined,* Hayward Gallery, London
1972	*The Modern Images,* High Museum of Art, Atlanta
1973	*The Zero Room,* Kunstmuseum, Dusseldorf
1974	*12 American Painters,* Virginia Museum, Richmond
	Inaugural Exhibition, Hirshhorn Museum, Washington, D.C.
1975	*American Art since 1945,* Museum of Modern Art, New York
1977	*20th National Print Exhibition,* Brooklyn Museum, New York
1980	*100 Artists, 100 Years,* Art Institute of Chicago
	American Sculpture: Gifts of Howard and Jean Lipman, Whitney Museum, New York

Collections:

Metropolitan Museum of Art, New York; Museum of Modern Art, New York; Whitney Museum, New York; Albright-Knox Art Gallery, Buffalo, New York; Baltimore Museum of Art; Indianapolis Museum of Art; Los Angeles County Museum of Art; San Francisco Museum of Modern Art; Art Gallery of Ontario, Toronto; Stedelijk Museum, Amsterdam.

Publications:

By INDIANA: articles—statement in *Art Now* (New York), 1969; "Pop: Interview with Robert Indiana," with Phyllis Tuchman, in *Artnews* (New York), May 1974; statement, and interview with D. B. Goodal, in *Robert Indiana,* exhibition catalogue, Austin, Texas 1977.

On INDIANA: books—*Robert Indiana: Graphics,* exhibition catalogue, by Richard Raymond, Notre Dame, Indiana 1969; *Robert Indiana: Prints and Posters 1961–71* by William Katz, Stuttgart and New York 1971, *Icons and Images of the 60's* by Nicolas and Elena Calas, New York 1971; *Pop as Art: A Survey of the New Superrealism,* by Mario Amaya, London

1972; *Robert Indiana,* exhibition catalogue with text by Marius B. Peladeau, Waterville 1982; *Wood Works: Constructions by Robert Indiana,* exhibition catalogue with essay by Virginia M. Mecklenburg, Washington, D.C. 1984.

Like other Pop artists, Robert Indiana has developed his own characteristic recipe or formula—in his case the use of sign lettering combined with bold hard-edge treatment. Essentially non-figurative, his simple geometric shapes are emblazoned with stencilled inscriptions in strong billboard colours. The work of other American pop artists such as Lichtenstein and Rosenquist also has an obvious affinity with the flat brilliance of a Hard Edge painter like Ellsworth Kelly, all having simple, uncompromising imagery and a common absence of any personality in the physical handling of the medium. Suzi Gablik has indeed tried to "redefine" Pop Art by limiting it to the particular variety with close affinities to Hard Edge abstraction—a redefinition which would exclude all the British pop artists, as well as such Americans as Jim Dine and Edward Kienholz.

At any rate the affinities of Indiana's work with Hard Edge abstraction are neither coincidental nor accidental, for in 1954 he settled in New York, living close to and becoming friendly with Ellsworth Kelly, who influenced his style. For several years Indiana painted Hard Edge pictures using the motif of the bilobed, fan-shaped Ginkgo leaf; for instance, "The Sweet Mystery" (1960–61), in which a double leaf is silhouetted on a dark rectangle, with the title stencilled below. The large "Crucifix" mural (1958–9) uses ginkgo and avocado as well as the circles which were to become so characteristic a motif in Indiana's work, and which seem to have been inspired by a circular stencil he had found in his sail loft. This also showed its influence on the geometric wood and metal constructions on which he stencilled insignia and slogans such as "Cuba."

American Pop art made its dramatic public debut in

1962 with exhibitions by Lichtenstein, Warhol, Rosenquist, Wesselman, and Indiana's first one-man show. And if his lettered signs and directional traffic symbols didn't have quite the same shock impact as the others' even more banal images, it was clear that he too had taken over crude commercial imagery and presentational technique. Indiana collaborated with Warhol on the film *EAT* in 1964, and for his first public commission he made a huge 20-foot *EAT* sign for the outside of the New York State Pavilion at the 1964 New York *World's Fair*.

Indiana's early water-colours reveal the influence of older American artists such as Hopper, Sheeler and Charles Demuth. The latter's "poster-portraits" incorporating the Cubist use of words, letters, and numerals as ready-made formal elements, have had a considerable influence on Pop Art, and his "I Saw the Figure 5 in Gold" (1928) inspired Indiana's use of numbers in such works as "The Demuth American Dream No. 5" (1963). The culmination of this use of numbers came with Indiana's vertical sequence of the numbers 1 to 10 hung in countdown to a height of over 50 feet for the American Pavilion at Montreal's *Expo 67*.

Indiana's LOVE paintings in 1966 were accompanied by LOVE sculptures made with Herbert Feuerlicht in carved aluminium. This and other typical Indiana slogans such as DIE, KILL, ERR, HUG, YIELD have been seen by some critics who long for a radical avant-garde as a satirical challenge to the naive optimism of the American dream, forcing an unwilling society to look at its underlying motivations, crude materialism, spiritual vacuity and ludicrously sexualized environment. Certainly Indiana's stencilled legends in their concentric rings of bright colour refer to Americana in all its forms, including history and also literature in his poetic evocations of Melville and Whitman. But only rarely does he make any outright social comment, as in his painting on the racial violence at Selma, Alabama, and his own comments on his EAT signs hardly suggest any satirical intent: "The word 'eat' is reassuring, it means not only food, but life. When a mother feeds her children, the process makes her indulgent, a giver of life, of love, of kindness." Indiana in fact shares the "cool," disinvolved style common to American Pop Art, which makes it not so much subversive but a straightforward reflection of American society as it is, which thus made Pop Art so immediately acceptable.
—Konstantin Bazarov

INSLEY, Will.

American. Born in Indianapolis, Indiana, 15 October 1929. Educated at Amherst College, Massachusetts 1951–55, B.A. 1955; Graduate School of Design, Harvard University, Cambridge, Massachusetts, 1955–58, B. Arch. 1958. Artist-in-Residence, Oberlin College, Ohio, 1966; Resident Critic, University of North Carolina, Greensboro, 1967–68; Visiting Critic, Cornell University, Ithaca, New York, 1969; taught at School of Visual Arts, New York, 1969–78; Lecturer, Cooper Union, New York, 1972. Recipient: National Foundation for the Arts and Humanities grant, 1966; Guggenheim Fellowship, 1969. Agents: Max Protetch, 37 West 57th Street, New York, New York 10019; Paul Maenz, Lindenstrasse 23, 5 Cologne 1, West Germany. Address: 231 Bowery, New York, New York 10002, U.S.A.

Individual Exhibitions:

1951 Museum of Fine Arts, Amherst College, Massachusetts
1965 Stable Gallery, New York
1966 Stable Gallery, New York
1967 Stable Gallery, New York
       Allen Art Museum, Oberlin College, Ohio
       Weatherspoon Art Gallery, University of North Carolina, Greensboro
1968 Stable Gallery, New York
       Walker Art Center, Minneapolis
       Albright-Knox Gallery, Buffalo, New York
1969 *Space Diagrams*, Institute of Contemporary Art, University of Pennsylvania, Philadelphia
       Insley/Mitchell/Poleskie, Andrew Dickson White Museum of Art, Cornell University, Ithaca, New York
       John Gibson Gallery, New York
1971 *Ceremonial Space*, Museum of Modern Art, New York
1972 Galerie Paul Maenz, Cologne
       Visual Arts Gallery, New York
1973 Fischbach Gallery, New York
       Plane für Eine Andere Welt, Museum Haus Lange, Krefeld, West Germany
1974 Fischbach Gallery, New York
       Württembergischer Kunstverein, Stuttgart
       Galerie und Edition Annemarie Verna, Zurich
1975 Allen Priebe Art Gallery, Arts and Communications Center, University of Wisconsin at Oshkosh
       College of the Arts, Ohio State University, Columbus
1976 Galerie und Edition Annemarie Verna, Zurich
       Fischbach Gallery, New York
       Museum of Contemporary Art, Chicago
1977 Max Protetch Gallery, New York
       Protetch-McIntosh Gallery, Washington, D.C.
1978 Galerie Orny, Munich
1980 Max Protetch Gallery, New York
1982 Max Protetch Gallery, New York
1984 Guggenheim Museum, New York

Selected Group Exhibitions:

1965 *Shape and Structure*, Tibor de Nagy Gallery, New York
1970 *L'Art Vivant aux Etats-Unis*, Fondation Maeght, St. Paul de Vence, France
1972 *Documenta 5*, Museum Fridericianum, Kassel, West Germany (and *Documenta 6*, 1977)
1974 *Recent Acquisitions*, Museum of Modern Art, New York
1976 *20 Jahre Museum Haus Lange*, Museum Haus Lange, Krefeld, West Germany (travelled to Max Protetch Gallery, New York)
1978 *Dwellings*, Institute of Contemporary Art, University of Pennsylvania, Philadelphia
1979 *Art and Architecture, Space and Structure*, Protetch-McIntosh Gallery, Washington, D.C.
1980 *Drawings—Structures*, Institute of Contemporary Arts, Boston
1981 *Amerikanische Zeichnungen der Siebziger Jahre*, Louisiana Museum, Humlebaek, Denmark
1984 *Dreams and Nightmares*, Hirshhorn Museum, Washington, D.C.

Publications:

By INSLEY: articles—interview with Elayne H. Varian in *Schemata 7*, exhibition catalogue, New York 1967; statement in "Hexagonal Channel Space" in *Art Now: New York* (New York), November 1969; "Fragments from the Interior Building" in *Will Insley: Space Diagrams*, exhibition catalogue, Philadelphia 1969; notes in *Will Insley: Ceremonial Space*, exhibition catalogue, New York 1971; "Janet Kardon Interviews Some Modern Mazemakers" in *Art International* (Lugano, Switzerland), April/May 1976; "Seriocomic Sp(i)eleology: Robert Smithson's Architecture of Existence" in *Arts Magazine* (New York), May 1978.

On INSLEY: books—*Will Insley: Space Diagrams*, exhibition catalogue, by Stephen Prokopoff, Philadelphia 1969; *Insley/Mitchell/Poleskie*, exhibition catalogue, Ithaca, New York 1969; *Will Insley: Ceremonial Space*, exhibition catalogue, text by Arthur Drexler, New York 1971; *Will Insley: Plane für Eine Andere Welt*, exhibition catalogue, Krefeld, West Germany 1973; *Will Insley*, exhibition catalogue, by Tilman Osterwold, Stuttgart 1974; *Unbuilt America* by Alison Sky and Michelle Stone, New York 1976; *Will Insley*, exhibition catalogue, Chicago 1976; *Will Insley: The Opaque Civilization*, exhibition catalogue with texts by Diane Waldman and Linda Shearer, New York 1984.

Will Insley: *Wall Fragments*, 1975

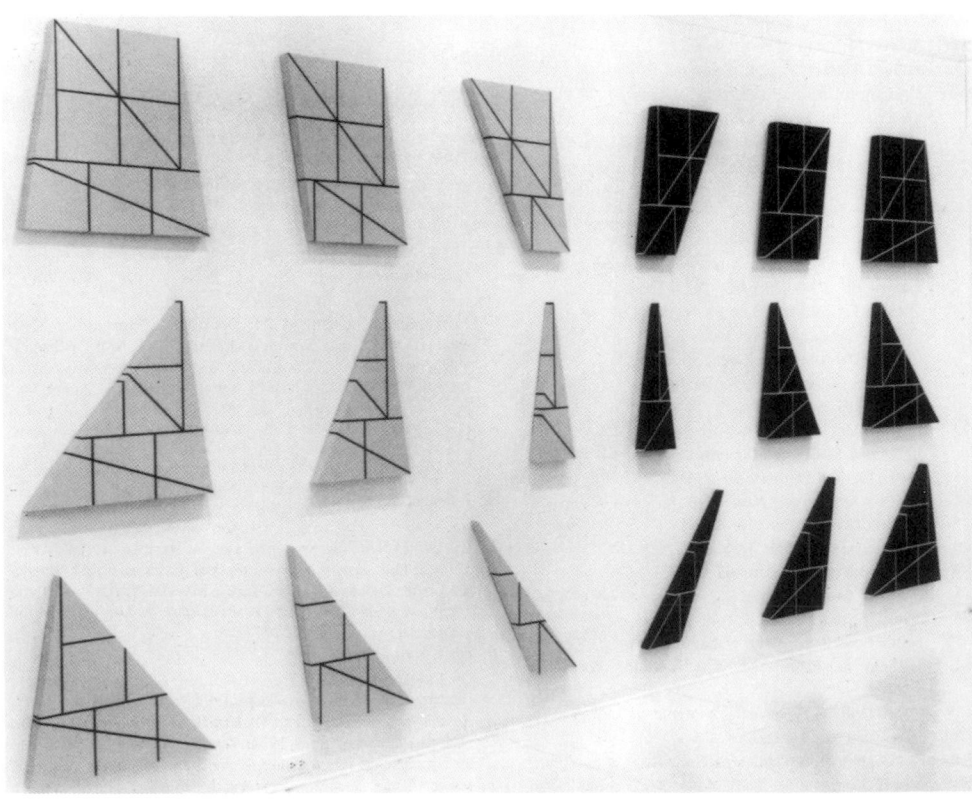

IPOUSTÉGUY, Jean (Robert).

French. Born in Dun-sur-Meuse, 6 January 1920.
Studied art at evening classes in the studio of Robert
Lesbounit, Paris, 1938. Independent artist in various
media, Paris 1938–48; sculptor, in Choisy-le-Roi,
Seine, since 1949: works in bronze, 1967–68, in Car-
rara marble, since 1968. Recipient: Prize, *Biennale*,
Venice, 1964; First Prize, *Kunstreferent*, Darmstadt,
1968; First Prize, *1st International Exhibition of
Original Drawings*, Rijeka, 1968; First Prize, *Inter-
national Biennale of Sculpture*, Budapest, 1973;
Grand Prix National des Arts, Ministère de la Cul-
ture, Paris, 1977. Address: 35 rue Chevreul, 94600
Choisy-le-Roi, France.

Individual Exhibitions:

1962	Galerie Claude Bernard, Paris
1964	Albert Loeb Gallery, New York
	Hanover Gallery, London
	Galerie Claude Bernard, Paris
1965	Städtisches Museum, Leverkusen, West Germany
1966	Galerie Thomas, Munich
	Galerie Claude Bernard, Paris
1967	Galleri Birch, Copenhagen
1968	Galleria Galatea, Turin
	Galleria Odyssia, Rome
	Pierre Matisse Gallery, New York
	Galleria La Nuova Pesa, Rome
	Galerie Claude Bernard, Paris
1969	Kunsthalle, Darmstadt
	Galerie Claude Bernard, Paris
1970	Badischer Kunstverein, Karlsruhe, West Germany
	Von-der-Heydt-Museum, Wuppertal, West Germany
	Galerie Veranneman, Brussels
1971	Galerie Claude Bernard, Paris
	Galleria Formi, Bologna
1972	Galerie Buchholz, Munich
	Galerie Claude Bernard, Paris
1973	Galleria Gabbiano, Rome
	Tolarno Galleries, Melbourne
1974	Galerie Claude Bernard, Paris
	Nationalgalerie, West Berlin
	Artel Galerie, Geneva
1975	Louisiana Museum, Humlebaek, Denmark
	Suite Prussienne: Berlin 1973–1974, Galerie Claude Bernard, Paris
1976	Galeria Juana Mordo, Madrid
	Galeria Trece, Barcelona
1978	Galleri Haaken, Oslo
	Sculptures et Dessins de 1957 à 1958, Fondation Nationale des Arts Graphiques et Plastiques, Paris
1979	*Werke 1956–1978*, Städtische Kunsthalle, West Berlin
	Galerie Alice Pauli, Lausanne
1981	*Dans le Noir et Sous la Lune: Fusains 1978–1979*, Galerie Claude Bernard, Paris
1982	Musée des Beaux-Arts, Lyons
1983	*Works on Paper*, Guggenheim Museum, New York
1985	*Natures Mortes*, Galerie Claude Bernard, Paris

Selected Group Exhibitions:

1958	*Exposition Internationale de Sculpture*, Galerie Claude Bernard, Paris
1964	*Biennale*, Venice
1968	*The Obsessive Image*, Institute of Contemporary Arts, London
1970	*Zeitgenossen*, Stadtische Kunsthalle, Recklinghausen, West Germany
1975	*Realismus und Realität*, Kunsthalle, Darmstadt
1976	*Boites*, Musée d'Art Moderne de la Ville, Paris (travelled to the Maison de le Culture, Rennes)
1977	*Les Mains Regardent*, Centre Georges Pompidou, Paris
1978	*Chemins de la Création*, Chateau d'Ancy le Franc, France
1981	*Anthropos*, at the *Festival of Vienna*, Austria
1987	*Rätsel Wirklichkeit*, Darmstadt, West Germany

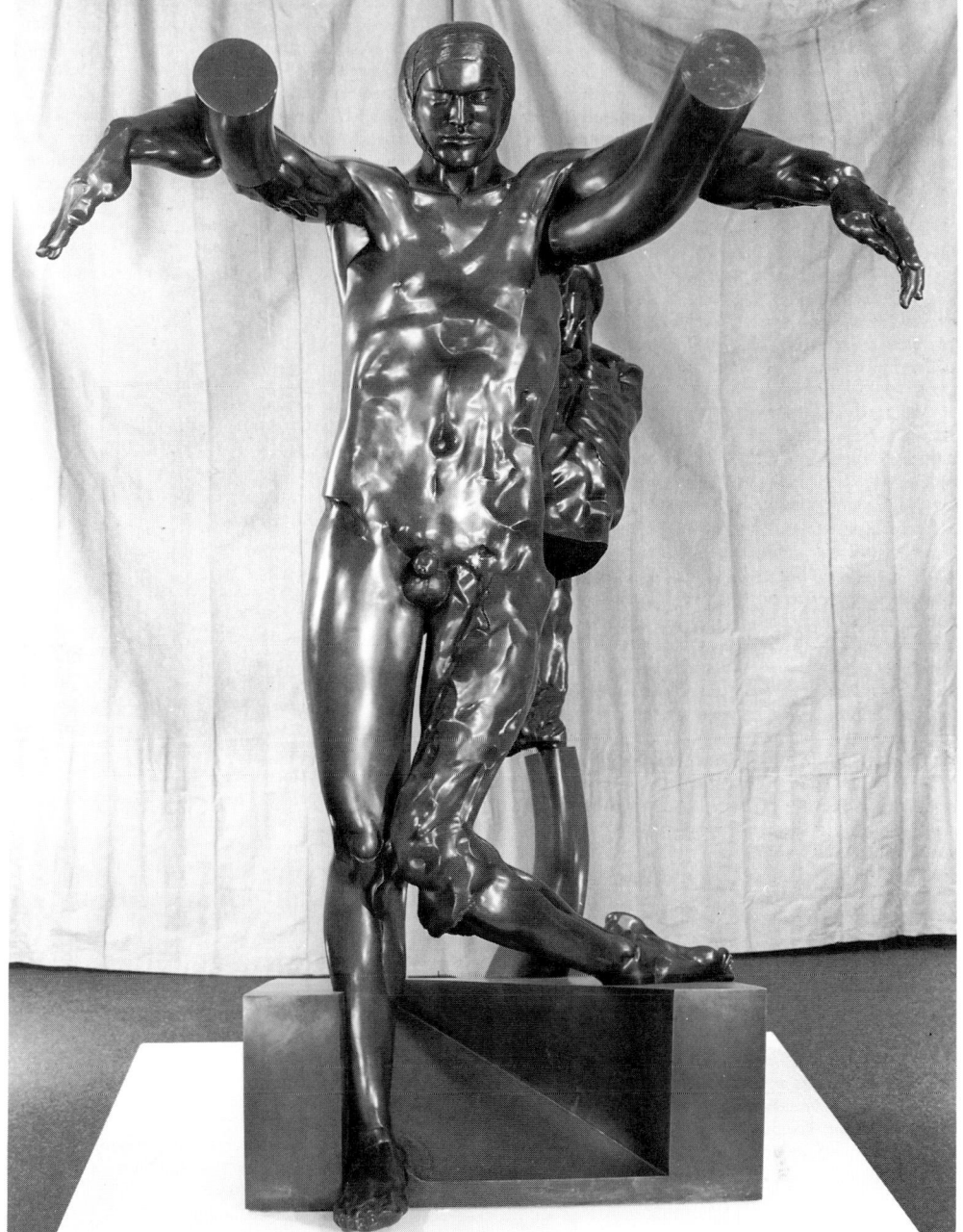

Jean Ipousteguy: *Val de Grace*, 1976

Collections:

Musée d'Art Moderne de la Ville, Paris; Fonds National
d'Art Contemporain, Paris; Nationalgalerie, West Berlin;
Tate Gallery, London; Museum Boymans-van Beuningen,
Rotterdam; Guggenheim Museum, New York; Museum of
Modern Art, New York; National Gallery of Canada, Ottawa;
National Gallery of Victoria, Melbourne.

Publications:

By IPOUSTÉGUY: books—*Procès*, with poem by Henri
Sylvester, Milan 1969; *Leaders et Enfants Nus*, book/object
in aluminium, Paris 1970; *Un Nouvel Archiviste*, with text by
Gilles Deleuze, Montpellier 1972; *Leonard ou la Fin de
l'Humilité*, with text by Robert Lebel, Paris 1974; *Von Kleist-
Ipousteguy*, with text by Heinrich Von Kleist, Heidelberg
1974; *Michelangelo*, portfolio, Munich 1975; *Ronds dens l'O
et le Pessimisme*, Rome 1976; *Sauve qui Peut, Robin*, or *Don
Heretique*, Paris 1978.

On IPOUSTÉGUY: books—*Ipousteguy*, exhibition catalogue,
with text by John Ashbery, London 1964; *Ipousteguy*, exhibition catalogue, with text by Jürgen Claus and Dagobert Frey,
Leverkusen, 1965; *Ipousteguy*, exhibition catalogue, with
text by Walter Lewino, Paris 1966; *Jean Ipousteguy*, exhibition catalogue, with text by Luigi Carluccio, Turin 1968; *Ipousteguy*, exhibition catalogue, with text by Bernd Krimmel,
Darmstadt 1969; *Ipousteguy*, exhibition catalogue, with text
by Jean Paget and Werner Haftmann, Geneva 1974; *Ipoustéguy: Suite Prussienne, Berlin 1973–1974*, exhibition catalogue, with text by Werner Haftmann, Paris 1975; *Jean
Ipousteguy*, exhibition catalogue, with text by Eduardo Chillida, Madrid 1976; *Ipousteguy: Sculptures et Dessins de
1957 à 1978*, exhibition catalogue, with text by Michel
Troche, interview by Jean Paget, Paris 1978; *Ipousteguy:
Werke 1956–1978*, exhibition catalogue, with interview by
Geneviéve Breerette, texts by Dieter Ruckhaberle, Walter Lewino and Bernd Krimmel, West Berlin 1979; *Ipousteguy:
Dans le Noir et Sous la Lune: Fusains 1978–1979*, exhibition
catalogue, Paris 1981; *Jean Ipousteguy: Natures Mortes*, exhibition catalogue with text by H. Sylvestre, Paris 1985; *Rat-
sel Wirklichkeit* by Elisabeth Krimmel, Darmstadt 1987.

"What does the analysis of a vocation yield?" Nothing very clear. The stronger the vocation, the more
difficult it is to explain. Man, generally speaking, answers everything by questions. And the artist compli-
cates the situation, moreover, by answering questions
that have not been asked. He is a relay of that which
cannot be expressed verbally.

While the world grows more and more dependent

on numbers, the artist expresses his efforts in their intervals. And these intervals are abysses. And you can see, palpitating at the bottom, writing that lets off a kind of perfume which defies analysis, as do the perfumes of color, of form and of sound. For the last twelve years or more, I have been preoccupied mainly with the theme of man accompanied by his first natural environment: his shadow.

—Jean Ipoustéguy

Originally a draughtsman and painter, Jean Ipoustéguy has devoted himself to sculpture since 1949. He belongs to the post-war humanist school, which in France includes Germaine Richier, and in England produced a series of artists who rejected abstraction to express the human condition through the human form.

Whilst Ipoustéguy has been largely concerned with the male torso, there are curious indications of fantasy and surrealism in some of his forms, objects which waver between reality and invention, symbolic suggestions of vague menace. Death has been a particular preoccupation, in which a faintly prehistoric, perhaps Etruscan, note appears in craggy, roughly hewn, hieratic monuments, on which rest primitively modelled heads. The upright male figures are powerfully created to suggest a rigid armature, in which the joints are openly displayed, areas of erosion frankly revealed. Whether this is a metaphor for skin, and therefore a symbol of inner erosion, or a covering of the body of precarious defence, is not made clear.

The Baroque mannerisms of these figures, and their universal pretensions, as faceless giants either blind or shielded, suggest god-like creatures, not human beings. There is no denying the audacity of these conceptions, the impressive handling of form, the powerful intellectual and spiritual questioning they propose. Even more perplexing is the famous "L'homme," a standing nude with outspread arms, clearly based on the famous fifth century B.C. bronze figure of Poseidon in the Athens National Museum. Ipoustéguy shows the figure not only with the seared and pitted skin of armature, but with a third leg, suggesting that we are not meant to look and judge this replica of a man in realistic terms but as a metaphorical symbol of some aspect of the human condition. Certainly it provokes a sense of mystery, and concern. The squat female figures with their exaggerated proportions and flattened, depersonalised faces, are even further removed from naturalism.

As a manipulator and architect of form, Ipoustéguy is an acknowledged master, and as a sculptor in bronze he has few modern equals. The problem which seems to beset him is the difficulty of evolving from the long tradition of the human form a manner and a message still potent and relevant. One is forced to face the question whether this has been possible since Rodin, without radical, symbolic distortion. Picasso, Matisse, Henry Moore have succeeded; Ipoustéguy has tried to evolve a passionate, expressionistic manner, especially in the symbolic violence and brutality of the armature-skins, and the exaggerations of the human form, whilst at the same time attempting to retain the detached archaism of distant civilisations.

—Charles Spencer

IRWIN, Robert.
American. Born in Long Beach, California 12 September 1928. Studied at the Otis Art Institute, Los Angeles 1948–50; Jepson Art Institute, Los Angeles, 1951; and Chouinard Art Institute, Los Angeles, 1951–53. Served in the United States Army, Heidelberg, Germany, 1946–48, California, 1951–53. Independent painter, since 1953: lives and works in San Diego, California. Instructor, Chouinard Art Institute, Los Angeles, 1957–58; University of California at Los Angeles, 1962; and University of California at Irvine, 1968–69; John J. Hill Professor, University of Minnesota, Minneapolis, 1981; J. Paul Getty Lecturer, University of Southern California, Los Angeles, 1986; Cullinan Professor, Rice University, Houston, 1988. Recipient: MacArthur Foundation Fellowship, Chicago, 1985–90. Agent: Pace Gallery, 32 East 57th Street, New York, New York 10022. Address: 1220 Rosecrans Street, Apt. 300, San Diego, California 92106, U. S. A.

Individual Exhibitions:

1957   Felix Landau Gallery, Los Angeles
1959   *Recent Paintings*, Ferus Gallery, Los Angeles
1960   Ferus Gallery, Los Angeles
        Pasadena Art Museum, California
1962   Ferus Gallery, Los Angeles
1964   Ferus Gallery, Los Angeles
1966   Pace Gallery, New York
        Robert Irwin/Kenneth Price, Los Angeles County Museum of Art
1968   Pasadena Art Museum, California
        Jewish Museum, New York
1969   Pace Gallery, New York
        72 Market Street, Venice, California
        Robert Irwin/Doug Wheeler, Fort Worth Art Museum, Texas
1970   Museum of Modern Art, New York
        Bell/Irwin/Wheeler, Tate Gallery, London
1971   Walker Art Center, Minneapolis
        Pace Gallery, New York
        Galerie Rudolf Zwirner, Cologne
1972   Sonnabend Gallery, Paris
        Ace Gallery, Los Angeles
        Fogg Art Museum, Harvard University, Cambridge, Massachusetts
        Mizuno Gallery, Los Angeles
1973   Pace Gallery, New York
1974   Mizuno Gallery, Los Angeles
        Pace Gallery, New York
        Wright State University, Dayton, Ohio
        University of California at Santa Barbara
1975   Fort Worth Art Museum, Texas
        Museum of Contemporary Art, Chicago
        Palomar College, San Marcos, California
1976   Walker Art Center, Minneapolis
        Mizuno Gallery, Los Angeles
1977   Whitney Museum of Art, New York (retrospective)
1978   *Mattrix*, University of California, Berkeley (installation)
        Scrim Wall, Portland Center for the Visual Arts, Oregon (installation)
1979   University of California, Berkeley (installation)
        Tumbling Glass Planes, Lake Placid, New York (installation)
        University of Kansas, Lawrence
        San Diego State University, California
        Palazzo Reale, Milan
1980   *Portal Park Slice*, Dallas, Texas (installation)
        Melinda Wyatt Gallery, Venice, California
        Window Transformation, Oberlin College, Ohio (installation)
1981   *Security Stairwell*, Project Studio One, New York
1982   *Light to Solid*, Louisiana Museum, Humlebaek, Denmark (installation)
1983   University of California, San Diego
        48 Shadow Planes, Old Post Office, Washington, D.C. (installation)
        9 Spaces/9 Trees, Arts Commission Plaza, Seattle, Washington (installation)
        Two Ceremonial Gates, San Francisco International Airport (installation)
        University of California, San Diego
1985   Pace Gallery, New York
        San Francisco Museum of Modern Art
1986   Museum of Contemporary Art, Los Angeles
1987   Wave Hill Gardens, Bronx, New York

Selected Group Exhibitions:

1970   *Kompass IV*, Van Abbemuseum, Eindhoven, Netherlands
1971   *Transparency, Reflections, Light, Space*, University of California at Los Angeles
1973   *Five Artists/Five Spaces*, San Francisco Museum of Art
1975   *History of American Sculpture*, Whitney Museum, New York
1976   *Projects for PCA*, Philadelphia College of Art
1978   *20th Century American Drawings*, Whitney Museum, New York
1980   *Aspects of the '70s: Siteworks*, Wellesley College, Massachusetts
1981   *Seventeen Artists in the Sixties*, Los Angeles County Museum of Art
1982   *Form and Function*, Pennsylvania Academy of Fine Arts, Philadelphia

Collections:

Museum of Modern Art, New York; Whitney Museum, New York; Art Institute of Chicago; Walker Art Center, Minneapolis; Fort Worth Art Museum, Texas; Los Angeles County Museum of Art; Norton Simon Museum of Art, Pasadena, California; San Francisco Museum of Modern Art; Tate Gallery, London.

Publications:

By IRWIN: book—*Being and Circumstances: Notes Toward a Conditional Art*, Larkspur, California 1985; articles—statement in *Artforum* (New York), June 1965; letter to the editor in *Artforum* (New York), February 1968; interview with Frederick S. Wight, in *Transparencey, Reflection, Light, Space: 4 Artists*, exhibition catalogue, Los Angeles 1971; "Robert Irwin: An Interview with Alistair Mackintosh" in *Art and Artists* (London), March 1972; "The State of the Real: Robert Irwin Discusses the Art of an Extended Consciousness," with Jan Butterfield, in *Arts Magazine* (New York), June 1972; "Reshaping the Shape of Things," with Jan Butterfield, in *Arts Magazine* (New York), September/October 1972.

On IRWIN: books—*Recent Paintings by Robert Irwin*, exhibition catalogue, Los Angeles, 1959; *Robert Irwin/Kenneth Price*, exhibition catalogue, by Philip Leider, Los Angeles 1966; *Robert Irwin*, exhibition catalogue, with text by John Coplans, Pasadena, California 1968; *Robert Irwin/Doug Wheeler*, exhibition catalogue by Jane Livingston, Fort Worth, Texas 1969; *Kompass IV*, exhibition catalogue, by Jean Leering, Eindhoven, Netherlands 1970; *Larry Bell/Robert Irwin/Doug Wheeler*, exhibition catalogue, by Norman Reid, London 1970; *Transparency, Reflection, Light, Space: 4 Artists*, exhibition catalogue, Los Angeles 1971; *Robert Irwin*, exhibition catalogue, Chicago 1975; *Robert Irwin*, exhibition catalogue, New York 1977; *Robert Irwin: Mattrix*, exhibition catalogue with essay by Lawrence Weschler, Berkeley 1978; *American Artists on Art: From 1940 to 1980*, edited by Ellen Johnson, New York 1982; articles—"Robert Irwin: The Artist's Premises" by Peter Plagens in *Artforum* (New York), December 1970; "The Searcher" by Douglas Davis in *Newsweek* (New York), 29 December 1975; "Robert Irwin: World Without Frame" by Edward Levine in *Arts Magazine* (New York), February 1976; "Robert Irwin: On the Periphery of Knowing" by Jan Butterfield in *Arts Magazine* (New York), February 1976; "Incredibly Beautiful Quandary" by Gordon Hazlitt in *Artnews* (New York), May 1976; "Robert Irwin's Line Paintings" by Peter Plagens in *Artforum* (New York), Fall 1978; "Taking Art to Point Zero" by Lawrence Weschler in *New Yorker*, 8–15 March 1982; "Like Water in a Glass" by Calvin Tomkins in *New Yorker*, 21 March 1983.

During the 1970's Robert Irwin joined the small group of Californians to have made a national reputation. Like that of other poetic, reductive artists, his work requires a slow and totally absorbed consideration by the viewer; and Irwin's own similar pace of conceptualization and realization has led to a small body of work. In his first museum retrospective, in 1977, the artist showed but 8 works—including his by-then well-known temporary installations where the space of the gallery itself was delineated only by taping, or by the boundaries and light effect created by

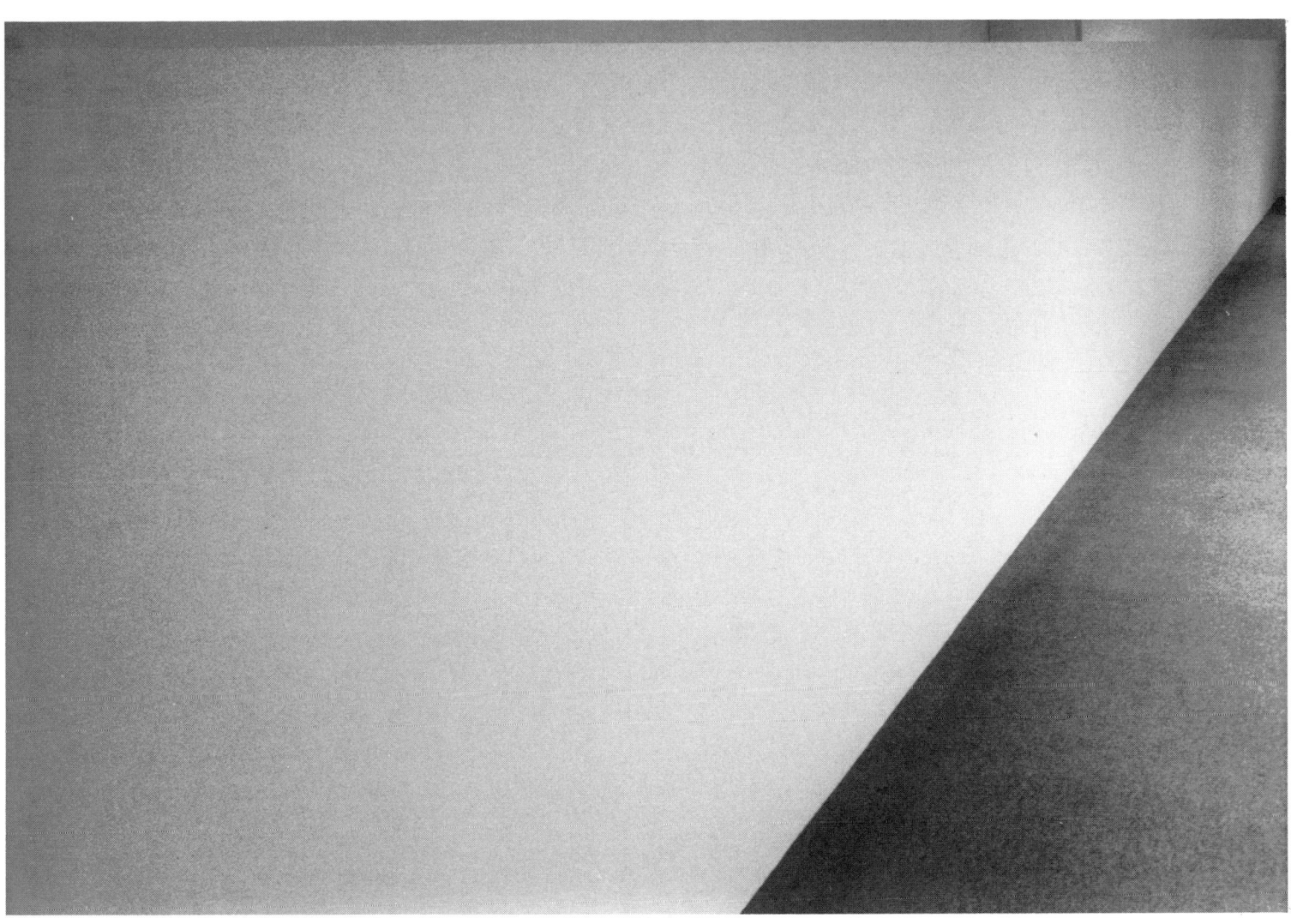

Christian Jaccard: *Toile Bleue Turquoise*, 1974

large expanses of nylon scrim. The contents of that exhibition easily reflected Irwin's highly self-critical evolution—not so much production-oriented but rather philosophical in its intent. Further demonstrating the strongly idealist, if not ascetic, character of his art—its closeness to his life patterns—was Irwin's refusal to allow photographs of his work to be reproduced during the 1960's since he wished no misconceptions of his art to be promulgated.

Like other Californians of that moment, he had worked during the later 1950's in Rico LeBrun-like figuration, followed then by an abstract-expressionist period. Then at the onset of the next decade, Irwin committed himself to a still on-going search for an anonymous, non-tactile, and light-evoking art. His paintings then became extremely spare—monochromatic grounds with four horizontal bars in a different color, ca. 1962, were followed by a further reduction, Rothko-like, to but two bars, ca. 1963-64.

If Irwin's "white style" of spiritual purity might align him with the '50's color-field artists, his desire for a non-sentimental clarity likewise aligns him with his California compatriots such as Valentine and Bell who similarly have sought an art of light—Orient-

influenced perhaps—yet without electronic means. In the late 1960's Irwin produced a series, which became well-known, of aluminum and then cast acrylic discs; when hung away from a supporting wall, and carefully lit, their sprayed surfaces seemed to dissolve into light itself. These were followed by some cast plastic columns which attempted in their translucence to order reflected light in the surrounding space.

No doubt decisive in Irwin's development, and due to his heightened fascination with perception itself, were his experiences—at the turn of the decade—along with the artist James Turrell and the psychophysicist Edward Wortz, in anechoic chambers and Ganzfelds designed for psychological sensory research. Irwin's installation which followed—both the temporary and more recently, several permanent outdoor works such as in Dallas and at Wellesley College, Massachusetts—are essentially "dematerialized" art objects where the spaces before the viewer, and their light, are the artist's goal. Those indoors have been accomplished by string, tape, and large expanses of scrim and light arrangements: demarcated areas, which the viewer was asked to observe, framed and intensified perception. Similarly,

outdoors, natural plantings and topographic manipulation together with, for example, large planar sheets of steel, wire fencing and aluminum were placed in both urban and pastoral settings, to accomplish parallel ends. These public works continued through the 1980's to number almost twenty.

Irwin has suggested four terms—now in wide-use—to define the relation of work to setting: site-dominant, site-adjusted, site-specific, and site-determined. In his desire for an art which, as unobtrusively as possible while still remaining a visible structure, offers the surrounding environment as the "work of art," Irwin has reduced his art to space almost alone. The fourth of these relationships is the ideal—and not for his art alone, but perhaps for the future of art as a larger activity of mankind. In his own words—"Breaking the frame was easy...but then where is the frame of reference? Understanding through historical context is what most people do. What is the larger frame of reference? Being and circumstance."

—Joshua Kind

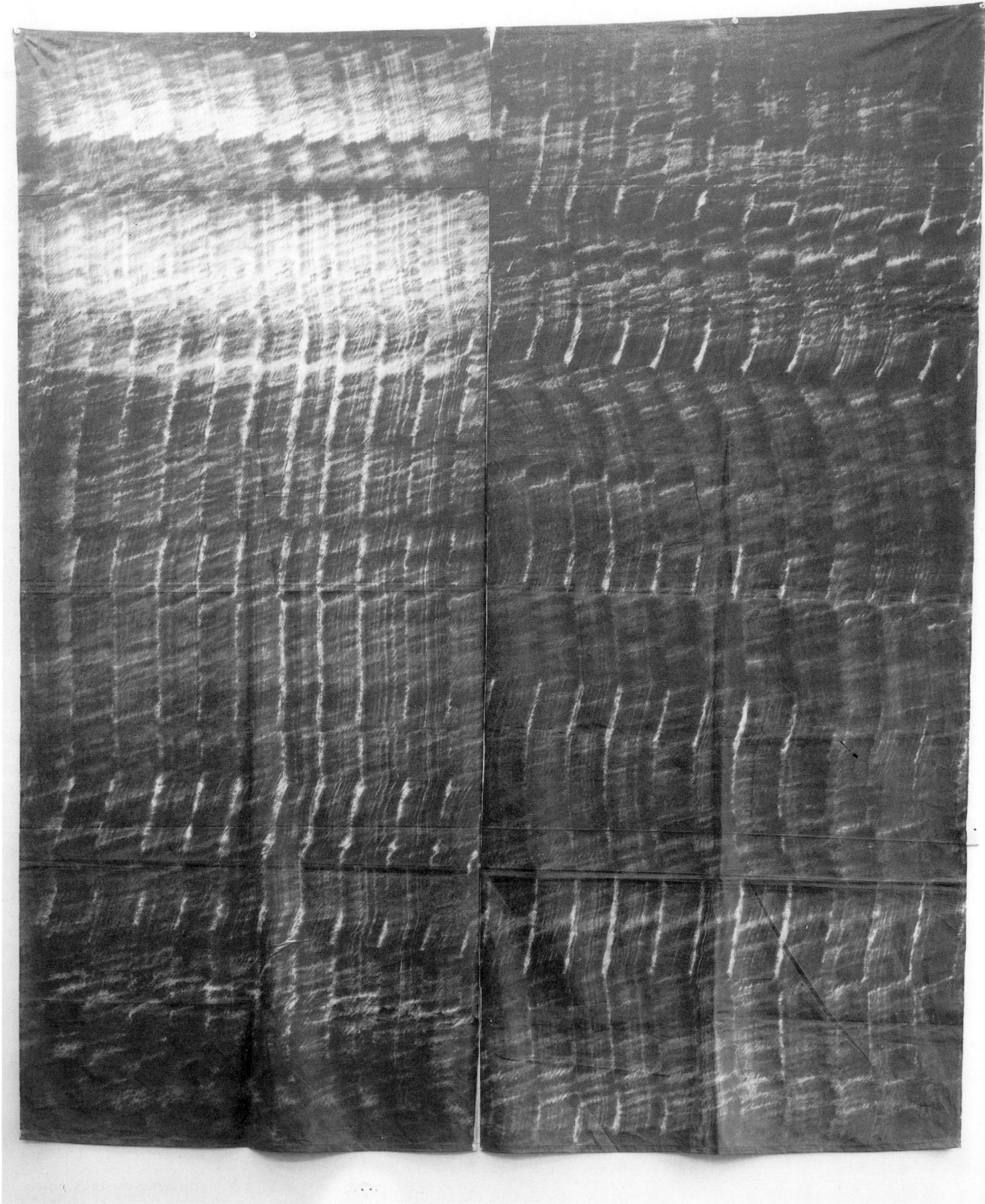

Robert Irwin: Installation at the Pace Gallery, New York, 1973

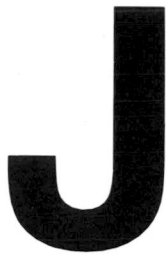

JACCARD, Christian.

Swiss/French. Born in Fontenay-sous-Bois, France, 2 April 1939. Educated at Ecole Nationale des Beaux-Arts, Bourges, France, 1956–60. Married Daniele-Louise Jaccard in 1964; sons: Clarence and Philippe. Independent painter, Paris, since 1964. Chevalier de L'Ordre des Arts et Lettres, France. Agent: Galerie Gilbert Brownstone, 9 rue Saint Gilles, 75003 Paris. Address: 5 rue Coetlogon, 75006 Paris, France.

Individual Exhibitions:

1962	Cabinet des Estampes, Geneva
	Galerie Cachet, Berne
1963	Cercle S.M.A., Geneva
	Galerie Valentine Descombes, Paris
1966	Cercle S.M.A., Geneva
1967	Maison de la Culture, Bourges
1972	Musée de l'Athénée, Geneva
1973	Institute of Contemporary Arts, London
1974	Galerie Lucien Durand, Paris
1975	Musée de l'Abbaye Sainte-Croix, Les Sables-d'Olonne, France
	Galerie d'Art T., Mulhouse, France
	Centre Nationale d'Art Contemporain, Paris (toured France)
	Musée des Arts Décoratifs, Nantes
	Musée d'Art Moderne, Ceret, France
1976	Galerie Gerald Piltzer, Paris
	Galerie Beaubourg, Paris
	Galerie B, Paris
	Musée d'Art et d'Industrie, Saint-Etienne, France
	Institut Francais, Stockholm
1978	Galerie La Hune, Paris
	Galerie Gerald Piltzer, Paris
	Galerie Madoura, Vallauris, France
	Galerie Arta, Geneva
1979	Suites Calcinées 1976–1978, Musée d'Art Moderne de la Ville, Paris
	Galerie Sapone, Nice
	Brannserier 1976–1978, Henie-Onstad Kunstkenter, Oslo
1980	Galerie Athanor, Marseilles
	Galerie Bernard, Geneva
1981	Center Culturel, Bretigny
1982	Galerie Jan Six, Paris
	Musée Cantini, Marseille
1983	Galerie des Ponchettes, Nice
1984	Galerie Bornand, Marseille
	Galerie Athanor, Marseille
	L'Autre Musée, Brussels
	Artothèque, Montpellier
	Atelier Bordas, Paris
	Galerie Gilbert Brownstone, Paris
1985	Centre d'Art Contemporain Pablo Neruda, Corbeil-Essonnes, France
	Institut Francais, Naples
	Pinacoteca, Foggia, Italy
	Museo Campano, Capoue, Italy
	Galleria Massimo Riposati, Rome
	Centre Culturel Français, Rome
	Galerie Sapone, Nice
1986	Galerie Gilbert Brownstone, Paris
1987	Maison de la Culture, La Rochelle, France
	Galerie Gilbert Brownstone, Paris
	Galerie Athanor, Nice

Selected Group Exhibitions:

1964	La Jeune Gravure, Cabinet des Estampes, Geneva
1972	12 Ans d'Art Contemporain, Grand Palais, Paris
1973	French Month, Institute of Contemporary Arts, London
1974	Nouvelle Peinture en France, Musée d'Art et Industrie, Saint-Etienne, France (toured France, Switzerland, Germany and Portugal)
1976	Artists from France, Warehouse Gallery, London
1977	Peinture sans Chassis, Musée des Beaux-Arts, Rouen (toured France and Great Britain)
1979	Tendance de l'Art en France 1968–79, Musée d'Art Moderne de la Ville, Paris
1981	Fran frankrike: 37 aktuella konstnarer, Liljevalchs Konsthall, Stockholm
1984	Ecriture dans la peinture, Centre National d'Art Contemporain, Nice
1986	Pictura Loquens, Centre National d'Art Contemporain, Nice (travelled to Palazzo Reale, Milan)

Collections:

Musée de l'Athénée, Geneva; Cabinet des Estampes, Geneva; Musée d'Art Moderne de la Ville, Paris; Bibliothèque Nationale, Paris; Musée d'Art et Industrie, Saint-Etienne; Musée des Sables-d'Olonne, France; Musée des Beaux-Arts, Dunkirk; Musée des Beaux-Arts, Grenoble; Bienal Corporation, Medellin, Colombia; Australian National Gallery, Canberra.

Publications:

By JACCARD: articles—"Reflexions/Motivations/Connotations" in Art Press (Paris), September 1976; "Ecrire sur l'Art" in Opus International (Paris), January 1979; "Christian Jaccard ou l'eloge de feu", interview with Anne Dagbert, in Art Press (Paris), September 1982; "Notion d'avant garde?" in Opus International (Paris), Autumn 1983; "Christian Jaccard", interview with Michel Giroud, in Kanal (Paris), January 1985.

On JACCARD: books—Art en France: Une Nouvelle Generation by Jean Clair, Paris 1972; Art Actuel en France by Anne Tronche and Hervé Gloaguen, Paris 1973; Christian Jaccard, exhibition catalogue, with text by Claude Fornet and Alfred Pacquement, Paris 1975; Christian Jaccard: Brannserier 1976–1978, exhibition catalogue, with text by Suzanne Page and Ole Henrike Moe, Oslo 1979; Christian Jaccard: Suites Calcinées 1976–1978, exhibition catalogue, with text by Suzanne Pagé and Gerard-Georges Lemaire, Paris 1979; Christian Jaccard l'Iconoclaste, exhibition catalogue by Achille Bonito Oliva and Gerard Georges Lemaire, Naples 1985; articles—review in Connaissance des Arts (Paris), January 1974; "Christian Jaccard et le Tissu de l'Empreinte" by Raoul Jean Moulin in L'Humanité (Paris), February 1974; "Christian Jaccard" in L'Art Vivant (Paris), May 1974; "La Defense" by Germain Viatte in L'Oeil, (Paris), October 1974; "Christian Jaccard ou l'Alphabetisation des Ficelles" by G. Brerete in Le Monde (Paris), April 1975; "L'Outil Fait le Peinture" by Raoul Jean Moulin in L'Humanité (Paris), April 1975; "L'Univers Fetichiste de Christian Jaccard" by Gerard-Georges Lemaire in Quotidien de Paris, 20 February 1978; "Ecrire sur l'Art" by G. Joppolo in Opus (Paris), January 1979; "Christian Jaccard, inconolatre/iconoclaste" by Alain Macaire in Kanal (Paris), June 1982; "Les papiers brules de Christian Jaccard" by France Borel in Pourquoi pas (Paris), 20 June 1984.

*   *   *

According to Nietzsche art carries the pleasure of destruction that then signifies the uneasiness of convention and the implicit need of linguistic regeneration perpetuated by the creative experience. This develops itself through the research of an image that doesn't already belong to the iconographical of the figurative culture but that for clarity and strength can always enter into the realm.

Christian Jaccard moves within a conception of art like the functions within a catastrophe, waiting like the intense unhinging of the tectonic equilibrium of language and like the unpredictable erosion of the imaginary. Until the 'seventies Avante-Garde art was produced under the influence of a linear evolution and then connected to a rectilinear development; as a result, the evolution became softer and less linear.

In this sense Jaccard works outside the schemes and expectations of a culture and uses materials and techniques that produce "an image of the regeneration of art" which is directly linked to the nietzschean idea of destruction and not only metaphorically.

In fact, the French artist uses the fire as a technique to determine the final image of the work and materials that evidently and dutifully fold and change form according to the temperature. The burnings become scars of a memory absolutely emotionless but already taken to an obvious formulation.

Interesting, at the same time, in Jaccards' works is the special installation of a painting that tends toward a bi-dimensionality and di-dramatization of every effect of depth. The fire becomes an element that purifies every strict symbolic valence with its use and acquires a modern and laical force within itself like connecting material and structure between various signs and materials that bend and adapt under the heat. Cold construction or projects that supplant the flagrant theme of the works don't exist.

At this point enters the creative process that adapts the typical temperature of the fire, progressive and at the same time non-linear, able to rise above the rigidness of the formal organization of the works that supplant the unpredictable climate that accompanies contemporary art. For this reason, we have works that in the end create images of contortion and calm that tend toward a figure that develops into a system of abstract and ornamental signs.

Everything passes under the regenerative force of the fire, even the history of the art and the images passed over and reheated by Jaccard at high temperatures. A temperature adapted to substract at a distance ancient historic languages that in this way are actualized and humanized by the pyromanic passion of an artist that works in balance between the desire to carry history into a state of ruin and that of giving back vitality to the exhibit.

—Achille Bonito Oliva

JACQUET, Alain (Georges Frank).
French. Born in Neuilly, Seine, 22 February 1939. Studied at University of Grenoble, baccalaureat 1959; studied architecture at the Ecole Nationale des Beaux-Arts, Paris, 1960. Independent painter and sculptor, Paris, since 1960. Recipient: Premio Marzotto, 1967. Agent: Galerie de France, Paris. Address: c/o Galerie de France, 52 rue de la Verrière, 75004 Paris, France.

Individual Exhibitions:

1961	Galerie Breteau, Paris
1962	Galerie Breteau, Paris
1963	Galerie Aujourd'hui, Brussels
	Robert Fraser Gallery, London
	Galerie Breteau, Paris
1964	Alexander Iolas Gallery, New York
1965	Galerie J, Paris
	Galerie Remy Audouin, Paris
	Galerie Lawrence Rubin, Paris
	Museo de Arte Moderno, Rio de Janeiro
	Galerie Bischofberger, Zurich
1966	Galerie M. E. Thelen, Essen
	Galerie 20, Amsterdam
1967	Galleria Apollinaire, Milan
	Galerie de Boog, Curacao, Dutch Antilles
	Galerie Heiner Friedrich, Munich
	French Section, at the *9th Bienal*, Sao Paulo
1968	Museum of Contemporary Art, Chicago
	Galerie Yvon Lambert, Paris
	Waddell Gallery, New York

1969	Galerie Bonnier, Geneva
	Museum Sztuki, Lodz, Poland
	Galeria Foksal, Warsaw
	Galerie Yvon Lambert, Paris
1970	Galleria Francoise Lambert, Milan
	Galeria Foksal, Warsaw
1971	Galleria La Salita, Rome
	Galerie Bonnier, Geneva
	Galleria Francoise Lambert, Milan
	Galerie René Block, West Berlin
1973	Galerie Bama, Paris
1974	Centre National d'Art Contemporain, Paris
1976	French Pavilion, at the *Biennale*, Venice
1977	Galleri Jacobson, Stockholm
1978	Musée d'Art et d'Histoire, Geneva
	Galerie Bonnier, Geneva
	Galerie Givaudan, Geneva
	Musée d'Art Moderne de la Ville, Paris
1981	Galerie de France, Paris

Selected Group Exhibitions

1961	*2nd Biennale de Paris*, Musée d'Art Moderne, Paris
1962	*Salon des Réalités Nouvelles*, Musée d'Art Moderne, Paris (and 1965)
1964	*Guggenheim International*, Guggenheim Museum, New York
1965	*Biennale de San Marino* (and 1967)
1966	*Art in the Mirror*, Museum of Modern Art, New York (toured the United States)
1968	*The Obsessive Image*, Institute of Contemporary Arts, London

	Documenta 4, Kassel, West Germany
1969	*When Attitudes Become Form*, Kunsthalle, Berne (toured Europe)
	Art by Telephone, Museum of Contemporary Art, Chicago
1970	*3 to Infinity*, Whitechapel Art Gallery, London

Collections:

Center Georges Pompidou, Paris; Musée d'Art Moderne de la Ville, Paris; Moderna Museet, Stockholm; Stedelijk Van Abbemuseum, Eindhoven, Netherlands; Kaiser Wilhelm Museum, Krefeld, West Germany; Louisiana Museum, Humlebaek, Denmark; Galleria Nazionale d'Arte Moderna, Rome; Musée d'Art Moderne, Geneva; Muzeum Sztuki, Lodz, Poland; Arts Council of Great Britain, London.

Publications:

By JACQUET: book—*Helen's Boomerang*, Geneva 1978.

On JACQUET: books—*Alain Jacquet*, exhibition folder, with text by John Ashbery, London 1963; *Alain Jacquet*, exhibition catalogue, with text by Otto Hahn, Zurich 1965; *Alain Jacquet*, exhibition catalogue, with text by Mario Barata, Rio de Janeiro 1965; *Alain Jacquet* by W. S. Childress, Paris 1968; *Alain Jacquet*, exhibition catalogue, with texts by Ryszard Stanislawski and Gregoire Müller, Lodz 1969; *Alain Jacquet*, exhibition catalogue, with texts by Pierre Restany and Suzanne Page, Paris 1978; *Alain Jacquet*, exhibition catalogue, with texts by Pierre Restany and René Ricard, Paris 1981; articles—"Alain Jacquet" by Otto Hahn in *Art International* (Lugano, Switzerland), October 1967; "Alain Jac-

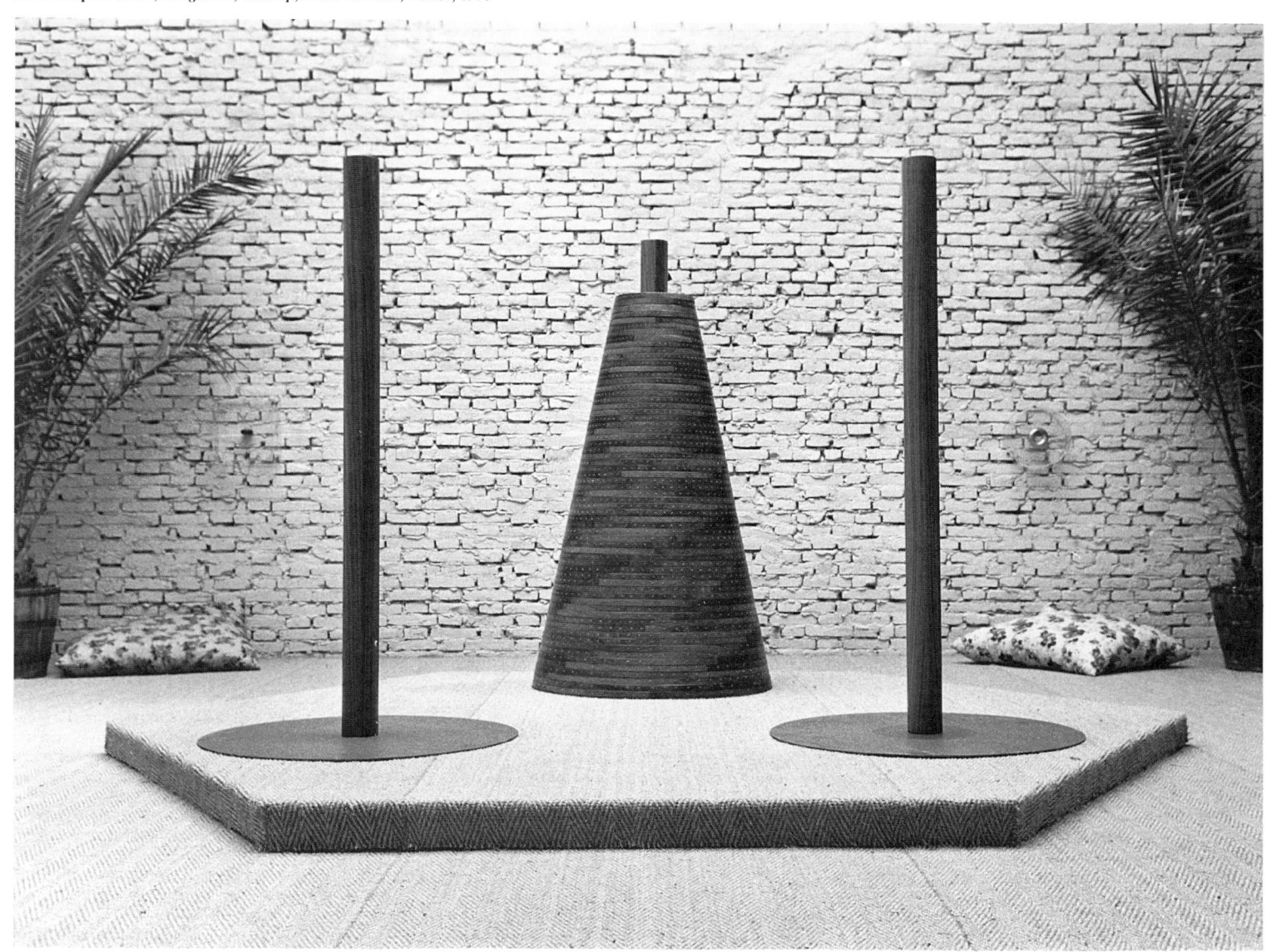

Alain Jacquet: *Churn*, *Doughknot*, and *Top*, at the *Biennale*, Venice, 1976

quet" by G. Pfeiffer in *Das Kunstwerk* (Baden-Baden, West Germany), October/November 1970; "Lettre de Suisse Romande: Alain Jacquet" by Jean-Luc Duval in *Art International* (Lugano, Switzerland), June 1971; "4 Artists in France" by D. Miller, in *Mundus Artium* (Athens, Ohio), vol. 7, no. 1, 1974; "Questions" by Otto Hahn, in *+ - 0* (Genval-Lac), January 1977.

Over something like a decade, Alain Jacquet (with a team of co-workers) set out to use the most sophisticated techniques employed by up-to-the-minute modern laboratories to bring into being what evolved as a kind of modern photographic silkscreen, greatly enlarged from the original; sometimes these enormous productions stretched in extent of height or width to dimensions of $1^3/4$ to 2 metres. Colours were bright and spectacular.

Those who remember these early works will recall that they were carried out in a most peculiar way (or most of them were). The huge enlargement included in its new magnification only too often in its transmogrification a 'blow-up' of the actual printed *frame* (in process block-engraving terms) so that the horizontal breaks (unobservable in the smaller version of the original) sprang into evidence giving a curious new meaning and accent to 'sunbathers' or whatever the subject's theme happened to be.

Without a struggle, it was as if Jacquet's picture had transported the viewer into a printing world which had never heard of rotogravure, but on other occasions, these silkscreens (usually applied on canvas laid down on plexiglass) would go off on a variant like the haunting "Gabrielle d'Estrée" in which the familiar Ecole de Fontainbleau faces of the beauties in the bath were replaced by Jacquet with modern counterparts in full maquillage.

It almost goes without saying that such a creative artist would not continue in this vein forever. One swallow, however enormous (and these silkscreens could and did go into printed editions of 2000 and more), does not make a Summer.

Today, Jacquet—the student who won his baccalaureat at Grenoble University and then went on to study architecture at the École des Beaux-Arts in Paris—has, ever experimenting, set his sights still wider, toying first with esoteric subjects, but now exercising his talents as a sculptor (another of the offcuts of his expansive art training) in mysterious crypto-memorials like the one he put on exhibit at the Venice Biennale—a simplified monolith flanked left and right by two verticals at a respectful distance and each set on a flat round base. The large centre-piece, entitled "Churn", on its righthand side has the pylon called "Dough-Knot"; the one to the left is described by its author as "Top".

—Sheldon Williams

JANSSEN, Horst.

German. Born in Hamburg, 14 November 1929. Educated in Oldenburg, 1937–40, and at the Napola Institute, Haselunne, 1941–45; studied art, under Alfred Mahlau, Staatliche Kunsthochschule, Hamburg, 1946–51. Married Verena von Bethmann-Hollweg in 1960. Painter and graphic artist, Hamburg, since 1952. Recipient: German Government scholarship 1950; Lichtwark Grant, 1952; Art Prize, City of Darmstadt, 1964; Edwin Scharff Award, Hamburg 1965; Grand Prize, *Biennale*, Venice, 1969; Schiller Award, Mannheim, 1975. Agent: Lefebre Gallery, 47 East 77th Street, New York, New York 10021, U.S.A. Address: Muhlenberger Weg 22, 2000 Hamburg 55, West Germany.

Individual Exhibitions:

1964	Kestner-Gesellschaft, Hannover
1965	Konstmuseum Gothenburg, Sweden
1966	Kunsthalle, Basle
1970	Marlborough Fine Art, London
1971	*Etsningar*, Goteborgs Konstmuseum, Gothenburg, Sweden
	Radierungen 1970–71, Galerie Kornfeld, Zurich
	Dommuseum, Lübeck, West Germany (with Paul Gavarni)
1973	Lefebre Gallery, New York
	Kestner-Gesellschaft, Hannover
	Kunsthalle, Hamburg (travelled to the Kunsthalle, Bielefeld, West Germany)
1974	Lefebre Gallery, New York
1976	Kunstverein, Mannheim
	Kunsthalle, Mannheim
1979	*Fruhe Arbeiter*, Kunstverein, Hamburg
1980	*Master Drawings*, International Exhibitions Foundation, Washington, D.C. (toured the United States)
1981	*Aquarelles, Dessins et Gravures*, Berggruen et Cie, Paris
1982	Albertina, Vienna
	Kamakura Museum, Tokyo
	Munch Museum, Oslo
1983	Lefebre Gallery, New York
1986	Berggruen et Cie, Paris

Selected Group Exhibitions:

1969	*Biennale*, Venice
1970	*Malerei nach Fotografie*, Münchner Stadtmuseum, Munich
1972	*4th Internationale Fruhjahrsmesse*, West Berlin
1973	*Kunst in Deutschland 1898–1973*, Kunsthalle, Hamburg (travelled to the Städtische Galerie im Lenbachhaus, Munich
1977	*Documenta 6*, Museum Fridericianum, Kassel, West Germany
1980	*Forms of Realism Today*, Musee d'Art Contemporain, Montreal (travelled to Ottawa and Toronto)

Collections:

Kestner Gesellschaft, Hannover; Goteborgs Konstmuseum, Gothenburg, Sweden.

Publications:

By JANSSEN: books—*Seid ihr alle da*, with poems by Rolf Italiaander, Hamburg 1948; *Plakate und Traktatchen*, Hamburg 1966; *Zehn Zeichnungen aus der Sammlung Poppe*, Hamburg 1966; *Zeichnungen von Horst Janssen und Fotos von Thomas Höpker*, Hamburg 1967; *Ballhaus Jahnke*, with text by Wieland Schmied, Frankfurt 1969; *Paul Wolf und die Sieben Zicklein*, Hamburg 1969; *Hensel und Gratel*, Hamburg 1969; *Horst Janssen Picture Book*, London 1970; *Zeichnungen*, West Berlin 1970; *Petty Fauer*, Hamburg 1970; *Radierungen 1970–1971*, West Berlin 1971; *Landschaftsradierungen 1970*, West Berlin 1971; *14 Biber*, Hamburg 1971; *Hokusai's Spaziergang*, Hamburg 1972; *Tessin*, Hamburg 1972; *Subversionen*, Hamburg 1972; *Fatter für Philip*, Hamburg 1972; *Norwegisches Skizzenbuch, September 1971*, West Berlin 1973; *Neue Zeichnungen 1970–1972*, West Berlin 1973; *Minusio*, West Berlin 1973; *Der Wettlauf zwischen Hase und Igel auf der Buxtehuder Heide*, Pfullingen 1973; *Carnevale di Venezia*, edited by Gerhard Schack, Hamburg 1973; *Missverstandnisse*, Hamburg 1973; *I. Ge-pferdte für Bettina*, Hamburg 1973; *Bettina*, Hamburg 1973; *Landschaft*, edited by Gerhard Schack, Hamburg 1974; *Kleines Geste-Buch*, edited by Gerhard Schack, Hamburg 1974; *Selbstbildnisse zu "Hanno's Tod,"* edited by Gerhard Schack, Hamburg 1975; *November*, West Berlin 1975; *"Ich Komme weiter" agte Laotse; "Wie das?" frog dieser*, with Wieland Schmied and Gerhard Schack, Hamburg 1976; *Umsoonst*, Hamburg 1976; *Die Kopie*, edited by Gerhard Schack, Hamburg 1977; *Nocturno*, with Birgit Jacobsen, Hamburg 1977; *Janssenhof*, with Theodor Storm, Hamburg 1977.

On JANSSEN: books—*Malerei nach Fotografie: von der Camera Obscura bis zur Pop Art, eine Dokumentation*, exhi-bition catalogue, Munich 1970; *Horst Janssen: Etsningar*, exhibition catalogue, with text by Jakob Brunn, Gothenburg, Sweden 1971; *Horst Janssen: Radierungen 1970–71*, exhibition catalogue, Zurich 1971; *Deutche Kunst der 60er Jahre: Malerie, Collage, Op-Art, Graphik* by Juliane Rohe, Munich 1971; *Vierte Internationale Fruhjahrsmesse*, exhibition catalogue, with introduction by René Block, West Berlin 1972; *Horst Janssen*, exhibition catalogue, with text by Thomas Mann, New York 1973; *Kunst in Deutschland 1898–1973*, exhibition catalogue, with text by Werner Hofmann, Hamburg 1973; *Zweihundert Jahre phantastische Malerei* by Wieland Schmied, West Berlin 1973; *Horst Janssen*, prints catalogue, Munich 1975; *Bucherkatalog Horst Janssen*, edited by Ursula Neufeldt and Wilfried Weber, Hamburg 1975; *Horst Janssen: Fruhe Arbeiter*, exhibition catalogue, with texts by Carl Vogel and Wolf Stubbe, Hamburg 1979; *Horst Janssen: Master Drawings*, exhibition catalogue, with an introduction by Alfred Hentzen, Washington, D.C. 1980; *Horst Janssen: Aquarelles, Dessins et Gravures*, exhibition catalogue, with a preface by Jean Clair, Paris 1981; *Horst Janssen: Retrospektiv auf Verdacht* by Heinz Spielmann, Hamburg 1982.

Horst Janssen currently occupies, I suppose, the leading position among artists who methodically keep their distance from the avant garde. The antinomy between preoccupation with nature and with the art of the past troubles him as little as other contradictions in himself. In eccentric fashion Janssen takes the individual movements as much for a motive of his art as for an ego repressing contemplation of the objectivity of appearance. Supported by a stupendous visual fantasy, a brilliantly dexterous talent for drawing, an adequate command of language for the purpose, he stands opposed to an intellectual aesthetic in which direct observation is no longer regarded as a quality.

The continuing veneration of his teacher Alfred Mahlau, whose influence still has its effect on him, is based on an understanding of nature and art which refuses a reflective interpretation, although Janssen possesses all the qualifications necessary for an intellectual interpretation of his own work.

In his early work the understanding of painters of the older generation is evident, above all of Kirchner in woodcuts, Picasso and Shan in lithography, of Klee and Dubuffet in etching, yet looking back we can see that his own hand was apparent even at an early stage. Janssen also turned to reality in abstract, satiric or paraphrastic drawing which, for him, remains an obligatory corrective. He uses his drawing ability in every medium, primarily in lithography and woodcuts, but also in tapestry and painting on glass, and later in his career in etchings which up to now in number and diversity can hardly be ignored. His work in posters and books has expanded since 1965. His style changes periodically and marks every area of his art. From the middle of the 1950's to the end of the 1960's planes, contours and hatching play a leading role, and later on bolder structures; since the late 1970's he has attached increasing importance to colour.

Janssen's development is reflected in countless self-portraits whose diversity is a demonstration of his creative fantasy and an interpretation of his own personality. There are cheerful sketches and poetic illustrations from his early years as a student, satiric and playfully erotic burlesques from "bachelor days," superbly drawn landscapes, paraphrases of European and Japanese drawing and large format graphic series in which the theme of death is ever more predominant. The etchings "Hanos death" and "Dance of death," in recent times the "Nigromontanus" series of drawings and etchings dedicated to Ernst Junger, number among his masterpieces, and not only within the suites representing death. Janssen shows death as a consequence of nature and Eros as the basis of his self knowledge.

Janssen comments, with pictorial and caricature like references to the final catastrophe, on the danger to society in its own faults, its lack of judgment and foresight. He reveals, always in relation to a concrete event, the practices of the art world and places them in direct relation to the crisis in society.

—Heinz Spielmann

JAUDON, Valerie.

American. Born in Mississippi, 6 August 1945. Studied at Mississippi State College for Women, Columbus, 1963–65; Memphis Academy of Art, 1965; University of the Americas, Mexico City, 1966–67; St. Martin's School of Art, London, 1968–69. Independent artist, New York, since 1973. Visiting Artist, Art Institute of Chicago, 1983; Philadelphia College of Art, 1985; Maryland Institute College of Art, 1985; Associate Professor, Hunter College, New York, 1986–87. Recipient: Creative Artists Public Service Grant for Graphics, New York, 1980; Art Award, Mississippi Institute of Arts and Letters, 1981; Special Commendation, Art Commission of the City of New York, 1987; National Endowment for the Arts Fellowship, Washington, D.C., 1988. Agent: Sidney Janis Gallery, New York. Address: c/o Sidney Janis Gallery, 110 West 57th Street, New York, New York 10019, U.S.A.

Individual Exhibitions:

1975   *Sonia Delaunay/Valerie Jaudon,* Livingston-Learmonth Gallery, New York
1977   Holly Solomon Gallery, New York
      Pennsylvania Academy of Fine Arts, Philadelphia
1978   Holly Solomon Gallery, New York
1979   Galerie Bischofberger, Zurich
      Holly Solomon Gallery, New York
1980   Galerie Hans Strelow, Dusseldorf
1981   Corcoran Gallery, Los Angeles
      Holly Solomon Gallery, New York
1983   Sidney Janis Gallery, New York
      Museum Quadrat, Bottrop, West Germany
      Amerika Haus, West Berlin
      Dart Gallery, Chicago
1985   Sidney Janis Gallery, New York
      Fay Gold Gallery, Atlanta, Georgia
      McIntosh/Drysdale Gallery, Washington, D.C.
1986   Sidney Janis Gallery, New York
1988   Sidney Janis Gallery, New York

Selected Group Exhibitions:

1977   *Critic's Choice 1976–1977,* Lowe Art Gallery, Syracuse, New York (travelled to the Munson-Williams-Proctor Institute, Utica, New York)
1978   *Pattern and Decoration,* Sewall. Art Gallery, Rice University, Houston

Valerie Jaudon: *File,* 1986

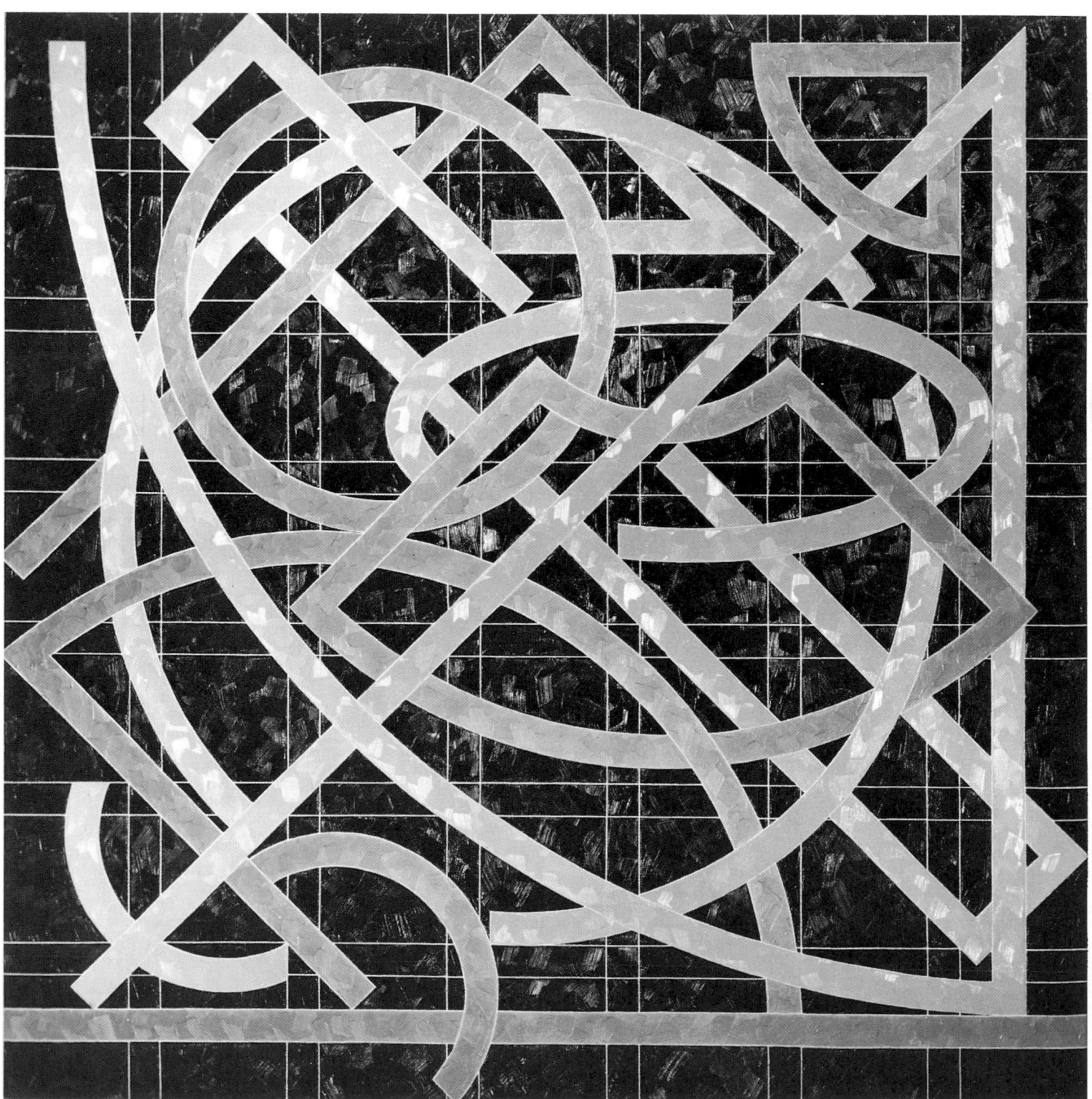

1979 *Black and White Are Colors: Paintings of the 1950's–1970's*, Lang Art Gallery, Claremont College, California
1980 *7 Young Americans*, Sidney Janis Gallery, New York
       Aspects of Printmaking in the 70's, State University of New York at Plattsburgh
1981 *New Directions*, Sidney Janis Gallery, New York
1983 *New Image/Pattern and Decoration*, Kalamazoo Institute of Arts, Michigan (toured the United States)
1984 *Abstract Painting Redefined*, Louis Meisel Gallery, New York (travelled)
1985 *Geometric Abstractions*, Bronx Museum of Arts, New York
1987 *Generations of Geometry*, Whitney Museum at the Equitable Center, New York

Collections:

Commodities Corporation Collection, Princeton, New Jersey; Indiana University Art Museum, Bloomington; Morton Neumann Collection, Chicago; Volvo Corporation Collections, Sweden; Ludwig Collection, Aachen, West Germany.

Publications:

On JAUDON: books—*Black and White Are Colors*, exhibition catalogue by David S. Rubin, Claremont, California 1979; *Valerie Jaudon*, exhibition catalogue with introduction by Sam Hunter, Bottrop, West Germany 1983; *Generations of Geometry*, exhibition catalogue by Kimmo Sarje, New York 1987; articles—"Approaching the Decorative" by Jeff Perrone in *Artforum* (New York), December 1976; "Valerie Jaudon" by Harold Olezarz in *Arts* (New York), December 1978; "The New Decorativeness" by John Perreault in *Portfolio* (New York), June 1979; "Pattern Painting" by Georges Boudaille in *Connaissance des Arts* (Paris), September 1979; "Cronaca dell'Arte a New York" by Tommaso Trini in *Domus* (Milan), January 1980; "Art: 7 Young Americans" by Hilton Kramer in the *New York Times*, 18 April 1980; "Allusive Depths: Valerie Jaudon" by John Perreault in *Art in America* (New York), October 1983.

*   *   *

Decoration and ornamentation have always been looked on as something secondary and inessential in the history of western art. History is no more than the narration made from it, and if only what is past can be narrated, the historic temporality is made clear to man in the telling, verbally or with pictures. History is as old as man; ever since he began, he has told his own story by means of figures, tokens or words. But ornament does not have the quality of history because (in the great majority of cases) it is abstract; it does not reproduce man and his exploits iconographically. A narration in pictures tells of something more than itself; ornament tells only of itself. Decoration has no history, describes no deeds or enterprises; it just happens; it is inarticulate, it produces patterns. Thus the practice of decorative art (which has never had any great master, any subject, any author) falls outside the logocentric project of subsuming within the field of pictorial reproduction all the external reality that man "controls," or thinks he can control. In the United States, pattern painting (regarded by most critics as part of a wider neo-decorative area) was considered objectively (even about the time it appeared, in 1975) as a reaction to mentalism and the formalism of minimal art, going back to the use of unusual materials and methods (cloth, textiles), the pleasures of pictorialism and the sensuality of colours. However, a typically minimal element is to be seen in the repetition of a plastic background shape (which is in any case part of the essence of decorative rhythm). And references are to be found also in the big United States abstractions of the 1950's and 60's (the recurrent use of a big format, the "all-over" employment of the surface of the picture), perhaps notably in the work of Newman, Agnes Martin and Frank Stella's shaped canvases and most recent metal reliefs. In this context Valerie Jaudon takes up again some decorative schemes using interlacing, typical of Arab and Middle Eastern culture and of the Celtic miniature.

Her compositions may be looked on as a number of grids applied to each other but never actually placed on top of each other. While the allusion to this progressive stratification is clear enough, there is still no suggestion of any depth of background. Or rather, the mental and psychological allusion to the third dimension that these networks might imply is firmly flattened on the surface by the distinct contraposition of dark and light making up the ribbons and by the flat versions of the knots and the background—though "background" is not the right term, for by "thinking" the canvas in negative it can be seen that the dark part is actually a dense, intricate juxtaposition of irregular triangles, lozenges and trapezoids. The flat, linear geometry of these works also arises from the fact that the brush always applies the paint (Valerie Jaudon uses metallic pigments and copper, to produce bright, reflecting surfaces) in the same direction as the edges of the ribbon (the "band" of colour), curved or straight according to the entire reticular composition.

—Massimo Carboni

JENKINS, Paul.

American. Born in Kansas City, Missouri, 12 July 1923. Studied at the Kansas City Art Institute, 1938–41; Art Students' League, New York, 1948–52. Served in the United States Naval Reserve Air Corps, 1943–45. Lives in New York since 1948, and in Paris since 1952. Independent artist, since 1953. Recipient: Film Prize, *Biennale*, Venice, 1964; Silver Medal, *Corcoran Biennial*, Washington, D.C., 1966; Golden Eagle Film Prize, New York, 1967. D.H.: Lindenwood College, St. Charles, Missouri, 1973; Humanitarian Award, National Committee of Arts for the Handicapped, U.S.A., 1982; Gold Medal, Art Directors Club of New York, 1983. Commander des Arts et Lettres, France, 1983. Agents: Gimpel and Weitzenhoffer Gallery, 724 Fifth Avenue, New York, New York 10019; Gimpel Fils, 30 Davies Street, London W1Y 1LG; Galerie Patrice Trigano, 4 bis rue des Beaux-Arts, 75006 Paris; Gallery Art Point, Yayoi Building, 6-19, 7-chome, Ginza, Chuo-ku, Tokyo 104. Address: 831 Broadway, New York, New York 10003, U.S.A.

Individual Exhibitions:

1954 Studio Paul Facchetti, Paris
       Zimmergalerie Franck, Frankfurt
1955 Zoe Dusanne Gallery, Seattle
1956 Martha Jackson Gallery, New York
1957 Galerie Stadler, Paris
       Martha Jackson Gallery, New York
1958 Martha Jackson Gallery, New York
       Arthur Tooth and Sons, London
1959 Galerie Stadler, Paris
1960 Martha Jackson Gallery, New York
       Esther Robles Gallery, Los Angeles
       Gallery of Realities, Taos, New Mexico
       Arthur Tooth and Sons, London
1961 Galerie Karl Flinker, Paris
       Martha Jackson Gallery, New York
       Esther Robles Gallery, Los Angeles
       Univeristy of Minnesota, Minneapolis
1962 Galerie Karl Flinker, Paris
       Galerie Charles Lienhard, Zurich
       Esther Robles Gallery, Los Angeles
       Galleria Toninelli Arte Moderna, Milan
       Galleria Odyssia, Rome
       Kunstverein, Cologne
1963 Arthur Tooth and Sons, London
       Galerie Eva de Buren, Stockholm
       Galerie Karl Flinker, Paris
       Gallery Moos, Toronto
1964 Tokyo Gallery
       Court Gallery, Copenhagen

Kumar Gallery, New Delhi
       Martha Jackson Gallery, New York
       Kestner-Gesellschaft, Hannover (retrospective; toured England, the United States, and Canada)
1965 Galerie Karl Flinker, Paris
       Gertrude Kasle Gallery, Detroit
       Court Gallery, Copenhagen
       Gallery of Modern Art, Scottsdale, Arizona
       American Embassy, Madrid
1966 Martha Jackson Gallery, New York
       Galerie Agnes LeFort, Montreal
       Hope Makler Gallery, Philadelphia
       Galerie Europa, West Berlin
       Savage Gallery, London
1968 Galerie D. Gervis, Paris
       Galerie Moos, Toronto
       Galerie Raber, Lucerne
       Martha Jackson Gallery, New York
       Seligmann Gallery, Seattle, Washington
1969 Martha Jackson Gallery, New York
1970 Martha Jackson Gallery, New York
       Gertrude Kasle Gallery, Detroit
1971 Martha Jackson Gallery, New York
       Richard Gray Gallery, Chicago
       Suzanne Saxe Gallery, San Francisco
       Museum of Fine Arts, Houston (retrospective)
       Dryden Gallery, Charlotte, North Carolina
       Gertrude Kasle Gallery, Detroit
1972 San Francisco Museum of Art (retrospective)
       Gimpel Fils, London
       Images Gallery, Toledo, Ohio
       Abrams Original Editions, New York
       Corcoran Gallery of Art, Washington, D.C. (toured the United States)
1973 Galerie Karl Flinker, Paris
       University of Notre Dame Art Gallery, Indiana
       Lindenwood College Art Gallery, St. Charles, Missouri
       Oklahoma Art Center, Oklahoma City
       Amarillo Art Center, Texas
       Santa Barbara Museum of Art, California
       Indianapolis Museum of Art
       Brooks Memorial Art Gallery, Memphis, Tennessee
       Martha Jackson Gallery, New York
       Louisiana Gallery, Houston
1974 Musée des Beaux Arts, Charleroi, Belgium (retrospective)
       Galerie Baukunst, Cologne
       Gimpel and Weitzenhoffer, New York
       Gimpel Fils Gallery, London
       Comsky Gallery, Los Angeles
       Kilcawley Centre Gallery, Youngstown State University, Ohio
       Gimpel Fils Gallery, London
       Comsky Gallery, Los Angeles
       Youngstown State University, Ohio
       North Texas State University, Denton
       Abrams Original Editions, New York
       Galerie Ulysses, Vienna
       Canton Art Institute, Ohio
       Zanesville Fine Arts Center, Ohio
       St. Clair County Community College, Port Huron, Michigan
       Witte Memorial Museum, San Antonio, Texas
       Fort Lauderdale Museum of the Arts, Florida
       Huntington Galleries, West Virginia
       University of Florida, Gainesville
       Hunter Museum of Art, Chattanooga, Tennessee
1975 Fort Lauderdale Museum of the Arts, Florida
       Galerie Tanit, Munich
       Galerie Farber, Brussels
       Ohio University, Athens
       Miami University, Oxford, Ohio
       Carone Gallery, Fort Lauderdale, Florida
       Closson Gallery, Cincinnati, Ohio
       Lauren Rogers Library and Museum of Art, Laurel, Mississippi
       Tampa Bay Art Center, Florida
       Montgomery Museum of Fine Arts, Alabama
       Columbia Gallery of Fine Arts, Columbus, Ohio
1976 Samuel Stein Gallery, Chicago
       Basel Art Fair
       Galerie Karl Flinker, Paris
       Gimpel and Weitzenhoffer Gallery, New York

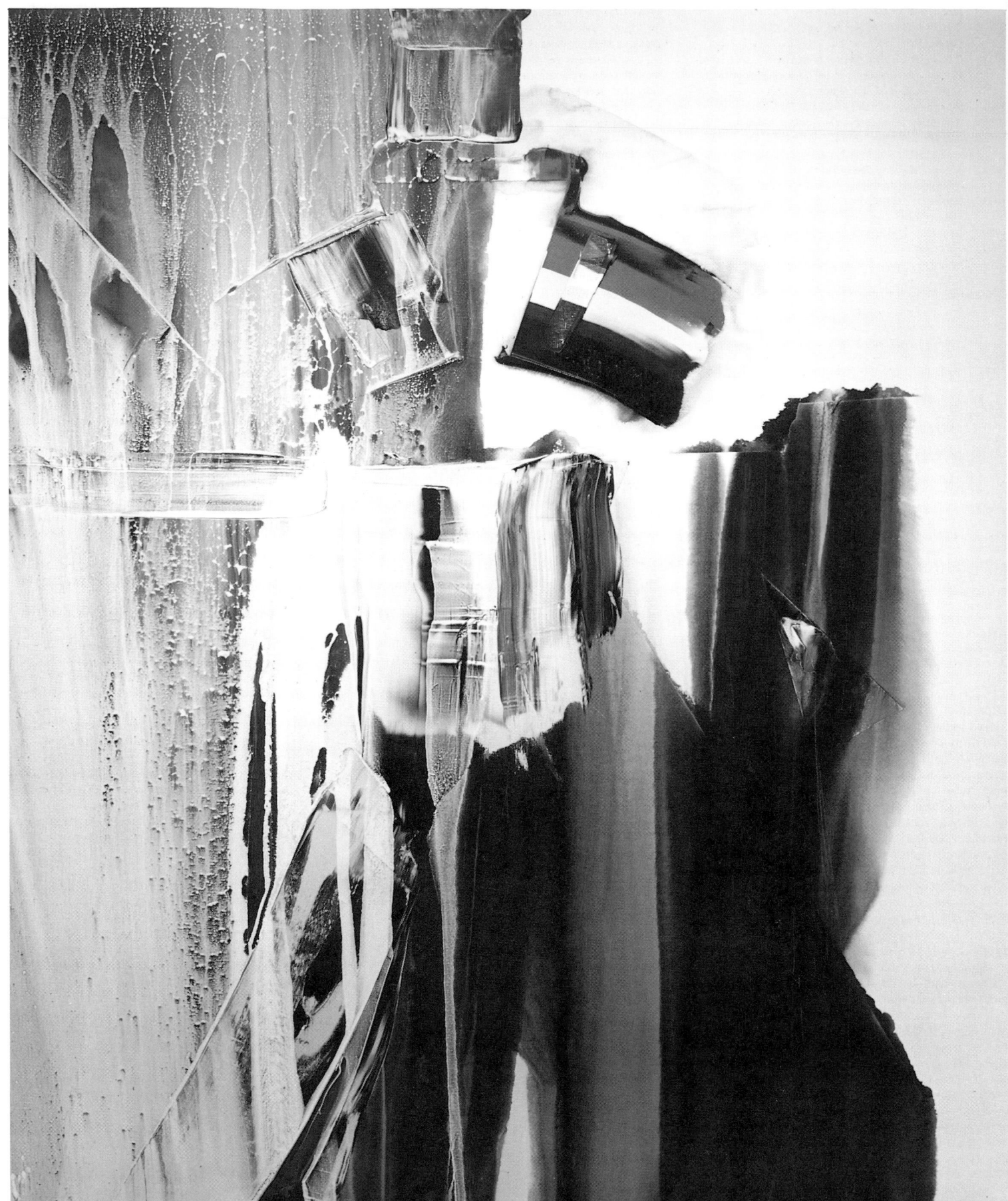

Paul Jenkins: *Phenomena Prism Emissary*, 1985

Jane Haslem Gallery, Washington, D.C.
The 24 Collection, Miami
Galerie Maillard, St. Paul de Vence, France
1977   Gimpel und Hanover Galerie, Zurich
La Galerie Cour St. Pierre, Geneva
Sears Bank and Trust Company, Chicago
Contemporary Gallery, Dallas
Philbrook Art Center, Tulsa, Oklahoma
Closson Gallery, Cincinnati, Ohio
Diane Gilson Gallery, Seattle
Martha Jackson Gallery, New York
Galerie d'Art de la MJC, Metz, France
1978   Galleria d'Arte Narciso, Turin
Gimpel and Weitzenhoffer Gallery, New York
1979   Gimpel and Weitzenhoffer Gallery, New York
1980   Elaine Horwitch Gallery, Scottsdale, Arizona
Gimpel Fils Gallery, London
Palm Springs Desert Museum, California
Samuel Stein Gallery, Chicago
Elaine Horwitch Gallery, Santa Fe, New Mexico
Balcon des Arts, Paris
Galerie Karl Flinker, Paris
1979   Gimpel and Weitzenhoffer Gallery, New York
Galerie Baukunst, Cologne
Galerie Charles Munchen, Luxembourg
Galerie Bronda, Helsinki
Elaine Horwitch Gallery, Scottsdale, Arizona
1980   Gimpel Fils Gallery, London
Elaine Horwitch Gallery, Scottsdale, Arizona
Contemporary Gallery, Dallas
Albert White Gallery, Toronto
Gallery Gwyn Hodges, Oxford
Galerie Karl Flinker, Paris
1981   Palm Springs Desert Museum, California (retrospective)
Irving Feldman Galleries, Sarasota, Florida
Western Carolina University, Cullowhee
Carone Gallery, Fort Lauderdale, Florida
Samuel Stein Gallery, Chicago
French Cultural Center, New York (and Theatre du Rond-Point, Paris)
Gimpel and Weitzenhoffer Gallery, New York
1982   Galerie Nicoline Pon, Zurich
Gimpel Fils, London
Irving Feldman Galleries, Detroit
Galerie Georges Fall, Paris
Contemporary Gallery, Dallas
1983   Mead Art Museum, Amherst, Massachusetts (retrospective)
Gimpel and Weitzenhoffer Gallery, New York
Galerie Georges Fall, Paris
Alex Rosenberg Gallery, New York
Contemporary Gallery, Dallas
1984   Carone Gallery, Fort Lauderdale, Florida
Musee d'Art Contemporain, Dunkerque, France
1985   Galerie Sapone, Nice
Gimpel and Weitzenhoffer Gallery, New York
Gallery Moos, Toronto
Galerie Georges Fall, Paris
Galleri Atrium, Stockholm
1986   Gimpel Fils, London
Gallery Art Point, Tokyo
Roswitha Haftmann Modern Art, Zurich
MR Galleria d'Arte Contemporanea, Rome
Galerie Michel Delorme, Paris
Butler Institute of American Art, Youngstown, Ohio
Focus Gallery, Lausanne
Elaine Horwitch Galleries, Santa Fe, New Mexico (and Scottsdale, Arizona)
Gimpel and Weitzenhoffer Gallery, New York
1987   Galerie 63, Klosters, Switzerland
Samuel Stein Gallery, Chicago
La Colomba Arte, Latina, Italy
Vismara Arte, Milan
Musee Picasso, Antibes, France
Galerie Regis Dorval, Paris

Selected Group Exhibitions:

1956   *41 American Watercolorists of Today,* Museum of Modern Art, New York
1958   *Nature in Abstraction,* Whitney Museum, New York (toured the United States)
1964   *Painting and Sculpture of a Decade,* Tate Gallery, London
1965   *Abstract Watercolors by 14 Americans,* Museum of Modern Art, New York
1972   *Abstract Expressionists,* Albright-Knox Art Gallery, Buffalo, New York
1974   *Inaugural Exhibition,* Hirshhorn Museum, Washington, D.C.
1977   *American Postwar Painting,* Guggenheim Museum, New York
        Quelques Americains a Paris, Centre Georges Pompidou, Paris

Collections:

Museum of Modern Art, New York; Guggenheim Museum, New York; Whitney Museum, New York; Corcoran Gallery of Art, Washington, D.C.; Hirshhorn Museum and Sculpture Garden, Washington, D.C.; Tate Gallery, London; Stedelijk Museum, Amsterdam; Fondation Maeght, St. Paul de Vence, France; Musee Picasso, Antibes, France; Centre Georges Pompidou, Paris.

Publications:

By JENKINS: books—*Observations of Michel Tapie,* with Esther Jenkins, New York 1956; lithographs for *Seeing Voice Welsh Heart* by Cyril Hodges, Paris 1965; *Strike the Puma,* play, Paris 1966; *The Sun in Scorpio,* with Joyce Wittenhorn, Venice 1959; *D. H. Lawrence and the Man Who Died,* lecture paper, Taos, New Mexico 1980; *Anatomy of a Cloud,* with Suzanne Donnelly Jenkins, New York and Paris 1985; articles—"A Cahier Leaf" in *It Is* (New York), Autumn 1958; "An Abstract Phenomenist" in *The Painter and Sculptor* (New York), Winter/Spring 1959; "American Abstract Painting" in *It Is* (New York), Winter/Spring 1959; "Panel: Non-American Painting" in *It Is* (New York), Winter/Spring 1959; "A Reply to Purity" in *It Is* (New York), Spring 1960; "Gustave Moreau: Moot Grandfather of Abstraction" in *Art News* (New York), December 1961; "Beauford Delaney: A Quiet Legend" in *Art International* (Lugano), 20 December 1962; "Conversation in the Studio with Paul Jenkins," interview by Michel Butler, in *Cimaise* (Paris), July/August 1963; "Jenkins Paints an Opinion" in *Art News* (New York), November 1966; "Jenkins on Matisse" in *Art World* (New York), November/December 1978; "Gustav Klimt Drawings" in *Art World* (New York), December/January 1980; "Tapies Paradox" in *Art World* (New York), September/October 1981; "Pour le Prisme du Chaman" in *Opera de Paris* (Paris), April 1987.

On JENKINS: books—*Dictionary of Abstract Painting* by Ferdinand Louis Berckelaers, New York 1957; *The Paintings of Paul Jenkins* by Kenneth B. Sawyer, Pierre Restany and James Fitzsimmons, Paris 1961; *Ein Halbes Jahrhundert abstrakte Malerie,* Munich and Zurich 1962; *Art U.S.A. Now,* edited by Lee Nordness and Allen S. Weller, New York 1962; *Paul Jenkins* by Jean Cassou, Paris 1963; *Lascaux and Jenkins: 14 Poems* by George P. Elliot, Lanthem, Maryland 1964; *A Dictionary of Contemporary American Artists* by Paul Cummings, New York 1966; *History of Modern Art* by H. H. Arnason, New York 1968; *The Joys and Sorrows of Recent American Art* by H. W. Janson, New York 1969; *Paul Jenkins Retrospective,* exhibition catalogue, by Gerald Nordland, Houston 1971; *Paul Jenkins* by Albert Elsen, New York 1973; *L'Art Abstrait* by Michel Seuphor, Paris 1974; *Paul Jenkins* by Alain Bosquet, Paris 1982.

*   *   *

The world of phenomena for me is involved with the capture of ever-changing reality, both in the act of painting and in the perceiving of reality. I am drawn to ever-changing realities not because they seem to be the evidence of a hazardous world but because they draw me closer to the wonders. Marvels incite me not just to accept change but to *induce* it. A phenomenon which springs forth from the real, that which happens, is something we must continually strive to perceive.

There are two kinds of light in painting which I move toward that become and relate form. One is radiant, luminous light, that element which has its light from *within,* as in an orb. Luminous light comes from a central source or place and exists independently. The other is reflected light which appears as a mysterious substance on the surface. It is a light coming from the outside source which creates constant reflection. When these two kinds of light interpene-

trate I discover unique forms which have a psychic substance, forms which build, hold on to one another, become alive and certain. Like psychic substances, they become caught in a state of abeyance. When this occurs, the color becomes what I call non-alternate color, color that cannot be any other color than what it is on the canvas. No other color can take its place. It becomes a constant not entirely dependent upon the color next to it.

Color is a fact of science: it is not an abstraction in itself. Color is the hidden fact of your psyche and you make it real or not. You make it your own or not. No two people have the same fingerprints. No two people have the same primary colors even if they should come out of the same Winsor Newton tube. Color becomes the factual evidence of the individual which is not discovered through theory or found through osmosis.

—Paul Jenkins

*   *   *

Aside from one brief aberration with black and white, Paul Jenkins was always a colourist obsessed by the accidental effects possible of achievement under the minimum of detailed control of the medium. His early experiences of working with glazes fired on clay in the ceramic factory where he worked for a short time undoubtedly left this feeling for the magical transformation that flow and heat can induce in colours. His travels from New York to Europe date from 1955 and took him away from the persuasive influences of the Abstract Expressionists that he felt too insistent. So much so that he destroyed all his work he had done prior to that year. Beginning afresh left him open none the less to ideas and impulses he could choose and deliberate on coolly. He took note of painters such as Moreau and Redon (Symbolists, it will be observed, who put colour high on their priorities), also Riopelle and Hokusai.

This was the date he began pouring paint and setting the course for the promised land he arrived at over the next few years. Another artist he found of common purpose was Wols, whose intuitional freedom struck sparks of sympathy. The "veils" that were developed from Wols by Frankenthaler, Louis and others in New York came to be of shared appeal though of subsequent individual evolution. Jenkins made his first works in acrylic around 1960, and the medium came to be employed along with oils and other synthetic paints to increase the limits to which he was committed. This activation of the vehicle by the gravity feed of colour involved manipulation of the canvas to direct the flow and direction of the pools of colours often in acts of physical complexity and resource. Large canvases would be laid on the floor and hooked up at one side to create valleys, and down them would flood full surges of red, ending on a verge like a tidal bore. The push-pull of linear white and luminous white left its mark. Indentations of ebb and flow were evident on the paintings that came to take a generic title of *Phenomenon.* Scale and variations of colours and strengths of tone conditioned the visual choreography.

Jenkins has made his charisma by his methods dictating their own form in colour to a large extent. But his colour is not invariably of negative purity. It gains and loses in its retinal impact through overpainting, mixing on surface level, opting for change by juxtaposition determined by gravitational flow rather than placing. Brushes are supplanted by an ivory blade in directing fluid paint on the support. Fusion without heat sets up optical stimulation of a subtle and delicate intensity. If many of the paintings and their prime choice of reds give a repeated suggestion of flower petals enlarged and isolated in their curving and elliptical outlines, in others the imagery is less determinate though allusions to other forms come through; butterfly wings in the iridescent glow and icebergs in the transparency of immense masses. Jenkins from the pure process of working the medium has come to distil an authentic spirit, staining instead of painting, colouring by flow rather than by application and in its potency having equal power to intoxicate the senses through the thirsty throat of the eye.

—G. S. Whittet

JENNEY, Neil.

American. Born in Torrington, Connecticut in 1945. Painter and sculptor; lives in New York. Agent: Blum Helman Gallery, New York. Address: c/o Blum Helman Gallery, 20 West 57th Street, New York, New York 10019, U.S.A.

Individual Exhibitions:

1968	Galerie Rudolf Zwirner, Cologne
1970	*Paintings*, Noah Goldowsky Gallery, New York
	Sculpture, David Whitney Gallery, New York
1975	Blum Helman Gallery, New York
	Wadsworth Atheneum, Hartford, Connecticut
1981	University of California Art Museum, Berkeley (retrospective; travelled to Corcoran Gallery of Art, Washington, D.C., and Contemporary Arts Museum, Houston; then a European tour organized by the Basel Kunsthalle)

Selected Group Exhibitions:

1969	*Anti-Illusion: Procedures/Materials*, Whitney Museum, New York
1978	*New Image Painting*, Whitney Museum, New York
1980	*Die Neue Wilden*, Neue Galerie-Sammlung Ludwig, Aachen, West Germany
	American Art from the 70's, Nordjyllands Kunstmuseum, Aalborg, Denmark
1982	*Attitudes-Concepts-Images 1960–80*, Stedelijk Museum, Amsterdam
1983	*Paintings and Sculpture from 8 Collections*, Museum of Contemporary Art, Los Angeles
1987	*Avant-Garde in the Eighties*, Los Angeles County Museum of Art

Publications:

On JENNEY: book—*Neil Jenney: retrospective*, exhibition catalogue with essay by Mark Rosenthal, Berkeley 1980; article—"Neil Jenney: Elegance With a Political Twist" by Hilton Kramer in the *New York Times*, 17 May 1981.

Jenney has insisted on the "mission" of his current work, and presents his art as a "social science." In such stance, he seemingly would align his production with the radical ethos of the 1960s; Jenney began his career in that decade, as a Minimalist, but left for a content-oriented, far more eclectic mode, the so-called Bad Paintings (1969–71). Long-known in N. Y. for his maverick personality, Jenney appears to share—along with fellow New Englanders Winsor and Grosvenor—an almost fierce independence, both in commercial control and production of their work: Jenney served as his own dealer for a long period.

His works at the onset of the 1970s already evinced the clearly directed humane and environmental concerns which would become his signature content. Although distinct from his still-active approach in their loosely drawn and finger-painterly surface effects, these simple narratives, with their verbal play as given in printed titles, and severe framing, carried some feeling of a Conceptual mode. In the following years, his older Minimalist allegiance would come into focus with an austere yet theatrical format: paint was now applied precisely, images presented close-up and only in fragments, and frames expanded to become architraval-like, black and massive, onto which the titles appeared in large stencilled characters. Through the early 1980s, these images were presented in exaggeratedly horizontal format (often with a proportion of 1:11, as in *Meltdown Morning*, 1975), which of course had a strong viewer effect. This has been phrased by reviewers as a fortress-like slit, tomb-like, and producing a mock-panoramic view, but all working as if to force a sense of both viewer frustration and intense involvment. Given the insistence upon subject formed by the highly abbreviated views and information, it might seem that a mock-didactic mode is intended.

Although described as reportorial, these paintings—especially given the artist's own language about them—present themselves as a call to action on the issues shown, i.e. *Acid Story*—the destruction of nature. Yet, by their generality and aloof removal (in his 1985 exhibition, Jenney had the gallery entirely dark except for spotlight upon the slit-like pictures, with an armed guard present) the work acknowledges the only stifled message of any art that would be "activist" and speak of issues of profound complexity and magnitude—but all within the minute artworld itself.

—Joshua Kind

JENSEN, Alfred.

American. Born in Guatemala City, 11 December 1903; attended primary school in Horsholm, Denmark; permanent resident of U.S. after 1934. Educated at San Diego High School, California, 1924–25; studied at San Diego Fine Arts School, 1925; also studied with Hans Hofmann, Munich, 1926–27, and at the Académie Scandinave, Paris, 1929. Married painter Regina Bogat in 1963; children: Anna and Peter. Art adviser to collector Sadie A. May, travelling in Europe and the United States, 1931–51; independent artist, New York, from 1951, known for diagrammatic paintings based on study of traditional and Western sciences. Taught at Maryland Institute, Baltimore, summer 1958. *Died* (in Glen Ridge, New Jersey) *4 April 1981.*

Individual Exhibitions:

1952	*Alfred Jensen: Experiments in Color*, John Heller Gallery, New York
1955	Tanager Gallery, New York
1957	Bertha Schaefer Gallery, New York
1959	*1st Exhibition of Murals*, Martha Jackson Gallery, New York
	Alfred Jensen and the Image of the Prism, Martha Jackson Gallery, New York
1961	*Magic Square*, Martha Jackson Gallery, New York
	Guggenheim Museum, New York
1963	Fairleigh Dickinson University, Madison, New Jersey
	Duality Triumphant, Graham Gallery, New York
	Kornfeld & Klipstein, Berne
	Divine Analogy and Time Reckoning, Graham Gallery, New York
1964	Kunsthalle, Basel
	Rolf Nelson Gallery, Los Angeles
	Stedelijk Museum, Amsterdam
1965	Graham Gallery, New York
	A Pythagorean Notebook, Rolf Nelson Gallery, Los Angeles
1966	Galerie Renée Ziegler, Zurich
	Works of Graphic/Alfred Jensen, Royal Marks Gallery, New York
1967	*The Acroatic Rectangle*, Cordier and Ekstrom, New York
	Royal Marks Gallery, New York
1968	*Treasures from Inventory III*, Martha Jackson Gallery, New York
	Cordier and Ekstrom, New York
	J. L. Hudson Gallery, Detroit
1970	*The Aperspective Structure of a Square*, Cordier and Ekstrom, New York
1972	*Paintings 1964–1972*, Pace Gallery, New York
	Galerie Kornfeld, Zurich
1973	Kestner-Gesellschaft, Hannover (toured Denmark and Germany)
	Recent Paintings, Pace Gallery, New York
1975	Kunsthalle, Basel
	Kornfeld & Klipstein, Basel
1976	*Selected Works 1961–1974*, Pace Gallery, New York

1977	Kornfeld & Klipstein, Basel
	Paintings and Diagrams from the Years 1957–1977, at the *14th Bienal*, São Paulo (toured the United States)
1981	Virginia Commonwealth University, Richmond
1983	Pace Gallery, London
	Studio School, New York
1985	Guggenheim Museum, New York
1988	Waddington Galleries, London

Selected Group Exhibitions:

1961	*American Abstract Expressionists and Imagists*, Guggenheim Museum, New York
1963	*Paintings from the Museum of Modern Art, New York*, Smithsonian Institution, Washington, D.C.
1964	*Post-Painterly Abstraction*, Los Angeles County Museum of Art (travelled to Walker Art Center, Minneapolis and the Art Gallery of Ontario, Toronto)
	Documenta 3, Museum Fridericianum, Kassel, West Germany (and *Documenta 5*, 1972)
1963	*Sammlung Marguerite Arp-Hagenbach*, Kunstmuseum, Basel
1971	*The Structure of Color*, Whitney Museum, New York
1973	*Biennial*, Whitney Museum, New York (and 1977)
1977	*Time*, Philadelphia College of Art
1980	*Aspects of the 70s: Mavericks*, Brandeis University, Waltham, Massachusetts

Collections:

Guggenheim Museum, New York; Museum of Modern Art, New York; Whitney Museum, New York; Albright-Knox Art Gallery, Buffalo, New York; Herbert F. Johnson Museum of Art, Cornell University, Ithaca, New York; San Francisco Museum of Modern Art; Kuntmuseum, Berne; Kunsthalle, Basel; Louisiana Museum, Humlebaek, Denmark; Seibu Museum of Art, Tokyo.

Publications:

By JENSEN: articles—"Statement" in *It Is* (New York), Autumn 1959; text in *Alfred Jensen*, exhibition catalogue, Berne 1963; text in *Alfred Jensen: The Aperspective Structure of a Square*, exhibition catalogue, New York 1970; "The Reciprocal Relation of Unity 20, 1969" in *Art Now: New York*, vol. 2, no. 4, 1970; text in *The Structure of Color*, exhibition catalogue, by Marcia Tucker, New York 1971; text in *Alfred Jensen: Recent Paintings*, exhibition catalogue, New York 1973.

On JENSEN: books (exhibition catalogues)—*Alfred Jensen: Experiments in Color*, New York 1952; *Alfred Jensen*, New York 1961; *Alfred Jensen* by Max Bill and E. W. Kornfeld, Zurich 1966; *Alfred Jensen* by Max Bill, Allan Kaprow and Wieland Schmied, Hannover 1973; *Alfred Jensen: Paintings and Diagrams from the Years 1957–1977* by Linda Cathcart, and Marcia Tucker, Buffalo, New York 1977; *Alfred Jensen: Paintings and Works on Paper*, exhibition catalogue with essays by Peter Schjeldahl and Maria Reidelbach, New York 1985.

The odyssey of Alfred Jensen is one that defies comparison. His idiosyncratic explorations into the dualities of universal truths, ancient theories and a specific, if not hermetic, methodology propelled him into a world of total independence. That artistic independence, in and of itself, was no small accomplishment.

Jensen embraced these concepts with such abandon, such conviction and such unordinary style that his paintings transcend the pomposity of his eccentric tales. The pictures, while their presence is stunning, are crude and strident enough to bring madmen to mind. Though Jensen was no closet lunatic, the obsessiveness of his work brings one perilously close to such an assumption.

And that is a large part of his power as an artist.

Like a cat-scan of intricate brainwork, his paintings portray a visual structure which attempts to elucidate the principles of solar energy, protons and neutrons,

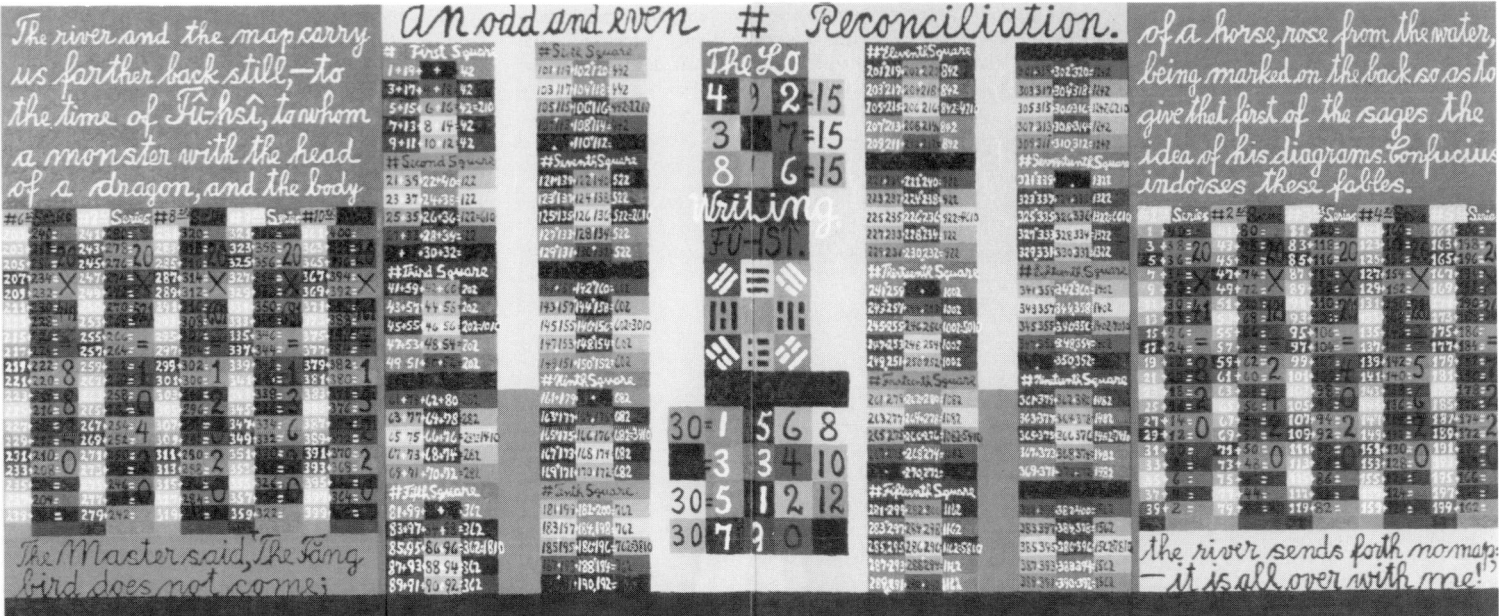

Alfred Jensen: *A Divine Mission*, 1976

heaven and earth, magnetic fields, Aztec calendars and much other lofty data, which marries with the often klutzy imperfection of the human mind and hand.

As if frosting a cake, Jensen painted in thick, dense blacks (on which was based, he believed, a "negative prism"), brilliant yellows, reds, blues, oranges and whites, loading his imagery of concentric circles and queer numerical patterns of squares and triangles with oscillating vitality. Embellished with handwritten phrases marked by a bookish resuscitation of ancient phenomena and presumably eternal truths—as explications, these numbers, quotes, equations and axioms dance on the surface like so much more imagery. Though each letter carries a weighty message, their handcraftedness and shaky script lends to each painting a sense of humility and bohemianism which overrides otherwise bombastic pronouncements. They are still authoritative and uncompromising, but, on a purely visual scale, they exist as juicy maps of one man's inspiration.

Though few of us could hope to unravel Jensen's tendentious ruminations completely, the real impact of his work exists in the visual dialogue he determined by following the abstruse patterns of his pursuits. Thus, whether we've read up on ancient China or the Pharaoh of Cheops or not, the work exudes a vitality which is undeniably penetrating.

—Janet Goleas

JIMENEZ, Luis (Alfonso, Jr.).

American. Born in El Paso, Texas, 30 July 1940. Assistant to his father in El Paso, 1946-58, then studied at the University of Texas at Austin, 1960-64, B.S. in art and architecture 1964, and Ciudad Universitaria, Mexico City, 1964. Married Vicky Cardwell in 1961 (divorced, 1966); daughter: Elisa; married Mary Wynn in 1967 (divorced, 1970); married Susan Brockman in 1985; son: Luis Adan. Sculptor: lived in New York City, 1966-73; assistant to Seymour Lipton, New York, 1965-67; Program Coordinator, New York City Youth Board, 1966-69; now lives and works in Hondo, New Mexico. Recipient: National Endowment for the Arts Fellowship, 1977. Agent: Hill's Gallery, 110 San Francisco, Santa Fe, New Mexico 87501. Address: P.O. Box 175, Hondo, New Mexico 88336, U.S.A.

Individual Exhibitions:

1969   Graham Gallery, New York
1972   O. K. Harris Gallery, New York
1973   Long Beach Museum, California
        Bienville Gallery, New Orleans
1974   Contemporary Arts Museum, Houston
1975   Hills Gallery, Santa Fe, New Mexico
        O. K. Harris Gallery, New York
        Bienville Gallery, New Orleans
1977   University of North Dakota, Grand Forks
        University of Santa Clara, California
1978   Yuma Fine Arts Association, Arizona
1979   Plains Art Museum, Moorehead, Minnesota
        Landfall Press Gallery, Chicago
        New Mexico Museum of Fine Arts, Santa Fe
        Hills Gallery, Santa Fe, New Mexico
1980   Joslyn Art Museum, Omaha, Nebraska
1981   Franklin Struve Gallery, Chicago
        Sebastian-Moore Gallery, Denver, Colorado
1982   Hydt-Blair Gallery, Santa Fe, New Mexico
1983   Candy Story Gallery, Folsom, California
        Yares Gallery, Scottsdale, Arizona
        Laguna Gloria Art Museum, Austin, Texas
1984   Phyllis Kind Gallery, New York
        Alternative Museum, New York
        Hammarskjold Plaza, New York
        Sculpture Plaza, New York
        Barnsdall Junior Arts Center, Los Angeles
        Art Attack Gallery, Boise, Idaho
        Roswell Museum and Art Center, New Mexico
1985   Dallas Museum of Art, Texas
        Sette Gallery, Tempe, Arizona
        Art Network, Tucson, Arizona
        University of Arizona, Tucson
1986   University of Texas / El Paso Art Museum, Texas
        Adair Margo Gallery, El Paso, Texas
1987   Moody Gallery, Houston
        Marilyn Butler Fine Arts, Santa Fe, New Mexico

Selected Group Exhibitions:

1969   *Human Concern / Personal Torment*, Whitney Museum, New York
1973   *The Male Nude*, Hofstra University, Hempstead, New York
1975   *Richard Brown Collects*, Yale University, New Haven, Connecticut
1977   *Ancient Roots / New Visions*, Tucson Museum of Art, Arizona (toured the United States)
1978   *Figure in the Landscape*, Wave Hill Sculpture Garden, New York

1979   *First Western States Biennial*, Denver Arts Museum, Colorado (toured the United States)
1982   *Recent Trends in Collecting*, Smithsonian Instituteion, Washington, D.C.
1983   *Myth of the Cowboy*, Library of Congress, Washington, D.C.
1985   *Power of Popular Image*, Queens College, Pennsylvania
1987   *Contemporary Hispanic Art in the United States*, Museum of Fine Arts, Houston (toured the United States)

Collections:

Witte Museum, San Antonio, Texas; Long Beach Museum, California; Roswell Museum and Art Center, New Mexico; Sheldon Memorial Art Gallery, University of Nebraska, Lincoln; Plains Art Museum, Moorehead, Minnesota; National Museum of American Art, Washington, D.C.; Art Institute of Chicago; Denver Art Museum, Colorado; Metropolitan Museum of Art, New York; Albuquerque Museum, New Mexico.

Publications:

On JIMENEZ: books—*Human Concern / Personal Torment*, exhibition catalogue by Robert Doty, New York 1969; *Humanist Art in the U.S.* by Barry Schwartz, New York 1971; *Plastic Sculpture* by Nick Roukes, Calgary, Alberta 1975; *Luis Jimenez*, exhibition catalogue, Austin, Texas 1984; *Luis Jimenez for Children*, Austin, Texas 1984; *Luis Jimenez: Sodbuster*, Dallas 1985.

My main concern is creating an "American" art: using symbols and icons. Sources for the work come out of popular art and esthetic (cowboys, western Indians, the Statue of Liberty, motorcycles), as does the material—plastic (surfboards, boats, cars). I feel I am a traditional artist working with images and materials that are of "my" time.

—Luis Jimenez

Luis Jimenez' sculptures are powerful, humorous, lusty and charged with explosive energy. They and the drawings communicate the artist's profoundly integrated understanding of classical form and inspired draughtsmanship. They also make visible his sources in the Mexican Renaissance expressions of J. C. Orozco which influenced some early murals which he painted as a student at the University of Texas. His

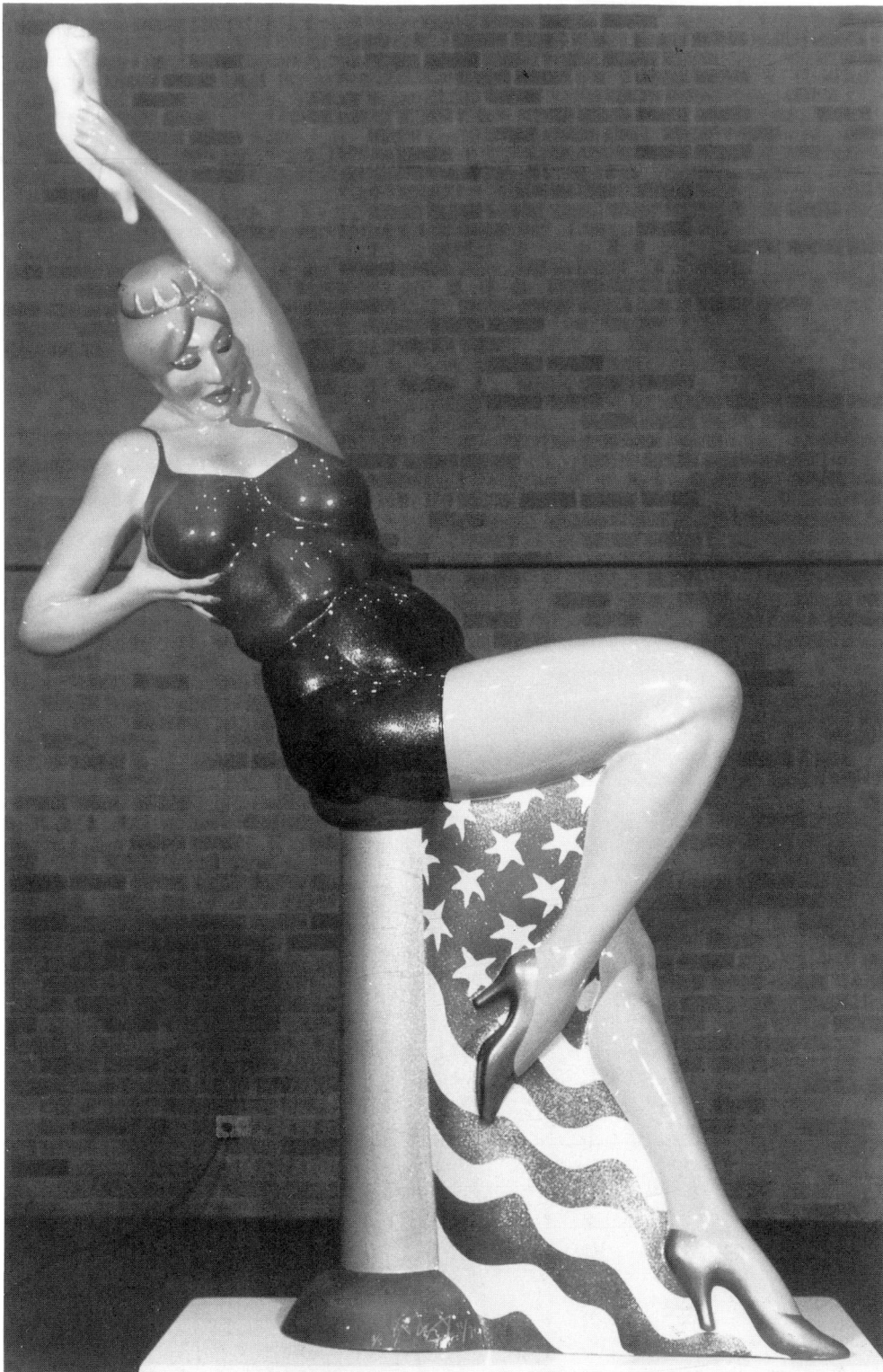

Luis Jimenez: *Barfly*, 1971

moral truth rather than exploits it for ulterior purposes.

"Progress" involves a series of monumental sculptures depicting the history of the West. The first of the series is a full-sized buffalo being attacked and killed by an Indian on horseback. It represents both the end of an historical era and its consequences as myth.

It would be unfair to Jimenez to regard his work as social comment alone or simply as a form of documentary. The sculpture goes further—making visible the processes and images which are basic to contemporary experience. Advanced plastic values and traditional subject-matter merge in a unique perspective. While the artist's sculpture identifies ubiquitous American symbols and myths, it also communicates the energy and form which are basic to a mature, passionate, and more humane existence. Jimenez' work is a turning point in American art, as it evokes fresh insights from native sources, giving new life to the tradition. Jimenez' "tastelessness," frequently discussed and admired by New York critics, presents a dramatic break with high fashion attitudes. It is central to subject-matter which more explicitly belongs to the native culture.

As a Chicano, Jimenez reveals his own powerfully self-contained background in each work and expresses his cogently moralistic view of contemporary America. The sculpture "Man on Fire" and the drawing "La Causa" refer specifically to the political expressions of the Chicano struggle to come to grips with the complex social dilemma facing America.

Throughout all the work Jimenez deals with essential metaphors. For example, "Birth Piece" depicts a stylised woman giving birth to a soul-less astronaut / robot, fully equipped for space travel; and "The End of the Trail" presents a dying Indian chief in an electric sunset. These expose a cultural orientation in which electrical or mechanical substitutes for natural phenomena and processes are transformed into sentimental myth.

The concept of the sex-object and its implications as cultural symbol is a logical theme for Jimenez' art, for it is in this arena that American fantasy reaches an apex of symbolic absurdity. In nearly all social activities, the exaggeration of an innate physical drive is precipitated into mythic substitutes which in turn affect attitudes about race, ethnicity, nationality, as well as about art and metaphysics. Jimenez succeeds in making the viewer intensely aware of these issues through an art from which he probes reality without isolating it from contemporary experience.

—James Harithas

subject-matter is folk art in the form of kitsch, involving border-town crafts: "Progress I" ultimately derives from this category of expression; "Barfly" is a politically charged reconstruction of the Statue of Liberty--a mythic "non-art" structure; "Rodeo Queen", "Rock Star" and "California Chick" are personifications derived from popular culture.

These subjects affirm Jimenez' incisive concern with popular myth. The artist challenges or redefines each myth by penetrating its meaning in order to release its power.

The use of fibreglass, neon, electric lights, and strong color derived from sign technology invests the sculpture with the immediacy of contemporary experience. It also reflects the artist's experience working in all phases of sign construction in his father's company in El Paso, Texas.

The above references and those involving the demolition derby, television, comics, the saga of the West, and commercial sexuality, not only focus on their own reality but express an absurdly riotous humor, which is quintessentially a part of an indigenous tradition—one which has declined under the influence of European fashion and its false ideals of "serious" decoration as high art.

Jimenez' images of women relate to those used in product promotion and also to the symbolic role which emphasizes woman's sexuality as beauty queen or rodeo queen. Significant to this area of his art is the "American Dream," the sexual confrontation between woman and Volkswagen, a new rendition of the theme "Mechanical Bride." Jimenez makes such obvious imagery in his subject-matter but, unlike popular pornographic literature, he states it as a dramatic

JOHNS, Jasper.
American. Born in Augusta, Georgia, 15 May 1930. Educated at University of South Carolina, Columbia; attended art school in New York, 1949. Served in the United States Army in Japan, 1949. Worked as bookstore salesman, New York, 1952–59; also worked as a window display artist, for various stores, including Tiffany's, New York. Director, Foundation for Contemporary Performance Arts Inc., New York, since 1963; Set and Costume Designer and Artistic Adviser, Merce Cunningham Dance Company, New York, since 1970; collaborated on *Un Jour ou Deux* ballet, with Merce Cunningham and John Cage, 1973. Recipient: First Prize, *Print Biennale*, Ljubljana, Yugoslavia, 1967; Prize, *Sao Paulo Bienal*, 1967; Skowhegan Award for Painting, 1972; Skowhegan Award for Graphics, 1977; Mayor's Award of Honor For Art and Culture, New York, 1978. Agent: Leo Castelli Gallery, New York. Resides in New York and St. Martin, French West Indies. Address: c/o Leo Castelli Gallery, 420 West Broadway, New York, New York 10012, U.S.A.

Individual Exhibitions

1958 Leo Castelli Gallery, New York
1959 Galerie Rive Droite, Paris
Galleria d'Arte del Naviglio, Milan
1960 Tweed Gallery, Minneapolis
Columbia Museum of Art, South Carolina (retrospective)
Leo Castelli Gallery, New York
1961 Leo Castelli Gallery, New York
Galerie Rive Droite, Paris
1962 Everett Ellin Gallery, Los Angeles (retrospective)
Galerie Ileana Sonnabend, Paris
1963 Leo Castelli Gallery, New York
1964 Jewish Museum, New York (retrospective)
Whitechapel Art Gallery, London (retrospective)
1965 Pasadena Museum of Art, California (retrospective)
Minami Gallery, Tokyo
American Embassy, London
Ashmolean Museum, Oxford
1966 Leo Castelli Gallery, New York
The Drawings of Jasper Johns, Smithsonian Institution, Washington, D.C.
1968 Galerie Ricke, Cologne
Galerie Buren, Stockholm
Museum of Modern Art, New York (circulating exhibit)
1969 Castelli Graphics, New York
Kunstmuseum, Basel
University of New Mexico, Albuquerque
Los Angeles County Museum of Art
Castelli-Whitney Gallery, New York
David Whitney Gallery, New York
1970 Leo Castelli Gallery, New York
New Gallery, Cleveland
Philadelphia Museum of Art
University of Iowa, Iowa City
Museum of Modern Art, New York
1971 Museum of Modern Art, New York
Castelli Graphics, New York

Kunsthalle, Bern
Minneapolis Institute of Arts
Dayton's Gallery 12, Minneapolis
Museum of the Sea, Hilton Head, South Carolina
Museum of Contemporary Art, Chicago
Marion Koogler McNay Art Institute, San Antonio, Texas
1972 Museum of Fine Arts, Houston
Museum of Modern Art, New York (circulating exhibition)
Galerie Buren, Stockholm
Heath Gallery, Atlanta
Johns / Stella / Warhol: Works in Series, South Texas Art Museum, Corpus Christi
Fendrick Gallery, Washington, D.C.
Jasper John's Decoy: The Print and the Painting, Emily Lowe Gallery, Hofstra University, Hempstead, New York
1973 Gertrude Kasle Gallery, Detroit
1974 Galerie de Gestlo, Hamburg
Knoedler Contemporary Prints, New York
Lo Spazil-Galleria d'Art, Rome
Lucio Amelio Modern Art Agency, Naples
Galerie Folker Skulima, Berlin
Museum of Modern Art, Oxford
Mappin Art Gallery, Sheffield
Herbert Art Gallery, Coventry
1975 Walker Art Gallery, Liverpool
City Art Gallery, Leeds
Serpentine Gallery, London
1976 Leo Castelli Gallery, New York
Janie C. Lee Gallery, Houston
Castelli Graphics, New York
1977 Castelli Graphics, New York (twice)
Brooke Alexander Inc., New York
Whitney Museum of American Art, Downtown Annex, New York
Whitney Museum of American Art, New York (retrospective)
1978 Museum Ludwig, Cologne (retrospective)

Georges Pompidou Center, Paris (retrospective)
Hayward Gallery, London (retrospective)
Seibu Museum of Art, Tokyo (retrospective)
San Francisco Museum of Modern Art (retrospective)
Margo Leavin Gallery, Los Angeles
Galerie Nancy Gillespie, Paris
Galerie Valeur, Nagoya
Prints 1970-77, Center for the Arts, Wesleyan University, Middletown, Connecticut (toured the United States)
John Berggruen Gallery, San Francisco
1979 Janie C. Lee Gallery, Houston
Galerie Valeur, Nagoya
Kunstmuseum, Basel
Staatliche Graphische, Munich
Stadtische Galerie, Stadelschen Kunstinstitut, Frankfurt
Kunstmuseum, Hannover
Tucson Museum of Art, Arizona
1980 Statens Museum for Kunst, Copenhagen
Moderna Museet, Stockholm
Castelli Graphics, New York
Tyler Museum of Art, Texas
1981 Tate Gallery, London
1982 Castelli Graphics, New York
L. A. Louver Gallery, Venice, California
1983 Akira Ikeda Gallery, Tokyo
Delahunty Gallery, Dallas
1984 Leo Castelli Gallery, New York
1985 Brooke Alexander Inc., New York
1986 Fondation Maeght, St. Paul de Vence, France
St. Louis Art Museum, Missouri
1987 Centro Reina Sofia, Madrid
1988 United States pavilion, *43rd Biennale*, Venice

Selected Group Exhibitions:

1958 *39th Biennale*, Venice

Jasper Johns: *Racing Thoughts*, **1983** Courtesy Whitney Museum, New York

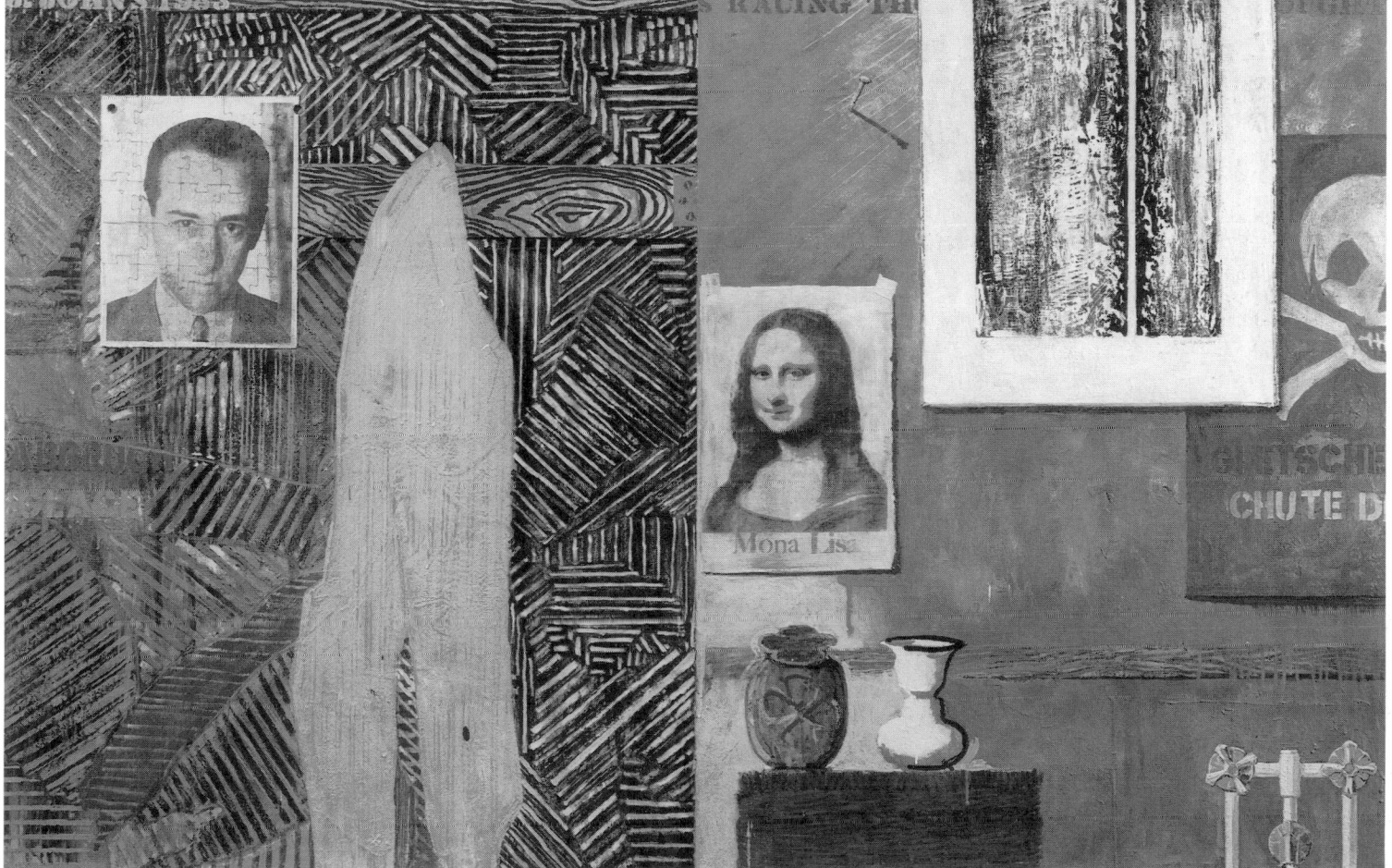

1964 *Painting and Sculpture of a Decade*, Tate Gallery, London
1969 *New York Painting and Sculpture 1940-1970*, Metropolitan Museum of Art, New York
1974 *American Pop Art*, Whitney Museum, New York
1975 *Sculpture: American Directions 1945-1975*, National Collection of Fine Arts, Smithsonian Institution, Washington, D.C.
1978 *Retrospective of the Biennales of Paris 1959-1975*, Seibu Museum of Art, Tokyo
1980 *Printed Art: A View of 2 Decades*, Museum of Modern Art, New York
1985 *Transformations in Sculpture*, Guggenheim Museum, New York
1987 *American Painting: Abstract Expressionism and After*, San Francisco Museum of Modern Art

Collections:

Museum of Modern Art, New York; Whitney Museum, New York; Guggenheim Museum, New York; Albright-Knox Art Gallery, Buffalo, New York; San Francisco Museum of Modern Art; Tate Gallery, London; Stedelijk Museum, Amsterdam; Kunstmuseum, Basel; Moderna Museet, Stockholm; Seibu Museum, Tokyo.

Publications:

By JOHNS: articles—statement in *16 Americans*, exhibition catalogue, New York 1959; "What Is Pop Art? Part II," interview with G. R. Swenson, in *Art News* (New York), February 1964; "Sketchbook Notes" in *Art and Literature* (Lausanne), Spring 1965; statement in *Art and Literature* (Lausanne, Autumn 1965; "Interview with Walter Hopps" in *Artforum* (New York), March 1965; "Marcel Duchamp (1887-1968): An Appreciation" in *Artforum* (New York), November 1968; "Sketchbook Notes" in *Juilliard* (New York), Winter 1968 / 69; "Sketchbook Notes" in *Art Now: New York* (New York), April 1969; "Thoughts on Duchamp" in *Art in America* (New York), July / August 1969; "Notes de Carnet" in *VH 101* (Paris), Autumn 1970; "Fragments According to Johns," interview with John Coplans, in *Print Collector's Newsletter* (New York), May / June 1972; "Interview," with David Sylvester, in *Jasper Johns' Drawings*, exhibition catalogue, London 1974.

On JOHNS: books—*4 Amerikaner*, exhibition catalogue, Berne 1962; *Jasper Johns*, exhibition catalogue, by Everett Ellin, Los Angeles 1962; *Amerikaner: Jasper Johns, Alfred Leslie, Robert Rauschenberg, Richard Stankiewicz*, exhibition catalogue, Stockholm 1962; *Jasper Johns* by Leo Steinberg, New York 1963: *6 Painters and Their Object*, exhibition catalogue, by Lawrence Alloway, New York 1963; *Jasper Johns*, exhibition catalogue, with essays by Alan Solomon and John Cage, New York 1964; *Jasper Johns*, exhibition catalogue, Japanese text by Yoshiaki Tono, Tokyo 1965; *The Drawings of Jasper Johns*, exhibition catalogue, with text by Stefan Munsing, Washington, D.C. 1966: *Jasper Johns* by Max Kozloff, New York 1967, rev. ed. 1969, 1972, 1974: *Die Graphik, Jasper Johns* by Carlo Huber, Berne 1970; *Jasper Johns* exhibition catalogue, San Francisco 1970; *Jasper Johns: Lithographs*, exhibition catalogue, with an essay by Riva Castleman, New York 1970; *Jasper Johns: Prints 1960-1970* by Richard S. Field, New York 1970; *Johns / Stella / Warhol: Works in the Series*, exhibition catalogue, Corpus Christi, Texas 1972; *Jasper Johns' Decoy: The Print and the Painting*, exhibition catalogue, text by Roberta Bernstein and Robert Lottman, Hempstead, New York 1972; *Jasper Johns' Drawings* exhibition catalogue, London 1974; *Foirades / Fizzles*, exhibition catalogue, text by Samuel Beckett introduction by Judith Goldman, New York 1977; *Jasper Johns* by Michael Crichton, New York 1977; *Jasper Johns: Prints 1970-77*, exhibition catalogue, by Richard S. Field, Middletown, Connecticut 1978; *Jasper Johns: Drawings and Prints 1975-1979*, Houston 1979; *Jasper Johns*, exhibition catalogue with essay by Judith Goldman, St. Paul de Vence 1986; *Jasper Johns: Obra Grafica 1960-1985*, exhibition catalogue with text by Riva Castleman, Madrid 1987.

Jasper Johns is with Rauschenberg the most influential of the American artists who followed Abstract Expressionism and reacted against it, raising some fundamental questions about art in the process. But in contrast to Rauschenberg's great variety, Johns has confined himself to much simpler means and a very small range of subjects. And unlike Rauschenberg he does not "act in the gap between art and life" or

relate to life in any way, but instead his formal enigmas constantly question the nature of art. His images are not merely simple and banal, but very, very cool, and often ironic as well, so they weren't so easily dismissed as mere neo-Dada, as Rauschenberg's could be.

The era of Pop art is usually dated from Johns' first one-man show early in 1958, which included paintings of flags, of targets, of numerals and letters of the alphabet, all chosen as familiar images from everyday life, which are not only simple but also essentially two-dimensional. Numbers and letters by their very nature have no depth, and the flags are painted flatly on the surface, covering the whole canvas, or set off against a simple border. But the encaustic (wax-based) paint is richly and vibrantly handled, focusing attention on the act of painting and bringing out the profound ambiguity between image and object, and the constant interplay between painted illusion and real object. These ordinary, banal images thus become thought-provoking, and since such formal problems of pictorial reality as flatness and the two-dimensional nature of paintings were the sort of intellectual problem American critics of the 50's and 60's loved to discuss, "Johns provided everything the New York critical intelligence requires to requite its own narcissism," as Brian O'Doherty aptly observed. These were in fact seminal influences, though ambiguous ones which could lead to such different lines of development as Pop and Minimalism, and which prompted one of the great critical axioms of the period, Leo Steinberg's dictum that "Whatever else it may be, all great art is about art."

Johns focuses attention on the painting as an object, a thing in its own right, rather than as representation. And this is made even clearer in those paintings which incorporate such things as rulers, brooms and spoons. Thus his target with four boxes over it, each containing a plaster model of a face cut off below the eyes, creates a powerful interplay of thwarted alternatives, making the human association and the formal geometry equally impersonal, and contradicting the flatness of the target with the spatial levels of the boxes. He breaks down and isolates the elements of painting itself and the ideas of illusion and literal fact in such paintings as "False Start" (1959), a series of visual puns in which patches of bright red, blue, orange or yellow are falsely identified by stencilling the names of other colours over them. Later paintings in which the public motifs such as flags and maps are replaced by more homely and domestic images such as coathangers and coffee cups are similarly relentless explorations of different ways of seeing.

The theme of illusion versus reality and the constant questioning of reality and identity is also basic to his sculptures. His bronze reproductions of beer cans, flashlights or cans with paint brushes in them are so carefully sculptured and painted that it is sometimes difficult to tell them from the originals, though they provide a highly ambiguous substitute. His irony directed towards art is seen in "The Critic Smiles," a toothbrush cast in sculptmetal, and "The Critic Sees," a pair of spectacles in the same material, with glass lenses reflecting opaquely back at the viewer.

Johns has regularly been compared with Duchamp, and certainly has the same sort of cool intelligence which has led him to challenge some cherished preconceptions about aesthetics and perception. But the limitations of an art so severely about art are seen all too clearly when carried to absurdity in the extreme reductivism of some of Johns' followers such as Frank Stella. Sir Karl Popper has mocked the reductive aridity of modern linguistic philosophy by comparing it to constantly polishing a pair of spectacles instead of ever looking through them at the world. Something similar might be said about the reductive path of much contemporary American art, and there may be greater irony in "The Critics Sees" than Johns himself ever intended.

—Konstantin Bazarov

JOHNSON, Lester.

American. Born in Minneapolis, Minnesota, 17 January 1919. Studied at the Minneapolis Institute School of Art, St. Paul Art School, Minnesota, and the School of the Art Institute of Chicago, 1942-47. Painter: moved to New York 1947; taught at St. Bernard School, New York, 1955-61, and at Ohio State University, Columbus, 1963; Summer Artist-in-Residence, University of Wisconsin, Milwaukee, 1964; with Yale University, New Haven, Connecticut: Adjunct Professor of Painting since 1964, Director of Studies, Graduate Painting, School of Art and Architecture, 1969-74, and Fellow of Trumbull College; fire destroyed home in Milford, Connecticut, and many of his works, 1967. Recipient: First Prize, Midwestern Artists Competition, 1942; Guggenheim Foundation Fellowship, 1973; Citation in Painting, Brandeis University Creative Arts Award, 1978. Agent: Gallery Moos Ltd., 133 Greene Street, New York, New York 10012. Addresses: 191 Milbank Avenue, Greenwich, Connecticut 06830, U.S.A.; School of Art, Yale University, New Haven, Connecticut 06520, U.S.A.

Exhibitions:

1951 Artists Gallery, New York
1953 Earl Pilgrim Gallery, Provincetown, Massachusetts
1954 Korman Gallery, New York
1955 Hansa Gallery, New York
     Zabriskie Gallery, New York
1956 Sun Gallery, Provincetown, Massachusetts
1957 Sun Gallery, Provincetown, Massachusetts
     Zabriskie Gallery, New York
1959 Sun Gallery, Provincetown, Massachusetts
     Zabriskie Gallery, New York
1960 H. C. E. Gallery, Provincetown, Massachusetts
     Sun Gallery, Provincetown, Massachusetts
1961 H. C. E. Gallery, Provincetown, Massachusetts
     Minneapolis Institute of Arts
     Zabriskie Gallery, New York
1962 B. C. Holland Gallery, Chicago
     Orton Museum, Ohio State University, Columbus
     Dayton Art Institute, Ohio
     Fort Worth Art Center, Texas
     Martha Jackson Gallery, New York
1963 Martha Jackson Gallery, New York
1964 Martha Jackson Gallery, New York
1965 Donald Morris Gallery, Detroit
     Yale University Art Gallery, New Haven, Connecticut
     Anderson-Mayer Gallery, Paris
1966 Martha Jackson Gallery, New York
1967 Martha Jackson Gallery, New York
     University of Wisconsin-Milwaukee
     Donald Morris Gallery, Detroit
1968 California College of Arts and Crafts, Oakland
1969 Martha Jackson Gallery, New York
     B. C. Holland Gallery, Chicago
1971 Martha Jackson Gallery, New York
1972 Alpha Gallery, Boston
1973 Richard Gray Gallery, Chicago
     Martha Jackson Gallery, New York
     Ruth S. Schaffner Gallery, Los Angeles
     Smith-Andersen Gallery, San Francisco
     Gallery Moos, Toronto
1974 Procter Art Center, Bard College, Annandale-on-Hudson, New York
     Donald Morris Gallery, Detroit
     Tyler School of Art, Philadelphia
     Ruth S. Schaffner Gallery, Los Angeles
1975 Livingstone-Learmouth Gallery, New York
     Martha Jackson Gallery, New York
     Jorgensen Gallery, University of Connecticut, Storrs
1976 Alpha Gallery, Boston
1977 Hurlbutt Gallery, Greenwich Library, Connecticut
     Gimpel and Weitzenhoffer Gallery, New York
     Gallery Moos, Toronto
1978 Ruth S. Schaffner Gallery, San Francisco
     Donald Morris Gallery, Detroit
     Peter M. David Gallery, Minneapolis
1979 Foster Gallery, Louisiana State University, Baton Rouge

	Gimpel Fils, London
1980	Gimpel-Hanover and André Emmerich Galerien, Zurich
	Gimpel and Weitzenhoffer Gallery, New York
1981	University of Virginia Art Museum, Charlottesville
	London Arts, Detroit
	Donald Morris Gallery, Detroit
1982	Alpha Gallery, Boston
	Gimpel and Weitzenhoffer, New York
1983	Paperwork Gallery, Larchmont, New York
	Zabriskie Gallery, New York
1984	Kansas City Art Institute, Missouri
	Munson Gallery, New Haven, Connecticut
1985	Zabriskie Gallery, New York
	Donald Morris Gallery, Detroit
	David Barnett Gallery, Milwaukee, Wisconsin
1986	Walter Moos Gallery, Toronto
	Munson Gallery, New Haven, Connecticut
1987	Westmoreland Museum of Art, Greensburg, Pennsylvania (travelled)
	Walter Moos Gallery, New York

Selected Group Exhibitions:

1957	*American Painting 1945-57*, Minneapolis Institute of Arts
1961	*Recent Painting, U.S.A.: The Figure*, Museum of Modern Art, New York (toured the United States and Canada)
1962	*Recent Trends in Painting, U.S.A.*, Art Institute of Chicago
1964	*Contemporary American Drawings*, Guggenheim Museum, New York
1972	*70th American Exhibition*, Art Institute of Chicago
1976	*Painting & Sculpture Today 1976*, Indianapolis Museum of Art
1979	*100 Years-100 Artists*, Art Institute of Chicago
1983	*American Realism 1930s-80s*, Summit Art Center, New Jersey
1985	*The Artist Celebrates New York*, Metropolitan Museum of Art, New York (travelled)
1987	*State of the Arts*, Aldrich Museum of Contemporary Art, Ridgefield, Connecticut

Collections:

Museum of Modern Art, New York; New School for Social Research, New York; Yale Gallery, New Haven, Connecticut; Albright-Knox Art Gallery, Buffalo, New York; Chrysler Museum, Norfolk, Virginia; Hirshhorn Museum, Washington, D.C.; Dayton Museum, Ohio; University of Ohio, Athens; Phoenix Museum, Arizona; California College of Arts and Crafts, Oakland.

Publications:

By JOHNSON: book—*Lester Johnson: Paintings 1970-74*, with an introduction by Burt Churnow, New York 1975.

On JOHNSON: books—*Mother and Child in Modern Art*, edited by Bruce Hooten and Nina N. Kaiden, New York 1964; *Artwork and Packages* by Harold Rosenberg, New York 1969; *Art on the Edge* by Harold Rosenberg, New York 1975; *The New York School: The Painters and Sculptors of the Fifties* by Irving Sandler, New York 1978; articles—"Lester Johnson Paints a Picture" by Lawrence Campbell in *Arts Magazine* (New York) March 1961; "Remarks of the Figure and Lester Johnson" by Priscilla Colt in *Art International* (Lugano, Switzerland) January 1964; "Lester Johnson, New Master" by James Mellon in the *New York Times*, March 14, 1971; "The Individual as a Crowd: Lester Johnson's Recent Paintings" by Barbara Thompsen in *Art in America*, (New York) November / December 1973; "Lester Johnson" by Burt Chernow in *Arts Magazine* (New York) November 1977; "Lester Johnson at Gimpel and Weitzenhoffer" by Robert Berlind in *Art in America* (New York) January / February 1978; "Lester Johnson" by Carter Ratcliff in *Art International* (Lugano, Switzerland) August / September 1981; "Lester Johnson's Strolling Players" by Dore Ashton in *Arts* (New York), April 1982; "Lester Johnson" by Ruth Bass in *Art News* (New York), December 1983; "Lester Johnson" in *Flash Art* (Milan), January 1984.

Lester Johnson's pictures of the 1970's are composed of crowds of stylized figures enlivened by a broad range of vibrant colors and patternings and further energized by the bulbous limbs which variously motion in twisting diagonals of impossible gesture. Johnson's figuration is based on abstract principles, specifically on the ideas underlying the gestural wing of American Abstract Expressionism as developed and practised during the 1940s and 1950s by painters such as Franz Kline, Jackson Pollock and Willem de Kooning.

Johnson developed his mature paintings of the 1970's through a long and logical process which began with his works of the 1950's, when he was working in a more abstract, "action painting" vein closely akin with the sweeping black and white compositions of Franz Kline. In Johnson's dark, ominous, directly and heavily worked canvases of this period, thick, black brushstrokes often curved to form oval, head-like shapes, signalling his urge toward a figurative element very like that of Pollock in his paintings of the early 1950's. By around 1964, distinct changes were occurring, Johnson's ovals now forming into still life, table top configurations which show a deliberate move away from former flatness into more three-dimensional realms. During the mid to late 60's, in Johnson's "Classical Figures" and "Street Scenes," dark and shadowy figures take over the scene, outlined in heavy black in near monochrome surroundings and frozen in agitated lateral movement. The dark, bowler-hatted men of this period are more fully modelled than ever before, but they remain crowded on frontal planes as they motion across and off the canvas surface. Compositions become more jam-packed, like modern-day, primitivizing friezes of horror-vacuii whose all-over structure is bursting beyond the framing edges. In 1972 women appear, bringing with them a range of colors and flashy patterned dresses which completes Johnson's evolution from the 1950's from somberly toned gestural abstraction to exuberantly energetic schematized figuration.

During the 1970's images of contemporary urban youth recur persistently. They are dressed in look-alike jeans, T-shirts and patterned garb which both set them off from other times and places and blend them into a stereotypical amalgam of interpenetrating anonymity. Hairdos and facial expressions are nearly interchangeable in Johnson's chosen types who stare off into the distances with firmly set mouths. Even while their huge and stiffened arms and legs are thrusting and bending in intertwining motions of mechanized vigour, their deepset eyes never meet nor search in the same direction. The jostling, close-packed activity of the densely overlapping bodies coupled with their seeming indifference to one another creates a powerful sense of the alienation which characterizes present-day urban living. Johnson makes what is usually semi-conscious into a hyper-conscious statement of the human state of crowded aloneness. The fullness of the scene, so heightened by colors, patterns and human bodies in transit, is utilized to convey a psychological reality, the vapid emptiness of all those rapidly-paced gestures which sweep outward into nowhere. Johnson is as much of the inheritor of Ernst Ludwig Kirchner or Fernand Léger as he is of gestural Abstract Expressionism. His pictures incorporate elements from each of these predecessors and turn them into an updated painterly vision of contemporary humanity mechanistically objectified.

—Barbara Cavaliere

JOHNSON, Ray.

American. Born in Detroit, Michigan, 16 October 1927. Studied at the Art Students League, New York, 1944-45, and at Black Mountain College, Beria, North Carolina, under Josef Albers, Robert Motherwell, Mary Callery, and Ossip Zadkine,

---

1945-48. Lives and works in New York. Member, American Abstract Artists, 1949-52; Founder Member, New York Correspondence School of Art, 1968-73. Recipient: National Institute of Arts and Letters Award, 1966; National Endowment for the Arts Award, 1976. Agent: Brooks Jackson Iolas Gallery, 52 East 57th Street, New York, New York 10022. Address: 44 West 7th Street, Locust Valley, New York 11560, U.S.A.

Individual Exhibitions:

1965	Willard Gallery, New York
1966	Willard Gallery, New York
	Richard Feigen Gallery, Chicago
1967	Willard Gallery, New York
	Richard Feigen Gallery, Chicago
1968	Richard Feigen Gallery, New York (toured Germany)
	Wooster Community Art Center, Danbury, Connecticut
	University of Virginia, Charlottesville
1969	Boylston Print Center, Cambridge, Massachusetts
1971	Angela Flowers Gallery, London
1972	Galleria Schwarz, Milan
1974	Rene Block Gallery, New York
1975	Galleria Massimo Valsecchi, Milan
	Gertrude Kasle Gallery, Detroit
1976	North Carolina Museum of Art, Raleigh (retrospective)
	Sid Deutsch Gallery, New York
1977	Sid Deutsch Gallery, New York
1978	Brooks Jackson Iolas Gallery, New York
1984	Nassau County Museum of Fine Art, Roslyn Harbor, New York

Selected Group Exhibitions

1949	*Annual Exhibition*, American Abstract Artists, New York (and 1950, 1951, 1952)
1962	*Gang Bang*, Batman Gallery, San Francisco
1967	*Pictures to Be Read / Poetry to Be Seen*, Museum of Contemporary Art, Chicago
1969	*Pop Art Redefined*, Hayward Gallery, London
1970	*New York Correspondence School*, Whitney Museum, New York
1972	*Document Show*, David Gallery, Houston
1974	*Invitation Correspondence*, Western Illinois University, Macomb
1977	*Words at Liberty*, Museum of Contemporary Art, Chicago
1981	*New Wave*, Project Studio One, Long Island City, New York
1983	*Ma Como Fanno i Mamai*, Galleria Borgobello, Parma, Italy

Collections:

Museum of Modern Art, New York; De Cordova Museum, Lincoln, Massachusetts; Art Institute of Chicago; Museum of Fine Arts, Houston.

Publications:

By JOHNSON: book—*The Paper Snake*, anthology, New York 1965; articles—"Follow Instructions" in *Arts Magazine* (New York), November 1971; "I Work Very Slowly" in *Arte Milano* (Milan), May 1972; "Abandoned Chickens" in *Art in America* (New York), November / December 1974.

On JOHNSON: books—*A Primer of Happenings and Time / Space Art* by Al Hansen, New York 1965; *Happenings, Fluxus, Pop, Nouveau Realisme* by Wolfgang Becker, Hamburg 1965; *Pop Art Redefined* by John Russell and Suzi Gablik, London 1969; *Mail Art* by Jean-Marc Poinsot, Paris 1972; *Ray Johnson*, exhibition catalogue with essay by David Bourdon, New York 1984.

Ray Johnson, the most celebrated figure in the Post-World War II international mailart movement, is also

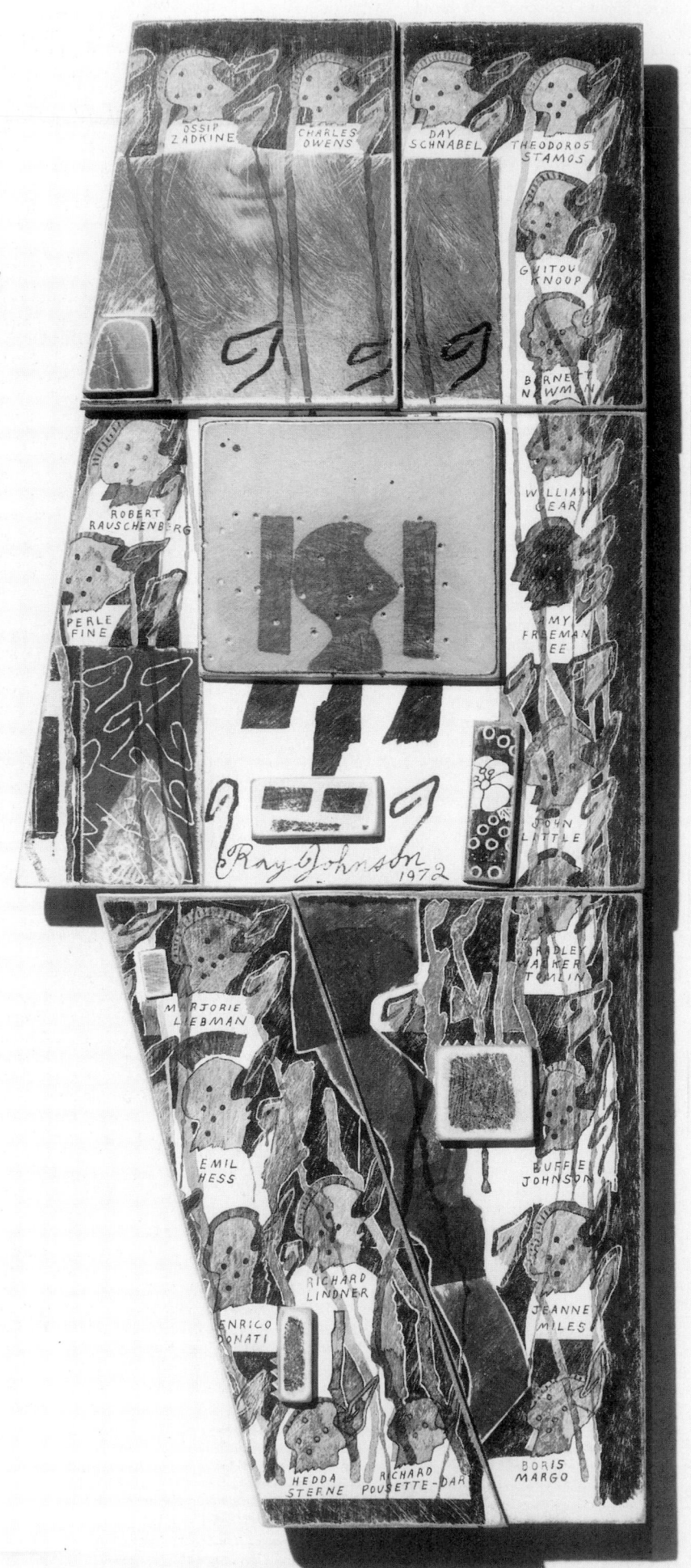

Ray Johnson: *Four Part Ad Reinhardt,* **1972** Courtesy Whitney Museum, New York

a talented collagist-painter who has interfaced life and art with provocative results in his lively and wondrously varied visual-verbal expression. He first developed a following for the letters, postcards, collages and small objects that he sent to friends and acquaintances in the New York art world soon after his arrival in the city in the early 1950's. By the late 1950's he was also making small collage paintings that ranged from abstract compositions with richly textured surfaces to pictures that featured rows of cut-up and painted letters, and portraits of famous popular culture figures. "Pink Circle" (1959), "Collage" (1959) and "Elvis Presley Collage" (1957) are examples. At the same time, he continued the mailings, and, filled with witty puns and drawings, his correspondence provided him with ample opportunity to display his hand as an orchestrator of art events. The receipt of a piece of mail from Ray Johnson was a special experience designed by him to turn the recipient into an active participant in a mailart piece. Instructions asked the recipient to do something further, whether it was to alter the original piece of mail and send it back to Johnson or to take part of the original piece of mail and send it on to a third party, often unknown to the original recipient. With his mail maneuvers, Johnson made the recipients and later the audiences who were able to read the mail in exhibitions conscious of the function and the rituals of the postal institution, a major aspect of contemporary industrial life, while he tested the definition of art, taking the art-is-idea-whatever-is-designated approach of Marcel Duchamp to the fullest extension.

From about 1968 to the spring of 1973, when he announced its death with a letter to the obituary column of the *New York Times*, the New York Correspondence School under Johnson's leadership held a series of meetings in New York. It was succeeded by two other organizations, Buddha University and the Asparagus Club. What made other artists as well as the leading critics and curators of the day respond enthusiastically to Johnson's correspondence and to participate in his planned activities were the twin elements of surprise and entertainment. At issue, also, in Johnson's work, both the correspondence and the collages, is an inquiring Pop attitude applied indiscriminately to life and art alike. This attitude animates the drawings and collage paintings of the late 1960's and early 1970's. Focusing on the "idols" of both the serious and popular culture, a group that included among others Virginia Woolf, Mondrian, Shirley Temple and actor Steve McQueen, Johnson made irreverent portraits of them, using photographs, intercut with drawn and painted motifs. He has also taken contemporary art events as subject: "The Ray Johnson History of the Betty Parsons Gallery" (1973).

In addition to continuing to send out mailart, Johnson since 1976 has been involved with a still on-going series of collages, based on silhouettes. And, in his recent work, the playful vitality of his unique vision is strongly evident.

—Ronny Cohen

JONAS, Joan.
American. Born in New York, 13 July 1936. Educated at Mount Holyoke College, Massachusetts; Boston Museum School; Columbia University, New York, M. F. A. Visiting Artist, Video School of Visual Arts, New York, 1972. Guest Lecturer, Princeton University, New Jersey, 1974; Yale University, New Haven, Connecticut, 1974; and Minneapolis College of Art, 1974; Visiting Artist, San Diego State University, California, 1975; Otis Art Institute, Los Angeles, 1975; and Kent State University, Ohio, 1977. Recipient: CAPS (Creative Artists Public Service Program), 1972, 1973 and 1975; National Endowment for the Arts Grant, 1973 and 1975; DAAD Artist's Fellowship, West Berlin, 1982. Agent:

Castelli-Sonnabend Videotapes and Films Inc., 142 Greene Street, New York, New York 10011. Address: 112 Mercer Street, New York, New York 10012, U.S.A.

Individual Exhibitions:

1968	St. Peter's Church, New York
1970	Alan Saret's Loft, New York
	University of California at San Diego
	Jones Beach, Long Island, New York
	14th Street YMCA, New York
1971	Loeb Student Center, New York
	University of California at Irvine
	Cape Breton Island, Nova Scotia
1972	LoGuidice Gallery, New York
	Documenta, Kassel, West Germany
	San Francisco Art Institute
	empty lots, New York
	The Tibur, Rome
	L'Attico, Rome
	Ace Gallery, Los Angeles
1973	Leo Castelli Gallery, New York
	Toselli Gallery, Milan
	Hofstra University, Hempstead, New York
	Galerie Musée, Paris
1974	The Kitchen, New York
	Contemporanea, Rome
	Galleria Schema, Florence
	Museum of Fine Arts, Boston
	Texas Gallery, Houston
	Walker Art Center, Minneapolis
	Kunsthalle, Cologne
	University of Massachusetts, Amherst
1975	Anthology Film Archives, New York
	Leo Castelli Gallery, New York
	San Diego State University, California
	Institute of Contemporary Arts, Los Angeles
	Womanspace, Los Angeles
	And/Or Gallery, Seattle
1976	San Francisco Museum of Modern Art
	Anthology Film Archives, New York
	Institute of Contemporary Art, Philadelphia (twice)
1977	Institute of Contemporary Art, Philadelphia
	Vanguard Theatre, Los Angeles
	Documenta, Kassel, West Germany
	The Kitchen, New York
	St. Mark's Church, New York
	Salle Patino, Geneva
	Kunsthalle, Basel
	Van Abbemuseum, Eindhoven, Netherlands
	School of Visual Arts, New York
1978	Van Abbemuseum, Eindhoven, Netherlands
	Vienna Performance Festival
1979	112 Mercer Street, New York
1980	Guggenheim Museum, New York
	University of California Art Museum, Berkeley
	University of California at Irvine
	Los Angeles Institute of Contemporary Art
1982	Kino Arsenal, West Berlin
1983	Whitney Museum, New York
	La Zattera de Babele, Genazzano, Italy
1984	DAAD-Galerie, West Berlin

Selected Group Exhibitions:

1973	*Festival d'Automne*, Paris
	Some Recent American Art, Australia (toured)
1974	*Xerox Corporation Show*, Rochester, New York
	Bienal, Sao Paulo
	Art Now '74, Washington
	Project '74, Cologne
1975	*The Video Show*, Serpentine Gallery, London
	Associated Students, University of California at Los Angeles
1982	*Documenta 7*, Museum Fridericianum, Kassel, West Germany

Collections:

Museum of Modern Art, New York.

Publications:

By JONAS: articles—"Paul Revere," with Richard Serra, in *Artforum* (New York), September 1971; "Organic Honey's Visual Telepathy" in *The Drama Review* (New York), vol. 16, no. 2, 1972; "Show Me Your Dances. . . ," with Simone Forti, interview with Carla Liss, in *Art and Artists* (London), October 1973: statement in *Dancescape*, New York 1973; documentation in *Castelli-Sonnabend Video Tape and Film Catalogue*, New York 1974; statement in "7 Years" in the *Drama Review* (New York), March 1975: statement in *Joan Jonas*, exhibition catalogue, West Berlin 1984; films—*Wind*, 1968; *Paul Revere*, with Richard Serra, 1971; *Veil*, 1971; *Songdelay*, 1973; video tapes—*Left Side, Right Side*, 1972; *Vertical Roll*, 1972; *Organic Honey's Visual Telepathy*, 1972; *2 Women*, 1973; *Barking*, 1973; *3 Returns*, 1973; *Glass Puzzle*, 1974; *Merlo*, 1974; *Disturbances*, 1974; *May Windows*, 1976; *Good Night, Good Morning*, 1976; *I Want to Live in the Country and Other Romances*, 1976.

On JONAS: articles—"Joan Jonas" by Laurie Anderson in *Art Press* (Paris), November/December 1973; "Joan Jonas: Making the Image Visable" by N. Carroll in *Artforum* (New York), April 1974; "Notes on Performance and the Arts" by A. Hayum in *Art Journal* New York), Summer 1975; "Joan Jonas's Performance Works" by D. Crimp in *Studio International* (London), July 1976; "Suspended in Shadow" in *Art News* (New York), April 1977; "View of Kassel" by D. Shapiro in *Artforum* (New York), September 1977; "Personal and Cultural Narratives" by Mary Stofflet in *Artweek* (Oakland, California), 26 January 1980; "Image of Silence" by A. Rosenthal in *Artweek* (Oakland, California), 17 May 1980; "Jonas's Futurism" by Mary Stofflet in *Artweek* (Oakland, California), 5 July 1980; "Wolf Calls and Frog Songs—Upside Down and Backwards" in *Artnews* (New York), September 1980.

*

My thinking about the medium of performance began in the late 60's. In saying that, I am pointing to a particular conceptual context that was fully developed when I began to work—one that concerned itself with discovering new forms of movement and totally new ways of structuring the temporal shape of an event. Yet, when I survey my work against that background of performances in the 60's, I realize that those specific concerns with movement and temporality are not my concerns. My own thinking and production has focused on issues of space—ways of dislocating it, attenuating it, turning it inside out, always attempting to explore it without ever giving to myself or to others the permission to penetrate it. I have returned again and again to specific set of formal/material metaphors with which to shape this space. The two most important of these are the mirror—with its capacity to interrupt and therefore to fragment deep space and its property of disorientation through left-right reversal—and the transmission of signals through a dislocating medium, such as very deep landscape that creates delays and relays of the signal, or the video feedback, which both dislocates and fragments the signal.

—Joan Jonas

*

Joan Jonas is one of the pioneering performance artists in America; her work inaugurated the synchronization of disciplines which previously had been developing along separate lines. Although educated as a sculptor, she was strongly influenced by new forms of dance and subsequently environments. All orchestrated to evoke archetypal images as in fairy tales and legends, her work is nevertheless completely contemporary and reflects the spirit and ambivalence of our time.

Born in 1936 in New York, Joan Jonas studied art in Massachusetts and in New York, thereafter dance with Trisha Brown, and in 1968, in collaboration with Peter Campus, she made her first film "Wind". In 1970, after a trip to Japan with Richard Serra and under the impact of the traditional Japanese theatre, she performed her "Mirror Piece", first in New York and later in California. In this work the artist examines details of her own naked body using mirrors. For Joan Jonas this piece was the breakthrough into a new phase of her own development. In "Organic Honey" of 1972 she incorporated video, and the number of performers widened; her goal was again female identity, but the mirror here was destroyed, burning the bridges to her past. In the same year two other performances, "Left Side-Right Side", concentrate on the face of the artist and on her bodily movements and their meaningful contorsions respectively. "Funnel" of 1974 extends the performance vocabulary, and video and participation of the audience are introduced. In "Twilight" of 1975, a haunting vision of woman, enclosed in a circular ring and confronted with a TV camera, is of archetypal significance.

After a tour to India she began performing with energies of previously unknown intensity, which can be seen in "Mirage" of 1975/1976. Her performances since 1976 have expanded into the area of fairy tales ("The Juniper Tree" of 1976 and "Upside Down and Backwards" of 1979) and science fiction ("Double Lunar Dogs" of 1978) and incorporate elements of music and dance as well as mirrors and light in order to create a new comprehensive universe of action. A culmination is reached in "He Saw Her Burning" of 1982/1983 in which Joan Jonas performs in combination with video, film and environmental ensembles. Based on a story about an American soldier in Germany and a woman in Chicago, two lines of narration are synchronized into a performance in which symptoms of our contemporary society are made transparent. In her 1987 performance "Volcano Saga", based on her trip to Iceland, she includes multimedia, simultaneous integration of film, music, dance, props and spoken narrative in a brilliant performance.

Reality is mysterious in the work of Joan Jonas, and a new and complex language has been inaugurated by the artist in which she has found appropriate means of communication for a contemporary theme. The artist in this sense is conceived as a shaman who opens a world which otherwise would remain closed for most people: "All the things I do seem to be signs or emblems against outside forces, like I was thinking of warding off the evil eye. They are ways of surviving, maintaining one's personality . . . not one's personality, one's existence." (Joan Jonas)

—Udo Kultermann

JONES, Allen.

British. Born in Southampton, Hampshire, 1 September 1937. Studied at Hornsey School of Art, London, 1955–59: N. D. D. 1959, A. T. D. 1961; and Royal College of Art, London, 1959–60. Married Janet Bowen in 1964 (divorced, 1978); daughters: Thea and Sarah. Painter, sculptor and graphic artist, London, since 1961. Instructor in Lithography, Croydon School of Art, 1961; Part-time Teacher, Chelsea School of Art, London, 1965; Visiting Instructor, Hochschule für Bildenden Künste, Hamburg, 1968–70; Guest Instructor in Painting, University of South Florida, Tampa, 1969, University of California at Irvine, 1973, and University of California at Los Angeles, 1977; Visiting Tutor in Painting and Drawing, Banff Centre School of Fine Arts, Albert, 1977; Guest Professor, Hochschule der Kunste, West Berlin, 1982–83. Recipient: Prix des Jeunes, *Biennale de Paris*, 1963; Tamarind Lithography Fellowship, Los Angeles, 1966. Associate, Royal Academy, London, 1981. Agent: Waddington Galleries, 2 Cork Street, London W1. Address: 41 Charterhouse Square, London EC1, England.

Individual Exhibitions

1963	Arthur Tooth and Sons, London
1964	Richard Feigen Gallery, New York
	Arthur Tooth and Sons, London
1965	Richard Feigen Gallery, Chicago
	Feigen-Palmer Gallery, Los Angeles
	Richard Feigen Gallery, New York

1966	Galerie Bischofberger, Zurich
	Museum of Modern Art, New York
1967	Galerie der Spiegel, Cologne
	Galerie Neuendorf, Hamburg
	Arthur Tooth and Sons, London
1968	Alecto Gallery, London
1969	Galleria Milano, Milan
	Museum Boymans-van Beuningen, Rotterdam (graphics retrospective; toured the Netherlands)
	Galerie Werigstatt, Bremen, West Germany
1970	Arthur Tooth and Sons, London
	Richard Feigen Gallery, New York
	Galerie Rudolf Zwirner, Cologne
	Studio Condotti 85, Rome
	Galerie Springer, West Berlin
	Galleria Milano, Milan
1971	Galerie de Spiegel, Cologne
	Galleria Il Fauno, Turin
	Galerie Richard Foncke, Ghent
	Galerie Delta, Rotterdam
	Galerie Bischofberger, Zurich
	Marlborough Graphics, London
1972	Studio Condotti 85, Rome
	Galerie Multi-Art, Antwerp
	Galleria Milano, Milan
	New Paintings and Sculpture, Marlborough Fine Art, London
1973	Tolarno Galleries, Melbourne
	Hogarth Galleries, Sydney
	Galerie Von Loeper, Hamburg
1974	Seibu Gallery, Tokyo
	Meitetsu Gallery, Nagoya, Japan
1975	Oriel Gallery, Cardiff (travelled to Glynn Vivian Gallery, Swansea; Arnolfini Gallery, Bristol; and Fruit Market Gallery, Edinburgh)
	Neue Galerie der Stadt, Linz, Austria
1976	Waddington Galleries II, London
	Waddington and Tooth Graphics, London
	Pander Kunstcentrum, The Hague
	Galerie Wentzel, Hamburg
1977	James Corcoran Gallery, Los Angeles
	Nova Gallery, Vancouver
	University of California at Los Angeles
1978	Institute of Contemporary Arts, London
	Kettles Yard, Cambridge
	Waddington Galleries, Montreal (travelled to the Waddington Galleries, Toronto)
1979	Walker Art Gallery, Liverpool (toured Britain and West Germany)
	Galerie Wentzel, Hamburg
1980	Waddington Galleries, London
1981	Galerie Engstrom, Stockholm
1982	Waddington Graphics, London
1983	Galerie Kammer, Hamburg
	Waddington Galleries, London
	Galeria Yerba, Murcia, Spain
1984	Galerie Wentzel, Cologne
	Galerie Kammer, Hamburg
1985	Waddington Galleries, London

Selected Group Exhibitions:

1960	Young Contemporaries, RIBA Galleries, London
1962	British Art Today, San Francisco Museum of Art
1963	Biennale de Paris, Musée d'Art Moderne, Paris (and 1965, 1971)
1965	The New Generation, Whitechapel Art Gallery, London
1969	Pop Art Redefined, Hayward Gallery, London
1974	Hyperréalistes Américains / Réalistes Européens. Centre National d'Art Contemporain, Paris
1977	British Painting 1952-1977, Royal Academy of Art, London
1980	Peinture Anglais 1960-80, Galerie de France, Paris
1983	The Folding Image, National Gallery of Art, Washington, D.C.
1985	Pop Art 1955-70, Museum of Modern Art, New York (and world tour)

Collections:

Arts Council of Great Britain, London; Tate Gallery, London; Wallraf-Richartz Museum, Cologne; Stedelijk Museum, Amsterdam; Musée Royal des Beaux-Arts, Ghent; Moderna Museet, Stockholm; Museum of Modern Art, New York; Norton Simon Museum of Art, Pasadena, California; Vancouver Art Gallery; Power Art Gallery, Sydney.

Publications:

By JONES: books—Allen Jones: das graphische Werk, with text by Hein Stunke, Cologne 1969; Allen Jones: Figures, edited by Galerie Mikro, West Berlin and Milan 1969; Allen Jones: Projects, with interview and texts by Ruth Messin and Bonnie Boston, London 1971; Waitress, with Tim Street-Porter, London 1971; Sheer Magic, New York 1979, London 1980; film—Manner wir Kommen, WDR television film, Cologne, 1970.

On JONES: books—Pop as Art: A Survey of the New Super-Realism by Mario Amaya, London 1965, 1972; Pop Art, edited by Lucy R. Lippard, New York and London 1966; Information: Tilson, Phillips, Jones, Paolozzi, Kitaj, Hamilton, exhibition catalogue, Basle 1969; Image as Language: Aspects of British Art by Christopher Finch, London 1969; Allen Jones, exhibition catalogue, with text by Enrico Crispolti, Milan 1970; British Painting and Sculpture 1960–1970, exhibition catalogue, with text by Edward Lucie Smith, London 1970; Erotic Art 2, compiled by Phyllis and Eberhard Kronhausen, New York 1970; Allen Jones: New Paintings and Sculpture, exhibition catalogue, London 1972; Allen Jones, exhibition catalogue / book, Tokyo 1974; Hypérréalistes Américains / Réalistes Européens, exhibition catalogue, with texts by Daniel Abadie, Jean Clair, Pierre Restany and others, Paris 1974; Allen Jones, exhibition catalogue, with text by Marco Livingstone, Liverpool 1979.

*

Allen Jones has explored many different media: lithography, watercolour, sculpture, photography, video, poster art and painting. In my opinion he is at his best when painting. Jones's style is instinctive; the brush is used in a masterly fashion, achieving superb variations of colour, memorable imagery, all executed with a tremendous clarity of thought and panache. "Thinking" painters are few and far between these days—in 1962 Jones entitled one of his paintings "The Artist Thinks." A symbol representing the artist appears regularly throughout his work, especially in the "Stage" series. A performance is taking place, and at the forefront of the canvas a figure almost always watches, encouraging the viewer to do the same and participate. In fact the viewer can identify with the seated figure, use it as a point of reference. Jones mixes abstract with figurative. Once I saw a painting before the figures had been added: it could have stood on its own without any additions, and John Hoyland wanted Jones to leave it as it was, but he instinctively added the figurative element.

Jones works from meticulous small sketches, with signs for ideas rather than completed images. He lets his feelings take over when he is painting. Unlike Kitaj, who feels that a painting is never finished, Jones considers a canvas completed if it tells a story with the traditional beginning, middle and end. Jones wants the points of reference to be contained only within the canvas. At one stage in his career he depicted a scene by using his own vocabulary made up of symbols—women were represented by the appearance of a bra, stocking tops or girdles. Jones admits that he did this owing to a lack of practice in modelling. In fact, later on he proved to be excellent at it, especially in painting such as "Leopard Lady" or "Bare me."

Female imagery has always played a major role in Jones's career. Those who know his work superficially always associate him with the Pirelli Calendar or else the woman on all fours with a sheet of glass on her back representing a table. It is sad that Jones is best known for this type of work. He defends it by saying that it is unreal, the proportions could never be attributed to real women. That may be, but one cannot help but find them offensive, particularly the fetishistic accoutrements. It is best to concentrate on Jones' paintings, because here he excels.

—Carine Maurice

JORN, Asger.

Danish. Born Asger Oluf Jorgensen in Vegrur, 3 March 1914; adopted name Jorn, in 1945. Educated privately, with Martin Kaaland-Jorgensen, 1930; studied at Silkeborg Teachers Training College, 1930-35; Art Academy, Copenhagen, 1938-40. Married Kirsten Lyngborg in 1939; married Matie van Domeslaef in 1951; married Nanna Enzenberger in 1973. Lived in Paris, 1935-37; worked in studios of Fernand Léger and Le Corbusier, Paris, 1937; collaborated with Le Corbusier, on World's Fair, Paris, 1937; Member, Linien group, Paris, 1937. Settled in Copenhagen, 1937; Founder, with Gjler Bille, Henry Heerup, Egill Jacobsen and Carl-Henning Pederson, Helhesten magazine, Copenhagen, 1941-44; secretly published monthly journal Lad og Folk during the war in Copenhagen, 1943-45; travelled in England and Holland, 1946; worked on tapestries, with Pierre Wermaere, France, 1947; Founder, with Arnault and Dotremont, Bureau Internationale du Surréalisme Révolutionnaire, Paris, 1947; spent six months in Djerba, Tunisia, 1947-48; Founder, with Karel Appel, Corneille and others, COBRA group, Paris, 1948-51; published Cobra Library; lived in Humlebaek, Denmark, 1949-50; spent six months in Suresnes, with Robert Jacobsen, 1950; worked on ceramics while recovering from tuberculosis, Silkeborg, 1951-53; lived in Switzerland, 1953; settled in Albissola, Italy, 1954; Founder, with Enrico Baj, Mouvement pour un Bauhaus Imaginiste, Switzerland, 1954-61, and Situationistes Internationales, Paris, 1953-57; produced experimental films, with Albert Mertz and Guy Debord, Munich, 1961, experimental music discs, with Jean Dubuffet, Paris, 1960; Founder, Scandinavian Institute for Comparative Vandalism, 1962-65. Recipient: Guggenheim Prize, New York, 1964 (declined). Honorary Citizen of Albissola, Italy, 1960. Died (in Aarhus, Denmark) 1 May 1973.

Individual Exhibitions:

1938	Dam and Fonss, Copenhagen (with Pierre Wemaere)
1942	Pustervig Kunsthandel, Copenhagen
1945	Macholms Kunsthandel, Copenhagen
	Maelholms Kunsthandel, Copenhagen (with Christofferson and Nielssen)
1948	Galerie Breteau, Paris
	Galerie Birch, Copenhagen
1949	Galerie Birch, Copenhagen
1950	Galerie Birch, Copenhagen
1951	Galerie Birch, Copenhagen
	Galerie Breteau, Paris
1953	Kunstforeningen, Copenhagen
	Tapel og Kunst, Odense, Denmark
1954	Galleria l'Asterisco, Rome
1955	Galerie Birch, Copenhagen
	Galleria del Naviglio, Milan
	Kunstindustrimuseet, Copenhagen
1956	Galerie Taptoe, Brussels
	Aarhaus Permanente, Denmark
	Galleria Notizie, Turin
1957	Galleria Cavallino, Venice
	Galerie Rive Gauche, Paris
	Galleria Il Prisma, Turin
	Institute of Contemporary Arts, London
1958	Institute of Contemporary Arts, London
	Galerie Rive Gauche, Paris
	Galleria La Tartaruga, Rome
	Galerie Alfred Schmela, Dusseldorf
	Galerie Sandner, Hamburg
	Galerie van de Loo, Munich
1959	Galleria Albissola Marina, Italy
	Galerie Rive Gauche, Paris
	Salone Annunciata, Milan
1960	Galerie Birch, Copenhagen
	Galerie Hybler, Copenhagen
	Galerie van der Loo, Munich (with Roel d'Haese)
	Galerie Rive Gauche, Paris
1961	Galleria Notizie, Turin
	Arthur Tooth and Sons, London
	Kunstforening, Viborg, Denmark
	Galerie Kobenhaven, Copenhagen

Galleria La Medusa, Rome
Gummesons Konstgalleri. Stockholm
Galerie Benador, Geneva
Lefebre Gallery, New York
1962 Galleria Cavallino, Venice
Galerie Rive Gauche, Paris
Lefebre Gallery, New York
1963 Jysk Kunst Galerie, Aarhus, Denmark
Galerie Birch, Copenhagen
Galerie Rive Gauche, Paris
Galerie van de Loo, Munich
1964 Galerie Birch, Copenhagen
Kunstforeningen, Copenhagen
Galerie Rive Gauche, Paris
Kunsthalle, Basle (toured the Netherlands and Denmark)
Silkeborg Art Museum, Denmark
Galeri Ateneum, Lund, Sweden
Danske Kunstforeningen, Hjorring, Denmark (toured Denmark)
Stedelijk Museum, Amsterdam
1965 Louisiana Museum, Humlebaek, Denmark
Galerie Buren, Stockholm
Kunstforening, Bergen, Norway (toured Norway)
Galerie Rive Gauche, Paris
Galerie van de Loo, Munich
1966 Arthur Tooth and Sons, London
Galerie van de Loo, Munich
Konstforening, Goteborg, Sweden (travelled to the Lunds Konsthall, Sweden)
1967 Lefebre Gallery, New York
Galerie Rive Gauche, Paris
Galerie im Erker, St. Gallen, Switzerland
Galerie Jeanne Bucher, Paris
Ars Studeo, Aarhus, Denmark
1968 Galerie van de Loo, Munich
1969 Galerie Jeanne Bucher, Paris
1970 Lefebre Gallery, New York
Galerie Jeanne Bucher, Paris
Galleria Arte Borgogna, Milan
1971 Arthur Tooth and Sons, London
Galerie im Erker, St. Gallen, Switzerland
1972 Lefebre Gallery, New York
Galerie Jeanne Bucher, paris
1973 Louisiana museum, Humlebaek, Denmark
Galerie van de Loo, Munich
Kestner Gesellschaft, Hannover
1974 Gruenebaum Gallery, New York
1976 Stedelijk Museum, Amsterdam
1979 Henie-Onstad Kunstscenter, Oslo
1981 Kunsthalle, Berne
1983 Royal Danish Embassy, London
1987 Musee d'Art Contemporarin, Nimes, France
Stadtisches Museum im Lenbachhaus, Munich

Selected Group Exhibitions:

1937 *Salon des Independants*, Paris
1939 *Skandinaverne*, Liljewaick, Stockholm (travelled to Charlottenburg and Copenhagen)
1941 *Dansk Kunst i dag*, Statens Museum for Kunst, Copenhagen
1947 *Abstrakt Kunst*, Reykjavik, Iceland
1954 *Contemporary Art in Scandinavia*, Brownstone Gallery, New York
1959 *Documenta 2*, Kassel, West Germany
1964 *Painting and Sculpture of a Decade 1954-1964*, Tate Gallery, London
1967 *Rosc 67: The Poetry of Vision*, Royal Dublin Society
1983 *Modern Art in the West*, Metropolitan Museum, Tokyo
1985 *Painterly Visions 1940-85*, Guggenheim Museum, New York

Collections:

Statens Museum for Kunst, Copenhagen; Kobberstiksamlingen, Copenhagen; Kunstindustrimuseet, Copenhagen; Louisiana Museum, Humlebaek, Denmark; Kunstmuseum Aarhus, Denmark; Nationalmuseum, Stockholm; Nasjonalgalleriet, Oslo; Henie-Onstad Kunstsenter, Oslo; Stedelijk Museum, Amsterdam, Museum of Modern Art, New York.

Publications:

By JORN: books—*Les Cornes d'Or et la Roue de la Fortune*, Copenhagen 1957; *Pour la Forme*, Paris 1958; *Critique de la Politique Economique*, Paris 1960; *Le Chevalure de Choses 1948-53*, with Christian Dotremont, Paris 1961; *On the Natural Order of things, Value and Economy, Luck and Chance, Ting and Polis*, 1962-64; *Signes Graves sur les Eglises de l'Eure et du Calvados*, Copenhagen 1964; *Gedanken eines Kunstlers*, Munich 1966; *Skanes Stenskulptur*, 1966; *La Langue Verte et la Cuite*, with Noel Arnaud, Turin 1968; *Au Pied du Mur*, with Noel Arnaud and Francois Dufrene, Paris 1969; *La Flute de Jade*, St. Gallen, Switzerland 1970; articles—"Peinture Detournée" in *Asger Jorn*, exhibition catalogue, Paris 1959; "The Fascinating Theme of the Tinker" in *XX Siecle* (Paris), June 1970; illustrated books—*The Girl in the Fire* by Genia Katz Rajchmann, 1939; *Chinese Poems*, 1943; *Occupation, 1939-45*, 1945.

On JORN: books—*Jorn a Venezia*, Venice 1963; *Asger Jorn's Aarhus Mural*, edited by Guy Atkins, Westerham, Kent 1964; *Asger Jorn's Writings to 1963*, edited by Guy Atkins and Erick Schmidt, Copenhagen 1964; *Asger Jorn by Virtus Schade*, Copenhagen 1965; *Jorn in Scandinavia* by Guy Atkins, London 1968; *Jorn: Cuba*, Turin 1970; *Jorn: Calui Qui* by Jean-Clarence Lambert, Paris 1972; *Jorn*, exhibition catalogue, by Wieland Schmied, St. Gallen, Switzerland 1973; *Jorn: Scultore* by Mario de Micheli, Milan 1973; *Jorn: Le Jardin d'Albissola*, Turin 1974; *Asger Jorn 1914-1973*, Silkeborg, Denmark 1974; *Asger Jorn: The Crucial Years 1954-1964* by Guy Atkins, London 1977; *Asger Jorn: The Final Years 1965-1973* by Guy Atkins, London 1980.

Son of parents who were teachers, Asger Jorn made his first landscapes and portraits at the age of 16. In Paris he studied painting with Léger from 1936 to 1937. He also assisted Le Corbusier in decorations for the Pavillon des Temps Nouveau. Another mural for Pierre Vermaere's house at Versailles saw him embarked on the large scale narratives he was to create in paint.

1948 was marked by his association with Dotremont, Appel, Constant and Corneille in the foundation of the Cobra movement. It lasted only three years, but they were intensely active. Jorn held exhibitions in Amsterdam and in Paris. In 1953 he travelled in France, Switzerland and Italy.

About 1956 Jorn had hit a peak of creative activity with colour taking an overwhelming effect on his compositions. His repertoire of figures was inexhaustible; only their definition varied. Weird denizens from unimaginable nightmares appeared in almost every canvas. Some expressed a supernatural phantasmagoria in an atmosphere of whirring menace. Others floated like witches in amorphous clouds of white.

Automatic paintings in animated sweeping compositions provoked riots of colour. Around 1961 he ventured on a phase of painting on the spread canvas having affinities with Sam Francis, laying trails of dots and pouring streams of paint. He also experimented with laying string covered in paint then removing it. 1962 saw his "Defigurations", when he painted his grotesque images on top of an old painted canvas carrying a straightforward landscape or conversation group from the 19th century.

Sculpture also attracted some of Jorn's daemonic energy, and he created a massive ceramic mural for a school in Denmark. He worked also on tapestries. Different media attracted Jorn throughout his life and he has exerted control of his strong colours, often pure and thickly textured, in large areas with a dominant impression of accident, providing solutions spontaneously and in improvised inspiration for resolution of a composition almost beyond organization. This deceptive rescue operation is built into his method of working, akin to action painting, and borne by the artist's powers of endurance and pre-thought results. Between 1965 and 1971 he completed large murals for a bank in Havana, Cuba.

Jorn took part in discussions on art theory and philosophy all his active life, and he wrote much about them; though his work, he claimed, became almost automatic in execution once it was in progress. Often it takes a humorous note as in "Jardin des Plaintes" where the pun is elaborated in the depiction of flower-like human heads. Jorn was a committed Expressionist whose analysis of his own works is contained in his statement: "I believe that colour immediately and totally transmits the content of a painting."

—G. S. Whittet

JOURNIAC, Michel.

French. Born in Paris, 7 October 1943. Educated at Lycée Voltaire, Paris; studied philosophy at St. Sulpice Seminary, Paris, and theology at the University of Paris; self-taught in art. Independent artist, Paris, since 1968. Agent: Galerie Stadler, Paris. Address: c/o Galerie Stadler, 51 rue de Seine, 75006 Paris, France.

Individual Exhibitions

1968 Cloitre des Billettes, Paris
1969 Galerie Daniel Templon, Paris
Galerie Martin-Malburet, Paris
Bonino Gallery, New York
1970 Galerie Daniel Templon, Paris
Galerie Martin-Malburet, Paris
1971 America-Center, Paris
1972 Galerie Stadler, Paris
U. E. R. des Arts Plastiques et Sciences de l'Art, Paris
Galerie Arges 2, Brussels
1973 Galerie Stadler, Paris
Espace 640, St. Jeannet, France
1974 Galerie Stadler, Paris
1975 Forum für Aktuelle Kunst, Innsbruck
Galerie Stadler, Paris
1976 Galleria Diagramma, Milan
Galleria Unimedia, Genoa
Galerie Stadler, Paris
1977 Galerie Artcurial, Paris
FIAC 77, Paris
1978 Galerie Sylvia Bourdon, Paris
Galerie Stadler, Paris
Galerie N R A., Paris
1979 Galerie Sylvia Bourdon, Paris
Galerie 32, Lyons
1980 International Cultureel Centrum, Antwerp

Selected Group Exhibitions:

1968 *Occupation des Lieux*, America-Center, Paris
1969 *Stand de Tir*, Musée Galliera, Paris (toured Japan)
1970 *Manifeste du Cheque*, Maison Francois Pluchart, Paris
1972 *Autopsie de la Venus de Milo*, Palais des Beaux-Arts, Brussels
1975 *Teyssedre: Art Sociologique*, Galerie Rencontres, Paris
1976 *Mythologies Quotidiennes 2*, Musée d'Art Moderne de la Ville, Paris
1977 *Le Corps*, Galerie Isy Brachot, Brussels
1978 *Lecon de Mots / Lecon de Maux*, Université de Nancy, France
1979 *Exposition Artitudes*, Galerie d'Art Contemporain, Nice

Publications

By JOURNIAC: book—*Le Sang Nu: recueil des poèmes*, Paris 1968; articles—"De la Censure à la Révolution Culturale", in *Artitudes* (St. Jeannet, France), March 1972; "Entretien avec Michel Journiac" in *Artitudes* (St. Jeannet, France), July 1972.

On JOURNIAC: books and pamphlets—*Journiac: piège pour une execution capitale*, exhibition leaflet, Paris 1971; *Journiac: contrat pour un corps*, exhibition leaflet, Paris 1972; *Il Corpo come Linguaggio* by Lea Vergine, Milan 1974; *Art,*

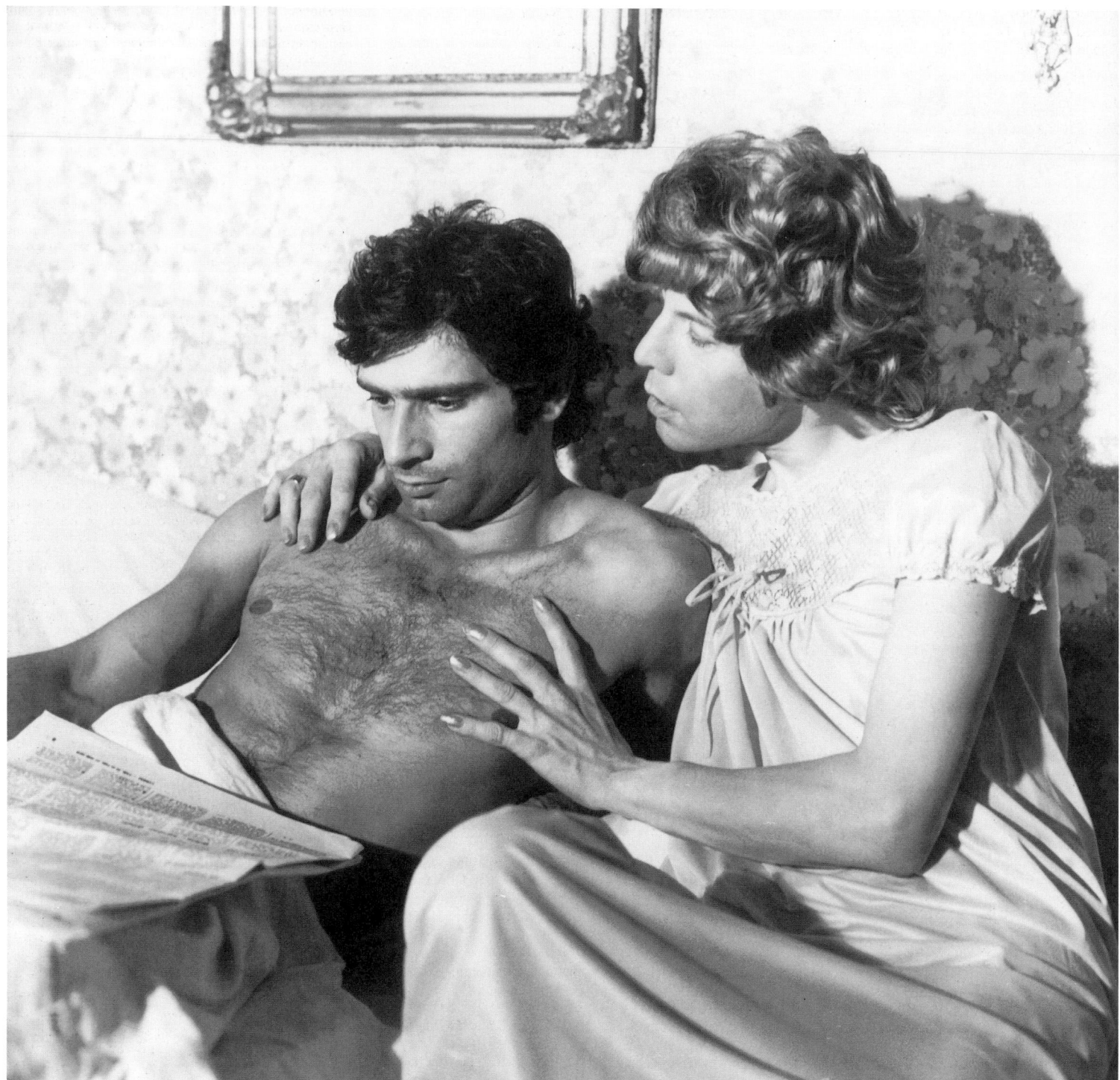

Michel Journiac: *24 Heures de la Vie d'une Femme Ordinaire,* 1980

Action, Participation by Frank Popper, Paris 1975; *Michel Journiac: L'Ossuaire de l'Egypte* by Marcel Pacquet, Paris 1977; *Michel Journiac,* exhibition catalogue, Antwerp 1980; articles—"Michel Journiac" by Catherine Millet, in *Flash Art* (Milan), November / December 1970; "Attitudes Critiques de Journiac" by Francois Pluchart, in *Combat* (Paris), February 1971; "Le Pièges de Michel Journiac" in *Opus International* (Paris), March 1973; "Les Pièges de Michel Journiac" in *Artitudes* (St. Jeannet, France), December 1973; "Dix Questions sur l'Art Corporel et l'Art Sociologique" in *Artitudes* (St. Jeannet, France), December 1973; "Adam ou Eve: Michel Journiac" by René Rozan in *Vie des Arts* (Paris), no. 80, 1975.

Six interrogative propositions

1. Ideologies, games which are no longer being played outside the pulsions of the word, have torn away the masks of promised liberties standing in the form of a scaffold of bodies.

2. Words which have become dead form the links in a chain of reasoning which erects the verbal trial of desire.

3. The inverted structure of a falsified language traps the naked body as a reified support to an economic production, chaining up of the gesture.

4. The bound body, tortured, reduced to being nothing but an instrument of work, object of production and end of a reified activity, is at the point of death.

5. The social rituals, work, family, fatherland, liberty, equality, fraternity are becoming alibis for oppressions, marking out of bodies.

6. From dead rationalisms are born a hidden fascism, out of which springs the pseudo-liberalism of a society which, conscious of not being unanimous, veils its lacerations and tries to restructure Man and his desire by subjugating him.

In the form of interrogative conclusion.

—Michel Journiac

JUDD, Donald.

American. Born in Excelsior Springs, Missouri, 3 June 1928. Educated privately in Omaha, 1939–40, then at Westwood High School, New Jersey, 1943–46; studied at the Art Student's League, New York, 1948, 1949–53; College of William and Mary, Williamsburg, Virginia, 1948–49; Columbia University, New York, 1949–53, 1957–62, B.Sc. 1953, M.A. 1962. Served in the United States Army, in Korea, 1946–47. Married Margaret Hughan (Julie) Finch in 1964; children: Flavin Starbuck, Rainer Yingling. Settled in New York; taught art part-time, Christadora Home and Police Athletic League, 1953; Reviewer, *Art News,* New York, 1959; Contributing Editor, *Arts Magazine,* New York, 1959–65; Reviewer, *Art International,* Lugano, 1965. Instructor, Brooklyn Institute of Arts and Sciences, New York, 1962–64; Visiting Artist, Dartmouth College, Hanover, New Hampshire, 1966; taught sculpture at Yale

University, New Haven, Connecticut, 1967; conducted Emma Lake Artists' Workshop, Lac La Ronge, Saskatchewan, 1968; Baldwin Professor, Oberlin College, Ohio, 1976. Recipient: Travel Grant, Swedish Institute, Stockholm, 1965; National Endowment for the Arts grant, 1967 and 1976; Guggenheim Fellowship, 1968. Agent: Leo Castelli Gallery, New York. Lives in west Texas and New York. Address: c/o Leo Castelli Gallery, 420 West Broadway, New York, New York, 10012, U.S.A.

Individual Exhibitions:

1956	*Don Judd and Nathan Raisen*, Panoras Gallery, New York
1957	Panoras Gallery, New York
1963	Leo Castelli Gallery, New York
1968	Whitney Museum, New York (retrospective)
	Irving Blum Gallery, Los Angeles
1969	Irving Blum Gallery, Los Angeles
	Leo Castelli Gallery, New York
	Galerie Ileana Sonnabend, Paris
	Galerie Rudolf Zwirner, Cologne
1970	Stedelijk van Abbemuseum, Eindhoven, Netherlands (toured Germany and the U.K.)
	Helman Gallery, St. Louis
	Leo Castelli Gallery, New York
	Galerie Konrad Fischer, Dusseldorf
	Janie C. Lee Gallery, Dallas
	Locksley Shea Gallery, Minneapolis
1971	Locksley Shea Gallery, Minneapolis
	Pasadena Art Museum, California (retrospective)
1972	Greenberg Gallery, St. Louis
	Richard Serra/Don Judd, Leo Castelli Gallery downtown, New York
	Galerie Ricke, Cologne
	Galerie Daniel Templon, Paris
1973	Leo Castelli Gallery downtown, New York
	Galleria Gian Enzo Sperone, Rome
	Konrad Fischer Galleria, Rome
	Locksley Shea Gallery, Minneapolis
	Galleria Gian Enzo Sperone, Turin
1974	Lisson Gallery, London
	Don Flavin/Don Judd/Sol LeWitt, Galleria La Bertesca, Milan
	Ace Gallery, Venice, California
	Galeria Aronowitsch, Stockholm
1975	Lisson Gallery, London
	Galerie Aronowitsch, Stockholm
	National Gallery of Canada, Ottawa (retrospective)
	Galerie Templon, Paris
1976	Heiner Friedrich Galerie, Munich
	Drawings 1956-1975, Kunstmuseum, Basel (travelled to Tübingen and Oxford)
	Skulpturen, Kunsthalle, Berne
	Janie C. Lee Gallery, Houston
	Anna Maria Verna Galerie, Zurich
	Sable Gallery, Toronto
	Leo Castelli Gallery, New York
1977	Museum of South Texas, Corpus Christi
	Heiner Friedrich Gallery, New York
	Max Protetch Gallery, Washington, D.C.
	Contemporary Arts Center, Cincinnati, Ohio
	Moderne Galerie, Bottrop, West Germany
	Heiner Friedrich Gallery, Cologne
	Ace Gallery, Venice, California
1978	Heiner Friedrich Gallery, New York
	Galerie Watari, Tokyo
	Leo Castelli Gallery, New York
	Vancouver Art Gallery
	Young Hoffman Gallery, Chicago
1979	Stedelijk van Abbemuseum, Eindhoven, Netherlands
	Leo Castelli Gallery, New York
	Akron Art Institute, Ohio
	Annemarie Verna Galerie, Zurich
	Lisson Gallery, London
	Thomas Segal Gallery, Boston
	Galerie Heiner Friedrich, Cologne
1980	Galerie Annemarie Verna, Zurich
1981	Leo Castelli Gallery, New York
	Newport Harbor Art Museum, California
1982	Larry Gagosian Gallery, Los Angeles

1983	Leo Castelli Gallery, New York
	Galerie Annemarie Verna, Zurich (twice)
	Carol Taylor Gallery, Dallas
	Spirit Square Art Center, Charlotte, North Carolina
	Blum Helman Gallery, New York
1984	Leo Castelli Gallery, New York
	Max Protetch Gallery, New York
	101 Spring Street, New York
	Margo Leavin Gallery, Los Angeles
	Neuberger Museum, Purchase, New York
1985	Galerie Annemarie Verna, Zurich
	Texas Gallery, Houston
	Galleria Lia Rumma, Naples
	Rhona Hoffman Gallery, Chicago
	Galerie Barbel Grasslin, Frankfurt
1986	Waddington Galleries, London
	Paula Cooper Gallery, New York
1987	Lawrence Oliver Gallery, Philadelphia

Selected Group Exhibitions:

1965	*Flavin/Judd/Morris/Williams*, Green Gallery, New York
1967	*American Sculpture of the 60's*, Los Angeles Country Museum of Art
1970	*Discovery of Harmony*, Expo Museum of Fine Arts, at the *World's Fair*, Osaka
1973	*Art 4*, at the *Basel Art Fair*
1974	*Choice Dealers—Dealers' Choice*, New York Cultural Center
1978	*American Art 1950 to the Present*, Whitney Museum, New York
1980	*Minimal Skulpturen: Sammlung Panza*, Kunstmuseum, Dusseldorf
1982	*Documenta VII*, Museum Fridericianum, Kassel, West Germany
1984	*The Languages of Geometry*, Kunstmuseum, Berne
1986	*Qu'est-ce que la sculpture moderne*, Musee d'Art Moderne, Paris

Collections:

Museum of Modern Art, New York; Whitney Museum, New York; Guggenheim Museum, New York; Hirshhorn Museum, Washington, D.C.; Art Museum of South Texas, Corpus Christi; Art Institute of Chicago; San Francisco Museum of Modern Art; National Gallery of Canada, Ottawa; Kunsthaus, Zurich; Stedelijk van Abbemuseum, Eindhoven, Netherlands.

Publications:

By JUDD: books—*Complete Writings 1959-1975*, Halifax and New York, 1975; *Complete Writings 1975-1986*, Eindhoven 1987; articles—reviews for *Art News* (New York), September-November 1959; reviews for *Arts Magazine* (New York), 1959–65; "New York City; A World Art Center" in *Envoy* (New York), Winter 1962; "Chamberlain: Another View" in *Art International* (Lugano, Switzerland), Christmas/New Year 1963/1964; "At the Fair" in *Art in America* (New York), August 1964; "Local History" in *Arts Yearbook 7*, New York 1964; "To Encourage Sculpture and Specific Objects" in *Arts Yearbook 8, New York 1965;* "John Chamberlain" in *7 Sculptors*, exhibition catalogue, Philadelphia 1965; reviews for *Art International* (Lugano Switzerland), April/May 1965; statement in *Primary Structure: Younger American and British Sculptors*, exhibition catalogue, New York 1966; "Questions to Stella and Judd," interview with Bruce Glaser, in *Art News* (New York), September 1966; response to question by Lawrence Alloway in *Arts Yearbook 9*, New York 1967; statement in "Sensibilities of the 60's" by Barbara Rose and Irving Sandler in *Art in America* (New York), January/February 1967; letter to the editor in *Arts Magazine* (New York), April 1967; statement in "Homage to the Square" by Lucy Lippard in *Arts in America* (New York), July/August 1967; "The Anti-Hierarchical American," interview with Amy Goldin, in *Art News* (New York), September 1967 statement in "Portfolio: 4 Sculptors" in *Perspecta* (New Haven, Connecticut), March–May 1968; statement in "La Sfida del Sistema" in *Metro* (Milan), June 1968; statement in *Art Now: New York* (New York), January 1969; "Complaints: Part I" in *Studio International* (London), April 1969; "Aspects of Flavin's Work" in *Don Flavin*, exhibition catational (London), February 1970; "Aspects of

Flavin" in *Art and Artists* (London), March 1970; "Don Judd: An Interview with John Coplans" in *Don Judd*, exhibition catalogue, Pasadena, California 1971; statement in *Newspaper-Lower Manhattan Township* (New York), January 1971; "WOHO" in *Newpaper-Lower Manhattan Township* (New York), April 1971; "Greater Westbeth" in *Newspaper-Greater Manhattan Township* (New York), May 1971; article in *George Segal*, exhibition catalogue, Paris 1972; "Complaints: Part II" in *Arts Magazine* (New York), March 1973; "Malevich: Independent Form, Color, Surface" in *Art in America* (New York), March/April 1974; interview with Jean Claude Lebensztejn in *Art in America* (New York), July/August 1975; "A Long Discussion Not About Masterpieces But Why There Are So Few Of Them" in *Art in America* (New York), September and October 1984, and in *Art Monthly* (London), February and March 1985; "Interview with Donald Judd", with Paul Taylor, in *Flash Art* (Milan), May 1987.

On JUDD: books—*Minimal Art*, edited by Gregory Battcock, New York 1968; *Don Judd*, exhibition catalogue, by William Agee, New York 1968; *Beyond Modern Sculpture* by Jack Burnham, New York 1968; *The New Sculpture: Environments and Assemblages* by Udo Kultermann, London 1968; *Don Judd*, exhibition catalogue, Pasadena, California 1971; *The Structure of Art* by Jack Burnham, New York 1971; *The Dedefinition of Art: Action Art to Pop to Earthworks* by Harold Rosenberg, London 1972; *Donald Judd*, exhibition catalogue, edited by Brydon Smith, Ottawa 1975; *Donald Judd: Zeichnungen/drawings 1956–1975*, exhibition catalogue, Basel 1976; *Profiles in American Art* by Barbara Rose, New York, 1981; *Artists Observed*, edited by Harvey Stein, New York 1986; *Donald Judd*, exhibition catalogue with essay by Ronald Jones, Philadelphia 1987; articles—"Donald Judd" by Barbara Rose in *Artforum* (New York), June 1965; "Allusion and Illusion in Donald Judd" by Rosalind Krauss in *Artforum* (New York), May 1966; "The Nart-Art of Donald Judd" by Martin Friedman in *Art und Artists* (London), February 1967; "Judd, Morris e Poons: Tre Nomi Nuovi" by Bruno Alfieri in *Metro* (Milan), no. 10, 1967; "The Serial Attitude" by Mel Bochner in *Artforum* (New York), December 1967; "Don Judd: The complexities of Minimal Art" by Barbara Rose in *Vogue* (New York), March 1969; "Don Judd" by Louwrien Wijers in *Museumjournaal* (Amsterdam), April 1969; "Judd and After" by Roelof Louw in *Studio International* (London), November 1972; "Donald Judd: 10 Years" by Gregoire Muller in *Arts Magazine* (New York), February 1973; "Ply Me with Judd" by Roberta Smith in *Village Voice* (New York), 23/29 September 1981; "Donald Judd: Early Work" by John Russell in the *New York Times*, 18 November 1983; "Sculture All-Over: La Casa di Don Judd a New York" in *Domus* (Milan), September 1985.

Somewhat new work is usually described with the words that have been used to describe old work. These words have to be discarded as too particular to the earlier work or they have to be given new definitions. Occasionally new terms have to be invented. I discarded "order" and "structure." Both words imply that something is formed. Material, area, volume, space or color are ordered or structured. The separation of means and structure—the world and order—is one of the main aspects of European or Western art and also of most older, reputedly civilized art. It's the sense of order of Thomist Christianity and of rationalistic philosophy which developed from it. Order underlies, overlies, is within, above, below or beyond everything.

I wanted work that didn't involve incredible assumptions about everything. I couldn't begin to think about the order of the universe or the nature of American society. I didn't want work that was general or universal in the usual sense. I didn't want it to claim too much. Obviously, the means and the structure couldn't be separate and couldn't even be thought of as two things joined. Neither word meant anything.

A shape, a volume, a color, a surface is something itself. It shouldn't be concealed as part of a fairly different whole. The shapes and materials shouldn't be altered by their context. One or four boxes in a row, any single thing or such a series, is local order, just an arrangement, barely order at all. The series is mine, someone's, and clearly not some larger order. It has nothing to do with either order or disorder in general. Both are matters of fact. The series of four or six doesn't change the galvanized iron or steel or whatever the boxes are made of.

—Don Judd

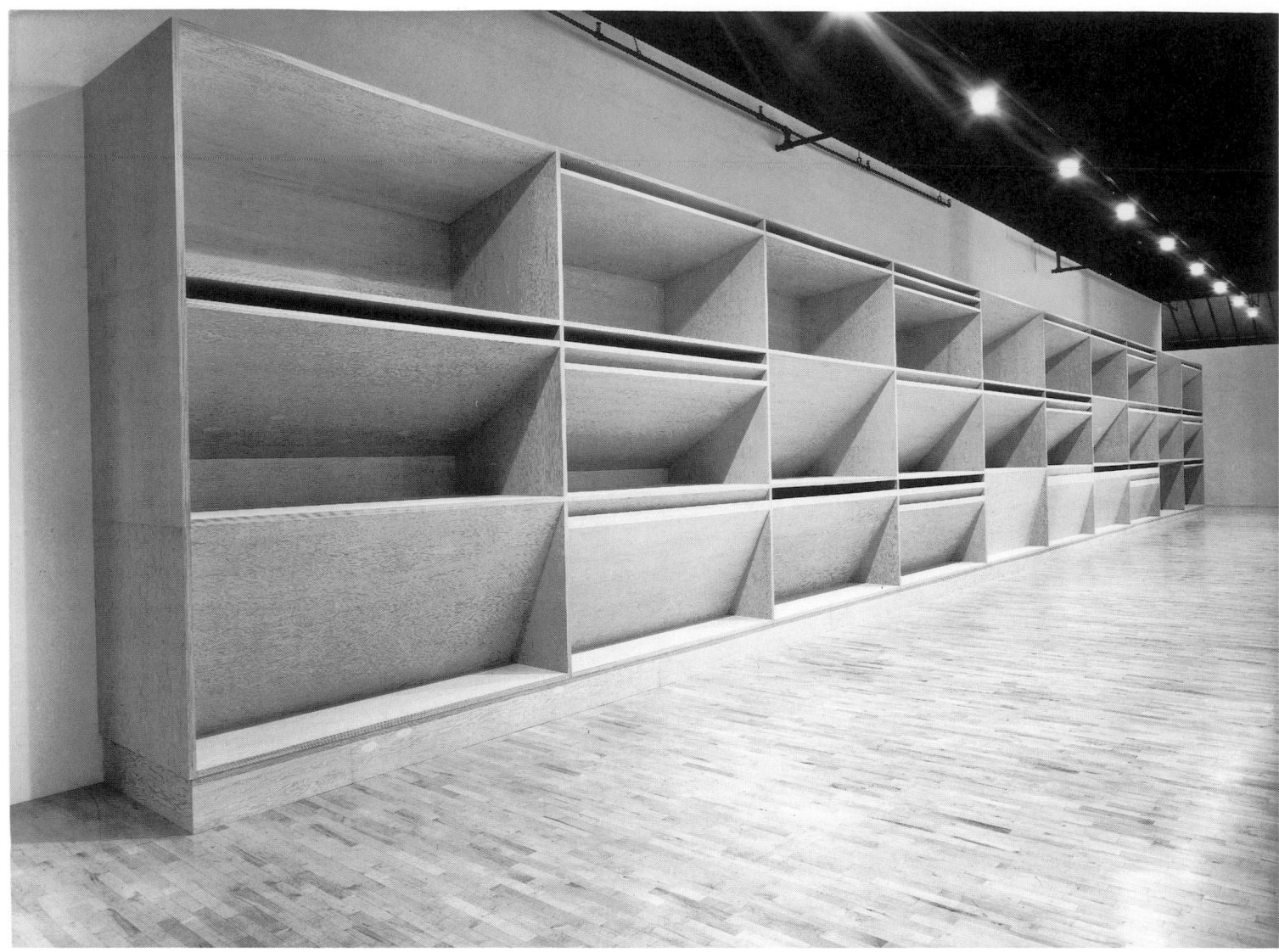

Donald Judd: *Untitled*, 1981

Donald Judd's mature art arose—like that of other major American artists in the mid-60's, and larger and continuing drives in literature and music even earlier—from the need to produce a muted and reductive art still clearly based upon a notion of the aesthetic and thus removed from life. All this reflected the exhaustion, as felt then, with art forms of high personal expression and complex internal construction, an uneasiness that extended easily into the nature of traditional materials, format, means of conception and construction. And so the real fascination of Judd's art, along with that of the others to be titled Minimalists in their geometric impulse, is that to satisfy itself, his work had to touch upon the boundary of anonymous object where whatever spiritual energy survived in the color field and geometric pictorial traditions was decisively nullified.

Yet now, in retrospect, Judd's first large body of mature work, that in metal (ca. 1965–73) and now ensconced in the textbooks, seemingly presents quite traditional visual conceits in their measured precision, material and textural distinctions, reliance upon color, light, and even, in some, a rhythm, for their aura. And, as such, even when felt as a part of the longer Western anti-Romantic' stance of elitist elegance, this formal manipulation may well be Judd's own Beckett-like device of play to keep the ultimate condition within the logic of his art—void—constantly at bay. When the entirety of the work is seen together, as in catalog reproduction, the artist's extensive use of "theme and variation" is clear, but not in any one single work. He has had fabricated extended series of variants of all of his well-known basic form-types: for instance, after arriving at the format of a signature

work in 1967, the vertical stack of wall-hung, frame-like boxes, at least 32 versions of such units, each usually numbering 10 elements, were made through 1973. Outwardly similar, the works differed in their use of many colors for the plexiglass sheets inserted into the metallic frames while the latter were produced in brass, copper, galvanized iron, copper, aluminum, with stainless steel the most frequently used.

After working as a painter in the later 1950's and into the first years of the 60's—to support himself at the time, Judd wrote art criticism—he then turned to free-standing sculptural forms which at first included both mixed media and found objects. He then executed a series of painted wooden objects—"harps," "bleachers," and slotted boxes—before, at mid-decade, his creative concept came to include industrial fabrication and a relatively small family of form types all centered about a box form, mostly open, and in metals. Constantly re-thought and reworked with no major external changes, the most characteristic types of this period centered upon this box-like-frame, horizontal, or vertical, singular or composed of multiple units, tied together with a bar form and wall-hung, or detached and floor-placed. (Judd has never titled his works, no doubt to further their anonymity and specificity—he himself uses the phrase "specific objects" to designate his work; ironically, this may have all the more personalized them, since by necessity they are referred to by the name of the collection in which they appear.)

Within the most recent decade of his career, from 1972 on, Judd has used untreated plywood for interior works—outdoor pieces have been executed in concrete and in steel. Both in larger ensembles,

whole gallery wall-length, and in smaller individual works exhibited together, as in 1981, the box form dominates and there are no color or material shifts; but the rhythmic changes available earlier only in the wall-hung horizontal bar form with its oft mathematiclly-based size and interval variance, can be easily seen in the plywood pieces. Especially in the smaller plywood works, where the external box-frame is visible, the work appears as a search for internal variety, softened by the wood-grain though still distinctly non-hierarchal. Recent work of the mid-80s has played variant upon earlier metal and tinted plexiglass rectangular construction. Critical complaint has spoken of their "old-fashioned" reliance upon craftsmanship, form, and chaste material; whereas more pointed views see the work as "archetype of corporate avant gardism" (J. Dechter) in its preciosity—use of copper, corten steel, brass, and mellifluous hues—and thus jewel-like seductiveness, and a "commodification" of Minimalist style. Others of course still admire without reservation such "stubborn orthodox Minimalism." And so Judd's art has continued as symbols representative of non-symbolic statement, which in their austerity and order can present thought if not feeling as well. But, as in any evolved creative idiom, there is a time when its emblem-value becomes more significant than its inventive flexibility. With such lessened contemporary adaptiveness, it is then a collector's art rather than the artist's; apparently for Judd, the minimalist mode is still under his control and operates without dilemma.

—Joshua Kind

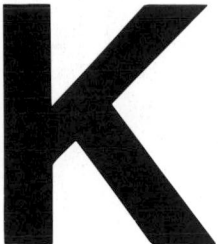

K

KALINOWSKI, Horst Egon.

German. Born in Dusseldorf, 2 January 1924. Educated at Staatliche Kunstakademie, Dusseldorf, 1945–48; Académie de la Grande Chaumiére, under Jean Dewasne, Paris, 1950–52. Travelled in Rome and Venice, 1949–50. Independent artist, since 1952: first collages and assemblages, 1956; first stage designs, 1959; first caisson sculptures, 1960; first lithographs, 1963. Professor, Kunstakademie, Karlsruhe, since 1968. Member, Preussische Akademie der Bildenden Künste, Berlin, 1968. Recipient: Carl Einstein Prize, Essen, West Germany, 1966; First Prize in Sculpture, Haus der Kunst, Munich, 1967; Burda Prize, 1967. Agent: Galerie Rothe, Werderplatz 17, Heidelberg. Address: c/o Staatliche Akademie der Bildende Künste, Reinhold Frankstrasse 81, 7500 Karlsruhe, West Germany.

Individual Exhibitions:

1953	Galerie Arnaud, Paris
1954	Galerie Arnaud, Paris
1955	Galerie Arnaud, Paris
	Galerie Franck, Frankfurt
1956	Galerie St. Laurent, Brussels
	Galerie Creuze, Paris
1957	Galerie Franck, Frankfurt
	Galerie Accent, Antwerp
	Galerie St. Laurent, Brussels
	Galerie Creuze, Paris
1958	Galerie Daniel Cordier, Paris
1959	Galerie 22, Dusseldorf
1961	Gallery Krzywe Kolo, Warsaw
1962	Robert Fraser Gallery, London (twice)
	Galerie Chave, Vence, France
	Galerie Daniel Cordier, Paris
1963	Galerie Daniel Cordier, Paris
1964	Robert Fraser Gallery, London
	Galerie Rothe, Heidelberg
	Galerie Miniature, Berlin
	Cordier-Ekstrom Gallery, New York
1966	Galerie Rothe, Heidelberg
	Cordier-Ekstrom Gallery, New York
1967	Städtische Kunsthalle, Mannheim (toured West Germany)
1969	*Caissons et Stèles 1961–1969,* Centre National d'Art Contemporain, Paris
	Galerie Rothe, Heidelberg
	Kestner-Gesellschaft, Hannover
	Kunst und Kunstgewerberverein, Pforzheim
	Lefebre Gallery, New York
1970	Makler Gallery, Philadelphia
1971	Galerie Charles Lienhard, Basle
	Caissons Ensachements 1970–71, Galerie Rothe, Heidelberg
1972	Kunstverein, Kassel
	Kunstverein, Cologne
1973	Chateau d'Ancy-Le-Franc, France
	Galerie Defet, Nuremberg
1974	Kunstverein, Trier, West Germany
	Goethe-Institut, Marseilles
	Galerie Athanor, Marseilles
	Goethe-Institut, Paris
	Galerie Marcel Billiot, Paris
	Galerie Rothe, Heidelberg
1975	Kunstforum, Bensheim, West Germany
1976	Galerie Rothe, Heidelberg
1977	Kunstmuseum, Dusseldorf
	Galerie Rothe, Heidelberg
1978	Neue Galerie, Aachen
	Kunsthalle, Mannheim
1979	Kunsthalle, Bremen
	Galerie Hilbur, Karlsruhe
1980	Galerie von Laar, Munich
1981	Galerie Rehklau, Augsburg
	Objekte 1975–80, Galerie Rothe, Heidelberg
1982	*Objekte, Reliefs, Ensachements, Termes,* Kunsthalle, Darmstadt
	Kleine Grafikgalerie, Bremen
	Kunstverein, Freiburg im Breisgau, West Germany
1983	Galerie Rothe, Heidelberg
1985	Galerie von Laar, Munich
	Deutsches Ledermuseum, Offenbach, West Germany
	Markuskirche, Francfort-Nied, West Germany
1986	Kunstverein, Kirchzarten, West Germany
1987	Arbeitskreis Galerie im Ganserhaus, Wasserburg, West Germany
	Galerie Rothe, at *FIAC 87,* Grand Palais, Paris
1988	Kunstverein, Albstadt, West Germany

Selected Group Exhibitions:

1956	*Divergences,* Stedelijk Museum, Amsterdam
1958	*Exposition Phases,* Galerie St. Laurent, Brussels
1959	*Phases,* Galerie Krzysztofory, Cracow
1963	*Art of Assemblage,* Museum of Modern Art, New York
1965	*Carnegie International,* Carnegie Institute, Pittsburgh
1968	*Art Vivant 1965–1968,* Fondation Maeght, St. Paul de Vence, France
1978	*Idee, Konzept und Werk,* Akademie der Bildenden Künste, Berlin
1981	*Dimensions des Plastischen,* Bildhauertechniken Neuer Berliner Kunsteverein in der Staatl. Kunsthalle, Berlin
1986	*Internationale Bildhauer Triennale,* Fellbach, West Germany
1987	*Europaischer Manierismus,* Kunsthaus, Vienna

Collections:

Neue Nationalgalerie, Berlin; Kunstmuseum, Dusseldorf; Galerie Rothe, Heidelberg; Städtische Kunstsammlungen, Bonn; Rheinisches Landesmuseum, Bonn; Wallraf-Richartz Museum, Cologne; Centre Georges Pompidou, Paris; Moderna Museet, Stockholm; Victoria and Albert Museum, London; Museum of Modern Art, New York.

Publications:

On KALINOWSKI: books—*Kalinowski,* exhibition catalogue, with text by Wieland Schmied and Frantisek Smejkal, Hannover 1969; *Kalinowski: Caissons et Stèles 1961–1969,* exhibition catalogue, with text by Frantisek Smejkal, Alain Bosquet, Heinz Fuchs and Gerard Gassiot-Talabot, Paris 1969; *Horst Egon Kalinowski,* exhibition catalogue, with text by Alain Bosquet, New York 1969; *Kalinowski: Caissons En-*

sachements 1970–71, exhibition catalogue, with text by Franz Josef van der Grinten, Heidelberg 1971; *Kalinowski,* with texts by Jean Dewasne, Pierre Bettencourt, and Pol Bury, Stuttgart 1975; *Kalinowski: Zeichnungen/Dessins, Bilder, Tableaux, Caissons,* exhibition catalogue with texts by Wolfgang Becker and Andreas Franzke, Aachen 1978; *Kalinowski: Objekte 1975–80,* exhibition catalogue, Heidelberg 1981; *Kalinowski: Objekte, Reliefs, Ensachements, Termes,* exhibition catalogue, with text by Heusinger von Waldegg and Dr. Sperlich, Darmstadt 1982; *Kalinowski: Collagen und Bildschreine,* with text by Hans Hoffstätter and Dr. Ludwig, Heidelberg 1982; *Kalinowski: papiers collés,* exhibition catalogue with text by Rainer Malkowski, Heidelberg 1983; *Kalinowski: Bandreliefs,* exhibition catalogue with text by Heusinger von Waldegg, Heidelberg 1985.

My caissons have always been containers as far as I was concerned. Their architecture enclosed a 'content', and their leather covering was intended to signify defence and protection. Leather has always possessed that function. Human beings used to protect themselves against the weather with animal hides; then came the loin cloth and the leather apron, the helmet, cuirass and glove. Water hose and bottle were made of leather; even tents were rooms made of leather. It is according to these particular qualities of leather that I have developed my caissons. The dimensions of the old bits of leather used in these designs determine the final form. The overall shape is simple and geometrical in order to accomodate flat surfaces and partitions on which the grained material is stuck and nailed. The spectator is thus presented with an empirical object to which he relates physically. The question I am frequently asked—what kind of leather do I use, or where do I find it?—is of no importance to me. I am primarily concerned with 'skin'. The experience and observation of the skin is my starting point.

The diverse forms of my objects, be they more geometric-static or more soft-organic, 'contain' within them IMAGINATION. They may be regarded as sexual, cryptic, repellent, sinister or magical, but such descriptions merely serve the spectator's need for associations, since only once he can name it does he banish the threat of an alien object. I do my best to achieve a direct, literally skin-tight relationship between the spectator and my objects so that they appear to him as part of an additional reality. They are meant to affect him physically, to disturb him. His hand should feel compelled to touch, but in the moment of advancing to hesitate, out of fear that the object, at present immobile, might suddenly move. The anatomy as the expression of symmetry and the forms of vegetative life support the conception on which my works are based. Awareness of form determines the first, while a fluent softness defines the second. Both obey the aim of assimilating the notion of life and death with that of untearable skin.

—Horst Egon Kalinowski

In one's mind it is hard to divorce Horst Egon Kalinowski from his leathern *caissons* and *steles*. It is for these works that he is best known and, in personal terms, they are the outward forms of his thought and being. Nevertheless, they represent a stage in his career that was reached after that sundry and perhaps

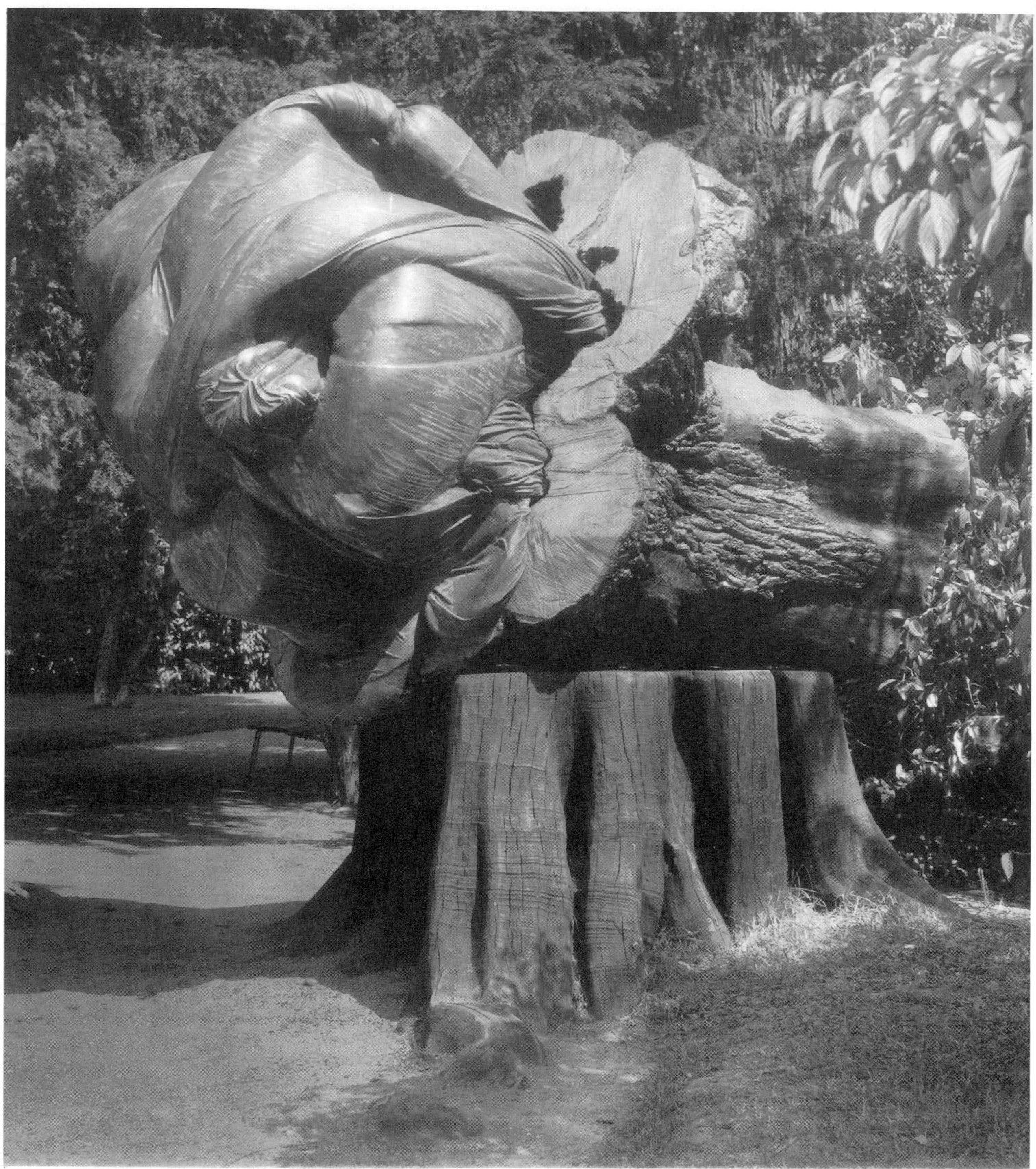

Horst Egon Kalinowski: *Baummark*, 1979

routine struggling through which the artist must pass before he finds his natural style.

By the time he was 26 Kalinowski had already become a non-figurative painter, but by 1956 he was at work upon collages and "objects." The cases and the sepulchral (?) tablets and portways first appeared in 1965, although evidence presaging their imminent arrival was seen in London in 1962 and 1964.

These caissons and steles are hermetic in character and in gestation. Kalinowski is not reticent about what they signify. These objects clad in leather are for him outside the debris of material existence. They are magical in the antique sense that emanates from the sacred paraphernalia of primitive societies. Messages from the unknown. As the artist puts it: "I want to get from this same magic presence that which flows from ritual objects." His work is his expression of his inner experiences. Intensely *human* (they frequently relate to torsos, backbone vertebrae, shoulders, eyes, tailbone, ears and sexual organs), they have, besides their mystery, a poetic resonance, and, well aware of this characteristic, Kalinowski gives to them poetic titles.

Those who seek here for a geometry will in many cases find it, but it is a geometry softened by its leather skin and invaded by the occult gravity of ancient secrets, all of which, in Kalinowski's work, take palpable form. The unity of monumentality, awesomeness, mystery and emotional contact makes these caissons and steles exceptionally tactile.

They have undoubtedly added their own (and new) vocabulary to the language of modern art.

—Sheldon Williams

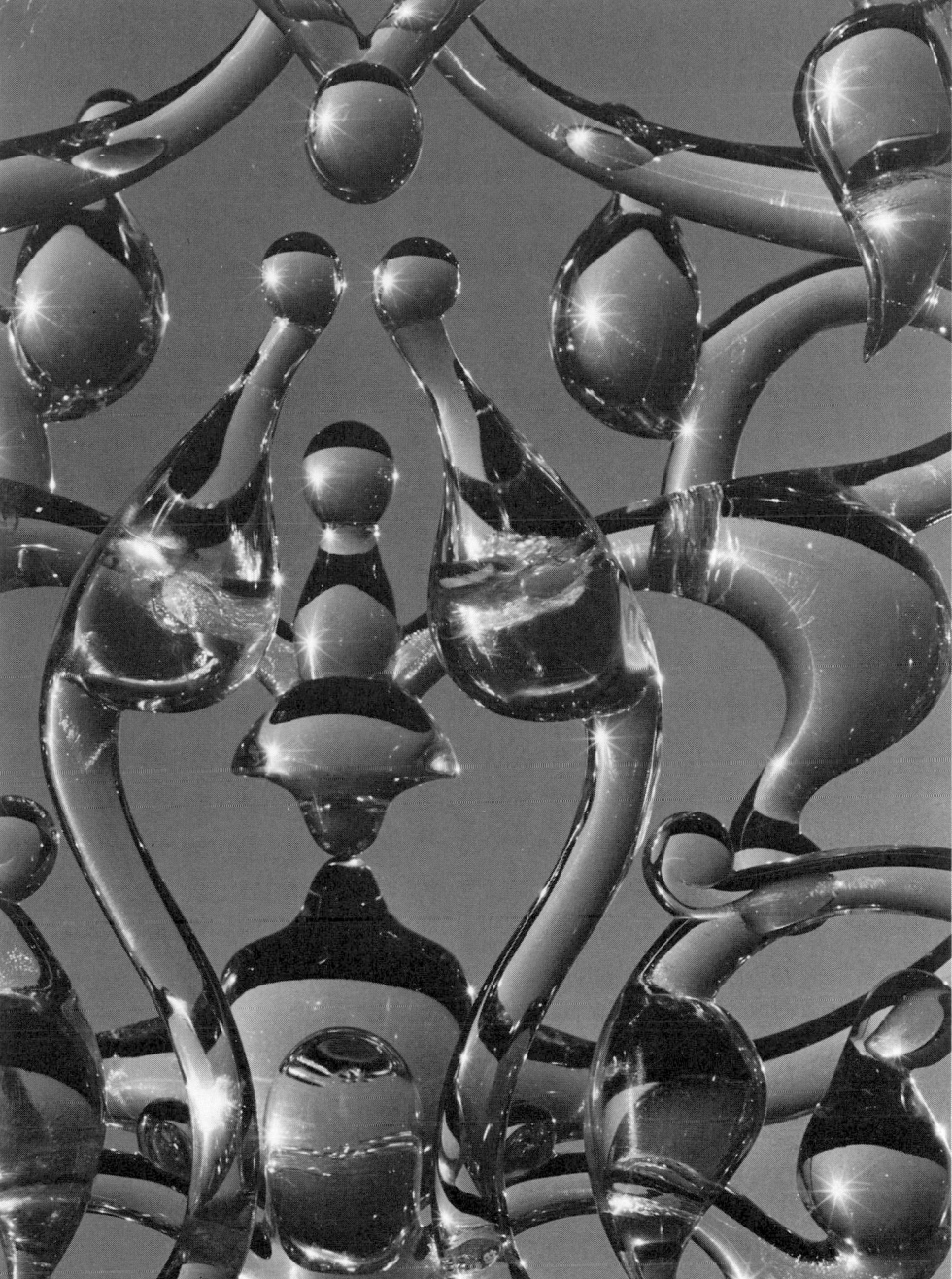

Stephen Kaltenbach: *Still Life*, 1975

KALTENBACH, Stephen.

American. Born in Battle Creek, Michigan, 5 May 1940. Educated at Analy High School, Sebastopol, California, 1958–61; studied at Santa Rosa Junior College, California, 1961–63; and the University of California at Davis, 1963–67, B.A. (honors) 1966, M.A. 1967. Served in the United States Navy, in Seattle, San Francisco, and Yokohama, Japan, 1959–60. Married Abi Allee in 1969. Painter: lives and works in California (lived in New York, 1967–70, and taught at the School of Visual Arts, 1968–70). Professor of Art, California State University at Sacramento, since 1970. Visiting Professor, University of Wisconsin, Madison, 1972–73. Address: Art Department, California State University, 6000 J Street, Sacramento, California, U. S. A.

Individual Exhibitions:

1966	Raymond College, University of the Pacific, Stockton, California
1967	San Francisco Museum of Art
1969	Whitney Museum, New York
1970	Reese Palley Gallery, San Francisco
1971	University of California at Davis
1972	Reese Palley Gallery, San Francisco
1979	Crocker Art Gallery, Sacramento, California

Selected Group Exhibitions:

1964	*Richmond Print and Sculpture Annual*, Richmond Art Center, California
1965	*New Ceramic Forms*, Museum of Contemporary Crafts, New York
1966	*New Modes in California Sculpture*, La Jolla Museum of Art, California
1968	*9 at Leo Castelli*, Castelli Warehouse, New York
1969	*Language 3*, Dwan Gallery, New York
	When Attitudes Become Form, Kunsthalle, Berne
	Concept Art. No Objects, Städtisches Museum, Leverkusen, West Germany
1970	*Information*, Museum of Modern Art, New York
	Biennale, Tokyo
1972	*Sacramento Artists*, Crocker Gallery, Sacramento, California

Collections:

Museum of Modern Art, New York; Oberlin College Art Museum, Ohio; Los Angeles County Museum of Art.

Publications:

By KALTENBACH: articles—text in *Studio International* (London), July/August 1970; "Interview with Stephen Kaltenbach by Cindy Nemser" in *Artforum* (New York), November 1970.

On KALTENBACH: books—*Arte Povera/Land Art* by Germano Celant, Turin 1970; *The Purposes of Art* by Doctor Elsen, New York 1970; *6 Years: The Dematerialization of the Art Object* by Lucy Lippard, New York 1972; *Conceptual Art* by Ursula Meyer, New York 1972.

I am interested in making art which is meaningful to people who haven't been trained to view art. In working toward an expression of this kind I am involved with both real and abstract visual elements. The Objective subject matter is drawn from human archetypes such as Father, Sky, death, earth, home. The abstract aspect of the work is derived through two principles. First there is the fact that on a fine scale reality is composed of abstract elements, and also that abstract and real form are distinguished by their degree of familarity. Both can exhibit the same visual characteristics. The visual qualities I work with on the abstract level of my painting are the same ones predominant in natural and man-made aesthetic archetypes such as the crown jewels, a sunset, the redwood forests. Those qualities are light broken by form: light, shade, shadow, reflection, and refraction; and light penetrating form: luminescence, translucency and transparency.

I am also interested in maintaining my art as a public visual statement, and avoiding its redefinition as a private possession of value or a financial investment. In working toward this goal I've considered various possibilities. The following agreement which was drawn up for my last painting is one such alternative.

Stone Maple

1. Ownership of this painting has been surrendered and relinquished. The painting carries with it no ownership rights. At no time shall it be owned by anyone.

2. No Monetary value shall be assigned or given to the painting for insurance or any other purpose.

3. Custody of the painting is subject to the following:
   a) Only museums open to the general public may exhibit the painting.
   b) Each museum shall retain the painting for a period of one year or longer as set forth below.
   c) Each museum, while in custody of the painting, shall notify as many other museums as possible that custody of the painting is available under the conditions specified herein. Such notification shall be made during the first three months of the above one year period. Custody shall pass to the museum first responding to the notification, and this museum shall pay the expenses of crating and shipping the painting to its next destination.
   d) If after making the painting available as set forth above, the museum in custody receives no request for the painting, the museum shall retain possession for additional successive one year periods during which it shall continue to offer possession to other museums.

4. No Museum shall incur any financial liability whatsoever on account of its custody of the painting nor shall any museum have any financial responsibility in connection with the condition of the painting or otherwise.

—Steve Kaltenbach

"Portrait of My Father" is an historical, personal painting by Stephen Kaltenbach, filled with references to the long decay of time, as evidenced in the seven years of painting Kaltenbach has thus far spent on the work. The father lies on his side, close to the ground, with a wide and long, whitish beard, eyes gazing outward. The painting, based on a photograph taken before his father's death, measures 9^1/$_2$ feet high by 14^1/$_2$ feet wide, thus beginning to impose the sadness of time into the distance and immensity of space. The sadness works itself from time into scale.

The painting has a photo-realistic effect, yet underneath the imagery is a more precise and difficult array of 10th century Islamic arabesque patterning, adding a layered, three-dimensional quality to the coloration. The colors therefore become more complex, shifting and transposing coloration in the interplay of layers of paint. Through the Islamic arabesque referencing, another culture is added to the father, a layer of emotional civilization is transferred to personal history. These arabesques, and this history, are not idle designs, but an intricate, fastidious alignment of imagery into history, of time directing itself toward the historical past, and thus working against the decay of future time.

The painting also marks for Kaltenbach a release of conceptual energies into a large, monumental work. His earlier pieces were all of a situational and ideational nature, serving to execute the type of actions mandated by the 1960's and early 1970's. One piece, for example, he chose to distribute from gallery to gallery, without ownership as a possible option. The work was to travel forever, from place to place. Here though, in "Portrait of My Father," he has chosen a large painting from which to anchor imagery, content and deep feeling. The complexity of his earlier activities remains, as does the scale.

—John Robinson

KANOVITZ, Howard.

American. Born in Fall River, Massachusetts, 9 February 1929. Educated at Providence College, Rhode Island, 1945–49, B.S. 1949; studied at Rhode Island School of Design, Providence, 1949–51; New School for Social Research, New York, 1951; and privately, with Franz Kline, New York, 1951–52. Married Mary Rattray in 1961; daughter: Cleo. Travelled as jazz musician in the United States, 1943–50; moved to New York, 1951; worked as window display artist, B. Altman, and freelance, New York, 1951–56; independent artist, since 1952: travelled extensively in France, Italy, Spain and Morocco, 1956–58; returned to New York, 1958; taught painting and design, Brooklyn College, New York, 1961–64; taught foundation design, Pratt Institute, New York, 1964–66; used air brush and spray gun designs, New York, 1967; lived in Cologne, 1971–72, and in London, 1972–73; returned to New York, 1974; produced, directed and narrated film *Hampton's Drive-In,* New York, 1974; taught painting, Southhampton College, Southhampton, New York, 1977–78; lived and worked in Berlin, 1979; taught painting, School of Visual Arts, New York, 1981–85. Recipient:DAAD Fellowship, to West Berlin, 1979. Agent: Marlborough Gallery, 40 West 57th Street, New York, New York 10019. Address: 463 Broome Street, New York, New York 10013, U. S. A.

Individual Exhibitions:

1962	Stable Gallery, New York
1964	Fall River Art Association, Massachusetts
1966	Jewish Museum, New York
1969	Waddell Gallery, New York (twice)
1970	Galerie M. E. Thelen, Cologne
	Benson Gallery, Bridgehampton, Long Island, New York
1971	Benson Gallery, Bridgehampton, Long Island, New York
	Waddell Gallery, New York
	Galerie Ostergren, Malmo, Sweden
	Everyman Gallery, New York
1973	Galerie M. E. Thelen, Cologne
	Hedendaagse Kunst, Utrecht
1974	Hedendaagse Kunst, Utrecht
	Wilhelm Lehmbruck Museum, Duisburg, West Germany
1975	Stefanotty Gallery, New York
1977	Galerie Jollenbeck, Cologne
	Benson Gallery, Bridgehampton, Long Island, New York
1978	Alex Rosenberg Gallery, New York
1979	Akademie der Künste, Berlin (retrospective)
	Kestner-Gesellschaft, Hannover (retrospective)
	Kunstverein, Freiburg (retrospective)
	Forum Künste, Rottweil (retrospective)
1982	Alex Rosenberg Gallery, New York
1986	Benson Gallery, Southampton, Long Island, New York
1987	Galerie Inge Baecker, Cologne
1988	Marlborough Gallery, New York

Selected Group Exhibitions:

1969	*Paintings from the Photo,* Riverside Museum, New York
1971	*Radical Realism,* Museum of Contemporary Art, Chicago
1972	*Sharp Focus Realism,* Sidney Janis Gallery, New York
1973	*Photo-Realism,* Serpentine Gallery, London

Howard Kanovitz: *Moonlit Wall,* 1984

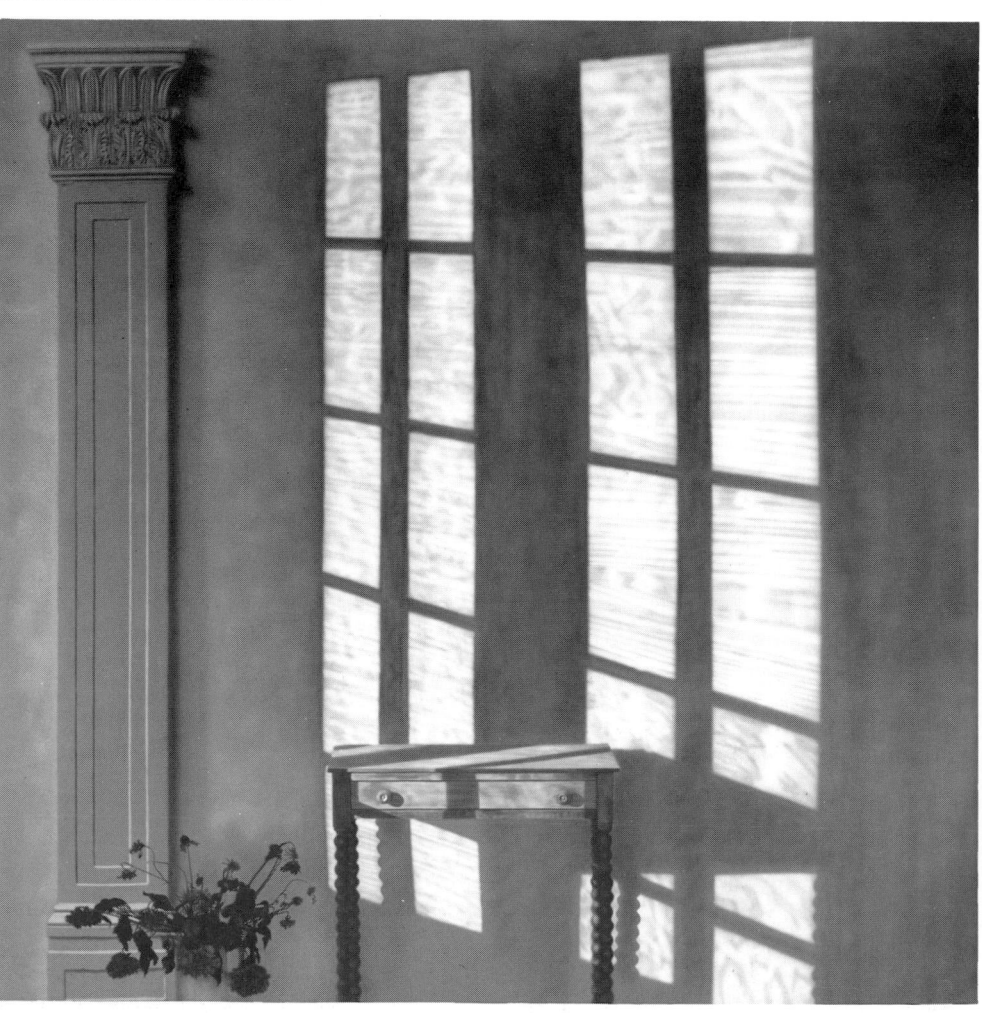

1974 *American Hyperrealists, European Realists,* Kestner-Gesellschaft, Hannover (toured Europe)

1977 *Documenta 6,* Kassel, West Germany

1978 *Aspects of Realism,* Guild Hall, East Hampton, New York

1980 *Portraits Real and Imaginary,* Guild Hall, East Hampton, New York

1982 *Spiegel-Bilder,* Wilhelm-Lehmbruck Museum, Duisburg, West Germany (travelled to West Berlin)

1984 *Automobile and Culture,* Los Angeles Museum of Contemporary Art

Collections:

Whitney Museum, New York; Guild Hall of East Hampton, New York; Museum of Art, Indianapolis; Neue Galerie der Stadt, Aachen; Wallraf-Richartz Museum, Cologne; Wilhelm Lehmbruck Muscum, Duisburg, West Germany; Museum Moderner Kunst, Vienna; Boymans van Beuningen Museum, Rotterdam; Museum of Contemporary Art, Utrecht; Sara Hilden Collection, Museum Atheneum, Helsinki.

Publications:

On KANOVITZ: books—*Howard Kanovitz,* exhibition catalogue, by Sam Hunter, New York 1966; *Neue Formen des Bildes* by Udo Kultermann, Tübingen, West Germany 1969; *Howard Kanovitz,* exhibition catalogue, by Sam Hunter, New York 1969; *Howard Kanovitz,* exhibition catalogue, by Udo Kultermann, Cologne 1970; *Radikaler Realismus* by Udo Kultermann, Tübingen, West Germany 1972; *The Painter and the Photograph, from Delacroix to Warhol* by Van Deren Coke, Albuquerque, New Mexico 1972; *Sign and Image* by Ichiro Haryu, Tokyo 1973; *Man-Made Nature* by Yusuke Nakahara, Tokyo 1973; *American Art of the 20th Century* by Sam Hunter, New York 1973; *Kanovitz,* exhibition catalogue, by Udo Kultermann, Duisburg, West Germany 1974; *Howard Kanovitz,* exhibition catalogue, by Wouter Kotte, Utrecht 1974; *Howard Kanovitz,* exhibition catalogue, by Dieter Wellershoff, Cologne 1977; *Super Realism* by Edward Lucie-Smith, London 1979; *Between Worlds: Howard Kanovitz,* exhibition catalogue by Jorn Merkert, Berlin and Hannover 1979; *Howard Kanovitz: Works of the 1980s,* exhibition catalogue with text by Peter Frank, New York 1988.

I have been turning my attention to figures recently and have a very big composition in mind, a group of three men and five women on a terrace. They are interestingly situated as regards my preoccupation with transparencies. The scene is set around a sliding glass door which is half open. Two figures are in front of the glass door, three are seen in the interior of the room, two are behind the glass, and one (myself) is reflected in it. There is something of Velasquez' "Meninas" in it, and now that I have seen the Picasso exhibition, I keep thinking that this work should be my "Demoiselles d'Avignon," a grand, firm composition but loaded with open-ended inquiry. I am just at the foothills of this mountain.

Now I am making paintings and sculptural works which involve my interest in appearance, illusion, and character. I use a precisionist approach, crystallizing my images so that they go beyond realism into an area that is similar to trompe-l'oeil. I use my own photography as the source of my painted images.

The relationship in my painting between light and subject becomes the basis of the character specific to each work, transforming the subject and sometimes merging it with the atmosphere of the painting. By emphasising the interaction of light and form, developed from my involvement with photography, I increase the overall intensity of the painting, thus heightening the form in its engagement with light.

My recent work is a new aspect of an idea which originally occupied me from 1967 to 1970, namely the depiction of such architectural subjects as windows, doors and walls, often with cut-out silhouetted life size figures. Together, these formed environments are partaking of real space. But these works, still fundamentally two-dimensional, could only suggest the prospect of sculpture. What is now evolving combines aspects of painted illusion with three-dimensional construction. The result places these new

works solidly in real space while asserting a specific mood in the context of an ethereal play of light.

—Howard Kanovitz

The work of Howard Kanovitz is one of the pioneering achievements toward the reintegration of the realist tradition into contemporary art. Along with parallel, but different, approaches by artists such as Philip Pearlstein, Alfred Leslie, Richard Estes, and Malcolm Morley, Kanovitz created a basis for a complex realism and the various facets that followed. His realism is a fresh reappraisal of the urban environment of New York in the 1960's and 70's and thus different from all the earlier types of realist painting. Among the several innovations of his artistic approach is the democratization of subject matter, which includes portraits of his friends, major figures of the New York art scene, banal objects taken from the daily environment of the artist, popular media imagery and objects from the world of advertising—all themes reflecting a specific and unique iconography and a real-life approach to the perception of a real environment.

Like the Florentine painters Masaccio, Andrea del Castagno and Uccello in their time, Kanovitz established methods by which it was possible to visually understand and represent the complex and sophisticated cultural milieu in his time. He developed a specific technique, including photography, opaque projection, and silk screen methods, and with these achieved an appropriate documentation of the multi-layered reality of the New York urban scene (*New Yorkers* of 1965; *The Opening* of 1967). In several of his works the process of the development of the painting remains visible to the viewer, while in other works, by means of human scale cut-out figures standing on the floor in front of the painting, the viewing itself becomes the theme (*The People* of 1968). In still other works he inaugurates a new and ambivalent approach of revitalizing the tradition of trompe l'oeil painting (*Projected Man* of 1977).

Since 1971/1972 Kanovitz's use of sophisticated forms of illusion has played an especially important role in his work, which becomes a philosophical challenge that questions the traditional vision of realism. The awareness of this dimension was articulated by Kanovitz himself: "Fidelity to the subject as seen begins to shift as elements not usually associated with subjects take on symbolic importance." The complex formal and iconographic range of Kanovitz's works since 1980 has furthermore increased, and encompasses images of memory, literary analogies and details of the cultural environment of Amagansett, in the State of New York, where Kanovitz lives after extensive travels in Europe during the late 'seventies. His works in recent years include landscapes, still-lifes and scenes with figures—not in the tradition of these categories, but often in a combination, thus constituting new pictorial forms. Consistently through all the various phases of his work Howard Kanovitz is concerned with the reality of seeing. Seeing and knowing, the problematic and human dimension of perception, are the main concern of the artist. The art of Howard Kanovitz reflects on the process and essence of painting, on the continuity of an art form which opens new perspectives not only for the eye but also for the mind, and thus is in line with the general reflected consciousness of our time. The eternal question of how reality can be perceived has been transcended into a creative and visual articulation of the unsolvable question of what reality is.

—Udo Kultermann

KANTOR, Tadeusz.

Polish. Born in Wielopole, 16 March 1915. Studied at the Academy of Fine Arts, Krakow, 1936-39: influenced by Stanislaw Ignacy Witkiewicz and Bruno

Schulz. Served in the Polish Resistance, directing underground theatre, Krakow, 1942-44. Married the painter and actress Maria Stangret in 1962. Worked as a stage designer in theatres in Krakow, Warsaw, and throughout Poland, 1944-55. Independent painter and graphic artist, Krakow and Warsaw, since 1948: organized first postwar exhibition of contemporary art, Krakow, 1948; founder-director, Cricot 2 theatre group, Krakow, 1956. Nominated Professor, Academy of Fine Arts, Krakow, 1949, 1968; Visiting Professor, Academy of Fine Arts, Hamburg, 1961. Recipient: Painting Prize, *Bienal de Sao Paulo,* Brazil, 1969; Premio Roma Medal, Galleria Nazionale d'Arte Moderna, Rome, 1969; Tadeusz Boy-Zelenski Theatre Critics' Prize, Warsaw, 1977; Comune di Roma Mayor's Medal, Rome, 1978; Cyprian Norwid Art Critics' Prize, Warsaw, 1978; Rembrandt Prize, Goethe Foundation, 1978; Comune di Milano Mayor's Prize, Milan, 1979; Comune di Firenze Mayor's Gold Medal, Florence, 1980; Gold Medal, City of Gdansk, 1980. Agent: Galeria Foksal, U1. Foksal l/4, Box 256, Warsaw 1. Addresses: Theatre Cricot 2 Centre (Cricoteca), Kanonicza Street 5, Krakow, Poland; and Elblaska Street 6/11, Krakow, Poland.

Individual Exhibitions:

1956 Galeria Po Prostu, Warsaw

1957 Galeria Krzysztofory, Cracow

1958 Muzeum Miejskie, Lublin, Poland

Galleri Samklaren, Stockholm

1959 Galerie Legendre, Paris

Kunsthalle, Dusseldorf

1960 Sandberg Gallery, New York

Galerie 54, Gothenberg, Sweden

1961 Galerie Legendre, Paris

1963 Galeria Krzysztofory, Cracow

1964 Galerie Alice Pauli, Lausanne, Switzerland

1965 Galeria Foksal, Warsaw (with Cricot 2)

1966 Galeria S. H. S., Cracow

Galerie Handschin, Basle

Galerie de l'Université, Paris

Galleri Pierre, Stockholm

Kunsthalle, Baden-Baden, West Germany

1967 Galeria Foksal, Warsaw

Osieke, Baltic shore, Poland (happening)

Galeria Krzysztofory, Cracow

1968 Kunsthalle, Nuremberg (2 performance-exhibitions)

Galeria Foksal, Warsaw

Kunsthalle, Nuremberg (tableau vivant)

Galeria Krzysztofory, Cracow

1970 Galeria Foksal, Warsaw

1971 Musée des Arts Décoratifs, Lausanne, Switzerland

Henie-Onstad Kunstsenter, Oslo

Atelier des Recherches Théatrales, Dourdan, France

Galeria Foksal, Warsaw

1972 Galeria Desa, Cracow

1973 Galeria Foksal, Warsaw

1975 *Emballages,* Museum Sztuki, Lodz, Poland

Kulturhuset, Stockholm

1976 Henie-Onstad Kunstsenter, Oslo

Galeria Zapiecek, Warsaw

Emballages 1960–1976, Whitechapel Art Gallery, London

Riverside Studios, Hammersmith, London (with Cricot 2)

1977 Galerie Ricard, Nuremberg, West Germany

1982 Galerie de France, Paris

Riverside Studios, Hammersmith, London

1986 Galerie Eva Poll, West Berlin

Selected Group Exhibitions:

1948 *Modern Art in Poland Since World War II,* Krakow

1957 *Grupa Krakowska,* Krakow

1958 *Documenta II,* Museum Fridericianum, Kassel, West Germany (and *Documenta 6,* 1977)

1960 *30th Biennale,* Venice

1963 *Polish Painting,* Museum Folkwang, Essen, West Germany

1965 *Kunst und Theater,* Kunsthalle, Baden-Baden, West Germany

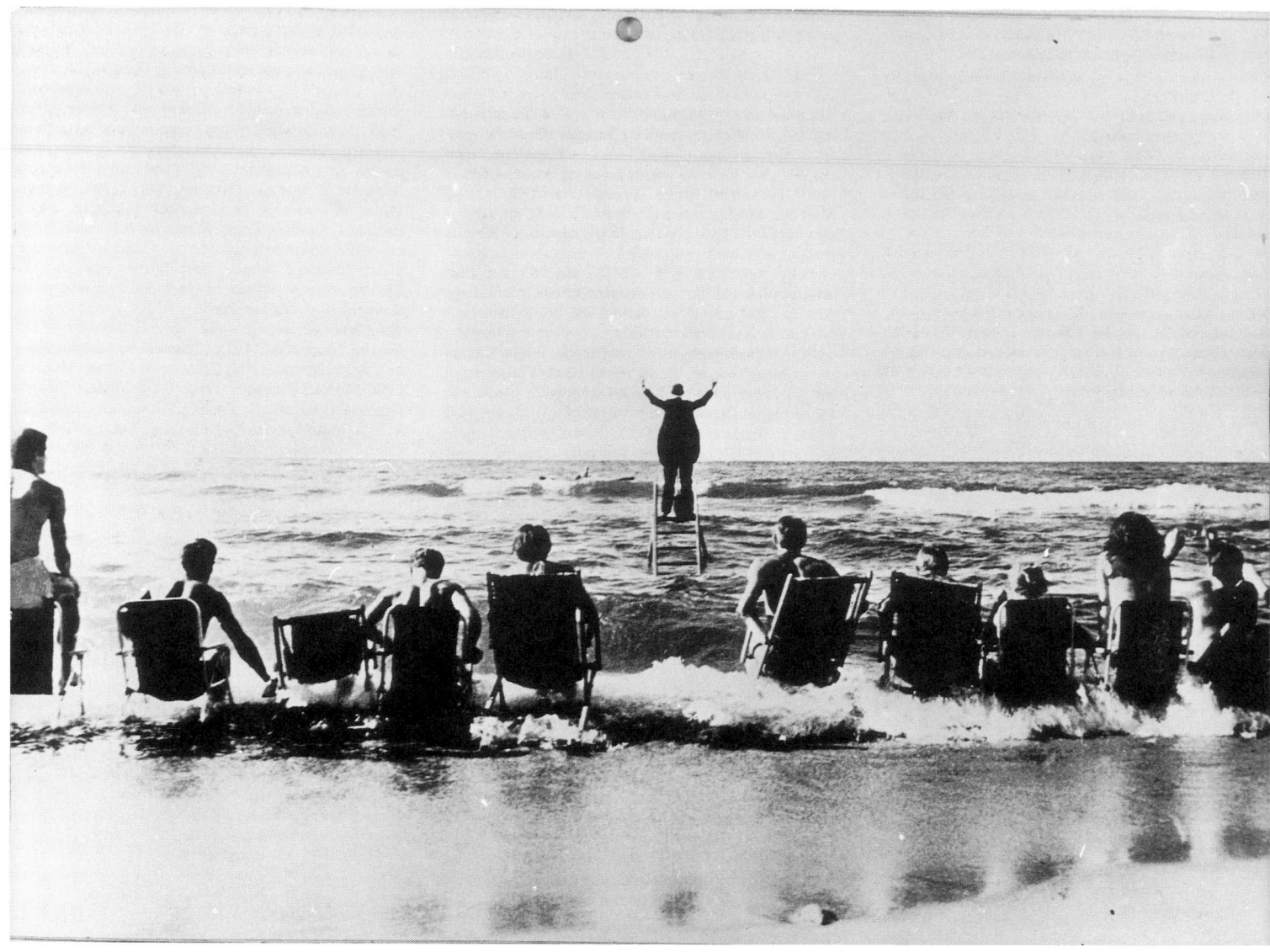

Tadeusz Kantor: *Panoramic Sea-Happening, Osieki, Baltic Seashore,* 1967

1967   *Bienal de Sao Paulo,* Brazil
1970   *Happening und Fluxus,* Kunstverein, Cologne
1978   *Painters from the Cricot 2 Theatre,* Rome

Collections:

Muzeum Sztuki, Lodz, Poland.

Publications:

By KANTOR: books—*Emballages,* Warsaw 1976; *Le Theatre de la Mort,* Paris 1978; *La Classa Morta,* with photos by Maurizio Buscarina, Milan 1981; *Wielopole Wielopole,* Milan 1981; *Metamorphosis,* Paris 1982; *Le Theatre Cricot 2,* Paris 1983.

On KANTOR: books—*Happening und Fluxus,* exhibition catalogue compiled by Hanns Sohm, Cologne 1976; *Tadeusz Kantor: Emballages,* exhibition catalogue with texts by Wieslaw Borowski and Ryszard Stanisklawski, Lodz 1975; *Tadeusz Kantor: Emballages 1960–76,* exhibition catalogue with essay by Ryszard Stanislawski, London 1976; *Tadeusz Kantor* by Wieslaw Borowski, Warsaw 1982.

In artistic development there are frequent moments when the vital creative act degenerates into a pursuit of a convention, when a work of art no longer involves any risk, adventure, revolt or uncertainty and becomes respectable and well established in its seriousness, dignity and prestige.

When this happens, the wisest thing to do is to leave the recognized stage and to shift to disinterested activities, on the verge of the ridiculous and shameful, deserving scorn and doomed to neglect.

Instinctively, I gave all my attention, and very soon all my passion, to objects of the "lower rank" that normally pass unnoticed, are skipped over, forgotten, and then simply dumped off. I started to collect my own notes, sketches, scraps of paper, hasty records of the "urgent" matters, those early discoveries when nothing is known for certain yet, when the "arrangements" are still under way and it doesn't even occur to make things that are "ready" for consumption, varnished, openly demonstrating the perfection of the work and its maker. . .

The imagination was suddenly no longer a store of materials for constructing and executing pictures, but a space into which objects from my own past were falling, in shape of wrecks or shams, but also not my own, strange, trite, schematic, accidental, mixed with important ones, valuable and negligible, facts, persons, letters, prescriptions, addresses, traces, dates, appointments. It was an inventory without any timing, hierarchy or location. Personally, I was in the midst of all this, without any definite role.

Such an adjustment of my own ambition to "create" near the zero point automatically brought about an essential shift in my attitude towards the past, with its relics and claims, as well as towards the object. For the aim was not to repeat it, but to recapture!

—Tadeusz Kantor

Tadeusz Kantor is one of the central figures of modern Polish art and is one of those whose activities are born from the continual polemics which inspire many artists. His creativity raises problems for debate, not only in the fields of painting and the theatre, but also in the new relationship created between author and audience in many other areas of activity.

Kantor developed artistically under the influence of two great Polish visionaries from the period between the wars: Stanislaw Ignacy Witkiewicz, painter, writer, philosopher and playwright, and Bruno Schulz, draughtsman and writer. Their work can be related very loosely to Surrealism.

Kantor's early artistic formation was completed by the experiences of the occupation of Poland and the terror of the Second World War. His independent theatrical activity began after the war with performances by his underground theatre, at which the audience was amazed by the non-conformity of the stage design and the anti-psychological interpretation of the hero's character. A similar non-conformity was the characteristic feature of his postwar paintings: they were dramatic but not literary compositions, revealing his deep knowledge of the Surrealist theory of painting. Through the work of Kantor and other Cracow painters, Surrealist theory became well known in Polish artistic circles. These same circles had faced moral defeat after the war and were searching for dramatic forms to express their personal nightmare memories. Kantor's independent attitude resulted from the fact that he always considered creativity to be a constantly regenerating phenomenon—that is, an inner pressure to consider one new problem after another.

In the years following 1955 Kantor was the first in Poland to suggest the existence of the unintentional, or spontaneous, gesture in painting: in other words that same improvisation which found its expressive meaning in Informal Art. Later he also realized that a similar shapeless structure could become the characteristic feature of theatrical performances. From 1956 he became, in many ways, a theatre reformer. In his successive productions of S. I. Witkiewicz's plays after 1961, this intentional shapelessness emphasized even more those elements in which we can recognize the origins of Theatre of the Absurd.

In the theatre this fascination with an object translated itself into the creation of wretched junk which disturbed both the course of action and the verbal contacts between the actors. In the Happenings of 1965, it produced a confusion of themes and simultaneous actions with accessories collected from various sources. The origins of this deliberate incoherence in Kantor's happenings can be traced to his earlier productions of Witkiewicz's plays, which contributed such elements as a lack of psychological contact between the actors, and a fragmentation of the script.

A similar incoherence appears in paintings executed at the same time and to some extent in Kantor's more recent works. His technique consists of mixing fragments of objects fixed to the canvas (for instance an umbrella) with traces of themes belonging to the former abstract Informal method.

In all his artistic manifestations, the presence of a letter or an envelope, a pocket, or a wretched traveling bag, plays a significant role. These symbols or keys represent the essence of the fate of a perpetual wanderer, the secrecy and the freedom which Kantor violates by tearing up envelopes and ripping out the inner linings of clothes. In other words, in his paintings and happenings, Kantor violates everyone's fundamental right to intimate secrecy. Moreover, Kantor often expects the audience to participate in this violation of privacy. During the course of a happening in 1967 (*A Letter*), the enthusiastic audience listened carefully to the reading of informal letters from unknown people and then destroyed a huge symbolic writing case. Similarly in *Multipart* the spectators had to complete an unfinished painting (using any free and unrestricted actions) by damaging or destroying it.

Is the *emballage* theme more significant than others and therefore sufficiently representative of Kantor's work? I think so, for several reasons. The most important is that the *emballage* theme is the starting-point for many of Kantor's artistic manifestations and therefore an exhibition with *emballage* as a *leit-motif* documents the work not only of the artist as a painter, but also as an author of happenings, theatrical productions, and events.

Kantor is particularly significant because not only is his vision the equal of other outstanding Polish artists, but he has also managed to bring together the disciplines of painting, theatre design, theatre direction, poetry and the theory of art, which are usually separated into rigid categories. The extraordinary result is in keeping with the power of his personality.

—Ryszard Stanislawski

KAPOOR, Anish.

Indian. Born in Bombay, 12 March 1954. Studied at Hornsey College of Art, London, 1973–77; Chelsea School of Art, London, 1977–78. Independent sculptor, London, since 1979. Instructor in sculpture, Wolverhampton Polytechnic, Staffordshire, 1979–82. Artist-in-Residence, Walker Art Gallery, Liverpool, 1982. Agents: Barbara Gladstone Gallery, 99 Greene Street, New York, New York 10012, U.S.A.; Lisson Gallery, 67 Lisson Street, London NW1 5DA. Address: 33 Coleherne Road, London SW10, England.

Individual Exhibitions:

1980	Studio Patrice Alexandre, Paris
1981	Coracle Press, London
1982	Lisson Gallery, London
	Walker Art Gallery, Liverpool
1983	Galerie 't Venster, Rotterdam
	Walker Art Gallery, Liverpool (travelled to Lyon, France)
	Lisson Gallery, London
1984	Barbara Gladstone Gallery, New York
	Galerie Paul Maenz, Cologne (with Bill Woodrow)
1985	Lisson Gallery, London
	Kunsthalle, Basle (travelled to Eindhoven, Netherlands)
	Institute of Contemporary Art, Boston

Anish Kapoor: *Wound*, 1988

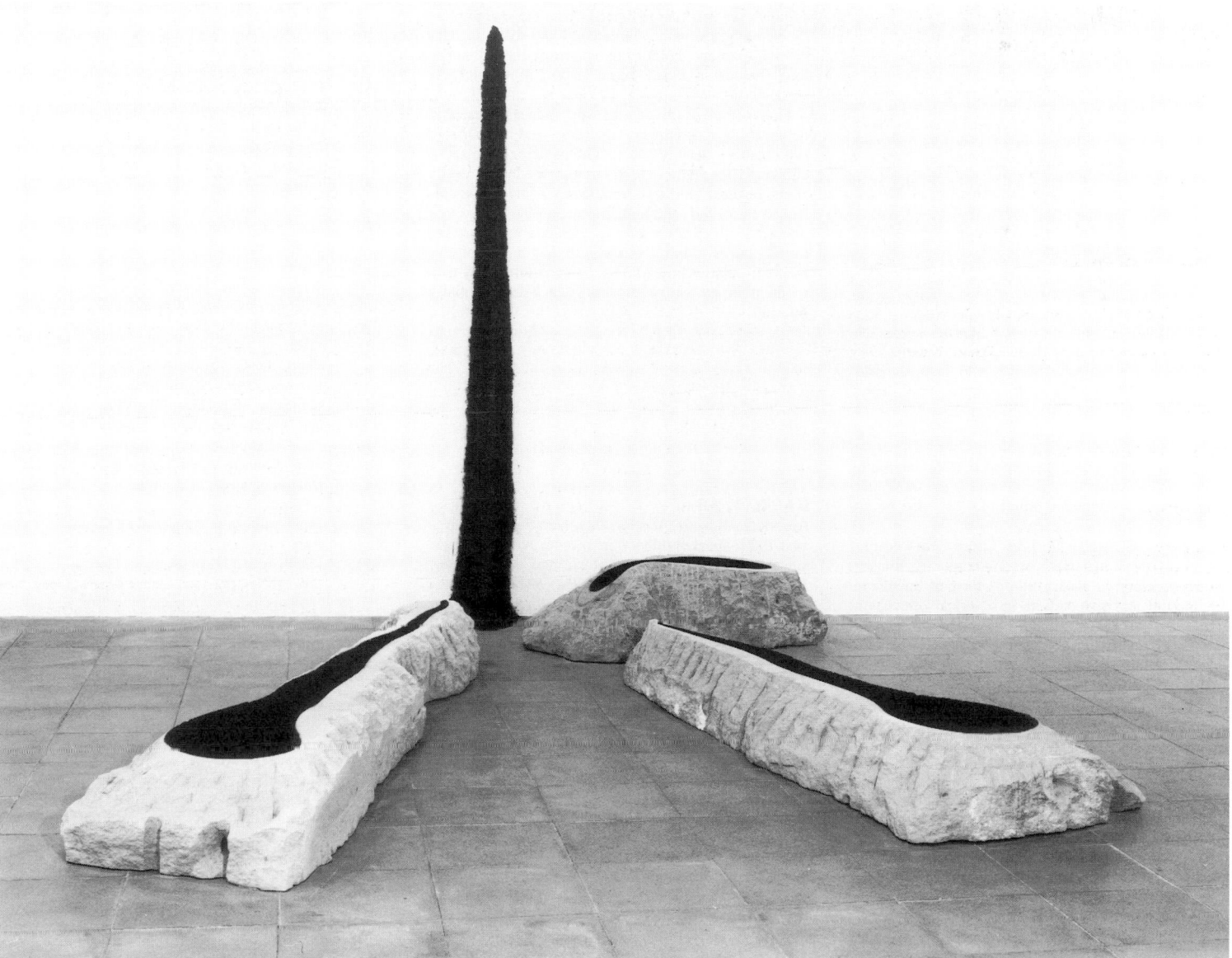

Donald Young Gallery, Chicago (with Bill Woodrow)
1986 Kunstnernes Hus, Oslo
Barbara Gladstone Gallery, New York
Albright-Knox Art Gallery, Buffalo, New York
University of Massachusetts, Amherst
1987 Ray Hughes Gallery, Sydney (travelled to Brisbane)
1988 Lisson Gallery, London

Selected Group Exhibitions:

1974 *Art Into Landscape I,* Serpentine Gallery, London
1975 *Young Contemporaries,* Royal Academy of Art, London
1978 *Northern Young Contemporaries,* Whitworth Art Gallery, Manchester
1981 *British Sculpture in the Twentieth Century: 1951–80,* Whitechapel Art Gallery, London
1983 *The Sculpture Show,* Hayward Gallery/Serpentine Gallery, London
1985 *The British Show,* Art Gallery of Western Australia, Perth (toured Australia and New Zealand)
1987 *A Quiet Revolution: British Sculpture Since 1965,* San Francisco Museum of Modern Art (travelled to Newport Beach, California; Washington, D.C.; Buffalo, New York)

Collections:

Museum of Modern Art, New York; Albright Knox Art Gallery, Buffalo, New York; Walker Art Center, Minneapolis; Stedelijk Museum, Amsterdam; Stedelijk Van Abbemuseum, Eindhoven; Rijkmuseum Kroller-Muller, Otterlo; Walker Art Gallery, Liverpool.

Publications:

On KAPOOR: books—*British Sculpture in the Twentieth Century: 1951–80,* exhibition catalogue edited by Sandy Nairne and Nicolas Serota, London 1981; *Anish Kapoor: Feeling into Form,* exhibition catalogue with essay by Marco Livingstone, Liverpool 1983; *The Sculpture Show,* exhibition catalogue with texts by Fenella Crichton, Stuart Morgan, Bryan Robertson and others, London 1983; *Anish Kapoor,* exhibition catalogue with texts by Jean-Christophe Ammann and Alexander von Graevenstein, Basle 1985; *Currents: Anish Kapoor,* exhibition catalogue with essay by David Joselit, Boston 1985; *The British Show,* exhibition catalogue with text by Stuart Morgan, Perth 1985; *Anish Kapoor,* exhibition catalogue with texts by Lynne Cooke and Arne Malmedal, Oslo 1986; *Anish Kapoor: Recent Sculpture and Drawings,* exhibition catalogue with essay by Helaine Posner, Amherst 1986; *Anish Kapoor,* exhibition catalogue with essay by Helen Raye, Buffalo 1986.

Within the group of so-called 'New Sculptors' brought to international prominence at the beginning of the 1980s, Anish Kapoor represents the most 'hermetic' artist, a characterization that can also be applied to Shirazeh Houshiary.

Kapoor, of Indian origin, does not employ commonly-used materials or contemporary images. On the contrary, he filters out any form of 'mundane' connotation and suspends it in a lyrical dimension. Since his first works around 1970, Kapoor has concentrated on assemblages and the installation of multiple elements in space, in the name of a certain stylistic and cultural eclecticism.

In his sculptures he expresses allegiance to two different cultural traditions—Western and Eastern. In so doing, he permeates his works with ideas gathered during frequent trips to India. These ideas stem from the rediscovery of art, philosophy, mythology, and even everyday life in India, transformed into mysterious plastic and visual equivalents, the origins of which are to be found in his prolific activity as a draughtsman. The precise correspondence between form and content, myth or architectural detail, is often completely accidental. It is the tendency of much Indian culture to express philosophical and spiritual concepts through sensual imagery. Kapoor's forms inherit that tendency: they almost invariably assume a biomorphic or phytomorphic aspect or, at any rate, allude to living organisms. In certain cases they suggest, by means of metaphor, a discourse on the imagery of the human body. Their form is the result of an interpenetration of different forms; it is a complexity of structures seeming to represent the idea of organic accretion, of endogenous proliferation—in a word, of vital rhythm.

In *Hole and Vessel* (1984), for instance, Kapoor accomplishes what can be termed a semantic displacement in the form of a vessel, one that can illustrate at the same time both the idea of a vessel and that of a hole as a container. But such elements, as well as designating items of common use, are treated as symbols of the maternal womb, of the vagina—and therefore of fecundation and birth. The vessel, moreover, alludes to the food that is preserved therein, and enlarges that micro-universe of the 'maternal' by indicating the nutrition and preservation of the species.

Kapoor's sculptures are not easily decoded: symbols are not employed in order to reveal a whole range of meanings, least of all those pertaining to a new definition of sculpture. The use of ensembles of sculptures rather than the single work (which takes on the character of a totem) is aimed at transfiguring the ordinary space of the exhibition into a sacred space. This aspect is then accentuated by the complexity—at times by the extravagance—of forms and of loud colours covering the surfaces of the work. His use of colour is particular and suggestive, since pigments are treated as highly significant elements.

The artist does not confine himself to painting his sculptures, very often made out of wood, cement or gypsum, but onto them he drops pigment in powder form. In such a way, the work is encompassed by colour, even seeming to emerge from the sculpture as its own aggregation. Alternatively, the work appears to sink into the colour: the pigment indeed forms thick haloes of richly hued matter all around the work.

This method of treating the work induces a dialectic between rigid complex structures and impalpable fluid matter—heavily loaded with meaning. The act of allowing pure pigment to fall around the forms recalls ritual gestures, and so accentuates the mysterious allusiveness of the sculpture. In such a way, the work is offered to the viewer not as a unique and absolute object, but is rather given as a dissemination of elements in relationship with space—and ultimately as a moment in a creative process, which is potentially infinite.

—Giorgio Verzotti

KAPROW, Allan.

American. Born in Atlantic City, New Jersey, 23 August 1927; spent childhood in Tucson, Arizona. Studied at the High School of Music and Art, Tucson, 1943–45, New York University, 1945–49, B.A. 1949, Hans Hofmann School of Fine Arts, New York, 1947–48, and New York University, 1949–50; studied art history at Columbia University, New York, under Meyer Schapiro, 1950–52, M.A. 1952, and studied at the New School for Social Research, New York, under John Cage, 1956–58. Married Vaughan Peters in 1955; children: Anton, Amy and Marisa. Performance Artist. Co-Founder, Hansa Gallery, New York, 1952, and Reuben Gallery, New York, 1960; Co-Director, Judson Gallery, New York, 1961. Instructor, 1952–56, and Assistant Professor, 1956–61, Fine Arts Department, Rutgers University, New Brunswick, New Jersey; Lecturer in Aesthetics, Pratt Institute, Brooklyn, New York, 1960–61; Associate Professor of Fine Arts, 1961–66, and Professor, 1966–69, Department of Fine Arts, State University of New York at Stony Brook; Director of Experimental Education, Institute of Contemporary Art, Boston, 1965–66; Co-Director, Project Other Ways, Berkeley, California Public Schools, 1968–69; Associate Dean, 1969–73, and Member of the Faculty, 1973–74, California Institute of the Arts, Valencia. Professor, Visual Arts Department, University of California at San Diego, since 1974. Founding Member, Advanced Placement Committee on Art and Art History, Educational Testing Service and College Entrance Examination Board, Princeton, New Jersey, 1969–72; Member, Board of Trustees, and Chairman of the Education Committee, Museum of Modern Art, Pasadena, California, 1973; Consultant Panelist, Visual Arts Program, National Endowment for the Arts, Washington, D.C., 1975. Recipient: Katherine White Award, New York, 1952; William and Noma Copley Foundation Award, 1963; Guggenheim Fellowship, 1967; Gold Medal, City of Milan, 1971; National Endowment for the Arts Award, 1974; Video Grant, University of California at San Diego, 1975; Annual Award and Gold Medal, Skowhegan School of Painting and Sculpture, Maine, 1975; D.A.A.D. Grant, West Berlin, 1975. Address: 1225 Linda Rosa Avenue, Los Angeles, California 90041, U.S.A.

Individual Shows/Environments/Happenings:

1953 Hansa Gallery, New York
Rutgers Art House, New Brunswick, New Jersey
Earle Pilgrim Gallery, Provincetown, Massachusetts (with L. Johnson)
1954 Hansa Gallery, New York
1955 Urban Gallery, New York
1956 Bernard-Ganymede Gallery, New York
Z & Z Delicatessen, New Brunswick, New Jersey (with George Segal)
The Jewish Community Center, Highland Park, New Jersey
Rutgers Art House, Rutgers University, New Brunswick, New Jersey
1957 Hansa Gallery, New York
Sun Gallery, Provincetown, Massachusetts
1958 Hansa Gallery, New York
Centaur Restaurant, New York
Untitled, Douglass College, New Brunswick, New Jersey
Untitled, Hansa Gallery, New York
1959 *Intermission Piece,* Reuben Gallery, New York
18 Happenings in 6 Parts, Reuben Gallery, New York
1960 *An Apple Shrine,* Judson Gallery, New York
1961 *A Spring Happening,* Reuben Gallery, New York
1962 *A Service for the Dead,* Maidman Playhouse, New York
Words, Smolin Gallery, New York
Chicken, YMHA, Philadelphia
Courtyard, Mills Hotel, New York
1963 *Bon Marché,* Bon Marché Department Store, Paris
1964 *Eat,* Old Ebling Brewery, The Bronx, New York
Birds, Southern Illinois University, Carbondale
Orange, unused citrus warehouse, Coral Gables, Florida
Paper, parking lot, University of California, Berkeley
1965 *Soap,* city and beach, Sarasota, Florida
Calling, New York and George Segal's woods, New Brunswick, New Jersey
1966 *Self-Service,* Boston, New York and Los Angeles areas
Gas, Hamptons area of Long Island (with Charles Frazier)
1967 *Interruption,* State University of New York at Stony Brook
Fluids, Los Angeles area
Moving, Chicago Area
Art Museum, Pasadena, California (retrospective; toured the United States)
Museum of Contemporary Art, Chicago (twice: once with Wolf Vostell)
1968 *Runner,* Washington University, St. Louis
Transfer, Wesleyan University, Middletown, Connecticut
Record I, University of Texas, Austin
Record II, University of Texas, Austin
Round Trip, State University of New York, Albany

	Arrivals, Nassau Community College, Hempstead, New York
	Population, Colby Junior College, New London, New Hampshire
	Overtime, University of California, San Diego
	Travelog, Fairleigh Dickinson University, Madison, New Jersey
	Refills, Hofstra University, New York
1969	John Gibson Gallery, New York
	Charity, Project Other Ways, Berkeley, California
	Pose, Project Other Ways, Berkeley, California
	Fine!, Project Other Ways, Berkeley, California
	Shape, Project Other Ways, Berkeley, California
	Hello, WGBH-TV, Boston
	Giveaway, Project Other Ways, Berkeley, California
	Purpose, Project Other Ways, Berkeley, California
	Transplant, University of Southern Nevada, Las Vegas
	Dial, San Francisco Art Institute
	Takeoff, U.S. International University, La Jolla, California
	Takeoff II, Sacramento State University, California
	Course, University of Iowa, Iowa City
	Homemovies, C. & D. Schmidt wedding, New Jersey and New York
1970	*Moon Sounds,* H. & R. Blau wedding, El Mirage Dry Lake, California
	Graft, Kent State University, Ohio
	Level, Aspen Institute of Contemporary Art, Colorado
	Don't, Los Angeles County Parks
	Publicity, California Institute of the Arts, Burbank
	Car Spaces, California Institute of the Arts, Burbank
	Tracts, California Institute of the Arts, Burbank
	Sweet Wall, Galerie René Block, Berlin
1971	Galerie Baecker, Bochum, West Germany
	Dial II, California Institute of the Arts, Valencia
	Good Morning!, San Francisco State University
	Print Out, Cultural Affairs Commission, Milan
	City Works, Galerie Baecker, Bochum, West Germany
	Calendar, California Institute of the Arts, Valencia
	Scales, California Institute of the Arts, Valencia
1972	*Message Units,* California Institute of the Arts, Valencia
	Baggage, Rice University, Houston
	Meters, California Institute of the Arts, Valencia
	Meteorology, Galerie Baecker, Bochum, West Germany
	Easy, California Institute of the Arts, Valencia
	Idea, Portland Center for the Visual Arts, Oregon
	Entr'acte, California Institute of the Arts, Valencia
1973	*Loss,* New York
	Highs, Kansas University, Lawrence
	Basic Thermal Units, Folkwang Museum, Essen
	Clockwork, California Institute of the Arts, Valencia
	Wink, California Institute of the Arts, Valencia
	Art Condition, California Institute of the Arts, Valencia
	Routine, Portland Center for the Visual Arts, Oregon
1974	*2nd Routine,* Stefanotty Gallery, New York
	Galleria La Bertesca, Milan
	Galerie Baecker, Bochum, West Germany
	Galleria Martano, Turin
	Galleria Martini & Ronchetti, Genoa
	On Time, Galerie Gerald Piltzer, Paris
1975	*Rates of Exchange,* Stefanotty Gallery, New York
	Echo-logy, Merrieworld West Gallery, Far Hills, New Jersey
	Comfort Zones, Galeria Vandres, Madrid
	Match, von der Heydt Museum, Wuppertal, West Germany
	Warm-Ups, Center for Advanced Visual Studies, Massachusetts Institute of Technology, Cambridge
	Likely Stories, Galleria Luciano Anselmino, Milan
	Useful Fictions, Galleria Schema, Florence
1979	University of Northern Iowa, Cedar Falls
	Ullrich Museum, Wichita, Kansas
1980	Pasadena Film Forum, California
1981	Provincetown Art Center, Massachusetts
1986	Museum am Ostwall, Dortmund, West Germany

Selected Group Exhibitions:

1957	*The New York School—Second Generation,* Jewish Museum, New York
1961	*Environments, Situations, Spaces,* Martha Jackson Gallery, New York
1965	*11 from the Reuben Gallery,* Guggenheim Museum, New York
1969	*Software,* Jewish Museum, New York
1970	*Happening und Fluxus,* Kölnischer Kunstverein, Cologne
1973	*Aktionen der Avant-garde,* Neue Berliner Kunstverein, Berlin
1974	*Poets of the Cities, New York and San Francisco, 1950–1965,* Museum of Fine Arts, Dallas (toured the United States, 1974–75)
1975	*Activity Dokumente 1968–76,* Kunsthalle, Bremen
1981	*California Performance: Now and Then,* Museum of Contemporary Art, Chicago
1987	*Berlinart 1961–87,* Museum of Modern Art, New York (travelled to San Francisco)

Collections:

Museum of Modern Art, New York.

Publications:

By KAPROW: books—*Assemblage, Environments and Happenings,* New York 1966; *Some Recent Happenings,* New York 1966; *Untitled Essay and Other Works,* New York 1967; *Echo-logy,* New York 1975; *Rates of Exchange,* New York 1975; *Warm-Ups,* Cambridge, Massachusetts 1975; *Sweet Wall Testimonials,* Berlin 1976; articles—"Rub-a-Dub, Rub-a-Dub" in *Anthologist* (New Brunswick, New Jersey), Spring 1957; "The Legacy of Jackson Pollock" in *Artnews* (New York), October 1958; "The Demiurge" in *Anthologist* (New Brunswick, New Jersey), Spring 1959; "One Chapter from 'The Principles of Modern Art' " in *It Is* (New York). Autumn 1959; "Happenings in the New York Scene" in *Artnews* (New York), May 1961, reprinted in *Design Annual* (Bombay), July 1962, and as "Happenings in New York" in *Randstad* (Amsterdam), 1966; "About Words" in *Randstad* (Amsterdam), 1966; "Impurity" in *Artnews* (New York), January 1963; "A Service for the Dead" in *Art International* (Zurich), 25 January 1963; "An Artist's Story of a Happening" in the *New York Times,* 6 October 1963; "The World View of Alfred Jensen" in *Artnews* (New York), December 1963; "Effect of Recent Art upon the Teaching of Art" in the *Art Journal* (New York), Winter 1963–64; "Nature in the Art of Irving Kriesberg" in *Art International* (Lugano, Switzerland), 16 January 1964; "Segal's Vital Mummies" in *Artnews* (New York), February 1964; "What Is an 'Environment' " in *Vogue* (New York), April 1964; "The Happening" in the *Ithaca Journal* (Ithaca, New York), 9 May 1964; "Should the Artist Be a Man of the World" in *Artnews* (New York), October 1964; "Eating" in *Second Coming Magazine* (New York), January 1965; "Eat" in *Tulane Drama Review* (New Orleans), Winter 1965; "Possibility of Contemporary Art" in *Mizue* (Tokyo), January 1966; "Hans Hofmann" in the *Village Voice* (New York), 24 February 1966; "The Happenings Are Dead, Long Live the Happenings" in *Artforum* (New York), March 1966, reprinted in *Aujourd'hui: Art et Architecture* (Paris), January 1967; "Experimental Art" in *Artnews* (New York), March 1966; "Female Art: No Games" in the *Village Voice* (New York), 28 April 1966; "Untitled Manifesto" in *Manifestos,* edited by Dick Higgins, New York 1966; "Self-Service" in *Soundings* (Long Island), Spring 1966; "Letter to the Editor" in *Tulane Drama Review* (New Orleans), Summer 1966; "Happenings: Interview mit Allan Kaprow" in *Magazin Kunst* (Mainz), 3rd quarter 1966; "Total Theatre" in *World Theatre 2,* Paris 1966; "The Sensibility of the 60's" in *Art in America* (New York), January/February 1967; "Death in the Museum" in *Arts Magazine* (New York), February 1967; "Jackson Pollock: An Artists Symposium, Part 1" in *Artnews* (New York), April 1967; "The End of the Concert Hall" in *The Statesman* (Long Island), 3 May 1967; "An Interview with Allan Kaprow," with Martin Fishgold, in *Cacophony* (Sea Cliff, New York), Spring 1967; "Pop Art: Past, Present and Future" in the *Malahat Review* (Victoria, British Columbia), July 1967; "What Is a Museum," with Robert Smithson, in the *Museum World Arts Yearbook,* New York 1967; "Gas" in *Theatre Experiment* by Michael Benedikt, New York 1967; "Pinpointing Happenings" in *Artnews* (New York), October 1967; "Happenings in the New York Scene" in the *Modern American Theatre: A Collection of Critical Essays,* edited by Alvin Kernan, New Jersey 1967; "The Happenings Are Dead, Long Live the Happenings" in *Arts in Society* (Madison, Wisconsin), 1968; interview, with Richard Kostelanatz, in *The Theatre of Mixed Means* by Kostelanatz, New York 1968; "Art and Education," with Jim Hinton and Herbert Kohl, in *Cultural Affairs* (New York), March 1968; "Extensions in Time and Space," interview, with Richard Schechner, in the *Drama Review* (New York), Spring 1968; "A Conversation with Allan Kaprow," with Donald J. Cyr, in *Arts and Activities* (New York), April 1969; "6 Ordinary Happenings" in *Aktionen* by Wolf Vostell, Hamburg 1970; "Home Movies" and "Moon Sounds" in *Arts in Society* (Madison, Wisconsin), Fall Winter 1970, "Days Off" in *Sipario* (Milan), March 1970; "Mid 20th Century Environments and Happenings" in *The Changing World and Man,* edited by Chandler M. Brooks, Stony Brook, New York 1970; "The Education of the Un-Artist, Part 1" in *Artnews* (New York), February 1971; "Publicity" in *Box* (Burbank, California), March 1971; interview, with Robert Filliou, in *Teaching and Learning as Performing Arts* by Filliou, Cologne and New York 1970; "The Education of the Un-Artist, Part 2" in *Artnews* (New York), May 1972; "The Education of the Un-Artist, Part 3" in *Art in America* (New York), January/February 1974; "L'Utilité d'un Passé Determinée" in *Opus International* (Paris), March 1974; "Easy" in *Art in America* (New York), July/August 1974; "Baggage" in *Source* (Sacramento, California), Spring 1974; "Old Wine, New Bottles" in *Artforum* (New York), June 1974; "Formalism: Flogging a Dead Horse" in *Quadrille* (Bennington, Vermont), Fall 1974; "Hello—Plan and Execution" in *Art Rite* (New York), Autumn 1974; "Routine" in *Journal of the Los Angeles Institute of Contemporary Art,* February 1974; "Animation: Stephan von Huene's Sound Sculptures" in *Sound Sculptures,* edited by John Grayson, Vancouver 1975; "Air Condition" in *Journal of the Los Angeles Institute of Contemporary Art,* June/July 1975; "Easy Activity" in *Art Studies for an Art Editor: 25 Essays in Memory of Milton S. Fox,* New York 1975.

On KAPROW: books—*Happenings* by Jürgen Becker and Wolf Vostell, Hamburg 1965; *A Primer of Happenings and Time/Space Art,* New York 1965; *Happenings* by Michael Kirby, New York 1965; *Le Happening* by Jean-Jacques Lebel, Paris 1966; articles—"Mr Kaprow's 18 Happenings" by J. H. Livingston in the *Village Voice* (New York), 7 October 1959; "Allan Kaprow" by Toshi Ichiyanagi in *Bijutsu Techo* (Tokyo), Fall 1965; "Allan Kaprow" by Dick Higgins in *Arts in Society* (Madison, Wisconsin), Spring/Summer 1968; "Allan Kaprow" by Kuniharu Akiyama and "Allan Kaprow" by Yusuke Narahara in *Bijutsu Techo* (Tokyo), August 1968; "Allan Kaprow" by Mirella Bandini in *Data* (Milan), June/August 1975; article by Jonathan Gray in *Arts Magazine* (New York), September 1976.

Allan Kaprow's stature as practitioner and theoretician in the field of Performance Art is well earned by his over 25-year-long creation and evolution from the late 1950's until the present. This respected pioneer in the field has a reputation and influence which covers New York, California and Europe.

Beginning around 1956, Kaprow began making large Assemblages incorporating a variety of found objects from the surrounding environment and also created Environments and Happenings. From these beginnings, he was expressing his intentions to delimit the boundaries between the arts, between art and life, and between the art maker and the viewer. Kaprow's view is expansionist, one which sees art in the streets and in the everyday environments of life, urban and country. It is not an anti-art Dada approach, but rather is geared toward separating art from the artificiality of the art world context, blurring categories to make art more an organic part of living experience. The Happenings were mostly "spectaculars" in which clusters of groups of people took part in situations which were not art derived and were carried out in varying time and place units. Many were ritualistic in theme such as the 1962 "Chicken" and "A Service for the Dead." Always interested in the audience getting more involved in the doing and seeing of the event, Kaprow moved away from the theatrical concept, omitting the audience as viewer and creating "non-theatrical", "participation" performance during the 1960's. By 1967 Kaprow was using the term Happening less and less, and after his 1967 piece "Fluids," the work became increasingly quieter, more intimate and more intimately involved with ordinary everyday routines. From 1967 to 1971 Kaprow did a series of "Work Pieces" in which physical labor became a kind of play, leisure situation. In "Sweet Wall" (1970), for example, participants built and subsequently destroyed a wall made with bricks held together by a "mortar" of bread and jam. The activity took place just a few steps away from the Berlin Wall, and like other works, called attention to the underlying symbolism of the task by removing the element of practical usefulness.

Around 1971 the works began to center on smaller groups, usually one, two or three, who performed routines which involve personal and interpersonal relationships. Kaprow named these works "Activities," a nomer meant to help convey the honing down of theatrics and centering in on the regular actions of everyday life which we often ignore and relegate to the semi-conscious of the "routine". As in all Kaprow's work, there is the interplay of choice and chance. The artist as director/participant remains in control but allows for and even welcomes chance and change by leaving choices open for the execution particulars which develop in the Activity's duration. The Activities follow this basic format: first, there is a preliminary gathering of the preselected participants during which Kaprow (always a participant) distributes and explains the "script" he has written. This script is an outline of the procedures to be followed; it tends to be spare and leave openings as to particulars in between designated actions. Second, participants split up into groups (2 or 3) and carry out the script's directions simultaneously and separately, with points of overlap along the route. Third, they regroup to discuss (Kaprow included, perhaps taping the talks) what has happened and put it in some perspective. There is no specific documentation of the work, but Kaprow produces what he calls "instruction manuals" which include the script and simulated photographs of the activity in process.

Actions and interactions which would normally be considered ordinary are brought into heightened consciousness, more powerfully so because they are gone through directly in real-life time and places by participants who are going through the motions in a tense state of choice between refusing or complying with each step along the way. The regular becomes strange and capable of fostering real anxieties and new insights alike. Beginning out of what Lawrence Alloway has called "a fertile misreading of Pollock," Kaprow has developed a body of work with potent psychological and social implications which can often affect people quite dramatically. They give apt pertinence to the active participation element in a time dominated more and more by the passivity induced by television. In recent works Kaprow is becoming less distanced personally, more introspectively meditative and willing to incorporate his personal experiences. As always, however, there is the persistently intellectual element of the creator at the controls, never to dominate answers but rather to bring to the fore possibilities of a unique nature. The Happening has become a term widely co-opted in popular culture, but Kaprow has reached far beyond the implications of his earlier work and is still searching for further penetration into his very fertile ideas and realizations.

—Barbara Cavaliere

KATZ, Alex.

American. Born in New York City, 24 July 1927. Studied at Cooper Union, New York, 1946–49; Skowhegan School of Painting and Sculpture, Maine, 1949–50. Served in the United States Navy, 1945–46. Independent artist, since 1950. Visiting Artist, Skowhegan School of Painting and Sculpture, Maine, 1960; Visiting Lecturer, Brooklyn Museum, New York, 1960; Visiting Lecturer, Yale University, New Haven, Connecticut, 1960–63; Instructor, Pratt Institute, New York, 1962–65; Visiting Critic, New York Studio School, 1967, and University of Pennsylvania, Philadelphia, 1973–74; Artist in Residence, Ameri-

can Academy, Rome, 1983. Recipient: Guggenheim Painting Grant, 1972; Cooper Union Professional Achievement Citation, 1972; St. Gauden's Medal in Art, Cooper Union, 1980; Skowhegan Award for Painting, 1980; *Art Direction* Magazine Award, New York, 1982; Graphic Design USA Award, New York, 1983; Art in Public Places Award, Chicago Bar Association, 1985. D.F.A.: Colby College, Waterville, Maine, 1984. Agents: Galerie Marguerite Lamy, 4 rue Beaubourg, 75004 Paris, France; Marlborough Gallery Inc., New York. Lives in New York. Address: c/o Marlborough Gallery Inc., 40 West 57th Street, New York, New York 10019, U.S.A.

Individual Exhibitions:

1954	Roko Gallery, New York
1957	Roko Gallery, New York
	University of Pennsylvania, Philadelphia
1958	Sun Gallery, Provincetown, Massachusetts
1959	Sun Gallery, Provincetown, Massachusetts
	Tanager Gallery, New York
1960	Stable Gallery, New York
1961	Stable Gallery, New York
	Mili-Jay Gallery, Woodstock, New York
1962	Tanager Gallery, New York
	Martha Jackson Gallery, New York
1963	Thibaut Gallery, New York
1964	Fischbach Gallery, New York (twice)
	Grinnel Gallery, Detroit
1965	Fischbach Gallery, New York
1966	David Stuart Gallery, Los Angeles
1967	Fischbach Gallery, New York (twice)
1968	Fischbach Gallery, New York
	Bertha Eccles Art Center, Ogden, Utah
	Towson State College, Baltimore
	Gotham Book Mart and Gallery, New York
1969	Mont Chateau Lodge, Morgantown, West Virginia
	Phyllis Kind Gallery
1970	Fischbach Gallery, New York
1971	Fischbach Gallery, New York
	Museum of Fine Arts, University of Utah, Salt Lake City (retrospective; toured the United States)
	University of California at San Diego
	Minnesota Museum of Art, St. Paul
	Wadsworth Atheneum, Hartford, Connecticut
	Galerie Dieter Brusberg, Hannover
	Phyllis Kind Gallery, Chicago
	Galerie Thelen, Cologne
1972	Reed College, Portland, Oregon
	Sloan-O'Sickey Gallery, Cleveland
1973	Carlton Gallery, New York
	Assa Galerie, Helsinki
	Marlborough Gallery, New York
1974	Picker Gallery, Colgate University, Hamilton, New York
	Davison Art Center, Wesleyan University, Middletown, Connecticut
	Marlborough Goddard Gallery, Toronto
	Marlborough Goddard Gallery, Montreal
	Alex Katz: Prints, Whitney Museum, New York (toured the United States)
1975	Marlborough Fine Art, London
	Galerie Marguerite Lamy, Paris
	Galerie Arnesen, Copenhagen
	Marlborough Graphics, New York
	Marlborough Goddard Gallery, Toronto
	American Foundation for the Arts, Miami
1976	Marlborough Gallery, New York
1977	Galerie Roger d'Amecourt, Paris
	Marlborough Galerie AG, Zurich
	Fresno Arts Center, California (toured western United States and Canada)
1978	*Recent Paintings,* Marlborough Gallery, New York
	Rose Art Museum, Brandeis University, Waltham, Massachusetts
1979	Brooke Alexander Gallery, New York
	Suzanne Hilberry Gallery, New York
	Robert Miller Gallery, New York
1980	*Scale and Gesture,* Queens Museum, Flushing, New York
	Marlborough Gallery, New York
	Hokin Gallery, Miami
1981	Portland Center for the Visual Arts, Oregon
	Robert Miller Gallery, New York
	Mira Godard Gallery, Toronto
	Contemporary Arts Center, Cincinnati
	University of California, Santa Barbara
1982	Hokin Gallery, Chicago
	Mira Godard Gallery, Chicago
	Brooke Alexander Gallery, New York
	Marlborough Gallery, New York
	John Stoller Gallery, Minneapolis
	Suzanne Hilberry Gallery, Birmingham, Michigan
	Marlborough Fine Art, London
1983	Suzanne Hilberry Gallery, Birmingham, Michigan
	Grace Hokin Gallery, Palm Beach, Florida
	Texas Gallery, Houston
	Marlborough Gallery, New York
	McIntosh/Drysdale Gallery, Houston
1984	Michael Lord Gallery, Milwaukee, Wisconsin
	Mira Godard Gallery, Toronto
	Colgate University, Hamilton, New York
	Suzanne Hilberry Gallery, Birmingham, Michigan
	Robert Miller Gallery, New York
	Asher-Faure Gallery, Los Angeles
	Benjamin Mangle Gallery, Philadelphia
1985	Robert Miller Gallery, New York
	Cooper Union, New York
	Marlborough Gallery, Tokyo
	Cleveland Center for Contemporary Art, Ohio (travelled to Colby College, Maine)
	Wichita State University, Kansas
	Farnsworth Museum, Maine
	O'Farrell Gallery, Brunswick, Maine
	Mario Diacono Gallery, Boston
1986	Whitney Museum, New York (retrospective)
	McIntosh/Drysdale Gallery, Washington, D.C.
	Marlborough Gallery, New York
	Texas Gallery, Houston
1987	Grace Hokin Gallery, Palm Beach, Florida
	Mira Godard Gallery, Toronto
	Suzanne Hilberry Gallery, Birmingham, Michigan
	Robert Miller Gallery, New York

Selected Group Exhibitions:

1960	*Young America 1960,* Whitney Museum, New York (toured the United States)
1967	*Large Scale American Paintings,* Jewish Museum, New York
1969	*Aspects of a New Realism,* Milwaukee Art Center (toured the United States)
1971	*Contemporary Realism,* Pennsylvania Academy of Fine Arts, Philadelphia
1973	*American Drawings 1963–1973,* Whitney Museum, New York
1975	*Portrait Painting 1970–75,* Allan Frumkin Gallery, New York
1979	*Printed Art: A View of Two Decades,* Museum of Modern Art, New York
1982	*The Human Figure,* Contemporary Arts Center, New Orleans
1984	*Visions of Childhood,* Whitney Museum Downtown, New York
1986	*The Painter-Sculptor in the 20th Century,* Whitechapel Art Gallery, London

Collections:

Museum of Modern Art, New York; Metropolitan Museum of Art, New York; Whitney Museum, New York; Fogg Art Museum, Harvard University, Cambridge, Massachusetts; Rose Art Museum, Brandeis University, Waltham, Massachusetts; Museum of Art, Rhode Island School of Design, Providence; Philadelphia Museum of Art; Hirshhorn Museum, Washington, D.C.; Art Institute of Chicago; Milwaukee Art Center.

Publications:

By KATZ: books—*Fragment,* with John Ashbery, New York 1968; *Interlocking Lives,* with Kenneth Koch, New York 1970; *Selected Declarations of Dependence,* with Harry Mathews, Calais, Vermont 1977; *Face of the Poet,* mono-

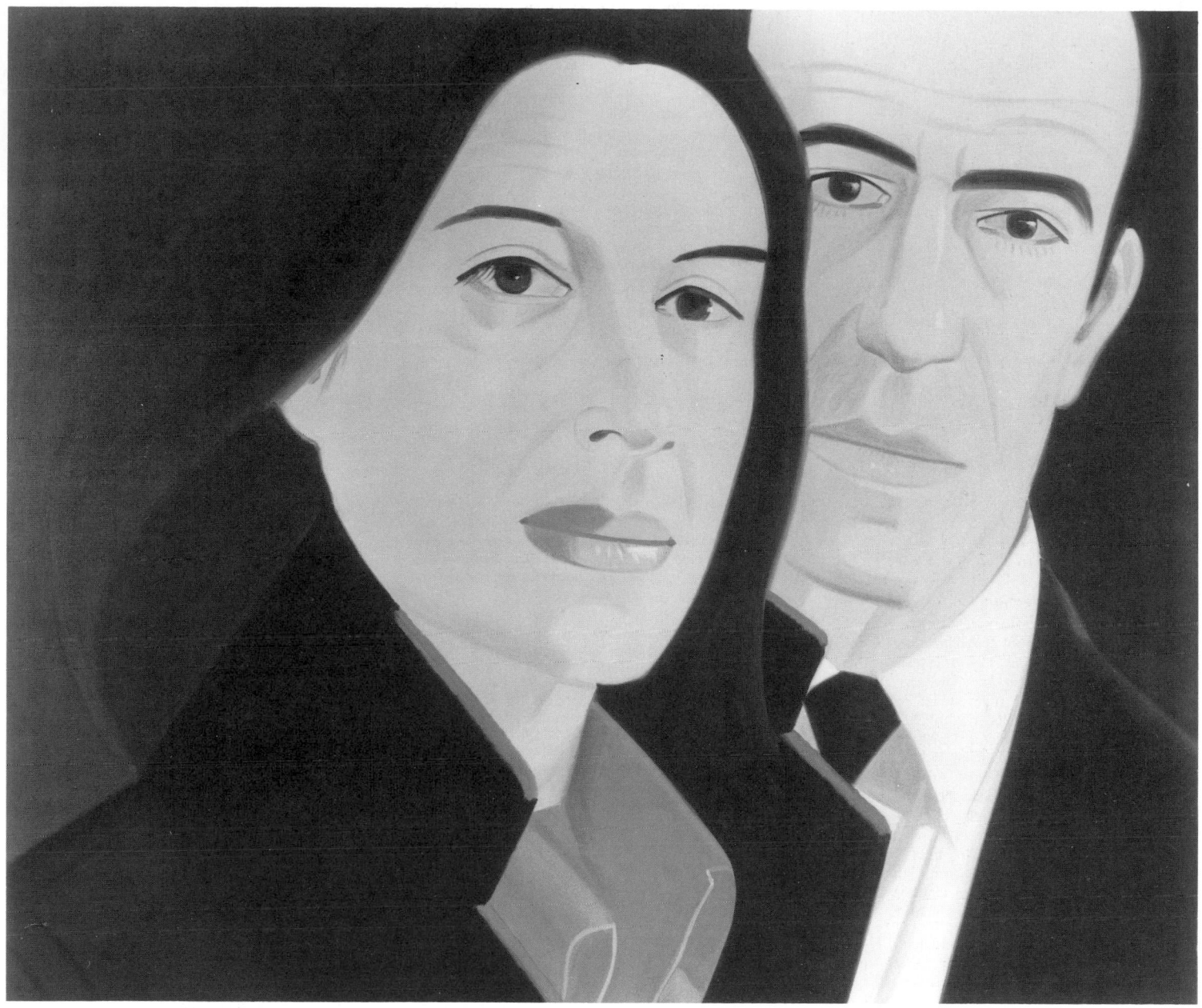

Alex Katz: *Ada and Alex*, 1980

graph, New York 1978; articles "Is There a New Academy?" in *Art News* (New York), September 1959; statement in *Art in America* (New York), January/February 1967; statement in *Art Now: New York* (New York), September 1970; "10 Portraitists," interview with Gerrit Henry, in *Art in America* (New York), January/February 1975.

On KATZ: books—*Minimal Art: A Critical Anthology,* edited by Gregory Battcock, New York 1968; *Alex Katz,* edited by Irving Sandler and William Berkson, New York 1971; *Alex Katz,* exhibition catalogue, New York 1973; *Alex Katz,* exhibition catalogue, Hamilton, New York 1974; *Alex Katz: Prints,* exhibition catalogue, text by Richard S. Field and Elke M. Solomon, New York 1974; *Art Chronicles 1954-1966* by Frank O'Hara, New York 1975; *Alex Katz,* exhibition catalogue, London 1975; *Alex Katz,* exhibition catalogue, New York 1976; *Alex Katz,* exhibition catalogue, with an essay by Robert Rosenblum, Fresno, California 1977; *Alex Katz: Recent Paintings,* exhibition catalogue, New York 1978; *Alex Katz: Curious,* exhibition catalogue, New York 1979; *Alex Katz* by Irving Sandler, New York 1979; *Alex Katz: Scale and Gesture,* exhibition catalogue, Flushing, New York 1980; *Alex Katz,* exhibition catalogue, New York 1980; articles—"Hipster" in *Newsweek* (New York), December 1965; "Art as Likeness" by Lawrence Alloway in *Arts Magazine* (New York), May 1967; "Alex Katz: Faces and Flowers" by Nicolas Calas in *Art International* (Lugano, Switzerland), December 1967; "Alex Katz" by Scott Burton in *Art Scene* (New York), March 1969; "Alex Katz and the Tactics of Representation" by David Antin in *Art News* (New York), April 1971; "The World of Alex Katz: Big Numbers . . . Fast Moves" by Hilton Kramer in the *New York Times,* January 1973; "Alex Katz at the Marlborough Gallery" by Sarah Kent in *Studio International* (London), March/April 1975; "Katz Advertises His Family" by David Bourdon in the *Village Voice* (New York), 7 September 1979; "Cool Katz" by John Perreault in *Soho News* (New York), 14 April 1980.

I work with gestures for one thing. It's in tight motion, and you can't do it with a camera. People accept the camera without thinking: the camera makes a nice sign of a dancer, for example, but it isn't a good symbol. So, a camera doesn't really help me with gestures.

How people stand . . . the paintings look like photographs because it looks like a specific instant, but the paintings are very carefully worked out and often they are part of that instant and made to appear like one instant. I work empirically in the beginning and then it gets enlarged, the lines get larger and the scale gets broader. Sometimes it will take 3 or 4 days to make one line of a large drawing. I'll take one line and make it stretch.

—Alex Katz

Early in his career Alex Katz began to swim upstream by painting portraits when no one was painting portraits. While abstract expressionism was still the leading style, Katz painted members of his family and his friends, and he made a further break with conventionality by making large rather than small to medium-sized realist paintings. The results were unusual. Katz responded to some of the same sources that influenced the abstract expressionists—Matisse (especially "The Red Studio") and the large flat color areas of Milton Avery—and devised a portrait style that resembles a precisionist landscape.

Katz often cuts off the figure or even a group of figures just below the shoulders, establishing an immediate association with antique portrait busts. Then he proceeds to assign qualities of monumentality to his subjects which in previous eras would have been apparent through dress, or by the mere existence of a portrait bust. Katz paints his figures on a grand scale, the sort reserved in earlier cultures for pharaohs and emperors. But, so far as we know, his subjects are not pharaohs and emperors, nor are they modern equivalents. Katz seldom provides a setting, and sometimes not even a costume, to help us understand why these people are bigger than life. Their features are reduced to simplified areas, so stylized that each reads as a separate element rather than as components of a physiognomy.

Certain art world individuals can be recognized among these subjects, but the anonymous faces take on a cinematic aura; their features are reduced to movie poster bluntness, and they are larger than life.

It is impossible to determine if Katz intended this movie star quality to envelop his subjects, but the associations with gigantic portrait busts these days have nothing to do with pomp and circumstance and everything to do with images found on the silver screen.

Alex Katz's work has achieved enormous visibility in the 1980s, as a result of a retrospective exhibition at the Whitney Museum of American Art in 1986 and the more recently (1987) published book on the artist by novelist Ann Beattie, for which Beattie made her own selections of work since 1980 on which to construct her essays. The essays appear in chapters with such titles as "A Reading of Alex Katz," "Ada," "Narratives," "Inanimate Portraits," and "Couples," and include references to films, literature, rock stars, other artists and the contemporary scene that Beattie and Katz both capture in their work. She concludes that, "Like Beckett, Katz had always been more interested in raising questions about what is meaningful and, by implication, how to live, than he is in attempting to offer interpretations of reality."

—Mary Stofflet

KAUFFMAN, (Robert) Craig.

American. Born in Eagle Rock, California, 31 March 1932. Studied at the School of Architecture, University of Southern California, Los Angeles, 1950-52; University of California at Los Angeles, 1952-56, B.A. 1959, M.A. 1956. Independent painter and sculptor, living in Paris, 1960-62, in California and New York since 1962. Instructor, University of California at Irvine, 1967-77; University of California, Berkeley, 1969; School of Visual Arts, New York, 1970-71. Recipient: United States Government Fellowship for the Arts, 1967; First Prize, *69th American Exhibition*, Art Institute of Chicago, 1970. Agents: Pace Gallery, 32 East 57th Street, New York, New York 10022; and Blum Helman Gallery, New York. Address: c/o Blum Helman Gallery, 20 West 57th Street, New York, New York 10019, U. S. A.

Individual Exhibitions:

1953	Felix Landau Gallery, Los Angeles
1958	Dilexi Gallery, Los Angeles
	Ferus Gallery, Los Angeles
1963	Ferus Gallery, Los Angeles
1965	Ferus Gallery, Los Angeles
1967	Ferus Gallery, Los Angeles
	Pace Gallery, New York
1969	Pace Gallery, New York
	Irving Blum Gallery, Los Angeles
1970	Pace Gallery, New York
	Pasadena Art Museum, California
	University of California at Irvine
1972	Irving Blum Gallery, Los Angeles
1973	Pace Gallery, New York
	Galerie Dorothea Speyer, Paris
1975	Riko Mizuno Gallery, Los Angeles
1976	Galerie Dorothea Speyer, Paris
	Robert Elkon Gallery, New York
	Comsky Gallery, Los Angeles
1977	*Moses, Delap, Kauffman*, Cassat Gallery, La Jolla, California
1978	Arco Center, Los Angeles
1979	Blum-Helman Gallery, New York
	Grapestake Gallery, San Francisco

Selected Group Exhibitions:

1965	*5 At Pace*, Pace Gallery, New York
1971	*Transparency, Reflection, Light, Space: 4 Artists*, University of California at Los Angeles (with Larry Bell, Peter Alexander, and Robert Irwin)
1975	*60 and 70: Trends of 6 California Artists*, Ruth Schaffner Gallery, Los Angeles
1976	*75 Years of California Art*, San Francisco Museum of Modern Art
	Recent Los Angeles Work, Museum of Modern Art, New York
1977	*Painting and Sculpture in California: The Modern Era*, Smithsonian Institution, Washington, D.C. (travelled to San Francisco Museum of Modern Art)
1978	*Works on Paper*, Margo Leavin Gallery, Los Angeles
1979	*Whitney Biennial*, Whitney Museum, New York
1986	*California Sculpture 1959-80*, San Francisco Museum of Modern Art

Collections:

Museum of Modern Art, New York; Whitney Museum, New York; Aldrich Museum, Ridgefield, Connecticut; Fort Worth Art Center Museum, Texas; Pasadena Art Museum, California; Los Angeles County Museum of Art; Santa Barbara Museum of Art, California; San Francisco Museum of Modern Art; Tate Gallery, London.

Publications:

By KAUFFMAN: articles—interview in *Transparency, Reflection, Light, Space: 4 Artists*, exhibition catalogue, Los Angeles 1971; "Interview with Jan Butterfield" in *Art in America* (New York), July 1976.

On KAUFFMAN: books—*5 At Pace*, exhibition catalogue, with an introduction by John Coplans, New York 1965; *Craig Kauffman*, exhibition catalogue, New York 1970; *Transparency, Reflection, Light, Space: 4 Artists*, exhibition catalogue, by Frederick Wight, Los Angeles 1971; *Painting and Sculpture in California: The Modern Era*, exhibition catalogue, San Francisco 1977; *Craig Kauffman*, exhibition catalogue, by Melinda Wortz, Los Angeles 1978; articles—"Notes on the Absorption of the Avant-Garde into the Culture" by Paul Stitleman in *Arts Magazine* (New York), May/June 1973; "New Paintings by Craig Kauffman" by Melinda Wortz in *Artweek* (Oakland, California), March 1975; "Kauffman's Subtle Joke" by Melinda Wortz in *Art News* (New York), June 1975; "The Trip from Abstract Expressionism" by Pamra J. King in the *Los Angeles Herald Examiner*, 16 April 1978; "Artists in the 70's—Free to See and Be Seen" by William Wilson in the *Los Angeles Times*, 30 April 1978; "Craig Kauffman's Interiors" by Melinda Wortz in *Artweek* (Oakland, California), 13 May 1978; "Unslick in L.A." by Peter Frank in *Art in America* (New York), September/October 1978; "A Passel of Patterners" by Peter Frank in the *Village Voice* (New York), 19 February 1979; "Painterly Surface, Architectonic Structure" by R. McDonald in *Artweek* (Oakland, California), 24 November 1979.

A native Californian, Craig Kauffman contributed at least as much as any other artist to the rise of the characteristic style which in the 1960's established Los Angeles as a major creative center. Kauffman's sophisticated works, and personal cosmopolitànism, are credited with having inspired in a generation of Southern California artists a level of professionalism that made possible the creation of an aesthetic expression no longer dependent upon New York and European examples. An exhibition of early abstract paintings at the avant-garde Ferus Gallery in 1958 was particularly critical in its influence, pointing the direction for other prominent artists such as Billy Al Bengston, Ken Price, and Robert Irwin. Laden with sexual imagery akin to that of still another colleague, John Altoon, these highly original works displayed a sophisticated union of the mechanical and biomorphic that invokes Duchamp and Picabia.

Kauffman began as a typical, albeit precocious, art-school Abstract Expressionist; by 1957 his paintings became more simplified, delineated, and hard-edged, incorporating the typical bulb and the tube shapes that provide the illusion of relief in the acrylic on plexiglass paintings of the early 1960's. These in turn led to the low-relief vacuum-formed wall paintings for which Kauffman is justifiably famous. Paradigmatic exemplars of the high-finish, reflective transparency, and sensual colorism of the L.A. look, these simple plexiglass shapes established the stylistic basis for an innovative group of Southern California artists.

In this respect, Kauffman's most important contribution began in 1964 with his experimentation with plastic. In works like "Yellow-Orange" (Los Angeles County Museum of Art), he distinguished himself as probably the first artist to "paint" in plastic using industrial techniques. This lesson was not lost on those fellow artists who turned to new materials, acquiring the technological skills necessary to manipulate them. Pursuing these interests, Kauffman produced into the early 1970's a series of plastic works in high-key transparent acrylic pigments. Maintaining a basic repertory of simple minimalist forms, he evolved by 1968 his large vacuum-formed half-bubbles in which light and color are magically suspended like yolks in translucent eggs. In these pieces the ovals and lozenges appear to be dematerialized by color: the viewer looks through the surface, into the painting itself. These perceptual interests were shared concurrently by several Los Angeles area artists, notably DeWain Valentine, who were also preoccupied with light and space. These concerns spawned another important regional phenomenon, the large-scale light and color installations of the "environmentalists," among them Irwin and James Turrell.

Although Kauffman's own process pieces of 1970 were clearly moving in the same direction, he opted for return to the object. From about 1972 to the present, Kauffman has created a series of closely related works, the content of which is the basic elements of a painting: an interpretation of structure, surface, color. The earlier pressed formed plexiglass versions resemble stained glass windows in which banded color has been applied to the "leading" rather than the glass. This linear architectural geometry reasserted itself further after 1974 (when Kauffman abandoned plexiglass) in paintings which bring to mind building construction framing or, most notably in works of 1976-77 such as "L'Atelier #1" and "Interior #2," the backs of canvases with unconventionally arranged stretcher bars.

Over the past years Kauffman has divided his time between studios in New York City and Laguna Beach, California. The recent acrylic paintings on paper and silk continue his interest in abstracted interiors, reintroducing the biomorphic shapes of his earlier work along with a more painterly and expressionistic technique. "Tell Tale Heart, 3rd Version" of 1980 (Blum Helman Gallery, New York) shares more than the title with its predecessor from 1958. Kauffman's continuity of vision and development lies not in the stylistic similarities between his early and most recent work but in his ability to apply the important lessons learned during the intervening years.

—Paul J. Karlstrom

KAWAGUCHI, Tatsuo.

Japanese. Born in Kobe, 15 February 1940. Studied at the Tama University of Fine Art, Tokyo, 1958-62, B. F. A. 1962. Married Chikako Kawaguchi in 1970; children: Yuki and Makiko. Lives and works in Kobe. Member, Group "i". Taught art in Yamada Junior High School, Kobe, 1962-64, and Komagabayashi Junior High School, Kobe, 1964-66; Assistant Professor, Art Department, Akashi Junior College, Akashi, 1968-78. Since 1978, Professor of Art, Kansai Art College, Osaka. Recipient: First Prize, and Collectors' Prize, *New Faces Exhibition*, Tokyo, 1965; Mainichi/French Government Scholarship Competition Prize, 1966; Prize for Excellent Work, *Japanese Art Festival*, Tokyo, 1968, 1973; Grand Prize, *Contemporary Space '68: Light and Environment*, Kobe, 1968; Prize for Excellence, First *Hakone Open-Air Exhibition*, 1973; Iue Cultural Prize,

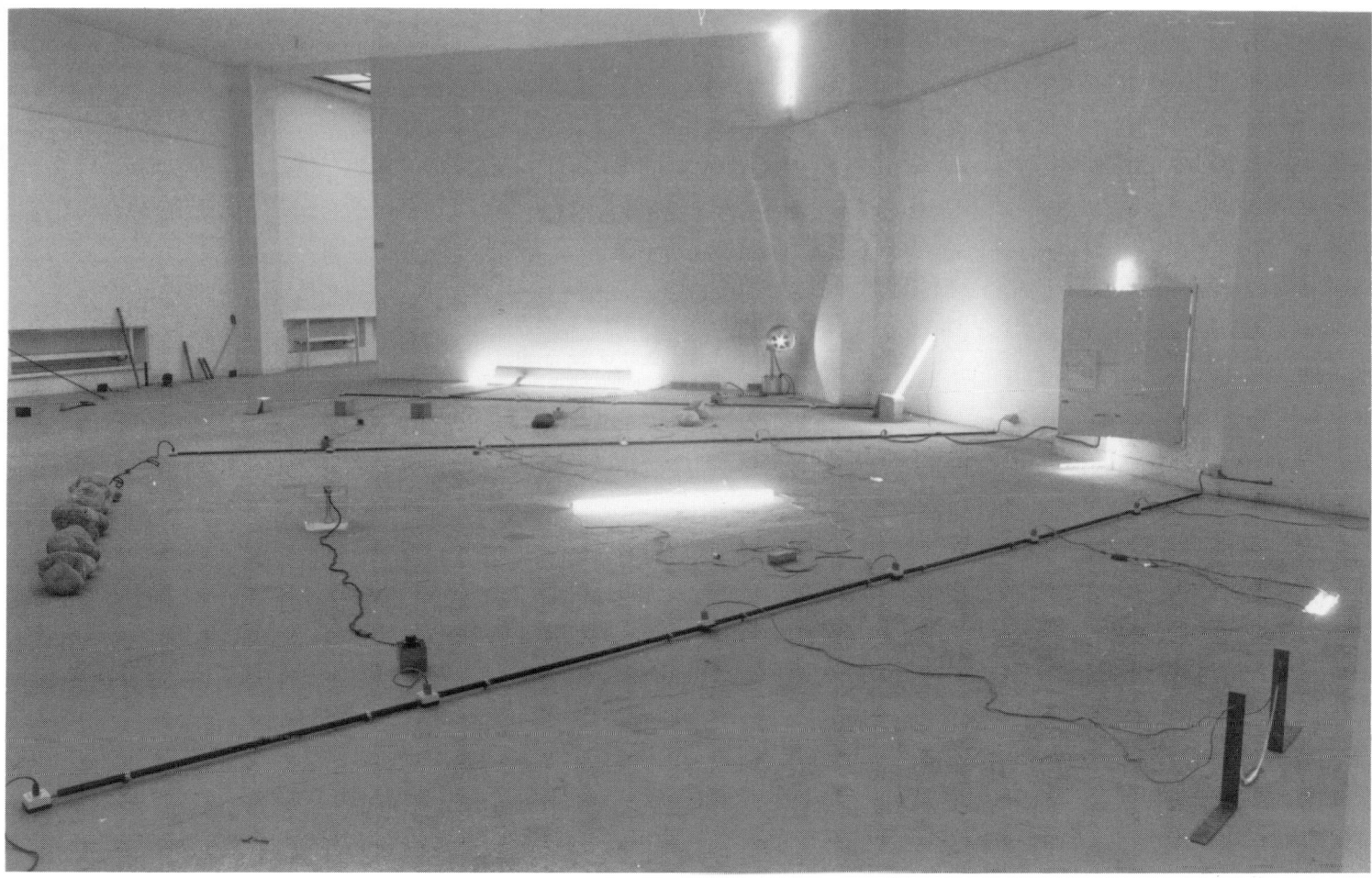

Tatsuo Kawaguchi: *Relation—Energy,* 1973

Kobe, 1974; Grand Prize, Osaka Citizens Gallery Opening Competition, 1974; Purchase Prize, *Biennale,* Sydney, 1976; Prize of the Museum of Modern Art, Hokkaido, at *International Biennale Exhibition of Prints,* Tokyo, 1979. Agents: Toa-Gallery, Miyaboshi Building, 3-12-16 Kitanagase-Dori, Chuo-ku, Kobe 650; Gallery 16, Sakurano-cho, Sanjo-Teramachi, Nakagyo-ku, Kyoto 604; Sakura Gallery, Fushimi Building 5F, 1-20-12 Nishiki, Naka-ku, Nagoya 460; and Art Front Gallery, 29-5 Sakuraoka, Shibuya-ku, Tokyo 150, Japan.

Individual Exhibitions:

1965 Gallery Anneau, Osaka
1966 Gallery 16, Kyoto
1967 Gallery 16, Kyoto
1968 *Dark,* Muramastu Gallery, Tokyo
1971 *172800 Seconds,* Gallery 16, Kyoto
1972 *Relation-Energy,* Gallery Piner, Tokyo
1975 *Tatsuo Kawaguchi's Recent Works,* Minami Gallery, Tokyo
      2 Artists: Tatsuo Kawaguchi and Keiji Uematsu, City Museum of Namban Art, Kobe
1977 Gallery Kitano Circus, Kobe
1978 *Works: Made of Parts,* Gallery 16, Kyoto
      Gallery U, Nagoya
      1968-1979: Tatsuo Kawaguchi, Art Center M, Obama
      Iron of Iron, Toa-Road Gallery, Kobe
1979 Toa-Road Gallery, Kobe
1980 *Relation-Quality,* Kobayashi Gallery, Tokyo
      Sakura Gallery, Nagoya
      Toa-Road Gallery, Kobe
1981 Toa-Road Gallery, Osaka
      Gallery Le Coin, Osaka
      Relation-Friction/Relation-Temperature, Art Front Gallery, Tokyo
1982 *Relation-Quality,* Sakura Gallery, Nagoya

Selected Group Exhibitions:

1968 *Fluorescent Chrysanthemum: Contemporary Japanese Art,* Institute of Contemporary Arts, London
1971 *Man and Nature,* Metropolitan Art Gallery, Tokyo
1973 *20 Years of Contemporary Art in Retrospective,* Metropolitan Art Gallery, Tokyo
      Bienal, Sao Paulo
1974 *Japan, Past and Present,* Kunsthalle, Dusseldorf
      Contemporary Japanese Art, Louisiana Museum, Humlebaek, Denmark (toured Denmark, Sweden, and Norway)
1977 *The Structure of Seeing,* Seibu Museum of Art, Tokyo
1981 *Art Now 1970-1980,* Hyogo Museum of Modern Art, Kobe
      Trends in Japanese Art in the 1970's, Institute of Culture and Arts, Seoul
1982 *Fifth Triennale: India 1982,* New Delhi

Collections:

National Museum of Modern Art, Tokyo; Ministry of Culture, Tokyo; Japan Foundation, Tokyo; Museum of Contemporary Art, Ngaoka, Japan; Okayama Cultural Center, Japan; Open-Air Museum, Ube, Japan; Osaka Prefectural Contemporary Art Center, Okayama, Japan; Museum of Modern Art, Hokkaido, Japan; Louisiana Museum, Humlebaek, Denmark; Art Gallery of New South Wales, Sydney

Publications:

By KAWAGUCHI: books—*Tokyo Biennale '70,* exhibition catalogue, Tokyo 1970; *Aspects of New Japanese Art,* exhibition catalogue, Tokyo 1970; *Sonzai,* editor, Kobe 1974; *Trends in Contemporary Art,* Tokyo 1977; articles—"The Starting Point of Creation" in *Mizue* (Tokyo), February 1972; "To Make a Photo an Object: The Distance Between Reality and the Photograph" in *Bijustu-Techo* (Tokyo), June 1972; preface to *Part,* exhibition catalogue, Osaka 1972; interview, with Yoshiaki Tono in *Mizue* (Tokyo), August 1974; "Sounding Out Conceptual Artists on Their Concepts," interview, with Shuji Terayama, in *Geijutsu-Club* (Tokyo), vol. 8, 1974; "Fragments of a Journey" in *Bijutsu-Techo* (Tokyo), February 1977; "Hand-Made Paper" in *Misho* (Osaka), May 1980.

On KAWAGUCHI: books—*172800,* exhibition catalogue, with preface by Yusuke Nakahara, Kroto 1971; *Relation-Energy,* exhibition catalogue, with preface by Ichiro Haryu, Tokyo 1972; *Thoughts on Photography* by Koen Shigemori, Tokyo 1972; *Tatsuo Kawaguchi's Recent Works,* exhibition catalogue, with an essay by Yoshiaki Tono, Tokyo 1975; *Japanese Contemporary Art 18: Art of Tomorrow,* Tokyo 1980; articles—"From Here to Here" by Toshiaki Minemura in *Bijutsu-Techo* (Tokyo), May 1972; "The Apocalypse of the Death of Art" by Jean Clair in *Bijutsu-Techo* (Tokyo), December 1973; "Tatsuo Kawaguchi" by Akio Fujieda in *Art in Japan Today,* edited by Suji Takashina, Yoshiaki Tono and Yusuke Nakahara, Tokyo 1984; "Tatsuo Kawaguchi" by Katuo Akane in *Way* (Osaka), April 1976; "Today, What is Technique in Art?" by Shigemitsu Hirano in *Mizue* (Tokyo), August 1977; "Tatsuo Kawaguchi's 'Relation-Quality' " by Toru Matsumoto in *Bulletin of the National Museum of Modern Art* (Tokyo), May 1982.

*

I have been lying on the beach for a long time, gazing at the sea and the sky.

On a fine day, in between the sea and the sky, we can see the mountains on the far shore. Today, however, they are obscured, as if scratched out, in the total grayness of clouds and mist.

The sea and the sky are the same color and have the same brightness. The horizon is nowhere in sight. There drifts in the grayness some quality that makes the sea the sea and some quality that makes the sky the sky. And where they meet, the sea and the sky blur indistinguishably, floating in the distant haze.

I stand up, looking at the distant vagueness. I drop my eyes to where I have been lying, and find that the weight of my body has left a slight depression in the sand.

—Tatsuo Kawaguchi

Suppose Tatsuo Kawaguchi, stopping over a large photocopy of the constellations spread out in front of him, checking each star carefully, keeps jotting down on it every figure of the light-hours that separate a star from the earth. Then, the photocopy of the starry heavens, when he is done with the job, becomes a figurative ruin that contains heaps of manifold times. Thus, however profound the thoughts you may entertain, or sweet the dreams you may be enraptured in, while looking wistfully at the starlit sky, what you think is that the light of each star is in fact the debris of the light that, having left the star several years, or even several centuries, ago, had just come down to meet your eyes, and the source of the light, that is, the star, might have perished ages ago. This is exactly why Buckminster Fuller had to define the universe as the "aggregate of nonsimultaneous . . . energy events." How interesting that the collection of lights observable from the earth simultaneously should involve such different lengths of time! Thus, Kawaguchi, having replaced the act of seeing with function of time, has virtually become a modern astrologist. (Professional astronomers don't usually bother to measure the light-hours of the stars that have no value for their research.)

Another time Kawaguchi will attempt to be a "carrier of darkness." For nothing but darkness is contained in the cast iron box which he closed up tight with bolts. Not even those little clatters, such as Duchamp's "Hidden Sounds," can be heard there. "But, certainly the air . . . ," you might suggest—but then I would have to call you an old-fashioned materialist. Because the thing sealed up in it is surely just "darkness."

It is the kind of "darkness" that, even if the box were opened, you wouldn't be able to see at all. This is a gracious contempt for the fact that the act of "seeing" is impossible without light. Furthermore, this box was crated in Kobe and carried to Tokyo by Shinkansen, the Bullet Train. Kawaguchi, with mischievous twinkles in his eyes, would ask you, "Is this Kobe darkness carried to Tokyo, or is it just Tokyo darkness?" This unanswerable question exists by itself as a pure conception of "darkness."

There is another cast metal box, cylindrical in shape and also closed up tight, inside which are blended two beams of light in different primary colors radiating from each end of the cylinder. But nobody can see exactly how the two colors blend there. The only thing you can be sure about is that there is no "hope" sealed in this Pandora's box. So, this time Kawaguchi becomes a Proteus who has sealed up his own eyes with a special kind of imagination.

The most distinctive feature of these works is that they are more or less severed from any circumstantial conditions; concepts are condensed and embodied in actual things that are sustained by themselves. As is clear in his works of stars, darkness and light—what the artist has been doing is to recapture the meaning of time, space and the act of seeing. But by working in this direction, he has been taking advantage of the given conditions in terms of time and place, producing in some respects a predominant effect that might be described as "environmental." When Kawaguchi participated, nearly 20 years ago, in a show called Group 'i' at Gifu, Japan, what he did was symbolic, for it was to dig up a huge hole on the river-bed of the Nagara and then fill it up again. The hole, like his starlights, existed for a certain length of time and then disappeared. At the show called 172800 Seconds (Gallery 16, Kyoto), placing an 8mm movie camera and a tape recorder in the showroom, the artist captured all the scenes and activities and sounds that occurred there during the show, and when the show was over, he sealed up in a box both films and tapes, just as he did with the "darkness" in those metal boxes, never showing anybody the results of the recording. The idea was to produce a canned time. In his work entitled Relation-Energy shown in 1972 Kawaguchi displayed all kinds of electrical gadgets to show how electric energy transforms itself into varied forms, sometimes just electric current running through inside the wire creeping on the floor, sometimes the heat in a nichrome wire, sometimes the light in a

fluorescent lamp, sometimes the wind coming forth through a fan, and so forth. In doing this, however, the artist's purpose was to weigh the balance between things seen and things unseen, showing how, in terms of energy, all those things, i.e. lights you can see, electric current you cannot see, an iron rod that doesn't move, are all identical after all.

Kawaguchi's more recent works, while still retaining a bit of "environmental" tendency, have added a new aspect, the emphasis on presenting objects. However, the degree of this new tendency in his works depends mainly upon how directly the specific concepts in his creative ideas can be expressed in the material on hand, after having gone through the process of condensation in the "thingness" of the given material. The movements of the conceptual world must come through the "thingness" of the material, as if they were dull, almost inaudible hums in the bottom of a deep sea, accompanied by tiny waves of a certain feeling—a feeling I might describe as something like the lyricism of slight flush concealed in the cool, distant expression of a face.

Conceptual art which had long seemed to refuse the world of things and objects so obstinately had reached, so to speak, the extreme of simply linguistically manipulating concepts. Is it too presumptuous to feel conceptual art has now arrived at the phase where it begins to reconsider the actual presentation of objects?

—Yoshiaki Tono

KAWARA, On.

Japanese. Born in Kariya, Aichi Prefecture, 2 January 1933. Educated at Kariya High School, until 1951; self-taught in art from 1951. First environmental sculptures, Tokyo, 1953; first date paintings, New York, 1966: travelled in the United States, Mexico and Europe, 1969–65; settled in New York City, 1965; travelled in South America and Mexico, 1968. Agent: Superone-Westwater-Fischer, 142 Greene Street, New York, New York 10012. Address: 140 Greene Street, New York, New York 10012, U.S.A.

Individual Exhibitions:

1971	Galleria Toselli, Milan
1972	Galerie Konrad Fischer, Dusseldorf
	Situation Gallery, London
1974	Kunsthalie, Berne
1976	Sperone Westwater Fischer, New York
1977	Date Paintings, Lisson Gallery, London
	Centre Georges Pompidou, Paris
1979	Yvon Lambert Gallery, Paris
1980	Continuity/Dicontinuity 1963–79, Moderna Museet, Stockholm (retrospective; travelled to Essen, Eindhoven and Osaka)
1982	Sperone Westwater Fischer, New York
1983	Akira Ikeda Gallery, Tokyo
1984	Akira Ikeda Gallery, Tokyo
1985	Lisson Gallery, London
1987	DAAD-Galerie, West Berlin

Selected Group Exhibitions:

1967	Language I, Dwan Gallery, New York
1968	Language II, Dwan Gallery, New York
1969	Language III, Dwan Gallery, New York
	557087, Seattle Art Museum
	Konception, Städtisches Museum, Leverkusen, West Germany
1970	An Opening Project, Socrates Perakis Gallery, Philadelphia
	Conceptual Art and Conceptual Aspects, New York Cultural Center
	Information, Museum of Modern Art, New York

1974	Andre: Broodthaers: Buren: Burgin: Gilbert & George: Kawara: Long: Richter, Palais des Beaux-Arts, Brussels
1980	Printed Art: A View of Two Decades, Museum of Modern Art, New York

Collections:

Kaiser Wilhelm Museum, Krefeld, West Germany

Publications:

On KAWARA: books—557087, exhibition catalogue, Seattle 1969; Concept Art, by Klaus Honnef, Cologne 1971; 6 Years: The Dematerialization of the Art Object by Lucy Lippard, New York 1973; articles—"On Kawara since Then" by Massayoshi Homma in Bijutsu-techo (Tokyo), December 1965; "The Dematerialization of Art" by Lucy R. Lippard and John Chandler in Art International (Lugano, Switzerland), February 1968; "Kawara" by Friedrichs in Kunstwerk (Baden-Baden West Germany), May 1972; "U.K. Commentary" by Richard Cork in Studio International (London), March 1972; "Borderlines in Art and Experience" by J. Bodolai in Artscanada (Toronto), Spring 1974; "Facteur chevals posttasche, die bild postkarte in der kunst" by S. Methen in Kunstwerk (Baden-Baden, West Germany), January 1974; "Carl Andre/Marcel Broodthaers/Daniel Burne/Victor Burgin/ Gilbert and George/On Kawara/Richard Long/ Gerhard Richter" by B. M. Reise in Art in America (New York), January 1975.

*

It is a paradox, but an intriguing paradox, that On Kawara, an extraordinary artist in such a seclusive, self-obliterative, impassive, and undiversified style, has been drawing considerable attention in America, in Europe as well as in Japan since the middle of the 1960's. He has been rarely visible as an artist in the traditional sense, but because of that, his art became literally universal. He reduced a myriad of unsettled discussions about the relationships between art and life to the simplest, the most explicit art form, namely, the 'date paintings', excluding every polysemous equivocations out of both form and content.

Individuality and universality became unified in his art through obliterating every semantic traces that lay between the two opposites. Kawara has been regarded as one of the most taciturn but thought-provoking Conceptual artists up to the present.

Born in 1933 at Kariya in Aichi Prefecture, Japan, he moved to Tokyo after he was graduated from a local high-school in 1951. His Bathroom series in 1953, the pencil drawing depicting odd, dismembered human bodies, brought the artist into public notice, though, later in life, he repudiated all his early representative styles. He went to America in 1959, traveled around Mexico and Europe, settled down in New York in 1965, and is a permanent resident of the city from then onward.

Kawara has been engaged in the 'date paintings' since 1966, simply recording the dates when he was at the work in such a way as 'June 22, 1979' with white letters on monochrome canvases. The I Read series, a collection of clippings from the daily newspapers assembled in loose-leaf binders, was started in 1966, followed by other two series, I Went and I Met, both started in 1968 in Mexico City. In the former series, he recorded his movements of each day, tracing his route of the day on a photo-copied map with a red ball-point pen. In the latter, the names of the people he met in a day were typewritten on a sheet of paper with the date.

In 1968, he also started his famous 'post-cards' series. He continued mailing the cityscape post-cards of the places he stayed in to his friends every day until September 1979 with the simple information of what time he got up in the day. There was a similar series by telegraph sent to his friends, telling just 'I Am Still Alive.' The minimum information about the date, time, and place carries no idiosyncrasy, making the artist On Kawara anybody as well as somebody. The artist becomes a liminous and anonymous body that flickers with the factual messages emitting to the world, so that the people who receive the messages question themselves about the meanings of the existence of the world, recalling what the 'date' really means.

Kawara's persistent concern about the continuity and momentariness of time led him to produce the *One Million Years,* a pair of 10-volume sets, each of which was filled with the record of one-million-years' dates; in the first 10 volumes, completed in 1971, was registered every dates of one million years up to 1969, and the second, brought out in 1980, was the future version, starting from 1981.

His major retrospective with the title 'On Kawara: continuity/discontinuity 1963–1979' was held in Stockholm, Essen, Eindhoven, and Osaka between 1980 and 1981.

—Tazmi Shinoda

KELLY, Ellsworth.

American. Born in Newburgh, New York, 31 May 1923. Studied at the Pratt Institute, Brooklyn, New York, 1941–42; Boston Museum School, 1946–48; Academie des Beaux-Arts, Paris, 1948. Served in the United States Army, 1943–46. Independent artist, since 1947. Taught evening classes, Roxbury, Massachusetts, 1947–48; travelled in France, 1948–54; taught at the American School, Paris, 1950–51; lived in New York, 1954–70; Graphic Artist, Gemini, G.E.L., Los Angeles, collaborated with Tyler, Graphics, Katonah, New York, 1976. Member, Park Sculpture Commission, Lincoln Park, Chicago, 1979. Recipient: Painting Prize, *Carnegie International,* Pittsburgh, 1961, 1964; Flora Mayer Witowsky Prize, Art Institute of Chicago, 1962; Brandeis University Creative Arts Award, Waltham, Massachusetts, 1963; Education Minister's Award, *International Art Exhibition,* Tokyo, 1963; Painting Prize, Art Institute of Chicago, 1974; President's Fellow Award, Rhode Island School of Design, Providence, 1980. Member, National Institute of Arts and Letters, 1974. Agents: Leo Castelli, New York; Blum-Helman Gallery, 20 West 57th Street, New York, New York 10022. Address: P.O. Box 151, Spencertown, New York 12165, U.S.A.

Individual Exhibitions:

1951   Galerie Arnaud, Paris
1956   Betty Parsons Gallery, New York
1957   Betty Parsons Gallery, New York
1958   Galerie Maeght, Paris
1959   Betty Parsons Gallery, New York
1961   Betty Parsons Gallery, New York
1962   Arthur Tooth Gallery, London
1963   Betty Parsons Gallery, New York
        Paintings, Sculptures and Drawings, Washington Gallery of Modern Art, Washington, D.C.
1964   Institute of Contemporary Art, Boston
        Galerie Maeght, Paris
1965   *27 Lithographies,* Galerie Maeght, Paris
        An Exhibition of Recent Paintings, Sidney Janis Gallery, New York

Ferus Gallery, Los Angeles
        Galerie Ricke, Kassel, West Germany
1966   Ferus Gallery, Los Angeles
        Knoll International, Dusseldorf
1967   Irving Blum Gallery, Los Angeles
        New Works, Sidney Janis Gallery, New York
1968   Irving Blum Gallery, Los Angeles
        An Exhibition of Paintings and Sculptures, Sidney Janis Gallery, New York
1971   Dayton's Gallery 12, Minneapolis
        Recent Paintings, Sidney Janis Gallery, New York
1972   *Paintings,* Galerie Denise René-Hans Mayer, Dusseldorf
        Albright-Knox Gallery, Buffalo, New York
        Galerie Ziegler, Geneva
1973   Museum of Modern Art, New York (United States touring retrospective)
        Leo Castelli Gallery, New York
        Irving Blum Gallery, Los Angeles
        Greenberg Gallery, St. Louis
1975   Ace Gallery, Venice, California
        Blum-Helman Gallery, New York
        Leo Castelli Gallery, New York (twice)
1976   Janie C. Lee Curtis Gallery, Houston
1977   Blum-Helman Gallery, New York
        Margo Leavin Gallery, Los Angeles
        Leo Castelli Gallery, New York
        Castelli Uptown Gallery, New York
1978   Museum of Modern Art, New York
1979   Metropolitan Museum of Art, New York
        Blum-Helman Gallery, New York
        Galerie Maeght, Zurich
        Paintings and Sculptures 1963–79, Stedelijk Museum, Amsterdam (toured Europe)

Ellsworth Kelly: *Black Panel II*, 1985

1981 Leo Castelli Gallery, New York
Leo Castelli Uptown, New York
Larry Gagosian Gallery, Los Angeles
Blum Helman Gallery, New York
1982 Margo Leavin Gallery, Los Angeles
John Berggruen Gallery, San Francisco
Thomas Segal Gallery, Boston
Castelli Graphics, New York
Whitney Museum, New York (travelled to St. Louis)
Blum Helman Gallery, New York
1984 Margo Leavin Gallery, Los Angeles
Leo Castelli Gallery, New York
Blum Helman Gallery, New York
Castelli Graphics, New York
1985 Blum Helman Gallery, New York
Leo Castelli Gallery, New York
Katonah Gallery, New York
Ann Weber Gallery, Georgetown, Maine
1986 Blum Helman Gallery, New York
1987 Fort Worth Art Museum, Texas (travelled to Boston; Toronto; Baltimore; San Francisco; Kansas City)
American Federation of Arts, New York (print retrospective; toured the United States, 1987-90)

Selected Group Exhibitions:

1949 *Premier Salon des Jeunes*, Galerie des Beaux Arts, Paris
1957 *Young America 1957*, Whitney Museum, New York
1964 *Post Painterly Abstraction*, Los Angeles County Museum of Art (toured the United States and Canada)
1970 *Kelly/Louis/Noland/Stella*, Museum of Contemporary Art, Chicago
1977 *Exposition Paris-New York*, Musée National d'Art Moderne, Paris
1979 *36th Biennial of American Painting*, Corcoran Gallery of Art, Washington, D.C.
1981 *Paris-Paris: Creations en France 1937-57*, Centre Georges Pompidou, Paris
1984 *La Grande Parade: Paintings after 1940*, Stedelijk Museum, Amsterdam
1985 *Transformations in Sculpture*, Guggenheim Museum, New York
1987 *The Barcelona Plazas*, Spanish Institute, New York

Collections:

Museum of Modern Art, New York; Whitney Museum, New York; Metropolitan Museum of Art, New York; Guggenheim Museum, New York; Washington Gallery of Modern Art, Washington, D.C.; Albright-Knox Art Gallery, Buffalo, New York; Art Institute of Chicago; Carnegie Institute of Art, Pittsburgh; Los Angeles County Museum of Art; Stedelijk Museum, Amsterdam; Tate Gallery, London.

Publications:

By KELLY: book—*Ellsworth Kelly*, exhibition catalogue, Los Angeles and New York 1984; articles—interview with Henry Geldzahler, in *Art International* (Lugano, Switzerland), February 1964; "Notes from 1969" in *Ellsworth Kelly: Paintings and Sculptures 1963-1979*, exhibition catalogue, Amsterdam 1979.

On KELLY: books—*Ellsworth Kelly*, exhibition catalogue, by Lawrence Alloway, London 1962; *Abstract Painting: 50 Years of Accomplishment from Kandinsky to the Present* by Michel Seuphor, New York 1962; *Paintings, Sculptures and Drawings by Ellsworth Kelly*, exhibition catalogue, with foreword by Adelyn D. Breeskin, Washington, D.C. 1963; *An Exhibition of Recent Paintings by Ellsworth Kelly*, exhibition catalogue, New York 1965; *Kelly: 26 Lithographies*, exhibition catalogue, by Dale McConathy, Paris 1965; *American Painting in the 20th Century* by Henry Geldzahler, New York 1965; *New Works by Ellsworth Kelly*, exhibition catalogue, New York 1967; *Constructivism: Origins and Evolutions* by George Rickey, New York 1967; *American Art since 1900* by Barbara Rose, New York 1967; *Minimal Art: A Critical Anthology*, edited by Gregory Battcock, New York 1968; *An Exhibition of Paintings and Sculpture by Ellsworth Kelly*, exhibition catalogue, New York 1968; *Ellsworth Kelly: Drawings, Collages and Prints* by Diane Waldman, Greenwich, Connecticut 1971; *Recent Paintings by Ellsworth Kelly*, exhibition catalogue, New York 1971; *Ellsworth Kelly: Paintings*,

exhibition catalogue, Dusseldorf 1972; *Ellsworth Kelly*, edited by E. C. Goossen, New York 1973; *Ellsworth Kelly* by John Coplans, New York 1973; *The Age of Avant-Garde* by Hilton Kramer, New York 1973; *Ellsworth Kelly: Recent Paintings and Sculptures*, exhibition catalogue, with an introduction by Elizabeth C. Baker, New York 1979; *Ellsworth Kelly: Paintings and Sculpture 1963-1979*, exhibition catalogue, with an introduction by Barbara Rose. Amsterdam 1979; *Ellsworth Kelly: Sculpture*, exhibition catalogue by Patterson Sims and Emily Pulitzer, New York 1982; *Ellsworth Kelly: Works on Paper*, exhibition catalogue by Diane Upright, Fort Worth 1987; *Ellsworth Kelly: A Print Retrospective 1949-1986*, exhibition catalogue by Rick Axom, New York 1987.

*

I have wanted to free shape from its ground, and then to work the shape so that it has a definite relationship to the space around it; so that it has a clarity and a measure within itself of its parts (angles, curves, edges, amount of mass); and so that, with color and tonality, the shape finds its own space and always demands its freedom and separateness.

In sculpture, the work itself is the form and the ground is the space around it. In painting, the form and the ground have always shared the same surface.

It was in the period from 1949 to 1954, when I lived in Paris, that I first achieved the separation of form and ground in a series of joined-panel paintings. The canvas panels were painted solid colors with no incident, lines, marks, brushstrokes or depicted shapes; the joined panels became a form, and thereby, transferred the ground from the surface of the canvas to the wall. The result was a painting whose interest was not only in itself, but also in its relation to things outside it.

From the time I returned to New York in 1954 and until 1965, I made few joined-panel works. The salient feature of my painting during that period was a large curved form that squeezed the ground to the edge of the canvas. Later, it was through the making of sculpture and cutting form out of metal, that I returned to making joined-panel works on canvas in which the ground was eliminated.

Since 1965, most of the painting and sculpture has been single or multiple monochrome panel works where the ground has moved to the wall or to the space around the free-standing pieces.

—Ellsworth Kelly

*

Ellsworth Kelly has been discussed in regard to Constructivist geometric abstraction, Abstract Expressionist scale and 1960's Minimalism, and he has been termed a "hard-edge," "systemic" and "post-painterly abstraction" painter. As is usually the case with such art historical relationships and labels, each seems to miss the overall intentions and effects of the work by stressing one or another element too strenuously. Kelly might be compared even more fruitfully with the American precisionists such as Georgia O'Keeffe or Charles Sheeler, whose basically hard-edge distillations from the contemporary landscape relate quite closely with Kelly's approach. He also equates with the elements of the color-field painters, especially Barnett Newman who, like Kelly, found inspiration in elements of Mondrian's contributions. The point is that, although all of these sources and overlaps may have credence in varying degrees, it is Kelly's early and unique synthesis and transformation of them which is the overriding feature in the body of work he has created beginning from about 1949.

It was in that year that Kelly painted a small oil on wood called "Kilometer Marker" in France. In this picture he visually realized the general characteristics which would continue to develop in his work over the following three decades. The generalized curved and rectangular shapes originate out of phenomena experienced personally. Along with the two-color combination of pale yellow and white, the crisply outlined shapes in juxtaposition work toward achieving a taut balance between positive and negative space which questions the nature of perception. Also in 1949, Kelly made a low relief construction titled "Window, Museum of Modern Art, Paris," anticipating his uses

of relief and sculpture in subsequent years to express his intentions in more literal terms.

In 1951-1952, Kelly made a group of pictures which used the grid as a basic structure to convey patterns of light and shadow, form and reflection, employing either rows of singly colored rectangles or combinations of curved wedges of one color together with a second color sharing the grid sections. By 1952, Kelly was juxtaposing squares or rectangular panels of one color each, distilling color and shape in drastically reduced terms which conveyed implications of perceived nature very different from the strictly purist readings of Malevich, and also from the energies of Mondrian's late works which seem the closest to Kelly's pictures of this period.

With his formal means and his visual intentions firmly in pace, Kelly proceeded to systematically analyze his possibilities, working to deduce the essential character of seen phenomena, using shape, color and proportion to visualize these essences more directly and simply. During the 1950's, curved and straight-edged shapes reach for the canvas edges, resting on the periphery, jutting in from the outside, butting or overlapping in various pictures. They seem to be both encroaching on the smoothly painted unitary surface and extending outward into the surrounding environment. In their elegant combinations of the sensuous and the pristine, they never lapse into either the decorative or the purely conceptual and always maintain hints at things seen, calling new attention to the ways solid objects and their shadows or reflections interact, examining the nature of physical phenomena and the effects of colored light. It is the perceived qualities of weight, perspective, fracturing which pervade the black and white works and the brightly colored ones as well.

Seen in the context of Minimalism, Kelly's works from the late 1960's to the present are often misinterpreted as fitting in with this formally based line of reductivism. It should not be forgotten that both his paintings and his sculptures of the 1950's had reached a level of distillation which was then radical in the context of the overriding expressionistic bent of the period and which had already achieved a statement of perceived essentials involving content outside the boundaries of the purely formal, both geometrically based and color based. Kelly's recent large, monochromatic shaped canvases and reliefs reiterate his intuitive capacities and his longtime practice, both of which combine to infuse his extremely distilled works with a distinctively individual understanding which never denies its roots in the memories of things seen.

—Barbara Cavaliere

KENNY, Michael.

British. Born in Liverpool, 10 June 1941. Studied at Liverpool College of Art, 1959-61; at Slade School of Fine Art, London, under Reg Butler, 1961-64. Married Rosemary Flood in 1968 (divorced); children: Dominic and Camilla; married Angela Fraser in 1978. Independent full-time sculptor, since 1965: lives and works in London. Part-time lecturer, Canterbury College of Art, Kent, 1964-65; Bristol College of Art, 1964-65; Goldsmiths College, London, 1968-72. Visiting Tutor, Slade School of Fine Art, London, 1972-82; External Assessor for the CNNA Diploma in Sculpture, since 1972; member of the Sculpture Faculty, British School, Rome, 1974-87. Recipient: Prize, Littlewoods' Sculptural Design Competition, 1964; Postgraduateship in Fine Art, University of London, 1964-65; Sainsbury Award, 1965; Major Award, Arts Council of Great Britain, 1975, 1977 and 1980. Associate, 1976, and Royal Academician, 1986, Royal Academy of Arts, London. Agent: Juda Rowan Gallery, 11 Tottenham Mews, London WIP 9PJ. Address: 71 Stepney Green, London EL 3LE, England.

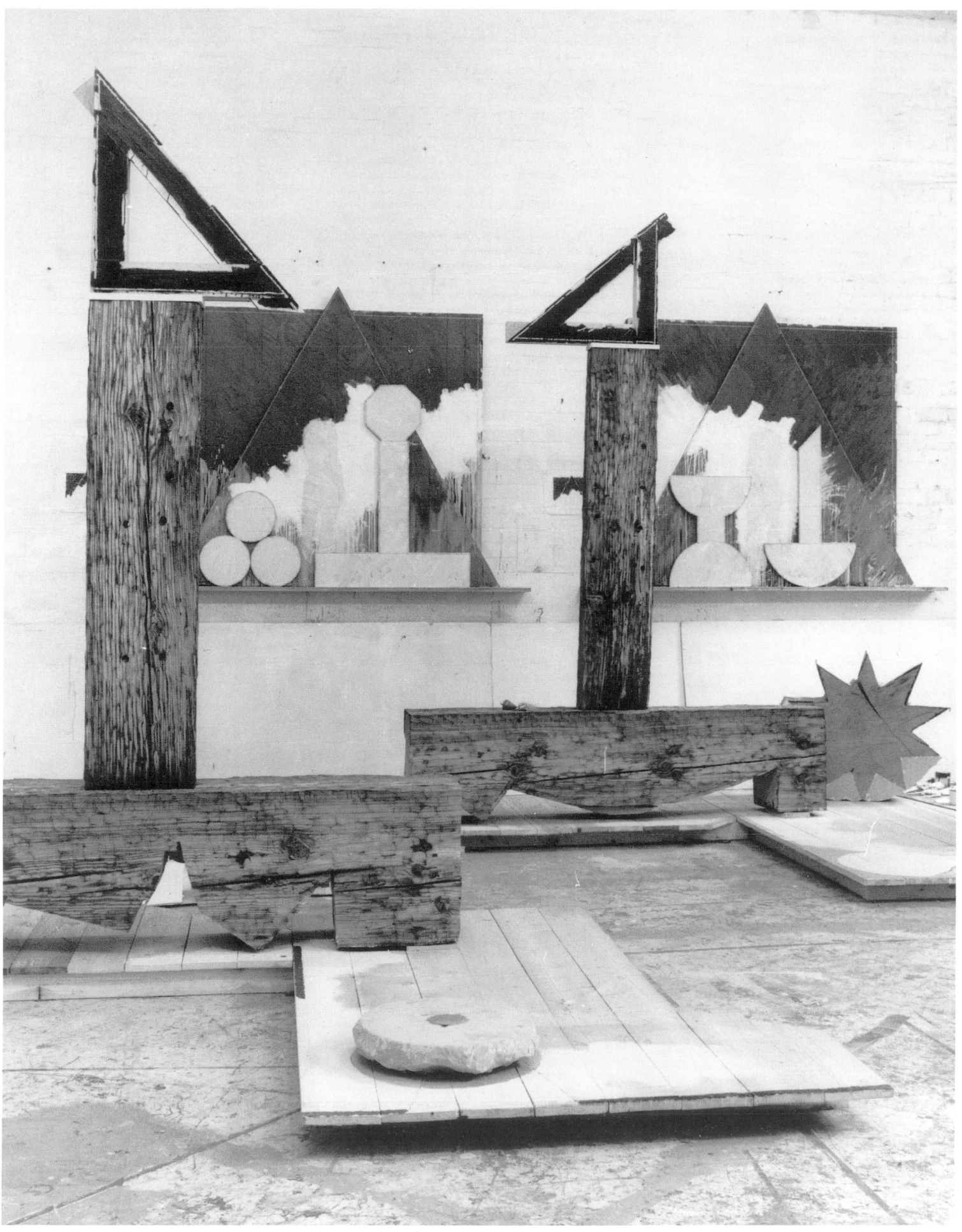

Michael Kenny: *In the Studio*, 1987

Individual Exhibitions:

1961	Walker Art Gallery, Liverpool
	Hope Hall Gallery, Liverpool
1964	Bear Lane Gallery, Oxford
1965	University of Southampton
1966	Hamilton Galleries, London
1969	Hanover Gallery, London
1977	Peterloo Gallery, Manchester
	Sculpture and Drawings, Serpentine Gallery, London
1978	Annely Juda Fine Art, London
1979	Roundhouse Gallery, London
1981	Annely Juda Fine Art, London
	Bluecoat Gallery, Liverpool (toured the U.K.)
1983	Tokyo Gallery, Tokyo
	Murdoch Lothian Fine Art, Liverpool
1984	Galerie Site, Paris
	Juda Rowan Gallery, London
	Arcade Gallery, Harrogate, Yorkshire
	Wilhelm-Lehmbruck-Museum, Duisburg, West Germany
1985	Galerie Lupke, Frankfurt
	Tokyo Gallery, Tokyo
1986	Royal Academy of Arts, London
1987	Galleria del Naviglio, Milan

Selected Group Exhibitions:

1966	*International Sculpture Exhibition,* Battersea Park, London
1968	*English Landscape Tradition in the 20th Century,* Camden Arts Centre, London
1976	*Arts' Council Collection 1975–1976,* Hayward Gallery, London
1977	*Silver Jubilee Exhibition of Contemporary British Sculpture,* Battersea, Park, London
1978	*Certain Traditions,* travelling exhibition (toured Canada and the U.K., 1978–80)
1979	*European Dialogue,* at the *Biennale,* Sydney (toured Australia and Tasmania, 1979–80)
1981	*British Sculpture in the 20th Century: Part II,* Whitechapel Art Gallery, London
1983	*Drawing in Air,* Sunderland Arts Centre, Cumbria (travelled to Swansea and Leeds)
1985	*Human Interest,* Cornerhouse Gallery, Manchester, Lancashire
1987	*The London Group,* Royal College of Art, London

Collections:

Arts Council of Great Britain, London; Tate Gallery, London; Jesus College, Oxford; Wilhelm Lehmbruck Museum, Duisburg, West Germany; Staatsgalerie, Stuttgart; British Council, London; British Museum, London; Victoria and Albert Museum, London; Leeds City Art Gallery, Yorkshire; Hara Museum of Contemporary Art, Tokyo.

Publications:

By KENNY: illustrated book—*I Know the Place,* poems by Harold Pinter, Warwick 1979; articles—statements in *Contemporary British Sculpture,* exhibition catalogue, London 1966; *Tate Gallery Acquisitions 1969,* London 1969; "Theory for Art: in *11 Sculptors: One Decade,* exhibition catalogue, London 1972; statements in *Art into Landscape,* exhibition catalogue, London 1974; *Directory of Artists: Space Open Studios,* London 1975; "The Crisis of Skill in Contemporary Painting and Sculpture" in *Fine Art Letter* (London), February 1982; "Michael Kenny interviewed by Adrian Lewis" in *Aspects* (Newcastle on Tyne), Summer 1982.

On KENNY: books—*Michael Kenny,* exhibition catalogue, by Andrew Forge, Oxford 1964; *Battersea Open-Air Exhibition,* exhibition catalogue, by Alan Bowness, London 1966; *English Landscape Tradition in the 20th Century,* exhibition catalogue, by Charles Spencer, London 1968; *Slade Centenary,* exhibition catalogue, London 1971; *11 Sculptors: One Decade,* exhibition catalogue, London 1972; *Michael Kenny: Sculpture and Drawings,* exhibition catalogue, by William Packer, London 1977; *The Sculpture of Michael Kenny,* exhibition catalogue with introduction by David Brett, Liverpool 1981.

Drawing is not a question of media, but of approach. For my own part, drawing is as important in my sculpture as it is in the works on paper, perhaps even more so for the drawing in the sculpture, because the structure of drawing is what holds it together.

My interest in drawing stems from the days as a student at the Slade where I was a reluctant draughtsman; nevertheless, it became the means by which I could hold together the content that I wanted to realize. The drawings which I do on paper are not "working drawings" as such. My working drawings I have never shown to anyone, certainly I have never exhibited them; they are made in a small sketchbook—about three inches by four which I carry around with me. The working drawings in these books are not only for sculpture, but also for the finished drawings that I exhibit.

I have mentioned the importance of drawing in my own work in order to affirm my strong belief that drawing is the cornerstone of the visual arts; it is the basic structure through which expression becomes possible. When Giorgio de Chirico spoke of "the terror of lines and angles" he was expressing that which in drawing is both primaeval and sophisticated—the existence of drawing as the profane image.

Animism, animation—I suppose that in recent sculptures and reliefs I have been concerned with the possibility of a material object, an actuality of material, containing a 'soul'. An enigmatic presence, an ambiguous duality, at one and the same time, an ethereal image and solid substance.

I can only make inconclusive statements—inconclusive in the Classical sense of cause and effect, that is. The titles are not descriptive; they extend the ambiguity. They are parallel to the images, *not* convergent on, or descriptive of, the image or substance. In the end the titles just add to the mystery and the confusion!

The Archaic and the Modern—the difference between an ancient and symbolic world view—the red rose as the blood of Christ—and the contemporary 'positivist' outlook is only one of attitude and viewpoint. In my sculpture there is no final 'truth' to be found—the whole Universe is only a part of *us.* The sculptures and reliefs and drawings are made of actual matter, but then the existence of matter is a degradation—a fall from perfection, from the purity of energy, the images fall into material existence. The fall—the degradation and the ultimate, hopeless quest for some whole truth is a pursuit that we seem to follow. We cannot perceive or understand the unknowable, all that remains is enigma. There is only image.

Stone, wood, charcoal are simply different manifestations of the same matter; they are interchangeable. To *draw* with stone—to *carve* with charcoal and paper. I believe my work is necessarily 'metaphysical'; it cannot have meaning any other way. Beyond the materiality of sculpture or painting there is only faith in something indefinable. I prefer to consider the fall of Adam and Eve from the point of view of the serpent. The Crucifixion from the point of view of Judas—and the creation of *anything* as the destruction of perfection. Change the viewpoint—it all remains the same.

—Michael Kenny

Outside the post-Caro school of English sculpture, Michael Kenny (a student of the Slade School, not St. Martin's, where Caro exerted so great an influence), shows none of the predilection for metal engineering forms or for the abstract Constructivist style. His works have a positive sense of realism to them, without being specifically tied to objects.

They are usually groups of separated forms, in mixtures of aluminium, marble, perspex and plastics, resembling, in some curious manner, the still-life paintings of Morandi. They seem to be searching for the same sense of interrelated balance as the great Italian artist sought in his rows of bottles or fruit. And like Morandi, Kenny infuses a disturbing sense of drama, almost of theatre, in formal confrontations. one is clearly invited to "read" these static groups,

which may not necessarily be pieces of sculpture, but serializations to be assessed as sequences of time and space, not single objects. They are meticulously arranged with elegance and positive directions to the viewer, all mounted on platforms which make the presentation all the more formal. Like the Morandi still-lifes they combine uprights, symbols of the human figure perhaps, with diverse quasi-geometrical shapes—square slabs of marble, pieces of aluminium arranged as pyramids, rows of metal rods bearing slabs of stone, variously suggesting tables, trestles, even gardens.

There is something speculative about these visual conundrums, as though the artist is challenging the preoccupations. The deceptive informality of Kenny's group of forms do not hide their premeditated planning and the sense of public occasion they suggest. The recent development from "still-life" to figure sculpture opens up interesting possibilities in Kenny's work; the new reclining figures retain the same sense of anonymity and enigma, with the body equating architectural linearity. This turn to overt reality is the result of the artist's fear of becoming too involved in an introverted, rarified world, the search for a direct human expression. It would be interesting and beneficial if the artist were afforded the opportunity to enlarge his scale and site them in a public place, where, whilst they might arouse doubt or hostility, it is unlikely they would be met with indifference.

—Charles Spencer

KIEFER, Anselm.

German. Born in Donaueschingen in 1945. Studied art, under Joseph Beuys, at the Staatliche Kunstakademie, Dusseldorf. Married to Julia Kiefer. Independent painter, in Dusseldorf, subsequently in Hornbach/Odenwald. Agent: Galerie Paul Maenz, Bismarckstrasse 50, 5000 Cologne 1. Address: Hornbach/Odenwald, West Germany.

Individual Exhibitions:

1969	Galerie am Kaiserplatz, Karlsruhe
1973	*Nothing,* Galerie Michael Werner, Cologne
	Der Niebelungen Leid, Goethe-Institut, Amsterdam
1974	*Alarichs Grab,* Galerie Felix Handschin, Basle
	Heliogabal, Galerie t'Venster, Rotterdam
	Malerei der verbrannten Erde, Galerie Michael Werner, Cologne
1975	*Unternehmen Seelowe,* Galerie Michael Werner, Cologne
1976	*Siegfried vergisst Brunhilde,* Galerie Michael Werner, Cologne
1977	Kunstverein, Bonn
	Galerie Helen van der Meij, Amsterdam
	Ritt an die Weichsel, Galerie Michael Werner, Cologne
1978	*Wege der Weltweisheit-Hermannsschlacht,* Galerie Maier-Hahn, Dusseldorf
	Bilder und Bucher, Kunsthalle, Berne
1979	Stedelijk Van Abbemuseum, Eindhoven, Netherlands
	Bucher, Galerie Helen van der Meij, Amsterdam
1980	*Verbrennen-Verholzen-Versenken-Versanden,* West German Pavilion, at the *Biennale,* Venice (with Georg Baselitz)
	Bilderstreit, Kunstverein, Stuttgart
	Württembergischer Kunstverein, Stuttgart
	Galerie Helen van der Meij, Amsterdam
	Bilder und Zeichnungen, Galerie Sigrid Friedrich-Sabine Kunst, Munich
	Holzschnitte und Bucher, Groninger Museum, Groningen, Netherlands
1981	*Und, Werdandi, Skuld,* Galerie Paul Maenz, Cologne

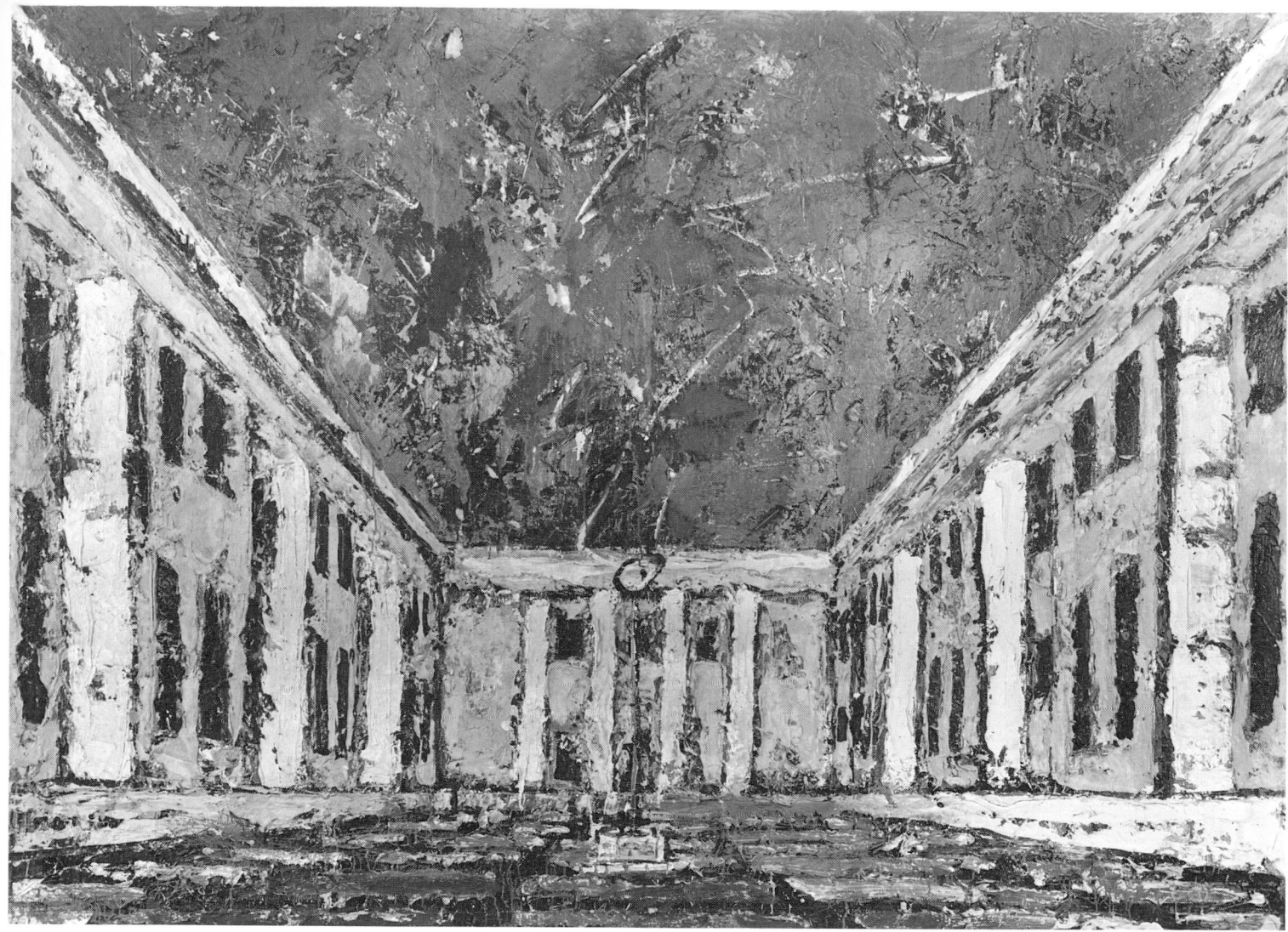

Anselm Kiefer: *Untitled,* **1983** Courtesy Anthony D'Offay Gallery, London

Marian Goodman Gallery, New York
Galleria Salvatore Ala, Milan
*Bucher,*Galerie Sigrid Friedrich-Sabine Kunst, Munich
Aquarelle 1970–1980, Kunstverein, Freiburg
Margarete—Sulamith, Museum Folkwang, Essen
(travelled to the Whitechapel Art Gallery, London)
1982   Galerie Paul Maenz, Cologne
Whitechapel Art Gallery, London
1983   CAPC/Musée d'Art Contemporain, Bordeaux, France
Anthony D'Offay Gallery, London
1984   Stadtische Kunsthalle, Dusseldorf
ARC/Musée d'Art Moderne de la Ville, Paris
Israel Museum, Jerusalem
Galerie Paul Maenz, Cologne
1985   Marian Goodman Gallery, New York
1986   Kunsthalle, Basle
1987   Galerie Foksal, Warsaw
Philadelphia Museum of Art, Pennsylvania (retrospective; toured the United States, 1987–88)

Selected Group Exhibitions:

1973   *14 mal 14,* Kunsthalle, Baden-Baden, West Germany
1976   *Beuys und seine Schuler,* Kinstverein, Frankfurt
1977   *Documenta 6,* Museum Fridericianum, Kassel, West Germany (and *Documenta 7,* 1982; *Documenta 8,* 1987)
1978   *The Book of the Art of Artists Books,* Museum of Contemporary Art, Teheran
1979   *Malerei auf Papier,* Badischer Kunstverein, Karlsruhe

1980   *Après le Classicisme,* Musée d'Art et d'Industrie, St. Etienne, France
1981   *A New Spirit in Painting,* Royal Academy of Art, London
1982   *60–80: Attitudes, Concepts, Images,* Stedelijk Museum, Amsterdam
1985   *The European Iceberg,* Art Gallery of Ontario, Toronto
1987   *Avant-Garde in the Eighties,* Los Angeles County Museum of Art

Collections:

Neue Galerie/Sammlung Ludwig, Aachen, West Germany; Stedelijk Van Abbemuseum, Eindhoven, Netherlands; San Francisco Museum of Modern Art.

Publications:

By KIEFER: book—*Die Donauquelle,* Cologne, 1978; articles—"Besetzungen 1969: in *Interfunktionen* (Cologne), no. 12, 1975; "Gilgamesch und Enkidu im Zederwald" in *Artforum* (New York), June 1981.

On KIEFER: books—*Anselm Kiefer,* exhibition catalogue, with texts by Dorothea von Stetten and Evelyn Weiss. Bonn 1977; *Anselm Kiefer: Bilder und Bucher,* exhibition catalogue, with texts by Johannes Gachnang and Theo Kneubuhler, Berne 18978; *Malerei auf Papier,* exhibition catalogue by Michael Schwarz and others, Karlsruhe 1979; *Anselm Kiefer,* exhibition catalogue, with text by Rudi H. Fuchs, Eindhoven, Netherlands 1980; *Biennale Venedig 1980: Deutscher Pavillon,* exhibition catalogue, with texts by Klaus Gallwitz and Rudi H. Fuchs, Stuttgart 1980; *Anselm Kiefer,* exhibition catalogue, with text by Rudi H. Fuchs,

Mannheim 1980; *Anselm Kiefer,* exhibition catalogue, with text by Tilman Osterwold, Stuttgart 1980; *Anselm Kiefer,* exhibition catalogue, with texts by Carel Blotkamp and Gunter Gercken, Groningen, Netherlands 1980; *Anselm Kiefer: Aquarelle 1970–1980,* exhibition catalogue, with text by Rudi H. Fuchs, Freiburg 1981; *Anselm Kiefer,* exhibition catalogue, with texts by Zdenek Felix and Nick Serota, Essen and London 1981; *Anselm Kiefer: Watercolours 1970–82,* with text by Anne Seymour, London 1983; *Anselm Kiefer,* exhibition catalogue with texts by Rudi Fuchs, Suzanne Page and Jurgen Harten, Dusseldorf and Paris 1984.

KIENHOLZ, Edward.
American. Born in Fairfield, Washington, 1927. Educated at Washington State College, Pullman; Eastern Washington College of Education, Cheney; Whitworth College, Spokane, Washington, 1945–52; self-taught in art. Married Nancy Reddin; children: Noah, Jenny and Chrisi. Independent artist known for life-sized sculptural tableaux: lived in Los Angeles, 1953–73; Director, Now Gallery, Los Angeles, 1956–57; Director, with Walter Hopps, Ferus Gallery, Los Angeles, 1957–63; moved to Berlin, 1973; now spends six months each year in Berlin and six months in Hope, Idaho; opened The Faith and Charity in Hope Gallery, Hope, Idaho, 1977; acknowledged collaboration of his wife in his work, 1981. Recipient: DAAD grant for residence in Berlin, 1973; Guggenheim grant, 1975. Agent: Galerie Maeght, Predigerplatz 10:12, 8000 Zurich, Switzerland. Addresses:

The Faith and Charity in Hope Gallery, Hope, Idaho 83836, U.S.A.; Meinekestrasse 6, 1 Berlin 15, West Germany.

Individual Exhibitions:

1955   Cafe Galleria, Los Angeles
1956   Syndell Studios, Los Angeles
1958   Ferus Gallery, Los Angeles
        Exodus Gallery, San Pedro, California
1959   Ferus Gallery, Los Angeles
1960   Ferus Gallery, Los Angeles
1961   Ferus Gallery, Los Angeles
        Pasadena Art Museum, California
1962   Ferus Gallery, Los Angeles
1963   Ferus Gallery, Los Angeles
        Iolas Gallery, New York
        Dwan Gallery, Los Angeles
1964   Dwan Gallery, Los Angeles
1965   Los Angeles Country Museum of Art
1966   Institute of Contemporary Art, Boston
        University of Saskatchewan, Regina
1967   Dwan Gallery, New York
        Washington (D.C.) Gallery of Modern Art
1968   Boise Art Museum, Idaho
        Vancouver Art Gallery
1970   *11 Tableaux*, Moderna Museet, Stockholm (toured Europe)
1971   Onnasch Galerie, Cologne
1972   Gemini G. E. L., Los Angeles
        Onnasch Galerie, Cologne
1974   Galerie Christel, Helsinki
        Galleria Bocci, Milan
        Galeria LPS, Turin
1975   *Roxys*, Ville de Strasbourg, France

1977   *The Art Show*, Galerie Folker Skulima, Berlin (travelled to the Centre Georges Pompidou, Paris, Städtische Kunsthalle, Dusseldorf, and Apollon Galerie Die Insel, Munich)
        The Volksempfangers, Nationalgalerie, Berlin (travelled to Galerie Maeght, Zurich, Städtischen Galerie im Lenbachhaus, Munich and Galleria Il Gabbiano, Rome)
1979   Louisiana Museum, Humlebaek, Denmark
        University of Idaho, Moscow
        University of Washington, Seattle
1981   Douglas Hyde Gallery, University of Dublin
        Galerie Maeght, Zurich
        Middendorf/Lane Gallery, Washington, D.C.
        L.A. Louver Gallery, Los Angeles
1982   GAK-Gesellschaft für Aktuelle Kunst, Bremen, West Germany
        Dibbert Gallery, Berlin
1983   Galerie Maeght, Paris
1984   San Francisco Museum of Modern Art
        Contemporary Arts Museum, Houston
        Walker Art Center, Minneapolis

Selected Group Exhibitions:

1961   *Art of Assemblage*, Museum of Modern Art, New York
1962   *50 California Artists*, Whitney Museum, New York
1968   *Dada, Surrealism and Their Heritage*, Museum of Modern Art, New York
1972   *Documenta 5*, Kassel, West Germany
1974   *ARS '74*, The Ateneum, Helsinki
1977   *Biennale*, Venice
1981   *Biennial*, Whitney Museum, New York
1982   *One Hundred Years of California Sculpture*, Oakland Museum, California

1984   *Salvaged: Altered Everyday Objects*, Project Studio One, Long Island City, New York
1987   *Berlinart 1961–87*, Museum of Modern Art, New York (travelled to San Francisco)

Collections:

Whitney Museum, New York; Los Angeles County Museum of Art; Stedelijk Museum, Amsterdam; Centre National d'Art Contemporain, Paris; Moderna Museet Stockholm; Louisiana Museum, Humlebaek, Denmark; Staatsgalerie, Stuttgart; Nationalgalerie, Berlin; Museum of Modern Art, Tokyo

Publications:

On KIENHOLZ: books—*Pop Art Redefined* by John Russell and Suzi Gablik, London 1969; *Edward Kienholz*, exhibition catalogue with texts by Lawrence Weschler and Ron Glowen, San Francisco 1984; articles—"A Portfolio of California Sculptors" by Donald Factor in *Artforum* (New York), August 1963; "The Savage Eye of Edward Kienholz" by John Coplans in *Studio International* (London), September 1965; "Crossing the Bar" by Suzi Gablik in *Artnews* (New York), October 1965; "Edward Kienholz" by Henry Hopkins in *Art in America* (New York), October/November 1965; "Edward Kienholz" in *Time* (New York), December 1965; "The Beanery" in *Newsweek* (New York), December 1965; "Beanery Built for Art" in *Life* (New York), January 1966; "The Underground Pre-Raphaelitism of Edward Kienholz En Vastkustrealist" by Beate Sydhoff in *Konstrevy* (Stockholm), January 1967; "68 High Art and Low Art" by Philip Leider in *Look* (New York), January 1968.

Edward Kienholz's assemblages and *tableaux vivants* possess at their core a moralist's critical assessment

Edward Kienholz: *Tadpole Piano Pool with Woman Attached*, 1973

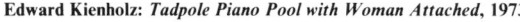

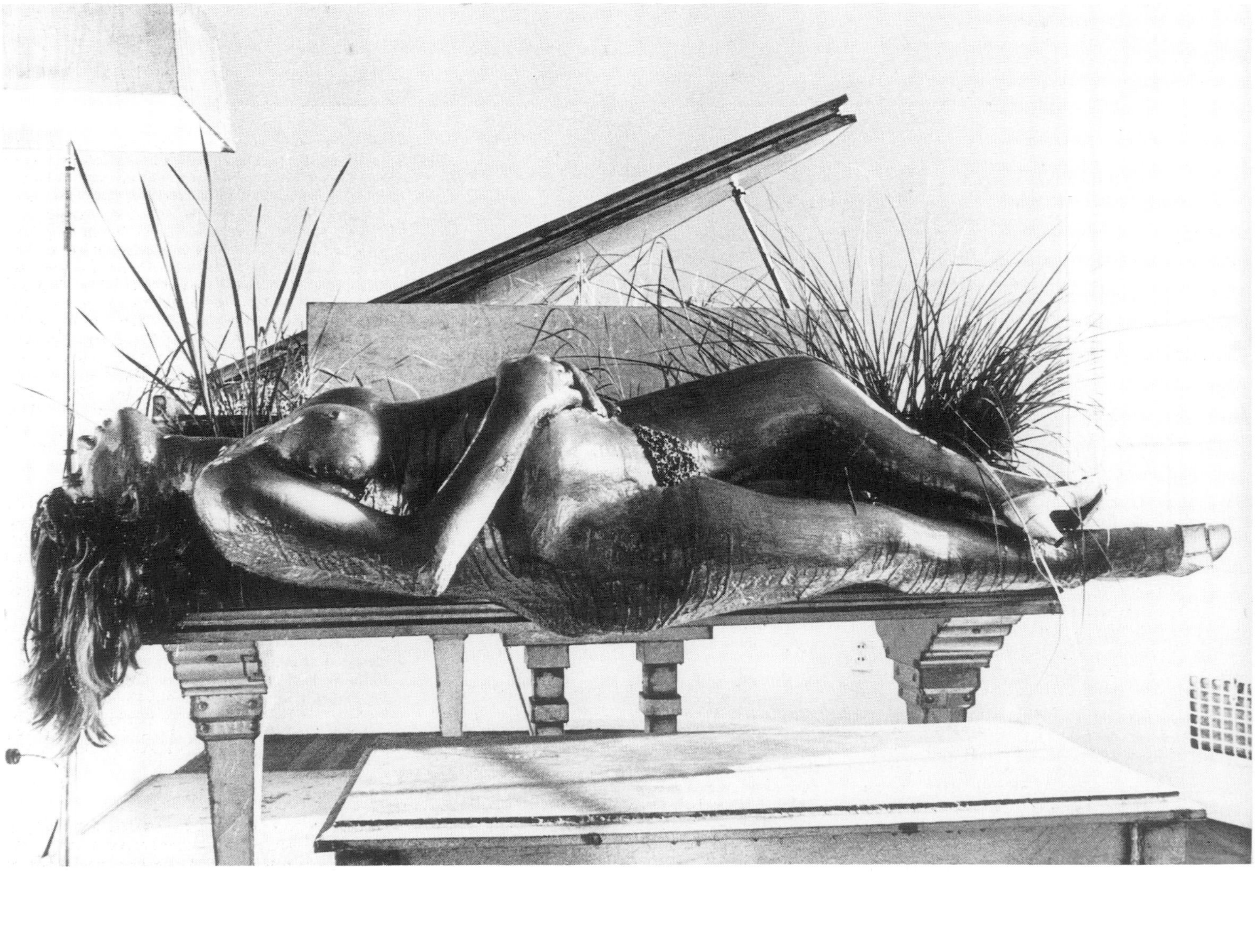

of contemporary society's conditions, institutions and values as they impact the life of the individual. Little escapes his scrutinizing gaze: sexual repression, social and political violence, racism, agism, the manipulation of social and sexual mores. His works are steeped in allegory and archetype, focused on the individual (either as figuration within the *tableau* or the viewer-as-participant) and commonplace objects and surroundings. A narrative often ensues as a direct means of quotation, but the implications of that narrative speak of a larger and more pervasive social phenomenon that conditions the story.

As an assemblagist, Kienholz has a remarkable eye for selective and suggestive detail, and an ability to imbue discarded common objects and consumer goods with metaphorical and allegorial significance. His "Volksempfangers" and "Tin TV" series of the 1970's invoke radios and television sets as a kind of human cipher (in the former) and as the vehicle for overt or covert propaganda purpose. A flophouse room, saved from the wrecking ball and re-assembled in all its sordid detail, becomes in "Sollie 17" a humanistic monument to loneliness and despair.

Kienholz's works agitate, but they are not agitational. They attack the repressiveness of complacency, particularly with respect to social and moral issues of our time. Thus a work like "Still Live" (1974), with its notorious randomly-activated and timed firing mechanism facing a chair in which the viewer is invited to sit, places the viewer in a life-and-death situation not for the sake of risk but as comment on the randomness and violence of terrorism and the inhumaneness of para-military means of political control.

Kienholz's art presents a dichotomy of familiarity and reproachment, often in direct extremes (the seat in "Still Live" is placed in comfortable and homey surroundings) to forcefully extract the symptomatic social cancer at the base of his commentary. Yet his art has also a poetic sensitivity: a respect for once-meaningful objects (such as old photographs and furniture), the *bricoleur's* facility of mechanical skills, the dramatist's eye for observation. At face value, Kienholz's works have the power to disturb and alienate. At a deeper level of meaning and intent, they force a confrontation with contemporary and universal aspects of society that manifest or conceal the foibles and imperfections of human nature. But, most importantly, they confront hypocrisy.

—Ron Glowen

KING, Phillip.

British. Born in Kheredine, Tunisia, 1 May 1934; moved with his family to London, 1946. Educated in primary schools in London; studied modern languages at Cambridge University, 1954–57, and sculpture at St. Martin's School of Art, London, 1957–58. Served in the Royal Signal Corps, 1952–54. Married Lillian Odelle in 1957; son: Anthony. Sculptor, living and working in London and Dunstable, Hertfordshire, since 1958. Worked as an assistant to Henry Moore, 1959–60; first fiberglass structures with colour, 1962; began working in steel, 1969. Lecturer, St. Martin's School of Art, 1959–80; Bennington College, Vermont, 1964; Slade School of Fine Art, London, 1967–70; Hochschule für Kunst, Berlin, 1979–80; Artist-in-Residence, Alexander Mackie College, Sydney, 1980. Since 1980, Professor of Sculpture, Royal College of Art, London. Trustee, Tate Gallery, London, 1967–69. Recipient: Boise Scholarship, Slade School of Fine Art, 1960; Peter Stuyvesant Travel Bursary, 1965; First Prize, *Socha Piestanskych Parkov*, Piestany, Czechoslovakia, 1969. Associate, Royal Academy of Arts, London, 1977. C. B. E. (Commander, Order of the British Empire), 1975. Agent: Mayor Rowan Gallery, London. Ad-

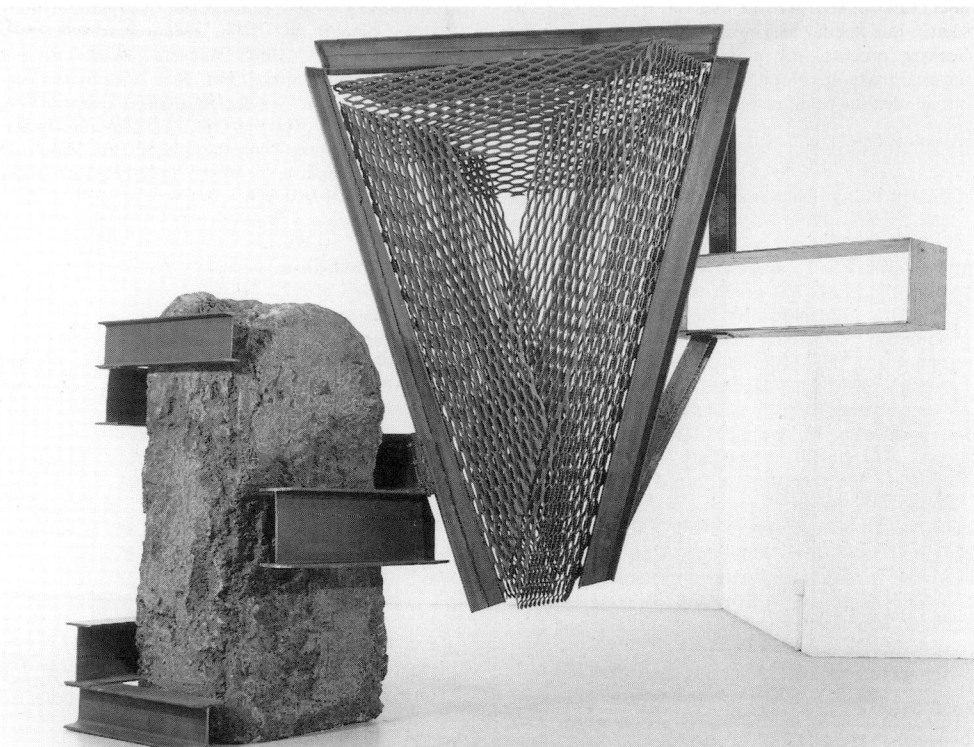

Phillip King: *Sculpture '74*, 1974

dress: c/o Mayor Rowan Gallery, 31A Bruton Place, London W1X 7AB, England.

Individual Exhibitions:

1957 Heffer's Gallery, Cambridge
1964 Rowan Gallery, London
1966 Richard Feigen Gallery, New York (travelled to Richard Feigen Gallery, Chicago)
    Isaac Delgado Museum of Art, New Orleans
1968 Galerie Yvon Lambert, Paris
    Biennale, Venice (with Bridget Riley; travelled to the Stadtgalerie, Bochum, West Germany, and Museum Boymans van Beuningen, Rotterdam)
    Whitechapel Art Gallery, London
1970 Rowan Gallery, London
1972 Rowan Gallery, London
1973 Rowan Gallery, London
1974 Rijksmuseum Kröller Müller, Otterlo, Netherlands (toured Europe, 1974–75)
1975 *Sculptures by Phillip King*, Rowan Gallery, London
    Mappin Art Gallery, Sheffield (toured the U.K., 1975–76)
1976 Third Eye Centre, Glasgow
    Oriel Gallery, Cardiff
1977 Rowan Gallery, London
1979 Rowan Gallery, London
1981 Hayward Gallery, London (travelled to the Fruit Market Gallery, Edinburgh)
1983 Juda Rowan Gallery, London
1987 Nishimura Gallery, Tokyo

Selected Group Exhibitions:

1961 *British Sculpture*, Jewish Museum, New York
1963 *International Biennale des Jeunes Artistes*, Paris
1965 *The New Generation*, Whitechapel Art Gallery, London
1969 *Contemporary Art: Dialogue Between the East and the West*, National Museum of Modern Art, Tokyo
1977 *Silver Jubilee Exhibition of Contemporary British Sculpture*, Battersea Park, London
1980 *British Art 1940–1980*, Hayward Gallery, London
1982 *British Sculpture in the 20th Century*, Whitechapel Art Gallery, London
1985 *Sculpture*, Fondation Cartier, Jouy-en-Josas, Fra
1987 *British Art in the 20th Century*, Royal Academy, London

Collections:

Arts Council of Great Britain, London; Tate Gallery, London; Ulster Museum, Belfast; National Gallery of Modern Art, Edinburgh; Rijksmuseum Kröller-Müller, Otterlo, Netherlands; Musée Royaux des Beaux-Arts, Brussels; Centre Georges Pompidou, Paris; Galleria d'Arte Moderna, Turin; Museum of Modern Art, New York; National Gallery of Victoria, Melbourne.

Publications:

By KING: articles—statement in *King*, exhibition catalogue, London 1964; "Phillip King, Young British sculptor Working Mainly in Plastics, Answers Some Questions by John Coplans" in *Studio international* (London), December 1965; statement in *Primary Structures*, exhibition catalogue, New York 1966; "British Artists at Venice: Phillip King Talks about His Sculpture" in *Studio International* (London), June 1968; "The Relevance of Matisse: A Discussion between Andrew Forge, Howard Hodgkin and Phillip King" in *Studio International* (London), July/August 1968; "Colour in Sculpture: Statements by Phillip King, Tim Scott, David Annesley and William Turnbull" in *Studio International* (London), January 1969; statements in *Phillip King*, exhibition catalogue, Otterlo, Netherlands 1974; "An Interview with Courturier" in *Art Press* (Paris), July/August 1975; "Phillip King", interview with Francis Spalding, in *Arts Review* (London), 10 April 1981; "Interview with Phillip King", with Richard Demarco, in *Studio International* (London), September 1982.

On KING: books—*Movements in Art since 1945* by Edward Lucie-Smith, London 1969; *Phillip King*, exhibition catalogue, by David Thompson, Otterlo, Netherlands 1974; *Sculptures by Phillip King*, exhibition catalogue, by Norbert Lynton, London 1975; *Phillip King*, exhibition catalogue, by Rudolf Oxenaar and others, London 1981 (includes bibliography); *Open Air Sculpture in Britain* by W. J. Strachan, London 1984; articles—"Phillip King" by William Feaver in the *Financial Times* (London), 12 March 1975; "Phillip King" by Norbert Lynton in *Art International* (Lugano, Switzerland), September 1977; "The Tree Within" by William Feaver in *The Observer* (London), 1 April 1979; "Phillip King in a Challenging Phase of Development" by John Russell in the *New York Times*, 28 June 1981; "Phillip King and Gottfried Honegger" in *Arts Review* (London), 10 June 1983.

I would like my work to be essentially something *of nature*, not parallel to it, nor evocation of nature but appearing as nature itself, by growing within its own laws, determined by our mutual reaction—for instance, our mutual near-ness and far-ness during the working process, my physical make-up equals its physical make-up. Not a metaphor for something else but an identity being revealed.

—Phillip King

Although Phillip King emerged among that group of young artists working with Anthony Caro at St. Martin's School of Art in London in the early 1960's, his art has always had a singularly individual flavour. A guiding concern of this group, the returning of sculpture to first principles after the excesses of 50's expressionism, produced a kind of minimal definition of sculpture as a self-sufficient three-dimensional object inhabiting space. They regarded abstraction as crucial for emphasizing these fundamental qualities, as was the positioning of the sculpture directly on the ground, without the intermediary of a pedestal. Only thus would the spectator be forced to confront and examine this "intruder" into his world. In a series of cone-based works, often vividly colored like the startling pink and green "Rosebud," King explored certain ways in which the viewer apprehends the object in front of him; how, by discerning its mass, volume, stability, structure and other such qualities, he constructs its "character."

Towards the end of the decade, in a series of multipartite works, like "Call," in which the emphasis has shifted from the sculptural object per se to the space it inhabits, King sought to define a sense of place, and invest it with a character. Although the various components articulate an area, such works are not installations, for they do not simply orchestrate a pre-existing space; rather, they segregate, then shape, a particular zone from within a larger arena: a sculpture is still a self-sufficient entity.

In the 70's King began using materials like slate, elm, steel and wiremesh in their raw states, exploiting their surface and textures for expressive effect. He reverted to the notion of a sculpture as a single entity, but continued to seek to define and characterize space and place, as titles like "Sure Place," "Open Bound," "Within," and "Ring Rock" indicate. Although the scale at times increased considerably, as in "Shogun," the sculptures were never removed from the realm of human dimensions. A confrontation between spectator and object remains central to his work, a confrontation in which the spectator learns something not only about the piece in front of him but about himself as well. This potentiality for increasing self-awareness is one of the essential justifications of sculpture for King. One of the constants in his art, it unifies a body of work which is very diverse in appearance.

—Lynne Cooke

KING, William (Dickey).

American. Born in Jacksonville, Florida, 25 February 1925. Educated at University of Florida, Gainesville, 1942–44; studied at Cooper Union Art School, New York, with John Hovannes and Milton Hebald, 1945–48 (Sculpture Prize, 1948); Skowhegan School of Painting and Sculpture, Maine, 1948; Brooklyn Museum Art School, New York, with Milton Hebald, 1949; Accademia di Belle Arti, Rome, 1949–50; Central School of Arts and Crafts, London, 1952. Married Lois Dodd in 1948; married Shirley Bowman in 1955; married Ann Kobin in 1965. Independent sculptor, since 1952. Instructor, Brooklyn Museum School of Art, New York, 1952–55; Lecturer in sculpture, University of California, Berkeley, 1965–66; Sculpture Instructor, Art Students League, New York, 1968–69; Instructor, University of Pennsylvania, Philadelphia, 1972–73. Recipient: Fulbright Travel Fellowship to Italy, 1949–50; Brooklyn Mu-

seum Prize, 1949; First Prize, Margaret Tiffany Blake Competition, 1951; Moorehead Patterson Sculpture Award, 1961; Augustus Saint Gaudens Medal, Cooper Union, 1964; New York State Creative Artists Public Service Award and Grant, 1974; Distinction Prize, Hakone Open-Air Museum, Japan, 1980. Agent: Terry Dintenfass, New York. Address: c/o Terry Dintenfass, 50 West 57th Street, New York, New York 10019, U.S.A.

Individual Exhibitions:

1954	The Alan Gallery, New York
1955	The Alan Gallery, New York
1958	The Alan Gallery, New York
1960	The Alan Gallery, New York
1961	The Alan Gallery, New York
1962	Terry Dintenfass, New York
1963	The Gallery, Norwalk, Ohio
1964	Donald F. Morris Gallery, Detroit
	Terry Dintenfass, New York
	Washington Federal Savings and Loan, Miami Beach
1965	Terry Dintenfass, New York
1966	Felix Landau Gallery, Los Angeles
	Berkeley Gallery, San Francisco
	Feigen-Palmer Gallery, Los Angeles
	Terry Dintenfass, New York
1967	Terry Dintenfass, New York
	William King: A Comprehensive Look, Lowe Art Gallery, University of Miami
1968	Terry Dintenfass, New York
1969	Terry Dintenfass, New York
	Guild Hall, East Hampton, New York
1970	Terry Dintenfass, New York
	Galerie Ann, Houston
	Berenson Gallery, Bay Harbor Island, Florida
	San Francisco Museum of Art
	Art Gallery, University of California at Los Angeles
	Santa Barbara Museum of Art, California
	University of New Mexico, Albuquerque
	Arkansas Art Center, Little Rock
1971	Terry Dintenfass, New York
	Alpha Gallery, Boston
	Dag Hammarskjold Plaza, New York
	Oklahoma Art Center, Oklahoma City
	University of Iowa, Iowa City
	Indianapolis Museum of Art
	Contemporary Arts Center, Cincinnati, Ohio
	Colby College, Waterville, Maine
	Syracuse University, New York
	Broward Community College, Ft. Lauderdale, Florida
	Ringling Museum, Sarasota, Florida
1972	Jacksonville Art Museum, Florida
	Hopkins Art Center, Dartmouth College, Hanover, New Hampshire
	Worcester Art Museum, Massachusetts
	Wadsworth Atheneum, Hartford, Connecticut
	Montgomery Museum of Fine Arts, Alabama
	Tennessee Fine Arts Center, Nashville
	Borough Hall, Brooklyn, New York
	Terry Dintenfass-Steel Gallery, Bridgehampton, Connecticut
1973	Terry Dintenfass, New York
	William Benton Museum, Storrs, Connecticut
	Aronson Gallery, Atlanta
	University of Georgia, Athens
	Elvehjem Art Center, University of Wisconsin
	Marion Koogler Mcnay Art Institute, San Antonio, Texas (travelled to Colorado Springs Fine Arts Center; Littleton Area Historical Museum, Colorado; Sangre de Cristo Arts and Conference Center, Pueblo, Colorado)
	State University of New York at Potsdam
	State University of New York at Fredonia
	State University of New York at New Paltz
	Terry Dintenfass, New York
	Moravian College, Bethlehem, Pennsylvania
	David Stuart Galleries, Los Angeles
1975	Amagansett Square, New York
1976	Terry Dintenfass, New York
1977	Terry Dintenfass, New York
	Zabriskie Gallery, New York

1979	University of Connecticut Library, Storrs
1980	Terry Dintenfass, New York
1981	Terry Dintenfass, New York
	Hoshour Gallery, Albuquerque, New Mexico
	Wingspread Gallery, Northeast Harbor, Maine
1982	Terry Dintenfass Gallery, New York
	Alpha Gallery, Boston
1983	Terry Dintenfass Gallery, New York
1984	Terry Dintenfass Gallery, New York
1985	Gallery Paule Anglim, San Francisco
1986	Hooks-Epstein Gallery, Houston
	Terry Dintenfass Gallery, New York
1987	Houshour Gallery, Albuquerque, New Mexico
	Gallery Paule Anglim, San Francisco
	David Heath Gallery, Atlanta, Georgia
	Montgomery Museum, Alabama
	Hunter Museum, Chatanooga, Tennessee

Selected Group Exhibitions:

1948	*Third International Sculpture Exhibition,* Philadelphia Museum of Art, Pennsylvania
1955	*Recent Sculpture U.S.A.,* Museum of Modern Art, New York
1962	*American Sculpture,* University of Tennessee, Knoxville (travelled to Conway, Arkansas; Tuscaloosa, Alabama)
1972	*Recent Figure Sculpture,* Fogg Art Museum, Harvard University, Cambridge, Massachusetts (toured the northeastern United States)
1973	*Sculpture in the Streets,* San Diego Fine Arts Gallery, California
1974	*WAVES: An Artist Selects,* Cranbrook Academy of Arts, Bloomfield Hills, Michigan (travelled to Grand Rapids Art Museum, Michigan)
1976	*Showhegan Retrospective,* Institute of Contemporary Art, Boston (travelled to Colby College, Waterville, Maine)
1978	*Human Figure in Contemporary Painting and Sculpture,* Genesis Gallery, New York
1980	*Sculpture in the 70s: The Figure,* Pratt Manhattan Center Gallery, New York (toured the United States)
1982	*Directions in Metal,* State University of New York at Potsdam

Collections:

Cornell University, Ithaca, New York; Syracuse University, New York; State University of New York at Potsdam; Addison Gallery of American Art, Andover, Massachusetts; Allentown Art Museum, Pennsylvania; Hopkins Art Center, Dartmouth College, Hanover, New Hampshire; First National Bank of Chicago; Fine Arts Center, Cheekwood, Tennessee; Weatherspoon Art Gallery, University of North Carolina, Greensboro; University of California, Berkeley.

Publications:

By KING: article—"Interview with William King," with Jack Graves, in *East Hampton Star* (East Hampton, New York), 17 July 1969, reprinted in *Time Magazine* (New York), 23 March 1970, and in *Artforum* (New York), May 1970.

On KING: books—*Sculpture: William King,* exhibition catalogue, New York 1954; *William King,* exhibition catalogue, Detroit 1964; *William King: A Comprehensive Look,* exhibition catalogue, text by August L. Reundlich, Miami 1967; *Recent Figure Sculpture,* exhibition catalogue, by J. L. Wasserman, Cambridge 1972; *Photography Year Book 1973* by John Sanders, London 1972; *An Artist in Residence: William King,* exhibition catalogue, with texts by Hilton Kramer and others, New York 1974; *The Age of the Avant-Garde* by Hilton Kramer, London 1974; articles—"San Francisco: William King" by P. D. French in *Artforum* (New York), May 1970; "The Witty Sculpture of William King" by John Canaday in the *New York Times,* 5 September 1971; "Something Funny's Going On" by Peter Scheldjhahl in the *New York Times,* 7 January 1973; "Many Small Grotesques in Sculpture by King" by Hilton Kramer in the *New York Times,* 1 December 1973; review by Jane Bell in *Arts Magazine* (New York), April 1976; "King's Woods" by S. Schwartz in *Art in America* (New York), September 1976; "King's Personalities" by W. Peterson in *Artweek* (Oakland, California), 13 January 1979.

A man of many parts—an experimenter with many materials. Rumour has it that William King was an unwilling pioneer, curiously unaware of the inherent value of his artifacts. Not surprisingly, when he first seriously considered becoming a sculptor, forgetting his previous ambitions in the field of architecture, he was quite prepared to sell his sculptures for $40–50 apiece. Budding artists of any sort have endured that sort of grind too often.

That was back in the late 40s when he had abandoned his home State of Florida and was moving on to New York and the Brooklyn Museum of Art School preparatory to spending a year at Rome's Accademia dei Belle Arti and another with the Central School in London: a respectable and extended period of varied tuition which did nothing to deflate his prying talents or their reflections on the recognizable quirks and behavioral performances of human types. So. What has transpired?

The 'thing' about William King is that he has essentially found a quizzical (without a hint of malice) vision of the OK well-heeled USA. The sculptural version of this keenly observed North American has been a telling factor in almost all of King's oeuvres over the past 40 years regardless of his adventures with different media and into their unexpected potentialities.

Here is a remarkably fluid interpreter of at least one strand of Americana from a local boy if one includes all the States of the Union as a locality. For those living outside the 'confines' of the Monroe Doctrine William King mirrors a world only seen by courtesy of Hollywood and the New Yorker. This means that psychological portrayal of *types* is not a cardinal message that his sculptures relate to most non-Americans. In the main they will not appreciate gentle nuances of gentlemen wearing the 'right' suits or of ladies carefully—and sometimes 'uncarefully'— posing in eternal *autre-jour* modish garb (except of course when they are naked, and even then they have a way of making their nudity privately stylish).

These remarks help underline the longlasting enthusiasm King has aroused amongst so many collectors in the States and how this confirms continuous success. Fortunately, there are more than one William King. He is a sculptor who, with increasing viability, is able to make his presence felt in the realms of novelty, ideas and inspirations. This is the *social* artist who, not content with the foibles of Mr. and Ms. America, yearns for another definition of the word *social;* maybe not the configuration of World problems, but certainly an imagery (often on a large scale) which spells out Personal Decisions. Taken together, these two aspects of William King emphasize why a captious dismissal of his work as 'humorous' is unacceptable. Whatever whims may appear, and unquestionably it does sometimes percolate through some of his ideas, the real approach to the output of this artist should be to size up his ability culturally, in order to pursue sculptural solutions which are visually appetizing without any psychological kickbacks or indulging in any mental parlour games.

Globally speaking, William King should be regarded as an artist rich in invention and with the insinuation of his personal style into a scarcely influenced number of subjects of humanity and their variants in widely differing raw materials.

Chipping away for hours with a blunt instrument at coral fragments when he was a child, he developed a love of creation that has never deserted him. Early application of carving craft to wood increased his understanding of the value of perfecting techniques (and time and again he has come back to timber as a sculptor's faithful ally), before he turned his attentions to exploring bronze (another material offering continuous promise). The next step was to investigate ways and means of operating with steel and aluminum, and here the very nature of the metals led him to concentrate on the assembly of shaped flat sheeting bolted and welded into constructions, tall in structure and frequently wide in extent. All these involvements with different raw elements, even if one seemed to succeed another, actually, once discovered, continued as part of his repertoire and co-existed with his aston-

ishing control of fashioning terracotta (the example of "Marilyn"—now unfortunately stolen—is supremely beautiful both in expression and execution).

In the 60s—and thereafter—King has also been vividly expanding sculptural developments in the uses of fabrics (including various examples of tailors' cloth and burlap) and metallics (naughahide, vinyl on linden wood and mylar), almost as if upon a quest to discover the philosopher's stone. Exotically 'alter-ego' collages and monotypes have followed.

Thus the tangled web of King's processes and the ingredients he has involved to achieve a happy outcome from those processes need to be examined before coming to descriptions of his actual completed works. "Forest Folk" (1978), 72″ high in wood, for instance, shows how he can fit together a wood jigsaw of boughs, while the 49″ high "Coat" of 1981 is a carefully carved work in wood, upright as the preferred majority of his single figures are. The bronze sculpture of the couple "Max and Peggy" of 1986 is adeptly worked and highly figurative except in the fashioning of the pair's faces. Sheet metal (cast aluminum) in a piece like "Magic" is in the form of a subtle chevron but betraying no sharpened angles in order to bring into being a female figure bent so that one extended hand almost touches the ground. The 3 striding figures of "Collegium" (1984) are a monument at Houston University, at least 6 times the height of a man and wrought in cast and plate aluminum. Even the trees are dwarfed by this towering eminence. As for the vinyl-covered figures, as opposed to all of King's other 'people', they are richly endowed with glossy colour-shining blacks and reds and gleaming opalescent whites.

In virtually every case where the carving or modelling is not scrupulously worked, limbs, outlines and features of men and women tend to be simplified or merely indicated—everything depends on stance. In such a manner William King, through his sculptures, stands astride the regionalisms of figuration and near-nonfiguration.

—Sheldon Williams

KIRILI, Alain.

French. Born in Paris in 1946. Associated with artist Philippe Sollers and "Tel Quel" literary group, Paris. Independent artist, Paris, since 1970, and New York, since 1975. Agent: Galerie Sonnabend, 12 rue Mazarine, 75006 Paris. Address: 13 rue Herold, 75001 Paris, France.

Individual Exhibitions:

1972	Galerie Sonnabend, Paris
1974	*Peintures, designs, sculptures, gravures*, Galerie Sonnabend, Paris
1976	Galerie Sonnabend, Paris
	Galerie Rencontres, Paris
1977	P.S. 1, Institute for Art & Urban Resources, Long Island City, New York
1978	*Sculpture: A Record of Past Work 1972–78*, Dartmouth College, Hanover, New Hampshire
	Geschmeidese Eisenskulpturen, Museum Haus Lange, Krefeld, West Germany
	Sonnabend Gallery, New York
	Galerie im Taxispalais, Innsbruck
1979	Galerie Schellmann + Kluser, Munich
	Galerie Sonnabend, Paris
	E. + O. Friedrich, Berne
	Sonnabend Gallery, New York
1980	Ernst Beyeler Galerie, at the *Art Fair '80*, Basle
1981	Sonnabend Gallery, New York
	Diane Brown Gallery, Washington, D.C.
	Recent Sculptures, Dallas Museum of Fine Arts
1982	Sonnabend Gallery, New York
	Storm King Art Center, Mountainville, New York

1983	French Embassy, New York
	Kunstverein, Frankfurt
	Bonnier Gallery, New York
1984	Galerie Adrien Maeght, Paris
	Centre d'Art Contemporain, Chateauroux, France
	Musée Saint-Pierre, Lyon, France
	Musée des Beaux Arts, Besancon, France
1985	Musée Rodin, Paris

Selected Group Exhibitions:

1975	*John Weber Invitational*, John Weber Gallery, New York
1976	*Soho Downtown Manhattan*, Akademie der Künste, West Berlin
1977	*Documenta*, Kassel, West Germany
1978	*Pour la Gravure*, Musée de l'Abbaye Sainte-Croix, Les Sables-d'Olonne, France
1979	*Contemporary Sculpture*, Museum of Modern Art, New York
1980	*Zeitgenossische Plastik*, Kulurhistorische Museum, Bielefeld, West Germany
1981	*Directions 1981*, Hirshhorn Museum, Washington, D.C.
1982	*Post Minimalism*, Aldrich Museum of Contemporary Art, Ridgefield, Connecticut
1985	*Maximal Implications of the Minimal Line*, Bard College, Annandale-on-Hudson, New York

Publications:

By KIRILI: books—*Die Yoni/Linga Plastiken*, Munich 1979; *Wer Hat Angst vor der Vertikalitat?*, Berne 1979; articles— "Philippe Sollers et Alain Kirili: texte aporistique" in *VH 101* (Paris), Spring 1971; "Thoughts on Samuel Yellin and Blacksmithing" in *Artforum* (New York), May 1978; "La Sculpture par l'Espirit", in *Art Press* (Paris), March 1980.

On KIRILI: books—*Mail Art, Communication à Distance, Concept* by Jean-Marc Poinsot, Paris 1971; *Conceptual Art* by Ursula Meyer, New York 1972; *Alain Kirili: peintures/dessins/sculptures/gravures*, exhibition catalogue, with text by Marcelin Pleynet, Paris 1974; *Alain Kirili: Sculpture: A Record of Past Work 1972–78*, exhibition catalogue, with text by Jan Van der Marck, Hanover, New Hampshire 1978; *Alain Kirili: Geschmiedete Eisenkulpturen*, exhibition catalogue, with text by Gerhard Storck, Krefeld, West Germany 1978; *Alain Kirili*, exhibition catalogue, with text by Peter Weiermair, Innsbruck 1978; *Pour la Gravure*, exhibition catalogue, with texts by Marcelin Pleynet and Christian Prigent, Les Sables-d'Olonne, France 1978; *Alain Kirili: Recent Sculptures*, exhibition catalogue, with text by Steven A. Nash, Dallas 1981; *Alain Kirili: Iron Sculptures*, exhibition catalogue with text by Monique Laurent, Paris 1985.

Alain Kirili, the sculptor, began his career on a theoretical note. In the late 1960's and early 1970's, he wrote texts on both the theory and practice of art influenced by his associations with the Tel Quel group in Paris. During this period he painted and drew; in 1972 he made his first sculptures in zinc, iron and terra cotta, and he often employed various mixed medium combinations. By 1975 his interests had narrowed to iron and the forge. Kirili's fascination with the rich, tradition-bound process of the forge, his deep-seated awareness of the importance of craft, as well as his recognition of the metaphorical associations implicit in the artist's manipulation of iron, are issues evident in his writings as well as in his sculptures.

The early iron sculptures were the product of a formally manipulated method, recalling the "drawing in space" approach of Julio Gonzalez. They consisted of metal rods hammered into tall, thin elements which Kirili joined by "threading" them through small loops and holes; whether standing or leaning against the wall, the inter-locking compositions appeared to shape the surrounding space, and they drew attention to the description of volumes among the parts. In certain examples—such as the ones in which a vertically disposed element can bring to mind an extended hand holding a triangle—figurative associations are tentative.

In the early 1980s, he turned to investigating simple geometric forms that have been encoded for centuries with religious significance. In the 17 variations of the cross it contains, the floor piece *Commandment V* (1981) is revealing of the sacred power of the Christian cross. Iconic traditions of statuary are wrestled with in a number of the abstract sculptures, in particular the examples of upright in forged iron with curved, indented or scooped out tops. In the "Kings" series, the reflective surfaces of these forged aluminum pieces, tall uprights with columnar shafts and crown-like capitals, are used to intensify the aura of majesty Kirili is seeking to convey.

In the recent bronzes, Kirili is making clear his enormous admiration for the powerful torsos of Rodin and their dynamically heaving surfaces which is such an outstanding trademark of them.

—Ronny H. Cohen

KIRKEBY, Per.

Danish. Born in Copenhagen, 1 September 1938.

Studied geology at the University of Copenhagen, 1957–64, Ph.D. 1964. Married Elisabeth Therkeisen in 1965 (separated, 1976); daughter: Rebecca; Married Vibeke Windelow in 1979; son: Sophus. Worked as a geologist in Greenland, 1958–72. Independent artist, Copenhagen, also working in New York, Greenland, and Central America, since 1965; Member, Fluxus group of artists, New York, 1966–67. Instructor, Staatliche Akademie der Bildenden Künste, Karlsruhe, from 1978. Recipient: Painting Scholarship, 1965, and Writing Scholarship, 1973, Statens Kunstfond, Copenhagen; Gold Medal, Royal Danish Academy of Art, Copenhagen, 1968; D.A.A.D. Fellowship, West Berlin, 1982. Member, Det Danske Akademi, Copenhagen, 1982. Agent: Galerie Michael Werner, Gertrudenstrasse 24, 5000 Cologne 1, West Germany. Address: Oscar Ellingersvel 11, 2000 Copenhagen F, Denmark.

Individual Exhibitions:

1964   Hoved-Bibliotek, Copenhagen
1965   Den Frie, Copenhagen
        Galerie Jensen, Copenhagen
1966   Galerie 101, Copenhagen (with Joseph Beuys, Bengt af Klintberg and Traakvogn 13)
1967   Galerie 101, Copenhagen
        St. Mark's, New York (with Nam June Paik, Takehisa Kosugi and Allen Kaprow)
        Neue Galerie, Aachen, West Germany (with Bjorn Norgard)
        Arkitektskolen, Aarhus, Denmark (with Bjorn Norgard)
1968   Studentersamfundet, Aarhus, Denmark (with Norgard and Nielsen)
        Jysk Kunstgaleri, Copenhagen
        Fyns Stifmuseum, Odense, Denmark
1969   Jysk Kunstgaleri, Copenhagen
1970   Jysk Kunstgaleri, Copenhagen
1972   Daner Galleriet, Copenhagen
        Gentofte Kunstbibliotek, Copenhagen
1973   Galerie St. Petri, Lund, Sweden
1974   Haderslev Museum, Denmark
        Galerie Michael Werner, Cologne
1975   Statens Museum for Konst, Copenhagen
        Henie-Onstad Kunstsenter, Oslo
        Daner Galleriet, Copenhagen
        Kunstbygningen, Aarhus, Denmark
1976   Gallery Cheap Thrills, Helsinki
        Ribe Museum, Ribe, Denmark
1977   Museum Folkwang, Essen
1978   Galerie Michael Werner, Cologne
        Kunstraum München, Munich

Per Kirkeby: *Untitled*, 1981

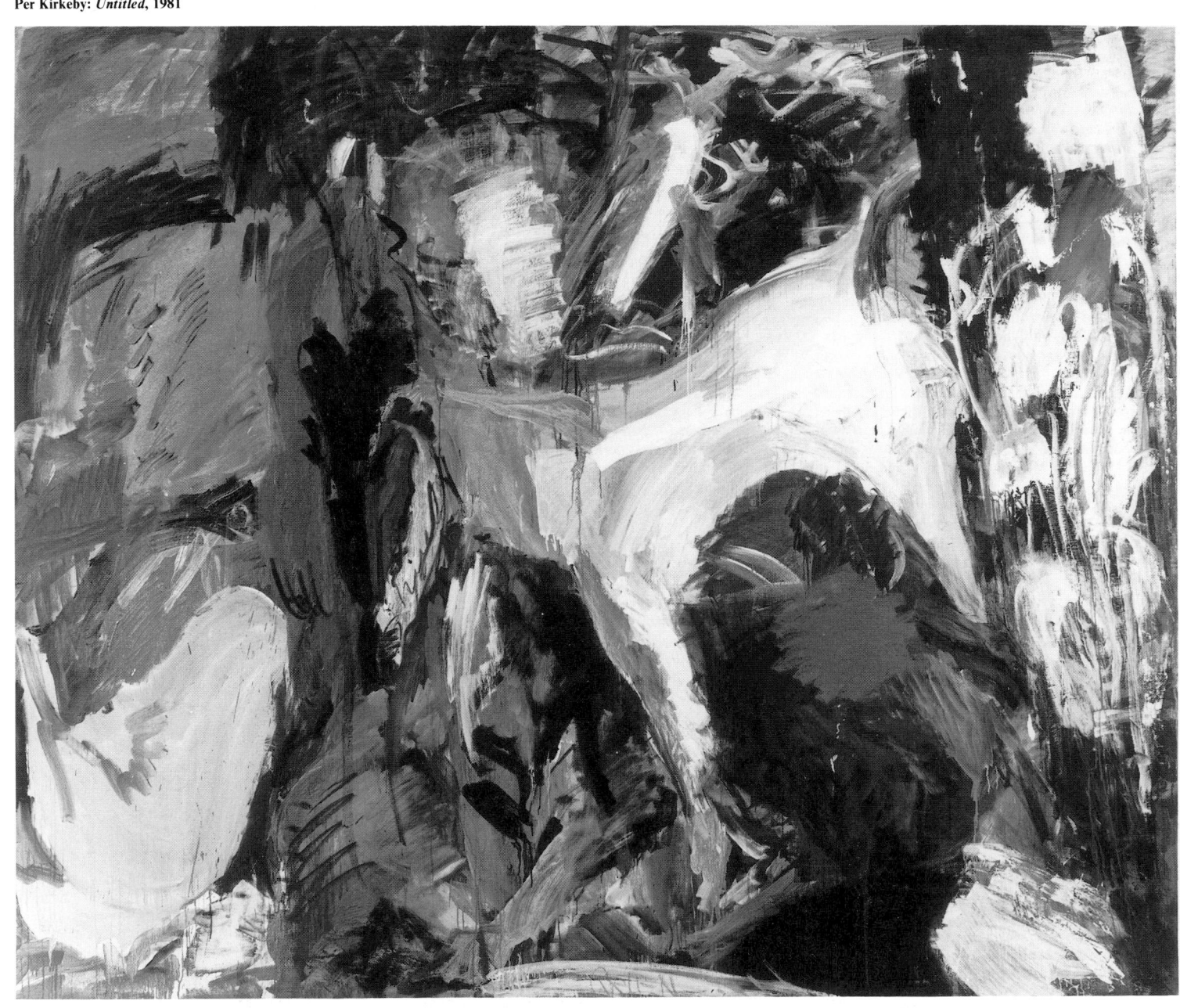

1979 Kunsthalle, Berne
1980 Galerie Fred Jahn, Munich
Galerie Helen van der Meij, Amsterdam
Galerie Michael Werner, Cologne
1981 Museum Ordrupsgaardsamlingen, Copenhagen
Galerie Fred Jahn, Munich
1982 Galerie Michael Werner, Cologne
Galerie Springer, West Berlin
Galerie Crone, Hamburg
Nigel Greenwood Gallery, London
Stedelijk Van Abbemuseum, Eindhoven, Netherlands
Galerie Fred Jahn, Munich
1983 Galerie Zwirner, Cologne
Galerie Sabine Knust, Munich
DAAD-Galerie, West Berlin
1984 Van Abbemuseum, Eindhoven
Strasbourg Museum, France
Galerie Thaddaeus Ropac, Salzburg, Austria
Kunstverein, Braunschweig, West Germany
Galerie Ulysses, Vienna
1985 Fruitmarket Gallery, Edinburgh
Douglas Hyde Gallery, Dublin
Galerie Knoedler, Zurich
Whitechapel Art Gallery, London
1986 Michael Werner Gallery, New York
Projekt fur Munster, West Germany
1987 Museum Boymans-van Beuningen, Rotterdam
Galerie Maeght Lelong, Zurich

Selected Group Exhibitions:

1962 *Den Eksperimenterende Kunstskole*, Galerie Gammel Strand, Copenhagen
1966 *Nordisk Ungdomsbienale*, Louisiana Museum, Humlebaek, Denmark
1968 *Anonymiteter*, Konsthall, Lund, Sweden
1970 *Happening und Fluxus*, Kunstverein, Cologne
1973 *Fluxshoe*, Midland Group Gallery, Nottingham (toured the U.K.)
1976 *Biennale*, Venice (and 1980)
1980 *A New Spirit in Painting*, Royal Academy of Arts, London
1982 *Documenta*, Kassel, West Germany
1983 *Erste Konzentration*, Galerie Boibrino, Stockholm
1985 *Promenades*, Parc Lullin, Genthod, Geneva

Collections:

Statens Museum for Konst, Copenhagen; Aarhus Kunstforeningen, Denmark; Silkeborgs Konstmuseum, Denmark; Odense Stiftsmuseum, Denmark; Louisiana Museum, Humlebaek, Denmark; Silkeborg Museum, Denmark; Moderna Museet, Stockholm; Van Abbemuseum, Eindhoven, Netherlands; Bavarian State Galleries, Munich; Henie-Onstad Kunstsenter, Oslo.

Publications:

By KIRKEBY: books—*Per Kirkeby Litt*, Morso, Denmark 1965; *Bla 5*, Copenhagen 1965; *Copyright*, Copenhagen 1965; *2.15*, Copenhagen 1967; *I Orkennen Moder Maigret Entropien*, Copenhagen 1968; *Bla, Tid*, Copenhagen 1968; *Billedforkafinger*, Copenhagen 1968; *Landskaberne*, Copenhagen 1969; *Bla, Ornament*, Copenhagen 1969; *Ornamentet er . . . .*, Copenhagen 1970; *Personerne*, Copenhagen 1970; *Jungling auf die Wanderschaft*, Copenhagen 1970; *Handlingen*, Copenhagen 1971; *Haandelser pa Rejsen*, Copenhagen 1971; *Vejret*, Copenhagen 1972; *Indianeriüv i regnskoven*, with Teit Jorgensen, Copenhagen 1973; *Mayalandet*, with Teit Jorgensen and Ib Michael, Copenhagen 1973; *Foyvende Blade*, Copenhagen 1974; *Gron Ornament*, Copenhagen 1974; *Under Duebla Himmel*, Copenhagen 1975; *Et Billedudvalg*, Copenhagen 1975; *Perspektivet*, Copenhagen 1975; *Naturens Blyant*, Copenhagen 1978; *Rejser*, Copenhagen 1978; *Serie*, Copenhagen 1978; *Naturstudiet*, Copenhagen 1979; *Billeder of Haderslev*, Copenhagen 1979; *Hus + Billede + Dekorations, 20'erne in Danmark* with Troels Andersen and Allan de Waal, Copenhagen 1978; *Bravura*, Copenhagen 1980; *Den Fortsatte Tekst*, Copenhagen 1982; *Tegninger II*, Copenhagen 1982; *Selected Essays from Bravura*, Eindhoven 1982; films—*Brigitte Bardot*, 1968; *Stevns Klint og Mons Kling*, 1969; *Gronlandsfilm I*, 1969; *Gronlandsfilm II*, 1970; *Fraendelos*, 1970;

Dyrehaven—den romantiske skov, 1970; *Tre piger og en gris*, 1971; *Wilhelm Freddie*, 1972; *Og myndighederne sagde stop*, 1972; *En erindring omet besog hos en lacandon-familie i regnskoven i Mexico*, 1975; *Normannerne*, 1975; *Asger Jorn*, 1977; *Carl Brumer*, 1980; *Thorvaldsen I*, 1980; *Geologi—er det egentlig videnskab?*, 1980.

On KIRKEBY: books—*Per Kirkeby: Danmark, Norge, Sverige* by Troels Andersen, Allan de Waal and Per Hovdenakk, Copenhagen 1975; *Fliegende Biatter*, exhibition catalogue, with text by Zdenek Felix and Troels Andersen, Essen 1977; *Kunstraum*, exhibition catalogue, with text by Hermann Kern, Munich 1978; *Per Kirkeby*, exhibition catalogue, with texts by Johannes Gachnang and Theo Kneubuhler, Berne 1979; *Per Kirkeby*, exhibition catalogue, with texts by Rudi H. Fuchs and Johannes Gachnang, Cologne 1980; *Per Kirkeby*, exhibition catalogue, with texts by Hanne Finsen and Rudi H. Fuchs, Copenhagen 1981; *Per Kirkeby*, exhibition catalogue with text by Johannes Gachnang, Eindhoven 1982; *Per Kirkeby: Projekt fur Munster*, exhibition catalogue with essay by Friedrich Meschedem, Munster 1986; *Per Kirkeby*, exhibition catalogue with text by Peter Schampers, Rotterdam 1987.

The world is outside language and outside writing. The world is material. Material thinks in material. Material you can handle is better material than that which you cannot handle. Writing is better material than language. Language is material too, and when that material thinks in that material we call it thoughts. The rest of the world cannot be translated into thoughts because thoughts are not thought in the rest of the world's material. That, for example, is the great problem of geology, that geologists do not express themselves on the material's material but in thoughts. The old ones were more at one with their material because at that time everything was unified even though they also said (even though they said it too)—yet Stensen became so aware of the problem by saying the geology that he stopped and became a Catholic bishop. All, all rocks from the oldest to the youngest were formed on the water, said Stensen, and later on the Neptunists, and from fire comes everything, all rocks have a volcanic origin, Moro said, and along with him the Plutonists. And in that way there was still something in the craft. Language has become arrogant because the world has been transformed into thoughts. But there is material writing that is pure because there is more material than in thoughts. *De solido intra solidum naturaliter contento dissertationis prodomus*, as Stensen said, even though in Latin and in that way it became more material and because of that just a little bit better geology too.

—Per Kirkeby

KITAJ, R(onald) B(rooks).
American. Born Ronald Brooks in Cleveland, Ohio, 29 October 1932; adopted name of stepfather, 1941; moved with his family to Troy, New York, 1943. Educated in Cleveland and New York primary schools; attended children's art classes, Cleveland Museum of Art, 1937–42; studied briefly at the Cooper Union, New York, under Sydney Delevante, R. B. Dowden, Paul Zucker and John Ferren, 1950–51; at Akademie der Bildenden Künste, Vienna, under Albert von Gutersloh and Fritz Wotruba, 1951–53; at Ruskin School of Drawing and Fine Art, Oxford, under Edgar Wind, 1957–59; at Royal College of Art, London, 1960–62. Served in the United States Army, 1955–57. Married Elsi Roessler in 1953 (died, 1969); son: Lem, and adopted daughter: Dominie Lee. Painter: worked on a Norwegian cargo ship, and travelled to Havana and Mexico, 1950; travelled as American seaman to Caribbean and Venezuela; visited Europe, 1951–53: lived in Vienna; joined the U.S. National

Maritime Union, and worked on ships travelling to South America; returned to Europe, 1953; travelled extensively in Europe and North Africa, then settled in England; formed close friendship with David Hockney and collaborated briefly with Eduardo Paolozzi; worked with Chris Prater on collage-prints, 1962–72; has spent summers in Sant Feliu de Guixols, Spain, since 1962; visited the United States, 1965–66; worked on drawings for *Sports Illustrated*, 1966; lived in California, 1967–68; formed close friendship with poet Robert Creeley, with whom he collaborated on two books, and painter Jess Collins; returned to England, 1968; lived in Hollywood, 1970–71; produced first life drawings, 1975; organized *The Human Clay* exhibition, London, 1976; lived in the United States, 1978–79. Lecturer, Ealing Technical College, 1961–63, and Camberwell School of Art and Crafts, London, 1961–63; Visiting Professor, University of California, Berkeley, 1967, and University of California at Los Angeles, 1970; Artist-in-Residence, Dartmouth College, Hanover, New Hampshire, 1978. Recipient: Arts Council Prize, London, 1960. Agent: Marlborough Fine Art, London. Address: c/o Marlborough Fine Art, 6 Albemarle Street, London WIX 4BY, England.

Individual Exhibitions:

1963 Marlborough New London Gallery, London
1965 Marlborough-Gerson Gallery, New York
Los Angeles County Museum of Art
1967 Cleveland Museum of Art
Stedelijk Museum, Amsterdam
1969 *Complete Graphics 1963–1969*, Galerie Mikro, Berlin (toured West Germany)
1970 Kestner-Gesellschaft, Hannover (travelled to the Museum Boymans-van Beuningen, Rotterdam)
1971 Graphics Gallery, San Francisco
1973 Amerika Haus, Berlin
Cincinnati Art Museum, Ohio (with Jim Dine)
1974 Marlborough Gallery, New York
1975 New 57 Gallery, Edinburgh
Petersburg Press, New York
1976 Petersburg Press, New York
Mala Galerija, Ljublijana, Yugoslavia
1977 Ikon Gallery, Birmingham, England
Marlborough Fine Art, London (travelled to Marlborough Galerie, Zurich)
1978 Beaumont-May Gallery, Hopkins Center, Hanover, New Hampshire
1979 Marlborough Gallery, New York
1980 Marlborough Fine Art, London
1981 Hirshhorn Museum and Sculpture Garden, Washington, D.C. (travelled to Cleveland Museum and the Kunsthalle, Dusseldorf, 1981–82)
1985 Marlborough Fine Art, London
1986 Marlborough Gallery, New York

Selected Group Exhibitions:

1963 *Towards Art?*, Graves Art Gallery, Sheffield (travelled to Laing Art Gallery, Newcastle upon Tyne, and the Municipal College of Art, Bournemouth)
1965 *Pop Art: Nieuwe Figuratie: Nouveau Realisme*, Palais des Beaux-Arts, Brussels
1967 *Visage de l'Homme dans l'Art Contemporain*, Musée Ruth, Geneva
1969 *Information*, Kunsthalle, Basle (travelled to the Badischer Kunstverein, Karlsrube)
1973 *Hommage à Picasso*, Nationalgalerie, Berlin (toured Europe)
1976 *The Human Clay*, Hayward Gallery, London (toured the U.K. and Belgium)
1981 *A New Spirit in Painting*, Royal Academy of Arts, London
1982 *Aspects of British Art Today*, Metropolitan Art Museum, Tokyo (toured Japan)
1984 *The British Art Show*, City Art Gallery, Birmingham (and Ikon Gallery, Birmingham; travelled to Edinburgh, Sheffield and Southampton)
1987 *A London School*, Louisiana Museum, Humlebaek, Denmark (travelled to Venice and Dusseldorf)

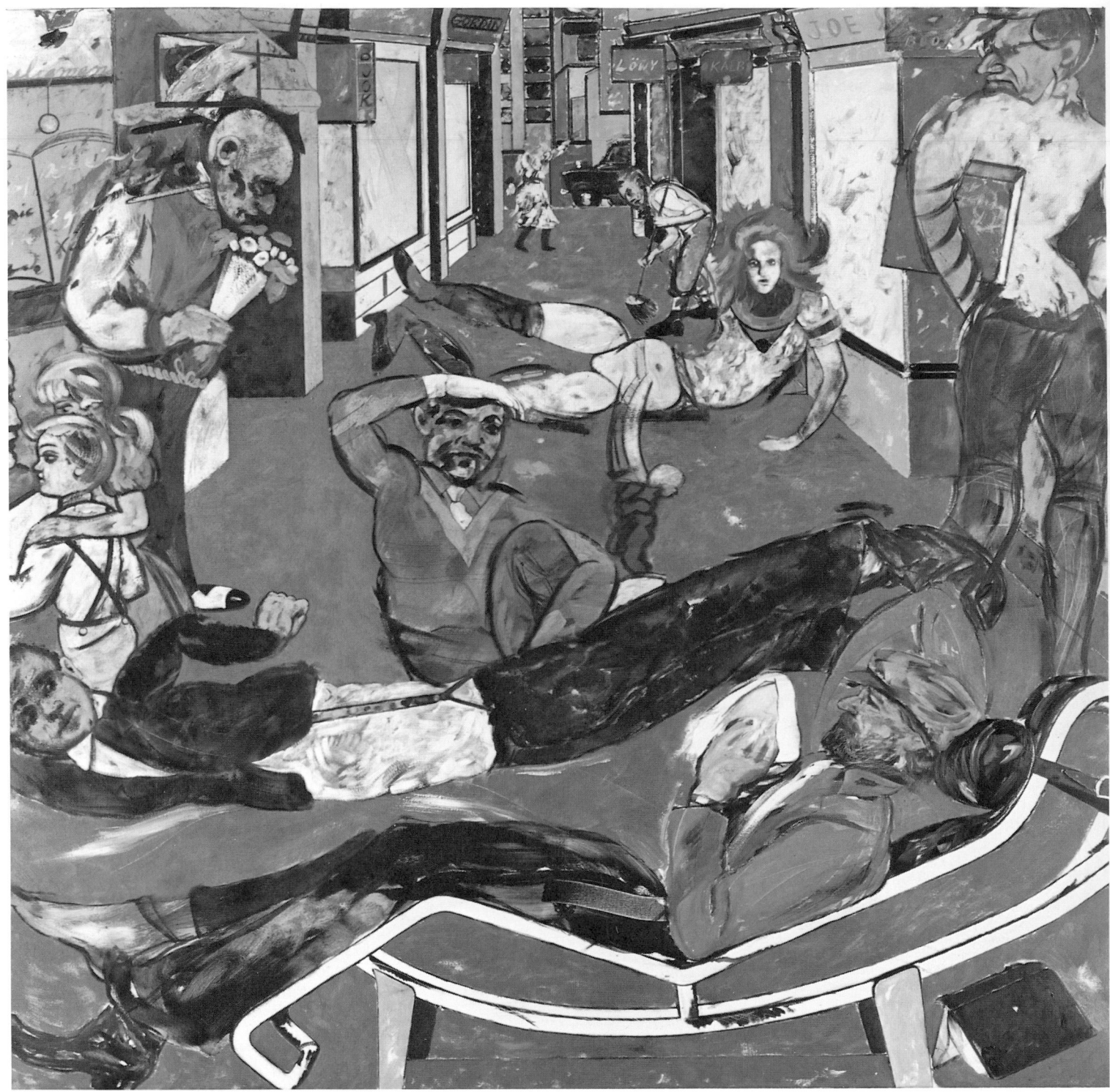

R. B. Kitaj: *Cecil Court, London WC2* (*The Refugees*), 1984

Collections:

Tate Gallery, London; Victoria and Albert Museum, London; Walker Art Gallery, Liverpool; Nationalgalerie, Berlin; Wallraf-Richartz Museum, Cologne; Kunsthalle, Hamburg; Stedelijk Museum, Amsterdam; Museu de Arte Moderna, Sao Paulo; Museum of Modern Art, New York; Art Institute of Chicago.

Publications:

By KITAJ: books—*Wings: A Collection of Works Produced at the Facilities of Lockheed, California,* Los Angeles 1971; *Open Photography, 1978,* exhibition catalogue, with John Szarkowski, Nottingham 1978; articles—"Two Paintings with Notes" in *London Gazette,* no.3, 1961; "Round the Art Galleries," letter to the editor, in *The Listener* (London), February 1963; "On Associating Texts with Paintings" in

Cambridge Opinion, January 1964; "Why Do Artists Make Prints?" answers to questions from Mark Glazebrook, in *Studio International* (London), June 1967; "Mainly about Using Photos" in *Art and Artists* (London), November 1969; "Letters from 31 Artists to the Albright-Knox Art Gallery" in *Gallery Notes* (Buffalo, New York), Spring 1970; "R. B. Kitaj: An Interview with Michael McNay" in *The Guardian* (London), 8 May 1970; "Painter's Reply" in *Artforum* (New York), September 1975; "R. B. Kitaj and David Hockney Discuss the Case for a Return to the Figurative" in *New Review* (London), February 1977; "Censorship of Erotic Art," letter to the editor, with Richard Hamilton and David Hockney, in the *Sunday Times* (London), 20 February 1977; "Commentary: World and Image" in the *Times Literary Supplement* (London), March 1977; "Dine . . . Some Historical Notes Apropos" in *Jim Dine: Works on Paper 1975-1976,* exhibition catalogue, London 1977; "A Love for Pictures and an Enthusiasm for Life," interview with Roger Berthoud, in *The Times* (London), 7 May 1977; "Chris . . . A Note Aproppos" in *Arts Review* (London), August 1977; "The

Horror! The Horror! . . . Conrad" in *Irving Petlin: Rubbings: The Large Paintings and the Small Pastels,* exhibition catalogue, Purchase, New York 1978; "The Autumn of Central Paris" in *Art International* (Lugano, Switzerland), March 1979; "A Return to London: R. B. Kitaj Replies to Some Questions Put to Him by Timothy Hyman" in *London Magazine,* February 1980; introduction to *The Artist's Eye,* exhibition catalogue, London 1980; "Glasgow Sale of Whistlers," letter to the editor, with John Golding and others, in *The Times* (London), 12 July 1980; introduction to *Leland Bell: Paintings,* exhibition catalogue, London, 1980; film—*R. B. Kitaj,* with Christopher Finch, directed by James Scott, London 1967.

On KITAJ: books—*R. B. Kitaj: Complete Graphics 1963-1969,* exhibition catalogue, by Werner Haftmann, Berlin, 1969; *R. B. Kitaj,* exhibition catalogue, with texts by John Ashbery, Joe Shannon and Jane Livingston, Washington, D.C. 1981; *R. B. Kitaj* by Marco Livingstone, Oxford 1985; articles—"An Eagerly Awaited First Exhibition" in *The*

Times (London), 7 February 1963; "Kitaj's Drawings from Life" by Jasia Reichardt in *Connoisseur* (London), October 1963; "R. B. Kitaj and the Scene" by Dore Ashton in *Arts and Architecture* (Los Angeles), April 1965; "Silkscreening—Any Number Can Play" by James R. Mellow in the *New York Times*, 30 January 1972; "Didactic and Dramatic" by Marina Vaizey in *Art News* (London), December 1974; "Kitaj Observed" by Michael Shepherd in *Arts Review* (London), April 1977; *R. B. Kitaj: Avatar of Ezra* by Timothy Hyman in *London Magazine*, August/September 1977; "Some Notes on Kitaj" by Michael Podro in *Art International* (Lugano, Switzerland), March 1979; "The Last History Painter: Expatriate, R. B. Kitaj Brings Home the Bacon" by Robert Hughes in *Time* (New York), April 1979; "Iconology as Theme in the Early Work of R. B. Kitaj" by Marco Livingstone in *Burlington Magazine* (London), July 1980; "The Kitaj Retrospective: Too Late or Too Early?" by Franz Schulze in *Artnews* (New York), January 1982; "Photomontage in the Early Work of R. B. Kitaj" by Catherine Klaus Schear in *Arts Magazine* (New York), September 1984: "Conversations with R. B. Kitaj" by Andrew Brighton in *Art in America* (New York), June 1986.

*   *   *

R. B. Kitaj has produced such a vast and varied body of work that the only way to give a notional idea of his oeuvre is to select specific paintings that I particularly admire.

"The Ohio Gang" is Kitaj at his most violent. A naked child/adult is pushed in its pram by a mad nurse; a human/animal scampers off into the distance; a naked woman is interrogated by a man and tortured by a woman. The painting functions on a variety of different levels: it tells stories that each viewer will interpret in his own way.

"Where the Railroad Leaves the Sea" is quite different. The stage is filled with only two people: a naked woman who bears a striking resemblance to Eva Braun and a man whose face is disintegrating à la Bacon. The goodbye kiss seems too particularly painful for the man whose hands are painted in such an expressive manner that they really seem to be cherishing the woman. The people are painted with fluid lines; the scenery is harsh and unbending. Kitaj is emphasizing the toughness of the world we have to survive in. In "Erie Shore" man is actually being destroyed. Fires are burning, naked torsos scream with terror, a prisoner looks pleadingly into a nurse's eyes, two bodies fall from a great height, and a walrus looks on unperturbed. Nature does not help man in his misfortune.

"Juan de la Cruz" is similar to the walrus. He remains passive while a woman is being sodomized in the background by a blob-like creature and then made to walk a gangplank by a gangster and a pirate.

"The Autumn of Central Paris" seems to be slightly more optimistic. Four people sit in the Tuileries discussing the problems of the world. The woman bears an uncanny resemblance to Virginia Woolf. One man cannot see well; the other has a hearing aid. In the foreground a revolutionary brandishes a sickle, and in the background an idyllic blue sky is savoured by a soldier, although hidden behind the tree is a building with shattered windows. Symbols of hope and despair are intermingled.

"To Live in Peace" for once seems to be of only hope. A group of people are sitting around a dining table listening to two members of their party singing. The figures are brilliantly painted. Fluid, free, and yet definite strokes. Sunlight is streaming in from the balcony which looks on to a vista of luscious greenery and deep blue sea. This is Kitaj at his most painterly, genuinely celebrating life.

"If Not, Not" is a masterpiece. The same flexibility and fluidity of colour is there, but the landscape is populated by suffering people. Yet again only Nature remains unscathed. Blue lagoons and giant palm trees are as resplendent as ever. Meanwhile a naked woman attempts to comfort and reassure a man who is running away, a wounded fighter crawls along the ground, a body lies immobile at the front of the canvas. At the top of the canvas loom the gates of Auschwitz.

In his portrait of "The Jew" Kitaj paints a character that could have easily come out of Bashevis Singer. A melancholy man still wearing the clothes he would have worn in Poland stares into the distance. One wonders what memories haunt him.

Kitaj has said: "Some books have pictures, some pictures have books." With many of his pictures the spectator is given enough material to write the book himself. Kitaj is a literary painter, deeply affected by his roots. He is haunted by the death of 26 million of his compatriots (20 million Russians, 6 million Jews). Kitaj paints with his heart and soul: at times, this makes the paintings go haywire, but when he hits the right notes, he produces perfection.

—Carine Maurice

*   *   *

KITATSUJI, Yoshihisa.

Japanese. Born in Osaka, 24 April 1948. Studied graphic design at Tama Art University, Tokyo, 1968–72, B.A. 1972. Worked as a display artist, Zeniya Company, Osaka, 1972–75; travelled to France, Germany, Holland and Italy, 1973; full-time artist, Osaka, since 1975. Recipient: Grant-in-Aid, *Biennale de Paris*, 1973. Agent: Galerie 16, Sakuranocho, Sanjo-Teramachi, Nakakyo-ku, Kyoto 604, Japan. Address: 36 Shakudo, Habikino-shi, Osaka 583, Japan.

Individual Exhibitions:

1974	Shinanobashi Gallery, Osaka
	Galerie 16, Kyoto
1975	Shirakaba Gallery, Tokyo
	Shinanobashi Gallery, Osaka
	Galerie 16, Kyoto
1977	Art Agency Company, Tokyo
1978	Galerie Kitano Circus, Kobe
1979	Tada Gallery, Osaka
1980	Shinanobashi Gallery, Osaka
1981	Galerie 16, Kyoto
1982	Muramatsu Gallery, Tokyo
	Shinanobashi Gallery, Osaka
1983	Galerie 16, Kyoto
1984	Shinanobashi Gallery, Osaka
	Galeria Graphica, Tokyo
	Galerie Krief Raymond, Paris
1985	Galerie 16, Kyoto
	Gallery Te, Tokyo
1986	Shinanobashi Gallery, Osaka
1987	Nabis Gallery, Tokyo
	National Museum of Art, Osaka

Selected Group Exhibitions:

1969	*9th Contemporary Exhibition of Japan*, Metropolitan Art Gallery, Tokyo
1970	*5th Japanese Art Festival*, National Museum of Modern Art, Tokyo
1972	*Kyoto Biennale*, Municipal Art Gallery, Kyoto
1973	*Biennale de Paris*, Musee National d'Art Moderne, Paris
1974	*Japan Past and Present*, Kunsthalle, Dusseldorf
1976	*International Biennial Exhibition of Prints*, National Museum of Modern Art, Tokyo
1982	*Internationale Jugendtriennale und Meister der Zeichung*, Kunsthalle, Nuremberg
1984	*Parallelism in Art No. 1*, Ohara Center, Tokyo
1985	*New Trends in Contemporary Japanese Art*, Walker Hill Art Center, Seoul
1987	*Art in Japan Since 1969*, Seibu Museum of Art, Tokyo

Publications:

BY KITATSUJI: articles—Memorandum" in *Art Criticism* (Tokyo), Autumn 1983; "Interview" in *Bijutsu-Techo* (Tokyo), December 1985.

On KITATSUJI book—*Yoshihisa Kitatsuji: Recent Works III*, exhibition catalogue with text by Akira Tatehata, Osaka 1987; articles—"Redactrice en Chef" by Daniel Treber in *Art Press* (Paris), September/October 1973; "10 Years for Tomorrow" by Arata Tani in *Bijutsu-techo* (Tokyo), November 1975; "Art Report" by Toshiakki Minemura in *TV Asahi* (Tokyo), May 1976; "Tenpyo" by Masaru Aguro in *Bijutsu-techo* (Tokyo), July 1978; "Yoshihisa Kitatsuji Exhibition" by Shigemitsu Hirano in *Yomiuri Shimbun* (Osaka), January 1979, "Tenpyo" by Kazuo Yamawaki in *Bijutsu-techo* (Tokyo), April 1979; "Tenpyo" by Izuru Otagi in *Bijutsu-techo* (Tokyo), July 1981; "Between Painting and Sculpture" by Yusuke Nakahara in *Ikebana Sogetsu* (Tokyo), August 1981; "Yoshihisa Kitatsuji's Etching as an Art" by Toshiaki Minemura in *Hangwa Geijutsu* (Tokyo), July 1982; "Yoshihisa Kitatsuji" by Toshiaki Minemura in *Japan Today II*, Tokyo 1984.

*   *   *

Iron: Iron man, iron heart and iron will (allegories of strength.) Hammer and pliers (imitations of hand.) Pistol and knife (revenge for the flesh.) The Eiffel Tower (philosophy of symbol.) Locomotive and ship (will of the mass.) Iron shaves off the outer shell of word by the flame of a gas burner. At first it is a red luminescence, and with higher temperature, it is red flowage that runs down. When cooled, it shows dry and sterile surface. Hammer it out, shave and polish, and a new word is born. Dried up sea. Murmur of a pot. A spider's web over the wall. A table amidst a desert. A shrivelled torso. A sword that absorbed memory.

Rust, a proof that iron is now alive. It is useless no matter how many words one scatters, or tries to pacify. It is a process for iron to return to its natural state.

Clay: Moist and doughy, a flexible substance which becomes hard ceramic after going through drying and baking. Perfect strength and dryness, with sterile surface like the one when red hot iron is cooled. Crisp lightness of a cardboard. Once baked the clay erases all trace of encumbering emotions no matter how much of these emotions one puts in, and it only becomes a form to distinguish from others, establishing its own status. The freshness of abandonment.

Paper: In regard to the height and the size within the visual scope, it is boundless. Its thinness and whiteness are not its first characteristic. A playground where stain and dyestuff play. As if to rub one's emotions the wrong way, it shaves off black powder from the tip of a pencil, and sprinkle it over the rough-textured surface. Furthermore, when you try to overcome iron's will forcibly, by pressing down, rubbing or squeezing it by the pad of your fingers, you always end up in defeat.

Feathers: Crows, eagles, pigeons, peacocks; feathers do not have a will of their own. The feathers of a live bird obey the movement of muscle; a feather is blown away by a breeze; a quill pen gives elegance to the movement of a hand; a feather-broom does not harm the bare skin, a feather quilt is a solid lump of air.

Resin (Plastic): Pine resin, starch syrup, tortoise shell, sea shell, colored-glass. These are nostalgic, sad and soft. Thin layer of translucence. Is it a crystallization of tears? Two butterflies soaring in the summer sky. A sudden nose dive. It is light but sharp.

Plaster: Endlessly cool and warm. Endlessly free and restrained. Endlessly soft and hard. Endlessly white. Its whiteness is like paper's and canvas's. When it meets with alien objects it becomes a support. But its whiteness does not vanish. A phantom screen enabling us to see the invisibles.

Greenish Blue: Pour red wine into a wide-mouthed bottle, hang a copper plate in the upper space of the bottle, and await for the copper plate to be corroded by the acid of wine. The cooper plate is gradually corroded and turns into dark green. When dried, its color changes into vivid greenish blue. When you put your nose close to the bottle, you can discern the faint odor of acid. If you dissolve the bubble and greenish blue in water, you may create a sea. Is the greenish blue a water sprite?

Book (Story), Photograph: An object to be easily held. The hours of turning the opened pages (or the

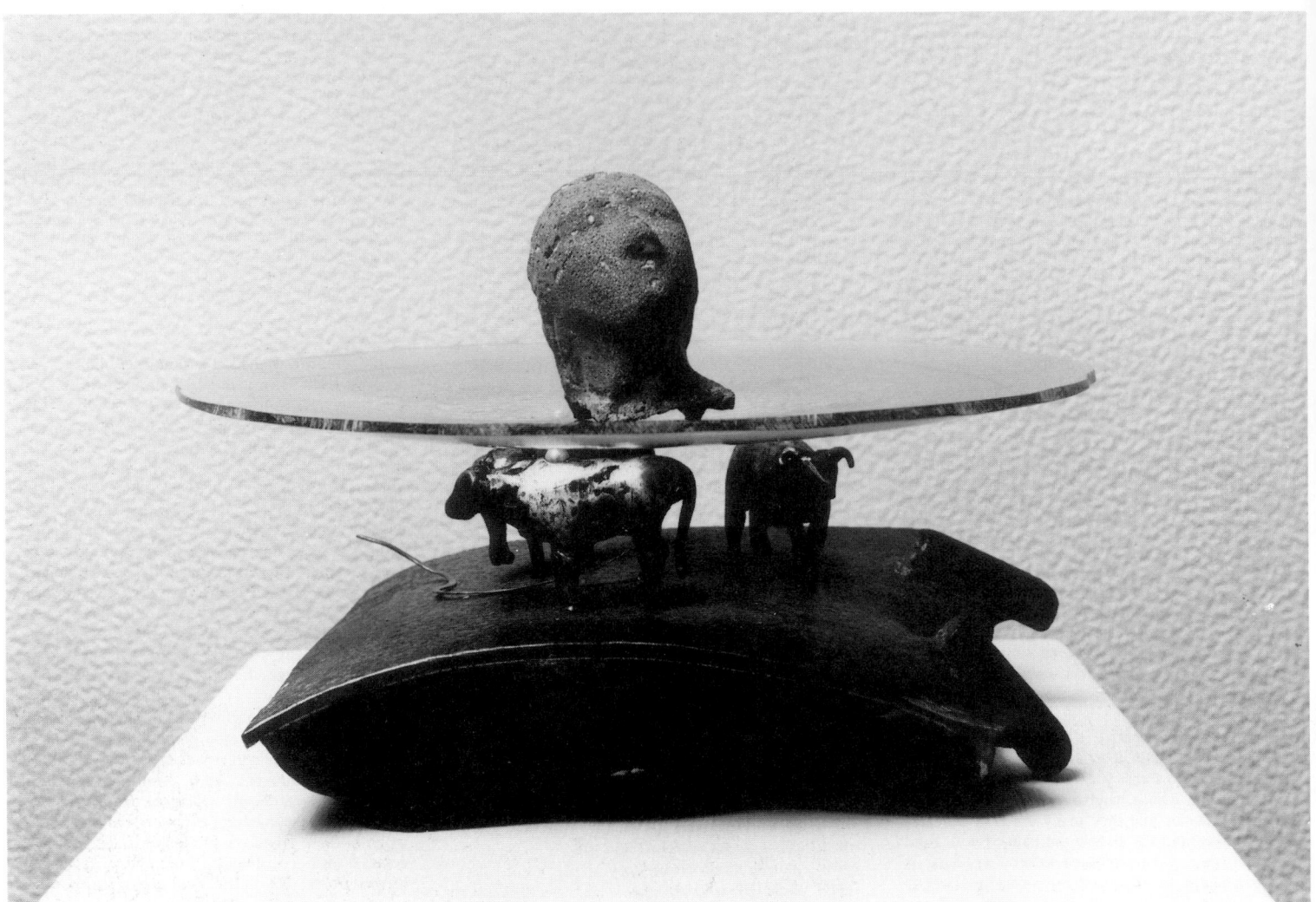

Yoshihisa Kitatsuji: *Basin,* 1986

pain caused by the chair-back.) The time of story makes you forget the hours and pain. The book leaves a photograph which is a concentrated image of the content hidden between the words. Also the photograph makes you see within the square framework. Words which should be uttered are overlaid. Words like a sigh, powerful words as a concept. The book drags in images, and photograph words.

Pleasure: A mood is always chaotic but quiet universe that brings a certain order and madness with an alien invader as stimulus. Thus dissimination process starts and sublimates it in a work. The image of work possesses different features depending on the mood it receives. Diversified materials cross each other during the process from reception to manifestation. It tolerates whatever form it turns out to be. There is no law. Confusion of images, chaotic sense for materials; they sympathize with each other and manifest according to my tolerance as the earth had created life with the cooling of the earth surface after its dramatic chaos within. A feeling of melancholy prevails in a work manifested with a calm and gray inner world.

—Yoshihisa Kitatsuji

KLAPHECK, Konrad.

German. Born in Dusseldorf, 10 February 1938. Educated at Humboldt Gymnasium, Dusseldorf, 1946–54; Staatliche Kunstakademie, Dusseldorf, 1954–58.

Married Lilo Lang in 1960 (died, 1987); children: Elisa and David. Independent painter, Dusseldorf, since 1958. Agents: Galerie Beyeler, Baumleingasse 9, 401 Basle, Switzerland; and Galerie Maeght, 13 rue de Teheran, 75008 Paris, France. Address: Kaiserswertherstr. 164, 4000 Dusseldorf 30, West Germany.

Individual Exhibitions:

1959   Galerie Schmela, Dusseldorf
1960   Galeria Schawarz, Milan
1962   Galerie Zwirner, Essen
1963   Galleria Schwarz, Milan
1964   Robert Fraser Gallery, London
1965   Galerie Ileana Sonnabend, Paris
        Palais des Beaux-Arts, Brussels
        Kestner-Gesellschaft, Hannover
1966   Kestner-Gesellschaft, Hannover
1968   Galleria Schwarz, Milan
1969   Sidney Janis Gallery, New York
1971   Galerie Rudolf Zwirner, Cologne
1972   Galleria Schwarz, Milan
        Galleria La Medusa, Rome
1974   Museum Boymans van Beuningen, Rotterdam (travelled to the Palais des Beaux-Arts, Brussels and the Städtische Kunsthalle, Dusseldorf)
1976   *Objekte Zwischen Fetisch und Libido,* Galerie Beyeler, Basle
1977   Galerie Rudolf Zwirner, Cologne
1980   *Derriere le Miroir,* Galerie Maeght, Paris
        Druckgraphik und Zeichnungen 1977–80, Kunsthandel Wolfgang Wittrock, Dusseldorf
1982   Galerie Maeght, Paris

1983   Kunstverein für die Rheinlande und Westfalen, Dusseldorf
1985   Galerie Maeght Lelong, Paris
        Kunsthalle, Hamburg (retrospective)
1986   Kunsthalle, Tubingen (retrospective)
        Haus der Kunst, Munich (retrospective)

Selected Group Exhibitions:

1962   *Phases,* Galerie de Université, Paris
1965   *Biennale de Paris*
1968   *European Painters Today,* Jewish Museum, New York
1971   *Contemporary German Art,* National Museum of Modern Art, Tokyo
1972   *Amsterdam: Paris: Dusseldorf,* Guggenheim Museum, New York
1974   *Réalism Européen, Hyperréalisme Americain,* CNAC, Paris
1977   *Documenta,* Kassel, West Germany
1980   *Dessins de la Fondation,* Fondation Maeght, St. Paul de Vence, France
1983   *Sammlung Wormland,* Haus der Kunst, Munich
1985   *Rheingold,* Plazzo Promotrice delle Belle Arti, Turin

Collections:

Musée Royaux de l'Etat Belge, Brussels; Neue Galerie, Aachen, West Germany; Kunstmuseum, Dusseldorf; Karl-Ernst-Osthaus Museum, Hagen, West Germany; Kunsthalle, Hamburg; Städtisches Museum, Leverkusen, West Germany; Museum von der Heydt, Wuppertal, West Germany; Centre National d'Art Contemporain, Paris; Museum Ludwig, Cologne; Staatsgalerie, Stuttgart.

Publications:

By KLAPHECK: articles—"La Machine et Moi" in *Opus International* (Paris), October 1970; statement in *Konrad Klopheck*, exhibition catalogue, Milan 1972; "Über meine Zeichnungen" in *Konrad Klapheck*, exhibition catalogue, Dusseldorf 1983; "Pourquoi je peint" in *Konrad Klapheck*, exhibition catalogue, Paris 1985.

On KLAPHECK: books—*Konrad Klapheck*, exhibition catalogue, with text by José Pierre, Milan 1960; *Konrad Klapheck*, exhibition catalogue, by André Breton, Paris 1965; *Konrad Klapheck*, exhibition catalogue, with text by Wieland Schmied, Hannover 1966; *Konrad Klapheck*, exhibition catalogue, with text by José Pierre, New York 1969; *Konrad Klapheck* by José Pierre, Cologne 1970; *Konrad Klapheck*, exhibition catalogue, with texts by Wieland Schmied, Edouard Jager, José Pierre and others, Rotterdam 1974; *Konrad Klapheck: Objekte Zwischen Fetisch und Libido*, exhibition catalogue, by Werner Schmalenbach, Basle 1976; *Konrad Klapheck: Werkverzeichnis der Druckgraphik 1977–1980*, exhibition catalogue, edited by Wolfgang Wittrock, text by Hans Kinkel, Dusseldorf 1980; *Konrad Klapheck: "Derriere le Miroir,"* exhibition catalogue, with text by Bernard Noel, Paris 1980; articles—review by J. A. Thwaites in *Art in America* (New York), Fall 1962; "El Mundo Mechanico de Konrad Klapheck" by Robert Altmann in *Islas 2* (Cuba), 1964; "Pop Art and Surrealism" by D. Irvin in *Studio International*, (London), May 1966; "Germany: The New Generation" by J. A. Thwaites in *Studio International* (London), October 1966; "The Machine and the Psyche: Klapheck's Exploration at Janis" by Gregory Battock in *Arts Magazine* (New York), February 1969; "Shift in Perspective" by F. Bowling in *Arts Magazine* (New York), Summer 1969; "Konrad Klapheck: Quotes and Comments" by Henry Martin in *Art International* (Lugano, Switzerland), December 1972; "Les Machines de Konrad Klapheck" by Georges Raillad in *La Quizaine Litteraire* (Paris), 1981; "Konrad Klapheck" by Peter Sager in *Zeit-Magazin* (Hamburg), November 1985; film—*Konrad Klapheck* by Elila Hershon and Roberto Guerra, premiered on German Television ARD, November 1980.

*   *   *

My pictures are to be seen as a whole, as an epic whose protagonists are embodied not in man but in his most important everyday objects. Perhaps the latter are more fitted than a portrait of their inventors to represent today's human comedy.

However clear and logical my pictures may look, it is chance I must thank for half their success. If at one point I can literally take over an image, at another I am forced by the unpredictable consequences of the size of the canvas to paint a picture that I did not have in mind to paint. Chance is the matter of inspiration.

I do not use things as symbols. I simply paint them as I can and let myself be surprised at what they have to say. Eventually the paintings must be cleverer than their creator and go beyond his intentions.

My chief weapons are humour and precision. It is only through the coldness of precision that you gain entry to the fires of the soul and only under cover of a joke that you can say outright what you have seen.

My subjectivity must be unrestrained for my pictures to become objective. It is in oneself that one finds the riddles of the world and their solution.

—Konrad Klapheck

*   *   *

Objects Between Fetishes and Libido was the title of the introduction that Werner Schmalenbach wrote to describe the art of Konrad Klapheck for the catalogue of his exhibition at the Galerie Beyeler, Basel, in 1976. Although the 46 exhibits were all new, they showed no shrinkage from the essential Klapheck, which goes back to his first painting of the typewriter in 1955.

Klapheck, the son of two art historians, twice went to art school in Dusseldorf (though at the first of these he entered as a scholarship boy in social studies). But everything that matters about Klapheck-as-artist began with that first painting of the typewriter.

The machine came late into the world of art, and at first it served merely to provide a variation in subject matter. Turner may have been fascinated by the locomotive rushing down the track through a fuzzy atmosphere, part mist, part steam, and the Impressionists may have been intrigued by the crowded scene at a mainline station with the big train playing a central *rôle*, but for the most part any pictorial imagery of the machine age cropped up in drawings and steel engravings produced by illustrators for magazines before the camera took over.

When the machine came into its own as art, it was ushered in with fanfares from iconoclastic trumpets blown by Malevich and his contemporaries in Russia or by the Futurists in Italy. Touches of witty sophistication were added to the "machine image" by the Dadaists, by Picabia, by Marcel Duchamp and in the early works by Max Ernst. But even these "modern art" interpretations had their pretensions. They were still the products of entrancement rather than understanding. Artists like Léger even took mechanics and altered their true appearance to the point where they become unrecognizable. Epstein might flirt with a conception like his "Rock-Drill," but it was a dalliance that did not turn into a love affair.

Against such a background Klapheck would not claim to be a father-figure of machine art, and he certainly has no connection with mec-artists like Bertini, but he did bring to fruition actual portraits of machines and machine parts, and did this in such a way that they became—for all their hyperreality—personalized, rather as the late Gnoli gave added personality to his perfected realism of subjects like the stretched bottom of a pair of skintight trousers (whose owner plainly had thick-fleshed buttocks).

Of all the artists of contemporary times, Gnoli comes closest to Klapheck in presentation. Thereafter, the relationship is not so close; Klapheck confines his paintings to machines. Unlike Gnoli, he is quite capable of suffusing areas in his paintings with luscious colour as background, if not in some manner introduced as part of the machine itself. But the greatest difference between the two—and it is difference which has played a large part in giving Klapheck his exceptional reputation—is there in the titles of so many of his pictures, titles that immediately bestow upon the machine portraits an extra dimension of drama or irony. The name of a picture ought to mean so little, but in Klapheck's case it is the key to the safe. The titles, he says, have to come from inspiration and, judging from their potency, this is probably an accurate statement.

For Klapheck, all machines are masculine or feminine, or both (never neuter!). The buzzer on the chair with its playful flex against a candy pink wall is called "The Pasha"; the row of rearing metal punches is called "Law and Order"; a flat iron is called "The House-Dragon"; the sewing-machine is called "Inquisition;" the bathroom spray is called "The Diva"; the schoolboy's all-purpose penknife is called "The Misanthrope"; and so on.

Just as the pictures without their titles are "nameless," so the titles without their pictures are without body. It is therefore difficult to underpin in cold print

Konrad Klapheck: *A Mother's Prayers I*, 1983

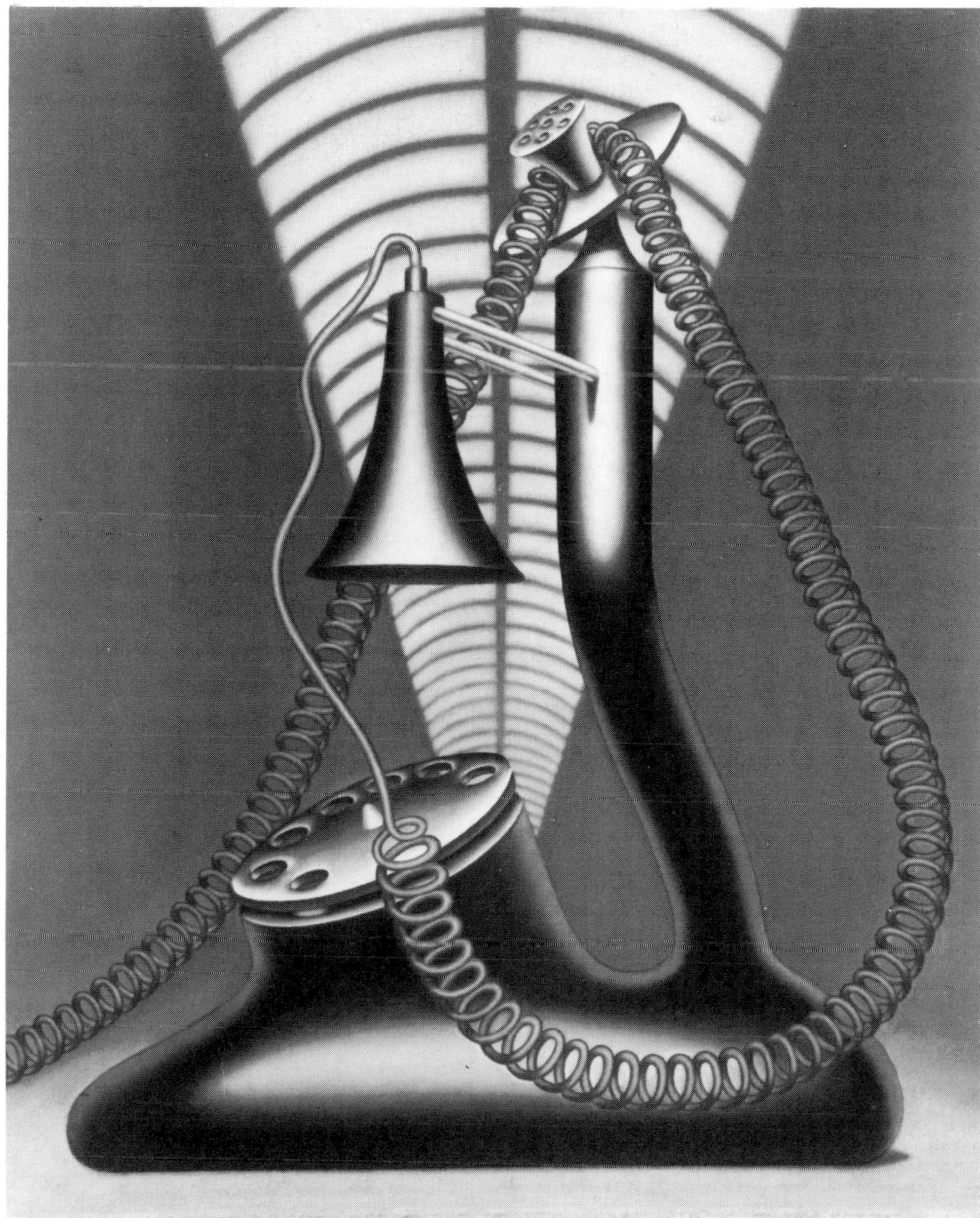

Schmalenbach's assertion that the subjects of this artist's pictures are fetishes or outright demands by libido. Klapheck injects "Life" into these inanimate objects, and it is a particularly exciting and unexpectedly alchemic performance. He really does change base metals into *gold*. Near to Surrealism, suggest Schmalenbach, but even closer to the psychologist's practice.

—Sheldon Williams

KNÍŽÁK, Milan.

Czechoslovakian. Born in Pilsen, 19 April 1940. Educated at Marienbad Primary School, 1946–54, Pianá High School, 1954–57, and the Pedagogic School, Prague, 1957–58; studied at the Art School, Prague, 1958–59, and the Art Academy, Prague, 1963–64; also studied mathematics, Prague, 1976–77. Served in the Czech Army, 1959–61. Married Sonia Svecová in 1967 (divorced, 1968); Jarka Charvátová in 1970 (divorced, 1974); and Maria Soudková in 1975. Worked as a road digger, carpenter, electrician, and stonemason's assistant, Prague, 1969–66; now a full-time artist; involved in musical activities, 1952–54, 1963–68, 1968–76, and 1978; in painting, objects, sculpture and environments, 1954–64; in fashion, 1962–70; in architecture, 1973–76. Founder, with Sonia Svecová, Jan Maria Mach, Vit Mach, Jan Trticek, and Robert Wittmann, Aktual group, Prague, 1964; associated initially with the Fluxus artists, Dick Higgins, Alison Knowles, and Ben Vautier, Prague, 1966. Imprisoned in Prague, 1966; travelled in Austria, Germany, Luxembourg, Iceland, 1968–70, in New York and throughout the United States, 1968–70; travelled in Holland, Switzerland, Belgium and Italy, 1980; Guest Professor, Summer Academy, Salzburg, 1987. Recipient: DAAD Scholarship, Berlin, 1974 (took up scholarship in Berlin, 1979–80); Kolar Prize, Czechoslovakia, 1977; Worpswede-Barkenhoff Award, West Germany, 1982; Schloss Bleckade Prize, West Germany, 1985. Agents: J. Dvorak, Art-Centrum, Nerudova 16, Prague 1; Galerie Inge Baecker, Zeughausstrasse 13, 5000 Cologne 1; Wewerka Gallery, Fasanenstrasse 41A, 1000 Berlin 15 (West). Address: Podskalska 7, 128 00 Prague 2, Czechoslovakia.

Individual Exhibitions:

1958   KASS, Marienbad, Czechoslovakia
1964   Galerie Viola, Prague
1968   Fluxus West, San Diego, California
1970   Galerie Art Intermedia, Cologne
1972   Museum am Ostwall, Dortmund
1976   Galerie A. Amsterdam
1980   Galerie Ars Viva, Berlin
        Galerie A, Amsterdam
        Galerie Baecker, Bochum, West Germany
        Museum Helmstedt, West Germany
        Kunstverein, Oldenburg, West Germany
1981   Private Apartment, Prague
1983   Galerie Ars Viva, West Berlin
        Galerie Gruppe Grun 1, Bremen
        Rank Xerox, Hannover
1984   Galerie Inge Baecker, Cologne
        Licht + Raumdesign, Cologne
1985   Galerie Camomille, Brussels
1986   Galleria UXA, Novara, Italy
        Kunsthalle, Hamburg
        Museum Alchimia, Milan
        Galerie OEKBZ, Cologne
1987   Galerie Potocka, Krakow, Poland
        Liget Galeria, Budapest
        Museum Sprengel, Hannover
        Galerie Wewerka, Hannover
        Ustav makromolekularni chemie CSAV, Prague
        Kunstmuseum, Bochum, West Germany

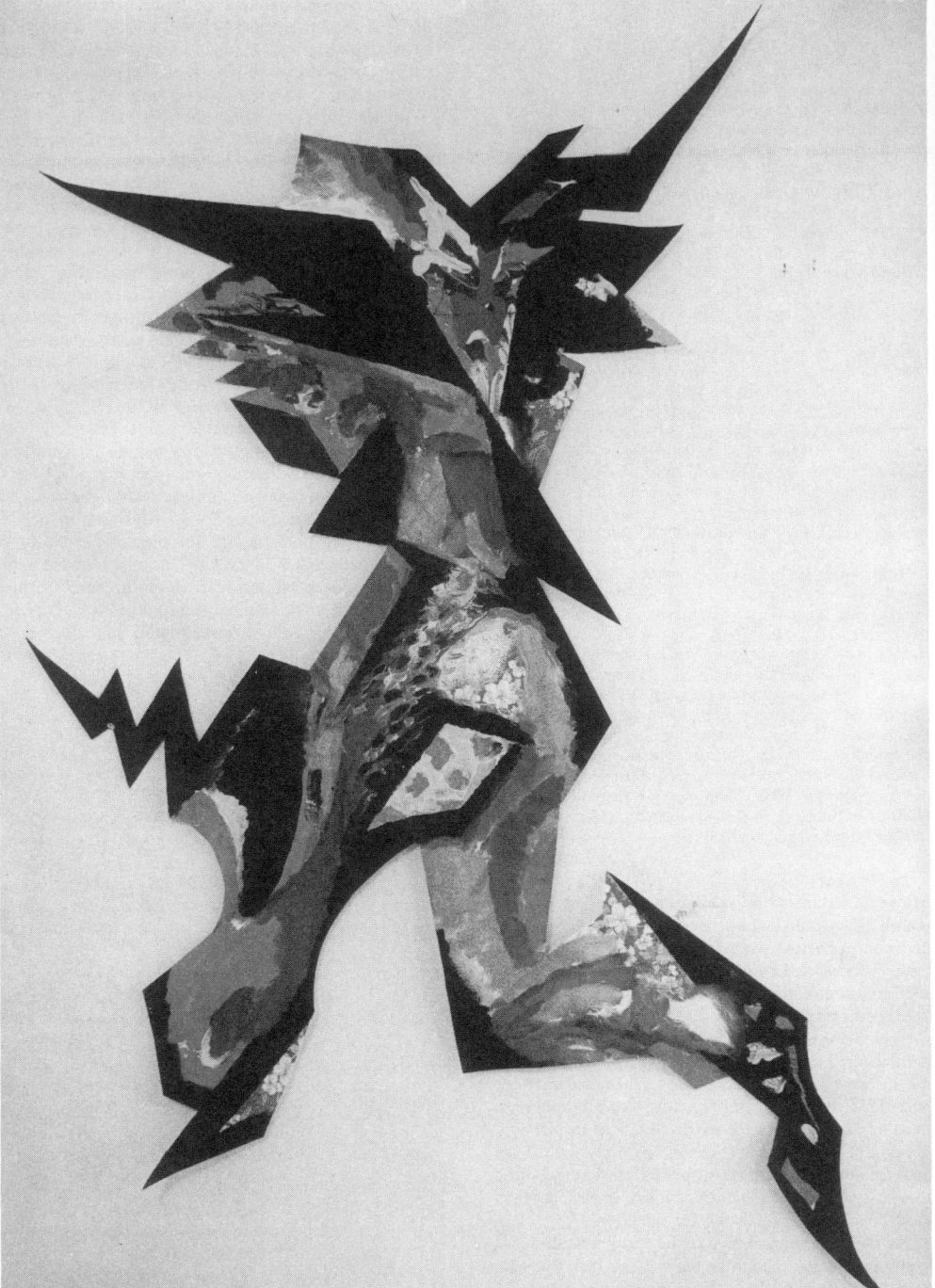

Milan Knížák: *Flat Sculpture*, 1987

Selected Group Exhibitions:

1967   *Aktual Art International,* San Francisco Museum of Art
1970   *Sammlung Feelisch,* Museum am Ostwell, Dortmund
1972   *Multiples: The First Decade,* Philadelphia Museum of Art
1974   *Biennale,* Musée d'Art Moderne, Paris
1976   *Monumente durch Medirn Resetzen,* Kunstmuseum and Kunstverein, Wuppertal, West Germany
1977   *Documenta,* Kassel, West Germany
1980   *Für Augen und Ohren,* Akademie der Künste, Berlin
1982   *Art Book Fair,* Akademie der Kunste, West Berlin
1984   *Multiples und Objekte,* Museum Wiesbaden, West Germany
1987   *Berlinart,* Museum of Modern Art, New York (travelled to San Francisco Museum of Modern Art)

Collections:

Museum am Ostwall, Dortmund; Cranbrook Museum, Bloomfield Hills, Michigan; Kunstmuseum, Stuttgart; Museum Sprengel, Hannover; Museo Mudima, Milan; Museo Vostell, Malpartida, Spain; Neuberger Museum, New York; Narodni Galerie, Prague; Muzeum Sztuki, Lodz, Poland.

Publications:

By KNÍŽÁK: books—*Flux White Meditation,* New York 1968; *Flux Dreams,* New York 1968; *Flux Snacks,* New York 1968; *Flux Papers,* New York 1968; *Zeremonien,* Remscheid, Germany 1971; *4 Objektes,* Berlin 1971; *Kurton,* Berlin 1971; *Aktual Schmuck,* editor, Cullompton, England 1973; *Flussiges Schweigen,* West Berlin 1983; *Mode/Fashion,* Worpswede, West Germany 1983; *Probable Poems,* Remscheid, West Germany 1983; *Die Korper-Prozesse 1982–*

85, Luneburg, West Germany, 1985; articles—in *Aktual Art* (Prague), nos. 1, 2 and 3, 1964–66; in *Aktual Newspaper* (Prague), nos. 1, 2 and 3, 1966–67; "Aktual in Czechoslovakia" in *Arts and Artists* (London), October 1972.

On KNÍŽÁK: books—*Assemblage, Environments and Happenings* by Allan Kaprow, New York 1966; *Umeni dnes* by J. Chalupecky, Prague 1966; *Notations* by John Cage, New York 1969; *Fluxfest Kit 2*, edited by George Maciunas, New York 1969; *Fantastic Architecture* by Wolf Vostell and Dick Higgins, New York 1969; *Sammlung Feelisch*, exhibition catalogue, Dortmund 1970; *Leben und Kunst* by Udo Kultermann, Tübingen 1970; *Multiples: The First Decade*, exhibition catalogue, Philadelphia 1972; *Milan Knížák* by Albrecht, Feelisch and Sohm, Stuttgart 1973; *Source No. 11*, edited by Kenneth S. Friedman, Sacramento, California 1973; *Environments and Happenings* by Adrian Henri, London 1974; *Documenta 6*, exhibition catalogue, Kassel, West Germany 1977; *Aktionskunst* by J. Schilling, Lucerne and Frankfurt 1978; *L'Art Aujourd'hui en Tchescoslovaquie* by Genevieve Benamon, Paris 1969; *Fluxus: The Most Radical and Experimental Art Movement*, edited by H. Ruhe, Amsterdam 1979; *Knížák*, exhibition catalogue, Berlin 1980; *Für Augen und Ohren*, exhibition catalogue, Berlin 1980; *Ecouter par les Yeux*, exhibition catalogue, Paris 1980; *Milan Knížák*, exhibition catalogue, Oldenburg, West Germany 1980; *The Art of Performance* by Gregory Battcock and Robert Nickas, New York 1984; *Milan Knížák: Action as a Life Style*, exhibition catalogue, Hamburg 1986; *Milan Knížák: Kleider auf den Korper Gemalt*, exhibition catalogue, Hannover 1987.

It is feeling and experience which shape my work, not any commitment to an aesthetic theory with its rules and regulations. In such theories there is always the seed of dogmatism, which can be dangerous to both art and life.

I do not believe, for example, that we can regard a statue as simply the result of the sculptor's efforts; or that we can regard a painting, novel, conceptual system, or indeed any human action, as a "product". Products are things which have an immediate usefulness, like shoes and pots and nails—although to look at them in this way will also raise some problems. If we think of human products as something different from and perhaps superior to natural things, then we should see such products as concrete stimuli which evoke or create the conditions for a response which will be different in kind and intensity for each individual (these matters can be demonstrated, although I will not stop to do so here). The result of artistic effort, then, is to cause a change in the inner life of the individual: it begins when we experience the work of art and is invisible; it cannot be measured or controlled.

It follows, then, that the work of art is not a fixed, static product, but a process which to some extent can make our lives richer and more intelligible, a process whose function, therefore, is didactic and ritualistic. Art is a kind of aid, like a vitamin, to the process of living. At its best it can enhance our individual lives and perhaps the quality of life in general. Once this ideal goal has been reached, the work itself simply disappears. It is no longer a necessary presence.

I emphasize this way of looking at art because it also defines the responsibility of the creative artist—his personal, moral obligations to the world he lives in and to the moral codes which govern it. Furthermore, I believe there is a close, causal connection between the artist's life and his work. Honor, responsibility, and all the other words which are losing their meaning in the modern world can regain their vitality in the work of the true artist. There is no difference between him and his work, and this is something which it is especially important for him to realize.

Thus the artist has a kind of duty to educate himself and this is not, of course, a question of attending schools and winning degrees. I mean self-education in the matters of ordinary everyday experience, the strengthening of a complete humility in the presence of even the most basic and primitive manifestations of life around us. This humility does not deify the things of the world; but it gives them a new significance, and in such a way that we can enjoy their presence and enter into their very being. If we can achieve this, the process of ordinary living becomes an absorbing, self-sufficient good.

For me art is not something I merely hear or see or touch. Art closes the gap between us and our dreams; it fills the space which separates us from a god who does not really exist except as the embodiment of our own ideals. The degree to which we can possess these ideals depends on our own abilities and efforts.

—Milan Knížák

Milan Knížák, the best known representative of Happenings and Fluxus in Eastern Europe, began his first "actions" in the streets of Prague in 1964, completely unaware of what was going on in western art. The first action, called "Demonstration of All the Senses," also performed in the street together with his friends in the Aktual group, which he formed, and a number of anonymous participants, was a follow-up to his earlier works, the paintings with piles of *objets trouvés* left out in the street for the casual, or not so casual, viewer.

Knížák's interest in the common people, in ordinary everyday things and doings, was in line with his idea of changing life, not merely art. Knížák intended his activities " . . . as a kind of primary illumination, or as hygiene, as the manifestation of a Messianism of a thousand heads."

His criticism was directed mainly at the sphere of the sentiments, which are fully realized in human life but suffocated and repressed by habits and platitudes. To unblock the fixed patterns he thought it important to acquire as wide and varied knowledge as possible, concentrating on the study not only of such sciences as mathematics, sociology and psychology, but also of architecture and of contemporary ideologies—and so also of the forms of entertainment.

His therapies are based at the same time on sacrifice and on hedonism, on asceticism and on free love—a synthesis, that is, of anti-materialism and a primitive paganism.

The performers in his actions had to learn how " . . . to love the fusion of two gases, to determine the qualities of a restaurant by its smell, to know how to stroke a cat's fur."

At the same time as his actions Knížák was also producing objects, or else suits of clothes and jewellery or even drawings and collages. All these came from his accumulation and collection of found images and images produced by his actions.

The actions in the street, open to everyone, and the life lived in common with his young followers were changed in the 1970's into private activities, and the only disciples that remained were his friends and relatives. The noise demonstrations gave way to silent acts based on more inward experiments, on imagination and evocation.

—Helena Kontova

KNOWLES, Alison.

American. Born in New York City, 29 April 1933. Educated in high schools in Scarsdale, New York, 1948–52; French school, Middlebury College, Vermont, 1952–54 (scholarship, 1952); studied illustration, Pratt Institute, Brooklyn, New York, 1954–57 (scholarship, 1954), B.F.A. 1957; painting, under Richard Lindner, Adolph Gottlieb, and Josef Albers, Syracuse University, New York, 1957–59; graphics, Manhattan School of Printing, New York, 1962. Married James Ericson in 1957 (divorced, 1959); Dick Higgins in 1963 (divorced, 1970; remarried, 1984); daughters: Hannah and Jessica. First involvement with the Fluxus artists, 1962. Independent artist, establishing Something Else Gallery, with Dick Higgins, New York, 1966; Director, Graphics Laboratory, California Institute of Arts, Valencia, 1970–72; Teacher, Douglass College, New Bruns-

wick, New Jersey, 1977; Founder, with Dick Higgins, Printed Editions publishing co-operative, New York, 1978–85; established shop/studio, Barrytown, New York, 1984. Recipient: Guggenheim Fellowship, 1968; National Endowment for the Arts Grant, Washington, D.C., 1981, 1985; Karl Sczuka Award, Westdeutscher Rundfunk, 1982; DAAD Grant, West Berlin, 1984. Agents: René Block Gallery, 409 West Broadway, New York, New York, 10012; Galerie René Block, Schaperstrasse 11, 1000 West Berlin 15, Germany; Galerie Inge Baecker, Berggate 69, 4630 Bochum, West Germany. Address: 122 Spring Street, New York, New York 10012, U.S.A.

Individual Exhibitions:

1958	Nonagon Gallery, New York
1962	Judson Gallery, New York
1972	*Artesian Festival of Art*, California Institute of Arts, Valencia
	Shoes for Ken Dewey, New York
	Proposition IV, Mercer Art Center, New York (travelled to Goddard College, Plainfield, Vermont)
1973	*Identical Lunch*, Galerie Inge Baecker, Bochum, West Germany
1974	*Collections from the Full Moon*, Galerie René Block, Berlin (travelled to De Appel, Amsterdam)
1976	*Objects in Hand*, De Appel, Amsterdam (travelled to Gallerie 38, Copenhagen)
	The Bean Garden, Vehicule Gallery, Montreal (travelled to the New School, New York; and Studio Morra, Naples)
1977	*Japanese Bean Garden*, St. Marks Church, New York
	Take a New Name, Whitney Museum, New York
	Sound and Image, Aarhus Kunstmuseum, Denmark
1978	*Leone D'Oro*, C-Space Gallery, New York
	I Am Festival, Remont Gallery, Warsaw (performance)
	3 Songs, Franklin Furnace, New York (performance)
	Bean Bag, 3 Mercer Street, New York
1979	*Jacob's Cattle*, Micro Gallery, University of California at Sacramento
	Inge Baecker Galerie, Bochum, West Germany
	Natural Assemblage and the True Crow Kitchen, New York (travelled to the School of Visual Arts, Rochester, New York)
	Natural Assemblages and the True Crow, Japanese Bean Garden, Fishes of the Philippine Seas, University of California at Sacramento (travelled to the University of California at San Diego and San Francisco State College)
1980	*The Bean Garden*, Walker Art Center, Minneapolis (travelled to School of Visual Arts, Rochester, New York)
	Coffin Gallery, University of Minnesota, Minneapolis
	House of Dust, Galerie A, Amsterdam
	20 Years of Performance Art: Dick Higgins and Alison Knowles, University of Massachusetts, Amherst
1983	*Leone d'Oro*, Moon Gallery, Mount Berry, Georgia
1984	*Bohnenweg*, Peter Schiller Galerie, West Berlin
1985	Galerie Inge Baecker, Cologne
1987	Nordyllands Kunstmuseum, Aalborg, Denmark

Selected Group Exhibitions:

1963	*Street Object Cologne*, Vostell Studio, Cologne
1967	*Artypo Exhibition*, Stedelijk Museum, Amsterdam
1970	*Happenings and Fluxus*, Kunstverein, Cologne
1974	*Fluxus Group*, Galerie Rene Block, West Berlin
1977	*03 23 03 Exhibition*, Museum of Fine Art, Montreal (travelled to National Gallery, Ottawa)
1978	*Fluxus Exhibition*, Ecart Gallery, Switzerland
1980	*Fluxus Group Show on Food Art*, Maison de la Culture, Chalon-Sur-Saône, France
1982	*Fluxus 1962–82*, Kunstverein, Wiesbaden, West Germany
1984	*Il Fascino della Carta*, Museo Civico, Reggio Emilia, Italy
1986	*Breath River Route*, 537 Artworks, New York

Collections:

Nordyllands Kunstmuseum, Aalborg, Denmark; Aarhus Museum, Denmark; Bibliothèque Nationale, Paris; René Block Gallery, New York and Berlin; Gilbert Silverman, Detroit; Galerie De Appel, Amsterdam; Inge Baecker, Bochum, West Germany; Hans Sohm Archives, Markgroeningen, West Germany; Kunstbibliotek, Hellerup, Denmark; Peppe Morra Gallery, Naples

Publications:

By KNOWLES: books—*Bean Rolls: A Canned Book,* New York 1963; *The T Dictionary in 4 Suits,* New York 1965; *By Alison Knowles,* pamphlet of performance scores, New York 1965; *The House of Dust,* computer score, programmed by James Tenney, Cologne 1969; *Journal of the Identical Lunch,* San Francisco 1970; *Proposition VI,* computer score, programmed by Mike Plesset, Los Angeles 1970; *Proposition IV,* computer score, programmed by Andrew Schloss, Benington, Vermont 1973; *Women's Work,* edited with Anna Lockwood, 1975; *More,* New York 1976; *Gem Duck,* Italy 1977; *7 Days Running,* Denmark, 1978; *Natural Assemblages and the True Crow,* Rochester, New York 1980; *The Red, the Green, the Yellow, the Black and the White,* with George Brecht, Brussels 1983; *A Bean Concordance, Vol. 1,* Barrytown, New York 1983; audiotapes—*3 Songs,* Copenhagen 1979; *Audiographics,* New York 1980.

On KNOWLES: books—*Musical America* by Tom Johnson and others, New York 1976; *The Amazing Decade,* edited by Moira Roth, New York 1983; articles—"Alison in Wonderland" by Emmett Williams in *Books* (New York), September 1966; "Follow Alice But . . ." by B. Hale in *The Telegram* (Toronto), September 1967; "Pandora's Book" in *Newsweek* (New York), April 1968; "En Bog at Bo i" by N. Barfoed in *Politiken* (Copenhagen), November 1968; "Your Guernica Is Very Good Looking" by Jill Johnston in the *Village Voice* (New York), February 1972; "Lunch ohne Mayonnaise" in *Ruhr Nachrichten-Bochumer Zeitung* (Bochum, West Germany), May 1973; "New Music" by Tom Johnson in *High Fidelity* (New York), June 1975; "The House of Dust" in *New Wilderness Letter* (San Francisco), no. 8, 1980; "The Book of Bean" in *Aperture* (Rochester, New York), Winter 1984; "Alison Knowles" by Franziska Brand in *Schattengrenze,* exhibition catalogue, Bremen, 1985.

The events I perform, the prints I have made and the environments I build are designed to put the spectator/performer in touch with him/herself and the real world. Natural sound, found objects and small familiar things are collected and investigated. Those things undergo considerable research to make a piece. It is useful to examine a button at great length. My personal investigations concern beans and shoes.
—Alison Knowles

Alison Knowles is sometimes known as "the woman in Fluxus," which, although Fluxus quite consciously included many women's work, is quite true in the sense that she was the only woman among the actual founders of Fluxus, the only woman who actually took part in all the original Fluxus Festivals in 1962-3.

Her earliest works were Abstract Expressionist, but by 1960 she began to include figurative elements usually based on found or everyday objects in her paintings, using radiator screens as stencils, blowing up objects found in the street with an opaque projector, etc. Since that time her work has remained, above all, as concrete as possible with daily living. The ongoing imagery in her work, which clarified in the early 1960's, is based on beans, books, fishes, shoes. Not only has she written a dozen or so visual books (or collected them), but she has also done several "editions" (that is, different versions) of a concept called *The Big Book,* collage environments with pages, usually about 2.5 meters high and 1.7 meters wide, the most recent of which uses bean folklore, imagery, science, stories and traditions as well as, for example, paper made by crushing beans into the pulp. Fishes, too, have featured prominently, from a series called *The Identical Lunch* (1966-81) in which a number of people ate tunafish sandwiches and buttermilk and described their experiences, or *Fishes of the Philip-*

pine Seas, a series of graphic works and performance works based on texts by the early 20th Century naturalist Barton Appler Bean.

The shoe series has been an ongoing one since the early days of Fluxus, when she did "Shoes of Your Choice" (1962) in which members of the audience came forward and described what the shoes they were wearing meant to them. It includes graphics made from photographs of found shoes and parts of shoes and several objects made from such parts.

Her major work in progress is *A Bean Concordance,* a book which contains as much as possible of the materials she has collected over 20 years concerning beans of all kinds. It was published in early 1983.
—Dean Higgins

KOCH, John.

American. Born in Toledo, Ohio, 18 August 1909. Self-taught in art. Married Dora Zaslavsky in 1935. Travelled in France and Britain, and lived in France, 1929-33; lived and worked in New York City from 1934. Instructor, Art Students League, New York, 1944-45. Chairman, School Committee, National Academy of Design; Member, Century Association, New York, and Lotus Club, New York. Recipient: Honorable Mention, *Salon de Printemps,* Paris, 1929; First Honorable Mention, Carnegie Institute, Pittsburgh, 1943; Award, 1952, Benjamin Altman Prize, 1959, and Saltus Gold Medal, 1966, National Academy of Design; Lotus Club Award, 1964; Century Club Medal, 1967; Samuel Finley Bresse Morse Medal, 1968. *Died 19 April 1978.*

Individual Exhibitions:

1927	Bonestell Gallery, Detroit
1935	Curt Valentine Gallery, New York
1939	Kraushaar Galleries, New York
1940	Nelson Gallery of Art, Kansas City, Missouri
1941	Kraushaar Galleries, New York
	J. L. Hudson Gallery, Detroit
1943	Kraushaar Galleries, New York
1944	Whyte Gallery, Washington
1945	Philadelphia Art Alliance
1946	Kraushaar Galleries, New York
1949	Kraushaar Galleries, New York
1951	Kraushaar Galleries, New York
	Portraits Inc., New York
	Suffolk Museum, Stony Brook, New York (retrospective)
	Everson Museum, Syracuse, New York
	Cowie Galleries, Los Angeles
1954	Kraushaar Galleries, New York
1958	Kraushaar Galleries, New York
1961	Kraushaar Galleries, New York
1962	Museum of Fine Arts, Richmond, Virginia (retrospective)
1963	New York Museum (retrospective)
	Berkshire Atheneum, Pittsfield, Massachusetts (retrospective)
1965	Kraushaar Galleries, New York
1969	Kraushaar Galleries, New York
1971	Speed Museum, Louisville, Kentucky (retrospective)
	Akron Art Institute, Ohio (retrospective)
1972	Kraushaar Galleries, New York
1973	New York Council Center
1975	Kraushaar Galleries, New York
1978	Columbia Museum of Art, South Carolina (retrospective)
1980	Kraushaar Galleries, New York

Selected Group Exhibitions:

1929	*Salon de Printemps,* Paris
	Salon des Tuileries, Paris
1939	*Group Exhibition,* National Academy of Design, New York

Collections:

Museum of Modern Art, New York; National Academy of Design, New York; Brooklyn Museum, New York; Newark Museum, New Jersey; Museum of Fine Arts, Boston; Museum of Fine Arts, Richmond, Virginia; Butler Institute of American Art, Youngstown, Ohio; Toledo Museum of Art, Ohio; Detroit Institute of Arts; Nelson Gallery, Kansas City, Missouri.

Publications:

On KOCH: articles—"John Koch" by Ernest Watson in *American Artist* (New York), December 1952; "Dali, Koch and the Academy" by Emily Genauer in the *New York Herald Tribune,* February 1958; "John Koch" by Alexander Eliot in *Time,* (New York), May 1962; "Back to the Nude: by John Canaday in *Horizon* (New York), September 1963; "The Crowded Eye" by John Canaday in *New York Times,* November 1963; "John Koch in New York" by Billi Boros in *Art Times* (New York), November 1963; "John Koch and His Glorious People" by Dorothy Parker in *Esquire* (New York), November 1964; "John Koch" by Ralph Fabri in *Today's Art* (New York), December 1964; "John Koch" by Douglas Davis in the *National Observer* (Chicopee, Massachusetts), December 1965; "The Realism of John Koch" in *American Artist* (New York), September 1966; "Art Doesn't Have to Be New" by Douglas Davis in the *National Observer* (Chicopee, Massachusetts), June 1968.

Superficially, John Koch could be thought of as nothing more than an illustrator, a sort of John O'Hara of the visual arts. Of course his subject matter allows for such a response: couples in bed watching television, cocktail parties, elegantly furnished rooms, musical recitals, and so forth. The way he paints, superficially, endorses this categorization.

I say "superficially" because, whether one agrees or not that he accomplished as much, Koch's ambition was to paint what he was interested in, knew intimately, and loved, in a clear and direct way, stemming from the masters although self-effacing on the surface. I'm back to that surface business again because, if taken only at its surface value, his art is indeed mere story-telling. But if one studies the way Koch handled light and the placement of figures and objects, his evident love of detail and texture, then I think the Dutch Masters come into the discussion. I am not arguing that Koch was trying for the marvelous "needlepoint" quality of Vermeer's application of paint, nor the "looseness" of Rembrandt's brushwork. Rather, I am referring to Koch's affinity to the spirit of Vermeer's handling of figures beside furniture in airy, light-flooded rooms, along with a bit of Rembrandt's genius for drama.

The difference is, of course, that these are domestic, modern dramas—nothing of Shakespeare's royals, just Eliot's cocktail drinkers. And Koch's sense of the rightness of things caused him to take a cooler approach, to subdue virtuoso brushwork, melodramatic lighting, violent gestures. Of course he didn't always succeed. Detail can become finicky, subject matter too literary. But in his best work he is in the line of painters such as Sargent and Fantin-Latour and the finest pictorial reporter of a certain domesticity that we have had.

—Ralph Pomeroy

KOCH, Pyke.

Dutch. Born in Ubbergen, 15 July 1901. Educated at Nutschoool, Nijmegen, 1907-13; Christelijk Gymnasium, Zeist, 1913-20; studied law, Rijksuniversiteit, Utrecht, 1920-26, B.A. 1926; mainly self-educated in art; influenced by German expressionist films and

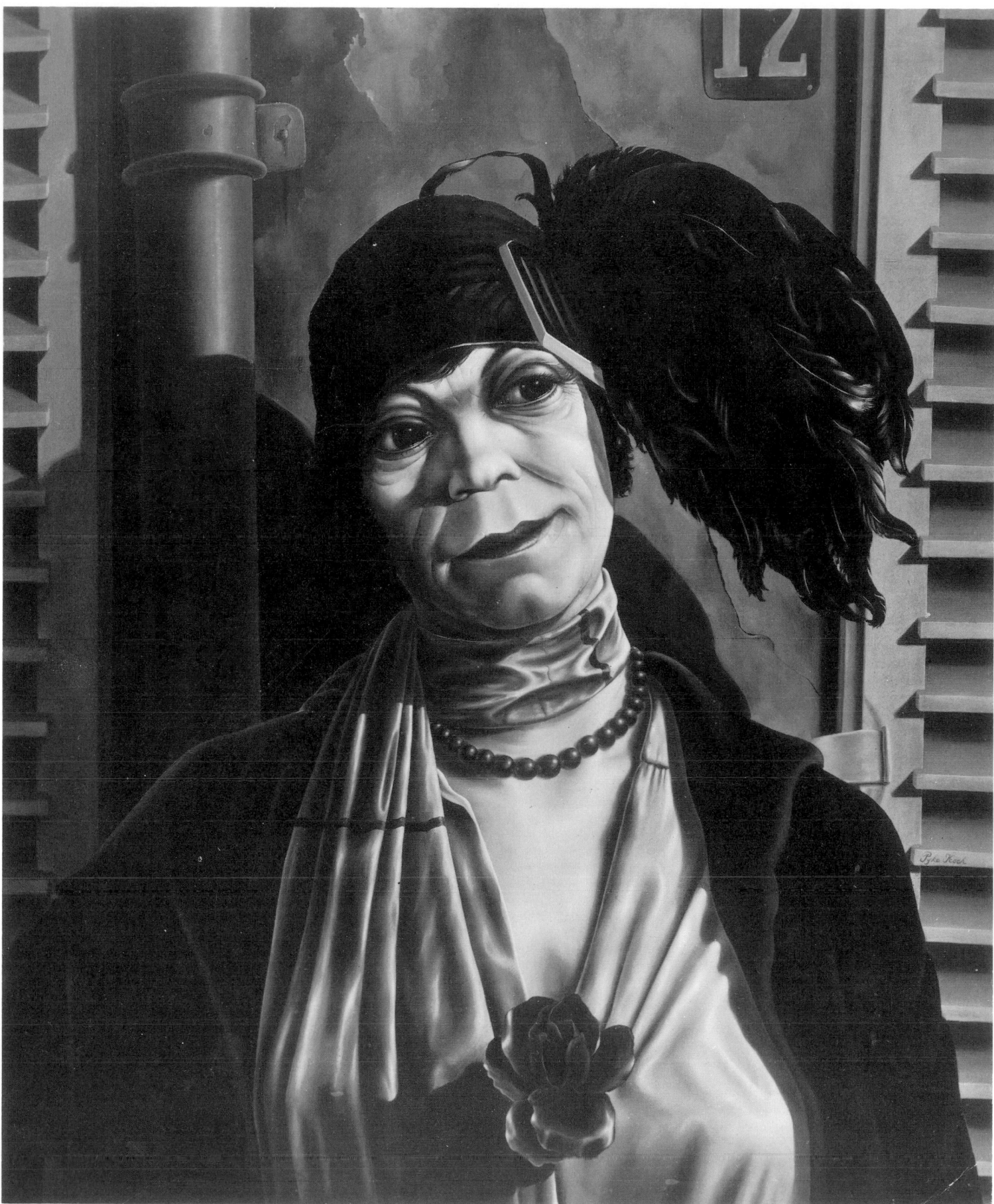

Pyke Koch: *Bertha van Antwerpen*, 1930

writings of Dostoyevsky, Baudelaire and Lautreamont. Married Hedwig Maria de Greer in 1934; children: Peter and Floris. Independent painter, Utrecht, 1927–82; worked occasionally in Florence, 1938–40. Address: Oude Gracht 341, 2500 Utrecht, Netherlands.

Individual Exhibitions:

1930	Kunsthandel P. de Boer, Amsterdam (with K. Postma and K. Willink)
1931	Rotterdamsche Kring, Rotterdam (with K. Postma and K. Willink)
	Voor de Kunst, Utrecht (with K. Postma and K. Willink)
1940	Genootschap Kunstliefde, Utrecht
1951	T. J. Botke House, Maastricht
1955	Stedelijk Museum, Amsterdam
1960	St. Paul Gallery and School of Art, Minnesota (travelled to Pensacola Art Center, Florida; University of Wisconsin, Madison; and the Walker Art Center, Minneapolis)
1964	Kunstzaal De Reiger, Utrecht (with William Kuik)
1965	Utrechtse Kring, Utrecht (with K. Willink)
1966	Gemeentemuseum, Arnhem
1969	Utrechtse Kring, Utrecht (with K. Postma and K. Willink)
1971	Koninklijke Museum voor Schone Kunsten, Antwerp (with R. Hynckes and K. Willink)
1972	Stedelijk Museum, Amsterdam
1980	Centraal Museum, Utrecht
1982	Institut Neerlandais, Paris

Selected Group Exhibitions:

1932	*Honderd jaar Nederlandse schilderkunst*, Koninklijke Museum voor Moderne Kunst, Brussels
1937	*International Exhibition of Painting*, Carnegie Institute, Pittsburgh
1938	*Biennale*, Venice
1960	*De bange jaren dertig*, Gemeentemuseum, Arnhem
1965	*Bienal*, Sao Paulo
1970	*L'Art en Europe autour de 1925*, Ancienne Douane, Strasbourg
1977	*Tendenzen der zwanziger Jahre*, Orangerie Charlottenberg, Berlin
1980	*Les Realismes 1919-1939*, Centre Georges Pompidou, Paris (travelled to the Staatliche Kunsthalle, Berlin)
1983	*Modern Dutch Painting*, National Gallery and Alexander Soutzos Museum, Athens (travelled to Amsterdam and Nuremberg)

Collections:

Stedelijk Museum, Amsterdam; Koninklijke Museum voor Schone Kunsten, Antwerp; Gemeentemuseum, Arnhem; Gemeentemuseum, The Hague; Gemeente Nijmegen, Netherlands; Museum Boymans-van Beuningen, Rotterdam; Centraal Museum, Utrecht; Rijksdienst Beeldende Kunst, The Hague; Stadhuis, Nijmegen, Netherlands; Minnesota Museum of Art, St. Paul.

Publications:

On KOCH: books—*Koch/Postma/Willink*, exhibition catalogue, Amsterdam 1930; *Pyke Koch* by Jan Engleman, Amsterdam 1941; *Pyke Koch*, exhibition catalogue, St. Paul, Minnesota 1960; *Pyke Koch*, exhibition catalogue, Arnhem 1966; *Pyke Koch* by Carel Blotkamp, Amsterdam 1972; *Pyke Koch*, exhibition catalogue, Utrecht 1980; *Pyke Koch*, exhibition catalogue, Paris 1982.

As my work is labelled "magic realism," it may be worthwhile to remember that, though magic realism was presented a few decades ago as if it were a new invention, it is as old as painting itself. For instance, a certain Piero della Francesca was a magic realist, and let us agree that he was not the worst one. If we, for the sake of convenience, keep using this label,

then we must first establish what is typical for the conception magic realism.

The surrealists created situations which are physically impossible; magic realism confronts us with situations that are possible, even commonplace, but contain an element of improbability or are improbable *tout court*. Magic realism exists by the grace of ambiguity, which is the source of a fascination on an entirely different level than that of beauty (or morality). It is brought about by the introduction of unobtrusive contradictory elements. Whereas the representations used by surrealism are separated from reality as if by the stroke of an axe, the same is achieved in magic realism as if by a hardly perceptible, cautiously executed cut with a razor blade, leaving reality intact on the outside but with an inner dislocation.

Piero della Francesca, for instance, combines extreme suffering or adoration with complete indifference—see the "Flagellation," the "Finding of the Cross" and so many other works. The element of improbability caused by this discrepancy raises the image above the reality depicted in it. The cool, unaffected acceptance of eternal iniquity and inequality is the basis of the mental power, of the "magic" of Piero's painting.

—Pyke Koch

The compact oeuvre of the Utrecht painter Pyke Koch shows virtually no stylistic changes over the years: what changes is his subject matter, not his manner of representation. His very first painting, "Dolores' Breakfast" (1927), is already characteristic, which is all the more remarkable when we consider that Koch had just given up the study of law for painting and was self-taught as an artist. For the rest of his life he continued to paint in the style generally referred to as "magic realism," probably because of his deep respect for the work of Charley Toorop, his fascination with film techniques, and the influence of Carel Willink. Around 1925 Willink moved from futuristic-constructivist abstractions to a kind of figurative work which served as a model for Dutch painters of the way in which a painter can encompass both people and things. With the help of Willink, Koch presented his early work in the *Spring Exhibition of the Independents*, held in the Municipal Museum of Amsterdam in 1928.

Throughout his entire career the image of woman served for Koch as the embodiment of puzzling and inexplicable truths. "Woman" in this sense, whatever different guises she may assume, is irresistible and commanding for him. In 1929, for example, he worked from a photograph of the German actress Astra Nielsen (the star of the great film *Dirnentrajödie*) and produced a portrait which is close to the work of the German Expressionists Dix and Grosz, particularly in their use of color. "Nocturnal" (1931) is lyrical: it represents a urinal in Utrecht, a place according to Koch which catches the atmosphere of the city. The year 1931 is a kind of highpoint in his career. His portrait of "Bertha van Antwerpen"—who is both whore and mother figure—is in part a fantasy: this woman will survive disaster and chaos. She is a born victor, not a victim. "The Shooting Gallery" from the same year would be overpowering if the pose of the young woman, despite its banality, did not also have a kind of sublimity: it is a repository of unambiguous sexual meanings. Koch's 1937 "Self-Portrait" stirred up some controversy, since it seemed to reveal fascist sympathies. According to the art historian Blotkamp, the head here radiates "a disconcerting mixture of will and power and defeatism."

Koch's admiration for painters of the Italian Renaissance such as Andrea Mantegna and Piero della Francesca is apparent in "The Chimney Sweep" (1943) and especially in his profile-portrait of Lady J. C. van Boetzelaer.

Koch reaches another highpoint in his 1955 canvas, "Contortionist." In "Resting Sleepwalker" (1965) he portrays a magical slumber which cannot be grasped in terms of the human or non-human alone. But in general Koch has a deep and vehement commitment

to reality, so that the adjective "magical" is never entirely appropriate.

—A. F. Wagemans

KOCMAN, J(iří) H(ynek).
Czechoslovakian. Born in Nové Město na Moravě, 6 August 1947. Studied at the University of Veterinary Medicine, Brno, Czechoslovakia, 1965–71. Has practiced as a doctor of veterinary medicine, working in clinical pharmacology, Brno, since 1971. Also an artist: has worked with graphics, poems, texts, since 1965; book-objects, reports, stamps, project/concepts, ecology, entomology, and studies of communication, since 1970; hand-sewn books, hand-made papers, paper re-making, and studies about paper and bookbinding, since 1975. Address: Vackova 64, 61200 Brno, Czechoslovakia.

Individual Exhibitions:

1966	Vysokoskolsky Klub, Brno
1968	*Tinktury*, Galerie Kluba A, Tryba, Brno
	Zamek, Bucovice, Czechoslovakia
1970	*Collyrie*, Galerie Mladých, Brno
1971	Psi Klub, Brno
	Trias Klub, Brno
1973	Stedelijk Museum, Amsterdam
1978	*Bücher und Stempel*, Galerie Learman, Dusseldorf
	17 Butterflies, Mala Galerie Cs. Spisovatale, Brno
	Rubber Stamp Works, Stempelplaats, Amsterdam
1981	Studio J. Gottschalk, Dresden
1983	Galerie für visuele Erlebnisse, Weddel, West Germany (retrospective)

Selected Group Exhibitions:

1969	*MAX* Dum Umĕni, Brno
1971	*Arte de Sistemas 1*, Centro Arte y Communicacion, Buenos Aires
1972	*Attention*, Galerie Impact, Lausanne, Switzerland
1973	*Texts*, Kapolna, Balatonboglar, Hungary
1974	*Tampons d'Artistes*, Institut de l'Environnement, Paris
1975	*Visual Poetry International*, Galerie de Doelen, Rotterdam
1976	*The Museum of Drawers*, Museumfoyer, Solothurn, Switzerland
1979	*Sprachen Jenseits von Dichtung*, Westfälischer Kunstverein, Munster
	3rd Trienále Umĕlecké Knízni Vazby, Karlovy Vary, Czechoslovakia
1980	*Von Aussehen der Wörter*, Kunstmuseum, Hannover
1982	*Young Fluxus*, Artists Space, New York
1986	*Turning Over the Pages*, Kettle's Yard Gallery, Cambridge

Collections:

Moravska Galerie, Brno; Schubladenmuseum für Moderne Kunst im 20, Jahrhundert, Berne; Kunsthaus, Zurich; Collection Hundertmark, Berlin; Fluxus West Archive, San Diego, California; Archiv Sohm, Stadtgalerie, Stuttgart; DAAD-Archiv, West Berlin; Sackner Archive, Miami Beach, Florida.

Publications:

By KOCMAN: books—*Europe-America: The Different Avant-Gardes*, edited by A. B. Oliva, Milan 1976; *Rubber No. 10*, edited by A. de Varbeneld, Amsterdam 1978; articles—visual poetry in *Lotta Poetica*, Brescia 1971; "Touch Activity" in *Aktuelle Kunst in Ost Europa*, edited by Klaus Groh, Cologne 1972; rubber stamp facsimiles in *Art et Communication Marginale*, edited by Hervé Fischer, Paris 1974; "Ceska vizualni poezie sedmdesatych let" in *Literarnevedny sbornik* (Prague), no. 1, 1983.

On KOCMAN: books—*Tinktury,* exhibition catalogue, by Jiri Valoch, Brno 1968; *Collyrie,* exhibition catalogue, by Jiri Valoch, Brno 1970; *JHK: My Activity 1965-73,* with text by Jiri Valoch, Brno 1973; *JHK: 17 Motýlku,* exhibition catalogue, with text by Jiri Valoch, Brno 1978; *JHK 1976-80,* with text by Jiri Valoch, Brno 1980; articles— "Künstlerstempel" by G. F. Schwarzbauer in *Magazin Kunst* (Mainz), no. 3, 1974; "The Stamp and Stamp Art" by Kenneth S. Friedman and G. M. Gugelberger in *Front* (San Francisco), no. 4, 1976; "Buchobjekte—das Buch als Kunstwerk" by A. Heibe in *Kunstnachrichten* (Zurich), no. 3, 1983; "The Contemporary Renaissance of Fine Bookbinding in Czechoslovakia" by E. Minar in *Fine Art* (New York), no 1, 1987.

I started to take an interest in paper at the time of my "graphic activities" (1965-70) when I got my first real experience with the material. In the first half of the 1970s I was engaged in Concept Art, Project Art, Stamp Art, Mail Art, etc. In 1976 I met the art-bookbinder master Professor Jindřich Svoboda, and had the opportunity to watch and learn the bookbinding processes. I feel that paper is a fantastic material and I am fascinated by paper's sensibilities.

In my book object made between 1970 and 1972 I placed different visual (especially coloured) aspects in the foreground. From 1977 on, I made "Hand-Sewn Books", book-concepts without text or illustration, books as material objects in themselves. In my bookbinding activity I like best to be able to work with various kinds of paper and to make something out of them: to be together with the paper. My first "Hand-Made Papers" were produced in January 1979. I employed a technique I called Paper-Re-Making.

Jiři Kocman: *Artist's Book of Handmade Paper*, 1982

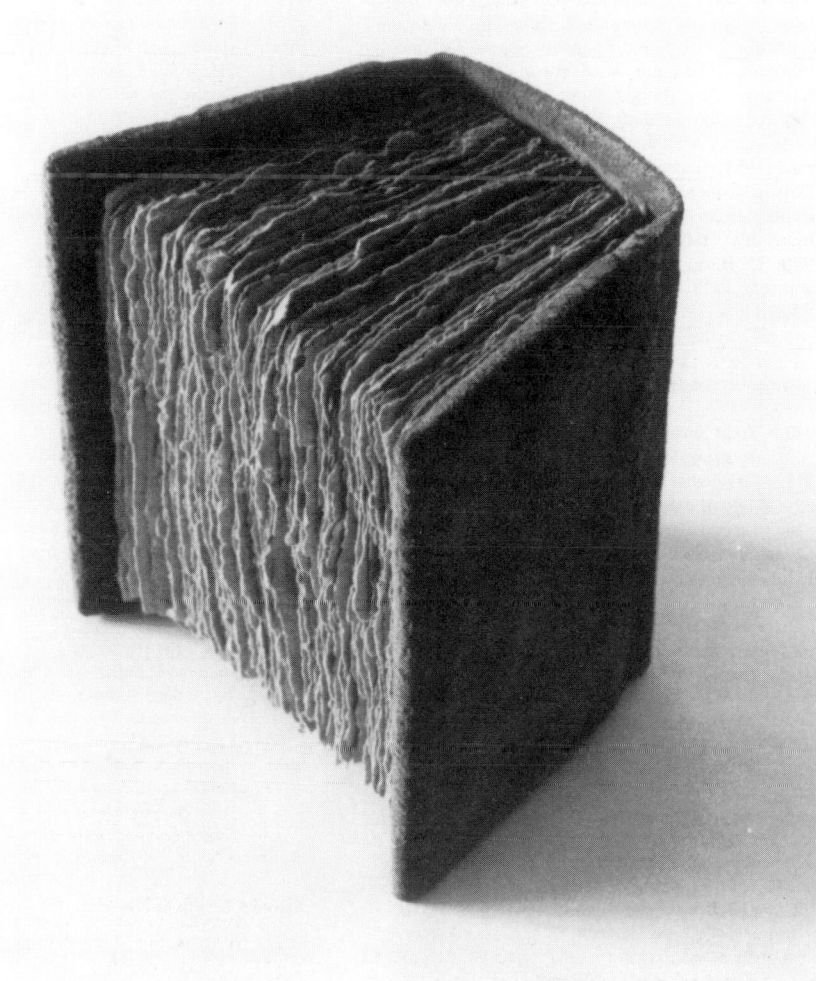

The papers I make are not for ordinary use: they are intended as pieces of work in themselves. I find it always exciting to make new paper, being especially interested in the fineness of its structure, transparency, the appearance of both sides of each sheet, the nature of its construction and individual character . . .

As important as its visual appearance are the tactile aspects: touching, feeling, tracing. Paper is made for the hands. All these notions are too "intimate" to talk much about.

—J. H. Kocman

The Czech artist, J. H. Kocman—best known as JHK—is concerned with systems. Kocman is not concerned with the cold, impersonal precision of systems, but rather with their poetry, with their musicality, with their suggestive valences.

Kocman is best known internationally for the seminal role he has had as a major developer of rubber stamp art. He organized some of the first international rubber stamp activities by contemporary artists, and edited the first true anthology of rubber stamp art. He is also known for his contributions to mail art and communications art, and to visual poetry.

The vast majority of his works walk the borderline between intimate art experience and science. Unlike many artists who organize data related to biological or astronomical processes, presenting them in good formats on large scale, Kocman presents his material in small, almost tender fragments. He takes one idea or process at a time, and uses its poetic, human potential to map lyrical aesthetic structures. In one regard, he removes from the idea of a system its rigid, systemic nature. In another, he heightens our consciousness of the fragile relationships which obtain in most systems which a scientist or an artist can investigate.

Many artists today employ scientific notions or the idea of systemic structures in their work. They often appear to do so simply to keep abreast of recent tendencies in the art world, despite the fact that the work itself is incapable of yielding interesting results. All too often, even the data, as science, and as systems, are invalid. As it is, therefore, the practitioners of these art forms take their art too seriously, and joke poorly with the science involved. Kocman takes an opposite and exemplary tack: his works frequently embody sly jokes on the history and practice of art, but his science is always accurate and serious, even though it may be presented in an intimate atmosphere of personalized poetics. This might perhaps be expected: after all, Kocman was trained as a scientist, and is a doctor of veterinary medicine. As a scientist, biological processes hold a fascination for him; as a practitioner of the healing arts, he holds life in high esteem. While he makes a playful or delightful art from the processes of science and life, therefore, it would be impossible for him to abuse them.

The key to Kocman's work is the intersection between the content of his systems and the delights which lie hidden within them. He is not concerned with the difference or similarity between art and life. The art/life battle has been well fought out by previous artists, and while it has some points left to be made, most of the art/life problems pursued by artists today are in reality retrograde tactics useful only in claiming career status. Even at that, the tactic is only useful in a provincial atmosphere where the arty world is not aware of the nature and discourse of art as it has played out over the recent decades of this century. Kocman's strategy is an appropriate international strategy: he accepts his position as a member of this generation of artists just come to prominence, a generation which accepts the results of the discourse between art and life, using those results as a platform from which new investigations may be launched.

Because he accepts his place in history, he is free to contribute to the next stages in art history. He is not trapped in any past doctrine, and will not be dismissed as an artist who spent his career re-stating the issues of the past for the benefit of tenure in an art school or academy. Instead, he takes the risk of his own search: the search for a personal style in a freshly-discovered world which accepts itself as having a dual nature, rooted equally in art and life. In a peculiar regard, he is the most free among artists. As a full professional in another discipline than art, he is able to make his living without any concern for the ups and downs of the art world. As an artist who draws on the disciplines of his profession, he is freed by the knowledge of his science to do work which does not demean itself by presenting its scientific content poorly.

Kocman's presentation is perhaps the most interesting phenomenon of his interaction with the art world. JHK does not prepare, as mentioned earlier, large-format explorations for exhibition and museum appreciation. Instead, he makes his works lovingly, individually, too personally, in fact, to be appreciated truly in the Byzantine atmosphere of most art situations. His works reach their audience in small, hand-made books, experiments, and individually-bound monographs. They include maps, plates, injected dye-samples, hand-cut pages, photographs, diagrams. They capture the pleasant spirit of correspondence art during its personalist phases of the '60's, and join it to the environmental and structuralist sensibilities of the '70's. When one acquires a Kocman piece, one does not have the feeling that one has outbid another collector of impersonally acquisitioned a new work. One feels that one is sharing part of an experiment which might have taken place recently in a friend's laboratory. Kocman's presentations summon up the image of a Royal Society as it might have been some centuries ago, a Society in which we are all colleague-scientists, working together to advance the frontiers of knowledge. We are content in this work together, and leave it to another group to bally-hoo the knowledge into fame and fortune. Kocman's work approaches the framework of the pure research end of research art in its tone, even though its content is warm and conversational.

Some artists succeed very well in the use of environmental and biological science for large-format presentations. Most notable, of course, are the Harrisons and Hans Haacke. In another way—particularly in the preparatory phases of his projects—we find Christo. The wonder and artful delight of the work of these artists is the fact that their use of science is not distorted in order to make it art, but that the science is managed properly as the art.

Kocman is unique in presenting scientific systems and their spinoff in intimate and poetic forms. His beautiful monograph, *Micro-Macro*, in fact, echoes in its title his role in the art world. Where others—some successfully, most badly—strive to fill out roles and careers on the macrocosmic scale, Kocman stands out as an artist whose work emerges beneath the microscope. Because of the intimacy of its presentation, in fact, even his non-microscopic work has a sensibly small scale, even when the ideas it presents are large, important ideas.

Success as an artist requires several facilities. One must be aware of that which has gone before, and play off it without repeating it. One must discover for one's work an authority of scale, tone and diction that is suitable to its content. One must develop a personal style of engagement and presentation which balances aesthetic concerns of content and the direct form of the work in a manner which is both unique to a great enough degree to be remarkable and which is congenial enough to enter into the dialogue of the art world. Kocman grapples well with these problems, and his growing success as an artist on the international scene bears witness to his talent and skill as a potentially major figure in contemporary art.

In some regards, Kocman's career is just freshly begun. He is considered by many to be the fourth major contemporary figure to emerge from Czechoslovakia, following the pioneers Kolar and Knizak, and following his better-known friend, Valoch. He is widely esteemed and has claimed a major place for himself in one field of art, rubber stamp art. Because his career rests more on poetic environmental concerns, however, his image is not as clearly defined as the other three—who are best-known for their major works, rather than for one or another career sidelight. In this regard, Kocman's stamp work is both a help and a hindrance to his total career. Because he is an intimist, as well, he is in some circles less well-known than Czech artists who have emerged more recently, but whose work is better given to wide exhibition and publication. In this regard, one thinks of the talented young Czechs such as Zorka Saglova, Olaf Hanel, Eugen Brikcius, Peter Stembera, and others. With Valoch, Kocman is seen as one of the first generation of Czechs of the post-Fluxus, post-Aktual period, and like Valoch, his work overlaps the activity of those movements in Czech contemporary art. As an intimist, he is also logically placed in context with Endre Tot and Jaroslav Kozlowsky—of Hungary and Poland respectively. It is to his credit, but a problem in publishing his work, that Kocman's work requires special printing techniques, many of which can only be done by hand, while many of the works of Tot and Kozlowsky can simply be reprinted photographically. It is, of course, for this reason, that his rubber stamp work is so much better than his biological or systematic works and process pieces.

In terms of his career, the greatest problem facing Kocman is the problem of scale. Can he retain his intimate tone and personalized qualities which so distinguish and enliven his use of systems, while translating them into a scale which will render them more visible to the world at large? This may well be a useless question, of course, since we have noted that Kocman is an extraordinary artist in relation to career concerns and art-world politics. Nevertheless, in viewing—or better put, in handling and contacting

Kocman's work, it is a question which is frequently asked.

That he, himself, is not overly concerned with such questions is part of the nature and character which makes him and his work so refreshing. The vitality and delight in Kocman's work arises from this spirit as much as from the way in which it handles important art issues in surprising and unique ways.

J. H. Kocman is a surprising and unique artist. A scientist who presents his work as a visual and intellectual poetics. A systematist who demonstrates the humanistic uses of systems, rather than using systems toward dehumanizing ends. A fresh voice out of the increasingly important art world of Eastern Europe which offers to engage and revitalize the often moribund West. J. H. Kocman is an artist who, through his intimate and personalized style, engages others in his work as colleagues, and as human beings.

—Kenneth Friedman

KOKOSCHKA, Oskar.

British. Born in Pöcklarn, Austria, 1 March 1886; emigrated to England in 1938: naturalized, 1947. Educated in Vienna primary schools; studied at the Kunstgewerbeschule, under Gustav Klimt, Vienna, 1905–09. Served in the Austrian Army, 1914–18; severely wounded on the Eastern Front, 1915; appointed official War artist, Isonzo, 1915–16. Married Olda Palkovska in 1951. Painter: lived in Switzerland, 1909–19, in Berlin, 1910–14; contributed illustrations for *Der Sturm,* Berlin; 1910; lived in Dresden, 1917–24; Lecturer, Dresden Akademie der Kunst, 1919–24; travelled extensively in Europe, 1924–30; lived in Vienna, 1930–34, in Prague, 1934–38; in London, 1938–53; visited the United States frequently from 1945; lived in Villeneuve, Switzerland, 1953–80; Founder, School for Seeing, International Summer Academy of the Plastic Arts, Salzburg, 1953 (taught there, 1953–63); designed sets for *Die Zauberflote,* Salzburg, 1955, and for the Bergtheater, Vienna, 1960–61. Recipient: Rome Prize, 1959; International Erasmus Prize, with Marc Chagall, Copenhagen, 1960; Order of Merit, West German Federal Republic, 1956. D. Litt.: Oxford University, 1963. Honorary Royal Academician, 1970. C. B. E. (Commander, Order of the British Empire), 1959. *Died* (in Villeneuve) *22 February 1980.*

Individual Exhibitions:

1910	Paul Cassirer Galerie, Berlin
	Folkwang Museum, Essen
1915	Galerie der Sturm, Berlin (with Heinrich Campendonk and Franz Marc)
1916	Galerie der Sturm, Berlin
1920	Galerie Lang, Darmstadt
1921	Galerie von Garvens, Hannover
	Galerie Caspari, Munich
	Kunstlervereinigung, Dresden
	Galerie Richter, Dresden
	Galerie Gurlitt, Berlin
1922	Graphisches Kabinett Erfuth, Dresden
1923	Kunstsalon Wolfsberg, Zurich
1924	Galerie Goldschmidt-Wallerstein, Berlin
	Galerie Goltz, Munich
	Neue Galerie, Vienna
1925	Kestner-Gesellschaft, Hannover
	Galerie Arnold, Dresden
1926	Kunsthandlung Goldschmidt, Frankfurt
	Galerie Caspari, Munich
1927	Gemeentemuseum, The Hague (toured the Netherlands)
	Kunsthaus, Zurich
	Kunsthaus Schaller, Stuttgart
1928	Leicester Galleries, London

1929	Kunsthaus Hermann Abels, Cologne
1931	Kunsthalle, Mannheim
	Galerie Georges Petit, Paris
1933	Galerie Feigl, Prague
1937	Osterreichisches Museum für Kunste und Industrie, Vienna
1938	Buchholz Gallery, New York
1939	Genootschap Kunstliefde, Ultrecht
1940	Gallery St. Etienne, New York
1941	Buchholz Gallery, New York
	Arts Club of Chicago
1942	City Art Museum, St. Louis
1943	Gallery St. Etienne, New York
1945	Neue Galerie, Vienna (with Gustav Klimt and Egon Schiele)
1947	Kunsthalle, Basle
	Stedelijk Museum, Amsterdam
	Kunsthaus, Zurich
1948	Institute of Contemporary Art, Boston (toured the United States)
1949	Feigl Gallery, New York
1950	Haus der Kunst, Munich
1951	Neue Galerie, Linz, Austria
	Wallraf-Richartz Museum, Cologne
	Schloss Charlottenburg, Berlin
1952	Institute of Contemporary Arts, London
1953	Kunstkabinett, Frankfurt
	Kunstnernes Hus, Oslo
1954	Gallery St. Etienne, New York
	Museum of Art, Santa Barbara, California (travelled to the California Palace of the Legion of Honor, San Francisco)
	Museu de Arte Moderna, Rio de Janeiro
	Kunstverein, Freiburg, West Germany
	Galerie Welz, Salzburg
1956	National Gallery, Prague
	Kunsthalle, Bremen, West Germany
1960	Marlborough Fine Art, London
1962	Tate Gallery, London
1966	Württembergischer Kunstverein, Stuttgart
	Marlborough-Gerson Gallery, New York
1967	Marlborough Fine Art, London
1968	Smithsonian Institution, Washington, D.C.
1969	Marlborough Fine Art, London
1971	Galerie Welz, Salzburg
	Osterreichische Galerie im Oberen Belvedere, Vienna
	Narodni Galerie, Prague
	Haus der Kunst, Munich
	Bethnal Green Museum, London
1974	Marlborough Fine Art, London
1975	Kunsthaus, Hamburg
1976	Roswitha Haftmann, Zurich
	Kunstlerhaus, Bregenz, Austria
	M. Fisher Gallery, London
	Victoria and Albert Museum, London
	Haus der Kunst, Munich
	Marlborough Fine Art, London
1978	Umetnostra Galerija, Maribor, Yugoslavia (toured Yugoslavia)
1981	Palais des Beaux-Arts, Brussels (with Gustav Klimt and Egon Schiele)
1982	Marlborough Fine Art, London
1984	Musee Jenisch, Vevey, Switzerland
	Snape Maltings, Aldeburgh, Suffolk
	Galerie Wurthle, Vienna
1984	Oskar Kokoschka Dokumentation Centre, Pocklarn, Austria
1986	Kunsthalle, Hamburg
	Kunsthaus, Zurich
	Tate Gallery, London
	St. Etienne Gallery, New York
	Los Angeles County Museum of Art
1987	Glyptothek, Munich
	Centro Mostre, Florence, Italy
	Santa Barbara Museum of Art, California
	Guggenheim Museum, New York

Selected Group Exhibitions:

1908	*International Kunstschau,* Vienna
1914	*Neue Sezession,* Munich
1922	*Biennale,* Venice

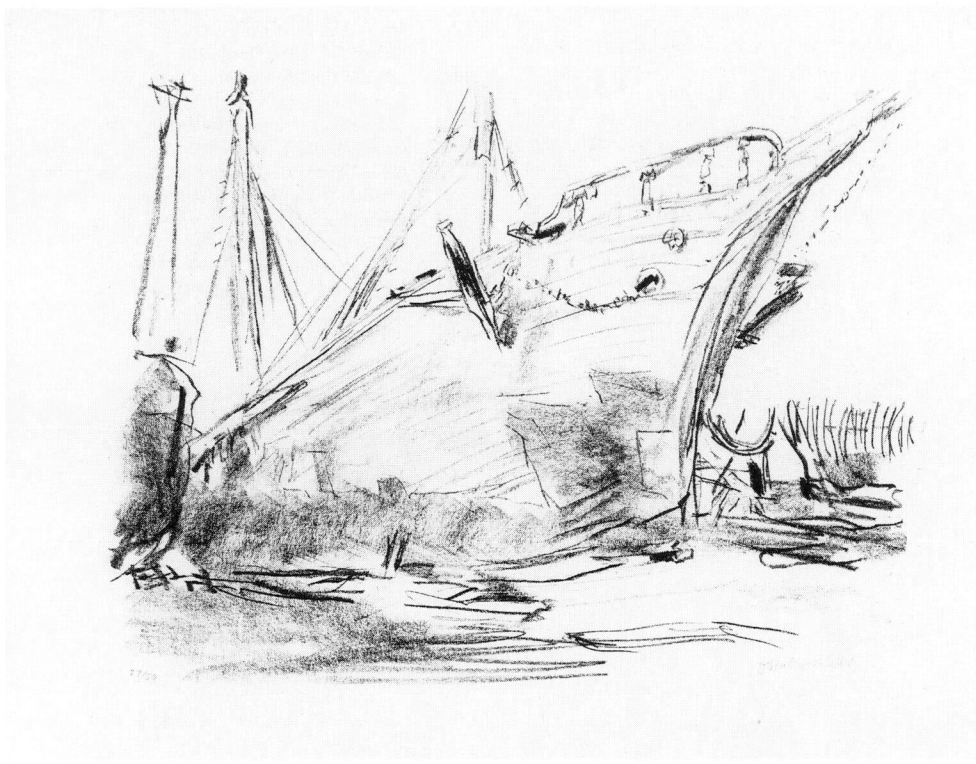

Oskar Kokoschka: *Apulian Journey: Ship Like a Dolphin*, 1963 Courtesy Guggenheim Museum, New York

KOLAR, Jiri.

French. Born in Protivin, Southern Bohemia (Czechoslovakia), 24 September 1914; emigrated to France, 1980: naturalized, 1984. Trained as apprentice carpenter, Protivin, 1928-34; mainly self-educated in art; influenced by writings of Marinetti and Surrealist artists. Married Bela Helclova in 1949. Worked as carpenter, laborer and waiter, Protivin, 1928-42; as independent artist/writer, as children's book author and translator, Kladno and Prague, 1942-80, in Paris, since 1980. Founder-Member, Group 42, Prague, 1942-48; Editor, Dilo Publishers, Prague, 1945-48. Recipient: *International Art Biennale* Prize, Lignano, Italy, 1968; Central Committee Prize, 50th Anniversary of the Czech Socialist Republic, Prague, 1968; International Joan Miro Drawing Prize, Barcelona, 1968; Czechoslovakia Prize, *Bienal*, Sao Paulo, 1969; Gottfried-von-Herder Prize, Vienna 1971; DAAD Fellowship, West Berlin, 1979. Agents: Galleria Schwarz, Via Gesu 17, 20121 Milan, Italy; Willard Gallery, 29 East 72nd Street, New York, New York 10021, U.S.A.; and Galerie R., Bismarckstrasse 45, Nuremberg, West Germany. Address: 61 rue Olivier-Métra, 75020 Paris, France.

Individual Exhibitions:

1937	Mozarteum, Theatre 37, Prague
1962	Club VU Manes, Prague
1963	Arthur Jeffers Gallery, London
	Museum of Modern Art, Miami
	Europaisches Forum, Alpbach, Austria
	Oblastni Galerie, Liberec, Czechoslovakia
1964	Galerie Gravura, Lisbon
	Metska Galerie, Louny, Czechoslovakia
	Schwitters/Kolar/Mesens, Grosvenor Gallery, London
1965	Die Kleine Galerie, Vienna
	Club VU Manes, Prague
	La Carabaga Club, Genoa
1966	Galerie Riquelme, Paris
	Galerie M. E. Thelen, Essen
	Galerie H., Hannover
	Centro Proposte, Florence
	Studio d'Informazione Estetica, Turin
1967	Klus Pratel Vytarneho Umeni, Prague
	Galerie Seyfried und Alten G. Neuhaus, Munich
1968	Galerie V. Spala, Prague
	Kunstlerhaus am Konigster, Nuremberg
1969	Kestner-Gesellschaft, Hannover
	Overbeck Gesellschaft, Lübeck, West Germany
	Junge Galerie, Kassel, West Germany
	Ulmer Museum, Ulm, West Germany
	Kunstverein, Munich
	Kleine Grafik Galerie, Bremen, West Germany
	Galerie am Klosterstern, Hamburg
	Galerie Hansjorg Mayer, Stuttgart
	Willard Gallery, New York
1970	Museum P. Bezruc, Opava, Czechoslovakia
	Galerie Wentdorf und Swetec, Dusseldorf
	Galerie Gmurzynska, Aachen, West Germany
1971	Librairie-Galerie La Hune, Paris
	ARC/Musée d'Art Moderne de la Ville, Paris
	Hofer Galerie H, Weinelt/Hof, West Germany
	Galerie K, Mainz, West Germany
1972	Galleria Schwarz, Milan
	Galerie M. Goebels, Kaiserslautern, West Germany
	Kleine Grafik Galerie, Bremen, West Germany
	Aktionsgalerie, Berne
1973	La Boetie Gallery, New York
	Collagen, Rollagen, Chiasmagen, Crumblagen, Museum Haus Lange, Krefeld, West Germany
	Museum Boymans-van Beuningen, Rotterdam
	Galerie Gunter Sachs, Hamburg
1974	Union des Arts Plastiques, St. Etienne-du-Rouvray, France
	Galerie R, Nuremberg
	Galerie Suzanne Bollag, Zurich
	Städtische Galerie, Siegen, West Germany
1975	Guggenheim Museum, New York
	Willard Gallery, New York
	Harriette Griffin Gallery, New York
	Jacques Caplan Gallery, New York

1933	*Pittsburgh International*, Carnegie Institute, Pittsburgh
1937	*Entartete Kunst*, Haus der Kunst, Munich (toured Germany)
1953	*Deutsche Kunst: Meisterwerke des 20. Jahrhunderts*, Kunstmuseum, Lucerne
1956	*100 Years of German Painting*, Tate Gallery, London
1962	*European Art: 1912*, Wallraf-Richartz Museum, Cologne
1969	*Gemaelde Bildwerke und Zeichnungen des 20. Jahrhunderts*, Nationalgalerie, Berlin
1977	*40 Modern Masters*, Guggenheim Museum, New York

Collections:

Stedelijk Museum, Amsterdam: Museum Boymans-van Beuningen, Rotterdam; Nationalgalerie, Berlin; Staatsgalerie, Stuttgart; Musée Royaux des Beaux-Arts, Brussels; Albertina Museum, Vienna; Scottish National Gallery of Modern Art, Edinburgh; Tate Gallery, London; Museum of Modern Art, New York; Carnegie Institute, Pittsburgh.

Publications:

By KOKOSCHKA: books—*Die Traeumende Knaben*, 1908; *Dramen und Bilder*, 1913; *Der Brennedne Dornbusch: Moerder Hoffnung der Frauen*, 1917; *Vier Dramen*, 1919; *Der Expressionismus Edvard Munch*, Vienna and Munich 1953; *Thermoplyae: Ein Triptychon*, Winterthur, Switzerland 1955; *Entwurfe für Gesamtaustatung zu W. A. Mozart's Zauberflote*, Salzburg 1955; *Shrifter: 1907-1955*, edited by Hans Maria Wingler, Munich 1956; *Spur im Treisand*, Zurich 1956; *Die Traemende Knaben und Andere Ditchtungen*, Salzburg 1956; *A Sea Ringed with Visions*, London 1962; *Word and Vision*, London 1967; *London Views: British Landscapes*, London 1972; *Saul and David*, London 1973; *My Life*, London 1974; articles—"Allos Maker" in *Zeit-Echo: Ein Kriegstagebuch der Kunstler*, Munich 1915; "Der Weisse Tiertoeter" in *Die Gefaehrten* (Vienna/Leipzig), no. 3, 1920; "Die Mumie" in *Frankfurter Zeitung*, December 1931; "An Approach to the Baroque Art of Czechoslovakia" in *Burlington Magazine* (London), November 1942; "Comenius: The English Revolution and Our Present Plight" in *Teacher of Nations*, Cambridge 1942; foreword to *The War as Seen by Children*, exhibition catalogue, London 1943; "Zum Expressoinismus" in *Freie Deutsche Kultur* (London), May/June 1944; "The Portrait in the Past and Present" in *Apropos* (London), March 1945; "Zu Meinem Denkengemaelde in London" in *Das Werk* (Winterthur, Switzerland), July 1952.

On KOKOSCHKA: books—*Oskar Kokoschka* by Paul Westheim, Potsdam and Berlin, 1918, 1925; *Oskar Kokoschka* by Hans Heilmaier, Paris 1929; *Kokoschka: Life and Work* by Edith Hoffmann, London 1947; *Oskar Kokoschka*, exhibition catalogue, by James S. Plaut, Boston 1948; *Oskar Kokoscha: The Work of the painter* by Hand Maria Wingler, London and Salzburg 1958; *Kokoschka: The Artist and His Time* by J. P. Hodin, London 1966; *Oskar Kokoschka: Drawings 1906-1965*, edited by Ernest Rathenau, Coral Gables, Florida 1966; *Das Druckgraphische Werk* by Hans Maria Wingler and Friedrich Welz, Salzburg 1975; *A Kokoschka Centenary: His Early Graphics*, exhibition catalogue with text by Victor Carlson, Los Angeles 1986; *Oskar Kokoschka*, exhibition catalogue with essays by Jaroslav Leshko and E. H. Gombrich, Santa Barbara 1987; *Oskar Kokoschka*, exhibition catalogue with essay by Werner Haftmann, Munich 1987.

*   *   *

Oskar Kokoschka never recognized any basis for his art other than his own experience. This included an increasing experience of the world; but his first of all there was his immediate surroundings, representatives of Viennese society before the First World War, and his friends; later on, European towns and landscape and the countries bordering the Continent; finally, the entire world entrusted to us the increasingly perilous situation which provoked his appeals.

All his life Kokoschka was critical of the period he lived in: in 1910 he provoked the wrath of the Austrian Crown Prince; in 1919 Communist zealots insulted him; after 1933 the National Socialist rulers threatened him; after 1945 the protagonists of the avant-garde reviled him. Kokoschka remained imperturbable, but also he did not hesitate to offer resistance with words and his own concrete actions. For ten years he concerned himself with the younger generation in his "School of Seeing." During the last decades of his life work other than painting occupied a larger place: tapestry, mosaic, finally the filming of his drama *Comenius*, begun in 1935 and completed in 1972, which contains the antinomy of political reformer and artist and so becomes also an interpretation of his own life.

—Heinz Spielmann

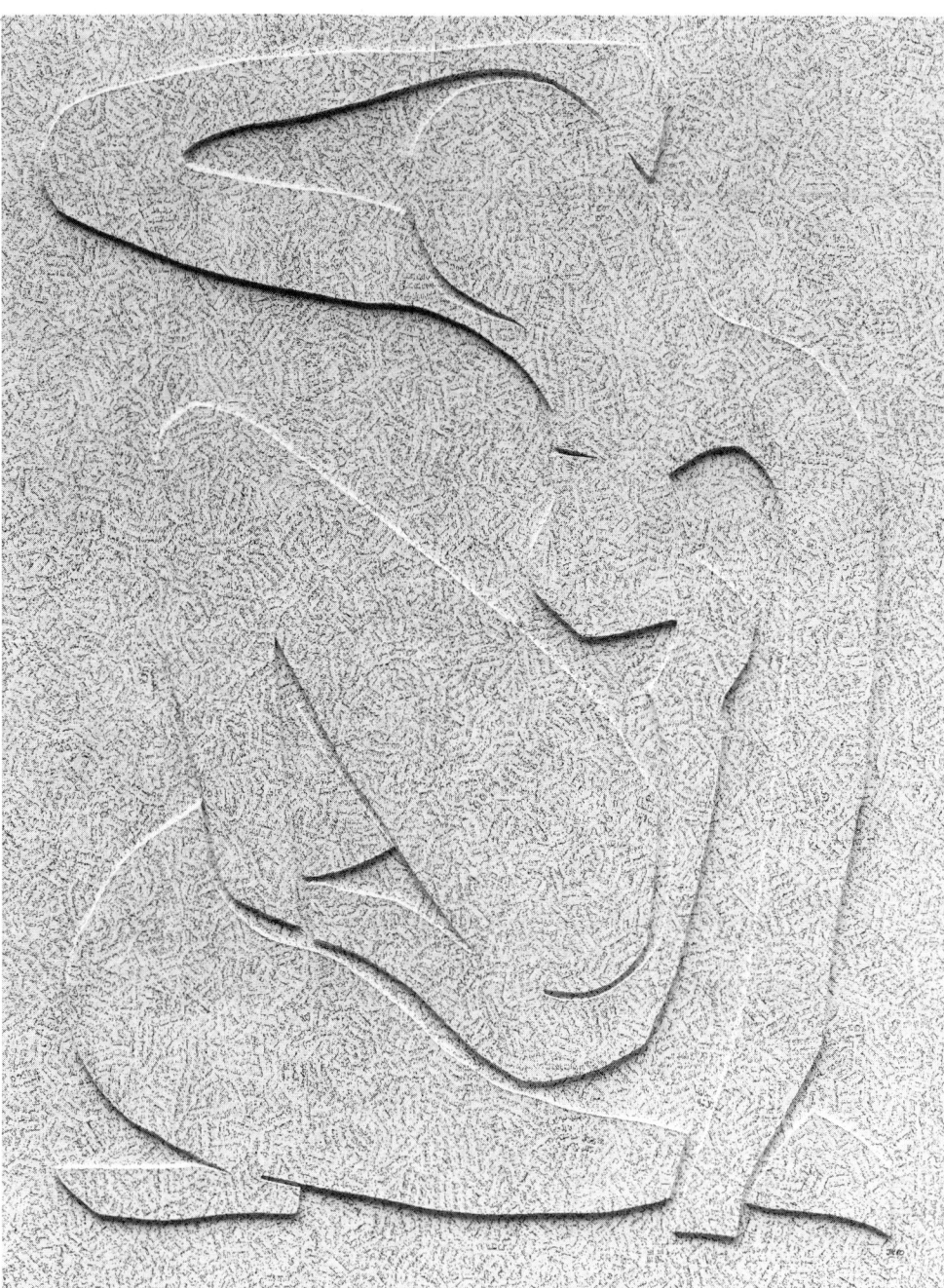

Jiri Kolar: *Hommage à Matisse*, 1981

Vancouver Art Gallery, British Columbia
Museum of Modern Art, Oxford
Galerie Schoeller, Dusseldorf
1985   Leopold-Hoesch-Museum, Duren, West Germany
Kunstverein, Heilbronn, West Germany
Galerie Rafay, Kronberg, West Germany
Galerie Svetlana, Munich
Centro d'Arte Contemporanea, Syracuse, Italy
Museum Rupertinum, Salzburg, Austria
Guggenheim Museum, New York
1986   Galerie Maeght Lelong, Paris
Galerie Grita Insam, Vienna
1987   Albemarle Gallery, London

Selected Group Exhibitions:

1963   *9 Europaische Kunstler,* Haus am Waldsee, Berlin
1965   *Between Poetry and Painting,* Institute of Contemporary Arts, London
1968   *Documenta 4,* Museum Fridericianum, Kassel, West Germany
1969   *Bienal,* Sao Paulo
1970   *Expo '70,* Osaka, Japan
1971   *Konkrete Poezie,* Stedelijk Museum, Amsterdam (toured Europe)
1973   *Hommage à Picasso,* Nationalgalerie, West Berlin (toured Germany)
1976   *20 Jahre Museum Haus Lange,* Museum Haus Lange, Krefeld, West Germany
1982   *International Air Fair* (Galerie Maeght display), Chicago

Collections:

Narodni Galerie, Prague; Kunsthalle, Nuremberg; Institut für Moderne Kunst, Nuremberg; Museum Haus Lange, Krefeld, West Germany; Museum der Kunst, Vienna; Museum Boymans-van Beuningen, Rotterdam; Muzeum Sztuki, Lodz, Poland; Musée National d'Art Moderne, Paris; Guggenheim Museum, New York; Museum of Modern Art, New York.

Publications:

By KOLAR: books—*Birth Certificate,* Prague 1941; *Night,* Prague 1943; *Limb and Other Poems,* Prague 1945; *7 Cantatas,* Prague 1945; *Odes and Variations,* Prague 1946; *Days of the Year,* Prague 1948; *One Day of Vacation,* Prague 1949; *Mister Sun on the Art of Poetry,* Prague 1957; *The Chance Witness,* Prague 1964; *In 7th Heaven,* Prague 1964; *Poems of Silence,* Prague 1965; *Poems R,* Copenhagen 1965; *The Plague in Athens, The Light of the World,* playtext, Prague 1965; *Aesop of Varsovice,* Prague 1966; *Signboard of Gersaint,* 1966; *Unser Taeglich Brot (Die Grube),* Vienna 1966; *New Epictetus,* Prague 1968; *Hinauf und Hinunter,* Hannover 1969; *Und 2: 10 Blatter aus Gersaints Auschaengeschild,* Kassel, West Germany 1969; *Poems of Silence,* Prague 1970; *The Liver of Prometheus,* Prague 1970; *Das Sprechende Bild,* Frankfurt 1971; *Hommage à Baudelaire,* Nuremberg 1972; *Wahlverwandschaften,* portfolio, Nuremberg 1972; *Dny v roce, Roky v dnech,* Prague 1975; *Suite* (poems), West Berlin 1980; *20 Gedichten* (poems), Rotterdam 1981; *Ocity Svedek,* Munich 1983; *Temoin oculaire,* Paris 1983; *Le Foie de Promethee,* Paris 1985; *Prometheova jatra,* Toronto 1985; *Jours de l'annee—Annees des jours,* Paris 1986; *Vrsovicky Ezop,* Munich 1986; film—*Attention, Mr. Veronese,* with Bohumil Musil, 1968.

On KOLAR: books—*Neue Dimension der Plastik* by Udo Kultermann, Tübingen 1967; *Concrete Poetry: A World View* by Mary Ellen Bolt, London and Bloomington, Indiana 1968; *Jiri Kolar* by Dietrich Mahlo and Miroslav Lamac, Cologne 1968; *Verso la Poesia Totale* by Adriano Spatola, Salerno 1969; *Jiri Kolar,* exhibition catalogue, with text by Wieland Schmied and Dietrich Mahlow, Hannover 1969; *Jiri Kolar* exhibition catalogue, with text by Jindrich Chalupecky, New York 1969; *Jiri Kolar* by Miroslav Lamac, Prague 1970; *Sign and Image* by Ichiro Haryu, Tokyo 1971; *Man-Made Nature* by Yusuke Narahara, Tokyo 1971; *Jiri Kolar: Collages,* exhibition catalogue, with text by Raoul-Jean Moulin, Paris 1971; *Jiri Kolar: L'Arte come Forma della Liberta,* edited by Arturo Schwarz, Milan 1972; *Jiri Kolar: Collagen Rollagen, Chiasmagen, Crumblagen,* exhibition catalogue, with text by Paul Wember, Krefeld, West Germany 1973; *Jiri Kolar: An Exhibition of Chiasmages, Rollages, Objects, Collages,* exhibition catalogue, New York 1975; *Jiri Kolar,* exhibition catalogue, with text by Thomas Messer and Jindrich Chalupecky, New

1976   Jasa Fine Art, Munich
Galerie Wentdorf und Swetec, Dusseldorf
Cheap Thrills Gallery, Helsinki
Halvat Hulit, Helsinki
Galerie Lowenadler, Stockholm
1977   Fairweather-Hardin Gallery, Chicago
Université de Genéve, Geneva
Galerie Yves Lambert, Paris
Galerie Schreiner, Basle
1978   Guggenheim Museum, New York
Albright-Knox Art Gallery, Buffalo, New York
Galerie Schoeller, Dusseldorf
Art Gallery of Ontario, Toronto
1979   Institut für Moderne Kunst, Nuremberg
1980   *Collagen, Rollagen, Chiasmagen, Materialbilder, Objekte,* Städtische Kunsthalle, Recklinghausen, West Germany
Unterwegs ins Paradies, Gutenberg Museum, Mainz, West Germany
Kunstverein, Wolfsburg, West Germany
Kunstmuseum, Dusseldorf
Neue Berliner Kunstverein, Berlin
Galerie Zellermayer-Lorenzen, Berlin
Galerie Inge Baecker, Bochum, West Germany

1981   Kassler Kunstverein, Kassel, West Germany
Genevieve and Serge Mathier, Besancon, France
Collagen und Objekte aus Berlin und Paris, Museum Folkwang, Essen
Galerie Maeght, Paris
Froissages, Galeria Metronom, Barcelona
1982   *Collages, Objectes,* Galeria Maeght, Barcelona
Galleria Primo Piano, Rome
Galleria Peccolo, Livorno
Die Welle Galerie, Iserlohn, West Germany
Galerie Schiessel, Munich
Centre Georges Pompidou, Paris
Southern Methodist University, Dallas
Padiglione d'Arte Contemporanea, Milan
Hokin Gallery, Palm Beach, Florida
1983   Stadtische Galerie, Bergisch Gladbach, West Germany
Galerie Maeght-Lelong, Paris
Galerie Slavia, Bremen, West Germany
Galleria Zarathustra, Milan
Galerie Kraus, Pfaffikon, Switzerland
1984   Galerie Praxis, Essen, West Germany
Stamparte Galleria, Bologna, Italy
Kunsthalle, Nuremberg, West Germany

York 1975; *Jiri Kolar: Collages* by Angelo Ripellino, Turin 1976; *Jiri Kolar: Transformations*, exhibition catalogue, with text by Charlotte Kotik, New York 1978; *Jiri Kolar*, exhibition catalogue, with texts by Wieland Schmied, Eberhard Roters and Lucie Schauer, Berlin 1980; *Kolar: Collagen, Rollagen, Chiasmagen, Materialbilder, Objekte*, exhibition catalogue, with texts by Thomas Grochowiak and Dietrich Mahlow, Recklinghausen, West Germany 1980; *Jiri Kolar: Unterwegs ins Paradies*, exhibition catalogue, with texts by Siglinde Hohenstein, Friedrich W. Heckmanns, Hans-Pieter Riese and Claus Groger, Mainz 1980; *Jiri Kolar: Froissages*, exhibition catalogue, with text by Gloria Picazo, Barcelona 1981; *Jiri Kolar: Collagen und Objekte aus Berlin und Paris*, exhibition catalogue, with texts by Helmut Heissenbuttel and Zdenek Felix, Essen 1981; *Jiri Kolar: Collages, Objectes*, exhibition catalogue, with text by Antonio Saura, Barcelona 1982; *Jiri Kolar: Poetry of Vision/Poetry of Silence*, exhibition catalogue with preface by Luke Romboudt, Vancouver 1984; *Jiri Kolar: Diary 1968*, exhibition catalogue with preface by David Elliott, Oxford 1984; *Jiri Kolar*, exhibition catalogue with introduction by Ronald Alley, London 1987; *Jiri Kolar* by Jindrich Chalupecky, Paris 1987.

Art is still capable of making its everyday discoveries of the world as a part of the general effort to achieve universality of knowledge, regardless of what field it takes place in—in science, for example. For this reason, the arbitrary has no place in art: there is no room for alien beginnings and processes, but only beginnings and processes which already belong, by their very nature, to the realm of art. It's the same as in science, where nothing can begin in isolation, but only when it's already inherent in the thing itself, as in mathematics. Of course, what matters is always a shift in things. Without this, no creative act has any meaning. Basically, it's impossible to think up anything entirely new . . .

Every new discovery in art, just as in science, expands the field of human perception and knowledge. This noetic aspect is for me the primary one. The same holds true for all the notions of so-called beauty with which some esthetics operate. If the idea of beauty is continually perfected, then the field of esthetic cognition in general is widened. If art produces a new view of the world, then the whole field of human perception is expanded. Of course, even today it's still possible to paint a beautiful portrait—but Leonardo's portraits were perfect. Van Dyck consummated this perfection such that subsequently it became necessary to begin a new way. Rembrandt had already abandoned all forms of idealization. Picasso enriched his painting with impulses inspired by Negro art, children's drawings, etc.

If art is the art of expanding human consciousness, then no form of this effort can be alien to it. One-sidedness is a great obstacle to such expansion, and may even retard it no matter what direction it may be going, even if it's heading forward. One-sidedness may be possible in times of crisis, but because crisis, it would seem, is something lasting, all the art of our time is somehow crisis-ridden, if not retrogressive, in spite of all the courage and the discoveries it has produced. I would say that one might even distrust it. It genuinely seems more against man than for him.

These questions perhaps aren't relevant to the artist himself, who needn't concern himself with them in the least, but it's a fact which I personally find essential to any further thinking. Even if art in itself is not something meaningless. Quite the contrary, it's surprising how necessary and useful it can be precisely for showing where modern man is. And this is immensely important. Art, and poetry in particular, is not the consequence of already expanded consciousness, but rather an outcome of the process of expansion. The aim of a picture, a poem, etc., is always to enthrall, and that is ultimately where the significance of all artistic enthusiasm lies. Such enthusiasm will bear fruit in relation to its strength and scope. There's an unwritten law—and it applies to poetry as well—that if one kind of art is no longer capable of expressing something, or if someone thinks a different kind might take him further, it can never be claimed that the new art is redundant. Because, on the contrary, precisely at that point in time, it may be indispensable for expressing the new idea, the new discovery. Today, it's unthinkable that a single approach to creation would be enough to insure development. Each way is no more than necessary, and this very necessity is a proof of its insufficiency. A certain type of art is capable of producing discoveries only as long as it doesn't claim a monopoly on development.

—Jiri Kolar

The pronunciation of Jiri Kolar's Czech name comes very close to *Collage*, the artist's predominant medium, but the similarity is altogether accidental, (In Czech, *Kolo* means wheel and *Kolar*, therefore, would be something like *Wheeler*.) It is a fact, however, that the collage and various variants have occupied Jiri Kolar intensively since the beginning of the 1960's and to some extent long before.

He got to this art form by indirection, since his first creative metier was not painting, or for that matter any of the plastic arts, but poetry. In a broader sense, Kolar remained, and thinks of himself even now, as a poet but one who has largely departed from reliance upon words in favor of forms, thus having in the main transferred communicative emphasis from verbal to plastic means.

This gradual transfer takes off from the printed page which Kolar initially covered with his own, compelling Czech poems. These derived partly from Kolar's interest in traditional and modern poetry written in his native tongue and partly from an intense preoccupation with symbolist, futurist and surrealist texts that have become accessible to him in translation. The latter shaped the artist's modern sensibility and awareness.

In any case his verse already in the 1950's showed a tendency towards letterism and developed from there toward concrete and "evident" poetry as his formally explicit verbal meanings receded in favor of a new plastic and visual presence. This process completed itself in the 1960's when screws and razor blades, nuts and bolts took the place of words, thereby creating a poetry of things. Such transformations confirmed Kolar's aspirations according to which in his own words, "The time may come when we shall be making poetry out of anything whatsoever . . . . "

Given Kolar's interest in placing objects on a flat surface it is not surprising that the collage medium (with which he had experimented early in the 1930's) would particularly recommend itself. He therefore not only accepted this cubist and surrealist device as his principal plastic expression but developed it toward highly original and personal ends. By controlled crumpling of reproduced images borrowed mostly from art history he created the *crumplage;* by introducing into the collage composition movable parts that could be lifted, the *ventilage;* and through the fragmentation and reconstitution of written and printed texts (which often used occult and arcane alphabets) he created his plastic style through the Greek lettered *chiasmage*. It is these alphabetic surfaces in black and white, sometimes interspersed with pictorial images, used two dimensionally or bulging into relief and sculpture, that have established Kolar's uniqueness and that have recommended him to a world-wide public, first at the 1968 *Documenta* and subsequently in 1969 in Sao Paulo where he carried away the first prize for Czechoslovakia.

His so-called *rollage* is Kolar's alternate, most prominent development. It is based on pictorial rather than lettered content. Here, superimpositions of thin stripes that carry one particular image are carefully spaced to make their impact felt over a ground projecting another. The result is a synthetic double or triple view that is not only witty and humorous but that also has the capacity to vitalize the reproduced material and raise it to the level of an original work of art.

The almost exclusive dependence upon secondary material, printed and reproduced, is characteristic for Kolar's work and sets the artist apart from his Dada and surrealist collage precursors. Disinterested in the cubist use of collage as a means to engage in a dialogue between formal and palpable reality and equally unconcerned with Dada and surrealist anti-art attitudes, Kolar seeks to recreate a "white humor" universe that combines a maximum of apparent irreconcilables and that casts its net widely across categoric limitations. His glue and scissors therefore assemble fragments from art together with those from life so that the newly created sequences contain (alternatively or occasionally even in a single work) quotations from the cultural heritage and from urban folkart. Art history spoofs thus intermingle with trivia drawn from our quotidian existence and both find a malleable common denominator in the printed matter that constitutes the material, pre-esthetic essence of Kolar's medium. One hardly needs to stress that such consistent reliance upon our printed universe also carries obvious symbolic overtones which, whether deliberately sought or not, sharpen the artist's profile as a witness of his time.

—Thomas Messer

KOSICE, Gyula.

Argentinian. Born in Kosice, Czechoslovakia, 26 April 1924. Emigrated to Argentina, 1928: subsequently naturalized. Studied at Academia de Bellas Artes, Buenos Aires, 1938–42. Married Diyi Laan in 1947; daughters: Vivian Luz and Irina Sol. Independent artist, Buenos Aires, from 1944: founder, *Arturo* magazine, 1944, and *Concrete Invention Art* magazine, 1945; founder-director, Madi art movement, Buenos Aires, 1946–58. Argentine commissioner for the *Bienal de Sao Paulo*, 1961; Venice *Biennale*, 1962; *Biennale de Paris*, 1963. Recipient: National Sculpture Prize, Instituto Di Tella, Buenos Aires, 1962; Acquisition Prize, Museo Nacional de Bellas Artes, Buenos Aires, 1966; Casa Argentina in Israel Prize, Museo de Arte Moderno, Buenos Aires, 1967; Award of Honour, Sociedad Argentina de Escritores, 1968; Fondo Nacional de Las Artes Prize, Buenos Aires, 1971; Hidronor Prize, Buenos Aires, 1972; Konex Prize, Buenos Aires, 1982; Book Prize, Asociacion Argentina de Criticos de Arte, 1982; Literature Prize, Municipality of Buenos Aires, 1986; Sculpture Prize, Museo Sivori, 1987. Addresses: (studio) Humahuaca 4662, Buenos Aires 1192, Argentina; (home) Republica de la India 3135-6°, Buenos Aires 1425, Argentina.

Individual Exhibitions:

1947	Galerias Pacifico, Buenos Aires
1953	Galeria Bonino, Buenos Aires
1960	Galerie Denise Rene, Paris
	Drian Gallery, London
1963	Galerie L'Oeil, Paris
1964	Galerie La Hune, Paris
1965	Terry Dintenfass Gallery, New York
1966	Galeria de Arte Moderno, Cordoba, Argentina
1967	Bonino Gallery, New York
1968	Instituto Di Tella/Galeria Bonino, Buenos Aires
1969	Galerie Lacloche, Paris
1970	Estudio Actual, Caracas
1971	Galeria Bonino, Buenos Aires
1972	Galeria de Arte del Banco Continental, Lima
1972	Museo Teatro San Martin, Buenos Aires
1973	Biblioteca Luis Angel Arango, Bogota, Colombia
1974	Israel Museum, Jerusalem
	Espace Cardin, Paris
1975	Galeria Pozzi, Buenos Aires
	Espace Cardin, Paris
1977	Galeria La Ciudad, Buenos Aires (retrospective)
	International Water Conference, Mar del Plata, Argentina
	Galeria Birger, Buenos Aires
1979	Galeria Unika, Punta del Este, Uruguay
	City Planetarium, Buenos Aires
1982	Hakone Open-Air Museum, Tokyo
	Plaza de la Ingenieria, La Plata, Argentina
	Secretaria de Cultura, Quilmes, Buenos Aires

1983	Casa de la Cultura, Cordoba, Argentina
1985	Centro Cultural, Buenos Aires
1988	Olympic Stadium, Seoul, Korea

Selected Group Exhibitions:

1948	*Salon des Realites Nouvelles*, Paris (and 1963)
1956	*38th Biennale*, Venice
1960	*Konkrete Kunst*, Helmhaus, Zurich
1964	*New Art from Argentina*, Walker Art Center, Minneapolis
1966	*Light in Art*, Contemporary Art Museum, Houston
1968	*Documenta 4*, Museum Fridericianum, Kassel, West Germany
1970	*Kinetics*, Hayward Gallery, London
1976	*2nd Triennale of Photography*, Israel Museum, Jerusalem
1981	*Operation Equinoxe 80*, Centre Georges Pompidou, Paris
1988	*International Sculpture Exhibition*, Garden of Sculpture, Seoul, Korea

Collections:

Museo Nacional de Bellas Artes, Buenos Aires; Museo de Arte Moderno, Buenos Aires; Instituto Di Tella, Buenos Aires; Museo Nacional de Bellas Artes, Montevideo; Centre Georges Pompidou/Musée National d'Art Moderne, Paris; Moderna Museet, Stockholm; Israel Museum, Jerusalem; Museum of Fine Arts, Houston; Aldrich Museum of Contemporary Art, Ridgefield, Connecticut; Hakone Open-Air Museum, Tokyo.

Publications:

By KOSICE: books—*Invencion*, Buenos Aires 1945; *Golsese*, Buenos Aires 1952; *Peso y medida de Alberto Hidalgo*, Buenos Aires 1953; *Antologia Madi*, Buenos Aires 1955; *Geocultura de la Europa de Hoy*, Buenos Aires and Paris 1959; *Poeme Hydraulique*, Paris 1960; *Arte Hidrocinetico*, Buenos Aires, 1968; *La Ciudad Hidroespacial*, Buenos Aires 1972; *Arte y Arquitectura del Agua*, Caracas 1974; *Arte Madi*, Buenos Aires 1982; *Obra Poetica*, Buenos Aires 1984; *Entrevisiones*, Buenos Aires 1985; *Teoria sobre el arte*, Buenos Aires 1987.

On KOSICE: books—*Non-figurative At Trends in Latin America*, edited by George Wittenborn, New York 1957; *Las esculturas hidraulicas de Kosice* by Guy Habasque, Santa Fe 1960; *Art in Latin America Today: Argentina* by Manuel Mujica Lainz, Washington, D.C. 1961; *Kosice* by Guy Habasque, Paris 1965; *Naissance de l'art cinetique* by Frank Popper, Paris 1967; *Escultura Argentina de Vanguardia* by Romualdo Brughetti, Buenos Aires 1970; *Madi y la vanguardia argentina* by Jorge B. Rivera, Buenos Aires 1976; *Science and Technology in Art* by Stewart Kranz, New York 1980; *Science + Art* by Ans van Berkum, Utrecht 1986.

The work of Gyula Kosice, one of the forerunners in the renewal of abstract forms in the post-war years, enlarges the field of kinetic research by its original use of an element virtually unexplored in plastic terms: water.

The wide range of the artist's interests, including sculpture and painting, poetry and theoretical essays, the monumental or architectural quality of some of his works, and the cosmic implications he draws from the dynamics of the creative process all make of Kosice a multi-faceted artist for whom the liberating function of the imagination finds its expression in the elaboration of a rational system.

Born in Czechoslovakia, Kosice was taken to Argentina at the age of four and received Agentinian citizenship. He studied at the Academy of Fine Arts in Buenos Aires and stayed on in Buenos Aires to pursue his artistic career. From 1944 he became involved with a group of young artists who were rebelling against establishment trends in Argentina—still dominated by the epigones of the Paris School—and drawing their inspiration from the Bauhaus, Constructivism and Max Bill in an attempt to develop an abstract language that was 'pure and hard'. With them Kosice founded the 'Madi' movement, becoming its leading theoretician and organiser. Bypassing the over-rigorous system of 'concrete' art, he developed what was to become the theoretical basis for his own researches: ' . . . to invent objects for a classless society which liberates energy and dominates space and time in all its fullness, and matter as far as its ultimate consequences' (extract from the Madi Manifesto, 1946). It was around this time too that he met the Italo-Argentinian sculptor Lucio Fontana and witnessed the publication of the first spatialist manifesto.

Open to all manner of technical experimentation, Kosice first exhibited a collection of paintings with irregular mounts, worked in blocks of colour; but it was to sculpture that he was to turn definitively, forcing dynamic effects from matter in order to create an impression of movement. His preference was for non-traditional materials, frequently of industrial origin, such as aluminum, plexiglass, glass and iron wire, and he executed two particularly innovatory works at this time: one, in wood, mobile, jointed and transformable; the other a 'luminary structure' of geometrical shape modelled out of a neon tube.

In 1948 he exhibited with the 'Madi' at the Salon des réalités nouvelles in Paris. This exhibition marked for him the beginning of an international career which would lead him, a few years later, to show his first hydrokinetic works at the Denise René gallery. One particular quality can help us to define the aesthetic of these sculptures: transparency, proceeding from a desire to appropriate the space without disturbing its visual unity. From now on, Kosice was to work principally with translucent materials (plexiglass, glass fibres) which asserted or effaced themselves under the spectator's gaze in a seductive play of appearances and reflections. The sculptures were composed in a subtle balance of fixed and mobile pieces. But it was through the use of water that the artist perfected the dynamisation of his sculptural system. The element of chance deriving from the displacement of liquid masses and from the very nature of water—which is intrinsically mobile and transformable—disrupted the traditional relationships of fullness—emptiness, depth—surface and container—content of the sculptural composition, leading Kosice to exercise scientific control over his materials. His formal language appropriated, by metaphorical transcriptions, the diverse forms which water can take: the bubbles, drops, jets, fountains, splashes, waves, pools . . . of the liquid part of the works became spheres, cylinders or planes in their solid representations.

Gyula Kosice: *Diyi All The Time*, 1967

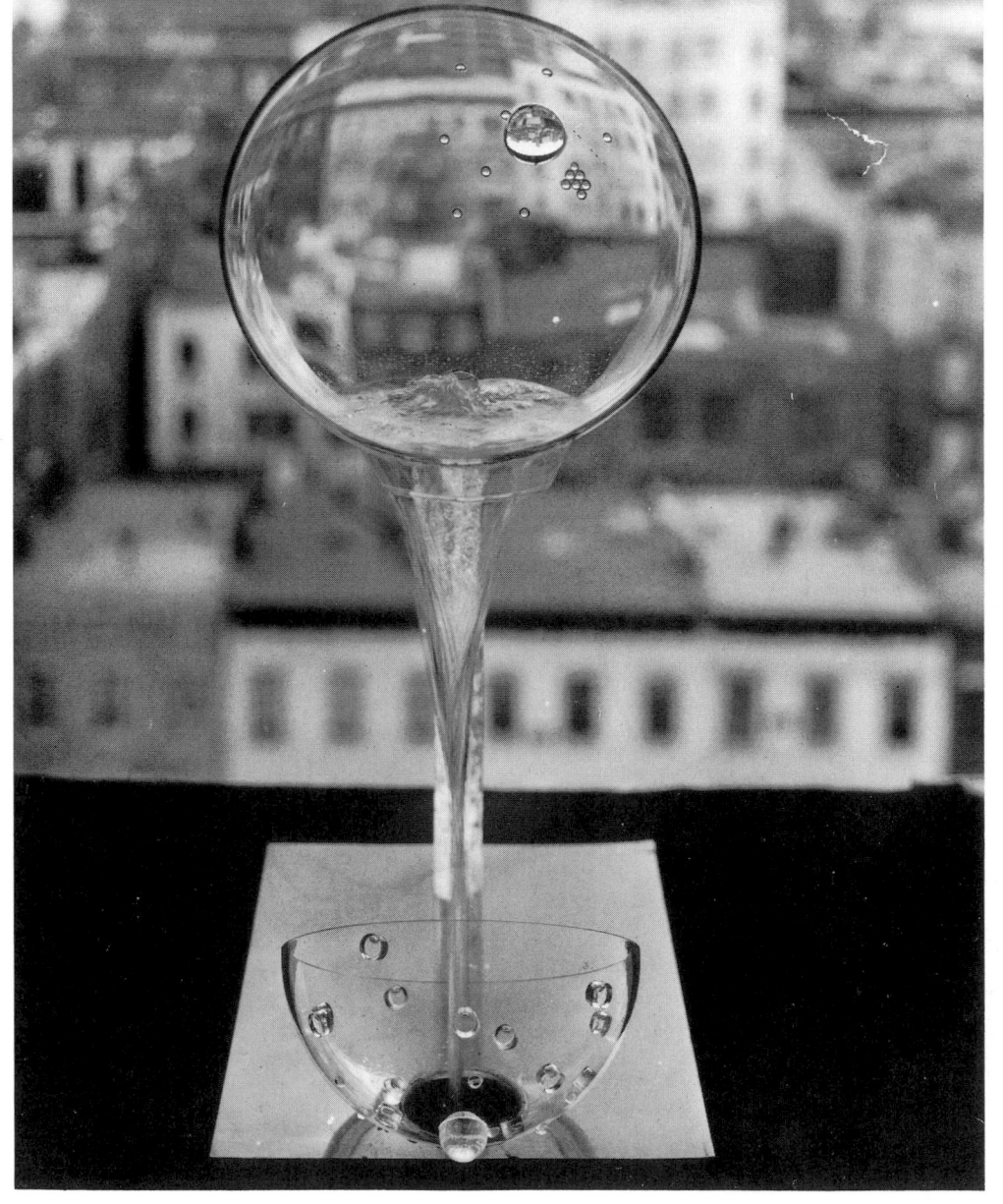

Gradually, the works were to expand in extent and complexity to become veritable polysensorial environments, bringing together over large surfaces, from the ground to the walls, luminous and sonorous elements which completed the hydraulic effects.

Naturally, Kosice also came to consider the architectural implications of his work, and its capacity to intervene directly in the transformation of the social environment. He realised a number of fountains and urban sculptures in various Latin American cities, as for example his impressive *Water Tower* (Buenos Aires, 1972), a hydraulic composition of monumental proportions which has as its base a long cylinder reaching up towards the sky.

Kosice's *Hydrospatial City,* shown in France in 1974, provided the synthesis of his architectural ideas. It consisted of the futurist projection in space of a revolutionary and liberating social structure so that "imprecise science becomes superhuman" (Kosice). Presented in the form of plans and models, the transparent cosmic city suppresses current divisions in living spaces, insisting on a necessary improvement in human relations. Its realisation is scientifically plausible thanks to the energy potential contained in the hydraulic power of clouds. Through this work the Argentinian artist developed "an invitation to take part in the supreme journey of technological humanism, an appeal to feel more acutely, to see higher and further, to live better" (Pierre Restany,Kosice exhibition catalogue at Espace Cardin, 1974).

—Dominique Liquois

KOSSOFF, Leon.

British. Born in London, 7 December 1926. Educated in London: studied at St. Martin's School of Art, London, 1949–53; also attended evening classes at the Borough Polytechnic, London, under David Bomberg, 1949–53; Royal College of Art, London, 1953–56. Served in the Jewish Brigade and Royal Fusiliers, in France, Belgium, Holland and Germany, 1945–48. Married Rosalind Pearl in 1954; son: David. Independent painter, London, since 1956; Member, London Group, 1962. Lecturer, Regent Street Polytechnic, London, 1959–64, Chelsea School of Art, London, 1959–64, and St. Martin's School of Art, London, 1966–69. Agent: Anthony D'Offay Gallery, 9 Dering Street, London, W1. Address: 147 Chatsworth Road, London NW2, England.

Individual Exhibitions:

1957   Beaux Arts Gallery, London
        Bruton Place Gallery, London
1959   Beaux Arts Gallery, London
1961   Beaux Arts Gallery, London
1963   Beaux Arts Gallery, London
1964   Beaux Arts Gallery, London
1968   Marlborough Fine Art, London
1972   *Recent Paintings,* Whitechapel Art Gallery, London
1973   Fischer Fine Art, London
1974   *Recent Drawings and Paintings,* Fischer Fine Art, London

1975   Fischer Fine Art, London
1979   Fischer Fine Art, London
1980   Riverside Studios, London
1981   *Paintings from a Decade 1970–1980,* Museum of Modern Art, Oxford (travelled to the Graves Art Gallery, Sheffield, Yorkshire)
1982   Louver Gallery, Los Angeles
1983   Hirschl and Adler Modern Gallery, New York
1984   Fischer Fine Art, London
        L. A. Louver Gallery, Los Angeles

Selected Group Exhibitions:

1963   *British Painting in the 60's.* Tate Gallery, London
1964   *Painting and Sculpture of a Decade 1954–64,* Tate Gallery, London
1967   *Recent British Painting,* Tate Gallery, London
1974   *Body and Soul,* Walker Art Gallery, Liverpool
1977   *British Painting 1952–1977,* Royal Academy of Arts, London
1979   *The British Art Show,* Mappin Art Gallery, Sheffield (toured Britain)
1981   *13 Britische Kunstler,* Neue Galerie, Aachen, West Germany
1985   *The British Show,* Art Gallery of Western Australia, Perth (travelled)
1987   *A School of London,* Kunstnernes Hus, Oslo (travelled)
1988   *The British Picture,* L. A. Louver Gallery, Venice, California

Leon Kossoff: *Hackney with German Hospital,* 1974

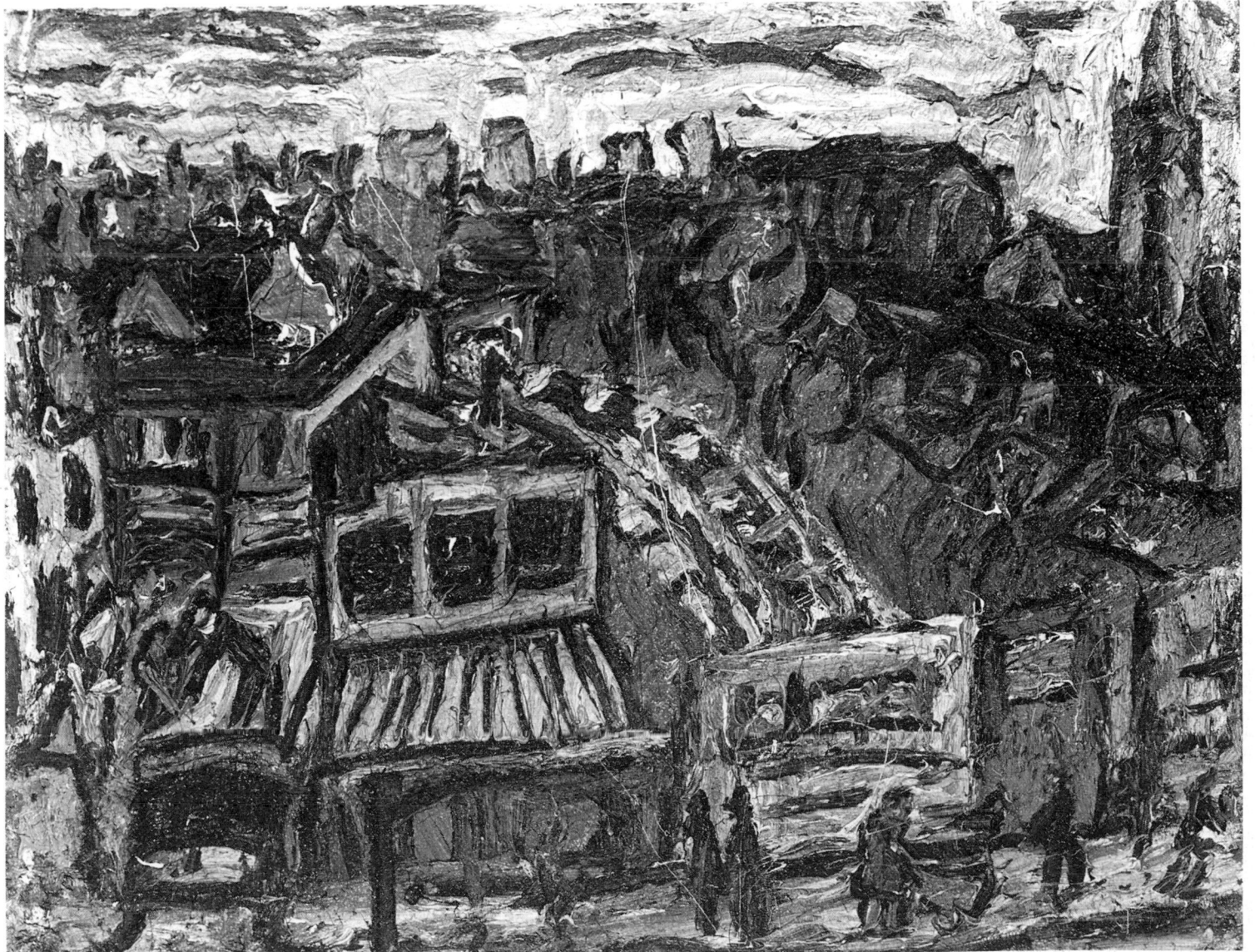

Collections:

Tate Gallery, London; British Museum, London; Fitzwilliam Museum Cambridge; Whitworth Art Gallery, Manchester; Thyssen-Bornemisza Collection, Lugano, Switzerland; Chrysler Museum, Provincetown, Massachusetts; National Gallery of Victoria, Melbourne.

Publications:

By KOSSOFF: articles—statement in *Leon Kossoff: Recent Drawings and Paintings*, exhibition catalogue, London 1974; "An Extract from a Letter" in *Leon Kossoff: Paintings from a Decade 1970–1980*, exhibition catalogue, by David Elliott, Oxford 1981.

On KOSSOFF: books—*Leon Kossoff: Recent Paintings*, exhibition catalogue, by David Mercer, London 1972; *Leon Kossoff: Paintings from a Decade 1970–1980*, exhibition catalogue, by David Elliott, Oxford 1981; *The British Picture*, exhibition catalogue with text by Marina Vaizey, Catherine Lampert and William Feaver, Venice, California 1988.

*

Although Leon Kossoff was born in England and a student at some of the country's best-known art schools, there is virtually nothing English about his art. His subjects are himself and his family and friends, or views from his home and studio in North London. This narrow field of vision reflects an intensely personal, almost autobiographical artform, whose emotional quality is rendered in an equally intense, mud-like impasto.

Kossoff is of Jewish origin, as is his friend and colleague Frank Auerbach, who shares his technical manner and also the narrow personal range of subject-matter. Both of them were deeply influenced by another Anglo-Jewish painter, David Bomberg, who, from analytical, cubist drawings and paintings, later developed a rich, Rembrandtesque style. Indeed, in considering this interesting group of painters, one must retrace artistic steps to artists like Rembrandt and Goya, to a concern for the human condition and the idea of the artist as an isolated representative of that universal situation.

Kossoff's work is of special interest since, whilst the medium and the subject always remain based in expressionism, by the use of cool, pleasant colour, and a refusal to be explicit as a portraitist or a painter of urban landscape, he refrains from over-dramatisation or sentimentality. The result is a dignified monumentality, which persuades the viewer that, whilst the painter starts from the particular, namely himself and his milieu, his aim is the general, even the universal. Equally surprising is that from the thick morass of churned-up pigment, Kossoff extracts forms and compositions of elegance, even charm, and has proved his ability to constantly extend and develop his range of technique and expression, without, in fact, adopting gimmicks or moving away from what is of personal significance.

—Charles Spencer

KOSUTH, Joseph.

American. Born in Toledo, Ohio, 31 January 1945. Studied at Toledo Museum School of Design, 1955–62 (also studied privately, under Belgian painter Line Bloom Draper, Toledo, 1956–62); studied painting, Cleveland Art Institute, 1963–64; C.A.S.A. Program, under Roger Barr, Paris, 1964–65; School of Visual Arts, New York, 1965–67; anthropology and philosophy, New School for Social Research, New York, 1971–72. Organized Visiting Artists Program (including Don Judd, Sol LeWitt and Ad Reinhardt), School of Visual Arts, New York, 1966–67; Founder-Director, Museum of Normal Art (formerly Lannis Gallery), New York, 1967; Reviewer, *Arts Magazine*, New York, 1967; Instructor, School of Visual Arts,

New York, 1968; Editor, Art and Language Press, Coventry, England, and New York, 1969–73; Lecturer, University of Chile, Santiago, 1971; Co-Editor, *The Fox* magazine, New York, 1975–76. Recipient: Cassandra Foundation Grant, New York, 1968. Agent: Leo Castelli Gallery, 420 West Broadway, New York, New York 10012, U.S.A. Address: 591 Broadway, New York, New York 10012, U.S.A.

Individual Exhibitions:

1967	Museum of Normal Art, New York
1968	Gallery 669, Los Angeles
	Bradford Junior College, Massachusetts (with Robert Morris)
1969	Douglass Gallery, Vancouver
	Instituto Torquato di Tella, Buenos Aires
	Nova Scotia College of Art, Halifax
	St. Martin's School of Art, London
	Museum of Contemporary Art, Chicago (in association with *Art by Telephone*)
	Art and Project, Amsterdam
	Coventry College of Art, England (in association with *Oxford Project*)
	Galleria Sperone, Turin
	A 37 90 89 Gallery, Antwerp
	Kunsthalle, Berne
	Pinacotheca, St. Kilda, Victoria
	Leo Castelli Gallery, New York
	Art Gallery of Ontario, Toronto
1970	Pasadena Art Museum, California
	Jysk Kunstgalerie, Copenhagen
	Aarhus Kunstmuseum, Denmark
	Kunstbiblioteket i Lyngby, Denmark
	Galerie Daniel Templon, Paris
	Galleria Sperone, Turin
1971	Galerie Paul Maenz, Cologne
	Protetch-Rivkin Gallery, Washington, D.C.
	Galerie Bruno Bischofberger, Zurich
	Centro de Arte y Comunicacion, Buenos Aires
	Lia Rumma Studio d'Arte, Naples
	Carmen Lamanna Gallery, Toronto
	Leo Castelli Gallery, New York
	Galleria Toselli, Milan
	Protetch-Rivkin Gallery, Convention Hall, Atlantic City, New Jersey (in association with *Boardwalk Show*)
1972	The New Gallery, Cleveland
	Leo Castelli Gallery, New York (2 shows)
	Sperone-Fischer Gallery, Rome
1973	Galerie Gunter Sachs, Hamburg
	Galerie Paul Maenz, Brussels
	Investigationen über Kunst und "problemkreise" seit 1965, Kunstmuseum, Lucerne
1974	Carmen Lamanna Gallery, Toronto
	Sperone-Fischer Gallery, Rome
	Claire S. Copley Gallery, Los Angeles
	Galerie La Bertesca, Dusseldorf
1975	Leo Castelli Gallery, New York
	Galleria Peccolo, Livorno, Italy
	Galerie MTL, Brussels
	Lia Rumma Studio d'Arte, Naples
	Galerie Liliane and Michel Durand-Desert, Paris (with Sara Charlesworth)
1976	Rennaissance Society, University of Chicago
	International Cultureel Centrum, Antwerp
1977	Kunstmuseum Van Hedeendagse, Ghent
1978	Van Abbemuseum, Eindhoven, Netherlands
	Museum of Modern Art, Oxford
	Carmen Lamanna Gallery, Toronto
1979	New 57 Gallery, Edinburgh
	Galerie Eric Fabre, Paris
	Galerie Paul Maenz, Cologne
	Galerie Rudiger Schottle, Munich
	Leo Castelli Gallery, New York
	Saman Gallery, Genoa
	Musée de Chartres, France
1980	P.S. 1, Institute for Art and Urvan Resources Inc., Long Island City, New York
1981	Staatsgalerie, Stuttgart
	Saman Gallery, Genoa, Italy
1982	Kunsthalle, Bielefeld, West Germany
1985	Centre d'Art Contemporain, Geneva

Selected Group Exhibitions:

1967	*Non-Anthropomorphic Art*, Lannis Gallery, New York
1969	*When Attitudes Become Form*, Kunsthalle, Berne (toured Europe)
1970	*Idea Structures*, Camden Arts Centre, London
1972	*Das Konzept ist die Form*, Westfalischer Kunstverein, Munster, West Germany
1973	*Art Investigations and Problematics since 1965*, Kunstmuseum, Lucerne, Switzerland
1974	*Painting and Sculpture Today*, Indianapolis Museum of Art (travelled)
1977	*Illusion and Reality*, Australian National Gallery, Canberra (toured Australia)
1979	*Concept/Narrative/Document: Recent Photographic Works from the Morton Neumann Family Collection*, Museum of Contemporary Art, Chicago (travelled to the Contemporary Arts Center, Cincinnati, and Joslyn Art Museum, Omaha, Nebraska)
1980	*Printed Art: A View of Two Decades*, Museum of Modern Art, New York
1981	*Westkunst*, Rheinhallen, Cologne

Collections:

Museum of Modern Art, New York; Guggenheim Museum, New York; Whitney Museum, New York; National Gallery of Canada, Ottawa; Tate Gallery, London; Van Abbemuseum, Eindhoven, Netherlands; Stedelijk Museum, Amsterdam; Kunstmuseum Van Hedendaagse, Ghent; Centre Pompidou, Paris; Australian National Gallery, Canberra.

Publications:

By KOSUTH: books—*January 5–31, 1969*, New York 1969; *Notebook on Water, 1965–66/Joseph Kosuth*, New York 1970; *Art and Language*, with Atkinson, Baingridge and others, Cologne 1972; *Joseph Kosuth*, exhibition catalogue, Stuttgart 1981; articles—"Four Interviews with Barry, Huebler, Kosuth, Weiner," with Arthur R. Rose in *Arts Magazine* (New York), February 1969; "Art After Philosophy" in *Studio International* (London), October–December 1969; "Picasso: A Synmposium," with others, in *Art in America* (New York), December 1980.

On KOSUTH: books—*Idea Structures*, exhibition catalogue, London 1970; *Joseph Kosuth*, Buenos Aires 1971; *Concept Art* by Klaus Honnef, Cologne 1971; *6 Years: The Dematerialization of the Art Object* by Lucy Lippard, New York 1973; *Joseph Kosuth: Investigationen über Kunst und "Problemkreise" seit 1965m*, exhibition catalogue, with texts by M. Ramsden and others, Lucerne 1973; articles—"Joseph Kosuth: 2 Shows" by Bruce Boice in *Artforum* (New York), March 1973; "Art Theory and Practice; Art Theory and the Decline of the Art Object" by Ian Jeffery in *Studio International* (London), December 1973; "10th Investigation: Proposition 5" by S. Buettner in *Arts Magazine* (New York), October 1975; "Long Night at the Movies" in *Art in America* (New York), March 1979; "Park Avenue Palazzo: Interior Design; Apartment in New York" by M. Filler in *Progressive Architecture* (New York), May 1979; "Joseph Kosuth" in *Flash Art* (Milan), June 1979; "Kosuth in Europa" in *Domus* (Milan), August 1979.

KÖTHE, Fritz.

German. Born in Berlin, 26 September 1916. Studied drawing at the Akademie für Angewandte Künste, Leipzig, 1936–38; mainly self-taught in painting; influenced by Neue Sachlichkeit artists, A. W. Dressler and Otto Nagel. Married Lieselotte Fenzlau in 1951; daughters: Cornelia and Regina. Independent painter, West Berlin; has also worked as a cartoonist and book illustrator, Berlin, 1939–41; as an instructor in drawing, Modeschule Wolf and Presseschule Skid, West Berlin, 1947–53; and as a designer and artist, Dorland Advertising Agency, West Berlin, and Blase Advertising Agency, Stuttgart, 1951–61. Agent: Galerie Wilbrand, Lindenstrasse 20, 5000 Cologne 1.

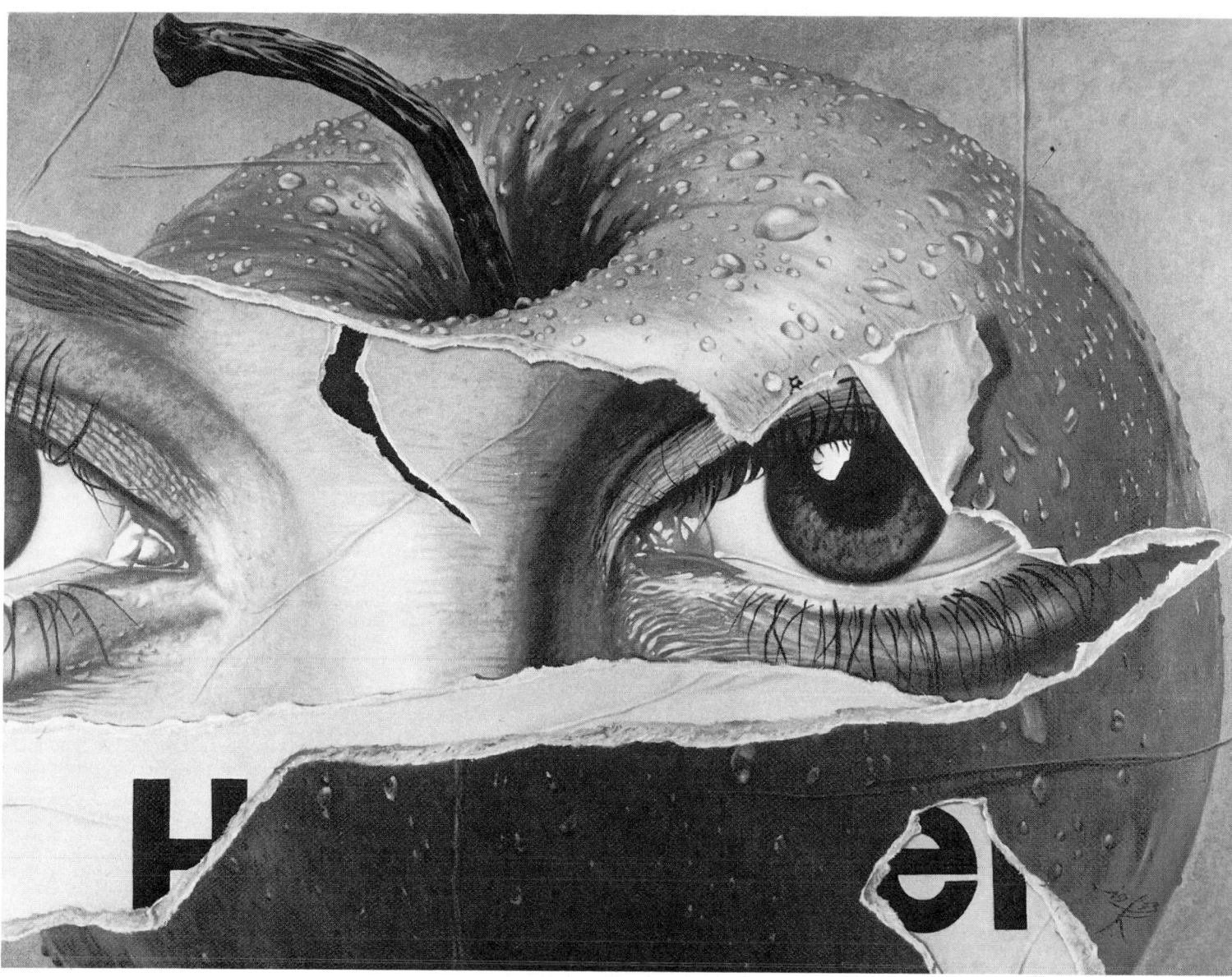

Fritz Köthe: *H*, 1973

Address: Branitzer Platz 3, 1000 Berlin 19, West Germany.

Individual Exhibitions:

1964	Galerie Springer, West Berlin
	Galerie Peithner-Lichtenfels, Vienna
1965	Galerie Tobies und Silex, Cologne
1966	Galerie Niepel, Dusseldorf
1967	Galerie Lichter, Frankfurt
	Galerie Passepartout, Copenhagen
1968	Galerie Tobies und Silex, Cologne
1969	Galerie Ben Wargin, West Berlin
	Galerie Niepel, Dusseldorf
1970	Galerie Lichter, Frankfurt
1972	Galerie Lietzow, West Berlin
	Gemalde, Aquarelle, Zeichnungen 1938–1972, Nationalgalerie, West Berlin
1973	Galerie 2, Stuttgart
1974	Galerie S, Deidesheim, West Germany
1975	Galerie Ketterer, Munich
	Galerie 2000, West Berlin
	Galerie Nordhorn, West Germany
	Galerie Villingen-Schwenningen, West Germany
	Galerie Passepartout, Copenhagen
1977	Galerie Wilbrand, Cologne
1978	Westfälischer Kunstverein, Münster
1979	Galerie Wilbrand, at *Art '79*, Basle
	Galerie Wilbrand, at *Kunstmarkt*, Cologne
	Galerie Wilbrand, Cologne

Kunstverein, Augsburg, West Germany
Kunstverein, Neustadt, West Germany
Leopold-Hoesch Museum, Duren, West Germany

Selected Group Exhibitions:

1967	*Neuer Realismus*, Haus am Waldsee, West Berlin
1968	*Galerie Passepartout*, Konsthall, Lund (toured Sweden)
1969	*The H. M. Moyens Collection*, Corcoran Gallery, Washington, D.C.
1970	*Pop Sammiung Beck*, Rheinisches Landesmuseum, Bonn
1971	*The German Art Scene*, Circle Gallery, London
1973	*Mit Kaméra, Pinsel und Spritzpistole*, Kunsthalle, Recklinghausen, West Germany
1974	*Liebe und Tod*, Burg Stolberg, Aachen, West Germany
1975	*Realitat und Realismus*, Kunsthalle, Darmstadt
1982	*Deutscher Kunstlerbund*, Cologne

Collections:

Nationalgalerie, West Berlin; Kupferstichkabinett, West Berlin; Museum Haus Lange, Krefeld, West Germany; Städtische Galerie, Mannheim; Leopold-Hoesch Museum, Duren, West Germany; Karl-Ernst-Osthaus Museum, Hagen, West Germany; Museum Witten, West Germany; Pop-Sammiung Beck, Dusseldorf; Achenbach Foundation for Graphic Arts, San Francisco.

Publications:

On KOTHE: books—*Fritz Kothe*, exhibition folder, with text by Carl Laszlo, Vienna 1964; *Pop Art*, by Lucy Lippard, New York 1966; *Pop und seine Folgen* by Heinz Ohff, Dusseldorf 1968; *Neue Sachlichkeit und Magischer Realismus* by Wieland Schmied, Hannover 1969; *Kunst in Berlin* by Ben Wargin, West Berlin and Zurich, 1969; *Neue Formen des Bildes* by Udo Kultermann, Tübingen 1969; *Fritz Kothe: Gemalde, Aquarelle, Zeichnungen 1938–1972*, exhibition catalogue, with texts by Heinz Ohff, Wieland Schmied, Carl Laszlo and Edouard Roditi, West Berlin 1972; *Neue Formen des Realismus* by Peter Sager, Cologne 1973; *Lens and Brush: A Stormy Liaison* by Gene Thornton, New York 1974; *Malerei Nach 1945* by Wieland Schmied, West Berlin 1974; *Le Pop Art* by José Pierre, Paris 1975; *Fritz Kothe: Das Malerische Werk 1963–1980* by Heinz Ohff and Wolfgang Saure, Cologne 1979.

My greatest inspiration came from the painters of the "New Objectivity." A. W. Dressler was my principal teacher even when my subjects in no way corresponded to his. In my earliest work from 1936 onwards, I expressed my interest in objective reality. At that time I drew and painted streets with crumbling facades and tattered posters. Later on I painted a reality critical of society (social critical realism) influenced by Käthe Kollwitz and Otto Nagel. I knew both of them personally.

So it was really only a short step to the paintings I have worked on since the end of the 1950's. Tyre-marked roads, torn-down posters, and cigarette stubs in gutters. Later on, from 1963/64, advertising posters, racing cars, and girls. I have always been fascinated by racing cars, motor racing, the Grand Prix sports. So I paint pictures with Stewart, Iycks, Fittipaldi, and their racing cars or parts of their cars. Torn, like posters pasted over one another. And the girls out of *Playboy* or *Lui* or from the covers of illustrated magazines. To me they are the modern, present day nude. I compose them into a picture with the racing cars. I deliberately use the colours, the photographs as models. The shape and colour of an exhaust pipe, a crash helmet, the mouth or body of a girl are my inspiration. In my paintings I want neither to criticise nor to praise, but merely to portray in what is to me a contemporary manner. In this way I tighten the picture, shift the important pieces to the foreground. They command the picture and produce an extra dimension. In the first half of the 1960's people associated my work with Pop Art. Later it counted as "New Realism" and "Photo Realism." I myself think of my paintings as a reality of our age.

—Fritz Köthe

Very different from those of Rotella or of Wolf Vostell are the curling edges of the peeling posters in Fritz Köthe's paintings. Not only are these photo-realistic versions of the real thing (re-constituted in Köthe's fantasizing) carried out with great sensitivity by his hyper-realist brush; they are also in the main reduced to two subjects (girls and cars) which come together in his translation of gatefold pin-ups or cover pictures from men's magazines, altered only to fall in line with Kothe's requirements—the visual association of girls with cars and urban destruction. In a variety of corporeal and mechanical tangles he points up the paradox of contemporary ecological carnage in contrast with the brightly polished threat of built-in obsolescence provided by racing cars and the paraphernalia of Grand Prix folie-de-grandeur. This, he claims, is the language of today and he himself is acutely conscious of being a contemporary artist in every sense that those two words can convey.

It can be seen that this painter's work has a pervading personal visual philosophy. If, for him, the artist's duty is to record as accurately as he can the imagery of Now, this also means coming to grips with the outstanding elements of raw material: cars and girls. Both have changed rapidly in appearance since the invention of the horseless *carriage* (now abbreviated to a *car* but in every other sense a more complicated contraption). Both have acquired, in their most exaggeratedly up-to-date versions, a shiny new look of conscious glamour and maquillage artificiality.

To prove that all this epidermic high finish and structural magnificence is ephemeral, Köthe gives the girls the fantasy of yesterday's soft porn sex mags blown up to billboard dimensions, but already coming adrift at the seams and the edges, if they have not suffered the destructive attentions of iconoclastic poster-rippers. The vehicles are more sturdy. Sometimes they feature in his paintings still in the prime of life, but often they show signs of wear or have even been victims of crash or collision.

The suggestion, certainly in some of the earlier work, is that girls and cars have achieved some kind of mystical union through the besmirching seminal fluids of grease and oil. This unnatural relationship is posed, if one can get beyond the crowded foreground of his pictures, in the clutter of urban fallout, the garbage, the disposables and the cigarette-butts.

—Sheldon Williams

KOUNELLIS, Jannis.

Greek. Born in Piraeus in 1936. Independent artist, Rome, since 1956; first stencilled number paintings, Rome, 1959; first tableaux vivants, Rome, 1966.

Agents: Sonnabend Gallery, 420 West Broadway, New York, New York 10012, U.S.A.; Galleria l'Attico, via Beccaria 22, Rome, Italy; Galleria Christian Stein, Via Lazzaretto 15, 20124 Milan, Italy. Address: Via del Banco de Santo Spirito 21, 00186 Rome, Italy.

Individual Exhibitions:

1960	Galleria la Tartaruga, Rome
1961	Galleria La Tartaruga, Rome (with Schifano and Twombly)
1964	Galleria La Tartaruga, Rome
1966	Galleria Arco d'Alibert, Rome
1967	Galleria l'Attico, Rome
1968	Galleria Iolas, Milan
1969	Galleria Enzo Superone, Turin
	Galleria l'Attico, Rome
	Galerie Alexandre Iolas, Paris
1970	Modern Art Agency, Naples
1971	Galleria Enzo Sperone, Turin
	Galleria l'Attico, Rome
	Galerie Folker Skulima, West Berlin
1972	Modern Art Agency, Naples
	Sonnabend Downtown Gallery, New York
1973	Galerie Sonnabend, Paris
	Galleria l'Attico, Rome
	Modern Art Agency, Naples
1974	Sonnabend Gallery, New York
	Galleria Stein, Turin, Italy
	Galleria l'Attico, Rome
	Galerie Folker Skulima, West Berlin
1975	Modern Art Agency, Naples
	Galerie Rudolf Zwirner, Cologne
	Galleria Mario Pieroni, Pescara, Italy
1976	Galleria l'Attico (Hotel Luneta), Rome
	Galleria Salvatore Ala, Milan
	Galerie Art-in-Progress, Dusseldorf
1977	Museum Boymans-van Beuningen, Rotterdam
	Kunstmuseum, Lucerne
	Galleria Tucci Russo, Turin
	Galeria Jean & Karen Bernier, Athens
	Villa Pignatelli, Naples
1978	Städtisches Museum, Mönchengladbach, West Germany
	Galleria Mario Diacono, Bologna (with Calzolari and Merz)
1979	Galerie Konrad Fischer, Dusseldorf
	Galerie Jean & Karen Bernier, Athens
	Salvatore Ala Gallery, New York
	Pinacoteca di Bari, Bari, Italy
	Museum Folkwang, Essen
1980	Galleria Lucio Amelio, Naples
	Galleria Mario Diacono, Rome
	Sonnabend Gallery, New York
1981	Galerie Durand-Dessert, Paris
	Galerie Karsten Greve, Cologne
1982	Galeria Obra Social, Madrid
	Whitechapel Art Gallery, London
	Staatliche Kunsthalle, Baden-Baden, West Germany
1983	Sonnabend Gallery, New York
	Galerie Konrad Fischer, Dusseldorf
	Galerie Durand-Dessert, Paris
1984	Galerie Schellmann und Kluser, Munich
	Sonnabend Gallery, New York
	Galleria Ugo Ferranti, Rome
	Galleria Lucio Amelio, Naples
1985	Galleria Christian Stein, Milan
	Stadtische Galerie im Lenbachhaus, Munich
	CAPC/Musée d'Art Contemporain, Bordeaux, France
1986	Kunstnernes Hus, Oslo
	Anthony D'Offay Gallery, London
	Kunsthalle, Basle
1988	Galleria Christian Stein, Milan

Selected Group Exhibitions:

1967	*6th Biennale de Paris*, Musée d'Art Moderne, Paris (and *7th Biennale*, 1971)
1968	*Recent Italian Painting and Sculpture*, Jewish Museum, New York
1969	*When Attitudes Become Form*, Kunsthalle, Berne (toured Europe)
1971	*Arte Povera*, Kunstverein, Munich
1976	*Ambiente/Arte*, at the *Biennale*, Venice
1977	*Documenta 6*, Kassel, West Germany (and *Documenta 7*, 1982)
1981	*Italians and American Italians*, Crown Point Gallery, Oakland, California
1982	*Vergangenheit-Gegenwart-Zukunft*, Wurttembergischer Kunstverein, Stuttgart
1985	*Promenades*, Parc Lullin, Genthod, Geneva
1987	*Avant-Garde in the Eighties*, Los Angeles County Museum of Art

Collections:

Galeria Nazionale d'Arte Moderna, Rome.

Publications:

By KOUNELLIS: articles—"Discorsi, Carla Lonzi e Jannis Kounellis," interview, in *Marcatre* (Milan), December 1966; "4 Domands (semiserie) a Jannis Kounellis" in *Flash Art* (Milan), November/December 1967; "Ponente, Volpi, Kounellis, una conversazione" in *Flash Art* (Milan) January/ February 1968; "Technique e Materiali," with M. Volpi in *Marcatre* (Milan), May 1968; "Jannis Kounellis: Pensierie osservazione," edited by G. Bartoiucci, in *Marcatre* (Milan), July/September 1968; "Per Pascali" in *Qui Arte Contemporanea* (Rome), March 1969; "Non per il teatro, ma con ilteatro," edited by Italo Moscati, in *Sipario* (Milan), April 1969; "Structure and Sensibility: An Interview with Jannis Kounellis," with Willoughby Sharp, in *Avalanche* (New York), Summer 1972.

On KOUNELLIS: books—*Jannis Kounellis*, exhibition catalogue, with text by Cesare Vivaldi, Rome 1964; *When Attitudes Become Form*, exhibition catalogue, edited by Harald Szeemann, Berne 1969; *7th Paris Biennale: Italy*, exhibition catalogue, edited by Achille Bonito Oliva, Paris 1971; *Jannis Kounellis*, exhibition catalogue, with texts by Jean-Christophe Ammann and Marlis Gruterich, Lucerne 1977; *Avanguardia di Massa* by Maurizio Calvesi, Milan 1978; *Jannis Kounellis*, exhibition catalogue, with texts by Zdenek Felix and Bruno Cora, Essen 1979; *Indians and American Italians*, exhibition catalogue, with introduction by Kathan Brown, Oakland, California 1981; *Vergangenheit-Gegenwart-Zukunft*, exhibition catalogue, with an introduction by Tilman Osterwold, Stuttgart 1982.

At Rome's Attico Gallery in 1969 Jannis Kounellis displayed his best-known work—a group of eleven live horses. In doing so Kounellis marked an important stage in his development as an artist and his concern for the relationship between the "natural" and the "artificial," for the relationship, that is, between elements which exist in nature and those things which the artist makes. For Kounellis, "nature" means not only earth, fire, water, minerals and the realms of animal and vegetable life, but coal and wool as well, which seem closer to the world of nature than to the world of man-made things. The "artificial," on the other hand, refers to things made by man's interventions: art can subvert nature; it is an organized cultural gesture. Two works from 1967, "Parrot" and "Daisy of Fire," clearly illustrate this interplay between art and nature. In the first piece, a live parrot sits on a perch which projects from a gray, monochrome canvas; in the second we have a large black-metal daisy with a tube at its center, from which a live flame issues.

But in fact Kounellis began his artistic experiments several years earlier. In one of his first works, for example (dating from 1958), we have a long, narrow table from which the word "oil" stands out in bold relief, while the words "wine" and "vinegar" shine through the varnished surface of the table. A few years later there were large canvases in which numbers and letters played an important role. In 1966 we have works like "Yellow," "Come" and "Night," which serve as a kind of conclusion to Kounellis' experiments with removing objects from their natural surroundings and subjecting them to new pressures. The word "yellow," for example, is actually painted

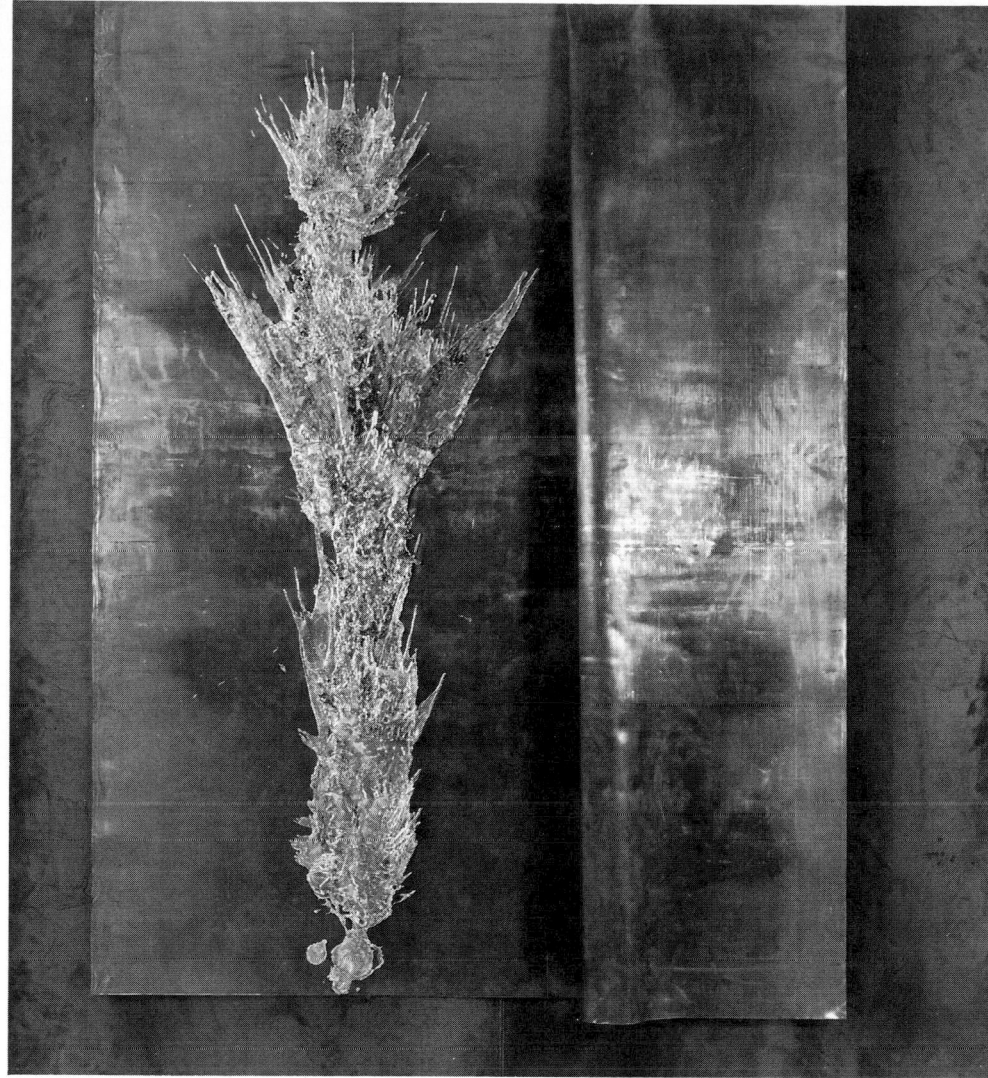

Jannis Kounellis: *Untitled,* 1986 Courtesy Anthony D'Offay Gallery, London

in red; the red roses are black, and so on. In such works Kounellis seems to express, in generalized terms, the relationship between artistic expression and formal qualities.

"Horses," referred to earlier, comes as the climax to Kounellis' first period of artistic development. In the mature works which follow, his aesthetic becomes complex, personal, and rich in tensions. In his 1971 exhibition at the La Tartaruga Gallery there were works from the 60's and new works which built upon them but went beyond them as well. And in his most recent work, displayed at a group show in Bologna in 1978, we have a work which can stand as a summary statement of his art to date: in front of a yellow canvas, a small ship rests on sacks of coal. Kounellis brings together elements which become parts of an intriguing whole which give ample evidence of his enduring vitality as an artist.

—Roberto G. Lambarelli

KOWALSKI, Piotr.

French. Born in Lvov, Poland (now in the U.S.S.R.), 2 March 1927; emigrated to Paris, 1953: naturalized, 1971. Educated in Poland and the United States; studied architecture, physics and mathematics, Massachusetts Institute of Technology, Cambridge, 1947–52, Dip. Arch. 1952. Worked as a mechanic in Poland, 1940–44; travelled in Europe and South America, 1946–47; architect in the office of I.M. Pei, New York, 1952–53, and with the Marcel Breuer team, Unesco Building Project, Paris, 1953–55; established own architectural practice, Paris, 1955; also, painter and sculptor, Paris, from 1954, subsequently in Montrouge, France: first paintings, 1954; first polyester sculptures, 1960. Founder, Atelier for Experimental Architecture, Paris, 1958. Recipient: First Prize, Rail Station Competition, Tunis, 1961; International Baumuseum Prize, Paris, 1962; Graham Foundation Award, Chicago, 1963; Chatelet Square Prize, Paris, 1969; DAAD Fellowship, West Berlin, 1972; Massachusetts Institute of Technology Fellowship, 1978–85; Rockefeller Grant, New York, 1979; Fulbright Fellowship, New York, 1979; French Ministry of Culture Scholarship (to the United States), 1982; Plaza at La Defense Prize, Paris, 1982; City Entry Prize, St. Quentin, France, 1983. Chevalier des Arts et Lettres, France, 1985. Agent: Ronald Feldman Fine Arts, 31–33 Mercer Street, New York, New York 10013, U.S.A. Address: 77 Avenue de la Republique, 92120 Montrouge, France.

Individual Exhibitions:

1961 Galerie des Beaux-Arts, Paris
1963 Kunsthalle, Berne
1966 Museu de Arte Moderna, Sao Paulo
Museu de Arte Moderna, Rio de Janeiro
1967 Galerie Claude Givaudan, Paris
1969 Musée d'Art Moderne, Paris
Galerie Claude Givaudan, Paris
Galerie X-One, Antwerp

1970 Stedelijk Museum, Amsterdam
Moderna Museet, Stockholm
Galerie Claude Givaudan, Paris
Amos Andersonin Taidemuseo, Helsinki
1971 Musée Picasso, Antibes, France (with Jean Dewasne)
1973 Galerie René Block, West Berlin
Galerie Edouard Loeb, Paris
1974 Musée Galliera, Paris
Galerie Eric Fabre, Paris
1975 Galerie Eric Fabre, Paris
1978 Galerie Eric Fabre, Paris
1979 Ronald Feldman Fine Arts, New York
Galerie Eric Fabre, Paris
Galerie Claude Givaudan, Geneva
1981 Galerie Eric Fabre, Paris
Centre Georges Pompidou, Paris
1983 Galerie Acapa, Angouleme, France
Hara Museum of Contemporary Art, Tokyo
1986 Galerie de Seoul, Korea

Selected Group Exhibitions:

1965 *Light and Movement,* Kunsthalle, Berne (travelled to Brussels, Baden-Baden, Dusseldorf and Paris)
1967 *Science Fiction,* Kunsthalle, Berne (travelled to Paris and Dusseldorf)
1969 *10th Middelheim Biennale,* Kunsthistorisches Museum, Antwerp
1970 *Kinetics,* Hayward Gallery, London
1972 *Documenta 5,* Museum Fridericianum, Kassel, West Germany
1975 *Les Machines Celibataires,* Kunsthalle, Berne (travelled to Venice, Brussels, Dusseldorf, Paris, Malmo, Amsterdam, Rennes and Vienna)
1976 *Museum of Drawers,* Museum Solothurn, Switzerland (travelled to Antwerp, Dusseldorf, Jerusalem, Washington, Los Angeles and Berne)
1983 *Electra,* Musee d'Art Moderne, Paris
1986 *XLII Biennale,* Venice

Collections:

Stedelijk Museum, Amsterdam; Centre Georges Pompidou, Paris; Bibliotheque Nationale, Paris; Moderna Museet, Stockholm; Kunstmuseum, Berne; Guggenheim Museum, New York; University of Southern California, Long Beach; Museum of Modern Art, Jerusalem; Hara Museum of Contemporary Art, Tokyo; Seoul Gallery, Korea.

Publications:

BY KOWALSKI: articles—"The Explosive Forms of Piotr Kowalski", interview, in *Architectural Forum* (New York), December 1965; "Sculpture a la dynamite" in *Le Nouvel Observateur* (Paris), 5 January 1966; "L'Art et la Technologie" in *Protee* (Quebec), no. 1, 1981; "Un point de vue peut etre aussi represente par une matrice" in *Alea* (Paris), March 1982.

On KOWALSKI: books—*Piotr Kowalski,* exhibition catalogue, with text by Harald Szeemann, Berne 1963; *A Concise History of Modern Sculpture* by Herbert Read, New York 1964; *Kowalski,* exhibition catalogue, with text by Harald Szeemann, Rio de Janeiro 1966; *Kowalski,* exhibition card folder, Paris 1967; *Kowalski,* exhibition catalogue, with text by Frank Popper, interviews by Gilbert Brownstone and Pierre Gaudibert, Paris 1969; *Piotr Kowalski,* exhibition catalogue, edited by Coosje Kapteyn and Ad Petersen, with an interview by Harald Szeemann, Amsterdam 1970; *Piotr Kowalski,* exhibition catalogue, with an interview by Harald Szeemann, Stockholm 1970; *Documenta 5: Befragung der Realität,* exhibition catalogue, edited by Harald Szeemann and others, Kassel, West Germany 1972; *12 Ans d'Art Contemporain en France,* exhibition catalogue, with texts by Francois Mathey, Daniel Cordier and Jean Clair, Paris 1972; *Piotr Kowalski: Time Machine + Projets,* exhibition catalogue with texts by Pontus Hulten, Dominique Bozo and Jean-Christophe Bailly, Paris 1981; *Kowalski,* exhibition catalogue with text by Alain Jouffroy, Tokyo 1983.

I do not find it comfortable to voice ideas underlining my work otherwise than in front of it or its illustra-

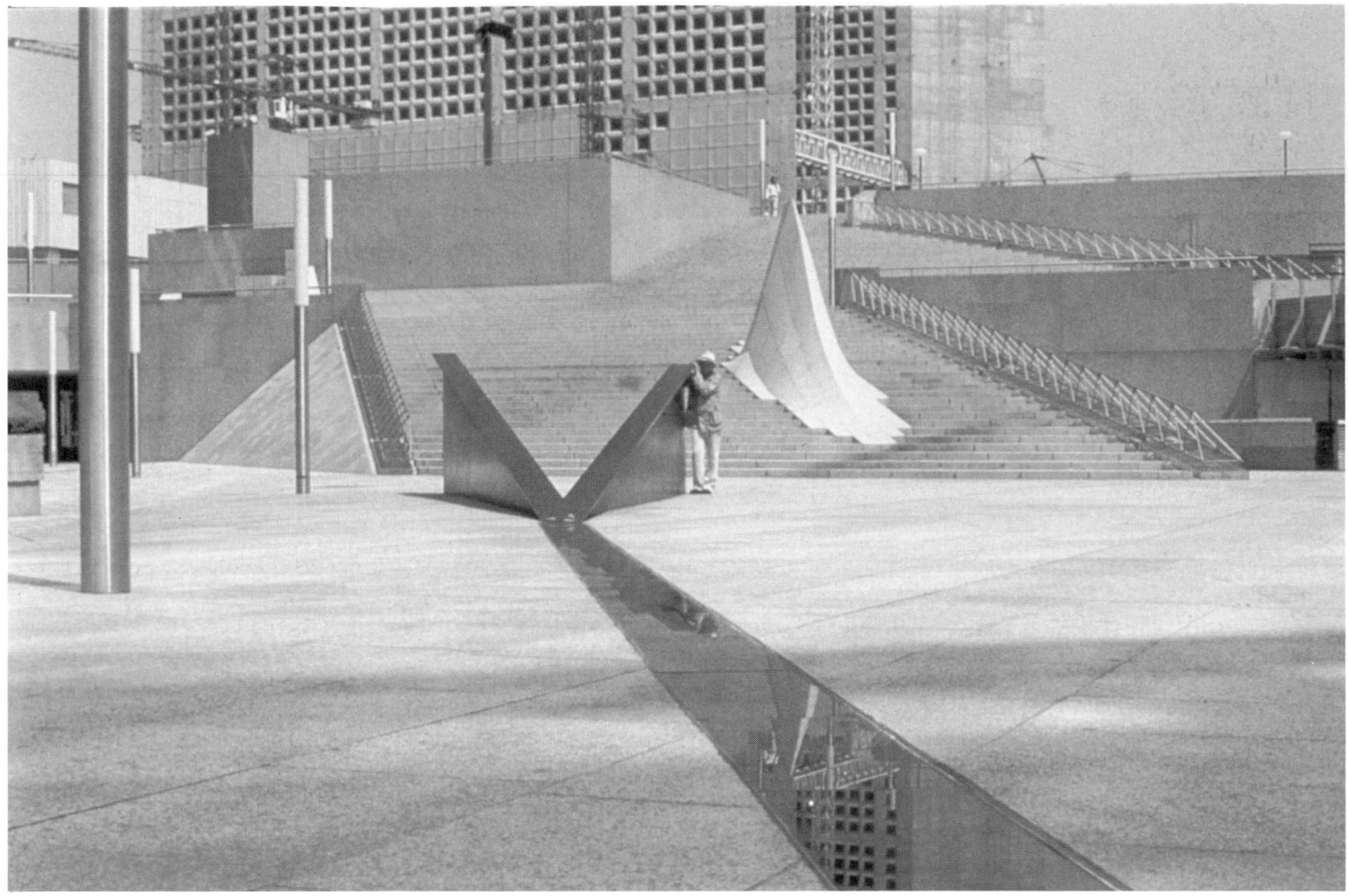

Piotr Kowalski: Plaza at La Defense, Paris, 1982–88

tion. So I chose the following text of a friend and critic, Jean-Christophe Bailly, which sums up my thoughts best now:

"How is space apprehended. How do we master data, mountains of scientific data, and how do we put them to use to shape our material world. How do we articulate experience within the given reference frames, frames that have to be made manifest in order to be changed? How sculpture is but an instant made evident of such an articulation.

It is all this that Kowalski seeks to render by linking again art with science as the notion of "cosa mentale" once proved, and seeks to render with no trace of nostalgia, with the elements of our time in all scales and variations, ordered with a demonstrative logic as a tool.

Pioneer of an encyclopedic issue in art, Kowalski appears today to be one of those rare artists that are conscious of the world they live in. World no more of frontal contemplation, nor that of linear times, but of infinite and aleatory production, where it became vital to place landmarks. Art becoming markings of portative knowledge and a vehicle for immediate poetics of experience such as Kowalski's 'sculpture.' "

—Piotr Kowalski

Piotr Kowalski throughout his career has aimed to achieve a wide scientific and artistic awareness through acting on the psychology of the spectator, who is invited to experience the elements of the technological universe and exploit certain of its meanings. In his "Grand Manipulateur" (1967), the spectator was impelled to act upon volumes of rare coloured gas within an overall electronic field, which caused it to light up and then become transparent once again in relation to the movements of the manipulator. Kowalski's "Mesures à prendre," exhibited at the 1972 Do-

cumenta, involved both a subtle use of neon light and the integral participation of the public, which illuminates the neon tubes through placing them next to electrically active screens. Kowalski's spatial preoccupations can be observed in a series of laconic pseudo-scientific statements that lend themselves to realization on a range of different scales: "ici" (The Point/Time/Sound on the threshold of perception), "La-bas" (a vector indicated by a red arrow), "XYZ" (three axes of coordinates defined by the three primary colours of light in a corner) and "Distance" (wire at red heat, stretched between two points in space and varying its length according to the degree of heating).

The time factor dominates in Kowalski's most recent constructions. "Time Machine I," a computer used as an art tool, transmits the immediate materiality of time, and its reversal manipulations. It treats time not as a trace or a memory but as a phenomenon in a real-time world accessible directly to the senses. "Time Machine II" is conceived as an open-ended system, capable of progressive upgradings. It adds to the sound treatment of the earlier work a video treatment. Both Time Machines are public-oriented and are interactive pieces which capture both the existing sound and the public's image and actions, and restitute them backward in real-time on television screens and through a sound system. The artist thus proposes to the spectator's enhanced attention, time events which move forward and backward.

For Kowalski, technological procedures are essentially linked to an acceptance of the present, while genuine scientific advance is always open to the future and cannot be technocratic. Although he dismisses any too facile notion of the inclusion of the public in the creative process, he holds that scientific and technological progress is basically mental in character and thus indissolubly linked with an aes-

thetic factor. And if art and science are connected as a result of the abolition of any hard and fast distinction, it is in man that all scientific and artistic preoccupations must reside.

—Frank Popper

KOZLOFF, Joyce.

American. Born Joyce Blumberg, in Somerville, New Jersey, 14 December 1942. Studied at the Art Students League, New York, 1959; Carnegie Institute of Technology, Pittsburgh, 1960–64, B.F.A. 1964; Rutgers University, New Brunswick, New Jersey, 1962; University of Florence, Italy, 1963; under Stephen Greene and Theodoros Stamos, Columbia University, New York, 1965–67, M.F.A. 1967. Married Max Kozloff in 1967; son: Nikolas. Instructor, elementary and secondary schools, Pittsburgh, 1964; junior high school, Cranford, New Jersey, 1964–65; Ox-Bow Summer School of Painting, Saugatuck, Michigan, 1972; Queens College, New York, 1972–73; and School of Visual Arts, New York, 1973–74; Visiting Artist, School of the Art Institute of Chicago, 1975; San Francisco Art Institute, 1975; Instructor, Syracuse University, New York, 1977; University of New Mexico, Albuquerque, 1978; Brooklyn Museum Art School, New York, 1978–79; Washington University, St. Louis, 1986. Advisory Board Member, Public Art Fund, New York, 1984–86; Board Member, College Art Association, 1985–89. Recipient: Tamarind Lithography Institute Grant, Albuquerque, New Mexico, 1972; Creative Artists Program Service Grant, New York, 1972–73 (printmaking), and 1975–76 (painting); American Association of University Women Grant in Painting, 1975; National Endowment for the Arts Grant, 1977, 1985; Yaddo Fellowship, Saratoga Springs, New York, 1984; Arts/Industry Program Award, John Michael Kohler Art Center, Sheboygan, Wisconsin, 1986–87. Agent: Barbara Gladstone Gallery, 99 Greene Street, New York, New York 10012. Address: 152 Wooster Street, New York, New York 10012, U.S.A.

Individual Exhibitions:

1970	Tibor de Nagy Gallery, New York
1971	Tibor de Nagy Gallery, New York
1973	Douglass College, New Brunswick, New Jersey
	Tibor de Nagy Gallery, New York
1974	University of Rhode Island, Kingston
	Tibor de Nagy Gallery, New York
1975	King Pitcher Gallery, Pittsburgh (with Howardena Pindell)
	San Francisco Art Institute
1976	Tibor de Nagy Gallery, New York (2 shows)
	Women's Building, Los Angeles
	Queens College, New York
1977	Watson de Nagy Gallery, Houston
	Jasper Gallery, Denver
	Tibor de Nagy Gallery, New York

1978	University of New Mexico, Albuquerque (with Max Kozloff)
1979	Everson Museum, Syracuse, New York
	Tibor de Nagy Gallery, New York
1980	Mint Museum, Charlotte, North Carolina
	The Renwick, Washington, D.C.
1981	Tibor de Nagy Gallery, New York (with Betty Woodman)
1982	Crown Point Gallery, Oakland, California
	Barbara Gladstone Gallery, New York
	Joslyn Art Museum, Omaha, Nebraska
1983	Berkshire Community College, Pittsfield, Massachusetts
	Barbara Gillman Gallery, Miami, Florida (with Miriam Schapiro)
	McIntosh/Drysdale Gallery, Houston (with Richard Haas and Ned Smyth)
	Institute of Contemporary Art, Philadelphia
	Lincoln Center for Performing Arts, New York (with Elizabeth Murray and Judith Murray)
1984	Delaware Art Museum, Wilmington
	Project Studio One, New York
1985	Barbara Gladstone Gallery, New York
1986	San Antonio Art Institute, Texas
	Boston University, Massachusetts (toured the United States, 1986–87)

Selected Group Exhibitions:

1972	*Painting Annual,* Whitney Museum, New York

1975	*Color, Light and Image,* Women's Inter-Art Center, New York
1977	*Pattern Painting,* Project Studio One, New York
1978	*Arabesque,* Contemporary Arts Center, Cincinnati
1979	*The Decorative Impulse,* Institute of Contemporary Art, Philadelphia
1980	*Printed Art: A View of Two Decades,* Museum of Modern Art, New York
1982	*Polychrome Sculpture,* Lever House, New York
1983	*Back to the U.S.A.,* Kunstmuseum, Lucerne, Switzerland
1985	*Working on the Railroad,* Whitney Museum, Stamford, Connecticut
1987	*Prints in Parts,* Crown Point Press, New York

Collections:

Museum of Modern Art, New York; Metropolitan Museum of Art, New York; Brooklyn Museum, New York; Vassar College, Poughkeepsie, New York; Albright-Knox Art Gallery, Buffalo, New York; Massachusetts Institute of Technology, Cambridge; Allen Memorial Art Museum, Oberlin, Ohio; Weatherspoon Gallery, University of North Carolina; Greensboro; Norton Gallery of Art, West Palm Beach, Florida; Neue Galerie Sammlung Ludwig, Aachen, West Germany. Commissioned works: Harvard Square Subway Station, Cambridge, Massachusetts; Wilmington Train Station, Delaware; Humboldt-Hospital Subway Station, Buffalo, New York; International Terminal, San Francisco Airport; 1 Penn Center Suburban Station, Philadelphia; Financial Station, Detroit; 7th and Flower Metro Rail Station, Los Angeles.

Joyce Kozloff: *Topkapi Pullman,* 1985

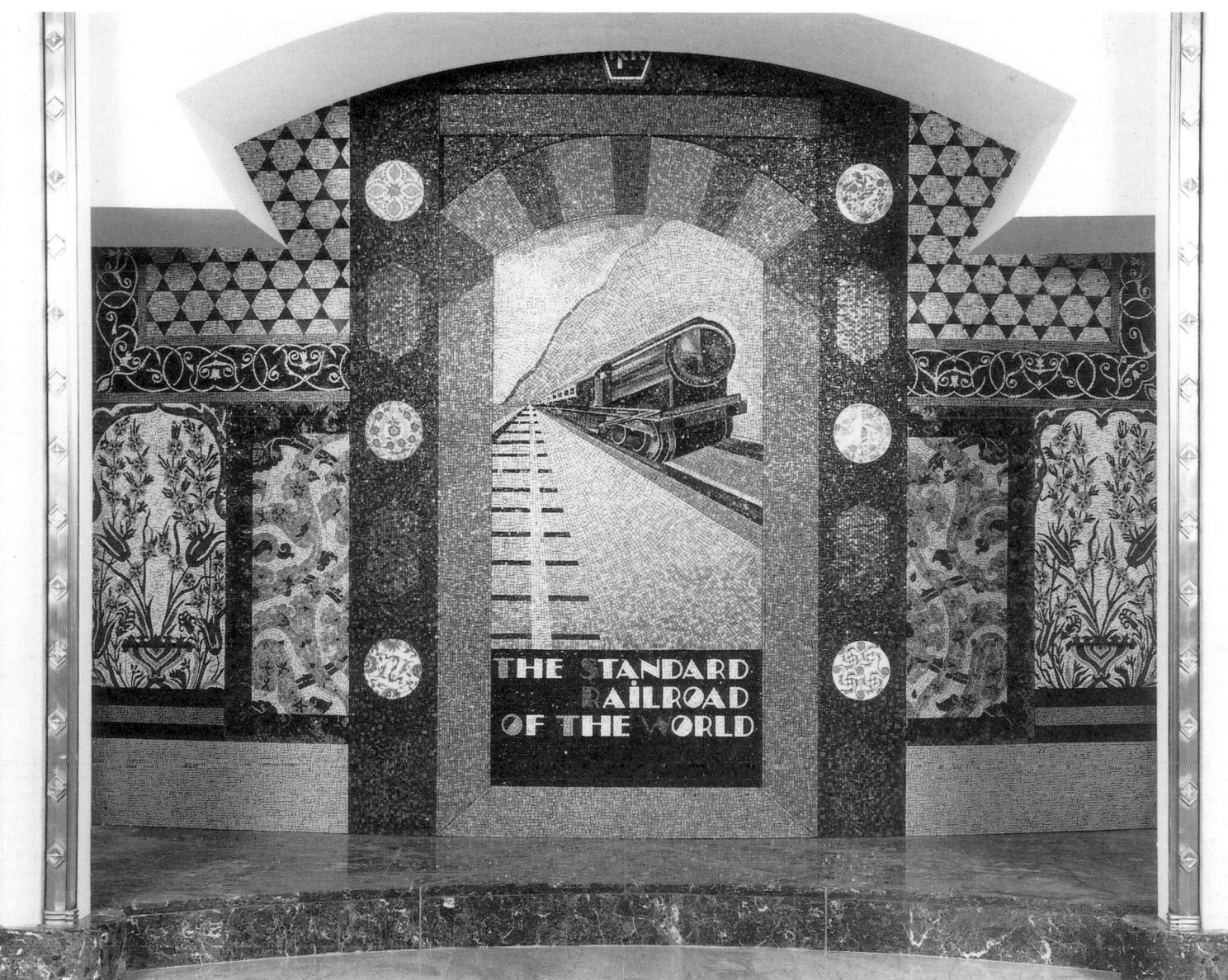

Publications:

By KOZLOFF; books—*Interviews with Women Artists*, editor, New York 1975; articles—"Letter to the Editor" in *Anonymous Was a Woman*, Valencia, California 1974; "Women Artists Speak on Women Artists," edited with May Stevens, in *Women's Studies* (New York), Fall 1976; "The Women's Movement: Still a Source of Strength or One Big Bore?," with Barbara Zucker, in *Artnews* (New York), April 1976; "Frida Kahlo" in *Women's Studies* (New York), vol. 6, no. 1, 1978; essay in *An Interior Decorated*, exhibition catalogue, New York 1979; "Frida Kahlo at the Neuberger Museum" in *Art in America* (New York), May/June 1979; "An Ornamented Joke" in *Artforum* (New York), December 1986.

On KOZLOFF: books—*From the Center* by Lucy Lippard, New York 1977; *Arabesque*, exhibition catalogue, by Ruth K. Meyer, Cincinnati, Ohio 1978; *Joyce Kozloff: An Interior Decorated*, exhibition catalogue, New York 1979; *I-80 Series: Joyce Kozloff*, catalogue with essay by Holliday T. Day, Omaha 1982; *Investigations 4: Joyce Kozloff*, with essay by Janet Kardon, Philadelphia 1984; *Working on the Railroad*, exhibition catalogue with text by Pamela Gruninger Perkins, New York 1985; *Joyce Kozloff: Visionary Ornament* by Patricia Johnston, Boston 1986; articles—"New York Letter" by Carter Ratcliff in *Art International* (Lugano), January 1978; "Atelierbeschuche" by Madeleine Stricler and Dominik Keller in *Du* (Zurich), June 1979; "Zurück and Hinzur 'Wurde des Dekorativen' " by Harald Szeemann in *Du* (Zurich), June 1979; "Decoration, Ornament, Pattern and Utility" by Carrie Rickey in *Flash Art* (Milan) June/July 1979; "The New Decorativeness" by John Perreault in *Portfolio* (New York), June/July 1979; "A Room with a Coup" by John Perreault in the *Soho Weekly News* (New York), 13 September 1979; "Joyce Kozloff" and "The Decorative Impulse" both by Jeff Perrone in *Artforum* (New York), November 1979; "Joyce Kozloff" by Nancy Stapen in *Artforum* (New York), Summer 1986; "Pattern and Decoration in the Public Eye" by Sally Webster in *Art in America*, (New York), February 1987.

My art of the last seven years or so has been for urban transportation systems. We city dwellers experience those systems daily. For me, the challenge has been to enhance and clarify their architecture without obstructing function, and to celebrate each city's visual and cultural history without alienating or pandering to a self-defined public.

—Joyce Kozloff

KRASNER, Lee.

American. Born Lenore Krassner, in Brooklyn, New York, 27 October 1908. Educated at Washington Irving High School, New York, 1922-25; Women's Art Schools of Cooper Union, New York, 1926-29; Art Students League, New York, 1928; National Academy of Design, New York, 1929-32; City College and Greenhouse House, New York, 1933; studied with Hans Hofmann, New York, 1933-40. Married the artist Jackson Pollock in 1945 (died, 1956). Worked as mural painter for the Public Works of Art Project, New York, 1934; Temporary Emergency Relief Administration, New York, 1934-35; Works Project Administration (W.P.A.) Federal Arts Project, New York, 1934; Federal Arts Project, Mural Division, 1938-42; Artists Union, 1939. Recipient: The Augustus St. Gaudens Medal, Cooper Union Alumni Association, New York, 1974; Lowe Fellowship for Distinction, Barnard College, New York, 1974. Agent: Pace Gallery, 32 East 57th Street, New York, New York 10022. *Died* (in New York) *19 June 1984.*

Individual Exhibitions:

1951	Betty Parsons Gallery, New York
1954	The House of Books and Music, East Hampton, New York
1955	Stable Gallery, New York
1958	Martha Jackson Gallery, New York
1959	Signa Gallery, East Hampton, New York
1960	Howard Wise Gallery, New York
1962	Howard Wise Gallery, New York
1965	*Paintings, Drawings and Collages*, Whitechapel Art Gallery, London (retrospective; toured the U.K.)
	Franklin Siden Gallery, Detroit
1967	*Paintings*, University of Alabama Art Gallery, Tuscaloosa
1968	Marlborough-Gerson Gallery, New York
1969	Marlborough-Gerson Gallery, New York
	Reese Palley Gallery, San Francisco
1973	*Recent Paintings*, Marlborough Gallery, New York
	Large Paintings, Whitney Museum, New York
1974	Miami-Dade Community College, Florida (travelled to Beaver College, Glenside, Pennsylvania)
1975	*Collages and Paintings 1933-1974*, Corcoran Museum of Art, Washington, D.C. (toured the United States)
	Marlborough Gallery, New York
1977	Pace Gallery, New York
	Susanne Hilberry Gallery, Birmingham, Michigan
1978	Janie C. Lee Gallery, Houston
1979	*Paintings 1959-1962*, Pace Gallery, New York
1980	Tower Gallery, Southampton, New York
1981	Pace Gallery, New York
	Janie C. Lee Gallery, Houston
1983	Museum of Fine Art, Houston (retrospective; toured the United States)
1986	Robert Miller Gallery, New York

Selected Group Exhibitions:

1974	*In den Unzähligen Bildern des Lebens: Surrealität/ Bildrealität 1924-1974*, Kunsthalle, Dusseldorf (travelled to Staatliche Kunsthalle, Baden-Baden 1975)
1975	*Subjects of the Artist: New York Painting 1941-1957*, Whitney Museum (Downtown Branch), New York
1977	*Women Artists: 1550-1950*, Los Angeles County Museum of Art, (travelled to the University of Texas at Austin; Museum of Art, Carnegie Institute, Pittsburgh; and the Brooklyn Museum, New York)
	New York WPA Artists, Then and Now, Parsons School of Design, New York
1978	*Abstract Expressionism: The Formative Years*, Herbert F. Johnson Museum, Cornell University, Ithaca, New York (travelled to Whitney Museum, New York, and Seibu Museum, Tokyo)
1979	*American Painting of the 1970's*, Albright-Knox Art Gallery, Buffalo, New York (travelled to Newport Harbor Museum, Newport Beach, California)
	Around Jackson Pollock, East Hampton, The 1950's, Centre Culturel Americain, Paris
1980	*17 Abstract Artists of East Hampton: The Pollock Years 1946-56*, Parrish Art Museum, Southampton, New York (travelled to the Benton Museum of Art, University of Connecticut, Storrs, and the Zabriskie Gallery, New York)
	The 50's: Aspects of Painting in New York, Hirshhorn Museum, Washington, D.C.
1981	*Tracking the Marvelous*, Grey Art Gallery, New York University

Collections:

Museum of Modern Art, New York; Whitney Museum, New York; Metropolitan Museum of Art, New York; Brooklyn Museum, New York; Neuberger Museum, State University of New York at Purchase; Philadelphia Museum of Art.

Publications:

By KRASNER: taped interviews—with Barbara Rose, in the Collection of the Archives of American Art, Washington, D.C., July 1966; with Dorothy G. Seckler, in the Collection of the Archives of American Art, Washington, D.C., December 1967 and April 1968; with Dolores Holmes, in the Collection of the Archives of American Art, Washington, D.C., Summer 1971; with Hermine Freed, videotape, in the Collection of Visual Resources, New York, 1973; with Barbara Novak, videotape, WGBH New Television Workshop Video-

tape Archives of the Arts, Boston, 1979; magazine interviews—"A Conversation with Lee Krasner," with Cindy Nemser, in *Arts Magazine* (New York), April 1973; with Cindy Nemser, in *Art Talk: Conversations with 12 Women Artists*, New York 1975; "A Conversation with Lee Krasner," with Richard Howard, in *Lee Krasner: Paintings 1959-1962*, exhibition catalogue, New York 1979; "Interviews with Lee Krasner," with Barbara Cavaliere, in *Flash Art* (Milan), January/February 1980; excerpts of interview with Barbara Novak, in *Lee Krasner: Recent Works*, exhibition catalogue, New York 1981.

On KRASNER: books—*Lee Krasner: Paintings, Drawings and Collages*, exhibition catalogue, with text by B. H. Friedman, London 1965; *Paintings by Lee Krasner*, exhibition catalogue, with text by D. McKinney, Tuscaloosa, Alabama 1967; *Lee Krasner: Recent Paintings*, exhibition catalogue, with text by D. McKinney, New York 1973; *Lee Krasner: Large Paintings*, exhibition catalogue, with text by Marcia Tucker, New York 1973; *Lee Krasner*, exhibition catalogue, Miami 1974; *Lee Krasner: Collages and Works on Paper 1933-1974*, exhibition catalogue, with text by Gene Baro, Washington, D.C. 1975; *Lee Krasner: 11 Ways to Use Words to See*, exhibition catalogue, New York 1977; *Abstract Expressionism: The Formative Years*, exhibition catalogue, by Robert Carleton Hobbs and Gail Levin, Ithaca, New York 1978; *Lee Krasner: Paintings 1959-1962*, exhibition catalogue, New York 1979; *Lee Krasner: Recent Work*, exhibition catalogue, New York 1981; *Lee Krasner: retrospective exhibition*, catalogue with essay by Barbara Rose, New York and Houston 1983; *Lee Krasner*, exhibition catalogue with texts by Robert Hughes and Bryan Robertson, New York 1986.

It is difficult for me to state the intentions of my painting. Some of my preoccupations are whether a canvas allows me to breathe or not. If it is earthbound, I find it difficult to breathe. I try to merge the organic with the abstract—whether that means male or female, spirit and matter, or the need for a totality rather than a separation are questions which I have not defined as yet.

—Lee Krasner (1983)

It was only in the later years of her life that Krasner received the credit she deserves as a first rate, first generation Abstract Expressionist painter. Krasner's pictures from the 1940's are informed by her understanding of the Abstract Expressionist idea: to infuse abstract painterly form with mysterious and significant content. The substantial body of work she created from that period until her death shows her continuous push into finer painterly expression of this idea and her particular abilities to attain freshness and spontaneity with a character and personality that never allow her work to rest pat on previous accomplishments.

During the 1930's, Krasner was working her way through major modernist painting of the earlier 20th century, especially that of Mondrian, Picasso and Matisse, and, with their help and her talents as a painter, she was beginning to locate the components for her personal route. Because she lacked money, the paintings Krasner made from 1943 to 1945 were mostly scraped down so that she could reuse the canvas. The first major evidence that Krasner had begun to visually realize her individual statement of Abstract Expressionist aims is in the group of paintings called the "Little Image" series which began in 1945 and continued until 1950. The densely painted, light-filled surfaces on these small pictures vibrate with abstract shapes, simultaneously readable as eyes, spirals, calligraphic hieroglyphs, microscopic organisms and/or constellations. These multi-referential signs are arranged in an allover manner over an underlying grid structure. Krasner had been painting for nearly two decades by this time, and she had reached the point when the painterly process was so well understood that she could work her way intuitively through layers of painted color until she reached the point at which everything seemed right, the signal that the picture was finished.

Krasner worked in cycles. Never content to stick to one series for more than four or five years, she continually seeks out new configurations of her vocabulary and syntax, each interconnected with her past

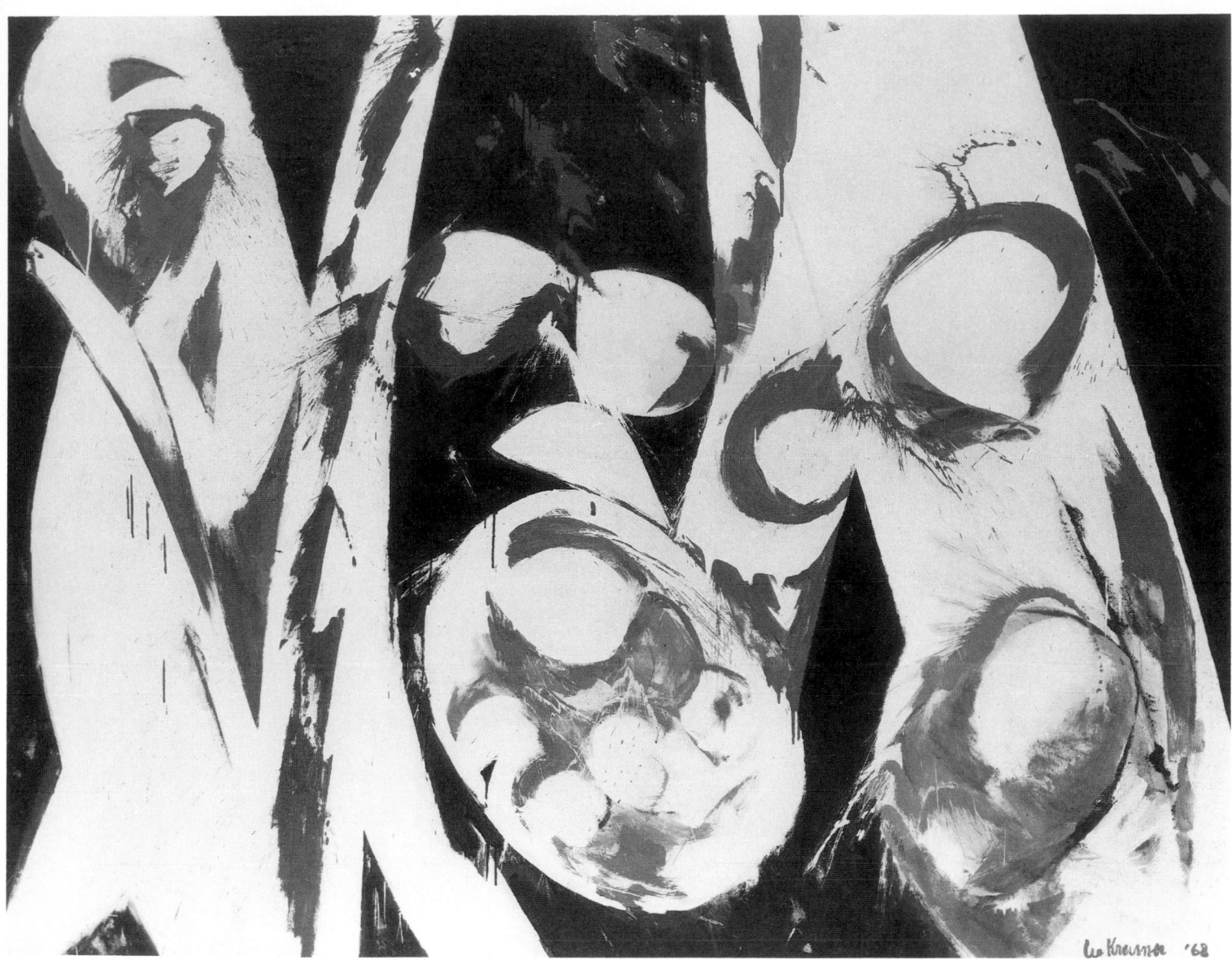

Lee Krasner: *The Green Fuse*, 1968

works but also building new syntheses for the present. In 1951, pictures became broader and thinner; vertical strips incorporate calligraphic shapes and painterly atmospheres. In 1953–55, she became discontent with these most recent works, and used all but two of them to make her first series of collages. Krasner used collage at times when she felt the need to revamp and make a move. They signify an experimental attitude which has produced many of Krasner's finest works. For this series, Krasner cut or tore up the works into strips and then arranged and pasted these fragments from her own past. Some of the resulting collages, such as "City Verticals" (1953), are composed of predominantly vertical motions which appear as if bars are holding from view some cryptic element subsumed beneath the surface. Others, such as "Bald Eagle" (1955), have clusters of irregular swatches which dance rhythmically across the surface, butting and overlapping while also cohabiting with overpainted areas. Krasner used similar configurations in her two murals for 2 Broadway in Manhattan (1958–59), colorful, light filled mosaics that still grace that area.

The group pictures which evolved in 1959–62 are closely related to her "Little Image" series, but are larger and more all-at-once and indicative of Krasner's increased ability to handle monumental scale with freer, more rugged and more rapidly painted gestures. Pictures of this group are well exemplified by the ruggedly painted, swirling patterns of organic shapes in almost monochrome tonalities which characterize "The Eye is the First Circle" (1960). In a further motioning shift of mood, pictures

from the late 60's and early 70's evolve Krasner's vocabulary into more monolithic, monumental shapes in more openly expansive atmospheres, using very high-key colors, combining pinks, grass greens and yellows with a more lighthearted quality that loses none of its thrusting, emotive energies.

In 1976, Krasner produced another series of collages, using pieces of charcoal drawings she had made in 1937–40 and subsequently put away. These works are among Krasner's finest, masterful in underlying structure and visually exciting in their mixed charcoal and oil textures and in their variously interacting areas of empty field and fragmented figural imagery. Titles are various tenses and moods of verbs, each suggestive of the state of mind implied in the title. "Imperative," for example, is packed full of imagery and sharply edged diagonals, while "Present Conditional" is more emptied of incident and arranged in a more regularized grid in which blacks, whites and grays are accompanied by a few arcs of ochre.

All of Krasner's pictures are the accumulations of her past experiences and memories, transformed by a painter's intuitions into statements of deeply emotional significance, and her series called "Solstice" (1980–81) carries yet another move deeper into this realization. These combinations of oil and collage on canvas contain sweeping statements which incorporate elements from each of Krasner's previous series to attain a gestural forcefulness which is very much in the present.

—Barbara Cavaliere

KRICKE, Norbert.

German. Born in Dusseldorf, 30 November 1922. Educated in Berlin; studied art, under Richard Scheibe, at the Hochschule für Bildende Künste, West Berlin, 1946–47. Served in the German Luftwaffe, 1941–45. Married Herta Kricke in 1946; daughter: Sabine. Sculptor, with studio in Dusseldorf, 1947–84; first "spatial" sculptures, 1949; first water sculptures, 1955. Professor, 1964–72, and Director, 1972–84, Staatliche Kunstakademie, Dusseldorf. Recipient: Graham Foundation Prize, Chicago, 1958; Grand-Prix, North Rhine-Westphalia 1963; Wilhelm-Lehmbruck Prize, Duisburg, West Germany, 1971. *Died* (in Dusseldorf) *26 June 1984.*

Individual Exhibitions:

1953	Ophir Galerie, Munich
1954	Galerie Parnass, Wuppertal, West Germany
1955	Kunsthalle, Dusseldorf
	City Gallery, Istanbul
1956	Galleri Sandaren, Stockholm
1957	Galerie Iris Clert, Paris
	Kunstverein, Freiburg im Breisgau, West Germany
1959	Galerie Iris Clert, Paris
1960	*Kricke/Luginbuhl/Tinguely,* Kunsthalle, Berne
1961	Museum of Modern Art, New York
	Lefebre Gallery, New York
	Galerie Karl Flinker, Paris
1962	Museum Haus Lange, Krefeld, West Germany
1963	Karl-Ernst-Osthaus Museum, Hagen, West Germany
	Galerie St. Stephan, Vienna

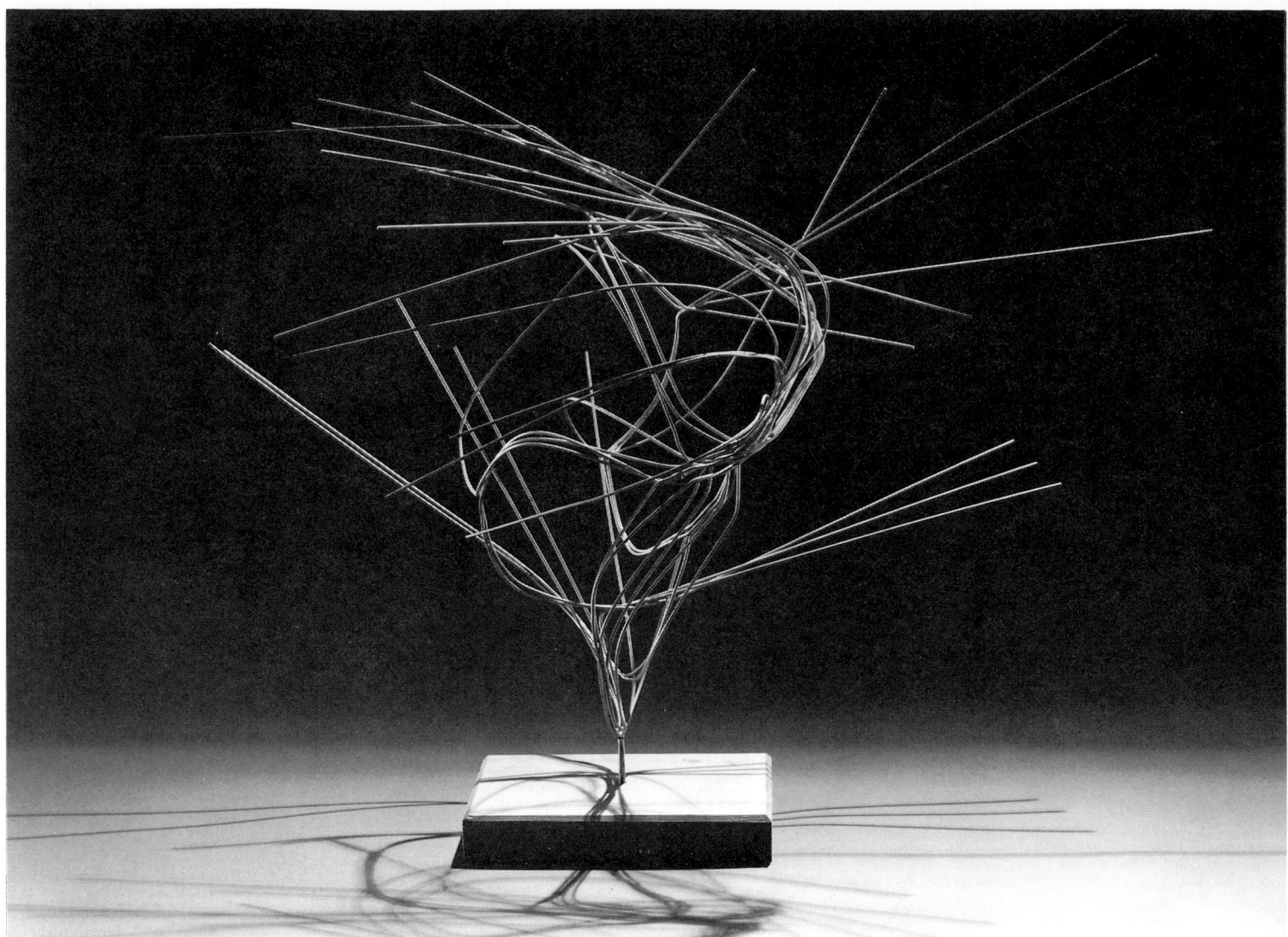

Norbert Kricke: *Raumplastik*, 1958

Selected Group Exhibitions:

Collections:

Wilhelm-Lembruck Museum, Duisburg, West Germany; Stadt Mönchengladbach, West Germany; Kunstmuseum, Dusseldorf; Karl-Ernst-Osthaus Museum, Hagen, West Germany; Kaiser Wilhelm Museum, Krefeld, West Germany; Städtisches Museum, Leverkusen, West Germany; Kunst-und Museumsverein, Wuppertal, West Germany; Museum of Modern Art, New York; Hirshhorn Museum and Sculpture Garden, Washington, D.C.

Publications:

By KRICKE: books—*Hommage à Kandinsky*, Dusseldorf 1956; *Forms of Water*, Dusseldorf 1956; articles—"Raum und Bewegung" in *Das Kunstwerk* (Baden-Baden, West Germany), March 1962; "Klein Fall für mich: in *Die Zeit* (Hamburg), 20 December 1968; "Mon Materiel est l'Espace" in *Skira Annual: Art Actuel*, Geneva 1976; "Integration von Kunst und Architektur" in *Frankfurter Allgemeine Zeitung*, 10 May 1977.

On KRICKE: books—*Norbert Kricke*, exhibition catalogue, with text by Carola Giedion-Welcker, Paris 1961; *Norbert Kricke*, exhibition catalogue, with text by Paul Wember, Krefeld, West Germany 1962; *Norbert Kricke* by Eduard Trier, Recklinghausen, West Germany 1963; *Kricke* by John Anthony Thwaites, Stuttgart, New York, London and Paris 1964; *Norbert Kricke: XXII Biennale di Venezia 1964*, exhibition catalogue, with text by Carola Giedion Welcker, Cologne 1964; *Norbert Kricke*, exhibition catalogue, with text by Carola Giedion-Welcker, New York 1968; *Norbert Kricke*, exhibition catalogue with texts by Jürgen Harten, Siegfried Salzmann and others, Dussseldorf 1975; *Norbert Kricke* by

Jürgen Morschels, Stuttgart 1976; *Kricke*, exhibition catalogue, with texts by Jürgen Morschel and Hannelore Kersting-Bleyl, Frankfurt 1980.

*   *   *

Of the generation of German sculptors who created their specific identities in the early 1950's, Norbert Kricke stands apart for the consistency and development of his non-objective space sculptures in metal. These first constructions were in bent metal rod, figures conceived in angular geometric equations. Proportions were of paramount importance in those profiles, defined in linear terms where movements were anticipated in the broad pyramidal base and the isosceles arrow zooming to the sky. Skeletal curves and straights of wire and tubing were accented in colour to emphasize the dematerialization of the whole. Space itself has always been at the heart of Kricke's conceptions, not without relevance to his intimate experience of it as a Luftwaffe pilot.

His second phase of development blossomed around 1955 when instead of single tubes of metal he grouped them in masses reminiscent of the weighty blacks in the paintings of Hartung. Those masses were arranged in planes that turned in dynamic arabesques. Climax to this period of activity was the space sculpture, 7 metres high, standing in symbolic eminence before the headquarters of the vast Mannesmann industrial empire in Kricke's native Dusseldorf, where I visited him in his challenging workshop area of an aircraft hanger. Succeeding this exploration, the artist built up his sculptures from rods welded into screens of different lengths angled in surfaces endowing them with wing-like analogies. One of the most successful of those is "Grosse Reux," the large space formation in the collection of the Baroness Alix de Rothschild at her Normandy chateau, where it is effectively sited against the full-volumed trees forming a natural backdrop.

This progression from linear silhouette to more subtle compositions involving varying masses has seen extraordinary advances, especially in "Wasserwalden" (water woods), formed of transparent plastic materials. Their function is as fountains complementary to architectural features; the water rises in vertical channels and descends the solid face, evoking a sensation of shimmering light. For Kricke steel rod and tubing have the advantage of forming their own armatures. His sense of the limits to which the load can be stretched gives his best works that tension that teeters on the brink of destruction with every strong wind while retaining the airy delicacy of a butterfly posed on the petal of a rose.

—G. S. Whittet

KRIEG, Dieter.

German. Born in Lindau, Bodensee, 21 May 1937. Studied art, under H. A. P. Grieshaber and Herbert Kitzel, at the Kunstakademie, Karlsruhe, 1958–62. Married Irene Kehne in 1970. Independent painter, in Karlsruhe and Baden-Baden, 1963–78, in Cologne from 1978. Guest Instructor, Kunstakademie, Karlsruhe, 1971–72; Stadelschule, Frankfurt, 1975–76; Professor, Kunstakademie, Dusseldorf, 1978. Recipient: Deutscher Kunstpreis der Jugend, Baden-Baden, 1966; Preis der Veranstalter, *Biennale Danuvius '68*, Bratislava, 1968; Kunstpreis der Bottscherstrasse, Bremen, 1969; Kunstpreis, City of Darmstadt, 1970. Agent: Galerie Heinz Herzer, Munich. Address: c/o Galerie Heinz Herzer, Maximilianstrasse 43, 8000 Munich 22, West Germany.

Individual Exhibitions:

1966	Badischer Kunstverein, Karlsruhe
1967	Galerie der Spiegel, Cologne
1968	Galerie der Spiegel, Cologne
1969	Galerie Thomas, Munich
	Gegenverkehr, Zentrum für Aktuelle Kunst, Aachen, West Germany
	Staatliche Kunsthalle, Baden-Baden, West Germany
1970	Galerie im Zimmertheater, Tübingen (with Hans Baschang)
	Württembergischer Kunstverein, Stuttgart
	Galerie Lauter, Mannheim
	Galerie Regio, Lorrach, West Germany
	Galerie der Spiegel, Cologne
1971	Neue Galerie, Baden-Baden, West Germany
	Galerie Stangl, Munich
1972	Kunsthalle, Darmstadt
	Westfalischer Kunstverein, Münster, West Germany
	Kunsthalle, Bielefeld, West Germany
	Städtischer Kunstpavillon, Soest, West Germany
	Frankfurter Kunstverein, Frankfurt
	Galerie Centro, Oldenburg, West Germany
1973	Galerie der Spiegel, Cologne
	Galerie Regio, Basle
	Galerie Schneider, Karlsruhe
	Städtische Galerie, Nordhorn, West Germany
1974	Bottcherstrasse, Bremen
	Galerie der Spiegel, Cologne
1976	Galerie Centro, Oldenburg, West Germany
	Galerie der Spiegel, Cologne
	Galerie am Promenadeplatz, Munich
1977	Galerie am Promenadeplatz, Munich
1978	Galerie am Promenedeplatz, in Weissadlergasse, Frankfurt

	Studio F, Ulm, West Germany
	German Pavillon, at the *Biennale*, Venice
	Galerie am Promenadeplatz, Munich
	Krutzraedthuis, Sittard, Netherlands
1979	Galerie am Promenadeplatz, Munich
1980	Galerie der Spiegel, Cologne
1981	Galerie Dibbert, West Berlin
	Galerie am Promenadeplatz, Munich
1982	Galerie Ha Jo Muller, Cologne
1983	Galerie Heinz Herzer, Munich
	Artothek, Cologne
1984	Badischer Kunstverein, Karlsruhe
1985	Galerie Heinz Herzer, Munich

Selected Group Exhibitions:

1967	*Wege 67*, Museum am Ostwall, Dortmund
	5th Biennale de Paris, Musée d'Art Moderne de la Ville, Paris
1968	*Krieg/Kriwet/Mavignier/Vostell*, Kunst und Museumverein, Wuppertal, West Germany
1970	*3rd Internationale der Zeichnung*, Mathildenhohe, Darmstadt
1971	*Aktiva '71*, Munich
1977	*Documenta 6*, Museum Fridericianum, Kassel, West Germany
1979	*Schlaglichter*, Rheinisches Landesmuseum, Bonn
1981	*Hartmann/Krieg/Kristiansen/Vogt*, Von der Heydt-Museum, Wuppertal, West Germany
1982	*Ansichten-Struckturen-Horizonte: Landschaften*, Bundeskanzleramt, Bonn
1983	*8 in Koln*, Kunstverein, Cologne

Collections:

Kunsthalle, Bielefeld, West Germany; Sammiung Schulza-Vellinghausen, Ruhr-Universitat, Bochum, West Germany; Städtisches Kunstmuseum, Bonn; Museum am Ostwall, Dortmund; Kunsthalle, Hamburg; Städtische Kunsthalle, Mannheim; Staatsgalerie Moderner Kunst, Munich; Staatsgalerie, Stuttgart; Von der Heydt Museum, Wuppertal, West Germany; Museum des 20. Jahrhunderts, Vienna.

Publications:

On KRIEG: books—*Tage, Tage, Jahre* by Marie Luise Kaschnitz, Frankfurt 1968; *Dieter Krieg*, exhibition catalogue, with text by Klaus Honnef, Aachen, West Germany 1969;

Dieter Krieg: *O.T.*, 1982

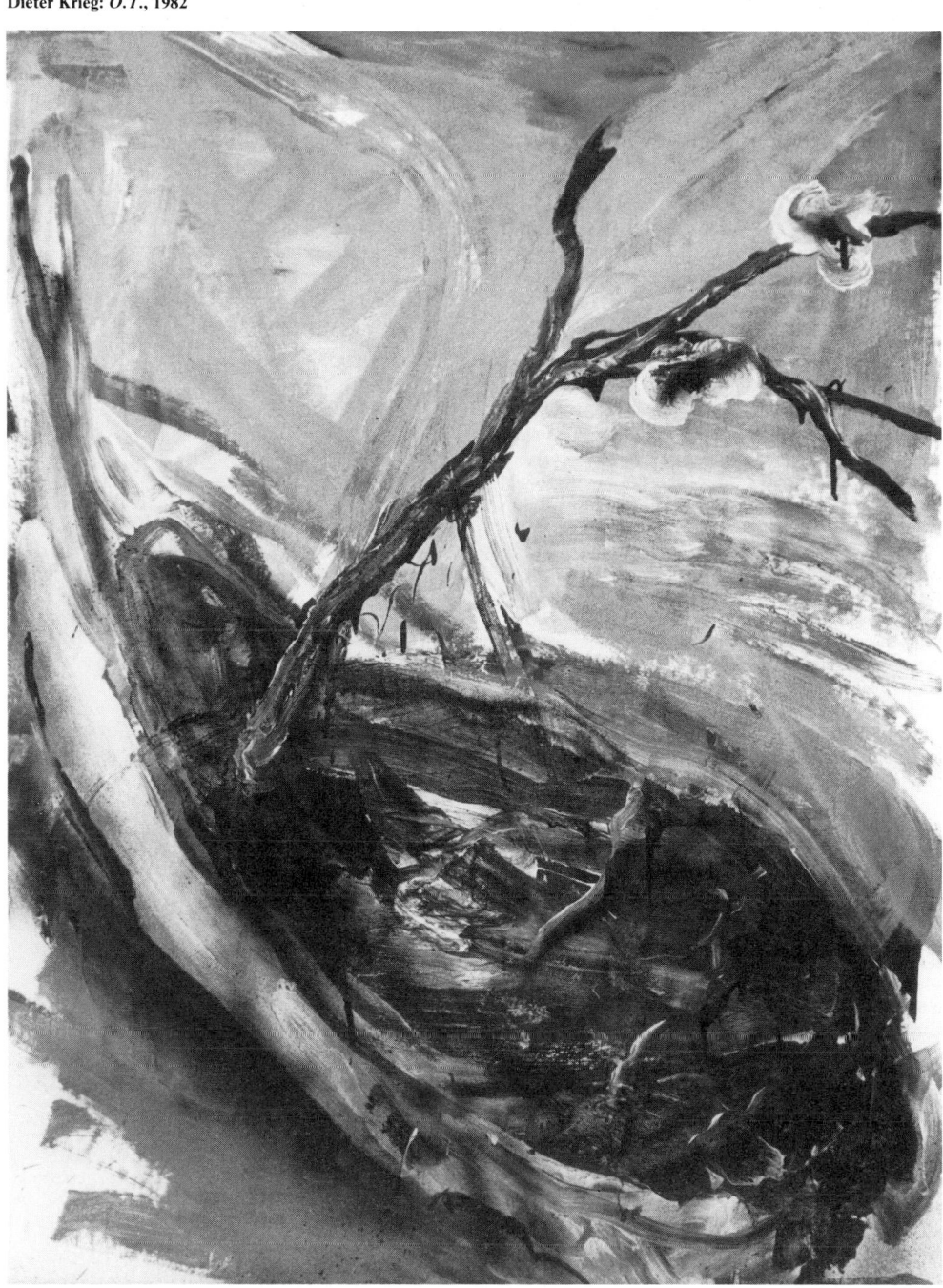

Deutsche Kunst—eine neue Generation by Rolf-Günter Dienst, Cologne 1970; *Deutsche Kunst der 60er Jahre* by Juiane Roh, Munich 1971; *Neue Formen des Realismus* by Peter Sager, Cologne 1973; *Deutsche Malerei nach 1945* by Weiland Schmied, Frankfurt 1974; *Biennale di Venezia 1978: Dieter Krieg,* exhibition catalogue, with texts by Klaus Gallwitz, Jürgen Morschel and Volker Klinnius, Cologne 1978; *Hartmann/Krieg/Kristiansen/Vogt: 4 beitrage zur neuen malerei,* exhibition catalogue, with text by Günter Aust, Wuppertal, West Germany 1981; *Dieter Krieg,* exhibition catalogue with essays by Hans Gunter Wachtmann and Andreas Vowinckel, Karlsruhe 1984.

In Dieter Krieg's painting the two factors which strike one straight away are permanent repetition and the increasing incorporation of illusionist techniques into the artistic calculation. Both features arise from Krieg's particular artistic methodology.

On the first point: Krieg's artistic activity is accomplished in stages, these being indicated by a series of identical picture themes. Thus ensued the quasi-experimental "Handchen" ("Little Hand") pictures of 1966, works which bring to the fore feet, reclining figures, cups, female acrobats, bandaged faces, trousers, little pipes, poles, troughs or boxes. In deciding on a serial treatment of different subject areas lies a fundamental principle.

Krieg, you see, subjects the chosen motif to a lengthy and exhaustive artistic test. He explores it again and again for its artistic load-bearing capacity and does not assimilate in this way until this has been thoroughly done. Moreover, continual repetition helps him to get the greatest possible distance from the projected content of the pictures so that he can formulate it more and more without emotional involvement.

And each time Krieg reaches the end of a series he literally paints the repeated picture-motif away. I mean this literally, for he overpaints it until only its rudiments are left visible. These he incorporates once more into the pictorial context, and makes it come to fruition in the overall effect.

Krieg, in common with many painters of his generation, abandons the picture, in the sense of an individual picture, in favour of a picture-series. This means that his artistic ideas are only manifested in a limited way in a single picture, that clarity about them is rather to be obtained via the combination of various different individual pictures. That way the individual picture retains, in another manner than in a picture-series, the definite movements afterwards as it did before its autonomy.

To that extent Krieg's picture sequences show no apparent consistency, particularly as the changes from picture to picture are extremely small, yet they demonstrate the process of a tenacious kinship with the most banal aspects of reality. In the forefront there stands the individual striving of an artist-personality to grasp reality by graphic means; and to convey objectivity the individual statement of reality, which pretends nothing. Hence also the insertion of handwritten interpolations, which have an entirely private character, and whose decoding delivers no essential information whatever. Hence also the insertion of very pictorial passages, which do not disown the touch of the painter's hand.

With regard to the second point: Krieg's ever more apparent penchant for illusionist effects invalidates subjective pretensions. However, in reality, it serves to emphasize them. Even in the "pole" paintings, in which thin metallic-looking sticks cast shadows, and produce a vague sense of spaciousness, there seems to be an attempt to express the objective reproduction of a cross-section of reality. On the other hand, in the "tank" and "box" pictures, illusionist techniques as such are brought conspicuously to the fore.

Whilst in the earlier works an illusionistic configuration is articulated within the compass of the picture, the picture consequently acting as a kind of "window" as it does in traditional naturalistic painting, in the more recent of the picture-series it is determined according to the proportions of the motif portrayed. Pictorial motive and creative representation show an identical frame; creative motive is not presented in a previously-determined frame. The pictorial frame has lost its function, the pictures have taken on the form of objects. This does not finally signalise its particular form of presentation: Krieg's works do not hang on walls, they stand on the floor, and lean against the wall. For all that, it is not a question of free-standing objects but of pictures which assert their objectness. Therewith Krieg to a certain extent carries illusionism to extremes, and distils from the exaggeration the admission of a consciously illusionistic procedure of production.

Krieg plays with the observer's ingrained expectations, and upsets them. While leading him directly to the illusionism of his work, he disconcerts also, and contrives a complex reflection about the relationship of reality and graphic representations of reality.

Just as Krieg reduces the formal content-factors to small specimens of elements, so also he represses their colourfulness. Certainly it is noticeable that a white, shading towards grey, predominates in his work, but it is almost always in juxtaposition with further, scarcely less strong colours. Whilst, however, in the "trouser" pictures white backgrounds and rich blue-grey colourful configurations confront one another, the chromatic opposition in the "stick" and "tank" pictures disappears in favour of an almost grey-on-grey constellation. The "box" pictures even use the indistinct colouring of unprimed canvas.

Krieg's manipulation of colour exerts a characteristic fascination. A disconcerting one. White diffuses a clinical, antiseptic atmosphere. It shimmers out in numerous gradations of colour, because Krieg does not camouflage his overpainting—he simply lets it stand; meanwhile, the grey brings about a metallically diffuse impression.

—Klaus Honnef

KRIESCHE, Richard.

Austrian. Born in Vienna, 28 October 1940. Studied at the Fine Arts Academy, Vienna, 1958–63. Served in the Austrian Army, 1965–66. Married Gerlinde Well in 1969; daughters: Sarah and Rosa. Artist, working with videotapes and performances, Graz, since 1971. Instructor, Technical School, Graz, since 1963. Art Director, Audio-Visual Centre, Graz, 1977–79; Founder, Kulturdata centre, Graz, 1984. Recipient: DAAD Fellowship, West Berlin, 1983; Research Grant, Massachusetts Institute of Technology, Cambridge, 1985–86. Address: Trautmansdorffgasse 1, 8010 Graz, Austria.

Individual Exhibitions:

1968	Forum Stadtpark, Graz
1970	Galerie im Griechenbeisl, Graz
1971	Sigi Krauss Gallery, London
1972	Galerie im Taxispalais, Innsbruck
1973	Neue Galerie, Graz
1975	Kölnischer Kunstverein, Cologne
	Galerie Stampa, Basle
1976	Galerie Nächst St. Stephan, Vienna
1977	Archivio Storico delle Arti Contemporanee, Venice
1980	Modern Art Galerie, Vienna
	Galerie Dr. Schurr, Stuttgart
1981	Hartmannsdorf, Austria
	Bob Adrian/Peter Hoffmann/Richard Kriesche, Galerija Suvremene Umjetnosti, Zagreb
1982	Kunsthaus, Zurich
	Forum Stadtpark, Graz
1983	Gedachtniskirche, West Berlin
1985	Massachusetts Institute of Technology, Cambridge
1987	Opera-Graz, Graz

Selected Group Exhibitions:

1971	*Situation Concepts*, Galerie Nächst St. Stephan, Vienna
2977	*Documenta 6*, Museum Fridericianum, Kassel, West Germany
1978	*Polar Crossing*, Los Angeles Institute of Contemporary Art
1981	*On Sculpture*, Museum im Lenbachhaus, Munich
1982	*Technology, Art and Advertising*, Hayden Gallery, Massachusetts Institute of Technology, Cambridge
1983	*Kunst und Photographie*, Nationalgalerie, West Berlin
1984	*Arte Austriacca 1960–84*, Galleria d'Arte Moderna, Bologna, Italy
1985	*Brainwork*, Municipal Art Gallery, Los Angeles
1986	*42nd Biennale*, Venice
1987	*Documenta 8*, Museum Fridericianum, Kassel, West Germany

Richard Kriesche: Video Performance at the Galerie im Taxispalais, Innsbruck, 1972

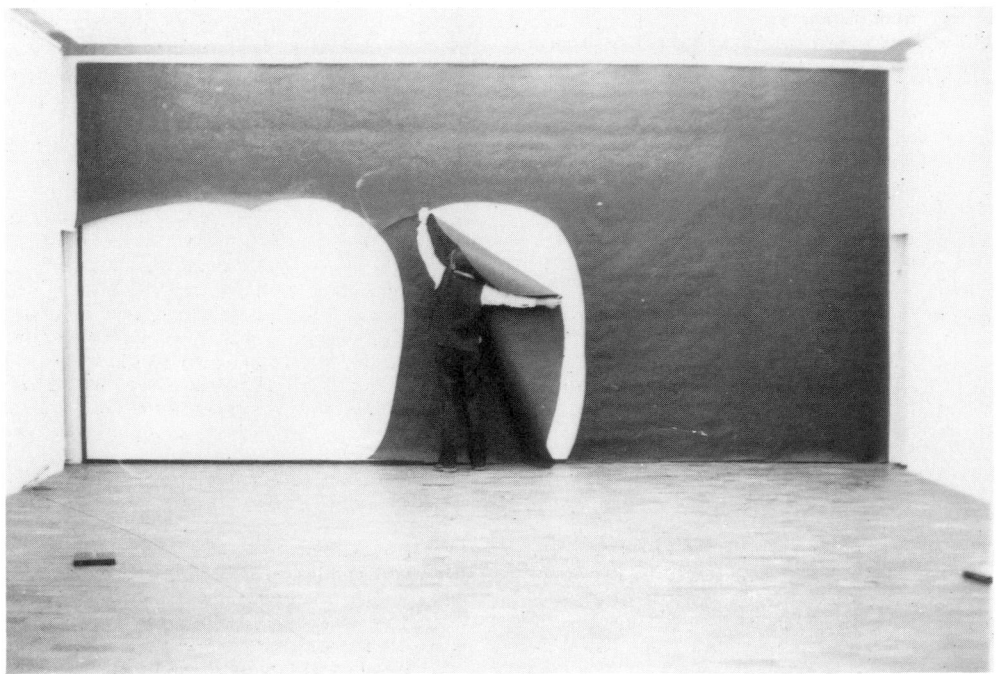

Collections:

Neue Galerie, Graz; Museum des 20. Jahrhunderts, Vienna; Kunsthalle, Hamburg.

Publications:

By KRIESCHE: books—*Life-video-sound-polaroid installation*, Graz 1973; *Video End, Graz Konzepte Theorien und Dokumente Osterreichischer Videoproduktionen*, Graz 1977; *Wirklichkeit gegen Wirklichkeit*, Kassel, West Germany 1977; *Kulturinitiative Weiz I*, Weiz 1977; *Kulturinitiative Weiz II*, Weiz 1978; *Kulturinitiative Bruck*, Bruck 1978; *Art, Artist and the Media*, Graz 1978; *Kinderfreundliches Kranzenzimmer*, Graz 1979; *Kunst Mikrokunst Makrokunst*, Graz and Zagreb 1981; *Humane Skulpturen*, Graz 1981.

On KRIESCHE: books—*Situation Concepts*, exhibition catalogue, Vienna 1971; *Bob Adrian/Peter Hoffmann/Richard Kriesche*, exhibition catalogue, Zagreb 1981; *Brainwork: Artificial Intelligence in the Arts*, exhibition catalogue, Los Angeles 1985.

*   *   *

The determining question for me is the question for the signification of an artist. If there are besides the important global issues (e.g., Peace) any others—the way of survival—then art is nothing else but a strategy for survival. The question remains: How does "survival strategy" look at any given moment? What is the task of the artist? What is the task of art? To me, it is solely a question of society needing new forms and languages to get through, over, under its barriers to solve its "home-made" contradictions. Specifically, in relation to the artist, it means that he himself has to overcome these barriers, has to get through the contradictions, and find an authentic formulation. It means that the artist has to abandon the secure and ritualized conditions of art-dialogue and involve himself in the risks of life-dialogue—to become again a *real* artist.

I am interested in farmers (project: humane skulpturen), prisoners (project: Karlau prison), small towns with a heavy provincialism (project: Weiz and Bruck), children in hospitals (project: Kinderfreundliches krankenzimmer), strikes (project: Dustmen's strike, London), etc., with a view to finding or developing a social language for learning forms for social living in and with the given reality, and for overcoming that reality. The penetration of the second—the media reality—counts in this as well. And so I am interested in 1 + 1 = 3, which I demonstrated electronically at the *Basle Art Fair*, or in "Technology as a Moral of the Ruling Class," which I have again demonstrated in Basle, at Galerie Stampa.

From the dialectics of both realities, my concern is to develop media-relevant references out of life, and life-relevance out of the media. I guess that's what "artworking" is about.

—Richard Kriesche

KRUGER, Barbara.

American. Born in Newark, New Jersey, 26 January 1945. Studied at Syracuse University, New York; Parsons School of Design, New York; School of Visual Arts, New York. Independent artist/photographer, New York, since 1972. Visiting Artist, California Institute of Art, Valencia; Art Institute of Chicago; University of California, Berkeley. Recipient: Creative Artists Public Service Grant, New York, 1976; National Endowment for the Arts Grant, Washington, D. C., 1983. Agents: Rhona Hoffman Gallery, 215 West Superior Street, Chicago, Illinois 60610; Larry Gagosian Gallery, 510 North Robertson Boulevard, Los Angeles, California 90048; Galerie Crousel-Robelin, 40 rue Quincampoix, 75004 Paris, France. Address: 55 Leonard Street, New York, New York 10013, U. S. A.

Individual Exhibitions:

1974	Artists' Space, New York
1975	Fischbach Gallery, New York
1976	John Doyle Gallery, Chicago
1979	Franklin Furnace, New York
	Printed Matter Window, New York
1980	Project Studio One, Long Island City, New York
1982	Larry Gagosian Gallery, Los Angeles
	Hallwalls Gallery, Buffalo, New York
1983	Annina Nosei Gallery, New york
	Galerie Chantal Crousel, Paris
	Institute of Contemporary Arts, London
1984	Le Nouveau Musee, Lyon-Villeurbanne, France
	Galerie Crousel-Hussenot, Paris
	Kunsthalle, Basle (with Jenny Holzer)
1985	Los Angeles County Museum of Art
1987	Galerie Monika Spruth, Cologne

Selected Group Exhibitions:

1973	*Whitney Biennial*, Whitney Museum, New York (and 1983)
1978	*False Face*, Name Gallery, Chicago
1980	*Four Different Photographers*, Padiglione d'Arte Contemporanea, Milan
1981	*19 Emergent Americans*, Guggenheim Museum, New York
1982	*Documenta 7*, Museum Fridericianum, Kassel, West Germany
1983	*The Revolutionary Power of Women's Laughter*, Protetch McNeill Gallery, New York

Publications:

By KRUGER: books—*Picture/Readings*, New York 1978; *No Progress in Pleasure*, New York 1982; *Beauty and Critique*, New York 1983; film—*Next to Nothing*, with Jane Weinstock, 1983.

On KRUGER: books—*Four Different Photographers*, exhibition catalogue with essay by Carol Squiers, Milan 1980; *19 Emergent Americans*, exhibition catalogue with text by Peter Frank, New York 1981; *Inespressionismo Americano*, exhibition catalogue with essay by Ingrid Sischy, Genoa 1981; *The Revolutionary Power of Women's Laughter*, exhibition catalogue with essay by Joanna Isaak, New York 1983.

*   *   *

Barbara Kruger is among those artists who seek filiation with other forms of expression for art. She employs written texts and images which are already functioning in public consciousness. She creates large tabloids with black-and-white women's, sometimes children's, faces and clashes them with short inscriptions running across the whole plate. Photographs are appropriated from posters, advertisements and various media images, that is, representations which have been already elaborated upon and many a time reproduced, so that it is impossible to detect the "original". What is more, in this procedure a traditional division into the original and a replica becomes immaterial; just as futile is the search for authorship of individual motifs. Instead, we have here a popular lexicon of images of contemporary American culture, loaded with images multiplicated by the media.

The same goes for the texts used by Kruger: they are fragments of various sentences, opinions, convictions and truisms functioning in public opinion, which are shaped not by different people in an individual intellectual effort but—like images—by the media (press, television, advertisements as well as film). Therefore, the texts also have no authors; they are replicas of replicas.

Therefore, Barbara Kruger's art refers to public space, but it draws its energy from subversion applied by the authoress towards this space. The tabloids make us realize that for a long time we have been surrounded with images and phrases that are used by "all". And we have grown accustomed to using them because we could no longer live and communicate otherwise. The inscription on one of the works: "We are obliged to steal language" (1980) tells us something about our condition in the world and about coercion we undergo while constructing our sentences, which we consider to be our own. We appropriate both sentences and images. In this world the identity of our "ego" is dispersed; it is everywhere and nowhere. Kruger's works tell us that we are not free in our thinking and perception, that it is not us at all; we live and express ourselves in a world staged by others and we do not know who the authors of this staging are.

However, Kruger not only undermines our consciousness of self; She also makes a subversion as regards the codes she appropriates. She does not use whole images but their fragments and combines them in such a way that they lose their original context. She does the same to the fragments of texts. She emulates the methods applied by the media themselves, which feed us only with fragments of unknown wholes. Therefore, she uses towards them the rule of mimesis in order to disclose their manipulations all the more effectively.

Image-and-text clashes created by Kruger have a strong feminist aspect; they refer to the situation of women in the men's world. In this world an individual appearance of a woman becomes obliterated in favour of "ideal" looks, in favour of a convention recorded by the media and served by advertisements. The authoress shows how all of us fall victim to a double falsification. Since we not only accept artificiality of the convention as the image of nature, but we fail to notice that the staging of a women's image is a doing of the men's world, which managed to impose this image on women as a binding one, what's more—as the one they desire. Kruger uses the tempting force of the advertisement image to disclose the fallacy of our identification with it. She refers to the trait so strongly functioning in the American culture to undermine its apparent rationality and hit the essence of power with which these images grasp public imagination.

Kruger's art is a plot against plots: against manipulations of the media and against the world subject to patriarchal organization. The authoress's plotting includes also visual forcefulness of her art, emulating graphic aggressiveness of American popular culture. This is an additional blow at the mechanisms of power exercised by this culture.

The destructive perception reaches even deeper. Destroying the primary context of appropriated images and texts, shifting their motifs in space and time, she pushes the viewer into a state of frustrating uncertainty. The viewer is not able to detect the original meaning of these motifs, although they are known to him in a way; he does not know what is the order of thinking behind it. The tension between what is known and what is unclear is a great force in Kruger's works. These works tell us that no image and no text have a permanent place in culture any longer, that points of view have become dispersed, that we have to live among contradicting categories and discrete choices, that motifs of the world become more and more illegible. Finally, that we can no longer expect either an ultimate code or an ultimate explanation. We gradually become—as Roland Barthes' "author"—nomads among images and meanings, none of which is privileged. And this is our new place in culture, the only one we can be sure of.

Barbara Kruger's art (both tabloids and books) strikes with the gravity of problems tackled by the authoress and the vastness of reflections aroused by these problems. This makes her one of the most important artists of the 1980s.

—Alicja Kepinska

KRUSHENICK, Nicholas.

American. Born in New York City, 31 May 1929. Educated at Dewitt Clinton High School, Bronx, New York, 1945–47; studied at Art Students League, New

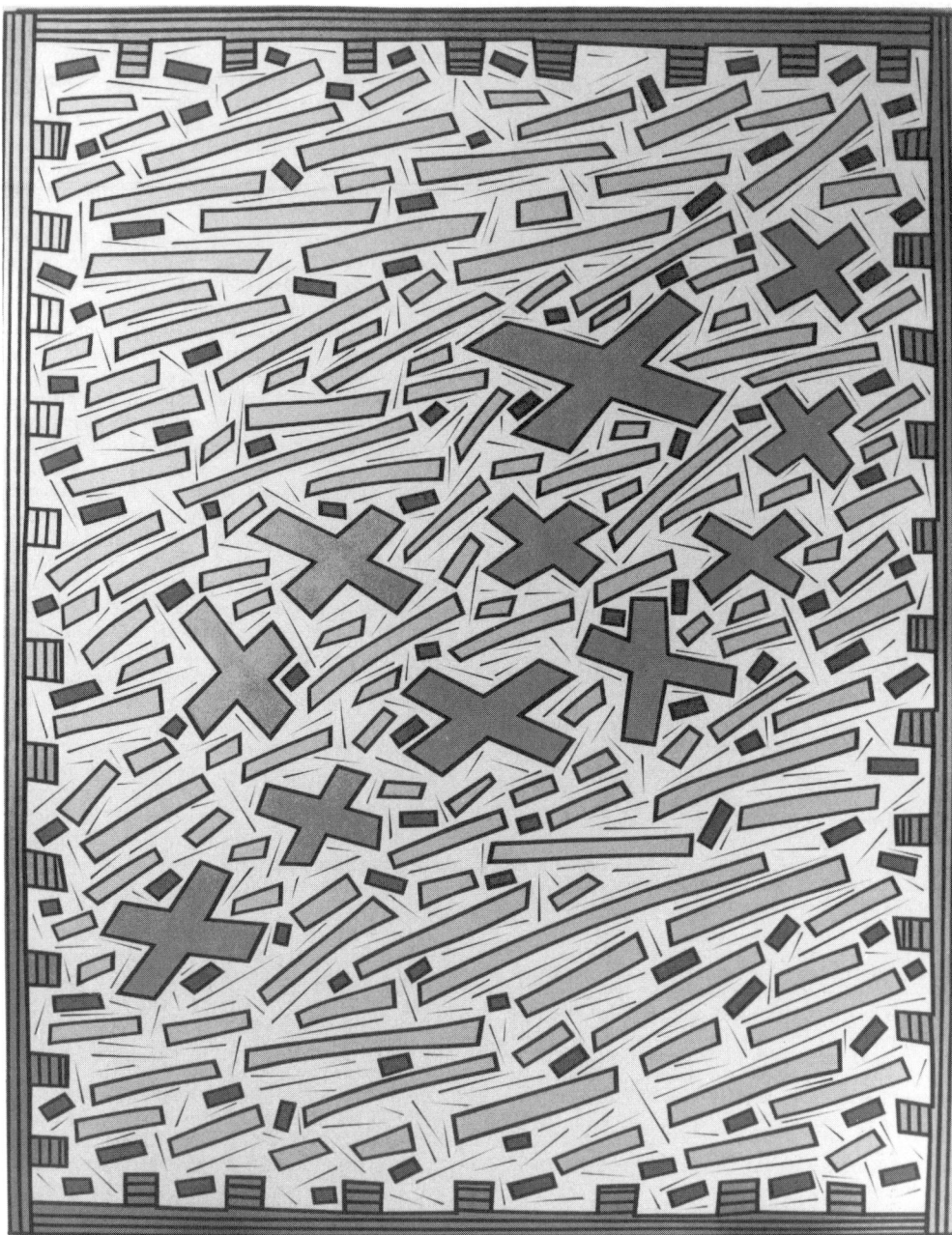

Nicholas Krushenick: *Second Glance*, 1986

York, 1948–50, Hans Hofmann School of Fine Arts, New York, 1950–51. Served in United States Army, 1947–48. Married Julia Greenfield in 1951; son: Shawn. Painter. Co-Founder of Brata Gallery, New York, 1958–61. Visiting Artist/Critic: School of Visual Arts, New York, 1965; Minneapolis School of Art, 1967; Cooper Union, New York, 1967–69; University of Wisconsin, 1968; Yale University, 1969, 1970; Cornell University, New York, 1970; Ball State University, Indiana, 1971; Lehmann College, New York, 1972; California State University, Long Beach, 1973; University of Alabama, 1973; St. Cloud State University, Minnesota, 1973; University of California, Berkeley, 1973, 1974; Ohio State University, 1974; University of Washington, 1974; California State College, San Bernardino, 1975; University of North Carolina, 1975; University of Kentucky, 1976; University of Delaware, 1976–77; Memphis Art Academy, 1978; Corcoran School of Art, Washington, D. C., 1978; Virginia Commonwealth University, 1982; Syracuse University, New York, 1982; Wilkes College, Pennsylvania, 1984. Assistant Professor, University of Maryland, College Park, since 1977. Recipient: Longview Foundation Award, 1962; Tamarind Fellowship, Los Angeles, 1965; Guggenheim Fellowship, 1967. Address: 140 Grand Street, New York, New York 10013, U.S.A.

Individual Exhibitions:

1957   Camino Gallery New York
1958   Brata Gallery, New York
1960   Brata Gallery, New York
1962   Graham Gallery, New York
1964   Graham Gallery, New York
1965   Fischbach Gallery, New York
1966   Galerie Muller, Stuttgart
1967   Galerie Sonnabend, Paris
       Pace Gallery, New York
       Franklin Siden Gallery, Detroit
       Galerie Nächst St. Stephan, Vienna
1968   Walker Art Center, Minneapolis (retrospective)
       Galerie Der Spiegel, Cologne
1969   Pace Gallery, New York
       Dartmouth College, Hanover, New hampshire
       Harcus-Krakow Gallery, Boston
       Galerie René Ziegler, Zurich
1970   University of South Florida, Tampa
       Galerie René Ziegler, Zurich
1971   Galerie Beyeler, Basel
1972   Lehman College, New York
       Galerie Kestner-Gesellschaft, Hannover
       Pace Gallery, New York
1973   Galerie Denise René-Hans Mayer, Dusseldorf
       University of Alabama, Birmingham

       Jack Glenn Gallery, Corona del Mar, California
       California State College, Long Beach
1974   ADI Gallery, San Francisco
       Portland Center for the Visual Arts, Oregon
       Henry Gallery, University of Washington, Seattle
       Reed College, Portland, Oregon
1975   Foster-White Gallery, Seattle
       California State University, San Bernardino
1976   Alfred University, New York
       University of Kentucky, Lexington
1977   Bucknell University, Lewisburg, Pennsylvania
       Newport Art Association, Rhode Island
1978   Pyramid Gallery, Washington
       Hokin Gallery, Chicago
       Elizabeth Weiner Gallery, New york
1979   Metropolitan Museum of Miami, Florida
1981   Aldrich Museum, Ridgefield, Connecticut
       Gallery K, Washington, D. C.
       Carnegie Mellon University, Piitsburgh
1982   Kaber Gallery, New York
       River Gallery, Westport, Connecticut
       Medici-Berenson Gallery, Miami, Florida
1984   18th Street Gallery, Santa Monica, California

Selected Group Exhibitions:

1963   *Drawing Exhibition*, Museum of Modern Art, New York
1964   *Post-Painterly Abstraction*, Los Angeles County Museum of Art (toured the United States and Canada)
1966   *Systemic Painting*, Guggenheim Museum, New York
1968   *Documenta 4*, Kassel, West Germany
1973   *Biennial*, Whitney Museum, New York
1978   *Homage to Hans Hofmann*, Metropolitan Museum of Art, New York
1983   *Art and Dance*, New York State University, Purchase
1985   *Exuberant Abstraction*, 100 Church Street, New York
1986   *Embellishment of the Statue of Liberty*, Cooper-Hewitt Museum, New York
1987   *Color Pure and Simple*, Stamford Museum, Connecticut

Collections:

Metropolitan Museum of Art, New York; Museum of Modern Art, New York; Whitney Museum, New York; Albright-Knox Art Gallery, Buffalo, New York; Walker Art Center, Minneapolis; Museum of Fine Arts, Dallas; Los Angeles County Museum of Art; Stedelijk Museum, Amsterdam; Folkwang Museum, Essen; Staatsgalerie, Stuttgart.

Publications:

By KRUSHENICK: article—statement in *Art Now* (New York), June 1970.

On KRUSHENICK: articles—"New York Letter" by Barbara Rose in *Art International* (Lugano, Switzerland), Summer 1964; review by Vivien Raynor in *Arts* (New York), May 1965; review by Sue Greene in *Art Voices* (New York), Spring 1965; "New York Letter" by Lucy Lippard in *Art International* (Lugano, Switzerland), September 1965; "Krushenick's Blazing Blazons" by John Perreault in *Artnews* (New York), March 1967; review by T. Mussman in *Arts* (New York), April 1967; review by J. Mellow in *Art International* (Lugano, Switzerland), May 1967; "Krushenick" by Dean Swanson, in *Art International* (Lugano, Switzerland) April 1968; "Krushenick's Cultural Revelations" by Gregory Battcock, in *Arts* (New York), April 1969; "The Artist Speaks" by Connie Robbins, in *Art in America* (New york), May 1969; "Nicholas Krushenick: New Paintings" by Connie Robbins in *Arts* (New York), December 1975.

The impact of Nicholas Krushenick's works is bold, brassy and belligerent. The imagery, very much his own invention, a kind of illegitimate offspring of pop and non-figuration, is a kind of rich pattern well defined by thick black outline, generally—but not always—against a plain primary background of scarlet, or yellow or ultramarine. There is nothing fussy about shapes or composition. The paint lies flat and unvaried. Some of the pictures have the flash reaction of op art upon the retina, but this is rendered by colour contrast, not by any mixed media tricks.

The paintings have names. Their titles usually relate to sociological phenomena—"Drop Out," "Moon Maid," "King Kong", "Malibu" and the like, but they are not without undertones that suggest an industrial world, an ambiance of technology. In a sense they are crude symbols, albeit expertly painted, of subliminal gossip. The pictures mean much more than their titles.

These are the paintings of Krushenick—a voice of contemporary times—but he also brings the same system of updated heraldry to his papier-collés and his graphics.

As one of the New York invaders, he has been able to exhibit in most of the European art centres and, of course, Tokyo. Unlike some of his compatriots of this genre, he has been able to relegate geometry to a back seat. The immediate impression is one of ineluctable flow in which the curvilinear takes precedence over the straight line. His shapes are fat, female and gaudy, but this first reaction—given time to mellow, as it should be—grows into an awareness that Krushenick has found a new and exciting way of turning random pattern into well organized programme.
—Sheldon Williams

KUDO, Tetsumi.

Japanese. Born in Osaka, 23 February 1935. Educated at Tokyo University, 1954–58, diploma in art 1958. Married Hiroko Kurihara in 1959. Taught in private art school for children, Tokyo, 1955–58. Independent artist, producing objects and performances, since 1958: has lived and worked in Paris since 1962. Recipient: Grand Prix, *International Young Artists Exhibition*, Tokyo, 1962; Grand Prix, *Festival International de la Peinture*, Cagnes, 1976; Special Citation, *Bienal*, Sao Paulo, 1977. Address: 30 rue Erard, Boite no. 57, 75012 Paris, France.

Individual Exhibitions:

1965	*Rien n'est laissé au hasard*, Galerie J, Paris
1966	Galerie 20, Amsterdam
	Galerie Thelen, Essen
1967	Galerie Mathias Fels, Paris
1968	Galerie Mickery, Amsterdam
1970	*Document 70*, Kunsthalle, Dusseldorf
1972	Stedelijk Museum, Amsterdam
1973	Galerie Beaubourg, Paris
	Galerie Mathias Fels, Paris
1975	Galleria Valsecchi, Milan
1977	Galerie Beaubourg, Paris
	Galerie Vallois, Paris
1978	Galerie Wunderland, Berlin
	Galerie Bellechasse, Paris
1979	Galerie Bellechasse, Paris
1981	Galerie Jöllenbeck, Cologne
	Sogetsu Museum, Tokyo
1982	UNAC, Tokyo
	Gallery 16, Tokyo
	Takagi Gallery, Nagoya, Japan
1983	Tenmaya Hall, Okayama, Japan
	Tamako Gallery, Tokyo
1984	Space Niki, Tokyo
	Shibuya Parco, Tokyo
	Espace Japon, Paris
1985	M. Gallery, Tokyo
	Galerie Brownstone, Paris
1986	Hirosaki City Museum, Japan
	Galerie Brownstone, Paris
	Galerie Claude Samuel, Paris

Selected performances: *Harakiri of Humanism* and *Bottled Humanism*, at the *Biennale*, Paris, 1963; *Instant Sperm*, Centre Americain d'Artistes, Paris, 1964; *For Nostalgic Purposes* and *For Your Living Room*, Musée d'Art Moderne, Paris, 1966; *Quiet Event*, Kassel, West Germany 1968; *Your Portrait*, Kunsthalle, Cologne, 1970; *Your Portrait in the Pollution*, at the *Bienal*, São Paulo, 1977; *Meditation-Buddha*, Theatre Diogenes and Galerie Wunderland, Berlin, 1978; *La Lumière non Perdue*, Centre Georges Pompidou, Paris. 1980; *Le Trou noir sacré*, Espace Japon, Paris, 1984.

Selected Group Exhibitions

1963	*Biennale*, Paris

Tetsumi Kudo: *Votre Portrait—Bonheur*, 1975

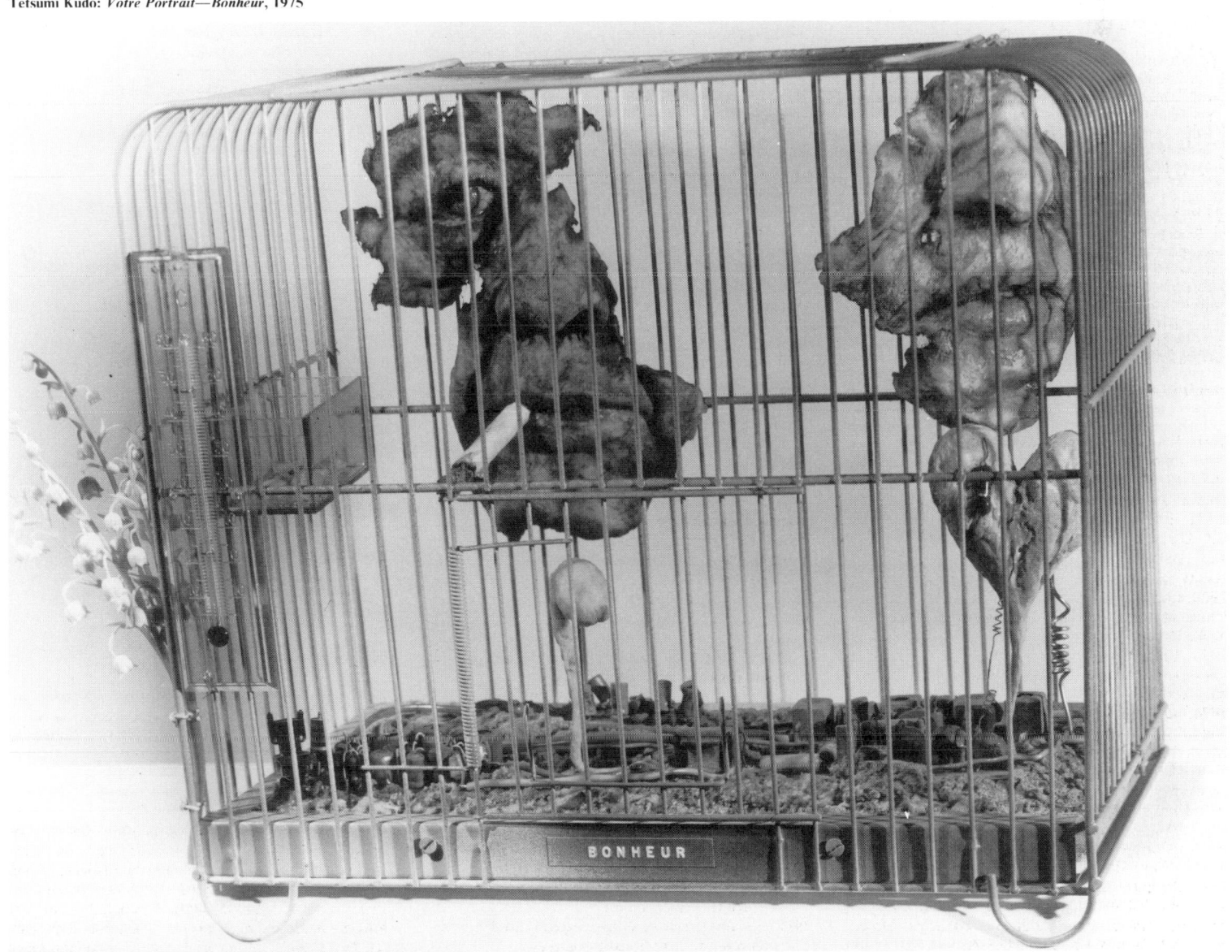

1965	*Les Objecteurs*, Paris
1970	*Happening & Fluxus*, Kunstverein, Cologne
1974	*Japan: Past and Present*, Kunsthalle, Dusseldorf
1976	*Boîtes*, Musée d'Art Moderne, Paris
1979	*Tendances de l'Art en France 1968-1979*, Musée d'Art Moderne, Paris
1981	*Contemporary Art of Japan—Year 1960*, National Museum of Modern Art, Tokyo
1984	*Electra*, Musée d'Art Moderne de la Ville, Paris
1985	*Reconstruction: Avant-Garde Art in Japan 1945-65*, Museum of Modern Art, Oxford
1986	*Japon des Avant-Gardes*, Centre Georges Pompidou, Paris

Collections:

Stedelijk Museum, Amsterdam; Centre Georges Pompidou, Paris; Musée d'Art Contemporain, Ghent, Belgium; Louisiana Museum, Humlebaek, Denmark; Museum des 20 Jahrhunderts, Vienna; Hara Museum, Tokyo; Sogetsu Museum, Tokyo; Musée d'Art Moderne de la Ville de Paris; Musée Cantini, Marseille; Tokyo Metropolitan Art Museum.

Publications:

By KUDO: books—*Pollution-cultivation-nouvelle ecologie*, exhibition catalogue, Amsterdam 1971; *La Lumière non perdue*, Paris 1980; *Satori*, exhibition catalogue, Tokyo 1981; articles—"Kudo: Dialogue et monologue", interview, with Ichiro Haryu, in *Opus International* (Paris), no. 47, 1973; "Boîte" and "Mythologies quotidiennes" in *Info Artitudes* (Paris), no. 15, 1977; "Meditation-Buddha in Berlin" in DAAD catalogue, Berlin 1978; films—*Votre Portrait*, with Van Zylen, 1967; *Monument of Metamorphosis*, 1969/70; *La Vase* by Ionesco, 1970; video—*Cérémonie de Kudo*, Berlin 1978.

On KUDO: books—*Tetsumi Kudo: Rien n'est laissé au hasard*, exhibition catalogue, by Pierre Restany, Paris 1965; *Tetsumi Kudo*, exhibition catalogue, by Udo Kultermann, Essen, West Germany 1966; *Assemblage, Environments and Happenings* by Allan Kaprow, New York 1966; *Kudo/Document 70*, exhibition catalogue, by Beeren, Nakahira, Jouffroy, and Gassiot-Talabot, Dusseldorf 1970; *Pop Art & Cie* by Francois Pluchart, Paris 1971; *Art en France une nouvelle generation* by Jean Clair, Paris 1973; *Art Actuel en France* by Anne Tronche and Hervé Gloaguen, Paris 1973; *Contemporary Art in Japan* by Ichiro Haryu, Tokyo 1977; *Kudo*, exhibition catalogue, by Yusuke Nakahara, Tokyo 1981; articles—"Art de détachment" by Shuji Takashina in *Art et Architecture* (Paris), January 1964; "Lettre de Paris" by Otto Hahn in *Art International* (Lugano, Switzerland), May 1965; "Objecteur avec conscience" by Otto Hahn in *L'Express* (Paris), December 1965; "Lettre de Paris—la nouvelle glaciation" by Gérald Gassiot-Talabot in *Art International* (Lugano, Switzerland), February 1966; "Miner la terrain" by Jean-Luc Godard and Alain Jouffroy in *L'Oeil* (Paris), May 1966; "Ils frappent au visage" by Pierre Cabanne in *Arts et Loisirs* (Paris), no. 85, 1967; "We Have Nothing to Lose But Our Brains" by John Lyle in *Art and Artists* (London), August 1969; "Kudo: Monument of Metamorphosis" by Ad Peterson in *Museumjournaal* (Amsterdam), June 1970; "Le monument de Kudo" by Gérald Gassiot-Talabot in *Opus International* (Paris), June 1971; "'Guérillero' du monde artistique" by Jacques Michel in *Le Monde des Arts* (Paris), October 1971; "Kudo: Ionesco et la décomposition de l'homme" by Jean-Clarence Lambert in *Opus International* (Paris), November 1971; "Kudo, ou fragments d'un paradis perdu" by Alain Jouffroy in *Sogetsu* (Tokyo), no. 128, 1980; "Kudo" by Anne Tronche in *25 Ans d'Art en France 1960-1985*, Paris 1985.

In my work I evoke not simply the mechanism, well known in the West, of Japanese society dominated by the Emperor, but rather the organisation which arose from the earliest times among the indigenous populations of the Japanese islands, the structure of an ancient community which was created through the formation of a number of concentric circles, with, at their centre, Mt. Fuji in eruption. It's a question of that same ancestral belief with regard to the spirits of the mountain, of the fox, the snake, the lightning . . . with regard to the structure of the spiritual life which emanates from the magic force of the Black Hole.

Westerners have a tendency to view this style of life based on animism as a total anachronism. And yet this structure continues to exist in Japan, unchanged since the Stone Age, through the era in which the imperial family was pre-eminent, up to our own technological era, the era of the mass media.

It is no doubt difficult for French people to understand the continuance of animism up to the present day. But if one thinks that our purpose is not animism, but the structure itself of this system and the (individual) elements which go to make it up, the research and the debate remain open.

I have attempted to carry out this research by constructing molecular models. I have invented separate curious elements, and in putting them together I have succeeded in making visible that particular Japanese structure which the French find it difficult to imagine. The mysterious energy emanating from Japan is represented by the rotation of circles surrounding the sacred black hole, by the multiplication and friction of these circles, and by the backward and forward motion of these rotating frictions.

I would be most happy to meet you in front of these models.

—Tetsumi Kudo

What characterizes Tetsumi Kudo's art is his intense concern for dismantling and dissolving away the human body and its parts. But it is also characteristic that there is a strong provocativeness inherent in Kudo's work. The year Kudo graduated from Tokyo University of Fine Art, 1958, he put on a performance in which he dumped raw eggs and tomatoes on a cloth spread upon the floor, and ran about over the mixture. This early work was as lucid as it was provocative. After that, Kudo, by making a series of works consisting of so many knots strung out so as to appear to extend into infinity, emphasized anti-human space; at the same time he took up the "philosophy of impotence" and emphasized both man's sexual relationships and collapse. In 1962 he gained the grand prize in the *Young Asian Artists Exhibition*, for one of his knotted string works, and used the prize money to go to France, where he has continued to live.

Kudo's activities after settling in Paris gradually became more radical. His series of happenings starting with "Philosophy of Impotence" in 1962 and "Harakiri of Humanism" in 1963 served to demonstrate by deed Kudo's thoughts, while the "Your Portrait" series depicted human bodies and parts of bodies which had been, it would seem, wrenched asunder, corroded by acid, and enlarged to greater than life size, to become grotesque fragments, barely held together by ragged skin and contraposed with ordinary articles used in daily life.

Provocative as Kudo is, he is not a sculptor. By his persistent orientation to the human body and his concern through his philosophy of impotence for Eros, Kudo's ultimate, underlying concern is for a New Man. The preoccupation with death is in fact a step toward a new life, and the philosophy of impotence is a sign of concern for the whole human being. Kudo cannot but be provocative, considering all this. Such works as "You Are Metamorphosing" and "Souvenir La Mue" or "Hommage à Jeune Génération" show clearly his concern for the twin principles of Life and Death. In 1971 Kudo cooperated in a production of a Eugène Ionesco film *La Boue*, during which he made a plaster replica of Ionesco, which he then cut to pieces to create a series of works.

How might man survive this age of electronics? Through his recent works on the theme "Electrocircuit," Kudo faces this very question. The art and death of man at the same time bespeak a concern for the life and death of art. It must be said that in his grotesque works there is this character.

—Tamon Miki

KUEHN, Gary.

American. Born in Plainfield, New Jersey, in 1939. Studied art history at Drew University, Madison, New Jersey, 1958–62, B. A. 1962, and Rutgers University, New Brunswick, New Jersey, 1962–64. Sculptor: lives and works in New Jersey. Instructor, Fairleigh Dickinson University, New Jersey, 1965; Drew University, 1965–68, School of Visual Arts, New York, 1968, Hochschule für Bildende Kunst, Braunschweig, West Germany, 1970, and Douglass College, Rutgers University, 1971–73; Visiting Lecturer, Princeton University, New Jersey, 1973. Since 1974, Instructor at Rutgers University Graduate School. Recipient: National Council on the Arts grant, 1967; Governor's Purchase Award, New Jersey State Museum, Trenton, 1972; National Endowment for the Arts grant, 1977; Louis Comfort Tiffany Foundation grant, 1977; DAAD Artist's Fellowship, West Berlin, 1979. Agent: Douglas Drake Gallery, Kansas City, Kansas. Address: c/o Douglas Drake Gallery, 4500 State Line, Kansas City, Kansas 66103, U. S. A.

Individual Exhibitions:

1966	*One Man/One Piece*, Douglass College, Rutgers University, New Brunswick, New Jersey
	Bianchini Gallery, New York
1967	Bianchini Gallery, New York
	Kunstverein, Cologne
	Galerie Ricke, at the *Kunstmarkt*, Cologne
	Galerie Ricke, Kassel, West Germany
1968	Galerie Ricke, Kassel, West Germany
	Milwaukee Art Center
	Galleria von Stein, Turin
1969	Fischbach Gallery, New York
	Galerie Ricke, Cologne
1970	Galerie Ernst, Hannover
	Galerie Thomas Borgmann, Cologne
1971	Fischbach Gallery, New York
1972	Galerie Ricke, Cologne
	Paley and Lowe Gallery, New York
1974	Stefanotty Gallery, New York
	Douglas Drake Gallery, Kansas City
	Galerie Carlsson I, Gothenburg, Sweden
1975	Galerie Arnesen, Copenhagen
1976	Landau Gallery, Los Angeles
	Douglas Drake Gallery, Kansas City
	Marion Locks Gallery, Philadelphia
	112 Greene Street Gallery, New york
1977	Galerie Ricke, Cologne
	Galerie Nothelfer, Berlin
	Eugenia Cucalón Gallery, New York
1978	Eugenia Cucalón Gallery, New York
	Drew University, Madison, New Jersey
1979	Eugenia Cucalón Gallery, New York
	Galerie Ricke, Cologne
	Galerie Zellermayer-Lorenzen, Berlin
1980	Württembergischer Kunstverein, Stuttgart
	Amerika Haus, Berlin
	Douglas Drake Gallery, Kansas City, Kansas
1981	Sergio Tosi Gallery, New York
1982	Sergio Tosi Gallery, New York
1986	Galerie Rudolf Zwirner, Cologne
	Galerie Julie Kewenig, Frechen, West Germany

Selected Group Exhibitions:

1967	*Painting and Sculpture Today*, Herron Museum, Indianapolis
1968	*Cool Art Today*, Larry Aldrich Museum, Ridgefield, Connecticut
1969	*Programm I*, Galerie Ricke, Cologne
	When Attitudes Become Form, Kunsthalle, Berne
1970	*Programm II*, Galerie Ricke, Cologne
1973	*Sculptors' Drawings*, Margo Leavin Gallery, Los Angeles
1977	*Documenta*, Kassel, West Germany
1980	*From Reinhardt to Christo*, Allen Memorial Art Museum, Oberlin College, Ohio
1985	*Clearly Stated*, Margarete Roeder Fine Arts, New York

Collections:

New Jersey State Museum, Trenton.

Publications:

On KUEHN: books—*Gary Kuehn*, exhibition catalogue, with text by Andreas Vowinckel, Stuttgart 1980; *From Reinhardt to Christo*, exhibition catalogue, Oberlin, Ohio 1980; articles—"Gary Kuehn's Pressure Principle" by Harris Rosenstein in *Artnews* (New York), December 1969; "Gary Kuehn" by Robert Pincus-Witten in *Artforum* (New York), January 1970; "Gary Kuehn, Fischbach Gallery" by Carter Ratcliff in *Art International* (Lugano, Switzerland), January 1970; "New York Letter" by April Kingsley in *Art International* (Lugano, Switzerland), January 1973; "Gary Kuehn, Stefanotty Gallery" by J. Gilbert-Rolfe in *Artforum* (New York), May 1974.

*   *   *

A feeling of impending doom and implosive psychological compression permeates the 20 years of work, first sculpture and now painting, of Gary Kuehn. What gives his work power is a sense of edgy uncertainty. Will the apocalyptical burdens portended in Kuehn's work actually dominate and terror reign? Or, will the warrior, implied or figuratively represented (the artist and/or the viewer), fend them off? Regardless of unacceptability in the art world, Kuehn has tenaciously persisted in a psychological exploration of the dark and light realms of psyche which has given him both feelings of exuberance and fear. He grapples with "large" metaphysical questions, taking the risk of being considered trite or being superficially understood. The compellingly primary tasks in his life/work have been working toward an integration of his soul, understanding/exploring the archetypes within him, and attempting to comprehend humanity's place in the universe. Formal concerns have always been secondary to the intentions and messages expressed.

The sculptures and paintings are wrought with struggles. His early work (sculptures) emotes this in more abstract and almost muddlingly but intriguingly unspecific way. Made of wood and steel with foam, the materials are very heavy and pliable. They transmute the pressures of living into formal metaphors, their internal tensions and squeezings conveying a free floating sense of humanity's impassivity and conformity to Fate. After working abstractly for a number of years, a particular sculpture, "Mythic Responsibility," was a shocking move into figuration and pivotal in his work. It is of three decapitated deer, joined in a triad by large hooks placed in the center of their necks. Considering Kuehn's lifelong examination of the psychological, an interest in the history and evolution of mythology is relevant. Historically, the symbol of a doe was known as a sacred moon animal; the lithe movement of deer correlated to moon dances, acts of ritual devotion. But, this sculpture brings isolation and misfortune. Regarding Fate, Kuehn's pessimistic belief at the time—"Nothing good comes from the sky"—is embodied in this piece.

After making "Mythic Responsibility," Kuehn felt at that time he had gone the limit (psychologically and artistically) with sculpture. Expanding the intensity of his art, he moved into painting. He has continued to be concerned with various animal images since.

Bird imagery is a recurring theme in his work—traditional symbols of spirituality and freedom. It is difficult to discern whether these birds are flying or static. Throughout Kuehn's career circles have been ever-present. Sometimes perfectly round and at others manipulated. Even, fluid, or constricted, this symbol could hold many meanings: the sun, the moon, and the earth (or other planets); of creativity and the artist's anima; or the mythological and complex Great Goddess. Most likely, they are any mixture of these things at different times. They seem to serve as spiritual guardians and enemies, images of birth and destruction. This would be fitting, considering that Kuehn has long been intrigued by the rela-

tionships between things which are only seemingly opposite.

Soon thereafter (c. 1979), he began to incorporate simply rendered stocky male figures. Then he began to add similar female figures. Sometimes they coexist in the same space and at others they are alone on a canvas. But, they never really seem to be together. The black and white figures represent the artist as well as humanity. Exuding silent but primitive power, they inhabit places without time in abandoned mindscapes of icy blues, greens, and reds (with some highlights of yellow).

One could describe the way Gary Kuehn works as mediumistic; unconsciously it flows through him. The ancient goddess, Mnemosyne, was the mother of the muses and guide of memory and journeys to oracular caves. The travels do not aid in memorization but in recalling entire stories and remembering all details of the narrative of one's life. It is Mnemosyne who partners with and protects Gary Kuehn. The process of moving beyond the apocalypse fore-shadowed in his work becomes a process of individuation.

—Elise LaRose

KUSAMA, Yayoi.

American. Born in Matsumoto City, Nagano, Japan, 22 March 1929, emigrated to the United States, 1960: naturalized, 1966. Educated at Arigasaki High School, Matsumoto, 1943–47; studied at the Arts and Crafts School, Kyoto, 1948–51; Art Students League, Brooklyn Arts School, and Washington Irving School, all in New York, 1957–58. Independent painter, sculptor and environmental artist, in Kyoto, 1951–57, in New York, 1957–74, in Tokyo since 1974: first monochrome pattern paintings, 1957; soft sculptures, 1961; infinity mirror works, 1964; happenings and kinetic works, 1965; films, 1966; ceramics and pastel collages, from 1974. Founder-director, Kusama Enterprises, Kusama Polka Dot Church, Kusama Musical Productions, Kusama Fashion Company Ltd., Kusama International Film Company Ltd., Body Paint Studio Company model agency, and KOK Homo Social Club, all in New York, 1968; Japan Edition Art Company publishing house, Tokyo, 1977. Founder-editor, *Kusama Orgy* weekly newspaper, New York, 1968; editorial board member, *Kindai Foudo (Modern Climate)* magazine, Tokyo, 1978. Recipient: Rockefeller Foundation Scholarship, New York, 1965; Film Prize, Belgian International Short Film Festival, Knokke-le-Zoute, 1968; Gold Award, Accademia di Belle Arti, Rome, 1982; Kadokawa Shoten Novelist Prize, Tokyo, 1983. Address: 1008 Ushigome Heim, Shinjuku-ku 30–2 chome, Haramachi, Tokyo, Japan.

Individual Exhibitions:

1952	Matsumoto Civic Hall, Japan
1954	Shirokiya Department Store, Tokyo
	Mimatsu Shobo Gallery, Tokyo
1955	Takemiya Gallery, Tokyo
	Kyuryudo Gallery, Tokyo
1957	Zoe Dusanne Gallery, Seattle, Washington
1959	Brata Gallery, New York
	Nova Gallery, Boston
1960	Gres Gallery, Washington, D.C.
	Stephen Radich Gallery, New York
1961	Detroit Gallery, Michigan
	Stephen Radich Gallery, New York
1962	Gertrude Stein Gallery, New York
1963	Castellane Gallery, New York (twice)
1964	Stedelijk Museum, Schiedam, Netherlands
1965	Orez Gallery, The Hague
	Stedelijk Museum, Schiedam, Netherlands
1966	Galleria del Naviglio, Milan
	Galerie M. E. Thelen, Essen, West Germany

1971	Orez Gallery, The Hague
1975	Nishimura Gallery, Tokyo
1976	Osaka Form Gallery, Tokyo
1977	Galerie Nikko, Tokyo
1978	Chamber of Commerce and Industry, Matsumoto, Japan
1979	Chugeki Art Salon, Matsumoto, Japan
	Inoue Department Store, Matsumoto, Japan
1980	Toho Gallery, Osaka, Japan
	American Center, Tokyo
	Tokyu Department Store, Nagano, Japan
	Yurakudo Gallery, Matsumoto, Japan
	Gallery Toshin, Tokyo (twice)
1981	Shibuya Seibu Department Store, Tokyo
	Gallery Kodosha, Ichinoseki, Japan
	Gallery Kumo, Tokyo
1982	Box Gallery, Nagoya, Japan
	Fuji Television Gallery, Tokyo
	Galleria del Naviglio, Milan
1983	Jardin de Luseine, Harajuku, Tokyo
	Supplement Gallery, Tokyo
	Video Gallery Scan, Tokyo
	Galerie Ornis, The Hague
1984	Fuji Television Gallery, Tokyo
	Video Gallery Scan, Tokyo
1985	Missoni Boutique, Yurakucho-Marion, Tokyo
1986	Tamagawa-Takashimaya, Tokyo
	Fuji Television Gallery, Tokyo
	Galerie Christian Cheneau, Paris
1987	Municipal Museum of Art, Kitakyushu, Japan

Major Happenings and Performances: *Mirror Ball Sale Happening*, Giardini della Biennale, Venice, 1966; *Self-Obliteration*, Black Gate Theater, New York, 1967; *Horse Play*, Washington Square, New York, 1967; *Body Festival*, Washington Square, New York, 1967; *Phallics Festival*, St. Patrick's Cathedral, New York, 1968; *Weekend Body Festival*, Central Park, New York, 1968; *Naked Demonstration*, Wall Street, New York, 1968; *Anti-War Happening*, United Nations Building, New York, 1968; *Nixon Orgy*, New School for Social Research, New York, 1968; *Polka Dot Happening*, Kusama Studio, New York, 1968; *Alice in Wonderland*, Central Park, New York, 1968; *Bust Out*, Sheepsmeadow, Central Park, New York, 1969, *Naked Orgy Performance*, Museum of Modern Art Garden, New York, 1969; *Happening for Venice*, Giardini Della Biennale, Venice, 1970; *Polka Dot Obliteration*, Video Gallery Scan, Tokyo, 1983; *Infinity Nets*, Video Gallery Scan, Tokyo, 1984; *The Flower of Basara*, Joshin Temple, Tokyo, 1985.

Selected Group Exhibitions:

1955	*International Biennial of Watercolor*, Brooklyn Museum, New York (and 1959)
1960	*Monochrome Malerei*, Stadtische Museum, Leverkusen, West Germany
1962	*Tentoonstelling Nul*, Stedelijk Museum, Amsterdam
1966	*The Object Transformed*, Museum of Modern Art, New York
1973	*American Art*, Civic Center, Philadelphia
1977	*Improbable Furniture*, Institute of Contemporary Art, Philadelphia
1979	*Soft-Art*, Kunsthaus, Zurich
1982	*Art Today—November Steps*, Yokohama City Hall, Japan
1985	*Reconstructions: Avant-Garde Art in Japan 1945–65*, Museum of Modern Art, Oxford
1986	*Le Japon des Avantgardes*, Centre Georges Pompidou, Paris

Collections:

Stedelijk Museum, Amsterdam; Chrysler Museum, Provincetown, Massachusetts; Oberlin College, Ohio.

Publications:

By KUSAMA: books—*Seven*, with Masataka Sekou and Masatoshi Tamaoki, Tokyo 1977; *Manhattan Suicide Addict*, Tokyo 1978; *Christopher Homosexual Brothel*, Tokyo 1983; *Fired St. Mark's Church*, Tokyo 1985.

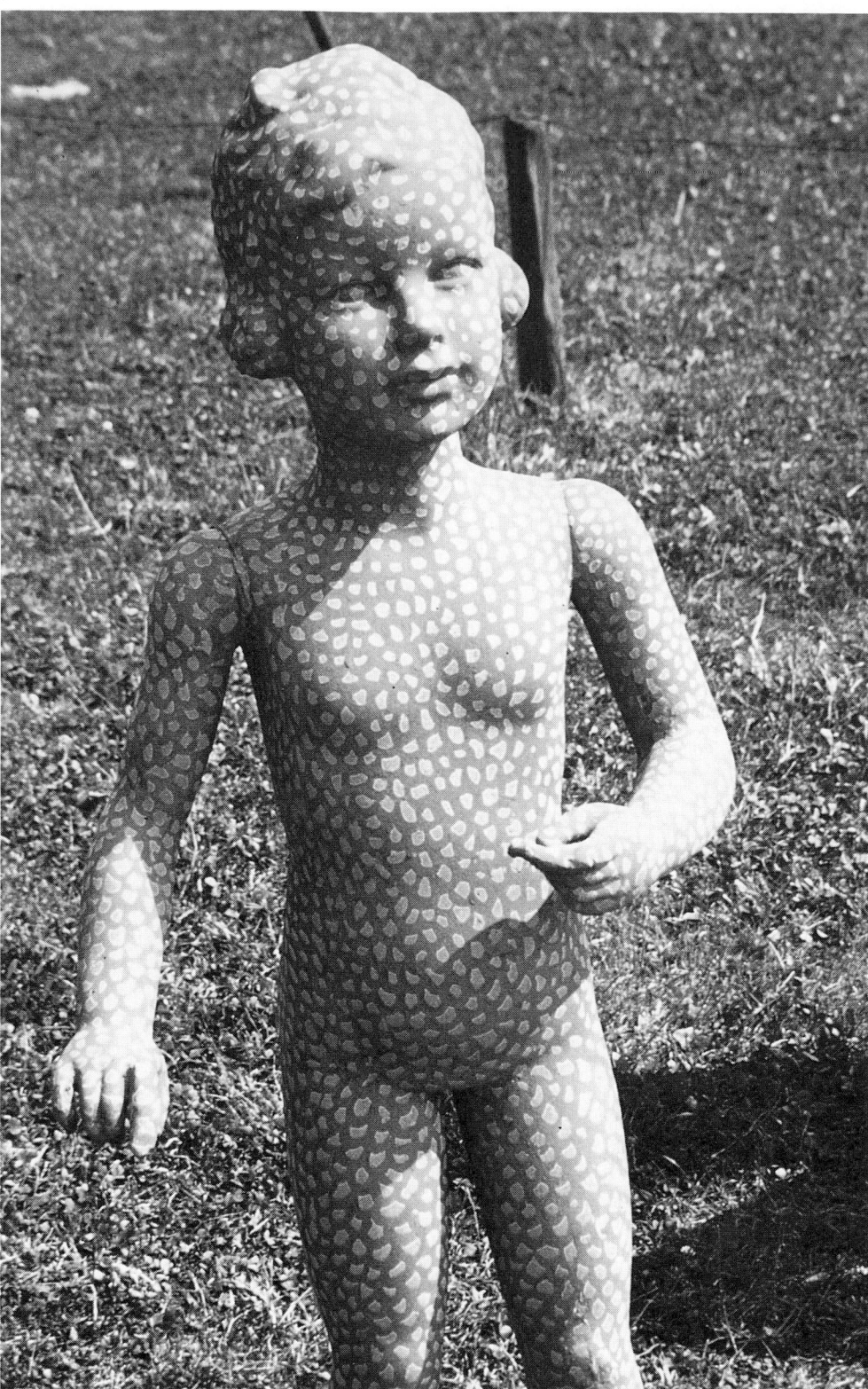

Yayoi Kusama: *Girl,* **1966**

She gradually aroused interest in New York by the end of the 1950's, creating paintings with multiplicative net pattern or polka-dotted overall surface. In 1961, she took up making soft sculptures which developed into perhaps one of her best known works in 1962, *1,000 boats;* boats made of thousands of phallic sacks with stuffing in each of them.

Kusama's activities in the 1960's depict the worldwide explosion and expansion of ideas in art of the decade, ranging over kinetic art, environmental art, Happenings, Pop art, film-making, fashion, publication and private enterprise.

In the early sixties, she began to create works with mirror and electricity which led the artist into making moving sculptures. Her shows were apt to be accompanied with Happenings around the middle of sixties, and she received the Rockefeller Foundation Scholarship in 1965. She staged an enterprising *Mirror Ball Sale Happening* at the première of the Venice Biennial, 1966, and made a film, *Kusama's Polka Dot Obliteration,* written and played by herself in 1967. The film was awarded at Belgian International Short Film Festival in 1968. In this period, she repeatedly performed artistic, anti-establishment and immoral Happenings in New York. She established her private enterprises for purposes of producing and selling her dresses and films.

After coming back to Japan in 1974, she began to make ceramic works and pastel collages. Her first novel came out in 1978, and the second novel in 1983, *Christopher Homosexual Brothel,* won a new novelist prize from Kadokawa publishing company. A golden prize was awarded to the artist in 1982 from Art Academy of Italy. She has never lost her energy in the 1980's, showing her works in a lot of exhibitions in and out of Japan.

Kusama's obsessive idea for self-obliteration (frequently the titles of her Happening shows), seems to have been derived from an inner desire to be emancipated from the psychopathic anguish which has been her old complaint. But it is obvious to anyone's eyes that the nightmarish beauty in Kusama's art claims a high reputation as one of the wondrous achievements created by an avant-garde artist regardless of her continuous endeavoring to conquer sufferings.

—Tazmi Shinoda

On KUSAMA: book—*Yayoi Kusama,* exhibition catalogue with essay by Toshiaki Minemura, Tokyo 1986.

What makes Yayoi Kusama's art notable is a kind of cosmological obsession integrated into art as forms of proliferating repetition and endless accumulation. She is a painter, sculptor, performing artist, film maker and novelist.

In her childhood in Matsumoto city in Nagano, Japan, where she was born in 1929 and graduated a local high school, Kusama was a great visionary; it was reported that she frequently saw aurora-fringed objects and heard animals and plants uttering human languages. She studied art at Kyoto Arts and Crafts School, and her extraordinary visions in paintings caught the interest of a psychopathologist, who reported her case at academic meetings.

She held her first one-person show with 240 paintings at Matsumoto city in 1952, and became known to the avant-garde art circles in Tokyo.

It was after 1957 when she went to New York and studied at Art Student League that her idiosyncratic vision and idea began to bloom as comprehensive art forms. Her repetitive pattern painting in monochrome starting in 1957 was one of the earliest examples of Systemic Painting which was to come out of New York in sixties, though Kusama's obsession for microbiological multiplication was quite different from the ideas of the Systemic painters.

KUSHNER, Robert.

American. Born in Pasadena, California, 19 August 1949. Educated at the University of California at San Diego, 1967–71, B.A. (honors) 1971. Independent artist, since 1971. Created costumes for *The Masque of the Red Death,* WGBH, Boston, 1971; costumes, with Jim Burton, for *Ballet Electronique,* 1973; costumes and set, with Sara Rudner, for *Dancing on View,* 1975; costumes, with Wendy Rogers, for *Gull's Meadow,* New York, 1976; costumes and set design for *November Duets* by Sara Rudner, 1977; costumes for *Oriental Dance* by Ellen Saltonstall, 1977; costumes and set for *Tropical Chenille* by Wendy Rogers, Berkeley and New York, 1978; sets for *Living Rooms* for Wendy Rogers, Berkeley, 1980; costumes and sets for *As Is* by Sara Rudner, 1980; costumes and sets for *The White Snake* by Ed Friedman, New York, 1982. Agent: Holly Solomon Gallery, New York. Address: c/o Holly Solomon Gallery, Inc., 724 Fifth Avenue, New York, New York 10019, U.S.A.

Individual Exhibitions:

1975 *Recent Works,* Rasdall Gallery, University of Kentucky, Lexington
1976 *Persian Line Part II,* Holly Solomon Gallery, New York

1977	Thorpe Intermedia Gallery, Sparkhill, New York
	Philadelphia College of Art
	Holly Solomon Gallery, New York
1978	Lunn Gallery, Washington, D.C.
	Mayor Gallery, London
1979	Daniel Templon Gallery, Paris
	Holly Solomon Gallery, New York (twice)
1980	Dart Gallery, Chicago
1981	*New Works,* Mayor Gallery, London
	The Question, The Answer, Another Question, Barbara Gladstone Gallery, New York
	Galerie Bischofberger, Zurich
	Paintings of Some Recent Acquaintances, Holly Solomon Gallery, New York
	Dreams and Visions, Holly Solomon Gallery, New York
	Asher/Faure Gallery, Los Angeles
	Akira Ikeda Gallery, Nagoya, Japan

1982	Galerie Rudolf Zwirner, Cologne
	University of Colorado Art Galleries, Boulder
	Holly Solomon Gallery, New York
	American Graffiti Gallery, Amsterdam
	Studio Marconi, Milan
	University of Southern California, Los Angeles
	Castelli-Goodman-Solomon, East Hampton, New York
1983	Dart Gallery, Chicago
	Holly Solomon Gallery, New York
1984	McIntosh/Drysdale Gallery, Houston
	Brentwood Gallery, St. Louis
	Galleria Giulia, Rome
	Brooklyn Museum, New York
1985	Holly Solomon Gallery, New York
	Galleria Capricorni, Venice
	Mayor Gallery, London
	Crown Point Press, New York

1986	Rugg Road, Boston
	Galerie Rudolf Zwirner, Cologne
1987	Holly Solomon Gallery, New York
	Fay Gold Gallery, Atlanta, Georgia
	Institute of Contemporary Art, Philadelphia

Performances: *Costumes for Moving Bodies,* University of California at San Diego, 1971; *An Evening of Theatre and Dance,* Parker 470 Gallery, Boston, 1972; *Costumes Constructed and Eaten,* Jack Glenn Gallery, Corona del Mar, California, and University of California at San Diego, 1972; *Robert Kushner and Friends Eat Their Clothes,* Acme Productions, New York, 1972; *The Orange County Book,* with Ed Friedman, Acme Productions, New York, 1973; *Hors d'Oeuvres Costumes,* Fairleigh Dickinson University, Teaneck, New Jersey 1973; *Demonstrations from the Wonderful World of Food,* St. Mark's Church, New York, 1973; *Masque of Clouds,* The Kitchen, New York, 1973; *The Masque of Monuments: Rocks and Water,* 98 Greene Street Loft, New York, 1973; *Food Fashion Show,* Art-Rite, New York, 1974; *The Persian Line,* The Kitchen, New York, 1975; *The New York Hat Line,* The Clocktower, New York, 1975; *Masque of Clouds: An Opera in Three Acts and 132 Variations,* with Tom Johnson, The Kitchen, New York, 1975; *Persian Line Part II,* Holly Solomon Gallery, New York, 1976; *That Kushner Look: One Size Fits All,* University of California at San Diego, California Institute of the Arts, Valencia, 541 Broadway, New York, Galleria Communale di Arte Moderna, Bologna, Fourmiere III, Zurich, and Philadelphia College of Art, 1977; *The New York Hat Line,* Thorpe Intermedia Center, Sparkill, New York, 1977; *Layers,* Galerie Alexandra Monett, Brussels; *Layers,* Holly Solomon Gallery, New York, Kunstverein, Vienna, Forum Stadtpark, Graz, Austria, University of California at San Diego, University of California at Irvine, and IDEA, Santa Monica, California, 1978; *The New York Hat Line,* Museum of Modern Art, New York, 1978; *That Kushner Look: One Size Fits All,* Soho TV, New York, 1978; *Hat Party,* Holly Solomon Gallery, New York, 1979; *Sentimental Fables,* Los Angeles Institute of Contemporary Art, 1979; *Sentimental Fables,* IMAC, Bayville, New York, and 87 Leonard Street, New York, 1980; *Hats for Tea,* Institute of Contemporary Art, Philadelphia, 1980; *Sentimental Fables,* Associate Council of the Museum of Modern Art, New York, 1981; *Travelling,* Institute of Contemporary Art, Boston, 1983.

Robert Kushner: *The Visitors—Genesis 18,* **1987**

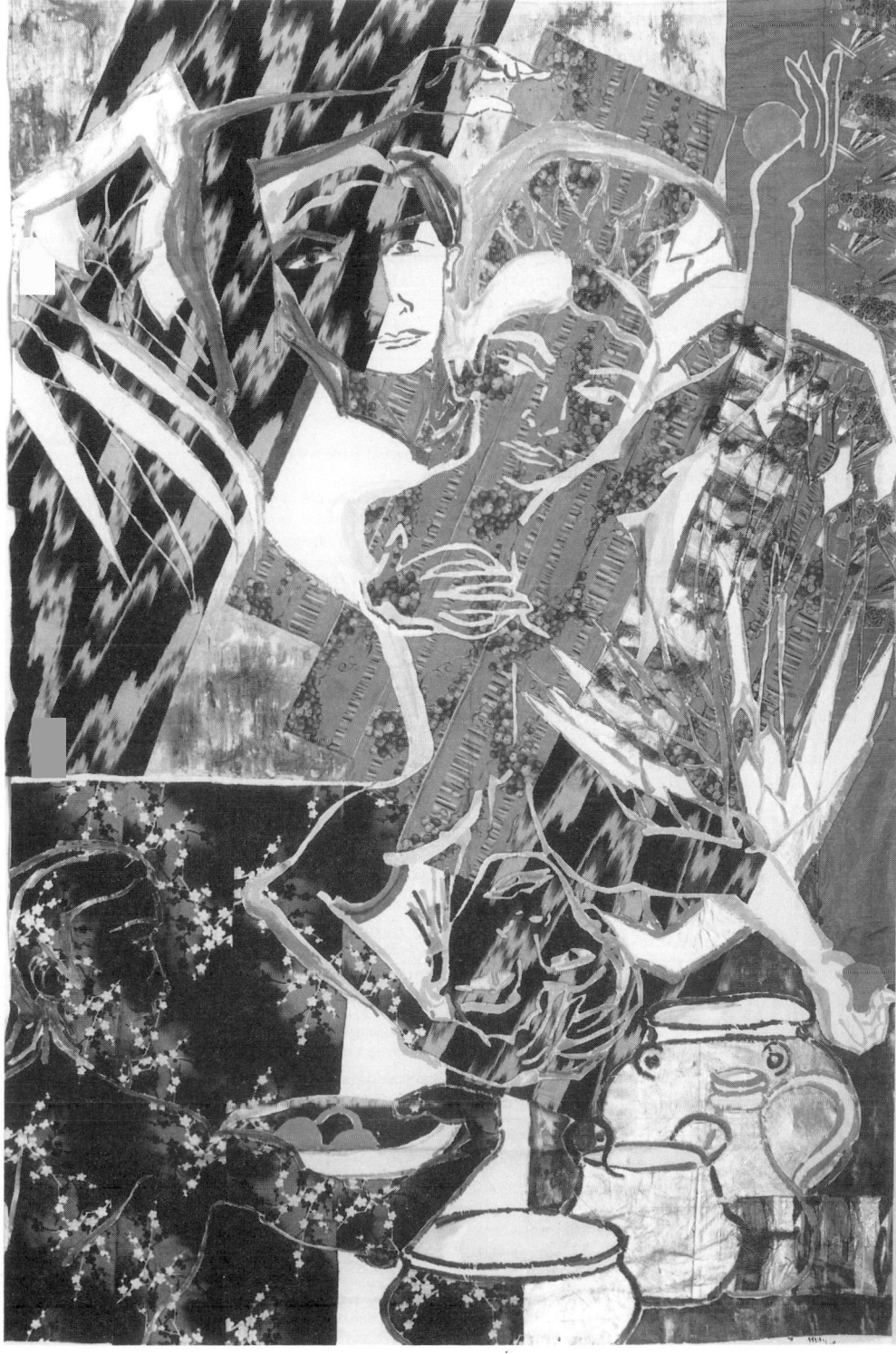

Selected Group Exhibitions:

1969	*Clouds,* Fahrenheit 451 Gallery, Laguna Beach, California
1975	*Biennial,* Whitney Museum, New York
1977	*Patterning and Decoration,* Museum of the American Foundation for the Arts, Miami
1978	*Patterning Painting,* Palais des Beaux-Arts, Brussels
1980	*Drawings: The Pluralist Decade,* at the *Biennale,* Venice (travelled to the Kunstforeningen, Copenhagen; Henie-Onstad Museum, Oslo; Biblioteca Nationale, Madrid; and the Gulbenkian Museum, Lisbon)
1981	*Alternatives in Retrospect: An Historical Overview 1969–1975,* New Museum, New York
1982	*New American Graphics,* Madison Art Center, Wisconsin (toured the United States, 1982–84)
1983	*Minimalism to Expressionism,* Whitney Museum, New York
1985	*Illuminating Color,* Pratt Institute, New York
1987	*Americana,* Groninger Museum, Groningen, Netherlands

Collections:

Museum of Modern Art, New York; Goldman Sachs and Company, New York; Morton G. Neuman Collection, Chicago; Rothschild Bank, St. Louis; Nelson Atkins Gallery, Kansas City, Missouri; Minneapolis Institute of Art; Neiman Marcus, Dallas; Koogler McNay Institute, San Antonio, Texas; Museum des 20 Jahrhunderts, Vienna; Neue Galerie, Aachen, West Germany.

Publications:

By KUSHNER: books—*Robert Kushner: New Bronze Sculp-*

ture, exhibition catalogue, New York 1987; illustrations for *Kathy Goes to Haiti* by Kathy Acker, New York 1977; *The Wonnerful World of Food*, with Amy Goldin, New York 1978; *The New York Hat Line*, with Ed Friedman and Katherine Landman, New York 1979; book cover and drawings for *The Telephone Book* by Ed Friedman, New York 1979; illustrations for *The Persian Poems by Janey Smith* by Kathy Acker, New York 1980; articles—"Conceptual Art as Opera" in *Artnews* (New York), May 1970; "Aida" in the *Paris Review* (New York and Paris), Fall 1979; "Letters to the Editor," with Kim MacConnel, in *Arts Magazine* (New York), January 1980; "Io, Kushner," interview with Francesca Alinovi, in *Bolaffiarte* (Turin), January 1981; "Things I Think about My Work" in *Flash Art* (Milan), Summer 1981; "Books: Man as Art" in *Artforum* (New York), March 1982.

On KUSHNER: books—*Art in the Seventies* by Edward Lucie-Smith, London and New York 1980; *Ornamentalism: The New Decorativeness in Architecture and Design* by Robert Jensen and Patricia Conway, New York 1982; *Trans Avant Garde International* by Achille Bonito Oliva, Milan 1983; *The New Image: Painting in the 1980's* by Tony Godfrey, New York 1986; *50 New York Artists* by Richard Marshall and Robert Mapplethorpe, New York 1986; articles— "Decoration Days" by John Ashbery in *New York Magazine*, 2 July 1979; "Art of the Whole Cloth" by Carrie Rickey in *Art in America* (New York), November 1979; "Robert Kushner" by Douglas Blau in *Flash Art* (Milan), January/February 1980; "Art: Kushner Exalts a Study in Goofiness" by Alan G. Artner in the *Chicago Tribune*, 14 March 1980; "The Joy of Ornament: The Prints of Robert Kushner" by Roberta Bernstein in the *Print Collector's Newsletter*, January/February 1981; "Artist and Printer" A Coincidence of Sympathies" by Deborah C. Phillips in *Artnews* (New York), March 1981; "Kim MacConnel and Robert Kushner at Mayor" by Stuart Morgan in *Artscribe* (London), March 1981; "Post-Modernist Painting" by Sam Hunter in *Portfolio* (New York), January/February 1982; "Robert Kushner" by Theodore F. Wolff in *Christian Science Monitor* (Boston), 10 June 1986.

Since his debut in the early 1970's, Robert Kushner has challenged the conventional notions of aesthetic suitability by creating fabric wall hangings and costumes flushing with ecstatically moody colours, unusual subject matter, old-fashioned motifs, and commercial designs. Seeking an alternative to the impersonal aspects of Minimalism and Formalism (then dominating the art world), he explored the neglected—however promising—area of decorative art. His main disagreement with these traditions stemmed from his refusal to regard art—or any of its components—as an isolated element. A decorative artist like Kushner is concerned with how the art adapts to and enhances an already established decor without demanding its refinement and the elimination of conflicting decorative detail (a special problem of minimalist sculpture.)

Since 1971 Kushner has succeeded in erasing the distinction between decoration and art. His emulation of the decorative is manifested in his ability to make art that is expansive and additive, embellished and exuberant. The images, colours, and patterns expand beyond the physical edge of the support, carrying the eye across the surface and implying an infinite continuation of the fluid and energetic line. He is unconcerned with illusionist spatial effects; instead, he fashions broad, flat outlines of the basic motif of each piece, applying colour to add tonal surrogates for modelled mass. It is a relatively fast method of working and one that discourages intricate brushwork. Except for the decorative appliques, there is no topology to his work. Content is of minimal importance; as a result, the formal aspects of his imagery are highlighted. He subjugates his forms and figures to decorative principles through cropping, non-naturalistic colours, and repetitive patterns. It is this use of pattern that establishes the artwork as a specimen of decoration.

Kushner's taste in colour has been central to his work, arresting, tropical hues freely positioned against flat, interior tones: mauves, gilts, oxblood, dark blues and reds, tertiary browns. The flat, inscribed nature of the drawing style and the physical flatness of the painting shift the considerable sensuality of the work onto its colour. The reflective ornamentation—glitter and metallic thread, for

instance—and the varieties of translucent fabrics that Kushner favours heighten this sensuality.

Kushner first produced fabric wall hangings in 1971. His early large-scale ink drawings emerged from a technique of copying intricate pattern motifs from historical fabrics and rugs onto paper. Consequently, he developed a vocabulary of forms, including the leaf, vine, seed pod, and floral images which recur in his work. A trip to the Middle East in 1974 left Kushner resolute to promote a continuity between his art and daily existence. The costumes which occupied him prior to his trip became, on his return, more than just props for performances. They became functionally androgynous—equally at home as shelter and as non-functional decoration—in a way that paralleled their deliberate sexual androgyny. Within a short time the paintings adopted the qualities of these costumes.

By 1975 he increased his scale and enlarged his repertory of images by selecting a wider range of subject matter—from books on European fabric and wallpaper design to advertising images and collections of Chinese commercial designs. *Bunnies Eating Bok Choy* (1977), *Empty Pagoda* (1977), and *Fishes and Lilies* (1977) were inspired by the Chinese line-drawing books. During the late '70s Kushner exhibited a series of multi-panel vertical works influenced by Matisse, among them: *Gisela* (1979), *Henrietta* (1979), and *Henri* (1978). In this series he achieved a continuation of the fluid line by carrying the viewer's eye across the zig-zag positioning of the faces in the paintings.

At that same time Kushner produced figural pieces which derived from newspaper and magazine photographs, images already composed and flattened. Not until 1982 did he begin drawing from a live model in the studio, a technique which prompted a series of ink drawings executed on oriental and handmade papers embedded with fibres, leaves, and sequins. Kushner fully integrated the figure into decorative style with his use of commercially produced wallpaper. The flattened components of the figure served to emphasize the ornamentation. The wallpaper pieces, such as *Wrapped* (1984) and *Contemplative* (1984), utilized the same technique as his large fabric paintings—the drawn image of the figure is viewed through cuts in the applied papers.

Kushner's genuine lack of self-consciousness, with its inherent sweetness and sincerity, sets him apart from the avant-garde tradition of the '80s. He likes to classify himself among the conservative artists, yet this category is equally unsuitable since there is neither verifiable, ordering structure to his work, nor a free permission to manifest the subconscious, as is required by the conservative tradition. Where does that leave Kushner? His work must rest somewhere between the two, welcoming loyalists from both sides to see something of themselves reflected in his gregarious, egalitarian, strikingly colourful drawings.

—Carrie Barker

Individual Exhibitions:

1961	Green Gallery, New York
1962	Swetzoff Gallery, Boston
	Green Gallery, New York
1964	Kornblee Gallery, New York
1965	Daniels Gallery, New York
1966	Red Carpet Gallery, Minneapolis
1967	Tokyo Gallery, Japan
	Gallery Bischofberger, Zurich
	Galerie Mutzenbach, Dortmund, West Germany
	Richard Gray Gallery, Chicago
	Franklin Siden Gallery, Detroit
1968	Gallery Del Leone, Venice
	Galerie Bischofberger, Zurich
	Galerie D'Aujourd'hui, Brussels
1969	Galerie Reckermann, Cologne
	Henri Gallery, Washington, D.C.
1972	Henri Gallery, Washington, D.C.
1973	Galerie Kowallek, Frankfurt
	Henri Gallery, Washington, D.C.
1974	Museum Folkwang, Essen
	Kaneko Art, Tokyo
1975	Galerie Denise René, New York
	Galerie Muller, Stuttgart
1977	Denise René Gallery, New York
1978	Koh Gallery, Tokyo
1979	Sakura Gallery, Nagoya, Japan
	Protetch-McIntosh Gallery, Washington, D.C.
1980	Akira Ikeda Gallery, Nagoya, Japan
1981	Akira Ikeda Gallery, Nagoya, Japan
1982	Galerie Reckermann, Cologne
	Gimpel-Hanover and Andre Emmerich Galleries, Zurich
1983	Akira Ikeda Gallery, Tokyo
	Sakura Gallery, Nagoya, Japan
1984	Akira Ikeda Gallery, Tokyo (and Nagoya)
1985	Kitakyushu Municipal Museum of Art, Japan
	Gallery, Yamaguchi, Osaka, Japan
	Kasahara Gallery, Osaka, Japan

Selected Group Exhibitions:

1961	*Carnegie International*, Pittsburgh, (and 1967)
1963	*Formalist Show*, Washington Gallery of Modern Art, Washington, D.C.
1964	*Motion and Movement*, Contemporary Art Center, Cincinnati, Ohio
1968	*First Indian Triennale of Contemporary World Art*, New Delhi
1973	*Art of Surface*, Art Gallery of New South Wales, Sydney
1974	*Japan: Tradition und Gegenwart*, Stadtische Kunsthalle, Dusseldorf
1979	*Constructivism and the Geometric Tradition*, Albright-Knox Art Gallery, Buffalo, New York
1982	*Kunst wird Material*, Nationalgalerie, West Berlin
1985	*Contemporary Japanese Painting*, National Gallery of Modern Art, New Delhi
1987	*Painting 1977–87*, National Museum of Art, Osaka, Japan

Collections:

Albright-Knox Art Gallery, Buffalo, New York; Larry Aldrich Museum, Ridgefield, Connecticut; Wadsworth Atheneum, Hartford, Connecticut; Worcester Art Museum, Massachusetts; Akron Art Institute, Ohio; Indianapolis Museum of Art; Texas University Art Museum, Austin; Museum Folkwang, Essen.

KUWAYAMA, Tadaaki.
Japanese. Born in Nagoya City, 4 March 1932. Studied at Tokyo University of Art, 1952–56, B.F.A. 1956. Married Rakuko Naito in 1958; children: Maki, Sono. Moved to New York in 1958; independent painter, since 1960. Recipient: *Art in America* New Talent Prize, New York 1964; National Endowment for the Arts Grant, Washington, D.C., 1969; Adolph and Esther Gottlieb Foundation Grant, New York, 1986. Agents: Akira Ikeda Gallery, 8–18, Kyobashi 2-chome, Chuo-ku, Tokyo, Japan; Galerie Reckermann, Albertusstrasse 16, 5000 Cologne 1, West Germany. Address: 136 West 24th Street, New York, New York 10011, U.S.A.

Publications:

By KUWAYAMA: articles—statement in *Art Now* (New York), September 1970; statement in *Flash Art* (Milan). June 1973; text in *Kunst wird Material*, catalogue, West Berlin 1982; statement in *Contemporary Painting*, catalogue, Tokyo 1987.

On KUWAYAMA: books—*Japan: Tradition und Gegenwart*, exhibition catalogue by Jurgen Harten Joseph Love and others, Dusseldorf 1974; *Tadaaki Kuwayama*, exhibition catalogue with text by Willy Rotzler, Kitakyushu, Japan 1985; articles—"Tadaaki Kuwayama: Green-White-Green" in *Art Now: New York*, (New York), no. 2, 1970; "Washington Letter" by David Bourdon in *Art International* (Lugano, Switzerland), December 1972; "Japan pa Louisiana" by Y. Tono and J. Love in *Louisiana Revy* (Humlebaek, Denmark), September 1974.

Born in Nagoya in 1932, Tadaaki Kuwayama is a 1956 graduate of the Nihon-ga-department of Tokyo University of Fine Art. In 1958 he moved to the United States, and settled in New York. He had his first one-man show at New York's Green Gallery in 1961, and has shown his works elsewhere in the United States, as well as in Europe and Japan. He has participated in group shows including the Guggenheim Museum's *Systemic Painting* (1966), Amersterdam's Stedelijk Museum's *New Forms and Shapes of Color* (1966), and Buffalo's Albright-Knox Gallery exhibition, *Plus by Minus: Today's Half-Century* (1968).

Kuwayama's paintings, at the outset, were based on a technique which permitted no variation, but since his monochrome paintings of the latter half of the 1950's, he has divided his paintings into symmetrical parts, and made paintings by bringing together panels of the same form. It may be said that the paintings appear to be pure abstracts, but they have no relationship to the traditional category of so-called abstract art. The framework of the paintings resists any formative positioning or arrangement, and presents a superficiality devoid of intervention by the spirit of the work. Although the paintings are beyond doubt the work of an artist, they have an existence quite remote from the artist. In other words, the works principally exist as objects, and are one manifestation of the subjects with which contemporary art is concerned.

Kuwayama has always been associated with the Minimalist painters in the United States, but his recent approach to the subtlety of the surface with exquisitely applied overall brushstrokes, as exemplified in his works of the 1980's, suggests his transcendental contemplation on the spiritual element that makes his paintings something more than deadpan art-objects.

—Yoshiaki Tono

LAING, Gerald (Ogilvie-).

British. Born in Newcastle upon Tyne, 11 February 1936. Educated at Berkhamsted School, Hertfordshire, 1945–53; Royal Military Academy, Sandhurst, Camberley, Surrey, 1953–55 (Commissioned Fifth Fusiliers, 1955–60); St. Martin's School of Art, London, 1960–64. Painter since 1962, and sculptor since 1965, in New York, 1964–69, in Ross-shire, Scotland, since 1969: concentrated on Pop paintings, 1962–65, abstract wall-pieces and three-dimensional sculptures, 1965–69, sculpture in the landscape, 1969–73, figurative sculpture since 1973; established a tapestry workshop, Conon Bridge, Ross-shire, 1970–74. Artist-in-Residence, Aspen Institute for Humanistic Studies, Colorado, 1966; Visiting Professor, University of New Mexico, Albuquerque, 1976–77; Professor of Sculpture, Columbia University, New York, 1986–87. Art Committee Member, Scottish Arts Council, Edinburgh, 1978–80; Commissioner, Royal Commission for Fine Art for Scotland, Edinburgh, 1987. Lives in Scotland and New York. Addresses: Kinkell Castle, Conon Bridge, Ross and Cromarty IV7 8AT, Scotland; 139 East 66th Street, New York, New York 10021, U.S.A.

Individual Exhibitions:

1963	Laing Art Gallery, Newcastle upon Tyne
1964	Institute of Contemporary Arts, London
	Richard Feigen Gallery, New York
	Feigen Palmer Gallery, Los Angeles
1965	Richard Feigen Gallery, New York
	Richard Feigen Gallery, Chicago
1966	Kornblee Gallery, New York (with Peter Phillips)
	Richard Feigen Galery, Chicago
1967	Richard Feigen Gallery, New York
	Galerie M. E. Thelen, Essen
	Pennsylvania State University, College Park
1969	Richard Feigen Gallery, New York
1970	Richard Feigen Gallery, Chicago
	Richard Demarco Gallery, Edinburgh
1971	Multiples Gallery, New York
	Center for Contemporary Art, Cincinnati, Ohio
	Aspen Institute for Humanistic Studies, Colorado
	Scottish National Gallery of Modern Art, Edinburgh
1973	Arthur Tooth and Sons, London
	University of New Mexico, Albuquerque
1974	Arthur Tooth and Sons, London
1975	Aberdeen Art Gallery, Scotland
1977	Max Hutchinson Gallery, New York
1978	Gladstone Court, Edinburgh
1979	Max Hutchinson Gallery, Houston
	Max Hutchinson Gallery, New York
1980	Scottish Gallery, Edinburgh
1981	Gallery Camino Real, Boca Raton, Florida
1982	Bacardi Gallery, Miami, Florida
1983	Herbert Art Gallery, Coventry, Warwickshire (retrospective)
	Joanne Lyon Gallery, Aspen, Colorado
1987	Albert Totah Gallery, London

Selected Group Exhibitions:

1963	*Young Contemporaries*, RBA Galleries, London
1964	*Contemporary British Painting and Sculpture*, Albright-Knox Art Gallery, Buffalo, New York
1966	*New Forms and Shapes of Colour*, Stedelijk Museum, Amsterdam
1967	*Bienal*, Sao Paulo
1968	*Annual Sculpture Exhibition*, Whitney Museum, New York
	Prospect '68, Dusseldorf
1969	*Contemporary American Painting and Sculpture*, Krannert Art Museum, University of Illinois, Champaign-Urbana
1970	*Monumental American Sculpture*, Museum of Art, Cincinnati, Ohio
1978	*Cubist Syntax in the '70s*, Ingber Gallery, New York

Collections:

Victoria and Albert Museum, London; Kunstmuseum, Gelsenkrichen, West Germany; Museum of Modern Art, New York; Whitney Museum, New York; Rose Art Museum, Brandeis University, Waltham, Massachusetts; Minneapolis Museum of Art; Tate Gallery, London; Scottish National Gallery of Modern Art, Edinburgh; Nagaoka Museum, Japan; Cornell University, Ithaca, New York.

Publications:

By LAING: book—*Kinkell: The Reconstruction of a Scottish Castle*, London 1974; articles—:"Notes Toward a Definition of U.S. Automobile Painting as a Significant Branch of Mobile Heraldry," with Reyner Banham, in *Art in America* (New York), September 1966; "How We Turned a Ruined Castle into a Home" in *The Observer* (London), November 1974.

On LAING: books—*Pop Art and After* by Mario Amaya, New York 1966; *Pop Art* by Lucy Lippard, New York 1966, London 1967; *Gerald Laing Retrospective*, exhibition catalogue, Edinburgh 1971; *Produktionsasthetische Probleme zeitgenossischer Schottischer Bildhauerei* by Babette Peters, Frankfurt and New York 1984; *Open Air Sculpture in Britain* by W. J. Strachan, London 1984; articles—:Hybrid: A Time of Life" by G. R. Swenson in *Art and Artists* (London), June 1966, "Gerald Laing" in *Catalyst* (London), January 1971.

My current work can be divided into four main categories—1. Figure sculpture. 2. Architectural commissions. 3. Portrait heads. 4. Applied art.

I intend that my sculpture should be accessible to as many people as possible, and to be recognizable as art if excavated 1,000 years from now. I divide my time between the Highlands of Scotland and Manhattan. This clash of cultural contrast ensures that I do not fall asleep at the wheel. I rely on my professional skill and education to preserve my endeavours. I am a professional artist in the sense that my work has provided my entire livelihood for more than twenty years, with only two brief interludes of teaching. I remain disturbed about some aspects of the contemporary art scene—an attitude which caused my initial departure from New York in 1979—and have adapted to working independently.

—Gerald Laing

The career of Gerald Laing illustrates very neatly one of the central problems of the present-day art system. The interested observer, who reads the views of the critics and catches up with one of those instant guides to contemporary art that appear every two or three years, will have the impression that art follows a logical course through history. Abstract Expressionism leads to Pop. Pop to Op. Op to Minimalism. Minimalism to Conceptualism and so on, and he might justifiably be under the impression that artists themselves follow the same course.

Art movements are created by critics, but artists are not. They pursue their own paths, waiting for the climactic moment when the searchlight of fashion sweeps across them and they "make it." The problem is that the searchlight does not stop, and in time it moves on, leaving them with expectations of a response that is no longer forthcoming. It may be that their best work is to come, but the tide of "art history" has swept past them and leaves them flapping on the beach, largely forgotten and without the supporting environment they have grown used to. More galling still, they find they are associated with work that they have long since surpassed.

Laing has been particularly affected by this process. His work became fashionable almost as soon as he left art college, and for five years he was associated with the Pop boom and sold widely. The irony is that this early and successful work, although stylish, has none of the depth and presence of the later sculpture which is hardly known at all.

Laing left St. Martin's School of Art in 1964 and with impeccable strategic instinct headed straight for New York, where the Pop boom was just beginning, and, thanks to the Beatles, anybody young and British was very much in demand. After a short period working with Robert Indiana, he landed a contract with Feigen and immediately began to sell.

The early work was mainly in the form of paintings and prints using the iconography of a confident and booming society: pin-up girls, dragster cars, free-fall parachutists, speed, flash, hard colour and bright style, the polished aluminium of a technological age coupled with a hint of Art Deco nostalgia—a winning combination for the mid-60's. And with the style went the life: custom painted cars, drinks at Max's Kansas City, smooth girls and sex on the studio floor. Move over Barnett Newman, 'cos we're going to rock n' roll right through the doors of the Metropolitan itself.

But an artist is not an ad-man. He has to follow his own vision or perish. Laing's work slowly crept down the wall onto the floor, the images faded and the works became abstract sculpture; and then there was Altamont and Kent State and Charlie Manson and Pop went pop! leaving nothing but a stain on the floor.

Most of the Pop artists took refuge in binding contracts with the hard men of 57nd Street, but Laing fled to Scotland, found a derelict castle, which he rebuilt, and then turned back to sculpture. What now emerged was very different: solid and massive, rusting steel, straight edged, hieratic presences that he grouped in the wild landscape around the castle, monuments to an older and more lasting reality than he found in New York. But the tide of art had by now moved into the arid desert of conceptualism and no one was interested in straightforward sculpture. Even his massive work for Strathclyde University in the heart of Glasgow passed virtually unnoticed, although, quite apart from being the largest single work of art in Britain including Stonehenge, it is an impressive and moving piece.

Since 1974, Laing has been experimenting with smaller works, usually based upon the human body and showing the influence of Matisse and other important sculptors of the early 20th century.

Whether Laing will surface again, in terms of fashionable success, will depend upon the justice of the art market. His current work is much superior to the Pop work, and one can only hope that soon dealers and public will recognize that fact.

—Alastair Mackintosh

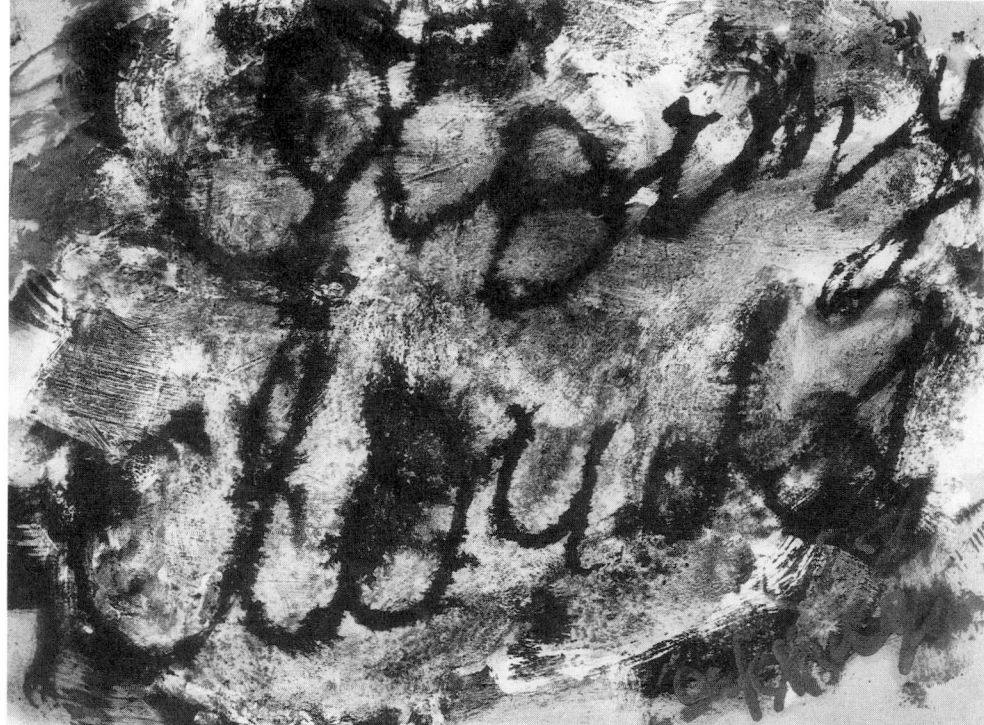

László Lakner: *Untitled*, 1984

LAKNER, László.

German. Born in Budapest, 15 April 1936; emigrated to West Germany, 1974: naturalized, 1980. Educated at Kepzo and Imparmuveszeti Gymnasium, Budapest, 1950–54; Fine Arts Academy, Budapest, 1954–60. Independent artist since 1960; has lived and worked in Berlin since 1974. Produced first photo-document paintings, and first book objects and book paintings, 1970. Artist-in-Residence, Museum Folkwang, Essen, 1972. Recipient: Museum Folkwang grant, 1968, 1972; D.A.A.D. Scholarship, Berlin, 1974; Roselius Foundation Prize, Bremen, 1976; German Critics Prize, 1976; P.S. 1 Scholarship, New York, 1980. Agents: Galerie Folker Skulima, Fasanenstrasse 68, 1 Berlin 15, Germany; Galerie Denise René-Hans Mayer, Dusseldorf; Galerie Georg Nothelfer, Berlin: and Galerie Isy Brachot, Brussels. Address: Wilmersdorferstrasse 69, 1 Berlin 12, West Germany.

Individual Exhibitions:

1969	Institute of Cultural Relations Galerie, Budapest
1974	*Found Documents*, Neue Galerie, Aachen, West Germany
	Overbeck-Gesellschaft, Lübeck
	Bilder, Bücher, Filme, Zettel, Neue Berliner Kunstverein
1975	Galerie Folker Skulima, Berlin
1976	Galerie Isy Brachot, Brussels
	Kasseler Kunstverein, Kassel, West Germany
1977	Galerie Denise René-Hans Mayer, Dusseldorf
	Galerie Folker Skulima, Berlin
1978	Galerie Art in Progress, Munich
	Book Works, Galerie ABF, Hamburg
1979	*Malerei 1974–1979*, Westfälischer Kunstverein, Münster
1980	*Small Sizes*, Galerie Zellermayer-Lorenzen, Berlin
1981	*Small Sizes*, Galerie Jaspers, Munich
1982	Galerie Heimeshoff, Essen, West Germany
1983	Bertha Urdang Gallery, New York
	Galerie Inge Baecker, Cologne (with Emmett Williams)
1984	Galerie Abras, Brussels
1985	Galerie 7, Freiburg, West Germany
	Galerie Nothelfer, West Berlin
1987	Galerie Heimeshoff, Essen, West Germany

Selected Group Exhibitions:

1968	*Modern Ungärische Kunst*, Museum Folkwang, Essen
1972	*Biennale*, Venice
1975	*8 from Berlin*, at the *Edinburgh Festival*, (travelled to the Kunstmuseum, Bonn, and the Neuer Berliner Kunstverein)
1977	*Documenta*, Kassel, West Germany
1979	*Biennale*, Sydney
1980	*Festa di Lettra*, Galleria Polygrapha, Barcelona
1981	*100 Jahre Kölner Dom*, Cologne
1983	*Neue Malerei in Deutschland*, Nationalgalerie, West Berlin
1985	*Rollbilder*, Kunstverein, Kassel, West Germany
1987	*Six Artists from Berlin*, Hara Museum, Tokyo

Collections:

Museum Folkwang, Essen; Museum Ludwig, Aachen, West Germany; Paula Modersohn-Becker Foundation, Bremen; University of Freiburg; Nationalgalerie, Berlin; Dahlem Museum, Berlin; Berlinische Galerie; National Gallery, Budapest; Museum of Modern Art, Lodz, Poland; Museum Boymans van Boeningen, Rotterdam.

Publications:

By LAKNER: films—*Toys*, 1968; *Spielzeug*, 1968; *Intervention*, with Geza Schnoller, 1969; *Ode*, 1973; *Video Program*, 1975; *Ode*, 1980; *Countenance*, 1981.

On LAKNER: books—*László Lakner*, exhibition catalogue, by György Kemèny, Budapest 1969; *Found Documents*, exhibition catalogue, by Dr. Wolfgang Becker, Aachen, West Germany 1974; *László Lakner: Bilder, Bücher, Filme, Zettel*, exhibition catalogue, with texts by Heinz Ohff and Karl Ruhrberg, Berling 1974; *László Lakner*, exhibition catalogue, with text by Heiner Stachelhaus, Dusseldorf 1977; *László Lakner: Malerei 1974–1979*, exhibition catalogue, with text by Thomas Deecke, Munster 1979; *László Lakner: Herliche Grusse aus Babel*, exhibition catalogue with text by Walter Grasskamp, Essen 1982; *László Lakner*, exhibition catalogue with texts by Manfred de la Motte and Roland Wiegenstein, West Berlin 1985: articles—article by Alain Jouffroy in *Opus International* (Paris), no. 1, 1971; article by Alain Jouffroy in *Opus International* (Paris), no. 5, 1972; article by Karl Ruhrberg in *Magazine Kunst* (Mainz), no. 1, 1976.

LAM, Wilfredo

Cuban. Born Wilfredo Oscar de la Concepcion Lam y Castilla, in Sagua la Grande, 2 December 1902. Studied at the Academia San Alejandra, Havana, 1920–23; Free Academy, Madrid, and in the studio of Fernando Alvarez di Sotomayor, Director of the Prado, Madrid, 1924–28. Married Eva Piris in 1929 (died, 1931); married Elena Holzer in 1944 (separated, 1950): married Lou Laurin in 1959: children: Eskil, Timour and Jonas. Painter: worked at the Academia de Quatre Gates, Barcelona, 1936–37; fought with the Republicans in the Spanish Civil War, then left Spain in 1938 and settled in Paris: close friendship with Oscar Dominguez and associated with Surrealists, especially André Breton and Max Ernst, Paris, 1938; during the occupation left France with Breton, Claude Levi-Strauss and others for Martinique, then via Santo Domingo to Cuba, 1941; after the war travelled frequently, spending long periods in New York, Cuba and Paris, 1946–52; settled again in Paris, 1952. Recipient: First Prize, Salone Nacionale, Havana, 1951; Gold Medal for Foreign Painters, Premio Lissone, Rome, 1953; Guggenheim Award, 1964; Premio Marzotto, Milan, 1965. *Died* (in Paris) *11 September 1982.*

Individual Exhibitions:

1928	Galerie Vilches, Madrid
1939	Galerie Pierre, Paris
	Peris Gallery, New York (with Pablo Picasso)
1942	Pierre Matisse Gallery, New York
1944	Pierre Matisse Gallery, New York

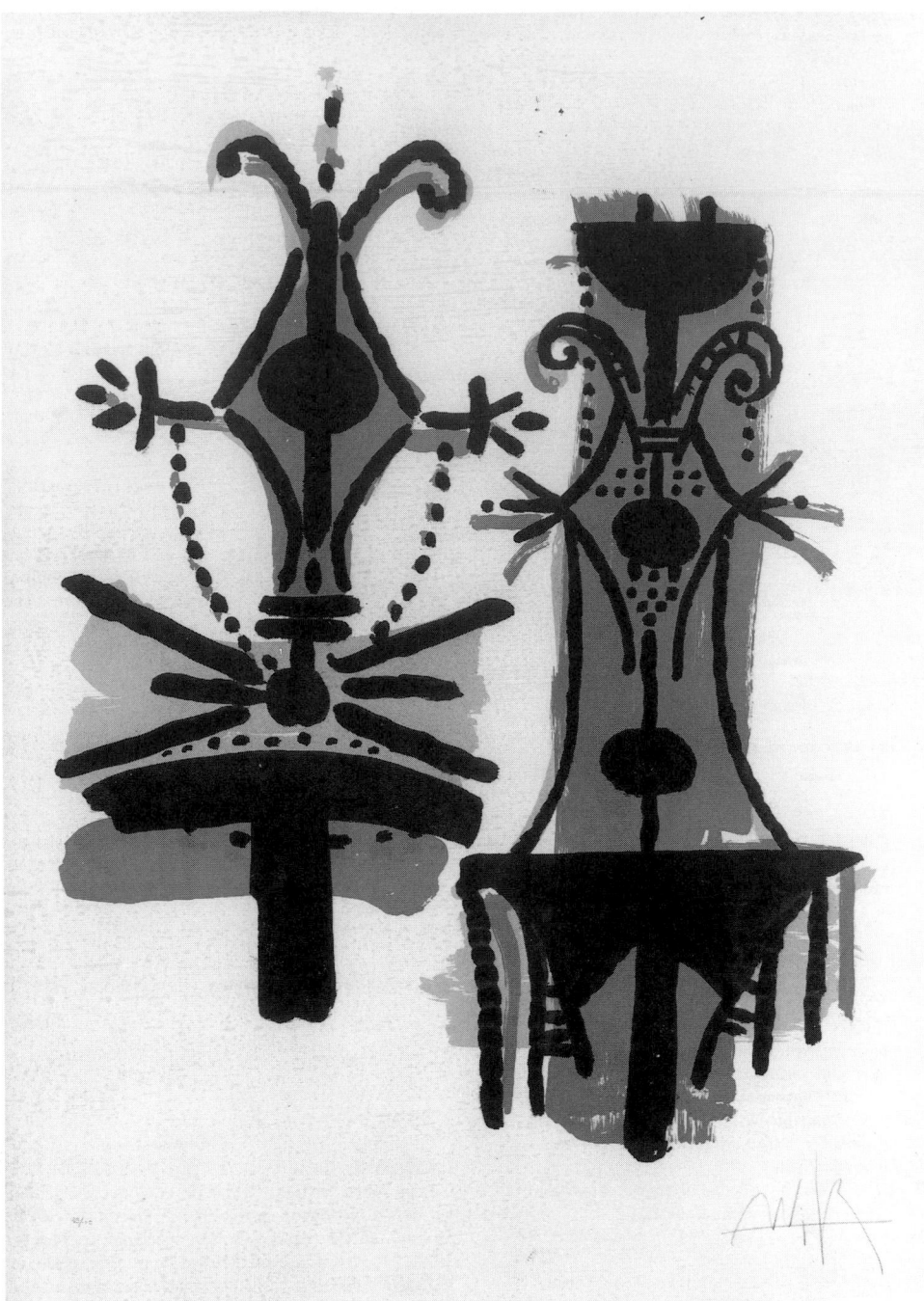

Wilfredo Lam: *Pour Jorn*, 1976 Courtesy Guggenheim Museum, New York

1945	Galerie Pierre, Paris	1964	Galleria Notizie, Turin
	Pierre Matisse Gallery, New York	1965	Museo de Arte Moderna, Havana
1946	Centre d'Art, Port-au-Prince, Haiti		Galerie Anderson, Malmo, Sweden
1948	Pierre Matisse Gallery, New York		Galerie Christine Aubry, Paris
1950	Pierre Matisse Gallery, New York	1966	Kunsthalle, Basle (with Vic Gentils)
1951	Ministry of Education, Havana		Kestner-Gesellschaft, Hannover
1952	Institute of Contemporary Arts, London	1967	Galerie Albert Loeb, Paris
1953	Galerie Maeght, Paris		Stedelijk Museum, Amsterdam
1955	Galerie Colibri, Malmo, Sweden		Moderna Museet, Stockholm
	University of Havana		Palais des Beaux-Arts, Brussels
	Museo de Bellas Artes, Caracas	1968	Musée d'Art Moderne de la Ville, Paris (with Matta
	Instituto Venezuela-Francia, Caracas		and Alicia Penalba)
1957	Palacio de Bellas Artes, Maracaibo, Venezuela		Galerie Villand et Galanis, Paris
	Galerie Cahiers d'Art, Paris	1969	Kunstkabinett, Frankfurt
1959	Galleria Grattacielo, Milan		Galleria Bergamini, Milan
1961	University of Notre Dame, Indiana	1970	Galleria Arte Borgogna, Milan
	Galerie La Cour d'Ingres, Paris		Galerie Krugier, Geneva
	Galleria del Canale, Venice		Gimpel Fils, London
	Galleria del Obelisco, Rome		Gimpel and Weitzenhoffer, New York
	Albert Loeb Gallery, New York	1971	Galerie Gimpel und Hanover, Zurich
1962	Salone Annunciata, Milan	1972	Galerie Tronche, Paris
1963	Galerie Krugier, Geneva		Studio Bellini, Milan
	Galeria de la Habana, Havana	1978	Ordrupgaard Samlingen, Copenhagen
	La Bibliteca Nacional, Havana	1979	Artcurial, Paris

1982	Pierre Matisse Gallery, New York
1987	Galerie Maeght Lelong, Zurich

Selected Group Exhibitions:

1947	*Exposition Internationale du Surrealisme*, Galerie Maeght, Paris
1958	*50 Ans d'Art Moderne*, Palais des Beaux-Arts, Brussels
1959	*Documenta*, Kassel, West Germany
1963	*Zeugnisse der Angst in der Modernen Kunst*, Darmstadt
1966	*Grands et Jeunes d'Aujourd'hui*, Musée d'Art Moderne de la Ville, Paris
1968	*Painting in France 1900–1967*, National Gallery, Washington, D.C. (toured the United States)
1978	*Cuba:Peinires d'Aujourd'hui*, Musée d'Art Moderne de la Ville, Paris

Collections:

Centre Georges Pompidou, Paris; Musée d'Art Moderne de la Ville, Paris; Moderna Museet, Stockholm; Tate Gallery, London; Nationalgalerie, Berlin; Museum Boymans-van-Beuningen, Rotterdam; Stedelijk van Abbemuseum, Eindhoven, Netherlands; Museum of Modern Art, New York; Art Institute of Chicago; Centro Medico, Havana.

Publications:

By LAM: articles—"Lettre de Wilfredo Lam" in *Opus International* (Paris). September 1971; discussion, with Anne Tronche, in *Wilfredo Lam*, exhibition catalogue, Paris 1972; "Lam della Giungla," interview, in *Bolaffiarte* (Turin), April 1974.

On LAM: books—*Lam*, exhibition catalogue, by André Breton, Port-au-Prince, Haiti 1946; *Wilfredo Lam y su Obra Vista a traves de Significados Criticos* by Fernando Ortiz, Havana 1950; *Lam* by Jacques Charpier, Paris 1960; *Lam* by Hubert Juin, Paris 1964; *Wilfredo Lam*, edited by Alex Grall, Paris 1970; *Servizi in Porcellana Decorati da Wilfredo Lam* by M. V. Ferrero, Turin 1970; *Wilfredo Lam* by Michel Leiris, Milan 1970; *Lam* by Alain Jouffroy, Paris 1972: *Wilfredo Lam*, exhibition catalogue with essay by Per Kirkeby, Zurich 1987.

Cuban Wilfredo Lam's father died at the age of 108 as the result of an accident. He was 84 when Wilfredo, the eldest of a family of 9, was born. The artist's mother was part African, part Indian, part European. Father was a Chinese trader.

Surely this was a romantic melting pot. The first of Wilfredo Lam's three children was the child of his third wife, and the painter was 59 years old when the boy was born. Not a patch on his father's extraordinary record, but Wilfredo Lam's reputation is global rather than domestic.

After time at the Havana Academie San Alejandra, he went to study painting in Spain, at that time still regarded by Cubans as a sort of mother country. In the mid-30's he saw his first Picasso exhibition and became associated with the *Quatre Gates* in Barcelona.

Franco's victory meant he had to leave Spain for Paris. Picasso was enthusiastic about Lam's work, and he introduced him to a number of surrealists--André Breton, Victor Brauner, Oscar Dominguez, Paul Eluard, Max Ernst, André Masson, Tanguy and Tristan Tzara.

It was against this kind of background and upbringing that the art of Wilfredo Lam developed, a kind of painting which never forgot the Caribbean but was able to weave such origins into the fabric of European contemporary art. In practical terms what this has meant is that Lam, one of the very few out of the West Indies to play a conspicuous role in the development of world culture, has refashioned Voodoo elements and the lush forbidden fruit of jungles in the Western hemisphere, while at the same time portraying these in a contemporary style acceptable to cultured Western eyes. Lam himself was familiar with the Haitian version of Voodoo, and no doubt also with the way in which the cult has been practised in Cuba. While he does not name *loas* (the Voodoo spirits) or accoutre them with their traditional attributes, he does describe them with dramatic line and with brooding dark pigment the esoteric "other world" whose West Indian and South American supporters regard as central to existence.

In his range of imagery, Lam scarcely altered over the years. If some of the "jungle" pictures are densely packed, this in no way inhibits the sparse style he uses for his *Personnages* and *Oiseaux* (potent in many of the paintings and drawings, even though slingshots have long since decimated the bird population of Haiti). Many of the *personnages* are horned, some wear the top hat of *Baron Samedi*, the loa in charge of the dead, beaks proliferate, and there are many sharp angles, triangles and empty eyes.

The special nature of Wilfredo Lam's art is its ability to bring West Indian Africa into Europe and into the United States.

—Sheldon Williams

LAMELAS, David.

Argentinian. Born in Buenos Aires, 12 December 1946. Studied at the Fine Arts Academy, Buenos Aires, 1960–65, and St. Martin's School of Art, London, 1968–69. Lived and worked in London from 1968; now lives in Los Angeles. Has lectured at the Nottingham School of Art, England; Slade School of Art, London; Royal College of Art, London; Académie des Beaux-Arts, Paris; University of California at Los Angeles; University of California at Irvine; Otis Art Institute, Los Angeles; California Institute of the Arts, Valencia; Hofstra University, Hempstead, New York; Rutgers University, New Brunswick, New Jersey; and the University of California at Santa Barbara. Recipient: Instituto Torcuato di Tella Prize, Buenos Aires, 1966; Sculpture Prize *Bienal,* Sao Paulo, 1967. Agents: Wide White Space, Molenstraat 81–83, Antwerp, Belgium; Galleria Francoise Lambert, Bastioni di Porta Nuova, Milan, Italy; and Galerie Yvon Lambert, 5 rue du Grenier-St.-Lazare, 75003 Paris, France.

Individual Exhibitions:

1965   Galeria Lirolay, Buenos Aires
1966   Galeria Lirolay, Buenos Aires
1970   Wide White Space Gallery, Antwerp
       Galerie Yvon Lambert, Paris
       Galleria Francoise Lambert, Milan
       Nigel Greenwood Gallery, London
1971   Galerie Yvon Lambert, Paris
1972   Galleria Lia Rumma, Naples
       Wide White Space Gallery, Antwerp
       Galleria Francoise Lambert, Milan
       Nigel Greenwood Gallery, London
1973   Wide White Space Gallery, Antwerp
       Wide White Space Gallery, Brussels
1974   Galleria Francoise Lambert, Milan
1975   Galerie Yvon Lambert, Paris
       Wide White Space Gallery, Antwerp
       Musée d'Art Moderne, Paris
       Palais des Beaux-Arts, Brussels
       Institute of Contemporary Arts, London
1976   Whitney Museum, New York
1978   Centro de Arte y Comunicacion, Buenos Aires

Selected Group Exhibitions:

1967   *Bienal,* Sao Paulo
1968   *Biennale,* Venice
       Wide White Space Artists, Wide White Space Gallery, Antwerp
1969   *Environmental Show,* Camden Art Centre, London

1970   *Information,* Museum of Modern Art, New York
1971   *Biennale de Paris,* Parc Floral de Vincennes, Paris
1972   *A Survey of the Avant-Garde in Britain,* Gallery House, London
1973   *Actualité d'un Bilan,* Galerie Yvon Lambert, Paris
       Documenta, Kassel, West Germany
1974   *Projekt 74,* Kunsthalle, Cologne

Collections:

Arts Council of Great Britain, London; Centre Georges Pompidou, Paris.

Publications:

By LAMELAS: book—*Publication,* London 1970; articles—"Self-Awareness" in *Art and Artists* (London), July 1969; "La lecture d'un film," with Lynda Morris, in *Art Press* (Paris), March 1973.

On LAMELAS: articles—"Un art d'analyse: Lamelas" by Catherine Millet in *Lettres Francaises* (Paris), May 1970; "David Lamelas" by Alain Jouffroy in *Opus International* (Paris), May 1970; "L'Effect:Ecran" by Severo Sarduy in *Art Press* (Paris), March 1973; "Self-Awareness" by Raul Escari in *Art and Artists* (London), July 1969; "David Lamelas: An Introduction to the Structural Development" by Lynda Morris in *Studio International* (London), January 1974; "David Lamelas" by Rosetta Brooks in *Studio International* (London), August 1975.

My first trip in 1958 is probably the most important and influential of all my moves since then; I travelled by boat from Buenos Aires to Spain, a 16 days trip in an English boat. From Galicia (where my parents come from) we travelled all over Spain. It was in Madrid at the El Prado Museum that I had a first major impact on my Art Consciousness with Velasquez' "Las Meninas." I do still have vividly the impact of when I first walked into "Las Meninas" room; no art experience has equalled yet the influence of that vision upon me. My second and again a definite influence was my move to London in 1968. The consequences of the move are equally permanent as my first view of Velasquez. And my third important move is my move from London to Los Angeles. I am not totally aware yet of the results of this move.

It may sound strange that I co-relate my evolution as an artist according to my geographical changes, but it is important to think of my work in reference to a particular *time* and *place* in which the work has been produced; I work as a response to the conditions of life in which I function at a particular moment and location.

David Lamelas: Stills from the film *The Desert People,* 1974

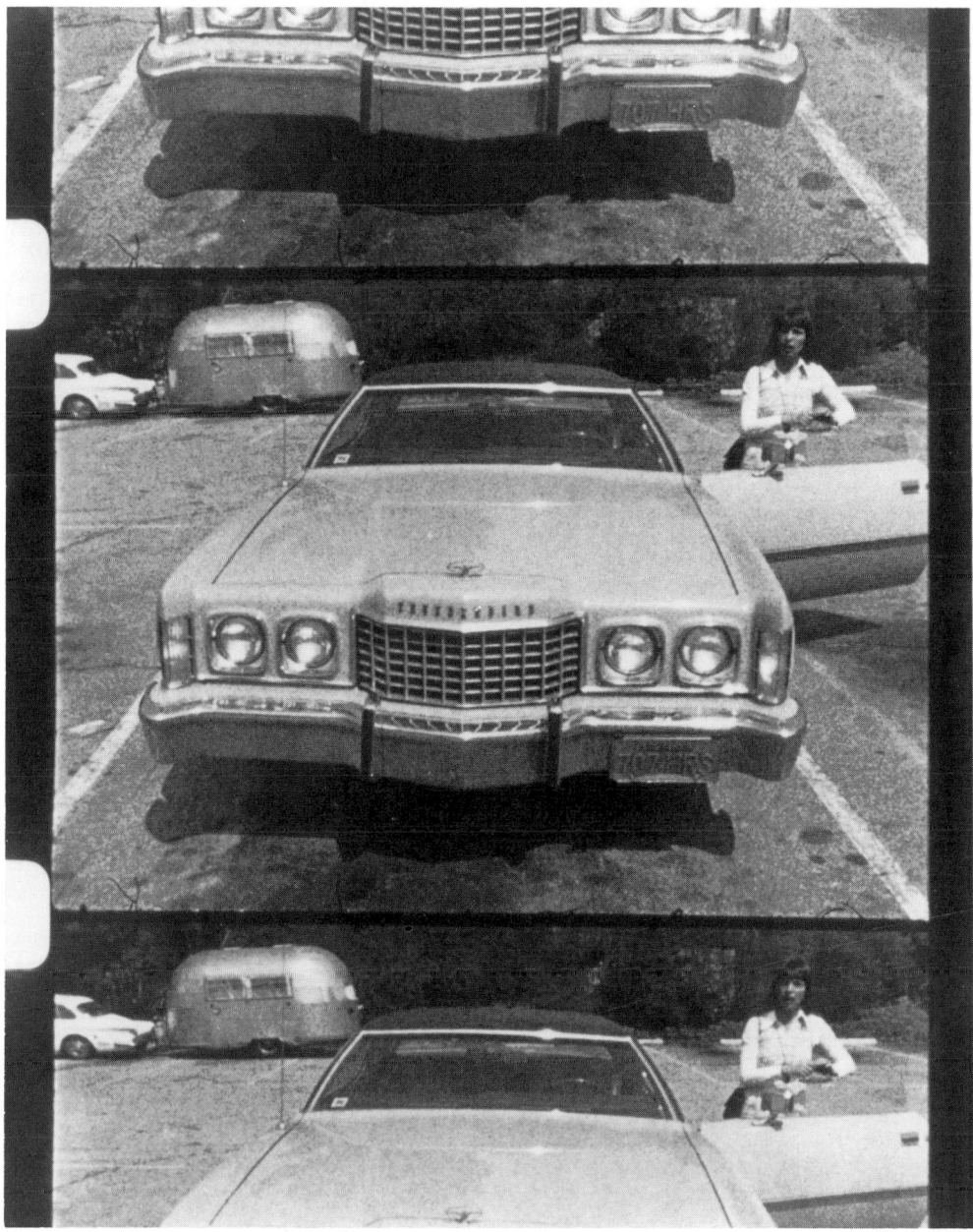

What I call my geographical positions on earth are carefully chosen according to a pre-plan of what I intuit my "art concerns" will be at a later state.

Generally about two to three years in advance it is possible to predict the development of my art interests; then I try as much as possible to place myself into the nearest to the perfect conditions for this work to be accomplished. Each piece represents the conclusion of the *conflict* created by my previous piece; the work I do in between the last piece and the next relates not only to an aesthetic framework but as wide as possible into other fields of experience of the "real" into the socio-economic-political context. I do consider all branches of human behavior into the field of the "real" (tangible) including the intellectual work, from where I depart on my *aesthetic reasoning*.

Since my framework is of the Visual Arts, I try to concentrate all of the complexities into the simplest possible common denominator of the Art Form, but since "art denominator" is constantly changing (as it should, otherwise it becomes an Academic product for market consumption, capitalized as merchandise of the Art World), each piece represents an entirely different conflict and also probably the use of a different media each time, from photographs to film to video, written form, drawing or any other.

And therefore to a different solution, giving place to create another conflict, to be resolved by the artist himself or herself, or any other artist who may be interested in following the new source.

—David Lamelas

The continuity of David Lamelas's work comes from the diversity of primary sources rather than stylistic devices of subject and image. The continuity emerges from the development of an intelligible structure, through which the viewer analyses his personal response to visual information. Image and structure are totally re-thought at the start of each new work; they are depersonalized to avoid all external connotations, except that of self reference.

Lamelas's early work was produced in Argentina between 1966 and 1968. A predominant interest was in the similarity of thought represented in disciplines as diverse as philosophy, psychology, literature and the visual arts. This interest provided an analytical background which approached the problems then presented by minimal art. Through the isolation of technical forms from any external content the work suggested a non-descriptive and non-physical art form.

These works developed towards an analysis of information, how people read a situation and its content.

The analysis of information developed into a concern with the relationship between time and vision. A similar attitude applies to *Publication*, the book published by Nigel Greenwood in 1970. Too much emphasis has been placed upon the statements in the book. The question of language is explicit because it is the subject of the texts, but the importance is the context, not the subject. *Publication* implies a syllogistic form; the book was the exhibition, but the exhibition was the actual work. Similarly the subject of the book was "oral and written language as an art form," which also dictated the structure of the piece as a book.

After *Publication* the function of language became incorporated in the work, a decision which was marked by the two *Reading* films. The first was a passage from Jose Luis Borges's *A New Dimension of Time*. The choice of Borges strengthened the implication that the film was a mirror-image of the person watching it. A very Borgian idea. The second film took a text from *Knots* by Ronald Laing. Both films are an analysis of reading, but not just reading a text. One also reads people, situations and visual information. The films reflect two ways of handling the same problem. There are not distinctions made between the two writers, only between the responses the writers produce. The difference between the two films is one of understanding and that is how the films connect.

The reduction which eliminated language after the *Reading* films is paralleled by the elimination of human action in *To Pour Milk into a Glass*. The camera position is constant throughout the film. In the first shot the glass is empty. In the second shot the empty glass is gradually filled to the rim. The third shot repeats the first two, until the milk overflows. Gradually the information is built up, extending the viewer's ability to read, repetition representing memory. The total simplicity, almost banality, of the images is intentional. The aim is to find an image which is the equivalent of one word, or one action—a total self-containment. The reality of a language description is different from the reality of a seen image but they both represent part of the same reality. The work attempts to bring the language of the film and the representation of the film to the same point.

The films are a conversation between the artist and the viewer; the abstracted structure allows the conversation to remain open-ended. In conversation a person says many things which are only relevant to the specific conversation; they do not relate to the subjects of the conversation. The films are about that area of communication. The only definitive statement is the visual response and individual understanding of the viewer.

—Lynda Morris

LANE, Lois.

American. Born in Philadelphia, Pennsylvania, 6 January 1948. Studied at Yale Summer School of Music and Art, New Haven, Connecticut, 1968; Philadelphia College of Art, B.F.A. 1969; Yale University, New Haven, Connecticut, M.F.A. 1971. Painter. Recipient: Creative Artists Public Service Program Grant, New York State Council on the Arts, 1977; Fellowship in painting, National Endowment for the Arts, 1978. Agent: Willard Gallery, New York. Address: c/o Willard Gallery, 29 East 72nd Street, New York, New York 10028, U.S.A.

Individual Exhibitions:

1977   Willard Gallery, New York
1979   Willard Gallery, New York
1980   *New Work by Lois Lane*, Willard Gallery, New York
         Greenberg Gallery, St. Louis
1981   Akron Art Museum, Ohio
1983   Willard Gallery, New York

Selected Group Exhibitions:

1978   *Ronald Greenberg Collection*, Brooks Memorial Art Gallery, Memphis, Tennessee
1979   *New Image Painting*, Whitney Museum, New York
         Biennial, Whitney Museum, New York
         10 Artists/Artists Space, Neuberger Museum, Purchase, New York
         American Painting: The 80's, Grey Art Gallery, New York University
1980   *Printed Art: A View of Two Decades*, Museum of Modern Art, New York
         American Prints 1960–1980, Bronfman Centre, Montreal

Since her inclusion in the well-publicized exhibition at the Whitney Museum of American Art, *New Image Painting*, Lois Lane's career has been surveyed in the critical literature. The phrase used in the title of that exhibition, the first "new trend" show in several years, has become a part of the critical discourse in the past few years: "new image" refers to artists who make little distinction between abstraction and figuration. Lane herself has said "I was never that inter-

ested in painting per se, I was much more interested in image making . . . ."

Characteristic of Lane's approach to the canvas have been large scale (5 by 8 feet is not uncommon), surfaces covered with a single color, or a contrast of matte and shiny variant of a color, and an extremely sparse array of figurative matter set against that ground. Reminiscent of Ron Gorchov's dual placement of similar marks against a large color field, for instance, were the paintings which Lane produced about 1977–78, where two bud-like forms and other clearly figurative shapes were placed at each side of the rectangle of the canvas.

In works from the early 1980's she used collaged pictures from magazines in a single line across the monochromatic rear color ground. It may be the overall modesty and humbled quality of their depiction whether drawn or collaged—despite their overall heroic size—that leads to an effect describable as enigmatic pathos. Lane's partisans insist on the intense and visionary significance of these images; and her commitment to an eclectic abstraction has remained unabated. More recently, there is a pleasure in the process and brushwork of her surfaces, while the domestic allusion—silhouetted forms of gowns, children, houses, et al.—remain as heretofore to set up the surreal expressiveness in her untitled paintings.

—Joshua Kind

LANG, Nikolaus.

German. Born in Oberammergau, 12 February 1941. Educated at the Volksschule, Oberammergau, 1948-53, and the Gymnasium, Ettal, Garmisch, 1953–56; studied woodcarving, under Julius Himpel, at the Staatliche Schnitzschule, Oberammergau, 1956–60, and art at the Akademie der Bildenden Künste, Munich, 1960–66, and the Camberwell School of Arts and Crafts, London, 1967–69. Married Celia Hewitt in 1974. Independent artist, Bayersoien, since 1969: associated with Rainer Wittenborn and "Gruppe Spur" artists, Munich, 1960–63; with artists Gilbert and George, Richard Hamilton, and Mark Boyle, London, 1966–68, Camberwell School of Arts and Crafts, London. Recipient: D.A.A.D. Stipendium, West Berlin, for travel to London, 1966–67, for travel to Japan, 1971–72; Staatlicher Bayerischer Forderungspreis, 1975; Villa Romana Prize, Florence, 1976; Glockengasse 4711 Art Prize, 1980; First Prize, Environment of the Free University Competition, West Berlin, 1982; Prinz Albrecht Palast Prize, West Berlin, 1983; Defet Prize, Kunstlerbund Deutschlands, 1986; Gabriele Munther-Johannes Eichner Stiftung Award, 1986; Kunstfonds Award, Bonn, 1986; Artist in Residence Award, South Australia College of Art, Adelaide, 1987. Address: Grundbauernhof, 8117 Bayersoien, West Germany.

Individual Exhibitions:

1968   Hagen Residence, London
1969   Kleine Galerie, Frankfurt
1970   Galerie Leonhardt, Munich
1971   Wimbledon Common, London
         Galerie de Gestlo, Hamburg (with Rainer Wittenborn)
         Galleri Ostergen AB, Malmo, Sweden
1972   Maltzahn Gallery, London
1973   Galerie de Gestlo, Hamburg
         Japanische Landschaften, Städtische Galerie im Lenbachhaus, Munich
1974   *Nikolaus Lang's Museum*, Neue Galerie, Aachen, West Germany
1975   Kunst Forum, Rottweil, West Germany
         Kestner-Gesellschaft, Hannover
1976   Wurttembergischer Kunstverein, Stuttgart
1978   Westfalischer Kunstverein, Munster
         Galerie Defet, Nuremberg, West Germany

Selected Group Exhibitions:

Collections:

Stedelijk Museum, Amsterdam; Tate Gallery, London; Nationalgalerie, West Berlin; Stadtische Galerie im Lenbachhaus, Munich; Australian National Gallery, Canberra; South Australia Art Gallery, Adelaide.

Publications:

On LANG: books—*Nikolaus Lang: Japanische Landschaften,* exhibition catalogue, with text by Armin Zweite, Munich 1973: *Nikolaus Lang's Museum,* exhibition catalogue, with text by Wolfgang Becker, Aachen, West Germany 1974; *Spurensicherung: Archaeologie und Erinnerung,* exhibition catalogue, with texts by Günter Metken and Uwe M. Schneede, Hamburg 1974; *5 from Germany,* exhibition catalogue, with text by Robert Kudielka, London 1974; *Nikolaus Lang,* exhibition catalogue, with texts, by Carl-Albrecht Haenlein and Günter Metken, Hannover 1975; *Vergangenheit-Gegenwart-Zukunft,* exhibition catalogue, with an introduction by Tilman Osterwold, Stuttgart 1982: films—*Nikolaus Lang,* television film by Dieter Wieland, 1970; *Nikolaus Lang und Ulrich Ruckriem,* television film by Jurgen Hohemeyer, 1975.

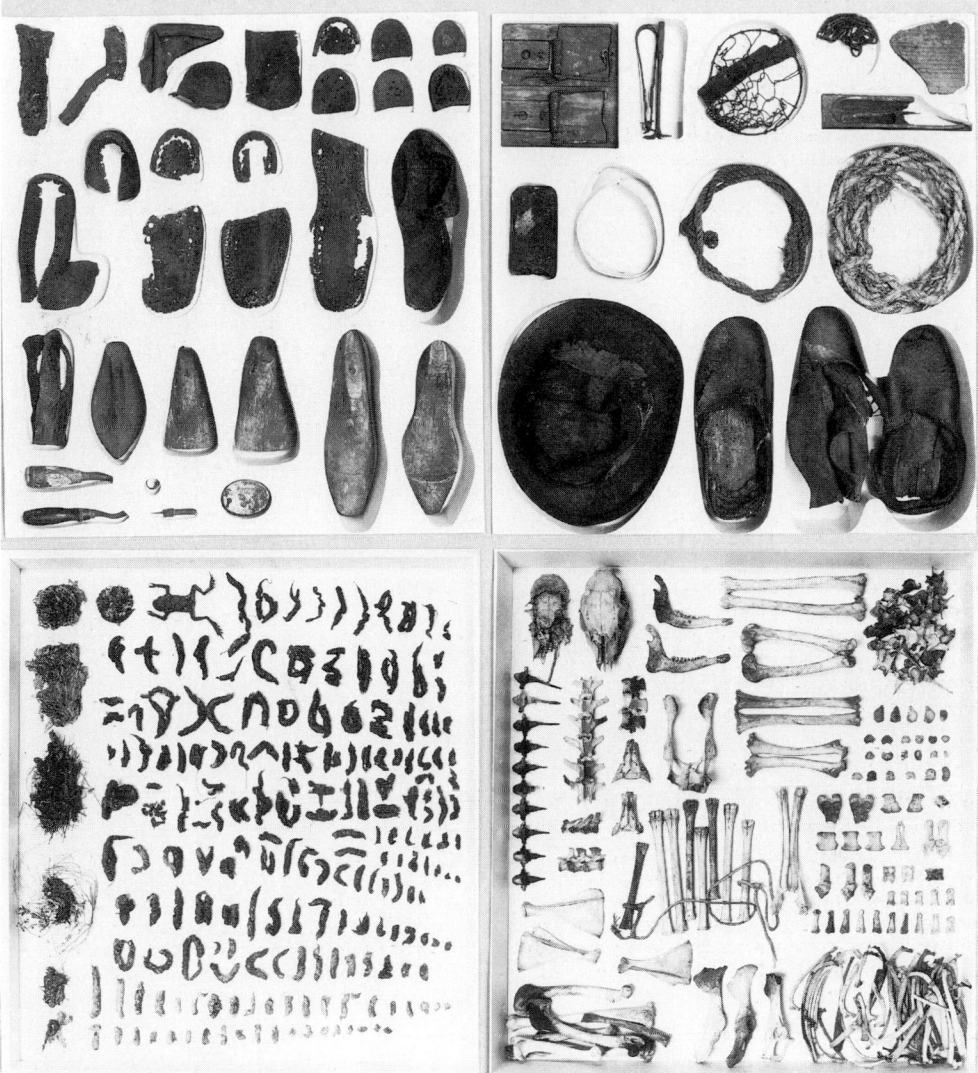

Nikolaus Lang: *Gotte Family*, 1973

Nikolaus Lang collects traces and remains. He preserves a situation which is both an objective detection and subjective finding, as well as a discovery of oneself. The investigation of the terrain imparts information about himself. Should one thus describe his activity as field research or a search for personal traces? Both apply, in my opinion, for ethnology too—at least according to Levi-Strauss' interpretation—involves a searching for oneself in others. A description of alien communities is of significance only in relation to our own; who could disregard himself in exploring remote circumstances?

Ethnology is concerned with groups whose relics can still be traced in our epoch. Nikolaus Lang found himself in a similar situation when he attempted to place the Gotte brothers and sisters. They were the children of a Swiss immigrant who purchased an isolated farmstead near Bayersoien, Germany. Four of the seven children were rejected by the old-established village community, so they built themselves cottages on the remote farm lands; they remained single and without progeny. One of the Gotte offspring emigrated to America.

These outsiders have since died. At the same time, the village community has begun to disintegrate due to the exodus from the land, tourism and mechanization. The distinct social division between the centre and the periphery, which determined the marginal, bachelor existence of the Gotte children as small farmers, cobblers and odd-job men, has become blurred and will probably soon be indistinguishable. This event provides the insight into the social structure of rural areas. Obvious are the problems of a brief happening and its far-reaching consequences, which is today the concern of historical researchers. Therefore over and above old customs and folklore, this case must be seen from many more perspectives; comparison with other phenomena of social rejection and non-integration could be illuminating.

Naturally, Nikolaus Lang is not concerned with comparative studies; although he proceeds in accordance with modern concepts in that he tackles a current problem and not a documented case, evaluates all the vestiges, even the most trivial, and not only documents or fashioned, possibly aesthetic objects. For example, he has collated villagers' statements about the Gotte family, searched their houses and, insofar as these have fallen into decay, the immediate vicinity. The discovered objects, which are partly clothing, household effects, religious items and tools, and partly paper, almanacs and farming catalogues, are displayed in the upper tray of a grain chest; its remaining two sections contain plants, fruit, snail shells, excrement of martens and the bones of deer found close to the houses, a mummified female hare, a roebuck skeleton, stones and fossil impressions discovered further afield. This leads to pages from the land register, geological maps, climatic charts and descriptions replete with photographs. However, in contrast to scientists, the artist consciously fails to exhaust all his sources; he selects a small section, limits himself to the tangible.

For here, in the middle of this apparently objective preservation of remains, we encounter the personal quintessence of his work.

Nikolaus Lang, who grew up near Oberammergau, was once a frequent visitor to the meadows where he met Ludwig Gotte. Now he has reacquainted himself with the terrain across which he once roamed so cursorily. It is a kind of magical taking possession ceremony when he defines the sources and other places, sets up walls of leaves and interwoven objects, breaks coal and stones, when he collects, gathers, patches up Joseph's house or paces off the field to check his cartographical data. "Ethnology" now probes into itself. "Objective" research becomes an inward-looking quest. By exploring the terrain he maps out his own dimensions, latent clues are activated, a link is forged between earlier recollections and present-day topographical reality, a continuity emerges from intervals of time and becomes immersed in the period of experience. Lang spent over one year working on the project which incorporates part of himself and his time. The search for apparently predeterminate phenomena becomes essentially an exploration of oneself, the search for a standpoint in our rapidly changing society.

Similar to his French colleagues, Lang is fascinated by natural history museums and herbariums, which emphasize both the creative and display aspects of collecting. This explains the painstaking arrangement and lettering of the trays, and the precise documentation. Combined with this is the feeling acquired in Japan for the sensuality of objects and the linguistic-semantic declarative force of their arrangement. Lang's trays thus contain hieroglyphics. They speak to the eyes and store time. One instant is preserved and codified. Their meaning is twofold, being related to the Gotte clan and those who investigate its traces. Finally, the brothers and sisters only sparked off a personal delimitation of a position—an impulse which appears to be transferable.

—Günter Metken

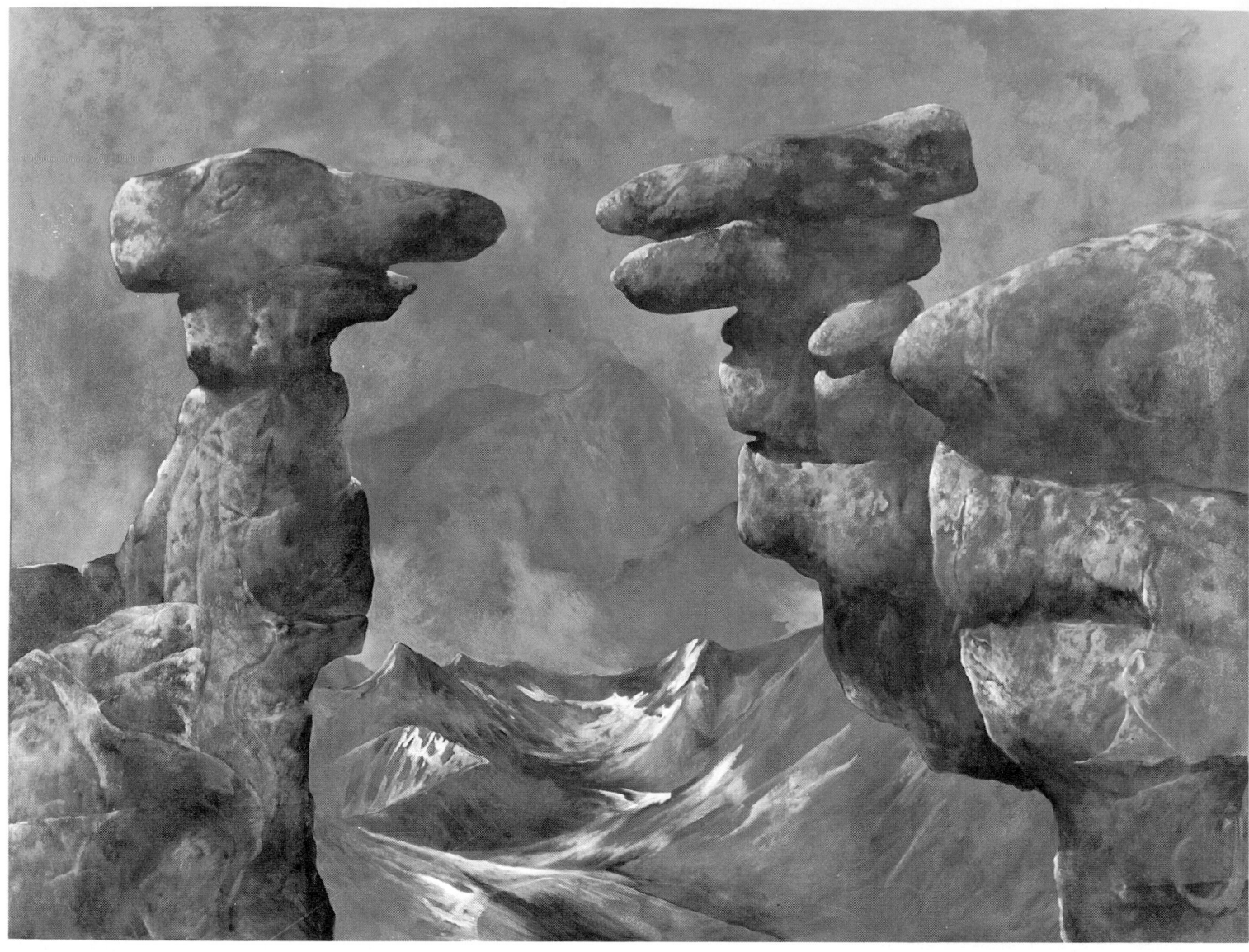

Ellen Lanyon: *Camel Rock Meets the Dartmoor Granite at Parmidgian Lake*, **1986**

LANYON, Ellen.

American. Born in Chicago, Illinois, 21 December 1926. Studied at the School of the Art Institute of Chicago, and Roosevelt University, Chicago, 1944–48, B.F.A. 1948; did graduate work at the University of Iowa, 1948–50, M.F.A. 1950; also studied at the Courtauld Institute, London, 1950–51. Married the artist Roland Ginzel; has two children. Independent painter since 1950: lives and works in New York City. Has taught at the Art Institute of Chicago, 1952–54, 1964-65, 1973, Rockford College, Illinois, 1954, Saugatuck Summer School of Painting, Michigan, 1961, 1962, 1967–69, University of Illinois, 1966, Oxbow Summer School, 1970, 1970–73, University of Wisconsin, 1972, Stanford University, California, 1973, University of California at Davis, 1973, Sacramento State University, California, 1973, Pennsylvania State University, University Park, 1974, Boston University, 1975, University of Iowa, Iowa City, 1975, Parsons School of Design, New York, 1979–80 and School of Visual Arts, New York, 1980; Associate Professor, Cooper Union, New York, since 1983. Recipient: Armstrong Prize, 1946, 1955, 1957, Town and Country Purchase Prize, 1947, Martin B. Cahn Award, 1961, and Vielehr Award, 1967, Art Institute of Chicago; Purchase Prize, Denver Art Museum, 1950; Pennell Purchase Prize, Library of Congress, 1950; Fulbright Fellowship, 1950; Dallas Museum of Fine Arts Award, 1965; Cassandra Foundation Grant, 1971; Yaddow Fellowship, Saratoga Springs, New York, 1974–76; National Endowment for the Arts Grant, 1974, 1987; Herewood Lester Cook Founda-

tion Grant, 1981; Logan Prize, Art Institute of Chicago, 1982. Agent: Richard Gray Gallery, 620 North Michigan Avenue, Chicago, Illinois 60611. Address: 138 Prince Street, New York, New York 10012, U.S.A.

Individual Exhibitions:

1952	Bordelon's, Chicago
1958	Superior Street Gallery, Chicago
1962	Stewart Rickard Gallery, San Antonio, Texas
	Fairweather Hardin Gallery, Chicago
	Zabriskie Gallery, New York
1964	Zabriskie Gallery, New York
1965	B. C. Holland Gallery, Chicago
1967	Fort Wayne Art Museum, Indiana
1968	B. C. Holland Gallery, Chicago
1969	Zabriskie Gallery, New York
1970	Richard Gray Gallery, Chicago
1972	Wabash Transit Gallery, Art Institute of Chicago
	Madison Art Center, Wisconsin
	National Collection of Fine Arts, Washington, D.C.
	Zabriskie Gallery, New York
1973	Richard Gray Gallery, Chicago
	Stephens College, Columbia, Missouri
1974	Kohler Center for the Arts, Sheboygan, Wisconsin
	University of California, Davis
	Pennsylvania State University, University Park
1976	Richard Gray Gallery, Chicago
	Galleria Odyssia, Rome
	Harcus Krakow Rosen Sonnabend Gallery, Boston

	Krannert Arts Center, University of Illinois, Champaign
	University of Missouri, Kansas City
1977	Women's Building, Los Angeles
	Lake Forest College, Illinois
1978	Fendrick Gallery, Washington, D.C.
	University of Houston, Texas
	Northern Illinois University, Dekalb
	Kentucky State University, Lexington
1979	Richard Gray Gallery, Chicago
	Bradley University, Peoria, Illinois
	Illinois Wesleyan University, Bloomington
1980	University of California, Davis
	Landfall Press, Chicago
	Odyssia Gallery, New York
1981	Alverno College, Milwaukee, Wisconsin
1982	Richard Gray Gallery, Chicago
	Rutgers University, Brunswick, New Jersey
1983	Susan Caldwell Inc., New York
	N.A.M.E. Gallery, Chicago
	St. Louis Community College, Missouri
1985	Richard Gray Gallery, Chicago
1987	Krannert Museum, University of Illinois, Champaign (retrospective; toured the United States)
	J. L. Becker Gallery, Provincetown, Massachusetts
	Barat College, Lake Forest, Illinois
1988	Richard Gray Gallery, Chicago

Selected Groups Exhibitions:

1945	*American Biennale*, Art Institute of Chicago

Collections:

Art Institute of Chicago; Krannert Museum, University of
Illinois, Champaign/Urbana; Museum of Contemporary Art,
Chicago; Metropolitan Museum of Art, New York; Brooklyn
Museum, New York; Library of Congress, Washington,
D.C.; National Museum of American Art, Washington,
D.C.; Denver Art Museum, Colorado; Madison Art Center,
Wisconsin; Walker Art Center, Minneapolis.

Publications:

By LANYON: articles—"Claire Zeisler" in *Art Scene* (Chicago), September 1967; "A Painter's Reply" in *Artforum*
(New York), September 1975; "Ellen Lanyon," interview
with David Elliott, in *Art News* (New York), May 1980; "Education of the Artist" in *Art Journal* (New York), Summer
1982.

On LANYON: books—*The Painter and the Photograph* by
Van Deren Coke, Albuquerque, New Mexico 1964, 1967;
Ellen Lanyon, exhibition catalogue, with text by Donn L.
Young, Fort Wayne, Indiana 1966; *Ellen Lanyon* by Franz
Schulze, New York 1972; *Ellen Lanyon*, exhibition catalogue
with texts by Dennis Adrian and Lucy Lippard, Chicago
1983; *The Art of Ellen Lanyon: A Retrospective Exhibition*,
catalogue with essays by Donald Kuspit and Stephen Prokopoff, Chicago 1987.

The approach has always been representational and
source material has been vital to the resolution of an
idea. Photographs from family albums, Rotogravure,
sports photography, nature guides, objects and an assortment of diverse printed matter constitute the inanimate inspiration while aviaries, conservatories,
humans, animals and natural environments provide
living stimulant.

From the earliest works, a sense of the amazing
phenomena of life as it manifests itself through cause
and effect has permeated the imagery . . . often making the results seem to be a studied surrealism or
metaphysical remark. Perhaps so, but, indeed, the
initial concept has been to illustrate the magical process of metamorphosis and transformation which occurs once a life process has begun. The drama of the
micro-scape as it expands to constitute the macro-
scape in a multitude of situations then becomes the
theme.

In recent works the incorporation of deep space,
landscape and the resemblance of natural formations
to an influenced human invention has predominated.
It is an ongoing adventure; a search for images which
can illustrate the predictability and incredible tolerance of nature.

—Ellen Lanyon

Ellen Lanyon's paintings represent two worlds. Although the images she uses reflect a detailed reality,
the combination of images provide insight into another world, a Pandora's box ruled by magic, transformations, and human fears and imaginings. Early in
her career, when other Chicago artists were captivated by the ethnographic collections at the Field Museum, Lanyon responded more directly to the
meticulous paintings done in 14th and 15th century
Siena which she found at the Art Institute. Although
she now paints on a larger scale, her fascination with
the meticulous continues, as does her use of distorted
perspective and disproportionate scale of objects. Her
subjects are anything but early Renaissance in concept. Using illustrations from a book on magic, and
other found objects, Lanyon assembles sophisticated
still-life groupings which she paints in acrylic on canvas or draws with prisma color pencils. Animals are
the main characters in Lanyon's mysterious, dream-
like dramas, but these are not pets nor are they an-
thropomorphized creatures of brawn or might. Frogs,
snakes, lizards, spiders, and birds, sometimes all in
the same painting, coexist or tumble out of containers
in the same way that ideas spill out of the mind when
released from subconscious confinement.

During the early 1970's Lanyon's work was created
in her studio, and the backgrounds of many paintings
are interiors or stylized landscapes. Even then, the
birds, animals, and insects dominated environments
to which they were interlopers. In "Xocolatyl," 1973,
animal life (tiny birds, enormous spiders) swarms
over a double valentine box, and in "Cobra," 1975, a
small but detailed house is possessed by a giant cobra
which coils in the background but sticks its head out
of the chimney. The house, and by implication its
inhabitants, worn like a medallion, is at the service of
the snake. Since the imagery is often rooted in personal experience, many of Lanyon's nightmarelike
works from this period lend themselves to a Freudian,
or paradoxically, a feminist interpretation.

In the mid-1970's Lanyon visited the Everglades
and began to integrate settings observed in nature into
her work. In "Egret," 1976, the swampy background
and large scale "real" egret dominate two smaller
foreground statues of the same bird. Nature has
grown more real and the manmade world less significant, a condition which, historically, has caused such
terror in man that, in his effort to gain control of the
world (earth), he has nearly succeeded in ending it.
The emphasis of images has shifted, and new and
different terrors abound in the recent work of Ellen
Lanyon.

—Mary Stofflet

LARDERA, Berto.

French. Born in La Spezia, Italy, 18 December 1911;
emigrated to France, 1947: naturalized, 1965. Educated at the Liceo Classico, La Spezia; studied classics at the University of Florence, 1926–32;
self-taught in sculpture and engraving. Married Cecile Corre in 1950; daughter: Aube. Sculptor, printmaker and graphic artist, Florence, 1933–46, in
Paris, since 1947. Critic, *La Nazionale del Popolo*
anti-fascist newspaper, Florence, 1944–46. Professor
of Sculpture, Hochschule für Bildenden Künste,
Hamburg, 1958–61. Officier, Ordre des Arts et Lettres, France; Chevalier, Légion d'Honneur, 1973.
Address: 9 Cité Falguière, 75015 Paris, France; and
18 rue de Seine, 75006 Paris, France.

Individual Exhibitions:

Selected Group Exhibitions:

Collections:

Galleria Nazionale d'Arte Moderna, Florence; Museum
Haus Lange, Krefeld, West Germany; Hochschule für
Bildenden Künste, Hamburg; Centre Technique, Paris; Cen-
tre Technique d'Etat, Le Mans, France; Conservatoire de
Musique et de Danse, Grenoble, France; Ecole d'Art et
Technique, Sens, France; Maison de France, Jerusalem;
Musée d'Art Contemporain, Montreal; Rhode Island Mu-
seum, Providence.

Publications:

On LARDERA: books—*Berto Lardera* by Michel Seuphor,
Milan 1933; *Berto Lardera: Sculptures, Dessins*, exhibition
folder, with text by Leon Degand, Paris 1948; *Berto Lardera*,
exhibition catalogue, with text by Paul Wember, Krefeld,
West Germany 1956; *Berto Lardera* by Michel Seuphor, Neu-
châtel, Switzerland 1960; *Berto Lardera: Plastik, Gouachen,
Collagen*, exhibition catalogue, with text by Alfred Hentzen,
Hamburg 1960; *Lardera*, exhibition catalogue, with text by
Michel Seuphor, Zagreb 1962; *Lardera: Jouet pour adultes*,
exhibition catalogue, with text by Jann Runnqvist, Stockholm
1964; *Lardera*, exhibition catalogue, with text by Guy Rob-
ert, Quebec 1965; *Lardera*, exhibition catalogue, with text by
Marc Netter, Le Havre, France 1966; *Berto Lardera*, by
Jouel Jianon and Marcel Brion, Paris 1968; *Berto Lardera:
La Rose des Vents*, exhibition catalogue, with text by Werner
Haftmann, New York 1969; *Berto Lardera*, exhibition cata-
logue, with texts by Manfred de la Motte, Harald Seiler,
Werner Haftmann and others, Hannover 1971; *Berto Lar-
dera: Plastiken, Collagen, Graphiken*, exhibition catalogue,
with texts by S. Salzmann, G. Gepts, J. Laude and others,
Duisburg, West Germany 1976.

In my first Two-Dimensional Sculpture in 1942 I
tried to use optical suggestions instead of volume,
weight and mass. This idea probably had an influence
on the experiments in op-art and kinetic art. These
are concerned with movement in its material aspect
whereas I study the dynamic of forms in space. The
essential thing is not movement as such, which is a
materialization of moving, but the inner drive. Optical suggestion offers a much greater variety of potential movements in the mind.

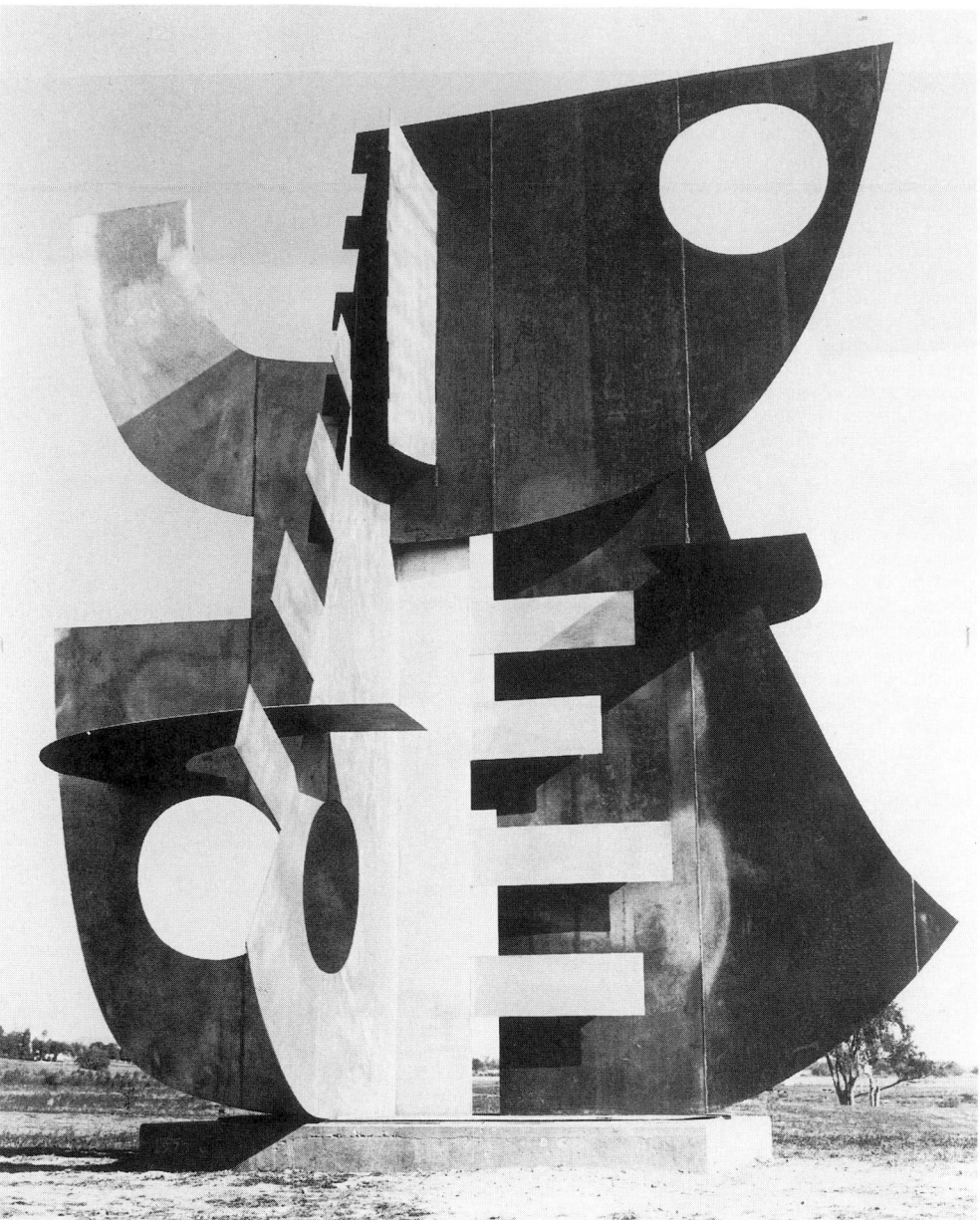

Berto Lardera: *Maryland Star*, 1970

By opposing two-dimensional forms one to another and reducing them to their essential expression, I obtained an infinite multiplicity of optical suggestions of space. That is the basic reason for two-dimensional sculpture.

—Berto Lardera

As if Domela or Hélion at his most non-figurative had become metal and 3-dimensional, the sculpture of Berto Lardera—through numerous vicissitudes—builds monuments to non-objectivity. Here is an "abstract" sculptor in the old 1930-ish sense of the word, but one who actually does not appear to have actually abstracted imagery from any recognizable object. This is not to suggest that his is a geometric style. On the contrary. The variety of his shapes and the angles at which they have been juxtaposed implies no such thing. Nor is he colour blind. Quite apart from the Kandinsky-like concern he shows for blacks and whites and primaries (other colours too) in his collages and crayon drawings, he has been known to insert areas of mosaic into iron bodies of some of his works, and he has a keen understanding of the contrast values that can be enhanced by the association of iron and steel and copper.

Michael Seuphor who, in his monograph on the artist, is adamant in his refusal to *explain* or analyse the Italian's work, still manages to give Lardera a special place in contemporary art when he describes him as a linkman, one who through his realization of the potentialities of "art" has gone a long way to reestablish the union between sculpture (and painting!) and architecture. Seuphor reminds his readers that in ancient times to build was regarded as the finest cultural achievement, and he goes on to declare that this canon of taste is bound one day to be revived and that therefore the Italian sculptor can be reckoned a precursor of a golden age yet to come.

Certainly Lardera, ever since he abandoned his early experiments (as a figurative artist!) when he believed that he was investigating the virtues of various sculptural media available, has exhibited a shrewd awareness of the architectural function that sculpture could fulfil. When he turned away from working in relief in favour of a new approach to sculptured "murals," he was already on course for his next development: 2-dimensional work. It was at this point that he seemed to have pirated abstract painting and turned pictures into objects—objects which could be viewed from two directions: front and rear.

For him, the natural extension of this activity was to re-involve himself with the three-dimensional; but his experience of the *flat* sculpture, free-standing or mural, made his understanding of the values promised by planes set at angles all the more potent. And throughout, the metals, like paint, were allowed to display varying surface characteristics to provide vis-

ual and tactile independence. Incisions, fretting, even surface engraving (and on rare occasions mosaic) all play their parts, where circumstance dictates, to allow a rich variety to permeate the body of his work.

—Sheldon Williams

LATHAM, John.

British. Born on Zambesi River, Rhodesia, 23 February 1921. Educated at Winchester College, Hampshire; studied at Chelsea School of Art, London, 1946–50. Served in the Royal Navy, 1940–46. Married Barbara Steveni in 1951; children: Noa, John Paul and Xenia. Lives and works in London: Founder-Member, Institute for the Study of Mental Images, London, 1954; executed first spray paintings, 1954; first book sculptures, 1958; first happenings and films, 1959; inaugurated Skoob Tower ceremonies, London, 1964; Founder-Member, Artists Placement Group, London, 1966; Part-time lecturer, St. Martin's School of Art, London, 1966–67. Address: 5 Boscombe Road, London W12 9HS, England.

Individual Exhibitions:

1948	Kingly Gallery, London
1955	Obelisk Gallery, London
1957	Obelisk Gallery, London
1960	Institute of Contemporary Arts, London
	Galerie Schmela, Dusseldorf
1962	Galerie International d'Art Moderne, Paris
1963	Bear Lane Gallery, Oxford
	Kasmin Gallery, London
	Alan Gallery, New York
1965	Bangor City Art Gallery, Wales
1970	Lisson Gallery, London
1974	Art Net, London
1975	Städtische Kunsthalle, Dusseldorf
1976	Tate Gallery, London
1978	Riverside Studios, London
1982	Riverside Studios, London
1983	Van Abbemuseum, Eindhoven, Netherlands
1986	Christ Church Picture Gallery, Oxford
1987	Lisson Gallery, London

Selected Group Exhibitions:

1959	*Group Exhibition*, Galleria dell'Ariete, Milan
1961	*Art of Assemblage*, Museum of Modern Art, New York (travelled to the Museum for Contemporary Arts, Dallas, and the Museum of Art, San Francisco)
1964	*Painting and Sculpture of a Decade 1954–64*, Tate Gallery, London
1967	*The 1950's* Museum of Modern Art, New York
1970	*Information*, Museum of Modern Art, New York
1971	*APG's Art and Economics*, Hayward Gallery, London
1975	*Structures and Codes*, Royal College of Art, London
1977	*APG's Incidental Personal Approach to Government*, at Documenta 6, Kassel, West Germany
1985	*Next Tomorrow*, Kettle's Yard Gallery, Cambridge
1986	*From a Broad Time Base*, Time Based Arts, Amsterdam

Collections:

Tate Gallery, London; Ulster Museum, Belfast; Städtische Kunsthalle, Dusseldorf; Museum of Art, Caracas; Museum of Modern Art, New York; Newark Museum, New Jersey; Gallery of Modern Art, Washington, D.C.

Publications:

By LATHAM: book—*Least Event, One Second Drawings,*

Blind Work, 24 Second Paintings, London 1970; articles—statement in *Alloway's Gazette* (London), 1960; "Time Base and Determination in Events" in *John Latham,* exhibition catalogue, Dusseldorf 1975; statement in *Arte Inglese Oggi,* exhibition catalogue, Milan 1976; interview, with Richard Dunares in *Studio International* (London), August 1982.

On LATHAM: books—*John Latham,* exhibition catalogue, by Lawrence Alloway, London 1960; *Art of Assemblage,* exhibition catalogue, by William C. Seitz, New York 1961; *John Latham,* exhibition catalogue, by Terry Measham, London 1976; *John Latham,* exhibition catalogue with text by Richard Hamilton, London 1987: articles—"In the Beginning Was the Word" by Eddie Wolfram in *Art and Artists* (London), August 1966; "10 Years of Conceptual Enquiring" by John A. Walker in *Studio International* (London), September 1976; article by Waldemar Janusz in *New Scientist* (London), February 1982.

Though it has taken many forms, John Latham's work always poses a deliberate and radical challenge, since he wants to use art as a polemical means of changing the world and the conceptual basis we use to think and talk about it. Behind his versatility of style is a consistently evolving philosophy, though one which he seems capable of expressing only in clumsy and obscure language, since he is certainly no master of the written word. Nevertheless he quotes approvingly James Joyce's well known saying "I go to forge . . . the conscience of my race," and this is obviously Latham's own aim. "The human being's root source of alienation is to be found in the concept whereby he relates to the rest of the 'material world,' " he declares. And he wants to heal the ever-widening split between intellect and emotions by giving much more emphasis to the intuitive and the non-rational.

Latham proposes that traditional thought based on the tangible, visible material world, on extendedness in space, with objects as the basic unit, should be replaced instead by a description based on extendedness in time, which would make events the basic unit. Latham is therefore a performance artist, his exhibited works being not independent aesthetic objects for their own sake but only the residue of events—events which pose questions and challenge assumptions. But their significance may change even for the artist himself, since his respect for intuitive processes means his acknowledgement that earlier works may express ideas which he hadn't consciously recognized at the time but which have surfaced later.

His obsession with finding "a language which shall copy Nature" began as early as 1954, when the paint-spray technique he was then using made droplets of paint pass through the air and settle on a surface. He was witnessing what appeared to be a statement of pure process, which seemed to him to offer the possibility of a language analogous to natural laws. But he really sprang into prominence with his SKOOB art—"Books" spelt backwards. This could mean painting on books, cutting books up, building great towers of them or burning them and sticking them on canvas to form highly emotive "matter" paintings. The desire to shock, the violation of a cultural taboo, was clearly a factor, as well as the stated desire to question books as "tools of the Mental Furniture Industry," to attack the tyranny of received opinion by mutilating these guided tours of intellectual knowledge. In the 1950's these SKOOB towers were fashionably neo-Dada, paralleling Rauchenberg's assemblages. But none of Latham's events, not even the scandal-provoking book and magazine burnings outside the British Museum in 1966 as part of the Destruction in Art Symposium, can compare in theatrical effect with the huge Nazi book bonfire outside the Reichstag in Berlin stage-managed by Dr. Goebbels, the greatest neo-Dadaist of them all. Latham's attitude to books, however, shows a characteristic ambivalence, since although he has poked fun at pretentious titles he is usually concerned with books as objects rather than with their actual content. The one exception is his chewing up page by page and fermenting a library copy belonging to the St. Martin's School of Art of a book which had been treated in the art world with ridiculous awe and reverence, Clement Greenberg's *Art and Culture,* the remains of which are decorously exhibited in the Museum of Modern Art in New York.

Body art and life-style art of the kind now most closely identified with Gilbert and George, the use of the artist's own person demonstratively, was also pioneered by John Latham as another means of shocking the public out of its normal complacency. Certainly one of the most effective of his attempts to relate his work directly to the everyday world was his 1971 exhibition recreating the experience of a car crash in which he was nearly killed. The documentation included the wrecked car itself, and a series of X-ray photographs showing his slow recovery in hospital. Here for once Latham's work was not overloaded with verbiage, but allowed to speak directly, creating a moving record of maiming and restoration to health, with the car as a potent symbol of destruction and death, as opposed to the Futurists' enthusiastic use of it as a symbol of progress.

Latham has become increasingly concerned with the artist's social responsibility, with the function and use of art in society. He likes to describe himself not as an artist but an Incidental Person, who can operate on the fringes of society, diagnosing its faults and bringing his specially developed intuition to bear on every conceivable aspect of it. This is the rationale behind the APG or Artists' Placement Group which Latham developed in 1966 with his wife Barbara as a means of placing artists within large industrial firms, hopefully for each other's mutual benefit by allowing the artist to bring his insight and fresh perception to bear in raising questions. In the mid-1970's Latham himself worked in this manner on environmental projects for the City of Glasgow, both on the urban renewal of a city which is running down and on trying to solve the problem of the colossal slag-heaps in the countryside resulting from coal-mining. His proposed solutions included turning these man-made mountains into tourist attractions by building huge SKOOB monuments on top of them, and altering attitudes to them by photographing some of them from angles which make them look like ancient fertility goddesses.

Other Latham projects range from paintings on roller blinds which change continuously through time as the blind is rolled, or one-second drawings, to "Spaceship Earth" type use of photographs of the earth from outer space. He is generally recognized as a valuable thorn in the flesh, pinpointing the tragic waste of human and earth's potential, raising all sorts of questions from trivial to fundamental, but sometimes weakening his own impact by surrounding his activities with too much of the incomprehensible verbiage of which he seems over-fond, while himself criticizing it.

—Konstantin Bazarov

John Latham: *The History of Skoob*

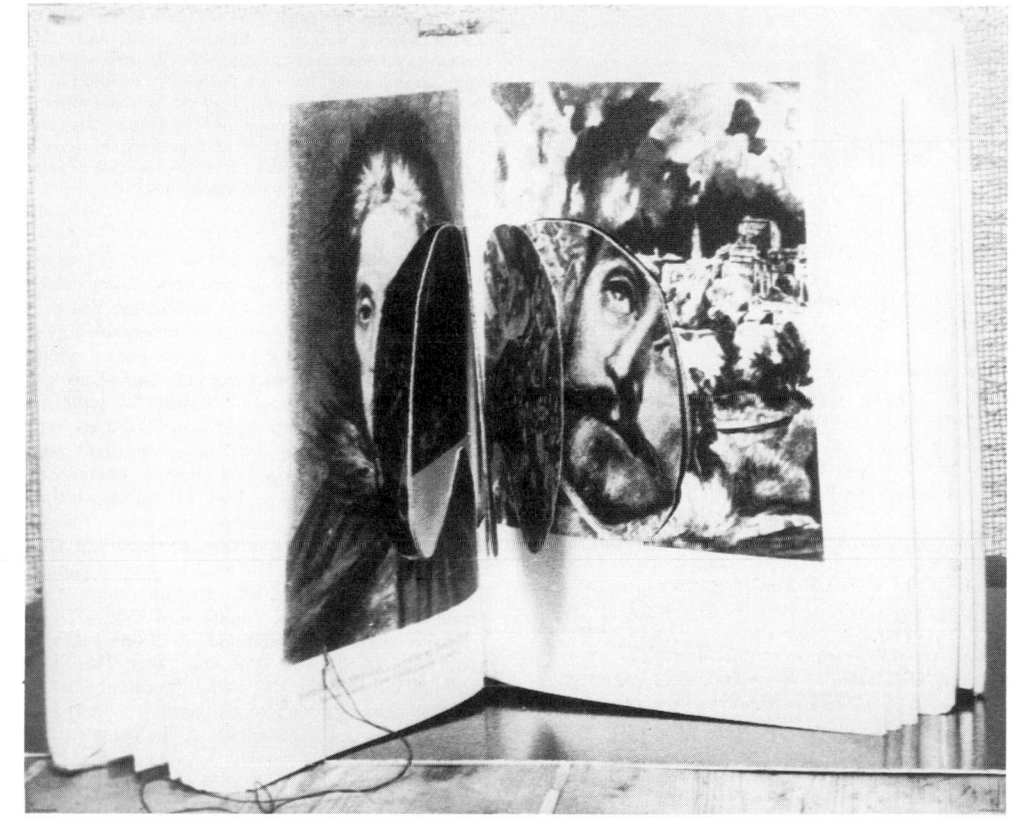

LAW, Bob.
British. Born in Brentford, Middlesex, 22 January 1934. Apprentice architectural designer: studied geometry, trignometry, perspective drawing and planning at night school, 1949; also studied ornithology and oology. Served in the British Army, in North Africa, 1952–54. Married Gina Cann in 1965; children: Vanessa and Daniel. Independent painter, since 1957: first "field" drawings and paintings, 1959, series of black paintings, 1964, white paintings, 1969, and sculpture, from 1980; lived in St. Ives, Cornwall, 1957–60, in Richmond, Surrey, 1960, 1964–69, in Froxfield, Hampshire, 1960–61, 1962–64, in Aix-en-Provence, France, 1961–62, in Twickenham, Surrey, since 1969. Has also worked as a carpenter, 1952, 1955–57, and furniture maker, 1962–64. Visiting Lecturer, Exeter School of Art, Devon, 1964–71. Recipient. French Government Scholarship, University of Aix, 1961; Purchase Award, 1967, and Major Award, 1978, Arts Council of Great Britain; Greater London Arts Association Award, 1981. Address: 17 Second Cross Road, Twickenham, Middlesex TW2 5QY, England.

Individual Exhibitions:

1962 Grabowski Gallery, London
1963 Christchurch College, Oxford

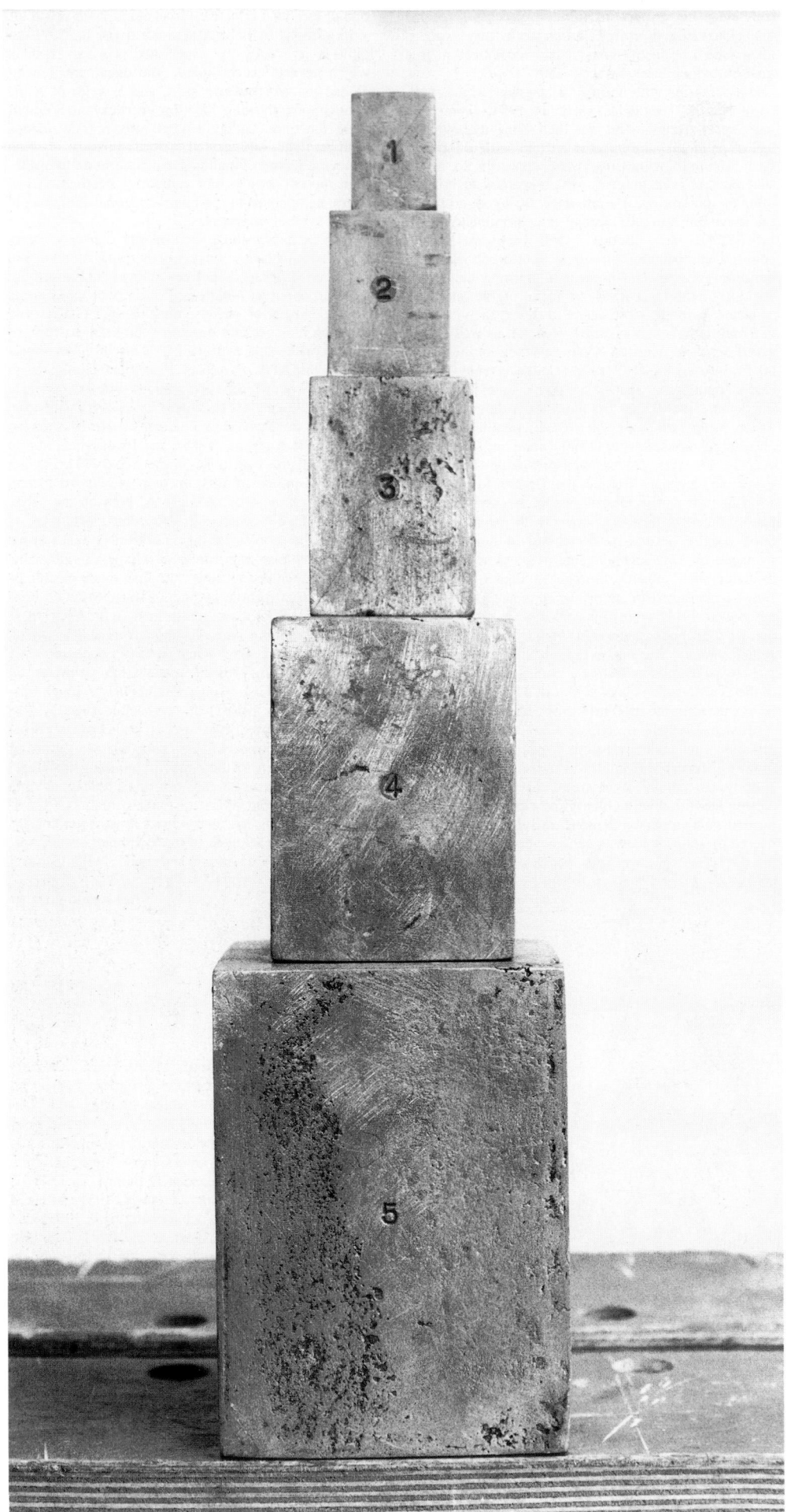

Bob Law: *1–2–3–4–5 Weighed Blue Series*, 1982

Selected Group Exhibitions:

Collections:

Tate Gallery, London; Arts Council of Great Britain, London; Victoria and Albert Museum, London; Southhampton Art Gallery, Hampshire; Worcester College, Oxford; Stedelijk Museum, Amsterdam; Museum of Modern Art, New York; City Art Gallery, Johannesburg.

Publications:

By LAW: book—*16 Drawings*, London 1971; articles—statements in *Bob Law*, exhibition catalogue, London 1962; *7 aus London*, exhibition catalogue, Berne 1973; *Arte Inglese Oggi*, exhibition catalogue, Milan 1976; *Contemporary British Artists*, London 1979; *ROSC 84*, exhibition catalogue, Dublin 1984.

On LAW: books—*Bob Law: 10 Black Paintings 1965–70*, exhibition catalogue with text by Richard Cork, Oxford 1974; *Bob Law: Paintings and Drawings 1959–78*, exhibition catalogue, London 1978; *Art in the Seventies* by Edward Lucie-Smith, London 1980; *St. Ives 1939–64* by David Brown, London 1985; *British Art Since 1900* by Frances Spalding, London 1986; *The Landscape of Experience* by Jeremy Hooker, London 1987; *British Art in the Twentieth Century* by Susan Compton, London and Munich 1987.

At first encounter one of Bob Law's "black" paintings appears just that—an uncompromising black square, pure geometry—but to an attentive and perceptive eye there is a gradual awareness of almost imperceptible nuances of rich, dense colour within the immaculate surface of a carefully crafted work.

The scale of his "black" paintings is, typically, 66" × 69", that of "a man with his arms outstretched, large enough to be peripheral when viewed." They may appear modest in comparison with the size of the New York School of Abstract Expressionists whose paintings dominated the art scene in the late 1950's and 60's when Law first commenced his own series. His work developed parallel to theirs but in a gentler, less expansive, more introverted and perhaps more English way.

He has used acrylic paint and has always paid meticulous attention to the edge conditions. There is a confining edge all the way round the colour field so that "the paintings don't go off edges . . . (and) start relating to the architecture outside the complete object."

A surface, which would when complete be violet/black/blue/black, is built up with a minimum of nine or ten coats, each having to be floated on with perfect evenness. In his obsessional search for the unflawed surface, Law rejects the canvas even after days of work if any irregularities or marks develop. Such is the delicacy of the final surface that it is extremely vulnerable to careless handling. His works are also practically unreproducable, as they photograph as simply black squares. To know his work, one has to know the real thing. That real thing, the almost-black, vibrant surfaces are essentially contemplative objects. The viewer cannot judge them by the sequential standards of traditional Western art. The response has to be totally subjective.

The artist has said that his works need time. He says that they may then start "to eat you up, grow on you. If you openly go to them and you are a receptive type of person for this sort of work, they may swallow you up and take you inside. If you don't like them, it's too bad: I don't care. They're just things."

—Mary Ellis

LEBENSTEIN, Jan.

French. Born in Brest-Litovsk, Poland, 5 January 1930; emigrated to France, 1959: naturalized, 1971. Educated at Lyceum, Warsaw, 1945–47; studied at the Academy of Fine Arts, Warsaw, 1948–54. Independent painter and graphic artist, Warsaw, 1954–59, in Paris since 1959. Recipient: Grand Prix de la Ville de Paris, 1959; International Forum Award, Tokyo, 1971. Address: 25 rue des Ecouffes, 75004 Paris, France.

Individual Exhibitions:

1956	Tarczynska Theatre, Warsaw
1958	Artists Association Gallery, Warsaw
1959	Galerie Lacloche, Paris
	Galerie Lambert, Paris
1960	Galleria Galatea, Turin
1961	Musée d'Art Moderne de la Ville, Paris
1962	Chalette Gallery, New York
	Cornell University, Ithaca, New York
1963	Galleria Profil, Milan
	Galleria dell'Obelisco, Rome
1964	Galerie D'Eendt, Amsterdam
	Palais des Beaux-Arts, Brussels
	Musée Grimaldi, Antibes, France
	Creatures Abominables de Jan Lebenstein et Carnet Intime, Galerie Lacloche, Paris
1965	*Monstrose Kreaturen und Carnet Intime*, Galerie Gmurzynska, Cologne
1966	Galleri Hammerslund, Oslo
	Galleri AP. Copenhagen
	Galerie Benjamin Katz, West Berlin
	Galleria Stendhal, Milan
1967	Galleri Moderna, Silkeborg, Denmark
1968	*Oeuvres 1966–1968*, Galerie Desbrière, Paris
	Galleria Il Fauno, Turin
1970	Galerie Kontakt, Antwerp
	Galerie Antiqua, Ghent
1971	Galleria Il Fauno, Turin
1972	GAlerie du Triangle, Paris
	Galerie Montjoie, Brussels
	Bodley Gallery, New York
1973	Hyman Gallery, Chicago
1974	Galerie Lambert, Paris
	Galleria Helioart, Rome
	Palazzo Giardine Mazzini, Macerata, Italy
	Theatre Oblique, Paris
1975	Galerie Altmann-Carpentier, Paris
	Galerie Lambert, Paris
	Théâtre National de l'Odéon, Paris
	Galerie L'Expression, Strasbourg
1976	Théâtre Oblique, Paris
	Galerie Montjoie, Brussels
	Galerie Presences, Brussels

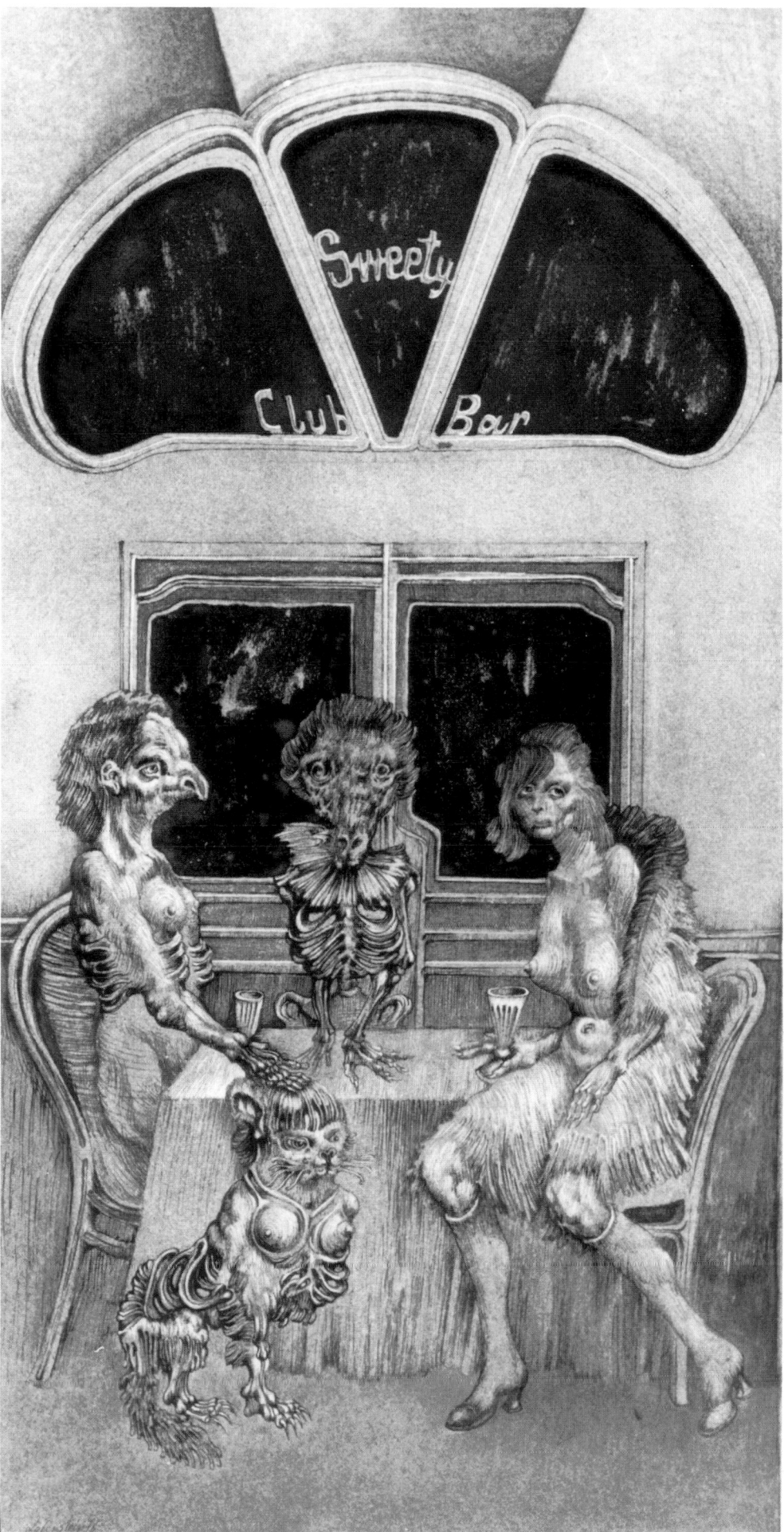

Jan Lebenstein: *La Nouvelle*, 1976

Galerie Saint-Remy, Liège, Belgium
Palais des Beaux-Arts, Brussels
1977 National Museum, Wroclaw, Poland
National Museum, Cracow, Poland
1978 Musée des Beaux-Arts, Angers, France
1980 Galerie Proscenium, Paris
L'Autre Musée, Brussels
1981 L'Autre Musée, Brussels

Selected Group Exhibitions:

1957 *2nd Exhibition of Modern Art*, Galerie Poprostu, Warsaw
1959 *Documenta 2*, Kassel, West Germany
1961 *15 Polish Painters*, Museum of Modern Art, New York
1964 *Figuration et Defiguration*, Musée des Beaux-Arts, Ghent
1965 *Contemporary Polish Painting*, Museum of Modern Art, Tel-Aviv
1966 *European Watercolours*, Museum of Modern Art, New York (toured the United States and Canada)
1967 *Carnegie International*, Carnegie Institute, Pittsburgh
1968 *Salon des Comparaisons*, Grand Palais, Paris
1971 *Japan Cultural Forum*, Tokyo
1977 *ROSC 77*, University College, Dublin

Collections:

Museum of Modern Art, New York: Carnegie Institute, Pittsburgh: Hirshhorn Museum, Washington, D.C.: Centre Georges Pompidou, Paris: Musée d'Art Moderne de la Ville, Paris: Narodowe Museum, Warsaw: Narodowe Museum, Cracow, Poland: Moderna Museet, Stockholm: Städtische Kunstgalerie, Bochum, West Germany: Museum of Modern Art, Tel-Aviv.

Publications:

On LEBENSTEIN: books—*Jan Lebenstein*, exhibition catalogue, with text by Clovis Eyraud and Raymond Cognat, Paris 1961; *Jan Lebenstein*, exhibition catalogue, with text by Jean Cassou, Antibes 1964; *Creatures Abominables de Jan Lebenstein et Carnet Intime*, exhibition catalogue, with text by Gérald Gassiot-Talabot, Paris 1964; *Jan Lebenstein*, exhibition catalogue, with text by Jean Cassou, Brussels 1964; *Jan Lebenstein: Monstrose Kreaturen and Carnet Intime*, exhibition catalogue, with texts by Jean Cassou and Gérald Gassiot-Talabot, Cologne 1965; *Jan Lebenstein*, exhibition folder, with text by Reidar Revold, Oslo 1966; *Lebenstein*, exhibition folder, with text by Jean Cassou, West Berlin 1966; *Lebenstein: Oeuvres 1966–1968*, exhibition catalogue, with text by Gérald Gassiot-Talabot, Paris 1968; *Erotic Art 2*, compiled by Phyllis and Eberhard Kronhausen, New York 1970; *Jan Lebenstein*, exhibition catalogue, with text by Janus, Turin 1971; *Jan Lebenstein: peintre des mythes de la nature humaine* by Constantin Jelenski, Pollenza 1981.

I feel that painting, at least in my own case, represents the best possible way in which to spend this period we call life.

What is important, I think, is to be able to believe, when years are gone and in spite of the results of one's work, that time was not lost in vain, that it was used to the utmost.

In the work of a painter, which is solitary by definition, satisfaction is gained by a feeling of being close to something which goes beyond the self, a feeling that abstract lines and colour on canvas create a second new reality.

Such moments are all too rare, though each painting represents an attempt at catching a glimpse of the "absolute."

Such moments are also moments of salvation, of escape from "nothingness," from limitations of self.

Painting, however, is not an act of contemplation, but an activity both mental and physical, directed at others. One does not paint for oneself but strives to establish a means of communication with the world.

—Jan Lebenstein

LE BROCQUY, Louis.

Irish. Born in Dublin, 10 November 1916. Educated in Irish primary shcools: studied chemistry at Trinity College, Dublin, 1936–37; self-taught in art. Married Jean Stoney in 1938 (divorced, 1948); one daughter; married the painter Anne Madden Simpson, in 1958; children: Alexis and Pierre. Independent painter, since 1938: worked in the family oil refining business, 1935–38: travelled in Europe, 1938–40, then returned to Dublin: organizer, with others, *Irish Exhibition of Living Art*, 1943; worked on Irish tinker paintings and theatre designs, stained glass and murals; settled in London, 1946; produced first tapestries, 1948; lived in France and Switzerland, 1958–60, and settled near Nice, 1960; destroyed many of his works, 1963; has worked on series of human head images, since 1964. Visiting Lecturer in paintings and mural design, Central School of Arts and Crafts, London, 1947–54; Visiting Tutor, Royal College of Art, London, 1955–58; Director, Kilkenny Design Workshops, 1965–77. Member, Irish Council of Design, 1963–65; Member of the Council, Society of Designers in Ireland, 1974–75. Recipient: Premio Prealpina, *Biennale*, Venice, 1956. D.Litt.: University of Dublin, 1962. Member, Royal Hibernian Academy, Dublin, 1949; Fellow, Society of Industrial Artists, 1960. Chevalier, Légion d'Honneur, 1974; Honorary Member, Royal Hibernian Academy, Dublin, 1983. Agents: Gimpel Fils, 30 Davies Street, London W1, England; Gimpel and Weizenhoffer Gallery, 1040 Madison Avenue, New York, New York 10021, U.S.A.; Taylor Galleries, 6 Dawson Street, Dublin 2, Ireland. Address: Domaine des Combes, 06510 Carros, France.

Individual Exhibitions;

1947 Gimpel Fils, London
1948 Leicester Galleries, London
1949 Gimpel Fils, London
1951 Waddington Galleries, London
Waddington Galleries, Dublin
Gimpel Fils, London
1955 Gimpel Fils, London
1956 Gimpel Fils, London
1957 Gimpel Fils, London
1959 Gimpel Fils, London
1960 Esther Robles Gallery, Los Angeles
1961 Gimpel Fils, London
Galerie Charles Lienhard, Zurich
1962 Dawson Gallery, Dublin
1966 Gimpel Fils, London
Dawson Gallery, Dublin
Municipal Gallery of Modern Art, Dublin
1967 Ulster Museum, Belfast
1968 Gimpel Fils, London
Galeria Kresler-Dos, Madrid
1969 Gimpel und Hanover Galerie, Zurich
Dawson Gallery, Dublin
1970 Oxford University Press, London
1971 Gimpel Fils, London
Dawson Gallery, Dublin
Gimpel and Weitzenhoffer, New York
1973 Dawson Gallery, Dublin
McClelland Gallery, Belfast
Fondation Maeght, St. Paul-de-Vence, France
1974 Dawson Gallery, Dublin
Gimpel Fils, London (travelled to the Galleria Le Bussola, Turin)
1975 Dawson Gallery, Dublin
Galerie Karl Flinker, Paris
Arts Council Gallery, Belfast
1976 Galerie Le Demeure, Paris
Municipal Gallery of Modern Art, Cork, Ireland
Musée d'Art Moderne de la Ville Paris
1977 Richard de Marco Gallery, Edinburgh
Galleria San Marco, Genoa
1978 Gimpel Fils, London
Municipal Gallery of Modern Art, Dublin
Gimpel und Hanover Galerie, Zurich
Gimpel and Weitzenhoffer, New York
Arts Council Gallery, Belfast
Waddington Galleries, Montreal

Galeria Maeght, Barcelona
1979 Galeria Kresler-Dos, Madrid
Galerie Jeanne Bucher, Paris
Bank of Granada, Spain
1981 Dawson Gallery, Dublin
Taylor Galleries, Dublin
Louis Le Brocquy and the Celtic Head Image, New York State Museum, Albany
1982 Palais des Beaux-Arts, Charleroi, Belgium
Galerie Jeanne Bucher, Paris
1983 Gimpel/Hanover/Emmerich, Zurich
Gimpel Fils, London
1985 Taylor Galleries, Dublin
1986 Brownstone Galeries, at *International Exhibition*, Chicago
Taylor Galleries, Dublin
1987 Arts Council Gallery, Dublin
Ulster Museum, Belfast
1988 National Gallery of Victoria, Melbourne (travelled to Adelaide and Sydney)

Selected Group Exhibitions:

1956 *Biennale*, Venice
1958 *50 Ans d'Art Moderne*, Palais des Beaux-Arts, Brussels
1987 *Painting Since World War II*, Guggenheim Museum, New York

Collections:

Tate Gallery, London; Victoria and Albert Museum, London; Arts Council of Great Britain, London; Leeds Art Gallery, Yorkshire; Ulster Museum, Belfast; Municipal Gallery of Modern Art, Dublin; Fondation Maeght, St. Paul-de-Vence, France; Albright-Knox Art Gallery, Buffalo, New York; Carnegie Institute, Pittsburgh.

Publications:

By LE BROCQUY: illustrated books—*The Táin*, translated by Thomas Kinsella, 1969; *The Playboy of the Western World*, 1970; *The Gododdin*, 1978; *Dubliners*, 1986.

On LE BROCQUY: books—*From Sickert to 1948* by John Russell, London 1948; *Art since 1945* by Herbert Read, London 1959; *A Letter to a Young Painter* by Herbert Read, London 1962; *A Concise History of Irish Art* by Bruce Arnold, London 1969; *Modern Masters* by Brahamer and Garner, Malmo, Sweden 1980; *Louis Le Brocquy* by Dorothy Walker, Dublin 1981, London 1982; *Louis Le Brocquy and the Celtic Head Image*, exhibition catalogue, by Proinsias Macrana and Anne Crookshank, Albany, New York 1981; *Le Brocquy: Images 1975–87*, exhibition catalogue, Dublin 1987.

Among the few extant early paintings by Louis Le Brocquy is one called "The Picnic" (1940), which, though very different from his later pictures, is a key to his future development as an artist. It has certain defects of draughtsmanship (the articulation of the limbs and their relationship with the ground, etc.) which were the sort of thing to be seized on by his critics and may have been an excuse for his work being rejected by the Royal Hibernian Academy in 1942 and again in 1943. It would have been the equivalent of refusing to print Joyce on the grounds that his spelling was bad and he made the occasional grammatical mistake. After all, Le Brocquy was self-taught and did not take up painting seriously until 1938. What is interesting and prophetic about this picture is the sadness and isolation of the figures. Each one is absorbed in his or her own thoughts. There is no communication, no human warmth, at least not on the surface. Isolation is a theme to which Le Brocquy constantly returns.

His next phase, however, was more fiery. The pictures of this period have been described as the "Traveller" series because of the predominance of tinkers, men and women who are euphemistically known in Ireland as "travelling people." In fact they are a hard, ruthless, mean and vindictive lot. It is thus Le Brocquy portrays them, in a Cubist idiom, similar to that

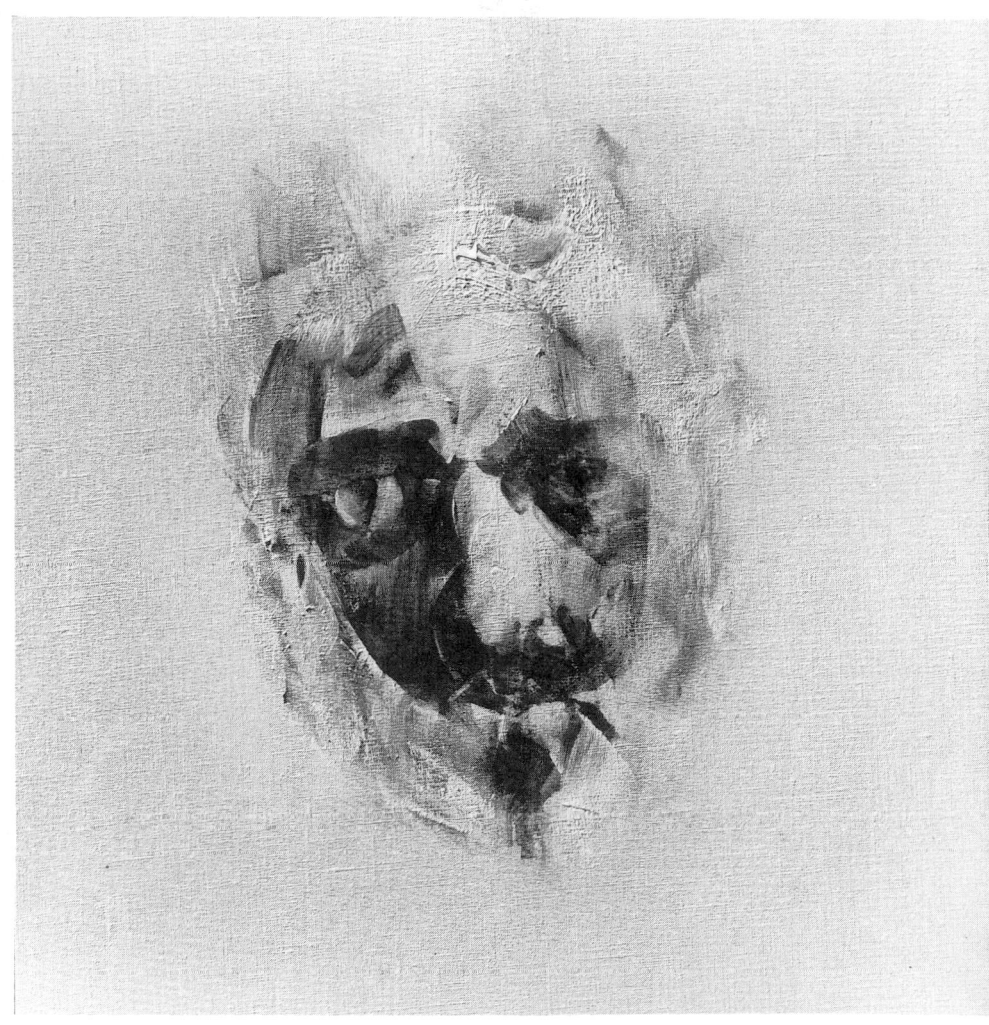

Louis Le Brocquy: *Image of August Strindberg*, 1981

LE GAC, Jean.
French. Born in Tamaris, Ales, 6 May 1936. Studied art, Section Preparatoire, Professorat de Dessin, Paris, 1954–58. Married Jacqueline Denoyel in 1958; children: Renaud, Agnes and Martine. Painter, Paris, 1958–68; has worked with photo-texts, Paris, since 1969. Has taught in various art schools in Paris, since 1958. Agent: Galerie Daniel Templon, 30 rue Beaubourg, 75003 Paris: John Gibson Gallery, 394 West Broadway, New York, New York 10012, U.S.A. Address: 67 Avenue Gambetta, 75020 Paris, France.

Individual Exhibitions:

1970	Galerie Daniel Templon, Paris
1971	Galerie Rive Droite, Paris
1972	Galerie Daniel Templon, Paris
	Galleria Daniel Templon, Milan
	Kunstmuseum, Lucerne
1973	Museum of Modern Art, Oxford
	Galerie 't Venster, Rotterdam
	Galerie Daniel Templon, Paris
	Galleria Daniel Templon, Milan
1974	John Gibson Gallery, New York
	Galleria Nuovi Strumenti, Brescia, Italy
	Israel Museum, Jerusalem
	Galerie Daniel Templon, Paris
	Galerie Loeb, Berne
	Galleria Daniel Templon, Milan
	Galerie Ricke, Cologne
1975	Galleria Cannaviello, Rome
	Galerie Daniel Templon, Paris
	Galleri St. Petri, Lund, Sweden
	Galleri Daner, Copenhagen
	Galerie Art in Progress, Munich
	Galleria Daniel Templon, Milan
1976	John Gibson Gallery, New York
	Galerie Daniel Templon, Paris
1977	Kunstverein, Hamburg (retrospective)
	John Gibson Gallery, New York
	Galerie Ricke, Cologne
	Städtische Galerie im Lenbachhaus, Munich
	Neue Galerie, Aachen, West Germany
	Galleria d'Arte Spagnoli, Milan
1978	Centre Georges Pompidou, Paris
	Cannaviello Studio d'Arte, Milan
1979	Galerie Daniel Templon, Paris
	John Gibson Gallery, New York
	Galerie Ricke, Cologne
	Kunstverein, Krefeld, West Germany
1980	Le Coin du Miroir, Dijon, France
1981	Galerie Daniel Templon, Paris
1982	Galerie France Morin, Montreal
	Galerie Catherine Issert, St. Paul-de-Vence, France
	Hal Bromm Gallery, New York
1983	Galerie Daniel Templon, Paris
	Galerie Le Chanjour, Nice, France
	Musée Municipal, La Roche sur Yon, France
1984	Studio Marconi, Milan
	Galerie Athanor, Marseille, France
	Galerie Catherine Issert, St. Paul de Vence, France
	ARC/Musée d'Art Moderne de la Ville, Paris
1985	Andata/Ritorno, Geneva
	Galerie Daniel Templon, Paris
	Chapelle des Carmelites, Toulouse, France
1986	Galerie Catherine Issert, St. Paul de Vence, France
1987	Galerie Daniel Templon, Paris
	Elisabeth Franck Gallery, Knokke-le-Zoute, Belgium
	Chapelle du Mejean, Arles, France
1988	Galerie Reckermann, Cologne

Selected Group Exhibitions:

1969	*Biennale de Paris*, Musée d'art Moderne, Paris
1972	*Pour Memoires*, Entrepots Laine, Bordeaux (toured France)
1976	*Artists from France*, Warehouse Gallery, Convent Garden, London
1979	*Origins of Recent European Art*, at the *Biennale*, Sydney
1981	*Westkunst*, Messehallen, Cologne

of Colquhoun and Keith Vaughan, admirably suited to his purpose. This, to my mind, was a splendid period of his work. Herbert Read had the good judgment to reproduce one of the masterpieces, "Man Creating a Bird" (1948), in his *Contemporary British Art* (1951).

There followed an equally fruitful period, known as the "Grey Series." Though faintly Cubist, these pictures were more suave and smooth, with subtle modulations of tone, whites, blacks, and, of course, grey. In this period there is a return, with greater emphasis, to the theme of isolation. Not only are humans—father, mother and child—isolated and cut off from one another, but they are cut off even from their domestic pets. At this time, Le Brocquy captured, as no one else has, the loneliness, isolation and bewilderment of being a child ("Child in a Yard," "Boy Behind a Door," 1954). All this was summed up in his prize-winning work, "A Family," which, not surprisingly, horrified the pious folk of Ireland, who have different views of family life; but, for all that, it is a superb work, which earned the somewhat fulsome remark: "the most ambitious attempt to trace and categorize the development of painting and sculpture from Cézanne and Rodin to our time."

There followed a period in which Le Brocquy's paintings became increasingly exiguous. The series has been called "Presences," but, insofar as the human figure progressively disappears into the semblance of a ghost or an X-ray photograph of a human form, they might more properly be described as absences. I do not say this in any derogatory sense. It is not my favourite Le Brocquy period, but it was a period in which his texture (*impasto*) became richer as detail became thiner and vaguer. It had a purity, simplicity, pared down quality which one associates with the plays of Beckett at that time and subsequently.

And it paved the way for his latest phase devoted to heads.

Some of the heads are of famous literary personages—W. B. Yeats, Joyce, Beckett, Lorca. Others are what he calls "ancestral heads," or heads of Irish heros or victims or martyrs. The impasted technique is used, but the brushlines have become more fluent and the whole effect is more painterly—and the psychological effect more horrendous. The "Presences" were isolated in that they were either views from the back or transparent views. The heads bring back the human presence, but only just. Even the faces of the living have a remote, deathlike look, as if seen behind frosted glass or through a mist. The mist of memory, perhaps; for these heads, though recognizable, are not strictly portraits: they are reconstructed. Some are sinister in the extreme: a mouth open in agony, a hidden face behind what seem to be blood-stained hands pressed against glass. It is Bacon country; not surprisingly: the two are friends, and there is a series of Bacon heads.

Le Brocquy's versatility as an artist is remarkable. Besides painting, he has been engaged in stage and costume design, textile design, book illustration, stained glass, mosaics and tapestry. What is most remarkable is his ability to adapt faithfully to each medium (a quality he shares with Beckett). His illustrations for Thomas Kinsella's translation of *The Táin* are masterly in capturing the spirit of the poem, though the style is quite different from that of his paintings. Again, in a series of designs for the Tabard tapestry factory, Aubusson, in a Cubist style, he exploits all the richness of colour and possibilities for the expression of joy in movement of which tapestry, unfettered by excessive naturalism, is capable.

—D. C. Barrett

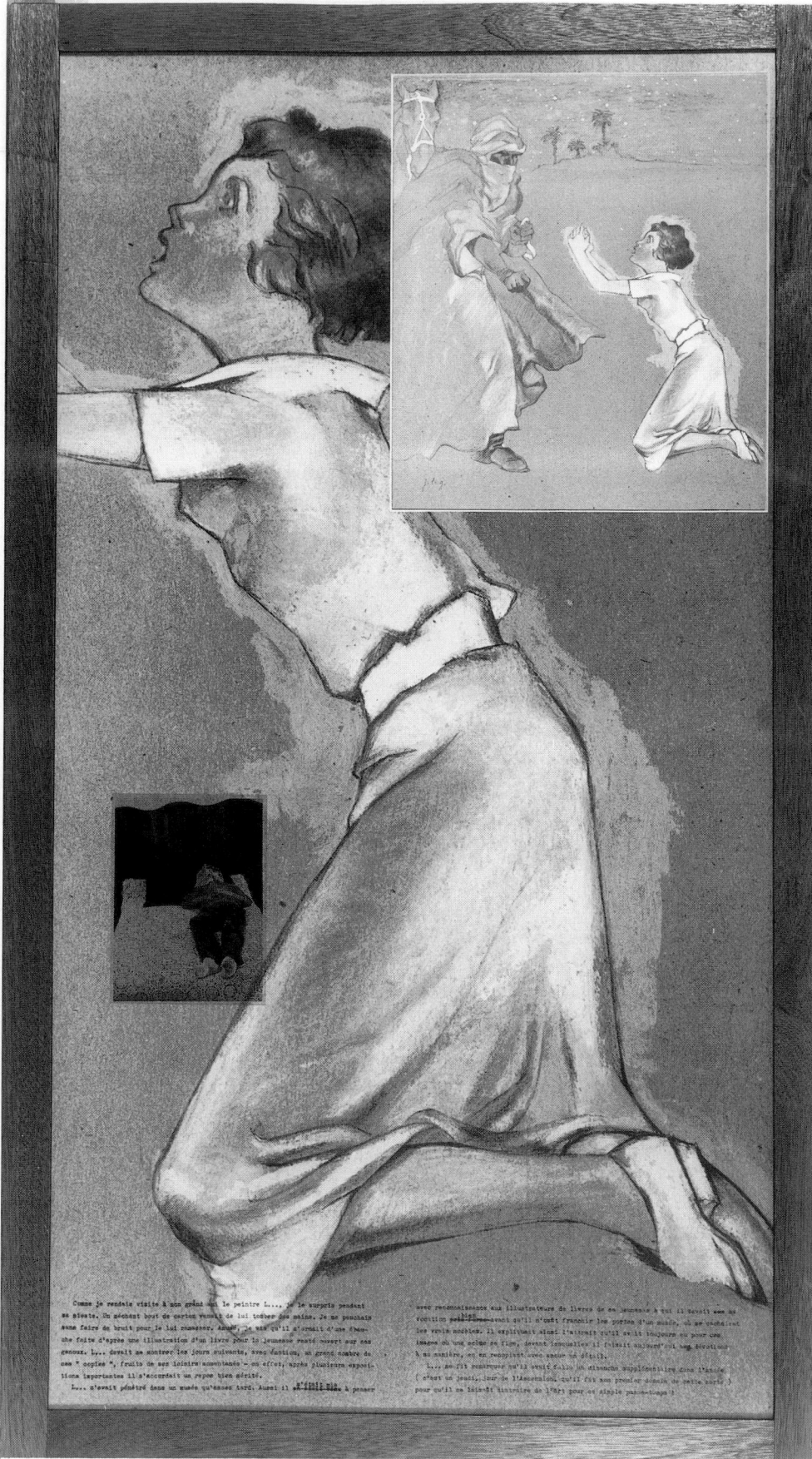

Jean Le Gac: *Le Délassement du Peintre (avec Touareg),* 1981

Collections:

Centre Georges Pompidou, Paris: Bibliothèque Nationale, Paris; Musée d'Art Moderne de la Ville, Paris; Fond National d'Art Contemporain, Paris; Musée d'Art et d'Industrie, St. Etienne, France; Neue Galerie, Aachen, West Germany; Museum Boymans-van Beuningen, Rotterdam; Museum of Modern Art, New York.

Publications:

By LE GAC: books—*Les Cahiers 1968-1971,* Lucerne 1972; *Jean Le Gac/Florent Max,* Paris 1972; *Le Recit,* Hamburg 1972; *Le Decor,* Paris 1972; *The Painter,* Rotterdam 1973; *The Imitation of Jean le Gac,* Oxford 1973; *Les Anecdotes,* Jerusalem 1974; *Le Fantome des Beaux-Arts,* Brussels and Hamburg 1975; *Le Professeur de Dessin,* Brussels and Paris 1976; *Der Maler,* with an introduction by Günter Metken, Brussels and Hamburg 1977; *Le Peintre—exposition romancée,* with an introduction by Günter Metken, Paris 1978; *Le Peintre de Tamaris près d'Ales,* Liège, Belgium 1980; *Image et Texte dans le Peintre de Tamaris près d'Ales de Jean Le Gac.* Bordeaux 1981; *Introduction aux oeuvres d'un artiste dans mon genre,* Arles, France 1987; films—*Signal,* 1970; *Jean Le Gac, artiste peintre,* with Michel Pamart and J and J. 1973; *La Fausse Ruine et le Peintre,* with Michel Pamart, 1979; *L'Hydravion et le Peintre,* with Renaud Le Gac, 1980; *Le Tour du Monde,* with Renaud Le Gac, 1982; *La sieste pittoresque,* with Renaud Le Gac, 1985; *Les statues,* with Renaud Le Gac, 1985-87; *L'absent et l'inconnu,* with Brigitte Cornaud and Philippe Gauthier, 1987; *Le peintre de la piscine Deligny,* with Christophe Loizillon, 1987.

On LE GAC: books—*Art en France, une nouvelle generation* by Jean Clair, Paris 1972; *Jean Le Gac* by Catherine Francblin, Paris 1984; *Jean Le Gac, un peintre de reve,* exhibition catalogue with texts by Catherine Francblin, Michel Nuridsany and Bernard Marcade, Paris 1984; *Jean Le Gac: les Fresques du Kursaal de Venise,* exhibition catalogue with text by Michel Gauthier, St. Paul de Vence 1986; *Jean Le Gac,* exhibition catalogue with text by Martine Le Gac, Knokke-le-Zoute 1987; articles—"Les Projets san Fin de Boltanski et de Jean Le Gac" by Gilbert Gatellier in *Opus International* (Paris), December 1969; "Les Activités Mysterieuses de Jean Le Gac" by Bernard Borgeaud in *Chroniques de l'Art Vivant* (Paris), June 1971; "Adventure Stories" by Effie Stephano in *Art and Artists* (London), May 1973; "Jean Le Gac et le Singulier Plural" by Claire Stoullig in *Art Press* (Paris), May 1974; "The Enigmatic Images of Jean Le Gac" by Kate Linker in *Arts Magazine* (New York), March 1977; "Jean Le Gac commentateur de Jean Le Gac" by Catherine Francblin in *Art Press* (Paris), March 1978; "Trouvez l'Artiste" by Anne Dagbert in *Art Press* (Paris), no. 59, 1982; "On the trail of Jean Le Gac" by Kate Linker in *Artforum* (New York), Summer 1986.

In 1980 I would have had nothing to add to that which I told you for your first edition: I was, quite simply, rather tired of the painter's role. The emotive strength I gained from his lightning appearance in my stories with photos had diminished by force of repetition. I had to make a major effort to invent new approaches. I lost all hope that the painter might again be able to appear in my eyes as "an early messenger of the meaning of the World" (Marcel Lecomte).

Fortunately in 1981 I discovered some pastels given to my daughter, a whole box which without me would have continued to wait impatiently in a drawer, and some poor quality cardboard which reminded me of my youthful years of poverty. I immediately reopened my books from childhood and, without respite, began to copy the illustrations which in the past had awakened me to Art. Since then I feel like a Far Eastern calligrapher or a monk illuminator of the Middle Ages, that is to say a painter whose "greatest pleasure is to recopy masterpieces indefinitely" until he reaches effusion by the simple means of spellbinding repetition.

1986/87: pursue my attempt at copying childhood images on large painted canvas connected with old movie-projectors. Ideally see my wide wall-decorations adorning a rich idle painter's home who has broken with Art History and the common species "contemporary artist".

—Jean Le Gac

Although Jean Le Gac has been active as an artist since the 1960's, it was not until 1973 that he became known internationally—the year that a name was given to the genre, "Narrative Art." What had been a formal tendency, paradoxically notable for the catholicity of its practitioners, became a "school," visible and coherent. Le Gac shares with his colleagues—Bill Beckley, David Askevold, Peter Hutchinson, and others—the concern with "story," mythic, frequently humorous, inverted parable, often without a point but replete with and dependent upon penetrating content. Like them, he binds text and photographic visual image indissolubly, neither assuming more significance than the other. Yet the oeuvre as a whole presents a deeper sense of intimate mystery than others in the same mode; he eschews the theatricality of Mac Adams, the deliberate twists of Beckley, and the expository tone of Hutchinson.

Le Gac, in fact, is a latter-day *intimiste*. Delving deep into his gentle and modest imagination, he "constructs" characters, unassuming and non-heroic, and places them in the French landscape, or static, comfortably unpretentious domestic interiors. They operate on a level of nostalgia or wistful fantasy, one which is sometimes explicitly autobiographical but which just as often is an inevitable function of the characters themselves, who seem to play out real or imaginary incidents almost separately from the artist who has created them. The consciousness at work here is hardly that of a naif, however, and concerns itself with a re-ordering and rendering of its own "flow," very much aware of both formal and mental parallels. In one of Le Gac's first major narrative series, "The Anecdotes" (1974), the artist's humorous modesty is inescapable, but a sharp and sophisticated edge comes to the surface in his introductory text: "An artist can become famous overnight. Therefore, it is no doubt wise to anticipate such an event by practicing at answering for your works in the presence of an interviewer . . . "This piece echoes the sly—but genuine—humility that underlies Le Gac's frequent references to his own profession, that of the artist, which emerge in such series as "The Painter" (1973), "The Drawing Master," and "The Phantom of the Beaux-Arts." Formally, this spirit is made palpable by the linear, active drawings presented in some of the photographic panels—executed, interestingly enough, not by Le Gac but by his wife, Jacqueline.

In his seminal essay on Narrative Art, originally printed in *Artforum* and later used as the catalogue essay for the first exhibition of this genre, James Collins likened Le Gac's work to that of Robbe-Grillet and Eric Rohmer, invoking, in particular, the film *Claire's Knee*. There is a certain inevitability to this comparison: Le Gac's work unravels themes, suggests at motivations, and meanders through an apparently unconnected series of incidents. Just as Rohmer's hero fixes his attention upon Claire's knee as erotic object—and subject—Le Gac displaces the banal and raises it to the level of significant myth. In the series of ten black and white and color panels called "The Painter," Le Gac surfaces this sensibility to great effect: he begins by likening the obsession with his principal character, the French painter himself, with his attempt to stop smoking, leads us through the painter's daughter's marriage to a local tradesman, and ends with a parenthetical comment on the resurrection of a certain hairstyle. What appears to be significant is mentioned, then tucked away; what appears to be insignificant at first takes on the aspect of great drama.

This is characteristic of all of Le Gac's work to date, and it is what enables it to operate on such a level of effectiveness (as well as the fact that the texts themselves are so brilliantly written and so superbly linked to the visual sign): the elegiac quality of revery and imagination, a mingling of multiple layers of past, present, future, an on-going search for what Baudelaire termed Correspondences.

—Jane Bell

LENICA, Jan.

Polish. Born in Poznan, 4 January 1928. Studied piano in Poznan, 1933–40, and architecture in Warsaw, 1947–52, Dip. Arch. 1952. Independent artist, known for posters, Warsaw, 1950–63, and in Paris, since 1963; also cartoon filmmaker, since 1957, and theatre decor designer, since 1972. Teaching assistant to Henryk Tomaszewski, Art Academy, Warsaw, 1954; Professor, Kunstakademie Gesamthochschule, Kassel, West Germany, 1979; Professor, Hochschule der Künste, West Berlin, since 1986. Recipient: Toulouse-Lautrec Prize, Paris, 1961; First Prize, *International Poster Biennale*, Warsaw, 1966; Bundesfilm Preis, West Germany, 1969; Preis der Stadt Essen, West Germany, 1980; Jules Cheret Prize, France, 1985; Alfred Kurzykowski Award, New York, 1987; Graphics Award, Childrens Book Fair, Bologna, 1987. Address: 3 rue St. Christophe, 75015 Paris, France.

Individual Exhibitions:

1948	Young Artists Club, Warsaw
1963	Stuck-Villa, Munich
1973	Poznan Gallery, Poland (retrospective)
1980	Centre Georges Pompidou, Paris

Selected Group Exhibitions:

1971	*Vier Polnische Plakatkunstler*, Deutsche Plakat-Museum, Essen
1980	*Triennale '80: Die Besten Plakate der Jahre 1977 bis 1980*, Deutsche Plakat-Museum, Essen

Collections:

Deutsches Plakat-Museum, Essen; Centre Georges Pompidou, Paris; Narodni Museum, Warsaw; Muzeum Narodowe, Poznan, Poland; Israel Museum, Jerusalem; Museum of Modern Art, New York.

Publications:

By LENICA: books—*The Train*, Munich 1969, London 1970; *The Magic Bird*, with text by Max Bolliger, London 1987; film—*Adam 2*, 1969.

On LENICA: books—*Vier Polnische Plakatkunstler*, exhibition catalogue, with text by H. Schardt, Essen 1971; *Graphic Designers in Europe*, volume I, edited by Henri Hillebrand, London 1971; *Art Without Boundaries 1950-1970*, edited by Gerald Woods, Philip Thompson and John Williams, London 1972; *Polish Poster Art Today* by Szymon Bojko, Warsaw 1972; *Triennale '80: Die Besten Plakate der Jahre 1977 bis 1980*. Exhibition catalogue, with text by Frieder Mellinghof, Essen 1980; *Jan Lenica*, edited by Frolich and Kaufmann, West Berlin 1981; articles—"Le plus important c'est l'oreille" in *Opus International* (Paris), April 1969; "Adam 2: A New Cartoon Film by Jan Lenica" by A. Brustellin in *Graphis* (Zurich), No. 145, 1969/70.

*

I have always liked moving on the outskirts of Art, on the borderline of various spheres, penetrating regions situated far from the main routes and others, less noble so to say. I used to find amusing an action against the rules which were considered in force in various fields, a combination of elements seemingly remote from, if not strange, to each other, the blurring of boundaries separating adjacent domains, grafting of nobler qualities onto "lower" species; in short—a quiet subversion. I have always been attracted to forms, sort of commonplace, held in disregard by those who work in more refined areas. These remarks may seem surprising today, at the time of the general integration of various arts, of the emancipation of such fields as graphic art, photography and many others. But I remember the time when painters despised graphic art, and when there was something contemptuous about the word "graphic artist". Where are those days? Art galleries are open to graphic art, and posters have been accepted into museums. Where is the boundary today between painting and graphic art? And who cares about the "purity of the species" these days? In the 'fifties I was accused of using in my posters non-graphic art techniques, which apparently disagreed with the printing technique; I was blamed for the introduction into my posters of subjects which originated straight from painting, such as portraits. Today there is no technique which has not been adapted by poster art which has disposed of the cramping cloak of graphic design and freed itself from an embarrassing isolation, has forgotten its service role so far as to make the mere definition of poster art impossible. Posters have returned to their sources: they are again multiplied pictures done on a "set subject".

The situation in films is somewhat different. I must admit that I have chosen a beastly uncomfortable position for myself. An action against the accepted rules brings about painful consequences. The ruling principles of supply and demand are ruthless in that they repudiate everything which does not find its place in the market. In the past I thought that the animated film could become an instrument of fantastic possibilities when dealt with by an artist. Film appeared to me as the most contemporary raw material, of unparalleled means of expression, as a vast and fruitful area of activity. I was not aware then of the enormous difficulties accumulating before those who do not want to bow to the commercial system of the cinema. The margin of creative freedom and experiment which existed until recently in the short film has virtually disappeared. No one needs it, there is no place for it in the picture houses, and festivals of short films are deserted, filled with the melancholy of past glamour. Apart from socialist countries, there is a *raison d'etre* for it only in the United States where the distribution and audience are assured by universities and film lending libraries. The development of film pursues a traditional line as a performance. Film as an object and manifestation of art in time and movement has not found either its sponsor or its recipient and collector. I see a chance for it in the development of modern techniques of reproduction, in the video cassettes and picture discs now appearing on the market. They may change the situation radically and result in a distribution of films which is now the privilege of works of literature and music.

—Jan Lenica

At one of the first interviews he gave, Jan Lenica gave the following reply in answer to the question, Who are you?: "I move on the fringes of fine art, film and literature. no dictionary has a name for this kind of occupation." But as art dictionaries are all in favor of subdivision into disciplines and media, any mention of Lenica must refer to him as a graphic artist, producer of posters, collages and drawings, and creator of animated films.

Apart from his characteristic traits—great self-irony, skepticism, and anger as a philosophical attitude—the intellectual and political climate of the period in which he grew up had a great influence on Lenica. Born into an artistic family, he inherited a traditional, political leaning towards the left, together with a certain sympathy for communism, from his father who was a known, non-conformist painter. Hence, it is easy to understand why the social changes in Poland, and revolutionary art like that of

Mayakowski, Grosz and Brecht, were so close to the artist's heart. He was fascinated by the Russian avant-garde of the 1920's—political theatre, agit-prop, revolutionary posters. Soon, however, like all of his generation, Lenica was to know the bitterness of disillusion. Their simplified view of life began to crack, revealing non-existent foundations. A period of moral and artistic reflection followed—a period of rational, lucid thinking, a farewell to the myths of youth. Criticism came to the fore, together with new values and motivation. Lenica began to search in art for that which exists universally, guides man's fate, explains his obsessions, fears—that which threatens him, his hopes and illusions. Lenica's mature work enters into a literary-artistic sphere, joining a sur-realistic vision of the world with a perversely absurd interpretation of human life. Romantic fantasy and a rationalistic, merciless hunting down of mystification and appearances are equally to be found in this kind of work. The movement made a name for itself in 20th century world culture through the works of famous writers like Witkiewicz, Gombiowicz, Mrozek, not to mention Ionesco, who was the scriptwriter for Lenica's film *Monseiur Tète* in 1959.

Lenica's romanticism and literary roots—they are the sources of his symbols and metaphoric images. They also originate in lay-culture, Polish folklore in particular. In spite of his having lived abroad since the middle of the 1960s, Lenica's imagination is still full of the naive and fantastic images of his compatriots. Images of people drawn into an urban, industrial way of life, viewing that Moloch of technology, the city, and in fact all innovations, from a distance, with an air of distrust. Bypassing stylization, Lenica skillfully draws on the experience of primitive art. He values coarse, unyielding materials and makes great use of a technique similar to folk cut-outs, fairground woodcuts and bazaar bric-a-brac in his workshop.

Over the years (Lenica's first poster appeared in 1953), he has not kept to any one cultural tradition. He likes mixing various methods and conventions in order to achieve his own style. The large monograph/catalogue printed in the German Federal Republic in 1981 contains all his work hitherto—posters and animated films; it also proposes subdivisions into periods for poster art; periode du realisme; recherches formelles; and signature trouvée.

Lenica's animated films share all the stylistic and ideological attributes of his graphics. One might call them an extreme, condensed form of graphics enriched by flexible narration and the length of time that the film runs. In *Adam 2*, Lenica's only feature film—which has subtitles as in a silent film instead of dialogue or commentary—the artist has gathered a kind of catalogue of visual ideas: autocollage, photocollage, assemblage, cut-outs, old engravings tastefully embedded in the crude contours of a drawing, pictures from 19th century prospectuses, and catalogues that recall Max Ernst's fantastic world.

"Film is a dream," says Lenica. Indeed, one watches his films as one would experience a dream—fantasies but of this world. In his surrealistic-secessional-grotesque cinema, whose sole author he is, Lenica leaves the moving pictures to speak of the greatness and the smallness of modern man.

—Szymon Bojko

LENK, (Kaspar) Thomas.
German. Born in Berlin, 15 June 1933. Studied for one term at the Kunstakademie, Stuttgart. Married Maria Bendig in 1959; daughters: Mira and Ilona. Sculptor, based in Stuttgart, since 1954; has worked on architectural sculpture projects, throughout West Germany, since 1968. Guest Professor, Heluwan University, Cairo, 1978. Recipient: Carnegie International Purchase Award, Pittsburgh, 1967; Third Prize, Socha Piestanskych Parkov, Bratislava, 1969; First Prize, *Norwegian Graphics Biennale*, Frederik-

stad, 1974. Agents: Manuspresse, Lieschingstrasse 6, 7000 Stuttgart; Galerie Holbein, Brouquierstrasse 6, 8990 Lindau; Fischbach Gallery, 29 West 57th Street, New York, New York. Address: 7171 Tierberg, Gemeinde Braunsbach, Schloss Tierberg, West Germany.

Individual Exhibitions:

1958	Galerie Boukes, Wiesbaden
1962	Galerie Mueller, Stuttgart
1963	Galerie Parnass, Wuppertal
1964	Studio F, Ulm
1965	Galerie Mueller, Stuttgart
1966	Galerie Handschin, Basle
	Galerie Bischofberger, Zurich
	Galerie Ricke, Kassel, West Germany
	Galerie Thomas, Munich
1967	Fischbach Gallery, New York
	Rowan Gallery, London
	Galleria del Naviglio, Milan
1968	Westfälischer Kunstverein, Münster
	Hessisches Landesmuseum, Darmstadt
	Städtische Galerie, Stuttgart
1969	Galerie Renée Ziegler, Zurich
1970	Galerie Mueller, Stuttgart
	Studio F, Ulm

Thomas Lenk: *Rotation 4*, 1985

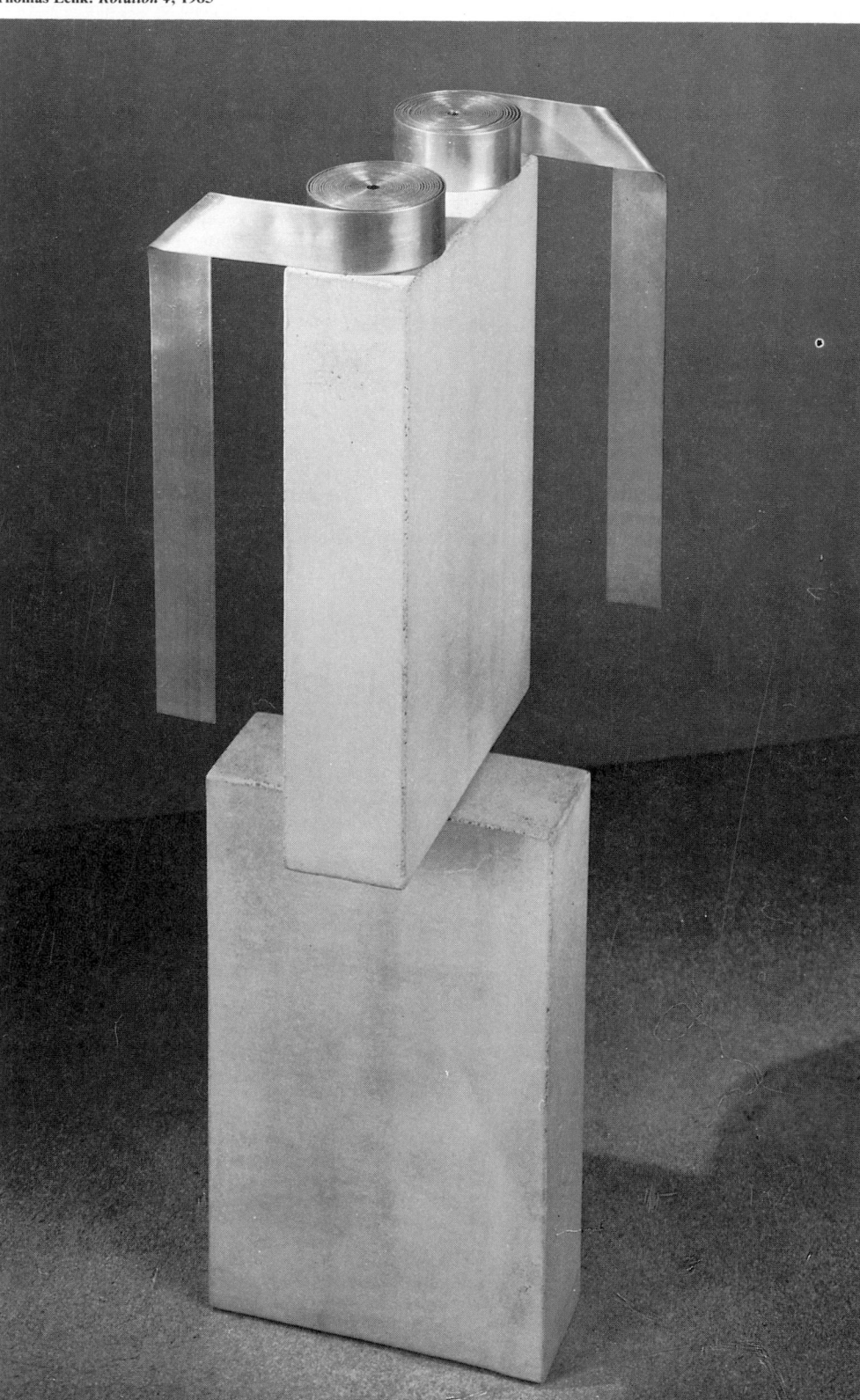

1971 Kunstmuseum, Bochum, West Germany
Museum Folkwang, Essen (German contribution to the 35th Venice *Biennale*)
Kunstmuseum, Dusseldorf
Galerie St. Johann, Saarbrucken
1973 Galerie Richard Foncke, Ghent
Museum Folkwang, Essen
1974 Württembergischer Kunstverein, Stuttgart
Kunsthalle, Dusseldort (with Ad Dekkers and Philip King)
1976 Kölnischer Kunstverein, Cologne (with Karl Pfahler and Hans Uhlmann)
1977 Staatsgalerie, Stuttgart
1978 Fikrum wa Fann Gallery, Alexandria, Egypt
1980 Städtische Kunsthalle, Dusseldorf (travelled to Kunsthalle, Tübingen, and the Westfälischer Kunstverein, Münster)
1983 Galerie Holbein, Lindau, West Germany
Kunsthalle, Nuremberg, West Germany
Galerie von Abercron, Munich
1984 Kunstverein, Heilbronn, West Germany
Galerie Cuenca, Ulm, West Germany
1985 Kunsthalle, Mannheim, West Germany
Erholungshaus Bayer AG, Leverkusen, West Germany
Neue Galerie de Stadt Linz, Austria
Galerie Holbein, Lindau, West Germany
1986 Staatsgalerie, Stuttgart
Kunstverein, Heilbronn, West Germany
1987 Manuspresse, Stuttgart

Selected Group Exhibitions:

1964 *Sculpture Allemande du Vingtième Siècle*, Musée Rodin, Paris
1967 *Sculpture from 20 Nations*, Guggenheim Museum, New York
1969 *1st Biennale Nurnberg*, Kunsthalle, Nuremberg
1971 *International Biennale of Prints*, Museum of Modern Art, Tokyo
1973 *12th Biennale Middelheim*, Middelheim, Antwerp
1975 *20th Century German Graphics*, The New School Art Center, New York (travelled to the Staatsgalerie, Stuttgart)
1979 *13th Graphics Biennale*, Ljubljana, Yugoslavia
1981 *Avantgarden retrospektiv*, Westfalishcer Kunstverein, Munster, West Germany
1985 *Kunst in der Bundesrpublik 1945-85*, Nationalgalerie, West Berlin
1987 *Mathematik in der Kunst*, Wilhelm-Hack-Museum, Ludwigshafen, West Germany

Collections:

Museum Folkwang, Essen; Kunstmuseum, Dusseldorf; Kunsthalle, Mannheim; Staatsgalerie, Stuttgart; Tate Gallery, London; Muzeum Narodowe, Warsaw; The Museum of Contemporary Art, Nagaoka, Japan; Soto Museum, Ciudad Bolivar, Venezuela; Museum of Modern Art, New York; Carnegie Institute, Pittsburgh.

Publications:

By LENK: books—*Nachbilder zu Mahler*, with Theodor W. Adorno, Stuttgart 1962; *Auseinandersetzen*, with Helmut Heissenbuttel, Stuttgart 1970; *Der Tod der Jugovic-Mutter*, with Johannes Wiedenheim, Stuttgart 1971; *Aufenthaltsraum*, with Franz Mon, Duisburg 1972; *Die Quatratur des Triptichons*, Stuttgart 1972; *Reminiszenzen*, Karlsruhe 1978; *Texte*, Stuttgart 1978; *Lob der Geometrie*, Karlsruhe 1980; *Grossvogel*, with Kuno Ulshofer, Schwabisch-Hall 1983; film—*Schichten*, with Walter Ruedel and Helmut Heissenbüttel, Essen 1973.

On LENK: books—*Lenk*, exhibition catalogue, with text by Samuel Reppenko, Stuttgart 1962; *Junge Deutsche Bildhauer* by Udo Kultermann, Mainz 1964; *Plastik der Gegenwart* by Ulrich Gertz, Berlin 1964; *Kaspar Thomas Lenk*, exhibition folder, Kassel, West Germany 1966; *Neue Dimensionen der Plastik* by Udo Kultermann, Tübingen 1967; *Positionen* by Rolf-Gunter Dienst, Cologne 1968; *Plastik der Gegenwart* by Heinz Fuchs, Baden-Baden 1970; *Deutsche Kunst: Eine Neue Generation* by Rolf-Günter Dienst, Cologne 1970; *Bis*

Heute by Karin Thomas, Cologne 1971; *Deutsche Kunst der 60er Jahre* by Jürgen Morschel, Munich 1972; *Thomas Lenk* by Dieter Honisch, Stuttgart 1976; *Bildende Kunst der BRD und Westberlins* by Hermann Raum, Leipzig 1977; *Werkverzeichnis der Serigrafien* by Dieter Honisch and Rolf Krauss, Karlsruhe 1979; *Thomas Lenk: Serie ADGA*, exhibition catalogue, with texts by Gotz Adriani, Jürgen Harten and Heiner Stachelhaus, Dusseldorf 1980; *Thomas Lenk: Werkverzeichnis der Seriegrafien*, with text by Helmut Heissenbuttel, Dieter Honisch, Franz Mon and others, Karlsruhe 1985; *Thomas Lenk: Skulpturen und Zeichnungen*, with text by Helmut Heissenbuttel, Dieter Honisch, West Berlin 1985; films—*Deutsche Bildhauer der Gegenwart* by Gerd Winkler, 1965; *Inn-Skulptur von Thomas Lenk* by Walter Rudel, 1969; *Thomas Lenk* by Frantiszek Kuduk, 1974.

In 1964 (via a casual game with beer tops) I made the significant discovery of 'layerings', and took a step towards serial, technological construction. The creation of vertical or horizontal layers with geometric base elements (square, circle, triangle or parallelogram) was no more than a stereotyped accumulation of volumes in graduated planes. I increased the unreality of such constructions by the use of luminous colours, which tend to destroy rather than strengthen the effect of a sculpture. I had soon amassed a whole collection of designs, models and sculptures which tested out the various possibilities of 'layering'—for which initially only my wife and few friends (how could it be otherwise?) had any understanding or regard. Following exhibitions in Stuttgart, Zurich, Mian, London and New York, and conversations with friends, colleagues and critics, I realized that my work had at last been accepted. Elsewhere too, people were thinking and working along similar lines.

—Thomas Lenk

Kaspar Thomas Lenk—or Thomas Lenk, as he currently prefers to be known—is an articulate engagierter Kunstler. He is fiercely and basically political, even if his politics have a personal flavour not usually identified with that area of thought and behavior. He believes that the true artist has an established place and pattern of production in society from which he should not deviate. He subscribes to many of the aims and objects of Malevich's *Suprematist Manifesto* of 1924 but thinks that they should be expanded and made more precise. He is particularly opposed to the sort of art that reflects in outrage-pictures activist political demos and taking to the streets, and he is equally against any respect for "fool's license" art (the cultural upgrading of the work of phantasists, eccentrics, naives, schizophrenics and any others who might be eligible for representation in Dubuffet's Art Brut museum).

Because Lenk goes to some lengths to give clear and direct associated definition to his opinions and cultural philosophy, all these attitudes are relevant to the way in which the work of this sculptor has developed. He not only holds his views with fanatical intensity; he also confirms the standpoints he has taken by translating them into practical visual form.

Like Malevich, he believes that art should be for the people—and hopefully, for the State as well—but unlike his Russian predecessor, he also maintains that art (in his case his sculpture and its related graphics) should be essentially *businesslike* and devised to be incorporated into business itself. In this sense Lenk's sculpture is intended to become part of the *business architecture* and its ambience.

Although he realizes the isolated character a work of art can express (in an art gallery, in a museum, even in a private collection), Lenk has tried to extirpate this element by making his sculpture ally itself to the space factor (and the non-space factor) instead of invading the same space and, in so doing, interfering with it. Thus in theory, although not visually recognizable, there is a strong affinity between his intentions and those of the Polish Jan Berdyszak. Both are seeking to ensure that their work, while it is a visible additive, is physically absorbed into the site expected for it.

Lenk would say that he is not an abstractionist but a concrete artist. His gradual approach to this position

has taken him from the personalized surrealism of his early days through a number of later stages all of which have led up to the style by which he is recognized today, a style that is still being expanded and variegated: "Heaps" (1957-61), "Stones" (1961), "Additions" (1961-64) and so on into the complex twists and turns in his work which he has introduced over the past two decades.

Those familiar with his sculpture are most likely to think of him as the creator of distorted columns composed of wood slates, aluminum (and sometimes plastics), each horizontal sliver matching its fellows, either quadri-rectangular or with rounded corners, or even circular—these are painstakingly built up, layer upon layer, and given a brilliant colour, often pillarbox red. Much variation on this central method of working has been carried out, and in some cases more than one colour has been employed. In recent years, besides the basic sprawl of the undulating columns, Lenk has investigated the opportunities of angling his sculptural forms to sprout from walls and, taking this experiment to still further extremes, he has actually constructed "independent rooms" through whose apertures, walls, windows and doors his inventions are able to spill out and make their "escape."

His claim to being a viable contributor to the contemporary art scene must surely rest upon his pragmatic ingenuity at adaptation, his ability to weld concrete art onto the mundane fabric of a technological age so that it ceases to be merely decorative or just evidence of high culture, but is actually an injected feature of the epoch it embellishes and encourages.

—Sheldon Williams

LE PARC, Julio (Alcides).
Argentinian. Born in Mendoza, 23 September 1928. Studied at the School of Fine Arts, Buenos Aires, under Lucio Fontana, 1942–54. Married Martha Garcia in 1959; children: Juan, Pablo and Yamil. Has lived and worked in France since 1958: Co-Founder, Groupe de Recherches d'Art Visuel (GRAV), Paris, 1960–68. Professor, Arts Plastiques et Sciences de l'Art, Université Paris I Pantheon/Sorbonne, 1972–73. Recipient: Gold Medal, with GRAV, *Biennale di San Marino*, 1963; Premier Prix Travail d'Equipe, with GRAV, *Biennale de Paris*, 1963; Special Di Tella Prize, Buenos Aires, 1964; International Grand Prix for painting, *Biennale*, Venice, 1966. Chevalier, Ordre des Arts et Lettres, France. Agent: Galerie Denise René. 124 rue la Boetie, 75008 Paris. Addresses: 29 rue Couste, 94230 Cachan, France; and 41 rue des Rabats, 92160 Antony, France.

Individual Exhibitions:

1966 Howard Wise Gallery, New York
Galerie Denise René (Rive Droite and Rive Gauche), Paris
Op Art Galerie, Esslingen, West Germany
1967 Halfmannshof, Gelsenkirchen, West Germany
Galerie Francoise Mayer, Brussels
Howard Wise Gallery, New York
Galerie Saint-Laurent, Saint-Laurent-du-Pont, France
Istituto di Tella, Buenos Aires
Istituto General Electric, Montevideo
Museo de Bellas Artes, Caracas
1968 Moderna Museet, Stockholm
Galerie Buchholz, Munich
Museu de Arte Moderna, Rio de Janeiro
Museo de Bellas Artes, Mexico City
Galleria del Naviglio, Milan
1969 Henie-Onstad Art Center, Oslo
Galleria de Foscherari, Bologna
Konsthallen, Gothenburg, Sweden
Galleria del Cavillino, Venice

1970   Galerie Denise René, Paris
       Casa de las Americas, Havana
       Ulmer Museum, Ulm, West Germany
1972   Galerie Antanona, Caracas
       Galerie Denise René, Paris
       Galerie Francoise Mayer, Brussels
       Städtische Kunsthalle, Dusseldorf (retrospective)
       Haus am Waldsee, Berlin-Zehlendorf
       Galerie Denise René-Hans Mayer, Dusseldorf
1973   Galleria La Polena, Genoa
       Denise René Gallery, New York
1974   Galerie Denise René, Paris
1975   Museo de Arte Moderno, Mexico City
       Galleria Lorenzelli, Bergamo, Italy
1976   Galeria Studium, Valladolid, Spain
       Galeria Rayuela, Madrid
       Modulations, Galerie Denise René, Paris
       Le Parc en la Coruna, Galeria Mestre Mateo, La Coruna, Spain
       Museo de Arte Moderno, Bogota
1977   *Festivals de Royan* at the *Quadriennale*, Rome
       Galeria Torques, Santiago de Compostela, Spain

Selected Group Exhibitions:

1965   *The Responsive Eye*, Museum of Modern Art, New York
       Lumière, Mouvement et Optique, Palais des Beaux-Arts, Brussels
1966   *Biennale*, Venice
1967   *Bienal*, Sao Paulo
1968   *Kinetische Kunst*, Haus am Waldsee, Berlin-Zehlendorf
1970   *Kinetics*, Hayward Gallery, London
1971   *Multiples: The First Decade*, Philadelphia Museum of Art
1973   *Electric Art*, Kunsthalle, Hamburg
1976   *Creadores Latinamericanos Contemporaneos 1950–1976*, Museo de Arte Moderno, Mexico City
1977   *L'Art et L'Automobile*, Centre Georges Pompidou, Paris

Publications:

By LE PARC: articles—"Propositions sur le Mouvement," with GRAV, in *Bewogen-Beweging*, exhibition catalogue, Stockholm 1961; text, with GRAV, in *Le Parc: XXXIII Biennale de Venise 1966*, Paris 1966; text and text with GRAV in *Lumière et Mouvement*, exhibition catalogue, Paris 1967; text and text with GRAV in *GRAV*, exhibition catalogue, Krefeld, West Germany 1968; "L'Art Valeur Bourgeoise au Travail Révolutionnaire" and interview, with Frederic Chaleuil, in *Politique d'Aujourd'hui* (Paris), no. 9, 1971; interview, with B. Breecken, in *Vendredi Hebdo*, January 1971; "Je me Déclare Incapable de Prendre une Décision pour Accepter ou Refuser l'Invitation de M. Lassaigne" in *Les Lettres Francaises* (Paris), April 1972; text and text with GRAV in *Le Parc*, exhibition catalogue, Dusseldorf 1972.

On LE PARC: book—*L'Art Actuel en France*, by Anne Tronche and Hervé Gloaguen, Paris 1973; articles—"Julio Le Parc: Recherches 1959–1971" by P. Kress in *Kunstwerk* (Baden-Baden, West Germany), March 1972; "Dusseldorf: Julio Le Parc" by A. Pohribny in *NAC* (Milan), April 1972; "52 interventi sulla Proposta di Comportamento di Enzo Mari" by Lea Vergine in *NAC* (Milan), August 1971; "Szene Rhein-Ruhr" by B. Kerber in *Art International* (Lugano, Switzerland), April 1972: "Julio Le Parc: The Laws of Chance" in *Studio International* (London), January 1973; "Arte Programmata: a cura di Lea Vergine" in *NAC* (Milan), March 1973.

From being an artist interested in kinetics and light, Julio Le Parc has gradually moved to environments and play, and become more and more politicized into what he calls a "cultural guerrilla." Coming to Paris from Argentina on a scholarship in 1958, he joined with Vasarely's son Yvaral and other like-minded artists the following year to found the Groupe de Recherche d'Art Visuel (GRAV), one of the many kinetic groups formed in Europe during the late 1950's and early 1960's. It was a deliberate reaction against the fashion for informal tachism, and was influenced by the ideas of Vasarely, with his belief in impersonality and the anonymity of the artist; these artists set up a communal studio and constructed some works under the group name alone.

At first the group's aim was scientific or pseudo-scientific research into visual problems, but gradually, as Le Parc became more and more dominant, it was led towards the other main tendency of kinetic art, the "game aesthetic" of building environments for play and spectator participation. The group built complex environmental *Labyrinths* through which the public had to crawl while playing visual games of many kinds, manipulating mirrors, or balls which run through labyrinths. Le Parc aims at *instability*, a situation in which any permanent form of a work becomes impossible to discern. His works are designed to disorientate the spectator, and he uses all sorts of devices like distorting glasses and spring-loaded shoes to achieve this disorientation.

Play and entertainment are basic even to his more serious mobiles and kinetic-light murals, which use simple suspended metallic elements to produce a constantly shifting play of light and shade. Other games demonstrate velocity, vibration or the way ping-pong balls are shot radially from a fast-spinning pivot to the sides of the box. The increasingly polemical and political nature of his work was shown when for a retrospective in Dusseldorf in 1972 he arranged a participative environment of large punch-me dolls, with faces painted to represent the pillars of established society: typically for him not only policemen, politicians, priests and journalists, but also the artist.

Le Parc has remarked that kineticism "runs the risk of becoming a new academicism," and he has increasingly become one of those artists who were seeking a new orientation for art as the direct manipulation of the environment. His own statements make clear the relationship of his political views to this earlier belief in artistic instability and disorientation: "One must become a kind of cultural guerrilla against the present state of things and point out all the contradictions. One must create new situations in which people may rediscover their capacity to bring about changes; fight any tendency towards stability, permanence, lastingness; fight anything that heightens the state of dependence, apathy, passivity which is linked to habits, established criteria and myths."

—Konstantin Bazarov

LESLIE, Alfred.

American. Born in the Bronx, New York City, 29 October 1927. Educated at DeWitt Clinton High School, New York, graduated 1945; studied at New York University, 1948–49, Pratt Institute, Brooklyn, New York, and the Art Students League, New York. Served in the United States Coast Guard, 1945–46. Independent painter, since 1946: lives and works in South Amherst, Massachusetts. Taught in the Adult Education Program, Great Neck, New York, 1956–57, and at the San Francisco Art Institute, Summer 1964. Recipient: Guggenheim Fellowship, 1969; First Prize, Butler Institute of American Art, Youngstown, Ohio. Agent: Oil and Steel Gallery, 30/40 Vernon Boulevard, Box 2218, Long Island City, New York 11102. Addresses: 8 West 13th Street, New York, New York 10011; 1641 South East Street, South Amherst, Massachusetts 01002, U.S.A.

Individual Exhibitions:

1951   Tibor de Nagy Gallery, New York
1952   Tibor de Nagy Gallery, New York
1953   Tibor de Nagy Gallery, New York
1957   Robert Keene Gallery, Southampton, New York
1958   Robert Keene Gallery, Southampton, New York
1960   Martha Jackson Gallery, New York
1961   David Anderson Gallery, New York
       Martha Jackson Gallery, New York
1962   Holland-Goldowsky Gallery, Chicago
       Martha Jackson Gallery, New York
1969   Noah Goldowsky Gallery, New York
1971   Noah Goldowsky Gallery, New York
       Leslie/Thiebaud/Pearlstein, Hayden Gallery, Massachusetts Institute of Technology, Cambridge
1975   *Paintings*, Frumkin Gallery, New York
1976   Museum of Fine Arts, Boston (travelled to the Hirshhorn Museum, Washington, D.C., and the Museum of Contemporary Art, Chicago)
1977   *Drawings*, Kilcawley Center Art Gallery, Youngstown State University, Ohio
1978   *Drawings by Alfred Leslie*, Jorgensen Gallery, University of Connecticut, Storrs

Selected Group Exhibitions:

1958   *Bienal*, Sao Paulo
1962   *Art since 1950*, at the *World's Fair*, Seattle
1963   *4 Americans*, Kunsthalle, Basle
1970   *22 Realists*, Whitney Museum, New York
1973   *American Drawings 1963–1973*, Whitney Museum, New York
1975   *3 Centuries of the American Nude*, New York Cultural Center
1976   *Bicentennial Exhibition: America '76*, Corcoran Gallery, Washington, D.C. (toured the United States, 1976–78)
1977   *Drawings of the 70's*, Museums of Modern Art, New York
       8 Contemporary American Realists, Pennsylvania Academy of Fine Arts, Philadelphia (travelled to the North Carolina Museum of Art, Raleigh, 1978)
1980   *The 50's: Aspects of Art in New York*, Hirshhorn Museum, Washington, D.C.

Collections:

Museum of Modern Art, New York; Whitney Museum, New York; Albright-Knox Art Gallery, Buffalo, New York; Hirshhorn Museum, Washington, D.C.; Art Institute of Chicago; Walker Art Center, Minneapolis; Stedelijk Museum, Amsterdam; Kunsthalle, Basle; Moderna Museet, Stockholm; Ludwig Collection, Aachen, West Germany.

Publications:

By LESLIE: articles—interview/statement in "Ten Portraitists" by Gerrit Henry in *Art in America* (New York), January/February 1975; statement in *Alfred Leslie: Paintings*, exhibition catalogue, New York 1975.

On LESLIE: books—*Alfred Leslie; Paintings*, exhibition catalogue, New York 1975; *Alfred Leslie*, exhibition catalogue, with an essay by Robert Rosenblum, Boston 1976; articles—"Paintings by Leslie: Is Modernism Dead?" by John Perreault in *Soho Weekly News* (New York), 13 November 1975; "Alfred Leslie: From MFA to Venice" by Robert Taylor in the *Boston Sunday Globe*, 9 May 1976; "Picking Up the Old Master's Options: A Look at Alfred Leslie" by Mark Mirsky in *The Real Paper* (Boston), 12 May 1976; "The Figure Paintings of Alfred Leslie: Larger Than Life and Scary" by Paul Richard in the *Washington Post*, 16 November 1976; "Alfred Leslie and American Realism" by Devonna Pieszack in the *New Art Examiner* (Chicago), February 1977.

The painting career of Alfred Leslie has proceeded exactly in reverse when compared with that of many contemporary artists. In the late 1950's Leslie was associated with the second wave of abstract expressionist painters, creating splashy gesture-ridden canvases filled with references to de Kooning and Motherwell. By the mid-1960's Leslie had abandoned abstraction but retained the large scale he achieved in geometric works done around 1962. Leslie was an independent thinker and, at a time when realist painting had a small following, transferred his interest in narration as an artistic form from films to painting. The artist had a number of objectives. He was inter-

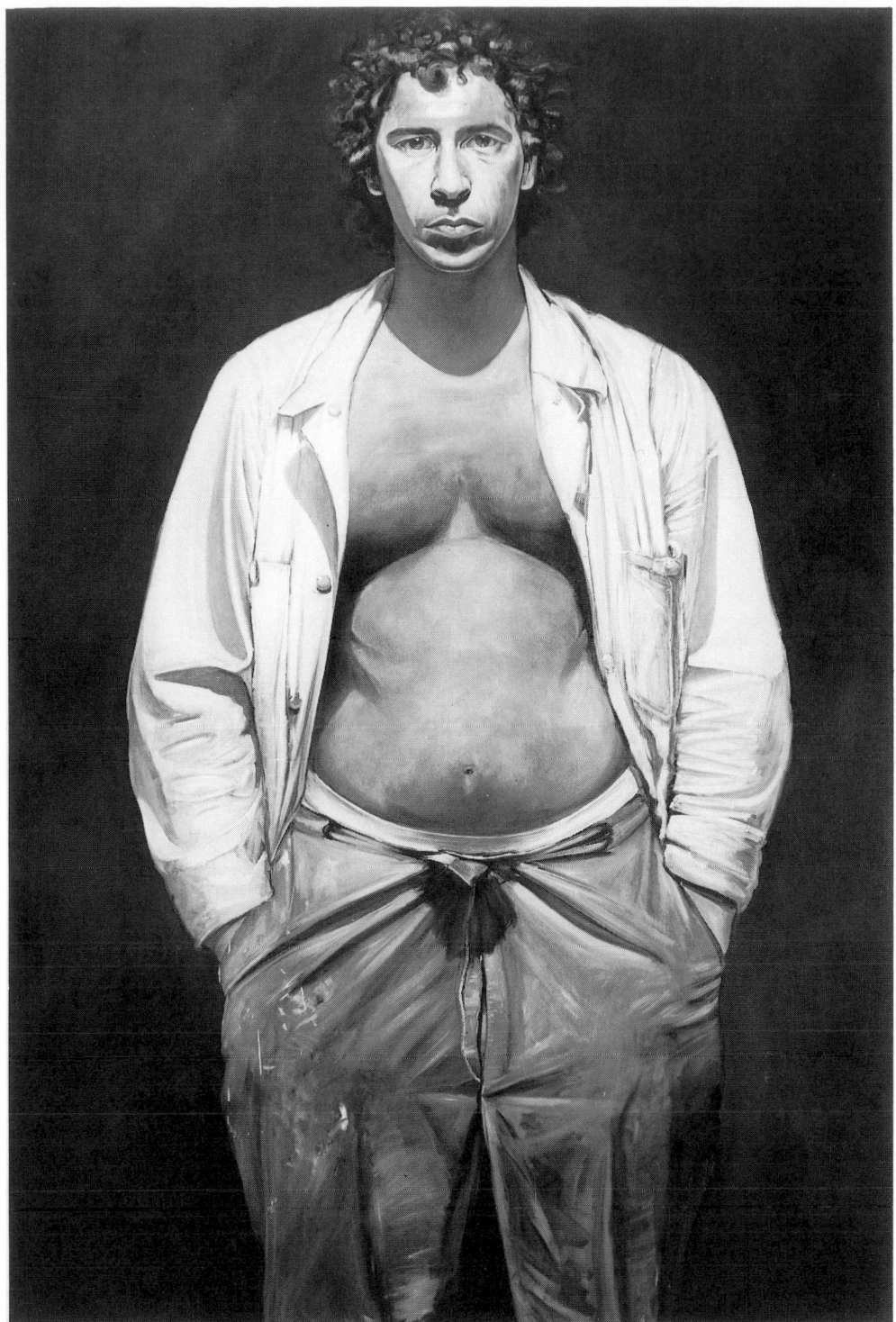

Alfred Leslie: *Self Portrait*, **1967** Courtesy Whitney Museum, New York

LE VA, Barry.

American. Born in Long Beach, California in 1941. Studied at California State University, Long Beach, 1960–63; Los Angeles College of Art and Design, 1963; Otis Art Institute, Los Angeles, 1963–67, BFA 1964, MFA 1967. Independent artist, since 1967: now lives and works in New York. Instructor, Minneapolis College of Art and Design, 1969–70, and Princeton University, New Jersey, 1973–74. Recipient: Young Talent Grant, Los Angeles County Museum of Art, 1968. Agent: Sonnabend Gallery, 420 West Broadway, New York, New York 10012. Address: 74 Grand Street, New York, New York 10013, U.S.A.

Individual Exhibitions:

1969	Walker Art Center, Minneapolis
	Institute of Fine Art, Minneapolis
	University of Wisconsin at River Falls
	Wisconsin State University at Menomonie
	Ohio State University, Columbus
1970	Galerie Ricke, Cologne
	La Jolla Museum of Art, California
1971	Nigel Greenwood Gallery, London
	University of Utrecht
1972	Galerie Projection, Cologne
	Galerie Ricke, Cologne
1973	Bykert Downtown Gallery, New York
	Rudolf Zwirner and Rolf Ricke, Cologne
1974	Bykert Gallery, New York
	Hartford Art School, Connecticut
	Galleria Toselli, Milan
1975	Weinberg Gallery, San Francisco
	Weinberg Gallery, New York
	Bykert Gallery, New York
	Claire Copley Gallery, Los Angeles
	Espace 5, Montreal
	Musée d'Art Contemporain, Montreal
1976	Galerie Ricke, Cologne
	Texas Gallery, Houston
	Weinberg Gallery, San Francisco
	Claire Copley Gallery, Los Angeles
	Sonnabend Gallery, New York
	Galerie Sonnabend, Paris
1977	Wright State University, Dayton, Ohio
1978	Texas Gallery, Houston
	Sonnabend Gallery, New York
1979	New Museum, New York (retrospective)
1980	Nigel Greenwood Gallery, London
1981	Sonnabend Gallery, New York
	New Gallery of Contemporary Art, Cleveland, Ohio
1982	Yarlow-Salzman Gallery, Toronto
1983	Sonnabend Gallery, New York
1985	Texas Gallery, Houston
1986	Daniel Weinberg Gallery, Los Angeles
	Sonnabend Gallery, New York

Selected Group Exhibitions:

1967	*Newcomers 1967*, Lytton Center of Visual Arts, Los Angeles
1969	*Anti-Illusion Procedures and Materials*, Whitney Museum, New York
1970	*Art in the Mind*, Allen Art Museum, Oberlin College, Ohio
1972	*Documenta 5*, Museum Fridericianum, Kassel, West Germany (and *Documenta 7*, 1982)
1975	*Bochner/Le Va/Rockburne/Tuttle*, Contemporary Arts Center, Cincinnati, Ohio
1976	*200 Years of American Sculpture*, Whitney Museum, New York
1978	*Contemporary Drawing: New York*, University of Santa Barbara, California
1979	*Drawings about Drawing Today*, University of North Carolina, Chapel Hill
1984	*Minding Measure: Measuring Mind*, Islip Art Museum, East Islip, New York
1986	*Art from Two Continents*, Helander Gallery, Palm Beach, Florida

ested in the story telling properties of painting as well as the moral interpretation of certain puzzling contemporary events; he was interested as well in portraiture and in traditional problems of lighting and composition. Leslie feels that film and photography have taken over the functions of storytelling and portraiture in our visual lives, and it is his intention to restore these elements. The portraits are often full length, and lighting is intensely angled, resembling a 17th century style made famous by Caravaggio.

In "The Killing of Frank O'Hara," 1966, a series Leslie painted to commemorate and explain the senseless death of his friend, the artist reverts to another earlier convention, a cycle of seven paintings to elucidate the entire action. The paintings are consciously dramatic—illuminated figures glow against darkened backgrounds and forms are acutely angled (O'Hara thrown, feet up, against the front of a beach taxi; O'Hara's body lowered on a stretcher at the loading pier) with references in the posed figures and faces to significant religious or mystical painters in art history—Blake, Mantegna, de la Tour. The final painting, of the cemetery where O'Hara's body lies, seems to establish the moral peace that Leslie, unlike most members of his generation, blatantly seeks through painting.

In 1982 Leslie completed a large (9′ × 11′) painting titled *The Thirteen Americans* as a commission for the Lyndon B. Johnson Library in Austin, Texas. The cross section of sitters seems to reflect and even momentarily revive L. B. Johnson's often called for concept of the Great Society, a sort of peaceable kingdom in which fellow Americans of all colors and ages would coexist without strife. Leslie puts it in an art-historical context by claiming "I wanted an art like the art of David, Caravaggio, and Rubens, meant to influence the conduct of people."

—Mary Stofflet

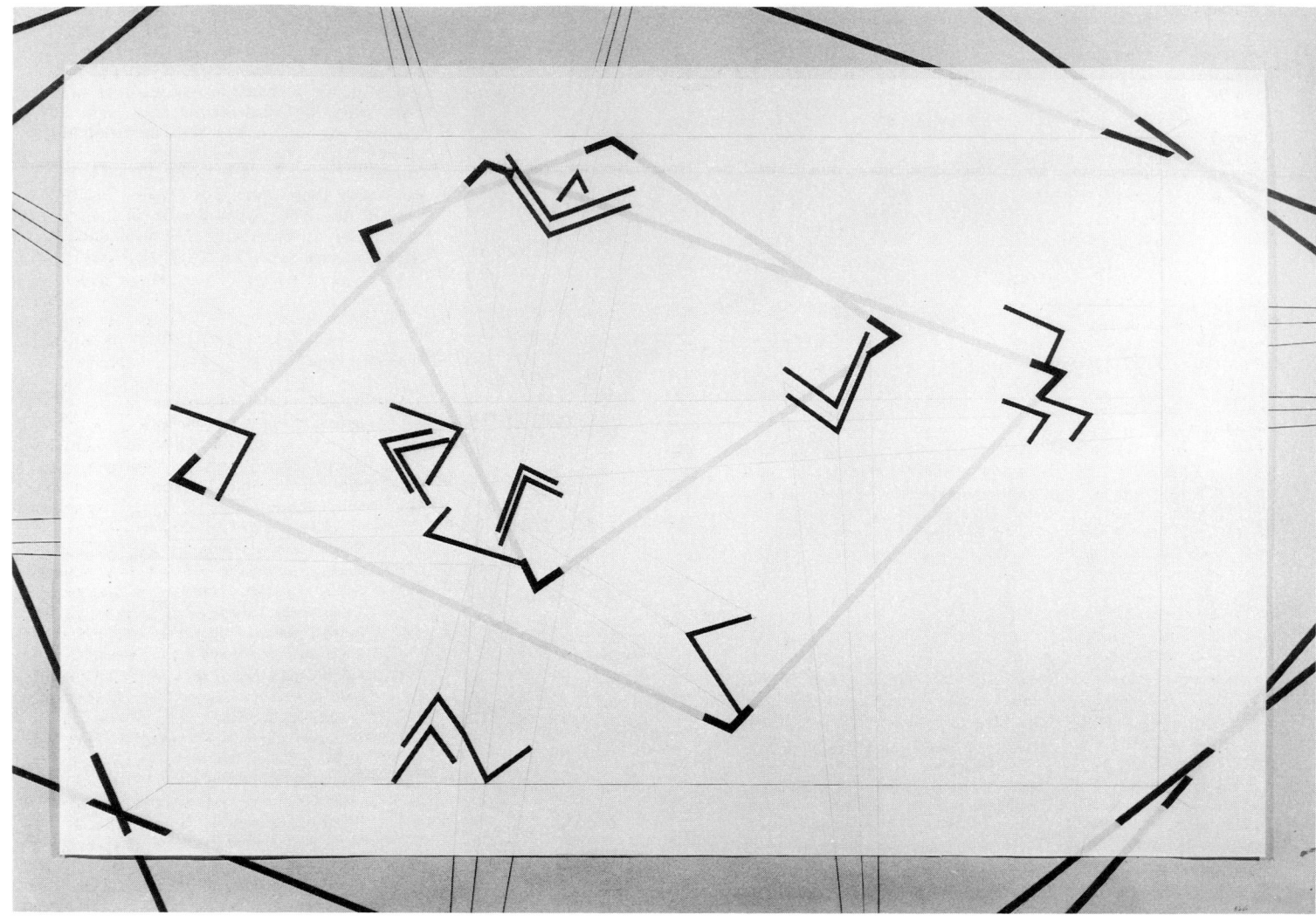

Barry Le Va: *Installation Study for Any Rectangular Space*, **1977** Courtesy Whitney Museum, New York

Collections:

Los Angeles County Museum of Art.

Publications:

By LE VA: articles—"Clocked Clown Outward" in *Studio International* (London), November 1971; "Discussions with Barry Le Va" in *Avalanche* (New York), Fall 1971.

On LE VA: articles—"Barry Le Va: Distributional Sculpture" by Jane Livingston in Artforum (New York), November 1968; "Barry Le Va and the Nondescript Description" by Larry Rosing in *Artnews* (New York), September 1969; "Notes on Piece by Barry Le Va" in *Studio International* (London), November 1971; review in *Artforum* (New York), June 1973; review in *Artforum* (New York), May 1975.

Beginning with his early scatter pieces of 1967–68, Barry Le Va's main intention has been to reject the "object aesthetic" and art tied to a "single glance" by creating works which are composed of widely dispersed arrangements of abstract elements. Usually termed a Postminimalist, Le Va rejects Minimalist rigorous geometrics, using open forms and eccentric materials and emphasizing process in compositional methods which apply expressionistic painterly ideas to sculptural forms. In Le Va's conceptually based works, visual structures are expressive of thinking processes, communicating ideas about the tension between seeming randomness and more coherent ordering principles. His scattered arrangements explore the perimeters of defined spaces as experienced by the viewer/participant who, through choice, moves through the environmental layout preordained by the artist to discover and perceive the underlying content.

In 1966–67, while Le Va was still in art school in Los Angeles, he began to develop what soon came to be known as "distributional pieces", using scraps lying around his studio which were meant to be elements in the pictures with cutout collage/elements he was making at that time. Separately from New York based artists such as Robert Morris and Richard Serra, Le Va was experimenting to find new possibilities based on ideas inherent in expressionist painting of the 1950s and in minimal structures of the 1960s. His methodology and syntax in place, Le Va proceeded to locate variations on his consistently held ideas through the 1970s.

Among Le Va's chosen materials have been felt, dust, flour, cement powder, paper toweling and wood. Determining his choices by the specific site in which his elements are to be dispersed, Le Va sets his limits, establishing the number, size and shape of his components. Because of the enlarged scale and summary dispersal of the elements, the plan underlying the piece is not at first visually apparent. To apprehend and decode the underlying schema, the viewer must move through the space, locating and perceiving elements such as direction, overlap and separation, filling in the gaps and recreating the situation set up by the artist in his or her own way. Memory becomes an important issue in the real time, physical experiencing of the participant of what at first seemed to be bunches of isolated forms. By the very nature of the scattered materials, permutations occur in the works' configurations, adding to the tension which already involved chance as well as choice. The physical experiencing of the ephemeral plan is suggestive of psychological states involving accumulation, continuities, discontinuities, expansion, dispersal, blockage. To my mind, Le Va's work is a kind of conceptualized methodology. As is true with much work of

this kind, Le Va has tended to the repetitive, and the result has been a lapsing into aestheticized dryness and esoterica which doesn't seem to hold much possibility by this time.

—Barbara Cavaliere

LEVERETT, David.
British. Born in Nottingham, 12 January 1938. Studied at Nottingham College of Art, 1957–61, at Royal Academy Schools, London, 1961–64. Married Sonia Loretta Wilhelmina Holme in 1961; sons: Jason and Simeon. Worked as builder-designer, London, 1954–57; scenic design assistant, Nottingham Repertory Theatre, 1956–57. Independent painter, since 1965: lives and works in London. Lecturer, Croydon College of Art, Surrey, 1965; Director of Studies, East Ham Technical College, London, 1966–69; Visiting Lecturer, Ravensbourne College of Art, Kent, 1969; Visiting Artist, Royal Academy Schools and Royal College of Art, London, and Visiting Lecturer, Hornsey College of Art, London, 1971–73; Visiting Lecturer, Slade School of Fine Art, London, since 1971; Visiting Artist, Norwich College of Art, Norfolk, 1972–74; Visiting Lecturer, Cooper Union, New York, 1974; and Dublin College of Art, 1980–82. Recipient: Arts Council Grant, 1974. Agent: Redfern Gallery, 20 Cork Street, London WIX 2HL. Address: 132 Leighton Road, London, NW5, England.

Individual Exhibitions:

Selected Group Exhibitions:

Collections:

British Council, London; Tate Gallery, London; Arts Council of Great Britain, London; Victoria and Albert Museum, London; Glasgow City Art Gallery; Museu de Arte Moderna, Sao Paulo; Museum of Modern Art, Zagreb; Modern Art Gallery, Koszalim, Poland; Museum of Contemporary Art, Athens, Art Gallery of New South Wales, Sydney.

Publications:

By LEVERETT: articles—"Artists Notebook" in *Art and Artists* (London), June 1969; statement in *Leverett*, exhibition catalogue, Verona 1974; "Fragments from the Laminates of Continuous Time" in *Words and Images*, Verona 1976; "Views from a Citadel" in *David Leverett*, exhibition catalogue, London 1985; "Sacred Gardens" in *David Leverett*, exhibition catalogue, St. Helier 1986.

On LEVERETT: books—*Play Orbit*, edited by Jasia Reichardt, London 1969; *Riflessioni sulla Pittura*, exhibition catalogue, Acireale, Italy 1973; *Colours in Painting: A European Situation*, exhibition catalogue, Rome 1976; article—"A Discussion of Multiples" by Paul Overy, in *Studio International* (London), September 1970.

The use of landscape as a metaphor is an important theme in my work. I use it as a means of exploring two important preoccupations that depend on the landscape for interpretation. The first takes the form of an inquiry into the way I perceive time and express it. The attempt to project a sensation of extended time that implies references to past, present and future is crucial to the inquiry. These various indicators of time invest the work with a sense of duration, with age, with perpetuity. References that reflect a sense of continuity that is carried in the formations of the land and the behavior of the seasons. The action of the weather, the motion of light are daily forces that confirm the histories of the Earth. In their effect they are the dynamics of change and turbulence that contrast against the durability of the rocks.

My second preoccupation is more difficult to describe because, ultimately, it is concerned with identity. It is the need to find and determine my position within the wider reaches of time. What I seek to do is to release this need by creating a primary sense of place through the work. The qualities of time that exist in the land allow this release to occur. The locations I choose on which to base my work are very important. They must contain features I can use to convey the sense of primary belonging to the earth. My views and perspective of the land are not just specific to its topographical characteristics. The spirit of place exists in the pervading wholeness of nature. The way we recognize it through a particular location only heightens its effect and draws our attention to it. The earth is our fundamental point of recognition to the vastness to which we belong. These considerations of time and space require forms of pictorial engagement that go much deeper than the surface landscape. They involve questions about the fragile state of one's identity as measured against time. Particular landscapes become for me a means of expressing the union which exists between the individual and nature. I believe the Earth is a sacred garden and that we are a part of it. We will interpret its mysteries with signs, symbols and images that affirm this union. Because of our primary link with the Earth, because we cannot be separated from it, we are its guardians too. Consequently, ignorance and abuse of this fact influences and damages the sacred gardens as much as it injures us.

—David Leverett

David Leverett's work can be described as concerned with narrative, in the sense of being less related to single, final images, than with communicating the process of creative thought and action. His work has gradually assumed a kind of manual serialization, so that each step is allowed its own clarity, no matter how complex the total structure. In fact, he describes his laminated, resin paintings as "Diaries of an event in time, the residue of remembrance of an event, as well as the activity whereby one records the event."

His development has been demonstrated in a series of paintings and prints which intimately interrelate, much of the experience derived from printmaking later being translated into paint. They begin with solid patterns in flat colours, positive and unconcerned with formative processes. A grid system then appeared, which seemed to undermine this positiveness, concerned with the structure beneath the solidity. The titles of these prints, referring to seasons, to shift and change, express the artist's growing concern with time and light, with the result that floating, rather than anchored form, and an image of a changeable world of sensations, began to emerge.

These prints required precise planning and control, but it was the overlaying of colour areas in the printing process which led to the first sprayed paintings. Here, even more than in the printing, Leverett became obsessed with the need to retain the narrative of creation, as a personal record and as a means of communication. Thus his pictures are not fixed points in time, but vortexes of creative time, inviting us into the intimacy of their structures. In recent years he has increasingly experimented with acrylics, firstly as the surfaces on which he projected spray techniques, and more recently laminated resins holding transparent sheets of drawn and painted paper. What emerges are living X-rays in which the artist describes time and experience.

—Charles Spencer

David Leverett: *Compilations*, 1981

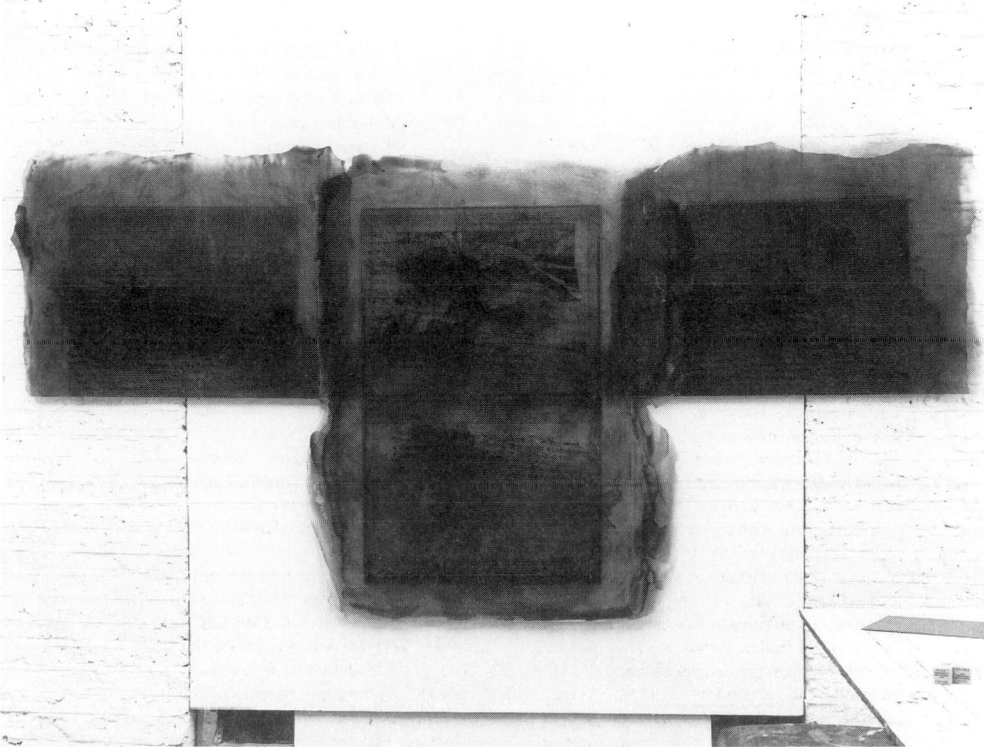

LEVINE, Les.

Canadian. Born in Dublin, Ireland, 6 October 1935; emigrated to Canada, 1957: naturalized, 1961. Studied at Central School of Arts and Crafts, London, 1953–55. Married Catherine Kanai in 1973. Independent artist, since 1959. Feature writer, *Aspen Times*, Colorado, 1967–68; Founder-Director, Levine's Restaurant, New York, 1968; Publisher and Editor, *Culture Hero*, New York, 1969; Founder, Museum of Mott Art Inc., New York, 1970. Artist-in-Residence, Design Conference, Aspen, Colorado, 1967, 1969; Associate Professor of Art, New York University, 1972–73; Artist-in-Residence, Nova Scotia College of Art and Design, Halifax, 1973; Distinguished Professor of Video Art, William Paterson College, Wayne, New Jersey, 1975; Artist-in-Residence, University of Illinois, Circle Campus, Chicago, 1975. Recipient: *Canadian Sculpture Biennale* Prize, Paris, 1969; Architectural League Grant, New York, 1972; Sculpture Fellowship, National Endowment for the Arts, 1974, 1980; Creative Artists Service Program Award for Video, New York, 1979. Address: 20 East 20th Street, New York, New York 10003. U.S.A.

Individual Exhibitions:

1964	Hart House, University of Toronto
	Blue Barn Gallery, Ottawa
	David Mirvish Gallery, Toronto
1965	The Isaacs Gallery, New York
	Book of Graphics, Toronto
1966	Blue Barn Gallery, Ottawa
	Fischbach Gallery, New York
	Art Gallery of Ontario, Toronto
	Lofthouse Gallery, Ottawa
	University of Western Ontario, London
1967	Walker Art Center, Minneapolis
	Museum of Modern Art, New York
	The Isaacs Gallery, New York
	Fischbach Gallery, New York
	Architectural League, New York
1968	Glendon Campus Art Gallery, York University, Toronto
	Fischbach Gallery, New York
	Gibson Gallery, New York
	New York State Council on the Arts
1969	Molly Barnes Gallery, Los Angeles
	Jack Burnham to Wed Judith Benjamin, Levin's Restaurant, New York
	New York Stock Market
	Museum of Contemporary Art, Chicago
	University of Michigan, Ann Arbor
	Rowan Gallery, London
	Phyllis Kind Gallery, Chicago
	Loeb Student Center, New York (and at West 4th Street, New York; New York City Department of Parks Show)
	Fischbach Gallery, New York
1970	Galerie de Gestlo, Bremen, West Germany
	The Isaacs Gallery, New York (2 shows)
	Fischbach Gallery, New York
1971	Protetch-Rivkin Gallery, Washington, D.C.
	Galerie M.E. Thelen, Cologne
	Galerie de Gestlo, Hamburg
1972	Finch College Museum of Art, New York
	Fischbach Gallery (Downtown), New York
	Harold Rivkin Gallery, Washington, D.C.
	Galerie M. E. Thelen, Cologne
1973	Galerie de Gestlo, Hamburg
	Michael C. Rockefeller Art Center Gallery, State University of New York at Fredonia
	The Isaacs Gallery, New York
	Seton Hall University, South Orange, New Jersey
	Anna Leonowens Gallery, Nova Scotia College of Art and Design, Halifax
1974	Galerie de Gestlo, Hamburg
	Vancouver Art Gallery
	University of California at San Diego
	Galerie Gerald Piltzer, Paris
	The Video Distribution Inc., New York
	Galleria Schema, Florence
	Stefanotty Gallery, New York
1975	A Space, Toronto

	Adler Castillo, Caracas, Venezuela
	Anthology Film Archives, New York
	Miami-Dade Junior College, Florida
1976	Galerie Gilles Gheerbrant, Montreal
	M. L. D'Arc Gallery, New York
	Lions Gallery of the Senses, Wadsworth Atheneum, Hartford
	California State University at Los Angeles
	Art Gallery of New South Wales, Sydney
	National Gallery of Victoria, Melbourne
	Paterson Ewing Gallery, University of Melbourne
	The Jam Factory, Adelaide, South Australia
1977	Everson Museum, Syracuse, New York
	Albright-Knox Gallery, Buffalo, New York
	Galerie de Gestlo, Hamburg
	The Isaacs Gallery, Toronto
	Vehicule Art, Montreal
	Galerie Arnesen, Copenhagen
	AIR/ZBS Foundation, Fort Edward, New York
	M. L. D'Arc Gallery, New York
1978	International Cultureel Centrum, Antwerp
	Rotterdamse Kunststichting
	The Station Gallery, Whitby, Ontario
	Laurentian University, Sudbury, Ontario
	Mary J. L. Black Library, Thunderbay, Ontario
1979	Parry Sound Public Library, Canada
	Paysages du Grand Nord, Canadian Cultural Centre, Paris
	Northern Illinois University, DeKalb
	Ronald Feldman Gallery, New York
	Galerie Jollenbeck, Cologne
	Philadelphia Museum of Art
	Video-As-Art, Myers Fine Arts Gallery, State University of New York at Plattsburgh
	Alberta College of Art, SAIT Campus, Calgary
1980	Marian Goodman Gallery, New York (2 shows)
	The Isaacs Gallery, Toronto
	Enzo Cannaviello Gallery, Milan
	Ronald Feldman Gallery, New York
1980	Studio d'Arte Cannaviello, Milan
1981	Ronald Feldman Gallery, New York
	Galerie Jollenbeck, Cologne
1982	Lower Manhattan Cultural Council, in New York subways
	Galleria del Cavallino, Venice
	Elizabeth Galasso Fine Arts, Ossining, New York
1983	N.A.M.E. Gallery, Chicago
	Isaacs Gallery, Toronto
	Ronald Feldman Gallery, New York
	80 Langton, San Francisco
	Honolulu Academy of Art, Hawaii
	Real Artways, Hartford, Connecticut
	Midtown Y Gallery, New York
1984	Lelia Ivy Gallery, Los Angeles
	Elizabeth Galsso Fine Arts, Ossining, New York
	Los Angeles Institute of Contemporary Art
	Ted Greenwald Gallery, New York
1985	Millennium, New York
	A Space, Toronto
	Mo David, New York
	Specacolor Lightboard, Times Square, New York
	Institute of Contemporary Arts, London
	Orchard Gallery, Londonderry, Northern Ireland
1986	Carpenter & Hochman, New York
	Trinity College, Dublin
	Ted Greenwald Gallery, New York
	Akademie der Kunst, Copenhagen

Selected Group Exhibitions:

1964	*Second Canadian Sculpture Exhibition*, National Gallery of Canada, Ottawa
1970	*Software*, Jewish Museum, New York
1977	*Documenta 6: Künstler*, Galerie de Gestlo, Hamburg
1978	*Projects*, Museum of Modern Art, New York
1979	*Journées Interdisciplinaries sur l'Art Corporel*, Centre Pompidou, Paris (traveled to Buenos Aires)
1980	*Printed Art: A View of Two Decades*, Museum of Modern Art, New York
1981	*Pictures and Promises*, The Kitchen, New York
1983	*Ten Years of Video*, Institute of Contemporary Art, Boston

1985	*Prozess und Konstruktion*, Stadtisches Museum im Lenbachhaus, Munich
1987	*Documenta 8*, Museum Fridericianum, Kassel, West Germany

Collections:

Museum of Modern Art, New York; Whitney Museum, New York; Philadelphia Museum of Art; National Gallery of Australia, Canberra; New Orleans Museum of Art, Louisiana; Institute of Contemporary Art, Boston; Corcoran Gallery of Art, Washington, D.C.; Honolulu Academy of Art, Hawaii; Art Gallery of Ontario, Toronto, Stadtisches Museum im Lenbachhaus, Munich.

Publications:

By LEVINE: books—*Poem Disposable*, co-author, New York 1969; *Museum of Mott Art Catalogue of Services*, New York 1970; *House*, Hilversum, Netherlands 1971, 1976; *After Art*, New York 1974; *Camera Art*, exhibition catalogue, Wayne, New Jersey 1974; *Bear News*, New York 1976; *Using the Camera as a Club/Not Necessarily a Great One*, New York 1976; *Five OHHH Disposable Sculptures*, Ontario 1977; *On Subjectivity*, portfolio, Cambridge, Massachusetts 1978; *Media: The Bio-Tech Rehearsal For Leaving The Body*, Calgary, Alberta 1979; *Hand Printed Etchings*, exhibition catalogue, New York 1980; *Les Levine: Large Format Polaroid Photographs*, exhibition catalogue, New York 1985; *Blame God: Billboard Projects*, exhibition catalogue, London 1986; television films—*The Last Sculpture Show* on META-TV, Arlington, Virginia 1972; "Les Levine Festival" on *Televisionaries* on Channel J Cable-TV, New York 1975; videotapes (all New York)—*Bum*, 1965; *Critic*, 1965; *The Nude Model*, 1966; *Slipcover*, 1966; *White Noise*, 1967; *Destruction in Art*, 1967; *Clothing and the Law*, 1967; *Architecture*, 1967; *The London Scene*, 1968; *Photon Strangeness*, 1968; *Electric Shock*, 1968; *The Big Eye*, 1968; *Iris*, 1968; *Contact*, 1969; *Columbia*, 1969; *Blank*, 1969; *Fashion Show Poetry Event*, 1969; *Paint*, 1969; *Topesthesia*, 1970; *John and Mimi's Book of Love*, 1970; *Mott Art Hearings*, 1970; *Body Control Systems*, 1970; *A.I.R. Software Show*, 1970; *Train*, 1971; *Stand-Up Cop*, 1971; *Mrs. Hunt*, 1972; *The Last Sculpture Show*, 1972; *The Troubles: An Artist's Document of Ulster*, 1972; *Outside the Republican Convention*, 1972; *Chain of Command*, 1972; *Supervision*, 1973; *The Last Book of Life*, 1973; *Topesthesia III*, 1973; *Gilbert and George*, 1973; *Christmas Card*, 1973; *Ritual*, 1973; *Language—Emotion + Syntax = Message*, 1973; *Space Walk*, 1974; *Script*, 1974; *The Story of Three Children*, 1974; *Spaghetti*, 1974; *Les Levin's Firenze*, 1974; *Visiting Artist*, 1974; *Brainwash*, 1974; *If I Graduate*, 1974; *Artistic*, 1974; *Les Levine's Greatest Hits*, 1974; *A Portrait of Anna*, 1974; *A Portrait of Les*, 1974; *Watergate Au Revoir*, 1974; *I Am an Artist*, 1975; *We Are Still Alive*, 1975; *An Interview with Bob Mulholland*, 1975; *Magic Carpet*, 1975; *Landscape I*, 1975; *Fortune Cookie*, 1975; *Cheap Thrill*, 1975; *One Gun*, 1975; *What Can the Federal Government Do for You?*, 1975; *Federal Fashions*, 1975; *Landscape II*, 1975; *Video Lecture*, 1975; *Starry Night*, 1975; *Mr. Abstract*, 1975; *The Last Art Student Has Been Eaten*, 1975; *I'm Lost*, 1976; *The Selling of a Video Artist*, 1976; *I Am Not Blind*, 1976.

On LEVINE: books—*Beyond Modern Sculpture*, by Jack Burnham, London 1968; *Minimal Art: A Critical Anthology*, edited by Gregory Battcock, New York 1968; *Recorded Activities*, exhibition catalogue, Philadelphia 1970; *The Structure of Art* by Jack Burnham, New York 1971; *Icons and Images of the 60's* by Nicolas and Elena Calas, New York 1971; *Great Western Salt Works* by Jack Burnham, New York 1974; *The Great American Chewing Gum Book* by Robert Hendrickson, Radnor, Pennsylvania 1976; *Art Actuel/Skira Annuel 1977*, Geneva 1977; *New Artists Video: A Critical Anthology*, edited by Gregory Battcock, New York 1978; *ZBS Foundation*, exhibition catalogue, Fort Edward, New York 1978; *The Great American Foot*, exhibition catalogue, with an introduction by Paul J. Smith, New York 1978; *Images of Self*, exhibition catalogue with an essay by Irving Sandler, Westfield, Massachusetts 1979; *Biennale de l'Association Belge des Critiques d'Art*, exhibition catalogue, Antwerp and Charleroi, Belgium 1979; *Journées Interdisciplinaires sur l'Art Corporel et Performances*, exhibition catalogue, with text by Pontus Hulten, Paris 1979; *Les Levine*, exhibition catalogue, Antwerp 1979; *Les Levine: Paysages du Grand Nord*, exhibition catalogue, with text by Mela Constantinidi, Paris 1979; *Video-As-Art by Les Levine*, exhibition catalogue, with an introduction by Judith K. Van Wagner, Plattsburg, New York 1979; *Time and Space Concepts in Art* by Marilyn Belford and Jerry Herman, New York 1980; *Museums by Artists*, edited by A.A. Bronson and Peggy Gale, Toronto 1983;

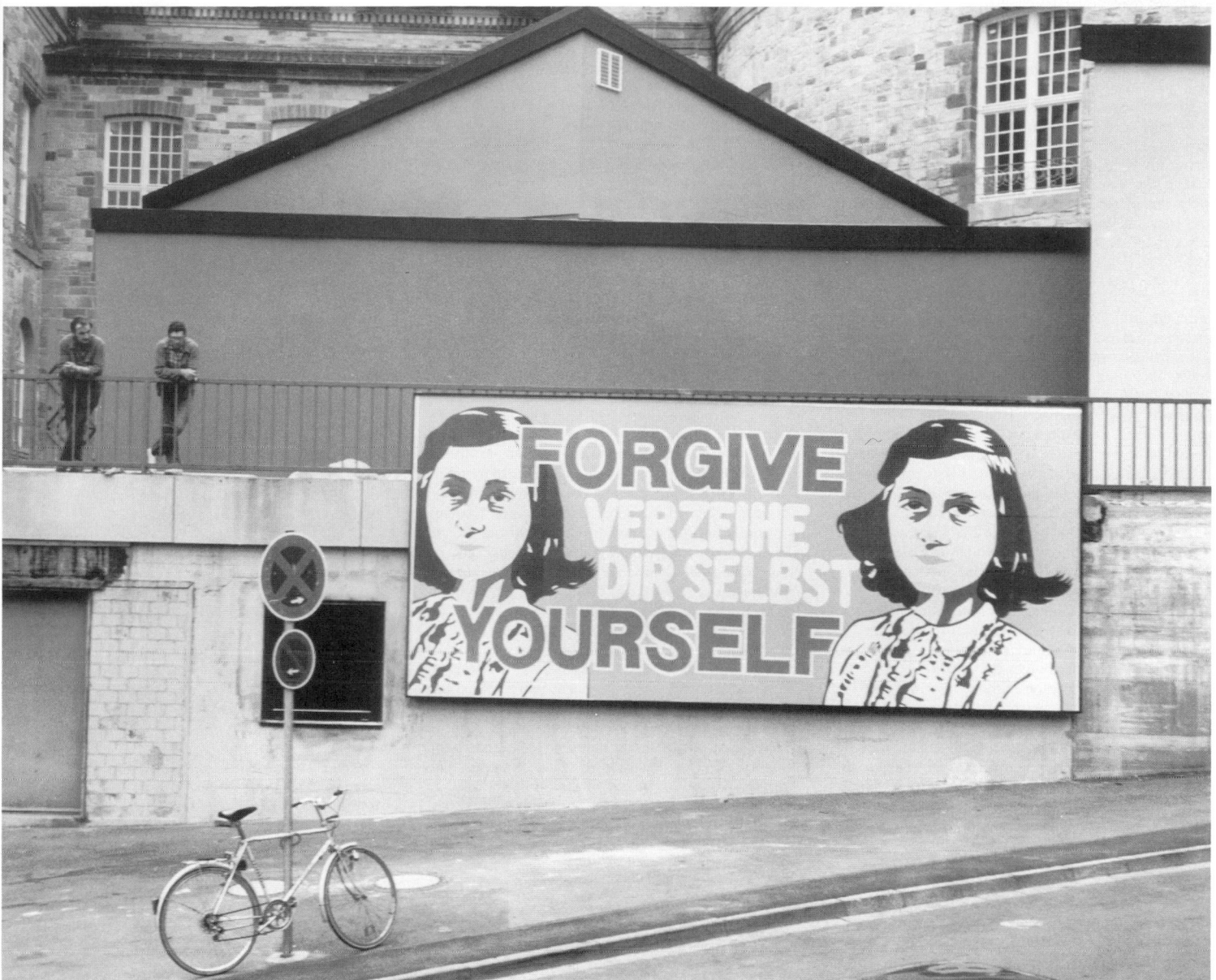

Les Levine: *Forgive Yourself*, billboard, Kassel, West Germany, 1987

Kunst und Video, by Bettina Gruber and Maria Vedder, Cologne 1983; *The Art of Performance*, edited by Gregory Battcok and Robert Nickas, New York 1984.

When an artist is asked why he does what he does, he is dumbfounded because he thinks he's already answered the question by doing what he does. He sees the question as a penalty and tries to imagine what rule he has broken so he can prove himself innocent.

For many years I've concerned myself with the systems of art as they relate to society in general, that is to say, the questions of the social values of art, and art's real service to society. I have been forced to ask myself, are the social and political problems of society a valid medium for art? The answer is, "Yes, of course." If art is to mean anything to society, it is the duty of the artist to employ his sensibilities in interpreting existing social systems.

I have on numerous occasions described myself as a media sculptor, a nomenclature which has puzzled the art world at large. Their difficulty in understanding seems to be the juncture between the word "sculpture" which is physical and the word "media" which is non-physical and ephemeral. The feeling amongst them seems to be that a non-physical medium, such as communications media, has no physical substance, shape or form, and so, therefore, to use the word "sculpture" which implies a shaping and forming technique would seem ridiculous.

However, in my case the media are my materials. I am interested in using my media to effect change and understanding of our environment; I want to consider media as a natural resource and to mold media the way others would mold matter. As with television the subject is the medium, i.e., if one has a politician on television, what we're really dealing with is the medium of politics. So in a sense, the subject of my work has to be considered the real medium. When I do a piece on Northern Ireland or games or the federal government no matter what technical medium I may be using, the real medium for the work is Northern Ireland, game rooms or the federal government. So I feel that communications media, particularly electronic media, have indeed a shape and form (though non-physical). My work deals with that shape and form and, therefore, I call myself a media sculptor. If media changes man, i.e., the television generation, then man must change media.

From where I stand, media is one of the few mysteries, both visual and audible, left for the 20th-century artist to decipher. By now, most formal problems connected with art production are a matter of academic knowledge. As a matter of fact, there is so much knowledge about color, form, shape, composition, relationships, esthetics, et al available that one has to assume that a lack of knowledge on the part of any individual amounts to not really wanting to know. It is also clear that making processes have revealed all of their secrets through industry. No one is going to

learn much about the making process by making art anymore. We know so much about art that it can now make itself.

Of course, some artists would say, "I only make art for myself. I don't care about the rest of society. I'm doing my own thing." A basic premise of my work is, "You can't do it for yourself." Why should anybody look at the wonderful experience you've produced for yourself? No, the artist's job is to show society the shape of what it's got and how it works.

Media is obviously the most viable for showing society anything as it is the most direct sub-carrier of language and culture. Simply, it is connected to more people than any other medium. It replaces talking. It replaces direct seeing, direct feeling, traveling. It moves the image through space instead of you having to move your body through space to see the image. It is more believable, less processed than any other medium. Being non-physical, television reaches the mind more directly than any physical medium. It affects knowledge and perception that understand and refer to realities in the environment that make us behave the way we do. It also does a lot more that one can't cover here, but it is clear to me that electronic media still holds many mysteries.

One other thing I like to think art does and that is to constantly re-process our understanding of what we think we already understand. For me, good art is like a growing up process in which one is constantly forced to re-assess the problem and re-evaluate the conditions of existence. A situation in which one is never quite sure of one's ground totally—in which nothing can be taken for granted completely—in which there is always something else to be understood about the situation.

In other words, I am for an art that develops new knowledge and understanding, without that new knowledge and understanding becoming an excuse or barrier for further understanding. The process of art-making can never become complacent. The artist is like a hunter who must be on his toes at all times, with eyes and ears fully open to respond to the anxious signals the world sends out.

—Les Levine

Since the mid-1960s, Les Levine, who has termed himself a "media sculptor," has produced more than 200 videotapes and a plethora of works in a variety of media including plastic· "disposable" sculptures, electronic environments, photographs, prints, and installations which combine all of these and other elements as well. Levine believes that art for and of the present must use the new electronic media and materials because of their pervasive and mystical powers as carriers of information, communicating directly, mind-to-mind, a specific and precise kind of knowledge about the moment. His work is based on a persistent analysis of the ideas which operate in the current communications systems and in art alike. His intention is to apprehend and maneuver them into ideas which, by redefining the meaning and functions of media and art, can send out signals to show people who and what we are and make us more conscious of our anxieties and our choices for survival.

Works such as "Photon: Strangeness 4" (1967), "Iris" (1968) and "Contact" (1969) use electronic equipment to provide us with a new perception of how we take in, digest and receive information fed to us by the cybernetic wonders of our post-industrial, "software society". "Iris" is a cybernetic eye which "sees" through three TV cameras located at the center of her bronze plastic facade. The cameras scan the viewer at close-up, medium and long range and show you your many sides, simultaneously, six at a time, live and moving in the multiple possibilities that you provide by placing them into her pre-coded system. It is a home entertainment video "humanoid" that portrays directly how television changes who we are.

It is in the field of Video Art that Levine has made his most pertinent contribution. Beginning as soon as the porta-pak became available to the individual, Levine made his 1965 videotape "Bum". From the start to the present, he has always opted to use the strategies and methods of television to attain the most direct message-making power. Levine's videotapes use the best high-tech means available, are edited for timing and incorporate special effects only as they are intrinsic to communication of the subject matter at hand. His video installations are visually colorful and complexly interwoven so as to simulate the ways we experience life in our rapidly paced electronic age.

Because Levine is a first generation video artist, he has made many works which examine the nature and techniques intrinsic to the video medium. Works such as "Brainwash" (1972), "Video Lecture" (1975), "Landscape I and II" (1971, 1975) and "The Selling of the Video Artist" (1976) both show and tell us the information we need to perceive more clearly the structural and psychological tactics which television uses to make us receive and believe. Some videotapes are about the role of the artist in the present, using the artist's direct presence in them as a model to portray what he feels and thinks as he is going through an experience. In "I Am an Artist" (1975) a video camera pursues Levine down the street, persistently asking him questions while the "celebrity" artist becomes increasingly annoyed and turns away with an above-it-all, "ivory tower" attitude. In "Artistic" (1974), Levine, writhing in a chair as if in a state of autism, rambles about the vulnerability of the artist who offers himself as model without heroics. Sarcasm, with and/or poignancy are employed as needed to convey the message of the artist's role as communi-

cator. When Levine is commenting on the state of the art, as in "The Last Sculpture Show" (1971), "Mr. Abstract" (1975) or "Cornflakes" (1976), a biting humor takes precedence, poking fun to convey the follies of formalist abstraction. It's the same in the art world as in the rest of the world, Levine transmits in works such as "Game Room: A Tribute to the Great American Loser" (1976) and "Deep Gossip" (1979), the conniving for psychological and sociological control.

Among Levine's most powerful and challenging video works are those which directly confront issues in the world, using interview and/or documentary formats to convey the ideas that what we've seen is different both from television and from formalized art alike. These include "The Troubles: An Artist's Document of Ulster" (1972), an intermix of moving and still images with captions and text about the conflicts and torments of Northern Ireland, and "We Are Still Alive" (1975), a moving document of the Innuits, an Eskimo tribe who depend on artmaking for their survival. Confronting and interacting with his subjects/participants in their own environments, Levine uses the specific powers of the video medium to artistically interpret our sociological and political systems.

In his 1978 video installation, "Diamond Mind," Levine proclaimed the necessity for always "moving on, continuing" if we are to survive in our age of global, instant information-giving via media, and he also implied his continuous intention not to become repetitive in his own work. Living up to this commitment, Levine took his video camera to Hawaii recently to create a video work titled "Visions from the God World" (1981) which is a kaleidoscopic view of that location where East meets West in a setting of mesmeric pleasure. Also in recent years Levine has made a series of Ads, large photographed and drawn images juxtaposed with captions which are meant to offer new ways to perceive the basic ideas underlying ordinary everyday experiences. One of these, "We Are Not Afraid," appeared in the Spring of 1982 in the advertising spaces on New York City subway cars, disguising its identity as to advertise an open-ended message concerning our anxieties. As in all Levine's works, the major concern is to harness the powerful methods and tactics of commercial media and make them the sources for artistic power.

—Barbara Cavaliere

LEVINE, Marilyn (Anne).

Canadian. Born Marilyn Hayes in Medicine Hat, Alberta, 22 December 1933. Studied chemistry at the University of Alberta, Edmonton, 1953–59, B. Sc. 1957, M. Sc. 1959; studied sculpture at the University of California, Berkeley, 1969–71, M. A. 1970, M. F. A. 1971. Married Sidney Levine in 1959. Ceramicist: now lives and works in the San Francisco area. Worked as a chemist on the geological survey of Canada, Ottawa, 1959–61; Instructor in Chemistry, Campion College, University of Saskatchewan, Saskatoon, 1962–64; Instructor in Ceramics, University of Regina, Saskatchewan, 1971–73; Assistant Professor of Art, University of Utah, Salt Lake City, 1973–76; Visiting Lecturer, University of California, Berkeley, 1975–80. Recipient: Gold Medal, Concorso Internazionale della Ceramica d'Arte, Faenza, Italy, 1969; Sculpture/Ceramics Prize, Louise and Adolf Schwenck Memorial, Montreal, 1969; Canada Council Arts Grant, 1969, 1973; International Academy of Ceramics Medal, Calgary, 1973; Research Fellowship, University of Utah, 1975; National Endowment for the Arts Grant, 1976, 1980. Agents: O. K. Harris Gallery, 383 West Broadway, New York, New York 10012; and Fuller Goldeen Gallery, 228 Grant Avenue, San Francisco, California 94108. Address: 950 61st Street, Oakland, California 94608, U. S. A.

Individual Exhibitions:

1966	The Craftsman, Regina, Saskatchewan
1967	Dunlop Art Gallery, Regina, Saskatchewan
	University of Calgary, Alberta
1968	Dunlop Art Gallery, Regina, Saskatchewan
1969	Dunlop Art Gallery, Regina, Saskatchewan
	Moose Jaw Art Museum, Saskatchewan
	University of Lethbridge, Alberta
1970	Canadian Guild of Potters, Toronto
1971	Northwest Handicraft House, North Vancouver
	University of California Art Museum, Berkeley
	Hansen Fuller Gallery, San Francisco
	University of Calgary, Alberta
1973	Bernard Danenberg Galleries, New York
1974	Norman McKenzie Art Gallery, Regina, Saskatchewan (retrospective)
	O.K. Harris Gallery, New York
	Morgan Gallery, Kansas City
1976	O.K. Harris Gallery, New York
1979	O.K. Harris Gallery, New York
1980	Fuller Goldeen Gallery, San Francisco
1981	O.K. Harris Gallery, New York
	Institute of Contemporary Art, Boston (retrospective)
1983	Fuller Goldeen Gallery, San Francisco
1984	O.K. Harris Gallery, New York

Selected Group Exhibitions:

1967	*Canadian Fine Crafts*, National Gallery of Canada, Ottawa
1970	*Survey 70: Realisms*, Museum of Fine Arts, Montreal
1971	*Clayworks: 20 Americans*, Museum of Contemporary Crafts, New York
1972	*Painting and Sculpture Today*, Indianapolis Museum of Art
1973	*Ceramic Objects*, Art Gallery of Ontario, Toronto (traveled to the New York Cultural Center)
1974	*Hyperrealisme*, Galerie Isy Brachot, Brussels
	New/Photo Realism: Painting and Sculpture of the 1970's, Wadsworth Atheneum, Hartford, Connecticut
1975	*Realism*, Wichita Museum, Kansas
1981	*Illusion and Reality*, Australian National Gallery, Canberra
1986	*California Sculpture 1959–80*, San Francisco Museum of Modern Art

Collections:

Saskatchewan Arts Board, Regina; University of Saskatchewan, Saskatoon; Norman McKenzie Art Gallery, Regina, Saskatchewan; Canada Council Art Bank, Ottawa; Museum of Fine Arts, Montreal; University of California Art Museum, Berkeley; Utah Museum of Fine Arts, Salt Lake City; Nelson Gallery, Kansas City; International Museum of Ceramics, Faenza, Italy; National Museum of Modern Art, Tokyo.

Publications:

By LEVINE: article—"The Photo Realists: 12 Interviews," with Nancy Foote, in *Art in America* (New York), November/December 1972.

On LEVINE: articles—"Ceramics 74: The Clay's the Thing" by Christopher Lowell in *Tactile* (Toronto), July/August 1974; "The Ceramics of Marilyn Levine" by Susan Peterson in *Crafts Horizons* (New York), February 1977; "American West Coast Artist Marilyn Levine" by Hiroshi Matsubara in *Contemporary Sculpture* (Tokyo), June 1978.

I am involved with both a sense of confrontation and a story in my work.

The confrontation results from the translation of a normally supple, changing material (leather, canvas, etc.) into an enduring, unyielding, rigid material (fired clay), giving it a stillness removed from the time-flux of everything around it. The conflict be-

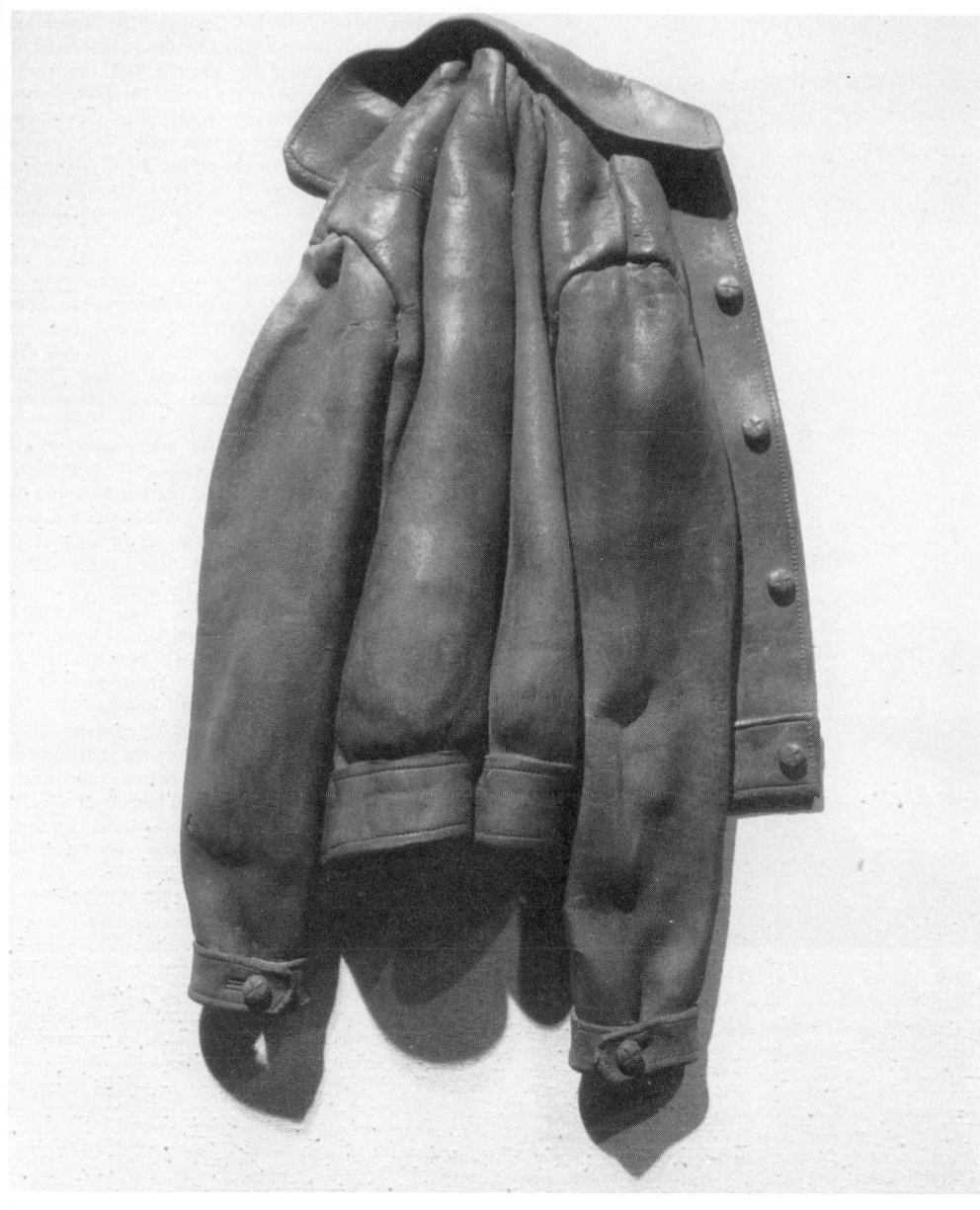

Marilyn Levine: *Blue Jacket*, 1974

tween visual and tactile clues disturbs one's sense of reality, with the result that one's relationship to the object can no longer be the same.

The story lies in the cracks, sags, tears, scuffs and stains. These non-conscious marks left on the object through its use are the trace of man acting and reacting in his environment.

—Marilyn Levine

Marilyn Levine arrived in California in 1969 and found herself in one of the most active ceramics environments in American art history. Peter Voulkos, John Mason, Jerry Rothman, Stephen De Staebler, Ron Nagle, and Jim Melchert had all established themselves as part of the force which propelled clay into the art world. Sculpture and ceramics began to merge as artists created large scale organic forms, some reaffirming and some denying the importance of vessels in ceramic art. Levine, who was influenced at first by California funk and later began to make bags and shoes from clay, chose an unusual direction for the time. Instead of concentrating on formalist issues in clay, as did many of her colleagues whose ceramics were influenced by the abstract expressionists, she chose everyday subjects akin to pop art or even an earlier trompe l'oeil sensibility, and constructed life, or slightly larger than life, sized objects.

Levine has added a multi-layered chapter to the history of ceramic art; her subjects, borrowed from pop and funk, seem avant-grade for her medium, yet in reality they are vessels, the oldest of clay forms. At the same time they possess the timeless quality that Levine consciously seeks in her art. They subtly embody the oldest of all clay arguments: is it art or craft? decorative or useful? Levine's shoes, bags, and brief cases are objects and vessels simultaneously, a dual identity which adds as much to the appreciation of her art as the carefully constructed age marks on the leatherlike clay add to the "history" of the object.

—Mary Stofflet

LeWITT, Sol.

American. Born in Hartford, Connecticut in 1928. Studied at Syracuse University, New York, 1945–49, B.F.A. 1949. Lives and works in New York. Instructor, Museum of Modern Art School, New York, 1964–67, Cooper Union, New York, 1967–68, School of Visual Arts, New York, 1969–70, and New York University, 1970. Agent: John Weber Gallery, 142 Greene Street, New York, New York 10012. Address: 117 Hester Street, New York, New York 10022, U.S.A.

Individual Exhibitions:

1965	Daniel Gallery, New York
1966	Dwan Gallery, New York
1967	Dwan Gallery, Los Angeles
1968	Dwan Gallery, New York
	Galerie Bischofberger, Zurich
	Galerie Heiner Friedrich, Munich
	Konrad Fischer Galerie, Dusseldorf
	Ace Gallery, Los Angeles
1969	Konrad Fischer Galerie, Dusseldorf
	Galerie L'Attico, Rome
	Galerie Ernst, Hannover
	Museum Haus Lange, Krefeld, West Germany
1970	Wisconsin State University at River Falls
	Dwan Gallery, New York
	Art and Project, Amsterdam
	Galerie Yvon Lambert, Paris
	Galleria Sperone, Turin
	Gemeemtemuseum, The Hague
	Museum of Art, La Jolla, California
1971	Dwan Gallery, New York
	Art and Project, Amsterdam
	Pasadena Art Museum, California
	Guggenheim Museum, New York
	John Weber Gallery, New York
	Lisson Gallery, London
	Museum of Modern Art, New York
	Galerie Stampa, Basle
	Galerie Konrad Fischer, Dusseldorf
1972	Kunsthalle, Berne
	Galerie Ernst, Hannover
	Walker Art Center, Minneapolis
	Massachusetts Institute of Technology, Cambridge
	California Institute of the Arts, Valencia
1973	Galerie Yvon Lambert, Paris
	John Weber Gallery, New York
	Lisson Gallery, London
	Museum of Modern Art, Oxford
	Galleria Toselli, Milan
1974	Galerie Yvon Lambert, Paris
	John Weber Gallery, New York
	Palais des Beaux-Arts, Brussels
	San Francisco Museum of Art (retrospective; toured the United States)
	Galleria Sperone, Turin
	Stedelijk Museum, Amsterdam
1975	Max Protetch Gallery, Washington, D.C.
	Konrad Fischer Galerie, Dusseldorf
	Galleria Gian Enzo Sperone, Turin
	Galleria Scipione, Macerata, Italy
	Israel Museum, Jerusalem
	Art and Project, Amsterdam
	Galerie Annemarie Verna, Zurich
	Kunsthalle, Basle
1976	Visual Arts Museum, New York
	Hammarskjold Plaza Sculpture Garden, New York
	Kunstverein, Cologne
1977	Konrad Fischer Galerie, Dusseldorf
	Lisson Gallery, London
	John Weber Gallery, New York
	National Gallery of Victoria, Melbourne
	Art Gallery of New South Wales, Sydney
	Galleria Genoa, Italy
1978	John Weber Gallery, New York
	Brooklyn Museum, New York
	Museum of Modern Art, New York (retrospective; toured the United States)
1979	Lisson Gallery, London
	Konrad Fischer Galerie, Dusseldorf
	Young-Hoffman Gallery, Chicago
	Galerie Yvon Lambert, Paris
1980	John Weber Gallery, New York
1981	*Wall Drawings 1968–81*, Wadsworth Atheneum, Hartford, Connecticut
	Paula Cooper Gallery, New York
	Weinberg Gallery, San Francisco
	RAW Gallery, Hartford, Connecticut
	Wadsworth Atheneum, Hartford, Connecticut
	Graphics I and II, Boston
	Paula Cooper Gallery, New York
1982	John Weber Gallery, New York
	Galleria Banco, Milan
1983	Lisson Gallery, London

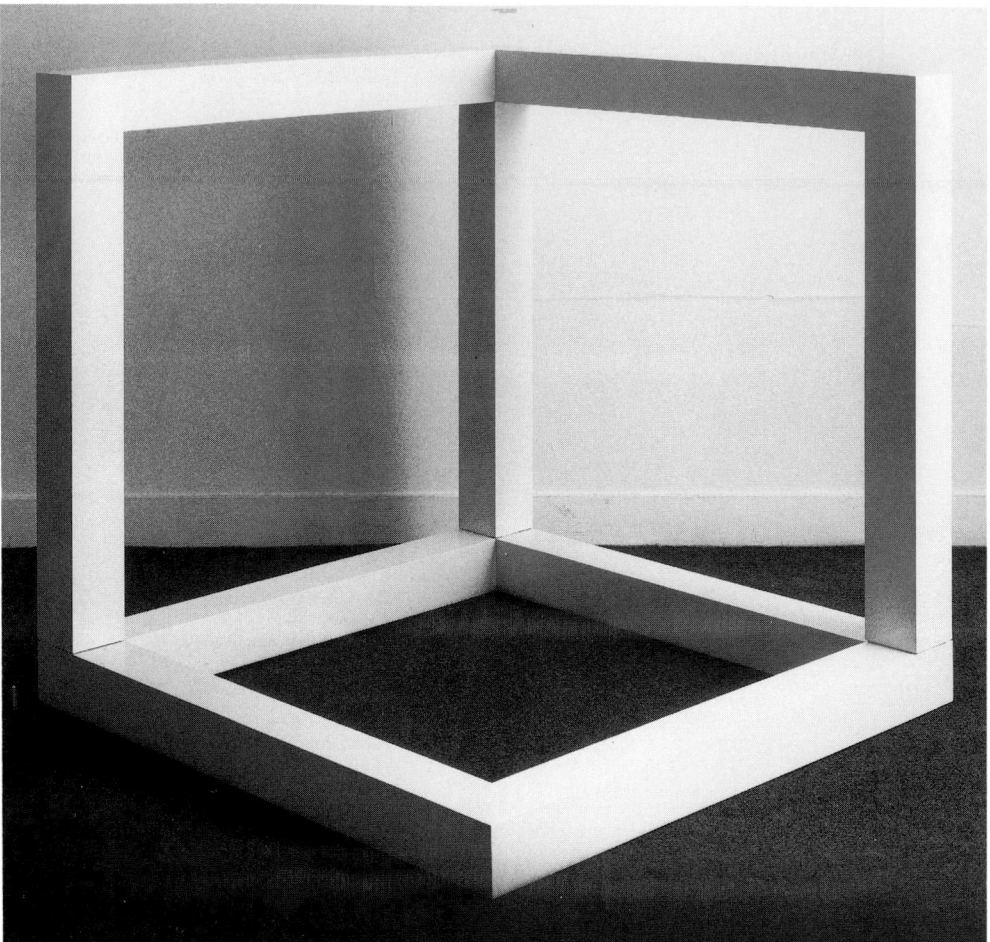

Sol LeWitt: *Structures*, 1973

1984	Stedelijk Museum, Amsterdam
	Van Abbemuseum, Eindhoven, Netherlands
	Wadsworth Atheneum, Hartford, Connecticut
1986	Tate Gallery, London
1987	ARC/Musée d'Art Moderne de la Ville, Paris
	Cleveland Museum of Art, Ohio
1988	Galerie Schiessel, Munich

Selected Group Exhibitions:

1965	*Box Show*, Byron Gallery, New York
1968	*Documenta 4*, Museum Fridericianum, Kassel, West Germany (and *Documenta 5*, 1972)
1971	*Guggenheim International*, Guggenheim Museum, New York
1974	*Kunst uber Kunst*, Kunstverein, Cologne
1978	*Book Art*, Cleveland Museum of Art
1979	*The Reductive Object*, Institute of Contemporary Art, Boston
1980	*Biennale*, Venice
1984	*Olympian Gestures*, Los Angeles County Museum of Art
1985	*Art Minimal I*, CAPC/Musee d'Art Contemporain, Bordeaux, France
1988	*Contemporary American Art*, Sara Hilden Art Museum, Tampere, Finland (traveled to Oslo)

Collections:

Museum of Modern Art, New York; Guggenheim Museum, New York; Albright-Knox Art Gallery, Buffalo, New York; Detroit Institute of Arts; Los Angeles County Museum of Art; Art Gallery of Ontario, Toronto; Tate Gallery, London; Centre National d'Art Contemporain, Paris; Stedelijk Museum, Amsterdam; Australian National Gallery, Canberra.

Publications:

By LeWITT: book—*Arcs, Circles and Grids*, Berne 1972; articles—"Ziggurats" in *Arts Magazine* (New York), November 1966; "American Sculpture" in special issue of *Artforum* (New York), Summer 1967; "Drawings Series 1968" in *Studio International* (London), April 1969; "I Am Still Alive: On Kawara" in *Studio International* (London), July/August 1970; "Sentences are Conceptual Art" in *Flash Art* (Milan), July 1971; "Page Drawings" in *Arts Magazine* (New York), February 1972; "Sol LeWitt" in *Flash Art* (Milan), June 1973; "Paragraphs on Conceptual Art" and "Sentences on Conceptual Art" in *Uber Kunst*, Cologne 1974.

On LeWITT: books—*Minimal Art: A Critical Anthology*, edited by Gregory Battcock, New York 1968; *Conceptual Art* by Ursula Meyer, New York 1972; *Incomplete Open Cubes*, exhibition catalogue, New York 1974; *Sol LeWitt*, exhibition catalogue, Amsterdam 1974; *Sol LeWitt 1968–84*, exhibition catalogue, Amsterdam 1984; *Sol LeWitt*, exhibition catalogue with text by Jeremy Lewison, London 1986.

*   *   *

Sol LeWitt's collaboration with choreographer Lucinda Childs and composer Philip Glass exhibited a tri-partite function of minimalism. Footage of larger-than-life dancers, previously shot at rehearsals, was shown simultaneously with the dance on the stage. A large scrim was hung in front of the stage to portray the film.

The film was a counterpart replica, in timing and spacing, of the dance, and for LeWitt an experiment in using a non-static grid patterning. A grid appears in the film, on the floor of the rehearsal stage, and serves to focus, spatially, an area from which the dance, unlike a film, appears to project itself back onto the audience. LeWitt's grids functioned to heighten the sense of immediacy in the dancing, while the filmic imagery became even more spectral. One filmic approach appeared to condense and shorten the grid, and therefore allow for an aspect of verticality in the dance movements. Another approach depicted an enlarged, spatially expansive grid, similar to the grids used to measure time and distance on a globe of the world, which produced a wider terrain for the movement of the dancers.

Outside of the exact functioning of the dancers on the film was the overall effect for the audience of live and danced movement, on the one hand, vs. static and filmic movement on the other. Particular movements were simultaneously enlarged as they swept past the smaller dancers on the stage. There was a sense of the filmic thought of the dancers hovering above them and images of dancers caught leaping in front of themselves. These produced always simple, not baroque, aspects of reflectivity.

Dance, movies, LeWitt's sculpture, and, as we know, painting all hunt for a style of active perspective, a field of perspective, a field of perceptive depth which belies the artificiality of art. Interestingly, in this collaboration, LeWitt is seen to cross into the physical dimensions of dance space, and Childs' dance to that equally physical, though permanent, world of sculpture.

For LeWitt, especially in his more recent works, the grid becomes the methodology of perception, rather than the product. In the "photogrid" books he shows photographs which are placed within a sectional grid pattern. The works take photography into a sculptural realm, attempting to make images spatial and physical. The particular imagery—his living room, bookshelf, his family, a trip taken—all create a sense of inward depth. The grid which frames the photos dismisses the actual distance between the objects in the separate photos and, therefore, perceptively appears to call the objects into a three-dimensional being.

"Dance 1," of the five part event held at the Brooklyn Academy of Music, appeared, to some, television-like, what with a dull-blue lighting cast over the stage. LeWitt also showed stills. Lucinda Childs was next to a giant image above herself on the screen and then the same image above her on a separate geometric plane. LeWitt's filming involved a high degree of technical definition, as in the progress of his own work in the composition of his cubistic models and sculptures. LeWitt's geometry in "Dance" was still sculptural, still planar, yet removed from an individuated aesthetic. Such an interesting place for minimalism to appear, at a junction of three divisional and distinct systems of minimalism.

—John Robinson

LIBERMAN, Alexander.
American. Born in Kiev, Russia, in September 1912; emigrated to the United States, 1941: naturalized, 1946. Studied at the Académie André Lhote, Paris, 1929-31; studied architecture, under Auguste Perret, at the Ecole des Beaux-Arts, Paris, 1930–32. Independent painter since 1936, and sculptor since 1959. Art Editor, *Vu* magazine, Paris 1933–37; Staff Member, 1941–43, and Art Director 1943, *Vogue* magazine, New York; Art Director, 1944, and Editorial Director, since 1962, Condé Nast Publications United States and Europe, New York. Recipient: D.F.A.: Rhode Island School of Design, Providence, 1980. Agent: André Emmerich Gallery, 420 West Broadway, New York, New York 10028. Addresses: Condé Nast Publications, 350 Madison Avenue, New York, New York 10017; 173 East 70th Street, New York, New York 10021, U.S.A.

Individual Exhibitions:

1959	Museum of Modern Art, New York
1960	Betty Parsons Gallery, New York
1962	Betty Parsons Gallery, New York
1963	Betty Parsons Gallery, New York
1964	Betty Parsons Gallery, New York
	Robert Fraser Gallery, London
	Paintings, Bennington College, Vermont

1965 Galleria dell'Ariete, Milan
Galerie Denise René, Paris
Galleria d'Arte, Naples
1966 Jewish Museum, New York
Betty Parsons Gallery, New York
1967 André Emmerich Gallery, New York (2 shows)
Betty Parsons Gallery, New York
1968 André Emmerich Gallery, New York
1969 Betty Parsons Gallery, New York
André Emmerich Gallery, New York
1970 *Painting and Sculpture 1950–1970*, Corcoran Gallery, Washington, D.C. (retrospective)
Museum of Fine Arts, Houston (retrospective)
1971 Hammarskjold Plaza, New York
1972 Honolulu Academy of Art (retrospective)
1973 André Emmerich Gallery, New York
1974 André Emmerich Gallery, New York (2 shows)
Janie C. Lee Gallery, Houston
1977 Van Straaten Gallery, Chicago
Storm King Art Center, Mountainville, New York (retrospective)
1978 Vernissage, Rome
1979 The Greenberg Gallery, St. Louis
Landau/Alexander Gallery, Los Angeles
The Arts Gallery, Baltimore
André Emmerich Gallery, New York
1980 André Emmerich Gallery, New York
1981 Hokin Gallery, Bay Harbor Island, Florida
André Emmerich Gallery, New York
1983 André Emmerich Gallery, New York
1985 Fort Worth Art Museum, Texas
Aldrich Museum of Contemporary Art, Ridgefield, Connecticut

Selected Group Exhibitions:

1954 *Younger American Painters*, Guggenheim Museum, New York

1965 *The Responsive Eye*, Museum of Modern Art, New York
1966 *New Shapes of Color*, Stedelijk Museum, Amsterdam
1968 *Art of the Real: 1948–1968*, Museum of Modern Art, New York
1972 *Contemporary Sculpture*, Phillips Collection, Washington, D.C.
Annual Exhibition of Contemporary American Painting, Whitney Museum, New York
1975 *Color as Language*, Museum of Modern Art, New York (and world tour)
1977 *Drawings for Outdoor Sculpture: 1946–1977*, John Weber Gallery, New York
1979 *Black and White Are Colors: Paintings of the 1950's–1970's*, Pomona College, Claremont, California (traveled to Scripps College, Claremont, California)
1981 *The Fine Art of Business*, De Cordova Museum, Lincoln, Massachusetts

Collections:

Guggenheim Museum, New York; Metropolitan Museum of Art, New York; Museum of Modern Art, New York; Whitney Museum, New York; Storm King Art Center, Mountainville, New York; Corcoran Gallery of Art, Washington, D.C.: Smithsonian Institution, Washington, D.C.; Art Institute of Chicago; Museum of Fine Arts, Houston; Tate Gallery, London.

Publications:

By LIBERMAN: books—*The Art and Technique of Color Photography*, New York 1951; *The Artist in his Studio*, New York 1960; *Steichen the Photographer*, exhibition catalogue, with others, New York 1961; *Greece, Gods and Art*, with Iris C. Love, New York 1968; articles—"Farewell to Hard Edge: Interview with Alexander Liberman," with Lawrence Alloway, in *Alexander Liberman: Paintings*, exhibition catalogue, Bennington, Vermont 1964; introduction to *Vogue Book of Fashion Photography 1919–1979* by Polly Devlin, New York 1979: film—*La Femme Francaise*, Paris 1936.

On LIBERMAN: books—*American Abstract Painters*, exhibition catalogue, with an introduction by Lawrence Alloway, London 1961; *Alexander Liberman*, exhibition catalogue, with introduction by Lawrence Alloway, New York 1962; *Alexander Liberman: Paintings*, exhibition catalogue, Bennington, Vermont 1964; *Hard Edge*, exhibition catalogue, Paris 1964; *Alexander Liberman*, exhibition catalogue, London 1964; *Pattern Art*, exhibition catalogue, with an introduction by Lawrence Alloway, New York 1966; *Alexander Liberman*, exhibition catalogue, with text by Sam Hunter, New York 1966; *Minimal Art: A Critical Anthology*, edited by Gregory Battcock, New York 1968; *Alexander Liberman: Painting and Sculpture 1950–1970*, exhibition catalogue, with an introduction by James Pilgrim, Washington, D.C. 1970; *Alexander Liberman*, exhibition catalogue, New York 1971; *Alexander Liberman*, exhibition catalogue, New York 1973; *Alexander Liberman: The Circle Paintings 1950–1964*, exhibition catalogue, with text by Thomas Hess, New York 1974; *Alexander Liberman*, exhibition catalogue, New York 1979; *Black and White Are Colors: Paintings of the 1950's–1970's*, exhibition catalogue, with an essay by David S. Rubin, Claremont, California 1979; *The Place of Art in the World of Architecture*, by Donald E. Thalacker, with a preface by Sam Hunter, New York 1980; *Handbook: The Guggenheim Collection 1900–1980* by Vivian Edicott Barnett, New York 1980; *Sculpture at Storm King*, with text by H. Peter Stern and David Collens, New York 1980; *Alexander Liberman* by Barbara Rose, New York 1982.

Since his arrival in the United States as a refugee from the war in Europe during the 1940s, Alexander Liberman has balanced the dual careers of designer for Condé Nast publications and fine artist of paintings, sculpture, and photographs. Born in Kiev, Russia, Liberman left his homeland with his parents during his adolescence, settling in Paris where he

Alexander Liberman: *Gate XIII*, 1981

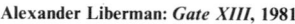

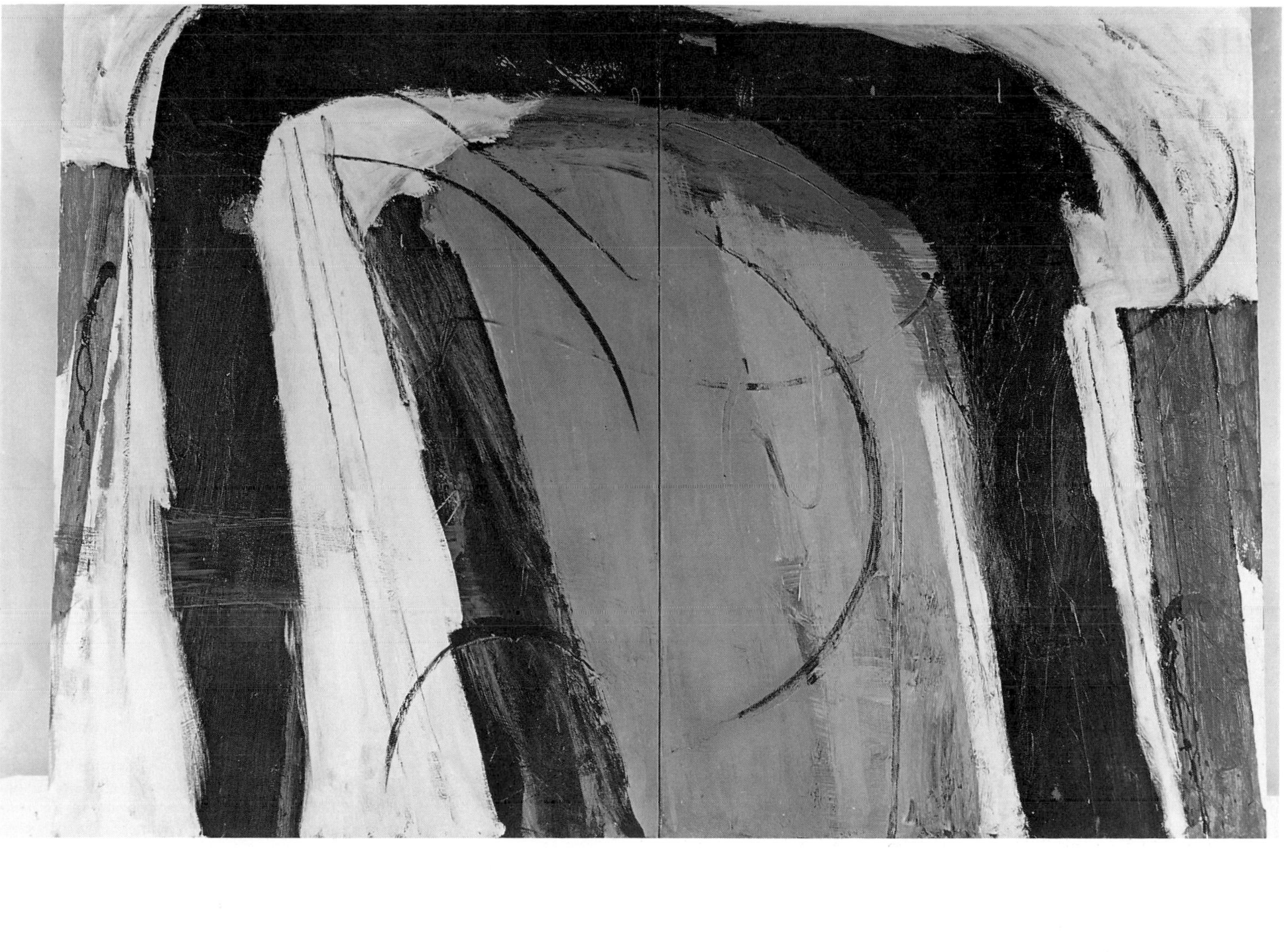

studied painting with Andre L'hote and architecture with August Perret at the Ecole des Beaux-Arts. He also received a baccalaureate degree in philosophy and mathematics from the Sorbonne. Liberman's design career began in 1933 when he was hired by *Vu* magazine. During the four years that he worked for *Vu* he rose quickly from art director to magazine editor. His innovative layouts reflected the avant-garde tendencies of contemporary European art, but his personal artistic talents were subordinated to his design interests until he returned to painting in 1945 in the United States. His initial gestural abstraction was quickly followed in the 1950s by hard edge paintings of two-dimensional geometric shapes that prefigure the minimal aesthetic of the 1960s. It is, however, in the construction of monumental abstract geometric metal sculptures that Liberman is best known to the art world.

In 1959 Liberman learned arc welding which led to his first welded metal sculpture. The following year he held his first one-man exhibition at Betty Parson's Gallery featuring both is painting and sculpture. His first large sculpture *Fire* was commissioned for the exhibition *The Responsive Eye* that was held at the Museum of Modern Art in 1965. Renowned American architect Philip Johnson commissioned Liberman's first large scale public sculpture in 1964 for the New York World's Fair. He titled the hanging aluminum construction, featuring a painted disk framed with curving bands of metal, *Prometheus*, indicating his interest in classical mythological subjects. Here the geometric shapes symbolize ancient and persistent human concerns translated into the abstract imagery characteristic of twentieth century thinking. As Barbara Rose has pointed out, Liberman is preoccupied "with the symbolic content of abstract work."

Since the early 1960s Liberman has worked in increasingly larger scale to fulfill his desire to create art that is epic and monumental. He has so frequently painted his constructions in a vivid scarlet hue that it has become a trademark of his sculpture. His giant metal constructions of abstract shapes complement large urban architectures as well as more the pastoral settings of sculpture parks where a number of his works are installed. They demonstrate the artist's use of industrial methods and materials as an expression of a particularly twentieth century artistic consciousness that relates in scale and technique to contemporary architecture.

Given his first camera when he was eight years old, Liberman has used photography as "a way of taking notes." He has also been involved in the artistic side of photography, which is attested to by his 1960 exhibition of photographs at the Museum of Modern Art titled *The Artist in his Studio*. In 1963 Liberman printed his first lithograph and since that time he has explored graphic art as another extension of his talent. In 1968 Liberman published his book *Greece, Gods and Art*. Although he began working as the art director for *Vogue* magazine in 1943, Liberman is currently editorial director of all Condé Nast publications, a position that would hardly seem to leave him time to produce art, yet he has managed to maintain a high level of artistic production.

—Percy North

LICHTENSTEIN, Roy.

American. Born in New York City, 27 October 1923. Studied at Ohio State University, Columbus, 1940-43, 1946-49, B.F.A. 1946, M.F.A. 1949; also studied at the Art Students League, New York, under Reginald Marsh. Served in the United States Army, 1943-46. Painter and sculptor; lives in New York City and Southampton, New York. Taught at Ohio State University, Columbus, 1946-51, New York State College of Education, Oswego, 1957-60, and Douglass College, Rutgers University, New Brunswick, New Jersey, 1960-63. Recipient: Skowhegan Award for Graphics, 1977. D.F.A., California Institute of the Arts, 1977. Agent: Leo Castelli, 420 Broadway, New York, New York 10012. Address: Post Office Box 1369, Southampton, New York 11968, U.S.A.

Individual Exhibitions:

1951	Carlebach Gallery, New York
1952	John Heller Gallery, New York
1953	John Heller Gallery, New York
1954	John Heller Gallery, New York
1957	John Heller Gallery, New York
1962	Leo Gallery, Los Angeles
	Galerie Sonnabend, Paris
1964	Leo Gallery, Los Angeles
	Galleria II Punto, Turin
	Leo Castelli Gallery, New York
1965	Galerie Sonnabend, Paris
	Leo Castelli Gallery, New York
1966	Cleveland Museum of Art
1967	Pasadena Art Museum, California (retrospective)
	Walker Art Center, Minneapolis
	Leo Castelli Gallery, New York
	Contemporary Art Center, Cincinnati, Ohio
1968	Stedelijk Museum, Amsterdam
	Tate Gallery, London (retrospective)
	Kunsthalle, Berne
	Kestner-Gesellschaft, Hannover
	Irving Blum Gallery, Los Angeles
1969	Irving Blum Gallery, Los Angeles
	Guggenheim Museum, New York (retrospective)
	Castelli Graphics, New York
1970	Galerie Sonnabend, Paris
	University of Puerto Rico, Mayaguez
	Nelson Gallery of Art, Kansas City
	Museum of Contemporary Art, Chicago
	Seattle Art Museum
	Columbus Gallery of Fine Arts, Ohio
	University of California at Irvine
1971	Leo Castelli Gallery, New York
	Irving Blum Gallery, Los Angeles
1972	Leo Castelli Gallery, New York
	Contemporary Art Museum, Houston
1973	Leo Castelli Gallery, New York
	Greenberg Gallery, St. Louis
	Galerie Beyeler, Basle
1974	Galerie Mikro, Berlin
	Margo Leavin Gallery, Los Angeles
	Current Editions, Seattle
	Mayor Gallery, London
	Leo Castelli Gallery, New York
1975	Centre National d'Art Contemporain, Paris
	Leo Castelli Gallery, New York
	Ace Gallery, Los Angeles
	Albert White Gallery, Toronto
1976	Mayor Gallery, London
	Galerie de Gestlo, Hamburg
	School of Visual Arts, New York
1977	Leo Castelli Gallery, New York
	Mayor Gallery, London
	California State University at Long Beach
	Städtische Kunsthalle, Mannheim
	Blum Helman Gallery, New York
1978	Leo Castelli Gallery, New York
	Ace Gallery, Los Angeles
	Institute of Contemporary Art, Boston
	Washington Gallery, Indianapolis
1979	Leo Castelli Gallery, New York
	University of Miami
	State University of New York at Stony Brook
1981	Leo Castelli Gallery, New York
	Whitney Museum Downtown, New York
	Whitney Museum, New York
	Fort Worth Art Museum, Texas
	Seattle Art Museum
	Blum Helman Gallery, New York

Selected Group Exhibitions:

1962	*New Paintings of Common Objects*, Pasadena Art Museum, California
1964	*Americansk Pop Konst*, Moderna Museet, Stockholm
1969	*New York Painting and Sculpture 1940-70*, Metropolitan Museum of Art, New York
1971	*Art and Technology*, Los Angeles County Museum of Art
1974	*Idea and Image in Recent Art*, Art Institute of Chicago
1976	*Drawing Now*, Museum of Modern Art, New York
1978	*About the Strange Nature of Money*, Kunsthalle, Dusseldorf
1979	*American Portraits of the 60's and 70's*, Aspen Center for the Visual Arts, Colorado
1984	*Olympian Gestures*, Los Angeles County Museum of Art
1985	*Painterly Visions 1940-84*, Guggenheim Museum, New york

Collections:

Whitney Museum, New York; Museum of Modern Art, New York: Guggenheim Museum, New York; Detroit Institute of Art; Art Institute of Chicago; Tate Gallery, London; Stedelijk Museum, Amsterdam; Wallraf-Richartz Museum, Cologne; Norton Simon Museum of Art, Pasadena, California.

Publications:

By LICHTENSTEIN: articles—"An Interview with Roy Lichtenstein," with John Coplans, in *Artforum* (New York), October 1963; "What Is Pop Art?", with Gene Swenson, in *Artnews* (New York), November 1963; "Oldernberg, Lichtenstein, Warhol: A Discussion," with Bruce Glaser, in *Artforum* (New York), February 1966; "Metamorphoses: L'Ecole de New York," with Jean Antoine, in *Quadram* (Paris), March 1966; "Interview with Roy Lichtenstein," with David Pascal, in *Giff Wiff* (Paris), May 1966; "Conversation with Roy Licthenstein," with Alan Solomon, in *Fantazaria* (Rome). July/August 1966; "Interview de Roy Licthenstein," with Colette Roberts, in *Aujourd 'hui* (Paris), December 1966; "Sensibility of the 60's," with Barbara Rose and Irving Sandler, in *Art in America* (New York). January/February 1967; "Talking with Roy Lichtenstein," in *Artforum* (New York), May 1967; "Le Classicisme du Hot Dog," with Raphael Sorin, in *La Quinzaine Litteraire* (Paris), January 1968.

On LICHTENSTEIN: books—*Pop Art and After* by Mario Amaya, New York 1965; *Happenings, Fluxus and Pop Art* by Jurgen Becker and Wolf Vostell, Hamburg 1965; *Pop Art One* by Dorothy Herzka, New York 1965; *The New Art*, edited by Gregory Battock, New York 1966; *Lichtenstein*, edited by Alberto Boatto and Giordano Falzoni, Rome 1966; *Pop Art* by Lucy Lippard, New York 1966; *Pop Art: Object and Image* by Christopher Finch, New York 1968; *Pop Art Redefined* by John Russell and Suzi Gablik, London 1969; *Roy Lichtenstein: Drawings and Prints* by Diane Waldman, New York 1969; *Roy Lichtenstein*, edited by John Coplans, New York 1972; *Roy Lichtenstein 1970-1980* by Jack Cowart, London 1987.

Roy Lichtenstein's work in the 1950's was concerned with the pioneer passages of American history, such as the opening of the West; he painted canvases recalling the cowboys and Indians in their figurative Remington style. From 1957 he went through a phase of Abstract Expressionism that by 1961 had broken into the imagery he has now made his own. Those pictures were crudely based on advertising illustration, strip comic characters, everyday objects and the adaptation of works by artists of the past. Prerequisite of the treatment was an overt reliance on line. The painting was not a direct blow-up of a newspaper detail, but the method of composing the motive including the lettered caption was simplified in bold two-dimensional terms linked to printing processes.

It goes without saying that the content of the picture had only incidental relevance to its treatment, the enlargement emphasizing its abstract qualities of design and rhythm. Painting *per se* was useful for its contrasting ability to bowdlerize commercial images con-

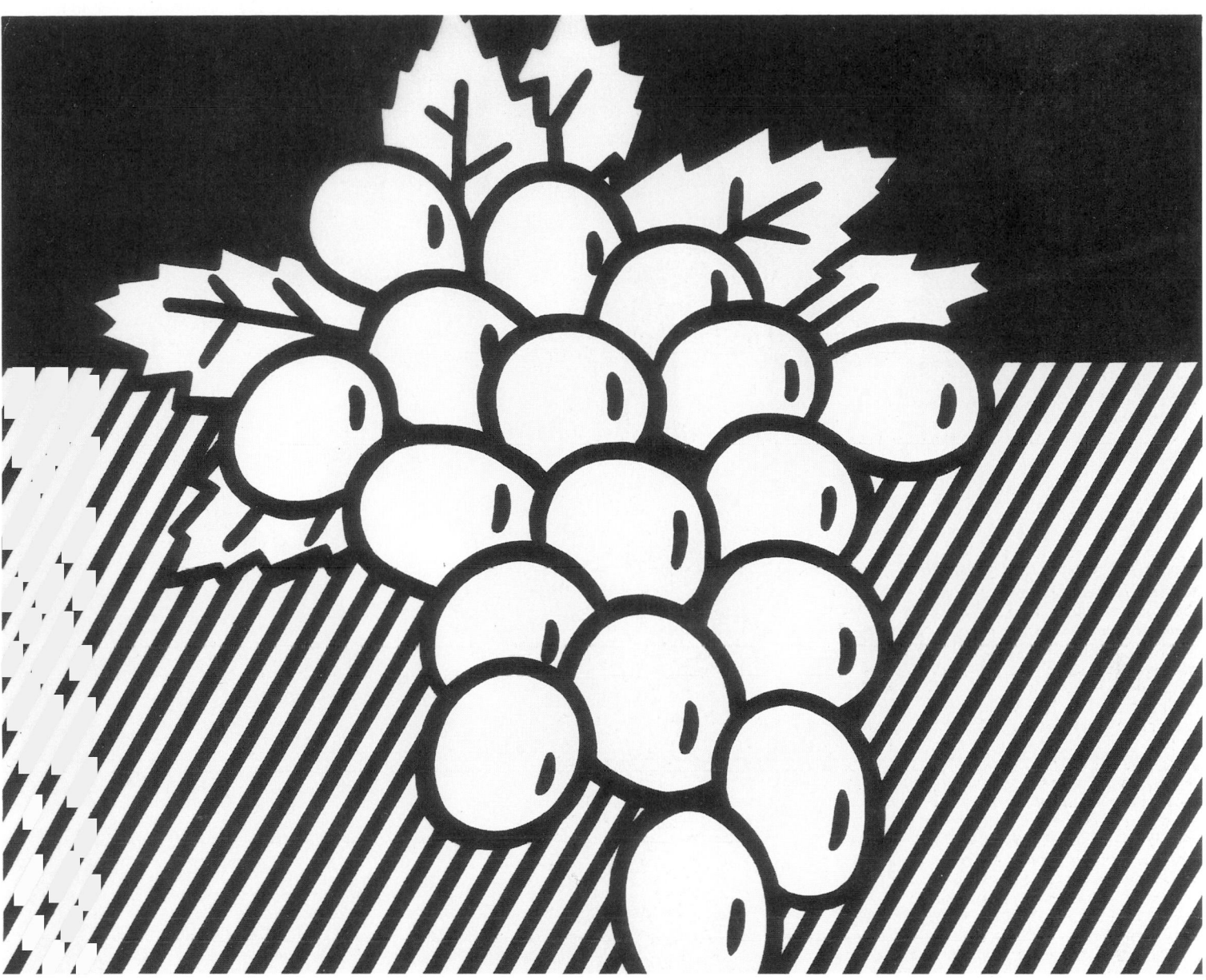

Roy Lichtenstein: *Grapes*, 1974

centrating on their banality. This calculated pastiche emphasized its throw-away life, and also depersonalized the artist's autographic quality.

In his brushstroke paintings of 1965/66 Lichtenstein seemed to send up the subjective concern for the working of the pigment that characterized Abstract Expressionism. Like the paintings, his sculptures are completely removed from the conventions of the art so that "Standing Explosion" of 1966 is a cut-out in enameled metal of a blown-up line drawing, suggesting an explosion such as might appear in a strip cartoon. Likewise, the so-called "Modern Sculptures" are no more in effect than copies of Art Deco interior design in the apartments of the 1930's. His "Modern paintings" series 1966-7 are based less upon the paintings themselves than on the proliferation of colour plates in art magazines and books.

The difficulty in placing Lichtenstein is not upon his self-contained identity as a painter but in the true personality of his work. By the act of pastiche he seeks to abdicate the right to be considered on his own terms. In their way, Lichtenstein's paintings and especially his sculptures enter the No Man's Land of Oldenburg, where the art is camouflaged to the point that imitation takes on an import and significance of its own. Like Picasso's "Maninas" after Velasquez, Lichtenstein's strip romances and vinyl seascapes are ready-made subjects after their commonplace reproductions.

—G. S. Whittet

LIJN, Liliane.

American. Born Liliane Segall in New York City, 22 December 1939; adopted name "Lijn," 1961. Educated at Solebury School, New Hope, Pennsylvania, 1950–54; at Liceo Cantonale di Lugano, Switzerland, 1955–57; studied archaeology at the Sorbonne, Paris, 1958–59; studied history of art, Ecole de Louvre, Paris, 1959–60; mainly self-taught in art, but influenced by Takis, Hundertwasser and Erro, Paris, 1958–64. Married the artist Takis in 1961 (divorced, 1967); children: Athanasios, Thanos. Independent artist, in Paris 1960–61, 1963–64, in London, since 1967; produced first light and kinetic sculptures, 1961; worked on house-building project, with Takis, in Athens, 1964–66. Recipient: Arts Council Award, 1976; Alecto Award, *Bradford Print Biennale*, 1976; Arts Council Publishing Award, 1981; Arts Council Holography Bursary, 1982. Agent: Fischer Fine Art Ltd., 30 King Street, St. James's, London SW1. Address: 99 Camden Mews, London NW1 9BU, England.

Individual Exhibitions:

1963	La Librairie Anglaise, Paris
1967	Indica Gallery, London
1970	Hanover Gallery, London
1972	Galerie Germain, Paris
1973	Jordan Gallery, London
1974	Great Georges Project, Liverpool
1976	Serpentine Gallery, London
1977	Alecto Gallery, London
	Durham Light Infantry Museum
	Mappin Gallery, Sheffield
	Walker Art Gallery, Liverpool (toured the U.K.)
1979	Central Art Gallery, Wolverhampton
1980	Eagle Walk Gallery, Milton Keynes
	Roundhouse Gallery, London
1982	Aberdeen Art Gallery, Scotland
1983	Paton Gallery, London
1985	Galerie Peter Ludwig, Cologne
1987	Fischer Fine Art, London

Selected Group Exhibitions:

1967	*Light and Movement*, Musée d'Art Moderne, Paris
	Science Fiction, Kunsthalle, Berne (traveled to Musée des Arts Décoratifs, Paris, and the Kunstmuseum, Dusseldorf)
1968	*Art Vivant*, Fondation Maeght, St. Paul-de-Vence, France
1970	*Kinetic Art*, Hayward Gallery, London
1975	*Internationale Vizuele Poezie*, Museum Boymansvan Beuningen, Rotterdam
1976	*Art of the 60's*, Tate Gallery, London
1978	*Hayward Annual*, Hayward Gallery, London
1981	*British Sculpture in the 20th Century*, Part 2, Whitechapel Art Gallery, London

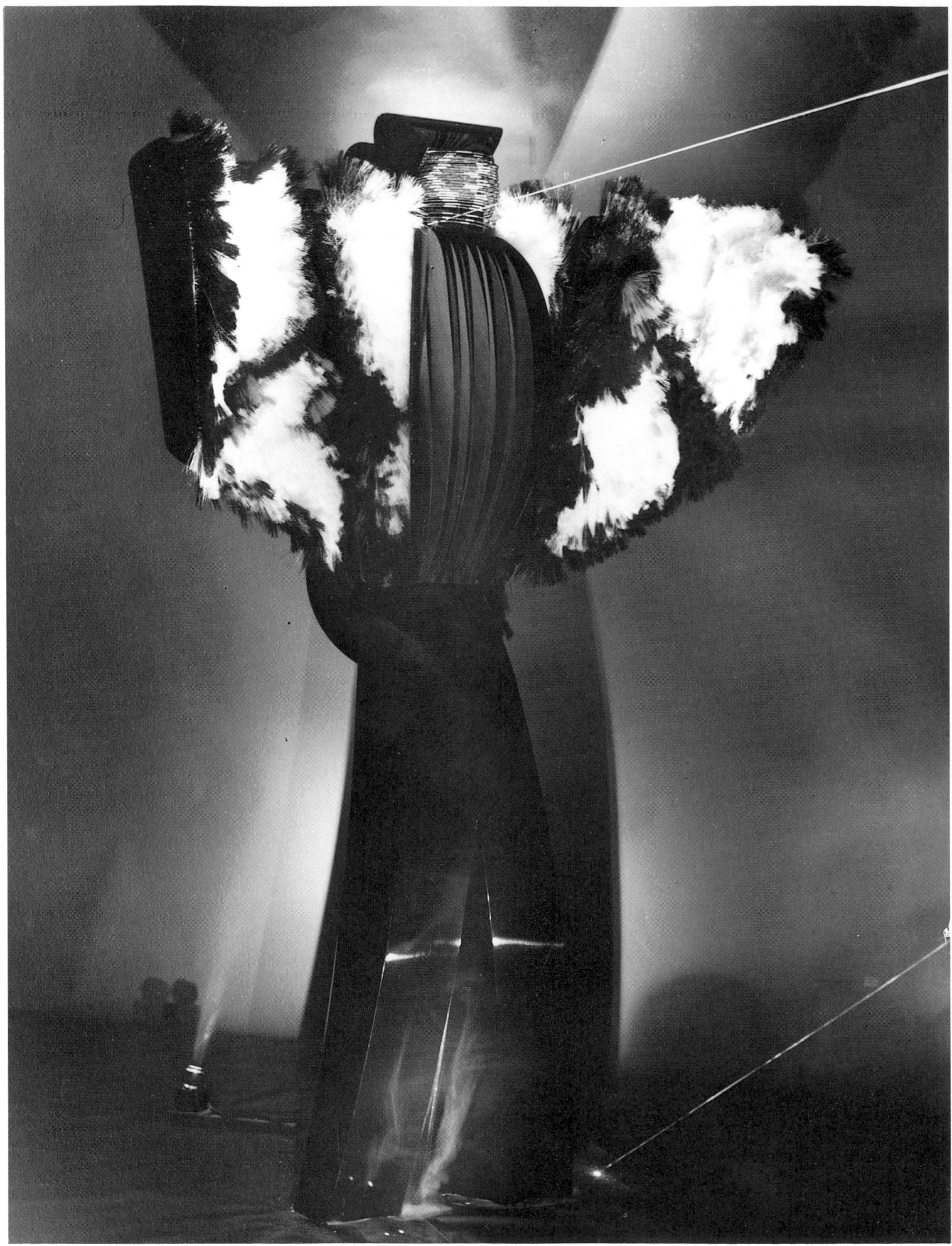

Liliane Lijn: *Woman of War*, 1986

1983 *Electra*, Musée d'Art Moderne de la Ville, Paris
1986 *Technologia e Informatica*, at the *Biennale*, Venice

Collections:

Tate Gallery, London; Arts Council of Great Britain, London; Victoria and Albert Museum, London; Graves Art Gallery, Sheffield; University of Warwick, Coventry; Bradford Art Gallery and Museum; Glasgow Museum; Musée de la Ville, Paris; Centre Georges Pompidou, Paris; Museum of Modern Art, New York; Art Institute of Chicago.

Publications:

By LIJN: books—*Crossing Map*, New York 1975, London 1983; *6 Throws of the Oracular Keys*, Paris 1982; articles—"The Takis Dialogues 2" and "1964 Electron Notes" in *Signals* (London), October 1964; "Poem Machines" in *Rohbo* (Paris), no. 4, 1968; "The Inside of a Work Is to Find Out" in *Art and Artists* (London), January 1971; "Inside and Out" and "Notes on Anti-Gravity Koans" in *Flash Art* (Milan), February 1971; "All People Are Artists" in *Ink* (London), September 1971; "Reflection," "3 Poems" and "Time Zone" in *Grosseteste Review* (Bicester), vol. 4, no. 2, 1971; "What Is Art?" in *Ostrich* (Whitley Bay), September 1973; "A Code of Form" in *Upstart* (New York), Spring 1978; "Hexagram" in *Harpers and Queens* (London), December 1980; "Receiving Change" in *Resurgence* (London), May/June 1981; "Artists on the 70's" in *Studio International* (London), vol. 1975, no. 991/2, 1981; "If" in *New Departures* (London), no. 14, 1982; "Imagine the Goddess!" in *Leonardo* (Oxford), no. 2, 1987; films and video—*What Is the Sound of One Hand Clapping?*, 1973; *The Power Game*, with Alastair Mackintosh, 1974.

On LIJN: books—*La Lune en Rodage* by Karl Lazlo, Basle 1964; *Kinetic Art* by Frank Popper, Paris 1967; *Kinetic Art* by Guy Brett, London 1967; *Movements in Art since 1945* by Edward Lucie Smith, London 1969; *Open Air Sculpture in Britain* by W. J. Strachan, London 1984; *British Art Since 1900* by Frances Spalding, London 1986; *Liliane Lijn: Imagine the Goddess*, exhibition catalogue with text by Jasia Reichardt, London 1987; articles—"Art as Research: The Experiments of Liliane Lijn" by Cyril Barrett in *Studio International* (London), June 1967; "Liliane Lijn in Discussion with Vera Lindsay" in *Studio International* (London), May 1969; "Functionalism of Art" by Alastair Mackintosh in *Art and Artists* (London), March 1973; "Beyond Light" by John Spurling in *New Statesman* (London), 24 December 1976; "Patterns of Light and Shadow" by Marina Vaizey in *The Sunday Times* (London), 2 January 1977; "Let There Be Light" by Michael Shepherd in *The Sunday Telegraph* (London), 9 January 1977; "Liliane Lijn" by Cyril Barrett in *Art Monthly* (London), February 1977; "Feminist Themes" by Richard Rush in *The Listener* (London), 28 September 1978; "Liliane Lijn" by Michael Sheperd in *Arts Review* (London), 19 December 1980; "Liliane Lijn at the Roundhouse" by Tam Giles in *Artscribe* (London), no. 27, 1981; "Interference in Plain Air" by Deanna Peterbridge in *Architectural Review* (London), April 1982; "Die Grosse Verfurhrung" by Friedmann Malsch in *Kunstforum International* (Mainz), October 1986.

In 1980 I came across a slide of an early (1959) painting of mine which I had almost completely forgotten. I was amazed to see a prismatic bird Goddess gigantic against a turbulent sky. She rises central, grounded and formal, surrounded by chaos in the form of flying creatures. I realized that the imagery of the painting was so complex and emotionally laden that I had been unable to deal with it as a whole. I had over the years to dismantle it, unconsciously to analyze it, and bit by bit to reconstruct, clarify and make real that chimera which had appeared to me on the 6th floor balcony of my apartment in Convention, a Polish quarter in Paris.

I was walking across the Place de la Bastille in the autumn of '82 when I began to hum a melody and the first words of a song came to me at such a pace that I hastened to look for a piece of paper and a pencil to scribble it down as I walked, not wishing to forget. Over and over I sang the threatening enigmatic words.

I've been armoured by your love
My house is your arsenal

My body your defense
I've been armoured by your love

In May I returned to Paris to give a performance at the Pompidou Centre of songs from *Crossing Map*. Although I was lured by the excitement of live performance, I was already thinking of making a performing sculpture. As usual the technical difficulties were discouraging, and that may be the reason why I did not immediately recognize that the *Woman of War* song was the song of a sculpture. Instead I thought of making a large winged female figure which would respond to the human voice and transform its vibrations into fluctuating patterns of light. A sculpture which would react to my voice, a sculpture with which I could perform. I began to imagine it as a female archetype. The archetype of the receptive. Robert Graves gave me the title *Lady of the Wild Things* which he mentions in his 'The Greek Myths' as a pre-patriarchal Greek Nymph Goddess.

Lady of the Wild Things is a Goddess of three aspects. Her light side, which is clothed in red and green (a constant reminder of opposites) is passive and still until activated by sound. Transforming sound into a luminous display, she reacts to her respondent. Her third aspect is her 'other side' which, as the moon's, is dark and all-embracing.

I've been armoured by your love
I've been blasted in your furnaces
And poured into your moulds
To fit the image to fit the image
I'm the image of woman
The image of She
A woman of war

Not unlike a shaman who chants concealed within an archetypal mask, I made *Woman of War* to embody the song which describes her. The words of the song are of a violence and an anger which I didn't think were mine. I felt as if the earth was singing through me.

Unlike *Lady of the Wild Things*, *Woman of War* is a female archetype of the creative. Since the act of creation is a battle, the creative archetype must be a warrior. It is part of the nature of this sculpture to perform specific actions, and for these to be properly timed to create a sense of suspense and awe. The performance of these symbolic steps enacts the ritual: the opening of her wings to reveal her soft and voluptuous interior, her song, the sudden billowing of smoke from beneath her, the thin red laser beam which shoots from her head to the prism-head of *Lady of the Wild Things*, ricocheting back in a faint pyramid of lines, her silence followed by the slow folding of wings across her ruffled black metallic breast concealing her head, transforming her appearance. Opposite, *Lady of the Wild Things* receives, transforms, reflects. If *Lady of the Wild Things* represents the contemplative peaceful side of human nature, *Woman of War* represents the violence we all carry inside ourselves.

Goddesses are creatures of a long forgotten past. Those who still remain belong to other cultures. In the West the archetypal female figures were destroyed long ago and divinity became a male principle. Spirit was claimed by man—spirit, sky, heaven, sun—and woman was left with the burden of body. The burden of a bearing body. Western woman for more than 2000 years has had no spiritual archetype, with the exception of the Virgin Mary, to which she could relate. The Virgin Mary epitomizes western man's physical and spiritual castration of women. She is the closest thing to a Goddess. She has conceived the Son of God but there has been no union, no carnal love, no dalliance, no play of powers, no sex. Chaste she conceives and bears Him. This is the miracle. Chastity. Her role is one of service. It naturally follows that female sexuality is a barrier to spiritual achievement. One look at the Hindu Goddesses is sufficient to ascertain that their sexuality was seen as a life-force, a power for good as well as for evil. Female sexuality is female power. To deny her sexuality is to deny her self. To divorce sex from spirit is to split self.

I want the Goddess to live again through my work. Embedded in my genetic memory lie fragments of her story which have surfaced over the years. Like the place names which in the United States are almost all that remain of the many indigenous tribes, her emblems punctuate both our diurnal and our nocturnal landscapes. Unknowingly, we have made her part of our industrial world.

Listen . . . my heart ticks like your bomb
Smell . . . the smoke of the mushroom on my breath
Look . . . I am the Medusa

—Liliane Lijn

Liliane Lijn is an artist who is fascinated by science, philosophy (particularly oriental philosophy) and words, that is, what one can do with words. She is not so much concerned with science itself or "art for a scientific age," as much the beauties and mysteries which science reveals and the possibilities for exploring these beauties which modern technology can offer the artist. And overriding all this is her oriental philosophical approach to the phenomena which science investigates.

Her approach to her work is intuitive, pragmatic and aesthetic. It has nothing to do with scientific research into optics, motion or related topics. This impression may have been given by the fact that, after a period of painting surrealist pictures (a not insignificant factor in her future development), she burst on the artistic scene as an optical-kinetic artist; and, like it or not, so, in part, she has remained, though by no means exclusively.

Among her early works in this field was a series of rotating perspex discs containing globules of water which acted as lenses and changed in size as the temperature and movement and the pressure of transparent spheres crossing the surface of the disc affected them. The moving spheres in turn reflected and magnified the globules or watery lenses, which, because of their liquidity, were alive and vibrant. A wonderful combination of rhythmic movement, light and vitality.

Light, pure white or refracted (coloured), as it traverses a prism, has been a persistent interest of hers since that time. So has the prism as a solid, crystalline object. The prisms, arranged in groups, bear a curious relationship to one another, like the monumental stones in a megalithic complex. Added to this, they produced spectral colours as one moves around them.

Another preoccupation of Lija's is with cones. She has to put them to all manner of artistic uses. At first they were used as a kind of kinetic concrete poetry. Letters were written on rotating cones. These could be formed into words. But, unlike static poetry, the spectator did not know (or could not remember) what letters were coming next: it was a new form of concrete poetry.

Subsequent uses to which the cones have been put include (a) their articulation, so that parts can swivel, and, in so doing, set up various kinds of relationships with other cones; (b) the insertion of tubes of neon light into the cones, which spiral upwards and downwards as the cones rotate; (c) dissected, transparent cones, made of wire mesh or metal sections. The latter two uses of the cone have been developed to form monumental works, such as the "White Koan," which now stands outside the Arts Centre of the University of Warwick, and "Split Spiral Spin" in the Birchwood Science Park, Warrington New Town. Both are objects of interest in their own right, that is, as static objects of contemplation; but they are interesting also for their kinetic effects, the liquid flow of light or the sounds of the wind in the mesh and the changing moiré patterns as one walks around the object.

Another device which Lijn has used to good effect is the rotating cylinder, unevenly coiled with wire (as on a resistance coil), which produces subtle ripples of light as it rotates. These come in various sizes and in combinations, usually groups of two or three. They may also be combined, to stunning effect, with "lenses," as in the "denslens" series, where a cylinder is embedded in a plexiglass hemisphere which refracts spectral colours as the cylinder rotates. These cylinders lend themselves to expansion, as in the 23 rotating columns forming a curved circle of 20 feet (6.1 m) in diameter in Milton Keynes; it can look magnificent at night.

In her more recent work Lijn has returned to the confrontation of objects and has begun to produce what she calls "totemic" objects. These "totems" usually consist of a lens, mounted on a metal stem and supported by two metal flanges. Sometimes they stand on their own, sometimes they confront "wave-guides" (a large group of rotating cylinders). They are called "figures of light." This might, uncharitably, be described as "science mysticism." So too might her "kori"—stone embedded with prisms and placed in a natural environment. But, if one has a puzzled interest in what she is now doing, the quality of the works (from a, perhaps, irrelevant aesthetic point of view) is as high as ever.

—D. C. Barrett

Richard Lindner: *Shoot*, 1968

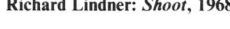

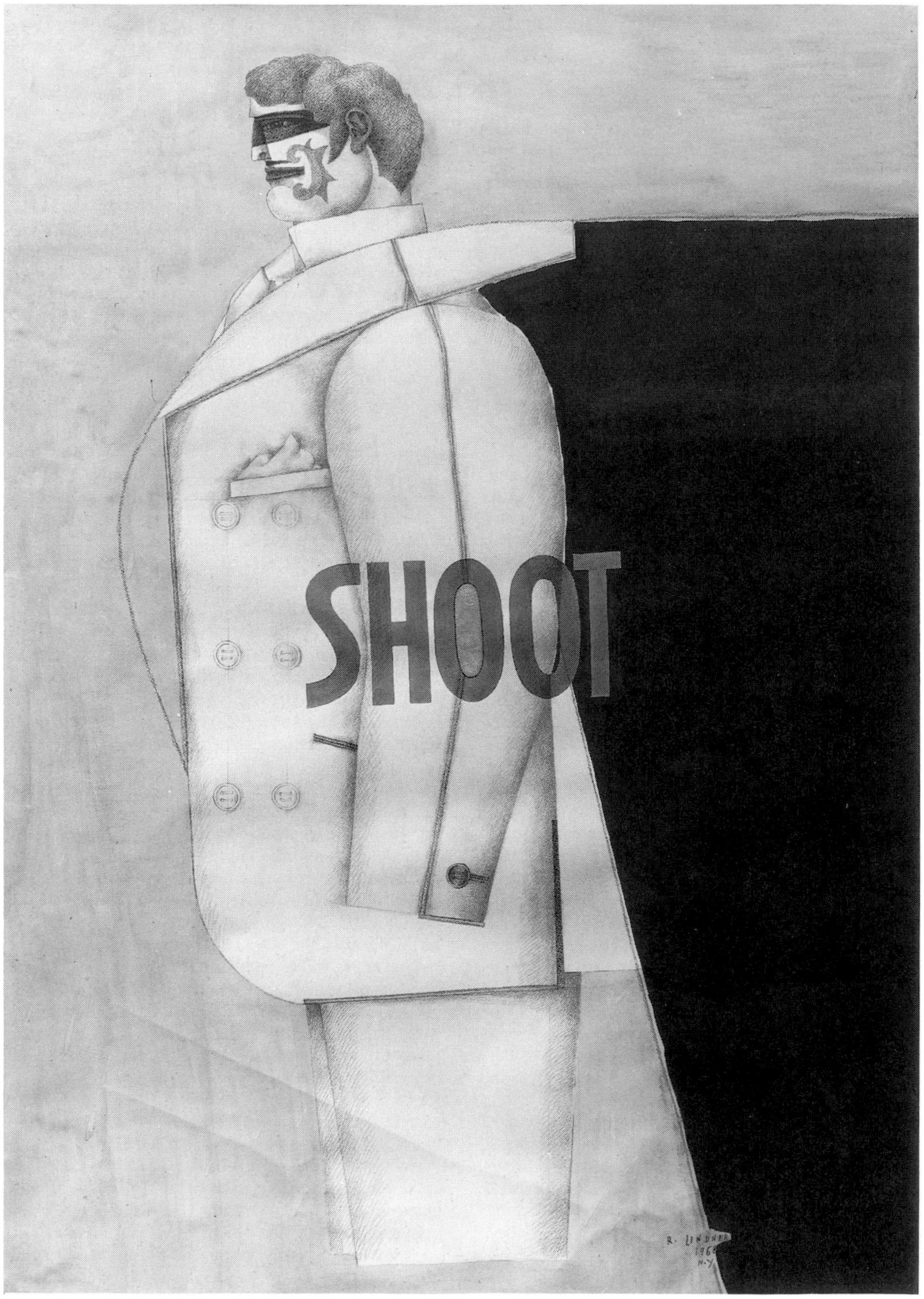

LINDNER, Richard.

American. Born in Hamburg, Germany, 11 November 1901; moved to Paris, 1933; emigrated to the United States in 1941: naturalized, 1948. Educated at Kunstgewerbeschule, Nuremberg, 1922–24; Kunstgewerbeschule, Munich, 1924–25; Akademie der Bildende Künste, Munich, 1925–27; Akademie der Künste, Berlin, 1927–28. Served in the British and French Armies during World War II. Married Denise Kopelman in 1968. Art Director, Knorr and Hirth publishers, Munich, 1929; subsequently worked as an illustrator and graphic designer for *Vogue, Fortune* and *Harper's Bazaar*; independent painter, 1950 until his death, 1978. Instructor, Pratt Institute, Brooklyn, New York, 1952–65 (originated course "Creative Expression"); Lecturer, Yale University School of Art and Architecture, New Haven, Connecticut, 1957; Visiting Lecturer, Hochschule für Bildende Kunst, Hamburg, 1965. Recipient: William and Noma Copley Foundation Award, 1957; Lichtwerk Award, Hamburg, 1970. Member, National Institute of Arts and Letters, 1972. Agent: Galerie Maeght, 13 rue de Téhéran, 75008 Paris, France. *Died* (in New York) *16 April 1978.*

Individual Exhibitions:

1954	Betty Parsons Gallery, New York
1956	Betty Parsons Gallery, New York
1959	Betty Parsons Gallery, New York
1961	David Cordier and Michel Warren Gallery, New York
1963	Robert Fraser Gallery, London
	Cordier and Ekstrom Gallery, New York
1964	Cordier and Ekstrom Gallery, New York
1965	Galerie Claude Bernard, Paris
	Galleria Galatea, Turin
	Cordier and Ekstrom Gallery, New York
1967	Cordier and Ekstrom Gallery, New York
	Galleria d'Arte Contemporanea, Turin
1968	Städtisches Museum Schloss Morsbroich, Leverkusen, West Germany
	Kestner-Gesellschaft, Hannover
1969	Staatliche Kunsthalle, Baden-Baden, West Germany
	Haus am Waldsee, West Berlin
	University of California, Berkeley (retrospective)
	Walker Art Center, Minneapolis (retrospective)
	Cordier and Ekstrom Gallery, New York
1970	Eat Art Gallery, Dusseldorf
1971	Galerie Boisseree, Cologne
	Spencer A. Samuels Gallery, New York
1972	Musée Nationale d'Art Moderne, Paris
1974	Musée Nationale d'Art Moderne, Paris
	Museum Boymans-van Beuningen, Rotterdam
	Städtische Kunsthalle, Dusseldorf
	Kunsthaus, Zurich
1975	Galerie Multiples, Paris
	Kunsthalle, Nuremberg
1977	Museum of Contemporary Art, Chicago (retrospective)
	Galerie Maeght, Paris
	Harold Reed Gallery, New York
1978	Sidney Janis Gallery, New York
	Museum of Modern Art, New York (retrospective)
	Fondation Maeght, Saint Paul de Vence, France (retrospective)
1979	Musée Saint Georges, Liège (retrospective)
	Galerie Maeght, Zurich
1980	Galerie Maeght, Barcelona
	Exposition d'Aquarelles, Stand de la Galerie Maeght, at F.I.A.C., Paris
1981	Galerie Maeght, Zurich

Selected Group Exhibitions:

1963	*Americans*, Museum of Modern Art, New York
	Documenta 3, Kassel, West Germany
1964	*Recent American Drawings*, Brandeis University, Waltham, Massachusetts
1965	*International Biennale*, Tokyo
	Color, Image and Form, Detroit Institute of Arts
1967	*Bienal*, de Sao Paulo
1968	*The Obsessive Image*, Institute of Contemporary Arts, London
1971	*The Poetry of Vision*, Royal Dublin Society
1972	*After Surrealism: Metaphors and Similes*, Ringling Museum of Art, Sarasota, Florida
1973	*25 Years of American Painting 1948–1973*, Des Moines Art Center, Iowa

Collections:

Museum of Modern Art, New York; Whitney Museum, New York; Rhode Island School of Design, Providence; Art Institute of Chicago; Cleveland Museum of Art; Tate Gallery, London; Musée National d'Art Moderne, Paris; Kunsthalle, Hamburg; Wallraf-Richartz Museum, Cologne; Museum Boymans-van Beuningen, Rotterdam.

Publications:

By LINDNER: books—*Tales of Hoffmann*, with Christopher Lazare, New York 1946; *Inleiding Door*, exhibition catalogue, with Alain Jouffroy and Peter Gorsen, Rotterdam 1974; articles—statement in *Americans 1963*, exhibition catalogue, New York 1963; interview, with Dore Ashton, in *Richard Lindner*, exhibition catalogue, Berkeley, California 1969; interview, with Wolfgang Georg Fischer, in *Richard Lindner*, exhibition catalogue, Paris 1974, and in *Art International* (Lugano, Switzerland), April 1974; interview, with John Gruen, in *Artnews* (New York), 14 April 1978.

On LINDNER: books—*Richard Lindner*, exhibition catalogue, with text by Sidney Tillim, New York 1960; *Richard Lindner*, exhibition catalogue, Paris 1965; *Richard Lindner*, exhibition catalogue, Hannover 1968; *Richard Lindner*, exhibition catalogue, Berkeley, California 1969; *Lindner* by Dore Ashton, New York 1969; *Richard Lindner* by Rolf Gunther Dienst, New York 1970; *Richard Lindner*, exhibition catalogue, with texts by Jean Leymarie and Jean-Hubert Martin, Peter Gorsen and Werner Spies, Dusseldorf 1974; *Richard Lindner* by Hilton Kramer, Boston, London and Berlin 1975, Paris 1978; *Richard Lindner*, exhibition catalogue, New York 1977; *Richard Lindner*, exhibition catalogue, Chicago 1977; *Richard Lindner 1901-1978*, exhibition catalogue, New York 1978; *Lindner*, exhibition catalogue, with text by Werner Spies, Saint Paul de Vence, France 1979; *Richard Lindner: Oils, Gouaches, Aquarelles 1954-1977*, exhibition catalogue, with text by James Lord, Barcelona 1980; *Richard Lindner*, exhibition catalogue, with text by Eugène Ionesco, Paris 1980; articles—"His Art Neither Pop nor Op but Lindner" by Helen Borsick in the *Cleveland Plain Dealer*, April 1966; "Richard Lindner" by Roland Penrose in *Art International* (Lugano, Switzerland), January 1967; "Lindner's Apocalyptic Honkytonk" by John Canaday in the *New York Times*, April 1969; "Richard Lindner" by Rolf Gunther Dienst in *Art and Artists* (London), August 1970; "Lindner" by Francis Gars in *Art Press* (Paris), February 1974; "Richard Lindner's Retrospective at the Musée National d'Art Moderne" by Michael Peppiatt in *Art International* (Lugano, Switzerland), March 1974; "Richard Lindner's Paintings and Drawings" by Pamela Leaderman in *Mid-West Art* (Milwaukee), vol. 4, no. 2, 1977; "Les Femmes de Richard Lindner" by Alain Jouffroy in *XXe Siècle* (Paris), June 1978; "Zum Tode von Richard Lindner" by Rolf Gunther Dienst in *Das Kunstwerk* (Stuttgart), June 1978; "A Send-Off by Richard Lindner" by Larry Rivers in *Art in America* (New York), November/December 1978; "El 'Contact' de Lindner" by Tomas Llorens in *Batik* (Barcelona), March/April 1980.

To understand something of the frisson that attaches itself to the work of Richard Lindner, it is necessary to take a look at the hectic and complicated life he led until he joined the Pratt Institute in Brooklyn in 1952.

Lindner makes dramas. All his pictures, from first to last, are imbued with black humour or outright shock tactics. In his own curious way he has updated the out-of-date. A picture by him leaves the viewer with an unresolved query in mind. Is it the artist who is some sort of *dernier cri* product or is he, the observer, no longer in touch with life as it is? Is Lindner an archaism, and is he, the man looking at the picture, the man of the 1980s? The corsets that have medieval structural defenses—strapping in in one sense and locking out in another, the men who like to wear their stetsons and who always seem dressed for an early evening stroll, the boys who look too old—too experienced—for their clothes; are these reflections of wild times in the Weimar Republic, or are they proper comment upon the fetishist sub-world of now?

Born in Hamburg, Lindner did not begin his formal art education until he joined Nuremberg's School of Fine and Applied Arts in 1922, after which he went on to the Academy of Fine Arts, in Munich. By this time he was beginning to find his feet in the world of culture and, after spending a year in Berlin, he went back to Munich to act as art advisor to a publisher until fleeing the Nazis for Paris where he started painting seriously.

After being interned as an alien at the outbreak of War he was released to join the French Army (and later work for the British), before finally leaving Europe for the United States.

In the U.S.A., Lindner first became well known through the illustrations he made for *Fortune*, *Vogue* and *Harper's Bazaar*, but when he was appointed a professor at the Pratt Institute he gave up illustration forever.

These brief notes do something to help explain the storyline of Lindner paintings. He knew the art world and, because he is an artist, he was able to carve himself a niche in the complex of modern art; but he also had long and professional experience as an illustrator and so, when he ceased to make illustrations, he transferred his narrative skill to painting.

They also act as a guide to the character of the imagery in his pictures. He was 19 when the First World War ended, he experienced the cumbersome inadequacy of the Stresemann regime, the madness of the German Inflation, and the coming of the Nazis.

If some of his early paintings recall Otto Dix at his most phlegmatic, if some of the later works suggest the early George Grosz (but in bass-clef), is this not to be expected from an artist who had a natural gift for telling tales? What is not so easy to place is the complicated "architecture" of the figures and their foundation garments in his contemporary works. These are not just composition trickery or artist's "patterns." They have a da Vinci practicality about them which in their brightest colours adds an extra resonance.

—Sheldon Williams

LINDOW, Christian.

German. Born in Altenburg, Thuringia (now in East Germany), 1 July 1945. Educated at Polytechnic High School, Altenburg, 1952-61; studied sculpture at the Werkkunstschule, Mannheim, 1962-65. Independent artist, Mannheim, 1965-69, in Berne, since 1969. Recipient: Louise Aeschlimann Stipendium, Berne, 1978-80. Agent: Galerie Toni Gerber, Gerechtigkeitsgasse 74, 3011 Berne. Address: Wasserwerkgasse 4, 3011 Berne, Switzerland.

Individual Exhibitions:

1969	Galerie Toni Gerber, Berne
1975	Galerie Toni Gerber, Berne
1977	Berner Galerie, Berne
1980	Neustadt 69, Schaffhausen, Switzerland
	Galerie M. L. Flammersfeld, Zurich
1981	Galerie Forme, Frankfurt
1982	Galerie Der Spiegel, Cologne
	Kunsthalle, Berne

Christian Lindow: *Sunset Boulevard*, 1983

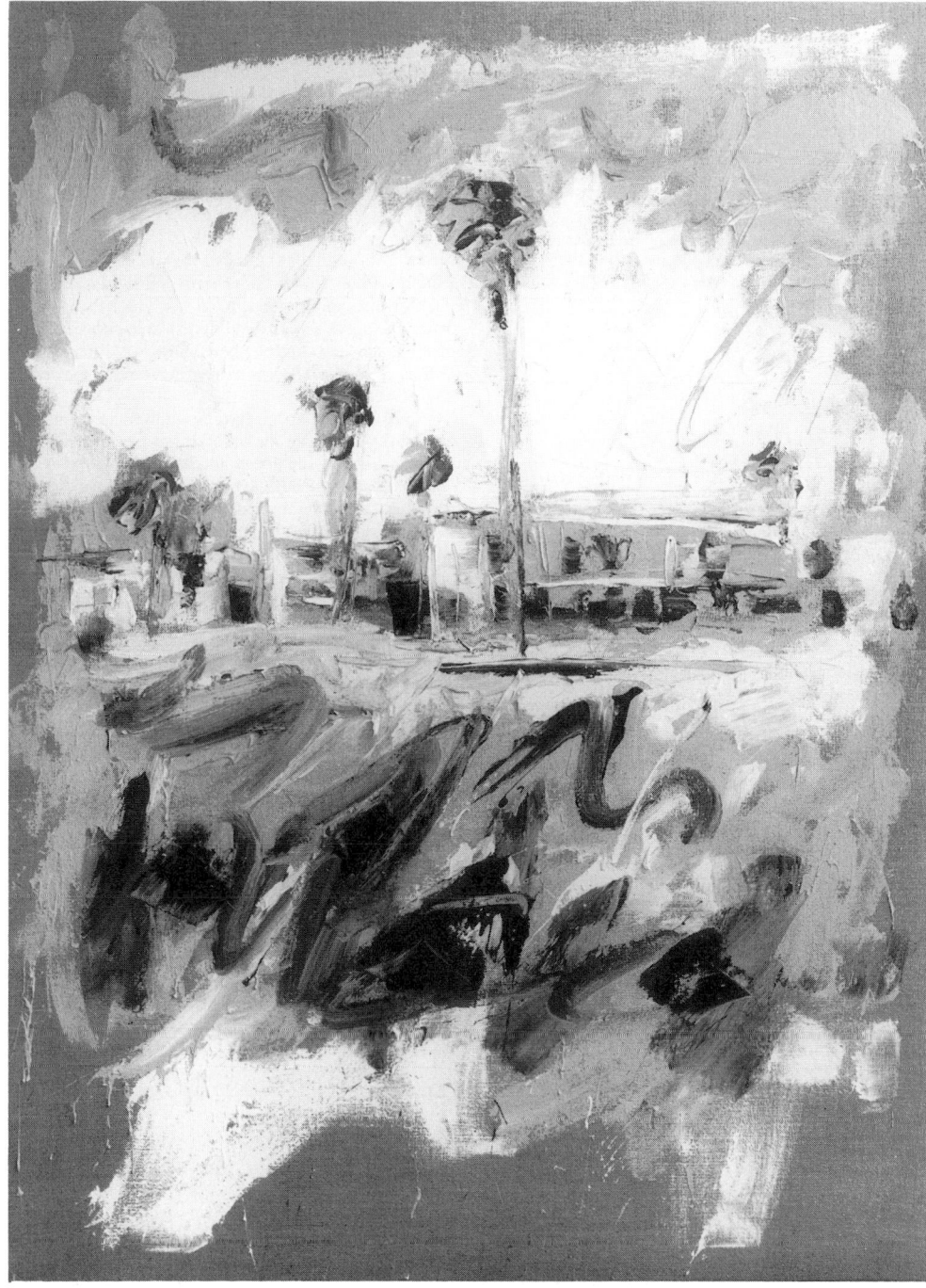

1983	Le Consortium, Dijon, France
1984	Galerie Der Spiegel, Cologne
1985	Association pour l'art contemporain, Nevers, France
	Suti Galerie, Berne
1987	Centre de Gravure, Geneva

Selected Group Exhibitions:

1968	*Deutscher Kunstpreis der Jugend*, Kunsthalle, Mannheim
1969	*Plaene und Projekte als Kunst*, Kunsthalle, Berne (traveled to the Kunstverein, Hamburg)
1971	*Situation-Concepts*, Galerie im Taxispalais, Innsbruck (traveled to the Galerie Nachst St. Stephan, Vienna)
1982	*Documenta 7*, Kassel, West Germany
1983	*Le paysage en quatre etats*, Maison de la Culture, Nevers, France
1984	*La peinture refiguree*, Musee de Brou, Bourg-en-Bresse, France
1987	*Europaische Biennale fur Druckgraphik*, Baden-Baden, West Germany

Collections:

Kunsthalle, Mannheim; Stadt Mannheim; Kunsthalle, Berne.

Publications:

By LINDOW: book—*I Believe in My Puberty*, Berne 1970; article—"Markierungsobjekt II", in *Das Kunstwerk* (Baden-Baden, West Germany), vol. 22, no. 11-12, 1969.

On LINDOW: books—*Situation-Concepts*, exhibition catalogue, Vienna 1971; *Christian Lindow*, exhibition catalogue with text by Marie-Louise Flammersfeld, Berne 1982; *Christian Lindow*, exhibition catalogue with text by Christian Besson, Nevers, France 1985.

LINDSTRÖM, Bengt.

Swedish. Born in Storsjo, Jamtland, 3 September 1925. Studied art at the Stockholm Academy 1944-45, Fine Arts School, Copenhagen 1945-46, and the Art Institute of Chicago, 1946-47. Painter and graphic artist, Paris, since 1947. Recipient: City of Stockholm Art Scholarship, 1950. Agent: Galerie Ariel, Paris. Address: c/o Galerie Ariel, 140 Boulevard Haussmann, 75008 Paris, France.

Individual Exhibitions:

1954	Gummensons Galleri, Stockholm
1958	Galerie Breteau, Paris
1960	Galerie Rive Gauche, Paris
1961	Manetan Galleri, Gothenburg, Sweden
	Galerie Le Zodiaque, Brussels
1963	Umea Museum, Sweden
1964	Gallery of Fine Arts, Boras, Sweden
	Anderson Gallery, Malmo, Sweden
	Museum of Fine Arts, Sundsvall, Sweden
1965	Galleri Birch, Copenhagen
	Galerie Rive Gauche, Paris
	Galerie Nord, Lille, France
1966	Museum of Fine Arts, Norrkoping, Sweden
1967	Galerie Veranneman, Brussels
	Galleri Medenius, Stockholm
	Galleri Norrland, Uppsala, Sweden
1968	Galerie Ariel, Paris
1969	Galerie la Pochade, Paris
1970	Galerie Ariel, Paris
	Galleri Birch, Copenhagen
1971	Galerie Nieuwe Stijl, The Hague
	Galerie Proteo, Toulouse

	Galleri Borgeson, Malmo, Sweden
	Galleri A. E., Gothenburg, Sweden
1972	Galleri Engelbrekt, Orebro, Sweden
	Galerie Ariel, Paris
1973	Galleria Cavini, Milan, Italy
	Galerie Veranneman, Brussels
1980	Edward Totah Gallery, London

Selected Group Exhibitions:

| 1971 | *Biennale*, Venice |
| 1972 | *Salon des Realités Nouvelles*, Musée d'Art Moderne, Paris |

Collections:

Konsthall, Malmo, Sweden; Lunds Konsthall, Lund, Sweden; Norrkoping Museum, Sweden; Sundsvall Museum, Sweden; Umea Museum, Sweden; Louisiana Museum, Humlebaek, Denmark; Museum van Hedendaagse Kunst, Ghent; Musée des Beaux-Arts, Ostend, Belgium; Carnegie Institute, Pittsburgh.

Publications:

On LINDSTRÖM: books—*Bengt Lindström*, exhibition catalogue, with texts by K. J. Geirlandt and Gita Brys-Schatan, Brussels 1967; *Bengt Lindström*, exhibition catalogue, with text by Jean Dypreau, Brussels 1973; *Bengt Lindström*, exhibition catalogue, London 1980; articles—"Bengt Lindström" by Georges Boudaille in *Cimaise* (Paris), September/December 1969; "Paris Letter" by E. Schwartz in *Art International* (Lugano, Switzerland), April 1972; "Tres Pintores Nordicos" in *Goya* (Madrid), January 1975.

From 1944 until 1947 Lindström was occupied with his art studies, first in Stockholm and subsequently at the Art Institute of Chicago. In 1948 he left for Paris where he spent a year dividing his time between Fernand Leger and André Lhote, although little of the influence of either seems to have survived in the art of their Swedish protege.

Lindström's paintings have a wildness in them that was never present in the art styles of Leger or Lhote, a ferocity more in tune with the angry vibrancy of adherents to the COBRA Group whose initial impact had been so far removed from his home country.

The desperate face of gangrene hue which peers out of a poisonous yellow background in his picture *Alpha and Omega* is perhaps more violent in temperament than the easy good-neighbourliness of *Les petits voisins* but the second painting also retains its mood of biting uncertainty. It is works like these that have led to a series of one-man exhibitions in Stockholm, Paris, Brussels, Cologne, Malmo, Copenhagen and the museums of Göteborg and Norrköping.

Torn between coarse figuration and utter figurative chaos pictures like *Viking*—a sort of fierce version of single combat, *Penelope* whose dark staring eyes dominate her pattern of stubby fingers in much the same way as those of *Femme à la Flute* with their black gaze piercing space as frantic fingertips explore the musical instrument, while in *Dejeuner sur l'Herbe* it seems as if Picasso has been thrown to the wolves.

Description of his pictures maybe best indicates the range and variety of Lindström's interpretations of even the most mundane subjects when they are jerked into unexpected conditions. COBRA has been given the license of Expressionism—Expressionism has been given full rein of the questing Kindermärchen of COBRA. An intriguing marriage.

—Sheldon Williams

LIPPOLD, Richard.

American. Born in Milwaukee, Wisconsin, 3 May 1915. Studied at the School of the Art Institute of Chicago, 1933-37; University of Chicago, 1933-37, B.F.A. in industrial design 1937; also studied music and dance in Chicago during the 1930's. Married Louise Greuel in 1940; children: Lisa, Tiana, and Ero. Industrial Designer, Cherry-Burrell Corporatin, Chicago, New York, Cedar Rapids, Iowa, and Baltimore, 1937-41; also worked in a freelance design partnership, Milwaukee, 1937-41; began to work in wire sculpture and wrote music, 1942; moved to New York, 1944; lives in Locust Valley, New York, since 1955. Instructor, University of Michigan, Ann Arbor, 1941-44, and Goddard College, Plainfield, Vermont, 1945-47; Head of the Art Department, Trenton Junior College, New Jersey, 1947-52; Part-time Teacher, Queens College, New York, 1947-48; Artist-in-Residence, Black Mountain College, Beria, North Carolina, 1948; Professor of Art, Hunter College, New York, 1952-65. Recipient: Third Prize, Sculpture Competition, Tate Gallery, London, 1952; Creative Arts Award, Brandeis University, Waltham, Massachusetts, 1958; Honor Award, American Institute of Architects, Chicago, 1959; Silver Medal, Architectural League of New York, 1960; Merit Award, Municipal Art Society, New York, 1963; Fine Arts Medal, American Institute of Architects, Chicago, 1970. D.F.A.: Ripon College, Wisconsin, 1968. Member, National Institute of Arts and Letters, 1963. Address: Post Office Box 248, Locust Valley, New York 11560. U.S.A.

Individual Exhibitions:

1947	Willard Gallery, New York
	Detroit Institute of Arts (with Peter Blume and David Smith)
1948	Willard Gallery, New York
1950	Willard Gallery, New York
1952	Willard Gallery, New York
1953	Arts Club of Chicago
	Layton Art Gallery, Milwaukee
1958	Brandeis University, Waltham, Massachusetts
1960	Corcoran Gallery, Washington, D.C.
1962	Willard Gallery, New York
1968	Willard Gallery, New York
1973	Willard Gallery, New York

Selected Group Exhibitions:

1946	*Origins of Modern Sculpture*, Detroit Institute of Arts
1947	*Whitney Annual*, Whitney Museum, New York
1954	*Salute to France*, Musée d'Art Moderne, Paris
	15 Americans, Museum of Modern Art, New York
1964	*New Members*, National Institute of Arts and Letters, New York
1979	*200 Years of American Sculpture*, Whitney Museum, New York
1980	*Photographs by Artists*, Los Angeles County Museum of Art
1981	*Contemporary Art Since 1939*, Kunsthalle, Cologne
1985	*Flying Tigers: Painting and Sculpture in New York*, Rhode Island School of Design, Providence (traveled to Worcester, Massachusetts)
1988	*43rd Biennale*, Venice

Collections:

Museum of Modern Art, New York; Metropolitan Museum of Art, New York; Whitney Museum, New York; Munson-Williams-Proctor Institute, Utica, New York; Wadsworth Atheneum, Hartford, Connecticut; Addison Gallery of American Art, Andover, Massachusetts; Virginia Museum of Fine Arts, Richmond; Detroit Institute of Arts; Milwaukee Art Center; Des Moines Art Center, Iowa; public installations—Inland Steel Building, Chicago; Lincoln Center, New York; Pan-Am Building, New York; St. Mary's Cathedral, San Francisco; Duomo, Viterbo, Italy; House of God Shinto Shrine, Kyoto, Japan; Deutsche World Bank Headquarters, Frankfurt; Darina Mandarin Hotel, Singapore.

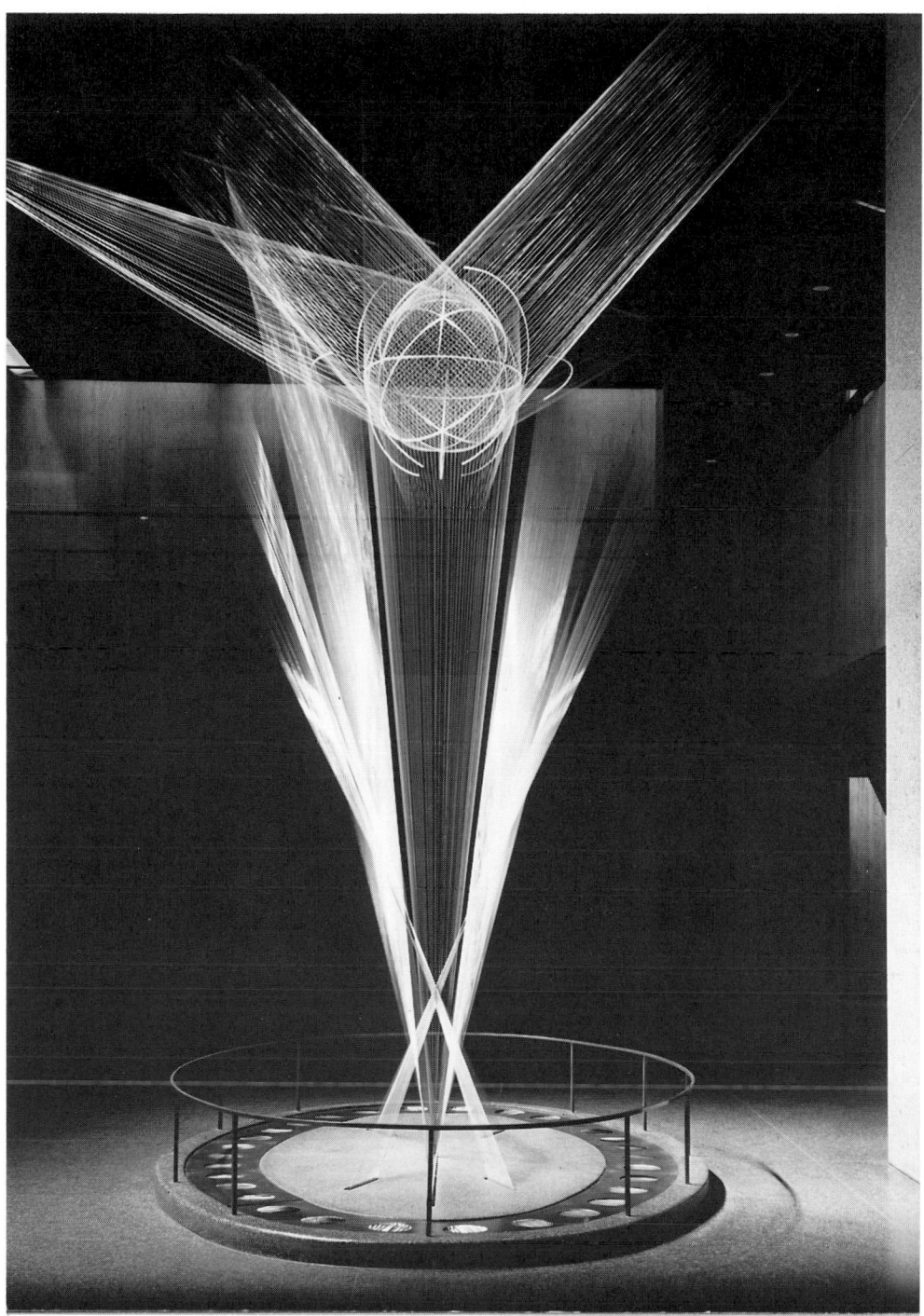

Richard Lippold: *Flight*, 1962

Richard Lippold may not be a pioneer, but he is definitely one of the most successful light experimentalists in the U.S.A. where interest in light sculpture increased suddenly during the 1960's as it took many different forms. Since the late 1940's Lippold has produced a series of impressive and memorable architectural/sculptural structures which are intricately composed of polished gold wires and plaques. His metallic creations have acquired over the years a philosophical-symbolic-religious bent which makes them even more relevant to our pragmatic society.

Although modernist in conception and style, Lippold's works often bring to mind the illusionistic virtuosity of the great Baroque decorators of the 17th century in Italy, for example his "Baldacchino" over the altar of St. Mary's Cathedral in San Francisco (1965-67). The great majority of his works shine with iridescent luminescence.

—Jean-Luc Bordeaux

LIPTON, Seymour.

American. Born in New York City, 6 November 1903. Educated at City College, New York, 1921-22; Columbia University, New York, 1923-27. Married Lillian Franzblau in 1930. Sculptor since 1928. Sculpture Instructor, New School for Social Research, New York, 1940-65; Instructor, Cooper Union, New York, 1942-43; Instructor, New Jersey State Teachers' College, Newark, 1944-46; Visiting Artist, Munson-Williams-Proctor Institute, Utica, New York, 1956; Visiting Critic, Yale University Art School, New Haven, Connecticut, 1957-59. Sculpture Chairman, Fine Arts Commission, New York, 1968. Recipient: Logan Award, Art Institute of Chicago, 1957; Guggenheim Award, 1960; Sculpture Award, Architectural League, New York, 1960, 1962; Purchase Award, New School for Social Research, New York, 1960; Sculpture in Architecture Award, Architectural League, New York 1962; Ford Foundation Grant, 1962; Perini Award, San Francisco, 1962; George Widener Gold Medal, Pennsylvania Academy of Fine Arts, Philadelphia, 1968. Agent: Marlborough Gallery, 41 East 57th Street, New York, New York 10022. Address: 302 West 98th Street, New York, New York 10025, U.S.A.

Individual Exhibitions:

1938	ACA Gallery, New York
1943	St. Etienne Gallery, New York
1948	Betty Parsons Gallery, New York
1951	American University, Washington, D.C.
1952	Betty Parsons Gallery, New York
1953	University of Teachers' College, New Paltz, New York
1954	Betty Parsons Gallery, New York
1956	Munson-Williams-Proctor Institute, Utica, New York
1958	Betty Parsons Gallery, New York
1961	Betty Parsons Gallery, New York
1962	Rensselaer Museum, Troy, New York
1964	Phillips Collection, Washington, D.C.
1965	Marlborough-Gerson Gallery, New York
1969	*The Creative Process*, Milwaukee Art Center University of Wisconsin, Madison
1971	Massachusetts Institute of Technology, Cambridge *Recent Works*, Marlborough Gallery, New York
1972	Virginia Museum of Art, Richmond
1973	Johnson Museum, Cornell University, Ithaca, New York
	Everson Museum, Syracuse, New York
1974	Marlborough Gallery, AG, Zurich
1976	*Recent Works*, Marlborough Gallery, New York
1979	National Museum of American Art, Washington, D.C.
	Jewish Museum, New York

Publications:

On LIPPOLD: books—*Contemporary American Sculptures*, by C. Ludwig Brumme, New York 1948; *Sculpture of the 20th Century* by Andrew Carnduff Ritchie, New York 1952; *Masters of Modern Art* by A. H. Barr, New York 1959; *The Sculpture of This Century* by Michel Seuphor, New York 1960; *Art and Life in America* by Oliver Lemkin, New York 1960; *Between the Fairs: 25 Years of American Art 1939-1964* by John I. H. Baur, New York 1964; *Direct Metal Sculpture* by Dona Z. Moilach, New York 1966; *Constructivism: Origins and Evolution* by George Rickey, New York 1967; *American Art since 1900: A Critical History* by Barbara Rose, New York 1967; *Form and Space: Sculpture in the 20th Century* by Eduard Trier, New York 1968.

Born into a place and an age in which space and time are our principal companions, I find it inevitable to love them more than the solid materials with which my ancestors were involved. We of this moment have learned to hurl ourselves through space, time, and energy with speeds and sensations beyond even the dreams of our forefathers. Yet for all the excitements of these experiences, the means of sensory perception, of intellectual contemplation, and of emotional response are unchanged; they continue to be responsible for all the tensions of human behavior, both within the individual and in his contact with all other beings; human, natural and artificial.

What a pleasure to be secure in the heart of all mankind and at once to be free in this security for exploration into aspects of earthly and cosmic realities which have been hidden to our knowledge until this instant! Courage to explore is not involved; it is simply a question of "doing what comes naturally" when one is free to find the form for his work in the challenge of new technologies and concepts—from suspension bridges to nuclear fission and space probes—from ancient yearnings for communication with the unknown. Wherein else lies the creative impulse?

—Richard Lippold

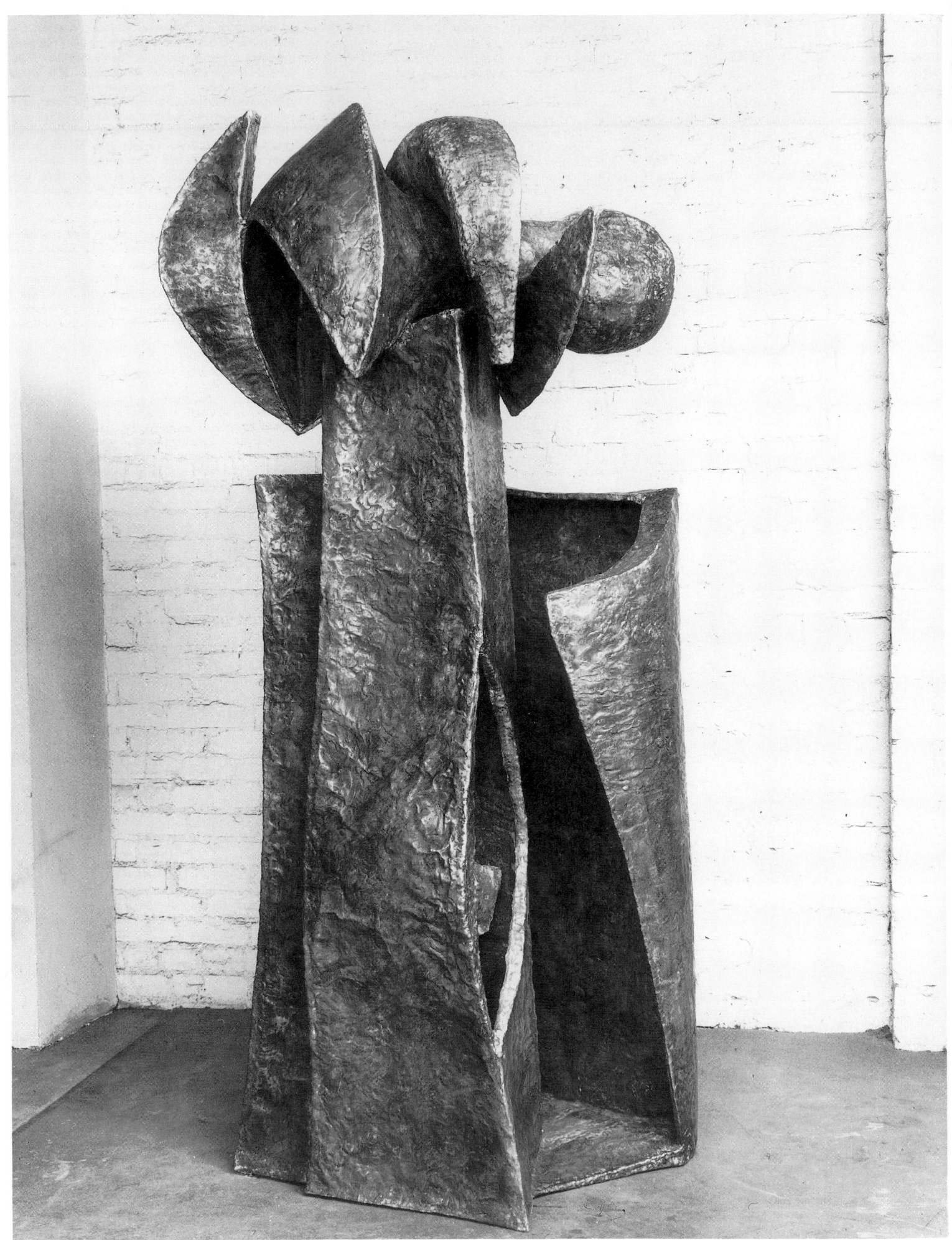

Seymour Lipton: *Empty Room*, 1964

Selected Group Exhibitions:

1959 *Nature in Abstraction*, Whitney Museum, New York
1960 *Documenta 2*, Kassel, West Germany
1962 *Spoleto Festival*, Italy
1965 *White House Festival of Arts*, Washington, D.C.
1966 *Art of the United States 1670-1966*, Whitney Museum, New York
1968 *Dada, Surrealism and Their Heritage*, Museum of Modern Art, New York
1969 *New American Painting and Sculpture*, Museum of Modern Art, New York
1971 *Antwerp Biennale*
1973 *Recent Sculpture 1964-1973*, Johnson Museum, Cornell University, Ithaca, New York
1975 *American Art since 1945 from the Collection of the Museum of Modern Art*, New York (toured the United States)

Collections:

Metropolitan Museum of Art, New York; Museum of Modern Art, New York; Whitney Museum, New York; Brooklyn Museum, New York; Albright-Knox Art Gallery, Buffalo, New York; Collection of Contemporary Art, Boston; Rhode Island School of Design, Providence; Phillips Collection, Washington, D.C.; Hirshhorn Museum, Washington, D.C.

Publications:

By LIPTON: articles—"Some Notes on My Work" in *Magazines of Art* (Washington, D.C.), November 1947; "Experience and Sculptural Form" in *College Art Journal* (New York), vol. 9, 1949; statements, in *12 Americans*, edited by Dorothy C. Miller, New York 1956; statement in *Nature in Abstraction* by John I. H. Baur, New York 1958; "Art in the USA: Artists Say: Seymour Lipton" in *Art Voices* (New York), Spring 1965; "Extracts from a Notebook" in *Arts* (New York), March 1971; "The Grotesque and Classical in Sculpture" in *Tracks* (New York), Spring 1977; statements, in "The 20th-Century Artists Most Admired by Other Artists" by Grace Glueck in *Artnews* (New York), November 1977.

On LIPTON: books—*Contemporary American Sculpture* by C. Ludwig Brumme, New York 1945; *Abstract Painting and Sculpture in America* by Andrew Carnduff Ritchie, New York 1951; *Sculpture of the 20th Century* by Andrew Carnduff Ritchie, New York 1952; *Seymour Lipton*, exhibition catalogue, New Paltz, New York 1955; *Nature in Abstraction* by John I. H. Baur, New York 1958; *American Art of the 20th Century* by Sam Hunter, New York 1959; *Modern American Painting and Sculpture* by Sam Hunter, New York 1959; *Looking Into Art* by Frank Seiberling, New York 1959; *Artists at Work* by Bernard Chaet, Cambridge, Massachusetts 1960; *Contemporary Sculpture: An Evolution in Volume and Space* by Carola Giedion-Welcher, New York, revised edition 1960; *Dictionary of Modern Sculpture*, edited by Robert Maillard, New York 1960; *A History of American Art* by Daniel M. Mendelowitz, New York 1960; *The Sculpture of This Century* by Michel Seuphor, New York 1960; *Seymour Lipton: A Loan Exhibition*, catalogue, Washington, D.C. 1964; *A Pictorial History of Western Art* by Edwin O. Christensen, New York 1964; *Seymour Lipton*, exhibition catalogue, by Sam Hunter, New York 1965; *Seymour Lipton* by Albert E. Elsen, New York 1968; *Seymour Lipton: The Creative Process*, exhibition catalogue, with an introduction by Tracy Atkinson, Milwaukee 1969; *Duncan Phillips and His Collection* by Marjorie Phillips, New York 1970; *Seymour Lipton: Recent Works*, exhibition catalogue, New York 1971; *Varities of Visual Experience* by Edmund Burke Feldman, New York 1972; *Recent Sculpture 1964-1973*, exhibition catalogue, with an introduction by Thomas W. Leavitt, Ithaca, New York 1973; *Seymour Lipton*, exhibition catalogue, with an essay by Nicholas Wadley, Zurich 1974; *American Art Since 1945* from the Collection of the Museum of Modern Art, exhibition catalogue, with an introduction by Alicia Legg, foreword by Richard E. Oldenburg, New York 1975; *Seymour Lipton: Recent Works*, exhibition catalogue, with an introduction by Thomas Leavitt, New York 1976; *Towards Sculpture* by W. J. Strachan, Boulder, Colorado 1976; *Aspects of Sculpture*, exhibition catalogue, by Harry Rand, Washington, D.C. 1979.

Seymour Lipton was a professional dentist before he began to interest himself in sculpture, and he has been entirely self-taught. He began about 1932 to design and make sculptures mostly in wood on figurative themes; then he became involved in the use of metal for his sculptures. In the 1950's he started fashioning works in sheet steel brazed edge to edge after he had cut out his shapes with metal shears. These heavy convoluted leaf-like forms that he has described as "outgrowing but not fully spread" have their insistent zoomorphic and floral analogies of an aggressive character which came to be varied by the application of melted nickel-silver and bronze over the surface of the sheet metal.

This organic symbolism with its ambivalent interpretations was integrated in the manipulated sheet and moulded metal with a strong dynamic thrust that took frequently a daemonic ferocity. In its interior rhythms as much as in the serrated edge of the silhouettes there was a fierce intensity of contortion and latching of forms, suggesting a serpentine pressure and the age-old interlinking of rocks through gravity and erosion. Lipton developed these smaller more monumental works, some of 8 feet in height, where the eternal motives of the seed, the protective womb and the contrasting model of a skeleton symbolize the theme "Struggle for Life" in various facets embracing sexual, botanical and metaphysical connotations.

"Pioneer" is such a work of major importance with branches and arms sprouting from the trunk or torso and a crown of barbed wire creating its telling allusion. Lipton had the unusual capacity to imply massive volumes by the most slender means, his thin metal forming contours and cliffs of tremendous power and presence. Later works took on more ambitious schemes in what has been described as "ideographic idioms." While in many of them the ideas have been confined to one base, their messages have been inscribed in terms demanding examination to trace their meanings. "The Ring" (1963), a resounding concept of two shield-like discs in bronze-coated metal 41 ins. high, has an evocative allusion to the life force evident in nature. The contemporary desire of artists working in three-dimensions to dictate the condition of the immediate environment in which their works can be seen is expressed by Lipton in conceptions such as "The Empty Room." This expansive wall is contextual and image-forming in the same setting with a vaguely articulated form contained and creating a relief on the surface of the metal. This magic sanctuary has nothing tender about it; it implies the active surge of regeneration in the phallic symbol superimposed on the bare expanse akin to the blossoming of beautiful flowers on a bomb site that our civilization has witnessed so often.

Lipton has forged arresting poetic entities in materials that emphasize their own harshness in the compulsory truth of their forms.

—G. S. Whittet

LOBDELL, Frank.
American. Born in Kansas City, Missouri in 1921. Studied at St. Paul School of Fine Arts, Minnesota, 1938-39; California School of Fine Arts, San Francisco, 1947-50; and Académie de la Grande Chaumière, Paris, 1950-51. Served as a Lieutenant in the United States Army, 1942-46. Painter: lived and worked in St. Paul and Minneapolis, 1940-42, and in Sausalito, California, 1945-48; established studio in the Mission District of San Francisco, 1948. Instructor, 1957-65, and Chairman of the Graduate Program, 1963, California School of Fine Arts, San Francisco. Artist-in-Residence, 1965, and since 1966 member of the faculty, Stanford University, California. Recipient: Artists Council Prize, 1948, and Purchase Prize, 1950, *Annual Drawing and Painting Exhibition*, San Francisco Museum of Art; San Francisco Bank Prize, *Annual Oil, Tempera and Sculpture Exhibition*, San Francisco Museum of Art, 1950; Adaline Kent Annual Award for a Californian Artist, 1960; Nealie Sullivan Award, San Francisco Museum of Art, 1960; Tamarind Fellowship, 1966. Agents: Oscarsson Siegeltuch and Company, 568 Broadway, New York, New York 10012; Smith-Anderson Gallery, 200 Homer Avenue, Palo Alto, California 94301, Address: 340 Palo Alto Avenue, Palo Alto, California 94301, U.S.A.

Individual Exhibitions:

1958 Martha Jackson Gallery, New York
1960 De Young Memorial Museum, San Francisco
 Martha Jackson Gallery, New York
1961 Pasadena Art Museum, California
 Drawings by Richard Diebenkorn and Frank Lobdell, Pasadena Art Museum, California
1962 Ferus Gallery, Los Angeles
1963 Martha Jackson Gallery, New York
 Pasadena Art Museum, California (retrospective)
 Drawings by Elmer Bischoff, Richard Diebenkorn and Frank Lobdell, Palace of the Legion of Honor, San Francisco
1964 Galerie D. Benador, Geneva
1965 Galerie Anderson-Mayer, Paris
1966 Pasadena Art Museum, California
1967 Marylhurst College, Oregon
1969 San Francisco Museum of Art
1970 St. Mary's College, Moraga, California
1972 Martha Jackson Gallery, New York
1978 Smith-Anderson Gallery, Palo Alto, California
1981 Reed College Art Gallery, Portland, Oregon
1983 San Francisco Museum of Modern Art

Selected Group Exhibitions:

1955 *Bienal*, Sao Paulo
1956 *California Artists*, Santa Barbara Museum of Art, California
1962 *The Artist's Environment: West Coast*, University of California at Los Angeles (traveled to the Oakland Art Museum, California, and the Amon Carter Museum, Fort Worth, Texas)
 50 California Artists, Whitney Museum, New York
1969 *Kompas 4*, Van Abbemuseum, Eindhoven, Netherlands
1972 *Painting Annual*, Whitney Museum, New York
1980 *Bay Area Art: Then and Now*, Suzanne Brown Gallery, Scottsdale, Arizona
1987 *American Painting: Abstract Expressionism and After*, San Francisco Museum of Modern Art

Collections:

Los Angeles County Museum of Art; Norton Simon Museum of Art, Pasadena, California; San Francisco; Stanford University, California.

Publications:

On LOBDELL: books—*Frank Lobdell*, exhibition catalogue with essays by Thomas Albright and Peter Boswell, San Francisco 1983.

A large, writhing biomorphic figure, evocative at once of a human being, enveloped by volcanic blacks in thick impastos, retreats toward the edge of the canvas, arms raised, with head thrown back and mouth open in a howl of anguish, pain, and despair. Such is the tenor of Frank Lobdell's early works which, as a statement of his existential vision, create figures with enormous legs and feet, engendering a feeling of earth-boundedness, of the futility of any attempt at physical flight from pain. His work can be seen as a powerful religious experience which, as in Dante's psychic journey through the *Divine Comedy*, charts the gradual evolution of the artist's own existential philosophy. Because of the fundamental unity between art and psyche in Lobdell's work, artistic maturation and personal growth go hand in hand, each contributing to the other's development. The tragic sense of elemental conflict which gives way to a lyrical and exalted liberation in his recent work illustrates Lobdell's personal transition.

Images of personal torment and spiritual pain stemming from unknown sources emerge during the brooding period of 1953–1954. The paintings frequently incorporate a smaller form alternately represented as a circle, or winged or armspread figure, usually shown in conjunction with a horizontal crescent shape. Lobdell then creates a larger figure which nearly always grasps for or surrounds the smaller form. Central to this period is the theme of the anguish caused by the discrepancy between human aspiration, symbolized by the circle or armspread figure, and human limitation, represented by the larger figure. Yet the cruciform, the armspread figure, the circle, and the crescent are all archetypal symbols, forms with associations deeply rooted in the human unconscious. Lobdell's early paintings seem to point towards an individual striving for spiritual fulfillment.

In the late '50s Lobdell begins to augment the torment of this large "pursuer" figure. His piece *April 1959* depicts a figure whose main features—head, arms, and hands—are emphasized with greater detail, yet they are assembled with no reference to the body as a whole. It is, in fact, no longer a figure at all, but an agglomeration of parts—howling mouths and rigid arms culminating in clenched fists all tied together in one inchoate mass, reflecting the pursuer's anguish, frustration, and impotence.

The body/spirit duality soon evolves into the juxtaposition of a single figure in the early '60s. The succession of figurally derived symbols of torment found in *April 1959* becomes increasingly attenuated, forming a serpentine meander which twists through the paintings with an elusive "spirit-figure" always at its head. As this form becomes less identifiable as a figure, a new figure emerges outside this chain with arms upraised and mouth howling. Essentially, the "pursuer" is a bystander witnessing the turmoil of his own internal struggle represented by the interaction between the ideal "spirit-figure" and the tormented forms of the serpentine trail. The paintings no longer express the juxtaposition of body and spirit, but of the self and the psychic forces which besiege it.

Lobdell's work toward the late '60s and early '70s incorporate nearly all the formal motifs he had developed until this time. Yet this period is distinguished by several traits which follow his subsequent career. The heavily outlined shapes that seemed to have tortuously struggled for so long for liberation from the protoplasmic environment to which they were bound, at last begin to free themselves. Lobdell achieves this by integrating symbolic and figurative forms. Inspired by Picasso's 1925 painting entitled *The Dance*, Lobdell composes a "Dance" series of 1970–71 which appears to be purely figurative. Yet his favorite forms and motifs embed themselves deep within the series. In *Dance V*, for example, the legs of the central figure cross to form a "spirit-figure," and the mouth and edge of the arm of the right figure, painted in white, combine to form a circle-and-crescent. Because of the incorporation of symbols stemming from the unconscious into these figures, the figures themselves are not only physical entities but psychic ones as well, with body and spirit integrated into a single form.

His piece *Fall 1971* resolves in two figures overlapping in a bewildering welter of lines, with the human figure even more distorted and difficult to identify. This trend to eliminate the central figure gradually continues through the late '70s and into the '80s. By 1977 all figural references are abstracted beyond recognition. The central images are dominated by crescents, spheres, and spirals. Lobdell also abandons his favorite motif, the cross or "spirit-figure." The paintings no longer represent the quest or yearning after the spirit. They are themselves expressions of this spirit.

From the beginning Lobdell has chosen to express himself through symbols. His career has been determined by a continuous effort to develop a visual vocabulary at once personal yet capable of achieving ever greater resonance and universality. His paintings appeal directly to the unconscious, and their power and life rests in their indefinability, their mutability, and their enigmatic persistence.

—Carrie Barker

LOHSE, Richard Paul.

Swiss. Born in Zurich, 13 September 1902. Educated in primary and secondary schools in Zurich, 1908–16; apprentice advertising designer, Zurich, 1918–22. Married Ida Duerner in 1942; daughter: Johanna. Worked in an advertising studio, 1922–27. Independent painter and graphic artist, Zurich, since 1928. Co-Founder, Allianz Vereiningung Moderner Schweizer Kunstler, Zurich, 1937; Co-Editor, *Bauen und Wohnen* magazine, Zurich, 1947–55; Zurich Branch Chairman, 1956–62, and Chairman of the Central Committee, 1962–64, Schweizerischer Werbund; Co-Editor, *Neue Grafik* magazine, Olten, 1958–65; Committee Member for Exhibitions, Kunsthaus, Zurich, 1962–70. Assistant Organizer, *Exhibition of 20th Century German Art*, London, 1938; Organizer, Swiss Section, *Salon des Réalités Nouvelles*, Paris, 1948, 1950. Recipient: Preis für Schweizer Malerei, Zurich, 1949; Sikkens Prize, Netherlands, 1971; Kunstpreis der Stadt, Zurich, 1973; Special Award, *World Print Competition*, San Francisco, 1977; Gold Medal, *Norsk Internasjonal*, Frederikstad, 1978; Drawing Award, *Euro-Biennale*, Heidelberg, 1979. Commandeur, Ordre des Arts et Lettres, France, 1986. Address: Stockerstrasse 32, 8002 Zurich, Switzerland.

Individual Exhibitions:

1957	Club Bel Etage, Zurich
1960	Kunstverein, Ulm, West Germany
	Galerie Charles Lienhard, Zurich
1961	Stedelijk Museum, Amsterdam
	Galerie 58, Rapperswil, Switzerland
1962	Kunsthaus, Zurich
1964	Galleria del Deposito, Genoa
	Galleria Cadario, Milan
1965	Galerie 58, Rapperswil, Switzerland
	Swiss Section, at the *Bienal*, Sao Paulo
1966	Instituto Torcuato di Tella, Buenos Aires
	Museu de Arate Moderna, Rio de Janeiro
1967	Galerie Renée Zeigler, Zurich
	Galerie Denise René, Paris
1968	Axiom Gallery, London
	Galerie Swart, Amsterdam
	Verfindustrie Jac Eyck NV, Heerlen, Netherlands
1969	Galerie Klubschule, Zurich
	Galleria Vismara, Milan
	Galerie Daedalus, Berlin
	Studio di Informazione Estetica, Turin
	Galerie Renée Zeigler, Zurich
1970	Galleria Il Fiore, Florence
	Galerie Zodiaque, Geneva
	Artestudio, Macerata, Italy
	Galleria Paolo Barozzi, Venice
	Kunsthalle, Berne
	Kunstverein, Munich
1971	Kunstverein, Hannover
	Moderna Museet, Stockholm
	Van Abbemuseum, Eindhoven, Netherlands
	Gemeentemuseum, the Hague
	2nd Biennale, Nuremberg
	Galleria La Polena, Genoa
	Galleria Peccolo, Livorno
1972	Galleria Vismara, Milan
	Swiss Pavilion, at the *Biennale*, Venice

Richard Paul Lohse: *30 Vertical Colour System Strokes with Horizontal Intervals*, 1972

Kunstmuseum, Dusseldorf
1973 Galerie Lydia Megert, Berne (opening exhibition)
1974 Galerie GE, Winterhur, Switzerland (opening exhibition)
1975 Kunsthalle, Dusseldorf
1976 Neue Galerie, Graz, Austria
      Kunsthaus, Zurich
      Modulare und Serielle Ordnungen, Moderne Gallerie, Bottrop, West Germany
      Galerie Renée Ziegler, Zurich
      Galerie Seestrasse, Rapperswil, Switzerland
      Multi Art Points, Amsterdam
      Galeria Cadaques, Cadaques, Spain
      Galeria Eude, Barcelona
1977 Galerie Swart, Amsterdam
      Galerie Media, Neuchátel, Switzerland
1978 Produzentengalerie, Zurich
      Van Abbemuseum, Eindhoven, Netherlands
1979 Galerie Lydia Megert, Berne
1980 Galerie Lydia Megert, at *Art 11, '80*, Kunstmeese, Basle
      Amos Anderson Museum, Helsinki
      Centro Culturale, Ascona, Switzerland
      Galerie Bossin, Berlin
1981 Galerie Christel, Stockholm
1982 Galerie Renée Ziegler, Zurich
      Galerie Teufel, Cologne
1983 Galerie Lydia Megert, Berne
      Ausbildungszentrum Wolfsberg, Ermatingen, Switzerland
      Kunstcentrum Badhuis, Gorinchem, Netherlands
      Wohnbedarf, Zurich
1984 Vrije Universiteit, Amsterdam
1985 Kunstmuseum, Lucerne, Switzerland
      Kunstverein, Braunschweig, West Germany
1986 Secession, Vienna
1988 Musée de Peinture et de Sculpture, Grenoble, France

Selected Group Exhibitions:

1936 *Zeitprobleme in der Schweizer Malerei und Plastik*, Kunsthaus, Zurich
1951 *Bienal*, Sao Paulo
1958 *Guggenheim International*, Guggenheim Museum, New York
1964 *Painting and Sculpture of a Decade 1954-64*, Tate Gallery, London
1966 *Vormen van der Kleur*, Stedelijk Museum, Amsterdam (traveled to the Württembergischer Kunstverein, Stuttgart, and the Kunsthalle, Berne)
1971 *The Swiss Avantgarde*, New York Cultural Center
1978 *Numerals 1924-77*, Yale University, New Haven, Connecticut (toured the United States)
1982 *Documenta 7*, Museum Fridericianum, Kassel, West Germany
1984 *Die Sprache der Geometrie im 20, Jahrhundert*, Kunstmuseum, Berne
1987 *Mathematik in der Kunst*, Wilhelm-Hack-Museum, Ludwigshafen, West Germany

Collections:

Kunstmuseum, Basle; Kunstmuseum, Dusseldorf; Kunsthas, Zurich; Kunstmuseum, Berne; Stedelijk Museum, Amsterdam; Van Abbemuseum, Eindhoven, Netherlands; Centre Georges Pompidou, Paris; University of East Anglia, Norwich; Museu de Arte Moderna, Sao Paulo, McCrory Corporation, New York.

Publications:

By LOHSE: book—*Almanach neuer Kunst in der Schweiz*, editor with Leo Leuppi, Zurich 1940; articles—"Die Flaeche" in *Abstrakt/Konkret* (Zurich), no. 1, 1944; "Die Mittel" in *Abstrakt/Konkret* (Zurich), no. 3, 1944; "Fortschrittlicher Bidinhalt und Konkrete Gestaltung" in *Abstrakt/Konkret* (Zurich), no. 4, 1945; "Bases Estructurales del Arte Concreto" in *Contemporaneo* (Buenos Aires), 1949; "A Revised Thematics for Progressive Art" in *Trans-Formation* (New York), no. 1-3, 1952; "A Step Farther: New Problems in Constructive Plastic Expression" in *Structure* (Amsterdam), no. 3/2, 1961; "Malerei als Zivilisations-arbeit," with

Fritz Billeter, in *Tagesanzeiger-Magazin* (Zurich), June 1972; "Normung als Strukturprinzip" in *Das Werk* (Winterhur, Switzerland), March 1974; "Das Reinhenphanomen in der Minimal Art" in *Kunstnachrichten* (Lucerne), May 1977; "Leserbriefe zu Outside" in *Archithese* (Zurich), no. 1, 1981; "Kunst im technologischen Raum" in *Basler Zeitung* (Basle), 14 May 1983.

On LOHSE: books—*Kalte Kunst* by Karl Gerstner, Teufen, Switzerland 1957; *Richard P. Lohse*, exhibition catalogue, with text by Hans Neuburg, Zurich 1960; *Richard P. Lohse* by Hans Neuberg, Ida Lohse, Konrad Wachsmann, Carola Giedion-Welcker, Siegfried Giedion and others, Teufen, Switzerland 1962; *Richard P. Lohse*, exhibition catalogue, with text by Jorge Romero Brest, Buenos Aires 1966; *Richard P. Lohse*, exhibition catalogue, with text by Harald Szeeman, Zurich 1967; *Constructivism: Origins and Evolution* by George Rickey, New York 1967; *Richard P. Lohse*, exhibition catalogue, with text by J. Leering, Heerlen, Netherlands 1968; *Richard P. Lohse*, exhibition catalogue, with text by Zdenek Felix, Berne 1970; *Richard P. Lohse*, exhibition catalogue, with text by Hans-Pieter Riese and Zdenek Felix, Hannover 1971; *Richard Paul Lohse*, with texts by Eugen Gomringer, F. W. Heckmanns, H. H. Holz, R. Kallhardt, J. Leering, H. P. Riese and W. Sandberg, Cologne 1973; Paris 1975; *Fabre als Sprache: Delaunay—Albers—Lohse* by Hans Joachim Albrecht, Cologne 1974; *Richard P. Lohse: Modulare und Serielle Ordnungen*, exhibition catalogue, with text by Jurgen Wissman, Bottrop, West Germany 1976; *Richard Paul Lohse*, exhibition catalogue, with text by Rudi H. Fuchs, Eindhoven, Netherlands 1978; *Richard Paul Lohse*, portfolio, with text by Rudi Fuchs, Zurich and Neuchâtel 1980; *Richard Paul Lohse*, exhibition catalogue with text by Andreas Brandt, Cologne 1983.

The history of modular and serial systems is not only one of the development of new structures, but a history of new methods.

Systematic organization is an analogous parallel to the structures of our present situation, of civilization. Although identical, it simultaneously throws doubt upon its social efficacy—through its use of objective means, the transparency of its methods, the possibility of prior calculation, the formation of lawfully unlimited structures. It is, in its methods of thought and practice, like a model directed to changing the environment.

A social basis corresponds to every cultural expression, a cosmology to every aesthetic. In no other form of art do the media and methods of a global technological strategy find a legitimate expression as they do in a constructive, logical, systematic or serial art, which is a sublimated and critical echo of the structures of civilization.

—Richard Paul Lohse

Looking at the paintings of Richard Paul Lohse today it is difficult to imagine him as a young artist going through all the stages that the time of his youth expected from him—portraits, landscapes, still lifes, a brief acquaintanceship with cubism, even a surrealist period. This kind of apprenticeship scarcely seems necessary for an artist who went on to become one of the key maneuverers in the sphere of op art, one who was not content simply to put his visual theories to the test but who also set out for his public detailed picture-analyses, explaining colour rhythms, the movement of colours round an axis, the systematic verticals of colour in relation to horizontals, and other yet more complex investigations. These diagrams were coded so that there should be no misunderstanding about colour relationships (0 for white, 1 for yellow, 2 for red-yellow, 3 for red, 4 for blue-red, 5 for violet, 6 for blue, 7 for green-blue, 8 for blue-green, 9 for green, 10 for green-yellow). Or the diagrams might be dispensed with altogether in favour of a bald formula like:

```
001000
002000
003142
314200
000300
000400
```

although in that case the code would be still further simplified (blue 1, green 2, red 3, yellow 4, white 0).

If these formulae sound cold, the actual paintings are not. The colours glow, plain and unvarnished, without the subtle decoration of a Vasarely.

—Sheldon Williams

LONG, Richard (J).
British. Born in Bristol, 2 June 1945. Studied at West of England College of Art, Bristol, 1962–65; St. Martin's School of Art, London, 1966–68. Produced first landscape artworks in England, 1967; and in Europe, North and South America, Mexico, Africa, Nepal, Australia and Japan, since 1969. Agents: Anthony d'Offay, London; Gallery Sperone Westwater Fischer, New York. Address: 121 York Road, Bristol BS6 5QG, England.

Individual Exhibitions:

1968 Galerie Konrad Fischer, Dusseldorf
1969 John Gibson Gallery, New York
      Galerie Konrad Fischer, Dusseldorf
      Museum Haus Lange, Krefeld, West Germany
      Galerie Yvon Lambert, Paris
      Galleria Lambert, Milan
1970 Dwan Gallery, New York
      Städtisches Museum, Mönchengladbach, West Germany
      Galerie Konrad Fischer, Dusseldorf
1971 Galleria Gian Enzo Sperone, Turin
      Museum of Modern Art, Oxford
      Art and Project, Amsterdam
1972 Whitechapel Art Gallery, London
      Museum of Modern Art, New York
      Galerie Yvon Lambert, Paris
1973 Stedelijk Museum, Amsterdam
      Wide White Space, Antwerp
      Galerie Konrad Fischer, Dusseldorf
      Lisson Gallery, London
1974 John Weber Gallery, New York
      Scottish National Gallery of Modern Art, Edinburgh
      Lisson Gallery, London
1975 Galerie Konrad Fischer, Dusseldorf
      Wide White Space, Antwerp
      Galerie Yvon Lambert, Paris
      Art and Project, Amsterdam
      Galerie Rolf Preisig, Basle
      Plymouth School of Art, Devon
1976 Galleria Gian Enzo Sperone, Rome
      Galerie Konrad Fischer, Dusseldorf
      Wide White Space, Antwerp
      Lisson Gallery, London
      Biennale, Venice
      Art Agency, Tokyo
      Arnolfini Gallery, Bristol
      Gallery Sperone-Westwater-Fischer, New York
      Corcoran Gallery, Washington, D.C. (with Carl Andre and Barry LeVa)
1977 Whitechapel Art Gallery, London
      Art and Project, Amsterdam
      Gallery Akumulatory, Poznah, Poland
      Galerie Rolf Preisig, Basle
      Lisson Gallery, London
      Kunsthalle, Berne
      Institute of Contemporary Art, Los Angeles (with David Askevold and Michael Asher)
      National Gallery of Victoria, Melbourne
      Art Gallery of New South Wales, Sydney
1978 Newlyn Art Gallery, Penzance, Cornwall (with Peter Joseph and David Tremlett)
      Art and Project, Amsterdam
      Galerie Yvon Lambert, Paris
      Galerie Konrad Fischer, Dusseldorf
      Lisson Gallery, London
      Park Square Gallery, Leeds, Yorkshire
      Gallery Sperone-Westwater-Fischer, New York

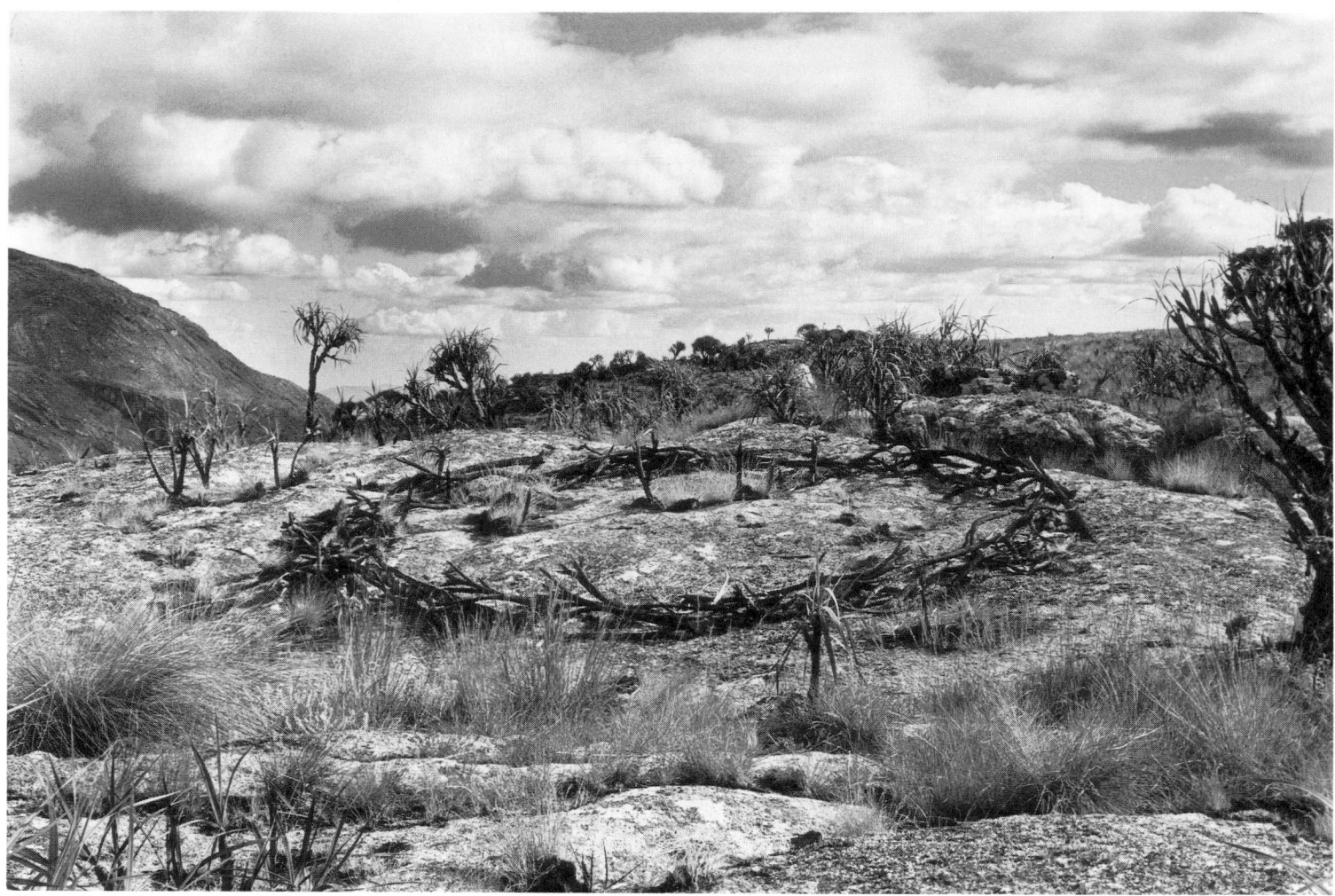

Richard Long: *Circle in Malawi, Africa,* **1978**

Austellungsraum Ulrich Ruckriem, Hamburg
1979   Tate Gallery, London (with Naum Gabo and Paul
       Nash)
       Ink, Zurich
       Anthony d'Offay Gallery, London
       Galerie Rolf Preisig, Basle
       Orchard Gallery, Londonderry, Northern Ireland
       Southampton University
       Stediljk van Abbemuseum, Eindhoven, Netherlands
       Lisson Gallery, London
       Art Agency, Tokyo
       Museum of Modern Art, Oxford
       Tate Gallery, London (with Paul Nash and Tom Phil-
       lips)
1980   Karen and Jean Bernier, Athens
       Art and Project, Amsterdam
       Fogg Art Museum, Harvard University, Cambridge,
       Massachusetts
       Gallery Sperone-Westwater-Fischer, New York
       Anthony d'Offay Gallery, London
       Galerie Konrad Fischer, Dusseldorf
1981   Anthony d'Offay, London (with Robert Bevan)
       Gallery Sperone-Westwater-Fischer, New York
       Graaeme Murray Gallery, Edinburgh
       Galerie Konrad Fischer, Zurich
       Anthony d'Offay, London
       David Bellman Gallery, Toronto
       Centre d'Arts Plastiques Contemporains, Bordeaux
1982   Anthony d'Offay, London (with Gilbert and George
       and Bruce McLean)
       Art and Project, Amsterdam
       Galerie Yvon Lambert, Paris
       Flow Ace Gallery, Los Angeles
       Sperone Westwater Fischer, New York
       National Gallery of Canada, Ottawa
1983   David Bellman Gallery, Toronto
       Arnolfini Gallery, Bristol
       Anthony d'Offay Gallery, London

       Antonio Tucci Russo, Turin
       Art Agency, Tokyo
       Century Cultural Center, Tokyo
       Galerie Konrad Fischer, Deusseldorf
1984   Coracle Press, London
       Galleria Lucio Amelio, Naples
       Galerie Crousel-Hussenot, Paris
       Jean Bernier Gallery, Athens
       Sperone Westwater, New York
       Dallas Museum of Art, Texas
       Butler Gallery, Kilkenny Castle, Ireland
       Orchard Gallery, Londonderry, Northern Ireland
       Anthony d'Offay Gallery, London
       Galerie Konrad Fischer, Dusseldorf
1985   Galerie Buchmann, Basle
       Anthony d'Offay Gallery, London
       Abbot Hall, Kendal, Westmoreland
       Konsthall, Malmo, Sweden
       Padiglione d'Arte Contemporanea, Milan
1986   Palacio de Cristal, Madrid
       Galerie Crousel-Hussenot, Paris
       Guggenheim Museum, New York
       Sperone Westwater, New York
       Anthony d'Offay Gallery, London
       Porin Taidemuseo, Finland
       Antonio Tucci Russo, Turin
1987   Musée Rath, Geneva
       Coracle Atlantic Foundation, Liverpool, Merseyside

Selected Group Exhibitions:

1966   *Group Exhibition,* Galerie Loehr, Frankfurt
1969   *When Attitudes Become Form,* Kunsthalle, Berne
1970   *Information,* Museum of Modern Art, New York
1972   *Documenta 5,* Kassel, West Germany
1976   *Arte Inglese Oggi,* Palazzo Reale, Milan

1979   *Matisse/Giacometti/Judd/Flavin/Andre/Long,* Kuns-
       thalle, Berne
1981   *British Sculpture in the 20th Century: Part 2: Sym-
       bol and Imagination, 1951–1980,* Whitechapel
       Art Gallery, London
1983   *Photography in Contemporary Art,* National Mu-
       seum of Modern Art, Tokyo
1985   *Transformations in Sculpture,* Guggenheim Mu-
       seum, New York
1987   *A Quiet Revolution: British Sculpture Since 1965,*
       Museum of Contemporary Art, Chicago (traveled
       to San Francisco; Newport Beach, California;
       Washington, D.C.; Buffalo, New York)

Collections:

Tate Gallery, London; Stedelijk Museum, Amsterdam;
Wallraf-Richartz Museum, Cologne; Louisiana Museum,
Humlebaek, Denmark; Museum des 20, Jahrhunderts, Vi-
enna; Musée d'Art Moderne de la Ville, Paris; Art Gallery of
Victoria, Adelaide, Melbourne; Art Gallery of Ontario, To-
ronto; Museum of Modern Art, New York; Art Institute of
Chicago.

Publications:

By LONG: books—*Richard Long: Skulptures,* Mönchenglad-
bach, West Germany 1970; *From Along a Riverbank,* Am-
sterdam 1971; *2 Sheepdogs Cross in and out of the Passing
Shadows, the Clouds Drift over the Hill with a Storm,* Lon-
don 1971; *South America,* Dusseldorf 1975; *From around a
Lake,* Amsterdam 1973; *John Barleycorn,* Amsterdam 1973;
Inca Rock Campfire Ash, Edinburgh 1974; *The North Woods,*
London 1977; *100 Stones,* Berne 1977; *A Straight 100 Mile
Walk in Australia,* Sydney 1977; *River and Stones,* Penzance,
Cornwall 1978; *River Avon Book,* London 1979; *Richard
Long,* Eindhoven, Netherlands 1979; *Aggie Weston's No. 16,*
London 1979; *A Walk Past Standing Stones,* London 1980;

Five, Six, Pick up Sticks, London 1980; *12 Works 1979–1981*, London 1981; *Mexico 1979*, Endhoven 1982; *Selected Works/Oeuvres Choisies 1979–1982*, Ottawaw 1982; *Touchstones*, Bristol 1983; *Countless Stones*, Eindhoven 1983; *Fango Pietre Legni*, Turin 1983; *Planes of Vision*, Aachen 1983; *Sixteen Works*, London 1984; *Mud Hand Prints*, London 1984; *River Avon Mud Works*, Londonderry 1984; *Postcards 1968–1982*, Bordeaux 1984; *Muddy Water Falls*, Noordwijk 1985; *Il Luogo Buono*, Milan 1985; *Richard Long in Conversation*, Bristol and Noordwijk 1985; *Piedras*, Madrid 1986; *Lines of Time*, Amsterdam 1986; *Stone Water Miles*, Geneva 1987.

On LONG: books—*Land Art: Long/Flanagan/Oppenheim/Smithson/Boezem/Dibbets/De Maria*, Berlin 1969; *Arte Povera* by Germano Celant, Turin 1970; *Richard Long: Land Art in Museum Haus Lange*, Krefeld, West Germany 1970; *The New Art*, exhibition catalogue, by Anne Seymour, London 1972; *Some Notes on the Work of Richard Long* by Michael Compton, London 1976; *Richard Long* by Rudi Fuchs, New York and London 1986; articles—"Some Recent Sculpture in Britain" by Charles Harrison in *Studio International* (London), January 1969; "Richard Long" by Willoughby Sharp in *Avalanche* (New York), no. 1, 1970; "Richard Long" by Jasia Reichardt in *Architectural Design* (London), March 1972; "Memories of Passing: A Note on Richard Long" by Rudi H. Fuchs in *Studio International* (London), April 1974; "Long Walks" by N. Foote in *Artforum* (New York), Summer 1980; "Richard Long at Anthony d'Offay" by Michael Craig-Martin in *The Burlington Magazine* (London), November 1980.

My art is about working in the wide world, wherever. It has the themes of materials, ideas, movement (walking), and time. The beauty of objects, thoughts, places and actions. I hope to make images and ideas which resonate in the imagination, that mark the earth and the mind. My work is about my senses, my scale, my instinct. I use the world as I find it, by design and by chance.

—Richard Long

Richard Long works lightly on the earth with great economy of means. His art is concerned with ideas about time, movement and places, with making marks on the earth, by walking or by re-arranging things that are found in a place, such as stones, sticks, pieces of brushwood or seaweed. He uses them to re-create simple basic shapes common to all mankind for many millennia: straight lines, circles, spirals, zig-zags, crosses and squares. These works may be as transient as walking a ten-mile straight line across a moor in England or splashing water onto rocks in Bolivia, or as long-lasting as a line of rocks placed together high in the wilderness of the Himalayas. Such anchors have a resonance partly because of their economy of image and partly because of the congruity between material, place and uninsistent calmness.

Long is a classical artist, imposing a configuration on the landscape. He shows his work in galleries in several ways. There are photographs of the marks and the places where they have been made. Others are presented in the form of maps, drawings or words sharing the routes and shapes of the walks.

There are also sculptures made from stone, slate, pieces of wood, or pine needles arranged in simple shapes on the floor, in form and medium to suit the ambiance. Recently Long has made circles of river mud on the walls of galleries.

—David Brown

LOPEZ GARCIA, Antonio.

Spanish. Born in Tomelloso, Ciudad Real, in 1936. Studied art at the Escuela de Bellas Artes de San Fernando, Madrid, 1950–55. Married the painter Maria Moreno. Independent painter, Madrid, since 1955. Recipient: Spanish Ministry of Education grant, to Italy, 1955; Kunstpreis der Stadt Darmstadt, 1975; Prince of Asturias Prize, Madrid, 1985. Address: Plaza de la Infancia 5, Madrid, Spain.

Individual Exhibitions:

1957	Ateneo, Madrid
1961	Galeria Biosca, Madrid
1968	Stampfli Gallery, New York
1970	Galerie Buchholz, Munich
1971	Galerie Claude Bernard, Paris
1972	Galleria Galatea, Turin

Selected Group Exhibitions:

1955	*Hernandez/Lopez/Lopez Garcia/Munoz*, Sala de la Direcion de Bellas Artes, Madrid
1968	*Spanische Kunst der Gegenwart*, Neue Galerie, Bochum, West Germany
1970	*Magischer Realismus in Spanien Heute*, Frankfurter Kunstkabinett H. Bekker von Rath, Frankfurt
1973	*Contemporary Spanish Realists*, Marlborough Fine Art, London
1974	*Ars '74*, Kunstmuseum Athenseum, Helsinki
1975	*Realismus + Realitat*, Kunsthalle, Darmstadt
1976	*5 Spanische Realisten*, Kunsthalle, Baden-Baden, West Germany
1977	*Documenta 6*, Kassel, West Germany
1978	*Internationaler Realismus heute*, Kunstverein and Kunsthaus, Hamburg
1980	*Spanische Realisten*, Kunstverein, Braunschweig, West Germany

Publications:

On LOPEZ GARCIA: books—*Magischer Realismus in Spanien heute*, exhibition catalogue, with text by Ernst Wuthenow, Frankfurt 1970; *Antonio Lopez Garcia*, exhibition catalogue, with text by Santiago Amon, Paris 1971; *Contemporary Spanish Realists*, exhibition catalogue, with text by Santiago Amon, London 1973; *5 Spanische Realisten*, exhibition catalogue with text by Ernse Wuthenow, Baden-Baden, West Germany 1976; *Spanische Realisten: Maria Moreno/Antonio Lopez Garcia/Isabel Quintanilla/Francisco Lopez*, exhibition catalogue, with text by Jürgen Schilling, Braunschweig, West Germany 1980.

LOUW, Roelof.

British. Born in Cape Town, South Africa, 17 February 1935; emigrated to England, 1961: naturalized, 1967. Educated at St. Martin's School of Art, London, under Anthony Caro, 1961–65. Served as sergeant, Royal Marines, Simonstown, Cape Town, 1954. Worked in architectural office, London, 1959 and 1961. Sculptor: lived in London, 1961–73; settled in New York, 1973. Lecturer in Sculpture, 1967–68, Director of the First Year Diploma Course, 1968–69, Director of the Third Year Diploma Course, 1969–70, and Director of Sculpture Projects of the Second Year Diploma Course, 1970–71, St. Martin's School of Art, London; Lecturer on Contemporary Sculpture, Maidstone School of Art, Kent, 1970–71; Lecturer in Painting and Sculpture, Royal College of Art, London, 1970; Visiting Lecturer, Victoria University, British Columbia, 1976–77; Visiting Artist, Rhode Island School of Design, Providence, 1977–78. Recipient: Prize, Sculpture Competition, Waterfront Project, Jane Street Pier, New York, 1981. Agent: Paul Maenz Gallery, 32 Lindenstrasse, 5 Cologne 1, West Germany. Address: 237 Lafayette Street, New York, New York 10012, U.S.A.

Individual Exhibitions:

1967	Arts Laboratory, London
1969	Museum of Modern Art, Oxford
1971	Nigel Greenwood Gallery, London
	Whitechapel Art Gallery, London
	Paul Maenz Galerie, Cologne
1974	392 West Broadway, New York

Selected Group Exhibitions:

1964	*Young Contemporaries*, FBA Galleries, London
1967	*Artist's Choice*, Kasmin Gallery, London
1968	*Abstract Sculpture Survey*, Camden Arts Centre, London
1969	*When Attitudes Become Form*, Kunsthalle, Berne (traveled to the Museum Haus Lange, Krefeld, West Germany, and the Institute of Contemporary Arts, London)
1970	*10th Tokyo Biennale*, Metropolitan Art Museum, Tokyo (toured Japan)
1971	*British Avant-Garde*, New York Cultural Center
1975	*Projects in Nature*, Merriewold West, Far Hills, New Jersey
1977	*Outdoor Exhibition*, Nassau County Museum of Fine Arts, Roslyn, Long Island, New York
1979	*The Artist's View*, Wave Hill Gardens, Bronx, New York
1980	*Drawings: Public Places*, Massachusetts Institute of Technology, Cambridge

Collections:

Tate Gallery, London; Victoria and Albert Museum, London.

Publications:

By LOUW: articles—"Symposium on Anthony Caro's Work," discussion with William Tucker, David Annesley and Tim Scott, in *Studio International* (London), January 1969; "Judd and After" in *Studio International* (London), November 1972; "Newman and the Issues of Subject Matter" in *Studio International* (London), December 1973; "Language and Perception: Victor Burgin" in *Artforum* (New York), February 1974; "Roelof Louw: An Interview, with Kenneth Baker, in *Art and Artists* (London), February 1974; "Sculpture in Nature" in *Projects in Nature*, exhibition catalogue, Far Hills, New Jersey 1975; "Working Procedures" in *The Artist's View*, exhibition catalogue, New York 1979.

On LOUW: articles—"The Sculpture of Roelof Louw" by Charles Harrison in *Studio International* (London), October 1968; "Roelof Louw" by Rosetta Brooks in *Flash Art* (Milan), February 1973; "Projects in Nature" by Jonathan Crary in *Arts Magazine* (New York), October 1975.

As a site sculptor my interests have developed into a concern not only with the localities of sculpture, but also with how works are generated by social circumstances—their subsequent use by society in these particular situations. In broad terms, this concern, with the positioning of artworks within the public domain, led me into initiating a specialized form of art consulting firm directed at responsible decision making by those most directly guiding the course of environmental issues: the corporations. Its purpose is not only to define business needs relative to art, but to consider these in terms of their potential value to dependent communities. As an instrument of this purpose, the firm is concerned with analysing and implementing these needs by recourse to the highly specialized and significant expertise that can be provided by academics within relevant fields. Alongside my commitment to researching social contexts for art, I have continued with my sculptural work. The influence of this concern with environmental problems, and its effect on my work, finds full definition in the sculptural project which recently won a Public Art Fund competition for a West Side waterfront site in New York.

—Roelof Louw

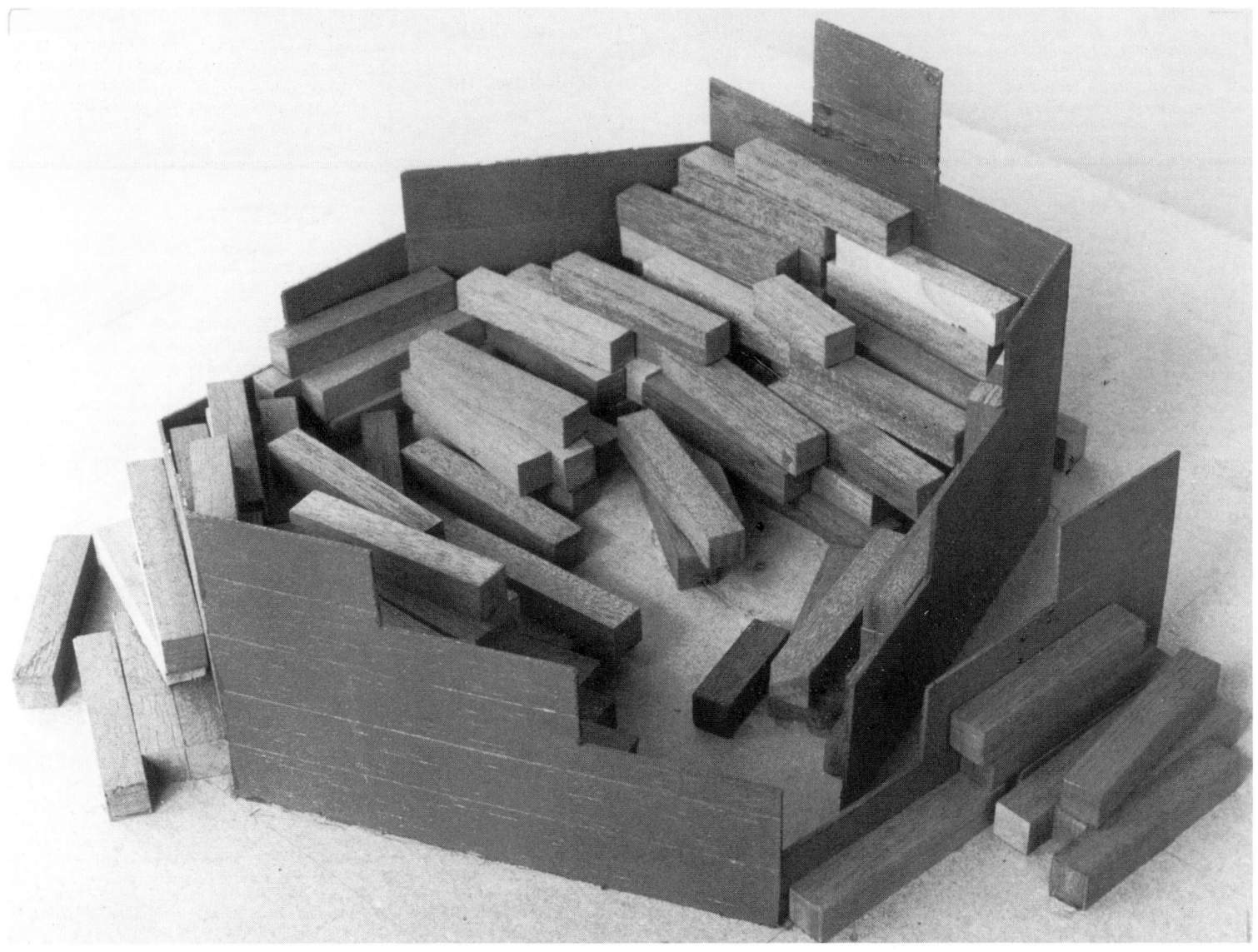

Roelof Louw: *Site Sculpture*, 1981

The development of Roelof Louw's sculpture falls into three periods. The site projects 1967–71, where specific materials (cast iron blocks, rubber bands, lead sheets, etc.) are used as a basis for physically relating to the "qualities" of a place. The tape recorder projects 1970–72, where a set of actions are carried out by participants, reported, and then played back as the "work". These projects explore the implicit structuring of space through "intentional" actions and the entry of the spectator into a work. The floor and site projects 1972–, using steel plates, where the above concerns are given a more concrete and unified form.

The consistent theme in Louw's projects has been the opening of the internal space of sculpture, so as to incorporate the "spectator" or "natural surroundings" into the work as a whole. He has identified the "private" and "inaccessible" space of Modernist sculpture with Idealism, and described his own work as an effort to "relocate" the concerns of sculpture.

To quote: "The Idealist attitude...lays claim to a search for essences. It supposes that to know the intrinsic nature of the self is also to know others. But this ethic is doubtful. Even if the recognition of 'attitudes or emotions' portends human understanding, it implies a self severed from the world at large. It stops short. For finally it is the tangible actions initiated by inner states that influence and maintain social life. If this responsibility is accepted, then it means to think not simply in terms of the display (or identity) of inner states, but more inclusively, to consider their social consequences.

"The capacities of sculpture, in my experience,

lead naturally towards this 'conviction'. Its brute materiality and ordering of physical distance, the shift and placement of masses over a ground area it permits (the very qualities rejected by Idealists) can be utilized to give direct account of how our physical actions impose upon and structure the space occupied by others. In Aesthetic purpose, these formal procedures move away from the introverted concern of the self-in-itself and towards a wider explication of conduct."

Similarly, Louw has described his site projects as an effort to employ sculpture as a means for directly relating to the physical "affects" of nature. While this area of concern has been germane to representational (landscape) painting it has been considered outside the formal scope of sculpture.

He says: "If the materials of sculpture are ordered by a structural scheme, then a different spatial freedom evolves. Without losing the mental sense of a whole, individual parts can be pulled apart, related across broad tracts of land and incorporate into a work the tangible features of a terrain. By doing this, the space of sculpture as a metaphor for directing physical response both encompasses and is disrupted by the raw experience of nature. In the process, as one distinct order is seen to initiate yet deconstruct another, mind and body, material order and landscape, mutually interpose. Firmly on the side of materialism, this approach bypasses representation, and more directly negotiates the rift between ideal (inner) physical responses and the pervasive surroundings of nature."

—Chryssa Zacharea

LUCASSEN, Reinier.

Dutch. Born in Amsterdam, 16 April 1939. Studied at the Rijksnormaalschool voor Tekenlaren and Rijksacademie voor Beeldende Kunsten, Amsterdam, 1957–60. Independent artist, Amsterdam, since 1960; worked on environmental paintings, with Etienne Elias, Raoul de Keyser and Roger Raveel, Beervelde Castle, Ghent, 1966; collaborated on paintings with Ger Van Elk, 1972. Founder Member, with Jan Dibbets and Ger Van Elk, International Institute for the Reeducation of Artists, Amsterdam, 1967. Artist-Instructor, Ateliers '63, Haarlem, since 1968. Recipient: Cassandra Foundation Award, 1970; David Roell Prize, Amsterdam, 1976. Agents: Lens Fine Art, Mechelse Steenweg 146, Antwerp; Galerie Espace, Keizersgracht 548, Amsterdam; and Galerie Grafiek 50, Wakken 0-6, Belgium. Address: Valeriusstraat 188 bv, 1075 GD Amsterdam, Netherlands.

Individual Exhibitions:

1966   Galerie 845, Amsterdam
1964   Galerie Espace, Amsterdam
1965   Stedelijk Museum, Amsterdam
1966   Galerie Espace, Amsterdam
        Markt 17, Enschede, Netherlands
        Groninger Museum, Groningen, Netherlands
        Galerie Kaleidoskoop, Ghent
1967   Galerie Espace, Amsterdam
1968   Galerie Espace, Amsterdam
1969   Rotterdamse Kunstkring, Rotterdam
        Dordrechts Museum, Dordrecht, Netherlands

	Galerie Espace, Amsterdam
1970	Tentoonstellingsdienst Den Bosch, Netherlands
	Galerie Espace, Amsterdam
1972	Stedelijk Museum de Lakenhal, Leiden
	Galerie Grafiek 50, Wakken, Belgium
	Tentoonstellingsdienst Den Bosch, Netherlands
1973	*Lucassen 63-73*, Frans Halsmuseum, Haarlem (toured the Netherlands)
	Galerie Grafiek 50, Wakken, Belgium
1974	Galerie Espace, Amsterdam
	Galerie Grafiek 50, Wakken, Belgium
1975	*Lucassen en de grote stijl*, Lens Fine Art, Antwerp
1976	Van Abbemuseum, Eindhoven, Netherlands
1977	*Lucassen 1977*, Galerie Espace, Amsterdam
1978	Lens Fine Art, Antwerp
1979	Stedelijk Museum, Amsterdam
	Galerie Espace, Amsterdam
1980	Gemeentemuseum, Aarnhem
1951	Galerie Espace display, *Fiac 81*, Paris
	Galerie Espace, Amsterdam
	Kunsthandel Lambert Tegenbosch, Heusden, Netherlands
1982	Lens Fine Art, Antwerp
1983	Galerie Espace, Amsterdam
	Museum Fodor, Amsterdam
1984	Galerie Espace, Amsterdam
1985	Lens Fine Art, Antwerp
1986	Dutch Pavilion, at the *Biennale*, Venice
	Galerie Espace, Amsterdam
	Museum Boymans-van Beuningen, Rotterdam

Selected Group Exhibitions:

1965	*Premio Lissone*, Italy
1967	*Junge Kunst aus Holland*, Kunsthalle, Berne
1969	*Profile 4*, Städtische Kunstgalerie, Bochum, West Germany
1971	*Stedelijk 60-70*, Ateneum, Helsinki (travelled to the Palais des Beaux-Arts, Brussels)
1973	*Fortunately There is Still Some Grass*, Camden Arts Centre, London
1976	*Reflektie en Realiteit*, Palais des Beaux-Arts, Brussels (toured Europe and Brazil)
1980	*Belgie-Nederland*, Palais des Beaux-Arts, Brussels (traveled to Museum Boymans-van Beuningen, Rotterdam)
1983	*Modern Dutch Painting*, National Gallery, Athens (traveled to Amsterdam and Nuremberg)
1985	*Aspecten van Nederlandse tekenkunst 1945-85*, Museum de Lakenhal, Leiden, Netherlands (traveled to Oberlin, Ohio)
1987	*Out of Holland*, Musée d'Art Contemporain, Montreal

Collections:

Stedelijk Museum, Amsterdam; Van Abbemuseum, Eindhoven, Netherlands; Museum Boymans-van Beuningen, Rotterdam; Gemeentemuseum, The Hague; Stedelijk Museum de Lakenhal, Leiden; Frans Halsmuseum, Haarlem; Groninger Museum, Groningen, Netherlands; Museum voor Hedendaages Kunst, Utrecht; Museum voor Schone Kunsten, Ghent; Galleria degli Uffizi, Florence.

Publications:

By LUCASSEN: articles—"Hommage san het einde van de schilderkunst" in *Lucassen*, exhibition catalogue, Amsterdam 1969; "Dagboekfragmenten" in *Reinier Lucassen*, exhibition catalogue, Haarlem 1973; "Dagboekfragmenten 2" in *Reinier Lucassen*, exhibition catalogue, Utrecht 1973; "Een appelte schillen" in *NRC-Handelsblad* (Amsterdam), 23 November 1974; "De mythe Sandberg is interessanter dan de werkelijkheid" in *Die Tijd* (Amsterdam), 7 November 1975; "Dagboek getekend Lucassen" in *De Revisor* (Amsterdam), 3 July 1975; "De kunstenaar heeft alleen verant-woording tegenover zichzelf" in *Keesings Reflector* (Amsterdam), 5 January 1976; "Dagboekfragment 11 Juli 1972" in *Reflectie en Realiteit*, exhibition catalogue, Brussels 1976; "Charchoune, meester van de schijnbare eevoud" in *Tableau II* (Amsterdam), March/April 1980; "De kunst en het geld" in *De Revisor* (Amsterdam), June 1980; "Nieuwe figuratie; een opvatting, geen stijl. Pop-Art; Een incident" in *Raster* (Amsterdam), no. 19, 1981; "De architect", in *De Gids* (Amster-

dam), no. 10, 1983; "Vraagen aan Lucassen" in *Jong Holland* (Amsterdam), no. 2, 1986.

On LUCASSEN: books—*Lucassen* by Roland Jooris, Hans Sizoo and Marchel Vos, Ghent 1969; *Lucassen*, exhibition catalogue, with text by Hans Sizoo, Leiden 1972; *Lucassen en Ger Van Elk...zogezegd* by Roland Patteeus, Tielt, Netherlands 1973; *Lucassen 63-73*, exhibition catalogue, with text by Hans Sizoo, Haarlem 1973; *Lucassen de grote stijl*, exhibition catalogue, with text by Hans Sizoo, Antwerp 1975; *Lucassen*, exhibition catalogue, edited by Rudi H. Fuchs, Eindhoven, Netherlands 1976; *Lucassen 1977*, exhibition catalogue, with text by Hans Sizoo, Amsterdam 1977; *Dutch Painting* by Rudi H. Fuchs, London 1978; *Lucassen*, exhibition catalogue, with text by Hans Sizoo, Amsterdam 1979; *Lucassen: schilderijen, tekeningen, assemblages 1960-1986*, with essays by Anna Tilroe, Hans Sizoo and Nicole Lasseel, Amsterdam 1986; *42. Biennale di Venezia: Lucassen*, exhibition catalogue with texts by Gijs van Tuyl and Karel Schampers, Amsterdam and The Hague 1986.

*   *   *

The essence of my work is determined by the fact that I do not care about notions, conceptions and forms such as figurative, non-figurative, rational, emotional, etc. I use (i.e., interpret) incompatible elements of style that should reject each other, in such a way that they assume a logical and organic form in the context of my work. When seen from the traditional notions of my style, my art has no style; I have turned the problem of style into a senseless problem.

Both in form and meaning this is a new aspect, possibly the only essentially new one in art since the great revolutions of the years 1900-1930.

—Reinier Lucassen

Reinier Lucassen: *Two 2*, 1985

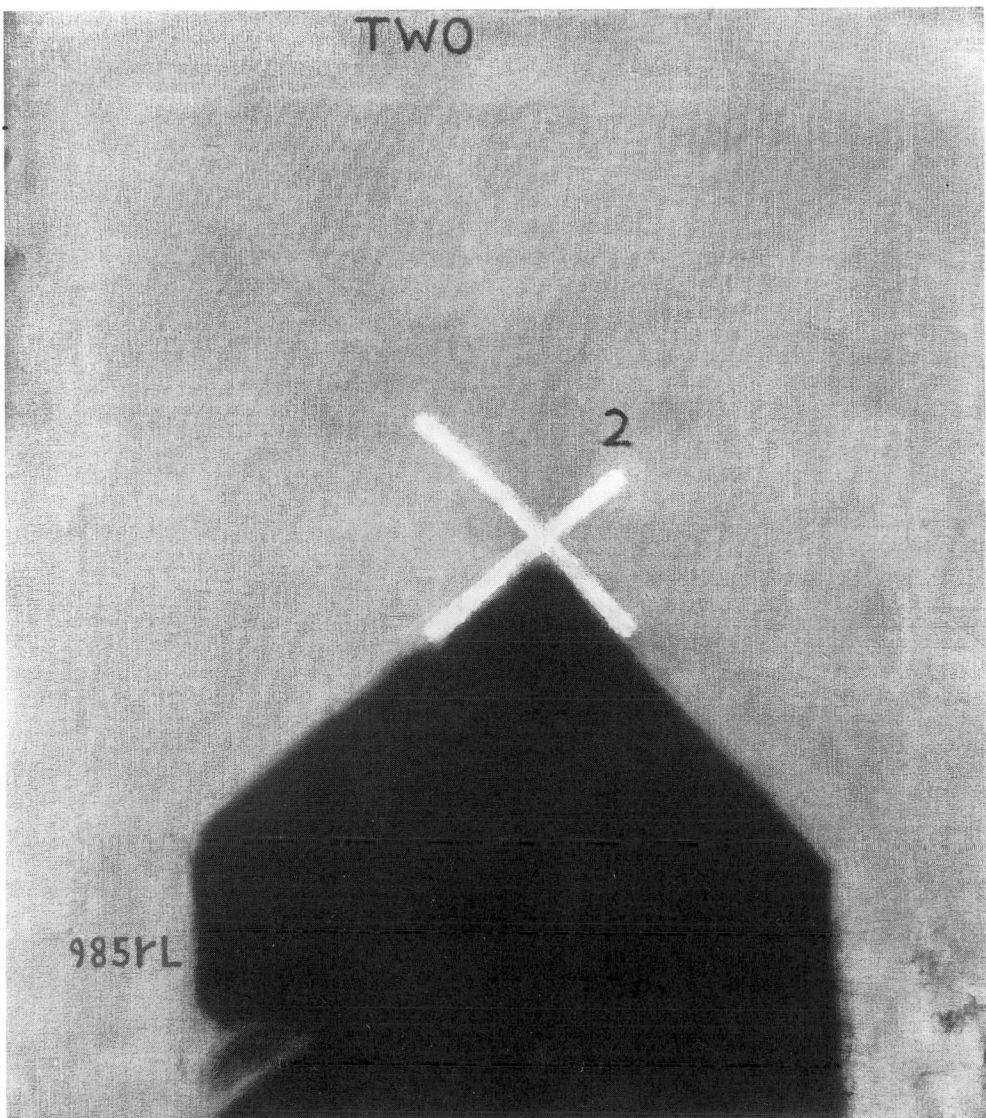

LUKIN, Sven.
American. Born in Riga, Latvia, 13 February 1934; moved to the United States. Studied at the University of Pennsylvania, Philadelphia. Painter: lives and works in New York. Recipient: Guggenheim Fellowship, 1966. Agent: Pace Gallery, 32 East 57th Street, New York, New York. Address: 807 Sixth Avenue, New York, New York 10001, U.S.A

Individual Exhibitions:

1959	Nexus Gallery, Boston
1961	Betty Parsons Gallery, New York
1962	Martha Jackson Gallery, New York
1963	Dwan Gallery, Los Angeles
	Pace Gallery, Boston
1964	Pace Gallery, New York
1966	Pace Gallery, New York
1968	Pace Gallery, New York
1981	Alex Rosenberg Gallery/Transworld Art, New York

Selected Group Exhibitions:

1961	*Carnegie International*, Pittsburgh
1962	*Whitney Annual*, New York
1964	*American Drawings*, Guggenheim Museum, New York
	The Shaped Canvas, Guggenheim Museum, New York
1966	*New Shapes of Color*, Stedelijk Museum, Amsterdam

1967   *Group Exhibition*, University of Colorado, Denver
1968   *Painting: Out from the Wall*, Des Moines Art Center, Iowa

Collections:

Whitney Museum, New York; Albright-Knox Art Gallery, Buffalo, New York; Larry Aldrich Museum, Ridgefield, Connecticut; University of Texas at Austin; Los Angeles County Museum of Art.

Publications:

On LUKIN: articles—review in *Arts Magazine* (New York), December 1968; review in *Artnews* (New York), January 1969; "New York Letter" by J. R. Mellow in *Art International* (Lugano, Switzerland), January 1969; review by Dore Ashton in *Studio International* (London), January 1969.

LUNDQUIST, Evert.

Swedish. Born in Stockholm, 17 July 1904. Educated in Stockholm, until 1920; studied at Carl Willhelmson's School of Painting, Stockholm, 1924; Académie Julian, Paris, 1924–25; Royal College of Fine Arts, Stockholm, 1925–31. Served in the Swedish Army, 1927. Married Ebba Reutercrona; sons: Hybner and Emanuel. Independent painter, Stockholm, since 1931. Professor of Painting, Royal College of Fine Arts, Stockholm, from 1960. Recipient: Swedish Association of Graphic Arts grant, 1959; Painting Prize, *Bienal*, Sau Paulo, 1961; Prince Eugene Medal, 1962; Artist Laureat, Stockholm 1964. Address: 17011 Drottningholm, Stockholm, Sweden.

Individual Exhibitions:

1934   Konstnarshuset, Stockholm
1938   Konstnarshuset, Stockholm
1941   Konstnarshuset, Stockholm
1944   Royal Academy of Fine Arts, Stockholm (retrospective)
1945   Konstnarshuset, Stockholm
1949   Samlaren, Stockholm
1953   Museum of Art, Eskildstuna, Sweden
       Konstnarushuset, Stockholm
1957   Royal Academy of Fine Arts, Stockholm
       Konsthalle, Gothenberg, Sweden
1960   Galerie Rive Gauche, Paris
       Beaux-Arts Gallery, London
1961   Little Studio Gallery, New York
       Renaissance Society, Chicago
1962   Gummeson Gallery, Stockholm
       Galleria del Cavallino, Venice
       Galerie Zodiaque, Brussels
       Beaux-Arts Gallery, London
1964   Swedish Pavilion, at the *Biennale*, Venice
1970   Royal Academy of Fine Arts, Stockholm
       Museum of Art, Gavle, Sweden
1971   *Malningar, Etsningar 1963–1971*, Lunda Konsthall, Lund, Sweden
       Museum of Art, Kalmar, Sweden
1974   Moderna Museet, Stockholm
1977   Royal Academy of Fine Arts, Stockholm
1979   *Peintures à l'Huile 1936–1979*, Centre Culturel Suedois, Paris
       Konsthall, Gothenburg, Sweden
1980   Centre Culturel, Suedois, Paris
       Thilska Galleriet, Stockholm
1982   Clocktower Gallery, New York
1985   Kunstnernes Hus, Oslo

Selected Group Exhibitions:

1952   *Carnegie International*, Carnegie Institute, Pittsburgh (and 1959)
1960   *Triennale*, Milan
1961   *Bienal*, Sao Paulo
1962   *Biennale*, Venice (and 1982)
1963   *Dunn International*, Fredericton, New Brunswick, Canada
1964   *Guggenheim International*, Guggenheim Museum, New York

Collections:

Moderna Museet, Stockholm; Svensk Nasjonalsgalleriet, Stockholm; Goteborgs Konsthall, Gothenberg, Sweden; Centre Georges Pompidou, Paris; Bibliothèque Nationale, Paris; Museum of Modern Art, New York; Tate Gallery, London; Museu de Arte Moderna, Sao Paulo; National Gallery of Victoria, Melbourne.

Publications:

On LUNDQUIST: books—*Evert Lundquist*, exhibition catalogue, Stockholm 1957; *Evert Lundquist: Malningar, Etsningar 1963–1971*, exhibition catalogue, with text by Oscar Reutersvard, Lund, Sweden 1971; *Evert Lundquist*, exhibition catalogue, with text by Philip von Schantz and Ulf Linde, Stockholm 1974; *Evert Lundquist*, exhibition catalogue, with text by Ulf Linde, Stockholm 1975; *Evert Lundquist: Peintures à l'Huile 1936–1979*, exhibition catalogue, with text by Ulf Linde, Paris 1979; *Lundquist*, exhibition catalogue with text by Erik Blomberg, Oslo 1985.

My personal and artistic taste and my temperament have always tended—in spite of many deviations and aberrations—to a predilection for classical art (from that day in 1922 when at the age of 19 I bought in London some photographic reproductions of the Elgin Marbles in the British Museum). This has now become ever more clearly my domain, and on this balanced, sound and largely universal art I exclusively feed; I feel at home in it, and its spirit I try to express in my work, in my own and my age's formal language. This is the way of the grand tradition, the way that endures in all ages and countries where the basic grounds of the Western spirit are still respected and revered. Particularly in this ravaged and in its artistic life so fragmented age, I believe this so-called 'reactionary' attitude of mine to be valuable as a counterweight to all that is fleeting, chaotic, primitive, artificial, and unfinished.

An artist can relate to his own work only to the extent to which he has mastered the language of others, the extent to which he is in a tradition. In certain respects, he may find himself incapable of adopting the tradition. He may feel a more or less compelling need to alter it, but the work he then creates cannot be understood by anyone, not even himself, other than in relation to the tradition that was to be changed. His deviations, and thus also his will, can be read off in this way.

What characterizes the art that rises above mere incidentals is its great and timeless nature. And this does not come about from new attitudes, fresh initiatives, etc., but is the result of a lifelong, devoted adherence to and entrenchment of a limited position. It is in his restriction, says Goethe, that the master reveals himself. It is not in absolute freedom, faithlessness and a desire for renewal that the strength of artistic creativity is expressed, but in an obstinate,

Evert Lundquist: *In the Window*, 1980

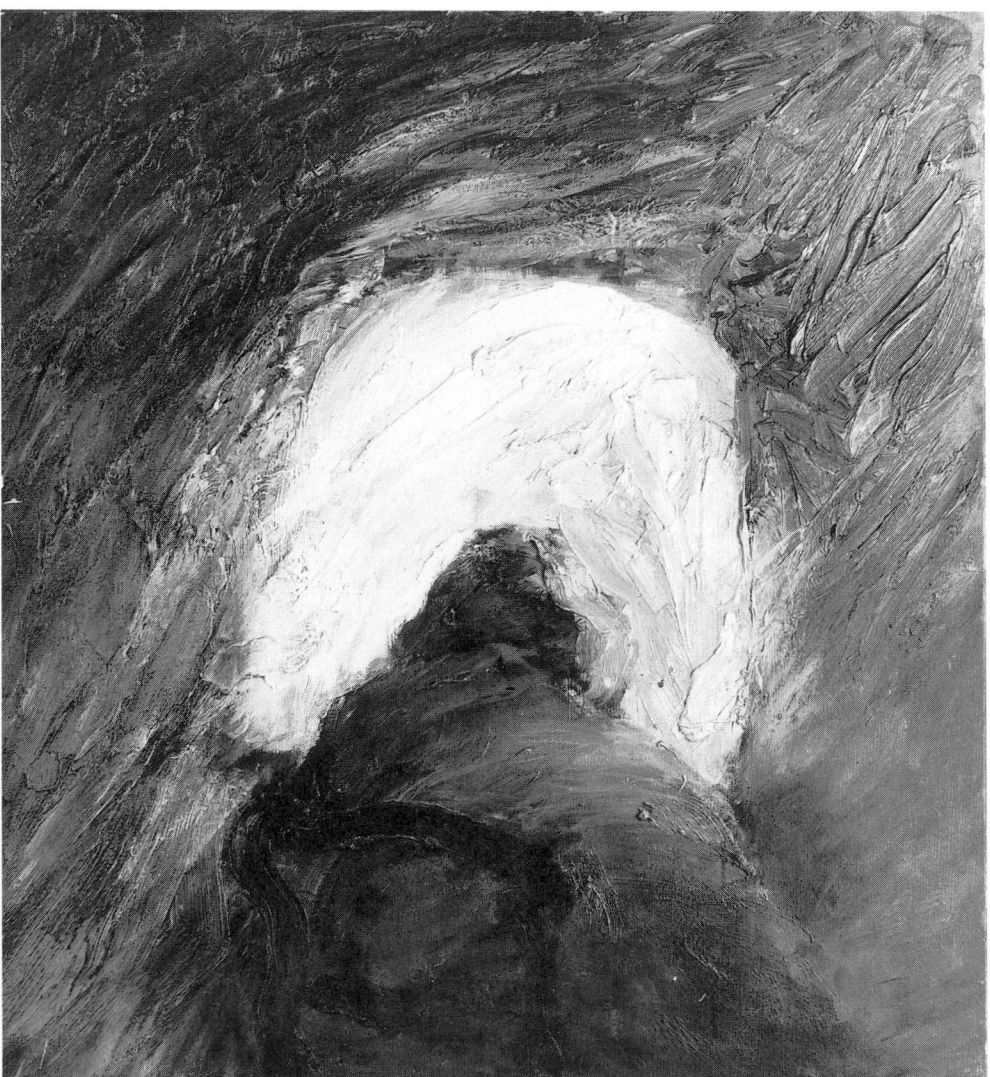

devoted limitation to a single field, in which one voluntarily renounces so-called freedom. There are examples in our own time. Take someone like Mondrian, or Brancusi!

—Evert Lundquist

Probably the most distinguished modern Swedish painter, and the best known outside his native country, Evert Lundquist had, for a while, a particular rapport with British art as a result of his meeting the painter Cliff Holden who lives in Sweden. Holden was a pupil of the important painter David Bomberg, who has decisively influenced an important area of post-war British art, including Auerbach and Kossoff, who paint in deep, heavy impasto, intimate, emotional or passionate views of their domestic circle or immediate physical surroundings. This group of artists exhibited regularly at the now defunct Beaux-Arts Gallery in London, and it was through Holden that Lundquist was introduced to this gallery and to the British art scene.

Lundquist was first influenced by a brand of realistic-impressionism, infused with a special sense of dynamic emotionalism, gradually thickening the impasto of the paint to almost relief proportions, in heightened colours. He developed more and more powerful and expressive pictorial forms. His subjects have always been landscape, still-life and figures in space, but whilst these remain the inspirational starting point, they became more and more abstracted, the outline of the forms merging into the heavy impasto, and at the same time he adopted an almost monochromatic palette, selectively and dramatically broken by well chosen reds, browns, and blue-greys.

There is something moving and heroic in Lundquist's work, a combination of anxiety, and understanding of the frailty of human flesh and human spirit, with an idealistic determination to battle through, to face life and the world with that mixture of sensitivity, pride and defiance, which, perhaps, reflects his nation's experience as a small, vulnerable community, surrounded by a sea and potential enemies.

Lundquist has exerted a considerable influence in his native country, as a result of his own achievements and stature, the dignified stance of an artist of communicable seriousness, and a teacher at the Stockholm College of Art. In the 1940's he was one of the founders of the Saltsjo Duvnas group of figurative painters, and although he soon outstripped most of his colleagues, developing a style combining stronger emotional and abstract elements than the artists of the group, he has retained his leading national position.

—Charles Spencer

LUPAS, Ana.

Rumanian. Born in Cluj, 30 August 1940. Studied at the Fine Arts Lyceum in Cluj and Bucharest, 1952–56; and at Ion Andreescu Fine Arts Institute, Cluj, 1956–62, Dip. 1962. Sculptor, performance and environmental artist, and writer, Cluj-Napoca, since 1962. Instructor, Fine Arts Lyceum, Cluj, 1967. President, Plastic Arts Union, Cluj, 1973. Recipient: Tapestry Prize, Rumanian Plastic Arts Union, 1969; Gold Medal, *International Kunsthandwerk Exhibition*, Stuttgart, 1969; Young Artist's Prize, Plastic Arts Union, Cluj, 1972; Silver Medal, *Triennale*, Milan, 1973; Honours Diploma, *Quadriennale des Kunsthandwerks*, Erfurt, Germany, 1974, 1978; Medal, *International Tapestry Triennale*, Lodz, Poland, 1975, 1981; Grand Prize, *1st Biennale of Drawing*, Lisbon, 1979; Grand Prize, *Biennale of Textiles*, Vichte, Belgium, 1982; Great Prize for Fine Arts, Rumania, 1982; Silver Prize, *1st Drawing Biennale*, Seoul, Korea, 1984. Address: Strada Pavlova 45, 3400 Cluj-Napoca, Rumania.

Individual Exhibitions:

1972 Galeria Apollo, Bucharest
National Theatre, Cluj, Rumania
1973 Galeria Wspolczesna, Warsaw
Flying Carpet Gallery, Margau, Rumania
Salon BWA, Wroclaw, Poland
Agence des Expositions Artistiques, Lublin, Poland
1974 The Coronets of August, Margau, Rumania
1982 Musée Cantonal des Beaux-Arts, Lausanne, Switzerland
1984 Espace 1, Cluj-Napoca, Rumania

Selected Group Exhibitions:

1969 *Internationales Kunsthandwerk*, Landesgewerbeamt, Stuttgart
1971 *Ekspozycja Tkaniny Artystycznej*, Galeria Zacheta, Warsaw
1972 *Rumanian Contemporary Art*, Central Museum of Art, Tokyo
1973 *Biennale de Paris*, Musée d'Art Moderne, Paris
1974 *Premi Internacional Dibuix Joan Miró*, Colegio d'Arquitectos, Barcelona
1975 *Miedzynarodowe Triennale Tkaniny*, Centralne Muzeum Wlokiennictwa, Lodz, Poland
1976 *Festival d'Anjou*, Abbaye du Ronceray, Angers, France
1979 *Biennale*, Art Gallery of New South Wales, Sydney
1982 *Rajz Drawing*, Pecs Gallery, Hungary
1984 *First International Drawing Triennale*, Fine Arts Centre, Seoul, Korea

Collections:

Council of Culture, Bucharest; Central Committee of the Rumanian Socialist Republic, Bucharest; Museum of Art, Cluj, Rumania; Babes Bolyai University, Cluj, Rumania; Museum of History, Iassy, Rumania; Museum of Contemporary Art, Galatzi, Rumania; Museum of Art, Ploiesti, Rumania; Centralne Museum Wlokiennictwa, Lodz, Poland.

Publications:

On LUPAS: books—*Pueblos, Hombres y Formas en Arte el Tapis* by Gratia Cutulli, Buenos Aires 1976; *Textile* by Keiko Fujioka and Mikiko Sakima, Tokyo 1980; *Die Kluge genossin* by Renate Windich, Freiburg 1984; articles—"Die kleine Triennale" by Anneliese Lehmann in *Heimtex* (Stuttgart), September 1969; "A Plastic Profile: Ana Lupas" by Negoita Laptoiu in *Tribuna* (Cluj, Rumania), February 1971; "Ana Lupas" by Georges Boudaille in *Les Lettres Francaises* (Paris), July 1971; "Ana Lupas" by Neaga Graur in *Contemporanul* (Bucharest), September 1972; "Ana Lupas" by Ion Frunzetti in *Romania Literara* (Bucharest), March 1972; "Ana Lupas/Warsaw" by Zbigniew Macarevicz in *Projekt* (Warsaw), no. 4, 1973; "Le Deuxième Souffle de la Biennale de Paris" by Daniel Abadie in *L'Oeil* (Paris), October 1973; "Tekstiile on Viesti" in *Omamarka* (Helsinki), no. 1, 1974; "Lodzban, a Triennalen" by Frank Ianos, in *Elet Es Irodalom* (Budapest), November 1975; "Rencontre avec Ana Lupas," by Francois Jaunin, in *Tribune du Matin* (Lausanne), January 1982.

The Meaning of my Work—Social Therapeutics

Our society—which in its course of wider removals, removals which revolutionized and revolutionize its structure, gives new dimensions to the universe of its material and spiritual values and generates changes in our mind and behaviour—henceforth needs people who integrate themselves creatively, and not in a conformist manner, in the life of society; I think that the problems which art sets, and which arise regarding its genesis, creative means, manifold consequences, finality and significance, exceed its own realm; and these problems oblige art to contribute, to shape, and to give new dimensions to the social existential universe, a universe indispensable to the individual who is to be formed and educated in order to express himself as a distinct personality, as a centre of initiative and creation.

My Task: Building-Site Worker, Hero of Thought

The artist should sink down his roots to the common source, to the general identify background. An identification with the essential facts of culture and work.

—Ana Lupas

There are very few artists in Eastern Europe who consciously take up the position of being Eastern European. Besides a few Polish and Hungarian ones, I know of only one in Moscow and two others in Kolozsvár (Cluj), Rumania. One of these two is Ana Lupas.

To be Eastern European means a certain state of mind. The borderline between East and West in European art is defined more by moral milestones than aesthetic ones. Here the artist always comes across the question of some kind of wholeness while working on any major concept, and he confronts the same question in the finished object too, with the desire to reconstruct the past and history. This is implicit in every affirmation and negation; it is always part of the work, always a principle. And we judge works from this moral point of view sometimes overemphasizing their values. We cannot imagine the personality and the thoughts of the avantgarde artist in any relation with the past, with history. We rather try to construct our own national traditions from the classic avantgarde—this is much more reassuring. We renationalize those who travelled from here to universal fame: Kandinsky, Kupka, Moholy-Nagy, Brancusi. . . . We prefer always to embrace illusions and historical paradoxes instead of the existing synthesis.

The works of Ana Lupas bear this historical consciousness too. Their means of expression reveal the signs of the 1970's, of freedom that cannot be shaped into any order: they are beyond any style. You cannot understand them without reference to the classic avantgarde and concept art; all art that wishes to exist in the present desires some heritage. But let me reiterate: the unique Eastern European touch of these works lies in the point of view from which they look at and judge history and the present scene, and it is to be found in their disposition to meet extremes.

But what exactly is this historical consciousness? Andrej Wajda puts it the following way: "To live in Eastern Europe means that for some obscure reason you find yourself trapped in historical events that happened a long long time ago but still haunt you as if you were responsible for them."

Ana Lupas is a textile artist. She makes experimental works: these pieces have in general been surfacing for the last 10 years, and although it may seem difficult to define what exactly they are, they form a very intensive and distinct entity. The prophets of the new textile—Abakanowicz and Buic—also come from Eastern Europe. And after the moveable feast of the new genre there is something more at the gates: some new, post-tactile innovations. And they will spring from the studios of artists like Ana Lupas. Post-textile textiles. Contemporary cultures could not integrate the applied, three-dimensional large textile works. There is no synthesis between the environment and autonomy. Thus we are left with sheer autonomy in this rootless process of creating objects and shaping the environment. This and the historical approach account for the fact that social responsibility and tragic possibilities are heavily marked here in Eastern Europe.

Ana Lupas is an optimist: in spite of all her social defeats and personal failures, she is still creating. She makes performances, she designs objects. (She used to teach, too: pottery, setting the sails for a very strong, new generation of artists.) Her works always emphasize the contradictions of reality. She makes a nest for the dove of peace in a time when the very word *war* too often howls above our heads. She sews a shirt in a time when our national identity is vanishing, and she draws the existential imprint of the owner on the surface of the shirt with the sewing machine. The grip is fierce: it is difficult to come to life given the conditions of our existence. She used to make children's toys tortured by other toys. Still, that was not the end. She selected some works of art, the

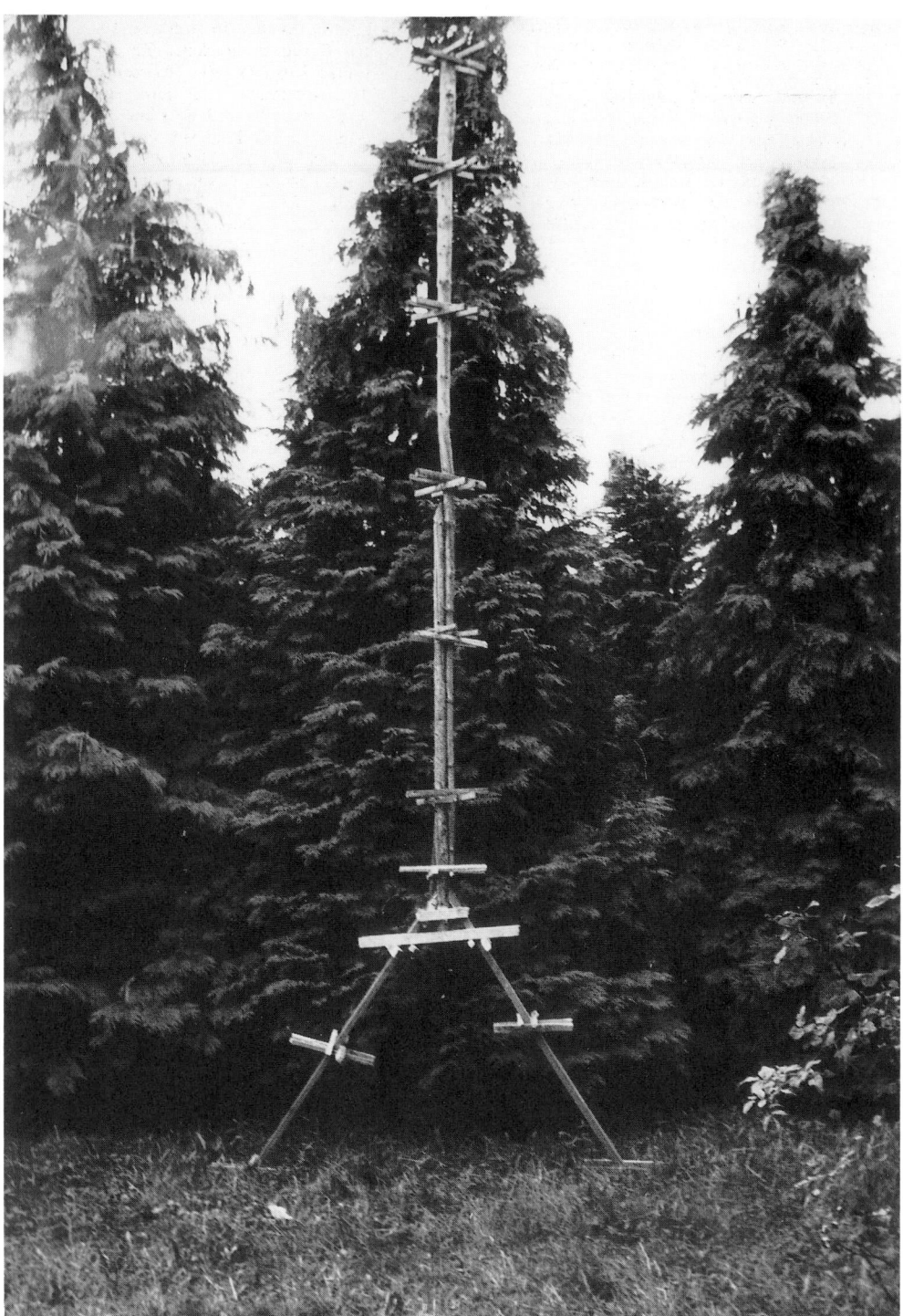

Ana Lupas: *Sculpture Installation*, 1986

documents of faith in social creativity, that proved false, and she declared them dead; she mourned them and buried them. And still that was not the end. It is still not clear enough that all good works by all good artists speak of death—of our death in Eastern Europe. Ana Lupas created her own way to the Calvary. She calls us to join her. Yet she is still an optimist.

There is a huge gobelin on the wall of her studio: tiny, soft, black patches against a piece of natural canvas. Fine work, naive, optimistic, of ten years ago. Below is the present: large bare pieces of textile, found objects of minimal aesthetics. Ana Lupas spreads a series of photos on the floor: her most important works are glued together in chronological order.

But what is the logic behind the succession of her works? The war-nest after the peace-work, the performance with wreaths of wheat after the tortured toys, the gesture pointing at the *objet trouvé* after the modulation of space, the creation of environments after the process-manipulation of time and events? Anyway, this is a truer logic than that of a sophisticated formal order. Or that of a more restrained way of thinking. Lupas is led on her way by the understanding of the present and of her personal emotions and feelings both good and evil. And she is well aware of the weight and meaning of her personal experience of history. And these experiences that have followed each other in close succession are extreme ones: the famous event when the people of a village made collective sculptures of wreaths of wheat, and hung white canvases to express a collective will of peace, and finally the tortured "Promethean-toys." The possibilities of the avantgarde approach and the way the artist understands his or her circumstances change like Brancusi's *Endless column*: they get wide, then narrow, then wide again, then narrow with the same proportions but always pointing upwards.

—Bán András

LUPERTZ, Markus.

German. Born in Liberec, Bohemia (now in Czechoslovakia), 25 April 1941. Educated in Rheydt, Rheinland, 1948–55; studied art under Laurens Goosens, Werkkunstschule, Krefeld, 1956–60; also studied at the Kunstakademie, Dusseldorf, 1960–61. Independent artist, in Krefeld, 1961, in West Berlin from 1962, and in Dusseldorf from 1986: first Dithyrambic paintings, 1962; first stage decors, 1982. Founder, Galerie Grossgorschen 35, West Berlin, 1964. Guest Instructor, 1974, and Professor from 1976, Staatliche Akademie der bildenden Kunst, Karlsruhe; Guest Professor, Summer Academy, Salzburg, 1983; Professor, Staatliche Kunstakademie, Dusseldorf, since 1986. Recipient: Villa Romana Prize, Florence, 1970; Deutscher Kritikerverband Prize, West Berlin, 1971. Agent: Galerie Michael Werner, Cologne. Address: c/o Galerie Michael Werner, Gertrudenstrasse 24–28, 5000 Cologne 1, West Germany.

Individual Exhibitions:

1964 Galerie Grossgorschen 35, West Berlin
1966 Galerie Grossgorschen 35, West Berlin
      Galerie Potsdamer, West Berlin
1968 Galerie Rudolf Springer, West Berlin
      Galerie Michael Werner, West Berlin
      Galerie Hake, Cologne
1969 Galerie Gerda Bassenger, West Berlin
      Galerie Benjamin Katz, West Berlin
      Galerie Hake, Cologne
1972 Galerie der Spiegel, Cologne
1973 Staatliche Kunsthalle, Baden-Baden, West Germany
      Galerie im Goethe-Institut/Provisorium, Amsterdam
1974 Galerie Michael Werner, Cologne
1975 Galerie Rudolf Zwirner, Cologne
      Galerie Michael Werner, Cologne
      Galerie Hans Neuendorf, Hamburg
1976 Galerie Michael Werner, Cologne
      Galerie Rudolf Zwirner, Cologne
      Galerie Seriaal, Amsterdam
1977 Kunsthalle, Hamburg
      Kunsthalle, Berne
      Van Abbemuseum, Eindhoven, Netherlands
      Galerie Hans Neuendorf, Hamburg
      Galerie Michael Werner, Cologne
1978 Galerie Heiner Friedrich, Munich
      Galerie Michael Werner, Cologne
      Galerie Helen van der Meij, Amsterdam
      Galerie Gillespie-Laage, Paris
1979 Whitechapel Art Gallery, London
      Barry Barker Gallery, London
      Josef-Haubrich-Kunsthalle, Cologne
1980 Galerie Michael Werner, Cologne
      Galerie Helen van der Meij, Amsterdam
      Galerie Rudolf Springer, West Berlin
      Galerie Heiner Friedrich, Munich
      Galerie Dr. Stober, West Berlin
1981 Galerie Rijs, Oslo
      Whitechapel Art Gallery, London
      Galerie Michael Werner, Cologne
      Galerie Rudolf Springer, West Berlin
      Marian Goodman Gallery, New York
      Waddington Galleries, London
      Galerie Fred Jahn, Munich
      Kunstverein, Freiburg, West Germany
      Galerie Dr. Stober, West Berlin
1982 Galerie Rudolf Springer, West Berlin
      Galerie Onnasch, West Berlin
      Galerie Michael Werner, Cologne
      Galerie Gillespie-Laage-Salomon, Paris
      Galerie Fred Jahn, Munich
      Marian Goodman Gallery, New York
1983 Van Abbemuseum, Eindhoven, Netherlands
      Musée d'Art Moderne, Strasbourg, France
      Galerie Thaddaeus Ropac, Salzburg, Austria
      Galerie Michael Werner, Cologne
      Waddington Galleries, London
      Galerie Maeght, Zurich
      DAAD-Galerie, West Berlin
      Galerie im Kornerpark, Neukolln-West Berlin
      Kestner-Gesellschaft, Hannover

Galerie Winter, Vienna
Marian Goodman Gallery, New York
Galerie Rudolf Springer, West Berlin
1984   Waddington Galleries, London
Galerie Gillespie-Laage-Salomon, Paris
Galerie Michael Werner, Cologne
Galerie Maeght-Lelong, Zurich
Galerie Fred Jahn, Munich
Galerie Winter, Vienna
Wiener Sezession, Vienna
Galerie Thaddeus Ropac, Salzburg, Austria
Mary Boone/Michael Werner Gallery, New York
Galerie Ascan Crone, Hamburg
Maximilianverlag Sabine Knust, Munich
1985   Galerie Ulysses, Vienna
Galerie Michael Werner, Cologne (twice)
Galerie Herbert Meyer-Ellinger, Frankfurt
Galerie Fred Jahn, Munich
Galerie Beaumont, Luxembourg
1986   Stadtische Galerie im Lenbachhaus, Munich
Kunstlerhaus, Salzburg, Austria
Galerie Thaddaeus Ropac, Salzburg, Austria
Galerie Sabine Knust, Munich
Galerie Gillespie-Laage-Salomon, Paris
Galerie Maeght Lelong, Paris
Galerie Reinhard Onnasch, West Berlin
Galerie Folker Skulima, West Berlin
Neuer Berliner Kunstverein, West Berlin
Galerie Rudolf Springer, West Berlin
Galerie Michael Werner, Cologne
Galerie Maeght Lelong, Zurich
Waddington Galleries, London
Mary Boone/Michael Werner Gallery, New York
1987   Museum Boymans-van Beuningen, Rotterdam
Galerie Michael Werner, Cologne
Kunstverein, Braunschweig, West Germany
Galerie Beaumont, Luxembourg
1988   Cleto Polcina Artemoderna, Rome

Selected Group Exhibitions:

1969   *Eskalation: 14 mal 14*, Kunsthalle, Baden-Baden, West Germany
1972   *The Berlin Scene*, Gallery House, London (travelled to Hamburg)
1974   *Erste Biennale der Kunst*, West Berlin
1976   *Zeichnungen-Tekeningen*, Galerie Seriaal, Amsterdam
1978   *Eleven Artists Workin in Berlin*, Whitechapel Art Gallery, London
1980   *Apres le classicisme*, Musée d'Art et d'Industrie, St. Etienne, France
1982   *Documenta 7*, Museum Fridericianum, Kassel, West Germany
1984   *Expressions: New Art from Germany*, Museum of Contemporary Art, Chicago
1986   *Raumbilder in Bronze*, Kunsthalle, Bielefeld, West Germany
1987   *Berlinart 1961-87*, Museum of Modern Art, New York (travelled to San Francisco)

Collections:

Nationalgalerie, West Berlin; Berlinische Galerie, West Berlin; Staatsgalerie moderner Kunst, Munich; Stadtische Museum im Lenbachhaus, Munich; Stadtisches Museum, Monchengladbach; Museum Ludwig, Cologne; Kunsthalle, Hamburg; Stadelsches Kunstinistitut, Frankfurt; Van Abbemuseum, Eindhoven; Museum Boymans-van Beuningen, Rotterdam; Australian National Gallery, Canberra.

Publications:

By LUPERTZ: books—*9 Gedichte, Zeichnungen*, West Berlin 1975; *Markus—Vogue*, Munich 1984; *Tagebuch New York 1984*, Berne and West Berlin 1984; *Bleiben Sie sitzen Heinrich Heine*, Vienna 1984.

On LUPERTZ: books—*Markus Lupertz: Kunst, die im Wege staht, Dithyrambisches Manifest*, exhibition catalogue, West Berlin 1966; *Markus Lupertz: Fasunenstr. 13*, exhibition catalogue with text by Christos Joachimides, West Berlin 1968; *Markus Lupertz: Bilder, Gouachen und Zeichnungen 1967-*

1973, exhibition catalogue with texts by Klaus Gallwitz and George Tabori, Baden-Baden 1973; *Markus Lupertz: Dithyrambische und Stil Malerie*, exhibition catalogue with texts by Johannes Gachnang and Theo Kneubuhler, Berne 1977; *Markus Lupertz: Stil Painting 1977-79*, exhibition catalogue with text by Siegfried Gohr, London 1969; *Markus Lupertz: Bilder 1970-83*, exhibition catalogue with texts by Carl Haenlein, Reiner Speck and others, Hannover 1983; *Markus Lupertz: Skulpturen 1981-86*, exhibition catalogue with texts by Lucie Schauer, Siegfried Gohr and others, West Berlin 1986; *Markus Lupertz: Arbeiten auf Papier, Bilder und Skulpturen*, exhibition catalogue with texts by Wilhelm Bojescul, Andreas Franzke and Remo Guidieri, Braunschweig 1987.

*   *   *

In the second half of the 1970s, Markus Lupertz's painting was already showing its dramatic dimension, particularly in the assemblage of form and space—as in *Interior III* (1974) and *Lupolis: Dithyrambic* (1975). The surface is thick with matter, and the forms seem 'imprisoned' in the very act of appearing or disappearing. A material abstraction where the surface appears in a spatial instability, almost surreal.

A forerunner of the German transvantgarde together with Baselitz, Immendorff, Penck and Kirkeby, Lupertz emerged as the most symbolic of all. His abstraction in the first place and his figuration in the second come from the dark depth of the unconscious, unleashing a kind of visionary ambiguity. In Lupertz's work, matter is constantly convulsed by striking, vivid colours and sharp, cutting marks. His symbolic expressionism, though, is also crosscut by ancestral energies forming a peculiar 'stylistic eclecticism' (Achille Bonito Oliva). The strangest forms are condensed, as in *Big Spoon* (1982), in which a diagonally placed spoon prevails upon the whole surface of the picture.

The language of painting, in order to be vital, has to deviate to measure itself against contradictory statements, as in Penck's primitive signs, in Immendorff's matter, in Baselitz's figurations, where the gestural action breaks into the surface in a 'narrative' guise, conquering spatiality. Lupertz seeks in art an edifying collision: he captures an oneiric vision, always stylistically different. Through this difference he mobilizes his 'gestural force', conquering the surface while his penetrating gaze leaves nothing untouched. The surface is the locus in which manifestations of the picture become the urgency of artistic language.

In this Lupertz is categorical: only matter in the very act of its making guarantees the mobility of the gesture, as much as of the artist's vision. The dramatic mobility which he deeply engraves into the surface strengthens the emotion.

Paraphrasing Gertrude Stein, one could say that in Lupertz's painting everything is destroyed and nothing really continues. For this reason it has a dramatic splendour of its own. The gesture, in its competitive and contingent urgency, takes hold of everything, making reality appear as kaleidoscopic, impossible to grasp, and so losing any referential human measure.

Therefore, in Lupertz's works—especially those of the 1980s—the inside and the outside are amalgamated (as in *Brooklyn*), a whole in which the visual plane is impenetrable. In works where monumental figuration prevails, this impenetrability is complete; the mark appears as if fragmenting the figure, almost always totally unrecognizable.

Lupertz is a painter of events. In his work everything must have a pictorial significance which can be found in the space of life. His 'expressionism' is humane. It is humane inasmuch as it loves painting as it appears to the painter's own gaze which enters inside the surface, modifying things and images. An 'essential solitude' prompts the artist to stand outside himself, to make contact with everyday, unforeseen events. Through his engagement with the exterior world, Lupertz violates the unknown, uncovers reality, abbreviates endless visual distances, to favour a kind of strategic osmosis. This advantage of penetration and gesture, which arrests the abstract/figurative instant, is apparent in Lupertz's most recent work.

—Italo Mussa

LÜTHI, Urs.
Swiss. Born in Lucerne, 10 September 1947. Studied art at the Kunstgewerbeschule, Zurich, 1963–64. Married Elke Kilga in 1974. Independent painter, 1965–69, performance and photographic artist, 1969–80, painter since 1980: lives in Zurich and Munich. Agents: Galerie Kaufman, Quellenstrasse 27, Zurich; Galerie Stadler, 51 Rue de Seine, 75006 Paris; Galerie Ernesto, Neusserstrasse 27, Cologne. Addresses: c/o Kaufmann, Kanzleistrass 105, 8004 Zurich, Switzerland; Wendl-Dietrichstrasse 17, 8000 Munich 19, West Germany.

Individual Exhibitions:

1966   Galerie Beat Mader, Berne
Galerie Palette, Zurich
1969   Galerie Junge Generation, Hamburg
Kabinett für Aktuelle Kunst, Bremerhaven, West Germany
Kunstverein, Bremen, West Germany
Galerie Palette, Zurich
1970   Galerie Toni Gerber, Berne
1972   Galleria Diagramma, Milan
Galerie Palette, Zurich
Galleria La Bertesca, Genoa
1973   Galerie Krinzinger, Innsbruck
Galerie Nachst St. Stephan, Vienna
Galleria Diagramma, Milan
Galleria Conz, Venice
1974   Studio Morra, Naples
Galerie Stadler, Paris
Galerie Stahli, Lucerne
Studio Marconi, Milan
Galleria Schema, Florence
1975   Galerie Stahli, Zurich
Galleria Diagramma, Milan
Studio Morra, Naples
Galerie De Appel, Amsterdam
Galerie Stadler, Paris
Galerie Stadler, at *Art '75*, Basle
Galerie Palette, Zurich
Modern Art Agency, Naples
Neue Galerie am Landesmuseum Joanneum, Graz, Austria
Musée d'Art et d'Histoire, Geneva
1976   Kunsthalle, Basle
Nishima Gallery, Tokyo
Galerie Gaetan, Geneva
Galerie Stahli, Zurich
Galerie Isy Brachot, Brussels
1977   Galerie Stadler, Paris
Galerie Krinzinger, Innsbruck
1978   Studio d'Arte Cannaviello, Milan
Museum Folkwang, Essen
Galerie Zellermayer, West Berlin
Galerie Stadler, Paris
1979   Galerie Stahli, Zurich
Galerie Isy Brachot, Brussels
Kunstmuseum, Aarau, Switzerland
Studio d'Arte Cannaviello, Milan
Galerie AK, Frankfurt
Galerie Gugu Ernesto, Cologne
1980   Galerie Krebs, Berne
Neue Galerie am Landesmuseum Joanneum, Graz, Austria
1981   *Bilder 1977-1980*, Kunstmuseum, Berne
1982   Studio d'Arte Cannaviello, Milan
Galerie Stahli, Zurich
Galerie Gugu Ernesto, Cologne
Galerie Nachst St. Stephan, Vienna
Galerie Krinzinger, Innsbruck
Kunstverein, St. Gallen, Switzerland
Galerie Buchmann, St. Gallen, Switzerland
1982   Kunstverein, Frankfurt
Galerie AK, Frankfurt
Studio d'Arte Cannaviello, Milan
Galerie Gugu Ernesto, Cologne
Kunstmuseum, Olten, Switzerland
1983   Galerie Anton Meier, Geneva
Kulturhaus Palazzo, Liestal, Switzerland
Wolfgang Gurlitt Museum, Linz, Austria

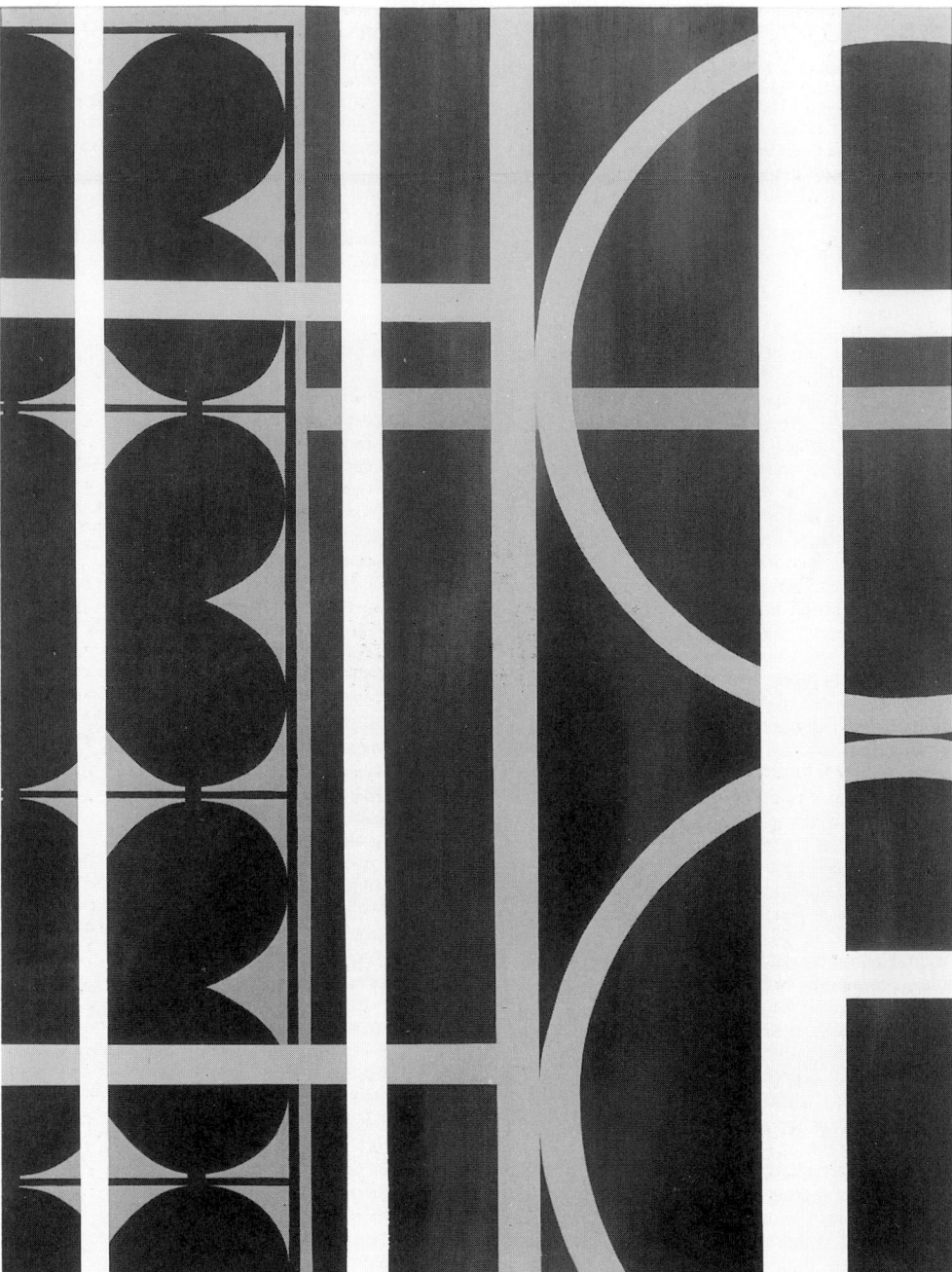

Urs Lüthi: *Selbstporträt aus der Serie der vertauschten Traume*, 1985

Wilhelm-Hack-Museum, Ludwigshafen, West Germany
Studio d'Arte Cannaviello, Milan
Galerie Gugu Ernesto, Cologne
1984 Galerie Stahli, Zurich
Abbaye de Fontevraud, Loire, France
Maison des Arts de Genas, France
1985 Maison de la Culture, St. Etienne, France
Galerie Stadler, Paris
Galerie Klein, Bonn
Galerie Gugu Ernesto, Cologne
1986 Kunstmuseum, Winterthur, Switzerland
Galerie Hubert Winter, Vienna
1987 Galerie Stadler, Paris
Galerie Gugu Ernesto, Cologne
Kunstverein, Munich
Galerie Elisabeth Kaufman, Zurich
Gesellschaft für Aktuelle Kunst, Bremen, West Germany

Selected Group Exhibitions:

1966 *Zurcher Kunstler*, Helmhaus, Zurich
1970 *Visualisierte Denkprozesse*, Kunstmuseum, Lucerne, Switzerland

1971 *Swiss Avantgarde*, Cultural Center, New York
1974 *Transformer*, Kunstmuseum, Lucerne, Switzerland
1976 *Identite, Identification*, Centre d'Art Plastique Contemporain, Bordeaux
1977 *Documenta 6*, Museum Fridericianum, Kassel, West Germany
1979 *Biennale of Sydney*, New South Wales, Australia
1981 *Autoportraits*, Centre Georges Pompidou, Paris
1983 *Kunst mit Fotografie*, Nationalgalerie, West Berlin
1984 *Ecritures dans la peinture*, Centre National des Arts Plastiques, Nice, France

Collections:

Kunsthaus, Zurich; Kunstmuseum, Winterthur; Kunstmuseum, Lucerne.

Publications:

By LÜTHI: books—*Just Another Story About Leaving*, Paris 1974; *The Personal Dissolves So Easily In The Typical*, exhibition catalogue, Innsbruck 1977; article—"Image as Emotion", interview with Effie Stephano, in *Art and Artists* (London), August 1974.

On LÜTHI: books—*Realismus* by Peter Sager, Cologne 1972; *Body Language* by Peter Gorsen, Graz 1973; *Transformer: Aspekte der Travestie*, exhibition catalogue with texts by Jean-Christophe Ammann and Peter Gorsen, Lucerne 1974; *Il Corpo Come Linguaggio* by Lea Vergine, Milan 1974; *Bodyworks*, exhibition catalogue by Ira Licht, Chicago 1975; *Some Day When My Longing Is Gone, I'm Gonna Take A Smile For A Walk In The Sun*, exhibition catalogue with texts by Wilfried Skreiner and Jean-Christophe Ammann, Graz 1975; *Urs Lüthi*, exhibition catalogue with texts by Jean-Christophe Ammann, Wilfried Skreiner, Maria Netter and Carlo Huber, Basle 1976; *Urs Lüthi*, exhibition catalogue with text by Zdenek Felix, Essen 1978; *Urs Lüthi: Bilder 1977–1980*, exhibition catalogue by Wilfried Skreiner, Rolf Winnewisser, Martin Disler and others, Graz 1980; *Ecritures dans la peinture*, exhibition catalogue by Francois Pluchart, Nice 1984; *Urs Lüthi: Sehn-Sucht*, exhibition catalogue with texts by Rudolf Koella and Annelie Pohlen, Winterthur 1986.

The theme of the self-portrait runs like a red ribbon through the work of the Swiss artist Urs Lüthi. The self-portrait in all its colourful variations accompanies him along the road to an unknown inner world, but also serves him as the expression of artistic egocentricity. This artistic self-centredness finally betrays his affinity with Picabia, whose spirit gently hovers over Lüthi's most recent pictures with their shifting chameleon-like quality.

An exhibition of his insignia and photo-portraits at the Museum of Art in Lucerne in 1970 first brought Lüthi before a wider audience. As a relentless self-portraitist he was already fascinated at that time by the myth of individual personality. To render in visual terms every facet of personal reality subsequently became his central creative aim. In order to emphasise their many-sidedness, he staged his photographic self-portraits in a varied sequence of inner landscapes which evoked changing moods and psychic aspects. And in the double pictures a tension between self-portrait and environment was effectively created.

Although he gained international recognition through Jean-Christophe Ammann's *Transformer* exhibition in Lucerne in 1974, Lüthi was not content merely to produce transformer works. He was more concerned in his relentless photo-series, to investigate the conceptual isolation of modern man and the contradictions inherent in individual personality; he even went so far as to set out in picture form his own physical death. At the beginning of the eighties he switched from photography to painting in the hope of capturing and projecting new aspects of his self-portrait. In these latest works he was aiming less at illustrating external features than at transposing onto canvas intangible factors such as feelings, desires and fears.

Urs Lüthi risked—successfully, it seems—the difficult switch to a second career: that of painting. In order to satisfy his obsession with his own mirror image, he began in 1984 a large, complex series whose allure lies in its mannered style, its fresh wit and irony—qualities generally seldom seen in Swiss artists. In these works he tries repeatedly to fathom his own 'I', demonstrating in the process his prolific creativity. His large exhibition at the Museum of Art in Winterthur in 1986 alone showed fifty new paintings in ten series, including large-format diptychs and triptychs. Each series revolved round a theme of self-portraiture from *Vague Memories* through *Dreams* and *Adventures* to *Pure Delivery*.

Lüthi transposes his multiple meanings and contradictions on to the canvas in a dry, only barely painterly manner. This brittle and in a certain sense analytical art links his paintings with his erstwhile photo-series. He manages to preserve his artistic anonymity and non-commitment by constantly changing his techniques and introducing references to recent art history. Out of a variety of influences—Cubism, Constructivism, Surrealism, Automatism and Abstract Expressionism—he constructs a personal, frequently strange and alienating amalgam. His *Self-Portraits from the Intense Feelings Series*, in which Eros triumphs, are reminiscent of Picabia, David Salle and Donald Baechler equally, *Vague Memories* are reminiscent of Gerhard Richter, and *Heads* of Sigmar Polke. A hint of Léger and Mondrian breathes through *Mistaken Dreams,* and Picabia's Constructivism of the late forties is mirrored in *Dream Pairs.*

The many-layeredness of Lüthi's paintings also recalls Picabia. Abstract blocks of colour are superimposed with several constructive layers; figurative representations are built up with abstract symbols; images are distanced and called into question by counter-images. Thus, out of an undefined area of colour the torso of a naked woman emerges, over which the outlines of a pin-up model and, painted with a thick brush, a sexually aroused matchstick man appear. Aesthetics are suggested, then immediately negated, trivialised with kitsch and the mundaneness of the day-to-day.

Lüthi's puzzle pictures are like a bottomless pit in which the eye can find no area to fix upon. The complex superimposition of ideas and planes, of drawing and painting, construction and free form runs through the whole of this latest work. From such perspectives the most disparate works are reconciled, and an area of sea, which at first sight produces a confusing effect, becomes intelligible. In this sea-landscape the various planes of colour, overtopped by a network of clouds and white foam, serve the ends of a pseudo-naturalism which at bottom is as abstract as any bare constructive painting. The single work has something banal about it; only in the context of the series as a whole does it gain its deeper meaning. And so, ultimately, Lüthi's self-portraits are the portrait in outline of the aspirations of our time.

—Roman Hollenstein

LYE, Len.

American. Born in Christchurch, New Zealand, 5 July 1901; emigrated to the United States, 1944; subsequently naturalized. Educated at H. Linley Richardson's evening classes, Wellington Technical Institute, 1915; studied briefly at Canterbury Art College, under Archibald Nicoll, 1919. Married. Worked as commercial artist for *Christchurch Sun,* 1919; moved to Australia and lived in Sydney, 1921–22; lived in Samoan Islands, 1923–24; returned to Sydney, 1924; produced first Kinetic Constructions, Samoa, 1923; worked as laborer in Australian outback, 1925; worked as stoker for passage to London, 1926; lived on barge on Thames River, London, 1927; guest exhibitor with 7 x 5 Society, London, 1927 and member from 1928; produced first film, *Tusalava,* 1928; worked with Eisenstein and Hans Richter, London Film Society Workshop, 1929; designed book covers for Seizen and Hours Press, for Robert Graves and Laura Riding, 1930–31; worked on numerous films, particularly for the General Post Office Film Unit and Ministry of Information, London, 1935; contributed to *London Bulletin,* 1940; settled in the United States, 1944; Director, *March of Time* news films, London, 1944–51; worked on experimental films using shadowgraph techniques; turned to kinetic sculpture, due to lack of funds for experimental films, 1958; visited New Zealand, 1968–69, 1977. President of Jury, *International Animation Festival,* Annecy, France, 1975. Established the Len Lye Foundation, 1980. Lecturer on Filmmaking, New York University, 1966; Visiting Lecturer, University of California, Berkeley, *2nd Buffalo Festival of the Arts Today,* Buffalo, New York, University of Edinburgh, and *Cambridge Animation Festival,* England, 1968. Recipient: Special Award, *Brussels International Film Festival,* 1935; New York Screen Directors' Guild Prize, 1953; Second Prize, Brussels World's Fair International Film Competition, 1958. *Died (in Warwick, New York) 15 May 1980.*

Individual Exhibitions:

1961   *Tangible Motion Sculpture,* Museum of Modern Art, New York
1965   Howard Wise Gallery, New York
        Contemporary Art Center, Cincinnati, Ohio
1977   Govett-Brewster Art Gallery, New Plymouth, New Zealand
1979   National Art Gallery, Wellington, New Zealand
1980   *A Personal Mythology,* Auckland City Art Gallery, New Zealand

Selected Group Exhibitions:

1936   *International Surrealist Exhibition,* New Burlington Galleries, London
1961   *International Kinetic Art Exhibition,* Stedelijk Museum, Amsterdam
        Festival of the Avant-Garde, Judson Hall, New York
1966   *Directions in Kinetic Sculpture,* University of California Art Museum, Berkeley
        68th American Exhibition, Art Institute of Chicago

1967   *American Sculpture of the 60's,* Los Angeles County Museum of Art
1976   *200 Years of American Sculpture,* Whitney Museum, New York
1978   *Dada and Surrealist Reviewed,* Hayward Gallery, London

Collections:

Museum of Modern Art, New York; Len Lye Foundation, Art Gallery of New South Wales, Sydney.

Publications:

By LYE: book—*No Trouble,* Deya, Majorca 1930; articles—"Voice and Color" in *Life and Letters Today* (London), Spring 1936; "Notes on a Short Colour Film" in *Life and Letters Today* (London), Winter 1936; "Film-making," with Laura Riding, in *Epilogue* (London), no. 1, 1938; "Song Time Stuff" in *Life and Letters Today* (London), Spring 1938; "Song Time Stuff, continued," in *Life and Letters Today* (London), Summer 1938; "Television—News Axes to Grind" in *Sight and Sound* (London), Summer 1939; "Knife Apple Sheer Brush" in *Tigers Eye* (New York), March 1948; "Tangible Motion Sculpture" in *Art Journal* (New York), Summer 1961; "When the Venutions sing 'Auld Lang Syne'" in *Film Book 2* by Robert Hughes, (New York), 1962; "Is Film Art?" in *Film Culture* (New York), Summer 1963; "Interview with Len Lye," with Gretchen Weinberg, in *Film Culture* (New York), Summer 1963; "Len Lye Speaks at the Film-maker's Cinematheque" in *Film Culture* (New York), Spring 1967; "The Tusalava Model" in *Experimental Animation* by Robert Russett and Cecile Starr, New York 1976; "Ray Thorburn Interviews Len Lye" in *Art International* (Lugano, Switzerland), April 1975; films—*Colour Box,* 1935; *Trade Tattoo,* 1937; *Musical Post, no. 1,* 1940; *Color Cry,* 1952; *Free Radicals,* 1958.

On LYE: books—*Directions in Kinetic Sculpture* by Peter Selz, Berkeley, Calfornia 1966; *Origins and Development of Kinetic Art* by Frank Popper, London 1968; *Icons and Images of the 60's* by Nicolas and Elena Calas, New York 1971; *Visionary Film* by P. Adams Sidney, New York 1974; *Published in Paris* by Hugh Ford, New York 1975; *Passages in Modern Sculpture* by Rosalind Krauss, London 1977; *Under the Influence: Recollections of Robert Graves, Laura Riding and Friends* by T. S. Matthews, London 1979; *Len Lye: A Personal Mythology,* exhibition catalogue, by Andrew Bogle and others, Auckland 1980; articles—"The Visionary Art of Len Lye" by Patricia Dandignae in *Craft Horizons,* May-June 1961; "The Artist as Film-maker: Len Lye" by Adrienne Mancia and Willard van Dyke in *Art in America* (New York), July-August 1966; "Len Lye in New Zealand" by Michael Dunn in *Art in Australia* (Sydney), March 1979.

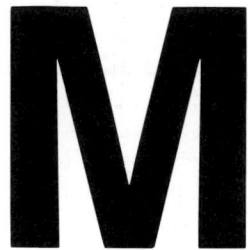

MACIUNAS, George.

American. Born in Lithuania in 1931. Studied architecture, musicology and art history. Worked for the United States Army on graphics and architecture, Wiesbaden, West Germany, 1960. Lived in New York, subsequently in Massachusetts. Inspirer of Fluxus—a name he gave to a series of multiples and other constructions produced from around 1962; also organized music groups of young Americans, using original instruments: arranged festivals in Wiesbaden and other European cities. *Died in 1978.*

Individual Exhibitions:

Numerous Fluxus Group exhibitions, including Kunstverein, Cologne, 1971; Palais des Beaux-Arts, Brussels, 1980; Cranbrook Academy of Art, Bloomfield Hills, Michigan.

Publications:

By MACIUNAS: article—"Tenthfluxleadanniversary-contents" in special issue of *Arts and Artists* (London), October 1972.

On MACIUNAS: book—*Happening und Fluxus* by Harald Szeemann and Hans Sohm, Cologne 1970; *Fluxus,* exhibition catalogue, by Jon Hendricks, Bloomfield Hills, Michigan 1981; articles—special issue of *Art and Artists* (London), October 1972; "Fluxus" by David Mayor in *Spanner* (London), May 1975; "George Maciunas" by Pierre Restany in *Domus* (Milan), January 1979; "George Maciunas" by Barbara Moore in *Artforum* (New York), October 1982.

GEORGE MACIUNAS left Lithuania (born there 1931)/moved to New York/wrote a manifesto* (or maybe Robert Watts did)

GEORGE MACIUNAS studied architecture/studied musicology/studied art history/met Dick Higgins Robert Watts Yoko Ono Alison Knowles George Brecht/and helped found Fluxus

GEORGE MACIUNAS became a coordinator/organized events/supported intermedia/designed *An Anthology*/and kept a low profile

GEORGE MACIUNAS published Flux kits, objects, multiples, games/created performances**/drew an Expanded Arts Diagram/nailed down each key of an entire keyboard starting with the lowest note and ending with the highest note/and maintained a Flux Center in New York

GEORGE MACIUNAS lived in Soho/supported co-operative housing for artists/expanded and contracted Fluxus

GEORGE MACIUNAS moved to Massachusetts (died there 1978)/left behind legends, unfinished battles, unresolved relationships, plans for the future/left behind a Fluxist saying "Whenever we get to wherever we're going, George will have the program organized for us."

*Manifesto

flux . . .

PURGE the world of bourgeois sickness, "intellectual,"
professional & commercialized culture, PURGE the world
of dead art, imitation, artificial art, abstract art, illusionistic art, mathematical art,—
PURGE THE WORLD OF "EUROPANISM"!

PROMOTE A REVOLUTIONARY FLOOD AND TIDE IN ART,
promote living art, anti-art, promote NON-ART REALITY to be
grasped by all peoples, not only critics, dilettantes and professionals,
FUSE the cadres of cultural, social & political revolutionaries into united front and action.

**A Performance

Homage to La Monte Young, by George Maciunas, Jan. 12, 1962 (preferably to follow performance of any composition of 1961 by L M Y.)

Erase, scrape or wash away as well as possible the previously drawn line or lines of La Monte Young of any other lines encountered, like street dividing lines, ruled paper or score lines, lines on sports fields, lines on gaming tables, lines drawn by children on sidewalks etc.

—Mary Stofflet

MACK, Heinz.

German. Born in Lollar, 8 March 1931. Studied art at the Staatliche Kunstakademie, Dusseldorf, 1950–53, and philosophy at the University of Cologne 1953–56, M.A. 1956. Married Michi Michaelis in 1973; daughters: Simone and Bettina. Independent artist, in Dusseldorf, from 1950, subsequently in Mönchengladbach: Founder, with Otto Piene, "Zero" movement, Dusseldorf, 1957; first light-works, 1958; first light pillar, 1961. Professor, Akademie der Künste, West Berlin, 1969. Editor, *MacKazin,* Dusseldorf, 1957–67, and, with Otto Piene, *Zero,* Dusseldorf, 1958–61. Recipient: City Art Prize, Krefeld, 1958; Premio Marzotto, 1963; Painting Prize, *Biennale de Paris,* 1965; Adolf-Grimme-Preis, 1970. Member, Akademie der Künste, West Berlin, 1968. Agents: Galerie Denise René, 196 Boulevard Saint-Germain, 75006 Paris, France; Galerie Alfred Schmela, Mutter-Ey-Strasse 3, 4000 Dusseldorf, West Germany; Galerie Semiha Huber, Talstrasse 18, 8001 Zurich, Switzerland; Galleria E, Ferruccio Fata, Bolzano, Italy. Address: Veddingerstrasse 232, Huppertzhof, 4050 Mönchengladbach, West Germany.

Individual Exhibitions:

1957	Galerie Alfred Schmela, Dusseldorf
1958	Galerie Alfred Schmela, Dusseldorf
1959	Galerie Iris Clert, Paris
	Galerie Behr, Stuttgart
	Galerie Dr. Griesebach, Heidelberg
1960	Galleria Azimut, Milan
	New Vision Centre, London
	Galerie Alfred Schmela, Dusseldorf
	Galerie Diogenes, West Berlin
	Studio F, Ulm, West Germany
1961	Galerie Nota, Munich
	Galerie Ad Libitum, Antwerp
	Galerie Dato, Frankfurt
	Galerie Stephan, Vienna
1963	Galleria Cadario, Milan
	Galerie Ad Libitum, Antwerp
1964	Galerie D, Frankfurt
	Galleria La Polena, Genoa
	Galleria Il Bilico, Rome
	Museum Haus Lange, Krefeld, West Germany
1965	Galleria L'Elefante, Venice
	Galerie Alfred Schmela, Dusseldorf
	McRoberts and Tunnard Gallery, London
	Kestner-Gesellschaft, Hannover
1966	Howard Wise Gallery, New York
1967	Op-Art Galerie, Esslingen, West Germany
	Galerie Rotloff, Karlsruhe
	Galerie Denise René, Paris
1968	Galleria dell'Ariete, Milan
	Galerie Handschin, Basle
	Gallerie Notizie, Turin
	Galerie Heseler, Munich
	Kunstlerhaus Halfmannshof, Gelsenkirchen, West Germany
1969	Galerie Ursula Lichter, Frankfurt
	Galerie Reckermann, Cologne
1971	Museum Folkwang, Essen
	Zacheta Museum, Warsaw
	Galerie Krinzinger, Bregenz, Austria
	Galerie Langer, Braunschweig, West Germany
	Galerie Reckermann, Cologne
	Galerie Jesse, Bielefeld, West Germany
	Kunstverein, Mannheim
	Galerie Dröscher, Hamburg
	Galerie Müller, Stuttgart
	Galerie Ursula Lichter, Frankfurt
1972	Galerie Denise René/Hans Mayer, Dusseldorf
	Modern Art Galerie, West Berlin
	Galerie Argelander, Bonn
	Akademie der Künste, West Berlin
	Städtische Kunsthalle, Dusseldorf
1973	Musée d'Art Moderne de la Ville, Paris
	Galerie Denise René, Paris
	Denise René Gallery, New York
	Galerie Lohri, Schiefbahn, West Germany
	Stedelijk Van Abbemuseum, Eindhoven, Netherlands
	Galerie Stoll, Cologne
1974	Bottcherstrasse, Bremen, West Germany
	Städtisches Museum, Mönchengladbach, West Germany
	Städtisches Museum, Dusseldorf
	Galleria E, Bolzano, Italy
	Galleria della Trinita, Rome

Galerie Reckermann, Cologne
Junior-Galerie, Hannover (toured Germany, Netherlands, Denmark and Switzerland)
1975 *Arbeiten aus den Jahren 1955-1975*, Galerie Denise René/Hans Mayer, Dusseldorf
Städtisches Museum, Mulheim/Ruhr, West Germany
Markisches Museum, Witten, West Germany
Nordjyllands Kunstmuseum, Aalborg, Denmark
Galerie Keller, Starnberg, West Germany
Städtisches Museum, Ravensburg, West Germany
Städtisches Palais, Linz, Austria
1976 Galerie Christa Bocker, Moens, Belgium
Galleria E, at *Arte Fiera*, Bologna
Kunstverein, Oldenburg, West Germany
Galerie Denise René/Hans Mayer, Dusseldorf (with Gunther Uecker)
1977 Junior-Galerie, Goslar, West Germany
Junior-Galerie, Dusseldorf
Galerie Brockstedt, Hamburg
Galerie St. Johann, Saarbrucken
Westdeutscher Landesbank, Münster, West Germany
Kunsthalle, Hamburg
Stadtmuseum, Munich
Städtisches Kunsthalle, Dusseldorf
Galerie Photo-Selection, Dusseldorf
Galerie Schoeller, Dusseldorf
Galerie Klaus Lincke, Dusseldorf
Kunstkabinett Dr. Griesebach-Grewenig, Heidelberg
Kunsthalle, Darmstadt
1978 Junior-Galerie, Hannover
Nikon Galerie, Zurich
Galerie Bossin, West Berlin
Kunstverein, Detmold, West Germany
Städtisches Museum, Mönchengladbach, West Germany
Rizzoli Gallery, New York
Amstutz Fine Art, Zurich
Unac Gallery, Tokyo
1979 Schlosspark, Stuttgart
1980 Kleine Grafik-Galerie, Bremen, West Germany
Galerie A, Munich
1981 Galerie Lauter, Mannheim, West Germany
Galerie Loehrl, Monchengladbach, West Germany
Galerie Reckermann, Cologne
Galerie Holtmann, Cologne
1982 Galerie Dibbert, West Berlin
Galerie Holtmann, Hannover
1983 Galerie der Deutschen Bank, Bielefeld, West Germany
Galerie der Deutschen Bank, Dusseldorf
Galerie der Deutschen Bank, Freiburg, West Germany
Galerie der Deutschen Bank, Hamburg
Galerie der Deutschen Bank, Cologne
Galerie Loehrl, Monchengladbach, West Germany
Galerie der Deutschen Bank, Wiesbaden, West Germany
1984 Skulpturenpark, Dusseldorf
Galerie Heseler, Munich
Deutsche Bank, Tokyo
1985 Galerie Denise René/Hans Mayer, Dusseldorf
Galerie Lauter, Mannheim, West Germany
Galerie Wack, Kaiserslautern, West Germany
Verein Deutscher Ingenieure, Dusseldorf
Galerie Babel, Heilbronn, West Germany
1986 Galerie Bossin, West Berlin
Galerie Hoffmeister West, Ludenscheid, West Germany
Galerie Schoeller, Dusseldorf
Kunsthaus Schaller, Stuttgart
Galerie Wahlandt, Stuttgart
Galerie Loehrl, Monchengladbach, West Germany
1987 Galerie Holtmann, Cologne

Selected Group Exhibitions:

1959 *Documenta*, Kassel, West Germany
1962 *NUL=Zero*, Stedelijk Museum, Amsterdam
1964 *Painting and Sculpture of a Decade*, Tate Gallery, London
1965 *The Responsive Eye*, Museum of Modern Art, New York
1968 *Biennale*, Venice (and 1970)

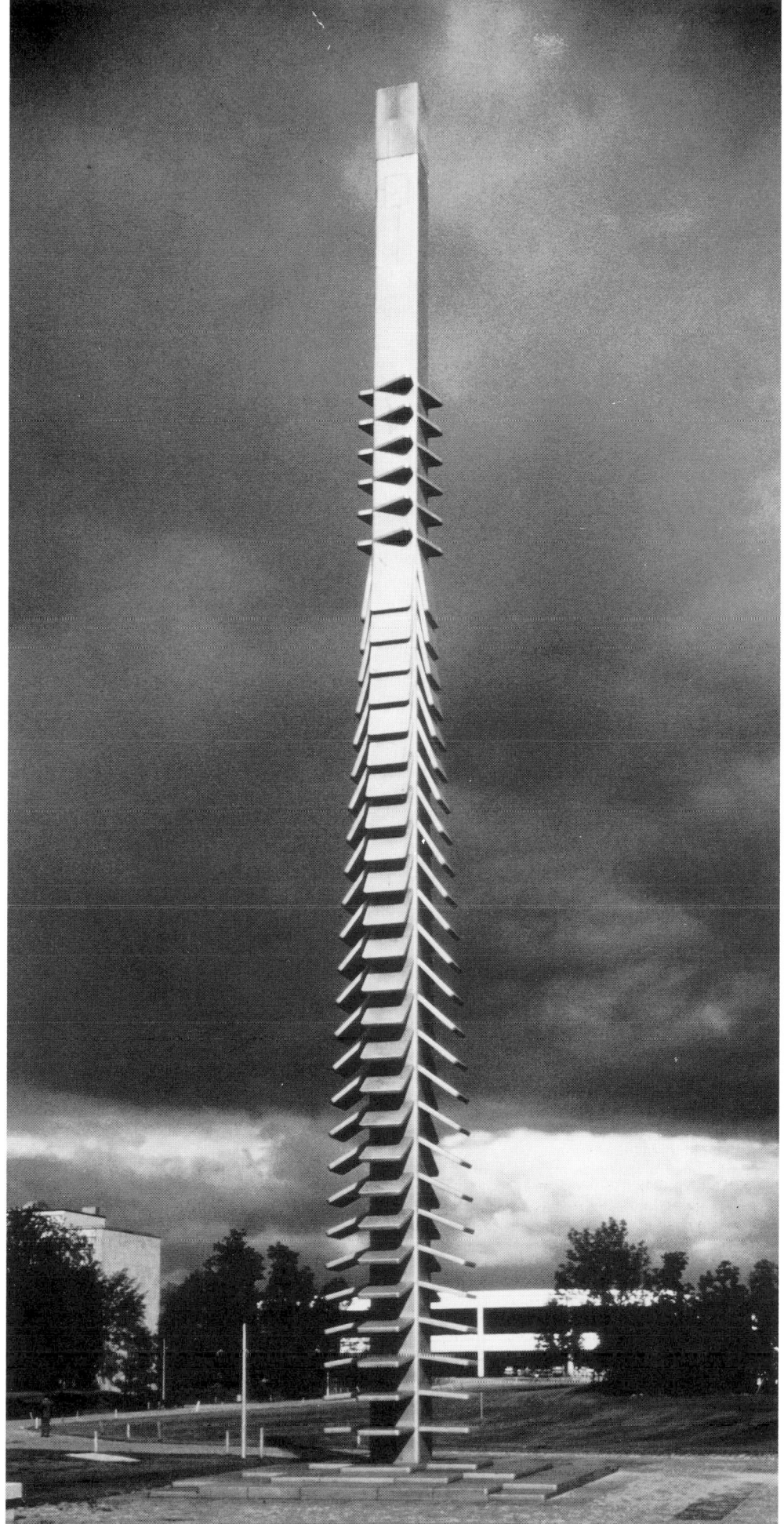

Heinz Mack: *Light Column*, Munich Airport, 1977

Collections:

Städtische Kunstsammlungen, Bonn; Städtisches Museum, Mönchengladbach, West Germany; Städtisches Kunstmuseum, Dusseldorf; Bauhaus-Archiv, West Berlin; Wallraf-Richartz Museum, Cologne; Kunstmuseum, Basle; Museum des 20. Jahhunderts, Vienna; Stedelijk Van Abbemuseum, Eindhoven, Netherlands; Musée Royal des Beaux-Arts, Brussels; Museum of Modern Art, New York.

Publications:

By MACK: books—*Movena*, Wiesbaden 1960; *Kinetische Kunst*, Zurich 1960; *Sahara-Projekt*, Dusseldorf 1960; *Fontana*, exhibition catalogue, Leverkusen, West Germany 1962; *Europaische Avantgarde*, exhibition catalogue, Frankfurt 1963; *Zero=Nul* exhibition catalogue, The Hague 1964; *Grosses Buch*, Dusseldorf 1964; *Plan 1—Integratie*, Antwerp 1964; *Kunst Heute*, Reinbek 1965; *De Nieuwe Stijl 2*, Amsterdam 1965; *Nul: Teil 1*, exhibition catalogue, Amsterdam 1965; *Zero in Bonn*, exhibition catalogue, Bonn 1966; *Jesus Rafael Soto*, exhibition catalogue, Hannover 1968; *Kunst seit '45*, Brussels 1969; *Zero*, with Otto Piene, Cambridge, Massachusetts, and Cologne 1973; *Strukturen*, Dusseldorf 1975.

On MACK: books—*Eine neue Konzeption in der Malerei* by Udo Kultermann, Milan 1960; *Ultime Tendenze dell'Arte d'Oggi* by Gillo Dorfles, Milan 1961; *The Development of Zero* by Otto Piene, New York 1964; *New Isms of Art* by Alan Bowness, London 1966; *Group Zero* by Cyril Barrett, London 1966; *Mack* by Margit Staber, Cologne 1968; *Deutsche Kunst: eine neue Generation* by Rolf-Günter Dienst, Cologne 1970; *Heinz Mack: Venice Biennale*, exhibition catalogue, with text by Dieter Honisch, Venice 1970; *Constructivist Tendencies from the Collection of Mr. and Mrs. George Rickey*, exhibition catalogue, with texts by George Rickey and Ala Story, Santa Barbara, California 1971; *Deutsche Kunst der 60er Jahre: Malerei, Collage, Op-Art, Graphik* by Juliana Roh, Munich 1971; *Mack: Objekte, Aktionen, Projekte*, exhibition catalogue, with texts by Wieland Schmied and Eberhard Roters, Eindhoven, Netherlands 1973; *Mack*, exhibition catalogue, with texts by Jacques Lassaigne, Wieland Schmied, Margit Staber and others, Paris 1973; *Heinz Mack: Arbeiten aus den Jahren 1955-1975*, exhibition catalogue, Dusseldorf 1975; *Mack*, exhibition catalogue, with text by Karin Thomas, Zurich 1978; *Mack: Skulpturen* by Dieter Honisch, Dusseldorf and Vienna 1986.

The discovery, taking place almost by accident, that art comes about unexpectedly, irritates our naive consciousness and makes it critical. Theoretical reflection is only a trap for the artist if it is speculative, that is to say if not preceded and again followed by the sensation of the picture which has come about. I have never hesitated to reflect on my own activity as an artist.

The shaping of forms in the existing sense can no longer be discussed. The conquering of colourfulness by colour itself corresponds to the abandonment of composition in favour of a simple structure zone, in other words the simple juxtaposition of all picture elements. The artist attains unity in his picture inter alia only to the extent that he is very well aware of the function of the individual picture elements; attractive detail is superseded by completely unattractive structure elements, meaningful only if they have a relationship to the picture, or represent such a relationship. By this means a structural element obtains its individuality, its unmistakable meaning; in itself, such an element is meaningless.

The physical-objective picture space must be rejected, even when it has abstract form. In the same way, the atmospheric picture space is naturalism.

An unexpected opportunity to make the aesthetic movement visible arose when I accidentally trod on a thin metal sheet lying on a sisal carpet. As I picked up the sheet the light was able to vibrate. Since the carpet was a mechanical product, the impression it left was also mechanical and decorative. The movement of the reflected light was entirely monotonous and boring. My metal reliefs, which I would prefer to call "light reliefs," are formed solely by finger pressure, and need light in place of colour to come alive. If given a mirror polish, even slight relief effect will suffice to disturb the peace of the light and cause it to vibrate. If these picture compositions are found attractive, then this is purely the expression of the beauty of light.

Luckily nature has not yet allowed the complete inventory of our world to be distributed evenly over the available space on the globe. Under the same sky we can still find nature reservations, unusual spaces which must be of large size, must create the impression that atom bomb explosions would dwindle and be lost inside them.

I admit that such spaces fill my imagination, and not least I admire the casual manner in which they spread out so untiringly. The deep, open space, not willing to stop even at the horizon, is the free sphere for my gaze, which hurries without purpose or direction over near and far, weightless, until it returns to me. The experience of the vastness remains in me then.

In such spaces the clarity of light and the fullness of calm can spread themselves permanently. Light gives the space its purpose, its atmosphere, its transparency. Light removes weight from space. Calm gives space its weight, through calm the space becomes audible, in such spaces we feel that our senses are finely tuned.

I desire to seek out ungraspable natural spaces in order to realize in them the second, comprehensible space, that of art. I call this artificial space the art of reservation. In this reservation, intended one day to be total, art shall find a new freedom. The Sahara project is intended to bring about freedom.

The problem of integration between architecture and pictorial art has been discussed a thousand times, but will not be shaken until patrons, architects and artists face up to the common task of producing an architecture entirely without purpose. Such architecture would require the same conditions as the fantastic classical architecture throughout the world still reveals: an irrational desire for beauty, expressed by all men, conveyed by the patron, realized by the builder and completed by the artist.

The most pleasant surprise for my eyes was the recognition that space and light are indeed more powerful than my artificial works, but that my relatively small constructions can reduce the endless expanse of space in themselves and can articulate and intensify the all embracing luminosity of light.

My art is not an abstraction of nature, and does not seek victory over nature. Nature is not my enemy. The museums are against me even though they buy my works. This has strengthened one of my convictions: my artistic expectations are best fulfilled by those works with a manifestation which causes the observer to forget the old guilty question as to whether what he sees is art or not. I am content with the unreality of fascination.

—Heinz Mack

Heinz Mack was one of the leading members of Group Zero, along with Otto Piene and Gunther Uecker. And like them he has been above all concerned with the use of light and movement in art, and with such new materials as glass and aluminum. Group Zero, of which Mack was co-founder in 1957, was one of the many groups and associations of kinetic artists formed during the late 1950's and early 1960's, all dedicated to using new means and new technologies in art. But in contrast to the scientifically purist approach of the French Groupe de Recherche d'Art Visuel, Zero was at the romantic end of the spectrum in adopting an intuitive relationship with technology and an individualist rather than a collectivist approach. These artists believed in light as *the* expansive medium, carrying energy from the artist to the spectator; and they also believed that the artist should help to change the environment on a large scale, which led them to the demonstrations and performances which Piene and Mack held in Dusseldorf, such as the one in 1960 when dozens of white balloons were set adrift in the night sky and their paths followed up into the heavens by searchlights.

"Movement is the true form of a work," Mack has said, and one form of such movement was the recurrent wave forms of his Cardiogram paintings. He found his conception of painting realized in Mondrian's late Boogie-Woogie paintings, which he saw as a profusion of little repetitive forms unified by the "all-over form" of the whole work. Increasingly, however, his work became involved in light play, and he has recounted how the fruitful accident of stepping on a thin piece of metal foil and thus imprinting it with the pattern of a mass-produced fibre mat led him to create the pieces that he called light reliefs. These depend on distorted reflectivity as light passes over the creased, rippled and slotted surfaces of aluminum sheets, producing sparkling, ever-changing landscapes of reflection.

Mack has also experimented with vibrating columns of light. And since 1958 he has been constantly developing the theme of rotating reliefs and light dynamos. These are metal plates driven by an electromotor so that they rotate behind a rippling plane of corrugated glass, so that light is reflected from it in changing patterns. The patterns are on the *moiré* principle also used by many purely Optical artists, the slow disturbance of the light rays reflected back at the viewer generating an optical illusion which gives a disturbing psychological effect of unbalance.

But like Otto Piene, Mack has also been turning to environmental art, dreaming of realizing works such as his "Sahara Relief" and "Light Pyramid" in some vast open space such as the Sahara desert where there is an abundance of calm, space and light to extend the "limitless stretch" of art.

—Konstantin Bazarov

MAGRITTE, René (Francois Ghislain).
Belgian. Born in Lessines, Hainault, 21 November 1898. Educated at Châtelet and Charleroi, Belgium, until 1914; studied, under Victor Servranckx, Académie des Beaux-Arts, Brussels, 1916–18; first experimental photomontages, 1929, but mainly self-taught in photography, from 1956. Served as infantryman, Belgian Army, Beverloo and Antwerp, 1921–22. Married Georgette-Marie-Florence Berger in 1922. Worked as a wallpaper designer and graphic artist, Peters Lacroix Company, Haren, 1919–21; poster designer and graphic artist, for Norine and Paul-Gustave Van Hecke fashions, and for Samuel Furs, etc., Brussels, 1923–27, 1930–31; painter and writer, associating with surrealist artists, in Brussels, 1923–27, 1931–67, in Le Perreux-sur-Marne, near Paris, 1927–30. Active as amateur photographer, Brussels, 1956–67. Editor, with E. L. T. Mesens, *Oesophage* and *Marie* reviews, Brussels, 1925–26; Contributor, *La Voix du Peuple* communist newspaper, Brussels, 1936. Recipient: Guggenheim Prize for Belgium, 1956. *Died (in Brussels-Schaerbek) 15 August 1967.*

Individual Exhibitions:

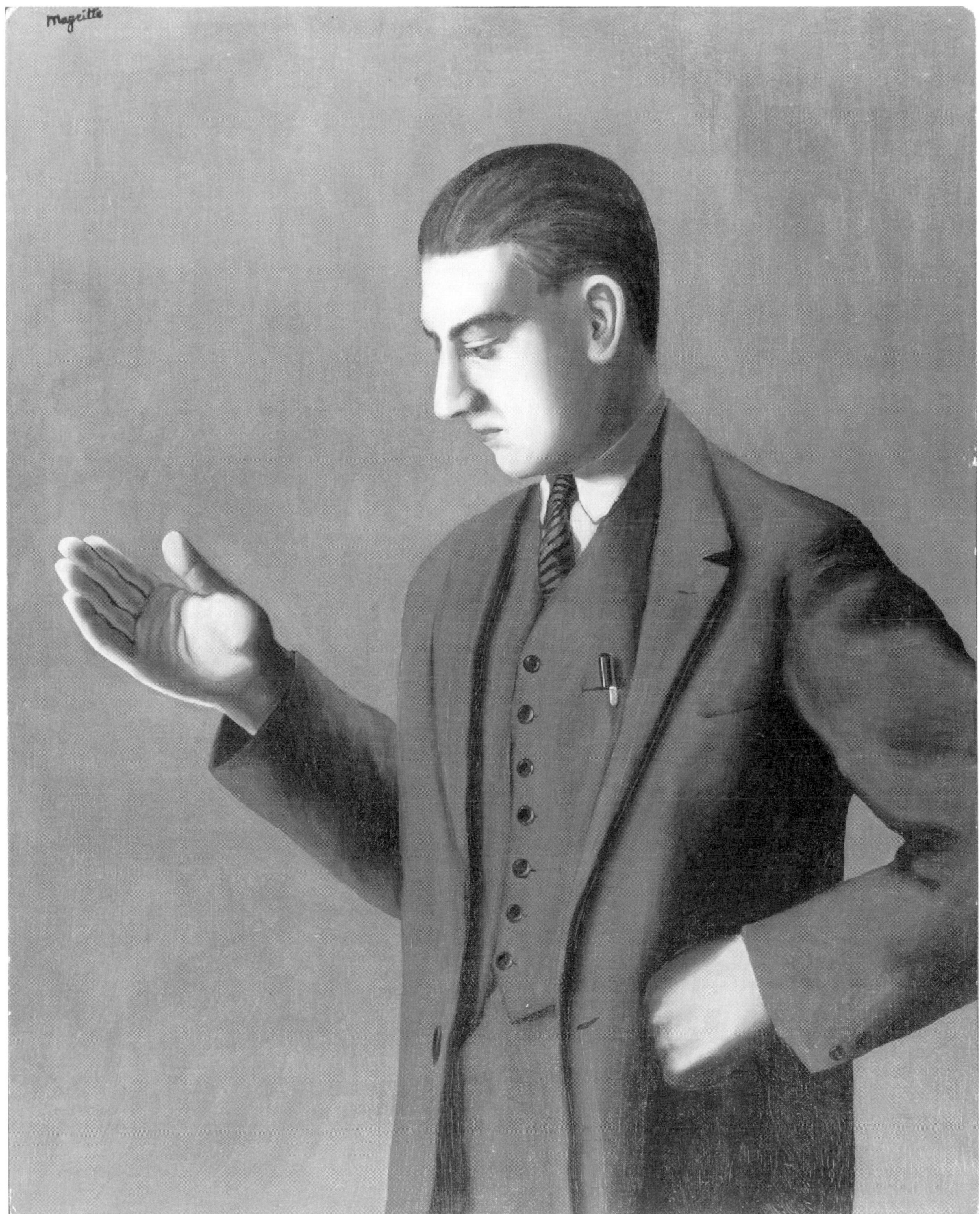

René Magritte: *Le Soupçon Mysterieux*, 1928

1941	Galerie Dietrich, Brussels
1943	Galerie Cosyn, Brussels
1944	Galerie Dietrich, Brussels
1946	Galerie Dietrich, Brussels
1947	Hugo Gallery, New York
	Société des Beaux-Arts, Verviers, Belgium
1948	Galerie Dietrich, Brussels
	Hugo Gallery, New York
	Galerie du Faubourg, Paris
	Copley Galleries, Hollywood, California
1949	Galerie Cosyn, Brussels
1950	Galerie Le Parc, Charleroi, Belgium
1951	Galerie Dietrich, Brussels
	Galerie Dietrich, Brussels
	Galerie Cosyn, Brussels
	Hugo Gallery, New York
1953	Galleria dell'Obelisco, Rome
	La Sirene, Brussels
	Temps Meles, Verviers, Belgium
	Galerie Le Carne, Liège
	Lefevre Gallery, London
	Sidney Janis Gallery, New York
1954	Galerie Dietrich, Brussels
	Maison des Loisirs, La Louviere, Belgium
	Sidney Janis Gallery, New York
1955	State Museum Luxembourg
	Galerie Pastoe, Brussels
	Galerie Cahiers d'Art, Paris
1957	Iolas Gallery, New York
1958	Galerie Cahiers d'Art, Paris
1959	Iolas Gallery, New York
	Musée des Beaux-Arts d'Ixelles, Brussels
	Bodley Gallery, New York
1960	Galerie Rive Droite, Paris
	Museum for Contemporary Art, Dallas (retrospective)
	Musée des Beaux-Arts, Liège
1961	Obelisk Gallery, London
	Grosvenor Gallery, London
	Albert Landry Gallery, New York
1962	Galleria Galatea, Turin, Italy
	Walker Art Center, Minneapolis
	Bodley Gallery, New York
	Iolas Gallery, New York
	Galleria Schwarz, Milan
	Casino Communal, Knokke-le-Zoute, Belgium
1963	Galleria l'Attico, Rome
1964	University of Chicago
	Arkansas Art Center, Little Rock
	Hanover Gallery, London
	University of St. Thomas, Houston
1965	Galerie Zwirner, Cologne
	Galleria Notizie, Turin, Italy
	Museum of Modern Art, New York (toured the United States)
	Iolas Gallery, New York
1966	Zwemmer Gallery, London
1967	Moderna Museet, Stockholm
	Museum Boymans-van Beuningen, Rotterdam
1969	Tate Gallery, London (retrospective)
	Kestner-Gesellschaft, Hannover (retrospective)
	Kunsthaus, Zurich (retrospective)
1971	Galerie Isy Brachot, Knokke-le-Zoute, Belgium
	National Museum of Modern Art, Tokyo (travelled to Museum of Modern Art, Kyoto, Japan)
1972	Gimpel and Hanover Galerie, Zurich
1973	Marlborough Fine Art, London
1975	Davlyn Gallery, New York
1976	Staatliche Kunsthalle, Baden-Baden
	Rice University, Houston (retrospective)
1977	Bibliothèque Municipale, Bordeaux
1978	Midland Group Gallery, Nottingham, England
	Palais des Beaux-Arts, Brussels (retrospective; travelled to Centre Georges Pompidou, Paris)
1979	Galerie Isy Brachot, Brussels
1982	Kunstverein, Hamburg
	National Museum of Modern Art, Tokyo
1983	Louisiana Museum, Humlebaek, Denmark
1984	Art Museum of Tampere, Finland
	Henie-Onstad Kunstsenter, Oslo
	Galerie Isy Brachot, Paris
	Centre Wallonie, Brussels
1986	Arnold Herstand Gallery, New York
1987	Fondation de l'Hermitage, Lausanne

Selected Group Exhibitions:

1923	*Ca Ira*, Cercle Royal Artistique, Antwerp
1928	*Surrealist Group*, Galerie l'Epoque, Brussels
1933	*Le Surrealisme*, Galerie Pierre Colle, Paris
1936	*Fantastic Art, Dada and Surrealism*, Museum of Modern Art, New York
1945	*Surrealist Diversity*, Arcade Gallery, London
1954	*Collages and Objects*, Institute of Contemporary Arts, London
1977	*Künstlerphotographien im XX. Jahrhundert*, Kestner-Gesellschaft, Hannover
1978	*Dada and Surrealism Reviewed*, Hayward Gallery, London
1979	*Photographic Surrealism*, New Gallery of Contemporary Art, Cleveland (travelled to Dayton Art Institute, Ohio; Brooklyn Museum, New York)
1984	*La Planète Affotée: Surrealisme 1938–47*, Centre de la Vieille Charité, Marseille, France

Collections:

Ministère de l'Education National et de la Culture, Brussels; Palais des Beaux-Arts, Brussels; Musée Royal des Beaux-Arts, Antwerp; Casino, Knokke-le-Zoute, Belgium; Palais des Beaux-Arts, Charleroi, Belgium; Kunsthaus, Zurich; Museum of Modern Art, New York; Los Angeles County Museum of Art; Art Gallery of Ontario, Toronto; National Gallery of Victoria, Melbourne.

Publications:

By MAGRITTE: books—*La Destination: Lettres à Marcel Marien*, Brussels 1971, 1977; *René Magritte: Manifestes et Autres Ecrits*, Brussels 1972; *Le Fait Accompli*, Brussels 1973; *La Belle Captive*, with text by Alain Robbe-Grillet, Lausanne, Switzerland and Paris 1975; *82 Lettres de René Magritte à Mirabelle Dors et Maurice Rapin*, Paris 1976; *René Magritte: Die Truglosen Bilder, Bioskop und Photographie*, with texts by Wolfgang Becker, Louis Scutenaire and Schuldt, Cologne 1976; *La Fidelité des Images: René Magritte, Le Cinematographe et la Photographie*, portfolio of 16 photos, with texts by Louis Scutenaire, Brussels and Hamburg 1976; *Les Couleurs de la Nuit*, Brussels 1978; *Croquer les Idées*, Brussels 1978; *Ecrits Complets*, compiled by André Blavier, Paris 1979; *Photographies de Magritte*, with text by Marcel Paquet, Paris 1982; *This is not a pipe*, with text by Michel Foucault, Berkeley and London 1983; articles—"Aux Quatre Chemins" in *Surrealist Drawings*, exhibition catalogue, Paris 1935; statement in *Le Bulletin* (London), no. 12, 1939; "James Ensor" in *Le Drapeau Rouge* (Brussels), 1945; "Dix Tableaux, Precedes de Descriptions" in *Le Miroir Infidèle*, Brussels 1946; statement in *René Magritte*, exhibition catalogue, Dallas 1960.

On MAGRITTE: books—*Magritte* by Marcel Marien, Brussels 1943; *René Magritte* by Louis Scutenaire, Brussels 1948; *Magritte* by James Thrall Soby, New York 1965; *René Magritte* by Patrick Waldberg, Brussels 1965; *Magritte*, exhibition catalogue, by David Sylvester, London 1969; *Magritte* by Suzi Gablik, London 1970; *Magritte: Poète Visible* by Philippe Robert-Jones, Brussels 1972; *René Magritte* by A. M. Hammacher, London 1974; *René Magritte: Signes et Images* by Harry Torczyner, Paris and New York 1977; *Magritte* by Jacques Dopagne, Paris 1977, London and New York 1979; *Avec Magritte* by Louis Scutenaire, Brussels 1977; *Künstlerphotographien im XX. Jahrhundert*, exhibition catalogue, edited by Carl-Albrecht Haenlein, Hannover 1977; *Retrospective Magritte*, exhibition catalogue, by Jean Clair, David Sylvester and others, Brussels and Paris 1978; *Magritte* by Richard Calvocoressi, London 1979; *Lettres à Magritte* by Joe Bousquet, Paris 1981; *Die Kunsttheorie René Magrittes* by Ralf Schieber, Munich 1981; *René Magritte: Life and Work* by Uwe M. Schneede, New York 1982; *Magritte, ou l'eclipse de l'etre* by Marcel Paquet, Paris 1982; *Magritte*, exhibition catalogue with texts by Camille Goemans, Martine Jaquet, Marcel Marien and others, Lausanne 1987.

Out of those artists selected by the general public as being the principal Surrealists (always a loose framework), the three names that stand out are Max Ernst (born German), Salvador Dali (Spanish) and René Magritte (Belgian) with the Catalan Joan Miró hovering somewhere on the edges. Of all the modern movements, Surrealism was/is the most international

and, despite its name, by no means Gallic in essence or even by adoption.

Its very ubiquitous incidence has proved that it will flower in any country, regardless of latitude or climate, although all these factors may help colour and fashion the form it takes.

In Magritte's case nearly all his imagery actually does take on the appearance of super-realism (sometimes, but not often, distorted). His colouring, generally sober, even if its brightest tints can be wayward, is never beyond the frontiers of superrealism.

Does this make his work unimaginative? On the contrary. The very contradictions with straight reality that pervade everything he ever did ensure shock, surprise, amazement and the arousal of keen interest, not doubts or enquiry. This matter of the outside viewers' reactions to his pictures and sculpture was of prime importance to him. He did not want those looking at them to say why? what? or how? For him every image, no matter what its relationship with the rest of the picture, had the right of symbols (to change arbitrarily in meaning). Such alchemy should brook no questions.

In its simplest form, the Magritte attitude to things and symbols is finitely set out in paintings where names are painted under objects and in which, from a straightforward point of view, either the name is in the wrong place, or the wrong object has been painted over the right name. The language of vision can play tricks with the same dexterity as the language of thought or indeed the language of any of the senses.

Magritte's style is nearly always operating at a relatively low temperature, but this does not mean that the latent drama cannot lurk in the shadows or the sunlight. In spite of the manner of his painting there is frequent evidence of secret excitement. Some of the pictures are serene, but they are the exception rather than the rule. Rock formations may be sombre and still take on the form of a bird in flight. His recamier couch, posed like a reclining woman, is a jointed coffin (after the style of David!). The canvas on the easel set before the window is transparent—an instant landscape. A horizontal flight of French loaves crosses the sky in disciplined array. Every Magritte tells another surrealist anecdote; and if he has a trademark, it is his own typically modest bowler hat.

—Sheldon Williams

MALER, Leopoldo (Mario).

Argentinian. Born in Buenos Aires, 2 April 1937. Studied social sciences at the New School for Social Research, New York, 1957–58; studied law at the University of Buenos Aires, 1958–60, University College, London, 1961–62, and the International Academy of Comparative Law, Helsinki, 1962. Married Silvia Oclander in 1967 (divorced, 1970); married Joyce Pieck in 1974. Practiced as a lawyer in Buenos Aires, 1960–61, 1965–67; Producer, External Services, British Broadcasting Corporation, London, 1961–64, 1968–74; also, Assistant Editor, *Talia* magazine and Announcer for Radio Municipal de Buenos Aires, 1965–67; Art Critic and Current Affairs Writer for *El Dia* newspaper, Buenos Aires, 1967–72; lived in Paris, 1973; created daily three-hour one-man program on Radio Belgrano, Buenos Aires, 1974–75; lived in London, 1975–77, and worked for the BBC and taught at Hornsey College of Art, London and Leeds Polytechnic, Yorkshire; moved to New York, and commenced work with lasers and synthesizers, 1977. Recipient: Special Prize, *Leipzig Film Festival*, 1964; Di Tella Institute Grant, Buenos Aires, 1965; Camden Arts Centre Grant, London, 1971–72; Grand Prize, *Biennal*, Sao Paulo, 1977; Guggenheim Foundation Fellowship, 1977–78. Address: 414 East 75th Street, New York, New York 10021, U.S.A.

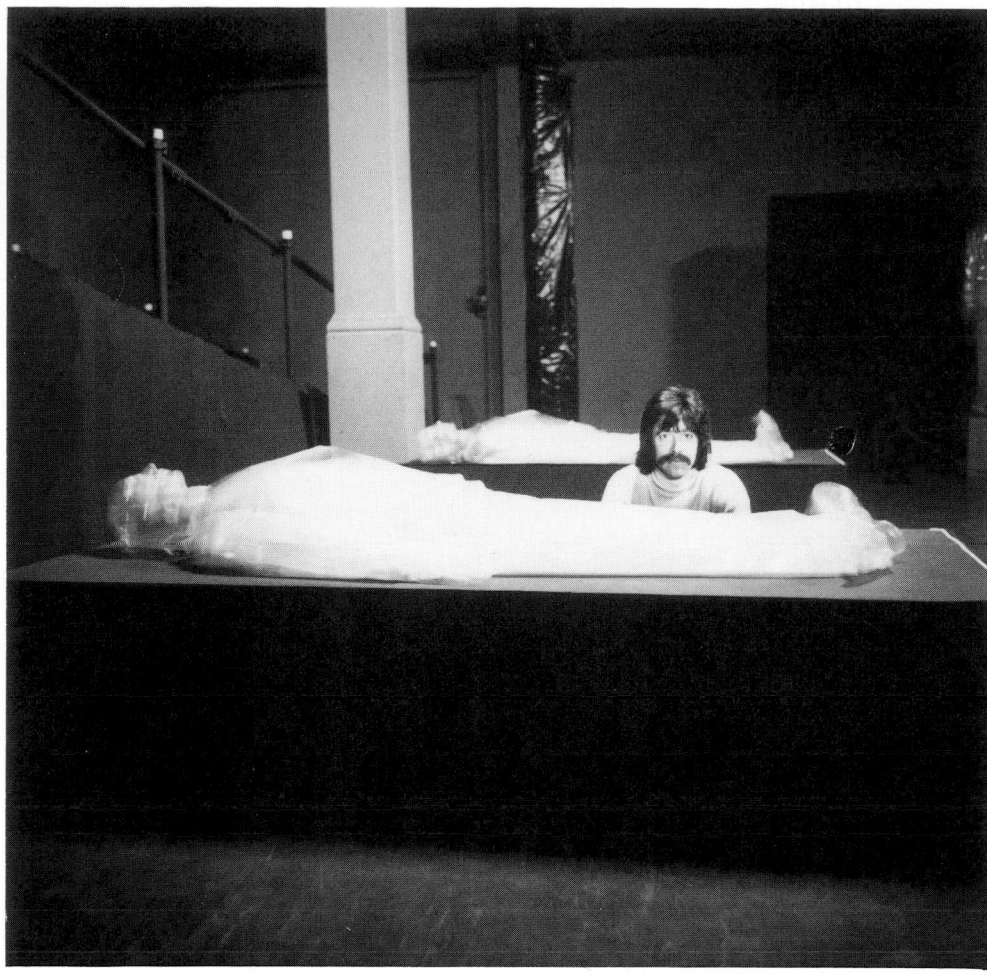

Leopoldo Maler: *Mortal Issues*, 1976

Individual Exhibitions:

1964   *Men in Silence*, National Film Theatre, London
1966   *Caperucita Rota*, Instituto Torcuato di Tella, Buenos Aires
1967   *Exhibition of an Opening*, Galeria Rubbers, Buenos Aires
1968   *Listen Here Now*, Arts Laboratory, Drury Lane, London
1969   *Outrage*, Roundhouse, London
        X-IT, The Place, London
1970   *X-IT2*, The Place, London
1971   *Silence*, Camden Arts Centre, London
        Crane Ballet, Kentish Town Playground, London
1972   *Q*, Camden Arts Centre, London
        Carnem et Cyclum, Great Georges Project, Liverpool
1975   *Mortal Issues*, Whitechapel Art Gallery, London
1976   Galeria Pecanins, Barcelona
1981   Gallery Watari, Tokyo

Selected Group Exhibitions:

1974   *Art Systems in Latin America*, International Cultureel Centrum, Antwerp (toured Europe)
1975   *Open Encounter on Video*, Espace Cardin, Paris (toured Europe)
1977   *Last Supper*, Fondation Miró, Barcelona
        Bienal, Sao Paulo
        21 Argentinos, Museo de Artes y Ciencias, Universidad Autonoma de Mexico, Mexico City
1978   *Grupo de los 13*, Museo de Arte Moderno, Rio de Janeiro
        Hayward Annual, London
1979   *3 Easy Pieces*, Centre Pompidou, Paris
        Bienal, Sao Paulo
1980   *Biennale*, Venice

Publications:

By MALER: article—"Silence" in *Art and Artists* (London), June 1971.

On MALER: book—*Q*, exhibition catalogue, with an introduction by Jasia Reichardt, London 1972; articles—"Visual Arts: June 1970-June 1971" by Charles Spencer in *Design in Greece* (Athens), no. 3, 1972; "Outside the Galleries" by Michael Shepherd in the *Sunday Telegraph* (London), November 1972; "Leopoldo Maler's Special Effects" by Guy Brett in *The Times* (London), November 1972; "Leopoldo Maler" by Georgina Oliver in *Arts Review* (London), November 1972; "Wring Out the Old" by Caroline Tisdall in *The Guardian* (London), December 1974; "Leopoldo Maler, o injusticado de CAYC" by Leonor Amarante in *O Estado de Sao Paulo*, 26 November 1978.

Excess as a source of creativity:

On experiencing "excess" one begins to explore limits of our knowledge. Excess demolishes ignorance and brings man closer to his inner nature . . . that of the unanswerable questions. Contemplation is a creative action. Any creative action implies an expansion. Expansion involves excess.

Choreographies:

I became interested in choreographies as a medium for the development of ceremonies. It deals with the kinaesthetical perfection and precision that other media lack for this purpose. It deals with action, and therefore one could plot a series of movements for either human beings, machines or any other object.

On working with a machine which has been designed to perform a specific series of industrial tasks, and including it in a creative event, we may experience NOT its liberation—as that would be irrelevant and unreal—but OUR own, from the standards of knowledge imposed by a productivitarian culture. To be able to play and to enjoy ourselves with a huge crane or lorry should—as an attitude—be as valid as any other social conquests. It involves the destruction of respect and fear for any utilitarian programming, and may help to convert the factories one day for other purposes, such as playgrounds. The day industrial plants may become useless and enjoyable will mark the real birth of a humane technology (same as when TV shall find its very raison d'etre).

Films:

(That strange medium recorded in the past and able to create the illusion of the present)

Same as in the case of the industrial machines I tried to liberate the film from its square screen and the multiplicity of objects and subjects inhabiting each single sequence.

In order to reach this purpose, I tried to recreate a magic environment, and "staged" films in art galleries and museums. They are frequently presented in the form of mixed media "tableaux" (e.g., "Silence", "Q" etc.). They are films of people—in full scale—projected into screens built in the same shape as the image, so there takes place a coincidence between it and the reflecting surface. You walk into a large dark room. There are several people looking at you, moving slowly and dreamlike. These people are in fact films watching YOU.

On another level these films are linked with the presence of a real object: a car, a preserved carcass, etc. So in this instance films act as a memory for the objects; a memory that visually manifests itself as an hallucinatory image. Memory acts here as an alternative possibility: what the film IS might or might not have happened.

Meanwhile, the spectator experiences two dimensions of time within the same spatial context.

SPACE is an all-important element of these exhibitions or "situations". The objects involved in these experiences, as sculptures in themselves, are perishable to some degree. But it is the emotional signalling of the space involved that most interests me, as I found that memory does not travel through the paths of time, but rather zigzags around spaces of our previous experiences.

In some ways I could describe my work in this field as that of "staging films." It may be explained more conceptually as a creative process which destroys that of the editing. It is a dismantling of images gathered in a single shot. I want the spectator to walk through the individual images of the film in order to experience them spatially. Why? I feel that one could—helped with the crutches of hallucination—start walking through the experiencing of large dark spaces which might finally give us the measure of our own beings. It is not by chance that religions put so much emphasis on the architectonics and grandeur of their prayer palaces.

Other of my past works, such as "Carnem et Cyclum"—a spectacular ritual produced in a deconsecrated Church in Liverpool—was intended to rescue the "original"—that is, the reawakening of the origins.

A ritualized act with choruses and 15 butchers trussing lamb carcasses hanging from a mechanized circular chain, aided by a conveyor belt which carried the meat pieces into the cooking area.

How many people have seen in their life a living lamb, a real animal whose meat they are going to chew and eat for the rest of their life? It is not unlikely that if a child were asked, what is a rump steak, he may well describe it as a "white poliurethane tray with a red solid substance on it" . . . as presented in its alienated form with the compliments of the local supermarket! One of the most striking views I ever had was on a visit to the largest meat packing factory in Argentina, where cattle walks in alive and well, just to be ready for export, tinned down the conveyor belt some 80 yards from its entering point. Miracles of consumer's excesses!

Human figure:

Few images awaken so much our feelings, anxieties or fears as the human presence. Only a body lying in a street can—even for a split second—slow down noises, speed and alienation, and make us consider our nature. It is the mortal presence which puts us back in touch with ourselves in times of deep alienation.

The human figure—sometimes in films, others as real people performing some action or sitting still; or life size inflatable bodies, etc.—is a recurring image in my work. Unlike other artists it is not the aesthetical proposition that is the content of my aim, but the secret ceremonial that the slow movement of a body may recall for us when contemplating it.
Fire:

Fire is extinguishable and therefore mortal. My most recent works include fire as a formal part of an object. Right, it is quite ephemeral, like life, and unlike stone, cast iron, or even papyrus.

The only possible permanence of these works is in the mind of some spectators, and past pieces could only be found in the intangible collection of man's own hallucinations.

—Leopoldo Maler

I would like to go through the world organizing feasts for weddings and births, ceremonies for leave-takings and welcomes. In a word, doing all that which, when there is celebration in common with other human beings, takes away from the word "artist" the meaning of a man isolated within society.

In a certain way, Leopoldo Maler accomplishes these desires. Although he has not yet gone all round the world, he travels every day. As an artist, many of his works are in fact feasts and ceremonies, that is, celebrations in dance, theatre, cinema, video; and all of these manifestations have to do with life and death, with the welcomes and leave-takings of the human being.

Maler prefers to call his works "situations," because—as he maintains—his interest is not directed to the creation of an object or the examination of a substance but to the elaboration of a "climate" by means of images. It is that he believes in the inventive power of contemplation as a form of participating—the best form possible. His images thus exercise the functions of catalysts, without necessarily supporting a narrative content. They are symbols of a personal ritual, and Maler develops them with the minutia of a person writing a book.

His situations, for these reasons, are in most cases ephemeral. However, Maler's message resides in this very transience. "Perhaps all work should be ephemeral," he has declared, "so that it will not constitute a burden for its creator, so that the creator may be reborn from the ashes of each experience." Nevertheless, there is more: man is by nature ephemeral, since none of his gestures, his motions, are ever repeated in the same way. Maler wishes precisely to redeem these gestures and movements as an uneven, secret and mysterious cipher of human happenings.

—Jorge Glusberg

MANESSIER, Alfred.

French. Born in Saint-Ouen, 5 December 1911. Studied architecture at the Ecole des Beaux-Arts, Amiens, 1926–29; studied at the Ecole des Beaux-Arts, Paris, 1929–33. Served as a technical draughtsman, Ministry of War, Paris, 1939. Married Therese Simonnet in 1938; children: Jean-Baptiste and Christine. Painter and graphic artist, Paris, since 1934. Recipient: Painting Prize, *Bienal*, Sao Paulo, 1953; First Prize, *Exhibition of Sacred Art*, Vienna, 1954; Grand Prix, *Carnegie International*, Pittsburgh, 1955; International Painting Prize, Valencia 1955; International Institute of Liturgical Art Prize, *Biennale*, Venice 1958, 1962; First Prize, *Print Biennale*, Grenchen, 1958; Painting Prize, *Biennale*, Venice 1962. Agent: Galerie de France, 52 rue de la Verrerie, 75004 Paris, France. Address: 20 rue Pierre Brossolette, 92140 Clamart, France.

Individual Exhibitions:

1949	Galerie Billiet Caputo, Paris
	Galerie Jeanne Bucher, Paris
1951	Galerie Apollo, Brussels
1952	Galerie de France, Paris
1953	Galleria Lattea, Turin
	Pierre Matisse Gallery, New York
1955	Galleri Blanche, Stockholm
	Institut Francais, Copenhagen
	Palais des Beaux-Arts, Brussels
	Stedelijk Van Abbemuseum, Eindhoven, Netherlands
1956	Galerie de France, Paris
1958	Kestner-Gesellschaft, Hannover
	Galerie de France, Paris
1959	Kunsthaus, Zurich
	Dienst voor Schone Kunsten, The Hague
	Museum Folkwang, Essen
	Haute Provence 1958–1959, Galerie de France, Paris
1961	Musée D'Amiens, France
1962	Galerie Tony Spinazzola, Aix-en-Provence, France
1964	Phillips Collection, Washington, D.C.
	University of Notre Dame, Indiana
	Forum Stadtpark, Graz, Austria
1965	Maison de la Culture, Caen, France
	Kunstnernes Hus, Oslo
	Konsthall, Lund, Sweden
1966	Galerie de France, Paris
	Galerie Wünsche, Bonn
	Galerie Emmy Widman, Bremen, West Germany
1967	Galerie Wünsche, Bonn
1968	Maison de la Culture, Amiens, France
	Maison de la Culture, Thonon-les-Bains, France
	Musée Fabre, Montpellier, France
	Maison de la Culture, Bourges, France
	Centre Culturel, Toulouse, France
1969	Musée de Metz, France
	Musée d'Art et d'Histoire, Luxembourg
	Städtisches Museum, Trier, West Germany
1970	Kunsthalle, Bremen, West Germany
	Mittelheim Museum, Koblenz, West Germany
	Musée de Dijon, France
	Oeuvres de 1935 à 1969, L'Abbaye de Ballelay, France
	Maison des Arts et Loisirs, Sochaux, France
	Galerie de France, Paris
1971	Galerie d'Art, Esche-sur-Alzette, Luxembourg
1972	Société des Arts, Mulhouse, France
	University of Notre Dame, Indiana
	Musée d'Art Moderne de la Ville, Paris
	Marais 19, Paris
	Musée de Metz, France
1973	Fundncao Calouste Gulbenkian, Lisbon
	Museu Soares des Reis, Porto, Portugal
1974	Musée Fabre, Montpellier, France
	Musée d'Art et d'Histoire, Neuchatel, Switzerland
	Librairie Feret, Bordeaux
	Neue Galerie am Wolfgang Gurlitt Museum, Linz, Austria
	Provincial Museum, Graz, Austria
	Provincial Museum, Kragenfurt, Austria
	Galerie de France, Paris
	Museum des 20. Jahrhunderts, Vienna
1975	Galleria Editalia, Rome
	Galerie de France, Paris
	Galerie Lafond, Chateauroux, France
1976	Musée Dynamique, Dakar, Senegal
	Galerie le Castrum-Rousillon, Gordes-Rousillon, France
	Galerie Candela, Cannes
	Hotel de Ville, Tours, France
	Galerie Municipale, Esch-sur-Alzette, Luxembourg
1977	Centre des Arts et Lettres, Saint-Nazaire, France (toured France)
	Hotel de Ville, Bayonne, France
1978	Galerie de France, Paris
	Palais de l'Europe, Le Touquet, France
	Centre Culturel Saint-Jacques, Lisieux, France
1979	*Manessier: Retrospective*, Palais des Beaux-Arts, Charleroi, Belgium
1981	*Schilderijen, Grafiek*, Gemeentemuseum, The Hague
	Musee de la Poste, Paris
1983	Galerie de France, Paris
	Galerie Patrice Trigano, Paris
1984	Galerie du Vieux, Chene, Geneva
	Mjallby Konstgard, Hamstad, Sweden
1986	Centre Noiroit, Arras, France

Selected Group Exhibitions:

1937	*Temoinage*, Galerie Breteau, Paris
1942	*Sous le Signe de l'Esprit*, Galerie Braun, Paris
1948	*New French Painting*, Kunstmuseum, Frankfurt
1953	*Bienal*, Sao Paulo
1958	*Biennale*, Venice
1969	*French Painting since 1900*, Royal Academy of Art, London
1972	*Paris et la Peinture Contemporaine*, Museo de Arte Moderno, Montevideo (toured South America)
1974	*Cent Ans de Peinture Francaise*, Musee des Beaux-Arts, Lille, France
1981	*Paris-Paris, 1937–57*, Centre Georges Pompidou, Paris
1984	*Sur Invitation*, Musee des Arts Decoratifs, Paris

Collections:

Centre Georges Pompidou, Paris; Neue Nationalgalerie, West Berlin; Museum Folkwang, Essen; Stedelijk Van Abbemuseum, Eindhoven, Netherlands; Sonia Henie-Nils Onstad Kunstsenter, Oslo; Moderna Museet, Stockholm; Kunsthaus, Zurich; Museu de Arte Moderno, Sao Paulo; Museum of Modern Art, New York; Carnegie Institute, Pittsburgh.

Publications:

On MANESSIER: books—*Manessier*, exhibition catalogue, with text by Edy de Wilde, Paris 1956; *Alfred Manessier*, exhibition catalogue, with text by Werner Schmalenbach, Hannover 1958; *Manessier: Haute Provence 1958–1959*, exhibition catalogue, Paris 1959; *Alfred Manessier*, exhibition catalogue, with texts by Fredrik Matheson and Ole Henrik Moe, Oslo 1965; *Alfred Manessier*, exhibition catalogue, with texts by Jacques Lassaigne and Don Alfonso Roig, Paris 1966; *Alfred Manessier: Oeuvres de 1935 à 1969*, exhibition catalogue with text by Bernard Dorival, Bellelay, France 1970; *Manessier*, exhibition catalogue, with an introduction by Michel Georges Bernard, and an interview by Leonie de la Grandville, Paris 1970; *Manessier* by J. P. Hoden, Bath and New York 1972; *Manessier*, exhibition catalogue, with text by Gaston Diehl, Lisbon 1973; *Manessier 1970–1974*, exhibition catalogue, with text by Camille Bourniquet, and an interview by Pierre Encrere, Paris, 1974; *Alfred Manessier: Retrospective*, exhibition catalogue, with text by Robert Rousseau, Charleroi, Belgium 1979; *Manessier: Schilderijen, Grafiek*, exhibition catalogue, with an introduction by John Sillevis, The Hague 1981; *Alfred Manessier 83*, exhibition catalogue with introduction by Pierre Encreue, Paris 1983; films—*Peintres d'Aujourd hui: Alfred Manessier* by Jacques Simonnet and Camille Bourniquet 1963; *Alfred Manessier* by Robert Essens, 1969; *Manessier* by Yvan Butler, 1971; *Manessier* by Pascal Bony, 1983.

Alfred Manessier came to maturity after the 1939–1945 war, following a period of spiritual retreat in a monastery. His beginnings date back to his study of architecture in Amiens until 1929 before he entered the Academies of Montparnasse to follow a figurative style of painting under Bissière and became friendly with Le Moal.

From 1934 to 1935, Manessier was painting Cubist pictures after meeting Picasso and Braque, then from 1935 to 1937 he experimented with pure abstraction. His isolation in Normandy during the war forced a fresh consideration of his aims. After some attempts at refinement, he decided that the transmission of the light from within the canvas itself was the major effect to be aimed for. Medieval stained glass, and the clarity and purity of their colours, were echoes in his compositions, where frameworks of thickened line conveyed the suggestion of the leading of window openings. Signs and symbols highly schematised became the rigging on which he flew the pennants of high-keyed colour. The linear structure often performed a two-fold purpose as in "Crown of Thorns" (1951), where the religious connotation is strikingly evident in a symbolism that is comparable to the use of emblems by Klee.

Klee, in fact, has the most obvious affinity in the animation of the picture plane, where Manessier's free employment of semaphors gives a two-dimensional elasticity. Light is in constant movement through and beyond the surface, controlled by the density and warmth of the pure hues in jewel-like juxtaposition. Manessier's spiritual involvement has contributed to his designs for stained glass windows, many of them for modern churches, and also to tapestries and lithographs.

Within his own highly inflected and rhythmic notation of a picture, Manessier has evolved his individual system of attack, lending each work its autographic identity inevitably expressive of its theme. There is something of the mystic semantics of Oriental calligraphy in a Manessier canvas, allied frequently to the abstract economy of a Chinese water-colour landscape. This esoteric content is revealed in the evocative disposition of signs, nonallusive to natural phenomena, but carrying in the arabesques a flatly painted choreography of silent import.

—G. S. Whittet

MANGOLD, Robert (Peter).

American. Born in North Tonawanda, New York, 12 October 1937. Educated at Cleveland Art Institute, 1956-59; Yale University, New Haven, Connecticut, 1960-63, B.F.A. 1961, M.F.A. 1963. Married the artist Sylvia Plimack (i.e., Sylvia Mangold, q.v.), in 1961; sons: James A. and Andrew P. Instructor, School of Visual Arts, New York, since 1963. Instructor, Hunter College, New York, 1964-65; Skowhegan Summer Art School, Maine, 1968; Yale-Norfolk Summer Art School, New Haven, Connecticut, 1969; and Cornell University Summer Art School, Ithaca, New York, 1970. Recipient: Summer Art Fellowship, Yale University, 1959; National Council for the Arts Award, 1966; Guggenheim Memorial Grant, 1969. Agent: John Weber Gallery, New York. Address: c/o John Weber Gallery, 142 Greene Street, New York, New York 10012, U.S.A.

Individual Exhibitions:

1964 Thibaut Gallery, New York
1965 Fischbach Gallery, New York
1967 Fischbach Gallery, New York
1969 Fischbach Gallery, New York
1970 Fischbach Gallery, New York
1971 Fischbach Gallery, New York
     Guggenheim Museum, New York
1973 Max Protetch Gallery, Washington, D.C.
     Daniel Weinberg Gallery, San Francisco
     Galerie Yvon Lambert, Paris
     Fischbach Gallery, New York
     Galleria Toselli, Milan
     Lisson Gallery, London
     Galerie Annemarie Verna, Zurich
     Galleria Mari-Lena Bonomo, Bari, Italy
1974 Museum of Contemporary Art, La Jolla, California
     John Weber Gallery, New York
     Galerie Konrad Fischer, Dusseldorf
     Daniel Weinberg Gallery, San Francisco
1975 Cusack Gallery, Houston
     Ace Gallery, Los Angeles
     Lisson Gallery, London
     Galerie Yvon Lambert, Paris
     Galerie Swart, Amsterdam
     Galleria D'Allessandro Ferranti, Rome
     Galerie Konrad Fischer, Dusseldorf
     John Weber Gallery, New York

1977 Four Large Works, Museum Hans Lange, Krefeld, West Germany
     Portland Center for the Visual Arts, Oregon
     Kunsthalle, Basle
     John Weber Gallery, New York
     Young-Hoffman Gallery, Chicago
1978 Galerie Annemarie Verna, Zurich
     Jean and Karen Bernier, Athens
     Yarlow-Salzman Gallery, Toronto
     Studio La Città, Verona
     Galerie Schellmann und Kluser, Munich
     Protetch-McIntosh Gallery, Washington, D.C.
1979 John Weber Gallery, New York
     Galerie Konrad Fischer, Dusseldorf
1980 Young-Hoffman Gallery, Chicago
     John Weber Gallery, New York
     Texas Gallery, Houston
     Gremälde, Kunsthalle, Bielefeld, West Germany
     Richard Hines Gallery, Seattle
1981 Galerie Annemarie Verna, Zurich
     Lisson Gallery, London
     Hoshour Gallery, Albuquerque, New Mexico
     Carol Taylor Gallery, Dallas
1982 Sidney Janis Gallery, New York
     Stedelijk Museum, Amsterdam
1983 Daniel Weinberg Gallery, Los Angeles
1984 Paula Cooper Gallery, New York
1985 Akron Art Museum, Ohio
     La Jolla Museum of Contemporary Art, California
     University of California, Berkeley
1986 Neuberger Museum, Purchase, New York

Selected Group Exhibitions:

1966 Systemic Painting, Guggenheim Museum, New York
1972 Documenta 5, Museum Fridericianum, Kassel, West Germany (and Documenta 6, 1977)
1975 Painting, Drawing and Sculpture of the 60's and 70's from the Dorothy and Herbert Vogel Collection, University of Pennsylvania, Philadelphia (travelled to the Contemporary Arts Center, Cincinnati)
1976 Drawing Now, Museum of Modern Art, New York
1977 Less Is More, Sidney Janis Gallery, New York
1978 American Painting of the 70's, Albright-Knox Art Gallery, Buffalo, New York
1979 Whitney Biennial, Whitney Museum, New York
1980 The Geometric Tradition in American Painting 1920-1980, Rosa Esman Gallery, New York
1984 American Art Since 1970, La Jolla Museum of Contemporary Art, California (travelled to Mexico City; Raleigh, North Carolina; Lincoln, Nebraska; Miami, Florida)
1985 Art Minimal I, CAPC/Musée d'Art Contemporain, Bordeaux, France

Collections:

Albright-Knox Art Gallery, Buffalo, New York; HHK Foundation of Contemporary Art, Milwaukee; Museum of Fine Arts, Houston; La Jolla Institute of Contemporary Art, California; Crex Collection, Zurich; Kunstmuseum, Basle; Städtisches Museum, Monchengladbach, West Germany; Museum Hans Lange, Krefeld, West Germany; Van Abbemuseum, Eindhoven, Netherlands; Museum Boymans-van Beuningen, Rotterdam.

Publications:

By MANGOLD: book—6 Arcs, New York 1978; articles—"Work Comments 1965 1966" in Systemic Painting, exhibition catalogue, New York 1966; "Robert Mangold: An Interview," with R. Krauss, in Artforum (New York), March 1974; "Interview with Robert Mangold," with Robin White, in View (Oakland, California), 1978.

On MANGOLD: books—Minimal Art: A Critical Anthology, edited by Gregory Battcock, New York 1968; Robert Mangold, exhibition catalogue, with an essay by Dianne Waldman, New York 1971; Robert Mangold, exhibition catalogue, with an essay by Naomi Spector, La Jolla, California 1974; Today/Tomorrow, exhibition catalogue, with an introduction by Paul E. Thompson, Miami 1976; Robert Mangold: Four Large Works, exhibition catalogue, Krefeld, West Germany 1977; Robert Mangold: Gemälde, exhibition catalogue, Bielefeld, West Germany 1980; Robert Mangold, exhibition catalogue with text by Alexander van Graevenstein, Amsterdam 1982; Robert Mangold, exhibition catalogue with essays by Mark Stevens and J. Michael Danoff, Akron, Ohio 1985.

Robert Mangold's career might be taken as a successful attempt to amalgamate some personal warmth and at times even dignified caprice within the larger Minimalist commitment to anonymity, literalism, and precise measure. Only his earliest works, in the mid-1960's, were three-dimensional forms, and resembled grayed and abstracted building wall parts. But at that time, the artist made a self-conscious decision not to follow a sculpture course; nonetheless, the general character of his painted art has appeared "architectural" in both the geometric clarity of his form-shapes and his continuing fascination with works composed of sections abutted together and comprising a single concept.

In the later 1960s, with Barnett Newman still an important influence, Mangold worked with oil sprayed on masonite surfaces such as the "Areas," 1966. More recently, he has used acrylic on canvas for works which became distinguished by large and clearly non-free-hand linear forms atop usually mellifously colored and monotonal grounds. These works have so developed during the course of the 1970's that at times the careful adjustment of the external shape edge to the internal patterns leads to the sensation that the normal neutrality of the outer edge of his works has become the real focus of the visual drama—or at least equally vital in establishing the significance of a single work. Where there appears to be error, as for instance "8 Circle Drawings," 1973, as if miscalculations of the regularized forms were unseen by the artist who then permitted such works to be exhibited, there is both the character of wit and as well Mangold's absorption with an uncompleted form—continually avoiding stasis by its suggestion of movement outside the boundaries of a particular work. He brings the old parlor game of visual illusion to bear upon images which have no apparent implication of such meaning at first glance.

Works of the later 1970s continued with internal linear marking but with a new emphasis on geometry, and went on to become shaped canvas as X and Plus, with clear allusion to De Stijl and Constructivism in a new kind of ease with European art traditions. As well, such visual play can be felt as a returning interest in compositional devices, and thus a leaving off of the negation of Minimalism. But then his work may have always conveyed more interest in internal relationships rather than developing a sense of objectness.

For the past decade, he has used a brush (rather than a roller, as earlier) to make his surfaces more available and turned to a lyric ensemble of color—chocolate brown, sky blue, et al. With the mid-1980s, the paintings have become marked with this-worldly suggestions—in fascinating counterpoint to the evolution of his wife's imagery (Sylvia Plimack Mangold) which has become more abstracted and diffused. In this time, in such a series as the Frame Paintings and the Irregular Areas, earlier motifs occur: the abutting of canvases, the play with curvilinear patterns within the geometry, and the emphasis on edge.

Although Mangold has said that he is much more interested in the preparation of his ideas than in the actual concretization of them in pictures, he is clearly an intuitive artist and does not work through formula or system.

—Joshua Kind

MANGOLD, Sylvia.

American. Born Sylvia Plimack in New York City, 18 September 1938. Studied fine arts at Cooper Union,

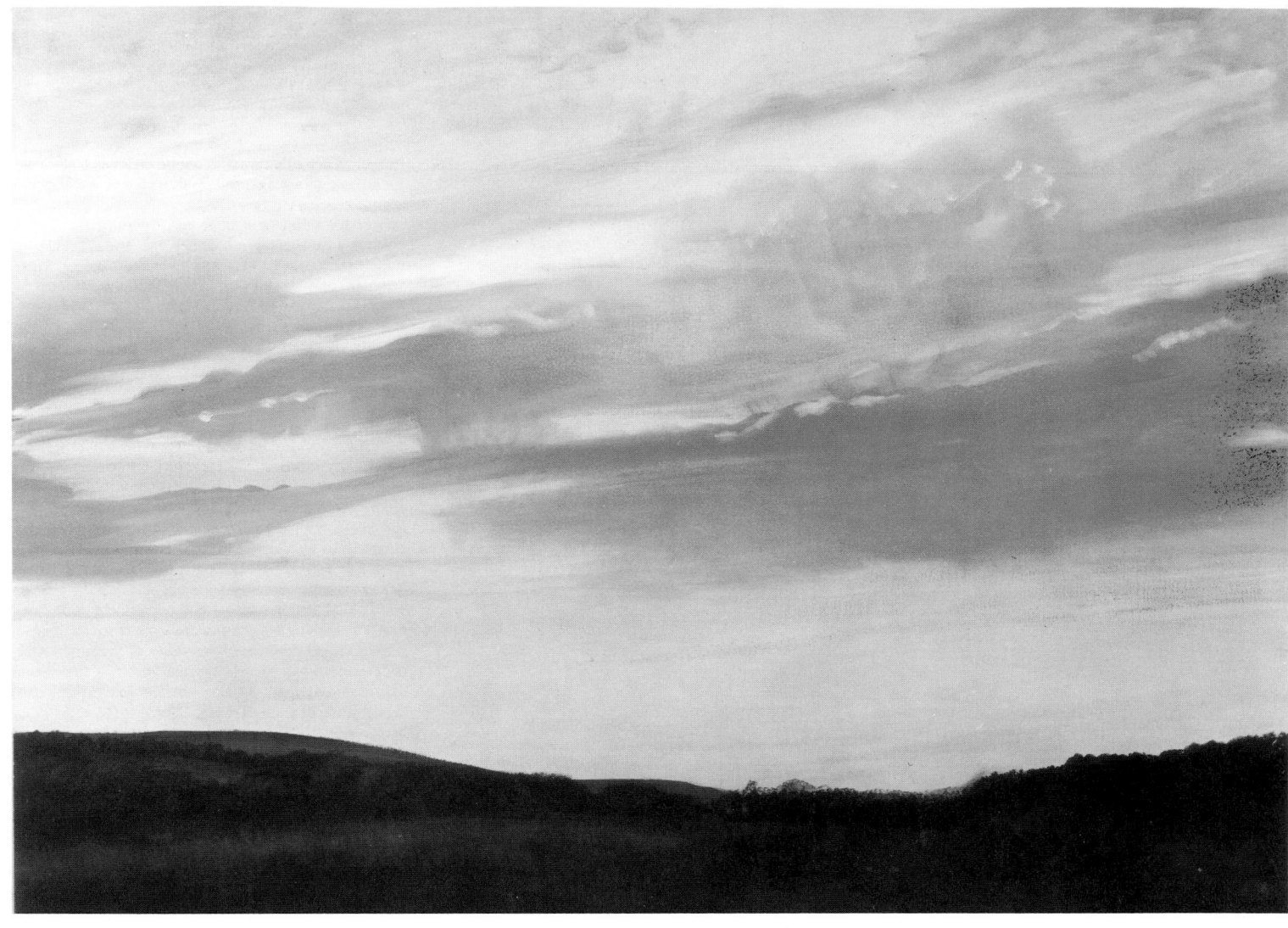

Sylvia Mangold: *Summer 1981*, 1981

New York, 1956–59; Yale University Art School, New Haven, Connecticut, 1959–61, B.F.A. 1961; influenced by Georgia O'Keeffe, Rene Magritte, Edward Hopper, John Haberle, John Peto, William Harnett, Robert Mangold, Jasper Johns and Phillip Pearlstein. Married the artist Robert Peter Mangold, *q.v.*, in 1961; sons: James A. and Andrew P. Worked (with Robert Mangold) as apartment house superintendent, New York, 1961–63. Instructor of Painting and Drawing, School of Visual Arts, New York, 1971–81. Recipient: National Endowment for the Arts Grant, 1974–75; Special Purchase Award, Davidson National Print and Drawing Competition, 1976. Agent: Brooke Alexander Inc., 20 West 57th Street, New York, New York 10019. Address: MD 1, Bull Road, Washingtonville, New York 10992, U.S.A.

Individual Exhibitions:

1974   Fischbach Gallery, New York
1975   Daniel Weinberg Gallery, San Francisco
        Fischbach Gallery, New York
1978   Droll-Kolbert Gallery, New York
        Galerie Annemarie Verna, Zurich
1980   Droll-Kolbert Gallery, New York
        Ohio State University, Columbus
        Young Hoffman Gallery, Chicago
1981   Matrix Gallery, Wadsworth Atheneum, Hartford, Connecticut
        Perspectives, Contemporary Arts Museum, Houston
1982   Brooke Alexander Inc., New York
1984   Brooke Alexander Inc., New York
1985   Rhona Hoffman Gallery, Chicago

1986   Texas Gallery, Houston
        Brooke Alexander Inc., New York

Selected Group Exhibitions:

1968   *Realism Now*, Vassar College, Poughkeepsie, New York
1971   *Twenty Contemporary Women Artists*, Aldrich Museum, Ridgefield, Connecticut
1973   *New York Realism*, Espace Cardin, Paris
1977   *Documenta 6*, Kassel, West Germany
1979   *The 1970's: New American Paintings*, New Museum, New York (toured Europe)
1980   *Drawings to Benefit the Foundations for Contemporary Performance Arts Inc.*, Leo Castelli Gallery New York
1981   *20 Artists: Yale School of Art 1950–1970*, Yale University Art Gallery, New Haven, Connecticut
1984   *New Vistas: Contemporary American Landscapes*, Hudson River Museum, Yonkers, New York
1986   *Drawings*, Spirit Square Arts Center, Charlotte, North Carolina

Collections:

Whitney Museum, New York; McCrory Corporation, New York; Yale University, New Haven, Connecticut; American Federation of Art, Washington, D.C.; Baltimore Museum of Art; Allen Memorial Art Museum, Oberlin, Ohio; Madison Art Center, Wisconsin.

Publications:

By MANGOLD: book—*Inches and Field*, New York 1978.

On MANGOLD: books—*Art on Paper*, exhibition catalogue, Greensboro, North Carolina 1968; *Realism Now*, exhibition catalogue, Poughkeepsie, New York 1968; *New Realism*, exhibition catalogue, Pottsdam, New York 1971; *26 Contemporary American Artists*, exhibition catalogue, Ridgefield, Connecticut 1971; *Still Life Today*, exhibition catalogue, New York 1971; *New Realism* by Udo Kultermann, Tübingen, West Germany 1972; *Contemporary American Painting Annual*, exhibition catalogue, New York 1972; *Objects and 8 Women Realists*, exhibition catalogue, Amherst, Massachusetts 1973; *Super Realism*, edited by Gregory Battcock, New York 1974; *Anonymous Was a Woman*, exhibition catalogue, Valencia, California 1974; *7 Realists*, exhibition catalogue, New Haven, Connecticut 1974; *Selections in Contemporary Realism*, Akron, Ohio 1974; *Works on Paper*, exhibition catalogue, Richmond, Virginia 1974; *A Woman's Sensibility*, Valencia, California 1975; *19th National Print Exhibition*, exhibition catalogue, Brooklyn, New York 1975; *60's/70's: Paintings, Drawings, Sculpture from the Vogel Collection*, Philadelphia 1975; *Spare*, exhibition catalogue, New York 1975; *Private Notions: Artists' Sketchbooks II*, exhibition catalogue, Philadelphia 1976; *Painting and Sculpture Today 1976*, exhibition catalogue, Indianapolis 1976; *Contemporary Images in Watercolor*, exhibition catalogue, Akron, Ohio 1976; *A View of a Decade*, exhibition catalogue, Chicago 1977; *Recent Works on Paper by American Artists*, exhibition catalogue, Madison, Wisconsin 1977; *Paintings '75/'76/'77*, exhibition catalogue, Bronxville, New York 1977; *Young Hoffman Gallery 1976–1979*, exhibition catalogue, Chicago 1970; *8 Artists: The Elusive Image*, exhibition catalogue, Minneapolis 1979; *Reality and Illusion*, exhibition catalogue, by Donald J. Brewer, Denver and Los Angeles 1980; *New York Realists 1980*, exhibition catalogue, by Roger Howrigan, Sparkill, New York 1980; *Sylvia Plimack Mangold* by Andrea Miller-Keller, Hartford, Connecticut 1980; articles— "Realism: The Painting Is Fiction Enough" by Hilton Kramer in the *New York Times*, 28 April 1974; "Sylvia Mangold: Light, Rules, Floors" by Judith L. Dunham in *Artweek* (Oakland, California), 27 September 1975; "Vogel Collection: They Pick Wisely, and Very Lovingly" by Victoria Donohoe in the *Philadelphia Inquirer,* 12 October 1975; "Painting Is as Painting Does" by John Perreault in the *Soho Weekly News* (New York), 12 May 1977; "Through the Looking Glass and What the Artist Found There" by David Mower in *Art International* (Lugano, Switzerland), September 1979; "Abstraction and Sensitivity" in *Artspeak* (New York), 31 January 1980; "Beautiful Deceptions" by Mark Stevens in *Newsweek* (New York), 24 March 1980; "Keep Up the Image" by William Zimmer in the *Soho Weekly News* (New York), 26 November 1980.

My paintings are a total of accumulated detail. The translation from the object to the canvas has a signature that is mine, and is the evidence of my efforts. I try for accuracy and illusion. Although I believe these qualities to be arbitrary, I need to strive for them.

—Sylvia Mangold

During the 1960's Sylvia Mangold established a realist painter's variant of one then favorite nonrepresentational image—grid-patterned, hard-edged, and measured. It was a complex and perhaps intellectualized, if not poeticized, realism that self-consciously incorporated a self-questioning attitude. Her precise, perspectival depictions of flooring—hardwood, grained boards—allowed her to become expert in the painting of their patterns. Aside from the physical materiality shown through her craft energy, these paintings were also about "measure": rulers and other devices of scale were included in these silent and usually otherwise empty room interiors. The images then became emblems of the irony within depiction—both the scale of actuality, and three-dimensional space, when illustrated pictorially. (Her work, interestingly enough, might be seen as the stylistic obverse of her painter-husband Robert's approach to scale and measure; both at that time and the present he has worked with two-dimensional geometric forms upon flat monochromatic fields.)

Since the mid-70's, Mangold has restricted the spatial extent of her former view, so that the surface of her canvas has become analogous to—in classic *trompe l'oeil* tradition—a flat wall plane; and the craft and zest that she once expended upon the wood graining now was given over to meticulous illusionist renderings of masking tapes, often much overlapped. Seemingly held in place by the tapes, centrally in the rectangle of the canvas, are landscape views. From the artist, we learn that these scenes are usually based upon those observed through her studio windows. Keeping this format intact, she has played many variants upon the relationship of the landscape views and the "wall area" outside the tapes, including images completely non-representational with the exception of the tapes. In such works, Mangold reveals the abstract force that has always clearly lain beneath her seemingly quiet mundane worlds. As well, it is not so much doubt about the efficacy of realism that distinguishes her work—no matter how powerful the depicted reality, it is all abstract.

—Joshua Kind

MAN RAY.

American. Born Emmanuel Rudnitzky, in Philadelphia, Pennsylvania, 27 August 1890. Studied art at evening classes in various schools, including the National Academy of Design, New York, 1908–12; studied life-drawing at the Francisco Ferrer Social Center, New York, 1912–13. Married Adon (Donna) Lacroix in 1914 (divorced, 1918); lived with Alice (Kiki) Prin, 1924–30; married Juliet Browner in 1946. Independent painter and sculptor, from 1911: worked as part-time designer in an advertising agency, New York, 1913–19; freelance photographer, filmmaker and painter, associating with Surrealist artists, Paris, 1921–40; freelance fashion photographer and painter, Hollywood, California, 1940–50; independent artist, concentrating on own photography and painting, Paris and Cadaques, Spain, 1951 until his death, 1976. Founder-Member, with Marcel Duchamp and Walter Arensberg, Society of Independent Artists, New York, 1915, with Marcel Duchamp and Francis Picabia, New York Dadaist movement, New York, 1917, and with Marcel Duchamp, Katherine Dreier and others, Société Anonyme, New York, 1920. Editor, with Henri S. Reynolds and Adolf Wolff, only issue of *TNT* magazine, New York, 1919, and with Marcel Duchamp, only issue of *New York Dada* magazine, New York, 1921. Instructor in Photography, Art Center School, Los Angeles, 1942–50. Recipient: Gold Medal for Photography, *Biennale,* Venice, 1961. *Died* (in Paris) *18 November 1976.*

Individual Exhibitions:

1915	Daniel Gallery, New York (and 1916, 1919)
1921	Librairie 6, Paris
1926	*Rayographs and Objects,* Galerie Surrealiste, Paris
	Photographs and Paintings, Daniel Gallery, New York
1927	Daniel Gallery, New York
1928	Galerie Surrealiste, Paris
1929	*Photographic Compositions by Man Ray,* Arts Club, Chicago
	Galerie Myrbor, Paris
	Rayographs and Paintings, Galerie Quatre Chemins, Paris
	Galerie Van Leer, Paris
1931	Galerie Alexandre III, Cannes
1932	Galerie Chez Dacharry, Paris
	Julien Levy Gallery, New York
	Galerie Vignon, Paris
1934	Lund Humphries and Company, London (and 1935)
1935	*Photographs and Rayographs,* Wadsworth Atheneum, Hartford, Connecticut
	Photographs and Drawings, Art Center School, Los Angeles
	Rayographs and Paintings, Galerie Adlan, Barcelona
	Galerie aux Cahiers d'Art, Paris
1936	Curt Valentin Gallery, New York
1937	Galerie Jeanne Bucher, Paris
	Palais des Beaux-Arts, Brussels (with Yves Tanguy und René Magritte)
1939	Galerie de Beaunne, Paris (travelled to the London Gallery)
1941	Frank Perls Galleries, Los Angeles
	M. H. de Young Memorial Museum, San Francisco
1943	Santa Barbara Museum of Art, California
1944	Pasadena Art Institute, California
1945	Los Angeles County Museum of History, Science and Art
1946	Circle Gallery, Los Angeles
1948	Copley Gallery, Hollywood, California
1951	Galerie Berggruen, Paris
1953	Paul Kantor Gallery, Los Angeles
1954	Galerie Furstenberg, Paris
1956	Galerie l'Etoile Scellée, Paris
	Musée de Tours, France (with Max Ernst and Dorothea Tanning)
1959	Galerie Rive Droite, Paris
	Alexander Iolas Gallery, New York
	Mayer Gallery, New York
	Galerie Larcade, Paris
	Institute of Contemporary Arts, London
1960	Esther Robies Gallery, Los Angeles
1962	*Man Ray: L'Oeuvre Photographique,* Bibliothèque Nationale, Paris
	Galerie Rive Droite, Paris
1963	Cordier and Ekstrom, New York
	Musée D'Amiens, France
	Cavendish Gallery, London
	Princeton University, New Jersey
	LGA Austellungsraum, Stuttgart
1964	Galleria Schwarz, Milan
1965	Cordier and Ekstrom, New York
1966	Los Angeles County Museum of Art (retrospective)
1968	Martha Jackson Gallery, New York
	Galerie der Spiegel, Cologne

1969	Hanover Gallery, London
	2 Generations of Photographs: Man Ray and Naomi Savage New Jersey State Museum, Trenton
	Galerie Alphonse Chave, Venice
	Studio Marconi, Milan
	Galleria Il Fauno, Turin
1970	Galerie Richard Foncke, Ghent
	Galleria del Cavallino, Venice
	Galerie XXme Siècle, Paris
	Galleria La Chioccoloa, Padua
	Noah Goldowsky Gallery, New York
	Museum Boymans-van Beuningen, Rotterdam (retrospective; travelled to Musé d'Art Moderne, Paris, and Louisiana Museum, Humlebaek, Denmark)
	Philadelphia Museum of Art
1971	Galleria Milano, Milan
	Salone Annunciata, Milan
	Galleria Il Fauno, Turin
	Galerie Suzanne Visat, Paris
1972	Galleria Gissi, Turin (travelled to Galerie Françoise Tournie, Paris, and Galleria dell'Arte Libreria Pictogramma, Rome)
	Galerie des 4 Mouvements, Paris
	Galleria Il Fauno, Turin
1973	Metropolitan Museum of Art, New York
	Galerie im Lenbachhaus, Munich (with Marcel Duchamp and Francis Picabia)
1974	New York Cultural Center (travelled to Institute of Contemporary Arts, London, and Galleria Il Fauno, Turin)
	Alexander Iolas Gallery, New York
	Galerie Alexandre Iolas, Paris
1975	Mayor Gallery, Athens
	G. Ray Hawkins Gallery, Los Angeles
	Palazzo dell'Esposizione, Rome
	Galleria Il Fauno, Turin, Italy
	Mayor Gallery, London
	Studio Marconi, Milan
1976	*Man Ray: Fotografia,* at the *Biennale,* Venice
1977	Kimmel/Cohn, New York
	Kiva Gallery, Boston
1978	*Vintage Photographs, Solarizations and Rayographs,* Allan Frumkin Gallery, Chicago
1979	*Man Ray: Inventionen und Interpretationen,* Kunstverein, Frankfurt (travelled to Kunsthalle, Basle)
1980	Prakapas Gallery, New York
	Galeria Eude, Barcelona (toured Spain)
1981	*Man Ray: Photographe,* Centre Pompidou, Paris
	Vintage Photographs, Knoedler Gallery, London
1982	Zabriskie Gallery, New York
	Meredith Long and Company, Houston
	Palau de la Virreina, Barcelona
1983	Robert Miller Gallery, New York
1985	Centre for Photography, Zagreb, Yugoslavia
	Muzoj Savremene Umetnosti, Belgrade
	Gemeentelijk Van Reekummuseum, Apeldoorn, Netherlands
	National Museum of American Art, Washington, D.C.
	Zabriskie Gallery, New York
	Museum Villa Stuck, Munich
1986	Galleria Vivita, Florence, Italy
1987	Galleria Editalia, Rome

Selected Group Exhibitions:

1928	*1st Independent Salon of Photography,* Salon de l'Escalier, Paris
1929	*Film und Foto,* Deutscher Werkbund, Stuttgart
1946	*Pioneers of Modern Art in America,* Whitney Museum, New York
1964	*The Painter and the Photograph: From Delacroix to Warhol,* University of New Mexico, Albuquerque
1966	*Dada,* Musée National d'Art Moderne, Paris
1967	*Photography in the 20th Century,* National Gallery of Canada, Ottawa (toured Canada and the United States, 1967–73)
1977	*The History of Fashion Photography,* International Museum of Photography, George Eastman House, Rochester, New York (travelled to Brooklyn Museum, New York; San Francisco Museum of Modern Art; Cincinnati Art Institute, Ohio; and Museum of Fine Arts, St. Petersburg, Florida)

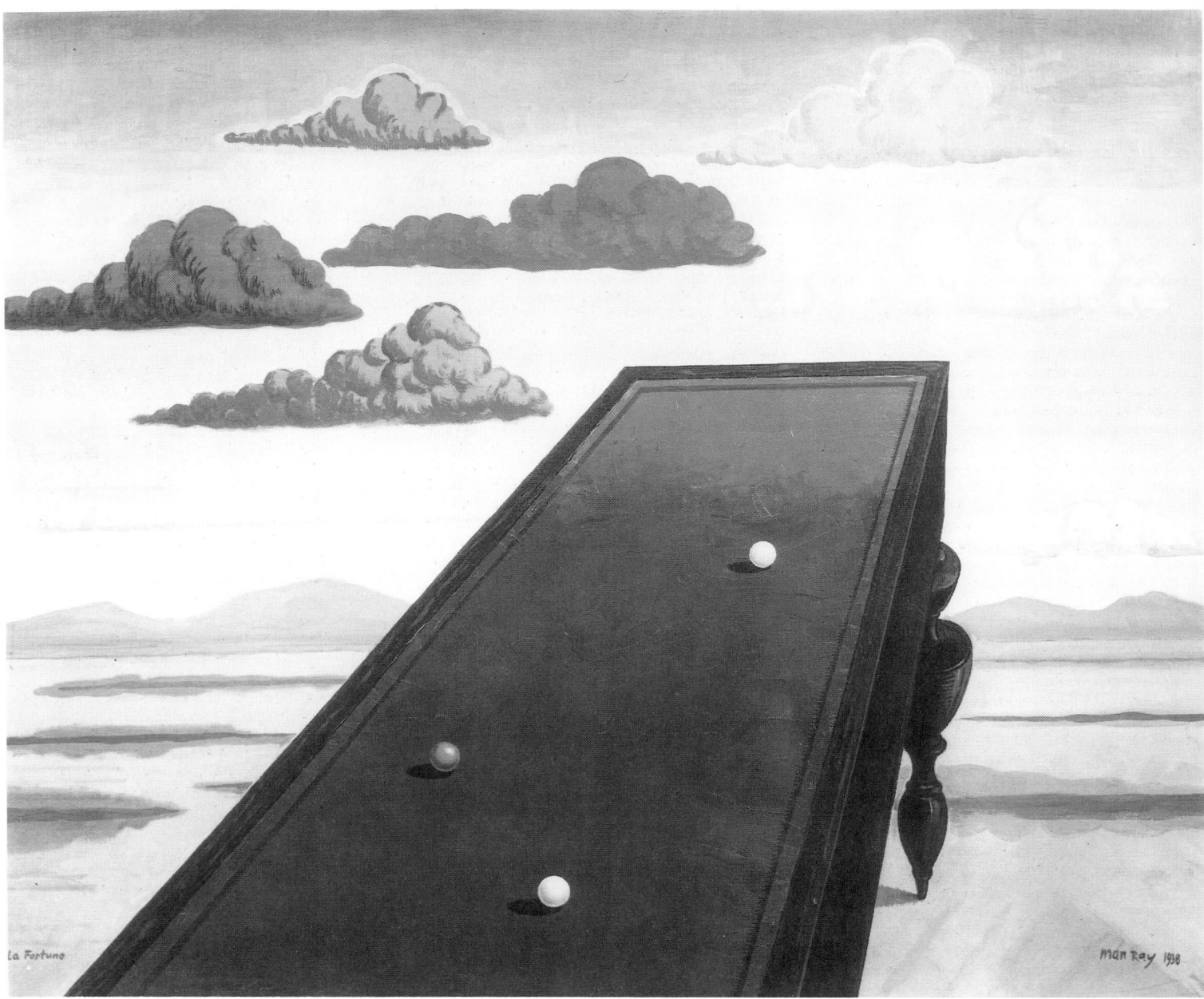

Man Ray: *La Fortune*, **1938** Courtesy Whitney Museum, New York

1979   *Photographie als Kunst 1879–1979*, Tiroler Landesmuseum Ferdinandeum, Innsbruck, Austria (travelled to Neue Galerie am Wolfgang Gurlitt Museum, Linz, Austria; Neue Galerie am Landesmuseum Joanneum, Graz; and the Museum des 20. Jahrhunderts, Vienna)

1980   *Experimental Photography*, Stills Gallery, Edinburgh (toured Britain)

1985   *L'Amour Fou: Photography and Surrealism*, Corcoran Gallery, Washington, D.C. (travelled to San Francisco; Paris; London)

Collections:

Museum of Modern Art, New York; International Museum of Photography, George Eastman House, Rochester, New York; Yale University, New Haven, Connecticut, Art Institute of Chicago; New Orleans Museum of Art; University of Kansas, Lawrence; University of New Mexico, Albuquerque; Oakland Museum, California; Provinciaal Museum voor Kunstambachten, Deurne-Antwerp; Musée d'Art Moderne, Paris.

Publications:

By MAN RAY: books—*Les Champs Délicieux: Album de Photographies*, portfolio of rayographs, with a preface by Tristan Tzara, Paris 1922; *Man Ray*, with text by Georges Ribemont-Dessaignes, Paris 1924; *Man Ray/George Hoyningen-Huene*, portfolio of fashion photos, Paris 1924–25; *Revolving Doors, 1916–17*, Paris 1926, Turin 1972; *Kiki Souvenirs*, Paris 1929; *Electricité*, portfolio of 10 rayographs, with an introduction by Pierre Bost, Paris 1931; *Man Ray Photographies, 1920–1934, Paris*, with text and poems by André Breton, Paul Eluard, Tristan Tzara and others, Paris 1934, reprinted as *Man Ray: Photographs, 1920–1934*, with an introduction by A. D. Coleman, New York 1975, and as *Man Ray: Photographien, Paris, 1920–1934*, with text by Andreas Haus, Munich 1980; *Facile*, with poems by Paul Eluard, Paris 1935; *Les Mains Libres*, with Paul Eluard, Paris 1937; *La Photographie n'est pas l'Art*, manifesto, with a foreword by André Breton, Paris 1937; *Alphabet for Adults*, Beverly Hills, California 1948; *To Be Continued Unnoticed*, Beverly Hill, California 1948; *Man Ray: L'Oeuvre Photographique*, exhibition catalogue, with text by Jean Adhemar and others, Paris 1962; *Man Ray: Self-Portrait*, Boston 1963; *Man Ray: 12 Photographs 1921–28*, portfolio, New York 1963; *Man Ray: Portraits*, with text by L. Fritz Gruber, Gutersloh, West Germany and Paris 1963; *Man Ray: Tous les Films que J'ai Realisé*, Paris 1965; *Les Mannequins*, Paris 1966; *Les Invendables*, portfolio, Vence, France 1969; *Mr. and Mrs. Woodman*, portfolio, Amsterdam 1970; *Oggetti d'Affezione: Rayographs*, with text by C. G. Argan, Turin 1970; *Man Ray: Les Voies Lactées*, New York 1974; *Man Ray: Femmes 1930–35*, portfolio of 26 photos, Milan 1981; articles—"Man Ray: Rayograms" in *Surrealisme A.S.D.L.R.* (Paris), December 1931; "Sur le Realisme Photographique" in *Cahiers d'Art* (Paris), no. 10, 1935; "La Photographie qui Console" in *XXme Siècle* (Paris), no. 2, 1938; "Is Photography Necessary?" in *Modern Photography* (New York), November 1957; "Man Ray: The Fiery Elf," interview with Morris Gordon, in *Infinity* (New York), October 1962; "Man Ray on the Future," interview with Ed Hirsch and Ben Zar, in *Popular Photography* (New York), January 1967; "Man Ray," interview with Paul Hill and Thomas Cooper in *Camera* (Lucerne), February 1975; films—*The Return to Reason*, 1923; *Emak Bakia*, 1926; *L'Etoile de Mer*, 1928; *The Mystery of the Chateau of Dice*, 1929.

On MAN RAY: books—*The History of Surrealist Painting* by Marcel Jean, London 1960; *Un Siècle de Photographie de Niepce à Man Ray*, exhibition catalogue, by Laurent Roosens, Paris 1965; *Man Ray*, with an introduction by Jules Langsner, Los Angeles 1966; *Man Ray: 60 Years of Liberties* by Louis Aragon, Jean Arp and others, Milan 1971; *The Painter and the Photograph: From Delacroix to Warhol* by Van Deren Coke, Albuquerque, New Mexico 1972; *Man Ray* by Janus, Milan 1973; *Photography in America*, edited by Robert Doty, with an introduction by Minor White, New York 1974; *Man Ray* by Roland Penrose, London 1975; *Man Ray: The Rigour of the Imagination* by Arturo Schwarz, Milan 1977; *Man Ray: L'Immagine Fotografica/Man Ray: The Photographic Image* by Janus, Milan 1977, London 1980; *Man Ray: Inventionen und Interpretationen*, exhibition catalogue, by G. Bussmann and others, Frankfurt 1979; *Man Ray: Photographe*, exhibition catalogue, with text by Jean-Hubert Martin, Paris 1981; *Man Ray*, exhibition catalogue with text by Merry A. Foresta, New York 1982; *Atelier Man Ray 1920–35*, exhibition catalogue by Alain Sayag, Paris 1982; *The Great Photographers: Man Ray* by Janus, London 1984; *Man Ray*, exhibition catalogue with texts by Andre Breton, Tristan Tzara and others, Florence 1986.

Man Ray was a rare individual. Possessed of an endlessly fertile imagination, he continued to create new and startling art works throughout his long career. Remaining at the forefront of the avantgarde, he experimented with every conceivable medium, invented a number of his own, and influenced several generations of artists. His major contributions fall into three categories: painting, sculpture, and photography (including film). Although his primary allegiance was to Dada, he also worked extensively with Surrealism. He was the only American dadaist to earn a major international reputation.

During his early years in New York, Ray painted in a variety of realistic and semi-realistic styles. In 1913 and 1914, spurred on by the Armory Show, he experimented with several Cubist styles and flirted with Expressionism. By 1915, however, he had become a fervent convert to Dada under the tutelage of his close friend Marcel Duchamp and was pursuing advanced experiments in abstraction. "The Rope Dancer Accompanies Herself with Her Shadows" (1916), which is related to Duchamp's "Bride Stripped Bare by Her Bachelors, Even," is a brilliant exercise in hard-edged precision. Here, as elsewhere, the artist displays an acute understanding of color and form. Like Duchamp, whom he resembled in many ways, Ray also delighted in readymades, assisted readymades, and assorted assemblages. Typically these are more complex than they seem, often involving complicated puns and hidden implication. Not all his work is intellectual, however, and much was cultivated for its shock value. In the best dadaist fashion he provokes the viewer via banality, paradox, and eroticism. Thus "Eighth Street" (1920) presents a dirty, battered tin can picked out of the gutter. One of his more famous pieces, "Gift" (1921), consists of a flat-iron with a row of tacks protruding from its underside, while in "Lampshade" (1919/21) he wraps a decomposed shade around a lamp-stand. Besides the fornicating "Mr. and Mrs. Woodman" (1947), one encounters objects such as the "Priapic Paper-Weight" (1920) and a whole series of provocative nudes.

Ray was equally ingenious in the realm of photography, where he concentrated on portraiture, nude studies, and special effects. Few of the literary or artistic luminaries residing in Paris escaped his camera. His best known nude is undoubtedly "Le Violon d'Ingres" (1924) which features a rear view of a seated woman (his mistress Kiki) with two f-shaped cut-outs superimposed on her waist. His experimental photography includes the celebrated rayographs—essentially negative impressions of objects—a number of abstract studies, and experiments with solarized images. With the advent of Surrealism Ray broadened his artistic base to include works in which dream played a role or which produced powerful unconscious vibrations. To this phase belong his experiments with painted masks and photographs like "Monument to D. A. F. de Sade" (1933). His interest in wrapped objects antedates Christo's by a great many years. In addition to illustrating numerous Surrealist texts he painted a whole series of pictures in the same mode. "At the Observatory Hour—The Lovers" (1934), which depicts an enormous pair of lips floating above a landscape with an observatory, dramatizes man's universal quest for love. Among his various essays in film Ray's *Starfish* (1928), based on a poem by Robert Desnos, has become a Surrealist classic.

—Willard Bohn

MANZÙ, Giacomo.

Italian. Born Giacomo Manzoni in Bergamo, 22 December 1908. Apprenticed to a wood carver and gilder and later to a plasterer, Bergamo, 1919; attended evening classes at the Fantoni School, Bergamo, 1921; studied briefly at the Accademia di Belle Arti, Verona, 1928; mainly self-taught in art. Served in the Italian Army, in Verona, 1927. Married Antonia Oreni in 1934 (separated, 1952); children: Carlo and Mileta (both died in 1937) and Pio; married Inge Schabel in 1958; children: Giulia and Mileto. Sculptor and painter since 1928; lived in Milan, 1930–33, then returned to Bergamo; worked on decorations for the chapel of the Catholic University, Milan, 1930; decorated main hall, Ardiano House, Selvino, near Bergamo, 1933; produced many drawings and paintings during the 1930's, also worked in chased copper; first bronzes, 1934; moved to Clusone, near Bergamo, 1942; settled in Milan, 1945; moved to Rome, 1958; worked on decorations of chapel in house of Don Giuseppe de Lucca, Rome, 1961; moved to the Vatican, 1963; settled in Campo del Fico, Ardea, near Rome, 1964; first theatre designs, for *Oedipus Rex* by Stravinsky, Rome, 1964; founded Raccolta Amici di Manzù, Ardea, 1969, which was donated to the Italian State, 1981. Professor of Sculpture, Brera Accademia di Belle Arti, Milan, 1941–54; Lecturer, Albertina Accademia, Turin, 1941–42; Lecturer, Kokoschka's International Summer School 1954–60. Recipient: Gold Medal, *Triennale*, Milan 1937; Grand Prize, *Quadriennale*, Rome, 1942; Italian Sculpture Prize, *Biennale*, Venice, 1948; International Lenin Prize, 1966; Via Condotti Award, Rome, 1981; Italian Gold Medal of Merit, Rome, 1981; Le Muse Medal, Academy of the Muse, Florence, 1981. Honorary doctorate: Royal College of Art, London, 1971. Corresponding Member, 1947, and Academician, 1954, Accademia di San Luca, Rome. Honorary Member: Académie Royale de Belgique, 1954; American Academy of Arts and Letters, 1964; Academia Nacional de Bellas Artes, Buenos Aires, 1964; Académie des Beaux-Arts, Paris, 1969; Academy of Arts of the U.S.S.R., 1969; American Academy of Arts and Sciences, 1978; European Academy of Sciences, Arts and Letters, Paris, 1981; Honorary Academician: Royal Academy of Arts, London, 1970. Address: Campo del Fico, 00040 Ardea, Rome, Italy.

Individual Exhibitions:

1933	Galleria del Milione, Milan
1934	Galleria delle Tre Arti, Milan
1937	Galleria Cometa, Rome
1938	Galleria Genova, Genoa (with Renato Birolli)
1941	Galleria Barbaroux, Milan
1942	Centro d'Azione per le Arti, Turin
1944	Galleria Galatea, Turin
1945	Galleria Galatea, Turin
1947	Palazzo Reale, Milan
	Galleria La Palma, Rome
1949	Instituto de Arte Moderno, Buenos Aires
1953	Hanover Gallery, London
1954	Galerie Welz, Salzburg (with Oskar Kokoschka)
1955	Galerie Welz, Salzburg (toured Europe)
1956	Hanover Gallery, London
	Kunsthaus, Winterthur, Switzerland (with Giorgio Morandi)
1957	World House Gallery, New York
	Palazzo Strozzi, Florence
1958	Opera Barilacqua di Musa, Venice
	American Federation of Arts, New York (with Giorgio Morandi)
	Galerie Welz, Salzburg
1959	Haus der Kunst, Munich (toured Europe, 1959–60)
1960	World House Gallery, New York
	La Nuova Pesa Galleria, Rome (with Renato Guttuso)
1962	Galerie Welz, Salzburg
	Palazzo della Pinacoteca Carrara, Bergamo
1964	Galleria Galatea, Turin
	Sala Napoleone, Venice
1965	Hanover Gallery, London
	Paul Rosenberg Gallery, New York
1966	Gallery Cube, Tokyo
	Academy of Art, Moscow (travelled to the Academy of Arts, Leningrad)
1967	Galleria Galatea, Turin
1968	Paul Rosenberg Gallery, New York
	Galleria Ciranna, Milan
	Museum Boymans-van Beuningen, Rotterdam
1969	Galerie des Beaux-Arts, Bordeaux

	Hanover Gallery, London
	Lumley Cazalet Gallery, London
	Academie der Künste, East Berlin
	Museum of Modern Art, New York
	Pushkin Museum, Moscow (travelled to the Hermitage Museum, Leningrad, and the Academy of Fine Arts, Kiev)
	Museo Nazionale, Reggio Calabria, Italy
1970	Galleria Odyssia, New York (with Giorgio Morandi and Ennio Morlotti)
	Teatro San Carlos, Naples
1971	Galleria Luigi Bellini, Florence
	Raccolta Amici di Manzù, Ardea, Rome
1972	Staatsgalerie Modernen Kunst, Munich
1973	National Museum of Modern Art, Tokyo
	Carolino Augusteum Museum and Galerie Welz, Salzburg
	Galleria Toninelli, Rome
	Galerie G, Berlin
	Piñacoteca Brera, Milan (travelled to the Galleria Civica d'Arte Moderna, Turin, and the Galleria Ghelfi, Verona)
	Belvedere Palace, Prague
	Palazzo Comunale, Pienza, Italy
	Galleria Idea, Florence
1974	Galerie am Hohen Markt, Krems-an-der-Donau, Austria
	Teatro Accademico del Bibbiena, Mantua, Italy
	National Gallery, Budapest
1975	Palazzo Diamanti, Ferrara, Italy
	Italo-Latin American Institute, Rome
1976	Universe Gallery, Tokyo
	Mariani Galleria, Ravenna, Italy
	Kunstmuseum, Münster, West Germany
	Raccolta Amici di Manzù, Ardea, Rome
1977	Palazzo della Ragione, Bergamo
	Carrara Academy, Bergamo
	San Bartolomeo, Bergamo
	Studio d'Arte A2, Rome
1978	Art Museum, Phoenix, Arizona (travelled to the Fine Art Museum, San Diego, California)
	Raccolta Amici di Manzù, Ardea, Rome
1979	Accademia delle Arti e del Disegno, Florence
	Galerie Nichide, Paris
	Universe Gallery, Tokyo
	Galleria Ellequadro, Genoa
	Gallery Tasende, La Jolla, California
1980	Galleria della Bezuga, Florence
	Centro Dantesco, Ravenna
	Pushkin Museum, Moscow
	Galleria Bergamini, Milan (travelled to the Galleria Forni, Bologna)
	100 Works 1938–1980, Art Gallery of Hamilton, Ontario (toured Canada, 1980–82)
1981	Galleria Ca' d'Oro, Rome
1986	Kunstnerforbundet, Oslo
	Bergen Billedgalleri, Norway
	Galleria l'Isola, Rome
1987	Carlsburg Glyptotek, Copenhagen
1988	Museum of Modern Art, Oxford

Selected Group Exhibitions:

1932	*Group Exhibition*, Galleria del Milione, Milan
1936	*Biennale*, Venice
1937	*International Exhibition*, Musée National d'Art Moderne, Paris
1939	*Italian Art, Ancient and Modern*, San Francisco Museum of Art
1951	*Bienal*, Sao Paulo
1955	*Biennale*, Open-Air Sculpture Garden, Antwerp
1958	*Pittsburgh International*, Carnegie Institute, Pittsburgh
1966	*20 Italian Sculptors*, Tate Gallery, London
1972	*Masters of Modern Italian Art*, Museum of Modern Art, Kyoto, Japan

Collections:

Raccola Amici di Manzù, Ardea, near Rome; Galleria Nazionale d'Arte Moderna, Rome; Tate Gallery, London; Middelheim Park, Antwerp; Wallraf-Richartz Museum, Cologne;

Kunstnernes Hus, Oslo; National Museum of Modern Art, Tokyo; Manzù Room, Open-Air Museum, Hakone, Japan; Museum of Modern Art, New York; Guggenheim Museum, New York.

Publications:

By MANZÙ: book—*Moscow*, 1972; illustrated books—*Il Falso e Vero Verde* by Salvatore Quadimodo, 1954; *Works and Days* by Hesiod, Rome 1966; *The New Testament*, Paris 1966; *King Oedipus* by Sophocles, New York 1966; *The Odyssey* by Homer, translated by Salvatore Quasimodo, Rome 1977; articles—"Dove va l'Arte Italiana? in *Domus* (Milan), February 1937; "La Disciplina dell'Arte" in *Pinifarina* (Turin), no. 5, 1964; "Paris Giacomo Manzu" in *Domenica del Corriere* (Milan), March 1970; "Il Disegno e sempre una Speranza" in *Didattica del Designo* (Brescia, Italy), March 1970.

On MANZÙ: books—*Manzù* by Giovanni Schweiller, Milan 1932; *Human and Religious Values in the Great Pietà of Giacomo Manzù for a Papal Monument* by Bruno Calzaferri, Milan 1943; *Giacomo Manzù; Sculptor* by Carlo Ludovico Ragghianti, Milan 1957; *Manzù* by John Rewald, London 1967; *Catalogue of the Graphic Work of Manzù 1929-1968* by Alfonso Ciranna, Milan 1968; *An Artist and the Pope* by Curtis Bill Pepper, New York 1968; *Manzù* by Mario de Micheli, Milan 1971 (includes bibliography); *Manzù and the Stage* by Blida Heynold von Graefe, Ardea, Italy 1972; *Manzù and the Theme of Peace* by Glauco Pellegrini, Florence 1976; *Giacomo Manzù*, exhibition catalogue, by M. Homma, J. P. Hodin and H. Kon, Tokyo 1973; *Manzù: 100 Works 1938-1980*, exhibition catalogue, Hamilton, Ontario 1980; film—*Giacomo Manzù* by Glauco Pellegrini, 1959.

"You have produced more than my portrait. You have told the story of my pontificate in bronze," said Pope John XXIII, the peasant's son from "Sotto il Monte" in the province of Bergamo, to Giacomo Manzù, the eleventh of a Bergamo shoemaker's twelve children. So the sculptor had again succeeded in what for him according to his own words is the most important element in sculpture: "The form should embrace what people have in them."

Manzù's sculptures, drawings and bas reliefs are always much more than an artist's perfect forms governed by the technique of his handicraft. The word handicraft in this instance is not accidental. Manzù is self-taught; he had been apprenticed as an 11 year old first to a wood carver, then to a plasterer. Only when he was 20 years of age, overwhelmed by his reaction to Impressionism in Paris, did he decide to become an artist. He was influenced by the Etruscans and the Roman and Gothic stonemasons of Lombardy but also by the great Medardo Rosso, much too little known outside Italy, who like Manzù modelled with light. But the impressionist Medardo almost dissolved his forms in the light, while the realist Manzù surrounds his with light, stresses their materiality as if with an inner light.

Manzù has always remained an outsider whose strengths grew with solitude. In 1954 he gave up the professorship at the Milan Brera Academy which he had held since 1941 so as to be able to work in peace.

Sensitivity and perceptive awareness dictate his work whose thematic breadth gives at first glance the impression of a contradiction. For it extends from the biblical themes of his bronze doors at St. Peter's in Rome, the cathedrals of Rotterdam and Salzburg to the almost ironically stylised Cardinals, from the sculptures and drawings for which his wife Inge and his children were models, to the erotic in the series of the lovers and of strip-tease.

Delicacy in him will never be feeble. The control of technique will never become routine. The handsome realism of his sculptures knows nothing of the smoothness of the neo-classic. His drawings are so little academic, like his bas reliefs which retain the sensitive freshness of his drawings. Only in the political caricatures of this ardent anti-fascist and anti-militarist does his soft line harden, is his otherwise lively sense of humour replaced by anger.

Manzù is the first Italian artist for whom a museum was established in his lifetime. The "Amici di Manzù" (Friends of Manzù) was inaugurated at the beginning of the 1970's near to his workshop in the "Fig-garden" of Ardea near to Rome. Grown solitary and continuing to work untiringly, the artist bequeathed the museum to the state in 1981. For he knows, in all grumbling modesty, that his works no longer belong to him but to the people.

—Monika von Zitzewitz

MARCA-RELLI, Conrad.

American. Born in Boston, Massachusetts, 5 June 1913; moved to New York City in 1926. Studied at the Cooper Union, New York, 1930. Served as a Private First Class in the United States Army, 1941-45. Married Anita Gibson in 1951. Painter, living and working in New York from 1930: influenced by associations with De Kooning, Pollock, Franz Kline and John Graham; Easel and Mural Painter, Federal Art Project, New York, 1935-38; lived in Rome and Paris, 1948-49; Organizing Member, 8th Street Club of painters and intellectuals, New York, 1949-50; lived in Easthampton, Long Island, New York, 1969-83, and in Sarasota, Florida, since 1983; also maintains a home in Ibiza, Spain. Guest Critic, Yale University, New Haven, Connecticut, 1954-55, 1959-60; Guest Professor, University of California, Berkeley, 1958; Artist-in-Residence, New College, Sarasota, Florida, 1966. Recipient: Logan Medal, Art Institute of Chicago, 1954; Ford Foundation Grant, 1959; Purchase Prize, Detroit Institute of Arts, 1960; Kohnstamm Prize, Art Institute of Chicago, 1963. Member, American Academy of Arts and Letters. Agent: Marisa del Re Gallery, 41 East 57th Street, New York, New York 10022. Address: 7337 Point of Rocks Road, Sarasota, Florida 33581, U.S.A.

Individual Exhibitions:

1947	Niveau Gallery, New York
1949	Niveau Gallery, New York
	Galleria Il Cortile, Rome
1951	New Gallery, New York
1953	Stable Gallery, New York
1955	Stable Gallery, New York
1956	Stable Gallery, New York
	Frank Perls Gallery, Hollywood, California
1957	Galleria La Tartaruga, Rome
	Galleria del Naviglio, Rome
1958	Stable Gallery, New York
1959	Kootz Gallery, New York
1960	Kootz Gallery, New York
	Playhouse Gallery, Sharon, Connecticut
1961	Kootz Gallery, New York
	Bolles Gallery, San Francisco
	Joan Peterson Gallery, Boston
	Istituto de Arte Contemporaneo, Lima, Peru
	Galerie Schmela, Dusseldorf
1962	Kootz Gallery, New York
	Galerie de France, Paris
1963	Galerie Charles Lienhard, Zurich
	Kootz Gallery, New York
	Tokyo Gallery
1964	Kootz Gallery, New York
1965	Galeria Bonino, Buenos Aires
1967	James David Gallery, Coral Gables, Florida
	Makler Gallery, Philadelphia
	Whitney Museum, New York (retrospective)
	Rose Art Museum, Brandeis University, Waltham, Massachusetts
1968	University of Alabama, Tuscaloosa
	Dorazio/Marca-Relli/Pasmore, Arts and Crafts Center, Pittsburgh
	Alpha Gallery, Boston
	Albright-Knox Members Gallery, Buffalo, New York
1969	Reed College, Portland, Oregon
	Seattle Art Museum
1970	Marlborough Gallery, New York
	University of Maryland Art Gallery, College Park
	Norton Gallery, West Palm Beach, Florida
	Gallery Van der Voort, Ibiza, Spain
1971	Museum of Fine Arts, Fort Lauderdale, Florida
	Lowe Art Museum, University of Miami
	Galerie Schmela, Dusseldorf
1972	Gallery Van der Voort, Ibiza, Spain
	Galeria Inguanzo, Madrid
1973	Galeria Inguanzo, Madrid
1974	Marlborough Galerie, Zurich
1975	Marlborough Goddard Gallery, Toronto
	Makler Gallery, Philadelphia
1981	Aronson Gallery, Atlanta
	Hokin Gallery, Chicago
1985	Marisa del Re Gallery, New York

Selected Group Exhibitions:

1959	*Documenta*, Kassel, West Germany
1960	*Segunda Bienal Interamericana de Mexico*, Mexico City
1961	*The Art of Assemblage*, Museum of Modern Art, New York
1966	*Art of the United States*, Whitney Museum, New York
1968	*American Painting: The 50's*, American Federation of Arts Gallery, New York (toured the United States)
1969	*American Drawings of the 60's*, New School Art Center, New York
1970	*Bienal de Arte Coltejer*, Medellin, Colombia
	American Painting 1970, Virginia Museum, Richmond
	Biennale, Venice
1976	*Newly Elected Members*, American Academy of Arts and Letters, New York

Collections:

Museum of Modern Art, New York; Metropolitan Museum of Art, New York; Guggenheim Museum, New York; Pennsylvania Academy of Fine Arts, Philadelphia; Detroit Institute of Arts; Art Institute of Chicago; High Museum of Art, Atlanta; Cleveland Museum of Art; Los Angeles County Museum of Art; San Francisco Museum of Modern Art.

Publications:

By MARCA-RELLI: article—"Collage Transformed: Interview with Marca-Relli," with Bernard Chaet, in *Arts Magazine* (New York), June 1959.

On MARCA-RELLI: books—*Marca-Relli*, exhibition catalogue, with a preface by William Rubin, New York, 1959; *Collage: Personalities, Concepts, Techniques* by Harriet Janis and Rudi Blesh, Philadelphia 1962; *Marca-Relli* by H. H. Arnason, New York 1963; *Marca-Relli*, exhibition catalogue, by William C. Agee, New York 1967; *Marca-Relli* by Gerard Miracle and Harold Rosenberg, Barcelona 1975; *Marca-Relli: New Works*, exhibition catalogue with essay by David L. Shirey, New York 1985.

Within the ambit of the New York School of Abstract Expressionism Conrad Marca-Relli evolved a highly personal style of his own. After working with broken shapes, jagged lines and smeared colour in a manner analogous to that introduced by Jackson Pollock and Willem de Kooning, he matured in the early 1950's a technique of collage painting in which cut-out shapes of painted canvas were attached to a canvas ground in expressive patterns with a thick black glue which emphasized their outlines. A characteristic example of his work in this style, which combined taut vigour with a certain gracefulness, is "The Battle" (1956), which combines oilcloth, toned canvas pieces, enamel and oil paint on a canvas ground. In *American Art of the 20th Century* Sam Hunter says of his work in this manner: "Using cut-out canvas shapes attached to a canvas base with a black glue line that both demarcated and blurred their separate identities,

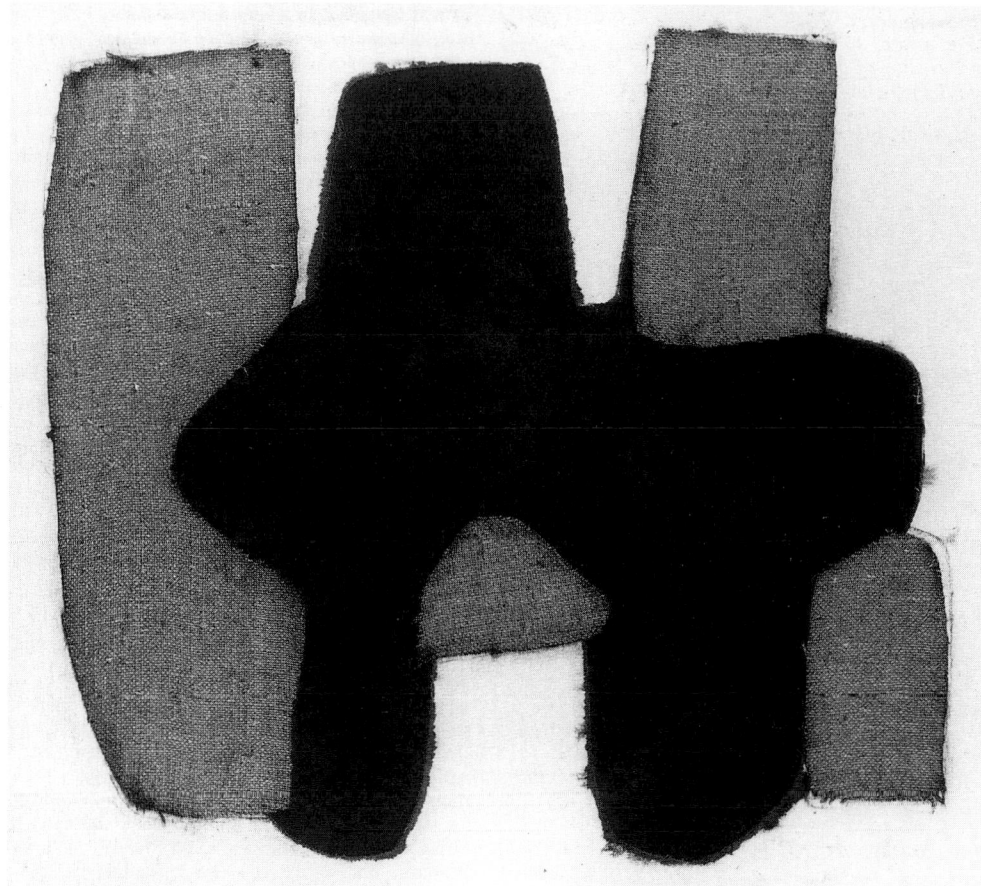

Conrad Marca-Relli: *M-7-71*, 1971

Marca-Relli developed new and dramatic modes of juxtaposition and structure in an original collage idiom. Qualities of the elementary were mixed with refinement, and, in an early figurative mode, metaphysical allusion poetically transformed the brute physical fact of his canvas fragments." His work in this manner has been likened to the painting of de Kooning at the end of the 1940's.

In the 1960's Marca-Relli experimented with three-dimensional constructions using white plastic or sheets of aluminium. These had a precision and purity of facture which approximated to the geometrical abstractions of certain of the Minimal school of artists, although they retained something of the spontaneity of his earlier work and usually avoided giving the impression of machine-like inevitability. He also experimented with a new type relief painting which approximated more closely to the objective and impersonal manner of Post-Painterly Abstraction. During the 1960's, indeed, his work contained features both of Expressionist and of Constructivist abstraction. If he failed to attain the highest peaks in either mode, his work had inventiveness, mastery and assured individuality in both.

—Harold Osborne

MARDEN, Brice.

American. Born in Bronxville, New York, 15 October 1938. Studied at Boston University School of Fine and Applied Arts, Massachusetts, 1952–61, B.F.A. 1961, and Yale University School of Art and Architecture, New Haven, Connecticut, 1961–63, M.F.A. 1963. Married Pauline Baez in 1960 (now divorced); son: Nicholas; married Helen Harrington in 1969. Painter: lives and works in New York. Instructor, School of Visual Arts, New York, 1969–73. Member, Board of Governors, Skowhegan School of Painting and Sculpture, Maine, 1972. Recipient: Third Prize, *American Exhibition,* Art Institute of Chicago, 1976. Agent: Pace Gallery, 32 East 57th Street, New York, New York 10022. Address: 105 Bowery, New York, New York 10002, U.S.A.

Individual Exhibitions:

1966	Bykert Gallery, New York
	Galerie Yvon Lambert, Paris
1968	Bykert Gallery, New York
1969	Bykert Gallery, New York
1970	Bykert Gallery, New York
	Galleria Francoise Lambert, Milan
1971	Galerie Konrad Fischer, Dusseldorf
	Galleria Gian Enzo Sperone, Turin
1972	Bykert Gallery, New York
	Locksley Shea Gallery, Minneapolis
1973	Galerie Konrad Fischer, Dusseldorf
	Galerie Yvon Lambert, Paris
	Galleria Francoise Lambert, Milan
1974	Contemporary Art Museum, Houston
	Webster College, St. Louis
	Bykert Gallery, New York
	Locksley Shea Gallery, Minneapolis
1975	Fort Worth Museum of Art, Texas
	Minneapolis Institute of Arts
	Knoedler Contemporary Prints Gallery, New York
	Galerie Konrad Fischer, Dusseldorf
	Galleria Alessandro/Ferranti, Rome
	Guggenheim Museum, New York
	Hester Royen Gallery, London
	Brice Marden/David Novros/Mark Rothko, Rice University, Houston
1976	Sperone-Westwater-Fischer Gallery, New York
1977	Galleria Sperone, Turin
	Brown University, Providence, Rhode Island
	Jean and Karen Bernier, Athens
	Max Protetch Gallery, Washington, D.C.
1978	Pace Gallery, New York
1979	Kunstraum, Munich
1980	Pace Gallery, New York

	Institut für Moderne Kunst, Nuremberg
1982	Pace Gallery, New York
1984	Pace Gallery, New York
1987	Galleria Stampa, Basle
1988	Anthony D'Offay Gallery, London

Selected Group Exhibitions:

1969	*Concept,* Vassar College Art Gallery, Poughkeepsie, New York
1970	*Modular Painting,* Albright-Knox Art Gallery, Buffalo, New York
1972	*Painting: New Options,* Walker Art Center, Minneapolis
	Documenta 5, Kassel, West Germany
1973	*Whitney Biennial,* Whitney Museum, New York
	Options and Alternatives: Some Directions in Recent Art, Yale University Art Gallery, New Haven, Connecticut
1974	*Some Recent American Art,* Museum of Modern Art, New York
	8 Contemporary Artists, Museum of Modern Art, New York
1976	*3 Decades of American Art,* Seibu Museum, Tokyo
1988	*Contemporary American Art,* Sara Hilden Art Museum, Tampere, Finland (travelled to Oslo)

Collections:

Museum of Modern Art, New York; Whitney Museum, New York; Walker Art Center, Minneapolis; Fort Worth Museum of Art, Texas; San Francisco Museum of Modern Art; Stedelijk Museum, Amsterdam.

Publications:

By MARDEN: book—*Suicide Notes,* Lausanne 1974; articles—"New in New York: Line Work" in *Arts Magazine* (New York), May 1957; "Points of View: A Taped Conversation with 4 Painters" in *Arts Magazine* (New York), December/January 1971; "Three Deliberate Greys for Jasper Johns" in *Art Now: New York,* March 1971; statement in *Arts Magazine* (New York), Summer 1972; "The Quality Problem" in *Artforum* (New York), October 1972; statement in *8 Contemporary Artists,* exhibition catalogue, New York 1974; "Conversations with Brice Marden," with Robinson de Ak Moore, in *Art Rite* (New York), Spring 1975.

On MARDEN: books—*Minimal Art: A Critical Anthology,* edited by Gregory Batteook, New York 1968; *Contemporary American Art,* exhibition catalogue with foreword by Peter Schjeldahl, Tampere 1988; articles—"New York: Brice Marden, Bykert Gallery" by J. Masheck in *Artforum* (New York), January 1971; "Ryman, Marden, Manzoni: Theory, Sensibility, Mediation" by Robert Pincus-Witten in *Artforum* (New York), June 1972; "Brice Marden's Paintings" by Roberta Smith in *Arts Magazine* (New York), May/June 1973; "Brice Marden's Paintings" by Jeremy Gilbert-Rolf in *Artforum* (New York), October 1974; "Brice Marden's Paintings" by Jeremy Gilbert-Rolfe in *Artforum* (New York), January 1975; "Brice Marden, David Novros, Mark Rothko: The Urge to Communicate Through Non-Imagistic Painting" by Janet Kutner in *Arts Magazine* (New York), September 1975; "Abstract Painting, Specific Spaces: Novros and Marden in Houston" by Carter Ratcliff in *Art in America* (New York), September/October 1975; "Vehicles for Rare Color" by William Zimmer in the *Soho Weekly News* (New York), May 1978; "Brice Marden" by Jane Bell in *Artnews* (New York), November 1978; review by Elizabeth Franklin in *Art in America* (New York), January 1981.

Brice Marden began to develop his reductivist abstract painting during the early to mid 1960s. From the beginning his technical proficiency and adeptness with color have been pronounced, and his studied comprehension of his art historical precedents is evident, stimulated, no doubt, by his training at Yale University.

By the time Marden left Yale in 1963, he had already begun to use two to four rectangular areas as the basic structure for his paintings. In 1965, he started to mix beeswax with oil to achieve a more physical, dense quality in his monochrome fields. Since his first one-man exhibition in 1966, Marden's

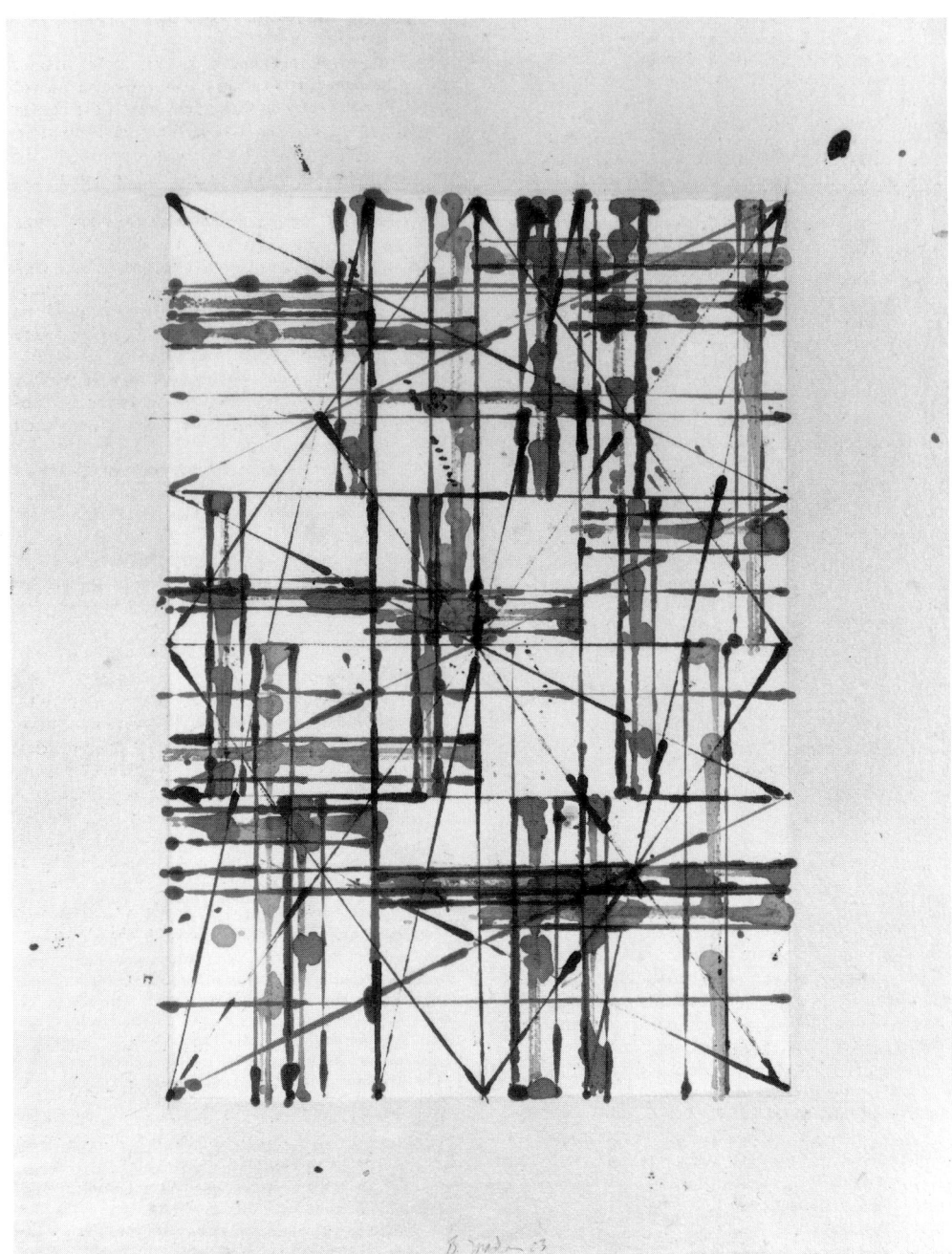

Brice Marden: *Basel Drawing*, 1983 Courtesy Anthony D'Offay Gallery, London

work has shown a continuous and persistent development of variations based on the limited format he had arrived at at that time. Marden seeks to achieve a balance by interrelating and distributing color, surface and shape. His is a slow process of refinement, a seeking out of subtler, more distilled expression of possibilities inherent in his set of purposeful limitations. After spending 1964 to 1967–68 concentrating on one-panel, one-color works, Marden worked for several years on the development of paintings which use various color combinations on two or three panels, joining single-colored panels in either vertical or horizontal formats.

Marden's color is highly individualistic and idiosyncratic. He achieves tones which are impossible to characterize through words which name colors, and it is his considerable ability as an intuitive inventor of color which helps give Marden's work an evocative, emotive quality which suggests content beyond the purely formal level. Although he is often characterized as a Minimalist, Marden does not fit in comfortably with minimalism's stress on the literal objecthood of the artwork. In Marden's pictures, abstract form as well as color are infused with a mysterious quality more associative with the mythic content undertones of Barnett Newman than with the reduc-

tivism of Donald Judd. To see Marden in a clearer historical context is to understand him as a second generation Abstract Expressionist of the color-field variety.

Also more in line with predecessors such as Newman and Mondrian is Marden's continual use of geometrical proportions which clearly show an involvement with the proportions of dynamic symmetry. (Interestingly enough, it was in a series of books by Jay Hambidge published by Yale University Press that both the construction of and the traditions involved with dynamic symmetry were brought to wide attention.) It has been written that Marden always prefers to measure his surfaces. Beginning with his early work, a number of Marden's panels have approximated the "golden section" rectangle and related proportions. A 1966 "Study," for example, measuring 30 x 48 inches, is in the proportion 1.6 (golden section is 1.618), and in Marden's large three panel painting, "Thira," (1979–80), each panel measures 1.6. The classical, intellectual nature of Marden's work finds another level in his uses of these shapes which places him in line with a long tradition of art ranging from the Parthenon to Renaissance painting and architecture to a number of abstract painters of the 20th century including Mondrian and

Barnett Newman. In addition, these shapes have long been thought to convey a sense of balance, stability, continuity and universality, qualities which are primary in Marden's paintings.

Working within his narrow range of elements, Marden has located a variety of possibilities. Underlying the seeming simplicity of the works are more complexities than meet the eye. The finely honed use of color relationships and panel divisions in "Thira" involve color, shape and number symbolisms which make the suggestion of classical temple architecture visually alive and capable of sustained contemplation. Marden's personal variant of modernist abstraction lies at the end of the line, but his talents and persistence have helped him create a body of work which has successfully fulfilled his conscientiously pursued intentions to pare down abstract elements and get closer to visualization of the structure of tense balance in universal terms.

—Barbara Cavaliere

MARINI, Marino.

Italian. Born in Pistoia, 27 February 1901. Studied painting, under Galileo Chini, and sculpture, under Domenico Trentacosta, at the Accademia di Belle Arti, Florence, 1917–22. Married Mercedes (Marina) Pedrazzini in 1938. Lived in Tenero, Locarno, Switzerland 1941–46; returned to Italy, and lived in Milan, 1946–53, and in Forte dei Marmi, 1953–80. Lecturer, Villa Reale Art School, Monza, 1929–40. Recipient: Diploma and Silver Medal, *5th Triennale,* Milan, 1933; Grand Prix, *International Exhibition,* Paris, 1937; Donatello Prize, City of Florence, 1961; Biancamono Prize, Milan, 1967; Gold Medal of Great Civic Merit of the Chamber of Commerce, Pistoia, Italy, 1967. Member, Accademia di San Luca, Rome, 1957. Honorary Member, Florentine Academy of the Arts, 1932, and Akademisches Kollegium, Munich, 1951; Corresponding member, Academia Nacional de Bellas Artes, Buenos Aires, 1969; Honorary Member, Akademie der Bildenden Künste, Nuremberg, 1962, and American Academy of Arts and Letters, 1968. *Died* (in Viareggio) *6 August 1980.*

Individual Exhibitions:

1932   Galleria Milano, Milan
      Galleria Sabatello, Rome
1933   Galleria Milano, Milan (with Massimo Campigli)
1937   Galleria Barbaroux, Milan
1941   Galleria Genova, Genoa
1942   Galleria dello Zodiaco, Rome
1945   Kunsthalle, Berne (with Germaine Richier and Fritz Wotruba)
      Galerie Aktuaryus, Zurich
1949   Galleria dell'Obelisco, Rome
1950   Watkins Gallery, Washington, D.C.
      Buchholz Gallery, New York
1951   Kestner-Gesellschaft, Hannover (travelled to the Kunstverein, Hamburg)
      Hanover Gallery, London
1952   Galerie Welz, Salzburg (with Henry Moore and Fritz Wotruba)
      Buchholz Gallery, New York
      Biennale, Venice
      Bayerische Staatsgemaldesammlungen, Haus der Kunst, Munich
1953   Curt Valentin Gallery, New York
      Svenska-Franska Konstgalleriet, Stockholm (travelled to the Kunsternes Hus, Oslo; Statens Museum for Kunst, Copenhagen, and the Konstmuseum, Gothenburg)
      Cincinnati Art Museum, Ohio
      Buchholz Gallery, New York
1954   Galerie Gerald Cramer, Geneva

Galerie Artek, Helsinki
Galerie der Spiegel, Cologne
1955   Kunsthalle, Mannheim
        Galerie Berggruen, Paris
        Martha Jackson Gallery, New York
        Pierre Matisse Gallery, New York
        Museum Boymans van Beuningen, Rotterdam
        Kunstverein, Dusseldorf
1956   Hanover Gallery, London
1957   Galerie Vömel, Dusseldorf
        Contemporaries Gallery, New York
1960   International Museum of Modern Art, Tokyo
        Orangerie, Erlangen, West Germany
1962   Kunsthaus, Zurich
1963   Toninelli Arte Moderna, Milan
1964   Kunsthalle, Munich
        Günther Franke Gallery, Munich
        Museum Boymans van Beuningne, Rotterdam
1965   Toninelli Arte Moderna, Milan (with Afro and Alberto Burri)
        Musée Royal des Beaux-Arts, Antwerp
        Galerie Obere Zaune, Zurich
        Museum of Art, Philadelphia
1966   Palazzo Venezia, Rome
        Kunsthalle, Darmstadt (travelled to Frankische Galerie, Nuremberg, and the Pfalzgalerie, Kaiserlauten, West Germany)
1968   Valiani, Pistoia, Italy
        Weintraub Gallery, New York
1969   Galleria Gissi, Turin (with Alberto Burri and Mattia Moreni)
        Bibliothéque Nationale, Paris
1970   Toninelli Arte Moderna, Milan
1971   Galerie XX Siècle, Paris
1972   Saletta Piero della Francesca, Milan
1974   Galleria San Fedele, Milan
1976   Patrick Seale Prints, London
1979   Musée d'Arte Moderne de la Ville, Paris
1984   Stadtische Kunsthalle, Mannheim, West Germany
1986   Galleria Pieter Coray, Lugano, Switzerland
        Galerie Patrick Cramer, Geneva
1987   Artcurial, Munich
        Staatsgalerie moderner Kunst, Munich

Selected Group Exhibitions:

1927   *3rd Mostra Internazionale delle Arti Decorative,* Monza, Italy
1930   *Die Entwicklung der Modernen Kunst in Italien,* Kunstmuseum, Berne
1932   *Biennale,* Venice
1940   *Ausstellung Zeitgenossischer Italienscher Maler und Bildhauer,* Kunsthaus, Zurich
1949   *20th Century Italian Art,* Museum of Modern Art, New York
1952   *Sculpture of the 20th Century,* Museum of Art, Philadelphia (travelled to the Art Institute of Chicago, and the Museum of Modern Art, New York)
1962   *Evidences of Fear in Modern Art,* Kunsthalle, Darmstadt
1966   *Arte Italiano Contemporaneo,* Museo de Arte Moderno, Mexico City
1971   *Scultori Italiani Contemporanei,* Palazzo Reale, Milan
1972   *Masters of Modern Italian Art,* National Museum of Modern Art, Kyoto (travelled to the National Museum of Art, Tokyo)

Collections:

Marino Marini Museum, Milan; Galleria Civica d'Arte Moderna, Milan; Musée Royal des Beaux Arts, Antwerp; Kunsthaus, Zurich; Kunstmuseum, Basle; Nationalgalerie, Berlin; Kunstmuseum, Dusseldorf; Rijksmuseum Kröller-Müller, Otterlo, Netherlands; Tate Gallery, London; Museum of Modern Art, New York.

Publications:

By MARINI: article—"Thoughts by Marino Marini on Art and Artists" in *Homage to Marino Marini,* special edition of *XX Siècle Review,* New York 1974.

On MARINI: books—*Marino Marini* by Paul Fierens, Paris and Milan 1936; *Marino Marini* by Filippo Pisis, Milan 1941; *Marino Marini* by Raffaele Carriere, Milan 1948; *Marino Marini* by Mario Ramons, Bologna 1951; *Marino Marini: Sculptor* by Douglas Cooper, Milan 1959; *Marino Marini* by Eduard Trier, Stuttgart, Milan, Neuchatel, and New York 1961; *The Sculpture of Marino Marini* by Eduard Trier, London 1961; *Marino Marini* by Hartmut Biermann, Berlin 1963; *Marino Marini* by Franco Russoli, London 1965; *Marino Marini: Lithographs 1942-1965* by Giovanni Carandente, New York 1968; *The Hand and the Eye of the Sculptor* by Paul Waldo Schwarz, London 1969; *Marino Marini: A Suite of 63 Recreations of Drawings and Sketches* by Werner Haftmann, New York 1969; *Marini* by Alberto Busignani, London 1971; *Complete Works of Marino Marini,* edited by Patrick Waldburg, Herbert Read and Giovanni de San Lazzaro, New York, Milan, and Berlin 1971; *Marino Marini: Sculpture, Painting, Drawing* by A. M. Hammacher, New York, and London 1971; *Marino Marini: Scultore* by Carlo Pirovano, Milan 1972; *Marino Marini alla Galleria d'Arte Moderna di Milano,* edited by Mercedes Percenutti Garberi, Milan, 1973 (includes bibliography); *Homage to Marino Marini,* special edition of *XX Siècle Review,* New York 1974; *Io sono un Etrusco* by Giorgio Ruggeri, Bologna 1978; *Marino Marini* by Ernesto Caballo, London and Milan 1980; *Marino Marini* by K. Azuma, Turin and London 1980; *Marino Marini: Disegni Inediti 1940-50,* with text by Erich Steingraber, Turin 1980; *Marino Marini: biografia per immagini,* Ivrea 1983; *Marino Marini,* exhibition catalogue with introduction by Manfred Fath, Mannheim 1984; *Marino Marini,* exhibition catalogue with texts by Carlo Pirovano and Erich Steingraber, Munich 1987.

*   *   *

In the six representatively arranged rooms of the Marini Museum which the artist has bequeathed to Milan's Gallery of Modern Art, all the platitudes and their opposites about Marino Marini are endorsed. There are the archaic and the modern, the early cheerful and the late tragic Marini, the "Etruscan" who once said "Etruscan art is not history but human truth," and the sculptor who blended ancient China, Crete and Egypt in works of the 20th century.

Faced with this work, the observer discovers that no arrangement, no itemization is of help, and current categories are unsuitable. Because Marini, the Mediterranean, the artist totally committed to the figurative, found his way to abstraction without contradicting himself. Because the beauty and serenity of his "Stagione felice" (happy phase) passed seamlessly into the tragic vision of the world of stumpy bodies, dissolved forms, the "Constructive Unreality" of his last decade. Describing this in words unquestionably smacks of the pathos that Marini could not bear.

He made no secret of his conviction that we are at the end of one civilization and that art in the traditional sense of beauty is no longer legitimate. An artist of Marini's rank could only react to this realization in two ways: grow silent or—this was his answer—search for the absolute form.

An anecdote in the photographic volume *Biography in Pictures,* told by his widow Marina, is typical of the early Marini and his sensuous delight in beauty. On his first visit to London he was waiting for a friend in Hyde Park. Some horses appeared accompanied by young English girls. As if bewitched by their cool blonde beauty, Marini flew at one of the girls and folded her in his arms. "It was as if I embraced the moon," he said to his friend who asked him to account for this outrageous behavior.

All his life Marino Marini was fascinated by the abstraction and coolness of the north, by its cathedrals, by the clear yet veiled regard of the Bamberg horseman.

In "Miracolo" and the archangels of 1934 a questioning about the reason for suffering appeared for the first time in Marini's art. He recorded later: "The agitation of my horses increases in each new work. The riders growing ever more powerless have lost control of the animals and the catastrophes to which they succumb resemble those that annihilated Sodom and Pompeii. I try to symbolize the last stage in the elucidation of a myth: the myth of the heroic, victorious individual, of the "Uomo di Virtu" (man of virtue) of the humanists." In the series of portrait heads begun in 1942 (almost all the originals are in the Milan Museum) he also destroyed myths and exposed souls.

Marini's work became more and more tragic, turned away from people and toward the static lines of architecture. Marini wrote on the socle of the bronze horseman for the Hague, which shows man and horse only as ideas—reason fallen, senses rearing: "We built, we destroyed, and a desolate song was left in the world."

A long road leads from the cheerfulness of the early jesters to the last tragic silhouettes which are still called jesters and so are like the crucified. From the sensual delight of the first "Pamona" to its later stumpy sisters. From the horseman in front of the Guggenheim Museum on the Grand Canal who with outstretched arms sings of man's mastery and equilibrium, to the fallen and broken horsemen of the last stages. It is Marino Marini's road out of the Eden of original creative force to the knowledge of sorrow and to the search for the absolute.

—Monika von Zitzewitz

MARIONI, Tom.

American. Born in Cincinnati, Ohio, 21 May 1937. Studied fine art at the Cincinnati Art Academy, 1955-59. Sculptor and percussionist, since 1959. Founder, Museum of Conceptual Art (MOCA), San Francisco, 1970. Editor and designer of *Vision* art journal published by Crown Point Press, Oakland, California, since 1975. Recipient: Artist Fellowship, National Endowment for the Arts, 1976, 1979, 1984; Guggenheim Fellowship, 1981; Asian Cultural Council Award, 1986. Address (studio): Apt. 805, 693 Mission Street, San Francisco, California 94105, U.S.A.

Individual Exhibitions:

1963   Bradley Memorial Museum of Art, Columbus, Georgia (sculpture)
1968   Richmond Art Center, California (sculpture)
1970   *The Act of Drinking Beer with Friends Is the Highest Form of Art,* Oakland Art Museum, California (sculpture installation)
1972   Richard Demarco Gallery, Edinburgh (drawing installation)
        DeSaisset Museum, University of Santa Clara, California (sculpture installation)
        Reese Palley Gallery, San Francisco (sculpture installation)
1975   Galeria Foksal, Warsaw (drawing installation)
1977   M. H. de Young Museum of Art, San Francisco (drawing installation)
        Paule Anglim Gallery, San Francisco (drawings and sculpture)
1978   Los Angeles Institute of Contemporary Art (drawings)
1979   *Museum of Conceptual Art,* San Francisco Museum of Modern Art (sculpture installation with free beer)
        Modern Art Gallery, Vienna (sculpture installation)
        Cochise Fine Arts Center, Bisbee, Arizona (sculpture installation)
1980   Felix Handschin Gallery, Basel (drawings)
        University of California Art Museum, Berkeley (drawing installation)
1981   Site Inc., San Francisco (sculpture installation)
1984   Gallery Paule Anglim, San Francisco
        A La Limit, Dijon, France
1985   Eaton/Shoen Gallery, San Francisco
1986   New Langton Arts, San Francisco
        Kuhlenschmidt/Simon Gallery, Los Angeles
1987   Museo Italo Americano, San Francisco
        Margarete Roeder Gallery, New York

Sculpture Performances: worked in night club, sketching nude model, San Francisco, 1966; "One Second Sculpture,"

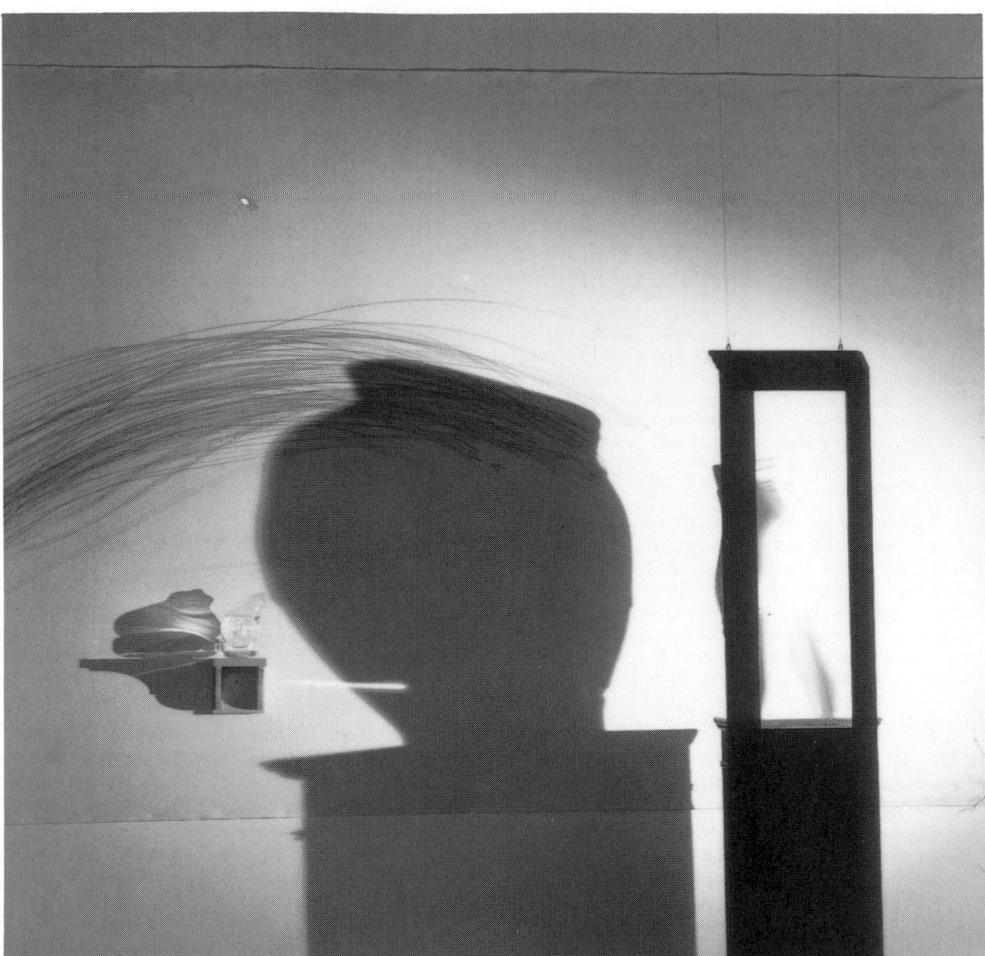

Tom Marioni: *Room for Interpretation*, 1987

San Francisco, 1969; "Chain Reaction," DeSaisset Museum, University of Santa Clara, California, 1971; "Identity Transfer," with Allan Fish, Berkeley Gallery, California, 1971; "The Creation of a Situation and Environment While Becoming Increasingly More Intoxicated," Reese Palley Gallery, San Francisco, 1971; "Sunday Scottish Landscape," Richard Demarco Gallery, Edinburgh, 1972; "The Creation: A 7-Day Performance," Reese Palley Gallery, San Francisco, 1972; "Christmas Poem," San Francisco, 1972; "A Talk," Project Inc., Boston, 1973; concert at St. Mary's Cathedral, *Edinburgh Festival*, 1973; concert at the Institute of Contemporary Arts, London, 1973, "Sculpture in 3/4 Time," San Francisco Museum of Art, 1973; "Concert/Lecture/Demonstration," University of California Art Museum, Berkeley, 1973; "The Sun's Reception," Marin County, California, 1974; "A Sculpture in 2/3 Time," Student Cultural Center, Belgrade, 1974; "One-Minute Demonstration," Gallery of Contemporary Art, Zagreb, 1974; "Drum Lecture," 63 Bluxome Street, San Francisco, 1974; "Lecture/Reception/Action," Indianapolis Museum of Art, 1974; "Duologue," with Terry Fox, Los Angeles, 1975; "Morning Action," Salon of the Museum of Modern Art, Belgrade, 1975; "East-West," with Peter Stembergh, Prague, 1975; "Thinking Out Loud," Galerie Foksal, Warsaw, 1975; "Bird in Space: A Psychic Sculpture," and/or Gallery, Seattle, 1976; "Yellow Is the Color of the Intellect," Portland Center for the Visual Arts, Oregon, 1977; "The Sound of Flight," M. H. de Young Museum of Art, San Francisco, 1977; "Now We'll Have a Party," at the *First International Performance Festival*, Vienna, 1978; "Freibier" at the *Vienna Performance Biennial*, 1979; "A Social Action," Dany Keller Galerie, Munich, 1979; "Praying with Chinese Firecracker," Krinzinger Gallery, Innsbruck, 1979; "'Liberating Light and Sound," Pellegrino Gallery, Bologna, 1979; "Talking-Drumming," Los Angeles Institute of Contemporary Art, 1979; "A Theatrical Action to Define Non-Theatrical Principles," Santa Barbara Museum of Art, California, 1979; "Studio," Kunst Museum, Berne, 1980; "Studio," Kunsthalle, Basel, 1980; "Bending Light," Berner Gallery, Berne, 1980;

"Atelier," Centre Georges Pompidou, Paris, 1980; "Studio," University of California Art Museum, Berkeley, 1980; "Spirit in the Dark," Crown Point Press, Oakland, California, 1980; "Drawing," Teahouse of the Saito Family, Kamakura, Japan, 1981; Museum of Contemporary Art, Chicago, 1981; Museum Folkwang, Essen, 1982; Kunstverein, Cologne, 1982; Ohara Shrine, Kyoto, Japan 1982; American Center, Kyoto, Japan, 1986.

Selected Group Exhibitions:

1972   *The San Francisco Performance*, Newport Harbor Art Museum, Newport Beach, California
1979   *Art as Photography*, Kunstverein, Salzburg, Austria
1980   *For Eyes and Ears*, Akademie der Kunst, Berlin
1981   *California Performance Now and Then*, Museum of Contemporary Art, Chicago
        Italians and American Italians, Crown Point Gallery, Oakland, California
1982   *100 Years of California Sculpture*, Oakland Museum, California
1983   *In Other Words*, Franklin Furnace, New York
1984   *The Sound Art Show*, Sculpture Center, New York
1985   *From Sound to Image*, Staatsgalerie, Stuttgart

Collections:

Oakland Museum, California; Santa Barbara Museum of Art, California; Museum of Art, Lodz, Poland; Newport Harbor Art Museum, Newport Beach, California; Museum of Modern Art, New York.

Publications:

By MARIONI: articles—"Tom Marioni", interview, in *Studio International*, (London), June 1972; "Activity as Sculpture", interview, in *Art and Artists* (London), August 1973.

On MARIONI: books—*Il Corpo Come Linguaggio* by Lea Vergine, Milan 1974; *The Painted Word* by Tom Wolfe, New York and London 1975; *Italians and American Italians*, exhibition catalogue with essay by Kathan Brown, Oakland, California 1981; *Art in the San Francisco Bay Area 1945-1980* by Thomas Albright, Berkeley, California 1985.

*

I see the world as a sculptor. I make tableau sculpture, installations, action/performances, video tapes, drawings and prints. I organize exhibitions and social events (the act of drinking beer with friends is the highest form of Art—1970). I make sound in my performance actions. I also use light reflection and shadow in my actions and installations. I use found-objects in my work and put them together to create new associations.

Many of my tableaux and installation sculptures are about a place, a city or a country, and usually they include objects from the music world and art world together, making a marriage of art and music.

The titles of my works usually are common expressions: *Thinking Out Loud* (1975), *The Power of Suggestion* (1979), *Room for Interpretation* (1987), *Birds of a Feather* (1986), and *Word of Mouth* (1980).

I love California and Europe; I love Leonardo and Marcel Duchamp; I love wine, women and song.

—Tom Marioni

*

On Friday the 13th of August, 1982, Tom Marioni created a café. The piece was called "A Social Action", and it contained elements which have characterized Marioni's work since 1970, when he performed "The Act of Drinking Beer with Friends Is the Highest Form of Art" at The Oakland Museum. The performance space was set as a still life, a roomscape which contained a table and chair, a bottle of beer, a refrigerator, and a record player. Area spotlights gave each element the heightened emphasis of individual installations, but the presence of Marioni the activator tied the elements and the space into a cohesive setting. The piece, which took place in North Beach, San Francisco, successfully duplicated the ambience of a North Beach café as it might exist in the mind of one who had never visited such a place, or, in other words, in an ideal state—no crowds, no noise, etc. This North Beach café of the mind had jazz on the record player and the kind of stillness in which one imagines the creation of great works. Marioni, dressed in jeans and red shoes, began to create the café by writing CAFE with red and green chalk on a dull black wall. He worked very hard, using enormous concentration, right down to the final crossbar on the E. Occasionally he stopped to photograph the work in progress. As he built up the chalk strokes, the letters became more three dimensional, more smudged, and more sculptural in effect. Powdered chalk dust dripped down the wall. Marioni's gestures were rhythmic, if not hypnotic. By the time the audience was approaching the same trance that governed the artist's activity, Marioni returned to the table in the center of the room, smiled, and spoke his only words: "Now we can have a party." He opened the door to the refrigerator, and everyone participated in the highest form of art.

Marioni, who has said that for him the act is the art and the documentation is just a record of the activity, treads such a thin line between life and art that even after a decade of intense performance activity in California, there are those who doubt the validity of his work. Perhaps it is the highest compliment that in a time when everything is accepted as art, Marioni still provokes the question: But is it art?

In 1986, two galleries in San Francisco simultaneously mounted exhibitions focusing on Marioni's work. One, at New Langton Arts, included *The Back Wall of MOCA 1970-1986*, an installation homage to the Museum of Conceptual Art that Marioni founded and directed in San Francisco. The other, at Eaton/Shoen Gallery, was a miniretrospective or work done since 1972 and included recent pieces on national identities, *The Italians, Part I,* and *The Germans, Part I.* Although Marioni protests that "I intend to hang onto the part—that's why I like San Francisco so much," he continues to expand the nations (in 1986 he added *The Japanese, Part I* to the series) and to record the ideas of art in stimulating and enlightening reifications.

—Mary Stofflet

MARISOL.

Venezuelan. Born Escobar Marisol in Paris, France, 22 May 1930. Studied at the Ecole de Beaux-Arts, Paris, 1949; Art Students League, New York, 1950; New School for Social Research, New York, 1951–54; Hans Hofmann School, New York, 1951–54. Sculptor, painter and graphic artist: lives and works in New York. Taught at Montana State University, Bozeman; designed sets for Martha Graham and Louis Falco dance companies. D.F.A.: Moore College of Art, Philadelphia. Agent: Sidney Janis Gallery, 110 West 57th Street, New York, New York 10019. Address: 427 Washington Street, New York, New York 10013, U.S.A.

Individual Exhibitions:

1958	Leo Castelli Gallery, New York
1962	Stable Gallery, New York
1964	Stable Gallery, New York
1965	Arts Club of Chicago
1966	Sidney Janis Gallery, New York
1967	Hanover Gallery, London
	Sidney Janis Gallery, New York
1968	Boymans-van Beuningen Museum, Rotterdam
1970	Moore College of Art, Philadelphia
1971	Art Museum, Worcester, Massachusetts
1973	*Prints 1961–1973*, Cultural Center, New York
1974	Estudio Actual, Caracas
1975	Sidney Janis Gallery, New York
	Makler Gallery, Philadelphia
1977	Contemporary Arts Museum, Houston
1981	Sidney Janis Gallery, New York
1984	Sidney Janis Gallery, New York

Selected Group Exhibitions:

1964	*Painting of a Decade*, Tate Gallery, London
1966	*Art of the U.S.A. 1670–1966*, Whitney Museum, New York
1967	*International der Zeichnung*, Darmstadt
	American Sculpture of the 60's, Los Angeles County Museum of Art
1968	*Biennale*, Venice
1969	*Pop Art*, Hayward Gallery, London
1970	*Women Artists*, Skidmore College, Saratoga Springs, New York
1975	*The Nude in America*, New York Cultural Center
1976	*The Dada/Surrealist Heritage*, Clark Art Institute, Williamstown, Massachusetts
1979	*The Opposite Sex*, University of Missouri, Columbia

Collections:

Whitney Museum, New York; Museum of Modern Art, New York; Albright-Knox Art Gallery, Buffalo, New York; Yale University Art Gallery, New Haven, Connecticut; Brandeis University, Waltham, Massachusetts; Arts Club of Chicago.

Publications:

On MARISOL: books—*Marisol* by Jack Mitchell, Caracas 1968; *Marisol* by José Ramon Medina, Caracas 1968; *The Autobiography and Sex Life of Andy Warhol* by John Wilcox, New York 1970; *Marisol: Prints 1961–1973*, exhibition catalogue, by John Loring, New York 1973; *Marisol*, exhibition catalogue, by Roberta Bernstein and Susan Hersch, Philadelphia 1975; articles—"Marisol's Magic Mixtures" by Law-

rence Campbell in *Artnews* (New York), March 1964; "Die elf Gesange der Marisol" by G. Guben in *Kunst* (Mainz, West Germany), 1969; "Marisol: Worcester Art Museum" by J. T. Butler in *Connoisseur* (London), January 1972; "Marisol" in *Mizue* (Tokyo), June 1972; "New York Letter" by April Kingsley in *Art International* (Lugano, Switzerland), October 1973; "Chers Maitres: Marisol's Homages to 20th Century Artists" by Joan Simon in *Art in America* (New York), October 1981.

Marisol became famous in the 1960's for her brilliantly satirical carvings and assemblages, which frequently incorporate her own striking features. When she arrived in New York in the 1950's she became part of the beat generation around Greenwich Village, and she was initially grouped with the Pop artists. But apart from her deadpan approach and sophisticated wit, she really had little in common with them, since her art has always criticized and reflected society and politics from her own very personal point of view.

Though her art is highly sophisticated, the influences on her early work include Pre-Columbian Mochica pottery, early American folk art, and Mexican boxes with pictures inside. The playful early sculptures she was making from about 1953 include roughly carved wooden figures of people and animals, and small erotic terra-cotta figures, sometimes placed behind glass in boxes. But in her mature work she has made use of such primitive, folk-like approaches to create sculptural tableaux satirizing social and political attitudes.

Her technique of painted wood sculpture stems from her association with the group around William King who bought some houses in Maine and furnished them with early American furniture. But she then extended these wood sculptures into assemblages by adding plaster casts or found objects, and by working skilfully in two and three dimensions by drawing and painting on her wood figures. She has great talent for evoking three dimensions by graphic techniques and unexpected projections, and the mixture of two- and three-dimensional effects in her works gives them an ambiguity and irony which make their satirical commentary on society even more potent.

These works are usually larger than life-size, and may be either single sculptures or arranged in groups. Her subjects range from socialites at a party to a poor family from the Dust Bowl migrating in search of work. They include celebrities like John Wayne and Andy Warhol, The Kennedy Family, and "LBJ Himself"—a giant figure holding three women, his wife and daughters, in the palm of his hand, which has been seen by supporters of women's liberation as a satire on male chauvinism. Yet her works also include constant references to the artist herself, such as many different types of women with her own features, or countless plaster casts of her face, hands or feet. Clearly one of her themes is an endless quest for her own identity, a search for the answer to the question "Who Am I?"

This quest becomes even more striking in more recent work, in which she withdrew from the external world of politics and society into identification with the mythic underwater world of the shark, barracuda and zebra fish. For these fish bodies in exquisitely carved, stained mahogany are given Marisol faces with pouting fish mouths. She has been at the centre of an enormous amount of mythmaking, but her art does remain enigmatic, mysterious and highly individual, even though it includes some direct and powerful social criticism.

—Lavinia Learmont

MARTIN, Agnes.

American. Born in Maklin, Saskatchewan, Canada, 22 March 1912; emigrated to the United States, 1932: naturalized, 1940. Educated in primary and secondary schools, Vancouver, British Columbia; Western Washington State College, Bellingham,

1935–38; Teachers' College, Columbia University, New York 1941–42, B.S. 1942; 1951–52, M.A. 1952; University of New Mexico, Albuquerque, 1946–47. Teacher, public schools in Washington, Delaware and New Mexico, 1937–46, 1948–50; Painting Instructor, University of New Mexico, Albuquerque, 1947–48; East Oregon College, La Grande, 1952–53. Independent painter, since 1957: joined Ruins Gallery group, with Louis Reiback, Bea Mandelbaum and Clay Spohn, Taos, New Mexico, 1956; associated with Ellsworth Kelly, Robert Indiana, Jack Youngerman and James Rosenquist, New York, 1957–67. Abandoned painting for 7 years and concentrated on writing, Cuba, New Mexico, 1967–73. Agent: Pace Gallery, 32 East 57th Street, New York, New York 10022. Address: Route 35, Galisteo, New Mexico 87540, U.S.A.

Individual Exhibitions:

1958	Betty Parsons Gallery, New York
1959	Betty Parsons Gallery, New York
1961	Betty Parsons Gallery, New York
	Robert Elkon Gallery, New York
1963	Robert Elkon Gallery, New York
1964	Robert Elkon Gallery, New York
1965	Robert Elkon Gallery, New York
1966	Robert Elkon Gallery, New York
	Nicholas Wilder Gallery, Los Angeles
1967	Nicholas Wilder Gallery, Los Angeles
1970	Robert Elkon Gallery, New York
	Nicholas Wilder Gallery, Los Angeles
1971	Visual Arts Center, New York
1972	Robert Elkon Gallery, New York
1973	Institute of Contemporary Arts, University of Pennsylvania, Philadelphia (retrospective; travelled to the Pasadena Museum, California)
	Kunstraum, Munich
1974	Kunsthalle, Tübingen, West Germany
	Kaiser Wilhelm Museum, Krefeld, West Germany
	Scottish National Gallery of Modern Art, Edinburgh
	Museum of Modern Art, New York
1975	Pace Gallery, New York
1976	Robert Elkon Gallery, New York
	Pace Gallery, New York
1977	Arts Council of Great Britain, Hayward Gallery, London (retrospective; travelled to the Stedelijk Museum, Amsterdam)
	Pace Gallery, New York
1978	Mayor Gallery, London
	Galerie Rudolf Zwirner, Cologne
	Pace Gallery, New York
	Harcus-Krakow Gallery, Boston
1979	Margo Leavin Gallery, Los Angeles
	Museum of New Mexico, Santa Fe
	Pace Gallery, New York
1980	Richard Gray Gallery, Chicago
	Pace Gallery, New York (toured the United States, and travelled to Glenbow Museum, Alberta, 1980–81)
1981	Pace Gallery, New York

Selected Group Exhibitions:

1976	*Aspects of Post-War Painting in America*, Guggenheim Museum, New York
	Biennale, Venice
	Drawing Now, Museum of Modern Art, New York (toured Europe)
1977	*Whitney Biennial*, Whitney Museum, New York
1978	*4 Contemporary Painters*, Cleveland Museum of Art
	American Painting of the 1970's, Albright-Knox Gallery, Buffalo, New York (toured the United States)
1979	*The Reductive Object: A Survey of the Minimalist Aesthetic in the 1960's*, Institute of Contemporary Art, Boston
	American Exhibition, Art Institute of Chicago
1980	*20 Americans*, San Francisco Museum of Modern Art
1987	*American Painting: Abstract Expressionism and After*, San Francisco Museum of Modern Art

Agnes Martin: *Untitled,* 1977

Collections:

Museum of Modern Art, New York; Whitney Museum, New York; Guggenheim Museum, New York; Hirshhorn Museum, Washington, D.C.; Art Institute of Chicago; Art Gallery of Ontario, Toronto; Tate Gallery, London; Stedelijk Museum, Amsterdam; Australian National Gallery, Canberra.

Publications:

By MARTIN: book—*On a Clear Day,* portfolio, 1971; article—"Reflections" in *Artforum* (New York), April 1973.

On MARTIN: books—*Systematic Painting,* exhibition catalogue, New York 1966; *Agnes Martin,* dissertation, by Frank Kolbert, Yale University, New Haven, Connecticut 1970; *Agnes Martin,* exhibition catalogue, by Lawrence Alloway and others, Philadelphia 1973; *Agnes Martin,* exhibition catalogue, by Herman Kern and others, Munich 1973; articles—"Agnes Martin: An Appreciation" by Kasha Linville in *Artforum* (New York), June 1971; "Agnes Martin" by Lawrence Alloway in *Artforum* (New York), April 1973; "Early Work" by Lizzie Borden in *Artforum* (New York), April 1973; "Agnes Martin and the Artificial Infinite" by Carter Ratcliff in *Artnews* (New York), May 1973; "Agnes Martin: The American Woman in Art" by Barbara Rose in *Vogue* (New York), June 1973; "Giving Art History the Slip" by Stephanie Barron in *Art In America* (New York), March/April 1974; "A Visit with Agnes Martin" by Anne Hillerman in *The New Mexican,* 26 July 1974; "An Art That's Almost a Prayer" by Hilton Kramer in the *New York Times,* May 1976; "Agnes Martin: 'Everything, Everything Is About Feeling . . . Feeling and Recognition'" by John Gruen in *Artnews* (New York), September 1976; "Whispers from Nature" by Adrienne Rosenthal in *Artweek* (Oakland, California), 28 April 1979.

Art work is a representation of our devotion to life. Everyone is devoted to life with an intensity far beyond our comprehe.· ion. The slightest hint of devotion to life in art work is received by all with gratitude.

In all the arts a performance without devotion is dead, and our conditioning in life is toward the absolutely dead, because prideful, performance.

Our whole inclination is to race forward. This racing is not an ordinary race to win over others. That is the prideful interpretation. It is an irresistible urge to win through to life. It is devotion to life.

The simplest devotion in the Pyramids and the most profound and complicated exultations of Beethoven are understood by all.

The enormous pitfall is devotion to oneself instead of to life. All works that are self devoted are absolutely ineffective. Even though they are often purchased by prideful people, they are soon recognized as dead.

Devotion to life is a feeling. Art work is made with this feeling, and response to art work is exactly the same feeling. This feeling of devotion literally carries us through life, past all distractions and pitfalls to a perfect awareness of life, to measureless happiness and perfection.

With no experience of real happiness, no conscious experience of devotion to life, one cannot be an artist. One must be lifted up, out of oneself, unconscious of self, as in the contemplation of beauty.

Life is consciousness of life itself. Our feelings of devotion are the measure of this consciousness. They are the measure of our lives and the measure of the effectiveness of our work.

The response to art work is unchanging, even in thousands of years, proving that it is of life.

—Agnes Martin

Delicate, powdery tonalities share the space with a thin linear all-over grid, transmitting a sense of vast spatial continuity which is both rigorously defined and subtly intangible. Agnes Martin reached her mature form and substance in 1961, and she has continued to find multiple variations based on her chosen schema during the subsequent two decades.

Martin is not a painter who came by her mature visualization either rapidly or easily. Although she achieved prominence in the decade of the 1960's, she had been working through her process of distillation since the 1940's, honing down each element through many levels and combinations. In the late 1940's Martin was making rather traditional still-lifes and portraits and by the early 1950's she had developed from these into an area of biomorphic abstraction related with the work of William Baziotes and Adolph Gottlieb during their 1940's phase. The linear quality of Arshile Gorky and Miró enters into works of around 1955, combining with a painterly atmosphere, translucent and palely toned, already suggestive of her mature pictures. Martin's felt relationship with the landscape, and particularly with the light quality, of the American Southwest is here already in evidence, and this connection was to persist throughout the years she lived in New York City.

Martin left New Mexico for New York in 1957. During the next few years her work became more geometric and unitary in form. Image and ground were coalescing in compositions which employed concentric rectangles and/or circles in symmetry. In "Lamp" (1959), a patterning of circles line up across an atmospheric surface, signalling Martin's imminent return to her characteristic grid format. Until around 1964, the grid was centered and framed within the canvas surface; on finely textured brown canvases, roughly drawn marks appear in repetitive patterns, showing a directness and handmade quality which would persist, finding levels of more refined subtlety in coming paintings. By 1964 the grid extends to the canvas edge, and Martin's system is complete.

Although Martin is often compared with the Hard-Edge abstractionists who became known, like herself, during the 1960's, her work is closer in feeling with first generation Abstract Expressionism, particularly with Ad Reinhardt's significative move into systematic, distilled form. Her visual development shows

her working through elements similar to this group of painters of her own generation, with whom she shares a commitment to exalted subject matter transmitted through the painterly abstract language. The difference between Martin and the Abstract Expressionists lies in her less outwardly heroic and intellectual nature. Her works are more directly based on the intuitive and informed by a fragile quality which is both stately and unobtrusive.

In 1967 Martin stopped painting and left New York to return to the Southwest. In the early 1970's she resumed working, her new pictures emitting a continued austerity and delicacy and moving more intently into the realm of self-identification with the space and light of her landscape environment. Finding the most nuanced of textual and tonal variations, Martin's recent paintings are a distinctive statement of authority and reserve, fusing elements of stability and change with an economy and touch achieved over many years of concentration and practice. In her systematic blending of fragile, graphic grid with light-filled washes of pale color, Martin has used rigorous ordering to make visual the mysterious interior reality of timeless, shadowy vibrations.

—Barbara Cavaliere

MARTIN, Kenneth.

British. Born in Sheffield, Yorkshire, 13 April 1905. Studied at Sheffield School of Art, 1921–23 and 1927–29; at Royal College of Art, London (Royal Exhibition), 1929–32. Married the painter Mary Balmford (i.e., Mary Martin) in 1930 (died, 1969); children: John and Paul. Independent painter and sculptor, London, 1932 until his death in 1984. Worked as a designer in Sheffield, 1923–29; produced first abstract paintings, 1948; first kinetic constructions, 1951; first "Chance and Order" works, 1969. Part-time Lecturer, Goldsmiths College of Art, London, 1946–68. Recipient: Gold Medal of the President of the Council of Ministers, Rome, 1965; Midsummer Prize, London, 1976. Honorary doctorate: Royal College of Art, London, 1976. Agent: Waddington Galleries, 33 Cork Street, London W1. Died (in London) 18 November 1984.

Individual Exhibitions:

1954	Heffer Gallery, Cambridge (with Mary Martin)
1960	Institute of Contemporary Arts, London (with Mary Martin)
1962	Lords Gallery, London
1967	Axiom Gallery, London
1970	Galerie M, Dusseldorf
	Museum of Modern Art, Oxford (with Mary Martin; toured the U.K., 1970–71)
	Waddington Galleries, London
1974	Waddington Galleries, London
	Galerie Swart, Amsterdam
1975	Retrospective, Tate Gallery, London
	Galerie M, Bochum, West Germany
1976	Galerie M, The Hague
	Scottish National Gallery of Art, Edinburgh (with Henry Moore)
1977	Museum of Modern Art, Oxford (toured the U.K.)
1978	Waddington Galleries, London
1979	Galerie Lydia Mergert, Berne
	Galerie Swart, Amsterdam
	Yale Center for British Art, New Haven, Connecticut
1980	Galerie M, Bochum, West Germany
	Gallery Gilles Gheerbrant, Montreal
	Sperone-Westwater-Fischer Inc., New York
1981	Galerie Lydia Mergert, Berne
	Waddington Galleries, London
1983	Leicester Polytechnic, Leicestershire
	Artek Gallery, Helsinki

1984	Waddington Galleries, London
1985	Serpentine Gallery, London
1987	Annely Juda Fine Art, London

Selected Group Exhibitions:

1951	British Abstract Art, AIA Gallery, London
1956	This Is Tomorrow, Whitechapel Art Gallery, London
1960	Konkete Kunst, Helmhaus, Zurich
1968	Documenta 4, Kassel, West Germany
1974	Art as Thought Process, Serpentine Gallery, London (toured the U.K. and France, 1974–75)
1976	Arte Inglese Oggi, Palazzo Reale, Milan
1980	Pier and Ocean, Hayward Gallery, London (travelled to the Rijksmuseum Kröller—Müller, Otterlo, Netherlands)
1982	Aspects of British Art Today, Metropolitan Museum, Tokyo (toured Japan)
1986	Forty Years of Modern Art 1945-85, Tate Gallery, London

Collections:

Tate Gallery, London; Arts Council of Great Britain, London; British Museum, London; Victoria and Albert Museum, London; Ulster Museum, Belfast; National Museum of Wales, Cardiff; Rijksmuseum Kröller-Müller, Otterlo, Netherlands; Folkwang Muscum, Essen; Wilhelm Lehmbruck Museum, Duisburg, West Germany; Museum of Modern Art, New York.

Publications:

By MARTIN: books—Abstract Art, London 1951; An Art of Environment, 1952; The Development of the Mobile, London 1975; Invention, London 1975; articles—"Architecture, Machine and Mobile" in Arts and Architecture (Los Angeles), February 1956; "Mobiles" in Architectural Design (London), October 1958; "Aim to Take Part in an Expressive Whole" in Architectural Design (London), November 1961; "Kinetics" in Architectural Design (London), December 1963; "Kinetics" in View (London), Spring 1966; "Kinetic as a Constructing Process" in Studio International (Lugano, Switzerland), Summer 1967; "Movement and Expression" in Data, edited by Anthony Hill, London 1968; "Richard Paul Lohse: An Appreciation" in Studio International (London), February 1968; "A Universal Kind of Art" in Perception (Birmingham, England), March 1969; "Scale and Change" in Studio International (London), January 1970; "The Martins," interview, with Conway Lloyd Morgan, in Isis (Oxford), May 1970; "City Sculpture Project" in Studio International (London), Summer 1972; "Chance and Order" in One (London), October 1973; thirteen texts written between 1955 and 1973 in Kenneth Martin: Retrospective, exhibition catalogue, by Andrew Forge, London 1975.

On MARTIN: books—9 Abstract Artists by Lawrence Alloway, London 1954; Collage: Personalities/Concepts/ Techniques by Harriet Janis and Rudi Blesch, Philadelphia and New York 1962; British Sculpture since 1945 by Denis Farr, London 1965; Modern English Sculpture by A. M. Hammacher, London 1967; Constructivism: Origins and Evolution by George Rickey, London 1967; Origins and Development of Kinetic Art by Frank Popper, London 1968; Art and the Machine by Alistair Grieve, Norwich, Norfolk 1968; Movements in Art since 1945 by Edward Lucie-Smith, London 1969; Mary and Kenneth Martin, exhibition catalogue, by Paul Overy, London 1970; Kenneth Martin: Retrospective, exhibition catalogue, by Andrew Forge, London 1975; Kenneth Martin, exhibition catalogue, by Andrew Forge, New Haven, Connecticut 1979; Kenneth Martin, exhibition catalogue with foreword by Andrew Dempsey, London 1985; Kenneth Martin, exhibition catalogue with text by Hilary Lane, London 1987.

I am interested in invention and naturalness. The study of, and active work with, the interrelationship of mathematics and the natural, should lead towards an art of imaginative naturalness. "Order" for me has primarily to do with the sequence of making. The use of mathematics or the unfolding of a mathematical idea in a sequence of time gives substance to the work.

One works in time, building with a sequence in which the study of mathematical and natural forces

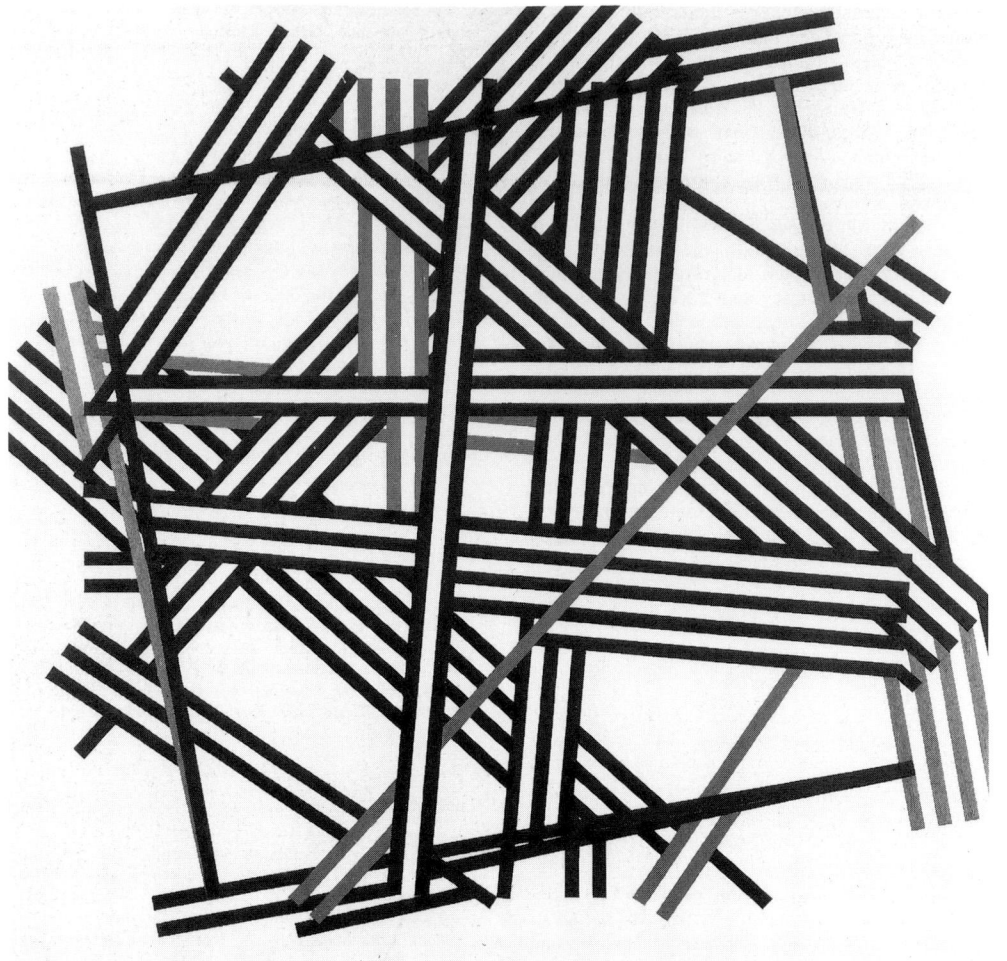

Kenneth Martin: *Chance Order Change 16,* 1981

takes command. Each step is a primitive act. Number sequence and development are intrinsic, giving character to the whole. The sequence is limited in the direction of the inventiveness of the artist and has to be governed by naturalness. That is a desire—natural, orderly invention into which disorder can enter too.

My drawings are invention with time; they are carried forward by time. My paintings are more contemplative. The act of drawing and the development of idea are concurrent. In painting I can contemplate these ideas and enjoy myself with the details which are coming into being again on the canvas.

The bonding of experience and information with which I am concerned I regard as truly organic.

It seems to me that the artist, in his activity of mental invention and inspiration, moves into further organic fields than those of D'Arcy Thompson in *Growth and Form.* In my earlier three-dimensional work I built outward from a nucleus, the nucleus being a forming idea. My recent work carries on that spatial enquiry.

—Kenneth Martin (1983)

Kenneth Martin belongs to the rare group of abstract artists in England who, once having made their break with figurative and objective motivation, were driven by the logic of their new position to adopt a pure and, at the same time, a flexible attitude towards their concepts. He was around the age of 44 when he made his first abstract paintings, and, while at that date (1949) they have an obvious debt to Mondrian, there is about them a depth of arrangement varied in pace and disposition of elements expressing spatial direction. His first kinetic constructions are dated 1951.

Martin's constructions were to be the chief vehicles of his art during the following 20 years. They had an elementary precept he summarized as follows: "A rational objective basis is necessary to the wildest flights of fancy, to improvisation and to the irrational

in order to create the work of art." In his screw mobiles, the motive was to create form from movement, and to do this he built up the expressive whole by a succession of apparently simple parts. Constructed in brass, bronze and steel, they embody additive processes, beginning as they do on paper, but in manufacture capable of taking on further logical permutations.

Serendipity is a bonus element. "Linkages" have the extended lengths and weighted blocks that weave delicate arabesques in which gravity and air currents play their intimate role. The linear constructions are based on triangulations built up in planar relations to each other. They have a solidity and rigidity of structure, though, like rocket launchers, they reveal their potential angles of trajectory.

"Oscillations" are twisting columns made up of short lengths of metal. Their sense of movement is stressed by the alternating rhythms induced by pendulum permutation. Preceded by mathematical calculations sometimes of complex variety, the constructions emerge often with an illusory imagery, giving a paradoxically unmaterial presence. Numerical permutations are called on by Martin as the preliminary steps for many of his Constructive artifacts, though aesthetic factors along with chance play their parts in the final decision of making.

"Chance and Order" was the name for the works he experimented on from 1969. The drawings and their following paintings and prints are based on a programme of parallel lines drawn from paired points of intersection on an imaginary grid of randomly chosen squares. This association of chance with a strictly calculated method of transcription has given to Martin's works an ascetic and emotively moving quality. From the precept that one circle represents perfection and (through long contemplation) ultimately boredom, Martin arrived at the inexorable conclusion: the permutation of perfection in conceived form produces multiplied and limitless variety.

—G. S. Whittet

MARTIN, Ron.
Canadian. Born in London, Ontario, 28 April 1943. Educated in commercial art at Beal Secondary School, London, Ontario, 1960–64. Contributing Editor, *20 Cents,* London, Ontario, 1967–70. Independent painter. Recipient: Best Oil Award, *Western Fair,* London, Ontario, 1966; Canada Council Centennial Purchase Award, Ottawa, 1967; Canada Council Arts Bursaries, Ottawa, 1968 through 1973; Visual Arts Grant, Ontario Arts Council, Toronto, 1973 through 1976. Agent: Carmen Lamanna Gallery, Toronto. Address: c/o Carmen Lamanna Gallery, 840 Yonge Street, Toronto, Ontario M4W 2H1, Canada.

Individual Exhibitions:

1965   Pollock Gallery, Toronto
1966   Pollock Gallery, Toronto
1967   Talbot College, University of Western Ontario, London
        20/20 Gallery, London, Ontario
1969   20/20 Gallery, London, Ontario
        York University, Toronto
1971   Carmen Lamanna Gallery, Toronto
1972   Carmen Lamanna Gallery, Toronto
1973   Carmen Lamanna Gallery, Toronto
1974   London Public Library and Art Museum, Ontario
        Carmen Lamanna Gallery, Toronto
        Forest City Gallery, London, Ontario
1975   Forest City Gallery, London, Ontario
        Carmen Lamanna Gallery, Toronto
1976   Forest City Gallery, London, Ontario
        Carmen Lamanna Gallery, Toronto
        World Paintings, Art Gallery of Ontario, Toronto
        Southern Alberta Art Gallery, Lethbridge, Alberta
1977   Carmen Lamanna Gallery, Toronto
1978   Galerie Michael Werner, Cologne
        Galerie Marielle Mailhot, Montreal
        Carmen Lamanna Gallery, Toronto
1979   Carmen Lamanna Gallery, Toronto
1980   Forest City Gallery, London, Ontario
        Carmen Lamanna Gallery, Toronto
1982   Carmen Lamanna Gallery, Toronto
1983   Carmen Lamanna Gallery, Toronto
1984   Carmen Lamanna Gallery, Toronto
1985   49th Parallel Gallery, New York
        Carmen Lamanna Gallery, Toronto
1986   Carmen Lamanna Gallery, Toronto
1989   Art Gallery of Ontario, Toronto

Selected Group Exhibitions:

1964   *Young Contemporaries,* London Public Library and Art Museum, Ontario
1967   *Centennial Exhibition,* National Gallery of Canada, Ottawa (toured Canada)
1968   *7th Biennale of Canadian Painting,* National Gallery of Canada, Ottawa
1971   *Contemporary Canadians,* Albright-Knox Gallery, Buffalo, New York
1973   *Boucherville, Montreal, Toronto, London,* National Gallery of Canada, Ottawa
1975   *Carmen Lamanna Gallery at the Owens Art Gallery,* Mount Allison University, Sackville, New Brunswick
1978   *Biennale,* Venice
1980   *10 Canadian Artists in the 1970's,* Art Gallery of Ontario, Toronto (international travelling exhibition)
1981   *20th Century Canadian Painting,* National Gallery of Canada, Ottawa (travelled to Japan)
1984   *Toronto Painting 84,* Art Gallery of Ontario, Toronto

Collections:

Art Gallery of Vancouver; Canadian Broadcasting Corporation, Vancouver; London Public Library and Art Museum, Ontario; McIntosh Art Gallery, University of Western Ontario, London; Art Bank, Canada Council, Ottawa; National Gallery of Canada, Ottawa; Art Gallery of Ontario, Toronto; Rothman's Art Gallery, Stratford, Ontario; Department of

External Affairs, Cultural Affairs Division, Ottawa; Agnes Etherington Art Centre, Queens University, Kingston, Ontario.

Publications:

By MARTIN: articles—contributions to *20 Cents* (London, Ontario), 1967–70; "Ron Martin Interview," with David Bolduc, in *For Proof Only*, Toronto 1974; "Ron Martin Interview," with Anne Garwood, in *Ron Martin*, exhibition catalogue, London, Ontario 1974; "Ron Martin Interview," with Joan Murray in *Ron Martin*, exhibition catalogue, London, Ontario 1974; recording—*Invisible Roots*, with London Experimental Jazz Quartet, 1974.

On MARTIN: books—*Diversity—Canada East*, exhibition catalogue, by N. E. Dillow, Edmonton, Alberta 1972; *Ron Martin: World Paintings*, exhibition catalogue, by Roald Nasgaard, Toronto 1976; articles—"Ron Martin's New Paintings" by David Rabinowitch in *Artscanada* (Toronto), August 1969; "Ron Martin at the 20/20 Gallery" by R. Woodman in *Artscanada* (Toronto), October/November 1970; "Toronto: Ron Martin, Carmen Lamanna Gallery" by G. M. Dault in *Artscanada* (Toronto), April/May 1971.

Ron Martin has been making one-colour paintings from the early 1970s red, blue, green, yellow, white. Since 1974 they have all been black. Most are characterized by broad sweeping traces, first of the brush, later of the fingers and the hand, moving the paint across the surface of the canvas to cover it. His recent paintings are less gestural and more anonymously made, but no less man-made for that.

Despite the marks of making in Martin's paintings, it would be a mistake to assume that he is engaged in some expressionist enterprise, because of our usual association of gestural painting with the intention of directly rendering personal emotions. The paintings are unambiguously the product of real physical and deeply felt human action. But once they have left the painter's studio, the works insist on being curiously autonomous. They are made of paint, as paintings are, but the paint has retained its own identity. It displays its mass. It has depth and extension. It glistens when light hits it; it even retains the look of its previous viscosity which yielded under, resisted and sometimes overruled the artist's hand or the tools he used to spread it. Nor do the paintings represent anything. They are not models of something, and they have no parts physically or visually separable. They simply exist as indivisible wholes which must be dealt with directly in terms of their measurable physical properties.

Yet the paintings continue to fascinate because each is like nothing that we have seen before, or that we can quite understand. Though the paint retains its literal integrity, it is not methodically applied, in the manner of Robert Ryman, for instance. It seems to be fixed where it is in one painting as a consequence of a heroic gesture of displacement, in another due to an act like that of stilling a turbulent sea. Thus read, the paintings become records of struggle against adversity, and of success, or relative success because the paint too has had its way, and are therewith in Martin's words, "a symbol, an analogy of the reality you and I exist in."

A Martin painting can also assume the aspect of another person openly facing one (unlike a Brice Marden painting which turns its back). Its size approximates the reach of a human being; its body of paint has organic unity. It has no ideal appearance, its surface is restive and changes under our scrutiny and with changing conditions, so that it yields only fragments of itself at the time. It has moods: or perhaps the viewer him/herself has put them there. And like a person it invites dialogue, but one which increasingly throws the viewer back on his/her own actions and reflections. Martin once stated his ambition to "make a painting that is primarily about the experience of the experiencer."

—Roald Nasgaard

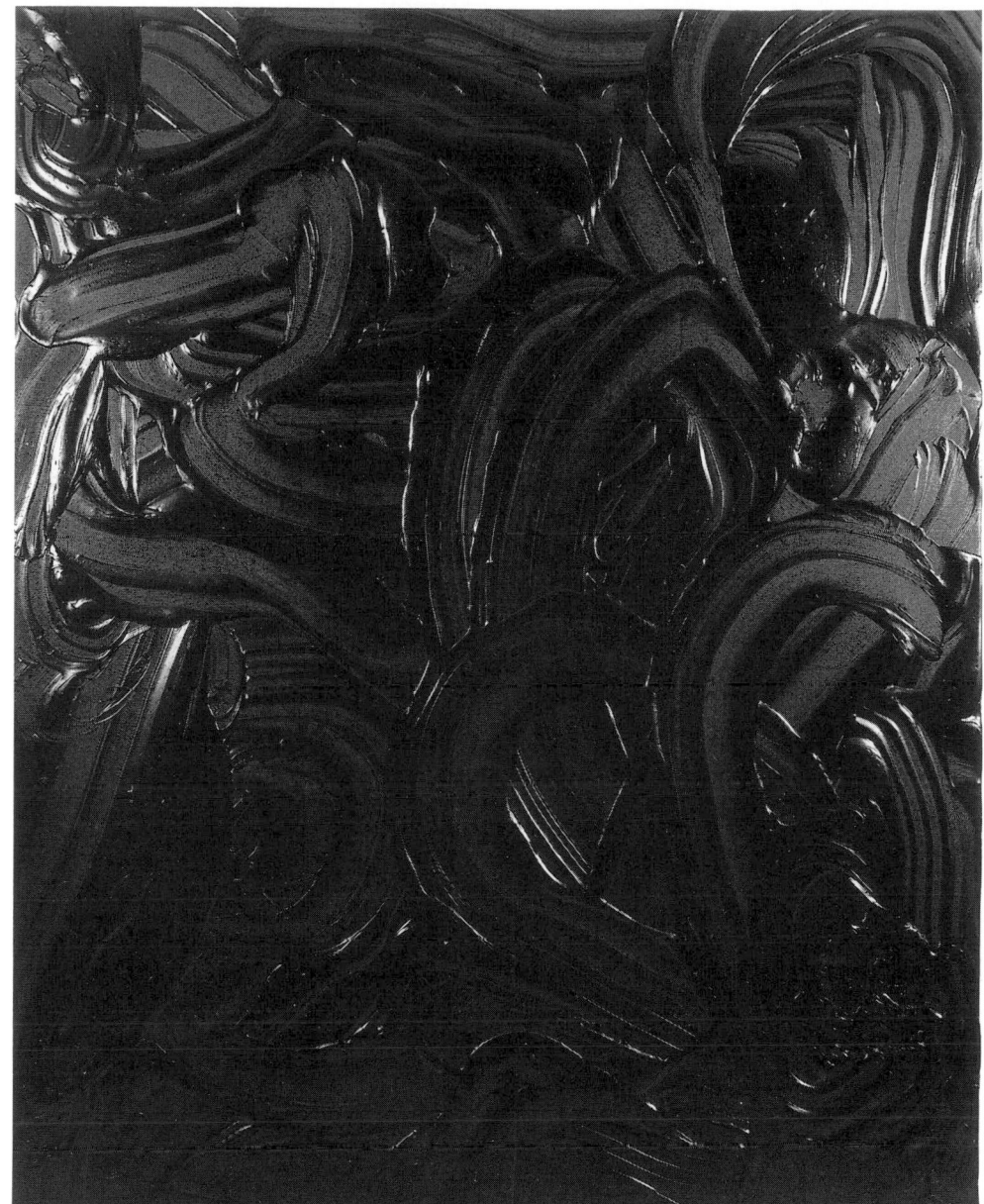

Ron Martin: *Lovedeath—Deathlove No. 15*, 1975

MASON, John.

American. Born in Madrid, Nebraska, 30 March 1927; moved to Nevada, 1937, and to Los Angeles, 1949. Studied at the Otis Art Institute, Los Angeles, 1949–52, and the Chouinard Art Institute, Los Angeles, 1953–54. Sculptor: has lived and worked in Los Angeles since 1954. Associate Professor of Art, 1967–73, and Professor and Chairman of Studio Art, 1973–74, University of California at Irvine. Since 1974, Professor of Art, Hunter College, New York. Recipient: Ford Foundation Award, Art Institute of Chicago, 1964; University of California Creative Arts Institute Award, 1969–70. Agents: Fuller Goldeen Gallery, 228 Grant Avenue, San Francisco, California 94108; Max Hutchinson Gallery, 138 Greene Street, New York, New York 10012. Address: Department of Studio Art, Hunter College, 695 Park Avenue, New York, New York 10021, U.S.A.

Individual Exhibitions:

1956	Gump's Gallery, San Francisco
1958	Ferus Gallery, Los Angeles
1959	Ferus Gallery, Los Angeles
1960	Pasadena Art Museum, California
1961	Ferus Gallery, Los Angeles
1962	Ferus Gallery, Los Angeles
1966	*Sculpture*, Los Angeles County Museum of Art (retrospective)
1974	*Ceramic Sculpture*, Pasadena Museum of Modern Art, California
1976	Hansen Fuller Gallery, San Francisco
1981	*Drawings, Sculpture and Proposals*, Max Hutchinson Gallery, New York

Selected Group Exhibitions:

1964	*Annual American Exhibition*, Art Institute of Chicago
	Annual Exhibition of Contemporary American Sculpture, Whitney Museum, New York
1967	*American Sculpture of the 60's*, Los Angeles County Museum of Art
1969	*West Coast 1945–1969*, Pasadena Art Museum, California
	Kompas 4, Van Abbemuseum, Eindhoven, Netherlands
1971	*Contemporary Ceramic Art Canada, U.S.A., Mexico*, National Museum of Modern Art, Kyoto, Japan
1974	*Public Sculpture/Urban Environment*, Oakland Museum, California
1976	*200 Years of American Sculpture*, Whitney Museum, New York
1977	*Foundations in Clay*, Los Angeles Institute of Contemporary Art
1986	*California Sculpture 1959–80*, San Francisco Museum of Modern Art

Publications:

On MASON: books—*John Mason: Sculpture,* exhibition catalogue, with text by John Coplans, Los Angeles 1966; *John Mason: Ceramic Sculpture,* exhibition catalogue, with text by Barbara Haskell and an introduction by R. G. Barnes, Pasadena, California 1974.

In the mid-1950's, John Mason, along with a talented group of Southern California artists, undertook a radical reorientation of the ceramic medium. Interested in exploring the physical properties of clay and its expressive potential, Mason embarked on a direct attack on traditional technique and craftsmanship. In participation with Peter Voulkos, Mason at first explored the expressionist possibilities inherent in the making of pottery. Playing on the innate qualities of clay (i.e., a malleable substance that requires quick and instantaneous working), the artist's gestural handling later evolved into a direct sculptural extrapolation of Abstract Expressionist painting. (Japanese pottery with its acceptance of asymmetry and imperfection was also an important influence.) Like Abstract Expressionism in general, these early sculptures, in their anthropomorphic or totemic bearing, never entirely relinquished figurative associations. At the verge of becoming primitive icons, they were suspended somewhere between pure expression and signification.

In its attention to the action of the hand and the processes that result in the transmutation of a volatile natural substance into a stable, culturally encoded object, Mason's work goes beyond expressionist assertion. After his Abstract Expressionist phase, the artist experimented with massive monolithic forms, creating primordial shapes reminiscent of crosses, double crosses, and spearheads. The increased size and homogeneity of these works combined with the general fragility of clay resulted in a number of complex technical problems. Standing between instability and permanence, Mason's primitive articulations, existing at the threshold of culture, echoed the concerns of his earlier expressionist work.

As Mason's work became increasingly smooth and monolithic throughout the 1960's, technical problems (such as cracking and breakage due to uneven shrinkage of the clay in the firing) became more severe. The artist's interest in a larger and more uniform format provoked an intense rethinking of the earlier concern with expressive handwork. After experimenting for several years with new materials, Mason settled on firebrick, a choice predicated on his increasing alienation from ceramic processes. Because the kiln is constructed from them, firebricks vestigially retain the mythology of the ceramic medium; within the furnace the clay undergoes a transition from nature to culture. Playing on firebrick's rich tonal and color variations, the artist created structures that were both systematic and sensuous. His early explorations were self-contained and more traditionally sculptural, such as his "Arch" (1976), a firebrick arch supported by the tension and pressure of its own weight. Since 1972, Mason has been working on floor pieces, deploying simple plinths of firebrick over large areas of gallery space. Under these special conditions, his elegant and beautiful structures assume a commanding territorial imperative in their reorientation of the spectator's sense of scale and place. Outside the domain of sculptural convention, works like "Hudson River Series" (1978) blast the logic of the self-contained monument, suggesting instead the conditions of landscape or architecture. Thus, in the traversal from the modernist sensibility of paradox, mysticism, and expression to the minimal, expansive, and temporal concerns of postmodernism, John Mason became one of the few artists to bridge, if not entirely reconcile, the often dissonant concerns of the two epochs.

—Maurice Berger

MASSON, André (Aimé René).

French. Born in Balagny, Oise, 4 January 1896; moved with his family to Brussels, 1904, settled in Paris, 1912. Studied at the Ecole Nationale Supérieure des Beaux-Arts, Paris, under Paul Baudouin, 1912. Served in the French Army, 1914–19: wounded and hospitalized for many months. Twice married. Painter: worked as a ceramic decorator, deliveryman for a glass factory, proof reader, etc., in Paris, in the 1920's; associated with the Surrealists, 1924–29; first book illustrations, 1925; first sculptures, 1928; Co-Founder, *Minotaure* review, Paris, 1930; moved to Grasse, Southern France, 1932; first theatre designs, for Ballet Russe de Monte Carlo, 1933; worked as an illustrator for *Acephale,* edited by Georges Bataille, 1933; lived in Tossa de Mar, Catalonia, Spain, 1934–36, and Lyons-la-Foret, France, 1937; produced theatre designs for Jean-Louis Barrault, Leonide Massine and Jean-Paul Sartre, from 1937; lived in Freluc, Auvergne, France, 1940–41; lived in Connecticut, 1941–45: organized the conference Origins of Surrealism at the Baltimore Museum of Art, 1941, and Mount Holyoke College, Massachusetts, 1943; associated with the exiled Surrealists, organizing conferences, lectures and exhibitions, New York, 1941–45; lived in Poitiers, France, and Aix-en-Provence, 1946–47; first lithographs, 1948; travelled extensively in Europe, particularly in Italy, from 1950; worked on designs for the ceiling of the Odéon: Théâtre de France, Paris, 1965; first tapestry designs, 1967; with Max Ernst and Dorothea Tanning, organized concerts with Karlheinz Stockhausen, 1970; participated in the film *Arts et l'Emphemere* by Pierre Schneider, 1971, and a televison film on Matisse, with Hans Hartung and Georges Mathieu, 1973. Member, Council of National Museums, 1962. Recipient: Grand Prix National des Arts, 1954. *Died* (in Paris) *28 October 1987.*

Individual Exhibitions:

1923	Galerie Simon, Paris
1929	Galerie Simon, Paris
1935	Pierre Matisse Gallery, New York
1936	Wildenstein and Company, London
	Galerie Simon, Paris
1941	Baltimore Museum of Art
1942	Buchholz Gallery and Willard Gallery, New York
	Arts Club of Chicago
1943	Buchholz Gallery, New York (with Paul Klee)
1944	Buchholz Gallery, New York
	Paul Rosenberg Gallery, New York
1945	Buchholz Gallery, New York
	Galerie Louise Leiris, Paris
1946	Palais des Beaux-Artx, Brussels
1947	Arts Council Gallery, London
	Buchholz Gallery, New York
	Galerie Louise Leiris, Paris
1948	Galerie Louise Leiris, Paris
1949	Landesamt für Museen, Fribourg, Switzerland
	Buchholz Gallery, New York
1950	Kunsthalle, Basle (with Alberto Ciacometti)
	Galerie Louise Leiris, Paris
1952	Galerie Louise Leiris, Paris
1953	Paul Rosenberg Gallery, New York
	Curt Valentin Gallery, New York
1954	Kunstverein, Dusseldorf (toured West Germany)
	Galerie Louise Leiris, Paris
1955	Kestner-Gesellschaft, Hannover
	Leicester Galleries, London
1956	Galerie Lucien Blanc, Paris
1957	Galerie Louis Leiris, Paris
	Galerie der Spiegel, Cologne
	Galerie R Hoffman, Hamburg
1958	Albertina Akademie, Vienna
	Saidenberg Gallery, New York
	Biennale, Venice
	Marlborough Fine Art, London
	Edgardo Acosta Gallery, Beverly Hills, California (travelled to the Pasadena Art Museum, California, and the Santa Barbara Museum of Art, California)
	Kunstkabinett Klihm, Munich

	Galerie Furstenberg, Paris
	Meijishobo, Tokyo
1959	Galleria Bussola, Turin
1960	Galerie Louise Leiris, Paris
	Galleria Il Segno, Rome
	Galerie Renée Ziegler, Zurich
	Svensk-Franska Konstgalleriet, Stockholm
1961	Saidenberg Gallery, New York
	Richard Feigen Gallery, Chicago
1962	Galerie Louise Leiris, Paris
	Marlborough Fine Art, London
1963	Galerie Gerald Cramer, Geneva
	Galerie du Perron, Geneva
1964	Stedelijk Museum, Amsterdam
	Akademie der Künste, Berlin
1965	Musée National d'Art Moderne, Paris
	Galerie Michael Hertz, Bremen, West Germany
	Tel Aviv Museum
	Galerie Gerald Cramer, Geneva
	Galerie Francoise Ledoux, Paris
1966	Galerie Les Contards, Lacoste, Vaucluse, France
	Saidenberg Gallery, New York
	Galerie Renée Ziegler, Zurich
	Galerie Wünsche, Bonn
1967	Musée des Beaux-Arts, Lyons
	La Nuova Loggia, Bologna
	Galerie Vincent Kramer, Prague
1968	Musée Cantini, Marseilles
	Galerie Louise Leiris, Paris
	Galerie Lucie Weil, Paris
	Musée, St. Etienne du Rouvray, France
1969	Galleria Il Fauno, Turin
	Galerie Sagot-le-Garrée, Paris
	Casino Comunal, Knokke-le-Zoute, Belgium
	Palazzo dei Diamanti, Ferrara, Italy
	Galleria del Milione, Milan
1970	La Nuova Loggia, Bologna
	Galleria Schwarz, Milan
	Galleria La Bussola, Turin
	Galerie Louise Leiris, Paris
	Museum am Ostwall, Dortmund (travelled to the Klingenmuseum, Solingen, West Germany, and the Pfalzgalerie, Kaiserlauten, West Germany)
1971	Centre d'Art, Beirut
	Basil Jacobs Fine Art, London
	Salle des Fêtes, Bobigny, France
	Galerie Andelt, Wiesbaden
	Galerie Gerald Cramer, Geneva (with Max Ernst)
	Galerie de l'Editeur, Paris
	Maison de la Culture, Amiens, France
1972	Maison des Arts et Loisirs, Montbeliard, France
	Galerie de Seine, Paris
	Waddington Galleries, London
	Galerie Michael Hertz, Bremen, West Germany
	Lerner-Heller Gallery and Blue Moon Gallery, New York
	Salon de la Quinzaine d'Art en Quency, Montauban, France
	Galerie Verrière, Paris
	Galerie Ariane, Gotbenburg, Sweden
1973	Galleria Zanini, Rome
	Galleria Schwarz, Milan
	Galleria San Sebastianello, Rome
	Galerie Louise Leiris, Paris
	Centre d'Art 2, Beirut
	Mayor Gallery, London
	Galerie Jacques Davidson, Tours, France
	Galerie du Lion, Paris
	Musée de l'Art et d'Histoire, Fribourg, Switzerland (travelled to the Galerie Gerald Cramer, Geneva)
	Lerner-Heller Gallery and Blue Moon Gallery, New York
1974	Galerie Benador, Geneva
	Opere 1925-1973, Il Collezionista d'Arte Contemporanea, Rome
	Galerie Claude Tchou, Paris
1975	Galerie de Seine, Paris
	Lerner-Heller Gallery and Blue Moon Gallery, New York
	Musée Grand-Palais de Malte, Aix-en-Provence
1976	Musée d'Art Moderne de la Ville, Paris
	Museum of Modern Art, New York
	Lerner-Heller Gallery and Blue Moon Gallery, New York

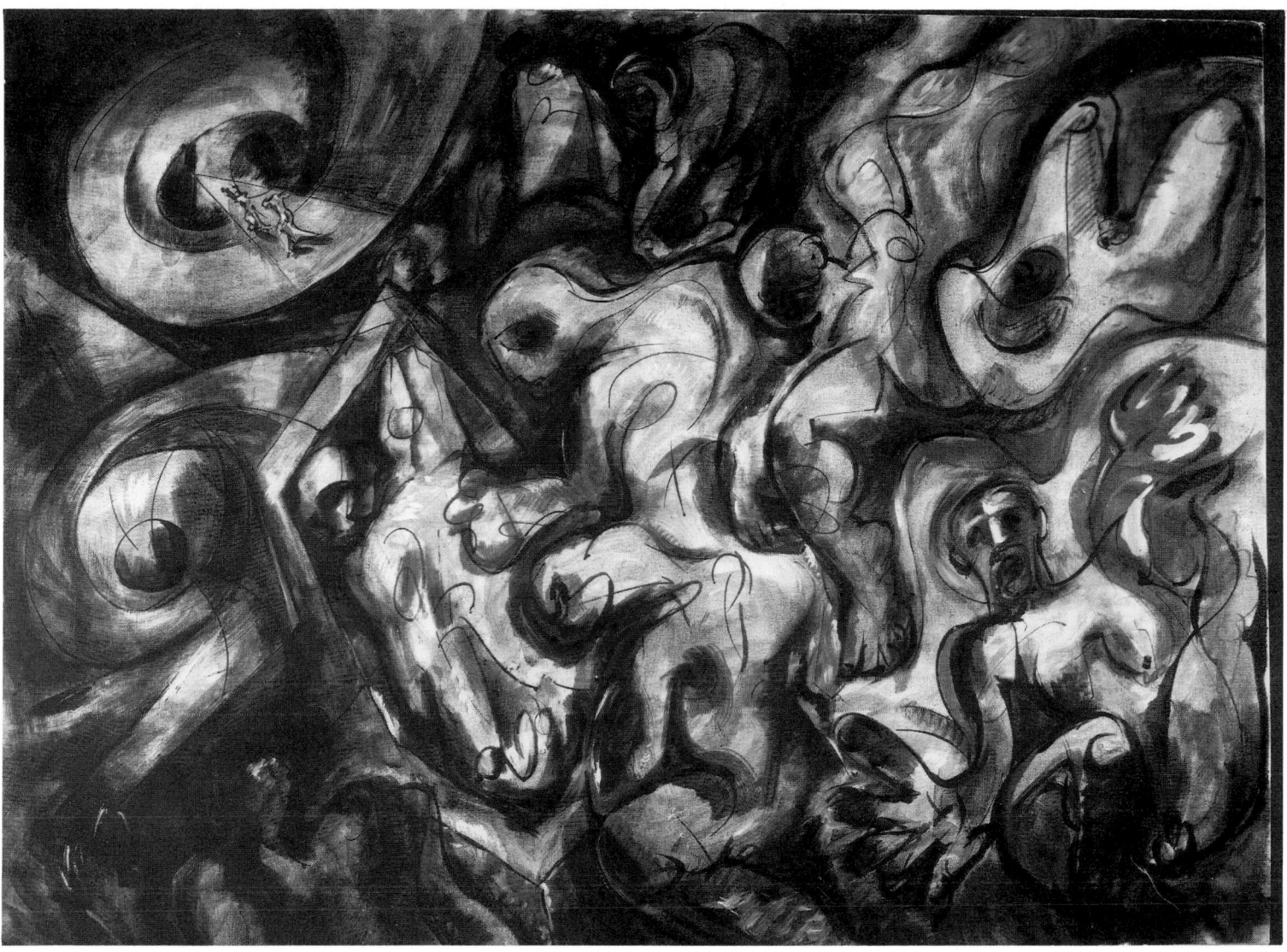

André Masson: *Catacombes (Suite Entrevisions)*, 1973

1977	Grand Palais, Paris
1978	Galerie Patrick Cramer, Geneva
1981	Orsanmichele, Florence
	Marisa del Re Gallery, New York
1983	Galerie Louise Leiris, Paris
1985	Fondation Royaumont, Belgium
1986	Artcurial, Paris
	Galerie Louise Leiris, Paris
1987	Marisa Del Re Gallery, New York
	Galerie Jade, Colmar, France
1988	Edward Totah Gallery, London

Selected Group Exhibitions:

1925	*Peintures Surrealistes*, Galerie Pierre, Paris
1936	*International Surrealist Exhibition*, Burlington Galleries, London
1937	*Fantastic Art, Dada, Surrealism*, Museum of Modern Art, New York
1942	*First Papers of Surrealism*, Reed Mansion, New York
1952	*Surrealistische Malerei in Europa*, Saarbrucken Museum, West Germany
1966	*Art Francais Contemporain*, Palais des Beaux-Arts, Brussels
1968	*Dada, Surrealism and Their Heritage*, Museum of Modern Art, New York (travelled to the Los Angeles County Museum of Art and the Art Institute of Chicago)
1973	*Futurism: A Modern Focus*, Guggenheim Museum, New York
1975	*Surrealism*, National Museum of Modern Art, Tokyo

| 1977 | *Neue Wirklichkeit: Surrealismus und Neue Sachlichkeit*, Orangerie, Schloss Charlottenburg, Berlin |

Collections:

Centre Georges Pompidou, Paris; Musée d'Art Moderne de la Ville, Paris; Wallraf-Richartz Museum, Cologne; Folkwang Museum, Essen; Nationalgalerie, Berlin; Tate Gallery, London; Museum of Modern Art, New York; Hirshhorn Museum, Washington, D.C.; National Gallery of Victoria, Melbourne.

Publications:

By MASSON: books—*Mythology of Being*, New York 1942; *Anatomy of My Universe*, New York 1943; *Nocturnal Notebook*, New York 1944; *Bestiaire*, New York 1946; *Mythologies*, Paris 1946; *Carnet de Croquis*, Paris 1950; *Le Plaisir de Peindre*, Nice 1950; *Voyage à Venise*, Paris 1952; *Metamorphose de l'Artiste*, Geneva 1956; *La Memoire du Monde*, Geneva 1974; books illustrated—*Soleils bas* by Georges Limbour, Paris 1924; *L'Anus Solaire* by Georges Bataille, Paris 1931; *Terre sur Terre* by Tristan Tzara, Paris 1946; *Le Dit du Vieux Marin, Christobel et Koubla Khan* by Samuel Taylor Coleridge, Paris 1948; *Un Saison en Enfer* by Rimbaud, 1960; *Oeuvres Completes: Essais Philosophiques* by Albert Camus, Paris 1962; *L'Idiot* by Dostoievsky, Paris 1966; articles—"Lettre à André Breton: in *La Révolution Surrealiste* (Paris), October 1925; "Tyrannie du Temps" in *La Révolution Surrealiste* (Paris), March 1926; "André Masson beantwortet einige Fragen: in *Das Kunstblatt* (Berlin), August 1931; "Du Haut de Montseratt" in *Minotaure* (Paris), June 1936; "Enquete" in *Les Cahiers d'Art* (Paris), vol. 14, nos. 1–4, 1939; "Mythologie de la Nature" in *Les Cahiers d'Art* (Paris), vol. 14, no. 56, 1939; "Peindre est une Ga-

geure" in *Les Cahiers du Sud* (Marseilles), March 1941, reprinted as "Painting Is a Wager" in *Horizon* (London), March 1943; "The Bed of Plato" in *View* (New York), October/November 1941; "Life and Liberty" in *Art in Australia* (Sydney), March/May 1942; "Re-Minotaure" in *View* (New York), May 1942; "L'Homme Emblématique" in *VVV* (New York), June 1942; "Mallarmé, Portraitist of Baudelaire and Poe" in *View* (New York), October 1942; "Page from a Notebook" in *View* (New York), vol. 3, no. 1, 1943; "Antille" in *Hemispheres* (New York), Autumn/Winter 1943/44; "Une Crise de l'Imaginaire" in *Fontaine* (Algiers), no. 35, 1944, reprinted in Masson's book *Le Plaisir de Peindre*, Nice 1950, and as "A Crisis of the Imaginary" in *Horizon* (London), July 1945 and in *Magazine of Art* (New York), January 1946; "Unité et Variété de la Peinture Francaise" in *Renaissance* (New York), vol. II–III, 1944–45; "Peinture Tragique" in *Les Temps Modernes* (Paris), Janurary 1946; "Eloge de Paul Klee" in *Fontaine* (Paris), June 1946, reprinted in Masson's book *Le Plaisir de Peindre*, and as "Homage to Paul Klee" in *Partisan Review* (New York), January/February 1947; "Le Peintre et le Temps" in *Les Temps Modernes* (Paris), July 1946; "Un Grand Siècle Pictural" in *Critique* (Paris), November 1946; "Notes" in *Les Cahiers du Sud* (Marseilles), vol. XXIII, no. 279, 1946; "Le Roi fou à la Couronne de Flammes" in *Les Cahiers du Sud* (Marseilles), vol. XXXIII, no. 275, 1946; statement in *11 Europeans in America* by James Johnson Sweeney, New York 1946; "Commentaires" in *Saisons* (Paris), Winter 1946/47; "L'Artiste et son Portrait: Corot reconte par lui-meme et par ses Amis" in *Critique* (Paris), March 1947; "Note sur l'Imagination Sadique" in *Les Cahiers du Sud* (Marseilles), vol. XXXIV, no. 285, 1947; "La Balance Faussée" in *Les Temps Modernes* (Paris), February 1949; "Color and the Lithographer" in *The Tiger's Eye* (New York), June 1949; "Divagations sur l'Espace" in *Les Temps Modernes* (Paris), June 1949; "Mouvement et Metamorphose" in *Les Temps Modernes* (Paris), October 1949; "L'Atelier de Calder" in *Les Cahiers d'Art* (Paris), vol. XXIV, no. 2, 1949; "Peinture et Rhétorique" in

Les Cahiers du Sud (Marseilles), vol. XXXVI, no. 295, 1949; "La Création Artistique est-elle affectée par les Événements Contemporains" in *Transition 49* (Paris), no. 5, 1949; "Courbet Le Réaliste Fabuleux" in *Critique* (Paris), January 1951; "The Instant Notes for a New Style" in *Artnews* (New York), October 1951; "Vue d'Ensemble: Fenise Retrouvé" in *Critique* (Paris), November 1951; "Proposition" in *Le Point* (Souillac, France), April 1952; "Monet: Le Fondateur" in *Verve* (Paris), nos. 27-28, 1952; "Notes sur la Peintures" in *Les Cahiers du Sud* (Marseilles), vol. XXXIX, no. 314, 1952; "Le Surrealisme et Après: Un Entretien au Magnétophone avec André Masson" in *L'Oeil* (Paris), May 1955; "L'Effusioniste" in *La Nouvelle Revue Francaise* (Paris), July 1955; "Une Peinture de l'Essentiel" in *Quadrum* (Brussels), May 1956; "Le Peintre es ses Fantasmes" in *Les Etudes Philosophiques* (Paris), October/December 1956; "Redon: Mystique with a Method" in *Artnews* (New York), January 1957; "L'Art commence ou le Réalisme finit," interview, with Alain Jouffroy, in *Arts Magazine* (New York), February 1958; "La Brume dans la Vallée de l'Arc" in *L'Arc* (Aix-en-Provence), Spring 1958; "Dialogues avec André Masson" in *Entretiens avec Georges Charbonnier*, Paris 1958; "Entretien avec André Masson" in *Le Monologue du Peintre* (Paris), vol. 1, 1959; preface to *Paris/New York: Arts Yearbook 3*, New York 1959; "Le Jardin des Délices" in *Critique* (Paris), May 1959; "Nicolas Poussin en 1960" in *La Nouvelle Revue Francaise* (Paris), June 1960; "Le Peintre et la Culture" in *Art de France* (Paris), vol. 4, 1964; "Some Notes on the Unusual Georges Bataille" in *Art and Literature* (Lausanne, Switzerland), Autumn/Winter 1964; "Mon Plafond à l'Odéon" in *Connaissance des Arts* (Paris), January 1966; "The Artist Speaks: André Masson" in *Erotic Art: A Survey of Erotic Fact and Fancy in the Fine Arts* by Phyllis and Eberhard Kronhausen, New York 1968; letter in "Letters from 31 Artists" by Ethel Moore in *Albright-Knox Art Gallery Notes* (Buffalo, New York), Spring 1970; "André Masson, Graveur et Illustrateur: histoire d'une de mes Folies" in *XXe Siècle* (Paris), June 1972; "Comment j'ai illustre des Livres" in *Bulletin du Bibliophile* (Paris), part 2, 1972; "Conversation avec Matisse: La Decoration Barnes" in *Critique* (Paris), May 1974; "A propos de Claude Monet" in *Paintings by Monet*, exhibition catalogue, Chicago 1975; "Interview with André Masson," with D. Rosenthal, in *Arts Magazine* (New York), November 1980.

On MASSON: books—*André Masson* by Jean-Louis Barrault, Georges Bataille, André Breton and others, Rouen 1940; *André Mason and His Universe* by Michel Leiris and Georges Limbour, Geneva 1947; *André Masson* by Hubert Juin, Paris 1963; *Masson* by Otto Hahn, Paris, New York and London 1965; *Mythologie d'André Masson* by Jean-Paul Clébert, Geneva 1971; *André Masson* by L. M. Sapphire, New York 1973; *André Masson: Opere 1925–1973*, exhibition catalogue, by Michel Leiris, Paul Elouard, André Breton and others, Rome 1974; *André Masson et les Puissances du Signe* by René Passeron, Paris 1975; *André Masson*, exhibition catalogue, by William Rubin and Carolyn Lanchner, New York 1976; *André Masson*, exhibition catalogue, by William Rubin, Carolyn Launchner and Michel Leiris, Paris 1977; *André Masson*, exhibition catalogue with text by Bernard Noel, Royaumont 1985; *André Masson*, exhibition catalogue with text by Claude Duthuit, Paris 1986; films—*André Masson et les Quatre Elements* by Jean Gremillon, 1959; *A la Source de la Femme Aimé* by Nelly Kaplan, 1966; *Perspectives Surrealistes: Les Metamorphoses*, ORTF-TV Film, 1971; *Le Monde Imaginaire d'André Masson*, with the sculptor Hansjorg Gesiger, TV Film, 1973.

*

Do fishes come at each other with knives? Does one praying-mantis stand flexing his knees while another prepares to duel with him to the death in an arena whose ringside is crowded with insect audience come to see battle done *mis-a-morte?* These have been the subjects of drawings and paintings by André Masson, carried out with figurative expertise that suggests spontaneous verve.

Such pictures seem remote in time and style from the artist's early juggling with a kind of classicist cubism, facetted works that looked only one remove from greco-roman culture, and which even shared with antiquity a palette of subdued hues and light-relief chiaroscuro, whereas the scenes of piscean and insect mortal combat were coloured in mid-day brilliance, only a shade more reserved than the lightning flashes of scarlet and yellow which set alight the "handwriting" pictures of the late 1930's. In that period, immediately before the War, Masson painted like one possessed. There was, for instance, a lithograph carried in one of the earlier copies of *Verve* where some stellar object in richest red was poised in a sky of

intensest blue and in a way so vivid that it made the eyes blink and, should they be closed a moment after, remained imprinted on the retina.

There have been many inventive pictures made by Masson since those days of 40 years ago. A wonderful and magical interior from a late stage of his development was bought not long ago for the Sztuka Museum in Lodz by Richard Stanislawsky. And there was an astonishing exhibition in Paris of Masson's *oriental* style and how this related to jewelry. But, nevertheless, probably his finest moments came before the War and one must be thankful that he was never idle for long.

At its best, Masson's line, and especially the painted line, is something never matched in the history of art, either before his time or since.

—Sheldon Williams

MATHIEU, Georges.

French. Born in Boulogne-sur-Mer, 27 January 1921. Educated at the Lycée Mariette, Boulogne, 1932; Lycée Hoche, Versailles, 1933–35; Lycée Corneille, Rouen 1936; studied law and English; mainly self-taught in painting. Painter, in Douai, Cambrai and Biarritz, 1942–47, in Paris, since 1947: first abstract works, 1944; developed lyrical abstraction/tachist work, from 1947. Instructor in English, Lycée de Douai, 1943; instructor for the United States Army, Cambrai 1944; instructor in French, American University, Biarritz, 1945–46; Head of Public Relations, United States Lines shipping company, Paris, 1947; Director/Editor, *Paris Review* (for United States Lines), Paris, 1953–63. Member, Académie des Beaux-Arts, Paris, 1975. Agent: Galerie Beaubourg, rue Pierre au Lard, 75004 Paris. Address: c/o Academie des Beaux-Arts, 23 Quai de Conti 75006 Paris, France.

Individual Exhibitions:

1950	Galerie Drouin, Paris
1952	Studio Paul Facchetti, Paris
	Stable Gallery, New York
1953	Galerie Marcel Evrard, Lille, France
1954	Kootz Gallery, New York
	Galerie Rive Droite, Paris
	Arts Club of Chicago
1955	Iolas Gallery, New York
	Kootz Gallery, New York
1956	Galerie Rive Droite, Paris
	Institute of Contemporary Arts, London
	Galerie Pierre, Paris
	Kootz Gallery, New York (2 shows)
1957	Palais des Beaux-Arts, Brussels
	Galerie Kleber, Paris
	Galleria dell'Naviglio, Milan
	Galerie Helios Art, Brussels
	Lyrical Abstraction in New Paintings by Mathieu, Kootz Gallery, New York
	Galleria Selecta, Rome
1958	Galerie Schmela, Dusseldorf
	Galerie d'Art Latin, Stockholm
	Galerie Grange, Lyons
	Galerie Chichio Haller, Zurich
	Galerie d'Art Moderne, Basle
	Galleria Castelnuovo, Ascona, Switzerland
	Kunstmuseum, Basle
	Galerie Internationale d'Art Contemporain, Paris
	Musée des Beaux-Arts, Liège, Belgium
	Galerie Rive Droite, Paris
	Hallwylska Museum, Stockholm
1959	Kunstverein, Cologne
	Iolas Gallery, New York (retrospective)
	Museum Haus Lange, Krefeld, West Germany
	Musée des Beaux-Arts, Neuchatel, Switzerland
	Musée de l'Athenée, Geneva

	Atelier Riehentor, Basle
	Galleria San Babila, Milan
	Galerie St. Stephan, Vienna
	Kootz Gallery, New York
	Galerie Jacques Dubourg, Paris
	Galerie Internationale d'Art Contemporain, Paris
	Museu de Arte Moderno, Rio de Janeiro
	Galeria Bonino, Buenos Aires
1960	Museu de Arte Moderno, Sao Paulo
	Museo del Ateneo, Madrid
	New London Gallery
	Kootz Gallery, New York
	Galerie Internationale d'Art Contemporain, Paris
	Galleria del Cavallino, Venice
1961	Palais de la Presidence, Beirut
	Galerie Schmela, Dusseldorf
	Galerie Rive Droite, Paris
	Galleria dell'Naviglio, Milan
	Galerie Jacques Dubourg, Paris
1962	Galerie Hilt, Basle
	18 Pientures, Bezalel National Museum, Jerusalem
	Neue Galerie im Kunstlerhaus, Munich
	Galleria Bussola, Turin
	Galleria dell'Ariete, Milan
	Galleria La Loggia, Bologna
	Tel-Aviv Museum
1963	Dominion Gallery, Montreal
	Musée d'Art Moderne de la Ville, Paris
	Galerie Internationale d'Art Contemporain, Paris
	Palais des Beaux-Arts, Brussels
1964	Gimpel Fils, London
1965	Galerie Charpentier, Paris
	Galerie Schmela, Dusseldorf
	Mostra dell'Opera Recente di Georges Mathieu, Galleria Il Milione, Milan
1967	Musee d'Art Moderne, Paris
	Gemalde-Gouachen-Aquarelle-Collagen, Kunstverein, Cologne
1968	Gimpel & Hanover Galerie, Zurich
	Gimpel Fils, London
1969	Manufacture Nationale des Gobelins, Paris
	Arts Council Gallery, Belfast
	Galerie Rive Droite, Paris
	Musée des Beaux-Arts, Rennes, France
	Opere Recenti di Georges Mathieu, Galleria Il Milione, Milan
1971	Galerie Veranneman, Brussels
	Musée Monetaire, Paris
1972	Gimpel Fils, London
	Galerie Stadler, Paris
1973	Berlin Oper, West Berlin
1974	*Oeuvres Anciennes 1948–1960,* Galerie Beaubourg, Paris
1976	Musée des Beaux-Arts, Antibes, France
1977	Casino Communal, Ostend, Belgium (retrospective)
	Chateau de Simiane, France
1978	Musee des Beaux-Arts, Aix-en-Provence, France (retrospective)
	Quelques Oeuvres Peintes de 1963 à 1978, Grand Palais, Paris
1979	Wildenstein Gallery, New York
	Dominion Gallery, Montreal
1980	*Bilder, Gouachen, Aquarelle und Zeichnungen von Georges Mathieu aus den Jahren 1944–1979,* Galerie Lauter, Mannheim
	Galerie Arts Contemporaine, at *Art 80,* Basle
	Musee de la Poste, Paris
1981	Galerie Protée, at *FIAC 81,* Grand Palais, Paris
1982	Hotel Meridien, Tunis
	Galerie Jade, Colmar, France
1983	Regency Intercontinental Hotel, Bahrain
	Chateau de Vascoeuil, France
	Galerie Pro Arte, Morges, Switzerland
1984	Hotel Meridien, Singapore
	Theatre Municipal, Brive, France
1985	Galerie Alain Moyon-Avenard, Nantes, France
	Wally Findlay Galleries, New York
	Galerie Rue Calvin, Geneva
	Palais des Papes, Avignon, France (retrospective)
1986	Findlay Gallery, Palm Beach, Florida
	Galerie du Luxembourg, Luxembourg
	Galerie Protée, Paris
1987	Findlay Gallery, New York
	Galerie Semiha Huber, Zurich

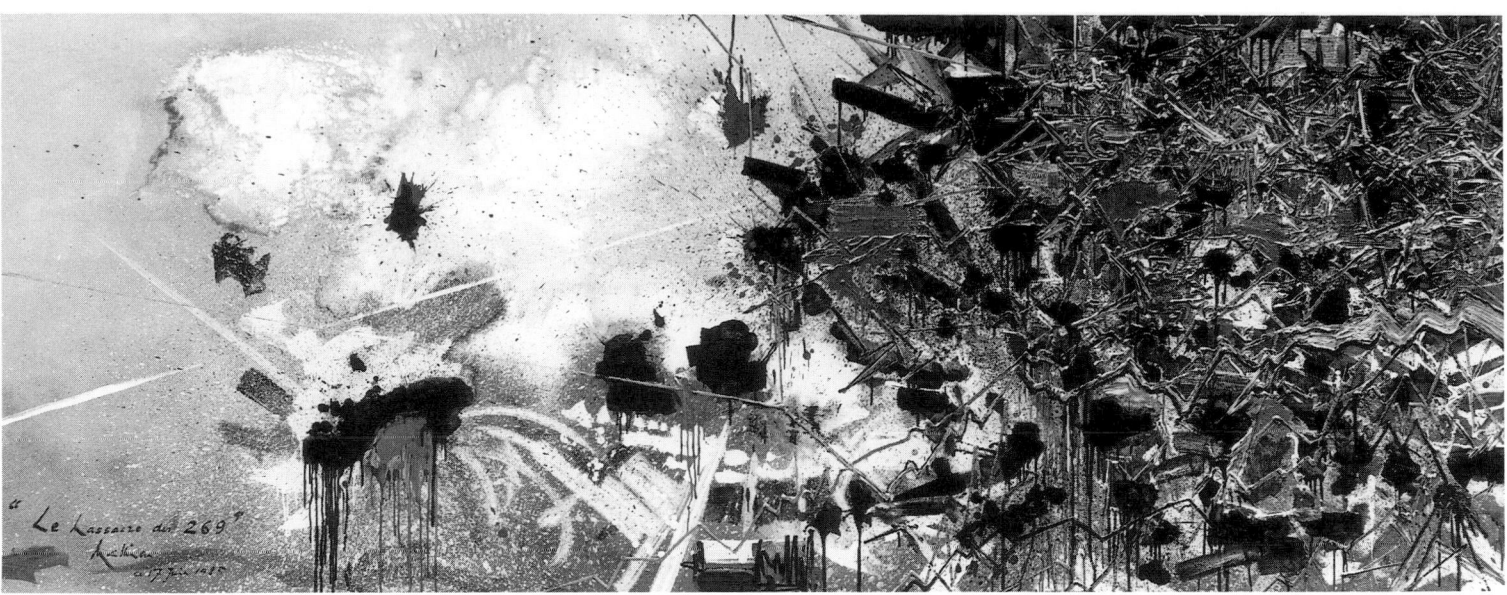

Georges Mathieu: *Le Massacre des 269*, 1985

Galerie Sapone, Nice, France
Galerie de Bellecour, Lyon, France
Galleria Tedia, Milan
Galerie Protée, Toulouse, France
Palazzo di Caserta, Italy

Selected Group Exhibits:

1947   *L'Imaginaire*, Galerie du Luxembourg, Paris
1948   *HWPSMTB*, Galerie Colette Allendy, Paris
1951   *Vehemences Confrontees*, Galerie Nina Dausset, Paris
1953   *Young European Painters*, Guggenheim Museum, New York
1957   *4 Paris Artists*, Otto Seligman Gallery, Seattle
1968   *Painting in France 1900–1967*, National Gallery of Art, Washington, D.C. (toured the U.S.A.)
1977   *Paris-New York*, Centre Georges Pompidou, Paris
1981   *Westkunst*, Messehallen, Cologne
1983   *Les Annees 60*, Musée de St. Etienne, France
1986   *Biennale*, Venice

Collections:

Centre Georges Pompidou, Paris; Museum des 20. Jahrhunderts, Vienna; Kaiser-Wilhelm Museum, Krefeld, West Germany; Kunstmuseum, Cologne; Kunsthaus, Basle; National Museum of Modern Art, Tokyo; Museum of Modern Art, New York; Guggenheim Museum, New York; Art Institute of Chicago; Art Gallery of Ontario, Toronto.

Publications:

By MATHIEU: books—*Anagogie de la non-figuration*, Paris 1949; *De l'Abstrait au Possible*, with introduction by Blaise Distel, Zurich 1959; *Au-dela du Tachisme*, Paris 1963; *Le Privilege d'Etre*, Paris 1967; *De la Revolte à la Renaissance*, Paris 1973; *La Response de l'Abstraction Lyrique*, Paris 1975; *L'Abstraction Prophetique*, Paris 1984.

On MATHIEU: books—*Georges Mathieu*, exhibition catalogue, with text by Michel Tapie, Paris 1952; *Georges A. Mathieu*, exhibition catalogue, with texts by Stephane Lupasco, Mark Tobey and Michel Tapie, Paris 1954; *Mathieu*, exhibition catalogue, with texts by Herbert Read and Toni del Renzio, London 1956; *Mathieu*, exhibition catalogue, with text by Toni del Renzio, Rome 1957; *Lyrical Abstraction in New Paintings by Mathieu* exhibition folder, with text by James Fitzsimmons, New York 1957; *Mathieu*, exhibition catalogue, with text by Julien Alvard, London 1960; *Georges Mathieu: 18 Peintures*, exhibition catalogue, with text by John Ashbery, Jerusalem 1962; *Mathieu*, exhibition catalogue, with texts by Julien Alvard and Pierre Restany, Munich 1962; *Mathieu*, exhibition catalogue, with texts by René Heron de Villefosse and Marie-Claude Dane, Paris 1963;

Mathieu, exhibition folder, with text by Werner Haftmann, Dusseldorf 1965; *Mostra dell'Opera Recente di Georges Mathieu*, exhibition catalogue, with text by Giulio Carlo Argan, Milan 1965; *Mathieu*, exhibition catalogue, with texts by Raymond Nacenta, Georges Schehade and Francois Mathey, Paris 1965, *Mathieu. Gemulde-Gouachen-Aquarelle-Collagen*, exhibition catalogue, with text by Werner Haftmann, Cologne 1967; *Mathieu*, exhibition catalogue, with text by Francois Bergot, Rennes 1969; *L'Art de Notre Temps: Georges Mathieu* by Francois Mathey, Paris and Milan 1969; *Opere Recenti di Georges Mathieu*, exhibition catalogue, Milan 1969; *Mathieu*, exhibition catalogue, with text by Pierre Dehaye, Paris 1971; *La Peinture, Le Geste, L'Action: l'Existentialisme en Peinture* by Margit Rowell, Paris 1972; *Mathieu*, by Dominique Quignon-Fleuret, Paris 1973; *Mathieu: Oeuvres Anciennes 1948–1960*, exhibition catalogue, with texts by Patrice Trigano and Dominique Quignon-Fleuret, Paris 1974; *Georges Mathieu et la poetica del Signo* by Maria Rosaria Mioni, Padua 1977; *Mathieu: Quelques Oeuvres Peintes de 1963 à 1978*, exhibition catalogue, with texts by Michel Hoog and others, Paris 1978; *Bilder, Gouachen, Aquarelle und Zeichnungen von Georges Mathieu aus den Jahren 1944-1979*, exhibition catalogue, with text by Rolf Lauter, Mannheim 1980; *Georges Mathieu: retrospective*, exhibition catalogue, Avignon 1985.

The only true creation is one which invents its means on the spot, calling everything into question. Who has lived those sublime, those tremendously heroic, moments when the artist, seeing the signs he recognises as his own appearing under his brush, butchers them like Cronos his children? Cronos whom the Romans foolishly identified with Saturn though he is the finest incarnation of Uranus! Oh! What a prodigy is this birth of new forms, this transition from Chaos to Cosmos, but what pain too in this birth unlike any other!

In that fundamental solitude, where security depends on speed and which has nothing to do with the work 'to measure' of those who relied on something real, or on an existing architecture, the painter, first spectator of the imaginary reality which he creates before living it, is an actor—hero by the same right as those rare military geniuses who have taken charge of events, creating challenges only to take them up, and traps only to defuse them. During the improvised execution of his works, the lyrical abstract artist initiates a strategy and a set of tactics similar enough to those of the great captains who, not content merely to win battles, left on them their own personal and original stamp, producing miracles rather than precedents. The artist ceases then to be the skilful executant of a vision composed by him in advance; he leads the action on his own account, an action in which the stake is not a victory over the enemy, but over himself.

That's where the drama lies. Every second it is his

duty to usher in not only forms, but techniques of whose efficacy and extent he knows nothing, blinding himself to the havoc he is causing, never able to go back, condemned to proceed in the dark until, after a thousand approaches, he gets a glimpse of the clearing from whence he will see the paths that lead to the light. What exhilaration in the gesture which suddenly transcends the whole past of Art, the whole of our own past!

From the soaked and folded towel dashed against the surface of *Hommage à Hideyoshi* on the roof of Osaka, to the white gashes of Stockholm, to the blood bath of Rio, to the luxuriant golden garlands of the *Election of Charles the Fifth*, born of the trajectory of the liquid pigment projected through space, landing on the canvas and flattening out there according to the laws of an unknown ballistics where speed, force, weight, fluidity and colour—the brush then ceasing to be in contact with the surface to be painted—all play their part, we witness as it were a liberating expansion of the artistic means, which would be as nothing if not accompanied at each step by a fresh sense of vertigo.

One has to have experienced the anguish which paralyses the arm at the very moment of the 'uncontrolled explosion' of which I spoke thirty years ago, if one is to understand the ill-timed intervention of reason and 'aesthetics' in this fight to the death which finds its resolution only in victory, not over three centuries of Cartesian orthopaedics, but over thirty years of pictorial awareness! Oh! If others could only know!

In this world where there is no help and no recourse, and where the most desperate cries fall on deaf ears, we must still reject every sort of buoy or life raft . . . and nor are we allowed to swim according to the established laws of swimming.

We must cross to the other side by walking on the water.

—Georges Mathieu

Georges Mathieu began painting in 1942, and in 1944 after reading a book on the novelist Joseph Conrad by Edward Crankshaw he adopted a nonfigurative style. 1947 was the year of decision, for then he moved to Paris and organised the first exhibition of Abstraction Lyrique. For him this was a protest against the retrogressive direction in art relating back to the classical tradition resurrected by the painters of the Renaissance. At first he was influenced by abstract surrealism as seen in the work of Wols. Later he went through a period when Pollock and de Kooning had their effect.

It was about 1948 when he developed his own individual style of painting that had its foundation in the gesture and a flow of spontaneous continuity of image across the canvas. Speed and improvisation have often been the foundation of some of his most successful paintings. He has painted a picture in front of an invited audience in a theatre within a few hours, a form of action painting that required confidence, energy and a total command of resources. Stage design, tapestries and mosaics as well as plans for the architecture of a new factory have issued almost ceaselessly from Mathieu's fertile imagination.

While much of his production is directed towards publicity, there is nevertheless a sound footing of competence in Mathieu's art that precludes its dismissal as facile. He has written much about art and philosophy. His admired masters of the past include El Greco, Goya, Rembrandt, van Gogh, and Le Brun. The choice of the last is not surprising, for Mathieu sees the role of the artist as a controller of the environment to the extent that he is architect, industrial designer, landscape gardener and consultant on all environmental problems as they demand visual consideration.

Mathieu sees contemporary painters as failing in their responsibility to the future because of a constant preoccupation with the art of the past. He endorses Pater's dictum that paintings should aspire to the condition of music. He believes that painting should exist in the same fashion as an autonomous art.

—G. S. Whittet

MATSUZAWA, Yutaka.

Japanese. Born in Shimosuwa, 2 February 1922. Studied architecture at Waseda Univeristy, Tokyo, 1941–46; contemporary poetry at Wisconsin State College, Superior, 1955–56; religious philosophy at Columbia University, New York, 1956–57. Married Misuzu Kamishima in 1948; child: Kumiko: married Haruo Takizawa; child: Yoko; married Yoji Nakamura. Worked as Architect, Azusa Architectural Office, Japan, 1946–48; now an independent artist pursuing spiritual and metaphysical explorations through both traditional and conceptual art-making, since 1952. Director, Data Center of Contemporary Art, Tokyo, since 1973; Lecturer, Bigakko Art School, Tokyo, 1971–81. Recipient: Fulbright Fellowship, 1955; Japan Society Fellowship, 1956; Painting Prize, Bienal, Sao Paulo, 1977. Permanent Member, Accademia Tiberina, Rome, 1978. Agents: Aoki Gallery, Ginza 3-3-10, Chuo-ku, Tokyo, Japan; Art & Project, Willemsparkweg 36, 1007 Amsterdam, Netherlands; Galerie Media, rue des Moulins 29, 2000 Neuchâtel, Switzerland. Address: 5370 Shimosuwa-machi, Nagano-ken 393, Japan.

Individual Exhibitions:

1963   Aoki Gallery, Tokyo
1964   Naika Gallery, Tokyo
1965   Naika Gallery, Tokyo
1966   Modern Art Center of Japan, Tokyo
1967   Ázuma Gallery, Tokyo
1970   Aoki Gallery, Tokyo
1971   Art & Project, Amsterdam
1974   Galeria Akumulatory 2, Poznán, Poland
1977   CAYC, Buenos Aires
1979   Ginza Kaiga Kan, Tokyo
1980   Podio del Mond Per L'Arte, Middelburg, Netherlands
1982   Galeria Media, Neuchâtel, Switzerland
      Okazaki Tamako Gallery, Tokyo
1983   Okazaki Tamako Gallery, Tokyo
1984   Galerie Christian Cheneau, Paris
      Okazaki Tamako Gallery, Tokyo
1985   Galerie Brigitte March, Stuttgart
      Okazaki Tamako Gallery, Tokyo
1986   Art Com, San Francisco
      Okazaki Tamako Gallery, Tokyo

Selected Group Exhibitions:

1953   *Yomiuri Independent Exhibition*, Metropolitan Art Gallery, Tokyo (and each subsequent year through 1963)
1970   *Nirvana*, Municipal Museum, Kyoto
      Contemporary Japanese Art, Guggenheim Museum, New York
1971   *Sonsbeek '71*, Netherlands
1976   *Biennale*, Venice
1977   *Bienal*, Sao Paulo
1981   *The 2nd International Drawing Triennale*, Wroclaw, Poland
1983   *New Trends in Japanese Art of the 1960s*, Metropolitan Gallery of Art, Tokyo
1985   *Reconstructions: Avant-Garde Art in Japan 1945–65*, Museum of Modern Art, Oxford
1987   *Nihon no Matsuri*, San Francisco Museum of Modern Art

Publications:

By MATSUZAWA: books—*Psi Black Box*, Tokyo 1982; *9 Mandalas*, Neuchâtel, Switzerland 1982; articles—"From Cybernetics to Mandala" in *Geijutsushincho* (Tokyo), no. 8, 1960; "Matter Vanishing" in *Gendaibijutsu* (Tokyo), no. 6, 1965; "Wander Around Tantra" in *Mizue* (Tokyo), no. 19, 1969; "About Sonsbeek '71" in *Bijutsu-techo* (Tokyo), no. 11, 1971; text in *Art and Strategy* by Walter Aue, Cologne 1972; "On Lawrence Weiner and Other Artists" in *Mizue* (Tokyo), no. 5, 1975; "Making Public Fine Art Works on the Radio" in *Gengo Seikatsu* (Tokyo), no. 2, 1981; "Biography Autographical" in *Kikan* (Tokyo), no. 13, 1982; "Fossa-Maguna Chinbotsu" in *Kaki no Ha*, Tokyo 1983.

On MATSUZAWA: books—*Deai wo Motomete* by U-Fan Lee, Tokyo 1971; *Art Now II* by Ichiro Haryu, Tokyo 1972; *Mirukoto no Shinwa* by Yusuke Nakahara, Tokyo 1972; *On Matsuzawa* by U-Fan Lee, Tokyo 1974; *P.S. Tokyo*, edited by Shuji Takashima, Yoshiaki Tono and Yusuke Nakahara, Tokyo 1974; articles—"Outside of Psi's Chamber" by Yoshie Yoshida in *Sansai* (Tokyo), no. 10, 1963; "On Matsuzawa" by Shuzo Takiguchi in *Yohaka ni Kaku*, Tokyo 1966; "A Self-Portrait of the Messiah—Yutaka Matsuzawa" by Ikuya Kato in *Bijutsu-techo* (Tokyo), no. 6, 1969; "Yutaka Matsuzawa—A Commune Penetrating the Dark" by Yoshie Yoshida in *Bijutsu-techo* (Tokyo), no. 11, 1972; "On Yutaka Matsuzawa" by Arata Tani in *Bijutsu-techo* (Tokyo), no. 2, 1974; "On Yutaka Matsuzawa" by Yusuke Nakahara in *Mizue* (Tokyo), no. 5, 1975; special number of *Yutaka Matsuzawa Kikan* (Shimosuwa, Japan), no. 3, 1982; "Matsuzawa Yutaka no Uchu" in *Suwa Genso Sha* (Suwa), 1985.

*Yutaka Matsuzawa: *Performance at Ilka Pass*, 1984*

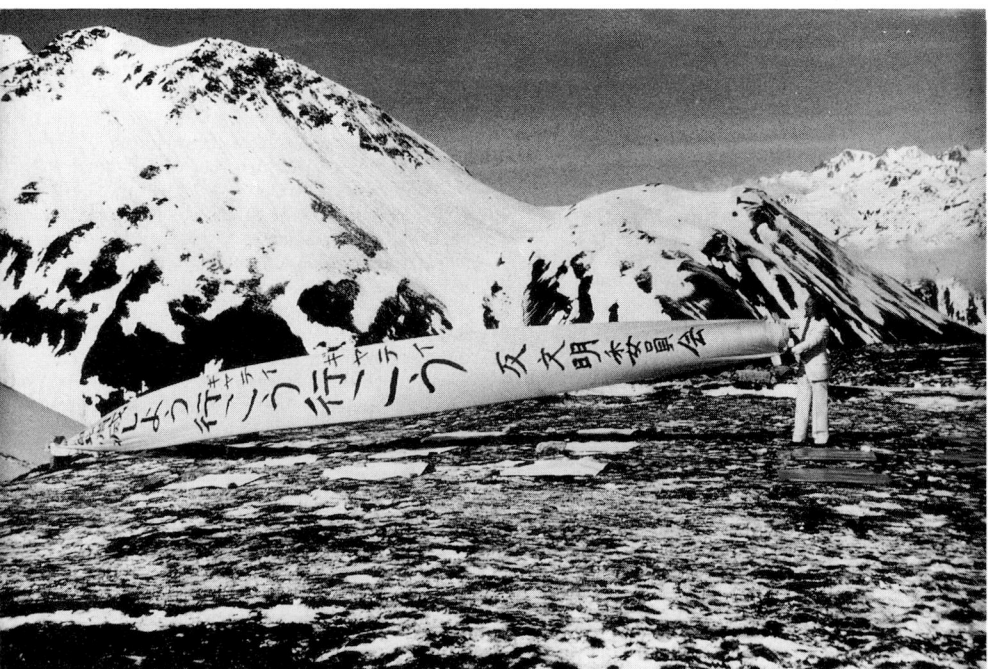

Nine Manifestos and Notifications
(for *Documenta 8*, Kassel, 1987)

1. I give a name to all exhibited pieces the catastrophe art. Because catastrophe is now close at hand.
2. I name all exhibited pieces the final fine art. Because fine art will soon come to an end.
3. Ah! We are the final human beings. Ah! We are the final human beings. Because human beings will soon vanish. Ah!
4. The catastrophe in the Compact Galaxy occurs after 3.10^{13} years.
5. The vanishing of the black hole in the galaxy occurs after 10^{100} years.
6. The cosmos after the vanishing of matter is serene light paradise with positrons and twilight after the collapse of the last proton of which the average life span is 10^{30} years.
7. The vanishing of the serene light paradise which is called positronium occurs after 10^{116} years.
8. The unstable hadron cuticle's span of life is 10^{23} seconds.
9. Ah! The remnant of your life is 15 years (by the vanishing of human beings in 2002).

—Yutaka Matsuzawa

Yutaka Matsuzawa was born in 1922, and graduated from the Department of Architecture of Waseda University in 1946. He spent 1955–1957 in America, but discarded his study of architecture in favour of the philosophy of religion, which he studied at Columbia University. It has been Matsuzawa's accomplishment that since then he has combined his perception and knowledge gained from the study of the philosophy of religion with his artistic work, becoming in the process a true original in contemporary Japanese art.

Matsuzawa first produced a series of works called "psi," and since performing a ceremony "All Being Disappear" (sic), in 1966, he has concentrated on painting. What identified Matsuzawa is his underlying, intense eschatological feeling in which all that is visible must become invisible. With such thought in mind, in 1967–1968 he persisted in dispensing information in the form of a succession of postcards. Typical titles of those postcards were "A Blank Sheet Picture for All Living and Non-Living Entities," and "The Picture Which Is Not Seen and Which Cannot be Seen," and "Picture Showing a Spirit in the Mist."

Matsuzawa's thinking thus is not aesthetic as much

as it is cosmic. He takes the invisible as being real, not the visible.

In the 1970 Tokyo *Biennal*, Matsuzawa gave to a gallery room in the museum the name "My Death," where he put on a performance and had this to say: "I exhibited my own death and the future. It was infinite existences in every mind of the contemplators, and it exists only in time. It is my death and your death, also his painting and her painting; it is involved in the Nirvana which does not increase nor decrease nor come nor go."

This Nirvana which neither increases nor decreases, neither comes nor goes, is Matsuzawa's Utopia.

Since the ceremony, "All Being Disappear," all of Matsuzawa's activities, in taking aim at this Utopia, are religious manifestations. Depending on one's viewpoint, it may be possible to classify this work as conceptual art. To identify accurately Matsuzawa's work, it must be called meta-art. That is because what Matsuzawa is aiming at is a plane at which distinctions cannot be made between concept and perception. In this, a critique of contemporary culture also emerges.

—Yusuka Nakahara

MATTA, Roberto (Sebastian Antonio Echaurren).

Chilean. Born in Chiloe, 11 November 1911. Educated at College of the Sacred Heart, Santiago, until 1928; studied architecture, Catholic University, Santiago, 1929-31. Dip. Arch. 1931; mainly self-taught in painting, from 1937. Married Germana Matta in 1940; children: Batan, Gordon, Paino, Federica, Remuntcho and Alisee. Worked as an interior decorator, Santiago, 1928; as merchant seaman, Compagnie Transatlantique ship, to Europe, 1933; as architectural assistant, Le Corbusier studio, Paris, 1934-36. Independent painter, Paris, 1938-39, in New York, 1939-48, Rome, 1950-54, and in Paris, since 1955. Member, with Federico Garcia Lorca, André Breton, Salvador Dali, Marcel Duchamp, Surrealist Group, Paris, 1937-48, and from 1959, founder, Etrusculudens, Etruscan crafts artisan group, 1972. Visiting instructor, Minneapolis School of Art, 1966. President, Cultural Congress, Havana, 1968. Recipient: Premio Marzotto, Rome, 1962. Address: 145 Boulevard Saint-Germain, 75006 Paris, France.

Individual Exhibitions:

1940	Julien Levy Gallery, New York (with Pavel Tchelitchew)
1942	Pierre Matisse Gallery, New York (and regularly until 1948)
1945	Sidney Janis Gallery, New York
1947	Galerie René Drouin, Paris
	Hugo Gallery, New York
1948	William Copley Gallery, Beverly Hills, California
1950	Galleria dell'Obelisco, Rome
	Galleria Schneider, Rome
	Galleria del Cavallino, Venice
	Galleri del Naviglio, Milan
1951	Institute of Contemporary Arts, London
1952	Allan Frumkin Gallery, New York
1953	Sala Napoleonica, Venice
	Alexander Iolas Gallery, New York
1954	Museo de Arte Moderno, Lima, Peru
	Museo de Arte Moderno, Santiago, Chile
	Galleria del Cavallino, Venice
1955	Galerie du Dragon, Paris
	Galleri Colibu, Malmo, Sweden
	Pan American Union, Washington, D.C.
	Alexander Iolas Gallery, New York
1956	*Matta: Terres Nouvelles*, Galerie du Dragon, Paris
1957	Museum of Modern Art, New York
	Ruth Moskin Gallery, New York
1958	Galleria Galatea, Turin

1959	Foundation Mendoza, Caracas
	Moderna Museet, Stockholm
	Galerie Daniel Cordier, Frankfurt
	Galerie Daniel Cordier, Paris
1960	Galleria del Naviglio, Milan
1961	Gimpel Fils Gallery, London
	Cordier and Warren Gallery, New York
1962	Galleria L'Attico, Rome
	Galerie Le Point Cardinal, Paris
	Gimpel Fils Gallery, London
1963	Allan Frumkin Gallery, New York
	Alexander Iolas Gallery, New York
	Galleria Schwarz, Milan
	Museo Civico, Bologna
	Galerie Edwin Engelberts, Geneva
	Casa de la Americas, Havana
	Auslander Gallery, New York
	University of Chicago
	Frank Perls Gallery, Los Angeles
	Kunsthalle, Dusseldorf
	Robert Fraser Gallery, London
	Museum des 20. Jahrhunderts, Vienna
	Galerie Le Point Cardinal, Paris
1964	Palais des Beaux-Arts, Brussels
	Stedelijk Museum, Amsterdam
	Städtische Kunsthalle, Mannheim, West Germany
	Galerie Michael Hertz, Bremen, West Germany
	Casa de la Americas, Havana
	Galerie Van de Loo, Munich
	Gimpel und Hanover Galerie, Zurich
1965	Kunstmuseum, Lucerne
	Galeria del Techo, Caracas
	Gimpel Fils Gallery, London
1966	Institute of Contemporary Arts, Lima, Peru
	Galerie Alexander Iolas, Paris
1967	Walker Art Center, Minneapolis
	Palais de Mutualité, Paris
	Galleria Senior, Rome
	Galleria S. Luca, Rome
	Casa de las Americas, Havana
	Musée d'Art et d'Histoire, Saint-Denis, France
1968	Alexander Iolas Gallery, New York
	Musée d'Art Moderne de la Ville, Paris (with Alfredo Lam and Alicia Penalba)
	Galleria La Medusa, Rome
1970	Nationalgalerie, Berlin
	Maison de la Culture, Amiens (with Claude Parent)
	Centre Culturel Municipal, Villeparisis, France
	Galerie Michael Hertz, Bremen, West Germany
1973	Galleria Il Fauno, Turin
	Palazzo dei Diamanti, Ferrara, Italy (toured Italy)
	Alexander Iolas Gallery, New York
	Museo Civico, Bologna
	Pinacoteca Comunale, Ravenna, Italy
	Centro Storico, Livorno, Italy
1974	Belle Ciao, Terni, Italy
	Kestner-Gesellschaft, Hannover (toured Germany)
	Office Culturel, St. Etienne du Rouvray, France
	Galeria Aele, Madrid
	Museo de Arte Moderno, Mexico City
	Museo de Arte Moderno, Bogota
	Museo de Bellas Artes, Caracas
1975	Andre Crispo Gallery, New York
	Alexander Iolas Gallery, New York
	L'homme Descend du Signe: Mattapastelli, Galleria dall'Orca, Rome
	Palazzo della Loggia, Brescia, Italy
	Kettles Yard Gallery, Cambridge
	Hotel de Ville, Venissieux, France
1976	Casa de las Americas, Havana
1977	Palazzo degli Alessandri, Viterbo, Italy
	Coigitum, Hayward Gallery, London
1978	Kettles Yard Gallery, Cambridge
	Galerie du Dragon, Paris
1979	Stamperia della Beauga, Florence
	Centre Culturel Municipal, Villeparisis, France
	Universita di Urbino, Italy
1980	Palazzo degli Alessandri, Viterbo, Italy
	Galerie Kinge, Paris
	Paintings and Drawings 1971-79, Tasende Gallery, La Jolla, California (travelled to Blanden Memorial Art Gallery, Fort Dodge, Iowa)
1982	*Roberto Matta: Architecte du Temps*, Theatre d'Ivry, Ivry-sur-Seine, France

	Riverside Studios, Hammersmith, London
1983	Palacio de Cristal, Madrid
1984	City Museum and Art Gallery, Plymouth, Devon (travelled to Oxford, Swansea, Sheffield, Bolton, and Newcastle-upon-Tyne)

Selected Group Exhibitions:

1937	*Surrealisme*, Galerie Wildenstein, Paris
1938	*Exposition Internationale du Surrealisme*, Galerie des Beaux-Arts, Paris
1942	*Artists in Exile*, Pierre Matisse Gallery, New York
1946	*5 Big Paintings*, Museum of Modern Art, New York
1955	*Bienal*, Sao Paulo
1958	*World's Fair*, Brussels
1959	*Documenta 2*, Museum Fridericianum, Kassel, West Germany
1968	*Dada, Surrealism and their Heritage*, Museum of Modern Art, New York
1974	*Biennale*, Venice
1981	*A New Spirit in Painting*, Royal Academy of Art, London

Collections:

Musée National d'Art Moderne, Paris; Nationalgalerie, Berlin; Stedelijk Museum, Amsterdam; Baltimore Museum of Art; City Art Museum, St. Louis, Missouri; Lawrence Art Museum, Williamstown, Massachusetts; Walker Art Center, Minneapolis.

Publications:

By MATTA: books—*Duchamp's Glass*, with Katherine S. Drier, New York 1944; *Come detta dentrovo significando*, Lausanne 1962; *Dialogo con Tarquinia*, Tarquinia 1975.

On MATTA: books—*Matta: Terres Nouvelles*, exhibition catalogue, with text by E. Glissant, Paris 1956; *Matta*, exhibition catalogue, with text by L. Hoctin, New York 1957; *Matta*, exhibition catalogue, with text by I. Gustafson, Stockholm 1959; *Histoire de la Peinture Surrealiste* by Marcel Jean, Paris 1959; *Matta*, exhibition catalogue, with text by Werner Hofmann, Vienna 1963; *Un Revolution du Régard* by Alain Jouffroy, Paris 1964; *Matta: Le Multiplicateur de Progrès* by José Pierre, Paris 1967; *Catalogue Raisonne de l'Oeuvre Gravée de Matta*, compiled by Ursula Schmitt, Silkeborg 1969; *Developpements sur l'infrarealisme de Matta* by Jean Schuster, Paris 1970; *Matta*, exhibition catalogue, with an introduction by Ursula Schmitt, Berlin 1970; *Matta*, exhibition catalogue, with text by Wieland Schmied, Hannover 1974; *L'homme Descend du Signe: Mattapastelli*, exhibition catalogue, with text by Giuliano Briganti, Rome 1975; *Matta: Catalogue Raisonne de l'Oeuvre Gravée 1943-1974*, compiled by Roland Sabatier, Stockholm and Paris 1975; *Matta: Opere dal 1939 al 1975* by Luisa Laureati, Rome 1976; *Matta: Coigitum*, exhibition catalogue, with interview by Peter de Francia, text by André Breton, London 1977; *Matta: Index dell'Opere Grafica dal 1969 al 1980*, edited by Germana Farrari, Viterbo, Italy 1980; *Roberto Matta: Paintings and Drawings 1971-1979*, exhibition catalogue, with texts by Peter Selz, J. M. Tasende and André Breton, La Jolla, California 1980; *Roberto Matta: Architecte du Temps*, exhibition catalogue, by Thierry Sigg and Jean-Pierre Faye, Ivry, France 1982; *Matta: The Logic of Hallucination*, exhibition catalogue with text by Paul Overy, London 1984.

In 1938, when the Surrealist movement seemed to be breaking up, new life was breathed into it by two new painters, the Chilean-born Roberto Matta and the Cuban Wilfredo Lam. And in contrast to the realistic or veristic surrealist imagery of Dali or Magritte, the surrealist aim of automatism, of painting out the inner impulses and tapping inner springs of energy in a spontaneous, improvisatory way, found a remarkable fulfilment in Matta's early paintings. He called them "inscapes" or "psychological morphologies" because he was trying in them to project visual metaphors for his inner feelings, impulses and passions. The results are violent, agitated explosions of luminous colour suggesting some cosmic creation or collapse—deep luminous space in whose shifting clouds float vaguely biomorphic or geological shapes, with everything in violent motion. Matta is above all

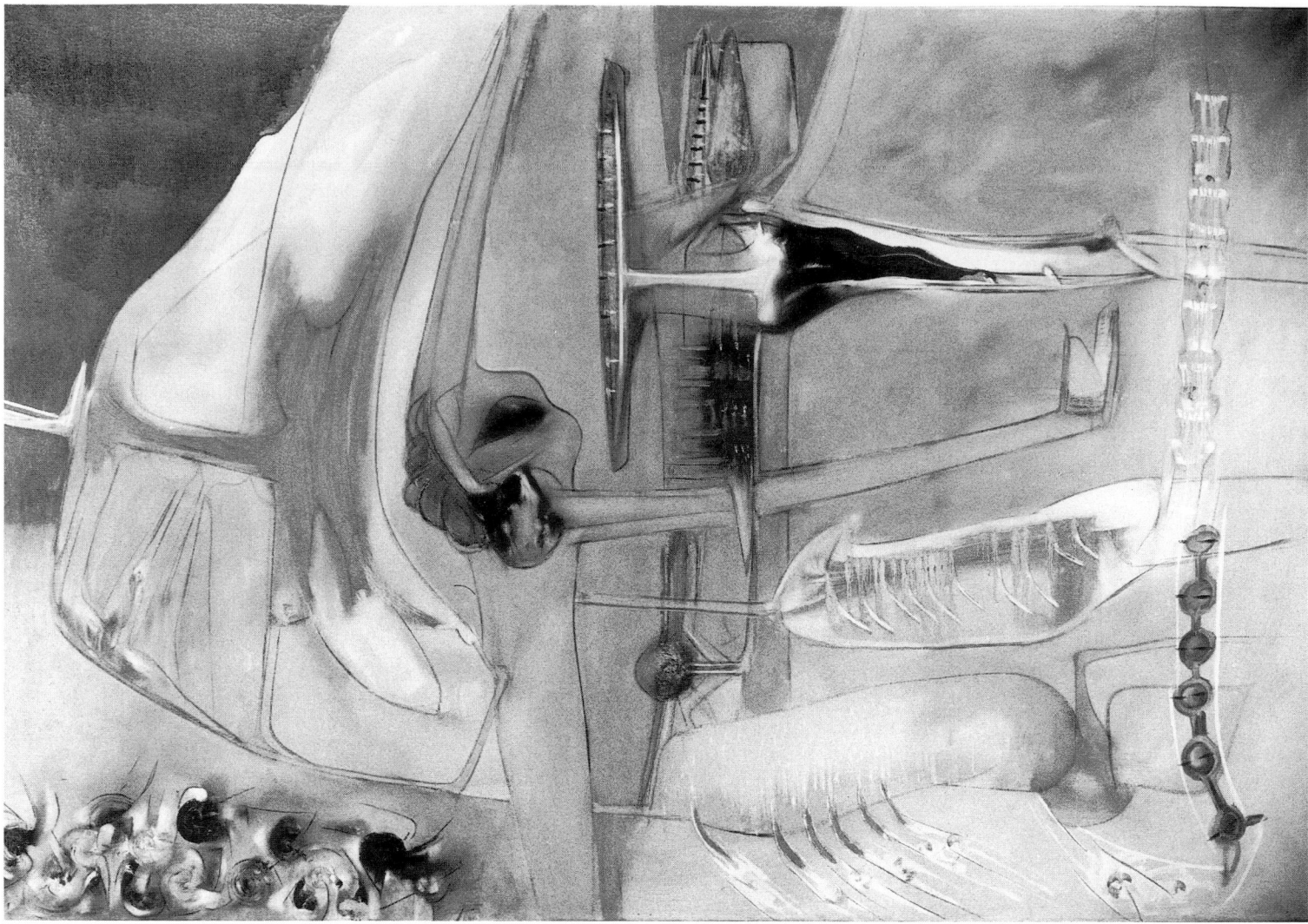

Roberto Matta: *Prime Ordeal*, c. 1946 Courtesy Museum of Contemporary Art, Chicago

the creator of imaginary worlds which manage to suggest the profound depths of the psyche simultaneously with the vastness of the universe.

When Matta fled to America during the 1939–45 war, along with other surrealists including Ernst, Tanguy, Breton and Masson, this sort of psychic automatism came like a revelation to American artists, and was one of the basic influences on the growth of Abstract Expressionism. Matta had a particularly profound influence on the work of Arshile Gorky, which shares a similar sort of lyricism, and on Robert Motherwell, who painted with Matta in Mexico in 1941.

Towards the end of the war, however, Matta's own style was undergoing a profound change: "My main preoccupation . . . was looking into myself. Suddenly I realized that while trying to do this I was *being with* a horrible crisis in society. My vision of myself was becoming blind for not being made one with people around me, and I sought to create a new morphology of others within my own field of consciousness." And so under the influence of the early machinist pictures of his friend Duchamp, man-like creatures with mechanical features began to appear in his works, in nightmare architectural settings, often amidst aggressive machinery and the crackling of high voltage electricity. Some of his bizarre anthropomorphs are like monstrous insects, lustful and erotic as they lunge aggressively at their female prey.

His mechanical monsters are painted on giant canvases, forming a wide-screen theatre in which his bizarre personages undergo transformation and struggle, tortured and torturing, reflecting the cruelty and destruction of war. Radical political aspirations were always an essential feature of surrealism, and some of Matta's more recent works have been more overtly political. But he is most successful when he poetically suggests rather than more specifically depicts "man's struggle against oppression and exposes the cruel constant of daily life," and the best of his later works reflect his own struggle to interpret the specific terrors and obsessions of contemporary humanity and to evolve a pictorial mythology for our technological age.

—Konstantin Bazarov

MATTA-CLARK, Gordon.

American. Born in 1945. Studied architecture at Cornell University, Ithaca, New York, 1963–68. Conceptual Artist: lived and worked in New York. *Died in 1978.*

Individual Exhibitions:

1971	Museo de Bellas Artes, Santiago, Chile
1972	112 Greene Street Gallery, New York
	98 Greene Street Loft, New York
1973	Mercer Street Gallery, New York
	Galerie 21, Amsterdam
	Galleria Forma, Genoa
1974	John Gibson Gallery, New York
	Museum, Aachen, West Germany
	Musée d'Art Moderne de la Ville, Paris
1975	Amerika Haus, Berlin
	Galleria Ala, Milan

1976	Holly Solomon Gallery, New York
	American Cultural Center, Paris
1977	Internationaal Cultureel Centrum, Antwerp
	Galerie Schmela, Dusseldorf
	Galerie Yvon Lambert, Paris
1978	Young-Hoffman Gallery, Chicago
1979	Städtische Kunsthalle, Dusseldorf
	Badischer Kunstverein, Karlsruhe, West Germany

Selected Group Exhibitions:

1971	*Pier 18*, Museum of Modern Art, New York
	Bienal, Sao Paulo
1972	*Photographic Portraits*, Moore College of Art, Philadelphia
	Documenta, Kassel, West Germany
1973	*Artists' Books*, Moore College of Art, Philadelphia
	New York in Chicago, Mies van der Rohe Plaza, Chicago
1974	*Questions-Answers*, Sarah Lawrence College, Bronxville, New York
1975	*Artists Make Toys*, The Clocktower, New York
1980	*Biennale*, Venice

Publications:

By MATTA-CLARK: books—*20th Century Sculptors*, New York 1971; *Wallspaper*, New York 1972, 1973; *Splitting*, New York 1974; films—*Pig Roast; Tree Dance; Fire Child; Open House; Automation House; Freshkill; Food;* video—*Chinatown Voyeur; Automation House; Profiles; Sauna View.*

On MATTA-CLARK: articles—articles by Robert Pincus-Witten in *Artforum* (New York), September 1970; article by Fred McDarrah in the *Village Voice* (New York), January

1971; "Gordon Matta-Clark: Jacks" by Liza Bear in *Avalanche* (New York), Fall 1971; article by John Perreault in the *Village Voice* (New York), October 1972; article by Germano Celant in *Casabella* (Milan), July 1974; "The Great Divide: Anarchitecture by Matta-Clark" by A. Brunelle in *Art in America* (New York), September/October 1974; article in *Artforum* (New York), November 1975.

MAURI, Fabio.

Italian. Born in Rome, 1 April 1926. Educated at the University of Milan, 1945–47; Faculty of Modern Literature, University of Rome, 1948–50. Married Adriana Asti in 1955 (separated, 1958). Independent artist, since 1956. Instructor of Painting and Drawing, Boys Town of Italy, Civitavecchia, 1947–53; Lecturer in Aesthetics, Academy of Art, L'Aquila, since 1979. Has written for the theatre, since 1958; General Manager, Editrice Valentino Bompiani and Editor, *Almanacco Letterario Bompiani* and *Sipario*, Rome, 1959–71; Editor, *Quindici*, Rome, 1967–68; and *La Città di Riga, nos. 1 and 2*, Macerata, Italy, 1976; President, Messaggerie Italiane books and periodicals, Rome, since 1982. Agent: Galleria Le Salita, Via Garibaldi 88, Rome. Address: Vicolo Febo 7, Rome, Italy

Individual Exhibitions:

1954	Galleria del Cavallino, Venice
1955	Galleria Apollinaire, Milan
	Galleria L'Aureliana, Rome
1956	Galleria San Babila, Milan
	Galleria Apollinaire, Milan
1960	Galleria San Marco, Rome
1963	Galleria La Salita, Rome
1965	Galleria Arco d'Alibert, Rome
1967	Galleria La Salita, Rome
1968	Galleria de Nieubourg, Milan
1969	Studio d'Arte Toninelli, Rome
1970	Palazzo Ricci, Montepulciano, Italy
	Stabilmenti Safa Palatino, Rome (performance)
	Galleria Barozzi, Venice (travelled to Galleria Acme, Brescia, Galleria La Steccata, Parma, and Galleria La Salita, Rome).
1972	Studio Barozzi, Milan
	Centro Multipli, Rome
	Galleria Seconda Scala, Rome
1974	Pilotta, Parma, Italy
1975	*Oscuramento*, Museo Civico, Bologna (with Piero Paolo Pasolini)
1976	*Senza*, Galleria Toselli, Milan
1977	*Brunelleschi e noi*, Chiostri di Santa Maria Novella, Florence
1978	*News from Europe*, A Space, Toronto
1979	*What is Fascism*, Performing Garage, New York
1980	*Muro d'Europa/La Barca*, De Appel, Amsterdam
1981	*Umanesimo/Disumanesimo nell'Arte Contemporanea*, Florence
1982	*1909–1930 Gran Serata Futurista*, Assessorato ala Cultura, Rome
	Galleria Il Falconiere, Ancona
1983	Facolta di Magistero, L'Aquila (performance)
	Assessorato alla Cultura, Florence (performance)
1984	Assessorato alla Cultura, L'Aquila (performance)
	University of Rome (performance)
	University of L'Aquila (performance)
	Palazzo Trinci, Foligno (performance)
1985	Civica Scuola Piccolo Teatro, Milan (performance)
	Galleria Mara Coccia, Rome
	Teatro Universitario, L'Aquila (performance)
	Marcati Traiani, Rome
1986	Palazzo Grassi, Venice
	Palazzo San Domenico, L'Aquila
1987	Studio Marconi, Milan (performance)

Selected Group Exhibitions:

1954	*11th Triennale*, Milan
1960	*Collettiva Internazionale*, Galleria La Tartaruga, Rome
1973	*Art around 70*, Philadelphia Museum of Art
1976	*032303*, National Gallery of Canada, Ottawa
1978	*I Numeri Malefici*, at the *Biennale*, Venice
1980	*Camere Incantate: Espansione dell'Immagine*, Palazzo Reale, Milan
1982	*Generazioni a Confronto*, University of Rome
1983	*Il Pop Art e l'Italia*, Castello Visconti, Milan
1985	*Arte Italiana degli anni '60*, Galleria Civica d'Arte Moderna, Turin
1987	*Sogno Italiano*, Castello di Genazzano, Italy

Collections:

Galleria Nazionale d'Arte Moderna, Rome; Museo Art Moderna, Turin; Museo Arte Moderna, Bologna; Instituto d'Arte Contemporanea, Parma; Museo d'Arte Moderna, Livorno; Museo d'Arte Moderna, Republic of San Marino.

Publications:

By MAURI: books—*Giro a Vuoto Cabaret*, Milan 1959; *Crack*, Milan 1960; *Artecronache*, with Pilnio de Martiis and Cesare Vivaldi, Rome 1961; *Giovanna di Io*, in *Potentissima Singora*, Milan 1965; *Der Politische Ventilator*, Rome 1970; *Osuramento*, exhibition catalogue, Rome 1975; *Manipolazione di Cultura*, Macerata, Italy 1976; *Dramophon*, Rome 1980; *Narcissus in the Cold*, Toronto 1982; *Blu Cobalto*, Rome 1985; *Storia di un Manifesto mancato*, Milan 1987; articles—"21 Modi per non pubblicare un Libro" in *Temp Presente* (Rome), September/October 1966; "Riflessioni in Apnea sulla Critica" in *Techne*, Florence 1968; "Azione Teoria e Illustrazione" in *La Città di Riga*, (Macerata, Italy), no. 1. 1976; "Intervista" in *Parachute* (Toronto), no. 14, 1978; "Appunti per un Elogio Assiomatico della Critica" in *Flash Art* (Milan), 1979; "Conferenza non fatta" in *Il Viandante e la sua Ombra*, edited by V. Artioli and F. Bartoli, Bologna 1981; "Nel 1970 gli anni '50 avevano 10 anni" in *Flash Art* (Milan), no. 112, 1983; "Dio e la scena" in *L'Immagine: arte, scienza, teoria*, Milan 1987; plays—*L'Isola*, Milan 1964; *Lezione Inglese*, Milan 1970 (appeared in *Sipario*, March 1970).

On MAURI: books—*Teatro delle Mostre* by Maurizio Calvesi, Lerici, Italy 1968; *Panorama di Pitture Interna-*

Fabio Mauri: *Muro d'Europa/La Barca*, 1979

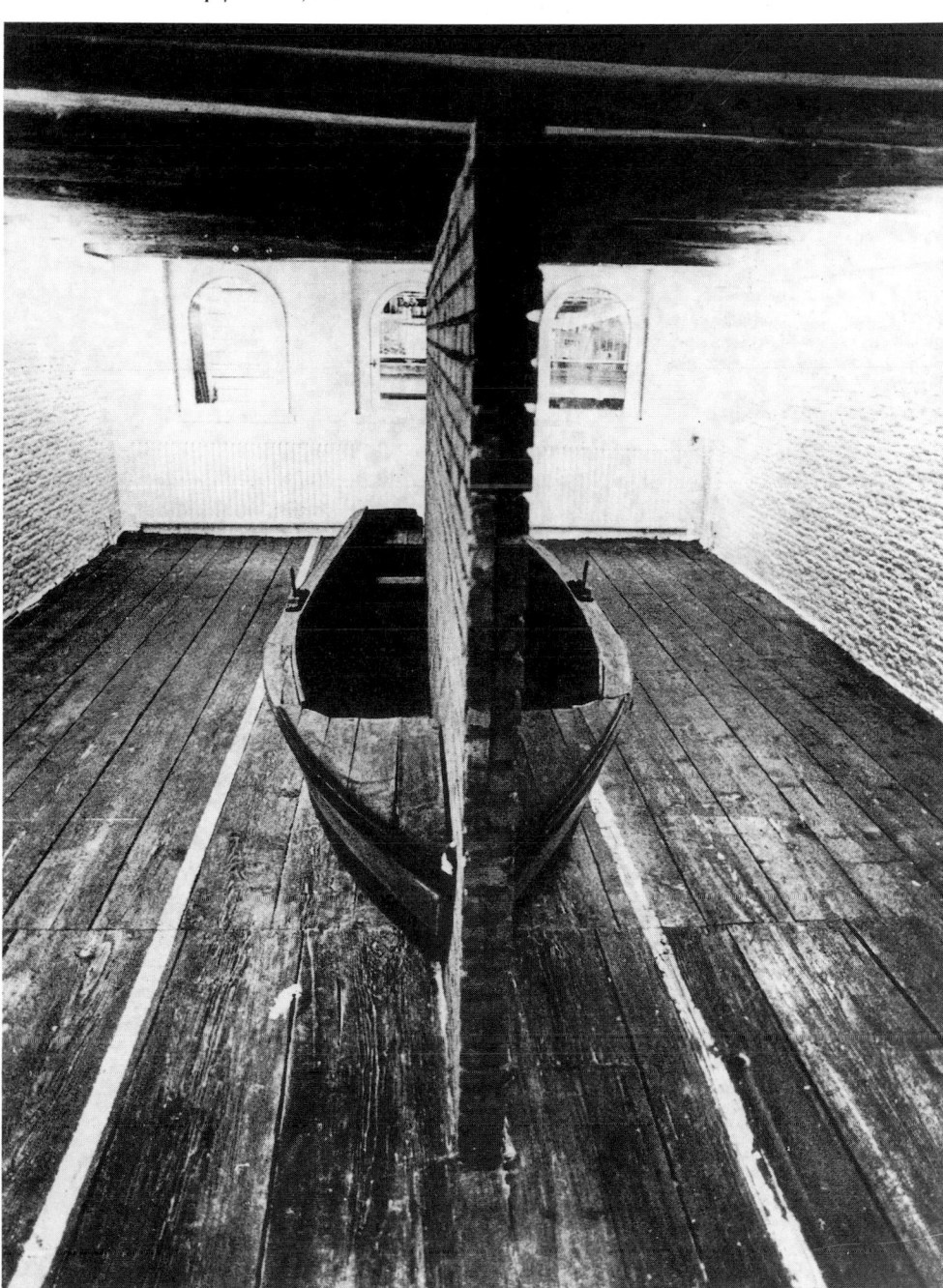

zionale by Udo Kultermann, Milan 1969; *Fabio Mauri 1959-1969* by Cesare Vivaldi, Rome 1969; *Amore mia* by Achille Bonito Oliva, Florence 1970; *Il Corpo come Linguaggio* by Lea Vergine, Milan 1974; *Nuove Prospettive della Critica* by Gillo Dorfles, Milan 1976; *Brunelleschi e noi*, exhibition catalogue, by Achille Bonito Oliva, Florence 1977; *Umanesimo/Disumanesimo nell'Arte Contemporanea*, exhibition catalogue, by Lara Vinca Masini, Florence 1980; *Fantasmi Italiani* by Alberto Arbasino, Rome 1980; *Fabio Mauri*, exhibition catalogue, Vancouver 1982; *Il Pop Art e l'Italia* by Bossaglia and Zatti, Pavia 1983; *Lo Spettacolo dell'Arte* by Lara Vinca Masini, Rome 1984; *Arte Italiana 1960–1985* by C. Christov Bakargiev, Milan 1987.

At this point, what I am interested in is expression, not art. Or rather, to avoid the limitations of paradox, poetry as illumination, born from an uninterrupted process of expression and moving towards knowledge of the objective expression of the world of appearances. This involves a complex theory which describes, in a logical, intuitive manner, the complex creative system of at least one individual: myself. It is obviously impossible to elucidate this theory in two lines. One can only indicate a couple of relatively simple derivatives:

1. No distinction between "genres," or perhaps, the reduction of all of them (music, painting, theatre, etc.) to single, exclusive "genre" of the mind which *had* to express itself to avoid obliteration at the hands of the "active" expression of the tangible world.

2. Knowledge, along with all forms of mental expression, should be considered an act of legitimate defense, as simple and natural as eating food; the only way of survival against the armies of error which are constantly nourished by the unqualifiable objectivity of the world.

—Fabio Mauri

During the 1950s, Fabio Mauri held a series of exhibitions in Milan, where he took part in, among other events, the Milan Triennale of 1954 and, in the following year, the Milan Biennale. In 1956 he returned to his native city of Rome. Towards the end of the 1950s, he produced a series of neo-dada works, a tendency then imposing itself on the Italian art scene.

Since then, Mauri's painting has a characteristic of its own, stemming from a combination of developed 'action painting' and new ways of expression linked to the mass media. *Autoritratto Cancellato* is dated 1959-60: inside a drawer a number of tentative brushstrokes are superimposed on a portrait. Atop the whole, a box of pasta is set. In that period, Mauri also produced the series *The End;* one example from the series is *Helzapopping,* where in an enclosure are made a number of marks, and the words, 'The End' appear.

Within this kind of poetic Mauri developed a theme that was to remain constant throughout his work. In time he would employ all possible expressive means. Cesari Vivaldi has written: "In his early work *The End* represents a cinema screen, whereas later on the screen will stand for the cinema itself." This applies to the artist's works up to the end of the 1960s, a period ending with *Cinema a luce solida.*

Mauri's interest in cinema is constantly declared in a more or less explicit way. In a later work of 1968 in which plexiglass is used, cinema is idealized and 'frozen' within the magic of a projection hall. A stand symbolizes the projector, and a pyramid connected to the side and base of the stand and fixed to the wall symbolizes the light beam from the projector. Mauri became so interested in cinema that he has never abandoned themes connected to projection, the film, etc.

Following important works such as *Che cosa e il Fascismo* (1971), *Ideology and Nature* (1973) and *Oscuramento* (1975), he produced *Senza*, a series of installations in which films are projected onto animated or still objects. In them, he was seeking a relationship between thought (concretized as film) and the real world. The result was a continuously changing event, revealing new aspects of filmic language contaminated by the outside world.

Between the period of *Solid Light Cinema* at the end of the 1960s and this new chapter in his production, a number of changes took place. Dominant among them is Mauri's increasing awareness of how impossible it was to crystallize the Core of European culture with the aim of affirming the validity of the work of art. The realization of this impossibility produced a reflection upon art and culture in an attempt to understand where such limitations originate. Mauri writes: "At the time I intuited that Europe contained invisible operating elements. The model of a consumer society in which Europe was caught was incapable of accounting for this. I decided to exhibit a series of readymades produced by recent history: Mussolini's megaphone which I had found, uniforms, military badges, and so on." So was born *What Is Fascism,* a work that concludes one epoch and opens another, where ideology takes on a fundamental role to reflect on this.

A theatrical element underlines *A Fest in Honour of General Ernest Von Hussel Passing Through Rome,* a complex sequence of performances simulating past reality, but a reality which nevertheless still has the power to influence people's current behaviour. It is such relationships between past and present, between fiction and reality that interest Mauri, and in such a light it is possible to see a common trend in his latest works, from *Ebrea* of 1971 to *Wall of Europe* of 1979. The latter work is an installation: a boat is divided into two equal halves along a longitudinal axis. The fundamental sense of the work is revealed in the author's own words: "The *Wall of Europe* alludes to the Berlin Wall, a scar that cuts across Europe, separating and splitting every thought and action."

—Roberto Lambarelli

McCOY, Ann.

American. Born in Boulder, Colorado, 8 July 1946. Studied philosophy, theology and the classics at the University of Colorado, Boulder, 1966-69, B.F.A. 1969; studied sculpture and drawing at the University of California at Los Angeles, 1969-72, M.A. 1972. Painter and printmaker, Los Angeles, 1972-77, in New York, since 1977. Art Instructor, School of Visual Arts, New York, since 1977; Barnard College, New York, since 1980; Columbia University, New York, since 1985. Recipient: New Talent Award, Los Angeles County Museum of Art, 1972; Norman Wait Harris Award, Art Institute of Chicago, 1974; American Association of University Women Award, 1976; D.A.A.D. Kunstlerprogramm Fellowship, West Berlin, 1977; National Endowment for the Arts Award, 1978. Agents: Brooke Alexander Inc., 20 West 57th Street, New York, New York 10019; Margo Leavin Gallery, 812 North Robertson, Los Angeles, California 90069. Address: 24 West 76th Street, New York, New York 10023, U.S.A.

Individual Exhibitions:

1970	Esther Bear Gallery, Santa Barbara, California
1974	Parrish Art Museum, Southampton, New York
	Fourcade Droll Inc., New York
	Nancy Hoffman Gallery, New York
1975	Institute of Contemporary Art, Boston
	Harcus-Krakow-Rosen-Sonnabend Gallery, Boston
	Betty Gold Fine Modern Prints, Los Angeles
1976	Margo Leavin Gallery, Los Angeles
1977	Wallraf-Richartz Museum, Cologne
1978	Brooke Alexander Inc., New York
	Chandler Coventry Gallery, Paddington, Australia
1979	Arts Club of Chicago
	Roy Boyd Gallery, Chicago
	Margo Leavin Gallery, Los Angeles
	Thomas Segal Gallery, Boston

	Brooke Alexander Inc., New York (travelled to the Portland Center for the Visual Arts, Oregon)
1981	Augen Galleries, Portland, Oregon
	Brooke Alexander Inc., New York

Selected Group Exhibitions:

1972	*15 Young Artists*, Pasadena Art Museum, California
1973	*New American Landscapes*, Vassar College, Poughkeepsie, New York
1974	*Drawings: Works by Contemporary Artists*, University of Miami
1975	*Both Kinds: Contemporary Art from Los Angeles*, University of California, Berkeley
1976	*America 1976*, Corcoran Gallery, Washington, D.C. (travelled to the Wadsworth Atheneum, Hartford, Connecticut, and the Fogg Art Museum, Cambridge, Massachusetts)
1978	*31st Annual Exhibition*, Brooklyn Museum, New York
1980	*Painting and Sculpture Today*, Indianapolis Museum of Art (travelled to the Contemporary Art Center, Cincinnati, Ohio)
1981	*Los Angeles Prints 1883–1980*, Los Angeles County Museum of Art
1985	*Memento Mori*, Moore College of Art, Philadelphia
1986	*Myths and Symbols*, Bruno Facchetti Gallery, New York

Collections:

Museum of Modern Art, New York; Whitney Museum, New York; Allen Memorial Art Museum, Oberlin, Ohio; Art Institute of Chicago; Denver Art Museum; Indianapolis Museum of Art; Los Angeles County Museum of Art; Houston Museum of Fine Art; National Gallery of Australia, Canberra.

Publications:

By McCOY: article—"The Demon and the Night Sea" in *Art International* (Zurich), no. 3-4, 1980.

On McCOY: articles—"The Rise and Decline of Younger Los Angeles Art" by Peter Plagens in *Artforum* (New York), May 1972; "The Strangeness of Reality" by Melinda Terbell in *Artnews* (New York), November 1973; "Artists in Love with their Art" by Peter Schjeldahl in the *New York Times*, 3 November 1974; "The Silent World of Ann McCoy" by Jean Luc Bordeaux in *Art International* (Lugano, Switzerland), January 1977; "Drawings from the Natural World" by Dorothy Burkhardt in *Artweek* (Oakland, California), 4 November 1978; "Looking for Ann McCoy" by John Loring in *Arts Magazine* (New York), December 1978; "Ann McCoy" by Jeff Perrone in *Artforum* (New York), December 1980; "Ann McCoy at Brook Alexander" by Carter Ratcliff in *Art in America* (New York), February 1980.

The works are concerned primarily with a kind of visual experience. At times in nature, I have felt like an instrument of perception, an optical lens viewing the scene before me in a non-judgemental, precognitive, mindless state. The visual experience becomes so intense, that what James referred to as the whirring-buzzing confusion of the mind stills, the lobe of the brain which is concerned with logic, discourse, reason, seems to be non-existent. It is a visual experience that is solely dependent upon the optical mind. I feel this is the visual experience that Stan Brakhage refers to in *Metaphors on Vision:* "Yet I suggest that there is a pursuit of knowledge foreign to language and founded upon visual communication demanding a development of the optical mind and dependent upon perception in the original and deepest sense of the word."

I wanted the works to be concerned with a kind of visual communication that was not dependent upon literal discourse, problematical thought, discursive symbolism . . . the intellect and its restrictive manifestations. I perceive nature in a particular way. All of the paintings of landscapes I have seen seemed re-

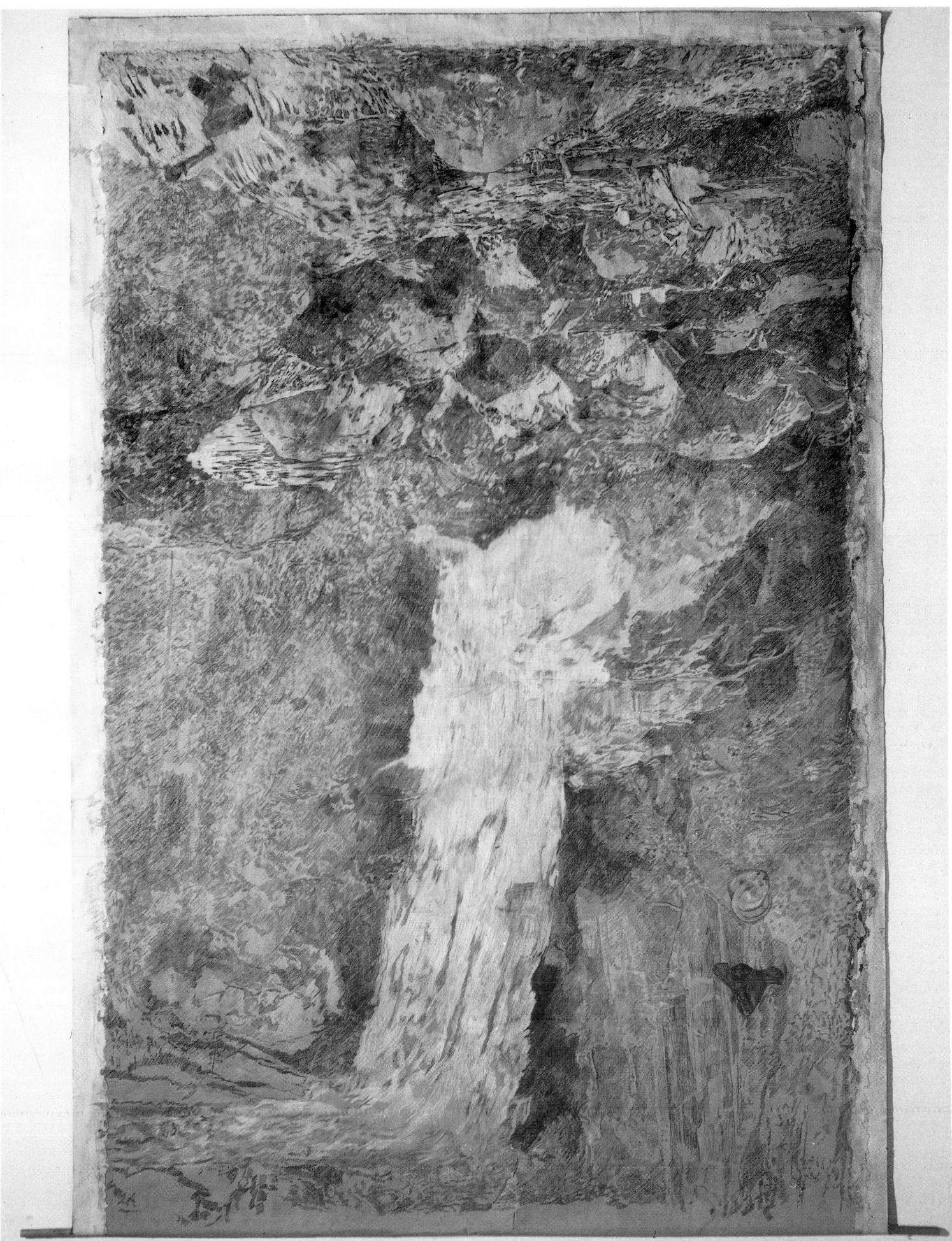

Ann McCoy: *Waterfall*, 1971

moved from this kind of perception. I wanted to draw the world as I perceived it.

The works are drawings. Four years ago I was working with transparency, luminosity and landscape; I was making sculptures that looked like Chinese jade mountains. I began to realize that I was more interested in the working drawings than in the sculptures. It was around that time that I also saw the first Sol Le Witt wall drawing. I liked the notion of drawing on such a large scale, drawing as an ultimate concern. I have always preferred drawings to paintings . . . liked old master's notebooks better than their paintings. My first drawings were very much like silver point drawings. My first drawing of Highland Mary Falls was all done with black and silver graphite . . . and had the same shimmering quality. The shimmering delicate quality of pencil seemed to capture the visual experience I had in nature.

Color became a concern about two years ago. I like the prismatic color sense one finds in Church and Bierstadt. I also like the kind of color one finds in film . . . color projected . . . has a transparent quality only found occasionally in watercolor paintings. The color in the drawings is determined by mood, weather and is generally the "natural" color of what is being drawn. I was interested in the work of Church for another reason . . . also in the work of Pollock. I like the general lack of emphasis on a particular area of the canvas. . . . I don't mean to confuse this with the notion of field painting generally. If one were to cut the canvas up into grid squares, one square would be no more important than another. When I am viewing a scene in nature, my visual field seems to defy the singling out of a particular object. I wanted to make the works, so that they, like nature, could not be perceived quickly. I have always liked the notion of complexity . . . gradual revelation . . . of several layers of perception of something being difficult to perceive or comprehend. This idea goes very much against much of the work of the sixties. . . . I often wonder if a viewer who is used to looking at Stellas can have the patience to spend several hours looking at one of my drawings.

The "cosmic landscape painters" felt that nature was man's salvation, a transcendental substitute for organized religion. They painted the world in a pre-Adamic state, a world without the hedgerow or structure of European thought. In the drawings I am indeed concerned with a kind of Garden of Eden world . . . but not a world viewed through the eyes of a noble savage or primitive man. I am concerned with an outer landscape . . . altered by consciousness . . . seen through the eyes of an inner part of one's being. I do not want the drawings to be thought of as the extension of an historical tradition . . . as a celebration of a kind of Yankee idealism. For me they are like shadow pictures of an inner world that bears a striking resemblance to an outer world. In many ways they are as mysterious to me as they are to the viewer. When I finish one, I am always totally surprised that I have drawn a place that I have not seen, that I have drawn it at all.

I work from photographs . . . often as many as fifty different photographs of different locations. *The Andes* was inspired by photographs of the Andes, and also by photographs of Yosemite. The underwater drawings are drawn from photographs usually of a particular place . . . like photographs of the Great Barrier Reef. I have often not seen the place I am drawing, but try to study a similar place to observe the lighting conditions. I drew *The Andes* after studying the light falling on the peaks where I ski. I drew the underwater works after driving in California, Mexico and Hawaii. The basic inspiration always comes from actually being out in nature. My studio is within a half hour of mountains, octopi, buffalos, starfish and swans . . . a situation that one could not duplicate in New York.

The works grow spontaneously. I never know what the work will look like in advance. I use photographs, some actual objects like sea shells and lantern slides to help create the weather effects. I sometimes do geological research and also study oceanography. I have always liked scientific textbooks with diagrams.

The drawings in the margins of the works are often notes or associations, that may or may not relate to the place in reality, but to places in my dreams. I like to combine scientific observation and detail with a dreamlike or unconscious element. The most recent works—*Le Pays Des Reves, Palou*—were aided by researching the ocean life in Australia, and also Palou, at the Sea Library.

Enough said. I hope that people will look at the works for themselves, and pay very little attention to anything that I have said about them. They are made to be seen without verbiage . . . are made for a part of the psyche that has nothing to do with the intellect.

—Ann McCoy

Influenced by Larry Bell, DeWain Valentine and Peter Alexander, Ann McCoy started her career by making cast resin sculptures of icebergs. Feeling there was a lack of support for her sculptures, she destroyed a great number of them and went on to experiment with drawing on a large scale. Water, however, continued to be (and still is) the main theme of her works, which are generally executed in colored pencil with acrylic ground on paper mounted on canvas.

The artistic world of Ann McCoy is located below the surface of the sea, which she explores and photographs herself. Since the early 1970's her drawings have been increasingly inhabited by sea ferns, shells, corals and fishes. Before her move from Venice, California to Berlin in January 1977 when she was awarded the coveted Berliner Kunstlerprogramm grant, her works were essentially luminous and calm. When she came back to the United States in 1978—to New York, where she now lives—her ocean drawings became more and more tormented and darker. McCoy called the drawings which she exhibited in 1979 "The Night Sea." She wrote that these works "have their origin in the unconscious . . . . Many of the images from these realms are primordial, pre-ancestral . . . ." The presence of threatening sea creatures such as voracious eels, octopus and serpents reflects the artist's current deep state of introversion. She wrote that the monsters she researched in oceanographic photo archives have been turned in her drawings into metaphors for the shadowy figures she has been encountering within herself. This journey into the sea of the unconscious takes her deeper and deeper, a dive which may partly explain the increasing darkness of the subaquatic element.

Unintimidated by any past or current fashions, McCoy offers the viewer a strong sensibility which is nourished by a great amount of reading ranging from St. Augustine, Thomas Aquinas, Irish poetry, St. John Perse and the Bible to art historical studies on, for example, 19th century American landscape painters. As the creator of a new form of visionary landscape (which also includes astronomical imagery), she has enjoyed great critical acclaim.

—Jean-Luc Bordeaux

McCRACKEN, John.
American. Born in Berkeley, California, 9 December 1934. Studied, under Gordon Onslow-Ford and Tony De Lap, California College of Arts and Crafts, Oakland, 1957-65, B.F.A. 1962. Served in the United States Navy, 1953-57. Instructor, University of California at Irvine, 1965-66; Assistant Professor, University of California at Los Angeles, 1966-68; Assistant Professor, School of Visual Arts, New York, 1968-69; Assistant Professor, Hunter College, New York, 1971-72; Lecturer, University of Nevada, Reno, 1972-73; Lecturer, University of Nevada, Las Vegas, 1973-75. Lecturer, College of Creative Studies, University of California at Santa Barbara, since 1975. Recipient: National Endowment for the Arts Grant, 1968. Agent: Nicholas Wilder Gallery, 82251

Santa Monica Boulevard, Los Angeles, California 90046. Address: 500 East Highway 41 (Sky Harbor Airport), Las Vegas, Nevada 89119, U.S.A.

Individual Exhibitions:

1965   Nicholas Wilder Gallery, Los Angeles
1966   Robert Elkon Gallery, New York
1967   Nicholas Wilder Gallery, Los Angeles
        Robert Elkon Gallery, New York
1968   Robert Elkon Gallery, New York
        Nicholas Wilder Gallery, Los Angles
1969   Ileana Sonnabend Gallery, Paris
        Sculpture 1965-1969, Art Gallery of Ontario, Toronto
1970   Sonnabend Gallery, New York
        Ace Gallery, Vancouver
1972   Robert Elkon Gallery, New York
1973   Robert Elkon Gallery, New York
1974   Seder-Creigh Gallery, Coronado, California
1978   Meghan Williams Gallery, Los Angeles
1979   Dobrick Gallery, Chicago
1980   Meghan Williams Gallery, Los Angeles
1982   Schaffner Gallery, Santa Barbara, California
1985   Flow Ace Gallery, Los Angeles
1986   Project Studio One, New York

Selected Group Exhibitions:

1967   *Biennale*, Paris (travelled to Pasadena Art Museum, California
        Guggenheim International Exhibition, New York
1968   *Options*, Milwaukee Art Center (travelled to Museum of Contemporary Art, Chicago)
1969   *Art of the Real*, Museum of Modern Art, New York (travelled to Paris and London)
        Kompas 4: West Coast USA, Van Abbemuseum, Eindhoven, Netherlands
1970   *Permutations: Light and Color*, Museum of Contemporary Art, Chicago
        American Exhibition, Art Institute of Chicago
1971   *5-Man Show*, Ace Gallery, Los Angeles (travelled to Edmonton Art Gallery, Alberta)
1975   *University of California at Irvine 1965-75*, La Jolla Museum of Contemporary Art, California
1978   *California Perspective: Light and Space*, California State University, Fullerton

Collections:

Museum of Modern Art, New York; Whitney Museum, New York; Guggenheim Museum, New York; Art Institute of Chicago; Milwaukee Art Center; Los Angeles County Museum of Art; Norton Simon Museum of Modern Art, Pasadena, California; San Francisco Museum of Art; La Jolla Museum of Contemporary Art, California; Santa Barbara Museum, California.

Publications:

On McCRACKEN: books—*5 Los Angeles Sculptors at Irvine*, exhibition catalogue, by John Coplans, Irvine, California 1966; *Primary Structures*, exhibition catalogue, by Kynaston McShine, New York 1966; *American Sculpture of the 60's* exhibition catalogue, by Maurice Tuchman, Los Angeles 1967; *A New Aesthetic*, exhibition catalogue, by Barbara Rose, Washington, D.C. 1967; *Guggenheim International Exhibition '67*, exhibition catalogue, by Thomas Messer and Edward Fry, New York, 1967; *Minimal Art: A Critical Anthology*, edited by Gregory Battcock, New York 1968; *Options*, exhibition catalogue by Lawrence Alloway, Milwaukee 1968; *Art of the Real*, exhibition catalogue, by E. C. Goossen, New York 1968; *Los Angeles 6*, exhibition catalogue, by John Coplans, Vancouver 1968; *Whitney Annual*, exhibition catalogue, New York 1968; *John McCracken: Sculpture 1965-1969*, exhibition catalogue, by Dennis Young and James Monte, Toronto 1969; *Late Modern: The Visual Arts Since 1945* by Edward Lucie-Smith, New York 1969; *James McCracken*, exhibition catalogue, Paris, 1969; *American Art of the 20th Century* by Sam Hunter, New York 1972; *University of California at Irvine 1965-75*, exhibition catalogue, by Melinda Wortz, La Jolla, California 1975; articles—"Rejective Art" by Lucy Lippard in *Art International* (Lugano, Switzerland), October 1966; "American Sculpture of the 60's" by Kurt Von Meier in *Art International* (Lugano, Switzerland), Summer 1967; "Sculpture of the 60's" by Edward Fry in *Art in America* (New York), September/October 1967; "Art Bloom" by John Coplans in *Vogue* (New York), 1 November 1967; "Los Angeles 1971" by Elizabeth Baker in *Artnews* (New York), September 1971; "Diversity in Unity: Recent Geometicizing Styles in America" by Lucy Lippard in *Art Since Mid-Century, Vol. 1: Abstract Art Since 1945*, Greenwich, Connecticut 1971; "Centering" by Emily Wasserman in *Arts Magazine* (New York), November 1972.

My sculptures have always tended to emphasize, it seems to me, a general outward simplicity, and, so far as my abilities and patience with the aspects of craft have gone, with a noticeable degree of material beauty. The making of "dumb but interesting things," or "just beautiful things," is more or less how I've thought of my attempts. Or to put it another way, I'd say that a consistent characteristic of my approach to art-making is that of trying to draw or put together, in the midst of earth-life experience, clear focusings, or centerings, in the form of concretized, archetypal-tending representations, or images, or objects that, I speculate, might function as "anchor points" in the sea of human consciousness, much as can a piece of wood, or stone, that one finds oddly or for some reason interesting and therefore keeps around somewhere in one's space.

Beyond a certain point, I feel I can, in relation to my own work, speak only as a viewer, with no more authority as to what's actually what than any other viewer. Therefore, I try to make as few claims as possible about it so as to avoid either preventing someone from seeing something they might have seen had I not suggested I knew what was there for everyone's perceptions, or, too, to avoid sounding too much like a pompous ass. This is one round-about way of saying that I wish my things to be not only engaging, but as open as possible in terms of how they are seen and felt and interpreted.

But I do nevertheless have some definite ideas, even things I might be insistent about—one being that an issue very central to my work is that of human (or psychic) self-realizing, self-transforming, self-imaging, self-illuminating. Not merely, that is, the so-called 'ego'-self, but the self that begins with something like ego-awareness and expands from there to fill all the space (and time) one might come to imagine. I tend to view the thing I make, and also all art objects—and, as a matter of fact, all objectifications of all kinds—as concentration or meditation devices. I try to make things which are, on the one hand, capable of drawing and sustaining one's interest, and on the other, of such a nature as to leave one free to enjoy whatever experiencing or dreaming or 'tripping'—or integrating—one might be inwardly inclined to do through them. I like the idea, for instance, of a person looking with such peculiar intensity at something that he then finds himself seeing "through" it, "beyond" it. To further distill this thought, or to risk an over-idealization, it seems in my view to be a matter of perceptually touching the infinite, the total universe "picture," through a finite device or three-dimensional object-point; it's the attempt at seeing and feeling something of the sphere that contains all time and all space through a particularly attuned chunk of the regular material stuff we live in and walk around in and make waves through.
—John McCracken

In the mid 1960's, John McCracken began making monochromatic columns and planks of wood and fiberglass covered with bright reflective color. His series of planks which lean against the wall were, at the time of their development during the sixties, a perceptive and inventive accomplishment, combining as they did a geometrical minimal rigor with flashy color and casual informality. They were also a nifty fusion of painting and sculpture, blending elements from the two and three dimensional with a stylistic emphasis very prominent in vanguard circles of that period.

McCracken's stated intentions are the desire to create unitary forms which are integrated dynamically with their environmental space. In all his works, the whole form is simply and directly perceptible, arriving at completion in relationship with the wall and floor. The element of interconnectedness (certainly neither a new nor a radical idea) is further aided by McCracken's scale, one just larger than humansize which is big enough to impress but not huge enough to encompass, and by the reflective quality of the light bouncing off laquer-like, glossy surfaces. By 1969, McCracken has begun using more neutral hues and more regular spacing in his installations, while continuing within the same general formal methodologies he had already come to prefer rather exclusively. His uses of chalky whites and matte grays attempt, it seems, to achieve a more integral energetic continuity between sculpture and surrounding environment. The regular ordering of congruent forms also serves as suggestive of ritualizing references, but these associations, as well as McCracken's intuited proportions, remain in the static realm, more dormant and classicizing than dynamic or mystical.

It is those leaning planks which use bright, hip colors such as lipstick red or plum, for instance, that attain the greatest degree of independence and character in McCracken's unitary oeuvre. His is a sort of success quotient which might be characterized by his choices of chic, L.A. flavored titles which he finds in fashion magazines. Although McCracken chooses not to acknowledge illusionistic relationships with seen objects such as diving boards or surfboards, it is such Pop-like connections which enliven his more openly seductive and flamboyant works with a personality that is capable of setting them apart from the more earnestly serious minimalisms of so many of his contemporaries.

Where McCracken went downhill was in his moves deeper and deeper into minimal aesthetics, taken too seriously and stripped of humor and of meaning outside the purely formalistic. He has continued to produce variation upon variation of his earlier works, pursuing them long past the time and context of their original potential, getting himself caught in a situation of endless repetition all too common among late blooming modernists whose variations on a single theme become more dry and obvious through years of overuse. McCracken has acknowledged a major debt to Barnett Newman in his similar search for the basic elemental form. In McCracken's case, as in too many others, emulation of Abstract Expressionism's less is more vocabulary and syntax tends to miss the point that each generation must find its own possibilities and instead leads the artist into a small corner of what was previously an open arena for big ideas.
—Barbara Cavaliere

McGARRELL, James.

American. Born in Indianapolis, Indiana, 22 February 1930. Educated at Indiana University, Bloomington, 1948-53; Skowhegan School of Painting and Sculpture, Maine, Summer 1953; University of California at Los Angeles, 1953-55, M.A. 1955; Academy of Fine Arts, Stuttgart, 1956. Married Ann Harris in 1955; children: Andrew and Flora. Painter. Worked as short order cook, bus boy, factory assembly-line worker, and door-to-door salesman, 1941-53. Independent artist, since 1955: travelled in Italy and Spain, 1955-56; resided in Paris, 1964-65, and in Grimaud, France, 1970-71. Artist-in-Residence, Reed College, Portland, Oregon, 1956-59; Professor of Fine Arts and Director of Graduate Painting Studies, Indiana University, Bloomington, 1959-80. Professor of Fine Arts, Washington University, St. Louis, since 1980. Recipient: Fulbright Fellowship, 1955-56; Tamarind Lithographic Workshop Grant, Los Angeles, 1962; Citation and Grant, National Institute of Arts and Letters, 1963; Guggenheim Fellowship, 1964; National Endowment for the Arts Grant, 1966, 1985. Foreign Correspondent Member, Académie des Beaux Arts de l'Institut de France, 1970. Agent: Allan Frumkin Gallery Inc., 41 East 57th Street, New York, New York 10022. Address: School of Fine Arts, Washington University, St. Louis, Missouri 63130, U.S.A.

Individual Exhibitions:

1955	Frank Perls Gallery, Beverly Hills, California
1957	Frank Perls Gallery, Beverly Hills, California
1958	Frank Perls Gallery, Beverly Hills, California
1959	Portland Art Museum, Oregon
1960	Indiana University, Bloomington
1961	Allan Frumkin Gallery, Chicago
	Allan Frumkin Gallery, New York
1962	Allan Frumkin Gallery, Chicago
	Salt Lake City Art Center, Utah
	Frank Perls Gallery, Beverly Hills, California
1963	Indiana University, Bloomington
	Portland Art Museum, Oregon
1964	Allan Frumkin Gallery, New York
	Berkshire Museum, Pittsfield, Massachusetts
	Florida State University, Tallahassee
	Frank Perls Gallery, Beverly Hills, California
1965	*The Graphic Works of James McGarrell*, Allan Frumkin Gallery, Chicago
	Galleria Galatea, Turin
1966	Allan Frumkin Gallery, New York
1967	Tragos Gallery, Boston
	Galerie Claude Bernard, Paris
	Galleria Galatea, Turin
	Galleria Il Fante di Spade, Rome
1969	Allan Frumkin Gallery, New York
1970	Galerie Claude Bernard, Paris
	Galleria dei Lanzi, Milan
1971	Allan Frumkin Gallery, New York
	Allan Frumkin Gallery, Chicago
	Quincy Art Center, Illinois (toured the United States)
	Galleria Il Fante di Spade, Rome
1972	Museum of Fine Art, Salt Lake City, Utah
	Galleria dei Lanzi, Milan
1973	Allan Frumkin Gallery, New York
1974	Galerie Claude Bernard, Paris
	Galleria Il Fante di Spada, Rome
1976	Galleria Il Fante di Spada, Rome
1977	Allan Frumkin Gallery, New York
	Clark-Benton Gallery, Santa Fe, New Mexico
1980	Allan Frumkin Gallery, New York
1981	Allan Frumkin Gallery, New York
	Eason Gallery, Santa Fe, New Mexico
	New Mexico Museum of Art, Albuquerque
1984	Allan Frumkin Gallery, New York
1985	Southern Methodist University, Dallas
	St. Louis Art Museum, Missouri
	Signet Arts Gallery, St. Louis, Missouri
1986	Allan Frumkin Gallery, New York
1987	Signet Arts Gallery, St. Louis, Missouri
	Charles Moore Gallery, Philadelphia
	Jane Haslam Gallery, Washington, D.C.
	Wichita State University, Kansas

Selected Group Exhibitions:

1956	*Whitney Annual*, Whitney Museum, New York (and 1958, 1960, 1963, 1967, 1969)
1959	*New Images of Man*, Museum of Modern Art, New York
1964	*Documenta*, Kassel, West Germany
1970	*The American Scene 1900-1970*, Indiana University Art Museum, Bloomington
1972	*Narrative Painting*, Kansas City Art Institute
1974	*American Prints 1913-63*, Museum of Modern Art, New York
1978	*Art about Art*, Whitney Museum, New York
1984	*Nueva Pintura Narrativa*, Museo Rufino Tamayo, Mexico City
1987	*Night Light, Night Life*, Sherry French Gallery, New York

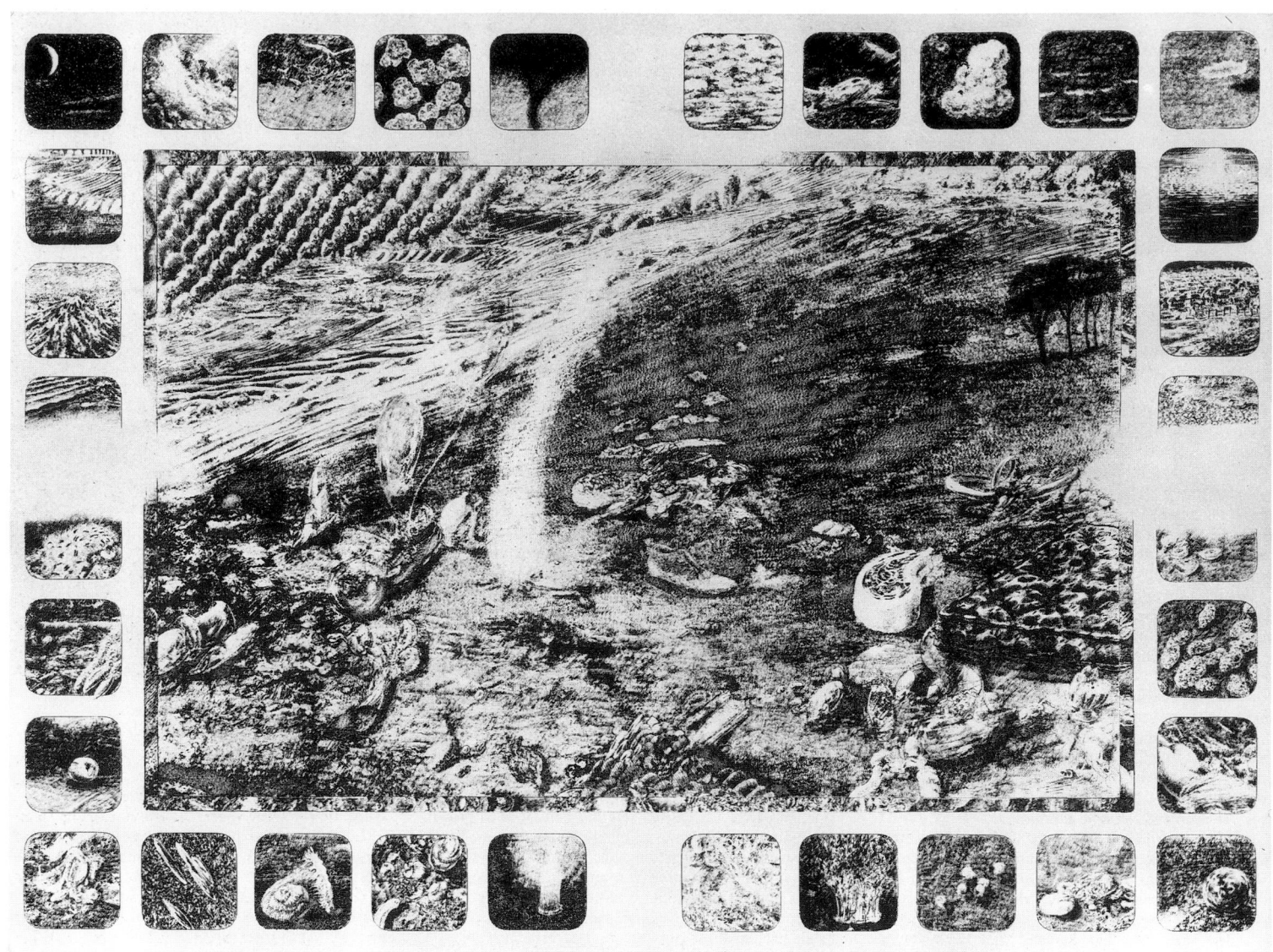

James McGarrell: *The Great Tufted Still Life, AII and BII*, 1975

Collections:

Museum of Modern Art, New York; Whitney Museum, New York; Brooklyn Museum, New York; Pennsylvania Academy of Fine Arts, Philadelphia; Baltimore Museum of Fine Art; National Gallery of Art, Washington, D.C.; Hirshhorn Museum and Sculpture Garden, Washington, D.C., Art Institute of Chicago; Kansas City Art Museum; Centre Georges Pompidou, Paris.

Publications:

By McGARRELL: article—"On Being a Provincial Artist" in *New Art Examiner* (Chicago), June 1986.

On McGARRELL: books—*The Graphic Works of James McGarrell*, exhibition catalogue, Chicago 1965; *James McGarrell*, exhibition catalogue, by Luigi Carluccio, Turin 1965; *James McGarrell*, exhibition catalogue, by Giovanni Testori, Paris, 1967; *The Quincy Inventions*, exhibition catalogue, text by Mark Strand, New York 1971; *James McGarrell*, exhibition catalogue, Paris 1974; articles—"James McGarrell" by Max Kozloff in *Art International* (Lugano, Switzerland) April 1964; "The Essence of Reality" by Paul Moses in the *Chicago Daily News,* 20 March 1965; "Art: Symbolism of the Quincy Inventions" by John Canaday in the *New York Times,* 15 May 1971; "James McGarrell" by Glenn O'Brien in *Artforum* (New York), May 1984; "James McGarrell's Universe" by Tom Bolt in *Arts Magazine* (New York), April 1986; "A Whirl of Ideas Spread on Canvas" by Victoria Donohoe in *Philadelphia Enquirer,* 17 January 1987.

I have always thought of painting as an artificial, synthetic construct which must, none-the-less, look organic, as inevitable as if it had grown, like a tree, according to natural processes.

In contradistinction with the great number of works being done in the past 25 years in the "less is more" tradition, my own seek to be inclusive. I like to get a lot going on, to paint over my head, to paint objects and visual complexes that are too difficult for me to understand entirely, or handle but which, when finally left on the canvas, have a sense of rightness or, again, inevitability.

Although I constantly study them, I have not, for several years, painted from direct visual sources or photographs.

—James McGarrell

Much of McGarrell's surreal-expressionist imagery appears the attempt to convey the poignance (if not the pathos as well) of the most specific, personal, and temporal of human moments, but transformed by the intrusive fantasy of the artificial and timeless realm of literary, historical, and intellectual inventions. And so the characteristic look of his work has been that of a complex amalgam of human figures—at times in spatially distorted environments—involved in interchange with other figures; the surroundings are often filled with emblematic-appearing accessories, and so an overall cast of the inexplicable is created.

The Expressionist aspect of his work, parallel to that of other mid-western American painters such as Robert Barnes, Seymour Rosofsky, and June Leaf, lies in his often loose and slurried paint-handling and aura of the foreboding. McGarrell has himself stated that in the mid-1960's " . . . salvation for me was to be found in the thickening of the plot rather than with simplification." But likewise that his multi-referential pictures " . . . do not stand for anything else, but represent themselves." If so, then McGarrell's dense visual and symbolic ambiguities are clearly his intention; and with his frequent reference, both hidden and overt, to the great works and eras of the European figurative tradition, his evolution may appear the technical exercises of an artist imbued with the pervasive Mannerism so often cited as characteristic of the post-modern period. McGarrell's largest work, exhibited in 1981, "*Travestimento,*" 8 by 20 feet, is both a summation of the previous two decades of work, and as well a new assertion of confidence in his approach.

With the decade of the 1980's, the artist has only increased the verve of his images, letting go any painterly qualities still remaining from the earlier work to perfect a more precise illusionism. Even with his continuing use of a large format, McGarrell has often presented multi-panel arrangements, with a predella and small vertical flanking pictures to produce a resemblance to the archaic polyptych; his narratives have remained as densely non-specific as heretofore, and so these surrounding images allow him more complex enigmatic weaves of space and sentiment. Another aspect of his mastery—perhaps like the sudden explosion of verbal nonsense in the midst of Dickens' narration—is his 'micro-abstraction,' little free-floating bits of non-representation which become an inexplicable part of the material density of the larger fictions depicted. The whole is then well-labelled "Illusionist Abstraction."

—Joshua Kind

McLAUGHLIN, John D.

American. Born in Sharon, Massachusetts, 21 May 1898. Educated in Maine and Andover, Massachusetts primary schools; self-taught in art. Served in the United States Army, in Military Intelligence, 1941–45; as major, Japanese Language Section, China, Burma and India, 1943–45. Married Florence Emerson in 1928. Travelled in Japan and the Far East; studied oriental languages and art, 1935–40; began painting in 1938; worked as dealer in oriental prints, Boston; moved to Dana Point, California, 1946. Recipient: Tamarind Lithography Fellowship, Los Angeles, 1963; Bronze Medal, *30th Corcoran Biennial,* Washington, D.C., 1967; Visual Arts Award, National Endowment for the Arts, 1967. *Died (in Dana Point) in March 1976.*

Individual Exhibitions:

1953   Felix Landau Gallery, Los Angeles
1958   University of California at Riverside
        Felix Laudau Gallery, Los Angeles
1960   Long Beach Museum of Art, California
1962   Felix Landau Gallery, Los Angeles
1963   Felix Landau Gallery, Los Angeles
        Pasadena Art Museum, California (retrospective)
1964   K. Kazimir Gallery, Chicago
1966   Felix Landau Gallery, Los Angeles
1968   Occidental College, Los Angeles
        Landau-Alan Gallery, New York
        Corcoran Gallery, Washington, D.C. (retrospective)
1970   Felix Landau Gallery, Los Angeles
1971   University of California at Irvine
1972   Nicholas Wilder Gallery, Los Angeles
1973   Corcoran and Corcoran Ltd., Coral Gables, Florida
        La Jolla Museum of Contemporary Art, California (retrospective)
1974   Whitney Museum, New York
        André Emmerich Gallery, New York
1975   Felicity Samuel Gallery, London
1976   Galerie André Emmerich, Zurich
1978   University of California at Santa Barbara
1979   Nicholas Wilder Gallery, New York
        André Emmerich Gallery, New York
1981   *Paintings 1950–1975,* Annely Juda Fine Art, London (travelled to Gimpel Hanover/André Emmerich Galerie, Zurich)
1982   James Corcoran Gallery, Los Angeles
        Ulmer Museum, Ulm, West Germany
        André Emmerich Gallery, New York
1983   Gatodo Gallery, Tokyo
1985   Thomas Babeor Gallery, La Jolla, California.
        Gatodo Gallery, Tokyo
1987   André Emmerich Gallery, New York

Selected Group Exhibitions:

1951   *Contemporary Painting in the United States,* Los Angeles County Museum of Art
1955   *Bienal,* Sao Paulo
1957   *American Painting,* Corcoran Gallery of Art, Washington, D.C.
1959   *1949–1959: A Decade,* Pasadena Art Museum, California
1962   *Geometric Abstraction in America,* Whitney Museum, New York
1965   *The Responsive Eye,* Museum of Modern Art, New York (toured the United States)
1969   *7 Decades,* Addison Gallery of American Art, Phillips Academy, Andover, Massachusetts
1970   *Looking West, 1970,* Joslyn Art Museum, Omaha, Nebraska

John McLaughlin: *Number 8,* 1971

1974   *Geometric Abstraction,* University of Nebraska, Omaha (toured the United States)
1977   *Los Angeles Hand-Edge Exhibition,* Los Angeles County Museum of Art

Collections:

Metropolitan Museum of Art, New York; Museum of Modern Art, New York; Addison Gallery of American Art, Andover, Massachusetts; Massachusetts Institute of Technology, Cambridge; Wadsworth Atheneum, Hartford, Connecticut; Smithsonian Institution, Washington, D.C.; Corcoran Gallery of Art, Washington, D.C.; Los Angeles County Museum of Art; Museum of Art, Long Beach, California.

Publications:

On McLAUGHLIN: books—*Geometric Abstraction,* exhibition catalogue, by Judith K. von Wagner, Omaha, Nebraska 1974; *John McLaughlin: Paintings 1950–1975,* exhibition catalogue, London 1981; *John McLaughlin,* exhibition catalogue with essay by Prudence Carlson, New York, 1987; articles—"The Californians" by Jan van der Marck in *Art International* (Lugano, Switzerland), May 1963; "McLaughlin and the Totally Abstract" by Gerald Nordland in *Frontier* (Chicago), January 1964; "John McLaughlin: Hard edge and American Painting" by John Coplans in *Artforum* (New York), January 1964; "Fact or Fiction? The Legacy of Oriental Art" by Constance Perkins in *Art in America* (New York), February 1965; "Color + Shape = Form: Equation for a New Aesthetic" by James Harithas in *Art Education* (Reston, Virginia), October 1967; "John McLaughlin" by S. C. Larsen in *Artweek* (Oakland, California), January 1979.

*   *   *

Since his death in 1976, John McLaughlin is increasingly being accorded the critical respect his uncompromisingly rigorous work warranted for him all along. For years, McLaughlin's reputation was for the most part limited to Southern California, where he worked by choice in semi-isolation in his small studio on the coast south of Los Angeles. Although the object of profound admiration on the part of a younger generation of artists, among them Ron Davis and Ed Moses, McLaughlin did not participate directly in the development of the L.A. "school" during the 1960's. Nonetheless, as much by his example and commitment as the work itself, McLaughlin is now acknowledged by critics and painters alike as the leading "Old Master" of California modernism.

In the 1930's McLaughlin had begun painting small landscapes in a manner somewhat reminiscent of Maurice Vlaminck. It was not until he and his wife settled in Dana Point that he was able to devote his full energies to painting. Within just a few years, certainly by 1948, he had adopted the geometric style upon which all his subsequent work was based. From the beginning McLaughlin charted and maintained an independent course with little regard for contemporary developments outside of his studio. The extent to which his reductive art developed independently from that of other geometric abstractionists such as Barnett Newman and Ad Reinhardt, to whom he is often compared, is open to some question. In his writings and correspondence (preserved at the Archives of American Art/Smithsonian Institution), McLaughlin consistently denied any direct connection between his paintings and those of other artists working in the Constructivist-de Stijl tradition. But at the same time he readily acknowledged a debt to the *ideas* of Mondrian and particularly Malevich. It was the theoretical and conceptual basis underlying works such as Malevich's *White on White* that attracted McLaughlin. Total elimination of the object and all symbolic overtones were means to the goals of anonymity and neutrality that McLaughlin sought in his art. To this end he employed a rigidly controlled imagery based on the rectangle firmly locked within a horizontal-vertical compositional matrix. McLaughlin was one of several Southern California painters working in a related manner in the 1950's. The 1959 exhibition *Four Abstract Classicists,* which opened in Los Angeles and later traveled to London, recognized this "indigenous" form of geometric abstraction in the Los Angeles area which was described for the first time in the catalogue as "hard-edged painting."

Although his exploration of geometrical forms places McLaughlin within a specific Western tradition, the philosophical basis for his art, and its ultimate goal, seems to have been largely Eastern. Most of what has been written about McLaughlin records his attraction to and contact with the Orient. His own statements further encourage an interpretation of his art within the context of Eastern thought. McLaughlin's apparent preoccupation with emptiness, neutrality, and absence of object stems from an Eastern concept of the "void." Evoked in his paintings through arrangements of rectangular shapes, the void represented for McLaughlin the most suitable "terrain" for the artist to confront himself and his relationship to nature. McLaughlin's art is, therefore, best understood in terms of modernist formal devices put directly to the service of Oriental philosophical objectives. This specific conceptual focus determined his direction as an artist and explains the consistency of his stylistic development. In general, the evolution was one of increasing reduction and simplification. Works dating from the late 1940's and early 1950's display a relatively complicated geometric vocabulary incorporating volume, shading, diagonals, line, and even texture—all of which were either eliminated or brought under the most rigorous control by about 1955.

Within a highly restricted format, McLaughlin patiently explored the compositional tensions created by the slightest adjustment of basic elements and color relationships. He proceeded by cutting colored bands and rectangles from construction paper and moved them about until satisfied with the arrangement, at which point the composition was set and the painting of the actual canvas involved no deviation from the "model." This practice was entirely in keeping with McLaughlin's desire to avoid subjective intrusions, evidence of the artist's presence which might compromise his goals of neutrality and anonymity. Intentions notwithstanding, there is a hand-made quality, a slight "scruffiness" of surface and edge, that in fact asserts the presence of the artist's hand and a dedication to simple craftsmanship. Despite their geometric severity, the paintings radiate a distinct warmth that contributes to their unique quality. McLaughlin's singular achievement was to imbue the disciplined conceptualism of his art with his own humility and a profound humanism.

—Paul J. Karlstrom

McLEAN, Bruce.

British. Born in Glasgow in 1944. Studied at the Glasgow School of Art, 1961-63; St. Martin's School of Art, London, 1963-66. Gave numerous performances, recorded by photographs, before forming the first Pose Band, Nice Style, with Paul Richards and Ron Carr, 1971. Lives and works in London. Lecturer, Maidstone College of Art, Kent, 1971. Recipient: Pratt Sculpture Bequest, 1965; Sainsbury Sculpture Award, 1966; Arts Council Award, 1975; Arts Council Bursary, 1978; DAAD Fellowship, West Berlin, 1981. Agent: Anthony D'Offay Gallery, 9 Dering Street, New Bond Street, London W1. Address: 34 Cleveland Road, London S.W. 13, England.

Individual Exhibitions and Performances:

1965	St. Martin's School of Art, London (performance)
1969	Konrad Fischer Galerie, Dusseldorf
	Royal College of Art, London (performance)
1970	Nova Scotia College of Art, Halifax
1971	Situation Gallery, London
	Yvon Lambert Galerie, Paris
1972	Galleria Francoise Lambert, Milan
	Tate Gallery, London (one day only)
	Sonja Henie Foundation, Oslo (with Nice Style)
1973	Tooth's Gallery, London (with Nice Style)
	Hanover Grand Hotel, London (with Nice Style)
	Royal College of Art, London (with Nice Style)
1974	Architectural Association, London (with Nice Style)
	Garage Gallery, London (with Nice Style)
1975	Robert Self Gallery, London (with Nice Style)
	Museum of Modern Art, Oxford
	Robert Self Gallery, Newcastle upon Tyne

1976	Battersea Art Centre, London (performance with William Furlong)
1977	Battersea Art Centre, London (performance with Sylvia Ziranek)
	Robert Self Gallery, London
1978	The Kitchen, New York (with Rosey McLean)
1979	Southampton University Gallery, Hampshire (performance with Rosey McLean, Sylvia Ziranek, and Peter Lacoux)
	Halle für Internationale Neue Kunst, Zurich
	Barry Barker Gallery, London
	Hayward Gallery, London (performance with Rosey McLean)
	Riverside Studios, London (performance with Paul Richards)
1980	Third Eye Centre, Glasgow (travelled to Fruit Market Gallery, Edinburgh and Arnolfini Gallery, Bristol)
	Basement Group, Newcastle upon Tyne (performance)
	Mikery Theatre, Amsterdam (performance with Paul Richards)
1981	Musée d'Art et d'Industrie, St.-Étienne, France
	Anthony D'Offay Gallery, London
	Art Project, Amsterdam
	Kunsthalle, Basle (travelled to the Whitechapel Art Gallery, London, and the Stedelijk van Abbemuseum, Eindhoven, Netherlands)
1982	Anthony D'Offay Gallery, London (with Gilbert and George and Richard Long)
	Galerie Chantal Crousel, Paris
	Galerie Greta Insam, Vienna
	Kanransha Gallery, Tokyo
	Mary Boone Gallery, New York
	Modern Art Galerie, Vienna
	Van Abbemuseum, Eindhoven, Netherlands
1983	Kanransha Gallery, Tokyo
	Galerie Kiki Maier-Hahn, Dusseldorf
	DAAD-Galerie, West Berlin
	Galerie Dany Keller, Munich
	Whitechapel Art Gallery, London
	Institute of Contemporary Arts, London
1984	Galerie Fahnemann, West Berlin
	Badischer Kunstverein, Karlsruhe, West Germany
	Galerie Dany Keller, Munich
	Art Palace, New York
	Kanransha Gallery, Tokyo
	Bernard Jacobson Gallery, New York
1985	Anthony D'Offay Gallery, London
	Bernard Jacobson Gallery, London
	Galerie Gmyrek, Dusseldorf
	Tate Gallery, London
1986	Bernard Jacobson Gallery, London
	Anthony D'Offay Gallery, London
	Scottish Gallery, Edinburgh
1987	Anthony D'Offay Gallery, London
	Galerie Fahnemann, West Berlin
	Hillman Holland Gallery, Atlanta, Georgia

Selected Group Exhibitions:

1965	5 Young Artists, Contemporary Arts, London
1966	Painting and Sculpture Today, Grabowski Gallery, London
1970	Information, Museum of Modern Art, New York
1979	Un Certain Art Anglais, Musée d'Art Moderne de la Ville, Paris
1980	Biennale, Venice
1981	A New Spirit in Painting, Royal Academy, London
1982	Vergangenheit/Gegenwart/Zukunft, Württembergischer Kunstverein, Stuttgart
1983	Thought and Action, Laforet Museum, Tokyo
1985	7000 Oaks, Kunsthalle, Tubingen, West Germany
1987	British Art in the 20th Century, Royal Academy of Arts, London

Collections:

Arts Council of Great Britain, London; British Council, London; Contemporary Arts Society, London; Tate Gallery, London; Victoria and Albert Museum, London; Glasgow Museums and Art Galleries, Scotland; University of South-ampton, Hampshire; Van Abbemuseum, Eindhoven, Netherlands; National Museum of Modern Art, Osaka, Japan; Tochigi Prefectural Museum of Fine Art, Japan.

Publications:

By McLEAN: books—King for a Day, exhibition catalogue, London 1972; Dream Works, London 1985; Ladder, London, 1987; Home Manoeuvres, London, 1987; articles—"Not Even Crimble Crumble" in Studio International (London), October 1970; "Nice Style at the Hanover Grand" in Audio Arts (London), no. 2, 1973; "Nice Style at Garage" in Audio Arts (London), supplement 1973; "Sorry: A Minimal Musical Parts" in Audio Arts (London), supplement 1977; "9 Works for Tape/Slide Sequence and a National Anthem" in Audio Arts (London), 1977; "I Want To Be a Seagull" in Salon Arts Magazine (Dusseldorf), 1978; "Ways of Viewing Mackerals and Mandolins" in Aspects (Newcastle), no. 4, 1978; "Titles: Teacups" in Salon Arts Magazine (Dusseldorf), 1979; "The Masterwork: Award Winning Fish Knife" in Audio Arts (London), supplement 1979; "Tape/Slide Piece" in Audio Arts (London), supplement 1979; interview with Nena Dimitrijevic in Bruce McLean, exhibition catalogue, London 1981; "Bruce McLean: Drawings" in Aspects (Newcastle), no. 16, 1981; films—6 Waiter Waiter Works, 1970; In the Shadow of Your Smile, Bob, 1970; The Elusive Sculptor: Richard Long, 1970; Wheedle, Deedle Work, 1970; A Million Smiles for One of Your Miles, Walter, 1971; Crease, Crisis (with Nice Style), 1973; The Masterwork, 1979.

On McLEAN: books—Performance 1909-709 by Roselee Goldberg, London 1979; Bruce McLean, exhibition catalogue, by Sarah Kent and David Brown, Glasgow, 1980; Bruce McLean, exhibition catalogue, by Nena Dimitrijevic, London 1981; Bruce McLean, exhibition catalogue with text by Mario Amaya, New York 1984; Bruce McLean, exhibition catalogue by Jean-Christophe Ammann, Basle and Florence 1984; Bruce McLean: Simple Manners or Physical Violence, exhibition catalogue, with text by Norman Rosenthal, Dusseldorf 1985; Bruce McLean, exhibition catalogue by Mary Rose Beaumont, Edinburgh 1986.

McLean studied at the Glasgow School of Art from 1961-63 and then went to St. Martin's School of Art in London to study sculpture from 1963-66. McLean went to St. Martin's at the time when Anthony Caro's teaching predominated in the sculpture department. The sculptural debates at this time revolved round subjects such as whether sculpture should sit on the ground or on plinths and the placement of abstract elements of metal and wood and colour arrangements. McLean and another student eventually, in 1965, responded to this with the placement of life-sized silhouettes of human figures, one on the roof and one in the street with the sculptors waving in the direction of Charing Cross Station—this was entitled "Mary Waving Goodbye to the Trains." This heralded McLean's sardonic style of art using a mixture of props and people in highly staged performances.

Since 1965 McLean's work has involved making sculpture using found materials, photography, performance and, most recently, paintings strongly influenced by his work with performance. He is probably best known for his 'pose works,' some of the earliest of which were produced in collaboration with Gilbert and George. To take an example, "Pose Work for Plinths" (1972), in a series of photographs, shows McLean posing in various awkward positions suggesting the stances of Henry Moore sculptures, on plinths of different heights. 'Nice Style: the World's First Pose Band,' was founded by McLean in 1971 with students from Maidstone College of Art, where he was teaching. They produced pose performances in a multi-media form, (with their roots in Dada and Futurism), and were highly complicated performances devoted to achieving the perfect post for a given context. For example, there were consumerism themes such as Freeze, an Opera Based on the Life-Style and Values of a Midwest American Vacuum Cleaner Company and Semi-Domestic Poses of 1973.

McLean developed various performances with an emphasis on irreverence and wit throughout the 1970's, climaxing in 1979 with the most ambitious: The Masterwork: Award Winning Fishknife, an elabo-

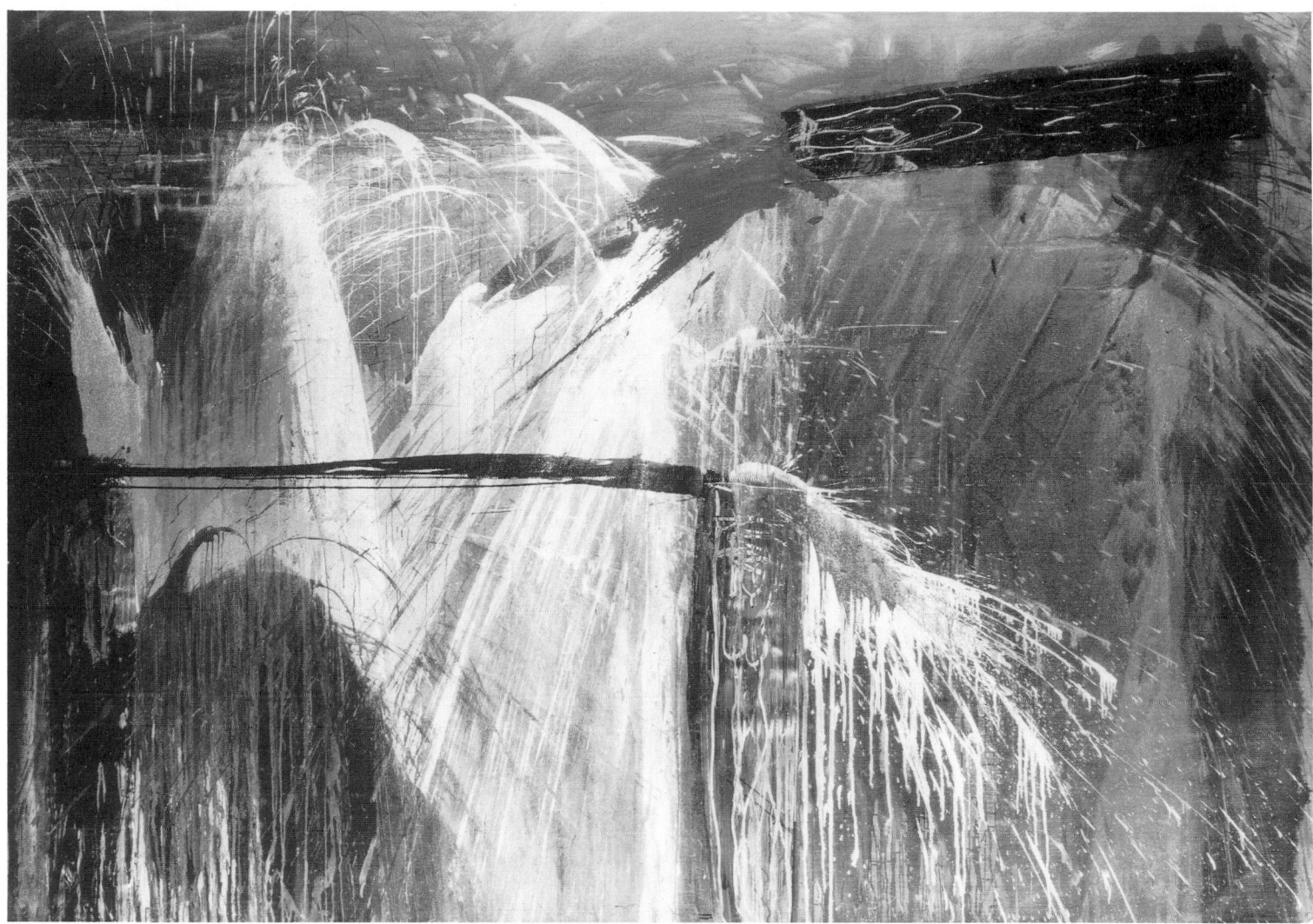

Bruce McLean: *Untitled,* 1986 Courtesy Anthony D'Offay Gallery, London

rate criticism of the consumer society and particularly the professions of architects and designers.

McLean has produced his performances round the world, and with the late 1970's these were becoming more often static installations. With the 1970's his 'Nice Style' drawings were closely linked to performance, but by 1977 his gouaches show thematic links only with performance—brightly coloured, simple, flat forms are acrobats against schematic drawings denoting space.

With the 1980's his paintings have become the dominant work of his output, (though there is still the occasional performance). His past interests are still evident in the organization of his picture surfaces. Backgrounds are divided up as he might have devised a score for a performance, and, in a painting of 1980, *Rock to Rock, Cheek to Cheek,* the dancing figures on the right of the picture are caught in a bright yellow triangle like a spotlight beam. Wording appears in the picture surface, yet the whole painting is dominated by an expressionistic brush style.

In the late 1980's he has been turning his attention to monumental stone sculpture. Yet as Richard Cork has written in the 1987 catalogue, *British Art in the 20th Century,* "McLean's sly, anti-heroic attitude is still there in the sculpture, and his debunking sense of humour is never very far away."

—Victoria Keller

McWILLIAM, F(rederick) E(dward).

Irish. Born in Banbridge, 30 April 1909. Studied at the Slade School of Art, London (Robert Ross Scholarship), 1928–31. Married Elizabeth Marion Crowther in 1932; daughters: Sarah and Bridget. Served in the Royal Air Force in Great Britain and the Far East, 1940–45. Sculptor: worked in Paris, 1931–32; has since then lived and worked in London: Member, British Surrealist Group, 1938; Member, Royal Academy, London, 1959 (resigned, 1962). Recipient: Prix de Concours, Unknown Political Prisoner Competition, London, 1953; Prize, *John Moore's Exhibition,* Liverpool, 1961; Oireachtas Prize, Trinity College, Dublin, 1961. Fellow, University College, London, 1962; D.Litt.: Queens University, Belfast, 1964. C.B.E. (Commander, Order of the British Empire), 1966. Address: 8A Holland Villas Road, London, W14 8BP, England.

Individual Exhibitions:

1939   London Gallery
1949   *Recent Sculpture,* Hanover Gallery, London
1952   Hanover Gallery, London
1953   Hanover Gallery, London
1956   Hanover Gallery, London
1958   Royal West of England Academy, Bristol
1960   Queens University, Belfast
1961   Waddington Galleries, London
1963   Waddington Galleries, London
        1st American Exhibition, Felix Landau Gallery, Los Angeles
1966   Waddington Galleries, London
1968   Waddington Galleries, London
1969   Travers Gallery, London

1973   *Sculpture 1972–73: Women of Belfast,* Waddington Galleries, London
        Women of Belfast: New Bronzes by F. E. McWilliam 1972–73, McClelland Galleries International, Belfast
        Dawson Gallery, Dublin
1975   Waddington Galleries, London
1976   Waddington Galleries, London
1977   Bell Gallery, Belfast
1979   Waddington Galleries, London
1980   Taylor Gallery, Dublin
1981   Ulster Museum, Belfast (retrospective; travelled to the Douglas Hyde Gallery, Dublin, and the Orchard Gallery, Londonderry)
1982   Warwick Arts Trust, London (retrospective)
1984   Waddington Galleries, London
        Gordon Gallery, Londonderry
1987   Gordon Gallery, Londonderry

Selected Group Exhibitions:

1939   *British Surrealist and Abstract Exhibition,* Northampton Art Gallery, England
1940   *Surrealism,* Zwemmer Gallery, London
1953   *2nd Biennale,* Middleheim Park, Antwerp
1961   *Carnegie International,* Pittsburgh
1964   *Painting and Sculpture of a Decade 1954–1964,* Tate Gallery, London
1972   *Decade 40,* Whitechapel Art Gallery, London
1978   *Dada and Surrealism Revisited,* Hayward Gallery, London
1980   *The Delighted Eye,* Earlham Street Gallery, London
1982   *Surrealism in England,* Galerie 1900/2000, Paris
1984   *English Contrasts 1950–60,* Artcurial, Paris (travelled to Serpentine Gallery, London)

against the older tradition. I have never seen any reason why representation should eliminate the formal design element which is the potent factor in abstract art. Perhaps what's needed now is another close look at the incredible diversity in Nature, bearing in mind John Fowle's words about creating "a world as real as but other than the world that is."

I've always welcomed commissions, even when the site or subject involved me in activity quite different from my current interests. But then, unlike the British Council, I have never set any store by consistency; life is too short for restrictive practices. Indeed, even if (as has often happened) the commission proves abortive, I enjoy having imposed upon me the *raison d'etre* for a new obsession. Nothing masochistic about that sort of provocation. Sometimes it has meant one off, finish; but more often it has led to variations on the theme. My dream remains to achieve a synthesis of classical and romantic, the romantic side providing the irrational element, as art that is public and private at the same time.

—F. E. McWilliam

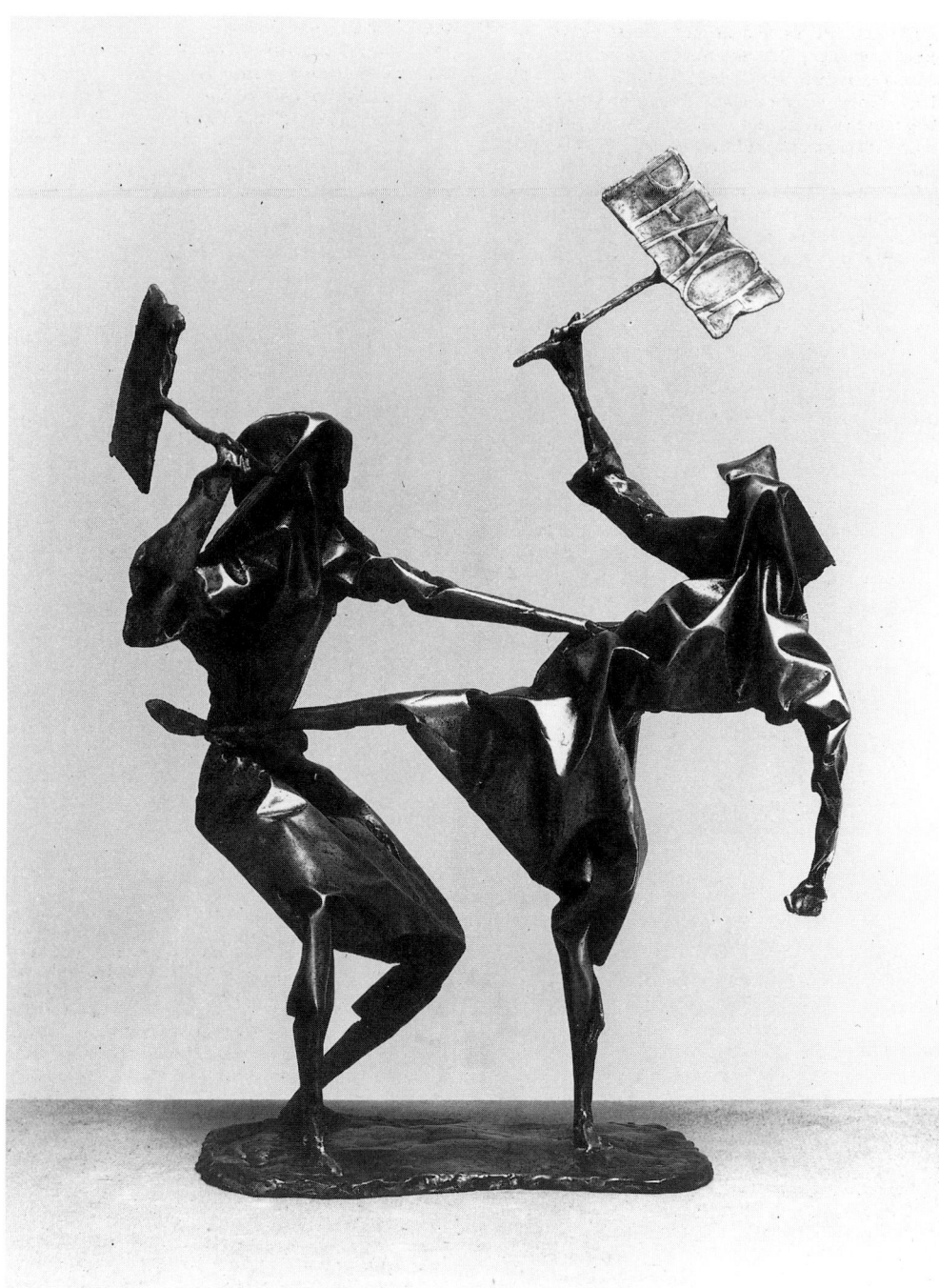

F. E. McWilliam: *Peace C.*, 1975

1986   *Sculpture in Britain Between the Wars,* Fine Art Society, London

Collections:

Tate Gallery, London; Museum of Modern Art, New York; National Portrait Gallery, London; City Art Gallery, Leeds; Belfast Museum and Art Gallery; Middelheim Park, Antwerp; Art Institute of Chicago; National Gallery of South Australia, Adelaide.

Publications:

By McWILLIAM: articles—article in *Architectural Design* (London), September 1958; interview, with William Gaunt, in *The Times* (London), 17 March 1960; "Harriet Cooke Talks to the Sculptor F. E. McWilliam" in the *Irish Times* (Dublin), Ocotber 1963; interview with Mel Gooding, in *Art Review* (London), 6 November 1981.

On McWILLIAM: books—*British Sculpture* by Eric Newton, London 1947; *F. E. McWilliam: Recent Sculpture,* exhibition catalogue, with text by Merlyn Evans, London 1949; *F. E.*

McWilliam: 1st American Exhibition, exhibition catalogue, Los Angeles 1963; *F. E. McWilliam: Sculpture 1972-73: Women of Belfast,* exhibition catalogue, London 1973; *Women of Belfast: New Bronzes by F. E. McWilliam 1972-73,* exhibition catalogue, with an introduction by Roland Penrose, Belfast 1973; *Towards Sculpture* by W. J. Strachan, London 1974; *F. E. McWilliam,* exhibition catalogue and book, by Judy Marle and T. P. Flanagan, Belfast 1981; articles—"The Sculpture of F. E. McWilliam" by Bryan Robertson in *Nimbus* (London), no. 2, 1954; "The Sculpture of F. E. McWilliam" by Albert Garnett in *Studio International* (London), November 1954; "F. E. McWilliam, ARA" by J. Wood Palmer in *Motif* (London), September 1959; "F. E. McWilliam, Waddington II" by J. Sexton in *Arts Review* (London), January 1971; "Art out of Torment" by Bruce Arnold in the *Irish Independent* (Dublin), October 1973; review by John Russell in *The Sunday Times* (London), November 1973.

I have rather lost my interest in abstract art, and looking back now it seems as though the "New Generation" movement was the last flowering before it got inbred and academic. I don't think it had much influence on my own work: my commitment was to sculpture of another kind. I worked within as well as

Not many artists go up so many avenues. Most of them, after their student days and their first experiences of comparative freedom, find a style of their own, improve upon it, modify it, perhaps even change it to a point approaching non-recognition, but never actually desert their chosen path. This is a general rule, of course; it is not always the case. The example of Picasso flashes before the eye, and even he was far from unique in this context.

F. E. McWilliam has made many changes, some of them radical. In the late 1940's he was exploring a kind of surrealism. A reassembly of the "immaculate corpse." Heads and limbs could be exact in academic terms, but the trunk would be missing. By 1950 he had moved on. This time he was associated with giant profiles, very 3-dimensional but sporting outsize nose and eyes. The figuration was utterly recognizable but distorted. And so on to a rough non-figuration in metal—for example, his "Witch of Agnesi" (1959) which might have claimed relationship with early Paolozzi or Peter King.

The tortuous route—for a sculptor—is set out here because it helps to explain how many things in sculpture the name McWilliam can mean. In 1956 he even made a striking full-length (6 ft.) portrait of Elisabeth Frink, a follow-up of the hieratic figures he had been making (one of which graces a cathedral in Wales).

By the early 1960's it seemed as if McWilliam had finally found the furrow he intended to plough. He gradually foreswore the semi non-figurative pieces he had been welding in metal and became absorbed in figures whose pyramid shoulders, knees and feet came together in physical contortions that at times grew close to abstraction. These were the "crankshaft" figures. A book was published by Tiranti which concentrated upon this phase of his work.

But then came more swift changes, including an astonishing re-jigging of the figures encrusted with miniature tiles of gold and blue mosaic. Then—all sorts of non-figurative shapes, rounded and tactile, the absolute opposite of the rough and gritty crankshaft works. Were polished bronzes such as "May Day" (1965) to be the terminal point in McWilliam's complex development? Indeed, no.

His "Women of Belfast" (1972-73) brought back figuration. Not the crankshaft type this time, although elbows and knees were once again dramatically angular. "Women of Belfast" had a terrible social significance. They gave the impression that they had been physically and mentally crumpled just as if these pathetic pliable females had been caught and crushed in a giant fist.

McWilliam has his admirers, but can they always be the same admirers? Did Picasso have fans who genuinely applauded his every change of tempo?

—Sheldon Williams

MEADOWS, Bernard.

British. Born in Norwich, 19 February 1915. Studied at the Norwich School of Art, 1934-36; Chelsea School of Art, London, 1936-37; Royal College of Art, London, 1938-40, 1945-47. Served in the Royal Air Force, 1941-46. Married Marjorie Payne in 1939; children: 2 daughters. Sculptor: worked as an assistant to Henry Moore, 1936-40: lives and works in London. Lecturer, Chelsea School of Art, London, 1948-60; Professor of Sculpture, 1960-80, and since 1980 Emeritus Professor, Royal College of Art, London. Address: 34 Belsize Grove, London NW3 4TR, England.

Individual Exhibitions:

1957	Gimpel Fils, London
	Paul Rosenberg Gallery, New York
1959	Gimpel Fils, London
1962	Paul Rosenberg Gallery, New YOrk
1963	Gimpel Fils, London
1965	Stedelijk Museum, Amsterdam
	Gimpel Fils, London
	Kunstamt, Reinickendorf, Berlin
	Museen der Stadt, Recklinghausen, West Germany
	Kunstverein, Braunschweig, West Germany
1966	Paul Rosenberg Gallery, New York
1967	Gimpel Fils, London
	Bear Lane Gallery, Oxford (with Robert Adams and Hubert Dalwood)
1975	Taranman Gallery, London
1977	Galerie Villand-Galanis, Paris
1978	Taranman Gallery, London
	Ecole d'Art, Angers, France
	Galerie de l'Ecole des Beaux-Arts, Rouen
1979	Fuji Television Gallery, Tokyo
1980	Taranman Gallery, London
1981	Taranman Gallery, London

Selected Group Exhibitions:

1955	*Young British Sculptors*, Arts Club of Chicago (toured the United States, 1955-56)
1956	*Biennale*, Venice
1957	*Bienal*, Sao Paulo
1958	*Pittsburgh International*, Carnegie Institute, Pittsburgh
1964	*Painting and Sculpture of a Decade 1954-64*, Tate Gallery, London
1966	*Contemporary Sculpture*, Musée Rodin, Paris
1972	*British Sculptors 1972*, Royal Academy of Arts, London

Collections:

Tate Gallery, London; Rijksmuseum Kröller-Müller, Otterlo, Netherlands; Middelheim Museum, Antwerp; Tel Aviv Museum, Israel; Museum of Modern Art, New York; Guggenheim Museum, New York; Albright-Knox Art Gallery, Buffalo, New York; San Francisco Museum of Modern Art; Museo de Bellas Artes, Caracas; National Gallery of New South Wales, Sydney.

Publications:

On MEADOWS: book—*Modern English Sculpture*, by A. M. Hammacher, London 1967; articles—"The Sculptor and His Drawings: Bernard Meadows" by W. J. Strachan in *The Connoisseur* (London), April 1974; "Bernard Meadows" by B. Phillpotts in *Arts Review* (London), December 1978.

*

Despite the influence of Henry Moore, to whom he was studio assistant for two years, Bernard Meadows developed a style of his own and a proficiency which ensured him a place of importance in British post War sculpture. In his first period he belonged to the generation of Kenneth Armitage, Lynn Chadwick and Reg Butler, all of whom enjoyed a considerable success during the 1950's, and his work had a generic simi-

larity with. He worked mainly in cast bronze, and these sculptures, although representational, imposed an image of their own distinct from the texture—like that of Lynn Chadwick and Ralph Brown—but was expressive in its impact in a way not unlike the Abstract Expressionist sculpture of Nakian and Roszak in America.

In the 1960's Meadows turned to abstraction, and the angular and spiky forms gave place to rounded and curved shapes often suggesting an organic origin and often with implicit or explicit erotic overtones. These near-spherical shapes were squeezed, balanced and grouped together to form sculptures of very varied expressive significance. Sometimes the cellular roundness suggests fertility or security, sometimes eroticism. His *Help* theme, the germ of which is represented by a pierced sphere squeezed between two flat surfaces, attracted particular attention, and a whole room was devoted to the genesis and evolution of this theme in the Royal Academy exhibition *British Sculptors 72*.

Meadows was particularly fond of fruit forms, which became something of an obsession with him at this time; he both used and exhibited casts made from actual fruits. As well as organic forms like fruits and breasts, his shapes sometimes suggest rocks and stones by their texture and compactness; sometimes they are jointed like bones. He continued to rely on an unchased surface of his cast for the expressive textures which he desired.

Meadows is in addition an accomplished draughtsman and his drawings, as shown by an exhibition staged in London in 1975, are a model of what sculptural drawing should be. The calligraphy is assured and the effect is solidly three-dimensional without being representational.

—Harold Osborne

MEDALLA, David.

Filipino. Born David Cortez de Medalla y Mosqueda, in Manila, 23 March 1942. Educated at Philippines Normal School, Manila, 1948-50; St. Mary's School, Sagada, Mountain Province, 1951-52; and University of the Philippines High School, Diliman, Quezon City, 1953; studied, under Mark Van Dorne and Moses Hadas, Columbia University, New York, 1954-55. Artist working with kinetic and participation projects, in Manila, 1956-63, in London since 1964. Arts Adviser, Keller Fine Arts, London, 1964; Editor, *Signals* magazine, London, 1964-66; Founder, Exploding Galaxy dance group, London, 1967-68; Co-Founder and Chairman, Arts Council of the Philippines, Manila, 1969; Founder-Secretary, Artists' Liberation Front, London 1971-74; Chairman, International Committee for Freedom in the Philippines, since 1973; Co-Founder and Chairman, Artists for Democracy, London 1974. Lecturer on Humanities and Oriental Culture, University of the Philippines, Manila, 1957-59; Staff/Student Adviser, Slade School of Art, London, 1971-72; Lecturer on Oriental Culture, St. Martin's School of Art, London, 1971-73; Lecturer on Chinese Culture and Civilization, University of Southampton, 1973-74; Lecturer in General Studies, Chelsea School of Art, London, 1973-75. Address: c/o Williams and Glyn's, Holts Branch, Kirkland House, Whitehall, London SW1, England.

Individual Exhibitions:

1955	616 West 11th Street, New York
1957	La Cave-Poetry Club, Manila
1961	Hotel des Quatre Nations, Paris
1962	*Paintings and Drawings 1954-1962*, Mayflower Barn, Jordans, Buckinghamshire, England
1965	Mercury Gallery, London
1967	Indica Gallery, London
1969	Arts Council Gallery, Manila
1970	Oriental Lodge, Kathmandu, Nepal
1971	Bateau *Mayflower II*, Paris
1972	Ikon Gallery, Birmingham, England
	Makibaka, Institute of Contemporary Arts, London (participation event)
	Toeval Shaw, University of Utrecht (participation event)
1974	Artists' Meeting Place, London
1975	Artists for Democracy, London

Selected Group Exhibitions:

1959	*500 Years of Philippine Art*, Department of Foreign Affairs, Manila
1964	*Soundings One*, Ashmolean Museum, Oxford
1965	*Art Cinetique*, Librairie Anglaise, Paris
1965	*Weiss auf Weiss*, Kunsthalle, Berne
1969	*When Attitudes Become Form*, Kunsthalle, Berne (toured Europe)
1970	*Multiples*, Whitechapel Art Gallery, London
1971	*Pioneers of Participation Art*, Museum of Modern Art, Oxford
1972	*Documenta*, Kassel, West Germany
1973	*The New Art*, Hayward Gallery, London
1974	*Art Festival for Chilean Resistance*, Royal College of Art, London

Collections:

National Museum of the Philippines, Manila; Museum of Modern Art, Quezon City, Philippines.

Publications:

By MEDALLA: books—*Codex Pacifica*, Manila 1961; *Commentary on the I Ching*, Manila 1962; *The Poet in Abyssinia: A Biography in Verse of Arthur Rimbaud*, Manila 1963; *Concerning Prometheus*, Manila 1971; *From the Masses to the Masses*, exhibition catalogue, Birmingham 1972; *Artists Liberation Manifesto*, with John Dugger, London, 1971; Articles—"Technological News" in *Signals* (London), vol. 1, no. 2, 1964; "Underground Voices" in *Circuit* (Cambridge), no. 1/15, 1968; "Kinetic Art: A Statement" in *Studio International* (London), March 1967; "Lu Hsun, Chief Commander of China's Proletarian Cultural Revolution: in *Friends of China News Bulletin* (London), vol. 1, no. 6, 1972; "Art for Whom," interview, with Alastair Mackintosh, in *Art and Artists* (London), June 1973; "David Medalla in Conversation with Brandon Taylor" in *Artscribe* (London), April 1977.

On MEDALLA: books—*Medalla: Paintings and Drawings 1954-1962*, exhibition catalogue, with texts by Paul Keeler, Guy Brett, Nicholas Snowden Willey and others, Jordans, Buckinghamshire 1962; *Kinetic Art* by Guy Brett, London 1967; *Naissance de l'Art Cinetique* by Frank Popper, Paris 1967; *The Heirs of Constructivism* by George Rickey, New York 1967; *Neue Dimensionen der Plastik* by Udo Kultermann, Tübingen 1967; *Kaleidoscope of Modern Art* by Kenneth Weston, London 1967; *Beyond Modern Sculpture* by Jack Burnham, New York 1968; *Documenta 5: Befragung der Realitat*, exhibition catalogue, edited by Harald Szeemann and others, Kassel, West Germany 1972; *Minimal Art*, edited by Gregory Battcock, New York 1968; *Environments and Events* by Frank Popper, Paris and London 1975.

*

Taken as a whole, my varied artistic creations can be considered as metaphorical explorations of the problems of necessity and freedom. My earliest paintings and watercolours were semi-imaginary records of daily life. As a boy I saw in common everyday events (my mother cooking, my sister at a sewing machine, friends climbing trees or bathing naked in the sea near my home, farmers planting rice, workers doing labour, etc), beautiful cosmic rhythms which moved me deeply and for which I sought the most immediate corresponding images by using a variety of experimental techniques. My experiments carried me forward into kineticism. My first bio-kinetic constructions examined the relationships between man, nature and machine. *Auto-creative sculpture*, which I discovered in 1963, gave me my first practical insights into the paradoxical problems of *chance and change,* and taught me the scientific principle of *the negation of negation.* I realized gradually that it was through the correct grasp and application of this principle (*negation of negation*) that all past generations of human beings have progressed and continue to progress from a lower to a higher stage of consciousness.

By the mid-60's, I had started to explore *Participation, production and performance art.* At first I tried to examine, through the medium of dance and through environmental sculpture, the different myths of different peoples of different lands. Intuitively at first, and subsequently guided by Marxism-Leninism-Mao Tse-tung thought, I was critically assimilating and finding modern ways of transmitting the diverse socialist and democratic elements in the cultures of the world's people. From the late 60's to the present, I have created a number of works which depend, for their realization, on the voluntary participation of masses of people. These works stem directly from my investigations of various social relations. Another set of works which I have evolved relate poetically to specific historical situations, such as my "Celebration of the Paris Commune" (1971). A third set of works are mass-participation propulsions for the future when humanity as a whole will realize its full spirituality after the abolition of classes has been effected (consequently, the abolition of all class contradictions) through a series of earth-shaking revolutions of which our enemy has witnessed the earliest tremors: Russia in 1917, China during the Great Proletarian Cultural Revolution, Vietnam, and the struggles for national liberation of the peoples of the Third World. According to Karl Marx, the first great teacher of the world's proletariat, "Freedom is the appreciation of necessity."

In making my artistic propulsions, which are metaphors of freedom, I strive consciously to find ways of integrating my artistic practice with the heroic struggle of the international working and all oppressed people of the world for emancipation. This process of integration is not an easy one and can only be accomplished in stages. It is not easy, but it is exciting, and it generates in me that enthusiasm which propels forward my artistic practice. I wrote the following statement for the catalogue of the 1972 *Documenta 5* exhibition in Kassel: "I create my art for people and all living things": this remains the guiding principle of all my varied artistic creations.

—David Medalla

All literature and art are for the masses of the people, and in the first place for the workers, peasants and soldiers; they are created for the workers, peasants and soldiers and are for their use.

—Mao Tsetung

O.K., alright, don't panic; I know this isn't China. I know we don't have peasants, and even if we did, well we do things differently in the West, don't we; we don't have that ability to subsume our individuality in the State. The crowning glory of Western Art is its individualism, isn't it, its many paths, its courageous struggle against the forces of mediocrity. I know all that stuff, you see, I really do.

A fat lot of bloody good it does, though, knowing that. There's nothing worse than a conforming individualist and it seems that the whole of the Western art world is crawling with them. Every gallery contains examples of Man's Courageous Search for Individual, no, let's put that in capitals, INDIVIDUAL Expression of Personal Truth. They even teach it at art schools now.

So what do we get? We get a system of individual works which have to be sold at a high price to sustain the individual artists with the result that the works are bought by individuals who happen to have a great deal of money, thanks to the work of a lot of other individuals who don't seem to have a great deal of money, and the end result is an elitist art, known about by perhaps 10,000 people around the world,

written about in the wooliest language, and worst of all so incredibly unutterably boring that it doesn't even have the virtue of decadence.

Let's have a look at Mao again:

"A society without culture is a dull-witted society and such a society cannot defeat the enemy."

The American army goes into the field against the Viet-Cong on a diet of The Man from UNCLE and John Denver. Only one outcome is possible.

Of course, Mao also says that there are two sets of criteria, political and aesthetic, and that neither should be lost for the sake of the other. Western art has no political criteria at all, though.

An artist like David Medalla is working in a framework that almost guarantees that his work will be misjudged. He tried to involve other people in his art, to make art for the people but still retaining aesthetic power. The only place where art can even be seen nowadays is right in the camp of the enemy, the dealers, the critics, the buyers. So he is accused by one side of making art that is too political and the other for supping with the devil. He can't win.

This perhaps explains why an artist of his stature has been largely ignored in the West. Although he made process and land art long before it was fashionable, although he invented forms of participation art five years before flower power and all that "we are all artists" stuff, although his work is remarkable for its gentle sanity, he is still considered some sort of eccentric maverick who might deserve a footnote or two.

At his best, and Medalla being a prolific artist is not always his best, he can make art which combines aesthetic qualities with political humility, art that resolves the edgy opposition between the individual and the people. In "A Stitch in Time," he arranged a large sheet of bare canvas hung in a gentle arc from two high poles and decorated with colourful hanks of wool. This was only the beginning of the piece; it was completed by the public who were invited to come and embroider any design they liked on the canvas. At any time, visiting the exhibition, one might find up to a dozen people sitting crosslegged, intently sewing in an atmosphere that was remarkable for its pleasant goodhumour and restfulness. The canvas slowly filled up with designs and images, some expertly executed, some very crude, but each one made with care and pleasure. The piece combined Maoist theory with traditional methods and imagery in a manner that is typical of Medalla's work.

This type of cultural literacy informs all Medalla's work. His wide ranging knowledge puts the ignorance of most western artists to shame and his concern for global politics shows up their parochialism. Medalla is a truly international artist, travelling continuously, learning delightedly from everything he meets, always remembering though that art is for the people. He is a challenge for those timid souls who characterize the Maoist as a humourless cultureless boor, and it is a sad reflection on liberalism that Britain and America have not made a greater effort to understand and support his work.

—Alastair Mackintosh

MEGERT, Christian.

Swiss. Born in Berne, 6 January 1936. Studied art at the Kunstgewerbeschule, Berne, 1952–56. Married Lydia Christoffel in 1964 (divorced, 1972); son: Boris; married Franzkiska Vogt in 1976. Independent artist, Berne, 1955–58, 1960–73; in Paris, 1958–60; in Dusseldorf, since 1973; produced monochrome black and white paintings, 1955–59; light-reflector works, 1959–63; light-kinetic works, since 1963. Founder Member, Nouvelle Ecole Européenne (N.E.E.) artists group, Lausanne, 1960; associated with Zero group, Copenhagen and Dusseldorf, 1960–63; Co-Founder and Art Director, Galerie Aktuell

artists' collective, Berne, 1964–69; Member, Cantonal Art Commission, Berne, 1970–73, and, Exhibitions Commission, Kunsthalle, Berne, 1974. Professor, Staatliche Kunstakademie, Dusseldorf, since 1976. Recipient: Swiss State Art Scholarships 1962–1964. Agent: Galerie Reckermann, Albertusstrasse 50, 5000 Cologne, West Germany. Addresses: Drakestrasse 7, 4000 Dusseldorf, West Germany; Schwarzenburgstrasse 17, 3007 Berne, Switzerland.

Individual Exhibitions:

1959	Club des 4 Vents, Paris
1960	Galleri Koepcke, Copenhagen (with Dieter Roth)
1961	Galerie Punt 31, Dordrecht, Netherlands
	Galerie St. Luc, Barcelona
	Galleri Koepcke, Copenhagen
1962	Galerie A, Arnhem, Netherlands
	Galerie Orez, The Hague
1963	Galerie D, Frankfurt
	Galerie Knoll, Basle
	Galerie Kasper, Lausanne
	Rijksuniversiteit, Leiden
1964	Schweizerische Landesausstellung, Lausanne
1965	Galerie Aktuell, Berne
	Halfmannshof, Gelsenkirchen, West Germany
1966	Galerie Loehr, Frankfurt
	Galerie Toni Gerber, Berne
1967	Op Art Galerie, Esslingen, West Germany
	Galleria Vismara, Milan
1968	Galerie Swart, Amsterdam
	Galerie Toni Gerber, Berne
	Galerie Reckermann, Cologne
1969	Galerie Bischofberger, Zurich
	Galerie Latzer, Kreuslingen, Switzerland
1970	Galerie Ernst, Hannover
	Galerie Lichter, Frankfurt
1971	Galerie Reckermann, Cologne
	Galerie Bernhard, Solothurn, Switzerland
	Galerie Thomas Keller, Starnberg, West Germany
1972	Stadtische Galerie, Berne
	Forum Kunst, Rottweil, West Germany
	Galerie Ernst, Hannover
1973	Galerie Media, Neuenberg
	Galerie Reckermann, Cologne
1974	Studio Casate, Milan
	Galerie Edith Wahlandt, Schwabisch Gmund, West Germany
1975	Lucy Milton Gallery, London
	Kunsthalle, Heilbronn, West Germany
	Galerie St. Johann, Saarbrucken
	Galerie 68, Rapperswil, West Germany
	Galerie Ubu, Karlsruhe
1977	Galerie G. Herzog, Buren an der Aare, Switzerland
1978	Galerie Edith Wahlandt, Schwabisch Gmund, West Germany
1979	*Werke 1956–1978, Bilder, Objekte, Zeichnungen,* Kunstverein, Dusseldorf
	Galerie Reckermann, Cologne
1980	Galerie Edith Wahlandt, Schwabisch Gmund, West Germany
1981	Galerie Schoeller, Dusseldorf
	Rosenthall Werk, Seib, West Germany
	Rosenthall Werk, Amberg, West Germany
1982	Galerie Edith Wahlandt, Schwabisch Gmund, West Germany
	Galerie Buhler, Biel, Switzerland

Selected Group Exhibitions:

1958	*Salon des Réalites Nouvelles,* Paris
1961	*Zero Group,* Institute of Contemporary Art, Philadelphia
1971	*The Swiss Avantgarde,* New York Cultural Center
1976	*Rationale Konzepte,* Galerie Pa Szepan, Gelsenkirchen, West Germany
1977	*Museum of Drawers,* Kunsthalle, Dusseldorf (travelled to the Israel Museum, Jerusalem)
1978	*Konkrete Kunst aus der Schweiz,* Kunstmuseum Badhuis, Gorinchem, Netherlands (travelled to Stedelijk Museum, Apeldoorn)

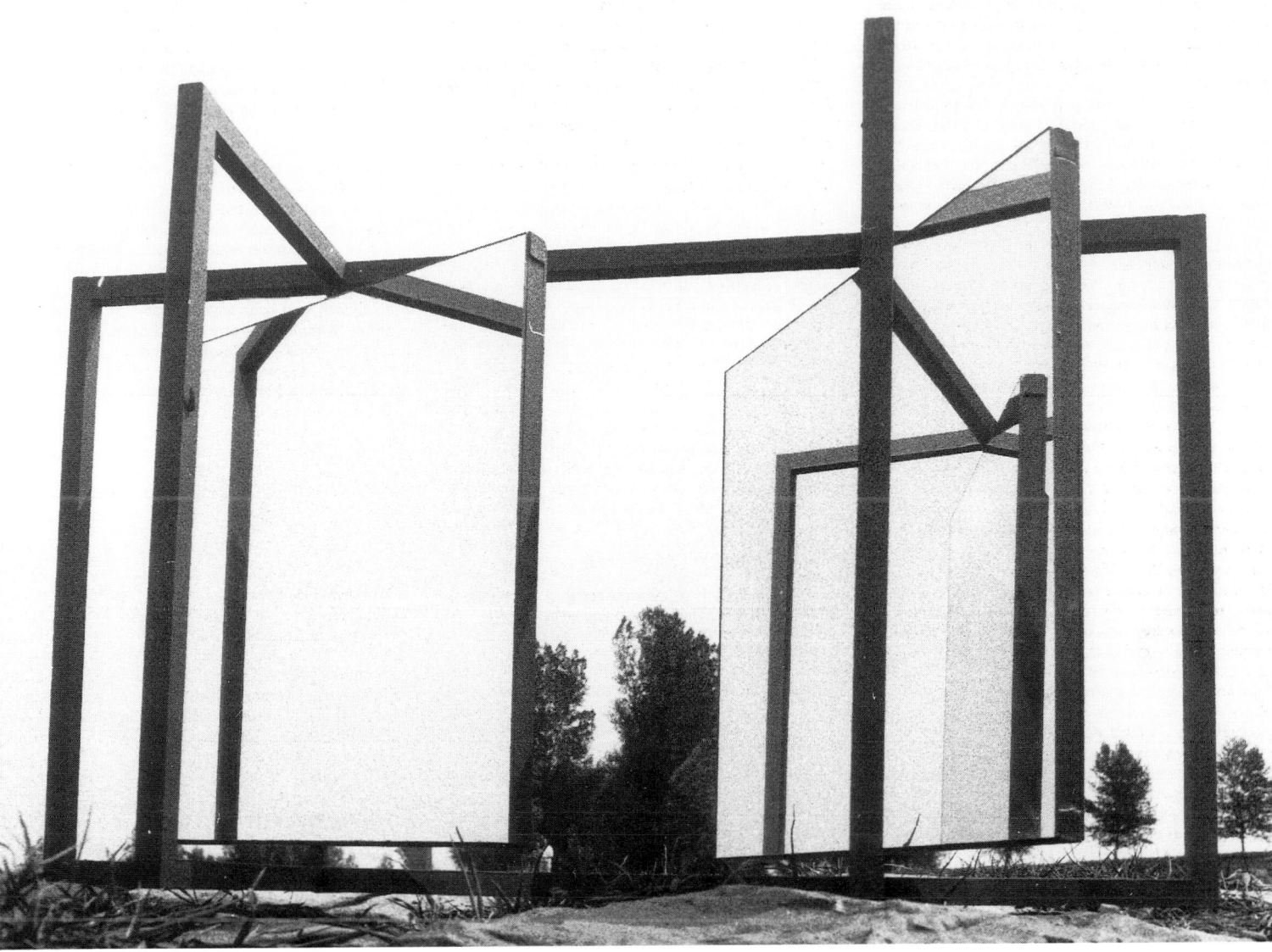

Christian Megert: *Kinetic Sculpture*, 1981

1979   *Lichtsculptures,* Informationszentrum, Eindhoven,
        Netherlands
1980   *Zero International,* Koninklijke Museum, Antwerp
1981   *Real und Irreal,* Galerie Schoeller, Dusseldorf
1982   *Spiegel,* Kunstverein, Hannover (travelled to Haus
        am Waldsee, West Berlin, and the Wilhelm
        Lehmbruck Museum, Duisburg, West Germany)

Collections:

Kunstmuseum, Berne; Progressives Museum, Basle; Städtische Sammlung, Berne; Landesmuseum, Hannover; Neues Landesmuseum, Münster; Städtische Kunsthalle, Recklinghausen, West Germany; Museum der Stadt, Dusseldorf; Museum der Stadt, Mönchengladbach, West Germany; Stadt Gorinchem, Netherlands; Albany Museum, New York.

Publications:

By MEGERT: books—*Ein neuer Raum,* Copenhagen 1961; *Glas und Spiegel Buch,* Berne 1962, 1974; *Wenn Sie einen Spiegel gegen einen Spiegel halten,* Cologne 1964; *Christian Megert,* Berne 1965; *Tam Tek,* Basle 1969; *Portfolio,* Starnberg, West Germany 1970; *Retro Megert,* Hinwil 1970; *Portfolio,* Zofingen 1974; *Der Raum und das Selbst,* with G. J. Lischka, Berne 1975.

On MEGERT: books—*Kunst unserer Zeit* by Will Grohmann, Cologne 1966; *Der Doppelte Masstab* by John Anthony Thwaites, Frankfurt 1966; *Licht Kunst Licht,* exhibition cata-logue, with text by Frank Popper, Eindhoven, Netherlands 1966; *Christian Megert,* exhibition catalogue, with text by Harald Szeemann, Esslingen, West Germany 1967; *Constructivism: Origin and Evolution* by George Rickey, New York 1967; *Neue Dimensionen der Plastik* by Udo Kultermann, Tübingen 1967; *Origins and Development of Kinetic Art* by Frank Popper, London 1968; *Kunst ist Revolution* by Louis Peters, Cologne 1969; *Op Art* by Cyril Barrett, London 1970; *Zero Raum,* exhibition catalogue, with text by Gerhard Storck, Dusseldorf 1974; *Christian Megert: Werke 1956-1978: Bilder, Objekte, Zeichnungen,* exhibition catalogue, with texts by Karl-Heinz Hering, Eugen Gomringer, Claus Bremer and Harald Szeemann, Dusseldorf 1979.

*   *   *

I will build a new space, a space without beginning and without end, in which everything lives and is called to live; which is at the same time quiet and loud, dynamic and static. It shall be high, as high as I want it and low if I want it low. It shall be constructable everywhere, on the smallest spot or big like a town, a country or even a thought.

A space which is merry, full of vitality, full of colour and movement, at the same time calmly calling for reflection without asking for anything, colourless and cold, which may change with the speed of thought after my desires, as I want it to be.

All the problems of space in the past and in the future will be found in my space, the solved ones and the unsolved ones, visible for everybody who is willing to see. It will contain only things existing in real-ity; everything unreal and unoriginal will no more be found in my space.

As it is real and surrealist and constructive and informal and colored and colorless, concrete and abstract, naive and intellectual and synchronized, it will also need no art, because it is art itself—and the inhabitants of this space become the greatest artists of our time, and everybody may become an inhabitant of this space. Try to find a space without beginning and end and limit; if you hold a mirror against a mirror you will find a space without end or limits, a space with unlimited possibilities—a new metaphysical space.

—Christian Megert

MELOTTI, Fausto.

Italian. Born in Roverto, Trento, 8 June 1901. Studied mathematics and physics, University of Pisa, 1918; electrical engineering, Milan Politecnico, 1924; sculpture, under Adolfo Widt, Brera Accademia di Belle Arti, Milan, 1929. Sculptor: lives and works in Milan; close friendship with Lucio Fontana from 1928; Founder, with Fontana, Antonasio Soldati and others, Gruppo del Milione, Milan, 1934–35;

Co-Founder, *Quadrante;* lived in Rome, writing poetry, 1941–43; after many of his works were destroyed by a bombing raid on Milan in 1943, he retired into obscurity for many years; worked on ceramics after the war and returned to sculpture in the 1960's. Lecturer, Scuola Artigana di Cantu, 1932. Recipient: Premio Internazionale, La Sarraz, Switzerland, 1937; Grande Medaglio d'Oro ad Artifice Italiano, Comune di Milano, 1958; Gold Medal, Prague, 1959; Gold Medal, Munich, 1964; Rembrandt Prize, Hamburg, 1974; Premio Diano Marina, 1975; Premio Biancamano, 1977; Premio Feltrinelli dell'Accademia dei Lincei, 1978. Address: Corso Magenta 66, 20123 Milan, Italy.

Individual Exhibitions:

1935	Galleria del Milione, Milan
1956	Galleria Annunciata, Milan
1967	Galleria Toninelli, Milan
	Galleria Notizie, Turin
	Palazzo del Comune, Reggio Emilia, Italy
1968	Galleria Il Segno, Rome
	Palazzo dei Diamanti, Ferrara, Italy
	Galleria Notizie, Turin
1969	Galleria dell'Ariete, Milan
1971	Galleria Martano, Turin
	Galleria Galatea, Turin
	Museum am Ostwall, Dortmund, West Germany
	Galleria dell'Ariete, Milan
1972	Galleria Civica d'Arte Moderna, Turin
	Galleria Galatea, Turin
1973	Galleria Il Segno, Rome
	Galerie Marlborough, Zurich (travelled to Marlborough Galleria d'Arte, Rome and Marlborough Fine Art, London)
1974	Galleria St. Luca, Bologna, Italy
	Galleria Il Sole, Bolzano,, Italy
	Galleria Morone, Milan
	Galleria Atena, Meda, Italy
1975	Galerie Schmela, Dusseldorf
	Galleria La Piramide, Florence
	Centro Rizzoli, Milan
	Galleria dell'Oca, Rome
	Galleria Beniamino, San Remo, Italy
	Galleria La Parisina, Turin
	Galleria Martini e Ronchetti, Genoa
1976	Galleria Rotta, Genoa
	Palazzo della Pilotta, Parma
	Galleria Editalia, Rome
	Galleria 3A, Turin
1977	Castello del Buonconsiglio, Trento, Italy
	Galleria Il Gabbiano, La Spezia, Italy
	Graphica Club, Milan
1978	Galleria Duchamp, Cagliari, Italy
	Galleria Morone 6, Milan
	Galleria Niccoli, Parma
1979	Galeria A 2, Rome
	Galleria Il Nome, Vigevano, Italy
	Galleria Pero, Milan
	Palazzo Reale, Milan
1980	Westend Galerie, Frankfurt
	Galerie Wintersberger, Cologne
	L'Uomo e l'Arte, Biella, Italy
	Villa Cicogna, Bologna San Lazzaro, Italy
1981	Musée des Beaux-Arts, La Chaux de Fonds, Switzerland (travelled to the Galerie Lopes, Zurich)
	Il Mercante di Stampe, Milan
	Forte di Belvedere, Florence
1982	Galleria Il Millennio, Rome
	Galleria Martano, Turin
1983	Galleria Nazionale d'Arte Moderna, Rome
	Galleria Pancheri, Rovereto, Italy
1985	Gallerie dell'Accademia, Venice
	Westend Galerie, Frankfurt
1987	Padiglione d'Arte Contemporanea, Milan

Selecteed Group Exhibitions:

1930	*Triennale,* Milan
1935	*Gruppo del Milione,* Galleria del Milione, Milan
1943	*Quadriennale,* Rome
1948	*Biennale,* Venice (and 1966)
1963	*Aspetti dell'Arte Contemporanea,* Castello Cinquecentesco, L'Aquila, Italy
1969	*Aspetti del Primo Astrattismo Italiano,* Galleria Civica d'Arte Moderna, Monza, Italy
1971	*Konkrete Kunst,* Westfalischer Kunstverein, Münster, West Germany
1973	*Sculpture Italienne Contemporanée,* Musée Royal d'Art et d'Histoire, Brussels
1977	*Gli Ultimi 15 Anni d'Arte in Italia,* Galleria Civica d'Arte Moderna, Turin
1980	*Anni Creativi al Milione, 1932–1939,* Palazzo Novellucci, Prato, Italy

Publications:

By MELOTTI: books—*Il Triste Minotauro,* Milan 1944; *Progetti di Melotti,* with Carlo Belli, Turin 1970; *Linée,* 1974; *Linée: Secondo Quaderno,* 1978; articles—"Idee sull'Insegnamento Artistico" in *Bolletino della Galleria del Milione* (Milan), June 1934; "L'Arte e Stato d'Animo Angelico Geometrico" in *Bolletino della Galleria del Milione* (Milan), May 1935; "Sculture Astratte del '35 e '65" in *Domus* (Milan), July 1962; "Cesar; Sculture e Disegni" in *Domus* (Milan), September 1962; "Un Gioco Che, Quando Nesce, e Poesia" in *Sculture Astratte,* Milan 1962; "Incertezza" in *Domus,* (Milan), March 1963; "Testimonianza" in *Homage to Gino Ghiringhelli,* exhibition catalogue, by Zeno Birolli, Milan 1964, reprinted in *Domus* (Milan), May 1965; "Bacon" in *Domus* (Milan), May 1966; "Un Gioco Che, Quando Riesce, e Poesia" in *Sculture Astratte,* Milan 1967; letter in *Esperienze dell'Astrattismo Italiano,* exhibition catalogue, Turin 1968; "Foglietti" in *Lo Spazio Inquieto,* edited by P. Fossati, Turin 1971; "L'Arte e Fenomeno dello Spirito" in *Fausto Melotti,* exhibition catalogue, Milan 1971; "The Consolation of Poetry" in *Arte Milano* (Milan), May 1972; "Fausto Melotti" in *Flash Art* (Milan), May/July 1972.

On MELOTTI: books—*Melotti,* exhibition catalogue, by Carlo Belli, Rome 1968; *Melotti: Sculture, Disegnie Pitture 1933–1968* by Carlo Belli, Reggio Emilia, Italy 1968; *Fausto Melotti,* exhibition catalogue, by Renato Barilli, Turin 1971; *Progetti di Melotti, 1932–36,* by Maurizio Fagioli, Turin 1971; *Fausto Melotti,* exhibition catalogue, by Zeno Birolli and Aldo Passoni, Turin 1972; *Melotti* by A. M. Hammacher, Milan 1975; *Fausto Melotti* by Maurizio Calvesi, Parma 1976; *Fausto Melotti,* exhibition catalogue, by Carlo Belli, Rome 1976; *Melotti: Fedele al Fantasma* by Gabriella Drudi, Rome and Milan 1979; *Fausto Melotti,* exhibition catalogue, by Carlo Pirovano and Erich Steingraber, Milan 1979; *Melotti,* exhibition catalogue, by A. M. Hammacher and Vanni Bramanti, Florence 1981; *Melotti: Ottantotto Disegni* by Carlo Pirovano, Florence 1981; *Fausto Melotti,* exhibition catalogue with texts by Mercedes Barberi and Giovanni Carandente, Milan 1987.

*

In front of one of Fausto Melotti's "Anti-Sculptures" one thinks of music by Mozart or of a Paul Klee who, instead of canvas, discovered thread, scraps of metal and shreds of material. For they are created out of poor material and out of the most expensive substances by an imagination which restricts itself to essentials in form and so returns to the happiness and significance of the world of childhood. Weightless, delicate metal creations which like musical notations make things heard visually perceptible. Fables made from thread with coloured spots of material, very cheerful and very serious stories mostly full of irony. His terracottas called "Teatrini," reminders of Etruscan house urns, conjure up metaphysical ideas behind a magical reality, as do the rare pictures and graphic works which survived the bombardment of Milan in 1943.

In 1974 in Hamburg, when the then 73 year old Fausto Melotti was honored with the Rembrandt prize, the donor A. Toepfer asked why this poet and musician was not greatly renowned among the sculptors of his native land. The answer was that he had indeed been well known for 40 years but that at his first exhibition in 1935 at the Milan Galleria del Milione, Carlo Carra had commented: "It is intelligent, but it is not sculpture."

Melotti was, like all his contemporaries, influenced by the Bauhaus and Constructivism, then silenced by fascism because such influences did not fit into any of the conventional rhetorical schemes. He remained si-

lent far into the post-war era and devoted himself, frequently distinguished by the *Triennale,* to ceramics, which he did not like. "Because there is always a little cheating in it and one never knows what the result will be. For the management above controls the fire."

On his 70th birthday Gillo Dorfles toasted him as the "youngest and most mature sculptor of Italy"; Maurizio Calvesi called him "the most consistent interpreter of the independence of the avant-garde, which also means independence from the gravity and rhetoric of sculpture." Franco Russoli, the now deceased director of Milan's Brera, wrote in 1975: "this fundamental poetic independence is the great moral and aesthetic quality which makes Melotti's art into one of the most supreme and genuine testimonies of the European cultural tradition." But Melotti is his own quietest and best interpreter. In 1935 he noted in his diary: "Art is an angelic geometric spiritual condition. It makes use of the intellect, not the senses." Another time he spoke of "the game which, when it succeeds, becomes poetry."

In his long life Fausto Melotti's game has often been successful.

—Monika von Zitzewitz

MEREDITH, John.

Canadian. Born in Fergus, Ontario, 24 July 1933. Educated at Brampton High School, Ontario; studied under J. W. G. Macdonald, Ontario College of Art, Toronto, 1950–53. Married Kyoko Hyashi in 1975. Independent painter, Toronto, since 1953. Agent: Isaacs Gallery, Toronto. Address: c/o Isaacs Gallery, 179 John Street, Toronto, Ontario M5T 1X3, Canada.

Individual Exhibitions:

1958	Gallery of Contemporary Art, Toronto
1959	Gallery of Contemporary Art, Toronto
1961	Isaacs Gallery, Toronto
1963	Isaacs Gallery, Toronto
1965	Isaacs Gallery, Toronto
	Blue Fern Gallery, Ottawa
1967	Isaacs Gallery, Toronto
	Wieland/Meredith, National Gallery of Canada, Ottawa
1973	Isaacs Gallery, Toronto
1974	*John Meredith: 15 Years,* Art Gallery of Ontario, Toronto (toured Canada)
1977	Isaacs Gallery, Toronto
1980	*John Meredith: Drawings, 1957–1980,* Art Gallery of Greater Victoria
	Isaacs Gallery, Toronto
1981	Isaacs Gallery, Toronto
1983	Isaacs Gallery, Toronto
1986	Region of Peel Art Gallery, Brampton, Ontario
1987	Isaacs Gallery, Toronto

Selected Group Exhibitions:

1965	*Biennal de Paris*
1967	*Painting in Canada,* Canadian Government Pavilion, at *Expo '67,* Montreal
	International Black and White Exhibition, Lugano, Switzerland
1968	*Canada: Art d'Aujourd'hui,* Musée National d'Art Moderne, Paris
	9 Canadians, Institute of Contemporary Art, Boston
1970	*8 Artists from Canada,* Tel Aviv Museum
1972	*Toronto Painting 1953–1965,* National Gallery of Canada, Ottawa
1976	*Abstractions,* Province of Ontario Exhibition, at the *Olympic Games,* Montreal
1978	*Modern Painting in Canada,* Edmonton Art Gallery
1981	*Linear Variables,* Winnipeg Art Gallery, Manitoba

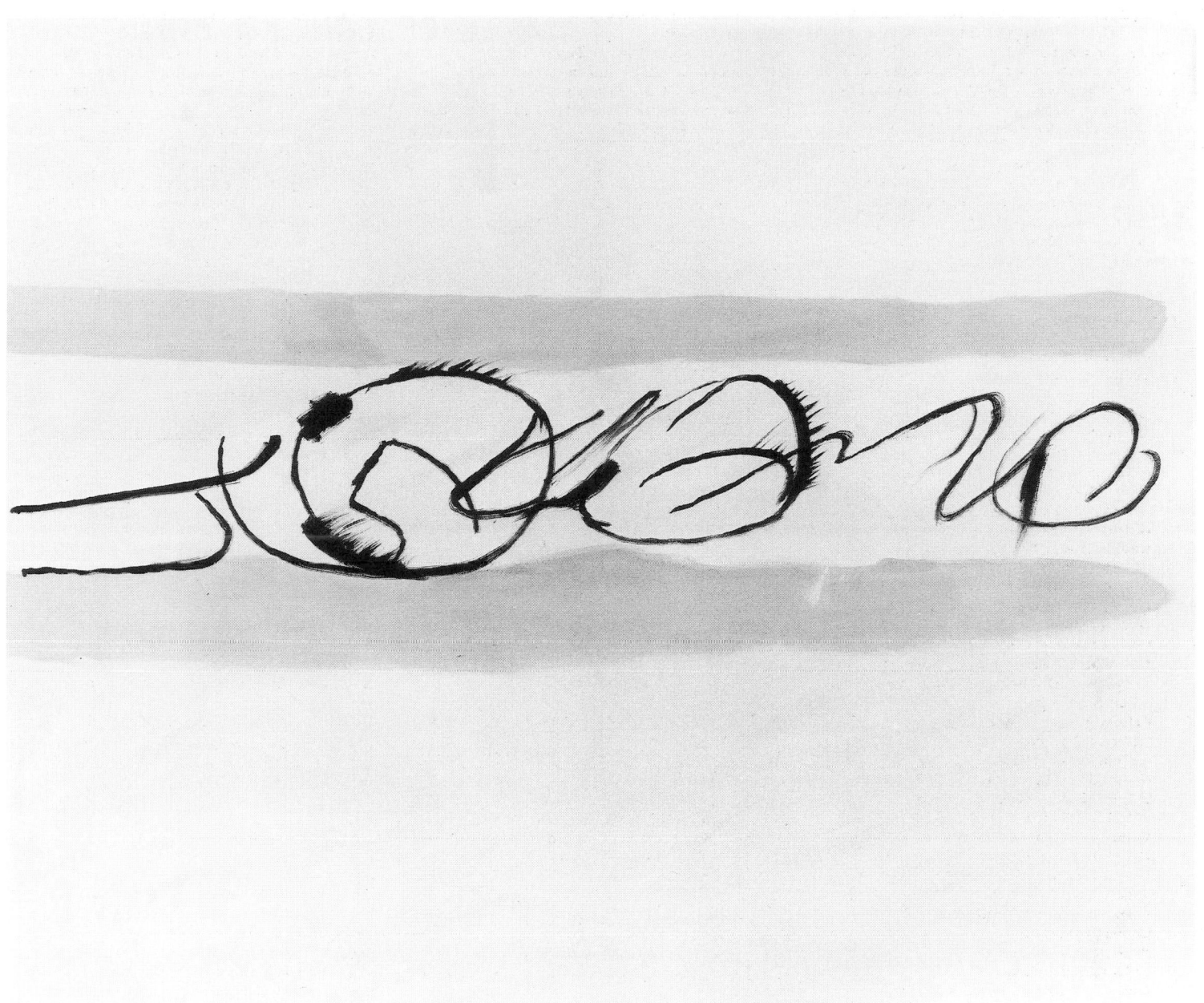

John Meredith: *Koto*, 1977

Collections:

Art Gallery of Greater Victoria; Art Gallery of Ontario, Toronto; Department of External Affairs, Ottawa; Museum of Fine Arts, Montreal; National Gallery of Canada, Ottawa; Toronto Dominion Bank; Vancouver Art Gallery; Winnipeg Art Gallery; Museum of Modern Art, New York; Philadelphia Museum of Art.

Publications:

On MEREDITH: books—*Contemporary Canadian Painting* by William Withrow, Toronto 1972; *A Concise History of Canadian Painting* by Dennis Reid, Toronto 1973; *John Meredith: 15 Years,* exhibition catalogue, by Marie Fleming, Toronto 1974; articles—"John Meredith: Painter" by Barry Lord in *Artscanada* (Toronto), April 1969; "The John Meredith Poems Untitled" by Barry Callaghan in *Exile* (Downsview, Ontario), June 1973.

For the last decade John Meredith has been one of the important, "big attack" painters on the Canadian scene. His "landscapes of the mind" have always been distinguished in the Toronto school by their use of line and deft handling of colour. Meredith is a "painter's painter." Younger members of the Toronto scene speak of him as the one they admire.

Painting for Meredith is a way of encompassing what he calls "the great mystery." In his early work, he explored flattened vertical bands of central images within a linear framework, sometimes with a semifigurative reference, in a shallow spatial depth. In 1964, he began to smudge the still wet lines in the paintings for a more lyrical, electrifying effect. At the same time his colour became higher in key.

Since 1966 (as in the Art Gallery of Ontario's "Seeker"), Meredith has been trying to transfer the spontaneous quality of his sketches to his canvases. Now in his work the sketch is more than ever a starting point. He takes liberties with it, transforming its vivacious qualities into a vigorous, broadly handled whole. These paintings, done very directly, recall fresh and exuberant watercolours. Big areas of cheerful, bustling colour predominate. But Meredith's idiosyncratic calligraphy, with its touch of Oriental influence, still shows up in works like "Black and White Painting May 1979."

Today, Meredith's work has turned a sharp colour. He's painting the female nude standing, reclining, or floating, using his smudged black line and glowing colour effect.

—Joan Murray

MERKIN, Richard (Marshall).

American. Born in Brooklyn, New York, 9 October 1938. Educated in New York City public schools, 1943–53; Erasmus Hall High School, Brooklyn, 1953–56; Syracuse University, New York, 1956–60, B.F.A. 1960. Married in 1960 (divorced, 1963). Worked as a department store stockboy, in a bindery, as a clothing salesman and as a chauffeur, while studying, 1953–60; Graduate Assistant, Michigan State University, East Lansing, 1960–61. Teaching Fellow, 1961–63, Assistant Professor of Painting, 1963–70, and since 1970 Adjunct Professor, Rhode Island School of Design, Providence. Visiting Artist-in-Residence, Syracuse University, New York, 1972. Recipient: Purchase Prize, *Printmaker's Show,* Washington, D.C., 1962, Tiffany Foundation Fellowship, 1962–63; Rosenthal Award, National Institute of Arts and Letters, 1975. Agents: Terry Dintenfass, 50 West 57th Street, New York; Harcus, Krakow, Rosen and Sonnabend, 7 Newbury Street, Boston; Kingpitcher Gallery, 303 South Craig, Pittsburgh; and Galleria dell'Ariete, via San Andrea 5, Milan. Address: 500 West End Avenue, Apartment 12D, New York, New York 10024, U.S.A.

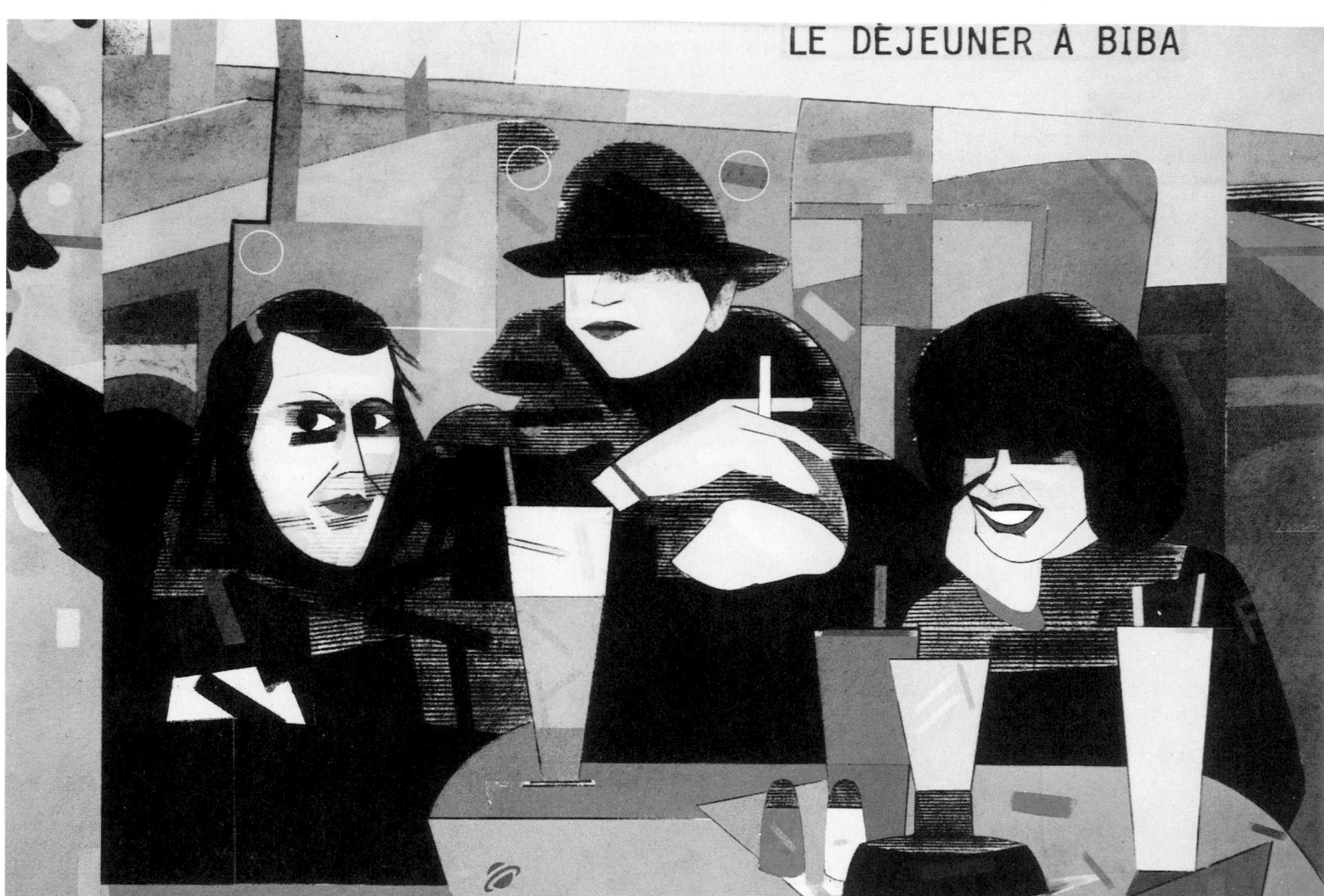

LE DÈJEUNER À BIBA

Richard Merkin: *Le Dejeuner à Biba*, 1976

Individual Exhibitions:

1965   Obelisk Gallery, Boston
1967   Byron Gallery, New York
1968   Obelisk Gallery, Boston (with James Melchert)
1969   Hayden Gallery, Massachusetts Institute of Technology, Cambridge
1971   Obelisk Gallery, Boston
         Galleria dell'Ariete, Milan
1972   Woods-Gerry Gallery, Rhode Island School of Design, Providence
1973   Terry Dintenfass Gallery, New York
1974   Terry Dintenfass Gallery, New York
1975   Harcus, Krakow, Rosen, Sonnabend Gallery, Boston
1976   Anhalt Barnes Gallery, Los Angeles
1978   Terry Dintenfass Gallery, New York
         Johnson Museum, Middlebury College, Vermont
1980   Chrysler Museum, Norfolk, Virginia
         Terry Dintenfass Gallery, New York
1981   Gallery Camino Real, Boca Raton, Florida
         Eric Makler Gallery, Philadelphia
         Terry Dintenfass Gallery, New York

Selected Group Exhibitions:

1965   *New England Contemporary Artists*, Northeastern University, Boston
1967   *Art in Process: Visual Development of a Collage*, Finch College Museum of Art, New York
1969   *Annual Exhibition*, Whitney Museum, New York
1970   *American Painting 1970*, Virginia Museum, Richmond
1974   *20th Annual Drawing and Small Sculpture Show*, Ball State University, Art Gallery, Muncie, Indiana
1976   *Painting and Sculpture*, Indianapolis Museum of Art

1979   *Alumni Artists Exhibition*, Syracuse University, New York
1988   *Figure It Out: Visual Body Language*, Helandes Gallery, Palm Beach, Florida

Collections:

Museum of Modern Art, New York; Whitney Museum, New York; Museum of Art, Rhode Island School of Design, Providence; Rose Art Museum, Brandeis University, Waltham, Massachusetts; Massachusetts Institute of Technology, Cambridge; Smithsonian Institution, Washington, D.C.; First National City Bank, Chicago; Minnesota Museum of Art; Fisk University Art Gallery, Nashville, Tennessee; Miami-Dade Junior College, Florida.

Publications:

By MERKIN: BOOK—*On Art and Perfume; or, Did Mondrian Use Masking Tape?*, catalogue, Cambridge, Massachusetts 1969.

John Gregory Dunne, the novelist, recently said, "I think you write to find out what you think." At the risk of not sounding particularly original, and perhaps a bit glib, I think that it is fair to say that I paint, I make pictures, to see what I saw.

—Richard Merkin

You can almost see him strutting the boulevard, bedecked and bejewelled as to fit the scenery. He pauses briefly to straighten his tie, smooth his hair, glance side to side with a casual indifference about the city. But the ambition in his inner eye is alarmingly stead-

fast; the smallest details of the scenery imbued with a life of their own call to him: a Turkish cigarette, a glove, a capped-toe shoe, a walking stick (and no artist has ever had a more exquisite eye for cigarettes, gloves, shoes, and walking sticks), not to mention tennis collars and boutonniers. Such details become a discreet element of design.

Richard Merkin is one of the few outstanding colourists and designers who exploits the energy and the dazzle of the boulevard, the city, the high-life, the low-life, even unto the sado-disco into his work. Rising out of the sixties, he employed his wholly maverick qualities to a technique polished by Rabelaisian and Gautierian mannerisms. In his exhibition "The Sins of New York on Simplicissimus Revisited," for example, the blocks of colour in his brilliant pastels remain flat, and yet are built up with a depth and chromatic density that defies every conventional notion of pastel. To create this effect, his pastels are custom-made with an extraordinary proportion of pigment.

Merkin takes great splendour in lushness. His paintings radiate with a warmth and opulence that is not easily found in modern art. Splashed with macaw greens, flamingo pinks, scuba blues and mimosa magentas, his is a palette bursting with a tropical joie de vivre. During a period in which modern art needs to be solved like riddles or deciphered like puzzles, Merkin remains loud, direct, disinterested in nostalgia or in a readily translatable language of symbols. In this respect he is a colourist in the tradition of French modernism excluding anything but the barest formal statement. With such wit and simplicity, he hardly has the right to be called artist when the ideal of the modern art world is both solemn and non-rational. In "Cafe Megalomania" Merkin again emerges as the "boulevardier," tipping his hat, as he loves to do, to the wits and antics kings of yesterday, in this case the satiric German artists, George Grosz and Edouard Thöny. His spirit is with Henry Lamb—or perhaps Warhol—artists who repeat the images of daily life, images that appear on the streets and on the breakfast table in newspapers. For repetition both celebrates and devalues. How large a gap do we habitually make between the image offered by a work of art and the real-life thing to which it refers? Such a question is at the centre of Merkin's work.

—Carrie Barker

MERZ, Mario.

Italian. Born in Milan in 1925. Married to the artist Marisa Merz. Independent artist, now living in Turin. Agents: Galleria Christian Stein, Piazza San Carlo 206, 10121 Turin; and Sperone Westwater, 142 Greene Street, New York, New York 10012, U.S.A. Address: Corso Tassoni 56, 10122 Turin, Italy.

Individual Exhibitions:

1953	Galleria Bussola, Turin
1956	Galleria del Milione, Milan
1962	Galleria Notizie, Turin
1967	Gian Enzo Sperone, Turin
1968	Gian Enzo Sperone, Turin
1969	Gian Enzo Sperone, Turin
	Galleria l'Attico, Rome
	Galerie Sonnabend, Paris
1970	Galerie Konrad Fischer, Dusseldorf
	Sonnabend Gallery, new York
	Galleria Francoise Lambert, Milan
1971	Gian Enzo Sperone, Turin
	Sonnabend Gallery, New York
	John Weber Gallery, New York
1972	Walker Art Center, Minneapolis
	Jack Wendler Gallery, London
1974	Haus am Lutzowplatz, Berlin
	Cassino Ova, Tortona, Italy
	Galleria Area, Florence
1975	Kunsthalle, Basle
1976	Galleria Mario Pieroni, Pescara, Italy
	Villa Pignatelli, Naples
	Gian Enzo Sperone, Rome
	Gian Enzo Sperone, Turin
	Galleria Tucci Russo, Turin
	Galerie Annemarie Verna, Zurich
	Galerie Konrad Fischer, Dusseldorf
1977	Galleria Salvatore Ala, Milan
	Galerie Annemarie Verna, Zurich
1978	Galerie Jean and Karen Bernier, Athens
	Galleria Lucio Amelio, Naples
	Galleria dell'Oca, Rome
	Galleria Tucci Russo, Turin
1979	Museum Folkwang, Essen
	Sperone Westwater Fischer, New York
	Institute of Modern Art, Brisbane, Australia
	Galerie Durand-Dessert, Paris
	Galerie Annemarie Verna, Zurich
	Galleria Franco Toselli, Milan
	Galleria Giuliana de Crescenzo, Rome
1980	Whitechapel Art Gallery, London
	Galleria Christian Stein, Turin
	Stedelijk van Abbemuseum, Eindhoven, Netherlands
	Galerie Albert Baronian, Brussels
	Sperone Westwater Fischer, New York
	Gian Enzo Sperone, Turin
	Galleria Salvatore Alan, Milan
1981	Konrad Fischer, Dusseldorf
	Musée d'Art Moderne de la Ville, Paris
	Kunsthalle, Basle
	Galerie Studio, Warsaw
	Konrad Fischer, Zurich

	Galleria Tucci Russo, Turin
	Galleria Christian Stein, Turin
	Joslyn Art Museum, Omaha, Nebraska
	Galleria Franco Toselli, Florence
	Galleria Lucio Amelio, Naples
1982	Sperone Westwater Fischer, New York
	Ackland Art Museum, Chapel Hill, North Carolina
	Galleria Mario Diacono, Rome
	Galerie Munro, Hamburg
	Galleria Marilena Bonomo, Bari, Italy
	Galleria Salvatore Ala, Milan
	Museum Folkwang, Essen, West Germany
	Staatsgalerie, Stuttgart
	Galleria d'Arte Moderna, Bologna, Italy
	Kestner-Gesellschaft, Hanover
1983	Anthony D'Offay Gallery, London
	Flow Ace Gallery, Venice, California
	Israel Museum, Jerusalem
	Galleria Pieroni, Rome
	Neuberger Museum, Purchase, New York
	Moderna Museet, Stockholm
	Galerie Nachst St. Stephan, Vienna
	Palazzo Congressi ed Esposizioni, Republic of San Marino
	Galerie Buchmann, Basle
1984	Galerie Konrad Fischer, Dusseldorf
	Albright-Knox Art Gallery, Buffalo, New York
	Hallwalls, Buffalo, New York
	Institute of Contemporary Art, Boston
	Galerie Sparta, Chagny, France
	Galeria Christian Stein, Turin
	Musée Toulouse-Lautrec, Albi, France
	Kunstverein, St. Gallen, Switzerland
	Sperone Westwater, New York
1985	Galerie Nachst St. Stephan, Vienna
	Galleria Christian Stein, Turin
	Kunsthaus, Zurich
	Galerie Durand-Dessert, Paris
	Galerie Munro, Hamburg
	Sperone Westwater/Leo Castelli Gallery, New York
	Musée d'Art et d'Industrie, Geneva
	Westfalischer Kunstverein, Munster, West Germany
	Galerie Pietro Sparto/Pascale Petit, Chagny, France
1986	Galleria Antonio Tucci Russo, Turin
1987	CAPC/Musée D'Art Contemporain, Bordeaux, France
	Galleria Toselli, Milan
	Chapelle de la Salpetriere, Paris
	Galerie Konrad Fischer, Dusseldorf
	Kunstverein, Munich
	Musée d'Art Contemporain, Montreal
1988	Anthony D'Offay Gallery, London

Selected Group Exhibitions:

1961	*International Art Exhibition*, Galleria Kaspers, Lausanne
1967	*Contemplazione*, Galleria Sperone/Galleria Stein, Turin
1969	*When Attitudes Become Form*, Kunsthalle, Berne (toured Europe)
1972	*Documenta 5*, Museum Fridericianum, Kassel, West Germany (and *Documenta 6*, 1977; *Documenta 7*, 1982)
1977	*Europe in the Seventies*, Art Institute of Chicago (travelled to Washington, D.C.; San Francisco; Fort Worth, Texas; Cincinnati, Ohio)
1979	*Third Biennale of Sydney*, Art Gallery of New South Wales, Sydney (travelled to Brisbane)
1981	*Identité Italienne: L'Art en Italie depuis 1959*, Centre Georges Pompidou, Paris
1983	*Arte a Torino 1946-53*, Accademia Albertina di Belle Arti, Turin
1985	*Transformations in Sculpture*, Guggenheim Museum, New York
1987	*Turin 1965-87: Arte Povera*, Musée d'Art et d'Histoire, Chambery, France (travelled to Lille)

Collections:

Galleria d'Arte Moderna, Turin; Stedelijk Museum, Amsterdam; Kaiser Wilhelm Museum, Krefeld, West Germany.

Publications:

By MERZ: books—*Fibonacci 1202-Mario Merz, 1970*, edited by Germano Celant and Pierluigi Pero, Turin 1970; *Fibonacci 1202-Mario Merz 1972*, edited by Pierluigi Pero, Turin 1972; *It is as possible to have a Space with Tables for 88 people as it is possible to have a Space with Tables for no-one: Tables from Drawings of Mario Merz*, New York 1974; *Tavole con le Zampe diventano Tavoli: Cascina Ova, Tortona*, Milan 1974; *La Frutta e qui . . .* , edited by Lucio Amelio, Naples 1976; articles—interview, with Richard Koshalek, in *Art and Artists* (London), June 1972; interview, with M. Haerditerin, in *Mario Merz*, exhibition catalogue, Berlin 1974; "L'immaginazione vivente e in Movimento continuo . . ." in *Mario Merz*, exhibition catalogue, Berlin 1974; "Annahern: Statistische Zeichnungen an Dynamische . . ." in *Projekt 74*, exhibition catalogue, Cologne 1975; "Texte 1970-1974" in *Mario Merz*, exhibition catalogue, Basle 1975; "Una Domenica Lunghissima dura approssimativamente dal 1966 e ora siamo al 1976" in *Citta di Riga I*, Rome 1977; "La Mancanza di Iconografia e la Nostra Conquista o la Nostra Dammazione?" in *Citta di Riga II*, Rome 1978; "April 1980, May 1980" in *Kunstforum International* (Mainz, West Germany), vol. 39, no. 3, 1980; "Interview mit Mario Merz," with Jean-Christoph Ammann and Suzanne Page, In *Mario Merz*, exhibition catalogue, Paris 1981; "Project for Artforum" in *Artforum* (New York), January 1985.

On MERZ: books—*Arte Povera* by Germano Celant, Milan 1969; *Mario Merz*, exhibition catalogue, by Ruhrberg and Schmeid, Berlin 1974; *Mario Merz*, exhibition catalgue, Essen 1979; *Mario Merz*, exhibition catalogue, by Zdenek Felix, Essen 1982; *Mario Merz*, exhibition catalogue with text by Carl Haenlein, Stockholm 1983; *Mario Merz*, exhibition catalogue with texts by Germano Celant and others, San Marino 1983; *Arte Povera, The Knot* by Germano Celant, New York 1985.

*

Mario Merz's art is a great profession of freedom. The artist always casts aside any effort to give his work titles like "arte povera," "assemblage," *objets trouvés*, etc. He wishes to discover and move all aspects of the imagination (consequently, as far as he is concerned, nothing in art is "outdated"). He also wishes never to become "classic" within his own art.

Merz's behavior cannot be related to any known mode; one can, however, approach it in the light of his general attitude towards culture and towards the dichotomy of culture-nature. The area of the artist's interest is European culture with a bent towards the Italian Renaissance. An intensive wish to "touch" culture at its origin is involved in this—in that one situation where it has not been radically opposed to nature.

This is why fruits of the earth often appear in Merz's work—faggots, fruit, vegetables, natural materials such as tar, earth, wax—and, with them, neon light, not in a technological sense but as a source of energy like the other substances. That is also why the prehistoric animals appear too. They are the representatives of times when man—the creator and carrier of culture—was still a participant in the "whole" of existence; he was integrally involved with nature. The igloo is an excellent example. In 1969 Merz created his first earthen igloo—an inhabitable construction in an almost natural organic shape. It is an elementary form, simultaneously concrete and conceptual, a union between the rational and the irrational, an expression of that which appears in the soul of man himself.

The table is also an important form for Merz: the subject has appeared since 1972. It represents in clear terms the basic needs of a person and his relationship to other people. The idea of "table" arose from a certain incident that took place in a restaurant, when a photographer took photographs with the following numbers of people—1, 2, 3, 5, 8—each number a sum of the previous two, the counting system of the medieval Italian mathematician Fibonacci. Merz used the system's refinements to build structures of a "natural height." The whole human dream of creating ideal structures that agree with the natural needs of man is contained in this mode. The shape of natural growth is, above all, the spiral, solved in accordance with nature's behavior, loaded down with ancient symbolic meanings because of its qualities (the field

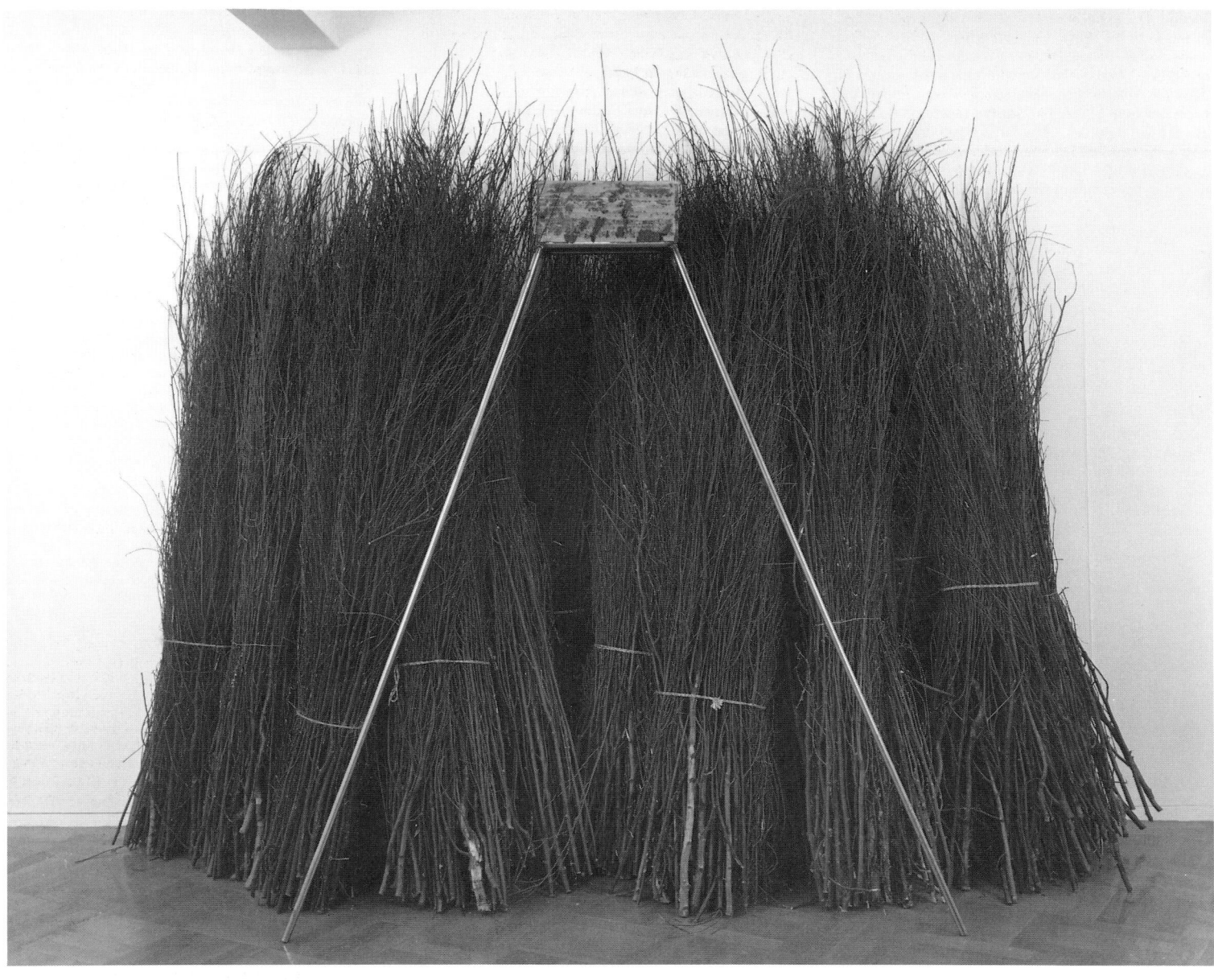

Mario Merz: *Lingotto*, **1968** Courtesy Anthony D'Offay Gallery, London

of meaning of the myth of Dionysus, the "dying" God, its lunar and aquatic affiliations). This shape thus appears in Merz's work in various ways—e.g., as spirals of paint squeezed straight from a tube or as a "golden spiral," inspired by the construction of a snail.

In such works the artist introduces the shape of the spiral in space and wishes to apply it to the idea of time. The expansion of space is similar to the idea of time—a concept that the Aztecs were aware of. The artist also expresses this idea in different ways—for example, he cuts the canvas with a neon rod, making two periods cross in the space produced in this way.

The problem of time is also expressed when the artist reaches back to prehistoric times, full of the most terrible monsters that nature, and the imagination that turns them into symbols, could create. Thus crocodiles, rhinoceroses, tigers, owls and other animals that "take part" in the history of man—i.e., in the evolution of time—appear in this kind of work.

When one reaches back to prehistory, one feels the enormousness of time—a kind of supertime. Animals, in particular ancient animals, are a reminder of the night of man, if one regards man himself as the day. To introduce one of the huge, ancient animals is to recall something very fundamental and timeless. That is exactly what Merz wishes to achieve—to find himself at the end of the present century and to understand that which is most basic in the existence of man.

This interest in the fundamentals of man's existence also expresses itself in the great thematic works that Merz undertakes. Examples are "living quarters" (the constantly elaborated formula of the igloo) and "food" (vegetables, fruit). The introduction of "food" came about as a result of a simple existential experience at an Autumn market: the artist was struck by nature's bounty . . . not only color and smell but also the quantity which in itself becomes a source of emotion. And a problem. One wishes to render "quantity" in art, but art is by definition an ideogram of that which is singular. One has to find in oneself a kind of innocence, naiveté or primordiality in order to recall the elementary form of the imagination, in order to cope with a vision like the enormousness (in all senses) of a pile of fruit.

In a similar manner, Merz introduces a faggot into the artistic plane: it "represents" not only the forest but also a quantity, a certain numerical continuity. As well, the fact that the twigs are tied up together produces a moving emotional situation: it creates the feeling of "togetherness," while at the same time wood is the symbol for loneliness.

The range of operations that Merz carries out between the existential plane and intellectual reflection and the artwork itself is very great indeed. The artist wishes to understand afresh all that was laid aside, abandoned, "lost" in the development of man. He is also interested in that which the 20th century avant-garde destroyed. He wishes to collect everything and

"put it back into place" once more. That is why his work encompasses faggots, fruit, animals, electricity, newspapers and igloos. It is not a kind of assemblage but a tidying up of the human landscape, which contains the forces of both expansion and concentration, and the strength of the dome, the igloo, which refers back to the ideas of the Renaissance, as that which holds it all together.

To tame once more the "human landscape" and to see it separated from all conventions within a linear understanding of time—this implies a recovery of man's dimension in a world that has lost or doubted it.

—Alicja Kepinska

MESENS, E(douard) L(eon) T(eodore).
Belgian. Born in Brussels, 17 November 1903. Studied music, 1918–24; self-taught in art. Started writing poetry and designing collages, 1924; Founder, with René Magritte and Paul Nouge, Belgian Surrealist Movement, Brussels, 1925; visited Paris, associated with the Surrealists, 1925; Editor, with Magritte, *Oesophage* review, Brussels, 1925; Editor, with Van

Hecke, *Variétés* and *Selection;* Editor, *Marie*, Brussels, 1928; served on the committee of the *International Surrealist Exhibition*, London, 1936; settled in London, 1938: Director, London Gallery, 1938–40 (Editor with Roland Penrose, *London Bulletin*, 1938–40). *Died* (in Brussels) *in 1971.*

Individual Exhibitions:

1958 Galerie Furstenburg, Paris
1959 Palais des Beaux-Arts, Brussels
1960 Galleria del Naviglio, Milan
1961 Grosvenor Gallery, London
1963 *Festival Belge d'Éré*, Salle La Reserve, Knokke-le-Zoute, Belgium
1965 Galleria del Naviglio, Milan
1970 Galleria Il Fauno, Turin
1971 Galerie Isy Brachot, Brussels
1974 *Collages 1957–71*, Acoris Surrealist Art Centre, London

Selected Group Exhibition:

1935 *Surrealist Exhibition*, Municipal Hall, La Louvière, Belgium
1936 *Fantastic Art: Dada: Surrealism*, Museum of Modern Art, New York
1961 *The Art of Assemblage*, Museum of Modern Art, New York
1971 *Britain's Contribution to Surrealism of the 30's and 40's*, Hamet Gallery, London

Collections:

Musée Royaux des Beaux-Arts, Brussels: Tate Gallery, London, Museum of Modern Art, New York

Publications:

By MESENS: books—*Poèmes 1923–58*, Paris 1959; *Le Cache-Sexe des Anges*, with others, Brussels 1978; articles—numerous contributions to Surrealist magazines, Brussels and London, 1925–70; "The Apprentice Magician in the Land of Plethora" in *Les Arts Plastiques*, Paris 1954.

On MESENS: books—*E. L. T. Mesens*, exhibition catalogue, Brussels 1971; *Britain's Contribution to Surrealism of the 30's and 40's*, exhibition catalogue, London 1971; *Antologie Grafica del Surrealismo*, by Maurice Henry, Milan 1972; *Le Surrealisme en Belgique* by José Vovelle, Brussels 1972; *Mon Ami Mesens* by Louis Scutenaire, Brussels 1972; *E. L. T. Mesens: Collages 1957–71*, exhibition catalogue, by Conroy Maddox, London 1974; *Rum, Bum and Concertina* by George Melly, London 1977.

The name of E. L. T. Mesens is just as likely to be remembered for his activities as an impresario and organizer of art as much as for his own production of paintings. He was an outstanding example of the century's versatile practitioner in various art forms, following each of them with enthusiasm. His first efforts were as a poet and a musician. He came under the influence of Satie, and worked as a composer until the early 1920's. His early acquaintance with Magritte and their joint friendship with members of the Surrealist movement in Paris was to have far-reaching effects for both men. Mesens took a great interest in painting, but for his own part he was largely self-taught, except in so far as his close contacts with artists such as Picabia, Tzara and Duchamp in Paris undoubtedly educated him in basic techniques like those of collage and water-colour he was to indulge in for most of his life. Duchamp as much as any one was a major influence in the poetic and irreverent attitudes he adopted in later years.

But Mesens found that the printed word and the propagation of the gospel of art in others' examples absorbed most of his time. For seven years he was secretary of the Palais des Beaux Arts in Brussels; he edited magazines as well as writing poetry. In 1936

he took part in the historic *International Surrealist Exhibition* in London, and two years later he settled in Britain. He ran his London Gallery and edited its much sought after *Bulletin* until 1940.

Just the same, he found time for his own work. Mainly the content was poetic and the visual aspect was formed by the slightest of materials, items such as used bus tickets, scraps of cigarette paper and cut-out card that were not only ready-made but were the readiest to hand to give form to his ideas. "Manhattan" (1960), for instance, presented a group of skyscrapers of various heights represented by pieces of printed tickets surmounted by the drawn shapes of dark bowler hats and walking canes around which blew streamers of wispy cloud. This kind of visual punning made its point quickly without leaving any great sensual impression of texture or colour.

It was the poet's gift for pointed choice, the selection of telling and frequently double-faced images that gave Mesen's work its special character. He shared the Dada contempt for tradition in a mild anti-art spirit but most of his work reflected a pocket theatre composed in scenes of witty transposition such as "Heureux menage au fond de la mer" (1961) where three bold types of the printers' ampersand are placed as in a family group against a broken water-colour ground, two of them seated on the back of a tipped-over capital E. This surprising investment of human characteristics and attributes into inanimate objects and signs was capable of cultivation to degrees of humorous relevance, sometimes acute but often no more than a mild indulgence.

—G. S. Whittet

MESSAGER, Annette.

French. Born in Berck, 30 November 1943. Studied at the Ecole Nationale Supérieure des Arts Décoratifs, Paris, 1962–66. Independent artist, working with photography and painting. Recipient: First Prize, *Kodak Photography International*, 1964. Address: 146 Boulevard Camelinat, 92240 Malakoff, France.

Individual Exhibitions:

1973 *Annette Messager Kunstlerin, Annette Messager Sammlerin*, Städtische Galerie im Lenbachhaus, Munich
      Musée de Grenoble, France
      Musée Rude, Dijon, France (with Boltanski and Le Gac)
      Galerie Yellow Now, Liège, Belgium
1974 Galleria Diagramma, Milan
      Galleri Daner, Copenhagen
      Galleri St. Petri, Lund, Sweden
      Musée d'Art Moderne de la Ville, Paris
1975 Galerie 't Venster, Rotterdam
      Galerie Ecart, Geneva
      Gallery of Contemporary Art, Zagreb
      Galerie Space, Wiesbaden, West Germany
1976 Galleria Multimedia, Erbusco, Italy
      Rheinisches Landesmuseum, Bonn
1977 Galerie Isy Brachot, Brussels
      Galerie Seriaal, Amsterdam
1978 Holly Solomon Gallery, New York
      Rheinisches Landesmuseum, Bonn
      Galerie Voksal, Warsaw
1979 Galerie Gillespie-Laage, Paris
1980 Galerie Gillespie-Laage, Paris
      St. Louis Art Museum
      Galerie le Coin du Mur, Dijon, France
1981 University of California at Irvine
      San Francisco Museum of Modern Art
      P.S. 1, New York
      Galerie Denise René-Hans Mayer, Dusseldorf
      Artists' Space, New York

1982 Artists' Space, New York
1983 Galerie Gillespie-Laage-Salomon, Paris
      Musée des Beaux-Arts, Calais, France
1984 ARC/Musée d'Art Moderne de la Ville, Paris

Selected Group Exhibitions:

1974 *Ils Collectionnent*, Musée des arts Décoratifs, Paris
1975 *New Media*, Konsthall, Malmo Sweden
1977 *Les Boites*, Musée d'Art Moderne de la Ville, Paris (travelled to Maison de la Culture, Rennes, France)
1978 *Biennale de Paris*, Musée d'Art Moderne de la Ville, Paris
1979 *Photography as Art*, Institute of Contemporary Arts, London
1980 *Works for Walls*, Cincinnati Art Center, Ohio
1981 *Szenen der Volkskunst*, Kunstverein, Stuttgart
1982 *Facons de Peindre*, Chalon-sur-Saône, France
1983 *New Art*, Tate Gallery, London
1984 *Biennale of Sydney*, Art Gallery of New South Wales, Sydney

Collections:

Centre Georges Pompidou, Paris; Musée d'Art Moderne de la Ville, Paris; Musée de Grenoble, France

Publications:

By MESSAGER: books-*Les Approches*, Hamburg 1973; *Mes Cliches Temoins*, Liège, Belgium 1974; *La Femme et . . .*, Geneva 1975; *Mes Jeux de Main*, Zagreb 1975; *Le Bonheur Illustre*, Bonn 1976; *Ma Collection de Proverbes*, Milan 1976; articles—"Dans l'Intimite d'Annette Messager" in *Chroniques de l'Art Vivant* (Paris), February 1974; "Annette Messager," interview with Barbara Radice, in *Flash Art* (Milan), June 1974; "Ma Collection d'Expressions et d'Attitudes Diverses" in *Chorus* (Paris), no. 12, 1975; "Annette Messager," interview with Aline Dallie, in *Les Cahiers du Griff* (Brussels), May 1976.

On MESSAGER: books—*Annette Messager Kunstlerin, Annette Messager Sammlerin*, exhibition catalogue, with text by Armin Zweite, Munich 1973; *Annette Messager*, exhibition catalogue, with text by Gosse Oosterhof, Rotterdam 1975; *Modellbilder*, exhibition catalogue, with text by Klaus Honnet, Stuttgart 1976; *Identité/Identifications*, exhibition catalogue, with text by Jacques Clayssen, Bordeaux 1977; *Annette Messager*, exhibition catalogue with text by Suzanne Pagé, Paris 1984.

As time goes by I feel less like talking about my work.

"My work," words that evoke research and effort, when actually I would like so much to have a light, mobile and flexible activity (and also go back and see all of Hitchcock's films; yes, I would like to be the "Hitchcock of painting"!).

I am an artist who would like to reconcile painting and photography—these two opposed media that hate each other, are jealous of one another or ignore each other . . . a rocky marriage. So, for this union, the two media must "explode." Photography must come out of its usual form, out of its small format anecdotal aspect. It must meet painting in the most unexpected forms and places. They must separate again to rejoin each other later, more freely, somewhere in space.

Photography, it is said, is cold, temporal, always linked to the present or the past (never to the future). United with painting which is physical, timeless, what disturbing disorder!

I don't have too much respect for the history of art and culture. Perhaps the weight of culture is less strong for women and that is our luck today. Let's go!

We live in history: the street, stores, advertisements, television, newspapers and the movies are a large part of our culture. This culture is a mixture of diverse elements, a big "do-it-yourself" arrangement of strange reminiscences, a "patchwork" of juxtaposed events which constitutes our identity. This is why the notion of "do-it-yourself" interests me so:

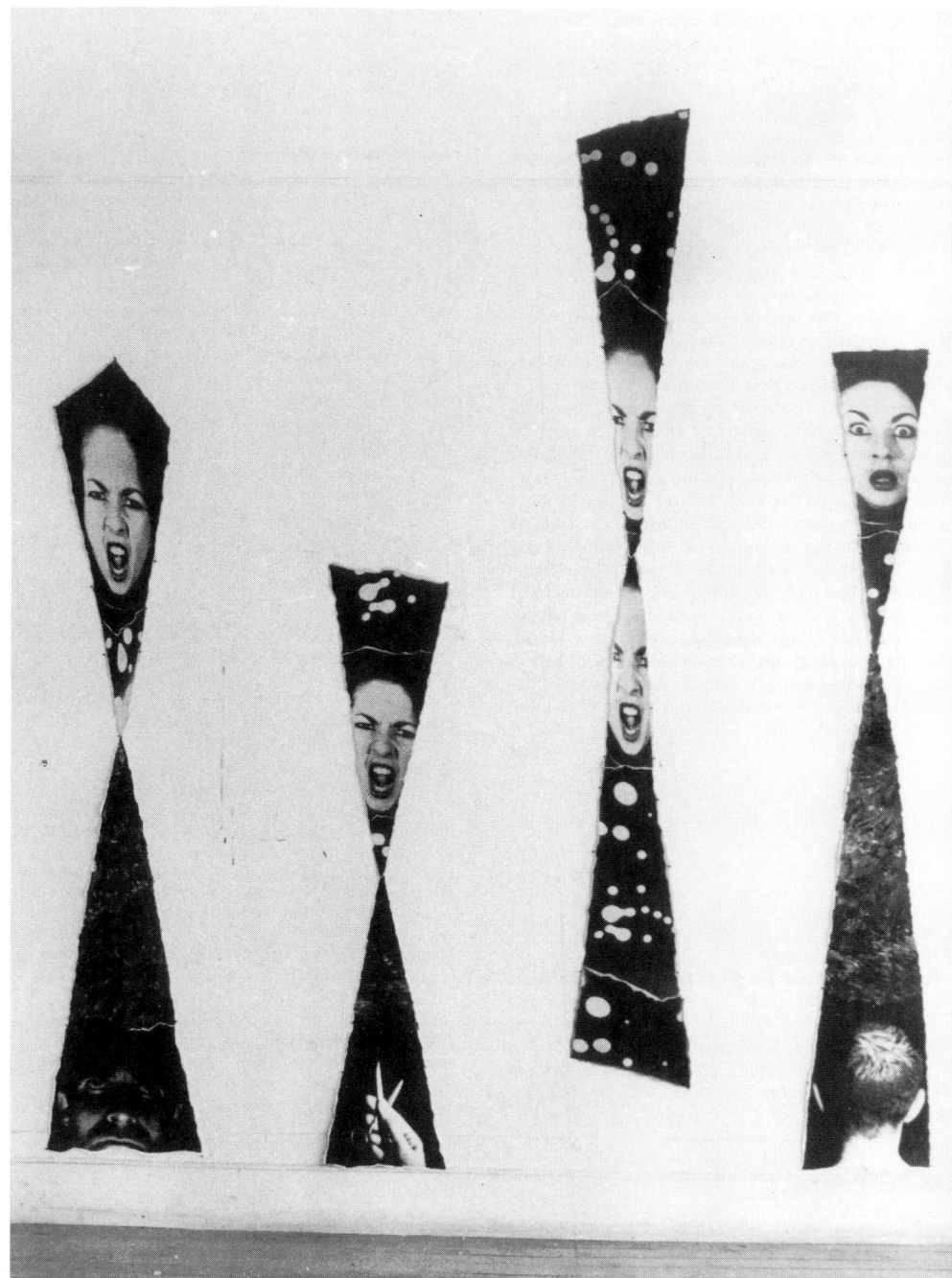

Annette Messager: *Les Variétés*, 1981

comes an additional part of the work, a work which in its essence is an analogy to the life process itself. In "La femme et l'operation" the same principle is applied to the drawing of her reproductive organs. Other works since the late 1970's are devoted to photographic series, such as "The Lover's Portraits" of 1977, "The Serials" of 1978 in which the behavioral cliches of man and woman in public and commercial media are the theme.

Works of this kind and those in the years to follow, such as "La femme-homme" of 1975, "Quel beau spectacle" of 1976, "Chimeres" of 1982/1983 and "Le piege Arachneen" of 1983 are pioneering for a new and authentic feminist art, which is not only a legitimate continuation of earlier tendencies in the art of women, but, in addition, exciting and often mysterious levels of reality are explored from an earlier unknown perspective. The fact that these endeavors manifest themselves in a newly created medium and in the programmatically crossing of existing borderlines between accepted media is significant for the necessity to challenge accepted cliches not only in art but also in life.

—Udo Kultermann

METZGER, Gustav.

Stateless. Born of Polish-Jewish parents, in Nuremberg, Germany, 10 April 1926; emigrated to Britain 1939. Studied woodwork, O.R.T.-O.S.E. Technical School, Leeds, 1941–42; part-time drawing studies, Cambridge School of Art, 1945; full-time art studies, Sir John Cass Institute, under David Bomberg at Borough Polytechnic, Anglo-French Art Centre, all in London, and at Antwerp Academy, Belgium, and Oxford School of Art, 1946–50; evening classes, under David Bomberg, Borough Polytechnic, London, 1950–53. Worked as furniture maker, joiner, farmer and gardener, 1942–44; as junk-dealer, King's Lynn, Norfolk 1953–58. Independent artist, London, since 1958, and in Frankfurt since 1980: first stone carvings, 1944; paintings, 1945–57; auto-destruction works from 1959. Secretary, Destruction in Art symposium, London, 1966; Editor, *PAGE,* bulletin of the Computer Arts Society, London, 1969–72; London Organizer, International Coalition for the Liquidation of Art, Tate Gallery Demonstration, London 1970; Vice-Chairman, Artists Union, London, 1972; Founder, with Cordula Frowein and Klaus Staeck, Kollektiv group and *Passiv-Explosiv* exhibition, Cologne, 1981. Address: c/o Cris Bittong, Oppenheimerlandstrasse 19, 6000 Frankfurt 70, West Germany.

"do-it-yourself" media, "do-it-yourself" assemblies of different cultures. These are our myths and our legends today.

—Annette Messager

The work of the French artist Annette Messager transcends borderlines between existing media and at the same time the borderlines between art and the social and political reality of women. Feminist argumentation is manifested on a level of artistic articulation, and both the intimate-private and the social-political are required components in this process. In terms of the making of her art the artist speaks of the unification of photography and painting, but this does not remain on the formalistic level of existing media, it is a basic crossing of borderlines of traditional taboo: and cliches of social behaviours.

In her earliest exhibitions of 1973 Annette Messager was directed toward a combined confrontation of painting and photography, corresponding to the theme of "Men-women and women-men." In these works photographs of couples are manipulated in regard to the domination within the individual couple so that as

a result masculine women and feminine men are documented in their accepted roles within the union.

In sequential works of 1972 and 1973 these tendencies toward a transcendence of media limitations are continued: in "Mes jalousies" of 1973 the artist manipulated photos of people in regard to aging; lines in the faces reveal the aging process specifically demonstrating the absurdities of eternal youth illusions in the media industry. Messager here successfully demonstrates the discrepancies between false ideals and a more accurate perception of reality.

In the works to follow the concentration on role behaviour and a conscious decision-making process is evident and the thematics are extended into areas such as commercials, comic strips and other forms of popular imagery, all re-evaluated under the insights of a radically feminist argumentation.

Since 1975 these endeavors more and more concentrate on the body of the artist which becomes her major medium. In "La femme et la mort" Messager outlines the skeleton of her body directly on her skin, and in "La femme et le dessin," using the same technique, she draws the anatomical details of her internal organs on her body. The process of the drawing be-

Individual Exhibitions (including lecture/demonstrations):

1959   *Paintings* 14 Monmouth Street, London W.C.2.
        Cardboards, 14 Monmouth Street, London W.C.2.
1960   *Paintings & Drawings 1945–60,* Temple Gallery, London
        Demonstration: Auto-Destructive Art, Temple Gallery, London
        Lecture/Demonstration, Heretics Society, Trinity College, Cambridge
1963   *Lecture/Demonstration,* Bartlett Society, School of Architecture, London University
1965   *Auto-Destructive Art,* Better Books, London (window-display)
        Lecture/Demonstration: Liquid Crystals, Society of Arts, Cambridge University
1966   *Liquid Crystals in Art,* Lamda Theatre Club, London
        Lecture/Demonstration, Ravensbourne College of Art, Kent
1968   *Extremes Touch,* University College, Swansea, Wales

1971 *Lecture/Demonstration*, National Film Theatre, London

1972 *Unrealizable Disintegrative Architecture*, Architectural Association, London

Executive Profile, Institute of Contemporary Arts, London

1981 *Faschismus Deutschland: Darstellung Analyse*, University of Berne

Selected Group Exhibitions:

1953 *Borough Bottega*, Berkeley Gallery, London

1969 *Event 1: Computer Arts Society*, Royal College of Art, London

1970 *Tendencije 4*, Galeria Suvremene Umjetnosti, Zagreb

1971 *Art Spectrum*, Alexandra Palace, London

1972 *3 Life Situations*, Gallery House, London

1974 *Art into Society/Society into Art*, Institute of Contemporary Arts, London

1977 *Towards Another Picture*, Midland Group Gallery, Nottingham

1981 *Vor dem Abbruch*, Kunstmuseum, Berne

Passiv-Explosiv, Hahnentorburg, Cologne, West Germany

Collections:

Archiv Hanns Söhm, Staatsgalerie, Stuttgart; Tate Gallery archive, London.

Publications:

By METZGER: books and pamphlets—*Auto-destructive art* manifesto 1, London 1959; *Auto-destructive art*, manifesto 2, London 1960; *Auto-destructive art, Machine art, Auto-creative art*, London 1961; *3 Manifestos*, London 1961; *Manifesto World*, London 1962; *Centre for Advanced Creative Studies*, with Marcello Salvadori, London 1963; *On Random Activity in Material/Transforming Works of Art*, London 1964; *Auto-Destructive Art*, London 1965; *DIAS Information*, 6 broadsheets, London 1967–78; *Passiv-Explosiv*, exhibition broadsheet, with Cordula Frowein and Klaus Staeck, Cologne 1981; articles—"3 Manifestos" in *De-collage* (Cologne), no. 6, 1967; "Machine Art, Auto-Creative Art, Auto-Destructive Art" in *Ark* (London), no. 32, 1962; "An Overwhelming Need for Shelter" in *Peace News* (London), 2 September 1966; "Automata in History," parts 1 and 2, in *Studio International* (London), March and October 1969; "Zagreb Manifesto," with Jonathan Benthall and Gordon Hyde, in *Studio International* (London), June 1969; "Kinetics" in *Arts and Artists* (London), September 1970; "Social Responsibility and the Computer Professional: The Rise of an Idea in America" in *PAGE* (London), October 1970; "A Critical Look at the Artist Placement Group" in *Studio International* (London), January 1972; "Art in Germany under National Socialism" in *Studio International* (London), March/April 1976.

On METZGER: books—*Mud Pie: the CND Story* by Herb Greer, London 1964; *4 Essays on Kinetic Art* by Stephen Bann, Reg Gadney, Frank Popper and Phil Steadman, London 1966; *Bomb Culture* by Jeff Nuttall, London 1968; *Origins and Development of Kinetic Art* by Frank Popper, London 1968; *Artworks and Packages* by Harold Rosenberg, London 1969; *The New Painting* by Udo Kultermann, London 1969; *Computers in Everyday Life* by Laura Tatham, London 1970; *Experimental Painting* by Stephen Dann, London 1970; *The Computer in Art* by Jasia Reichardt, London 1971; *Science and Technology in Art Today* by Jonathan Benthall, London 1972; *Environments and Happenings* by Adrian Henri, London 1974; *Art-Action and Participation* by Frank Popper, London 1975; *Art of the 60's* by Hugh Adams, London 1978; *Rubbish Theory: The Creation and Destruction of Value* by Michael Thompson, Oxford 1979.

Gustav Metzger himself traces the auto-destructive art of which he is the founder back to roots in Dadaism, Russian revolutionary art, and the work of Moholy-Nagy. But his own practice of destruction in art is a reflection of his extreme political and social radicalism, of feelings of a world in crisis which have been with him ever since he arrived in Britain in 1939 as a refugee from the menace of Hitler, and which the atom bomb and environmental pollution have only served to strengthen. He is repelled by the threat of technology, arguing that it has built a "self-destroying society," which demands an auto-destructive art in response. With other pioneers like Tinguely he was one of the first to theorize about and to practise destruction in art around 1960. And he has been one of the influences behind the emphasis on art as action and process, radically questioning consumer society, with the consequent withering away of the consumable art object which has been a marked feature of recent avant-garde activity.

Metzger was a painter until 1957, though he had long been dissatisfied with painting, having told his

Gustav Metzger: *Passiv-Explosiv* exhibition, Cologne, 1981

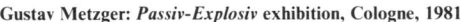

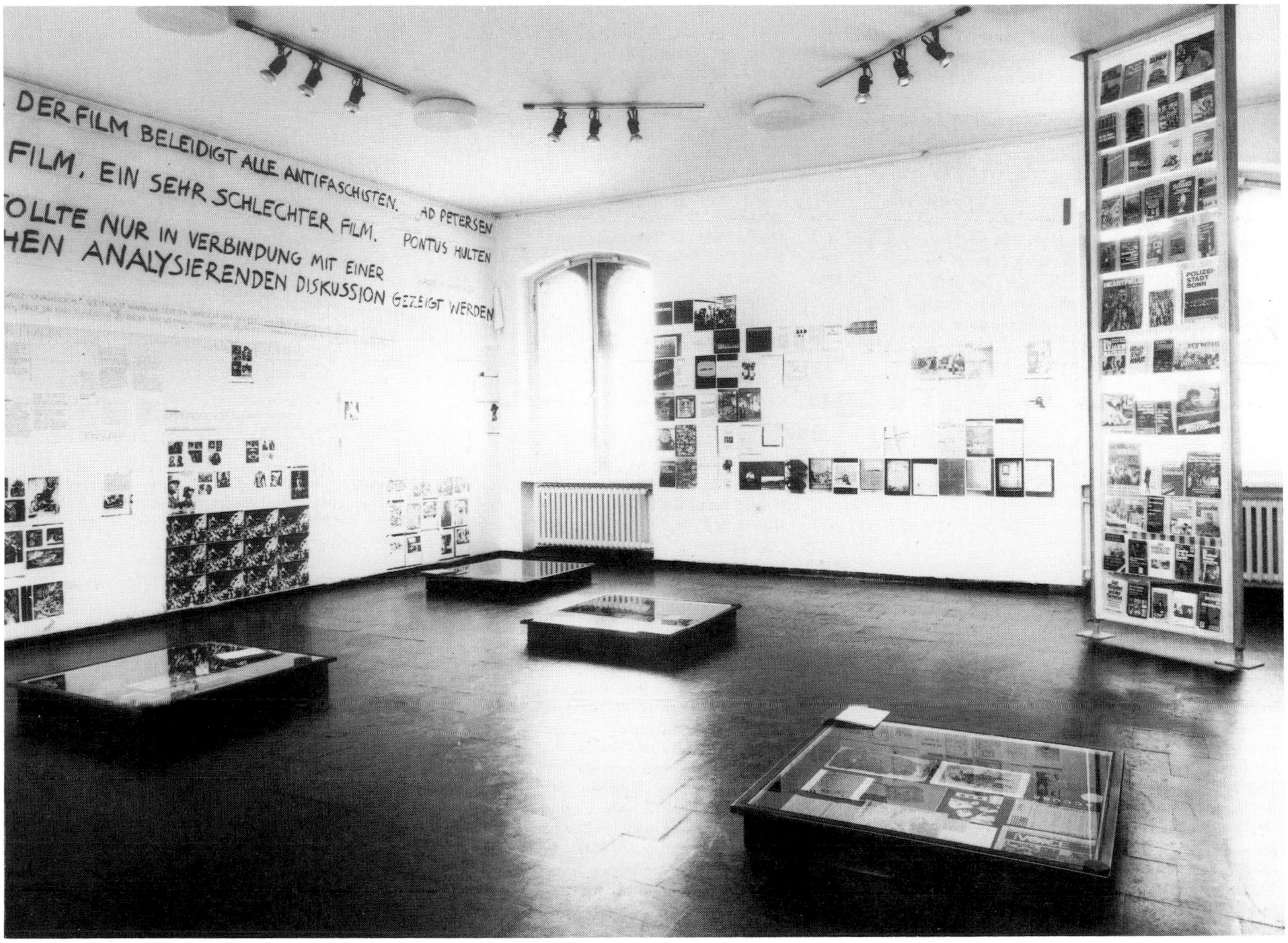

teacher Bomberg that he was looking for something "extremely fast and intense. About ten years later I saw Pollock's drip paintings. They came nearest to that conception of painting I had in 1946." Thinking this fast, intense vision couldn't be captured with paint on canvas, he tried painting and scraping on mild steel. In 1960 he at last found what he was looking for by painting with acid on sheets of nylon stretched in a frame. This has the opposite effect from building up paint on canvas, for the acid dissolves the nylon, so that the artist actually destroys the work in the process of creating it. Such auto-destructive art is material that is undergoing a transformation in time, so that Metzger converted the act of painting into a performance at which the audience participated. And he was also hoping to involve his audience in the "aesthetic revulsion" that he was thus trying to express for the self-destructive course of Western society.

The tension between an auto-creative art of change, growth and movement and auto-destructive decay as the natural forces run their course was even more dramatic when Metzger started demonstrating the colour changes of chemicals. Always eager to get closer to the transformation processes of nature, Metzger used liquid crystals between polaroid screens. By heating them and letting them cool, he was able to project a constantly changing image of translucent colour as the chemical broke down.

Yet Metzger is really interested less in such demonstrations than in what at first sight may seem a contradiction in terms, more "permanent" forms of auto-destructive art. In the lecture *Auto-Destructive Art* (1965) that he delivered to the Architectural Association he outlines several such monumental or sculptural projects. One for instance would be a construction of three slabs of mild steel, 18 feet high with a base about 24 feet by 18 feet which when exposed to the corrosion of an industrial atmosphere would decay over a period of about ten years. Much more complex and expensive is his idea for a sculpture of five walls, each about 30 feet high and 40 feet long, each wall composed of 10,000 uniform elements, square in one, rectangular or hexagonal in another. Each element is ejected under the control of a digital computer, so that again over a period of about 10 years the work would cease to exist.

Metzger is thus not averse to using technology in his own works. And he has indeed been an active and ardent supporter of the British Society for Social Responsibility in Science, dedicating himself to redirecting science and technology towards less destructive and militaristic ends. The final purpose of his auto-destructive art is to transform social attitudes through an aesthetic of revulsion. However, though like the performance artists who create happenings one of Metzger's aims has been to get away from the privileged situation of easel painting in galleries, his audiences have been small and elitist, and he has never been one of those artists eagerly courted by the press.

—Konstantin Bazarov

MICHAUX, Henri.
French. Born in Namur, Belgium, 24 May 1899; emigrated to France, 1924: naturalized, 1955. Educated at Putte-Grasheide, 1906–11; at Jesuit College, Brussels, 1911–17; studied medicine, Brussels, 1919; mainly self-educated in painting and drawing, from 1937. Married Louise Ferdiere in 1941 (died, 1948). Travelled as ship's stoker to Holland, United States, Argentina, Brazil and France, 1920–21. Worked as freelance writer and poet, Brussels, 1922–24; in Paris and on travels throughout Europe and Far East from 1924; painter and draughtsman, Paris, 1937 until his death in 1984; produced first mescaline-influenced paintings, Paris, 1956. Editor-in-Chief, *Hermes* quarterly review, Paris and Meudon, 1937–39. Recipient:

Prix Einaudi, Venice, 1960; Grand Prix National des Lettres, Paris, 1965 (refused). *Died* (in Paris) *17 October 1984.*

Individual Exhibitions:

1937	Librairie de La Pleiade, Paris
1938	Galerie Pierre, Paris
1942	Galerie de l'Abbaye (Galerie Zack), Paris
1944	Galerie Rive Gauche, Paris
1946	Galerie Rive Gauche, Paris
	Librairie-Galerie La Hune, Paris
1947	Galerie du Livre, Basle
1948	Galerie René Drouin, Paris
1949	Galerie René Drouin, Paris
1951	Galerie Rive Gauche, Paris
1952	Galerie du Dragon, Paris
1954	Galerie René Drouin, Paris
	Dussane Gallery, Seattle
1956	Librairie-Galerie La Hune, Paris
	Galerie René Drouin, Paris
	Ruth Moskin Gallery, New York
	Galleria d'Arte Selecta, Rome
1957	Palais des Beaux-Arts, Brussels
	Studio Paul Facchetti, Paris (with Jean Dubuffet and Wols)
	Gallery One, London
1958	Galleria dell'Ariete, Milan
1959	Galerie Daniel Cordier, Paris
	Aquarelle, Temperabilder, Federzeichnunge, Mescalinerzeichnungen, Galerie Daniel Cordier, Frankfurt
	Galerie Charles Lienhard, Zurich
	Galerie Andre Droules, Rheims
1960	French Pavilion, at the *Biennale,* Venice
	Galleri Blanche, Stockholm
1961	Cordier-Warren Gallery, New York
	Palais des Beaux-Arts, Brussels
1962	*Oeuvres Récentes,* Galerie Daniel Cordier, Paris
	Silkeborg Museum, Denmark
	Galleria Notizie, Turin
1963	Robert Fraser Gallery, London
	Cordier and Ekstrom Gallery, New York
	Libreria Einaudi, Rome
	Galleri De Buren, Stockholm
	Galerie Van de Loo, Munich
1964	*Gouachen/Tuschen,* Stedelijk Museum, Amsterdam (retrospective)
	Galerie Motte, Geneva (retrospective)
1965	Musée d'Art Moderne, Paris (retrospective)
1966	Galerie Le Point Cardinal, Paris (with Antonin Artaud and Max Ernst)
	Henri Michaux 1946–1966, Galerie Edwin Engelberts, Geneva
	Aquarelle, Frottagen und Zeichnungen von 1946–1966, Galerie Rudolf Zwirner, Cologne
1967	*Choix d'Oeuvres des Années 1946–1966,* Galerie Le Point Cardinal, Paris
	Palazzo Grassi, Venice
1968	Université de Rouen
	Galerie d'Art Moderne, Basle
	Galerie Van de Loo, Munich
	Galerie Le Point Cardinal, Paris (with Viseux and Louis Pons)
1969	Von der Heydt Museum, Wuppertal, West Germany
	Musée d'Art et d'Industrie, St. Etienne, France
	Galleri De Buren, Stockholm
1970	Galerie Maya, Brussels
	Galerie Melisa, Lausanne
	Galerie Artek, Helsinki
1971	Galerie Le Point Cardinal, Paris
	Henri Michaux: Retrospective, Palais des Beaux-Arts, Charleroi, Belgium
	Musée des Beaux-Arts, Ghent
1972	Palais des Beaux-Arts, Brussels
	Kestner-Gesellschaft, Hannover
1973	Galerie S. Mamede, Lisbon
1974	Galerie Erker, St. Gallen, Switzerland
	Oeuvres Nouvelles, Galerie Le Point Cardinal, Paris
1975	Lefebre Gallery, New York
	Galerie Melisa, Lausanne
	Galerie Jacques Davidson, Tours, France
	Galerie Loeb, Berne

	Galerie Gilles Gheerbrant, Montreal
1976	*Peintures,* Fondation Maeght, St. Paul de Vence, France (retrospective)
	Stadtmuseum, Graz, Austria (retrospective)
	Museum des 20, Jahrhunderts, Vienna (retrospective)
	Galerie Edwin Engelberts, Geneva
	Galerie Maya, Brussels
	Galerie Le Point Cardinal, Paris
1977	Institut Francais, Athens
	Galerie Van de Loo, Munich
	Galerie Thomas Borgmann, Cologne
1978	Musée d'Art Moderne, Paris (retrospective)
	Guggenheim Museum, New York (retrospective)
	Musée d'Art Contemporain, Montreal (retrospective)
	Galerie Le Point Cardinal, Paris
	Galerie Hubert Winter, Vienna
	Galerie Heike Curtze, Vienna
	Galerie Gilles Gheerbrant, Montreal
1979	Galerie Pudelko, Bonn
	Galerie A, Munich
1980	Galerie Renée Ziegler, Zurich
	Galerie Le Point Cardinal, Paris
1981	Kaneko Art Gallery, Tokyo
	Institut Francais, Athens
1982	Galleri Olsson, Stockholm
	Oeuvres Récentes 1980–1982, Galerie Le Point Cardinal, Paris
1983	Seibu Museum, Tokyo
	Kitakyushu Municipal Museum, Ohtsu, Japan
1984	Galerie Olsson, Stockholm
	Edward Thorp Gallery, New York
	Studio d'Arte, Turin
	Galerie Artek, Helsinki
1985	Abbaye de Beaulieu, France (retrospective)
	Galerie Le Point Cardinal, Paris
	Galerie Baudoin Lebon, Paris
	Galerie Reckermann, Cologne
	Galerie Limmer, Freiburg, West Germany
1986	Galerie Patrice Trigano, Basle
1987	Galerie Patrice Trigano, Paris
	Galerie Lelong, Zurich

Selected Group Exhibitions:

1962	*Presencias 1945–1962,* Galerie René Metras, Barcelona
	Summer Group Show, Robert Fraser Gallery, London
1963	*Corneille/Gaar/Gleghorn/Kodra/Michaux/Millares/Saura/Schneider,* Stone Gallery, Newcastle upon Tyne, England
1965	*Dubuffet/Matta/Michaux/Requichot,* Robert Fraser Gallery, London

Collections:

Musées Royaux des Beaux-Arts, Brussels; Centre Georges Pompidou, Paris; Silkeborg Museum, Denmark; Moderna Museet, Stockholm; Stedelijk Museum, Amsterdam; Museum des 20, Jahrhunderts, Vienna; Guggenheim Museum, New York.

Publications:

By MICHAUX: books—*Fable des Origines,* Paris 1923; *les Rêves et la Jambe,* Antwerp 1923; *Qui je fus,* Paris 1927; *Eduador,* paris 1929; *Mes Propriétés,* Paris 1929; *Un certain plume,* Paris 1930; *Un Barbare en Asie,* Paris 1933; *La Nuit remue,* Paris 1935; *Voyage en Grande Carabagne,* Paris 1936; *Entre centre et absence,* Paris 1936; *Sifflets dan le temple,* Paris, 1936; *Lointain interieur/Plume,* Paris 1938; *Peintures,* Paris 1939; *Au pays de la magie,* Paris 1941; *Arbres des Tropiques,* Paris 1941; *Exorcismes,* Paris 1943; *Tu vas être père,* Paris 1943; *Labyrinthes,* Paris 1944; *Le Lobe des monstres,* Paris 1944; *L'espace du dedans,* Paris 1944; *Epreuves, Exorcismes,* Paris 1945; *Liberté d'Action,* Paris 1945; *Apparitions,* Paris 1946; *Peintures et Dessins,* Paris 1946; *Ici, Podema,* Lausanne 1946; *Arriver à se réveiller,* Paris 1947; *Nous deux encore,* Paris 1948; *Ailleurs (Voyage en Grande Garabagne, Au pays de la magie, ici Podema),* Paris 1948; *Meidosems,* Paris 1948; *Poésie pour pouvoir*, with engravings, by M. Tapie, Paris 1949; *La vie dans les plis*, Paris 1949; *Lecture*, with lithographs by Zao-Wou-Ki, Paris 1950; *Passages*, Paris 1950; *Tranches de savoir*, with cover design by Max Ernst, Paris 1950; *Mouvements*, Paris 1951; *Veille*, Paris 1951; *Nouvelles de l'etranger*, Paris 1952; *Face aux Verrous*, Paris 1954; *Quatre cents hommes en croix*, Paris 1956; *Miserable miracle*, Paris 1956; *L'Infini turbulent*, Paris 1957; *Paix dans les brisements*, Paris 1959; *Vigies, sur cible*, with engravings by Matta, Paris 1959; *Connaissance par les gouffres*, Paris 1961; *Vents et Poussières*, Paris 1962; *Les grandes epreuves de l'esprit*, Paris 1966; *Parcours*, portfolio of etchings, with introduction by René Bertele, Paris 1967; *Vers la completude (Saisie et Dessaisies)*, Paris 1967; *Facons d'endormi, Facons d'eveille*, Paris 1969; *Poteaux d'angle*, Paris 1971; *Emergences—Resurgences*, Geneva 1972; *En revant à partir de peintures enigmatiques*, Paris 1972; *Moments*, Paris 1973; *Bras Casse*, Paris 1973; *Quand tombent les toits*, Paris 1973; *Par la voie des rhythmes*, Paris 1974; *Moriturus*, Paris 1974; *Ideogrammes en Chine*, Paris 1975; *Coups d'arret*, Paris 1975; *Les Ravages*, Paris 1976; *Choix de poèmes*, Paris 1976; *Jours de silence*, Paris 1978; *Saisir*, Paris 1979; *Une Voie pour l'insubordination*, Montpellier 1980; *Comme un ensablement*, Montpellier 1981; *Affrontements*, Montpellier 1981; *Chemins cherches, Chemins perdus, Transgressions*, Paris 1981; *Les Commencements*, Montpellier 1983; *Par surprise*, Montpellier 1983; film—*Images du monde visionnaire*, with Eric Duvivier, 1963.

On MICHAUX: books—*Decouvrons Henri Michaux* by Andre Gidé, Paris 1941; *Poètes d'Aujourd'hui* by René Bertele, Paris 1946, 1980; *Henry Michaux, poète de notre société* by Philippe de Coulon, Paris 1949; *Michaux* by Robert Brechon, Paris 1959; *Henri Michaux: Aquarelle, Temperabilder, Federzeichnunge, Mescalinerzeichnungen*, exhibition catalogue, with text by Max Bense, Frankfurt 1959; *Henri Michaux*, exhibition catalogue, with text by Max Bense, Zurich 1959; *Henri Michaux* by Alain Jouffroy, Paris 1961; *Henri Michaux: Oeuvres Récentes*, exhibition catalogue, with text by Genevieve Bonnefoi, Paris 1962; *Henri Michaux*, exhibition catalogue, with text by Carl Lonzi, Turin 1962; *Le Poète Henri Michaux et les Drogues Hallucinogenes* by De Ajuriaguerra and F. Jaeggi, Basle 1963; *Henri Michaux: Gouachen/Tuschen*, exhibition catalogue, with text by Genevieve Bonnefoi and René Bertele, Amsterdam 1964; *Henri Michaux ou une mesure de l'etre* by Raymond Bellour, Paris 1965; *Henri Michaux au Silkeborg Museum* by René Bertele, Silkeborg and Paris 1965; *Henri Michaux*, exhibition catalogue, with text by Jean Cassou, Paris 1965; *Henri Michaux 1946-1966*, exhibition catalogue, with text by Jean Starobinski and René Bertele, Geneva 1966; *Aquarelle, Frottagen und Zeichnungen von 1946-1966 von Henri Michaux*, exhibition catalogue, with text by Kurt Leonhard, Cologne 1966; *Michaux* by N. Murat, Paris 1967; *Henri Michaux: Choix d'Oeuvres des Années 1946-1966*, exhibition catalogue, with texts by Jean Grenier and René Bertele, Paris 1967; *Henri Michaux* by Kurt Leonhard, Stuttgart 1967; *Henri Michaux*, exhibition catalogue, with texts by Michael Durafour, Hermann Herberts and René Bertele, Wuppertal, West Germany 1969; *Henri Michaux: Retrospective*, exhibition catalogue, by Robert Rousseau and Jean Dypreau, Charleroi, Belgium 1971; *Henri Michaux*, exhibition catalogue, with texts by Wieland Schmied and others, Hannover 1972; *Michaux, peintre* by Wieland Schmied and Kurt Leonhard, St. Gallen, Switzerland 1973; *Henri Michaux: A Study of His Literary Work* by Malcolm Bowie, Oxford 1973; *Henri Michaux, esclave et demiurge* by M. Beguelen, Lausanne 1974; *Henri Michaux: Oeuvres Nouvelles*, exhibition catalogue, with text by Jean-Dominique Rey, Paris 1974; *Henri Michaux: peintures*, exhibition catalogue, with texts by Jacques Dupin, Genevieve Bonnefoi, Jean Starobinski and others, St. Paul de Vence, France 1976; *Athlone French Poets: Henri Michaux* by Peter Broome, London 1977; *Henri Michaux*, exhibition catalogue, with texts by Pontus Hulten, René Bertle, Octavio Paz and others, Paris 1978; *Henri Michaux: Oeuvres Récentes 1980-1982*, exhibition catalogue, with text by Yves Peyre, Paris 1982; *Henri Michaux*, exhibition catalogue with preface by Jean-Christophe Bailly, Paris 1987; film—*Henri Michaux ou l'espace du dedans* by Genevieve Bonnefoi and Jacques Veinat, 1965.

The Belgian poet Henri Michaux achieved a particular notoriety with the drawings he made under the influence of the drug mescalin. These had a distinct style close in appearance and manner to automatic writing. This freak activity which captured the public imagination was far more important than recalling it might suggest.

It began with the creation of high density. Paper or card would be thickly packed with rhythmic script. Michaux himself declared that he was *realising*

rhythms, some of them "electronically small." But he took his rhythmic systems (about which he insisted he had so much more to learn) into more free, less compact rivers of energetic cursive scrawls. When he spoke about the introduction of further colours and a better conception of how they can be most effective, he was modestly overlooking the great corpus of work. A recent exhibition at Le Point Cardinal did include works which tentatively employed earth colours, and these, like the prevailing blacks, were applied with water techniques, so that one was left wondering how safe the reliable black would be against the putative incursion of more and brighter colours in the future.

Unlike Kolar, also at one time a poet and also one who subsequently turned to the visual arts (first by making visual poems out of assemblages, but thereafter delving deep into the propensities he felt were offered him by collage itself), Michaux made his sortie into the visual arts by concentrating upon the potentialities of line and script. Of the two, Kolar is the most disciplined. Despite the wide range of variants which the printed assemblages and collages make possible for him, they cannot match the anarchic freedom of Michaux's fluid line.

—Sheldon Williams

MIKI, Tomio.

Japanese. Born in Tokyo in 1937. Educated at the Tokyo School of Hygiene Technology, Dental Technician's Diploma 1957. Independent artist known for exclusive preoccupation with depicting the human ear. Recipient: Prize, *6th Mainichi Contemporary Art Exhibition*, Tokyo 1964; Frontier Prize, *9th Mainichi Contemporary Art*, Tokyo 1967; Sculpture Prize, *V Jeune Biennale de Paris*, 1967; Rockefeller Foundation Grant, 1971. *Died in 1977.*

Individual Exhibitions:

1959   Kunugi Gallery, Tokyo
1961   Bunshun Gallery, Tokyo

1963   Naika Gallery, Tokyo
1965   Minami Gallery, Tokyo
1968   Minami Gallery, Tokyo
1972   Minami Gallery, Tokyo

Selected Group Exhibitions:

1957   *Yomiuri Independent*, Metropolitan Museum, Tokyo
            (annually until 1963)
1964   *Young 7*, Minami Gallery, Tokyo
            6th Mainichi Contemporary Art Exhibition, Tokyo
1965   *Tokyo Biennale*
            Contemporary Trends in Japanese Paintings and Sculptures, National Museum of Modern Art, Tokyo
            New Japanese Painting and Sculpture, Museum of Modern Art, New York
1966   *7th Mainichi Contemporary Art Exhibition*, Tokyo
            Modern Art of Japan, Galleria del Cavallino, Venice
1967   *Jeune Biennale de Paris*
1968   *Biennale*, Venice

Collections:

Louisiana Museum, Humlebaek, Denmark; Dentsu Building, Tokyo.

Publications:

On MIKI: *Japan: Tradition und Gegenwart*, exhibition catalogue, Dusseldorf 1974.

After graduating from a vocational school in Tokyo in 1957, Tomio Miki began to submit works to the Yomiuri Independent Exhibitions, which had been gathering artists' works rejected by the "official" art world. In 1962 he showed his first aluminum casting of an ear, which was the start of his "Ear" series, a theme he pursued relentlessly for years. "I didn't select the ear," he explained, "It selected me."

The amputated ears fuse in them the loneliness of noncommunication and the aspiration for oral communication. Miki's ears have included: an array of rows of life-size ears; an ear almost twice as tall as a man; a cannabalistic ear with an elongated lobe

Tomio Miki: *Ears* **installation at the Minami Gallery, Tokyo, 1972**

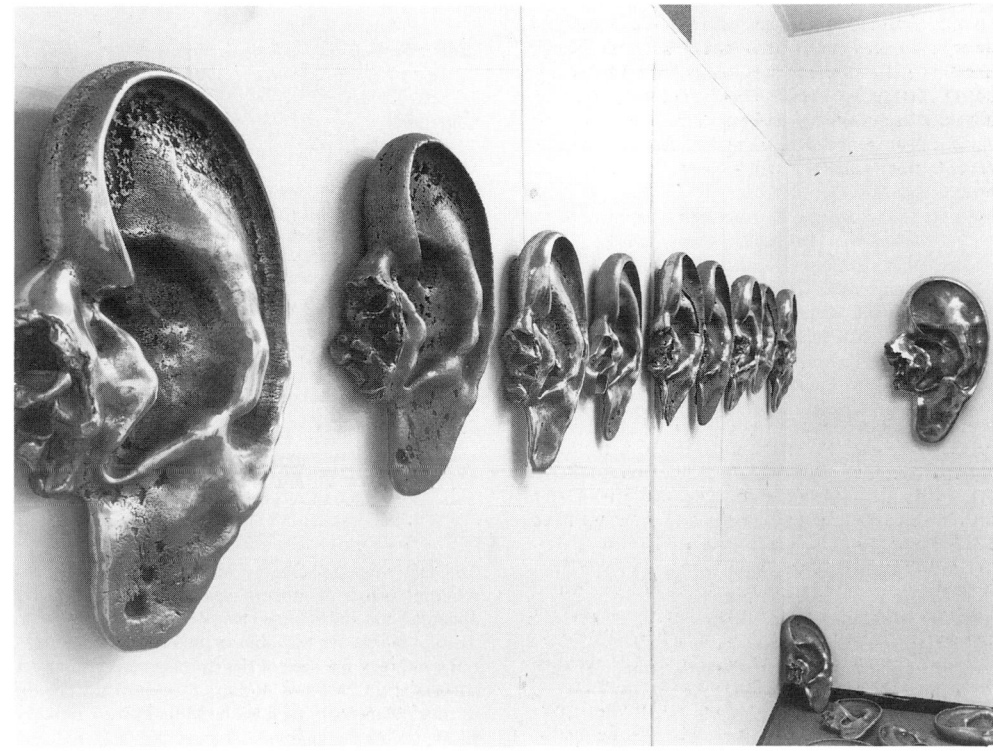

pierced by a spoon; and ears illuminated with red and blue neon lights. And there have been ears as in a great complex, curved mirrors, with cracks and placed in a box. These variations of all kinds resist appearing to be objects which man has severed from the human body; they are predestined self-limitations of the artist.

In 1966 Miki made a huge abstract version by carrying the shape of the ear to extreme limits; he also cooperated with the art staff working on director Hiroshi Teshigahara's film *The Face of Another*. In 1968 he participated in the Venice *Biennale*. He made a monumental ear for the Plaza of the Seven Days at the *World's Fair* in Osaka in 1970. Shortly thereafter he was awarded a Rockefeller Foundation grant which enabled him to spend a year in the United States. He returned to Japan in December 1972 and again began to display his works in a comprehensive exhibition of his ear series.

After a six month trip to New York in 1976, he completed a series of large drawings executed, as it were, by an anonymous person. He made huge pieces of ear in rather complicated forms. His "twin" had been sketching various states of the work, and after Miki destroyed the completed ear, the twin produced a series of drawings depending on sketches and memory. Miki declared that all of these drawings constituted his "Ear Sculptures."

Miki died in 1977.

—Yoshiaki Tono

MILLARES, Manolo.

Spanish. Born in Tenerife, Canary Islands, 17 February 1926. Self-taught in art. Married Elvireta Escobio. Painter: started career as landscape artist; associated with Surrealist group, Tenerife, 1948; produced first abstract paintings, 1949; Co-founder, *Planos de Poesia* magazine; Editor, *Aqueros, Problemas de Arte Contemporanea* and *Plus* magazines; Founder-Member, El Paso group, Madrid, 1957. *Died* (in Madrid), *14 August 1972.*

Individual Exhibitions:

1945	Circulo Mercantil, Las Palmas, Canary Islands
1947	Gabineto Literario, Las Palmas, Canary Islands
1948	El Museo Canario, Las Palmas, Canary Islands
1949	Gabineto Literario, Las Palmas, Canary Islands
1950	La Laguna, Tenerife, Canary Islands
1951	Galeria Jardin, Barcelona
	El Museo Canario, Las Palmas, Canary Islands
	Clan, Madrid
1952	Galeria Jardin, Barcelona
1953	Circulo Artistico, Gerona, Spain
	Galeria Wiot, Las Palmas, Canary Islands
1954	Galeria Buchholz, Madrid
	Instituto de Estudios Hispanicos, Puerto de la Cruz, Tenerife, Canary Islands
1955	Sindicato de Inicitaive, Tarragona, Spain
	Instituto de Estudios Hispanicos, Puerto de la Cruz, Tenerife, Canary Islands
	Museo Ballester de Arte Contemporaneo, Tortosa, Spain
	Clan, Madrid
1957	Ateneo, Madrid
1960	Galerie Daniel Cordier, Frankfurt
	Pierre Matisse Gallery, New York
1961	Galerie Daniel Cordier, Paris
1962	Galeria Biosca, Madrid
	Galerie Aujourd'hui, Brussels
1963	Ateneo, Madrid
	Galleria Odyssia, Rome
1964	Circulo de la Amistad, Cordoba, Spain
	Museo dé Arte Moderno, Buenos Aires
	Galeria Grises, Bilbao, Spain
	Galeri Latina, Stockholm

1965	Galeri 54, Gothenburg, Sweden (with Pucciarelli and Molinier)
1966	Galeria René Metrás, Barcelona
	Galerie Buchholz, Munich
	Galeria Ivan Spence, Ibiza, Spain
1967	Galeria Juana Mordó, Madrid
	Galeria Sur, Santander, Spain
1968	Galeria La Pasarela, Seville
	Galerie Buchholz, Munich
1969	Galeria Latina, Palma de Mallorca
1970	Galeria Val i 30, Valencia
	Galeria Juana Mordó, Madrid
1971	Pierre Matisse Gallery, New York (with Antonio Saura)
	Galeria Goldeano, Zaragoza, Spain
	Galerie Messine, Paris
	Galerie Lauter, Mannheim
	Kunstverein, Wolfsburg, West Germany (with Amadeo Gabino and Manuel Rivera)
	Galeria Egam, Madrid
	Musée d'Art Moderne de la Ville, Paris
1972	Galeria Juan de Aizpura, Seville
	Galerie Herbert Meyer-Ellinger, Frankfurt (with Jean Dubuffet)
1973	Galeria Aritza, Bilbao, Spain
	Galeria Tassili, Oviedo, Spain
	Casa de Colon, Las Palmas, Canary Islands
	Sala Lonca, Tenerife, Canary Islands
	Galeria René Metrás, Barcelona
	Galeria Juana Mordó, Madrid
	Galeria 42, Barcelona
1974	Galeria René Metrás, Barcelona
	Centro de Arte M 11, Seville
	Galeria Eduine, Madrid
	Galeria Val i 30, Valencia
	Homage to Manolo Millares: His Last Paintings 1969-1971, Pierre Matisse Gallery, New York
1975	Galeria Vegueta, Las Palmas, Canary Islands
1976	Galeria Trece, Barcelona

Selected Group Exhibitions:

1953	*Semana Internacional*, Santander, Spain
1956	*Biennale*, Venice
1959	*European Art Today*, Minneapolis Institute of Art
1960	*New Spanish Painting and Sculpture*, Museum of Modern Art, New York
1961	*Carnegie International*, Carnegie Institute, Pittsburgh
1965	*Contemporary Spanish Artists*, Contemporary Art Museum, Houston
1968	*Spanische Kunst Heute*, Akademie der Bildenden Künste, Berlin
1970	*Biennale International de Menton*, France

Collections:

Museo Casa de Colon, Las Palmas, Canary Islands; Museo Español de Arte Contemporaneo, Madrid; Tate Gallery, London; Galleria Nazionale d'Arte Moderna, Rome; Israel Museum, Jerusalem; Museu de Arte Moderna, Rio de Janeiro; Museum of Modern Art, New York; Minneapolis Institute of Art; Museum of Fine Arts, Houston.

Publications:

On MILLARES: books—*Millares* by Vicente Aquilera Cerni, Madrid 1957; *Millares* by José Ayllon, Madrid 1962; *Millares* by José Maria Moreno Galvan, Barcelona 1970; *Manolo Millares* by Carlos Areán, Madrid 1972; *Homage to Manolo Millares: His Last Paintings 1969-1971*, exhibition catalogue, by José Augusta Franca, New York 1974.

The late Manolo Millares was one of the most astounding artists of modern Spain. Without using the apparent and indifferent chance effects employed by Antoni Tapies, he was able in his mixed-media creations to break the area of the canvas and refashion its surface with a kind of organized openwork webbing of rope. Many such pictures by Millares were fiercely painted with the anarchist colours of black, red and white, but whether this could have been a political allusion, at this time (over a decade after his death) it would be difficult to confirm. What is not an unanswerable question is how much his roped imagery related to the social conditions in which he lived in Spain. At best, this might have been described as ultramontane.

The wounds in his canvases are gashes, not slashes (like those of Fontana). The ropes are symbols of bondage, natural or imposed. The careless expertise of the way in which the paint has been added, whilst it has none of the "Act-of-God" immediacy to be found in Tapies' work, also keeps well away from the kind of control exercised by Saura.

Moreno Galvan, the Spanish critic (himself something of a rebel, and twice apprehended by the police for undiplomatic lectures he gave on the subject of the work of Picasso) asserts that "men were always not only the object, but also the subject of his pictures. The others, the puppets, the red-painted rags, the rents, are in him like a sign of the perishable, the passing of life . . . and of time . . . . "

With Galvan's emphasis upon the human element in this artist's work it is not always easy to agree. In so many cases, the mere redolence of the image is so passionate in outcry that it might be the shriek of any creature, tethered and inflicted, with pain. Perhaps the presence of man was made more apparent in the series of "Antropofaunas" he began painting in 1969. To the black, red and white were added other colours, albeit of muted dramatic impact. The title given to these pictures is exact and descriptive. They portray the tangle of man and beast.

—Sheldon Williams

MILOW, Keith (Arnold).

British. Born in London, 29 December 1945. Educated in Baldock, Hertfordshire primary schools; studied at Camberwell School of Art, London, 1962-67; Royal College of Art, London, 1967-68. Painter: now lives and works in New York; travelled to Morocco, 1965, Rome, 1966, and Amsterdam, Paris and Kassel, 1968; worked on experimental projects for the Royal Court Theatre, London, 1968. Lecturer in Printmaking, Ealing School of Art, London, 1968-70; Artist-in-Residence, University of Leeds, 1970-72; Lecturer, Reading University, Berkshire, 1971. Lecturer, Royal College of Art, London, since 1974; Visiting Lecturer in Painting, Canterbury School of Art, Kent and Chelsea School of Art, London, since 1975. Recipient: Gregory Fellowship, University of Leeds, 1970; Harkness Fellowship, London, 1972; Calouste Gulbenkian Foundation Visual Arts Award, 1976; First Prize, *Tolly Cobbold Eastern Arts National Exhibition*, 1979. Agent: Nigel Greenwood Inc., London. Address: c/o Nigel Greenwood Inc., 4 New Burlington Street, London W1, England.

Individual Exhibitions:

1968	Axiom Gallery, London
1970	Nigel Greenwood Inc., London
1971	Arnolfini Gallery, Bristol
	Institute of Contemporary Arts, London
1972	King's College, Cambridge
	Leeds City Art Gallery
	Utrechtkring, Utrecht
	Nigel Greenwood Inc., London
1973	J. Duffy and Sons, New York
	Nigel Greenwood Inc., London
1974	Nigel Greenwood Inc., London
1975	Hester van Royen Gallery, London
	Arnolfini Gallery, Bristol
	Galerie Jacomo Santiveri, Paris
	Nigel Greenwood Inc., London

Selected Group Exhibitions:

Collections:

Arts Council of Great Britain, London; Tate Gallery, London; Victoria and Albert Museum, London; Contemporary Arts Society, London; Art Gallery of Ontario, Toronto; Museum of Modern Art, New York; Oberlin College, Ohio.

Publications:

By MILOW: articles—"Choice States," interview, with Anne Seymour, in *Studio International* (London), March 1972; statement in *Keith Milow: Drawings,* exhibition pamphlet, Liverpool 1977.

On MILOW: books—*6 at the Hayward,* exhibition catalogue, by Michael Compton, London 1969; *Keith Milow,* exhibition catalogue, by J. Grosfed. Utrecht, 1972; *The New Art,* exhibition catalogue, by Anne Seymour, London 1972; *From Henry Moore to Gilbert and George,* exhibition catalogue, by Anne Seymour, London 1973; *Art as Thought Process,* exhibition catalogue, by Michael Compton, London 1974; *Keith Milow,* exhibition catalogue, by William Feaver, Cambridge 1976; articles—"Keith Milow" by Marina Vaizey in the *Financial Times* (London), August 1972; "Keith Milow" by William Feaver in *Art International* (Lugano), September 1972; "Keith Milow" by William Feaver in the *Financial Times* (London), November 1974; "Keith Milow" by Donald Kuspit in *Artforum* (New York), January 1983.

Keith Milow is a painter whose pictures are by no means confined to the two dimensional surface of a canvas. Early works included printed images, usually of architecture, that were divided and rearranged or spaced out regularly across the surface. The breaking down and reconstruction of an image soon invaded the third dimension. Milow would take a drawing of work he revered, such as a Caro sculpture, and turn that drawing into a sculpture by partially slicing it into strips and folding each strip, imbued with resin, back so that its end would adhere to the previous strip. The overall silhouette was that of a hyperbole.

The strategy of taking an image, usually of a work of art but sometimes that of the real space around the work, and reconstructing or recycling it in one or more stages, has been a constant one in his art. It is related to that of several other British artists and may be considered a British tradition, including for example, Michael Craig Martin and Stephen Buckley. Its doyen is Richard Hamilton. However, the character of Milow's work, as of himself, is very different from that of any of these other artists. It is exemplified in his most recent and persistent series.

For more than five years he has taken as his starting point that most central image of the western culture,

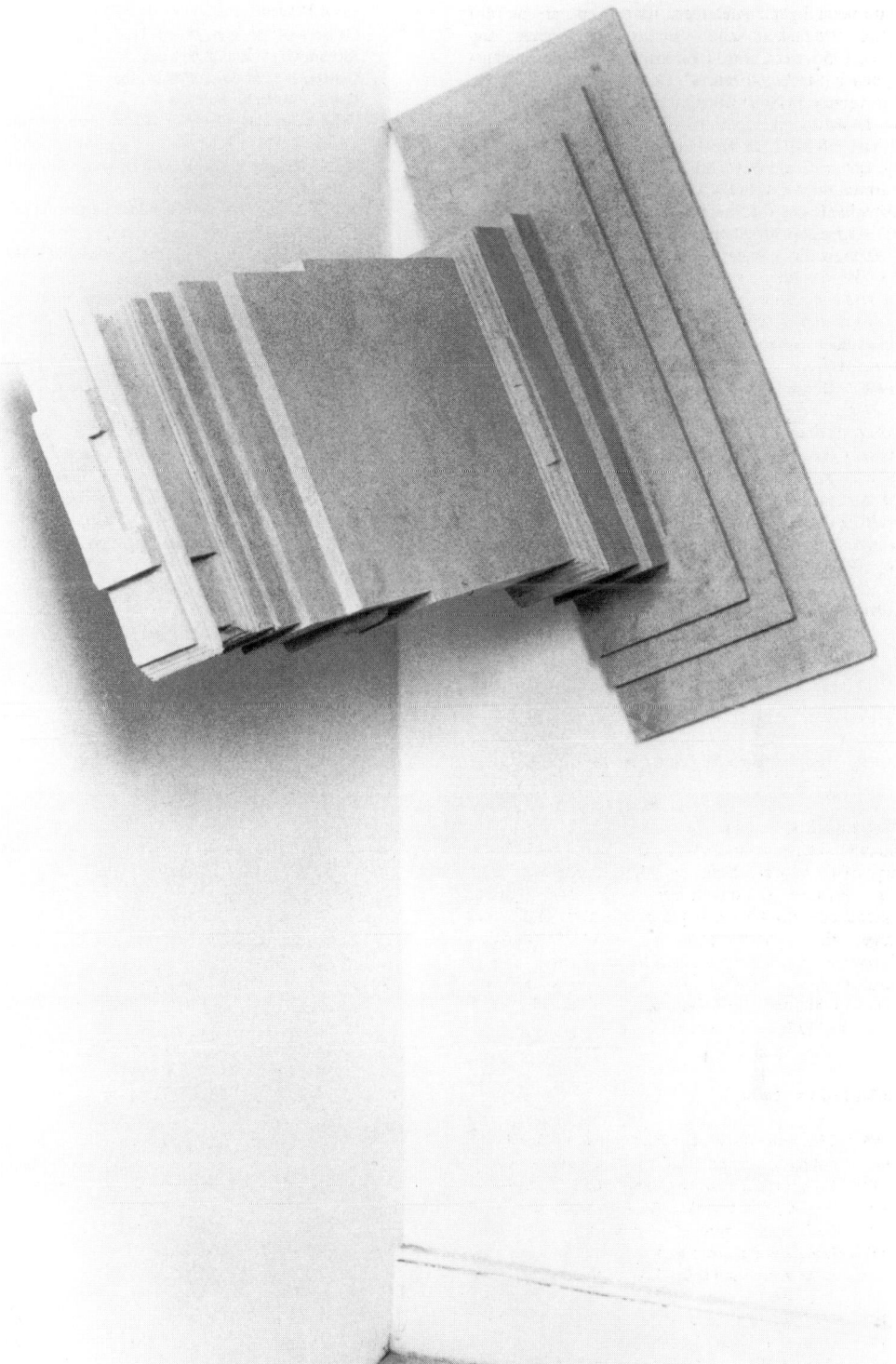

Keith Milow: *First Cenotaph* (detail), 1979

the Latin cross. The image remains always quite recognizable and is most often intact in outline. However, its surface is divided by orthogonal and diagonal shifts of plane. Surfaces are offset, staggered or rebated. This simple, powerful configuration has served as the basis of hundreds of variations not only of form but of surface. Milow employs wood, resin, paint, metal powders, plaster and cement. Very often the first impression, of great weight for example, may be subtly contradicted by the slightest indication that the object is hollow and somehow provisional. Though real, the object has the effect of being an illusion. The shadows cast by or on the piece are integrated with the arises that denote the changes of level and both appear pictorial.

Architecture is one of Milow's recurrent themes. It may appear in the form of synecdoche: the *beton brut* of one of his crosses recalling the chapel of Corbusier; of quotation: the photograph of Stirlings History Library in prints of the late 60's or in the real life relationship of the image in paintings to one's perception of them and of the space around them in the "Split Definitive" series of 1977.

—Michael Compton

MIRALDA, Antoni.

Spanish. Born in Tarrasa, Barcelona, 2 October 1942. Studied at School of Textile Engineers, Tarrasa, 1956–61; Centre International d'Etudes Pedagogiques, Sèvres, France, 1962–64. Served in the University Militia. Married the artist Dorothée Selz in 1966. Independent artist, Barcelona, 1959–62, in Paris, 1963–72, in New York and Paris, since 1972. Teacher, Children's Studio, Barcelona, 1959–61; fashion photographer, *Elle* magazine, Paris, 1964–68. Recipient: City of Barcelona bursary, to Paris, 1962–63; laureate, *5th Biennale de Paris,* 1969. Address: 262 West 73rd Street, New York, New York 10023, U.S.A.

Individual Exhibitions:

1964	Centre International d'Etudes Pedagogiques, Sèvres, France
	Galerie Makum, Amsterdam
1965	New Art Centre, London
	Peintures, Galarie Zunini, Paris
1966	Institute of Contemporary Arts, London
1967	Galerie Zunini, Paris
1969	Aronowitsch Gallery, Stockholm (with Dorothée Selz)
	Galerie Aspects, Brussels
1970	Galerie Claude Givaudan, Paris (with Dorothée Selz)
	Hanover Gallery, London

	Schloss Georghausen, Cologne (with Dorothée Selz)
1971	Eat-Art Galerie, Dusseldorf (with Dorothée Selz)
	Galleria del Naviglio, Milan
	Richard Gray Gallery, Chicago
	Galleria II Segnapassi, Pesaro, Italy
	Galleria Duemila, Bologna
	Galerie-Boutique Germain, Paris (with Dorothée Selz)
	Kurten Festival, Cologne (with Dorothée Selz and J. Xifra)
	Fête de L'Ecole Laique, Chatillon, Bagneux, France (with Dorothée Selz and J. Xifra)
	228 West Broadway, New York (with Antonio Muntadas)
1972	Museum of Contemporary Crafts, New York
	Illinois Center, Chicago
1973	Galerie Liliane Francois, Paris
	Henry Gallery, Seattle
	International Design Conference Center, Aspen, Colorado
	John Kaldor Showrooms, Sydney
	Art Gallery of New South Wales, Sydney
	Galeria Palaires, Palma de Mallorca, Spain
	Metropolitan Museum of Art, New York (with Antonio Muntadas)
	Fete des Enfants, Chatillon, Bagneux, France (with J. Xifra)
1974	Florida State University, Tallahassee (with Antonio Muntadas)
	Edgemont High School, New York (with Antonio Muntadas)

	9th Avenue International Festival, New York
1975	Galeria Pecanins, Mexico City
	Centre Georges Pompidou, Paris (with J. Xifra)
	Centre Culturel, Villeparisis, France
	Galeria Noire, Paris
1976	Galeria G, Barcelona
	Kunst Kontakte, Vienna
	Fine Arts Building, New York
1977	Contemporary Arts Museum, Houston
1978	International Cultureel Centrum, Antwerp

Selected Group Exhibition:

1965	*4th Biennale de Paris,* Musée d'Art Moderne de la Ville, Paris (and *6th Biennale,* 1969)
1968	*The Obsessive Image,* Institute of Contemporary Arts, London
1969	*Salon du Mai,* Musée d'Art Moderne, Paris
1971	*Collection de M. et Mme. B.,* Centre National d'Art Contemporain, Paris
1972	*Bread Show,* Deson-Zaks Gallery, Chicago
1973	*New York Avant-Garde Festival,* Grand Central Station, New York
1974	*Prospectiva 74,* Museu de Arte Contemporanea, Sao Paulo
1975	*Art Sociologique,* Centre d'Art et Communication, Liechtenstein
1976	*Such Werke,* Kunsthalle, Nuremberg
1977	*Trois Musées: Marseille/Lyon/Grenoble,* Centre Georges Pompidou, Paris

Antoni Miralda: *Moveable Feast, New York,* 1974

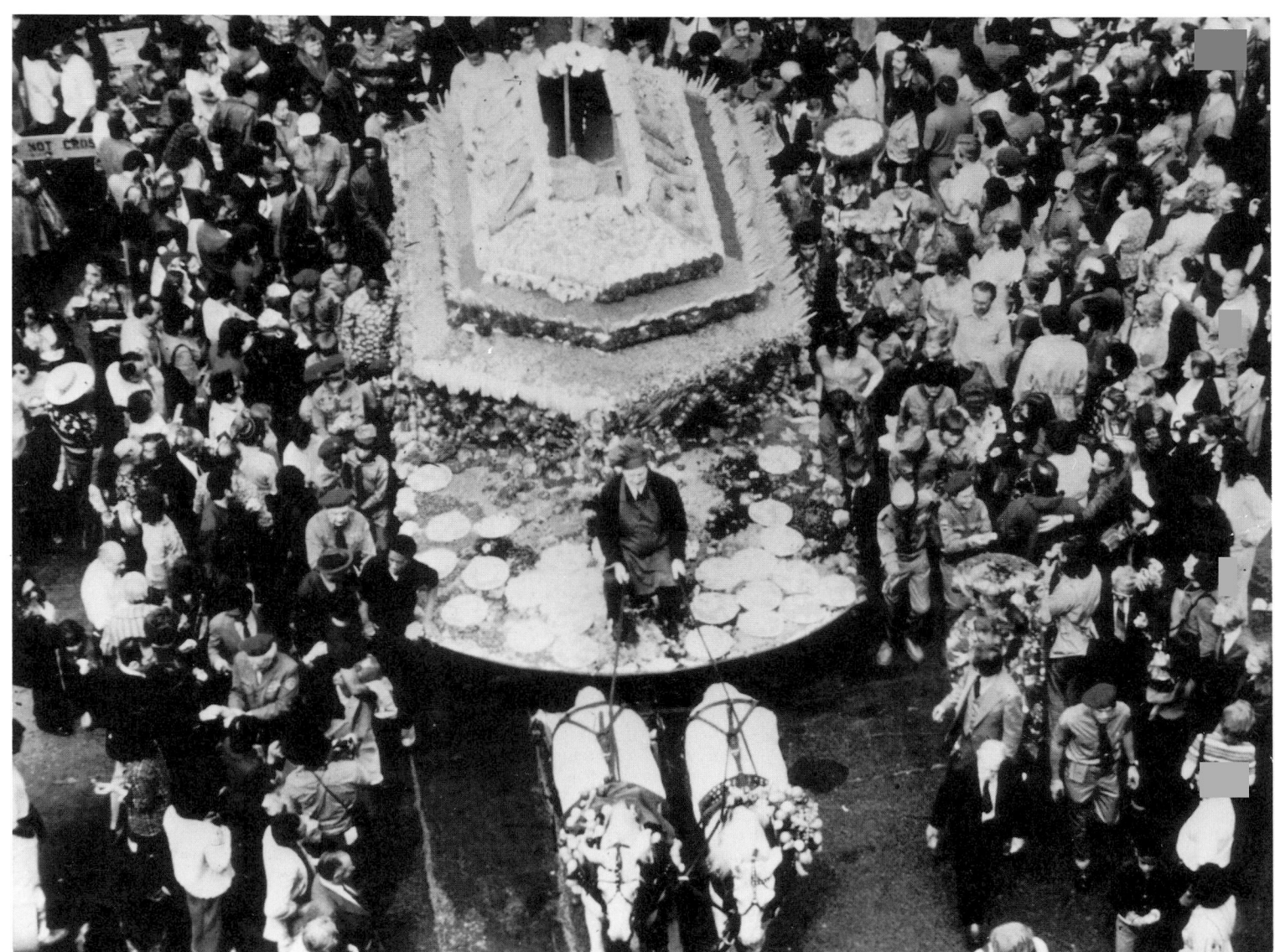

Collections

Moderna Museet, Stockholm; Centre Georges Pompidou, Paris; Musée Cantini, Marseilles; Art Gallery of New South Wales, Sydney.

Publications:

By MIRALDA: books—*Album*, privately printed 1973; *Memorials*, Paris 1975.

On MIRALDA: books—*Antoni Miralda: Peintures*, exhibition catalogue, with text by Jeanine Lipsi, Paris 1965; *Dictionnaire Abreges des Cendriers-Tombeaux* by Gilbert Lascault, Paris 1975; *Antoni Miralda*, exhibition catalogue, with text by Pierre Restany, Antwerp 1978; articles— "Soldats Saldats, Art Menjable" by A. Cirici Pellicer in *Serra d'Or* (Barcelona), September 1969; "Amerlioration de la Facade du Musée Galliera" by J. Claude de Feugas in *Opus International* (Paris), December 1969; "A. Miralda—Hanover Gallery" by Paul Overy in *The Financial Times* (London), December 1969; "War in a Spanish Garden" by Beate Sydhoff in *Art and Artists* (London), January 1970; "Events by Miralda and Selz" in *Studio International* (London), April 1971; "Antoni Miralda et l'Art Cannibale" by Pierre Restany in *Chroniques de l'Art Vivant* (Paris), May 1971; "Le Banquet et la Battaille" by Claude Bouyere, in *Opus International* (Paris), November 1973; "Galerie Notre—Miralda" by Otto Hahn in *L'Express* (Paris), April 1975.

Brilliantly juxtaposed colors—in his personal dress, habitat and edible art—are now virtually a trademark of Antoni Miralda. But absence of color played as large a part in his early work: the transformation of clichés of French culture into obsessional pseudo-monuments. Stark white, thousands of cheap toy plastic soldiers, guns and bayonets in hand, climb the drapery folds and poised wings of a full-size plaster cast of the Victory of Samothrace or imitate the bas-relief of an ornate Empire pedestal. Hundreds more of the three-inch figures line up along the medallion borders of *toile*-painted fabrics.

He has said that his choice of military image was a direct result of his (non-combative) army service in Spain; however it seems to appear here not as a political or pacifist statement, but as a catharsis of the regimented monotony of military life. In his privately printed book, *Album* (1973), Miralda reinvents his personal history to prove that he was born with the *idée fixe*. Tiny toy soldiers turn up in baby pictures; miscellaneous military group photos and doughboy routines from Busby Berkeley films are reprinted alongside his own real, somewhat campy, portraits in uniform.

In both the sculptures and the book the device of repetition metamorphoses one single pictorial and sculptural element into highly decorative patterns and shapes—the specific figurative outline becomes evident only on close inspection. What appears at a distance to be a spherical sculpture, for example, reveals itself to be composed of multitudes of figures swarming over the convex surface; the book's ornamental borders break down into half-inch high silhouettes of the same military figures.

The repetitive motifs, the pedestals, the aura of traditional heroic statues reached its culmination in a series of models expressly meant to be monuments (for which no full-scale versions were ever built), but utilizing other small plastic toys such as trees and animals. Some of these date from as recently as 1975, but the transition from monuments (symbolic objects) to celebrations (symbolic events) had been going on since 1967.

In that year Miralda created his first food pieces, in collaboration with Dorothée Selz. Playing in the associations of food with ritual and ceremony, he fashioned ornate celebratory cake sculptures, the most spectacular of which was "L'anniversaire de l'amour" (1969), exhibited at the *Salon de Mai* at the Musée D'Art Moderne in Paris. Tiers of cakes, each representing a particular environment, were delineated in detail with doll-house furniture and frosting decor. Among others were a music room cake, a bathroom cake, a zoo cake and a landscape cake.

1969 also marked his first extension of food-object into food-event with "Memorial," a ceremonial feast in purple and black, to commemorate the French "Day of Death!" Later pieces (often in collaboration with Selz and/or other Paris-based artists) include "Diner en quatre couleurs" (1970) for 400 costumed participants and food in red, blue, yellow and green, and "La fête en blanc" (1970) for 300 guests and food in white. In each work the formal ceremonial (sometimes processional) use of costumed celebrants, heightened by the psychological implications of color, reinforced the link between ritual and food, whether somber or festive.

For the edible art accompanying each of these events, Miralda perfected a system of achieving colors in dyed food as brilliant as any paint used by Matisse. Normally pale foodstuffs, such as bread, rice and pasta, are transformed into an incredible rainbow—rolls in bright primaries, french loaves in swirls of magenta, yellow and aquamarine (the breads have their color baked in), steaming bowls of grain arranged in spectrum order. White wine takes on sparkling transparent hues that match the meal. Where called for, natural colors are manipulated, such as for the all-white feasts or the "Edible Landscape" (1972) with its foundation of chocolate mountains.

In 1974 a "Moveable Feast" was commissioned by the City of New York as the grand finale to a two-day *International Food Festival* held on the streets of the Ninth Avenue market area. Merchants from up and down this mile-long gourmet paradise donated materials for a float drawn by two horses. Among the symmetrical patterns of multi-colored foods, dye-saturated rice formed the flags of all 20 countries represented by the festival. As the float proceeded down the avenue, wending its way through thousands of festival-goers and punctuated by the enthusiastic speeches of city officials, Miralda's work took on a particularly joyous relevance, a paean to food itself—his ultimate festive celebration.

—Barbara Moore

MIRÓ, Joan.

Spanish. Born in Barcelona, 20 April 1893. Educated in Barcelona primary schools; attended evening classes, with Senor Civil, Barcelona, 1900; studied at the Escuela Oficial de Bellas Artes de la Lonja, under Modesto Urgell and José Pasco, Barcelona, 1907, briefly at the Commercial School, Barcelona, 1907, and at Francesco Gali's Escuela d'Arte, Barcelona, 1912–15; attended life nude drawing classes, Grand Chaumière, Paris, 1937. Married Pilar Joncosa in 1929; daughter: Dolores. Painter and sculptor: associated with the Saint Lluch circle, Barcelona, 1913; shared studio with E. C. Ricart, Barcelona, 1915; Member, Agrupacio Courbet, Barcelona, 1918; visited Paris, 1919, and settled there in 1920; produced poster for *L'Instant* periodical, Paris, 1920; stayed summers in Montroig, 1919–33; associated with Surrealists, Paris, 1924; designed sets for Diaghilev's *Romeo and Juliet* ballet, with Max Ernst, 1926; executed first "papiers colles," 1928; designed sets, costumes, curtains and toys for *Jeux d'Enfants* ballet, choreographed by Massine, for Ballet Russe de Monte Carlo, 1932; returned to Barcelona, 1932–36; lived again in Paris, 1936–40; designed poster for Aidez l'Espagne, for the Spanish Loyalists, Paris, 1937; stayed summer in Varengeville, Normandie, with the architect Paul Nelson, 1938; lived in Paris and Barcelona, 1940–50; settled in Barcelona, 1956; built studio, designed by Josep Lluis Sert, Palma de Majorca, 1956. Recipient: Grand Prix for Graphics, *Biennale*, Venice, 1954; Guggenheim International Award, 1958; Painting Prize, *Pittsburgh Interna-* tional, 1967. Honorary doctorate: Harvard University, Cambridge, Massachusetts, 1968. *Died* (in Palma de Majorca) *25 December 1983*.

Inidividual Exhibitions:

1918	Galerie Dalmau, Barcelona
1921	Galerie La Licorne, Paris
1925	Galerie Pierre, Paris
1928	Galerie Georges Bernheim, Paris
1929	Galerie Le Centaur, Brussels
1930	Curt Valentin Gallery, New York
	Galerie Pierre, Paris (with Alberto Giacometti and Hans Arp)
1931	Arts Club of Chicago
	Galerie Pierre, Paris
1932	Pierre Matisse Gallery, New York
	Galerie Pierre Colle, Paris
1933	Pierre Matisse Gallery, New York
	Mayor Gallery, London
	Galerie Pierre, Paris
	Galerie Georges Bernheim, Paris
1934	Galerie Percier, Paris (with Julio Gonzalez and Pablo Picasso)
	Galerie Cahiers d'Art, Paris
1935	Pierre Matisse Gallery, New York
1936	Pierre Matisse Gallery, New York
1937	Zwemmer Gallery, London
1938	Mayor Gallery, London
	Pierre Matisse Gallery, New York
1940	Pierre Matisse Gallery, New York
	Museum of Modern Art, New York
1945	Pierre Matisse Gallery, New York
1947	Pierre Matisse Gallery, New York
1948	Pierre Matisse Gallery, New York
	Galerie Maeght, Paris
	Museum of Art, San Francisco (with Pablo Picasso and Juan Gris; travelled to the Portland Art Museum, Oregon)
1949	Pierre Matisse Gallery, New York
	Galerie Blanche, Stockholm
	Kunsthalle, Berne
	Kunsthalle, Basle
1951	Pierre Matisse Gallery, New York
1952	Moderne Galerie Otto Stangl, Munich (with Alexander Calder)
1953	Galerie Maeght, Paris
	Pierre Matisse Gallery, New York
1954	Kaiser Wilhelm Museum, Krefeld, West Germany
1956	Pierre Matisse Gallery, New York
	Galerie Maeght, Paris
	Palais des Beaux-Arts, Brussels (travelled to the Stedelijk Museum, Amsterdam, and the Kunsthalle, Basle, 1956–57)
1958	Pierre Matisse Gallery, New York
1959	Museum of Modern Art, New York
1961	Musée de l'Athenée, Geneva
	Galerie Maeght, Paris
1962	Musée National d'Art Moderne, Paris
	National Museum of Western Art, Tokyo
1963	Galerie Maeght, Paris
	Galleria del Naviglio, Milan
1964	Tate Gallery, London
	Kunsthaus, Zurich
1966	Philadelphia Museum of Art
	Museum of Western Art, Tokyo (travelled to the Museum of Modern Art, Kyoto)
1968	Fondation Maeght, St. Paul-de-Vence, France (travelled to the Ancien Hospital de la Santa Cruz, Barcelona)
1969	Haus der Kunst, Munich
1970	Galleria Arte Borgogna, Milan
1971	Galerie Hachette, London
	Casino Municipal, Knokke-le-Zoute, Belgium
	Walker Art Center, Minneapolis (travelled to Cleveland Museum of Art, and the Art Institute of Chicago)
1972	Hayward Gallery, London
	Kunsthalle, Zurich
	Acquavella Galleries, New York
	Guggenheim Museum, New York
	Pierre Matisse Gallery, New York
	Sala Gaspar, Barcelona

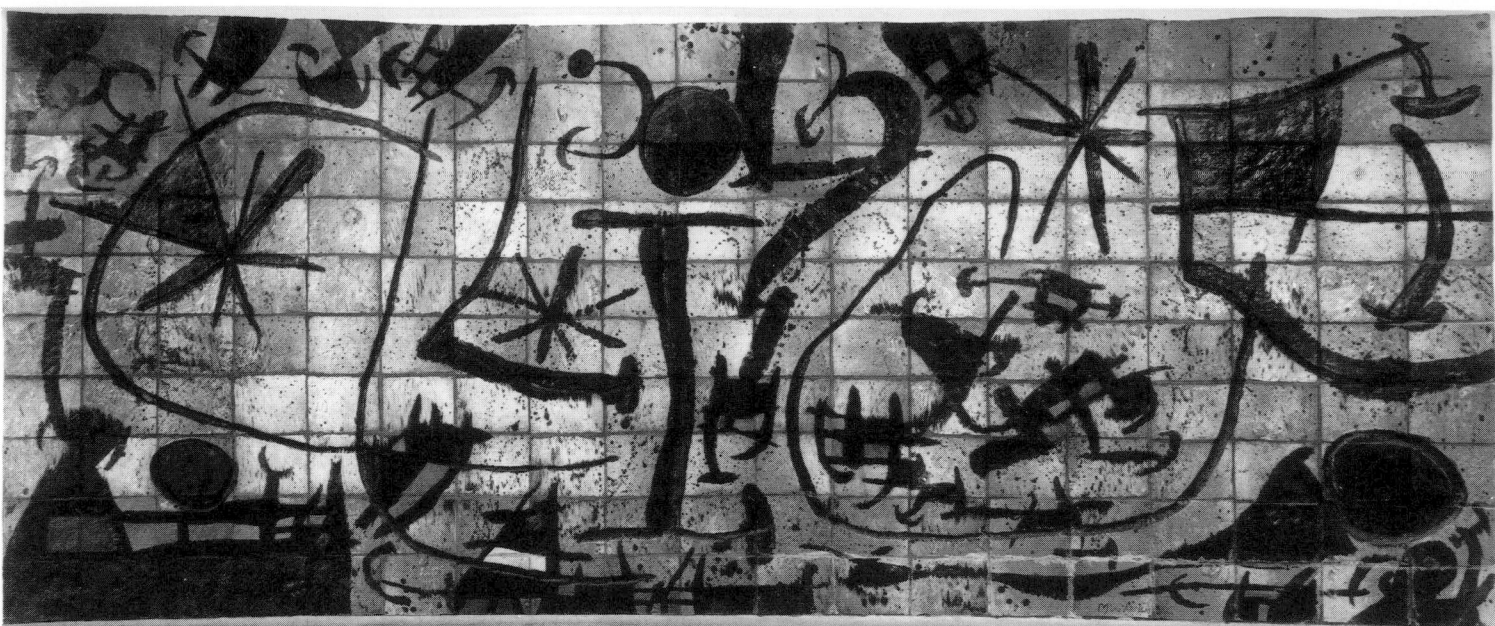

Joan Miró: *Alicia,* **1967** Courtesy Guggenheim Museum, New York

Fuji TV Gallery, Tokyo (with Alexander Calder; travelled to the Galerie Beyeler, Basle, 1973)

1973 Fondation Maeght, St. Paul-de-Vence, France
Museum of Modern Art, New York
Galerie Maeght, Paris

1974 Gallery 21, London
Sala Gaspar, Barcelona
Galerie Melki, Paris
Tate Gallery, London
Grand Palais, Paris
Musée d'Art Moderne de la Ville, Paris

1975 Pace Gallery, New York
Knoedler Gallery, New York
Mayor Gallery, London
Galeria Dau al Set, Barcelona
Galerie Maeght, Paris
Los Angeles County Museum of Art
Pierre Matisse Gallery, New York

1976 Fundacio Joan Mió, Barcelona
Pierre Matisse Gallery, New York

1978 Galerie Maeght, Barcelona
Museo Espanol de Arte Contemporanea, Madrid
Pierre Matisse Gallery, New York
Musée National d'Art Moderne, Paris

1979 Palazzo Pretoria, Prato, Italy
Orsanmichele, Florence
Seibu Museum of Art, Japan
Galerie Maeght, Zurich
Gallery Moos, Toronto
Galerie Patrick Cramer, Geneva

1980 *Selected Paintings,* Hirshhorn Museum and Sculpture Garden, Washington, D.C.
Galerie 2, Zurich
Pierre Matisse Gallery, New York

1981 Harcourts Gallery, San Francisco
Waddington Galleries, London

1982 Museum of Fine Arts, Houston
Scottish National Gallery of Modern Art, Edinburgh

1983 Galeria Joan Prats, Barcelona
Galerie Maeght, Paris
Guggenheim Museum, New York
Riverside Studios, Hammersmith, London (with photos by J. Gomis; travelled to Oxford)

1984 Israel Museum, Jerusalém
Pace Gallery, New York
Musee d'Art Moderne, Paris
Fuji Television Gallery, Tokyo
Center for Fine Arts, Miami, Florida

1985 Pierre Matisse Gallery, New York
Hayward Gallery, London
Galerie Maeght Lelong, Zurich

1986 Fundacio Joan Miro, Barcelona
Museum of Fine Arts, Montreal
Kunsthaus, Zurich

1987 American Federation of Arts, New York (toured the United States)

1988 Fabian Carlson Gallery, London

Selected Group Exhibitions:

1919 *Agrupacio Courbet,* Barcelona
1923 *Salon d'Automne,* Paris
1926 *International Exhibition of Modern Art,* Brooklyn Museum, New York
1936 *Fantastic Art: Dada and Surrealism,* Museum of Modern Art, New York
1964 *Documenta 3,* Kassel, West Germany
1968 *Dada, Surrealism and Their Heritage,* Museum of Modern Art, New York
1971 *The Non-Objective World 1924–1939,* Galerie Jean Chauvelin, Paris (travelled to Annely Juda Fine Art, London, and Galleria Milano, Milan)
1972 *Der Surrealismus 1922–1942,* Haus der Kunst, Munich (travelled to Musée des Arts Décoratifs, Paris)
1983 *Modern Art in the West,* Metropolitan Museum, Tokyo
1985 *Painterly Visions 1940–84,* Guggenheim Museum, New York

Collections:

Fundacio Joan Miro, Barcelona; Nationalgalerie, Berlin; Tate Gallery, London; Stedelijk Museum, Amsterdam; Kunsthaus, Zurich; Centre Georges Pompidou, Paris; Foundation Maeght, St. Paul-de-Vence, France; Guggenheim Museum, New York; Museum of Modern Art, New York; Los Angeles County Museum of Art.

Publications:

By MIRÓ: articles—"Propos" in *La Publicat* (Barcelona), 1928; "Je reve d'un Grand Atelier" in *XXe Siècle* (Paris), May 1938; "Le Carnaval d'Arlequin" in *Verve* (Paris), January/February 1939; "Jeux Poetiques" in *Cahiers d'Art* (Paris), vol. 10–21, 1946; "Ma Dernier Oeuvre est un Mur" in *Derriere le Miroir* (Paris), June/August 1958; "Je travaille comme un Jardinier" in *XXe Siècle* (Paris), February 1959; "Propos" in *Daedalus* (Cambridge, England), vol. 89, no. 1, 1960; "Propos recueillis par Rosamond Bernier" in *L'Oeil* (Paris), July/August 1961; "The Creative Spirit in Art and Science: An Interview with Bruno Friedman" in *Impact of Science on Society* (Paris), October/December 1969; "Joan Miro: Interview par Otto Hahn" in *Art Press* (Paris), June/August 1974; "Ceci es la Couleur de mes Reves" in *Entretiens avec Georges Raillard,* Paris 1977; illustrated books—*Il etait une Petit Pie* by Lise Hertz, Paris 1928; *Enfrances* by

Georges Hugnet, Paris 1933; *L'Antitete* by Tristan Tzara, Paris 1947.

On MIRÓ: books—*Joan Miro* by James Johnson Sweeney, New York 1941; *Le Surrealisme et la Peinture* by André Breton New York 1945; *Joan Miro* by Clement Greenberg, New York 1948; *Joan Miro: His Graphic Work* by Sam Hunter, New York 1958; *The Miro Atmosphere* by Joaquim Gomis and Joan Prats, New York 1959; *Joan Miro* by Walter Erben, Munich and London 1959; *Joan Miro* by James Thrall Soby, New York 1959; *Miro* by Jacques Lassaigne, Paris 1963; *Miro: Etude Biographique et Critique* by Jacques Lassaigne, Geneva 1963; *Miro* by Umbro Apollonio, London 1969; *Miro* by Mario Bucci, London 1970; *Miro* by Roland Penrose, London 1970; *Miro: L'Artiste et L'Oeuvre* by Michel Chilo, Paris 1971; *Miro: Magnetic Fields* by Rosalind Krauss and Margit Rowell, New York 1972; *Hommage à Joan Miro,* special edition of *XXe Siècle,* Paris 1972; *Joan Miro: Lithographs* by Michel Leiris, 3 vols. New York 1972–75, Paris 1977; *Miro in the Collection of the Museum of Modern Art,* exhibition catalogue, by William Rubin, New York 1973; *Joan Miro: Carnets Catalans,* 2 vols. by Gaeton Picon, Geneva 1976; *Miro: Selected Paintings,* exhibition catalogue, by Charles W. Millard and others, Washington, D.C., 1980; *Miro Lithographe IV, 1969–1972* by Nicolas and Elena Calas, Paris 1981; *Joan Miro,* exhibition catalogue with essays by Jacques Dupin, Barbara Rose and others, Zurich 1984; *The Captured Imagination: Drawings by Joan Miro,* exhibition catalogue with essay by Margit Rowell, New York 1987.

* * *

It is not easy to summarize in a few lines an *oeuvre* so complex, so rich in invention, as that of Joan Miró. Perhaps the best way of doing it, and certainly the most concise, will be to look for what are the "aesthetic constants" in his work that appear throughout the whole series of his paintings, his engravings and his sculpture.

I believe, then, that among the outstanding elements that may be singled out as most typical of those works are the following: (1) his continual pursuit of the abolition of the symmetrical element in composition, both in his paintings and in his sculptures, with the resulting tendency towards a markedly asymmetrical kind of composition; (2) the search for the "void," even in the confusion of figures and symbols characteristic of his work; (3) the distinct prevalence in his paintings and engravings of a timbric rather than a tonal colour; (4) the abolition of volumetric spatiality and search for a new spatiality different from those both of naturalistic and of surrealistic art; (5) the creation of an alphabet of special symbols; a genuine idiolectic vocabulary used in the creation of zoomorphic and anthropomorphic forms and of emblems that recur throughout his work; and (6) in his sculpture, the volumetric and plastic transfer of some of the constants that I have listed; in particular the construction of fantastic figures like those in his paintings and the use in some of his sculptures of "found objects," at a later time actually fused into the bronze.

Despite the highly convulsive variety of Miró's "inventions," these figures of his—it might be better to describe them as "form-figures"—are found in almost all his works and are the key to an important position: an ever-present marriage of figuration and abstraction. Almost more than any other artist in this century, Miró was able to free himself early from the traditional type of figurativeness; he was able to avail himself of the conquests of Cubism, Surrealism and Dadaism, to by-pass "volumetric" and naturalistic figuration and, while himself almost always "figurative," to take over the conquests and formal innovations of abstractism.

What, in fact, are the images that recur most often in his pictures and graphic work? Stars, suns, moons, creatures with a human or animal appearance, elements of sexual character—emblems suggesting the phallus and the vulva—symbols shaped like commas, asterisks.

To divide all this work into clearly separated periods involves a risk of becoming pedantic. None the less, it must be borne in mind that the Catalan artist's greatest students (notably Jacques Dupin) have suggested more than once a division into the following fundamental periods: Catalan Fauvism (1915–17), poetic realism (1918–19), ultimate realism (1920–23), dream pictures and composition of the void (1925–27), plastic concentration (1932–34), tragic realism (1937 38), constellations (1939 41), the invention of an "alphabet" (1942–46), followed, from the 1950s on, by the final stages of his activity, which remained constant and continually renewed.

—Gillo Dorfles

MITCHELL, Joan.

American. Born in Chicago, Illinois, 12 February 1926. Educated at Francis Parker School, Chicago, graduated 1942; Smith College, Northampton, Massachusetts, 1942–44; Art Institute of Chicago, 1944–49 (on travel fellowship in Europe, 1948–49), B.F.A. 1947, M.F.A. 1950; Columbia University, New York, 1950. Independent painter, since 1950; established studio at St. Mark's Place, New York, 1950, and attended meetings at The Club, frequenting Cedar Tavern (with Willem de Kooning, Philip Guston, Franz Kline and others); travelled to Paris, 1955, and established studio, 1959, working in the circle of Jean-Paul Riopelle, Kimber Smith and Shirley Jaffe. Recipient: Brandeis Creative Arts Award Medal, Waltham, Massachusetts, 1973. Honorary doctorate: Ohio Wesleyan University, Delaware, Ohio, 1971. Agent: Xavier Fourcade Inc., New York. Address: c/o Xavier Fourcade Inc., 36 East 75th Street, New York, New York 10021, U.S.A.

Individual Exhibitions:

1951	New Gallery, New York
1953	Stable Gallery, New York
1954	Stable Gallery, New York
1955	Stable Gallery, New York
1957	Stable Gallery, New York
1958	Stable Gallery, New York
1960	Galerie Neufville, Paris
	Galleria dell'Ariete, Milan
1961	Stable Gallery, New York
	B.C. Holland Gallery, Chicago
	Dwan Gallery, Los Angeles
	Southern Illinois University, Carbondale
1962	Massachusetts Institute of Technology, Cambridge
	Galerie Jacques Dubourg, paris
	Galerie Lawrence, Paris
	Galerie Klipstein und Kornfeld, Berne

1965	Stable Gallery, New York
1967	Galerie Jean Fournier, Paris
1968	Martha Jackson Gallery, New York
1969	Galerie Jean Fournier, Paris
1971	Galerie Jean Fournier, Paris
	Martha Jackson Gallery, New York
1972	*Fresh Air School: Sam Francis/Joan Mitchell/ Walasse Ting*, Carnegie Institute, Pittsburgh (toured the United States)
	Martha Jackson Gallery, New York
	Everson Museum, Syracuse, New York
1974	Whitney Museum, New York
	Arts Club of Chicago
1976	Galerie Jean Fournier, Paris
	Xavier Fourcade Inc., New York
1977	Xavier Fourcade Inc., New York
1978	Galerie Jean Fournier, Paris
	Ruth Schaffner Gallery, Los Angeles
	Webb and Parsons Gallery, Bedford Village, New York
1979	Paula Anglim Gallery, San Francisco
1980	Galerie Jean Fournier, Paris
	Xavier Fourcade Inc., New York
	Richard Hines Gallery, Seattle
1981	Gloria Luria Gallery, Florida
	Xavier Fourcade Inc., New York
	Janie C. Lee Gallery, Houston
1982	Musée d'Art Moderne de la Ville, Paris
1983	Xavier Fourcade Inc., New York
1984	Galerie Jean Fournier, Paris
1985	Xavier Fourcade Inc., New York
1986	Xavier Fourcade Inc., New York
	Keny and Johnson Gallery, Columbus, Ohio
1987	Galerie Jean Fournier, Paris

1988	Corcoran Gallery of Art, Washington, D.C. (travelled to San Francisco; Buffalo, New York; San Diego, California; Ithaca, New York, 1988–89)

Selected Group Exhibitions:

1959	*Documenta 2*, Kassel, West Germany
1961	*American Abstract Expressionists and Imagists*, Guggenheim Museum, New York
1962	*40 Artists Under 40*, Whitney Museum, New York (toured the United States)
1967	*Large American Paintings*, Jewish Museum, New York
1971	*Younger Abstract Expressionists of the 50's*, Museum of Modern Art, New York
1974	*5 American Painters: Recent Works*, Ruth Schaffner Gallery, Santa Barbara, California
1978	*American Painting of the 1970s*, Albright-Knox Art Gallery, Buffalo, New York
1980	*The Fifties: Painting in New York 1950–60*, Hirshhorn Museum, Washington, D.C.
1984	*Action the New Direction: Precision in New York 1955–60*, Newport Harbor Art Museum, Newport Beach, California (toured the United States)
1987	*Prints of Contemporary American Artists*, Mount Holyoke College, South Hadley, Massachusetts (travelled)

Collections:

Museum of Modern Art, New York; Guggenheim Museum, New York; Whitney Museum, New York; Rockefeller Insti-

Joan Mitchell: *A Few Days (After James Schuyler)*, 1985

tute, New York; Carnegie Institute, Pittsburgh; Corcoran Gallery, Washington, D.C.; Phillips Collection, Washington, D.C.; Walker Art Center, Minneapolis; Art Institute of Chicago; Musée d'Art Moderne, Paris.

Publications:

By MITCHELL: articles—"Reply to Irving H. Sandler" in *Artnews* (New York), September 1958; statement in *Nature in Abstraction,* exhibition catalogue, New York 1958; "Statement" in *Artnews* (New York), May 1967.

On MITCHELL: books—*40 Artists Under 40,* exhibition catalogue, New York 1962; *Fresh Air School: Sam Francis/Joan Mitchell/Walasse Ting,* exhibition catalogue, Pittsburgh 1972; *Joan Mitchell: My 5 Years in the Country,* with an introduction by James Harithas, Syracuse, New York 1972, introduction reprinted as "Weather Paint" in *Artnews* (New York), May 1972; *Joan Mitchell,* exhibition catalogue, by Marcia Tucker, New York 1974; *5 American Painters: Recent Works,* exhibition catalogue, Santa Barbara, California 1974; *Joan Mitchell: New Paintings,* exhibition catalogue, New York 1976; *Joan Mitchell* by Judith E. Bernstock, New York 1988; articles—"Mitchell Paints a Picture" by Irving Sandler in *Artnews* (New York), October 1957; "Joan Mitchell" by Irving H. Sandler in *School of New York: Some Younger Artists,* edited by B. H. Friedman, New York 1959; "An Expressionist in Paris" by John Ashbery in *Artnews* (New York), April 1965; "Joan Mitchell: To Obscurity and Back" by Peter Schjeldahl in the *New York Times,* April 1972; "Joan Mitchell's Envisionments" by Carter Ratcliff in *Art in America* (New York), July/August 1974; "Sensations of Landscape" by Thomas B. Hess in *New York Magazine,* 20 December 1976; "New York Letter: Joan Mitchell" by Carter Ratcliff in *Art International* (Lugano, Switzerland), January 1978; "On Winter's Traces" by John Ashbery in *New York Magazine,* 24 March 1980; "Joan Mitchell: Art and Life at Vetheuil" by Linda Nochlin in *House and Garden* (New York), November 1984; "Joan Mitchell" by John Russell in the *New York Times,* 25 April 1986.

Joan Mitchell has been true all along to abstract expressionism. Historically she is one of the so-called second generation painters belonging to that movement. Originally from the American Midwest, she has spent the greater part of her career working in Paris. I mention this fact because I think it is important. Perfectly aware of and friendly with many of the painters of the New York scene, she has nevertheless been able to "keep her distance" from much of the merely fashionable and trendy that infects so many New York artists (not that Paris doesn't produce its own dangers!). By absenting herself from the hot center, so to speak, of abstract expressionism, she has been able to develop in a steady and consistent way—to follow her own nose. Much the same could be said of Sam Francis who also spent considerable time in France.

A case could even be made for the larger view one often experiences living amid an older culture—and the clearer vision sometimes experienced in looking on from afar. In any event, the paintings that have resulted from Mitchell's independence are wonderfully fresh and individual while clearly within the abstract expressionist idiom. There is definitely a kind of Joan Mitchell painting.

Much of the time it has to do with her response to nature—to streams, ponds, rocks, trees, hills, etc.—to places, to landscapes. There is even something of Cezanne's passion of blues and greens although little of his geometry. Mitchell's paintings are gutsy, lavish, exhilarating works full of grace notes. They are both lyric and robust and "work" splendidly at every scale.

Unlike many artists of her generation, Mitchell has not opted for successive art movements, for Pop or Op or Minimalism or New Realism. At the same time her steadfastness is not merely a form of stubbornness or the result of being locked-in. Rather it is expressive of the nature of her talent and indicative of the quality of her art—which it would appear is mined from a deep and inexhaustible vein.

—Ralph Pomeroy

MOHR, Manfred.

German. Born in Pforzheim, 8 June 1938. Studied tenor saxophone and oboe, Pforzheim, 1955–59; studied art, Kunst-und Werkschule, Pforzheim, 1957–61; self-taught in computer science, from 1968. Married Estarose Wolfson in 1976. Independent artist, in Paris, 1963–81, and in New York since 1982. Recipient: Print Prize, 10th Graphics Biennale, Liubliana, 1973; Prize, World Print Competition, San Francisco, 1973. Agents: Galerie Teufel, Auf dem Rothenberg 13, 5000 Cologne 1, West Germany; Galerie Gilles Gheerbrant, 4060 St. Laurent, Suite 604, Montreal, Quebec H2W Y19, Canada; Galerie Weiller, 5 rue Git-le-Coeur, 75006 Paris, France. Address: 20 North Moore Street, New York, New York 10013, U.S.A.

Individual Exhibitions:

1968	Galerie Daniel Templon, Paris
1969	Galerie Annemarie Verna, Zurich
1971	ARC/Musée d'Art Moderne de la Ville, Paris
	Galerie Mangelgang, Groningen, Netherlands
1972	Galerie Swart, Amsterdam
1973	Galerie Edith Wahlandt, Schwäbisch Gmünd, West Germany
1974	Galerie Weiller, Paris
	Gallerie Gilles Gheerbrant, Montreal
1975	Galerie Weiller, Paris
	Galerie Swart, Amsterdam
1976	Galerie D + C Mueller-Roth, Stuttgart
	Galerie Média, Neuchâtel, Switzerland
	Galerie Disque Rouge, Brussels
	Galerie Gilles Gheerbant, Montreal
	Galerie Situation 2, Hamburg
1977	Galerie Edith Wahlandt, Schwäbisch Gmünd, West Germany
	Galerie Weiller, Paris
1978	Galerie Teufel, Cologne
	Galerie St. Petri, Lund, Sweden
1979	Galerie D + C Mueller-Roth, Stuttgart
	Galerie Gilles Gheerbant, Montreal
	Galerie Weiller, Paris
1980	Galerie Teufel, Cologne
1981	Galerie Gilles Gheerbrant, Montreal
1982	Galerie D + C Mueller-Roth, Stuttgart
	Galerie Weiller, Paris
	Galerie Teufel, Cologne
1983	Art Research Center, Kansas City, Missouri
1985	Galerie Gilles Gheerbrant, Montreal
	Galerie Teufel, Cologne
1986	Galerie D + C Mueller-Roth, Stuttgart
	Galerie Charley Chevalier, Paris
	Galerie Jeanne Buytaert, Antwerp
1987	Wilhelm-Hack-Museum, Ludwigshafen, West Germany
1988	Galerie Teufel, Cologne
	Reuchlin Museum, Pforzheim, West Germany

Selected Group Exhibitions:

1965	*Noir et Blanc,* Galerie Facchetti, Paris
1969	*Salon de Mai,* Musée d'Art Moderne, Paris
1972	*Computerkunst und Musikalische Texturen,* Staatsgalerie, Stuttgart
1975	*ICCH/2,* Museum of Modern Art, Los Angeles
1978	*Recherche et Creation,* Centre Georges Pompidou, Paris
1980	*Printed Art: A View of Two Decades,* Museum of Modern Art, New York
1983	*Electra,* Musée d'Art Moderne de la Ville, Paris
1985	*Emerging Expression,* Bronx Museum of the Arts, New York
1987	*Mathematik in der Kunst,* Wilhelm-Hack-Museum, Ludwigshafen, West Germany

Collections:

Museum Ludwig, Cologne; Nationalgalerie, West Berlin; Stadtische Kunstmuseum, Bonn; Wilhelm-Hack-Museum, Ludwigshafen; Stadtisches Museum Abteiberg, Monchengladbach; Stedelijk Museum, Amsterdam; Bibliotheque Nationale, Paris; Victoria and Albert Museum, London; Tel Aviv Museum, Israel; Musee d'Art Contemporain, Montreal.

Publications:

By MOHR: books—*Artificiata I,* Paris 1969; *Petit Livre de Nombres au Hasard,* Paris 1971; film—*Cubic Limit,* 1975.

On MOHR: books—*Future's Fictions* by Richard Kostelanetz, New York, 1970; *Computergraphik—Computerkunst* by Herbert W. Franke, Munich 1971; *Apparative Kunst,* edited by Herbert W. Franke and Gottfried Jager, Cologne 1973; *Manfred Mohr: Cubic Limit,* exhibition catalogue, Paris 1975; *Manfred Mohr: Generative Drawings,* exhibition catalogue, Paris and Pforzheim 1977; *Manfred Mohr: Dimensions,* exhibition catalogue, Stuttgart 1979; *Manfred Mohr: Werkubersicht 1965–1980,* exhibition catalogue, Cologne 1980; *Manfred Mohr: Divisibility,* exhibition catalogue, Montreal 1981; *Manfred Mohr: Algorithmische Arbeiten 1967–1987,* exhibition catalogue with texts by Bernhard Holeczek and Richard W. Gassen, Ludwigshafen 1987.

In my artistic development I did not have the typical constructivist background. I was an action painter and jazz musician. Through a development of consciousness, I detached myself from spontaneous expressions and turned myself to a more constructivist and, therefore, geometric expression (1964).

Beyond this, my art developed into an algorithmic art in which inventing rules (algorithms) is the starting point and basis of my research. These "compositional rules" are not necessarily based on already imaginable forms, but on abstract and systematic processes. My rules are parametic rules, which means that at certain points in the process, conditions have to be set for which, in some cases, random choices can be employed.

In my work, similar to a journey, only the starting point and a theoretical destination is known. What happens during the journey is often unexpected and surprising. Even though my work process is rational and systematic, as well as controlled by visual criteria at all times, it is always open to surprises. With such parametric rules, the actual image is created as the result of a process.

Since 1973, in my research, I have been concentrating on fracturing the symmetry of a cube, without questioning the structure of the cube as a 'system'. This disturbance or disintegration of symmetry is the basic generator of new constructions and relationships. What I am interested in are the two-dimensional signs (etresgraphiques) resulting from the projection of the lines of a cube. I describe them as unstable signs because they evoke visual unrest.

My art is not a mathematical art, but an expression of my artistic experiences. I invent rules which reflect my thinking and feelings. These algorithms can become very complex, that is to say, complicated and difficult to survey. In order to master this problem, the use of a computer is necessary in my work. Only in this way is it possible to overlay as many rules as necessary without losing control. It is inevitable that the results—that is, my images—are not readable at first glance. The information is deeply buried and a certain participation is demanded from the spectator, a readiness to interrogate this material.

In principal, all my work can be verified and rationally understood. This does not mean that there is no room for associations and imagination. On the contrary, the rational part of my work is limited basically to it's production. What one experiences, understands, learns, dreams . . . or interprets because of the presence of the art work rests solely in the mind of the spectator.

An art work is only a starting point, a principle of order, an artist's statement, intended to provoke the spectator to continue his investigations.

—Manfred Mohr

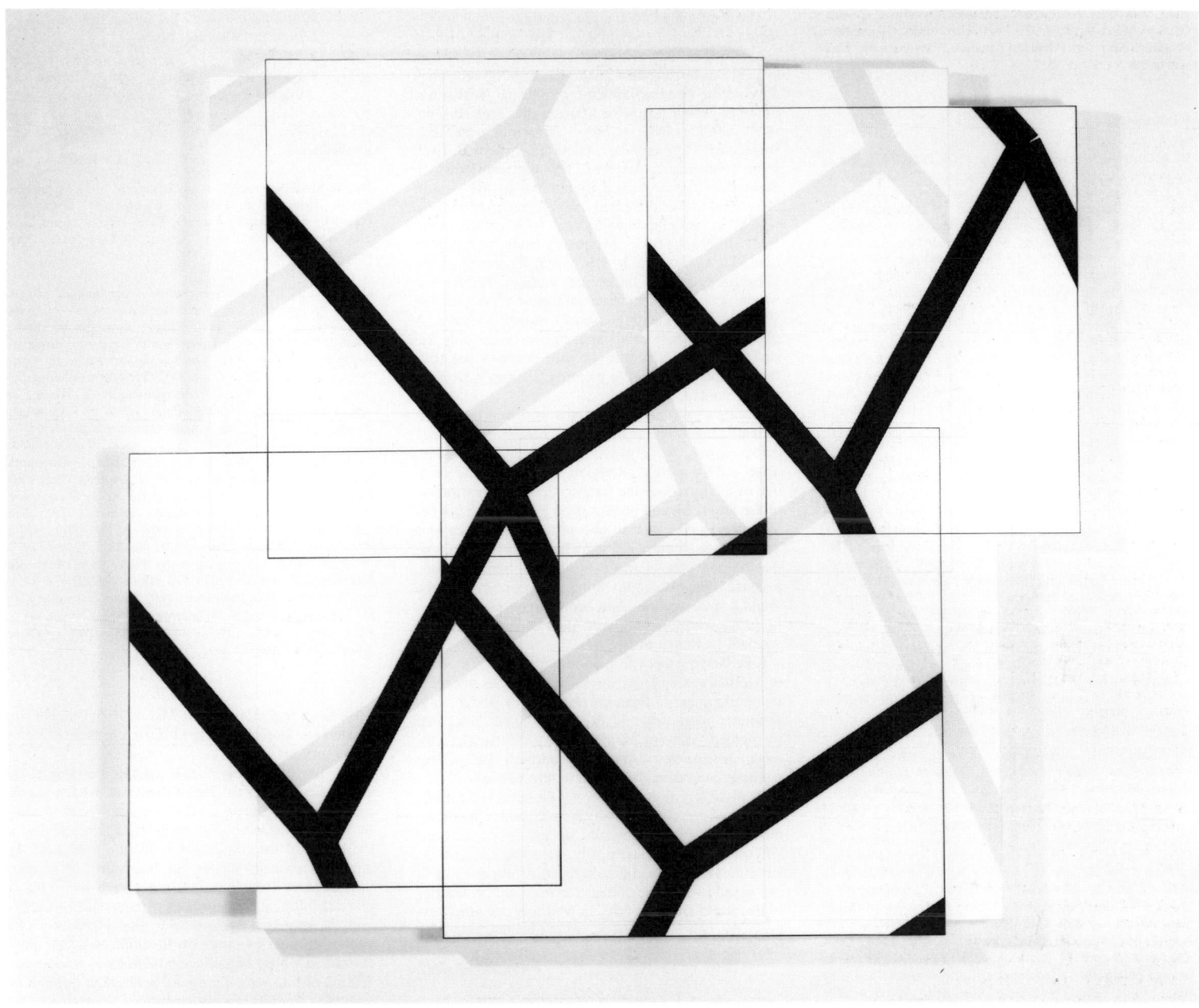

Manfred Mohr: *P 407 H*, 1987

MOLINARI, Guido.

Canadian. Born in Montreal, Quebec, 12 October 1933. Studied at Ecole des Beaux-Arts, Montreal, 1948–51, and under Marian Scott and Gordon Webber, Musée des Beaux-Arts, Montreal, 1951. Painter: Director, Galerie l'Actuelle, Montreal, 1955–57. Chairman, Department of Painting, Sir George William University, Montreal, since 1970. Jury Member, *91st Annual Exhibition,* Royal Academy of Arts, Montreal, 1971. Recipient: Laureat, Province of Quebec Artistic Competition, 1961; Jessie Dow Award, Musée des Beaux-Arts, Montreal, 1962; Buyer's Awards, *Biennial,* Winnipeg Art Gallery, 1962; Samuel and Ayala Zacks Purchase and Gift Award, Montreal, 1964; Grand Award, *Annual Spring Exhibition,* Musée des Beaux-Arts, Montreal, 1965; Guggenheim Fellowship for Creative Painting, New York, 1967. Address: 3290 Sainte Catherine Street East, Montreal, Quebec H1W 2C6, Canada.

Individual Exhibitions:

1954 Galerie l'Echourie, Montreal
1956 Galerie l'Actuelle, Montreal
1958 Galerie Artek, Montreal

1962 Galerie Nova et Vetera, College de St.-Laurent, Quebec
1963 Galerie Libre, Montreal
     East Hampton Gallery, New York
1964 Jerrold Morris International Art Gallery, Toronto
     Norman MacKenzie Art Gallery, University of Saskatchewan, Regina
     Vancouver Art Gallery
     Galerie du Siècle, Montreal
1965 East Hampton Gallery, New York
1966 Edmonton Art Gallery, Alberta
     Galerie du Siècle, Montreal
1967 20/20 Gallery, London, Ontario
     Galerie Nova et Vetera, College de St.-Laurent, Quebec
     East Hampton Gallery, New York
1968 Galerie du Siècle, Montreal
     Canada: Ulysse Comtois, Guido Molinari, at the *Biennale,* Venice
1971 Galerie Campo, Antwerp
1972 *Paintings,* Dalhousie University, Halifax, Nova Scotia
1976 National Gallery of Canada, Ottawa (retrospective; toured Canada)
1979 Musée d'Art Contemporain, Montreal
     York University, Toronto

Selected Group Exhibitions:

1955 *Espace 55,* Musée des Beaux-Arts, Montreal
1959 *Biennial Exhibition of Canadian Painting,* National Gallery of Canada, Ottawa.
1961 *Guido Molinari and Claude Tousignant,* Musée des Beaux-Arts, Montreal
1965 *The Responsive Eye,* Museum of Modern Art, New York
1967 *9 Canadians,* Institute of Contemporary Art, Boston
1968 *Canada: Art d'Aujourd'hui,* Musée National Art Moderne, Paris
1970 *Grands Formats,* Musée d'Art Contemporain, Montreal
1977 *Contemporary Canadian Painters,* Canadian Department of External Affairs travelling exhibition (world tour)
1984 *Reflections: Contemporary Art Since 1964,* National Gallery of Canada, Ottawa

Collections:

Musée des Beaux-Arts, Montreal; Sir George Williams University, Montreal; Art Gallery of Ontario, Toronto; Winnipeg Art Gallery, Manitoba; Norman MacKenzie Art Gallery, Regina; Vancouver Art Gallery; National Gallery of Canada, Ottawa; Museum of Modern Art, New York; Guggenheim Museum, New York; Chrysler Museum, Provincetown, Massachusetts.

Publications:

By MOLINARI: book—*Ecrits sur l'Art 1954-1975,* edited by Pierre Theberge, Ottawa 1976; articles—"Sans Titre" in *Le Petit Journal* (Montreal), September 1954; "L'Espace Tachiste ou Situation de L'Automatisme" in L'Autorite (Montreal), April 1955; "L'Affaire du Musée, G. Molinari Demandé la Demission de M. Steegman" in *Le Devoir* (Montreal), August 1958; "Le Langage de l'Art Abstrait" in *Art Abstrait,* exhibition catalogue, Montreal 1959; "Notes sur la Peinture, Re-evaluation de Wassily Kandinsky" in *Situations* (Montreal), March 1959; "Le Salon et les Peintres" in *Situations* (Montreal), April 1959; "Les Automatistes au Musée," "Huit Dessins de Claude Tousignant," and "A Nui Cri" in *Situations* (Montreal), September 1959; "Reflexions sur l'Automatisme et le Plasticisme" in *Situations* (Montreal), March/April 1961; statement in *Prize Winner Paintings: Book III* by Margaret Harold, Fort Lauderdale, Florida 1963; "Sans Titre" in *Guido Molinari,* exhibition catalogue, Regina, Saskatchewan 1964, reprinted in *Molinari,* exhibition catalogue, Montreal 1964; "Sans Titre" in *Canadian Art* (Toronto), January 1966; "Sans Titre: in *Statements: 18 Canadian Artists,* exhibition catalogue, Regina 1967; "La Perception des Structures" in *La Presse* (Montreal), December 1967; "L'Ecrivain a des Antennes" in *Liberté* (Montreal), December 1967; "Molinari," interview, with Pierre Theberge, in *Artscanada* (Toronto), March 1969; "L'Ecrivain a des Antennes" in *Liberté* (Montreal), May/July 1969; "Molinari: Pour un Art de Participation" in *La Presse* (Montreal), January 1970; "Sur: Le Choix de Peintre sur de Grandes Surfaces" in *Grands Formats,* exhibition catalogue, Montreal 1970; "Molinari: Un Geste Social" in *La Presse* (Montreal), April 1971; "Sans Titre" in *Paintings by Guido Molinari,* exhibition catalogue, Halifax, Nova Scotia 1972; "Sans Titre" in *Contemporary Canadian Painting* by William Withrow (Toronto), 1972.

On MOLINARI: books—*Guido Molinari,* exhibition catalogue, Regina, Saskatchewan 1964; *Molinari,* exhibition catalogue, Montreal 1964; *Statements: 18 Canadian Artists,* exhibition catalogue, Regina, Saskatchewan 1967; *Paintings by Guido Molinari,* exhibition catalogue, Halifax, Nova Scotia 1972; *Guido Molinari,* exhibition catalogue with text by David Burnett, Montreal 1979; articles—"Du Molinarisme au Plasticisme avec Guido Molinari" by Robert Millet in *Le Nouveau Journal* (Montreal), April 1962; "Molinari, Intuition Rationalisée!" by Paul Borduas in *Le Laurentien* (Montreal), October 1962; "Une Heure avec Guido Molinari" by Robert l'Heureux in *Le Droit* (Ottawa), October 1964; "Molinari on Molinari" by Rea Montbizon in *The Gazette* (Montreal), October 1964; "Molinari à Quitte l'Aureole pour une Ancre d'une Tonne" by Robert Millet in *Le Magazine Maclean* (Montreal), February 1968; "Molinari et le Serie Verticale" by Yves Robillard in *La Presse* (Montreal), February 1968; "Sans Titre" by Pierre Theberge in *Canada: Ulysse Comtois, Guido Molinari,* exhibition catalogue, Venice 1968; "An Artist Unites Man and Environment" by Gail Dexter in *The Toronto Star,* March 1969; "Molinari—The Medium Is Colour" by Michael White in The Gazette (Montreal), October 1971; "The Precociousness of Guido Molinari" by François Gagnon in *Artscanada* (Toronto), December 1976.

By the mid-1960s a number of Montreal painters including Guido Molinari had emerged whose central concern was the engagement of the viewer's perceptual faculties in the experience of duration. This concern has remained active into the 1980's, and the work can now be accepted as a heroic contribution to post-war painting without real parallels in either Europe or the rest of North America.

Molinari, despite some important automatist and tachist experiments, entirely eschewed painterliness or gesture in favour of the impersonal application of colour with precise and rectilinear edges on a white gesso ground. In this he was more rigorous than New York School painting when in the 1960s it rejected painterliness in favour of flatter, more regular and geometric modes of organization. A Noland colour stain painting will always be both more lyrically expressive and more illusionistically deep than a Molinari, which obliterates any evidence of paint texture, masks the canvas support and closes off any penetration by the eye into a potentially evocative space.

The majority of Molinari's paintings of the 1960's were composed of rows of equal vertical bands whose colour was serially arranged. They did not find much critical favour outside Canada, perhaps because they appeared to embrace something from the idealist tradition of geometric abstraction and thus seemed separate from other North American painting, suspiciously European and therefore regressive. Even more problematic, however, was the way in which these paintings presented themselves to the viewer. New York taste preferred holistic compositions in which "at every moment the work itself is fully manifest" (Michael Fried). Molinari's tended to function like an event caused by the visual dynamics of the juxtaposed colours under the scrutiny of the eye which was invited to read and reread the painting from side to side with constantly changing results. A painting whose variable appearances were only revealed as it was seen through time offered a very different experience from a painting, such as a Noland, seen instantaneously.

Molinari early defined his own work within the historical continuity of Malevich, Mondrian, Pollock and Newman, working with the objectivity of Mondrian and the scale of Newman, but without the idealism of the former or the transcendental expressionism of the latter. Instead he advanced his painting out beyond the canvas surface into what he describes as a "painting environment" which "sucks you in" so that "a new type of space is created—fictional space because it happens in the mind and yet it involves the totality of perception. You become conscious of getting into something and you then cannot distinguish yourself from that thing."

Like North American painting in general, the work of Molinari, despite its formal rigour, does not trace its development to preconceived plan or design. It is generated intuitively and existentially and "anchored in pigment and not in ideology" (Elderfield). Molinari nevertheless shares Mondrian's belief that painting can reveal "the true nature of reality." The dynamism of vision whereby a painting reveals itself, the acts of perception in which we consider the movements of the coloured masses, up and down, right and left, in and out, centrifugally, centripetally, and attempt to seize them and hold them are comparable to the ways in which we come to terms with the realities of the world and therefore, in Molinari's words, "express the new relationships we are establishing with the world."

—Roald Nasgaard

MOLINIER, Pierre.
French. Born in Agen, Lot-et-Goronne, 13 April 1900. Educated in Agen primary schools; studied at the Ecole des Beaux-Arts, Agen, 1918-20. Lived in Paris, 1920-23; settled in Bordeaux, 1923; Founder-Member, Artistes Indépendants de Bordeaux, 1927; first Fantasy and Allegory paintings, Bordeaux, 1936; first autobiographical works, 1946; met André Breton, and associated with Surrealist group, Paris, 1955-56. *Died* (by suicide; in Bordeaux) *3 March 1976.*

Individual Exhibitions:

1955 L'Etoile Scellée, Paris
1979 Centre Georges Pompidou, Paris
1980 Konsthall, Malmo, Sweden

Selected Group Exhibitions:

1928 *Société National des Beaux Arts,* Paris
     Artistes Indépendants, Bordeaux
1959 *Exposition International du Surrealisme,* Paris

1961 *Mostra Internazionale del Surrealismo,* Milan
1966 *Festival de l'Erotisme,* Bordeaux
1967 *A Phalla,* Sao Paulo
1974 *Transformer,* Kunstmuseum, Lucerne (toured Austria and Germany)

Publications:

By MOLINIER: articles—"Le Striptease" in *Le Surrealisme Même* (Paris), no. 4, 1958; "L'Art Magique" in *Molinier,* edited by Jean-Jacques Pauvert, Paris 1969; "Pierre Molinier: Interview with Thierry Agullo" in *Artitudes* (St. Jeannet, France), no. 21-23, 1975.

On MOLINIER: books—*Pierre Molinier,* exhibition catalogue, by André Breton, Paris 1955; *Mostra Internazionale del Surrealismo,* exhibition catalogue, by André Breton and Alain Joubert, Milan 1961; *Molinier* by Raymonde Borde and André Breton, Paris 1964; *Erotique du Surrealisme* by Robert Benayoun, Paris 1965; *Festival de l'Erotisme,* exhibition catalogue, Bordeaux 1966; *Le Surrealisme et la Peinture* by André Breton, Paris 1966; *Molinier,* edited by Jean-Jacques Pauvert, Paris 1969; *Surrealism: Permanent Revelation* by Roger Cardinal and Robert Stuart Short, London 1970; *Pierre Molinier lui-même: Essay on the Surrealist Hermaphrodite* by Peter Gorsen, Munich 1972; *Antologie Grafica del Surrealismo* by Maurice Henry, Milan 1972; *Transformer: Aspekte der Travestie,* exhibition catalogue, by Jean-Christophe Ammann, Martine Lanini and Peter Gorsen, Lucerne 1974; *Molinier,* edited by Bernard Letu, Geneva 1979; *Molinier,* exhibition catalogue, by Pierre Paret, Francoise Molinier and others, Paris 1979; films—*Molinier* by Raymond Borde and André Breton, 1964; *Satan bouche un Coin* by J. P. Bouyzou and R. V. Marongui, 1967; *Chrono Sud* by R. Etienne and O'Leary, 1968; *Pierre Molinier 7 rue des Faussets* by Pierre Sitnsolo, 1975.

Molinier's tragic suicide in March 1976 brought to a sudden end one of the most bizarre characters of contemporary art.

The life of Molinier began on Good Friday at the commencement of the 20th Century in the Lot. Looking at his subsequent development, it is hard to see—by parental decision—his early education received at the hands of the Jesuit Order. A little pointless? But strangely enough it was the way the holy fathers crossed over from ordinary male garb to a kind of clerical habit, a robe instead of coat-and-trousers, a sort of monkish transvestism that introduced the young Molinier to a taste for this kind of sexual transformation whose beguiling influence was to take possession of him with increasing persuasion through his adult life and in his art inventions through the last dozen of his years on earth.

The easygoing lightheartedness of a mixture of Jesuit education (!) leading him to art school at Agen where he in the first place devoted his talents to painting landscapes from nature came to an end in 1920 when he left for Paris. In the French capital he spent three years studying the styles and techniques of the Old Masters, before leaving to take up residence in Bordeaux where he lived the rest of his life. During the next four years he evolved his own version of Impressionism, later turning to probing the possibilities of colour abstractions (which 20 years after were to be repeated by others in what came to be known as the 'Informel'). These he painted alongside experiments directed at making Böcklin-esque nature studies and producing his own investigations into Jugendstil portraits.

All these art activities amount to what could be a long drawn-out curtain raiser to the arrival of a genuinely unique artist. The Molinier of 1956 emerged as the painter of the 'oeuvre-secret' pictures of an artworld burgeoning with menageries and communities gouged out of myth and legend, sphynxes, chimeras and sirens wrought immaculately in an amazing manner owing its ancestry to erstwhile Mannerism and which could also claim a mixed relationship with Josephson, Moreau and even Redon. With suitable personal transformation, Molinier found inspiration for a number of his esoteric paintings from studying works in Paris at the Musée Moreau, an early cultural nudge in the direction of Surrealism.

Back home in Bordeaux, stern in its unyielding conservatism and traditionalism, taste was appalled by the strong implication of pornography with which Molinier was able to infuse the eroticism of his pictures.

In 1951, his painting "Le grand combat" became the launching-pad of a fierce scandal provoking a charge of obscenity because it emphasized a homage to voluptuousness.

Within four years this astonishing contester of the moral status-quo came into direct contact with the surrealiste movement when he wrote to André Breton enclosing photos of his latest works. The response was immediate and enthusiastic. Breton promptly called on him to join the Surrealists and a year after invited him to open the new surrealist gallery "Ètoile Scellée" with a one-man show of his pictures with the grand old man of the movement describing him as close in spirit to Munch and Moreau.

This short analysis of Molinier's entry into the World of Art, an arrival which put him in touch with a rich and varied company of the famous and infamous already established in the couloirs of culture, is but an overture before his grand opera.

It was in 1966 that Molinier began his auto-statement in photomontage. (The 'fictitious' tombstone in his memory he had already erected in a neglected garden 16 years earlier. It was in 1966 that the stage was set; no scenery, perhaps just the odd piece of comfortable characterless 'good-taste' furniture with or without decorated screen as required 'props' if necessary, stray female accessories strewn with abandon (if considered apt) and often, for dramatic purpose the relentless *godmiché*. Most frequently all of these 'extras' did not find a place, leaving the picture area empty except for one or more 'glamour girls', puppets clad in corsetry to the waist, suspender belts in evidence to fasten sleek black silk stockings terminating in stiletto-heeled black footwear. Also, in a number of these skilfully executed photographs the lead-player would be Pierre Molinier himself in complementary transvestite attire either masked to match his puppet companion or companions or, his face deftly disguised in calculated make-up and sporting a wig to claim twinship with hs carefully posed dolls. Buttocks were always bare and so, usually depending on circumstance, were breasts.

Many times Molinier and Hans Bellmer have been classed as artistic cousins. Both, of course, did have recourse to photography of puppets whose limbs and other body parts—Molinier also had a big collection of *spare* legs, arms, hips and heads—could, if the occasion arose, be patterned into elaborate anatomical jigsaws. This remodelling of the human form occurred more in the case of Bellmer's puppetry, but it was also present in the paintings of Molinier, and such physical juggling was brought into play in the drawings and paintings from both of them.

As with bits and pieces of human bodies, coming together in realistic or fanciful and fantastic assembly, so with the basic sexuality which all of Molinier's mature oeuvres display, his pluralism and melange-ability also extended into thought processes and study. For him, frontiers melted between heterosexuality, homosexuality, bisexuality, narcissism, lesbianism and the transvestite element that could invade all of them.

Nor did he confine his research into Sex as a subject to his art-investigatory phantasies. It could be said, with some accuracy, that his bookshelves were bursting with learned and technical volumes (old and new) concerned with this physical manifestation stretching from the amoeba to humans in thought and language scientific, philosophical, theoretical, literary and poetic. Such a panoply of print could, and did, go into and examine—sometimes in romantic, sometimes lyrical, sometimes horrific, sometimes *verboten*, sometimes psychological, sometimes medical—aspects of his much written, but not so often spoken, detailed appraisals: sadism, masochism, bondage, masturbation, fetishism, every natural or extreme condition, none of these was a closed book to Molinier. Agreement with their contents did not always obtain. Indeed, some of them, the reputa-

tion and flavour of which he already knew, were never read.

As already asserted, here was one of *the most bizarre characters of contemporary art;* a surrealist flirt, a friend of literary giants, somewhat of an eccentric (but only in his lifestyle at his Bordeaux Atelier du Grenier St. Pierre and the art products that poured out of it). His admirers were from many walks of life, but were chiefly intellectual comprising a formidable corps, including not only Breton, but also the author of *Histoire d'O,* the French writer Georges Bataille and many others in the forefront of aesthetics and the arts.

—Sheldon Williams

MONORY, Jacques.

French. Born in Paris, 25 June 1934. Studied at the Ecole Technique des Arts Appliques, Paris, 1951–55. Served in French transport company, attached to the United States Army, 1955–56. Married Sabine Monirys in 1960 (divorced, 1968); son: Antoine. Director, Editions Delpire publishing company, Paris, 1956–64; independent painter and graphic artist, Paris, since 1964; first paintings, 1952; first films, 1968. Agent: Galerie Lelong, 13 rue de Teheran, 75008 Paris. Address: 9 Villa Carnot, Cachan 94230, France.

Individual Exhibitions:

1955	Galerie Kleber, Paris
1959	Galerie La Hune, Paris
1965	Galerie Henriette Legendre, Paris
1966	Galleria Schwarz, Milan
1967	Galerie Blumenthal-Mommaton, Paris
	Galleria Il Punto, Turin
1968	*Meurtres,* Galerie Blumenthal-Mommaton, Paris
1969	Galleria Forni, Bologna
	Studio d'Arte Condotti 85, Rome
	Galleria Il Punto, Turin
1971	Galerie Klang, Cologne
	Velvet Jungle/N.Y., Musée d'Art Moderne de la Ville, Paris (travelled to the Palais des Beaux-Arts, Brussels)
1972	Stedelijk Museum, Amsterdam
	Musée d'Art et d'Histoire, Saint-Etienne, France
	Neue Galerie, Aachen, West Germany
1973	Galleria Borgogna, Milan
1974	*Les Images Incurables,* Centre National d'Art Contemporain, Paris
1975	Louisiana Museum, Humlebaek, Denmark
	Galerie Maeght, Zurich
	Galerie Lanzenberg, Brussels (with Erro)
1976	*Operas Glaces,* Galerie Maeght, Paris
1977	Fondation Maeght, St. Paul-de-Vence, France
	Images Incurables/Opera Glaces, Palais des Beaux-Arts, Charleroi, Belgium
	Recits tremblants, Galerie de Larcos, Paris
	Hommage à C. D. Friedrich, Kunsthall, Hamburg
1978	*Technicolor,* Galerie Maeght, Paris
	Galerie Maeght, Zurich
	Figuration, Musée des Beaux-Arts, Grenoble, France (with Peter Klasen)
1979	Maison de la Culture, Rennes, France
1980	*Monory 3,* Galerie Maeght, Barcelona
	Lunds Konsthall, Lund, Sweden
1981	*Ciels, Nebuleuses et Galaxies,* Galerie Maeght, Pairs
	Galerie Claude Riedel, Paris (with Jean Dupuy)
1982	Musée de la Chartreuse, Douai, France
	Maison de la Culture, Nevers, France
	Musée des Beaux-Arts, Pau, France
1983	Maison de la Culture, Grenoble, France
1984	ARC/Musée d'Art Moderne de la Ville, Paris
	Galerie Fuji TV, Tokyo
	Galerie Pierre Hubert, Geneva
	Galerie Andate/Ritorno, Geneva
1986	Musée des Sciences de La Villette, Paris
1987	Musée Gare D'Orsay, Paris
	Galerie Maeght Lelong, Paris

Selected Groups Exhibitions:

1964	*Mythologies Quotidiennes,* Musée d'Art Moderne de la Ville, Paris
1968	*European Painters Today,* Musée des Arts Décoratifs, Paris (toured the United States)
1972	*Douze Ans d'Art Contemporain en France,* Grand Palais, Paris
1973	*Hyperrealistes Americains/Realistes Europeens,* Centre National d'Art Contemporain, Paris
1977	*Guillotine et Peinture,* Centre Georges Pompidou, Paris
1979	*De la Nature Etrange de l'Argent,* Kunsthalle, Dusseldorf (travelled to Eindhoven and Paris)
1982	*Alea,* ARC/Musee d'Art Moderne de la Ville, Paris
1983	*1960,* Musee d'Art et Industrie, St. Etienne
1986	*Espace* at the *Biennale,* Venice

Collections:

Centre Georges Pompidou, Paris; Musée d'Art Moderne de la Ville, Paris; Musée Cantini, Marseilles; Musée d'Art et d'Industrie, St. Etienne, France; Musée des Beaux-Arts, Genoble, France; Museée des Beaux-Arts, Pau, France; Stedelijk Museum, Amsterdam; Museum Boymans-van Beuningen, Rotterdam; Neue Galerie, Aachen, West Germany; Louisiana Museum, Humlebaek, Denmark.

Publications:

By MONORY: books—*Document bleu,* Paris 1970; *Deux,* with Franck Venaille, Paris 1973; *USA 76, Bicentenaire Kit,* book/object, with Michel Butor, Paris 1975; *Hommage à C. D. Friedrich,* with Jean-Christophe Bailly, Paris 1977; *Recits tremblants,* with Jean-Francois Lyotard, Paris 1977; *Poètes charcutiers,* Paris 1978; *Diamondback,* Paris 1979; *Rien ne bouge assez vite au bord de la mort,* Paris 1984; *Quick,* Paris 1987; books illustrated—*La mort sans phrase* by Charles Autrand, Paris 1968; *La baignoire verte* by Francoise Thieck, Paris 1974; *La Victoire à l'Ombre des Ailes* by Stanislas Rodanski, Paris 1975; *Eternité, zone tropicale* by Alain Jouffroy, Paris 1976; films—*Ex,* 1968; *Brighton Belle,* 1974; *La Voleuse,* 1986.

On MONORY—*Jacques Monory,* exhibition catalogue, with text by Gérald Gassiot-Talabot, Paris 1967; *Art et Contestation* by Gérald Gassiot-Talabot, Brussels 1968; *Depuis 45* by Gérald Gassiot-Talabot, Brussels 1970; *Monory* by Pierre Gaudibert and Alain Jouffroy, Paris 1972; *Jacques Monory,* exhibition catalogue, with text by Wolfgang Becker, Aachen, West Germany 1972; *Art en France, une nouvelle generation* by Jean Clair, paris 1972; *L'Art Actuel en France* by Anne Tronche and Hervé Gloaguen, Paris 1973; *Monory: Les Images Incurables,* exhibition catalogue, with text by Alain Jouffroy, Paris 1974; *Jacques Monory: Operas Glaces,* exhibition catalogue, with text by Gilbert Lascault, Paris 1976; *Figures de l'Art Contemporain* by M. LeBot, Paris 1977; *Guillotine et Peinture* by Alain Jouffroy, Paris 1977; *Monory: Images Incurables/Operas Glaces,* exhibition catalogue, with text by Jean-Christophe Bailly, Charleroi, Belgium 1977; *Monory: Technicolor,* exhibition catalogue, with text by Alain Jouffroy, Zurich 1978; *Monory* by Jean Christophe Bailly, Paris 1979; *Monory 3,* exhibition catalogue, with texts by Jacques Adelin Brutaru and Marianne Nanne-Brahmmar, Lund, Sweden 1980; *Monory: Ciels, Nebuleuses et Galaxies,* exhibition catalogue, with text by Jean-Francois Lyotard, Paris 1981; *Monory: l'Assassinat de l'Experience par la Peinture* by Jean-Francoise Lyotard, Paris 1981; *Monory et la Peinture-Avion* by H. F. Debailleux, Paris 1983; *Jacques Monory en Dandy* by H. F. Debailleux Paris 1984; *Entretien presque imaginaire avec Jacques Monory* by Georges Charbonnier, Paris 1987.

*

My work has always been a catharsis for the anguish of death. Very directly in MEUTRES (Murders), always more or less slyly, a taste of CATASTROPHE throughout my extremely cinematographic subjects. Personal obsessions at play with collective obsessions, an impassioned pessimist, my painting, films, texts, make me a pertinent witness of our times.

Painting in its substance has only concerned me re-

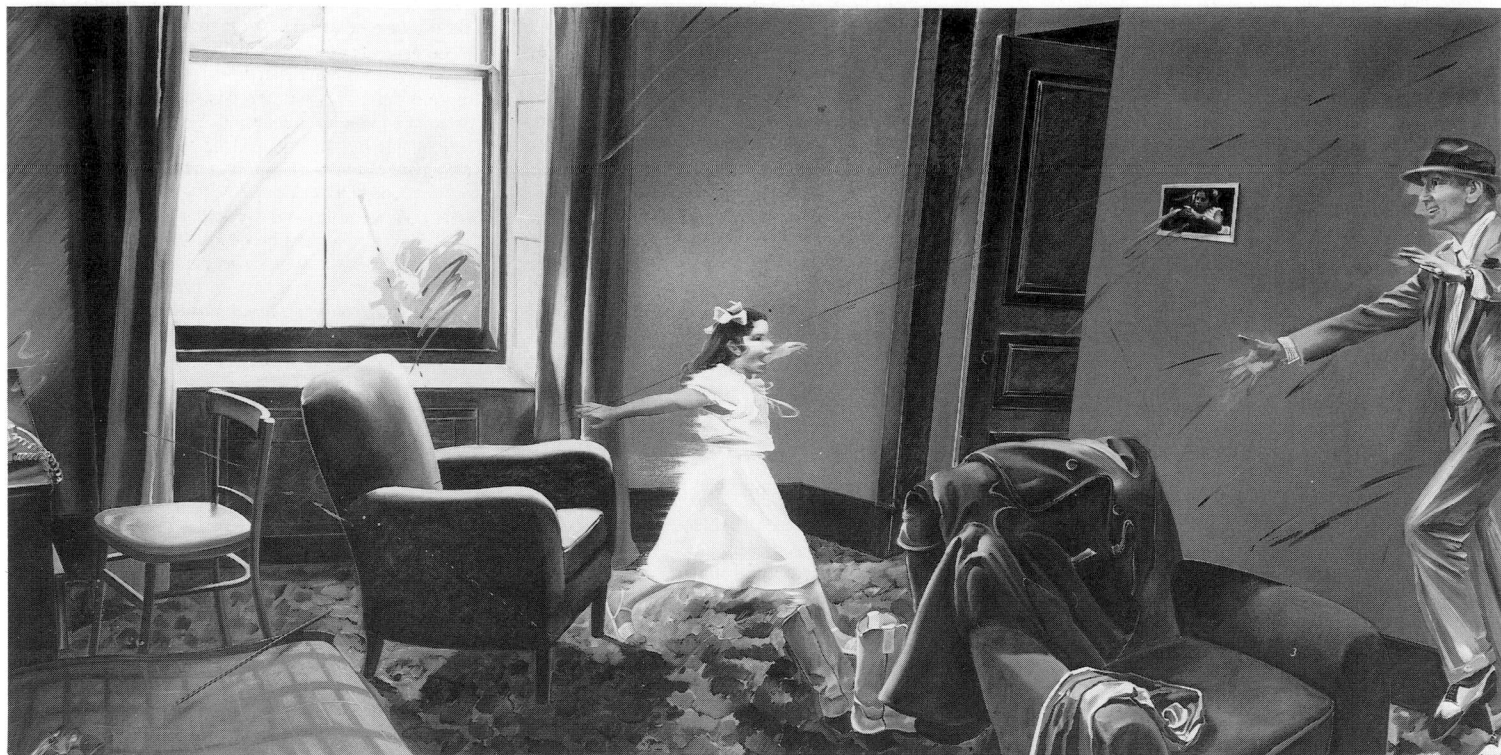

Jacques Monory: *La Voleuse No. 9*, 1986

cently after my series CIELS, NEBULEUSES ET GALAXIES (Skies, nebulae and galaxies), and the recent series FRAGILE, TOXIQUE, LE PEINTRE, and LA VOLEUSE. I work with it to question the pleasure of painting.

I am a romantic at a time when my expression can only appear as realistic dandyism, if possible with a little humour.

—Jacques Monory

There can be little doubt, after one's first encounter with the 'pictures' of Jacques Monory, that this artist—who did not take seriously the creation of works of art from his own hand until 1952 when he was still a student at the Ecole Technique des Arts Appliqués, was from the outset an accomplished performer, strange in his imagery but nonetheless amazingly adept.

A picture like *Meutre Novi* (at a time when he was making a series of 'meutres'), oil painted on canvas under plexiglass, declares a total bleakness. Three-quarters of this work shows—at an angle—a relentlessly undecorated tiled wall and, only at the bottom left-hand corner, a crouching half-figure of a man posed with his bald cranium bowed towards the picture-viewer, his hands clutched across his breast, the bent left arm caught by three out of four tracer bullets that have pierced the overall covering of plexiglass creating small starshapes at the point of impact. The dramatic perplexity of such a pictorialised situation attracts and repels simultaneously. Perhaps this is the predominant message of Monory's terrifying appeal.

What, after all, is so sinister about a sort of classic young homburgered American-style "Daddy" in correspondent shoes charging with outstretched hand into a characterless sitting-room to greet a kind of Hollywood girl-child type, neat white bow in hair, faultless knee-length white dress, her arms thrown wide in exaggerated welcome, careering towards him? All this against a tedious duplex background. The huge boring window behind has a large scribble over the lower edge of one of its immense panes, the stuffed easy chair is supremely uncluttered, making furniture and fittings seem like props on a stage for an acting company who could afford nothing better. Admittedly, to one side of the window there is a door ajar, and jackboots slouch beside another armchair

which is casually slipping out of the front of the picture, clothes strewn with unconcerned abandon over one of its tightly upholstered arms and across a well-padded back. But where is the Drama? Although this work is 19 years younger than the *Meutre Novi* of 1967, it still conveys a sense of alarm—albeit without the bullet-holes showing.

Maybe it was his dalliance with films and filming in the late seventies that gave him this quixotic Cartier-Bresson flavour of the normal couched in abnormal terms (although actually he provides nothing like the photos of the great cameraman, except in his capacity to evoke the magnetism of a chance happening helping him to build up such a knack for portraying unusual at its most usual—or vice-versa).

In fairness, not all the works of Monory are quite so worrying in their reticence. Sometimes the murder weapon and the one holding it are only too vivid in visual italics. The *usual* in a world steeped in violence? Happily, not for most of us. But then, if not in style, in intent Monory is a *realist*.

Not surprisingly, besides making his chilling picture inventions, he is also an author and essayist, and he has been able to turn his dauntless talent as an artist to illustrations for books written by others as well. He is a Jack-of-all-Trades, but Master of many, even enhancing a melange of these abilities to transform photography—very much his own photography, of course—into an art-form.

—Sheldon Williams

MONRO, Nicholas.

Born in London in 1936. Studied at the Chelsea School of Art, London, 1958–61. Sculptor. Lecturer, Swindon School of Art, Wiltshire, 1963–68. Lecturer, Chelsea School of Art, London, since 1968. Recipient: Arts Council of Great Britain Award, London, 1969; City Sculpture Project Prize, Peter Stuyvesant Foundation, London, 1972. Address: Potters Cottage, Shefford Woodlands, near Newbury, Berkshire, England.

Individual Exhibitions:

1968   Robert Fraser Gallery, London
        Galerie Pribaut, Amsterdam
1969   Galerie M. E. Thelen, Essen
1971   Waddington Galleries, London
1972   City Art Gallery, Bristol (travelled to Municipal Art Gallery, Wolverhampton, Staffordshire)
1977   Fruit Market Gallery, Edinburgh
1978   Felicity Samuel Gallery, London

Selected Group Exhibitions:

1968   *Mostra Mercato d'Arte Contemporanea*, Florence
        Salon des Jeunes Peintres, Paris
        Prospect, Dusseldorf
1969   *Pop Art*, Hayward Gallery, London
1970   *Klischee und Antiklischee*, Suermondt Museum, Aachen, West Germany
1972   *Art Around 1970*, Neue Galerie, Aachen, West Germany
1975   *New Work*, Hayward Gallery, London
1976   *New Work II*, Hayward Gallery, London

Collections:

Arts Council of Great Britain, London.

Publications:

By MONRO: article—statement in *Ark* (London), no. 39, 1965.

On MONRO: books—*Nicholas Monro*, exhibition catalogue, by Udo Kultermann, Essen 1969; *Image as Language: Aspects of British Art 1950–1968* by Christopher Finch, London 1969; *Art Around 1970*, exhibition catalogue, by Wolfgang Becker, Aachen, West Germany 1972; articles—"Formalism and Informality in the Visual Arts" by P. Flore in *Sculpture International* (London), no. 2, 1968; "Monro's Menagerie" by E. Wolfram in *Art and Artists* (London), January 1975.

To a certain extent Nicholas Monro is a pioneer of figurative art. During his college years Tucker and King were attracting a great deal of attention whilst he was quietly sculpting figures. He went through a very brief abstract phase but not long enough to make any impact. Monro has always investigated the comical/satirical side of life. Even his choice of subject matter brings a grin to your face.

All the sculptures are executed in fibreglass as it is a light, durable, easy and strong material to work with. Monro's best known tableau is the "Waiters' Race." For many years it has been an annual tradition for all the big London hotels to enter their waiters in a race which takes place in the heart of Soho in Dean Street. There is a spaghetti eating competition, a cigar smoking contest and so on. Monro has never attended this event, but the concept fired his imagination and he has created an ensemble of sculptures appearing in hilariously contorted stances. From a more literary point of view the piece can be linked to Muybridges' first photographs in which an animal's mode of walking was recorded by setting up a series of trip wires which then set off a camera. Monro equals the camera, but he is a distorting camera.

Apart from the waiters, Monro also presented us with a wonderfully bland herd of sheep; they were somewhere between Pop and Minimal. Strangely enough, when Monro was half way through completing his sheep, Paul Lalanne introduced his herd to the world. The big difference was that Lalanne's could be used as chairs whilst Monro's could only be visually appreciated!

Monro's sculptures are unforgettable for a variety of reasons. The selected images are powerful, comical, and immaculately executed. He is an artist who has a unique vision and will bend to no authority to change it. In 1972 the Peter Stuyvesant Foundation gave 12 different artists a choice of a city for which they were to prepare a sculpture. Monro created King Kong for Birmingham. Although Monro was supposed to present an image with a direct link to the city, he deliberately chose to be obtuse—though maybe he thinks of Birmingham as a concrete jungle.

Monro has also presented us with Falling Giraffes, Quasimodo, Max Wall and Douglas Fairbanks Jr. Sadly, the humour must now temporarily disappear, for Monro is working on a commission which requires him to sculpt a group of dancers from various countries, all wearing national costume. Gone will be the wild colours; the sculptures will be made to look like Portland stone; the crazy stances will also disappear. One can only hope that Monro will soon be able to unleash his wildness again.

—Carine Maurice

MOON, Jeremy.

Born in Altrincham, Cheshire, 29 August 1934. Educated in Shrewsbury primary schools; studied law at Christ's College, Cambridge, 1955–58; studied briefly at the Central School of Art, London, 1961; mainly self-taught in art. Served in the British Army in Korea and Japan, 1952–54. Married Elizabeth (Beth) Bryant in 1963; children: Robert, Benedick and Georgina. Worked as advertising executive, 1958–62. Full-time painter from 1963. Lecturer, St. Martin's School of Art, London, 1963–68, and Chelsea School of Art, London, 1963–73. Recipient: Associated Electrical Industries Prize for Sculpture, 1962. *Died* (in motorcycle accident) *30 November 1973.*

Individual Exhibitions:

1963	Rowan Gallery, London
1965	Rowan Gallery, London
1966	Rowan Gallery, London
1967	Galerie Müller, Stuttgart
1968	Rowan Gallery, London
1969	Rowan Gallery, London
1970	Rowan Gallery, London
1971	Rowan Gallery, London
1973	Rowan Gallery, London
1974	Rowan Gallery, London
1976	Serpentine Gallery, London (travelled to City Art Gallery, Manchester, and Kettle's Yard Gallery, Cambridge)
1978	Rowan Gallery, London

Selected Group Exhbitions:

1962	*Young Contemporaries,* FBA Galleries, London
1964	*Contemporary British Painting and Sculpture,* Albright-Knox Gallery, Buffalo, New York
1965	*London: The New Scene,* Walker Art Center, Minneapolis
1966	*John Moore's Liverpool Exhibition,* Walker Art Gallery, Liverpool
1967	*5th Biennale des Jeunes,* Musée National d'Art Moderne, Paris
1968	*Britische Kunst Heute,* Kunstverein, Hamburg
1969	*Marks on Canvas,* Museum am Ostwall, Dortmund, West Germany
1970	*Colour and Structure,* Farmers Blaxland Gallery, Sydney

Collections:

Tate Gallery, London; Victoria and Albert Museum, London; Fitzwilliam Museum, Cambridge; Scottish National Gallery of Modern Art, Edinburgh; Ulster Museum, Belfast; Albright-Knox Art Gallery, Buffalo; Walker Art Center, Minneapolis; Institute of Contemporary Art, Sydney.

Publications:

By MOON: articles—statement in *Studio International* (London), September 1967; "Enemies of Painting" in *Studio International* (London), December 1971; "Interview with Barry Martin" in *One* (London), April 1974.

On MOON: articles—"Mr. Jeremy Moon Experiments" in *The Times* (London), 9 June 1965; "Jeremy Moon's Recent Paintings" by Charles Harrison in *Studio International* (London), March 1968; "Jeremy Moon" by Peter Fuller in *Arts Review* (London), June 1970; "Obituary" in *The Times* (London), 4 December 1973; "Jeremy Moon" by Charles Harrison in *Studio International* (London), January 1974; "Moon Paintings" by William Feaver in *The Guardian* (London), 19 January 1974; "Jeremy Moon" by Marina Vaizey in the *Financial Times* (London), 29 January 1974; "Jeremy Moon" by Lavinia Learmont in *Arts and Artists* (London), March 1976.

*   *   *

Jeremy Moon's paintings look carefully planned and are cleanly executed. Everything in them is stated unambiguously. Here are alternative bands of colour, that is a right angle, this is a vertical-horizontal grid, there are red, yellow, blue, white, green, etc. His colours are often bright and always active, and they run unmodulated from edge to edge of the shape they make. There is no modelling, no shadow, no transition. Everything is painted flatly with a neat, impersonal technique that produces a skin of paint thick enough to obscure the texture of the supporting surface, wood or canvas. He avoided the pleasurable accidents that thin paint on cloth or wood can bring, principally because he wanted his colours unqualified by anything other than their inter-relationships. His paintings thus present themselves as utterly factual and self-evident.

One imagines him preparing each composition fully on paper, and then, carrying it out on the larger scale carefully but mechanically. But that is not how his paintings were done. For one thing, a difference in scale means a fundamental difference in effect; for another Moon's pastels on papers are no equivalent to acrylics on canvas.

In answer to the question "How do you know when you have finished a painting?" he wrote: "I usually have a fairly clear idea when I start a painting of how I want it to look when it's finsihed. But once I start

work, the more the painting develops, the more I become aware of the difference between what I planned to do and what I have actually done. The process of finishing the picture therefore is to a certain extent a question of coming to terms with what I've actually done and relinquishing the original conception. The final stage—getting the picture to work as I want it to—always goes on longer than I expect. I just keep looking at it and working on it week by week until I have taken it as far as I can—which is sometimes too far—then it's finished." He was always ready to discard finished and over-finished paintings; for example, he spent the summer of 1969 on twelve large canvases all of which he soon after destroyed as worthless.

So making each painting involved a process of readjustment, both of his plans and of his expectations, and thus each painting starts from his previous experience but also enlarges his experience while it comes into being. Moon often worked in series, producing a number of paintings of similar format and organization. When he did so it would seem likely that the ratio of foreknowledge as against adjustment and discovery must have shifted in favour of the former, but even here we must guard against short-circuiting the process; it is precisely when small changes are made within a tried system that surprising transformation can occur. Then also there comes the point when the painter knows that a series has ended and his work has to find another starting point. The new start may or may not be implied in the work just done; the new idea may or may not be ready and waiting for realization. Again, it would be a mistake to see a change of appearance in Moon's work as representing a change of direction within himself. Just as small changes within a known framework can have fundamental effect, so all-over changes may be made in order to embody ideas that had become dominant in what came before.

This is apparent in the paintings themselves. Furthermore, it is proved by Moon's sketches and working drawings for his paintings. I have looked through a great quantity of rough sketches as well as more finished drawings, and they taught me what witnessing Moon's one-man exhibitions over the years had not made clear. Beth Moon says that Jeremy sketched and doodled incessantly at home, whilst chatting, watching television (which he did quite a lot), listening to music (he was passionate about jazz, and very interested in avant-garde music), and so on, and I have seen the results, on all sorts of bits of paper and done with pencil, biro or crayon, with cars, motor bikes and extreme female footwear appearing among pictorial jottings. I learned from them that (1) he worked amid a buzz of ideas, even when the paintings emerging from his studio all belonged to one series; (2) each painting, singleton or part of a series, started as the preferred project among several variations jotted down; and (3), although the succession of a series gives one the impression of a steady and sequential programme, Moon's ideas existed in no sequence but leapt over the years and reappeared in new guises.

—Norbert Lynton

MOORE, Henry.

British. Born in Castleford, Yorkshire, 30 July 1898. Educated in Castleford primary schools; studied at Teachers Training College, 1915–16, and at Leeds College of Art, 1919–21, and Royal College of Art, London, 1921–24. Served as a Lance-Corporal in the 15th London Regiment, in France and England, 1916–19, and as an official war artist, London, 1940–45. Married Irina Radetzky in 1929; daughter: Mary. Sculptor: lived in London, 1921–40; produced first Mother and Child sculptures, influenced by pre-Columbian art, 1922; Lecturer in Sculpture, Royal College of Art, 1924–32; Founder-Member, with

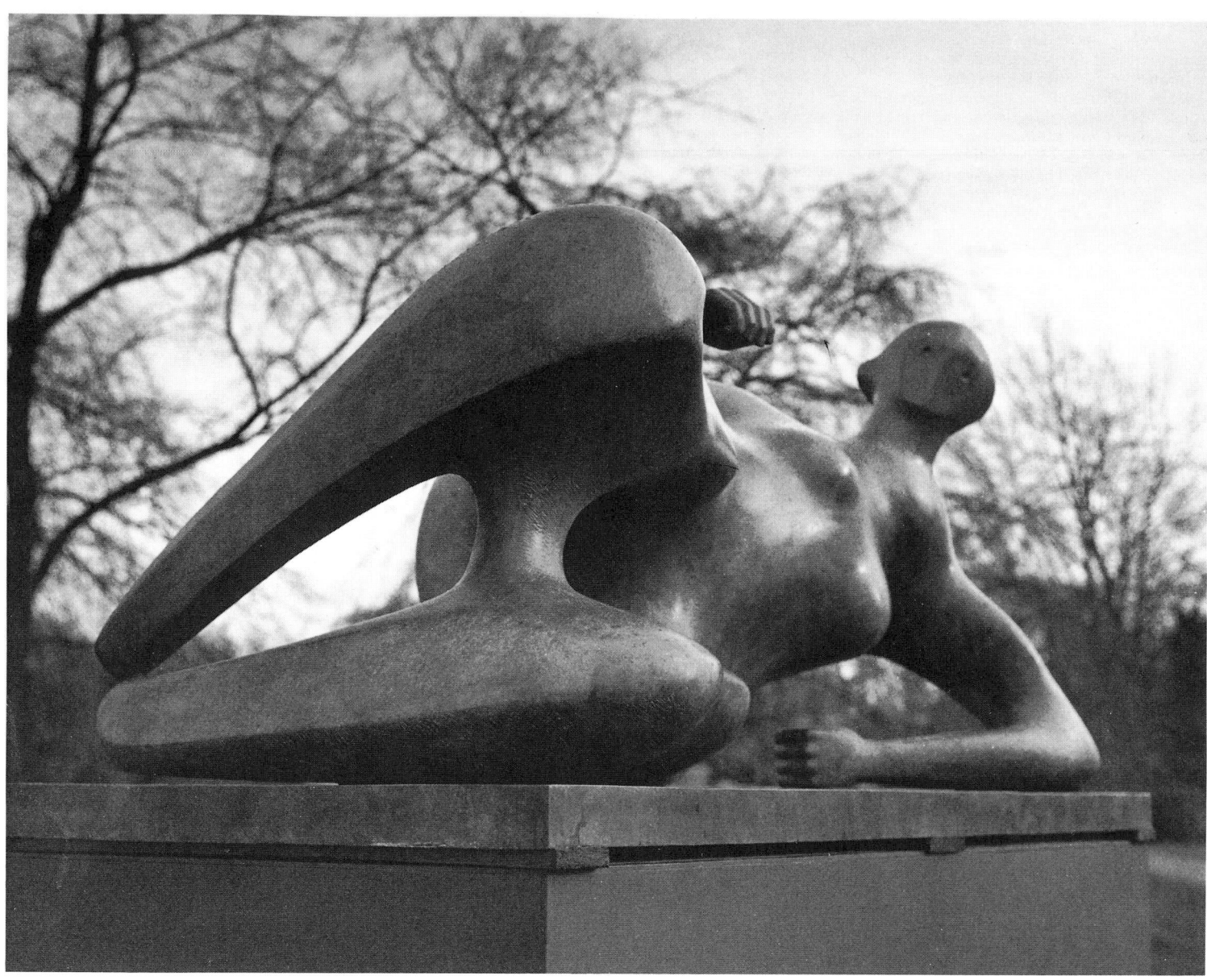

Henry Moore: *Large Reclining Woman*, 1981

Barbara Hepworth, Ben Nicholson and others, Unit One, London, 1931; Founder of the Department of Sculpture, 1932, and Lecturer in Sculpture, 1932–39, Chelsea School of Art, London; settled in Much Hadham, Hertfordshire, 1940; also worked in Forte dei Marmi, Italy, from 1977; founded Henry Moore Foundation, Much Hadham, 1977. Trustee, Tate Gallery, London, 1941–56; Member, Art Panel, British Council, 1945; Member, Royal Fine Art Commission, 1948–71; Trustee, National Gallery, London, 1955–71; Chairman, Auschwitz Memorial Committee, 1958. Recipient: International Prize for Sculpture, *Biennale,* Venice, 1948; Sculpture Prize, *Bienal,* Sao Paulo, 1953; Second Prize, *Carnegie International,* Pittsburgh, 1957; Stefan Lochner Medal, Cologne, 1957; Commemorative Award for the Arts, Yeshiva University, New York, 1968; Erasmus Prize, Netherlands, 1968; Gold Medal, Society of the Friends of Art, Cracow, Poland, 1969; Grosse Goldene Ehrenzeichen, Veinna, 1978; Grand Cross of the Order of Merit, Federal German Republic, 1980. Honorary doctorate: University of London, 1953; Harvard University, Cambridge, Massachusetts, 1958; Oxford University, 1961; University of Sussex, Brighton, 1965; Yale University, New Haven, Connecticut, 1966; University of Toronto, 1968; University of Durham, 1970; and Columbia University, New York, 1974; Honorary Fellow, Churchill College, Cambridge, 1965. Honorary Fellow, Royal Institute of British Architects, 1971; Member, Royal

Scottish Academy of Painting, Sculpture and Architecture, 1974. Corresponding Member, 1948, and Associate, 1975, Académie Royal Flamande des Sciences, Lettres et Beaux-Arts de Belgique; Foreign Member, Swedish Royal Academy of Fine Arts, 1950; Foreign Member, American Academy of Arts and Sciences, 1955; Corresponding Academician, Academia Nacional de Bellas Artes, Buenos Aires, 1959; Member, Wiener Secession, Vienna, 1969; Member, L'Institut of the Académie de Beaux-Arts, Paris, 1975; Member, Academie Européene des Sciences des Arts et des Lettres, 1981; Commandeur de l'Ordre des Arts et des Lettres, Paris, 1973; Cavaliere di Gran Croce dell'Ordine al Merito della Repubblica Italiana, 1972. Companion of Honour, 1955; Member, Order of Merit, 1963. *Died* (in Much Hadham, Hertfordshire) *31 August 1986.*

Individual Exhibitions:

1928	Warren Gallery, London
1931	Leicester Galleries, London
1933	Leicester Galleries, London
1935	Zwemmer Gallery, London
1936	Leicester Galleries, London
1939	Mayor Gallery, London
1941	Temple Newsam, Leeds, Yorkshire
1943	Buchholz Gallery, New York
1945	Berkeley Galleries, London
1946	Leicester Galleries, London
	Phillips Memorial Gallery, Washington, D.C.
	Museum of Modern Art, New York
1947	Art Institute of Chicago (travelled to the San Francisco Museum of Art)
	National Gallery of New South Wales, Sydney (toured Australia)
1948	Arts Council Gallery, Cambridge
	Galleria d'Arte Moderna, Milan
	Roland Browse and Delbanco, London
1949	Wakefield City Art Gallery, Yorkshire
	Galerie de Arte Mexicano, Mexico City
1951	Tate Gallery, London
	Leicester Galleries, London
	Haus am Waldsee, Berlin
	Buchholz Gallery, New York
	Albertina, Vienna
1952	National Gallery of South Africa, Cape Town
	Academian, Stockholm (toured Europe)
	Neue Galerie der Stadt, Linz, Austria
	Boymans-van Beuningen Museum, Rotterdam
	Institute of Contemporary Arts, London
	Comite voor Artisticke Werking, Antwerp
	Kestner Gesellschaft, Hannover (toured West Germany)
	Galerie Welz, Salzburg (with Marino Marini and Fritz Wotruba)
1954	Leicester Galleries, London
	Kunsthalle, Mannheim (toured West Germany)
	Stadverwaltung, Göttingen, West Germany

	Curt Valentin Gallery, New York
1955	Leicester Galleries, London
	Kunsthalle, Basle
	University of Colorado, Boulder (toured the United States)
	Museum of Fine Arts, Montreal (toured Canada and New Zealand)
1958	Hatton Gallery, Newscastle upon Tyne
	Marlborough Fine Art, London
	Ashmolean Museum, Oxford
1959	Palacio Foz, Lisbon (toured Spain)
	Metropolitan Art Gallery, Tokyo (toured Japan)
	Middelheim Park, Antwerp
	Marlborough Fine Art, London
	Zachenta Gallery, Warsaw (toured Poland)
1960	Kunsthalle, Hamburg (toured West Germany)
1962	Arts Council Gallery, Cambridge
	Marlborough Fine Art, London
1963	Marlborough Fine Art, London
	Wakefield City Art Gallery, Yorkshire
	Ferens Art Gallery, Hull, Yorkshire
	La Jolla Art Center, California (toured California)
1964	Marlborough Fine Art, London
	Palacio de Bellas Artes, Mexico City (toured South America)
1965	Marlborough Fine Art, London
	Orleans Gallery, New Orleans
	Marlborough Galleria d'Arte, Rome
	University of Arizona Art Gallery, Tucson
	Arkansas Art Center, Little Rock
	Museum des 20, Jahrhunderts, Vienna (with Jean Dubuffet and Mark Tobey)
1966	Marlborough Fine Art, London
	City Museum and Art Gallery, Folkstone, Kent (travelled to the Museum and Art Gallery, Plymouth, Devon)
	Philadelphia College of Art
	Israel Museum, Jerusalem
	Sala Delles, Bucharest (toured Eastern Europe)
	Cordova Museum, Lincoln, Nebraska
	Sheffield Art Gallery and Museum, Yorkshire
	Trinity College, Dublin
	Smithsonian Institution, Washington, D.C.
1967	Marlborough Fine Art, London
1968	Tate Gallery, London
	Rijksmuseum Kröller-Müller, Otterlo, Netherlands (toured West Germany and the Netherlands)
1969	National Museum of Modern Art, Tokyo (toured Japan and travelled to Hong Kong)
	York Univerity
	Norwich Castle Museum, Norfolk
1970	Marlborough Gerson Gallery, New York
	Knoedler Gallery, New York
	Galerie Beyeler, Basle
	Galerie Cramer, Geneva (toured Europe and travelled to New York)
	Marlborough Fine Art, London (with Pablo Picasso and Graham Sutherland)
1972	Forte di Belvedere, Florence
1973	Fischer Fine Art, London
1974	Los Angeles County Museum of Art
	Wilhelm Lehmbruck Museum, Duisburg, West Germany (toured West Germany and Belgium)
1976	Zürcher Forum, Zurich
	Imperial War Museum, London
	Scottish National Gallery of Modern Art, Edinburgh (with Kenneth Martin)
	Fischer Fine Art, London
	Grafton Gallery, Bury St. Edmonds, Suffolk
	Lillian Heidenberg Gallery, New York
1977	Orangerie des Tuilleries, Paris
	Bibliothèque Nationale, Paris
	Gracefield Arts Centre, Dumfries, Scotland
	Art Gallery of Ontario, Toronto (toured Japan and travelled to London 1977–78)
1978	Cartwright Hall and Lister Park, Bradford, Yorkshire
	Serpentine Gallery, London
	Tate Gallery, London
	Bayerischen Staatsgemaldesammlungen, Munich
	Galeria Joan Prats, Barcelona
	Festival Gallery, Aldeburgh, Suffolk
	Gallery Kasahara, Osaka, Japan
	Stiftung Landis und Gyr, Zug, Switzerland

	Schlossgut Wolfsberg, Ermstigen, Switzerland
	Galeria Pieter Coray, Lugano, Switzerland
1979	Prince Henry's High School, Evesham, Worcestershire
	Wildenstein Gallery, New York
	Jersey Museum, Channel Islands
	Bundeskanzleramt, Bonn (travelled to William Hack Museum, Ludwigshafen, West Germany)
	Umetnosti Pavilijon, Slovenj Gradec, Yugoslavia (travelled to the Serbian Academy, Belgrade)
1980	Il Bisonte, Florence
	Victoria and Albert Museum, London
	Galerie Levy und Forderkreis, Hamburg
	Campus West Library, Welwyn Garden City, Hertfordshire
	Fischer Fine Art, London
	Galerie Patrick Cramer, Geneva
1981	125 Raskowsky, Sofia, Bulgaria
	Retire Park, Madrid
	Gulbenkian Foundation, Lisbon
	Royal Museum, Folkestone, Kent
	Galleria Bergamini, Milan
	Wildenstein Gallery, London
	Contemporary Sculpture Center, Tokyo
	Gallery Welz, Salzburg
	Alex Rosenberg Gallery, New York
1982	Joan Miró Foundation, Barcelona
	Fine Arts Center, Colorado Springs
	Galleria Comunale, Forte dei Marmi, Italy
	Hoam Art Museum, Seoul, Korea
	Durham Light Infantry Museum, County Durham
	Fischer Fine Art, London
	Linda Goodman Gallery, Sandton, South Africa
1983	Galerie Maeght, Paris
	Alex Rosen Gallery, New York
1984	Marlborough Fine Art, London
	Marlborough Graphics, London
	Kunstmuseum, Herning, Denmark
	Columbus Museum of Art, Ohio
1985	San Francisco Museum of Modern Art
	Art Gallery of Ontario, Toronto
1986	Kent Fine Art, New York
	Galerie Patrick Cramer, Geneva
	Thomas Gibson Fine Art, London
1987	Marlborough Fine Art, London
	Fischer Fine Art, London
	Vallecchi Editore, Florence, Italy
	Hofstra University, Hempstead, New York
1988	Art Gallery of Ontario, Toronto

Selected Group Exhibitions:

1936	*Fantastic Art, Dada and Surrealism*, Museum of Modern Art, New York
1948	*Biennale*, Venice
1962	*Art since 1950*, Ca'Pesaro, Venice
1967	*Guggenheim International*, New York
1968	*British Sculpture of the 50's*, Musée des Augustins, Toulouse
1973	*Henry Moore to Gilbert and George*, Palais des Beaux-Arts, Brussels
1982	*Gauguin to Moore: Primitivism in Modern Sculpture*, Art Gallery of Ontario, Toronto
1983	*Aspects of British Art*, Guggenheim Museum, New York

Collections:

Tate Gallery, London; Victoria and Albert Museum, London; Henry Moore Foundation, Much Hadham, Hertfordshire; Stedelijk Museum, Amsterdam; Israel Museum, Jerusalem; National Gallery of Victoria, Melbourne; Art Gallery of Ontario, Toronto; Hirshhorn Museum and Sculpture Garden, Washington, D.C.; Museum of Modern Art, New York; Experimental Museum, Mexico City.

Publications:

By MOORE: books—*Henry Moore's Sheep Sketchbook*, London, New York and Paris 1980; *Henry Moore: Sculpture*, edited by David Mitchinson, Barcelona, London, New York and Stuttgart 1981; articles—statement in *Architectural Asso-*

ciation Journal (London), May 1930; statement in *Unit One: The Modern Movement in English Architecture, Painting and Sculpture*, London 1934; "Mesopotamian Art" in *The Listener* (London), June 1953; "The Sculptor Speaks" in *The Listener* (London), August 1937; "Primitive Art" in *The Listener* (London), April 1941; "The Living Image: Art and Life" in *The Listener* (London), November 1941; "Note on the Madonna and Child Statue" in *Transformation* (London), no. 3, 1945; "Message de la Sculpture" in *XXe Siècle* (Paris), 1951; "Interview with Ark Magazine" in *Ark* (London), November 1952; "The Sculptor in Modern Society" in *Artnews* (New York), November 1952; "Henry Moore Talking to David Sylvester" in *The Listener* (London), August 1963; statements in *Henry Moore at the British Museum*, London 1981.

On MOORE: books—*Henry Moore, Sculptor* by Herbert Read, London 1934; *Henry Moore: Sculpture and Drawings*, volume I and II by Herbert Read, volume III by Herbert Read and Alan Bowness, volumes IV and V by Alan Bowness, London and New York 1944–82; *Meaning and Symbolism in Three Modern Artists: Edvard Munch, Henry Moore, Paul Nash* by George Wingfield-Digby, London 1955; *The Archetypal World of Henry Moore* by Eric Neuman, New York 1959; *The Art of Henry Moore* by Will Grohmann, London 1960; *Henry Moore: A Study of His Life and Work* by Herbert Read, London 1965; *Henry Moore: Carvings 1923–1966* by Robert Melville, London 1967; *Henry Moore: Sculpture and Drawings 1921–1969* by Robert Melville, London 1970; *Henry Moore in America* by Henry J. Seldis, London 1973; *Henry Moore: Catalogue of Graphic Work*, 3 volumes, by Gerald and Patrick K. Cramer, Alistair Grant and David Mitchinson, Geneva 1973–80; *Henry Moore: Drawings* by Kenneth Clark, London and New York 1974; *Henry Moore: Sculpture and Environment* by David Finn, New York and London 1977; *With Henry Moore: The Artist at Work* by Gemma Levine, London and New York 1978; *Henry Moore: Sculptures in Landscape* by Geoffrey Shakerley and Stephen Spender, London, Oslo and New York 1978; *The Moore Collection in the Gallery of Ontario* by Alan G. Wilkinson, Toronto 1979; *Henry Moore: Portrait of an Artist* by John Read, London 1979; *Henry Moore: The Reclining Figure*, exhibition catalogue with essays by Steven W. Rousen, Ann Garrould and others, Columbus, Ohio 1984; *Henry Moore's Photographs of his Sculpture*, exhibition catalogue with essay by Van Deren Coke, San Francisco 1985; *The Life of Henry Moore* by Roger Berthoud, London 1986; *Henry Moore Remembered* by Alan G. Wilkinson, Toronto 1988; films—*Henry Moore, Sculptor*, directed by John Read, 1951; *Henry Moore: London 1940–42*, directed by Nancy Thomas, 1963; *Henry Moore: Man of Form*, directed by Anthony Roland, 1965; *Henry Moore: at Home*, directed by John Read, 1973; *A Henry Moore for Moline*, directed by Arthur Wolf, 1975; *Henry Moore at 80*, directed by John Read, 1978.

Owing to his service in the First World War, Henry Moore was a late starter in art. On demobilization from the army in 1919, he went to Leeds School of Art. He stayed two years and went on to the Royal College of Art till 1925, when he visited Italy. He joined the staff of the Royal College and later transferred to the Chelsea School of Art till 1939.

The human figure has always been at the root of Moore's work and, as he has said, he found principles of form and rhythm from the study of natural objects. From his earliest productions there existed a formal difference between the carved and the modelled work. From 1922 his carvings in wood and stone follow an intense interest in extra-European sculptures: the Egyptian, the Sumerian, the African and chiefly the Mexican pre-Columbian epitomised in the Aztec Chacmool. The chunky solidity of the last contrasted with the more naturalistic flow of the few bronzes from the female life modes. After 1930 he was clearly coming to terms with the amalgam of form and feeling. An abstraction of shape in the figure carvings lends them an added warmth.

There followed a flirtation with forms owing something to the example of Picasso in their distorted imagery, and also to the surrealist juxtapositions of Giacometti. Hollowing out of the centred mass of his figures occurred in the 1930's, when Moore was experimenting in various directions, some to be abandoned quickly, others continuing profitably, such as the opened-out interiors of a torso in clay, concrete and subsequently wood. Developing from the opening-out came the stringed and enclosed objects as seen through the aperture in the outer shell.

During the 1940's Moore returned to a more figurative idiom best known in his "Madonna and Child" for St. Matthew's Church, Northampton. This carving in stone has obvious debts to Massaccio and Michelangelo in its simple dignity and broad fullness of form that were to be stylised in the family groups and standing figures of the period. In parallel to his sculptures came the exciting activity between 1940 and 1942 as an official war artist, when he made his famous Shelter Drawings. Undeniably the most monumental to emerge from the hostilities, they have a strong similarity to the iconography of Mantegna.

Moore always worked in a continuous and varied investigation of glyptic possibilities, going back to ideas begun 20 or 30 years before, and making new works taking up from the previous ones as departure points. Relationships of man and woman, and mother and child, as well as the free-standing single figures, make the 1950's a productive and important phase of Moore's career. Bronzes predominate with occasional exceptions, like the grand "Internal and External Forms," 1953/4, almost nine feet high, carved like a mammoth peapod pierced to reveal its figure sheltering symbolically within. "King and Queen" of a year earlier is separate yet unified by its stylised affinity. In an outdoor setting the bronze group has an imposing character when seen from a distance. In the 1960's Moore produced some of his most telling abstract works, developing the separation and locking-together motives that underlined the unified concepts of the whole. More than any other sculptor before him, though acknowledging the pioneering example of Brancusi, Moore revealed an extensive vocabulary of form symbols that he employed in the creation of significant total images.

Paraphrases of human anatomy presence found in rocks and pebbles, and even in the contours of mountain ranges, have been enlarged and enhanced by Moore in numinous artifacts that carry their intrinsic proportions of scale acceptable in any size from maquette to massive cast. While he may instil into an inert bronze some of the overpowering atmosphere of its theme, like "Atom Piece" (1964), or endow the warmth of the glowing red Soroya marble "Three Rings" of 1966/7 with a purified balance of mass and distanced voids, it is man in the universe that dominates Moore's prodigious and prolific output. He fulfils his contemporary role as explorer of continents never before examined, recycling inherited universal visual experiences in catalytic fusion of imagination and eminent tactile reality.

—G. S. Whittet

MORANDI, Giorgio.

Italian. Born in Bologna, 20 July 1890. Studied at the Accademia di Belle Arti, Bologna, 1907–13. Served in the Italian Army briefly; discharged due to illness. Painter: lived and worked in Bologna: associated with Giorgio de Chirico, Carlo Carra and the Scuola Metafisica, 1916–18; stayed summers in Grizzana and settled there in 1938. Lecturer in drawing, Scuola Elementaria, Bologna, 1914–30; Director of Elementary Schools, Reggio Emilia and Modena provinces, 1926–27; Professor of Engraving, Accademia di Belle Arti, Bologna, 1930–56. Recipient: Prize, *Quadriennale,* Rome, 1931; First Prize, *Collectionist Exhibition,* Cortina d'Ampezzo, 1941; Italian Painting Prize, *Biennale,* Venice, 1948; Grand Prize for Painting, *Bienal,* Sao Paulo, 1957; Rubens Prize for Painting, Siegen, West Germany, 1962; Gold Medal, Municipality of Bologna, 1963. Member, Accademia Nazionale de San Luca, Rome, 1948, and Swedish Academy, 1951. *Died* (in Grizzana) *18 June 1964.*

Individual Exhibitions:

1945	Galleria Il Fiore, Florence
	Galleria La Palma, Rome
1948	Calcografia Nazionale, Rome
1949	Palais des Beaux-Arts, Brussels
1954	Gemeentemuseum, The Hague (travelled to New Burlington Gallery, London)
1955	Delius Gallery, New York
1956	Kunstmuseum, Winterthur, Switzerland (with Giacomo Manzu)
1957	World House Galleries, New York
	Galleria Galatea, Turin
1958	The American Federation of Art, New York (with Giacomo Manzu)
1962	Hans Seel am Markt, Siegen, West Germany
1963	Galerie Krugier, Geneva
1964	*8th Mostra Nazionale di Arti Figurative,* Ancona
	Kunsthaus, Bielefeld, West Germany
	Kunstverien, Karlsruhe
	Kestner-Gesellschaft, Hannover
1965	Kunstverein, Wuppertal, West Germany
	Scottish Gallery of Modern Art, Edinburgh
	Kunsthalle, Berne
	Fundacion Eugenio Mendoza, Caracas
1966	Calcografia Nazionale, Rome
	Galleria Nazionale Arte Moderna, Rome
	Biennale, Venice
	Palazzo dell'Archiginnasio, Bologna
	Scuola Comunale, Grizzana, Italy
1968	Galerie Krugier, Geneva
	Galleria De'Foscherai, Bologna
	National Gallery, Copenhagen
	Nasjionalgalleriet, Oslo
	Galerie Villand et Galanis, Paris
	Busch-Reisinger Museum, Harvard University, Cambridge, Massachusetts
1969	Centro d'Arte Dolomiti, Cortina d'Ampezzo, Italy
1970	Galleria Annunciata, Milan
	Galleria Odyssia, New York (with Giacomo Manzu and Ennio Morlotti)
	Royal Academy of Arts, London
	Galleria del Milione, Milan (with Ennio Morlotti)
1971	Musée National d'Art Moderne, Paris
	Ripartizione Istituzioni Iniziative Culturali, Milan
1972	Stedelijk Museum, Amsterdam
1973	Hermitage Museum, Leningrad (travelled to the Pushkin Museum, Moscow)
	Galleria Nazionale d'Arte Moderna, Rome
1975	Galleria d'Arte Moderna, Bologna
1977	Israel Museum, Jerusalem (travelled to Tel Aviv Museum, 1978)
1978	Western Australian Art Gallery, Perth
	Acqueforti, Cabinetto Disegni e Stampe degli Uffizi, Florence
	Musée des Beaux-Arts, Lyons
	Lumley Cazalet Gallery, London
	Grand Palais, Paris
	Galleria Civica d'Arte Moderna, Palazzo dei Diamonti, Ferrara, Italy
	Marie-Louise Jeanneret Art Moderne, Geneva
1981	Haus der Kunst, Munich
	San Francisco Museum of Modern Art (travelled to the Guggenheim Museum, New York, and the Art Center, Des Moines, 1981–82)
1982	Galleria d'Arte Moderna, Bologna
1983	Palazzo della Permanente, Milan
	Guggenheim Museum, New York
1984	Hirshhorn Museum, Washington, D.C.
	Pinacoteca Nazionale, Bologna
	Galleria Mara Coccia, Rome
	National Museum of Wales, Cardiff
1985	Kunstverein, Frankfurt
	Musée Cantini, Marseille, France
	Musée des Augustins, Toulouse, France
	Galleria dell'Oca, Rome
1986	Galleria Comunale d'Arte Moderna, Bologna

Selected Group Exhibitions:

1921	*Valori Plastici,* Nationalgalerie, Berlin
1926	*Primo Mostra Novecento,* Milan
1930	*Exhibition of Engravings,* Bibliothèque Nationale, Paris
1935	*Ancient and Modern Italian Art,* Jeu de Paume, Paris
1939	*Golden Gate Exhibition, San Francisco*
1940	*Exhibition of Italian Art,* Kunsthaus, Zurich
1949	*20th Century Italian Art,* Museum of Modern Art, New York
1950	*Modern Italian Art,* Tate Gallery, London
1953	*Bienal,* Sao Paulo
1962	*Grand Prize Winners from the Biennale 1948–1960,* Ca'Pesaro, Venice

Collections:

Galeria d'Arte Moderna, Turin; Galleria Nazionale d'Arte Moderna, Rome; Centre Georges Pompidou, Paris; Tate Gallery, London; National Gallery of Modern Art, Edinburgh; Gemeentemuseum, The Hague; Stedelijk Museum, Amsterdam; Israel Museum, Jerusalem; Hermitage Museum, Leningrad; Museum of Modern Art, New York.

Publications:

On MORANDI: books—*Morandi* by C. Brandi, Florence 1952; *Giorgio Morandi,* exhibition catalogue, by Vitale Bloch and Lamberto Vitali, London 1954; *Pittori Italiani dal Futurismo a Oggi* by Guido Ballo, Rome 1956; *Ritratto di Morandi* by C. Brandi, Milan 1960; *Giorgio Morandi: Pittore* by Lamberto Vitali, Milan 1964; *L'Opera Grafica di Giorgio Morandi* by Lamberto Vitali, Turin 1964; *Morandi* by Marco Valsecchi, Milan 1964; *Morandi* by Guido Guiffre, Florence and London 1970; *Giorgio Morandi,* exhibition catalogue, by Andrew Forge, London 1970; *Il Tempo di Morandi* by Valerio Zurlini, Reggio Emilia, Italy 1975; *Morandi: Drawings* by Neri Pozza, Rome 1977; *Morandi: Catalogo Generale* by Lamberto Vitale, Milan 1977; *Giorgio Morandi: Acqueforti,* exhibition catalogue, by Anna Maria Petrioli Tofani, Florence 1978; *Morandi,* exhibition catalogue, by Luigi Magnani and others, New York 1981; *Giorgio Morandi,* exhibition catalogue, by Franz Armin and others, Munich 1981; *Morandi in Galleria,* exhibition catalogue edited by Franco Solmi, Bologna 1985; *Morandi: 100 Opere su Carta,* with texts by Rosalba Tardito, Franco Solmi and Marilena Pasquali, Milan 1986.

Some years ago I asked one of the directors of New York's Museum of Modern Art why they didn't mount a Morandi retrospective. He replied that the subject had been brought up a number of times at meetings, but the idea had always been rejected—"too many bottles" was the consensus. This nearly incredible over-simplification from an institution responsible for more than one display of repetitious work on one note, gives some idea of the peculiar prejudices that can crop up at any one time in the art establishment. Could one have submitted at the same time "too many squares" (Albers)? or "too many fuzzy rectangles" (Rothko)? Surely the point was being begged: it is the *painting* that makes Morandi's pictures of value, not their subject matter. Having evidently to paint *something,* Morandi found bottles more malleable than people. And, if one is to make an effort at accuracy, he was a superb and subtle landscape painter as well.

The Chardin of our epoch, or perhaps, closer (he included no people), the Zurburan (of the still lifes), Morandi shares with these masters that captivity of pearly still-ness that encloses their works. Close tonalities, even light, the treatment of shadow as substance, complex suggestions of metaphysical dramas—all serve to enlarge the "narrowness" of what we are shown. On the surface, some boxes, bottles, containers a slab of wall, pale trees; suggestively, a walled town, a holy compound, a sacred grove.

As a painter in love with the art of painting, in search of a subject neither "abstract" or "real," Morandi found the cubes and volumes of his beloved Cézanne in everyday tea tins, vases, bottles. These he transformed through the application of paint, the accumulation of dust, and the actions of time, into symbols of themselves so that they could be painted "impersonally" as it were. And the lessons these still lifes taught him he applied to his landscapes of sun-patinaed houses and silvery olive farms. In the end his simplifications led to a way of seeing as limited and as large as that of Mondrian.

—Ralph Pomeroy

MORELLET, François.

French. Born in Cholet, 30 April 1926. Educated at College Colbert, Cholet, 1932–36, 1940–41; at the Lycée Charlemagne, Paris, 1937–39, 1942–44; at Ecole des Langues Orientales, Paris, 1945–47; received degree in Russian, 1947; mainly self-taught in art from 1947; influenced by meeting Almir Mavignier, 1950, and Max Bill, 1954. Married Danielle Marchand in 1946; children: Frederic, Christophe and Florent. General Manager, Morellet-Guerineau toy factory, Cholet, 1948–75. Artist, working with kinetic and optical experiments, Cholet, since 1950. Founder, with Sobrino, Le Parc, Stein, Yvaral and Rossi, Groupe de Recherche d'Art Visuel, Paris, 1960–68. Recipient: First Prize (with G.R.A.V.), *4th Biennale di San Marino,* 1963; Ohara Museum Prize, *Tokyo Print Biennale,* 1974; First Prize, *Bienal,* Sao Paulo, 1975; Will Grohmann Prize, West Berlin, 1979; Silver Medal, *2nd Triennale of Drawing,* Wroclaw, 1981; Grand Prix National de la Sculpture, France, 1986; Superior Prize and 5th Henry Moore Grand Prize, Hakone, Japan, 1987. Agents: Galerie Liliane et Michel Durand-Dessert, 3 rue des Haudriettes, 75003 Paris, France; Galerie M, Haus Weitmar, 4630 Bochum, West Germany. Address: 83 rue Porte-Baron, 49300 Cholet, France.

Individual Exhibitions:

1950	Galerie Crouze, Paris
1958	Galerie Colette Allendy, Paris
1960	Galerie Aujourd'hui, Palais des Beaux-Arts, Brussels
1961	Galerie Nota, Monaco
	Galerie Studio F, Ulm, West Germany
1962	Studio G, Zagreb
1966	Galerie der Spiegel, Cologne
1967	Galerie Denise René Rive Droite, Paris
	Galerie Denise René Rive Gauche, Paris
	Indica Gallery, London
1969	Galerie Plus Kern, Ghent
	Galerie Swart, Amsterdam
	Halfmannshof, Gelsenkirchen, West Germany
1970	Galerie M, Bochum, West Germany
	Galerie Denise René-Hans Mayer, Dusseldorf
	Galerie Swart, Amsterdam
	Galleri Artestudio, Macerata, Italy
1971	Galleria Cenobio-Visualita, Milan
	Van Abbemuseum, Eindhoven, Netherlands
	Centre National d'Art Contemporain, Paris
	Galerie Denise René Rive Gauche, Paris
	Kunstverein, Hamburg

	Städtisches Museum, Leverkusen, West Germany
	Eat Art Galerie, Dusseldorf
	Galerie M, Bochum, West Germany
	Kunstverein, Frankfurt
	Galerie Thomas Keller, Starnberg, West Germany
	Galerie Lichter, Frankfurt
1972	White Gallery, Lutry, Switzerland
	Palais des Beaux-Arts, Brussels
	Galerie Plus Kern, Ghent
	Kunstmuseum, Bochum, West Germany
	Lucy Milton Gallery, London
	Musee des Beaux-Arts, Grenoble, France
	Kunstmuseum, Dusseldorf
	Galerie Media, Neuchâtel, Switzerland
1973	Galerie Zodiak, Geneva
	Musée des Beaux-Arts, Nantes, France
	Galeria Arte Contacto, Caracas
	Museum Sztuki, Lodz, Poland
	Galerie Swart, Amsterdam
	Galerie Le Disque Rouge, Brussels
	Galerie D + C Muller-Roth, Stuttgart
	Centre Culturel, St. Pierre des Corps, France (toured France)
1974	Lucy Milton Gallery, London
	Galerie Lydia Megert, Berne
	Studio Plus Kern, Brussels
	Galleria Cavallino, Venice
	Galleria Trinita, Rome
	Galleria Uxa, Novara, Italy
	Galerie 58, Rapperswil, Switzerland
	Studio Casati, Merate, Italy
	Galerie Ernst, Hannover
	Gallerie 2B, Bergamo, Italy
	Musée Bargoin, Clermont Ferrand, France (toured France)
1975	Studio Marconi, Milan
	Galleria Sincron, Brescia, Italy
	Galleria Il Centro, Naples
	Galleria E, Bolzano, Italy
	Galerie M, Bochum, West Germany
	Galerie M, The Hague
	Galerie A, Parma
	Galerie Swart, Amsterdam
	Art Research Center, Kansas City
1976	Verfindustrie, Heerlen, Netherlands
	Club 44, La Chaux de Fonds, Switzerland
	Galerie Hermanns, Munich
	Galerie 13, Angers, France
	Galerie Müller-Roth, Stuttgart
	Galerie F. L., Rome
	Multipla de Arte, Sao Paulo
	Galleria Beniamino, Sanremo, Italy
	Lichtobjekte, Westfälischer Kunstverein, Münster, West Germany

	Galleria Giuli, Lecco, Italy
	Centro Serre Ratti, Como, Italy
1977	Nationalgalerie, West Berlin
	Staatliche Kunsthalle, Baden-Baden, West Germany
	Musée d'Art Moderne de la Ville, Paris
	Kunsthalle, Kiel, West Germany
	Galerie Swart, Amsterdam
	Annely Juda Gallery, London
	Galerie Nancy Gillespie-Elisabeth De Laage, Paris
	Centro del Portello, Genoa
	Galerie Le Disque Rouge, Brussels
	Studio Casati, Merate, Italy
	Galerie Latzer, Kreuzlingen, Switzerland
	Galerie Dritte, Zofingen, Switzerland
	Atelier de Recherche Esthetique, Caen, France
1978	Commanderie van St. Jan, Nijmeegs Museum, Netherlands
	Electric Gallery, Toronto
	Galerie Gilles Gheerbrant, Montreal
	Cloitre St. Trophime, Arles, France
	Galeria Cadaques, Cadaques, Spain
	Galerie Seestrasse, Rapperswil, Switzerland
	Galerie Lydia Megert, Berne
	Galerie Nancy Gillespie-Elisabeth De Laage, Paris
	Galerie Lachowsky, Brussels
	Galerie Magazijn, Groningen, Netherlands
	Studio Marconi, Milan
	Galleria Piero Cavellini, Brescia, Italy
	Galleria Uxa, Novara, Italy
1979	Galeria Eude, Barcelona
	Galerie Swart, Amsterdam
	Galerie Morner, Stockholm
1980	Galerie Nordenhake, Malmo, Sweden
	Galerie Le Coin du Miroir, Dijon, France
	Galerie Genevieve et Serge Mathieu, Besancon, France
	Galerie Hermanns, Munich
	Galerie Müller-Roth, Stuttgart
	Musée des Beaux-Arts, Toulon
	Galleria La Bottega del Quátro, Bergamo, Italy
	Galerie Fritz Buhler, Biel-Bienne, Switzerland
	Galerie M, Bochum, West Germany
1981	Centre Jean Vilar, Angers, France
	Helsingin Kaupungin Taidesmuseo, Helsinki
	Galerie Gilles Gheerbrant, Montreal
	East Gallery, London
	Annely Juda Gallery, London
	Galerie Durand-Dessert, Paris
1982	Galerie Lydia Megert, Berne
	Musée Savoisien, Chambery, France
	Kunstcentrum Badhuis, Gorinchem, Netherlands
	Centre Culturel, Cherbourg, France
	Musée des Beaux-Arts, Angers, France
1983	Galerie Convergences, Nantes, France

François Morellet: *Courbe Fragmentée,* **1954**

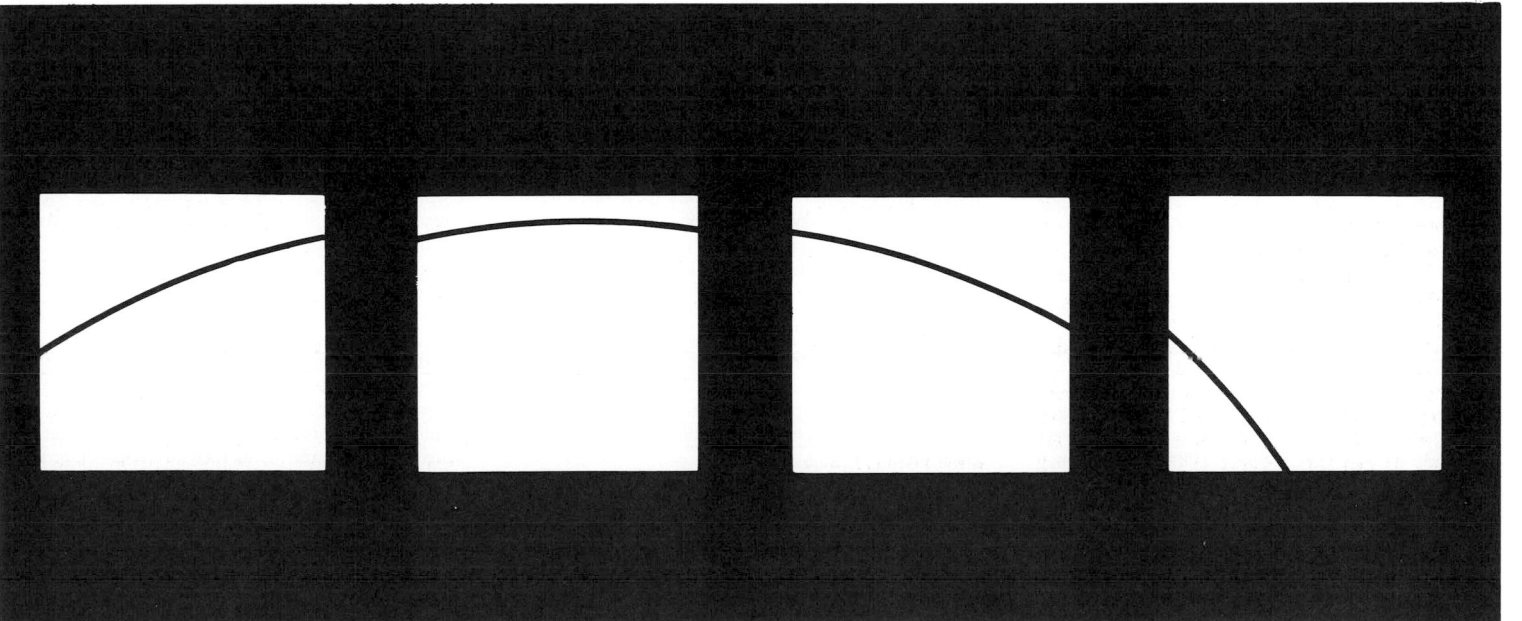

Musée Municipal, La Roche sur Yon, France
Tours Narbonnais, Carcassonne, France
Galerie au Fond de la cour a droite, Chagny, France
Ecole d'Architecture Saint Luc, Ghent
Stadtmuseum Quadrant, Bottrop, West Germany

1984 Wilhelm-Hack-Museum, Ludwigshafen, West Germany
Galerie Nordenhake, Malmo, Sweden
Albright-Knox Art Gallery, Buffalo, New York (travelled to Montreal, New York and Miami)

1985 Galerie Durand-Dessert, Paris
Musée Saint Pierre, Lyon, France
Galerie M, Bochum, West Germany
Galerie Zographia, Bordeaux, France
Galerie Kunst + Architektur, Hamburg
Abbaye Royale de Fontevraud, France

1986 Centre Georges Pompidou, Paris (retrospective; travelled to Amsterdam)
Galerie Plus-Kern, Brussels
Artothèque, Montpellier, France
Musée des Arts, Cholet, France
Galerie Steendrukkerij, Amsterdam
Galerie Oniris, Rennes, France
Musée Fabre, Montpellier, France
Galerie Blanche, Stockholm
Bruno Facchetti Gallery, New York
Oscarsson-Siegeltuch Gallery, New York
Galerie Emmerich/Margrit Bauman, Zurich
Centre d'Art Contemporain, Dijon, France

1987 Bruno Facchetti Gallery, New York
Rijksmuseum Kröller-Müller, Otterlo, Netherlands
Groninger Museum, Groningen, Netherlands

Selected Group Exhibitions:

1961 *Movement*, Moderna Museet, Stockholm (travelled to Stedelijk Museum, Amsterdam)

1965 *The Responsive Eye*, Museum of Modern Art, New York (toured the United States)

1967 *Lumière et Mouvement*, Musée d'Art Moderne, Paris

1975 *Bienal*, Sao Paulo

1977 *Documenta 6*, Kassel, West Germany

1980 *Printed Art since 1965*, Museum of Modern Art, New York

1982 *60–80: Attitudes/Concepts/Images*, Stedelijk Museum, Amsterdam

1983 *Concepts in Construction 1910–80*, Tyler Museum of Art, Texas (toured the United States and Canada)

1985 *Vom Zeichen: Aspekte der Zeichnung 1960–85*, Kunstverein, Frankfurt (travelled to Kassel and Vienna)

1987 *Mathematik in der Kunst*, Wilhelm-Hack-Museum, Ludwigshafen, West Germany

Collections:

Centre Georges Pompidou, Paris; Musée d'Art Moderne de la Ville, Paris; Tate Gallery, London; Stedelijk Museum, Amsterdam; Nationalgalerie, West Berlin; Kunstmuseum, Dusseldorf; Kunsthaus, Zurich; Moderna Museet, Stockholm; Albright-Knox Gallery, Buffalo, New York; Musée des Beaux-Arts, Montreal.

Publications:

By MORELLET: books—*Pour une peinture experimentale programmee*, with Groupe de Recherche d'Art Visuel, Paris 1962; *Pour un Art Abstrait Progressif*, with F. Molnar, Zagreb 1963; *90°*, Cholet, France 1970; articles—"Für eine programmierte experimentelle Malerei" in *Francois Morellet*, exhibition catalogue, Cologne 1966; "Mise en condition du spectateur" in *Lumière et Mouvement*, exhibition catalogue, Paris 1967; "The Choice in Present-Day Art" in *Data*, edited by Anthony Hill, London, 1968; "Zur Situation des Kunstbetrachters" in *Fordererkreis Wilhelm Lehmbruck Museums*, exhibition catalogue, Duisburg, West Germany 1970; "Du spectateur au spectatuer ou l'art de deballer son pique-nique" in *Morellet*, exhibition catalogue, Eindhoven, Netherlands 1971; "Auto-critique/Autokritika" in *10. Biennale de Gravure*, exhibition catalogue, Ljubljana 1973; "1st History—2nd, The Moral" in *Morellet*, exhibition

catalogue, London 1974; "Fragen an Francois Morellet," with Gislind Nabakowski, in *Heute Kunst* (Dusseldorf), June/August 1975; "Die direkten Lichtquellen" in *Francois Morellet: Lichtobjekte*, exhibition catalogue, Münster 1976; "Les Années 70" in *Skira Annuel*, Geneva 1980; "Pourquoi ai-je ete incapable d'ecrire un article dans Quad" in *Quad* (Paris), July 1980; "Apropos d'Oeuvres Ephemeres et d'Integrations Architecturales" in *Mise en Pieces, Mise en Place, Mise au Point*, exhibition catalogue, Chalon-sur-Saône, France 1981; "La Geometrie des Contraintes" in *Media 81*, exhibition catalogue, Neuchâtel, Switzerland 1981; "J'ai realise depuis 1968 de nombreuses oeuvres ephemeres . . ." and "Nota . . ." in *Murs*, exhibition catalogue, Paris 1981; "Doctor de Stijl and Mister Bonset" in *Colloque International: Theo van Doesburg*, Dijon 1982; "Geometrees" in *Francois Morellet: Geometrie*, exhibition catalogue, Fontevraud 1985; interview with Serge Lemoine in *CNAC Magazine* (Paris), January/February 1986; "Au secours la droite revient" in *Francois Morellet: Geometrie dans les spasmes*, exhibition catalogue, Dijon 1987.

On MORELLET: books—*A la Recherche d'une Base—Peintures de Morellet* by Francois Monar, Nantes, France 1958; *Constructivism: Origins and Evolution* by George Rickey, New York 1967; *L'Art CInetique* by Frank Popper, Paris 1967; *Kinetic Art* by Guy Brett, London and New York 1968; *Optical Art* by René Parola, New York and London 1969; *Op Art* by Cyril Barrett, London and New York, 1970; *Human Information Processing* by P. H. Lindsay and D. A. Norman, New York and London 1972; *Francois Morellet—Les regles du jeu* by Michel Baudson, Brussels 1972; *L'Art Actuel en France* by Anne Tronche and Hervé Gloaguen, Paris 1973; *Beyond Modern Sculpture* by Jack Burnham, New York 1973; *Geschichte der abstrakten Kunst 1900–1960* by Cor Blok, Cologne 1975; *Art—Action and Participation* by Frank Popper, London 1976; *Le Declin de l'Objet* by Frank Popper, Paris 1975; *Concepts of Modern Art*, edited by Tony Richardson and Nikos Stangos, New York and London 1979; *Francois Morellet: Systems*, exhibition catalogue with texts by Jan Van der Marck and Charlotta Kotik, New York 1984; *Francois Morellet: retrospective*, exhibition catalogue with texts by Dominique Bozo, Catherine Millet and others, Paris 1986; *Francois Morellet: Lichtinstallaties*, exhibition catalogue with text by Frans Haks, Groningen 1987.

*

Part 1—History.

1926–1952 Nothing of interest. From 1952 onwards I have been making useless, therefore artisitc, objects with the constant purpose of reducing to a minimum my arbitrary decisions. I have suppressed composition, removed all interest in the execution, and above all I have applied rigorously systems which are both simple and obvious. The only elements of "fantasy" are brought about by genuine chance or by the spectator's participation. All this has been done in an atmosphere of total apathy as regards the general public.

Recently, however, the specialists have discovered in my "work", according to their particular temperament, severity, mirth, nihilism, anguish, virtuosity, asceticism, etc. It has reminded them of planetary constellations, rain on puddles, 'la petite madeleine' of Proust and so on.

Part 2—The Moral.

They are right in thinking all this, for the plastic arts must allow the spectator to find in them what he wants—that is to say what he brings to them himself. Works of art are like picnic areas or Spanish Inns, where one consumes what one takes there oneself.

Art is meant to say nothing (or everything). Specialists who respect each other experience each of them a different picnic, in opposition to one another and often contrary to the intentions which the artist would himself have formulated. When, during their life-time, artists seem to agree with certain of their commentators, it is in most cases because they have accepted, with astonishment and delight the significance given by these people to their work. Even more they have then sought to resemble the image, now given them.

The impossibility of conveying 'messages' is evident, for example, in politics. How well I understand the distrust felt by dictators towards the artists of the 'avant-garde'—even those of the same political turn of mind! (I cannot on the other hand conceive why those obsessed by politics choose, to express themselves, something so ambiguous and corrupt as art).

It is the great fraternity, the great conspiracy of the 'great men' to make the 'little men' believe that if Pasteur, Karl Marx, de Gaulle, Cezanne, had died at birth, no one would have been saved from rabies, capitalism, nazism, or impressionism. Of course, the cult of personality is natural. It was natural that we should worship Jesus Christ, Hitler or Elvis Presley. It is those who are worshipped who commit the fault in allowing themselves to be worshipped. They are the real reactionaries, those artists who, voluntarily or not, cultivate the arbitrary, allow one to believe in the existence of some secret justification, play the unknown despot, all the while considering themselves to be the revolutionary element in art. Since Duchamp, all the numerous revolutionary artists have been equally skillful in destroying the art of their predecessors as they have been in building up their own brilliant image.

All this will never change unless the geniuses cease being brilliant and concern themselves with becoming simply the awakeners, the masters of ceremony of the general public—that public which still does not realise that it is itself a genius (see Filliou).

Alternatively perhaps, the spectators might come to realise that, as in that tale by Hans Christian Andersen—'The Emperor's New Clothes'—it is they, the spectators, thanks to their brilliant imagination, who invest with splendour the Emperors and the artists. It would be a marvellous entertainment (but it would all the same be ironic that it should happen just as the picnickers begin to invest me with brilliance).

—Francois Morellet

*

Prominent in the activities of the Groupe de Recherche d'Art Visuel, of which he was a founding member, and a constant exhibitor with the Nouvelle Tendance, Franeois Morellet combined aesthetic proclivities with a scientific interest in new and out-of-the-way avenues of perception. His activities in this field were extremely versatile. He sought new applications for graphic techniques, explored new effects of light, and made important uses of scientific investigations into the effects of cyclical rotation.

From the early 1950's he explored the possibilities of the statistical distribution of identical elements over a picture surface in order to create an impression of complete homogeneity vibrant with optical energy. At the same time he was working with the superimposition or partial superimposition of uniform grills in order to create unexpected or semihallucinary effects in space. Particular attention was attracted by his *Sphéres-trames*, which were cellular spheres built up of metal rods and tubes set at right angles to each other and sometimes measuring as much as 6 feet in diameter, and by his *Grillagés*, which were metal frames and meshes set one above the other with different axes. Many of them were hung as mobiles for the sake of their curious properties in regard to the reflection of light and for the optical illusions they effected. Later they were sometimes given an architectural context by being designed for a particular site. These were considered to mark the early stages in the passage from static to kinetic Op art. In 1970 Morellet collaborated with the architect Claude Parent in designing a room with "oblique space" for the French Pavilion at the 35th Venice *Biennale*. And in 1970–71 he applied his earlier techniques to a large-scale commission for the Plateau Beaubourg, Paris, designing decorations in blue and red on the blind walls of houses to give the impression of superimposed grills. Both these works were considered to be important landmarks of Op art.

From about 1963 Morellet also turned his attention to the creation of rhythmical effects by the use of a light source, working first with white light and later with white and red neon rods or tubes in order to produce rhythmic accents in space. In this, as also of course in his mobiles, stochasticism or the element of chance, played a significant part. Morellet was also among the foremost of those who advocated spectator participation. In his light structures the spectator was allowed to initiate and control the rhythmical processes by means of buttons and switches. Morellet's theory was that the artist provides the basic elements, but the work of art emerges only with the collaboration of the spectator—together with the play of chance. In a small publication of 1971 entitled *Du Spectateur au spectateur ou l'art de déballer son pique-nique* he wrote: "For roughly 20 years I have obstinately continued to produce works which have been based on the guiding principle of reducing my arbitrary decisions to a minimum. To put limits on my 'artist's' sensibility, I among others have made use of simple and obvious systems, of pure chance, and of spectator participation." He concludes the spectator should "cease to be the humble vassal of the great genius. Let him recover his dignity, his activity before those who should be no more than the leaders of the game."

—Harold Osborne

MORLEY, Malcolm.

British. Born in London in 1931; moved to New York, 1964. Educated at Royal College of Art, London, 1954–57. Independent painter, living in New York, since 1957. Worked as a waiter, Longchamps Restaurant, New York, 1964. Associated with Barnett Newman, New York, 1964–65. Instructor, Royal College of Art, London, 1956; Instructor, Ohio State University, Columbus, 1965, 1966, and School of Visual Arts, New York, 1967–69. Instructor, State University of New York at Stony Brook, since 1972. Recipient: Turner Prize, Tate Gallery, London, 1984. Agent: Xavier Fourcade Inc., New York, Address: c/o Xavier Fourcade Inc., 36 East 75th Street, New York, New Yor, 10021, U.S.A.

Individual Exhibitions:

1957	Kornblee Gallery, New York
1964	Kornblee Gallery, New York
1967	Kornblee Gallery, New York
1969	Kornblee Gallery, New York
1973	Galerie Gerald Piltzer, Paris
	Stefanotty Gallery, New York
1974	Stefanotty Gallery, New York
1976	Clocktower Gallery, New York
1977	Galerie Jurka, Amsterdam
	Galerie Jollenbeck, Cologne
1979	Nancy Hoffman Gallery, New York
	Suzanne Hilberry Gallery, Detroit
1980	Wadsworth Atheneum, Hartford, Connecticut
1981	Xavier Fourcade, Inc., New York
1982	Akron Art Institute, Ohio
	Xavier Fourcade Inc., New York
1983	Whitechapel Art Gallery, London (travelled to Basle)
	Corcoran Gallery of Art, Washington, D.C.
1984	Museum of Contemporary Art, Chicago
	Brooklyn Museum, New York
1985	Piccadilly Gallery, London
	Fabian Carlsson Gallery, London
1987	Piccadilly Gallery, London

Selected Group Exhibitions:

1966	*The Photographic Image*, Guggenheim Museum, New York
1969	*Aspects of a New Realism*, Milwaukee Art Center (travelled to the Museum of Contemporary Arts, Houston, and Akron Art Institute, Ohio)
1972	*Contemporary American Painting*, Whitney Museum, New York
	Sharp Focus Realism, Sidney Janis Gallery, New York
1973	*Photo-Realism*, Serpentine Gallery, London
1974	*Projekt 74*, Cologne
	Dealers' Choice/Choice Dealers, New York Cultural Center
1977	*Painting in the Age of Photography*, Kunsthaus, Zurich
1980	*One Major Work Each*, Xavier Fourcade Inc., New York
1981	*A New Spirit in Painting*, Royal Academy, London
1987	*The Long Perspective*, Thomas Agnew and Sons, London

Collections:

Metropolitan Museum of Art, New York; Whitney Museum, New York; Fordham University, New York, Hirshhorn Museum, Washington, D.C.; Detroit Institute of Arts; Museum of Contemporary Art, Chicago; Louisiana Museum, Humlebaek, Denmark; Utrecht Museum, Netherlands; Neue Galerie der Stadt Aachen, West Germany.

Malcolm Morley: *M.A.S.H.*, 1978 Courtesy Museum of Contemporary Art, Chicago

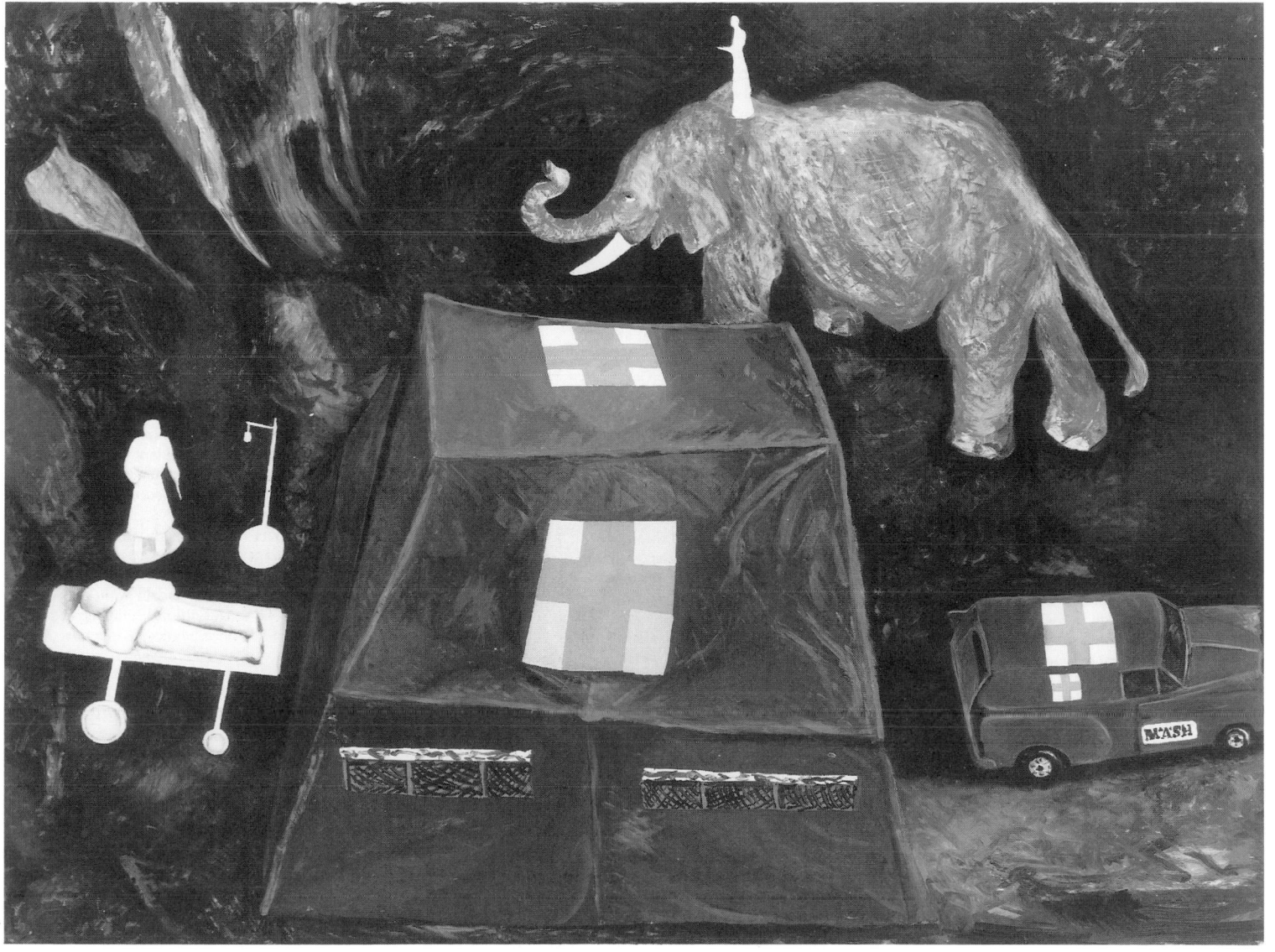

Publications:

On MORLEY: books—*Pop Art Redefined* by John Russell and Suzi Gablik, New York 1969; *Pop Art* by Michael Compton, London 1970; *Icons and Images of the 60's* by Nicholas and Elena Calas, New York, 1971; *New Realism* by Udo Kultermann, New York 1972; *Super Realism: A Critical Anthology,* edited by Gregory Battcock, New York 1975; *Photorealism* by Louis K. Meisel, New York 1980; *Malcolm Morley,* exhibition catalogue with texts by Michael Compton and Nicholas Serota, London 1983; articles—"New Names This Month" by Jill Johnston in *Artnews* (New York), October 1964; "Morley Paints a Picture" by Lawrence Alloway in *Artnews* (New York), Summer 1968; "The Reception of Figurative Art" by Sidney Tillim in *Artforum* (New York), February 1969; "New York: Super-Real Is Back in Town" by Ralph Pomeroy in *Art and Artists* (New York), May 1969; "Pop Reappraised" by John Russell in *Art in America* (New York), July/August 1969; "Real and the Artificial: Painting of the New Environment" by William C. Seitz in *Art in America* (New York), November 1972; "Malcolm Morley: Post Style Illusionism" by Kim Levin in *Arts Magazine* (New York), February 1973; "Malcolm Morley: Toward Erotic Painting" by Valentine Tatransky in *Art International* (Lugano, Switzerland), October 1979; "Malcolm Morley: Talking About Seeing" by Klaus Kertess in *Artforum* (New York), Summer 1980.

*

As a result of the paintings he made from 1965 to 1969–70 Malcolm Morley became known as the first Photo-Realist. The title is a well deserved one, and yet Morley is much more than this label implies. Never satisfied to rest on previous accomplishments, he has continued to develop a body of work during the 1970's which prove him to be one of the most astute painter's painters practicing at the present time.

Morley's abstract paintings from the early 60's made use of the grid system. In a 1964 picture titled "High July" he introduced representational imagery arranged in a composition of striated pattern which reads from top to bottom as clouds, sky, sea and beach. Extracting and combining from these two elements, Morley began, in 1965, to use the grid to paint handmade enlargements of reproduced images which originated out of posters and photographs of contemporary scenes and events as well as from the paintings of masters such as Vermeer. During this period Morley stated that he had no interest in subject matter as such, and that he accepted it "as a byproduct of surface." Painting square by square and often upside down, Morley questioned perceptions of literalness and reduplication. He was exploring the character of the confusions about meaning which occur through time and changing context. These paintings were a new kind of synthesis of painterly expression and content gleaned from the mass-produced sources through which we see most visual information from past and present, from art and life alike. From the start, there is a painterly quality which differs from the character of the photographic precursor. His use of devices such as the white border and the three-dimensional foldout form amplify these issues.

On his incredibly detailed painting titled "Racetrack" (1969–70), Morley superimposed a large red "X" in a gesture which destroyed, in effect, the literalness of the photo-real image and communicated the reality of paint as paint. "LA Yellow Pages" (1971, acrylic in wax) integrates into the work the rough tears Morley had made in his pocketbook source, not as collage but as painted surface. Paintings of the next few years become even rougher and denser in paint quality. "Rotterdam" (1974) is exemplary of this period; folds from the photographic source become painted elements in this picture which, in effect, negates Morley's earlier, more photo-real depiction of the same image in "SS Rotterdam in Rotterdam" (1966).

Among Morley's most effective pictures to date is "The Ultimate Anxiety" (1978). The model is a postcard showing part of a painting by the 18th century Venetian scene painter Francesco Guardi. Morley transforms this reproduced image into a painterly rendition of color and light which, on close inspection, breaks up the scene into gestural strokes. Over the scene, Morley paints a colorful toy train which moves diagonally across the composition in a swipe of defiance towards the idea of meaning in literal depiction. "Christmas Tree (The Lonely Ranger in the Jungle of Desires)" (1979) mixes images of toys with those of parrot, snake and woman's legs, all of which cohabit in their jungle setting. It is a move further penetrating into Morley's continual concerns, dealing with what he had earlier called the "pornographic" element in the two-dimensional surface which controls "because you can't penetrate it."

Morley's recent pictures of animals in the landscape seem to come more directly from memories of seen experience, incorporating beside Morley's homage to Delacroix and Cezanne the hint that perhaps an unencumbered perception of things seen directly is in order at this time if we are to understand the nature of meaning as it really is, in paint and in life. In addition to Morley's investigations into the nature of his medium, the strength in his work lies in his ability to communicate the anxieties felt by the individual always on the edge of continuing or being destroyed, hovering, as it were, on the beach, ship or train, in the jungle or the city. He has accomplished much to convey the continued relevancy of the painter for the present by maintaining a fierce independence and persistence, refusing to be waylaid by trendiness or stylishness.

—Barbara Cavaliere

MORLOTTI, Ennio.

Italian. Born in Lecco, 21 September 1910. Studied at the Accademia di Belle Arti, Florence, 1936–37; Brera Accademia de Belle Arti, Milan, 1939. Served with Parisian troops during World War II. Painter: lives and works in Milan; visited Paris, 1937; settled in Milan, 1939; collaborated, with Corrente movement, Milan; Member, Fronto Nuovo delle Arti, Milan, 1946. Recipient: Travel Scholarship to France, 1947; Prize, *Biennale,* Venice, 1962, and *Dunn International,* Fredericton, New Brunswick, 1963. Address: via Mussi 9, 20154 Milan, Italy.

Individual Exhibitions:

1943	Galleria di Corrente, Milan (with Bruno Cassinari and Ernesto Treccanni)
1946	Galleria del Camino, Milan
1949	Galleria del Milione, Milan
1951	Gatherine Viviano Gallery, New York
1953	Catherine Viviano Gallery, New York (with Afro and Renato Birolli)
	Galleria del Milione, Milan
1957	Centro Culturale Olivetti, Ivrea, Italy (with Alberto Burri and Emilio Vedova)
1959	Italia Francia, Turin
	Catherine Viviano Gallery, New York
1963	Ente Turismo, Lecco, Italy
	Galleria Annunciata, Milan
1964	Odyssia Gallery, New York
1965	Gissi Galleria d'Arte, Turin
1966	Ente Primi, Rome
	Kunsthalle, Darmstadt
	Salon Annunciata, Milan
1967	Kunsthalle, Basle
1968	Galleria Bergamini, Milan
	Galleria Odyssia, Rome (with Alberto Burri and Renato Guttuso)
1970	Galleria del Milione, Milan (with Giorgio Morandi)
	Galleria Odyssia, New York (with Giorgio Morandi and Giacomo Manzu)
1971	Marlborough Fine Art, London
	Commune di Acqui Terme, Italy
1972	Galleria Cocorrocchia, Milan (with Alberto Burri and Renato Guttuso)
	Comune di San Gimignano, Italy
	Marlborough Gallery, New York
	Biennale, Venice
1973	Palazzo Strozzi, Florence
	Galleria Cocorrocchia, Milan
1974	Pinacoteca Tosio Martinengo, Brescia, Italy
	Marlborough Fine Art, London
	Pinacoteca Carrara, Bergamo, Italy
	Disegni 1960–1973, Museo Poldi Perroli, Milan
1975	Palazzo della Pilotta, Parma, Italy

Selected Group Exhibitions:

1958	*Carnegie International,* Carnegie Institute, Pittsburgh
1962	*Biennale,* Venice
1963	*Dunn International,* Beaverbrook Art Gallery, Fredericton, New Brunswick (travelled to the Tate Gallery, London)
1965	*5 Artisti Milanesi,* Kunsthalle, Winterhur, Switzerland
1974	*Graphics of the 20th Century,* Marlborough Fine Art, London

Publications:

On MORLOTTI: books—*Ennio Morlotti* by Mario de Micheli, Milan 1947; *Morlotti* by Giovanni Testori, Milan 1951; *Morlotti* by Antonio Manfredi, Milan 1958; *Morlotti* by Francesco Arcangeli, Milan 1962; *Morlotti* by Carlo Volpi, Rome 1963; *Morlotti* by Douglas Cooper and Franco Russoli, Rome 1966; *Morlotti e l'Informale* by Flavio Caroli, Ph.D. Thesis, University of Bologna, 1968; *Morandi/ Morlotti* by Roberto Tassi, Milan 1970; *Morlotti* by Francesco Biamonti, Milan 1972; *Morlotti* by Marco Valsecchi, Milan 1972; *Morlotti: Disegni 1960–1973.* exhibition catalogue, by Marco Valsecchi, Milan 1974; *Morlotti: Figure 1942–1975* by Roberto Tassi, Milan 1975; *Morlotti: Teschi 1974–1977* by Giovanni Testori, Busto Arisizio, Italy 1978; films—*Il Verde di Morlotti* by Pier Paolo Ruggerini and Roberto Tassi, RAI, 1968; *Ennio Morlotti* by Pier Paolo Ruggerini and Francesco Arcangeli, RAI, 1970.

*

Ennio Morlotti belongs to a group of Italian artists, which includes Guttuso and Birolli, who were impressed and moved by the art of Picasso, and in particular by the direct, socio-political involvement of "Guernica". In fact, this led to a curious misconception about realism, so that when, in 1945, Morlotti joined a group of Italian artists in the *Manifesto del Realismo,* it was the art of Picasso and Léger which they hailed as ideal representations. The confusion here was between naturalism and representation, as a means of distinguishing their work from abstraction.

Commitment and symbolism were more relevant elements in the work of the so called Italian "realists," who, in 1946 joined with Morlotti to form the Fronto Nuova dell'Arte—including Guttuso, Turcato, Cassinari, Santomaso and Vedova. All these artists tended towards abstraction, although human and social references remained important in their work. It was really a resistance to complete abstraction which united them, far more than any common, social commitment or stylistic unity.

Another important influence can be traced in Morlotti's paintings, the intense gesturalism of German Expressionism, and a dense colour harmony derived from a romantic involvement with landscape.

In his mature work Morlotti has foregone any direct realistic or even human reference in a series of still-lifes and landscape studies, rendered with utmost economy in short, vigorous jabs of rich, juicy pigment, limited to a few heavy colours. A draughtsman of elegant, involved complexity, he continues this sense of clarity into even the most abstracted canvases. His spiritual quality is pantheistic and dionysiac in its intense sense of pleasure, conveyed in the paintings by a rich sensuality. The delineation of fruit and vegetables, with their feminine fullness and roundness, are the notes of a lover, whilst the immediate, quick, profound awareness of the delicious forms and colour and nature is the response of infatuation.

Expressive qualities of painting have more and more dominated Morlotti's needs, and his handling of paint, with its mixture of purposeful jabbing and the magic of chance relationships, identifies him with the Tachiste movement. In recent years he has occasionally moved to flower-pieces and nudes, but he remains most impressive in the heavy, ponderous still-life and landscapes, with their low, blue, Ernstlike skies.

—Charles Spencer

MORRIS, Michael. Has also worked as Marcel Idea, Marcel Dot and Miss General Idea.

Canadian. Born in Saltdean, Sussex, England, 16 May 1942; emigrated to Canada in 1946. Educated at Victoria University, Toronto, 1960–62; Vancouver School of Art, British Columbia, 1962–64; Slade School of Fine Art, London University, 1964–65. Independent painter and installation artist, from 1967, and video artist from 1971; lived in Vancouver, 1967–81, and in West Berlin, since 1981. Acting Curator, Vancouver Art Gallery, 1967; Instructor-Coordinator for Special Events, Centre for Communication and the Arts, Simon Fraser University, Burnaby, British Columbia, 1967–68; Coordinator, Media Workshops for National Film Board of Canada, 1969; developed concept of Image Bank, with Vincent Tarsov, 1970, and Founder, Image Bank archives, 1972; founder, Image Bank Video Editions, 1981. Guest Lecturer, Fine Arts Department, University of Victoria, 1970; Artist-in-Residence, University of Saskatchewan, Regina, 1972; Guest lecturer, University of British Columbia, Vancouver, 1973–74. Recipient: Canada Council Short Term Travel Grant, 1965; Purchase Award, Vancouver Art Gallery, 1966; Canada Council Arts Bursary, 1967, 1969 and 1972; Award for Painting, *Perspective '67*, Art Gallery of Ontario, Toronto, 1967; Purchase Award, Montreal Museum of Fine Arts, 1967 and 1969; Senior Canada Council Grant, 1974–75, 1982–83; DAAD Artist Fellowship, West Berlin, 1981. Agent: Gallery Allen, 3025 Granville Street, Vancouver, British Columbia V6H 3J9. Address: Mommsenstrasse 9, 1000 Berlin 12 (West), Germany.

Individual Exhibitions:

1964	New Design Gallery, Vancouver
1965	Victoria Art Gallery, British Columbia
1967	Fine Arts Gallery, University of British Columbia, Vancouver
	Douglas Gallery, Vancouver
1969	Marlborough Godard Gallery, Montreal
1970	Ace Gallery, Vancouver
1980	Musée d'Art Contemporain, Montreal
1981	Centre Culturel Canadien, Brussels
1982	Galerie Ars Viva, West Berlin
1983	Galerie Janssen, West Berlin
	Galerie J. J. Donguy, Paris
	Backroom Gallery, Victoria
1984	De Fabriek, Eindhoven, Netherlands
1985	Victoria Art Gallery, British Columbia
1986	Vancouver Art Gallery, British Columbia
	Or Gallery, Vancouver
1987	Eisenbahnstrasse Galerie, West Berlin

Selected Group Exhibitions:

1967	*Spring Show*, Museum of Fine Arts, Montreal
1968	*Canada 101*, at the *Edinburgh Festival*
1969	*Biennale*, Paris
1971	*Image Bank Post Card Show*, Fine Arts Gallery, University of British Columbia, Vancouver
1973	*Trajectore Canadian*, Musée d'Art Contemporain, Paris
1974	*Environmental Communications*, Institute of Contemporary Arts, London
1979	*Cibachrome*, National Film Board, Ottawa
1983	*Museums by Artists*, Art Gallery of Ontario, Toronto
1986	*Das andere Land*, Schloss Charlottenburg, West Berlin

Collections:

National Gallery, Ottawa; Canada Council, Ottawa; Department of External Affairs, Ottawa; Vancouver Art Gallery; Art Gallery of Ontario, Toronto; Museum of Fine Arts, Montreal; Winnipeg Art Gallery; Art Gallery of Greater Victoria, British Columbia; Edmonton Art Gallery, Alberta; Museum of Modern Art, New York.

Publications:

By MORRIS: books—*Image Bank Post Card Show*, exhibition catalogue, Toronto 1971; *Image Bank Annual Report*, Vancouver 1972; *Image Bank Image Exchange Directory*, Vancouver 1972; article—"Alex and Roger" in *B. C. Almanac* (Vancouver), 1970; numerous contributions to magazines and books, including: *Concrete Poetry*, Vancouver 1963; *Space Atlas*, Victoria, British Columbia 1971; *Art Work No Commerical Value*, New York 1971; *Pages Magazine* (London), 1972; *File Magazine* (Toronto), 1972 and 1973; *Vice Magazine* (San Francisco), 1973; *Source: Music for the Avant Garde* (Sacramento), 1974; *Strange Feces*, Vancouver 1975; film and videotape—*Light On*, 3 minute, 16mm film, 1973; *Image Bank Colour Research 1972–74*, 27 minute videotape, 1974; *Video Narcissus*, 1979/80; *Lil Picard: End of the Bowtie*, 1982; *Fluxus Constructivism*, 1983; *Video Wannsee*, 1984; *Female Voices*, 1985; *Female Feet*, 1986; *Siren of Girona*, 1987.

MORRIS, Robert.

American. Born in Kansas City, Missouri, 9 February 1931. Studied engineering, University of Kansas City; art, Kansas City Art Institute, 1948–50; California School of Fine Arts, San Francisco, 1951; Reed College, Portland, Oregon, 1953–55; art history, Hunter College, New York, 1961–62, M.A. 1962. Served in Corps of Army Engineers in Arizona and Korea, 1951–52. Worked in theatre improvisation, San Francisco, 1955–60; collaborated in performance works with Yvonne Rainer, New York 1963. Contributor, *Artforum*, New York, since 1966. Assistant Professor, Hunter College, New York, since 1967. Recipient: Prize, Walker Art Center, Minneapolis, 1966; First Prize, International Institute, Torcuato di Tella, Buenos Aires, 1967; Guggenheim International Award, 1967; Guggenheim Fellowship, 1969; Sculpture Award, Society Four Arts, 1975; Skowhegan Medal for Progress and Environment, Maine, 1978. D.F.A.: Williams College, Williamstown, Massachusetts, 1986. Agent: Leo Castelli Gallery, 420 West Broadway, New York, New York 10012. Address: R.D. 1, Box 444, Gardiner, New York 12525, U.S.A.

Individual Exhibitions:

1957	Dilexi Gallery, San Francisco
1958	Dilexi Gallery, San Francisco
1963	Green Gallery, New York
1964	Green Gallery, New York
	Galerie Schmela, Dusseldorf
1965	Green Gallery, New York
1966	Dwan Gallery, Los Angeles
1967	Leo Castelli Gallery, New York
1968	Leo Castelli Gallery, New York
	Galerie Ileana Sonnabend, Paris (2 shows)
	Van Abbemuseum, Eindhoven, Netherlands
1969	Leo Castelli Gallery, New York
	Galleria Enzo Sperone, Turin
	Irving Blum Gallery, Los Angeles
	Corcoran Gallery, Washington, D.C.
	David Gallery, Houston
1970	Irving Blum Gallery, Los Angeles
	Detroit Institute of Arts
	Whitney Museum, New York
	Stedelijk Museum, Amsterdam
	Castelli Graphics, New York
1971	Tate Gallery, London
	Galerie Ileana Sonnabend, Paris
1972	Leo Castelli Gallery, New York
	David Gallery, Houston
1973	Galerie Ileana Sonnabend, Paris
	Konrad Fischer Gallery, Dusseldorf
	Max Protetch Gallery, Washington, D.C.
	Galleria Forma, Genoa
	Lucio Amelio Modern Art Agency, Naples
	Ace Gallery, Venice, California
1974	*Projects*, Institute of Contempoary Art, University of Pennsylvania, Philadelphia
	Sonnabend-Castelli Gallery, New York
	Galerie Art in Progress, Munich
	Alessandra Castelli Gallery, Milan
	Grand Rapids Project, Belknap Park, Grand Rapids, Michigan
1975	Galleria D'Allesandro-Ferranti, Rome
	Carlson Gallery, University of Bridgeport, Connecticut
1976	Leo Castelli Gallery, New York
	Sonnabend-Castelli Gallery, New York
1977	Louisiana Museum, Humblebaek, Denmark
	Williams College, Williamstown, Massachusetts
	James Corcoran Gallery, Los Angeles
	Portland Center for the Visual Arts, Oregon
	Stedelijk Museum, Amsterdam
	Het Observatorium in Oostelijk Flevoland Netherlands
	Galerie Art in Progress, Dusseldorf
	Galerie Ileana Sonnabend, Paris
1978	Florence Wilcox Gallery, Swarthmore College, Pennsylvania
	Beaver College, Glenside, Pennsylvania
	Galleria Civica d'Arte Moderna, Comune di Ferrara, Italy
1979	Leo Castelli Gallery, New York
	Ileana Sonnabend Gallery, New York
	Wright State University, Dayton, Ohio
1980	Waddington Galleries II, London
	Richard Hines Gallery, Seattle
	Art Institute of Chicago
	Leo Castelli/142 Greene Street Gallery, New York
1981	Contemporary Arts Museum, Houston
1982	Williams College, Williamstown, Massachusetts (travelled to Boston, Seattle, Austin and Grand Rapids)
1983	Leo Castelli Gallery, New York
	Sonnabend Gallery, New York
	University of Illinois, Champaign
	Galerie Daniel Templon, Paris
	Rijkmuseum, Amsterdam
1984	Konsthall, Malmo, Sweden
	Galerie Nordenhake, Malmo, Sweden
	Contemporary Arts Museum, Houston
	Padiglione d'Arte Contemporanea, Milan
	Portland Center for the Visual Arts, Oregon
1985	Sonnabend Gallery, New York
	Leo Castelli Gallery, New York
1986	Galerie Daniel Templon, Paris
	Museum of Contemporary Art, Chicago

Selected Group Exhibitions:

1963	*Black, White and Grey*, Wadsworth Atheneum, Hartford, Connecticut
1966	*The Other Tradition*, Institute of Contemporary Art, Philadelphia
1970	*Information*, Museum of Modern Art, New York
1975	*Sculpture, American Directions 1945–1975*, National Collection of Fine Arts, Smithsonian Institution, Washington, D.C.
1978	*Art About Art*, Whitney Museum, New York (toured the United States)
1979	*The Reducive Object: A Survey of the Minimalist Aethetic in the 1960's*, Institute of Contemporary Art, Boston
1980	*Biennale*, Venice

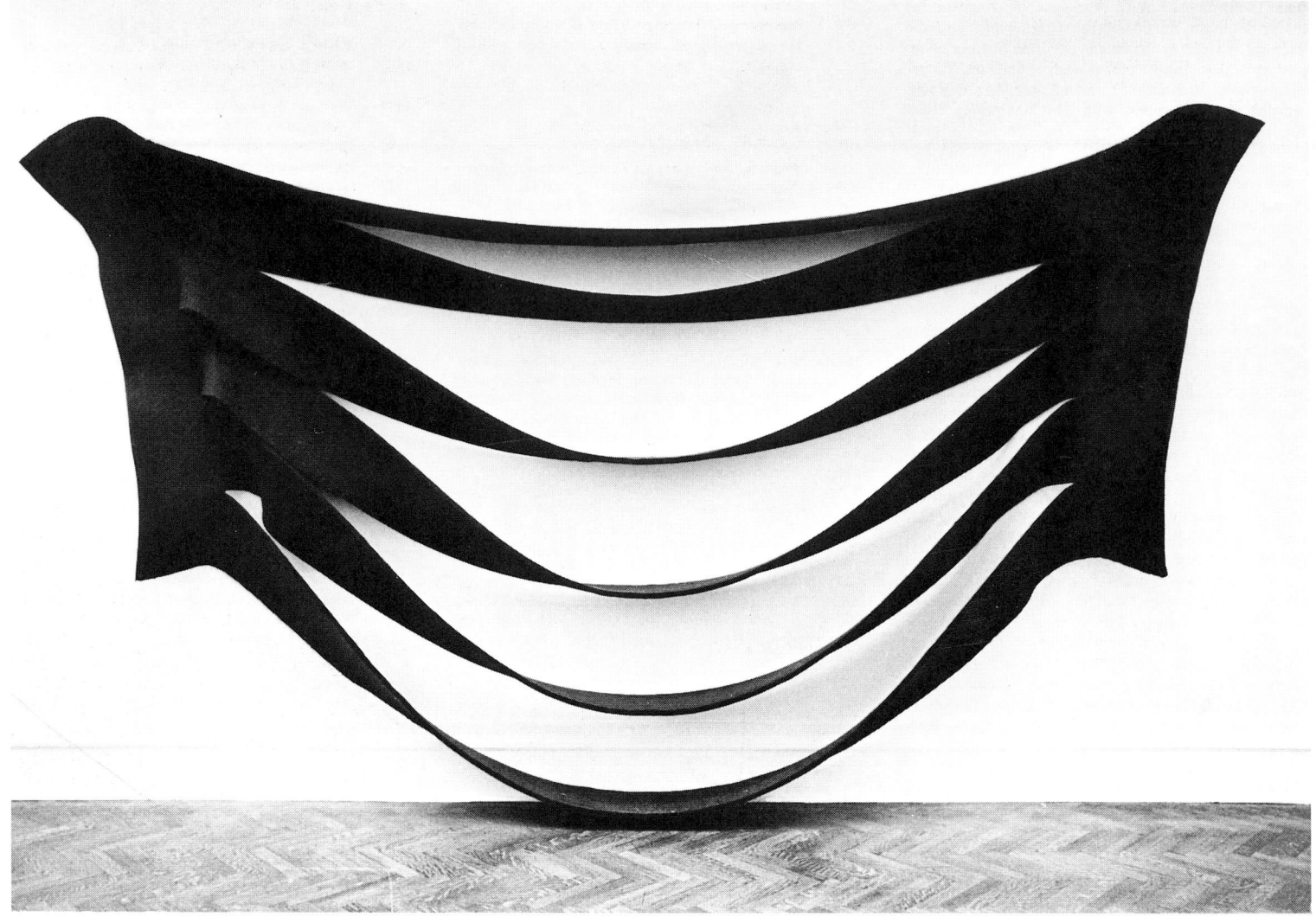

Robert Morris: *Untitled,* 1970

1982   *Postminimalism,* Aldrich Museum, Ridgefield, Connecticut
1984   *Content: A Contemporary Focus 1974–84,* Hirshhorn Museum, Washington, D.C.
1987   *Avant-Garde in the Eighties,* Los Angeles County Museum of Art

Collections:

Museum of Modern Art, New York; Whitney Museum, New York; Wadsworth Atheneum, Hartford, Connecticut; Allen Memorial Art Museum, Oberlin College, Ohio; Walker Art Center, Minneapolis; Dallas Museum of Fine Arts; National Gallery of Canada, Ottawa; Tate Gallery, London; Moderna Museet, Stockholm; National Gallery of Victoria, Melbourne.

Publications:

By MORRIS: book—*Continuous Project Altered Daily,* 1969; articles—"Notes on Sculpture, Part 1" in *Artforum* (New York), February 1966; "Notes on Sculpture, Part 2" in *Artforum* (New York), October 1966; "Notes on Sculpture, Part 3" in *Artforum* (New York), June 1967; "Anti-Form" in *Artforum* (New York) April 1968; statement in *Art Now: New York* (New York), June 1969; "Some Notes on the Phenomenology of Making: The Search for the Motivated" in *Artforum* (New York), April 1970; "Pace and Process" in *Avalanche* (New York), Fall 1970; "A Method of Sorting Cows" and "A Dialogue," with David Sylvester, in *Robert Morris,* exhibition catalogue, London 1971; "The Art of Existence: 3 Extra Visual Artists, Work in Process" in *Artforum* (New York), January 1971; "Interview mit Robert Morris," with Lil Picard, in *Kunstwerk* (Baden-Baden, West Germany), January 1972; "Robert Morris Interviewed by A. B. Oliva" in *Domus* (Milan), November 1972; "Some Splashes in the Ebbtide" in *Artforum* (New York), February 1973; "Aligned with Nazca" in *Artforum* (New York), October 1975; "The Present Tense of Space" in *Art in America* (New York), January/February 1978; "Looking Back: An Interview," with J. Fineberg, in *Arts Magazine* (New York), September 1980.

On MORRIS: books—*Robert Morris,* exhibition catalogue, Eindhoven, Netherlands, 1968; *Robert Morris,* exhibition catalogue, Washington, D.C. 1969; *Robert Morris,* exhibition catalogue, by Marcia Tucker, New York 1970; *Robert Morris,* exhibition catalogue, by Michael Compton and David Sylvester, London 1971; *Robert Morris: Felt Pieces,* exhibition catalogue, by Walter Kambartel, Stuttgart 1971; *Robert Morris: Projects,* exhibition catalogue, with text by Edward Fry, Philadelphia 1974; *Line As Language: Six Artists Draw,* exhibition catalogue, by Rosalind Krause, Princeton, New Jersey 1974; *Robert Morris: Grand Rapids Project,* Grand Rapids, Michigan 1975; *Het Observatorium von Robert Morris in Oostelijk Flevoland,* exhibition catalogue, with text by E. de Wilde and others, Amsterdam 1977; *Structures for Behavior,* exhibition catalogue, by Roald Nasgaard, Toronto 1978; articles—"Robert Morris: Une Esthetique de Transgression" by A. Michelson in *Art Press* (Paris), July/August 1973; "Robert Morris: The Complication of Exhaustion" by J. Gilbert-Rolfe in *Artforum* (New York), September 1974; "Minimalism and Critical Response" by P. Tuchman in *Artforum* (New York), May 1977; "Authoritarian Abstraction" by D. B. Kuspit in *Journal of Aesthetics and Art Criticism* (Cleveland), Fall 1977; "Earthworks as Reclamation: Problems and Promises" by R. Glowen in *Artweek* (Oakland, California), 25 August 1979; "Monument-Sculpture-Earthwork" by N. Foote in *Artforum* (New York), October 1979; "Morris: Prisoner of Modernism" by Carter Ratcliff in *Art in America* (New York), October 1979; "Artist (Neo-Dandy) Stripped Bare by His Critic (Neo-Careerist) Almost" by D. B. Kuspit in *Arts Magazine* (New York), May 1980; "Space of the Self: Robert Morris in the Realm of the Carceral" by S. F. Eisenman in *Arts Magazine* (New York), September 1980; "Work for Landscape and Gallery" by R. Glowen in *Artweek* (Oakland, California), 4 October 1980.

> I seem to speak, it is not I, about me, it is not about me.
> Samuel Beckett, *The Unnamable*

In its ironic relationship to representation, Robert Morris' "I-Box" (1962) invokes Beckett's drained vision of the world, where "I" is simply a word, a verbal sign that is seeking to assume an "eloquent silence" while still clinging to the vestiges of life. The work, a small box with a door in the shape of the letter "I," is not as much "about" an "I" as it is "about" the futility of representation itself. The door opened, the phonetic "I" yields to a silent one—a photograph of the artist naked and grinning. The polemic waged in "I-Box," on the pre-eminence of one category of signs over the other, is ironic; the signs themselves, never able to be the represented object, are trapped on the surface, engaged in a self-directed and incestuous dialogue.

Like Beckett, Morris wished to divest the art object of the kind of *a priori* intellectual determination rooted in logical, rationalist thought. "Disengagement with preconceived enduring forms and orders for things," Morris has said, "is a positive assertion. It is part of the work's refusal to continue estheticizing form by dealing with it as a preconceived end." After his early, Duchamp-inspired work, Morris explored the possibilities of process and experience. Concentrating on temporal states, Morris produced pieces such as "Metered Bulb" (1963), in which a meter records a light bulb's expenditure of electricity, or "Site" (1963), a performance piece (with Carolee Schneeman) in which various tasks were acted-out around an updated tableaux-vivant of Manet's "Olympia." Later, sculptures composed of simple geometric forms (L-beams, cubes) or of interchangeable units constituted an immediate, self-referential presence that forced the spectator to confront his physical (and psychological) situation. Eventually, Morris employed freely formed materials such as thread and felt in order to defeat the resolute Gestalt of the earlier minimalist works (i.e., a cube is a shape the mind already knows). These "anti-form" pieces further asserted the work's independence from the sacred hegemony of art history.

Morris' divestment of the art object of predetermined psychological content is tempered by his understanding that "experience" is never entirely free of historical or psychological nuances. The philosopher Jacques Derrida has observed that while "experience has always designated the relationship with a presence . . . it always corresponds to a certain type of factual or regional experience (historical, psychological, physiological, sociological, etc.)." Underlying many of Morris' projects is an almost "archaeological" awareness of concomitant art historical situations: in "Observatory" (1971), a monumental earthwork consisting of sloped circular walls, a seemingly self-referential situation is charged with allusions to Stonehenge and other neolithic buildings. "Hearing" (1972) juxtaposes an arrangement of heat-activated objects (a copper chair, a zinc table, and a lead bed) with a 3-and-a-half hour recording of a hypothetical interrogation between a council, a witness, and an investigator, a self-reflexive drama of ideas on "various questions about art history and about the relation of perception to language." In "Box with the Sound of Its Own Making" (1961), a 9-inch walnut cube containing a 3-hour recording of the sounds of its being constructed, Morris literally interposes a temporal historical supplement into the viewer's experience. More recently in "Preludes (for A.B.)" (1980), crosses, skulls, and inscribed marble slabs are placed in a darkened gallery as morbid commentaries on various cultural phenomena (eg. "Roller Disco: Cenotaph for a Public Figure" or "Cenotaph for Cancer"). The representational statement implied in Morris' coffin-like "I-Box" is recast two decades later by his cenotaphs, cynical gravestones that mark the bankruptcy of much of the modernist utopian vision.

—Maurice Berger

MOSER, Wilfrid.

Swiss. Born in Zurich, 10 June 1914. Studied painting at the André Lhote studio and the Ecole Fernand Léger, Paris, 1945. Married to Eva Puig; son: Gabriel. Painter, Paris and Zurich, since 1946: tachiste paintings, 1950–59; collages and assemblage reliefs, 1959–69; 3-dimensional objects and models, 1963–77; returned to figurative landscape painting, 1974. Central President, Swiss Painters, Sculptors and Architects' Society, Zurich, 1964–71; Member, Federal Commission for Fine Arts, Zurich, 1964–72. Agents: Galerie Jeanne Bucher, 53 rue de Seine, 75006 Paris; Galerie Louis Carre, 10 Avenue de Messine, 75008 Paris; and Galerie Semiha Huber, Talstrasse 58, 8001 Zurich. Address: 19 Avenue de Tourville, 75007 Paris, France; and 89 Seestrasse, 8002 Zurich, Switzerland.

Individual Exhibitions:

1958	Galerie Jeanne Bucher, Paris
1961	Galerie Jeanne Bucher, Paris
1963	Galleri Haaken, Oslo
1964	Kunstmuseum, Lucerne
1965	Galerie Jeanne Bucher, Paris
1967	Galerie Alice Pauli, Lausanne
1970	Galerie Jeanne Bucher, Paris
	Kunsthaus, Zurich
1971	Kunsthaus, Chur, Switzerland
	Galerie Scheidegger and Maurer, Zurich
1973	Kunstmuseum, Thun, Switzerland
1974	Kunstverein, Bienne, Switzerland
	Galerie 57, Bienne, Switzerland
	Musée de Metz, France
1975	Galerie G4, Winterthur, Switzerland
	Musée de Metz, France
1977	Galerie RB, Fribourg, Switzerland
1978	Galerie E. Schiedegger, Zurich
	Galerie G4, Winterthur, Switzerland
	Galerie Jeanne Bucher, Paris
1979	Museum Schaffhausen, Switzerland
1980	Swiss Pavilion, *Biennale*, Venice
	Kunsthkeller, Berne
1981	Galerie Jeanne Bucher, Paris
	Galerie Semiha Huber, Zurich
1982	Kunsthkeller, Berne
1983	Galerie G4, Winterthur, Switzerland
	Galerie Jeanne Bucher, Paris

Selected Group Exhibitions:

1951	*6 Young Paris Painters*, Galleri Blanche, Stockholm
1957	*The Molzau Collection*, Kunsthaus, Zurich (travelled to Copenhagen and The Hague)
1958	*Carnegie International*, Carnegie Institute, Pittsburgh
1959	*Bienal*, Sao Paulo
1961	*Kompas-Paris: Carrefour de la peinture*, Van Abbemuseum, Eindhoven, Netherlands
1968	*Premio Marzotto*, Museo di Valdagno, Italy
1972	*31 Swiss Artists*, Grand Palais, Paris
1977	*Artistes Zurichois*, Musée Rath, Geneva
1978	*Beginn des Tachismus in der Schweiz*, Kunsthaus, Zurich
1982	*Salon de Mai*, Paris

Wilfrid Moser: *L'Autre d'Ophide*, 1982

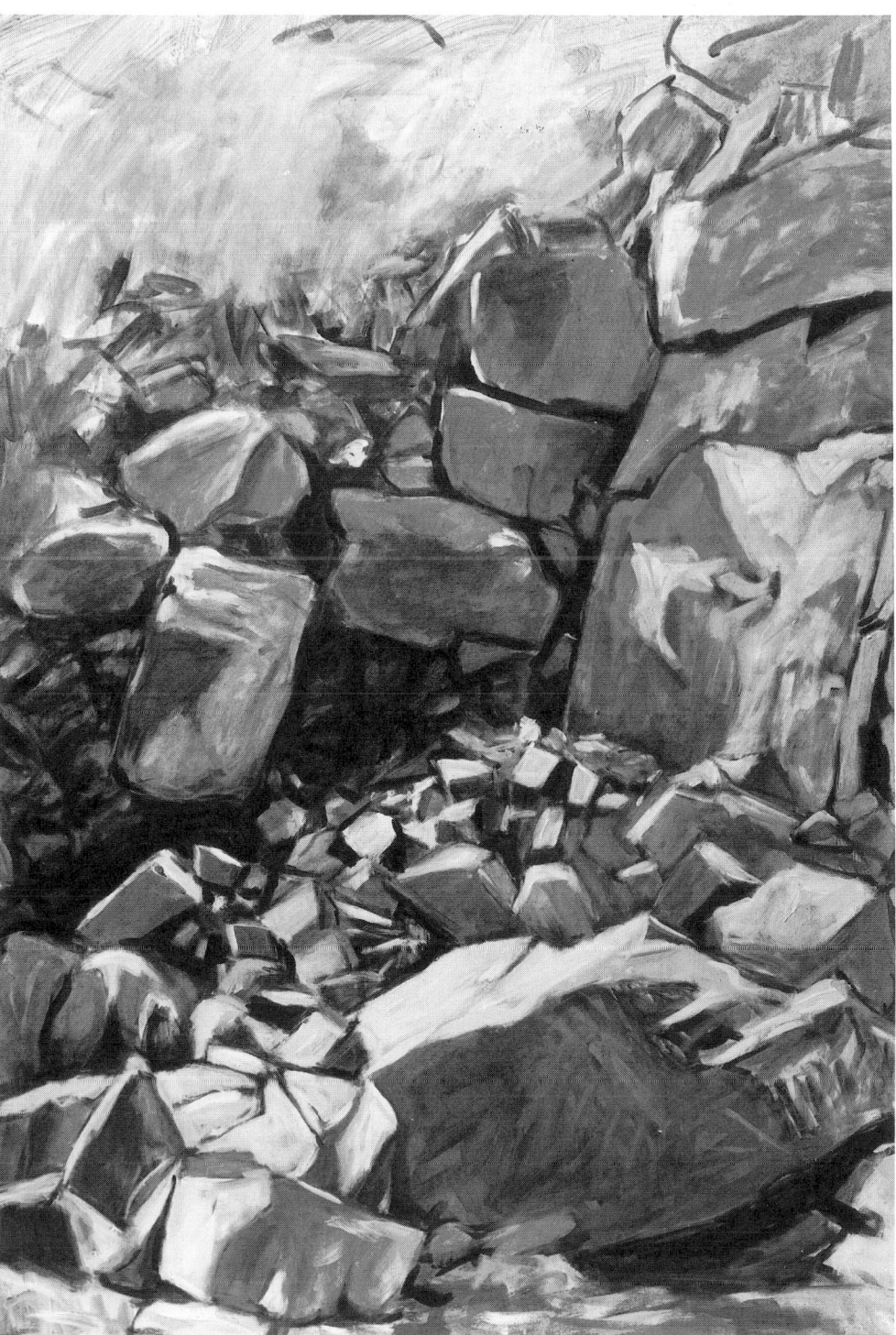

Collections:

Kunsthaus, Zurich; Kunsthalle, Kunstmuseum, Lucerne; Kunstmuseum, St. Gallen; Kunstmuseum, Thun, Switzerland; Museo d'Arte Contemporaneo, Locarno; Musée National d'Art Moderne, Paris; Musée de Peinture et Sculpture, Grenoble; Musée de Metz, France; Sonja Henie/Niels Onstad Foundation, Oslo; Museum of Contemporary Art, Chicago.

Publications:

On MOSER: books—*Premier Bilan de l'Art Actuel* by R. Lebel, Paris 1953; *Propos sur la Peinture Actuelle* by R. V. Gindertael, Paris 1955; *Musée de Poche: 16 Peintres de la Jeune Ecole de Paris* by H. Wescher and H. Juin, Paris 1956; *Dictionnaire de la Peinture Abstraite* by Michel Seuphor, Paris 1957; *Moser*, exhibition catalogue, with preface by Franz Meyer, Paris 1961; *Moser*, exhibition catalogue, with text by P. F. Althaus, Lucerne 1964; *Ecloe de Paris* by Raymond Nacenta, Neuchâtel, Switzerland 1969; *Wilfrid Moser*, exhibition catalogue, with text by F. A. Baumann, Zurich 1970; *Moser*, exhibition catalogue, with text by P. F. Althaus, Chur, Switzerland 1971; *Swiss Made* by Paul Nizon, Zurich 1971; *Moser*, exhibition catalogue, with text by Fritz Billeter, Bienne, Switzerland 1974; *Actualité 77*, edited by Skira Verlag, Geneva 1977; *Moser* by F. A. Baumann, Zurich 1978; *Moser*, exhibition catalogue, with interview by Dominique Bozo, Paris 1978; *Moser*, exhibition catalogue, with text by M. Freivogel, Schaffhausen, Switzerland 1979; *Moser*, exhibition catalogue, with text by Daniel Abadie, Paris 1981; *Wilfrid Moser: Kitharou*, exhibition catalogue, with text by P. Killer, Zurich 1981; films—*Moser*, television film, by W. Bolliger and P. F. Althaus, 1970; *Moser*, television film, by P. K. Wehrli, 1977.

The dramatizing of the third dimension, that is, space as a factor of expression, takes place on a flat surface, canvas, paper, etc; and this dramatization of space which strikes the onlooker, disturbs and attracts him, has been neglected since the Renaissance. Artists such as Grünewald, later Piranesi and some romanticists like the German Caspar David Friedrich or the French Theodore Géricault, had based their art on the dramatizing of space. Dürer had tamed space into perspective, brought a convention, formal rendering of the third dimension.

It is only after the destruction of the old visual habits through new forms of expression like cubism or constructivism, that the following generations were put in the situation of formulating anew the problem of the third dimension and reflecting fundamentally upon the possibilities of its realization.

—Wilfrid Moser

Painting without image, if not without subject, is the paradoxical proposition of the latest works of Wilfrid Moser. Not that distinctly portrayed elements of reality are not recognizable therein. (Some might even say: Moser paints stones or Moser paints trees.) It is however a question of nothing less than what we call certainty. Masses of fallen stones, confusion of stripped branches: in this world stricken with indescribable disaster is heard again the echo, from now on devoid of meaning, of the great romantic themes—the forest, solitude in the mountains, the dream of communion with natural forces. But our age is no longer one of innocence. It is of the world *after* to which Moser has for some years begun to call attention.

The obvious "difference" in his latest works has naturally led commentators to search for that which made the break in his work. The passage, in 1968, from painting to sculpture seems to be the indisputable turning point. Nothing, however, separates Moser's sculpture from his former painted work: both share the same confidence of expression. It is rather a matter of a different degree in the understanding of forms. It was in fact in portraying sculptures among heaps of stones in works on paper, completed between 1973 and 1975, that Moser established a different relationship to the object and to his style.

Until then art for Moser had an absolute value. His urban images, just as much as his abstract works or his sculptures, affirm the reality of the world, the power of the painter to recognize and convey it. The works in volume—assemblages of planks or constructions—go so far as to deny the fiction of the image so as to register directly in the inventory of reality. Portraying them, as he did in the works on paper which mark his return to expression in paint, no doubt led him to perceive the accepted character of every image, its value directly in tune with that of the language which expresses it. Truth, touchstone of his experience, reveals itself, he discovers, not in the image but in the form. The warm confidence of his works, their generous aesthetic, is followed by an ethic of parsimony. Metaphor for a collapsed language, the stones of Moser are also the very materials for its reconstruction. From this point on, all his work will be a slow and careful experiment to name the unnameable.

Moser's works on paper are in a way the laboratory for his painting and also for his language. Preparatory to and in parallel with his paintings, they experiment with problems, give rise to solutions, prepare in their multiplicity the successful route. According to the material used—gouache or pastel—they seek more to define the image or to invent its plastic transcription. Everything reflects the major problem of Moser's painting: the creation of violent spatial tension, of a *dramatization of space*. Even more than in the paintings, one can follow in the juxtaposition of the works on paper the incessant search to render present and palpable a non figurative subject. Tension will often result from only minute modifications: a more accentuated curve emphasizing a plane, the different value of a colour suddenly giving the necessary density to a block of stone. As in two versions of an identical drawing, like "Caved-in Wall," each shows a different truth by the sole play of colour: one, an opalescent white, emphasizes the structure of the blocks until it is transformed into a coagulation of signs close to his former abstract paintings; the other, a constant ochre, tends to accentuate reliefs and cavities, to hollow out intervening space. In Moser's work it is no longer a question of a motive to paint, but of a motive of painting. In fact these works display a veritable "rage of expression".

It is true that the margin between their intention and the dangers of a dull naturalism is narrow. The damp squib of the "new objectivity" has clearly demonstrated what confusion could reign among figuration, post modernism and academic reaction. Moser is not looking for a nostalgic return to tradition, a desire to paint according to the masters, but rather the establishment of another tradition where without hesitation he blazes the trail: the Master E.S., Altdorfer, Géricault, Caspar David Friedrich or the Picasso of "Blue Train". As for all of these painters, Moser's realism is an anti-naturalism. Without doubt the various "Undergrowths" are the extreme example of this attitude. A constantly repeated subject, banished from modern art and left to commercial artists, it was impossible at the beginning to imagine a worse example. It is true that vegetal nature according to Moser is not more appealing than his "Ends/Bits/Scraps of the World" or his masses of fallen stones: dead trees, defoliated copses, inextricable confusion of branches—and it would be difficult to reproach him his choice of subject for its pleasing character. But it is in the very method of painting that the "difference" is first established.

Painting without a model, whether stones or trees, he cannot be said to "imitate," and the veracity of his branches owes more by contrast to the abstract space on which they are inscribed than to realistic observation. For Moser does not site his derisory trophies of the forest, unless by a coloured shore which takes the place of both light and space. What is important to him is to introduce in parallel to the concise drawing of the stones, curve and intertwinings, to play, in the face of overlapping and stacked arrangements, an involved and complex game, to work the empty space in the place of the full. In order to hem in more closely these creations of space Moser invents in this series a genuine negative writing: what he does show is less the branches than that which they define, less

the bars of the cage than concretely its interior dimension.

Truth puts out one's eyes. Moser's painting hollows out the canvas. Nothing is apparently more in contradiction to the lesson of modern art than this evident will to open up space; nothing, in reality, is more customary. The "Sainte-Victoires" of Cezanne do not suppress the display in depth of the planes but affirm, in opposition to reviving conventions, the pictural equality of the foreground and the background, the primacy of the painting over the illusion of perspective. The landscapes of Le Cannet by Bonnard are surrounded by foliage, for that which encloses them in the foreground, sets the surface, renders the view of the subject more distant by the contrast of colours. The problem of space remains inherent in figuration, even if by modernist theories deny it, and one could envisage a history of thought which would be that of successive spatial transcriptions and their invention.

Affirmation of the picture plane and creation in its interior of genuine pockets of space is the very stuff of Wilfrid Moser's work. Temporary equilibrium, of opposing principles, each of his works, in its frenzied search, calls to mind the Frenhofer of "Unknown Masterpiece." They intend to determine an imperceptible certainty.

—Daniel Abadie

MOSES, Ed.

American. Born in Long Beach, California, 9 April 1936. Educated at the University of California at Irvine, M.A. 1958. Independent painter, in Venice, California, since 1958. Instructor, University of California at Irvine, 1968–71. Instructor, University of California at Los Angeles; Visiting Instructor, Skowhegan School of Painting and Sculpture, Maine, 1983. Recipient: Tamarind Lithograph Grant. Agent: L. A. Louver Gallery, 55 North Venice Boulevard, Venice, California 90291. Address: 1233 Palms Boulevard, Venice, California 90291, U.S.A.

Individual Exhibitions:

1958	Ferus Gallery, Los Angeles
	Dilexi Gallery, San Francisco
1959	Area Gallery, New York
	Ferus Gallery, Los Angeles
	Dilexi Gallery, San Francisco
1960	Dilexi Gallery, San Francisco
1961	Ferus Gallery, Los Angeles
1963	Ferus Gallery, Los Angeles
1969	Mizuno Gallery, Los Angeles
1970	Mizuno Gallery, Los Angeles
1971	Hansen-Fuller Gallery, San Francisco
	Ronald Feldman Fine Arts, New York
1972	Nicholas Wilder Gallery, Los Angeles
	Dayton's Gallery 12, Minneapolis
	Felicity Samuel Gallery, London
1973	Ronald Feldman Fine Arts, New York
	Art in Progress, Zurich
	Dayton's Gallery 12, Minneapolis
1974	Art in Progress, Munich
	André Emmerich Gallery, New York
1975	André Emmerich Gallery, New York
1976	University of California at Los Angeles
	Los Angeles County Museum of Art
1979	Sidney Janis Gallery, New York
1982	Jacobson-Hochman Gallery, New York
	James Corcoran Gallery, Los Angeles
1981	James Corcoran Gallery, Los Angeles
1982	Musee d'Art Moderne, Paris
	Jacobson-Hochman Gallery, New York
1983	Dorothy Rosenthal Gallery, Chicago
1984	Larry Gagosian Gallery, Los Angeles
1985	L.A. Louver Gallery, Venice, California
1988	Ianetti-Lanzone Gallery, San Francisco

Selected Group Exhibitions:

Collections:

Corcoran Gallery of Art, Washington, D.C.; Art Institute of Chicago; Walker Art Center, Minneapolis; San Francisco Museum of Modern Art; Norton Simon Museum of Art, Pasadena, California.

Publications:

By MOSES: article—interview, with Stephanie Barron, in *Moses*, exhibition catalogue, Los Angeles 1976.

On MOSES: articles—"Los Angeles: Ed Moses, Mizuno Gallery" by Peter Plagens in *Artforum* (New York), September 1970; "New York: Edward Moses, Ronald Feldman Fine Arts" by Joseph Masheck in *Artforum* (New York), February 1972; "Ed Moses: The Problem of Regionalism" by Peter Plagens in *Artforum* (New York), March 1972, "London Commentary" by Bernard Denvir in *Studio International* (London), September 1972; *Documenta 5*, exhibition catalogue, Kassel, West Germany 1972; "Print as Surface" by J. Loring in *Arts Magazine* (New York), September 1973; "New York Letter" by P. Derfner in *Art International* (Lugano, Switzerland), April 1974.

*   *   *

Ed Moses—exhibiting originally as Edward Moses y Branco—did not receive the early acclaim enjoyed by his younger Ferus Gallery (1957-1966) colleagues, Larry Bell, Billy Al Bengston, Robert Irwin and Craig Kauffman, although director Walter Hopp's singular eye undoubtedly saw the seeds of vanguard work in his New York-inspired Abstract Expressionism. He seemed to lag behind the others who abandoned that style soon after the turn of the decade to venture boldly and directly into "finish fetish" and the "L.A. Look." Unlike their work Moses' *Rose* drawings and paintings of the early 60s were not easily identified with rising national movements like Pop—despite their source in the design on cheap Mexican oilcloth—or with Minimalism. It wasn't until the late 70s, when his flat, deceptively smooth, monochrome planes emerged that Minimalism was ascribed to the paintings which actually evolved from diagonal grids, densified by layering and smoothed by scraping and sanding. The *Roses* however, cut out, with the spaces in between filled with shimmering graphite hatchings, can now be seen by hindsight to forecast the later trend in pattern painting.

Moses, earlier a premedical student, drew schematized landscapes of the Venice boardwalk in 1952 revealing the propensity for structure that came to underlie even the gestural work that followed. The outer frame of *Rafe* (1958), reminiscent of Philip Guston, whose abstract style, as well as De Kooning's and Milton Resnick's, marked his work at the time, is reiterated inside the edge and echoed in the predominantly right-angled disposition of bright skeins of paint weaving over the center. In drawings of erotically suggestive organic forms much like those of Kauffman, whose work made a significant impact, and John Altoon, spontaneous marks exist in a structured framework.

Moses' constructive bent was given full rein outside the province of studio art—he worked as a technical draftsman, 1954-56, then briefly served as a design engineer for solar aircraft. Later, he designed the Chapellet Winery at St. Helena, California (1969).

Those skills came into play in the creation of an environment at the Mizuno Gallery (1970). By cutting a rectangle out of the roof, leaving the rafters to permit sunlight to fall on the floor in slanted stripes of light and dark, he elegantly introduced rough lumber and other raw materials into the realm of light and space art.

Prior to that, the *Roses* had given way to geometric abstraction, by no means rigidly drawn, but as loose and intuitively rendered grids, at first tending to horizontal lines recalling Agnes Martin, whom he came to know while maintaining a studio at Coenties Slip in New York City (1958-60).

While Moses' grids have also reflected the influence of Mondrian—even a Mondrianesque *Chrysanthemum* emerged in drawings (1961)—they became characteristally diagonal, sometimes like tartans but more often suggesting designs on Navajo blankets, a phenomenon the artist has intensively researched within a lifelong interest in fabric and pattern. *Loom* (1971) is a testimonial to this pursuit, a fiber and resin painting with loosely tied threads extending from the warp.

The use of resin as a support came about in the late 60s, at first joined to unstretched canvas: his *Indian Blanket Series* (1970-71) awarded him critical acclaim. The loose-hanging "soft" paintings also cast him in the role of guru to many younger artists involved in creating "meditative" surfaces and sharing the interest in Tibetan Buddhism to which he was drawn in 1971.

That engagement is reflected in a 1981 series, the "Raw Wood Paintings," which, at first glance, appear to be diametrically opposed to the monochromes which preceded them, but, unlike those, they expose, rather than conceal his process. Here, multipatterned constructions of rectangular boards incorporate different sizes of finished and unfinished woods, rough and finish carpentry procedures. Strident in color and varied in gesture, bearing strong references to primal and non-Western cultures, they ultimately suggest altarpieces; the right-angled *Ohbo*, partly wood-finished and partly painted, embraces cornering walls, kimono-like in exterior shape.

Moses has since returned to canvas, tending to alternate between somewhat more structured diagonally "woven" grids, predominantly red, gold and black, and the more spontaneous, organic "worm" paintings, whose serpentine forms tend to neutral tones.

Both series are executed with oil and acrylic pigments which were poured together into a bucket and applied to canvases stretched horizontally on a wooden platform out of doors. Often incorporating a stenciled spider, the diagonal grids are executed with large brushes sweeping over the canvas alongside a board rotated to a 45 degree angle serving as a straight-edge, the diagonal format maintained even as successive layers of pigments, each cancelling out the one preceding, tend to undermine it.

All control is abolished in the organic paintings. There, intention and preconception give way entirely to the unconscious automatist mark. With a household mop rapidly swabbing the layers onto the soaked canvas, membranous strands collide and separate before the oil finally floats to the top and the acrylic bleeds into the support, their action forming lightning-like streaks and misty, atomized implosions, with the artist acting merely to "distribute" paint over the support. On occasion, that process overtakes rejected or incomplete gridded canvases so that throbbing and surging linear elements penetrate and overlay the existing organization, both demolishing it and becoming one with it.

Moses' drawings, which reveal the full extent of his researches, are, like his prints, no less valuable in their own right. They complete a body of work, which, he confesses, is frequently "as much a surprise to me as it is to anyone else." A dialogue between structure and spontaneity, and between medium and maker, his oeuvre records the progress of a career in which intuition, always open to provocation but never submitting to fashion, has been an unfailing guide.

—Merle Schipper

MOSSET, Olivier.
Swiss. Born in Berne, 11 May 1944. Educated in several Swiss schools, until 1965; also worked with the artists Jean Tinguely, Daniel Spoerri and Arman, 1962-65. Independent painter, in Paris, 1965-77, in New York, since 1977. Member, with Daniel Buren, Michel Parmentier and Niele Toroni, Groupe BMPT, Paris, 1966-68. Agents: John Gibson Gallery, 205 East 78th Street, New York, New York 10021; Tony Shafrazi Gallery, 328 East 11th Street, New York, New York 10003; Galerie Gilbert Brownstone, 17 rue Saint Gilles, 75003 Paris. Address: 476 Broadway, New York, New York 10013, U.S.A.

Individual Exhibitions:

Selected Group Exhibitions:

Collections:

Musée d'Art Moderne de la Ville, Paris; Centre Georges Pompidou, Paris. Kunstmuseum, Berne; Museum of Modern Art, New York.

Olivier Mosset: *Agent*, 1986

Publications:

By MOSSET: book—*Ecrits et Entretiens*, with John Armleder and Helmut Federle, Grenoble 1987; articles—"Armleder and Mosset in Conversation" in *Artscribe* (London), November/December 1986; "Oliver Mosset", interview with Robert Nickas, in *Flash Art* (Milan), February/March 1987.

On MOSSET: books—*Olivier Mosset: Catalogue no. 1*, with text by Serge Bard, Paris 1967; *Mosset*, exhibition catalogue, with text by Jean-Paul Dolle, Paris 1969; *Art Actuel en France* by Anne Tronche, Paris 1973; *I Colori della Pittura*, exhibition catalogue, with text by Italo Mussa, Rome 1976; *Fracture du Monochrome*, exhibition catalogue, with text by Bernard Lamarche-Vadel, Paris 1978; *Tendances de l'Art en France*, exhibition catalogue, with text by Marcelin Pleynet, paris 1979; *Painting about Painting*, exhibition catalogue, with text by Nancy Einreinhofer, Wayne, New Jersey 1981; *Olivier Mosset*, exhibition catalogue with text by Maurice Besset, Chateauroux 1985; *Olivier Mosset*, exhibition catalogue with texts by Ulrich Loock and Adelina von Furstenberg, Geneva 1986; articles—"BMPT" by Gregoire Muller in *Robho* (Paris), Autumn 1967; "Olivier Mosset" by Otto Hahn in *L'Express* (Paris), November 1968; "BMPT" by Michel Claur in *VH 101* (Paris), Spring 1971; "Le Groupe BMPT" by Otto Hahn in *Art Press* (Paris), June/August 1974; "Olivier Mosset" by Otto Hahn in *+-0* (Genval-Lac), September 1976; "Olivier Mosset" by Bernard Lamarche-Vadel in *Artistes* (Paris), June/July 1980; "Getting on with Painting" by Marcia Hafif in *Art in America* (New York), April 1981; "Armleder, Mosset, Toroni" by Dieter Schwarz in *Noema* (Zurich), Summer 1987; film—*Fun and Games for Everyone* by Serge Bard, 1968.

Even though nothing escapes the laws of history, the main problem remains a praxis, material and formal, that of applying color on the canvas, that of painting. Far from cutting the work off from reality, such practice should indeed give painting its full meaning: to make it be what it is, instead of being a reflexion upon reality which, though not preventing it from being, would, nevertheless, obfuscate its own reality.

I have difficulties speaking about my work: in fact, I have difficulties speaking about painting, and frankly, I am slightly disturbed by this conversation. Of course, we do talk about these things, and more or less in this way, but what bothers me is to be in a position to defend the conceptions we have of our work, because as I see it, such conceptions are not defendable. If I entertain a relationship of rightness to my work, it is a private relationship. It is up to others to say something.

—Olivier Mosset

Olivier Mosset's painting began in 1965 with a series of canvases carrying minimal images, such as a full

stop mark or a letter 'A'. From 1967 to 1968 Mosset belonged to the group BMPT (Buren, Mosset, Parmentier, Toroni) in which he pursued and radicalized his choice of a neutral and anonymous intervention in painting. Each artist chose and repeated his own 'distinctive' mark. Buren's vertical stripes equalled Mosset's circle painted in the middle of the canvas.

The group produced a number of 'actions' intended to 'present' the work: a way of "giving itself to the public" in codified places. The group also transgressed a central artistic convention—the instance of recognizability, the 'personal mark' that renders the work identifiable as produced by a particular artist.

The repetition of a visual element is also in contrast to the logic of chronological evolution within a body of work, and thus the needs of the market. But the constant repetition of a constant element itself became a 'stylistic cipher' bringing the artist back to his own subjectivity, and so once more the repetition itself had to be rejected.

Mosset's gesture in that period was still highly ideological, while his aim was directed at producing an analysis of the material reality of painting, from which both biography and ideology were to be banned. For this reason, in 1972 a move was made towards a series of paintings of 'constant dimensions', marked by vertical bands (seldom diagonal), firstly white and grey, later of different colours, at times tonally consistent, on other occasions dissonant. The passage from series to the next is dependent on purely accidental causes determined by practical considerations: running out of a supply of a particular colour, the commission of a particular kind of picture, or simply the will to experiment with new pigments.

In this way Mosset's work is qualified by an investigation into colour, which is progressively reduced to a two-tone analysis—whereas later on he concentrates on tone alone in paintings where the vertical bands are delimited only by thin graphic lines (1977). Later on, this delineating element is also discarded, and the artist then engaged himself with a poetic of monochrome only, a kind of work that has absorbed him up to the present day.

Mosset is inspired by the work of Ad Reinhardt, though he does not posit the painting as an absolute, or the monochrome choice as an extreme statement at the core of a reflection which is purely metalinguistical as the American master does. Mosset deconstructs the system of painting, moving away from the absolute to the contingent.

The monochrome stands metonymically for the whole painting and represents the most appropriate vehicle for research into the signifying potentialities of colour. In any case, the monochrome is considered by its nature as an event bearing a 'zero degree' potential for expression. It is the very matter of painting of which Mosset analyses the mechanisms.

—Giorgio Verzotti

MOTHERWELL, Robert.
American. Born in Aberdeen, Washington, 24 January 1915. Studied painting, California School of Fine Arts, San Francisco, 1932; studied philosophy, Stanford Institute, California, 1932–37, B.A. 1937; Harvard University Graduate School of Arts and Sciences, Cambridge, Massachusetts, 1937–38; studied, under Meyer Shapiro, Columbia University, New York, 1940; studied engraving, under Kurt Seligman, 1941, and under Stanley William Hayter, 1945. Married Maria Emilia Ferreira y Moyers in 1941; daughters: Jeannie and Lise; married Helen Frankenthaler in 1958; married Renate Ponsold in 1972. Art Instructor, University of Oregon, Eugene, 1939; Black Mountain College, Beria, North Carolina, 1945–51; Co-Founder, with William Baziotes, Barnett Newman and David Hare, Subject of the Artist School, New York, 1948 (closed, 1949); Founder, School of Fine

Arts, New York, 1949 (closed, 1950); Painting Instructor, 1951–58, and Distinguished Visiting Professor, 1971–72, Hunter College, New York; Instructor, Graduate Seminar, Oberlin College, Ohio, 1952; Instructor, Colorado Springs Fine Arts Center, Summer 1954; Visiting Critic, 1964–65, and Advisor on Art, 1972, Graduate Program of the Arts, Columbia University, New York; Co-Chairman of Seminar, with Anthony Caro and Alex Colville, University of Toronto, Ontario, 1970; Instructor of seminars at Provincetown Art Workshop, Massachusetts, and at Calhoun College, Yale University, New Haven, Connecticut, 1971. Advisor, Bliss International Study Center, Museum of Modern Art, New York, 1968; Education Advisor, Guggenheim Foundation, New York, 1968–75; Special Advisor, National Council on the Arts, Washington, D.C. 1969; Consultant, National Collection of Fine Arts, Smithsonian Institution, Washington, D.C., 1971. Editor, *Documents of Modern Art* series, from 1944; Editor, with John Cage, Pierre Chareau, and Harold Rosenberg, only issue of *Possibilities,* New York, 1947; General Editor, *Documents of 20th Century Art,* New York and London, 1968; Advisory Editor, *American Scholar,* Washington, D.C., 1968–75. Recipient: Guggenheim Award, 1964, and Fellowship, 1969; Belgian Art Critics Prize, 1966; National Council on the Arts Grant, 1966; Fellowship in Perpetuity, Metropolitan Museum of Art, New York, 1967; Torcuato di Tella Prize, Buenos Aires, 1967; Benjamin Franklin Fellow, Royal Society of Arts, London 1968; Award for Distinction in Visual Arts, University of South Carolina, Columbia, 1974; Grande Medaille de Vermeil, Paris, 1977; Gold Medal, Pennsylvania Academy of Fine Arts, 1979; Medal of Merit, University of Salamanca, Spain, 1980; Skowhegan Award for Printmaking, Maine, 1981; Mayor's Award of Honor, New York, 1981; Gold Medal, National Arts Club, New York, 1983; Great Artists Award, New York University/Guggenheim Museum, 1985; MacDowell Colony Medal, 1985; Medalla d'Oro de Bellas Artes,

Madrid, 1986. D.F.A.: Bard College, Annandale-on-Hudson, New York, 1973; Maryland Institute, Baltimore, 1974; Southeastern Massachusetts University, North Dartmouth, 1974; University of Connecticut, 1979; Rhode Island School of Design, 1980; Otis Art Institute/New School for Social Research, 1985; Brown University, 1985; Hunter College, 1985. Member, National Institute of Arts and Letters, 1969; American Academy of Arts and Letters, New York American Academy of Arts and Sciences, Cambridge, Massachusetts; Royal Society of Arts, London. Agent: Knoedler Gallery, 19 East 70th Street, New York, New York 10021. Address: 909 North Street, Greenwich, Connecticut 06830, U.S.A.

Individual Exhibitions:

1939	Raymond Duncan Gallery, Paris
1944	Art of This Century Gallery, New York
1946	Kootz Gallery, New York
	Museum of Art, San Francisco
1947	Kootz Gallery, New York
1949	Kootz Gallery, New York
1950	Kootz Gallery, New York
1952	Allen Memorial Art Museum, Oberlin College, Ohio
1953	Kootz Gallery, New York
1957	*Paintings and Collages,* Sidney Janis Gallery, New York
1959	*First Retrospective Exhibition,* Bennington College, Vermont
	Sidney Janis Gallery, New York
1961	*Recent Paintings and Collages,* Sidney Janis Gallery, New York
	Collages (1958–60), Galerie Berggruen, Paris
1962	Pasadena Art Museum, California
	I Collages di Motherwell, Galleria Odyssia, Rome
	Galerie Der Spiegel, Cologne
	A Retrospecitve Exhibition, Sidney Janis Gallery, New York

1963	Smith College, Northampton, Massachusetts
	Massachusetts Institute of Technology, Cambridge
1965	*Collages,* Phillips Collection, Washington, D.C. (retrospective)
	Museum of Modern Art, New York
	Galerie Schmela, Dusseldorf (with Conrad Marc-Relli)
1966	Contemporary Art Museum, Houston
	Baltimore Museum of Art
	Stedelijk Museum, Amsterdam
	Whitechapel Art Gallery, London
	Folkwang Museum, Essen
	Palais des Beaux-Arts, Brussels
	Museo Civico, Galleria d'Arte Moderna, Turin
	Museum of Art, San Francisco
	Indiana University Art Museum, Bloomington
	University of California at Riverside
1968	Whitney Museum, New York
	Museum of Art, Richmond, Virginia
	Marlborough Galleria d'Arte, Rome
	Museum of Modern Art, New York
1970	David Mirvish Gallery, Toronto
1971	*Bilder und Collagen 1967–70,* Galerie im Erker, St. Gall, Switzerland
	Kunstverein, Freiburg, West Germany
1972	Walker Art Center, Minneapolis
	Dayton's 12 Gallery, Minneapolis
	Lawrence Rubin Gallery, New York
	Metropolitan Museum of Art, New York
	University of Iowa Art Museum, Iowa City
	Frederick Gallery, Washington, D.C.
	Gertrude Kasle Gallery, Detroit
	The Collages of Robert Motherwell: A Retrospective Exhibition, Museum of Fine Arts, Houston
1973	Cleveland Museum of Art
	Recent Works, Princeton Museum, New Jersey
	Current Editions, Seattle
	Wadsworth Atheneum, Hartford, Connecticut
	John Berggruen Gallery, San Francisco
	Museum of Fine Arts, Boston
	David Mirvish Gallery, Toronto

Robert Motherwell: *Elegy to the Spanish Republic No. 70,* 1961

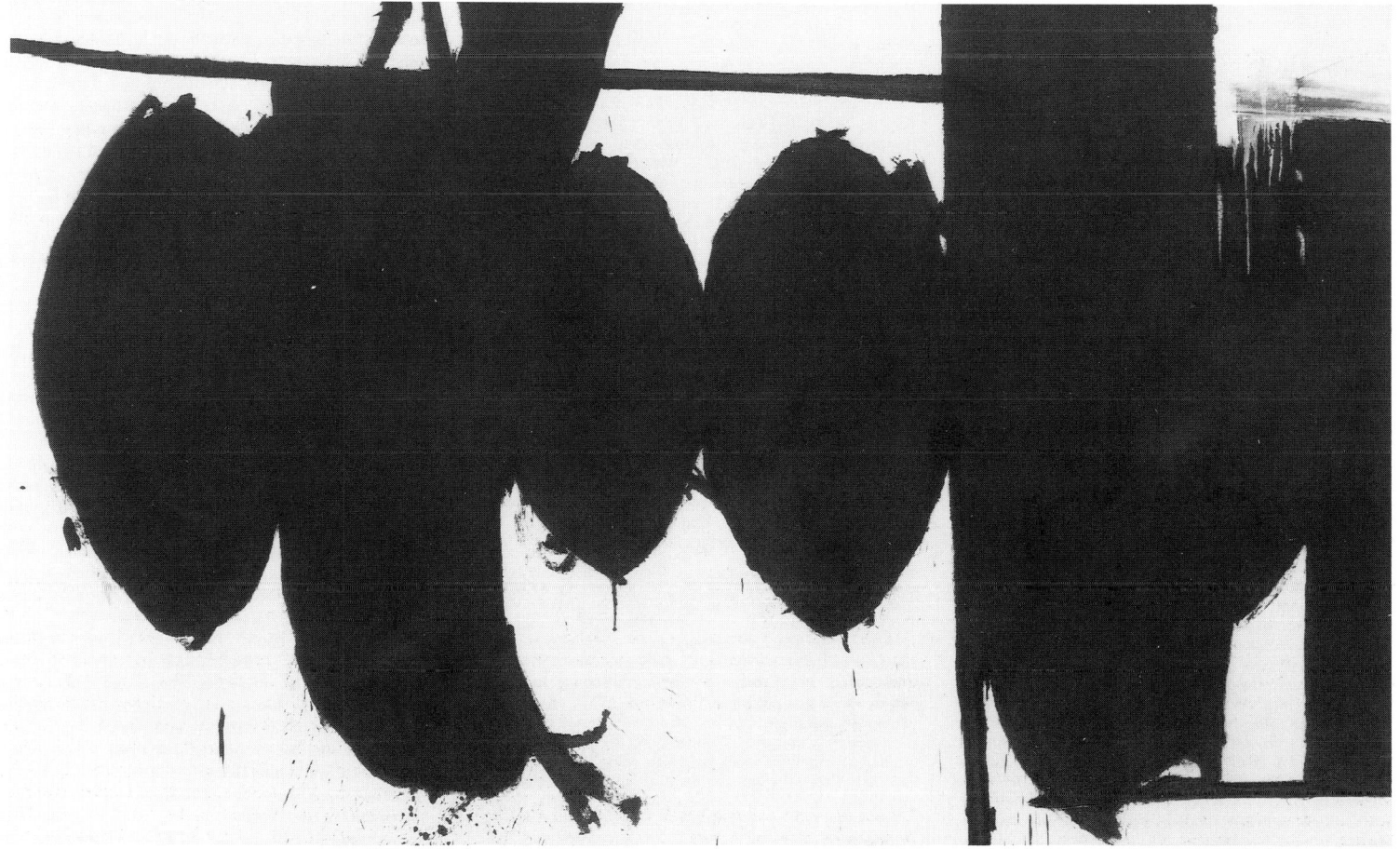

1974 Knoedler Contemporary Art Gallery, New York
Brooke Alexander Inc., New York
1975 Waddington Gallery, London
Retrospective del Gran Pintor Norteamericano, Museo de Arte Moderno, Mexico City
1976 Knoedler Contemporary Art Gallery, New York
1977 Museum des 20. Jahrhunderts, Vienna (retrospective: travelled to Musée d'Art Moderne, Paris; Royal Scottish Academy, Edinburgh; and the Royal Academy of Arts, London)
1978 *David Smith/Robert Motherwell*, Museo de Arte Contemporaneo de Caracas, Venezuela
1979 *Robert Motherwell and Black*, William Benton Museum of Art, Storrs, Connecticut
William Ehrlich Gallery, New York
Janie C. Lee Gallery, Houston (retrospective)
Brooke Alexander Gallery, New York
1980 Centre Cultural de la Caix de Pensions, Barcelona (retrospective; travelled to Fundación Juan March, Madrid)
1981 American Federation of Arts, New York (retrospective)
1983 Albright-Knox Art Gallery, Buffalo, New York (retrospective; travelled to Los Angeles, San Francisco, Seattle, Washington, and New York 1983–85)
Bavarian State Museum of Modern Art, Munich

Selected Group Exhibitions:

1958 *Biennale*, Venice
1959 *Documenta 2*, Kassel, West Germany
1964 *Dunn International*, Tate Gallery, London
1968 *Carnegie International*, Pittsburgh
1969 *New American Painting and Sculpture*, Museum of Modern Art, New York
1972 *Abstract Painting in the 70's*, Museum of Fine Arts, Boston
1974 *Prints from Gemini G.E.L.*, Walker Art Center, Minneapolis
1978 *American Art at Mid-Century: The Subjects of the Artist*, National Gallery of Art, Washington, D.C.
1985 *Painterly Visions 1940–84*, Guggenheim Museum, New York
1987 *American Painting: Abstract Expressionism and After*, San Francisco Museum of Modern Art

Collections:

Museum of Modern Art, New York; Metropolitan Museum of Art, New York; Whitney Museum, New York; Albright-Knox Art Gallery, Buffalo, New York; National Gallery of Art, Washington, D.C.; Smithsonian Institution, Washington, D.C.; Cleveland Museum of Art; Art Institute of Chicago; San Francisco Museum of Modern Art; Stedelijk Museum, Amsterdam.

Publications:

By MOTHERWELL: books—*Plastic Art and Pure Plastic Art* by Piet Mondrian, editor, New York 1945; *Robert Motherwell: Collages 1943–1949*, with Marianne Moore, New York 1949; *The Dada Painters and Poets: An Anthology*, editor, New York 1951; *Modern Artists in American*, edited with Ad Reinhardt, New York, 1951; *Robert Motherwell's "A la Pintura": The Genesis of a Book*, exhibition catalogue, with John McKendry and Diane Kelder, New York 1971; articles—"Notes on Mondrian and Chirico" in *VVV* (New York), June 1942; "The Modern Painter's World" in *Dyn* (Coyoacán, Mexico), November 1944; "Painter's Objects" in *Partisan Review* (New York), Winter 1944; "Henry Moore" in *New Republic* (New York), 22 October 1945; "Beyond the Aesthetic" in *Design* (London), April 1946; statement in *14 Americans*, exhibition catalogue, New York 1946; statement, and editorial preface, with Harold Rosenberg, in *Possibilities: An Occasional Review* (New York), Winter 1947; preface to *Arp, On My Way: Poetry and Essays 1912–1947*, New York 1948; preface to *Beyond Painting and Other Writings by the Artist and His Friends* by Max Ernst, New York 1948; "The Ideas of Art: A Tour of the Sublime" in *Tiger's Eye* (New York), 15 December 1948; preliminary notice to *The Rise of Cubism* by Daniel-Henry Kahnweiler, New York 1949; preface to *Black or White: Paintings by European and American Artists*, exhibition catalogue, New York 1950, reprinted in *Black and White*, exhibition catalogue, New York 1963; preliminary notice to *Baudelaire to Surrealism*, New York 1950; preface to *The Fauvist Painters* by Georges Duthuit, New York 1950; preface to *David Smith*, exhibition catalogue, New York 1950; "What Abstract Art Means to Me" in *Museum of Modern Art Bulletin* (New York), Spring 1951; "The Public and the Modern Artist" in *Catholic Art Quarterly* (Boston), Easter 1951; "The Rise and Continuity of Abstract Art" in *Arts and Architecture* (Los Angeles), September 1951; preface to *The School of New York: 17 Modern American Painters*, exhibition catalogue, Beverly Hills, California, reprinted in *The School of New York*, exhibition catalogue, Santa Barbara, California 1951; "Artists' Sessions at Studio 35 (1950)" in *Modern Artists in America* (New York), no. 1, 1951; preface to *Motherwell*, exhibition catalogue, New York 1952; "The Painter and the Audience" in *Perspectives USA* (New York), Autumn 1954; "A Painting Must Make Human Contact" in *New Decade* (New York), 1955, reprinted in *Painters on Painting*, edited by Eric Protter, New York 1963; statement in *Bradley Walker Tomlin*, exhibition catalogue, New York 1957; "The Significance of Miró" in *Artnews* (New York), May 1959; "Painting as Self-Discovery," recorded interview, with David Sylvester, for the BBC, October 1960; "In Support of the French Intellectuals," with others, in *Partisan Review* (New York), January/February 1961; "What Should a Museum Be?" in *Art in America* (New York), vol. 49, no. 2, reprinted in *VI Bienal de Museo de Arte Moderna*, exhibition catalogue, Sao Paulo 1961; and in *Robert Motherwell: A Retrospective Exhibition*, catalogue, Pasadena, California 1962; statement, in *The Cubist Painters: Aesthetic Meditations* by Guillaume Apollinaire, New York 1962; "A Conversation at Lunch" in *An Exhibition of the Work of Robert Motherwell*, exhibition catalogue, Northampton, Massachusetts 1963; statement, in "The Creative Use of the Unconscious by the Artist and the Psychotherapist" in *Annals of Psychotherapy: Journal of the American Academy of Psychotherapists*, vol. 5, no. 1, 1964; interview, with Bryan Robertson, in *Art: New York* (New York), 15 December 1964; "A Major American Sculptor: David Smith" in *Vogue* (New York), February 1965, reprinted in *People and Things in 'Vogue,'* edited by Allene Talmey, Englewood Cliffs, New Jersey 1970; "A Letter from Robert Motherwell to Frank O'Hara, Dated August 18, 1965" in *Robert Motherwell*, exhibition catalogue, New York 1965; "The Motherwell Proposal" in *Seminar on Elementary and Secondary School Education in the Arts*, edited by Howard Comant, New York 1965; "An Interview with Robert Motherwell," with Max Kozloff, in *Artforum* (New York), September 1965; article in *Robert Motherwell*, exhibition catalogue, by Luigi Mallé, Turin 1966; interview, with Sidney Simon, in *Art International* (Lugano, Switzerland), Summer 1967; statement in *Art Now: New York* (New York), May 1969; "Addenda to the Museum of Modern Art Lyric Suite Questionnaire: From Memory . . . with Possible Chronological Slips" in *Museum of Modern Art Newsletter* (New York), Fall 1969; "David Smith: Erinnerungen" in *Robert Motherwell: Bilder und Collagen 1967–1970*, exhibition catalogue, St. Gall, Switzerland 1970; "The Universal Language of Children's Art and Modernism" in *The American Scholar*, (Washington, D.C.), Winter 1970; "The Artist Speaks" in *Robert Motherwell at Saint Paul's School*, Concord, New Hampshire, 1970; preface to *Dialogues with Marcel Duchamp* by Pierre Cabanne, New York 1971; "Robert Motherwell," interview, with Irmelin Lebeer, in *Chroniques de l'Art Vivant* (Paris), July/August 1971; introduction to *The Journal of Eugene Delacroix*, New York 1972; "Robert Motherwell: Words and Images," interview with Heidi Golsman-Freyberger, in *The Print Collector's Newsletter* (New York), January/February 1974, reprinted in *Art Journal* (New York), Fall 1974; "A Talk with Robert Motherwell," interview, with Vivian Raynor, in *Artnews* (New York), April 1974; "Interview with Robert Motherwell, June 14, 1974," with Richard Wagener, in *Robert Motherwell in California Collections*, exhibition catalogue, Los Angeles 1974; "The Humanism of Abstraction" in *Tracks* (New York), November 1974; "A Conversation with Robert Motherwell, Painter," with Janet Baker-Carr, in *Harvard Magazine* (Cambridge, Massachusetts), October 1975; "Correspondence" in *Art Press* (Paris), January/February 1976.

On MOTHERWELL: books—*Robert Motherwell*, exhibition catalogue, with a preface by James Johnson Sweeney, New York 1944; *Abstract-Expressionist Painting in America: An Interpretation Based on the Work and Thought of 6 Key Figures*, dissertation, by William C. Seitz, Princeton University, New Jersey 1955; *Robert Motherwell: Paintings and Collages*, exhibition catalogue, New York 1957; *Motherwell: First Retrospective Exhibition*, catalogue, with text by Eugene C. Goosen, Bennington, Vermont 1959; *Recent Paintings and Collages*, exhibition catalogue, New York 1961; *American Abstract Expressionists and Imagists*, exhibition catalogue, with text by H. H. Arnason, New York 1961; *Robert Motherwell Collages (1958–60)*, exhibition catalogue, with text by Sam Hunter, Paris 1961; *VI Bienal de Museo de Arte Moderna*, exhibition catalogue, with text by Sam Hunter, Sao Paulo 1961; *I Collages di Motherwell*, exhibition catalogue, with text by Sam Hunter, Rome 1962; *Robert Motherwell: A Retrospective Exhibition*, catalogue, with texts by T. W. Leavitt, Frank O'Hara and Sam Hunter, with a poem by Barbara Guest, New York 1962; *An Exhibition of the Work of Robert Motherwell*, exhibition catalogue, Northampton, Massachusetts 1963; *Collages by Robert Motherwell*, exhibition catalogue, with text by Sam Hunter, Washington, D.C. 1965; *Robert Motherwell*, exhibition catalogue, with an introduction by Frank O'Hara, New York 1965; *Robert Motherwell*, exhibition catalogue with text by Frank O'Hara, Amsterdam 1966; *Robert Motherwell*, exhibition catalogue, by Luigi Mallé, Turin 1966; *Robert Motherwell: Bilder und Collagen 1967–70*, exhibition catalogue, St. Gall, Switzerland 1970; *The Collages of Robert Motherwell: A Retrospective Exhibition*, catalogue, with an introduction by Philippe de Montebello, text by E. A. Carmean, Jr., Houston 1972; *Robert Motherwell: Recent Works*, exhibition catalogue, with an introduction by Sam Hunter, Princeton, New Jersey 1973; *Robert Motherwell: Selected Prints 1961–74*, exhibition catalogue, with a foreword by Arthur A. Cohen, New York 1974; *Robert Motherwell in California Collections*, exhibition catalogue, with texts by Emerson Woelffer, Gifford and Joanne Philipps, Los Angeles 1974; *Robert Motherwell's 'Elegics to the Spanish Republic,' Including an Explanation of the Artist's Theory*, dissertation, by Robert C. Hobbs, University of North Carolina, Chapel Hill 1975; *Robert Motherwell: Retrospectivea del Gran Pintor Norteamericano*, exhibition catalogue, with text by Dore Ashton, Mexico City 1975; *Robert Motherwell* by H. H. Arnason, New York 1977; *Inside New York's Art World* by Barbara Diamonstein, New York 1979; *Robert Motherwell: Reconciliation Elegy*, paper, presented by E. A. Carmean, Jr., New York 1980; *Robert Motherwell and Black*, exhibition catalogue, with text by Stephanie Terenzio, Storrs, Connecticut 1980; *Robert Motherwell: The Painter and the Printer* by Stephanie Terenzio, New York 1980; *Robert Motherwell* by Jack Flam and Dore Ashton, New York 1983; *Stephen's Iron Crown and Other Related Works* by E. A. Carmean, Fort Worth 1985.

Robert Motherwell is unique among the New York School Abstract Expressionists in his ability to change with the times yet remain relevant. Instead of developing a single "trademark" image, like Mark Rothko's soft rectangles or Jackson Pollock's dripped-line maze, Motherwell has allowed his image world to evolve naturally, feeding on itself while taking additional nourishment from the art ideas that are in the air around him. Finding himself surrounded by European artists-in-exile, particularly Surrealists, at the outset of his career, he took inspiration from Cubist collage, and Surrealist automatism and their trust in the unconscious, to produce some of the most ambitiously scaled and daring collages of the early 1940's. In addition, he produced some of the most perversely austere abstractions—such as "Little Spanish Prison," 1941—ever painted by an Abstract Expressionist. He also created a few marvelously crude, brutalized little paintings which have turned out to be a rich vein to mine in recent years as he explores the depths of atavism and the primitive impulse.

Toward the end of the 1940's, in paintings such as the Museum of Modern Art's "Voyage," his collages were transformed into monumental canvases. In the "Elegy to the Spanish Republic" series the juxtaposition of repeated columnar verticals with organic ovoid masses, all painted in stark black and white, created a somber, processional mood that underlined the psychological profundity of his imagery. He continued to explore the structural potential of the early collages in the paintings of the 1950's and emphasized the calligraphic aspects of paint handling in paintings like "Je t'aime," 1955. A series of small oils on panel, where raw, personnage-like forms seemed to emerge from the inchoate calligraphy like matter in a void, led him to attempt monsterish images in a huge scale. "Monster (for Charles Ives)," 1959 and "Spanish Painting with the Face of a Dog," 1958 are among the few survivors of this period; he destroyed most of the others—much to his regret, since they both harked back to some of his earliest, and perhaps most personal, images, and prefigured the primitivizing painting that enthralls him today.

He continued to work out of the ideas of the Elegy series during the 1960's, and he enlarged the scale of his collages as well as the scope of his printmaking and the freedom of his drawing. Even more daringly, he began to explore the possibilities of acrylic paint and huge expanses of pure color in the "Open" series. These monochromatic canvases were activated more often than not by only a single charcoal or painted line signifying a window. The spare geometry of "Little Spanish Prison" resurfaced in paintings as did the Matissean notion the "more blue is bluer than less blue." But the 60's were a cool period when emotionalism was a low priority in the visual arts, and Motherwell's life and career were at an especially smooth and untroubled passage. In the following decade severe illness, emotional upheavals, a change of physical surroundings, plus the repeated reassessments of his life's work and his aims that have been demanded by numerous major monographs and retrospective exhibitions, have all worked to upset the status quo for him, and he's painting more unevenly, more energetically, more freely than he ever has. He's taking more and greater risks, but when he brings the painting off—as he did his "Elegy to the Spanish Republic No. 100" after 12 years of intermittent effort in 1975—he hits some of the highest points of his more than two score long artistic life.

—April Kingsley

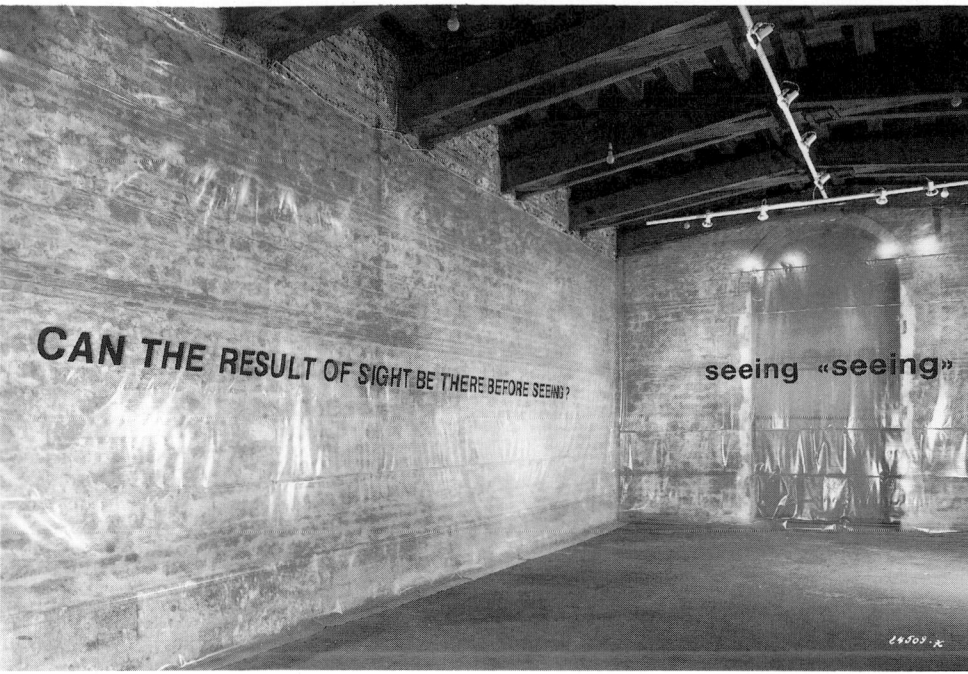

Tania Mouraud: *Art Space No. 2*, at Bordeaux, 1976

MOURAUD, Tania.

French. Born in Paris, 2 January 1942. Educated at Pensionnat des Jeunes Filles, Voisenon, 1952–56; Institution Jeanne d'Arc, Fontainebleau, 1956–57; and St. Martin's School, Solihull, Warwickshire, 1957–58; studied art, Académie de la Grande Chaumière, Paris 1965–66, and mathematics and logic, at the Université de Vincennes, Paris, 1970–71. Married Jamal Autun in 1962 (divorced, 1969); daughter: Saphira. Worked as baby-sitter, car-washer, journalist, secretary, laboratory assistant, interviewer, decorator and interpreter, in France and Germany, 1958–76; French language instructor, Berlitz Schools, Dusseldorf and Duisburg, 1961; assistant to sculptor Kurt Link, Dusseldorf, 1963–64; assistant to photographer Daniel Aron, Paris, 1974–75. Independent artist, in Paris, since 1966. Professor of Environmental and Conceptual Art, Ecole des Beaux-Arts, Tourcoing, 1976. Recipient: Research Grant, Ministry of Culture, Paris, 1976. Agent: Galerie La Remise du Parc, 2 impasse des Bourdonnais, 75001 Paris. Address: 62 rue de Montreuil, 75011 Paris, France.

Individual Exhibitions:

1966	Galerie Zunini, Paris
	Galerie Mensch, Hamburg
1970	Galerie Rive Droite, Paris
	Galleria Apollinaire, Milan
1971	Galerie Ben Vautier, Nice
	Galleria LP 220, Caliche Liguria, Italy
	Galerie Rive Droite, Paris
1972	Galleria Francoise Lambert, Milan
1973	Musée d'Art Moderne de la Ville, Paris
1974	Galerie Yellow Now, Liège, Belgium
1975	Galerie Anka, Paris
1976	Chez Malabar et Cunegonde, Nice, France
1977	Project Studio One, New York
1978	Franklin Furnace, New York
	Street billboards, Paris
1980	Street billboards, Lyon, France
1981	Studio 666, Paris
1983	Galerie Wilde, Cologne
	Galerie Samia Saouma, Paris
	Maison du temps libre, Torcy, France
1986	Musée de la Photographie, Charleroi, Belgium
	Maison de la Culture, Amiens, France

Selected Group Exhibitions:

1966	*Festival de Chateauvallon*, France
1967	*Festival d'Avignon*, France
1970	*Art Concepts from Europe*, Galeria Bonino, New York
1972	*Douze Ans d'Art Contemporain en France*, Grand Palais, Paris
1974	*Grandes Femmes, Petits Formats*, Galerie Iris Clert, Paris
1976	*Identité/Identification*, Centre d'Art Plastique Contemporain, Bordeaux
1979	*Words*, Museum Bochum, West Germany (travelled to Palazzo Ducale, Genoa)
1982	*Une autre photographie*, Maison de la Culture Andre Malraux, Creteil, France
1984	*Le Temps du Regard*, Hopital de Rheims, France (toured France)
1985	*Nouvelles Acquisitions*, Musée Carnavalet, Paris

Collections:

Centre National d'Art Contemporain, Paris; Biblothèque Nationale, Paris; Fonds National d'Art Contemporain, Paris; Bibliothèque Historique de la Ville de Paris; Musée Carnavalet, Paris; Fondation Camille, Paris; CAPC/ Musée d'Art Contemporain, Bordeaux.

Publications:

By MOURAUD: books—*Focale ou la Fonction de l'Art*, exhibition catalogue, Paris 1973; *Waking Up*, Liège, Belgium 1974; *Revisited*, Lyon 1980.

On MOURAUD: books—*Mouraud: One More Night*, exhibition catalogue, with text by Pierre Restany, Paris 1970; *Mouraud*, exhibition catalogue, with text by Tomasso Trini, Milan 1970; *Art, Action, Participation* by Frank Popper, London 1975; *From the Center: Feminist Essays on Women's Art* by Lucy Lippard, New York 1977; *Tania Mouraud; Vitrines*, exhibition catalogue with text by Jean-Francois Chevrier, Torcy 1983; articles—"Blanc jusqu'au vertige" by Bernard Bourgeaud in *Pariscope* (Paris), no. 95, 1970; "Tania Mouraud" by Tomasso Trini in *Flash Art*, (Milan), May/June 1970; "Les Meditations de Mouraud" by Francois Pluchart in *Combat* (Paris), 22 February 1971; "Tania Mouraud" by Catherine Millet in *Les Lettres Francaises* (Paris), 3 March 1971; "L'Experience Spirituelle" by Bernard Bourgeaud in *Pariscope* (Paris), no. 146, 1971; "Tania Mouraud" in *Art Press* (Paris), March/April 1973; "Occupation Textuelle de Tania Mouraud" in *Le Monde* (Paris), 25 January 1978; "Tania Mouraud" by Anne Dagbert in *Art Press* (Paris), no. 76, 1983; "Tania Mouraud" by Guy Mandery in *Photomagazine* (Paris), September 1985.

Our difficulty with the analysis of form starts with the fundamental fact that we take the visualized object as a single entity. We experience an object and give it a name. But all the same, we are sure, even from a non-philosophical standpoint, that the name is given to a group of sensations and that each sensation when viewed separately would demand a "single name". Thus, it can be said that what we call "one object" is in fact a group of objects. This group of objects (or sensations) belongs to the central object to which the "single name" was originally given.

Aesthetics, like the innumerable media (already employed, or to be employed in the future) would be just a medium to give us a vision of the focal centre. In formal Art this fact is often forgotten and unnecessary emphasis is given to the means rather than the end.

Quoting a statement of Joseph Kosuth, "works of Art are analytical proposition", I add that art should analyze and reach the "focal centre", or at least, try to near it. In my view, Art is a dialogue introducing the viewer to newer values, and leading him to a focus beyond the scope of morphology. Through my work I am showing that Philosophy and Art must merge to lead us to Knowledge.

—Tania Mouraud

MUEHL, Otto.

Austrian. Born in Grodnau, Burgenland, 16 June 1925. Studied German culture and History, University of Vienna, 1947–52, B.A., 1952; studied art at the Akademie der Bildenden Künste, Vienna, 1952–57. Served in the German Army, 1943–45; Lieutenant; Infantry Storm Decoration and Iron Cross, 1944. Married Friedrike Neiss in 1965 (divorced, 1970); son: David. Worked as teacher in a high school, Vienna, 1952; drawing therapist, Therapie Heim, Vienna, 1953; tutor in mathematics, Vienna, 1953–68. Independent artist, working with psychoanalytic actions, in Vienna, from 1960, and subsequently also in Gols, Burgenland: Founder, with Gunter Brus, Direct Art Institute, Vienna, 1966; AA Kommune, Gols, 1970; and AAKK Actions Analytical Kommune children's group, Gols, 1974; Editor-Publisher, *AA Kommune News* quarterly, Gols, 1974; worked with phylogenetic and onthogenetic parabolas, Gols, from 1975. Adopted occasional pseudonyms Uni Ferkel, Franz Knoedl and AA OO, from 1970. Recipient: Dirty Old Man Prize, *Wet Dream Festival*, Amsterdam, 1971. Agent: Karl Heinz Hein, Progressive Art Productions, Foehrenstrasse 11A, 8031 Groebenzell, Austria. Addresses: Praterstrasse 32/2/12, 1020 Vienna, Austria; AA Kommune, Friedrichshof, Gols, 7122 Burgenland, Austria.

Individual Exhibitions:

1961 Galerie Junge Generation, Vienna
1963 *Swamping the Venus*, Vienna
Mama & Papa, Vienna
Penis Action, Vienna
Breading an Ass, Vienna
Leda & the Swan, Vienna
Rumsti Bumsti, Vienna
Bimmel Bimmel, Vienna
Silver Ass, Vienna
1964 *2 Human Heads and a Cow Head*, Dusseldorf
Still-Life with Horse's Heads, Perinetgasse, Vienna
O Tannenbaum, Augartenstrasse, Vienna
1965 *Gymnastics Class in Food*, Perinetgasse, Vienna
1966 *Grimoid*, Perinetgasse, Vienna
1967 *Defense-Training*, Perinetgasse, Vienna
Psycho-Motoric Sound Action, Perinetgasse, Vienna
1969 *Christmas Action: Pig Slaughtered in Bed*, Braunschweig, West Germany
1970 *Investment Fund*, Vienna
Action, Bremen, West Germany
Action, Berne
1971 *Action with Goose*, at the *Wet Dream Festival*, Amsterdam
1973 *Last Art Action*, University of Ohio, Columbus

Selected Group Exhibitions:

1962 *Blut Orgel Actions*, Perinet Keller, Vienna
1963 *Festival of Psycho-Physical Naturalism*, Vienna
1966 *Action Concert for Al Hansen*, Galerie St. Stephen, Vienna
1967 *Zock Festival*, Grunen Tor, Vienna
1968 *Revolution and Art*, University of Vienna
1970 *Happening und Fluxus*, Kunstverein, Cologne
1976 *Weiner Aktionistenszene um 1960*, Stichting De Appel, Amsterdam
1977 *The Spirit of Vienna*, René Block Gallery, New York
1978 *Paris-New York*, Centre Georges Pompidou, Paris
1984 *Arte Austriacca 1960–84*, Galleria d'Arte Moderna Bologna, Italy

Publications:

By MUEHL: books—*Mama and Papa*, Frankfurt 1969; *Zock: Aspects of a Total Revolution 1966–1971*, Vienna 1971; *History and Development of Human Consciousness*, Gols, Austria 1975; films—*Amose*, 1968; *Sodonna*, 1969; *Scheiss Kerl*, 1970; *The Cherries in Papa's Garden*, 1974; *Selbstdarstellungs Aktions*, 1975; disc—*AA Selbstdarstellungs Musik*, Vienna 1975.

On MUEHL: books—*Wein* by Peter Weibel, Frankfurt 1970; *Film as Subversive Art* by Amos Vogel 1974; *Paris-New York*, exhibition catalogue, edited by K. G. Pontus Hulten, Paris 1978; articles—"Return to Reason: On Experimental Film in West Germany and Austria" by B. Hein in *Studio International* (London), November/December 1975; "L'Art Corporel" by Francois Pluchart in *Artitudes* (St. Jeannet, France), January/March 1975; "L'Art Corporel" by Arthur McIntyre in *Art and Australia* (Sydney), July/September 1976; "Einbruche unreflektier Wirklichkeit: Wiener Aktionismus in Amsterdam" by g. F. Schwarshauer in *Kunstmagazin* (Mainz), vol. 17, no. 1, 1977; "Wiener Aktionismus" by J. Willink in *Museumjournaal* (Amsterdam), April 1979.

i am convinced that only people become artists who have been physically damaged through their upbringing in the small family. seen in this way, my actions as an artist were actually an attempt to resolve these damages. at first i tried it with painting, but i soon noticed that it wasn't making me healthier. painting was not a strong enough medicine for me; my fever remained. i noticed that beneath the mask of my good-citizen conformity, a very aggressive guy was hiding, a fact that i had previously kept secret even from myself. this was my sickness. the problem at this point was to find ways and means of fitting this aggressive guy into art. i succeeded. i discovered for this purpose the junk sculpture. he acted like a murderer against sheet metal, wood, against all possible useful objects of our civilization. i smashed everything. i smashed it into junk art. my tools were no longer the paintbrush, they were the pick-axe and hatchet. but even this wasn't enough for me, i invented the material action. this gave me the possibility of coming out with my aggressions much more directly and intensively. i worked with women and men, i showered and smeared them with food, i literally buried them in consumer products. this produced an extension, a social aspect came into the foreground.

i understood that it is the assignment of the artist to destroy art, that means coming closer to reality. the artist has the social responsibility to change himself and eventually society as well. only after many years did i realize that this is impossible through art, that the artist himself is nothing other than one of the socially accepted professional roles. because i didn't know this and knew no way other than art to get to reality, i intensified my actions to extremely aggressive undertakings. in the end it brought me fines and jail sentences but at the same time fame.

in spite of this, these actions had a happy result for me personally. they made it possible for me to destroy my still conservative existence, although i defended myself against the change, at that time i was still married, had a family, and lived by tutoring mathematics. one action at the university of vienna got me into jail for two months. a professor of early history ran distracted out of the lecture hall in which my action took place, broke down, crying and tearing his hair, in the arms of colleagues. he sobbed "this disgrace, this disgrace! it is unbearable! the honour of the university is ruined!" the minister of education called out during an assembly "i am ashamed to be austrian!" overnight i was styled into a scandal figure. i became known as the university pig. mothers did not dare send their children to me for tutoring. for the leftists who helped organize the action with me, i was a bourgeois pig who had destroyed their successful political work. i had scared away the working class.

in any case, suddenly i stood there alone. it dawned on me that there was nothing more to be done with art as i had practised it up to this point. i could not abolish the discrepancy between art and reality, i couldn't achieve an identity through art, i couldn't unify art with reality, i had failed in my attempt. aside from that i noticed that it wasn't my personal fault, that the gap between artist and social reality could not be resolved and had never been resolved by any artist in the world. for this reason i gave up the picture surface, the sculptures, and finally the art action as well. i changed to a new medium and had the idea of using, instead of paints or food, the direct social reality as modelling material. in 1970 i started to set up the experiment of living art work, a continuous living experiment, developing and advancing with time. this environment has been growing and expanding without interruption. this living environment, i would like to speak of life as art, has now developed itself into art once again. it is art in art. whereby, instead of the word art, the word reality can be interpolated. therefore reality in reality, art in reality, reality in art.
reality art—art reality.
real reality, real art, artificial reality.
identity of art and reality.
art unmasks itself here as a derivative of reality.
reality without art is only half-reality. art without reality is no art.

—Otto Muehl

Otto Muehl calls his Material Action a kind of representational painting, a form of visual self-therapy using edible substances. To the audience, these actions often appear to be complete self-alienation, accidentally produced. In fact, they are planned to the last detail, and their effects are entirely calculated.

Many of Muehl's actions evoke associations of human birth. Beaten eggs, a slimy substance, tomato ketchup, flour, powder, paint and buttermilk are poured over the bodies of the women who take part; a balloon explodes. Such symbolism is easily explained. Associations of death, of violence, are called forth by the slaughtering of animals. Sexuality is directly expressed within the actions. Fundamental experiences which are not consciously noticed play an essential role in the actions. These are such everyday things as eating, drinking, urinating, shitting and vomiting.

Muehl's defencelessness vis-a-vis the press and his audiences is indicated by the criticism that he has got stuck in the phase of anal fixation. This seems quite mistaken, for as everyone knows from developmental psychology, too-early toilet training and an abrupt transition from the anal period causes children irreparable damage. Such criticisms of Muehl rebound on those who make them. For one cannot but make the presumption that such people have themselves been considerably affected by too-early toilet training.

Life within society is governed by countless norms which are only consciously perceived by very few individuals. Life begins with birth in the labour ward, and ends with fully-automated cremation. If we consider our own sexuality, we notice the difficulties which are put in the way of expressing it fully according to our desires. Perhaps it was considerations such as these which led to Muehl's style of action. Muehl had very negative experiences with the Austrian authorities, experiences which directly incited them to continue and intensify his actions. Muehl has had nearly 70,000 schillings worth of fines and legal costs, and spent 77 days in prison.

By the end of the 1960's Muehl's actions were attended almost exclusively by voyeurs. Perhaps this was the reason for Muehl's withdrawal from the art scene. His experiences with actions form the basis of the work of the AKTIONSANALYTISCHEN ORGANISATION, a kind of community based on free love and communal possessions. Within the AAO a form of therapy has been developed, self representation in groups or individually. The high point of the self-portrayal consists of recounting one's birth experiences. The goal of the self-portrayal is to eliminate the damage wreaked by the nuclear family. Muehl is the sovereign-master, the emperor of the AAO.

—Albrecht D.

MULLER, Robert.

Swiss. Born in Zurich, 17 May 1920. Educated at the Handelsschule, Zurich; studied art, under Charles-Otto Banninger and Germaine Richier, Zurich, 1939–45; under Germaine Richier, Paris, 1949; studied metal-casting, Paris, 1952–53. Sculptor and graphic artist, in Zurich, 1940–45; in Lonay, Lake Leman, 1945–47; in Genoa, 1947–49; in Paris, 1949–60; in Villiers-le-Bel, Val d'Oise, France, since 1960. Associated with war-time avant-garde artists, Galerie Gasser, Zurich, 1940–45; influenced by *Marino Marini* exhibition, Zurich, 1943; associated with painters Fieschi and Scanavino, cineaste Ribulsi, and sculptor Alfieri, in Genoa, 1947–49; with artists Geist, Rivers, Sugarman and Tajiri, in Paris, 1949; with Surrealist group, Paris, 1959. Produced first works in steel, Paris, 1951; wood engravings, Paris, 1958. Recipient: Sculpture Prize, *Biennale*, Venice, 1956; Regina-Feigel Prize, *Bienal*, Sao Paulo, 1957; Jean Arp Prize, Biel, 1966; Kunstpreis, City of Zurich, 1971; Foundation for Graphic Arts Prize, Switzerland, 1981. Agents: Galerie Renée Ziegler, Zurich; and Galerie Ernst Scheidegger, Wettingerweis 2, 8032 Zurich. Address: c/o Galerie Renée Ziegler, Ramistrasse 34, 8001 Zurich, Switzerland.

Individual Exhibitions:

1954	Galerie Craven, Paris
1955	Galerie de France, Paris
1959	Kunsthalle, Basle (retrospective)
1960	Galerie d'Eendt, Amsterdam
1962	Albert Loeb Gallery, New York (with Jean Ipousteguy and Miguel Berrocal)
1963	Albert Loeb Gallery, New York
1964	Galerie Renée Zeigler, Zurich
	Galerie de France, Paris
	Plastiken, Stedelijk Museum, Amsterdam (retrospective; travelled to Kunsthalle, Berne; Kunsthalle, Dusseldorf; and the Museum des 20. Jahrhunderts, Vienna, 1964–65)
1967	Galerie de France, Paris
1968	*Tekeningen*, Stedelijk Museum, Amsterdam
	Zeichnungen von Robert Muller, Jean Tinguely, Bernard Luginbuhl, Kunstmuseum, Basle
1971	Galerie de France, Paris
	Werke 1967–71, Kunsthalle, Basle
	Helmhaus, Zurich
	Galerie Renée Ziegler, Zurich
1972	Galerie Renée Ziegler, Zurich
	Plastik, Zeichnungen und Graphik, Galerie Bernard, Solothurn, Switzerland
1974	Galerie Scheidegger, Zurich
1977	Galerie Scheidegger, Zurich
1978	*Robert Muller/Bruno Muller: Skulpturen, Zeichnungen, Malerei, Graphik*, Kunsthaus, Aarau, Switzerland
1979	*Dessins 1937–1978*, Musée Rath, Geneva
1982	Galerie Scheidegger, Zurich
	Galerie Renée Ziegler, Zurich
	L'Oeuvre Grave, Musée d'Art et d'Histoire, Geneva

Selected Group Exhibitions:

1946	*Nationale Kunstausstellung*, Geneva
1956	*Biennale*, Venice
1958	*World's Fair*, Brussels
1961	*Bewogen Beweging*, Stedelijk Museum, Amsterdam (toured Denmark and Sweden)
1964	*Painting and Sculpture of a Decade 1954–1964*, Tate Gallery, London
1967	*Expo '67*, Montreal
1970	*Carnegie International*, Carnegie Institute, Pittsburgh
1973	*Contemporary French Sculpture*, National Art Gallery, Wellington, New Zealand (toured Australia and South America)
1975	*60 Ans d'Art Abstrait*, Maison de la Culture, Rheims
1981	*Zeichnungen von 13 Schweizer Eildhauern*, Tiroler Kunstpavillon, Innsbruch, Austria (travelled to the Modern Art Galerie, Vienna; and the Karntner Landesgalerie, Klagenfurt, Austria)

Collections:

Kunsthaus, Zurich; Kunstmuseum, Basle; Kunstmuseum, Winterthur, Switzerland; Kunstverein, Hannover; Stedelijk Museum, Amsterdam; Centre Georges Pompidou, Paris; Musée d'Art Moderne de la Ville, Paris; Museu de Arte Moderna, Sao Paulo; Museum of Modern Art, New York; Hirshhorn Museum and Sculpture Garden, Smithsonian Institution, Washington D.C.

Publications:

On MULLER: books—*Sculpture Moderne en Suisse* by Marcel Joray, Neuchâtel, Switzerland 1955; *Robert Muller: Plastiken*, exhibition catalogue, with texts by Karl-Heinz Hering and Harald Szeeman, Dusseldorf 1965; *Robert Muller: Plastiken*, exhibition catalogue, with text by Werner Hofmann, Vienna 1965; *Robert Muller: Tekeningen*, exhibition catalogue, with foreword by Jan Martinet, Amsterdam 1968;

Zeichnungen von Robert Muller, Jean Tinguely, Bernhard Luginbuhl, exhibition catalogue, with foreword by Dieter Koepplin, Basle 1968; *Robert Muller, Werke 1967–71*, exhibition catalogue, with texts by Peter F. Althaus and Dorothea Christ, Basle 1971; *Robert Muller* by Gregoire Muller, Paris 1971; *Robert Muller* by Pierre Descargues, Brussels 1971; *Robert Muller: Plastik, Zeichnungen und Graphik*, exhibition catalogue, with a preface by Peter F. Althaus, Solothurn, Switzerland 1972; *Robert Muller, Bruno Muller: Skulpturen, Zeichnungen, Malerei, Graphik*, exhibition catalogue, with texts by Paul Nizon and Heiny Widmer, Aarau, Switzerland 1978; *Robert Muller: Dessins 1937–1978*, exhibition catalogue, with texts by Rainer Michael Mason and Paul Nizon, Geneva 1979; *Robert Muller: L'Oeuvre Grave*, exhibition catalogue, with text by Rainer Michael Mason, Geneva 1982.

MUNARI, Bruno.

Italian. Born in Milan, 24 October 1907. Sculptor, filmmaker and designer: lives and works in Milan: associated with the Secondo Futurismo Group, Milan, 1927–33; executed first Fotogrammi works, after Man Ray and Moholy-Nagy, Milan, 1932; first Macchine Inutili, Milan 1933; co-signed. *Manifesto Tecnico dell'Aeroplastica Futurista*, 1934; worked on large abstract mosaic for *6th Triennale*, Milan, 1937; first kinetic works, 1945; "Libri Illeggibili" and children's books, 1949; published *Manifesto del Meccanismo*, 1949; Co-Founder, Movimento d'Arte Concreta, Milan, 1949; created animated wind mobile for Societá Motta, *Milan Fair*, 1950; worked with polarized light from 1953; with films from 1962; first Xerox works from 1965. Recipient: Compasso d'Oro, Milan. Agent: Bruno Danese, Milan. Address: Via Vittoria Colonna 39, 20149 Milan, Italy.

Bruno Munari: *Our Forefathers' Presence*, 1970

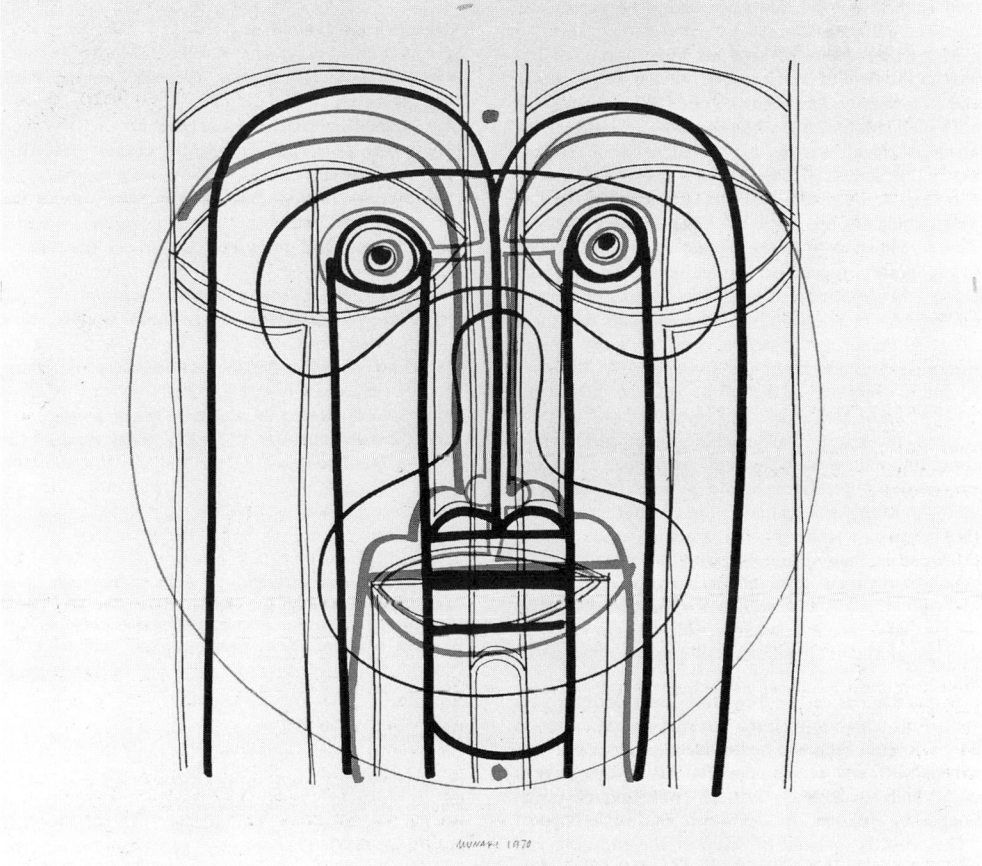

Individual Exhibitions:

1933	Galerie Tre Arti, Milan
1934	Galleria Milano, Milan
1954	Museum of Modern Art, New York
1966	Museum of Modern Art, Tokyo
1967	Howard Wise Gallery, New York
1971	Galleria San Fedele, Milan
1973	Galerija Suvremene Umjetnosti, Zagreb
1979	University of Parma, Italy

Selected Group Exhibitions:

1927	*Secondo Futurismo*, Galleria Pesaro, Milan
1929	*Trentate Futuristi*, Galleria Pesaro, Milan
	Peintres Futuristes Italiens, Galerie 23, Paris
1930	*Biennale*, Venice
1932	*Secondo Futurismo*, Galerie Renaissance, Paris
1933	*Triennale*, Milan
1951	*Arte Astratta e Concreta in Italia*, Galleria Nazionale d'Arte Moderna, Rome
1955	*Mouvement*, Galerie Denise Renée, Paris

Collections:

Galleria Nazionale d'Arte Moderna, Rome; Kunstmuseum, Krefeld, West Germany; Museum of Modern Art, New York.

Publications:

By MUNARI: books—*Design as Art*, Harmondsworth, Middlesex 1971; *Alfabetiere*, Turin 1972; *Cappucetto Verde*, Turin 1972; *Cappucetto Giallo*, Turin 1972; articles—"Un Metodo di Progettizione" in *Ottagono* (Milan), September 1970; "Statements by Munari" in *Studio International* (London), October 1970; "L'Equilibrio degli Opposti" in *Ottagono* (Milan), March 1971; "Che cose'e un Abitacolo" in *Domus* (Milan), March 1971; "Libri per Bambini: Intervista con Bruno Munari" in *NAC* (Milan), June/July 1971; "L'Autorita Offi" in *Ottagono* (Milan), September 1971; "Strutturazione Interna di Spazii Cubici" in *Ottagono* (Milan), January 1972; "L'Uomo a piu Dimensioni" in *Ottagono* (Milan), March 1972; "La Machine Antropomorfa" in *Ottagono* (Milan), June 1972; "Le Luci-spia" in *Ottagono* (Milan), September 1972; "Compasso d'Oro a Ignoti" in *Ottagono* (Milan), December 1972; "Moduli Combinabili in Strutture Quadrale" in *Ottagono* (Milan), June 1973; "Bruno Munari Interview" by I. Lebeer in *Chroniques de l'Art Vivant* (Paris), November 1974; films—*Colori della Luce*, 1963; *Moiré* 1964.

On MUNARI: books—*Munari 71*, exhibition catalogue, by Paulo Fossati and others, Milan 1971; *Munari*, exhibition catalogue, by Paolo Fossati, Zagreb 1973; *Bruno Munari*, exhibition catalogue, by Giulio Carlo Argan and Alessandro Mendini, Parma 1979; *L'Arte Anomala di Bruno Munari* by A. Tanchis, Bari, Italy 1981.

I search for a balance between the case and the rule. The case makes me discover some new aspects of life both inside and outside of myself. The rule helps me to construct the images with art. With these images I search to communicate, with exactness, the way I happen to do it and to let others also know.

—Bruno Munari

Sculptor, film maker and designer, Bruno Munari has been active in kinetic art, the art of luminism, machine art, the art of the multiple and Ludic art. In tribute to his great versatility he was called by Picasso "the new Leonardo."

After a brief association with the later school of Futurists—he contributed to the *Aeropittura* exhibition of 1931—he began making wire mobiles and kinetic sculpture in 1933. With these he anticipated and influenced Tinguely, whom he met in 1954. He called them "machines inutiles," and the best known of them is his "L'Ora X," a clock constructed during the 1940's in which the hands move mechanically round a clock face without numbers. After the war he made his mark at the important exhibition *Mouvement* staged by the Denise René Gallery, Paris, in 1955.

As a founding member of the Movimento per l'Arte Concreta in 1949, he began to investigate the problems of the fragmentation of light, displaying the aesthetic applications of fragmented light in his series of "Projections" and in "Direct Applications of Polarized Light" in 1957. He also made transparent and coloured collages from plastic materials.

Munari has made perhaps his most important impact in the field of Machine Art, which he pioneered and of which he has been the chief theoretician. He published *Manifesto de Meccanismo* in 1949 and a series of manifestos on this theme in 1952. He believes that industrial design has a social function to reawaken in the general public that sensibility for fine form which, in the words of Gillo Dorfles, "otherwise threatens to be overwhelmed by the widespread contemporary pseudo-art disseminated by the machine." In opposition to the subjectivism inherent in our heritage of Romanticism, Munari holds that there exists a genuinely objective code of good design which can be understood and appreciated by ordinary people in every part of the world. It is the duty of the artist to know and understand machines and by their designs to ensure that machine-made productions conform to these standards of good taste. In close conjunction with this he was a pioneer of the art of the "Multiple"—called in Italy "Arte Programmata"—that is, the machine-made article produced in many examples with no other function than to exist as a work of art for appreciation and contemplation. It has been his view that industrial design can do more than handicraft or fine art to educate the public to appreciation of genuine artistic values.

In pursuances of the foregoing ideas Munari also turned his attention to Ludic art and in collaboration with Giovanni Belgrado he produced a series of "Visual Games" and a "Composable ABC" designed to evoke and encourage a critical awareness of visual images in children. In the words of Frank Popper: "The child is induced to discover the meaning and value of forms and colours, and to recognize their logical development in the interests of his own thought processes and critical judgment."

There is something of the social apostle in all Munari's artistic activities and interests.

—Harold Osborne

MUNDY, Henry.

British. Born in Birkenhead. Cheshire, 13 January 1919. Studied at the Laird School of Art, Birkenhead, 1933–37; Camberwell School of Art, London, 1946–50. Married Gillian Ayres in 1951; children: James Stephen and Sam George. Painter: lives and works in London. Lecturer in Painting, Bath Academy of Art, Corsham, Wiltshire, and St. Martin's School of Art, London. Recipient: William Frew Prize, Pittsburgh, 1961; First Prize, *John Moore's Exhibition*, Liverpool, 1961; Edwin Austin Abbey Award, London, 1975; Arts Council of Great Britain Grant, London, 1975. Address: 23 Wellesley Road, London, W4, England.

Individual Exhibitions:

1955	Gallery One, London
	AIA Gallery, London
1957	Gallery K.B., Oslo
1960	Stone Gallery, Newscastle upon Tyne
	Hanover Gallery, London
1961	Stone Gallery, Newcastle upon Tyne
1962	Hanover Gallery, London
1963	Stone Gallery, Newcastle upon Tyne
	Arts Council Gallery, Cambridge (with Carl Richards and Peter Lanyon; toured the U.K.)
1965	Hanover Gallery, London
1967	Bear Lane Gallery, Oxford (with Benedict Rubbra)
1972	Kasmin Gallery, London
1980	Serpentine Gallery, London (with Colin Cina and Dennis Creffield)

Selected Group Exhibitions:

1958	*Carnegie International*, Carnegie Institute, Pittsburgh
1960	*Situation*, RBA Galleries, London
1961	*New London Situation*, Marlborough Fine Arts, London
1962	*British Painting Today*, San Francisco (toured the Untied States)
1964	*Painting and Sculpture of a Decade*, Tate Gallery, London
	Englische Maler und Bildhauer, Stuttgart
1966	*European Drawings*, Guggenheim Museum, New York
1967	*Aspects of New British Art*, Queensland Art Gallery, Brisbane
1974	*British Painting 74*, Hayward Gallery, London
1977	*British Painting, 1952-1977*, Royal Academy of Arts, London

Collections:

Tate Gallery, London; Laing Art Gallery, Newcastle upon Tyne; National Gallery of Victoria, Melbourne; Art Gallery of Ontario, Toronto; San Francisco Museum of Modern Art; Brooklyn Museum, New York, Carnegie Institute, Pittsburgh.

Publications:

On MUNDY: book—*Painting and Sculpture of a Decade*, exhibition catalogue, London 1964; articles—"7 Exhibitions at the Tate" by William Tucker in *Studio International* (London), April 1972; "London Letter" by William Feaver in *Art International* (Lugano, Switzerland), April 1972.

With Irish blood in his veins, Henry Mundy who grew up in Birkenhead had managed to exert enough cultural pressure to get himself a scholarship to the Laird School of Art when he was 14 years old, but in some ways it was a bit of a Pyrrhic victory, notably because the award covered only fees—no subsistence allowance. The year was 1933, not an auspicious one for those of tender years but possessing no financial resources.

In those days, the young and unknown potential artist had few courses open to him. One of these, a hardy perennial for painters and sculptors, was teaching. Mundy tried teaching for a while after leaving the Laird School of Art, but his first effective incursion into the contemporary art world did not come until 15 years after the war when, following his one-man show in Newcastle (Stone Gallery), he was taken up by Erica Brausen of the Hanover Gallery in London. The two international prizes which he subsequently won brought him to the attention of a world public, and his name today is generally included amongst those who gave British art a new face in the postwar period.

In its way, the work which first won him recognition was both subtle and subliminally diplomatic. At a time when a public searching for something "new" was prepared to relegate the romantic—and often sentimental—paintings by artists like Keith Vaughan, John Craxton, John Minton (even Colquhoun and McBride) and the sculptural carryings-on of Michael Ayrton—at such a time, with pop art in its infancy, the enthusiasm was for nonfiguration, allowing for some small tachiste legacies, and perferably not too hard-edge. Mundy met this new requirement on two levels. Not only did his painting fit neatly into the conception of what modern British art at that time should be; it also carried with it a poetic flavour of very fine sensibility. This lyrical quality had nothing to do with the heavy-handed style to be found in the works of so many of the British wartime romantics, yet it could, in its nearly hidden leger-de-main manner, be seen as a bridging style, aware of the recent past, but fully involved with the modern postwar era. For those pining, however discreetly, for what had gone, Henry Mundy's oeuvres of those days were acceptable primarily for their unquestionable quality but also because they contained links, never mind how slight, with the "isolationist" art of Britain during the war years. (It needs to be emphasized, lest there should be any false impressions, that Mundy's paintings at that time *in no way resembled* those of the wartime artists. It was the accent of his visual communication rather than its vocabulary which makes such an assessment viable; and even this accent was extremely sotto voce.)

Today, his work presents a totally different appearance. Apart from the artist himself and his signature, the new pictures share only one element with the old. Poetry may have been sent into exile, colours have retired to an extent which frequently almost leaves the paintings to the mercies of monochrome, the grid replaces the elegy, but the same stern auto-discipline continues to ensure a ruthless censorship that has been with him from the start and whose outcome is works of discriminatory and subtle taste.

It is not without significance that "Henry Mundy, Float III 61" at the Tate is the sole survivor of the three Float paintings that were exhibited in Newcastle at the Stone Gallery in 1961 and a year later at the Hanover Gallery in London. Mundy destroyed Floats I and II.

The variations on the grid principle began about 1969, but imagery hung in the balance in many of his paintings for several years.

Mundy is now certain that the essential virtue of a painting is its relation with *surface*; not the tactile surface but the area (could be stretches of sand, limitless sky, the flat sea) of single character which tempts the artist (the creative mind) to take action—make a mark, do something that will give the surface greater puissance without introducing any sense of external elements.

Mundy is an artist who does not care for the finite. A canvas for him can lose its edge because the "image" does not reach its side. Or it can become continuous, its huge quadrilaterals joining each other so that the final work is like the four vertical insides of a box.

When asked if this kind of "picture" is not fulfilling a kind of wallpaper function, Mundy says No. For want of a better description, they make up a *situation*.

Henry Mundy asserts that painting is not dead; it is just that in contemporary times we have seen a lot of rubbish cleared away so that results are much cleaner.
—Sheldon Williams

MURPHY, Catherine

American. Born in 1946. Studied at the Pratt Institute, Brooklyn, New York, B.F.A.; also studied at the Skowhegan School of Painting and Sculpture, Maine. Free-lance artist. Recipient: National Endowment for the Arts grant, 1979; Guggenheim Fellowship, 1982. Agent: Xavier Fourcade Inc., New York. Address: c/o Xavier Fourcade Inc., 36 East 75th Street, New York, New York 10021, U.S.A.

Individual Exhibitions:

1972	First Street Gallery, New York
	Piper Gallery, Massachusetts
1975	*Recent Paintings*, Fourcade, Droll Inc., New York
1976	*Catherine Murphy: A Retrospective Exhibition*, Phillips Collection, Washington, D.C. (travelled to the Institute of Contemporary Art, Boston)
1979	*Recent Paintings*, Xavier Fourcade Inc., New York
1985	Xavier Fourcade Inc., New York

Selected Group Exhibitions:

1972	*Annual Painting and Sculpture Exhibition*, Whitney Museum, New York
1973	*Biennial*, Whitney Museum, New York
1974	*Painting and Sculpture Today*, Indianapolis Museum
1976	*A Selection of American Art: The Skowhegan School 1946–76*, Institute of Contemporary Art, Boston (travelled to the Colby Museum of Art, Waterville, Maine)
1977	*A View of a Decade*, Museum of Contemporary Art, Chicago
1979	*Awards Exhibition*, American Academy and Institute of Arts and Letters, New York
1981	*Real, Really Real and Super Real*, San Antonio Museum Association, Texas
1982	*Lower Manhattan from Street to Sky*, Whitney Museum, Downtown Branch, New York
1983	*American Still Life 1945–83*, Contemporary Arts Museum, Houston (travelled to Buffalo, New York; Columbus, Ohio; Purchase, New York; Portland, Oregon)
1986	*The Window in 20th Century Art*, Neuberger Museum, Purchase, New York (travelled to Houston)

Collections:

Whitney Museum, New York; Chase Manhattan Bank, New York; The Newark Museum, New Jersey; New Jersey Art Museum, Trenton; Phillips Collection, Washington, D.C.; Hirshhorn Museum and Sculpture Garden, Washington, D.C.; Weatherspoon Art Gallery, University of North Carolina at Greensboro; Security Pacific National Bank, Los Angeles.

Publications:

By MURPHY: article—"Catherine Murphy: Art Is My Lifestyle," interview, in *The Woman Artist*, special issue of *Art and Man* (New York), November 1974.

On MURPHY: books—*Catherine Murphy*, exhibition catalogue, Washington, D.C. and Boston 1976; *Catherine Mur-*

Catherine Murphy: *Scrub*, 1987

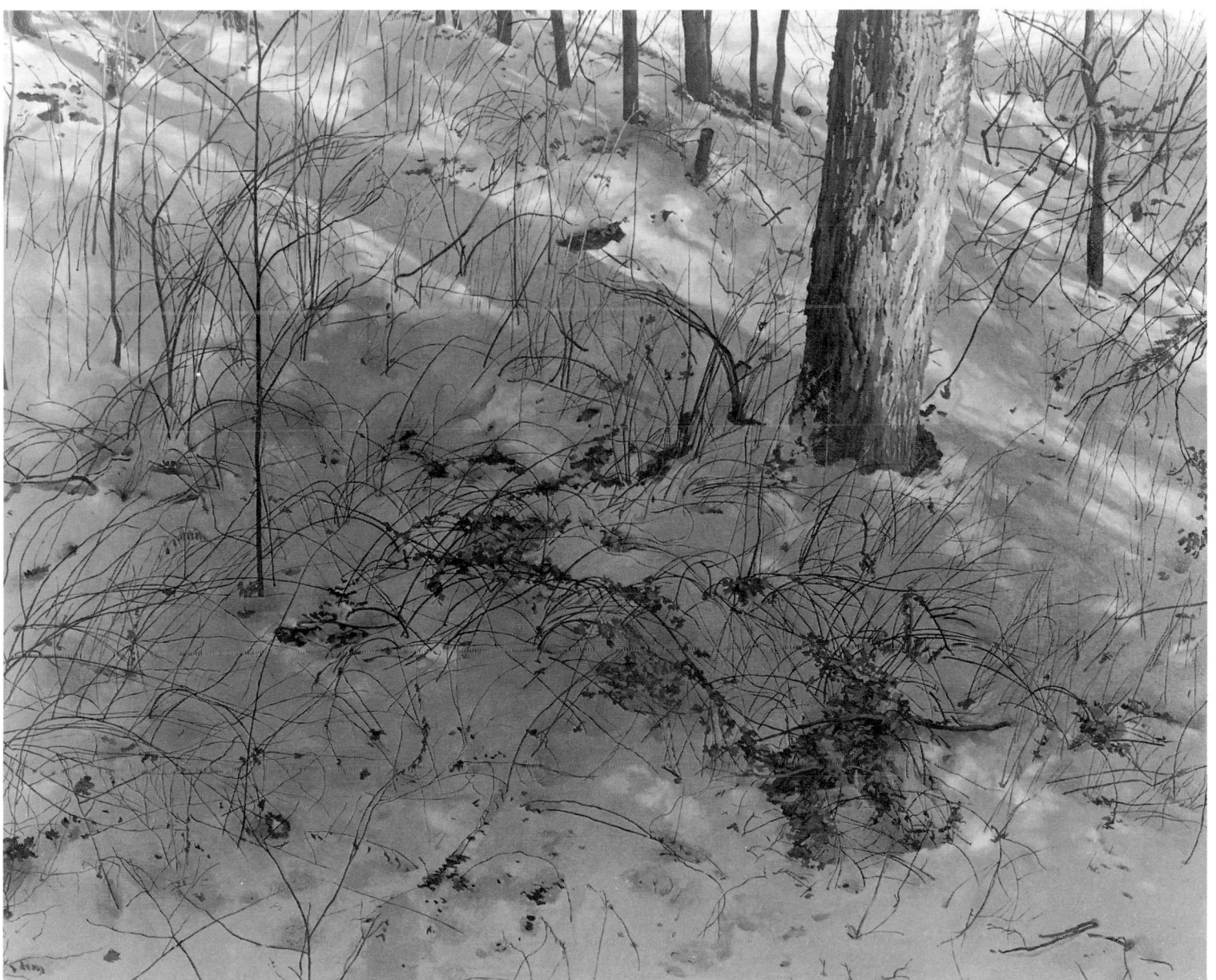

phy: New Paintings and Drawings 1980–85, exhibition catalogue, New York 1985; articles—"The Art of Survival (and Vice Versa)" by Vivien Raynor in *The New York Times Magazine*, 17 February 1974; "Arts Reviews: Catherine Murphy" by Allen Ellenzweig in *Arts Magazine* (New York), February 1975; "An Uncommon Painter of the Commonplace" by Hilton Kramer in *New York Times*, 9 March 1975; "Painter with a Novelist's Eye" by Piri Halasz in the *New York Times*, 11 January 1976; "Catherine Murphy: The Rise of a Cult Figure" by John Gruen in *Artnews* (New York), December 1978; "Catherine Murphy" by Hilton Kramer in the *New York Times*, 11 May 1979; "The Magic of the Commonplace" by John Gruen in *Quest* (New York), January 1980; "Revival of Realism" by Mark Stevens in *Newsweek* (New York), 7 June 1982; "Catherine Murphy" by Kay Larson in *New York*, 16 December 1985; "Catherine Murphy" by Jeanne Silverthorne in *Artforum* (New York), February 1986.

Rightly enough, Murphy's images have been labelled "biographical vision," and in this regard, they clearly parallel the creative efforts of, for instance Andrew Wyeth (and all others imbued with such existential need). Her art seems as if it were able only to arise from the necessity to comment upon the intimate and mysterious immediacy of her human and physical surroundings. Her 1985 exhibition was but the third solo show of her entire career, and its contents indicated that her production in the six years since her previous exhibition was about 8 pencil drawings and 11 oil paintings. Not only were all those works intimately related to her outwardly placid life in Duchess County, N.Y., but as if to buttress even more intensively the personal time that we may intuit in such a slow-paced professional creative pace, the artist and her artist-husband Harry Roseman, had moved into her parents' home during this time so as to rid them of any distractions from mundane personal up-keep.

Even though she had only a debut exhibition, Murphy became widely known in 1976 through a travelling exhibition arranged by the Philips Collection, Washington, D.C. Her work continues to be held in high regard as an import and contribution to the realist resurgence of the past two decades. While her images with large foreground figures have been considered relatively life-less, her landscapes and interior views—still life essentially—comprise her best work. Her paintings verge on Photo-Realism with their deft sine-sable brushwork, and yet they are "warmer" both in touch and feeling; and may well be taken as "post-modern" in their insistence upon an unembarrassed and clearly nonsarcastic Romantic nuance. Huddled figures, for instance, may converse in a dark corner at the base of a stair case—in an image which is ostensibly focused upon a cluster of window ledge objects. Another special characteristic in her finest work appears as an emphasis on the artifice of art making: Murphy may display obviously self-conscious chords of color; or present a clearly arbitrary compositional pattern which is a match, or foil, to some other part of the pictorial design. Murphy's realism then may be felt as synthesizing—a second wave encompassing older attitudes beyond the '70s phenomenological objectification.

—Joshua Kind

MURRAY, Elizabeth.

American. Born in Chicago, Illinois, in 1940. Educated at the Art Institute of Chicago, B.F.A. 1962, and at Mills College, Oakland, California, M.F.A. 1964. Independent artist. Instructor, Bard College, Annandale-on-Hudson, New York, 1974–75, 1976–77; Princeton University, New Jersey, 1977; Yale University, New Haven, Connecticut, 1978–79. Visiting Instructor, Wayne State University, Detroit, 1975; California Institute of the Arts, Valencia, 1975–76, and School of the Art Institute of Chicago, 1975–76. Recipient: Walter M. Campana Award, Art Institute

of Chicago, 1982; American Academy and Institute of Arts and Letters Award, 1984; Skowhegan Medal for Painting, Maine, 1986. Agent: Paula Cooper Gallery, New York. Address: c/o Paula Cooper Gallery, 155 Wooster Street, New York, New York 10012

Individual Exhibitions:

1974	Jacobs Ladder Gallery, Washington, D.C. (with Joseph Zucker)
	Elizabeth Murray/Marilyn Lenkowsky/John Torreano, Paula Cooper Gallery, New York
1975	Paula Cooper Gallery, New York (with James Dearing)
	Jared Sable Gallery, Toronto
1976	Paula Cooper Gallery, New York
1978	Ohio State University, Columbus
	Phyllis Kind Gallery, Chicago
	Paula Cooper Gallery, New York
1980	Galerie Mukai, Tokyo
	Susanne Hilberry Gallery, Birmingham, Michigan
1981	Paula Cooper Gallery, New York
1982	Smith College, Northampton, Massachusetts
	Daniel Weinberg Gallery, Los Angeles
1983	Portland Center for the Visual Arts, Oregon
	Paula Cooper Gallery, New York
1984	Knight Gallery, Charlotte, North Carolina
	Paula Cooper Gallery, New York
	Brooke Alexander Inc., New York
1985	University of New Mexico, Albuquerque
1986	Carnegie-Mellon University, Pittsburgh
1987	Dallas Museum of Art, Texas (toured the United States, 1987–88)
	California State University, Long Beach (travelled to Berkeley)
	Paula Cooper Gallery, New York

Selected Group Exhibitions:

1974	*American Abstract Painting Today*, Whitney Museum Downtown, New York
1977	*9 Artists*, Guggenheim Museum, New York
	Paintings 1975–77, Sarah Lawrence College Gallery, Bronxville, New York (travelled to the American Foundation for the Arts, Miami, and the Contemporary Arts Center, Cincinnati, Ohio)
1978	*8 Abstract Painters*, Institute of Contemporary Art, University of Pennsylvania, Philadelphia
1979	*New Painting: New York*, Hayward Gallery, London
1980	*American Drawing in Black and White 1970–80*, Brooklyn Museum, New York
1981	*1981 Painting Invitational*, Oscarsson Hood Gallery, New York
1983	*Minimalism to Expression: Painting and Sculpture Since 1965*, Whitney Museum, New York
1985	*Correspondence: New York Art Now*, Laforet Museum, Tokyo (travelled to Tochigi and Kobe, Japan)
1987	*Prints in Parts*, Crown Point Press, New York

Collections:

Museum of Modern Art, New York: Guggenheim Museum, New York; Whitney Museum, New York; Museum of Fine Arts, Boston; Art Institute of Chicago; Dallas Museum of Art, Texas; Walker Art Center, Minneapolis; Philadelphia Museum of Art; Saint Louis Art Museum, Missouri; Hirshhorn Museum, Washington, D.C.

Publications:

On MURRAY: books—*Early Work by Five Contemporary Artists*, exhibition catalogue with texts by Marcia Tucker and Allan Schwartzman, New York 1977; *American Painting: The Eighties*, exhibition catalogue by Barbara Rose, New York 1979; *La Peinture Americaine: Les mythes et la matiere* by Madeleine Deschamps, Paris 1981; *Elizabeth Murray: Recent Paintings and Drawings*, exhibition catalogue, Portland, Oregon 1983; *The Pluralist Era: American Art 1968–1981* by Corinne Robins, New York 1984; *American Art Now* by Edward Lucie-Smith, New York 1985; *Elizabeth Murray:*

Drawings 1980–1986, exhibition catalogue with essays by Elaine A. King and Ann Sutherland Harris, Pittsburgh 1986; *Elizabeth Murray: Paintings and Drawings*, exhibition catalogue with essays by Roberta Smith and Clifford S. Ackley, Dallas and New York 1987.

Elizabeth Murray, since 1974, has emerged as a leading practitioner of emotively loaded, ambiguously abstract color painting. She found her mature direction after having investigated various other issues: a funky, Pop-inspired imagist painting along with three-dimensional reliefs dominated her work during the 1960's. In the early 1970's she was exploring single forms and repetitive structures like steps and waves in oil painting. Then in about 1974 she changed her direction, and eradicating any direct representational associations, instituted, instead, a back-to-basics constructive approach to making pictures. Stressing the clear and specific presentation of line, plane and color, the paintings from the mid-1970s reveal the elaboration of a personal vocabulary of motifs and compositional devices as well as scalar relationships.

In 1975 the first shaped paintings offered the viewer even more dynamic experiences of colors and forms. Her ability to break the rules by making irregular and regular as well as local and disharmonious colors work together by working against each other is strongly evident in such examples as *Singing School* and *Rise*, both 1976. The evocative qualities of the imagery is underscored in the examples from 1977–78 in which complex and choreographed interplays among the pictorial elements impress as equivalential statements about feelings and even human relationships. *Parting and Together* (1978) and *Daybreak* (1977–78) are examples.

In the late 1970's the paintings had become larger and took on more aggressive shapes. In 1980 the strong pictorial forces generated by the imagery caused Murray, finally, to burst apart the canvas and to adapt multiple format that ranged anywhere from two to more than 20 pieces. By freeing certain thematic impulses earlier present as undercurrents, Murray has worked from the early 1980s toward broadening the scope of her vision. In *Yikes* (1982) she lets her keen sense of humor out, in an amusing painting of a broken cup, in which the title gives fitting voice to the exclamatory qualities of the bold cartoonish imagery and the physically fragmented structure of the canvas on which it appears. In *Kitchen Painting* (1985) she shows her imaginative depths in the affective way that color, shape and representational motifs come together to convey the complex family feelings often suffusing, if not suffocating domestic space. *Kitchen Party* is also an example of multiple shaped canvases arranged into a relief structure with elements jutting off, which the artist has favored in this period.

—Ronny Cohen

MURRAY, Robert.

Canadian. Born in Vancouver, British Columbia, 2 March 1936. Educated at Saskatoon Teachers College, Saskatchewan, 1954–55 (scholarship, 1955); studied art, under Jack Shadbolt, Will Barnet, Barnett Newman, John Ferren and Clement Greenberg, Emma Lake Artists Workshop, Saskatchewan, 1955, 1957, 1961; studied at Regina College School of Art, University of Saskatchewan, 1956–58, and Institute Allende, San Miguel, Mexico, 1958 (scholarship). Served in the Royal Canadian Air Force Auxiliary, 1951–54. Married Diana Armatage in 1959 (divorced, 1969); children: Megan and Becca; married Cintra Wetherill Lofting in 1971; children: Claire and Hillary. Independent sculptor, since 1960. Art Instructor, Buena Vista School, Saskatoon, Saskatchewan, 1955–56; Assistant Art Instructor, University of Saskatchewan, Saskatoon, Summer 1958; Art In-

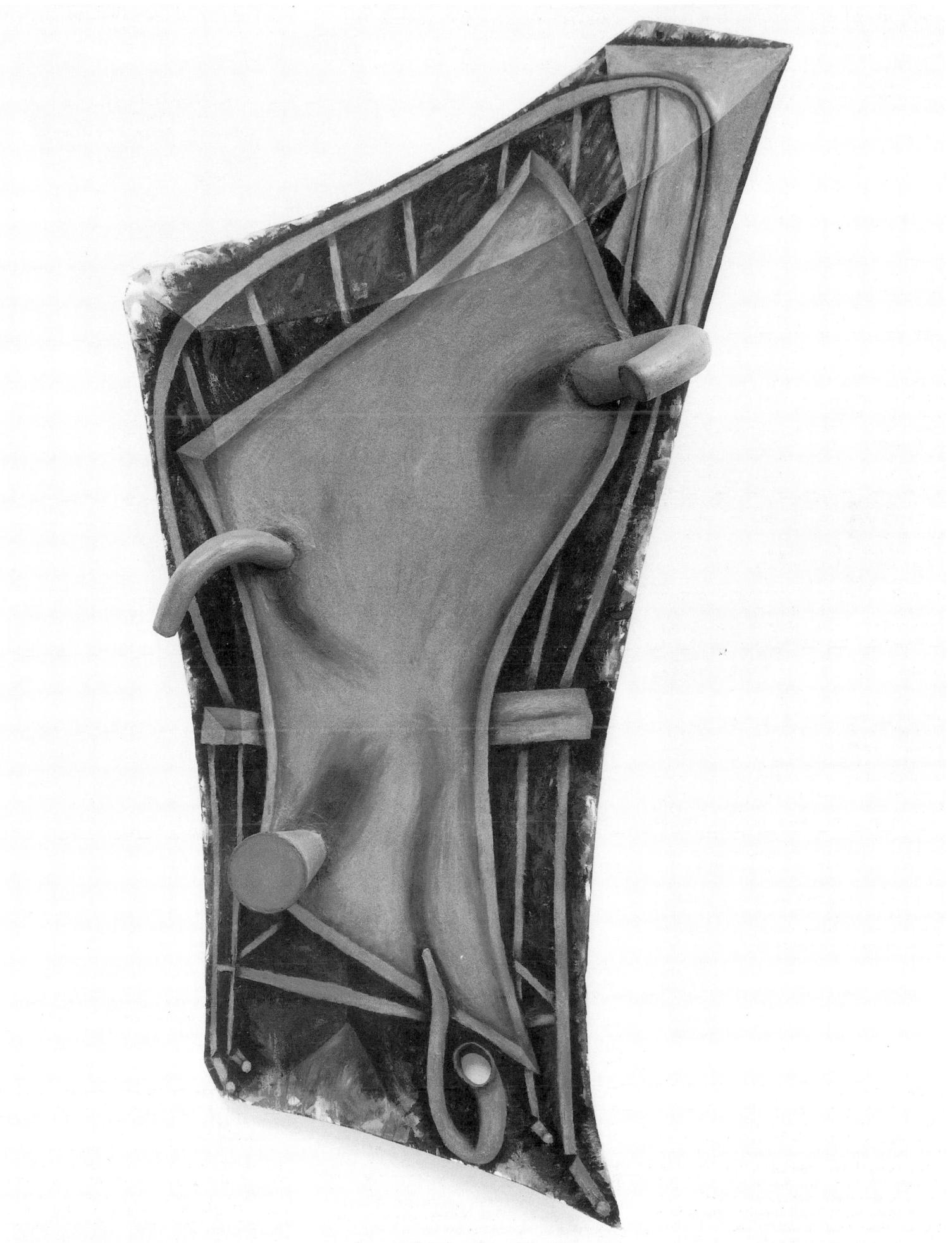

Elizabeth Murray: *The Hunger Artist*, 1987

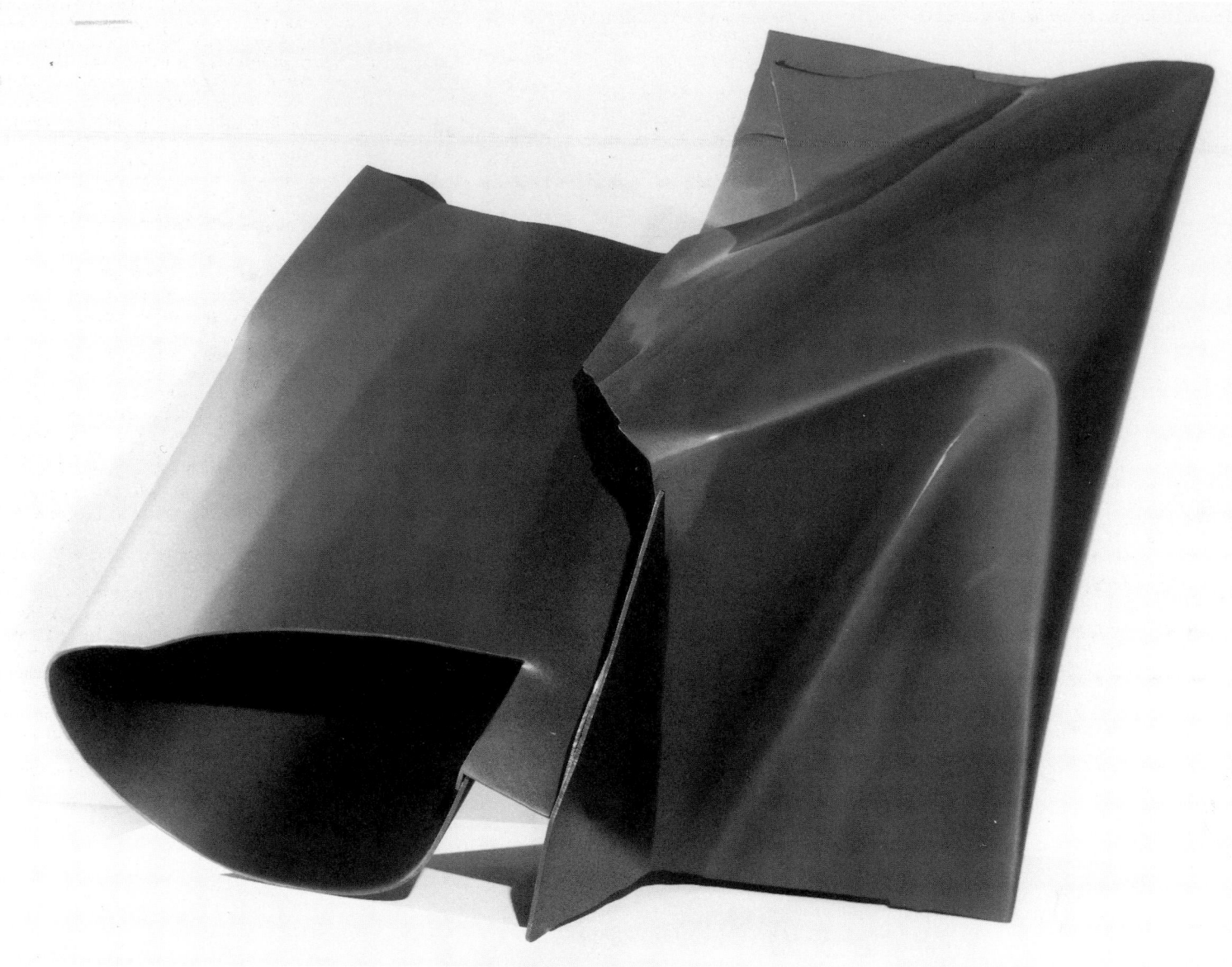

Robert Murray: *Susquehanna*, 1980

structor, Technical Collegiate, Saskatoon, 1959-60; Art Instructor, Hunter College, New York, 1965-69; Artist-in-Residence, Yale University, New Haven, Connecticut, 1968; Art Instructor, School of Visual Arts, New York, 1971-78; Artist-in-Residence, University of Regina, Saskatchewan, 1978; University of Alberta, Edmonton, 1978; and University of Manitoba, Winnipeg, 1978. Recipient: Recognition Award, Saskatchewan Arts Board, Regina, 1958; Arts Scholarship, 1960, and Bursary, 1969, Canada Council, Ottawa; National Endowment for the Arts Grant, 1969; Second Prize, *Bienal,* Sao Paulo, 1969; Allied Arts Medal, Royal Architectural Institute of Canada, 1977. Agent: Richard Green Gallery, 152 Wooster Street, New York, New York 10012. Address: First Floor, 66 Grand Street, New York, New York 10013, U.S.A.

Individual Exhibitions:

1965   Betty Parsons Gallery, New York
1966   Betty Parsons Gallery, New York
1967   David Mirvish Gallery, Toronto
        Jewish Museum, New York
1968   Betty Parsons Gallery, New York
        David Mirvish Gallery, Toronto
1969   Bettery Park, Cultural Affairs Department, New York
1970   *Robert Murray/Ronald Bladen,* The Gallery, Vancouver

1971   Dag Hammarskjold Plaza, New York
1972   David Mirvish Gallery, Toronto
1974   Paula Cooper Gallery, New York
        David Mirvish Gallery, Toronto
1975   Mendel Art Gallery, Saskatoon, Saskatchewan
        The Gallery, Stratford, Ontario
        David Mirvish Gallery, Toronto
1976   *Watercolors by Robert Murray and Toni Onley,* Olympia Galleries, Philadelphia
1977   Janie C. Lee Gallery, Houston
        Hamilton Gallery of Contemporary Art, New York
1978   Sewall Art Gallery, Rice University, Houston
1979   Dayton Art Institute, Ohio
        Columbus Museum, Ohio
        Hamilton Gallery of Contemporary Art, New York
        Klonaridis Gallery, Toronto
1980   Hamilton Gallery of Contemporary Art, New York
        Klonaridis Gallery, Toronto
1981   Klonaridis Gallery, Toronto
1982   Hamilton Gallery of Contemporary Art, New York
        Klonaridis Gallery, Toronto
1983   Phillips Academy, Andover, Massachusetts
        Sam Houston Gallery, Vancouver
        Art Gallery of Greater Victoria, British Columbia
1984   The Esplanade, New York
1985   Centro Culturale Canadese, Rome
        Gallery One, Toronto
1986   Gallery 291, Atlanta, Georgia
        Richard Green Gallery, New York
1987   Richard Green Gallery, Los Angeles

Selected Group Exhibitions:

1971   *49th Parallel: New Canadian Art,* Museum of Contemporary Art, Chicago
        Lithographs from the Nova Scotia College of Art Workshop, Museum of Modern Art, New York
1972   *Masters of the 60's,* Edmonton Art Gallery, Alberta (travelled to the Winnipeg Art Gallery, Manitoba, and David Mirvish Gallery, Toronto)
1973   *Contemporary American Art,* Whitney Museum, New York
1975   *Artist and Fabricator,* Fine Arts Center Gallery, University of Massachusetts, Amherst
        Condition of Sculpture, Hayward Gallery, London
1976   *American Salon des Refuses,* Stamford Museum, Connecticut
1977   *Project, New Urban Monuments,* Akron Art Institute, Ohio (toured the United States)
1978   *In Small Scale,* Hamilton Gallery of Contemporary Art, New York (travelled to Marion Locks Gallery, Philadelphia)
1981   *Bronze Show,* Hamilton Gallery of Contemporary Art, New York

Collections:

Saskatchewan Arts Board, Regina; Mendel Art Gallery, Saskatoon; Canada Council Art Bank, Ottawa; Art Gallery of Ontario, Toronto; National Gallery of Canada, Ottawa; Whitney Museum, New York; Metropolitan Museum of Art, New

York; Hirshhorn Museum, Washington, D.C.; University of Massachusetts, Amherst; Dayton Art Institute, Ohio.

Publications:

By MURRAY: articles—"The Education of 12 Practicing Artists" in *Canadian Art* (Toronto), December 1965; "10 Artists in Search of Canadian Art" in *Canadian Art* (Toronto), January 1966; interview, with Barbara Rose, in *Canadian Art* (Toronto), July 1966; interview, in "Design and Expression in Minimal Art" by James S. Pierce in *Art International* (Lugano, Switzerland), May 1968; "Barnett Newman 1905-1970: An Appreciation" in *Artscanada* (Toronto), August 1970; films— *Art Is,* New York 1970; *Vision U.S.A.,* New York 1971.

On MURRAY: books—*Robert Murray/Ronald Bladen,* exhibition catalogue (includes statement by Murray), Vancouver 1970; *Artist and Fabricator,* exhibition catalogue, by Hugh Marlais Davies (includes interview with Murray), Amherst, Massachusetts 1975; *Robert Murray,* exhibition catalogue, Toronto 1975; *Watercolors by Robert Murray and Toni Onley,* exhibition catalogue, with critical notes by Ruth Fine Lehrer, Philadelphia 1976; *Robert Murray,* exhibition catalogue, Dayton, Ohio 1979; *Robert Murray: Sculpture and Working Models,* exhibition catalogue by Greg Bellerby, Victoria 1983; articles—"Canada: Art d'Aujourd'hui" by Bernard Teyssedre in *Vie des Arts* (Montreal), Spring 1968; "Blow-Up: The Problem of Scale in Sculpture" by Barbara Rose in *Art in America* (New York), July 1968; "Robert Murray/Canada" by Brydon Smith in *Artscanada* (Toronto), October 1969; "Bladen and Murray: The Giants of Canadian Sculpture" by Joan Lowndes in *Vie des Arts* (Montreal), Summer 1970; "Sculpture: A Rebirth of Humanism" by Joe Bodolai and "Robert Murray: Against the Monument" by M. Greenwood in *Artscanada* (Toronto), Autumn 1974; "Living with Sculpture" by John L. Taylor in *Artnews* (New York), October 1974; "The Giant Size Art of Robert Murray" by Robert Fulford in *Saturday Night* (Toronto), December 1975; "Where the Monumental Sculptors Go" by Roy Bongartz in *Artnews* (New York), February 1976; "Robert Murray: Generating Sculpture from the Metal Plate" by Hugh M. Davies in *Arts Magazine* (New York), October 1977; "Robert Murray: On Being a Sculptor" by Lowry Sims in *Artscanada* (Toronto), April 1979; "Robert Murray" by Anna Babinska in *Vanguard* (Vancouver), September 1981.

Robert Murray is known as a maker of constructed metal sculpture which uses simple geometric forms and industrial materials and methods, unified by colored industrial finishes. On the strength of that description, Murray sounds like one of the many followers of Anthony Caro, but in fact, the Canadian sculptor is something of an anomaly, since he arrived at his kind of painted metal construction about the same time that Caro first began to work in steel.

Like Caro, Murray developed his steel works from David Smith's example. This is made clear by one of Murray's earliest mature pieces, a fountain sculpture for the City Hall of Saskatoon, Saskatchewan, where he went to art school. The piece is deceptively simple: two similar cut-out metal shapes, with curving projections, reach towards one another. But there is a Smith-ian animation and personality in each of the arching forms, particularly in the way they stand erect on stylized "feet."

Like any intelligent young sculptor, Murray was aware of what Caro was doing in the '60's, but he was also aware of minimalism and other contemporary ideologies. Perhaps in response to these influences, his work became noticeably simplified during that decade. His sculptures of the '60's and early '70's insist on the primacy of vertical-horizontal relationships and logical geometric configurations of lucid, angular shapes. The structure of each piece is readily apparent; nothing is hidden. Murray exploits the possibilities of mechanical processes in these works. They involve folding and bending on a very large scale, so that we immediately think about machinery and the factory, while their smooth, saturated surfaces are as impassive as industrial coatings.

Since about 1974 Murray's sculpture has become more playful and more lyrical. He has evolved a new vocabulary of irregularities and curves, to supplement the austere geometry of his earlier work. He is still fascinated by process and the effects that technology affords, and this can sometimes cause problems. When the technical aspects of fabricating a fluttering handkerchief of steel become too apparent, the sculpture suffers, but when the finished form seems more important than how it was made, the piece can be both powerful and delicate, apparently unaffected by concerns of gravity and weight. The slightly iridescent surfaces of some recent works emphasize the fragility of curling edges and swelling planes and, at the same time, returns us to the physicality of the metal itself, recalling as they do custom car bodies.

Since the early 1980s, Murray has worked in an intermediate, more intimate scale which seems to suit him very well. The works in this middle size include some bronzes, made from sheets (not cast). The malleable metal and its ability to assume color through patination give Murray full scope for his new interest in more elaborate surfaces and forms. If the severities and geometric purity of his earlier work could be called Classical, in Wölfflin's sense of the word, then the sumptuous curves, complex profiles and inflected surfaces of these sculptures can only be termed Baroque.

Since about 1985, Murray's sculpture has once again dealt with severe geometric forms, but at the same time has become more complex in terms of surface and texture, since he often combines a variety of materials—metal and wood, for example—in a single piece. He continues to work in a range of sizes, but to date there is the risk of the small sculptures seeming precious or like maquettes for larger works because of their new complexity of construction. The expressive possibilities of the of contrasting materials seems clearest and most effective in the larger works.

—Karen Wilkin

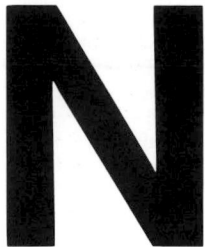

NAGASAWA, Hidetoshi.

Japanese. Born in Manchuria, China, 30 October 1940. Studied at Tama University of Fine Arts, Tokyo, 1959–63. Independent artist, since 1966: lived in Tokyo, 1966–67, and in Milan, since 1967. Agents: Galleria Arte Borgogna, via Borgogna 7, 20122 Milan; Galleria Francoise Lambert, Bastioni di Porta Nuova 11, 20121 Milan. Address: Via Bramante 29, 20154 Milan, Italy.

Individual Exhibitions:

1969	Galleria Sincron, Brescia, Italy
1970	Galleria Francoise Lambert, Milan
1971	Galleria Toselli, Milan
	Galleria l'Attico, Rome
	Galleria La Bertesca, Milan
1972	Galleria Art Borgogna, Milan
	Galleria Nuova Muse, Bologna
1974	Galleria Arte Borgogna, Milan
	Galleria Acme, Brescia, Italy
1975	Galleria Christian Stein, Turin
	Galleria L'Attico, Rome
1976	Galleria Christian Stein, Turin
1977	Galerie t'Venster, Rotterdam
1978	Galleria Piero Cavellini, Brescia, Italy
	Galleria L'Attico, Rome
	Galleria Arco d'Alibert, Rome
1979	Galleria Cesare Manzo, Pescara, Italy
1980	Galleria Wirz, Milan
1981	Tokyo Gallery, Tokyo
1982	Galleria Piu Due Cannaviello, Milan
	Galleria Piero Cavellini, Brescia, Italy
1985	Galleria Piero Cavellini, Milan
1987	Galleria Studio G7, Bologna

Selected Group Exhibitions:

1970 *Japan Art Festival,* Guggenheim Museum, New York
1973 *Biennale,* Paris
1974 *Japan: Tradition und Gegenwart,* Städtische Kunsthalle, Dusseldorf
1976 *Sette Italiani e sette Giapponesi,* Istituto Italiano di Cultura, Tokyo
1979 *Italy and Japan in the Last Ten Decades,* National Museum of Art, Osaka, Japan
1982 *30 Anni d'Arte Italiana 1950–80,* Villa Manzoni, Lecco, Italy
1984 *Trends of Contemporary Japanese Art 1970–84,* Metropolitan Art Museum, Tokyo
1986 *Chambres d'Amis,* Museum van Hedendaagse Kunst, Ghent, Belgium
1987 *Drei Japanische Kunstler,* Stadtgalerie, Saarbrucken, West Germany

Collections:

National Museum of Art, Osaka, Japan; Museum van Hedendaagse Kunst, Ghent, Belgium.

Publications:

By NAGASAWA: articles—in *Nagasawa,* exhibition catalogue, Rome 1975; *Sette Italiani e sette Giapponesi,* exhibition catalogue, Tokyo 1976; *Nagasawa,* exhibition catalogue, Tokyo 1981; and in *Casabella* (Milan), no. 390, 1974; *Flash Art* (Milan), no. 50, 1974, no. 111, 1983, no. 137, 1983; *Ohara Magazine* (Tokyo), no. 12, 1976, no. 1, 1977, no. 2, 1977; *Domus* (Milan), no. 605, 1980, no. 618, 1981, no. 631, 1982; *Panorama Lombardia* (Milan), no. 14, 1984; *Gran Bazaar* (Milan), no. 5/7, 1984, no. 4/5, 1985; films and videotapes—untitled film, Milan 1971; *No. 1,* Milan 1971; untitled videotape, Milan 1972.

On NAGASAWA: books—*Nagasawa* by Salvadori Trotta, Milan 1972; *Japan: Tradition und Gegenwart,* exhibition catalogue with text by T. Minemura and others, Dusseldorf 1974; *Nagasawa,* exhibition catalogue with text by L. M. Venturi, Milan 1974; articles—review in *Domus* (Milan), November 1968; review in *Flash Art* (Rome), May 1971; review in *Data* (Milan), September 1971; review in *Flash Art* (Rome), May/June 1972; review in *Bijutsu-Techo* (Tokyo), August/September 1972; "Milan in Autumn" by Henry Martin in *Art International* (Lugano, Switzerland), January 1973; *8th Biennale de Paris,* exhibition catalogue, by J. Cahen-Salvadori, G. Boudaille, J. M. Poinsot and others, Paris 1973.

Born in Manchuria in 1940, Nagasawa began exhibiting his work in his adopted town of Milan in 1971. In the same year he held exhibitions in Rome, at which he showed several works including an aluminium plaque on which two arrows were juxtaposed. Alongside were bronze panels on which male members were represented on a tondo together with the names of great artists of the past. It was in 1972 that, with Trotta and Salvadori, Nagasawa published a catalogue (from the Toselli Gallery) documenting a performance piece. In it, the artist is touching various bodily parts of a naked woman who is located at the centre of a large white canvas. The artist touches the woman until she disappears. As he continues to touch the canvas, the impression of the woman reappears.

In these early experiments, a poetic based on the contrasts between 'To Be' and 'To Appear' are outlined, in addition to the idea of the fragment as part of the whole, the relationship between East and West, and—most importantly—between past and present. This is the poetic which informs the work *Piroga* (Open Boat) of 1973; as published in the magazine *Flash Art,* it was accompanied by the caption: this open boat, constructed in chestnut wood, was made in Ortisei, following the plan of an original dating from 1800–1200 BC, found in Molina di Ledro and now in the collection of the Trento Museum of Natural Science. The current structure was made using only those techniques available to neolithic cultures, such as fire and appropriate metal instruments. In a later interview (1975), Nagasawa expressed his interest in ethnology: "For man, the most difficult situation is to lose his own culture in place of a new one in which he does not find his roots. That means death . . . "

Nagasawa is profoundly interested in the fusion of his own Japanese culture with that of Latin races, particularly that of Italy where he now lives. A series of works produced between 1975 and 1976 recall a love and skill the Japanese have for working with pa-per, as in origami. Here is how Nagasawa describes his own work in this field: "to use paper in the sense of cooking food. I say 'cooking', as I do not mean to find new ways of interpreting a particular material, but rather to aim at making it take over many different flavours while remaining itself." It is in this way that Nagasawa is interested in the direct relationship with matter—be it paper, wood or stone—following the natural characteristics of the material.

He is also concerned with finding the lowest common denominator of an aesthetic kind for natural objects, either subjecting them to modifications prompted by human intervention, or simply arranging them as part of a composition. A statement of 1975 reveals this deep involvement: "If the designer of a beautiful garden happens to see a magnificent Bernini sculpture, he will immediately understand it and will apprehend the degree of beauty in the work although expressed in a different language to his own. So Bernini would himself have done, without any mediation, when faced with a beautiful garden."

Boat, a work of 1980–81, well illustrates this idea. The shell of a boat is carved out of a single block of marble, and the inside filled with earth. In the soil, a willow tree (Caprea Pendula) has been planted. The boat's shape is reminiscent of the basin of a seventeenth-century fountain with a rounded rim. The prow of the boat, like a little crest, suggests the waves of the sea. But then the tree occurs with its characteristic pendulous branches to remind the viewer that, after all, the boat is a fountain, the tree trunk is a water jet, and the branches are the spray. It was five years earlier that Nagasawa had spoken of Bernini and the Garden, and here his words are materialized in the natural fountain of this work. Such an equation not only supports his words but makes explicit the roots of the Oriental in his work and the influence of what has been absorbed during his years in Italy.

—Roberto Lambarelli

NAGEL, Peter.

German. Born in Kiel, 6 April 1941. Educated in Kappeln/Schiei, until 1959; studied art, under Wienert, Kluth, Gecelli and Mavignier, at the Hochschule für Bildenden Künste, Hamburg 1960–65. Married Hanne Axelsen in 1966; children: Tina and Christoph. Figurative "realist" painter, in Hamburg and Kleinflintbek, since 1965: Founder-Member, with Dieter Asmus, Nikolaus Stortenbecker and Dietmar Ullrich, Zebra group of painters, Hamburg, 1965. Professor of Painting, Kunstakademie, Kiel, 1985. Recipient: Deutschen Akademie/Villa Massimo Prize, Rome, 1968, 1976; Premio Fiorino, Deutsche Bundesregierung für Malerei, Florence, 1969; First Prize, *International Triennale of Coloured Prints,* Grenchen, 1970; Kulturpreis, Bundesverband der Deutschen Industrie, 1971; City of Freiburg Prize, *European Print Biennale,* Mulhouse, 1976; Kulturpreis, City of Kiel, 1977; *Kunstlerflag-*

gen fur Europa Prize, Mannheim, 1983. Honorary Member, Freie Akademie, Hamburg, 1981; Honorary Guest Member, Deutsche Akademie, Rome, 1981. Agent: Fischer Fine Art, 30 King Street, London SW1, England. Address: Klein Flintbeker Weg 24, 2302 Kleinflintbek, West Germany.

Individual Exhibitions:

1965   Galerie 14, Aarhus, Denmark
1966   Galerie 13, Hamburg
1967   Landesmuseum Schloss Gottorf, Schleswig, West Germany
        Galerie Patio, Frankfurt
        Museum of Art, Vejen, Denmark
1968   Galerie 68, Kiel
        Niederfriesisches Museum, Husum, West Germany
1969   Städtische Kulturamt, Soest, West Germany
1970   Galerie Schmucking, Braunschweig, West Germany
        Galerie Defet, Nuremberg
1971   Galerie Musterbert, Basle
        Bilder, Graphik, Galerie van de Loo, Munich
        Galerie Dierks, Aarhus, Denmark
        Kunstschau Bottcherstrasse, Bremen, West Germany
        Galerie Kafsack, Paderborn, West Germany
        Galerie Walther, Dusseldorf
1972   Galleri Haaken, Oslo
        Galerie Schlegl, Zurich
1973   Werkverzeichnis 1965–72: Bilder, Zeichnungen, Grafik, Projekte, Galerie Hoeppner, Hamburg
        Galerie Hoeppner, Munich
1974   Galerija Krystofory, Cracow
1975   Fischer Fine Art, London
        Grafik-Forum, Lübeck
        Architektenkammer, Kiel
        Galerie Lornsentrasse, Kiel
1976   Galleria II Nuovo Torcoliere, Rome
        Galerie Kammer, Hamburg
        Galleri Dierks, Aarhus, Denmark
        Schloss Clemenswerth, Sogel, West Germany
        Studio Jaeschke, Bochum, West Germany
1977   Galerie Kafsack, Paderborn, West Germany
        Kunstkreis, Nordenstadt, West Germany
        Galerie Die Welle, Iserlohn, West Germany
        Gambro, Hechingen, West Germany
        Rathaus, Kiel
        Palais des Arts et de la Culture, Brest, France
        Galerie Schmucking, Braunschweig, West Germany
1978   Dragerwerk, Lübeck
        Galerie Walther, Dusseldorf
        Galerie Nouvelle, Horsens, Denmark
        Schloss Homburg, West Germany
        Werkverzeichnis 1972–78: Gemalde, Zeichnungen, Grafik, Projekte, Kunsthalle, Kiel
1979   Galleri Haaken, Oslo
        Tel Aviv Museum, Israel (travelled to Haifa and Beer Sheva)
1981   Kunstverein, Mannheim
        Galerie Remmele, Giefgen, West Germany
1982   Radicke Gallery, Washington, D.C.
        Studio Jaeschke, Bochum, West Germany
        Freie Akademie, Hamburg
1983   Kunstverein, Langenhagen, West Germany
1984   Kunstverein, Augsburg, West Germany
        Galerie Nemo, Eckenforde, West Germany
        Oberhessisches Museum, Giefgen, West Germany
1985   Kulturkreis, Rendsburg, West Germany
        Kunstkreis, Hameln, West Germany
        Randers Kunstmuseum, Denmark
1987   Museum Tallin, Estonia, U.S.S.R.

Selected Group Exhibitions:

1965   Internationale Osterausstellung, Kunstforeningen, Aarhus, Denmark
1966   Gruppe Zebra, Landesmuseum, Oldenburg, West Germany
1969   5 Maler unter 30, Ulmer Museum, Ulm, West Germany
1970   Gruppe Zebra, Westfälischer Kunstverein, Münster, West Germany
1971   Biennale, Paris

1975   Zehn Jahre Gruppe Zebra, Fischer Fine Art, Stuttgart
1976   Sport in der Kunst, Kulturkreis der BDI, Dusseldorf
1978   Realisten aus Hamburg, Expositiezaal De Delen, Rotterdam
1983   Realist Graphics from the BRD, Havana, Cuba
1986   Sport und Kunst, Madrid

Collections:

Städtische Sammlung, Kiel; Sammlung Deutscher Ring, Hamburg; Staatsgemaldesammlungen, Stuttgart; Städtische Sammlungen, Karlsruhe; Neue Galerie/Sammlung Ludwig, Aachen, West Germany; Bayerische Staatsgemaldesammlung, Munich; Kunstmuseum, Dusseldorf; Deutsche Akademie, Rome; Kunstmuseum, Basle; Musée Cantonal des Beaux-Arts, Lausanne, Switzerland.

Publications:

On NAGEL: books—Deutsche Kunst; eine neue Generation by Rolf-Günter Dienst, Cologne 1970; Peter Nagel: Bilder, Graphik, exhibition catalogue, Munich 1971; Galerie der neuen Künste by Heinz Ohff, West Berlin 1971; Deutsche Kunst der 60er Jahre: Malerei, Collage, Op-Art, Graphik by Julian Roh, Munich 1971; Bis Heute: Stilgesschichte der Kunst des 20. Jahrhunderts by Karin Thomas, Cologne 1971; Deutsche Kunst der 60er Jahre by J. W. von Moltke, Kapstadt, West Germany 1972; Deutsche Kunst seit 1945 by Wieland Schmied, Milan 1972; Peter Nagel: Verkverzeichnis 1965–72: Bilder, Zeichnungen, Grafik, Projekte, exhibition catalogue, edited by Hans Hoeppner, text by J. Kruse, Hamburg 1973; 10 Jahre Gruppe Zebra exhibition catalogue, Stuttgart 1975; Peter Nagel: Werkverzeichnis 1972–78; Gemalde, Zeichnungen, Grafik, Projekte, exhibition catalogue, with texts by Jens Christian Jensen, Bernhard Kerber and Duilio Morosini, Kiel 1978.

As a contemporary painter I often find myself facing a conflict. Much as, on the one hand, people, things and my immediate surroundings have an intrinsic interest for me, which I would like to represent as much as possible, without compromise, yet I am also restricted by my intimacy with the creative materials, the exacting patterns of thought which arise in so ordering a surface that the picture is "right."

Of course I know that these two interests are not entirely incompatible, but a voluntary limitation to purely aesthetic problems might simplify many things. If I did without realistic appearances and made my motifs accessible through abstraction and deformation, I would have greater freedom to introduce what means I wished.

I know these methods from my student years. At that time, as a reaction to tachistic unconnectedness, I had already undertaken the attempt to bring the object once more into play. And yet the object was always only secondary, in that it acts to certain extent as a peg on which to hang an artistic fantasy garment (compare the first printed graphics Nr. 1–3).

The more I committed myself to the object, and recognized its intrinsic worth, the more difficult became the formal solution of a painting. This heightened degree of difficulty is something which I have always found attractive; indeed from time to time I consciously set up new trip-wires for myself. Thus it pleases me to incorporate creatively or in a thematically significant way motifs which conceal within themselves the danger of the literary, kitsch or reportage. A painting full of risks interests me more than an assured programme. Occasional sorties into the realm of the fantastical or decorative demonstrate my need to work now and then in a playful manner. To these groups belong the balloon-blowers and the still-lifes with brightly coloured cloths, where the cloths have the advantage that they are able to be deformed, without having to work realistically any the less.

It can be asked why I have not made use of the opportunity of greater creative freedom and escaped from the confusions of motifs. What have I gained?

There are amongst other things the following advantages. The realistic picture offers a stronger possibility of identification and can facilitate access by the

usually unskilled observer. Formal processes in the picture can be checked and subsequently evaluated.

Unrelated formalism on the one hand and plain naturalism on the other are the extreme dangers. The goal can only be to allow neither formal nor thematic decisions to be dominant over the other. The happiest case is a fluctuation of the two, demonstrating their mutual interdependence. Herein lies one of the most useful criteria of artistic quality. The intensity of the reciprocal action of the connection of form and reality constitutes in my opinion the substance of an artistic product. That is not something that can be said of bland realism.

—Peter Nagel

In the mid-sixties objective artistic representation was widely regarded as suspect. A group of young painters, who were then studying at the Technical School of Applied Arts in Hamburg and who were unable to envisage a form of painting that lacked objective content, formally rejected the (in their eyes) unacceptable stance of non-objective art. Calling themselves the 'Zebra' group, they were initially widely known—for the first five years or so—as a group rather than as individual artists. Eventually, however, the individuality of the group's various members became apparent. Peter Nagel, a member of the group from its inception, soon distinguished himself from his friends by a high degree of critical and mathematical awareness. The latter is evident in the sharpness and precision of his drawing, in the almost glaring clarity of his colours, in the carefully selected moment of representation and the sharp fixing of the artistic process. Nagel's critical ability is apparent in his satirical distance from the scenes and people he represents (including himself). The coolness of the representational method and the objectivity of the criticism provide a reciprocal stimulus.

Besides painting and graphics Nagel has devoted himself equally—and with equal success—to printmaking, an area in which he has received several marks of distinction. During the last decade he has regularly applied himself to practical work, designing theatre sets and doing well paintings. He is a member of the Free Academy of Arts in Hamburg and professor of art at the technical college in Kiel. His latest artistic work is based on the tension between rigid contours and illusionistic plasticity and the written characters that appear in sections of the picture; the artistic element remains here an aspect of illusionistically represented objectivity.

—Heinz Spielmann

NAKAZATO, Hitoshi.

Japanese. Born in Tokyo, 15 March 1936. Studied painting, Tama College of Art, Tokyo, 1956–60, B.A. 1960; painting and printmaking, University of Wisconsin, Milwaukee, 1962–64, M.S. 1964; painting, Graduate School of Fine Arts, University of Pennsylvania, Philadelphia, 1964–66, M.F.A. 1966. Independent painter, in New York, since 1966. Recipient: John D. Rockefeller Scholarship, New York, 1966; Painting Prize, Cheltenham Art Center, Pennsylvania, 1967, 1968; Drawing Prize, Moore College of Art, Philadelphia, 1968; Award of Excellence, 5th Japan Art Festival, Tokyo and New York, 1970; Fine Work Prize, Shell Art Exhibition, Tokyo, 1970; Creative Artists Public Service Grant, New York, 1974; Color Print Prize, American Color Print Society, Philadelphia, 1975; Japan/U.S. Consortium for Environmental Planning and Design Education Grant, Ohio, 1982. Agents: Muramatsu Gallery, 7-1 Ginza, Chuo-ku, Tokyo; Tokyo Gallery, 6–18, 8-chome Ginza, Chuo-ku, Tokyo 104. Address: 361 West 36th Street, New York, New York 10018, U.S.A.

Individual Exhibitions:

1964	St. James Gallery, Milwaukee
1966	Alverno College, Milwaukee
1968	Cheltenham Art Center, Pennsylvania
1970	Pinar Gallery, Tokyo
1976	University of Pennsylvania, Philadelphia
	Upstairs Gallery, San Francisco
1977	Print Club, Philadelphia
	University of Pennsylvania, Philadelphia
	Tokyo Gallery, Tokyo
1978	Mercer College, Trenton, New Jersey
	Muramatsu Gallery, Tokyo
	Newman Gallery, Philadelphia
	West Chester College, Pennsylvania
1979	Soker-Kaseman Gallery, San Francisco
	Eric Makler Gallery, Philadelphia
	Pennsylvania Academy of Fine Arts, Philadelphia
1980	Muramatsu Gallery, Tokyo
	Gross McLeaf Gallery, Philadelphia
1981	Mei Gallery, Tokyo
	Bridgeport University, Connecticut
1982	Tokyo Gallery, Tokyo
1983	Ten Gallery, Fukuoka, Japan
	Tochigi Prefectural Museum of Fine Arts, Utunomiya, Japan
1986	AIP Gallery, Philadelphia
	Muramatsu Gallery, Tokyo
1987	Hara Museum of Contemporary Art, Tokyo

Selected Group Exhibitions:

1963	*Wisconsin Painters and Sculptors*, Milwaukee Art Center, Wisconsin
1968	*American Drawing 1968*, Moore College of Art, Philadelphia
1970	*Expo Art*, Furakawa Pavilion, Osaka, Japan
1973	*Japanese Artists in America*, National Museum of Modern Art, Kyoto, Japan (travelled to Tokyo)
1975	*Young Artists*, Union Carbide Building, New York
1977	*Prints in Series: Idea to Image*, Brooklyn Museum, New York
1979	*Contemporary Drawing*, Philadelphia Museum of Art
1984	*Japanese Contemporary Paintings 1960-80*, Gunma Prefectural Museum of Modern Art, Maebashi, Japan
1986	*Contemporary Japanese Art*, Taipei Fine Arts Museum, Taiwan
1987	*Painting 1977-87*, National Museum of Art, Osaka, Japan

Collections:

Museum of Modern Art, New York; Philadelphia Museum of Art; Pennsylvania Academy of Art, Philadelphia; Brooklyn Museum, New York; National Gallery of Art, Washington, D.C.; Tokyo Metropolitan Art Museum; Hara Museum of Contemporary Art, Tokyo; National Museum of Modern Art, Kyoto; Hyogo Prefectural Museum of Modern Art, Kobe; National Musem of Art, Osaka.

Publications:

On NAKAZATO: books—*Hitoshi Nakazato: Today and Yesterday*, exhibition catalogue with texts by Gerald Silk and Akira Tatehata, Tokyo 1987.

My image making is concerned with using neutral shapes, lines and colors to define a chosen space. This results in an immediate and simple image which, at the same time, is perceptually complex and intense. And in this process of image making, I seek to achieve an original and personal experience.

Last summer for a solo exhibition in Tokyo, I painted a number of diptychs. Each diptych combined two paintings utilizing different color systems. In addition, I devised a small panel as a diagram to be attached on the side. The diagram which I called "common piece" dealt with a certain aspect of the diptych and allowed written words and numbers to be

included to expand the scheme of expression. It gave me an exit from the abstract painting within one level of activity at the same time it offered the viewers an entry into my paintings.

During most part of the time that I worked in my studio for the Tokyo show, the Iran-Contra Hearings were on television. I also watched from my loft window the police raid crack dealers on 9th Avenue. Could this be called a perfect painting background? Art cannot be made without social context. My continuous wonder has been what exists beyond the thinking frame of "what has been done and what not" and the art climate.

—Hitoshi Nakazato

Hitoshi Nakazato, having been reputed as a deft, excellent system-oriented painter in the sixties and seventies, became known as one of the most sophisticated Japanese artists who has succeeded in producing extraordinary works by making the best use of both Western modernist ideas for painting and the Japanese sensibilities, especially to color, in the 1980's. He was born in Tokyo in 1936, studied painting at Tama College of Art in Tokyo. He went to the United States when he was 26, and continued studying painting and printmaking at University of Wisconsin and the Graduate School of Fine Arts in University of Pennsylvania until 1966. He settled down in New York in 1971, and lives and works there.

In the late sixties, Nakazato was engaged in pattern paintings with various combinations of identical forms in different colors; V shapes, for instance, in the *Penn Series, on Yellow* in 1966, each of them being comprised of one waved arm and its vertical or horizontal counterpart jointed to one another. He worked by predetermined system, exploring manifold but limited possibilities of color/shape combinations. Throughout the seventies, he produced series of impressive paintings, mainly characterized by the rigorous lines. In the paintings such as *Chi Su Ma* and *Ma Su Chi* in 1970, he took advantage of the traditional carpenter's technique of line making. Stretching a length of cord, dipped in China ink, across a raw canvas, the artist picked up the cord, hit the canvas with it, marking a line with some slightly splashed smudges. The procedure was repeated several times and the painting appeared like a musical score without notes.

His idea of doing it seemed to be derived, for one thing, from the urge that he wanted his paintings free from any personal gestures of brushstrokes. More or less, it was the widely supported idea among painters in that period, for the purpose of guaranteeing the autonomy of the painting. There was, however, a more important concern for him since the beginning of his career. It was 'flatness', a different approach to ensure the autonomy of the paintings. It was only through the flatness that he could show his true gift as a stunning color-field painter.

It should be underlined that he never lost his faith in both 'flatness' and 'objectivity', while bringing out the outstanding paintings with the extremely delicate, soft, unaffected, angelic, and tactile colors. But some slightest nuances of subjectivity could be traced in his paintings in the middle of the eighties and from then onward. He rendered the boundaries between two color areas the gentle undulations with suggestive blurs, or applied the carefully-weighted, smudgy brushstrokes at the edges of the canvases. The grids, rectangular outlines, and sometimes diagonals, drawn deftly by hand on the color areas, are characteristic of his works. They seem to act as if giving a definition to the pictorial surface in a clear, logical way, while making it easier for each of the applied colors to reveal its own, interacting nature in correspondence with other elements. Still, the undulating, blurred boundaries or smudgy brushstrokes succeeded in activating not only the adjoining color fields but also the painting itself.

In 1987, he invented an intriguing, unprecedented device to reinforce both 'definition' and 'activation' at the same time. Nakazato made small paintings,

what he calls the 'companion pieces,' with diagrammatic figures and hand-written words such as "One Forth and One Forth" or "Four and a Half" on gray backgrounds, and placed them beside the larger paintings.

They are physically apart, but conceptually related, as the diagrams and words on the 'companion pieces' hint or pretend that they act as determinative agents for the larger canvases. The viewer might not elicit any relevant information from those diagrams and words, but cannot deny that they work as if defining something according to the unknown system, and activate the larger canvases next to the small canvases. It is notable that Nakazato achieved his outstanding, unprecedented color-field paintings in combination with the conceptual activators.

—Tazmi Shinoda

NANNUCCI, Maurizio.
Italian. Born in Florence, 20 April 1939. Educated at the University of Florence, 1957-61; studied art, in Berlin and Florence, 1959-62. Married Ughetta Dani in 1969; children: Simone and Matteo. Independent artist, Florence, since 1962: concentrated on operative methodologies, 1962-65; concrete verbal structures, visuals and semantics, 1964-65; phonological and electronic music, and uses of verbal communications, 1965-70; environments and sensory processes, 1967-71; neon as writing, computer-aided visuals and music, from 1967; tautological procedures, 1970-72; photographic researches on color in nature, 1973-74; multimedia practices, from 1975. Editor, *Exempla Editions*, Florence, 1970; *Mela* art magazine, Florence, 1976, and Mela Recordings, 1978; co-ordinator, "Zona Archives" non-profit organization, Florence, since 1974. Lecturer and Visiting Artist: Ecole Superieure des Arts Visuels, Geneva; Maryland Institute College of Art, Baltimore; Helsinki Kuvataideakatemia; New York University; Fine Arts Academy, Reykjavik, etc. Recipient: Artist of the City of Florence, 1970; Austrian Government Artist Fellowship, Graz, 1970. Agents: Galerie Walter Storms, Kaulbachstrasse 6, Munich; Studio Grossetti, Via dei Piatti 9, Milan. Address: Via Marsala 4, 50137 Florence, Italy.

Individual Exhibitions:

1965	Galleria Vigna Nuova, Florence
1966	Galleria L'Elefante, Venice
1968	Centro Arte Viva, Trieste
1969	Galleria Vismara, Milan
1970	Galleria Barozzi, Venice
	Galleria La Polena, Genoa
1971	Galerie Thomas Keller, Munich
1972	Galleria Segnapassi, Pesaro, Italy
	Galleria Flori, Florence
1973	Galerie Historial, Nyon, Switzerland
	Salone Annunciata, Milan
	Galleria Nova/Arte Moderna, Prato, Italy
	Galleria Christian Stein, Turin
	Galerie Thomas Keller, Munich
1974	Galleria La Bertesca, Genoa
	Neue Galerie am Landesmuseum Joanneum, Graz, Austria
	Galerie Denise René-Hans Mayer, Dusseldorf
	Galleria Schema, Florence
1975	Banco Galleria, Brescia, Italy
	Galeria Lydia Megert, Berne
	Galerie Ecart, Geneva
1976	Galerie Muller-Roth, Stuttgart
	Galleria Area, Florence
1977	Galleria Forma, Genoa
1978	*Biennale*, Venice
	Galerie Im Taxispalais, Innsbruck

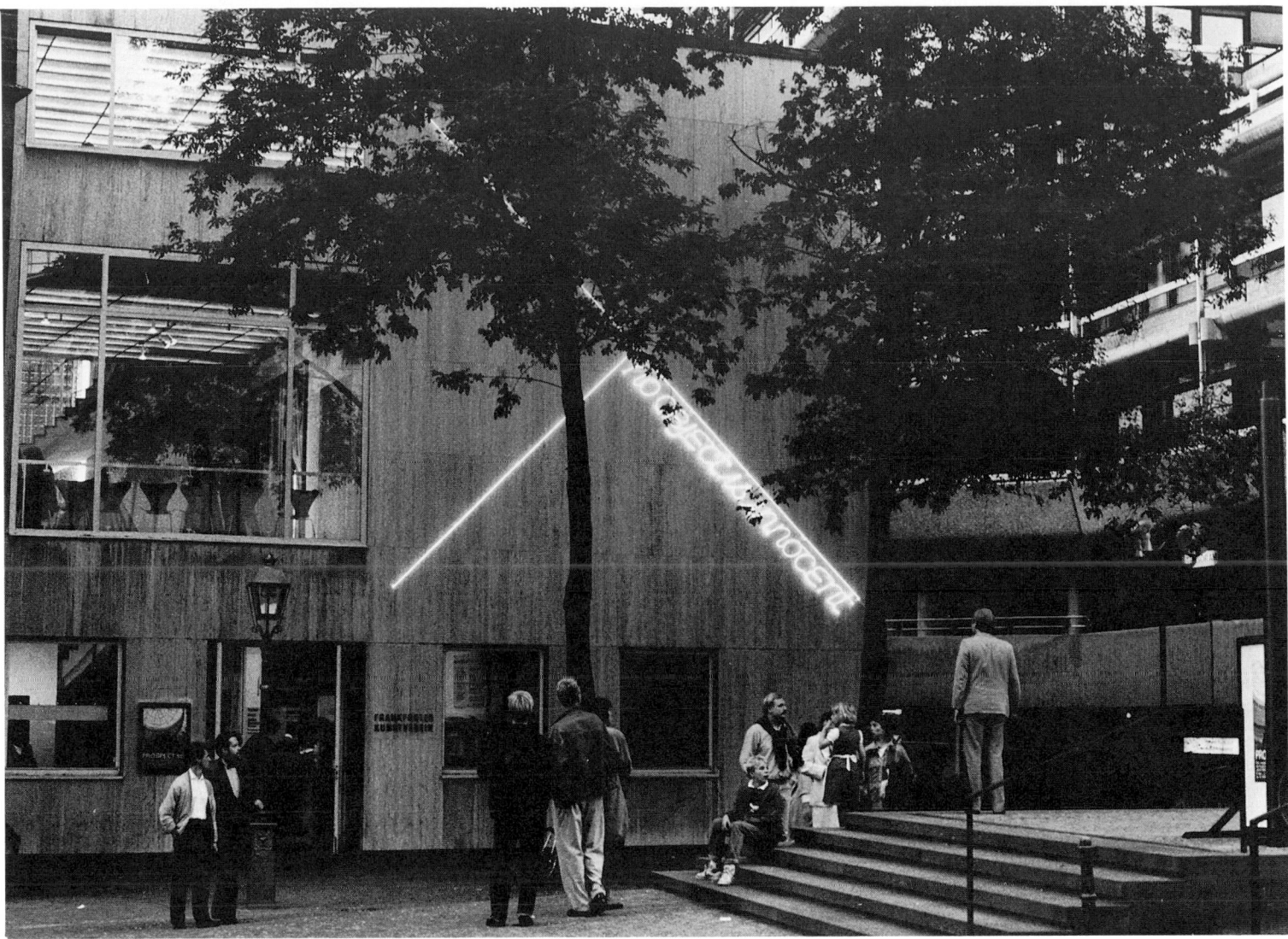

Maurizio Nannucci: *No Object Is Innocent*, neon installation, Frankfurt, 1986

1979	International Cultureel Centrum, Antwerp
	Galerie Walter Storms, Munich
	Galerie Sudurgata, Rekyavik, Iceland
1980	Galerie Lydia Megert, Berne
	Kunstverein, Braunschweig, West Germany
1981	Coracle Gallery, London
1982	Vleeshal, Middelburg, Netherlands
1983	Palazzo Vecchio, Florence
1984	Kunstverein, Frankfurt
1985	Galerie Beatrix Wilhelm, Stuttgart
1987	Art Metropole, and Instituto Italiano di Cultura, Toronto (toured Canada, 1987–88)

Selected Group Exhibitions:

1969	*Nova Tendencija 4*, Galerie Suvremene Umjetnosti, Zagreb
1971	*Art Systems*, Museo de Arte Moderno, Buenos Aires
1973	*Fluxshoe*, Museum of Modern Art, Oxford (toured the U.K.)
1974	*Contemporanea*, Parcheggio Villa Borghese, Rome
1976	*Artists' Books*, Institute of Contemporary Arts, London (toured the U.K.)
1977	*Documenta 6*, Museum Fridericianum, Kassel, West Germany
1979	*Kunst als Photographie 1949–1979*, Tiroler Landesmuseum Ferdinandeum, Innsbruck (toured Austria)
1981	*Identité Italienne*, Centre Georges Pompidou, Paris
1985	*Sul linguaggio e l'ecstasi*, Alvar Aalto Museum, Jyvaskyla, Finland (toured Finland)
1986	*Aspects of Italian Art 1960–85*, Kunstverein, Frankfurt

Collections:

Stedelijk Museum, Amsterdam; Neue Galerie am Landesmuseum Joanneum, Graz, Austria; Museo d'Arte Contemporanea, Milan; Museo Progressivo d'Arte, Livorno; Galerija Suvremene Umjetnosti, Zagreb; Bibliothèque Nationale, Paris; Centre Georges Pompidou, Paris; Museum of Modern Art, New York.

Publications:

By NANNUCCI: books—*Play Texte*, with Jochen Gerz, Paris 1968; *Universum*, Florence 1969; *9 Colors*, Florence 1970; *Exempla*, Florence 1970; *My/dum/my*, Florence 1970; *Definitions*, Zurich 1971; *Poemi Cromatici*, Florence 1971; *Nomenclature*, Oldenburg 1972; *Schema Informazione*, Florence 1973–74; *Writings*, Graz, Austria 1974, *Poem/Poesie*, Naples 1975; *Rose aux*, Geneva 1975; *Provisoire et definitif*, Geneva 1975; *The Medium Is the Word*, Rome 1975; *M-40*, Amsterdam 1976; *Small Press Scene*, Florence 1976; *Sessanta verdi naturali*, Innsbruck and Florence 1977; *Art as Social Environment*, Lugo and Amsterdam 1978; *Star/scrivendo camminando*, Hinwil 1978; *Parole*, Florence 1979; *Mela Postcard Book*, Florence 1979, *Some Texts*, *Pages in Motion*, Florence 1980; *Some Texts*, Florence 1980; *To Cut a Long Story Short*, exhibition catalogue, Middelburg 1982; *Up Above the World*, Florence 1982; *Some Texts*, Frankfurt 1983; *Image du Ciel*, exhibition catalogue, Frankfurt 1984; *L. H.*, Toronto and Aachen 1987; video—*The Missing Poem is the Poem*, Florence 1973; *Sometexts*, Vancouver 1987; record—*Audio Intellect*, Florence 1983.

On NANNUCCI: books—*Anthology of Concrete Poetry*, edited by Emmett Williams, New York 1967; *Neue Formen der Bilder* by Udo Kultermann, Tübingen 1969; *International Malerwochen Graz* by Wilfried Skreiner, Graz, Austria 1970; *L'Azione Concreta*, exhibition catalogue, by Paolo Fossati, Como, Italy 1971; *Datilogrammi* by Carlo G. Argan, Graz 1974; *Konkretedichtung* by Siegfried Schmidt, Munich 1974; *Art et Communication* by Hervé Fischer, Paris 1974; *La Escritura en Libertad* by F. Millan and G. Sanchez, Madrid 1975; *La Piramide Capovolta* by Luigi Ballerini, Padua 1975; *Parlare e Scrivere* by Renato Barilli, Marcerata 1977; *Autocritico Automobile* by Achille Bonito Oliva, Milan 1977; *Art Aktuell/Skira* by Jean Lue Duval, Geneva 1977; 1979; *Offmedia* by Germano Celant, Bari, Italy 1977; *The Record as Artwork*, exhibition catalogue, by Germano Celant, Fort Worth 1978; *Spatialisme et Poesie Concrete* by Pierre Garnier, Paris 1978; *Extra Media* by Enrico Crispolti, Turin 1978; *Maurizio Nannucci*, exhibition catalogue, by Fulvio Salvadori, Antwerp 1979; *Poesie Sonore* by Henry Chopin, Paris 1979; *Parola/Immagine* by Flavio Caroli, Milan 1979; *Identité Italienne*, exhibition catalogue, by Germano Celant, Paris 1981; *Books by Artists*, exhibition catalogue, by Tim Gest and Germano Celant, Toronto 1981; *Maurizio Nannucci: To Cut a Long Story Short*, exhibition catallgue with text by Pier Luigi Tazzi, Middelburg 1982; *Maurizio Nannucci: Unus ex Curiosis*, exhibition catalogue with text by Flaminio Gualdoni, Florence 1983; *Snow, Weiner, Nannucci*, exhibition catalogue by Peggy Gale, Toronto 1987; articles—"Anthology of Concretism" by Eugene Wildmann in *Chicago Review*, no. 9, 1967; "Poetry as a Means for the Structuring of Social Environment" by Eugene Gomringer in *Visible Language* (Cleveland), vol. 10, no. 3, 1976; "Quando l'arte si facon la T.V." by Daniela Palazzoli in *La Republica* (Rome), 31 May 1977; "Un Libro fatto di Marmo" by Renato Barilli in *L'Espresso* (Rome), 26 February 1978; "Risoma e Struttura, intervista" by Lino Centi in *Data* (Milan), March/May 1978; "On Fluxus" by Ken Friedman in *Flash Art* (Milan), October/November 1978; "The Italian Art Scene" by Henry Martin in *Art News* (New York), March 1981; "Maurizio Nannucci" by Sandro Procati in *Segno* (Pescara) no. 34, 1984; "Talking with Nannucci" by Pier Luigi Tazzi in *Wetstuff* (Florence), no. 2, 1985.

After the "Dattilogrammi," which were channeled into research work on concrete poetry, I became involved in situations that made me understand that there was another territory to explore, It could be called "intermedia," and it includes a host of experiences that stretch from mail art to all of the Fluxus situations to concrete poetry. These experiences were not easy to classify. However, my attitude, once I had investigated interdisciplinary activities, was to respect my origins as a visual artist. I never thought of proposing myself as a poet or as a musician. I always considered myself as an artist coming from another discipline and trying to widen his references, all the while reducing them to experiences I had already faced visually—a different specific context that could be, say, electronic music or concrete poetry.

At times I have applied an idea from one discipline to a different discipline. At first, I'd elaborate on the idea visually, later with sound, and finally in terms of language. Sometimes the whole thing turned out to be smooth enough, sometimes really different things came out: what actually mattered was the method, never the result. Again, at times my interest would shift toward utilization of the media, which somehow suggested their conditions to me.

My work with media and different other materials was done round about the mid-1960's. It was the time of success of great art shows. A new situation with people looking for new propositions was created. These people were active the world over and acted as a magnet for identification and ideas. It was felt that the artist's work needed a new interpretation: it wasn't simply a matter of "producing artwork" but looking for a better system for a wider diffusion of ideas. I kept in touch with a number of artists who were motivated by the same stimuli. I think I forwarded something like a thousand single, typed pages. It was a way to give out correct information on my work, in an unassuming way.

—Maurizio Nannucci

Maurizio Nannucci is an artist whose work could be (and has been) almost endlessly theorized, since almost all of his widely differing pieces are marked by both a single-mindedness and a lack of physical substance that critics (especially friendly critics) can easily be uncomfortable with: they feel called upon to beef the work up into full-fledged intellectual respectability, and they usually start with Saussure. But Nannucci, as a "concept artist," is far from "hard-core": his spirit is romantic, if not downright baroque (as evidenced, perhaps, in his motto, which is itself a work. "Always Endeavor to Find Some Interesting Variation"), and one does well to remember that the paternity of the concept of "concept art" is to be attributed not to Kosuth and Art & Language, but rather to Henry Flint and Fluxus. Nannucci is an inveterate wanderer in the realms of what Dick Higgins (one of the Fluxus theoreticians) has defined as "inter-media"—the little almost empty spaces that lie *between* the media and that allow a witty and playful mind to deal sometimes with nonsense and sometimes with a very clear perception of the way all rational and verbal systems are as though afloat in a fluid of silent and pre-rational, if not spiritual, pre-suppositions—pre-suppositions, in any case, whose very possibility of existence is never explained by the systems of rational explanation that are built on top of them. The fundamental perception, perhaps, is that mind is precedent to mental instrumentation.

Nannucci's very earliest works came out of concrete poetry: he called them *dattilogrammi*, and they consisted of images made with typewriters. The word "red" (*rosso*), for example, was typed a thousand or so times in red ink on a square of red paper. *Idem*, of course, for the colors (or the words) "yellow," "blue," "black," and "white." It's typical of Nannucci to have used only the primary colors. In 1967, he did an object called "Poem." It's a rubber stamp of the word "poem." In photographs of this work, one notices the obvious fact that the word on the stamp and the word as stamped are upside-down mirror images each of the other. A little later, Nannucci began

to work with neon tubing: the illuminated script entitled "Phonetic Alphabet" spells itself out as *Abicidieeffegiacca*, etc., which translates into English's more precarious orthography as *eighbeseedeeeeefjeeaich . . . .* and on to *zee*. The neon writing called "Corner" bends in its center at right angles and is of course exhibited in a corner. "Universum," from 1969, is a book that can't be opened because it's bound with a back rib down both its right and left sides. "Sixty Natural Greens" is described as a proposal for a more accurate and scientific color nomenclature and consists of that many photos of that many different kinds of green plants, completed with a list of their Latin names, from Mirabilis Jalapa Green to Azalea Hortensis Green. A work from 1973 shows a sequence of nine photos of the artist's hand as it writes a word on a pool of water. Another photo work shows 90 images of the artist as he walks through the streets of Florence; it's completed by a map and an overhead photo of the area involved as well as by the list of the names of the streets that are strolled through. The path being followed spells out the word "star." At the Venice *Biennale* in 1978, Nannucci presented a work that consisted of a Piper Cub that flew through the skies trailing a series of blue letters that spelled out the message "image du ciel." While the plane was doing this, the artist sat in a beautiful old wicker chair beneath a potted palm which was set up inside the Italian pavillion. On the wall next to the chair was a small framed photograph.

Nannucci has also been active in mail art, computer art, record making, book production, posters and postage cards. A descriptive list of his works could extend to considerable length, but even a partial list is proof that no form other than the list can deal with them: Nannucci's work won't yield to easily formulable generalizations.

—Henry Martin

NASH, David.

British. Born in Esher, Surrey, 14 November 1945. Studied at Kingston College of Art, Surrey, 1963-67; Chelsea School of Art, London, 1969-70. Married Claire Langdown in 1972; children: William and Jack. Independent sculptor, living in Blaenau Ffestiniog, North Wales, since 1967: sculptor-in-residence, Grizedale Forest, Cumbria, 1978, and at Yorkshire Sculpture Park, Wakefield, 1981-82. Visiting instructor, Newcastle Polytechnic, Royal College of Art, Newport College of Art, Dublin College of Art, etc., since 1967; also workshop projects in the United States, 1980, 1983, 1987, Japan, 1982, 1984, and the Netherlands, 1982. Recipient: Welsh Arts Council bursary, Cardiff, 1975; Prize, *International Drawing Biennale*, Middlesborough, Yorkshire, 1979. Agent: Annely Juda Fine Art, 11 Tottenham Mews, London W1P 9PJ. Address: Capel Rhiw, Blaenau Ffestiniog, Gwynedd, Wales.

Independent Exhibitions:

1973	St. William's College, York
	Oriel Gallery, Bangor, Wales
1976	Arnolfini Gallery, Bristol
	Oriel Gallery, Bangor, Wales
1978	Air Gallery, London
	Chapter Gallery, Cardiff
	Chester Arts Centre, Cheshire
1979	Arnolfini Gallery, Bristol
	Parnham House, Dorset
1980	Elise Meyer Gallery, New York
	Southampton University, Hampshire
	Galleria del Cavallino, Venice
1981	St. Paul's Gallery, Leeds, Yorkshire
1982	Elise Meyer Gallery, New York
	Oriel Gallery, Bangor, Wales

	Rijksmuseum Kroller-Muller, Otterlo, Netherlands
	Yorkshire Sculpture Park, Wakefield
	Kilkenny Art Gallery, Ireland
	Midland Group Gallery, Nottingham
1983	Third Eye Centre, Glasgow (travelled to Edinburgh, Llandudno, Swansea, Stoke-on-Trent)
	Douglas Hyde Gallery, Dublin
	South Hill Park Arts Centre, Bracknell, Berkshire
1984	Kamakura Gallery, Tokyo
	Nagisa Park, Moriyama City, Japan (toured Japan, 1984-85)
1985	Washington University, St. Louis, Missouri
	Rijksmuseum Kroller-Muller, Otterlo, Netherlands (with Sjoerd Buisman)
	Heide Art Gallery, Melbourne, Victoria
	Aveago Gallery, Sydney
	Galerij S65, Aalst, Belgium
1986	Juda Rowan Gallery, London
1987	L. A. Louver Gallery, Los Angeles
	Andrew Knight Gallery, Cardiff

Selected Group Exhibitions:

1975	*The Condition of Sculpture*, Hayward Gallery, London
1977	*From Wales*, Fruitmarket Gallery, Edinburgh
1980	*British Art Now: An American Perspective*, Guggenheim Museum, New York
1981	*British Sculpture in the 20th Century: Part II*, Whitechapel Art Gallery, London
1982	*Aspects of British Art Today*, Metropolitan Art Museum, Tokyo (toured Japan)
1983	*The Sculpture Show*, Hayward Gallery/Serpentine Gallery, London
1984	*Haarlem Hout*, Frans Hals Museum, Haarlem, Netherlands
1985	*Transformations in Sculpture 1945-85*, Guggenheim Museum, New York
1986	*Focus on British Art*, International Cultureel Centrum, Antwerp
1987	*A Quiet Revolution: British Sculpture Since 1965*, Museum of Contemporary Art, Chicago (travelled to San Francisco, Newport Harbour, Washington and Buffalo, 1987-88)

Collections:

Arts Council of Great Britain, London; Tate Gallary, London; Guggenheim Museum, New York; Walker Art Center, Minneapolis; Rijksmuseum Kroller-Muller, Otterlo, Netherlands; Metropolitan Art Museum, Tokyo; Hiroshima Fine Art Museum, Japan; Tochigi Prefectural Museum of Fine Arts, Japan; Scottish National Gallery of Modern Art, Edinburgh; National Museum of Wales, Cardiff.

Publications:

By NASH: books—*Briefly Cooked Apples*, York 1973; *Loosely Held Grain*, Bristol 1976; *Fletched Over Ash*, London 1978; *Wood Quarry*, New York 1980; *Fellowship*, Wakefield 1982; *Stoves and Hearths*, London 1982; *Wood Quarry Otterlo*, Otterlo 1982; *Sixty Seasons*, Glasgow 1983; *Ki No Katachi Ki No Inochi*, Tokyo 1984; *Elm Wattle Gum*, Melbourne 1985; *Hole Veluwe Otterlo*, Otterlo 1985; *Tree to Vessel*, London 1986; *Wood Primer*, San Francisco 1987.

On NASH: books—*The Condition of Sculpture*, exhibition catalogue with essay by William Tucker, London 1975; *British Art Now: An American Perspective*, exhibition catalogue with text by Diane Waldman, New York 1980; *A Sense of Place: Sculpture in Landscape*, edited by Peter Davies and Tony Knipe, Sunderland 1984; *Earthworks and Beyond: Contemporary Art in the Landscape* by John Beadsley, New York 1984; *Artists in Wales: Second Nature* by Eric Rowan, London 1984.

Earlier, I used woodmill wood, regular, standard units; later, greenwood, fresh from the tree; now, the tree itself. The more I look at the tree, the more I see that tree: its space and location, its volume and structure, its engineering and balance. More than that, I see the uniqueness of each single tree, and beyond

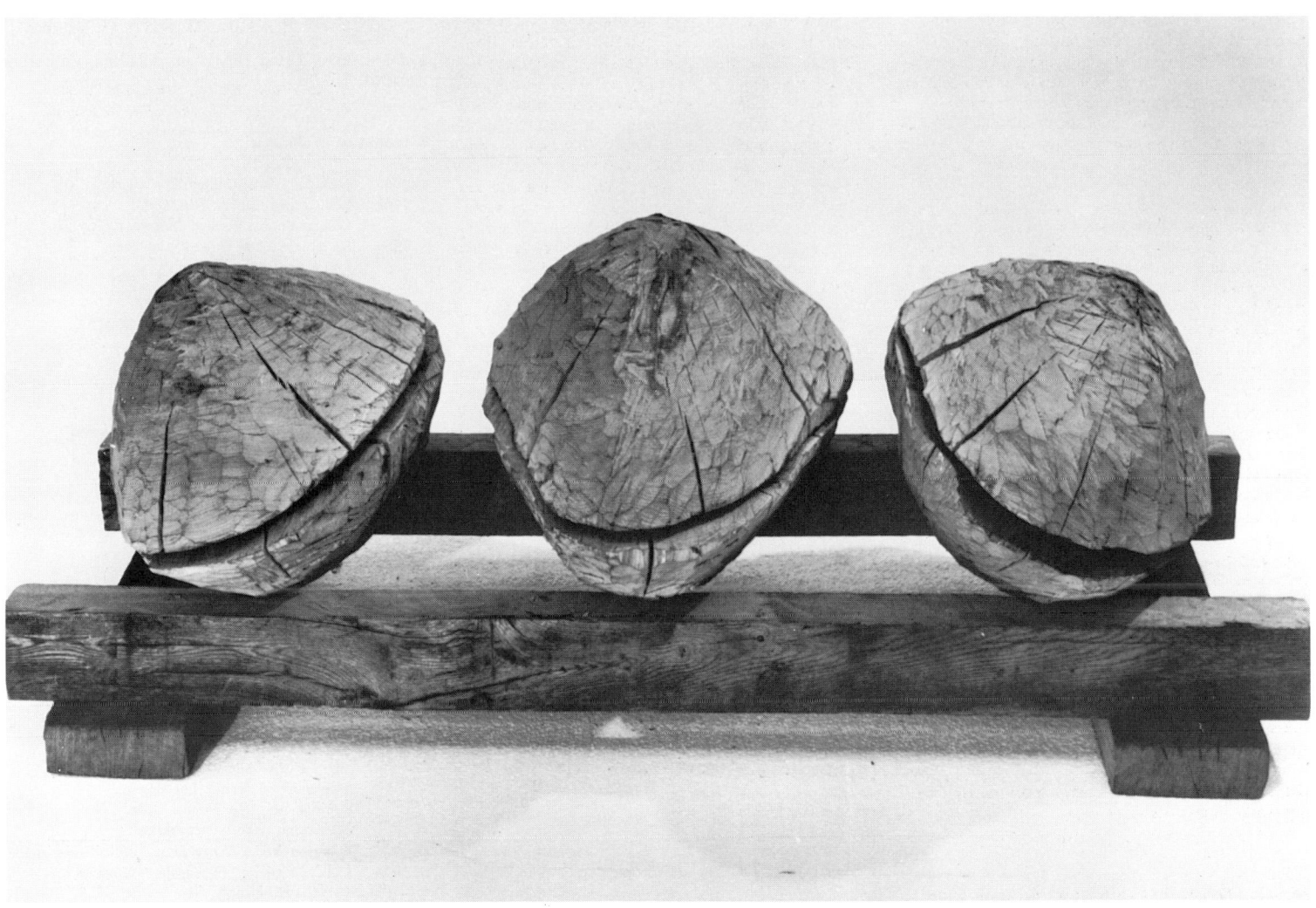

David Nash: *Three Clams on a Rack*, 1979

that still I see it as a great emblem of life. A potent vibrant tower, a whirling prayer wheel of natural energy.

I want a simple approach to living and doing. I want a life and work that reflects the balance and continuity of nature. Identifying with the time and energy of the tree and with its mortality, I find myself drawn deeper into the joys and blows of nature.

Worn down and regenerated; broken off and reunited; a dormant faith revived in the new growth on old wood.

—David Nash

Though David Nash was born in Surrey and went to art school at Kingston Upon Thames and Chelsea he very deliberately opted out of the London art scene shortly after leaving college and has lived and worked in North Wales, in the little town of Blaenau Ffestiniog ever since. This is his spiritual home, the place where he has developed his own highly personal and idiosyncratic art.

Trees are his main source of inspiration and he works with them sometimes as a woodman; sometimes as a forester; felling and hewing; planting and fletching; burning and charring; stacking and making rough carpentry. His has not been a reclusive, Thoreau-like existence, however, for his work is as approachable as the man himself and has aroused widespread interest both in Europe and as far afield as Japan. In the years he spent as Resident Sculptor in the Grizedale Forest and the Yorkshire Sculpture Park (the only time he has lived away from North Wales) he started several major projects and stimulated much local interest and participation.

He works in a very British organic naturalist tradition—the tradition of Gainsborough and Constable and in our own day that of Hepworth. Wordsworth advised—"Let Nature be your teacher" and John Constable sought the "pure apprehension of natural fact" and counselled that "the landscape painter must walk in the fields with an humble mind" and should study Nature with all the seriousness of a scientist. Nash would seem to be in sympathy with Constable's approach with the reservation that he "takes exception to the land being referred to as 'landscape', referring to the land as 'landscape' is the same as referring to people as 'portraits'." The term 'landscape' he says implies a "view instead of an organic reality."

Some of Nash's tree sculptures consist of working on existing saplings, young and pliant enough to be manipulated into strange and suggestive shapes. In this he does no more than nature herself in some of the tortured distortions resulting from prolonged exposure to strong winds, for example. He may conceive and commence a project of planting which after a period of years will be tended to form domes or arches or other architectural shapes, being created and conditioned over time by the particular space in which they are sited. Trees, as he often points out, are 90% space.

Smaller, moveable pieces which can be set up in a gallery are often quirky and lighthearted. Running Table, for example, is a rectangular block supported on four spindly, splayed, branches so that the whole contraption appears to be scampering away. He often uses green wood which changes as it gradually dries out or is exposed to variations of temperature—a Museum Conservationist's nightmare!—but Nash accepts any accidents which occur both in the making and afterwards as intrinsic to the work. In another piece, a roughly constructed box which inevitably commenced to split in random places is called "Cracking Box", and in his titles, both of the sculptures and of his drawings, there is a playful and witty use of words.

Nash's drawings are an important side of his work and are simple, direct and uncluttered. They too are often made from 'found' materials such as earth, leaves, fruit juice, grass or charcoal from a fire, and show in diagrammatic form the evolution of his sculptures from their origin in the felled tree.

Nash's attitude to his trees is anthropomorphic—he responds to the personality of the different species seeing some as aggressive and brutal and others as passive and gentle and watches their individual characteristics developing over the years in his own plot of land 'Ca'en-y-Coed' (the Field in the Trees).

His art may be seen as a response to the widespread and rapidly being articulated alarm about environmental and ecological problems. One can but welcome such a direct and popular art which helps to focus on these anxieties and in so doing may lead us on to some solutions.

—Mary Ellis

NAUMAN, Bruce.
American. Born in Fort Wayne, Indiana, 6 December 1941. Studied mathematics, and art under Italo Scanga, University of Wisconsin, Madison, 1960–64, B.S. 1964; art, under William Wiley, Robert Arneson, Frank Owen and Stephen Kaltenbach, University of California at Davis, 1965–66, M.F.A. 1966. Independent artist and filmmaker, since 1966. Instructor, San Francisco Art Institute, 1966–68; Sculpture Instructor, University of California at Irvine, 1970. Recipient: National Endowment for the Arts Grant, 1968; Aspen Institute for Humanistic Studies Grant,

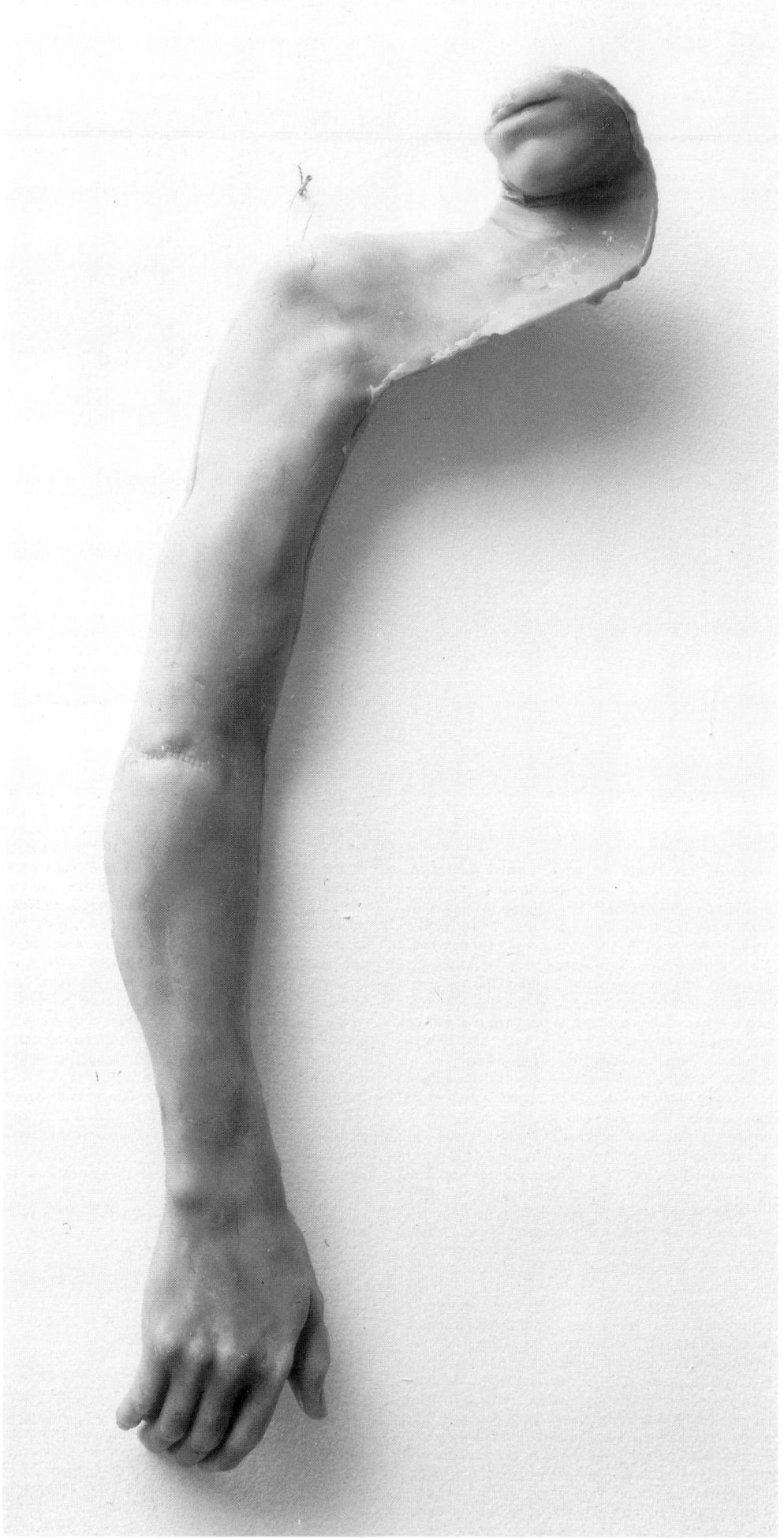

Bruce Nauman: *From Hand to Mouth*, 1967

Colorado, 1970. Agent: Leo Castelli Gallery, 420 West Broadway, New York, New York 10012. Address: 4630 Rising Hill Road, Altadena, California 91001, U.S.A.

Individual Exhibitions:

1966 Nicholas Wilder Gallery, Los Angeles
1968 Leo Castelli Gallery, New York
      Galerie Konrad Fischer, Dusseldorf
1969 Sacramento State College, California
      Leo Castelli Gallery, New York
      Nicholas Wilder Gallery, Los Angeles
      Galerie Sonnabend, Paris
1970 Nicholas Wilder Gallery, Los Angeles
      Galerie Konrad Fischer, Dusseldorf
      Galleria Sperone, Turin
1971 Galerie Sonnabend, Paris
      Galerie Konrad Fischer, Dusseldorf
      Leo Castelli Gallery, New York (2 shows)
      Joseph Helman Gallery, St. Louis
      Ace Gallery, Vancouver
1972 *Work from 1965–1972*, Los Angeles County Museum of Art (retrospective; toured the United States and Europe)
1973 Leo Castelli Gallery,Nnew York
      University of California at Irvine
1974 Ace Gallery, Vancouver
      Galerie Art in Progress, Munich
      Galerie Konrad Fischer, Dusseldorf
      Wide White Space, Antwerp
1975 Leo Castelli Gallery, New York
      Galerie Konrad Fischer, Dusseldorf
      Albright-Knox Art Gallery, Buffalo, New York
1976 Ace Canada, Vancaouver
      Leo Castelli Gallery, New York
      University of Nevada, Las Vegas
      Sperone-Westwater-Fischer Gallery, New York
      Sonnabend Gallery, New York
1977 Nicholas Wilder Gallery, Los Angeles
1978 College Gallery, Minneapolis Institute of Arts
      Leo Castelli Gallery, New York
      Galerie Konrad Fischer, Dusseldorf
      Galerie INK, Zurich
      Ace Gallery, Vancouver
1979 Galerie Schmela, Dusseldorf
      Marianne Deson Gallery, Chicago
      Portland Center for the Visual Arts, Oregon
      Hester van Royen Gallery, London
1980 Leo Castelli Gallery, New York
      Hill's Gallery, Sante Fe, New Mexico
      Galerie Konrad Fischer
      Carol Taylor Art Gallery, Dallas
      Bruce Nauman/Barry Le Va, Nigel Greenwood Inc., London
1981 INK: Halle fur internationale neue Kunst, Zurich
      Nigel Greenwood Inc., London
      Rijksmuseum Kroller-Muller, Otterlo, Netherlands
      Staatliche Kunsthalle, Baden-Baden, West Germany
1982 Leo Castelli Gallery, New York
      Sperone-Westwater-Fischer, New York
1983 Baltimore Museum of Art, Maryland
1985 Museum of Modern Art, New York
1986 Kunsthalle, Basle
      ARC/Musée d'Art Moderne de la Ville, Paris
1987 Whitechapel Art Gallery, London

Selected Group Exhibitions:

1975 *Drawing Now*, Museum of Modern Art, New York, (toured Europe and Norway)
1976 *The Artist and the Photograph*, Israel Museum, Jerusalem
      Painting and Sculpture in California: The Modern Era, San Francisco Museum of Modern Art (travelled to the Smithsonian Institution, Washington, D.C.)
1977 *Drawings for Outdoor Sculpture: 1946–1977*, John Weber Gallery, New York (toured the United States)
1978 *20th Century American Drawings: 5 Years of Acquisitions*, Whitney Museum, New York

1979 *Made by Sculptors*, Stedelijk Museum, Amsterdam
1979 *The Broadening of the Concept of Reality in the Art of the 60's and 70's*, Museum Haus Lange, Krefeld, West Germany
American Portraits of the 60's and 70's, Aspen Center for the Visual Arts, Colorado
1980 *Contemporary Sculpture: Selections from the Collection of the Museum of Modern Art*, New York
1987 *Avant-Garde in the Eighties*, Los Angeles County Museum of Art

Collections:

Museum of Modern Art, New York; Whitney Museum, New York; Guggenheim Museum, New York; Museum of Holography, New York; Albright-Knox Art Gallery, Buffalo, New York; Fogg Art Museum, Cambridge, Massachusetts; Art Institute of Chicago; City Art Museum, St. Louis; Stedelijk Museum, Amsterdam; Museum Haus Lange, Krefeld, West Germany.

Publications:

By NAUMAN: books—*Pictures of Sculptures in a Room*, Davis, California 1966; *Clear Sky*, San Francisco 1968; *Burning Small Fires*, San Francisco 1968; *L.A. AIR*, Los Angeles 1970; articles—"Way Out West," interview, with Elizabeth Baker and Joe Raffaele, in *Artnews* (New York), Summer 1967; "Nauman," interview, with Willoughby Sharp, in *Arts Magazine* (New York), March 1970; "Bruce Nauman," with Willougby Sharp, in *Avalanche* (New York), Winter 1971; "Body Works" in *Interfunktionen* (Cologne), September 1971; films and videotapes—*Manipulating the T-Bar*, 1966; *Opening and Closing*, 1966; *Revolving Landscape*, 1966; *Fishing for Asian Carp*, with William Allan, 1966; *Building a New Slant Step*, with William Allan, 1966; *Abstracting the Shoe*, with William Allan, 1966; *Playing a Note on the Violin While I Walk Around the Studio*, 1968; *Bouncing Two Balls Between the Floor and Ceiling with Changing Rhythms*, 1968; *Wall-Floor Positions*, 1968; *Violin Tuned D.E.A.D.*, 1968; *Slow Angle Walk*, 1968; *Stamping in the Studio*, 1968; *Bouncing in a Corner*, 1968; *Manipulating a Fluorescent Tube*, 1968; *Slo-Mo (Black Balls, Bouncing Balls, Gauze, Pulling Mouth)*, 1969; *Walk Dance*, 1969; *Violin Film No. 1*, 1969; *Violin Film No. 2* 1969; *Art Makeup No. 1 White*, 1969; *Art Makeup No. 2 Pink*, 1969; *Art Makeup No. 3 Green*, 1969; *Art Makeup No. 4 Black*, 1969; *Pulling Mouth*, 1969; *Walking in Contraposto*, 1969; *Bouncing in a Corner*, 1969; *Lip Sync*, 1969; *Revolving Upside Down*, 1969; *Pacing Upside Down*, 1969; *Studio Problems No. 1*, 1971; *Studio Problems No. 2*, 1971.

On NAUMAN: books—*Bruce Nauman*, exhibition catalogue, with text by David Whitney, New York 1968; *Bruce Nauman: Work from 1965-1972*, exhibition catalogue, with essays by Jane Livingston and Marcia Tucker, Los Angeles 1972; *Spiralen und Progressionen*, exhibition catalogue, Lucerne 1975; *Bruce Nauman*, exhibition catalogue with text by Katharina Schmidt, Baden-Baden 1981; *Bruce Nauman: Neons*, exhibition catalogue with essay by Brenda Richardson, Baltimore 1983; *Bruce Nauman: Werke von 1965 bis 1986*, exhibition catalogue with essays by Jean-Christophe Ammann, Nicholas Serota and Joan Simon, Basle 1986.

NEAGU, Paul.

British. Born in Bucharest, 22 February 1938; emigrated to England in 1969; naturalized, 1976. Educated in Bucharest and Timisoara primary schools; studied at the Academy of Fine Arts, Institute "N Grigorescu," Bucharest, under Professor Ghitescu and C. Cracium, 1959-65. Married Sybilla Oarcea in 1967 (divorced, 1974). Worked as accountant, draftsman, topographer and electrician, Timisoara and Bucharest, 1954-59. Now lives and works in London: works and exhibits as the Generative Art Group. Part-time Lecturer, Hornsey College of Art, Chelsea School of Art, and Royal College of Art, London, 1972-81. Recipient: Award, Centre Internationale de Recontres, Nice, 1972; Arts Council of Great Britain Award, 1973, 1978; Prize, *Tolly Cobbold Exhibition*,

1976; Northern Arts Fellowship, 1979. Agent: Curwen Gallery , 4 Windmill Street, London W1. Address: 31c Jackson Road, London N7, England.

Individual Exhibitions:

1969 Amphora Gallery, Bucharest
Richard Demarco Gallery, Edinburgh
Bauzentrum, Hamburg
1970 Sigi Krauss Gallery, London
1971 Compass Gallery, Glasgow
Sigi Krauss Gallery, London (with Horea Bernea; travelled to the Compass Gallery, Glasgow)
1972 Galerie Rivolta, Lausanne
1975 Compass Gallery, Glasgow
Museum of Modern Art, Oxford
Sunderland Arts Centre, County Durham
1976 Leeds Polytechnic Gallery
1978 Newcastle Polytechnic Gallery
1979 Élise Meyer Inc., New York
Third Eye Centre, Glasgow
Institute of Contemporary Arts, London
1980 Norwich Arts Centre
Project Gallery, Dublin
DLI Museum, Durham
Liverpool Academy of Art
1981 Galerie Rivolta, Lausanne
Ceolfrith Gallery, Sunderland
1982 Laing Art Gallery, Newcastle upon Tyne
1983 Liverpool University, Merseyside
Gallery K, Tokyo
Olga Korper Gallery, Toronto
Kamakura Gallery, Tokyo
1984 Curwen Gallery, London
Galerie Rivolta, Lausanne
1985 London Business School, London
1986 Gallery K, Tokyo
1987 Serpentine Gallery, London
Curwen Gallery, London

Selected Group Exhibitions:

1971 *Rumanian Art Today*, Richard Demarco Gallery, Edinburgh
1973 *Earth Images*, Scottish National Gallery of Modern Art, Edinburgh (travelled to the Whitechapel Art Gallery, London)
1975 *The Condition of Sculpture*, Hayward Gallery, London
1976 *6 Times*, Serpentine Gallery, London

1977 *Silver Jubilee Exhibition of British Sculpture*, Battersea Park, London
1981 *Baroques '81*, Musée d'Art Moderne de la Ville, Paris
1982 *Aspects of British Art Today*, Metropolitan Art Museum, Tokyo (toured Japan)
Inner Worlds, E. M. Flint Gallery, Walsall, Staffordshire (toured the U.K. 1982-83).
1984 *Time and Space*, Visual Arts Center, Anchorage, Alaska
1985 *Attitude*, Guildhall Gallery, Northampton, England

Collections:

Victoria and Albert Museum, London; Tate Gallery, London; Arts Council of Great Britain, London; Scottish National Gallery of Modern Art, Edinburgh; Stedelijk Museum, Amsterdam; Kulturbehorde, Hamburg; Musée Cantonal des Beaux-Arts, Lausanne; Ministry of Culture, Bucharest; Philadelphia Museum of Art; Art Institute of Chicago.

Publications:

By NEAGU: books—*Guide to Generative Arts*, 1977; articles—"Palp Art," with others, in *Arta Plastica* (Bucharest), vol. 5, 1970; "Objets-Gateaux" in *Leonardo* (Paris), no. 3, 1970; "Le Diner Neagu," interview, with Andrei Doicescu, in *Opus International* (Paris), April 1970; "The Janus Effect," interview, with Stewart Scotney, in *Art and Artists* (London), October 1974.

On NEAGU: books—*Romanian Art Today*, exhibition catalogue, Edinburgh 1971; *Paul Neagu*, exhibition catalogue, by Paul Overy, Glasgow 1979; *Paul Neagu* by Paul Overy, Sunderland 1981; articles—"Letter from Bucharest" by Radu Varia in *Studio International* (London), July/August 1971; "Products of the Split Personality" by Paul Overy in *The Times* (London), 4 March 1975; "Crossbearings and Stars" by Hugh Adams in *Art and Artists* (London), September 1980.

For most of my art life I have been interested in three interlocking principles: THE MOUNTAIN, the TEMPLE and the FLIGHT or, otherwise geometrically speaking, *The Triangle* (pyramid), *the Rectangle* (pseudo-labyrinth) and *the Spiral*. The Mountain, or better still, the *Volcanic Mound*, is a metaphor for the *Force of Nature;* the *Temple* for the *Human Building* or mentality of the mind, while the third symbol, the *Spiralling Flight*, expresses the desired spiritual quality of the *realized fusion*, fruition or "crown of vic-

Paul Neagu: *Open Monolith*, 1981

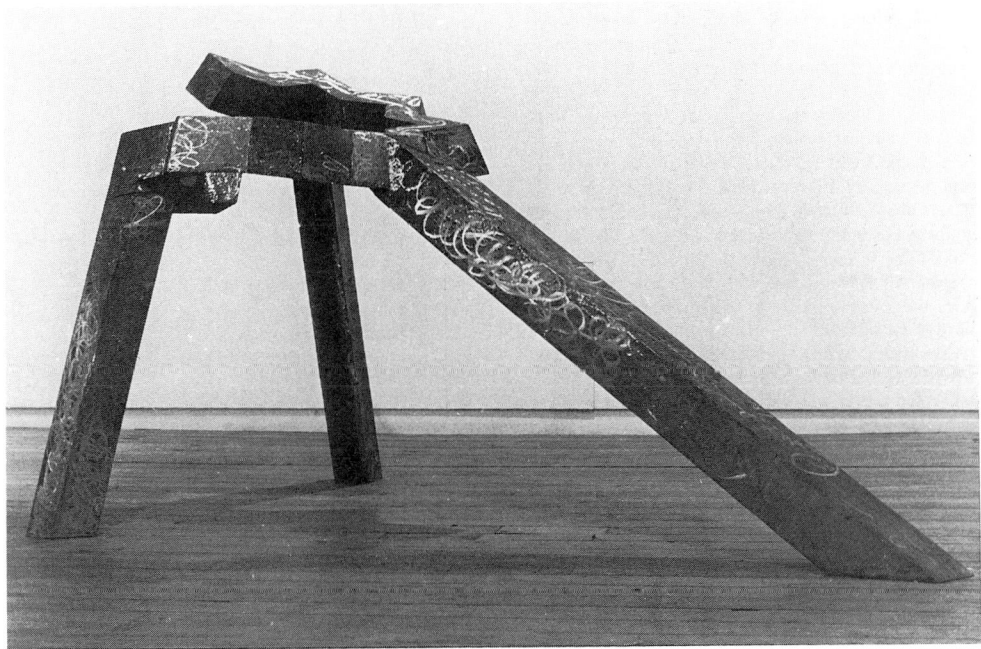

tory" . . . . These three levels of concern and approach are the lining of my works: graphic, painting and sculpture. Each department according to its own characteristic language. Sculpturally, therefore, I am trying to say, if translated from verbiage into form, volume, space, surface, substance, the same thing; the same epic ideas collaborating and interlocked in one object, as "OPEN MONOLITH" for instance.

A synthesis of particularly sculptural idioms by which one can sense the roots, the branching as well as the fruit itself (Earth, flesh and flight).

—Paul Neagu

The difficult feat of vanishing up one's own rear end has been achieved not once but infinitely many times by artists of the late 20th century. Furthermore, the manner in which this has been achieved would have greatly pleased Thomas Aquinas or any other of those medieval metaphysicians with a taste for calculating the number of angels able to dance upon a pinhead or the exact date of the Creation, for the artists have carried out the exercise entirely conceptually.

The abstract noun, once the prerogative of theologians and radical reformers, has now become the cornerstone of visual art; edge-information-system-paradigm-process, the list is endless; and these are not words used only by critics. The great majority of contemporary artists employ these words automatically and unconsciously, so pervasive is the orthodoxy, and their art is often no more than illustration of their ideas.

This tendency represents one pole of contemporary art; the fashionable pole. It retains its spotlit position by comparing itself with the opposite extreme, that of the anti-intellectual, it's-better-not-to-ask-questions type of art mysticism, and, of course, it's no contest.

That both positions share the same, highly debatable premises is not understood by many who have had to struggle through the British system. We must look for salvation to the eccentrics, the fetishists, and the foreigners. Which brings me to Paul Neagu.

Neagu makes sculpture, not that it looks anything like most contemporary sculpture; he does performances which abide by none of the conventions of "Performance Art," and as for his drawing and painting . . . well, let us consider his drawing and painting for a moment.

It is a truism of contemporary art that a painter must establish his territory, become known for a style which he can then repeat with minute variations for the rest of his career. He has to do this so that buyers and critics can recognize his work. The fact that this leads to sterility and boredom is irrelevant in the face of economic pressure.

It is also a truism that a group with an impressive sounding name is a useful weapon in picking up public money and critical esteem. The name gives respectability, the group allows choice within a certain dialectical pattern.

Neagu belongs to the Generative Art Group. There are four other artists. So far, so good.

The trick is that the four other artists are all Neagu, painting under different names and different styles. He was able to sustain this fiction long enough for the group to become established and go into the history books. The hunter is hunted; that is real radicalism for you. It also enabled Neagu to investigate other styles without the irritation of critics trying to reconcile them all for him.

Most British artists, the serious ones, which means most British artists, find Neagu's attitude puzzling, and prefer not to talk about him. He does not fit into the system; he does not frown when he works.

I doubt myself if Neagu is particularly interested in art at all. He *makes* things, using anything that comes to hand. His favorite materials are wood, leather, and string, but he does not limit himself to them. None of his objects follows on logically from any other, but they are all related. They are tactile and cerebral, simple and complicated, in a word—paradoxical, which is the essence of knowledge.

Enough has been written of the influence on Neagu

of his native Rumanian folk-art to save me the trouble; I doubt if it's important anyway. Such comments on stylistic influence are a method of dis-associating an artist from the reality of his actual time and place. It would be comforting to explain Neagu's art as being Rumanian and showing the influence of Brancusi: doing so would remove him as a challenge to British and American art. The fact is that his origins have precious little to do with his quality, except in the negative sense that he has avoided the Western orthodoxy.

My first memory of Neagu was at the Demarco Gallery in Edinburgh. He had just come over from Rumania and had unerringly headed for the only outpost of artistic illogic in the British Isles. He had taken over a basement room and hung it with objects, of wood, of leather, of fur. It was lit only by a single light, and one had to feel one's way around, from texture to texture. In the middle of the web sat Neagu, while a tape recorder twittered and squeaked in the background. I thought at the time that he would be able to design a magnificent set for *The Tempest*. There aren't many British artists I would trust with Shakespeare.

—Alastair Mackintosh

NEGRET, Edgar.

Colombian. Born in Popayan in 1920. Educated in Popayan primary and secondary schools; studied at the Escuela de Bellas Artes, Cali, Colombia, 1938–43; studied, with Jorge de Oteiza, Popayan, 1944–46, and in Madrid, 1953; at Clay Club Cultural Center, New York, 1948–50; influenced by Henry Moore. Independent sculptor, since 1937: visited Bogota, then travelled to Europe, 1950; lived in Paris, 1950–52; travelled in Spain and Mallorca, 1953; in Paris and the United States, 1955; painted original posters, graphics and sets for La Mama Theatre, New York, 1963; founder, La Mama Bogota Theatre, Colombia, 1970. Instructor, New School for Social Research, New York, 1958. Museo Negret founded by the Colombian Government, Popayan, 1986. Recipient: First Prize, *Salon Nacional*, Bogota, 1949; Travel Fellowship, Paris, 1958; Silver Medal, *Bienal*, Sao Paulo, 1965; Gran Premio a las Artes, *Salon Nacional*, Bogota, 1967; David E. Bright Foundation Prize, *Biennale*, Venice, 1968; Guggenheim Foundation Fellowship, 1975. Agent: Humphrey Fine Art, New York City. Address: c/o Humphrey Fine Art, 242 East Fifth Street, New York, New York 10003; and 37 East 7th Street, New York, New York 10003, U.S.A.

Individual Exhibitions:

1943	Palacio de Bellas Artes, Cali, Colombia
1944	Convento de San Francisco, Popayan, Colombia
1946	Biblioteca Nacional, Bogota
1948	*Edgar Negret/Eduardo Ramirez*, Sociedad de Ingenieros, Bogota
1950	Peridot Gallery, Nnew York
1951	Galeria de Arte, Bogota
	Galerie Arnaud, paris
1953	Museo de Arte Contemporaneo, Madrid
1955	Peridot Gallery, New York
1956	Pan-American Union, Washington, D.C.
1957	*Edgar Negret/Jack Youngerman*, Gres Gallery, New York
1958	Biblioteca Nacional, Bogota
1959	David Herbert Gallery, New York
1962	Museo de Bellas Artes, Caracas
	Biblioteca Luis-Angel Arango del Banco de la Republica, Bogota
1963	Galeria de Arte El Callejon, Bogota
1964	*Edgar Negret/Eduardo Ramirez*, Graham Gallery, New York

1965	Museo de Arte Moderno, Bogota
1966	Graham Gallery, New York
	Museu de Arte Moderna, Rio de Janeiro
	Galeria Siglo XX, Quito
	Casa de la Cultura, Guayaquil, Ecuador
	Museo de Zea, Medellin, Colombia
1967	Richard Demarco Gallery, Edinburgh
	Axiom Gallery, London
	Negret/Rojas, Galeria Nacional, Cali, Colombia
1968	Biblioteca Nacional, Bogota
	Negret/Cicero, Galerie Simone Stern, New Orleans
1969	Museo La Terulia, Cali, Colombia
1970	Stedelijk Museum, Amsterdam
1971	Galerie Buchholz, Munich
	Städtische Kunsthalle, Dusseldorf
	Museo de Arte Moderno, Bogota (retrospective)
1972	Galerie Bonino, New York
	Arts Club of Chicago
1974	Galeria Bonino, New York
	San Juan Museum of Fine Arts, Puerto Rico
	Corcoran Gallery of Art, Washington, D.C.
	Negret, Ramirez, Rojas, Galeria Monte Avila, Bogota
1975	University of Texas at Austin
	Museo d'Arte Moderno, Bogota
1976	Galeria Belarca, Bogota
	Center for Inter-American Relations, New York (retrospective)
	Sala de Exposiciones, Caracas
1977	Galeria San Diego, Bogota
1978	La Galeria, Quito, Ecuador
1979	Galeria Garcés Velásquez, Bogota (retrospective)
	Museo de Arte Moderno, Bogota
	Galeria San Siego, at *FIAC 79*, Grand Palais, Paris
1980	Galeria Quintero, Barranquilla, Colombia
	Galeria 9, Lima, Peru
1981	Fondacion Joan Miro, Barcelona
	Sala Caja de Ahorros, Alava, Vitoria, Spain
1982	Galeria Atenea, Barranquilla, Colombia
	Contemporary Sculpture Center, Tokyo
1983	Museo Espanol de Arte Contemporaneo, Madrid
	Galeria Casa Negret, Bogota
1984	Galeria Avianca, Barranquilla, Colombia
1985	Museo Casa Negret, Popayan, Colombia
1986	Humphrey Fine Art, New York
1987	Museo de Arte Moderno, Bogota (retrospective)
	Humphrey Fine Art, New York

Selected Group Exhibitions:

1950	*Sculptures and Paintings from Colombia*, New School for Social Research, New York
1952	*Salon des Réalités Nouvelles*, Paris
1956	*Carnegie International*, Carnegie Institute, Pittsburgh
1958	*Biennale*, Venice
1961	*Geometrics and Hard Edge*, Museum of Modern Art, New York
1968	*Documenta*, Kassel, West Germany
1975	*Latin American Artists Today*, University of Texas at Austin
1976	*El Arte Colombiano a Través de los Siglos*, Palacio de Velázquez, Madrid
1979	*Twenty-Five Years Afterwards: Nevelson, Kelly, Negret*, Museo de Arte Moderno, Bogota
1985	*Works of Botero, Grau, Negret*, Museum of Modern Art of Latin America, Washington, D.C.

Collections:

Museo Casa Negret, Popayan, Colombia; Museo de Arte Moderno, Bogota; Museo de Arte Moderno, Caracas; Museo de Arte Moderno, Santiago, Chile; Museum of Modern Art, New York; Albany Institute of History and Art, New York; Pan-American Union, Washington, D.C.; University of Nebraska, Lincoln; Guggenheim Museum, New York; Stedelijk Museum, Amsterdam.

Publications:

On NEGRET: books—*Negret*, exhibition catalogue, with text by Franklin Konigsberg, London 1967; *Contemporary Art in*

Latin America by Gilbert Chase, New York 1970; *Negret: A Retrospective Catalogue* by Eduardo Serrano, Bogota 1987; articles—"Reviews and Previews: Negret" by Frank O'Hara in *Artnews* (New York), November 1955; "Reflexiones sobre la Edad de los Metales" by Marta Traba in *Vinculo Shell* (Buenos Aires), 1957; "Reviews and Previews: Edgar Negret" by Lawrence Campbell in *Artnews* (New York), November 1959; "News and Views from New York: Edgar Negret at the David Herbert Gallery" by Marvin D. Schwartz in *Apollo* (London), December 1959; "The World of Art: Pan-America: 5 Contemporary Colombians" by Marta Traba in *Art in America* (New York), Spring 1960; "Edgar Negret" by Maria-Rosa Gonzales in *Dictionnaire de la Sculpture Moderne* (Paris), 1960; "Fabricacion del Silencio" by Jorge de Oteiza in *Aparatos Magicos*, exhibition catalogue, Caracas 1962, reprinted in *6th Bienal*, exhibition catalogue, Sao Paulo 1965; "The Sculpture of Edgar Negret" by Douglas Hall in *Studio International* (London), September 1967; "Reviews and Previews: Edgar Negret" by Rosalind Brown in *Artnews* (New York), April 1969; "Der Bildhauer Edgar Negret" by E. Trier in *Art International* (Lugano, Switzerland), Summer 1970.

*   *   *

Edgar Negret is a Colombian sculptor who the more he was introduced to modern idioms and nonobjective concepts, the more he seemed paradoxically to reflect in his work something of the silent dialogue between ancient monolithic style and a communal memory not yet overlaid by the superfluous data of intervening civilizations.

He was slow in maturing, though by 1949 while relating to figurative tradition he had assimilated Moore's penetration of the mass. From 1954 he switched his attitude towards metal constructions, and from this point they assumed the open situation rising from flat ground rather than the top of a pedestal. This integration with environment none the less concentrated the axis on a central base and profiles strongly marked by cut-out shapes—signals, arms, slots and brackets—set up systems of iconic semaphores. As an admirer of both Gaudi and Calder, he simulated a style of metallic rococo, and the illumination of his flat metal by bright reds and oranges instilled a note of carnival to static constructions, while breaking up the tonal mass in light.   :

"Emblem for an Aquarium" (1954) has its abstract simplicity, while its polychrome shells project unstressed affinities with fish. In the 1960's he operated with large structures of sheet metal, chiefly aluminum, symbolizing the mechanical power of screws and propellers as they might be embodied in entities of morphological character. Negret found an apt concrete weight to his formal syntax, placing the sheer planes and flanged girders as physical embodiments of abstract relationships that were sums of simplified complexity. They took poetic solidities economically in reduced dimensions of architectural scope. In works such as "The Bridge" and "Stanchion 2" of 1968-70 the massive rivetted and bolted girders are patterned by the repetition of the fastening nuts and heads in the way a cathedral is ornamented by its functional buttressing, Gothic effects being heightened by the lozenge shaped holes.

This identification with architecture continues alongside the airborne spirit of much of Negret's metaphoric imagery. "Cape Kennedy" (1966) has its obvious connection with space travel in its crude simplicity yet by that fact implying untold energy in its suggestion of upward angled thrust. "Navigators" also combines the helmeted astronaut image with the centrifugal spirit of automotive power. "Temple" (1971) is a structure conceived in voided grandeur, defining impressive proportions of space and converting straight-edged girders into contemporary capitals bearing measured architectural decoration in their flanges and bolt-heads.

Negret is singularly outstanding for his affirmation of contemporary man-released power transfigured to optimist paraphrase in organic poetry. His complex yet simple monoliths celebrate man's capacity to evolve for good instead of evil, for exploration rather than for destruction; his clean-cut constructions stand for classical order of tensed proportion and inhabited dignity.

—G. S. Whittet

NEIZVESTNY, Ernst.

Russian. Born in Sverdlovsk, Urals, in 1925. Studied at the Academy of Art, Riga, Latvia, 1947-48, and Surikov Art Institute, Moscow, 1948-54; influenced by work of Michelangelo, Henry Moore and Jacques Lipchitz. Served as volunteer paratrooper in the Red Army, 1942 (wounded and hospitalized in Bratislava and Brno, Czechoslovakia, 1943-45). Worked as assistant to several sculptors, Moscow, 1948-54; foundry-worker in rolling stock yards, Urals, 1954-55; independent sculptor, Moscow, 1955-75, in Vienna, 1976-77, and in Zurich, since 1977. Recipient: Silver Medal, *International Youth Festival*, Moscow 1957; Red Star, for war-time gallantry, Moscow, 1964. Address: c/o Bolschoi Sergijewsky Pereulok 18, Moscow, U.S.S.R.

Individual Exhibitions:

1961	Druzhba Club, Moscow
1962	University of Moscow (with Y. Yankilewsky)
1964	Grosvenor Gallery, London
	Zentral Buchhandlung, Vienna
1965	Museum of Modern Art, Belgrade
	Grosvenor Gallery, London
1969	Galleria La Barcaccia, Montecatini, Italy
1971	Galleria Il Gabbiano, Rome
1972	Tel-Aviv Museum
1975	New York Cultural Center

Selected Group Exhibitions:

1954	*Young Moscow Artists*, Moscow
1961	*The Nine*, Moscow
1962	*The Belyutin Studio Group*, Bolshaya Kommunisticheskaya Street, Moscow
1964	*Aspects of Contemporary Soviet Art*, Grosvenor Gallery, London
1965	*Young Moscow Kinetic Artists*, Viola Gallery, Prague
1966	*Festival of Fine Arts*, Sopot-Poznan, Poland
1970	*The Russian Avant-Garde in Moscow Today*, Galerie Gmurzynska, Cologne
1974	*Progressive Tendencies in Moscow 1957-1970*, Städtisches Museum, Bochum, West Germany
1975	*The Glezer Collection of Russian Art*, Kunstlerhaus, Vienna (toured Austria and Germany)
1977	*Unofficial Art from the Soviet Union*, Institute of Contemporary Arts, London

Collections:

Russian Art Museum, Leningrad; Alexander Glezer Collection, Vienna.

Publications:

On NEIZVESTNY: books—*Ernst Neizvestny*, exhibition catalogue, with text by D. Cosic and N. Stripoevic, Belgrade 1965; *Ernst Neizvestny*, exhibition catalogue, with text by John Berger, Tel-Aviv 1972; *Soviet Art and the Tasks of the Struggle Against Bourgeois Ideology* by V. Vanslov, Moscow 1969; *Ernst Neizvestny*, exhibition catalogue, with text by Franco Miele, Montecatini, Italy 1969; *Art and Revolution: Ernst Neizvestny and the Role of the Artist in the U.S.S.R.* by John Berger, London 1969; *Ernst Neizvestny*, exhibition catalogue, with texts by John Berger and Renato Guttuso, Rome 1971; *The Glezer Collection of Russian Art*, exhibition catalogue, with texts by Hans Mayr, Alexander Glezer and Viktor Tupizin, Vienna, 1975; *Unofficial Art from the Soviet Union*, exhibition catalogue, with texts by Igor Golomshtok and Alexander Glezer, London 1977.

*   *   *

Before leaving the Soviet Union in 1976 Neizvestny had occupied an ambiguous position as the best-known Soviet artist of his generation, whose work nevertheless could not be publicly shown. For years he had consistently opposed the enforced new academicism of Socialist Realism, courageously arguing as well as working to demonstrate that official Soviet art had no right to its claims. Yet the idea of an art truly serving a whole society is as central to his thinking as it was to that of the Constructivists at the time of the Revolution, for he maintains that only art can make people fully conscious of themselves in time and history.

And the starting point of all Neizvestny's work, in both sculpture and drawing, is the tragic history of his own times and the sufferings his country has endured during them. He expressed this suffering in terms of the human body; his works, in plaster, stone or bronze, are all concerned with endurance and the growth and transformation this brings about. Thus the recurring theme of his art is human strength to survive and grow, depicted in some heroic, anguished metamorphosis of the human figure. As John Berger has put it "For Neizvestny the human body is the field of all possible metaphors. All that he has to say can be said in terms of the human body. It represents the quintessence of all that is not death . . . his interest . . . begins with an insatiable curiosity about the body. He is not concerned with its beauty but with its workings, its power, its resistance, its limits and its mysteries." And it was literally through his own body that Neizvestny became so keenly aware of life, having been severely wounded and left for dead in the Second World War.

But though he is an artist of tremendous energy, power and ambition, the isolation in which he has been forced to work means that there has sometimes been a contrast between the sheer force of his abilities and their proper realization. Thus his writhing forms, immense shoulders and clenched fists have been criticized by Hilton Kramer as being over-rhetorical: "The enormous hands in dramatic gestures, the twisted mouths, the orotund musculature of his larger-than-life male figures and their altogether massive stance—these and other characteristic features of his sculpture, while clearly the work of a sizable talent, are closer in feeling to the clichés of Socialist Realism than to the more critical spirit of modern art."

But if Neizvestny sometimes is guilty of lapsing into a rather debased rhetoric, this may be because he is desperately struggling to express not outward appearance but interior feelings. Even in the case of a single simple form like the sphere he has claimed a distinction between inner and outer truth: "Two sculptors are carving a sphere out of stone. One of them wants to achieve the most perfect form of sphere and sees the meaning of his work in turning a mass of stone into a perfect sphere. The other is also carving a sphere, but only in order to convey the inner tension expressed in the form of a sphere filled to bursting point. The first sphere will be the work of a craftsman, the second that of an artist."

Neizvestny is also a prolific graphic artist, for instance in his voluminous series of etchings illustrating Dante's *Divine Comedy*. Again the appeal of the *Inferno* is that it offers splendid opportunities for an artist whose main concern is to express human anguish and suffering, as in the lovers whirled along in their whirlwind of passion, or the woman suicide in the Forest of Suicides, crouching with a tree growing violently through her.

Obsessed with Michelangelo, Neizvestny has also been influenced by Henry Moore and by the Lipchitz of the late, massive baroque figures. He similarly aspires to a monumental statement, a kind of heroic humanism, thinking of sculpture as being essentially a public art, so that he has made maquettes for very large-scale public monuments, though very few have actually been put up. He sees many of his figures of giants or prophets as potentially capable of being assembled together to make one vast work which he thinks of as a *Gigantomachia*. But his opposition to the official hierarchy means that most of his bronzes have had to be cast by himself in primitive conditions in his small overcrowded shop, thus limiting their size.

However, he did receive some state commissions such as the large sculpture for a children's summer colony in the Crimea, as well as some private commissions for memorials on the graves of some prominent men, most notably Khrushchev. The two men had a famous argument in November 1962 when

Khrushchev denounced modern art after seeing an exhibition in Moscow that Neizvestny had helped to arrange. Later, after Khrushchev's fall from power, the two men began a friendly coorespondence. So after the former leader's death, his family asked the sculptor to design a memorial for his grave—a realistic head of Khrushchev on a platform, with two intertwined forms of black and white stone behind, locked in perpetual struggle. But Neizvestny's own struggle with the Soviet authorities continued, and in the harsher climate once the Thaw under Khrushchev had receded he found it more difficult to express himself, until in March 1976 he was given permission to leave Russia, moving to the West and conducting negotiations for the export of some of his sculpture.

—Konstantin Bazarov

NESBITT, Lowell (Blair).

American. Born in Baltimore, Maryland, 4 October 1933. Educated at Tyler School of Fine Art, Philadelphia, 1950-55, B.F.A. 1955; studied stained glass and etching, Royal College of Art, London, 1955-56. Served in the United States Army, 1956-58. Designed theatre sets, 1948-54; Art Director, closed circuit television, Walter Reed Army Medical Center, Bethesda, Maryland, 1957-60; worked at Phillips Collection, Washington, D.C., 1959-63. Independent artist, associating with Robert Indiana, Louise Nevelson, Jasper Johns and Andy Warhol, New York, since 1963. Instructor of Printmaking, Baltimore Museum of Art, 1961-63; Instructor, School of Visual Arts, New York, 1973. Address: 69 Wooster Street, New York, New York 10012, U.S.A.

Individual Exhibitions:

1958	Baltimore Museum of Art
1963	Franz Bader Gallery, Washington, D.C.
1964	Corcoran Gallery, Washington, D.C.
1965	Rolf Nelson Gallery, Los Angeles
	Henri Gallery, Washington, D.C.
	Howard Wise Gallery, New York
1966	Gertrude Kasle Gallery, Detroit
	Rolf Nelson Gallery, Los Angeles
	Henri Gallery, Washington, D.C.
	Howard Wise Gallery, New York
1967	Jefferson Gallery, San Diego
	Louisiana Gallery, Houston
	Henri Gallery, Washington, D.C.
	Gertrude Kasle Gallery, Detroit
1968	Stable Gallery, New York
1969	Stable Gallery, New York
	Baltimore Museum of Art
	Henri Gallery, Washington, D.C.
	Gertrude Kasle Gallery, Detroit
	Galerie M. E. Thelen, Essen
1970	Galerie M. E. Thelen, Cologne
	Stable Gallery, New York
	Gertrude Kasle Gallery, Detroit
1971	Gertrude Kasle Gallery, Detroit
	Gimpel Fils, London
	Gimpel and Weitzenhoffer, New York (2 shows)
	Lambert Studios, Los Angeles
	Pyramid Gallery, Washington, D.C.
	Galerie de Gestio, Bremen
1972	Galerie M. E. Thelen, Cologne
	Gimpel und Hanover Galerie, Zurich
	Fabian Carlson Galerie, Göteborg, Sweden
	Galerie Ostergren, Malmo, Sweden
	Kunstverein, Freiburg, West Germany
	Galerie Arneson, Copenhagen
	Galerie Aronowitch, Stockholm
	Hansen Fuller Gallery, San Francisco
	Corcoran and Corcoran Gallery, Miami
1973	*The Flower Series 1964-73*, Corcoran Gallery, Washington, D.C.
	Marion Locks Gallery, Philadelphia

	Kunstverein, Freiburg, West Germany
	Galerie Arneson, Copenhagen
	Gertrude Kasle Gallery, Detroit
	Gimpel and Weitzenhoffer, New York
	Galerie John Craven, Paris
	Stefanotty Gallery, New York
	Gimpel Fils, London
1974	Gimpel Fils, London
	Stefanotty Gallery, New York
	Gertrude Kasle Gallery, Detroit
	Galerie Arneson, Copenhagen
	Fendrick Gallery, Washington, D.C.
	Brooke Alexander Inc., New York
	Walton Gallery, San Francisco
	Galerie HM, Brussels
	Museo de Bellas Artes, San Juan, Puerto Rico
1975	Pyramid Gallery, Washington, D.C. (2 shows)
	Andrew Crispo Gallery, New York
	Pace Gallery, New York
	Memorial Art Gallery, Rochester Museum, New York
	Corcoran Gallery, Washington, D.C.
	Josef Gallery, New York
1976	Galerie HM, Brussels
	Andrew Crispo Gallery, New York
	Hokin Gallery, Palm Beach, Florida
	Hokin Gallery, Chicago
	Hayden Gallery, Massachusetts Institute of Technology, Cambridge
	Treasure Island, Bicentennial Museum, San Francisco
1977	Graphis Gallery, Toronto
	Gumps Gallery, San Francisco
	Andrew Crispo Gallery, New York
	Edwin A. Ulrich Museum of Art, Wichita, Kansas
	Janus Gallery, Venice, California
	Galeria Arte/Contacto, Caracas, Venezuela
	Galerie Jollen, Cologne
1978	Strong's Gallery, Cleveland
	Intown Club, Cleveland
	Kent State University, Ohio
	B. R. Kornblatt Gallery, Baltimore
	Art Contact, Miami, Florida
	Still Lifes, Andrew Crispo Gallery, New York
1979	Selby Museum, Sarasota, Florida
	Flowers, Andrew Crispo Gallery, New York
1980	McNay Art Institute, San Antonio, Texas
	Lyford Cay Gallery, Nassau, Bahamas
	Galerie Jerome, Copenhagen
	Galeria Arte/Contacto, Caracas, Venezuela
	Profile Gallery, New York
	Aldrich Museum of Contemporary Art, Ridgefield, Connecticut
	B. R. Kornblatt Gallery, Baltimore
	Galleri Herder, Falsterbo, Sweden
	Hull Gallery, Washington, D.C.
1981	Hokin Gallery, Palm Beach, Florida
	General Electric Corporation, Connecticut
	Andrew Crispo Gallery, New York
	Fay Gold Gallery, Atlanta
	Southwest II Galeries, Dallas
1982	Butler Institute of American Art, Youngstown, Ohio
1983	Oklahoma Art Center, Oklahoma City
	Institute of Contemporary Art, Philadelphia
1984	Oklahoma Art Center, Oklahoma City
1985	G. Sander Fine Art, Daytona Beach, Florida
	Temple University, Philadelphia
	Long Island University, New York
	Bourne Gallery, Surrey, England

Selected Group Exhibitions:

1971	*Target Moon*, Wallraf-Richartz Museum, Cologne
1972	*Hyperrealistes Americaines*, Galerie des Quatres Mouvements, Paris
1973	*Johanssen Collection*, Museum Folkwang, Essen
1974	*Flowertime at Lincoln Center*, New York
1977	*30 Years of American Print Making*, Brooklyn Museum, New York
	The Bicycle, Museum Boymans-van-Beuningen, Rotterdam
1978	*Collector's Choice*, Mississippi Museum of Art, Jackson
1979	*Selected Paintings from the Andrew Crispo Gallery Collection*, New York
1985	*American Realism*, San Francisco Museum of Modern Art (toured the United States)

Collections:

Museum of Modern Art, New York; Baltimore Museum of Art; Corcoran Gallery, Washington, D.C.; National Gallery of Art, Washington, D.C.; National Aeronautic and Space Administration, Washington, D.C.; Art Institute of Chicago; Milwaukee Art Center; Cleveland Museum; Bibliothéque Nationale, Paris; National Art Gallery, Wellington, New Zealand.

Publications:

By NESBITT: book—*Loweel Nesbitt: An Autobiography*, exhibition catalogue, New York 1975; article—"An Interview with Lowell Nesbitt," with Adam Drewnowki, in *Interview* (New York), December 1975.

On NESBITT: books—*Lowell Nesbitt*, exhibition catalogue by Morris Graves, Los Angeles 1965; *Flowers, Facades and IBM Machines*, exhibition catalogue, by Henry Martin, New York 1965, reprinted in *Collage* (Palermo, California), October 1965; *Lowell Nesbitt*, exhibition catalogue, by Anders Bergh, Malmo, Sweden 1972; *Lowell Nesbitt*, exhibition catalogue, by Udo Kultermann, Zurich 1972; *Lowell Nesbitt*, exhibition catalogue, by Roy Slade, San Juan, Puerto Rico 1973; *The Flower Series 1964-73*, exhibition catalogue, with text by Henry T. Hopkins, Washington, D.C. 1973; *Lowell Nesbitt: Still Lifes*, exhibition catalogue, New York 1978; *Lowell Nesbitt: Flowers*, exhibition catalogue, New York 1979; *Lowell Nesbitt*, exhibition catalogue, Ridgefield, Connecticut 1980; articles—"Lowell Nesbitt" by Cindy Nemser in *Arts Magazine* (New York), December 1966/January 1967; "Lowell Nesbitt's Photographic Approach" by Hilton Kramer in the *New York Times*, March 1970; "Sharp Focus Realism" by Denise Wolmer in *Arts Magazine* (New York), March 1972; "The Male Nude Arrives at Last" by Cindy Nemser in *Changes* (New York), July 1972; "Lowell Nesbitt's Autobiography" by Gene Baro in *Arts Magazine* (New York), December 1975; "Lowell Nesbitt" in *Artnews* (New York), April 1976; "Background for an Artist" by Peter Carlson in *Architectural Digest* (New York), April 1977; "Lowell Nesbitt" by Noel Frackman in *Arts Magazine* (New York), June 1977; "Haus Lowell Nesbitt" by Anja Veg in *Architektur und Wohnen* (Stuttgart), November 1977; "Home Is Where the Art Is" by John Dorsey in the *Baltimore Sun*, 4 March 1979; "Lowell Nesbitt" by Gerrit Henry in *Art in America* (New York), November 1979; "I Fiori Humani de Lowell Nesbitt" in *Harpers Bazaar Italia*, July/August 1980.

Lowell Nesbitt is one of the multifarious group of painters who helped bring Realism back into prominence more than a decade ago. He is best known for his magnified, close-up views of flowers, shoes and other ordinary objects which he paints with meticulous care for detail. Although he starts with photographic models, Nesbitt paints on the canvas without the aid of the projected image which many of the other Realists use, which lends his pictures a feeling very like the Dutch still-life painters and also like the American Precisionists such as Charles Sheeler and particularly Georgia O'Keefe.

Since 1964 Nesbitt has produced about 15 to 20 series of works whose subject matter ranges from building facades in Lower Manhattan, to still lifes, studio interiors, shoes, bridges around Manhattan, his dog Echo, animals and fruits and vegetables. In each case, the articles in the work are arranged somewhat schematically to convey something beyond the literal, seen image for its own sake. In the most arresting works, little things, treated with tender loving care, transmit an aura of mysterious importance. In his shoe pictures, for example, attention is given to the individual qualities of the object, down to the wrinkles from wear and the brand names.

About one-third of Nesbitt's total output has concentrated on huge, blowups of flowers such as irises, lilies, tulips and roses, which Nesbitt endows with a life-of-their-own nature and a cold beauty far beyond their natural appearances in the garden or wilderness. Zeroing in on this subject and painting it in all its

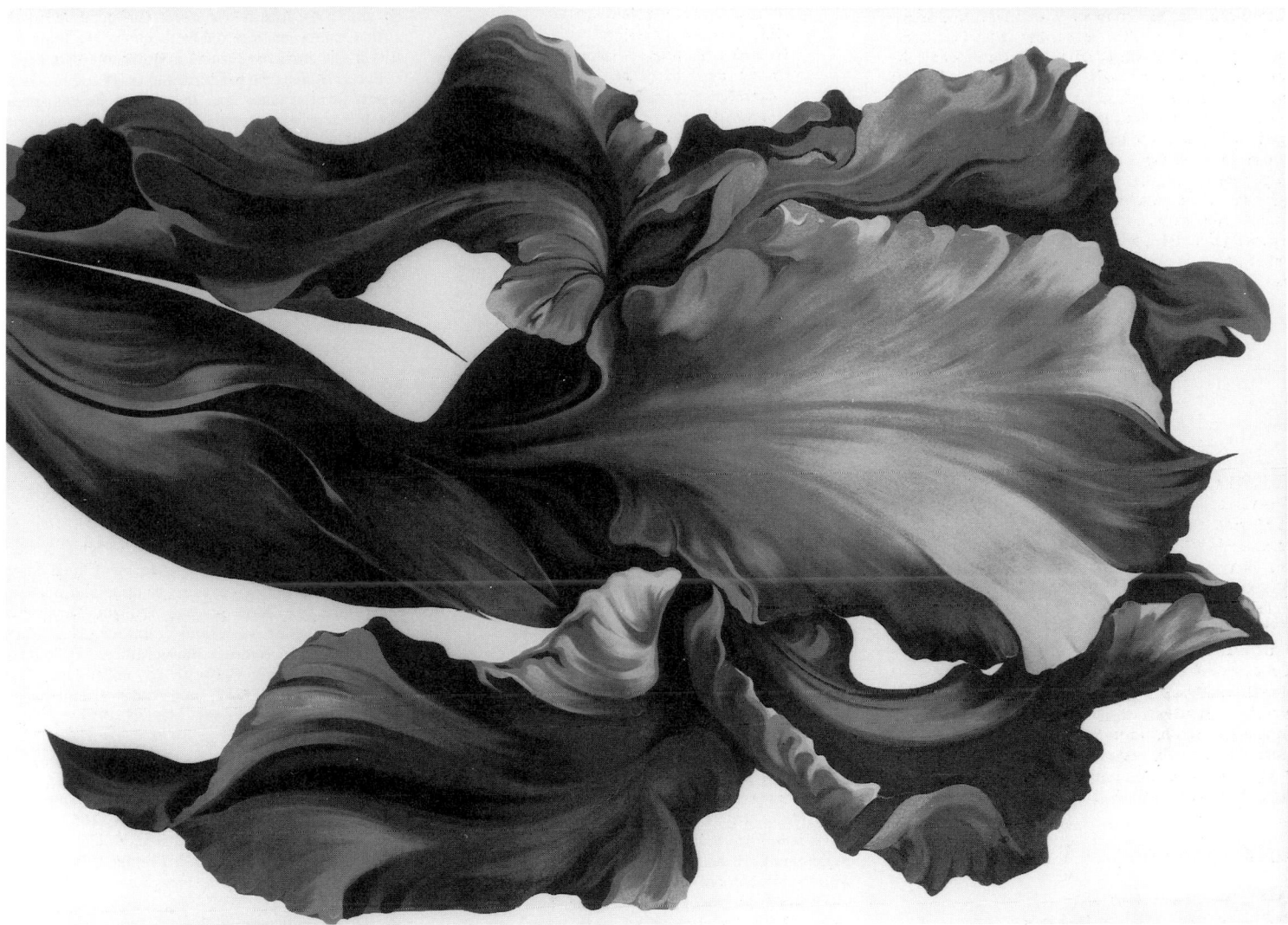

Lowell Nesbitt: *Dark Brown Iris on White*, 1979

literal details in firm, unbroken contour and exquisite colorings, Nesbitt transforms the explicit into a monumental, almost metaphysical presence of cold sensuousness. In recent works such as "Bird Flying over Orchid" (1981), the image of the bird's wingspan while in flight hovers above and behind that of the exotic bloom, echoing form and color to create a composition with implications beyond that of the photographic reproduction. As in many of his earlier works, the new series of fruits and vegetables play on asymmetrical balancing of shapes which share their space with crisply rendered patterns. There is a similar mix of ordered structure and sensuous mysticism in all his still lifes, which is especially successful in works of 1976 such as "Amber Beads and Mask," a tabletop grouping in which things lying around the studio attain a drama and lushness which make them seem eerie and organic. Nesbitt transforms the usually unnoticed details of life into something special and bigger than life.

—Barbara Cavaliere

NEUSTEIN, Joshua.

Israeli. Born in Danzig, Germany (now Gdansk, Poland), 16 October 1940; displaced person and political prisoner, with his family, in Poland, the U.S.S.R. and Germany, 1949; settled in the United States, 1950; emigrated to Israel, 1964. Educated at the Yeshiva Rabbi Jacob Joseph, New York, 1951–56; College of the City of New York, under Professor Hans Kohn, 1957–61, B.A. 1961; Art Students League, New York, 1959–61; Pratt Institute, Brooklyn, New York, 1960–63; studied privately with Arieh Aroch and Zwi Mairowich, Jerusalem, 1964–68. Served in the Israeli Army as a 2nd Lieutenant in the Tank Division, 1964–66. Painter: worked as a waiter in Monticello, New York and Lakewood, New Jersey, 1955–58, as a baker in New York, 1958–59, as a real estate broker and in the Department of Welfare, New York, 1959–61, as a furrier, New York, 1961–63, and as a croupier, Brooklyn, 1961–62; ordained as a rabbi, 1962; settled in Jerusalem, 1964; now lives and works in New York City and Jerusalem. Editor, *Art en Garde*, Jerusalem, since 1975. Lecturer, Ramaz Yeshiva, Brooklyn, 1962–64. Lecturer, Bezalel Academy, Jerusalem, since 1974. Recipient: Jerusalem Prize, 1971; Willem Sandberg Prize, Jerusalem, 1973. Agents: Rina Gallery, 23 East 74th Street, New York, New York 10020; Yod Fat Gallery, 190 Dizengorf, Tel Aviv, Israel. Address: 300 West 108th Street, New York, New York 10023, or 7 Hamavak Street, French Hill, Jerusalem.

Individual Exhibitions:

1966   Rina Gallery, Jerusalem
1969   *Boots*, Jerusalem Artists House
1970   *Road Piece*, Helena Rubinstein Pavilion, Tel Aviv
         Jerusalem River Project, Israel Museum, Jersualem
1971   Gallery House, London
         Galerie Yvon Lambert, Paris
1972   Yod Fat Gallery, Tel Aviv
         Haifa Museum, Israel

1973   Rina Gallery, New York
         Yod Fat Gallery, Tel Aviv
1974   *The Sound of Pines Opening in the Sun*, Yod Fat Gallery, Tel Aviv
1975   Rina Gallery, New York
         Worcester Art Museum, Massachusetts (with Gross and Kupferman)
         Julie M. Gallery, Tel Aviv
         Territorial Imperative, Golan Heights, Israel (travelled to Krusa, Denmark and Belfast, 1975–78)
1977   Pollock Gallery, Toronto
         Gallery Birch, Copenhagen
         Tel Aviv Museum
         Velar Gallery, Carnegie-Mellon University, Pittsburgh
1979   Mary Boone Gallery, New York
1980   Givan Fine Arts, Tel Aviv
         Quintessence, Dayton, Ohio
1981   Tel-Hai, Upper Galilee, Israel
1983   Cornell University, Ithaca, New York
1984   Galerie X+, Brussels
         Givon Gallery, Tel Aviv
         Israel Museum, Jerusalem
1987   Exit Art, New York

Selected Group Exhibitions:

1970   *Israel on Paper*, High Museum of Art, Atlanta
1971   *Concepts + Information*, Israel Museum, Jerusalem
1972   *Documenta 5*, Museum Fridericianum, Kassel, West Germany
1974   *Beyond Drawing*, Israel Museum, Jerusalem
1978   *Seven Artists in Israel*, Los Angeles Coutny Museum of Art

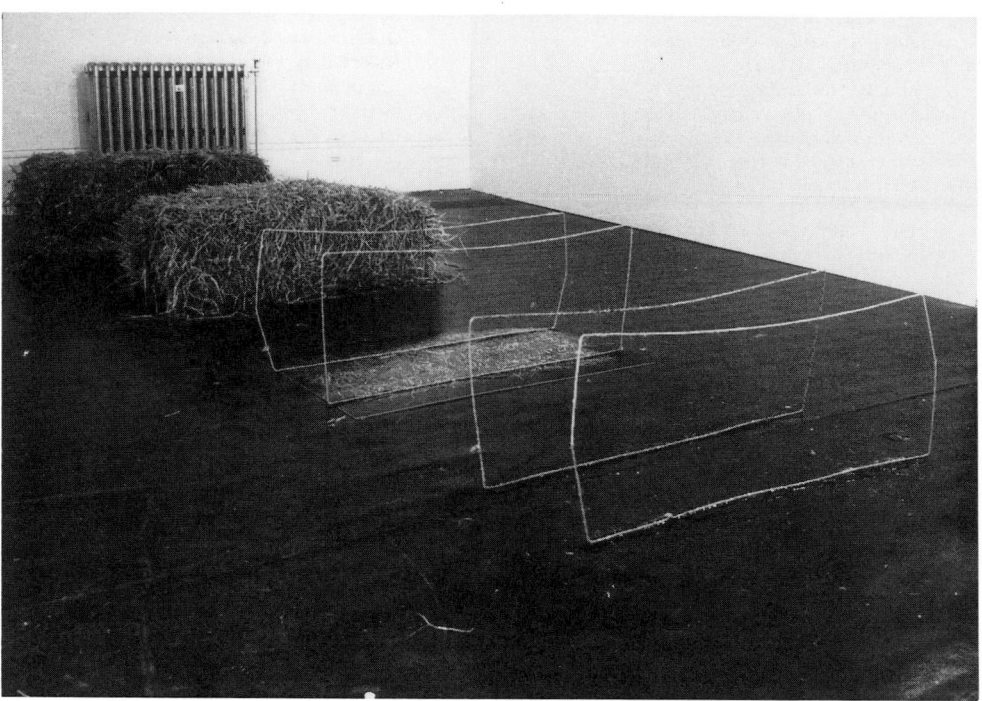

Joshua Neustein: *Hay Bales and Binding*, 1971

1980   *With Paper: About Paper*, Albright-Knox Art Gallery, Buffalo, New York
1982   *Bilder Sind Nicht Verboten*, Kunsthalle, Dusseldorf
1985   *The American Experience*, Bass Museum, Miami, Florida (toured the United States)
1987   *Immigrants and Refugees/Heroes or Villains*, Exit Art, New York

Collections:

Israel Museum, Jerusalem; Tel Aviv Museum; Museum of Modern Art, New York; Guggenheim Museum, New York; Albright-Knox Art Gallery, Buffalo, New York.

Publications:

By NEUSTEIN: books—*Affidavit*, exhibition catalogue, co-editor, London 1972; articles—"I Remember George Grosz" in *Flash Art* (Milan), November 1972; "On Aroch and Mairowich" in *Jerusalem Post*, December 1974.

On NEUSTEIN: books—*Concepts + Information*, exhibition catalogue, by Yona Fischer, Jerusalem 1971; *Abstraction to Nature to Landscape*, exhibition catalogue, by Yona Fischer, Jerusalem 1972; *4 Draughtsmen*, exhibition catalogue, by Ammon Barzel, Tel Aviv 1974; *Definition of Art* by Gideon Ofrat, Tel Aviv 1974; *Seven Artists in Israel*, exhibition catalogue with texts by Maurice Tuchman and Stephanie Barron, Los Angeles 1978; *With Paper: About Paper*, exhibition catalogue with essay by Charlotta Kotik, Buffalo 1980; *Bilder sind nicht verboten*, exhibition catalogue with text by Jurgen Harten, Dusseldorf 1982; *Joshua Neustein: Maps*, exhibition catalogue with introduction by Yigal Zalmona, Jerusalem 1983; *Joshua Neustein: The Bethlehem Series*, exhibition catalogue with essays by Joseph Masheck and Pierre Restany, New York 1983; *The American Experience*, exhibition catalogue with essays by Cynthia McCabe and Tuan Yi-Su, New York 1985; *Joshua Neustein*, exhibition catalogue with texts by Carlo McCormick, Irit Rogoff and Klaus Ottmann, New York 1987.

Joshua Neustein has a love affair with paper. He folds it, tears it, pleats it, cuts it; it is often left un-severed. *Stella* (1971) resembles a maze—follow the paper through from one end to the other, along the surfaces with the torn edges on either side—you will come to the end without a break on the way. His paper works are positive, secure, un-wavering. The first ten years of Neustein's life were insecure, miserable, unstable and, must have been at times, negative.

His native Danzig had already suffered its own vicissitudes before he was born; a free state under the protection of Poland from 1920 until annexed by Hitler in 1938. With his family he was displaced by the Germans to Poland, then by way of the USSR and Austria arrived in the United States, settling in Brooklyn.

His father had been forced to cut wood in Siberia—could this have been the beginning of his romance with the structure of the paper that was to become so important in his work twenty years later? His involvement with the materials of his trade is total; his understanding of the structure of paper (he has observed its manufacture in the mills) and the myriad methods of treatment available to him are his language.

During his time of study at yeshiva (rabbinical school) he would draw in the margins of the commentaries of the Torah (Jewish law) horrifying his teachers who compelled him to erase his doodles and restore the pages to their original condition. This was soon after his arrival in the United States, possibly his introduction to the printed page—the blank margins were too much of a temptation. The second Commandment forbidding representational art may have directed him in his early work to the influences of American Abstract Expressionism and his work has been compared to that of Larry Rivers (a fellow Jew).

Some of his presentations bring to mind the sufferings and deprivations of the wondering masses of European refugees immediately following World War II. *Boots* (1969) composed of 17000 pairs of old boots, and Barriers (1971), *River Project* (1970), *Landscapes with Bales of Hay* (1970), *Earth, Air, Fire Water: Elements of Art* (1971 Group Exhibition)—reminiscent of what lay outside, where nature was there for the having.

Paper—a common commodity—accessible, inexpensive, diverse, beautiful: Its bare form asking to be clothed; straight lines to be curved; the whole to be divided. He avoided the strongest colours in his more youthful works and was attracted to beiges, whites, tans, some yellows, pinks and greens, leaving the texture of the paper to be observed; by the 1980's, still handling the paper in his own particular style, he is concerned with creating a further dimension and produces large-scale works, with the undersides of the paper, though not entirely seen, covered in paint, now in much stronger colours, but with a continuing fondness for the pearly whites. Unframed, unstretched, not even attached to a wall, they hang—islands (or almost) isolated in space. His work has a mystery and

an ability to disturb. He does with paper what the 17th Century masters did with cloth. He folds and lifts it—he curls the corners in order to create depth.

Recently Neustein has turned to maps and produced a new form of landscape. In so doing he has spread his horizons to encompass international boundaries and the political, social and territorial problems facing the world today. The basic map is the truth (the discovered form), man makes and constantly changes the boundaries—Neustein adds imagination. His attached objects, in metal, sticks, glass, form obliterating or semi-obliterating platforms disturbing the marked borders. Is it his wish to blot out and start again? He is never didactic—yet his paintings do inform.

—Muriel Emanuel

NEVELSON, Louise.
American. Born Louise Berliawsky, in Kiev, Russia, 23 September 1900; emigrated to the United States with her family, 1905. Studied painting and drawing, under Theresa Bernstein and William Meyerwitz, New York, 1920; voice and dramatics, New York, 1920; art, under Kenneth Hayes Miller, Art Students League, New York, 1929-30; art, under Hans Hofmann, Munich, 1931-32; modern dance, under Ellen Kearns, 1932; archaeology, Mexico, 1951-52. Married Charles Nevelson in 1920 (separated, 1931) son: Myron. Worked as film extra, Berlin and Vienna, 1931; assistant to Diego Rivera, Mexico City, 1932-33; worked at the Sculpture Center, New York, 1949-50, and at Atelier 17, New York, 1953-55. Instructor of Art, Educational Alliance School, 1937; Great Neck Adult Education Program, New York, 1950's. Chapter President, New York, 1957-59, and National President, 1962-64, Actor's Equity; Vice President, Federation of Modern Painters and Sculptors, 1962-64; Member, Sculptor's Guild, 1962-64; Participant, National Council on Arts and Government, Washington, D.C., 1965. Recipient: Grand Prize, *Art: U.S.A.*, New York, 1959; Mr. and Mrs. Frank G. Logan Prize, Chicago, 1960; Tamarind Fellowship, 1963, 1967; Medal, MacDowell Colony, Peterborough, New Hampshire, 1969; Skowhegan Medal for Sculpture, Maine, 1971; Creative Arts Award in Sculpture, Brandeis University, Waltham, Massachusetts, 1971; American Institute of Architects Award, 1977. D.F.A.: Western College for Women, Oxford, Ohio, 1966; Smith College, Northampton, Massachusetts, 1973; D.H.L.: Hobart and William Smith College, Geneva, New York, 1971; Columbia University, New York, 1977; Boston University, 1978. Agent: Pace Gallery, 32 East 75th Street, New York, New York 10022, U.S.A. *Died* (in New York) *17 April 1988.*

Individual Exhibitions:

1941   Karl Nierendorf Gallery, New York
1942   Karl Nierendorf Gallery, New York
1943   Karl Nierendorf Gallery, New York
         Norlyst Gallery, New York
1944   Karl Nierendorf Gallery, New York
1946   Karl Nierendorf Gallery, New York
1950   Lotte Jacobi Gallery, New York
1954   Lotte Jacobi Gallery, New York
         Marcia Clapp Gallery, New York
1955   Grand Central Moderns, New York
1956   Grand Central Moderns, New York
1958   Grand Central Moderns, New York
         Esther Stuttman Gallery, New York
1959   Martha Jackson Gallery, New York
1960   Galerie Daniel Cordier, Paris
         David Herbert Gallery, New York
         Deborah Sherman Gallery, New York

1961 Galerie Daniel Cordier, Paris
Pace Gallery, Boston
Martha Jackson Gallery, New York
Tanager Gallery, New York
Staatliche Kunsthalle, Baden-Baden, West Germany
1963 Sidney Janis Gallery, New York
1964 Pace Gallery, New York
Pace Gallery, Boston
Galerie Gimpel-Hanover, Zurich
Galleria d'Arte Contemporanea, Turin
Kunsthalle, Berne
1965 David Mirvish Gallery, Toronto
Pace Gallery, New York
Galerie Schmela, Dusseldorf
1966 Ferus-Pace Gallery, Los Angeles
1967 *Prints and Drawings 1953–1966,* Whitney Museum, New York
Rose Art Museum, Brandeis University, Waltham, Massachusetts
1968 Arts Club of Chicago
Pace Gallery, New York
1969 *Louise Nevelson 1959–1961,* Bürgermeister-Ludwig-Reichert-Haus, Ludwigshafen, West Germany
Museo Civico, Turin
Recent Wood Sculpture, Pace Gallery, New York
Harcus-Krakow Gallery, Boston
Sculptures 1959–1969, Rijksmuseum Kröller-Müller, Otterlo, Netherlands
Museum of Fine Arts, Houston
Galerie Jeanne Bucher, Paris

Pace Columbus Gallery, Ohio
Akron Art Institute, Ohio
1970 Martha Jackson Gallery, New York
Whitney Museum, New York
University of Texas at Austin
1971 Makler Gallery, Philadelphia
Pace Gallery, New York
1972 Dunkelman Gallery, Toronto
Pace Gallery, New York
Parker 470 Gallery, Boston
1973 Studio Marconi, Milan
Wood Sculptures, Walker Art Center, Minneapolis
Modern Museet, Stockholm
1974 San Francisco Museum of Art
Musée d'Art Modern de la Ville de Paris
Palais des Beaux-Arts, Brussels
Neue National Galerie, West Berlin
Museum of Fine Arts, Dallas
Pace Gallery, Columbus, Ohio
Makler Gallery, Philadelphia
C. W. Post Center, Long Island University, Greenvale, New York
High Museum of Art, Atlanta
William Rockhill Nelson Gallery of Art, Kansas City, Missouri
Pace Gallery, New York
Louise Nevelson as Printmaker, Cincinnati Art Museum
1975 Minanu Gallery, Tokyo
Galleria d'Arte Spagnoli, Florence
Cleveland Museum of Art

Harcus-Krakow-Rosen-Sonnabend Gallery, Boston
Galleria d'Arte l'Arcipelago, Turin
Hokin Gallery, Palm Beach, Florida
1976 Makler Gallery, Philadelphia
Dawn's Presence-Moon Garden + Two 1969–1975, Pace Gallery, New York
1977 *The Metal Sculptures,* Neuberger Museum, Purchase, New York
1978 Pace Gallery, New York
Pace Gallery, Columbus, Ohio
Recent Works, Richard Gray Gallery, Chicago
Linda Farris Gallery, Seattle
1979 Makler Gallery, Philadelphia
Farnsworth Museum, Rockland, Maine
Norton Gallery, West Palm Beach, Florida
Jacksonville Art Museum, Florida
1980 Pace Gallery, New York
Wildenstein and Co., New York
Whitney Museum, New York
Scottsdale Center for the Arts, Arizona
The 4th Dimension, Phoenix Art Museum, Arizona
Seattle Art Museum
Winnipeg Art Gallery
Museum of Art, University of Iowa, Iowa City
Dayton Art Institute, Ohio
1981 Wildenstein and Co., London
Pace Gallery, New York
Makler Gallery, Philadelphia
Galerie de France, Paris
1982 Harcus/Krakow Gallery, Boston
Richard Gray Gallery, Chicago

Louise Nevelson: *Mirror Shadow XXIV,* 1986

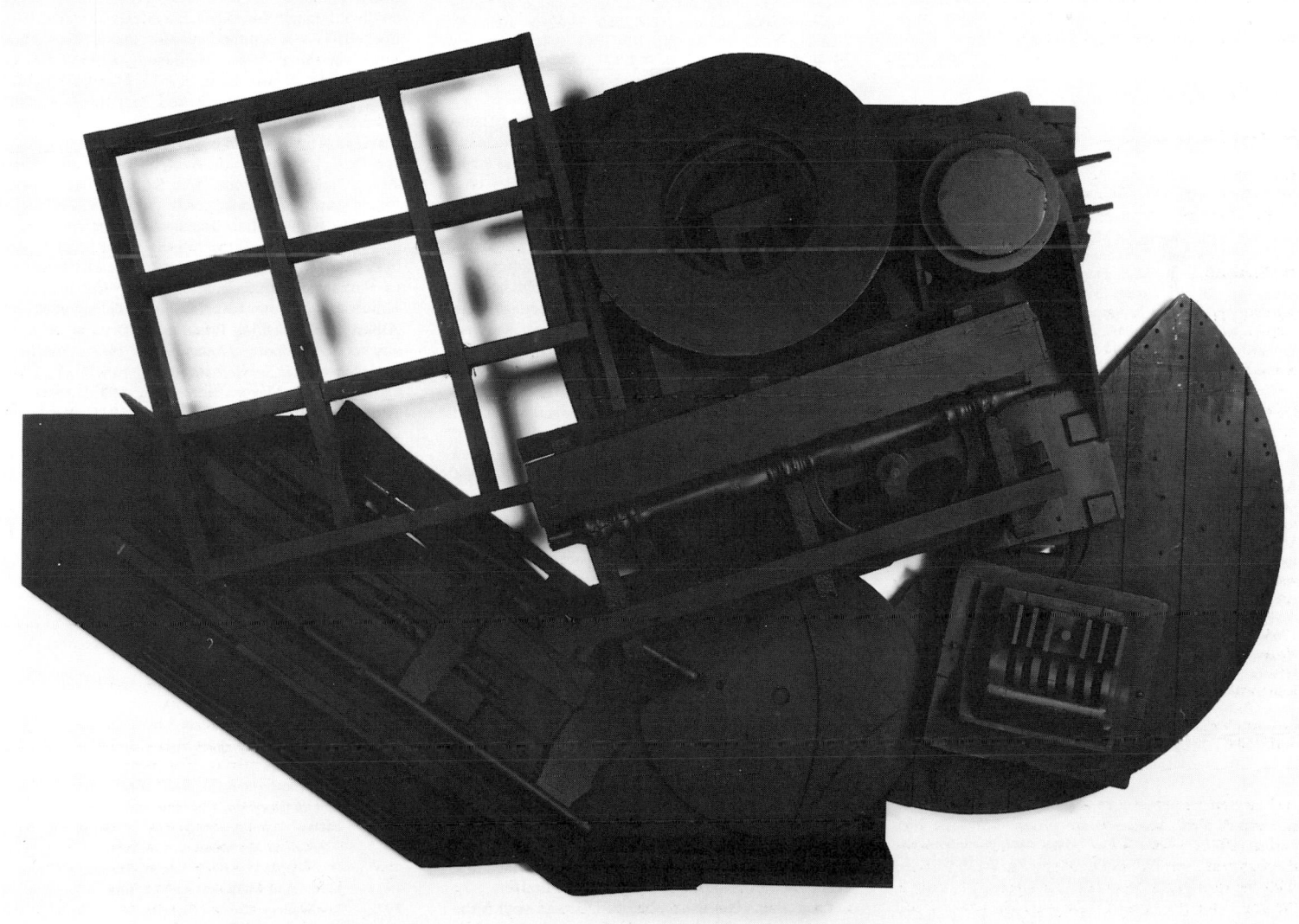

	Fay Gold Gallery, Atlanta, Georgia
	Wildenstein and Co., Tokyo
1983	Pace Gallery, New York
	Grey Art Gallery, New York University
1984	Barbara Krakow Gallery, Boston
	Grace Hokin Gallery, Miami
	Makler Gallery, Philadelphia
	Storm King Art Center, Mountainville, New York
	State University at Buffalo, New York
1985	Hokin Gallery, Miami
	Pace Gallery, New York
	Farnsworth Museum, Rockland, Maine
1986	Galerie Claude Bernard, Paris
	Galerie Alice Pauli, Lausanne, Switzerland
	Guggenheim Museum, New York
	Pace Gallery, New York
	Massachusetts Institute of Technology, Cambridge
1987	Whitney Museum, Fairfield County, Connecticut
1988	Centre Georges Pompidou, Paris

Selected Group Exhibitions:

1935	*Young Sculptors*, Brooklyn Museum, New York
1946	*Whitney Annual*, New York (and 1947, 1950, 1953, 1956, 1957, 1958, 1960, 1962, 1964, 1966, 1969)
1964	*Painting and Sculpture of a Decade*, Tate Gallery, London
1969	*Tamarind: Homage to Lithography*, Museum of Modern Art, New York
1973	*American Art at Mid-Century*, National Gallery of Art, Washington, D.C.
1976	*200 Years of American Sculpture*, Whitney Museum, New York
1979	*Vanguard American Sculpture: 1913-1939*, Rutgers University, New Brunswick, New Jersey
1981	*Sculpture and its Related Drawings*, Marisa del Re Gallery, New York
1985	*Transformations in Sculpture*, Guggenheim Museum, New York
1986	*Relief Sculpture*, Hirshhorn Museum, Washington, D.C.

Collections:

Guggenheim Museum, New York: Metropolitan Museum of Art, New York: Museum of Modern Art, New York; Whitney Museum, New York; Corcoran Gallery, Washington, D.C.; Hirshhorn Museum, Washington, D.C.; Art Institute of Chicago; Los Angeles County Museum of Art; Tate Gallery, London; Musée d'Art Moderne de la Ville de Paris; and numerous public installations including Federal Courthouse, Philadelphia; Pepsico World Headquarters, Purchase, New York; World Trade Center, New York; Madison Plaza, Chicago; Crocker Center, Los Angeles.

Publications:

By NEVELSON: books—*Nevelson: Facade—Twelve Original Serigraphs in Homage to Edith Sitwell*, with text by Edith Sitwell, New York 1966; *Dawns and Dusks*, edited by Diana MacKown, New York 1976; articles—"Queen of the Black Black" in "The Private Myth" by Philip Pearlstein in *Nevelson* by Colette Roberts, Paris 1964; statement in "Period Rooms: The 60's and 70's" in *Art in America* (New York), November/December 1970; "Do Your Work" in "Why Have There Been No Great Women Artist?" in *Artnews* (New York), January 1971; "Nevelson on Nevelson" in *Artnews* (New York), November 1972; recorded interview, with Arnold Glimeher, in *Archives of American Art*, New York 1973; interview, in *Art Talk: Conversations with 12 Women Artists* by Cindy Nemser, New York 1975; statement in "Is New York Still the Artistic Place to Be?" By Gerrit Henry in *Artnews* (New York), November 1976.

On NEVELSON: books—*Nature in Abstraction* by John I. H. Bauer, New York 1958; *16 Americans*, exhibition catalogue, (includes statement by Nevelson), by Dorothy C. Miller, New York 1959; *Louise Nevelson*, exhibition catalogue with text by Hilton Kramer, New York 1960; *Nevelson*, exhibition catalogue, New York 1961; *The Art of Assemblage*, exhibition catalogue, by William Seitz, New York 1961; *Nevelson*, exhibition catalogue, with text by Kenneth Sawyer and others, New York 1961; *Nevelson* by Colette

Roberts, Paris 1964; *Nevelson*, exhibition catalogue, New York 1964; *Louise Nevelson* by John Gordon, New York 1967; *Louise Nevelson: Prints and Drawings 1963-1966*, exhibition catalogue, by Una E. Johnson, New York 1967; *Louise Nevelson*, exhibition catalogue, Chicago 1968; *Nevelson: Recent Wood Sculpture*, exhibition catalogue, New York 1969; *Louise Nevelson*, exhibition catalogue, Paris 1969; *Louise Nevelson*, exhibition catalogue (includes statement by Nevelson), with text by Mary Hancock Buxton, Houston 1969; *Louise Nevelson, 1959-1961*, exhibiton catalogue, with text by Manfred Fath, Ludwigshafen, West Germany 1969; *Louise Nevelson: Sculptures 1959-1969*, exhibition catalogue, with text by R. Oxenaar, Otterlo, Netherlands 1969; *Louise Nevelson* by Arnold Glimcher (includes prologue by Nevelson), New York 1972; *Louise Nevelson* by Germano Celant, Milan 1973; *Nevelson*, exhibition catalogue, with text by Franco Russoli and Arnold B. Glimcher, Milan 1973; *Louise Nevelson*, exhibition catalogue, Stockholm 1973; *Nevelson: Wood Sculptures*, exhibition catalogue, by Martin Friedman, Minneapolis 1973; *Nevelson*, exhibition catalogue, with text by Joan V. Miller, Greenvale, New York 1974; *Nevelson: Skygates and Collages*, exhibition catalogue, New York 1974; *Louise Nevelson as Printmaker*, exhibition catalogue, with text by Kristin L. Spangenberg, Cincinnati 1974; *Nevelson: The Prints*, exhibition catalogue, by Gene Baro, New York 1974; *Art in Boxes* by Alex Mogelon and Norman Laliberte, New York 1974; *Louise Nevelson*, Exhibition catalogue (includes statement in Japanese by Nevelson), Tokyo 1975; *Nevelson: Dawn's Presence-Moon Garden + Two at Purchase: The Metal Sculptures*, exhibition catalogue, Purchase, New York 1977; *Nevelson: Recent Wood Sculptures*, exhibition catalogue, New York 1977; *Louise Nevelson: Recent Works*, exhibition catalogue, Chicago 1978; *Louise Nevelson*, exhibition catalogue, Rockland, Maine 1979; *Louise Nevelson: Atmospheres and Environments*, exhibition catalogue, with an introduction by Edward Albee, New York 1980; *Nevelson: Maquettes for Monumental Sculpture*, exhibition catalogue, (includes interview with Nevelson by Barbaralee Diamonstein), New York 1980; *Nevelson: Wood Sculpture and Collage*, exhibition catalogue, with text by David L. Shirey, New York 1980; *Louise Nevelson: The Fourth Dimension*, exhibition catalogue, with text by Laurie Wilson, Phoenix, Arizona 1980; *Louise Nevelson*, exhibition catalogue by Carter Ratcliff, New York 1981; *Nevelson's World* by Jean Lipman, London 1987.

From her beginnings the conditioning of the frame was to recur for Louise Nevelson. It doubled in its way with the proscenium arch, for she came to art in several aspects, and this breadth of approach to some extent was never relinquished; voice and drama seemed complementary to the three dimensions that claimed her finally. Working at the Art Students League gave her the rudiments, and Hans Hofmann in Munich in 1931 taught her something, though her European experience in acting and seeing collage were no less durable influences. The same year saw her start collecting African and Amerindian art. Her drawings then have a great volume of form, being concrete linear images. 1932 saw her working with Diego Rivera on a mural painting. Her sculptures had a solidity with affinities to Lipchitz and Cubism, though her first one-man show in 1941 revealed traces to Mayan and Near Eastern imagery. By 1944 she was into ceramics and modelling sculptures in terra cotta with more and more concern for the blocked-in masses.

For the next ten years Nevelson was working out her dynamic, now concerned almost exclusively with the assemblages that took the forms of compartments, one of the first being a more or less straight adaptation of a liquor crate tipped on end. By 1960 the concepts were reaching their peak of significant authority. Large low relief panels in boxwood, some more than eight feet tall, offered their black presences with mystery and an aura of religious solemnity not denied by the evidence of their source materials—cheap boxes with fitted ingredients of newel posts, chair legs and bevelled shelf edgings and, now and then, a rude hunk of unplaned wood. This compartmentalization of the relief wall emphasized the multiplicity of the contained detail so that on each shelf appeared what seemed the miniature furnishings of a chapel in an overcrowded baroque cathedral.

Then after 1963 the mood changed and with it the colour scheme. Gold replaced the unreflecting black; colour lent a Byzantine splendour to the iconic facades that took greater strength from simplicity and

economy of shape; now she had boxes made to order for her assemblages instead of relying on the chance of ready-made. In the 1960's the sculptures took a simpler abstract phase often with spheres of wood arranged in repeated groups across the squared divisions of the wooden wall. Other materials were introduced, mirrors and Plexiglass opening up the ribbed structure to the light. In those the strong paraphrase of music made itself apparent especially in the large vertical traceries, baroque in arched symphonic rhythms. In the 1970's the works are more individually conceived—flowers and trees in welded aluminium and Plexiglass are freestanding and unenclosed.

Architectural and musical in span, Nevelson's works have the ultimate universal quality of the image formed by emotion and character catching its unique idiom from time and place. Simultaneously primeval and sophisticated, they escape the dating of fashion by their triumph of atavistic magic over the irrelevance of material.

—G. S. Whittet

NEWMAN, Barnett.

American. Born in New York City, 29 January 1905. Educated at the National Hebrew School, New York, and DeWitt Clinton High School, New York; studied art, under Duncan Smith, John Sloan and William von Schlegell, at the Art Students League, New York, 1922, 1929; City College of New York and Educational Alliance, New York, 1923-27, B.A. 1927; studied botany, Brooklyn Botanical Gardens, New York, 1939-41; ornithology, Museum of Natural History, New York, 1941; ornithology, Cornell University, Ithaca, New York, 1941. Married Annalee Greenhouse in 1936. Worked in father's clothing manufacturing business, New York, 1927-29. Independent artist, associating with Clyfford Still, Jackson Pollock, Tony Smith, Adolph Gottlieb and Milton Avery, New York, from 1930. Substitute Art Instructor in various schools, New York, 1931-40; Co-Founder, with William Baziotes, Robert Motherwell and Mark Rothko, Subject of the Artist School, New York, 1948 (closed, 1949); Art Instructor, University of Saskatchewan, Saskatoon, 1959; Art Instructor, University of Pennsylvania, Philadelphia, 1962-63; Albert Dorne Visiting Professor of Drawing, University of Bridgeport, Connecticut, 1968. Published *America's Civil Service Magazine*, New York, 1936. Candidate for Mayor, New York, 1933. Associate, American Ornithologist's Union, 1941. Recipient: Creative Arts Medal in Painting, Brandeis University, Waltham, Massachusetts, 1969. Agent: Xavier Fourcade Inc., 36 East 75th Street, New York, New York 19921, U.S.A. *Died* (in New York) *4 July 1970.*

Individual Exhibitions:

1950	Betty Parsons Gallery, New York
1951	Betty Parsons Gallery, New York
1958	Bennington College, Vermont (retrospective)
1959	French and Company, New York
1962	*Barnett Newman and Willem de Kooning*, Allan Stone Gallery, New York
1965	Nicholas Wilder Gallery, Los Angeles
1966	*The Stations of the Cross*, Guggenheim Museum, New York
1969	M. Knoedler and Co., New York
	22 Lithographien, Kunstmuseum, Basle
1970	*Barnett Newman: January 29, 1905–July 4, 1970*, Pasadena Art Museum, California
	Das Graphische Werk, Kammerkunsthalle, Berne
1971	Museum of Modern Art, New York
1972	Tate Gallery, London (travelled to the Stedelijk Museum, Amsterdam, and the Galeries Nationales du Grand Palais, Paris)
1979	Baltimore Museum of Art, Maryland

1981 Kunstmuseum, Basle
Museum Ludwig, Cologne
Centre Georges Pompidou, Paris
1982 Dia Art Foundation, New York
1983 Barnett Newman Foundation, New York

Selected Group Exhibitions:

1957 *American Paintings 1945–1957,* Minneapolis Institute of Arts
1958 *The New American Painting,* Kunsthalle, Basle (toured Europe and the United States)
1959 *Documenta 2,* Kassel, West Germany
1964 *'54–'64: Painting and Sculpture of a Decade,* Tate Gallery, London
1967 *Kompas 3,* Van Abbemuseum, Eindhoven, Netherlands (travelled to the Kunstverein, Frankfurt)
1968 *Dada, Surrealism and Their Heritage,* Museum of Modern Art, New York (travelled to Los Angeles and Chicago)
1969 *Prints by 4 New York Painters,* Metropolitan Museum of Art, New York
1976 *20th Century American Drawing: 3 Avant-Garde Generations,* Guggenheim Museum, New York
America As Art, National Collection of Fine Arts, Smithsonian Institution, Washington, D.C.
1978 *The Subject of the Artist,* National Gallery of Art, Washington, D.C.

Collections:

Museum of Modern Art, New York; Longview Foundation, New York; Walker Art Center, Minneapolis; Tate Gallery, London; Centre Georges Pompidou, Paris; Kunstmuseum, Basel; Kunsthalle, Basel; Moderna Museet, Stockholm, Museum Folkwang, Essen.

Publications:

By NEWMAN: books—*On the Need for Political Action by Men of Culture,* unpublished manifesto, New York 1933; *Can We Draw,* exhibition catalogue, New York 1938; *American Modern Artists,* exhibition catalogue, New York 1943; *Adolph Gottlieb,* exhibition catalogue, New York 1944; *Pre-Columbian Stone Sculpture,* exhibition catalogue, New York 1944; *Northwest Coast Indian Painting,* exhibition catalogue, New York 1946; *The Ideographic Picture,* exhibition catalogue, New York 1947; *Stamos,* exhibition catalogue, New York 1947; *Herbert Ferber,* exhibitionc catalogue, New York 1947; *Amlash Sculpture from Iran,* exhibition catalogue, New York 1963; *18 Cantos 1963–64,* West Islip, New York 1964; articles—"The Answer" in *America's Civil Service Magazine* (New York), January 1936; "Globalism Pops into View" in the *New York Times* 13 June 1943; "Escultura Pre-Colombina en Piedra" in *La Revista Belga,* August 1944; "Sobre el Arte Moderno: Examen y Ratificacion" in *La Revista Belga,* November 1944; "La Pintura de Tamayo y Gottlieb" in *La Revista Belga,* April 1945; "Teresa Zarnower" in *Art of This Century* (New York), April 1946; "Las Formas Artisticas del Pacifico" in *Ambos Mundos,* June 1946, reprinted in English as "Art of the South Seas" in *Studio International* (London), February 1970; "The First Man Was an Artist" in *Tiger's Eye* (New York), October 1947; "Contemporaneousness" in *Tiger's Eye* (New York), December 1947; "The Object and the Image" in *Tiger's Eye* (New York) March 1948; "The Sublime Is Now" in *Tiger's Eye* (New York), December 1948; "To Be or Not: 6 Opinions on Trigant Burrow's 'The Neurosis of Man' " in *Tiger's Eye* (New York), October 1949; "Letter to the Editor" in *Art Digest* (New York), 15 March 1950; "Studio 35" in *Modern Artists in America,* edited by Robert Motherwell and Ad Reinhardt, New York 1952; "Letter to the Editor" in *Art Digest* (New York), 15 February 1954; "Critic or Commissar," letter to the editor, in the *New Republic* (New York) 28 October 1957; "Letter to the Editor" in *Artnews* (New York), May 1961; "Letter to the Editor" in *Artnews* (New York), September 1961; "Frontiers of Space," interview, with Dorothy Gees Seckler, in *Art in America* (New York), Summer 1962; "Embattled Lamb," book review, in *Artnews* (New York), September 1962; "The New York School Question," inverview, with Neil A. Levine, in *Artnews* (New York), September 1965; statement in *United States of America,* exhibition catalogue, Sao Paulo 1965; "Letter to the Editor" in *Artnews* (New York), November 1965; "The Case for 'Exporting' National Avant-Garde Art," interview, with Andrew Hudson, in the *Washington Post,* 27 March 1966; "The 14 Stations of the Cross" in *Artnews* (New York), May 1966; "A Conversation: Barnett Newman and Thomas B. Hess," unpublished interview, typescript in the *Museum of Modern Art,* New York, 1 May 1966; "The Museum World" in *Arts Yearbook 9,* New York 1967; "Jackson Pollock: An Artists Symposium" in *Artnews* (New York), April 1967; "Letter to the Editor" in *Art Internationals* (Lugano, Switzerland), November 1967; "Letter to the Editor" in *Art International* (Lugano, Switzerland), January 1968; introduction to *Memoirs of a Revolutionist* by Peter Kropotkin, New York 1968; "Letter to the Editor" in *Artnews* (New York), February 1968; "Letter to the Editor" in *Artforum* (New York), March 1968; "For Impassioned Criticism" and "Letter to the Editor" in *Artnews* (New York), Summer 1968; "Who's Afraid of Red, Yellow and Blue" in *Art Now: New York* (New York), March 1969; "Chartres and Jericho" in *Artnews* (New York), April 1969, reprinted in *Studio International* (London), February 1970; "In Front of the Real Thing" in *Artnews* (New York), January 1970; films—*Barnett Newman, American Painter,* interview, by Frank O'Hara on *Art New York* series, WNDT-TV, Newark, New Jersey, 8 December 1964, in Television Archive of the Arts, Museum of Modern Art, New York; *Barnett Newman on U.S.A. Artists* series, National Educational Television, 12 July 1966, in Television Archive of the Arts, Museum of Modern Art, New York; interview, in *Painters Painting New York,* directed by Emile de Antonio, New York, 4 April 1970.

On NEWMAN: books—*Barnett Newman and Willem de Kooning,* exhibition catalogue, with text by Allan Stone, New York 1962; *Barnett Newman: The Stations of the Cross,* exhibition catalogue (includes statement by Newman), New York 1966; *Barnett Newman: 22 Lithographien,* exhibition catalogue, by Carlo Huber, Basle 1969; *Barnett Newman* by Thomas B. Hess, New York 1969; *Prints by 4 New York Painters,* exhibition catalogue, New York 1969; *Barnett Newman: January 29, 1905–July 4, 1970,* exhibition catalogue, Pasadena, California 1970; *Barnett Newman: Das Graphische Werk,* exhibition catalogue, by Berne 1970; *Barnett Newman,* exhibition catalogue, by Thomas B. Hess, New York 1971; *Who's Afraid of Red, Yellow and Blue III* by Max Imdahl, Stuttgart 1971; *Broken Obelisk and Other Sculptures* by Harold Rosenberg, Seattle and London 1971; *Barnett Newman,* exhibition catalogue, by Thomas B. Hess, London, Amsterdam and Paris 1972; *Barnett Newman* by Harold Rosenberg, New York 1978; *Barnett Newman: The Complete Drawings,* Baltimore 1979; *Barnett Newman,* exhibition catalogue with essays by Hugh M. Davies and Riva Castleman, New York 1983.

In his life and work Barnett Newman personifies the dichotomy of the artist in society—how to be himself and, by denying association with external reality and previous artifacts, how to achieve a valid communication with the general public. Over many years—from the 1940's, when New York was finding itself as the place for a painter to be—Newman's polemical stimulus was not only the basis of his pedagogical programme but was also his vital reason for being.

How to dematerialize the subject was his first objective, and in retrospect it can be seen that the crisis developed in 1948 when he painted "Onement I" as a field of cadmium red bisected vertically by a stripe of orange. It symbolized the Holy Grail that he and his fellow knights had been questing: the painting became its own justification, and by the absence of discernible allusions, conventional or otherwise, it established its own terms. Yet even in his search for the perfect immaculate conception, Newman could not forswear the spiritual and metaphorical interpretation of the coloured canvas. The stripe down the centre of the painting was more than the division of the field: it epitomised the separation of life from darkness in God's creation.

Colour had the supreme role for Newman. Red especially had its own grandeur and complemented by another colour or by another shade produced the most symphonic passages. From 1940 onwards scale was to exert a dominant power in the painting, though not necessarily by extent. To some degree Newman overcame the problems of context. His "Cathedra" (1951) by its immensity—about 8 feet by 18 feet—became object and setting at the same time.

Newman was continuing until the moment of his premature death to conceive different views from the road he was travelling. For, although he did not envisage ever arriving at a conclusive end, he was happy to have found the route, and following it gave him stimulation and satisfaction. A series of triangular paintings was one important stage of the journey. Another was the sculpture "Broken Obelisk" in which a steel pyramid supports a truncated and inverted obelisk apex to apex in dramatic suspense.

If New York was a School, Newman was a key member as pupil, master and leader. He set a standard of self-confidence: he believed in the indestructibility of the artist's destiny as maker of material spirit and revealer of mysteries. By the catharsis of concentrated means in an expanded area, and above all by the enveloping volume of colour flooding the mind, Newman conceived his art as experience in a public environmental existence. Painting in his hands at last moved away from the wall.

—G. S. Whittet

NICHOLSON, Ben.

British. Born in Denham, Buckinghamshire, 10 April 1894; son of the painter Sir William Nicholson. Educated in London primary schools; studied at the Slade School of Fine Art, London, 1910–11; studied French in Tours, 1911–12; studied Italian in Milan, 1912–13. Married the painter Winifred Dacre in 1920; children: two sons and daughter; married the sculptress Barbara Hepworth in 1934; children: triplets, married the journalist-photographer Felicitas Vogler in 1957. Painter: lived in Pasadena, California for health reasons, 1917–18; returned to England and lived in Cumbria and London, 1920–31; stayed winters in Castagnola, Switzerland, 1920–24; visited Paris frequently from 1920; Member and President, Seven and Five Society, London, 1925–36; visited Cornwall, with Christopher Wood, 1928; stayed summer in Norfolk, with Barbara Hepworth, Henry Moore and Ivan Hitchens, 1931; shared studio in Hampstead, London with Hepworth, 1932–39; associated with Hampstead artists, Henry Moore, Naum Gabo and others; visited France, with Hepworth, 1932–33. Member, Abstraction-Creation group, Paris, and Unit One, London, 1933–35; Editor, with the architect J. L. Martin and Naum Gabo, *Circle: International Survey of Constructivist Art,* London, 1937; moved to Cornwall, 1939; lived in Carbis Bay, 1939–43, in St. Ives, 1943–58; Founder-Member, Penwith Society of Arts, St. Ives, 1949; visited Italy and Greece frequently from 1950; worked on mural commission, Regatta Restaurant, *Festival of Britain,* London, 1951; lived near Ascona, Switzerland, 1958–72; worked on concrete relief commission for *Documenta 3,* Kassel, West Germany, 1964; returned to England: lived in Cambridge, 1972; moved to Hampstead, London, 1975. Recipient: First Prize for Painting, *Pittsburgh International,* 1952; Belgian Critics Prize, 1954; Ulysses Award, *Biennale,* Venice, 1954; Governor of Tokyo Award, *International Exhibition,* Tokyo, 1955; Grand Prix, *International Bianco e Nero Exhibition,* Lugano, Switzerland, 1955; Grand Prix, *International Exhibition,* Lugano, 1956; Guggenheim International Painting Prize, 1956; International Prize for Painting, *Bienal,* Sao Paulo, 1957; Rembrandt Prize, 1974. Order of Merit, 1968. *Died* (in London) *6 February 1982.*

Individual Exhibitions:

1923 Patterson's Gallery, London (with Winifred Nicholson)
1924 Adelphi Gallery, London
1927 Beaux Arts Gallery, London (with W. Staite Murray and Christopher Wood)
1929 Alex Reid and Lefevre Gallery, London (with W. Staite Murray and Winifred Nicholson)
1930 Alex Reid and Lefevre Gallery, London
Galerie Georges Bernheim, Paris (with Christopher Wood)

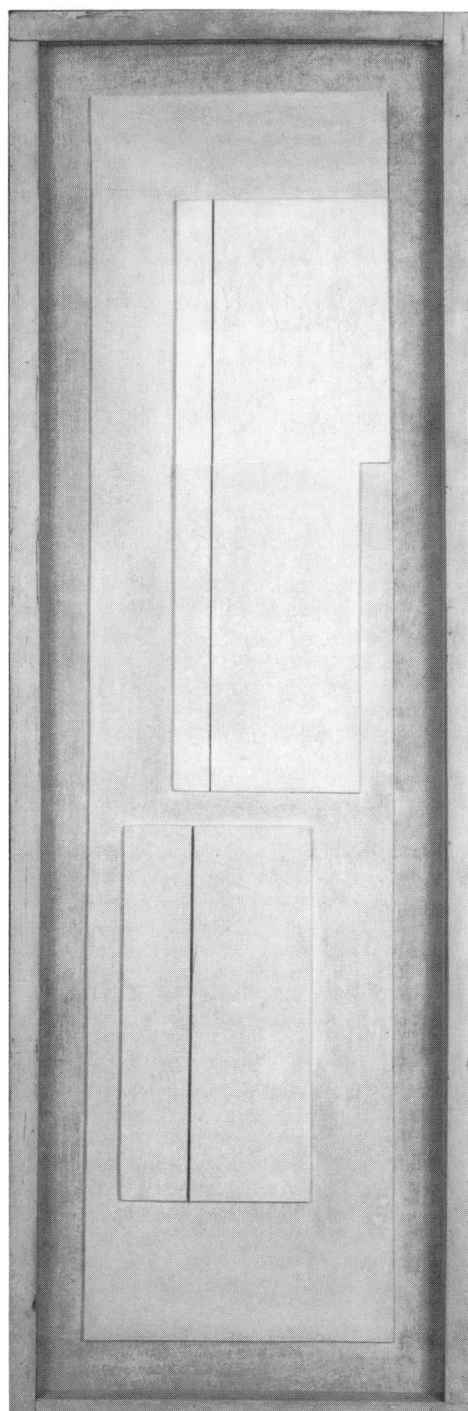

Ben Nicholson: *February 1956*, **1956** Courtesy Guggenheim Museum, New York

1931	Bloomsbury Gallery, London (with W. Staite Murray and Barbara Hepworth)
1932	Alex Reid and Lefevre Gallery, London
	Tooth Gallery, London (with Barbara Hepworth)
1933	Alex Reid and Lefevre Gallery, London (with Barbara Hepworth)
	Alex Reid and Lefevre Gallery, London
1935	Alex Reid and Lefevre Gallery, London
1937	Alex Reid and Lefevre Gallery, London
1939	Alex Reid and Lefevre Gallery, London
1944	Leeds City Art Gallery
1945	Alex Reid and Lefevre Gallery, London
1946	Alex Reid and Lefevre Gallery, London (with Graham Sutherland)
1947	Alex Reid and Lefevre Gallery, London
1948	Alex Reid and Lefevre Gallery, London
1949	Framestop, Boston
	Durlacher Gallery, New York
1950	Penwith Society of Arts, St. Ives, Cornwall (with Barbara Hepworth and Victor Pasmore)

	Alex Reid and Lefevre Gallery, London
1951	Swetzoff Gallery, Boston
	Durlacher Gallery, New York
	Phillips Gallery, Washington, D.C.
1952	Alex Reid and Lefevre Gallery, London
	Durlacher Gallery, New York
1954	*Biennale,* Venice (with Francis Bacon and Lucian Freud)
	Galerie Apollo, Brussels
	Alex Reid and Lefevre Gallery, London
	Stedelijk Museum, Amsterdam (travelled to the Musée National d'Art Moderne, Paris, and the Kunsthaus, Zurich, 1954–55)
1955	Durlacher Gallery, New York
	Palais des Beaux-Arts, Brussels
	Samlaren Gallery, Stockholm
	Ben Nicholson: A Retrospective Exhibition, Tate Gallery, London
	Gimpel, Fils, London
1956	Galerie de France, Paris
1957	Gimpel Fils, London
	Bienal, Sao Paulo (travelled to Museo Nacional del Bellas Artes, Buenos Aires)
1959	Gimpel Fils, London
	Kestner Gesellschaft, Hannover (toured Germany)
	British Council Gallery, London
	Galerie Charles Lienhard, Zurich
	Laing Art Gallery, Newcastle upon Tyne
	Galerie Schmela, Dusseldorf
1960	Galerie Charles Lienhard, Zurich
	Galleria Lorenzelli, Milan
1961	André Emmerich Gallery, New York
	Kunsthalle, Berne
1962	Galerie Charles Lienhard, Zurich
	Galerie der Speigel, Cologne
1963	Gimpel Fils, London
	Kunstmuseum, St. Gallen, Switzerland
	Marlborough Fine Art, London
1964	Dallas Museum of Fine Arts
	Richard Gray Gallery, Chicago
	Crane Kalman Gallery, London
1965	Marlborough-Gerson Gallery, New York
1966	Galerie Gimpel-Hanover, Zurich
1967	Marlborough Fine Art, London
	Galleria Antonelli, Milan
	Kestner-Gesellschaft, Hannover (toured Germany)
	Galleria La Bussola, Turin (travelled to the Galleria Marlborough, Rome)
1968	Galerie Beyeler, Basle
	Marlborough New London Gallery
	Crane Kalman Gallery, London
1969	Tate Gallery, London (retrospective)
	Tokyo Gallery
1970	Marlborough Fine Art, London
1971	Marlborough Fine Art, London (travelled to the Marlborough Galerie, Zurich, and Marlborough Galleria d'Arte, Rome, 1971–72)
1973	Gimpel Fils, London
	Galerie Beyeler, Basle
	Galleria Castelnuovo, Ascona, Switzerland
1974	*Works on Paper,* André Emmerich Gallery, New York
	Crane Kalman Gallery, London
	Tate Gallery, London
	Galleria Narcisso, Turin
	Galerie Georges Moos, Geneva
	Fischer Fine Art, London
	Redfern Gallery, London
1975	Andé Emmerich Gallery, New York
	Galerie André Emmerich, Zurich
	Victoria and Albert Museum, London
1976	Tate Gallery, London
	Waddington Galleries, London
	Arts Club of Chicago
	Galerie Yngvanzo, Madrid
1978	Galerie André Emmerich, Zurich (with Anthony Caro)
	Ben Nicholson: 50 Years of His Art, Albright-Knox Art Gallery, Buffalo (travelled to the Hirshhorn Museum and Sculpture Garden, Washington, D.C., and the Brooklyn Museum, New York, 1978–79)
1980	Waddington Galleries, London
1982	Waddington Galleries, London

1983	Kettles Yard Gallery, Cambridge (travelled to Bradford, Canterbury and Plymouth)
	Waddington Gallery, London
1984	Kunsthalle, Mannheim, West Germany
1985	Gallery Kasahara, Osaka, Japan
1987	Fundacion Juan March, Madrid

Selected Group Exhibitions:

1931	*Recent Developments in British Painting,* Arthur Tooth and Sons, London
1935	*These, Antithese, Synthese,* Kunsthalle, Lucerne
1936	*Cubism and Abstract Art,* Museum of Modern Art, New York
1938	*Tentoonstelling Abstracte Kunst,* Stedelijk Museum, Amsterdam
1939	*World's Fair,* New York (toured the United States and Canada)
1946	*Unesco International Exhibition,* Musée National d'Art Moderne, Paris
1952	*Pittsburgh International,* Carnegie Institute, Pittsburgh
1962	*British Art Today,* San Francisco Museum of Art (travelled to the Dallas Museum for Contemporary Arts, and the Santa Barbara Museum of Art, California)
1973	*Henry Moore to Gilbert and George,* Palais des Beaux-Arts, Brussels
1977	*Aspekte Konstruktiven Kunst,* Kunsthaus, Zurich

Collections:

Tate Gallery, London; Arts Council of Great Britain, London; Scottish National Gallery of Modern Art, Edinburgh; Nationalgalerie, West Berlin; Stedelijk Van Abbemuseum, Eindhoven, Netherlands, Kunsthaus, Zurich; Art Gallery of Ontario, Toronto; Museum of Modern Art, New York; Guggenheim Museum, New York; Los Angeles County Museum of Art.

Publications:

By NICHOLSON: articles—"The Aim of the Modern Artist" in *The Studio* (London), December 1932; "The Modern Movement in English Architecture, Painting and Sculpture," edited by Herbert Read, in *Unit One,* London 1934; "Quotations" in *Circle: International Survey of Constructive Art,* edited by Ben Nicholson, J. L. Martin and Naum Gabo, London 1937; "Notes on Abstract Art" in *Horizon* (London), October 1941, reprinted in *Art of This Century,* New York 1942, and in *Ben Nicholson: Paintings, Reliefs and Drawings,* London 1948, "Alfred Wallis," with Sven Berlin, in *Horizon* (London), January 1943, reprinted in *A Retrospective Exhibition of Paintings by Alfred Wallis,* exhibition catalogue, Bournemouth, Hampshire 1950, and in *Alfred Wallis,* exhibition catalogue, London 1968; "Further Notes on Abstract Art" in *Ben Nicholson: Painting, Reliefs and Drawings,* London 1948; "Defending Modern Artists" in the *Daily Mail* (London), 7 August 1951; "Notes" in *Ben Nicholson: A Retrospective Exhibition,* exhibition catalogue, London 1955; statements in *A Review of British Abstract Art in 1956,* London 1957; "Architecture and the Artist" in the *Architects Journal* (London), January 1958; "Mr. Ben Nicholson Answers Some Questions about His Work and Views" in *The Times* (London), 12 November 1959; "More or Less about Abstract Art: A Reply to Victor Pasmore" in *London Magazine,* July 1961; statement in *Ben Nicholson: Art in Progress* by David K. Baxandall, London 1962; "The Life and Opinions of an English Modern," interview with Vera and John Russell, in the *Sunday Times* (London), 23 April 1963; "Mondrian in London" in *Studio International* (London), December 1966; statements in *Ben Nicholson,* exhibition catalogue, Basle 1968; "Tribute to Herbert Read" in *Studio International* (London), January 1969, reprinted in *Herbert Read: A Memorial Symposium,* edited by Robin Skelton, London 1970; "Extracts from Letters" in *Ben Nicholson: Studio International: Special Edition,* London 1969; statements in *Ben Nicholson: Works on Paper,* exhibition catalogue, New York 1974.

On NICHOLSON: books—*Ben Nicholson: Paintings, Reliefs, Drawings,* edited by Herbert Read, London 1948; *Ben Nicholson* by John Summerson, London 1948; *Contemporary Painters—Ben Nicholson* by James Thrall Soby, New York 1949; *Ben Nicholson,* 2 volumes, by Herbert Read: Volume 1, *Works from 1911–1947,* London 1955, Volume II, *Works since 1947*, London 1956; *Masters of British Painting 1800–1950* by Andrew C. Ritchie, New York 1956; *Ben Nicholson: The Meaning of His Art* by J. P. Hodin, London 1957; *Ben Nicholson* by Ronald Alley, London 1962; *Ben Nicholson: Art in Progress* by David K. Baxandall, London 1962; *Ben Nicholson: Paintings* by Herbert Read, London 1962; *Ben Nicholson: Architectural Suite* by Herbert Read, London 1966; *Ben Nicholson: Drawings, Paintings and Reliefs 1911–1968* by John Russell, London 1969; *Ben Nicholson*, exhibition catalogue, by Norman Reid and Charles Harrison, London 1969; *Ben Nicholson: Paintings, Reliefs, and Drawings*, exhibition catalogue, London 1974; *Ben Nicholson: 50 Years of His Art*, exhibition catalogue, by Steven A. Nash, Buffalo, New York 1978 (includes bibliography); *Ben Nicholson: The Years of Experiment 1919–39*, exhibition catalogue with introduction by Jeremy Lewison, London 1983; *Ben Nicholson*, exhibition catalogue with essay by Jeremy Lewison, Madrid 1987.

In 20th century art Ben Nicholson ranks as a phenomenon since he was as much a two-dimensional painter as a sculptor in panels of low relief. He solved to his own satisfaction, at different periods of his career, the problems of rendering retinal sensations in space, often with no more assistance than the geometrical perspectives of line on one plane. What seems at first glance to present a conflict of naturalistic scenes and seemingly non-objective shapes is often no more than the telling juxtaposition of form in mass and in outline. Regarded as the leading British abstract artist between the wars, he followed the logic of his convictions, paradoxically embodying a romantic attitude towards the classic.

He was a late convert to Constructivism. He despised art schools and spent only a term or two at the most at the Slade in 1911 before travelling to Italy, the United States and France. In Paris he absorbed the ideas of abstraction after meeting Mondrian who had a great influence. But even before that meeting he had produced paintings some incorporating collage having their direct links with Cubism of Gris and the Purism of Ozenfant.

Articulate about his aims and the functions of art in general, Nicholson believed in the validity of any medium whether canvas and oil paint or rock face and chisel; he was co-editor with J. L. Martin and Naum Gabo of the review *Circle* in 1937 that set out the views of the movement towards an abstract constructivism in England. His White Reliefs of the 1930's imposed their authority by their variations of the circle and the rectangle raised and sunk in a shadow-casting and subtle refinement distinctive in its aggressive delicacy.

1939 and the move to Cornwall where he was to live for the next 20 years were considerable factors affecting his art. Here, beside the wide bay of St. Ives and the low curving skyline, details of the panorama came to be part of the vision he transcribed on paper and canvas. The concern with purity continued, but it was now shared with the presence of symbols of reality in nature. The silhouettes, frequently in line alone, of full-bosomed objects such as amphoras, jugs and goblets came to be balanced with sensuous and balanced tones of arbitrary colour composing paintings of remarkable if reticent presence.

His move to Switzerland meant for Nicholson continuity and also another direction of intensely personal importance. His reliefs took on a greater affinity with rock faces and the textured patinas of wood; they developed a flexibility and a tense equilibrium between recessed shapes and their non-reflective colour and surfaces. This opening of new and stimulating achievements at a late stage marked Nicholson as a unique artist in austere discipline and pure refinement of coloured form.

—G. S. Whittet

NIGRO, Mario.

Italian. Born in Pistoia, 28 June 1917. Studied music in Arezzo, 1923–29; studied chemistry and mineralogy at the University of Pisa, 1936–45; self-taught in art. Married Violette Talentoni in 1948 (divorced, 1976); son: Gianni. Painter: first Abstract and Cubist works, Livorno, Italy, 1945; worked as chemist in Department of Pharmacy, Livorno Hospital, 1945–58; Member, Movimento Arte Concreta, Milan, 1949; settled in Milan, 1955; visited Paris, 1956 and 1957. Address: via Brera 23, 20121 Milan, Italy.

Individual Exhibitions:

1949	Libreria Salto, Milan
1951	Libreria Salto, Milan
	Galleria La Vigna Nuova, Florence
1952	Galleria Giraldi, Livorno
	Galleria Numero, Florence
	Le Quattro Pipe, Turin
1953	Studio B 24, Milan
1954	Casa della Cultura, Livorno
1955	Galleria Numero, Florence
1959	Galerie Kasper, Lausanne, Switzerland
	Salone Annunciata, Milan
	Galleria del Cavallino, Venice
1962	Galleria Numero, Milan
1965	Casa della Cultura, Livorno, Italy
1966	Galleria Rizzato-Witworia, Milan
1967	Galleria La Polena, Genoa
	Galerie Suzanne Bollag, Zurich
	Galleria Notizie, Turin
1968	*Biennale*, Venice
1970	Galleria dell'Ariete, Milan
1971	Galleria Toselli, Milan
	Galleria Sincron, Brescia, Italy
	Zentrum für Aktuelle Kunst, Aachen, West Germany
	Galleria del Mille, Bergamo
1972	Galerie Loehr, Frankfurt
	Galleria La Polena, Genoa
	Galleria Toselli, Milan
	Galleria Peccolo, Livorno
	Galerie M, Bochum, West Germany
1973	Galleria La Cappellatta, Osnago, Italy
	Studio Barozzi, Venice
	Studio Maddalena Carioni, Milan
1974	Multicentre, Milan
	Galleria Il Sole, Bolzano, Italy
	Galleria La Nuova Citta, Brescia, Italy
	Galleria Marlborough d'Arte, Rome
	Galleria Peccolo, Livorno
1975	Galleria dell'Ariete, Milan
	Galleria La Polena, Genoa
1977	Galleria Seno, Milan
	Galleria Lorenzelli, Milan
1978	Galleria Editalia, Rome
	Galleria Milano, Milan
	Galleria Martano, Turin
1979	Studio Grossetti, Milan
	Padiglione d'Arte Contemporanea, Milan
	Galleria Plurima, Udine, Italy
1981	Studio d'Arte Contemporanea Dabbeni, Lugano, Switzerland
1982	Studio Grossetti, Milan
1983	Galerie Loehr, Frankfurt
	Studio Grossetti, Milan
1984	Galerie Teufel, Cologne
1985	Galleria Il Sole, Bolzano, Italy
	Galleria Plurima, Udine, Italy
1986	Galleria L'Isola, Rome

Selected Group Exhibitions:

1951	*Arte Astratta in Italia*, Galleria Nazionale d'Arte Moderna, Rome (toured Europe)
1952	*Gruppo Arte Concreta di Milano*, Kulturinstitut, Vienna (toured Austria and South America)

Mario Nigro: *Perche mi hai lasciato?*, 1974

1959	*Grafik der Gegenwart*, Salzburg
1964	*Biennale*, Venice (and 1982)
1971	*Konkrete Kunst*, Westfälischer Kunstverein, Münster, West Germany
1972	*The Non-Objective World*, Annely Juda Fine Art, London
1975	*Italian Painting Today*, Galerie Espace, Montreal (travelled to the Galerie Daniel Templon, Paris)
1981	*Arte e Critica*, Galleria Nazionale d'Arte Moderna, Rome
1982	*Rassegna del Movimento Arte Concreta*, Rieti, Italy
1985	*De Maria/Merz/Nigro/Paladino*, Galleria Toselli, Milan

Collections:

Pinacoteca, Livorno; Galleria Nazionale d'Arte Moderna, Rome; Galleria Civica d'Arte Moderna, Turin; Museu d'Arte Moderna, Sao Paulo; Museu d'Arte Moderna, Rio de Janeiro.

Publications:

By NIGRO: books—*Mario Nigro*, with Vanni Schweiller, Milan 1968; *Lettera di un Raro Amore*, exhibition catalogue, Genoa 1972; article—"Non c'e pui la Figa" in *Domus* (Milan), April 1979).

On NIGRO: books—*Arte Astratta e Concreta*, exhibition catalogue, by Carlo Giulio Argan and Gillo Dorfles, Rome 1951; *Alte und Moderne Kunst* by Walter Zettl, Vienna 1964; *Mario Nigro*, exhibition catalogue with text by Tommaso Trini, Rome 1986.

*

From a superficial point of view Mario Nigro's work could be defined as being post-Constructivist; however, it possibly represents the most successful example of the "bridge" between that experience and the very recent analytical researches interpreting the latter in the widest sense.

In fact, throughout his whole career, there is cohesion: a subtle but robust thread links the vigorous works of the early 1950's to the ultimate rarefied present-day works: from "Ritmi" in 1950-51, to "Spazi Totali," of 1953-60, to the environmental researches of the 1960's, up until "Tempo Totale" of the late 1960's and the "Metafisica di Colore," Nigro focused his attention on the unveiling of the ultimate elements of art, those that go beyond sign, colour, rhythm, to unite the concepts of space and time. It is a progressive ratification of signs and colour almost to the point of having exhausted and proved the potential of particular forms and particular lines. Today, Nigro tends to go for an absolute and perfect idea that will coincide with the elimination of every action and every sign in favor of the contemplation of the clear surface, uncut and untouchable.

However, such a formal progression does not simply imply a nihilist conceptualization of creating art, an interest in the starting point of the work of art rather than an attempt to comprehend the totality—of space, time—in the fragment of the surfaces without renouncing for this a theme of tenuous poetry, of a semi-metaphysical mystery. There are profound suggestions that slowly emerge from his surfaces, that grip the eye with the sensation of infinite whiteness of the canvas, that involve even the mythical and elusive titles that the artist has given his works, particularly in the last few years.

Nigro's geometry, while rising to the peak of concept, also involves all those psychological and cultural values that modify the initially assumed traditional rationale. In 1979 the artist wrote: "My post-rationalism is born in this dimension: it does not consist of being less rigorous geometrically because then one would automatically arrive at and therefore bring about the imperfect and informal in romantic decadence, also the rigidity is vital—but the external vision is more complicated, thus one can have the sense of an 'ambiguous' geometry.

—Marco Meneguzzo

NIIZUMA, Minoru.

Japanese. Born in Tokyo, Japan, 29 September 1930; moved to New York, 1959. Studied, under Tsuruzo Ishii, at the National University of Arts, Tokyo, 1952-55, B.F.A. 1955. Served in the Japanese Imperial Army, 1945. Married; children: Ta and Andre. Art Therapist, New York, since 1974. Instructor, Brooklyn Museum Art School, New York, 1964-70; Assistant Professor, Columbia University, New York, 1972-84. Organized First New York Sculpture Symposium, 1971. Trustee of International Graduate University, Lugano, Switzerland, since 1974; Director, Stone Institute, New York, since 1983. Member, and Permanent Juror since 1957, Modern Art Association of Japan; Member, Sculptors Guild. Recipient: Modern Art Association Award, Japan, 1955, 1956. Agent: Gimpel and Weitzenhoffer Gallery, 1040 Madison Avenue, New York, New York 10021. Address: 463 West Street, New York, New York 10014, U.S.A.

Individual Exhibitions:

1955	Takemiya Gallery, Tokyo
1956	Fugetsudo Gallery, Tokyo
1957	Fugetsudo Gallery, Tokyo
1958	Sato Gallery, Tokyo
1966	Howard Wise Gallery, New York
1967	Flair Gallery, Cincinnati
1968	Howard Wise Gallery, New York
	Flair Gallery, Cincinnati
1971	Westbeth Gallery, New York
	Rockefeller University, New York
1972	Gimpel and Weitzenhoffer Gallery, New York
1973	Galerie Gimpel and Hanover, Zurich
	Gimpel and Weitzenhoffer Gallery, New York
1974	Gimpel and Weitzenhoffer Gallery, New York
1976	Centre for International Arts, New York
	Seibu Museum of Art, Tokyo
1977	Umeda Museum of Modern Art, Osaka, Japan
	Gimpel and Weitzenhoffer Gallery, New York
1978	Gimpel and Weitzenhoffer Gallery, New York
1983	Mekler Gallery, Los Angeles

Selected Group Exhibitions:

1965	*The New Japanese Paintings and Sculptures*, Museum of Modern Art, New York
	Howard Wise Gallery, New York (and annually until 1971)
	Exhibition of Japanese Artists Abroad: Europe and America, National Museum of Modern Art, Tokyo
1966	*Whitney Biennial*, Whitney Museum, New York (and 1968)
1967	*Carnegie International*, Pittsburgh
1969	*2nd Flint Invitational*, Flint Institute of Art, Michigan (and annually, 1972-75)
1972	Gimpel and Weitzenhoffer Gallery, New York (and annually until 1975)
1975	*Biennale of Middleheim*, Antwerp
	10 Artists: A Selection of Contemporary Japanese Art, Center for International Arts, New York

Collections:

National Museum of Modern Art, Tokyo; National Museum of Modern Art, Kyoto; Museum of Modern Art, New York; Guggenheim Museum, New York; Rockefeller University, New York; Chase Manhattan Bank, New York; Albright-Knox Art Gallery, Buffalo, New York; Smith College Museum of Art, Northampton, Massachusetts; Hirshhorn Museum, Washington, D.C.; Des Moines Art Center, Iowa.

*

In creating my work, I always have the feeling of harmony—the harmony of nature and the harmony of man with nature. To emphasize the harmony I have always made a contrast between the rhythms and highly polished surfaces of the work and the surfaces which I have made rough and crude. This symbolizes

to me the duality of nature, its beauty and its cruelty, and also, the duality of man.

—Minoru Niizuma

Minoru Niizuma's stone sculptures result from his meditation of the relationship between landscape and sculpture. Born in Tokyo in 1930, he graduated the sculpture class of Tokyo University of Fine Art. In 1959 he went to New York with a grant of the school attached to the Brooklyn Museum of Art, where after graduation he taught stone carving from 1964 to 1970. He has established his career as a sculptor in New York, and lives and works in the city until now.

Since his early stage in 1960's up to the middle stage in the late 70's, his idea had been characteristically articulated in forms based on cubic marble. *Castle of the Eye* series or *Fortress* series consists of a single cube or several identical cubes vertically arranged one by one like skewered dice. Each cube has concave surfaces with parallel grooves so that the form looks as if it produces or receives the mysterious echoes of the outer world.

Another cube series in this period is *Nest*. Those are works with a single cube standing on one corner. A *Nest* sculpture usually has a hole through the sides as if it is an eye of the stone spirit looking through a human soul. Sometimes a *Nest* has parallel grooves on the concave sides, and the series can be regarded as evolved from or developed simultaneously with other two series. Niizuma gave the works other than those three cube series titles suggesting natural phenomena like *Rainbow, Silent Sea, Autumn Moon, Whisper in the Mountain* or *Star Dust*. And any of these works with such naturalistic titles shows the artist's attitude toward sculpture that harmonizes, not copes, with the natural world. It is one of the ideas traditionally fostered in Japanese art history.

In the late 70's, he put the idea further in such works as *Moonshadow of Mountain, Horizon, Shallow and Murmuring Brook, Volcano in Summer, Mountainous* and *Cloudy Bluff*, though he retained quasi-cubic forms even in those works. These sculptures have polished surfaces, clear-cut sides, sometimes with a ditch, dent or bump on them, sometimes with narrow parts retaining rough chiseling traces. It is no wonder that anyone who experiences his works in this period can be caught with an idea that the works were made by natural power; polished by moonlight, smoothed by the wind, hollowed by rain water or cut off by a landslide.

The artist has been diminishing smooth surfaces, presenting more and more unpolished texture and rough furrows in the works in the 80's such as in *Black Mountain, Volcano, Black Stream* and *Pyramid*. Those recent works look as though ancient relics have survived for thousands of years without uttering a single word. They are reminiscent of old garden stones in Buddhist temples. He had been an assistant professor at Columbia University in New York from 1972 to 1984, and is the director of the Stone Institute in New York since 1983.

—Tazmi Shinoda

NITSCH, Hermann.

Austrian. Born in Vienna, 29 August 1938. Studied at the Graphische Lehr-und Versuchsanstalt, Vienna, 1953-57; mainly self-taught in art, from 1956. Married Eva Krannich in 1965 (divorced, 1966); Beate Konig in 1968 (died, 1977). Independent artist, working in Vienna, 1957-69, and in Schloss Prinzendorf, near Vienna, since 1971; also lived in West Berlin, 1969-70, and Munich, 1977-84; first orgy-mystery-theatre works, 1957; first action paintings, 1960; first actions, 1962. Founder, with Bauer, Brus, Ruhm and Wiener, Osterreichisches Exilregierung, West Berlin, 1969. Guest Instructor, Stadelschule, Frankfurt, 1971, 1973; Kunsthochschule, Frankfurt, 1979,

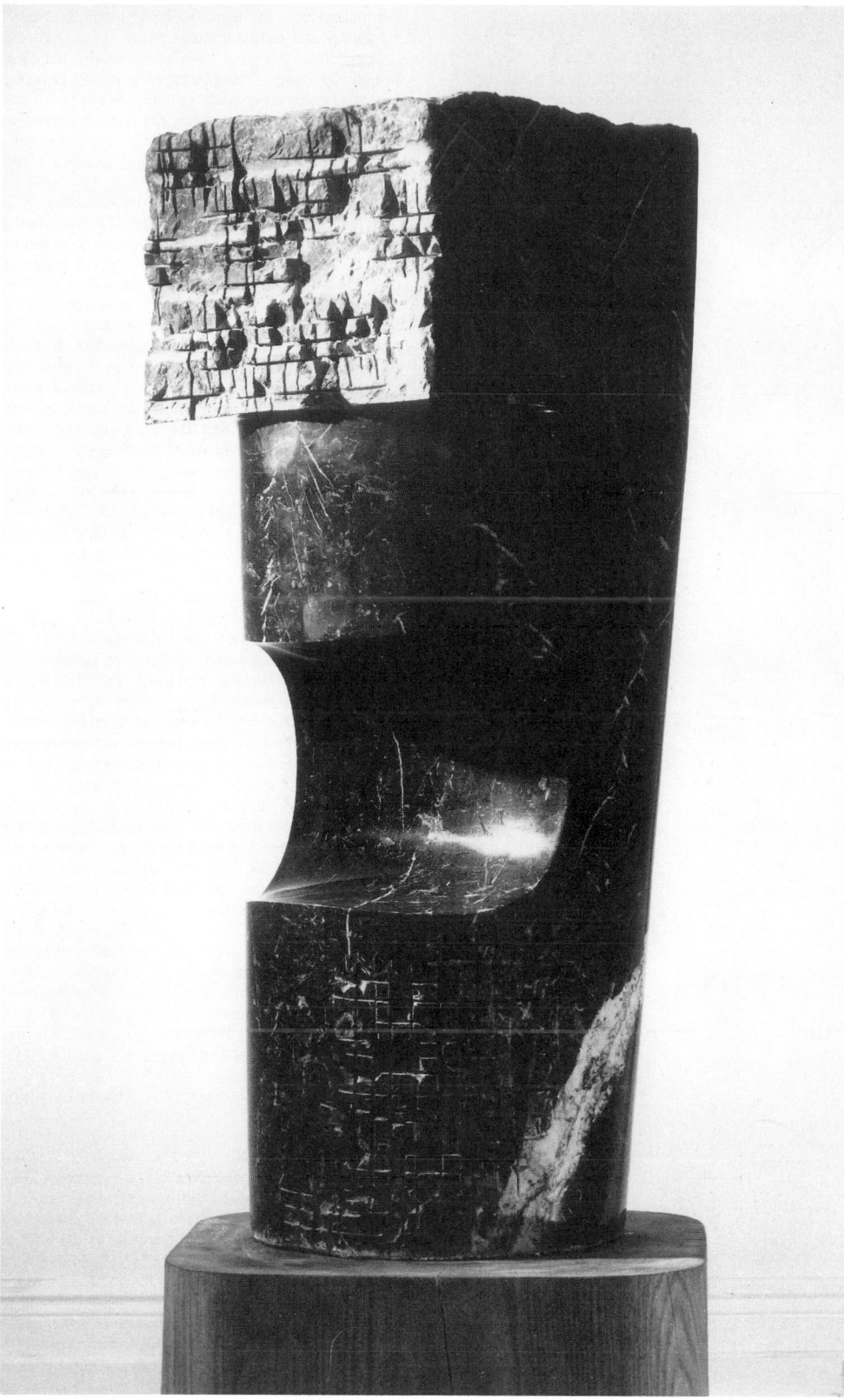

Minoru Niizuma: *Whisper in Mountain*, 1979

1980, 1981; Kunstschule, Reykjavik, 1980. Agents: Galerie Fred Jahn, Maximilianstrasse 10, 8000 Munich; Kunstandel Kurt Kalb, Backerstrasse 3, 1010 Vienna; Galerie Heike Curtze, Seilerstatte 15, 1010 Vienna; Studio Morra, via Calabritto 20, 80121 Naples. Address: Schloss 1, 2185 Prinzendorf an der Zaya, Austria.

Individual Exhibitions:

1960	Loyalty Club, Vienna
1961	Galerie Fuchs, Vienna
1963	Galerie Dvorak, Vienna
1964	Galerie Junge Generation, Vienna
1966	Galerie Dvorak, Vienna
1969	Galerie Casa, Munich
1970	Aktionsraum 1, Munich
	Cinematheque, New York
1971	Galerie Schottle, Munich
1972	Galerie Matala, Tubingen, West Germany
	Galerie Grunangergasse, Vienna (retrospective)
1973	Stadelschule, Frankfurt
	Galerie Grunangergasse, Vienna
	Galerie Werner, Cologne
	Galerie Klewan, Vienna
1974	Studio Morra, Naples
	Galleria Diagramma, Milan
1975	Galerie Krinzinger, Innsbruck
	Galerie Stadler, Paris
	Schloss Prinzendorf, Lower Austria
1976	Kunstverein, Kassel, West Germany
1977	Galerie de Appel, Amsterdam
	Studio Morra, Naples
1978	Modern Art Galerie, Vienna (retrospective)
	Western Front, Vancouver
	Galerie Klein, Bonn
1979	Galerie Heike Curtze, Dusseldorf
	Galerie Ollave, Lyon, France
	Galerie Petersen, West Berlin
	Schloss Prinzendorf, Lower Austria
1981	Galerie Klewan, Munich
	Galerie Pakesch, Vienna
	Kulturhaus, Graz, Austria (retrospective)
1982	Galerie Zell am See, Austria
1983	Galerie Heike Curtze, Vienna
	Galerie Armstorfer, Salzburg
	Van Abbemuseum, Eindhoven, Netherlands (retrospective)
1985	Galerie Maeght Lelong, Zurich
	Mercato di Sale, Milan
	Galerie Heike Curtze, Vienna
1986	Galerie Fred Jahn, Munich
	Studio Morra, Naples
	Galerie Heike Curtze, Dusseldorf
1987	Secession Galerie, Vienna
	Villa Pignatelli, Naples (retrospective)
	Galerie Fred Jahn, Munich
	Galerie Hans Christian Hoschek, Graz, Austria
	Galerie Harald Behm, Hamburg
	Galerie Heike Curtze, Vienna

Actions and Concerts: Nitsch has performed 84 Actions in Vienna, Prinzendorf, Graz, London, New York, Cincinnati, New Brunswick, Los Angeles, Munich, Cologne, Stuttgart, Frankfurt, West Berlin, Florence, Turin, Naples, Bologna, Milan, Trieste, Paris, Vancouver, Arnhem, and Eindhoven, 1962–87; he has performed or conducted 9 of his own musical compositions in galleries, museums and concert halls in Prinzendorf, Vienna, Innsbruck, Linz, Graz, Munich, Hamburg, and Basle, 1974–86.

Selected Group Exhibitions:

1961	*Geist und Form*, Galerie Ebendorferstrasse, Vienna
1962	*Die Blutorgel*, Perinet-Keller, Vienna
1970	*Happening und Fluxus*, Kunstverein, Cologne
1972	*Documenta 5*, Museum Fridericianum, Kassel, West Germany
1979	*Sydney Biennale*, New South Wales, Australia
1981	*Westkunst*, Messehallen, Cologne
1982	*Wiener Aktionismus*, Galerie Heike Curtze, Dusseldorf
1984	*Arte Austriacca 1960–84*, Galleria d'Arte Moderna, Bologna, Italy
1986	*Rennweg*, Castello di Rivoli, Turin (travelled to Madrid)

Collections:

Museum of Modern Art, New York; Tate Gallery, London; Stadtisches Museum im Lenbachhaus, Munich; Staatsgalerie, Stuttgart; Kunsthalle, Hamburg; Kunstmuseum, Berne; Stedelijk Van Abbemuseum, Eindhoven; Castello di Rivoli, Turin; Wolfgang Gurlitt-Museum, Linz; Museum Moderner Kunst, Vienna.

Publications:

By NITSCH. books—*Orglen Mysterien Theater—Orgies Mysteries Theatre*, Darmstadt 1969; *Das Orgien Mysterien Theater II*, Naples and Munich 1976; *O. M. Theater*, Naples 1976; *Partitur der 50. Aktion*, West Berlin 1976; *Die Eroberung von Jerusalem*, Naples and West Berlin 1976; *3 Ty poskriptbande*, 3 vols., Naples 1976; *Das Orgien Mysterien Theater—die Partituren aller aufgeführten Aktionen, 1960–79*, Naples, Munich and Vienna 1979; *45. Aktion*, Naples 1980; *Behauptungen und Beschreibungen zum Projekt des O. M. Theaters*, Altona 1981; *Projekt Prinzendorf—ein Sonderband der Protokolle das O. M. Theater*, Vienna and Munich 1981; *Die Wortdichung des Orgien Mysterien Theaters*,

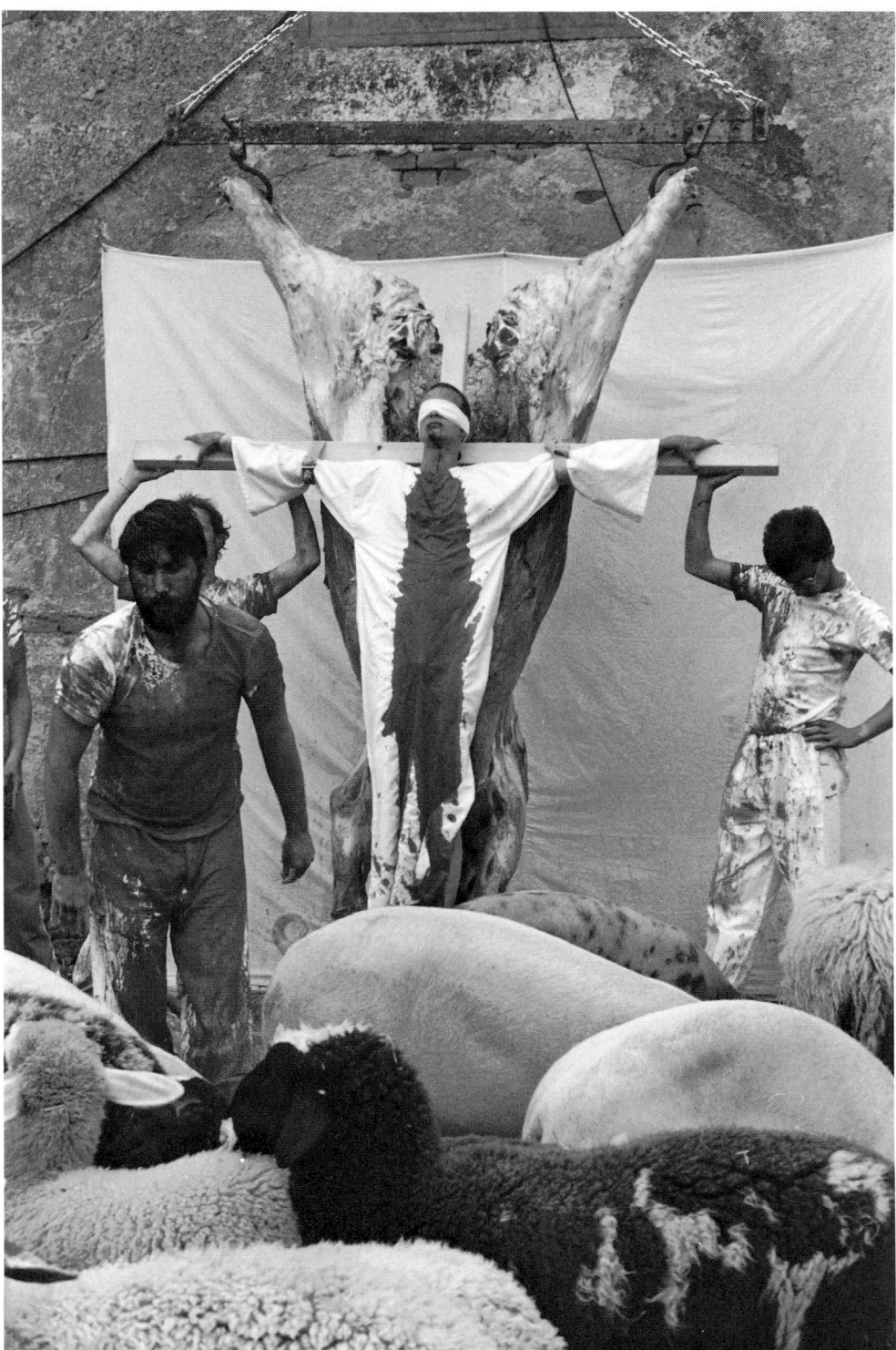

Hermann Nitsch: 80th Action, Prinzendorf, 1984

Form condenses the surrounding world in the enjoying senses and moves it closer to us, drives us more strongly into our own liveliness, drives us more strongly into being. Practice of art = mystic of being. Aesthetic even deep into cruelty. Aesthetic of the cruel.) Establishing synesthetically relations between: perception of touch,
perception of taste,
perception of smell,
perception of acoustic and visual registrations
shall inspire our senses orgiastically. The accelerating activation of all senses can be compared to psychoanalysis. Instead of associating, actions are instituted which heighten the perceptions of the senses until the endpoint of orgiastic "abreaction". (Evaluation of elemental sensuous aggressive-sadistic perceptions, dilacerating of raw meat, disembowelment of slaughtered animal cadavers and trampling on the entrails. The use of cry—and noise actions/noise music). The result is a descent into subconscious regions. We have a sex drive originating which reaches to the very bottom of sado-masochistic excess. The basic excess = endpoint of the "abreactive" experience, sado-masochistic acting; breakthrough as well as demonstrable and conciousness of the subconscious regions, catharsis. Dramatic climax of the play. The "abreactive" events become automatically playacting. Through thorough "abreaction" this playing contributes to overcome excessive experiencing, and replaces it with sublimated experience. The events which are presented at the O. M. Theatre are not acted as in the case of classical theatre, but are occurring in reality. The spectator is placed into the event. He is himself occurring, he shall reach his own self—reach the mystic of being. The action of the play brings the spectator to the realization of his own existential reality. Through the explanation of mystic symbolism originates a demythologized awareness of mythic projections. (Dispute with the collective unawareness). After the "abreaction" provoked by the play, the excessive can be overcome. There comes a quiet, meditative understanding of existence. Sublimation, the mystic of being instead of "abreaction". As a result, the actions only provoke contemplation and submersion into the world of phenomena. The excessive, sad-masochistic "abreaction" is sublimated to the dispute with colour (colour reactions, colourgames, colour-projections). The concentrated aesthetic liturgy of the O. M. Theatre can expand over the entire human life and can transform the process of living into a positive, life-enjoying, aesthetic ritual.

—Hermann Nitsch

It is possibly still available: a portrait-photo of Hermann Nitsch—in limited edition—the man himself, blindfolded (with white bandage) blood streaming down from his mouth and left shoulder to the base of his stomach (totally naked, of course) from Studio Morra, Via Calabritto 20, 80121 Napoli for D. Mark 30—a souvenir of 1977.

A leader-member of the *Destruction in Art* Vienna-based movement which went into voluntary exile for a while in Germany, Hermann Nitsch has never evaded exhibitionism. The group's output took the form of performance art and generally all four Destruction in Art members Gunter Brus, Otto Mühl, Rudolf Schwarzkögler and Hermann Nitsch himself (other enthusiasts as well if they could be recruited in time for 'rehearsals' and be available at the time and for the place of display) were all employed, singly or in concert, in the 'Action'.

The DIA group tended to concentrate—with their own bodies and behavior—upon the unsavoury aspects of human life. Special attention would be given to the cruel side of eroticism, exaggerated themes of pornography, the nastier guilts masked by middle-class propriety with invasions of sexual ambiguity and exhibitionism whenever appropriate. They also set great store on enactments of physical torture, castration and other forms of emasculation, together with the shadier inferences of bestiality. Nudity and

Vienna 1982; *Asolo II, Fest*, Naples 1983; *Das Orgien Mysterien Theater*, Vienna 1983; *Das Orgien Mysterien Theater 1960–1983*, exhibition catalogue, Eindhoven 1983; *Das Orgien Mysterien Theater, die Partituren aller aufgefuhrten Aktionen*, vol. 4, Vienna 1984; *O. M. Theater—Lesebuch*, Vienna 1985; *Das Orgien Mysterien Theater, die Partituren aller aufgefuhrten Aktionen*, vol. 2, Vienna and Naples 1986; sound discs and cassettes—*Akustisches Abreaktionsspiel*, Vienna 1973; *Musik der 45. Aktion*, Naples 1974; *Requiem fur meine Frau Beate*, Naples 1977; *Musik der 60. Aktion*, West Berlin 1978, Stuttgart 1979; *5. Sinfonie Basel, 23 Oktober 1980*, Stuttgart 1980; *Musik der 66. Aktion*, Stuttgart 1980; *6, Sinfonie*, Stuttgart 1980; *Musik der 68. Aktion*, Stuttgart 1980; *Island*, Lucerne 1980; *Musik der 80. Aktion*, Basle and Munich 1984.

On NITSCH: books—*Happenings* by Jurgen Becker and Wolf Vostell, Reinbeck 1965; *Aus der Theorie des O. M. Theaters*, edited by F. Mauthner, Vienna 1965; *Happening und Fluxus*, exhibition catalogue compiled by Hanns Sohm, Cologne 1970; *Wien—Bildkompendium Wiener Aktionismus und Film* by Peter Weibel and Valie Export, Frankfurt 1976; *Aktionskunst* by Jurgen Schilling, Lucerne and Frankfurt 1978; *Herman Nitschs O. M. Theater* by Eckenhart Sterk, Freiburg 1982; *Der Wiener Aktionismus—das O. M. Theater, eine Performance—Theoretische Studie*, thesis by Hubert Klocker, Vienna 1983.

The O. M. Theatre (orgies-mysteries theatre) is the attempt of an absolute "Gesamtkunstwerk". The world of the phenomena is understood through synesthesia. Drama (lyric, epic), painting and music combine themselves in a six-day feast of glorification of existences. The spectator (participant, player) is thrown into a more intensified aesthetic-mystic understanding of the surrounding world.

(Form/aesthetic—essential aim of practice of art. Intensified registration of the world through the form.

the profuse flow of gore combined to make the usual signature of their works.

Not surprisingly they were seen to be the stars and the centre of attention for the DIAS (Destruction in Art Symposium) at St. Bride's Hall off London's Fleet Street only three years before Schwarzkögler in an access of self-mutilation inadvertently managed to kill himself. At the London DIAS two journalists from United Press called the police on the grounds that the 'performances' were an affront to public decency, a step which eventually led to the Symposium's organization being arraigned and brought to London's supreme court, the Old Bailey, on charges of trying to deprave and corrupt members of the DIAS audience. After a 4-day hearing Judge Rogers, having asked the 12-person jury to reach a decision, spoke in open court to those attending the trial to advise them that he had had a most extraordinary communication from the foreman of the jury—to wit: the twelve had agreed to bring in a joint verdict for the two accused of Guilty, but only if the twelve jurors could have assurance from the Judge that he would act leniently towards them both if the Jury took that course. If, on the other hand, they received no such promise, they would pronounce both prisoners Innocent. Judge Rogers added that he would now speak to both counsels, prosecuting and defending and alert them to this strange situation. In 'consequence' the jury brought in a unanimous verdict of Guilty for both the accused. One was fined £200 (which was immediately collected from visitors attending the court) and the other was bound over to be of exemplary behaviour for 12 months.

As has been implied, members forming the Viennese 'Destruction in Art' group (none of whom were present at the Old Bailey trial although they had all agreed to play their part there). Both Defence and Prosecution were somewhat terrified by what they might resort (if given such a chance and opportunity to demonstrate in such a 'theatre') Hermann Nitsch, as a general organizer, promoter and ideas-man has appeared to be in the forefront of the group's prosecution of aims—to shock, disgust, horrify and bring to light the ugly backgrounds of human behaviour. But it should be emphasized that the movement, acting together, in pairs or as single performers, display a recognizable independence from their colleagues exemplified in character and appearance. Each has his own line of specialities of 'performance'. Mühl, for instance, laces his insults with a disturbing sense of humour, black or purple, depending upon the viewer's character.

—Sheldon Williams

NIVOLA, Constantino.

American. Born in Orani, Sardinia, 5 July 1911; emigrated to the United States in 1939; subsequently naturalized. Learned from his father, masonry, plastering, stucco work and woodcutting; studied at Istituto Superiore d'Arte, Milan, M.A. 1936. Married Ruth Guggenheim in 1938; has 2 children. Sculptor: Art Director, Olivetti Company, Milan, 1936; Art Director, *Interiors* magazine, New York, 1940–45; invented sand casting technique to make bas-relief sculpture for large-scale murals. Director, Design Workshop, 1954–57, and Visiting Professor, Carpenter Center for the Visual Arts, 1970 and 1973, Harvard Graduate School of Design, Cambridge, Massachusetts; Instructor, Columbia University, New York, 1961; Instructor, International University of Art, Florence, 1971; Artist-in-Residence, American Academy in Rome, 1972; Visiting Instructor, University of California at Berkeley, 1978. Recipient: Philadelphia Decorators Club Award, 1959; Carborundum Major Abrasive Marketing Award, Certificate of Merit, Municipal Art Society of New York, 1962; Silver Medal of Honor in Sculpture, Architectural League of New York, 1962; Gold Medal, *Regional*

Exhibition of Figurative Art, Cagliari, Italy; Certificate of Commendation, Park Association of New York, 1965; Fine Arts Medal, American Institute of Architects, 1968. Diploma, Federation of Graphic Arts. Honorary Fellow, Royal Academy of Fine Arts, The Hague; Member, Architectural League of New York; Member, National Institute of Arts and Letters, 1972. Agent: Staempfli Gallery, 44 East 77th Street, New York, New York 10021. Address: 410 Stone Road Springs, East Hampton, New York 11937, U.S.A.

Individual Exhibitions:

1927	Sassari Gallery, Sardinia
1940	*Constantino Nivola/Saul Steinberg,* Better Parsons Gallery, New York
1950	Tibor de Nagy Gallery, New York
1954	Peridot Gallery, New York
1956	Harvard University, Cambridge, Massachusetts
1957	Peridot Gallery, New York
1958	Architectural League of New York
1959	Galleria del Milione, Milan
	Arts Club of Chicago
1960	American Federation of Arts, travelling exhibition
1962	Galleria dell'Ariete, Milan
1963	Andrew-Morris Gallery, New York
1965	Byron Gallery, New York
1966	Byron Gallery, New York
1973	Marlborough Galleria d'Arte, Rome (moved to Galleria II Segno, Rome)
	Università di Cagliari, Italy
	Willard Gallery, New York
1974	Institute of Contemporary Art, Boston
1978	Paule Anglin Gallery, San Francisco
	Jaffe-Friede Gallery, Dartmouth College, Hanover, New Hampshire
1979	*Mythology on the Pot,* Quay Gallery, San Francisco
1987	Washburn Gallery, New York

Selected Group Exhibitions:

1950	*Art Quadriennial,* Rome
1957	*Whitney Annual,* Whitney Museum, New York
1958	*Carnegie International,* Carnegie Institute, Pittsburgh
1966	*Sculptor's Guild Annual Exhibition,* New York
1980	*American Sculpture: Gifts of Howard and Jean Lipman,* Whitney Museum, New York

Collections:

Museum of Modern Art, New York; Whitney Museum, New York; Philadelphia Museum of Art; Hirshhorn Museum and Sculpture Garden, Washington, D.C.

Publications:

By NIVOLA: articles—statement in *Zodiac* (Milan), no. 4, 1959; statement and preface in *Constantino Nivola,* exhibition catalogue, by Jan van der Marck, Hanover, New Hampshire 1978.

On NIVOLA: article—"Sculpture ambiente" by Ernesto N. Rogers in *Casabella Continuità* (Milan), January 1959.

NOGUCHI, Isamu.

American. Born in Los Angeles, California. 17 November 1904; moved, with family, to Tokyo, 1906. Educated at Morimura Gakuen Kindergarten Tokyo, 1908–10; Chigasaki Grammar School, Japan, 1910–17; semi-apprenticed to cabinet maker, Chigasaki, 1917; studied at St. Joseph's College, Yokohama, Japan, 1917–18; Rolling Prairie Public School, Indi-

ana, 1918–22; sculpture apprentice, to Gutzon Borglum, Stamford, Connecticut; studied art and sculpture, under Onorio Ruotolo, Leonardo da Vinci Art School, New York, 1923–26; medicine, Columbia University, New York, 1924–27; drawing, Academie Grande Chaumiére and Colarossi School, Paris, 1927; brush drawing, under Chi Pai Shi, Peking, China, and pottery, under Uno Jinmatsu, Kyoto, Japan, 1931. Married Yoshiko (Shirley) Yamaguchi in 1953 (divorced, 1955). Independent sculptor and artist, since 1926. Worked in restaurant, New York, 1924; influenced by seeing Brancusi exhibition, Brummer Gallery, New York, 1926; moved to Paris, working with Brancusi, 1927; met Alexander Calder, Stuart Davis, Fouijita, Morris Kantor, Pascin and André Ruellen, Paris and London, 1927; travelled between New York and Paris, 1928–30, travelled to Berlin, Moscow, Peking, Tokyo and Kyoto via the Trans-Siberian Railway, 1931–32; created first set design, for *Frontier* ballet by Martha Graham, leading to numerous collaborations, New York, 1935; lived and worked in Mexico, 1935–36, in Hawaii, 1939; drove across the United States, with Arshile Gorky, 1941; voluntary intern, relocation camp for Japanese-Americans, Poston, Arizona, 1942; designed coffee table for Herman Miller and table lamp for Knoll, New York, 1944; travelled throughout the world, 1949–50; designed sets and costumes for Gielgud's *King Lear,* London, 1955; established studio, Long Island, New York, 1961; established studio, Island of Shikoku, Japan, 1971. Recipient: Guggenheim Fellowship, 1927, and Travel Fellowship, 1931; Bollingen Foundation Grant, 1950; Second Prize, Society of Four Arts Sculpture Competition, Palm Beach, Florida, 1974; Albert Einstein Commemorative Award, 1978; Mayor's Award of Arts and Culture, New York, 1978; MacDowell Medal, Peterborough, New Hampshire, 1982; New York State Governor's Award, 1984; Japanese American Citizens League Award, 1984; Israel Museum Fellowship, Jerusalem, 1985; President's Medal, U.S.A., 1985; Kyoto Prize, Inamori Foundation, Japan, 1986; National Medal of Arts, Washington, D.C., 1987. D.F.A.: New School for Social Research, New York, 1974; University of Southern California, Los Angeles 1979; D.H.L.: Columbia University, New York, 1984. Member, American Academy of Arts and Letters; American Academy of Arts and Sciences. Agents: Pace Gallery, 32 East 57th Street, New York, New York 10022; Gimpel Fils, 30 Davies Street, London W1Y 1LG, England. Address: 32–37 Vernon Boulevard, Long Island City, New York 11106, U.S.A.

Individual Exhibitions:

1928	Marie Sterner Gallery, New York
1929	Eugene Schoen Gallery, New York
1930	Harvard Society for Contemporary Art, Cambridge, Massachusetts
	Arts Club of Chicago (toured the United States)
	Albright Art Gallery, Buffalo, New York
1931	Rochester Memorial Art Gallery, New York
	John Becker Gallery, New York
	Demotte Galleries, New York
	Reinhardt Galleries, New York
1932	John Becker Gallery, New York
1933	Mellon Galleries, Philadelphia
1934	Honolulu Academy of Fine Arts, Hawaii
	Sidney Burney Gallery, London
1935	Marie Harriman Gallery, New York
1939	Honolulu Academy of Fine Arts, Hawaii
	John Becker Gallery, New York
1942	Museum of Modern Art, San Francisco
	John Becker Gallery, New York
1947	Museum of Modern Art, New York (retrospective)
1950	Mitsukoshi Store, Tokyo
1952	Museum of Modern Art, New York
1953	Museum of Modern Art, New York
1954	Stable Gallery, New York
1963	Cordier and Ekstrom Gallery, New York
1965	Cordier and Ekstrom Gallery, New York
1967	Cordier and Ekstrom Gallery, New York

1968 Gimpel Fils Gallery, London
Galerie Gimpel und Hanover, Zurich
Whitney Museum, New York (retrospective)
1969 Cordier and Ekstrom Gallery, New York
1970 *Noguchi/Rickey/Smith,* University of Indiana, Bloomington
1972 Gimpel Fils Gallery, London
Galerie Gimpel und Hanover, Zurich
1975 *Steel Sculptures,* Pace Gallery, New York
1977 Museum of Modern Art, New York
1978 *Noguchi's Imaginary Landscapes,* Walker Art Center, Minneapolis (toured the United States)
1979 *Drawings and Sculptures: Noguchi/Calder/Smith,* Storm King Art Center, Mountainville, New York
1980 Whitney Museum, New York
Pace Gallery, New York
André Emmerich Gallery, New York
1981 Galerie Maeght, Paris
1983 Pace Gallery, New York
1985 Arnold Herstand Gallery, New York
Seibu Department Store, Tokyo
1986 Pace Gallery, New York
American Pavilion, *Biennale,* Venice

Selected Group Exhibitions:

1939 *World's Fair,* New York
1946 *14 Americans,* Museum of Modern Art, New York
1970 *Expo '70,* Osaka, Japan
1974 *Japan: Tradition und Gegenwart,* Städtische Kunsthalle, Dusseldorf
1976 *200 Years of American Sculpture,* Whitney Museum, New York
1979 *A Century of Ceramics in America 1878–1978,* Everson Museum of Art, Syracuse, New York
1980 *Perceiving Modern Sculpture: Selections for the Sighted and Non-Sighted,* Grey Gallery, New York University
1983 *Abstract Painting and Sculpture in America 1927–44,* Carnegie Institute, Pittsburgh (travelled to San Francisco and New York)
1985 *Transformations in Sculpture,* Guggenheim Museum, New York
1986 *Le Japon des Avant-Gardes,* Centre Georges Pompidou, Paris

Collections:

Metropolitan Museum of Art, New York; Museum of Modern Art, New York; Whitney Museum, New York; Guggenheim Museum, New York; Garden Commission, Chase Manhattan Bank, New York; Storm King Art Center, Mountainville, New York; National Gallery of Art, Washington, D.C.; Hirshhorn Museum, Washington, D.C.

Publications:

By NOGUCHI: books—*A Sculptor's World,* New York 1968; *The Isamu Noguchi Garden Museum,* New York 1987; articles—interview in *The Artist's Voice: Talks with 17 Artists* by Katherine Kuh, New York 1962; "Noguchi on Brancusi" in *Craft Horizons* (New York), August 1976; interview in *Artists in Their Own Words: Interviews,* by Paul Cummings, New York 1979.

On NOGUCHI: books—*Art in America: A Complete Survey* by Holger Cahill and Alfred H. Barr, New York 1935; *Modern Art in America* by Martha Chandler Cheney, New York 1939; *La Surrealisme in 1947* by André Breton, Paris 1947; *Tradition and Experiment in Modern Sculpture* by Charles Seymour, Washington, D.C. 1949; *Abstract Painting and Sculpture in America* by Andrew C. Ritchie, New York 1952; *Noguchi* by Shuzo Takiguchi, Tokyo 1953; *Modern Art U.S.A.: Men, Rebellion, Conquest 1900–1956* by Rudi Blesh, New York 1956; *Nature in Abstraction* by John I. H. Baur, New York 1958; *American Art since 1900: A Critical History* by Barbara Rose, New York 1967; *Isamu Noguchi* by John Gordon, New York 1968; *Isamu Noguchi: The Life of a Sculptor* by Tobi Tobias, New York 1974; *Noguchi: Steel Sculptures,* exhibition catalogue, New York 1975; *Isamu Noguchi* by Sam Hunter, New York 1978; *Noguchi's Imaginary Landscapes,* exhibition catalogue, Minneapolis 1978; *The Sculpture of Isamu Noguchi 1924–1979* by Nancy Grove and Diane Botuick, New York 1980; *Isamu Noguchi: 75th Birth-*

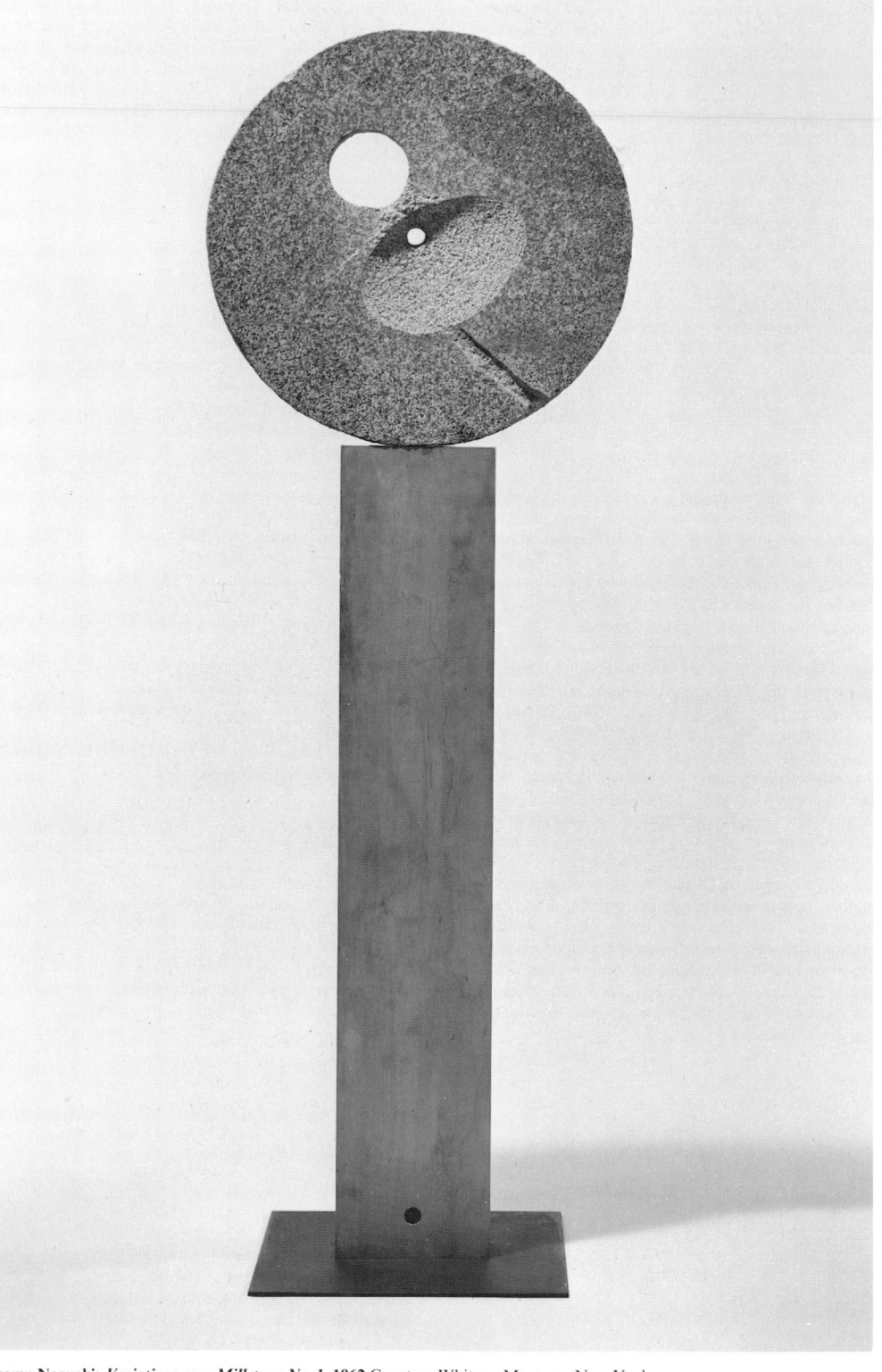

Isamu Noguchi: *Variations on a Millstone No. 1,* 1962 Courtesy Whitney Museum, New York

day Exhibition, catalogue, New York 1980; *Sculpture of Spaces,* exhibition catalogue, New York 1980; *75th Birthday Exhibition: Landscape Tables 1968–1979,* exhibition catalogue, New York 1980; articles—"Noguchi's Recent Marbles" by Dore Ashton in *Art International* (Lugano, Switzerland), October 1972; "Noguchi's Vision Shakes Up Young Japanese" by Joseph Love in *Artnews* (New York), September 1973; "Isamu Noguchi's Elegant World of Space and Function" by Benjamin Forgey in *Smithsonian* (Washington, D.C.), April 1978; "Noguchi's Multiplicities" by Franz Schulze in *Art in America* (New York), January/February 1979; "Sense and Subtlety in Stone" by Robert Hughes in *Time* (New York), 7 March 1980; "Rocks" by Calvin Tomkins in *The New Yorker,* 24 March 1980.

One of the great sculptors of this century, Isamu Noguchi has married his easternism to the west and produced an art enriched and enlarged by both cultures. A perfect example of this happy worldliness are the paper lamps he has designed. Aimed at a commercial market, they reflect the design attitudes of Europe and America while harking back to ancient Japanese craft.

This doubtless has been true of Noguchi's work throughout his career. Again and again one is reminded of orientalisms while looking at something undeniably western. Some of this has to do with a genius for simple means such as the extraordinary white silk curtain that represents the tide of furies who seize Orpheus in the great ballet by Balanchine/ Stravinsky. The same inspired economy is characteristic of Noguchi's sets for dances by Martha Graham. He is a master at establishing symbols for things while remaining an abstractionist. Certainly a number of his finest sculptures are like calligraphy taken into the third dimension.

Everything is grist to his mill: the way in which polished marble forms interlock and mesh becomes curiously erotic in his hands. There are strong suggestions of exotic cults and unknown cultures whose signs and totems gleam in exquisitely worked stone. Noguchi is a marvellous carver rather than a modeler and he likes to take his material all the way to a highly finished state. This does not mean that he substitutes finish for expressiveness. He knows, too, when to suggest the *unfinished*, the broken, the hacked. Think of Michelangelo's uncompleted slaves. Then think of his extremely finished Pieta.

Noguchi, committed to the art of our time, is at the same time an inspired re-inventor of much that is ancient. This movement back and forth in time, together with an aesthetic play between east and west, has produced a new art of classical timelessness.

—Ralph Pomeroy

NOLAN, Sidney (Robert).

Australian. Born in Melbourne, Victoria, 22 April 1917. Educated in Melbourne schools until 1932; studied part-time at the Prahran Technical College, Melbourne, 1932–34, and at the National Gallery School, Melbourne (full-time), 1934–36; studied engraving and lithography with S. W. Hayter at Atelier 17, Paris, 1957–59. Served in the Australian Army, 1941–45. Married Elizabeth Patterson in 1939 (divorced, 1942); the author Cynthia Hansen in 1948 (died, 1976); Mary Boyd in 1978. Designer, Fayrefield Hats factory, Melbourne, 1934–38; Illustrator, Reed and Harris publishers, Melbourne, 1945–47. Full-time painter, in Sydney, 1950–51, Cambridge, England, 1951–53, various towns throughout Europe, 1954, in London and Hereford since 1955, and in New York, 1965–66, 1969; also stage designer, from 1941. Recipient: Dunlop Painting Prize, Sydney, 1950; Painting Prize, *Biennale*, Venice, 1954; National Art Gallery Scholarship, Melbourne, 1956; Italian Government Scholarship, 1956; Commonwealth Fund Fellowship, 1958; Australian National University Fellowship, 1965. Honorary doctorate: Australian National University, Canberra, 1968; Bavarian University, Munich, 1971; University of Leeds, 1974; University of Sydney, 1977. C.B.E. (Commander, Order of the British Empire), 1963; Knighted, 1981; Order of Merit, 1983. Agent: Marlborough Fine Art Ltd., 6 Albemarle Street, London W1X 3HF. Address: 61 Deodar Road, Putney, London SW15, England.

Individual Exhibitions:

1940	Sidney Nolan Studio, Melbourne
1943	Contemporary Art Society, Melbourne
1946	University of Melbourne
1948	Moreton Galleries, Brisbane
1949	David Jones Art Gallery, Sydney
	Macquarie Galleries, Sydney
	Maison de l'Unesco, Paris
1950	Stanley Coe Gallery, Melbourne
	Libreria di Quattro Venti, Rome
	David Jones Art Gallery, Sydney
	Maquarie Galleries, Sydney
1951	Redfern Gallery, London
	Maquarie Galleries, Sydney

1952	Stanley Coe Gallery, Melbourne
	Redfern Gallery, London
1955	Redfern Gallery, London
1956	Johnstone Gallery, Brisbane
	Durlacher Gallery, New York
	Gallery of Contemporary Art, Melbourne
1957	*Paintings 1947–57*, Whitechapel Art Gallery, London, (toured the U.K.)
	Johnstone Gallery, Brisbane
1958	Durlacher Gallery, New York
1960	Phoenix Art Museum, Arizona
	Leda and the Swan and Other Recent Works, Mattiesen Gallery, London
1961	Hatton Gallery, Newcastle upon Tyne (retrospective: toured the U.K.)
	Bonython Gallery, Adelaide
	Austrian Galleries, Melbourne
1962	Durlacher Gallery, New York
	Institute of Contemporary Arts, London
	Skinner Galleries, Perth
1963	Marlborough Fine Art, London
	Georges Gallery, Melbourne
1964	Bonython Gallery, Adelaide
	The 1946–47 Ned Kelly Paintings, Qantas Gallery, London
	At the *Aldeburgh Festival*, Suffolk (toured the U.K.)
1965	Marlborough-Gerson Gallery, New York
	Recent Work, Marlborough Fine Art, London
	David Jones Art Gallery, Sydney
	Menzies Library, Australian National University, Canberra
	Albert Hall, Canberra
	Australian Galleries, Melbourne
1966	Shepparton Gallery, Melbourne
	Qantas Gallery, Sydney
	Marlborough New London Gallery (with John Piper and Ceri Richards)
1967	*Retrospective Exhibition: Paintings from 1937 to 1967*, Art Gallery of New South Wales, Sydney (retrospective toured Australia)
	Qantas Gallery, Sydney
1968	At the *Aldenburgh Festival*, Suffolk
1970	National Gallery of Victoria, Melbourne
1971	*Gemalde und Druckgraphik*, Kunsthalle, Darmstadt
	Ashmolean Museum, Oxford
1972	Tate Gallery, London
	Institute of Contemporary Arts, London
	Marlborough Fine Art, London
1973	*Paintings and Prints*, Fuji Television Gallery, Tokyo
	At the *Ilkley Literature Festival*, Yorkshire (retrospective)
	David Jones Art Gallery, Sydney
	Royal Dublin Society
	Farmers Blaxland Gallery, Sydney
1974	Art Gallery of South Australia, Adelaide
	Shepparton Gallery, Melbourne
1975	*Some Notes for Oedipus*, Marlborough Fine Art, London
	David Jones Art Gallery, Sydney
1976	Rudy Komon Gallery, Sydney
1977	Institute of Modern Art, Brisbane
	Rudy Komon Gallery, Sydney
1978	Institute of Modern Art, Brisbane
	Australian Galleries, Melbourne
	Rudy Komon Gallery, Sydney
	War Memorial Gallery, Canberra
	Australian Embassy, Paris
1979	*Sidney Nolan 1937–1979*, Folkestone Arts Centre, Kent, England
1980	Rudy Komon Gallery, Sydney
1982	Thomas Agnew and Sons, London
1983	Grosvenor Museum, Chester, Cheshire
	National Gallery of Victoria, Melbourne
	Windsor Community Arts Centre, Australia
1987	National Gallery of Victoria, Melbourne
	Art Gallery of New South Wales, Sydney
	Art Gallery of Western Australia, Perth
	Art Gallery of South Australia, Adelaide

Selected Group Exhibitions:

1952	*Carnegie International*, Carnegie Institute, Pittsburgh
1954	*Biennale*, Venice
1959	*Documenta*, Kassel, West Germany
1961	*Recent Australian Painting*, Whitechapel Art Gallery, London
1962	*Rebels and Precursors: Painting in Melbourne 1937–47*, National Gallery of Victoria, Melbourne (travelled to the Art Gallery of New South Wales, Sydney)
1963	*British Painting in the 60's*, Tate Gallery, London
1965	*The English Eye*, Malborough-Gerson Gallery, New York
1966	*Animal Painting: Van Dyck to Nolan*, Queen's Gallery, London

Collections:

Tate Gallery, London; Gulbenkian Foundation, London; Arts Council of Great Britain, London; National Gallery of Australia, Canberra; National Gallery of Victoria, Melbourne, Western Australian Art Gallery, Perth; Tom Collins Memorial Gallery, Perth University; Museum of Modern Art, New York.

Publications:

By NOLAN: books—*Paradise Garden*, with an introduction by Robert Melville, London 1971; books illustrated—*Outrider*, by R. Stow, London 1962; *Near the Ocean* by Robert Lowell, London 1966; *A Sight of China* by Cynthia Nolan, London 1969; *The Voyage* by Charles Baudelaire, London 1968; *Children's Crusade* by Benjamin Britten, London 1973.

On NOLAN: books—*Place, Taste and Tradition: A Study of Australian Art since 1788* by Bernard Smith, Sydney 1945; *Art Here: Buvelot to Nolan* by C. Turnbill, Melbourne 1947; *A Study of Australian Art* by H. Badham, Sydney 1949; *A Gallery of Australian Art* by H. Badham, Sydney 1954; *Sidney Nolan: Paintings 1947–57*, exhibition catalogue, with text by Colin MacInnes, London 1957; *Modern Australian Painting and Sculpture 1950 to 1960*, edited by Kim Bonython, Adelaide 1960; *Sidney Nolan: Leda and the Swan and other recent works*, exhibition catalgoue, with text by Stephen Spender, London 1960; *Sidney Nolan* by Kenneth Clark, Colin MacInnes and Bryan Robertson, London 1961; *Nolan*, exhibition catalogue, with text by John Russell, Newcastle upon Tyne 1961; *Australian Painters: 40 Profiles* by J. Hetherington, Melbourne 1963; *Conversations with Painters* by N. Barber, London 1964; *The 1946–47 Ned Kelly Paintings by Sidney Nolan*, exhibition catalogue, with text by Elwynn Lynn, London 1964; *Ned Kelly: 27 Paintings by Sidney Nolan* by Robert Melville, London 1964, as *The Legend of Ned Kelly*, New York 1964; *Ballet in Australia* by Peggy van Praegh, Melbourne 1965; *Australian Landscape Painting* by J. Reed, Melbourne 1965; *Sidney Nolan: Recent Work*, exhibition catalogue, with text by Robert Melville, London 1965; *Sidney Nolan: Myth and Imagery* by Elwynn Lynn, London 1967; *Open Negative: An American Memoir* by Cynthia Nolan, London 1967; *Sidney Nolan: Retrospective Exhibition: Paintings from 1937 to 1967*, exhibition catalogue, with text by Hal Missingham, Sydney 1967; *Sidney Nolan: Gemalde und Druckgraphik*, exhibition catalogue, with texts by Hans G. Sperlich and Bernd Krimmel, Darmstadt 1971; *Sidney Nolan: Paintings*, exhibition catalogue, with text by Robert Melville, London 1972; *Sidney Nolan: Paintings and Prints*, exhibition catalogue, with an introduction by Kenneth Clark, Tokyo 1973; *Sidney Nolan: Some Notes for Oedipus*, exhibition catalogue, with text by Robert Melville, London 1975; *Sidney Nolan 1937–1979*, exhibition catalogue, with text by Colin MacInnes, Folkestone, Kent 1979; *Sidney Nolan: Australia* by Elwynn Lynn, Sydney and London 1980, *Sidney Nolan*, exhibition catalogue with text by Richard Haese, Melbourne 1983; *Sir Sidney Nolan*, exhibition catalogue with essay by Elwynn Lynn, Windsor 1984; *Sidney Nolan: Landscapes and Legends*, exhibition catalogue with text by Jane Clark, Melbourne 1987.

Sir Sidney Nolan is probably Australia's best-known living artist both in his homeland and internationally. but I doubt if he is Australia's most popular artist. He has always been more of a painter's painter than a people's painter. Despite his often quite immediately appealing subject matter (bushrangers, animals and wondrous landscapes), his interpretations have been extremely personal, exploiting a symbolic language owing something to established contemporary masters such as Paul Klee and Kasimir Malevich.

A retrospective exhibition of *Works on Paper* by Nolan covering a period of approximately forty years toured Australia in the early 1980's. Many of the works included were borrowed from the artist's personal collection and were especially insightful. The dominating features were intimacy of scale, the use of rather subdued colours generally, a readiness to explore unusual media combinations and an emphasis on self-expressive techniques. Nolan has worked consistently and prolifically for most of his professional life which has been marked by exceptionally energetic outbursts of creative activity—as many as 13 drawings and 12 paintings in three days. Rapid execution would tend to indicate that emotional intensity, rather than technical facility (in the more conventional sense), has been Nolan's underlying priority.

Never a very responsive or co-operative art student in his younger Melbourne years, he determinedly broke with local artistic taste-makers and puzzled the critics. In the *Works on Paper* retrospective there was plenty of early evidence that Nolan was always determined to convincingly speak his own artistic language. His drawings and media experiments of the late 1930's and early 1940's took the form of an intensely-felt personal diary. History and myth have often been interpreted by Nolan to reveal elements of a decidedly autobiographical nature. Early (and, by local standards, boldly daring) explorations of collage (using rectilinear breakups and complex tonal interplays) were accompanied by voyages of discovery employing a wide range of inks and paints on unlikely papers. The monotype process was one which accommodated Nolan's early graphic flair where linear emphasis dominated. Smudged pastels and soft water colours helped create dream-like, semi-abstract landscape imagery (part fact, part fiction), inspired by Dimboola, the Grampians and Heidelberg (1942-45). During these war years Nolan commonly used broad washes of background colour with heavy black ink calligraphy superimposed ("Desert, Morning, Plane Crash," 1942). A sketch for Max Harris's *The Vegative Eye* (1943) revealed an approach to head studies (psychological states) which he was to develop further in his rivetting Burke and Wills portraits of the early 1950's and the powerfully disturbing Gallipoli war visages of the 1960's.

The stylized Ned Kelly heads first emerged in 1946 both in drawing and paint. Masked in a rectangular black helmet the infamous Irish-born bushranger was to become Nolan's most beloved and recognizable creation and the source of inspiration for a seemingly endless series of paintings and prints (etchings and lithographs) which continues to the present with varying degrees of success.

An inveterate traveller, Nolan has ventured into the desert wastelands of Central Australia, Africa, the Greek Islands and Antarctica. Although seldom painting on location, Nolan has always been inspired by the many places he has visited, and, blessed with extraordinary powers of recall, he has created some of his most intriguing works on his return to more "civilized" climes. The Greek series from the mid 1950's paid homage to the mythology of an ancient culture. A combination of water-based dyes and oil crayons resulted in some hypnotically beautiful and appropriately theatrically flavoured works.

During the 1970's Nolan seemed to go into a decline, relying increasingly on clichéd reworkings of his past symbols and themes. Numbers of minimal crayon drawings (from 1978) and a suite of drawings based on an episode in Dante's *The Divine Comedy* gave rise to speculation that the once sophisticated child-like (pseudo-naive) elements in Nolan's work may have tripped over into mere childishness.

During the 1980's Sir Sidney Nolan continues to design for the theatre and divide his time between Australia and Europe. He visits Australia for special projects, such as his series of paintings executed in conjunction with the film 'Burke and Wills', starring Nigel Havers. Nolan worked on location with the film crew and the resulting paintings were among his finest for years.

He has been the subject of a vast touring retrospective, sponsored by his loyal supporter, Rupert Murdoch. This retrospective, shown in State galleries throughout Australia during 1987-1988, has confirmed his place as one of Australia's most innovative artists and the artist who has most successfully exploited the Australian mythology.

Recent paintings have explored the possibilities inherent in spray aerosol painting, reinforcing Nolan's belief in the 'reality' of the spontaneous gesture or mark, using comparatively unconventional means.

Now that the public feuding with his fellow Australian, Nobel Prize winning author Patrick White, has subsided, Nolan seems to have directed his energies to more satisfying ends, as he has extended the range of his earlier preoccupations. He is recharging his batteries in his seventies.

—Arthur McIntyre

NOLAND, Kenneth.

American. Born in Asheville, North Carolina, 10 April 1924. Studied art, under Ilya Bolotowsky, Black Mountain College, North Carolina, 1946-48, summer 1950; studied sculpture, under Ossip Zadkine, Paris, 1948-49; student-teacher, Institute of Contemporary Arts, Washington, D.C., 1949-50. Served as glider pilot and cryptographer in the United States Air Force, 1942-46. Married Cornelia Langer in 1950 (divorced, 1957); children: William, Lyndon and Cady; married Stephanie Gordon in 1967 (divorced, 1970). Independent artist, since 1950. Instructor, Institute of Contemporary Arts, Washington, D.C., 1950-51, and Catholic University, Washington, D.C., 1951-60; Instructor of night classes, Washington Workshop Center of the Arts, Washington, D.C., periodically, 1952-56; conducted Emma Lake Artists' Workshop, University of Saskatchewan, Regina, 1963; Instructor, Bennington, College, Vermont, summer 1966; Guest, Tel Aviv Foundation of Literature and Art, 1971; Guest Lecturer, in Australia and New Zealand, 1975. Now lives and works in South Salem, New York. Recipient: International Prize, Centro de Artes Visuales, Instituto Torcuato di Tella, Buenos Aires, 1964; Citation in Creative Arts, Brandeis University, Waltham, Massachusetts 1965; Copper Medal, William A. Clark Prize, Corcoran Gallery of Art, Washington, D.C., 1967. Member, American Academy of Arts and Letters, 1977. Agent: André Emmerich Inc., New York, New York. Address: c/o André Emmerich Inc., 41 East 57th Street, New York, New York 10022, U.S.A.

Individual Exhibitions:

1949	Galerie Creuze, Paris
1956	Tibor de Nagy Gallery, New York
1958	Tibor de Nagy Gallery, New York
	Jefferson Place Gallery, Washington, D.C.
1959	French and Company, New York
1960	Jefferson Place Gallery, Washington, D.C.
	Galleria dell'Ariete, Milan
	Galerie Lawrence, Paris
	André Emmerich Gallery, New York
1961	Galerie Neufville, Paris
	André Emmerich Gallery, New York
	Bennington College, Vermont
1962	Galerie Charles Lienhard, Zurich
	Galerie Schmela, Dusseldorf
	André Emmerich Gallery, New York
1963	Kasmin Gallery, London
	André Emmerich Gallery, New York
	Galerie Lawrence, Paris
1964	Jewish Museum, New York
	Galerie Schmela, Dusseldorf
1965	Kasmin Gallery, London
	David Mirvish Gallery, Toronto
1966	Nicholas Wilder Gallery, Los Angels
	André Emmerich Gallery, New York

1967	André Emmerich Gallery, New York
1968	Kasmin Gallery, London
	David Mirvish Gallery, Toronto
1969	Lawrence Rubin Gallery, New York
1971	André Emmerich Gallery, New York
1972	Galerie Mikro, West Berlin
1973	André Emmerich Gallery, New York
1974	David Mirvish Gallery, Toronto
	Jack Glenn Gallery, Corona del Mar, California
	Janie C. Lee Gallery, Houston
	Rutland Gallery, London
1975	School of Visual Arts, New York
1976	André Emmerich Gallery, Zurich
	Leo Castelli Gallery, New York
1977	*Kenneth Noland: A Retrospective*, Guggenheim Museum, New York (toured the United States, 1977-78)
	André Emmerich Gallery, New York
1978	André Emmerich Gallery, New York
1979	Waddington Graphics, London
	André Emmerich Gallery, Zurich
1980	André Emmerich Gallery, New York
	Castelli Graphics, New York
1981	Waddington Galleries, London
1982	Douglas Drake Gallery, Kansas City, Missouri
	Downstairs Gallery, Edmonton, Alberta
1983	Hokin Gallery, Bay Harbor Island, Florida
	Galeria Joan Prats, Barcelona
1984	Galerie de France, Paris
	Makler Gallery, Philadelphia
1985	Galeria joan Prats, Barcelona
1986	André Emmerich Gallery, New York

Selected Group Exhibitions:

1959	*Biennial of Contemporary American Painting*, Corcoran Gallery, Washington, D.C.
1964	*Post-Painterly Abstraction*, Los Angeles County Museum of Art (toured the United States and Canada)
1969	*New York Painting and Sculpture 1940-70*, Metropolitan Museum of Art, New York
1976	*Aspects of Postwar Painting in America*, Guggenheim Museum, New York
1977	*New Ways with Paper*, National Collection of Fine Arts, Smithsonian Institution, Washington, D.C.
1978	*American Painting of the 1970's*, Albright-Knox Art Gallery, Buffalo, New York (toured the United States)
1979	*International Biennial Exhibition of Prints in Tokyo*, National Museum of Modern Art, Tokyo (toured Japan)
1980	*Aspects of the 70's: Painterly Abstraction*, Brockton Art Museum, Massachusetts
1982	*A Private Vision*, Museum of Fine Arts, Boston
1986	*An American Renaissance*, Fort Lauderdale Museum of Art, Florida

Collections:

Museum of Modern Art, New York; Whitney museum of American Art, New York; Albright Knox Art Gallery, Buffalo, New York; Fogg Art Museum, Harvard University, Cambridge, Massachusetts; Baltimore Museum of Art; National Gallery of Art, Washington, D.C.; Hirshhorn Museum, Washington, D.C.; Milwaukee Art Center; Art Institute of Chicago; Australian National Gallery, Canberra.

Publications:

By NOLAND: articles—"Letter to the Editor" in *Artnews* (New York), November 1962; "Jackson Pollock: An Artist's Symposium, Part 2" in *Artnews* (New York), May 1967; "Color, Format and Abstract Art: An Interview with Kenneth Noland," with Diane Waldman, in *Art in America* (New York), May/June 1977; interview in *Artists in Their Own Words: Interviews* by Paul Cummings, New York 1979.

On NOLAND: books—*A Concise History of Modern Painting* by Herbert Read, London 1968; *Minimal Art: A Critical Anthology*, edited by Gregory Battcock, New York 1968; *History of Modern Art* by H. H. Arnason, New York 1969; *A Reading of Modern Art* by Dore Ashton, New York 1969; *The New Painting* by Udo Kultermann, New York 1969; *Late*

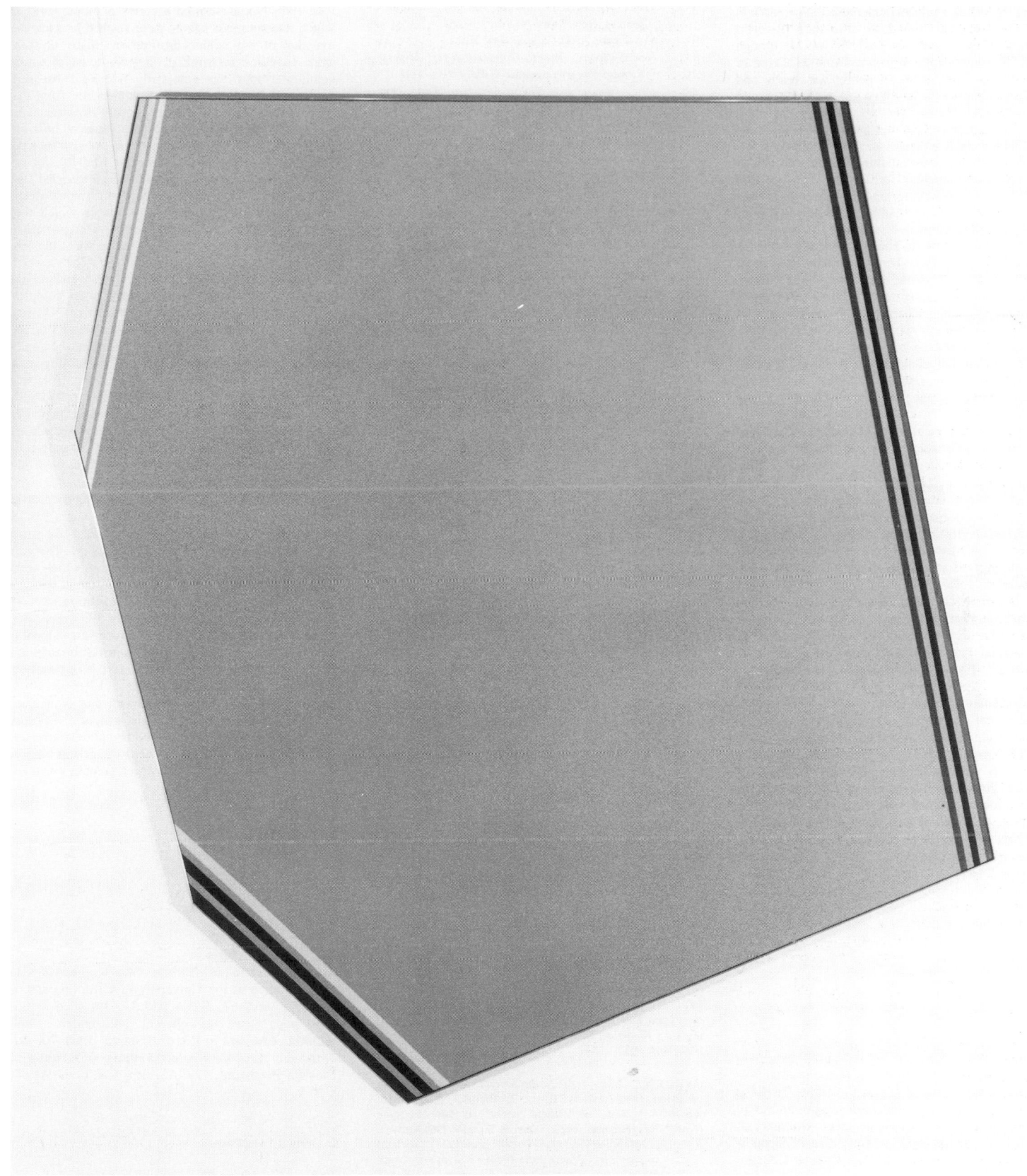

Kenneth Noland: *Knit*, 1978

Modern by Edward Lucie-Smith, New York 1969; *On the Future of Art* by Jack Burnham, New York 1970; *10 Washington Artists*, exhibition catalogue, Edmonton, Alberta 1970; *La Pittura Americana Dopoguerra* by Daniel M. Mandelowitz, New York 1970; *Icons and Images of the 60's* by Nicolas and Elena Calas, New York 1971; *Kenneth Noland* by Kenworth Moffett, New York 1977; *Kenneth Noland: A Retrospective*, exhibition catalogue, by Diane Waldman, New York 1977; *Kenneth Noland Handmade Papers* by Judith Goldman, Bedford Village, New York 1978; *The New School: Painters and Sculptors of the 50's* by Irving Sandler, New York 1978; *A World History of Art: Painting, Sculpture,* *Architecture and Decorative Arts* by Gina Pischel, New York, revised edition 1978; *Louisiana: Pictorial Reportage,* Humblebaek, Denmark 1979; *Handbook: Guggenheim Museum Collection 1900–1980* by Vivian Endicott Barnett, New York 1980; *With Paper, About Paper*, exhibition catalogue, Buffalo, New York 1980; articles—"Notes on American Painting of the 60's" by Walter Darby Bannard in *Artforum* (New York), January 1970; "Noland's New Paintings" by Walter Darby Bannard in *Artforum* (New York), November 1971; "Noland" by Kenworth Moffett in *Art International* (Lugano, Switzerland), Summer 1973; "To Re-Examine the Work of Kenneth Noland" by Ken Carpenter in *Studio Inter-* *national* (London), July/August 1974; "Kenneth Noland" by R. J. Rees in *Studio International* (London), January/February 1975; "Kenneth Noland's New Paintings and the Issue of the Shaped Canvas" by Kenworth Moffett in *Art International* (Lugano, Switzerland), April-/May 1976; "Landmarks on the Color Field" by Hilton Kramer in the *New York Times*, 22 April 1977; "Kenneth Noland and Quality in Art" by Alwynne Mackie in *Art International* (Lugano, Switzerland), Summer 1979; "Teaching Modernism: What Albers Learned in the Bauhaus and Taught to Rauschenberg, Noland and Hesse" by Carl Goldstein in *Arts Magazine* (New York), December 1979.

The highly formal work that emerged in New York in the 60's as "minimal" found one of its most powerful practitioners in Kenneth Noland. It was as though what he had been working toward came to a kind of timely climax so that the art public was ready and able to see what he, along with a group of artists, was exploring.

The minimal artists, as the tag implies, are concerned with reductive means, dealing with only a few of the elements that are available to an artist, such as color, structure, singular forms, etc. Noland first worked with targets of color and chevrons along with the shape of the stretched canvas, then moved toward a very direct and narrow statement of horizontal bands of color in beautiful and inventive relationships like musical chords. Gene Davis was painting vertical bands of color, but Noland's horizontal bands were refreshingly not the same. Their scale was different and the tension much more relaxed, stretching as it did outwards apparently without end. The forms were of course the bands of color and the "spaces between" them which could be seen either as other bands or a ground depending on the way an observer chose to see them and the emphasis Noland gave any given color.

The sheer act of painting, I suspect, then led Noland through compositional means—that is, the balancing out of tensions produced not only by the play of color but also by the relationships between forms. The next set of paintings by Noland bears a strong resemblance to plaids with vertical and horizontal bands of color crossing over one another and acting as "frames" for the central field of color. This concern with edges is shared by a number of contemporary artists.

The balancing-out of vertical and horizontal in terms of compositional give-and-take has since led Noland to the further compositional step of dealing with diagonals and their relationship to the edge of the painting. He is back to shaped canvases, but whereas symmetry was his answer in the earlier diamonds and tondos, now the diagonals throw the structure off-center and the shapes of the canvases are highly irregular and asymmetrical. This has resulted in a very complex structure where the activity going on within the stretched canvas in joined by the activity *outside* its form—the relationship of the work to its surroundings. In his most successful new work Noland has been able to control all this relational activity in such a way as to continue to produce easel paintings of great integrity.

—Ralph Pomeroy

NONAS, Richard.

American. Studied cultural anthropology. Worked as an archeologist in Georgia and Alabama; spent two years as ethnographer in Northern Mexico Indian village; conducted Indian research in Yukon Territory and northern Ontario; visited Indian communities in the Grand Canyon and Lapland; spent two years in Paris. Sculptor since 1967. Instructor in Anthropology, University of North Carolina; Queens College, New York; Lecturer, University of Rochester, New York; Lecturer, School of the Visual Arts, Cooper Union and Hunter College, New York; Visiting Artist, Sarah Lawrence College, Bronxville, New York, and Fresno State College, California, 1974. Recipient: Change Inc. Grant, 1972; Guggenheim Foundation Fellowship, 1974; National Endowment for the Arts Grant, 1976. Address: 14 Harrison Street, New York, New York 10003, U.S.A.

Individual Exhibitions:

1972	10 Bleecker Street Gallery, New York
	112 Greene Street Gallery, New York
1973	The Clocktower, Institute for Art and Urban Resources, New York
	112 Greene Street Gallery, New York
	New Sculpture: Robert Grosvenor/Forest Meyers/ Richard Nonas, Loguidice Gallery, New York
	New Sculpture: Jene Highstein/Richard Nonas, University of Rhode Island, Kingston
1974	Galleria Forma, Genoa
	Galleria d'Allesandro, Rome
	Galerie Schöttle, Munich
	Daniel Weinberg Gallery, San Francisco
	383 West Broadway, New York
1975	Marilena Bonomo Galleria, Bari, Italy
	Idea Warehouse, New York
	Holly Solomon Gallery, New York
1976	*New Sculpture/Old Tower*, Spoleto, Italy
	Galleria St. Fidele, Milan
	Dartmouth College, Hanover, New Hampshire
	Galerie Hetzler-Keller, Stuttgart
	Art Gallery, Wright State University, Dayton, Ohio
	Salvatori Ala Galleria, Milan
1977	PS1, Institute for Art and Urban Resources, Long Island City, New York
1981	Oil and Steel Gallery, New York
	Hudson River Museum, Yonkers, New York
	Studio La Citta, Verona, Italy
1982	University of Massachusetts, Amherst
	Franklin Furnace, New York (retrospective)

Selected Group Exhibitions:

1972	*5 Sculptors/7000 Sq. Ft.*, 10 Bleecker Street Gallery, New York
1973	*Sculpture Annual*, Whitney Museum, New York
	Mass '73, Chicago
1974	*Anarchitecture*, 112 Greene Street Gallery, New York
1976	*Holz-Kunst-Stoff*, Staatliche-Kunsthalle, Baden-Baden, West Germany
1977	*Documenta*, Kassel, West Germany
1978	*Sculpture*, Hal Bromm Gallery, New York

Collections:

Sony Corporation, New York; Sarah Lawrence College, Bronxville, New York; Aldrich Museum, Ridgefield, Connecticut; Dartmouth College, Hanover, New Hampshire; University of Pennsylvania, Philadelphia; Bryn Mawr College, Pennsylvania; Wright State University, Dayton, Ohio; Walker Art Center, Minneapolis; Moderna Museet, Stockholm.

Publications:

By NONAS: books—*Details from the Excavation of Wooster Street*, New York 1972; *Summer, 1906*, New York 1973; *Northern/Southern*, Genoa 1974; *Sonora Cows*, New York 1974; *My Life on the Floor*, New York 1975; *Making Sculpture*, New York 1975; *Lost in Spoleto*, New York 1976; *Montezuma's Breakfast*, New York 1977; radio play—*Goats Itch*, New York 1982.

On NONAS: book—*New Sculpture/Old Tower*, exhibition catalogue, with text by Panza di Biumo, Milan 1976; articles—"4 Works by Richard Nonas" in *Arts Magazine* (New York), February 1973; essay by Suzanne Delahauty in *6 Visions*, exhibition catalogue, Philadelphia 1973; "Richard Nonas" in *Flash Art* (Milan), June 1974; "3 Sculptors: Mark di Suvero, Richard Nonas, Charles Ginnever" by Nancy Foote in *Artforum* (New York), June 1976; "Richard Nonas" in *Flash Art* (Milan), April 1976; "Richard Nonas: Field Works" by Jan van der Marck in *Art in America* (New York), January 1977; "Montezuma and the PS1 Kids" by Grace Glueck in the *New York Times*, 15 April 1977; review by Donald Kuspit in *Art in America* (New York), March 1981.

Closely associated with Minimalist and Postminimalist sources, the sculpture produced by Richard Nonas in the 1970's uses simple forms and rough, heavy industrial materials to construct horizontal structures which manipulate and redefine the spaces for which they are specifically made.

In 1973 Nonas showed a series of floor works in which rough timber beams were stacked in a manner like that of log cabin construction. Many of these were dedicated to Mark di Suvero, some of whose qualities Nonas has emulated. Nonas's subsequent work, however, is quite different formally from that of di Suvero, becoming less ruggedly expressionistic and more concerned with slender, attenuated horizontality and deceptive simplicity. In works such as "Atumosis" (1974) and "Crocodile" (1976), for example, long, thin steel beams form an inverted "L" and a capital "I" respectively, their shapes determined by the particular gallery spaces which they were made to alter. Nonas's sculpture characteristically tends to both fill the space and at the same time defer bringing undue attention to itself. The viewer is urged to become a participant, to move in and out and through the work in order to perceive its complete relationship with its symbiotic environment. On first glance, Nonas's forms seem quite simple and direct, yet, on sustained interaction, they assume a complex task in the subtleties of placement and arrangement which serve to reshape their surroundings. If there is deeper meaning in Nonas's work, it lies in its ability to communicate perceptions of the complexities concealed in deceptively simple forms. His is a statement which seems to proclaim that what is outwardly "minimal" can be made "maximal" through the viewer's efforts.

In 1980 Nonas did an installation composed of an arrangement of 12 rough lumber structures resembling primitive chairs and 12 steel plateau-like structures resembling primitive tables or altars. The aura is one of a modernist/primitivizing urge which seeks to reinvent some primitive ceremony by reinventing a specific city space with multiple repetition of modernly abstracted yet still primitively allusive shapes. Nonas's background as an anthropologist is evident in this work which, like his others, aims at broaching a hint at the complex devices underlying minimal abstraction's misleading simplicity.

Note should be made of the fact that Nonas, although primarily known for his sculpture, has also produced a number of artists' books, photographs and narrative works. Among his newest works is a radio play titled *Goats Itch* (1982) which he both wrote and performed.

—Barbara Cavaliere

NORDMAN, Maria.

American. Born in Görlitz, Silesia, Germany in 1943. Studied at the University of California at Los Angeles, 1961-67, B.F.A., M.A.. Travelled in Europe, and researched coherent light models, 1968. Editorial Assistant to Richard Neutra, 1969-70. Address: c/o Rosamund Felsen Gallery, 669 North La Cienaga Boulevard, Los Angeles, California 90069, U.S.A.

Individual Exhibitions:

1967	University of California at Los Angeles
1972	Pasadena Museum of Modern Art, California
	12 South Raymond Street, Pasadena, California
	20th and Idaho, Santa Monica, California
1973	*Saddleback Mountain*, University of California at Irvine
1974	Galleria Franco Toselli, Milan
1976	Museo d'Artista, Florence
1978	*5 Public Proposals for an Open Place*, Rosamund Felsen Upstairs Gallery, Los Angeles (travelled to Galerie Saman, Geneva, 1979)
1981	Fogg Art Museum, Harvard University, Cambridge, Massachusetts
1983	Westfalischer Kunstverein, Munster
1985	La Jolla Museum of Contemporary Art, California

Selected Group Exhibitions:

1976	*Biennale*, Venice
1977	*Documenta 6*, Heckerstrasse, Kassel, West Germany
1979	*Andre/Buren/Nordman: Space as Support*, University of California, Berkeley
1980	*Pier and Ocean: Construction in the Art of the 70s*, Hayward Gallery, London (travelled to Rijksmuseum Kroller-Muller, Otterlo, Netherlands)
1983	*The First Show*, Museum of Contemporary Art, Los Angeles
1984	*Nel mezzo della primavera*, Galleria Pieroni, Rome
1985	*Promenades*, Parc Lullin, Genthod, Geneva

Publications:

By NORDMAN: books—*Fragment from the Notes of Maria Nordman*, Munich 1977; *Unpublished Notes*, Santa Monica, California 1979; *Poiema, Notes 1970-*, Cologne 1982; article—interview with Barbara Haskell and Hal Glicksman, in *Maria Nordman: Saddleback Mountain*, exhibition catalogue, Irvine, California 1973.

On NORDMAN: book—*Andre, Buren, Irwin, Nordman: Space as Support*, exhibition brochure with essay by Jan Butterfield, Berkeley, California 1979; articles—"Art Walk" by William Wilson in *Los Angeles Times*, 20 October 1978; "Lux Lucis" by Corinna Ferrari in *Domus* (Milan), April 1979; "Maria Nordman" in *Bijutsu Techo* (Tokyo), April 1979; "The Work of Maria Nordman" by Germano Celant in *Artforum* (New York), March 1980; "Review: Maria Nordman" by Annelie Pohlen in *Artforum* (New York), March 1984.

Maria Nordman occupies herself with works which concern people in relation to their surroundings. She works with spaces which can be light and dark, noisy and silent, broad and narrow, which she conceives however in such a manner that the interior is brought to the outside and in counter-movement the exterior comes inside. But the "natural aspects" of the gradual transition of day into night, of light into darkness, of breadth into narrowness, of noise into silence, can also be included as surroundings.

Space, light and sound are the most important components in Maria Nordman's work, not as material entities but as elements of our world perceptible and experiential in time. Space and light are closely linked; neither the one nor the other exists in isolation. Maria Nordman sees light as a determinant, elementary presence. Light comes from the sun, the planet revered by all early cultures: in this sense it is to be understood as myth. But it can also be interpreted otherwise: as a neutral, omnipresent power, as man's companion, as a constant which not only acts as a yardstick in our perception of the world, but also "it defines any place to unpredictable degrees from the same points of departure."

We all move from space to space, from place to place, from light to darkness; these are elements which can be experienced in the relationship of man to man. Light opens up space, space reflects light. Maria Nordman investigates these relationships in discovering, adapting and opening up places or spaces in which the "natural aspects" of light and the "boundlessness" of space are present. She gives intellectual and spiritual effect to these relationships in her restrained, poetic and peaceful works.

—Zdenek Felix

NOVELLI, Gastone.

Italian. Born in Vienna, Austria, 1 August 1925. Studied political and social science at Florence University, 1945–47; self-taught in art. Joined partisans, arrested in 1943, and imprisoned until 1945. Painter: lived in Brazil, 1948–54; returned to Italy, 1955, and settled in Rome, 1956; visited Greece, 1961; worked on decor for *Papà, Povero Papà* by Kopit, Teatro La Cometa, Rome, 1963; Founder, with Giuliani, Manganelli and Perilli, *Grammatica* magazine, Rome, 1964. Lecturer in Design and Theory of Communication, Institute of Art, Sao Paulo, 1951–54; Lecturer, Accademia di Belle Arti di Brera, Milan, 1968. Recipient: Premio, *Festivale dei Due Mondi*, Spoleto, 1958; First Prize for Painting, Castello Svevo, Termoli, Italy, 1962; First Prize for White and Black, Rassegna Arte Figurativa di Roma e Lazio, 1962; Premio Capogrossi, *Biennale*, San Marino, 1965; Premio Gollin, *Biennale*, Venice, 1964. *Died* (in Milan) *22 December 1968*.

Individual Exhibitions:

1950	Galeria Domus, Sao Paulo
1952	Galeria Teurenio, Rio de Janeiro
1953	Museu d'Arte Moderna, Sao Paulo
1955	Studio B 24, Milan
1957	Galleria La Salita, Rome
1959	Galleria dell'Ariete, Milan
1960	Galleria La Tartaruga, Rome
1961	Galleria Il Tragheto, Venice
	Galleria Il Gattocielo, Milan
	Galerie du Fleuve, Paris
1962	Alan Gallery, New York
1963	Galleria Levi, Milan
	Galleria Pogliani, Rome
	Tokyo Gallery
1964	*Biennale*, Venice
	Kunstverein, Freiburg, West Germany
	Galerie Thomas, Munich
	Arco d'Alibert, Rome
1965	Alan Gallery, New York
1966	Marlborough Galleria d'Arte, Rome
	Court Gallery, Copenhagen
1967	Galleria Rotta, Genoa
	Galleria Barozzi, Venice
	Galleria Flori, Montecatini, Italy
1968	Musée des Beaux-Arts, La Chaux de Fonds, Switzerland
	Galleria Toninelli, Milan
	Galerie Semiha Huber, Zurich
	Biennale, Venice
	Galerie Espace, Amsterdam
1969	Landau-Alan Gallery, New York
	Grafica Romero, Rome
1970	Galleria Marlborough d'Arte, Rome
	Querini Stampalia, Venice
1971	Studio Marconi, Milan
	Marlborough Galleria d'Arte, Rome
1972	Studio La Città, Verona
	Galleria Civica d'Arte Moderna, Turin
	Studio Marconi, Milan
	Museum of Modern Art, New York
1973	Studio St. Andrea, Milan
1974	Galleria 3 A, Turin
	Studio Marconi, Milan
1975	Galleria Il Sole, Bolzano, Italy
1976	Galleria del Milione, Milan
	Marlborough Galleria d'Arte, Rome
	Studio Marconi, Milan (with Bruno di Bello)
1979	Galleria Editalia, Rome

Selected Group Exhibitions:

1951	*Bienal*, Sao Paulo
1958	*Italian Painters of Today*, Museum of Modern Art, Tokyo
1960	*The New Generation in Italian Art*, Federation of Art, New York
1961	*Carnegie International*, Carnegie Institute, Pittsburgh
1965	*Italienische Kunst Heute*, Kunsthalle, Munich (toured Europe)
1966	*Miniature Sculptures*, Marlborough-Gerson Gallery, New York
1967	*Expo '67*, Montreal
1968	*Recent Italian Paintings and Sculptures*, Jewish Museum, New York

Collections:

Galleria Nazionale d'Arte Moderna, Rome.

Publications:

By NOVELLI: books—*Viaggio in Grecia*, Rome 1966; *Mais Si Vous Voulez Pourir en Paix*, Rome 1966; articles—"La Macchina Totem" in *L'Esperienza Moderna* (Rome), April 1957; "Analizzare il Processo Creativo" in *L'Esperienza Moderna* (Rome), August 1957; "La Creazione di un Opera Plastica . . ." in *Gastone Novelli*, exhibition catalogue, Rome 1957; "Scritto sul Muro" in *L'Esperienza Moderna* (Rome), January 1958; "Roma 1958" in *L'Esperienza Moderna* (Rome), March 1959; "PPQ" in *Crack* (Milan), 1960; "Tutto e Come Una di Quelle Notti Bianche" in *Antologia del Possibile* (Milan), 1962; "Pittura Procedente da Segni" in *Grammatica* (Rome), November 1964; "La Parola a Gastone Novelli" in *Che Fare* (Milan), Winter 1968–69; "Il Linguaggio Figurativo e la Sua Funzione" in *Civilta delle Macchine* (Rome), January 1969; "Dipingere e Anche Esprimere per Segni" in *Grammatica* (Rome), July 1969; statement, in *Gastone Novelli*, exhibition catalogue, Rome 1970; book illustrated—*Histoire de l'Oeil* by Georges Bataille, 1959.

On NOVELLI: books—*Novelli*, exhibition catalogue, by Guido Ballo, Milan 1969; *Gastone Novelli*, exhibition catalogue, by Guido Ballo, Rome 1970; articles—"Gastone Novelli" by Gianni Novak in *D'Ars* (Milan), March-July 1969; "Novelli" in *Flash Art* (Milan), September/October 1970.

After he returned to Italy from Brazil, where he had been living between 1948 and 1954, Gastone Novelli continued during the 1960's to conduct those experiments which were necessary to his development as an artist. He had started out in the 50's as a kind of Neo-Cubist ("A Cube Develops into np," for example, comes from 1953), and at the same time worked on a technique which was based on Paul Klee's abstract lyricism. In the middle of the 50's Novelli also experimented with kinetic art ("Antithesis of Movement," 1954, and "Motion of a Sculpture," 1955, illustrate this phase of his development). And after a brief rebellion against formalism, he reached his maturity as an artist.

In 1957 Novelli and Achille Perilli founded the review *L'Esperienza Moderna*, and it was Perilli who helped him with his further experiments, particularly with regard to the tensions involved in the art of painting. By 1960 Novelli's poetic world was fully realized: his painting was now characterized by a shrewd use of form and the content it expresses.

Novelli's art consists mainly in establishing relationships between dots of color and gestures which are transformed into a kind of sign-language or symbolic writing. Both color and sign-language are important here, but the language itself also becomes an integral part of the pictorial surface. This dialectical interplay of colors and signs is the main characteristic of his work up to the moment of his untimely death in 1968.

Novelli's dialectic involves two parallel movements. On the one hand he achieves coloristic effects by his use of white on white and of white and red or blue. On the other hand he continues to use a language of signs which owes something to his anti-formalist phase and to the automatic writing of the surrealists. The result is not so much an intimate diary as it is a documentation or transcript of things Novelli encountered in everyday life—things which in turn give his work its effortless freedom and spontaneity.

Novelli's visual "writing" is not obtrusive but plays its own role in establishing a balance among his different color areas, delicately controlling those areas in geometric forms. It is this equilibrium which marks his mature work.

—Roberto G. Lambarelli

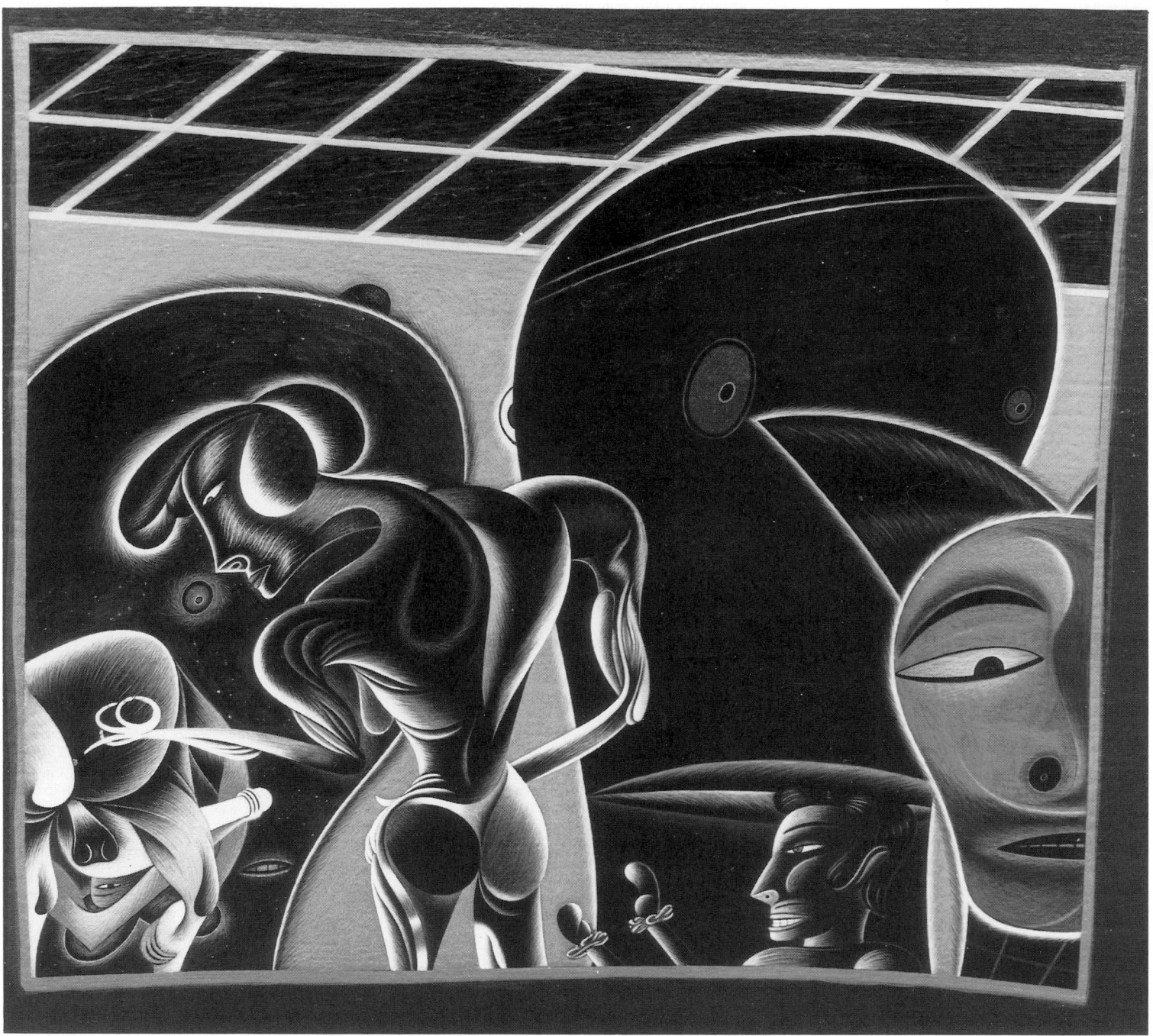

Jim Nutt: *Ah ha* (*It is!*), 1980

NUTT, Jim.

American. Born in Pittsfield, Massachusetts, 28 November 1938. Studied at the Art Institute of Chicago, B.F.A. 1965. Independent artist, working in Chicago. Agent: Phyllis Kind Gallery, Chicago and New York. Address: c/o Phyllis Kind Gallery, 313 West Superior Street, Chicago, Illinois 60610, U.S.A.

Individual Exhibitions:

1970	Phyllis Kind Gallery, Chicago
1971	Candy Store Gallery, Folsom, California
1972	Phyllis Kind Gallery, Chicago
	Candy Store Gallery, Folsom, California
1973	Candy Store Gallery, Folsom, California
1974	Museum of Contemporary Art, Chicago
	Walker Art Center, Minneapolis
	Whitney Museum, New York
1975	San Francisco Art Institute
	Portland Center for the Visual Arts, Oregon
	Phyllis Kind Gallery, Chicago
1976	Phyllis Kind Gallery, New York

1977	Phyllis Kind Gallery, Chicago
	Phyllis Kind Gallery, New York
1979	Phyllis Kind Gallery, Chicago
1980	Rotterdamse Kunstichting, Rotterdam
	Phyllis Kind Gallery, New York
1981	Phyllis Kind Gallery, Chicago
1982	Phyllis Kind Gallery, Chicago
1983	James Mayor Gallery, London
1984	Phyllis Kind Gallery, New York
1985	Phyllis Kind Gallery, Chicago

Selected Group Exhibitions:

1966	*The Hairy Who*, Hyde Park Art Center, Chicago
1969	*Spirit of the Comics*, Institute of Contemporary Art, Philadelphia
1972	*Chicago Imagist Art*, Museum of Contemporary Art, Chicago
1973	*American Drawings 1963–1973*, Whitney Museum, New York
1977	*View of a Decade*, Museum of Contemporary Art, Chicago

1979	*Chicago Currents*, National Collection of Fine Art, Washington, D.C. (and subsequent tour)
1980	*Who Chicago?: An Exhibition of Contemporary Imagists*, Sunderland Art Centre, England (toured the U.K. and travelled to the Institute of Contemporary Art, Boston, and the Contemporary Art Center, New Orleans, 1980–82)
1983	*The Comic Art Show*, Whitney Museum, New York
1984	*Contemporary Focus 1974–84*, Hirshhorn Museum, Washington, D.C.
1987	*Chicago Figurative Imagery*, Northern Illinois University, Dekalb

Collections:

Whitney Museum, New York; Metropolitan Museum of Art, New York; Philadelphia Museum of Art; Anne D'Harnancourt Rishel Collection, Philadelphia; Sydney and Frances Lewis Collection, Richmond, Virginia; New Orleans Museum of Art; Art Institute of Chicago; Museum of Contemporary Art, Chicago; Morton Neumann Collection, Chicago; Museum des 20. Jahrhunderts, Vienna.

Publications:

By NUTT: article—"An Interview with Jim Nutt," with Russell Bowman, in *Arts Magazine* (New York), February 1978.

On NUTT: books—*Artworks and Packages* by Harold Rosenberg, New York 1969; *Chicago Imagist Art*, exhibition catalogue, with an essay by Franz Schulze, Chicago 1972; *Fantastic Images: Chicago Art since 1945* by Franz Schulze, Chicago 1972; *Made in Chicago*, exhibition catalogue, with an essay by Whitney Halstead, Sao Paulo 1973; *Jim Nutt*, exhibition catalogue, with an essay by Whitney Halstead, Chicago 1974; *Jim Nutt*, exhibition catalogue, with an essay by Phil Linhares, San Francisco 1975; *Who Chicago?: An Exhibition of Chicago Imagists*, exhibition catalogue, Sunderland, England 1980; *From Chicago*, exhibition catalogue, with an essay by Russell Bowman, New York 1982; *Focus on the Figure*, exhibition catalogue, with an essay by Barbara Haskell, New York 1982; articles—"Whimsical Amalgam of Pop Art and Surrealism" by Peter Schjeldahl in the *New York Times*, 15 September 1974; "Jim Nutt at the Whitney" by Dennis Adrian in *Art in America* (New York), September/October 1974; "Chicago: The Look" by April Kingsley in *Art Express*, (New York), January/February 1982; "Painting in Chicago" by Reagan Upshaw in *Portfolio* (New York). May/June 1982.

*   *   *

Nutt studied at the School of the Art Institute, Chicago from 1960-65. From 1966-69 he took part in the series of "Hairy Who" shows in Chicago which launched his career as one of the so-called "Chicago Imagists".

Nutt's drawings and paintings are full of strong linear elements, with cartoon-like imagery, highly inventive with a predilection for strong and brilliant colour and a highly refined technique. Dennis Adrian, in his essays on Chicago art, has written that Nutt's "careful finish gives the image a high degree of resolution, enhancing its visionary force".

Within these settings nude figures, widely distributed across the picture surface engage in erotic encounters, (though sex is never depicted). These are menacing fantasies, with a measure of scatalogical humour thrown in for good measure. Nutt also emphasises the object-like character of his works by incorporating the frame into the picture, or as Adrian writes: "Many of Nutt's paintings are painted on both sides (on plexiglass), so that there is no aspect of the painting *as an object* which does not manifest the artist's interest and concerns."

Since the early 1970s Nutt has taken part in major international exhibitions: in 1972 he was a featured artist at the Venice Biennale; in 1973 he was shown at the Sao Paulo Bienal; and in 1980–82 he was represented in the exhibition "Who Chicago", which toured America and Britain.

—Victoria Keller

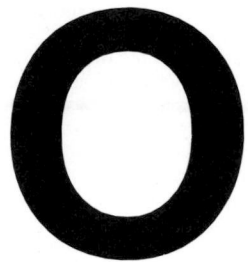

OITICICA, Helio.

Brazilian. Born in Rio de Janeiro, 26 July 1937.
Studied under the painter Ivan Serpa, Museu de Arte
Moderna, Rio de Janeiro, 1954. Lived and worked in
Rio until 1970, in New York City, from 1970. Member, Frente group, Rio de Janeiro, 1955, and Neo-Concrete group, 1959. Joined Magueira Samba dance
school: advanced to Passista (one of the lead
dancers), 1965. *Died in 1980.*

Individual Exhibitions:

1964   *Environment of Nuclei and Bolides*, Galeria G4, Rio
        de Janeiro
1967   *Collective Parangole*, Aterro Park, Rio de Janeiro
1968   *Apocalipopotesis*, Aterro Park, Rio de Janeiro
1969   Whitechapel Art Gallery, London
1980   Galeria Chaves, Porto Alegre, Brazil

Selected Group Exhibitions:

1965   *Opinion 65*, Museu de Arte Moderna, Rio de Ja-
        neiro
1967   *Brazilian New Objectivity*, Rio de Janeiro

Publications:

By OITICICA: book—*Carlos Vergara*, exhibition catalogue
text, Rio de Janeiro 1978; article—"On the Discovery of Cre-
leisure" in *Art and Artists* (London), April 1969.

On OITICICA: books—*Projectos de Helio Oiticica*, exhibition catalogue, by Mario Pedrosa, Rio de Janeiro 1960; *Kinetic Art* by Guy Brett, London 1967; articles—"Arte
Moderna, Arte Pos-Moderna, Helio Oiticica" by Mario Pedrosa in *Correio da Marha* (Brazil), July 1966; "Oiticica
Talks to Guy Brett" in *Studio International* (London), March
1969; "Helio Oiticica's People" By Jacqueline Barnitz in
Arts Magazine (New York), September/October 1972;
films—*Arte Publica* by Sirito, Rio de Janeiro 1965; *Apocali-
popotese* by Raimundo Amado and Leonardo Bartucci, Rio
de Janeiro 1968.

Sick and worried in London in 1969. Sitting uncomfortably in an office room at the Whitechapel Gallery
before his exhibition there began to take final shape,
Helio Oiticica made an instant recovery when his
friend came in with his magic necklaces. He had been
upset that very morning by a strange look—perhaps
the evil eye? He had been wearing no protection and
had been feeling ill ever since—maybe a mortal illness? In a strange country, so far from home, who
can tell? These reminiscences are set down to try and
help explain the dichotic nature of the man: part so-
phisticate, part primitive. And what else . . . ?

During his stay in London, Helio Oiticica's main
concern was not the progress of his exhibition, or
even the effect it was having on the outside world.
No. His central worry was over the fate of two "tropi-
calia" musicians—young men who had been arrested
in his native Brazil without reason and whose future
was in grave jeopardy unless someone did something
about them . . . something quickly.

At that time Oiticica himself was involved in Tropi-
calia, the name given for the whole syndrome of life
and its manifestations in a country with a hot climate,
an underdeveloped social conscious, and a legacy of
culture inherited in almost equal proportion from Portuguese merchant adventurers (who came in the main
from the peasantry) and from the imported slave populations from Africa. It is indeed a mixed birthright,
so perhaps it should not seem so strange that it has
spawned such dissident talents as those of Mario
Cravo, di Cavalcanti, Kracjberg, and—the most difficult to place—Helio Oiticica.

For him, life of the *favelas* (the shanty towns on the
hillsides), the dance, music, poetry, the magic of
Candomble/Macumba, stone, earth, water, and his
fire boxes (the *Bolides*) were all inextricably in combination to form the basis of valid art.

That kind of thinking is not welcome in a country
that for good or ill is run on philosophies more in
tune with those of the Medicis and the Borgias than
with contemporary thinking. It is not surprising that
Helio Oiticica left home for the United States; the
wonder was that he did not do so many years earlier.
Perhaps he was without fear. He certainly had no mis-
givings when he enjoined the Brazilian Ambassador
to the Court of St. James's to take off socks and shoes
so that he could wade through the narrow channel of
water that led to the *bolides* and the poetry deposited
in them, nor did he think it unusual that a young girl
should be induced to ease herself into an aperture and
climb into a box *bolide*, there to lie like a body
stretched out for burial. The participation of the spectator.

And besides the *bolides*, there were the capes (offering another opportunity for the visitor to join in
and help Oiticica create art), and—of course—there
was the dance.

—Sheldon Williams

O'KEEFFE, Georgia.

American. Born in Sun Prairie, Wisconsin, 15 November 1887. Studied art, under John Vaderpoel, Art
Institute of Chicago, 1905–06; under William Merritt
Chase, F. Luis Mora and Kenyon Cox, Art Students
League, New York, 1907–08 (Chase Still Life Scholarship, 1908); under Alan Bement, University of Virginia, Charlottesville, 1912; under Arthur Dow and
Alan Bement, Teachers College, Columbia Univer-
sity, New York, 1914–16. Married the photographer
Alfred Stieglitz in 1924 (died, 1946). Worked as
commercial artist, drawing lace and embroidery for
advertisements, Chicago, 1908–1910. Art Supervi-
sor, public schools, Amarillo, Texas. 1913–16; In-
structor, Summer Art School, University of Virginia,
Charlottesville, 1913–16; Columbia College, South
Carolina, 1915; Chairman, Art Department, West
Texas State Normal School, Canyon, 1916–18. Met
Alfred Stieglitz, New York, 1916, moved to New
York to concentrate on painting, 1918; travelled to
Taos, New Mexico, with Mrs. Paul (Rebecca) Strand

and Mabel Dodge Luhan, 1929; travelled extensively
in the United States, from 1932; travelled in Mexico,
1951, and in Europe, Asia, India, Middle East, Pacific Islands and North America, 1953–69. Worked
on exhibitions from the Stieglitz estate for the Museum of Modern Art, New York, and the Art Institute
of Chicago, 1947–1949. Recipient: Woman of Distinction Award, *World's Fair* Tomorrow Committee,
New York, 1939; Creative Arts Award, Brandeis University, Waltham, Massachusetts, 1963; Gold Medal
for Painting, National Institute of Arts and Letters,
New York, 1970; M. Carey Thomas Award, Bryn
Mawr College, Pennsylvania, 1971; Edward Macdowell Medal, 1972; Gold Medal, Skowhegan School
of Painting and Sculpture, Maine, 1973; First Annual
Governor's Award, New Mexico, 1974; Presidential
Medal of Freedom, Washington, D.C., 1977; National Medal of Arts, Washington, D.C., 1985.
D.F.A.: College of William and Mary, Williamsburg,
Virginia, 1938; University of New Mexico, Albu-
querque, 1964; Randolph-Macon Women's College,
Ashland, Virginia, 1966; Brown University, Provi-
dence, Rhode Island, 1971; Minnesota College of Art
and Design, Minneapolis, 1972; D.H.L.: University
of Wisconsin, Madison, 1942; Mt. Holyoke College,
South Hadley, Massachusetts, 1971. Member, Na-
tional Institute of Arts and Letters, 1947; American
Academy of Arts and Letters, 1963; and American
Academy of Arts and Sciences, 1966. Estate: Georgia
O'Keefe Foundation, Albiquiu, New Mexico 87510.
Died (in Santa Fe, New Mexico) 6 March 1986.

Individual Exhibitions:

1917   291 Gallery, New York
1923   *Alfred Stieglitz Presents 100 Pictures, Oils, Water-
        Colors, Pastels, and Drawings by Georgia
        O'Keeffe, American*, Anderson Galleries, New
        York
1924   *Alfred Stieglitz Presents 51 Recent Pictures, Oils,
        Water-Colors, Pastels and Drawings by Georgia
        O'Keeffe, American*, Anderson Galleries, New
        York.
1926   Intimate Gallery, New York
1927   Brooklyn Museum, New York (retrospective)
        Intimate Gallery, New York
        Anderson Galleries, New York
1928   Intimate Gallery, New York
        Anderson Galleries, New York
1929   Anderson Galleries, New York
        Intimate Gallery, New York
1930   An American Place, New York
1931   An American Place, New York
1932   An American Place, New York
1933   An American Place, New York
1934   An American Place, New York
1935   An American Place, New York
1936   *Exhibition of Recent Paintings, 1935*, An American
        Place, New York
1937   University of Minnesota, Minneapolis
        An American Place, New York
1938   College of William and Mary, Williamsburg, Vir-
        ginia
        An American Place, New York

1939 *Exhibition of Oils and Pastels*, An American Place, New York

1949 *Exhibitions of Oils and Pastels*, An American Place, New York

1941 An American Place, New York

1942 An American Place, New York

1943 An American Place, New York
Art Institute of Chicago (retrospective)

1944 *Paintings, 1943*, An American Place, New York

1945 An American Place, New York

1946 An American Place, New York
Museum of Modern Art, New York (retrospective)

1950 An American Place, New York

1952 Downtown Gallery, New York

1953 Museum of Fine Arts, Dallas

1955 Gibbes Art Gallery, Charleston, South Carolina
Downtown Gallery, New York

1958 Downtown Gallery, New York
Pomona College, Claremont, California

1960 Worcester Art Museum, Massachusetts (retrospective)

1961 Downtown Gallery, New York

1965 *An Exhibition of the Work of the Artist from 1915 to 1966*, Amon Carter Museum, Fort Worth, Texas (retrospective; travelled to Houston and Albuquerque)

1970 Whitney Museum, New York (retrospective; travelled to Chicago and San Francisco)

1978 Metropolitan Museum of Art, New York

1981 Whitney Museum, New York

1985 Museum of Fine Arts, Boston
Museum of New Mexico, Santa Fe

1986 Gerald Peters Gallery, Dallas

Selected Group Exhibitions:

1916 *New Paintings and Drawings*, 291 Gallery, New York

1917 *Annual Exhibition*, Society of Independent Artists, New York

1925 *7 Americans*, Anderson Galleries, New York

1929 *Paintings of 19 Living Americans*, Museum of Modern Art, New York

1937 *5 Painters*, University of Minnesota, Minneapolis

1955 *Contemporary American Painting*, Whitney Museum, New York

1958 *The Stieglitz Circle*, Pomona College, Claremont, California
Nature in Abstraction, Whitney Museum, New York (toured the United States)

1976 *20th Century American Drawing: Three Avant-Garde Generations*, Guggenheim Museum, New York

1985 *American Realism*, San Francisco Museum of Modern Art (travelled to Lincoln, Massachusetts; Austin, Texas; Evanston, Illinois; Williamstown, Massachusetts; Akron, Ohio; Madison, Wisconsin)

Collections:

Metropolitan Museum of Art, New York; Museum of Modern Art, New York; Brooklyn Museum, New York; Albright-Knox Art Gallery, Buffalo, New York; National Gallery of Art, Washington, D.C.; Phillips Collection, Washington, D.C.; Art Institute of Chicago; Carl Van Vechten Gallery of Fine Art, Fisk University, Nashville, Tennessee; Museum of Fine Arts, Dallas; Tate Gallery, London.

Publications:

By O'KEEFFE: books—*The Work of Georgia O'Keeffe*, portfolio, 1937; *Georgia O'Keeffe: Drawings*, New York 1968; *Some Memories of Drawings*, New York 1974; *Georgia O'Keeffe*, New York 1976; articles—statement, in *Manuscripts* (New York), December 1922; "Letters to Alfred Stieglitz" in *Georgia O'Keeffe* exhibition catalogue, New York 1938; "About Painting Desert Bones" in *Georgia O'Keeffe: Paintings, 1943*, exhibition catalogue, New York 1944; "Stieglitz: His Pictures Collected Him" in the *New York Times*, December 1949; interview in *The Artist's Voice: Talks with 17 Artists* by Katharine Kuh, New York 1962; letters in *Letters from 31 Artists to the Albright-Knox Art*

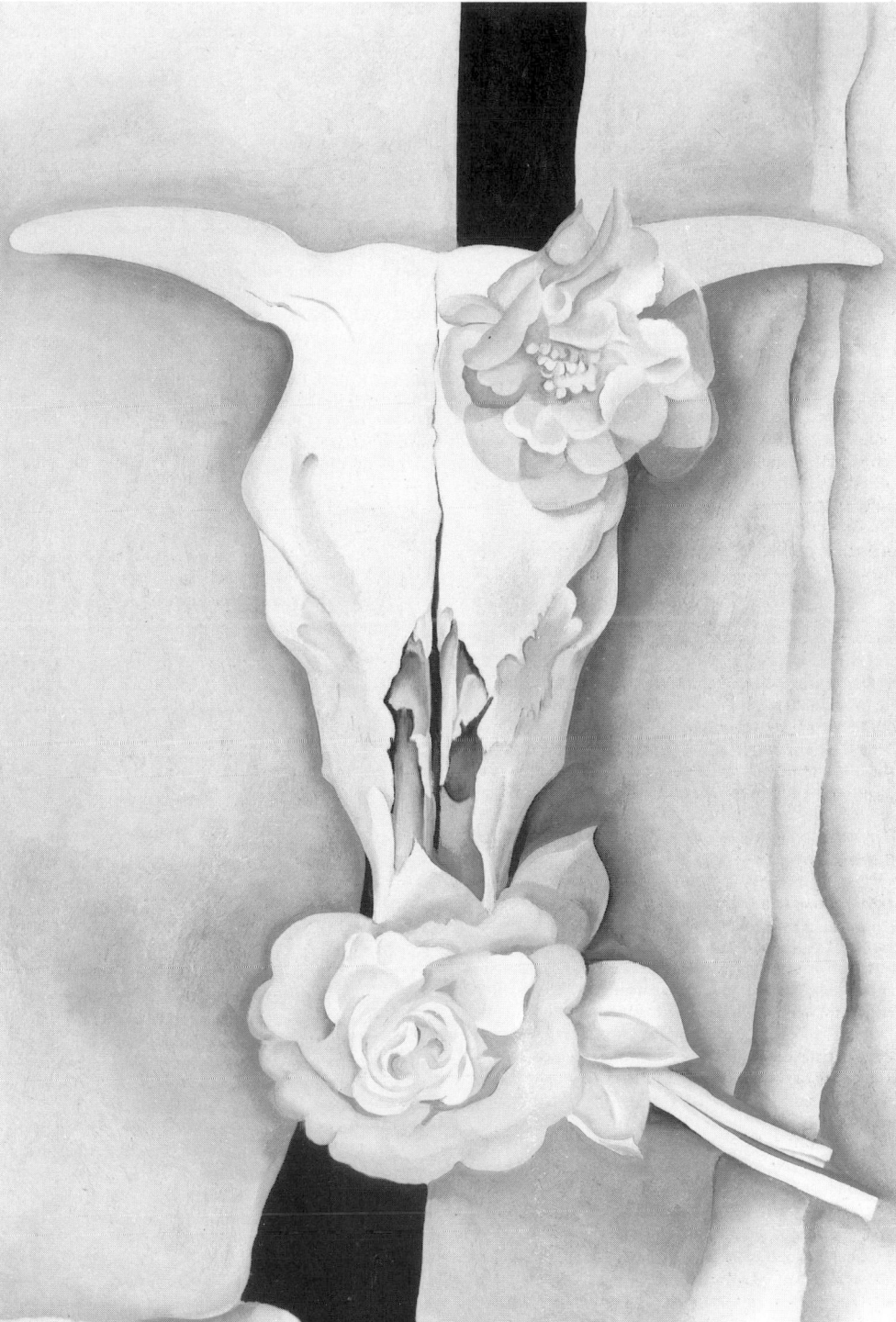

Georgia O'Keeffe: *Cow's Skull with Calico Roses*, 1931 Courtesy Art Institute of Chicago

Gallery, edited by Ethel Moore, Buffalo, New York 1970; introduction to *Georgia O'Keeffe: A Portrait by Alfred Stieglitz*, exhibition catalogue, New York 1978; "Georgia O'Keeffe: An American Original," interview, with M. L. Kotz, in the *Reader's Digest* (New York), May 1979.

On O'KEEFFE: books—*Alfred Stieglitz Presents 100 Pictures, Oils, Water-Colors, Pastels and Drawings by Georgia O'Keeffe, American*, exhibition catalogue (includes statement by O'Keeffe), New York 1923; *Alfred Stieglitz Presents 51 Recent Pictures, Oils, Water-Colors, Pastels and Drawings by Georgia O'Keeffe, American*, exhibition catalogue (includes statement by O'Keeffe), New York 1924; *Paintings By 19 Living Americans*, exhibition catalogue, New York 1929; *Georgia O'Keeffe: Exhibition of Recent Paintings, 1935*, catalogue, with text by Marsden Hartley, New York 1936; *The Work of Georgia O'Keeffe: A Portrait of 12 Paintings* by James Lane and Leo Katz, New York 1937; *Georgia O'Keeffe*, exhibition catalogue, New York 1938; *Georgia O'Keeffe: Exhibition of Oils and Pastels*, catalogue (includes

statement by O'Keeffe), New York 1939; *Georgia O'Keeffe: Exhibition of Oils and Pastels*, catalogues (includes statement by O'Keeffe), New York 1940; *Georgia O'Keeffe* by Daniel Catton Rich, Chicago 1943; *Abstract and Surrealist Art in America* by Sidney Janis, New York 1944; *Georgia O'Keeffe: Paintings, 1943*, exhibition catalogue, New York 1944; *Catalogue of the Alfred Stieglitz Collection for Fisk University*, Nashville, Tennessee 1949; *Georgia O'Keeffe: 40 Years of Her Art* by Daniel Catton Rich, Worchester, Massachusetts 1960; *Georgia O'Keeffe: An Exhibition of the Work of the Artist from 1915 to 1966*, catalogue, edited by Mitchell Wilder, Fort Worth, Texas 1966; *The Art of the Real: U.S.A. 1948-1968* by E. C. Goossen, New York 1968; *Georgia O'Keeffe* by Lloyd Goodrich and Doris Bry, New York 1970; *Georgia O'Keeffe: The Development of an American Modern*, dissertation, by Charles Child Eldredge, University of Minnesota, Minneapolis 1971; *The Students of William Merritt Chase* by Ronald G. Pisano, Huntington, New York 1973; *Early American Moderns: Painters of the Stieglitz Group* by Mahanri Sharp Young, New York 1974; *Alfred Stieglitz and* the American Avante-Garde by William Innes Homer, Boston 1977; *The Eye of Stieglitz*, exhibition catalogue, New York 1978; *Georgia O'Keeffe: A Portrait by Alfred Stieglitz*, exhibition catalogue, New York 1978; *A Recognizable Image: William Carlos Williams on Art on Artists*, edited by Bram Dikstra, New York 1978; *The Collection of Alfred Stieglitz* by Weston J. Naef, New York 1978; *Originals: American Women Artists* by Eleanor Munro, New York 1979; *Portrait of an Artist: A Biography of Georgia O'Keeffe* by Laurie Lisle, New York 1980; *Georgia O'Keeffe*, exhibition catalogue with text by Patterson Sims, New York 1981; *Georgia O'Keeffe*, exhibition catalogue with essay by Barbara Haskell, Santa Fe 1985; *Georgia O'Keeffe: One Hundred Flowers*, edited by Nicholas Callaway, London 1987.

Like several other American painters—John Marin and Edward Hopper to name two—Georgia O'Keeffe painted both New England and the Southwest. Her paintings of New York City are powerful semiabstractions which relate her to the "Precisionist" painters with their preoccupation with simplification, design, hard-edges, omitted or stylized shadows, areas of even color. But her real love affair is with the mountains, desert landscapes and enormous skies of places like New Mexico.

She can be called a realist in the way she depicts things we can read as known to us, but her editing of forms to serve her formal needs as a painter reveals an artist of acute and profound gifts of abstracting. She was really not much like any other painter. Her best work is charged with the mysterious. In her hands, flowers, looked at so closely and presented so out of natural scale, become worlds threatening to engulf us in sensual floods of shape and color as though we are bees about to become drunk on nectar. She turns sun-bleached skulls into icons for some unknown cult. Hills heave and spread like bodies. High-altitude clouds could be ice floes in a thin blue sea. The architecture of the adobe is shown so pure in line as to vie with Mies or Mondrian.

This mystery is partially created by a surreal sensibility—earth as flesh, small things become gigantic—but it also has something to do with subject matter of place—the flower in the desert skull—along with the effect light has on vision. True artists respond deeply to what they are looking at and how it is lighted. Whistler could never have painted the way he did if he'd lived in New Mexico. And when Gauguin journeyed to the South Seas his *color* changed along with his imagery, although his way of depicting forms did not alter radically from those of his Normandy paintings.

Nor do O'Keeffe's forms change that much from Big Town to small *arroyo*. But somehow the *air* does. No doubt it has something to do with the space between things and between those things and the sky. And perhaps, if sound has anything to do with visual responses, the availability of silence has something to do with it too.

—Ralph Pomeroy

OLDENBURG, Claes (Thure).

American. Born in Stockholm, Sweden, 28 January 1929; emigrated to the United States: naturalized, 1953. Studied literature and art, Yale University, New Haven, Connecticut, 1946–50, B.A. 1950; art, under Paul Weighardt, Art Institute of Chicago, 1952–54. Married Pat Muschinski in 1960. Worked as an apprentice reporter, City News Bureau, Chicago, 1952–54; illustrator, *Chicago Magazine*, 1955–56; operated Ray Gun Manufacturing Company, New York and worked part-time in Cooper Union Museum School Library, New York, 1956–61; met Jim Dine, George Brecht, Allan Kaprow, George Segal and Robert Whitman, New York, 1959; collaborated with Lippincott Environmental Arts Inc., now Lippincott Inc., New York, 1969; established studio in New Haven, Connecticut, 1969–70. Recipient: American Institute of Architects Award, 1977. Agent: Leo Castelli Gallery, 420 West Broadway, New York, New York 10012. Address: 556 Broome Street, New York, New York 10013, U.S.A.

Individual Exhibitions:

1959	Cooper Union Art School Library, New York
	Judson Gallery, New York
1960	*Snapshots from the City*, Judson Gallery, New York
	Reuben Gallery, New York
1961	*Ironworks Fotodeath (Circus)*, Reuben Gallery, New York
1962	Ray Gun Theater, New York
	Museum of Contemporary Art, Dallas
	Green Gallery, New York
1963	Richard Feigen Gallery, Chicago
	Gayety, University of Chicago
	Dwan Gallery, Los Angeles
1964	Sidney Janis Gallery, New York
	Galerie Sonnabend, Paris
	Pace Gallery, Boston
1965	Sidney Janis Gallery, New York
1966	*New Work*, Sidney Janis Gallery, New York
	Claes Oldenburg; Skulpturer och Techningar, Moderna Museet, Stockholm
	Robert Fraser Gallery, London
1967	Museum of Contemporary Art, Chicago
	Sidney Janis Gallery, New York
	Dine/Oldenburg/Segal: Painting/Sculpture, Art Gallery of Ontario, Toronto
1968	*Notes*, Irving Blum Gallery, Los Angeles
	Sidney Janis Gallery, New York
1969	*Constructions, Models and Drawings*, Richard Feigen Gallery, Chicago
	Sidney Janis Gallery, New York
	Drawings and Prints, Museum of Modern Art, New York (retrospective; toured Europe)
1970	University of California at Los Angeles Art Gallery
	Sidney Janis Gallery, New York
	Stedelijk Museum, Amsterdam
	Kunsthalle, Dusseldorf
	Tate Gallery, London
1971	*Object into Monument*, Pasadena Art Museum, California (toured the United States and Japan)
	New Work, Sidney Janis Gallery, New York
	Margo Leavin Gallery, Los Angeles
1972	University of California Art Museum, Berkeley
	Philadelphia Museum of Art
	Des Moines Art Center, Iowa
	Fort Worth Art Center, Texas
	Nelson-Atkins Museum, Kansas City, Missouri
1973	Art Institute of Chicago
	Minami Gallery, Tokyo
	Recent Prints, Knoedler and Company, New York
	New Gallery, Cleveland
1974	Leo Castelli Gallery, New York
	Hammarskjold Plaza, New York
	Notes in Hand, Lo Spazio Gallery, Rome
	The Lipstick Comes Back, Yale University Art Gallery, New Haven, Connecticut
1975	*Zeichnungen*, Kunsthalle, Tübingen
	Kunstmuseum, Basle
	Städtische Galerie in Lenbachhaus, Munich
	Nationalgalerie, West Berlin
	The Alphabet In L.A., Margo Leavin Gallery, Los Angeles
	6 Themes, Walker Art Center, Minneapolis
	Denver Art Museum
	Seattle Art Museum
	Erotic Fantasy Drawings, Mayor Gallery, London
	Museum Haus Lange, Krefeld, West Germany
	Petersburg Press, New York
	Dootson-Calderhead Gallery, Seattle
	Zarvan Gallery, Teheran
1976	Kaiser Wilhelm Museum, Krefeld, West Germany
	Museum des 20. Jahrhunderts, Vienna
	Städtisches Kunstinstitut, Frankfurt
	Kestner-Gesellschaft, Hannover
	Notes in Hand, Galeria 42, Barcelona
	Institute of Contemporary Art, Boston
	Hayden Gallery, Massachusetts Institute of Technology, Cambridge
	Art Gallery of Ontario, Toronto
	Sable-Castelli Gallery Limited, Toronto
	Margo Leavin Gallery, Los Angeles
	John Berggruen Gallery, San Francisco
	Kestner-Gesellschaft, Hannover
	Leo Castelli Gallery, New York
	Multiples Gallery, New York
1977	Louisiana Museum, Humblebaek, Denmark
	Tekeningen, Aquarellen en Grafiek/Drawings, Watercolors and Prints, Stedelijk Museum, Amsterdam
	Dessins, Aquarelles et Estampes, Centre Georges Pompidou, Paris
	Richard Gray Gallery, Chicago
	Social Security Administration, Chicago (installation)
	The Inverted Q, Akron Art Institute, Ohio
	Mouse Museum/Ray Gun Wing, 2 Collections/2 Buildings, Museum of Contemporary Art, Chicago
1978	Phoenix Art Museum, Arizona
	St. Louis Art Museum
	Museum of Fine Arts, Dallas
	Whitney Museum, New York
	Margo Leavin Gallery, Los Angeles
1979	Rijksmuseum Kröller-Müller, Otterlo, Netherlands
	Museum Ludwig, Cologne
1980	Leo Castelli Gallery, New York
	Prints by Howard Hodgkin 1977–1979 and Claes Oldenburg 1971–1979, Waddington Graphics, London
1983	Margo Leavin Gallery, Los Angeles

Selected Group Exhibitions:

1960	*New Forms/New Media I*, Martha Jackson Gallery, New York
1964	*Painting and Sculpture of a Decade 1954–64*, Tate Gallery, London
1968	*The Obsessive Image 1960–1968*, Institute of Contemporary Arts, London
1974	*American Pop Art*, Whitney Museum, New York
1976	*Drawing Now*, Museum of Modern Art, New York (toured Europe and Scandinavia)
1978	*Drawings for Outdoor Sculpture 1946–1977*, Amherst College, Massachusetts (toured the United States)
1979	*American Portraits of the 60's and 70's*, Aspen Center for the Visual Arts, Colorado
1980	*Printed Art: A View of 2 Decades*, Museum of Modern Art, New York
1981	*Selections from Castelli: Drawings and Works on Paper*, Neil Ovsey Gallery, Los Angeles
1987	*American Painting: Abstract Expressionism and After*, San Francisco Museum of Modern Art

Collections:

Museum of Modern Art, New York; Whitney Museum, New York; Art Institute of Chicago; Los Angeles County Museum of Art; National Gallery of Canada, Ottawa; Tate Gallery, London; Victoria and Albert Museum, London; Stedelijk Museum, Amsterdam; Kunstmuseum, Basle; Moderna Museet, Stockholm.

Publications:

By OLDENBURG: books—*Store Days, Documents from The Store (1961) and Ray Gun Theater (1962)*, with Emmett Williams, New York 1967; *Injun and Other Stories (1960)*, New York 1966; *Some Program Notes About Monuments, Mainly*, supplement catalogue, New York 1967; *Claes Oldenburg: Notes*, exhibition catalogue, Los Angeles 1968; *Proposals for Monuments and Buildings 1965–1969*, Chicago 1969; *Notes In Hand*, New York and Basle 1971; *Raw Notes*, Halifax, Nova Scotia 1973; *More Ray Gun Poems (1960)*, Philadelphia 1973; *Photo Log, May 1974–August 1976*, Stuttgart 1976; *Press Log, May 1974–August 1976*, Stuttgart 1976; articles—"The Artist Says: Claes Oldenburg" in *Art Voices* (New York), Summer 1965: "The Object: Still Life," interview, with Jan McDevitt, In *Craft Horizons* (New York), September/October 1965; "Claes Oldenburg: Extracts from the Studio Notes, 1962–64," selected by Max Kozloff, in *Artforum* (New York), January 1966; "Oldenburg, Lichtenstein,

Warhol: Discussion," edited by Bruce Glaser, in *Artforum* (New York), February 1966; "Eftertankar" in *Konstrevy* (Stockholm), no. 5/6, 1966; "Oldenburg's Monuments," interview, with Gene Baro, in *Art and Artists* (London), December 1966; comments in *Perspecta 11* (New Haven, Connecticut), 1967; "Take a Cigarette Butt and Make It Heroic," interview, with Suzi Gablik, and "Egomessages About Pollock" in *Artnews* (New York), May 1967; "America: War and Sex, Etc." in *Arts Magazine* (New York), Summer 1967; conversations, with others, in *Theatre of Mixed Means* by Richard Kostelanetz, New York 1968; "The Artist Speaks: Claes Oldenburg," interview, with John Coplans, in *Art in America* (New York), March/April 1969; "The Bedroom Ensemble, Replica 1" in *Studio International* (London), July/August 1969; "How to Keep Sculpture Alive, In and Out of a Museum," interview, in *Arts Magazine* (New York), September/October 1969; "Eigen Statement" in *Art Now: New York* (New York), October 1969; "Chronology of Drawings" in *Studio International* (London), June 1970; "Claes Oldenburg, An Interview," with A. W. Reaves, in *Artforum* (New York), October 1972; "Oldenburg on Multiples," interview, with John Loring, in *Arts Magazine* (New York), May 1974; "History of the Alphabet/Good Humor" and "The Letter Q" in *The Alphabet in L.A.*, exhibition catalogue, Los Angeles 1975; interview, with Martin Friedman, in *Oldenburg: 6 Themes*, exhibition catalogue, Minneapolis 1975; "About California" in *Vision* (Oakland, California), no.1, 1975; "Interview mit Claes Oldenburg," with Friedrich Bach, in *Das Kunstwerk* (Baden-Baden, West Germany), May 1975; "Added Comments" in *The Soft Screw*, exhibition catalogue, Los Angeles 1976; "Collecting Ray Guns in New York" in *Vision* (Oakland, California) no.3, 1976; "The Double-Nose/Purse/Punching Bag/Ashtray" in *Tracks* (New York), Winter 1976; radio broadcasts—discussion, with Roy Lichtenstein and Andy Warhol, moderated and edited by Bruce Glaser, on WBAI-FM, New York, June 1964; interview, with J. Seigel, on WBAI-FM, New York, 5 October and 10 October 1969.

On OLDENBURG: books—*Exhibition of Recent Work by Claes Oldenburg*, catalogue, New York 1964; *Claes Oldenburg*, exhibition catalogue, Paris 1964; *New Work by Claes Oldenburg*, exhibition catalogue, New York 1966; *Claes Oldenburg, Skupturer och Techningar*, exhibition catalogue, Stockholm 1966; *Oldenburg*, exhibition catalogue, New York 1967; *Dine/Oldenburg/Segal: Painting/Sculpture*, exhibition catalogue, with a foreword by Brydon Smith, text by Ellen H. Johnson, Toronto and Buffalo, New York 1967; *American Sculpture of the 60's*, exhibition catalogue, Los Angeles 1967; *Claes Oldenburg: Drawings and Prints*, with an introduction and commentary by Gene Baro, New York and London 1969; *Claes Oldenburg: Constructions, Models and Drawings*, exhibition catalogue, Chicago 1969; *Claes Oldenburg*, exhibition catalogue, by Barbara Rose, New York 1969; *Claes Oldenburg*, exhibition catalogue, Amsterdam 1970; *Claes Oldenburg*, exhibition catalogue, London 1970; *New Work by Claes Oldenburg*, exhibition catalogue, New York 1970; *Claes Oldenburg: Object into Monument*, exhibition catalogue by Barbara Haskell, Pasadena, California 1971; *Experiment in Grafiek: Gemini GEL*, exhibition catalogue, by J. Leering, Eindhoven, Netherlands 1971; *Claes Oldenburg* by Ellen Johnson, Baltimore 1971; *Claes Oldenburg: Recent Prints*, exhibition catalogue, New York 1973; *Notes In Hand*, exhibition catalogue, Rome 1974 ; *The Lipstick Comes Back*, exhibition catalogue, with an introduction by Alan Shestack, essay by Susan B. Casteras, New Haven, Connecticut 1974; *Claes Oldenburg: The Alphabet in L.A.*, Los Angeles 1975; *Claes Oldenburg: 6 Themes*, exhibition catalogue, with an introduction by Martin Friedman, Minneapolis 1975; *Zeichnungen von Claes Oldenburg*, Tübingen, West Germany 1975; *Erotic Fantasy Drawings*, exhibition catalogue, with essay by Richard Morphet, London 1975; *Drawing Now*, exhibition catalogue, with text by Barbara Rose, New York 1976; *The Soft Screw*, exhibition catalogue, Los Angeles 1976; *Notes in Hand*, exhibition catalogue, Barcelona 1976; *Mouse Museum/Ray Gun Wing, Two Collections/Two Buildings*, exhibition catalogue, Chicago 1977; *Claes Oldenburg: Tekeningen, Aquarellen en Grafiek/Drawings, Watercolors and Prints*, exhibition catalogue, Amsterdam 1977; *Oldenburg: The Inverted Q*, exhibition catalogue, by Robert Doty, Akron, Ohio 1977; *Monuments and Monoliths, A Metamorphosis*, exhibition catalogue, Roslyn, New York 1978.

After graduating from Yale, Claes Oldenburg worked as a reporter for a time. Then he took classes at the Art Institute of Chicago and opened a studio where he made magazine illustrations and easel paintings. The first three-dimensional objects did not appear until 1957 after he had moved to New York and met with artists working there in environmental and theatrical projects and happenings.

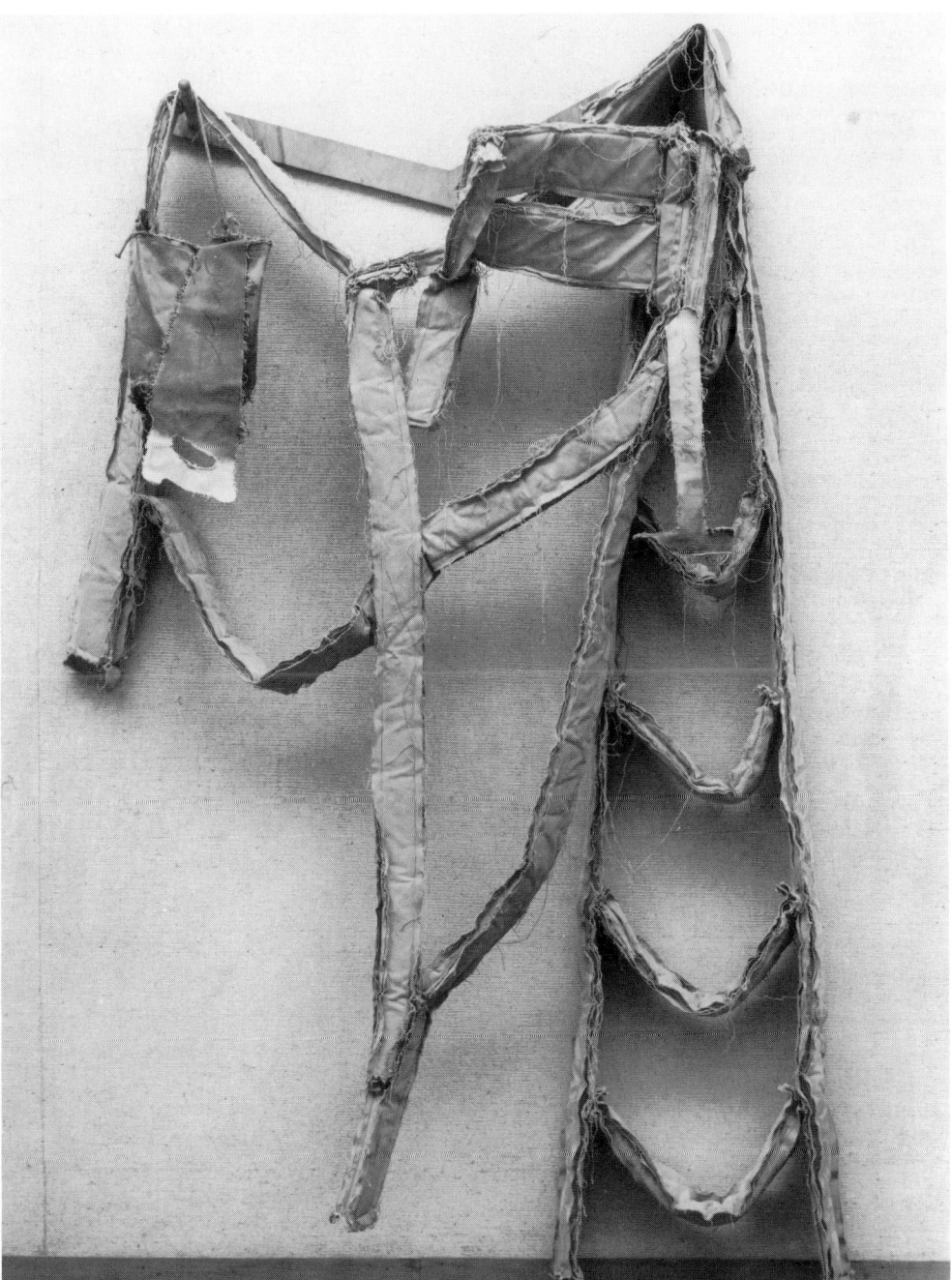

Claes Oldenburg: *Giant Soft Ladder*, 1967

This was the fertilising ambiance where he began to produce his art objects in relation to what surrounded him. From deep sessions of drawing the still lifes of daily existence, he went into their reconstitution in flat constructions of hessian, cardboard and other ready-made materials. Collage and papier mache were used to compress some of the images he drew as grafitti on the walls of the Bowery and other streets of downtown Manhattan. They were shown for the first time as "The Street" at the Judson Gallery in 1960 and later at Reuben. Next came the Flags he produced from flotsam gathered on the Massachusetts beaches.

In 1961, after contributing to a group show at the Martha Jackson Gallery replicas in reliefs, signs and advertisements copied from actual goods on display in neighbourhood shops, he opened "The Store" in his studio. Here he added some free-standing pieces in the form of a roast joint and a two-piece bathing suit in plaster. From these modest starts Oldenburg moved up next year with his first offering of giant soft sculptures taking a part of the Pop Art then flowering in profusion.

The mammoth cheeseburgers and ice cream cones by their size made a new dimension in art that Oldenburg saw as a softening, a flaccidity in attitude as well as appearance. Oldenburg continued to work on constructions that fitted naturally into themes. After the Store came the Home, Electrical and Mechanical Objects and the Car. "Bedroom Ensemble" (1964), originally installed at Sidney Janis Gallery, was based on a motel on the way to Malibu. The aim was to remove emotive and personal attitudes so that it presented only formal attributes like the Pyramids.

This attempt to introduce a time lag in advance in the contemplation of contemporary objects of everyday use had its surrealist shock especially when embodied in such projects as "Hats Blowing in the Wind" as a feasible monument for a city square.

Oldenburg acknowledged Duchamp's theory of art as a special way of regarding objects by his "Soft Engine for Airflow with a Can and Transmission". Like Goeritz's emotional architecture and Christo's draped mountains, Oldenburg's soft monuments take on the inspirational fantasy of proportional surprise as much by juxtaposition as by transformation from still life to robot character. He engages outrage to activate the apathetic.

—G. S. Whittet

OLITSKI, Jules.

American. Born Jevel Demikovosky in Snovsk, Russia, 27 March 1922; emigrated with family to the United States, 1924; naturalized, 1942. Studied at Beaux Arts Institute, New York, 1940–42; National Academy of Design, New York, 1940–42; Zadkine School of Sculpture, Paris, 1949; Académie de la Grande Chaumière, Paris, 1950–51; New York University, New York, 1951–56, B.S. 1952, M.A. 1954. Served in the United States Army, Special Training Unit, Purdue University, Lafayette, Indiana, 1942–45. Married Gladys Katz in 1944 (divorced, 1951); married Andrea Hill Pearce in 1956 (divorced, 1975); daughters: Eve and Lauren; married Joan Forges Gorby in 1980. Independent painter and sculptor, since 1951: lives and works in New York City, and in New Hampshire and Florida. Associate Professor of Art, State University of New York at New Paltz, 1954–55; Curator, New York University Art Education Gallery, New York, 1955–56; Art instructor and Fine Arts Department Coordinator, C. W. Post College, Long Island University, Greenvale, New York, 1956–63; Instructor in Art, Bennington College, Vermont, 1963–76; Sally and Milton Avery Professor, Bard College, Annandale-on-Hudson, New York, 1987. Recipient: Purchase Prize, Ford Foundation, 1964; First Prize and Gold Medal, *30th Biennial Exhibition,* Corcoran Gallery, Washington, D.C., 1967; Distinction in the Arts Award, University of South Carolina, 1975. Agents: Knoedler Contemporary Art, 19 East 70th Street, New York, New York 10021; David Mirvish Gallery, 596 Markham Street, Toronto, Ontario, Canada; Kasmin Ltd., 10 Clifford Street, London W1X1RB, England. Address: 207 Fifth Avenue, Brooklyn, New York 11215; or R.D. No. 1, Bear Island, Lovejoy Sands Road, Meredith, New Hampshire 03253, U.S.A.

Individual Exhibitions:

1950	Galerie Huit, Paris
1958	Alexander Iolas Gallery, New York
1959	French and Company Inc., New York
1960	French and Company Inc., New York
1961	Poindexter Gallery, New York
1962	New Gallery, Bennington College, New York
	Poindexter Gallery, New York
1963	Galleria d'Arte Santa Croce, Florence
	Galleria Trastevere di Topazia Alliata, Rome
	Galleria Toninelli, Milan
	Poindexter Gallery, New York
	3 American Painters: Lewis, Noland, Olitski, Norman Mackenzie Gallery, Regina, Saskatchewan
1964	Richard Gray Gallery, Chicago
	David Mirvish Gallery, Toronto
	Kasmin Gallery, London
	Galerie Lawrence, Paris
	Poindexter Gallery, New York
1965	Poindexter Gallery, New York
	David Mirvish Gallery, Toronto
	Kasmin Gallery, London
	3 American Painters: Noland, Olitski, Stella, Fogg Art Museum, Harvard University, Cambridge, Massachusetts
1966	Nicholas Wilder Gallery, Los Angeles
	André Emmerich Gallery, New York
	David Mirvish Gallery, Toronto
	Kasmin Gallery, London
	Frankenthaler, Noland, Olitski, New Brunswick Museum, Fredericton (toured Canada)
1967	Corcoran Gallery, Washington, D.C. (retrospective; toured United States)
	David Mirvish Gallery, Toronto
	André Emmerich Gallery, New York
	Kasmin Gallery, London
1968	Institute of Contemporary Art, Philadelphia
	David Mirvish Gallery, Toronto
	Kasmin Gallery, London
1969	French and Company Inc., New York
	Metropolitan Museum, New York
	Lawrence Rubin Gallery, New York
	David Mirvish Gallery, New York

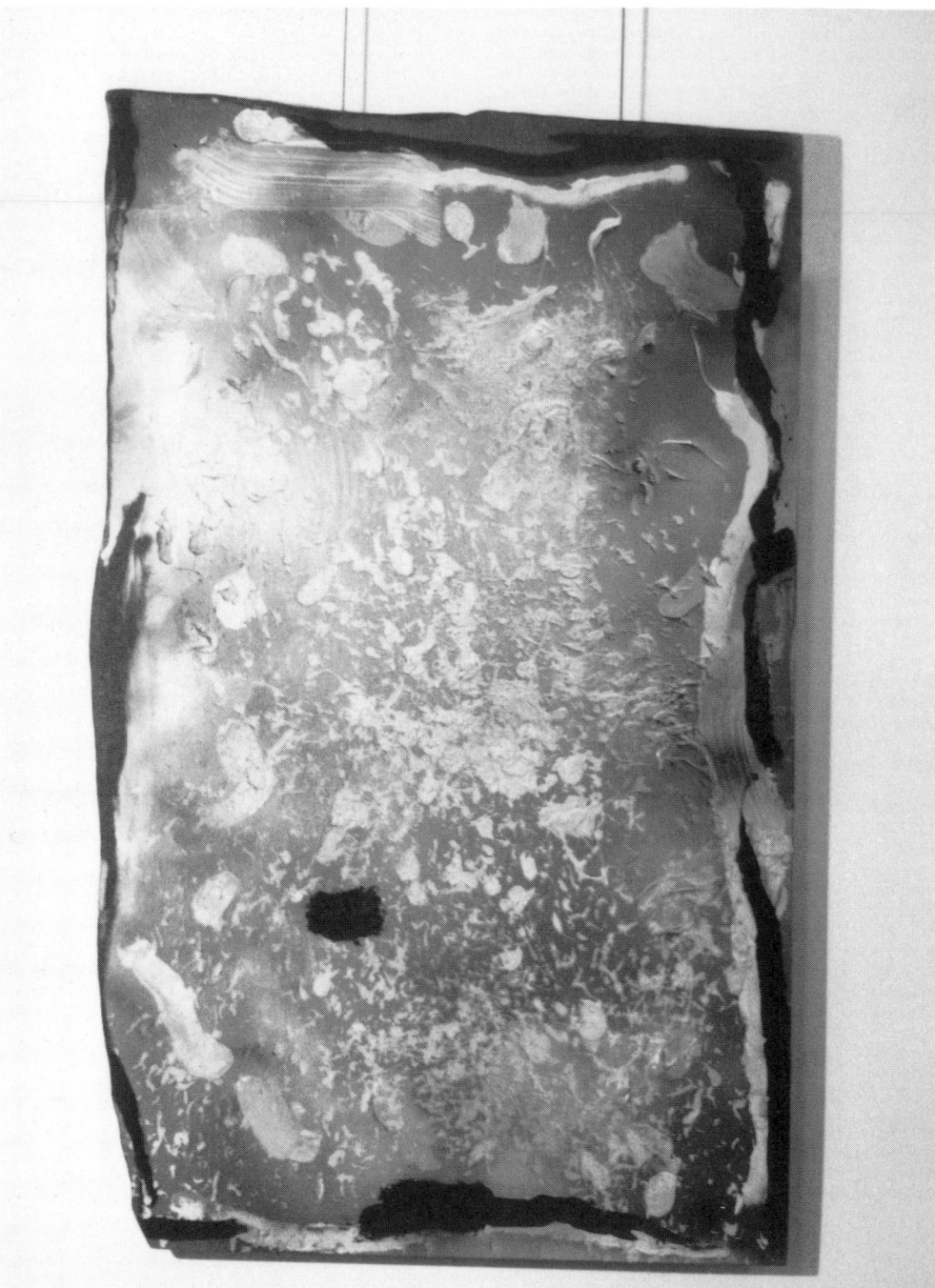

Jules Olitski: *Lakshmi Steam,* 1986

	Kasmin Gallery, London
1970	Lawrence Rubin Gallery, New York
	David Mirvish Gallery, Toronto
	Kasmin Gallery, London
1971	Lawrence Rubin Gallery, New York
	David Mirvish Gallery, Toronto
	Kasmin Gallery, London
1972	Lawrence Rubin Gallery, New York
	David Mirvish Gallery, Toronto
	Kasmin Gallery, London
1973	Lawrence Rubin Gallery, New York
	Nicholas Wilder Gallery, Los Angeles
	André Emmerich Gallery, Zurich
	Knoedler Contemporary Art, New York
	Museum of Fine Arts, Boston (retrospective; toured the United States)
	David Mirvish Gallery, Toronto
1974	Corcoran Gallery, Washington, D.C. (toured the United States, Canada, and Europe)
	David Mirvish Gallery, Toronto
	André Emmerich Gallery, New York
	Knoedler Contemporary Art, New York
1975	David Mirvish Gallery, Toronto
	Knoedler Contemporary Art, New York

	Galerie Wentzel, Hamburg
	Dart Gallery, Chicago
1976	Knoedler Contemporary Art, New York
	Watson/deNagy Gallery, Houston
1977	André Emmerich Gallery, New York
	Knoedler Contemporary Art, New York
	Galerie Wentzel, Hamburg
	Museum of Fine Arts, Boston
	Amerika Haus, West Berlin
	Hirshhorn Museum, Washington, D.C.
1978	David Mirvish Gallery, Toronto
	Knoedler Gallery, London
1979	Knoedler Contemporary Art, New York
	Edmonton Art Gallery, Alberta
1981	Janus Gallery, Los Angeles
	André Emmerich Gallery, New York
	Paintings from the 60's, M. Knoedler and Company, New York
	Gallery One, Toronto
	Galerie Wentzel, Hamburg
	Knoedler Gallery, London
	Harcus/Krakow Gallery, Boston
	The Downtown Gallery, Edmonton, Alberta
	Meredith Long and Co., Houston

1982   Gallery One, Toronto
Downstairs Gallery, Edmonton, Alberta
Harcus/Krakow Gallery, Boston
Meredith Long and Co., Houston
Martha White Gallery, Louisville, Kentucky
1983   Gallery One, Toronto
M. Knoedler and Co., New York
Yares Gallery, Scottsdale, Arizona
Galerie Wentzel, Cologne
Harcus Gallery, Boston
1984   André Emmerich Gallery, New York
Yares Gallery, Scottsdale, Arizona
Gallery One, Toronto
Chateau de Jau, Perpignan, France (retrospective)
Galerie Daniel Templon, Paris
1985   Musée de Valence, France
Duke University, Durham, North Carolina
M. Knoedler and Co., New York
Galerie Wentzel, Cologne
Phillips Exeter Academy, New Hampshire
1986   André Emmerich Gallery, New York
Yares Gallery, Scottsdale, Arizona (retrospective)
Gallery One, Toronto
Galerie Wentzel, Cologne
Yares Gallery, Scottsdale, Arizona
1987   M. Knoedler and Co., New York
Meredith Long and Co., Houston
Gallery Camino Real, Boca Raton, Florida
Galerie Wentzel, Cologne
André Emmerich Gallery, New York
Gallery One, Toronto

Selected Group Exhibitions:

1968   *L'Art Vivant 1965–1968*, Fondation Maeght, St. Paul-de-Vence, France
1969   *New York Painting and Sculpture 1940–1970*, Metropolitan Museum of Art, New York
1973   *11 Artistes Américains*, Musée d'Art Contemporain, Montreal
1974   *The Great Decade of American Abstraction: Modernist Art 1960–1970*, Museum of Fine Arts, Houston
1977   *Drawings of the 70's*, Art Institute of Chicago
1979   *American Painting of the 1970's*, Albright-Knox Art Gallery, Buffalo, New York
1981   *Frankenthaler/Louis/Noland/Olitski*, Centre d'Arts Plastiques Contemporains, Bordeaux
1983   *Early Works by Contemporary Masters*, André Emmerich Gallery, New York
1985   *Grand Compositions*, Fort Worth Art Museum, Texas
1987   *Abstract Painting '57–'87*, Gallery Camino Real, Boca Raton, Florida

Collections:

Museum of Modern Art, New York; Whitney Museum, New York; Albright-Knox Art Gallery, Buffalo, New York; Corcoran Art Gallery, Washington, D.C.; Hirshhorn Museum and Sculpture Garden, Smithsonian Institution, Washington, D.C.; Chrysler Museum, Norfolk, Virginia; Cleveland Museum of Art; Art Institute of Chicago; Norton Simon Museum of Art, Pasadena, California; Norman Mackenzie Art Gallery, Regina, Saskatchewan.

Publications:

By OLITSKI: articles—"Painting in Color" in *33rd Biennale of Art*, exhibition catalogue, Venice 1966; "On Sculpture" in *Metropolitan Museum of Art Bulletin* (New York), April 1969; "First Chapter (A Short Story)" in *Partisan Review* (New Brunswick), no. 2, 1978; "Reflections on Masterworks" in *Update* (Edmonton), July/August 1985; essay in *The Courage of Conviction*, edited by Phillip L. Berman, New York 1985; essay in *Jules Olitski: A Retrospective View*, exhibition catalogue, Scottsdale 1986.

On OLITSKI: books:—*3 New American Painters: Louis, Noland, Olitski*, exhibition catalogue, By Clement Greenberg, Regina, Saskatchewan 1963; *3 American Painters: Noland, Olitski, Stella*, exhibition catalogue, by Michael Fried, Cambridge, Massachusetts 1965 *Jules Olitski*, exhibition catalogue, by Kenworth Moffett, Boston 1973; *Great Drawings of All Time: The Twentieth Century*, edited by Victoria Throson, New York 1979; *Jules Olitski*, by Kenworth Moffett, New York 1981; *Jules Olitski*, exhibition catalogue by Dominique Fourcade, Perpignan 1984; articles—"Jules Olitski's New Paintings" by Michael Fried in *Artforum* (New York), November 1965; "Frankenthaler, Kelly, Lichtenstein, Olitski: A Preview of the American Selection at the 1966 Venice Biennale" by Henry Geldzahler in *Artforum* (New York), June 1966; "The Sculpture of Jules Olitski" by Kenworth Moffett in *Metropolitan Museum of Art Bulletin* (New York), April 1969; "Painterliness Redefined: Jules Olitski and Recent Abstract Art" by John Elderfield in *Art International* (Zurich), December 1972, April 1973; "Jules Olitski as Post-Raphaelite" by Vivien Raynor in the *New York Times*, 31 March 1978; "Jules Olitski" by Jeanne Silverthorne in *Artforum* (New York), May 1984; "Jules Olitski" by Valentin Tatransky in *Arts Magazine* (New York), May 1985.

*

I was not at all on the scene in the forties and barely, if at all, in the late fifties. I don't really feel on the scene today either. Concerning present taste and sensibility, I am bemused by collectors and museum people who dote equally, at one and the same time, upon their David Smith *and* their George Segal, upon their Kenneth Noland *and* their James Rosenquist, upon their Anthony Caro *and* their Alexander Calder. When did it begin? Did the few collectors twenty or thirty years ago of Pollock and Still also go for Ben Shahn and Corbino? In the latter nineteenth century the collectors and critics who went for Monet and Picasso didn't go for Bouguereau and Meissonier too. (This easy acceptance in our time of high art alongside lesser or even meretricious art was first brought to my attention by Clement Greenberg in a talk he gave at Bennington College eight or nine years ago.)

Attitude toward money? Maybe what's new is the expectation of artists that real money is to be made in the making and selling of art. Art dealers are quite properly out to make a profit. I doubt there has been any change in their area. An art maker of one sort or another has existed for at least several centuries, which certainly hasn't prevented great art from being made, or great artists from practicing their art. Artists always hope that one day they will find their Kahnweiler. But the sad truth is there are no Kahnweilers. Even Kahnweiler wasn't Kahnweiler, at least not as he has been pictured in retrospect. Money in itself doesn't corrupt. One has to be accessible to corruption. Money can be a help, especially when you have a family. That ought to be obvious.

As to the kind of painting and sculpture being done, I don't think a time that has produced a Nolan, a Caro, among at least an armful of younger and older artists, has anything to be apologetic for.

I suppose one enormous difference, maybe unique to recent times, is the emergence of artists in their twenties and early thirties (there may even be some in their teens, though I don't know any) who are given major shows in respectable galleries and museums and are taken very seriously by the art public, art critics, collectors, and maybe most damaging of all, by themselves. The young artist who feels that every move he makes is being watched by critics and collectors, by his peers and the public, not unnaturally may come to have a vested interest in maintaining his success. One painter I know—one who survived his youthful success and is now working better than ever—said to me one day, rather plaintively, "It was like growing up in public." There is value in long years of obscurity, if one doesn't go insane or become suicidal, in that, simply because nobody is looking, the habit of fooling around and trying things out gets ingrained. This seems to be true for painters and sculptors (with some exceptions) in a way that it isn't for poets, composers, mathematicians, or chess masters.

It's hard to take risks if you feel you have something to lose. And it's that much harder if you have something to lose at about the same time as you've begun to shave. I don't think it occurred to serious young artists of my generation (I am fifty-six years old now) that money and fame would be there at the very outset of our careers. At least I myself never

thought it. It simply wasn't a part of the reality of my twenties, thirties, or early forties.

There are, of course, other differences between then and now. There is an increasing emphasis on the tying of art and the marketplace to social causes, politics, certain groups or blocs of people. To my mind art is a democratic situation; anyone can look at it and make it, and everyone should have his or her chance to be seen, if the work has anything to it. That's just it. Quality must remain the paramount concern. The quality of the art and the quality of the viewer.

—Jules Olitski

*

Jules Olitski is one of the leading American post-painterly abstractionists, a colour field painter who in the wake of Morris Louis developed his own methods of using colour to provide a voluptuous sensual experience. His sprayed paintings are completely devoid of depicted shape, and represent a radical and thoroughgoing attempt to make art out of nothing but colour. This has meant that for those American critics who see colour field abstraction as the quintessence of contemporary art, Olitski has become the undisputed living master, whose innovations have placed him at the farthest outpost of progress in art. Thus for Kenworth Moffett, who directed the 1973 Olitski retrospective and wrote its catalogue, the essence of Olitski's greatness and of his novelty lies in his having "developed and revised Jackson Pollock's central innovation, the over-all picture, in order to make it serve color."

Olitski's early work, between 1952 and 1959, had thick encrusted surfaces built up from smears and trails of paint in the expressionist manner of Hans Hofmann. But by 1960 he was producing stained paintings, organized around cores, such as ovals ringing each other or clustering in one corner of the field, with large areas of bare canvas, the shapes making their impact through their rich saturated colours.

But his interest in the primary of colour rather than shape led him by 1965 to abandon drawings and composition and to spray paint in tiny particles on to soaked unprinted canvas, using contrasting hues to produce rich optical effects. These sprayed paintings consist of nothing but colour, abandoning shape entirely. Michael Fried has argued that much of the motivation behind Olitski's first sprayed paintings sprang from his desire to oppose the kind of structure at work in the paintings of Noland and Stella. But his paintings do depend on the shape of their supports, and more recently he has been contrasting the sprayed center with an outer edge of more thickly painted or sprayed bands which establish the literal existence of the canvas, while the more delicately sprayed centre creates an illusory, dissolving space.

For these effects the paintings are necessarily on a large scale, usually huge, and the paradox of Olitski's work is this vastness of scale compared with the limitation of content. Sweetly pretty, like so many attractive candy boxes, they seem to be the decorative product of an essentially hedonistic vision. The successive sprayings cause the colours to melt into one another, producing brilliant atmospheric effects which have led Olitski's work to be not inaptly described as the first fully abstract version of Impressionism, which as Barbara Rose puts it, "like Olitski's mist and hazes, delighted in effects of light, atmosphere and movement."

Unfortunately, however, much of the American critical talk about these paintings offers fine examples of the higher drivel, exposing the absurd overpraise lavished on American post-war art in general, which some critics try to present as a matter of uninterrupted advance from Pollock into higher and higher realms of excellence. Not only does this involve the claim that all painting must revolve around a single elementary aesthetic issue, but as Harold Rosenberg has acidly observed, the irony of Moffett's elevation of Olitski is that he praises him not for opening new paths but for acting as "a bloc, *the* influence that has to be gone through or overcome if any fundamental innovation or breakthrough is to be achieved."

—Konstantin Bazarov

OLIVEIRA, Nathan.
American. Born in Oakland, California, 19 December 1928. Educated at Mills College, Oakland; California College of Arts and Crafts, Oakland, M.F.A., 1952. Served in the United States Army, 1953-55. Independent painter, since 1953: lives and works in Northern California. Instructor, San Francisco Art Institute and California College of Arts and Crafts, Oakland, 1955-56; University of Illinois, 1961-62; University of California at Los Angeles, 1963-64; Cornell University, Ithaca, New York, 1964; University of Colorado, Boulder, 1965; University of Hawaii, Honolulu, 1971; Cranfield Academy of Art, Bloomfield Hills, Michigan, 1972; Baltimore Art Institute, 1972; Herron Art Institute, Indianapolis, 1972; and Kent State University, Ohio, 1972. Instructor, Stanford University, since 1964. Recipient: Tiffany Award for Graphic Arts, 1957; Guggenheim Foundation Fellowship, 1958; N. W. Harris Bronze Medal, Art Institute of Chicago, 1960; Special Prize, El Retiro Parquet, Arte de America y España, Madrid 1963; Tamarind Fellowship, 1964; National Endowment for the Arts Award, 1974. Associate, National Academy of Design, New York. Agent: Charles Cowles Gallery, 420 West Broadway, New York, New York 10012. Address: 785 Santa Maria Avenue, Stanford, California 94305, U.S.A.

Individual Exhibitions:

1957	Eric Locke Gallery, San Francisco
1958	Alan Gallery, New York
1959	Alan Gallery, New York
	Paul Kantor Gallery, Beverly Hills, California
1960	Alan Gallery, New York
	Paul Kantor Gallery, Beverly Hills, California
1961	*Recent Works*, Krannert Art Museum, University of Illinois, Urbana (travelled to the University of Minnesota, Minneapolis)
	Walker Art Center, Minneapolis
	Paul Kantor Gallery, Beverly Hills, California
1962	Paul Kantor Gallery, Beverly Hills, California
1963	*Major Comprehensive Exhibition of 5 Years of Work*, Dickson Art Center, University of California at Los Angeles (travelled to the San Francisco Museum of Art; Fort Worth Art Center, Texas; and the Colorado Springs Fine Art Center, Colorado, 1963-64)
1964	*12 Intimate Fantasies*, R. E. Lewis Gallery, San Francisco
1965	*10 Years of Printmaking*, Stanford University, California (travelled to the San Francisco Museum of Art)
	Alan Gallery, New York
	Felix Landau Gallery, Los Angeles
1967	*Watercolors and Drawings*, Landau-Alan Gallery, New York
1968	Galerie Bleue, Stockholm
	Gump's Gallery, San Francisco
	Stanford University, California
	Felix Landau Gallery, Los Angeles
1969	*Works on Paper*, Martha Jackson Gallery, New York
	San Francisco Museum of Art
	Martha Jackson Gallery, New York
1970	Terry Dintenfass Gallery, New York
	Wisconsin State University, Oshkosh
1971	Michael Smith Gallery, Los Angeles
	Smith-Anderson Gallery, Palo Alto, California
	Stanford University, California
	Terry Dintenfass Gallery, New York
1972	Southwestern College, Chula Vista, California
	Charles Campbell Gallery, San Francisco
	Jack Glenn Gallery, Corona del Mar, California
	Terry Dintenfass Gallery, New York
1973	Fullerton Junior College, California
	Anderson Art Corridor, Sacred Heart Schools, Menlo Park, California
	15 Years Survey of Paintings 1958-1973, Oakland Art Museum, California
	Spirit Paintings, Jack Glenn Gallery, Corona del Mar, California
1974	Smith-Anderson Gallery, Palo Alto, California

1975	Dorsky Gallery, New York
	Charles Campbell Gallery, San Francisco
1976	Jorgensen Gallery, University of Connecticut, Storrs
	Smith-Anderson Gallery, Palo Alto, California
	University of California at Santa Cruz
	Wichita State University, Kansas
1977	El Camino College, Torrance, California
	Charles Campbell Gallery, San Francisco
	John Berggruen Gallery, San Francisco
1978	*20 Years' Work on Paper*, Santa Rosa Community College, California
	Carpenter Center for the Visual Arts, Harvard University, Cambridge, Massachusetts
	Dorsky Gallery, New York
	Cheney Cowles Memorial Museum, Spokane, Washington
	Galerie Veith Turske, Cologne
1979	Charles Campbell Gallery, San Francisco
	Galerie Veith Turske, Cologne
	John Berggruen Gallery, San Francisco
	Oliveira: Survey of Monotypes 1973-78, Baxter Art Gallery, Pasadena, California
1980	Alan Gallery, New York
	Print Retrospective, California State University, Long Beach
	Charles Cowles Gallery, New York
1981	Arts Club of Chicago
1982	John Berggruen Gallery, San Francisco
1983	Honolulu Academy of Arts, Hawaii
	John Berggruen Gallery, San Francisco
	Charles Cowles Gallery, New York
1984	San Francisco Museum of Modern Art (retrospective, travelled Laguna Beach, California; Madison, Wisconsin; Lincoln, Nebraska; Norman, Oklahoma)
1985	Honolulu Academy of Arts, Hawaii
1986	Stanford University, California
	Richard Gray Gallery, Chicago
	Galleria II Bisonte, Florence

Selected Group Exhibitions:

1952	*Annual Exhibition of Watercolors, Prints and Decorative Arts*, Richmond Art Center, California
1956	*10 Years of American Prints 1947-1956*, Brooklyn Museum, New York
1957	*4 Leading Printmakers of the Bay Area*, Eric Locke Gallery, San Francisco
1958	*Recent American Prints*, University of Illinois, Urbana
1963	*Arte Actuale de America Y España*, Los Palacios de Valázquez y Cristal de Retiro, Madrid (toured Europe)
1975	*National Exhibition of Prints*, Smithsonian Institution, Washington, D.C.
1980	*Bay Area Art: Then and Now*, Suzanne Brown Gallery, Scottsdale, Arizona
1982	*Drawings by Painters*, Long Beach Museum of Art, California
1984	*The Figurative Mode: Bay Area Painting 1956-66*, Grey Art Gallery, New York University
1987	*American Painting: Abstract Expressionism and After*, San Francisco Museum of Modern Art

Collections:

Museum of Modern Art, New York; Brooklyn Museum, New York; National Collection of Fine Arts, Smithsonian Institution, Washington, D.C.; Butler Institute of American Art, Youngstown, Ohio; Des Moines Art Center, Iowa; Art Institute of Chicago; Oakland Museum, California; Grunwold Center for the Graphic Arts, University of California at Los Angeles; Honolulu Academy of Art.

Publications:

By OLIVEIRA: article—interview, with Andrew de Shong in *Artweek* (Oakland, California), 13 October 1973.

On OLIVEIRA: books—*Nathan Oliveira* by Frederick Wight, Los Angeles 1963: *The Tamarind Book of Lithography: Art and Techniques* by Garo Z. Antreasian and Clinton Adams,

New York 1971; *Nathan Oliveira: 15 Year Survey of Paintings, 1958-73*, exhibition catalogue, by Harvey L. Jones and George Neubert, Oakland, California 1973; *Nathan Oliveira*, exhibition catalogue, by Fred Ploeger, Spokane, Washington 1978; *Nathan Oliveira: A Survey Exhibition 1957-1983*, exhibition catalogue with essays by Thomas H. Garver and George W. Neubert, San Francisco 1984; articles—"Nathan Oliveira" by Dan Tooker in *Art International* (Lugano, Switzerland), December 1973; "Nathan Oliveira: Strength in Art" by Susan Ackerman in *Stanford Daily* (California) 29 November 1977; "Nathan Oliveira and the Monotype" by Maudette Balle in *Artweek* (Oakland, California), 3 October 1979; "Nathan Oliveira: Survey of Monotypes 1973-78" by Harry Jaffe in *Peninsula Times Tribune* (California), 16 January 1980.

*

Nathan Oliveira has been closely identified with the so-called Bay Area Figurative School which emerged in Northern California during the 1950's. Reacting against the prevalent Abstract Expressionist style, David Park, Richard Diebenkorn, and Elmer Bischoff concurrently developed a variation in which painterly gesture and spontaneity were applied to landscape and the human figure. Oliveira's own figurative art matured in close contact with these and other painters working in a similar manner, but there are fundamental differences in attitude that set him apart. Bay Area Figurative painting was primarily concerned with formal matters; light, color, and the nature of paint. The figure was introduced as another composition element, and this basic objectivity stands in direct contrast to Oliveira's subjective romanticism.

Central to Oliveira's work is a humanistic vision that focuses on the figure. Typically female and nude, Oliveira's isolated figures appear to be emerging from the pigment in which their forms have been discovered. Appearing and reappearing in vaporous landscapes of shadow and mist, they embody an artistic and philosophical concept of transformation. Indistinct, faceless or masked, Oliveira's generalized images are symbolic presences rather than individuals. The "Spirit Women" of 1971, for example, are recognized as female figures only by their pubic triangles. Ghostlike, they are depicted in the process of materializing or dematerializing.

Despite their striking other-worldliness, these images are not entirely invented from imagination. Although the paintings are not done directly from the model, individual models and Oliveira's feelings about them do provide the essential memories upon which his preternatural, "recalled" images are based. Oliveira's visionary imagery, with all its mythical, mystical, and supernatural evocations, is in fact firmly grounded in personal experience of actual human beings—including studio nudes recalled in tranquility. The importance of this contact is evidenced by Oliveira's recent return to drawing directly from the model.

Oliveira's rich, painterly style has encompassed near non-objectivity as well as figuration. In the 1959 "Standing Man with Stick" or the "Dance" and "Bathers" series of the same year, stylized figures are all but obliterated in a thickly painted Abstract Expressionist surface. And the highly abstracted "Ryan Sites" (1981) share certain similarities with Diebenkorn's "Ocean Park" series. Nonetheless, Oliveira's commitment to nature and the figure precludes excursions into pure abstraction, post-painterly or otherwise. A group of "Sites" are actually landscapes painted in tribute to Monet. The most recently exhibited figurative works again bear witness to the consistency of Oliveira's vision and goals along figurative lines.

Oliveira enjoys a growing international reputation as a painter; but he is also a widely respected printmaker. His influence as a teacher at Stanford and particularly his experimentation with monotypes constitute important aspects of his career. The same basic themes appear throughout the graphic work where his sources and inspirations are perhaps most evident: the mysterious, symbolic imagery of Eugene Carrière and Odilon Redon is encountered in Oliveira's dark Lithographic "portraits" and disembodied heads such as "Black Christ I," 1963. His profound admiration for Goya led to a dryprint version of "Disasters of War." But perhaps the most important influence was that acknowledged in a major suite of lithographs entitled "To Edgar Allan Poe" (1970-1971). Like Poe, Oliveira seeks to uncover the realms of dreams, the unconscious, and the supernatural, deeply hidden truths about spirituality and the human condition.

—Paul J. Karlstrom

OLIVIERI, Claudio.

Italian. Born in Rome, 28 November 1934. Studied at the Accademia di Belle Arti di Brera, Milan, 1952–56. Married Anna Lusenti in 1963; daughter: Elenora. Worked as art director of media agency, Milan, 1959–62. Full-time painter, since 1978: lives and works in Milan. Recipient: Morgan Painting Prize, Ravenna, 1972; Michetti Award, Francavila Are, Italy, 1972. Agent: Galleria del Milione, via Biali 21, Milan. Address: Via Ausonio 8, 20123 Milan, Italy.

Individual Exhibitions:

1959	Salone Annunciata, Milan
1960	George Lester, Rome
1963	Salone Annunciata, Milan
1967	Salone Annunciata, Milan
1969	Galleria del Milione, Milan
1970	Galleria La Loggia, Bologna
1971	Galleria del Milione, Milan
	Galleria Contini, Rome
1973	Galleria 3b, Bolzano, Italy
	Galleria San Luca, Bologna
1974	Galleria Peccolo, Livorno, Italy
	Kunstverein, Münster, West Germany
	Galleria La Piramide, Florence
1975	Galleria del Milione, Milan
1977	Galleria del Banco, Brescia, Italy
	Galleria Capricorno, Venice
1978	Galerie Stevenson Palluel, Paris
1980	*Biennale,* Venice
1982	Padiglione d'Arte Contemporanea, Milan
1983	Galleria Civica, Modena, Italy
1984	Galerie E Edition, Munich
	Galleria Lorenzelli, Milan
1985	Galerie Von Loe, Bonn
1987	Galerie Schafer, Giessen, West Germany

Selected Group Exhibitions:

1966	*33rd Biennale,* Venice
1972	*10th Quadriennale,* Rome
1973	*Tempi di Percezione,* Galerie Merian, Krefeld, West Germany
1974	*Geplante Malerei,* Kunstverein, Münster, West Germany (travelled to the Galleria Milione, Milan)
1975	*New Italian Painting,* Galerie Espace 5, Montreal
1977	*Documenta 6,* Kassel, West Germany
1981	*Arte e Critica,* Galleria Nazionale d'Arte Moderna, Rome
1982	*Exploration in Italian Art,* National Gallery of New South Wales, Sydney
1985	*On Language and Ecstasy: A Generation in Italian Art,* Museum of Fine Art, Pori, Finland (travelled to Helsinki)
1987	*Italienische Kunst,* Kunstverein, Frankfurt

Collections:

Museo d'Arte Contemporanea, Parma, Italy; Galleria Communale d'Arte Moderna, Livorno, Italy; Washington University, St. Louis; Museo Civico d'Arte Contemporanea, Milan; Galleria Civica, Bologna, Italy.

Publications:

By OLIVIERI: article—statement in *Flash Art* (Milan), October/November 1974.

On OLIVIERI: books—*Geplante Malerei,* exhibition catalogue by Klaus Honnef, Munster, West Germany 1974; *Claudio Olivieri,* exhibition catalogue with essay by Paolo Fossati, Modena, Italy 1983; articles—"Claudio Olivieri" by Daniela Palazzoli in *Kunst Forum* (Mainz), February 1975; "Gli Occhi di Atlantide" by Luigi Ballerini in *Yale Italian Studies* (New Haven, Connecticut), Spring 1980.

Before painting is the unthought, the completely opaque place of non-relation. From this irrelationship "before" painting traverses the invisible towards a visible no longer blind, capable not so much of revealing the hidden, but of disconnecting the sensing of habitual evidence.

The surface of painting, the fine veil upon which the encounter occurs, is the point where the infinitesimal subtraction of the tangible is affected, where that which is subtracted from materiality is restored to the glance.

But, I do not wish to speak of a before painting, nor

an after; painting remains there, in that which is missing in word, in its indescribable pure being, which cannot respond because, perhaps, in it all is a questioning.

I have never worked toward setting up cultural deterrents, or toward a conjuring of collateral circumstances; I consider extraneous any descriptive collusion, any anticipation.

Painting is, in itself, an outshining which does not play with the catalogue of cultural components, which cannot, in the attempt to refer itself back to a casuality, expect to recognize itself in its reflection.

Painting is "seen," but not in the act of showing the illusion of something; painting "sees," but not from a "where" definable as distance.

Painting is nothing other than the purely and solely visible, is that which, suspending all connotative inclines, introduces the non-mediated but infinite distance which makes of space a memory.

—Claudio Olivieri

To "place" the work of Claudio Olivieri somewhere between the formation of the so-called New Painting and Analytical Painting is reductive, perhaps even di-

Claudio Olivieri: *Teleogale,* 1987

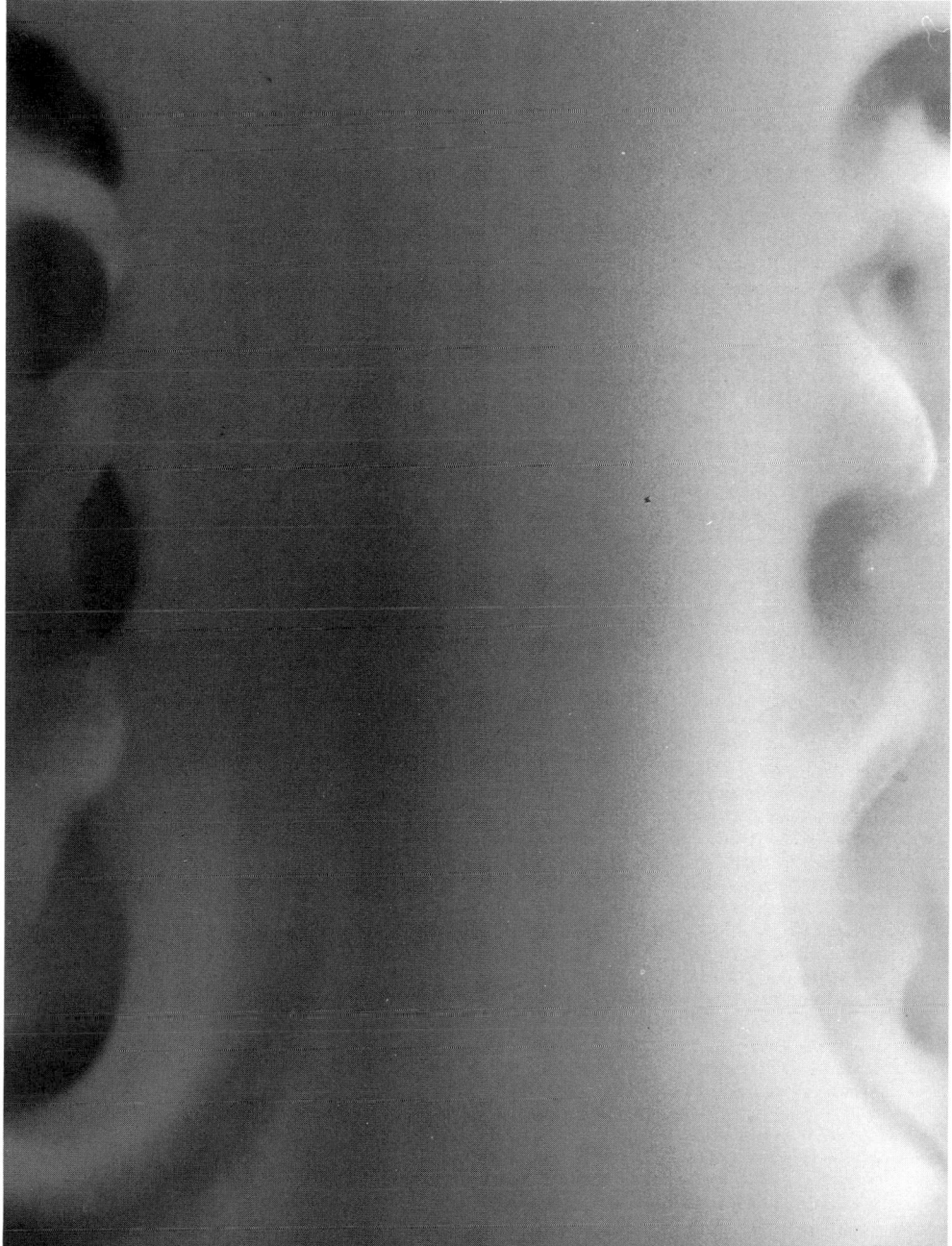

versionary. Even if the inquiry is based on such concerns as the structure of painting, on colour, surface, the ultimate elements of the artistic discipline, one must nevertheless carefully distinguish between those artists who have admired pictorial negation and those who, though interested in the determination and definition of specific pictorial space, do not actually believe in its destruction. Olivieri belongs to the latter category.

His large actual canvases—large surfaces suit this artist—are played on such minimal chromatic grids that at first they seem to be monochrome, yet they make the eye travel across the canvas; they grasp the internal chromatic states; and the almost invisible colored curves and spectral pulsations metaphysically attract the observer to look "inside" the painting. At this point the colour, the surfaces, and the chromatic vibrations are no longer only elements of investigation; they become "other"; they involve the artist and the spectator in a series of cultural links, mnemonically and symbolically evoked through colour.

But naturally symbol and memory in Olivieri's paintings remain inside the field of the painting: in fact, one is not talking about literary symbols that need only be "represented," the fruition of which belongs to a world outside painting; something more is involved. The colour itself is a symbol, an evocation, a memory, the space of which exists alongside the physical space of the canvas. It is this *mental* space that, instead of negating, the painting enhances.

In 1981, Olivieri wrote: "Painting remains there, in that lack of speech; it cannot reply; but perhaps everything in it is a question" and "colour does not narrate; it is the end of the future, the uterus, the dream to come, the tale that began with history."

—Marco Meneguzzo

ONOSATO, Toshinobu.

Japanese. Born in Iida, 8 June 1912. Educated at Nihon University, Tokyo, 1931; Atelier Tsuda Seifu, Tokyo, 1931–33. Served in the Japanese Army in Manchuria, 1942–45. Married Tomoko Onosato in 1951; children: Rokumaru and Toumaru. Independent artist, 1935 until his death in 1986. Member, Black Exhibition Group (Kokushokuten), Tokyo, 1935–37, and Jiyu Bijitsuka Kyokai, Tokyo, 1938–56. Recipient: Mainichi International Grand Prize, Tokyo, 1963. Agents: Franell Gallery, Okura Hotel, 3 Akasaka Aoi-Cho Minato-ku, Tokyo 107; Katsura Gallery, 165 Main Street, Northport, New York 11768, U.S.A. *Died* (in Kiryu City) *30 November 1986.*

Individual Exhibitions:

1953 Takemiya Gallery, Tokyo
1955 Mimatsu Gallery, Tokyo
1958 Kabutoya Gallery, Tokyo
1961 Gress Gallery, Washington, D.C.
1962 Minami Gallery, Tokyo
1969 Minami Gallery, Tokyo
1971 Honma Museum, Sakata, Japan
1972 Galerie Kornfeldt, Zurich
1976 Wako Print Gallery, Tokyo
1980 Soker-Kaseman Gallery, San Francisco
1981 Katsuyama Educational and Welfare Hall, Fukui, Japan
1982 Mikimoto Hall, Tokyo
1984 Siebu Contemporary Art Gallery, Tokyo

Selected Group Exhibitions:

1953 *Abstraction and Fantasy*, National Museum of Modern Art, Tokyo
1956 *Art of the World Today*, Takashimaya, Tokyo
1964 *Guggenheim International*, Guggenheim Museum, New York
1965 *New Japanese Painting and Sculpture*, Museum of Modern Art, New York
1966 *Japan Art Festival I*, Cultural Center, New York
1968 *Ornamental Tendencies in Contemporary Painting*, Haus am Waldsee, Berlin (toured West Germany)
1974 *Japan Past and Present*, Museum of Modern Art, Dusseldorf
1977 *Modern Painting of Japan*, Takashimaya Gallery, Tokyo
1983 *Movements of Modern Art*, Metropolitan Art Museum, Tokyo
1986 *Japon des Avant-Gardes*, Centre Georges Pompidou, Paris

Collections:

National Museum of Modern Art, Tokyo; Contemporary Art Museum, Nagáoka; Galleria Nazionale d'Arte Moderna, Rome; Guggenheim Museum, New York; Ohara Museum, Kurashiki, Japan; Honma Museum, Sakata, Japan; Public Museum of Modern Art, Gunma, Japan; Public Art Museum, Fukuoka, Japan; Metropolitan Art Museum, Tokyo; Louisiana Museum, Humlebaek, Denmark.

Publications:

By ONOSATO: book—*Fight for Existence*, edited by Teijirou Kubo, Tokyo 1978; articles—"Space Concept of Picture" in *Mizue* (Tokyo), October 1935; "Circle and Egg" in *Geijytsu Shincho* (Tokyo), March 1961; "Secret" in *Mizue* (Tokyo), July 1963; "Artist's Opinion and His Work" in *Bijitsu Techo* (Tokyo), October 1963; "Absolute and Universal" in *Bijitsu Techo* (Tokyo), January 1965.

On ONOSATO: books—*Works of Toshinobu Onosato*, exhibition catalogue, by Teijirou Kubo, Tokyo 1958; *Toshinobu Onosato*, by Shuzo Takiguchi, Tokyo 1964; *Art in Japan Today* by Yoshiaki Tono, Tokyo 1974.

*

People sometimes ask me why I paint the "circle," but I myself think nothing is more natural than that. From primitive ages innumerable circles must have been painted by men. The circle is the most fundamental one among the forms which reconstruct nature, and I chose it just like matter did when it wanted to become form. This is the perfect form, having neither direction nor inclination. It lies there always in state of "direct front."

At first it was a mass of clay itself. So I discovered the "circle" in a pure state. Then I put on it minute squares in succession, filling eventually the whole surface of tableau. And I began from there a science of colour and form. The clay was scraped off little by little and directed in search of possibilities of a different kind.

The circle is an enriched plane without contour, and its dimension can be recognized more concretely by dividing in small areas. Division is born from the piling up of colour planes, and created psychological and optical unevenness, transforming abstract plane into a state of being.

Assuredly "circle" is "form," but in fact I don't recognize it as "form." What is needed then when I, wanting no restriction by "form," continue wishing to fix there something definite? Something unlimited which nevertheless must always be there, something which can at the same time be the expression of my thought and the most clear state of being itself.

These processes of thinking must have been at the source of my act of construction of my paintings which consists of putting the large "circle" at the centre of tableau, dividing it progressively by squares and finally making it simple ground of endless patterns. "Circle" seems to be neither my final object nor my principal subject. I think painting constitutes a world similar to the world of human beings. Don't you say "white and black," "man and woman?" To be similar, there must never be imitations.

—Toshinobu Onosato (1983)

Toshinobu Onosato: *Vary Hexagon*, 1984

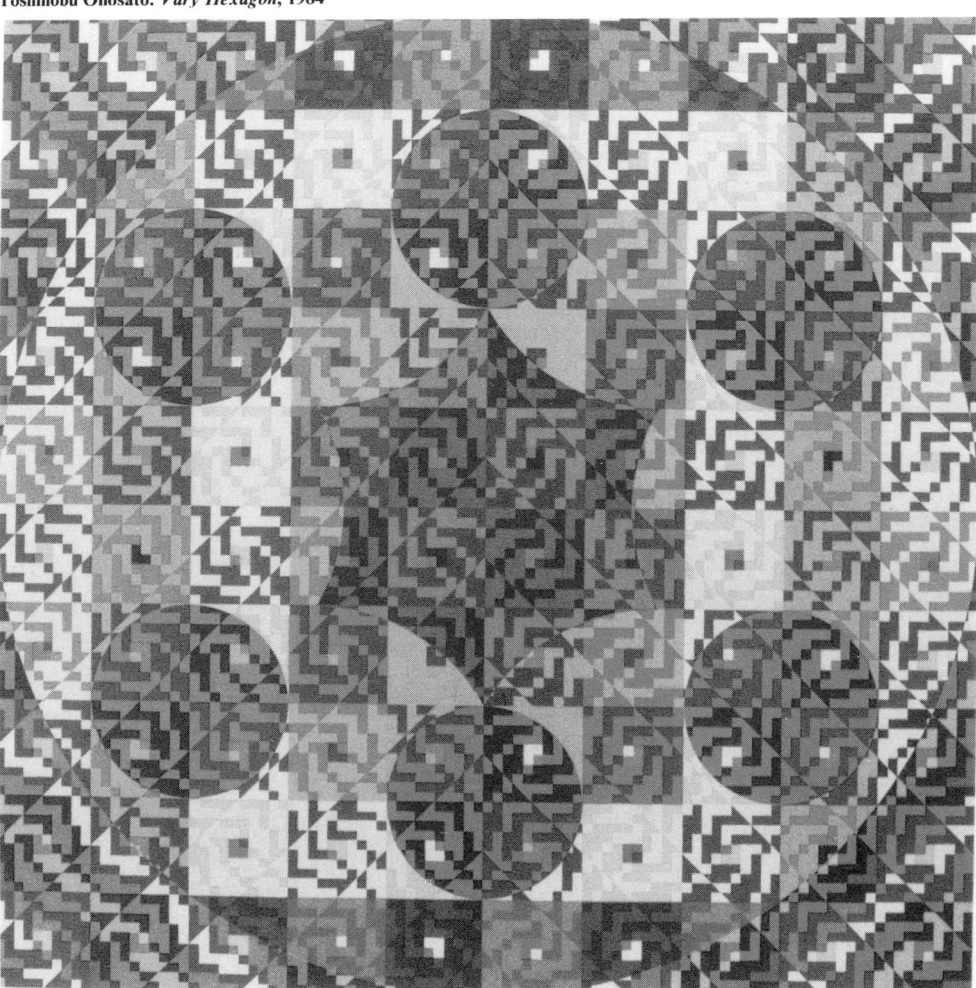

Toshinobu Onosato, a Japanese painter born in 1912 in Nagano, was an outstanding geometric abstractionist who, until his death in 1986, had produced an exquisitely intricate cosmos with never-exhausting combinations of circles and squares.

He moved to Kiryu in Gunma when he was ten, and lived and worked there for the rest of his life. In 1931, he studied art under Seifu Tsuda and his painting was accepted by Nika Exhibition in 1935. He joined the Liberal Artists Association, one of the most productive avant-garde artist's groups in Japan, in 1938, since then creating challenging paintings in Constructivist style, and began to stand out as a pioneering abstract painter in Japan.

He was drafted into the Army in 1941, went to the front, spent three years from 1945 to 1948 in Siberia as a prisoner of war.

His first one-person show took place at Takemiya Gallery in Tokyo in 1953 under the curatorship of a renowned Japanese Surrealist-critic, Shuzo Takiguchi. His geometric style was established when he introduced circle motifs into his painting in 1955, and then his canvas grew more and more elaborate with mosaic pattern in red, blue, and yellow.

In his painting *Work* in 1962, the canvas assumed a collective array composed of a number of small squares and rectangles with blue and yellow frames. A full and large circle comes out in the middle of the canvas, not with an outline but with an optical effect created by changing colors of frames of the smaller squares in the array.

Onosato put down his idea in 1963: I don't like "illusion." What is most important to my work is "existence." It is to array and pile up pure objects (colors) as signs according to the directions from my brain system. Existent senses have equal value with natural objects, and they settle on canvas as area of the brain map. It is something before you can call it painting. It stays symmetrical as it is free from pictorial manipulation. Vibration of my senses expands out of a circle, and then it contracts and breathes.

He represented Japanese artists in the Venice Biennials in 1964 and 1966, and attained an international fame in sixties and seventies. His paintings in eighties achieved a splendor with geometrical forms breaking into multi-faceted complexity in red, blue, yellow and black, making the canvas a feast of color sheds. Uniqueness in Onosato's art lies in his transcendental idea that induces the viewer to sense something beyond the formal intricacy through purely optical experience.

—Tazmi Shinoda

ONTANI, Luigi.

Italian. Born in Montovolo, Bologna. Self-taught in art. Lives and works in Rome. Agent: Galleria l'Attico, Via del Paradiso 41, Rome. Address: Via Angelo Brunnetti, 37, 00100 Rome, Italy.

Individual Exhibitions:

1970   Centro Culturale, San Fedele, Milan
        Florence Festival
        Galleria Diagramma, Milan
        Palazzo Diamanti, Ferrara, Italy
1973   Galleria Contemporanea, Rome
1974   Modern Art Agency, Naples
        Galleria l'Attico, Rome
        Lp. 220, Turin
1975   Galleria l'Attico, Rome
        De Appel, Amsterdam
1976   Galleria l'Attico, Rome
        Galerie Sonnabend, Paris
        Galleria Sperone, Milan
        Sonnabend Gallery, New York

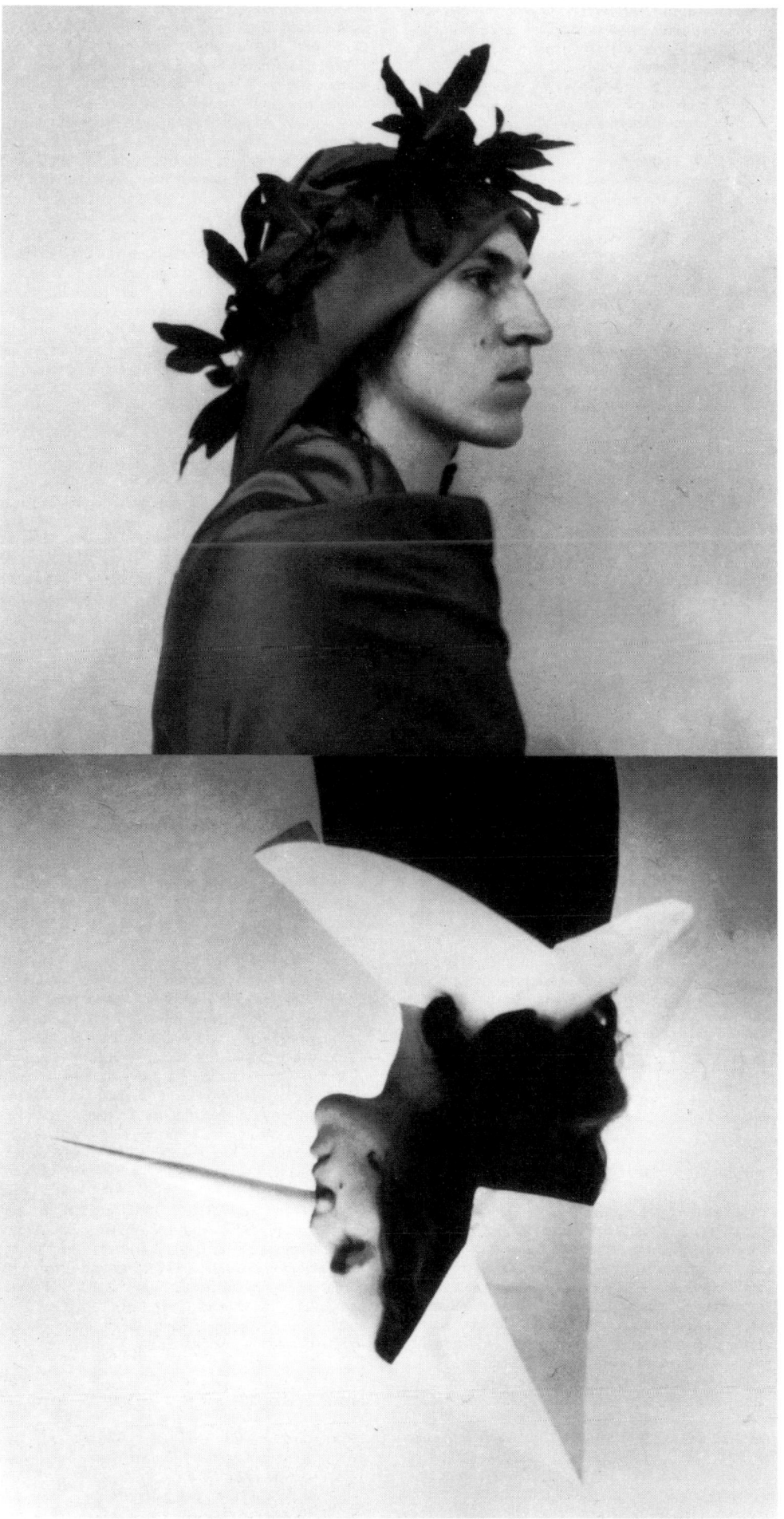

Luigi Ontani: *Dante/Pinocchio*, 1974

1977	Galleria d'Arte Moderna, Bologna
	Koepelzaal, Amsterdam
1978	Galleria l'Attico, Rome
	Franz Paludetto, Turin
1979	Mario Diacono, Bologna
	Palazzo Ducale, Genoa
	Kitchen Center, New York
	A Space, Toronto
1980	Lucio Amelio, Naples
	Galleria Minini, Brescia, Italy
1981	*Galleria Minini, Milan*
	Galleria Diacono, Rome
	Galleria Evan Menzio-Elena Pron, Turin

Selected Group Exhibition:

1973	*April Festival,* Belgrade
1974	*Photomedia,* Museum am Ostwall, Dortmund, West Germany
	Transformer, Kunstmuseum, Lucerne
1975	*Selbsportrat als Selstdarstellung,* Innsbruck
1977	*Arte in Italia, 1960-1977,* Galleria Civica d'Arte Moderna, Turin
1980	*Dieci Anni Dopo,* Galleria d'Arte Moderna, Bologna
1981	*Arte Critica,* Galleria Nazionale d'Arte Moderna, Rome
1982	*Italian Art Now,* Guggenheim Museum, New York
	Italian Art 1960-1982, Hayward Gallery, London
1986	*Aspects of Italian Art 1960-85,* Kunstverein, Frankfurt

Collections:

Galleria Nazionale d'Arte Moderna, Rome

Publications:

By ONTANI: articles—"Luigi Ontani: Continua-O" in *Flash Art* (Milan), April 1974; "Continua-8" in *Data* (Milan) Autumn 1974; "Continua-3" in *Photo 13* (Milan), November 1974; "Continua-1" in *Il Corpo come Linguaggio* by Lea Vergine, Milan 1974.

On ONTANI: books—*Il Comportamento* by Renato Barilli, Rome 1973; *Transformer,* exhibition catalogue, by Jean Christophe Ammann, Lucerne 1974; *Fotomedia: Video,* exhibition catalogue, Dortmund, West Germany 1974; *Il Corpo come Linguaggio* by Lea Vergine, Milan 1974; *Europa: America* by Achille Bonita Oliva, Milan 1976; *Live Art: 1909 to the Present* by Roselee Goldberg, London 1979; *De Chirico tra Duchamp a Malevitch* by Francesco Poli, Bologna 1980; *Italian Art Now: An American Perspective,* exhibition catalogue, by Diane Waldman and Lisa Dennison, New York 1982; articles:—"Ontani" by Barbara Reise in *Annual of New Art and Artists,* Amsterdam 1974; "Process, Concept and Behaviour in Italian Art" by Achille Bonita Oliva in *Studio International* (London), February 1976; "Performance Art in Italy" in *Studio International* (London), February 1976.

The art and life of Luigi Ontani are divided into three distinct periods that only communicate with each other in secret. First, performance, next photography, and finally painting. The arch of this subtly magic time starts from 1970 and reaches to the present day. The absolute protagonist is always the artist himself (his body as the image and likeness of art), the exhausting aestheticism of his sensibility and sensuality and imagination, often with a vein of humour.

Luigi Ontani's work is thus always rather precious, either when he represents an historic personage ("Dante") or a mythical figure ("Bacchus," "Leda and the Swan," "Self Portrait"), or when he depicts the imaginary creations of mythology, using watercolour technique. The artist is present or absent (it is no matter); the "fiction" of art demands this extraordinary service. Painting itself is to him a sort of projection "outwards" of the everyday; it means "inside" the incorruptible unreality of beauty, without which art would be like an extinct sun. Luigi Ontani loves all that belongs to the sun; in the nuances of his water-colours he seems, Narcissus-like, to see his own ecstatic fantasies. His great desire is to capture them; but art is the dream that makes possible the strangest and most remote desires in the spatiality of memory.

The "mythical" space of his work seems almost non-existent; it appears and disappears in a transparent remoteness flooded in unreal light. But it is in that space that the artistic effect is made, sheltered from the descriptive clamour of everyday experience. A case in point is a work of 1981, "Self Portrait." Here Luigi Ontani has represented the ideal clothing of the artist—of himself, of course. The individual parts of which it is composed, made from white paper, have been fixed to the walls of the gallery (Mario Diacono, Rome) with pins. Two self-portraits (delicate photographs retouched with paint) face one another like images in a mirror on two opposite walls, while a third photograph (also retouched in paint) shows the artist's feet. Everything was arranged in advance, as if for a ceremony. The "ideal clothing" is the fantastic vestment of art: the artist hides in it, he is somewhere else—in the mythical and unreal space of beauty.

For Luigi Ontani as for Oscar Wilde before him, there is no difference between art and life. Excess is his aesthetic, incomprehensible harmony his exhausting contemplation of beauty, at once sublime and ironic. The technique of the water-colour used in recent works renders clearly the concept of the mirror image that unveils memories and fancies that have by now become uncontrollable. It is this, perhaps, that makes Luigi Ontani a "libertarian" artist, unpredictable and open even to the splendors of the absurd.

—Italo Mussa

OPALKA, Roman.

Polish. Born of Polish parents, in Hocquincourt, Abbeville, France, 27 August 1931. Educated in Poland, 1935-39, and in Germany 1939-45; studied art, Walbrzych School, Nowa Roda, 1946-49; School of Fine Arts, Lodz, 1949-50; Academy of Fine Arts, Warsaw, 1957-60. Served as art instructor to army officers, House of Culture, Polish Army in Warsaw, 1957-60. Lives with Marie-Madeleine Gazeau since 1976. Independent artist, Warsaw, 1960-75, in West Berlin, 1975-1977, in Paris, 1977-79, and in Tournon d'Agenais, France, since 1979. Recipient: Young Polish Painters Prize, Sopot, 1965; Grand Prize, First Bradford Print Biennale, Yorkshire, 1968; Gold Medal for Graphics, Golden Grapes Exhibition, Zielona Gora, 1969; K. C. Norwid Critics' Prize, Warsaw, 1969; First Prize, 3rd Graphics Biennale, Krakow, 1970; Prize, 2nd Bradford Print Biennale, Yorkshire, 1970; Prize, 7th International Graphics Biennale, Tokyo, 1970; Ohara Art Museum Prize, Tokyo, 1970; Ministry of Arts and Culture Prize, Warsaw, 1971; Graphics Prize, International Art Exhibition, Le Mans, 1977; Painting Prize, 14th Bienal de Sao Paulo, Brazil, 1978. Agent: John Weber Gallery, 142 Greene Street, New York, New York 10012, U.S.A. Address: Manoir de Bazeraz, Thezac, 47370 Tournon d'Agenais, France.

Individual Exhibitions:

1966	Dom Artysty Plastyka Gallery, Warsaw
1969	Wspolczesna "Ruch" Gallery, Warsaw
1971	Galleria LP220, Turin
	Galleria Il Punto, Calice-Turin
1972	Galleria Annunciata, Milan
	Galleria LP220, Turin
	Galleria La Bertesca, Genoa
	William Weston Gallery, London
1973	Museum Folkwang, Essen

1974	Galerie Bruno Bischofberger, Zurich
	John Weber Gallery, New York
1975	Galeria 72, Chelm, Poland
	John Weber Gallery, New York
1976	Palais des Beaux-Arts, Brussels
	Museum Boymans-van Beuningen, Rotterdam
1977	Musée d'Art et d'Histoire, Geneva
	Galerie René Block, West Berlin (2 shows)
	John Weber Gallery, New York
	16 Details of the Work, Museum Haus Lange, Krefeld, West Germany
1978	Amherst College, Massachusetts
	Columbus Museum of Art, Ohio
1979	Allentown Museum of Art, Pennsylvania
	Muhlenberg College, Allentown, Pennsylvania
	John Weber Gallery, New York (travelled to Toronto)
	Minneapolis Institute of Art, Minnesota
	Grand Rapids Art Museum, Michigan
1980	Galerie Art in Progress, Dusseldorf
	La Jolla Museum of Contemporary Art, California
	Galerie Walter Storms, Munich
	Studio Carlo Grossetti, Milan
	Hessisches Landesmuseum, Darmstadt, West Germany
	Rice Museum, Houston
1981	Westfalischer Kunstverein, Munster, West Germany
	Musée des Beaux-Arts, Montreal
	Galerie Walter Storms, Villingen, West Germany
1982	Galerie Isy Brachot, Paris
	Erker-Galerie, St. Gallen, Switzerland
	John Weber Gallery, New York

Selected Group Exhibitions:

1965	*Young Polish Painting,* Sopot, Poland
1968	*1st International Biennale of Graphic Art,* Bradford Museum, Yorkshire (and *2nd Biennale,* 1970)
1969	*Bienal,* Sao Paulo (and *14th Bienal,* 1978)
1970	*Biennale,* Venice
1973	*Painting and Sculpture Today,* Indianapolis Museum of Art
1975	*Empirica,* Museo Castelvacchio, Verona
1976	*Today/Tomorrow,* University of Miami
1977	*Documenta 6,* Kassel, West Germany
1981	*Soundings,* Neuberger Museum, Purchase, New York

Collections:

National Museum, Warsaw; Muzeum Sztuki, Lodz, Poland; Galleria Nazionale d'Arte Moderna, Rome; Bibliothèque Nationale, Paris; Nationalmuseum, Stockholm; Sammlung Albertina, Vienna; Museum Folkwang, Essen; Museum Boysman-van Beuningen, Rotterdam; Ohara Museum, Tokyo; Museum of Modern Art, New York.

Publications:

By OPALKA: books—*Travel Sheets 508325-527089,* Turin 1972; *1965/1-Detail 1602183-1728670,* Mediolan 1975; *Opalka 1965/1-00,* photographs and disc, Munich 1980.

On OPALKA: books—*Roman Opalka,* exhibition catalogue, with text by W. Jaworska, Warsaw 1966; *ModernPrints* by Pat Gilmour, London 1970; *Roman Opalka:Descrizione del Mondo,* exhibition catalogue, Turin 1971;*Roman Opalka,* exhibition catalogue, with text by Luigi Carluccio, Cracow 1972; *Polska Awangarda Malarska 1945-1970,* exhibition catalogue, with text by Bozena Kowalska, Warsaw 1975; *Roman Opalka,* exhibition catalogue, with text by Bozena Kowalska, Chelm Lubelski, Poland 1975; *Empirica: L'Arte tra Addizione e Sottrazione,* exhibition catalogue with text by G. Cortenova, Verona 1975; *Today/Tomorrow,* exhibition catalogue, with text by Paul E. Thompson, Miami 1976; *Roman Opalka,* exhibition catalogue, with text by Rainer Michael Mason, Geneva 1977; *Roman Opalka: 16 Details of the Work,* exhibition catalogue, with text by Gerhard Storck, Krefeld, West Germany 1977; *14. Bienal de Sao Paulo 1977: Poland,* exhibition catalogue, with an introduction by Mariusz Hermansdorfer, Warsaw 1977; *Roman Opalka: 1965/1-16 Details,* exhibition catalogue/book, with texts by Jeffrey Deitsch and David Shapiro, New York 1978; *Opalka 1965/1-00,* exhibition catalogue with texts by Denys Riout and David Shapiro, Paris 1982.

Roman Opalka: *1965/1–00 (detail 1684726–1687479)*, 1965

In my atttude, which constitutes a programme for my lifetime, progression registers the process of work, documents and defines time.

Only one date appears—the date of the coming into being of the first detail—1965, opened by the sign of infinity, as well as the first and last number of the given detail.

I am counting progressively from one to infinity, on details of the same size (voyage notes excluded), by hand, with a brush, with white paint on a grey background, with the assumption that every following detail will have 1% more white than the preceding one. In connection with this I anticipate the arrival of the moment when details will be identified in white on white.

Every detail is accompanied by a phonetic registration on a tape recorder and phoographic documentation of my face.

—Roman Opalka

Roman Opalka's artistic development since the 1960's has been unusually consistent. Seeking a system that would have "validity for one's entire life," he decided to explore the phenomenon of time—time, that is, as a linear phenomenon, as it appears to us in our daily lives. The basis for formulating this idea was his cycle "Chronemes," canvases closely covered with small dots (1963) and his cycle of etchings "Description of the World" (inspired by Marco Polo) begun in 1968. The pictures in this latter cycle show a limitless antheap of humanity; the structure of this pulsating mass is, however, interpreted metaphorically. Man is but a part of a species, starting (symbolically) with Adam and Eve and reaching to infinity via the constant addition of basic units. The multiplicity caused by this additive system reveals the concept of number as the basis of constant evolution.

The problem of linear time is explored within this context. The artist is intensely conscious of time as a component of his life; he sets out to measure this time—however long it may last—precisely.

From 1965 onwards Opalka has recorded sequential numbers from one onwards on consecutive canvases (and also on his "Postcards from a Journey"). These works completely lack nostalgia for the time that has passed; this indifference, however, is not that of a lifeless recording mechanism. This sequence of numbers records all the artist's emotional upheavals, his periods of fatigue and rest: the record rises and falls, it waxes and wanes, pauses, intensifies, stretches or contracts. The networks thus obtained become a personal affirmation of life, "the secrets of mental concentration." The artist himself repudiates all automization: "I carry on a dialogue in the name of man, not in the name of a machine."

An important component of the process is its aural record—a taped recording of the count. The artist enunciates each written figure loudly, and the recorded voice exhibits the mental state of the speaker, the signs of effort, the difficulty in pronouncing the fearsomely interwoven, rustling consonants in Polish figures.

In spite of the simplicity of this method, its character and mechanism do not become fully clear. One of its mysteries is the very instinct of counting and the fascination that it holds for all of us. Not only is this peculiar compulsion of interest but also the fact that occasionally numerical values take on psychological meaning.

It is true that in this work all numbers are equally important in the sense that they are all numbers of a set, but certain numbers will become prominent from a different perspective. Among these there will be numbers formed by the repetition of a single digit and, most importantly, numbers invested with the aura of ancient symbolism. This is why Opalka says: "I dream of reaching seven sevens."

The number "7" is particularly important in mysticism as an apocalyptic, prophetic, secret number. It arises from the union of two basic numbers: "3" (the element of spirit, masculinity) and "4" (the material world, femininity). Together 3 and 4—i.e., 7—represent the universe and all its phenomena.

Opalka's yearned-for 7 was known to Pythagorean mysticism, which considered numbers to be the heart of the world. "4" symbolizes a square, "3" a triangle. The square divides into two triangles—it is thus divisible, transcendable (matter). The triangle, however, divides only into triangles, i.e. into itself. It is thus indivisible, eternal (spirit).

The basis of activity in Opalka's system is movement in time. Time, however, changes, but like the triangle, only into itself. It continues instead of ending. It is eternity itself.

Using this simple counting system, Opalka reaches many of the cultural layers comprising human thought. His numbers contain all the content of the numbers comprising the substance of mathematics.

Opalka's operations even have a mathematical aspect: the works show a mathematical continuity that returns by the addition of ones. In this way, a continuum is delineated which contains the elements of infinity. Although this is absurd both logically and mathematically, its psychological aspect is not so absurd. Logically, infinity is unattainable, but psychologically it lies within our grasp. This is why it can be symbolized by a single sign, the horizontal eight. It seems so easy to grasp, to hold. Only when one tries to grasp its components, to reach it via some chosen path, does it become unreachable, beyond comprehension.

Opalka counts the uncountable. The recorded voice accompanying the count becomes particularly meaningful: it adds nothing mathematically, but by turning the continuation into a psychological action, it interiorizes it. Further, it is only by vocal repetition—i.e., by identification—that one understands this continuation to be an individual's concrete drama, developed by the psyche, which is concentrated in the heart of one problem.

—Alicja Kepinska

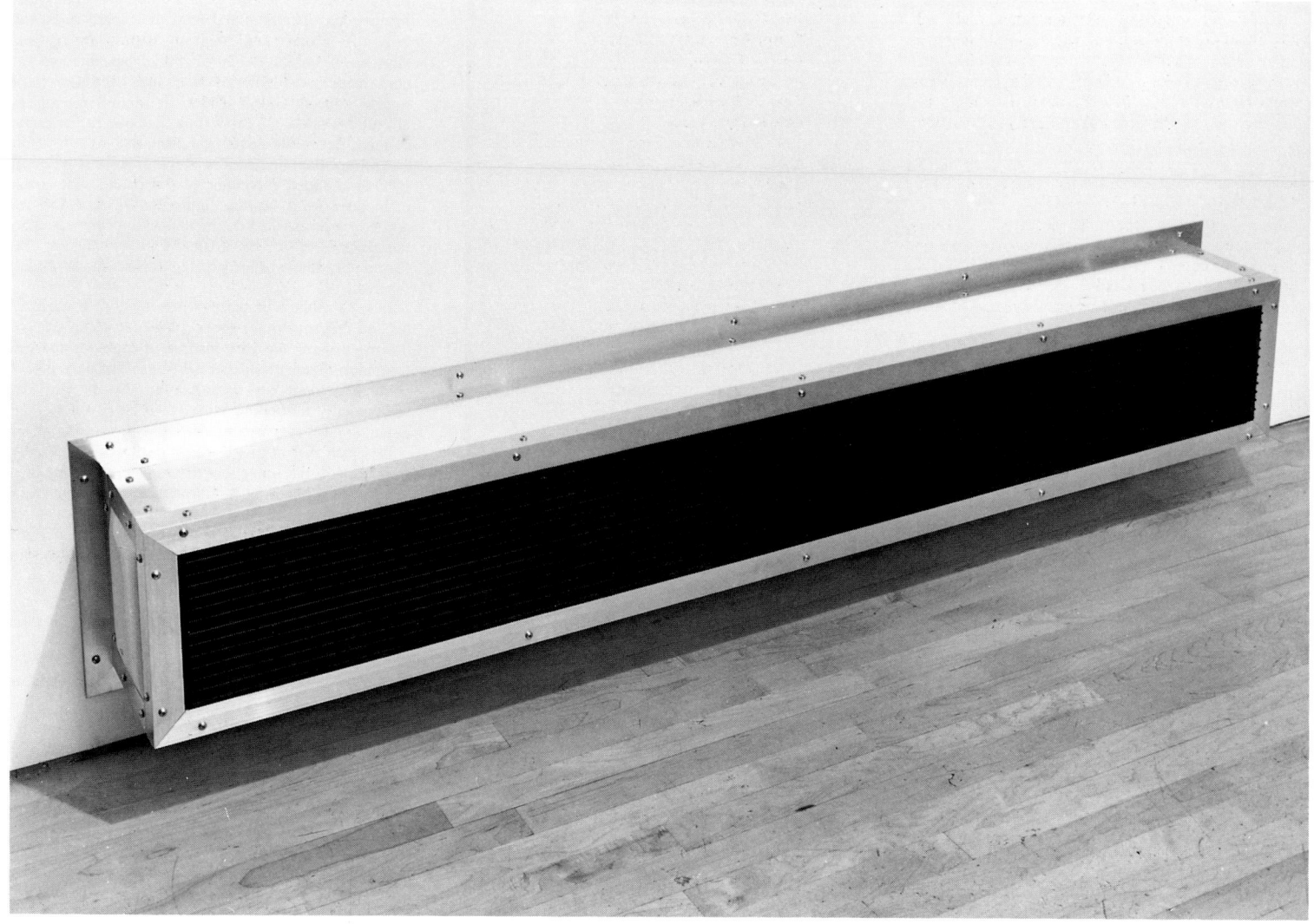

Julian Opie: *E.*, **1987** Courtesy Lisson Gallery, London

OPIE, Julian.

British. Born in London, in 1958. Studied at Goldsmith's College of Art, London, 1979–1982. Independent sculptor, London, since 1982. Agent: Lisson Gallery, London. Address: c/o Lisson Gallery, 67 Lisson Street, London NW1 5DA, England.

Individual Exhibitions:

1983	Lisson Gallery, London
1984	Kolnischer Kunstverein, Cologne
1985	Groninger Museum, Groningen, Netherlands
	Institute of Contemporary Arts, London
	Lisson Gallery, London
1986	Galleria Franco Toselli, Milan
	Lisson Gallery, London
1988	Lisson Gallery, London

Selected Group Exhibition

1983	*The Sculpture Show*, Hayward Gallery/Serpentine Gallery, London
1984	*Metaphor and/or Symbol*, National Museum of Modern Art, Tokyo (travelled to Osaka)
1985	*The British Show*, Art Gallery of Western Australia, Perth (toured Australia and New Zealand)
1986	*Forty Years of Modern Art 1945–1985*, Tate Gallery, London
	Sculpture: 9 Artists from Britain, Louisiana Museum, Humlebaek, Denmark
1987	*British Art of the 1980s*, Liljevalchs Konsthall, Stockholm (travelled to Tampere, Finland)
	Focus on the Image, Phoenix Art Museum, Arizona (toured the United States, 1987–90)

Collections:

Arts Council of Great Britain, London; Contemporary Art Society, London: Tate Gallery, London; Stedelijk Museum, Amsterdam; Neue Galerie-Sammlung Ludwig, Aachen; Israel Museum, Jerusalem.

Publications:

By OPIE: articles—"Julian Opie Interview," with Lynne Cooke, in *Flash Art* (Milan), April 1987.

On OPIE: books—*Julian Opie*, exhibition catalogue with texts by Wulf Herzogenrath and Kenneth Baker, Cologne 1984; *Julian Opie*, exhibition catalogue with texts by Michael Craig-Martin and others, London 1985; *Julian Opie: Drawings 1982 to 1985*, exhibition catalogue, London 1985.

*

Similarly to his contemporaries Tony Cragg and Bill Woodrow, the young English sculptor Julian Opie has returned to the city from the countryside. This was a significant move, considering that the work of these artists includes everyday objects of man-made materials in an elaborate visual vernacular which employs banal urban images.

Opie's early works were more concerned with the image and its definition outside the picture plane than with neo-avantgarde sculpture and its heritage. Opie did not hesitate to give up three-dimensionality in order to achieve an iconic dimension. The problems pertaining to the relationship between mass and volume do not in any way qualify his work. Sculpture demands an involvement additional to the requirements of painting. The defining role of painting was earlier clearly evident in Opie's work: he was then working with very thin steel sheets, easily modelled to created a simulacra of objects and words made concrete and realizable through painting.

A pile of books on the verge of falling to the ground (*Incident in the Library II,* 1983) was identified by the strokes of colour which designated and differentiated each part of the whole. The painting was 'handwritten', almost rudimentary in this respect, demonstrating that the painting itself was based on irony—as in *Personal Effects* (1984), for example, where Opie skilfully 're-made' identity documents, credit cards, cheques, envelopes and metro tickets, each painted onto sheets of steel.

All Opie's works had this character of parody, the remaking of everyday objects inserted into a spectacular universe which, in turn, parodies the universe of mass-media, their realm as signifying objects. Copies of masterpieces (*Cultural Baggage,* 1984), as well as enormous typographic letters in the form of words grouped in improbable assemblage (*Lonely,* 1984), reproduce the banality of mass-media while simultaneously capturing the semantic wealth of its messages. The work could not avoid measuring itself against the power of the connotations induced by the media industry; painting and sculpting, in order to affirm themselves as non-obsolete systems of communication, had to find some sort of relationship with them.

In that phase, a status of the work art as 'pure' was denied. To stress this, Opie built solid figures which he then applied to a kind of 'fake' canvas of foreshortened perspective, each figure being denominated by a number. Without this minimal level of denomination, the figures would have remained unimaginable, Opie was declaring that the abstract form in sculpture is no longer sufficient unto itself unless it makes a reference to the parody of its own history.

With the sculptures of 1986 and after, Opie radically alters the sense of his works. They are now concerned with a subtle and ironic minimalism. His recent pieces are large, vividly coloured bas-reliefs, variously inserted one into the other, or simply laid near each other. The very colour itself, the irregularity of the figures, and the estranging sense implied by the titles (*We'll Be Dead Soon*, 1986) promote the idea of an ironic detachment which shares a definitely non-figurative, non-objective character.

Even shrewder are the most recent works (1987), which camouflage distinctions between sculpture and apparatus of common use—for instance, a pair of air conditioner outlets, or a radiator. Here the artist ridicules our faulty observation and awareness through the device of displacement.

—Giorgio Verzotti

OPPENHEIM, Dennis.

American. Born in Electric City, Washington, 6 September 1938. Studied art, California College of Arts and Crafts, Oakland, California, 1959-64, B.F.A. 1964; Stanford University, California, 1964-65 (Teaching Assistant, 1965), M.F.A. 1965. Married Karen Erwin in 1959 (divorced, 1961); children: Eric, Kristin and Chandra. Professor of Art, Yale University, New Haven, Connecticut, 1969; Professor of Art, State University of New York at Stony Brook, 1969. Lives and works in New York City. Recipient: Guggenheim Foundation Sculpture Grant, 1972; National Endowment for the Arts Sculpture Grant, 1974. Agents: Yvon Lambert Galerie, 5 rue Grenier, St. Lazare, Paris, France; Sonnabend Gallery, 420 West Broadway, New York, New York 10012; Ace Gallery, 185 Windward Avenue, Venice, California. Address: 54 Franklin Street, New York, New York 10013, U.S.A.

Individual Exhibitions:

1968 John Gibson Gallery, New York
1969 Yvon Lambert Galerie, Paris
John Gibson Gallery, New York
Galleria Lambert, Milan
A Report: 2 Ocean Projects, Museum of Modern Art, New York
1970 Resse Palley, Gallery, San Francisco
John Gibson Gallery, New York
Pennsylvania Art Museum, Erie
Galleria Lia Rumma, Naples
Crossman Gallery, Wisconsin State University at Whitewater
1971 Yvon Lambert Galerie, Paris
Galleria Lambert, Milan
Harcus-Krakow Gallery, Boston
Galerie 20, Amsterdam
1972 *Outdoor Projections*, Sonnabend Gallery, New York
Projections, Nova Scotia College of Art, Halifax
Mathias Fels Galerie, Paris
2000 Shadow Projections, Tate Gallery, London
L'Attico, Rome
Galerie D, Brussels
1973 Sonnabend Gallery, New York
Chandra Oppenheim, Rivkin Gallery, Washington, D.C.
Galerie Sonnabend, Paris
Galleria Forma, Genoa
Galerie D, Brussels
Mayor Gallery, London
Museum of Conceptual Art, San Francisco
1974 Galleria Forma, Genoa
Galerie D, Brussels
Stedelijk Museum, Amsterdam
John Gibson Gallery, New York
Galerie Oppenheim, Cologne
Galerie Oppenheim, Brussels
Galleria Paolo Barrozzi, Milan

1975 Galleria Lambert, Milan
John Gibson Gallery, New York
Galerie Oppenheim, Cologne
Galleria Castelli, Milan
Retrospective, Palais des Beaux-Arts, Brussels
Galleria Schema, Florence
Galerie Vega, Liege
P.M.J. Self Gallery, London
Yvon Lambert Galerie, Paris
The Kitchen, New York
Anthology Film Archives, New York
1976 Museum Boymans-van Beuningen, Rotterdam (retrospective)
Bo Alveryd Gallery, Kavlinge, Sweden
Framartstudio, Naples
M.L. D'Arc Gallery, New York
1977 M.L. D'Arc Gallery, New York
CARP, Los Angeles
HM Gallery, Brussels
Hans Meyer Gallery, Dusseldorf
John Gibson Gallery, New York
Multiples Gallery, New York
University of Rhode Island, Kingston
University of Montana, Missoula
Wright State University, Dayton, Ohio
Yvon Lambert Galerie, Paris
Yaki Kornbilt Gallery, Amsterdam
1978 Musée d'Art Contemporain, Montreal (retrospective)
Art Gallery of Ontario, Toronto (retrospective)
University of Iowa, Iowa City
Marian Goodman Gallery, New York
Visual Arts Musem, New York
State University of New York at Plattsburgh
Marianne Deson Gallery, Chicago
1979 Kunsthalle, Basle
University of Massachusetts, Amherst
John Gibson Gallery, New York
The Kitchen, New York
Israel Museum, Jerusalem

Herron Gallery, Indianapolis
Winnipeg Art Gallery
Eels Gallery, Kent State University, Ohio
Musée d'Art Moderne, Paris
Northern Illinois University, DeKalb
Galleria François Lambert, Milan
Kunstverein, Stuttgart
Paul Robeson Center, Rutgers University, Newark, New Jersey
1980 Bruce Gallery, Edinboro, Pennsylvania
Cranbrook Academy of Art, Bloomfield Hills, Michigan
Ace Gallery, Venice, California
Portland Center for the Visual Arts, Oregon
Yvon Lambert Galerie, Paris
Pasquale Trisorio, Naples
Association Musée d'Art Moderne, Geneva
Morris/Acconci/Oppenheim, Sonnabend Gallery, New York
1981 Sonnabend Gallery, New York
Graduate Center, City University of New York
Contemporary Arts Center, Cincinnati
Galerie Marika Malacorda, Geneva
Galleria François Lambert, Milan
Lowe Art Museum, Miami
Richard Hines Gallery, Seattle, Washington
1982 Marianne Deson Gallery, Chicago
Rijksmuseum Kröller-Müller, Otterlo, Netherlands
Mills College, Oakland, California
Galerie Stampa, Basle
Ikon Gallery, Birmingham, England
Lewis Johnstone Gallery, London
Musée d'Arte et d'Histoire, Geneva
Olsen Gallery, New York
Bonlow Gallery, New York
Vancouver Art Gallery, British Columbia
Taub Gallery, Philadelphia
Ohio State University, Columbus
1983 Akira Ikeda Gallery, Tokyo
Flow Ace Gallery, Venice, California

Dennis Oppenheim: *Newton Discovering Gravity*, 1984

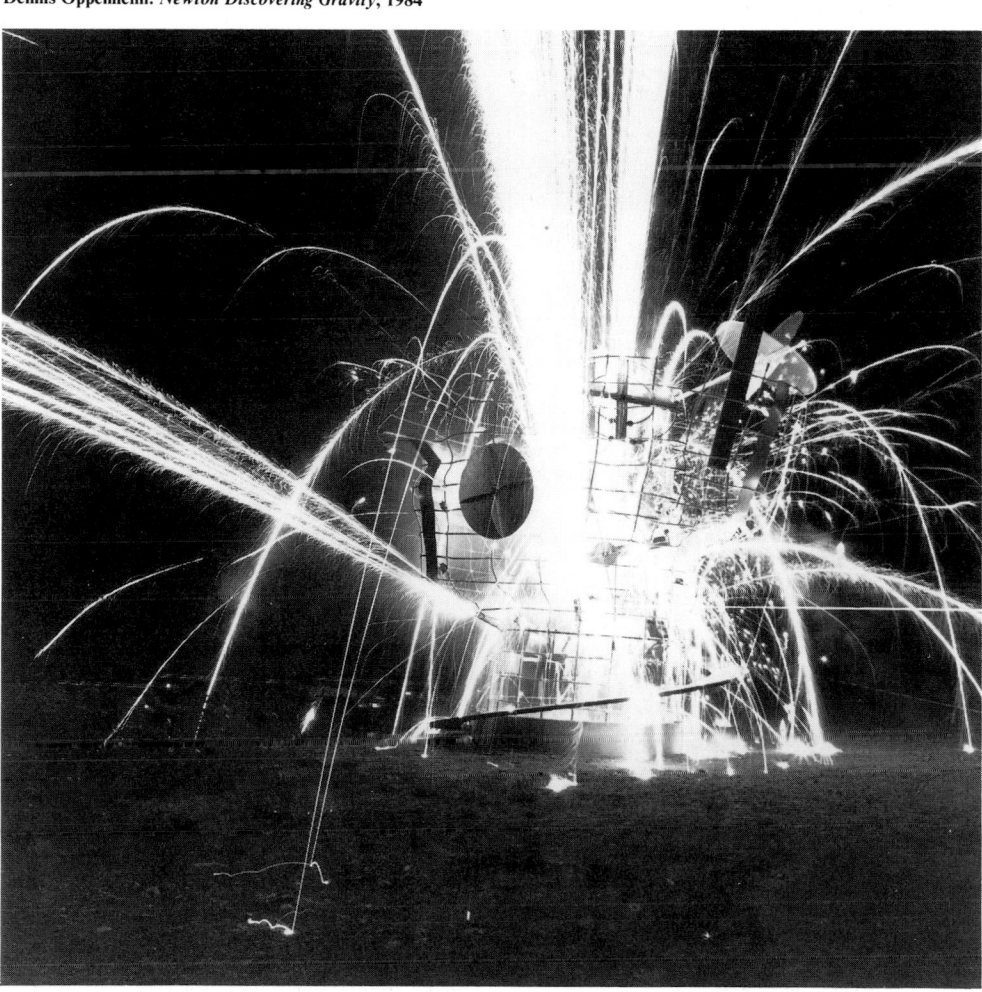

Galerie Schurr, Stuttgart
Serra Di Felice Gallery, New York
Seattle Art Museum, Washington
Munson-Williams-Proctor Institute, Utica, New York
Yorkshire Sculpture Park, West Bretton
Whitney Museum, New York
1984   Braunstein Gallery, San Francisco
Galerie Hans Mayer, Dusseldorf
Sander Gallery, New York
Philadelphia Art, Alliance, Pennsylvania
San Francisco Museum of Modern Art
La Jolla Museum of Contemporary Art, California
ZHTA-MI Gallery, Thessaloniki, Greece
Visual Arts Center, Anchorage, Alaska
Tel Aviv Museum, Israel
1985   Sander Gallery, New York
Grand Rapids Art Museum, Michigan
Alan Brown Gallery, Hartsdale, New York
Knight Gallery, Charlotte, North Carolina

Selected Group Exhibitions:

1968   *Earthworks,* Dwan Gallery, New York
1970   *Information,* Museum of Modern Art, New York
1973   *Aspects de l'Art Actuel,* Musée Galliera, Paris
1975   *Body Art,* Museum of Contemporary Art, Chicago
1977   *Documenta 6,* Kassel, West Germany
1978   *Sculpture/Nature,* Centre d'Arts Plastiques, Bordeaux
1981   *Machineworks,* Institute of Contemporary Art, University of Pennsylvania, Philadelphia
1983   *Kunst mit Photographie,* Nationalgalerie, Wesst Berlin
1985   *Modern Machines: Recent Kinetic Sculpture,* Whitney Museum, New York
1987   *Large Scale Photography,* Ringling Museum of Art, Sarasota, Florida

Collections:

Museum of Modern Art, New York; Detroit Institute of Arts, Art Gallery of Ontario, Toronto; Tate Gallery, London; Musée d'Art Moderne de la Ville de Paris; Centre Georges Pompidou, Paris; Stedelijk Museum, Amsterdam; Boymans-van Beuningen Museum, Rotterdam; Kunsthaus, Zurich; Louisiana Museum, Humlebaek, Denmark; public installations include: Fattoria di Celle, Pistoia, Italy; Tel-Hai, Upper Galilee, Israel; Bundesgarten, West Berlin; University of New Mexico, Albuquerque; Ville de Thiers, France.

Publications:

By OPPENHEIM: books—*Catalyst 1967-70,* reprinted from *Artscanada,* Toronto 1970; *Indentations,* Amsterdam 1974; articles—"Interview with Dennis Oppenheim," with Willoughby Sharp, in *Studio International* (London), November 1971; "Interaction: Form/Energy/Subject" in *Arts Magazine* (New York), March 1972; "Interview with Dennis Oppenheim," with Lynne Herschman, in *Studio International* (London), November 1973; "I Shot the Sheriff" in *Impulse* (Toronto), Spring 1979; "Interview," with D. Wall, in *New Jersey Architecture,* July/August/September 1979; "Interview," with D. Talley, in *Altanta Art Workers Coalition Newspaper,* September/October 1979; "Interview with Dennis Oppenheim" in *Studio International* (London), no. 999, 1983.

On OPPENHEIM: books—*Pop Art et Cie* by François Pluchart, Paris 1972; *6 Years: The Dematerialization of the Art Object* by Lucy Lippard, New York 1973; *Icons and Images of the 60's* by Nicolas and Elena Calas, New York, 1971; *Il Corpo Come Linguaggio* by Lea Vergine, Milan 1974; *Great Western Salt Works* by Jack Burham, New York 1974; *Dennis Oppenheim,* exhibition catalogue, Amsterdam 1974; *Man Creates Art, Art Creates Man,* by Dwayne Preble, New York 1974; *Proposals 1967-1974* by Lebeer-Hossman, Brussels 1975; *Whitney Biennial '77,* exhibition catalogue, New York 1977; *Individuals: Post Movement Art in America* by Alan Sondheim, New York 1977; *16 Projects/4 Arts* by William Spurlock, Dayton, Ohio 1978; *American Artists Talk on Art, 1940-1980,* edited by E. H. Johnson, New York 1982; *Dennis Oppenheim,* exhibition catalogue, Tokyo 1983; *Dennis Oppenheim,* exhibition catalogue, Tel Aviv 1984; articles—"Artist as Shaman" by Jack Burnham in *Arts Magazine* (New

York), May 1973; "Dennis Oppenheim, Myth and Ritual" by Lenore Goldberg in *Art and Artists* (London), August 1973; "Projekt" By I. Lebeer in *L'Art Vivant* (Paris), July/August/September 1974; "Madness in the Arena" by Nicolas Calas in *Artforum* (New York), September 1977; "It Ain't What You Make, It's What Makes You Do It" By A. Ramsden in *Parachute* (Montreal), Winter 1978; "D.O.: Post Performance Works" by Kim Levin in *Arts Magazine* (New York), September 1978; "Dennis Oppenheim's Delirious Operations" by Jonathan Crary in *Artforum* (New York), November 1978; "Gut Reaction" by S. Morgan in *Artscribe* (London), Spring 1979; "Image and Object in Contemporary Sculpture" by Grace Glueck in the *New York Times,* 11 January 1980; "Dennis Oppenheim and the Eternal Machine" by C. Simmons in *Artweek* (Oakland), 19 May 1984.

OPPENHEIM, Meret.

Swiss. Born in Berlin, Germany, 6 October 1913; emigrated to Switzerland, 1948, and subsequently naturalized. Educated at various German and Swiss schools, 1918–30; studied at the Kuntstgewerbeschule, Basle, 1929–30, 1938–40, and at the Academie de la Grande Chaumière, Paris, 1932–33. Married Wolfgang La Roche in 1949 (died, 1967). Independent artist, associating with surrealists Alberto Giacometti, Sophie Taeuber and Hans Arp, in Paris, from 1932, and in Berne, from 1948; also worked as a picture-restorer, Paris, 1940–48. Recipient: Kunstpreis, City of Basle, 1974; Grand Art Prize, City of Berlin, 1982. Agent: Renée Ziegler, Minervastrasse 33, 8000 Zurich. *Died, (in Basle) 15 November 1985.*

Individual Exhibitions:

1936   Galerie Schultess, Basle
1952   Galerie d'Art Moderne, Basle
1959   *La Festin,* Chez Daniel Cordier, Paris
Galerie Riehentor, Basle
1960   Galleria Schwarz, Milan
Galleria Serodine, Ascona, Switzerland
1965   Gimpel and Hanover Galerie, Zurich
1967   Moderna Museet, Stockholm
1968   Galerie Krebs, Berne
1969   Galerie der Spiegel, Cologne
Galleria La Medusa, Rome
Editions Claude Givaudan, Paris
1970   Galleria Il Fauno, Turin
1971   Galerie Bonnier, Geneva
Galerie d'Art Moderne, Basle
1973   Galerie Suzanne Visat, Paris
Galerie Renée Ziegler, Zurich
1974   Galerie Ziegler S.A., Geneva
Galerie Muller, Stuttgart
Jeu d'Été, Galerie Arman Zerbib, Paris (with Anna Boetti and Roberto Lupo)
City Museum, Solothurn, Switzerland
1975   City Museum, Winterthur, Switzerland
Wilhelm-Lehmbruck-Museum, Duisberg, West Germany
Galleria San Lucca, Bologna, Italy
Galerie 57, Biel, Switzerland
1976   Galerie Carmen Casse, Paris
1977   Galerie Elisabeth Kaufmann, Basle
Galerie Loeb, Berne
Galerie Nothelfer, West Berlin
Galerie Gerhild Grolitsch, Munich
Galerie Boulakia, Paris
1978   Eugenie Cucalon Gallery, New York
Galerie Levy, Hamburg
1979   Stadtische Galerie, Moers, West Germany
Kunstverein, Wolfsburg, West Germany
1980   Galerie 57, Biel, Switzerland
Marian Goodman Gallery, New York
1981   Galerie Claude Givaudan, Geneva
Galerie Nachst St. Stephan, Vienna (travelled to Innsbruck; Klagenfurt; Salzburg)
1982   Galleria Pieroni, Rome

Selected Group Exhibitions:

1933   *Salon des Surindépendants,* Musée d'Art Moderne, Paris
1936   *International Suurealist Exhibition,* New Burlington Galleries, London
Fantastic Art, Dada and Surrealism, Museum of Modern Art, New York
1942   *Allianz,* Kunsthaus, Zurich
1959   *Exhibition Internationale de Surréalisme,* Galerie Daniel Cordier, Paris
1961   *The Art of Assemblage,* Museum of Modern Art, New York
1968   *Dada, Surrealism and their Heritage,* Museum of Modern Art, New York
1972   *Le Surréalisme,* Musée des Arts Décoratifs, Paris
1978   *Dada and Surrealism,* Hayward Gallery, London
1982   *Documenta 7,* Museum Fridericianum, Kassel, West Germany

Collections:

Kunstmuseum, Basle: Kunsthaus, Zurich; Stadtmuseum, Winterhur, Switerland; Stadtmuseum, Solothurn, Switzerland; Centre National d'Art Contemporain, Paris; Moderna Museet, Stockholm; Museum of Modern Art, New York.

Publications:

By OPPENHEIM: books illustrated—*La Lune en Rodage* by Carl Laszlo, Paris 1954; *Sansibar: Geditche und Serigraphien,* Basle 1981; articles—"Enquêtes" in *Le Surréalisme Même* (Paris), no. 3, 1957; "Cahiers d'Ecoliers" in *Le Surréalisme Même* (Paris), no. 2, 1957; "Le Striptease, enquête" in *Le Surréalisme Même* (Paris), no. 5, 1959; "Don't Cry—Work," interview, with Lynne Tillman and Carla Liss, in *Art and Artists* (London), October 1973; "Meret Oppenheim—Kunstpreis" in *Kunstbulletin* (Basle), February 1975; "Io Meret" in *Bolaffiarte* (Turin), no. 103, 1980; recording—*Meret Oppenheim spricht Meret Oppenheim,* tape-recording, Hattingen 1974.

On OPPENHEIM: books—*Fantastic Art, Dada and Surrealism* by Alfred H. Barr, New York 1936; *Almanach neuer Kunst in der Schweiz,* Zurich 1939; *Histoire de Surréalisme* by Maurice Nadeau, Paris 1945; *Histoire de Surréalisme: Documents Surréalistes* by Maurice Nadeau, Paris 1948; *Meret Oppenheim,* exhibition catalogue, with text by André Pieyre de Mandiargues, Milan 1960; *Der Surréalismus* by Patrick Waldberg, Cologne 1965; *Erotique du Surréalisme* by Robert Benayoun, Paris 1965; *Meret Oppenheim,* exhibition catalogue, with texts by K. G. Pontus Hulten, Max Ernst, Carl-Fredrick Reutersvard and others, Stockholm 1967; *Meret Oppenheim,* exhibition catalogue, with text by Marcel Jean, Rome 1969; *Dada and Surrealist Art* by William S. Rubin, New York 1969; *Meret Oppenheim,* exhibition catalogue, with text by Janus, Turin 1970; *Objekt-Kunst von Duchamp bis Kienholz* by Willy Rotzler, Cologne, 1972; *Meret Oppenheim,* exhibition catalogue, with text by Hans Christophe von Tavel, Solothurn, Switzerland 1974; *Meret Oppenheim et ses Jeux d'Été,* exhibition catalogue, with text by Patrick Waldberg, Paris 1974; *Meret Oppenheim: Arbeiten von 1930-1978,* exhibition catalogue, with text by Jürgen Glaesemer, Hamburg 1978; *Meret Oppenheim: Catalogue Raisonné,* Zurich 1983.

Some artists achieve a particular notoriety for a single work. Picasso made "Guernica" as a monument to the whole Spanish obloquy of Franco and the Nazis. Duchamp could hardly improve upon his "great glass" demonstration of the Bride traversed by her Bachelors. How much homage can Josef Albers pay to the Square?—and so on.

Meret Oppenheim made Surrealism palpable with her fur-enveloped teacup and saucer. To her credit, a large sector of the world has never forgotten this extraordinary invention even though it first reached public scrutiny over 50 years ago. It was in the great international surrealist exhibition which reached London in 1936.

A modicum of intelligence and understanding will be enough to realize that here was an innovator, a surrealist Columbus of considerable and unusual power. Society does not take easily to brilliant dislocation of accepted values, but Meret Oppenheim's cup-and-saucer became almost a trademark for the surrealist movement worldwide.

In the interim, her ability to fabricate the unexpected continued, and it is unchivalrous for those who have had an opportunity of seeing her subsequent inventions not to recognize that one can get further than fur crockery. One has only to remember the gardenia mirror of the dressingtable (Galerie Charpentier—1964—"Le Surréalisme") with its convex glass, a vagina in reverse, to realize how this kind of genius for originality does not tire.

How does such an artist start? What are her inspirations and what about the materials she uses? Even the untitled and undated woodcuts from long ago have a freak individuality about them. Whatever connection with reality they may have has been totally obliterated both by the casualness of the image and by the haphazard tinting of the prints. Each pull is different from its fellow because of independent colouration.

Perhaps the encounter with so many and such distinct surrealists of the early 30s—Giacometti, Kurt Seligmann, Hans Arp and Sophie Täuber-Arp—was sufficient of itself to fire her imagination and take her into the heart of the surrealist world with which she has never lost touch.

—Sheldon Williams

OSSORIO, Alfonso.

American. Born in Manila, Philippines, 2 August 1916; emigrated to the United States: naturalized, 1939. Educated at St. Richard's School, Malvern, Worcestershire, England, 1924–30; Portsmouth Priory, Providence, Rhode Island, 1930–34; Harvard University, Cambridge, Massachusetts, 1934–38, B.A. 1938; Rhode Island School of Design, Providence, 1938–39. Served in the United States Army, 1943–46. Married Bridget Hubrecht in 1940. Lived in Taos, New Mexico, 1940–42, then settled in New York City; spent summers in East Hampton, New York, met Lee Krasner and Jackson Pollock, 1949: visited Victorias, Philippines, returned briefly to New York, and travelled to Paris, 1949; met Jean and Lili Dubuffet; introduced by Dubuffet to Michel Tapie; visited briefly in East Hampton, New York, and purchased home there, 1951; travelled to Chicago with the Dubuffets; introduced to Clyfford Still, 1952: installed l'Art Brut collection in his East Hampton house, 1952; organized exhibition series at Executive House, New York, 1956–58; Co-Founder, with Elizabeth Parker and John Little, Sigma Gallery, East Hampton, and organized summer exhibitions there, 1957–60; exhibited l'Art Brut collection at Cordier and Warren Gallery, New York, before returning it to Dubuffet, 1962; spent summers in Greece and Turkey, from 1964. Agent: Oscarsson Hood Gallery, 41 West 57th Street, New York, New York 10019. Address: Post Office Box 70, Wainscott, New York 11975, U.S.A.

Individual Exhibitions:

1941 Wakefield Gallery, New York
1943 Wakefield Gallery, New York
1945 Mortimer Brandt Gallery, New York
1951 Studio Paul Facchetti, Paris
 Betty Parsons Gallery, New York
1953 Betty Parsons Gallery, New York
1956 Betty Parsons Gallery, New York
1958 Betty Parsons Gallery, New York
1959 Betty Parsons Gallery, New York
1960 Galerie Stadler, Paris
1961 Betty Parsons Gallery, New York
 Galerie Stadler, Paris
 Selection, Cordier and Warren Gallery, New York
 Galerie Cordier-Stadler, Frankfurt
1963 Cordier and Eckstrom Gallery, New York

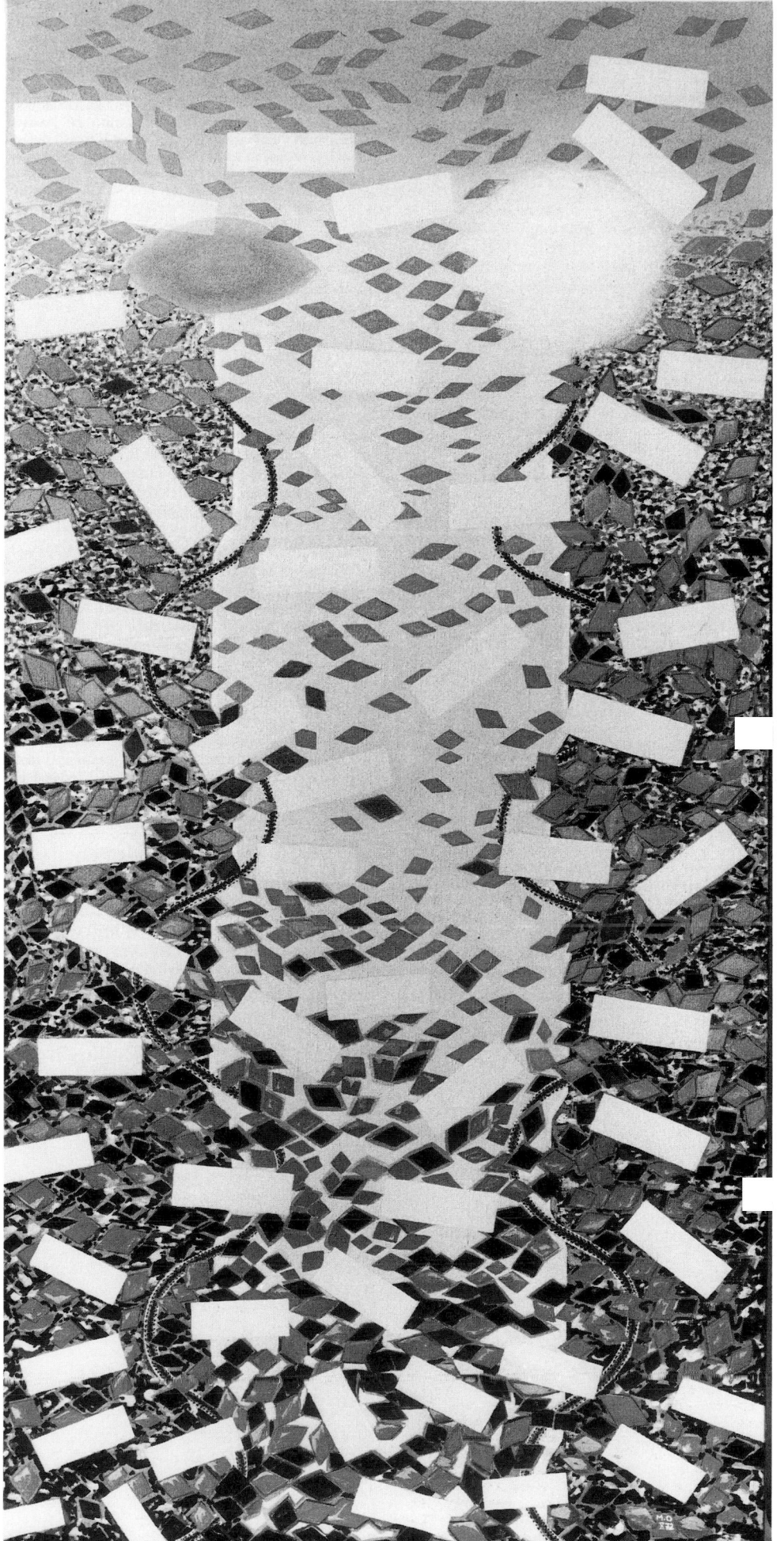

Meret Oppenheim: *Le Secret de la Végétation,* 1972

1965	Cordier and Eckstrom Gallery, New York
1967	Cordier and Eckstrom Gallery, New York
1968	Cordier and Eckstrom Gallery, New York
1969	Cordier and Eckstrom Gallery, New York
1972	Cordier and Eckstrom Gallery, New York
1980	Guild Hall Museum, East Hampton, New York
1984	Oscarsson Hood Gallery, New York

Selected Group Exhibitions:

1958	*International Sky Festival*, Osaka, Japan
1968	*The Door*, Museum of Contemporary Crafts, New York
1976	*14 Paintings: De Kooning, Dubuffet, Ossorio, Pollock, Still*, Thomas Gibson Fine Art, London

Collections:

Museum of Modern Art, New York; Whitney Museum, New York; Guggenheim Museum, New York; Metropolitan Museum of Art, New York; New York University; Wadsworth Atheneum, Hartford, Connecticut; Brandeis University, Waltham, Massachusetts; Philadelphia Museum of Art; International Center of Aesthetic Research, Turin; Boymans-van Beuningen Museum, Rotterdam.

Publications:

By OSSORIO: books—*Poems and Wood Engravings*, London 1934; *Exhibition of Recent Paintings by Lee Krasner*, exhibition catalogue, New York 1960; *John Little Paintings*, exhibition catalogue, New York, 1961; *Art Brut*, exhibition catalogue, New York 1961; articles—"Jackson Pollock in *Pollock*, exhibition catalogue, New York 1951, reprinted in *Pollock*, exhibition catalogue, Paris 1952, and in *15 Americans*, exhibition catalogue, New York 1952, and in *The New American Painting*, exhibition catalogue, New York 1959; "One Man's Art U.S.A." in *Artnews* (New York), October 1956; "Michael Lekakis" in *Americans 1963*, exhibition catalogue, New York 1963; "The House of the Hourloupe" in *Artnews* (New York), May 1968; "Notes" in *14 Paintings: De Kooning, Deubuffet, Ossorio, Pollock, Still*, exhibition catalogue, London 1976; interview, with Judith Wolfe, in *Ossorio*, exhibition catalogue, East Hampton, New York 1980.

On OSSORIO: books—*Les Peintures Initiatiques d'Alfonso Ossorio* by Jean Dubuffet, Paris 1951; *Ossorio* by Michael Tapie, Turin 1961; *Ossorio: A Selection*, exhibition catalogue, New York 1961; *Art in Progress: The Visual Development of a Collage* by Alfonso Ossorio by B. H. Friedman, New York 1972; articles—"The Eastern Long Island Painters" by Patsy Southgate in *Paris Review*, Spring/Summer 1959; "We Visit the Artist Alfonso Ossorio" by Louise Elliot Rago in *School Arts* (Worchester, Massachusetts), April 1960; "Alfonso Ossorio: A Biography, Mostly of His Work" by B. H. Friedman in *Art International* (Zurich), April 1962; "Ossorio" by Simone Frigerio in *Aujourd'hui: Arts et Architecture* (Paris), May 1963; "The Artist as Collector: Alfonso Ossorio" by Kenneth B. Sawyer in *Studio International* (London), March 1965; "5 Famous Artists in Their Personal Backgrounds" in *House and Garden* (New York), December 1965; "The Diabolic Craft of Alfonso Ossorio" by Richard Howard in *Craft Horizons* (New York), January/February 1967; "Alfonso Ossorio" by B. H. Friedman in *Art International* (Lugano, Switzerland), February 1967; "Ossorio the Magnificent" by Francine de Plessix in *Art in America* (New York), March/April 1967; "Alfonso Ossorio: La Mia Collezione e una Fabbrica di Idee" in *Bolaffiarte* (Turin), January 1974; "Ossorio" by Peter Blake in *Architecture Plus* (London), January/February 1974; films—*Galaxy* by Gregory Markopoulous, 1966; *The Artist: His Work and His Studio* by Terry Krumm, 1969.

*   *   *

During a career that has spanned four decades, Alfonso Ossorio has had his work approached critically from two viewpoints, neither of which is incorrect but rather overlapping. First, he has been historically placed among the first generation of Abstract Expressionists, a view supported by Ossorio's close enduring friendship with Jackson Pollock, whose influence can indeed be seen in the surrealist ink drawings Ossorio produced during the 1940's. Second, much has been rightly made of the artist's relationship with French artist Jean Dubuffet, whose abiding fascination with *Art Brut* ("raw art") closely paralleled Ossorio's, if it did not precisely influence it. Ossorio's development has incorporated these elements into his work—but it is not, as has been suggested, derivative of them.

In fact, Alfonso Ossorio occupies a unique position in contemporary art, one which has frequently aroused controversy, no matter what medium or style he engaged: combinations of wax, watercolor and collage, white lead and plaster, diagrammatic, neo-Constructivist paintings which used and twisted the physical pigment itself into ropelike reliefs, and, from the 50's until now, complex, sculptural wall-constructions and freestanding pieces incorporating such specialized detritus as bones, glass eyes, pieces of tree trunk and mirrors. The work has been described as "primitive," "barbaric," "voodoo-like". The critical emphasis has been placed almost entirely upon the materials themselves—not by the artist, although he is well aware of their connotations of violence, mutilation, and death—rather on the iconography, frequently anthropomorphic, that subsume them. When Ossorio uses the term "congregated imagery," he does so advisedly, to separate his work from the more popular and possibly inaccurate genre of assemblage, or relief construction. The term implies a *cerebral* gathering of materials, not a celebration of the found object. These congregations are often highly decorative, but motivated by an intellectual—even mystical—concern, rather than a purely visual one. If his colors are violent, and his use of materials visceral, it is because he is attempting to give, in Dubuffet's words, "body to conceptual ideas—to the point of making them pass completely into the field of material objects—and at the same time preventing the real things he wants to represent from materializing too much . . . ." The final product is, of course, frequently horrifying, although presenting more declarations of hope than have often been seen in his work. It is also an immensely sophisticated body of work, "borrowing" from Oriental art, sometimes testing new industrial materials (like the plastic sheeting experimented with in 1968), at others re-interpreting the Christian, and pagan, myths of death and resurrection. Although bearing similarities to the best of Art Brut, as practiced by the insane and the imprisoned, Ossorio's work indicates a calculated thoughtfulness that can only come from a professional draughtsman and an artist learned in mythic and formal history. The content is demanding, compelling; it is not automatic at all, but complicated, difficult "to read," frequently relying on a *combinatoire* of a visual vocabulary specifically chosen to evoke atavistic responses and an ordered control that "masks" these very emotive elements through complicated design.

Although Ossorio's style and materials have altered throughout the past thirty years, these concerns have bound all the different phases of his work indissolubly. In fact, he will frequently use elements from earlier pieces in new "congregations," a "reclamation," as he terms it. He will return from time to time generalized figuration, using a piece of tree-trunk or a glass eyeball from another, earlier piece; similar components echo each other from separate periods of his evolution as an artist. Starfish, bones, feathers, fragments of anatomical photographs emerge, disappear, and re-emerge from work to work. Past, present, and even future combine, dissipate, and reassemble, in an esoteric yet somehow recognizable fashion, in an insinuating blend of repulsion and attraction.

—Jane Bell

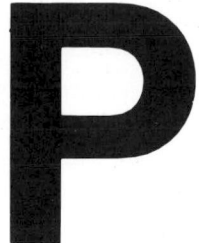

PAGE, Robin.

Canadian. Born in London, England, 2 November 1932. Studied at the Vancouver school of art, 1952–1954. Married Carol Page in 1960; daughter from earlier marriage: Rachel. Independent artist, since 1954: lived in Vancouver, 1954–59, in London and Leeds, Yorkshire, 1959–69, in Dusseldorf and Cologne, 1970–78, in West Berlin, 1978–80, and in Munich since 1981; has also worked in Paris, 1960, 1976. Guest Lecturer, High Wycombe College for Further Education, Buckinghamshire, Leicester College of Art, and Coventry College of Art, 1963–1965; Senior Lecturer, Leeds College of Art, 1965–70; Visiting Professor, University of Essen, 1978; Professor of Painting and Graphics, Akademie der Bildenden Kunste, Munich, since 1981; Professor of Painting, Internationale Sommerakademie fur Bildenden Kunste, Salzburg, 1986. Recipient: Canada Council Senior Arts Grant, Ottawa, 1975; DAAD Artists Fellowship, West Berlin, 1978. Address: c/o Akademie der Bildenden Kunste, Akademiestrasse 2, 8000 Munich 20, West Germany.

Individual Exhibitions:

1969	Art Intermedia, Cologne
1971	Eat Art Gallery, Dusseldorf
1972	Galerie Müller, Cologne
1973	Kunstverein, Cologne
	Galerie Müller, Stuttgart
	Galerie Gunter Sachs, Hamburg
1974	Galerie Foncke, Ghent
	Salon de Mai, Paris (travelled to Braunschweig, West Germany, and the Lijnbaancentrum, Rotterdam)
1975	Galerie Allen, Vancouver
1977	Junior Galerie, Goslar, West Germany
	Galerie Vallois, Paris
1979	Galerie Redmann, Sylt, West Germany
	Akademie der Kunste, West Berlin
1980	Galerie Redmann, West Berlin
	Galerie Redmann, at *Art '80*, Basle
	Kunsthalle, Darmstadt, West Germany
1982	Kunstverein, Augsburg, West Germany

Selected Group Exhibitions:

1953	*Young West Coast Painters*, Vancouver
1962	*Festival of Misfits*, Gallery One, London
1964	*Cross Section*, City Museum, Leicester
1969	*Amadou in A*, Antwerp
1970	*Happening and Fluxus*, Kunstverein, Cologne
1972	*Documenta*, Kassel, West Germany
1973	*6th International Triennal of Coloured Graphic Prints*, Grenchen, Switzerland
1976	*Holz-Kunst-Stoff*, Staatliche Kunsthalle, Baden-Baden, West Germany
1978	*Museum des Geldes*, Stadtische Kunsthalle, Dusseldorf
1979	*Ten Artists from the DAAD Programme*, DAAD-Galerie, West Berlin

Collections:

Museum Folkwang, Essen; Staatsgalerie, Stuttgart.

Publications:

By PAGE: article—"Robin Page" in *Flash Art* (Milan) May 1972.

On PAGE: books—*Mail Art: Communication à Distance: Concept* by Jean-Marc Poinsot, Paris 1971; *Robin Page: Bildparabeln*, exhibition catalogue, Augsburg 1982: articles—"A Note on Robin Page" by E. Lynn in *Art International* (Lugano, Switzerland), May 1973; "Robin Page, Galerie Müller" by G. Wirth in *Das Kunstwerk* (Baden-Baden, West Germany), July 1973; "Everybody Invited" by John Anthony Thwaites in *Art and Artists* (London), November 1973; "Artist Dips His Brush in Canadian Wry" by Art Perry in *Vancouver Province*, November 1974; "I Am a Unique Idiot" by Marq de Villiers in *Weekend Magazine* (Montreal), February 1975; "Art in a Brown Paper Bag" in *Weekend Magazine* (Montreal), May 1975.

*

Art is Hell!

—Robin Page

On the surface Robin Page is the archetypal frontier Canadian—big, brash, tough-talking, hard-drinking, gravel-voiced, complete with beard and denim coveralls. Almost a caricature. He even hangs tree-felling saws on the walls of his Munich home. Yet beneath the gruff protective exterior lives a dedicated, articulate artist and teacher.

Page's work presents a similar dichotomy. At first glance it is jokey, fun. But the artistic wit of Page is only a tool he uses to make serious statements about art, life and communication.

Page originally trained as a cartoonist, progressing perhaps unexpectedly to hard-edge painting. The lure of Europe brought him to the stimulus of Paris—so often an artist's catalyst—and London life gave him access to surrealism and the anti-art of Fluxus. Page was associated with Fluxus almost from the beginning, contributing major and minor Happenings throughout the 1960's. The 1970's found Page in Germany where he was able to function totally as an artist for the first time with his first one-man exhibition and artist-in-residence positions providing studio space and stability.

Images, in good art, can not merely represent themselves. The guitar in Page's work is one of his multi-layered autobiographical images which give depth and continuity to his oeuvre. Page played the guitar in a Vancouver-based band (one of more than 60 jobs which have supported him over the years); the guitar was the central object to one of his earlier Happenings—at the Misfits Concert in 1962 he kicked his guitar from the ICA through the streets of London with the help of audience members, returning with a few shreds to the concert stage; later the guitar appears in a painting and an actual object in "The Blind Man" of 1970, one of his "Parables."

The Parables began in Germany; they are Page's statements about art, conservation, politics, modern life. Central to each Parable is an action self-portrait. Painted from a photograph, the painting is highly detailed, technically skilled. Page uses his own image as an object, raw material, just as he incorporates work of other artist's—Picasso, Brancusi, Duchamp, De Chirico. A Charlie McCarthy-like dummy named Whildon (well-done?) acts as occasional comic to Page's straight-guy. The action in the painting does not, however, remain on the two-dimensional canvas. It thrusts into space in front, completing the artist's statement with a three-dimensional object. Expectations of reality are fulfilled.

Indications are that Page's Parables have all been written and new work is about to emerge from this artist who asks "Hey, Whildon, why has humor never replaced seriousness as the most respected cultural attitude?" Answer: "Because the people can't fake it!"

—Marlee Robinson

PAIK, Nam June.

Korean. Born in Seoul in 1932. Educated at the University of Tokyo, 1952–56; studied music, with Stockhausen, Darmstadt; art history and philosophy in Germany, 1956–58. Video artist: lives and works in New York; worked in electronic music studio for Radio Cologne, 1958–61; associated with the Fluxus group, New York, during the 1960's; Artist-in-Residence, WGBH-TV, Boston, 1969; Artist-in-Residence, WNET-TV, New York, 1971; works closely with Japanese artist Shigeko Kubota. Agent: Holly Solomon Gallery, 724 Fifth Avenue, New York, New York 10019. Address: P.O. Box 846, Canal Street Station, New York, New York 10013, U.S.A.

Individual Exhibitions:

1959	Galerie 22, Dusseldorf
1960	Mary Bauermeister Studio, Cologne
1961	*Simultan*, Galerie Lauhus, Cologne (with Wolf Vostell and Stefan Wewerka)
1962	Kammerspiele, Dusseldorf
1963	Galerie Parnass, Wuppertal, West Germany
1965	Bonino Gallery, New York
1971	Bonino Gallery, New York
1972	Museum of Modern Art, New York
1973	The Kitchen, New York
1974	Everson Museum of Art, Syracuse, New York
	Bonino Gallery, New York
1975	René Block Gallery, New York
1976	Bonino Gallery, New York
	René Block Gallery, New York
1982	Whitney Museum, New York
	Museum of Contemporary Art, Chicago (retrospective)
1984	Metropolitan Art Museum, Tokyo
	DAAD-Galerie, West Berlin

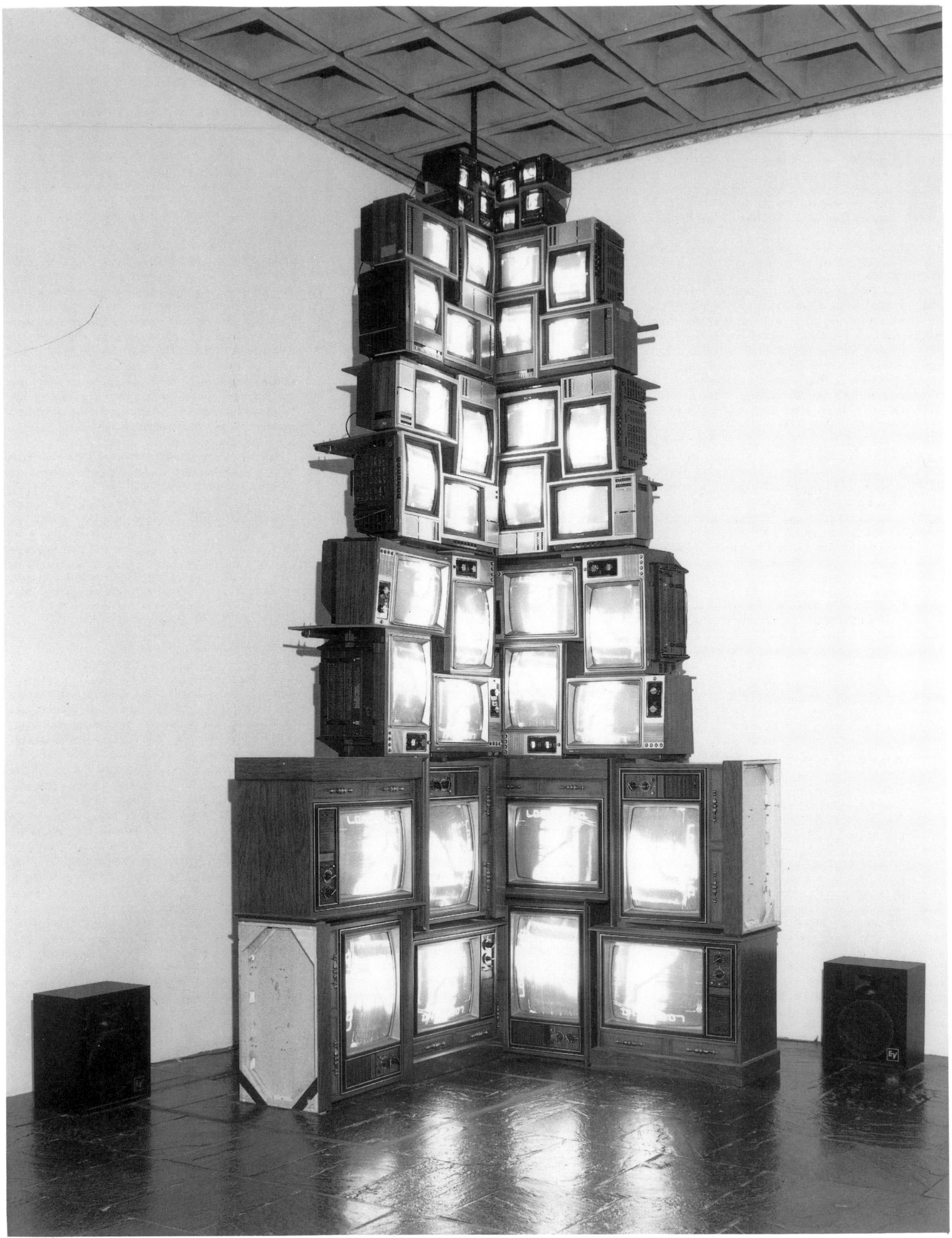

Nam June Paik: *V-yramid*, **1982** Courtesy Whitney Museum, New York

Selected Group Exhibitions:

1962   *Fluxus Festival*, Wiesbaden, West Germany
1968   *Cybernetic Serendipity*, Institute of Contemporary Arts, London
1969   *TV as a Creative Medium*, Howard Wise Gallery, New York
1971   *St. Jude Video International*, de Saisset Art Gallery and Museum, University of Santa Clara, California
1973   *Circuit: A Video Invitational*, Everson Museum of Art, Syracuse, New York
1975   *Open Circuits: The Future of Television*, Museum of Modern Art, New York
1975   *Video Art*, Institute of Contemporary Art, Philadelphia
1987   *Avant-Garde in the Eighties*, Los Angeles County Museum of Art
1988   *The Arts for Television*, Museum of Contemporary Art, Los Angeles (travelled)

Publications:

By PAIK: book—*An Anthology of Nam June Paik*, exhibition catalogue, West Berlin 1984; articles—"Expanded Education for the Paperless Society" in *Interfunktionen* (Cologne), no. 7, 1971; article in *Flash Art* (Milan), May/June 1972; television broadcasts—*Video Commune*, WGBH-TV, Boston 1970; *The Selling of New York*, WNET-TV, New York 1972; *Tribute to John Cage*, WNET-TV, New York 1974.

On PAIK: book—*Nam June Paik: Mostly Video*, exhibition catalogue with essay by Hohn G. Hanhardt, Tokyo 1984; articles—"Patricia Sloane Discusses the Work of Nam June Paik" in *Art and Artists* (London), March 1972; "Video Art's Guru" By D. C. Denison in the *New York Times*, 25 April 1982; review by Grace Glueck in the *New York Times*, 7 May 1982.

In the big exhibition next to the "Bachelor Machines" show on the Zattere quay in Venice for the baby *Biennale* of 1975, the fantastic Nam June Paik TV performance was not only the most amusing (funny?) activity, it was also the best put together. Its connection with the "Proposte per il Mulino Stucky" (a proper use for warehouse property which was lying empty and rotten) was not easily apparent, but there are more things in Heaven and Earth . . . .

Perhaps the solution to NJP's ubiquitous appeal lies in the paradoxical fact that he does not like television, does not even own a set (at least he did not have one when he was intriguing visitors to the Audio-Video tent in the park in Sonsbeek in 1971). His attitude to the whole communications systems summed up in the big part he plays as creator of international hook-up programmes—coupled with his inventive skill that has even led to the magic button that puts the person who presses it on the screen.

Of Korean origin, with university background in Tokyo, Munich, and Freiburg, NJP is a good example of the contemporary artist-cum-technician. His concern with screen imagery is to treat it as might a painter. What *is* can be given new existence and can join phantasies that do not exist. A sequence can be interrupted, up-ended. Sound is not constant, it can have its character entirely altered, or it can be silenced, or it can dance up and down in volume. Voice, music, clatter can all be mingled or transposed. The range of colour variations and exchanges seems limitless.

These descriptive facts about NJP's work are not offered to suggest that they are unique. Others have made similar experiments. NJP differs from them because his standards are so high and when there is something to be discovered, he so often discovers it before anyone else.

His abilities are so great that even established authority (in California, for instance) is nervous about his scope. Apprehensive, yes—but short on action because the person with whom they are concerned is too valuable to the medium professionally to be even lightly harassed.

NJP's finished works are one thing, but he is a worker of great fluidity. At Sonsbeek, for example, he used visitors to the Audio-Video tent as raw material. They saw themselves on screen and they saw their normal appearance could be set in motion by the artist. Nor did everything with which they were concerned stay in Sonsbeek. The 1971 festival in Holland, called with typical Dutch language-play *Beyond Lawn and Order* stretched nationwide so that the images thrown upon NJP's screens could be picked up all over the country.

—Sheldon Williams

PALADINO, Mimmo.
Italian. Born in Paduli, near Benevento, 18 December 1948. Painter: lives and works in Milan. Agents: Waddington Galleries, 2 Cork Street, London WIX 1PA, England. Address: Largo La Foppa 5, 20121 Milan Italy.

Individual Exhibitions:

1976   Nuovi Strumenti, Brescia, Italy
1977   De Ambrogi-Cavellini, Milan
        Galleria dell'Ariete, Milan
        Galleria Lucio Amelio, Naples
1978   Galleria Persano, Turin
        Galerie Paul Maenz, Cologne
        Galleria Franco Toselli, Milan
        Galerie Tanit, Munich
1979   Galleria Lucio Amelio, Naples
        Galerie Anne Marie Verna, Zurich (with Francesco Clemente and Nicola de Maria)
        Centre d'Art Contemporain, Geneva
        Galerie t'Venster, Rotterdam
        Galleria Mazzoli, Moderna, Itlay
        Art and Project, Amsterdam
1980   Galleria dell'Ariete, Milan
        Galleria Persano, Turin
        Galerie Paul Maenz, Cologne
        Galerie Anne Marie Verna, Zurich
        Kunstverein, Karlsruhe
        Marian Goodman Gallery, New York
        Galleria Franco Toselli, Milan
1981   Galleria Lucio Amelio, Naples
        Galleria Mario Diacono, Rome
        Galleria d'Arte Moderna, Bologna
        Galerie Bischofberger, Zurich
        Galerie Daniel Templon, Paris
        Marian Goodman Gallery, New York
        Galleria Franco Toselli, Milan
        Galerie Tanit, Munich
        121 Art Galerie, Antwerp
        Zeichnungen 1976-1981, Kunstmuseum, Basle (toured West Germany and Denmark, 1981-82)
1982   Waddington Galleries, London
        Kunstmuseum, Wuppertal, West Germany
        Marian Goodman Gallery, New York
        Galerie Buchmann, St. Gallen, Switzerland
1983   Galleria Medusa, Capodistria, Italy
        Galerie Engstrom, Stockholm
        Galerie Thomas, Munich
        Sperone-Westwater, New York
1984   Waddington Galleries, London
        Musée St. Pierre d'Art Contemporain, Lyon, France
        Galerie Thaddeus Ropac, Salzburg, Austria
1985   Galerie Michael Haas, West Berlin
        Galleria Lucio Amelio, Naples
        Kunstnernes Hus, Oslo
        Galerie Holtmann, Cologne
1986   James Corcoran Gallery, Los Angeles
        Sperone-Westwater, New York
        Waddington Galleries, London
        Galerie Bernd Kluser, Munich
        Galeria Comicos, Lisbon
1987   Galleria Franco Toselli, Milan
        Fuji Television Gallery, Tokyo

Moderne Galerie Rupertinum, Salzburg, Austria
Kulturhaus, Graz, Austria
Galerie Thaddeus Ropac, Salzburg, Austria

Selected Group Exhibitions:

1975   *Da Mezzo giorno al Tramonto*, Villa Colpicelli, Naples
1977   *Fotografia come Analisi*, Teatro Gobetti, Turin
1978   *International Drawing Triennale*, Warsaw
1979   *Europa '79*, Kunstmuseum, Stuttgart
1980   *Die Enthauptete Hand: 100 Zeichnungen aus Italien*, Kunstverein, Bonn
1981   *A New Spirit in Painting*, Royal Academy of Arts, London
1982   *Documenta 7*, Kassel, West Germany
1984   *Det Italienska Transavantgardet*, Lunds Konsthall, Sweden
1985   *The European Iceberg*, Art Gallery of Ontario, Toronto
1987   *Avant-Garde in the Eighties*, Los Angeles County Museum of Art

Publications:

By PALADINO: articles—"Vincitorio intervista Mimmo Paladino" in *L'Expresso* (Milan), July 1981.

On PALADINO: books—*Fotografia come Analisi*, exhibition catalogue, by Mirella Bandini, Turin 1977; *The Italian Trans-Avantgarde* by Achille Bonito Oliva, Milan 1980; *En De Re* by Achille Bonito Oliva, Modena, Italy 1980; *Mimmo Paladino*, exhibition catalogue, by Michael Schwarz, Andreas Franzke and Wolgang Max Faust, Karlsruhe 1980; *Mimmo Paladino*, exhibition catalogue, by Mario Diacono, Rome 1981; *Mimmo Paladino: Zeichnungen 1976-1981*, exhibition catalogue, by Jean-Christophe Ammann and others, Basle 1981 (includes bibliography); *Mimmo Paladino*, exhibition catalogue, Wuppertal, West Germany 1982; *Mimmo Paladino: Works on Paper*, exhibition catalogue with texts by Otto Breicha, Dieter Koepplin and others, Salzburg 1987.

The works of Mimmo Paladino rely predominantly on thin strokes, essential even when the formal elaboration is very dense. The symbols in his paintings are intimate, of the greatest intensity, containing the essence of Mediterranean culture. His blue has a sense of depth, as do his black, yellow or red, which moves us to silence.

Paladino expresses an idea of living, inherent Grecianness, an existential condition that only a man of the south possesses. Such an idea, born as it is of the meeting of different cultures, leads naturally enough to an eclectic activity. With more vigour and sensibility than others, he has been able to restore art to such remote themes as death, the infinite, longing; as the ego that looks at itself in the mirror to read the id there; the mystery. The view of the world derived from this, while markedly subjective, is a broad one; in the end things are seen to be internal to an organic whole. His Grecianness thus becomes evident in his presentation of the *single whole*; man, nature and depth coincide, and the whole combines to show a complex image of life as a perceptible presence. Thus in these works death, in its tragic essence, tends to reinforce its opposite by being presented as confirmation of the fact that the unfathomable mystery of life still persists.

A mysterious wisdom lies at the origin of the object of art. Paladino has shown that he possesses that wisdom, in creating a language that appears in its universal form, of symbols freed from the classical categories of reading. Symbols and metaphors are transformed in order to attend the Sacred Rite undisturbed; skeleton figures are present in silence at the coitus of reason with the lost sense.

Paladino has given substance to the expression of a free eclecticism which restores to the physical act of painting and drawing, as a poetic phenomenon internal to the crisis of reason, a poetry that desires neither to cure nor to create crises. In its appearance the work refutes any scientific approach, in that everything is restored to a pristine, uncompleted, gesture; phantasms, enigmatic presences, in every case presences, declare their existence within the system of contemporary troubles.

—Demetrio Paparoni

PALAZUELO, Pablo.

Spanish. Born in Madrid in 1916. Studied architecture at the Escuela Superior de Bellas Artes, Madrid, and the School of Arts and Crafts, Oxford, 1934–36; studied lithography at the Ecole des Beaux-Arts, Paris. Painter, Madrid, 1939–47, Paris, 1947–63, and Madrid, since 1963; produced first purely abstract works, Paris, 1948; sculptor, Paris, 1954, 1962–63; in Madrid, since 1963. Member, with Lara, Lago, Valdivieso, Guerrero and Olmeda, Grup El Paso, Madrid, 1945–47. Recipient: Study-Travel grant to Paris, Institut Francais, Madrid, 1947; Kandinsky Award, Paris 1952; Purchase Prize, *International Graphics Exhibition*, Ljubljana, 1969. Agents: Galeria Maeght, Montcada 25, 08003 Barcelona, Spain; Galerie Maeght Lelong, 13–14 rue de Teheran, 75008, Paris, France. Address: Garcia de Paredes 78, Madrid, Spain.

Individual Exhibitions:

1948	Galerie Denisé Rene, Paris
	Art Gallery of Ontario, Toronto
1955	Galerie Maeght, Paris
1958	Galerie Maeght, Paris
1963	Galerie Maeght, Paris
1966	Galeria Juana Mordo, Madrid
1968	City Art Museum, St. Louis
	Kunstverein, West Berlin
	Louisiana Museum, Humlebaek, Denmark
	Museum Boymans-van Beuningen, Rotterdam
	University of Puerto Rico
1969	Konsthall, Lund, Sweden
1970	Galerie Maeght, Paris
1972	Musée des Beaux-Arts, La Chaux de Fonds, Switzerland
	Olbilder Gouachen, Galerie Maeght, Zurich
1973	Galerie Iolas-Velasco, Madrid
1977	Galeria Maeght, Barcelona
	Galeria Theo, Madrid
1978	Galerie Maeght, Paris
	Sculptures, Peintures, Galerie Maeght, Zurich
1979	Galerie Art in Progress, Munich
1981	Galeria Theo, Madrid
	Herning Kuntsmuseum, Angligarden, near Copenhagen (with Pol Bury)
1984	Galeria Maeght, Barcelona
1985	Galeria Theo y Sala Celini, Madrid
1986	Galeria Maeght Lelong, Paris
1987	Galeria Theo, Madrid
	Museo de Arte Contemporaneo, Madrid

Selected Group Exhibitions:

1945	*Escuela Jovene de Madrid*, Galeria Buchholz, Madrid
1948	*Salon de Mai*, Paris
1952	*Peintres d'Aujourd'hui à Paris*, Kunsthaus, Zurich
1954	*Young European Painters*, Guggenheim Museum, New York
1959	*13 Peintres Espagnols Actuels*, Musée des Arts Décoratifs, Paris
1966	*Grandes et Jeunes d'Aujourd'hui*, Musée d'Art Moderne de la Ville, Paris
1968	*L'Art Vivant*, Fondation Maeght, St. Paul-de-Vence, France
1975	*Spanish Contemporary Painting*, New York Art Center
1979	*Otra Dimension*, Galeria Theo, Madrid
1987	*Espacios Urbanos*, Fundacio Miro, Barcelona

Collections:

Museo de la Castellana, Madrid; Fundacion Juan March, Madrid; Bankinter, Banco de Santander, Madrid; Museo de Vitoria, Spain; Museo de Arte Abstracto Espanol, Cuenca, Spain; Kunsthaus, Zurich; Musée des Beaux-Arts, La Chaux de Fonds, Switzerlands; Fondation Maeght, Saint Paul-de-Vence, France; Guggenheim Museum, New York; Carnegie Museum, Pittsburgh.

Publications:

By PALAZEULO: book—*Palazuelo*, with Claude Esteban, Paris 1980, Madrid 1981; articles—"Poems" in *Trece de Nieve* (Madrid), no. 7, 1963; "Cles pour des Espaces Inextricables" in *Chroniques de l'Art Vivant* (Paris), April 1970; "Notes de Travail" in *Derrière le Miroir* (Paris), no, 184, 1970; "La Geografia Visionaria de Luis Canelo" in *Luis Canelo*, exhibition catalogue, Madrid 1974; "En el Camino de Grodillo" in *Luis Grodillo*, exhibition catalogue, Barcelona 1976; "Materia, Forma y Lenguaje Universal," Interview with Santiago Amon, in *Revista de Occidente* (Madrid), no.7, 1976; illustrated books—*Lunariae*, with poems by Max Holzer, Paris 1972; *L'Ablatif Absolu*, with text by Michel Couturier, Paris 1976; *Soldadesca*, with text be José Miguel Ullan, Valencia 1978; *Ancres*, with texts by Pierre Reverdy, Paris 1978; *Exercises*, with text by Jean Daive, Paris 1980.

On PALAZUELO: books and catalogues—*Spanish Art Now* by William Dyckes, Madrid 1966; *Modern Paintings, Drawings and Sculpture Collected by Louise and Joseph Pulitzer, volume 3*, with introduction by Agnes Moran, Cambridge, Massachusetts 1971; *Pablo Palazuelo*, exhibition catalogue, with text by Paul Seylaz, La Chaux de Fonds, Switzerland 1972; *Palazuelo: Olbilder Gouachen*, exhibition catalogue, with text by Max Holzer, Zurich 1972; *Palazuelo*, exhibition catalogue, with texts by Max Holzer and Julian Gallego, Madrid 1973; *Palazuelo*, exhibition catalogue, with texts by Santiago Ammon and Daniel Giralt-Miracle, Barcelona 1977; *Palazuelo*, exhibition catalogue, with text by Jose-Miguel Ullan and others, Madrid 1977; *Palazuelo: Sculptures, Peintures*, exhibition catalogue, with text by Max Holzer, Zurich 1978; *Palazuelo: Pinturas, Esculturas y Gouaches*, exhibition catalogue with introduction by Miguel Logrono, Madrid 1987.

PALERMO.

German. Born Peter Schwarze in Leipzig, 23 June 1943; adopted by Heisterkamp family, renamed Peter Heisterkamp, Leipzig, 1943; assumed artist pseudonym "Palermo" from Mafia boxing-promoter Blinky Palermo, Dusseldorf, 1964. Educated at 49th Grundschule, Leipzig, 1949–52; Gymnasium in Münster, 1954–59; boarding school, Burgsteinfurt, 1959–61; studied art, Werkkunstschule, Münster, 1961–62; painting, under Bruno Goller and Joseph Beuys, Kunstakademie, Dusseldorf, 1962–67. Married Ingrid Denneborg, 1965 (divorced); married Kristin Hanigk in 1969 (divorced, 1975). Painter: Dusseldorf, 1964–69; shared studio in Mönchengladbach with sculptor Ulrich Ruckriem, 1969–76. Agent: Thordis Moeller, Dia Art Foundation, 107 Franklin Street, New York, New York 10013, U.S.A. *Died* (in Sri Lanka) *17 February 1977.*

Individual Exhibitions:

1966	Galerie Friedrich und Dahlem, Munich
1967	Galerie Heiner Friedrich, Munich
1968	Galerie Konrad Fischer, Dusseldorf
	Von der Heydt Museum, Wuppertal, West Germany
	Galerie Heiner Friedrich, Munich
1969	Kabinett für Aktuelle Kunst, Bremerhaven, West Germany
	Galerie René Block, Berlin
	Galerie Ernst, Hannover
1970	Galerie Rudolf Zwirner, Cologne
	Galerie Konrad Fischer, Dusseldorf
	Galerie Thomas Borgmann, Cologne
	Galerie Ernst, Hannover
1971	Kabinett für Aktuelle Kunst, Bremerhaven, West Germany
	Galerie Heiner Friedrich, Munich
	de Utrechtse Kring, Utrecht
	Galerie Heiner Friedrich, Cologne (with Gerhard Richter)
1972	Galleria Diagramma, Milan
	Galerie Klein, Bonn
	Galerie Heiner Friedrich, Cologne (with Gerhard Richter)
	Galerie Heiner Friedrich, Munich
1973	*Objekte*, Städtisches Museum, Mönchengladbach, West Germany
	Wandmalerei, Kunstverein, Hamburg
	Galerie Heiner Friedrich, Cologne
1974	Kunstlersiedlung Halfmannshof, Gelsenkirchen, West Germany
	Zeichnungen 1963–73, Kunstraum, Munich (travelled to Institut für Moderne Kunst, Nuremberg, and the Städtisches Kunstmuseum, Bonn)
	Galerie Heiner Friedrich, Munich
1975	*Druckgraphik 1970–1974*, Städtisches Museum, Leverkusen, West Germany
	Galerie Günter Sachs, Hamburg
	Galerie Heiner Friedrich, Munich
	Galerie Heiner Friedrich, Inc., New York
1976	Galerie Heiner Friedrich, Cologne
1977	Galerie Centro, Oldenburg, West Germany
	Stoffbilder 1966–1972, Museum Hans Lange, Krefeld, West Germany
	Galerie Heiner Friedrich, New York
1978	Galerie Heiner Friedrich, Munich
	Galerie Heiner Friedrich, New York
1979	Galerie Foerster, Münster, West Germany
	Galerie Heiner Friedrich, Cologne
1980	Kunstverein, Bremerhaven, West Germany
	Galerie-Verein in Haus der Kunst, Munich
	Dia Art Foundation, Cologne
	Galerie Art in Progress, Dusseldorf
	Galerie Kubinski, Stuttgart
1981	Städtisches Kunstmuseum, Bonn
1984	Kunstmuseum, Winterthur, Switzerland
1985	Kunsthalle, Bielefeld, West Germany
	Van Abbemuseum, Eindhoven, Netherlands

Selected Group Exhibitions:

1965	*Weiss/Weiss*, Galerie Schmela, Dusseldorf
1968	*Prospekt '68*, Kunsthalle, Dusseldorf
1969	*Sammlung Stroeher*, Nationgalerie, Berlin
1970	*Strategy: Get Arts*, Richard Demarco Gallery, Edinburgh
1972	*Documenta 5*, Museum Fridericianum, Kassel, West Germany
1975	*Bienal*, Sao Paulo
1976	*Biennale*, Venice
1981	*Art Allemagne Aujourd'hui*, Musée d'Art Moderne de la Ville, Paris
1982	*German Drawings of the 60s*, Yale University, New Haven, Connecticut
1984	*Neue Deutsche Kunst in Dusseldorf*, Messegelande, Dusseldorf

Collections:

Dia Art Foundation, New York; Städtisches Kunstmuseum, Bonn; Städtisches Museum, Mönchengladbach, West Germany; Museum Ludwig, Cologne; Neue Galerie, Kassel, West Germany; Galerie der Stadt, Stuttgart; Galerie Verein München in Haus der Kunst, Munich; Museum Haus Lange, Krefeld, West Germany; Städtisches Museum, Leverkusen, West Germany; Kunstmuseum, Dusseldorf.

Publications:

On PALERMO: books—*Deutsche Kunst: Ein neue Generation* by Rolf-Günter Dienst, Cologne 1970; *14 x 14*, exhibition catalogue, with text by Klaus Gallwitz, Baden-Baden, West Germany 1970; *Documenta 5*, exhibition catalogue, with texts by Harald Szeeman, Jean-Christophe Ammann and others, Kassel, West Germany 1972; *Palermo: Objekte*, exhibition catalogue, with text by Johannes Cladders, Mön-

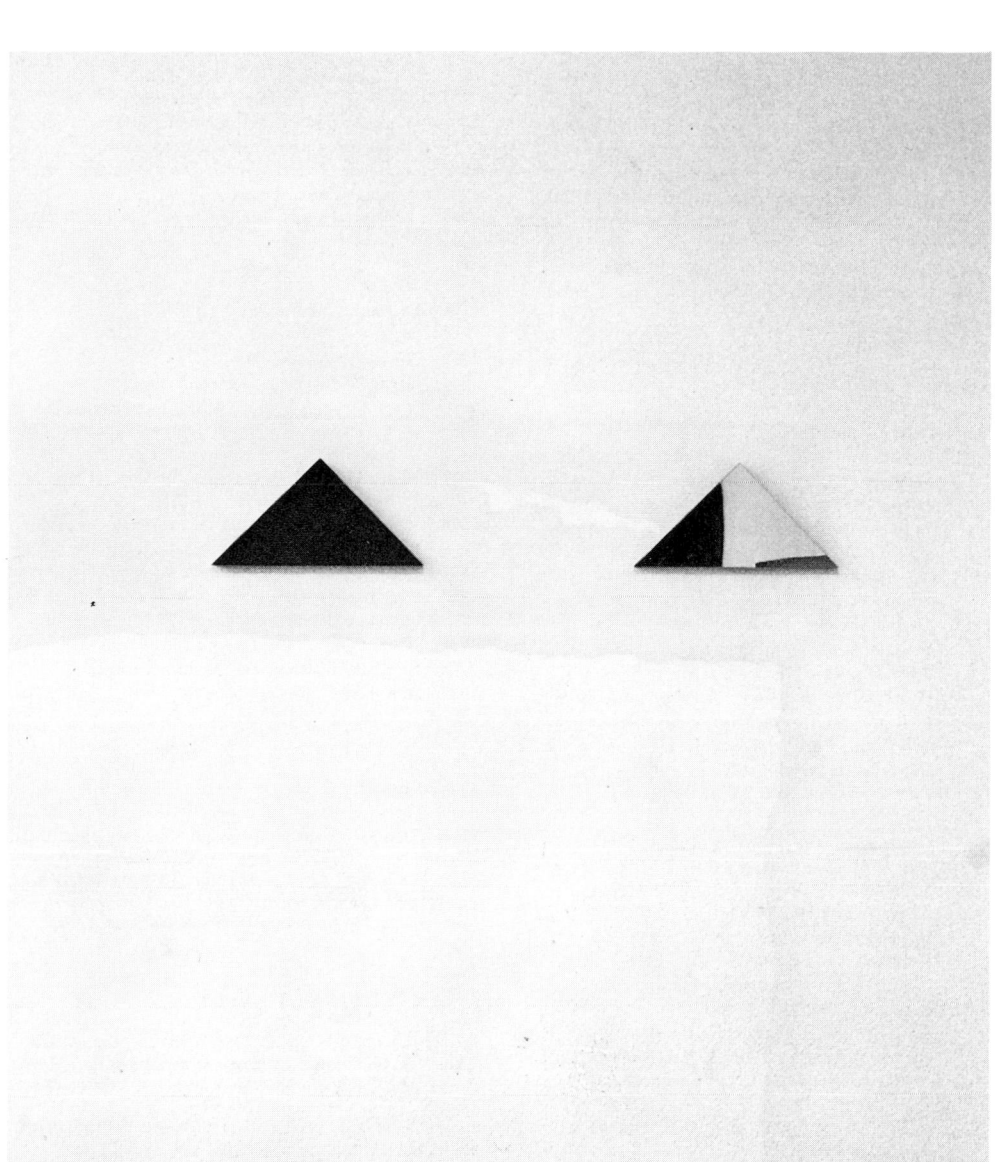

Palermo: *Objekt mit Spiegel,* 1969

PANAMARENKO.
Belgian. Born in Antwerp in 1940. Studied at the Koninklijke Academie voor Schone Kunsten, Antwerp, 1955-1960; National Hoger Instituut, Antwerp, 1962-64. Served in the Belgian Army, 1961-62. Independent artist, Antwerp since 1964; first happenings, 1964; first aeroplanes, 1967; first airship consruction, 1969; work on magnetic fields and magnetic airships, since 1977. Editor, with Hugo Heyrman, Bernd Lohaus and Wout Vercammen, *Happening News,* Antwerp, 1964-65; Founder, with Anny de Decker, Bernd Lohaus and Hugo Heyrman, Wide White Space Gallery, Antwerp, 1966: Member, Vrije Aktie Groep Antwerpen (V.A.G.A.), Antwerp, 1968. Agent: Anny de Decker, Wide White Space, Molenstraat 81-83, 2000 Antwerp. Address: Bierkorfstraat 2, 2000 Antwerp, Belgium.

Individual Exhibitions:

Selected Group Exhibitions:

chengladbach, West Germany 1973; *Palermo Wandmalerei,* exhibition catalogue, Hamburg 1973; *Palermo: Zeichnungen 1963-73,* exhibition catalogue, with text by Ludwig Rinn, Munich 1974; *Palermo: Druckgraphik 1970-1974,* exhibition catalogue, with text by Walter Ehrmann, Leverkusen, West Germany 1975; *Palermo: Stoffbilder 1966-1972,* exhibition catalogue, with text by Gerhard Storck, Krefeld, West Germany 1977; *Blinky Palermo 1964-1976,* with texts by Dierk Stemmler, Bonn 1981; *Palermo: Werke 1963-1977,* exhibition catalogue with texts by Laszlo Glozer, Max Wechsler and others, Winterthur 1984.

Palermo (actually Peter Heisterkamp) belongs to the "silent" artists of his generation in Germany. His early death in 1977 brought to an end a sensitive work which is gaining increasing appreciation.

Palermo, who studied from 1962-67 at Dusseldorf Academy with Bruno Goller and Joseph Beuys, was a painter. His interest concerned specific painterly problems even when he occupied himself with objects or spatial organization, or with pictures which—instead of painting—he created from strips of cloth. To Palermo colour and form were the fundamental elements of painting. He dedicated himself to the investigation of their interchangeable relationships with a persistence which with constant checking of points of departure continually led him to new discoveries.

Acting more from intuition than from reason, Palermo hardly bothered about a style. The preference for simple geometric forms like quadrilaterals, triangles, squares and ovals, for horizontal and vertical lines and for a closely legible division of areas, based mainly on colour relationships, did not develop in him from the constructivist tradition. And even when there are suggestions of Malevich or Newman in some of his works, we are not here concerned with an art of metaphysical content.

To Palermo the world of colours and basic forms possessed such powers of expression and offered so many possibilities that he was able, almost without limitation, to create his pictures from them. This vision is particularly evident in a series of pictures in white or coloured cloths sewn together (begun in 1966-1967): here Palermo demonstrates that he knew how to use non-painterly means in the interpretation of colour and space effects without distancing himself from the intentions of painting. The "Wall Drawings and Wall Paintings" with which he was occupied from 1968 prove it even more clearly: each of these solutions presents an individual answer to the needs of the concrete room (gallery, dwelling, etc.). Whether of the "free" subjective or "strict" rational tendency, Palermo's working method always went from sensible weighing up and intuitive intervention to supposed harmony.

—Zdenek Felix

1982 *Vergangenheit-Gegenwart-Zukunft*, Württembergischer Kunstverein, Stuttgart
1983 *17a. Bienal de Sao Paulo*, Brazil

Collections:

Kaiser-Wilhelm-Museum, Krefeld, West Germany; Ministry of Culture, Brussels; Fonds Regional d'Art Contemporain du Nord/Pas de Calais, Lille.

Publications:

By PANAMARENKO: book—*De Mechanism van de Zwaartekracht*, Antwerp 1975.

On PANAMARENKO: books—*Boezem/Panamarenko* exhibition catalogue with text by Jan Leering, Eindhoven, Netherlands, 1970; *Panamarenko: Automobile und Flugmaschinen*, exhibition catalogue, with text by Jean-Christophe Ammann, Jürgen Harten, L. Schirmer and others, Lucerne 1972; *Panamarenko*, exhibition catalogue, with texts by Suzanne Page and Jean-Christophe Ammann, Paris 1973; *Panamarenko: Flugobjekte und Zeichnungen*, exhibition catalogue, with texts by Werner von Mutzenbecher, Felix Philipp Ingold and Dietrich Helms, Basle 1977; *Panamarenko*, exhibition folder, with texts by Bernard Ceysson and Anne Dary, St. Etienne, France 1977; *Panamarenko: Umbilly I*, exhibition catalogue, with texts by Paul Hefting and Felix Philipp Ingold, Eindhoven, Netherlands 1977; *Panamarenko*, exhibition catalogue, with text by Rudi Oxenaar, Lucius Grisebach, Piet van Daalin and others, West Berlin 1980; *Vergangenheit-Gegenwart-Zukunft*, exhibition catalogue, with an introduction by Tilman Osterwold, Stuttgart 1982; *Panamarenko: Arbeiten 1966–1985*, exhibition catalogue, with texts by Wolfgang Rech, Bernd Wiedmann and others, Friedrichshafen 1985.

Panamarenko began his art career as a student in Antwerp's Koninklijke Academy of Fine Arts. Few of his colleagues and tutors can have imagined the complex and weaving course to which a training would lead him.

This elusive artist, so varied in his fabrication of 'objects' and his adventures with assemblages—taking time off to co-edit *Happening News* (which, of course, included 'news' and information about his own happenings), and—above all—his investigations into magnetism, first its fields and later his discovery of its application to magnetic airships . . . such description of the ways and inspirations of such an artist can only help to suggest a Galileo-stature.

Panamarenko once wrote: "I proudly present my new Aeroplane prototype. From different recent inventions and improvements, a new combination is made. The safest, economic and low-cost plane ever designed. It is also very beautiful." He then goes on to give all measurements, materials involved, performance—including lift-off, range and speed. And—classic provision—you don't have to be a pilot to fly it.

Panamarenko is an artist searching for unexpected associations on images, neo-realist conceptions as exemplified in his strange (and detailed) lithographs, such as *The Aero Modeller*—his translation from 'plane' to 'airship'.

An outstanding oddity in the world of contemporary art, he is one of those artists usually (or, at least, frequently) included in important international exhibitions such as *Metamorphosis of the Object*, for example, an enormous museum show, first seen at the Brussels Palace of Fine Arts before its tour of Rotterdam, Berlin, Basle and Paris.

—Sheldon Williams

PANE, Gina.

French. Born in Biarritz, to Italian parents, 24 May 1939; acquired French nationality in 1975. Educated in Valle del'Orco and Turin primary schools; studied at Ecole des Beaux-Arts, under André Chastel, Paris, 1960–65. Lived in Turin, 1944–60; worked as information-processor, IBM, Turin, 1959–60; settled in Paris, 1960; concentrated on painting, lithography and sculpture, Paris 1965–68; abandoned plastic activities, and began first body actions and performances, Turin, 1968; multi-media works, from 1980. Lecturer in Painting, Ecole des Beaux-Arts, Le Mans, France, 1980. Agent: Galerie Christine et Isy Brachot, 62a Avenue Louise, 1050 Brussels, Belgium. Address: 22 rue Quincampoix, 75014 Paris, France.

Individual Exhibitions:

1968 Galerie Heller, Paris
Fenestrelle, Turin
Pierres Déplacées, Valle de l'Orco, Italy
Lecture dans un Jardin Potager, Ecos, France
La Peche endeuillé, Galleria LP 220, Turin (travelled to the Galleria Diagramma, Milan)
1969 *Autocritique*, Turin
Work in Progress, Paris
Alignement infini, Deauville, France
Situation Ideale, Ecos, France
Table de Lecture, Turin
Premier Projet du Silence, Galleria Franzp, Turin
Deplacements, Ospedale San Giovanni, Turin
Streap-rake, Galleria Franzp, Turin
Desert Traces, Grands et Jeunes, Paris
Palo-Acqua Alta, Galerie Rive Droite, Paris
1970 *Terre Protégée 2*, Turin
Continuation d'un Chemin de Bois, Ury, France
Mon Corps, Ury, France
Semences de Graines de Chanvre, Ury, France
Narcisse, Jarcy, France
Hommage à Yves Klein, Paris
Deuxième Projet du Silence, Ury, France
Le Riz, Galerie Rive Droite, Paris
1971 *L'Escalade*, Pane Atelier, Paris
Hommage à un Jeune Drogue, Bordeaux
Quatrième Projet du Silence, Musée Galliera, Paris
Nourriture: Actualités TV: Feu, Fregnac, Paris
1972 *Le Lait Chaud*, Boutan, Paris
Lecture d'un Certificat Medical de Madame R.S., Paris
Action Posthume, Paris
Vie-Mort-Reve, Belgrade
Je, Bruges, Belgium
1973 *Autoportrait(s)*, Galerie Stadler, Paris
Transfert, Space 640, St. Jeannet, France
Azione Sentimentale, Galleria Diagramma, Milan
1974 *Psyche*, Galerie Stadler, Paris
Death Control, Galerie Diagramma, Basle
Action Melancolique 2 x 2 x 2, Studio Morra, Naples
1975 *Le Corps Presenti*, Galerie Krinzinger, Innsbruck
Discours mou et mat, Galerie de Appel, Amsterdam
Death Control 2, Galerie Stadler, Paris
1976 *La Mise en Action Imagée d'une Sequence: Le Secret*, Galerie Stadler, Paris
Il Caso Numero 2 sul Ring, Galleria Diagramma, Legnano, Italy
Io Mescolo Tutto, Museo d'Arte Moderna, Bologna
1977 *Action Theorique*, Libero Per, Naples
Laure, Galerie Isy Brachot, Brussels
A Hot Afternoon, at Documenta 6, Kassel, West Germany
1978 *Little Journey 1*, Vienna
A Hot Afternoon 2, Galeria Quadrum, Lisbon
Mezzogiorno a Alimena 2, San Francisco Art Institute
Little Journey 2, Los Angeles Institute of Contemporary Art
1979 *Mezzogiorno a Alimena 3*, Centre Georges Pompidou, Paris
Little Journey 3, Goethe Institut, Paris
1980 *Travail d'Action*, Galerie Isy Brachot, Paris
1981 *Partition d'Action: Action de Chasse: C'est la Nuit, Cherie*, Franklin Furnace, New York
Partition d'Action: Petit Voyage Oh! Oh! Oh! en couleurs, Kunstlerhaus Bethanien, Berlin (travelled to GEDOK, Hamburg)
1983 *Partition*, Galerie Arapède, Tours, France
Partition, Galerie Isy Brachot, Paris
1984 *Guerre-Partizioni*, Galleria Marginalia, Turin
1985 Ecole Nationale d'Art Decoratif, Limoges, France
Padiglione d'Arte Contemporanea, Milan
1986 *La legende dorée*, Musée d'Art Moderne, Villeneuve d'Ascq, France
1987 *Travaux recents*, Galerie Christine et Isy Brachot, Brussels

Selected Group Exhibitions:

1968 *Grands et Jeunes*, Paris
1969 *Biennale des Jeunes*, Paris
1970 *Form Concept*, Bonino Gallery, New York
1975 *Body Works*, Museum of Contemporary Art, Chicago
1977 *L'Art Corporel by Francois Pluchart*, Galerie Isy Brachot, Brussels
1978 *6th Biennale Internazionale della Grafica d'Arte*, Florence
1981 *Typisch Frau*, Galerie Magers, Bonn
1983 *Panorram d'Art Contemporain en France 1960–80*, Centre Culturel, Coutances, France
1985 *Ceci n'est pas une photographie*, Fonds Régionale d'Art Comtemporain, Aquitaine, France
1987 *Les Années 70—Les Années Memoire*, Centre d'Art Contemporain, Meymac, France

Collections:

Centre Georges Pompidou, Paris; Centre National d'Art Contemporain, Paris; Musée d'Art Contemporain, Epinal, France; Musée d'Art Contemporain, Villeneuve d'Ascq, France; Fondation Camille, Paris; Fonds Régional d'Art Contemporain, in Bordeaux, Lyon and Toulouse, France.

Publications:

By PANE: films—*Solitrak*, 1968; *Parcours Identification*, with Denis Gherbrand, 1970; *Action: Vie: Mort: Reve*, 1972; *Action Melancolique*, with Anne Marchand 1974; *Death Control*, with Francoise Masson, 1975; videotapes--*Nouriture: Feu: A*, 1971; *Le Lait Chaud*, with Daniel Orsi, 1972; *Autoportraits*, 1973; *Psyche*, 1974.

On PANE: books—*Art en France, une Nouvelle Generation* by Jean Clair, Paris 1973; *L'Art Actuel en France* by Anne Tronche, Paris, 1974; *Body-Art et Storie Simili* by Lea Vergine, Milan 1974; *L'Arte Moderna—La Body Art* by Gillo Dorfles, Milan 1977; *Gina Pane*, exhibition catalogue with texts by L. Vergine and G. Manganelli, Milan 1984; *Gina Pane: La Legende Dorée*, exhibition catalogue with texts by Gilbert Perlein and Michel Baudson, Lille 1986; articles—"Gina Pane" by Claude Bouyeur in *Les Lettres Francaises* (Paris), May 1971; "Gina Pane, faire reflechir" by Bernard Borgeaud in *Pariscope* (Paris), June 1971; "Gina Pane en Action" by Claude Bouyeur in *Plaisir de France* (Paris), June 1972; "Gina Pane" by J. J. Leveque in *Opus International* (Paris), November 1972; "La Response Sanglante de Gina Pane" by Francois Pluchart in *Combat* (Paris), January 1973; "Performance of Concern" by Effie Stephano in *Art and Artists* (London), April 1973; "Gina Pane ou la Debacle des Agnes" by Bernard Teyssedre in *Opus International* (Paris), no. 51, 1974: "The TV Aesthetic" by Tony del Renzio in *Art and Artists* (London), 1974; "Feminismus Kunst" in *Heute Kunst* (Dusseldorf), February/March 1975; "Short Trip" by L. Lewis In *Artweek* (Oakland, California), September 1978; "Gina Pane: Wounded as Sign" by Helena Kontova in *Flash Art* (Milan); October/November 1979; "Gina Pane en toute urbanité" by Anne Dagbert, and "Gina Pane: l'instant du ravissement" by J. M. Touratier in *Opus International* (Paris), no. 94, 1984.

My work corresponds to different methods of approach to a material reality and seeks to show that the very manner in which "we" experience the body is never completely "ours" because all bodily experience reflects the body of others—in other words, My Body in Action is not only in RELATION but RELATION itself.

It is not a surface with a centre (a flat picture) nor a socle (a support of something else), but the whole, the exterior, the interior: the very BODY of the dis-

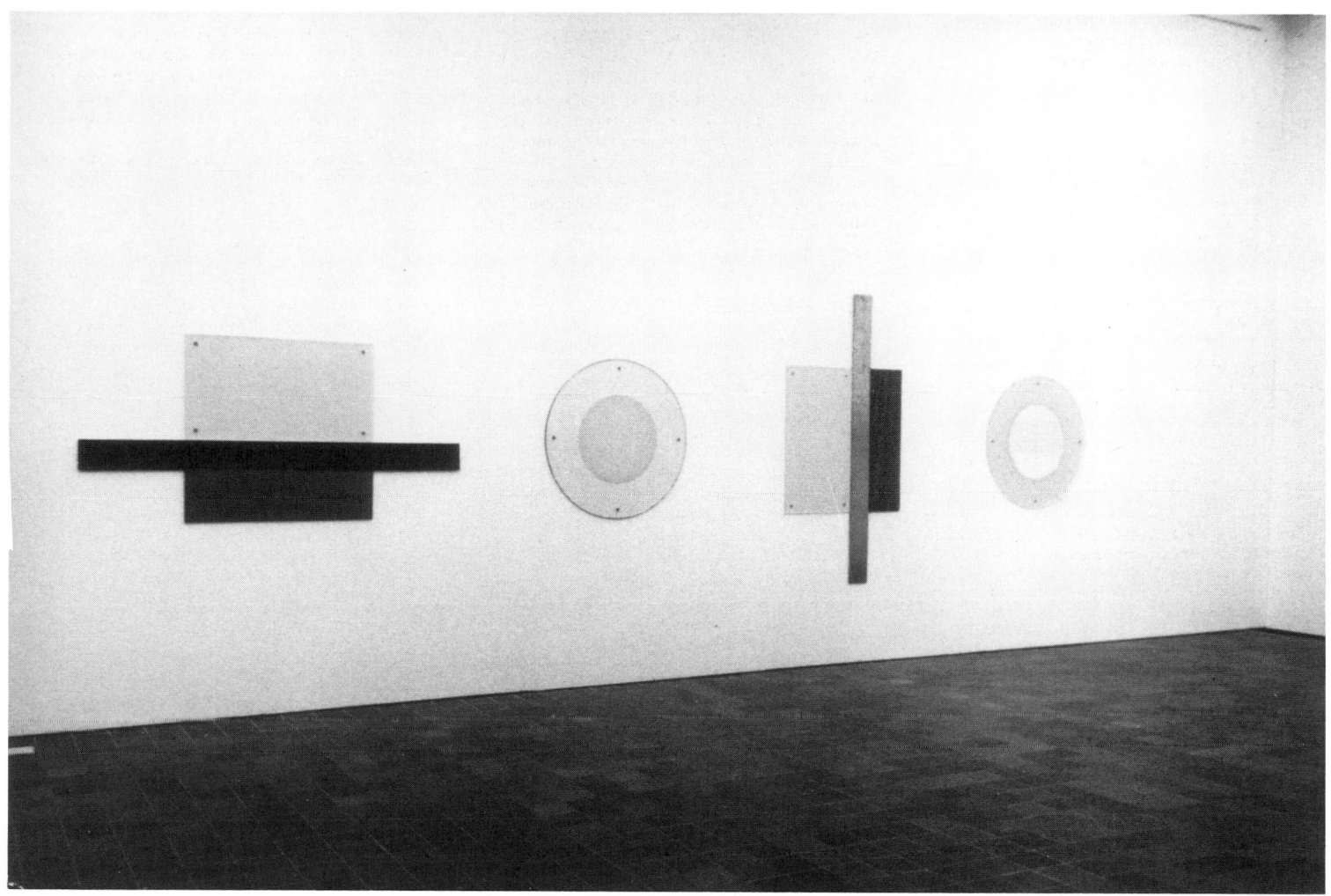

Gina Pane: *Le Martyre de St. Laurent, No. 2,* 1986

course. It achieves a "proximity" because it is not enclosed: its completeness is seen on all sides embracing the theory of significance in the production of re-actuation. One has to understand "My Body in Action" not as the skin of a painting enclosing its interior but as a WRAPPING/UNFOLDING bringing back depth to the edge of things.

—Gina Pane

Before becoming a protagonist of Body Art, Gina Pane was a painter and sculptor. Her painting was, however, growing more and more like an "action," to a point where her pictures were produced by the mark left by brushes let fall on the canvas.

In 1968 came her first actions and installations in nature, like "The Displaced Stones" and "Continuation of a Woodland Path," in which the artist existed solely as a performer of simple acts, such as for instance the moving of materials or objects. Her body, which was simply an instrument, became from 1970 the protagonist of her actions.

In one of her first body actions, "Protected Earth," Gina Pane simply shielded a part of the ground with her own body, the ground having been first, in an action with the same title ("Protected Earth, No. 1"), been covered (protected, in the artist's words) with cement objects fastened together with belts. In this phase, therefore, the body passed from being an instrument to being a medium of expression.

From 1971 on, the main image in the actions became the wound, which with Gina Pane, unlike other more radical Body Art artists, was not only something personal, a psycho-physical act, but also a sign ". . . through which I can communicate the loss of strength . . . a gesture of fracture and breaking."

After some actions concentrating purely on the gesture of wounding herself, from 1972 this action became only one element in a spectacle of growing richness and complexity, both visually and in its content, full of metaphysical and imaginary references. A small paper boat might serve to suggest the idea of travel, the wound might become an act of magic, as it did for the doctor-healers in ancient Greece, who inflicted on their own bodies the same wounds that they wished to heal.

At the same time Gina Pane still expresses herself by other means, such as photography, objects, drawing and video, which represent other aspects of her actions.

From the latest years come the musical scores painted for the performances. These are paintings composed of big panels with scenes from an imaginary story, which have to be acted by the performers, not now by the artist. The performers in this case become simply actors, instruments to create a living image.

—Helena Kontova

PAOLINI, Giulio.

Italian. Born in Genoa, 5 November 1940. Independent artist, since 1964: lives and works in Turin. Produced costumes and scenic designs for *Bruto II,* Turin, 1969, *Manfred,* Turin, *Colloquio con Malcolm X,* Genoa, and *Atene Anno Zero,* Turin, 1970; *Laborninthus II,* Genoa, 1971; *Hierapolis,* Turin, 1983; *Rosenist,* West Berlin, 1984; *Il combattimento di Tancredie e Clorinda,* Turin, 1985. Recipient: Television Scenography Prize, RAI Television, Rome, 1971; Premio Fontana, 1975; DAAD Fellowship, West Berlin, 1981. Agent: Galleria Christian Stein, via Lazzaretto 15, 20124 Milan. Address: Piazza Vittorio Veneto 10, 10123 Turin, Italy.

Individual Exhibitions:

1964   Galleria La Salita, Rome
1965   Galleria Notizie, Turin
1966   Galleria dell'Ariete, Milan
1967   Sala delle Colonne, Teatro Stabile, Turin
         Una Poesia, Libreria Stampatori, Turin
         Galleria del Leone, Venice
         Galleria Christian Stein, Turin
1968   Libreria dell'Oca, Rome
         Galleria Notizie, Turin
1969   Galleria de Nieubourg, Milan
         Una Copia della Luce, Studio La Tartaruga, Rome
         Galleria del Leone, Venice
1970   *Vedo,* Qui Arte Contemporanea, Rome (travelled to the Galleria Notizie, Turin)
1971   *Un Quadro,* Galleria dell'Ariete, Milan (travelled to the Galleria La Salita, Rome)
         Appolo e Dafne, Libreria Stampatori, Turin (travelled to Studio C, Brescia)
         Galerie Paul Maenz, Cologne
1972   Galleria Notizie, Turin
         Apoteosi di Omero, Galleria Marilena Bonomo, Bari, Italy, (travelled to the Modern Art Agency, Naples)
         Sonnabend Gallery, New York
1973   *Idem,* Galleria Notizie, Turin
         Galleria Toselli e Francoise Lambert, Milan
         La Doublure, Galleria L'Attico e Sperone Fischer, Rome
         Royal College of Art, London
         Galerie Annemarie Verna, Zurich
         Studio Marconi, Milan

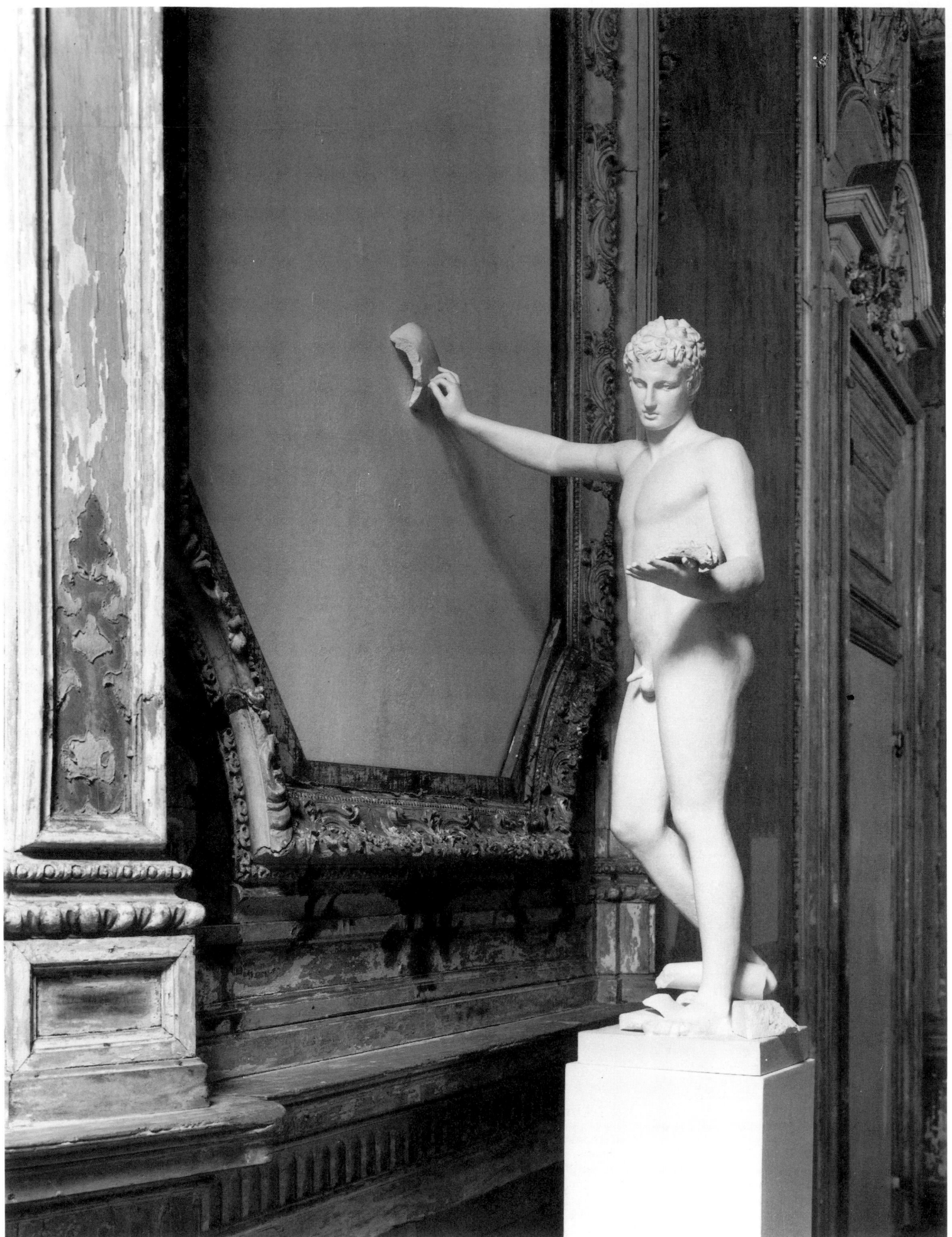

Giulio Paolini: *L'Altra Figura* **(detail), 1986**

1974	Modern Art Agency, Naples
	Museum of Modern Art, New York
	Galleriaforma, Genoa
	Galerie Paul Maenz, Cologne
	Galleria Marilena Bonomo, Bari, Italy
	Galleria Il Sole, Bolzano, Italy
1975	*Museo*, Galleria Notizie, Turin
	Galerie Annemarie Verna, Zurich
	Galerie Art in Progress, Munich
	Galerie Paul Maenz, Cologne
	Galleria D'Alessandro-Ferranti, Rome
	Studio G7, Bologna
	Galleria Ferrari, Verona
1976	Samangallery, Genoa
	Galleria Multipli, Turin
	Studio Marconi, Milan
	Galerie Yvon Lambert, Paris
	University of Parma
	Galleria Area, Florence
	Galerie Paul Maenz, Cologne
	Banco, Brescia, Italy
1977	Sperone Westwater Fischer Gallery, New York
	Galerie Annemarie Verna, Zurich
	Städtisches Museum, Mönchengladbach, West Germany
	Lisson Gallery, London
	Galerie Paul Maenz, Cologne
	Kunstverein, Mannheim
	Annali 1961–1976, Galleria Ugo Ferranti, Rome
1978	Museo Diego Aragona Pignatelli Cortes, Naples
	Galerie Yvon Lambert, Paris
	Gallera Christian Stein, Turin
	Galleria Marilena Bonomo, Spoleto, Italy
	Galerie Albert Baronian, Brussels
	Galleria Mario Diacono, Bologna
	Del Bello Intelligibile, Musée d'Art Moderne de la Ville, Paris
	Galerie Paul Maenz, Paris
1979	Galleria dell'Oca, Rome
	Liber Veritatis, Lisson Gallery, London
	Galerie Jean et Karen Bernier, Athens
	Atto Unico in Tre Quadri, Studio Marconi, Milan
1980	*Pendant*, Galerie Annemarie Verna, Zurich
	Stedelijk Museum, Amsterdam (travelled to the Museum of Modern Art, Oxford)
	Instituto Nazionale per la Grafica, Rome (with Michelangelo Pistoletto and Patella)
	Ritratto dell'Artista come Modello, Galleria Ugo Ferranti, Rome
1981	Galleria Christian Stein, Turin
	Hortus Clausus, Kunstmuseum, Lucerne
	Galerie Paul Maenz, Cologne
	Casa di Lucrezio, Banco, Brescia, Italy
	La Caduta di Icaro, Padiglione d'Arte Contemporanea, Milan
	Del Bello Intelligibile, Kunsthalle, Bielefeld, West Germany (travelled to the Museum von der Heydt, Wuppertal, West Germany)
	Galleria Marilena Bonomo, Bari, Italy (travelled to Galleria Francoise Lambert, Milan)
	Raum für Kunst, Hamburg
	Nouveau Musée, Lyon-Villeurbanne, France
	Laforet Museum, Tokyo
	Galerie Yvon Lambert, Paris
1983	Galleria Christian Stein, Turin
	Galerie Paul Maenz, Cologne
	Galleria Lucrezia De Domizio, Pescara, Italy
1984	Los Angeles Institute of Contemporary Art
	Nouveau Musée, Lyon-Villeurbanne, France
	Studio Marconi, Milan
	Direction Régionale de Culture de Bourgogne, Dijon, France
	Giulio Paolini, at the *27. Festival di due mondi*, Spoleto, Italy
	Galerie Annemarie Verna, Zurich
	Studio G7, Bologna
1985	Galleria Pieroni, Rome
	Galerie Maeght Lelong, Paris
	Guggenheim Museum, New York
	Pinacoteca Comunale, Ravenna, Italy
	Arti Visive, Ravenna, Italy
	Art Gallery of Vancouver, British Columbia
	Musée d'Art Contemporain, Montreal
	Marian Goodman Gallery, New York

	Galleria Locus Solus, Genoa, Italy
	Galleria Marilena Bonomo, Bari, Italy
1986	Palais des Beaux-Arts, Charleroi, Belgium
	Galerie Albert Baronian, Brussels
	Galerie Paul Maenz, Cologne
	De Vleeshal, Middelburg, Netherlands
	Staatsgalerie, Stuttgart
	University of California, Berkeley
1987	Galleria Pieroni, Rome
	Galleria Christian Stein, Milan
	Marian Goodman Gallery, New York
	Institute of Contemporary Art, Nagoya, Japan
	Musée des Beaux-Arts, Nantes, France

Selected Group Exhibitions:

1966	*Aspetti dell'Avanguardia in Italia*, Galleria Notizie, Turin
1969	*Biennale*, Paris
1970	*Information*, Museum of Modern Art, New York
1971	*New Italian Art: 1953–1971*, Walker Art Gallery, Liverpool
1973	*Italy Two: Art Around '70*, Philadelphia Civic Center
1974	*Kunst bleibt Kunst: Projekt '74*, Kunsthalle, Cologne
1976	*Biennale*, Sydney
1981	*Identité Italienne*, Centre Georges Pompidou, Paris
1985	*Transformations in Sculpture*, Guggenheim Museum, New York
1987	*Avant-Garde in the Eighties*, Los Angeles County Museum of Art

Collections:

Galleria Civica d'Arte Moderna, Turin; Tate Gallery, London; Centre Georges Pompidou, Paris; Stedelijk Museum, Amsterdam; Museum Haus Lange, Krefeld, West Germany; Staatsgalerie, Stuttgart; Museum of Modern Art, New York; Guggenheim Museum, New York; Musée d'Art Contemporain, Montreal; Australian National Gallery, Canberra.

Publications:

By PAOLINI: books—*Idem*, with text by I. Calvino, Turin 1975; *Del bello intelligibile*, with text by S. Page, Paris 1978; *Atto unico in tre quadri*, with C. Bertelli and C. Vattimo, Milan 1979; *Hotus Clausus/Werke und Schriften 1960–1980*, with M. Kunz and M. Wechsler, Lucerne 1981; *De bouche a orielle*, with R. Denizot, Paris 1982; *Casa di Lucrezio*, with texts by B. Man and others, Bologna 1984: *Voix off*, with text by A. Coulan, Macon 1986; *Ancora un libro*, with text by B. Cora, Rome 1987; articles—interview, with M. Pistoi, in *Marcatre* (Rome), no. 19–22, 1966; interview in *Centroarte* (Turin), no. 1, 1967; "Il Quadro di sempre" in *B't* (Milan), no. 5, 1967; "Una Lettera sul Tempo" in *Paolini*, exhibition catalogue, Turin 1968: "Happening" in *Qui Arte Contemporanea* (Rome), no. 5, 1969; "Note per le Scene e i Costumi del Bruto II" in *Qui Arte Contemporanea* (Rome), no. 6, 1969; interview, with C. Lonzi, in *Autoritratto*, Bari, Italy 1969; interview in *Bolaffiarte* (Turin), no. 1, 1970; "Intenzioni su Don Chisciotte" in *Rivista Rai* (Turin), July 1970; "Vedo" in *Vedo*, exhibition catalogue, Turin 1970; "un Quadro" in *Un Quadro*, exhibition catalogue, Milan 1971 and in *Data* (Milan), no. 2, 1972; interview, with Klaus Staeck in *Befragung der Documenta*, Göttingen 1972; interview, with M. Volpi Orlandini, in *Futuribili* (Rome), no. 42–43, 1972; interview, with M. Bandini, in *Prospects* (Milan), no. 1, 1972; "Note di Lavoro" in *Nac* (Milan), no. 3, 1973; "Dipingere la Pittura," interview, with N. Orengo, in *Fuoricampo* (Turin), no. 2, 1973; "La Doublure" in *La Doublure*, exhibition catalogue, Rome 1973; "Dentro il Linguaggio," interview, with Achille Bonito Oliva, in *Paolini*, exhibition catalogue, Genoa 1974; "Una Domanda Discreta," interview, with N. Orengo, in *Libri Nuovi* (Turin), June 1975; interview, in *Nuova Societa* (Turin), no. 71, 1976; interview, with L. M. Venturi, in *Studio International* (London), January/February 1976; "Offlentiche Diskussion," with Maurizio Calvesi, in *Galleria Nazionale d'Arte Moderna* (Rome), April 1976; "Ma L'Artista non e un Computer," interview, with F. Minervino, in *La Republica* (Rome), September 1976; interview in *Nuova Societa* (Turin), no. 90, 1976; "Bilanci e Programmi: La Parola agli Artisti," interview, in *Qui Arte Contemporanea* (Rome), no. 17, 1977; "Moderno: Post Moderno: Millenario," interview, in *Data* (Milan), no. 29–29, 1977; "Cos'e L'Avanguardia," interview, in *Noti-*

ziario (Milan), no. 6, 1977; "Lezione di Pittura" in *Imprinting*, Rome 1979; "Incontro con l'Artista," with Bruno Cora, in *Accademia di Belle Arti*, (Perugia, Italy), April 1981; "Conversazione con gli Studenti," with A. Charre, in *Ecole Nationale des Beaux-Arts* (Lyons), May 1981.

On PAOLINI: books—*Giulio Paolini* by Germano Celant, New York and Paris 1972; *Giulio Paolini* by Maurizio Fagioli and A. C. Quintavalle, Parma, Italy 1976; *Giulio Paolini*, exhibition catalogue, by J. Cladders, Mönchengladbach, West Germany 1977; *Giulio Paolini*, exhibition catalogue, by Harald Szeemann and D. Elliott, Amsterdam 1980; *Giulio Paolini: Del Bello Intelligibile*, exhibition catalogue, by E. Franz, Bielefeld, West Germany 1982, (includes bibliography); articles—"Giulio Paolini: Recent Works" in *Domus* (Milan), November 1972; "Giulio Paolini" by Tomassa Trini in *Art Press* (Paris), May/June 1973; "Image of the Image: The Work of Giulio Paolini" by Germano Celant in *Art and Artists* (London), May 1974; "Giulio Paolini" by Leo Rubinfien in *Artforum* (New York), April 1977; "Seeing Things Right" by Marina Vaizey in *The Sunday Times* (London), 17 April 1977; "Spatial Imagery" by Paul Goldberger in *Architectural Digest* (New York), no. 4, 1979.

*

Art in its character is by definition new. When it appears not to be so, it is only because we experience no suitable expectancy in ourselves. But even if this were not so, it is in fact all we can say for art; it does not admit of diagnosis, let alone therapies.

Any statements that one can make about art are necessarily *a posteriori* reflections, are therefore conclusions, never predictions. We call present-day art analytic, but nothing would be further from the truth than to present the artist as a computer programmed for art analysis. He does not know the stations of his search but he gives it absolute and mysterious obedience. We learn what this obedience demands of him only when we find in him something "new" (that which, in the ancients, still surprises us). That is why today everything new seems to me as old as the idea of the new.

—Giulio Paolini

*

Giulio Paolini has been conducting his artistic experiments for more than 20 years and has now developed an aesthetic based on a few characteristic elements which he combines and re-combines in new ways, to produce new, complex wholes. At the start of his career, in 1960, he was already interested in the principles which he was later to develop and refine. Two works from 1960, "Geometric Design" and "Design of the Letter," record his quest for what it is in the nature of things which can give a work of art value. Here we can no longer think of the work as a mechanical synthesis but must see it as an analytical process in which the artist scrutinizes the elements he uses and resolves the problems they present.

Paolini's early work demonstrates this conception of art: his first documented piece, for example (the "Geometric Design" referred to above), is a small canvas on which he has made a preliminary squaring-off of the surface before him ("all drawing," he has explained, "is preliminary drawing"). This is followed by other works in which Paolini emphasizes the fundamental elements available to the painter and the problems involved in combining them. Thus in one we have an empty canvas-frame which bravely displays a can of varnish; in another work, a set of canvases joined together but their backs to the viewer; and in still another he has assembled many little pieces of colored cardboard. From the start of his career he was always concerned with the material the artist must use to construct his expressive wholes.

During the next phase of his development Paolini became interested in the role space plays in painting. The 1963 "Horizontal," for example, is a work in which he strives to find the best optimal axis for viewing works which are hung 160 cm. from the floor. At the same time he is also concerned with the ways in which the art of the past affects the present. Thus we have such works as "A Young Man Looking at Lorenzo Lotto" (1967) and "The Invention of Ingres" (1968). In the latter work Paolini has superimposed over Raphael's self-portrait the slightly distorted image of the same portrait as realized by Ingres. This juxtaposition produces an unsettling effect whch boldly proclaims Paolini's own artistic presence. In "Mimesis" (1975) we have two identical plaster casts of classical busts placed opposite each other, in mirror-like fashion.

After having made all of these experiments, Paolini has entered into a mature, reflective phase which encompasses all of his earlier interests in material, space, the art of the past and, now, his own past. His work is fundamentally a way of questioning which changes but always seeks the true, existential nature of art itself.

—Roberto G. Lambarelli

PAOLOZZI, Eduardo (Luigi).

British, Born in Leith, Scotland, of Italian parents, 7 March 1924. Educated in schools in Leith and Edinburgh; studied at the Edinburgh College of Art, 1943, and the Slade School of Fine Art, London, 1944–47. With family interned as enemy alien in 1940; released after three months and conscripted to Pioneer Corps, 1940–44. Married Freda Madge Eliot in 1951; children: Louise, Anna, and Emma. Sculptor: lived in Paris and met Alberto Giacometti, 1947–50; acted, with Michael Andrews, in *Together* by Lorenza Mazzetti, London, 1954; lived in Hamburg, 1960–62, and Berlin, 1974; lives and works in London and Thorpe-le-Soken, Essex. Lecturer in Textile Design, Central School of Art and Design, London, 1949–55; Lecturer in Sculpture, St. Martin's School of Art, London, 1955–58; Visiting Professor, Hochschule für Bildende Kunst, Hamburg, 1960–62; Professor of Ceramics, Fachhochschule, Cologne, 1977–82; Professor, International Summer Academy, Salzburg, 1981, 1982. Since 1968, Tutor in Ceramics, Royal College of Art, London; since 1981, Professor of Sculpture, Akademie Bildenden Künste,

Munich. Recipient: British Critics Prize, 1953; Norma and William Copley Foundation Award, 1956; David Bright Foundation Award, *Biennale*, Venice, 1960. Watson F. Blair Prize, Chicago, 1961; DAAD Fellowship, Berlin, 1974; Purchase Prize, *Guggenheim International Sculpture Exhibition*, 1967; First Prize for Sculpture, *Carnegie International*, Pittsburgh, 1967; First Prize, Closed Competition for the Development of the Rhinegarten, Cologne, 1980; Saltire Society Award, 1981; Grand Prix d'Honneur, Print Biennale, LiublJana 1983. Honorary doctorate: Royal College of Art, London, 1979; University of Glasgow, 1980. Associate, Royal Academy of Arts, 1972; Royal Academician, 1979. Honorary Member, Architectural Association, London, 1981. Fellow, University College, London, 1986. Her Majesty's Sculptor in Ordinary for Scotland, 1986. C.B.E. (Commander, Order of the British Empire), 1968. Address: 107 Dovehouse Street, London SW3 6JZ, England.

Individual Exhibitions:

1947	Mayor Gallery, London
1948	Mayor Gallery, London
1949	Mayor Gallery, London
1950	Hanover Gallery,London (with Kenneth King and William Turnbull)
1958	Hanover Gallery, London
1960	Betty Parsons Gallery, New York
	Manchester City Art Gallery
	Biennale, Venice
1961	Palais des Beaux-Arts, Brussels (with Victor Pasmore)
1962	Betty Parsons Gallery, New York
1963	Waddington Galleries, London
1964	Robert Fraser Gallery, London
	Museum of Modern Art, New York
1965	Hatton Gallery, Newcastle upon Tyne
	Chelsea School of Art, London
	Editions Alecto, London
1966	Scottish National Gallery of Art, Edinburgh
	Robert Fraser Gallery, London
	Pace Gallery, New York

1967	Pace Gallery, New York
	Hanover Gallery, London
	Alecto Gallery, London
	Rijksmuseum Kröller-Müller, Otterlo, Netherlands
1968	Worth Ryder Art Gallery, University of California, Berkeley
	Galerie Neuendorf, Hamburg
	Stedelijk Museum, Amsterdam
	Plastik und Graphik, Städtische Kunsthalle, Dusseldorf
	Kunstverein, Stuttgart
	Galerie Mikro, Berlin
	Kunstmuseum, Gothenburg, Sweden
1970	Pollock Gallery, Toronto
1971	Tate Gallery, London
1972	St. Katherine's Gallery, London
1973	Victoria and Albert Museum, London (toured the U.K.)
1974	Galerie Wentzel, Hamburg
	Kestner-Gesellschaft, Hannover
1975	Nationalgalerie, Berlin (travelled to the Kunstverein, Karlsruhe, and the Kunsthall, Bremen)
	The Need to Draw, Fruit Market Gallery, Edinburgh (toured the U.K., 1975–76)
1976	Laing Art Gallery, Newcastle upon Tyne (toured the U.K., 1976–77)
	Sculpture, Drawings, Collages and Graphics, Marlborough Fine Art, London
	National Exhibition Centre, Swift Current, Saskatchewan (toured Canada)
1977	Victoria and Albert Museum, London
	Galerie Renate Fassbender, Munich
	Anthony d'Offay Gallery, London
1978	Kunstverein, Kassel, West Germany
1979	Kunstverein, Cologne
	Glasgow Print Studio Gallery
	Talbot Rice Art Centre, University of Edinburgh
1980	Kunstverein, Münster, West Germany (toured West Germany)
1982	Museum für Kunst und Gewerbe, Hamburg
1983	Aedes Gallery, West Berlin
1984	Architectural Association, London
	Royal Scottish Academy, Edinburgh
	Städtische Galerie im Lenbachhaus, Munich
1985	Museum Ludwig, Cologne
	Moderna Galerija, Liubljana, Yugoslavia
	Centre for Contemporary Art, Breda, Netherlands
	Ivan Dougherty Gallery, Paddington, New South Wales
	Espace Lyonnais d'Art Contemporain, Lyon, France
	Crawford Municipal Art Gallery, Cork, Ireland
	Museum of Mankind, London
1986	Royal Academy of Art, London
	Glaskasten, Marl, West Germany
1987	Serpentine Gallery, London

Selected Group Exhibitions:

1948	*Group Exhibition,* Galerie Maeght, Paris
1952	*Biennale,* Venice
1953	*Parallel of Life and Art,* Institute of Contemporary Arts, London
1957	*Bienal,* Sao Paulo
1959	*Documenta, 2,* Kassel, West Germany
1969	*Pop Art Redefined,* Hayward Gallery, London
1976	*Arte Inglesi Oggi 1960–1976,* Palazzo Reale, Milan
1981	*British Sculpture in the 20th Century,* Whitechapel Art Gallery, London
1982	*Aspects of British Art Today,* Metropolitan Art Museum, Tokyo (toured Japan)
1984	*The Automobile and Culture,* Museum of Contemporary Art, Los Angeles

Collections:

Tate Gallery, London; Victoria and Albert Museum, London; Arts Council of Great Britain, London; Art Museum and Gallery, Glasgow; University of St. Andrews, Scotland; Nationalgalerie, Berlin; Kunsthalle, Hamburg; Rijksmuseum Kröller-Müller, Otterlo, Netherlands; Museum of Modern Art, New York; Guggenheim Museum, New York.

Eduardo Paolozzi: *Piscator,* **1981**

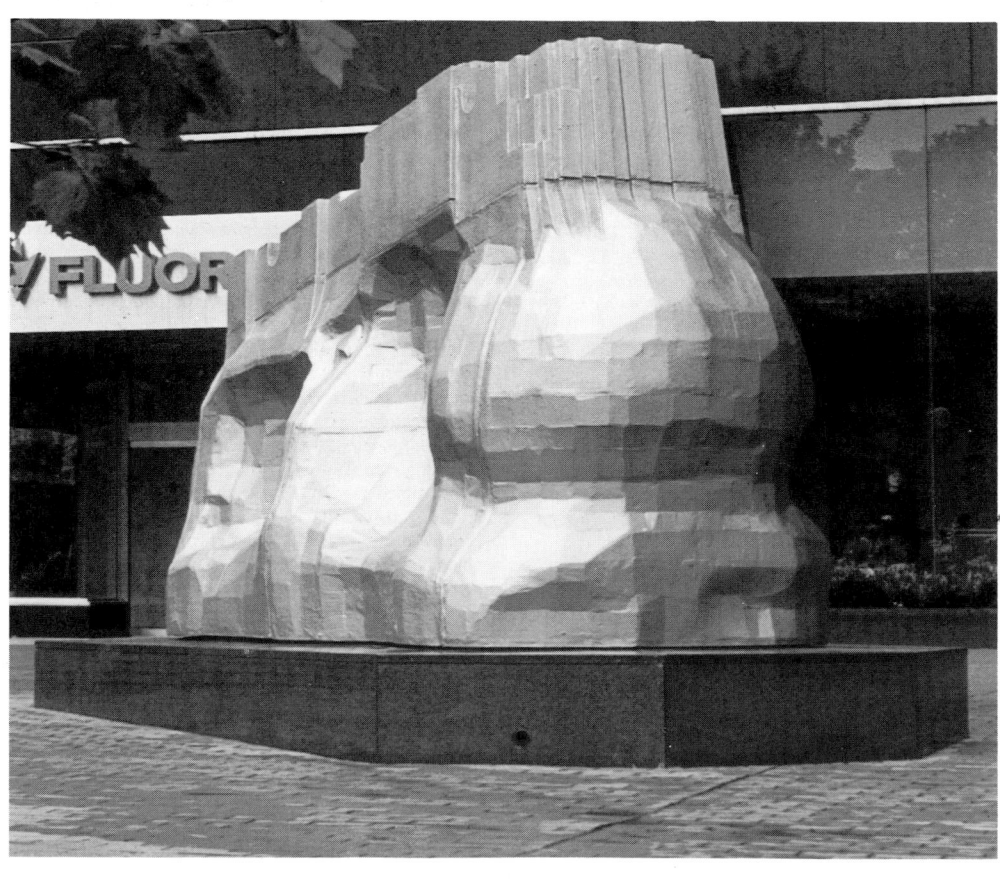

Publications:

By PAOLOZZI: books—*Metaphysical Translations*, London 1960; *The Metallization of a Dream*, London 1963; *Kex*, New York 1966; *Abba-Zaba*, London 1970; articles—"Metamorphosis of Rubbish: Mr. Paolozzi Explains His Process" in *The Times* (London), 2 May 1958; "Interview with Eduardo Paolozzi," with E. Roditi, in *Arts Magazine* (New York), May 1959; statement in *New Images of Man*, exhibition catalogue, New York 1959; "Mein Diktionaer" in *Blatter und Bilder* (Wurburg, West Germany), March/April 1960; "The Sculptor Speaks: The Enchanted Forest" in *The Observer* (London), 24 April 1960; "Interview with Eduardo Paolozzi," with Richard Hamilton, in *Contemporary Sculpture Arts Yearbook*, New York 1965; "Moonstrips: General Dynamic FUN" in *Ambit 33*, London 1967' "Analysis of Domains of the Spectrum of Alternatives" in *Eduardo Paolozzi: Plastik and Grafik*, exhibition catalogue, Dusseldorf 1968; "Why We are in Vietnam" in *Ambit 40*, London 1969; "Moonstrips" in *Neue Englische Prosa*, (Cologne), 1970; "Speculative Illustrations: Eduardo Paolozzi in Conversation with J. G. Ballard and Frank Whitford" in *Studio International*, (London), October 1971; "10 Questions to Eduardo Paolozzi" by Diane Kirkpatrick in *Ambit 51*, London 1972; "The Iconography of the Present" in *The Times Literary Supplement* (London), December 1972; "About the Prints: The Artists Talking at an Interview" by E. Bailey and C. Hagben in *Bunk*, London 1973; "Conversation with Jim Waugh" in *Eduardo Paolozzi*, exhibition catalogue, Glasgow, 1979.

On PAOLOZZI: books—*Eduardo Paolozzi* by Michael Middleton, London 1963; *Paolozzi* by U. M. Schneede, Stuttgart and New York 1970; *Eduardo Paolozzi* by Diane Kirkpatrick, London 1970; *Eduardo Paolozzi: Sculpture, Drawings, Collages and Graphics*, exhibition catalogue, by Wieland and Schmied and others, London 1976; *Eduardo Paolozzi*, exhibition catalogue, by Rosemary Miles, London 1977; *Eduardo Paolozzi* by Winfried Konnertz, Munich; *Eduardo Paolozzi: Underground*, exhibition catalogue edited by Richard Cork, London 1986; *Paolozzi: Sculptures from a Garden*, exhibition catalogue with text by Frank Whitford, London 1987.

Divine ambiguity is possible with collage—flesh robots marred by object or object masquerading as flesh. There is nothing astonishing in that—witness the great portraits of Arcimboldo. We have learned to define collage as a process where dreams can be rejected and the victims exposed to ridicule. The word "collage" is inadequate as a description because the concept should include "damage, erase, destroy, deface and transform"—all parts of a metaphor for the creative act itself. Preconscious elaboration must have a relationship to chance, therefore the permutations of 101 figures on 40 landscapes and interiors represent a process of endless destruction until finalization.

—Eduardo Paolozzi

Eduardo Paolozzi was outstanding among post-war British sculptors to make their reputations beyond the shadow of Moore. Born exactly one day before Caro in 1924, he studied at Edinburgh College of Art before going into the Slade in London. He was at the Slade until 1947; then he moved to Paris where he met, and saw the works of, the avant garde sculptors, including Giacometti. By 1950 he was back in England and embarked on a programme of personal investigation into the role of sculpture in a world where Renaissance ideals seemed ill at ease. This quest had its origins in his days at the Slade when he was to find more fascinating subjects to draw at the Science Musem in South Kensington than in the life class.

Despite the compulsive interes in the shape and organization of mechanical processes, Paolozzi did not admire them for the abstract appearances or functional symmetry, as did the Constructivists. He saw analogies between the engineered and anatomical image and struck a forceful surrealist note between them, a contrast he exploited in the 1950's by incorporating "ready-mades" in the composition of grotesque heads. Those and the larger figures were conceived as forms encrusted and embossed in decorative relief patterns. Semi-abstract in character they were regarded in the light of science-fiction robots retaining an upright human stance.

About 1961 Paolozzi began some of his most extraordinary sculptures, designed and cast in steel and alloy. He has expressed his view that idols representing rational order of technology can be as fascinating as the fetishes of a Congo witch doctor. Elements of precast metal were adapted and assembled within schemes of impressive architectural significance developing their own original iconography, suggestive of the transformation of the visible world, in machinery that became monumental and capable of transmitting a mystical presence.

Similarly the animistic metaphors latent in the contorting spirals of steel tubing were spun into a Laocoon-like struggle embodied in unyielding metal. In recent years Paolozzi has produced a series in silkscreen and other media containing literary and scientific data in variable colour schemes. The composing of the minuscule cuneiform motives reduce the unified impact to an esoteric literary reading.

In Paolozzi's sculpture the idol and the unique shapes with their superimposed decoration have surrealist mystery. Some of the latter constructions bear the delicate trivialisation of the process reflective of neo-Dada tendencies of the 1960's, lacking however any of the self-destructive desperation of a Tinguely.

—G. S. Whittet

PARMIGGIANI, Claudio.

Italian. Born in Luzzara, Reggio Emilia, 1 March 1943. Studied at the Istituto Statale di Belle Arti, Modena, 1959-61. Married Silvia Guberti in 1963; son: Cosimo. Lives and works in Bologna. Lecturer in Paiting and Drawing, Accademia di Belle Arti, Macerata, Italy, 1971-73. Editor, with Mario Diacono and Achille Maramotti, *Tau Ma*, Bologna, since 1975. Recipient: Premio Bolaffi, Turin, 1976. Agents: Galleria Christian Stein, Piazza San Carlo 206, 10121 Turin; Galleria Mario Diacono, Piazza Magnanelli 24, 00187 Rome. Address: Via Guido Reni 4, 40125 Bologna, Italy.

Individual Exhibitions:

1965	Libreria Feltrinelli, Bologna
	Sala Di Cultura, Modena, Italy
1966	Libreria Feltrinelli, Milan
1969	Galleria Christian Stein, Turin
1970	Galleria Diagramma, Milan
	Galleria Paolo Barozzi, Venice
1971	Galleria Flori, Florence
1972	Galleria L'Uomo e l'Arte, Milan
	Galleria Christian Stein, Turin
1974	Gallerio Piero Cavellini, Brescia, Italy
	Galleria Alessandra Castelli, Milan
1975	Galleria Schema, Florence
	Natural History Museum, Lazzaro Spallanzani, Reggio Emilia, Italy
1976	Galleria La Tartaruga, Rome
	Galleria d'Arte Moderna, Bologna
	Galerie im Taxipalais, Innsbruck
	Galleria Forma, Genoa
1978	Galleria Civica d'Arte Moderna, Portofino, Italy
	Studio Mario Diacono, Bologna
	Galerie Albert Baronian, Brussels
1979	Galleria Christian Stein, Turin
	Galerie Annemarle Verna, Zurich
	Studio Carlo Grossetti, Milan
1981	Galleria Mario Diacono, Bologna
	Kunstverein, Frankfurt
1982	Galleria Christian Stein, Turin
	Galerie Liliane et Michel Durand-Dessert, Paris
	Padiglione d'Arte Contemporanea, Milan
	Biennale, Venice
1983	Galleria Mario Diacono, Rome
1984	Italian Pavilion, *40th Biennale*, Venice
	Stadtische Kunsthalle, Dusseldorf
1986	Galleria Christian Stein, Turin
	Italian Pavilion, *41st Biennale*, Venice
	Albert Totah Gallery, New York
1987	Mario Diacono Gallery, Boston
	Kunstverein, Salzburg, Austria
	Museum Moderner Kunst, Vienna
1988	Kunstverein, Frankfurt

Selected Group Exhibitions:

1967	*Segni nello Spazio*, Castello di San Giusto, Italy
1970	*Exhibition of Contemporary Concrete Poetry*, Geijutsu Seikatsu Gallery, Tokyo
1972	*Biennale*, Venice
1974	*Fotomedia*, Museum am Ostwall, Dortmund, West Germany
1975	*Selbstportrait als Selbstdarstellung*, Galerie im Taxipalais, Innsbruck
1977	*Biennale*, Paris
1979	*Sistina: Società per Arte*, Galleria d'Arte Moderna, Bologna
1980	*Arte e Critica*, Galleria Nazionale d'Arte Moderna, Rome
1984	*Der Traum des Orpheus*, Stadtische Galerie im Lenbachhaus, Munich

Collections:

Galleria Nazionale d'Arte Moderna, Rome

Publications:

By PARMIGGIANI: books, with Mario Diacono—*Delocazione*, Modena, Italy 1970; *Malanngan*, Modena, Italy, 1972; *Deiscrizione*, Modena, Italy 1973; *Daphnephoria*, Modena, Italy 1974; *Annunciazione*, Rome 1972.

On PARMIGGIANI: books—*Tavole Temporali* by Vincenzo Agnetti, Modena, Italy 1967; *Blanc* by Corrado Costa, Milan 1968; *Yang Yin* by Daniela Palazzoli, Genoa 1973; *Ultime Tendenze nell'Arte d'Oggi* by Gillo Dorfles, Milan 1973; *Claudio Parmiggiani*, exhibition catalogue, by Giorgio Celli, Bologna 1976; *Claudio Parmiggiani: Tavole: Teatri: Riti* by Paolo Fossati, Bolzano, Italy 1976; *L'Arte Moderna* by Renato Barilli, Milan 1977; *Informale: Oggetto: Contemportamento* by Renato Barilli, Milan 1979; *L'Immaginazione Alchemica* by Maurizio Calvezi, Frankfurt 1981; *Claudio Parmiggiani: Ikonostase*, exhibition catalogue with text by Dieter Ronte, Vienna 1987.

Robert Musil has written: " . . . pictures are divided into two big, contrasting classes. The first class comes from being written within a thing, the other from looking at a thing from outside; the concave feeling and the convex feeling, the spatial condition as well as the objective condition, penetration and contemplation, are repeated equally in experimental antitheses and in so many linguistic images that it is legitimate to infer an origin in an ancient dualistic form of human experience." The inside and the outside, the full and the empty, revelation and concealment, presence and absence—these are the key to the understanding of Claudio Parmiggiani's work. Starting from the monochromatic zeroing of the picture, he then went further, shifting the plan of his interests from painting to space, regarded as a place for projection, for fantasy, for scene. On a cyclic-labyrinthine course the matrix painting of the invention becomes sculpture, in the sense of material that becomes space and has to be extracted from the light, material that is still the vector of light and colour.

In his first works Parmiggiani made great use of photographic media as an instrument that could give him the maximum both of objectivity and at the same time of separation from the materiality of the objects. This was at the end of the 1960's, when many of the most thoughtful artists, now that the orgy of "poor art" was exhausted, were to be found on the conceptual front of the post-avantgarde. Parmiggiani—and the experience of Paolini, Lumaca, Piruca and Di Be-

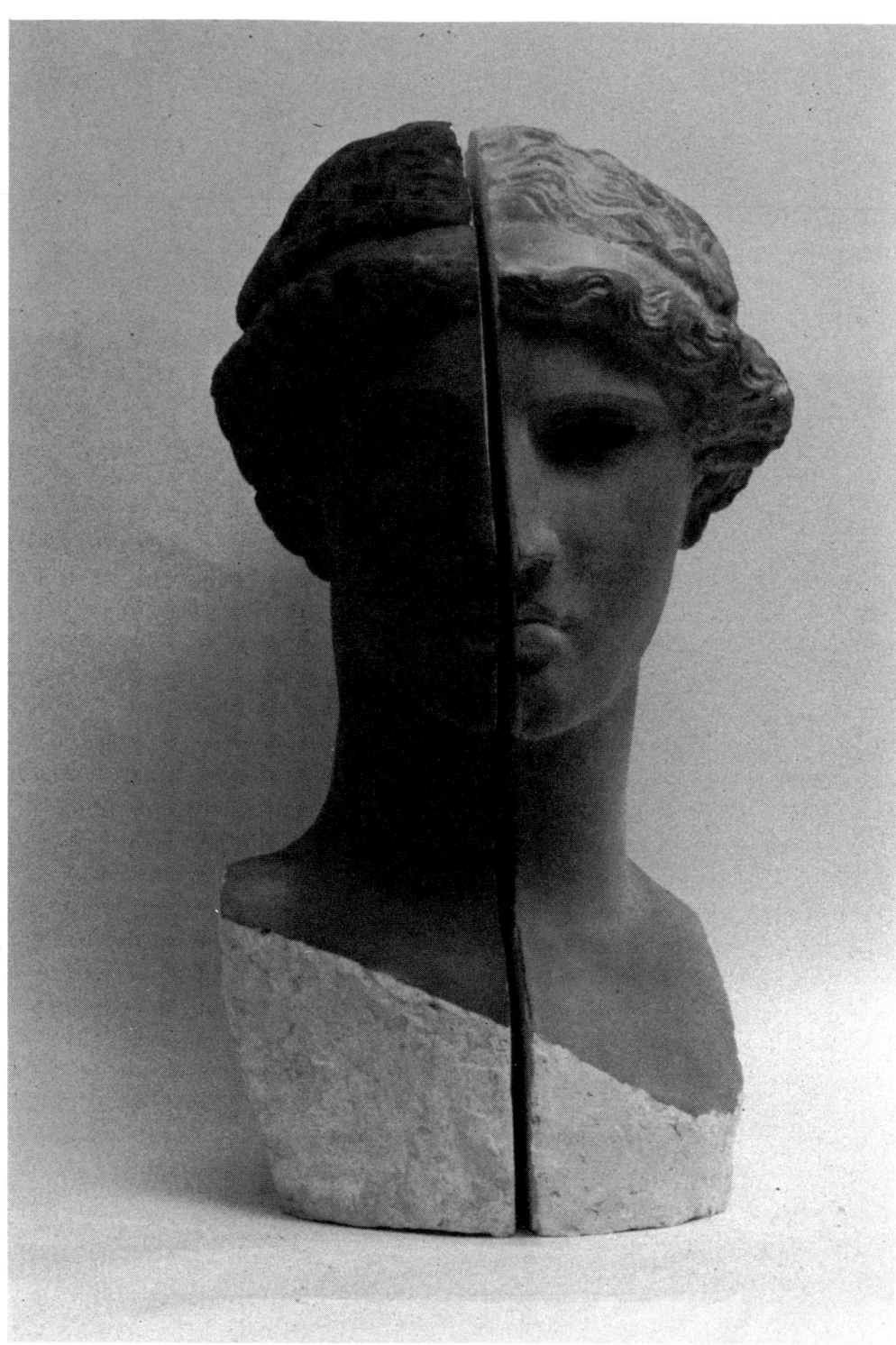

Claudio Parmiggiani: *Atena Ermetica*, 1980

those of literary linguistics. The operation of strict semiotics becomes poetic again, the metaphorical design becomes oneiric, and at last the picture becomes independent and the research comes out of the historical archives and returns to decoration. The archaeology of the images is abandoned, and the interest is shifted to a more recent past; something of Mondrian's analysis appears, but the themes are developed and matured with the rarest of characteristics. In a complex system, alternating play and elegant irony, the work unfolds through the coinvolvement of space and time. The artist marries "the imaginary and the symbolic" in a "meeting of opposed principles" in a sythesis of "plenum and form" (in the sense given by E. Panofsky in his text *Perspective as Symbolic Form*, in which "the principle of the plenum corresponds to the intuitive forms of time and the principle of form to the intuitive form of space"). The work is endlessly discovering possible confrontations in space and time, in relation to the antique as a source for intervention and as a place where the epiphany of form is established.

As long ago as 1584, Borghini distinguished between two types of artistic invention, that "derived from others" and that "which comes from the artist himself." The first corresponds with representation, which is always based on reality, The other to fantasy, which can make and break its own rules. But fantasy cannot be considered independent of the iconographic heritage; if anything, it is a departure from the logic of the rules, but as such it is subject in turn to other rules. Look for example at the paintings of Dosso Dossi, which Parmiggiani refers to in more than one work: "inflated, weightless masses with widened surfaces; bright, brilliant colours, strange lights like fireworks; extraordinary inventions and fantasies side by side with passages of a surprising truthfulness; sacred and profane themes treated with the same gay lightness" (G. C. Argan).

The mass of references and occasional quotations becomes so rich as to be lost in the narration. Nothing comes before the moment of surprise; the image, with no origin, shows the inverted depth of the work; the eye, as if entrapped by the oscillation of the play between what is real and what is virtual, between what comes from others and what is the artist's own, follows the infinitesimal movements, the disconnections, the appearances. But the suspense is short-lived; between illusion and transformation the visual metaphor vanishes again in the actual dimension of reality. And the cycle begins again.

—Carmine Benincasa

llo was not so different—turned towards the recovery of past art. "The Student of Letters" is a work of those years, in which, by means of obliterations, substitutions, fading out, he acted as "corrector" of the work of the same name by Rembrandt. "In penetrating Rembrandt's work," writes M. Calvesi, "he makes its significance clear." He removes the painting to the historical period of his own iconography, and makes it as it were reflected in a different imagination. This imagination becomes the fluid, continuous meeting point or bridge, suspended across time as a bridge suspended across a river, between Rembrandt and his modern interlocutor . . . it is an enquiry into the essence of art which, apart from the differences in language, seems to appear at one in the desire to reduce complexity to unity, the piece to the whole. An essence, therefore, that transcends time."

Cultured reminiscences and dreams, illusion and irony that critical argument converts into metaphor. It

was Magritte who created the separation between meaning and representation, dissociating and condensing metaphor and metonymy: "My pictures look like pictures. My painting is thought that sees." It is from this proliferation of monuments of dismantling and reinterpretation, aspects of Musil's dialectic of the inside and the outside, that there comes the recovery of the "remote," the hidden and all those "phobias" connected with the "loss of centre." Parmiggiani works on everything that the artist had kept secret, hidden or rejected; he works on the picture at its heart, in the recesses of the mind, so as to purge every residue. It matters little if the cutting and reassembly lead to diffuseness; dross is added to dross, remoteness to remoteness. With each excision, each substitution, the range of metaphor grows broader.

To enable him to interpret, the artist makes use of a widest choice of instruments, which are, after all,

PARR, Mike.

Australian. Born in Sydney, New South Wales, 19 July 1945. Educated at University of Queensland, Brisbane, 1965–66; studied at National Art School, Darlinghurst, New South Wales, 1968. Married Tess Stefanitsch in 1977; daughter: Adrian. Independent artist, Newton, New South Wales, since 1970. Cofounder, with Peter Kennedy, Inhibodress Cooperative Gallery, Sydney, 1970–73. Lecturer in Art, Sydney University Art Workshop, 1974–78; Lecturer in Sculpture, Sydney College of Arts, 1978–82. Recipient: Australian Government Study Grant, for study in Europe, 1977. Agent: Roslyn Oxley 9 Gallery, 13–21 Macdonald Street, Paddington, Sydney, New South Wales. Address: Post Office Box M56, Newtown South, New South Wales 2042, Australia.

Individual Exhibitions:

1970   Reid Gallery, Brisbane
1971   Inhibodress Gallery, Sydney
           Pinacotheca Gallery, Melbourne (with Tim Johnson)
           Inhibodress Gallery, Sydney
           Inhibodress Gallery, Sydney (with Peter Kennedy)

Selected Group Exhibitions:

Collections:

National Art Gallery of New South Wales, Sydney; Visual Arts Board of the Australian Council, Sydney; National Art Gallery of Victoria, Melbourne; National Art Gallery of South Australia, Adelaide; National Art Gallery of Australia, Canberra; National Library, Canberra; Flinders University, South Australia; Art Gallery of Western Australia, Perth; Chase Manhattan Bank, New York; First National Bank, Chicago.

Publications:

By PARR: books—Black Box of Word Situations No. 1, Sydney 1971; 150 Programmes and Investigations, Sydney 1971, Wall Definitions, Sydney 1973; Black Box of Word Situations No. 2, Sydney 1978; articles—"Other Dimensions" in Aspect (Sydney), Winter 1975; "3 Questions" in Aspect (Sydney) vol.2, no. 1, 1976; "Ahasex to Zymasex" in Art in Australia (Sydney), April/June 1976; "Notes on Recent Work" in Flash Art (Milan), February/April 1978; "Artist's Statement" in 3rd Biennale of Sydney: European Dialogue, exhibition catalogue, Sydney 1979; "Notes on the Structure of Content: Black Box/Theatre of Self Correction—Parts 1 and 2" in Venice Biennale 1980: Australia, exhibition catalogue, Sydney 1980; "Notes on my Work" in The 1st Australian Sculpture Triennale, exhibition catalogue, Melbourne 1981; "Artist's Statement" in Eureka! Artists from Australia, exhibition catalogue, London 1982; "A-Atrophy" in Aspect (Sydney), June 1983; "Le moi createur et l'autre", interview with Catherine Millet, in Art Press (Paris), October 1983; "The Art of John Nixon" in Australia and International Art Monthly (Sydney), August 1987; films—Idea Demonstrations, with Peter Kennedy, 1972; Rules and Displacement Activities Part 1, 1974; Rules and Displacement Activities, Part 2, 1976; Rules and Displacement Part 3, 1977; Rules and Displacement Activities, Part 3, 1983.

On PARR: books—Videotapes from Australia, exhibition catalogue, with text by Bernice Murphy and Stephen Jones, Sydney 1979; Venice Biennale 1980: Australia, exhibition catalogue, with introduction by Elwyn Lynn, Sydney 1980; The Visual Arts, edited by M. K. Symonds, C. Portley, R. E. Phillips, Sydney 1980; Australian Perspecta, exhibition catalogue, with introduction by Bernice Murphy, Sydney 1981; Self-Portrait/Self Image, exhibition catalogue, with text by Janine Burke, Sydney 1981; Eureka! Artists from Australia, exhibition catalogue, with texts by Nancy Underhill, Ian Burn and Paul Taylor, London 1982; An Australian Accent, exhibition catalogue with texts by Daniel Thomas and Jonathan Fineberg, New York 1984; Mike Parr: Portage, exhibition catalogue with introduction by Jonathan Holmes, Hobart 1985; Mike Parr: The Satellites of Death, exhibition catalogue with essay by Anthony Bond, Brisbane 1986; articles—"Idea Demonstrations: Body Art and 'Video Freaks' in Sydney" by Donald Brook in Studio International (London), June 1973; "Art and Sanctuary" by Patrick McCaughey in Aspect (Sydney), Spring 1975; "Videotapes from Australia: A Top Collection from Down Under" by Victor Ancona in Videography (New York), February 1980; "Films by Artists" by Jennifer Phipps in Art in Australia (Melbourne), Spring 1980; "Venice Biennale 1980" by Suzanne Davies in Art Network (Sydney), Spring 1980; "Report from Australia" by Suzi Gablik in Art in America (New York), January 1981; "Australian Art: Beyond the Cringe", special issue of Studio International (London), October 1983; "Mike Parr at Ruth Siegel" by Eleanor Heartney in Art in America (New York), January 1987.

All of my work since my first conceptual pieces and performances in 1970-71 at Inhibodress Cooperative Gallery, Sydney, is an organic whole. Continuity and vertical structure are the essence of my approach because in many ways the "meaning" derives from the linkage between works; the works themselves are intense moments, ephiphanies in the sense that James Joyce speaks of inspiration and illumination. These intense moments are either "actual," where my performance pieces are a revelation of personal obsessions based on real behaviour, or else symbolic. However, I am not interested in literary symbolism or literary devices; these symbols are unconventional and function in ways similar to the symbolism of the Abstract Expressionists which was simultaneously abstract in its unitary reductionism but universal in its ambience.

The symbols of the Abstract Expressionists gelled out of process and had no a priori structure. They were arrived at; recognized at the moment of their fusion—they were signs isolated against a field. This is exactly how my "actions" or "gestures" work. The great bulk of my work is based on the performance. I perform myself (I mean I act out my own intensity). The records of many of these performances have been made into films or else portfolios of prints. The films, the prints and even the recent installations are more often a revelation of process; the linkage between images—they record the alternative nature for the personalism of the world I want to reveal, but their status is different to the actual performance.

The performance lifts me and audience into real time; into a continuous present tense; each performance, existing at the edge of the present tense, is suffused with an existential realism of peculiar intensity. Between my behavior and the behavior of the audience, there is a formative osmosis—it is a peculiarly miasmic world of mirror images. The intensity

Mike Parr: *The Polar Sea*, 1986

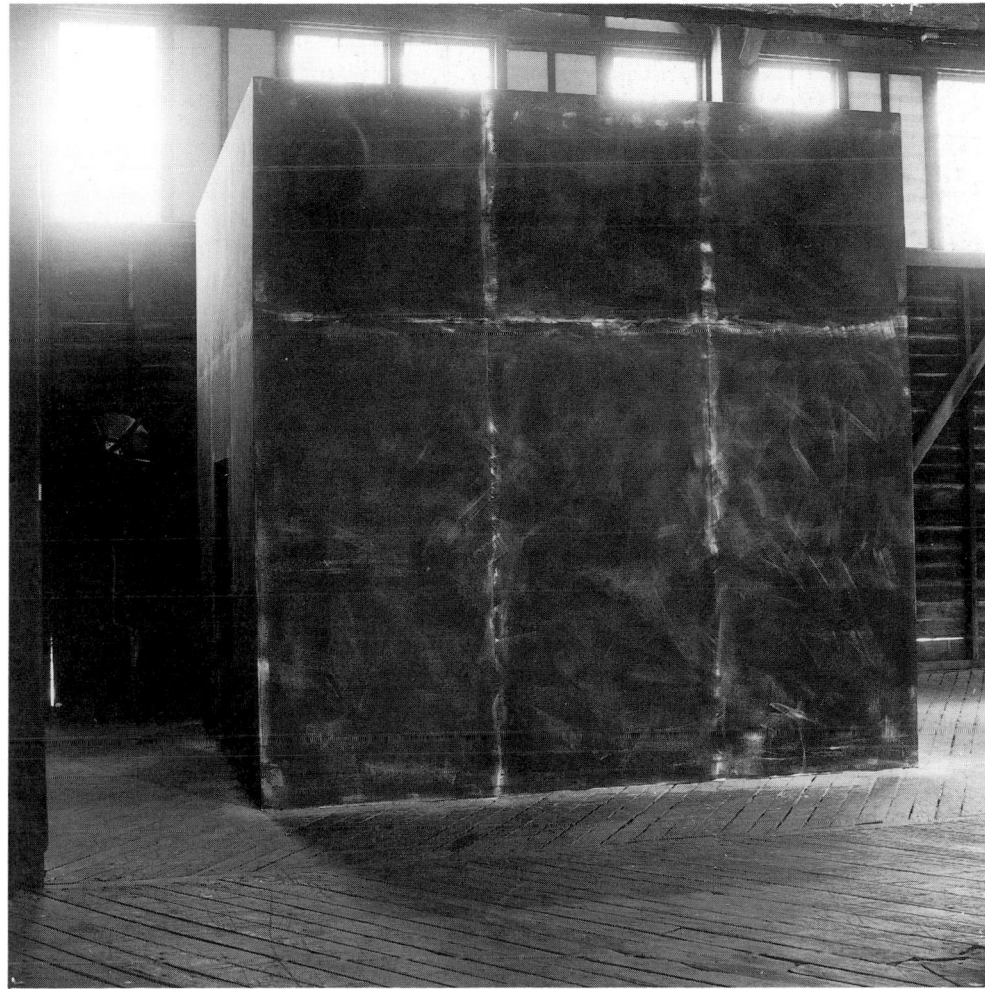

and the immediacy of this world constitutes itself as a sign, but existing at the edge of the present tense; it is a sign of absolute abstraction and realism. This is a peculiar contradiction, the consequence of tautological reduction. The chair on which I sit is nominated as the chair on which I sit. The event to occur is described as the event to occur: i.e. "Sitting before an audience . . . bare your shoulder . . . let a friend bite into your shoulder . . . until your friend's mouth is filled with blood." In 1972 this was displayed on the wall of Inhibodress like a print—an art object. One night, after the audience had become used to the instruction for an event as an object, it was performed before them. It was an event without apparent reason—a sign of itself. As a sign of itself it expanded to become a kind of chasm into which we all disappeared. The fact that it was an event without meaning stimulated the audience to search their memories and reasons. Insofar as the event demanded a meaning, it extracted from the self-consciousness of the audience. It was as though the room was filled with dead albatrosses—one for each member of the audience.

Anyway, the peculiarity of my work is that all these events as events fuse together—gradually a "parallel fiction" to the fiction of memory emerges. It is cancerous, like the supernatural, because it extracts its parameters from the real (it is my view that every event is attached to its shadow, in the same way that objects are; every shadow is the antidote to its meaning, but simultaneously the prerequisite for it). So the process is omnipresent and endless, like paranoia, and yet discrete.

The recent "Black Boxes" and room installations reassemble process, tinker with its organic continuity, fabricate elaborate fictions. The mirror images deployed in the installations compound the "fictions," tautologize perception and fix the glutinous extensibility of the process. Therefore, it is hard not to look. The audience tends to look too hard. Looking hard they see themselves. This complication of the mirror images as metaphor is the "meaning" of the "Black Boxes" and installations.

The cibachrome records and cibachrome graphics that I make are actual mirrors. In this respect, they are a subversive extension of the process.

Recent installations have extended all these ideas in the absence of performers. I have become very interested in problems of anamorphic distention and of incorporating images of extreme anamorphic distortion back into rooms and space, that extend two-dimensional perspective literally, three-dimensionally. I should add that these images are always self portraits and that the initial source of the image was photographs from performances. These problems of sight-line and the position of the viewer (the relativity of all representational codes and by implication the attendant problems of psychological distance) continue and extend all my earlier notions of breaking down and articulating the space between viewer and artwork. The black/white photograph is of a piece called *The Polar Sea (In the Wings of the Oedipal Theatre Part 3)*. It was presented at the 1986 Biennale of Sydney. The tension between inner and outer was very marked in this work. The sanding of the exterior revealed structure, as well as opening an illusionistic, painterly space. The interior of the room was completely black. In fact, the interior had been completely charred by fire. The piece was located in a huge warehouse space—on a pier. The audience entered the darkness of the room in fear and trepidation. In the contained blackness and silence of this room they could smell the dead smell of fire and distantly below them they could hear the movement of the sea.

—Mike Parr

Mike Parr first came to the attention of the Australian art scene in a significant way during 1970 when he helped initiate an artists' co-operative in Sydney. He was the principal organizer of Inhibodress Gallery, which provided a genuine alternative for innovative artists who were seeking to work without the limitations normally imposed by commercial gallery directors. Inhibodress encouraged video-performance art experiments as well as offering display spaces for more conventional forms of expression such as painting and sculpture. Freedom from profit-making incentives resulted in the development of an art centre which defied establishment tastes.

During the comparatively short-lived Inhibodress venture (1970–1972) Parr worked with film-makers Aggy Read and Ian Stocks who edited ideas and performances by Parr and his fellow-artist Peter Kennedy resulting in *Idea Demonstrations* (black, white and colour with optical sound) which was later shown at the Sydney Film Festival (1973) with added material by Parr. Film was always an important part of Parr's activities as a performance artist, providing him with a viable means of documentation. Photographic stills of his performance pieces have assumed the status of artworks in themselves and pose interesting questions related to art-photography issues. By employing the services of outstanding local photographers, such as John Delacour, the artist has guaranteed documentation of the highest technical order.

The content of Parr's works has been primarily autobiographical, and he has used his body as other artists might have used paint or stone as an essential medium for self-expression. Because Parr's left arm is congenitally unformed he has had to cope with a physical liability which has radically influenced his life both personally and as an artist. In a series of performances Parr attempted to exorcise his feelings of physical inadequacy (or incompleteness) by literally chopping off a life-like prosthesis created from various materials and packed with animal livers. The action culminated with some of the artist's family gathering up the dismembered parts and replacing the severed artificial arm with another knitted from pink yarn.

It is tempting to interpret Parr's obsessive concern with his missing arm in Freudian terms related to castration fears. Confrontation might lead to acceptance in much the same way as electro shock therapy. Parr's often brutal treatment of his body as a ground for experiment (including various forms of self-mutilation and induced vomiting) is meant to offer a form of catharsis. Self-mutilation, it is hoped, will lead to self-liberation.

To many observers (and critics) his activities appear sado-masochistic and incomprehensible in any art context. But Parr's works have obvious precursors in a host of performance pieces by European artists such as Chris Burden, Yves Klein, Piero Manzoni, Arnulf Rainer and Rudolph Schwarzkogler. The latter committed a form of ritual suicide in 1969 by methodically amputating sections of his anatomy (penis et al) in an ultimate gesture of liberation which makes Parr's endeavours appear quite tame.

In the context of "theatre of cruelty" Parr's performances have not been altogether successful. His attempts to involve audiences have led more often to their retreat into civilised passivity. Success should, perhaps, be measured in more personal (or self-indulgent) terms.

From the mid 1970s much of Parr's work divorced itself from the audience of outsiders, although some of his *Primary Vomit* actions took place in public viewing areas such as Watters Gallery (Sydney) in 1977, (section of a series *Rules and Displacement Activities*, Part 3, *I Am Sick of Art.*) The more intimate explorations were highly erotic encounters involving naked bodies and a variety of touching experiences incorporating such disparate materials as blood, feathers and honey. Family and close friends participated in his *Performance Room* (1978) pieces and at the Venice Biennale (1980), when a series of tableaux vivants combined with live performances further extended the *Performance Room* possibilities.

At the 4th Biennale of Sydney (1982) Parr was represented by a visually stunning photographic installation (*Parapraxis 3*) exploiting images of the human head in a manner which indicated possible new departures in Parr's ongoing voyage of self-discovery and enlightenment.

Concepts of 'photo-death' have recurred in Parr's work since 1982, culminating in a series of Xeroxed self-portraits which gradually 'dissolve' or 'eradicate' recognisable features of the artist's face.

In 1984, Parr's work was included in a highly acclaimed group exhibition (together with contributions from contemporary Australian artists Imants Tillers and Ken Unsworth), called *An Australian Accent,* sponsored by fabric manufacturer John Kaldor, which debuted at New York's P.S.I. Gallery and toured to the Corcoran and state galleries in Australia. It was a privately-funded initiative which established a role model for overseas exhibitions of contemporary Australian art.

The international influences of the Italian Trans-Avant-Garde were echoed in local variations on large-scale, neo-figurative painting-drawing. Parr's huge self-portraits in charcoal (and other media) on sheets of paper pinned directly onto the gallery walls extended notions of drawing as performance art and drawing as a 'thinking aloud' process, whereby finished 'statements' were as significant in scale and concept as anything traditionally classified as painting and sculpture.

The drawing as art object aspect of Parr's Eighties activities, while acknowledging its roots in earlier performance art, seems at odds with Parr's earlier rejection of commercial gallery marketing processes. Parr has very recently moved into the area of limited edition artist's prints, indicating that his acceptance of the place of the art object in the overall scheme of things is now a *fait accompli.*

One of the most interesting features of Parr's drawings (not so much in evidence in his *Green Self-Portraits,* shown at the Rosyln Oxley 9 Gallery in Sydney in mid-1987) has been his division of the working area into two assymetrical sections, importing a symbolic left-hand, right-hand side of the brain significance. Parr's 'landscapes of the mind' are reinforced by portraits of the artist's face, often distorted into forms of extravagant metamorphosis.

The most striking irony concerning Parr's drawings has been their execution by a one-armed artist. Their technical virtuosity and mammoth scale would be daunting for an artist with two arms, and half Parr's age.

—Arthur McIntyre

PARTRIDGE, David (Birdie).

Canadian. Born in Akron, Ohio, 5 October 1919; emigrated to Canada: naturalized, 1944. Educated at Radley College, Berkshire, England, 1933–35, and Trinity College School, Port Hope, Canada, 1935–38; studied geology and paleontology, Trinity College, University of Toronto, 1938–41, B.A. 1941; painting, under Carl Schaeffer, Hart House, Toronto, 1939–41, under André Bieler, Carl Schaeffer and Will Ogilvie, Queen's University Summer Art School, Kingston, Canada, 1946–47, under Harry Stenberg, Art Students League, New York, Summer 1948; Slade School, London, 1950–51 (British Council Scholarship); etching under Stanley William Hayter, Atelier 17, Paris, 1958. Served as Flying Instructor/Flight Lieutenant, Royal Canadian Air Force, 1942–45. Married Helen Rosemary Annesley in 1943; children: Katharine and John. Independent artist, since 1961. Instructor, Appleby College, Oakville, Ontario, 1945–46; Art Instructor, Ridley College, St. Catharines, Ontario, 1946–65; St. Catharines Collegiate Institute and St. Catharines Art Association, 1953–56; Queen's Summer School, Kingston, Ontario, 1955, 1959–60; Ottawa Civic Centre, 1958–61; Ontario College of Art, Toronto, 1974–75. Member of London Group, living in England, 1962–74. Co-Founder, 1954, and Curator, 1954–56, St. Catharines Public Library, Ontario; Docent, National Gallery of Canada, Ottawa, 1959–61; Trustee, Art Gallery of Canada, Toronto. Recipient: Sculpture Purchase Award, Museum of Fine Arts, Montreal, 1962; Toronto Aviva Sculpture Prize,

1976, 1979; First Place, Toronto City Hall Mural Competition, 1977; First Place, Royal Canadian Academy Sculpture Competition, 1978. Member, Royal Canadian Academy, 1962. Fellow, Royal Society of Arts and Sciences, London, 1971. Agents: Nancy Poole's Studio, 16 Hazelton Avenue, Toronto, Ontario; Moore Gallery Ltd., 34 Hess Street, Hamilton, Ontario. Address: 77 Seaton Street, Toronto, Ontario M5A 2T2, Canada

Individual Exhibitions:

1956	St. Catharines Art Gallery, Ontario
1957	Rose and Crown, Fletching, Sussex, England
1959	St. Catharines Art Gallery, Ontario
	Robertson Gallery, Ottawa
	Gallery of Contemporary Art, Toronto
1960	Robertson Gallery, Ottawa
1961	Queen's University, Kingston, Ontario
	Here and Now Gallery, Toronto
1962	Robertson Gallery, Ottawa
	Agnes LeFort Gallery, Montreal
	Jerrold Morris International Gallery, Toronto
1964	The New Vision Centre, London
1965	Agnes LeFort Gallery, Montreal
	Commonwealth Institute, London (with Toni Onley)
	New Charing Cross Gallery, Glasgow
1966	University of Sheffield, England
1967	Hamilton Gallery, London
1968	Richard DeMarco Gallery, Edinburgh
1970	Convent Garden Gallery, London
1973	Roberts Gallery, Toronto
1974	Alwin Gallery, London
1975	Willstead Gallery, Windsor, Ontario
	Roberts Gallery, Toronto
1977	Roberts Gallery, Toronto
1979	Atikokan Centennial Museum, Ontario
1982	Gallery Quan, Toronto
1984	Gallery Quan, Toronto
1986	Nancy Poole's Studio, Toronto
1987	Moore Gallery, Hamilton, Ontario

Selected Group Exhibitions:

1962	*Spring Show,* Museum of Fine Arts, Montreal
1964	*2nd Exhibition of Canadian Sculpture,* National Gallery of Canada, Ottawa
	Carnegie International, Pittsburgh
1965	*Art and Engineering,* Art Gallery of Toronto
1966	*Art of the Commonwealth,* Nottingham, England
1967	*Sculpture '67,* City Hall, Toronto
	Canadian Biennial, National Gallery of Canada, Ottawa
1969	*Canada Council Collection,* National Gallery of Canada, Ottawa
1977	*Rehearsal,* Harbourfront Art Gallery, Toronto
1978	*Sculpture 1978,* City Hall, Toronto (travelled to London and Brussels)

Collections:

National Gallery of Canada, Ottawa; Art Gallery of Ontario, Toronto; Art Gallery of Windsor, Ontario; University College, Trinity College, and Hart House, at the University of Toronto; Ridley College, St. Catharines, Ontario; Montreal Museum of Fine Art; Tate Gallery, London; Victoria and Albert Museum, London; Art Gallery of New South Wales, Sydney; Library of Congress, Washington, D.C.

Publications:

By PARTRIDGE: article—"Printmaking" in *Canadian Art* (Ottawa), March/April 1961.

On PARTRIDGE: articles—"Profile on David Partridge" by Philip Pocock in *Canadian Art* (Ottawa), March/April 1962; "The Nailman" in *Time* (New York), 27 July 1962; "David Partridge" by Pierre Rouve in *Arts Review* (London), May 1964; "Profile" by Majorie Bruce Milne in the *Christian Science Monitor* (Boston), 1 October 1974; "David Partridge" by Kenneth Coutts-Smith in *Quadrum* (Brussels), no.

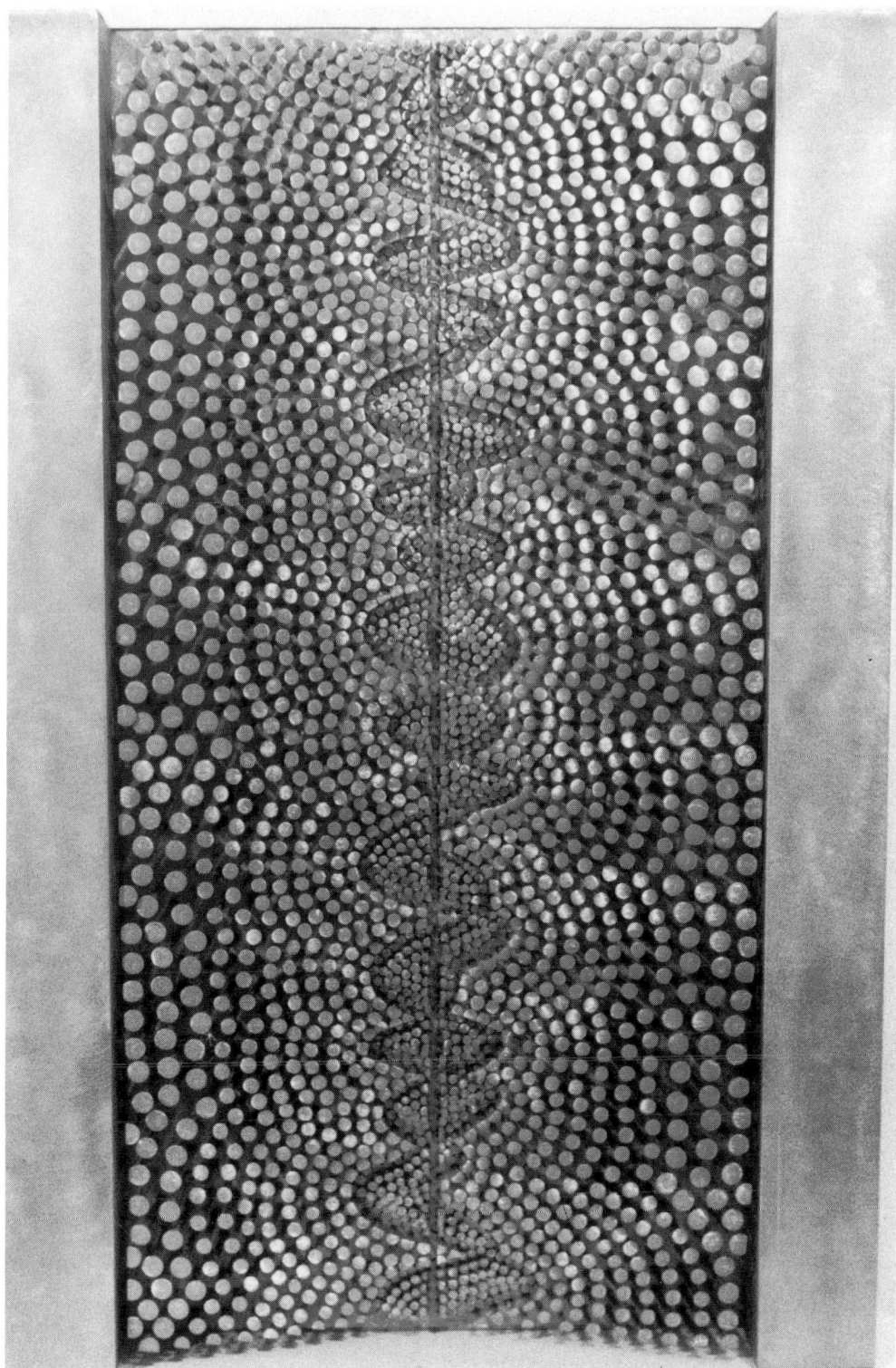

David Partridge: *Sound Valley No. 2,* 1983

18, 1964; "David Partridge's Nail Mosaics" by Charles Spencer in *Studio International* (London), July 1965; "Profile" by Max Wykes-Joyce in *Arts Review* (London), July 1965; "Alchemy of the Nail Artist" by Edward Gale in the *Scotsman* (Edinburgh), 11 December 1967; "Common Nail Makes Unique Sculpture" by Kay Kritzwiser in *Globe and Mail* (Toronto), 13 October 1973; "Nailman's Lament" by Stephen Godfrey in *Globe and Mail* (Toronto), 6 May 1978; article by David Quinter in the *Windsor Star* (Ontario), 19 September 1979; article by James Tiley in *Vanguard* (Vancouver), Spring 1982.

Although first a teacher-painter and printmaker, I feel I actually started my professional career in 1958 when I produced my first "Nail" configuration. The inspiration for this came from a show of Zoltan Kemeny's welded angle iron reliefs at Studio Fachetti in Paris in 1958. Later that year—lacking welding equipment but, due to remodeling a house in Ottawa, I hammered out my first *Naillie* as I have come to call them affectionately. In 1962 I won a sculpture prize in Montreal with one and got a commission to do a mural. By 1965 I had pretty well stopped painting and printmaking and was devoting all my time to hammering nails. Uecker of Zero Group must have started his nail things about the same time I did—but I didn't see his work until I came to England in 1962, and certainly mine have developed in a completely different way. My work is influenced by early studies in geology and paleontology and by hours of flying over Northern Ontario during the war. Latterly archaeology has had a strong influence. However I have always worked intuitively rather than from preconceived designs or drawings. Currently I am becoming involved in the sound qualities of nails often struck, stroked or dropped through. Several of the 'musical' naillies have been used by composers (J. Bethens at the University of Western Ontario, and the Canadian percussion group Nexus have used several during world tours of China and Asia and Europe).

During the last three years I have made a return to painting—based on experiences of flying in an ultralight (microlight) aircraft I built in 1982. A successful show of "Ultralight Approach Series" at Nancy Poole's Studio in 1986 was of basically skyscapes with a suggestion of landing area at the bottom.

—David Partridge

It was in Paris, studying etching under Hayter, that the Canadian artist David Partridge first saw the metal reliefs of Zoltan Kemeny. At this time Partridge was a painter and print-maker, with little involvement in three-dimensional form. Having studied art largely in England, he lived in London for ten years, from 1962, developing his fascinating technique of nail-reliefs. He continued to paint, however, solid rock-like shapes, reminiscent of Ernst's landscapes, and curiously enough it is the transference of these forms to the pointilliste technique of nail-heads, which gives his work its unique character.

Partridge relates the origin of his method to the rebuilding of a small family house in Ottawa, eighteen months after having seen Kemeny's reliefs. Pulling down a wooden wall, he revealed a group of nails, forming a relief composition, and immediately began to experiment, treating the nails as elements of design, only later exploiting the third-dimension. This led to further variations: different length nails, or undulating forms resulting from the nails being driven in at different lengths, with different heads. An infinite variety of texture, density and spatialism, became possible. Colour was introduced by varying galvanized steel with copper and zinc, and then polishing or lacquering.

A neat balance between decoration and the exploration of rhythmic space saves his work from repetitive banality, but it is by no means denigratory to affirm that the technique is best suited to large, architectural murals. Fortunately, Partridge has secured many of these, in different parts of the world.

—Charles Spencer

PASCHKE, Ed(ward).

American. Born in Chicago, Illinois, 22 June 1939. Educated at the School of the Art Institute of Chicago, B.F.A. 1961, M.F.A. 1970. Painter: lives and works in Chicago. Instructor, Meramac College, St. Louis, 1970–71; Barat College, Lake Forest, Illinois, 1971–77; School of the Art Institute of Chicago, 1974–76; Columbia College, Chicago, 1976–78. Professor of Drawing, Northwestern University, Evanston, Illinois, since 1977. Recipient: Cassandra Foundation Grant, 1972: Logan Medal, Art Institute of Chicago, 1972. Agent: Phyllis Kind Gallery, 313 West Superior Street, Chicago, Illinois 60610. Adress: 1629 North Killburn, Chicago, Illinois 60646, U.S.A.

Individual Exhibitions:

1970	Deson Zaks Gallery, Chicago
1971	Hundred Acres Gallery, New York
1972	Deson Zaks Gallery, Chicago
1973	Richard DeMarco Gallery, Edinburgh
	Deson Zaks Gallery, Chicago
1974	Contemporary Arts Center, Cincinnati, Ohio
	Galerie Darthea Speyer, Paris
	Hundred Acres Gallery, New York
1975	Pyramid Gallery, Washington, D.C.

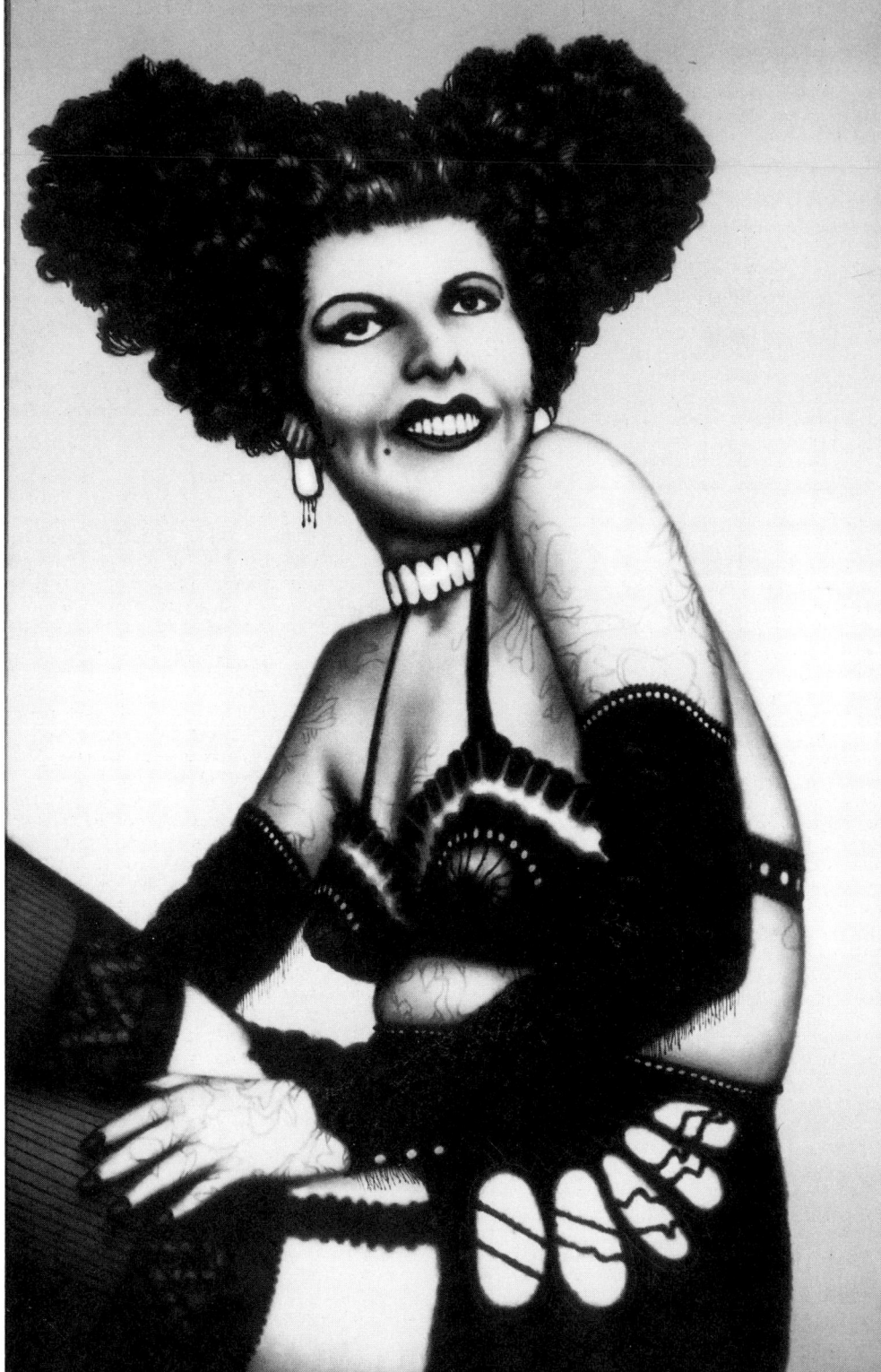

Ed Paschke: *Elcina,* **1973** Courtesy Museum of Contemporary Art, Chicago

	Contemporary Art Center, Cincinnati, Ohio (retrospective)
	Deson Zaks Gallery, Chicago
1976	Marion Locks Gallery, Philadelphia
	Galerie Darthea Speyer, Paris
1977	Phyllis Kind Gallery, Chicago
1978	Galerie Darthea Kind Gallery, Paris
	Phyllis Kind Gallery, Chicago
1979	Phyllis Kind Gallery, Chicago
1981	Phyllis Kind Gallery, Chicago
1982	Phyllis Kind Gallery, Chicago
	Renaissance Society, University of Chicago
1986	Witney Museum, New York
	Metropolitan Museum of Art, New York

Selected Group Exhibitions:

1962	*Chicago and Vicinity Show,* Art Institute of Chicago (and 1967, 1969, 1973)
1969	*Don Baum Sez "Chicago Needs Famous Artists,"* Museum of Contemporary Art, Chicago
1972	*Chicago Imagist Art,* Museum of Contemporary Art, Chicago
	What They're Up to in Chicago, National Gallery of Canada, Ottawa (travelling show)
1973	*Biennial,* Whitney Museum, New York
	Made in Chicago at the Bienal, Sao Paulo, (toured South America, and travelled to the National Collection of Fine Arts, Smithsonian Institution,

Washington, D.C. and Museum of Contemporary Art, Chicago)
1977 *View of the Decade*, Museum of Contemporary Art, Chicago
New in the 70's, University of Texas at Austin
Masterpieces of Chicago Art, Chicago Public Library Cultural Center
1980 *100 Artists, 100 Years*, Art Institute of Chicago

Collections:

Brooklyn Museum, New York; Baltimore Museum of Art; Museum of Contemporary Art, Chicago; Art Institute of Chicago; Centre Georges Pompidou, Paris; Museum des 20. Jahrhunderts, Vienna; Museum Boymans-van Beuningen, Rotterdam.

Publications:

On PASCHKE: article—review in the *New York Times*, 19 March 1982.

Edward Paschke is one of the representatives of the so-called 60's Chicago School—the figurative movement, i.e., the "Imagists." He is of a group comprised of Roger Brown, Edward C. Flood, Philip Hanson, Gladys Nillson, James Nutt, Christina Ramberg and Karl Wirsum who are (close enough) his contemporaries, not to mention the much older H. C. Westermann who led them. These artists introduced a certain amount of ferment into the American art scene, occasionally even shocking the public.

At first the group appeared informally, giving their exhibitions names taken from an underground vocabulary: *The Hairy Who, Non-Plussed Some, Marriage Chicago Style*. These artists also emulated people on the fringes of the community in their behavior and lifestyle. It was fashionable to display artistic bad taste, even vulgarity. Their anti-aestheticism also embraced subjects that Pop Art had treated with discretion—sexual deviation, the kinds of pictures that one sees in porn shops, kitsch, obscene magazines, etc.

Paschke was born in 1939 in Chicago to a family of Polish-German descent. Although he spent his childhood and youth in the country, nature did not play a great part in the development of the artist's imagination. He visited doubtful bars, used slang, occasionally picked fights, and penetrated the hidden life of the metropolis. From material taken from reality itself, he began to build his images. Albeit theatrical, these were closer to reality than real theatre. Fetishes turned into pictures appeared in his first works. Such a fetish might be a man's or woman's shoe of absurdly exaggerated proportions.

In his next phase, the artist concentrated on eccentric portraits. His gallery of archetypes—models of the 1960's and early 70's, popularized by mass-produced underground magazines—may one day be considered a study of the night fauna of the great city. These persons wear gaudy clothes, ingenious Afro hairstyles or exotic hair coverings. Their bodies are covered in heavy make-up or even tattoos. They are grotesque, stunted, sexually ambiguous.

In his later paintings social provocation has dissipated: erotic perversion, travesty, hermaphrodism and the various dark inhabitants from the city underworld disappear. Now the sitters appear to be wearing the theatrical masks that take away their individuality. They are shadows of real people—singers, guitarists, circus people, pleasure seekers. Their contours are erased, softened, washed and blurred like a photograph that is out of focus. A ghostly masquerade in ghostly colors—electric green, orange, red and yellow—appears on the canvas in an aureola of flickering light impulses that bring into pictures from the television screen. Streaks that appear to be glowing with moonlight cut across the ground, breaking up its cohesion and artistic illusion. Inspired by falsely produced reality—electronic images made up of dots—Paschke now poses new problems in art. He also poses new problems in communicating through painting that reveals static, deformations and malformations.

—Szymon Bojko

PASMORE, Victor.
British. Born in Chelsham, Surrey, 3 December 1908. Educated in London primary schools; attended evening classes at the Central School of Arts and Crafts, London, 1927–30, while working in local government service, 1927–37. Married the painter Wendy Lloyd Blood in 1940; has two children. Painter: Member, London Artists Association, 1932, and the London Group, 1934; abandoned abstract experiments and returned to visual realism, 1936; Founder, with Claude Rogers and William Coldstream, Euston Road School, London, 1937–40; returned to abstract painting, 1948; with Robert Adams, Adrian Heath, Anthony Hill and Kenneth Martin, organized first post-war abstract painting and sculpture exhibition, London, 1951; Consultant for Urban Design, Peterlee New Town, County Durham, 1954–77; associated with Ben Nicholson and Barbara Hepworth in the Penwith Society of Art, St. Ives, Cornwall, 1951; organized summer school in Scarborough, Yorkshire as experimental center for "The Developing Process," 1955–57; organized *The Developing Process* exhibition, Newcastle upon Tyne and London, 1959; worked in graphics, with Kelpra Studios, London, 1964, and 2RC Workshop, Rome, 1971; now lives and works in Malta. Visiting Lecturer, Camberwell School of Art, London, 1943–49, and Central School of Arts and Crafts, London, 1949–54; Director of Painting, Department of Fine Art, University of Durham at Newcastle upon Tyne, 1954–61. Trustee, Tate Gallery, London, 1963–66. Recipient: Carnegie Prize for Painting, *Pittsburgh International*, 1964; Gold Medal, *Graphics Biennale*, Frederikstad, Norway, 1972; Graphics Prize, 1971, and Grand Prize, 1977, *Biennale*, Ljubljana; Charles Wollaston Award, Royal Academy, London, 1983. Honorary doctorate: University of Newcastle upon Tyne, 1967; University of Surrey, 1969; Royal College of Art, London, 1972; University of Warwick, 1985. Royal Academician, London, 1984. C.B.E. (Commander, Order of the British Empire), 1959; Companion of Honour, 1981. Agent: Marlborough Fine Art, 6 Albemarle Street, London W1X 3HF, England. Address: Dar Gamri, Ta Kazzina, Gudja, Malta.

Individual Exhibitions:

1932 London Artists Association Cooling Gallery, London
1940 Wildenstein Gallery, London
Redfern Gallery, London
1942 Wildenstein Gallery, London
1947 Redfern Gallery, London
1948 Redfern Gallery, London
1950 Redfern Gallery, London
Penwith Society, St. Yves, Cornwall (with Ben Nicholson and Barbara Hepworth)
1951 Redfern Gallery, London
1954 Institute of Contemporary Arts, London
1955 Redfern Gallery, London
Arts Council Gallery, Cambridge
1958 O'Hara Gallery, London
1960 Hatton Gallery, Newcastle upon Tyne
Biennale, Vienna (toured Europe, 1960–62)
1961 Palais des Beaux-Arts, Brussels (with Eduardo Paolizzi)
Marlborough New London Gallery, London
Kunstgalerie, Bochum, West Germany
1962 Kestner-Gesellschaft, Hannover
1963 Galerie Charles Leinhardt, Zurich
Kunsthalle, Berne

1964 Galleria Lorenzelli, Milan
Marlborough New London Gallery, London
1965 Tate Gallery, London (travelled to the Scottish National Gallery of Art, Edinburgh, and the Walker Art Gallery, Liverpool)
Bienal, Sao Paulo (toured South America)
1966 Marlborough New London Gallery, London
1967 Marlborough-Gerson Gallery, New York
Ranger's House, Blackheath, London
1968 Hatton Gallery, Newcastle upon Tyne
Whitworth Art Gallery, Manchester
Ulster Museum, Belfast (travelled to Trinity College, Dublin)
1969 Marlborough New London Gallery, London
1970 Galleria Lorenzelli, Milan
Arts Club of Chicago (travelled to Allentown Art Museum, Pennsylvania)
Palazzo de la Salle, Valletta, Malta
1971 Arnolfini Gallery, Bristol
1972 Marlborough Fine Art, London
1973 Marlborough Galerie, Zurich
Villiers Pty, Paddington, New South Wales, Australia
1974 Galleria Lorenzelli, Milan
Marlborough Galleria d'Arte, Rome
Marlborough Graphics, London
1975 Museum of Fine Art, Valletta, Malta
1977 Marlborough Fine Art, London (travelled to the Marlborough Galerie, Zurich)
1978 Galleria 2RC, Rome
Grafica '78 Internzionale, Messina, Sicily
Musée des Beaux Arts, La Chaux de Fonds, Switzerland (travelled to the Gentof Radhus, Copenhagen)
1979 *Graphics International Biennale*, Ljubljana
Burstow Gallery, Brighton College, Sussex
Galleria Lorenzelli, Milan
1980 Royal Academy of Arts, London
Tate Gallery, London
Marlborough Fine Art, London
Cartwright Hall, Bradford, Yorkshire
1981 Amane Gallery, Osaka, Japan
Woodlands Art Gallery, Greenwich, London
National Gallery, Oslo (toured Scandinavia, 1981–82)
1982 Galleria Lorenzelli, Milan
Galerie Carinthia, Klagenfurt, Austria
Galerie Nicoline Pon, Zurich
1983 Marlborough Fine Art, London
1985 Musée des Beaux-Arts, Calais, France
1986 Marlborough Fine Art, London

Selected Group Exhibitions:

1942 *Euston Road Group*, London
1951 *Abstract Art*, A1A Gallery, London
1956 *Masters of British Painting*, Museum of Modern Art, New York
1958 *Documenta 2*, Kassel, West Germany
1960 *Biennale*, Venice
1962 *Premio Marzotto*, Valdagno, Italy
1964 *Painting and Sculpture of a Decade*, Tate Gallery, London
1965 *Bienal*, Sao Paulo
1970 *Expo '70*, Osaka, Japan
1977 *International Biennale of Graphic Art*, Ljubljana, Yugoslavia

Collections:

Tate Gallery, London; Scottish National Gallery of Art, Edinburgh; National Gallery of Victoria, Melbourne; National Gallery of New South Wales, Sydney; Rijksmuseum Kröller-Müller, Netherlands; Museum Boymans-van Beuningen, Rotterdam; Galleria Nazionale d'Arte Moderna, Rome; National Gallery of Canada, Ottawa; Museum of Modern Art, New York; Albright-Knox Art Gallery, Buffalo, New York

Publications:

By PASMORE: books—*A Developing Process in Art Teaching*, Newcastle upon Tyne, 1959; *Colour as a Function of*

Multi-Dimensional Space, London 1976; articles—"The Artist Speaks" in *Art News and Review* (London), February 1951; "Abstract Painting and Structure in England" in *The World of Abstract Art* (New York), 1957; "Connections Between Painting, Sculpture, and Architecture" in *Zodiac* (Brussels), no. 1, 1957; "Drawings as an Organic and Autonomous Activity" in *London Magazine,* March 1964; "The Artist on His Work" in *Christian Science Monitor* (Boston), December 1965; "The Developing Process" in *Data* (London), 1968; "Re-establishing the Individual Factor" in *Art and Artists* (London), March 1969; "The Concrete Picture-Plane and the Multi-Dimensional Space" in *The Structurist* (Saskatoon, Canada), no. 9, 1969; "Picasso's Debt to Turner" in *The Sunday Times* (London), 8 December 1974; "Turner's Influence on Me" in *Turner Society News* (London), October 1978; "Turner and Impressionism" in *Turner Society News* (London), April 1979; "A Crisis in Function" in *London Magazine,* April 1979.

On PASMORE: books—*Victor Pasmore* by Clive Bell, London 1944; *Victor Pasmore,* exhibition catalogue, by Werner Smalenbach, Hannover, 1962; *Victor Pasmore* by Jasia Reichardt, London, 1963; *Victor Pasmore* by Herbert Read, Paris 1964; *Victor Pasmore,* exhibition catalogue, by Ronald Alley, London 1965; *The Space Within,* exhibition catalogue, by Dennis Duerden, New York 1967; *Victor Pasmore: Catalogue Raisonnee* by Alan Bowness and Luigi Lambertini, London, New York and Milan 1980; *Victor Pasmore 1950-1967,* exhibition catalogue with text by Evelyne-Dorothee Allemand, Calais 1985.

*   *   *

Revolution in the form and imagery of the visual arts has either followed or accompanied critical changes in the evolution of human consciousness—Greece, Byzantine, the Renaissance, etc. Now again, in the 20th century, when the conceptual implications of modern science have been pointing to a new metamorphosis of the mind, a new revolution has taken place. The dedication of painting and sculpture to a logical and extraneous relation between man and nature, which has formed their content since the Renaissance, has been challenged by a new copernican revolution in which man, as well as the earth, is the relative factor. As a result, man and nature have begun to merge in a relationship which is not only more integrated, but also irrational and more individual. It is perhaps in the independent forms, intrinsic images and individual freedom of modern art that this new humanism and new cosmology has found its most potent expression.

—Victor Pasmore

*   *   *

Victor Pasmore: *Brown Symphony,* 1975

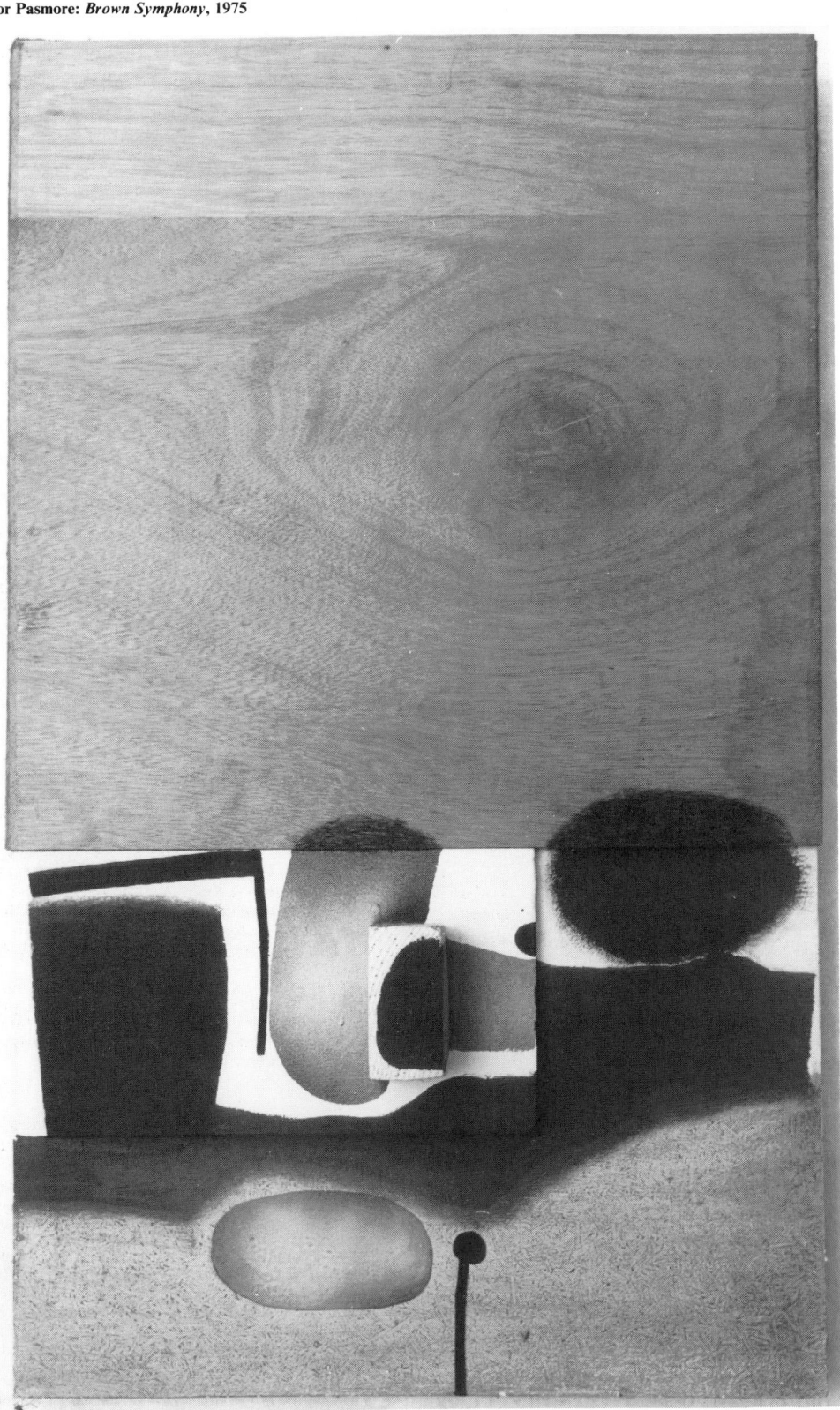

Victor Pasmore is that rare thing in English culture, an artist-theoretician. It therefore comes as surprising to discover that he is self-taught as an artist; his mother was a Sunday painter and his father a doctor, but for 10 years he worked as a clerk for the London County Council before being rescued by his first patron, Sir Kenneth Clark. His special gifts as a teacher contributed to the Euston Road School, founded by William Coldstream, Graham Bell and Claude Rogers, and from 1954 to 1961 he was Master of Painting at Durham University, at which time Richard Hamilton was his assistant, later his successor. It was at Durham that Pasmore was able to develop his theories of art, the integration of aesthetics and town planning and then develop his own brand of English Constructivism.

It is some measure of his independence and individuality, that despite brilliant gifts and early fame, it is only since 1962 that he has been able to support himself by his art. As early as 1934 he had experimented with abstract forms, which he regards more as an outburst of youthful high spirits rather than a serious effort. But this period clearly contributed to the beautiful neo-Impressionistic paintings of the 40's, landscapes and scenes of the Thames, in which highly selected, near abstracted details, are rendered with Whistlerish delicacy. This reference to Whistler is all important, since Pasmore's work at this time (and since) is compounded of influences derived from Impressionism and Japanese art, as well as Cézannesque-Cubist analyses of space.

Although his break from poetic naturalism to constructive abstraction forms one of the most dramatic incidents in modern British art, it was not as immediate as is generally supposed. There was a period of gestation and transience, especially connected with his association with Cornwall, in the early 50's, during which he also organized important post-war exhibitions of purely abstract art. "Abstraction White, Brown, Grey and Ochre," 1949 (in the Tate Gallery) might easily be mistaken for a typical cubist collage of Ben Nicholson, and suggests the same sea-coast formation to be found in that artist's Cornish works. Pasmore's drawings of the Cornish coast, less cubistically formal, explore rhythmic, spiral motifs, which relate both to his interest in Japanese art, and his later organic paintings. One must not fail to note Pasmore's reverence for Constable and Turner, who, he feels, raised English nostalgia for nature to unsurpassed levels of poetic expression. In his own transient period the drawings and paintings of natural phenomena (snowstorms, clouds, and the like) are clearly related to the preoccupations of these two English masters, and the involvement with nature which has produced some of our finest art and poetry.

Pasmore's more disciplined Constructivist period may have been an attempt to restrict the means whereby the understanding of nature, of space and light, could be formulated into severely limited expressive means. As in all his work, but particularly in the Constructions of the late 50's/60's, a striking balance of mind and emotion is aimed at, in which elegance, taste and scholarship play their parts.

Above all Pasmore has the special gift of conveying physical energy, a quality necessary to all great works of art. His work is exhilarating and exciting, never passive or depressive; one is conscious of the quality of thought and planning behind it, as well as the dexterous craftsmanship of its expression. Control, formality, rationality do not in any way inhibit passion, so that no matter how direct and positive the statement, it never lacks poetic resonance.

Although the early abstract studies led to three—dimensional constructions, Pasmore later conceded that his basic interest was painting: "I am quite prepared to accept that my own bent and training is not as a sculptor or architect. I am returning to painting because I find I can go further with it." Since the mid 60's Pasmore has evolved a body of work, paintings and prints, which finally reconcile his love of nature, his love of paint and the delightful mixture of influences which range from Turner and Constable, Whistler, the Impressionists, and especially Japanese art. His knowledge of oriental art goes back to his schooldays, and his early acquaintance with the orientalist Laurence Binyon. He would spend holidays in the British Museum, carefully examining Chinese landscape painting and the prints of Utamaro.

In his mature paintings he has clearly returned to the lessons learned and impressions received as a youth. His work has once again become organic, rhythmic compositions of large monochrome forms, like huge land-masses, linked by channels in which islands and isthmuses create interlocking shapes. Some paintings use flat areas of solid colour, others in a pointillist style which goes back to his early Impressionist landscapes. They are beautiful, satisfying works, relaxed and at ease; not concerned with the tensions set up by the Constructivist reliefs, and in a sense no longer suggesting radical views or solutions. They embody the Turneresque or Japanese acceptance of life and nature, as phenomena to be studied, sources of pleasure and inspiration.

—Charles Spencer

PEARLSTEIN, Philip.

American. Born in Pittsburgh, Pennsylvania, 24 May 1924. Studied, under Sam Rosenberg, Robert Lepper and Balcomb Greene, Carnegie Institute of Technology, Pittsburgh, 1946–49, B.F.A. 1949; Institute of Fine Arts, New York University, 1951–55, M.A. 1955. Independent painter, since 1955. Instructor, Pratt University, New York, 1959–63; Visiting Critic, Yale University, New Haven, Connecticut, 1962–63; Professor of Art, Brooklyn College, New York, 1963. Recipient: Fulbright Travel Fellowship, to Italy, 1958; National Endowment for the Arts Grant, 1969; Guggenheim Fellowship, 1971, 1972; American Academy of Arts and Letters Award, 1973; Painting Prize, *First International Biennal of Figurative Painting*, Tokyo, 1974; Artist-in-Residence Fellowship, American Academy, Rome, 1982. Agent: Hirschl and Adler Modern, New York City. Address: c/o Hirschl and Adler Modern, 851 Madison Avenue, New York, New York 10021, U.S.A.

Individual Exhibitions:

1955	Tanager Gallery, New York
1956	Peridot Gallery, New York
1957	Peridot Gallery, New York
1959	Tanager Gallery, New York
	Peridot Gallery, New York
1960	Allan Frumkin Gallery, Chicago
1962	Kansas City Art Institute
	Allan Frumkin Gallery, New York
1963	Allan Frumkin Gallery, Chicago
1965	Allan Frumkin Gallery, New York
	Allan Frumkin Gallery, Chicago
	Ceeje Gallery, Los Angeles
	Reed College, Portland, Oregon
1966	Ceeje Gallery, Los Angeles

1967	Allan Frumkin Gallery, New York
	Bradford Junior College, Massachusetts
1968	Carnegie-Mellon Institute, Pittsburgh
1969	Allan Frumkin Gallery, New York
1970	Chatham College, Pittsburgh
	Georgia Museum of Art, Athens (retrospective; toured the United States)
1971	Graphics I and II Gallery, Boston
	Leslie/Pearlstein/Thiebud: Contemporary Views of Man, Hayden Gallery, Massachusetts Institute of Technology, Cambridge
1972	Galerie M. E. Thelen, Cologne
	Galleri Ostergren, Malmo, Sweden
	Galerie Kornfeld, Zurich
	Staaliche Museen-Kupferstichkabinett, West Berlin
	Kunstverein, Hamburg
	Donald Morris Gallery, Detroit
	Hansen Fuller Gallery, San Francisco
	Allan Frumkin Gallery, New York
1973	Parker 470 Gallery, Boston
	Editions La Tortue, Paris
1974	Allan Frumkin Gallery, New York
	Finch College, New York (retrospective; toured the United States)
1975	*The Human Figure*, Gimpel Fils, Ltd., London
	Neuberger Museum, Purchase, New York
	Marianne Friedland Gallery, Toronto
1976	Barbara Fendrick Gallery, Washington, D.C.
	Donald Morris Gallery, Detroit
1978	Springfield Art Museum, Missouri (toured the United States)
	Harcus-Krakow Gallery, Boston
1980	Allan Frumkin Gallery, New York
	Association of American Artists, New York
	FIAC, Paris
1981	*Landscape Aquatints 1978–1980*, Brooke Alexander Inc., New York
	Ringling Museum of Art, Sarasota, Florida
	Columbus College, Georgia
	Reynolds/Minor Gallery, Richmond, Virginia
	Marianne Friedland Gallery, Toronto
	North Dakota State University, Fargo
	University of North Carolina, Greensboro
	Springfield Art Museum, Missouri
	Graphics I and II, Boston
1982	Allan Frumkin Gallery, New York
	Summit Art Center, New Jersey
	Donald Morris Gallery, Birmingham, Michigan
1983	Galleria Il Ponte, Rome
	American Academy, Rome
	University of Northern Iowa, Cedar Falls (toured)
	Milwaukee Art Museum, Wisconsin (retrospective; travelled to Brooklyn, New York; Philadelphia; Toledo, Ohio; Pittsburgh)
1984	Marianne Friedland Gallery, Toronto
	Fay Gold Gallery, Atlanta, Georgia
	Richmond University, Virginia
1985	Hirschl and Adler Modern, New York
	Graphics I and II, Boston
1986	James Madison University, Harrisonburg, Virginia
	Palace Theatre of the Arts, Stamford, Connecticut
	Atlantic Center for the Arts, New Smyrna Beach, Florida
	Amherst College, Massachusetts
1987	Art Gallery in Chicago
	Marianne Friedland Gallery, Toronto
	State University of New York, Binghamton
1988	Hirschl and Adler Modern, New York

Selected Group Exhibitions:

1954	*Emerging Talent*, Kootz Gallery, New York
1962	*The First Five Years*, Whitney Museum, New York
1968	*Realism Now*, Vassar College, Poughkeepsie, New York
1974	*7 Realists*, Yale University, New Haven, Connecticut
1977	*8 Contemporary Realists*, Pennsylvania Academy of Fine Arts, Philadelphia (travelled to the North Carolina Museum of Art)
1979	*6 Painters of the Figure*, University of Colorado Museum, Boulder
1980	*Realism/Photorealism*, Philbrook Art Center, Tulsa, Oklahoma
1982	*Contemporary American Realism Since 1960*, Pennsylvania Academy of Fine Arts, Philadelphia
1985	*American Realism: The Precise Image*, Isetan Museum, Tokyo (travelled to Osaka and Yokohama, Japan)
1987	*Visions of America*, ACA Galleries, New York

Collections:

Museum of Modern Art, New York; Whitney Museum, New York; Metropolitan Museum of Art, New York; Brooklyn Museum, New York; Vassar College, Poughkeepsie, New York; Hirshhorn Museum, Washington, D.C.; Corcoran Gallery, Washington, D.C.; Art Institute of Chicago; Cleveland Museum of Art; Milwaukee Art Center.

Publications:

By PEARLSTEIN: articles—"The Symbolic Language of Francis Picabia" in *Arts Magazine* (New York), January 1956; "Futurism and Some Other Impure Forms" in *Artnews* (New York), Summer 1961; "The Private Myth" in *Artnews* (New York), September 1961; "The Figure Paintings Today Are Not Made in Heaven" in *Artnews* (New York), Summer 1962; "Whose Painting Is It, Anyway?" in *Arts Yearbook*, New York 1964; statement in *Art Now: New York* (New York) March 1971; "Why I Paint the Way I Do" in the *New York Time*, August 1971; "A Conversation with Philip Pearlstein," interview, with Ellen Schwartz, in *Art in America* (New York), September/October 1971; "Pearlstein Portraits," interview, with Ralph Pomeroy, in *Art and Artists* (London), September 1973; interview, with Paul Cummings, in *Artists in Their Own Words: Interviews*, New York 1979.

On PEARLSTEIN: books—*Philip Pearlstein*, exhibition catalogue, with an essay by Linda Nochlin, Athens, Georgia 1970; *Leslie/Pearlman/Thiebaud: Contemporary Views of Man*, exhibition catalogue, with text by Sidra Stich, Cambridge, Massachusetts 1971; *Philip Pearlstein*, exhibition catalogue, Detroit 1972; *Neue Formen des Realismus* by Peter Plagens, Cologne 1973; *The Age of the Avant-Garde* by Hilton Kramer, New York 1973; *7 Realists*, exhibition catalogue, New Haven, Connecticut 1974; *Philip Pearlstein: The Human Figure*, exhibition catalogue, London 1975; *Returns of Realism*, Part 1, exhibition catalogue, with essays by Allan Frumkin and Charlotte Stokes, Rochester, Michigan 1978; *Philip Pearlstein: Landscape Aquatints 1978–1980*, exhibition catalogue, New York 1981; *Philip Pearlstein: A Painter's Progress*, exhibition catalogue with essay by Paul Master-Karnik, Summit, New Jersey 1982; *Philip Pearlstein: A Retrospective*, exhibition catalogue with texts by Russell Bowman and Irving Sandler, Milwaukee 1983; articles—"Confronting the Solemn Nude" by John Perreault in the *Village Voice* (New York), 14 February 1974; "What the Flesh on Real Humans Looks Like" by Peter Schjeldhal in the *New York Times*, 17 February 1974; "Pearlstein: Portraits at Face Value" by Hayden Herrera in *Art in America* (New York), January/February 975; "Art View" by Hilton Kramer in the *New York Times*, 15 February 1976; "Philip Pearlstein: Is He the Enemy of Realism?" by Robert Duffy in the *St. Louis Post-Dispatch*, 27 February 1977; "Philip Pearlstein: Naked Nudes, A Profile" by John Perreault in the *Soho Weekly News* (New York), 20 April 1978; "An Artist Who Likes the Body" by Franz Schulze in the *Chicago Sun Times*, 17 June 1979; "The Evolution of Philip Pearlstein, Part 1" by L. Wallin in *Art International* (Lugano, Switzerland), Summer 1979; "The Evolution of Philip Pearlstein, Part 2" by L. Wallin in *Art International* (Lugano, Switzerland), September 1979; "Philip Pearlstein: The Complete Paintings" by Lawrence Alloway in *Art in America* (New York), February 1985; "Artist and Model: Why the Tradition Continues" by Grace Glueck in the *New York Times*, 8 June 1986.

Most artists reach maturity when they consciously decide what kind of art they do not want to make. They are then free to go on to invent an attitude that opens new technical and stylistic possibilities. Around 1960, I felt a sudden revulsion to the expressionism that had been the dominant characteristic of art of the New York painters during the preceding decade. My own works then had taken off from the Abstract Expressionists. I was determined to start from a zero position to pragmatically depict the forms of the models I hired. The models took poses that provided me with picture structure possibilities. I rejected self-expression, psycho-drama and all other story-telling, letting the implications of such fall as

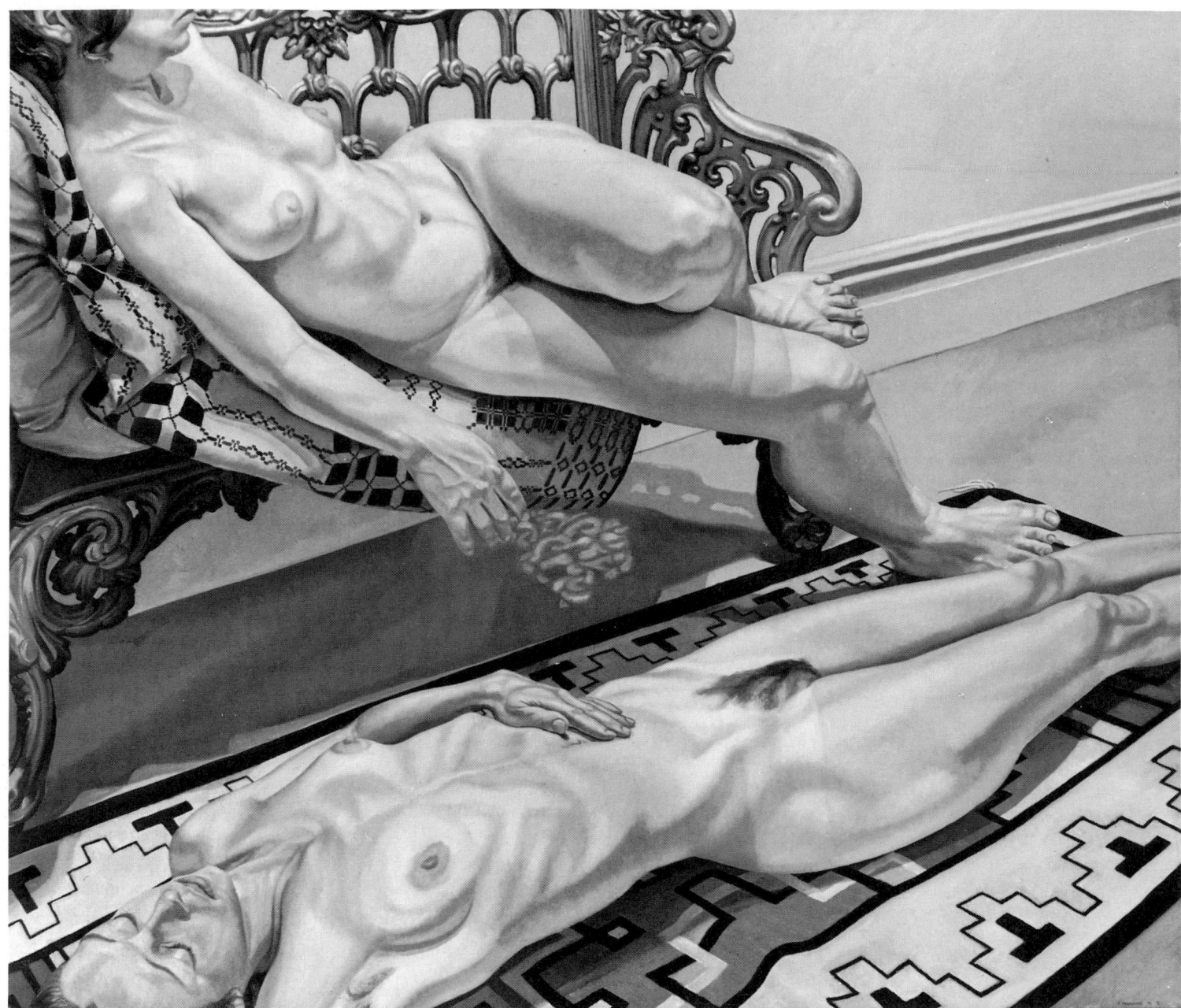

Philip Pearlstein: *Two Reclining Female Models*, 1973

they would. I concentrated on the exploitation of creating the illusions of form in space, that to me remains the most intriguing of painting problems. Along the way I have been charged with being pornographic, or worse, anti-humanistic, etc. However, my intent has been to ignore all that, and, supported by the figurative traditions of Western art, to explore the aesthetics inherent in one possible way of painting.

—Philip Pearlstein

Philip Pearlstein's preoccupation with the human figure enriches his visual utterance, but it is not, as one might think, the over-riding element in his compositions. Rather the *forms* of such figures are the shapes he chooses to work with as the areas and edges within the compositional limits of a rectangle. The way parts of the figures move right off the canvas does not greatly concern him as he has established a module for the entire work from the very beginning—a hand, say, or perhaps a foot. Once chosen, this module is completely realized before the next form is worked on, and this working out or away from the initial module sets the scale against which successive forms are measured. As a result, the cropping—so characteristic of his work—has a quality of surprise about it;

even he doesn't always know where it will occur. But control is maintained, and a satisfying sense of balance, through the establishment of the right scale over the whole painting. As for the going-off, Pearlstein shares the compositional novelty achieved by a number of contemporary artists in that he does not structure his work in relation to the edge of the canvas. He enjoys the increased struggle this creates for the picture plane in trying to maintain itself.

Pearlstein has come up with a revealing statement to describe what he does with his nude figures—he calls his manipulation of bodies "a sort of stilled-action choreography." He has no interest in the psychological overtones of the relationships exposed in his work. It is only as a subject for painting that he considers his models, rather like the way Morandi utilized his bottles. Pearlstein wants the movement of the forms, their directional thrust, to create the structure of the painting. He also wants to put down what it is he sees as a way of re-iterating the innate dignity of the human body.

—Ralph Pomeroy

PENALBA, Alicia (Perez).

Argentinian. Born in San Pedro, Buenos Aires, 9 August 1913. Educated at Escuela Materna, Valparaiso, Chile, 1919; various schools in Patagonia, 1921-23; Escuela Municipal San Cristobal, Sante Fe, 1924; Anfunes, Cordoba, 1925; Escuela de Bella Obreros del Porvenir, San Juan, 1926; Escuela Nacional de Bellas Artes, Buenos Aires, 1930-34; Escuela Superior de Bellas Artes Ernesto de la Carcova, Buenos Aires, 1934, 1944-46; Ecole Nationale Supérieure des Beaux-Arts, Paris, 1949-50; Académie de la Grand Chaumière, Paris, 1950-53; Married Amadeo Binci in 1940 (divorced, 1963). Worked at various jobs in Buenos Aires and Paris, until 1956. Independent sculptor, Paris, since 1956. Recipient: Sculpture Prize, *6th Bienal,* Sao Paulo, 1961; Hakone Special Prize, Ninotaira, Japan, 1969; Gulbenkian Foundation Prize, 1974. Agents: Galerie Alice Pauli, 7 Avenue Runine, Lausanne, Switzerland; and Artcurial, Paris. Address: c/o Artcurial, 9 Avenue Matignon, 75008 Paris, France.

Individual Exhibitions:

1957   Galerie Du Dragon, Paris

1960	Galerie Claude Bernard, Paris
	Otto Gerson Gallery, New York
1961	Galerie Charles Lienhard, Zurich
1962	Museu de Arte Moderna, Rio de Janeiro
	Devorah Sherman Gallery, Chicago
1964	Stedelijk Van Abbemuseum, Eindhoven, Netherlands
	Rijksmuseum Kröller-Müller, Otterlo, Netherlands
	Stadtisches Museum Schloss Morsbroich, Leverkusen
1965	Galerie Creuzevalt, Paris
1966	Galerie Bonino, New York
	The Phillips Collection, Washington, D.C.
1967	Galerie d'Art Moderne, Basle
	Galerie Alice Pauli, Lausanne, Switzerland
1969	*Sculptura*, Galleria Nuovo Carpine, Rome
	Toninelli Arte Moderna, Milan
1971	Galerie Alice Pauli, Lausanne, Switzerland
	Galerie d'Arte Moderne, Basle
1975	Artel Galerie, Geneva
	Galerie de France et du Benelux, Brussels
1976	Arte/Contacto, Caracas
	Galleria Stendhal, Milan
1977	Galerie Carmen Martinez, Paris
	Musée d'Art Moderne de la Ville, Paris
	Villand-Galanis, Paris
1978	Museo de Bells Artes, Caracas
1980	Galleria Pieter Coray, Lugano, Switzerland
	Parc Municipal de Vernier, Geneva
	Stadtpark, St. Gallen, Switzerland
	Artcurial, Paris
	Galleria M. Ferrari, Brescia, Italy
1981	Jardins de la Ville d'Evian, France
	Jardins de la Ville de Lucerne
1982	Musée des Beaux-Arts, La Chaux de Fonds, Switzerland

Selected Group Exhibitions:

1958	*Carnegie International*, Carnegie Institute, Pittsburgh (and 1964,1967, 1970)
1959	*3 Bildhauer aus Paris*, Museum Haus Lange, Krefeld, West Germany
	Documenta 2, Kassel, West Germany (and *Documenta 3*, 1964)
1964	*Meisterwerke der Plastik*, Musem des 20. Jahrhunderts, Vienna
1967	*Dix Ans d'Art Vivant*, Fondation Maeght, St. Paul-de-Vence, France (and 1968)
1968	*Totems et Tabous*, Musée d'Arte Moderne de la Villa, Paris
1969	*1st Exhibition of Modern Sculpture*, Hakone Open Air Museum, Ninotaira, Japan
1973	*Masters of Modern Sculpture*, Seibu Takatsuki Shopping Center, Tokyo (toured Japan)
1977	*Fiberworks*, Cleveland Museum of Art
1982	*Hans und Walter Bechtler Sammlungen*, Kunsthaus, Zurich

Collections:

Centre Georges Pompidou, Paris; Rijksmuseum Kröller-Müller, Otterlo, Netherlands; Handels Hochschule, St. Gallen, Switzerland; Hakone Open Air Museum, Ninotaira, Japan; Museo de Bells Artes, Caracas; Albright-Knox Art Gallery, Buffalo, New York; Phillips Collection, Washington, D.C.; Hirshhorn Museum and Sculpture Garden, Smithsonian Institution, Washington, D.C.; Carnegie Institute, Pittsburgh; Dallas Museum of Fine Arts.

Publications:

By PENALBA: articles—statement in *Bilan de l'Art Actuel*, Paris 1953; "Genachten van Penalba" in *Penalba*, exhibition catalogue, Otterlo, Netherlands 1964; "Reflexions sur la Sculpture" in *Quadrum* (Brussels), no. 17, 1964; "Letters from 31 Artists to the Albright-Knox Art Gallery" in *Gallery Notes* (Bufflao, New York), Spring 1970; statement in *Penalba*, exhibition catalogue, Lausanne and Basle 1971; "Y el vuelo," poem, in *Nouveiles Images* (Lombreuil), October 1974.

On PENALBA: books—*Penalba*, exhibition catalogue, with text by Patrick Waldberg, Paris 1957; *La Sculpture de ce Siècle* by Michel Seuphor, Neuchâtel, Switzerland 1959; *Penalba* by Michel Seuphor, St. Gallen, Switzerland 1960; *Mains et Merveilles* by Patrick Waldberg, Paris 1961; *Scultura Francese Moderna* by Giuseppe Marchiori, Milan 1963; *Penalba: Scultura*, exhibition catalogue, with text by Giovanni Carandente, Rome 1969; *Vingt-Cinq Ans d'Art Vivant* by Michel Ragon, Paris 1969; *The Evolution of Modern Sculpture* by A. M. Hammacher, New York 1969; *L'Art Abstrait*, vols. 3 and 4, by Michel Seuphor, and Michel Ragon, Paris 1973-74; *Penalba* by Jorn Merkert, Paris 1977; *Interventi sull'Arte Figurativa Contemporanea 1970-76* by Giuseppe Marchiori, Treviso 1977; *Penalba*, exhibition catalogue, with text by André Berne-Joffroy, Paris 1977; *Penalba*, exhibition catalogue, with text by Jean-Louis Ferrier, Lucerne 1981.

There is only one material that submits itself entirely to my desires: that is clay. Any other material, one finds that from the very start certain limitations are imposed which shackle the total desire for expression. By their very nature, stone, wood, iron and other materials subject the artist to a mystification. Not so with clay. It does not impose any beauty or any *a priori* expression. It yields itself entirely to my researches; it is for me, the only truly plastic material.

When I make use of other materials, I do so because I am forced to in order to work . . . .

As I see it, the form to which I wish to give a material existence cannot resemble anything which exists, unless it be that unknown interior of oneself which only seeks to speak its message of its own being.

What is of importance is ordering, rhythm, like in music which only expresses itself in its totality; dissociated from this soul anything materialised resembles a form already created by nature.

. . . Far too much has been said about vegetable forms on the subject of my early sculptures. This period of my work, which people have called "totemic," was guided by a need to spiritualize the symbols of eroticism, the source of all creation, the most pure and sacred state of life of man. This whole content of the mystery of procreation rose up towards heaven in solid and intricate forms protecting the delicate fruit deposited on the interior, suggesting the idealisation of the flesh as much as its birth. This world of forms thus came neither from leaves nor branches, nor from a direct reference to nature forms which makes the work, but the setting of order of these forms, given a rhythm by the individual. A language which expresses the very depths of being, this need to poeticise unveils that which is most unknown in man.

This first period (from 1952 to 1957) emptied an interior necessity. Thus exorcised, my sculpture took other routes which rise from a more civilised, more complex era to the search for a perfection of sculptural means. This is how my sculptures have started to be more airy, pierced with light, looking for plastic equilibrium in all directions. I think that equilibrium is the only thing which leads to the successful outcome of a work. I do not believe in the temperamental gesture, which has not been wholeheartedly adopted, nor, in the sculptures of the bizarre—creatures which have been damaged, burnt or mimiced, batrachian or insectiform. A Musée Dupuytreit (a pathology museum in Paris, similar to the Hunter collection, Royal College of Surgeons) of sculpture holds no attraction for me.

—Alicia Penalba

Alicia Penalba: *Sirène*, 1981

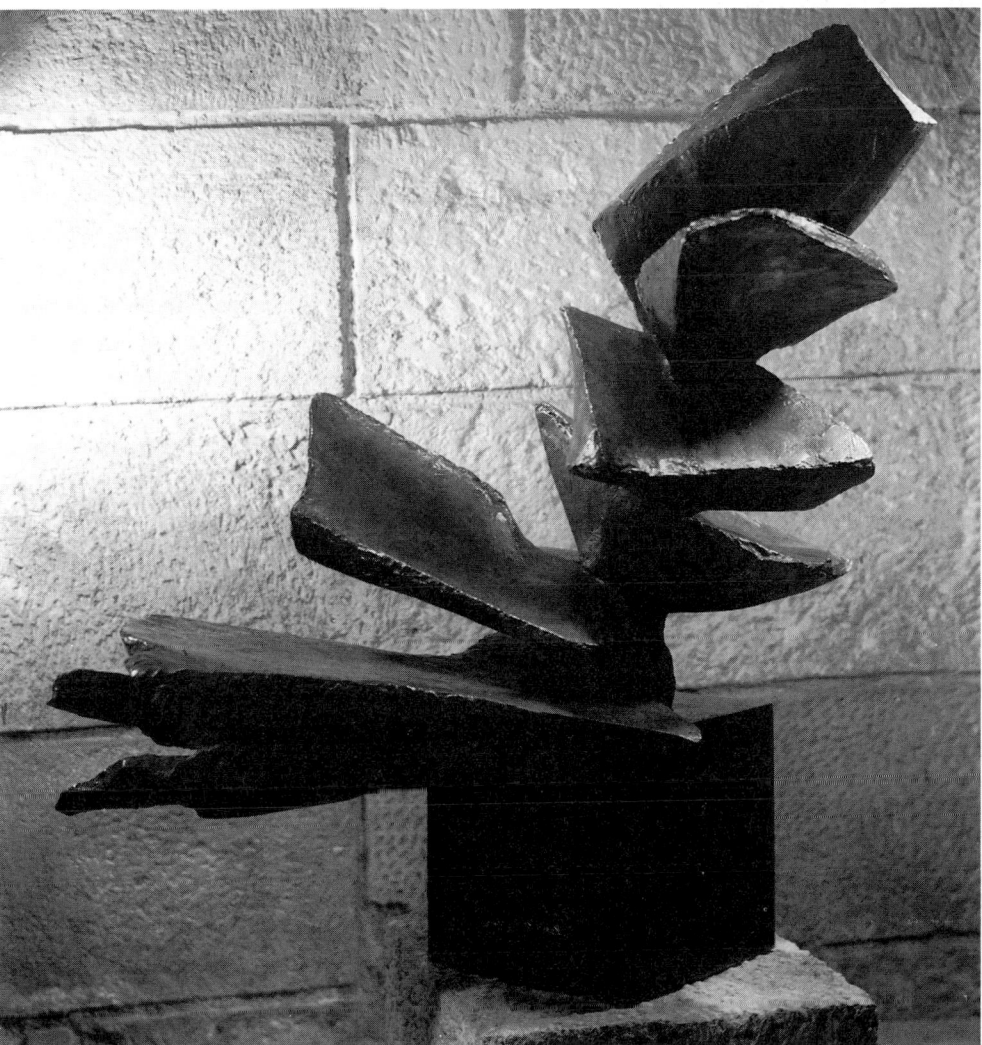

Alicia Penalba occupies an exceptional position among contemporary artists. Her art lies in testing the limits of the possible. Long before the demand for an expressly feminine aesthetic was advanced, the artist had brought ideas of independence into effect in her life and work, freed herself from ties of family, country and religion and from the isms, groups and concepts of the art world.

Penalba came relatively late to that means of artistic expression which enabled her to bring her immense talent for haptic form to perfection. The Argentinian born artist turned from painting to sculpture in Paris at the age of 35 and gained in Ossip Zadkine's atelier the missing dimension necessary for her self realization in the art. She acquainted herself with Brancusi's exacting standards of craft, occupied herself with Giacometti's conception of space, took Hans Arp's lively flowing forms as an ideal and adopted his concept of the art as movement in parallel with events in nature. At the beginning of the 1950's the sculptress had discovered her own path which she took to the limits of form, towards an experience of the limits of time and space.

The poetic titles that Penalba gives to her works are like boundary stones marking the stages which the artist covered on a rectilinear path off the beaten track. The only early work that the sculptress did not destroy before her fresh start on abstraction in 1951 she called "The Fruitful Goddess". With her first abstract sculptures on the theme of nature-mysticism she created growing forms in space, in whose shapes flow reminiscences from a childhood rich in experiences of fantasy in the exotic Patagonian landscape. The priestess of the "Vegetal Liturgy" erects the idol-like symbols of "Totems of Love." Without doubt, her preoccupation with Mayan culture was also of importance in the development of the interior images which the artist forms in clay in order to perpetuate them in monumental size in metal. The bud-like closed forms of "Chrysalid" are followed by the broken open forms of "Dialogue" with its open interior space. In the alternating play of foreground and distance, of attraction and repulsion, Penalba forms the contrast between heavy and light, hard and soft, masculine and feminine, closed and open, into a unity of space in which the spectator is also included. The sculptures, often composed directly within a landscape, make spatial relationships visible as structural elements dovetailed architeconically with nature. After the sculptress had directed the raising of "Great Cathedral" a new "Sign" testifies to the fragility of equilibrium in creation. Penalba does not remain unchanged in "Great Refuge"; she pursues one of the oldest human ideas for experiencing time and space, the dream of flying.

"Flying ones" is the point of departure into the fourth dimension, the dimension of time, which is now of essential significance in the artist's creative work. Besides the elements of earth and water, air appears in increasing measure: as an element in which soaring "Birds of Passage" rise from the earth and disregard the laws of gravity, in the great spirit of a purified language of form in metaphorical high flight.

—Dagmar Sinz

PENCK, A. R.

German. Born Ralf Winkler, in Dresden, 5 October 1939; adopted name A. R. Penck, 1969. Educated at the 38th Grundschule, Dresden, 1945–53; self-taught in art, from 1953. Served in the DDR Volksarmee, 1957, 1973–74. Trainee design draughtsman, Dresden, 1956; worked as a newspaper delivery-boy, night watchman, postman, stoker, etc, Dresden, 1957–60. Independent artist, working with intuitive and sym-

bolic imagery, from 1963, establishing his own studio in the Lange Strasse, East Berlin, 1963, and in the Gostritzer Strasse, Dresden, 1977: lived in East Berlin, 1963–72, in Lindenau, 1972–76, in Dresden, 1976–80, and in Kerpen, near Cologne, from 1980. Currently lives and works in Cologne, London and Dublin. Recipient: Print Prize, *International Triennale,* Grenchen, 1974; Will-Grohmann Prize, 1976; Rembrandt Prize, Basle, 1980. Agent: Galerie Michael Werner, Cologne. Address : c/o Galerie Michael Werner, Gertrudenstrasse 24–28, 5000 Cologne 1, West Germany.

Individual Exhibitions:

1969	Galerie Michael Werner, Cologne
1970	Galerie Michael Werner, at the *IKI Art Fair,* Cologne
1971	Galerie Heiner Friedrich, Munich
	Museum Haus Lange, Krefeld, West Germany
	Galerie Michael Werner, Cologne
1972	Wide White Space Gallery, Antwerp
	Kunsthalle, Basle
	Goethe-Institut, Amsterdam
	Galerie Stampa, Basle
	Galerie Michael Werner, Cologne
	Galerie Grafikmeyer, Karlsruhe
	Galerie Beck, Erlangen, West Germany
1973	Galerie Loehr, Frankfurt
	Nova Scotia College of Art and Design, Halifax
	Daner Galleriet, Copenhagen
	Galleria L'Uomo e l'Arte, Milan
1974	Galerie Michael Werner, Cologne
	Galerie Stampa, Basle
	Galerie Nachst St. Stephan, Vienna
	Galerie Heiner Friedrich, Munich
	Städtisches Galerie "Altes Theater," Ravensburg, West Germany
	Wide White Space Gallery, Antwerp
1975	Galerie Neuendorf, Hamburg
	Kunsthalle, Berne
	Galerie Seriaal, Amsterdam
	Stedelijk Van Abbemuseum, Eindhoven, Netherlands
	Galerie Michael Werner, Cologne
	Kunsthalle, Basle
1977	Galerie Seriaal, Amsterdam
	Kunstverein, Mannheim
	Museum Ludwig, Cologne
1978	*Zeichnungen bis 1975,* Kunstmuseum, Basle
	Galerie Helen van der Mey, Amsterdam
	Galerie Rudolf Springer, West Berlin
1979	*Concept Conceptruimte,* Museum Boysman-van Beuningen, Rotterdam
	Galerie Michael Werner, Cologne
1980	Galerie Fred Jahn, Munich
	Städtisches Museum Schloss Morsbroich, Leverkusen, West Germany
	Galerie Michael Werner, Cologne
	Kunstmuseum, Basle
1981	Galerie Helen van der Mey, Amsterdam
	Gemalde, Handzeichnungen, Josef-Haubrich-Kunsthalle, Cologne
	38 neue bilder, Galerie Neuendorf, Hamburg
1982	Sonnabend Gallery, New York
	Galleria Lucio Amelio, Naples
	Galleria Toselli, Milan
	Studio d'Arte Cannaviello, Milan
	Galerie Gillespie-Laage-Salomon, Paris
	Waddington Galleries, London
	Edition Sabine Knust, Munich (with Korg Immendorf)
	Galerie Michael Werner, Cologne
	Kunstmuseum, Basle
	Kunstmuseum, Bonn
1983	Galleria Lucio Amelio, Naples
	Yarlow/Salzmann Gallery, Toronto
	Galerie Michael Werner, Cologne
	Galerie Springer, West Berlin
	Galerie Sabine Knust, Munich
	Galerie Gillespie-Laage-Salomon, Paris
1984	Mary Boone/Michael Werner Gallery, New York
	Watari Gallery, Tokyo
	Studio d'Arte Cannaviello, Milan

	Galerie Maeght Lelong, Zurich
	Waddington Galleries, London
	Galerie Alma, Lyon, France
	Ulrike Kantor Gallery, Los Angeles
	Tate Gallery, London
	A. R. Penck, at the *Biennale,* Venice
	Akira Ikeda Gallery, Tokyo
	Galerie Sabine Knust, Munich
	Galerie Michael Werner, Cologne
	Temple Bar Studios, Dublin
1985	Musée d'Art et d'Industrie, St. Etienne, France
	Brody's Gallery, Washington, D.C.
	Arnolfini Gallery, Bristol, Avon
	Galerie Michael Werner, Cologne
	Stadtisches Museum, Monchengladbach, West Germany
	Mary Boone/Michael Werner Gallery, New York
	Galerie Herbert Meyer-Ellinger, Frankfurt
	Neue Galerie-Sammlung Ludwig, Aachen, West Germany
	Kunstverein, Braunschweig, West Germany
1986	Deweer Art Gallery, Zwevegem-Otegem, Belgium
	Galleria Christian Stein, Milan
	Galerie Maeght Lelong, Zurich
	Galerie Springer, West Berlin
	Galerie und Edition Stahli, Zurich
	Galerie Gillespie-Laage-Salomon, Paris
	Kunstverein, Freiburg, West Germany
	Maximilian Verlag/Sabine Knust, Munich
	Galerie Collection d'Art, Amsterdam
	Cabinet des Estampes, Geneva
	Barbara Toll Fine Arts, New York
	Galerie Michael Werner, Cologne
	Galerie Dobele, Ravensburg, West Germany
	DAAD-Galerie, West Berlin
	Galerie de Ganzerik, Eindhoven, Netherlands (with Johannes Brus)
	Kunsthalle, Bielefeld, West Germany (with P. Kirkeby and M. Lupertz)
1987	Orchard Gallery, Londonderry, Northern Ireland
	Stadtisches Museum, Monchengladbach, West Germany
	Douglas Hyde Gallery, Dublin
	Edinburgh College of Art, Scotland
	Fruitmarket Gallery, Edinburgh
	Galerie Michael Werner, Cologne
	Ulmer Museum, Ulm, West Germany
	Galerie Steinmetz, Bonn
	Galerie Chobot, Vienna
	Galerie und Edition Stahli, Zurich
	Musée de Strasbourg, France
	Galerie Jule Kewenig, Frechen-Bachem, West Germany
	Kettle's Yard Gallery, Cambridge, England
	Galerie Thaddeus Ropac, Salzburg, Austria
	Galerie Springer, West Berlin
	Galerie Gillespie-Laage-Salomon, Paris (with G. Baselitz and M. Lupertz)
1988	Galerie Van de Loo, Munich

Selected Group Exhibitions:

1971	*Prospekt '71,* Kunsthalle, Dusseldorf (and *Prospekt '73,* 1973)
1972	*Documenta 5,* Kassel, West Germany (and *Documenta 7,* 1982)
1974	*Projekt '74,* Kunsthalle, Cologne
1975	*Functions of Drawing,* Rijksmuseum Kröller-Müller, Otterlo, Netherlands
1978	*Werke aus der Sammlung Crex,* Ink, Zurich, Switzerland (travelled to the Louisiana Museum, Humlebaek, Denmark; Städtische Galerie im Lenbachhaus, Munich; and the Kunstverein, Hamburg)
1979	*European Dialogue,* At the *3rd Biennale of Sydney,* Art Gallery of New South Wales, Sydney
1981	*A New Spirit in Painting,* Royal Academy of Art, London
1983	*Expressions: New Art from Germany,* St. Louis Art Museum, Missouri (travelled to Philadelphia; Chicago)
1985	*The European Iceberg,* Art Gallery of Ontario, Toronto

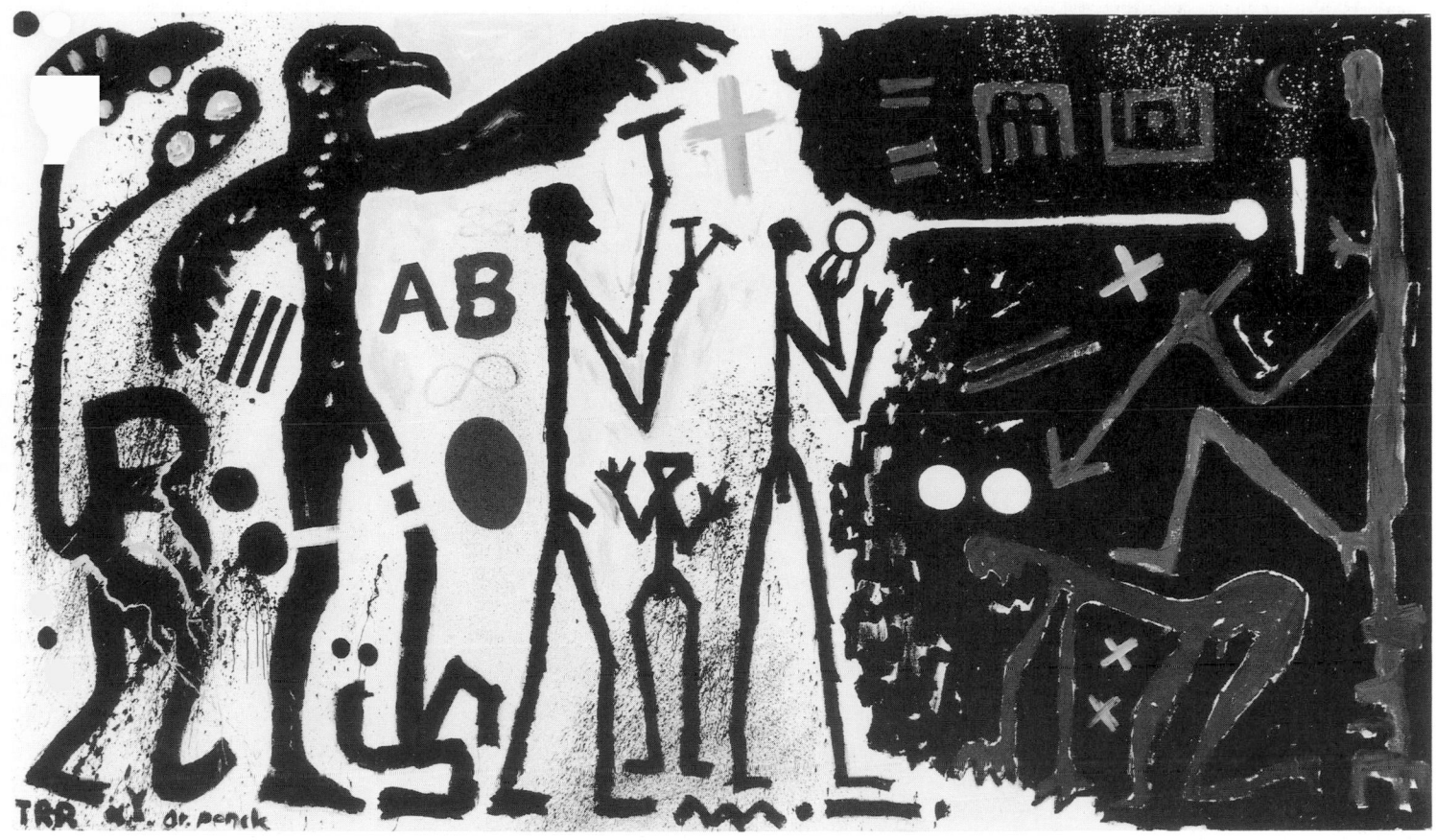

A. R. Penck: *T R R*, 1982

1987   *Mathematik in der Kunst,* Wilhelm-Hack-Museum,
        Ludwigshafen, West GErmany

Collections:

Stedelijk Museum, Amsterdam; Van Abbemuseum, Eindhoven; Kaiser-Wilhelm-Museum, Krefeld; Neue Galerie-Sammlung Ludwig, Aachen; Kunsthalle, Basle; Museum of Fine Arts, Boston.

Publications:

By PENCK: books—*Standart Making,* Munich 1970: *Was ist Standart,* Cologne and New York 1970; *Ich. Standart Lieratur,* Paris 1971; *Zeichen als Verstandigung,* exhibition catalogue, Krefeld, West Germany 1971; *Standart: Deskriptive Einfuhrung 1 + 2,* Milan 1973; *Europaische Sonette,* Antwerp 1974; *Sanfte Theorie über Arsch, Asche und Vegetation,* Groningen 1979; *Immendorff besucht y. Deutschland mal Deutschland—Ein Deutsch-Deustcher Vertrag,* with Jorg Immendorff, Munich 1979; *Kneipen und Kneipentexte,* Dresden 1980; *Je suis un livre: achetez-moi maintenant,* Paris 1981; *Ende im Osten: 98 Zeichnungen,* West Berlin 1981; *A. R. Penck: Paris Graphik* Munich 1984; *Welt des Adlers,* West Berlin 1985; *Standart-Modelle 1973/74,* Cologne 1985; *Standart 1971/73,* West Berlin 1985; *Mein Denken,* edited by Klaus Gallwitz, Frankfurt 1986; articles—"Der Adler" in *Interfunktionen* (Cologne), no. 1, 1974; "Ich über Mich Selbst" in *Kunstforum International* (Mainz), December/January 1975; editor, *Krater und Wolke* (Cologne), no. 1, 1982.

On PENCK: books—*A. R. Penck,* exhibition catalogue, with texts by Johannes Gachnang and Dieter Koepplin, Basle 1975; *A. R. Penck,* exhibition catalogue, with text by Günther Gercken, Hamburg 1975; *A. R. Penck: Zeichnungen bis 1975,* exhibition catalogue, with texts by Johannes Gachnang and Dieter Koepplin, Basle 1978; *A. R. Penck: Concept Conceptruimte,* exhibition catalogue, with texts by Wim A. L. Beeren, Johannes Gachnang, M. Visser and others, Rotterdam 1979; *A. R. Penck: Gemalde, Handzeichnungen,* exhibition catalogue, with text by Siegfried Gohr, Cologne 1981; *A. R. Penck,* exhibition catalogue, with text by Johannes Gachnang, Berne 1981; *A. R. Penck: 38 neue bilder,* exhibition catalogue, with text by Günther Gercken, Hamburg

1981; *A. R. Penck,* exhibition catalogue, with text by Richard Calvocoressi, London 1982; *A. R. Penck: 45 Zeichnungen,* exhibition catalogue with text by Dieter Koepplin, Basle and Bonn 1982; *A. R. Penck: Brown's Hotel and Other Works,* exhibition catalogue with text by Richard Calvocoressi, London 1984; *A. R. Penck: Mike Hammer—Konsequenzen,* exhibition catalogue with text by Johannes Cladders, Monchengladbach 1985; *A. R. Penck: Graphik Ost/West,* exhibition catalogue with text by D. Bojescul, Braunschwieg 1986; *Penck West in Berlin—Zeichnungen aus den Jahren 1980–1982,* exhibition catalogue with text by Wieland Schmied, West Berlin 1987.

*   *   *

Penck received no formal artistic training and was given his first public exhibition in East Germany in 1956. Shortly before the building of the Berlin Wall in 1961 he exhibited at the Akademie der Kunst in East Berlin. Penck gave up painting for two years, going back to it in 1963 on being given a commission by an architects' co-operative to paint a mural for four walls of a Dresden cellar. He painted a black line representing the border between East and West with soldiers shown shooting each other and sprawled on the ground. This has been described as resembling the prehistoric hunting scenes found on the walls of caves in Southern France and Northern Spain. By 1965 when Penck participated in an exhibition at the Pushkin House, Dresden, he was falling out with the authorities which made it difficult for him to exhibit publicly. His pictures were smuggled to the West for his first solo show at Galerie Michael Werner in Cologne in 1969. In 1973 Penck's name was found to be a pseudonym, which had been successfully used to hide his name while his work was on show in the west. By 1980 his position had become extremely difficult in Dresden where he could not sell his pictures legally. He was "bought out" and allowed to immigrate to the west. In 1983 he moved to London.

In the 1982 Waddington Gallery and 1985 Tate Gallery catalogues of Penck exhibitions Richard Calvocoressi has explained the paintings as an elaborate method of picture writing which the artist uses to communicate his bleak understanding of human behavior. His picture surfaces have, scattered across

them, "geometric or archetypal forms, symbols from mathematics or logic, hieroglyphs, emblematic objects (orb, eagle, death-mask, flower), the occasional face or head, often in pictorial shorthand, and large, anonymous, stick-like figures, singles or in pairs . . . . The key to all this is Penck's interest in cybernetics, information theory, codes and cyphers, imaginatively and humorously exploited." The paintings are not to be seen though as the kind of "automatic writing" as used in Surrealism, but carefully thought out in advance.

Since coming to the west, Penck has explored a great variety of artistic outlets, such as sculpture, book making, prints, music and the occasional film. Such is his mistrust, though, of the artist's recognizable style, the artist's "handwriting", (and in this he is not alone among his generation), that he still uses various pseudonyms, (such as Mike Hammer, TM, Ypsilon, Alpha), to correspond to different areas of his artistic output.

—Victoria Keller

PENONE, Giuseppe.
Italian. Born in Garessio Ponte, 3 April 1947. Independent Artist, Turin, since 1967. Agents: Galerie Paul Maenz, Bismarkstrasse 50, 5000 Cologne 1, West Germany; Galleria Christian Stein, Turin and Milan. Address: c/o Galleria Christian Stein, Piazza San Carlo, 10121 Turin, Italy.

Individual Exhibitions:

1968   Deposito d'Arte Presente, Turin
1969   Galleria Sperone, Turin
1970   Aktionsraum 1, Munich
        Galleria Toselli, Milan
1972   Galerie Paul Maenz, Cologne

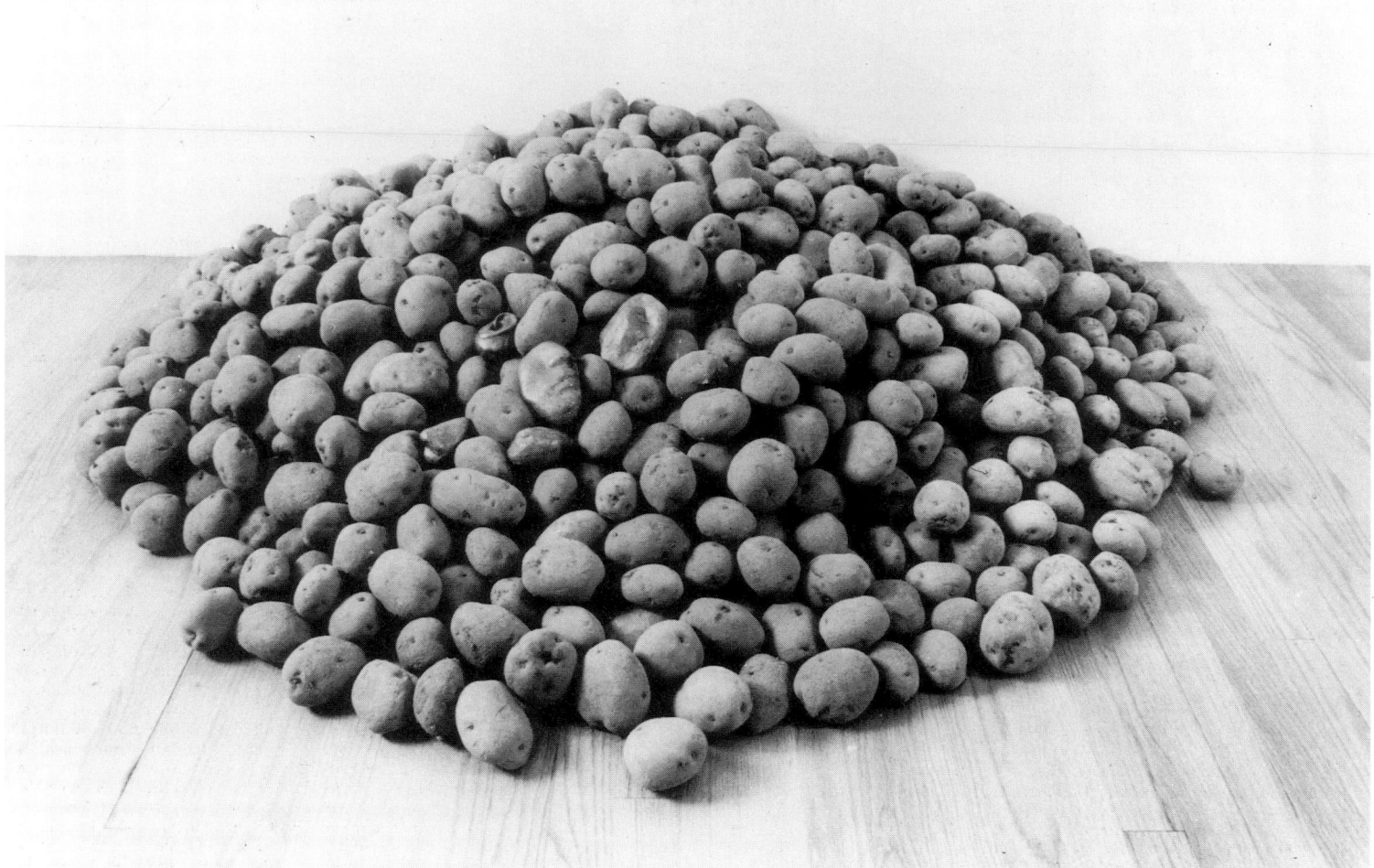

Giuseppe Penone: *Potatoes*, 1977

1973	Galleria Multipli, Turin
	Galleria Sperone, Turin
	Galleria Toselli, Milan
	Galerie Klaus Lupke, Frankfurt
	Galerie Paul Maenz, Cologne
1974	Galleria Sperone/Fischer, Rome
	Galerie 't Venster, Rotterdam
	Galleria Schema, Florence
1975	Galerie Paul Maenz, Cologne
	Samangalleria, Genoa, Italy
	Galleria Sperone, Turin
	Sperone Gallery, New York
1976	Nuovi Strumenti, Brescia, Italy
	Studio De Ambrogi, Milan
1977	Kunstmuseum, Lucerne
1978	Galerie Paul Maenz, Cologne
	Galerie Rudolf Zwirner, Cologne
	Staatliche Kunsthalle, Baden-Baden, West Germany
	Galleria Salvatore Ala, Milan
	Museum Folkwang, Essen, West Germany
	Galleria De Crescenzo, Rome
1979	Galerie Durand-Dessert, Paris
	Studio G7, Bologna
	Halle fur Internationale Neue Kunst, Zurich
1980	Galerie Helen van der Meij, Amsterdam
	Stedelijk Museum, Amsterdam
	Kabinett fur Aktuelle Kunst, Bremerhaven, West Germany
	Ausstellungsstudio, Mochengladbach, West Germany
	Galleria Christian Stein, Turin
	Lisson Gallery, London
	Galerie Gewad, Ghent, Belgium
1981	Salvatore Ala Gallery, New York
	Galerie Konrad Fischer, Zurich
1982	Stadtisches Museum, Monchengaldbach, West Germany
	Salvatore Ala Gallery, New York
	Galerie Konrad Fischer, Zurich

1983	Galleria Salvatore Ala, Milan
	Galleria Christian Stein, Turin
	Galerie Durand-Dessert, Paris
	National Gallery of Canada, Ottawa
1984	Fort Worth Art Museum, Texas
	Museum of Contemporary Art, Chicago
	Musée d'Art Moderne de la Ville, Paris
1986	Galerie Buchmann, Basle
1987	Galleria Christian Stein, Milan

Selected Group Exhibitions:

1969	*Konzeption-Conception*, Stadtisches Museum, Leverkusen, West Germany
1970	*Conceptual Art, Arte Povera, Land Art*, Galleria Civia d'Arte Moderna, Turin
1972	*Documenta 5*, Museum Fridericianum, Kassel, West Germany
1974	*Die verlorene Identitat*, Stadtisches Museum, Leverkusen, West Germany
1976	*Identite-Identification*, Centre d'Art Plastique Contemporain, Bordeaux, France
1978	*XXXVIII Biennale*, Venice (and *XXXIX Biennale*, 1980)
1981	*Identite Italienne: l'art en Italie depuis 1959*, Centre Georges Pompidou, Paris
1982	*Italian Art Now: An American Perspective*, Guggenheim Museum, New York
1984	*Il Modo Italiano*, Los Angeles Institute of Contemporary Art

Publications:

By PENONE: books—*Svolgere la propria pelle*, Turin 1971; *Rovesciare gli occhi*, with Jean-Christophe Ammann, Turin 1977.

On PENONE: books—*Arte Povera: Conceptual, Actual or Impossible Art* By Germano Celant, Milan 1969; *Giuseppe Penone*, exhibition catalogue with texts by Jean-Christophe Ammann and Ugo Castagnotto, Lucerne 1977; *Giuseppe Penone*, exhibition catalogue with texts by Jean-Christophe Ammann, Renato Barilli and Hans Albert Peters, Baden-Baden 1978; *Giuseppe Penone*, exhibition catalogue with essay by Germano Celant, Amsterdam 1980; *La Vision Poetique de Giuseppe Penone*, exhibition catalogue with essay by Jessica Bradley, Ottawa 1983.

From the beginning of 1968, Penone's work has been marked by a radical departure from traditional artistic movements towards a natural, almost 'artless' ambience. Through a direct physical contact with nature, Perone has interacted with the processes of physical growth to represent these elements and processes in the form of photographic documentation. These interactions were later effected in the studio. In many works, Penone emphasized the presence of the body—of the hand, for instance, by means of imprints pressed onto a wide range of materials, thus creating a metaphor for psycho-physical energy or a metonym for the universe.

Penone is searching for indices in the sense that American philosopher Charles Peirce describes: the index is a sign "which attracts attention towards a particular object without actually describing it" while maintaining "a direct physical connection" with that object. Thus the image in its early stages of formation is still linked to organic phenomena. Works such as *To Unfold One's Own Skin, Gypsum Print and Projections*, or *Coincidence of Images* promote a tactile reading of the object, of space, of a part of the body or corporeal substance. At the root of the work is a direct connection between the psychological and the physical, between the artist and the materials upon which the epidermis of the skin leaves its traces.

In other cases, again it is the body which generates forms, as in the terracottas that bear the imprint of the hand or of the inside of the mouth—or in an evocative projection of the body in the form of his breath affecting the surface of archaic 'vases' in a work of 1978. Whenever Penone evokes the image via the standpoint or 'topos' of the self-portrait, he does so in order to negate its role as a privileged route of information.

Central to the group Arte Povera, of which Penone is one of the foremost representatives, form and image are integrated outside traditional systems. Penone's most recent works empathise with nature to a lesser extent. On the one hand are installations in which the image is recognizable and distinct, and on the other is an 'activation' of metaphor which comes very close making the message redundant. Penone rarely uses the customary artists' materials, preferring to work with earth, vegetables, vases and bronze castings which continue to take on the character of plant life—tree forms, bark and branches—and the anthropomorphic, thus imposing the natural event within the very heart of artifice.

—Giorgio Verzotti

PEPPER, Beverly.

American. Born Beverly Stoll in Brooklyn, New York, 20 December 1924. Studied industrial and advertising design at the Pratt Institute, Brooklyn, New York, 1939–41, B.A. 1941; Art Students League, New York, 1946; Atelier André Lhote, Paris, 1948; Atelier Fernand Léger, Paris, 1949. Married Lawrence Gussin in 1941 (divorced, 1948); son: John Randolph; married Curtis Gordon (Bill) Pepper in 1949; son: Jorie Sheppard Graham. Worked as art director for numerous advertising agencies, New York, 1942–48. Independent artist, since 1949, travelling extensively in Europe and North Africa; lived in Paris and Haut du Cagnes, France, 1949–50, and in Positano, Italy, 1951–52, settling in Rome in 1952; travelled in Far East and India, being especially influenced by Cambodian Khmer sculpture, 1960; concentrated on sculpture, Rome, 1961; moved to Torre Gentile di Todi, Perugia, Italy, 1972. Recipient: Gold Medal and Sculpture Purchase Award, *Mostra Internazionale Fiorino*, Italy, 1966; First Prize and Purchase Award, Jacksonville Art Museum, Florida 1970; Best Art in Steel Award, Iron and Steel Industry, New York, 1970; Central Service Administration Grant, Washington, D.C., 1974; National Endowment for the Arts Award, 1975. D.F.A.: Pratt Institute, New York, 1982; Maryland Institute, Baltimore, 1983. Agent: André Emmerich Gallery, 41 East 57th Street, New York, New York 10022, U.S.A. Addresses: 84 Thomas Street, New York, New York 10015, U.S.A.; Torre Gentile di Todi, Perugia 06059, Italy.

Individual Exhibitions:

1952	Galleria dello Zodiaco, Rome
1954	Barone Gallery, New York
1955	Obelisk Gallery, Washington, D.C.
1956	Galleria Schneider, Rome
	Barone Gallery, New York
1958	Barone Gallery, New York
1959	Galleria dell'Obelisco, Rome
1961	Galleria Pogliani, Rome
1962	Thibaut Gallery, New York
1965	Marlborough Galleria d'Arte, Rome
1966	McCormick Place, Chicago
1967	Jewish Museum, New York
1968	Marlborough Galleria d'Arte, Rome
	Galleria La Bussola, Turin
	Galleria Paolo Barozzi, Venice
1969	Marlborough Gallery, New York
	Museum of Contemporary Art, Chicago
	Hayden Court and Plaza, Massachusetts Institute of Technology, Cambridge
	Albright-Knox Art Gallery, Buffalo, New York
1970	Everson Museum, Syracuse, New York
	Piazza della Rotonda, Milan
	Studio Marconi, Milan
1971	Galerie Hella Nebelung, Dusseldorf
	Piazza Margana, Rome
	470 Parker Street Gallery, Boston
1972	Qui Arte Contemporanea, Rome
	Marlborough Galleria d'Arte, Rome
1973	Tyler School of Art, Temple University Abroad, Rome
1975	Hammarskjold Plaza Sculpture Garden, New York
	André Emmerich Gallery, New York
1976	San Francisco Museum of Modern Art
1977	André Emmerich Gallery, New York
	Rosa Freudenheim Gallery, New York
	Seattle Museum of Contemporary Art
	Indianapolis Museum of Art
	Hopkins Art Center, Dartmouth College, Hanover, New Hampshire
1978	Princeton Art Museum, New Jersey
	Indianapolis Museum of Art
1979	André Emmerich Gallery, New York
	Hofstra University, Hempstead, New York
	Piazza Mostra, Todi, Perugia, Italy
	Piazza Maggiore, Todi, Perugia, Italy
1980	Nina Freudenheim Gallery, Buffalo, New York
	Thomas Segal Gallery, Boston
	André Emmerich Gallery, New York
	André Emmerich Gallery, Zurich
	Ronald Greenberg Gallery, St. Louis
1981	Makler Gallery, Philadelphia
	Linda Farris Gallery, Seattle, Washington
	Davenport Gallery, Iowa
	Hansen Fuller Goldeen Gallery, San Francisco
1982	André Emmerich Gallery, New York
	Laumeier Sculpture Park, St. Louis
	Yares Gallery, Scottsdale, Arizona
	Galleria Il Ponte, Rome
1983	Gimpel-Hanover and André Emmerich Galerien, Zurich
	André Emmerich Gallery, New York
	Huntington Galleries, West Virginia
	John Berggruen Gallery, San Francisco
1984	André Emmerich Gallery, New York
1985	Adams-Middleton Gallery, Dallas
	John Berggruen Gallery, San Francisco
1986	André Emmerich Gallery, New York
	Albright-Knox Art Gallery, Buffalo, New York (travelled to San Francisco; Columbus, Ohio; Brooklyn, New York; Miami, Florida, 1986–88)

Selected Group Exhibitions:

1961	*The Quest and the Quarry*, Rome/New York Art Foundation, Rome
1968	*Plus by Minus: Today's Half-Century*, Albright-Knox Art Gallery, Buffalo, New York
1972	*XXIII Biennale*, Venice
1976	*Women Artists '76*, McNay Art Institute, San Antonio, Texas
1978	*Drawings for Outdoor Sculpture 1946–1977*, John Weber 3, New York
1980	*Drawings*, Nina Freudenheim Gallery, Buffalo, New York
1981	*All in Line: An Exhibition of Linear Drawing*, Lowe Art Gallery, Syracuse University, New York (travelled to Terry Dintenfass Gallery, New York)
1985	*The Artist as Social Designer*, Los Angeles Institute of Contemporary Art

Collections:

Fogg Art Museum, Harvard University, Cambridge, Massachusetts; Massachusetts Institute of Technology, Cambridge; Albright-Knox Art Gallery, Buffalo, New York; Vassar College, Poughkeepsie, New York; Dartmouth College, Hanover, New Hampshire; Hirshhorn Museum, Washington, D.C.; Indianapolis Museum of Art,; Walker Art Center, Minneapolis; Galleria Civica d'Arte Moderna, Turin; installations include:—Richard J. Hughes Justice Complex, Trenton New Jersey; Four-Leaf Towers, Houston; Phoenix Center, Pontiac, Michigan; Johns Hopkins Hospital, Baltimore; First Interstate Center, Seattle; Sol y Ombra Park, Barcelona, Spain.

Publications:

By PEPPER: pamphlet—*Public Sculpture and Its Public*, for the National Council on Arts Administration, Washington, D.C., March 1979; article—"Space, Time and Nature in Monumental Sculpture" in *Art Journal* (New York), Spring 1978.

On PEPPER: books—*Passages in Modern Sculpture* by Rosalind Krauss, New York 1977; *Originals: American Women Artists* by Eleanor Munro, New York 1979; *Beverly Pepper in Todi*, exhibition catalogue, with an introduction by Roberto Abbondanza, texts by Marisa Volpi Orlandini and Sam Hunter, Todi, Perugia, Italy 1979; *Acquisitions 1974–78*, exhibition catalogue, Jan van der Marck, Hanover, New Hampshire 1979; *Contemporary Artists at Work: Sculptors, Vol. 2*, New York 1980; *Beverly Pepper: The Moline Markers*, exhibition catalogue with essay by Phyllis Tuchman, Davenport, Iowa 1981; *Currents: Contemporary Trends in the Visual Arts* by Howard Smagula, New York 1983; *Beverly Pepper*, exhibition catalogue with text by Ronny Cohen, New York 1986; *Beverly Pepper: Sculpture in Place*, with texts by Douglas G. Schultz and Rosalind E. Krauss, New York 1986; articles—"Beverly Pepper" by Virgilio Guzzi in *Il Tempo* (Milan), December 1952; "Beverly Pepper" by Lawrence Campbell in *Artnews* (New York), December 1954; "Beverly Pepper" by E. M. Munroe in *Artnews* (New York), December 1956; "Beverly Pepper" by Giovanni Carandente in *Arte Oggi* (Milan), October 1961; "Plus by Minus" by Douglas McAgy in *Art Gallery* (Ivoryton, Connecticut), 1968; "Beverly Pepper, Galleria Hella Nebelung" by Y. Friedrichs in *Das Kunstwerk* (Baden-Baden, West Germany), July 1971; "Art" by Robert Hughes in *Time* (New York), June 1975; "A Space Has Many Aspects" by Jan Butterfield in *Arts Magazine* (New York) September 1975; "New York Letter" by Carter Ratcliff in *Art International* (Lugano, Switzerland), no. 6, 1977; "Arte Actuel" by Jean-Luc Daval in *Skira Annual*, Geneva 1978; "Beverly Pepper's New Sculpture" by Margaret Sheffield in *Arts Magazine* (New York), September 1979; "Monument/Sculpture/Earthwork" by Nancy Foote in *Artforum* (New York), October 1979; "The Sculpture of Beverly Pepper" By Will Ameringer in *Arts Magazine* (New York), October 1983; "Interconnections: Beverly Pepper" by Kenneth Baker in *Art in America* (New York), April 1984; "Beverly Pepper" by Jane Bell in *Art News* (New York), February 1985.

If I talk about the formal problems that involve me, it is because the abstract language of form that I have chosen has become a way to explore an interior life of feeling. In this way, my forms mirror emotional reality. The problems to which I have consistently linked my work concern the question of sculptural illusion. Put briefly, I wish to make an object that has a powerful physical presence, but is at the same time inwardly turned, seeming capable of intense self-absorption.

The works I made of highly polished stainless steel in the late 1960's achieved this kind of dualism primarily through the mirror-like finish of their surface. Those surfaces acted to emphasize the actual weight and density of the steel. At the same time they made the physical bulk of the sculpture withdraw behind a screen of reflections.

Under certain light conditions and from certain angles this reflectivity picks up the sculpture's environment—sky, grass, earth. This causes the work almost to disappear, so that all that remains visible is the network of blue enamel lines that indicates the interior faces of the forms. From other angles, the surfaces reflect into one another, causing geometries to appear which are not part of the physical format of the work. But even though these internal reflections are illusions, they do in fact prefigure the actual shape the crystalline forms will appear to have, when viewed from another angle. In this way the reflected illusions seem to be sculptor's "anima"—appearing to generate its total being, from within the shifting depths of the mirror.

Reflection may be the most obvious way to generate illusions; but there are other ways that are equally direct. One of these is forced (and therefore false) perspective, which I began to concentrate on in the

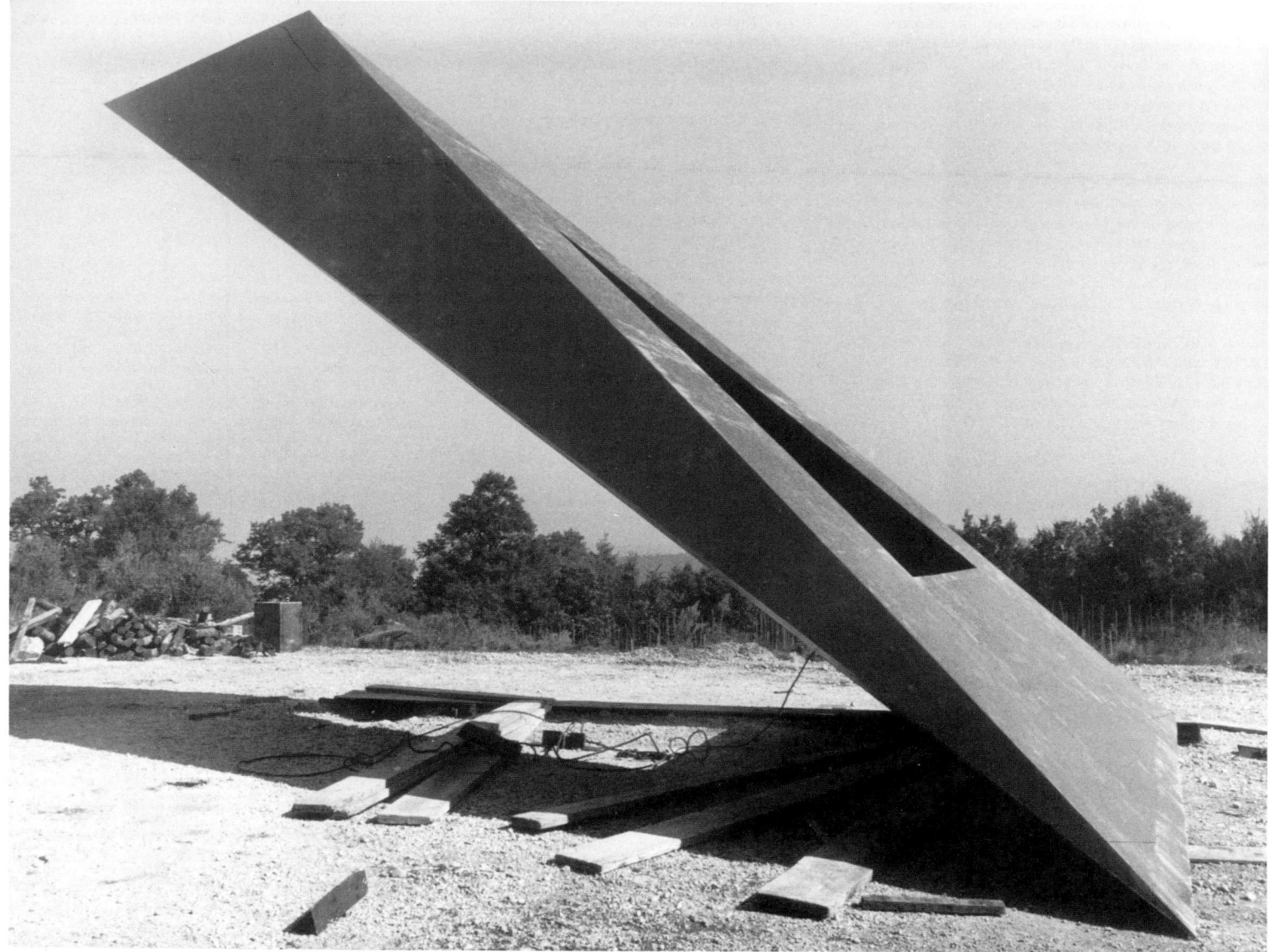

Beverly Pepper: *Phaedra*, 1976

early 1970's. "Exodus" (1972), for example, is a large stainless steel pyramid which contains a pyramidal void. Because of the eccentric relationship between solid and void, the position of the void appears to be tunneling in a different direction from the one revealed by the other side of the sculpture. So when the viewer actually moves around to the other side of the work and sees another triangular opening, it is not clear that the two openings into the inside of the volume are related. The illusion is that somewhere inside the sculpture the continuity of the inner form has been disrupted, or diverted from one configuration to another.

It is the perspective relationship between mass and void that causes this apparent shift. The effect of this is that the inner reaches of a very simple geometrical form appear mysteriously able to create relationships whose logic is not clear to the viewer but is instead very private. And a result of this mysteriousness is that the massiveness of the physical form is suspended—or made to seem quite thin—as the viewer tries to correlate the flat shapes formed on the front and back of the sculpture.

In my recent work I have tried to maintain this precarious balance between the physically self-evident and the sense of an elusive inner logic. In "Alpha" (1974) I used four triangular sheaths—joined to form two pairs—to give an intense experience of the generative power of the interior, from which the sheaths develop or peel away. As in "Exodus," we have here

two parts of a work that are obviously related to one another but are puzzlingly incapable of logical fusion. Looking back at the decisions I made while working on "Alpha," I realize now they came from the same emotional source that has formed all my work. I want the sculptures to seem to be creating relationsips which are very simple, yet at the same time are beyond the viewer's grasp. I want it to seem as though an inexplicable coherence works inside the sculpture to generate external aspects of its physical being which are always unexpected because they are unpredictable.

In my work, the image comes from within me—an "emotion" that is released. I then apply whatever critical abilities I possess to allow the intermingling of the intellect and emotion. Even if there is a conflict and contradiction among these two, I allow them to feed into one another and eventually merge into one being.

—Beverly Pepper

Since the early 1960s Beverly Pepper's sculpture has undergone significant formal changes. The monumental steel columns of the early 1980's mark a radical departure from the geometric steel sculpture and environmental works of the 1970's. Yet the columns, with their strong references to architectonic structures like obelisks and memorial stones, share with the earlier work an intrinsic power that significantly alters

whatever environment in which they are situated. Pepper's sculpture has the power to retain its integrity as sculpture but the graciousness to understand its location in a place. Significant examples of this aspect of her art are "Thel," installed at Dartmouth College, New Hampshire in 1977, and "Amphisculpture" of 1974–75 at the AT&T Long Lines Center, Bedminister, New Jersey. Both works are monumental in their proportions yet literally become part of the landscape. Scale for Pepper is a human quality and one she tempers with a consciousness of geography and place.

Few sculptors have been as successful as Pepper in avoiding the blankness of geometry characterized by decorative forms that have meaning only as pure form. Pepper's art is insistently meaningful and devoid of superfluous moments and gestures. There has always been a sense of mystery in the massive forms she constructs, but the columns of recent vintage are perhaps the richest in a sense of history and time. First exhibited in the piazza at Todi, Italy, the columns are as monumental as the earlier horizontal sculptures, yet have a vocabulary which permits experience, time and history to become dominant elements. The piazza at Todi provided a superb location for the columns, but their intrinsic power is such that even in other less historically rich locations, there is a quality of self-absorption and mystery about the work which suggests a new form for the term "monument."

—Katharine Smith

PERILLI, Achille.

Italian. Born in Rome, 28 January 1927. Studied history of art at the University of Rome, 1945–46. Painter: Founder-Member, with Pietro Consagra, Piero Dorazio and others, Forma I, Rome, 1947; visited Paris, and met Hans Arp, Francis Picabia, Alberto Magnelli and Antoine Pevsner, 1948; Member, Movimento Arte Concreta, Rome 1948; travelled in Austria and Germany, 1949, and lived in Paris, 1950–51; Founder, with Dorazio, *Arte Visive* magazine, Rome, 1952; travelled in Spain and Germany, 1954–55; Associated with Hannah Höch, and influenced by the Dada group, Berlin, 1955; Founder, with Gastone Novelli, *L'Esperienza Moderna* magazine, Rome, 1957–59; worked on theatrical designs, including *Collage* ballet, Teatro Elisco, Rome, 1961; Founder, with Novelli and others, *Grammatica* magazine, Rome, 1964, and, with others, Altro group, Rome, 1973; worked on theatrical designs for Rome Opera, *Dies Irae*, 1978. Lecturer in Visual Communications, School for Industrial Design, Rome, 1965. Recipient: Premio Fontana, *Biennale di San Marino,* 1963; Premio Comune di Roma, *Quadriennale di Roma,* 1965; Premio Lugano, Switzerland 1968; Prize for Drawing, *International Exhibition of Graphics,* Rijeka, Yugoslavia, 1970. Agent: Frankfurter Westend Galerie, Arndtstrasse 12, 6000 Frankfurt am Main, West Germany. Address: Largo Arenula 34, 00186 Rome, Italy.

Individual Exhibitions:

1956	Galleria Strozzina, Florence
1957	Galleria La Tartaruga, Rome
1958	Galleria del Naviglio, Milan
1959	*Bienal,* Sao Paulo
	Galleria del Cavallino, Venice
1960	Galleria La Tartaruga, Rome
	Galleria del Naviglio, Milan
	Galleria Souza, Mexico City
1962	*Biennale,* Venice
	Galerie Creuze, Paris
1963	Bonino Gallery, New York
1964	Kunstverein, Freiburg
	Galerie Baier, Mainz
	Galleria del Deposito, Genoa
1965	Felix Landau Gallery, Los Angeles
	Galleria La Tartaruga, Rome
1966	Galleria del Naviglio, Milan
	Court Gallery, Copenhagen
	Galleria Il Segno, Rome
1967	Marlborough Galleria d'Arte, Rome
1968	*Biennale,* Venice
	Galleria La Sfera, Modena, Italy
	Galleria Rotta, Genoa
1969	Gallery, Foksal, Warsaw
	Galleria Alfieri, Venice
1970	Grafica Romero, Rome
	Galleria m'Arte, Milan
	Narodni Gallery, Prague
1971	Galerie Forum, Zagreb
	Jacques Baruch Gallery, Chicago
	Galerie Espace, Amsterdam
	Marlborough Galleria d'Arte, Rome
	Galleria La Bussola, Turin
	Galleria Rotta, Milan
	West End Galerie, Frankfurt
1972	Galerie Grondahl, Copenhagen
	Grafica Romero, Rome
	Marlborough Galleria d'Arte, Rome
	Galleria Quattro Venti, Palermo
1973	Marlborough Galerie, Zurich
	10th Quadriennale Nazionale d'Arte, Rome
	Nova Arte Moderne, Prato, Italy
	Musée des Beaux-Arts, La Chaux de Fonds, Switzerland
1974	3A Galleria d'Arte Moderna, Turin
	Galleria Spagnoli, Florence
	Galleria Il Milione, Milan
	Galleria Ravagnan, Venice
1975	Marlborough Galleria d'Arte, Rome
	La Tavolozza, Palermo, Sicily
	La Permanente, Cesena, Italy

1976	Circolo della Stampa, Messina, Sicily
	Galleria Rotta, Genoa
	Studio Soldano, Milan
	Galleria Linea 70, Verona
1977	Palazzo dei Diamanti, Ferrara, Italy
	Lo Spazio della Pittura 1947–1977, Trissino, Italy
	Palazzo Tomitano, Feltre, Italy
1978	Galleria Lo Spazio, Naples
1980	Studio F22, Palazzolo sull-Oglio, Italy
	Galleria Vismara, Milan
	Galerie d'Art International, Paris
1981	West End Galerie, Frankfurt
1982	Studio F22, Palazzolo sull'Oglio, Italy
	Galleria Giuli, Lecco, Italy
	Galleria Bluart, Varese, Italy
	Galleria d'Arte, Republic of San Marino
1983	Galleria Editalia, at the *Fiera di Bari,* Italy
	Galleria Editalia, Rome
	Galleria Arte Duchamp, Cagliari, Italy
1984	Galleria Il Segno, Pordenone, Italy
	Paris Art Center, Paris
	Studio F22, Palazzolo sull'Oglio, Italy
	Galleria Le Pietre, Arenzano, Italy
	Galleria Ariele, Vicenza, Italy
	Galleria Il Millennio, Rome
	Galleria Peccolo, Livorno, Italy
	Galleria Spriano, Omegna, Italy
1985	Galleria La Panchetta, Bari, Italy
	Galerie d'Art International, Paris
	Studio Mara Coccia, Rome
	Galleria La Scaletta, Matera, Italy
	Free Time Club, Cesena, Italy
	Galleria Luce, Venice
	Galleria Fioretto, Padua, Italy
	Galleria Maurizio Corradini, Mantua, Italy
1986	Studio Mara Coccia, at the *Fiera dell'Arte,* Bologna, Italy
	Galleria Morone 6, Milan
	Galleria Emiclea, Gaeta, Italy.

	Studio F22, Palazzolo sull'Oglio, Italy
	Galerie d'Art International, at *FIAC 86,* Grand Palais, Paris
	Accademia dei Concordi, Rovigo, Italy
1987	Free Time Club, at the *Fiera di Bologna,* Italy
	Galleria Maurizio Corradini, at the *Fiera di Bari,* Italy
	Galleria Meta, Bolzano, Italy
	Spazio Studio d'Arte, Bologna, Italy
	Studio Santandrea, Savona, Italy

Selected Group Exhibitions:

1948	*Quadriennale,* Rome
1950	*Biennale,* Venice
1957	*Painting in Post-War Italy 1945–1957,* Columbia University, New York
1961	*Art Italien Aujourd'hui,* Galerie International d'Art Contemporain, Paris
1968	*Recent Italian Paintings and Sculpture,* Jewish Museum, New York
1971	*20 Artistas Italianos,* Museo de Arte Moderna, Mexico City
1980	*Italian Graphic Abstract Art,* Museum of Modern Art, Haifa
1982	*Goethe und Italien,* West End Galerie, Frankfurt
1985	*Nouvelles Tapisseries,* Paris Art Center, Paris
1987	*L'Informale in Italia,* Kunstmuseum, Lucerne, Switzerland

Collections:

Galleria Nazionale d'Arte Moderna, Rome; Galleria Comunale, Rome; Ca' Pesaro, Venice; National Gallery, Prague; Musée des Beaux Arts, La Chaux de Fonds, Switzerland; Washington University, St. Louis, Missouri.

Achille Perilli: *La Sommossa Ergonomica,* 1986

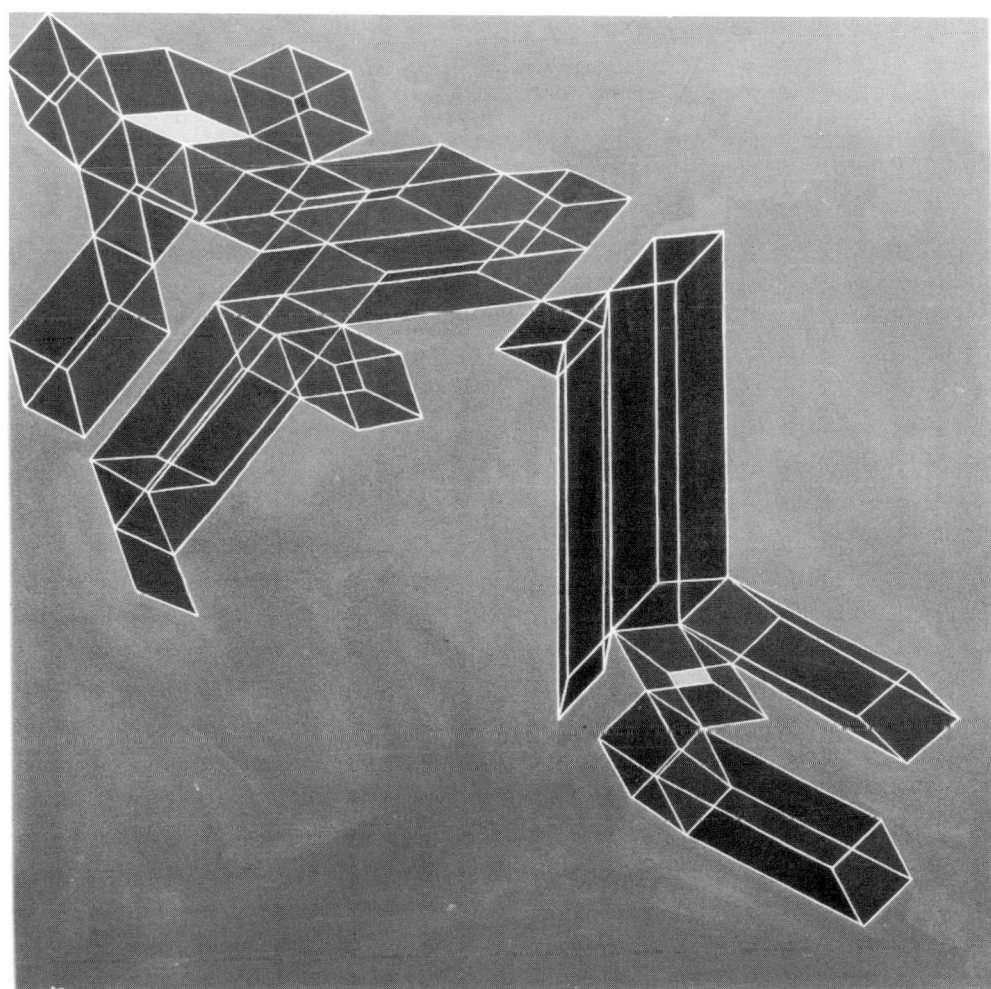

Publications:

On PERILLI: books—*Achille Perilli*, exhibition catalogue, by Umbro Apollonio, Venice 1962; *Achille Perilli*, exhibition catalogue, by Margit Stabler, Zurich 1973; *L'Arte in Italia dopo la seconda guerra mondiale* by Giorgio De Marchis, Turin 1982; *Achille Perilli—Continuum 1947/1982*, exhibition catalogue by Francesco Vincitorio, San Marino 1982; *Achille Perilli: L'irrazionale geometrico*, exhibition catalogue by G. C. Argan, Paris 1984; articles—"Perilli e la Comunicazione Efficace" by Bruno Alfieri in *Metro* (Milan), no. 6, 1962; "Achille Perilli: Immagine e Organizzazione" by Nello Ponente in *Civiltà delle Macchine* (Rome), March 1967; "Achille Perilli" by Milton Gendel in *Art International* (Lugano, Switzerland), vol. 15, no. 9, 1971; "The Painting Thought of Achille Perilli" by Roger Bordier in *Cimaise* (Paris), 1982.

In re-examining those visual experiences which, during the course of the century, have been generically labelled as abstractionism, one seems to perceive, amongst the few theoretical certainties and the many poetic uncertainties, a thread linking the attainment of rationalist truth to the decadence of the same and its formal dissolution.

The slow but constant shift from representation to presentation, based on the "linguistic" values of the code and the denial of iconographical communication, undoubtedly freed the artist from various influences which bound him to the idea of reality. The visual factor acquired a degree of autonomy with respect to the concept of reproduction and was no longer intended as evidence, a record or window on history, but as a manner of investigating the nature of the world and of mankind's existence. Thus it becomes an analysis of the structure of the visual world; as Klee wrote, "Art does not copy visible objects, but renders them visible."

This progress and occasional regression, this lengthy voyage was meant to illuminate, uncover and reveal the most subtle workings of vision; to reproduce the procedure of focusing the image; to communicate it by means of an analytical methodology; and, above all, to extract from the depths of our memory, the richest and most complex forms of knowledge. This process knew both absolute certainties and shattering failures, due to the difficulties of carrying out an enquiry comprehensive of the many possible interpretations available to investigators. One of the absolute certainties was the belief that to proceed on the basis of pure perception (the retina) was enough to rediscover the essential laws of vision; all other approaches were dismissed as spurious or insufficiently pure. This was a certainty which derived from the conviction that everything could be reduced to the essence of painting, which coincided with the essence of geometrical form—the fundamental crossing of the horizon with a vertical line on a white surface.

To reach this point it was necessary to reduce painting, or the investigation of painting, to an absolute. Beyond this absolute, the value of representation was no longer intended as a transcription of reality, or continuated by the necessity of transmitting a specific message (landscape, still life, portrait): it became a free component of pictorial activity, strengthened by the multiplication of "languages" through the ambiguity of speech (De Chirico, for instance, or Pop Art).

The equally drastic alternative was the re-examination of the possibilities inherent in media understood as material (canvas, paper, wood, burlap, glass and so forth): see Schwitters and most informal art. But when absolute certainty, the unchanging values of the horizontal and vertical, of the primary values, were recognized, then the feeling arose that the approach adopted had been mistaken from the start and should be corrected. The error, that of identifying the eye as the instrument of understanding, derived from centuries of habit and mental sloth which restricted visual perception to Durer's maxim: "First, the eye that sees; second, the object that is seen; third, the intervening distance."

It was not enough to remove the object and the distance in order to achieve the optimum effect, known as abstraction. Malevitch, having recognized the law of geometrical absolution, was able to admit: "This is why we are obliged to clarify that—there is a difference—and indeed a great contradiction between the creative work of the painter and pure optical activity." He continued: "Therefore we must conclude that the mutation of form and colour in artistic activity does not take place on the basis of visual optical perceptions, but as a consequence of their alterations in our mind; that is, in the creative imagination of the painter in whose mind the pictorial image has arisen."

The black square on the white square has a slight variation in measurement: it is an irregular square. The certainty of geometry has begun to yield to and to transform itself into the Suprematist painting of 1917—a geometric yellow form bathed in a light which dissolves into space. Certainty has by now completely given way to geometrical uncertainty, the conception of a geometrical form that is no longer determined by laws of mathematics or optics, but by slight dislocations and displacements produced by memory on the data of visual perception. Geometric irrationality has come into being as a result of the dissolution of geometricl form, its loss of weight, its escape from two-dimensionality: the instruments of enquiry have shifted decisively from perception to memory, together with all the knowledge, both conscious and unconscious, that the contemporary world has acquired. It is a shift so great as to produce a fundamental change in the visual world and in all future discoveries pertaining to it. It means "shaping imaginary space through a material object," as El Lissitskij foresaw.

What then is the imaginary space, if not a new mode of visual structure, a more complex contribution to our definition of knowledge which is no longer linked to the activity of the eye alone, but related to a series of more complex sensations and different perceptions? And, with respect to history, does not this shift from the certainty of reason to the the uncertainty of madness, reveal the decadence and dissolution of the utopia of technology, the safety of the megalopolis, faith in progress? Vantongerloo during his last years followed Malevitch's example, substituting the mysticism of form with the mysticism of mathematics.

The result was the same: the slow dissolution of geometrical certainty in favour of an open form permitting language to perceive the mysteries of the visual world through investigation.

In 1939 Variant seems to have extended its lines of force in space with an extraordinary essentiality of tension. For it is formal tension which causes the dissolution of form: it is tension which takes the place of order, certainty, safety.

Visual tension may only be achieved when several opposing forces are able to discharge themselves contemporaneously. When this takes place in a concentrated and "tense" space, such as geometrical space, the shifting of forces, the lessening of certainty—which interests me—then occurs. Form loses certainty and is transformed into a field of rapid motion, violent struggle, unbelievable deformations defining new, unknown and complex structures governed by laws which I defined in my 1975 manifesto *Machinerie, ma chere machine*: "From the relation between two geometric modules, occasionally in contrast, occasionally similar with slight variations, a sequence is born which tends to shift in space until . . . it spreads from picture to picture, evolving, associating with other factors, constantly increasing the complexity of the investigation of Imaginary Space. The interpretation of such sequences suggests passages which shatter the idea of central space, or superficial space or light space. To enter within or to stay without, to advance or to halt, are all acts of vision, not of perception, which require independent choices for each of the various possibilities suggested by the image. It is not necessary to alter or change the order of sequence: alteration, transformation are inherent in the manner of seeing the structure, in the ambiguity created by the shift from one level to another, from one chromatic law to another, from volume to void. Interpretation and observation must be extended in time to include successive stages of memorization, to analyze possible interpretations without being limited to formal structure, but taking into account all these materials belonging to the collective unconscious which inform the deepest levels of human consciousness.

It is a process which tends to broaden rather than restrict, to shift the field of enquiry from the perceptual to the mental; it rejects any minimalization of the uncertainties concentrated in the visual, expanding them so as to affect those uncharted areas between one code and another, and to implicate alien linguistic structures.

Such implications deny the severity of an absolute code, or a primary code and its unchangeable "linguistic" laws, since that code has already been transformed into *Another (Altro)* through a methodology which I call intercode: by working on areas which are affected by a law, but are not subject to it. Although these areas are sensitive to its presence and reality, the law itself is perceived with the greatest ambiguity possible, with respect to meaning and value, so as to allow all manner of deformations and transformations. Only then is creative imagination able to build a new utopia: geometrical non-form.

—Achille Perilli

Achille Perilli is one of the large group of talented Italian artists who came to maturity in the post-war period, and retained considerable attachment to and influence from Paris. He is one of the most diversely active and successful of his generation, embodying typical native brilliance as designer, graphic artist and polemicist; and also exceptionally successfully in his work the theatre. He is what might loosely be called a gestural artist, which gives him some attachment to Tachisme, most easily compared with the French painter Georges Mathier. Perilli, however, is much more truly "informal" than his French contemporary, saved by excellent technique and taste from the exhibitionistic excesses common to artists of his genre. Among the most attractive of his early works was a series entitled "Picture Stories," comic-strip compositions based on insect-like linear figures, arranged in sequences, contrasted with coloured zones, bands and right-angles. He usually works on monochrome backgrounds, pale, reticent colours on which graffiti-like motives are "scratched." They have connotations of cave-drawings, whilst at the same time conveying contemporary humor, part cynicism, part fear of the very thing made fun of. He later developed large-scale versions of these figures, entitlted "trasformazione della spazio," in which the relationship of the insect-like form to the space it occupied became important.

A brilliant draughtsman and designer, Perilli has produced splendid etchings, and other prints, as well as practising as a teacher of design. Work in the theatre ties in with his involvement with story-telling and the depiction of figures in space. He has designed ballets for La Scala, Milan and has worked with the Teatro Gruppo 63 of Palermo and other companies. Efforts to relate art objects to theatrical presentations have resulted in a number of fascinating productions—"Collage," 1961, which combined mobile sculpture, projections and music, and in 1967 "Grammatica No Stop Teatro." As an aesthetic activist, Perilli founded the group Forma I, in 1947, and has helped launch three important art magazines, *Art Visive*, 1952, *L'Esperienze Moderna*, 1957 and *Grammatica*, 1964.

—Charles Spencer

PETLIN, Irving.

American. Born in Chicago, Illinois, 17 December 1934. Educated at the Art Institute of Chicago, 1952–

56, B.F.A.; Yale University, with Josef Albers, New Haven, Connecticut, M.F.A. 1959. Served in the United States Army, 1957–59. Painter: lived in France, 1959–63; now lives and works in New York. Instructor, University of California at Los Angeles, 1963–66; Rhode Island School of Design, Providence, 1978; Cooper Union, New York, 1977–80; Artist-in-Residence, Dartmouth College, Hanover, New Hampshire, 1983. Recipient: Ryerson Fellowship, 1956; Copley Foundation Grant, 1961; Guggenheim Foundation Fellowship, 1971. Agent: Marlborough Gallery, 40 West 57th Street, New York, New York 10019. Address: 257 West 11th Street, New York, New York 10014, U.S.A.

Individual Exhibitions:

1956	Dilexi Gallery, San Francisco
	Cliffdwellers Gallery, Chicago
1960	Galerie du Dragon, Paris
1962	Galerie du Dragon, Paris
	Galleria Galatea, Turin
1963	Galerie du Dragon, Paris
1964	Galerie du Dragon, Paris
	Hanover Gallery, London
1965	Palais de Beaux-Arts, Brussels (retrospective)
1966	Rolf Nelson Gallery, Los Angeles
1967	Odyssia Gallery, New York
1968	Galerie du Dragon, Paris
	Galleria Il Fante di Spade, Rome
	Odyssia Gallery, New York
1969	Odyssia Gallery, New York
	Galleria Odyssia, Rome
1970	Odyssia Gallery, New York
1971	Odyssia Gallery, New York
	Galleria Odyssia, Rome
1973	Galleria Odyssia, Rome
1974	Galleria Documenta, Turin
	Galleria Bergamini, Turin
1975	Galerie du Dragon, Paris
1976	Galleria Odyssia, Rome
	Rebecca Cooper Gallery, Washington, D.C.
1977	Galleria Bergamini, Milan
1978	State University of New York at Purchase
	Arts Club of Chicago
1979	Odyssia Gallery, New York
1981	Odyssia Gallery, New York
1982	Odyssia Gallery, New York
1983	Dart Gallery, Chicago
	Odyssia Gallery, New York
	Dartmouth College, Hanover, New Hampshire
1984	Marlborough Gallery, New York
1986	Marlborough Gallery, New York
1987	Simms Fine Art Gallery, New Orleans
	Galerie Jean Briance, Paris
	Kent Fine Art, New York

Selected Group Exhibitions:

1972	*Chicago Imagist Art*, Museum of Contemporary Art, Chicago
1980	*100 Artists, 100 Years*, Art Institute of Chicago
1982	*Jewish Themes*, Jewish Museum, New York
1983	*Bodies and Souls*, Artists Choice Museum, New York
1984	*Art Americain*, Centre Georges Pompidou, Paris
1985	*Narration Drawing*, New York Studio School
1986	*American Myths*, Kent Fine Art, New York

Collections:

Museum of Modern Art, New York; Centre Georges Pompidou, Paris.

Publications:

On PETLIN: book—*Irving Petlin: Weisswald*, exhibition catalogue with text by Edwawrd F. Fry, New York 1987.

PHILLIPS, Peter.

British. Born in Birmingham, 21 May 1939. Educated at Birmingham primary schools; Birmingham College of Art, 1955–59; Royal College of Art, London, 1959–62. Married Marion-Claude Xylander in 1970. Travelled in France, Switzerland and Italy, 1959; in France, 1961; in Spain, the United States and North Africa, 1964. Worked on Entrance Hall, and machine designs, *Shakespeare Exhibition*, Stratford-on-Avon, Warwickshire, 1964; lived in New York, 1964–66; travelled extensively in the United States and Canada, 1965; settled in Zurich, 1966. Guest Professor, Hochschule für Bildende Künste, Hamburg, 1968–69. Recipient: Harkness Fellowship, 1964. Address: Im Ostgarten 5, 8044 Gockhausen, Zurich, Switzerland.

Individual Exhibitions:

1965	Kornblee Gallery, New York
1966	Kornblee Gallery, New York
1967	Galerie Bischofberger, Zurich
1968	Galerie der Spiegel, Cologne
	Kornblee Gallery, New York
	Galleria del Leone, Venice
	Alecto Gallery, London
	Galerie Bischofberger, Zurich
1969	Galerie Bischofberger, Zurich
1970	Studio d'Arte Condotti Rome
	Galleria Milano, Milan
1971	Galerie Leonhart, Munich
	Galleria d'Arte Vinciana, Milan
	Studio d'Arte Condotti, Rome
1972	Westfälischer Kunstverein, Münster (retrospective)
1973	Galerie Bischofberger, Zurich
1974	Galleria Plura, Milan
	Galerie Bischofberger, Zurich

Peter Phillips: *Autokustomotive*, 1964

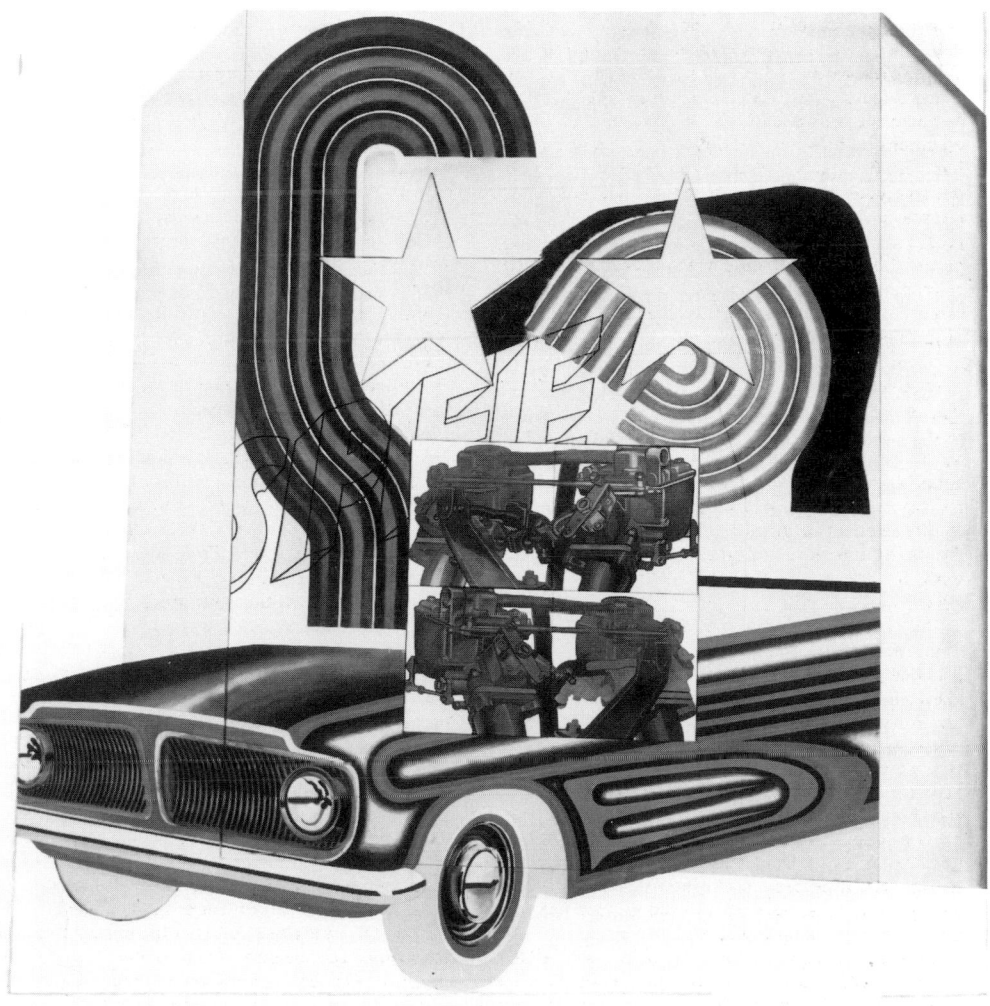

1976	Tate Gallery Coffee Shop, London
	Waddington Galleries, London
1982	*Retrovision*, Walker Art Gallery, Liverpool (toured the United Kingdom)
1987	Galerie Jamileh Weber, Zurich

Selected Group Exhibitions:

1961	*Young Contemporaries*, RBA Galleries, London
1962	*The New Realists*, Sidney Janis Gallery, New York
1964	*The New Generation*, Whitechapel Art Gallery, London
1965	*Op and Pop*, Moderna Museet, Stockholm
1966	*Primary Structures*, Jewish Museum, New York
1968	*Junge Generation Grosbrittannien*, Akademie der Bildenden Künste, Berlin
1971	*Around the Automobile*, Hofstra University, Hempstead, New York
1976	*Pop Art Redefined*, Kunstverein, Hamburg
1981	*Avantgarden Retrospektiv: Kunst nach 1945*, Westfälischer Kunstverein, Münster, West Germany
1986	*British and American Pop Art*, Tate Gallery, London

Collections:

Tate Gallery, London; Victoria and Albert Museum, London; Museum voor Schone Kunsten, Ghent; Neue Pinakothek, Munich; Albright-Knox Art Gallery, Buffalo, New York; Museum of Modern Art, New York.

Publications:

On PHILLIPS: books—*Private View* by Bryan Robertson, John Russell and Lord Snowdon, London 1965; *Pop Art* by Günter Dienst, Weisbaden 1965; *Pop as Art* by Mario Amaya, London 1965; *Pop Art* by Lucy Lippard, London

1965; *Peter Phillips*, exhibition catalogue, by Christopher Finch, London 1966; *Pop Art: Object and Image* by Christopher Finch, London 1968; *Image as Language* by Christopher Finch, London 1969; *Pop Art Redefined* by John Russell and Suzi Gablik, New York and London 1969; *Peter Phillips*, exhibition catalogue, by Enrico Crispolti, Rome 1970; *Peter Phillips*, exhibition catalogue, by Roberto Sanesi, Milan 1971; *Peter Phillips* by Enrico Crispolti, Milan 1975; *Retrovision: Peter Phillips*, exhibition catalogue, by Marco Livingstone, Liverpool 1982.

From his final months at the Royal College of Art in 1962, Peter Phillips felt moved to reject completely the time-worn formulae for painting pictures. After studying at the Birmingham College of Art before coming to London, Phillips had trained in technical drawing. His views were conditioned by the employment of painting media for the purposes of illustration and description, rather than for the creation of "Fine Art." In 1964 he was one of the youngest exhibitors in *The New Generation* exhibition at the Whitechapel Gallery. He received a Harkness stipend from the Commonwealth Fund and spent the next two years in New York. While he was there, he perfected his performance with the air brush and used photography extensively in his graphics. He held his first one-man show in New York in 1965 with the Kornblee Gallery. Since 1966 he has lived in Zurich, where he exhibits at the Galerie Bischofberger.

Of the younger Pop generation Phillips composes his pictures almost exclusively from the second-hand imagery of publicity, either the glossy advertisements in magazines, billboards or the flashing lights on one-arm bandits and jukeboxes. Treated in a disintegrated cutaway sectional format, the large canvases become decorative data-charts of recognizable views of automobile interiors over-painted in zigzags and parallel stripes, that give the work a feeling of dynamic abstraction. This absorption in the intricacies of mechanics as they affect modern living is formalized in pictures apart from a sense of realism in the bland description of parts. It is the still life of consumer durables. The motives, such as the inset power units of internal combustion engines, exploratory if not beautiful, reveal the vicarious nature of their source, almost deserving the title Post-Photo Collage Jazz Painting.

Brilliant metallic colours mark rejection of the oil palette for acrylics and instil a chromatic dazzle, as in his "Pneumatics," where an air-line whips and coils through an arrangement of tyres, headlights, and exploded engine and star-stickers bearing a petrol company's selling symbol. The elements that take their place in Phillips's work pay no regard to aesthetic appeal or geometric design. Overall flatness of the picture plane eliminates perspective, so that details complete in themselves emerge from their backgrounds like the paper legends of an amusement arcade. Phillips has developed subject to a new variety by the substitution of the painting itself composed in eye-catching design of decorative publicity style, dynamic and brightly abstract.

—G. S. Whittet

PHILLIPS, Tom.

British. Born in London, 24 May 1937. Educated at St. Catherine's College, Oxford, 1957–60; studied painting at the Camberwell School of Art, London, under Frank Auerbach, Charles Howard and Euan Uglow, 1961–63. Married Jill Purdy in 1961; children: Eleanor and Conrad. Painter, since 1963; also a poet and composer (composed opera *Irma*, first performed at York University, 1973): lives and works in London. Lecturer in English and Music, Brixton, London, 1960–61; Lecturer, Ipswich School of Art, 1966–67, and Wolverhampton College of Art, 1967–70; Part-time Lecturer, Royal College of Art and Slade School of Fine Art, London, 1975. Recipient:

Second Prize for Painting, *John Moore's Exhibition*, Liverpool, 1969; First Prize for Painting, Artists International Association, 1969; Book Design Award, Victoria and Albert Museum, London, 1983. Associate, Royal Academy, London, 1984. Agent: Angela Flowers Gallery, 11 Tottenham News, London W1. Address: 57 Talfourd Road, Peckham, London SE15 5NN, England.

Individual Exhibitions:

1965	Artist's International Association Gallery, London
1968	Ikon Gallery, Birmingham
	Elizabeth Gallery, Coventry
1970	Angela Flowers Gallery, London
1971	Angela Flowers Gallery, London
	Bear Lane Gallery, Oxford
	City Art Gallery, Wolverhampton
	Welsh Arts' Council Gallery, Cardiff (travelled to the Arnolfini Gallery, Bristol, and Dartington Hall, Devon)
1972	Galerie Rudolph Zwirner, Cologne
	Bear Lane Gallery, Oxford
1973	Hatton Gallery, Newcastle upon Tyne
	Marlborough Fine Art, London
	Marlborough Graphics, London
	Institute of Contemporary Art, London
1974	Gallery 101, Johannesburg
	Marlborough Gallery, New York
	Downtown Gallery, New York
1975	Gemeentemuseum, The Hague
	Nova Spectra Gallery, The Hague
	Kunsthalle, Basle
	Galleria Massimo Valsecchi, Milan
	Galerie BA-MA, Paris
	Centre d'Art et Communication, Vaduz, Lichtenstein
	Musée d'Art Moderne de la Ville, Paris
	Palais d'Athenée, Geneva
1976	Angela Flowers Gallery, London
	Serpentine Gallery, London
	Fabian Fine Art, Capetown
	Municipal Art Gallery, Durban, South Africa
	University of Witwatersrand, Johannesburg
	National Museum and Art Gallery, Gaberone, Bechuanaland
	Midland Group Gallery, Nottingham
	City Art Gallery, Wolverhampton
	Arts Centre, Durham
	Mappin Art Gallery, Sheffield
	Oriel Gallery, Cardiff
	Fabian Fine Art, Capetown (toured South Africa)
1977	Waddington Galleries, London
	Kunstverein, Mannheim
	AIFACS, New Delhi
	Oriel Gallery, Cardiff
	Ferens Art Gallery, Hull
1978	Lefevre Gallery, New York
	Galerie BA-MA, Paris
1979	Centre Cultural du Marais, Paris
	Marlborough Fine Art, London
	Tate Gallery, London (with Richard Long and Paul Nash)
	Galleria Massimo Valsecchi, Milan
	Galerie BA-MA, Paris
1982	Galleria d'Arte Moderna, Bologna
	Waddington Galleries, London
1983	Victoria and Albert Museum, London
1985	Wingfield College, Suffolk
1986	Center for Book Arts, New York
1987	Angela Flowers Gallery, London
	Mappin Art Gallery, Sheffield
	Turnpike Gallery, Wigan, Yorkshire

Selected Group Exhibitions:

1964	*Young Contemporaries*, Fine Art Society Galleries, London
1967	*Summer Exhibition*, Royal Academy of Art, London
1970	*Biennale*, Venice
1973	*La Peinture Anglaise d'Aujourd'hui*, Musée d'Art Moderne de la Ville, Paris
1976	*Arte Inglese Oggi*, Palazzo Reale, Milan
1978	*Art for Society*, Whitechapel Art Gallery, London
1980	*The Open and Closed Book*, Victoria and Albert Museum, London
1984	*The Hard Won Image*, Tate Gallery, London
1985	*Livres d'Artistes*, Centre Georges Pompidou, Paris
1987	*New Faces at the Gallery*, National Portrait Gallery, London

Collections:

Victoria and Albert Museum, London; Tate Gallery, London; Boymans-van Beuningen Museum, Rotterdam; Gemeentemuseum, The Hague; National Museum, Stockholm; Neue Galerie der Stadt, Aachen, West Germany; National Gallery of Australia, Canberra; Musée d'Art Moderne de la Ville, Paris; Museum of Modern Art, New York; Philadelphia Museum of Art.

Publications:

By PHILLIPS: books—*Control Magazine No. 2*, London 1966; *The Directions*, with Jerome Rothenberg, London 1970; *Correspondence*, with Roy Fisher, London 1970; *Metamorphosis*, with Roy Fisher, London 1970; *Trailer*, Stuttgart 1971; *A Humument, Volumes I and II*, London 1971; *Anthology of Concrete Poetry*, London 1971; *Images Words and Words Images*, New York 1971; *Future Fiction*, New York 1971; *This Book is a Movie*, New York 1971; *In One Side and Out the Other*, with André Crozier and John James, London 1971; *A Humument, Volumes III, IV and V*, London 1972; *The Birth of Art*, London 1972; *4 Artists*, London 1972; *A Humument, Volume VI, London 1973*; *Breakthrough Fictioneers*, New York 1973; *The Recollection*, Exeter 1973; *The Source of the Dove*, London 1973; *Introduction to Works in Johannesburg*, Johannesburg 1974; *A Humument, Volume VII, London 1974*; *A Humument, Volumes VIII and IX*, London 1974; *Tom Phillips: Works and Texts to 1974*, London and Stuttgart 1975; *Imaginary Postcards*, with Jonathan Williams, 1975; *A Humument, Volume X*, London 1976; *A Humument, Volume X, London 1980*; *Dante's Inferno: Livre d'Artiste*, London 1983; *Dante's Inferno*, London 1985; *The Heart of a Humument*, Stuttgart 1985; illustrations to Malcolm Bradbury's *Cuts*, London 1987; *Works/Texts to 1987*, Stuttgart 1988; articles—"The Seafarer" in *Pause Magazine* (Oxford), no. 2, 1970; "On 'A Humument'" in *London Magazine*, February 1970; "Extracts from 'A Humument'" in *Poetry Review* (London), April 1971; "Postcard Composition" in *Pages* (London), nos. 1–3, 1971; statement in *Tom Phillips*, exhibition catalogue, London 1982; illustrated books—*The Coherence* by Anselm Hollo, London 1968; *The Wolverhampton Wanderer* by Mike Horowitz, London 1972; film—*Drawing*, 1977; musical scores—*Ornamentik, Opus 9*, 1968; *Harmonia Praestrabilita*, 1968; BBC Publications, Sessions 1, 1969; *Irma*, opera, 1969; *Ein Deutsches Requiem*, 1972; *Lesbia Waltz*, 1972; *Scratch Music*, 1972; *Variations on Opus 85*, 1977.

On PHILLIPS: books—*Tom Phillips*, exhibition catalogue, by Richard Morphet, London 1971; *Tom Phillips* by Charles Spencer, London 1973; *Tom Phillips*, exhibition catalogue, by John Russell, London 1973; *Late Modern* by Edward Lucie-Smith, London 1977; *Fifty Years of Tom Phillips*, exhibition catalogue with text by Michael Tooby, Sheffield 1987; articles—"Tom Phillips" in *Studio International* (London), October 1971; "A Book of Bits or a Bit of a Book" by Alan Woods in *Cambridge Quarterly*, Spring 1982; "The Layered Look" by Nancy Soloman in *Afterimage* (London), Spring 1983; "Tom Phillips: Renaissance Man in the Twentieth Century" by Mike von Joel in *Artline* (London), April-May 1987.

Tom Phillips has spent the past six years translating and illustrating Dante's *Inferno*. The translation is the element he most enjoys, because at that he considers himself an amateur and therefore finds it a challenge. A few of the 40 out of the 140 images I have seen are excellent—for example, "Dante in His Study," which is based on one of the best known portraits of Dante thought to be by Signorelli. Phillips has eliminated unnecessary details and portrays Dante's remarkable chiselled and aquiline features with great simplicity. "The Dark Wood" illustrates the beginning of the Inferno. Here Phillips employs a technique he has used since 1969—words or letters emphasize meaning. Thus the words "Selva Oscura" repeated many times as in Tantra create a claustrophobic forest. Repetition

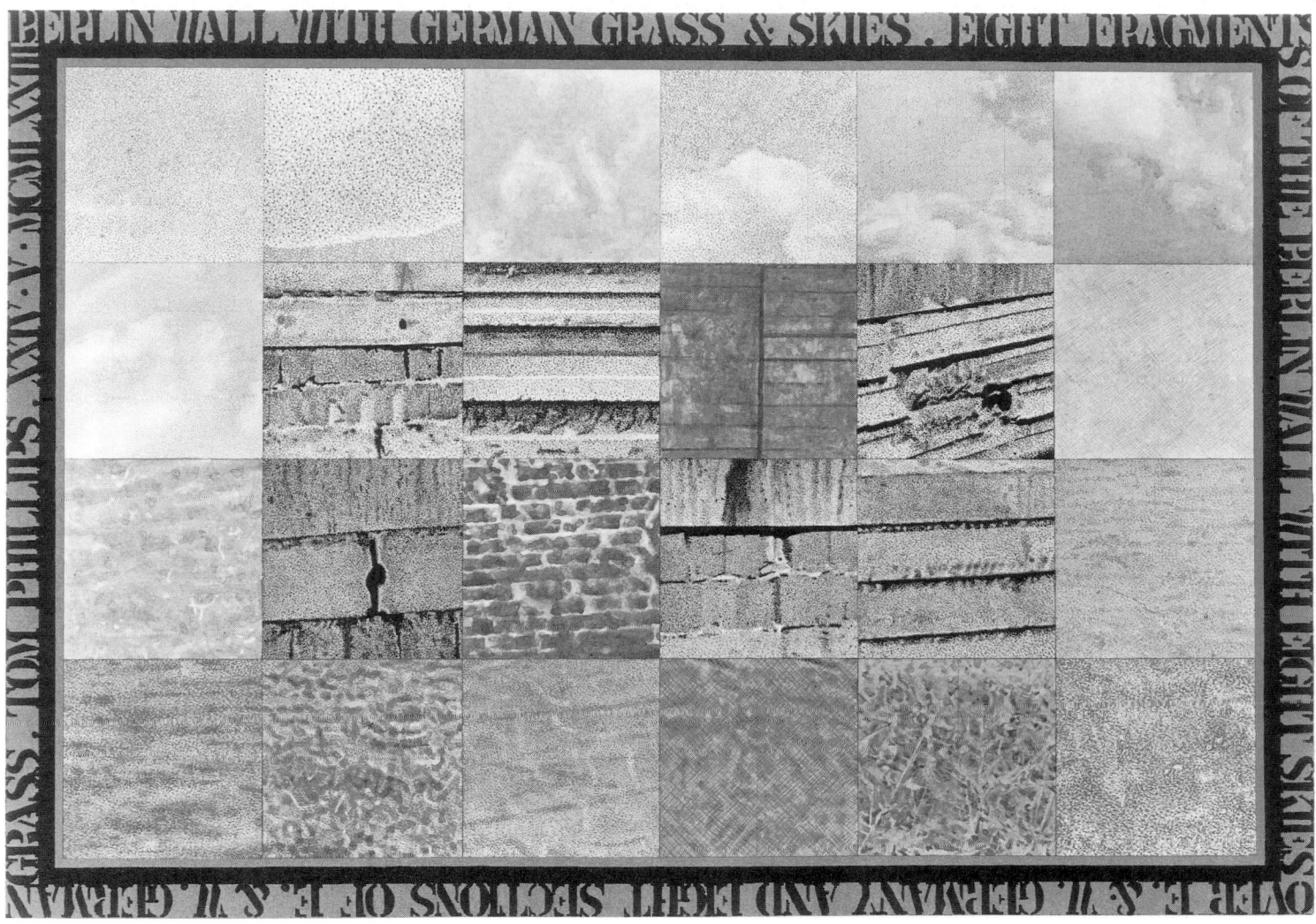

Tom Phillips: *Berlin Wall*, 1973

is also present in "I had not thought death had undone so many." A print of 517 heads drawn between December 1977 and December 1978 represents the crowds inhabiting hell.

Spending such a long time on this print admirably demonstrates Phillips' obsessive patience and ability to focus on one particular theme for a long period of time. In the 60's he came across a turgid Victorian novel called *A Human Document* by W. H. Mallock. The discovery of this work has led to its introduction in almost everything Phillips does (even poor Dante); he considers its use to be inexhaustible. The first direct result was "The Humument," which he worked on from 1966 to 1975. Mallock's text became a backdrop for Phillips' own creation, and snippets of the actual text were highlighted. Levi-Strauss has called this technique "Bricolage"—in other words, how to "Mess About." The value or meaning of this exercise is incomprehensible.

Occasionally Phillips has involved himself in projects of interest such as the conjectured pictures based on a postcard of the interior of a room in the Mappin Art Gallery, Sheffield. His ability in portraiture is remarkable: it is difficult to understand why he plays games and often wishes to be unnecessarily obscure. A story his mother told encapsulates his persona perfectly. When he was a small boy he brought back old bones from a first visit to France. Why he chose old bones in preference to cheese or bread, for example, must remain a question for some speculation. The anecdote does, however, relate to his work, which often requires some highly speculative processes and can defy interpretation!

—Carine Maurice

PICASSO, Pablo.

Spanish. Born in Malaga, Andalusia, 25 October 1881; moved with his family to La Coruna, 1891, and to Barcelona, 1895. Educated in La Coruna; studied at La Llonja Art School, under his father, Barcelona, 1896–97; studied briefly at the Royal Academy of San Fernando, Madrid, 1897; in Cordona's studio, Barcelona, 1899–1900. Lived with Fernande Ulivier, 1905–1911; married Olga Koklova in 1918 (divorced, 1935); son: Paul; lived with Marie Therese Walter; daughter: Maria, lived with Francoise Gilot, 1946–53; children: Claude and Paloma; married Jacqueline Rogul in 1958. Painter and Sculptor: maintained first studio, Barcelona, 1896; contributed illustrations to periodicals, Barcelona, 1900; visited Paris, and shared studio with Carlos Casagemas, 1900; Founder, with Francisco de Assis Soler, Arte Jove, Madrid, and became art editor and illustrator, 1901; settled in Paris, 1904; spent summers in Southern France, from 1911; associated with Juan Gris, Georges Braque, Max Jacob and André Derain; visited Rome, with Jean Cocteau, and met Diaghilev, 1917; subsequently associated with Igor Stravinsky and Leonide Massine; designed costumes and scenery for Diaghilev's *Parade*, Paris, 1917, and *Le Tricorne*, London, 1919; continued work on theatrical designs, until 1924; Director, Prado, Madrid, 1936; committed to Republican cause during Spanish Civil War, and sold artwork to raise funds; exhibited "Guernica" at the *World's Fair*, Paris, 1937; lived near Paris during the occupation; joined French Communist Party, 1944; moved to the South of France, 1948; settled near Aix, 1958; moved to Mougins, France, 1961. Recipient: Honorable Mention, *Exhibition of Fine Arts*, Madrid, 1897; Painting Medal, Customs of Aragon, Madrid and Malaga 1898; First Prize, *Carnegie International*, Pittsburgh, 1930. *Died* (in Antibes, France) *8 April 1973.*

Individual Exhibitions:

1900	Els Quatre Gats, Barcelona
1901	Salon Parés, Barcelona
	Galerie Ambroise Vollard, Paris
1982	Galerie Berthe Weill, Paris
1904	Galerie Berthe Weille, Paris
1909	Galerie Ambroise Vollard, Paris
	Galerie Thannhauser, Munich
1911	Photo Secession, New York
	Galerie Thannhauser, Munich
1912	Stafford Gallery, London
	Dalman Galerie, Barcelona
1913	Neue Galerie, Berlin
	Galerie Thannhauser, Munich
1918	Paul Guillaume Galerie, Paris (with Henri Matisse)
1919	Leicester Galleries, London (with Henri Matisse)
	Galerie Rosenberg, Paris
1922	Galerie Thannhauser, Munich
1924	Galerie Rosenberg, Paris
1931	Musée d'Art Francais, Paris (with Fernand Léger and Georges Braque)
1932	Galerie Georges Petit, Paris
	Kunsthaus, Zurich
1934	Galerie Percier, Paris (with Julio Gonzalez and Juan Miró)
1935	Mayor Gallery, London (with Juan Gris and Fernand Léger)

1936	Galerie Rosenberg, Paris
	Renou et Colle Galerie, Paris
1937	Zwemmer Gallery, London (with Giorgio de Chirico)
1938	Kunstnernes Hus, Oslo (with Henri Matisse and Georges Braque; toured Scandinavia)
	New Burlington Galleries, London
1939	Arts Club of Chicago
	Museum of Fine Arts, San Francisco
	London Gallery
	Museum of Modern Art, New York
1940	Art Institute of Chicago
1941	Bignou Gallery, New York
1945	Victoria and Albert Museum, London (with Henri Matisse; travelled to the Palais des Beaux-Arts, Brussels)
	Buchholz Gallery, New York
	Louis Carré Galerie, Paris
1948	Galerie Louise Leiris, Paris
	Arts Council Gallery, London
	Kestner-Gesellschaft, Hannover (with Juan Gris and Joan Miró)
	Museum of Art, San Francisco (travelled to the Portland Art Museum, Oregon)
1950	Maison de la Pensée Francaise, Paris
1951	Saidenberg Gallery, New York (with Fernand Léger)
1953	Musée des Beaux-Arts, Lyons
	Galleria Nazionale d'Arte Moderna, Rome
	Palazzo Reale, Milan
	Museo de Arte Moderna, Sao Paulo
1954	Maison de la Pensée Francaise, Paris
1955	Musée des Arts Décoratifs, Paris
	Bibliothèque Nationale, Paris
	Haus der Kunst, Munich
1956	Arts Council Gallery, London
1957	Galerie Louise Leiris, Paris
	Museum of Modern Art, New York
	Musée Reattu, Arles, France
1958	Philadelphia Museum of Art
1959	Musée Cantini, Marseilles
	Galerie Louise Leiris, Paris
1960	Le Musée, Vallauris, France (with Fernand Léger)
	Tate Gallery, London
	Galerie Motte, Paris
1962	Museum of Modern Art, New York
1966	Bibliothèque Nationale, Paris
	Grand Palais, Paris
	Petit Palais, Paris
1968	Staatliche Kunsthalle, Baden-Baden, West Germany
1970	Marlborough Fine Art, London (with Henry Moore and Graham Sutherland)
1971	Musée National d'Art Moderne, Paris
1972	Museum of Modern Art, New York
1973	Israel Museum, Jerusalem
	Kunsthalle, Bremen, West Germany
	Galerie Louise Leiris, Paris
	Palais des Beaux-Arts, Brussels
	Museu Picasso, Barcelona
	Palais des Papes, Avignon
	Fischer Fine Art, London
	Galleria Levi, Milan
	Museo Nacional de Bellas Artes, Buenos Aires
	Kunstverein, Hannover
	Leslie Waddington Prints, London
1974	Fuji TV Gallery, Tokyo
	Leslie Waddington Prints, London
	Galerie Jankrugier, Geneva
	Galerie Gerald Cramer, Geneva
	Marlborough Galleria d'Arte, Rome
	Badisches Landesmuseum, Karlsruhe
	Kunstverein, Hamburg (toured West Germany)
1975	Marina Gallery, Weybridge, Surrey
	Neue Gesellschaft für Bildende Kunst, Berlin
1976	Kunstmuseum, Basle
	Centro Annunciata, Milan
1977	Fundacion Juan March, Madrid
	Galerie Patrick Cramer, Geneva
	E. Jan Wissleingh and Company, Amsterdam
	Museu Picasso, Barcelona
1978	Museum der Bildenden Künste, Leipzig
	Museu Picasso, Barcelona
1979	Kestner Gesellschaft, Hannover
	Kunsthalle, Bielefeld, West Germany (with Juan Gris and Georges Braque)

	Museu Picasso, Barcelona
	Galerie Kornfeld, Berne
	Grand Palais, Paris
1980	Galerie Claude Bernard, Paris
1981	Art Gallery of Ontario, Toronto
	Museo Espanol de Arte Contemporaneo, Madrid (travelled to the Museu Picasso, Barcelona)
1982	Staatliche Museen Pruessischer Kulturbesitz, Berlin
1983	Galleria Seno, Milan
	Galerie Gianna Sista, Paris
	Edward Totah Gallery, London
1984	Kunsthalle, Bielefeld, West Germany
	National Gallery of Victoria, Melbourne
	Art Gallery of New South Wales, Sydney
	Fischer Fine Art, London
	Museo Rufino Tamayo, Mexico City
	Guggenheim Museum, New York
	Los Angeles County Museum of Art
1985	Museum Het Kruithuis, Hertogenbosch, Netherlands
	Kunstmuseum, Berne
	Richard Gray Gallery, Chicago
1986	Lumley Cazalet, London
	Galerie Thomas, Munich
	Stephen Muzoh and Company, New York
	Galerie Beyeler, Basle
	Kunsthalle, Tubingen, West Germany
	Kunstverein, Dusseldorf
	Pace Gallery, New York
	Royal Academy of Art, London (toured the United States and Canada, 1986–88)
1987	Waddington Galleries, London
	Sala Gaspar, Barcelona

Selected Group Exhibitions:

1913	International Exhibition of Modern Art (Armory Show), Armory of the 69th Infantry, New York (travelled to the Art Institute of Chicago, and Copley Hall, Boston)
1937	International Exhibition, Petit Palais, Paris
1944	Salon d'Automne, Paris
1947	The Cubist Spirit and Its Time, Tate Gallery, London
1950	Biennale, Venice
1952	Salon de Mai, Paris
1961	The Art of Assemblage, Museum of Modern Art, New York
1983	Modern Art in the West, Metropolitan Art Museum, Tokyo

Collections:

Museu Picasso, Barcelona; Museum of Modern Art, Barcelona; Centre Georges Pompidou, Paris; Musée Picasso, Antibes, France; Tate Gallery, London; Hermitage Museum, Leningrad; Museum of Modern Art, New York; Philadelphia Museum of Art; Art Institute of Chicago.

Publications:

By PICASSO: books—*Le Desir attrape par la Queue*, play, Paris 1945, as *Desire Caught by the Tail*, translated by Ronald Penrose, London 1970; *Picasso: Poemas y Declaraciones*, Mexico City 1944; *Picasso et a Poesie*, Rome 1953; *Tout le Fatras Immonde*, Paris 1954; *The Four Little Girls*, translated by Ronald Penrose, London 1970; *Picasso on Art*, edited by Dore Ashton, London 1972; articles—"Picasso Poete" and "La Literature de Picasso" in *Cahiers d'Art* (Paris) no. 7–10, 1935; "Textes de Picasso" in *Cahiers* (Paris), 1948; illustrated books—*Saint Matorel* by Max Jacob, Paris 1911; *Le Chef d'oeuvre inconnu* by Honoré de Balzac, Paris 1931; *Lysistrata* by Aristophanes, Paris 1934.

On PICASSO: books—*Catalogue d'Oeuvres de Picasso* by Christian Zervos, 33 volumes, 1932–78; *Picasso: 50 Years of his Art* by A. H. Barr, Jr., New York 1946; *Homage to Paris* by Ronald Penrose, London 1951; *Pablo Picasso* by Maurice Reynal, Geneva 1953; *Pablo Picasso* by Jean Cassou, Paris 1954; *Pablo Picasso: 55 Years of His Graphic Work* by B. Geiser, London 1955; *Pablo Picasso* by Wilhelm Boeck and Jaime Sabartés, London 1955; *Picasso* by F. Elgar and R. Maillard, Paris and London 1955; *Portrait of Picasso* by Ronald Penrose, London 1956; *The Private World of Pablo Picasso* by David Douglas Duncan, New York 1957; *Picasso:*

His Life and Work by Ronald Penrose, London 1958; *Picasso: The Formative Years* by Anthony Blunt and Phoebe Pool, London 1962; *Picasso and His Women* by Jean-Paul Gespelle, London 1967; *Picasso 1930–1968* by Pierre Dufour, Geneva 1969; *Picasso: Birth of a Genius* by Juan-Eduardo Girlot, London 1972; *Picasso in Retrospect* by Ronald Penrose and Daniel-Henry Kahnweiler, New York 1973; *Good-bye Picasso* by David Douglas Duncan, London 1974; *Sunshine at Midnight; Memories of Picasso and Cocteau* by Genevieve Laporte, London 1975; *Picasso's Mask* by André Malraux, London 1976; *Picasso: A Comprehensive Bibliography* by Ray Anne Kibbey, London 1977; *Picasso: The Cubist Years 1907–1916* by Pierre Daix, Paris 1977, London 1979; *Picasso: Art as Autobiography* by Mary M. Gedo, Chicago 1980; *Picasso and His World* by Terry Measham, London 1980; *Picasso's Guernica: The Labyrinth of Narrative and Vision* by Frank D. Russell, London 1980; *Picasso* by Pierre Cabanne, Neuchâtel, Switzerland 1981; *Picasso: The Last Years 1963–1973*, exhibition catalogue with essay by Gert Schiff, New York 1984; *Je Suis Le Cahier: The Sketchbooks of Picasso*, edited by Arnold and Marc Glimcher, New York 1986; *Picasso's Concrete Sculpture* by Sally H. Fairweather, London 1987.

Pablo Picasso has often been compared with Stravinsky as one of the great artistic chameleons of the 20th century, each reacting to the crisis of expression in modern art by constantly exploring, thus passing through a whole series of phases of creative activity. It has indeed been said that Picasso painted each of his pictures as if he were trying to discover the art of painting all over again. But though Stravinsky and Picasso both shared an immense capacity for absorbing and reshaping other men's styles, and have thus both been called "eclectic," it is no longer so easy as it once seemed to pigeon-hole their careers into neat if necessarily overlapping periods, for it is becoming much clearer in retrospect that each was an integral talent, and that mere magpies could hardly have played the crucial role they did in enlarging the meaning of art in the 20th century.

But how far is Picasso still a "contemporary" artist, eligible for inclusion in this book? Whereas Mondrian, Matisse and Duchamp have all been clearly major influences on the art of the last three decades, it might be said that Picasso's own direct influence on the development of art came to an end in the 1920's, and that in his final phase after the war he had already completely lost touch with contemporary art, even though he himself was as productive as he had been in his earlier career. But he no longer seemed the great innovator and explorer that he had been during the artistic revolution of the first 30 years of this century, when he was constantly disrupting traditional concepts of art and extending its boundaries, while tremendously influencing other artists, many of whom founded whole careers on ideas Picasso had explored for a year or two of his.

Picasso had an almost immediate success with his first really personal and original paintings, those of the so-called Blue and Pink periods, which in some ways show him as the last great Symbolist painter, though with their mood-creating colours and emotive distortions of forms they also relate to the earlier phases of Expressionism. And it was this search for force of expression which led to his interest in primitive, particularly African, art. The tremendous expressive power of African masks and sculptures was a sensational demonstration that naturalism was not the only way an artist could express himself. And these exotic sculptures offered solutions to Picasso and other painters who were trying to break away from naturalism because they recognized that African sculptors were not concerned to represent the superficial appearance of the world, but were instead striving to represent a completely different reality, to make visible the invisible world of the instincts and emotions. Picasso was not the first painter to discover tribal art—Vlaminck, Derain, Matisse and Braque had all done that a year or so earlier. But it was he who made the most potent use of it in the proto-cubist "Desmoiselles d'Avignon," a painting which shocked even friends like Braque when they saw it in his studio.

This was a curtain-raiser to Cubism, which was

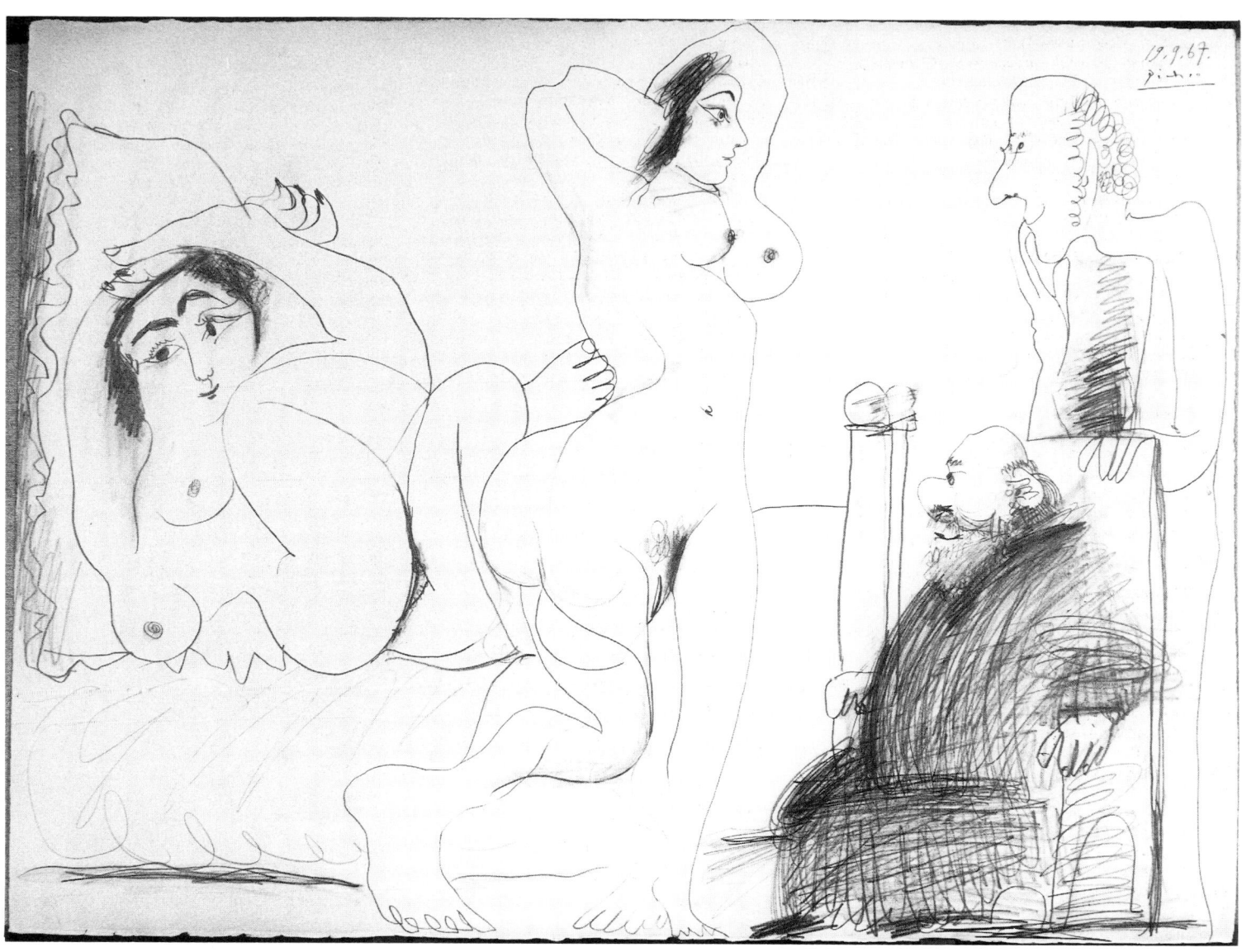

Pablo Picasso: *Femmes Nues et Vieillards*, 1967

also a working-out of Cézanne's radical discoveries about the nature of space. In spite of its short duration, cubism became and has remained perhaps the most important and influential movement of the century. With this fundamental reassessment of the nature of visual perception Picasso's direct influence on other artists was at its height, including more currently fashionable artists like Mondrian and Duchamp. Nor was this influence only on painting, for Picasso has had just as profound an influence on sculpture, and his collages and constructions have played a large part in breaking down the boundaries between painting and sculpture which has been such a feature of contemporary art. Picasso himself was already using the idea of assemblage, and the collage technique of extending the surface of the picture outwards has been explored in different ways by many subsequent artists from Schwitters' collages to Rauschenberg's combines, all attempts to incorporate "reality" into the work without actually imitating it in the old representational way. And the astonishing streams of cubist "guitars" and "still-lifes" made of wood or sheet-metal have had such a profound influence on later sculptors as different as David Smith and Cesar that a younger sculptor like William Tucker can write: "There is no doubt, to my mind, that the most totally revolutionary of all modern sculptures in concept, material, and execution, are in Picasso's Cubist constructions."

Cubism was a consistent passion with Picasso for some five years, but an exploratory passion in which every work revealed new variations and new possibilities. But while continuing to explore these possibili-

ties, he was now also painting in a severely classical naturalistic style, and from now on he always worked in various styles concurrently. Neoclassicism was in many ways a personal style for Picasso, an idealist dream which was the fruit of his direct contact in 1917 with Italy and the classical tradition while working on the Diaghilev ballet *Parade,* and of the first, happy phase of his marriage to a young ballerina. But it was also partly a general change of mood which was affecting all the arts, with neoclassical music being pioneered by Stravinsky in his Diaghilev ballets of this time. With surrealism Picasso was part of a movement which he helped to develop though he had no part in initiating it, and after this he seems to be less and less a direct influence on the mainstream of contemporary art. The main recent critical fashion, from supporters of Abstract Expressionism like Clement Greenberg to much younger critics like Timothy Hilton, has been one of antipathy to most if not all of Picasso's post-Cubist works, as though Picasso's main role in art had been to prepare the way for an allegedly higher American post-war and abstract supremacy, so that his return to the figure and hostility to abstract art are "obtuse." Thus Hilton loftily dismisses "Guernica": "The American Artists—Pollock above all—well understood that 'Guernica' was not, in itself, a progressive painting . . . Clement Greenberg, uniquely qualified to understand that American response to Picasso, was precise and damning about the picture. His criticism is eloquent of the way that, as far as the new art was concerned, 'Guernica' was felt to be irrelevant and even reactionary."

What this whole nonsensical argument does do, however, is condemn not Picasso, but the whole degenerate, mannerist formalism into which the American and most other contemporary art has slid. The argument goes back to the whole development of art since Cubism. Did Picasso misunderstand the nature of Cubism, as Otto Hahn has suggested: "Picasso, though he was among the founders of Cubism, never drew the right conclusions from it. He sent Art off along a highly cerebral track as a business of conceptual painting, yet stuck to his belief in 'temperament.' " On the contrary, I would argue that it was Picasso's followers who completely misunderstood the nature of Cubism, right from the very first book on the new art, *Du Cubisme,* by the minor Cubist followers Gleizes and Metzinger, who insisted on treating it as a code, a systematic and standardized technique for representing objects. Picasso was never a formula artist of this type, but an explorer, and an essential part of his art was the continual search for an expressive style through which to communicate his highly-charged feelings and energy. An experimental period in the arts is harvest-time for the charlatan, and Picasso's mannerisms can be imitated all too easily. But his own supreme gift was that marvellous natural draughtsmanship, that marvellous fluency of line with which he is seen drawing a bull in the films which show him in action, a personal style which however goes right back to the very sources of art and which he shares with the paleolithic cave artists. And this sort of fluent brush drawing can never be an *intellectual* activity whose results can be dissected with pseudo-Wittgensteinian pretentiousness of a fashionable art critic, but a personally expressive, emotional, indeed an erotic activity. Roland Penrose has claimed that it is largely due to Picasso "that the conception of art as a powerful emotional medium, rather than a speech for the perfection of ideal forms of beauty, has become accepted among the artists of our time. The return to a fundamental belief that art should spring from a primitive need to express our feelings towards the world around us in strong emotional terms makes us more prone to value a work of art for its vitality than for its perfection. It is the exceptional power of Picasso's work that compels us, in return, to discover in it the mysterious presence of beauty."

The tragedy is that this has *not* been so. How prophetic Herbert Read now seems when he writes: "That Picasso has been the most influential artist of the first half of the 20th century is obvious, but not all influences are good influences, and indeed for an age to be dominated by the idiosyncrasies of a single personality is a sign of weakness. The example of Michelangelo in the past is a melancholy witness to this fact." Michelangelo's creativity was, like Picasso's, a profound and constant struggle to express the emotional intensity of his own inner tensions, but it was because his Mannerist followers merely made hollow imitations of him that Ruskin could describe Michelangelo as "a great fellow, but the ruin of art." "Guernica" is one of a frightening series of pictures with which Picasso reacted to his personal crisis and to the political events of the inter-war years, and hanging—as it did in New York it remained a constant reproach to the mannerist degeneracy of so much American painting and criticism, from the formalist sterility of Frank Stella's paintings, which demand to be seen only as object, to the trivial minimalism of Carl Andre's pile of bricks.

Picasso's last phase after 1945 still shows the same extraordinary productivity, though with these late works he seems to withdraw from contemporary art movements altogether in order to plunge into a kind of retrospective re-working of his former inventions. For this last work is notable for the way in which it ranges back and forth in its preferences to earlier styles, as though commenting on the processes of its own evolution. Yet there were no new radical inventions of his own, and even though he still showed something like his old versatility, his output was notably uneven. It has been rightly remarked that Picasso is one of the few truly great artists to have lived to a very old age and yet failed to produce a distinctive late manner and a deepening of profundity. Yet he rightly felt himself closer spiritually to the Old Masters than to any of the modern avant-garde painters who made whole careers of flogging one small formula to death. And he was still obsessively at work, still refusing to stand still, and even this final phase of his activity was influential, since most of his best post-war work was in the field of ceramics, and Picasso helped to promote a new flourishing of poetry and a revival of the moribund ceramics industry in the South of France. Much of the late work of the ageing artist is also charged with an obsessive sexuality, a high erotic content which may because of his great public charisma as an artist have contributed to the current liberating view of eroticism. Roland Penrose tells the story of Jean Leymarie asking Picasso to define the difference between art and eroticism: "But there is no difference," said Picasso with great seriousness. And it is precisely because he *was* an erotic artist that Picasso is, and will remain, such a great one.

—Konstantin Bazarov

PICHÉ, Roland.
British. Born in London, 21 November 1938. Studied at the Hornsey School of Art, London, 1956–60; with the sculptor, Gaudia, in Montreal, 1956–60; and at the Royal College of Art, London, 1960–64. Married Wendy Peacock in 1959 (divorced); son: Remus; married San-San in 1966; daughters: Tanya and Charmaine. Sculptor: assistant to Henry Moore, Much Hadham, Hertfordshire, 1962–63; settled in Tollesbury, Essex, 1964. Principal Lecturer in charge of Sculpture, Maidstone College of Art, Kent, since 1964. Member, Fine Arts Panel, Council for National Academic Awards, 1976–78. Recipient: Walter Neurath Prize, London, 1961; Young Contemporaries Prize, London, 1964; Silver Medal, Royal College of Art, London, 1964; Peter Stuyvesant Foundation Travel Bursary, 1965; Prix de la Ville de Paris, *Biennale*, Paris, 1965; First Prize, *Structure '66*, Welsh Arts Council, 1966; Commission Prize, Moorgate Sculpture Competition, London, 1968; Arts Council of Great Britain Award, 1977; Eastern Arts Association Award, 1978, 1980. Agent: Marlborough Fine Art, 6 Albemarle Street, London W1X 4BY. Address: Victorios Studios, Tollesbury, Essex, England.

Individual Exhibitions:

1967 Marlborough New London Gallery
1969 Galerie Ad Libitum, Antwerp
     Middelheim Biennale, Antwerp
1968 Gothenburg Museum, Sweden (with Jack Smith)
1975 Canon Park, Birmingham, England
1980 *Spaceframes and Circles*, The Minories Gallery, Colchester, Essex
     Ikon Gallery, Birmingham

Selected Group Exhibitions:

1964 *Young Commonwealth Artists*, Whitechapel Art Gallery, London
1965 *Towards Art II*, Royal College of Art, London
     The New Generation 1965, Whitechapel Art Gallery, London
     The Summer Exhibition, Marlborough New London Gallery
1966 *The English Eye*, Marlborough-Gerson Gallery, New York
1967 *Pittsburgh International*, Carnegie Institute, Pittsburgh
1970 *British Sculpture out of the 60's*, Institute of Contemporary Arts, London
1972 *British Sculptors '72*, Royal Academy of Arts, London
1977 *Silver Jubilee Exhibition*, Battersea Park, London
1980 *British Sculpture of the 20th Century*, Whitechapel Art Gallery, London

Collections:

Royal College of Art, London; British Council, London; Arts Council of Great Britain, London; Whitworth Art Gallery, Manchester; Gothenburg Museum, Sweden; Western Australian Art Gallery, Perth; Museum of Modern Art, Sao Paulo; Museum of Modern Art, New York.

Publications:

By PICHÉ: articles—statement in *Roland Piché*, exhibition catalogue, London 1967; "Conversation with Keith Reeves" and "A Selection of Notes and Meditations Collected from Sketchbooks, 1975–79" in *Spaceframes and Circles*, exhibition catalogue, Colchester 1980.

On PICHÉ: books—*British Sculpture Out of the 60's*, exhibition catalogue, by Gene Baro, London 1970; *British Sculptors '72*, exhibition catalogue, by Thomas Monnington and Bryan Robertson, London 1972; *Spaceframes and Circles*, exhibition catalogue, by A. Dunlop, Colchester 1980.

My work recreates experience within an expanding awareness of traditional and contemporary dimensions. My main concern being to evolve a sculptural language into a synthesis in which contradiction and paradox are apparent. To transcend the independence of "situation" into a more "universal state" through an experience of physical matter towards a collective awareness in which basic contradictions are understood. My interest in qualities of vulnerability, internal rather than external situations, softness and fluid forms, reflects a reaction to stability and "complete statement". However, the interrelationship between fragmentation of, and totality, are part of a total concern. The "process of forming" reveals the structure beneath the visual experience and is one ingredient that developed the notion of the "container" and "spaceframe" idea. The evolution and use of the spaceframe resulted from an increasing awareness of "spatial relationship," "fragmentation of form," "change" and qualities of violation and symbolic interpretation. My central concern has been to develop a concept founded on reason and to increase its powers of meaning and communication through a more perceptive process.

—Roland Piché

One of the most talented and interesting of the odd-men-out in British sculpture, Roland Piché, like, in some respects, Michael Sandle, combines expressionistic and sensuously tactile involvements, with positively sur-realistic images, and an emotional intensity which almost belies his national origins. He came to prominence in the *New Generation* show at the Whitechapel Gallery, London, in 1965, when his isolation from the post-Caro-St. Martin's School of young sculptors added distinction to an already personal manner.

It would be unfair to suggest that Piché is out to shock with his sculpture; it would be equally unfair to deny that, as with Francis Bacon, or before him Van Gogh, he has the knack of disturbing the viewer, whilst at the same time involving him in the strange imagery. Piché works in a mixture of materials, fibreglass, resin, wood, plaster; a distinctive feature to his work is the Bacon-like cage or frame in which he sets his strange, organic, enlargements of physical organs, many of them overspilling the cage in almost frightening engagement. The word "Frame" often appears in his titles, but on occasions he uses names which both describe the physical movement of the structure, and suggest more complex emotional or spiritual states; "Desposition," for the instance, descending through the cage, linked with another blood-red organ, which either denotes umbilical attachment or the literal spilling out of guts.

Other works suggest a highly romantic nature, given to illustrative, theatrical imaginings, although more recently Piché has severely attempted to formalise his imagery, so that the cageframe assumes dominant importance with oblique references, in round and oval forms of varying sizes, oddly placed within or round the structure, suggesting human, interior organs.

Whereas Michael Sandle, his nearest contemporary sculptor, displays an elegant wit, similar to the surrealistic fantasies of Victorian writers and illustrators, Piché has an altogether rougher, tougher personality, with little apparent humour in his art. Drama, energy, daring are his stylistic characteristics, in a complex metaphorical, illustrative sculpture suggesting both an intense autobiographical concern, as with Bacon, as well as a misanthropic view of life.

—Charles Spencer

PIENE, Otto.
German. Born in Laasphe, Westphalia, 18 April 1928. Educated in Lubbeckke, Westphalia, until 1948; studied art at the Blochererschule, and Hochschule der Bildenden Künste, Munich, 1948–50; and at the Staadtliche Kunstakademie, Dusseldorf, 1950–53; studied philosophy at the University of Cologne, 1953–57. Independent artist, in Cologne 1957–61, in

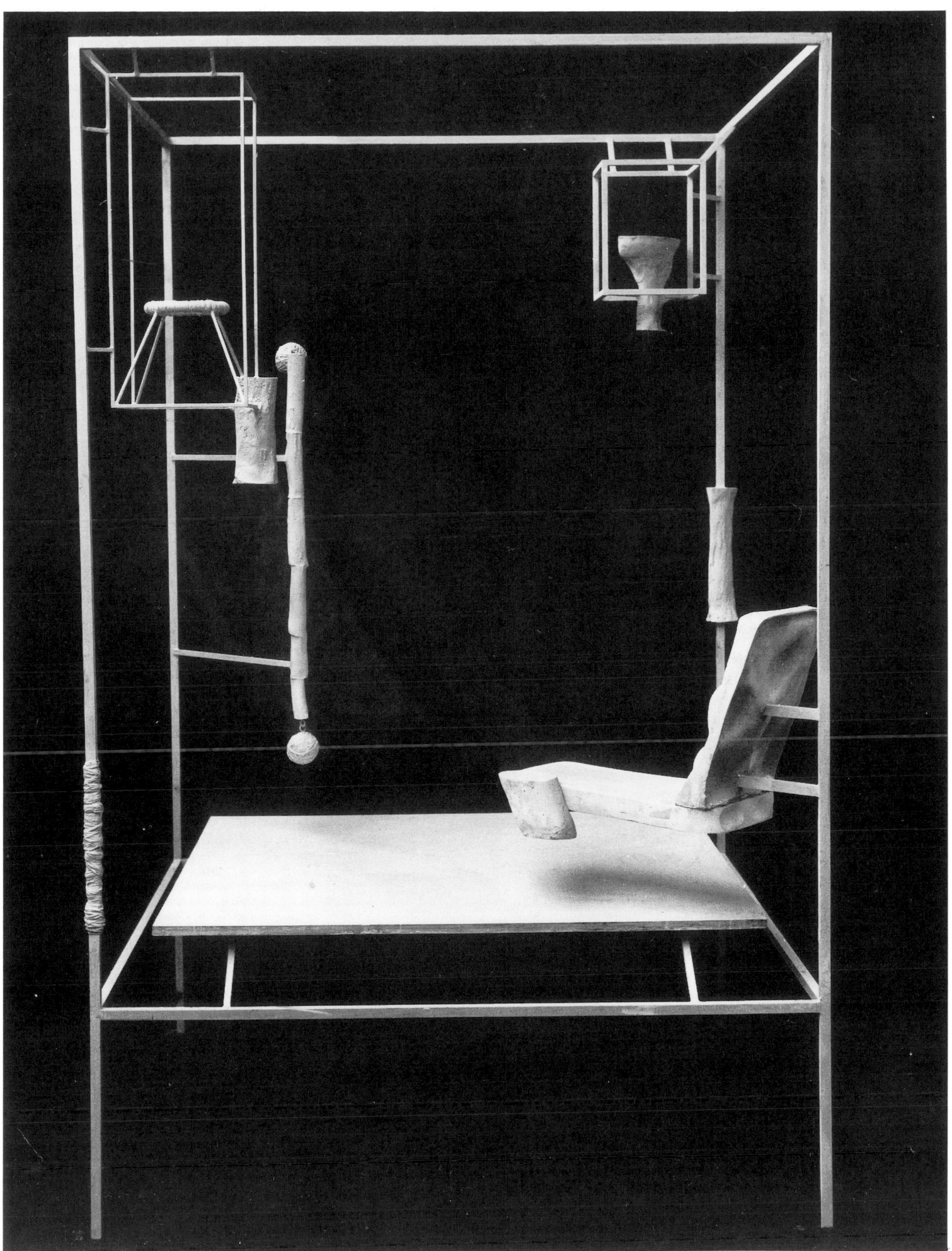

Roland Piché: *White Spaceframe,* 1979

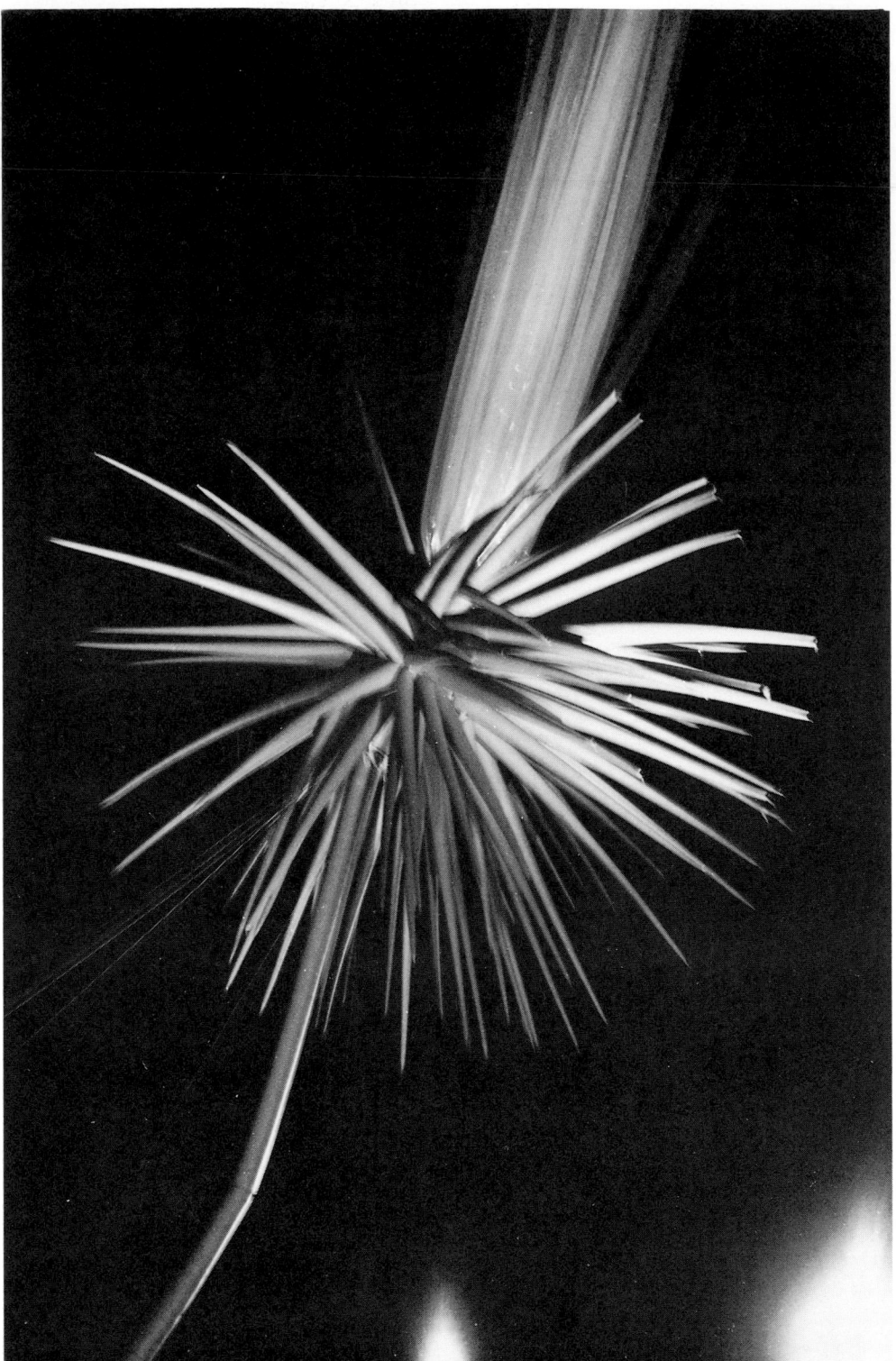

Otto Piene: *Blue Star Linz*, aerial sculpture, 1981

Dusseldorf, since 1961, in Cambridge, Massachusetts, since 1968, and in Brewster, New York, since 1970: first light performances and environments, 1959; automated light sculptures and fire-paintings, 1960. Founder, with Heinz Mack, Group Zero, Cologne 1957; Co-Publisher, magazines *Zero 1* and *Zero 2*, Cologne, 1958, and *Zero 3*, 1961. Visiting Professor of Art, University of Pennsylvania, Philadelphia, 1964; Resident Fellow, 1968–70, Non-Resident Fellow since 1970, and Professor of Environmental Art since 1972, Massachusetts Institute of Techology, Cambridge. Recipient: Josef Pankofer Preis, Baden-Baden, West Germany 1959; Cultural Relations Prize, *Graphic Art Biennale*, Ljubljana 1967; Konrad von Soest Prize, Münster, 1968; Tamarind Lithography Fellowship, Los Angeles, 1968; Purchase Prize, *International Graphics Exhibi-*tion, Ljubljana 1969; Purchase Prize, *International Drawings Exhibition*, Rijeka, 1970; National Museum of Modern Art Prize, *8th Biennale*, Tokyo, 1972. Address: c/o Massachusetts Institute of Technology, 40 Massachusetts Avenue, Cambrigde, Massachusetts 02139, U.S.A.

Individual Exhibitions:

1959   Galerie Alfred Schmela, Dusseldorf
1960   Galerie Diogenes, West Berlin
         Galerie Alfred Schmela, Dusseldorf
         Studio F, Ulm, West Germany
1961   Galerie Ad Libitum, Antwerp
         Galerie Nota, Munich
         Galerie Dato, Frankfurt

Galerie St. Stephan, Vienna (with Heinz Mack)
         Galerie Muller, Stuttgart
1962   *Licht und Rauch/Graphik*, Städtisches Museum Schloss Morsbroich, Leverkusen, West Germany
         Galerie Alfred Schmela, Dusseldorf
         McRoberts and Tunnard Gallery, London
         Studio F, Ulm, West Germany (with Heinz Mack and Günther Uecker)
1963   *Permanentes Lichtballet*, Galerie Müller, Stuttgart
         Obilder und Gouachen, Galerie Alfred Schmela, Dusseldorf
         Die Feuerblume, Galerie Ad Libitum, Antwerp
         Galleria Cadario, Milan
         Galleria La Polena, Genoa
         Museum Haus Lange, Krefeld, West Germany (with Heinz Mack and Günther Uecker)
         Kaiser-Wilhelm-Museum, Krefeld, West Germany (with Heinz Mack and Günther Uecker)
1964   Galerie Lawrence, Paris (with Günther Uecker)
         Galleria Il Bilico, Rome (with Heinz Mack)
1965   Galerie Rottloff, Karlsruhe
         Howard Wise Gallery, New York
         Kestner-Gesellschaft, Hannover (with Heinz Mack and Günther Uecker)
1966   Galerie Alfred Schmela, Dusseldorf
1967   *Fire Flower Power*, Museum am Ostwall, Dortmund, West Germany
         Galerija Centar, Zagreb
         Galerie Seyfried, Munich
1968   Westfalisches Landesmuseum, Münster, West Germany
         Studio F, Ulm, West Germany
1969   *Elements*, Howard Wise Gallery, New York
         Yale University, New Haven, Connecticut
1971   *Bilder, Feuergouachen und Graphik 1957–1967, Skyart Portfolio 1969, Bilddokumentation 1967–1971*, Galerie Heseler, Munich
1972   Galerie Wentdorf und Swetec, Dusseldorf
         Sloane O'Sickey Gallery, Cleveland
         Centro de Arte y Communicacion, Buenos Aires
         Galerie Heseler, Munich
         Westfalisches Landesmuseum, Münster, West Germany
1973   Galerie Heseler, Munich
         Galerie Wentdorf und Swetec, Dusseldorf
         Kölnischer Kunstverein, Cologne
         Museo Genero Perez, Cordoba, Argentina
1974   Galerie Heimeshoff, Essen
         Kunstverein, Ingolstadt, West Germany
         Galerie Lohrl, Willich, West Germany
1975   Kleine Grafik-Galerie, Bremen, West Germany
         Paintings, Gouache, Drawings, Massachusetts Institute of Technology, Cambridge
         Galerie Lauter, Mannheim
         Galerie Heseler, Munich
         Galerie Lohrl, Willich, West Germany
         Galerie Ehrensperger, Zurich
1976   Galerie Schoeller, Dusseldorf
         88 Pine Street, New York
1977   Galerie Heseler, Munich
         Fitchburg Art Museum, Massachusetts
         Galerie Heimeshoff, Essen, West Germany
         Galerie Schoeller, Dusseldorf
1978   Galerie Heseler, Munich
1979   Galerie Heseler, Munich
1980   Galerie Schoeller, Dusseldorf
         State University of New York, Stony Brook
1984   Guggenheim Museum, New York

Selected Group Exhibitions:

1959   *Vision in Motion*, Hessenhuis, Antwerp
1961   *The Movement Movement*, Stedelijk Museum, Amsterdam (travelled to the Moderna Museet, Stockholm)
1964   *Zero: European Experimental Art*, Institute of Contemporary Art, Philadelphia
1969   *Inflatable Sculpture*, Jewish Museum, New York (travelled to the De Witte Memorial Museum, San Antonio, Texas)
1970   *Kinetic Art*, Hayward Gallery, London
1973   *Westphalian Art*, Westfälisches Landesmuseum, Münster, West Germany

1977 *Documenta 6*, Museum Fridericianum, Kassel, West Germany

1981 *Centervideo*, American Center, Paris (travelled to the Kunstverein, Cologne)

1983 *Electra*, Musée d'Art Moderne de la Ville, Paris

1985 *Mehr Licht*, Kunsthalle, Hamburg

Collections:

Kunstmuseum, Dusseldorf; Museum om Ostwall, Dortmund, West Germany; Westfälisches Landesmuseum, Münster, West Germany; Städtische Kunstsammlungen, Bonn; Stedelijk Museum, Amsterdam; Stedelijk Van Abbemuseum, Eindhoven, Netherlands; Musée Royal des Beaux-Arts, Brussels; National Gallery of Canada, Ottawa; Museum of Modern Art, New York; Philadelphia Museum of Art.

Publications:

By PIENE: Books—*More Sky*, Cambridge, Massachusetts 1973; *Arttransition, You Are Here*, Cambridge, Massachusetts 1975; *Centerbeam*, Cambridge, Massachusetts 1980; *Centervideo*, exhibition catalogue, editor, with Elizabeth Goldring and Vin Grabill, Cambridge, Massachusetts 1981; *Sky Art Conference '81*, catalogue, editor, with others, Cambridge, Massachusetts 1981.

On PIENE: books—*Piene: Licht und Rauch/Graphik*, exhibition catalogue, Leverkusen, West Germany 1962; *Piene: Die Fleuerblume*, exhibition folder, Antwerp 1963; *Otto Piene: Permanentes Lichtballet*, exhibition catalogue, Stuttgart 1963; *Piene: Olbilder und Gouachen*, exhibition catalogue, Dusseldorf 1963; *Piene: Fire Flower Power*, exhibition folder/poster, with text by Eugen Thiemann, Dortmund, West Germany 1967; *Otto Piene: Elements*, exhibition catalogue, New York 1969; *Deutsche Kunst: Eine Neue Generation* by Rolf-Günter Dienst, Cologne 1970; *Hommage à Fontana* by Günter Aust, Wuppertal, West Germany 1969; *Deutsche Kunst der 60er Jahre: Malerei, Collage, Op-Art, Graphik* by Juliane Roh, Munich 1971; *Otto Piene: Bilder, Feuergouachen und Graphik 1957-1967, Skyart Portfolio 1969, Bilddokumentation 1967-1971*, exhibition catalogue, Munich 1971; *Otto Piene Lichtballet und Kunstler der Gruppe Zero*, exhibition catalogue, Munich 1972; *Otto Piene*, exhibition catalogue, with texts by Wulf Herzogenrath, Gerhard Storck and Lawrence Alloway, Cologne 1973; *Otto Piene: Paintings, Gouache, Drawings*, exhibition catalogue, with text by Lawrence Alloway, Cambridge, Massachusetts 1975; *Ars Electronica*, exhibition catalogue edited by Christine Schopf, Linz 1980.

What is painting?

A painting is a field of forces, the arena where its author's impluses all come together, there to be transformed, reformed into a movement of color. Energies which the painter has received out of the fullness of the universe are now directed into channels open to the spirit of the onlooker.

What is color?

Color is articulation of light.

And what is light?

Light is the sphere of everything that lives, the element in which the trialogue of painter, painting and spectator must take place; it is caught and intensified into a continuous vibration which contains all three.

What is vibration?

Vibration is nuance come alive; it outlaws contrast, shames tragedy and dismisses drama. It is the vehicle of the frequencies, the life-blood of color and the pulse of light. Vibration is pure emotion and pure energy, that which gives the picture its radiance.

What is pure energy?

The undisturbed continuum, never ending, unquenchable, the stuff of life.

What are they all, painting, color, light, vibration and pure energy?

Life. And the free spirit.

—Otto Piene

Otto Piene has used many different media, from Light Ballets to Smoke pictures and to performances and events involving balloons and kites. But they are linked by a fascination with light which runs through all his work, whether kinetic art which consists essentially of light sculptures or performances which are projected, programmed light manifestations.

In 1957 he was co-founder with Heinz Mack of Group Zero, one of the many groups and associations of kinetic artists formed during the late 1950's and early 60's, all dedicated to the use of new means in art. In contrast to the French Groupe de Recherche d'Art Visuel, with their scientific purism, Zero was at the romantic end of the spectrum in adopting an intuitive relationship with technology. They believed in light as *the* expansive medium, carrying energy from the artist to the spectator; they also believed that man has to live *with* rather than against technology, and that artists today should help to change the environment on a large scale, as opposed to a petty scale.

This desire to work on a scale large enough to "reharmonize . . . the relation beween man and nature" led Piene to go beyond the production of conventional art objects such as painting, to create works directed towards the aim of articulating light and making it real and perceptible as a natural force. The light paintings which he began making in 1957 were projected on to a wall, ceiling or floor by placing a precut stencil over a light source, Piene then developed these static light paintings into Light Ballets, using hand-operated lamps whose light he directed through the stencils in a series of different projections choreographed by accompanying sound such as jazz. The solo then turned into a group performance, with each member of the ensemble holding individual lamps and contributing different shapes and colours to the projection. A later stage was to mechanize the light ballet, using motors and other machines, with the use of revolving perforated discs to produce changing and overlapping light patterns. Piene has also used multitudes of tiny incandescent lamps to establish volumes in space, with shapes indicated by titles such as "Onion Flower" (1965), "Milky Way" (1965) or "Corona Borealis" (1965), and with their own spectrum of colour depending on the current running through them. He has also used walls of light as architectural installations, such as a facade of "sculptured" light operated by a programme for a store in Cologne.

But Piene has also been involved with light in the form of fire, and with the other traditional "elements" of earth, air, and water. His "elemental" art however includes also the "human elements" of the active participation of the spectators in his varied performances. His "fire pictures" involve the display of smoke and other effects of combustion, for instance by placing paper over a meshed screen with a candle under it, fixing the smoke and soot and indicating the kinship of these smoke vibration patterns with other natural forces in such titles as "Fire Flower." For his "air" art he has used flags, kites and streamers in various city spaces, a giant red balloon or windsock which dominated the 1970 Kinetics exhibition at London's Hayward Gallery, and all sorts of other inflatables. In 1961 Group Zero staged a series of demonstrations in the streets or on the banks of the Rhine, flying huge transparent hot-air balloons. Piene later developed such performances on an even more gigantic scale, as in his "Field of Hot Air Sculpture over a Fire in the Snow" in 1969 on an athletic field at M.I.T., composed of 30 transparent polythene balloons of different shapes and sizes, raised repeatedly with hot air from tanks spaced around the field, and all lit up by arc lights.

Piene's "sky events" of the late 1960's and early 70's thus drew together both environmental and participatory tendencies, and he has argued that "by exposing artists' work in places that are open to many peoples' eyes such as the sky—and by the use of broadcasting and televising techniques , . . the artist could be very helpful in rebuilding, reshaping, humanizing CITIES old and new." His book *More Sky* is a plea for more scope and space for art, for freeing it from museums and galleries and the making of objects in order to enable future artists to accept the challenge of taking on city planning and shaping tasks on a large scale, an environmental art for social use, with art and architecture, the city and the open landscape, all interacting in a total ecological and elemental aesthetics.

—Konstantin Bazarov

PIGNON, Edouard.

French. Born in Bully, Pas-de-Calais, 12 February 1905. Mainly self-taught in art, Paris, from 1927. Miner and stonemason, Bully, 1921-27; worked at various jobs while studying drawing and sculpture, Paris, 1928-38; independent artist, Paris, since 1938; concentrated on painting, from 1940; on theatrical decors, from 1948. Recipient: Grand Prix, *Bienal*, Sao Paulo, 1951; Guggenheim Prize, 1958; Gold Medal/Prix Leonardo da Vinci, 1973; Grand Prix des Arts, City of Paris, 1976. Agent: Galerie Beaubourg, 23 rue du Renard, 75004 Paris. Addresses: Le Moulin de la Colline, 399 rouade du Belvedere, 83140 Six-Fours, France; 26 rue des Plantes, 75014 Paris, France.

Individual Exhibitions:

1939 Maison de la Culture, Paris

1946 Galerie de France, Paris

1948 Galerie Apollo, Brussels

1949 Galerie de France, Paris

1951 Galerie Evrard, Lille, France
       Leicester Galleries, London

1952 Galerie de France, Paris

1953 Galerie de France, Paris

1954 University of Louisville, Kentucky

1955 Galerie de France, Paris (2 exhibitions)

1956 Perls Galleries, New York

1959 Galerie Rauch, Monte Carlo

1960 Galerie de France, Paris
       Musée de Metz, France
       Musée de l'Histoire et de l'Art, Luxembourg

1961 Galerie Spinazzola, Aix-en-Provence, France
       Musée des Beaux-Arts, Nantes, France

1962 Galerie de France, Paris
       Galerie du Passeur, France
       Galerie Cavalero, Cannes
       Galerie Parti Pris, Grenoble, France

1963 Galerie Spinazzola, Aix-en-Provence, France
       Maison de la Culture, Le Havre, France
       Guilde du Disque, Lausanne, Switzerland
       Kunsthandel M. L. de Boer, Amsterdam

1964 Galerie Desire, St. Etienne, France
       Galleria Nuova Milano, Milan
       Maison de la Culture, Caen, France
       Kunstmuseum, Lucerne
       Musée d'Art et d'Histoire, Geneva

1965 Musée des Beaux-Arts, Valenciennes, France
       Musée des Beaux-Arts, Lille, France
       Maison de la Culture, Namur, Belgium
       Palais des Beaux-Arts, Charleroi, Belgium

1966 Msuée d'Art Moderne, France
       Maison de la Culture, Rheims, France (toured France)

1968 Galerie de France, Paris

1969 Galerie La Proue, Rennes, France
       Galerie Argens, Strasbourg
       Galleria Nuova Pesa, Rome
       Centre Culturel, La Seyne, France
       Maison de la Culture, St. Etienne, France
       Abbye St. Hugues, Cluny, France
       Hotel de Ville, St. Etienne du Rouvray
       Galerie Municipale, Esch-Alzette, Luxembourg

1970 Galerie Philippe Reichenbach, Paris
       Galerie de France, Paris
       Musée Galliera, Paris
       Theatre du VIII, Lyons
       Centre Culturel, Venissieux, France
       Maison des Arts et Loisirs, Sochaux, France
       Group Scolaire Henri-Wallon, Trappes, France
       Musée d'Ingres, Montauban, France

1971 Seibu Newspaper Gallery, Tokyo

1972 Galerie Aspect, Brussels
       Galleria Tokrbandena, Trieste
       Théâtre du Parvis, Brussels

1973 Galerie de France, Paris
       Galleria Hausammann, Cortina d'Ampezzo, Italy
       Maison de la Culture, Paris (toured France)
       Galleria Pace, Milan
       Dalles Rooms, Bucharest (retrospective; toured Rumania, Hungary, Poland and Luxembourg)
       Establissements Usinor, Denain, France

1974	Galerie Protee, Toulouse
	Galleria Verrocchio, Pescara, Italy
	Hotel de Ville, Douai, France
	Musée de Calais, France
	Musée de St. Pol, France
	Hotel de Ville, St. Pol, France
	Hotel de Ville, St. Maxim, France
1975	Galleria Giorgio de Cillia, Udine, Italy
	Galerie Nicole Fourrier, Lyons
	Galerie Protee, Toulouse
	Chateau de Simiane, Valreas, France
	Galleria Civica d'Art Moderna, Bologna
	Fondatin Noroit, Arras, France
	Maison de la Culture, Saint-Genevieve des Bois, France (toured France)
	Musée de Seret, Pyrenées Orientales, France
1976	Musée d'Art Moderne de la Ville, Paris
1977	Galerie Anne et Albert Prouvost, Paris (retrospective)
	Hotel de Ville, St. Etienne du Rouvray, France
	Galerie Govaerts, Brussels
1978	Maison de la Culture, Nanterre, France
	Salle des Fetes Jean Vilar, Argenteuil, France
	Centre Culturel, Corbeil, France
	Hotel de Ville, Bayonne, France
	Musée des Beaux-Arts, Beziers, France (retrospective)
1979	Musée de Saint-Denis, France
	Galerie Armorial, Brussels
	Air-France Office, Roissy, France
1980	Centre des Telecommunications, La Londe-les-Maures, France
	Fondation Paul Ricard, Paris
	La Galerie du Verger, Touquet, France
	Palais des Arts et de la Culture, Brest, France
1981	Musée de la Seita, Paris (retrospective)
	Galerie d'Art Municipale, Esch-sur Alzette, Luxembourg
	Galerie des Granges, Geneva
	Galleria Villata, Cerina Monferrato, Italy
	Musée de la Poste, Paris
1982	Galleria La Gradiva, Rome
	Galerie Beaubourg, Paris
	Galleria Maggiore, Bologna, Italy
1983	Hôtel de Ville, Villeurbanne, France
	Maison de la Culture, Bourges, France
1984	Musée Picasso, Antibes, France
	Galleria La Gradiva, Rome
1985	Grand Palais, Paris (retrospective)
	Théâtre Jean-Louis Barrault, Paris
	Galerie Trigano, Paris
	Galerie Beaubourg, Paris
	Galerie Regis Dorval, Lille, France
	Galleria La Gradiva, Rome
1986	Musée de Dieppe, France
	Musée de Issoudun, France
	Musée de Lens, France
	Galleria Il Fante di Spada, Milan
	Galerie Condillac, Bordeaux
	Galerie Gastaud, Clermont-Ferrand, France
	Galerie de Luxembourg, Luxembourg
1987	Musée de Sète, France
	Galerie Beaubourg, Paris

Selected Group Exhibitions:

1932	*Salon des Indépendants*, Paris (regularly from 1932)
1944	*Salon de Mai*, Paris (regularly from 1944)
1955	*New Decade*, Museum of Modern Art, New York
1961	*Post-War European Art*, Stedelijk Van Abbemuseum, Eindhoven, Netherlands
1971	*Painters of Paris since 1950*, Fundacao Gulbenkian, Lisbon
1978	*Paris des Années 50*, Galerie Ariel, Paris
1979	*Celebration en Bleu*, Manege Royal, Saint-Germain en Laye, France
1980	*Les Années 30 en France*, Musée d'Art et d'Industrie, St. Etienne, France
1982	*Le Paysage Revolutionnaire de Cezanne à nos Jours*, Action Artistique Francaise Galerie, Tokyo
1986	*Cinquantenaire du Front Populaire*, Musée de Saint-Brieuc, France

Collections:

Centre Georges Pompidou, Paris; Centre National d'Art Contemporain, Paris; Tate Gallery, London; Musée d'Histoire et de l'Art, Luxembourg; Musée des Beaux-Arts, La Chaux de Fonds, Switzerland; Museum of Contemporary Art, Skopje, Yugoslavia; National Museum of Modern Art, Tokyo; Museu de Arte Moderna, Sao Paulo; Johannesburg Museum, South Africa; Museum of Moderna Art, New York.

Publications:

By PIGNON: books—*Battages et Pousseurs de Ble*, with Georges Bataille, Paris 1962; *La Quete de la Réalité*, Paris 1966; *Contre Courant*, Paris 1973; illustrated books—*Les Blason* by Maurice Sceve, Paris 1945; *Noir sur Blanc* by Helene Parmelin, Paris 1955; *Dialogues de l'Arbre* by Paul Valery, Paris 1958; *Jacques le Fataliste* by Diderot, West Berlin 1967; *Lumière de Beatrice* by Gerald Mourgue, Paris 1974; *Cinquante de Poesie* by Eugenio Montale, Paris 1974; *Mascarade* by Ronsard, Paris 1976; *Poèmes* by Daniel Gelin, Paris 1979.

On PIGNON: books—*Cinq Peintres d'Aujourd'hui* by Frank Elgar, Paris 1943; *Pignon* by Henri Lefebre, Paris 1956; *Cinq Peintres et le Théâtre* by Helene Parmelin, Paris 1957; *Edouard Pignon* by Helene Parmelin, Paris 1960; *Edouard Pignon: 50 peintures de 1936 à 1962*, edited by Jean-Louis Ferrier, Paris 1962; *Edouard Pignon* by Henri Lefebre, Paris 1970; *Pignon* by Raoul-Jean Moulin and André Calles, Paris 1970; *50 Nus de Pignon* by Giuseppe Marchiori, Paris 1973; *Rencontre avec Pignon* by E. Maurizi, Paris 1974; *Pignon* by Jean-Louis Ferrier, Paris 1976; *Histoire des Nus* by Helene Parmelin, Paris 1976; *Pignon*, exhibition catalogue, Paris 1981; *Pignon*, exhibition catalogue, Rome 1982; *Poesimage numero special: Pignon*, Savigny-le-Temple 1983; *Pignon*, exhibition catalogue, Paris 1985; *Pignon: touches et zigzag pur un portrait* by Helene Parmelin, Paris 1987; films—*Pignon* my Mitrani, 1961; *Pignon* by Michel Chapuis, 1962; *Edouard Pignon* by Guy Suzuki, 1964; *Pignon: Peintre du Nord* by Bernard Claeys, 1965; *Pignon* by Michel Chapius and Charles Chaboud, 1966; *Pignon* by Pierrer Dumayet, 1970; *Pignon: Courte Biographie Cinematographique* by Guy Gilles, 1970; *Les Seigneurs de la Guerre de Pignon* by Fleurent, 1970; *Pignon* by Josiane Serror, 1973; *Edouard Pignon* by Alain Leroy, 1974; *Edouard Pignon* by Michel Lacelot, 1978; *Pignon* by Patrick Barberis, 1982; *Pignon* by Pierre Daix, 1985; *L'Homme debout, Edouard Pignon* by Jean-Luc Ardouin and Gabrielle Althen, 1985.

*   *   *

Throughout a long artistic life, the hallmark of Pignon has been durable continuity. The son of a miner from Marles-les-Mines whose family had been employed in deep mining man and boy for nearly three centuries, Edouard Pignon was one of several children growing up in poor circumstances.

In 1912, Èdouard Pignon saw the horrors of the pit disaster at La Clarence which killed close on 100 workers. The tragedy imprinted itself on his mind and was many years later made by him the subject of two of his important paintings each entitled "Ouvrier mort". At the local school, Pignon was awarded a 'certificate' for the promise he showed in his art studies. He loved drawing. During the years of the First World War, his mother ran a bar while his father worked in the mine and, when a soldier, on his way to the battle-front, stopped at Mme. Pignon's estaminet for a drink, the young Pignon drew a portrait of him and was so fascinated by the likeness contained in the result that, for the first time he felt in touch with the magic of Art. Even after the armistice the havoc wreaked in France by the War seemed inescapable. In the year of 1919 his father fell ill with silicosis. At 14 Edouard himself went to work in the mines, a job he hated because of the pervading darkness.

Against such a background, he continued to occupy himself with his drawings whenever the opportunity presented itself. And within him the determination to one day entirely devote himself to becoming an artist grew and grew. Because of this obsession, in 1922 he enrolled in a drawing correspondence course and, by now, was buying books dealing with Fine Art, writing to Paris for one such book about Matisse and another concerned with the art of La Fresnaye and was able to lay hands on a thesis called 'Le Metier de Rubens'

which told him a great deal about oil painting techniques; he also came across a small publication about Van Gogh and was able to purchase a large reproduction of Picasso's *Moissonneurs*. But it was not until a year later that he made his first trip to Paris, spending a few days in the capital which enabled him fit in a day trip to Lille and discover the marvels of Goya's "Les Vieilles et les Jeunes".

This account to contain and expand his artistic ambitions and struggles continued and continued (even during his military service when he was able to complete his first oil paitning—*Portrait of Uncle Edouard*).

The early years were hard indeed. They involved switching from one job to another just to survive and escape unemployment. At one point, he even obtained a 'licence' to make 'pignons dentés' and join evening classes in the Boulevard Montparnasse. Nevertheless, despite penury, his social horizon was broadening. In Paris, he was meeting many new friends, a kaleidoscope of intellectuals and artists (including the artist Arpad Szenes). It was these contacts that encouraged him to visit the Paris galleries specializing in 'contemporary' (1929) art—the cubism of Picasso, the works by La Fresnaye, Braque, Bonnard, Matisse and Lèger.

While in employment with the Renault Company, he became a member of l'AEAR—*The Association of Revolutionary Artists and Writers*, a prelude to his membership of the Communist Party for which he was blacklisted and sacked by Renault. L'AEAR organized a large exhibition of art works, including among them three of Pignon's latest paintings, touched in style a little with cubist influence and owing something of their strength to Lèger.

During the 1930s, the scale of his acquaintances continued to increase. He could now number amongst his friends and colleagues Lèger, Lhôte, Szenes, Vieira da Silva, the Prevért brothers, Malraux, Hèlion, Herbin, Lipschitz, Marcel Duhamel and Robert Delaunay, amongst whom there was a constant series of interplays of ideas all helping to transform the peasant boy from the mines into an active participant in the Art World of France. As a Party Member of the Communists, taking his place alongside of Picasso, Lèger and Lhôte, his art gravitated towards acquisition of a steady revolutionary accent, soon to become strongly evident in his work, a factor which has persisted (acceptable or—more frequently—unacceptable because it was so remote from Social Realism by hardline Communists) from that day to this.

With pictures now being accepted for exhibition from him by numerous galleries in Paris (including temporary exhibitions in museums and set up by organizations) it can still prove difficult to discover in these early works the actual *trend* (however mixed at various stages of his development in style) leading to what has come to be recognized today in whatever form as typical flavour of Pignon's oeuvre. This realization of how we have come to expect the Pignon artistic personality to register in pictorial expression on his canvases so that the artist's signature is assumed before it is read had to wait until after the Second World War. (Even then it was much cooler and less strident than his painting was to become later.)

Pignon did not sell one of his pictures until 1939. This was a painting he had made during his time in the French airforce, stationed at Villacoublay, a 'maternité' titled *La Toilette*, now in the permanent collection of the Musée d'Art Moderne de la Ville de Paris.

Pignon joined the French Resistance. Some twelve months later, at the request of Jeanne Bucher (the founder of the Paris gallery which bears her name) he moved into the home of Lipschitz, evacuated by the sculptor who left for the USA when he realized the danger in which he stood from the Nazis. At the Lipschitz home in Boulogne where Pignon set up house he made a point of burying the sculptor's bronzes in the garden where they remained undetected until they were dug up after hostilities and the occupation of France ended.

The 'history' of Pignon—there is much more to it—

ought to end without more ado because it is time to give a proper examination of the artwork of this fierce rebel. Even so, it should be borne in mind that he had become in his way a sort of proto-Eurocommunist, rejecting Stalin (but not the Soviet Union), rejecting 'social-realism' (but not Communism), rejecting 'engagierter Kunst' (but not the politics it sought to promote), against the occupations of Hungary and Czechoslovakia (preferring to declare support for those who resisted the Russian invasions of those two States). Pignon was permanently in opposition to the War in Vietnam, General de Gaulle, all forms of Fascism and anything that smacked of Conservatism and Centrism. All these attitudes he sought to express in his pictures.

At the outset of 1949, he was painting pictures which somehow managed to combine the quiet composition qualities of André Lhôte with a loosely designed atmosphere of Raoul Dufy at his casual best with perhaps even a hint—in figuration, not in colouring—of Marquet. Vigour and violence of brush strokes and a sort of suppressed temper were in strong evidence 1958 onwards. Trees and other vegetation raged in swirling contortions. Imagery steadily became more ferociously and markedly coherent. Colours, with Pignon reservations, took on alarming aggression often in direct contrast with messages implied by the subjects.

In the 1960s, it was as if the wonderful harvesting scenes he had once painted were all forgotten. Now the fields and woods were full of battle and the bleeding heart of struggle.

Then, another switch. From 1966 to 1980 war was virtually swept into the background to be replaced by Divers. The *plongeurs* were rich in brilliant colours. The erstwhile blacks and greens and dark blues gave way to vibrant pinks, emeralds, and maroons. And they were interspersed with other subject matter that this tireless and violent painter pressed into service to give his paintings still greater intensity of feeling-cumdisruption.

By the late 1970s, after the vicious paintings of the 'Cockfights' came a special tribute to flamboyant womanhood; sometimes these nudes, in all their unashamed pulchritude, would let themselves curve or pose in statuesque stance, but more often their happy abandonment sheds any accent of modesty into a careless oblivion.

Where can one place the endless career of this turbulent artistic dissenter, this active co-operator in his lonely antagonism, an artist and a man at total odds with anything which allies itself to the status-quo, fundamentally against all other kinds of revolt but his own, way to the Left but the indomitable foe of the aparatchik? Where indeed? The very length of the list of his artist and intellectual friends—such a close relationship with Picasso first in Vallauris and Sanary for instance—fails not to assure one of his status as an extraordinary and exceptional artist on the contemporary scene. To select one of his recent inspirations—one can only suppose that the uncategorisable Pignon will just continue to plunge on and on.

—Sheldon Williams

PIPER, John.
British. Born in Epsom, Surrey, 13 December 1903. Educated at Epsom College, 1917–21; articled clerk in his father's law office, Piper, Smith and Piper, London, 1921–26; studied under Raymond Coxon, Richmond School of Art, Surrey, 1926–27; under Morris Kestelman and Francis Spear, Royal College of Art, London, 1927–29; and at the Slade School of Fine Art, London 1930. Served as Official War Artist, with Ministry of Information, London 1940–45; recorded bomb damage, communications and marshalling yards. Married Eileen Holding in 1929 (divorced 1937); married Myfanwy Evans in 1937.

Painter, in Betchworth, Surrey, 1927–35, and in Hammersmith, London, 1929–35, in Henley, Oxforshire, since 1935: contributed criticism to *Nation, Atheneum, New Statesman* and *The Listener*, London, 1928–30; visited Paris, 1933; Founder, with Myfanwy Evans, *Axis* magazine, London, 1935–37; Founder, with Robert Wellington and Baynard and Curwen Presses. *Contemporary Lithographs,* London, 1936; designed sets and costumes for *The Quest* ballet, with music by William Walton, London, 1943; Founder Member, English Opera group, London, 1947; worked on lithographs at Mourlot's Studios, Paris 1953, and on designs for the Baptistry window, Coventry Cathedral, 1957–62. Trustee, Tate Gallery, London, 1944–61. Member, Royal Fine Art Commission, since 1959. Recipient: Lithography Prize, Vietnamese Government, 1963. Honorary doctorate: University of Leicester, 1960; Oxford University, 1964; University of Sussex, Brighton, 1974. Honorary Associate, Royal Institute of British Architects, 1957, and Royal College of Art, 1959. Companion of Honour, London, 1972. Agent: James Kirkman Limited, 46 Brompton Square, London SE3 2AF. Address: Fawley Bottom Farm House, Henley on Thames, Oxfordshire, England.

Individual Exhibitions:

1927	Arlington Galleries, London (with David Birch)
1933	Zwemmer Gallery, London
1938	London Gallery
1940	Leicester Galleries, London
1941	Temple Newsam, Leeds (with Graham Sutherland and Henry Moore)
1945	Leicester Galleries, London
1946	Leicester Galleries, London
1948	Curt Valentin Gallery, New York
1950	Curt Valentin Gallery, New York
1951	Leicester Galleries, London
1953	*Aldeburgh Festival,* Suffolk
	Arts Council Gallery, Cambridge
1955	Curt Valentin Gallery, New York
1956	Kunstsaal Magdelene Sothman, Amsterdam
1957	Durlacher Gallery, New York
	Leicester Galleries, London
1959	Leicester Galleries, London
1960	Arthur Jeffress Gallery, London
	Gloucester Art Gallery, London (with Lynn Chadwick)
	Durlacher Gallery, New York
1962	Arthur Jeffress Gallery, London
1963	Marlborough Fine Art, London
1964	Marlborough Fine Art, London
1966	Marlborough Fine Art, London (with Sidney Nolan and Ceri Richards)
1967	Marlborough Fine Art, London (toured the U.K.)
	Marlborough Fine Art, London (with Ceri Richards)
1969	Marlborough Fine Art, London
	Bear Lane Gallery, Oxford
1970	Hammet Gallery, London
	Derwent College, University of York
	Century Galleries, Sonning, Berkshire
	Pieter Wenning Gallery, Johannesburg
	Folkstone Adult Education Centre, Kent
1972	Marlborough Fine Art, London
1973	Marjorie Parr Gallery, London
	Compendium Galleries, Birmingham
	Paintings, Drawings, Prints and Illustrated Books, Frank Gadsby Gallery, Leicester
	Pieter Wenning Gallery, Johannesburg
	9th Century Festival, Lincoln Cathedral, Lincolnshire
1974	Parc Howard Gallery, Llanelli, South Wales
1975	University of York
1976	School of Art and Design, Sheffield, Yorkshire
	Gallery Kasahara, Osaka
1977	Marlborough Fine Art, London
	Hambledon Gallery, Blandford Forum, Dorset
1978	University of Cardiff
	Bohum Gallery, Henley-on-Thames, Oxfordshire
	The Maltings, Snape, Aldeburgh, Suffolk
	Glynn Vivian Art Gallery and Museums, Swansea, South Wales

1979	*50 Years of Work,* Museum of Modern Art, Oxford (travelled to The Minories, Colchester, Essex)
1980	Regimental Chapel, Manchester Chatedral
	Rufford Craft Centre, Ollerton, Nottinghamshire
1981	Maclean Gallery, London
	Dorchester Abbey, Dorset
	Marlborough Fine Art, London
1982	Solomon Gallery, Dublin
	Blackman Harvey, London
	Newlyn Art Gallery, Cornwall
	Kettle's Yard Gallery, Cambridge
1983	*John Piper,* at the *Aldeburgh Festival,* Suffolk
	Marlborough Fine Art, London
	Tate Gallery, London (retrospective)
1984	*John Piper,* at the *Lichfield Festival,* Staffordshire
	Marlborough Gallery, New York

Selected Group Exhibitions:

1932	*New English Art Society: 7 and 5,* Zwemmer Gallery, London
1935	*Abstract-Concrete,* Zwemmer Gallery, London
1942	*New Movements in Art,* London Museum, Lancaster House, London
1951	*Festival of Britain,* London
1955	*Aldeburgh Festival,* Suffolk
1965	*Axis, Circle, Unit One,* Marlborough Fine Art, London
1970	*International Art Fair,* Kunsthalle, Basle
1973	*Contemporary British Painters and Sculptors,* Marlborough-Godard Gallery, Toronto
1977	*British Painting 1952–1977,* Royal Academy of Arts, London
1981	*Drawings and Watercolours of 13 British Artists,* Marlborough Fine Art, London

Collections:

Tate Gallery, London; Victoria and Albert Museum, London; Guggenheim Museum, New York; Museum of Modern Art, New York; Phillips Collection, Washington, D.C.; National Gallery of Canada, Ottawa; Museum of Modern Art, Sao Paulo.

Publications:

By PIPER: books—*The Wind in the Trees,* 1924; *Shell Guide to Oxfordshire,* London 1938; *Shell Guide to Shropshire,* with John Betjeman, London 1939, 1951; *British Romantic Artists,* London 1942; *Murray's Architectural Guide to Buckinghamshire,* with John Betjeman, London 1948; *Murray's Architectural Guide to Berkshire,* with John Betjeman, London 1949, articles—"Obituary: Adrian Stokes" in *Architectural Review* (London), March 1973; "A Piper Portfolio," interview, with M. Margetts, in *Crafts* (London), January/February 1979; books—illustrated *Wordsworth's Guide to the Lakes,* edited by W. Moelwyn Merchant, London 1952; *Selbourne* by Gilbert White, London, 1962.

On PIPER: books—*John Piper* by John Betjeman, London 1944; *John Piper: Paintings, Drawings and Theatre Designs 1932–54,* London 1955; *John Piper: European Topography 1967–69, Oil Paintings and Gouaches,* London 1969; *The Painter's Object,* edited by Myfanwy Evans, London 1970; *Paintings, Drawings, Prints and Illustrated Books by John Piper,* exhibition catalogue, by R. Graham, Leicester 1973; *John Piper: 50 Years of Work,* exhibition catalogue, by John Betjeman, J. Hoole and others, Oxford 1979; *John Piper* by A. West, London 1979; *John Piper: Paintings in Coloured Light,* exhibition catalogue with introduction by Martin Harrison, Cambridge 1982; *Piper's Places* by Richard Ingrams, London 1983; *John Piper: Retrospective Exhibition,* catalogue with texts by David Fraser Jenkins, John Russell and others, London 1983; articles—"The Sitwells Tuscan Castle: Watercolours by John Piper" by Gervaise Jackson-Stops in *Country Life* (London), January 1981.

At the Royal College of Art, John Piper cultivated the traditional English concern for drawing that he has consistently used in the several branches of art he has practised since, including painting in oils and watercolour, engraving, designing for theatrical production and stained glass design. His intense interest in look-

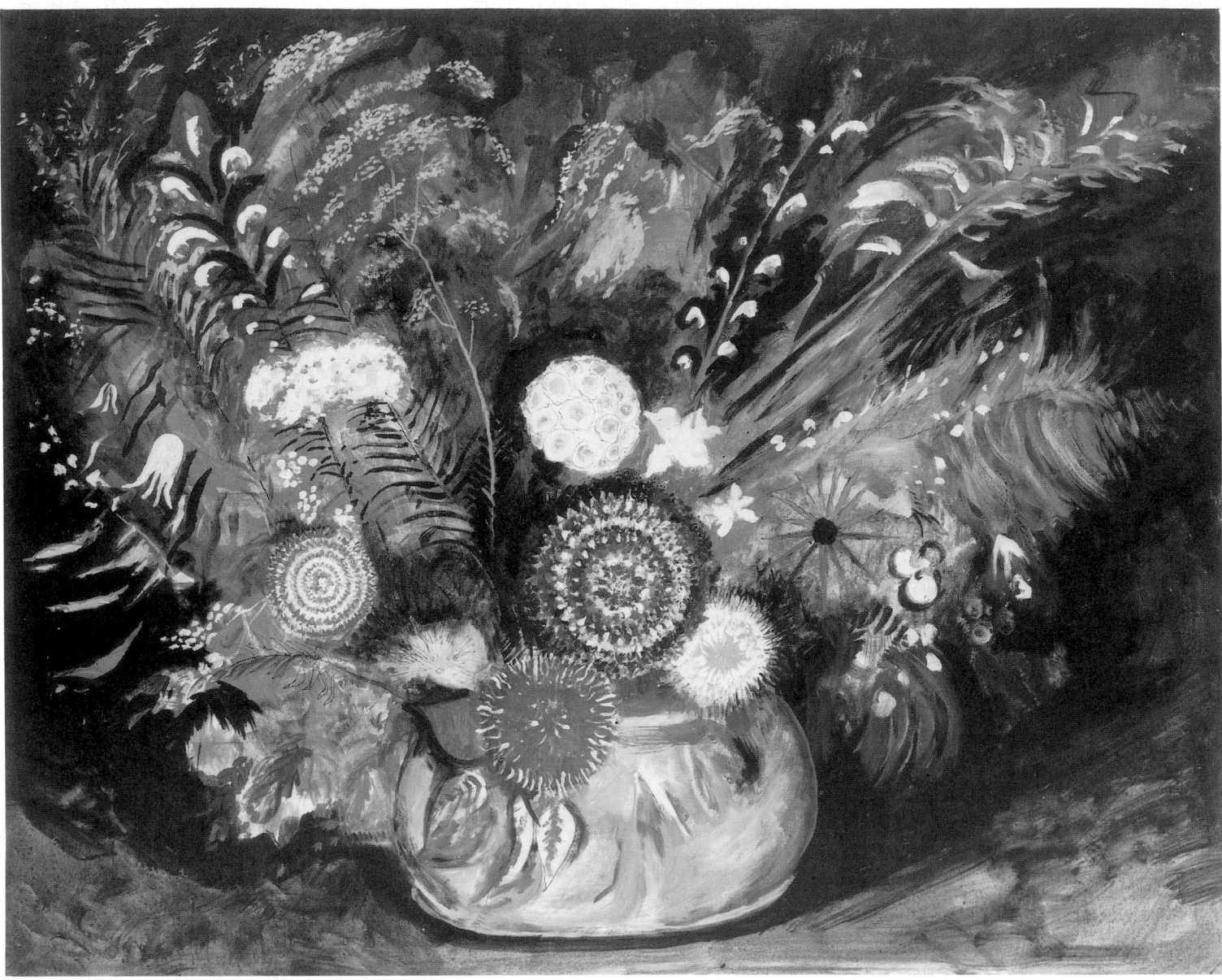

John Piper: *Summer Flowers I*, 1986

ing at art, and reading and discussion, led him to write discerning art criticism. He had also a great love for music and the theatre, also for archaeology and architecture, a profession he once thought of entering.

Piper's early pictures were more or less straightforward renderings of picturesque views of the landscape of the South Coast. Then in 1933 he visited Paris and met some of the leading figures then veering towards the abstract; they included Braque, Léger, Brancusi and Hélion. For a time, Piper composed landscapes that reflected this abstract influence. Observation of natural phenomena has always been at the root of Piper's art, followed by architecture taking a high place in subject matter.

Lively stylization enlivened his treatment of given scenes, especially during the Second World War, in which he served as an official war artist with a special interest in recording the damage to historic buildings. He also worked on preserving in pictorial form records of Britain's distinctive visual character in its town and villages. After the war, Piper made frequent trips on the Continent by car and exhibited series of the oils and water-colours he made of the buildings and landscapes of France and Italy. In particular Venice provided him with much material, and his dark palette of the 1939–1945 period was replaced by a scheme of warmer hues. While the figure is almost totally absent from his paintings, there is consistent reflection of man's presence in the many pictures of churches and inhabited communities. He has been de-

scribed as a 20th century Piranesi, though he lacks the Italian's theatrical drama.

To some degree Piper is perhaps the victim of his own versatility in that some of his slighter topographical works do not quite live up to the reputation won by his larger and more impressive oils. He invests his paintings with a significant atmosphere that can be immensely evocative. Light is a vital ingredient of his art and he will be remembered also for the brilliantly incandescent stained-glass window he designed for Coventry Cathedral.

—G. S. Whittet

PISANI, Vettor.

Italian. Born in Bari, 14 June 1935; lived on the Island of Ischia until 1945, then moved to Naples. Studied architecture at a Jesuit School, Naples, c. 1950. Founder, Rosa Croce Theatre and School of Art, Rome. Recipient: Premio Pino Pascali, Bari, Italy, 1970. Address: via A. Poliziano 78, 00184 Rome, Italy.

Individual Exhibitions:

1970   *Maschile, Femminile e Androgino: Incesto e Cannibalismo in Marcel Duchamp*, Galleria La Salita, Rome
       Galleria Arte Contemporanea, Rome
       Amoremio, Palazzo Ricci, Montepulciano, Italy (with Michelangelo Pistoletto)
       Premio Nazionale Pino Pascali, Castello Svevo, Bari, Italy
1973   Galleria L'Attico, Rome
1976   *Incontri Internazionale d'Arte*, Rome (with Michelangelo Pistoletto)
1982   *Vettor Pisani: R. C. Theatrum*, Museum Folkwang, Essen

Selected Group Exhibitions:

1970   *Vitalita del Negativo*, Palazzo delle Esposizioni, Rome
1971   *Bienal*, Sao Paulo
       Arte Povera, Kunstverein, Munich
1972   *Documenta*, Kassel, West Germany
1977   *Settimana della Performance*, Bologna
1980   *Italian Art Now: An American Perspective*, Guggenheim Museum, New York
1982   *Arte Italiana 1960–82*, Hayward Gallery, London
1986   *Esculturas sobre la Pared*, Galeria Juana de Aizpuru, Madrid

Publications:

By PISANI: articles—"Il Teatro a Coda" and "Per Coerenza: in *Vettor Pisani: R. C. Theatrum,* exhibition catalogue, Essen 1982.

On PISANI: books—*Vettor Pisani,* exhibition catalogue, by Achille Bonito Oliva and others, Bari, Italy 1970; *La Performance,* Macerata, Italy 1978; *Vetto Pisani: R. C. Theatrum,* exhibition catalogue, by Maurizio Calvesi, Essen 1982; articles—"L'Arte Povera" by Renato Barilli in *L'Arte Moderna,* Milan 1975; "Vettor Pisani" by Tommaso Trini in *Data* (Milan), October/November 1976; "Vettor Pisani" in *Data* (Milan), Summer 1978.

Since the 1970's the art of Vettor Pisani has founded its true alchemical significance in its language, which has a closed/open oscillation rich in dark, symbolic areas; he proceeds by hermeneutic antitheses, brooding on indirect references, he assumes different attitudes in his work, revealing complex, sometimes actually irreconcilable, paths. He does not possess a single technique through which the work of art appears diversified, as if isolated from the global contest of the discourse. Pisani uses a language that is inexorably deductive, which forces the viewer to be suspicious of a deductive interpretation of the cause-and-effect type. Its course is thus a sort of spiral, winding round the same violent alchemical significance.

With its orientative power, the language of Pisani's art continually displaces the real to unveil it internally through obscure poetic differences in level. Its secret space ends where nature begins, an alchemical nature, as we see in the work "The Hero's Bedroom" of 1970. But his evocative power is oedipal; thus, while the artist identifies himself with the materials that compose the work of art, he discovers disconcerting elective affinities in them which take the work to the origin of creativity, of existence as an artist. The mystery of art remains mysterious; only bright or dark whirlpools are revealed within it. The work of art hints at the dazzling conceptual truth present in the alchemical significance. In the work called "The Stuggle of Light and Darkness" (1980) Pisani prefigures his own birth as an artist; the island of Ischia, where he lived as a child, is lit by a brilliant light, the symbolic image of art's creativity.

A theatrical production unites Vettor Pisani's works. They are linked because they have in common the flowing, circular birth of the representation itself. The alchemical significances never upset their own contents, because they are initial premises, unchanted and undulating. Within its theatricality (regardless of the everyday environment) the work of art jealously guards the complexity of its own (masculine/feminine) origin. The revelation of it depends on the intellectual paths taken by the observer's eyes, in which the visual-mental possibilities of interpretation are vigorously intertwined. Out of the depths they rise up to the light, to the subtle, changing play of nature, to the imagination's ornamentation. There is no superstition in art, but remote, mysterious beauty, which the artist transforms with amazement and alarm because he knows that he has eternity before him—eternity violated by poetry and imagination, spectres of the imprecision and obscurity of art. In the "Orient" as in the "Occident," says Pisani, the artist loves nature and its labyrinths. And so it all starts again from the beginning, in a circle, through new indefinite identifications. Art is the eternal Eden.

—Italo Mussa

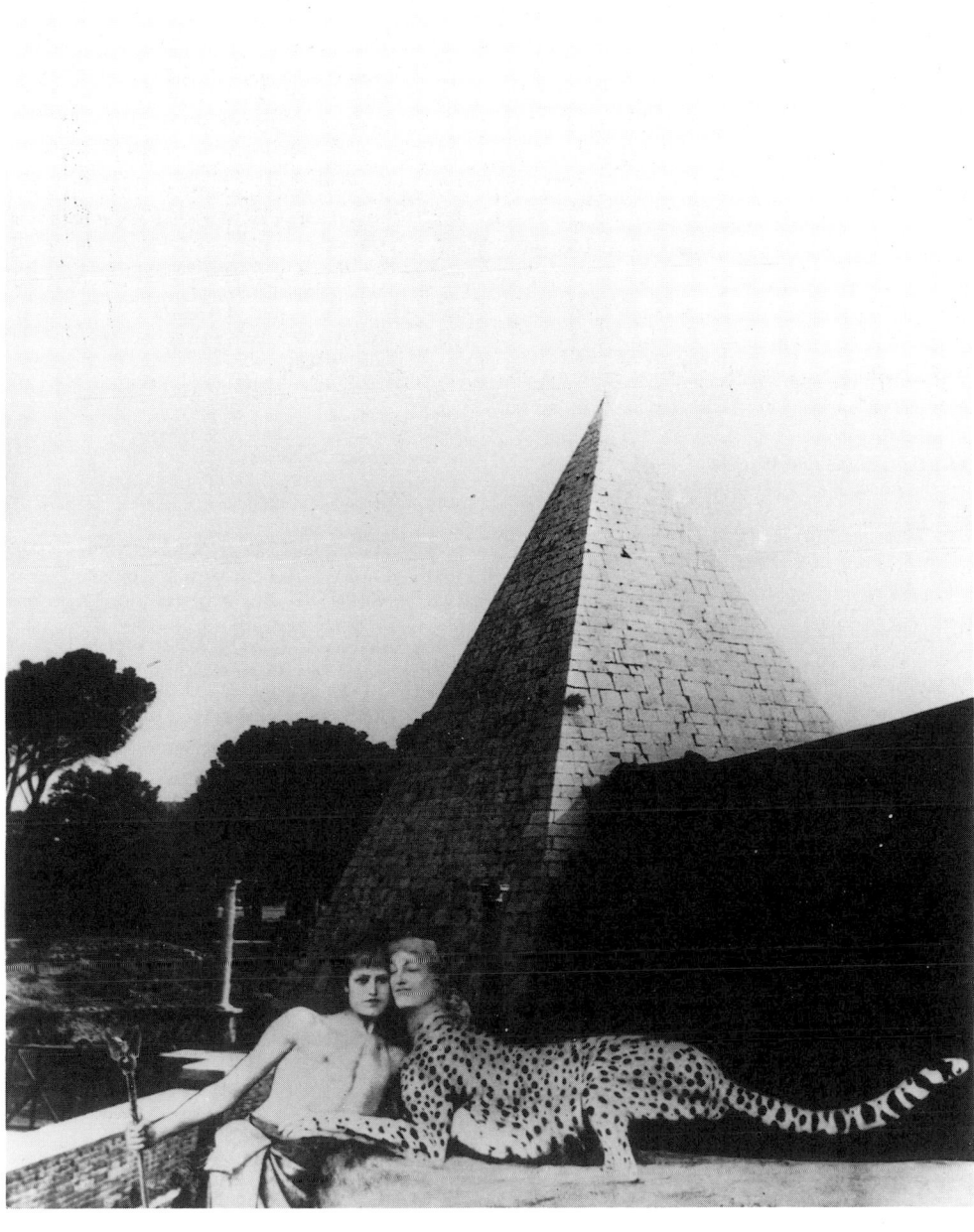

Vettor Pisani: *Oedipus and the Sphinx,* 1980

PISTOLETTO, Michelangelo.
Italian. Born in Biella, 23 June 1933; moved with his family to Turin, 1934. Self-taught in art; assistant to father in picture restoration business, Turin, 1957. Executed first painting, 1956; first sculptures, 1964; actions and happenings, 1970; worked in Berlin 1978; travelled for two years in the United States giving performances, 1979–81. Recipient: DAAD Grant, 1978. Agent: Galleria Lucio Amelio, Piazza dei Martiri 58, 80121 Naples, Address: Via Argonne 1, 10133 Turin, Italy.

Individual Exhibitions:

1960	Galleria Galatea, Turin
1963	Galleria Galatea, Turin
1964	Galerie Ileana Sonnabend, Paris
	Galleria Sperone, Turin
	Galleria del Leone, Venice
1965	Ideal Standard, Milan
	Galerie Heiner Friedrich, Munich
1966	Walker Art Center, Minneapolis
	Galleria del Leone, Venice
	Galleria Sperone, Turin
	Galleria La Bertesca, Genoa
	Studio Pistoletto, Turin
1967	Galleria Sperone, Turin
	Galerie Zwirner, Cologne
	Hudson Gallery, Detroit
	Palais des Beaux-Arts, Brussels
	Galleria Naviglio, Milan
	Galerie Ileana Sonnabend, Paris
	Kornblee Gallery, New York
	Museum Boymans-van Beuningen, Rotterdam
	Badischer Kunstverein, Karlsruhe, West Germany
	Albright-Knox Art Gallery, Buffalo, New York
1969	*Warhol/Pistoletto,* New Gallery, Cleveland
1970	Palazzo Ricci, Montepulciano, Italy (with Vettor Pisani)
	Modern Art Agency, Naples
	Galleria dell'Ariete, Milan
	Galleria Sperone, Turin
1972	Galleria dell'Ariete, Milan
	Kunstverein, Frankfurt
	Galleria Toninelli, Rome
1973	Galleria Sperone, Turin
	Marlborough Galleria d'Arte, Rome
	Kestner-Gesellschaft, Hannover
1984	Sidney Janis Gallery, New York
	Kestner-Gesellschaft, Hannover
	Galerie Mathildenhohe, Darmstadt
	Galerie Günther Sachs, Hamburg

1975 Galleria Sperone, Rome
Modern Art Agency, Naples
Galleria Multipli, Turin
Galleria Christian Stein, Turin
Castelli Graphics Gallery, New York
1976 Galleria Christian Stein, Turin
Galleria Salvatore Alan, Milan
Galerie Saman, Genoa
Incontri Internazionale d'Arte, Rome (with Vettor Pisani)
Palazzo Grassi, Venice
1977 Galerie Marie Louise Jeanneret Art Moderne, Geneva
1978 Nationalgalerie, West Berlin
1979 Institute of Arts, Rice University, Houston
Georgia Museum of Arts, Athens
1980 *Nazionale per la Grafica,* Rome (with Giulio Paolini and Luca Patella)
1981 Westfalischer Landesmuseum, Munster, West Germany
1982 Galleria Pieroni, Rome
Galerie Tanit, Munich
1983 Galleria Giorgio Petano, Turin
Galleria La Polena, Genoa, Italy
Italian Cultural Institute, Madrid
1984 Centre d'Art Contemporain, Geneva
Centro d'Art Contemporanea, Syracuse, Italy
1985 Palacio de Velazquez, Madrid
Galerie de France, Paris
1986 Kunstnernes Hus, Oslo
1987 Montevideo Galerie, Antwerp, Belgium

Selected Group Exhibitions:

1958 *Premio San Fedele,* Milan
1964 *Niewe Realisten,* Gemeentemuseum, The Hague
1966 *The Object Transformed,* Museum of Modern Art, New York
1969 *Information,* Museum of Modern Art, New York
1970 *Land Art/Arte Povera/Conceptual Art,* Museo Civico d'Arte Moderna, Turin
1975 *Realismus und Realität,* Kunsthalle, Darmstadt
1977 *La Traccia del Racconto,* Villa Comunale Ormand, San Remo, Italy
1982 *Documenta,* Kassel, West Germany
1985 *The European Iceberg,* Art Gallery of Ontario, Toronto
1986 *Aspects of Italian Art 1960–86,* Kunstverein, Frankfurt

Collections:

Albright-Knox Art Gallery, Buffalo, New York; Kaiser Wilhelm Museum, Krefeld, West Germany; Kunstmuseum, Dusseldorf.

Publications:

By PISTOLETTO: books—*Le Ultime Parole Famose,* Turin 1967; *L'Uomo Nero: Il Lato Insopportabile,* Salerno, Italy 1970.

On PISTOLETTO: books—*Michelangelo Pistoletto: A Reflected World* by M. Friedman, Minneapolis 1966; *Pistoletto,* exhibition catalogue, by Henry Martin, Rotterdamn 1969; *Michelangelo Pistoletto,* exhibition catalogue, by Wieland Schmied, Hannover 1973; *Michelangelo Pistoletto,* exhibition catalogue, by Bernd Krimmel, Darmstadt 1974; *Michelangelo Pistoletto: Les Quatre Saisons,* exhibition catalogue with preface by Guiseppe Conte, Paris 1985; articles—"Pistoletto" by Henry Martin in *Art International* (Lugano, Switzerland), February 1969; "Pistoletto Traverse le Miroir" by A. Boatto in *Opus International* (Paris), March 1972; "Michelangelo Pistoletto" by Tommaso Trini in *Data* (Milan), July/September 1976; "Pistoletto's American Campaign" by M. Welish in *Art in America* (New York), February 1981.

Michelangelo Pistoletto's early work dates from the mid-1950's, but it was a 1961 painting which marked a truly significant point in his development as an artist. After completing a series of large self-portraits

but this time done on an acrylic base coated with plastic varnish so that the surface became extremely mirror-like. The effect was striking—so much so that Pistoletto changed the entire direction of his work. What now interested him was the possibility of establishing a reciprocal relationship between the images painted in the canvas and the images reflected on its highly polished surface. Thus Pistoletto was setting up a relationship between art and life, between reality and pictorial invention, an artistic intention which provided the key to his work during this period.

The early self-portraits and "reflecting" paintings were followed by completely mature works in which mirror-like surfaces still played an important role. Pistoletto now drew and then photographed images which he then attached to polished metal surfaces, thus moving from a kind of formalism to a kind of reporting: painting becomes photography. The earlier relationships between reality and invention are now replaced by relationships established between reality and its reflected image, thus affording two levels of interpretation: we have the relationships of image to reflection, and the image itself. In three works from 1965, "No Higher Fares on the Train," "Vietnam" and "Coming," a pattern is set: the viewer is not passive but interacts with the images which reflect his own presence.

Pistoletto also created *trompe l'oeil* works with plexiglass surfaces where invention replaces the reflection of "reality." There is none of the interaction referred to above, but a kind of arbitrary substitution, imposed by the artist himself. These too are characteristic works, but there are others as well, which express different aesthetic intentions. "A Cubic Meter of the Infinite" (1966), for example, is a work in which six mirrors, tied together by a cord, turn inwards toward each other and create an infinite series of reflections, some barely perceptible to the eye. And still later, after producing some works which come close to being minimalist, he went on to produce important pieces such as "Venus of the Rages" in which he takes on new formal motifs which enrich and animate the expressive quality of his work.

—Roberto G. Lambarelli

1975 Galerie Sonnabend, Paris
Daner Galleriet, Copenhagen
Galerie Paul Maenz, Cologne
1977 Galerie Sonnabend, Paris
Galerie Paul Maenz, Cologne
Galleria Massimo Valsecchi, Milan
Centre d'Art Plastique Contemporain, Bordeaux
Maison de La Culture, Rennes, France
Neue Berliner Kunstverein, West Berlin
1978 Galerie Sonnabend, Paris
Centre Georges Pompidou, Paris
Kunstverein, Bonn
Palais des Beaux-Arts, Brussels
Kunstverein, Mannheim
Museum of Modern Art, New York
Sonnabend Gallery, New York
1979 Galerie Sonnabend, Paris
Palazzo dei Diamanti, Ferrara, Italy
Carpenter Center, Harvard University, Cambridge, Massachusetts
Philadelphia College of Art
Galerie Paul Maenz, Cologne
1980 Studio G7 (Ginevra Grigolo), Bologna
Carpenter Center, Harvard University, Cambridge, Massachusetts
Sonnabend Gallery, New York
P.S. 1, New York
Galleria Massimo Valsecchi, Milan
1981 Maison de la Culture, Chalon-sur-Saône, France
Villa Romana, Florence
Musée de Nice, France
Galerie Daniel Templon, Paris
1982 Sonnabend Gallery, New York
Studio G7, Bologna, Italy
Galleria Massimo Valsecchi, Milan
1983 Chapelle St.-Louis de la Salpetriere, Paris
Chiesa di San Carpoforo, Milan
1984 Galerie Daniel Templon, Paris
Sonnabend Gallery, New York
1985 Studio G7, Bologna, Italy
Galleria Arco d'Alibert, Rome
Brooklyn, Museum, New York
Newport Harbor Art Museum, Newport Beach, California
Maison de la Culture, Grenoble, France
Musée Montelimar, France
1986 Forum Middelburg, Netherlands
Neuberger Museum, Purchase, New York
Villa Pratolino, Italy
Artiste Gallery, Bath, Avon

POIRIER, Anne and Patrick.

French. Anne: born Anne Houllevigue in Marseille, 31 March 1942. Patrick: born in Nantes, 5 April 1942. Both studied at the Ecole Nationale Superieure des Arts Decoratifs, Paris, 1963–66. Married in 1968; son: Alain-Guillaume. Anne and Patrick Poirier have worked together on archaeological reconstruction and documentation projects, in Paris and Rome, since 1967. Recipients: Villa Medici Fellowships, Rome, 1967, 1973, 1974; D.A.A.D. Fellowship, West Berlin, 1977–78. Agents: Galerie Paul Maenz, Bismarckstrasse 50, 5000 Cologne 1, West Germany; Galleria Massimo Valsecchi, Via Santa Marta 11, 20123 Milan, Italy; Sonnabend Gallery, 420 West Broadway, New York, New York 10012, U.S.A.; and Galerie Daniel Templon, 30 rue Beaubourg, 75004 Paris. Address: 65 rue St. Charles, 75015 Paris, France.

Individual Exhibitions:

1970 Galleria Arco d'Alibert, Rome
1972 Galerie Paul Maenz, Cologne
1973 Neue Galerie, Aachen, West Germany
Sammlung Ludwig, Cologne
Galerie Paul Maenz, Cologne
Galerie Sonnabend, Paris
1974 Sonnabend Gallery, New York
Sonnabend Gallery, Geneva
Galleria Forma, Genoa
Galerie Yellow-Now, Liège, Belgium

Selected Group Exhibitions:

1970 *Contemporary Art,* French Pavilion, at *Expo 70,* Osaka, Japan
1972 *Grands et Jeunes d'Aujourd'hui,* Grand Palais, Paris
1973 *Biennale de Paris,* Musée d'Art Moderne, Paris
1975 *Memoire d'un Pays Noir,* Palais des Beaux-Arts, Charleroi, Belgium
1976 *Biennale,* Venice (and *Biennale,* 1980)
1977 *Documenta 6,* Kassel, West Germany
1979 *European Dialogue,* at *Biennale of Sydney,* Art Gallery of New South Wales, Sydney
1982 *Vergangenheit-Gegenwart-Zukunft,* Württembergischer Kunstverein, Stuttgart
1985 *Promenades,* Centre d'Art Contemporain, Geneva
1987 *Avant-Garde in the Eighties,* Los Angeles County Museum of Art

Collections:

Sammlung Ludwig, Aachen, West Germany; Nationalgalerie, West Berlin; Museum of Ghent, Belgium; Tate Gallery, London; Musée d'Art Moderne de la Ville, Paris; Australian National Gallery, Canberra; Musée des Beaux-Arts, Montreal.

Publications:

By the POIRIERS: books—*A la Memoire de Romulus,* Liège, Belgium 1974; *Les Paysages Revolus,* Paris 1975; *Les Réalités Incompatibles,* Copenhagen 1975; *Domus Aurea,* Brus-

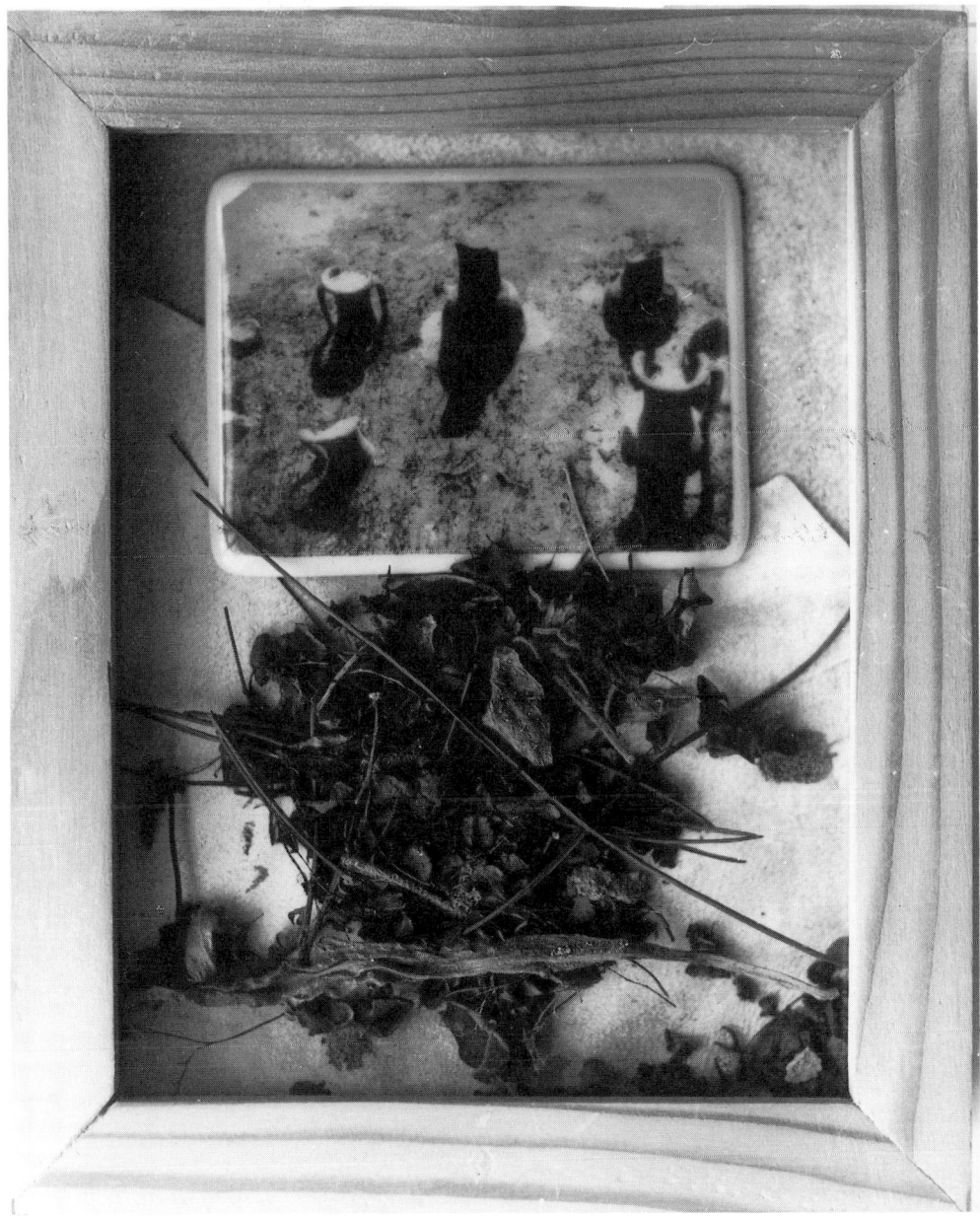

Anne and Patrick Poirier: *Urnes—Isola Sacra*, 1973

sels and Paris 1977; *Petit Guide à l'Usage des Voyageurs*, Brussels 1978; *140 Notes Around a Round Utopia*, Paris 1979.

On the POIRIERS: books—*Art en France: une nouvelle generation* by Jean Clair, Paris 1972; *Anne and Patrick Poirier*, exhibition catalogue, with texts by Wolfgang Becker and Günter Metken, Aachen, West Germany 1973; *Spurensicherung* by Günter Metken, Cologne 1977; *Anne and Patrick Poirier: Domus Aurea—Fascination des Ruines*, exhibition catalogue, with texts by Gilbert Lascault, Daniel Sallenave, Günter Metken, Denis Roche and Renaud Camus, Paris 1978; *Anne and Patrick Poirier*, exhibition catalogue, with texts by Christian Besson and Marie Lapalus, Chalon-sur-Saóne, France 1981; *Anne and Patrick Poirier: Lost Archetypes*, exhibition catalogue with text by Stuart Morgan, Bath 1986.

The death of Ephialtes

Art is perhaps a privileged way for understanding not only our participation in the society in which we live, but also our roots in the whole human adventure. This understanding is not gained in logical but in purely intuitive fashion. At least that, for our part, is what we look for in our work: the entry into a discourse which would be that of the subconscious, a discourse using a language which would escape the tyranny of Time and the rigid codes of logic.

And it is not by accident that the two most permanent themes in our work are Architecture and Mythology, which, since the beginning, return alternately, echo and complete each other. They are only metaphors, approaches to this Unknown Continent, the subconscious, that we clumsily try to explore with our makeshift means.

For us it is a matter of geographical wandering, of physical drift which conditions and stimulates the mental drift: we journey not only into the site through texts and images, but above all on the site through architecture, ruins and gardens peopled with mythical figures. Without this physical and palpable contact with the actual places we could not truly capture the "genius loci" which will stimulate our subsequent work.

Architecture and Archaelogy have often served, since Antiquity, as a metaphor for Memory or an attempt to explain subconscious phenomena.

We could talk at length about this theme which fills us with enthusiasm and which has guided all our work on Architecture: namely the relation of Archae ology and Architecture with the mental universe. Or, put in another way, the relation of a four dimensional (three dimensions of Space and one dimension of Time) physically perceptible and penetrable world with an imperceptible and physically impenetrable world whose space-time dimensions are of another quality, an other essence. And how these spaces inter-

communicate by hidden doors which we have to discover.

Another approach to this subconscious universe is by Mythology. Our encounter with mythological figures in Angkor and Rome stimulated our first truly "archaeological" work. "The Gardens of the Villa Medici," Rome 1970: 15 casts in Japanese paper, 15 manuscripts, 15 photographs on porcelain. Centre Georges Pompidou, Paris.

Mythological figures, representing the intemporal and permanent in the human psyche, have not ceased to fascinate us and particularly the myth of the Gorgon, directly linked to the idea of the gaze. In 1979 at the Palazzo di Diamanti in Ferrara, we carried out "La Stanza dello Sguardo," where the gaze of 8 identical gorgons meet.

The idea of gigantism also particularly interested us—a work presented at the Villa Romana in Florence consisted of a series of paper casts of giant statues as well as herbaria—and heralded our later work at CELLE, where we tried to produce an episode suggested by the mythological struggle between earthly powers (the giants) and cosmic forces (the gods).

We retained only a few signs of the struggle: the EYE of the giant Ephialtes, modelled on an anonymous sculpture magnified 12 times; Zeus's THUNDERBOLTS and the ARROWS of Heracles, Apollo or Artemis buried in the eye.

Time and Nature are called on to play an essential role in this work which remains incomplete without their intervention. If they manage to transform this giant eye, making it resemble one day the tumbled rocks which surround it, they could, however, never change the direction of this regard.

—Anne and Patrick Poirier

Among the artists whose theme was summarized at the fifth Kassel *Documenta* in 1972 under the designation "individual mythologies," the "Spurensicherer" (those who secure a trail/protect vestiges) form a particular group. Within this group Anne and Patrick Poirier occupy a distinguished and exceptional position by virtue of their collaboration and their search for the collective vestiges of culture.

The decisive stimulus for the direction of their work came to this artists during their visit to the Villa Medici in Rome. They realized that while a wealth of evidence from the past was still available in the eternal city, the significance of ruins and archaeological finds was not currently understood and that this required an intervention. Anne and Patrick Poirier made this role of mediator their business. They start from the idea that, in order that it may survive, the connection with the roots of our culture must again be made visible. While they place the present in a parallel relationship to the past, they disassociate themselves in their work from any belief in a progressive artistic avant-garde. The couple start from the assumption that historical development does not occur in linear mode, rather that the past can be placed in parallel to the present. The Poiriers' activity consists in demonstrating this connection with specific historical buildings or sites as examples—recording, understanding and making them visible. They employ their own intuition and sensitivity and their artistic abilities and attempt in the union of their creative abilities to increase the potential for understanding and for making visible.

In the collaborative work of this couple there is no strict division of labour. Each partner could carry out the other's activity. The work of the individual first achieves its full effect, however, in combination with that of the other. The work begins with the idea of an archaeological adventure on which they at first embark intuitively. They trace past reality in viewing its monuments, the eventual study of available documents and the restoration of associations with things seen and known. They take photographs, collect fragments, look for plant remains, take casts, prepare plans and inventories. After an intensive investigation of the locality and a mutual exchange of impressions and ideas, there results a deeper understanding of past reality which is now to be made visible once more. In spite of the extreme precision of the work it compares less with an account of scientific research than with an historical novel.

When the joint preparatory works have provided an overall picture, the creative activity of reconstruction begins. Tools, herbariums, plans, casts, implements recreate the historic site in miniature. Artistic creation culminates in the installation when, with the simplest of materials, water and sand, brush and paper, complex thought processes are set in motion and the vision which preceded the work assumes intelligible form. For instance the ruined city of "Ostia Antica" mentioned by Herodotus can be resurrected as a new reality on 40 square metres. At an exhibition the reduced scale allows the spectator a general view which, by virtue of a certain shock effect, should arouse his own associations and awaken those memories already almost lost to modern man. The couple's collaborative work that brings visible reality to the Domus Aurea (Golden House) has its full effect in that moment when the viewers react to the display and themselves introduce collective reminiscences in relation to Nero's palace. In this way Anne and Patrick Poirier's creation is of artistic significance for the future, both in the originality of the production process and in its metaphysical extensions.

—Dagmar Sinz

POLKE, Sigmar.

German. Born in Oels, Niederschlesien, now Olesnicka, German Democratic Republic, 13 February 1941; moved to West Germany, 1953. Studied glass-painting in Dusseldorf-Kaiserswerth, 1959–60; studied painting, under Gerald Hoehme and Karl-Otto Goetz, Staatliche Kunstakademie, Dusseldorf, 1961–67. Independent painter, in Dusseldorf, 1967–70, in Willich bei Krefeld, 1971–79, and in Cologne since 1980. Founder, with Konrad Fischer-Lueg and Gerhard Richter, Capitalist Realist painting group, Dusseldorf, 1963. Guest Instructor, 1970–71, and Professor since 1977, Adakemie der bildenden Kunste, Hamburg. Recipient: Painting Prize, *Bienal*, Sao Paulo, 1975. Agents: Galerie Konrad Fischer, Platanenstrasse 7, Dusseldorf, West Germany; Galerie Toni Gerber, Berne. Address: c/o Galerie Toni Gerber, Gerechtigkeitsgasse 74, 3011 Berne, Switzerland.

Individual Exhibitions:

1966	Galerie H, Hannover
	Galerie René Block, West Berlin
	Galerie Alfred Schmela, Dusseldorf
1967	Galerie Heiner Friedrich, Munich
1968	Galerie René Block, West Berlin
1969	Galerie Rudolf Zwirner, Cologne
	Galerie René Block, West Berlin
1970	Galerie Heiner Friedrich, Munich
	Galerie Konrad Fischer, Dusseldorf
	Kabinett für Aktuelle Kunst, Bremerhaven, West Germany
	Galerie Toni Gerber, Berne
	Galerie Thomas Borgmann, Cologne
1971	Galerie Michael Werner, Cologne
	Galerie Ernst, Hannover
	Galerie Konrad Fischer, Dusseldorf
	Galerie Toni Gerber, Berne
1972	Galerie Rochus Kowallek, Frankfurt
	Galerie Grafikmeyer, Karlsruhe
	Goethe-Institut, Amsterdam
	Galerie Michael Werner, Cologne
1973	Galerie Konrad Fischer, Dusseldorf
	Westfälischer Kunstverein, Münster, West Germany
1974	Galerie Dorothea Loehr, Frankfurt

	Galerie Cornels, Baden-Baden, West Germany
	Galerie Toni Gerber, Zurich
	Galerie Thomas Borgmann, Cologne
	Galerie Michael Werner, Cologne
	Galerie Rudolf Zwirner, Cologne
	Stadtisches Kunstmuseum, Bonn
	Galerie Klein, Bonn
	Galerie Springer, West Berlin
1975	Kunsthalle, Kiel
	Galerie Michael Werner, Cologne
	Galerie Klein, Bonn
1976	*Bilder, Tucher, Objekte*, Kunsthalle, Tübingen
	Kunsthalle, Dusseldorf
	Stedelijk Van Abbemuseum, Eindhoven, Netherlands
	Galerie Toni Gerber, Berne
1981	Galerie Toni Gerber, Berne
	Rheinisches Landesmuseum, Bonn
1977	Kunstverein, Kassel, West Germany
1978	Halle fur Internationale Neue Kunst, Zurich
1980	Galerie Klein, Bonn
1981	Galerie Toni Gerber, Berne
	Galerie Bama, Paris
	Galerie Klein, Bonn
1982	Galerie Bama, Paris
	Holly Solomon Gallery, New York
1983	Galerie Michael Werner, Cologne
	Studio d'Arte Cannaviello, Milan
	Galerie Thomas Borgmann, Cologne

1984	Stadtisches Kunstmuseum, Bonn
	Galerie Klein, Bonn
	Kunsthaus, Zurich
	Kunsthalle, Cologne
	Marian Goodman Gallery, New York
1985	Mary Boone Gallery, New York
	Galerie Schmela, Dusseldorf
	Anthony D'Offay Gallery, London
1986	Galerie Thomas Borgmann, Cologne
	Mary Boone Gallery, New York
	Galerie Klein, Bonn
1987	David Nolan Gallery, New York

Selected Group Exhibitions:

1963	*Demonstrative Ausstellung*, Kaiserstrasse, Dusseldorf
1965	*Tendenzen*, Städtisches Museum, Trier, West Germany
1969	*Konzeption-Conception*, Städtisches Museum Schloss Morsbroich, Leverkusen, West Germany
1970	*New Multiple Art*, Whitechapel Art Gallery, London
1972	*Documenta*, Kassel, West Germany (and 1982)
1975	*Bienal*, Sao Paulo
1982	*Vergangenheit-Gegenwart-Zukunft*, Württembergischer Kunstverein, Stuttgart
1987	*Avant-Garde in the Eighties*, Los Angeles County Museum of Art

Sigmar Polke: *Dürerhase*, 1968

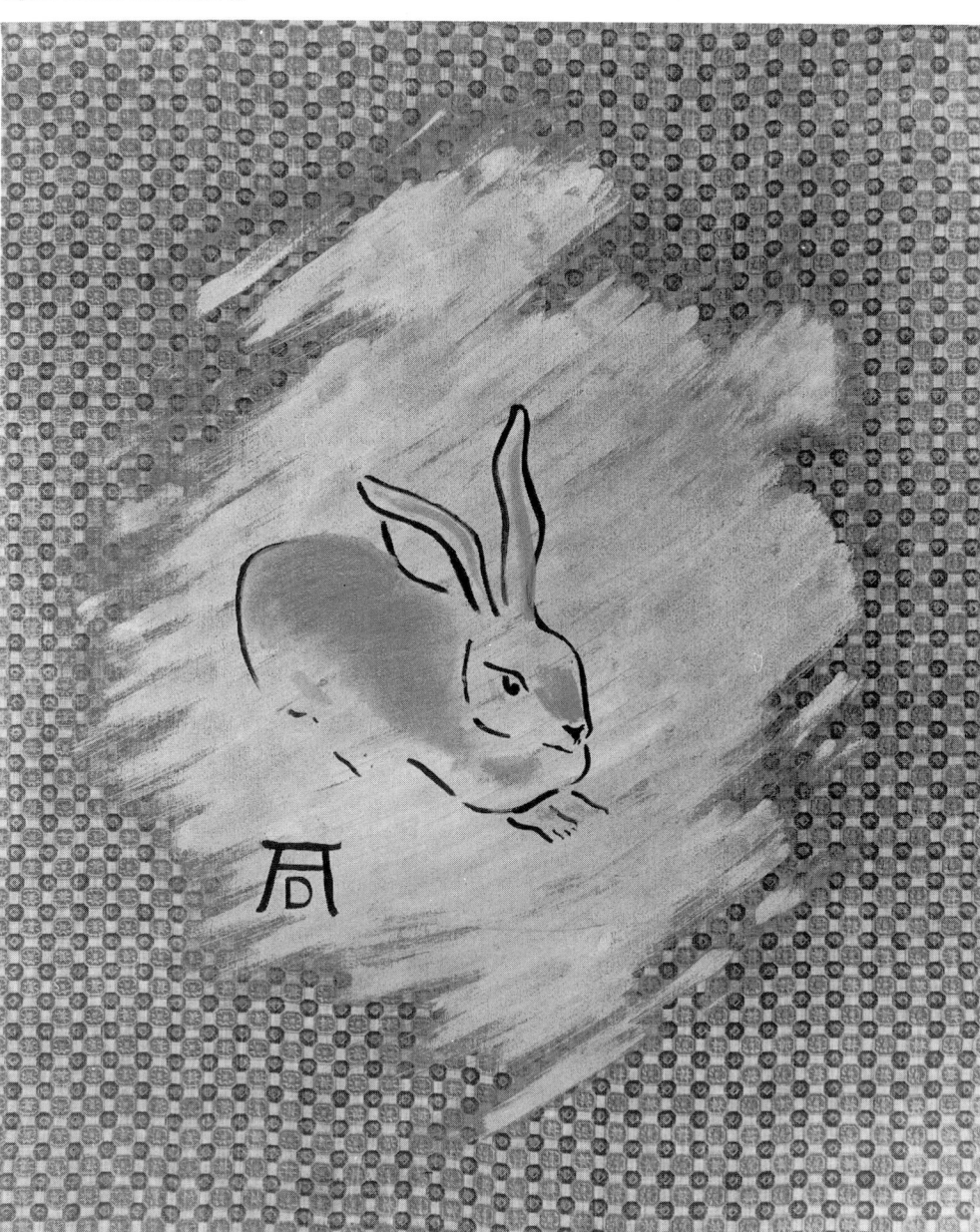

Collections:

Städtisches Kunstmuseum, Bonn; Kunstmuseum der Stadt, Dusseldorf; Kunsthalle, Tübingen; Landesmuseum, Darmstadt; Museum Boymans-van Beuningen, Rotterdam; Stedelijk Van Abbemuseum, Eindhoven; Centre Georges Pompidou, Paris; Museum of Modern Art, New York.

Publications:

By POLKE: books—*Hohere Wesen befelhlen*, West Berlin 1968; *. . . der ganze Korper fuhlt sich leicht und mochte fliegen*, Dusseldorf 1969; *Die Grafik der Kapitalistischen Realismus* with others, edited by René Block, West Berlin 1971; *Bizarre*, Heidelberg 1972; *Original und Falschung*, with Achim Duchow, Münster, West Germany 1973.

On POLKE: books—*Pop und die Folgen* by Heinz Ohff, Dusseldorf 1968; *Deutsche Kunst: eine neue Generation* by Rolf-Günter Dienst, Cologne 1970; *Noch Kunst: Neuestes aus Deutschen Ateliers*, Dusseldorf 1970; *Bis Heute* by Karin Thomas, Cologne 1971; *Deutsche Kunst der 60er Jahre* by Jürgen Morschel, Munich 1972; *Documenta 5: Befragung der Realitat*, exhibition catalogue, edited by Harald Szeemann and others, Kassel, West Germany 1972; *Six Years: The Dematerialization of the Art Object* by Lucy R. Lippard, New York 1973; *Sigmar Polke: Bilder, Tucher, Objeckte*, exhibition catalogue, with texts by Joseph Beuys, Gerhard Richter, F. W. Heubach and Benjamin D. Buchloh, Tübingen 1976; *Vergangenheit-Gegenwart-Zukunft*, exhibition catalogue, with text by Tilman Osterwold, Stuttgart 1982; *Sigmar Polke: Drawings from the 1960s*, exhibition catalogue with text by Prudence Carlson, New York 1987.

*

Polke studied at the Kunstakademie in Düsseldorf from 1961–67, where one of his teachers was Joseph Beuys. Over the past twenty-five years Polke has not adhered to any single style or theme; nor has he evolved any new style or theme. At different times, and sometimes simultaneously he has been involved with installations, painting and photography. His work has encompassed abstraction and figuration and certain motifs do recur at irregular intervals in his output.

In the mid 1960s, while still a student he, and others in Düsseldorf, produced a series of works which they styled "Capitalist Realism". Polke's contribution can be seen as wry tributes to the pleasures of consumerism, for example, in *Plastik-Wannen* (1964) the subject is plastic food-storage containers which are the sort of goods difficult to obtain in Eastern Block countries. Much of Polke's work of the later 1960s was a response to the mechanical self-assured nature of American Pop Art. A typical picture might begin at the top of the canvas with Lichtenstein's Ben Day dot method, but by the middle of the canvas the dots begin to disintegrate.

With the early 1970s came Polke's selection of Francis Picabia as a guiding light. However, it was not Picabia's most well thought of work of the Dada period that he was interested in but the later works. With paintings like *Nude with Salamander* (1971) Polke adopted Picabia, (as the essay in the Warhol/Beuys/Polke catalogue, Milwaukee, 1987, has it), "at his most *debased* as his own formal ground. [His] Picabia-based paintings do not simply promote or perpetuate the *fetishes* and idiosyncratic *decadence* of a wayward minor master. It is rather as if Polke, through these works, is saying: 'This is what it all finally came to in Europe with paintings. So I'll pick things up right here, and see how far I get.' " Also at this time Polke's admitted impulse towards the baroque manifested itself. Works of the 1970s, such as *Menschkln* (1972), employ layers of overdrawing and the use of miscellaneous fabrics. These interests enlarged Polke's range of techniques and devices and intensified the content of his pictures. *Menschkin* is a picture of a group of grey faces superimposed on snakeskin pattenred fabric. The subject is thereby intensified by this non-painterly yet aggressive ground.

By the late 1970s, Polke's wide-ranging use of materials, (which has been called chaotic), and urgent tone appealed to many younger artists looking for alternatives to the current vogue for Conceptual Art.

Particularly appealing was his incorporation of "found objects" in the tradition of Dada, into his canvases.

With the 1980s Polke's pictures have become dominated by what could be called historical themes: prison bars, prison camps and watch towers. In *Hochstand* (1984) for example, a watchtower is superimposed on two fabrics, one a tweed, the other overblown flowers. Perhaps with maturity Polke is now settling into a style, but like many German artists his work remains dominated by the division of his country.

—Victoria Keller

POMODORO, Arnaldo.

Italian. Born in Morciano di Romagna, Pesaro, 23 June 1926. Studied architecture and jewelry-making; mainly self-taught in sculpture. Worked as stage-designer and jewelry-maker in Pesaro, 1950–54; thereafter, independent sculptor in Milan: Founder-Director, with Giorgio Perfetti and his brother Gio Pomodoro, Studio 3P, Pesaro and Milan, 1958. Artist-in-Residence, Stanford University, California, 1966–67; Guest Instructor, University of California, Berkeley, 1968, 1970. Recipient: First Prize, *Mostra di Disegni*, Lodi, 1958; Foreign Ministry Travel Scholarship, Rome, 1959; Premio del Libro, *Mostra della Bronzetta*, Padua, 1959; Sculpture Prize, *Biennale d'Arte Triveneta*, Venice, 1959; *Spoleto Festival* Prize, with Garelli, 1960; Sculpture Prize, *Bienal*, Sao Paulo, 1963; Gran Premio di Scultura, *Biennale*, Venice, 1964; Sculpture Prize, *Carnegie International*, Pittsburgh, 1967; Graphics Prize, Florence, 1972. Agent: Studio Marconi, via Tadino 15, 20124 Milan. Address: via Vigevano 31, 20144 Milan, Italy.

Individual Exhibitions:

1954	Galleria Numero, Florence
	Galleria Montenapoleone, Milan
1955	Galleria dell'Obelisco, Rome
	Galleria del Cavallino, Venice
	Galleria del Naviglio, Milan (with Gio Pomodoro)
1956	Galleria del Cavallino, Venice (with Gio Pomodoro)
1957	Galeria Bonino, Buenos Aires
	Galleria Prisma, Turin
	Galleria dell'Obelisco, Rome
1958	Galeria del Naviglio, Milan
	Kunstverein, Cologne
	Galerie Helios Art, Brussels (with Gio Pomodoro)
	Metallreliefs, Galerie 22, Dusseldorf (with Gio Pomodoro)
1959	Galerie Internationale d'Art Contemporain, Paris (with Gio Pomodoro)
	Galerie Internationale d'Art Contemporain, Brussels (with Gio Pomodoro)
1961	Palazzo Masimo, Rome
1062	*Recent Sculpture*, Felix Landau Gallery, Los Angeles
	Musée de l'Athenée, Geneva
	Galerie Internationale d'Art Contemporain, Paris
1963	Palais des Beaux-Arts, Brussels (with Gio Pomodoro)
1965	Kunstverein, Cologne
	Galleria Marlborough, Rome
	Marlborough-Gerson Gallery, New York
	Louisiana Museum, Humlebaek, Denmark
1966	Galleria del Deposito, Genoa
1968	Marlborough New London Gallery
	Galerie Pierre, Stockholm
	Studio Marconi, Milan
1969	*Work 1959–1969*, Museum Boymans-van Beuningen, Rotterdam
	Kunstverein, Cologne
	Galerie Semiha Huber, Zurich
	Galleria Marlborough, Rome
1970	University of California at Berkeley (toured the United States)
	Galleria La Città, Verona
	Fine Arts Gallery, San Diego, California
	Portland Art Museum, Oregon
	Studio Marconi, Milan
1971	University of Texas at Austin
	Wadsworth Atheneum, Hartford, Connecticut
	Galleria Quattro Venti, Palermo, Sicily
	Immagine della Città di Pesaro, con le Sculture di Arnaldo Pomodoro, Open-air street exhibition, Pesaro, Italy
	Un Centesimo di Secondo, Studio Marconi, Milan
1972	Galerie Stangl, Munich
	Westend Galerie, Frankfurt
	Grosplastiken, Stadttheater, Darmstadt
	Galleria Verde, Florence
1973	Galerie Fontana Morose, Geneva
1974	Rotonda di Via Besana, Milan
1976	Marlborough-Gerson Gallery, New York
1978	Museo de Bellas Artes, Caracas
1984	Forte di Belvedere, Florence
1987	Marisa del Re Gallery, New York

Selected Group Exhibitions:

1954	*Triennale*, Milan (and 1957)
1956	*Biennale*, Venice
1958	*10 Contemporary Italian Sculptors*, Museum of Fine Arts, Houston
1959	*Documenta*, Kassel, West Germany
1962	*Schrift und Bild 1*, Staatliche Kunsthalle, Baden-Baden, West Germany (travelled to the Stedelijk Museum, Amsterdam)
1963	*Bienal*, Sao Paulo
1968	*Recent Italian Paintings and Sculptures*, Jewish Museum, New York
1971	*New Italian Art 1953–71*, Walker Art Gallery, Liverpool
1972	*Contemporary Italian Sculptors*, Hakone Open-Air Museum, Nihotaira, Japan

Collections:

Galleria Nazionale d'Arte Moderna. Rome; Museo Revoltella, Trieste; Wallraf-Richartz Museum, Cologne; Musée Royal des Beaux-Arts, Brussels; Tate Gallery, London; Museum of Modern Art, New York; Albright-Knox Art Gallery, Buffalo, New York; University of California Art Museum, Berkeley; Museu de Arte Moderno, Rio de Janeiro; Museo de Bellas Artes, Buenos Aires.

Publications:

By POMODORO: articles—"Notes on My Work, 1966" in *Arnaldo Pomodoro: Work 1959–1969*, exhibition catalogue, Rotterdam 1969; "Correspondence," with Tom Freudenheim, in *Arnaldo Pomodoro*, exhibition catalogue, Berkeley, California 1970; "Interview," with Franceso Leonetti, in *Arnaldo Pomodoro: Un Centesimo di Secondo*, exhibition catalogue, Milan 1971; interview, with Sam Hunter, in *Arnaldo Pomodoro*, exhibition catalogue, Milan 1974; essay in *Arnaldo Pomodoro*, exhibition catalogue, New York 1987.

On POMODORO: books—*Gio e Arnaldo Pomodoro*, exhibition catalogue, with text by Gio Ponti, Milan 1955; *Gio e Arnaldo Pomodoro*, exhibition catalogue, with text by Alfonso Gatto, Venice 1956; *Gio e Arnaldo Pomodoro*, exhibition catalogue, with text by Guido Ballo, Brussels 1958; *Gio e Arnaldo Pomodoro: Metallreliefs*, exhibition folder with text by Guido Ballo, Dusseldorf 1958; *Gio e Arnaldo Pomodoro*, exhibition catalogue, with texts by Stephane Lupasco, Georges Mathieu, Abraham A. Moles, and Guido Ballo, Paris 1959; *Dalla Poetica del Segno all Presenze Continuita: Arnaldo e Gio Pomodoro* by Guido Ballo, Milan 1962; *Recent Sculpture by Arnaldo Pomodoro*, exhibition catalogue, with texts by Theodore Roethke and Kynaston McShine, Los Angeles 1962; *Arnaldo Pomodoro/Gio Pomodoro*, exhibition catalogue, with text by Giulio Carlo Argan, Brussels 1963; *Arnaldo Pomodoro*, exhibition catalogue, with texts by Francesco Leonetti, Roberto Sanesi, and Umbro Apollonio, Rome 1965; *Arnaldo Pomodoro*; exhibition catalogue, with text by Frank O'Hara, New York 1965; *Arnaldo Pomodoro*, exhibition pamphlet, with text by Nello Ponente, Genoa 1966; *New Italian Art 1953–1971*, exhibition catalogue, with text by

Giovanni Carandente, Liverpool 1971; *Immagine della città di Pesaro, con le Sculture di Arnaldo Pomodor,* exhibition folder, Pesaro 1971; *Arnaldo Pomodoro: Grosplastiken,* exhibition catalogue, with texts by H. W. Sabais and Bernd Krummel, Darmstadt 1972; *Arnaldo Pomodoro,* exhibition catalogue, with texts by Gonzalo Castellanos and Giulio Carlo Argan, Caracas 1978; *Arnaldo Pomodoro at the Belvedere Fort,* with texts by Giulio Carlo Argan and Italo Mussa, Florence 1986.

Italy, a country of artists and artisans, is almost unique in producing distinguished artists from single families; the brothers Arnaldo and Gio Pomodoro can be compared with the Cascellas, or the two Legnaghi, and many others. Curiously enough this fraternal tradition seems to be particularly strong in sculpture.

Unlike the strict preferences of the Cascellas for natural marble, Arnaldo Pomodoro is a master of bronze casting, working on a gigantic scale with an almost theatrical sense of drama, yet at the same time a meticulous concern for detail. It comes, therefore, as no surprise to learn that, in fact, he started his career as a stage designer and that he has often created remarkable jewelry.

Pomodoro's characteristic forms are either huge spheres or free-standing columns, somewhat phallic as they rise from semi-spherical bases. One might assess these two forms as female and male, and indeed, on occasions, the columns include, in their incisions, a penetrating hole, or a relief-like, inverted sphere, whilst the globes are broken through to reveal rigid thrusting prongs.

As an artist Pomodoro shares the Italian love for the monumental, as well as a delight in brilliant, decorative materials, plus an openly communicative manner. Pomodoro's work is certainly impressive, beautifully fashioned and cast, assertive and self-assured, positive, demonstrative and entertaining. Stylistically, apart from the interplay of round and upright forms, there are reminders of Fontana in the anxiety to penetrate the outer skin of the sculptures in order to erode the surfaces and to reveal complex inner forms. It is difficult to know whether these bruises and incisions are symbols of violence or tragedy, or of passion, and whether the interior analysis is an anxiety to penetrate life's mystery, or merely to playfully reveal "the works of the clock," so to speak.

One of the problems of Italian artists like Pomodoro, brilliant, gifted, capable of working on a large, public scale, is that the native sense of craftsmanship and wit predominates, often obscuring more serious pretensions. Pomodoro's work does, however, often look like gigantic, charming pieces of jewelry.

—Charles Spencer

POMODORO, Gio.
Italian. Born in Morciano di Romagna, Pesaro, 17 November 1930. Studied with Professor Caponetto, Istituto Tecnico per Geometria, Pesaro, 1946–51; thereafter, mainly self-taught in art, but influenced by writings by Kafka, Pound, Apollinaire, Eluard, and Auden, and by paintings of Franz Kline. Served in the Italian Army, 1952–53. Married Gigliola Gagnoni in 1958; son: Bruto. Sculptor, and artist in jewelry and graphics: lived in Florence, 1951–52 and 1953–54, and in Milan and Querceta since 1954, when he began to concentrate on architectural sculptures; Member, with Enrico Baj, Sergio Dangelo, Asger Jorn and others, Arte Nucleare group, Milan, 1954–57; Founder-Director, with Giorgio Perfetti and brother Arnaldo Pomodoro, Studio 3P, Pesaro and Milan, 1958. Recipient: Sculpture Prize, *Biennale,* Paris, 1959; David E. Bright Prize, *Biennale,* Venice, 1959. Agent: Galleria Stendhal, via Gesu 5, 20121 Milan. Address: via Rucellai 20, 20126 Milan, Italy.

Individual Exhibitions:

1954	Galleria Numero, Florence
1955	Galleria del Cavallino, Venice
	Galleria dell'Obelisco, Rome
	Galleria del Naviglio, Milan (with Arnaldo Pomodoro)
1956	Galleria del Cavallino, Venice (with Arnaldo Pomodoro)
1957	Galeria Bonino, Buenos Aires
1958	Galerie Helio Art, Brussels (with Arnaldo Pomodoro)
	Metallreliets, Galerie 22, Dusseldorf (with Arnaldo Pomodoro)
1959	Galerie Internationale d'Art Contemporain, Paris (with Arnaldo Pomodoro)
	Galerie Internationale d'Art Contemporain, Brussels (with Arnaldo Pomodoro)
1960	Galerie Internationale d'Art Contemporain, Paris
1962	Galleria Blu, Milan, Italy
	Musée de l'Athenée, Geneva
1963	Palais des Beaux-Arts, Brussels (with Arnaldo Pomodoro)
1964	Galleria Marlborough, Rome
	Galerie Semiha Huber, Zurich
1965	*Opere Grafiche 1957–1964,* Galleria del Naviglio, Milan
	Musée des Beaux-Arts, La Chaux de Fonds, Switzerland
	Dom Galerie, Cologne
	Louisiana Museum, Humlebaek, Denmark
1966	Kunstverein, Wuppertal, West Germany
	Galleri a Buffalmacco, Piacenza, Italy
1967	Marlborough-Gerson Gallery, New York
	Galleria Marlborough, Rome
	Gimpel Fils Gallery, London
1968	Galerie Rothe, Heidelberg
	Galleria Martano Due, Turin
	Galerie de France, Paris
	Galleria dell'Ariete, Milan
1969	Galleria La Bussola, Turin
	Galerie Pierre, Stockholm
	Sculpture, Felix Landau Gallery, Los Angeles
1970	Martha Jackson Gallery, New York
	Galleria Blu, Milan
1971	Galerie Françoise Mayer, Brussels
	Galleria dell'Ariete, Milan
	Martha Jackson Gallery, New York
	Galleria L'Uomo e l'Arte, Milan
1972	Galleria La Bottega, Ravenna
	Galeria Documenta, Sao Paulo
1973	Galleria Il Giorno, Milan
	Galleria Forum, Trieste
1974	Galleria Cavour, Milan
	Galleria Niccoli, Parma
	Galleria del Naviglio, Milan
	Sculture dal 1958 al 1974, Pinacoteca, Ravenna
	Galerie Farber, Brussels
1975	Galleria Lorenzelli, Bergamo, Italy
	Galleria La Bottega, Ravenna
	Galleria Il Segnapassi, Pesaro, Italy
	Galleria Ricerche, Turin
1976	Musée d'Ixelles, Brussels
	Opere in Pietra dal 1974 al 1976. Galleria Stendhal, Milan
	Sculture in Pietra 1973–1976. Castello dell'Imperatore, Prato, Italy
1977	Museo Ca Pesaro, Venice
1978	Galleria CIAC, Udine, Italy
	Galleria 3A, Turin
	Arte Incontri, Fara d'Adda, Italy
1979	Kunsthalle-Libreria Fermo di Cavallo, Rome
1980	Galleria San Carlo, Naples
	Luogo di Misure 1977–1978, Cassa di Risparmio, Verona
1981	Galleria Fioretto, Padua, Italy
	Studio Melotti, Ferrara, Italy
	Sculture 1968/1981, Galleria Farsetti, Focette (Lucca), Italy
1982	*Parete di Misure,* Direzione del Partito Comunista Italiano, Rome
1983	Bank fur Gemeinwirtschaft, Frankfurt
	Galleria Il Salotto, Como, Italy
1984	Galleria Stendhal, Milan
1985	Studio Melotti, Ferrara, Italy
	Studio Dabbeni, Lugano, Switzerland
	Palazzo Civico, Lugano, Switzerland
1986	Circolo Nuova Italsider, Taranto, Italy
	Palazzo Ducale, Pesaro, Italy
1987	Studio Saudino, Viareggio, Italy
	Basilica San Ambrogio, Milan
	Galleria Denisi Fiorani, Piacenza, Italy
	Galleria L'Isola, Rome

Selected Group Exhibitions:

1976	*Print Biennale,* National Museum of Modern Art, Tokyo
1967	*10 Ans d'Art Vivant,* Fondation Maeght, St. Paul-de-Venice, France
1970	*British Print Biennale,* City Museum and Art Gallery, Bradford, Yorkshire
1974	*Martha Jackson Collection,* Albright-Knox Art Gallery, Buffalo, New York (toured the United States)
1976	*Grafica Sperimentale,* Palazzo Strozzi, Florence
1977	*Private Images: Photos by Sculptors,* Los Angeles County Museum of Art
1979	*Gravura Abstracta Italiana,* Fundacao Gulkenkian, Lisbon
1982	*Arte Italiana 1960–82,* Hayward Gallery, London
1984	*Die Sprache der Geometrie,* Kunstmuseum, Berne
1987	*Ipotesi per un Museo,* Parco di Versiliana, Italy

Collections:

Galleria Nazionale d'Arte Moderna, Rome; Palais des Beaux-Arts, Brussels; Wilhelm-Lehmbruck Museum, Duisburg, West Germany; Kusntverein, Wuppertal, West Germany; Musée des Beaux-Arts, La Chaux de Fonds, Switzerland; Tate Gallery, London; Hirshhorn Museum and Sculpture Garden, Smithsonian Institution, Washington, D.C.; Phoenix Museum of Art, Arizona.

Publications:

By POMODORO: articles—"Devenir de la Necessité." in *Gio et Arnaldo Pomodoro,* exhibition catalogue, Paris 1959; "A Conversation with Gio Pomodoro," with Luce Hoctin, in *Gio Pomodoro,* exhibition catalogue, Rome 1964; "Interview" in *Borba* (Zagreb), October 1970; "Gio Pomodoro," in *Margutta* (Rome), no. 7/8, 1971; "Conversazione con Gio Pomodoro," with Guido Ballo, in *Gio Pomodoro,* exhibition catalogue, Milan 1974; "Note per Isla Negra" in *Gio Pomodoro,* exhibition catalogue, Milan 1976; interview, with Guido Ballo, in *Gio Pomodoro: Sculture in Pietra 1973–1976,* exhibition catalogue, Prato, Italy 1976.

On POMODORO: books—*Gio Pomodoro,* exhibition catalogue, with text by L. Sinisgalli, Rome 1955; *Gio et Arnaldo Pomodoro,* exhibition catalogue, with text by Guido Ballo, Brussels 1958; *Gio et Arnaldo Pomodoro,* exhibition catalogue, with texts by Stephane Lupasco, Georges Mathieu, Abraham a. Moles, and Guido Ballo, Paris 1959; *Arnaldo Pomodoro/Gio Pomodoro,* exhibition catalogue, with text by Giulio Carlo Argan, Brussels 1963; *Gio Pomodoro: Opere Grafiche 1957–1964,* exhibition catalogue, with text by Guido Ballo, Milan 1965; *Gio Pomodoro,* exhibition catalogue, with texts by Nello Ponente, Patrice Seylaz, and Michel Tapie, La Chaux de Fonds, Switzerland 1965; *Gio Pomodoro,* exhibition catalogue, with text by Günter Aust, Wuppertal, West Germany 1966; *Sculpture: Gio Pomodoro,* exhibition catalogue, Los Angeles 1969; *Gio Pomodoro: Sculture dal 1958 al 1974,* exhibition catalogue, with texts by Raffaele De Grada and Giulio Guberti, Ravenna 1974; *Gio Pomodoro: Sculture in Pietra 1973–1976,* exhibition catalogue, with texts by Paolo Fossati and Antonio Del Guercio, Prato, Italy 1978; *Gio Pomodoro: Opere in Pietra dal 1974 al 1976,* exhibition catalogue, with text by Paolo Fossati, Milan 1976; *Gio Pomodoro: Luogo di Misure 1977/1978,* exhibition catalogue, with texts by Antoni Del Guercio and Giuseppe Marchiori, Verona 1980; *Gio Pomodoro: Sculture 1968/ 1981,* exhibition catalogue, with text by Carlo L. Ragghianti, Focette, Italy 1981; *Gio Pomodoro: Parete di Misure,* exhibition catalogue, with text by Enrico Berlinguer and Antonio Del Guercio, Rome 1982; *Gio Pomodoro: Marmi e Bronzi 1984–87,* exhibition catalogue with text by Giovanni Carandente, Rome 1987.

With his elder brother Arnaldo, and Giorgio Perfetti,

Gio Pomodoro was one of a remarkable group of artist-jewellers in the early 1950's; the two Pomodoro brothers produced a series of miniature sculptures and experiments from which many of their mature ideas emerged. Whilst the elder Pomodoro went on to produce massive bronze sculptures, monumental in the best Italian manner, yet at the same time basically concerned with the same problems as were examined in the small jewelry, Gio has proved to be a rather more quizzical and experimental artist.

He still works as a jeweller, one of the most inventive among a fine group of artists who devote themselves to this pursuit, and who, it should be added, are usefully supported by a long artisan tradition, and an interested public. Gio Pomodoro's concern with space is both more infinite and more diverse than his brother's involvement with global or tower structures. His early works in bronze had a far more tough, visceral character than the smooth, polished forms of his brother; he was clearly not so concerned with interior space as the definition of line and volume. The reliefs were based on undulating masses with internal tensions, vitalized by typical Pomodoro exuberance and assurance, marked by the same Baroque energy and movement as is evident in his brother.

His development has denied a concentration on bronze and a greater concern for rigid and contained forms, as well as a dialectic between solids and fluids. For these reasons he has switched to fibre-glass which permits him to obtain a positive outward skin, in the manner of his brother's bronze surfaces, which, without penetration, allows considerable enquiry and registration of a variety of shapes and pressures. The effect is almost that of upholstery,

although without the formal programme of furniture.

Pomodoro avoids complacency and decorative order by treating each side of the huge oblong shapes or cubes as separate entities, to be inflated or deflated, inscribed or defaced. The result is more indefinite and subtle than his brother's entertaining bronzes.

—Charles Spencer

POONS, Larry.

American. Born in Tokyo, Japan, 1 October 1937; moved to United States in 1938. Educated at the New England Conservatory of Music, Boston, 1955–57; Museum of Fine Arts School, Boston, 1959. Independent artist, New York, since 1960. Artist-in-Residence, Institute of Humanistic Studies, Aspen, Colorado, 1966–67; Visiting Instructor, New York Studio School, New York, 1967. Agent: André Emmerich Gallery, 41 East 57th Street, New York, New York 10022. Address: 831 Broadway, New York, New York 10003, U.S.A.

Individual Exhibitions:

1963	Green Gallery, New York
1964	Green Gallery, New York
1965	Green Gallery, New York

Larry Poons: *Affetso*, 1987

1967	Leo Castelli Gallery, New York
1968	Kasmin Gallery, London
	Leo Castelli Gallery, New York
1970	Lawrence Rubin Gallery, New York
1971	Lawrence Rubin Gallery, New York
	Kasmin Gallery, New York
1972	Lawrence Rubin Gallery, New York
	David Mirvish Gallery, Toronto
1973	Lawrence Rubin Gallery, New York
	Knoedler Gallery of Contemporary Art, New York
1974	*Recent Paintings,* Edmonton Art Gallery, Alberta
	Galerie La Bertesca, Dusseldorf
	Knoedler Gallery of Contemporary Art, New York
1975	Ace Gallery, Los Angeles
	Galerie André Emmerich, Zurich
	Knoedler Gallery of Contemporary Art, New York
1976	David Mirvish Gallery, Toronto
	Galerie Daniel Templon, Paris
	M. Knoedler and Co., New York
1977	Ace Gallery, Los Angeles
	Watson-de Nagy Gallery, Houston
	M. Knoedler and Co., New York
1978	Galerie Ninety-Nine, Bay Harbor Islands, Florida
	M. Knoedler and Co., New York
1979	André Emmerich Gallery, New York
	Gemälde, Amerika Haus, West Berlin
	Amerika Haus, Hannover
1980	Galerie Ulysses, Vienna
	Theo Waddington Gallery, Toronto
	Hett Gallery, Edmonton, Alberta
1981	Galerie Ninety-Nine, Bay Harbor Islands, Florida
	Andre Emmerich Gallery, New York
	Gallery One, Toronto
	Galerie Artline, The Hague
	Museum of Fine Arts, Boston (retrospective)
1982	Andre Emmerich Gallery, New York
	Meredith Long and Co., Houston
	Gallery One, Toronto
	Theo Waddington Gallery, Montreal
1983	Andre Emmerich Gallery, New York
1984	Gallery One, Toronto
1985	Andre Emmerich Gallery, New York
1986	Andre Emmerich Gallery, New York

Selected Group Exhibitions:

1963	*Formalists,* Washington Gallery of Modern Art, Washington, D.C.
1966	*Systemic Painting,* Guggenheim Museum, New York
1968	*The Art of the Real: USA 1948–68,* Museum of Modern Art, New York (travelled)
1970	*Color and Field 1890–1970,* Albright-Knox Art Gallery, Buffalo, New York (travelled to Dayton, Ohio; Cleveland, Ohio)
1972	*Masters of the Sixties,* Edmonton Art Gallery, Alberta (travelled to Winnipeg, Manitoba
1974	*The Great Decade of American Abstraction: Modernist Art 1960–1970,* Museum of Fine Arts, Houston
1977	*Surface, Edge and Color,* Whitney Museum, New York
1980	*Aspects of the 70's: Painterly Abstraction,* Brockton Art Museum, Massachusetts
1985	*Pre Postmodern,* St. Lawrence University, Canton, New York
1987	*The Great Decade: American Abstraction Modernist Art 1960–70,* Museum of Fine Arts, Houston

Collections:

Museum of Modern Art, New York; Whitney Museum, New York; American Federation of Art, New York; Metropolitan Museum of Art, New York; Guggenheim Museum, New York; Museum of Fine Arts, Boston; Philadelphia Museum of Art; Hirshhorn Museum, Washington, D.C.; Tate Gallery, London; Stedelijk Museum, Eindhoven, Netherlands.

Publications:

By POONS: article—"An Interview with Larry Poons," with Phyllis Tuchman, in *Artforum* (New York), December 1970.

On POONS: books—*The United States of America VIII*, exhibition catalogue, by W. Hopps, Sao Paulo 1965; *The Structure of Color*, exhibition catalogue, by Marcia Tucker, New York 1971; *Larry Poons: Recent Paintings*, exhibition catalogue, by Terry Fenton, Edmonton, Alberta 1974; *15 Sculptors in Steel Around Bennington 1963-1978*, exhibition catalogue, by Andrew Hudson, North Bennington, Vermont 1978; *A Century of Ceramics in the United States 1878-1978* by Garth Clark and Margie Hughto, New York 1979; *Larry Poons: Gemälde*, exhibition catalogue, by Terry Fenton, West Berlin 1979; *Color Abstractions: Selections from the Museum of Fine Arts, Boston*, exhibition catalogue, with an introduction by Kenworth Moffett, Boston 1979; *L'Amérique aux Indépendants*, exhibition catalogue, Paris 1980; *Aspects of the 70's: Painterly Abstraction*, exhibition catalogue, with text by Marilyn Friedman Hoffman, Brockton, Massachusetts 1980; *Larry Poons: Paintings 1971-1981*, exhibition catalogue with text by Kenworth Moffett and Terry Fenton, Boston 1981.

*   *   *

Larry Poons' early maturity centered around his educational preparation for a career as composer; his growing sense that he was "capable of painting" which came to him at the 1959 Barnett Newman exhibition (Newman was as well an important personal influence at that time); and Poons' working through, in the late 1950s, a group of geometric-abstract images related to DeStijl and Constructivist style. He would then become well-known in the '60s decade with paintings which combined the reductivist novelty of that time—the retinal play of Optical Art and the expansive flat color fields of post-painterly abstraction—with a seemingly modernist visualization of musical form play (akin perhaps to Kupka and Kandinsky). Poons invented an ellipsoidal ('lozenge') shape, itself combining geometric and organic nuance, and displayed it in interacting lines built up upon a non-visible grid formation often called Systemic. Poons' career-long search had come into view: the creation of a design flow that would appear random (he had studied with John Cage), but was in reality calculatedly composed.

From that moment flowed a long progress—and is no doubt still the artist's controlling device—to derive the essential significance of image-making from what is outwardly an improvisatory approach. The elliptical forms became loose-edged towards the close of the 1960s, and from the next decade to the present, Poons has been a virtuoso painterly painter. From the post-painterly evolution, he adopted a pour technique, together with staining, dripping, and canvas folding with all the attendant paint manipulation as well as long dragged brush strokes. And from all of this, he often allowed a thick crust to build up. It was as if the European modernist residue of Bauhaus and Constructivist thought displayed in his earlier hard-edge pictures was displaced by the need to produce a more indigenous and rhapsodic American landscape easily recalling in its synthesis the work of Still and Newman, and more at hand, Jules Olitsky, together with the energy of the abstract-expressionist gestural tradition.

In the matter of technique, the Poons hallmark became the great swinging pour of paint, at first with the onset of the 1970s, with the canvas placed, Pollock-like, on the studio floor; and then within a year to produce the almost sculptural effect of the so-called monochromatic 'Elephant Skin' paintings. And then, within a year, he began to direct paint-filled buckets onto often gigantic canvas stapled to the studio wall, with the resultant drip pattern controlled and used, in the final state of the picture, both down-and upwards. The great size and unusual rectangular shapes oft found in Poons' oeuvre seem to imply both great compositional fascination as well as Romantic ardor, a sense only increased by the at times corruscating density of color and the deep crust formed by the flowing paint. Yet it may be that the overall effect is restrained, and if so, such sensation would arise from the mellifluous, Impressionist pastel hues favored by Poons, and the relatively traditional movement and closure patterns of the formal dispositions. His clearly heroic scale and masterful control of color and surface in his return to painterly abstraction may have led to a lessened critical acceptance of his art—held sentimental and conservative during the 70s dec-

ade when other standards of achievement and fashion were held foremost in the high art world. Nonetheless Poons' persistence in upholding a warm, yet controlled improvisatory art has outlasted that swing of taste; and now, seen in post-modern light, his paintings well suit the eclectic spectrum which can easily embrace both their craft and their mood.

—Joshua Kind

POSEN, Stephen.

American. Born in St. Louis, Missouri, 27 September 1939. Educated at Washington University, St. Louis, 1957-62, B.F.A. 1962; studied painting at Yale University, New Haven, Connecticut, 1962-64, M.A. 1064. Served in the United States Army, 1957-58. Married Susan Orzack in 1966; daughter: Alexandra. Independent painter, New York, since 1967. Professor of Painting and Drawing, Cooper Union, New York, since 1970. Visiting Critic, Brooklyn Museum Art School, New York, 1975. Recipient: Milliken Travel Scholarship, New Haven, 1964; Fulbright Travel Grant, 1964-66; Creative Artists Program Service Grant, New York, 1973. Agent: Jason McCoy Gallery, 19 East 71st Street, New York, New York 10021. Address: 115 Spring Street, New York, New York 10013, U.S.A.

Individual Exhibitions:

1969	O.K. Harris Gallery, New York
1970	O.K. Harris Gallery, New York
1971	O.K. Harris Gallery, New York
1974	O.K. Harris Gallery, New York
1978	Robert Miller Gallery, New York

Selected Group Exhibitions:

1972	*Documenta 5*, Kassel, West Germany
1973	*Realism Now*, New York Cultural Center, New York
1974	*7 Realists*, Yale University Art Gallery, New Haven, Connecticut
	New Realism, Art Institute of Chicago
	Biennale '74, Tokyo
	71st American Exhibition, Art Institute of Chicago
1975	*Trompe l'Oeil*, Taft Museum, Cincinnati, Ohio
1977	*Illusion and Reality*, Australian National Gallery, Canberra (toured Australia)
	Malerei und Photographie im Dialog, Kunsthaus, Zurich
	8 Contemporary Realists, Pennsylvania Academy of Fine Arts, Philadelphia

Collections:

Chase Manhattan Bank, New York; Museum of Fine Arts, Richmond, Virginia; Pennsylvania Academy of Fine Art, Philadelphia; Guggenheim Museum, New York

Publications:

On POSEN: books—*Radical Realism* by Udo Kultermann, Tübingen, West Germany 1972; *Neue Formen des Realismus* by Peter Sager, Hamburg 1973; *Super Realism*, edited by Gregory Battcock, New York 1975; articles—"New York Galleries" by Willis Domingo in *Arts Magazine* (New York), May 1971; "Neue Formen des Realismus" by Peter Sager in *Magazin Kunst* (Mainz, West Germany), Winter 1971; "Rent Is the Only Reality" by Ivan Karp in *Arts Magazine* (New York), December 1971/January 1972; "The Art World, Reality Again" by Harold Rosenberg in *The New Yorker*, February 1972; "New Wrinkles in Realism" by John Perreault in the *Village Voice* (New York), March 1974; "On Art" by Peter Frank in the *Soho Weekly News* (New York), March 1974; "Realism: The Fiction Is Enough" by Hilton Kramer in the *New York Times*, April 1974; "Polsen's Two Paintings

a Year Are Well Worth Waiting For" by John Canaday in the *New York Times*, September 1975; "Stephen Posen and the Mixed Metaphor" by Dore Ashton in *Arts Magazine* (New York), November 1978; "Dialectic in Modernism: The Paintings of Stephen Posen" by A. Mackie in *Art International* (Lugano, Switzerland), January 1980.

*   *   *

My painting involves the meeting and fluidity of exchange between life, illusion and the demands of the medium.

—Stephen Posen

*   *   *

Before artistic innovation can be valid, the artist has to confront, and ultimately challenge, past artistic conventions. Imbued with an impressive knowledge of art history, Stephen Posen's paintings exist as modern interpretations of traditional themes. Much of his work speaks with the visual language of his age-old favorites: the spiritual freedom encompassed in a large Rothko canvas; the solidity of reality in Cezanne's still lifes; the spatial structure in a Giotto and Vermeer painting; the sensitivity to paint in a Monet; and the bluntness and honesty in American folk paintings. Yet rather than a cheap facsimile of historic monuments, Posen struggles to use these qualities to produce a painting that is, in his words, "a state of mind (fluid, structured, expressive, and accessible.)"

Posen's "state of mind" largely depends on his understanding of reality. Consequently, his work since 1973 has been a study of illusion. He denies the importance of illusionism to his paintings, although he is considered essentially an abstract artist. More than anything his use of the photographic image has pushed him into abstraction. The photograph, taken by an associate under the artist's directions, is enlarged to a one-on-one scale to the eventual painting's size. The photograph allows him to explore the nature of reality and the difference between reality and art. Because photographs designate the picture plane, and thus the space behind and in front of it, his paintings achieve the same equilibrium. This heightened definition of space in his work raises questions about the reality of the photograph in the context of the external world. For Posen it represents a combination of object, document, and space, and thus helps him establish relationships in levels of reality. In this sense, painting to Posen becomes an explanation of reality to himself.

Onto the enlarged photograph Posen superimposes coloured pieces of cloth, stapled to its surface. The coloured cloth either hangs as strips on the surface or covers boxes underneath. The arrangement of the cloth with the context and information of the photograph becomes the "subject" of his painting. The success of his work rests on his ability to hold the number of directional movements in the canvas in rhythmic equilibrium. His 1976 piece, "Variations on a Millstone," illustrates Posen's care in creating a balance.

He models the pieces of cloth, the scaffolding, intuitively, after proloned contemplation. He draws his inspiration from one visual source, the photograph, until a point in the painting where he "abandons the model and the painting takes over, meaning that it exerts demands formal and expressive which are not visible in the construction itself." These details give Posen's work its vital energy; their subtleties demand from the viewer the same degree of contemplation required to create the painting. Posen is asking for involvement in his work on both intellectual and sensory levels. He wants the reality of the painting to help explain reality.

—Carrie Barker

POUSETTE-DART, Richard.

American. Born in St. Paul, Minnesota, 8 June 1916; son of the writer and painter Nathaniel Pousette-Dart.

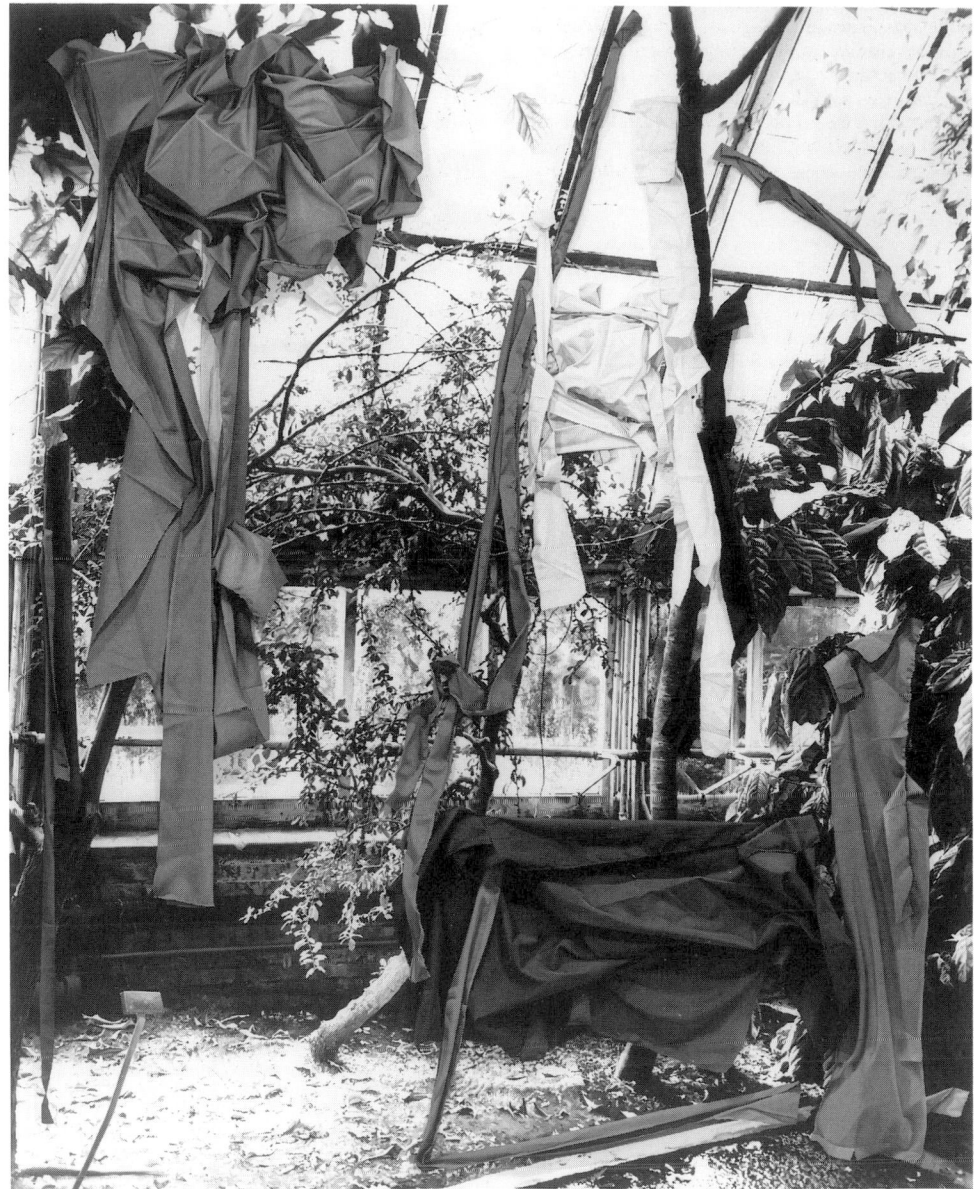

Stephen Posen: *Untitled*, 1974

Educated at Scarborough School, Scarborough-on-Hudson, New York, 1928–35; studied at Bard College, Annandale-on-Hudson, New York, 1936. Married Evelyn Gracey in 1946; children: Joanna and Jonathan. Full-time painter, New York, since 1940: associated with the Abstract Expressionists and Studio 35, New York. Taught at the New School for Social Research, New York, 1959–61, and the School of Visual Arts, New York, 1965; Guest Critic, Columbia University, New York, 1968–69; taught at Sarah Lawrence College, Bronxville, New York, 1970–74; Professor, Art Students League, New York, 1980–86. Recipient: Guggenheim Fellowship, 1950; Ford Foundation Grant, 1959; Cornstock Prize, Art Institute of Chicago, 1961; Silver Medal, *Corcoran Biennial,* Washington, D.C., 1965; National Endowment for the Arts Grant, 1967; Distinguished Lifetime Award, Tiffany Foundation, New York, 1981. D.H.L.: Bard College, 1965. Agent: Marisa del Re Gallery, 41 East 57th Street, New York, New York 10022. Address: 286 Haverstraw Road, Suffern, New York 10901, U.S.A.

Individual Exhibitions:

1941	Artists Gallery, New York
1943	Marion Willards Gallery, New York
1945	Marion Willards Gallery, New York
1946	Marion Willards Gallery, New York
1947	Art of This Century Gallery, New York
	Howard Putzel Gallery, New York
1948	Betty Parsons Gallery, New York
1949	Betty Parsons Gallery, New York
1950	Betty Parsons Gallery, New York
1951	Betty Parsons Gallery, New York
1953	Betty Parsons Gallery, New York
1955	Betty Parsons Gallery, New York
1958	Betty Parsons Gallery, New York
1959	Betty Parsons Gallery, New York
1960	Betty Parsons Gallery, New York
1961	Betty Parsons Gallery, New York
1963	Whitney Museum, New York
1964	Betty Parsons Gallery, New York
1967	Katonah Art Gallery, Katonah, New York
1969	Museum of Modern Art, New York (toured the United States)
	Obelisk Gallery, Boston (toured the United States)
	University of Washington, Seattle
1974	Whitney Museum, New York (retrospective)
	Andrew Crispo Gallery, New York
1975	Allentown Art Museum, Pennsylvania
	Wichita State University, Kansas
1976	Andrew Crispo Gallery, New York
1978	Andrew Crispo Gallery, New York
	Arts Club of Chicago
1981	Marisa del Re Gallery, New York
1983	Marisa del Re Gallery, New York
1986	Marisa del Re Gallery, New York

Selected Group Exhibitions:

1944	*Abstract Painting and Sculpture in America,* Museum of Modern Art, New York
1949	*Whitney Annual,* New York (and 1951, 1953)
1955	*Young Americans,* Museum of Modern Art, New York
1958	*Nature in Abstraction,* Whitney Museum, New York
1959	*Documenta,* Kassel, West Germany
1961	*The Art of Assemblage,* Museum of Modern Art, New York
1973	*American Art at Mid-Century,* National Gallery of Art, Washington, D.C.
1978	*Abstract Expressionists: Formative Years,* Cornell University, Ithaca, New York
1981	*Decade of Transition 1940–50,* Whitney Museum, New York
1986	*An American Renaissance,* Fort Lauderdale Museum of Art, Florida

Collections:

Museum of Modern Art, New York; Metropolitan Museum of Art, New York; Whitney Museum, New York; Guggenheim Museum, New York; Albright-Knox Art Gallery, Buffalo, New York; Addison Gallery of American Art, Phillips Academy, Andover, Massachusetts; Newark Museum, New Jersey; Philadelphia Museum of Art; Corcoran Gallery of Art, Washington, D.C.; National Collection of Fine Arts, Smithsonian Institution, Washington, D.C.

Publications:

By POUSETTE-DART: articles—"What Is the Relationship Between Religion and Art?" in *Union Theological Seminary* (New York), 1952; statements in *The New York School: The First Generation: Paintings of the 1940's and 1950's,* exhibition catalogue, by Maurice Tuchman, Los Angeles, 1965.

On POUSETTE-DART: books—*Richard Pousette-Dart,* exhibition catalogue, by John Gordon and Lloyd Goodrich, New York 1963; *Richard Pousette-Dart,* exhibition catalogue, by James K. Marne, New York 1974; *Richard Pousette-Dart: Presences, Black and White 1978–80,* exhibition catalogue with essay by Lawrence Campbell, New York 1981; *Richard Pousette-Dart (E Series) 1981–83,* exhibition catalogue with essay by Lowery Sims, New York 1983; *Richard Pousette-Dart: Recent Paintings,* exhibition catalogue with texts by Robert C. Hobbs and Sam Hunter, New York 1986; articles—"Inside Nature" by Thomas B. Hess in *Artnews* (New York), February 1958; "Richard Pousette-Dart: Transcendental Expressionist" by Jack Kroll in *Artnews* (New York), April 1961; "Transcending Shape, Richard Pousette-Dart" in *Arts Magazine* (New York), November 1974; "Concerning the Spiritual in Pousette-Dart" by Carter Ratcliff in *Art in America* (New York), November/December 1974.

Richard Pousette-Dart began painting around 1939, and by the mid-1940's he had already developed the vocabulary of forms and the scale which is characteristic of many other first generation Abstract Expressionists developing during the same period of time. Perhaps his rapid evolution owes something to the fact that his father was a painter and writer about American art and his mother was a poet, and certainly it owes a lot to Pousette-Dart's involvement with mystical ideas from a youthful age. His sculpture and painted primitivizing heads from the late 1930's and early 1940's connect with Picasso, who was a "father figure" most of this generation of American artists had to face up to at that time.

The point is that Pousette-Dart was working in his individual and continually developing form in pictures such as "Symphony Number 1, The Transcendental" (1942), employing an all-over grid as infrastructure and painting many layers of thick colored pigments to arrive at a sign language composed of humanoid shapes of multi-referential association. In the works of the mid-1940's, such as "Comprehension of the Atom, Crucifixion" (1945), one can still make out some figural references of specific nature, cross and fish here, totemic and densely painted, not unlike the more abstracted signs which continue to appear in various combinations for years to come. These include spirals, circles, lozenges, writing marks, diamonds and rectangles, variously subsumed and peeking through up to 30 or 40 layers of heavily worked paint. Most of Pousette-Dart's pictures of the next two decades are all-over fields, some shimmering with a calmer, more evenly dispersed quality, others peopled with swarms of cell-like shapes which are arrived at and illuminated through his skillful manipulation of color in various states of hue, value and intensity.

Always Pousette-Dart strives for a rhythmic, harmonic balance, a vibrating state in which flickering tension is heightened by the haloing and blending of shapes merging gradually with their surrounding field. It is a meditative art, achieved by a kind of slow automatism and requiring a continuous perception through time to achieve the desired effects. The artist's intention is to communicate a spiritual state evocation of the interrelatedness of the continuum which stretches across time and space.

With pictures such as "Presence, Red" (1968–69) and "Merging Presences" (1972–73) Pousette-Dart explores the field inhabited by one or two large shapes, most often orbs which achieve their balancing edge in relationship with fields of differing color relationships. His works of the past few years continue this basic format, now limited to black and white for the purpose of setting limits which can free newer possibilities out of purposeful abstinence. There continues to be lots of thickness in the pigment, an element always predominant throughout Pousette-Dart's development. Either one or a balanced repetition of circle, spiral, rectangle are used to create a variety of combinations which would seem impossible within such strict limitations of means. What predominates is a classical, silent, almost eerie calm enlivened by the illumination of black/white light which draws you closer and invites contemplation of the mysteries in universals, both microscopic and galactic. In his fifth decade of Abstract Expressionist painting, Pousette-Dart portrays a vigor and mastery of his means which responds to his intention for mystical meanings with continued commitment.

—Barbara Cavaliere

POZZI, Lucio.

American. Born in Milan, Italy, 29 November 1935; emigrated to the United States in 1962; naturalized, 1972. Studied under the sculptor Michael Noble, Milan, 1955–59; also studied architecture, Rome, 1958–59. Served in the Italian Cavalry, Montebello Regiment, Rome, 1959–60: Lieutenant. Art Director and Designer, Studio Gramma, and Design Consultant, Architeti Urbanisti Associazione, Rome, 1959–62. Visiting Lecturer in Art History, Marlboro College, Vermont, 1969–71; Lecturer in Art History, 1970–71, and Professor of Art, 1970–75, Cooper Union, New York; Visiting Professor of Art, Princeton University, New Jersey, 1976. Instructor in Art, School of Visual Arts, New York, since 1978; Visiting Professor, University of Arkansas, Little Rock, 1986. Agent: John Weber Gallery, New York. Address: c/o John Weber Gallery, 142 Greene Street, New York, New York 10012, U.S.A.

Individual Exhibitions:

1961	Topazia Alliata Gallery, Rome
1962	Topazia Alliata Gallery, Rome
1963	Topazia Alliata Gallery, Rome
1964	New York Six Gallery, New York
1965	20th Century West Galleries Ltd., New York
1971	Galleria dell'Ariete, Milan
1973	Marian Locks Gallery, Philadelphia
	Ariete Grafica, Milan
1974	John Weber Gallery, New York
	Galleria Forma, Genoa
	Clocktower, New York
1975	John Weber Gallery, New York
	Galleria Sperone, Turin
	Galleria Sperone, Rome
	Galleria Peccolo, Livorno, Italy
	Galerie December, Münster, West Germany
	Galleria Area, Florence
	Galerie Yvon Lambert, Paris
	Kazuo Akao Art Agency Co. Ltd., Tokyo
	Galerie Art in Progress, Munich
1976	Galerie Yvon Lambert, Paris
	Galerie Recontres, Paris
	Galerie Aronowitsch, Stockholm
	Galleria Françoise Lambert, Milan
	Galerie Albert Baronian, Brussels
	Fine Arts Building, New York
	Julian Pretto Gallery, New York
	Galerie Charles Kriwin, Brussels
	Rush Rhees Gallery, University of Rochester, New York
1977	Galleria Françoise Lambert, Milan
	Institute for Art and Urban Resources, P.S.1, Queens, New York
	Salone Annunciata, Milan
	Galerie Marika Malacorda, Geneva
	Lucio Pozzi: Works and Ideas 1960-1977, Dartmouth College Art Galleries, Hanover, New Hampshire
	Diego Cortex, New York
1978	John Weber Gallery, New York (2 shows)
	Hal Bromm Gallery, New York
	Fine Arts Center, C. W. Post College, Greenvale, New York
	Marika Malacorda, Basle
	Museum of Modern Art, New York
	Mario Diacono, Bologna
	Kazuo Akao Art Agency Co. Ltd., Tokyo
	Julian Pretto Gallery, New York
1979	Galerie Yvon Lambert, Paris
	Galerie Albert Baronian, Brussels
	Farideh Cadot, Paris
	Hal Bromm Gallery, New York (2 shows)
	Young Hoffman Gallery, Chicago
1980	Texas Gallery, Houston
	P.S.1, Queens, New York
	John Weber Gallery, New York
	Musée du Parc de la Boverie, Liège
	Galleria Françoise Lambert, Milan
	Marian Locks Gallery, Philadelphia
	Marika Malacorda, Basle
	Galerie Albert Baronian, Brussels
	Art Gallery, University of Massachusetts, Amherst
1981	Ariete Grafica, Milan
	Carol Taylor Art, Dallas
	Galleria Peccolo, Livorno, Italy
	John Weber Gallery, New York
1982	Kunsthalle, Bielefeld, West Germany
	Carol Taylor Art, Dallas
	Image Gallery, Stockbridge, Massachusetts
1983	Badischer Kunstverein, Karlsruhe, West Germany
1984	Leo Castelli Gallery, New York
	John Weber Gallery, New York
	Susan Caldwell Gallery, New York
	Cava Gallery, Philadelphia
1985	Studio Grossetti, Milan
	M-13 Gallery, New York
	Gerald Just Gallery, Hannover
	Gloria Luria Gallery, Bay Harbor Island, Florida
	Galerie Liesbeth Lips, Amsterdam
1986	Mario Diacono Gallery, Boston
	John Weber Gallery, New York
	Studio E, Rome
	American Academy, Rome
	Galerie Albrecht, Munich

Selected Group Exhibitions:

1965	*New York Six*, Loeb Center, New York University
1973	*La Riflessione sulla Pittura*, Palazzo Comunale, Acireale, Italy
1975	*Tendances Actuelles de la Nouvelle Peinture Américaine*, Musée d'Art Moderne de la Ville de Paris
1976	*Rooms*, Institute for Art and Urban Resources, P.S.1, Queens, New York
1977	*Words*, Whitney Museum-Downtown, New York
1979	*Wall Painting*, Museum of Contemporary Art, Chicago
1980	*Drawing: The Pluralist Decade*, Institute of Contemporary Art, University of Pennsylvania, Philadelphia
1983	*American Abstract Artists*, University of North Caroline, Greensboro (travelled to University, Alabama)
1985	*Biennale des Friedens*, Kunstverein, Hamburg
1987	*Reconnecting*, Detroit Institute of Arts, Michigan

Collections:

Museum of Modern Art, New York; Chase Manhattan Bank, New York; Dartmouth College Galleries, Hanover, New Hampshire; University of Massachusetts, Amherst; University of Kentucky Art Museum, Lexington; Kunstmuseum, Basle; Australian National Gallery, Canberra.

Publications:

By POZZI: books—*5 Stories*, New York 1974; *Unwritten*, with David Shapiro, New York 1977; *Hender*, 1978; articles—"Super Realisti USA" in *Boffiarte* (Turin), March 1972; article in *Art-Rite* (New York), no. 3, 1973; "Adesso La Pitture Dipinge La Pitture" in *Bolaffiarte* (Turin), May 1974; "La Pittura" in *Europa*, April 1975; "Il Gruppo 'Level' 1975" in *Flash Art* (Milan), May 1975; "Painting Matters" in *Art-Rite* (New York), Spring 1975; "Instruction Manual" in *Tracks* (New York), Fall 1975; "Max Neuhaus" in *Data* (Milan), September/October 1975; "What is Proper Training of the Artist?" in *American Artist* (New York), March 1976; "Avangardia USA" in *Bolaffiarte* (Turin), May/June 1976; "A Discussion Continued" in *Central Hall Artists Newsletter* (Port Washington, New York), no. 6, 1976; "Artist's Books" in *Art-Rite* (New York), no. 13, 1977; article in *Documenta 6*, exhibition catalogue, Kassel, West Germany 1977; article in *Kunst und Media: Materialien zur Documenta 6*, exhibition catalogue, Kassel, West Germany 1977; "Project for a Short Theatrical Action in Three Parts" in *Premieres Recontres Internationale d'Art Contemporain*, Montreal 1977; "Fare Ate e un Fatto Politico" in *Data* (Milan), March/May 1977; "Burgtheater bei Tag und bei Nacht" in *Mela* (Florence), Autumn/Winter 1978; "Eleven Drawings" in *Whitewalls*, (Chicago), Winter/Spring 1979; "An Interview with Lucio Pozzi," with David Shapiro, in *New York Arts Journal*, no. 15, 1979; statement and interview in "Lucio Pozzi" by Thierry de Duve in *Parachute* (Montreal), Spring 1979; "We Were Four . . ." in *Mela* (Florence), Autumn/Winter 1979/1980; statement in "Situation Esthetics: Impermanent Art and the 70's Audience," edited by Nancy Foote, in *Artforum* (New York), January 1980; "A Letter to Peder Bonnier" in *Artforum* (New York), Summer 1980; "The When" in *Whitewalls* (Chicago), Winter 1981; "475 Years" in *New Observations* (New York), no. 12, 1983; "Critical Point" in *Art Criticism* (Stony Brook, New York), no. 3, 1986; films and videotapes—*Plus*, 1974; *Portrait #1*, 1975; *2 Times*, 1975; *Updownleftright #1*, 1975; *A Boetti Suggestion*, 1975; *Portrait #2*, 1975; *Updownleftright #2*, 1975; *Comin from Reading #1, Interview with Lucio Pozzi and Philip Smith*, with Paul Michael Shavelson, 1976; *CEAC*, 1976; *Onetwothreefour*, 1976; *Dialogue*, 1976; *Study for "Dialogue"*, 1976; *Patchameena*, 1977; *Little Chief*, 1977; *Yesno*, 1978; *Index*, 1978; *Walk*, 1978; *Snow*, 1978.

On POZZI: books—*Due Dimensioni*, Milan 1962; *Tendances Actuelles de la Nouvelle Peinture Américaine*, exhibition catalogue, Paris 1975; *Photographical Process as Medium*, exhibition catalogue, New Brunswick, New Jersey 1976; *New York, New York*, exhibition catalogue, Los Angeles 1976; *Rooms*, exhibition catalogue, Queens, New York 1976; *Collection in Progress: The Collection of Milton Brutten and Helen Herrick*, exhibition catalogue, Philadelphia 1977; *Lucio Pozzi: Works and Ideas 1960-1977*, exhibition catalogue, by Jan Van Der Marck, Hanover, New Hampshire 1977; *'75 '76 Painting*, exhibition catalogue, Bronxville, New York 1977; *Works for the Collection of Dorothy and Herbert Vogel*, exhibition catalogue, Ann Arbor, Michigan 1977; *Aphoto*, exhibition catalogue, Milan 1977; *Bilder Ohne Bilder*, exhibition catalogue, Bonn 1978; *Disseminazione*, exhibition catalogue, Varese, Italy 1978; *Lucio Pozzi*, exhibition catalogue, by Mario Diacono, Bologna 1978; *Words*, exhibition catalogue, by Isabella Puliafito, Bochum, West Germany 1979; *Wall Painting*, exhibition catalogue, by Judith Russi Kirsch-

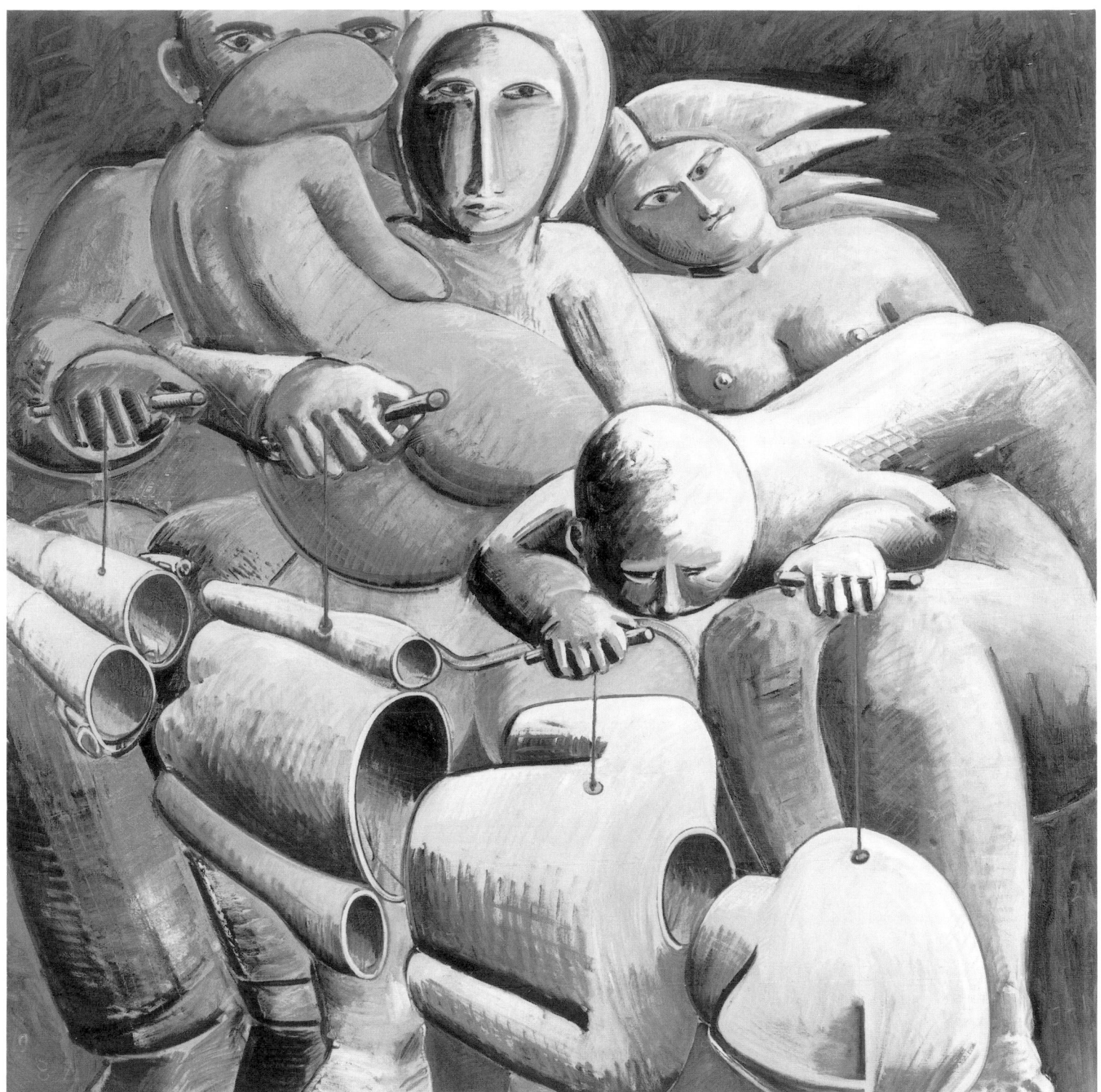

Lucio Pozzi: *Orpheus Re-Membered*, 1987

ner, Chicago 1979; *Painting in Environment*, exhibition catalogue, essays by Renato Barilli and Francesca Alinovi, Milan 1979; *Painting: 5 Views*, exhibition catalogue, by Nancy Einreinhofer, Wayne, New Jersey 1979; *Abstract Painting, New York City 1981*, exhibition catalogue, with an introduction by Tiffany Bell, Hempstead, New York 1981; *Lucio Pozzi*, exhibition catalogue with texts by David Ebony, David Shapiro and others, Bielefeld 1982, *Lucio Pozzi. Figurative Malerei 1980–1982* by Heribert Heere, Munich 1983.

I am involved in a continuing investigation of the art of painting, which I consider a most important component of modern culture. The procedures of painting, its language, its speculative and environmental context, its contemplative and emotional content are the matrix of my work. I devote much of my time to painting, but I also continually probe into different dimensions. Materials and situations, other than pigment applied by hand onto static surface, offer me the opportunity of dealing with a variety of perceptual codes.

While developing a logical structure common to all my activities, I regard each as a specific operational methodology, the inherent characteristics of which I reveal and respect.

I try to base my work on a systematic, analytical approach so that I may then, in every project, leap beyond the describable, and combine in each piece factors of spontaneous improvisation.

I write about art. I work with words alone, or combined with images. I work with photography. I compose concerts of acoustic situations. I organize performances and make films and videotapes.

All the separate activities I have so far brought forward seem at this point to be merging into one single flux, with parts, images and symbols freely interchanging from work to work.

—Lucio Pozzi

PRASSINOS, Mario.

French. Born of Greek parents, in Istanbul, 12 August 1916; emigrated to France, 1922: naturalized, 1949. Educated at Lycée Condorcet, Paris, 1923–31; studied at Atelier Clement Serveau, Paris, 1932–33; Ecole des Langues Orientales Vivantes, Paris, 1933–

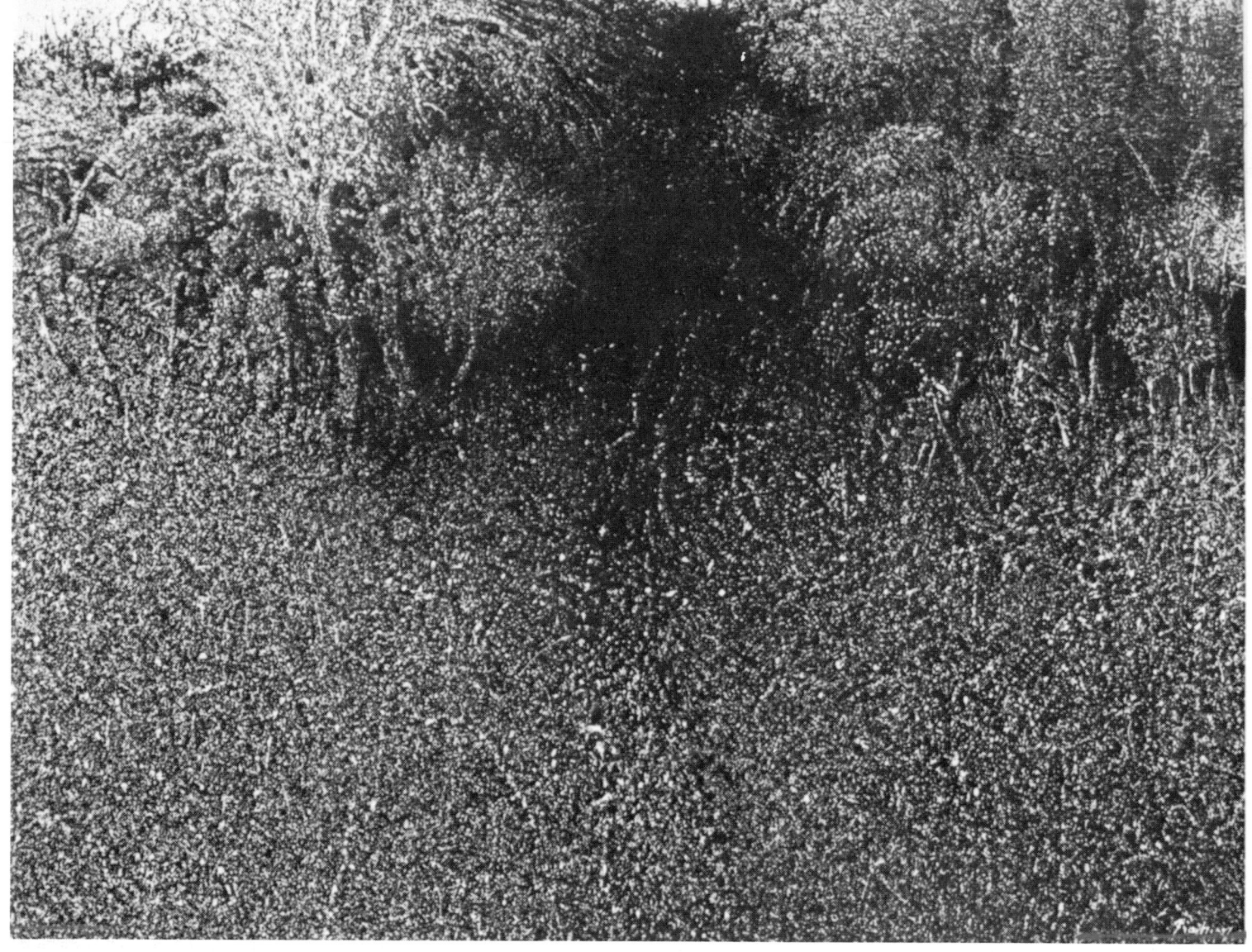

Mario Prassinos: *Le Printemps*, 1981

36. Served as a volunteer corporal, 22nd Regiment des Volontaires Etrangers, Alsace and Somme, 1939: Croix de Guerre, 1940. Married Yolande Borelly in 1938; daughters: Catherine and Emmanuelle. Painter, living and working in Paris, since 1932 until his death in 1985: associated with surrealists André Breton, Paul Eluard, René Char, Benjamin Peret, Max Ernst, Jean Arp and Marcel Duchamp, 1934-36; created first theatre decors, 1947; first tapestries, 1951; worked as scenographist for theatres, Paris, and for La Scala, Milan, 1948-72. Recipient: First Prize for Tapestry, *Biennale,* Milan 1957, and *World's Fair,* Brussels, 1958; Grand Prize for Tapestry, Fondation Robert Four, Paris, 1979. Chevalier, Order des Arts et Lettres, 1960; Chevalier de la Légion d'Honneur, 1966. Agents: Galerie de France, 3 Faubourg Saint Honore, 75008 Paris; Galerie La Demeure, 6 Place Saint Sulpice, 75006 Paris. *Died* (in Paris) *23 October 1985.*

Individual Exhibitions:

1938	Galerie Billiet-Vorms, Paris
1944	Galerie de la Pleiade/N.R.F., Paris
1945	Librairie l'Amour des Arts, Paris
1946	Detroit Public Library
1947	Galerie Billiet-Caputo, Paris
1948	Galerie Billiet-Caputo, Paris
1949	Librairie-Galerie La Hune, Paris
1950	Perspectives Gallery, New York
1951	Kunstring, Rotterdam

Kunsthandel Santee Landweer N.V., Amsterdam
Galerie Appollo, Brussels

1953	*Drawings, Monotypes and Engravings,* Hanover Gallery, London
	Librairie-Galerie La Hune, Paris
	Editions Gallimard, Paris
	Galerie de France, Paris
	Galleria Latte, Turin
1955	Galerie de France, Paris
1956	Galerie La Demuere, Paris
1957	Galerie de France, Paris
1958	Galleria Blu, Milan
1960	Galerie de France, Paris
	Librairie-Galerie La Hune, Paris
	Kunstverein, Wuppertal, West Germany (toured Germany)
1961	Städtisches Museum, Gelsenkirchen, West Germany
	Kunsthalle, Kiel, West Germany
	Oeuvre Tisse, Galerie La Demeure, Paris
	Galleri Haaken, Oslo
	Musée Chateau Grimaldi, Antibes, France
1962	Galerie Spinazzola, Aix-en-Province, France
	Galerie Miroir, Montpellier, France
1963	Galerie La Demeure, Paris (with Singier and Tour-liere)
	Gemeentemuseum, Arnhem, Netherlands
	Cultureel Centrum, Breda, Netherlands
	Galerie Orangerie Verlag, Cologne
	Kunsthalle, Basle
	Musée, La Chaux de Fons, Switzerland
	Galerie Gregoire, Marseilles
1964	Maison de la Culture, Caen, France

	Galerie de France, Paris
	Galerie La Demeure, Paris
	Galerie Numaga, Auvernier-Neuchfel, France
	Galerie Colette Ryter, Zurich
1965	Akademie der Bildende Künste, Munich
	Musée des Beaux-Arts, Le Havre, France
	Galerie Du Castel, Avignon
1966	Gallery 8, Athens
	Galerie La Demeure, Paris
	Galerie de France, Paris
1967	Galerie Colette Ryter, Zurich
	Ecole Normale Supérieure, St. Cloud, France
	Faculté des Lettres, Nanterre, France
	Maison de la Culture, Amiens, France
	Maison de la Culture, Rheims, France
1968	*Polyptiques,* Galerie La Demeure, Paris
	Maison de la Culture, Thonon, France (toured France)
	Musée Cantini, Marseilles
1969	Arts Club of Chicago
	Union des Arts Plastiques, St. Etienne du Rouvay, France
	Galerie Wallet-Fouque, Amiens, France
1970	Musée Reattu, Arles, France
	Centre Culturel, Toulouse
	Maison des Arts, et des Loisirs, Sochaux, France
1971	Galerie Colette Ryter, Zurich
	Galerie Noella Gest, St. Remy, France
	La Galerie, Nimes, France
	Empreindre, Galerie de France, Paris
	Musée, La Chaux de Cossonay, Switzerland
	Salle des Ecuries de St. Hughes, Cluny, France

Centre Culturel Communal, Corbeil-Essones, France
1973 Théâtre Jean Vilar, Suresnes, France
Galerie Colette Ryter, Zurich
Centre Culturel, Arcueil, France
Liacopoulos Gallery, Athens
Galerie Nicole Fournier, Lyons
1974 Ecole des Beaux-Arts, Angers, France
Théâtre, Angers, France
Oeuvre Tisse, Galerie La Demeure, Paris
Greniers St. Jean, Angers, France
Travaux Noir et Blanc, Estampes, Ancien Couvent Royal, St. Maximin, France
Galerie Noella Gest, St. Remy, France
Abbaye de Monmajour, Arles-Montmajour, France
Galleria Il Segnapasso, Pesaro, Italy
Galerie Nicole Fournier, Lyons
1975 Ecole Polytechnique, Paris
Chateau de Boussac, France
Ancienne Saline Royale, Arc et Senans, France
1976 Galerie de France, Paris
Galerie Candela, Cannes
Galerie l'Enseigne du Cerceau, Paris
1977 Galerie de l'Ours, Tours
Schloss Ingelheim, West Germany
Centre Culturel, Aubagne, France
Galerie Le Balcon des Arts, Paris
1978 Galerie d'Athenes, Athens
Galerie les Trois Ormeaux, Aix-en-Province, France
Salon de l'Enclave, Valreas, France (with Gence and Alessandri)
1979 Institut Francais, Athens
1980 Galerie Protee, Toulouse
Peintures et Dessins Recents, Grand Palais, Paris
Galerie Noella Gest, St. Remy, France
1981 Maison Jean Vilar, Avignon
Palais des Arts et de la Culture, Brest
1983 College d'Echanges Contemporains, St. Maximin, France
Archives de la Ville de Marseilles, Frances
Cloitre St. Louis, Aix-en-Province, France (retrospective)
1984 Centre d'Art Plastique, Villefranche sur Saone, France
Chapelle Ile du Grand Couvent, Cavaillon, France
Institut Francais, Athens
Palais des Grands Maitres, Athens
Museum of Salonika, Greece
Galerie Simoncini, Luxembourg
1986 Chapelle Notre Dame de Pitié, St. Remy de Provence, France
Hotel de Sade, St. Remy de Provence, France
Hotel Estrine, St. Remy de Provence France
Galerie Noella Gest, St. Remy de Provence, France
1987 Chappelle Notre Dame de Pitié, St. Remy de Provence, France
Hotel de Sade, St. Remy de Provence, France
La Malmaison, Cannes, France
Bibliothèque Municipale, Cannes, France

Selected Group Exhibitions:

1938 *L'Art Cruel,* Galerie Billiet-Vorms, Paris
1952 *11 Painters from Paris,* Stedelijk Museum, Amsterdam
1959 *Documenta 2,* Kassel, West Germany
1961 *Carnegie International,* Carnegie Institute, Pittsburgh
1965 *10 Ans d'Art Vivant 1955-1965,* Fondation Maeght, St. Paul-de-Vence, France
1971 *Paris Painters since 1950,* Fondacao Gulbenkian, Lisbon
1977 *26 French Artists,* Kunstforening, Aarhus, Denmark (travelled to Nordjyllands Konstmuseum, Aalborg, Kontspavillion, Esbjerg, and Kunstforening, Svendborg, Denmark; and Galerie Pesch, Cologne)
1981 *Portraits d'Arbres,* Centre Culturel, Boulogne-Billancourt, France
1985 *La Tapisserie en France,* Ecole Nationale Superieure des Beaux-Arts, Paris
1987 *40 Ans de Festival,* Maison Jean Vilar, Avignon, France

Collections:

Fondation Mario Prassinos, St. Remy de Provence, France; Centre Georges Pompidou, Paris; Musée Picasso-Chateua Grimaldi, Antibes, France; Musée Cantini, Marseilles, Musée d'Art Contemporain, Dunkirk, France; Palais de Justice, Lille, France; Kunst und Museumsverein, Wuppertal, West Germany; Museum für Kunst und Gewerbe, Hamburg; Arts Club of Chicago; Musée de Quebec, Canada.

Publications:

By PRASSINOS: books—*Petit Traite de Tapisserie,* Paris 1967; *Les Pretextats,* Paris 1973; *Invention de la Photographie,* Paris 1980; *La Colline Tatouée,* Paris 1983; articles—"Hommage à Jean Lurcat" in *Galerie des Arts* (Paris), January 1968; "Le Carton de Tapisserie sera pas" in *Galerie des Arts* (Paris), no. 74, 1969; "L'Artiste aurait Besoin qu'on l'Aime" in *Les Lettres Francaises* (Paris), 7 September 1970; "Preface" in *Douze Photographies de Lucien Clergue,* Arles, France 1970; "Le Carton de Tapisserie" in *Graphics* (Zurich), no. 151, 1970; "Le Carton" in *Cahiers Ciba-Geigy* (Basle), March 1973; "Lucien Clergue" in *Camargue Secrete,* album of Clergue photos, Paris 1976; "Le Clair et l'Obscur" in *Vagabondages* (Paris), no. 13, 1979; "Picasso en Prison" in *L'Arch* (Paris), no. 82, 1981.

On PRASSINOS: books—*Mario Prassinos: Drawings, Monotypes and Engravings,* exhibition catalogue, with text by W. J. Strachan, London 1953; *La Tapisserie Francaise et les Peintures Cartonniers* by Jean Cassou, Paris 1957; *Le Monologue de Peintre* By G. Charbonnier, Paris 1959; *Mario Prassinos: Arbes et Bouquets,* exhibition catalogue, with texts by Gisele Prassinos and Myriam Prevot, Paris 1960; *Mario Prassinos: Oeuvre Tisse,* exhibition catalogue, with text by Jean Louis Ferrier, Paris 1961; *Ces Peintures Vous Parlent* by Louis Goldaine and Pierre Astier, Paris 1964; *Mario Prassinos: Tentative de Portrait de Bessie Smith,* exhibition catalogue, Paris 1964; *Le Grand Livre de la Tapisserie* by P. Verlet and M. Florisonne, Lausanne, 1965; *Les Pretextats: Prassinos,* exhibition catalogue, Paris 1966; *Tapisseries de Notre Temps,* Geneva 1967; *La Tapisserie des Origines à nos Jours* by Madeline Jarry, Paris 1968; *Polytechniques: Prassinos,* exhibition catalogue, Paris 1968; *Mario Prassinos,* exhibition catalogue, with text by Jean-Jacques Leveque, Chicago 1969; *Prassinos,* exhibition catalogue, with text by Marc Alyn, Arles, France 1970; *Mario Prassinos: Empreindre,* exhibition catalogue, Paris 1971; *Mario Prassinos: Travaux Noir et Blanc, Estampes,* exhibition catalogue, with text by Jean Salusse, René Char and others, Saint-Maximin, France 1974; *La Tapisserie: Art de Notre Temps* by Madeleine Jarry, Paris 1974; *Mario Prassinos: Oeuvre Tisse,* exhibition catalogue, with text by Catherine Prassinos, Paris 1974; *Mario Prassinos: Noir et Blanc,* exhibition catalogue, Paris 1976; *Mario Prassinos: Peintures et Dessins Recents,* exhibition catalogue, with text by Raymond Queneau, Francois Nouirissier, Pierre Cabanne and others, Paris 1980; films—*Prassinos* by Max-Pol Fouchet, 1960; *L'Image et le Moment* by Robert Lapoujade, 1961; *Prassinos* by E. Tybo, 1963; *Un Quart d'Heure avec Mario Prassinos* by Jean L'Hote, 1967; *Revue des Arts 5: Prassinos* by P. Schneider, 1968; *Actualités Pathe-Journal, May 1968,* by Max Damain, 1968; *Prassinos* by Lucien Clerque, 1969; *A Livre Ouvert* by Jean Manceau, interview with Robert Ytier, 1974; *Dieu et le Monde* by Peter Bermbach, 1979; *Ombre et Lumière* by Daniel Le Comte, 1979; *Mario Prassinos,* interview by Jean Louis Ferrier, 1980; *Boite aux Lettres* by J. Garcin, 1983.

I would like the spectator to look at my paintings in two ways. First from three or four metres, that is to say far enough away for the subject (the surface image) to be clear. Then he should go towards it progressively until he sees nothing more than the texture (the white points and the black points and their variously concentrated arrangement). Then, having only a memory of the subject, he will take the place of the painter and, as close to the painting as the painter was when he painted, he will discover that there is a beyond of the image. That is where I would like to lead him.

When one enlarges a photograph to a maximum, far from rendering the detail more precise, one reaches a point where a reading of the subject becomes impossible and it seems that one has crossed a threshold as if passing from the visible and tangible universe which is apparently ours to that of matter and the atom, to the unknown which we know is there but of which we have no knowledge.

The technique of black pointillism projected onto a canvas laid flat on the ground or by jet onto a vertically held canvas, is destined, in giving an ambiguous reading, to encourage the birth of images which are unexpected (but revealed as if they already existed elsewhere) and also to suppress the specific outline of things, to fuse the tree with the sky and the sky with the earth in a corpuscular mist. There is a point in my work where all sorts of images are possible. And in certain pictures several images coexist, superimposed.

—Mario Prassinos (1983)

Born in Istanbul Mario Prassinos came to France when he was a boy and studied at the Sorbonne. His first experiments with art were in graphic media and embraced surrealist themes from his contacts with followers in the movement around 1938. He became a French citizen and has lived in France continuously since then, making his name primarily as an etcher and engraver. The basic strong outlines and profile forms of his figures are strong elements in the tapestries that he began to make in 1951 and which subsequently became major productions in his oeuvre.

For a painter or a graphic artist to become successful as a tapestry designer requires a certain abandonment of principles to the extent that space must be represented by contrasts of colour areas rather than any suggestions of aerial perspective. At the same time it was possible for Prassinos to continue to rely heavily on the linear patterns that were characteristics of his most impressive prints. Thus *Trois oiseaux et un soleil,* (1952), a large strongly drawn tapestry, is an effective transposition into the soft material of woven wool of the semi-abstract rendering of the identifiable motives. His construction of the various parts—head, beak, body and tail—is formed in the typical parallel contours of light and dark tones, the enclosures of form that dart across the surface in vivid equivalents of the flying birds.

Consistent in his earlier work is the predominance of black; the framework of forms assume a hieratic frieze through which the light and colour shine in the mystic figures like those in a stained glass window of a medieval cathedral. This double function of the black as the cloisonné division of colour areas and as the outline of the dominant figures has a peculiarly powerful and stimulating presence when Prassinos creates his evocative flower pieces where the compositions simulate the effect of effulgent blooming in the glow of the wool threads illuminating the total width of the tapestry. Yet gradually in his tapestries he reaches toward a spontaneity where the unique qualities of the textured wool varies from the unbroken stretches of pure colour to the singing accents of red and yellow with the persistent rigid enclosure of black anchoring the design to its solid base.

In his painting of *Bessie Smith* (1962) he approached the charisma of the legendary blues singer through 15 canvases each presenting her essence in individual images that were as reflective of her personality as if she were singing 15 different songs. But the singer was the same, a funambulist symphony neither abstract nor yet figurative as in his later landscapes of 1970 in which he adopts a splatter technique to suggest the arid territory of Turkey where he was born, only its lonely trees on the skyline breaking the even bareness of the land mass.

In his changing styles Prassinos maintained the serene consistency of his art, using motives of flowers and nature, sometimes humans playfully transformed, always musical in colour and tonal harmonies, rhythmic and moving in euphoric gracefulness.

—G. S. Whittet

PRENT, Mark (George).
Canadian. Born in Montreal, Quebec, 23 December 1947. Educated at Logan School, Strathcona High,

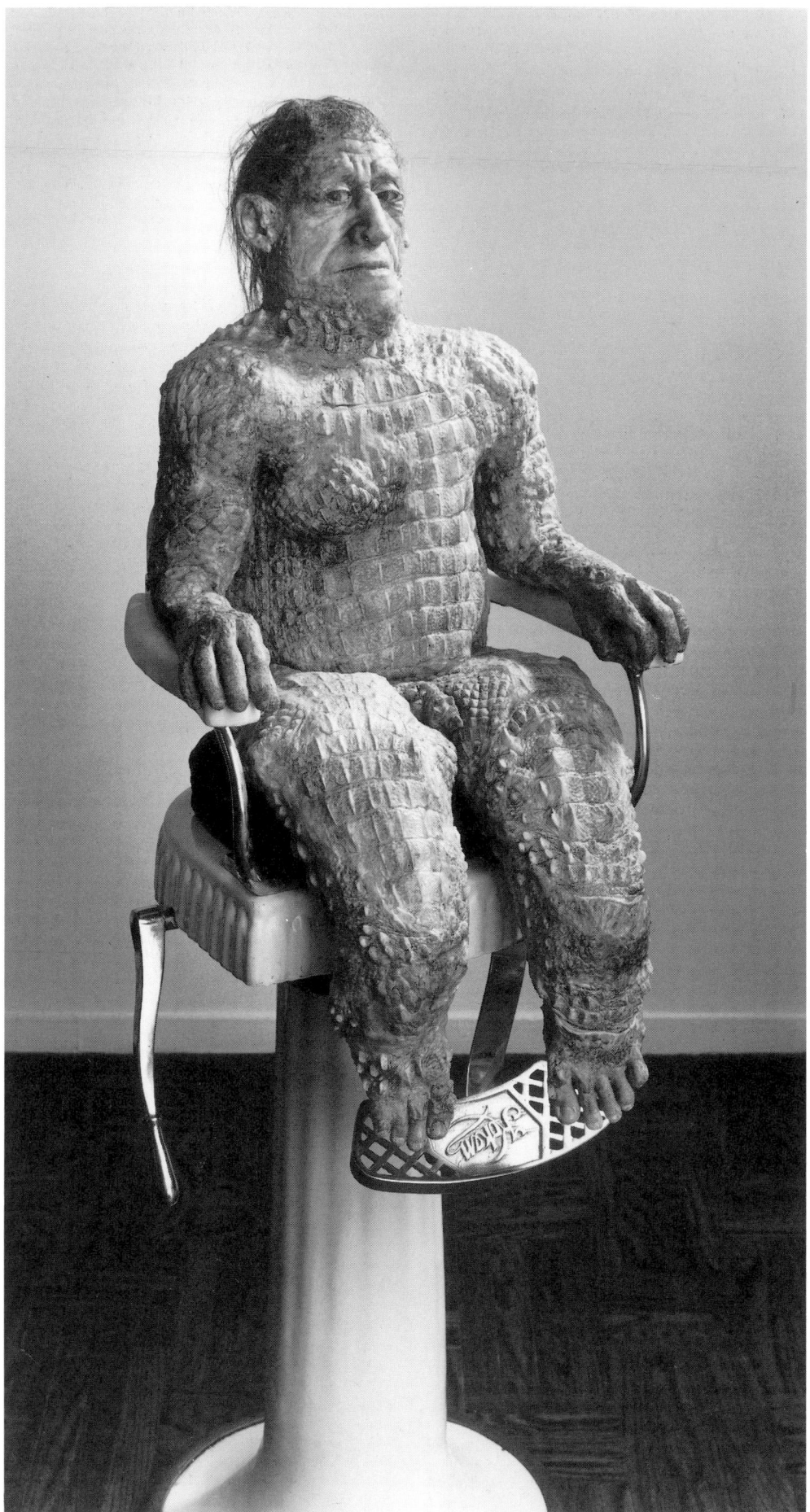

Mark Prent: *The Incurable Romantic*, 1981

Montreal, 1962–63; Outremont High School, Montreal, 1963–66; studied under John Ivor Smith, Sir George Williams University, Montreal, 1966–70, B.F.A. 1970. Independent artist, Montreal, since 1969. Recipient: Canada Council Arts Grant, 1971, 1972, 1973, 1975, 1977; DAAD Stipendium, West Berlin, 1975; Guggenheim Fellowship, 1977; Victor M. Lynch-Staunton Award, 1978; Canada Council Senior Arts Grant, 1978, 1980, 1981, 1985; Ludwig Vogelstein Foundation Fellowship, 1985. Agent: Isaacs Gallery, 179 John Street, Toronto, Ontario M5T 1X3. Address: 35 Bank Street, St. Albans, Vermont 05478, U.S.A.

Individual Exhibitions:

1971   Wiseman Gallery, Sir George Williams University, Montreal
1972   Isaacs Gallery, Toronto
       Warren Benedek Gallery, New York
1974   Art Gallery of York University, Toronto
       Isaacs Gallery, Toronto
1975   *Mark Prent: Extended Realism*, Akademie der Künste, West Berlin
1976   Kunsthhalle, Nuremberg
1978   Stedelijk Museum, Amsterdam
       Isaacs Gallery, Toronto
       Wiseman Gallery, Sir George Williams University, Montreal
1979   Musée d'Art Contemporain, Montreal
       Art Space, Peterborough, Ontario
       Saw Gallery, Ottawa
1981   Isaacs Gallery, Toronto
       Prince/Prent/Whiten, Agnes Etherington Art Center, Kingston, Ontario
1982   Salle Tremble, Alma, Quebec
1984   Galerie Fucito, Montreal
1985   Forest City Gallery, London, Ontario
1986   Galerie Esperanza, Montreal

Selected Group Exhibitions:

1970   *Survey '70*, Montreal Museum of Fine Arts
       Biennial, Winnipeg Art Gallery
1972   *Realism: Emulsion and Omission*, Agnes Etherington Art Center, Queen's University, Kingston, Ontario (travelled to the University of Guelph Art Gallery, Ontario)
1973   *Biennale*, Musée d'Art Moderne de la Ville de Paris
1974   *The Isaacs Gallery at the Owens Art Gallery*, Mount Allison University, Sackville, New Brunswick
1978   *Performance*, Harbourfront Art Gallery, Toronto
1979   *Birmingham Festival of the Arts*, Alabama
1980   *11th International Sculpture Conference*, Dupont Center, Washington, D.C.

Collections:

Art Bank of Canada, Ottawa; Art Gallery of Ontario, Toronto; Sir George Williams University Art Galleries, Montreal; Musée d'Art Contemporain, Montreal.

Publications:

By PRENT: articles—"Freedom and the Artist," interview, with Joyce Zemans, in *The Canadian Forum* (Toronto), August 1974; "Extended Realism," interview, with Thomas Deecke, in *Was Ist Wann*, West Berlin 1975.

On PRENT: books—*Mark Prent: Extended Realism*, exhibition catalogue, West Berlin 1975; *Mark Prent*, exhibition catalogue, Nuremberg 1976; *Mark Prent*, exhibition catalogue, Amsterdam, 1978; *Mark Prent*, exhibition catalogue, Montreal 1979; articles—"Justice: What is Disgusting" in *Time* (Toronto), 13 March 1972; "Mark Prent" by Michael Greenwood in *Artscanada* (Toronto), Spring 1972; "The Arts Macabre-Vision" by Geoffrey James in *Time* (Toronto), 4 February 1974; "Mark Prent's Macabre Manipulation" by Werner Rode in *Kunst* (Mainz, West Germany), no. 3, 1975; "Mark Prent und das Skandalose" by Karl Huhrberg in *Mark Prent: Extended Realism*, exhibition catalogue, West Berlin 1975; "Schock, Dekadenz, Oder . . . ?" by Heinz Neidel in

Du Zurich), May 1976; "Mark Prent" by Henry Lehmann in the *Montreal Star,* 11 December 1976; "Mark Prent: De Nachtmerrie Is Kunst" by Jan Bart Klaster in *Het Parool* (Amsterdam), 25 February 1978; films—*If Brains Were Dynamite, You Wouldn't Have Enough to Blow Your Nose* by Tom Burstyn, Montreal 1976; *Mark Prent: Overmood* by Brian McNeil, Montreal 1978.

I display my work in environments for several reasons. First of all, the environment can be used to force the viewer to become involved with the piece by making it impossible to see it successfully without purposeful contact with the piece. For example, to see my *Death in the Chair* in operation, a viewer must mount the stairs to the *Death Chamber* and pull the switch that "electocutes" a figure in the chair (the figure jolts). In another piece the viewer must peer through scratches in the painted-out surface of a small window on a door in order to see the figure inside the room. Very often, the only way the public can see one of my pieces is by climbing stairs which have not been erected purely for spectator purposes, but are visually necessary to complete the environment.

I like to think that a viewer cannot be indifferent to a piece if he must, when he encounters it, decide whether to make the effort required to view the piece or not. He cannot just "pass by" the piece and "see it."

The enviromental form is the only way to adapt an exhibition area to allow the piece displayed full impact. Nothing can disturb or detract from the mood of a closed environment that can only be viewed from the outside, looking in. This brings me to my final reason for working in environments—a very practical one.

My work can occasionally be very fragile and easily damaged. When I know that the work is safely displayed with four walls, a ceiling, and a floor between it and the public, I sleep a lot better at night. They are "my" environments, really. I, and I alone, can unlock them, enter, and play with them at will.

—Mark Prent

The word most often applied to the sculpture of Mark Prent is "controversial." In contrast to the sensational and shock elements others find in his work, Prent remarks on the sense of humour he finds there. His images are often figures in impossible situations—like his woman/pig spread-eagled on an operating table. Prent uses horror as a formal approach.

Prent was trained in a traditional way at Montreal's Sir George Williams University. But he is fascinated with found objects, particularly pieces of leather and metal more than 50 years old, and he likes to utilize their form, texture, material and colour. Often he uses his own face and body in his sophisticated, questioning work. His earlier pieces, such as "And Is There Anything Else You'd Like Madam?" (1971) and "Hanging Is Very Important" (1972), were often environments: in fantastic room settings, different parts of the human body are substituted for pieces of meat. Today he has become interested in making kinetic pieces. In his "The Incurable Romantic" (1981) the eyes of a shrunken, wizened "alligator-man" seated in a Victorian child's barber chair, rove constantly to confront the viewer.

Prent's "extended realism" lends itself to excessive reactions. He himself stresses the aesthetic involved in his use of the horrific, and the beauty of his work is in terms of texture, colour, and form.

—Joan Murray

PRICE, Kenneth.
American. Born in Los Angeles, California, in 1935. Studied at the Chouinard Art Institute, Los Angeles; Los Angeles County Art Institute; University of Southern California, Los Angeles, B.F.A. 1956; State University of New York at Alfred, M.F.A. 1959. Recipient: Tamarind Fellowship, Los Angeles, 1968-69. Agent: Willard Gallery, 29 East 72nd Street, New York, New York 10021. Address: Box 1356, Taos, New Mexico 87571, U.S.A.

Individual Exhibitions:

1960	Ferus Gallery, Los Angeles
1961	Ferus Gallery, Los Angeles
1964	Ferus Gallery, Los Angeles
1966	Los Angeles County Museum of Art (with Robert Irwin)
1968	Kasmin Gallery, London
1969	Whitney Museum, New York
	Mizuno Gallery, Los Angeles
1970	Gemini G.E.L., Los Angeles
	Kasmin Gallery, London
1971	David Whitney Gallery, New York
	Mizuno Gallery, Los Angeles
	Galerie Neuendorf, Cologne
	Galerie Neuendorf, Hamburg
1972	Gemini G.E.L., Los Angeles
1973	Nicholas Wilder Gallery, Los Angeles
	Galerie Neuendorf, Hamburg
1974	Willard Gallery, New York
	Felicity Samuel Gallery, London
1976	Ronald Greenberg Gallery, St. Louis
	James Corcoran Galleries, Los Angeles
1978	Los Angeles County Museum of Art
	Gallery of Contemporary Arts, Taos, New Mexico
1979	Willard Gallery, New York
	Texas Gallery, Houston
	Hansen-Fuller-Goldeen Gallery, San Francisco
1981	James Corcoran Galleries, Los Angeles
	Modernism, San Francisco
	Betsy Rosenfield Gallery, Chicago

Selected Group Exhibitions:

1962	*50 California Artists,* Whitney Museum, New York
1963	*Sculpture of California,* Oakland Art Museum, California
1966	*10 from Los Angeles,* Seattle Art Museum
1967	*American Sculpture of the 60's,* Los Angeles County Museum of Art
1971	*Gemini: Technics and Creativity,* Museum of Modern Art, New York
1975	*Sculpture: American Directions 1945-75,* National Collection of Fine Arts, Washington, D.C.
1976	*30 Years of American Printmaking,* Brooklyn Museum, New York
	200 Years of American Sculpture, Whitney Museum, New York
1979	*A Century of Ceramics in the U.S. 1878-1978,* Everson Museum of Art, Syracuse, New York
	Whitney Biennial, Whitney Museum, New York

Collections:

Museum of Modern Art, New York; Whitney Museum, New York; Hirshhorn Museum and Sculpture Garden, Smithsonian Institution, Washington, D.C.; Art Institute of Chicago; San Francisco Museum of Art; Los Angeles County Museum of Art; Norton Simon Museum of Art, Pasadena, California; Victoria and Albert Museum, London; Stedelijk Van Abbemuseum, Eindhoven, Netherlands.

Publications:

On PRICE: articles—"Painting and Sculpture: The Los Angeles Scene" by Jules Langsner in *Craft Horizon* (New York), July/August 1962; "Sculpture in California" by John Coplans in *Artforum* (San Francisco), August 1962; "Kenneth Price" by Henry T. Hopkins in *Artforum* (San Francisco), August 1963; "Out of Clay" by John Coplans in *Art in America* (New York), December 1963; "The Sculpture of Kenneth Price" by John Coplans in *Art International* (Lugano, Switzerland), March 1964; "Specific Objects" by Donald Judd in *Arts Yearbook,* New York 1965; "London: Stop Press-Nature Survives" by Simon Watson Taylor in *Art and Artists* (London), March 1968; "Two Good Deeds" by Bryan Roberton in *The Spectator* (London), May 1968; "Kenneth Price" by Jim Crumrine in *Craft Horizons* (New York), November/December 1969; "London Letter" by Bernard Benvir in *Art International* (Lugano, Switzerland), March 1970; "London" by David Russell in *Arts Magazine* (New York), March 1970; "Los Angeles" by Peter Plagens in *Artforum* (New York), October 1970; "The Revival of Prints" by Robert Hughes in *Time* (New York), January 1971; "Art" by Thomas Hess in *New York Magazine,* December 1974; "Kenneth Price—Willard" by Judith Tannenbaum in *Arts Magazine* (New York), February 1975; "Kenneth Price at Willard" in *Art in America* (New York), May/June 1975.

The dominant characteristic of post-war American art has been a search for significance, or to be more precise, Significance. To many American artists, European art seemed too modest in its methods; a small canvas, however radical its contents could easily be lost in the huge and complicated arena of contemporary life; chamber music drowned by the roar of traffic.

To achieve the sensation of Significance, painters and sculptors employed scale, forcing the viewer to concentrate upon the work to the exclusion of all else. Blasted by the visual equivalent of a 400,000 amp sound system it was impossible not to notice the things, to look willy-nilly for meaning. Although the technique of scale was first used in the era by Abstract Expressionists it was taken over by the successors. Pop artists, while rejecting all other tenets of Expressionism retained the scale, as did Op and Minimal artists, while the tendency reached its apotheosis in Land Art. Whatever else could be overthrown, Significance was fundamental.

The art of Kenneth Price and other West Coast artists is a direct challenge upon this orthodoxy. His work is deliberately unsignificant (the common negative, insignificant, means something quite different) and one of its most typical qualities is a throw-away nonchalance.

Price made his name with works in ceramic, the choice of material being crucial. There is no limit to the scale on which one can use wood, steel, fiberglass or earth, but ceramic needs a kiln and kilns can never be very large. In addition, ceramic is traditionally used either for small ornaments or functional objects, both concepts which would be anathema to the Great American Artist in his search for unsullied Significance. As a result Price's work was first greeted with hostile bewilderment.

Which is not surprising. A generation gorged on vast washes of colour, or monolithic wedges of orange steel, was suddenly faced with a room of small ceramic CUPS. Some of them were adorned with animals, (frogs usually) and other motifs, and none of them could be called beautiful in a traditional sort of way. In fact, some of them were down-right ugly.

Many "admirers" of Price have tried to pretend that his work still adheres to the traditionally American values; thus Maurice Tuchman refers to "a significant movement in the use of ceramics as a major sculptural medium" and goes on to suggest that the "minorness" of Price's work is an illusion. In fact, Price's work is an attempt to exclude such terminology from art, and to make work which cannot really be discussed at all.

Indeed there is not much one can say about small, greyish green turds of ceramic, the style of his more recent works. Even his cups defy much interpretation; they are there and that is that. To wax eloquent about his "painterly" use of colour is to wrap the shroud of dead terminology around his living work, and, anyway, those who do so are made ridiculous by his very unpainterly paintings. There is no useful interpretation possible.

This is a negative virtue, albeit one of fundamental importance in an age when art is threatened by a tidalwave of logorrhoea. The discovery of the positive virtues must be left to the individual when he sees the actual work, an event for which words can never be a substitute. Speaking personally, I found that, on first acquaintance, Price's work irritated and even repelled

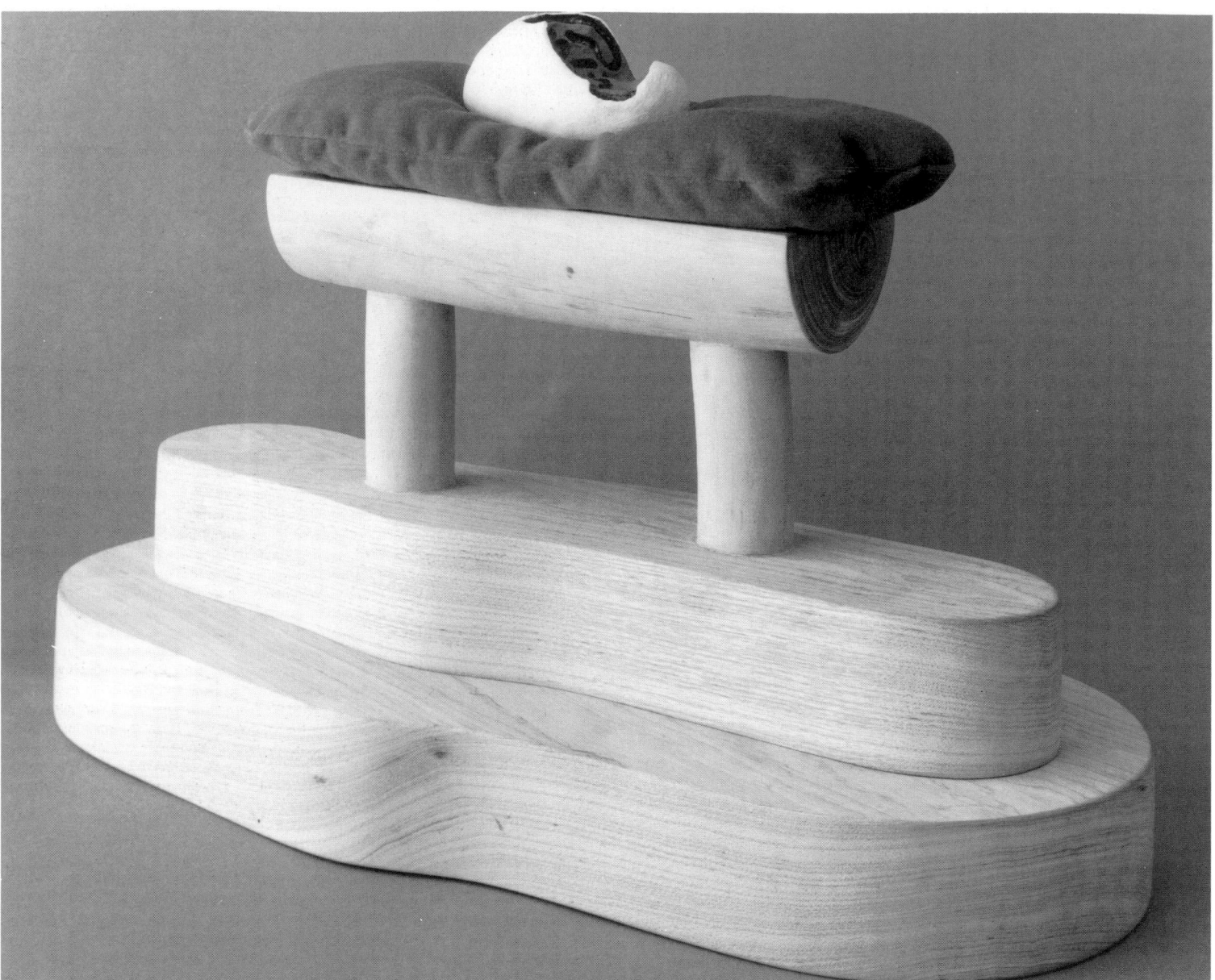

Kenneth Price: *Specimen B 1520.06,* 1964

me, seeming to be a blind alley in the triumphant march of America art towards, well I was never quite sure what it was towards, but the band played and the crowds cheered and I felt sure it must be going somewhere. Now, when all we have left is the confetti on the streets, Price's back road looks more and more promising.

But don't ask me why . . .

—Alastair Mackintosh

PROCKTOR, Patrick.

British. Born in Dublin, 12 March 1936. Educated in London primary schools; studied Russian at London University, 1954–56; studied at the Slade School of Fine Art, London, under John Aldridge, Frank Auerbach, Keith Vaughan, Claude Rogers, Reg Butler, William Townsend, William Coldstream and Richard Beer, 1958–62. Served as a Sub-Lieutenant, Royal Navy, in Combined Services School for Linguists, Cornwall, London and Fife, Scotland, 1954–56. Married Kirsten Bo Andersen in 1973 (died, 1984): son: Nicholas Bo. Independent painter, since 1963. Worked as apprentice builder's merchant, London,

1952–54; as Russian interpreter, British Council, Russia and the United Kingdom, 1956–61; as omelette chef, Academy Restaurant, London, 1956; as clerk, Thomas Cook Travel Bureau, London, 1956; as art therapist, Fulham Western Hospital, London, 1960–63; as art broadcaster, BBC Russian Service, London, 1960–65; as Russian interpreter, San Francisco-Moscow Peace March, 1961; as fashion model, London, 1968; as set and costume designer for *Bed Bug* by Mayakowsky, London University, 1960; as set designer for *Saint's Day* by John Whiting, Theatre Royal Stratford, London University, 1960; as set designer for *Cage of God* ballet, Sadlers Wells Theatre, London 1967; designed decor, British Pavilion, *Expo '67,* Montreal; set and costume designer for *Twelfth Nigh,* 1968, and *Total Eclipse,* Royal Court Theatre, London 1969; designed background, *The Greatest Show on Earth,* Coliseum, London, 1972. Lecturer, Camberwell School of Art, London, 1962–67, and Maidstone College of Art, Kent, 1962–67; Color Consultant (sculpture), 1965–67, and Lecturer in Painting, 1968–72, Royal College of Art, London. Recipient: Murray Landscape Scholarship, Royal Academy of Art, London, 1959 and 1961; Abbey Minor Travelling Scholarship, 1962. Honorary Member, Royal Watercolour Society, London, 1978. Agent: Redfern Gallery, London. Address: c/o Redfern Gallery, 20 Cork Street, London W1, England.

Individual Exhibitions:

1963	Redfern Gallery, London
1965	Redfern Gallery, London
1967	Redfern Gallery, London
1968	Redfern Gallery, London
	Lee Nordness Gallery, New York
1969	Redfern Gallery, London
	Alecto Gallery, London
	Alecto Gallery, New York
1970	Clare College, Cambridge
	Alecto Gallery, London
	Alecto Gallery, New York
1971	Studio La Città, Verona
1972	Galleria del Cavallino, Venice
	Galleria di Piazza Galvani, Bologna
	Galleria L'Approdo, Turin
	Redfern Gallery, London
1973	Galleria Henze, Campione d'Italia, Switzerland
	Salisbury Festival, Wiltshire
1974	Redfern Gallery, London
	Galleria Tinoghelfi, Vincena, Italy
	Gallery 101, Johannesburg (toured South Africa)
1975	Rochdale Art Gallery, Lancashire
1976	Redfern Gallery, London
	Galerie Biedermann, Munich
	Alecto Gallery, London
1977	Galleria L'Approdo, Turin
	Gallerina del Cavallino, Venice

Selected Group Exhibitions:

Collections:

Tate Gallery, London; Arts Council of Great Britain, London; New College, Oxford; National Gallery of Victoria, Melbourne; Sao Paulo Museum of Art; Museum of Modern Art, New York; Los Angeles County Museum of Art.

Publications:

By PROCKTOR: books and portfolios—*One Window*, Venice 1974; *Venice Suite* aquatints, London 1977; *China Suite*, aquatints, London 1980; *Chateau de Bordeaux*, aquatints, London 1986; article—"Why Do I Paint?" in *New Society* (London), May 1963, illustrated books—*Poems by Rimbaud and Verlaine*, London 1968; *The Rime of the Ancient Mariner* by Samuel Coleridge, London 1978.

On PROCKTOR: books—*Patrick Procktor* by Patrick Kinmonth, London 1985; *Patrick Procktor: Prints 1959-1985*, catalogue raisonné, Birmingham 1985; articles—"Against the Rimless Men" by Bryan Robertson in *London Magazine*, July 1963; "Patrick Proctor's New Paintings" by Robert Hughes in *Studio International* (London), May 1967; "Patrick Procktor" by Paul William White in *Connoisseur* (London), July 1974; "Stylish Rebel" by William Packer in *Art*

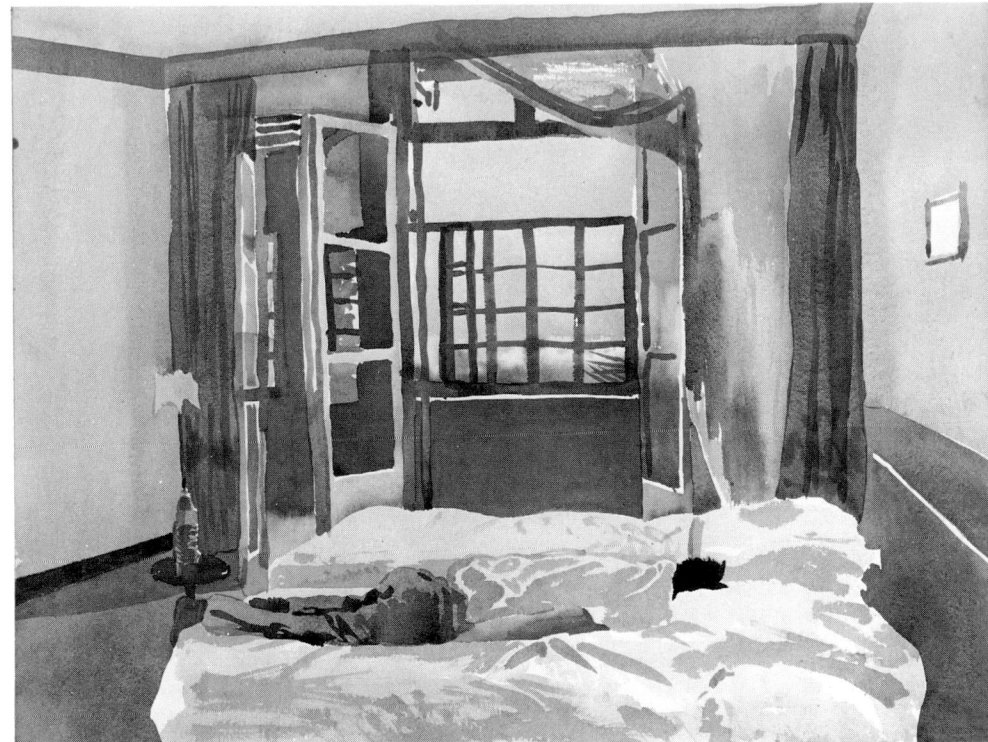

Patrick Procktor: *Zonked, Aswan*, 1984

and Artists (London), August 1974; "The Master of Marylebone" by William Green in the *Sunday Telegraph* (London), November 1980.

You ask me for about 300 words or so—I paint, watercolour, draw and etch in line and aquatint. That's 10 words. But to write it out 30 times . . . think of the time it would take when I could be painting, watercolouring, drawing or etching in aquatint and line.

—Patrick Procktor

Patrick Procktor has numerous shows to his credit at the Redfern Gallery, and he cannot be pidgeon-holed. At the beginning of his career he was criticized for varying his style too much, but as a young artist he was discovering his range; he continues to do so. His painting career is similar to his non-painting career, in which he went from being an omelette chef to a Russian interpreter. Some of his paintings are like runny omelettes—not well thought out; others are as well structured and beautiful as Russian grammar.

An important group of paintings is that of the London Philharmonic Orchestra. The brush is used like a conductor's baton, at times giving a hint of an image, at others becoming much more forceful. These black and white brush paintings are successful because of the simple calligraphic strokes. The accompanying etchings are disappointing. The intimacy and vivacity is lost. The double etching of the left and right hand side of the orchestra is weighed down by the deep orange background. Procktor is attempting to convey the sense of heat and depth on stage, but fails to do so.

The paintings resulting from the sketches are far more abstract, with heavy stippled backdrops and very strong colours. Procktor is at his best when painting familiar and treasured objects—such as a still life entitled "Stubbs Jigsaw"—on the jigsaw are casually strewn an ashtray, a vase filled with white anemones, an exquisite antique desk light, and so on. The image is painted with light delicate brushstrokes. The pots of Morning Glory in "Road Works Ahead" are superbly painted—a crisp, clear cut, watercolour that has the same kind of flourish as the brilliant portrait of gondolier Bruno Palmarin. In this portrait Procktor demonstrates his skill: he is capable of manipulating watercolour with extraordinary dexterity and achieves remarkable variations of shading, but that is only when he chooses to.

—Carine Maurice

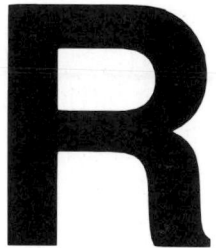

RADICE, Mario.

Italian. Born in Como, 1 August 1898. Studied veterinary medicine; attended evening and Sunday painting classes at local art schoool and studied privately with a Como painter, 1912–18. Served in the Italian Army, 1918–20. Worked in Como paper mill, and in Buenos Aires, 1924–30; thereafter devoted himself to painting: lived and worked in Como, 1930 until his death in 1987. Travelled in France, Germany, and Switzerland, 1930–32; visited Paris and associated with Fernand Léger, 1931–32, Co-Founder-Editor of *Quadrante*, Milan, 1932; worked on architectural projects, murals, bas-reliefs and mosaics, Como, 1933–38; organized, with Maulio Rho and Alberto Sartoris, *Exhibition of Modern Art* at Villa Olmo, Como 1936; Founder-Member, with Terragni and Ciliberti, *Valori Primordiali*, group and periodical, Rome, 1938; worked on various church projects with Cesare Cattaneo, 1939–43 (unrealized, due to death of Cattaneo in 1943). Recipient: Painting Prize, Città di Gallarate, Italy, 1950; Primo Michetti, Francavilla al Mare, Italy, 1954; First Prize, Morgan's Paint, Rimini, Italy 1957; Primo Einaudi, Milan, 1958; Gold Medal of Artistic Merit, Como, 1964; Ambrogino d'Oro Medal, Milan, 1973; Abbondino d'Oro Prize, Como, 1985; U. Biancamano Prize, Pavia, 1987. Agent: Marlborough Galleria d'Arte, via Gregoriana 5, 00187 Rome. *Died (in Como) 25 July 1987.*

Individual Exhibitions:

1936	Moody Gallery, Buenos Aires
1943	Galleria Bergamini, Milan
1953	Galleria San Fedele, Milan
1954	Galleria Del Fiore, Milan
1956	National Gallery of Victoria, Melbourne (toured Australia)
1962	Galleria Lorenzelli, Bergamo, Italy
1965	Galleria Agrati, Monza, Italy
1968	Centro Culturale Rosmini, Trento, Italy
	Galleria Vismara, Milan
	Galleria Martano Due, Turin
	Galleria La Colonna, Como
1970	Galleria Peccolo, Livorno
1971	Deutsches Vonderau Museum, Fulda, West Germany
	Marlborough Galleria d'Arte, Rome
1972	Galleria Quattro Venti, Palermo
	Galleria Annunciata, Milan
1973	Associazione Amici dell'Arte, Modena
	Università di Messina, Italy
1974	Westend Galerie, Frankfurt
	Galleria Spagnoli, Florence
1975	Galleria Pellegrino, Bologna
1976	Musée des Beaux Arts, La Chaux de Fonds, Switzerland
1977	Galleria La Promotrice, Turin
1979	*Mario Radice,* at the *Biennale,* Venice
1980	Galleria Il Salotto, Como
1981	Galleria Pantha Arte, Como
1982	Villa Malpensata, Lugano, Switzerland
1985	Galleria Lorenzelli, Milan
	Galleria Italia, Naples

Selected Group Exhibitions:

1940	*Biennale,* Venice
1947	*Quadriennale,* Rome
1950	*Art Vivant Italienne,* Palais des Beaux Arts, Brussels
1969	*Aspetti del Primo Astrattismo Italiano 1930–1940,* Galleria Civica d'Arte Moderna, Monza, Italy
	Bienal, Sao Paulo
1970	*Arte Italiana 70/70,* Museo Poldo Pezzoli, Milan
	Konkrete Kunst, Westfälischer Kunstverein, Münster, West Germany
1971	*Mostra Arte Lombarda,* Museo Civico, Cremona, Italy
1972	*4th Biennale of Italian Graphic Art,* Faenza, Italy

Collections:

Galleria Nazionale d'Arte Moderna, Rome; Galleria Civica d'Arte Moderna, Turin.

Publications:

On RADICE: books—*Pittura Italiana del Dopoguerra* by Tristan Sauvage, Milan 1957; *Venti Disegni di Mario Radice* by Franco Russoli, Milan 1962; *La Linea dell'Arte Italiana* by Guido Ballo, Rome 1964; *Il Viaggiatore in Arte* by Marcello Venturoli, Milan 1966; *Pittura e Scultura degli Anni 60* by Raffaele de Grada, Milan 1967; *Occhio Critico 2* by Guidi Ballo, Milan 1968; *Gli Astrattisti de Gruppo Como dagli Anni Trenta ad Oggi* by Alberto Longatti, Milan 1972; *Mario Radice: Gli Affreschi della Casa Terragni 1932–36* by Guido Ballo, Como 1973; *Lettera sulla Nascita dell'Astrattismo in Italia* By Carlo Belli, Rome 1978; *Who is Mario Radice?* by Angelo Maugeri, Como 1986; articles—"Il Pittore Mario Radice" by F. T. Marinetti in *Meridiano di Roma* March 1939; "Radice" by G. J. Kasper in *Art Actuel* (Lausanne, Switzerland), no. 4, 1958.

A self-taught painter, Mario Radice played a distinguished late role in the Futurist movement and was one of the principal promoters of Italian abstract paintings from 1930. More than most of his Italian colleagues he was deeply concerned with the relationship between abstraction and rational architecture, closer to the philosophy and outlook of the Dutch de Stijl group, which sought to relate the aesthetic analysis of space to practical, public purpose.

With the painters Maulio Rho and Carla Badiali, who, like Radice, lived in Como, and the architect Terragni, who came from the same town, he formed a group to promote these ideas, also expressed in the magazines *Quadrante* and *Valori Primordiali,* which he edited.

His paintings were deeply affected by Mondrian, logically and clearly arranged as assemblies of geometrical forms, built up with clear, pure purpose, exploiting a structural basis which immediately relates to architecture and town planning. Radice displays a fine sense of space and a much lighter touch than his Dutch mentor. There is little sense of mortality in his work, or, indeed, of meditation. The form floats in the space rather as they do in the dream fantasies of Paul Klee or the surrealist sequences of Joan Miró. His colour is charming and gay, blues, greens, grays, neither the stern primary colours of Mondrian, nor the strident, over-anxious brightness of many of his Italian contemporaries.

Radice saw his works as mural decorations, integral to the architecture they enhance, as well as immediately communicative to the public they serve. In some ways they serve as backdrops to human movement, and could, indeed, do so to advantage in the theatre.

—Charles Spencer

RAETZ, Markus.

Swiss. Born in Berne, 6 June 1941. Studied at teacher-training college in Berne, 1957–61. Independent painter, influenced by Tachisme and Action-Painting, in Berne, 1960–69, Amsterdam, 1969–73, Carona (Ticino), 1973–76, and again in Berne since 1976: first three-dimensional works, 1964; first concept-art works, 1968. Recipient: D.A.A.D. Fellowship, West Berlin, 1981–82. Agents: Galerie Stahli, im Bahnhof Enge, 8002 Zurich; Galerie Farideh Cadot, 77 rue des Archives, 75003 Paris, France. Address: Engestrasse 7, 3012 Berne, Switzerland.

Individual Exhibitions:

1966	Galerie Toni Gerber, Berne
1967	Galerie Toni Gerber, Berne
	Galerie Felix Handschin, Basle
1969	Galerie Bischofberger, Zurich
	Galerie Toni Gerber, Berne
	Galerie Mickery, Loenersloot, Netherlands
1970	Centrum voor Coomunikatie, Utrecht
	Galerie René Block, West Berlin
	Markt 17, Enschede, Netherlands
	Galerie Toni Gerber, Berne
	Galerie Mickery, Loenersloot, Netherlands
1971	Galleria Diagramma, Milan
	Galerie Herzog, Buren an der Aare, Switzerland
	Galerie Loeb, Berne
	Galerie Mollenhoff, Cologne
1972	Galerie Renée Ziegler, Zurich
	Zeichnungen, Objekte, Kunstmuseum, Basle
	Galerie Renée Ziegler, Geneva
	Musée d'Art de l'Histoire, Geneva
	Galerie Toni Gerber, Berne
	Galerie Seriaal, Amsterdam
1973	Galerie Stahli, Zurich
	Goethe-Institut, Amsterdam
1974	Galerie Toni Gerber, Berne (2 shows)
1975	Kunstmuseum, Lucerne
	Amsterdam Fruhjahre 1973; Arbeiten aus einem Monat und einer Nacht von Markus Raetz, Kunthaus, Zurich
	Neue Galerie am Landsmuseum Joanneum, Graz, Austria
1976	Galerie Toni Gerber, Berne (2 shows)
	Galerie Seriaal, Amsterdam
1977	Galerie Herzog, Buren an der Aare, Switzerland
	Galerie Toni Gerber, Berne

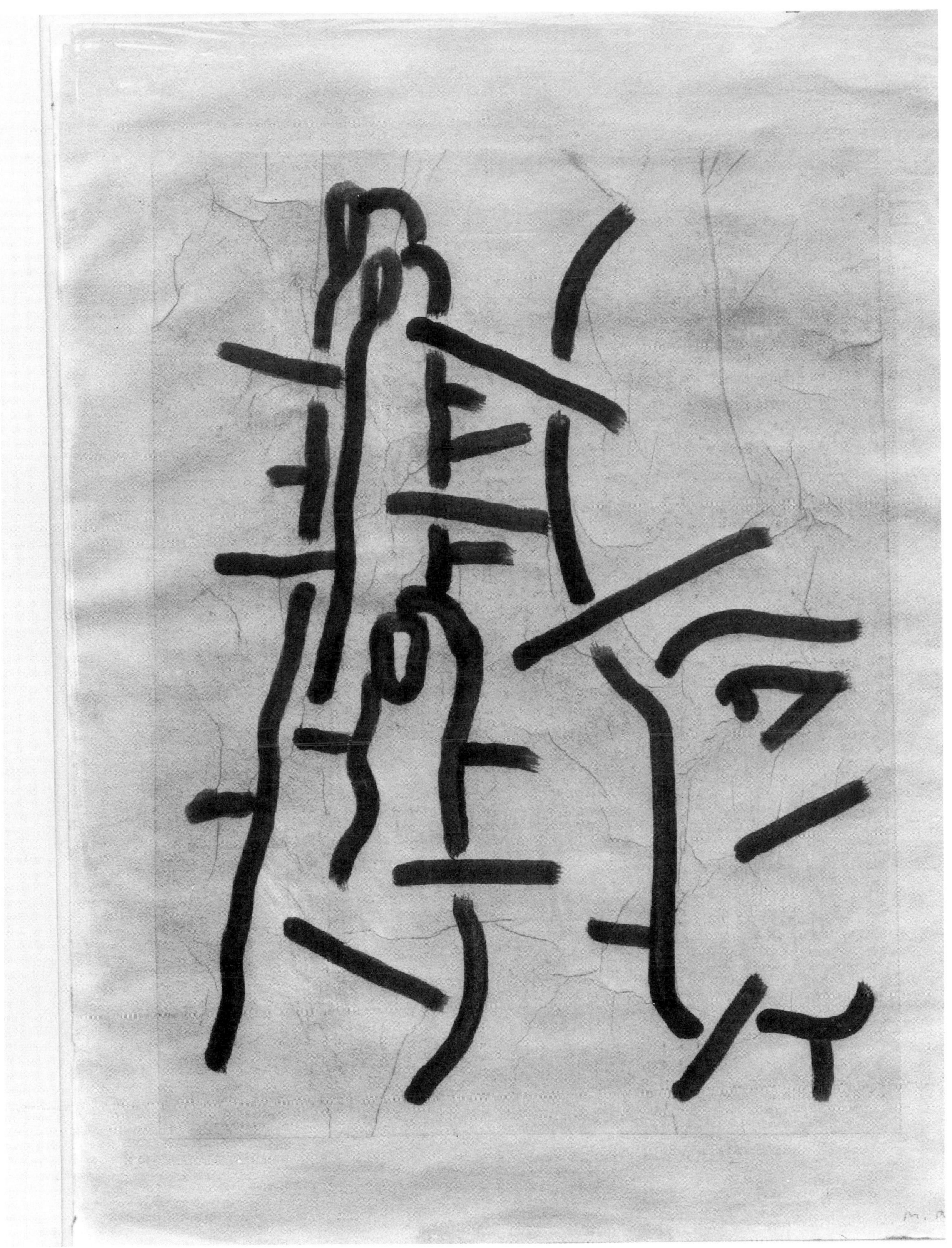

Markus Raetz: *Untitled*, 1981

Kunstmuseum, Berne
Kunsthalle, Berne
1979 Galerie Herzog, Buren an der Aare, Switzerland
Galerie Stahli, Zurich
1980 Stedelijk Museum, Amsterdam
Galleria Lucio Amelio, Naples
1981 Kunsthaus, Aarau, Switzerland
Galerie Krinzinger, Innsbruck
Galerie Nächst St. Stephan, Vienna
Kunstverein, Kassel, West Germany
1982 DAAD-Galerie, West Berlin
Kunsthalle, Basle
1983 Musée d'Art Moderne de la Ville, Paris
Nouveau Musée, Lyon-Villeurbanne, France
Kunstverein, Frankfurt
1984 Galerie Pablo Stahli, Zurich
1986 Kunsthaus, Zurich
Kunstverein, Cologne
1987 Moderna Museet, Stockholm

Selected Group Exhibitions:

1965 *Biennale*, Musée d'Art Moderne, Paris (and 1970)
1968 *Documenta*, Kassel, West Germany (and 1972, 1982)
1969 *When Attitudes Become Form*, Kunsthalle, Berne (toured Europe)
1970 *Information*, Museum of Modern Art, New York
1972 *31 Artistes Suisses Contemporains*, Grand Palais, Paris
1977 *Bienal*, Sao Paulo
1979 *Schweizer Kunst*, Fundatie Kunsthuis, Amsterdam
1981 *Le Dessin Suisse 1970-1980*, Musée Rath, Geneva
1984 *An International Survey of Painting and Sculpture*, Museum of Modern Art, New York
1985 *Cross-Currents in Swiss Art*, Serpentine Gallery, London

Collections:

Tate Gallery, London; Stedelijk Museum, Amsterdam; Centre Georges Pompidou, Paris; Musée de Toulon, France; Kunstmuseum, Basle; Kunstmuseum, Berne; Kunsthaus, Aarau, Switzerland; Kunsthaus, Zurich; Kunstmuseum, Lucerne; Musée d'Art et d'Histoire, Geneva.

Publications:

By RAETZ: books—*Plans and Projects 1965-1969*, Loenersloot 1969; *27 Reproduktionen von Zeichnungen*, Lucerne 1970; *Notizbuchlein 27.8-17.9.1971*, Berne 1971; *Buch mit 138 Xeroxkopien nach dem Projekt 1969*, Lucerne 1971; *Von diesem Blatt eine Kopie machen; die Kopie wieder koperien; diesen Prozess nach belieben Fortsetzen*, Amsterdam 1971; *Die Bucher*, 3 vols. in cassette, Zurich 1975; *Notizbuch*, Zurich 1975; *Seiben Geschichten der sieben Prinzessinnen*, Lucerne 1975; *-& u. & + &*, with others, Berne 1977; *Mimi*, Aarau 1981; *CH '70- '80*, Lucerne 1981; *Notizen 1981-82*, West Berlin 1982.

On RAETZ: books—*Electronic Art: elektronische und elektrische objekte und environments, neon objekte*, Dusseldorf 1969; *Documenta 5: Befragung der Realitat*, exhibition catalogue, edited by Harald Szeeman and others, Kassel, West Germany 1972; *Markus Raetz: Zeichnungen, Objekte*, exhibition catalogue, with text by Dieter Koepplin, Basle 1972; *Amsterdam Fruhjahre 1973: Arbeiten aus einem Monat und einer Nacht von Markus Raetz*, exhibition catalogue, with text by Erik Gysling-Billeter, Zurich 1975; *Markus Raetz*, exhibition catalogue, with text by Johannes Gachnang, Berne 1977; *Das Beobachten des Beobachtens: Markus Raetz—Zeichnungen*, exhibition catalogue, with text by Jürgen Glaesemer, Berne 1977; *Markus Raetz*, exhibition catalogue with introduction by Ad Petersen, Amsterdam 1980; *Markus Raetz*, exhibition catalogue, with text by Jean-Christophe Ammann, Basle 1982; *Markus Raetz*, exhibition catalogue, with text by Peter Weiermair, Frankfurt, 1983; *Markus Raetz: Arbeiten 1962-1986*, exhibition catalogue, Zurich 1986.

The Swiss artist Markus Raetz is the creator of a labyrinth-like universe of meanings and irritations. He is at the same time an indefatigable investigator of the possibilities of expression offered him by his method combining thought and fantasy. Behind this method lies the question about the limits and reliability of perception, an old if no less topical problem.

Raetz prefers to tackle this problem through drawing. It seems that he has a command of all the conceivable styles and refinements of this classical technique, so easily and naturally flow the lines in his drawings, so naturally do the forms and images take shape. Yet first impressions are deceptive. Some of Raetz's drawings are playful and simple; many others, on the other hand, are confused and complex. They force us, not unlike a puzzle or rebus, to reflect and to decipher, for they often employ sensory perceptibility only as a pretext for an intellectual operation.

Raetz links the questioning of reality with the questioning of the creative process; each to him is equally important. So the ideas develop into motifs and form chains from which new motifs and images arise. When Raetz for example replaces lines with points or dashes, the "old" image gains a "new" dimension whose renewed possibilities of association can be investigated. The way from a "simple" to a "multi-layered" motif is thereby pre-programmed.

This is also the case in other works by Raetz: photographs, sculptures, objects and painted cloths. He has a particular preference for books, since the character of a book allows the reproduction of a series of drawings which have arisen on a pad without alteration to sequence and so to authenticity. Raetz understands how to use in constantly new variations the principle of metamorphosis as a means for perception of the world.

—Zdenek Felix

RAFFAEL, Joseph. (Joe Raffaele).
American. Born in Brooklyn, New York, 22 February 1933. Educated at Cooper Union, New York, 1951-54; Yale University School of Fine Arts, New Haven, Connecticut, under Josef Albers, 1954-56, B.F.A. 1956; Fulbright Fellow, Italy, 1958-59. Married Judy Collins in 1968; children: Robert, Matthew, Rachel and Reuben. Worked for the New York Public Library, 1952-54; Layout Artist, *Yale Daily News*, New Haven, 1955-56; travelled in England, France and Italy, 1956. Full-time Artist since 1956: currently lives in Cap d'Antibes, France. Art Instructor, University of California at Davis, 1966; Instructor, School of Visual Arts, New York, 1967-69; Associate Professor of Art, University of California, Berkeley, Summer 1969; Professor of Art, California State University, Sacramento 1969-74; Art Instructor, University of Utah, Snowbird, 1976. Recipient: Louis Comfort Tiffany Fellowship, 1960; First Painting Prize, *International Biennal*, Tokyo, 1974; Purchase Prize, *Concours d'Antiques*, Oakland Museum, California, 1975. Agent: Nancy Hoffman Gallery, New York. Address: c/o Nancy Hoffman Gallery, 429 West Broadway, New York, New York 10012, U.S.A.

Individual Exhibitions:

1958 Kanegis Gallery, Boston
1959 Galleria Numero, Florence
1963 D'Arcy Gallery, New York
1965 Stable Gallery, New York
1966 Stable Gallery, New York
1968 Stable Gallery, New York
Berkeley Gallery, San Francisco
1969 Sacramento State College, California
Worth Ryder Gallery, University of California, Berkeley
1970 Wichita Art Museum, Kansas
1971 Reese Palley Gallery, San Francisco
University of California Art Gallery, San Diego
1972 Reese Palley Gallery, New York
Nancy Hoffman Gallery, New York
1973 Nancy Hoffman Gallery, New York
Water Painting, University of California Art Museum, Berkeley
Museum of Contemporary Art, Chicago
1974 Barbara Okun Gallery, St. Louis
3 Realists: Close/Estes/Raffael, Worcester Art Museum, Massachusetts
Nancy Hoffman Gallery, New York
1975 University of Nevada Art Gallery, Las Vegas
Norman MacKenzie Art Gallery, University of Saskatchewan, Regina
1976 Nancy Hoffman Gallery, New York
Ruth Braunstein's Quay Gallery, San Francisco
1977 Museum of Fine Arts, St. Petersburg, Florida
ARCO Center for Visual Art, Los Angeles
Roy Boyd Gallery, Chicago
1978 Barbara Fendrick Gallery, Washington, D.C.
Valpraiso University, Indiana
John Berggruen Gallery, San Francisco
San Francisco Museum of Modern Art
Des Moines Art Center, Iowa
Joslyn Art Museum, Omaha, Nebraska
Newport Harbor Art Museum, Newport Beach, California
Denver Art Museum
1979 Nancy Hoffman Gallery, New York
Louise Himelfarb Gallery, Watermill, New York (with Robert Dash)
Stewart Center Gallery, Purdue University, West Lafayette, Indiana (with Judy Raffael)
Wenger Gallery, La Jolla, California (with Judy Raffael)
1980 Nancy Hoffman Gallery, New York
Wake Forest University, Winston-Salem, North Carolina
Columbus Museum of Arts and Science, Georgia
Birmingham Museum of Art, Alabama
Mint Museum of Art, Charlotte, North Carolina
Mississippi Museum of Art, Jackson
Images Gallery, Toledo, Ohio
Redding Museum, California
1981 John Berggruen Gallery, San Francisco
Elvehjem Art Center, Madison, Wisconsin
University of Connecticut, Storrs (travelled to Lincoln, Nebraska; Grand Forks, Dakota; Racine, Wisconsin; Calgary, Alberta; Boise, Idaho)
1982 Saddleback Community College, Mission Viejo, California
Santa Ana Community College, California
Allport Associates Gallery, Larkspur, California
John Berggruen Gallery, San Francisco
Delaware Art Museum, Wilmington
Jacksonville Museum, Florida (travelled to West Palm Beach, Florida)
Nancy Hoffman Gallery, New York
1983 University of Austin, Texas
Richard Gray Gallery, Chicago
Nancy Hoffman Gallery, New York
1984 Nancy Hoffman Gallery, New York
1985 Gibbes Art Gallery, Charleston, South Carolina
New York Academy of Sciences
Salt Lake Art Center, Utah (travelled to Billings, Montana; Casper, Wyoming)
1986 Nancy Hoffman Gallery, New York
Woltjen/Udell Gallery, Edmonton, Alberta
1987 Nancy Hoffman Gallery, New York

Selected Group Exhibitions:

1966 *Art in the Mirror*, Museum of Modern Art, New York
1969 *Paintings from the Photo*, Riverside Museum, New York
1973 *Separate Realities*, Los Angeles Municipal Art Gallery
1976 *Illusions of Reality and Realists' Prints*, Australia Council, North Sydney (toured Australia)
1977 *8 Contemporary American Realists*, Pennsylvania Academy of Fine Arts, Philadelphia

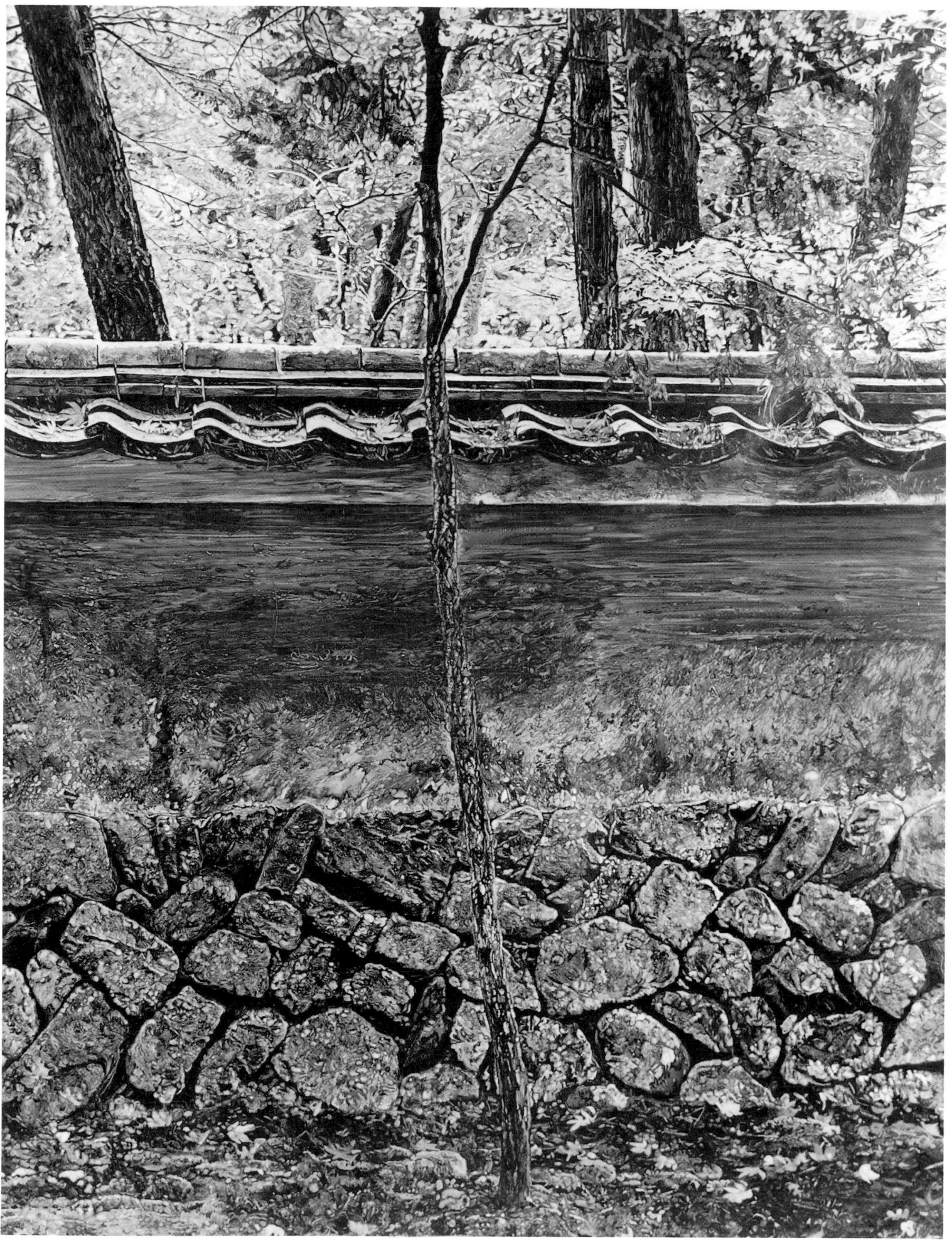

Joseph Raffael: *Haven*, 1986

1979   *Late 20th Century Art: The Sydney and Frances Lewis Foundation Collection,* Virginia Commonwealth University, Richmond (travelled to Institute of Contemporary Art, University of Pennsylvania, Philadelphia)

1980   *The Print Club Invitational 1980,* Print Club, Philadelphia

1983   *West Coast Realism,* Laguna Beach Museum, California

1985   *Art in the San Francisco Bay Area 1945–80,* Oakland Museum, California

1987   *Modern American Realism,* National Museum of American Art, Washington, D.C.

Collections:

San Francisco Museum of Modern Art; University of California Art Museum, Berkeley; Santa Barbara Museum of Art, California; Los Angeles County Museum of Art; Library of Congress, Washington, D.C.; National Collection of Fine Arts, Smithsonian Institution, Washington, D.C.; Hirshhorn Museum and Sculpture Garden, Smithsonian Institution Washington, D.C.; Museum of Contemporary Art, Chicago; Metropolitan Museum of Art, New York; Whitney Museum, New York.

Publications:

On RAFFAEL: books—*Joseph Raffael,* exhibition catalogue, San Francisco 1970, *Joseph Raffael,* exhibition catalogue, New York 1972; *Water Painting,* exhibition catalogue, Berkeley, California 1973; *Separate Realities,* exhibition catalogue, by Laurence Drieband, Los Angeles 1973; *3 Realists: Close/ Estes/Raffael,* exhibition catalogue, by Leon Shulman, Worcester, Massachusetts 1974; *Contemporary Landscape Painting,* exhibition catalogue, by George Keubler, Oklahoma City 1975; articles—"Oh, To Be Born Under Pisces, with Saggitarius Rising" by Grace Glueck in the *New York Times,* 29 December 1968; "In Art with Joseph Raffael" by Lynne Zickerman in *Daily California Arts Magazine* (Berkeley), October 1972; "The Paintings of Joseph Raffael" by William S. Wilson in *Studio International* (London), May 1974; "Nature Upclose" by Jerome Tarshis in *Horizon* (New York), September 1978; film—*The Eyes Have It,* by Gloria Smith for National Broadcasting Corporation (NBC-TV), 1972.

Painting is the subject of my work, and nature the inspiration. Wallace Stevens has written: "The subject of the poem is poetry." I believe that too: painting, for me, is the subject of the painting. The process of painting the work. What happens from moment to moment. What occurs. The events that take place before my eyes.

I want the paintings to be like nature. Nature is always changing. I want the work to be always changing. In the sense that each time they are looked at they are different. I want to encourage people to look at my paintings in different light situations. They always look different.

—Joseph Raffael

The lyrical paintings of Joseph Raffael sing of nature, expressed in the ebb and flow of a subject matter wedded intrinsically and naturalistically to the medium. The substance is water: the icy, bubbling riffles of a shallow coursing stream; limpid pools with gracefully swirling trout and Japanese trout below calm surfaces decked with lilypads and punctuated by blossoms and buds. His medium is as fluid as his subject—thinned luminescent colors in droplets, blobs and stains, with contours emphasized to make each appear as a discrete, atomic unit. The large scale canvases and watercolors are realist in mode, but that reality is built on the accretion of myriad abstract particles and shapes. Light glistens, sparkles, and reflects off the surfaces in the watery images and the fluid texture of paint. It is the incident of light that brings into being the form and substance of water.

Raffael works from photographs, a convenience for capturing those momentary and spontaneous occurrences in nature. External references to natural scale and distance are cropped; the image in isolation fills the picture plane and intensifies the fragmentation of object and substance. Rather than a faithful copy of a photograph, Raffael re-constructs a timeless and meditative image with scintillating color, gesture and fluid texture. The momentary incident is captured, and provides for silent reverie and contemplation.

For Raffael, nature is in the constant act of becoming. He portrays not the fact of natural experience, but its painterly equivalent. Raffael's practice of the Chinese meditative concept of *ch'i* is reflected in these considerations. The boundlessness of nature, time and thought coalesce on canvas. Water and light, emblematic of nature's omnipresence, are the vehicles for its perception.

—Ron Glowen

RAINER, Arnulf.

Austrian. Born in Baden, near Vienna, 8 December 1929. Studied art briefly at the Akademie der Bildenden Künste, Vienna, 1950; mainly self-taught. Married three times (divorced). Independent artist, living and working in Vienna, since 1947; produced surrealist drawings, 1947–51; random-images and proportion studies, 1951–52; surreal works influenced by hallucinogenic drugs, 1964–65; Grimace-photos, 1968–73; cooperative works, with artist Dieter Roth, 1974; mortuary images, 1977–87. Instructor, master class for painting, Akademie der Bildenden Künste, Vienna, and Guest Professor, Staatliche Akademie der Bildenden Künste, Stuttgart, since 1981. Recipient: Artist Prize, Vienna, 1974 (rescinded by Mayor Gratz of Vienna); Grosser Osterreichischer Staatspreis für Malerei, Vienna, 1978; Max Beckmann Preis, Frankfurt, 1981. Member, Akademie der Künste, West Berlin, 1981. Agent: Galerie Ulysses, Opernring 21, 1010 Vienna. Address: Mariahilferstrasse 49, 1060 Vienna, Austria.

Individual Exhibitions:

1951   Galerie Kleinmayr, Klagenfurt, Austria
1952   Galerie Franck, Frankfurt
         Art Club Gallery, Vienna
         Galerie Springer, West Berlin
1954   Galerie Würthle, Vienna
1956   Galerie St. Stephan, Vienna
1957   Wiener Secession, Vienna
1958   Galerie 33, Berne
         Galerie St. Stephan, Vienna
         Galerie Boukes, Wiesbaden, West Germany
1960   Galerie St. Stephan, Vienna
1961   Galleria del Cavallino, Vienna
         Galerie St. Stephan, Vienna
         Galerie Dato, Frankfurt
         Galerie Seide, Hannover
1962   Galerie Schmela, Dusseldorf
         Galerie Rottloff, Karlsruhe
         Minami Gallery, Tokyo
         Galerie 61, Klagenfurt, Austria
1963   Galerie St. Stephan, Vienna
1964   Galerie Springer, West Berlin
1965   Galerie Rottloff, Karlsruhe
1966   Galerie Peithner-Lichtenfels, Vienna
1967   Galerie Grossgorchen, West Berlin
1968   Osterreichisches Kulturinstitut, Warsaw
         Galerie Steinbacher-Hohl, Frankfurt
         Museum de 20. Jahrhunderts, Vienna
         Galerie St. Stephan, Vienna
1969   Galerie Hake, Cologne
         Galerie im Taxispalais, Innsbruck
         Galerie Ariadne, Vienna
         Galerie Rewolle, Bremen, West Germany
         Forum 67, Linz, Austria
         Galerie Casa, Munich
         Galerie Springer, West Berlin
         Galerie Tams, Munich

1970   Galerie Müller, Stuttgart
         Galerie Van de Loo, Munich
         Galerie Müller, Cologne
         Forum Stadpark, Graz, Austria
         Galerie Lichter, Frankfurt
         Galerie St. Stephan, Vienna
         Galerie Schottle, Munich
         Kunsteverein, Frieburg, West Germany
1971   Museum des 20. Jahrhunderts, Vienna
         Kunstverein, Hamburg
         Galerie Ariadne, Vienna
         Galerie Müller, Cologne
1972   Galerie Ariadne, Cologne
         Galerie Grunangergasse, Vienna
         Austrian Institute, New York
         Galerie Van de Loo, Munich
         Busch-Reisinger Museum, Cambridge, Massachusetts
         Galerie Klein, Bonn
1973   Galerie Müller, Stuttgart
         Graphische Sammlung Albertina, Vienna
         Galerie Ariadne, Cologne
         Galerie Schöttle, Munich
1974   Galerie Klein, Bonn
         Studio Santandrea, Milan
         Galerie Grunangergasse, Vienna
         Kunstverein, Bremerhaven, West Germany
         Galerie Ariadne, Cologne
         Ariadne Gallery, New York
         Abis Gallery, West Germany
         Gestische Handmalerein, Kunstraum München, Munich
         Galerie Greve, Cologne
1975   Galerie Grunangergasse, Vienna
         Superpaintings 1954–64, Ariadne Gallery, New York
         Galerie Stadler, Paris
         Retrospektive, Hessische Landesmuseum, Darmstadt
         Galerie Aktuelle, Kunst, Frankfurt
1976   Galerie Heiner Friedrich, Munich
         Galerie Winterberger, Cologne
         Galerie Shapira, Vienna
         Galerie Stadler, Paris
         Kunstverein, Mannheim
         Centre d'Arts Plastiques Contemporains, Bordeaux
         Galerie Aktuelle Kunst, Frankfurt
         Grimaces, Neue Galerie, Linz, Austria
         Kunstverein, Frankfurt
1977   Kunsthalle, Berne
         Städtische Galerie im Lenbachhaus, Munich
         Kestner-Gesellschaft, Hannover
1978   Osterreichischer Galerie, Vienna
1980   Van Abbemuseum, Eindhoven, Netherlands
         Whitechapel Art Gallery, London
         Retrospective, Nationalgalerie, West Berlin
         Als Van Gogh als . . . Uberarbeitungen von Photos und Reproduktionen von Van Gogh Selbstportraits, Galerie Curtze, Vienna
         Galerie Springer, West Berlin
         Galerie AK, Frankfurt (toured Germany)
1981   Galerie Droschl, Graz, Austria
         Kunstverein, Heidelberg
         Galerie Freund, Klagenfurt, Austria
         Galeria Erhardt, Madrid
         Galerie Turske, Zurich
         Galerie Ulysses, Vienna
         Galerie Holtmann, Cologne
         Stadtische Galerie, Frankfurt
         Galerie Academia, Salzburg
         Galerie Curtze, Vienna
         Galerie Hummel, Vienna
         Galerie Munro, Hamburg
         Sala Parpallo, Valencia, Spain
         Dossi Arte Contemporanca, Bergamo, Italy
         Galerie Holtmann, Hannover
         Graphikubermalungen, Galerie Klein, Bonn
         Galerie Curtze, Dusseldorf
         Galerie Friedrich-Kunst, Munich
1982   Louisiana Museum, Humlebaek, Denmark (retrospective)
         Suermondt Museum, Aachen, West Germany
         Galerie M, Bochum, West Germany
1983   Kunstmuseum, Hannover

Konsthall, Malmo, Sweden
Ulmer Museum, Ulm, West Germany
Wilhelm Hack Museum, Ludwigshafen, West Germany
Museum van Hedendaagse Kunst, Ghent, Belgium
Westfalischer Landesmuseum, Munster, West Germany
1984   Neuer Berliner Kunstverein, West Berlin
Stadtisches Museum, Monchengladbach, West Germany
Centre Georges Pompidou, Paris
Van Abbemuseum, Eindhoven, Netherlands
Kunstmuseum, Dusseldorf
Kunsthaus, Zurich
1985   Museum of Modern Art, Oxford
Castello di Rivoli, Turin
Kunsthalle, Nuremberg, West Germany
Groninger Museum, Groningen, Netherlands
Museum Boymans-van Beuningen, Rotterdam
Galerie Maeght Lelong, Zurich
1986   Florida Atlantic University, Boca Raton
University of South Florida, Tampa
Grey Art Gallery, New York University
Neue Galerie-Museum Ludwig, Aachen, West Germany
Kunsthalle, Hamburg (with Gunter Brus)
Abbazia di San Gregorio, Venice
Kunsthalle, Bremen, West Germany
Musée Cantonal des Beaux-Arts, Lausanne (with Louis Soutter)
Schirn Kunsthalle, Frankfurt
Provinciaal Museum, Hasselt, Belgium
Museum Moderner Kunst, Vienna
North Carolina Museum of Art, Raliegh
1987   Centre National d'Art Contemporain, Grenable, France
Saidye Bronfman Center, Montreal
Neue Galerie im Wolfgang Gurlitt Museum, Linz, Austria
Galerie Ulysses, Vienna
1988   Galerie Sabine Knust, Munich

Selected Group Exhibitions:

1951   *Hundsgruppenausstellung,* Institut fur Wissenschaft und Kunst, Vienna
1953   *German Graphics,* Art Institute of Chicago
1959   *Documenta,* Museum Fridericianum, Kassel, West Germany (and 1972, 1977)
1963   *Schrift und Bild,* Stedelijk Museum, Amsterdam (travelled to Baden-Baden)
1967   *9th Tokyo Biennale,* Metropolitan Musem of Art, Tokyo
1973   *Kunst aus Photographie,* Kunstverein, Hannover
1975   *Bodyworks,* Museum of Contemporary Art, Chicago
1979   *European Dialogue,* at the *Biennale of Sydney,* New South Wales
1983   *Aspects of Postwar Painting in Europe,* Guggenheim Museum, New York
1987   *Berlinart 1961–87,* Museum of Modern Art, New York (travelled to San Francisco)

Collections:

Museum of 20. Jahrhunderts, Vienna; Osterreichische Galerie, Vienna; Nationalgalerie, West Berlin; Staatsgalerie, Stuttgart; Kunstmuseum, Dusseldorf; Kunstmuseum, Bonn; Kunstmuseum, Basle; Tate Gallery, London; Art Institute of Chicago; Guggenheim Museum, New York.

Publications:

By RAINER: books—*TRRR-Early Drawings, 1947–51,* Vienna 1969; *Face Farces,* Vienna 1971; *Uberdeckungen,* with text by Otto Breicha, Vienna 1971; *Vermachtnis uber meinene Nachlass,* Cologne 1972; *Blindzeichnungen 1951–73,* Cologne 1973; *Hirndrang,* edited by Otto Breicha, Salzburg 1980; films and video—*Verlegenes und Vergebliches-Selbstbeschaftigungen, 1974; Confrontation with My Video Image: Mouth Piece and Slow Motion,* 1974; *Doppeldruck,* with Dieter Roth, 1976; *Duell in Schloss,* with Dieter Roth, 1976.

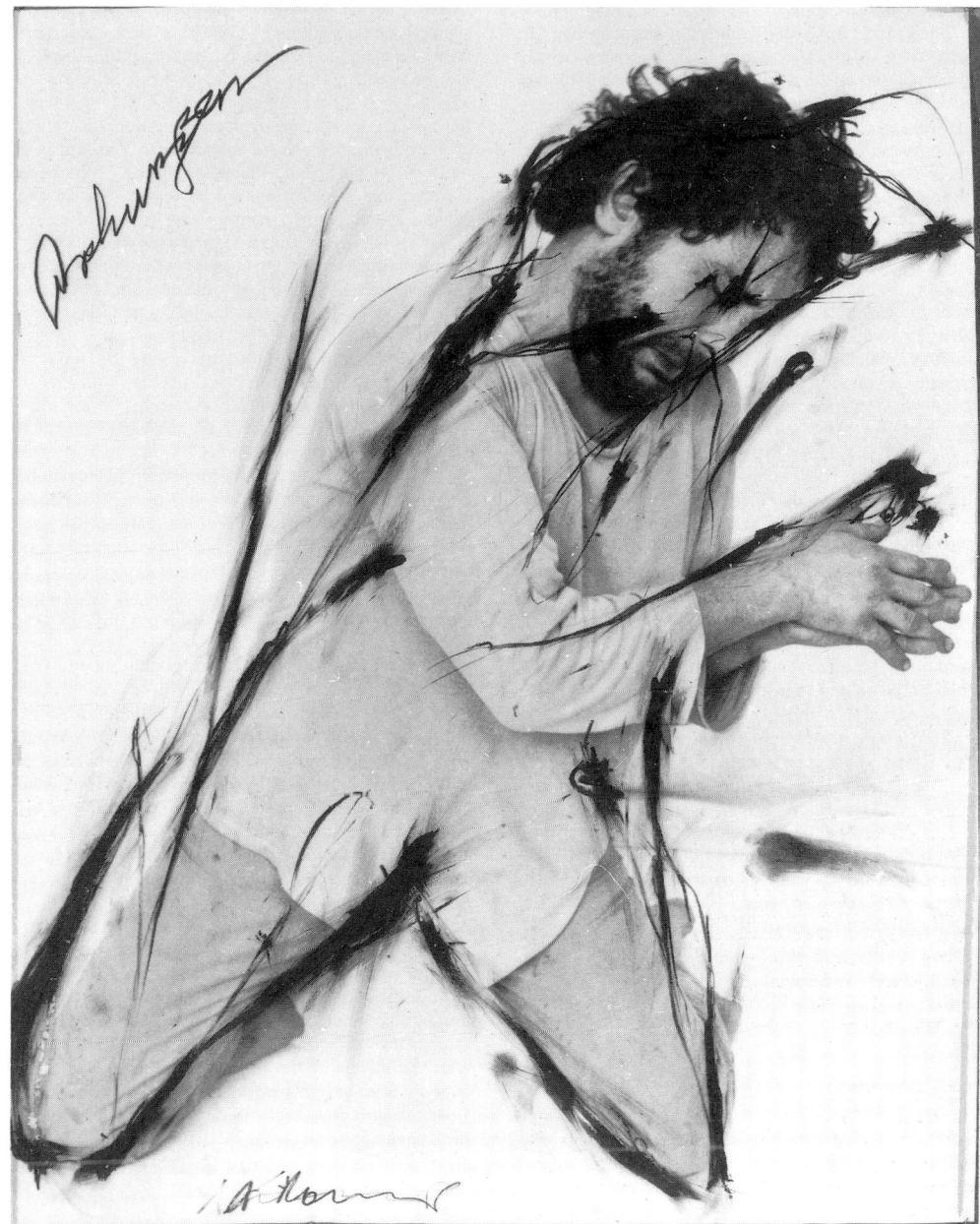

Arnulf Rainer: *Body-Language,* 1973

On RAINER: books—*Arnulf Rainer,* exhibition catalogue, with texts by W. Hofmann and H. Kern, Hambuerg 1971; *Documenta 5,* exhibition catalogue, edited by Harald Szeeman and Jean-Christophe Ammann, Kassel, West Germany 1972; *Arnulf Rainer: Gestische Handmalerein,* exhibition catalogue, Munich 1974; *Ranier: Superpaintings 1954–64,* exhibition catalogue, New York 1975; *Arnulf Ranier: Retrospektive,* exhibition catalogue, with text by Dieter Honisch and Hermann Kern, West Berlin 1980; *Arnulf Rainer: Als Van Gogh..Uberarbeitungen von Photos und Reproduktionen von Van Gogh Selbstportraits,* exhibition catalogue, Vienna 1980; *Arnulf Rainer: Graphikubermalungen,* exhibition catalogue, with text by I. Kern, Bonn 1981.

When I produce my own image, then it is also an attempt to expand—visual formulation of the possible, the imagined. I grab my hair and pull, I jump without reason, mimic discoveries, draw visions, lie and lie, until it could become true. I make no attempt at a one-to-one correspondence, I let it happen through an act of reproduction.

My own ideas, corrections, idealizations, develop in three phases: first scenic, extracted photographically. It must be reduced as much as possible, since it is concentrated in the instant that the camera records. Corrections aren't possible, only the instant counts. Most often I use a mirror, not as a control, but as a stimulation, to achieve a kind of extroverted commu-

nication with myself. Well defined, motivated performances, known typecastings—as practised by actors—don't interest me. It is only in the realising that I can find, that I can look for, whatever it is that wants to activate itself within me.

My two second scribbles were a first step towards 1/10 of a second exertion of being photographed. The second phase: selection from hundreds of moments. The identification with one, the rejection of another. Criteria: intensity of facial transformation and nervous tension. I don't trust myself to destroy the great deal of residue, perhaps the criteria within me will change themselves.

Categories of expression such as peace, relaxation, maturity, eventemperedness, don't, for the while, excite my attention: without doubt an expressive formalistic visagism dominates.

The third phase: afterwards, often weeks later, when nothing remains but a flat piece of paper, there follows a further correction and selection. I draw over them and exert myself to discover new, more important, more meaningful lies. Only when I begin to believe myself do I give up. The stronger the physiognomic quality, the faster the graphic accentuation is accomplished. I end the work quickly and don't slide into complete overpainting.

Were there really such a thing as photographic documentation the overdrawing wouldn't be necessary. I am often more aware at the instant of being photographed than I can ever be while overdrawing. On the paper only a dull reflection remains that needs to be accentuated and fattened out. That is why the mixture of mediums is necessary, from the inadequacy of what is left over from the photo sessions. Often I think of a combination of paintings, movements, three dimensional photography. In order to be able to work with complete sequences, rapidly changing scenes, I am now buying a camera with an automatic release mechanism.

It is not at all clear to me where this physiognomism will lead. I have gained another vantage point. Because of the many lies I no longer know where borders are to be drawn. I lose myself in the possible, catch impossibilities: vectors that burst; growths, swollen in anger; breaks, cracks, split from irritation, flowers or wounds produced in pain. Agglomerations that destroy themselves.

The first stages of working with my own body before a camera were drawings with physiognomic themes; but equally the forming of traces of my body or movements. To these belong drawing with closed eyes, smearing of the face, painting with fingers and toes, with the left hand etc., all forms of a psychophysical reproduction upon a pictorial surface. In addition, for the last few years, I have been making use of photography. At first just for grimaces, afterwards for gestures and body-motoric expressions. Photography alone, however, is not able to communicate adequately a moving or statically concentrated tension. For a closer approximation I draw over the photograph. This isn't retouching, but rather accenting, the reawakening of the dynamic aspect of the frozen moment. In this way my work became a mixture of performing and visual art.

Well defined human forms—I couldn't find myself among them. Only when their strictness and confinement were enunciated, could I grab hold of myself.

Facit: I begin to forget, I don't try to save face; I only want transformations, changes, jumps, things not formulated. Identity seems so sure that I no longer pay attention to it. But the cage is always there. Caught in my own production, I stand with my back to the wall, planning a new escape.

—Arnulf Rainer

Today Arnulf Rainer is best known for the astonishing embellishments he adds to the photographic image of his face (and sometimes his body as well). A few years have helped the public forget that he is also an expert in many graphic fields, notably that of drypoint. Before he began work upon the strange range of autoportraits he had already been experimenting with imagery that, a bit further West than Vienna, might have been seen as yet another diversion of Cobra Art. He managed a permanent if eccentric figuration engulfed in scrawls and busy linear explosions in these earlier works and, in its way, elements of this style have survived to be injected into the photographic self-portraits. But even so, this sweeping generalisation overlooks his surrealist drawings of 1948–50, also the Central-Horizontal- and Vertical-visions, and his Black Pictures—all of which also, one way or another, have led up to his latest work.

The violence exhibited in Rainer's oeuvre over the past decade suggests that he should be associated with the Direct Action school of Vienna; but this would be wrong. Both philosophically and creatively he has nothing to do with Nitch and Muehl. Actually, he is far closer to Dieter Roth with whom he has shared a number of exhibitions.

Peter Baum, Director of the Galerie der Stadt Linz Wolfgang-Gurlitt-Museum, goes as far as to say (March 1976) that "in the past few years Rainer has altered the face of painting." This artist has made himself familiar with many aspects of creativity, including some of the least considered (the drawings and paintings by schizophrenics and the mentally sick, and it is possible with their tantalizing inspirations in mind that he has investigated with such zest the challenge of extending opportunities offered by the self-portrait).

Baum implies that Rainer is "singular" in the dictionary sense of the word, and this view could certainly be maintained on the basis of an exhibition like the one held at the Wolfgang-Gurlitt-Museum in March/April 1976, although Wilfried Skreiner writing about the artist's *Grimaces* exhibition saw things differently because, as he pointed out, "the language of faces" is part of the "language of art." Skreiner's belief is that Rainer must not be regarded as in any sense *isolated;* on the contrary, he is one of many, albeit an important example, of those who in a thoroughly accepted manner—the self-portrait—have changed the appearance of modern art. Hans M. Schmidt in his introduction to the Rainer Retrospective Exhibition (Hessische Landesmuseum, Darmstadt, 1975) goes still further, comparing Rainer's traditional concern with the self-portrait with that of van Gogh, Rembrandt and Kokoschka . . . "the originality of his self presentation is the manner in which he seeks the core of personality."

What started as a re-interpretation of passport-photographs has now become much more sophisticated. Rainer's photo-portraits are carefully staged today so that they leave out every other suggestion of imagery outside Rainer himself. His expressive face, sometimes bearded, sometimes unshaven, sometimes completely beardless, assumes all sorts of *grimaces*. His body, too, when it is in evidence, takes up all kinds of unexpected poses. The photos themselves, large (175 x 122cm) or small (50 x 60cm) are printed onto a variety of grounds—china, aluminium sheet, photo-canvas and photographic paper. Once his image is in place, he begins to decorate it. Swift flashes of colour (red, yellow, orange and black) may be added as dramatic incidentals or, as in the case of one of the "Ohne Titel" pictures in the Neue Galerie der Stadt Linz (1976 exhibition), the entire area of the photograph has been overpainted and worked upon. The ultimate reaction experienced from such a show is one of quickened enthusiasm. A single person, a single face can suddenly opened up a completely new frontier of vision rich in emotionally uninhibited exhibitionism which is at the same time a personal triumph of communication with the outside world, even though this "communication" today is often fraught with the effects of the swing of the artist's creative pendulum which can take his inventive activities from clear recognizable "realism" to almost total black obliterations of the image.

—Sheldon Williams

RAJLICH, Tomas.

Dutch. Born in Jankov, Czechoslovakia, 5 March 1940; emigrated to the Netherlands 1969: naturalized, 1977. Studied at the School of Decorative Arts, Prague, 1954–58, and Academy of Fine Arts, Prague, 1958–64. Married Hanusova Rajlich in 1963. Painter and sculptor, Prague, 1964–68, in The Hague, since 1969. Instructor, Vrije Academie, The Hague, 1971–80. Agents: Galerie Yvon Lambert, 5 rue du Grenier St. Lazare, Paris, France; and Art and Project, Prinsengracht 785, Amsterdam, Netherlands. Address: Sirtemastraat 144, 2513 SR The Hague, Netherlands.

Individual Exhibitions:

1961	Galerie Mladych, Prague
1971	Stedelijk Museum, Schiedam, Netherlands
	Gemeentemuseum, The Hague
1972	Haagse, Kunstkring, The Hague
	Galerie Collection d'Art, Amsterdam
1973	Städtisches Museum, Bochum, West Germany
1974	Galerie Yvon Lambert, Paris
	Galerie Seriaal, Amsterdam
	Galleria Francoise Lambert, Milan
	Art and Project, Amsterdam

1975	Groninger Museum, Groningen, Netherlands
	Jaap Berghuis/Tomas Rajlich/Martin Rous, Westfälischer Kunstverein, Münster, West Germany
1976	Stedelijk Museum, Schiedam, Netherlands
	Galerie Yvon Lambert, Paris
1978	Gemeentemuseum, The Hague
	Centraal Museun, Utrecht
1979	Galleria Peccolo, Livorno, Italy
	Haags Gemeentemuseum, The Hague
	Art and Project, Amsterdam
1980	Artline, The Hague
1982	Artline, The Hague
1983	Art and Project, Amsterdam
1985	Artline, The Hague
1986	Galerie im Winter, Bremen, West Germany
1987	Galleria Peccolo, Livorno, Italy
	Galeria Aale, Madrid
	Gallery Hatanaka, Tokyo

Selected Group Exhibitions:

1968	*Sculpture Tchecoslovaque*, Musée Rodin, Paris
1973	*Lof der Tekenkunst*, Stedelijk Van Abbemuseum, Eindhoven, Netherlands
	8th Biennale de Paris, Musée d'Art Moderne, Paris
1975	*Fundamentele Schilderkunst*, Stedelijk Museum, Amsterdam
1976	*I Colori della Pittura*, Istituto Italo-Latino-Americano, Rome
1977	*Trois Villes-Trois Collections*, Musée de Grenoble, France (travelled to Marseilles, St. Etienne and Paris)
1978	*Fracture du Monochrome*, Musée d'Art Moderne de la Ville, Paris
	Bilder ohne Bilder, Rheinisches Landesmuseum, Bonn
1979	*Unga Hollandare*, Liljevalchs Konsthall, Stockholm
1983	*Von der Ungleichheit des Ahnlichen in der Kunst*, Stadtische Galerie, Ludenscheid, West Germany (travelled to Gelsenkirchen and Unna)

Collections:

Musée de Grenoble, France; Musée Cantini, Marseilles; Gemeentemuseum, The Hague; Museum Boymans-van Beuningen, Rotterdam; Centraal Museum, Utrecht; Stedelijk Museum, Schiedam, Netherlands; Stedelijk Museum, Amsterdam; Stuyvesant Collection, Amsterdam; Narodni Galerie, Prague; Museum of Modern Art, New York.

Publications:

On RAJLICH: books—*Tomas Rajlich*, exhibition catalogue, The Hague 1971; *Jaap Berghuis/Tomas Rajlich/Martin Rous*, exhibition catalogue, with text by Klaus Honnef, Münster, West Germany 1975; *Fundamentele Schilderkunst/Fundamental Painting*, exhibition catalogue, with text by Rini Dippel, Amsterdam 1975; *Elementary Forms of Contemporary Painting and Drawing in the Netherlands*, exhibition catalogue, with texts by Guys van Tuyl, Hans Sizoo and Klaus Honnef, Amsterdam 1975; *Tomas Rajlich*, exhibition catalogue, with text by L. Brozek-Dolezal, Utrecht 1978; *Rajlich*, exhibition catalogue, The Hague 1979; *De Nederlandse Indentiteit in de Kunst na 1945* by Geurt Imanse, Amsterdam 1984; *Tomas Rajlich*, exhibition catalogue with texts by Flip Bool, Livorno 1987.

The painter Tomas Rajlich, who was born in Czechoslovakia, works and lives in The Hague, Holland, from 1969 onwards. In his new country he found an artistic climate that welcomed the views he already had developed in his native Prague.

Within a short time his work met the critical attention of some of the leading writers on art. The art historian Carel Blotkamp wrote an introduction for the exhibition-catalogue *3 Konkretisten aus Prag* (Museum Bochum, 1973) in which he put Rajlich's typical grid-structure in a strikingly convincing perspective. Blotkamp describes this type of organization as unpersonal and as aiming at a clear relation between the external, physical existence of a canvas and its internal structure.

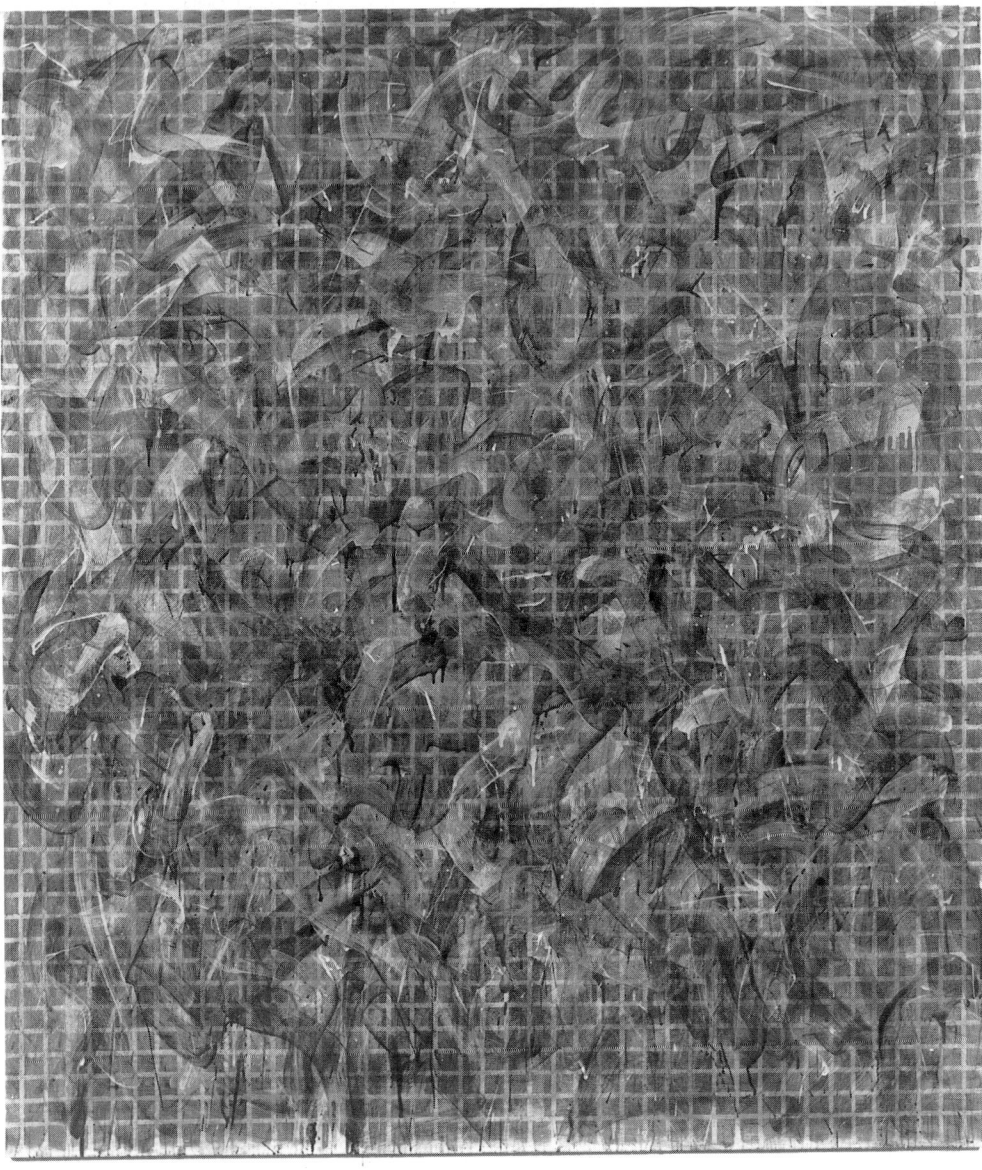

Tomas Rajlich: *Untitled*, 1975

According to Blotkamp the visual formulation in Rajlich's work is lucid and convincing in its objective to demonstrate a 'minimal disruption of regular structure.' Rajlich wants to provide painterly gesture with a ground that cannot be discussed and that offers no terms for speculation, with a background that is concrete.

A change occurs from about 1976 on when the gridstructures are seen to disappear from sight. This development starts with gesturely strokes loosely laid over the grid in a transparent paint. Hereafter, the surface they cover tends to become larger and larger while at the same time the paint itself gets more opaque. The next phase is marked by a series of paintings in which the underlying grid is only to be discovered at the extreme ends of the canvas. Finally, in 1979, the paintings are almost black. A rectangled part of the canvas, however, has been overpainted with a shining material that adds a reflection to the skin of the painting's surface. Also from the years 1976–77 dates a series of collages in which the theme of transparency is dealt with.

Rajlich's work appears to be methodical and uncompromising. The self-imposed restrictions lead him to a continuous reflection on his own premises. The general context of this research is a concrete, late-constructivist tradition of painting, of which the exhibition title *Fundamental Painting* (Stedelijk Museum, Amsterdam, 1975) seems to be a variation. In The Netherlands there has always been a special attention towards these strict views in painting, possibly because the artistic debate since De Stijl's early 20th century emergence ordinarily focused on the conflicting ideas of painting as rational intention versus painting as individual product.

Rajlich's inflexible gridstructures contradict the viewer's need of a personal, subtly formulated composition. Additionally, the complementary painterly gesture as well is given in well measured quantities. Taken together these assure a position on one's own in The Netherlands.

—A. F. Wagemans

RAMOS, Mel(vin John).

American. Born in Sacramento, California, 24 July 1935. Studied, under Wayne Thiebaud, at Sacramento Junior College, California, 1953–54; at San Jose State College, California 1954–55; Sacramento State College 1955–58, B.A. 1957, M.F.A. 1958. Married Leta Alice Helmers in 1955; children: Bradley, Scot and Rochelle. Independent painter, since 1955; lives and works in California. Taught at Elk Grove High School, California, 1958–60; Mira Loma High School, California, 1960–66; Sacramento State College, California, 1965–66; and Arizona State University, Tempe, 1967; Artist-in-Residence, University of Southern Florida, Tampa, 1970, and Syracuse University, New York, 1970; Visiting Artist, University of Wisconsin, Madison, 1973, and Pacific Lutheran University, Tacoma, Washington, 1973. Associate Professor of Painting, 1966–1980, and since 1980 Professor of Painting, California State University at Hayward. Recipient: Purchase Prizes: San Francisco Museum of Art, 1948, and Oakland Art Museum, 1959; Artists Fellowship, National Endowment for the Arts, Washington, D.C., 1986. Agent: Louis Meisel, 141 Prince Street, New York, New York 10012. Address: 5941 Ocean View Drive, Oakland, California 94618; or Moragrera 38, Horta de San Juan, Tarragona, Spain.

Individual Exhibitions:

1964	Bianchini Gallery, New York
1965	Bianchini Gallery, New York
	David Stuart Gallery, Los Angeles
1966	Galerie Ricke, Kassel, West Germany
1967	San Francisco Museum of Art
	Berkeley Gallery, San Francisco
	Galerie Tobies-Silex, Cologne
1968	Mills College Art Gallery, Oakland, California
	David Stuart Gallery, Los Angeles
1969	David Stuart Gallery, Los Angeles
	Gallery Reese Palley, Los Angeles
	Stadtsmuseum, Aachen, West Germany
1970	Artists Contemporary Gallery, Sacramento, California
1971	French and Co., New York
	Graphics Gallery, San Francisco
	Galerie Bruno Bischofberger, Zurich
	Galerie Richard Foncke, Ghent
1972	Utah Museum of Fine Arts, Salt Lake City
1973	Dickinson College, Carlisle, Pennsylvania
	Madison Art Center, Wisconsin
	Pacific Lutheran University, Tacoma, Washington
1974	Meisel Gallery, New York
	David Stuart Gallery, Los Angeles
1975	Museum Haus Lange, Krefeld, West Germany (retrospective)
1976	Meisel Gallery, New York
1977	Morgan Gallery, Shawnee Mission, Missouri
	Oakland Museum, California (retrospective)
1978	University of Nevada at Reno
1979	California State University, Chico
1981	Meisel Gallery, New York
	Modernism, San Francisco
	California State University at Chico
1982	Route 66 Gallery, Philadelphia
	Melinda Wyatt Gallery, Venice, California
1985	Louis K. Meisel Gallery, New York
1986	Hokin Gallery, Chicago
1987	Studio Trisorio, Naples

Selected Group Exhibitions:

1963	*Pop Goes the Easel*, Contemporary Art Museum, Houston
1969	*Pop Art Revisited*, Hayward Gallery, London
1973	*The Super Realist Vision*, De Cordova, Museum, Lincoln, Massachusetts
1975	*3 Centuries of the American Nude*, New York Cultural Center
1976	*California Painting and Sculpture: The Modern Era*, San Francisco Museum of Modern Art
1978	*Art about Art*, Whitney Museum, New York
1981	*American Drawings in Black and White 1970–80*, Brooklyn Museum, New York
1983	*Modern Nude Paintings 1880–1980*, National Museum of Art, Osaka, Japan
1984	*Automobile and Culture*, Museum of Contemporary Art, Los Angeles
1985	*Pop Art 1955–70*, Art Gallery of New South Wales, Sydney (travelled to Brisbane and Melbourne)

Collections:

Museum of Modern Art, New York; University Museum,

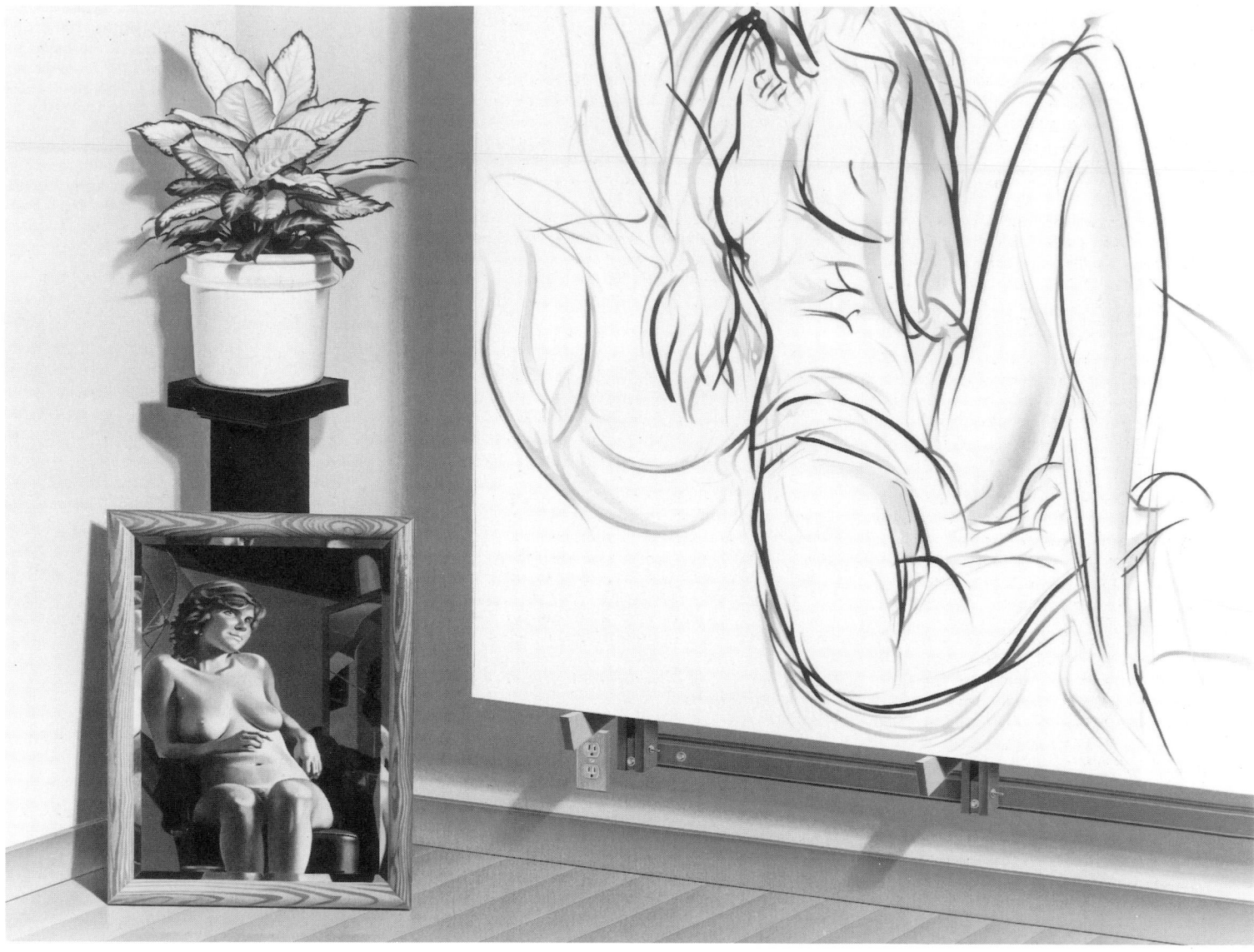

Mel Ramos: *The Artist's Studio, No. 1*, 1987

Potsdam, New York; Chrysler Museum of Art, Norfolk, Virginia; San Francisco Museum of Modern Art; Oakland Museum, California; Museen der Stadt, Aachen, West Germany; Kaiser Wilhelm Museum, Krefeld, West Germany; Guggenheim Museum, New York.

Publications:

By RAMOS: book—*Mel Ramos: Watercolors,* Berkeley, California 1979; article—"Interview with Mel Ramos," with Dan Tooker, in *Art International* (Lugano, Switzerland), December 1973.

On RAMOS: books—*Pop Art* by John Rublowsky, New York 1965; *La Pop Art* by Enrico Crispolti, Milan 1966; *Invitation to Vision* by Earl Linderman, Dubuque, Iowa, 1966; *Pop Art* By Lucy Pippard, New York 1966; *New Tendencies in Art* by Aldo Pellegrini, New York 1966; *Pop Art* by Michael Compton, London 1969; *Neue Formen des Bildes!* by Udo Kulterman, Berlin 1969; *Pop und die Folgen* by Heinz Ohff, Dusseldorf 1969; *Creativity and Communication* by Colin Forbes, London 1970; *Erotic Art 2* by Phyllis and Eberhard Kronhausen, New York 1970; *Erotic Art Today* by Volker Kahmen, Greenwich, Connecticut 1971; *Art Now/New Age: The Pop Image of Man* by Yoshiaki Tono, Tokyo 1971; *Woman as Sex Object* by Thomas Hess and Linda Nochlin, New York 1972; *Art as Image and Idea* by Edmund B. Feldman, New York 1972; *Kitsch* by Jacques Sternberg, London 1972; *Pop* by Simon Wilson, London 1974; *Mel Ramos* by Elizabeth Claridge, London 1975; *20th Century Masters of Erotic Art* by Bradley Smith, New York 1980; *Art in the San Francisco Bay Area 1945-80* By Thomas Albright, Berkeley, California 1985.

The subject of my painting is the figure. The object of my painting can be anything and usually is. I sometimes think that everything is instantaneous except my work, and I get the feeling that the best figuration is in the movies. Nevertheless, despite the rampant self-consciousness about "formal" concerns that seems to characterize 20th century art, the best painting still announces itself in this manner, and I am not particularly interested in becoming an exception. I am for an art that hangs on the wall and asserts itself.

—Mel Ramos

Mel Ramos' new landscapes, introduced in New York a few years ago, ostensibly seem to represent a major departure from the blunt figurative Pop paintings that brought him fame in the 1960's. In reality, however, the fundamental issues that formed the basis of his earlier aesthetic investigations—exploration of forms, a search for complete objectivity in representation—also inform the new work. "I have never been interested in dealing with art from an esoteric point of view," he says. "I do not think of objects as symbols, but as temporal, formal entities, as shapes to be explored purely on a formal basis."

A major California figure of the first generation of Pop artists, Ramos came to the attention of the art world when Pop art was at its apogee. He participated in a movement that in celebration of the banal, the commonplace, the vulgar, often gently parodied familiar icons of American popular culture. His first

mature works were a sort of hard-edge figurative paintings that documented as well as mimicked comic book heroes and *Playboy* sex symbols, using a limited palette of flat colors and hard precise drawing. Then, in a series of salutes to art history executed in the 1970's Ramos turned his attention from the lowly to the mighty with reconstructions of traditional and modernist masterpieces which he infused with a new eroticism drawn from the heroic images of contemporary folklore. Unfortunately, because of the notoriety fostered by their subject matter (beautiful nude bodies—mostly female), the ideas behind the works from these two decades were overshadowed by journalistic sensationalism, and often misunderstood. Central to Ramos' aesthetic are the modernist principles of both "objectness" and autonomy of the painted surface that depersonalize a subject. Thus, for him, the figures were never anything but objects—plastic shapes to be studied and recreated with paint on canvas, or paper, according to his particular vision—and to regard them as anything else was to miss the point of the art entirely.

Ramos' approach to the landscape is a similar one. His images may have changed to monuments, cacti, bridge supports, and palm trees, but they are treated with a like impersonal neutrality. That they are an outgrowth of the artist's art historical "Homage Series" of the 70's, particularly De Kooning's, is evident from the lushly brushed surfaces and what he calls "the gesticulated backgrounds." In allegiance to Morris Louis' famed unfurled canvases, they are organized around a central void flanked by angled rows of colored travel-related objects depicted in a worm's eye perspective, the way a tourist would look at those objects. "The landscape came about mainly through my travels," Ramos explains, "and the way one looks at things, as tourists look at the facades of buildings, as palm trees . . . . " In keeping with his preference for the mundane, the iconography of these new paintings is derived from postcards, travel posters, and other popular media images, thus marking the opening of a new chapter rather than a change in the narrative.

"My primary concern has always been ART; I am interested in ART, and the subject matter of my work is, and will always be, ART." With these words, Mel Ramos recapitulates two very successful decades. On the strength of the interest generated by the new landscapes, one might hazard the prediction that the third will be as important.

When Mel Ramos showed his landscapes for the first time in 1982, a controversy that had simmered for two decades was put to rest. Ramos, his critics proclaimed, may not be a male chauvinist painter after all; he may just have been a misunderstood artist who was manipulating the female form to satirize the worst aspect of American advertising. Speculations were rife about the cause of the switch from figures to landscapes, but the move was a good one, everyone agreed, and as one Los Angeles reviewer declared, "Sex's loss (was) art's gain."

In point of fact, Mel Ramos was not then, nor has he ever been, a male chauvinist, or a satirist, or anything but an artist concerned with art and its history. "Although I have been accused of being a sexist, or of exploiting women, I really have never had any politics," he said five years ago. With a perspective of nearly three decades, despite assertions to the contrary, it is now clear that militancy has never been Ramos' posture, and that the change in subject matter was but another means of exploration—of research into new ways to make this the same individualistic statement in as many forms as possible.

And where did the research into the landscape lead to? . . . As demonstrated by Ramos' new series, *The Artist in the Studio:* right back to the figure and the history of art! In this series and its corollary, *The Drawing Lesson,* De Kooning and Manet make way for Ingres and Matisse; a "nude descending a staircase" takes on a new look; soft-focus mirror reflections and family memorabilia are added to the repertoire; and, most importantly, Ramos is now drawing from his own past, as in the restated *Kellog* painting he turned into a composition centered around a drawing by Ingres. "My new paintings are more narcissistic," he said during a recent interview. "I use some of my old works in my compositions, showing them reflected in mirrors, and this is what I mean by narcissistic. This is not a new device: artists have shown mirror-reflected images for ages, ever since the mirror was invented in the fifteenth century, when Jan Van Eyck painted *Giovanni Arnolfini and his Bride* (1434)."

The significance of the new *Artist in his Studio* series goes far beyond reconsiderations of imagery, however. In his art historical "Homages" works of the seventies, Ramos relied upon well-known modernist masterpieces which he recast according to his own aesthetic vocabulary—parodying or celebrating, as the cases may have been. In the current *Studio* paintings and drawings, he continues to pay tribute to the heroes from the past, but the prototypes are less obvious. Matisse, Ingres, Bonnard, Duchamp are all part of the cast of characters, but there is no question as to the identity of the protagonist. In addition, the images from which he draws are not as renowned, and if they are rendered just as faithfully, they are now but one segment of a complex compositional scheme. This, in turn, gives the works an irrefutable stamp of Ramos authenticity that establishes them firmly within the stream of art history—lending truth once more to the timeless French adage: "The more things change, the more they stay the same."

—Andree Marechal-Workman

RAUSCHENBERG, Robert.

American. Born in Port Arthur, Texas, 22 October 1925. Studied at the Kansas City Art Institute and School of Design, 1946–47; Académie Julian, Paris, 1947; Black Mountain College, North Carolina, with Joseph Albers, 1948–50. Married Susan Weil in 1950 (divorced, 1952); son: Christopher. Served in the United States Navy Reserve, as a neuropsychiatry technician, at California Naval Hospital, 1942–45. Independent artist, New York, since 1950. Taught at Black Mountain College, 1952, mounting first "happening" with John Cage and others. Has worked with the Merce Cunningham Dance Company, New York, as a stage and costume designer, since 1955: Technical Director since 1960. President of the Board of Directors, Change Inc., New York, 1970; Member, Board of Directors, Public School #1, New York, 1977; President, Trisha Brown Dance Company, New York, 1978. Recipient: Art Institute of Chicago Prize, 1960; Ohara Prize, National Museum of Modern Art, Tokyo, 1962; First Prize, 1963, and Grand Prix d'Honneur, 1979, *International* Exhibition of Graphic Art, Ljublijana, Yugoslavia; First Prize, *Biennale,* Venice, 1964; William A. Clark Gold Medal and Prize, *Corcoran Biennial Exhibition of Contemporary American Painters,* Washington, D.C., 1965; Logan Award, Art Institute of Chicago, 1976; Mayor's Award of Honor in Arts and Culture, New York, 1977; Creative Arts Medal in Painting, Brandeis University, Waltham, Massachusetts, 1978; Chicago Arts Award, 1978; Special Award, *Graphic Arts Biennale,* Cracow, Poland, 1979; Skowhegan Medal for Painting, Maine, 1982; Grammy Award, New York, 1984; Jerusalem Prize for Arts and Letters, Friends of Bezalel Academy, 1984. D.H.L.: Grinnell College, Iowa, 1967; D.F.A.: University of South Florida, Tampa, 1976. Fellow, Rhode Island School of Design, Providence, 1978. Member, American Academy of Arts and Sciences, 1978. Foreign Member, Royal Academy of Fine Arts of Stockholm, 1980; Officier, Ordre des Arts et Lettres, France, 1981. Agents: Leo Castelli Gallery, 4 East 77th Street, New York, New York 10021; and Sonnabend Gallery, 420 West Broadway, New York, New York 10012. Addresses: Laika Lane, P.O. Box 54, Captiva Island, Florida 33924; and 381 Lafayette Street, New York, New York 10003, U.S.A.

Individual Exhibitions:

1951	Betty Parsons Gallery, New York
1953	The Stable Gallery, New York
	Galleria d'Arte Contemporanea, Florence
1955	Charles Egan Gallery, New York
1958	Leo Castelli Gallery, New York
1959	Leo Castelli Gallery, New York
	Galleria La Tartaruga, Rome
	Galerie 22, Dusseldorf
1960	Leo Castelli Gallery, New York
1961	Leo Castelli Gallery, New York
	Galerie Daniel Cordier, Paris
	Galleria dell'Ariete, Milan
1962	Dwan Dallery, New York
1963	Leo Castelli Gallery, New York
	Jewish Museum, New York (retrospective)
	Galleria del'Obelisco, Rome
	Galerie Ileana Sonnabend, Paris
1964	Galerie Ileana Sonnabend, Paris
	Galleria Civica d'Arte Moderna, Turin
	Paintings, Drawings and Combines 1949–1964, Whitechapel Art Gallery, London (retrospective)
1965	Leo Castelli Gallery, New York
	Amerika Haus, Berlin
	Contemporary Arts Society, Houston
	Paintings 1963–1964, Walker Art Center, Minneapolis
	Moderna Museet, Stockholm
1966	Museum of Modern Art, New York
1967	Leo Castelli Gallery, New York
	Douglas Gallery, Vancouver
1968	Leo Castelli Gallery, New York
	Museum of Modern Art, New York
	Stedelijk Museum, Amsterdam

	Peale House, Philadelphia
	Kunstverein, Cologne
	Musée National d'Art Moderne, Paris
1969	Leo Castelli Gallery, New York
	Fort Worth Art Center, Texas
	Douglas Gallery, Vancouver
1971	Galerie Ileana Sonnabend, Paris
1972	Leo Castelli Gallery, New York
	Galerie Ileana Sonnabend, Paris
	Galerie Buren, Stockholm
1973	Galerie Ileana Sonnabend, Paris
	Leo Castelli Gallery, New York
	Ace Gallery, Venice, California
	Mitchell Gallery, Southern Illinois University, Carbondale
	Israel Museum, Jerusalem
1974	Graficstudio Tampa, University of South Florida, Tampa
	Galerie Buren, Stockholm
	Galerie Mikro, West Berlin
	Lucio Amelio Modern Art Agency, Naples
	Museum Haus Lange, Krefeld
	Castelli-Sonnabend Galleries, New York
	Castelli Graphics, New York
	Gemini, G.E.L., Los Angeles
	Galerie Sonnabend, Geneva
	Jared Sable Gallery, Toronto
1975	Castelli Graphis, New York
	Gemini, G.E.L., Los Angeles
	Visual Arts Gallery, New York
	Ace Gallery, Venice, California
	Museo d'Arte Moderna ca'Pesaro, Venice
	Art Association, Newport, Rhode Island
1976	Ace Gallery, Venice, California
	Galerie de Gestlo, Hamburg
	Greenberg Gallery, St. Louis
	Galerie H. M., Brussels
	Galleria Civica d'Arte Moderna, Ferrara, Italy
	Leo Castelli Gallery, New York
	Fort Belvidere, Florence
	Ace Gallery, Vancouver
	National Collection of Fine Arts, Washington, D.C. (retrospective)
	Alberta College of Art, Calgary
	Galleriet, Lund, Sweden
1977	Ace Gallery, Venice, California
	Galleriet, Lund, Sweden
	Galerie Sonnabend, Paris
	Museum of Modern Art, New York (retrospective)
	Leo Castelli-Ileana Sonnabend Galleries, New York
	San Francisco Museum of Modern Art (retrospective)
	John Berggruen Gallery, San Francisco
	Albright-Knox Art Gallery, Buffalo, New York
	Art Institute of Chicago
	Linda Farris Gallery, Seattle
	Janie C. Lee Gallery, Houston
	Galerie Rudolf Zwirner, Cologne
1978	Galerie Sonnabend, Paris
	Mayor Gallery, London
	Vancouver Art Gallery
	Gemini, G.E.L., Los Angeles
	Castelli Graphics, New York
	Fort Worth Art Museum, Texas
1979	Sonnabend Gallery, New York (twice)
	Akron Art Institute, Ohio
	Richard Gray Gallery, Chicago
	Ace Gallery, Venice, California
	Richard Hines Gallery, Seattle
	Gloria Luria Gallery, Miami
	Portland Art Center, Oregon
	Kunsthalle, Tübingen (retrospective)
	Art in Progress, Cologne
	Castelli Uptown, New York
	Kunstmuseum, Hannover (retrospective)
	Musée de Toulon, France
	Multiples-Goodman, New York
	Institute of Contemporary Art, Virginia Museum, Richmond
	Gloria Luria Gallery, Bay Harbor Islands, Florida
1980	Conejo Valley Art Museum, Thousand Oaks, California
	Edison Community College, Fort Myers, Florida
	Visual Arts Museum, New York

Staatliche Kunsthalle, Berlin (retrospective)
Leo Castelli Gallery, New York
Galerie Sonnabend, Paris
Ace Gallery, Venice, California
Ace Gallery, Los Angeles (twice)
Staatliche Kunsthalle, Dusseldorf
Sanibel Photo Gallery, Florida
Louisiana Museum, Copenhagen (retrospective)
Cranbrook Academy of Art, Bloomfield Hills, Michigan
Balitmore Museum of Art
Fendrick Gallery, Washington, D.C.
Children's Hospital, Washington, D.C.
Magnuson-Lee Gallery, Boston
Ace Gallery, Vancouver
Galleriet, Lund, Sweden
Equitable Trust, Baltimore
1981   Stadtische Kunstinstitut, Frankfurt (retrospective)
New Gallery of Contemporary Art, Cleveland
Gemini Gallery, Palm Beach, Florida
Stadtische Galerie im Lenbachhaus, Munich (retrospective)
Colorado State University, Denver (toured the western United States and Canada)
Tate Gallery, London (retrospective)
Fay Gold Gallery, Atlanta
Centre Georges Pompidou, Paris (retrospective)
Sonnabend Gallery, New York
Sable-Castelli Gallery, Toronto
Gallery Watari, Tokyo
Styria Gallery, New York
Institute of Contemporary Art, Boston
Mayor Gallery, London
Gibbes Art Gallery, Charleston, South Carolina
Magnuson-Lee Gallery, Boston
Grimaldis Gallery, Baltimore
Rosamund Felsen Gallery, Los Angeles
1982   Sonnabend Gallery, New York
Photographers' Gallery, Sanibel Island, Florida
Edison Community Collge, Fort Myers, Florida
Hara Museum of Contemporary Art, Tokyo
Castelli Graphics, New York
Lunds Galleriet, Lund, Sweden
Long Beach Museum of Art, California
Flow Ace Gallery, Paris
Van Straaten Gallery, Chicago
Museum of Modern Art, New York
1983   Sonnabend Gallery, New York
Castelli Gallery, New York
Thomas Babeor Gallery, La Jolla, California
Louisiana Museum, Humlebaek, Denmark (travelled to Copenhagen and Oslo)
Prince Hotel, Tokyo
KBS Kaikan, Kyoto, Japan
Flow Ace Gallery, Los Angeles
Daytona Beach Community College, Florida
Jinxian, Anhui Province, China
Edison Community College, Fort Myers, Florida
Galleria di Franca Mancini, Pesaro, Italy (travelled to New York; Houston; Cleveland, Ohio; Raleigh, North Carolina; West Palm Beach, Florida; Long Beach, California)
Douglas Elliott Gallery, San Francisco
Castelli Graphics, New York
Dalsheimer Gallery, Baltimore
Maryland Institute, Baltimore
Susanne Hilberry Gallery, Birmingham, Michigan
Marianne Friedland Gallery, Toronto
Australian National Gallery, Canberra
1984   Port Arthur Public Library, Texas
Harcourts Contemporary Gallery, San Francisco
Galerie Beyeler, Basle (retrospective)
Heland Thorden Wetterling Galleries, Stockholm
Miami Center for Fine Arts, Florida
Fondation Maeght, St. Paul de Vence, France
Adagio Gallery, Bridgehampton, New York
Gemini G.E.L., Los Angeles
Allen Street Gallery, Dallas
Objects Gallery, San Antonio, Texas
Edison Community College, Fort Myers, Florida
Scheinbaum and Russek Gallery, Santa Fe, New Mexico
Sonnabend Gallery, New York
Castelli Graphics, New York

1985   Fundacion Juan March, Madrid (retrospective; travelled to Barcelona)
B. R. Kornblatt Gallery, Washington, D.C.
Ringling Museum of Art, Sarasota, Florida
Muso Rufino Tamayo, Mexico City (and world tour)
Galerie Daniel Templon, Paris
Contemporary Arts Museum, Houston (travelled to San Antonio, Dallas and Corpus Christi)
1986   Moosart Gallery, Miami, Florida
Contemporary Arts Museum, Houston
Espace Nicois d'Art et de Culture, Nice, France
Larry Gagosian Gallery, New York
Edison Community College, Fort Myers, Florida
Acquavella Galleries, New York
School of Visual Arts, New York
Castelli Gallery, New York
Setagaya Art Museum, Tokyo
Sogetsu Kaikan, Tokyo
Dallas Museum of Art, Texas
1987   Metropolitan Museum of Art, New York
Heland Thorden Wetterling Galleries, Stockholm
Kaj Forsblom Gallery, Helsinki
Blum-Helman Gallery, New York
Galerie Denise Rene/Hans Meyer, Dusseldorf
Galleria Lucio Amelio, Naples
Edison Community College, Fort Myers, Florida
Castellia Graphics, New York

Selected Group Exhibitions:

1957   *Collage in America,* American Federation of Arts, New York (toured the United States)
1961   *American Vanguard,* Guggenheim Museum, New York (toured Europe)
1964   *Black, White and Gray,* Wadsworth Atheneum, Hartford, Connecticut
1968   *Dada, Surrealism and their Heritage,* Museum of Modern Art, New York
1973   *Fotografia Creativa,* Centro La Capella, Trieste, Italy
1978   *Art About Art,* Whitney Museum, New York
1980   *Printed Art of the 60s and 70s,* Museum of Modern Art, New York
1983   *Photography in America 1910–83,* Tampa Museum, Florida
1985   *Painterly Visions 1940–84,* Guggenheim Museum, New York
1987   *American Painting: Abstract Expressionism and After,* San Francisco Museum of Modern Art

Collections:

Museum of Modern Art, New York; Guggenheim Museum, New York; Whitney Museum, New York; Stedelijk Museum, Amsterdam; Los Angeles County Museum of Art; Museum Ludwig, Cologne; Kaiser Wilhelm Museum, Krefeld; Kunsthaus, Zurich; Art Gallery of Ontario, Toronto; National Gallery of Canada, Ottawa.

Publications:

By RAUSCHENBERG: articles—interview, with Dorothy Seckler, for *Archives of American Art* (Washington, D.C.), 21 December 1965 (transcript, unpublished); "Carnal Clocks" in *Art Now: New York,* May 1969; "A Collage Comment by Robert Rauschenberg in His Latest Suite of Prints" in *Studio International* (London), December 1969; "Robert Rauschenberg Talks to Maxime de la Falaise McKendry" in *Interview* (New York), May 1976; film—*Canoe,* New York 1966.

On RAUSCHENBERG: books—*Rauschenberg,* exhibition catalogue, with an essay by Gillo Dorfles, Milan 1961; *Rauschenberg,* exhibition catalogue, with essays by John Cage, Lawrence Alloway, and others, Paris 1963; *Robert Rauschenberg: Paintings, Drawings and Combines 1949–1964,* exhibition catalogue, with essays by Henry Geldzahler, John Cage, Max Kozloff, London 1964; *4 Germinal Painters, United States of America: 32nd International Biennial Exhibition of Art,* exhibition catalogue, with an essay by Alan R. Soloman, New York, 1964; *Robert Rauschenberg: Paintings 1953–1964,* exhibition catalogue, with an introduction by Dean Swanson, Minneapolis 1965; *Robert Rauschenberg,* exhibition catalogue, by Andrew Forge, Amsterdam 1968; *Robert*

Rauschenberg by Andrew Forge, New York 1969; *Rauschenberg: Black Market* by Jürgen Wissman, Stuttgart 1970; *Rauschenberg at Graphic Studio,* exhibition catalogue, with an introductory by Willard McCracken, and a foreword by Donald Saff, Tampa, Florida 1974; *The Bride and the Bachelors: 5 Masters of the Avant Garde* by Calvin Tomkins, New York 1974; *Rauschenberg's Pages and Fuses,* exhibition catalogue, with an introduction by Joseph E. Young, Los Angeles 1974; *Robert Rauschenberg,* exhibition catalogue, with essays by Guido Perocco, Daniel Abadie, David Bourdon, Venice 1975; *Robert Rauschenberg,* exhibition catalogue, with essays by Paola Serra Zanetti, Daniel Abadie, David Bourdon, Ferrara, Italy 1976; *Robert Rauschenberg* by Gotz Adriana, Munich 1979; *Off the Wall* by Calvin Tomkins, New York 1980; *Photography and Art 1946–1986* by Andy Grundberg and Kathleen Gauss, Los Angeles 1987.

Rauschenberg is with Jasper Johns the most influential of the artists who reacted against the high seriousness and solemn introspection and spirituality of Abstract Expressionism and the critical reverence accorded to it, and in the process raised some fundamental questions about art and its relation to life. In comparison to Johns, Rauschenberg's work is much more varied, and he has shown a constant zest for exploration which sharply distinguishes him from the narrow formula or recipe type of modern artist. In fact he has pioneered or anticipated many of the subsequent movements in American art, and he has also been a truly eclectic artist in his use of different techniques, so that the extraordinary variety of his work makes it a microcosm of the artistic developments of the last two decades.

John Cage has quoted as Rauschenberg's central "message" his now famous statement that "Painting relates to both art and life. Neither can be made—I try to act in the gap between the two." It was in fact Cage's example that caused Rauschenberg to formulate that remark, for Cage had already been breaking down the distinction between art and life with his random noises and chance events, so that instead of offering artistically structured and ordered experiences he was trying to "unfocus" the spectator's mind and so to make him more open, more aware of himself and his environment. For Cage's off-beat, Zen-oriented mind had led him right away from the Western tradition of art as personal expression to a belief in the complete depersonalization of creativity by chance procedures like throwing dice—thus proposing the revolutionary overthrow of the whole basic assumption of Western art since the Renaissance, that the artist by individual self-expression creates order and communicates feelings and emotions.

Similarly Rauschenberg started attacking the inflation of the artistic ego that had been an integral part of Abstract Expressionism by saying that being an artist was no different spiritually from being a cargo humper, a file clerk, or anything else. And if his famous erased De Kooning drawing was at least in part an act of homage, he was certainly attacking the idea of highly subjective action painting when he made two Abstract Expressionist pictures which reproduce each other identically in every splash and dribble. Having the same sort of quirky, off-beat, mind as Cage, a mind which works in angular ways full of ricochets and inventions, Rauschenberg studied under the rigorous Albers to give himself discipline. And among the works which resulted were his own explorations of minimalism in all-white and all-black paintings. All sorts of interpretations have been advanced for these, but it is clear from Rauschenberg's own statements that these are a far cry from Malevich's suprematist *White on White,* but a continuation of his own dialogue between art and life by letting life and the environment enter directly into art: "I always thought of the white paintings as being not passive but very—well, hypersensitive, so that one could look at them and almost see how many people were in the room by the shadows cast, or what time of day it was."

The comparison is therefore rather with the monochromatic paintings that Yves Klein had begun painting two years earlier, and both artists moved on in the direction of actuality, towards methods and attitudes that incorporate the outside world within the work of

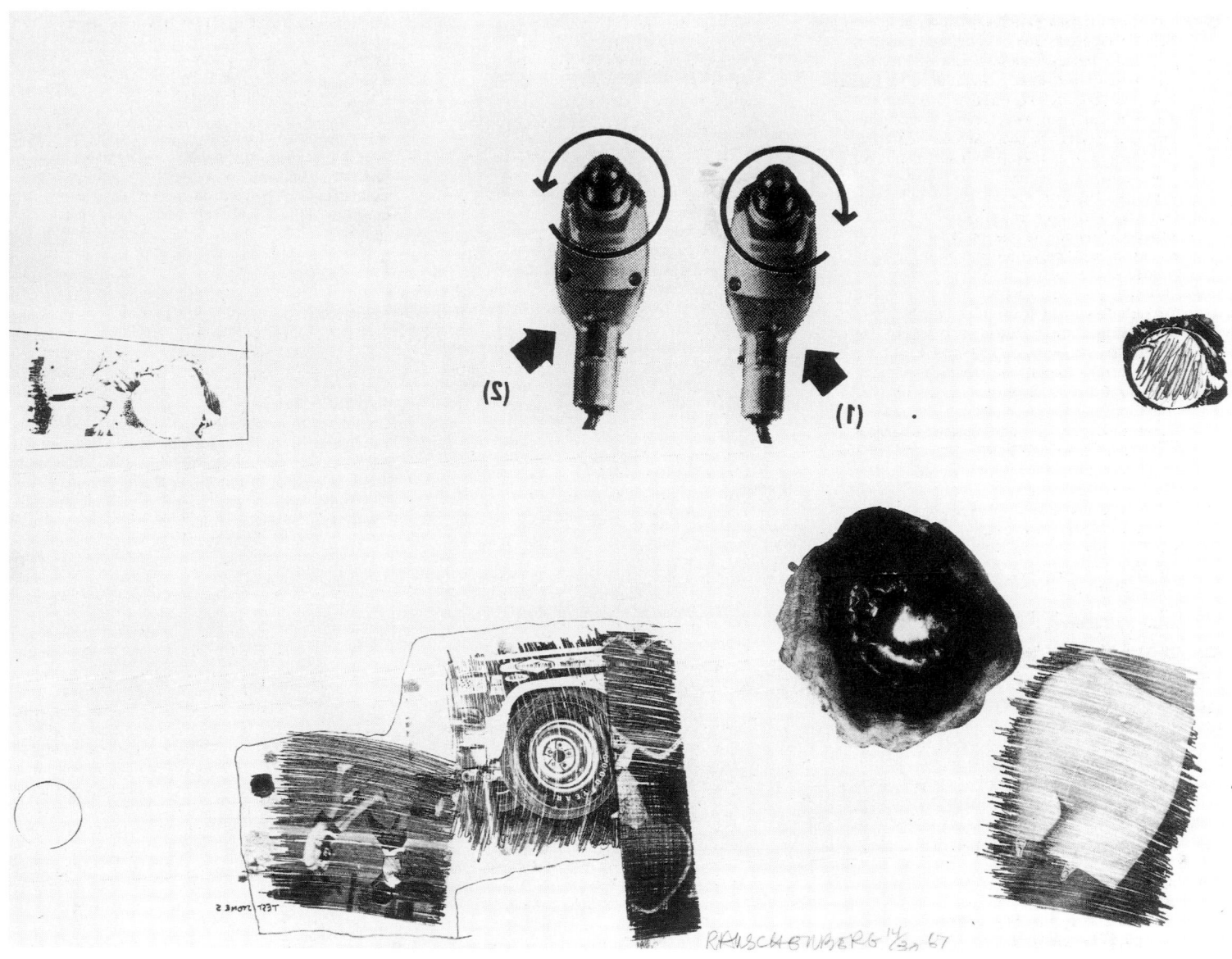

Robert Rauschenberg: *Test Stone 5,* 1967

art. Using the free brushwork of Abstract Expressionist painting, Rauschenberg began to load his canvases with rags and tatters of cloth and other collage elements of discarded junk. He incorporated ladders or chairs into the painting, and broke down the distinctions between painting and sculpture, so that many of his "combines" are free-standing works which can include any junk material, from Coca-Cola bottles and old radios to stuffed birds or a stuffed goat wearing an automobile tyre, and even a full-sized made-up bed. John Cage has stressed that the essential point of these "combines" is their multiplicity, their lack of any unitary subject. Like the work of Duchamp they do abound in puns, parallels and hidden meanings, but there is no unitary meaning, only a flux of images in which the dialogue between art and everyday reality is kept open and unresolved. In his "combines" Rauschenberg is the complete city artist, collaborating with his environment with that open receptive attitude advocated by Cage.

Rauschenberg was thus helping to open up the tracts of popular and junk imagery that were to become the basis of Pop art. But such assemblages also provided the jumping-off point for environmental art and for the happening, both of which Rauschenberg was himself exploring. The theatre pieces which have been as important in his work as his visual art grew out of his close association with Cage and with the innovative choreographer Merce Cunningham, with whose Dance Company Rauschenber has had a long association not only as a designer but as a dancer too. And just as the "combines" include collages of all sorts of found and ready-made objects, so Rauschen-

berg's Theatre Pieces and Happenings are essentially collages, though instead of being static they include the added dimensions of time and event, allowing things to happen, including anything which happens to take place by chance. Again there is no meaning in the usual sense, but simply a bringing together of disparate images, as in his earlier paintings and combines, and in his later lithographs and silk screens.

By the late 1950's Rauschenberg had begun to think of his work as a kind of reporting, and action photographs from magazines and newspapers were cropping up more and more frequently in his works. He then found that newsprint, when wetted with lighter fluid and then rubbed, transfers a grey ghost of itself to paper, and this opened his work to a whole stream of image-quotation from newspapers and magazines. He used this technique in his set of illustrations to Dante's *Inferno,* Dante being a character in a towel from *Sports Illustrated,* while Virgil appears alternately as Adlai Stevenson and as a baseball umpire. The resulting combination of diverse images was aptly described by Cage as "like many television sets working simultaneously, all tuned differently." Rauschenberg then adopted Andy Warhol's technique of making silk-screens of photographs and stencilling them on to the surfaces of silk-screen paintings whose trapped images in electronic colours have a brilliantly heightened documentary flavour. Similarly his lithographs, such as the two series devoted to the American space programme "Booster" (1967) and the "Stoned Moon" series (1970) are a rich, complicated mix of diverse images.

It was logical that Rauschenberg should one day

incorporate not merely the thrown-away junk of industrial society in his works, but its active technology too, as he began to do when he incorporated an electric clock, a blinking light, or three working radiosets into his combines. One of his long-standing collaborations has been with the laser-scientist Billy Kluver, with whom in 1966 he started the non-profit foundation EAT (Experiments in Art and Technology), whose intention was "to catalyze the inevitable active involvement of industry, technology and the arts." Among Rauschenberg's own forays into art works making use of technology are the series of "Revolvers," round paintings using characteristic assemblages of disparate images, but on plexiglass discs which can be driven by motors, so that they revolve and prevent any definite conclusions about the "right way" of viewing the works. "Soundings" (1968) is an environment work using the same basic idea as the early white paintings which had invoked the space of nothingness in which the disparate objects of the surroundings could be reflected and seen afresh. Basically it is a plexiglass wall hanging in the centre of a room to make a sort of hall of mirrors, with microphones picking up the spectator's talk and triggering the projection of changing images, including the viewers themselves, onto the mirror sufaces.

Despite his seeming multiplicity, therefore, Rauschenberg's activities have behind them a consistent set of developing ideas, ideas very similar to those of John Cage. Schoenberg said of Cage that he was "not a composer but an inventor—of genius," and that phrase could easily be adapted to fit Rauschenberg. But whereas very few composers indeed have been prepared to accept Cage's extreme position in abandoning the personal expression of composed music in favour of listening to the random noises of life, the world of the visual arts, already conditioned by Duchamp to accept that anything may be selected and displayed as art, has been more ready to be influenced along such lines. Recent American art has offered two extreme courses, both of them reductive—the insistence that there is no boundary between art and life found in Rauschenberg and Cage, or the Hard Edge insistence on art deriving from art alone, with the exaltation of the painting as object which reaches its *reductio ad absurdum* in the work of Frank Stella. But whatever its ultimate value may prove to be, Rauschenberg's work, with its constant questioning of the nature of art itself and the nature of reality, has challenged most artistic concepts, so that Robert Rosenblum can justly say of him: "Every artist after 1960 who challenged the restrictions of painting and sculpture and believed that all of life was open to art is indebted to Rauschenberg—forever."

—Konstantin Bazarov

RAYNAUD, Jean-Pierre.

French. Born in Colombes, 20 April 1939. Studied at Versailles Horticultural School, France, 1955-57; mainly self-taught in art, 1962. Served in the French Army, 1959-61. Worked at various jobs, including architectural assistant and floral decorator, Paris, 1961-66. Independent artist, since 1962: first exhibited art works, Paris, 1964; opened his house in Colombes to the public, 1974; first stained glass commission, Noirlac, 1976; garden-commission, Grenoble, 1977. Address: 25 rue des Robichons, 78000 La Celle-St.-Cloud, France.

Individual Exhibitions:

1965	Galerie Jean Larcade, Paris
1966	*Jean-Pierre Raynaud et la Conscience de Soi*, Galerie Mathias Fels, Paris
1967	Galleria Apollinaire, Milan
1968	Stedelijk Museum, Amsterdam
	Galerie Mathias Fels, Paris
	Moderna Museet, Stockholm
	Württembergischer Kunstverein, Stuttgart
1969	Centre National d'Art Contemporain, Paris
	Galerie Alexandre Iolas, Paris
1970	Palais des Beaux-Arts, Brussels
	Galerie Alexandre Iolas, Paris
	Alexandre Iolas Gallery, New York
1971	Israel Museum, Jerusalem
	Galleria LP220, Turin
	Galerie Smith, Brussels
	Hyde Park, London
	Open-Air Exhibition, Hannover
1972	Salone Annunciata, Milan
	Musée des Arts Décoratifs, Paris
	Galerie D, Brussels
1973	Galerie Alexandre Iolas, Paris
1974	Galerie D, Brussels
	Galerie Alexandre Iolas, Brussels
1975	Galerie Alexandre Iolas, Paris
	Palais des Beaux-Arts, Brussels
1978	Musée des Beaux-Arts, Ghent
1979	Centre Georges Pompidou, Paris
1981	Galerie Jean Fournier, Paris
	Hara Museum of Contemporary Art, Tokyo
1982	Galerie L'Hermitte, Coutances, France
1983	Grand Palais, Paris
1984	Newport Harbor Art Museum, Newport Beach, California
	Galerie Daniel Varenne, Zurich
1985	ARC/Musee d'Art Moderne de la Ville, Paris
	Seibu Museum, Tokyo

	Galerie Gilbert Brownstone, Paris
	Fondation Cartier, Jouy-en-Josas, France
	Daniel Varenne Gallery, Chicago
1986	Carpenter and Hochman Gallery, New York

Selected Group Exhibitions:

1964	*Salon de la Jeune Sculpture*, Paris
1965	*4th Biennale de Paris*, Musée d'Art Moderne de la Ville, Paris
1966	*Salon de Comparaisons*, Paris
1967	*Expo '67*, Montreal
	Superlund, Lunds Konsthall, Lund, Sweden
	Bienal, Sao Paulo
1972	*Douze Ans d'Art Contemporain en France*, Grand Palais, Paris
	Amsterdam-Paris-Dusseldorf, Guggenheim Museum, New York
1977	*Paris-New York*, Centre Georges Pompidou, Paris
1981	*Opening Exhibition*, Museum of Modern Art, Toyama, Japan

Collections:

Centre Georges Pompidou, Paris; Musée Cantini, Marseilles; Stedelijk Museum, Amsterdam; Musée des Beaux-Arts, Ghent; Kaiser Wilhelm Museum, Krefeld, West Germany; Israel Museum, Jerusalem; Hara Museum of Contemporary Art, Tokyo; Rhode Island Museum of Art, Providence; de Menil Foundation, Houston; Museum of Modern Art, New York.

Publications:

On RAYNAUD: books—*Jean-Pierre Raynaud et la Conscience de Soi*, exhibition catalogue, with text by Pierre Restany, Paris 1966; *Superlund*, exhibition catalogue, with text by Pierre Restany and others, Lund, Sweden 1967; *Douze Ans d'Art Contemporain en France*, exhibition catalogue, with texts by F. Mathey, J. Clair, D. Cordier and others, Paris 1972; *Amsterdam-Paris-Dusseldorf*, exhibition catalogue, with text by Blaise Gautier, New York 1972; *Jean-Pierre Raynaud* by Emmy de Martelacre, Paris 1975; *Abbaye Cistercienne, Noirlac: Vitraux de Jean-Pierre Raynaud*, Paris 1977; *Jean-Pierre Raynaud*, exhibition catalogue, New York 1986.

*

Jean-Pierre Raynaud started exhibiting his sculptures and objects at the Galerie Creuze (*Salon de la jeune sculpture*) in 1964, but his first effective show, one in which he was able to spread himself and be properly seen, did not occur until a year later when he had his big one-man exhibition at the Galerie Jean Lacarde for which Alain Jouffroy wrote his catalogue *Une Laboratoire Mental*.

The Raynaud toilet with its lifted seat in white!

No need for him, like Duchamp, to up-end the porcelain and scribble a fake signature across its edge in thick black paint.

In fact it is the shock impact of Rayaud's creations that is so impressive. To make "matter-of-fact" all the fetishes of horror, whether in the home, in the prison or in the hospital, is alarming enough in its mental magnetism, but when the *facts*, the bits and pieces, the random introduction of photographs, the elements of everyday drama (like the fire buckets) are combined in a sterile colour scheme of red, white and occasional black (almost the official anarchist colours!), the eye becomes literally *brain-washed*. Thought becomes cerebral instead of visual. His "psycho-objects" really are psycho-objects. Chains, and numbers, and boxes, and doors and bolts stand alone in an hysterical isolation, or are brought together in *assemblages* which are none the less telling because the uncompanioned monologue has been replaced by a script for more than one voice.

The clean terror of Raynaud's fixtures and fittings is one of the most eccentrically arresting records of the contemporary situation.

"Psycho-Objet Cailloux A," with its modern instrument of multi-pronged torture, hanging like a lavatory brush above the pile of pebbles on the shelf, is

supported by the grim poster with message at the top reading

Premieres: Portes 14, 15, 16
Secondes: Portes 12, 13

above the photo of a white-coated stooping man, arms akimbo, his eyes censored by a white rectangle, alone in front of the warehouse doors with only a fire hydrant (figure 3 painted on it in white) to keep him company. This is a Kafka vignette made visual.

—Sheldon Williams

RAYSSE, Martial.

French. Born in Golfe-Juan, 12 February 1936. Independent artist, in Paris, subsequently in Beaulieu-sur-Mer, France; first theatre designs, 1966, first films, 1967. Recipient: David Bright Award, *Biennale*, Venice, 1969. Address: c/o Galerie Iolas, 8 rue Perronet, 75007 Paris, France.

Individual Exhibitions:

1957	Galerie Longchamp, Nice
1959	Galerie d'Egmont, Brussels
1961	Galleria Schwarz, Milan (with Arman)
1962	Galerie Alfred Schmela, Dusseldorf
	Alexander Iolas Gallery, New York
1963	*Mirrors and Portraits*, Dwan Gallery, Los Angeles
	M. H. de Young Memorial Museum, San Francisco
	Galleria del Leone, Venice
1964	Galerie Alexandre Iolas, Paris
	Maitre et Esclave de l'Imagination, Stedelijk Museum, Amsterdam
	Dwan Gallery, Los Angeles
1965	*L'Obsession Solitaire*, Galerie Alexandre Iolas, Paris
1966	Alexander Iolas Gallery, New York
1967	Galleria Alexandre Iolas, Milan
	Palais de Beaux-Arts, Brussels
	Dwan Gallery, Los Angeles
	Galerie Der Spiegel, Cologne
	Svensk-Franska Konstgalleriet, Stockholm
	Galerie Alexandre Iolas, Paris
1968	Museum of Contemporary Art, Chicago
1969	Galerie Alexandre Iolas, Paris
	Galerie Der Spiegel, Cologne
	Galerie Alexandre Iolas, Geneva
	Narodini Galerie, Prague
1970	Alexander Iolas Gallery, New York
	Moderner Kunstmuseum, Munich
	Galleria Alexandre Iolas, Milan
1972	25 rue du Dragon, Paris
1975	Galerie Benador, Geneva
	Galeria Der Spiegel, Cologne
1976	Galerie Karl Flinker, Paris
1977	Galerie Eva de Buren, Stockholm
	Centre d'Art, Flaine, France
1978	Galerie Karl Flinker, Paris
1980	Galerie Claude Givaudan, Geneva
	Fondation Veranneman, Kruishoutem, Belgium
1981	*Martial Raysse 1970–1980*, Centre Georges Pompidou, Paris
	Stedelijk Museum, Amsterdam

Selected Group Exhibitions:

1961	*The Art of Assemblage*, Museum of Modern Art, New York
1964	*40 Ans de Collage*, Musée d'Art Moderne, Paris (travelled to Musée d'Art et d'Histoire, St. Etienne, France)
1969	*Biennale*, Venice (and 1976)
1970	*Pop Art, Nouveau Réalisme, Nouvelle Figuration*, Casino Municipal, Knokke, Belgium
1973	*L'Art du 20eme Siècle*, Musée Rath, Geneva

1977   *Paris-New York*, Centre Georges Pompidou, Paris
1979   *Biennale of Sydney*, Art Gallery of New South Wales, Sydney
1980   *Le Reel en Question*, Maison des Arts, Montbeliard, France (travelled to Galerie Athanor, Geneva)

Collections:

Musée de la Ville, Paris; Musée National d'Art Moderne, Paris; Neue Galerie/Sammlung Ludwig, Aachen, West Germany; Staatsgalerie, Stuttgart; Kaiser-Wilhelm-Museum, Krefeld, West Germany; Stedelijk Museum, Amsterdam; Stedelijk Van Abbemuseum, Eindhoven, Netherlands; Louisiana Museum, Humlebaek, Denmark.

Publications:

By RAYSSE: book—*I Had a Thousand Things to Put in Order*, exhibition catalogue, New York 1966; *J'Ai Mille Choses à Classer*, Palermo 1966; articles—"Geometri Variable" in *Paris Review*, February 1967; "La Beauté c'est le Mauvais Gout" in *Jeune Afrique* (Paris), February 1968; films—*Jesuscola*, 1967; *Portrait Electro Machin Chose*, 1967; *Homero Presto*, 1968; *Camembert Martial Extra-Doux*, 1969; *Le Grand Depart*, with Lucienne Hamon, Anne Wiazemsky and Sterling Hayden, 1970; *Pig Music*, 1971; *L'Hotel des Folles Fatmas*, 1976; *Intra Muros*, 1977-80; *La Petite Danse*, 1978-80.

On RAYSSE: books—*Martial Raysse: Mirrors and Portraits*, exhibition catalogue, with text by John Ashbery, Los Angeles 1963; *Martial Raysse: Maitre et Esclave de l'Imagination*, exhibition catalogue, with texts by Otto Hahn and Pierre Restany, Amsterdam 1964; *Martial Raysse ou l'Obsession Solaire*, exhibition catalogue, with text by Otto Hahn, Paris 1965; *Martial Raysse*, exhibition catalogue, with text by Otto Hahn, Los Angeles 1967; *Martial Raysse*, exhibition catalogue, with text by Pierre Restany, Brussels 1967; *Minimal Art: A Critical Anthology*, edited by Gregory Battcock, New York 1968, London 1969; *Martial Raysse*, exhibition catalogue, edited by Ad Petersen, Amsterdam 1981; *Martial Raysse 1970-1980*, exhibition catalogue, with texts by Pontus Hulten, Jean-Yves Mock, Gilbert Lascault and others, Paris 1981.

An early painting of a detergent packet by Martial Raysse sums up his attitude to the world of art in a way that has nothing to do with the kitchen sink or socialist realism. It would be better to remember that he was born in Golfe-Juan than to think about washing-up. Better still, think about both at the same time.

Raysse has a weird kind of bruderschaft with the American Tom Wesselmann. However different the end-product of their work, both are, albeit with dissimilar emphases, concerned with and absorbed in the real (artificial!) portrait of contemporary life. Wesselmann's great American nudes bask in air-conditioned apartments, and their dish-washer machines need detergents too. A chemical cleanliness pervades their world with just the same pertinacity as the Prisunic svelte make-up that displaces dirt and mops up perspiration for the girls of Martial Raysse. If Wesselmann's models look more at ease and better organized than the chic Raysse clotheshorses, it is only because their niche in the American Way of Life is that much more cosily secure. One notices that they have a tendency to stay indoors (a drive or a trip to the beach is obviously a carefully planned break in continuity), whereas the Raysse beauties, whether demonstrating luminous lipstick or plundered from Ingres or Cranach, are definitely on parade. No subdued table lamps for them; they have to face the uncertain illumination of Neon or the hard glare of Cote d'Azur sunshine.

Wesselmann stays with the time and place of a modern dream America. His fancy and magpie-collecting culpability take Raysse far and wide even if the raw strip lighting, the chemical colours and the band-box perfection of his figures do not deviate. In *Paradise Lost*, Nureyev and Fonteyn must contend with Raysse sets that make the serpent light up! For most of the Covent Garden audience the Garden of Eden drama was a long time ago; even Milton has

celebrated a few centenaries; but for Raysse the story belongs to Now and should be dressed accordingly.

He is a creator of the artificialdom of contemporary times, and he gives to a manmade fabricated existence absolute veracity. Neon is true, and so are aniline dyes. The best buys from the supermarket look well on the right girl.

Because he is adept, inventive and has confident modish taste, Raysse belongs comfortably in the arena of contemporary art. No vieux-jeux! He does not mirror modern times: he italicises them. His control of assemblages, collages, distortions, situations and technical gimmickry hardly falters.

—Sheldon Williams

REBEYROLLE, Paul.
French. Born in Eymoutiers, Haute-Vienne, 3 November 1926. Educated in Limoges until 1944; mainly self-taught in art from 1944, but attended Académie de la Grande Chaumière, Paris 1944-45; influenced by work of Soutine, Léger, Chagall and Picasso. Independent painter, Paris, since 1945. Committee Member, *Salon du Mai*, Paris, 1957. Member, French Communist Party, 1950-56. Recipient: Prix de la Jeune Peinture, Paris, 1950; Prix Feneon, Paris, 1951; Painting Prize, *Biennale*, Paris, 1959; First Prize (French section), *John Moores Exhibition*, Liverpool, 1959; Grand Prix de la Ville de Paris, 1982. Agent: Galerie Maeght Lelong, 13 rue de Teheran, 75008 Paris. Address: 2 Passage Dantzig, 75015 Paris, France.

Individual Exhibitions:

1951   Galerie Drouant-David, Paris
1954   *Recent Paintings*, Marlborough Fine Art, London
1956   Maison de la Pensée Francaise, Paris
1958   Galerie Saint-Germain, paris
1959   Galerie Creuzevalt, Paris
1961   *Recent Paintings*, Marlborough Fine Art, London
        Galerie André Schoeller, Paris
1962   Janvier Nitta Gallery, Tokyo
        Galerie André Schoeller, Paris
1964   Marlborough-Gerson Gallery, New York
        Galerie André Schoeller, Paris
1966   Galerie André Schoeller, Paris (with Fautrier and Messagier)
1967   Galerie Maeght, Paris
1969   Galerie Maeght, Paris
1970   Galerie Maeght, Paris
1971   *Grands Formats*, Fondation Maeght, St. Paul-de-Vence, France
1972   Studio Marconi, Milan
1973   *Prisonniers*, Galerie Maeght, Paris
1974   Galerie Maeght, Zurich
1976   Galerie Maeght, Paris
        Galerie Larcos, Paris
1979   Galerie Maeght, Paris
        Grand Palais, Paris
1982   Hospice Saint-Louis, Avignon, France
        Galerie Maeght, at *FIAC 82*, Grand Palais, Paris
        Galerie Editart, Geneva
        Galerie Art Contemporain, Limoges, France
        Galerie Maeght, Zurich

Selected Group Exhibitions:

1945   *Grands Formats*, Galerei du Bac, Paris
1948   *Salon des Jeunes*, Paris (and regularly to 1957)
1952   *5 Young French Realists*, Arcade Gallery, London
1957   *Bienal*, Sao Paulo
1962   *Grands et Jeunes d'Aujourd'hui*, Grand Palais, Paris
1969   *Festival d'Avignon*, France
1970   *L'Art dans la Ville*, Maison de la Culture, Arceuil, France
1978   *Kunstmesse*, Basle

Collections:

Musée d'Art Moderne de la Ville, Paris; Fondation Maeght, St. Paul-de-Vence, France.

Publications:

By REBEYROLLE: books illustrated—*Eloge du Socialisme* by Samir Amin, Paris 1975; *Conte Rouge pour Paloma* by André Velten and Serge Sartreau, Paris 1976.

On REBEYROLLE: books—*Rebeyrolle: Recent Paintings*, exhibition catalogue, with text by Neville Wallis, London 1954; *Rebeyrolle*, exhibition catalogue, with text by Georges Besson, Paris 1956; *Recent Paintings by Rebeyrolle*, exhibition catalogue, with text by Herbert Read, London 1961; *Rebeyrolle* by Pierre Descargues, Paris 1970; *Rebeyrolle: Grands Formats*, exhibition catalogue, with text by Jean-Louis Prat, St. Paul-de-Vence, France 1971; *Paul Rebeyrolle: Prisonniers*, exhibition catalogue, with text by Ricardo Porro and Michel Foucault, Paris 1973; *Paul Rebeyrolle*, exhibition catalogue, with text by Peter F. Althaus, Zurich 1974; *Paul Rebeyrolle: Natures Mortes et Pouvoir*, exhibition catalogue, with text by Carlos Franqui, Paris 1976; *Rebeyrolle: Peintures 1968-1978*, exhibition catalogue, with texts by Michel Tronche, Carlos Franqui, and others, Paris 1979; *Rebeyrolle: Les évasions manquées*, exhibition catalogue with preface by Jacques Dupin, Zurich 1982.

When the Galeria Maeght opened in the Calle Moncada in Barcelona in 1974, works by 27 International artists were chosen to celebrate the event. The list started with ADAMI, BAZAINE, BRAQUE, BURY, CALDER, and CHAGALL. Paul Rebeyrolle, low on the catalogue because the artists were arranged in alphabetical order, came near the end with a grand triptych called "De la grande baleine" (1973), but one can see by the company he keeps that he is held in high esteem. When an important sale was held in London in aid of Vietnam war prisoners and wounded, John Berger without hesitation picked out Rebeyrolle's painting of a frog as the best—and most important—work on show.

As an artist Rebeyrolle is a creator of frequent changes. In fact, as a contradiction in terms, the one constant in all his work is change. Figuration flits in and out of his painting. He is an artist of conscience (in "Coexistences," a black dragon's jaws close on a red boot). Mixed media is engulfed in paint, slats of wood that look as if they were fugitives from Tapies are only casually interrelated by some random old chickenwire, while the tachiste pigment swirls round about and the early swatches of brown at the base of a canvas 4m. wide show that the imprints of cat's paws were made while the thick paint was still wet.

Rebeyrolle has just enough individuality to prevent him ever becoming submerged in any art movement. The charisma of his works is magnetic, a personal magic that sets him aside as one of the lone wolves of contemporary painting.

—Sheldon Williams

REINHARDT, Ad(olph Dietrich Friedrich).
American. Born in Buffalo, New York, 24 December 1913. Studied art history at Columbia University, New York, under Meyer Schapiro, 1931-35 and 1936-37; also studied at the National Academy of Design, under Carl Holty and Francis Criss, 1936-37, and at New York University Institute of Fine Arts, under Alfred Salmony and Guido Schoenberger, 1946-50. Served as photographer in the United States Navy, 1944-45. Painter: lived and worked in New York; worked in the Easel Division, Works Progress Administration, Federal Art Project, 1936-39; Member, American Abstract Artists Group, 1937-47; artist-reporter for *P.M.*, New York, 1944 and 1946-47; Editor, with Robert Motherwell,

only issue of *Modern Artists in America*, New York, 1952. Assistant Professor, Brooklyn College, New York, 1947-67. Lecturer, California School of Fine Arts, San Francisco, 1950, University of Wyoming, Laramie, 1951, Yale University, New Haven, Connecticut, 1952-53, and Hunter College, New York, 1954-67. *Died* (in New York) *30 August 1967*.

Individual Exhibitions:

1943	Columbia University, New York
1944	Artists Gallery, New York
1945	Mortimer Brandt Gallery, New York
1946	Brooklyn Museum School, New York
	Betty Parsons Gallery, New York
1952	Betty Parsons Gallery, New York
1953	Betty Parsons Gallery, New York
1956	Betty Parsons Gallery, New York
1957	Syracuse University, New York
1959	Betty Parsons Gallery, New York
1960	Galerie Iris Clert, Paris
	Betty Parsons Gallery, New York
1961	Städtisches Museum, Leverkusen, West Germany (with Francesco Lo Savio and Jef Verheven)
1963	Galerie Iris Clert, Paris
	Dwan Gallery, Los Angeles
1964	Institute of Contemporary Arts, London
1965	Graham Gallery, New York
	Betty Parsons Gallery, New York
1966	*Painting*, Jewish Museum, New York
1970	*25 Years of Abstract Painting*, Marlborough Gallery, New York
1972	Städtisches Kunsthalle, Dusseldorf (toured Europe, 1972-73)
1973	Stable Gallery, New York
	Stedelijk van Abbemuseum, Eindhoven, Netherlands
1974	Marlborough Gallery, New York
	Marlborough Gallery, Zurich
1980	Guggenheim Museum, New York

Selected Group Exhibitions:

1939	*World's Fair*, New York
1951	*Abstract Painting and Sculpture in America*, Museum of Modern Art, New York
1955	*The New Decade*, Whitney Museum, New York
1958	*World's Fair*, Brussels
1961	*Abstract Expressionists and Imagists*, Guggenheim Museum, New York
1963	*Americans, 1963*, Museum of Modern Art, New York
1964	*Painting and Sculpture of a Decade 1954-1964*, Tate Gallery, London
1966	*2 Decades of American Painting*, National Museum of Modern Art, Tokyo

Collections:

Whitney Museum, New York; Museum of Modern Art, New York; Metropolitan Museum of Art, New York; Albright-Knox Art Gallery, Buffalo, New York; Carnegie Institute, Pittsburgh; Yale University, New Haven, Connecticut; Los Angeles County Museum of Art; Tate Gallery, London; Städtisches Museum, Leverkusen, West Germany; Nasjional Galleriet, Oslo.

Publications:

By REINHARDT: articles—"Abstract Art Turns Over" in the *New Republic* (New York), May 1940; "How to Look," series, in *PM* (New York), 1944-46; "Stuart Davis" in *New Masses* (New York), November 1945; "Political Cartoon" in *Critique* (New York), October 1946; texts in *Ad Reinhardt*, exhibition catalogue, New York 1946; "Letter to L. Redmond" in *Artnews* (New York), Summer 1950; "Our Favorites" in *Artnews* (New York), March 1952; "Artist in Search of an Academy" in *College Art Journal* (New York), Spring 1953; "Part II Who are the Artists?" in *College Art Journal* (New York), Summer 1954; "Letter" in *Artnews* (New York), November 1956; "12 Rules for a New Academy" in *Artnews* (New York), May 1957; "25 Lines of Words on Art" in *It Is* (New York), Spring 1958; "Is Today's Artist With or

Against the Past?" in *Artnews* (New York), June 1958; "Panel: All-Over Painting," with Elaine de Kooning and Martin James, in *It Is* (New York), Autumn 1958; "Letter" in *Artnews* (New York), January 1959; "Letter" in *Artnews* (New York), April 1959; "Discussion: Is There a New Academy?" in *Artnews* (New York), June 1959; "7 Quotes" in *It Is* (New York), Autumn 1959; "Timeless in Asia" in *Artnews* (New York), January 1960; "Documents of Modern Art" in *Pax* (New York), no. 13, 1960; "Letter" in *Artnews* (New York), April 1961; "How to Look at Modern Art in America" in *Artnews* (New York), Summer 1961; "Angkor and Art" in *Artnews* (New York), December 1961; "3 Texts 1955-1961" in *Pax*, (New York), no. 18, 1962; "Interview with Irving Sandler" in the *New York Post*, August 1962; "What Is Ugly?" in *ICA Bulletin* (London), August/September 1964; "Art as Art" in *Art International* (Zurich), December 1962; "Letter" in *Dissent* (New York), Spring 1963; "Autocritique du Reinhardt" in *Iris-Time* (Paris), June 1963; "The Next Revolution in Art: Art-as-Art Dogma Part II" in *Artnews* (New York), February 1964; "Reinhardt Paints a Picture" in *Artnews* (New York), March 1965; "The Artists Say . . . Ad Reinhardt: 30 Art Planks" in *Art Voices* (New York), Spring 1965; "Art in Art Is Art as Art" in *Lugano Review*, no. 5-6, 1966, and in *Sign, Image, Symbol* by Gregory Kepes, New York 1966; "Art vs. History: The Shape of Time by George Kubler" in *Artnews* (New York), January 1966; "Ad Reinhardt: 3 Statements" in *Artforum* (New York), March 1966; interview with Bruce Glaser in *Art International* (Lugano, Switzerland), December 1966.

On REINHARDT: books—*Ad Reinhardt: Paintings*, exhibition catalogue, by Lucy Lippard and Sam Hunter, New York 1966; *Ad Reinhardt: Black Paintings 1951-1967*, exhibition catalogue, New York 1970; *Ad Reinhardt: 25 Years of Abstract Painting*, exhibition catalogue, New York 1970; *Ad Reinhardt*, exhibition catalogue, Dusseldorf 1972; *Ad Reinhardt*, exhibition catalogue, by D. McConathy, Zurich 1974; *Ad Reinhardt*, exhibition catalogue, by Margit Rowell, New York 1980; *Ad Reinhardt* by Lucy Lippard, New York 1981 (includes bibliography).

*   *   *

It is irresistible not to quote the phrase (used in another context and applied to insects) "the dark is light enough" when speaking of Ad Reinhardt's mature paintings. These last paintings represent one of the extremes of modernist purism. They repeat the same form—a cross-like structure—within a square painted so evenly and so dark, in colors so close in value, as to appear to be nothing more than black squares. They are *tours de force* of subtlety demanding careful and close scrutiny from the viewer in order to discover the beauty, even poetry, of the color shifts. Think of the visual adjustments one makes on entering a dark room or walking in a wood on a starless night.

Reinhardt's colleague and close friend, Mark Rothko, shared his great interest in "lightless" color, in darkness and blackness. The philosophical aim appears to be how far one can go toward the depiction of absence without entirely giving up presence. Such pursuits could be called typical of end-of-the-road modernism. The minimal again. In a way the effort is reflective of Gertrude Stein's re-definition of the rose only in terms of itself: where she wrote, "a rose is a rose is a rose," Reinhardt says, "a nearly black square is a nearly black square is a nearly black square."

Interestingly, Reinhardt did not just decide to reduce his means out of the blue. His work evolved from complex abstractions often of bright, even gay, color like visual jazz riffs. His precursors were the *de Stijl* painters—above all Mondrian. Reinhardt brought to their formal explorations a peculiarly American wit and crankiness. He was famous for his idiosyncratic attitude toward art and the practice of painting. And once he truly listened to himself it became impossible to separate the ideas from the painting. So the uncompromising journey into the dark.

—Ralph Pomeroy

RENOUF, Edda.

American. Born in Mexico City, 17 June 1943; emigrated to the United States, 1957; naturalized, 1978. Educated at Putney School, Vermont, 1957-1961; studied at Sarah Lawrence College, Bronxville, New York, 1961-65, B.A. 1965; Académie Julian, Paris, 1963-64; Art Students League, New York, 1967-68; Columbia School of the Arts, New York, 1968-71; M.F.A. 1971. Independent artist, since 1972. Lived in Paris, from 1971; taught in Paris for Sarah Lawrence College program, 1974; now lives and works in New York. Recipient: Printing Fellowship, National Endowment for the Arts, Washington, D.C., 1978. Agent: Blum Helman Gallery, 20 West 57th Street, New York, New York 10019. Address: 20 West 30th Street, New York, New York 10001, U.S.A.

Individual Exhibitions:

1972	Galerie Yvon Lambert, Paris
1973	Galleria Francoise Lambert, Milan
1974	Konrad Fischer Gallery, Dusseldorf
	Galerie Yvon Lambert, Paris
	Galerie MTL, Brussels
1975	Galerie Yvon Lambert, Paris
	Galleria Francoise Lambert, Milan
	Galleria Marilena Bonomo, Bari, Italy
1976	Julian Pretto and Co., New York
	Galleria Francoise Lambert, Milan
	Rolf Preisig Gallery, Basle
	Allessandro Ferranti Gallery, Rome
1977	Kathryn Markel Fine Arts, New York
	Weinberg Gallery, San Francisco
	Galerie MTL, Brussels
1978	Blum Helman Gallery, New York
	Wadsworth Atheneum, Hartford, Connecticut
	Young-Hoffman Gallery, Chicago
	Margo Leavin Gallery, Los Angeles
	Galerie Yvon Lambert, Paris
	Graeme Murray Gallery, Edinburgh
	Galleria Francoise Lambert, Milan
	Ugo Ferranti Gallery, Rome
1979	Blum Helman Gallery, New York
	Weinberg Gallery, San Francisco
	Konrad Fischer Gallery, Dusseldorf
1980	Blum Helman Gallery, New York
	Ronald Greenberg Gallery, St. Louis
	Galerie Yvon Lambert, Paris
	Margo Leavin Gallery, Los Angeles
	Thomas Segal Gallery, Boston
1981	Graeme Murray Gallery, Edinburgh
1982	Carol Taylor Gallery, Dallas
	Blum Helman Gallery, New York
1983	Galleria Francoise Lambert, Milan
1984	Galerie Yvon Lambert, Paris
1985	Blum Helman Gallery, New York
1986	Martina Hamilton Gallery, New York
1987	Liesbeth Lips Gallery, Amsterdam
	Blum Helman Gallery, New York

Selected Group Exhibitions:

1972	*Actualité d'un Bilan*, Galerie Yvon Lambert, Paris
1973	*Drawings*, Museum of Modern Art, Oxford
1973	*Biennale*, Paris
1974	*Geplante Malerei*, Kunsthalle, Münster, West Germany
1975	*International Print Exhibition*, at the *Jyvaskyla Arts Festival*, Alvar Aalto Museum, Jyvaskyla, Finland
1977	*Extraordinary Women*, Museum of Modern Art, New York
1978	*Contemporary Drawing/New York*, University of California at Santa Barbara
1979	*Whitney Biennial*, Whitney Museum, New York
1985	*Livres d'Artistes*, Centre Georges Pompidou, Paris
1987	*New York Scene*, Liesbeth Lips Gallery, Amsterdam

Collections:

Museum of Modern Art, New York; Whitney Museum, New York; Metropolitan Museum of Art, New York; Philadelphia

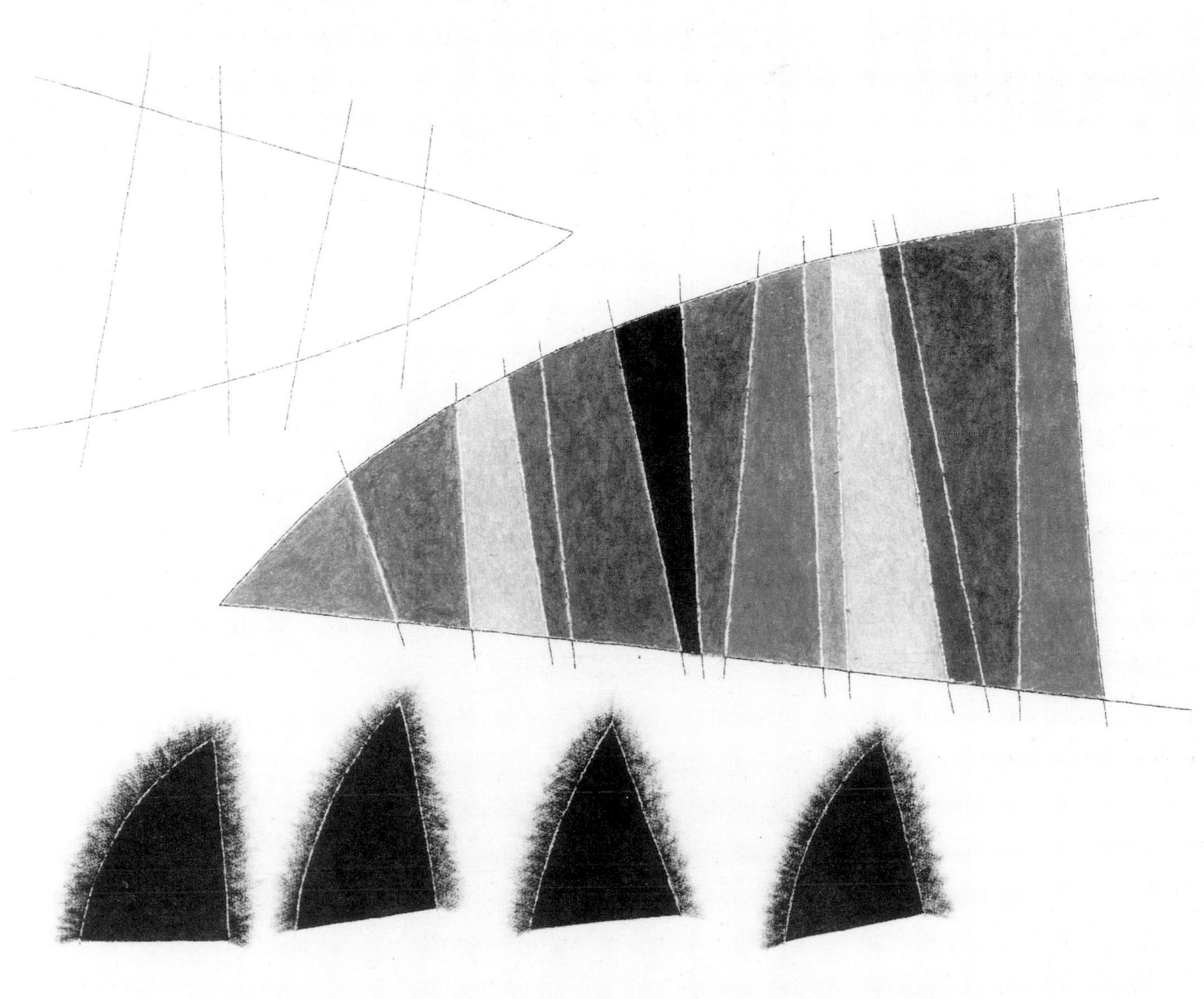

Edda Renouf: *New York Song No. 2*, 1985

Museum of Art; Art Institute of Chicago; Museum of Fine Arts, Dallas; Centre Georges Pompidou, Paris; Musée des Beaux-Arts, Grenoble, France; St. Louis Art Museum, Missouri; Australian National Gallery, Canberra.

Publications:

By RENOUF: books—*Lines*, Milan 1974; *Lines and Non-Lines*, New York 1977; *Echoes*, Edinburgh 1979; articles—"Entretiens avec Edda Renouf", with C. Beret, in *Art Press* (Paris), January 1973; "Edda Renouf," statement, in *Flash Art* (Milan), Aprile 1974.

On RENOUF: book—*Matrix 36: Edda Renouf,* exhibition brochure with text by Peter O. Marlow, Hartford, Connecticut 1978; articles—"Edda Renouf" in *Peinture Cahiers Theoriques* (Paris), January 1973; "Flash Art: France—Edda Renouf" in *Flash Art* (Milan), April 1974; "Edda Renouf" by France Morrin in *Parachute* (Montreal), Winter 1977/78; "Intimate Mathematics" by Susan Larsen in *Art News* (New York), December 1978; "Edda Renouf" by Anne Dagbert in

Art Press (Paris), February 1981; "Edda Renouf at Blum Helman" by Steven Henry Madoff in *Art in America* (New York), May 1982; "Edda Renouf chez Galerie Yvon Lambert" in Regis Durand in *Art Press* (Paris), September 1984.

*   *   *

There is a life, an energy in every material. The thing is to sense this energy and to reveal it by the most direct path.

Changing the structure of the base, I add, scrape or sand. Not covering, but uncovering—not closing, but opening—it is then what it is.

There is a mixture of both logical, mathematical structures and organic randomness in the materials. As I work, the materials make me aware of archetypal signs and forms, both structured and random within my unconscious. It is as a silent flow of sound, a silent conversation between the materials and my imagination, an intuitive listening out of which the work of art grows.

—Edda Renouf

REUSCH, Erich.

German. Born in Lutherstadt, Wittenberg, 26 June 1925. Educated at Melanchthon-Gymnasium, Lutherstadt until 1946; studied sculpture and architecture, under Richard Scheibe and Hans Uhlmann, at the Hochshule für Bildende Kunst, West Berlin, 1947–53. Served in German Army, 1944–45. Married Sonja Dietzler in 1969; daughter: Simone. Worked in an architect's office, Dusseldorf, 1953–56; free-lance architect, Dusseldorf, designing housing estates in Dusseldorf, Hannover and Frankfurt, and initiating Bonn-Heckenheim/Merl stellite town, 1956–64. Independent artist, Dusseldorf, since 1964; first sculpture reliefs and paintings, 1954; first electro-static objects, 1968. Professor, Staatliche Kunstakademie, Dusseldorf, since 1974. Agents: Galerie Hans Mayer/Denise Rene, Grabbeplatz 2, 4000 Dusseldorf; and Galerie Rupert Walser, Fraunhoferstrasse 19, 8000 Munich. Address: Breddeweg 4, 5982 Neuenrade 5, West Germany.

Individual Exhibitions:

1966   Von-der-Heydt Museum, Wuppertal, West Germany
1967   Galerie H, Hannover
        Haus am Lutzowplatz, West Berlin
        Galerie im Europa Center, West Berlin
1968   Galerie Swart, Amsterdam
        Galerie Loehr, Dusseldorf
1969   Galerie Swart, Amsterdam
1970   Galerie M, Bochum, West Germany
        Kunstverein, Aachen, West Germany
1971   Galerie Ernst, Hannover
        Kabinett für Aktuelle Kunst, Bremerhaven, West
        Germany
1972   Galerie Wilbrand, Cologne
        Hommage à McCready, Museum am Ostwall, Dort-
        mund, West Germany
        Lucy Milton Gallery, London
1973   *Elektrostatische Objekte,* Kunsthalle, Kiel, West
        Germany
1974   Galerie M, Bochum, West Germany
        Galerie Müller-Roth, Stuttgart
        Galerie Falazik, Neuenkirchen, West Germany
1976   Galerie Müller-Roth, Stuttgart
        Salone Annunciata, Milan
        Kunsthalle, Dusseldorf
        Galerie St. Johann, Saarbrucken
1978   Karl-Ernst-Osthaus Museum, Hagen, West Germany
1979   *Skulpturen, Reliefs, Zeichnungen, Collagen,* Galerie
        Müller-Roth, Stuttgart
1981   Galerie Hans Mayer/Denise Rene, Dusseldorf
1984   Gallery 44, Kaarst, West Germany
        Galerie Monochrome, Aachen, West Germany
        Galerie Linie, Moers, West Germany
1986   Stadtische Galerie, Ludenscheid, West Germany
1987   Skulpturen Museum Glaskasten, Marl, West Ger-
        many
        Galerie Rupert Walser, Munich

Selected Group Exhibitions:

1965   *Das Relief,* Landesmuseum, Darmstadt
1968   *Junge Deutsche Plastik,* Wilhelm-Lehmbruck-
        Museum, Duisburg, West Germany (toured Ger-
        many)
1969   *Raume,* Städtisches Museum Schloss Morsbroich,
        Leverkusen, West Germany
1970   *Strategy: Get Arts,* Richard Demarco Gallery, Edin-
        burgh
1972   *Szene Rhein-Ruhr,* Museum Folkwang, Essen
1975   *Empirica,* Commune di Rimini, Italy (travelled to
        Museo Castelvecchio, Verona)
1980   *Reliefs,* Westfalisches Museum, Munster, West Ger-
        many
1981   *Schwarz,* Kunsthalle, Dusseldorf
1985   *Kunst in der Bundesrepublik 1945-85,* Nationalgale-
        rie, West Berlin
1986   *Bodenskulptur,* Kunsthalle, Bremen, West Germany

Collections:

Städtisches Museum Schloss Morsbroich, Leverkusen, West
Germany; Kunstmuseum, Mönchengladbach, West Ger-
many; Wilhelm-Lehmbruck-Museum, Duisburg, West Ger-
many; Museum am Ostwall, Dortmund, West Germany;
Kunstmuseum, Ludwigshafen, West Germany; Kunsthalle,
Kiel, West Germany; Städtisches Museum, Bochum, West
Germany; Staatsgalerie, Stuttgart.

Publications:

By REUSCH: film—*Kunst und Architekur: chancen vertran,*
television film, 1975.

On REUSCH: books—*Park und Bildwelt* by Eugen
Thiemann, Dortmund, West Germany 1969; *Projekte, Kon-
zepte, Aktionen* by Walter Aue, Cologne 1971; *Bis Heute* by
Karin Thomas, Cologne, 1971; *Neue Konkrete Kunst* by
Bernhard Kerber, Bochum, West Germany 1972; *Erich
Reusch: Hommage à McCready,* exhibition catalogue, with
text by Eugen Thiemann and Bernhard Kerber, Dortmund,
West Germany 1972; *Erich Reusch,* exhibition folder, Lon-

don 1972; *Erich Reusch: Elektrostatische Objekte,* exhibition
catalogue, with text by Jens Christian Jensen, Kiel, West Germany 1973; *Bildhauer heute: Erich Reusch* by Bernhard Kerber, Hildescheim 1977; *Erich Reusch,* exhibition catalogue,
with text by Clara Weyergraf, Hagen, West Germany 1978;
Erich Reusch: Skulpturen, Reliefs, Zeichnungen, Collagen,
exhibition folder, Stuttgart 1979; *Erich Reusch,* exhibition
catalogue by Jurgen Wissman, Ludenscheid 1986. film—
Erich Reusch by Heiner Hepper and Hubert Neuerburg,
1974.

In 1956 at the beginning of my independent artistic
career, I designed the first ground-related sculptures.
Some of them were conceived in such a manner that
they could not immediately be appreciated to their
full extent but were only to be experienced in their
diverse constellations and their changing relation to
surrounding space if one traversed them. The concept, conditioned by the considerable outlay, was first
realized in the sculpture at the WBV grounds in Munich, which had a maximum dimension of around
500 metres (1979-1982). In 1963 reliefs were created
whose flat steel plates projected vertically in space.
My work was interrupted by my profession as architect (projects for housing estates in Dusseldorf, Hannover and Frankfurt, and for the satellite town
Meckenheim-Merl), and the sculptures which lie
flush with the ground, exclusively composed of
planes, originated at the beginning of 1965. These
sculptures were the very first spatial forms without
vertical elevation and, similarly decentralized, were
conceived for large dimensions.

The first electrostatic objects were carried out in
1968. Corresponding to the electrostatic charge,
black pigment settles on plexiglass. The constellation
of the deposit varies. The pigment lying on the floor

Erich Reusch: Fountain Disk Design of the Rathausplatz, Bochum, 1980

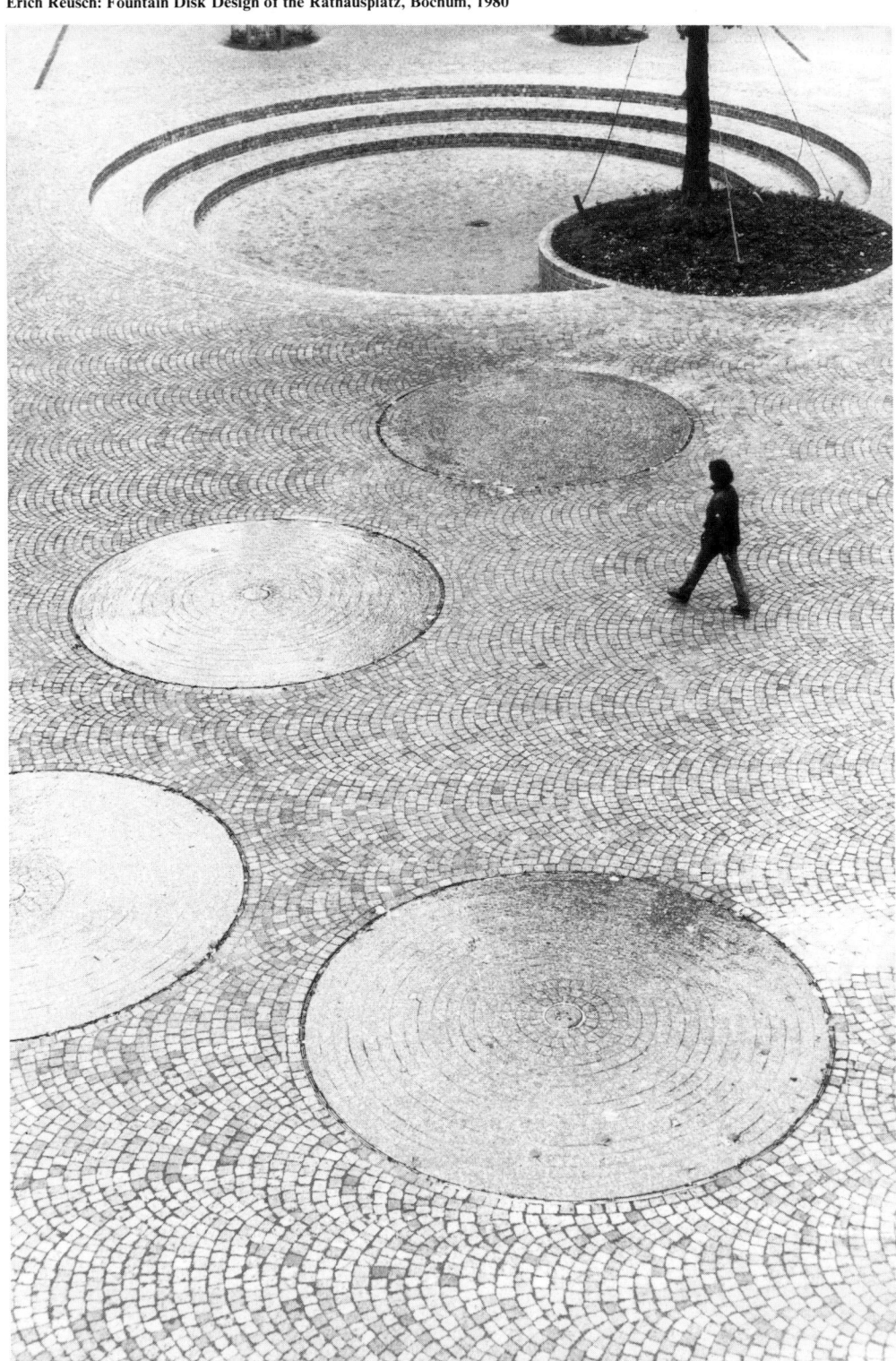

demonstrates this variability.

In 1974 the first decentralized sculptures originated, whose individual forms were disproportionately small. Without oppressive monumentalism they hold a dialogue with the surrounding space. The expansion of this concept forms part of my future work. At the same time, in recent years, apart from many drawings, coloured decentralized objects have originated, accomplishing a relationship not only within themselves but also searching for a relation with surrounding space.

—Erich Reusch

REUTER, Hans Peter.

German. Born in Schwenningen am Neckar, 3 September 1942. Studied at the Akademie der Künste, Karlsruhe, 1963–64, 1966–67, and, under Albrecht von Hancke, Franz Nagel and Emil Schumacher, at the Akademie der Künste, Munich, 1965. Married Hildegard Fuhrer in 1969. Painter, Karlsruhe, since 1967. Instructor, Karlsruhe High School, 1969–75; Professor, Akademie der Künste, Nuremberg, since 1985. Recipient: Villa Romana Prize, Florence, 1973; Deutsche Industrie Stipend, 1975; Cité des Arts Fellowship, Paris, 1976–77; Wilhelm Morgner Prize, Soest, 1977; Annemarie and Will Grohmann Stipend, Stuttgart, 1977; Villa Massimo Prize, Rome, 1980. Agents: Galerie Denise René-Hans Mayer, Grabbeplatz 2, 4000 Dusseldorf, West Germany; Staempfli Gallery, 47 East 77th Street, New York, New York 10021, U.S.A. Address: Am Steinhausle 8, 7500 Karlsruhe 41, West Germany.

Individual Exhibitions:

1969 Galerie am Kaiserplatz, Karlsruhe
1971 Neue Galerie, Baden-Baden, West Germany
      Galerie Herzog, Ladenburg, West Germany
      Galerie 2, Stuttgart
1972 Forum Kunst, Rottweil, West Germany
      Galerie Denise René-Hans Mayer, Dusseldorf
1974 Galerie Denise René-Hans Mayer, Dusseldorf
1975 Städtische Galerie, Nordhorn, West Germany
1976 Sudwest Galerie, Karlsruhe
      Galerie Edith Wahlandt, Schwabisch Gmund, West Germany
1980 *Olbilder, Zeichnungen, Gouachen,* Galerie Denise René-Hans Mayer, Dusseldorf
      Rheinisches Landesmuseum, Bonn
1981 Goethe Institut, Brussels
      Recent Paintings, Staempfli Gallery, New York
      Kunsthalle, Heilbronn, West Germany
      Landesgirokasse, Stuttgart
      Sudwest-Galerie, Karlsruhe
1984 Galerie Hofstee, Frankfurt
      Galerie Denise Rene/Hans Mayer, Dusseldorf
1985 Stadtische Galerie, Villingen, West Germany
1986 Galerie Schloss Rimsingen, West Germany
      Galerie Loehr, Frankfurt
1987 Galerie Haus Geiselhard, Reutlingen, West Germany
      Stadtische Galerie, Ravensburg, West Germany
1988 Villa Merkel, Esslingen, West Germany
      Wilhelm-Hack-Museum, Ludwigshafen, West Germany

Selected Group Exhibitions:

1967 *Kunstpreis der Jugend,* Kunsthalle, Mannheim (travelled to the Städtisches Museum, Enschede)
1971 *Aktiya 71,* Haus der Kunst, Munich
1973 *14 x 14,* Kunsthalle, Baden-Baden, West Germany
1975 *Contemporary German Art,* Art Gallery of New South Wales, Sydney (toured Australia)
1977 *Documenta,* Kassel, West Germany

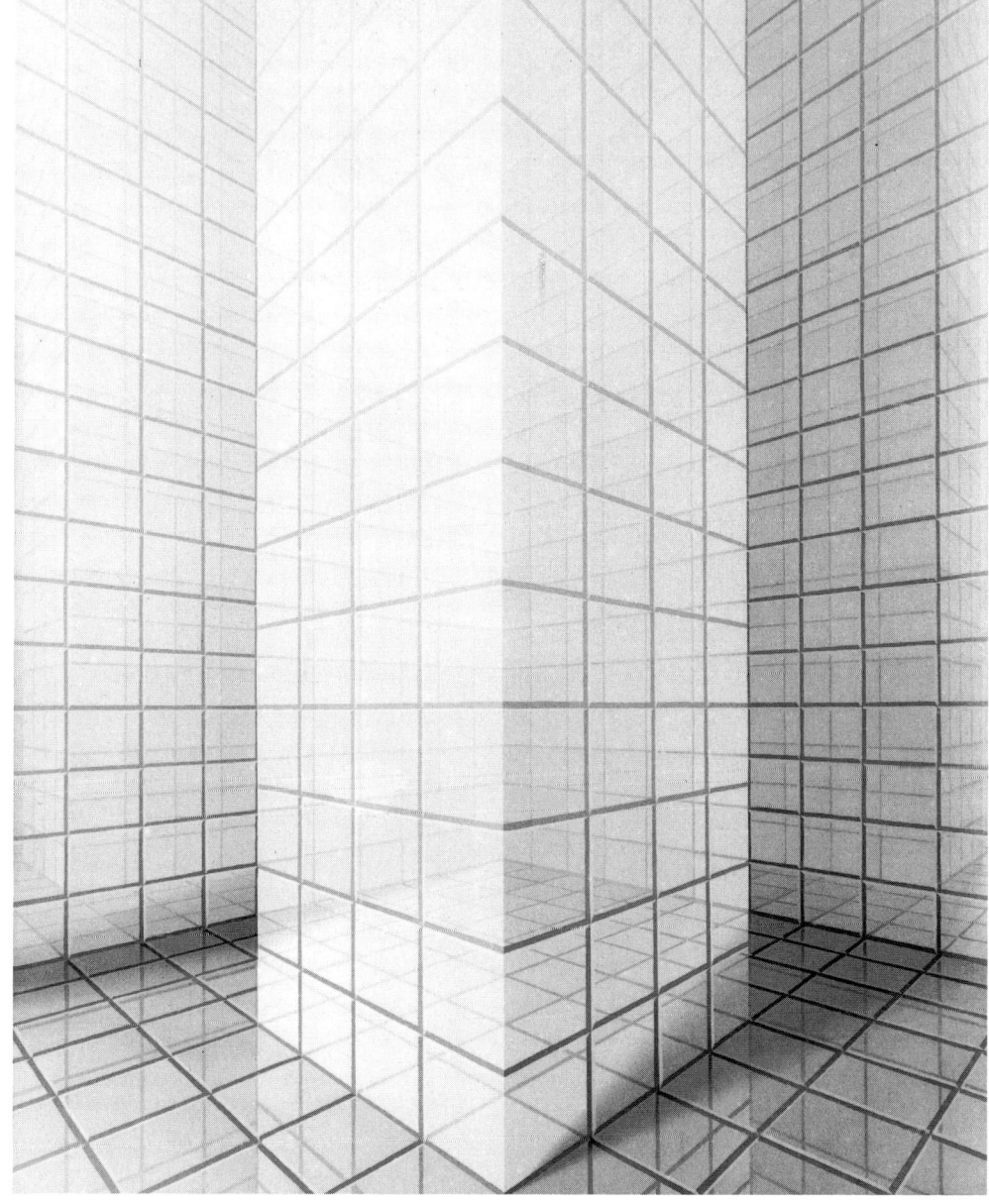

Hans Peter Reuter: *Spiegel-Raum,* 1985

1979 *Karlsruhe-Chicago,* Schloss Ettlingen, West Germany
1980 *Mediterranean Biennale,* Alexandria, Egypt
1983 *Kunst-Landschaft-Architektur,* Nationalgalerie, West Berlin
1985 *Raum und Mythos,* Villa Vauban, Luxembourg
1986 *Symmetrie,* Mathildenhohe, Darmstadt, West Germany

Collections:

Bundesrepublik Deutschland, Bonn; Staatliche Kunsthalle, Karlsruhe, Kunsthalle, Kiel, West Germany; Bayerische Staatsgemaldesammlungen, Munich; Staatsgalerie, Stuttgart; Galerie der Stadt, Stuttgart; Städtische Kunsthalle, Recklinghausen, West Germany; Stadtische Sammlungen, Soest, West Germany; Ulmer Museum, Ulm, West Germany; Städtisches Museum, Heilbronn, West Germany.

Publications:

On REUTER: books—*Hans Peter Reuter,* exhibition catalogue, Ladenburg, West Germany 1971; *5 from Germany,* exhibition catalogue, with text by Robert Kudielka, London 1974; *Documenta 6,* exhibition catalogue, with texts by Klaus Honnef, Evelyn Weiss and others, Kassel, West Germany 1977; *Neue Formen des Realismus* by Peter Sager, Warsaw and Recklinghausen, West Germany 1979; *Hans Peter Reuter: Olbilder, Zeichnungen, Gouachen,* exhibition folder, Dusseldorf 1980; *Hans Peter Reuter,* exhibition catalogue, Bonn 1980; *Hans Peter Reuter: Recent Paintings,* exhibition folder, with text by George W. Staempfli, New York 1982; *Hans Peter Reuter,* exhibition catalogue, Esslingen 1988; articles—"Deutsche Kunst: Eine neue Generation" by Rolf-Günter Dienst in *Das Kunstwerk* (Baden-Baden, West Germany), no. 6, 1971; "Hans Peter Reuter" by Klaus Honnef in *Architektur und Wohnen* (Hamburg), no. 2, 1976; "Hans Peter Reuter" by Marie Hullenkremer in *Art 8/1980,* exhibition catalogue, Basle 1980.

*

My pictures have changed following, and as a result of, my stay at the Villa Massimo in Rome. Space in the picture has become simplified. There are no vanishing points any more, no empty spaces; there are merely details, corners and in parts simply walls. Colour has evolved from blue to white with a lighted effect, and in the watercolours to a spectrum of red, green, black and blue. Through the play of light over its surface and its at times disconcerting mirror effects the picture appears to me as an independent spatial system and no longer as the representation of space. Colour, especially in the watercolours, no longer represents something (e.g. a blue wall), but is only itself. It creates its own colour space.

I had been trying to achieve this for years, but only in Rome did I understand that I had to give up perspectives in large measure in order to attain a depth of colour. Leading a strongly modulated life of its own, colour seems to take over the role which 'things' played in my paintings before 1970, functioning as a sort of emotional antithesis to the logical system of the grid. This grid structure, which appears in my works in the form of jointed squares, seems to be an indispensable part of my pictures to date.

I have often tried to paint pictures without reference to this framework—usually under provocation from awkward critics who reproached me for allegedly clinging to a 'trademark'—but I have never been satisfied with the results. The pictures always struck me as imprecise, washed out, insufficiently defined; in short they made me nervous. I link 'grid', 'structure', 'schema' and 'system' with the idea of being surveyable, clear, certain, calm, logical, comprehensible, overseeable and comforting. It's the same in everyday life: if I find myself confronted with a confused and chaotic situation in which I can't see my way forward, I feel anxious. Only when I have gained a certain overview, recognized what principle is involved and given the whole matter some structure, can I make a correct assessment and possibly even take a positive view.

In my pictures exactly the same thing happens. They begin from an amorphous feeling, which then precipitates certain effects of colour, light or space. I don't think about what's happening; I simply wait for it to happen. Only then do I begin to structure the usually imprecise design, defining it and giving it a clear form. There are a number of verbal analogies that one might apply here, such as 'clarifying what is obscure' or 'imposing order on chaos'. It seems to me, however one describes it, that with my pictures I am trying to make my own heaving emotions intelligible through clarity and logic.

In this respect the concept of beauty is also important to me. A concept that art avoids if it can and which I can obviously not define either. For me it links in with the composition, another type of system or structure, where what is at stake is the relationship of individual components one to another. Now, if the individual components of a whole are linked to one another in a clear order and the 'how' nevertheless remains an inexplicable mystery, then, to me, the whole is at least fascinating, if not beautiful.

Pure systematics is often pure boredom. Pure emotionalism can be equally stultifying if prolonged. The linking of the two is an exciting thing for me, an endless source of new pictures.

—Hans Peter Reuter

RICHTER, Gerhard.

German. Born in Dresden, 9 February 1932. Studied art at the Hochschule für Bildende Künste, Dresden, 1952–57, and, under Karl-Otto Gotz, at the Staatliche Kunstakademie, Dusseldorf, 1961–64. Married the artist Isa Genzken in 1982; daughter: Betty. Worked as scenery-painter, Stadttheater, Zittau, East Germany, 1949–50; commercial artist for several firms, Zittau, 1950–51; photolaboratory technician, Dresden, 1957–60. Full-time painter, Dusseldorf, since 1963. Guest lecturer, Hochschule für Bildenden Künste, Hamburg, 1967; Lecturer in Fine Arts at a gymnasium, Dusseldorf, 1968–69; Professor, Staatliche Kunstakademie, Dusseldorf from 1971. Recipient: Kunstpreis Junger Westen, Recklinghausen, 1967; Arnold Bode Prize, Kassel, 1982. Agent: Galerie Konrad Fischer, Platanenstrasse 7, 4000 Dusseldorf. Address: Kaiserwerther Strasse 115, 4000 Dusseldorf 30, West Germany.

Individual Exhibitions:

1963	Mobelhaus Berges, Dusseldorf (with Konrad Lueg)
1964	Galerie Heiner Friedrich, Munich
	Galerie Alfred Schmela, Dusseldorf
1965	Galerie René Block, West Berlin
1966	Galerie Friedrich und Dahlem, Munich
	Galerie Alfred Schmela, Dusseldorf
	Galleria La Tartaruga, Rome
	Galerie Bishofberger, Zurich
	Galleria del Leone, Venice
	Galerie René Block, West Berlin
1967	Wide White Space gallery, Antwerp
	Galerie Heiner Friedrich, Munich
1968	Galerie Ricke, Kassel, West Germany
	Galerie Rudolf Zwirner, Cologne
1969	*Arbeiten 1962 bis 1971*, Galerie Gegenverkehr, Aachen, West Germany
	Galleria del Naviglio, Milan
	Galerie René Block, West Berlin
1970	Palais des Beaux-Arts, Brussels
	Galerie Konrad Fischer, Dusseldorf
	Museum Folkwang, Essen
	Galerie Jorg Schellmann, Munich
	Galerie Heiner Friedrich, Munich
1971	Kunstverein, Dusseldorf
	Kabinett für Aktuelle Kunst, Bremerhaven, West Germany
	Galerie Thomas Borgmann, Cologne
1972	Galerie Heiner Friedrich, Munich
	Galerie Rudolf Zwirner, Cologne
	Galerie Konrad Fischer, Dusseldorf
	Museum van Hedendaagse Kunst, Utrecht
1973	Galerie Seriaal, Amsterdam
	Onnasch Gallery, New York
	Kunstverein, Bremerhaven, West Germany
	Galleria La Bertesca, Milan
1974	Galerie René Block, West Berlin
1975	Städtisches Museum, Mönchengladbach, West Germany
	Kunstverein, Braunschweig, West Germany
	Galerie Rolf Preisig, Basle
	Galerie Konrad Fischer, Dusseldorf
	Bilder aus den Jahren 1962–1974, Kunsthalle, Bremen, West Germany
1976	Kaiser-Wilhelm-Museum, Krefeld, West Germany
	Museum Haus Lange, Krefeld, West Germany
	Galleria Renzo Spagnoli, Florence (travelled to the Galleria La Bertesca, Genoa)
	Galerie Durand-Dessert, Paris
	Galleria Lucio Amelio, Naples
1977	Centre Georges Pompidou, Paris
	Galerie Konrad Fischer, Dusseldorf
1978	*Abstract Painting*, Stedelijk Van Abbemuseum, Eindhoven, Netherlands
	48 Portraits, Midland Group Gallery, Nottingham
	Sperone-Westwater-Fischer, New York
	Nova Scotia College of Art, Halifax
1979	Whitechapel Art Gallery, London
1980	Sperone-Westwater-Fischer, New York
	Museum Folkwang, Essen, West Germany
	Van Abbemuseum, Eindhoven, Netherlands
	Galleria Mario Pieroni, Rome
1981	Kunsthalle, Dusseldorf
1982	Kunsthalle, Bielefeld, West Germany
	Kunstverein, Mannheim, West Germany
	Galerie Hetzler, Stuttgart
	Galerie Fischer, Zurich
	Padiglione d'Arte Contemporanea, Milan
1983	Sperone-Westwater-Fischer, New York
	Galleria Lucio Amelio, Naples
	Galleria Mario Pieroni, Rome
	Galerie Konrad Fischer, Dusseldorf
1984	Musee d'Art et d'Industrie, St. Etienne, France
	Galerie Thomas Borgmann, Cologne
	Galerie Wilkens-Jacobs, Cologne
1985	Marian Goodman Gallery, New York
	Sperone-Westwater, New York
1987	Museum Overholland, Amsterdam
1988	Anthony D'Offay Gallery, London
	Art Gallery of Ontario, Toronto (retrospective; toured the United States)

Selected Group Exhibitions:

1965	*14 Aspekte Moderner Malerei*, Haus der Künste, West Berlin
1968	*Junge Deutscher Kunstlerbund*, Kunsthalle, Nuremberg
1969	*9 Young Artists*, Guggenheim Museum, New York
1972	*Documenta 5*, Museum Fridericianum, Kassel, West Germany (and *Documenta 7*, 1982)
1971	*New Multiple Art*, Whitechapel Art Gallery, London
1975	*Fundamental Painting*, Stedelijk Museum, Amsterdam
1976	*Projekt Retrospekt*, Kunsthalle, Dusseldorf
1981	*A New Spirit in Painting*, Royal Academy of Art, London
1984	*Ein anderes Klima*, Kunsthalle, Dusseldorf
1987	*Avant-Garde in the Eighties*, Los Angeles County Museum of Art

Collections:

Kunstmuseum, Dusseldorf; Neue Galerie/Sammlung Ludwig, Aachen, West Germany; Museum Folkwang, Essen; Stedelijk Van Abbemuseum, Eindhoven, Netherlands; Stadtisches Museum, Monchengladbach; Nationalgalerie, West Berlin; Stadtisches Kunstmuseum, Bonn; Louisiana Museum, Humblebaek, Denmark; Kunstmuseum, Basle; Guggenheim Museum, New York.

Publications:

By RICHTER: books—*Bericht über eine Demonstration*, Dusseldorf 1963; *Gerhard Richter: Atlas van de foto's en schetsen*, exhibition catalogue, Utrecht 1972; *Gerhard Richter: Atlas der Fotos, Collagen und Skizzen*, exhibition catalogue, Krefeld, West Germany 1976.

On RICHTER: books—*Pop Art* by Rolf-Günter Dienst, Wiesbaden 1965; *Schlussel zur Modernen Kunst* by Karl Ruhrberg, Dusseldorf 1966; *Gerhard Richter*, exhibition catalogue, with text by Klaus Honnef, Aachen, West Germany 1969; *Gerhard Richter: Arbeiten 1962 bis 1971*, exhibition catalogue, with texts by Karl-Heinz Hering and Dietrich Helms, Dusseldorf 1971; *Gerhard Richter*, exhibition catalogue, with text by Jean-Christophe Ammann, Munich 1972; *Neue Formen des Realismus* by Peter Sager, Cologne 1973; *Projekt '74: Aspekte Internationaler Kunst am Anfang der 70er Jahre*, exhibition catalogue, with texts by Dieter Ronte, Evelyn Weiss, Manfred Schneckenburger and others, Cologne 1974; *Gerhard Richter: Bilder aus den Jahren 1962–1974*, exhibition catalogue, with texts by Manfred Schneckenburger and Marlis Gruterich, Bremen 1975; *Gerhard Richter*, exhibition catalogue, with texts by K. G. Pontus Hulten and Benjamin Buchloh, Paris 1977; *Gerhard Richter: 48 Portraits*, exhibition catalogue, edited by Lynda Morris, Nottingham 1978; *Gerhard Richter: Abstract Paintings*, exhibition catalogue, with texts by Rudi H. Fuchs and Benjamin Buchloh, Eindhoven, Netherlands 1978; *Gerhard Richter: Zweigelbe Striche*, exhibition catalogue, with text by Zdenek Felix, Essen 1980; *Gerhard Richter: Abstrakte Bilder 1976 bis 1981*, exhibition catalogue, with texts by Rudi H. Fuchs and Heribert Heere, Munich 1981; *Gerhard Richter*, exhibition catalogue, with text by Bruno Cora, Milan 1982; *Gerhard Richter*, exhibition catalogue with text by Benjamin Buchloh, New York 1985; *Gerhard Richter: The London Paintings*, exhibition catalogue with essay by Jill Lloyd, London 1988; *Gerhard Richter Retrospective*, exhibition catalogue with essays by Michael Danoff and Roald Nasgaard, Toronto 1988.

Every time we describe an event, add up a column of figures or take a photograph of a tree, we create a model; without models we would know nothing about reality and would be like animals.

Abstract paintings are fictitious models because they visualize a reality which we can neither see nor describe but which we may nevertheless conclude to exist. We attach negative names to this reality: the unknown, the un-graspable, the in-finite, and for thousands of years we have depicted it in terms of substitute images like heaven and hell, gods and devils. With abstract painting we created a better means of approaching what can be neither seen nor understood because abstract painting illustrates with the greatest clarity, that is to say with all the means at the disposal of art, 'nothing'. Accustomed to recognizing real things in paintings we refuse, justifiably, to consider color alone (in all its variation) as what the painting reveals, and instead allow ourselves to see the unseeable, that which has never before been seen and indeed is not visible. This is not an artful game,

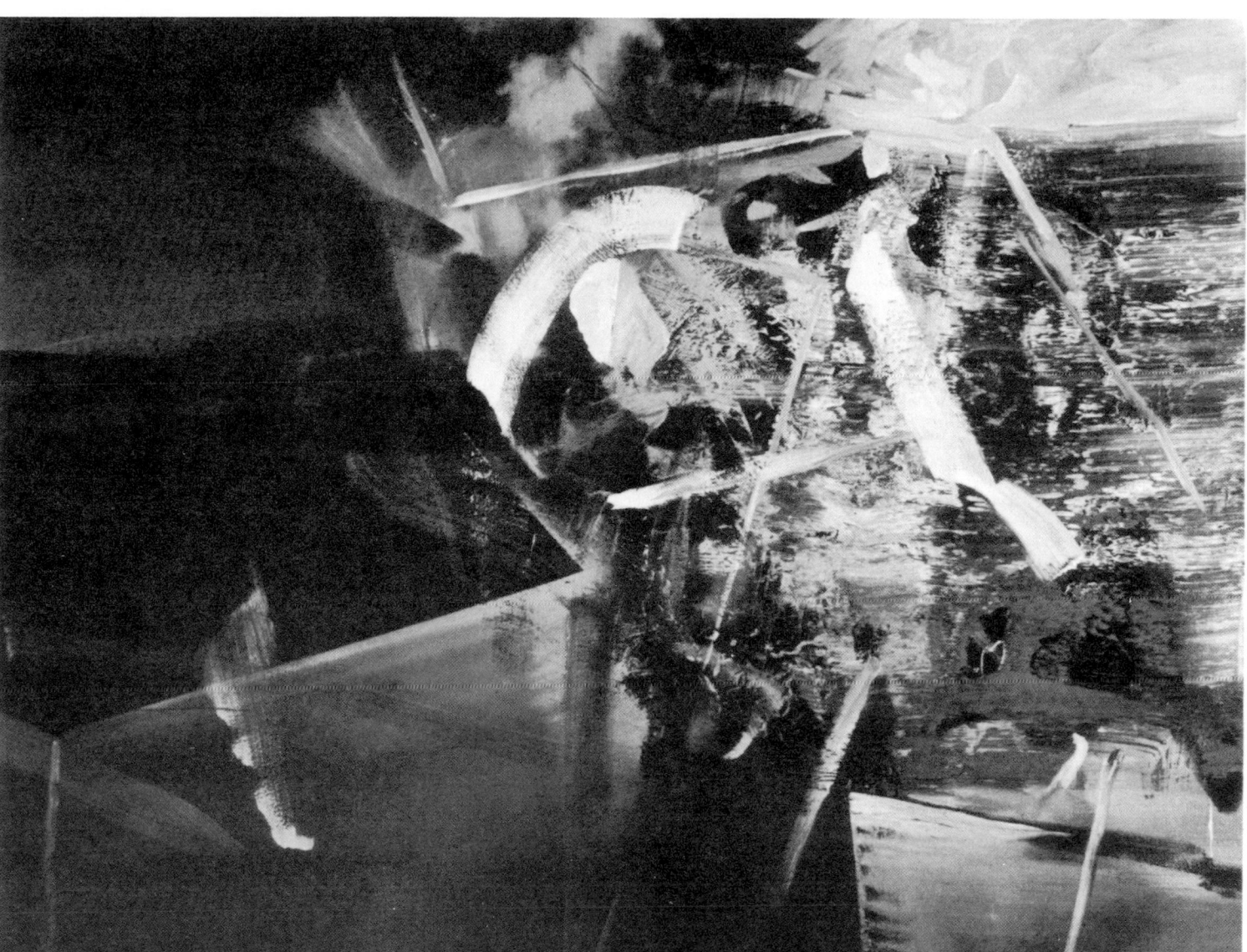

Gerhard Richter: *Number 508,* 1982

it is a necessity; and since everything unknown frightens us and fills us with hope at the same time, we take these images as a possible explanation of the inexplicable or at least as a way of dealing with it.—Of course even representative paintings have this transcendental aspect; since every object, being part of a world whose last and first causes are finally unfathomable, embodies that world, the image of such an object in a painting evokes the general mystery all the more compellingly the less 'function' the representation has. This is the source of the continually increasing fascination, for example, that so many old and beautiful portraits exert upon us.—Thus paintings are all the better, the more beautiful, intelligent, crazy and extreme, the more clearly perceptible and the less decipherable metaphors they are for this incomprehensible reality.

Art is the highest form of hope.

—Gerhard Richter

Richter's work is characterized by a pervasive heterogeneity, its parts refusing to be linked together into easily unified structures or developmental overviews. This is true of its chronological development, in which disparate streams of work overlap, of the relation between individual kinds of work produced at any one time, and within the depth of the individual works themselves. A chronological examination of the work therefore hides what is revealed by a thematic approach according to subject matter, and

vice-versa. Nevertheless the work may be divided into three broad sections: the Figurative—all the paintings based on found, or Richter's own photographs, from the earliest Photo Paintings beginning in 1962, to the latest landscapes and still lifes; the Constructive—the more theoretical work, produced primarily between 1966 and 1976, such as the Colour Charts, the "Inpaintings" and the Gray Paintings, and *Forty-eight Portraits,* but also including pictures of windows and doors, and objects like the Glass Panes, and the Mirrors; and the Abstract—encompassing all the work since 1976 except for the landscapes and the still lifes, but also reaching back to a number of small, gray, experimental paintings from the late 1960s.

Thus Richter has never sought a recognizable style, and has never used consistent techniques. His development has followed no clear rules that can be analyzed in terms of formal development, and, if he has not actually backed away from them, he has certainly taken a subversive attitude toward most of the historical tasks of Modern painting: subjective expression, symbolic or metaphysical representation, the production of Utopian models, the description of reality, etc. He has acted contradictorily, delighting, or despairing, in abrupt juxtapositions, and has unhesitatingly tested issues evoked by painting through reaching outside it, to conceptual projects, occasionally to object-making, and especially to photography. Nor can we ever be quite sure about his high-mindedness, especially when he serves up what looks dangerously kitschy and nostalgic in the photo-based landscapes

and *memento mori* still lifes that are so seductively pleasing.

But if Richter assumed a critical attitude to painting and to abstract art at a time when both were long in crisis, he has also become, during the past decade, the most consummate maker of abstract paintings investing them with the power progressively to explore reality. When in 1976 Richter made an abrupt about face in his work, breaking free (one can never say forever with Richter) from the severe painterly impassive and personally aesthetic bounds of his Constructive work, not even he was sure of the implications. In little "sketches," as he called them at first, he suddenly rallied the full arsenal of his painting trade, and with abandon, trying it all out, laid the groundwork for the compositionally complicated, heavily impastoed and richly polychromatic abstract paintings that have since dominated his work.

The transition was not easy, and had first to be mediated through photography, as in the "smooth" abstract pictures from between 1977 and 1980; and underlying premises needed to be redoubted, as in the gray-painted Glass Panes in 1977, and the Mirrors from 1981. Nevertheless abstract painting has come to constitute the largest single body of work within an apparently many-sided career. Yet it is not a little surprising—despite some twenty-five years of painting, and an oeuvre catalogue of over six hundred paintings at last count—to recall how exclusively Richter has been a painter, and a rather traditional one, choosing few new materials, working almost always with oil on canvas. It is as if the critical thrust of the work, and the context in which it was produced and has been shown calls for another order of categorization. Accordingly criticism has tended to stress the skeptical aspects of Richter's work, and more recently, perhaps a little embarrassed by the sheer beauty and optimistic sensuality of the Abstract Paintings of the 1980s, has preferred to address the conceptual basis of the work, focusing on the deconstructivist job it does on expressionist painting's belief in unmediated subjectivity, rather than on Richter's own professed desire to be producing something positive and constructive out of his contradictory moves. In any case as Richter always stresses, surveying the body of his work: "The paintings do not differ from each other, I change my method of approach only whenever I think it appropriate."

From the first catalogued painting, *Table* from 1962, to the Abstract and Figure Paintings of the 1980s, the heterogeneity of the work is also its truthfulness. If Richter upholds "art as the highest form of hope" (as in his much quoted statement from *Documenta 7*), he does so with a reserved optimism that may echo Modernism, but not with Modernism's expectation of discovering final harmonies, visions or unities. The character of the individual works, most clearly stated in the Abstract Paintings, is not their resolution but in the dispersal of their elements, their coexistant contradictory expressions and moods, their opposition of promises and denials. They are complex visual events, suspended in interrogation, and "fictive models" for the reality which escapes direct address, eludes conceptualization and description, but resides inarticulate in our experience.

—Roald Nasgaard

RICKEY, George (Warren).

American. Born in South Bend, Indiana, 6 June 1907. Educated at Trinity College, Glenalmond, Scotland, 1921–26; Balliol College, Oxford, 1926–29, B.A. 1929, M.A. 1941; Ruskin School of Drawing, Oxford, 1928–29; Académie André Lhote, Paris, 1929–30; Académie Moderne, Paris, 1929–30; Institute of Fine Arts, New York University, 1945–46; State University of Iowa, with Mauricio Lasansky, 1947; and the Institute of Design, Chicago, 1948–49. Married Edith Leighton in 1947; children: Stuart and Philip. Served in the United States Army Air Corps, 1940–45; Staff Sergeant. Painter in the 1930's and 40's, sculptor since the early 1950's. History Instructor, Groton School, Massachusetts, 1930–33; worked in the Editorial Department of *Newsweek* magazine, New York, 1936; Artist-in-Residence, Olivet College, Michigan, 1937–39; part-time faculty member, Art Department, Kalamazoo College, Michigan, 1938–40; Director, Institute of Arts, Kalamazoo, 1938–40; Chairman, Art Department, Muhlenberg College, Allentown, Pennsylvania, 1946–48; Instructor, University of Washington, Seattle, 1948; Associate Professor, Fine Arts Department, Indiana University, Bloomington, 1949–55; Professor of Art, Newcomb College, Tulane University, New Orleans, 1955–61; Professor, University of California at Santa Barbara, 1960; Professor, School of Architecture, Rensselaer Polytechnic Institute, Troy, New York, 1961–66. Visiting Artist, Dartmouth College, Hanover, New Hampshire 1966; Regents Lecturer, University of California at Santa Barbara, 1967. Recipient: Carnegie Grant, 1940, 1941; Guggenheim Fellowship, 1960, 1961; DAAD Stipendium, Berlin, 1968; Fine Arts Honor Award, American Institute of Architects, Houston, 1972; Medal for Sculpture, Skowhegan School of Painting and Sculpture, Maine, 1973; Creative Arts Award in Sculpture, Brandeis University, Waltham, Massachusetts, 1979; Citation, National Association of Schools of Art, 1981; New York State Governor's Arts Award, Albany, 1986; Urban Design Commission Award, Atlanta, 1986. Honorary

doctorates: Knox College, Galesburg, Illinois, 1970; Williams College, Williamstown, Massachusetts, 1972; Union College, Schenectady, New York, 1973; Indiana University, Bloomington, 1974; Kalamazoo College, Michigan, 1977; York University, Toronto, 1978; Tulane University, New Orleans, 1983; State University of New York, Purchase, 1986. Member, National Institute of Arts and Letters, 1974; Akademie der Künste, West Berlin, 1987. Address: R.D. 2, Box 235, East Chatham, New York 12060–9739, U.S.A.

Individual Exhibitions:

1933	Caz-Delbo Gallery, New York
1935	Denver Art Museum
1943	Denver Art Museum
1945	Denver Art Museum
1948	Denver Art Museum
1950	Associated American Artists, Chicago (with Reginald Neal)
1953	*Mobile Sculpture*, John Herron Art Museum, Indianapolis
1955	Kraushaar Gallery, New York
1956	Isaac Delgado Museum, now New Orleans Museum of Art
1957	Amerika Haus, Hamburg
	School of Architecture, Rensselear Polytechnic, Troy, New York
1959	Kraushaar Gallery, New York
1960	Museum of Art, Santa Barbara
1961	Kraushaar Gallery, New York
	Museum of Art, University of Oklahoma, Norman
1962	Primus-Stuart Galleries, Los Angeles
	Kinetische Skulpturen, Galerie Springer, Berlin
	Kunstverein, Hamburg
1963	Williams College Museum of Art, Williamstown, Massachusetts
	Rush Rhees Fine Arts Center, University of Rochester, New York
	Hopkins Center Art Galleries, Dartmouth College, Hanover, New Hampshire
1964	Kalamazoo Institute of Arts, Michigan
	Kinetic Sculptures, Boston Institute of Contemporary Art
	Staempfli Gallery, New York
	David Stuart Gallery, Los Angeles
1966	Corcoran Gallery of Art, Washington, D.C.
1967	Walker Art Center, Minneapolis
	Staempfli Gallery, New York
	Fort Wayne Art Museum, Indiana
	Musée d'Art Contemporain, Montreal
1968	Halfmannshof, Gelsenkirchen, West Germany (with Heinz Mack)
1969	*Mobile Skulpturen*, Haus am Waldsee, Berlin
	Kunstverein, Munich
	Museum Boymans-van Beuningen, Rotterdam
	Kunsthalle, Nuremberg
	New Jersey State Museum, Trenton
	Staempfli Gallery, New York
1970	Whatcom Museum of History and Art, Bellingham, Washington
	Henry Gallery, University of Washington, Seattle
1971	Staempfli Gallery, New York
	Retrospective Exhibition 1951–1971, at University of California at Los Angeles (toured the United State)
1972	Museum of Art, University of Iowa, Iowa City
1973	Kestner Gesellschaft, Hannover
	Neue Nationalgalerie, Berlin
1974	Galerie Bucholz, Munich
	Galerie Espace, Amsterdam
1975	Staempfli Gallery, Fordham University Plaza, New York
	College of St. Rose, Albany, New York
	Gimpel and Hanover, Zurich
	Gimpel Fils, London
1976	Kunsthalle, Bielefeld, West Germany
	Kresge Art Center, Michigan State University, East Lansing
	Ball State University, Muncie, Indiana
1977	Gimpel and Hanover, Zurich
	Galerie Espace, Amsterdam

	Galerie Buchholz, Munich
	Galerie Kasahara, Osaka
	Städel Museum, Frankfurt
	Dag Hammarskjold Plaza, New York
	Makler Gallery, Philadelphia
1979	*Skulpturen Material Technik*, Amerika Haus, Berlin
	Guggenheim Museum, New York (retrospective)
1981	Musée d'Art Contemporain, Montreal
1982	Scottish Sculpture Trust, Glasgow (travelled to Yorkshire Sculpture Park)
1983	Tulane University, New Orleans
1984	Bauhaus Archiv, West Berlin
	Josef Albers Museum, Bottrop, West Germany
1985	Art Center of South Bend, Indiana (also at Indiana University, South Bend; St. Mary's College, South Bend; Snite Museum of Art, South Bend; University of Notre Dame, Indiana)
1986	Bryant Park, New York
	Maxwell Davidson Gallery, New York
	Zabriskie Gallery, New York
	Neuer Berliner Kunstverein, West Berlin
1987	Carl Schlosberg Fine Arts, Sherman Oaks, California
	Galerie Pels Leusden, West Berlin
	State University of New York, Purchase

Selected Group Exhibitions:

1951	*American Sculpture*, Metropolitan Museum of Art, New York
1959	*Recent Sculpture USA*, Museum of Modern Art, New York
1964	*Documenta 3*, Kassel, West Germany
1965	*Licht und Bewegung*, Kunsthalle, Berne (toured Belgium and West Germany)
1970	*Kinetic Art*, Hayward Gallery, London
1974	*The Non-Objective World*, Annely Juda Fine Art, London
1976	*Sculpture '76*, Greenwich Arts Council, Connecticut
1980	*Pier and Ocean*, Hayward Gallery, London
1983	*Sculpture: The Tradition in Steel*, Nassau County Museum of Fine Art, New York
1987	*Nothing But Steel*, Cold Spring Harbor Laboratory, Long Island, New York

Collections:

Museum of Modern Art, New York; Yale University Art Gallery, New Haven, Connecticut; Hirshhorn Museum, Washington, D.C.; National Collection of Fine Arts, Washington, D.C.; Tate Gallery, London; Nationalgalerie, Berlin; Kunsthalle, Hamburg; Auckland City Art Gallery, New Zealand; Rijksmuseum Kroller-Muller, Otterlo, Netherlands; Modern Art Museum, Senri Hills, Osaka, Japan. Numerous public installations in the United States and Europe.

Publications:

By RICKEY: articles—"Scandale de succès" in *Art International* (Lugano, Switzerland), May 1965; "Kinesis Continued" in *Art in America* (New York), December 1965; "Origins of Kinetic Art" in *Studio International* (London), February 1967; interview, with Frederick S. Wight, in *George Rickey, Retrospective Exhibition 1951–1971*, exhibition catalogue, Los Angeles 1971; statement in *George Rickey*, exhibition catalogue, New York 1975; "Naum Gabo" in *Artforum* (New York), November 1977; "Ich bin ein Berliner" in *Artgallery* (Berlin), June/July 1978; ten brief essays in *Georges Rickey: Skulpturen Material Technik*, exhibition catalogue, West Berlin 1979; "Less is Less" in *Art Journal* (New York), Fall 1981; "South Bend: Seven Decades Later" in *George Rickey in South Bend*, exhibition catalogue, South Bend, Indiana 1985; three brief essays in *George Rickey*, exhibition catalogue, New York 1986; "In the Fullness of Time" in *George Rickey*, exhibition catalogue, West Berlin 1987.

On RICKEY: books—*Kinetische Skulpturen*, exhibition catalogue, with an introduction by Henry R. Hope, West Berlin 1962; *George Rickey—Kinetic Sculptures*, exhibition catalogue, with a foreword by Susan M. Thurman, Boston 1964; *George Rickey*, exhibition catalogue, with an introduction by Peter Selz, Washington, D.C. 1966; *Mack—Rickey*, exhibition catalogue, with an introduction by Wieland Schmied,

Gelsenkirchen, West Germany 1968; *George Rickey: Mobile Skulpturen*, exhibition catalogue, with an introduction by Wieland Schmied, West Berlin 1969; *George Rickey: Ein Porträt Kunstler Als Gaste in Berlin* by Eberhard Roters, West Berlin 1969; *George Rickey* by Nancy Rosenthal, New York 1977; *George Rickey . . . 1979*, exhibition catalogue, New York 1979; *George Rickey: Kinetic Sculpture on Clydeside*, exhibition catalogue with foreword by Robin Spencer, Glasgow 1982; *George Rickey: New Orleans Plus 30*, exhibition catalogue with essay by Marilyn Brown, New Orleans 1983; *George Rickey in South Bend*, exhibition catalogue with text by Hayden Herrera, South Bend, Indiana 1985.

Looking back over the twenty-four years since I began seriously to compose with movement *itself* as my medium, I would say that my objectives have become clearer and simpler, though not necessarily easier to achieve. The shape of components has been reduced to a more austere geometry, while my view of the vocabulary and syntax of movement has been enormously extended. I have learned a great deal about material and about techniques for working it. I have moved my sculptures outdoors into the wind and have found Nature, both as power and as environment, to be a benign ally. This permitted much larger sculptures and the satisfaction (as well as the anxiety) of mounting large pieces in public places.

I have worked with linear elements of all of these 24 years, in the last 12 with tapered, slender blade-like forms balanced on knife edges. In the last 5 years I have also proceeded from moving lines to moving planes to moving volumes. These volumes could be between surfaces as in cubes, tetrahedra or columns of planes, or within imaginary surfaces whose edges were indicated by moving lines. I have also varied the axes of rotation to arrive at conical, rather than linear, paths. I have at the same time continued to search through the possibilities of earlier themes; an old motif can sprout new branches. I have solved, in the last two years or so, the problem of hanging a moving part on a moving part, a kind of "elbow linkage", with three moving parts depending one on another. Art historians separate periods in an artist's life but the artist himself is free to overlap them.

I am sometimes asked what will come next? In retrospect I do not find that I have often done what I thought I was going to do, though each step now seems consistent with the previous one, and none of my excursions (even 20 years of painting, before I made sculpture) seems wasted.

—George Rickey

George Rickey's introduction to modernism in art occurred in Paris where he studied painting with André Lhote, Léger and Ozenfant in the early 1930s. Subsequently he went back to the U.S. and taught in various academies while pursuing an active career as a painter of Social Realist pictures in styles reflective of Cézanne and Cubism. During his war service with the Army Air Corps he amused himself constructing little mobiles, but it was not until 1948–49 when he went back to school at the Institute of Design, Chicago, listening to Gabo lecture and reading Moholy-Nagy's *The New Vision* that he became immersed in sculpture at first allowing a kind of figurative element to exist but soon being completely captivated by outright constructivist concepts.

The mobiles of Alexander Calder were a source of inspiration in the early 1950's, though Rickey progressed away from the playful if limited circuits executed by the little cut-out leaves in the older man's constructions. From about 1957 his work grew more ambitious in both size and in setting, and he created series where the basic forms were concentrated within the one orbit.

First works were inspired by natural shapes and were designed to be hung on a wall, thus limiting their viewpoint to the frontal. Then he extended the aspects from which the work was visible so that "Sedge Variation IV" (1961–64) was composed of two counter weighted planes that assumed two angles of vision.

Rickey's reputation became widespread chiefly

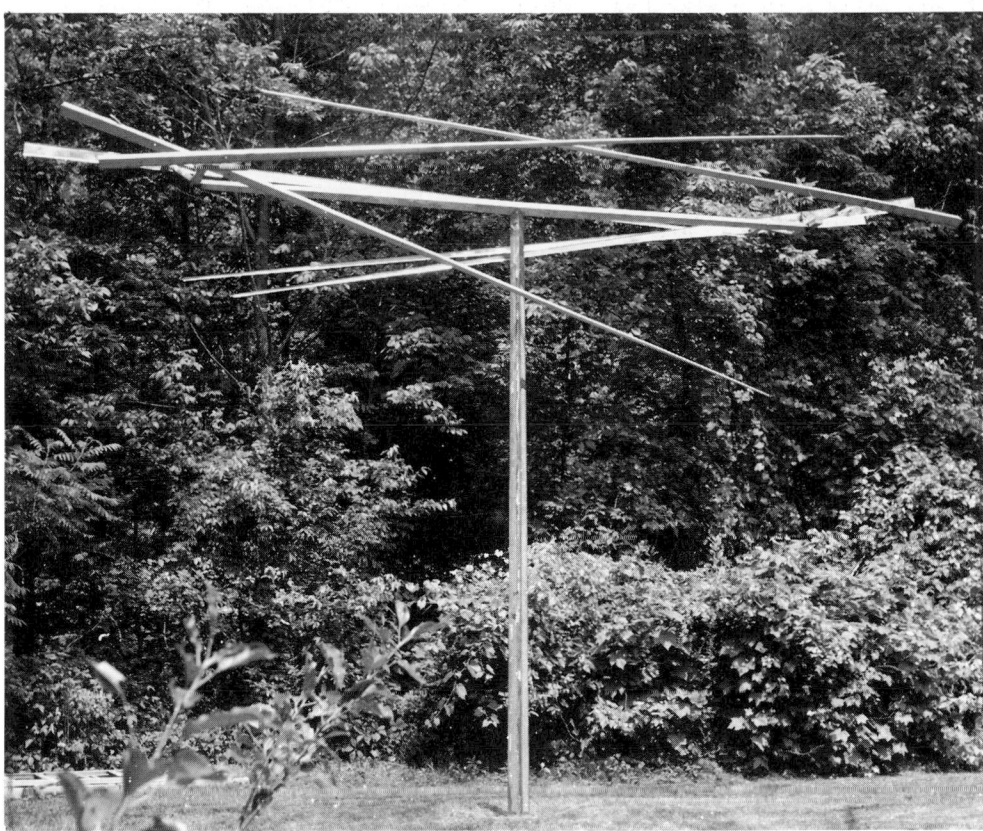

George Rickey: *Six lines in a T Var II*, 1979

when his work was exhibited in Europe, where kinetics were appreciated more widely than in the U.S. His recognition was expedited by the inclusion of his "Two Lines Temporal" in the 1964 *Documenta*. This massive construction of stainless steel rods of triangular section tapering from 8 ins. wide at the base to a point 35 ft. high achieved an impressive symmetry leaning, falling and moving in parallel rhythms and oscillating in independent axes.

The bearings and the gearing of the axles on which Rickey's constructions pivot and dance are designed with an exactitude in calculation of effect, while wind-strength remains the unpredictable factor; the fail-safe mechanisms are built in so that even gale force winds cannot overbalance or capsize the whole. Variation in the speed of the independent and correlated tracks of motion produced only by wind currents is an integral part of each construction. The momentum that leads to the tipping of a blade rises to a climax in the apex of the swing, then is suspended by the force of gravity exerted while the weight of each blade falls slowly to its seemingly pre-ordained pause at its nadir.

From 1964 to 1969 Rickey evolved a series of closely related sculptures comprising either three or five elements that were free-standing and required a circumambulatory inspection to appreciate their complete operation. At one point the edges of the planes only are apparent so that the volume is negative, then as the permutation of planned movement changes the flatness of the blade faces combine to present a surface almost continuous in expanse. One of Rickey's greatest public sculptures is his "Two Rectangles Vertical Gyratory" (1969) in a shopping centre in Rotterdam. These long planes of stainless steel go through see-saw movements and move at angles to each other.

Movement is at the root of Rickey's work since it is the motion of large planar areas or rods rather than their forms which creates the unique sensations on the spectator. Time too is of the utmost, for it plays its dramatic role in the pace and suspenseful pauses in the choreography of the abstract light-reflecting surfaces in space.

—G. S. Whittet

RILEY, Bridget (Louise).

British. Born in London, 25 April 1931. Educated in Cornwall, Buckinghamshire, and Cheltenham: studied under Sam Rabin, at Goldsmiths College of Art, London, 1949–52; also studied at Royal College of Art, London, 1952–55, and under Maurice de Sausmarez, at Thubron's Summer School, Norfolk, 1959. Painter: has lived and worked in London since 1956; worked for J. Walter Thompson Advertising Agency, London, 1958–59; visited Spain and Portugal, 1959; and spent Summer 1960 in Italy; has worked partly in Vaucluse, France, since 1961; visited Greece, 1967; collaborated with Peter Sedgley on *Space*, a scheme for the organization of studios for artists, St. Katherine's Dock, London, 1969–71; travelled in Europe and the United Kingdom, 1971–75, and in India, Japan, and elsewhere in the Far East, 1977. Lecturer in Art, Convent of the Sacred Heart, London, 1957–58; Part-time Lecturer in Art, Loughborough College of Art, Leicestershire, 1959–61, Hornsey College of Art, London, 1960, and Croydon College of Art, Surrey, 1962–64; Trustee, National Gallery, London, since 1981. Recipient: Peter Stuyvesant Foundation Travel Bursary, 1964; Grand Prize for Painting, *Biennale*, Venice, 1968; Prize, *International Print Biennale*, Tokyo, 1972; Gold Medal, *Grafik-Biennale*, Fredrikstad, Norway, 1980. Commander, Order of the British Empire (CBE), 1972. Agent: Mayor Rowan Gallery, 31a Bruton Place, London W1A7AB. Address: 7 Royal Crescent, London W11, England.

Individual Exhibitions:

1962   Gallery 1, London
1963   Gallery 1, London
        University of Nottingham
1965   Richard Feigen Gallery, New York
        Feigen/Palmer Gallery, Los Angeles
1966   Robert Fraser Gallery, London (with Harold Cohen)
        Museum of Modern Art, New York (toured the United States)
        Richard Feigen Gallery, New York

1967 Richard Feigen Gallery, New York
1968 *Biennale*, Venice (with Phillip King: travelled to the Städitsche Kunstgalerie, Bochum, West Germany, and the Museum Boymans-van Beuningen, Rotterdam)
1969 Rowan Gallery, London
Bear Lane Gallery, Oxford (travelled to the Midland Group Gallery, Nottingham, and the Arnolfini Gallery, Bristol)
1970 Richard Feigen Gallery, Chicago
Kunstverein, Hannover (toured Eastern and Western Europe
1971 Rowan Gallery, London
1972 Rowan Gallery, London
1973 *Paintings and Drawings 1961-73*, Whitworth Art Gallery, Manchester, (toured the U.K.)
1974 MacRobert Centre, University of Stirling, Scotland (travelled to Collins Exhibition Hall, Strathclyde, Scotland, and the Aberdeen Art Gallery, Scotland)
1975 Galerie Beyeler, Basle
Sidney Janis Gallery, New York
1976 Rowan Gallery, London
Coventry Gallery, Sydney
1977 Minami Gallery, Tokyo
1978 Sidney Janis Gallery, New York
Albright-Knox Art Gallery, Buffalo, New York (toured the United States, Australia, and Tokyo)
1979 Australian Galleries, Melbourne
Bonython Gallery, Adelaide
1980 Artline, The Hague
Silkscreen Prints 1965-78, Arts Council, London (toured Britain)
1981 Rowan Gallery, London
Warwick Arts Trust, London
1983 Nishimura Gallery, Tokyo
Juda Rowan Gallery, London
Arcade Gallery, Harrogate, Yorkshire
Newcastle Polytechnic, Northumberland
Queens hall Art Centre, Hexham, Northumberland
1984 Royal Institute of British Architects, london
Galerie Reckermann, Cologne
Durham Light Infantry Museum, England (toured Britain)
1985 Goldsmith's College, London
Nina Freudenheim Gallery, Buffalo, New York
1986 Maclaurin Art Gallery, Ayr, Scotland (toured)
Jeffrey Hoffeld and Co., New York
1987 Galerie Konstruktiv Tendens, Stockholm
Galerie und Edition Schlegl, Zurich
Mayor Rowan Gallery, London

Selected Group Exhibitions:

1955 *Young Contemporaries*, London
1962 *Towards Art*, Arts Council Gallery, London (toured the U.K.)
1965 *The Responsive Eye*, Museum of Modern Art, New York (toured the United States)
1967 *Jeunes Peintres Anglais*, Musée des Arts Décoratifs, Paris
1973 *La Peinture Anglaise Aujourd'hui*, Musée National d'Art Moderne, Paris
1976 *Arte Inglese Oggi 1960-76*. Palazzo Reale, Milan
1978 *British Santidskunst*. Kunstnernes Hus. Oslo (travelled to Trondheim and Bergen, Norway)
1982 *Aspects of British Art Today*, Metropolitan Museum, Tokyo (travelled to Tochigi, Osaka, Fukuoka and Sapporo, Japan)
1984 *A Different Climate*, Stadtische Kunsthalle, Dusseldorf
1986 *XLII Biennale*, Venice

Collections:

Tate Gallery, London; Victoria and Albert Museum, London; Fitzwilliam Museum, Cambridge, Scottish National Gallery, of Modern Art, Edinburgh; Stedelijk Museum, Amsterdam; Museum of Modern Art, New York; Albright-Knox Art Gallery Buffalo, New York; Museum of Fine Arts, Dallas; Australian National Gallery, Canberra; Art Gallery of New South Wales, Sydney.

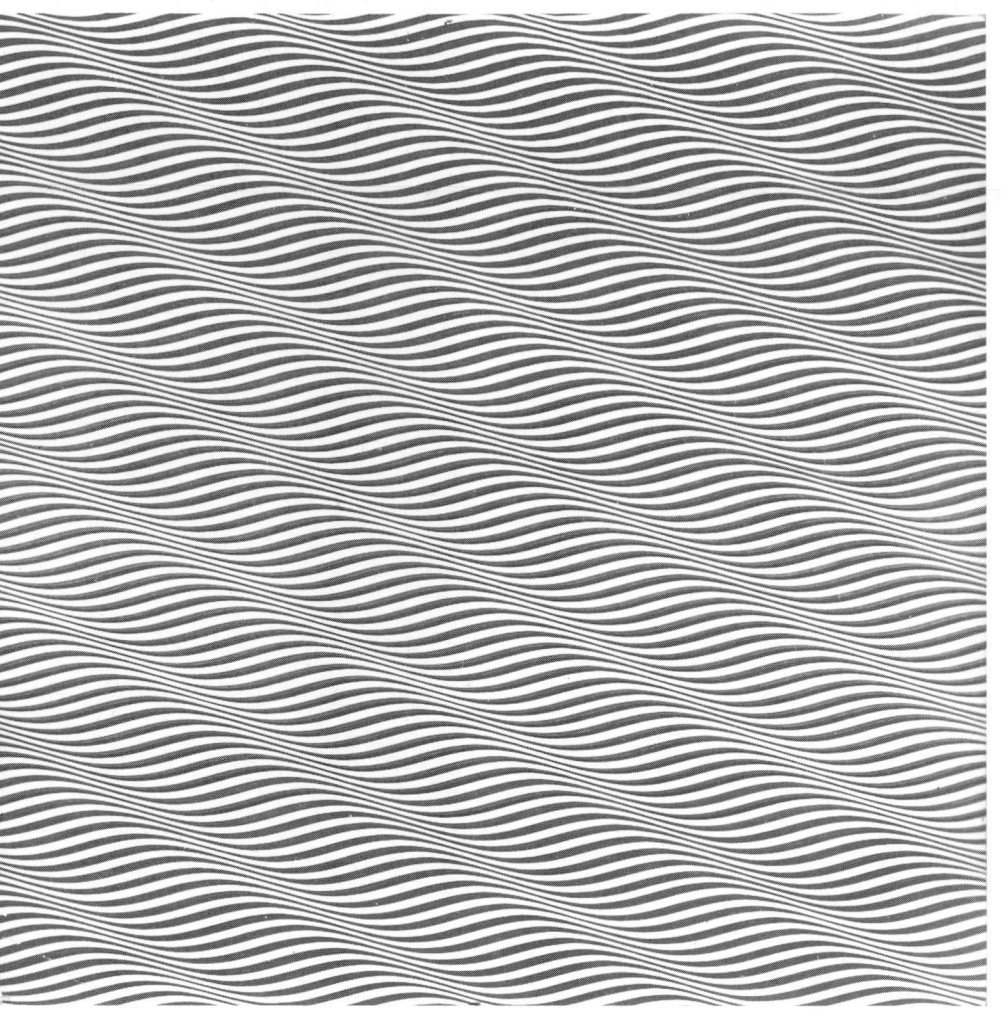

Bridget Riley: *Cataract 3*, 1967

Publications:

By RILEY: articles—statement in *The New Generation*, exhibition catalogue, London 1964; "Bridget Riley Answers Questions about Her Work" in *Monad I* (London), 1964; "Perception Is the Medium" in *Artnews* (New York), October 1965; "Bridget Riley Interviewed by David Sylvester" in *Studio International* (London), March 1967; "Bridget Riley and Maurice de Sausmarez; A Conversation" in *Art International* (Lugano, Switzerland), April 1967; "Notes on Some Paintings" in *Art and Artists* (London), June 1968; "Bridget Riley in Conversation with Robert Kudielka" in *Bridget Riley: Paintings and Drawings 1961-73*, exhibition catalogue, London 1973; "On Travelling Paintings" in *Art Monthly* (London), no. 39, 1980; "Bridget Riley on Swimming Through a Diamond" in *Vogue* (London), March 1984.

On RILEY: books—*Bridget Riley*, exhibition catalogue with introduction by Maurice de Sausmarez, London 1962; *Optical and Kinetic Art* by Michael Compton, London 1967; *Movements in Art Since 1945* by Edward Lucie-Smith, London 1969; *Bridget Riley* by Maurice de Sausmarez, London 1970; *Modern English Painters* by John Rothenstein, London 1974; *Art Since Pop* by John A. Walker, London 1975; *Bridget Riley*, exhibition catalogue with text by Robert Kudielka, Tokyo 1977; *Art of the Sixties* by Hugh Adams, London 1978; *Bridget Riley: Works 1959-78*, exhibition catalogue with introduction by Robert Kudielka, London 1978; *Women Artists from Antiquity to the Twentieth Century* by Wendy Slatkin, New York 1983.

*

My paintings are not concerned with the romantic legacy of expressionism, nor with fantasies, concepts or symbols.

I draw from nature, I work with nature, although in completely new terms. For me nature is not landscape, but the dynamism of visual forces—an event rather than an appearance—these forces can only be tackled by treating colour and form as ultimate identities, freeing them from all descriptive or functional roles.

The context of painting provides an arena in which to tap these visual energies—to unlock their true potential and latent characteristics. Once released they have to be organized in new pictorial terms, every bit as much, though quite differently, as when painting nature in landscape or still life.

The new motif determines the size, the proportion, even the "way up" of the painting just as the old natural motif determined these factors before. In working on a painting I choose a small group of colours and juxtapose them in different sequences, to provide various relationships and to precipitate colour reactions. These colour *events* are delicate and elusive, they have to be organized to make them more *present*—more *there* more *real*. I take for example three colours, say magenta, ochre and turquoise plus black and white, a situation which then triggers off airy irridescent bursts of colour.

I choose a form and a structure in which to repeat these colour clouds, to accumulate them, to mass them until each painted unit is submerged in a visual rhythm which, in turn, collectively generates a shimmering coloured haze. This luminous substance is completely meshed with the actual coloured surface and together they provide the experience of the painting.

—Bridget Riley

*

Bridget Riley has the distinction of being one of the few British artists (and the only British woman) to win the *premio* at the Venice *Biennale*. She thus enjoys an enormous international reputation. She is one of the pioneers of Op Art, not *the* pioneer.

Her early work was divisionist in technique. It enabled her to capture the intensity of light and colour, the visual equivalent of energy, even the pulsations of heat, from a shimmering landscape.

This preoccupation with light, heat and pulsating

energy persisted into the next phase of her work, which marked the beginning of those pictures by which she has come to be known. In this phase she worked in black and white with very simple elements—small triangles or ovals, curved lines, vertical lines, horizontal lines. She discovered that a systematic repetition of these small elements could generate the visual equivalent of energy very powerfully. In "Static" (which refers to an electric charge, not absence of movement), for instance, tiny ovals assault the optic nerves in such a way as to suggest the bombardment of heat and light from the shale on a mountain on an intensely hot summer's day.

In the early 1960's her pictures fell roughly into three types: systematic repetitions of simple elements such as triangles, as in "Straight Curve," in which triangles of varying proportions are arranged in straight rows in such a way that an impression of curved lines is produced; broken concentric figures, such as "Disfigured Circle," in which there is a continuous shift of perspective, or the "Blaze" series, in which counterflow hatched lines forming eccentric circles grind into one another; and undulating curved lines, like waves, which heave and billow, as in the appropriately named "Current."

What is remarkable about these early pictures, apart from the technical brilliance, and the suavity and rhythm of undulating lines, is the intensity of feeling they generate and the way their effects are achieved with such economy of means. The aggressiveness of some of these works may reflect certain feelings which Riley had at the time and transferred to canvas. The economy of means is connected with a belief (which she inculcated in her teaching) that restraints on an artist lead to greater, not less, richness of invention and individuality of expression. In this connection, she had a practice, which she called "pacing," in which a circle or triangle is "put through its paces," moved from full circle, through various ovals, to almost a straight line, with unforseeable and stimulating results.

From the stark and dramatic contrasts of black and white Riley turned to the modulation of tones.

This gave her greater scope, since tone can modify and produce form. Thus, not only were the elements "paced" by an alteration of shape, but also by alteration of tone. Moreover, variations in tone created overall patterns which black and white on their own could not do.

By the late 1960's Riley was working in colour, at first two colours (red and blue), then three, four, five, with white, or, more recently, black intervening. Superficially they may seem to be no more than strips of colour juxtaposed. The perceptive spectator, however, will notice how these colours react on one another to "induce" other ethereal, aerial colours through the "spread" of the pigment colours into the areas of white. Thus, in an early work, "Late Morning," a sense of the opulence of a late summer morning, with its golden-green glow, when the sun has all but dispersed the morning mists and the air is still cool, is induced by the juxtaposition of orange, various shades of green and white.

In those early colour works Riley had not quite mastered the principle of colour induction. She thought that it consisted in inducing colour into a white area. It is, of course, partly that. But in her recent work she has discovered that the "inhibitive" effect of black may lead to a far richer induction of colour. It seems that in these recent works she has finally achieved the goal she has been aiming for. These recent works are both entirely individual, canvas by canvas, but rich in coloration, suggesting the richness of oriental colours.

Critics of Bridget Riley's work have said that her pictures are nothing more than exercises in perceptual psychology or designs for commercial advertising. Ironically she did work for an advertising agency, and, it could be said, that the so-called "woolmark" is a plagiarism of one of her "Fragments." And some of her work is of interest to perceptual psychologists. It is also true that her method of work is perhaps more blatantly "experimental" than that of most artists—sketch, cartoon, etc.—and that she employs

assistants to produce the final work. Space does not allow a proper discussion of these matters. Suffice it to say that the use of assistants is in the grand tradition of painting; artistic experimentation has nothing to do with scientific experimentation (though scientists may use works of art as material for their investigations); and, what advertisers do with works of art should not reflect on the works themselves. Art is art, neither science nor advertising; and Bridget Riley is an artist pure and simple.

—D. C. Barrett

RINKE, Klaus.

German. Born in Wattenschied, 29 April 1939. Educated in Wattenschied, 1945-54; apprentice painter/decorator in Westphalian department store, Gelsenkirchen, 1954-57; studied painting and free pictorial expression, Folkwangschule, Essen-Werden, 1957-60. Independent artist, in Paris 1960-62, Rheims 1962-64, and in Dusseldorf since 1964: abstract paintings and drawings, 1960-66; polyester sculptures, 1965-68; first sculptures with water, 1968; first body-works and "demonstrations," 1969; first films and videos, 1969. Professor of Free Pictorial Expression, Staatliche Kunstakademie, Dusseldorf, 1974. Recipient: Prize, with Nancy Graves and Pierpaolo Calzolari, *Biennale*, Paris, 1971; Landespreis, Nordrhein-Westfalen, Dusseldorf, 1973; Konrad-von-Soest Prize, Landeschaftsverbandes Westfalen, Dusseldorf, 1974. Agents: Reese Palley Gallery, 550 Sutter Street, San Francisco, California 94102, U. S. A.; and Galerie Alfred Schmel, Dusseldorf. Address: c/o Galerie Schmela, Mutter-Ey-Strasse 3, 4000 Dusseldorf, West Germany.

Individual Exhibitions:

1962	Galerie Le Portulan, Le Havre, France
1963	Galerie Haut-Pave, Paris
1964	Centre Culturel St. Severin, Paris
1965	Galerie Butterbach, Luxembourg
1969	Galerie Konrad Fischer, Dusseldorf
1970	Städtisches Museum Schloss Morsbroich, Leverkusen, West Germany
	Galerie Konrad Fischer, Dusseldorf
1971	Galleria Toselli, Milan
	Galerie Ricke, Cologne
	Videogalerie Gerry Schum, Dusseldorf
	Gegenverkehr, Aachen, West Germany
1972	Situation Gallery, London
	Galleria L'Attico, Rome
	Reese Palley Gallery, New York
	Reese Palley Gallery, San Francisco
	Kunsthalle, Tübingen
1973	Kunsthalle, Recklinghausen, West Germany
	At the *Bienal*, Sao Paulo
	Württembergischer Kunstverein, Stuttgart
	Galerie Ricke, Cologne
	Universitat, Kiel
	Museum of Modern Art, New York (outdoor action)
1974	The Clocktower, New York
	Galerie Schmela, Dusseldorf
	Westfalischer Kunstverein, Münster, West Germany
1975	Galerie Hetzler + Keller, Stuttgart
	Galerie Defet, Nuremberg
	Objekte, Photoserien, Zeichnungen 1969-1975, Kunstverein, Dusseldorf
	Galerie Schmela, Dusseldorf
1976	Museum of Modern Art, Oxford
	Städtisches Museum, Wiesbaden, West Germany
	Reuchlinhaus, Pforzheim, West Germany
	Travaux 1969-1976, Musée d'Art Moderne de la Ville, Paris
1978	*Meine Plastik ist Zeichnung*, Kunsthalle, Hamburg
1981	*Die Autonomen Werke von 1957 1980*, Staatsgalerie, Stuttgart
1982	Kunstmuseum, Dusseldorf
	Flow Ace Gallery, Vancouver, British Columbia
1983	Flow Ace Gallery, Paris
1984	Museum Neandertal, Mettmann, West Germany

Selected Group Exhibitions:

1968	*12 Environments*, Kunsthalle, Berne
1969	*14 x 14 Escalation*, Staatliche Kunsthalle, Baden-Baden, West Germany
1970	*Information*, Museum of Modern Art, New york
1971	*Prospekt*, Kunsthalle, Dusseldorf
1972	*Documenta*, Kassel, West Germany (and 1977)
1973	*Kunst aus Fotografie*, Kunstverein, Hannover (travelled to Städtische Kunstsammlungen, Ludwigshafen, West Germany)
1974	*Projekt 74*, Kunsthalle, Cologne
1975	*Bodyworks*, Museum of Contemporary Art, Chicago
1977	*Europe in the 70's*, Art Institute of Chicago (travelled to the Hirshhorn Museum, Washington, D.C.)
1983	*Sculpture Biennale*, Middelheim Park, Antwerp, Belgium

Collections:

Nationalgalerie, West Berlin; Museum Folkwang, Essen; Städtisches Museum Schloss Morsbroich, Leverkusen, West Germany; Museum Ludwig, Cologne; Neue Galerie/Sammlung Ludwig, Aachen, West Germany; Kaiser-Wilhelm Museum, Krefeld, West Germany; Staatsgalerie, Stuttgart; Kunsthalle, Tübingen; Kunstmuseum, Bonn; Tate Gallery, London.

Publications:

By RINKE: book—*Klaus Rinke: Zeit Time-Raum Space-Korper Body—Handlungen Transformations*, edited by Gotz Adriani, Cologne 1972; *Klaus Rinke: Skulpturen und Zeichnungen*, exhibition catalogue, Mettmann 1984; articles—"Kunstwater van Klaus Rinke" in *Museumjournaal* (Amsterdam), September 1970; "Between Spring and Ocean" in *Studio International* (London), March 1971; "Statement" in *Avalanche* (New York), March 1971; "Phenomenology of a Time, Space System," edited by Evelyn Weiss, in *Studio International* (London), April 1974; films and videos—*Zwoelf Fass Geschoeppftes*, 1969; *41 Polyesterelement Verteilt und Zusammen Gezogen*, 1969; *Wasser Hippen*, 1970; *Fernost-/Far East German Buddha*, 1970; *Inhalation I + II*, 1971; *Wasser Holen Bringen Schulten*, 1971; *Mutation*, 1971; *Galerie Konrad Fischer*, 1971; *Energiegrenzen*, 1971; *Distant und Zeitrelation*, 1971; *Boden-Raum*, 1971; *Elliptisch*, 1971.

On RINKE: books—*Klaus Rinke*, exhibition catalogue, with text by Rolf Wedewer, and an interview by Jacques Laval, Leverkusen, West Germany 1970; *Klaus Rinke: 12th Bienal de Sao Paulo 1973*, exhibition catalogue, with text by Manfred Schmalriede, Cologne 1973; *Klaus Rinke: Objekte, Photoserien, Zeichnungen 1969-1975*, exhibition catalogue, with a foreword by Karl-Heinz Hering, text by Manfred Schmalriede, Dusseldorf 1975; *Klaus Rinke: Travaux 1969/1976*, exhibition catalogue, with texts by Suzanne Page, Evelyn Weiss and Pierre Guyotat, Paris 1976; *Klaus Rinke: Meine Plastik ist Zeichnung*, exhibition catalogue, with text by Werner Hofmann and Helmut R. Leppien, Hamburg 1978; *Rinke: Die autonomen Werke von 1957-1980*, exhibition catalogue, with texts by Stephan von Wiese and Klaus Heinz, Stuttgart 1981.

Klaus Rinke has sought in the most vigorous way at his command to eliminate every vestige of the past from his work. Not like the Futurists who wanted to replace heritage with a new imagery based upon the contemporary world of their times, but like an extended conceptualist, he has cauterised imagery to the point of non-existence. The world is permitted only in terms of temporal theory or physics. Aids like the camera and engineering make these practices visible, tangible even, but the burden of proof is upon the brain rather than upon the eye or the hand. Actions—demonstrations he calls them—are also an appeal to cerebral ratiocination rather than emotion. Rinke looks for the viability of his work in Situations like

Landscape, Space or in the abstract systems of Physics and Geometry.

Beyond the conceptual frontiers, and to demonstrate time and space, he builds systems which spell out the magic of computers but always in the series order he has ordained. He is particularly obsessed with two elements, both of which can play their parts in these fields—expansion and gravitational pull. In the former, to take one specific example, he has shown with his drawing "Circular Expansion" that he can enter the realms of optics that less sophisticated eyes might assume were the prerequisites of Bridget Riley and Victor Vasarely. This is a fairly primitive demonstration of visual truth by Rinke. The *"Measuring Instrument for Eternity"* (an engineering construction) of 1972/73 shows how far he can pursue his theories when he wishes.

—Sheldon Williams

RIOPELLE, Jean-Paul.

Canadian. Born in Montreal in 1923. Painter: travelled France, Germany, and New York, 1946; settled in Paris, 1947; associated with the Automatistes group led by Paul-Emile Borduas, Recipient: Prix Unesco, Paris, 1962. Companion of the Order of Canada, 1969. Agents: Pierre Matisse Gallery, 41 East 57th Street, New York, New York 10022; and Galerie Maeght Lelong, 13–14 rue de Teheran, 75008 Paris. Address: 10 rue Fremincourt, 75015 Paris, France.

Individual Exhibitions:

1949	Galerie Nina Dausset, Paris
1950	Galerie Greuse, Paris
1951	Galerie Springer, Berlin
1952	Galerie Hachette, Paris
	Galerie Henriette Niepoe, Paris
1953	Galerie Pierre Loeb, Paris
1954	Pierre Matisse Gallery, New York
	Galerie Rive Droite, Paris
	Galerie Evrad, Lille, France
1955	Pierre Matisse Gallery, New York
1956	Gimpel Gallery, London
	Galerie Jacques Dubourg, Paris
	Kunstverein, Cologne
	Kunst-und Museumverein, Wuppertal, West Germany
	Kestner Gesellschaft, Hannover
1959	Kunsthalle, Basle
	Richentor, Basle
	Svensk-Franska Konstgalleriet, Stockholm
	Galerie Anne Abels, Cologne
	Arthur Tooth and Sons Gallery, London
1960	Galerie Jacques Dubourg, Paris
	Galleria l'Ariete, Milan
	Assosiazione Arti Figurative, Turin
1962	National Gallery of Canada, Ottawa
1963	Galerie d'Art Moderne, Basle
	Arthur Tooth and Sons Gallery, London
1965	Pierre Matisse Gallery, New York
1967	Musée de la Province, Quebec
1972	Galerie Maeght, Paris
1974	Galerie Maeght, Paris
	Pierre Matisse Gallery, New York
1975	Pierre Matisse Gallery, New York
	Galeria Maeght, Barcelona
	Galleria d'Arte Narciso, Turin
	Gallery Moos, Toronto
1977	*Jean-Paul Riopelle: Grands Formats 1952–75,* Pierre Matisse Gallery, New York
1980	Musée d'Art et d'Industrie, St.-Etienne, France
	Galerie Maeght, Zurich
1981	Raydon Gallery, New York
	Gimpel Fils Gallery, London
	Centre Georges Pompidou, Paris
1983	Galerie Maeght Lelong, Paris
1985	Pierre Matisse Gallery, New York

Selected Group Exhibitions:

1951	*Bienal*, Sao Paulo (and 1955)
1954	*Biennale*, Venice (and 1962)

Jean-Paul Riopelle: *Feu Follet*, **1951** Courtesy Gimpel Fils, London

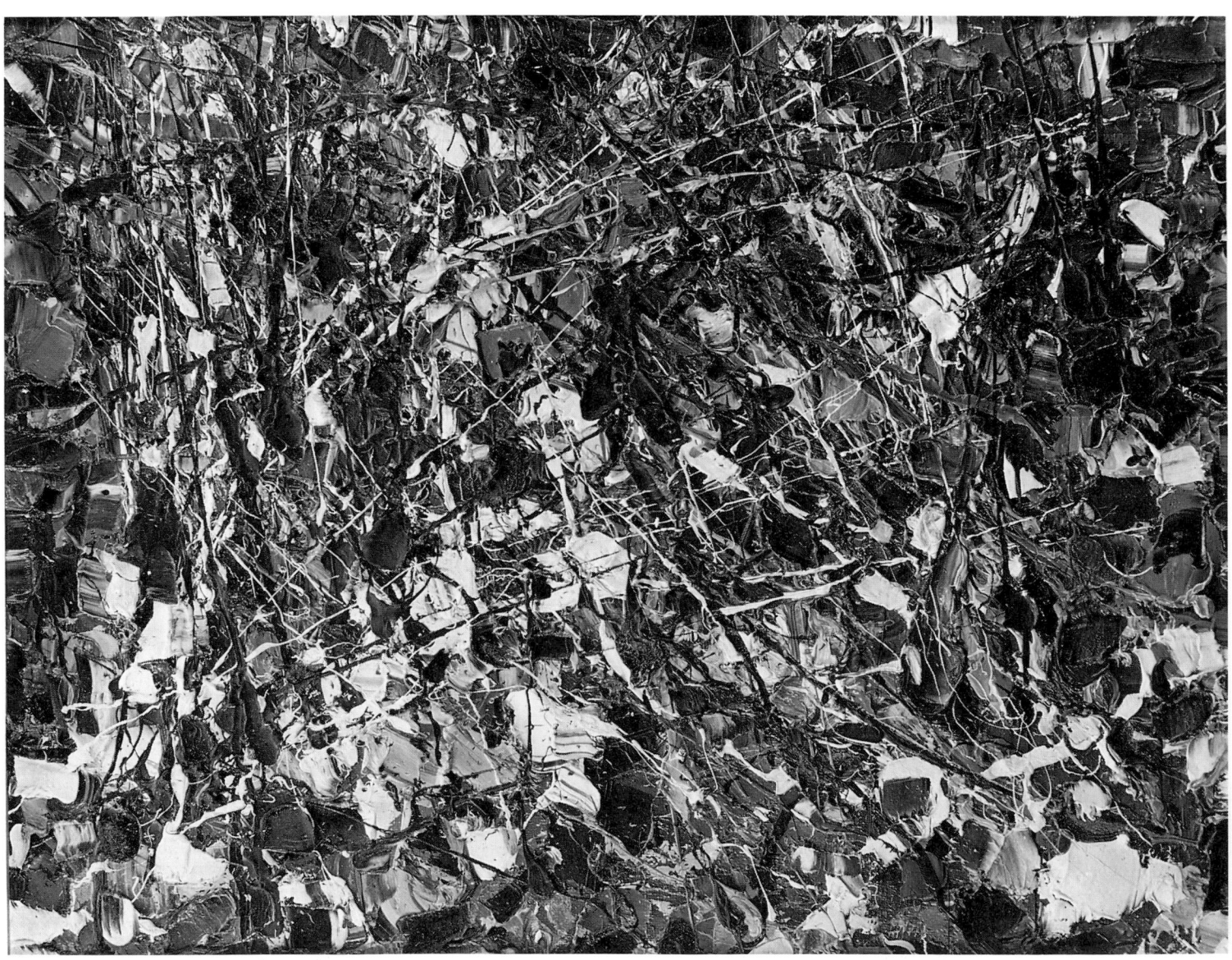

1956	*Internationale Sezession*, Leverkusen, West Germany
1958	*World's Fair*, Brussels
1959	*Documenta*, Kassel, West Germany
1960	*Salon de Mai*, Paris
1961	*Carnegie International*, Pittsburgh
1970	*8 Artists from Canada*, Museum Haaretz, Tel Aviv

Collections:

National Gallery of Canada, Ottawa; Art Gallery of Ontario, Toronto; Los Angeles County Museum of Art; Scottish National Gallery of Modern Art, Edinburgh; Neue Nationalgalerie, Berlin; National Gallery of Victoria, Melbourne.

Publications:

On RIOPELLE: books—*Riopelle*, exhibition catalogue, Paris 1954; *Riopelle: Reperes*, exhibition catalogue with preface by Lise Gauvin, Paris 1983; *Jean-Paul Riopelle: Les Oies Sauvages*, exhibition catalogue, New York 1985; articles—"Two Answers" by Neville Wallis in *The Observer* (London), June 1959; "A Painter of Awakening—Jean-Paul Riopelle" by Georges Duthuit in *Canadian Art* (Ottawa), October 1959; "La Sculpture de Peintre: Bronzes de Riopelle" in *Quadicum* (Paris), no. 11, 1961; "Riopelle" by Franco Russoli in *Derrière le Miroir* (Paris), April 1970; "Riopelle ou la Pensée Sauvage" in *Chroniques de l'Art Vivant* (Paris), May 1970; "Jean-Paul Riopelle: A Poet of the Sign" by M. Greenwood in *Artscanada* (Toronto), August 1971; "Lettre de Suisse" by J. L. Daval in *Art International* (Lugano, Switzerland), March 1973; special issue of *Derrière le Miroir* (Paris), March 1976.

Nicolas de Staël and Jean-Paul Riopelle have proved themselves the masters of thick-paint applied impasto in contemporary times. Unlike de Staël, whose only non-figurative work veered towards exact and tight abstract compositions, the Canadian was able to spread his squares and deluges of colours in a far more amorphous mass. For those who can tease their eyes through the strife of colours and the stodgy pigment there are at least two surprises in store: a) under and running through the lumpy scales of paint there is a well-tuned discipline of composition which draws the whole painting together in much the same way as the open eye in one of Lee Bontecou's constructions will give cohesion to the entire apparatus; and b) out of this emerges a kind of architecture not so far removed from that of Vieira da Silva, except that in Riopelle's case there is no instance of nervous *schadenfreude* that can haunt some of the more daunting canvases of Vieira da Silva.

Of course a talent like that of Riopelle could never stay still. At some stage the embattled frontage presented by his painting would be bound to yield to change, however characteristic. But it was not actually the expected transition from one kind of fortresslike wall of paint to another that took place. Instead the areas of paint began to isolate themselves and assume the individuality of independence. Brightly coloured areas, although free-flocking, took on something of the intensity of those to be found in the flower paintings of Ernst Wilhelm Nay. This was particularly true of the watercolours. The paintings tended to stay more closely integrated, although the "pattern" (or subject) in them became clear cut, more sculptural; and the gouaches and the pastels-and-charcoal drawings have, in many cases, given the central image a distinct outline, placing it like a jewel on black velvet.

Are all these demonstrations of inventive skill anything to do with change of ambience? Riopelle has been living and working in Paris since 1947. Does any artist carry his personal creativity with him into a new atmosphere and not expect to be affected by a different climate? Riopelle fits so comfortably into the Ecole de Paris and he plainly has added to its lustre—but do he and his work owe anything to Paris?

—Sheldon Williams

RIVERS, Larry.

American. Born Larry Grossberg in the Bronx, New York, 17 August 1923; changed name to Rivers at start of career as jazz saxophonist, 1940. Studied at the Julliard School of Music, New York, 1944–45; Hans Hofmann's School, New York and Provincetown, Massachusetts, 1947–48; New York University, 1948–51, B.A. 1951. Served in the United States Army, 1942–43. Married Augusta Burger in 1945 (separated, 1946); children: Steven and Joseph; married Clarice Price in 1960 (separated, 1967); children: Gwynne and Emma. Played in jazz bands, New York, in the early 1940's; began painting, 1945; travelled in Europe, then returned to New York and began painting full time, 1950; lived with his mother-in-law, Berdie Burger, his favorite model, Southampton, Long Island, 1953–57; began working in welded metal sculpture, 1957; visited Paris, 1961–62; Set and Costume Designer, *Oedipus Rex*, New York, 1966; travelled to Africa and collaborated with Pierre Gaisseau on the television film *Africa and I*, 1967–68; began work with videotape, 1970; collaborated with Jean Tinguely on multimedia work, Paris, 1979. Artist-in-Residence, Slade School of Fine Art, London, 1964; Instructor, University of California at Santa Barbara, 1972; Lecturer on Contemporary American Art, in various Russian Cities, at invitation from Union of Soviet Artists, 1976. Recipient: Third Prize, Corcoran Museum, Washington, D.C., 1955. Agent: Marlborough Gallery, New York. Address: c/o Marlborough Gallery Inc., 40 West 57th Street, New York, New York 10019, U.S.A.

Individual Exhibitions:

1949	Jane Street Gallery, New York
1951	Tibor de Nagy Gallery, New York
1953	Tibor de Nagy Gallery, New York
1954	Tibor de Nagy Gallery, New York
	Stable Gallery, New York
1956	Tibor de Nagy Gallery, New York
1957	Tibor de Nagy Gallery, New York
1958	Tibor de Nagy Gallery, New York
1959	Tibor de Nagy Gallery, New York
1960	Tibor de Nagy Gallery, New York
	Martha Jackson Gallery, New York
1961	Dwan Gallery, Los Angeles
	Tibor de Nagy Gallery, New York
1962	Tibor de Nagy Gallery, New York
	Gimpel Fils, London
	Galerie Rive Droite, Paris
	Dwan Gallery, Los Angeles
1963	Dwan Gallery, Los Angeles
1964	Gimpel Fils, London
1965	Rose Art Museum, Brandeis University, Waltham, Massachusetts (retrospective)
	Pasadena Art Museum, California (retrospective)
	Jewish Museum, New York (retrospective)
	Detroit Institute of Arts (retrospective)
	Minneapolis Institute of Arts (retrospective)
1970	*Drawings 1949–1969*. Art Institute of Chicago
	Larry Rivers 1965–70, Marlborough Gallery, New York
1973	*Larry Rivers 1970–73*, Marlborough Gallery, New York
	Palais des Beaux-Arts, Brussels
1974	*From the Coloring Book of Japan*, Marlborough Gallery, New York
1975	Marlborough Gallery, New York
1976	*Works of the 60's and 70's*, Gimpel Fils, London
1977	Marlborough Gallery, New York
	Robert Miller Gallery, New York
	Hokin Gallery, Chicago
1978	ACA Gallery, New York
1979	*Recent Works, Golden Oldies*, Robert Miller Gallery, New York
1980	Museo de Arte Contemporanio de Caracas, Venezuela
1981	Marlborough Fine Art, London
1982	Marlborough Gallery, New York
	Studio Marconi, Milan
1983	Elaine Horwich Gallery, Phoenix, Arizona
	Guild Hall Museum, East Hampton, New York
1984	Kouros Gallery, New York
	Jewish Museum, New York
1985	University of Pennsylvania, Philadelphia
	Marlborough Fine Art, Tokyo
1986	Aselphi University Center, Garden City, New York
	Marlborough Gallery, New York

Selected Group Exhibitions:

1950	*New Talent 1950*, Samuel Kootz Gallery, New York
1956	*12 Americans*. Museum of Modern Art, New York
1958	*Carnegie International*, Pittsburgh
1960	*Business Buys American Art*, Whitney Museum, New York
	Painting and Sculpture of a Decade 1954–64, Tate Gallery, London
1966	*2 Decades of American Painting*, Museum of Modern Art, New York (travelled to Japan, India, and Australia)
1968	*Documenta 4*, Kassel, West Germany
1970	*American Painting 1970*, Virginia Museum of Art, Richmond

Collections:

Metropolitan Museum of Art, New York; Museum of Modern Art, New York; Whitney Museum, New York; Corcoran Gallery of Art, Washington, D.C.; Hirshhorn Museum and Sculpture Garden, Washington, D.C.; Chrysler Art Museum, Provincetown, Massachusetts; Brandeis University, Waltham, Massachusetts; Art Institute of Chicago; Tate Gallery, London.

Publications:

By RIVERS: books-drawings for *Coloring Book of Japan 1973; The Donkey and the Darling*, with Terry Southern, New York 1977; *Drawings and Digressions*, with Carol Brightman, New York 1979; articles—"Young Draftsman or Master Draftsman" in *Art News* (New York). January 1955; "An Interview with Larry Rivers," with James Thrall Soby, in *Saturday Review* (New York), 3 September 1955; statement in *12 Americans*, exhibition catalogue, by Dorothy C. Miller, New York 1956; "Why I Paint as I Do," interview with Frank O'Hara, in *Horizon* (New York), September/October 1959; "Monet: The Eye Is Magic" in *Art News* (New York), April 1960; interview in *Conversations with Review* (New York), July/August 1961; "We Hitch Our Wagons to a Star" in *Mademoiselle* (New York), August 1961; "6 Poems by Larry Rivers" in *Locus Solus* (New York), vol. 1, no.3/4, 1962; "My Life Among the Stones" in *Location* (New York), vol. 1, no. 1, Spring 1963; introduction to *Larry Rivers*, exhibition catalogue, London 1964; "Dear Teen-age Audience" in *Seventeen Magazine* (New York), November 1964; "A Memoir" in *Larry Rivers*, exhibition catalogue, Waltham, Massachusetts 1965; "Sensibility of the 60's" in *Art in America* (New York), January 1967; "Blues for Yves Klein" in *Artnews* (New York), February 1967; statement in "What Is Pinter Up To?" in the *New York Times*, 5 February 1967; "Jackson Pollock: An Artists' Symposium" in *Artnews* (New York), April 1967; statement in *Art Now: New York*, May 1970; "If You Can't Draw, Trace: Frank Bowling Talks with Larry Rivers" in *Arts Magazine* (New York), February 1971; interview in *Arts Chronicles 1954–1966* by Frank O'Hara, compiled by D.M. Allen, New York 1975; "Golden Oldies: An Interview with Larry Rivers," with Jeffery H. Loria, in *Arts Magazine* (New York), November 1978.

On RIVERS: books—*Modern Art and the New Past* by James Thrall Soby, Norman, Oklahoma 1958; *Some Younger Artists*, edited by B.H. Friedman, New York 1959; *Rivers*, exhibition catalogue, text by John Ashbery and Thomas B. Hess, London 1962; *Larry Rivers*, exhibition catalogue, with text by Sam Hunter, Waltham, Massachusetts 1965; *Larry Rivers* by Sam Hunter, New York 1969; *Rivers* by Sam Hunter, 1972; *Larry Rivers: Drawings 1949–1969*. exhibition catalogue, Chicago 1970; *Larry Rivers 1970–1973*, exhibition catalogue, New York 1973; *Larry Rivers: From the Coloring Book of Japan*, exhibition catalogue, New York 1974; *Larry Rivers: Works of the 50's and 60's*, exhibition catalogue, London 1976; *Larry Rivers: Recent Works, Golden Oldies*, exhibition catalogue, New York 1979; *Larry Rivers*, exhibition catalogue, text by David Joel Shapiro. Caracas 1980; *Larry Rivers: Relief Paintings*, exhibition catalogue, New York 1986.

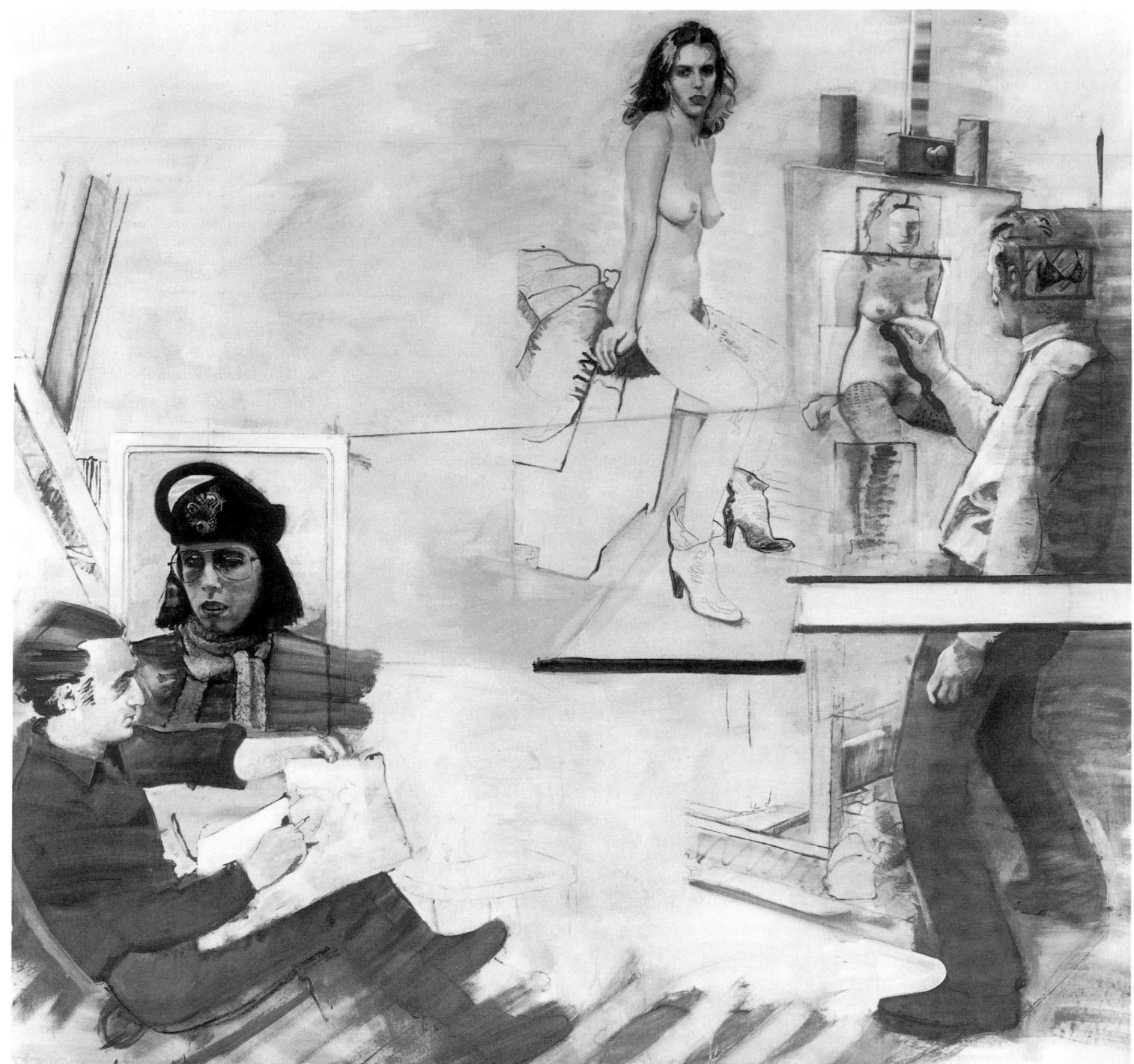

Larry Rivers: *The Continuing Interest in Abstract Art*

Larry Rivers is one of those American artists who followed De Kooning in adapting the freedom of the Abstract Expressionist technique towards figurative ends. And in painting bank notes, cigarette packets and advertisements he was along with Rauschenberg one of the first Americans to use ready made vernacular images, thus paving the way for Pop Art. But Rivers differs from the Pop Artists in using given imagery, whether popular commercial clichés or his copies of Old Masters, as the basis of painterly variations in his freely expressionistic style.

Rivers has shown considerable versatility, beginning his career as a professional jazz saxophonist, writing poetry, and making constructions, sculptures, graphics and stage designs as well as painting. He has also been very eclectic in the subject matter he has reworked in his paintings. History, folklore and popular myth all combined in his painting of "George Washington Crossing the Delaware" (1953), in which he used the currently accepted mode of Abstract Expressionism not for purely abstract painterly purposes

but to transform a scorned and banal image from the past. His variations of familiar themes, in which he humorously played with transformations of visual clichés, range from well-known old master paintings to objects from daily life like his cigarette packets. And in such pictures as "Dutch Masters and Cigars II" (1963) he combines the two in a composition of an open cigarbox with a reworking of Rembrandt's "Syndics" as the picture on the lid.

Thus Rivers introduced recognizable subject matter into abstract Expressionism in far more explicit terms than had De Kooning, adapting that style to a montage-like combination of images taken both from the urban commercial environment and from fine art. His human figures may like "O'Hara" be variations on other paintings, in this case a famous Géricault standing male nude, or they may be taken directly from life as are his candid portraits of his mother-in-law Birdie in the nude. His "Double Portrait of Birdie" (1955), shows her in two different poses, simulating movie montage. In other cases he uses the

human figure to project an ironic image derived from instructional graphics, with a head having parts of the face all neatly labelled in French, or a female nude similarly labelled with the French names for the parts of the body. Other paintings are fragmented accounts of a particular experience such as a street accident, treated in out-of-focus, multiple views.

Rivers' use of urban and commercial images anticipates Pop Art, but his playful and painterly treatment of them is very different from the cool, deadpan approach of the Pop artists, and he has never been influential in the way that Rauschenberg has. He isn't an artist who fits neatly into any category. Edward Lucie-Smith has said of him that the outstanding characteristic of all his paintings is "a kind of glancing obliqueness, as if the artist were unable to focus on the actual subject for very long at a time." His subjects are secondary to the treatment he gives them, and he himself has described his variations on familiar themes as "a smorgasbord of the recognizable, and if being the chef is no particular thrill, it was as much as I could cook up." Barry Ulanov has called him "a superior entertainer." The wit which is in his writing is even more substantial than in his painting. But one would like to see his facility and humor reach beyond virtuoso twirls and twists to more demanding material, though it is something in a time when the surfaces of pop art and the emblems of easy identification absorb so many painters to find even entertainment that requires a little thought, a brief pause.

—Konstantin Bazarov

ROCKBURNE, Dorothea.

Canadian. Born in Verdun, Quebec, Canada. Studied at the Ecole de Beaux-Arts, Montreal, 1947–50; Black Mountain College, North Carolina, 1951–56, B.F.A. Painter: lives and works in New York. Taught Art Theory, School of Visual Arts, New York. Recipient: Guggenheim Fellowship, 1972–73; Painting Award, Art Institute of Chicago, 1972; National Endowment for the Arts fellowship, Washington, D.C., 1974; Creative Arts Award, Brandeis University, Waltham, Massachusetts, 1985. Agents: Xavier Fourcade, Inc., 36 West 75th Street, New York, New York 10012; Texas Gallery, 2012 Peden, Houston, Texas 77019; Richard Gray Gallery, 620 North Michigan Avenue, Chicago, Illinois 60611; David Bellman Gallery, 134 Peter Street, Toronto, Ontario, Canada. Address: 140 Grand Street, New York, New York 10013, U.S.A.

Individual Exhibitions

1970	Bykert Gallery, New York
1971	Galerie Ileana Sonnabend, Paris
1972	New Gallery, Cleveland
	Bykert Gallery, New York
	Galleria Toselli, Milan
	University of Rochester Art Gallery, New York
	Galleria d'Arte, Bari, Italy
1973	Bykert Gallery, New York
	Galleria Toselli, Milan
	Lisson Gallery, London
	Hartford College of Art, Connecticut
	Daniel Weinberg Gallery, San Francisco
	Galleria Schema, Florence
1974	Galleria Toselli, Milan
1975	Galleria Schema, Florence
	Galerie Charles Kriwin, Brussels
1976	John Weber Gallery, New York
1978	John Weber Gallery, New York
1979	Texas Gallery, Houston
1981	Texas Gallery, Houston
1982	Contemporary Art Museum, Houston
	Whitney Museum, New York
1983	Museum of Fine Arts, Houston
1985	Denver Art Museum, Colorado (toured the United States, 1985–87)

Selected Group Exhibitions

1976	*Drawing Now,* Museum of Modern Art, New York
1977	*Biennial,* Whitney Museum, New York
	Documenta 6, Kassel, West Germany
1978	*HHK Foundation for Contemporary Art,* Brumder Gallery, Milwaukee Art Center
1979	*Biennial,* Whitney Museum, New York
1980	*Explorations in the 70's,* Pittsburgh Plan for Art
	With Paper, About Paper, Albright-Knox Gallery, Buffalo, New York (travelled to Museum of Fine Arts, Springfield, Massachusetts)
1983	*A Century of Modern Drawing,* Museum of Fine Art, Boston
1985	*An American Renaissance,* Fort Lauderdale Museum of Art, Florida

Collections:

Whitney Museum, New York; Museum of Modern Art, New York; Fogg Art Museum, Harvard University, Cambridge, Massachusetts; Corcoran Gallery of Art, Washington, D.C.; Philadelphia Museum of Art; High Museum of Art, Atlanta; Minneapolis Art Institute; Museum of Fine Arts, Houston; HHK Foundation for Contemporary Art, Inc., Milwaukee, Wisconsin.

Publications:

By ROCKBURNE: articles—"Works and Statements," edited by Robert Pincus-Witten, in *Artforum* (New York), March 1972; "Interview with Dorothea Rockburne," with Jennifer Licht, in *Artforum* (New York), March 1972; "Notes to Myself on Drawing" in *Flash Art* (Milan), April 1974; "An Interview with Dorothea Rockburne," with Roberta Olson, in *Art in America* (New York), November/December 1978.

On ROCKBURNE: books—*Dorothea Rockburne* by Bruce Boice, Hartford, Connecticut 1973; *6 Years: The Dematerialization of the Art Object* by Lucy R. Lippard, New York 1973; *Biennial Exhibition,* exhibition catalogue, New York 1979; *Exploration in the 70's,* exhibition catalogue, with an essay by Robert Rosenblum, Pittsburgh 1980; *With Paper, About Paper,* exhibition catalogue, essay by Charlotta Kotik, Buffalo 1980; *Art in the 70's* by Edward Lucie-Smith, Ithaca, New York 1980.

ROMBERG, Osvaldo.

Argentinian. Born in Buenos Aires, 28 May 1938; emigrated to Israel in 1973. Studied architecture at Buenos Aires University, 1956, 1959–62. Served in the Argentine Army, Buenos Aires, 1957–59. Married Anya Avram in 1970. Painter: lives in Israel and in New York. Instructor, University Art School, Còrdoba, Argentina, 1963–66, and Puerto Rico University, San Juan, 1966–69; Visual Art Instructor, Fine Arts Department, Tucumàn University, Argentina, 1971–72. Visual Art Instructor, Fine Arts Department, Bezalel Academy, Jerusalem, from 1973; Sculpture Instructor, 1974–75, and Professor of Aesthetics from 1975, State Teachers College, Herzyla, Israel. Recipient: First Printmaking Prize, Architectural Hall, Buenos Aires, 1961; First Printmaking

Dorothea Rockburne: *Disjunction/Or*, 1970

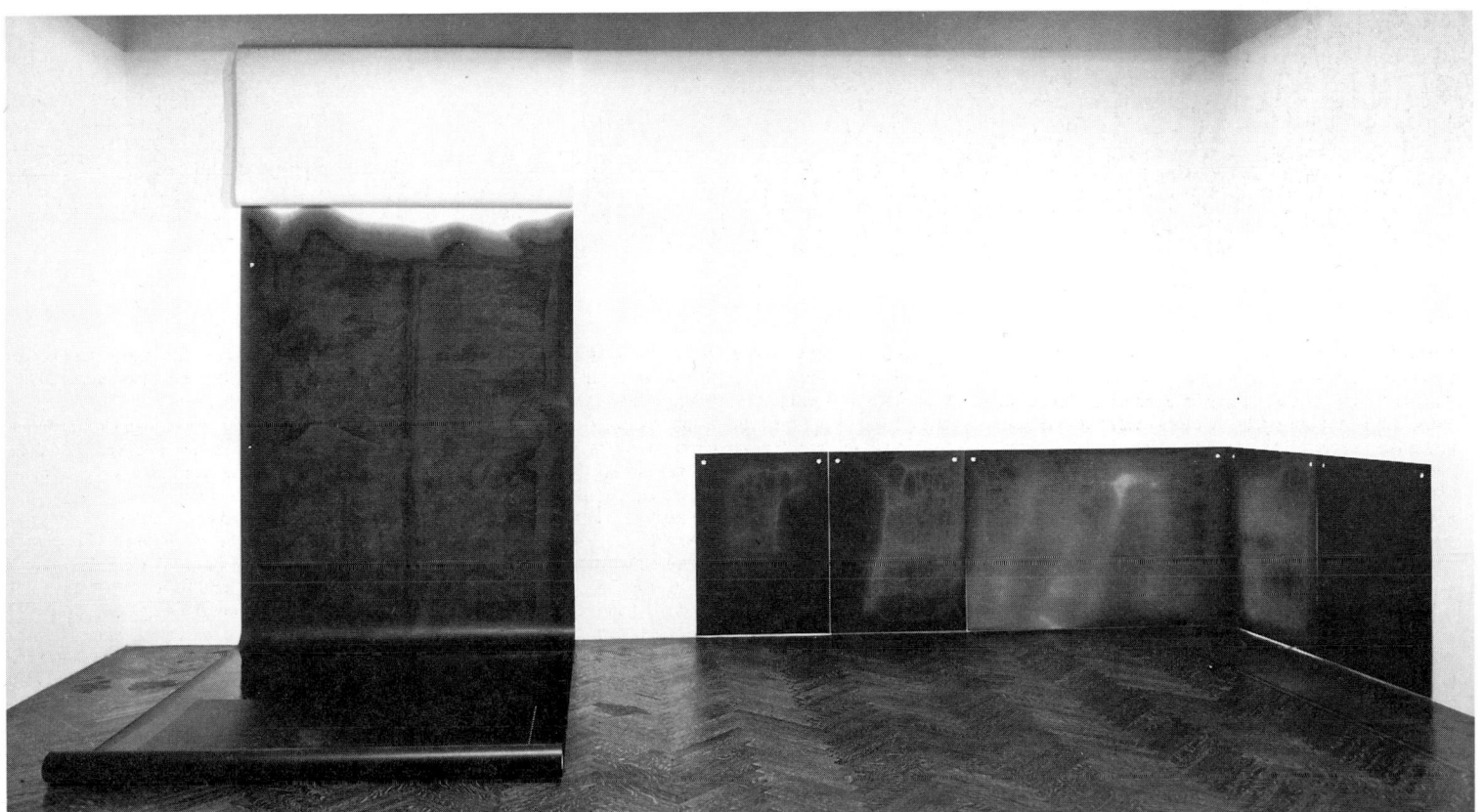

Prize, Hebraica Hall, Buenos Aires, 1965; National Collage Award, Còrdoba, Argentina, 1967; National Printmaking Award, Argentine National Hall, Buenos Aires, 1968; Gold Mannequin Design Prize, Buenos Aires, 1969; First Sculpture Prize, *Park Competition,* Buenos Aires, 1971. Agents: Galerie Stadler, 51 rue de Seine, 75006 Paris, France; Galerie Linssen, Prinz-Albert-Strasse 47, 5300 Bonn, West Germany. Address: 88 Prince Street, New York, New York 10012, U.S.A.

Individual Exhibitions:

1961	Central Society of Architects, Buenos Aires
1962	Contemporary Art Institute, Lima
	Galeria Galatea, Buenos Aires
1963	Art Center, Lima
	Galeria Nueva, Buenos Aires
1964	Pan American Union, Washington
	Museum of Modern Art, Miami
1965	Galeria Lirolay, Buenos Aires
1966	Galeria El Sol, Buenos Aires
	Panamanian Art Institute, Panama City
	Galeria Dinasty, Buenos Aires
	Modern Art Gallery, Cordoba, Argentina
1967	Foussats Gallery, New York
	Casa del Arte, San Juan, Puerto Rico
1968	XX2 Gallery, Caracas
	Print Club of Philadelphia
	Galeria Makarius, Buenos Aires
	Galeria Rubbers, Buenos Aires
1969	Galeria Contemporànea, Buenos Aires
1970	Sala de Artes y Letras, San Jose, Costa Rica
	El Cafe Literario, Guatemala City
	National Art Gallery, El Salvador
	Art Museum, Lima
	Art Gallery, Managua, Nicaragua
1971	Studio Farnese, Rome
	Galeria del Triangulo, Buenos Aires
1972	Center of Art and Communications, Buenos Aires
	Tucumàn Museum of Art, Argentina (retrospective)
1974	Center of Art and Communications, Buenos Aires
1975	*Typologies,* Yodfat Gallery, Tel Aviv (travelled to the International Cultureel Centrum, Antwerp)
1976	Galerie Keller, Starnberg, West Germany
	Galerie Julie M, Tel Aviv
	Galerie Yaki Kornblit, Amsterdam
	Kunstverein, Laiphein, West Germany
1977	Galleria Peccolo, Livorno, Italy
	Galerie Krohn, Konstanz, West Germany
	Delson-Richter Galleries, Old Jaffa, Israel
1979	Galerie Stadler, Paris
1980	Galerie Linssen, Bonn
	Centro de Arte y Comunicacion, Buenos Aires
1981	Musee d'Art Moderne, Strasbourg, France
	Galerie Stadler, Paris
1982	Gimel Gallery, Jerusalem
	Galerie Linssen, at the *International Art Fair,* Chicago
1983	Richter Gallery, Jaffa, Israel
	Galleri Bellman, New York
	Galerie Stadler, Paris
1984	Galerie Springer, West Berlin
	Kunstmuseum, Hannover
	Linssen Gallery, Bonn
1985	Tibor de Nagy Gallery, New York

Selected Group Exhibitions:

1967	*Biennale,* Tokyo
1969	*Art and Cybernetics,* Bonino Gallery, Buenos Aires
1971	*Argentine Art,* Camden Art Centre, London
1972	*Biennale,* Venice
1973	*Introduction to Design,* Jerusalem Museum
1974	*Latin American Art System,* International Cultureel Centrum, Antwerp (toured Europe)
1976	*Works on Paper,* Galerie Keller, Starnberg, West Germany
1979	*The Artists Choice,* Tel Aviv Museum, Israel
1980	*Art about Art,* Galerie Nouvelles Images, The Hague
1982	*Here and Now,* Israel Museum, Jerusalem

Collections:

Museo de Bellas Artes, Buenos Aires; Institute of Contemporary Art, Lima; Casa del Arte, San Juan, Puerto Rico; Instituto Panameno de Arte, Panama City; Museum of Modern Art, New York; Brooklyn Museum, New York; Philadelphia Museum of Art; Museum of Modern Art, Miami; Pan American Union Collection, Washington, D.C.; Library of Congress, Washington, D.C.

Publications:

By ROMBERG: books—*Introduction to Graphic Art,* Tucumàn, Argentina 1972; *Journeys into Visual Experience,* Tucumàn, Argentina 1972; films and videotapes—*Interview with Ran Schechori* by Jorge Glusberg, Buenos Aires 1974; *Typologies of My Body,* Bezalel, Israel 1975; *Typologies of the Wailing Wall,* Bezalel, Israel 1975.

On ROMBERG: books—*Osvaldo Romberg,* exhibition catalogue, with an introduction by Sam Hunter, New York 1967; *Retrospective View of Argentine Art* by J. Romero Brest, Buenos Aires 1971; *Osvaldo Romberg,* exhibition catalogue, by Edmundo Concha, Tucumàn, Argentina 1972; *Landscape as Idea,* exhibition catalogue, by Jorge Glusberg, Buenos Aires 1972; *Art in Israel* by Ran Schechori, Tel Aviv 1974; *Osvaldo Romberg: Typologies,* exhibition catalogue, with an introduction by Florent Bex, Antwerp 1975; *Osvaldo Romberg: Kunst uber Kunst,* exhibition catalogue with text by Michael Erlhoff, Hannover 1984; *Osvaldo Romberg, Recent Works,* exhibition catalogue with text by Carter Ratcliff, New York 1985.

*   *   *

During recent years my interest in results has decreased on the one hand while my concern with preparatory process has considerably increased on the other. Since the *Space verificator* of 1970's running through 1971–72 landscape projects, we can observe a permanent search after classification of space, providing it with a frame of reference. Sometimes dialectical concepts, like rational-irrational, are counter poised.

Then the search moves on the field of the basic possibilities inherent in the pictorial medium and in the human being as executive agent.

The most frequent questions are: what is a painting, a drawing, a sculpture, in its ultimate meaning?

The colour classification, the graphic proofs on paper or tridimensional objects emphasized the artistic gesture before form, before composition, before the dictionary's morphological definition of what is correct.

A kind of process esthethics is thus generated; these processes are elevated to a degree of results by "super exercises" exhibited on the walls of the gallery.

Osvaldo Romberg: *Untitled,* 1981

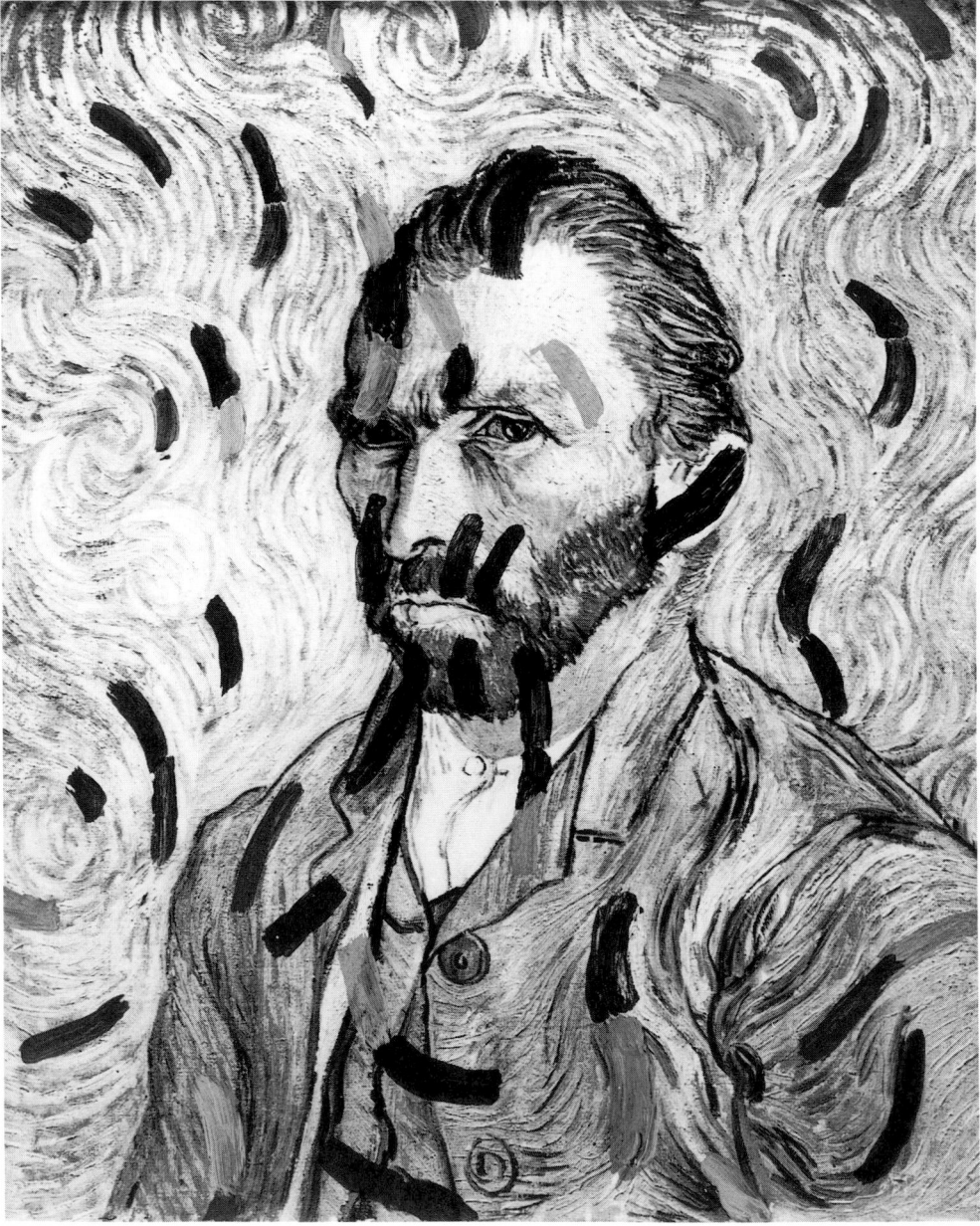

This means, in some way, to begin anew, to sense again the pleasure of painting, to paint the painting, to try and define again and again in each work, what is the essence of painting.

Art is unverifiable; we can merely approach it through exercises, which sometimes surmount their own limits and provide us with a mystique of expression if we are artists, and a mystique of perception if we are observers.

—Osvaldo Romberg

For many years, Osvaldo Romberg has been trying to penetrate into the essence of the work of art and its components, at the same time analysing the creative act in its most elementary form. This investigation implies that the painting process, the relationship between the pictorial medium and the artist, the relationship perception-expression is much more important than the resulting product (the painting).

Romberg's structural analysis of "painting" focuses on the three basical elements: colour, line, act. These are reduced to their most elementary forms.

Romberg uses only five principal colours (white, black, ultramarine blue, vermilion red, medium yellow), from which all other tones and tonalities are derived. Spots or touches are produced on the canvas, usually in a determined scheme of rectangular spaces. For some works, Romberg has chosen not to use a brush. These works consist of casual spots, which are all given a number as may be the case in other works as well.

While analysing the act of "painting," Romberg just draws primary forms as e.g. line, circle, spiral in a neutral tone. These forms are produced through elementary movements of right or left hand, right or left foot, mouth etc. (cf. a work entitled: "Typology Through Three Parts of My Body"). Notwithstanding the discipline and the mathematical progress of the investigation, irrational and aesthetical values can be recognized within the results of these experiments. The duality between head and senses comes plainly into the open, even in the slightest interventions of the artist. The analysis of one colour, the classifications of a series of colours, the subtle trace of the hand, sometimes sure, sometimes clumsy, have a pure and primitive charm, even if they refer to the limitation of human action, or-by numbering and ordering-to the relativity of a spatial and temporal perception.

The aesthetical dimension is probably clearest in those works in which Romberg applies his colour analysis to famous painters. He leaves the strict logical scheme to produce a series of analytical colour impressions on the canvas. (cf. "I Remember Malevich" etc.)

Romberg paints the painting process. His oeuvre being part of the "New Painting," it is important to point out that it should not be seen as the concrete form of a theoretical program. Instead, it has grown from the practice of painting and it requires or refers to a new theory.

—Florent Bex

ROSENBACH, Ulrike.
German. Born in Salzdetfurth, Germany in 1943. Studied under Joseph Beuys, at the Akademie für Bildende Künste, Dusseldorf, 1964-69. Independent artist, since 1970: first video works, 1972; first action-performances, 1973. Founder, Schule für kreativen Feminismus private school, Cologne, 1976-83. Instructor, California Arts Institute, Valencia, 1976; Fachhochschule, Cologne, 1977; Staatliche Kunstakademie of Dusseldorf, Munster, 1984. Recipient: Art Prize, Nordthein-Westfalen, 1977; Study Award for Video Art and Feminist Art, California Institute of Art, Valencia, 1976; Artist's Stipend, City of Cologne, 1978. Address: Lochnerstrasse 10, 5000 Cologne 1, West Germany.

Individual Exhibitions:

1972	Galerie Ernst, Hannover
1975	Oppenheim Studio, Cologne
	Galerie Magers, Bonn
1976	*Foto, Video, Aktion*, Sammlung Ludwig, Aachen, West Germany
1978	Galerie Stampa, Basle
1979	Kulturmuzentrum für Frauen, Stuttgart
1980	Galerie Meier-Hahn, Dusseldorf
	Ulrike Rosenbach/Valie Export, Sedelijk Museum, Amsterdam
1981	*Video, Foto, Serije*, Centar za Fotografiju, Film i TV, Zagreb
1982	Museum Schwarzes Kloster, Freiburg, West Germany
1983	Institute of Contemporary Art, Boston
1984	Galerie Philomene Magers, Bonn
	Galleria Stampa, Basle
1985	Galerie Grita Insam, Vienna
1986	Galerie Meier-Hahn, Dusseldorf
	Neue Galerie/Sammlung Ludwig, Aachen, West Germany
1987	Galleria Stampa, Basle

Selected Group Exhibitions:

1973	*1,000 Miles Fram Here*, Gallery House, London (travelled to the Kunsthalle, Dusseldorf)
1974	*Videoshow*, Museum of Modern Art, New York (travelled to the Institute of Contemporary Art, Philadelphia)
1975	*Magna-Feminismus*, Galerie Nächst St Stephan, Vienna
1978	*Frauen Machen Kunst*, Galerie Magers, Bonn
1980	*Mythen und Zeichen*, Kunstverein, Bonn
	Biennale, Venice
1981	*Videokunst*, Baden-Baden, West Germany
1983	*The Video History Show*, Museum of Modern Art, New York
1985	*Kunst nach 45*, Nationalgalerie, West Berlin
1987	*Documenta 8*, Museum Fridericianum, Kassel, West Germany

Publications:

By ROSENBACH: article—"Haubenkunst" in *Avalanche* (New York), no. 8, 1973.

On ROSENBACH: books—*Video Art: An Anthology*, edited by Ina Schneider and Beryl Korot, New York and London 1976; *Ulrike Rosenbach: Foto, Video, Aktion*, exhibition catalogue, with text by Lucy Lippard and others, Aachen, West Germany 1977; *5 in Köln: Michael Buthe, Sigmar Polke, Ulrike Rosenbach, Gerhard Ruhm, Alf Schuler*, exhibition catalogue, with text by Wulf Herzogenrath and others, Cologne 1979; *Ulrike Rosenbach/Valie Export*, exhibition catalogue, with text by P. M. Pickshaus, Amsterdam 1980; *Ulrike Rosenbach: Video-Foto-Serije*, exhibition catalogue, with text by Mangelos, Zagreb 1981; *Videokunst in Deutschland* by Wulf Herzogenrath, Cologne 1983; *Ulrike Rosenbach: Video and Performance Art*, exhibition catalogue, Boston 1983; *Feminist Aesthetics* by Gisela Ecker, London 1985; *Bis Heute* by Karin Thomas, Cologne 1986; *Spuren des Heiligen in der Kunst 2: Ulrike Rosenbach*, exhibition catalogue by Wolfgang Becker, Aachen 1986.

The work of Ulrike Rosenbach is a radical and artistically convincing manifestation of contemporary feminist art. It is a critical and dialectical confrontation with a historical continuity which it—at the same time—continues and challenges. From her earliest beginnings the artist worked on a polemical level and articulated polarities and tensions which are inherent in the patriarchially dominated traditional and contemporary culture.

After her studies with Joseph Beuys, Ulrike Rosenbach began creating works around 1970 in which social roles of women were the theme, among others *Hauben fuer verheiratete Frauen*; clichés of the traditional society were attacked and the authentic reality of women newly constituted. In 1971 the artist included video tapes in her work, which continuously was dealing with the activity of feminist politics, but within this establishing an authentic artistic articulation. In works such as *Bindemaske, Einwicklung mit Julia* (Involvement with Julia) and *Eine Frau ist eine Frau* (A Woman is a Woman), all of 1972, she demonstratively constituted a new image of woman in intermedia.

Works in the years to follow, such as *Der Mann sei das Haupt der Frau* (Man is the Head of Woman) of 1973 and *Madonna of the Flowers* of 1974/1975 give artistic reinterpretations of existing literary and painterly historic documents on the basis of a feminist consciousness. It is not the individual work of art which is the target of destruction, but the partriarchal projection of the passive image of woman which does not correspond with reality.

These tendencies culminate in *Glauben Sie nicht, dass ich eine Amazone bin* (Don't Believe that I am an Amazon) of 1975 in which the painting by Stefan Lochner *Madonna im Rosenhag* is incorporated into a performance in which Ulrike Rosenbach shoots fifteen arrows into a reproduction of the historical image and at the end of the performance superimposes her own image into that of the Gothic madonna. The action *Reflektionen ueber bie Geburt der Venus* (Reflections on the Birth of Venus) of 1976 also refers to and uses a historical precedent, here Botticelli's painting *The Birth of Venus*, but again Rosenbach re-constitutes her own interpretation of woman, rejecting the historical cliché and the social and cultural degradation documented in Botticelli's work.

Ulrike Rosenbach continued these actions in 1976 with *Zehntausend Jahre habe ich geschlafen und nun bich ich erwacht* (I Have Slept Ten Thousand Years and now Awoke), one of the masterpieces of contemporary international performance art. Sleep and awakening here become analogous with death and rebirth in a ritual-like action. Prehistoric symbolism and the reality of contemporary life, both seen from a radical feminist perspective, are united, and a powerful new form of performance art is created. In the same year the artist created other forms of performances, among them *Female Energy Exchange*, as well as the manifesto *Hexenmuetter*, which was published in 1977.

Several actions since 1977 concentrate on male imagery: *Herakles-Herkules-King Kong* of 1977 contrasts historic role behaviour in men with contemporary reality. In other works such as *Die einsame Spaziergaengerin-Hagazussa* (The Lone Walker-Hagazussa) of 1979, using a reproduction of Caspar David Friedrich's painting *Gebirgslandschaft mit Regenbogen*, Rosenbach combines action and video.

Most of Rosenbach's works are aimed at the release of contemporary female energy in a creative artistic manifestation. This is evident in other works in 1981, *Psyche aber, sie irrte gaenzlich umher* (But Psyche wandered About), and *Psyche und Eros* (Psyche and Eros), partly in collaboration with her daughter Julia. In *Frauenkultur—Kontaktversuch* (Women's Culture—Attempt at Contact) and *JudoFrauen haben als Hilfe Boten* (Judo Women have Messengers as Help), both of 1981, again in a creative confrontation of live action and video, the artist re-constitutes the reality of women in contemporary culture. Performances in recent years, such as *Ewa and Adam* of 1982/1983, *Im Garten der Goettin* (In the Garden of the Goddess) of 1986 and *ANA'L HAQ—I am God* of 1986—expand the earlier thematics into escatological and cosmological dimensions in regard to the meaning of women's contribution to contemporary culture.

The essence of Ulrike Rosenbach's work is the transformation of female consciousness by means of an authentic artistic creation. This is, as all art, multi-levelled, rationally not understandable and open for various views of interpretation, as Rosenbach wrote in 1974: "Life is complicated and an art that is simplifying it, is just a complicated lie." Rosenbach's art is not on the level of feminist propaganda, it is, quite the opposite, on the level of a complex and irrational, often mysterious and inexplainable new art form, which was newly constituted and in this sense continued the art tradition of the past, enriching it by a new dimension.

—Udo Kultermann

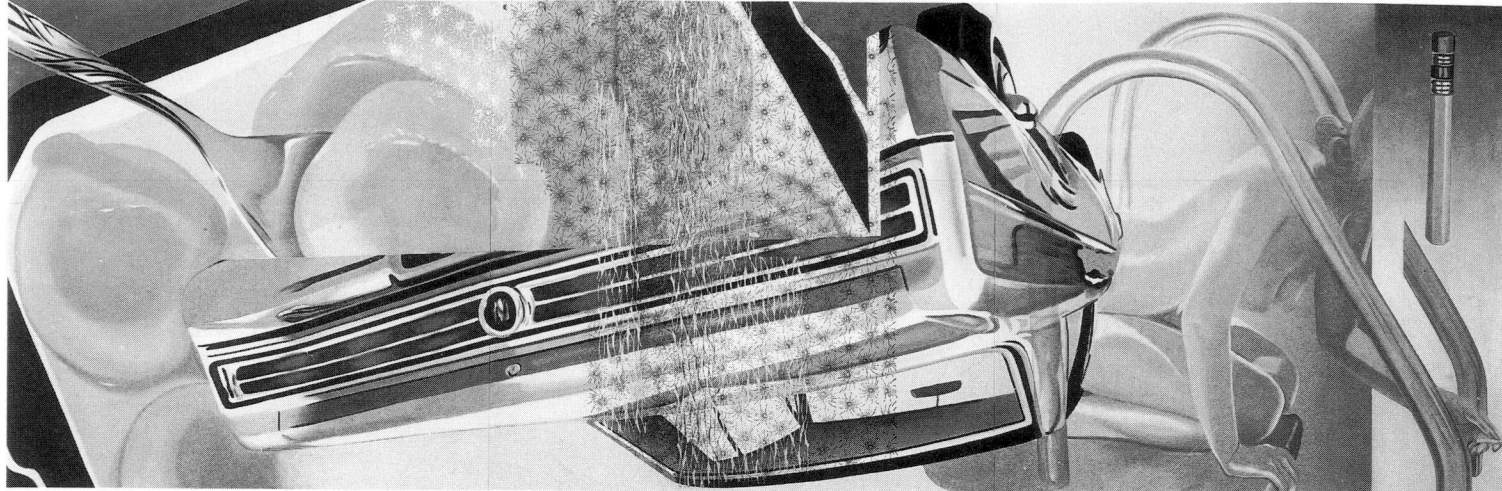

James Rosenquist: *Lanai*, 1964

ROSENQUIST, James.

American. Born in Grand Forks, North Dakota, 29 November 1933. Studied art, under Cameron Booth, at the University of Minnesota, Minneapolis, from 1948 (on scholarship), and at the Art Students League, New York, 1954-55; attended drawing classes organized by Jack Youngerman and Robert Indiana, New York, 1957-58; studied Eastern philosophy and history, Apsen Institute of Humanist Studies, Colorado, 1965. Married Mary Lou Adams in 1960; son: John. Painter, printmaker, and "Pop" artist. Commercial display artist, General Outdoor Advertising Company, 1952-54; chauffeur, Winchester, New York, 1955; met Robert Indiana, Chuck Hinman, Robert Rauschenberg, Jasper Johns, and Jack Youngerman, New York, 1956; Member, International Pictorial Painters Union, New York, 1957; commercial display artist, Bonwit Teller, and Tiffany and Company, New York, 1959; began series of lithographs, with Donald Saff, Graphics Studio, University of South Florida, Tampa, 1971; completed 11 graphic works for the Petersburg Press, London, 1972; rented studio, and completed lithographic series, Tampa, 1973-74; lobbied, with Marion Javits and Robert Rauschenberg, to amend tax laws regarding artists and their estates, Washington, D.C., 1975; prepared sets for the Joffrey Ballet's *Deuce Coupe*, New York, 1975; spent summer in California, and began collaboration on prints with Susan Hall, 1976; built house and studio with architect Gilbert Flores, 1976; continued collaboration with Susan Hall, at Gemini Workshops, Los Angeles, 1977; bought property in Soho, New York, and designated a floor each for painting, graphics, and living; returned to Florida to paint, 1979. Visiting Lecturer, Yale University, New Haven, Connecticut, 1964. Member, Board of Directors, National Endowment for the Arts, 1978. Recipient: Torcuato di Tella International Prize, Buenos Aires, 1965. Agent: Leo Castelli Gallery, 420 West Broadway, New York, New York 10012. Address: Box 4, Aripeka, Florida 33502; or 162 Chambers Street, New York, New York 10007, U.S.A.

Individual Exhibitions:

1962	Green Gallery, New York
1963	Green Gallery, New York
1964	Dwan Gallery, Los Angeles
	Galerie Ileana Sonnabend, Paris
	Galleria Sperone, Turin
1965	Leo Castelli Gallery, New York
	Moderna Museet, Stockholm
	Museo d'Arte Moderna, Turin
	Galerie Ileana Sonnabend, Paris
1966	Leo Castelli Gallery, New York
	Moderna Museet, Stockholm
	Staatliche Kunsthalle, Baden-Baden, West Germany
	Louisiana Museum, Humlebaek, Denmark
	Stedelijk Museum, Amsterdam

1967	Musée des Arts Décoratifs, Paris
1968	National Gallery of Canada, Ottawa
	Galerie Ileana Sonnabend, Paris
	Galleria Sperone, Turin
	Metropolitan Museum of Art, New York
1969	Leo Castelli Gallery, New York
1970	Galerie Ricke, Cologne
	Leo Castelli Gallery, New York
1972	*Gemaälde, Räume, Graphik*, Wallraf-Richartz Museum, Cologne (retrospective)
	Whitney Museum, New York
	Museum of Contemporary Art, Chicago
	Galleria del Milione, Milan
	Margo Leavin Gallery, Los Angeles
1973	Galerie Hans Hoeppner, Hamburg
	Galerie Hans Hoeppner, Munich
	Amerika Haus, West Berlin
	Jack Glenn Gallery, Corona del Mar, California
	Center of the VisuaL Arts, Portland, Oregon
	Courtney Jules Gallery, Dallas
	Stedelijk Museum, Amsterdam
	Leo Castelli Gallery, New York
1974	Max Protetch Gallery, Washington, D.C.
	Margo Leavin Gallery, Los Angeles
	Galerie Michael Pabst, Vienna
	Prints, Scottish Arts Council Gallery, Edinburgh (travelled to the Art Gallery and Museum, Aberdeen, and the City Museum and Art Gallery, Dundee, Scotland)
	Jared Sable Gallery, Toronto
	Paintings 1961-1973, Mayor Gallery, London
1975	Leo Castelli Gallery, New York
1976	Gallery A, Sydney
	Berenson Gallery, Bay Harbor Islands, Miami Beach
	Corcoran and Greenberg Inc., Coral Gables, Florida
	Mayor Gallery, London
	Paule Anglim Associates, San Francisco
	Ronald Greenberg Gallery, St. Louis
1977	Leo Castelli Gallery, New York
	Sable-Castelli Gallery, Toronto
	National Gallery of Victoria, Melbourne
	Institute of Modern Art, Brisbane
1978	Mayor Gallery, London
	Multiples Gallery, New York
1979	*Graphics Retrospective*, Ringling Museum of Art, Sarasota, Florida (travelled to the Fort Lauderdale Museum of the Arts, Florida)
1981	Leo Castelli Gallery, New York
1982	*Paintings from the 60's*, Mayor Gallery, London

Selected Group Exhibitions:

1967	*Whitney Annual*, Whitney Museum, New York (and 1969)
1968	*Documenta*, Kassel, West Germay
1969	*Pop Art*, Hayward Gallery, London
	New York Painting and Sculpture 1940-1970, Metropolitan Museum of Art, New York

1974	*American Pop Art*, Whitney Museum, New York
1978	*American Painting of the 1970's*, Albright-Knox Art Gallery, Buffalo, New York
1979	*Black and White Are Colors: Paintings of the 1950's-1970's*, Scripps College, Claremont, California
1980	*Printed Art: A View of 2 Decades*, Museum of Modern Art, New York
1984	*Reflections: Contemporary Art Since 1964*, National Gallery of Canada, Ottawa

Collections:

Museum of Modern Art, New York; Whitney Museum, New York; Albright-Knox Art Gallery, Buffalo, New York; Chrysler Museum of Art, Norfolk, Virginia; Hirshhorn Museum and Sculpture Garden, Smithsonian Institution, Washington, D.C.; Museum of Contemporary Art, Chicago; Norton Simon Museum of Art, Pasadena, California; National Gallery of Canada, Ottawa; Tate Gallery, London; Centre Georges Pompidou, Paris.

Publications:

By ROSENQUIST: portfolio—*Rosenquist: 6 Etchings*, Tampa, Florida 1976; articles—statement in *Art in America* (New York), June 1963; statement in *Artnews* (New York), February 1964; statement in the *Partisan Review* (New York), Fall 1965; statement in *Rosenquist*, exhibition catalogue, Paris 1968; interview, with G. R. Swenson, in *Metropolitan Museum of Art Bulletin* (New York), vol. 26, 1968; interview, with J. Siegel in *Artforum* (New York), June 1972; "Pop," interview, with Phyllis Tuchman, in *Artnews* (New York), May 1974; statement in *James Rosenquist: An Exhibition of Paintings 1961-73*, exhibition catalogue, London 1974.

On ROSENQUIST: books—*Rosenquist*, exhibition pamphlet, with an introduction by Tommaso Trini, Paris 1968; *James Rosenquist*, exhibition catalogue, with text by Marcia Tucker, New York 1972; *James Rosenquist: Gemälde, Räume, Graphik*, exhibition catalogue, with text by Evelyn Weiss, Cologne 1972; *James Rosenquist*, exhibition catalogue, with text by Wim A. L. Beeren, Amsterdam 1973; *James Rosenquist: An Exhibition of Paintings 1961-1973*, exhibition catalogue, with an introduction by David Sylvester, London 1974; *Black and White Are Colors: Paintings of the 1950's-1970's*, exhibition catalogue, with a foreword by David Steadman, and text by David S. Rubin, Claremont 1979; *James Rosenquist: Graphics Retrospective*, exhibition catalogue, with an introduction by Elayne H. Varian, Sarasota, Florida 1979; *Printed Art: A View of 2 Decades*, exhibition catalogue, New York 1980; *American Prints 1879-1979*, exhibition catalogue, New York 1980; *American Prints 1879-1979*, exhibition catalogue, London 1980; *Print Publishing in America*, exhibition catalogue, Schiedam, Netherlands 1980; *James Rosenquist: Paintings from the 60's*, exhibition catalogue, with text by Richard Shone, London 1982.

Of all Pop artists, James Rosenquist was one who emerged from inside the commercial advertising scene rather than approaching it as a spectator. He had spent time working actually as a billboard painter in the mid-West before arriving in New York and meeting up with Rauschenberg, Johns and Kelly. Ever conscious of the brainwashing effect of giant images on the public mind, his paintings are frequently exposures of the means adopted. This often appears as an erotic sales punch embodied in a woman's lips—they can be Marilyn Monroe's, and the make-up shades will be specified, but the motive is not heightening the punch but illuminating its exploitation. Combination of images, often in large scale, parade the vocabulary of persuasive identifications in publicity campaigns. This painting-out of television or movie drama on the scale of billboard give a monumental "still" effect more oblique than Lichtenstein's and in the early works such as "The Light That Won't Fail" (1961) the monochrome finish accentuates the projected "soap opera" association.

Paint on single surface was not to be exclusive for Rosenquist's image transmission. He added wooden and Plexiglass structures to illustrate an "exploded" picture idea filched from commercial advertising pages. Often the source of his human faces appears by the inclusion of a section of the television tube and of sundry montage effects. Other giant compositions such as "F-111" (1965), the colossal panorama of a jet fighter hurtling across 86 feet of unrelated motives, including a Firestone tyre, electric light bulbs, the atomic dust plume and Shirley Temple when young, inside a hairdryer with a background of blown-up spaghetti, is a fourwall wrap-around mural of contemporary authenticity. The large scale montage is given extra dimension by the inclusion of sections of moulded aluminium panels so the spectator and passers-by are reflected, giving surprise elements of movement and colour.

This activation of the picture by the spectator provides the ready-made kinetic ingredient very much at the heart of contemporary art exemplified by Rosenquist, for thus the picture-assemblage is an instant happening for whoever comes into its orbit. Dayglo and lead-based colours, designed to carry across city squares, at closer range have saturating power on the retina. How the Renaissance connection has been eliminated from painting completely is evident at its highest degree in Rosenquist for, as far as he is concerned, it was never there.

The overall even strength in Pop compositions is basic in all Rosenquist's work—not "this is how it is" but "this is how I make it": bright, deadpan, noncommittal, uncommitted, it can be a close-up of a film star's "facescape"; she is not a person, she is an apparatus for selling something, the cosmetic accessories or the smokes or a movie but only to the naive or the retarded a symbol of sex or feminine attraction and then not for real; it glorifies devitalised life.

—G. S. Whittet

ROSS, Charles.

American. Born in Philadelphia, 17 December 1937. Studied at the University of California, Berkeley, 1958-62, A.B. Mathematics 1960, M.A. Sculpture 1962. Independent artist known for utilizing solar energy; lives and works in New York. Instructor, University of California, Berkeley, 1962 and 1965; Associate Professor of Sculpture, Cornell University, Ithaca, New York, 1964; Co-Director, Dancers' Workshop Company, San Francisco, 1964-66; Instructor, School of Visual Arts, New York, 1967 and 1970-71; Visiting Architecture Professor, University of Utah, Salt Lake City, 1972-73. Recipient: National Endowment for the Arts Grant, 1974, 1976, 1977; Center for World Game Studies Grant, 1975. Address: 383 West Broadway, New York, New York 10012, U.S.A.

Individual Exhibitions:

1961	Dilexi Gallery, San Francisco
1962	Museum of Art, Richmond, California
1964	White Art Museum, Cornell University, Ithaca, New York
1965	University of Kentucky, Lexington
	Dilexi Gallery, San Francisco
1966	Dilexi Gallery, San Francisco
1968	Dilexi Gallery, San Francisco
	Daytons Gallery 12, Minneapolis
	Dwan Gallery, New York
1969	Dwan Gallery, New York
1971	Dwan Gallery, New York
1972	John Weber Gallery, New York
1974	The Clocktower, New York
1975	University of Utah, Salt Lake City
1976	*The Substance of Light*, La Jolla Museum of Contemporary Art, California
1977	Museum of Contemporary Art, Chicago
	Institute of Contemporary Art, Philadelphia
	John Weber Gallery and Susan Caldwell Gallery, New York (joint exhibition)
	Hayden Gallery, Massachusetts Institute of Technology, Cambridge
1979	John Weber Gallery, New York
1981	John Weber Gallery, New York
	Portland Center for the Visual Arts, Oregon
1982	Heydt/Blair Gallery, Santa Fe, New Mexico
1985	Plaza of the Americas Gallery, Dallas

Selected Group Exhibitions:

1963	*Biennale*, Paris
1968	*Magic Theater*, Atkins Museum, Kansas City, Missouri
1969	*Whitney Annual*, Whitney Museum, New York
1975	*Drawings III*, Städtisches Museum, Leverkusen, West Germany
1977	*Probing the Earth: Contemporary Land Projects*, Hirshhorn Museum, Smithsonian Institution, Washington, D.C. (travelled to the La Jolla Museum of Contemporary Art, California and the Seattle Art Museum)
1980	*Cartes et Figures de la Terre*, Centre Georges Pompidou, Paris

1983	*Sky Art*, BMW Museum, Munich
1984	*The Dilexi Years 1958-70*, Oakland Museum, California
1986	*Lo Spazio*, at the *Biennale*, Venice

Collections:

Whitney Museum, New York; Towson State University, Maryland; Grand Rapids Art Museum, Michigan; Indianapolis Museum of Art; Nelson Atkins Museum, Kansas City, Missouri; University of California Art Museum, Berkeley; Walker Art Center, Minneapolis; Albuquerque Museum, New Mexico.

Publications:

By ROSS: book—*Sunlight Convergence/Solar Burn*, Salt Lake City, Utah 1975; articles—"Charles Ross," interview, with Ward Jackson, in *Art Now* (New York), Fall 1971; "Solar Burns/Sunlight Convergence" in *Arts Magazine* (New York), December 1973/January 1974; "Star Axis" in *Whole Earth Review* Menlo Park, California), Winter 1985; films— *Sunlight Dispersion*, New York 1972; *Arisaig July 10, 1972*, New York 1972.

On ROSS: books—*The Art of Time* by Michael Kirby, New York 1969; *On Sight On Energy*, edited by Alison Sky, New York 1974; *The Substance of Light: Sunlight Dispersion, The Solar Burns, Point Star/Star Space*, exhibition catalogue, by Steve Katz, La Jolla, California 1976; *Probing the Earth*, exhibition catalogue, by John Beardsley, Washington, D.C. 1977; *The Place of Art in the World of Architecture*, by Donald Thalacker, New York 1979; *Overlay: Contemporary Art and the Art of Prehistory* by Lucy Lippard, New York 1983; articles—"Special Rights" by David Lee in *Artnews* (New York), December 1967; "Richard Van Buren, David Novros, Charles Ross" by Emily Wasserman in *Artforum* (New York), Summer 1968; "Schemata 7" by Elaine Varian in *Minimal Art*, edited by Gregory Battcock, New York 1969; "Charles Ross" by Ward Jackson in *Art Now* (New York), Fall 1971; "Charles Ross, The Substance of Light" by Fran Priesman in *Artweek* (Oakland, California), 6 March 1976; "Charles Ross" by David Shapiro and Lindsay Stamm in *Arts Magazine* (New York), June 1977; "Charles Ross: Light's Measure" by Donald Kuspin in *Art in America* (New York), March/April 1978; "A Bright Idea" by Mary Cowen in the *Christian Science Monitor* (Boston), 16 May 1979; "New Landscapes in Art" by Kay Larson in the *New York Times Magazine*, 13 May 1979; cover article in *Architecture Record*

Charles Ross: *Light, Rock, Water*, 1986

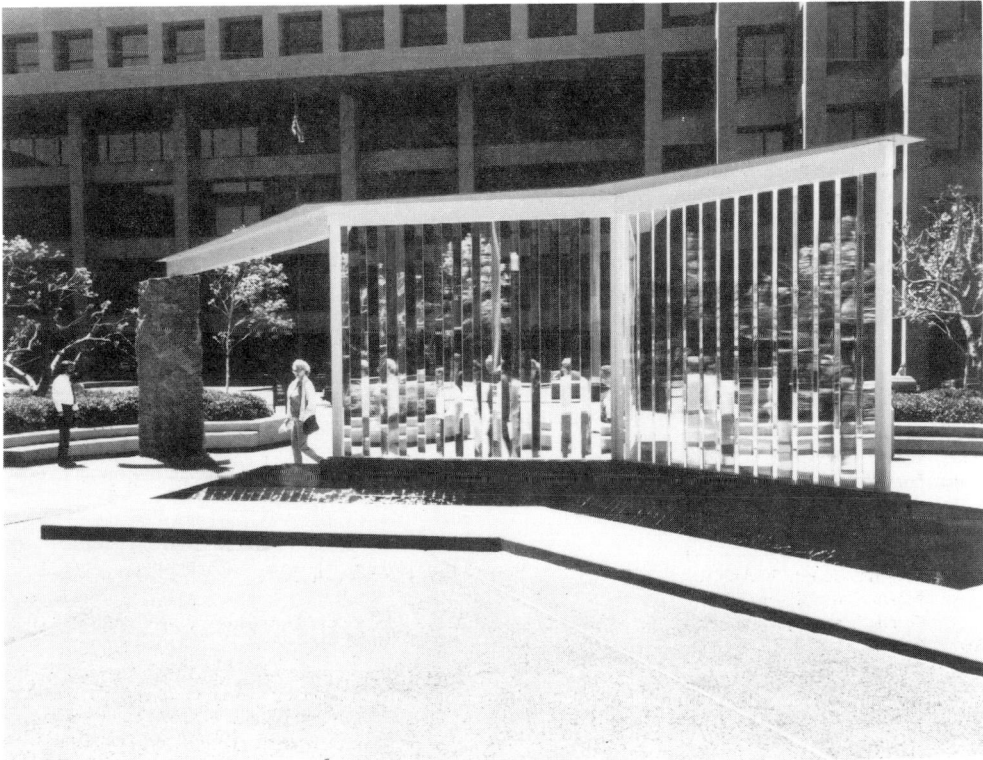

(New York), August 1981; "Charles Ross" by Katherine Chafee and "Prism Behavior in Indiana" by Steve Katz in *Artspace* (New York), Fall 1981; "Western Spaces: Excavating the Present" by Edward Ranney in *Aperture* (Millerton, New York), Spring 1985; "Gestures and Creations" by Georg Gerster in *Wochenende Neue Zurcher Zeitung* (Zurich), 9/10 May 1987.

. . . discrete, tangible images drawn by light . . . manifesting elements of light's structure, solar power, the combined motions of the earth in space and the geometry of the stars.

The work is not directed toward information about light energy, but rather toward knowing the core and contexts of this energy—toward achieving a sense of its sources. The works are windows through which cosmic elements reveal themselves: forms whose content telescopes back into space . . . .

The work looks beyond art as self-referential self-contained artifact to art as a point of contact with the universe energy system.

—Charles Ross

Charles Ross has described each of his works of art as "a facet of a larger work whose subject is the totality of light energy." While light has traditionally been associated with the work of painters, its role as an element and concern of sculpture has become a central issue in the work of several artists in recent years. Among those artists, Ross is a pivotal figure recognized for his exploration of light separated into its spectrum of color. The rich, clear prismatic color that is integral to his sculpture adds a sensuous richness to art that is based on observation and analysis of physical phenomenon and its expression in mathematics, physics and philosophy.

Ross's work is notable for the concerns he assiduously avoids as well as the ones that dominate his thinking. Unlike much contemporary sculpture, Ross's work exhibits little interest in geometric forms or materials. His principal interest is the experience of art, and his sculpture is dominated by a sense of duration and time. It is the mutable experience of light and color affecting an environment, and our response to that experience, that forms the art, rather, than the object or installation that creates the experience.

Ross's interest in mathematics and philosophy form the conceptual and theoretical core of his art, an interest that dates from the early 1960's. While the nature of his interests suggest a didactive quality, the work itself, particularly the permanent installations in office buildings in Nebraska and Colorado, has a lyrical sort of beauty as the pure color of the light moves from surfaces in response to the changing angles of the sun's rays on the prism mounted in skylights. Major installations of Ross's work are spatially expansive yet are only one aspect of his inquiry into the nature and experience of light. "Solar Burns" are works created by the effect of light burning sections of paper. Other recent work has included large columns which act as prisms and create spectrums of color within an enclosed space. Perhaps the most ambitious work, however, is the "Star Axis," a monumental earthwork begun in the New Mexico desert in 1971. Monumentally scaled to explore the relationship between the earth and the sun, "Star Axis" represents the fullest measure of the artist's involvement in witnessing, participating and experiencing light and its genesis.

—Katharine Smith

ROSZAK, Theodore.
American. Born in Poznan, Poland, 1 May 1907; emigrated (with parents) to the United States, 1909: naturalized, 1921. Studied at the Art Institute of Chicago, 1922–26; National Academy of Design, and Columbia University, New York, 1926–27; University of Illinois, Urbana, 1927; did graduate work at the Art Institute of Chicago, 1927–29 (European Travel Fellowship, 1927–28; American Travel Fellowship, 1928; Raymond Fellowship, 1929). Married Florence Sapir in 1931; daughter: Sara. Worked as Marine Engineer and Draftsman, Stevens Institute of Technology, Hoboken, New Jersey, 1932–45. Instructor, Art Institute of Chicago, 1926–28; Design Laboratory, New York, 1938–40; Teacher of Aircraft Mechanics, Delehanty Institute, New York and built aircraft for Brewster Aircraft, Newark, New Jersey, 1940–45; Instructor, Sarah Lawrence College, Bronxville, New York, 1940–55; Visiting Professor and Art Critic, Columbia University, New York, 1970–73. Member, Advisory Council of Art and Architecture, Yale University, New Haven, Connecticut, 1959–62; U.S. Delegate, International Art Congress, Vienna, 1960–61; Member, Advisory Committee on Cultural Presentations Program, State Department, Washington, D.C., 1961–67; Member, Fine Arts Commission, Washington, D.C., 1962–68; Member, Board of Trustees, Tiffany Foundation, New York, 1962–81; Member, Board of Governors, Skowhegan School of Painting and Sculpture, Maine, 1962–81; Charter Member, Drawing Society, 1965–81; Member, New York Arts Commission, New York, 1969–81; Member, Board of Trustees, Academy in Rome, 1970–72. Recipient: Silver Medal, Poznan, Poland, 1929; Tiffany Foundation Fellowship, New York, 1931; Eidendrath Award, Chicago, 1934; Frank G. Logan Medal, Chicago, 1947, 1951; International Award, Tate Gallery, London, 1951; Faculty Fellowship, Sarah Lawrence College, Bronxville, New York, 1951; International Award, *Bienal*, Sao Paulo, 1956; George E. Widener Gold Medal, Philadelphia, 1956; Ford Foundation Fellowship, 1959; Campangna Award, Chicago, 1961; Griner Award, Indiana, 1962; Century Association Medal, New York, 1967. Honorary Fellow, Vienna Secession, 1960. Fellow, National Institution of Arts and Letters, 1964. *Died* (in New York) *3 September 1981.*

Individual Exhibitions:

1928	Allerton Galleries, Chicago
1935	Roerich Museum, New York (retrospective)
1936	Albany Institute of Art, New York
1940	Julien Levy Gallery, New York
	Artist Gallery, New York
1951	Pierre Matisse Gallery, New York
1953	Pierre Matisse Gallery, New York
1956	Whitney Museum, New York (retrospective; toured the United States)
1957	Walker Art Center, Minneapolis
	San Francisco Museum of Art
1958	Seattle Art Museum, Washington
	Fairweather-Hardin Gallery, Chicago
1959	Institute of Contemporary Art, Boston
	Museum of Art, Richmond, Virginia
	Museum of Fine Arts, Houston
	University of Wisconsin, Madison
1962	Pierre Matisse Gallery, New York
1971	Century Association, New York
1973	*Early Paintings*, Harold Ernst Gallery, Boston
1974	*Graphics: Lithographs and Drawings 1971–1974*, Pierre Matisse Gallery, New York
1976	*Recent Works*, Arts Club, Chicago
	Fairweather-Hardin Gallery, Chicago
1978	*Constructions 1932–1945*, Zabriskie Gallery, New York
1979	Hayden Gallery, Massachusetts Institute of Technology, Cambridge
1981	Fort Lauderdale Museum of Art, Florida
	Carrone Gallery, Fort Lauderdale, Florida
1984	Whitney Museum, New York

Selected Group Exhibitions:

1932	*Chicago Artists*, Art Institute of Chicago
1933	*Whitney (Museum) Biennale*, New York
1935	*American Abstract Art*, Whitney Museum, New York
1947	*14 Americans*, Museum of Modern Art, New York
1953	*International Exhibition*, Tate Gallery, London
1962	*International Exhibition of 20th Century Sculpture*, Vienna
1963	*International Sculpture*, Darmstadt, West Germany
1964	*American Annual*, Philadelphia Academy of Fine Arts
1979	*Vanguard American Sculpture 1913–1939*, Rutgers University Art Gallery, New Jersey
1981	*Sculpture and Related Drawings*, Marisa Del Re Gallery, New York

Collections:

Guggenheim Museum, New York; Museum of Modern Art, New York; Whitney Museum, New York; Hirshhorn Museum, Washington, D.C.; Smithsonian Institution, Washington, D.C.; Pennsylvania Academy of Art; Art Institute of Chicago; Walker Art Center, Minneapolis; Museum of Fine Arts, Houston; Tate Gallery, London.

Publications:

By ROSZAK: book—*Theodore Roszak Exhibition*, New York 1962; articles—"Some Problems in Modern Sculpture," with Robert Goldwater, in *Magazine of Art* (New York), February 1949; "A Theodore Roszak Profile," interview, with Belle Krasne, in *Art Digest* (New York), 15 October 1952; "In Pursuit of an Image" in *Chicago*, no. 2, 1955, reprinted in *Quadrum* (Brussels), November 1956; "Statements and Documents: Artists on Art and Reality, on Their Work, and on Values," with others, in *Daedalus*, vol. 89, no. 1, 1960.

On ROSZAK: books—*Theodore Roszak Exhibition*, catalogue, New York 1935; *Tradition and Experiment in Sculpture* by Charles Seymour, Washington, D.C. 1948; *Modern Sculpture* by Frederic Puma, New York 1953; *Masters of Modern Art*, exhibition catalogue, by Alfred A. Barr, New York 1954; *Sculpture of the 20th Century*, exhibition catalogue, by Andrew C. Ritchie, New York 1954; *Theodore Roszak*, exhibition catalogue, by H. H. Arnason, New York, 1956; *Theodore Roszak*, exhibition catalogue, by H. H. Arnason, Minneapolis 1957; *Sculpture of the 19th and 20th Century* by Fred Licht, New York 1967; *Roszak: Early Paintings*, exhibition catalogue, by Dudley C. Watson and Emily Genauer, Boston 1973; *Theodore Roszak: Graphics: Lithographs and Drawings, 1971–1974*, exhibition catalogue, by D. C. Rich and B. S. Meyers, New York 1974; *Theodore Roszak: Recent Works*, exhibition catalogue, Chicago 1976; *Theodore Roszak: Constructions 1932–1945*, exhibition catalogue, New York 1978; *Varieties of Visual Experience* by Edmund Burke Feldman, Englewood Cliffs, New Jersey 1978; *The Sculpture of Theodore Roszak 1932–1952*, dissertation, by J. F. Seeman, Stanford, California 1979; articles—"About Theodore Roszak" by Harry Salpeter in *Coronet* (New York), November 1937; "Three Who Carry the Acetylene Torch of Modernisme" by Belle Krasne in *Art Digest* (New York), 15 April 1951; "Roszak's Moral Lesson" by Henry McBride in *Artnews* (New York), February 1953; "Solo Show Opens Whitney Year" by Emily Genauer in the *New York Herald-Tribune Book Review*, 23 February 1956; "Modern Sculpture" by Howard Devree in the *New York Times*, 23 September 1956; "Art: Two Against the Current" by Hilton Kramer in the *New York Times*, 7 December 1974; "Roszak Evokes Spirit of Bauhaus" by Hilton Kramer in the *New York Times*, 1 December 1978; "Roszak's Early Constructions" by Joan M. Master in *Arts Magazine* (New York), November 1979; "Notes on Roszak: The Last Laugh" by J. Kind in *New Art Examiner* (Chicago), April 1976; "Theodore Roszak, Sculptor of Eagle at London Embassy" by Bernard Holland in the *New York Times*, 4 September 1981.

Theodore Roszak is famous for spiky metal sculptures which, with their highly personal idiom and tormented symbolism, combine fantasy with plant and animal forms to produce a feeling of surrealistic menace. But these metallic fantasies came only after two earlier phases of development during which he had been successively a painter and then a Constructivist sculptor in wood.

He began his career as a draughtsman and lithographer, then became a painter. On a trip to Europe in 1929 he came under the influence of the Surrealists, above all de Chirico, whose fantastic perspective he absorbed into his own romantic realist paintings. He was still producing paintings and lithographs through

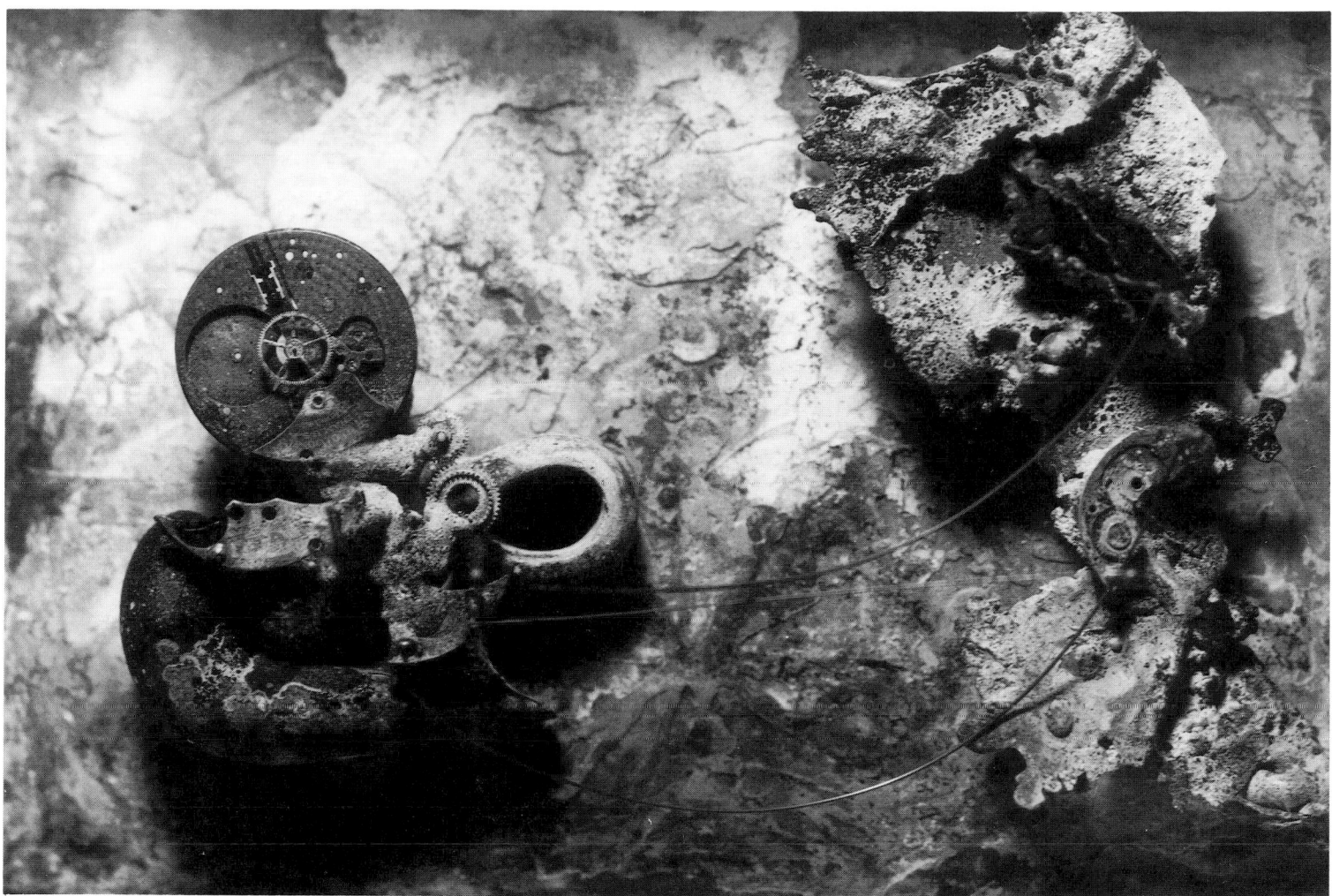

Theodore Roszak: *Vigil*, 1975

the 1930's, but by 1931 he had started to make sculptures, at first experimenting with clay and plaster.

Constructivist theories of Moholy-Nagy, under whom Roszak taught at the Design Laboratory in New York from 1938–40, a project intended to advance Bauhaus techniques and principles in America, inspired him to explore the problems of structure and sculptural form. This he did in a series of wood and plastic constructions cased on the geometry of pure forms such as the straight line and the cone, from 1936–1943.

But having saturated himself in Constructivist ideas, he then moved on from geometric abstraction to become one of the pioneer welder-sculptors, including David Smith and Seymour Lipton, whose innovations are intimately associated with those of the Abstract Expressionist painters. The sculptors too were trying to break away from European prototypes by exploring untraditional materials and methods, and Roszak and Lipton both felt the need to move beyond casting and carving into a form of addictive constructions which would escape from the formal limitations of Constructivism. Since 1945 Roszak had concentrated exclusively on metal sculpture, using his extensive technical knowledge of welding and the making of alloys to create dramatic, thoroughly romantic works which are a mixture of figuration and symbolism. But he was convinced of the very real unity of techniques, working by first making a drawing of a basic idea. This establishes an interrelation between lines, colours and tensions which is then given a three-dimensional interpretation in iron wire, which is then further developed into the final metal sculptures. All Roszak's early interests have in fact coalesced into his mature work, since these recapture the romantic freedom of his earlier approach to painting and combine surrealist improvisation and addiction to accident in their discovery of fascinating effects of eroded surfaces and variations in texture.

He drew his themes for these welded steel sculptures not only from personal experience and an intense involvement with society, but also existential ideas, and literature such as *Moby Dick*, which inspired the aggressively pursuing "Whaler of Nantucket." The language of potent new sculptural symbols which emerges is full of organic analogies, predatory or threatening natural forms such as clutching tree roots, or the bone-like skeletal structures of "Iron Gullet," or the harsh world of "Thorn Blossom," where the delicate opening flower has a shield of thorns thrown over it. The figurative element remains only a suggestion, but Roszak's organic abstractions in welded steel are bold and urgent personal images which made an important contribution to the expressionist vitalism which was the parallel in postwar American sculpture to the development of Abstract Expressionist painting.

—Lavinia Learmont

ROTELLA, Mimmo.
Italian. Born Domenico Rotella in Catanzaro, Calabria, 17 October 1918. Studied at the Academy of Fine Art, Naples. Independent artist, living in Rome, 1949–61, in Paris, 1961–80, and in Milan since 1980: first "epistaltici" phonetic poems, 1949; first torn paper works, 1954; first Mec Art (mechanically-produced) works, 1963. Member, Pierre Restany's Nouveaux Réalistes group of artists, Paris, 1961. Artist in Residence, University of Kansas City, Missouri, 1951–52; Visiting Lecturer: Theresa College, Kansas City, 1952; School of Visual Arts, New York, 1962; University of Havana, Cuba, 1986. Recipient: Fulbright Fellowship, 1951. Agent: Studio Marconi, Via Tadino 15, 21024 Milan. Address: Viale Lombardia 9, 20131 Milan, Italy.

Individual Exhibitions:

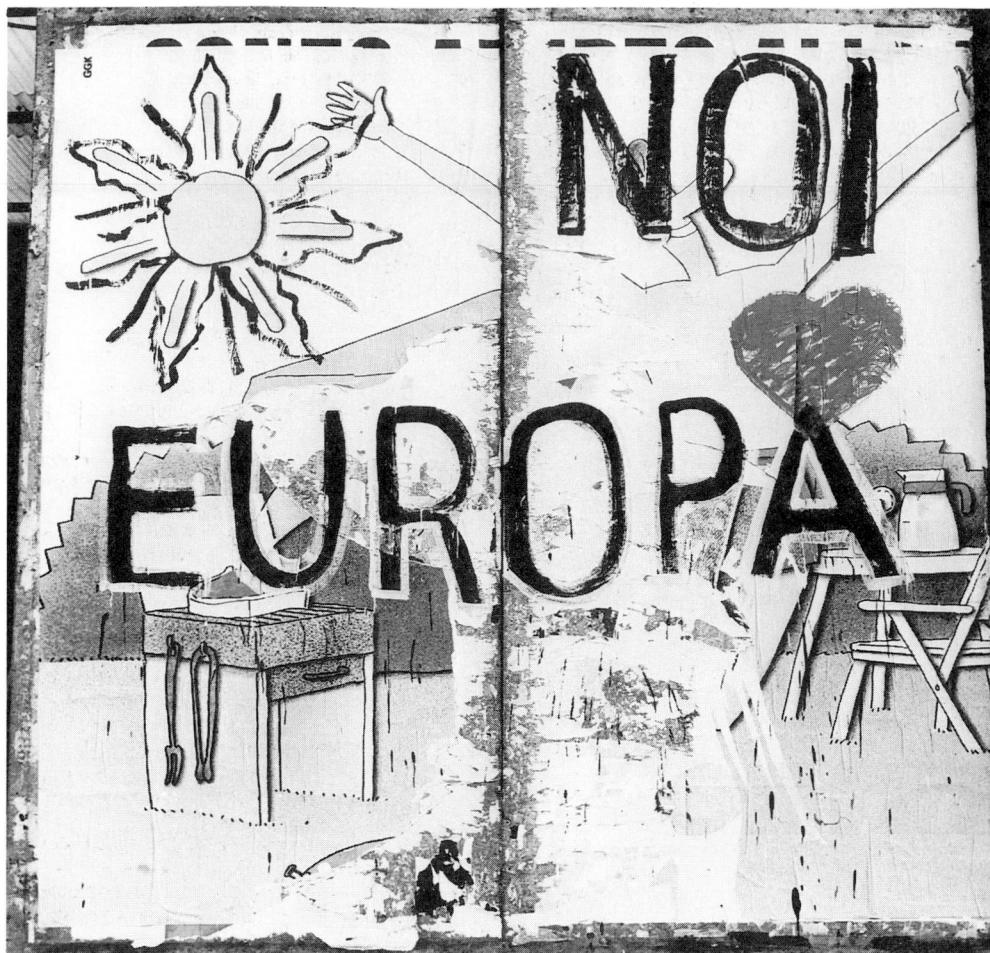

Mimmo Rotella: *Noi Europa*, 1987

Galleria Il Punto, Turin
1967 Galerie 20, Amsterdam
Galerie Ricke, Cologne
1969 Galleria del Naviglio, Milan
Galleria Arco d'Alibert, Rome
Rotella 1954–1968, Galerie Fitzroy, Brussels
Studio San Andrea, Milan
1971 Galerie Mathias Fels, Paris
1973 Studio Bellini, Milan
Galerie Marquet, Paris
1974 Galerie Craven, Paris
Galerie J. Ferrero, Paris
Galerie Inter Arts, Lyons
Galleria dell'Ariete, Milan
1975 Galerie des Deux Rues, St. Tropez, France
Rotonda della Besana, Milan
1978 *Opere dal 1958–75*, Galleria Civica d'Arte Moderna, Castello di Portofino, Italy
Padiglione d'Arte Contemporanea, Ferrara, Italy
1981 Studio Marconi, Milan
Galerie Denise René, Paris
1984 Studio Marconi, Milan
1985 Galerie Reckermann, Cologne
1986 Galleria Niccoli, Parma, Italy

Selected Group Exhibitions:

1949 *Salon des Réalités Nouvelles*, Paris
1959 *International Print Biennale*, Ljubljana, Yugoslavia
1961 *The Art of Assemblage*, Museum of Modern Art, New York (travelled to the Museum of Contemporary Art, Dallas, and the San Francisco Museum of Art
1963 *L'Art et L'Ecriture*, Staatliche Kunsthalle, Baden-Baden, West Germany (travelled to the Stedelijk Museum, Amsterdam)
1964 *Pop Art/Nouveau Réalisme*, Palais des Beaux-Arts, Brussels
1971 *Décollages*, Staatsgalerie, Stuttgart

1977 *3 Villes/3 Collections*, Centre Georges Pompidou, Paris
1982 *Registrazione di Frequenze*, Galleria d'Arte Moderna, Bologna
1984 *Ecritures dans la peinture*, Villa Arson, Nice, France
1986 *Arte italiana degli anni Sessanta*, Castello di Rivoli, Turin

Collections:

Galleria Nazionale d'Arte Moderna, Rome; Centre Georges Pompidou, Paris; Museu de Arte Moderna, Sao Paulo; Museum of Contemporary Art, Chicago; Fort Lauderdale Museum of Art, Florida; Stedelijk Museum, Amsterdam; Museum Ludwig, Cologne; Museum Moderner Kunst, Vienna; Museum of Modern Art, Tel Aviv; Museo d'Arte Moderna, Milan.

Publications:

By ROTELLA: book—*Autorotella*, Milan 1972; articles—"Cosi" in *Rotella*, exhibition catalogue, Rome 1957; "Il Mondo di Immagini Violentissime che i Circonando" in *Alternative Attuali*, exhibition catalogue, L'Aquila, Italy 1962; "Caro le Noci" in *Rotella: Dal Décollage alla Nuova Immagine* by Pierre Restany, Milan 1963; recording—*Poemi fonetici 1949–75*, LP disc, Milan 1975.

On ROTELLA: books—*Rotella*, exhibition catalogue, by Paul Garner, Kansas City, Missouri 1952; *Rotella*, exhibition catalogue, by Nello Ponente, Milan 1958; *Rotella*, exhibition catalogue, by Emmilio Villa, Rome 1959; *Rotella*, exhibition catalogue, by Pierre Restany, Rome 1961; *Rotella: Dal Décollage alla Nuova Immagine* by Pierre Restany, Milan 1963; *Les Nouveau Réalistes* by Pierre Restany, Paris 1968; *Rotella 1954–1968*, exhibition catalogue, by Otto Hahn, Brussels 1969; *Rotella* by Tommaso Trini, Milan 1974; *Rotella: Opere dal 1958–75*, exhibition catalogue, by Pierre Restany, Portofino, Italy, 1978; *Vitalità del negativo nell'arte italiana*

1960–70 by M. Calvesi, G. Dorfles and A. Bonito Oliva, Turin 1980; *Le Blanks de Rotella*, exhibition catalogue with text by Pierre Restany, Milan 1984; *1960: Les Nouveaux Réalistes*, exhibition catalogue by Pierre Restany, Paris 1986.

*

Collage, unfortunately, has a place in history and an origin and a development in both earlier and contemporary art. I say unfortunately, because I should have wished to have invented collage myself. In my childhood the gray skies, the gray houses, the faces, the roads, the dust, the feeling, all the immense gray things of the South filled me with a sense of urgency, a rage, to invent colors and to paste them on certain restricted spaces of my fantasy. Then I began to express myself with tissue paper. All this about memories of childhood is an ingenuous reference, a literary presumption. But the rage remains. To rip posters from the walls is the only act of real evaluation, the only protest against a society that has lost its taste for the mutations and transformations of the extraordinary.

I paste posters together, then I rip them: new forms are born, unforeseeably. I have abandoned easel-painting in order to make this protest. If I had the powers of Samson, I would paste Piazza di Spagna with certain of its morbid and tender autumnal tints, on the red squares of the Gianiculum at sunset. You will say: "This is all rambling. Explain your work, rather, for it is not very intelligible." Very well; it is concerned with a research, a research which places its reliance not in the aesthetic, but in the unforeseeable, in the very humors of the texture. It is like a trumpet, a drum, a saxophone that play by themselves. I place my reliance in the trumpet, the drum, and the saxophone. I have no wish to be eccentric, otherwise I would dress in the street clothes of the Napoleonic Era. Eccentricity in our time is reactionary; the truth lies, instead, in a hope for the future. Were I to paste up colors in various shapes on pieces of cardboard, selecting them as if from an easel, I should then be resolving simple problems of taste with the help of an artisan's technique. I rip posters, first from the walls, then from the base of the composition: how much taste, how much fantasy, how much interest accumulates, thrusting forward and drawing near from the first to the last rip. It is not a matter of juxtaposing abstract colors, but of colors with a life of their own, with a spirit, with—so to speak—a vitality. If I pass from researches into the nature of color to researches into the nature of texture, then the meanings transform themselves and become dramatic. How will the earth be after the end of the world? It may be as smooth and as cold as a surface of marble, rigged by canals as contorted as trails in the wilderness. Collage suggests a yellow or a yellowish patina for this geography of the deluge: and the patina is a hope.

—Mimmo Rotella

*

Mimmo Rotella's contribution to modern art has been the development of the Cubist collage technique to a formula known as "decollage," or double collage, also followed by the French "affichistes," by which posters stripped from walls are transferred onto the canvas, reduced or decomposed by further mutilation. This was a comparatively late development, when the artist was over thirty, working and living in Rome after a period of study in the United States under a Fulbright Scholarship.

In America he had experimented with phonetic poems, painted a huge mural at the University of Missouri in Kansas City and held an exhibition in the same town. It may be that this contact with the United States influenced his interest in urban poster sites, whilst, back in post-war Italy, these mutilated, processed images presented both a symbol of contemporary conditions and the means of expressing them.

The earliest decollages were really substitutes for abstract painting, using the colour and texture of the papers to establish a sensitive, carefully balanced, atmospheric image, not unlike the work of Schwitters. There was little of the social comment of a collagist such as Raoul Hausmann, or the psychological, sur-realistic exploitation of Max Ernst. Rotella's work, at this stage, was colourful and dramatic, growing more and more assured, intricate, brilliant, exploiting to the full the maximum potential of the medium. It is interesting, for instance, to note the transitions from hot colours to futuristic rhythmic detail, and then changes to broad areas of tone.

By 1960 he reverted to a calmer, less active for-mula, of broad areas of single colours, and large ges-tural shapes, rather than the busy intricacy of the first period. At this stage he also invoked direct narrative or moral messages; this invoked the exploitation of photographic images which were allowed to dominate and direct the picture, whereas in the past he had remained strictly abstract. Suggestions of American pop-art, notably Andy Warhol, were inevitable, espe-cially in the manipulation of film-star faces, but Ro-tella always remained more complex and painterly than the American artist.

In the mid 60's a major change of style and purpose resulted in direct simplicity, single, powerful, news-paper images of the death of a Pope, or a Vietnam soldier, reproductions of magazine covers, portraits of fellow artists, advertisement still-lifes. This relied far more on single photographic or reproducible im-ages, heralding the new photo-realistic school of fel-low painters. Rotella's "nouveau realism" of "Photo-reportages" represent a further break-away from traditional Western techniques, and an anxiety to artistic statement to both the methods and images of urban society. He therefore involved himself in mass mythology and mechanical operations, indeed he is credited with inventing the term "mecart" to describe this aesthetic philosophy.

At one period of his career, in the early 60's, he involved himself in the assemblage of objects, a form of junk-art, extending the process of *object trouvés* from the city walls to its streets. This Duchamp-like process ranged from manufactured ready-mades, like toy balls and window models displaying brassieres, to complex, semi-realistic assemblages of flea-market rubbish. These works appeared, in fact, at the turning point in Rotella's career, when he was about to aban-don the painterly, sensitive, often brilliant manipula-tions of colour and texture, for the sober, restrained, direct "mechanical" photo-reportage.

—Charles Spencer

ROTH, Dieter.

Swiss. Born Karl-Dietrich Roth, of Swiss and Ger-man parents, in Hannover, Germany, 21 April 1930; moved with his parents to Switzerland, 1943. Edu-cated in Hannover, 1936-43; in classical secondary school in Zurich, 1943-46, and in St. Gallen, 1946-47; apprentice graphic designer, Studio Friedrich Wuthrich, Berne, 1947-51; studied lithography, un-der Eugen Jordi, Kehrsatz, 1950: associated closely with artists Franz Eggenschwiler and Paul Talman, Berne, 1947-51. Married Sigridur Bjornsdottir in 1957 (separated, 1964); children: Karl Bjorn and Vera. Independent artist, in Berne, 1951-56, Copen-hagen, 1956-59, subsequently in Reykjavik, Mos-fellssveit, Iceland, Stuttgart, and in Mols, Switzerland, 1958-84, lives in Basle since 1984; first collages and woodcuts, 1949; first films and baked food sculptures, 1954; works with goldsmiths and archi-tects, 1957-58; with editions Hansjorg Mayer, Stuttgart, London and Reykjavik, 1968-1981; collab-orations with artists Stefan Wewerka, 1970, Arnulf Rainer, 1973-76, Richard Hamilton, 1975-77; sound recordings and concerts, with Gerhard Ruhm, Os-wald Wiener and others, since 1973. Also worked occasionally as builder/decorator, Berne, 1951-60; graphic and textile designer, Berne and Copenhagen, 1954-58; graphic designer, Geigy Corporation, New York, 1959; in Ragner Kjartansson's ceramic work-

shop, Reykjavik, 1960; and in Karl Gerstner/Markus Kutter advertising agency, Basle, 1960 and 1968. Founder-Editor, *Spirale* magazine, Berne, 1953; Di-rector, with Rolf Iseli, Peter Meier and Walter Vogeli, Gallery 33, Berne, 1954; Founder, with Einar Bragi, Forlag editions, Reykjavik, 1957-58; Founder/designer, with Magnus Palsson and Manfred Vilh-jamsson, Kula furniture shop, Reykjavik, 1960; co-publisher, Edition Hansjorg Mayer, Stuttgart, London and Reykjsavik, 1968-81; Founder, with Karl Schulz, Schepperts Press, Braunschweig, 1970-77; Founder, Dieter Roth's Family Press, and Dieter Roth Pictures, 1974; Founder *Review for Everything*, 1975; Founder, *Kopiks* magazine, Bali, 1984. Visit-ing Critic 1959, and Instructor 1964, Yale University, New Haven, Connecticut; Instructor, Rhode Island School of Design, Providence, 1965; Watford School of Art, London, 1968; and Staatliche Kunstakademie, Dusseldorf, 1968-70. Recipient: Kiefer-Hablitzel Painting Prize, Berne, 1954; Gold Medal, *San Fran-cisco Textile Fair*, 1956; William and Norma Copley Award, Chicago 1960; Kunstpreis der Stadt Iserlohn, 1969; First Prize, *International Print Biennale*, Gren-chen, 1973; Rembrandt Prize, Goethe-Foundation, Basle, 1982; Kunstpreis der Nord/LB, Hannover, 1984; Charles Nypels Prize, Maastricht, 1986. Ad-dress: Hegenheimerstrasse 24, 4055 Basle, Switzer-land.

Individual Exhibitions:

1958	Mokka Kaffi, Reykjavik
1960	Galerie Koepcke, Copenhagen (with Christian Me-gert)
1963	Galerie Koepcke, Copenhagen
1964	Philadelphia Museum School of Art
1967	Galerie Zwirner, Cologne (with Dorothy Iannone)
	Galerie der Edition Hansjorg Mayer, Stuttgart
1968	Galerie Zwirner, Cologne
	Galerie Handschin, Basle
	Galerie Neuendorf, Hamburg
	Galerie René Block, West Berlin
	Galerie Tobies und Silex, Cologne (with Stefan We-werka)
1969	Galerie Ernst, Hannover
	Eugenia Butler Gallery, Los Angeles
	Galerie Hake, Cologne
	Art Intermedia Cologne
	Galerie Muller, Stuttgart
1970	Galerie Werner, Copenhagen
	Galerie Kummel, Cologne (with Stefan Wewerka)
	Galerie Mikro, West Berlin (with Stefan Wewerka)
1971	Galerie Toni Gerber, Berne
	Art Intermedia, Cologne
	Ziegler Editionen und Graphik, Zurich
	Eat-Art Galerie, Dusseldorf
	Universitat, Kiel
	Langenbacher und Wankmiller, Lucerne
	Museum Haus Lange, Krefeld, West Germany
	Von-der-Heydt Museum, Wuppertal, West Germany (with Stefan Wewerka)
1972	Haags Gemeentemuseum, The Hague
	Kunsthalle, Basle
	Helmhaus, Zurich
	Kunsthalle, Baden-Baden, West Germany
	Galerie Grunangergasse, Vienna
	Richard Foncke Gallery, Ghent
	Museum Haus Lange, Krefeld, West Germany
	Galerie 2, Stuttgart
	Galerie Kammer, Hamburg
	Eat-Art Galerie, Dusseldorf
1973	Hayward Gallery, London
	European Gallery, San Francisco
	Galerie Meyer-Ellinger, Frankfurt
	Galerie Steinmetz, Bonn
	Vancouver Art Gallery
	Kunstverein, Braunschweig, West Germany
	Akademie der Künste, West Berlin
	Kunsthalle, Dusseldorf
1974	Kunstverein, Mannheim
	Galerie Steinmetz, Bonn
	Galerie Kammer, Hamburg
	Langenbacher und Wankmiller, Lucerne

	Manus-Presse, Stuttgart
	Kestner-Gesellschaft, Hannover
	Kunstverein, Hamburg
1975	Stedelijk Museum, Amsterdam
	Galerie Steinmetz, Bonn
	Galerie Bama, Paris
	de Moriaan, den Bosch, Netherlands
	Galleria il Capricorno, Venice
	Galerie Grunangergasse, Vienna
	Dieter Roth Pictures, Hamburg
	Galerie Renee Ziegler, Zurich
	Gallery Ariadne, New York (with Arnulf Rainer)
	Galerie Hoss, Stuttgart
1976	Galleri Dierks, Aarhus, Denmark
	Kulturhaus, Graz, Austria (with Arnulf Rainer)
	Galerie Kalb, Vienna
	Galerie Buchmann, St. Gallen, Switzerland
	Galeria Cadaques, Cadaques, Spain (with Richard Hamilton)
	Kaiser-Wilhelm-Museum, Krefeld, West Germany
	British Council Institute, Barcelona (with Richard Hamilton)
	Galerie im Reuchlinhaus, Pforzheim, West Germany
	Galerie am Jakobsbrunnen, Stuttgart
	Stadtmuseum, Solothurn, Switzerland
	Turnpike Gallery, Leigh, Lancashire, England (with Richard Hamilton)
1977	Institute of Contemporary Arts, London (with Rich-ard Hamilton)
	Pari e Dispari, Cavriago, Italy
	Galerie Fassbender, Munich
	Galerie Handschin, Basle
	Galerie Stahli, Zurich
	Galery 44, Kaarst, West Germany
	Galerie Steinmetz, Bonn
	Haags Gemeentemuseum, The Hague (with Richard Hamilton)
	Junior-Galerie, Dusseldorf (with Richard Hamilton)
	Galeria Cadaques, Cadaques, Spain (with Karl and Bjorn Roth)
	Print Gallery Pieter Brattinga, Amsterdam
	Galeria Eude, Barcelona (with Richard Hamilton)
	Aargauer Kunsthaus, Aarau, Switzerland (with Richard Hamilton)
	Fundacio Joan Miró, Barcelona (with Richard Ham-ilton)
1978	Carl Solway Gallery, New York (with Richard Ham-ilton)
	Waddington and Tooth Galleries, London (with Richard Hamilton)
	Galerie Buchmann, St. Gallen, Switaerland
	Galerie Anton Meier, Geneva
	Galerie Handschin, Basle
	Whitworth Art Gallery, Manchester (with Richard Hamilton)
	Galeria Cadaques, Cadaques, Spain (with Richard Hamilton)
	Galeria Maeght, Barcelona (with Richard Hamilton)
	Galerie Nothelfer, West Berlin
	Galerie Handschin, Basle
	Ulmer Museum, Ulm, West Germany
1979	Backworks, New York
	Stempelplaats, Amsterdam
	Kunsthalle, Bielefeld, West Germany (with Richard Hamilton)
	Galerie René Block, West Berlin (with Richard Hamilton)
	Galerie Klewan, Munich (with Arnulf Rainer)
	Staatsgalerie, Stuttgart
	Galerie Holtmann, Hannover
1980	Kunstmuseum, Lucerne
	Langenbacher und Wankmiller, Lucerne
	Galerie Holtmann, Hannover (with Richard Hamil-ton)
	Haags Gemeentemuseum, The Hague
	Galerie Buchmann, St. Gallen, Switzerland (with Arnulf Rainer)
1981	Galerie Buchmann, St. Gallen, Switzerland
	Galerie Holtmann, Cologne
	Helmhaus, Zurich
	Galerie Littman, Basle
1982	Galerie Bama, Paris
	Kunstmuseum, Basle
	Bahnhof Buffet SBB, Basle

Galerie Klewan, Munich
Swiss Pavilion, at the *Biennale*, Venice
Galerie Toni Gerber, Berne
Buchhandlung Niedlich, Stuttgart
Galerie Kurt Kalb/Kunstbuchhandlung Judith Ortner, Vienna
Galerie Hummel, Vienna
Nýlistasafnid, Reykjavík
Roosenhaus, Hamburg

1983 Reinhard Onnasch Ausstellungen, West Berlin
Holderbank Management und Beratung, Holderbank, Switzerland
Antiquariat Walter Wögenstein, Vienna
Kunstverein, Bonn
Galerie Handschin, Basle
Institut für Kunstgeschichte, Vienna University

1984 Museum of Contemporary Art, Chicago
Petersen Galerie, West Berlin (with Björn Roth and others)

1985 Herzog Anton Ulrich Museum, Braunschweig, West Germany
Petersen Galerie, West Berlin (with D. Roth Verlag)
Loft, Munich (with D. Roth Verlag)
Hegenheimerstrasse 24, Basle (with D. Roth Verlag)
Burckhardt und Partner, Basle
Galerie Priska Meier, Zell, Switzerland (with Björn and Vera Roth)
Hegenheimerstrasse 24, Basle (with Björn Roth)

1986 Galerie Marlene Frei, Zurich
Museum für Gegenwartskunst, Basle
Nigel Greenwood Books, London
Rhode Island School of Design, Providence
Galerie Marlene Frei, Zurich (with Björn Roth and Ingrid Wiener)
Holderbank Management und Beratung, Holderbank, Switzerland
Centre Régional d'Art Contemporain Midi-Pyrenees, Labège, France
Hegenheimerstrasse 24, Basle
Galerie Portikus, Frankfurt

Selected Group Exhibitions:

1953 *Berner Kunstler*, Galerie Schindler, Berne
1955 *Junge Berner Kunstler*, Kunsthalle, Berne
1959 *Edition MAT*, Société d'Art St. Germain-de-Près, Paris
1965 *Between Poetry and Painting*, Institute of Contemporary Arts, London
1968 *Documenta 4*, Museum Fridericianum, Kassel, West Germany (and *Documenta 6*, 1977)
1972 *Amsterdam-Paris-Dusseldorf*, Guggenheim Museum, New York
1974 *Artists' Books*, University of California Art Museum, Berkeley
1982 *Westkunst*, Messenhallen, Cologne
1984 *Von Hier Aus*, Messenhallen, Dusseldorf
1986 *Bein i köldu ofni*, Nordiskt Konstcentrum, Sveaborg, Finland

Collections:

Kunsthaus, Zurich; Kunsthalle, Hamburg; Stedelijk Museum, Amsterdam; Bibliothèque Nationale, Paris; Museum Haus Lange, Krefeld, West Germany; Tate Gallery, London; Moderna Museet, Stockholm; Louisiana Museum, Humlebaek, Denmark; Museum des 20. Jahrhunderts, Vienna; Museum of Modern Art, New York.

Publications:

By ROTH: books—*Bilderbuch*, Reykjavik 1956; *Kinderbuch*, Reykjavik 1957; *Book*, Reykjavik and Paris, 1968; *Ideogramme*, Darmstadt 1959; *Bok 1956–59*, Reykjavik 1959; *Bok 2a*, Reykjavik 1960; *Bok 2b*, Reykjavik 1961; *Bok 4a*, Reykjavik 1961; *Bok 5*, Reykjavik 1961; *Bok 3a*, Reykjavik 1961, 1981; *Bok 3b*, Reykjavik 1961; *Bok 3c*, Reykjavik 1961, Mosfellssveit 1981; *Bok 3d*, Reykjavik 1961; *Daily Mirror Book*, Reykjavik 1961; *Literaturwurst*, book/object, Reykjavik 1961, West Berlin 1970; *Daglegt Bull/Daily Bul, no. 8*, La Louvière, Belgium 1961; *Book AC 1958–64*, New Haven 1964; *Quadratblatt*, Hilversum, Netherlands 1965; *Kölner Divisionene: 7 August 65*, Cologne 1965; *Schneewittchen*, Cologne 1965; *Quick von Diter Rot 1961–65*, Reykjavik 1965; *Scheisse: Neue Gedichte von Diter Rot*, with an appendix by Al Fabri Providence, Rhode Island 1966; *Copley Buch*, Chicago 1966; *Die Blaue Flut*, Stuttgart 1967; *Mundunculum—Band 1: Das rot'sche Videum*, Cologne 1967; *Poetrie nr. 2*, Stuttgart 1967; *80 Wolken, 1965 bis 1967*, Stuttgart 1967; *A Look into the Blue Tide part 2*, New York 1967; *Snow*, West Berlin 1967; *Stempelkasten*, Dusseldorf 1967, rev. ed. Stuttgart 1972; *Poeterei 3–4*, editor, with Rudolf Rieser, Stuttgart 1968; *Poemetrie*, editor, with Rudolf Reiser, Cologne 1968, rev. ed. Cologne 1970; *Noch mehr Scheisse: Ein Nachlese*, Stuttgart 1968; *Sonntagsbeigabe der Zeitung für Kaukausen und Umgebung*, Stuttgart 1968; *Die gesamte Scheisse: Gedichte und Zeichnungen von Diter Rot*, West Berlin 1968; *246 Little Clouds*, with an introduction by Emmett Williams, New York, Cologne, Paris 1968; *Little Tentative Recipe by Diter Rot and Students of Watford School of Art*, Stuttgart 1969; *Gesammelte Werke*, first series, 20 vols, Stuttgart, London, and Reykjavik 1969–1976; *Islandisch Leder*, Reykjavik 1970; *Postkartenblock*, Cologne and London 1971; *Franz Eggenschwiler, der Junglin, der Mann, die Zeit, das Werk: Ein Essay von Diter Rot*, Stuttgart 1971; *2 Probleme unserer Zeit: ein Essay von Dieter Rot*, Reykjavik 1971; *Wer war Mozart: ein Essay von Dieter Rot*, Reykjavik 1971; *Wer ist der Nicht Weiss wer Mozart war*, Reykjavik 1971; *Dieter Rot: ein Frage?*, Reykjavik 1971; *Ein Essay uber das Verhalten de Allgemeinen zu oder Gegenuber dem Besonderen BZW des Besonderen zu Order Gegenuber dem All-gemeinen*, Reykjavik 1971; *Frische Scheisse (eine Nachlese)*, Reykjavik 1972; *Die Schastrommel nr. 9: Ergebnisse des ersten Berliner Dichter-Workshops (30.10–7.11.1972)* with Friedrich Achleitner, Günter Brus, Gerhard Ruhm and Oswald Wiener, Stuttgart 1973; *Das Tranenmeer*, Stuttgart 1973; *Der Tranensee*, Reykjavik 1973; *Die Gesamte Scheiss von Diter Rot*, West Berlin and Stuttgart 1973; *Das Tranenmeer: Band 2*, Stuttgart 1973; *Fruhe Schriften und typische Scheiee ausgewahlt-und mit einem Haufen Teilverdautes von Oswald Winer*, Darmstadt 1973, Stuttgart, London and Reykjavik 1975; *Murmel*, 1974; *Bucher*, Hannover 1974; *Dars Wahnen: Das Wahnen Band 1 (Tranenmeer 3)*, Stuttgart 1974; *Die Die Die Gesamte Scheisse von Dietrich Roth*, West Berlin, Stuttgart, London and Reykjavik 1974; *Das Original oder Kann das Gemalde der Maler sein? Eine Bastel-Novelle von Max Plunderbaum*, Stuttgart 1974; *Boeken*, Amsterdam 1975; *Neo Nix and Neo-Mix*, with Arnulf Rainer, Stuttgart 1975; *Das Riginal=Das Original, Bastelnovelle nr. 2*, Stuttgart 1975; *Die Die Die DIE Gesamte verdammte Scheisse von Karl-Dietrich Roth*, West Berlin, Stuttgart, London and Reykjavik 1975; *Roth and Rainer: Misch-u. Trennkunst*, with Arnulf Rainer, Graz, Austria 1976, Stuttgart and London 1979; *Ratiobrief, 1. Auflage*, with Arnulf Rainer, Vienna 1976; *Ratiobrief, 2. verbesserte Auflage, Saugpost, Auslandsverkehr u.a.m.*, with Arnulf Rainer, Vienna 1976; *Ratiobrief 3* with Arnulf Rainer, Vienna 1976; *Collaborations of Ch. Rotham*, with Richard Hamilton, Stuttgart and Cadaques, Spain 1977; *Interfaces*, with Richard Hamilton, New York 1977; *Complete Works (Part 2)*, 5 vols., Stuttgart and London 1977-; *Interfaeces*, with Richard Hamilton, London 1978; *150 Speedy Drawings: nrs. 1501–1650, 2-handed, made in Cadaques on the 1st + 2nd of oktober 1977*, Cadaques and Zug 1978; *Von Blau ins Grau: Zwei Aber kein Saldot*, with Arnulf Rainer, Zug and Vienna 1978; *Das Wahnen Band 2A (Tranenmeer 4)*, Stuttgart, London and Zug 1978; *Das Original nr. 3: Das Fatal-Orininal (Baselnovelle nr. 3)*, Stuttgart and Zug 1978; *Trophies: 125 Two-Handed Speedy Drawings*, Stuttgart and London 1979; *Unterm Plunderbaum-(die Sonetten 195?–1979)=Das Weinen no. 2=Das Wahnen, bd. 2B (Tranenemeer 5)*, Stuttgart and London 1979; *Dieter Roth: Ein Lebenslauf von 50 Jahren*, Lucerne 1980; *Telefonzeichnungen 1976–78*, Stuttgart and London 1980; *Antwoorden op Vragen*, with Krees Broos, The Hague 1980; *Der Moralist: Essay nr. 7*, Zurich, London, Stuttgart and Lucerne, 1981; *Bats: 130 Zweihandige Schnellzeichnungen*, West Berlin 1981; *Dogs: 128 zweihandige Schnellzeichnungen*, West Berlin 1981; *Biennale Venezia 1982*, Berne 1982; *4 Dutzend schnelle Weichzeichnungen*, Hamburg 12982; *2 Schock schnelle Weichzeichnungen 1982*, West Berlin 1983; *Holderbank*, Holderbank 1983; *Landenhuter (aus den Jahren 1965–1983)*, West Berlin 1983; *Holderbank*, Holderbank 1983; *A Diary (from the year 1982)*, Basle 1984; *20 Zeichnungereihen*, with Björn Roth, Basle 1984; *150 Schnellzeichnungen 1977*, West Berlin 1984; *Kopiks no. 1*, With Björn, Karl and Vera Roth, and others, West Berlin 1985; *(untitled)*, with Michael Seeger and Dorothea Baumer, Stuttgart 1985; *Bone in a Cold Oven*, with Björn Roth, and others, Basle 1986; *Katalog zur Austellung des grossen Teppiches*, Zurich and Basle 1986; *Bilder-und Teppichausstellung*, Holderbank and Basle 1987; films and videos—*Pop 1. dock 1 N 2. letter. dot*, 1956–61; *Dieter Roth/Scheissegedichtlesung/Wien, Juli 1975*, 1976; *Arnulf Rainer und Dieter Roth: Doppeldruck*, 1976; *Arnulf Rainer und Dieter Roth: Duell im Schloss*, 1976; *Arnulf Rainer und Dieter Roth: Der Kranke*, 1977; *Arnulf Rainer und Dieter Roth: Ein truber Nachmittag (Rainer)/Wer hatte das gedacht, dass auch das Verwerfen nichts macht! (Roth)*, 1977; *Arnulf Ranier und Dieter Roth: Fuzzle-Piece (Rainer)/ Wer hatte das nicht gedacht, dass alles nichts macht! (Roth)*, 1977; *Arnulf Rainer und Dieter Roth: Gesprach am Morgen (Rainer)/(varying title)(Roth)*, 1979; *Arnulf Rainer und Dieter Roth: Stanfotos (Rainer)/(varying title)(Roth)*,, 1979; *Arnulf Rainer und Dieter Roth: Umgriffe (Rainer)/(varying title)(Roth)*, 1979; *Arnulf Rainer und Dieter Roth: Uble Stunden (Rainer)/Was Ekelhaftes (Roth)*, 1979; *Ballet*, with Beatrice Cordua and Peter Schonherr, 1979; records and tapes—*3. Berliner Dichterworkshop, 12/13.7.73*, with Gerhard Ruhm and Oswald Wiener, Stuttgart, London and Reykjavik 1973; *Novembersymphonie (Doppelsymphonie)*, with Gerhard Ruhm and Oswald Wiener, Stuttgart 1974; *Selten geharte musik, munchner Konzert mai 1974* with Günter Brus, Hermann Mitsch, Gerhard Ruhm and Oswald Wiener, Stuttgart, London and Reykjavik 1975; *Islenskra Fjalla (Kalli live at Danneckerstrasse)*, with Karl Roth, Zug 1975; *Selten gehorte musik, Streichquartett 55 81 71 (Romenthalquartett)*, with Günter Brus, Hermann Nitsch and Gerhard Ruhm, Stuttgart, London and Reykjavik 1976; *Canciones de Cadaques* with Richard Hamilton and Chispas Luis, Cadaques and Stuttgart 1976; *Selten gehorte Musik, Tote Rennen, Lieder*, with Oswald Wiener, Stuttgart and London 1977; *Selten gehorte Musik, Musica che si Ascolta Rarmente, Das Berliner Konzert*, with Attersee, Günter Brus, Hermann Nitsch, Arnulf Rainer, Gerhard Ruhm, Dominik Steiger and Oswald Wiener, Reggio Emmilia, Naples and Stuttgart 1977; *Collaborations: Readings*, with Richard Hamilton, London 1978; *Tibidabo*, Zug and Cadaques 1978; *Lorelei: The Long Distance Sonata*, with Björn Roth and Vera Roth, Stuttgart and London 1978; *Radiohous-Klage=Musik, Die Radiosonate*, Brussels, Hamburg and Stuttgart 1978; *Misch-und Trennkunst: Autonom-Dialog-ische Thermatik*, Arnulf Rainer, Brussels, Hamburg and Zug 1978; *Rainer-Roth oder "Ratio-Konditio"* with Arnulf Rainer, Hamburg and Stuttgart 1979; *Thy Quatsch est min Castello*, Stuttgart 1979; *Selten gehorte Musik. Munich, Mai 1979: Abschoepfsymphonie. Die Abschoepfung*, with Attersee, Heinz Cibulka, Herbert Hossman, Hansjorg Mayer, Hermann Nitsch, and Paul Renne, Björn Roth, Gerhard Ruhm, Dieter Schwarz, André Thompkins, and Oswald Wiener, Stuttgart, Brussels and Hamburg 1979; *Autofahrt No. 1. 15–16 h, 17. Apr. 79*, with Björn Roth, Stuttgart 1979; *The Kuemmerling Trio Plays Kuemmerling Trios no. 1 & 2*, with Hansjorg Mayer and Emmett Williams, Stuttgart 1979; *Fernquartett*, with Björn Roth, Karl Roth and Vera Roth, Stuttgart 1980; *Harmonica Curse*, London 1981.

On ROTH: books—*Books and Graphics 1947–1971*, exhibition catalogue, edited by Hansjorg Mayer, Stuttgart 1971; *The Story of Bern (or) Showing Colors* by Dorothy Iannone, Dusseldorf 1970; *Dieter Roth Gewurz-Objekte, Gummiband-Bilder etc . . .* , exhibition catalogue, with text by Paul Wember, Krefeld, West Germany 1971; *Danger in Dusseldorf (or) I Am Not What I Seem* by Dorothy Iannone, Stuttgart, London and Reykjavik 1973; *Dieter Roth*, anthology, edited by Galerie Steinmetz, Bonn 1974; *Dieter Roth: Werke von 1973/ 1975*, exhibition catalogue, with text by Peter F. Althaus, Solothurn, Switzerland 1976; *An Titils. Skaldverk* by Einar Gudmundsson, Reykjavik 1978; *Auf der Bogen Bahn: Studien zum litararischen Werk von Dieter Roth* by Dieter Schwarz, Zurich 1981; *Johann Wolfgang von Goethe Stiftung: Verleihung des Rembrandt-Preises 1982 an Dieter Roth*, with text by Emmett Williams, Basle 1982; *Dieter Roth*, exhibition catalogue with text by Ann Goldstein, Chicago 1984; *Dieter Roth: Arbeiten auf Papier 1974–1984*, exhibition catalogue with text by Dietrich Helms, Hannover and Braunschweig 1985; *Dieter Roth* by Kees Broos, Labège 1987.

When I was born, I found myself, so I have been told, at a place in Germany, which I found the most horrible place to be, early or later in life. Horribly screaming Germans everywhere, scolding beating me up all the time, and when I grow up to be able to look around me, I found them engaged not only in war with me, but also with those horrible bombs and grenades throwing, terrible cruel madmen called the English and those insane massmurders, throwing bombs and blasts from the sky out of terrifying manmade monsters called airplanes or airoplanes, the so-called Americans, horribly adept killers and massmurderers. All three, Germans, Englishmen, Americans from Northamerica, as bloodthirsty at that time, the time of my little boyhood, as the silly French, thirsting for blood, the Russians, killers of the first order, Italians, Poles, murderous bunch of monsters as ugly themselves as their horrible inventions and imaginations. There, among them Fighters and Slaughterers, I grow up pissing in my timid pants, shitting into my pisswet trousers all the time and weeping all the time like a poor little dogturd. Then I was brought to Switzerland my horribly Christian Home Country. There were those murderous, butchering people, called soldiers and defenders of Freedom, everywhere. I survived there 12 years and then got away to friendly wonderful Copenhagen. But I fell into that awfully black hole called Matrimony, and I struggled there, horribly kicking, fucking and pissing in my timid little pants for seven years. Hell! But I got away to the United States of Northamerica, full of horrifying Maneaters, Butchers, Christians and other stuff. Pissing and shitting in my awfully wet pants, I survived, a strong and screaming cannibal myself now, a bastard of terror and fear, kicking, fucking, drinking and pissing. Running around different countries, all the same time, I find myself a dweller of butchershops, cannibal of fate, rage, tears, fears, and shit, piss, blood and shit, a bastard of fear, murderous Hangover from Hell. Pissing in his awfully shitting, pissing, shitting trousers, called his pants, of fears and tears. Hangover from shitfucking places like Hell, Germany, U.S.A., England, France, China, Russia, Heaven, God, Angels, Christ, Buddha, Shit, Piss and Fear.

—Dieter Roth

"Good bye! Good bye!" was Dieter Roth's return of thanks when he received the *Rembrandt prize* in the Basle Art Museum in February 1982. This farewell accompanying a friendly and eloquent retreat and holding out hope for the future, runs like a motto through Dieter Roth's work. Alarmed by the aesthetic and moral demands directed at the artist Roth never makes more than a small bow to convention and looks for the exit. "He quickly leaves this place and betakes himself apace," as Wilhelm Busch, one of his artistic ideals, wrote.

It was also "Good bye" at the beginning of his *Quadruple Concert* in the Basle Academy of Music where Roth was to play on four instruments, accompanied by a battery of strong drinks on the long grand piano. The concert had in fact already taken place in the two hours before the time announced by the poster. What followed were musical intermezzi, accompanied by counter-orders, drowned in playbacks of the music played earlier this evening. "As broke as when I came-/as broke I now must go,/and say in modest blame:/Farewell, forever so!" was the last poem of his volume *Still More Shit* from 1968, although this solemn declaration was followed in the same year by *The Complete Shit*. Roth does not simply disappear but conceals behind the modest gesture a performance powerful already in its extent.

Like the magician he shows that his hands are empty before pulling rabbits out of the air—there are pictures hidden under his cap, and in his jacket pocket a diary with entries which could go directly into his volumes of poetry without any alteration. In appearance Roth represents the discreet style of the Bourgeois, grey three piece suit and light grey shirt. A business man on his travels, the cap gives a sportsmanlike touch. Today, when industrialists follow fashion, these clothes are a reminder of pre-war days, manufacture and small industries. The diary bulging his pocket is not merely order book and agenda for the production which Roth calls "positive, therefore civilising," but also a repository for emotions and reflections, "Junk and Waste."

For more than two years junk and waste really filled his pockets when Roth decided to collect all the flat rubbish that passed through his hands, packing it into transparent bags for filing. In the autumn of 1981 he built them into two pyramids in Zürich's Helmhaus, a melancholy still life of a civilisation's dead remains. In its strict method (collecting everything flat during a year) this collection recalls Roth's artistic beginnings among the Swiss concrete artists of the 1950s. As his father was a Swiss living abroad, Roth came to Switzerland in 1943 from bomb-destroyed Hanover as a foster child, and after grammar school and apprenticeship as a graphic artist he made his first etchings (on tea-box tin instead of copper plate, due to lack of money) and poems. He made

ends meet with occasional work and soon met with harsh criticism of his works when his friends Eugen Gomringer and Marcel Wyss rejected his poems as dreadfully sentimental. He rescued himself into minimal texts, reduced in part to dashes and dots, and constructivist pictures which he carried so far that finally he exchanged the brush for a knife and cut books out of coloured paper so that slits offered views of the following pages, producing subtle optical effects.

As a textile designer Roth was invited to a Danish firm, worked for a year in Copenhagen and met a girl from Iceland whom he followed to Reykjavík and married. Because he lived so far away and most of his contacts with Europe were broken, Roth was not able to devote himself to a simple artistic career but had to support himself working for a goldsmith and in furniture design. That changed his art: "When you go down, this concrete poetry and Mondrian painting doesn't help at all; only shit and rage." So Roth accepted everything that, while making a picture, got onto the picture's surface and gave up all claim to neat clarification of forms. This no longer pleased the purists in Switzerland and elsewhere, and it took years for Roth to succeed in making this (often under rich colour) hidden lament palatable to the public. Roth had already overtaken the postwar belief in a progress in which art and advertising would form an alliance for the future of consumerism, even before this joined an all inundating flood of merchandise. Roth saw under the cleanly prepared surface the hidden "War of living creatures" production as a raging contest: "I understand civilisation as everybody eating everybody." Letting himself go is a moral gesture with which Roth demonstrates against all those who draw up regulations and use them against others, and yet he knows that he too must take part in this struggle. His large graphics and book exhibition opened in Stuttgart on September 1979, forty years after the outbreak of the second world war; "Over such talk one often forgets the dreary things that are happening outside, that nobody sees, where one thinks there is only open air acrobatics going on (and in the worst case, football).—No, outside, it is war!, there's marching, bleeding and bombing!"

Great tension stems from the fact that Roth always tackles his work with the ambition necessary to hold his ground against the competition, yet speaks for amateurish work, or stuff quickly made. It is more than an easy moral creed, for it leads, for example, to a time and energy consuming project like the *Review For Everything*. Roth founded it in 1975 under the motto "Review For Everything accepts and publishes everything that comes." In the seven issues published so far, Roth and notable artists join with amateurs, children, all who have the courage to collaborate. The editor does not select, but tries to put up whatever comes to him and to defend all possible options. Only when criteria fall is there something new to see. On similar grounds Roth, whose list of own books contains over a hundred titles, founded his *Familien Verlag*, publishing books and records initially of his children and relatives, then of friends and acquaintances. Publishing these works he apologizes for the extent of his own production which threatens to push others to the wall,—at the same time these published works become part of the Roth-ian work, a circle from which there seems to be no way out.

Even when Roth takes new paths, approaches music for example, invents *Rarely Heard Music,* and demonstrates the non-command of instruments, he wins a throw. It is true that what happens is not the norm in concert halls—when he, for instance, places next to musical time the minutes and seconds which he must see through to an end,—music as the living of a prescribed lifetime. In the concerts which he initially gave with a few, later with an increasing number of friends, harmony gradually drowns in the sea of individual expressions, the music expresses its own destruction, and by the side of Haydn's symphony *Die Schöpfung* appears *Die Abschöpfung.* To enhance these sounds Roth left his own music-making aside and recorded in a large kennel on Mount Tibidado near Barcelona twenty four hours of continual dog

barking; to him the strongest music of all, the perfect lament. Comparison with the sorrowful angry howling and whining degrades art but it elevates the despised animals, depending on the point of view the spectator wants to adopt.

So that such enterprises should not end only as anecdotes Roth published the results as records or tapes, above all in the *edition hansjörg mayer,* Stuttgart. His *Collected Works* have also appeared there, a first part with twenty volumes and a second part with, so far, three volumes. Whether this second part and a projected third part (that is sixty volumes in all) will ever be completed, is not certain. Roth has proved that his work can establish itself on the bookshelves. Where logical consequence threatens, it is better to stop or to turn, for otherwise Roth could just as well have stayed with the Concrete Painting of his father's generation. "You poor and lonely man and arise, don't get caught by your contemporaries, flee, beetle, flee!"

—Dieter Schwarz

ROTHENBERG, Susan.
American. Born in Buffalo, New York, 20 January 1945. Educated at Cornell University, B.F.A. 1966; George Washington University, 1967; studied at the Corcoran Museum School, Washington, D.C. Painter. Recipient: CAPS Grant for Painting, 1976–77; Guggenheim Fellowship for Painting, 1980. Agent: Willard Gallery, New York. Address: c/o Willard Gallery, 29 East 72nd Street, New York, New York 10021, U.S.A.

Individual Exhibitions:

1975   *3 Large Paintings,* 112 Green Street, New York
1976   Willard Gallery, New York
1977   Willard Gallery, New York
        Susan Rothenberg/Judith Ornstein, Willard Gallery, New York
1978   *Matrix,* University Art Museum, Berkeley, California
        Recent Work, Walker Art Center, Minneapolis
        Greenberg Gallery, St. Louis
1979   Willard Gallery, New York
1979   *Recent Paintings,* Mayor Gallery, London (travelled to Galerie Rudolf Zwirner)
1981   *5 Heads,* Willard Gallery, New York
        Akron Art Museum, Ohio
        Robert Moskowitz, Susan Rothenberg, Julian Schnabel, Kunsthalle Museum, Basle (travelled to the Frankfurt Kunstverein, and Louisiana Museum, Humlebaek, Denmark, 1981–82)
1982   Stedelijk Museum, Amsterdam
1983   Willard Gallery, New York
        Los Angeles County Museum of Art
        Institute of Contemporary Art, Boston
1984   Barbara Krakow Gallery, Boston
1985   California State University, Long Beach
        Des Moines Art Center, Iowa

Selected Group Exhibitions:

1974   *New Talent,* Sachs Gallery, New York
1976   *Animals,* Solomon Gallery, New York
1978   *7 Artists: Contemporary Drawings,* Cleveland Museum of Art
1979   *New Image Painting,* Whitney Museum, New York
        American Painting: The 80's, Grey Art Gallery, New York University (travelled to the Contemporary Art Museum, Houston, and the American Center, Paris, 1979–80)
1980   *Biennale,* Venice
1981   *A New Bestiary: Animal Imagery in Contemporary Art,* Institute of Contemporary Art, Virginia Museum, Richmond

1982 *Focus on Figure,* Whitney Museum, New York
1985 *Horses in Twentieth Century Art,* Nicola Jacobs Gallery, London
1987 *Avant-Garde in the Eighties,* Los Angeles County Museum of Art

Collections:

Museum of Modern Art, New York; Whitney Museum, New York; Albright-Knox Art Gallery, Buffalo, New York; Akron Art Museum, Ohio; Walker Art Center, Minneapolis; Art Museum of South Texas, Corpus Christi; Museum of Fine Arts, Houston.

Publications:

On ROTHENBERG: articles—"From Primary Structures to Primary Imagery" by Mark Rosenthal in *Arts Magazine* (New York), October 1978; "Art: What's New, Whitney Style," by Vivien Raynor in the *New York Times,* 8 December 1978; "Art for '79 Eyes" by Barbara Rose in *Vogue* (New York), January 1979; "The Abstract Image" by Roberta Smith in *Art in America* (New York), March/April 1979; review by Hilton Kramer in *New York Times,* 13 April 1979; review by Peter Schjeldahl in *Artforum* (New York), Summer 1979; "Neo-Modernists—A Sense of Deja-Vu" by Hilton Kramer in *New York Times,* 23 September 1979; "Painting in New York: An Illustrated Guide" by Thomas Lawson in *Flash Art* (Milan), October/November 1979; review by Sarah Kent in *Time Out* (London), 28 February 1980; "All Roads Head to the Venice Biennale" by Carrie Rickey in *The Village Voice* (New York), 9 June 1980; "Bravery in Action" by Peter Schjeldahl in *Village Voice* (New York), 29 April-5 May, 1981; "An Audacious Inaugural Exhibition" by Hilton Kramer in the *New York Times,* 20 September 1981; "Susan Rothenberg" by Michael Danoff in *Akron Art Museum Newsletter* (Ohio), 21 November 1981; "Post Modernist Painting" by Sam Hunter in *Portfolio Magazine* (New York), January/February 1982; "Robert Moskowitz, Susan Rothenberg and Julian Schnabel" in *Flash Art* (Milan), February/March 1982.

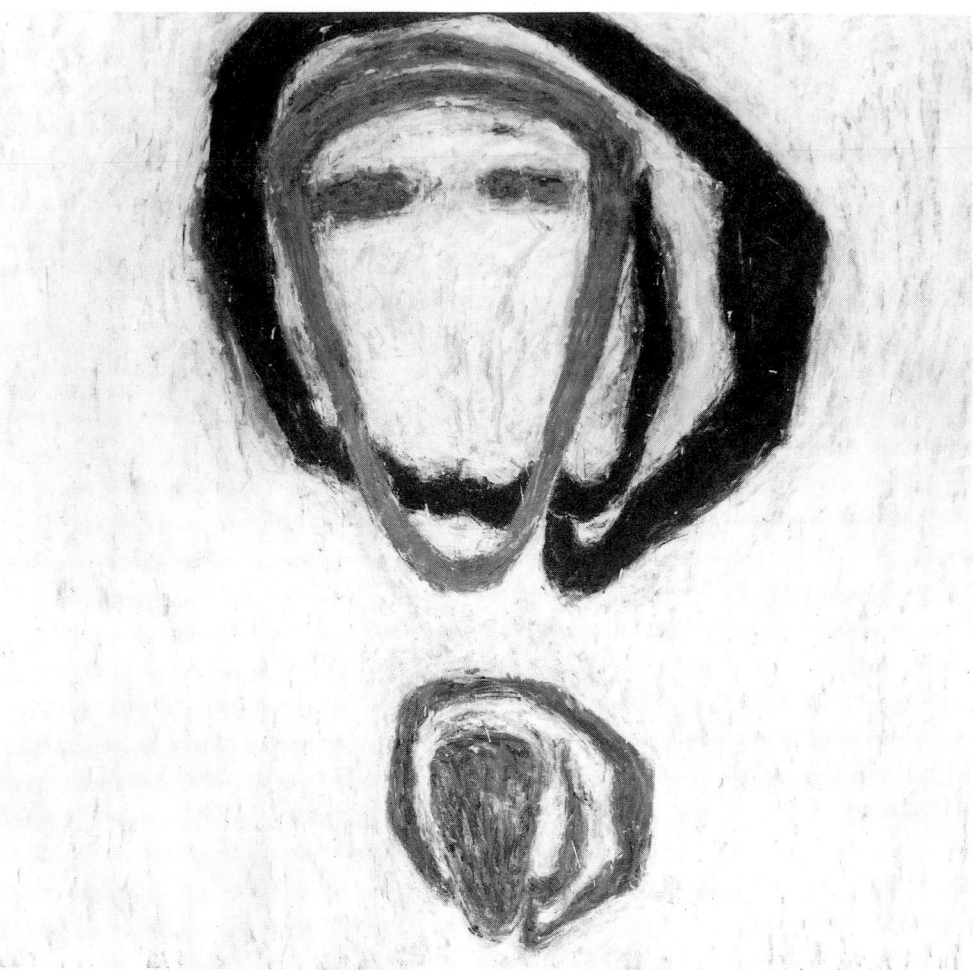

Susan Rothenberg: *Untitled Number 147*

Susan Rothenberg, born in Buffalo, New York, was educated at the universities of Cornell and George Washington and the Corcoran Museum in the then prevalent abstract style of painting with its emphasis on 'process' and on maintaining the flatness of the picture plane. She commenced her career as an artist painting in this purely abstract mode. However, in 1973 the first horse image, shadowy and phantom-like, appeared in her work, and over the next few years she achieved an international reputation with a series of canvases featuring these horse portrayals. Rothenberg herself says that the horse figure appeared accidentally as a dividing device, but it is undoubtedly an image that has had powerful associations in art over the centuries. It can stand both for unbridled force or as a tamed but potentially violent source of energy, and thus as a symbol for human sexuality. At that time her introduction of a representational element into an abstract painting was an unusual and startling contribution. The paintings were nearly all in monochrome, using blues, greys, blacks and whites—cold colours which enhanced the curious other-worldly quality of her canvases. The compositional devices were simple; using the horse as a centering element on a scaffolding of diagonals or horizontal and vertical grids integrated into a thick, brushy, all-over textured background. The ghostly horse figures sometimes merged and sometimes appeared separate from the surface. Rothenberg was still, at this time, endeavouring to maintain one plane but found that spatial illusions did not necessarily destroy the unity of the whole. At the beginning of the eighties a general loosening up of her brushwork became noticeable and the horse gradually began to fade out to be replaced, first of all by anatomical parts—hands, limbs, bones—and then human and humanoid shapes. The emotional content of her art also deepened, the images giving a feeling of extreme anguish. These fragments of humanity are touching in their eroded fragility, speaking of a desperate clinging to survival in an encroaching darkness. Now handling

the paint much more freely and expressively her interest in the geometric scaffolding lessened.

Whole figures started to appear in her work in the mid-eighties, seeming to emerge from a flurry of feathery brushstrokes. She works on a large scale, (280 x 220 cm. is an average size for her painting on canvas) and the cumulative effect of seeing her works in quantity, as in an exhibition, is of a collapsing, imploding world. Lately she has made tentative excursions into colour. In a late work of truly massive scale, *Vertical Spin* (1986/7), there is a tumble of raw, red figures down the center of the painting against a dark, striated background. The effect is of viewing through coarse netting. At the base, there is a cluster of half naked male figures, one behind the other, as though clinging to a raft. Long verticals widen from the top—one could be looking down into a dark canyon with rushing rapids. In an upper corner a face gradually reveals itself—much larger in scale than the other figures, colourless as a skull with dark eye sockets and a black gaping mouth. The brushwork is dry and applied with a coarse hogshair brush, at least an inch in width and the paint is built up very thickly in places. Her achievement, in this huge canvas, is that the details have meanings in themselves, but form parts of a whole which can convey to a receptive viewer, a totally different meaning or meanings. Sadly, like so many of her generation, Rothenberg is hampered by her deficiency in draughtsmanship from realising to its full potential her powerful and original imagery.

—Mary Ellis

ROTHKO, Mark.

Born Marcus Rothkowitz in Dvinsk, Russia, 25 September 1903; emigrated with family to the United States in 1913: naturalized, 1938; adopted name Rothko, 1940 (changed legally, 1958). Educated in Russia and Portland, Oregon primary schools; attended drawing and painting classes at local art school; studied liberal arts, Yale University, New Haven, Connecticut, 1921–23; studied anatomy, under George Bridgemen, and still life and figure drawing, under Max Weber, at the Art Students League, New York, 1924–26; and printmaking, briefly, under Will Barnet, Art Students League, 1931. Married Edith Sacher in 1932 (divorced, 1945); married Mary (Mell) Alice Beistle in 1945; children: Kate and Christopher. Painter: lived and worked in New York from 1925. Member, Art Students League of New York, 1926–29; Inaugural member, Artists Union, New York, 1933; friendly with Milton Avery and Adolph Gottlieb, with whom he spent vacations; Founder, with Gottlieb, Ilya Bolotowsky, Louis Harris and others, The Ten, abstract-expressionist group, New York, 1935–40; worked in Easel Division, Works Progress Administration, Federal Art Project, New York, 1936–37; signed statement, with Avery, Gottlieb and others, seceding from the American Artists Congress, and founded Federation of Modern Painters and Sculptors, New York, 1940; became active member of Cultural Committee of the Federation; worked closely with Gottlieb, 1941–43; Founder, with Clyfford Still, Robert Motherwell, William Baziotes and others, Subjects of the Artist teaching group, New York, 1948–49; worked on monumental canvases for 4 Seasons Restaurant, Seagram Building, New York (now in Tate Gallery, London), commissioned by Philip Johnson, 1958; disassociated himself from abstract expressionism in lecture at Pratt Institute, Brooklyn, 1958. Part-time children's teacher, Center Academy, Brooklyn Jewish Center, New York, 1929–52; Guest Lecturer, California School of Fine Arts, San Francisco, 1947 and 1949; Assistant Professor, Department of Design, Brooklyn College, 1951–54; Guest Lecturer, University of Colorado, Boulder, 1955; Visiting Artist, Tulane University, New Orleans, 1956; Visiting Lecturer, University of California, Berkeley, Summer 1967. Recipient: Brandeis University Creative Arts Award, 1965. Honorary doctorate: Yale University, New Haven, Connecticut, 1969. Member, National Institute of Arts and Letters, 1968. *Died* (by suicide; in New York) *25 February 1970.*

Individual Exhibition:

1933	Art Museum, Portland, Oregon
	Contemporary Arts Gallery, New York
1940	Neumann-Willard Gallery, New York (with Marcel Gromaire and Joseph Solman)
1945	Art of This Century, New York
1946	San Francisco Museum of Art (travelled to the Museum of Art, Santa Barbara, California)
	Mortimer Brandt Gallery, New York
1947	Betty Parsons Gallery, New York
1948	Betty Parsons Gallery, New York
1949	Betty Parsons Gallery, New York
1950	Betty Parsons Gallery, New York
1951	Betty Parsons Gallery, New York
1954	Art Institute of Chicago (travelled to the Rhode Island School of Design, Providence)
1955	Sidney Janis Gallery, New York
1957	Contemporary Arts Museum, Houston
1958	Sidney Janis Gallery, New York
1960	Phillips Gallery, Washington, D.C.
1961	Museum of Modern Art, New York (toured Europe, 1961–63)
1963	Guggenheim Museum, New York
1964	Marlborough New London Gallery, London
1965	Galleria Nazionale d'Arte Moderna, Rome
	Marlborough New London Gallery
1970	Museum of Modern Art, New York
	Museo d'Arte Moderna Ca Pesaro, Venice (travelled to the Marlborough Gallery, New York)
1971	Galleria Martano, Turin
	Marlborough Galleria d'Arte, Rome
	Kunsthaus, Zurich (toured Europe)
	Galleria Lorenzelli, Bergamo, Italy
	Yale University Art Gallery, New Haven, Connecticut
1972	Hayward Gallery, London
1974	Newport Harbour Art Museum, Newport Beach, California
1975	Cleveland Museum of Art (with Milton Avery and Jon Schueler)
1977	Galleria Civica d'Arte Moderna, Mantua, Italy
1978	Pace Gallery, New York
	Guggenheim Museum, New York
1981	Pace Gallery, New York
1984	National Gallery of Art, Washington, D.C. (toured the United States, 1984–86)
1987	Tate Gallery, London

Selected Group Exhibitions:

1928	*Group Exhibition,* Opportunity Galleries, New York
1933	*Paintings by Selected Americans,* Uptown Gallery, New York
1944	*Abstract and Surrealist Art in the United States,* Cincinnati Art Museum, Ohio (toured United States)
1948	*Biennale,* Venice
1951	*Surrealisme and Abstraction,* Stedelijk Museum, Amsterdam (travelled to the Palais des Beaux-Arts, Brussels, and the Kunsthaus, Zurich)
1958	*The New American Painting,* Kunsthalle, Basle (toured Europe, 1958–59)
1966	*2 Decades of American Painting,* Museum of Modern Art, New York (toured the Far East)
1970	*Malerei des Zwanzigsten Jahrhundrets,* Kunsthaus, Zurich
1985	*Painterly Visions 1940–84,* Guggenheim Museum, New York
1987	*American Painting: Abstract Expressionism and After,* San Francisco Museum of Modern Art

Collections:

Museum of Modern Art, New York; Whitney Museum, New York; Art Institute of Chicago; Tate Gallery, London; Centre Georges Pompidou, Paris; Nationalgalerie, Berlin; Kunsthaus, Zurich; Stedelijk Museum, Amsterdam; Boymans-van Beuningen Museum, Rotterdam; Museu de Arte Moderna, Rio de Janeiro.

Publications:

By ROTHKO: books—*Clyfford Still,* exhibition catalogue, New York 1946; *Milton Avery,* with Adelyn D. Breeskin, New York 1969; articles—statement, with Bernard Bradden, in *The 10: Whitney Dissenters,* exhibition catalogue, New York 1938; letter, with Adolph Gottlieb, in the *New York Times,* 13 June 1943; "Personal Statement" in *A Painting Prophecy, 1950,* exhibition catalogue, Washington, D.C. 1945; "Ides of Art," with Gottlieb, Newman and others, in *Tiger's Eye* (New York), December 1947; "Romantics Were Prompted" in *Possibilities* (New York), October 1949; letter, with William Baziotes, Adolf Gottlieb, Wilhem de Kooning and others, in *Artnews* (New York), Summer 1950; "How to Combine Architecture, Painting and Sculpture," with others, in *Interview* (New York), May 1951; interview in *Conversation with Artists,* New York 1957; "Lecture at Pratt Institute, Brooklyn, Fall 1958" in *The New York School, 1965,* Los Angeles 1965; essay in *Milton Avery,* exhibition catalogue, Washington, D.C. 1970; broadcast—*The Portrait and American Artist,* on WYNC, 13 October 1943.

On ROTHKO: books—*Modern Art U.S.A.* by Rudi Blesh, New York 1956; *From Realism to Reality* by Virgil Barker, Lincoln, Nebraska 1959; *Mark Rothko,* exhibition catalogue, by Peter Selz, New York 1961; *Modern Painting and the Northern Romantic Tradition: Friedrich to Rothko* by Robert Rosenblum, New York 1975; *American Art Since 1900: A Critical History* by Barbara Rose, New York and Washington D.C. 1975; *Mark Rothko* by Diane Waldman, New York and London 1978; *The Legacy of Mark Rothko* by Lee Seldes, London 1978; *Marden, Novros, Rothko: Painting in the Age of Actuality* by Sheldon Nodelman, Houston 1978; *Mark Rothko: Works on Paper,* with essay by Bonnie Clearwater, New York 1984, London 1986.

The Sublime, the dialectic of the tragic and the transcendental: this basically romantic idea describes the myth surrounding both Rothko, the artist, and Rothko, the man. How does one go about evaluating the art of a myth second in recent American painting only to that of Jackson Pollock? Mark Rothko is very often discussed in purely poetic terms and solely aligned with his full blown paintings of the 1950's and 1960's.

It is, of course, in these mature paintings that Rothko made his major statement and contribution. But his mature pictures are not a miraculous "breakthrough" out of the perennial void. They are the offspring of many years of painting, looking, thinking, analyzing, synthesizing and condensing. In them are the memories transmuted from elements of his expressionistic figures and landscapes from the early 1930's, of his simplified and flattened subway scenes which closely followed, and of his formative pictures of the early to late 1940's. It was during the mid-1940's that many of Rothko's most magical pictures took form, many of them watercolors and others oils with titles such as "The Source," "Aquatic Dreams," "Prehistoric Memory," and "Slow Swirl at the Edge of the Sea." In these works, singular or small groupings of multi-associational shapes hover, writhe or quiver in painterly liquid atmospheres of subtle tonalities; they are both more abstract and more painterly than the works of European Surrealism, and they intimate a more spiritually based idea as well. Rothko's grasp of the painting process and his synthesis from many sources from psychology, philosophy, primitive art and mythic themes among others, had brought him to the point at which he could release the substance and feeling of his inner self into his art directly. By about 1947, Rothko was further developing his subject and form in a series of shifting abstract shapes called "Multiforms." In these, he started using names of colors, numbers or untitled as his titles as a further attempt to make associations more generalized and open-ended. By 1949, Rothko had arrived

at the basic two or three soft-edged rectangles which were to form the works of the next 20 years. These hovering shapes, fuzzy and soaked into their translucent environments, are bathed in diversely colored light and shadow ranging from the most high-keyed to the darkest and coolest of hues and values to transmit barely perceptible presences from within the fields. During the following two decades, Rothko sought and found multiple variations out of the elements he had distilled from the previous 20 years of painting. I, among other writers, believed all of Rothko's pictures constitute one work in many variations. His paintings are as interconnected as are our memories and our present experiences in the mind's eye.

There is a temptation to view Rothko's art purely in terms of formal prowess or sensual appeal, especially in light of his considerable painter's skills, and it is equally possible to dwell too exclusively on his ethical, spiritual intentions. It was a high ambition which Rothko and his contemporaries held, as Rothko himself put it in 1945, "to make concrete the purposes of the spirit's varied quickness and stillness." It is in the way that painterly prowess fuses with visual realization of underlying intention that the real nature of the work is revealed. In this fusion, meaning is conveyed directly through painterly process and form, abstract because that was the most advanced contemporary language of Rothko's generation and is therefore seen as the best route to express the human tensions which persist through time in present terms.

In his last works, Rothko reached his ultimate expression of the tragic sublime. Their only close parallel to me are the Nocturnes of Whistler. All semblances from the seen are subsumed in the nuances of grays, while motions of the horizons fluctuate like our grasp of above and below, earth and spirit. If I have any criticism of Rothko's work, it is that they sometimes carry us too far from the early end of the spectrum, but in these last pictures we are returned to cope with the realm with a deeper sense of the spiritually activated beyond.

—Barbara Cavaliere

RÜCKRIEM, Ulrich.

German. Born in Dusseldorf, 30 September 1938. Trained as an apprentice stonemason, Dusseldorf, 1957–59; studied briefly at the Werkkunstschule, Cologne, 1959. Independent sculptor, in Norvenich, near Cologne, since 1962: first stone-splitting works, 1968; worked in Mönchengladbach, 1969. Professor of Sculpture, Hochschule für bildende Kunste, Hamburg, 1975–84; Professor of Sculpture, Kunstakademie, Dusseldorf, since 1984. Lives in Anrochte-Klieve and in Cologne. Recipient: Forderpreis des Landes Nordrhein-Westfalen, 1973; Kunstpreis der Stadt Krefeld, 1973; Forderpreis, Bundesverband der deutschen Industrie, 1975; Lichtwark-Preis, Hamburg, 1983; Konrad-von-Soest Preis, Münster, 1984; Verband der deutschen Kritiker Preis, West Berlin, 1985; Arnold Bode Preis, Kassel, 1985. Address: Mainzer Strasse 77, 5000 Cologne 1, West Germany.

Individual Exhibitions:

1964	Domgalerie, Cologne
	Leopold-Hoesch-Museum, Duren, West Germany
1967	Galerie Ad Libitum, Antwerp
1968	Galerie Tobies und Silex, Cologne
1969	Galerie Ernst, Hannover
	Galerie Konrad Fischer, Dusseldorf
1970	Museum Haus Lange, Krefeld, West Germany
	Galerie Ricke, Cologne
1971	Kabinett für Aktuelle Kunst, Bremerhaven, West Germany
	Galerie Ernst, Hannover

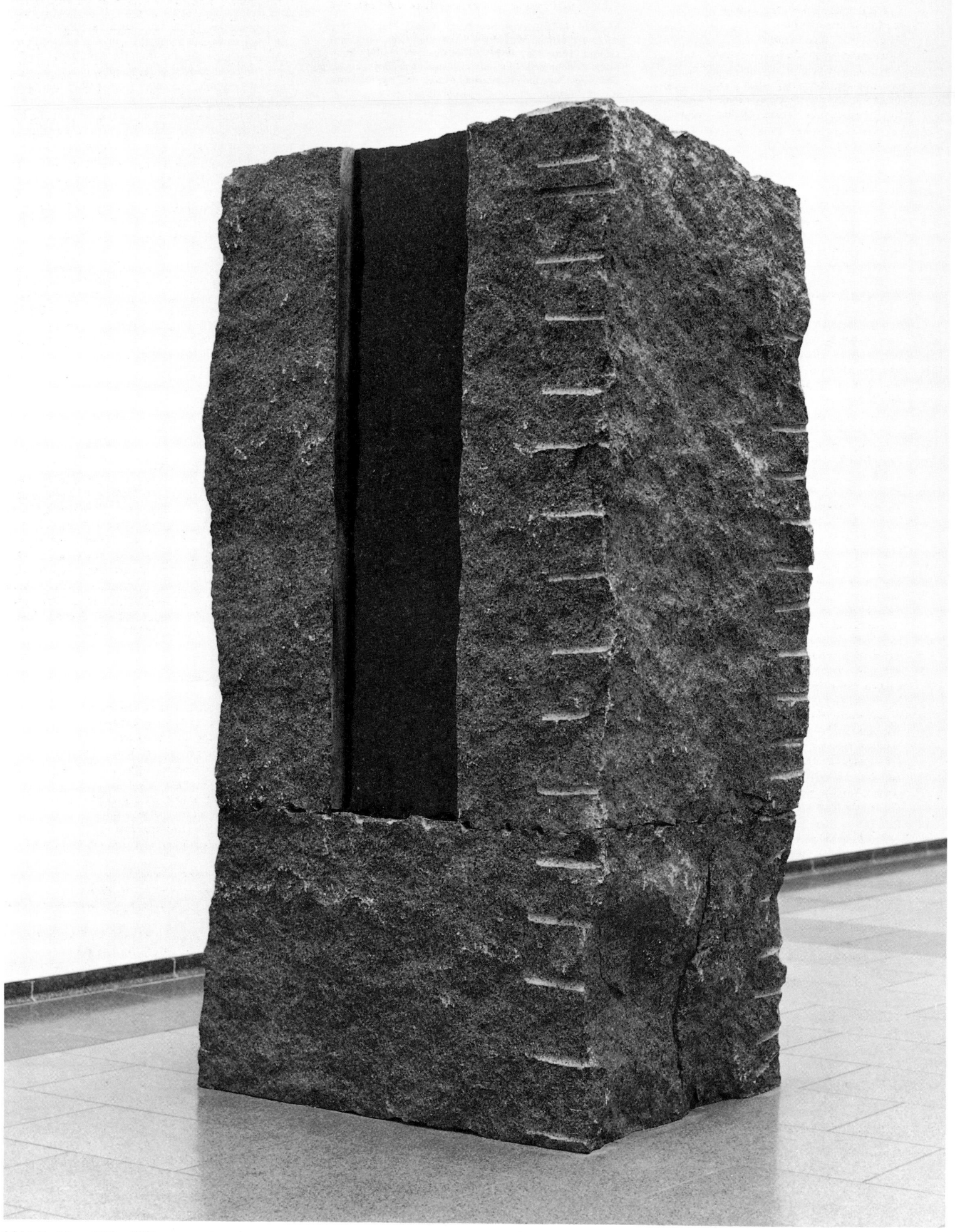

Ulrich Ruckriem: *Pfeiler*, 1986

Galerie Konrad Fischer, Dusseldorf
Mayfair Gallery, London
Galerie Paul Maenz, Cologne
Videogalerie Gerry Schum, Dusseldorf
1972 Paula Cooper Gallery, New York
Staatliche Kunsthalle, Baden-Baden, West German
1973 Kunsthalle, Tübingen, West Germany
Stadtisches Museum, Mönchengladbach, West Germany
1974 Kunstverein, Frankfurt
Kunstraum München, Munich
Galerie Preisig, Basle
Galerie Paul Maenz, Cologne
Galerie Konrad Fischer, Dusseldorf
1975 Lisson Gallery, London
Galerie Preisig, Basle
Galerie Durand-Dessert, Paris
Art and Project, Amsterdam
1976 Museum of Modern Art, Oxford
Stadtisches Museum, Mönchengladbach, West Germany
Galerie Klein, Bonn
1977 Van Abbemuseum, Eindhoven, Netherlands
Galerie Konrad Fischer, Dusseldorf
1978 Galerie Hetzler und Keller, Stuttgart
Museum Folkwang, Essen, West Germany
West German Pavilion, at the *Biennale,* Venice
Galerie Klein, Bonn
Stadtisches Kunstmuseum, Bonn
1979 Kunsthalle, Bielefeld, West Germany
Kabinett für Aktuelle Kunst, Bremerhaven, West Germany
Westfalischer Kunstverein, Münster, West Germany
Stichting Eindhoven, Netherlands
Sperone-Westwater-Fischer, New York
Graeme Murray Gallery, Edinburgh
Galerie Durand-Dessert, Paris
1980 Galerie Konrad Fischer, Dusseldorf
Kunstraum München, Munich
Galerie Hetzler, Stuttgart
Galerie Klein, Bonn
Galerie Loehrl, Mönchengladbach, West Germany
1981 Fort Worth Art Museum, Texas
Galerie Konrad Fischer, Zurich
1982 Galleri Nordenhake, Malmo, Sweden
1983 Centre Georges Pompidou, Paris
Raum für Kunst, Hamburg
1984 Galerie Konrad Fischer, Dusseldorf
Stadelgalerie, Frankfurt
Skulpturprojekt im offentlichen Raum, Hamburg
Produzentgalerie, Hamburg
Kamakura Gallery, Tokyo
1985 Galerie Wilkens und Jacobs, Cologne
Westfalisches Landesmuseum, Münster, West Germany
Galerie Klein, Bonn
Staatliche Kunstsammlungen Neue Galerie, Kassel, West Germany
1986 Rijksmuseum Kröller-Müller, Otterlo, Netherlands
Galerie Konrad Fischer, Dusseldorf
Galerie Loehrl, Mönchengladbach, West Germany
Kunstverein, Freiburg, West Germany
1987 Galerie Klein, Bonn
Kunstsammlung Nordrhein-Westfalen, Dusseldorf
Abteiberg-Museum, Mönchengladbach, West Germany
Kölnischer Kunstverein, Cologne
Halle Rückriem, Cologne-Höningen
Victoria Miro Gallery, London
Donald Young Gallery, Chicago

Selected Group Exhibitions:

1967 *Wege 67,* Museum am Ostwall, Dortmund, West Germany
1969 *17 deutsche Kunstler,* Kunstverein, Hannover
1972 *Documenta 5,* Museum Fridericianum, Kassel, West Germany (and *Documenta 7,* 1982; *Documenta 8,* 1987)
1975 *The Condition of Sculpture,* Hayward Gallery, London
1978 *38th Biennale,* Venice

1981 *Art Allemagne Aujourd'hui,* Musée d'Art Moderne, Paris
1984 *Von hier aus,* Messehallen, Dusseldorf
1985 *Kunst in der Bundersrepublik 1945-85,* Nationalgalerie, West Berlin
1986 *Wild, Visionary, Spectral: New German Art,* Art Gallery of South Australia, Adelaide

Collections:

Westfalisches Landesmuseum, Munster; Kunstmuseum, Bonn; Museum Haus Lange, Krefeld; Museum Ludwig, Cologne; Nationalgalerie, West Berlin; Neue Galerie und Stadtische Kunstsammlungen, Kassel; Rijksmuseum Kröller-Müller, Otterlo; Stedelijk Van Abbemuseum, Eindhoven; Fort Worth Museum of Art, Texas; Art Gallery of South Australia, Adelaide.

Publications:

On RÜCKRIEM: books—*Jahresbericht 1971,* edited by Paul Maenz, Cologne 1971; *Documenta 5: Befragung der Realität,* exhibition catalogue, edited by Harald Szeemann and others, Kassel, West Germany 1972; *Ulrich Rückriem: Skulpturen 1968-1973,* with an introduction by Günter Ulbricht, Cologne 1973; *Projekt 74: Aspekte internationaler Kunst am Anfang der 70er Jahre,* exhibition catalogue, with texts by Dieter Ronte, Evelyn Weiss, Manfred Schneckenburger and others, Cologne 1974; *Ulrich Rückriem,* exhibition catalogue, Oxford 1976; *Ulrich Rückriem: Skulpturen 1968-1976,* exhibition catalogue, with text by Rudi H. Fuchs, Eindenhoven, Netherlands 1977; *Ulrich Rückriem* by Hermann Kern, Munich 1977; *Ulrich Rückriem: Venezia 1978,* exhibition catalogue, with texts by Rudi H. Fuchs and Klaus Gallwitz, Stuttgart 1978; *Ulrich Rückriem: Skulpturen 1968-78,* exhibition catalogue, with text by Rudi H. Fuchs, Essen 1978; *Ulrich Rückriem: Skulpturen 1977-78,* exhibition catalogue, with text by Thomas Deecke, Münster, West Germany 1979; *Ulrich Rückriem,* exhibition catalogue, with text by Michael Pauseback, Bielefeld, West Germany 1979.

*

Contact with works of Rückriem, in the basic sense, is like straying into a stonemason's yard. A sudden confrontation with well-chined rock, sometimes cloven, sometimes pitted, but always with a definitive impression of well-tuned 3-dimensional geometry. Not surprisingly, his craft as a sculptor springs from two sources, each in its way as significant as the other.

Ulrich Rückriem was, for a short while, a student of carving at the Dusseldorf Staatliche Kunstakademie, but then he also derived experience in its most practical form as assistant to a professional stonehewer in what might for others have proved a prosaic setting. Such was far from the case with Rückriem.

Looking at his sculpture to-day, one is aware of two fundamental virtues: his undeviating love of his raw materials (showing the same sort of affection for stone as a draughtsman like Titus-Carmel bestows upon the qualities and characters of paper); and secondly, the straight-and-narrow path which he has adapted in his sculpture throughout showing up in his unyielding decisions never to allow any temptation of even the least touch of figuration to enter into the nature and spirit of his works, nor to listen to the siren-voices of beguiling romanticism (to both of which failings a sculptor like Jacob Epstein too easily fell prey). Nor should it be overlooked that here is an artist who particularly favours extremely tough materials—like large blocks of granite—for the execution of his works which strongly implies that clearly any diversion from puritanical intentions would wreak havoc upon any goal in view for his finished pieces).

A typical instance of his unadulterated sense of creative mission was shown at Hannover's Galerie Ernst. Examining this upright rectangular eminence (10 small blocks to one side, and 10 larger blocks matching them in careful exactitude on the other, all clasped together with roughly implanted short strips of a metallic substance like medals on the chest of a monument), one is overwhelmed by the crude (simple in meaning, rather than in execution) power of this artist's vision tempered by such a strict discipline.

Rückriem's main work-centre as an independent sculptor was since 1962 in Nörvenich, a small village just outside Cologne where, some 6 years later, he began his splitting processes (leading to *geschliffen* and polishing), after which he transferred his work-life as a sculptor to his studio in Monchengladbach where his wall-reliefs and freestanding sculptures now reach completion.

There should be no misunderstanding about the kind of status this artist has been able to achieve during the past 25 years. Apart from showing his works in the main art centres and galleries of West Germany, Switzerland, Italy, Sweden, Holland, Japan, Australia, Austria, the United States, Britain and Eire, it should be noted that he was an official participant at the Venice Biennale and the 1987 Kassel Dokumenta. As can be realised, Ulrich Rückriem is no stranger when it comes to invitations to take part through his works in important accrochages and anthologies of Modern Art in international events, frequently in museums (where he has appeared either as an isolated exhibitor or in company with respected elders and contemporaries in his chosen field).

—Sheldon Williams

RUPPERSBERG, Allen.

American. Born in Cleveland, Ohio, 5 January 1944. Studied at the Chouinard Art Institute, Los Angeles. Independent artist, working in Los Angeles, Santa Monica and New York, since 1969. Recipient: National Endowment for the Arts grant, Washington, D.C., 1976; Theodoron Award, Guggenheim Museum, New York, 1982. Agents: Patty Aande, 660 Ninth Avenue, San Diego, California 92101; Marian Goodman Gallery, 24 West 57th Street, New York, New York 10019. Address: 1314 Second Street, Santa Monica, California 90401, U.S.A.

Individual Exhibitions:

1969 Eugenia Butler Gallery, Los Angeles
1970 Pasadena Art Museum, California
1971 Art and Project, Amsterdam
1972 Market Street Program, Venice, California
      Pomona College Art Gallery, California
1973 Situation Gallery, London
      Galleria Francoise Lambert, Milan
      Stedelijk Museum, Amsterdam
      Galerie Yvon Lambert, Paris
      Information Gallery, University of California at Irvine
1974 Art and Project, Antwerp
      Claire Copley Gallery, Los Angeles
      Kabinette für Aktuelle Kunst, Bremerhaven, West Germany
1977 *Projects,* Museum of Modern Art, New York
1982 Los Angeles County Museum of Art
1985 Museum of Contemporary Art, Los Angeles (retrospective; travelled to New York)

Selected Group Exhibitions:

1969 *When Attitudes Become Form,* Kunsthalle, Berne (toured West Germany and the U.K.)
      955.000, Vancouver Art Gallery
1970 *Art in the Mind,* Allen Memorial Art Museum, Oberlin College, Ohio
      Whitney Annual, Whitney Museum, New York
1971 *24 Young Los Angeles Artists,* Los Angeles County Museum of Art
      Pier 18, Museum of Modern Art, New York
1972 *Documenta,* Kassel, West Germany
1973 *Videotapes by Artists,* Allen Memorial Art Museum, Oberlin College, Ohio
      Artists' Books, Moore College of Art, Philadelphia
1974 *Group Show,* Art and Project, Antwerp

Collections:

Los Angeles County Museum of Art; Norton Simon Museum of Art, Pasadena, California; Stedelijk Museum, Amsterdam; Guggenheim Museum, New York.

Publications:

By RUPPERSBERG: books—*23 Pieces*, Los Angeles 1969; *24 Pieces*, Los Angeles 1970; *Al's Grand Hotel*, exhibition catalogue, Los Angeles 1970; *Greetings from L.A.*, Los Angeles 1972; *Allen Ruppersberg*, Amsterdam 1973; *Fifty Helpful Hints on the Art of Everybody*, Los Angeles 1984; video—*A Lecture on Houdini*, Los Angeles, 1973.

On RUPPERSBERG: books—*Allen Ruppersberg*, exhibition catalogue with essay by Helen Winer, Pomona 1972; *Allen Ruppersberg: The Secret of Life and Death*, with essay by Howard Singerman, Los Angeles and Santa Barbara 1985; articles—"Scenarios/Documents/Images II" by Helene Winer in *Art in America* (New York), October 1973; "Wilde about Harry" by Peter Plagens in *Artforum* (New York), April 1975.

Now entering his twentieth year on the exhibition scene, Allen Ruppersberg continues to uphold the stance which began when he rejected his art school background of traditional formal study of studio art to engage in the conceptually oriented "post-studio" school of thinking in 1969. Located by Peter Plagens in 1985 as "somewhere between Rauschenberg and Ruscha"—both have influenced his work—he was early inspired by artists for whom Duchamp had pointed the way, by Yves Klein and the Nouveaux Réalistes as well as by Jasper Johns.

Ruppersberg's first solo exhibition in 1969 opened the Eugenia Butler Gallery in Los Angeles, that city's first venue for Conceptual Art, which showed William Wegman, William Leviton and others. Included in Seth Segelaub's catalogue, *One Month* (1969), he was in touch with New York Conceptualists such as Robert Barry, Joseph Kosuth and Lawrence Weiner; his meeting with Ger van Elk and Dutch conceptualists led to a solo show in Amsterdam, *Art and Project* (1971).

Indeed, until 1974, despite a 1970 exhibition at the Pasadena Art Museum, his work found its primary response in Europe, more receptive to Conceptual Art in those early years. With that interest still continuing, the American art audience has caught up and joined.

Living in the Los Angeles area for over a decade furnished setting, and often subject, for his work. *23 Pieces*, the first of a series of three books, asserted his conviction that art could reveal the beauty and mystery that lies in the ordinary, indeed, the banal. There, twenty-three black and white snapshots; from park benches to tacky coffee shops, from hotel lobbies to the Museum of Natural History Diorama, we find portraits of emptiness, the pedestrian artlessness of the photography endowing them with mystery and poignancy. In *Greetings from L.A.* (1972)—a "lucid and powerful examination of the tawdry, tarnished truth of Tinseltown"—the empty pages that comprise the greater part of the book are the most telling. (The orange-covered volume floats, overscaled, over the ocean-side, California-sunset landscape on the 1973 painting, *Greetings from L.A.*)

From Venice, where he lived briefly in 1970, Ruppersberg moved to Hollywood. His own image began to enter his work on frequent occasions; as the reader—narrating in a strait-jacket—in the 1973 video piece *A Lecture on Houdini (for Terry Allen)*; seated at a table on which objects gradually accumulate in the series of incongruously captioned snapshots which end with his "suicide," in *To Tell the Truth* (1973), and as negative silhouettes; cut-outs of his profiled head, in *Personal Art* (1973).

A lover of reading, Ruppersberg's work has been nourished by both Great Books and screaming tabloids, by poetry and by pornography. While continuing to produce original books he appropriates favorite authors—among them, Oscar Wilde, whose *Portrait*

of *Dorian Gray* he diligently, meticulously and laboriously handprinted on twenty six-by-six-foot canvases in 1974. Fusing literature with painting, he layers it with new meaning. Other pieces join the world of lofty ideas with the world of ordinary objects. In the 1979 *Rare Books (Baudelaire)* an announcement of exhibition of the poet's *oeuvres posthumes* resides in a cigar box. With such wry and unexpected juxtapositions, his work abounds in paradox and contradiction, in irony and ambiguity.

In 1985, The Museum of Contemporary Art, Los Angeles, held a survey of Ruppersberg's work, 1969-1984, the exhibition traveling to the New Museum of Contemporary Art, New York, later in the same year. The book, *Allen Ruppersberg: The Secret of Life and Death* (Los Angeles and Santa Barbara: Museum of Contemporary Art and Black Sparrow Press, 1985), with a penetrating essay by Howard Singerman, accompanied the show, with reproductions and texts by the artist including, "Where's Al," (1972) consisting of 121 typed index cards and 150 instamatic prints, "A Lecture on Houdini," and in part, "The Secret of Life and Death" (1977), with text printed over images of natural and man-made objects, together with other writings.

The MOCA survey fully revealed the pungency of Ruppersberg's dry, deadpan wit and the depth of his quirky, sidelong vision in a body of work that is complex yet accessible, profound yet lucid. One critic, Peter Plagens, cited *Dorian Gray* as "one of Ruppersberg's masterpieces," in his engaging article on the show. Back in 1970, Plagens had pronounced the Pasadena Museum show "the worst exhibition I've ever seen," then, five years later acclaimed the *Lecture on Houdini* the "best 40 minutes in five-odd hours inside the world's smallest Twin-Vue walk-in east of the Hudson, the video chamber of the Whitney Museum's Biennial." Plagens' view of the survey convincingly confirmed that earlier about-turn!

In "Fifty Helpful Hints on the Art of Everybody," (1984) a kind of artist's credo illuminating and explicating his position. Ruppersberg sums up the essence of his vision in a brief sentence: "Art should be familiar and enigmatic, like human beings." Indeed, that axiom underscores a body of work that is accessible yet complex, lucid yet profound.

After fifteen years of dividing his time between Santa Monica and New York, Ruppersberg now lives and works in New York.

—Merle Schipper

RUSCHA, Edward (Joseph).
American. Born in Omaha, Nebraska, 16 December 1937. Educated in Classen High School, Oklahoma City, 1954-56; studied at Chouinard Art Institute, Los Angeles, under Richard Rubin, 1956-60. Served in the United States Navy, 1956-60. Married Danna Knego in 1967 (divorced, 1972); son: Edward. Painter, photographer and book creator, Los Angeles, since 1960. Lecturer in Painting, University of California at Los Angeles, 1969-70. Recipient: National Council on the Arts Award, 1967, 1978; National Endowment for the Arts Grant, 1969, 1978; Guggenheim Foundation Fellowship, 1971-72; Skowhegan Medal in Graphics, Maine, 1974. Agent: Leo Castelli Gallery, 420 West Broadway, New York, New York 10012. Address: 1024-3/4 North Western Avenue, Hollywood, California 90029, U.S.A.

Individual Exhibitions:

1963	Ferus Gallery, Los Angeles
1964	Ferus Gallery, Los Angeles
1965	Ferus Gallery, Los Angeles
1967	Alexander Iolas Gallery, New York
1968	Irving Blum Gallery, Los Angeles
	Galerie Rudolf Zwirner, Cologne
1969	Irving Blum Gallery, Los Angeles
1970	Alexander Iolas Gallery, New York
	Alexander Iolas Gallery, Paris
	Galerie Heiner Friedrich, Munich
	Nigel Greenwood Inc., London
1971	Contract Graphics Gallery, Houston
1972	University of California at Santa Cruz
	Janie C. Lee Gallery, Dallas
	Corcoran and Corcoran Gallery, Miami
	Minnesota Institute of the Arts
	DM Gallery, London
1973	*Projection*, Projection Ursula Wevers, Cologne
	University of California at San Diego
	Leo Castelli Gallery, New York
	Galerie Francoise Lambert, Milan
	Nigel Greenwood Inc., London
	John Berggruen Gallery, San Francisco
	Ronald Greenberg Gallery, St. Louis
	Ace Gallery, Los Angeles
	Picker Gallery, Colgate University, Hamilton, New York
1974	Leo Castelli Gallery, New York
	Galerie Francoise Lambert, Milan (twice)
	Root Art Center, Hamilton College, Clinton, New York
	Golden West College, Huntington Beach, California
	Texas Gallery, Houston
	H. Peter Findlay Works of Art, New York
1975	Galerie Ricke, Cologne
	Sable-Castelli Gallery, Toronto
	University of North Dakota, Grand Forks
	University of Arizona, Tempe
	Glaser Gallery, La Jolla, California
	Leo Castelli Gallery, New York
	Fox Venice Theatre, California
	Prints and Publications 1962–1974, Arts Council of Great Britain, London (toured the U.K.)
	Northern Kentucky State College, Highland Heights
	Ace Gallery, Los Angeles
1976	Ace Gallery, Los Angeles
	Los Angeles Institute of Contemporary Art
	Matrix Gallery, Wadsworth Atheneum, Hartford, Connecticut
	Stedelijk Museum, Amsterdam
	Dootson-Calderhead Gallery, Seattle
	Paintings, Drawings and Other Works, Albright-Knox Art Gallery, Buffalo, New York
	Institute of Contemporary Arts, London
	Sable-Castelli Gallery, Toronto
1977	University of Lethbridge, Alberta (travelled to the University of Calgary Art Center, Alberta)
	Fort Worth Art Museum, Texas
	David Hockney: Photographic Pictures; Edward Ruscha: Photographic Books, Nova Gallery, Vancouver
	Ace Gallery, Los Angeles
	Ace Gallery, Venice, California
1978	Galerie Ricke, Cologne
	MTL Galerie, Brussels
	Galerie Rudiger Schöttle, Munich
	Art Gallery, University of Redlands, California
	Castelli Gallery, New York
	Ace Gallery, Vancouver
	Graphics Works, Auckland City Art Gallery, New Zealand
	Gelter-Pall, New York
1979	Richard Hines Gallery, Seattle
	Texas Gallery, Houston
	Ink, Zurich
1980	Portland Center for the Visual Arts, Oregon
	Ace Gallery, Venice, California
	Leo Castelli Gallery, New York
	Foster Goldstrom Gallery, San Francisco
1981	Arco Center for Visual Art, Los Angeles
	The Works of Edward Ruscha, San Francisco Museum of Modern Art (toured the United States 1982–83)
	John Berggruen Gallery, San Fancisco
	Flow Ace Gallery, Los Angeles
	Castelli Graphics, New York
	Jacobson/Hochman Gallery, New York
	Castelli-Feigen-Corcoran, New York

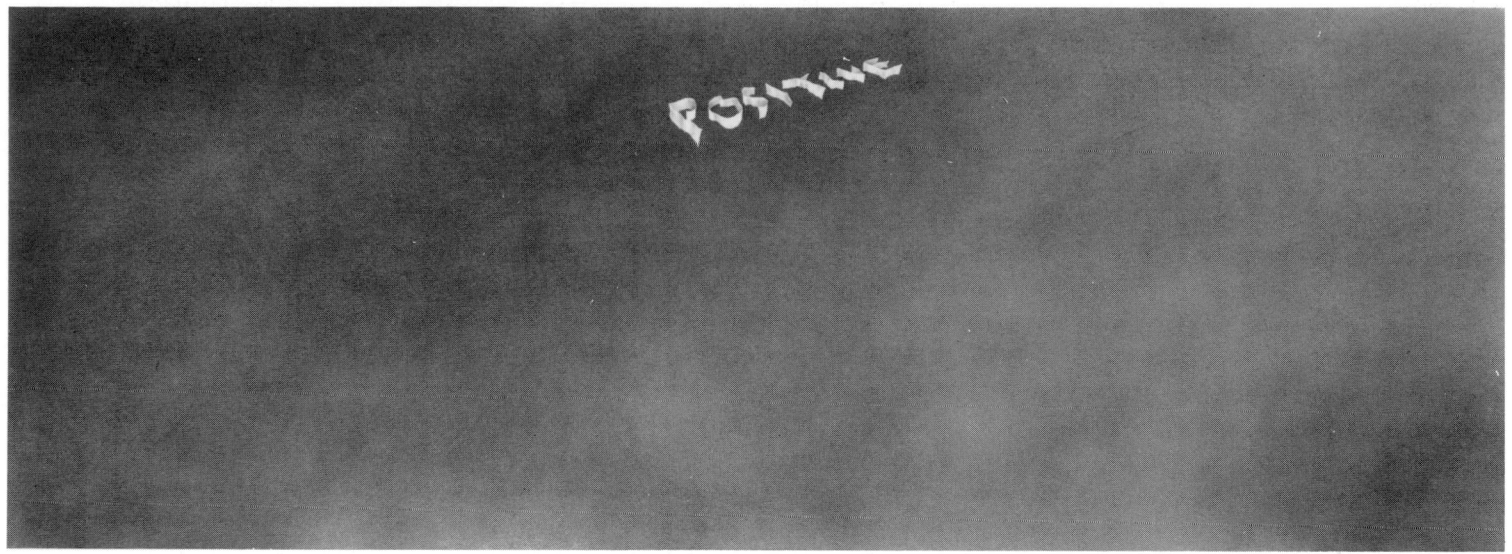

Edward Ruscha: *Positive*, 1972

1983   Route 66, Philadelphia
       Bernard Jacobson Gallery, Los Angeles
       Cirrus Editions, Los Angeles
       Galleria del Cavallino, Venice
1984   Leo Castelli Gallery, New York
       Morgan Gallery, Kansas City, Missouri
1985   James Corcoran Gallery, Los Angeles
       Galerie Gilbert Brownstone, Paris
       Musée St. Pierre, Lyon, France
       University of Southern California, Los Angeles
       Galerie Tanja Grunert, Cologne
1986   Leo Castelli Gallery, New York
       Janie Beggs Fine Arts, Aspen, Colorado
       Texas Gallery, Houston
       Westfälischer Kunstverein, Munster, West Germany
       Galerie Susan Wyss, Zurich
       Fuller-Goldeen Gallery, San Francisco
1987   Robert Miller Gallery, New York
       Leo Castelli Greene Street, New York
1988   Lannan Museum, Lake Worth, Florida
       Texas Gallery, Houston
       James Corcoran Gallery, Los Angeles

Selected Group Exhibitions:

1962   *New Paintings of Common Objects*, Pasadena Art Museum, California

1965   *Words and Images*, Guggenheim Museum, New York

1969   *Pop Art*, Hayward Gallery, London

1973   *American Drawings 1963–73*, Whitney Museum, New York

1976   *Painting and Sculpture in California: The Modern Era*, San Francisco Museum of Modern Art

1980   *Printed Art: A View of Two Decades*, Museum of Modern Art, New York

1982   *Contemporary Los Angeles Artists*, Nagoya City Museum, Japan

1984   *The Automobile and Culture*, Museum of Contemporary Art, Los Angeles

1985   *Americanische Zeichnungen 1930–80*, Stadtische Galerie im Stadel, Frankfurt

1986   *Spectrum: In Other Words*, Corcoran Gallery of Art, Washington, D.C.

Collections:

Museum of Modern Art, New York; Whitney Museum, New York; Hirshhorn Museum, Washington, D.C.; Contemporary Art Foundation, Oklahoma City; Institute of Arts, Minneapolis; Meadow Brooks Art Gallery, Oakland University, Rochester, Michigan; Los Angeles County Museum of Art; Norton Simon Museum of Art, Pasadena, California; Oakland Art Museum, California; Stedelijk Museum, Amsterdam.

Publications:

By RUSCHA: books—*26 Gasoline Stations*, Hollywood 1962; *Various Small Fires*, Hollywood 1964; *Some Los Angeles Apartments*, Hollywood 1965; *The Sunset Strip*, Hollywood 1966; *34 Parking Lots*, Hollywood 1967; *Royal Road Test*, with Mason Williams and Pat Blackwell, Hollywood 1967; *Business Cards*, with Billy Al Bengston, Hollywood 1967; *9 Swimming Pools*, Hollywood 1967; *Crackers*, with Mason Williams, Hollywood 1968; *Babycakes*, New York 1969; *Real Estate Opportunities*, Hollywood 1969; *A Few Palm Trees*, Hollywood 1970; *Records*, Hollywood 1971; *Colored People*, Hollywood 1971; *Dutch Details*, Rotterdam 1972; *Hard Light*, with Lawrence Weiner, Hollywood 1972; *Guacamole Airlines*, New York 1980; articles—"An Interview with Edward Ruscha," with John Coplans, in *Artforum* (New York), February 1965; contribution in *Design Quarterly* (Minneapolis), vol. 78/79, 1970; contribution in *Aspen Magazine* (Aspen, Colorado), Fall/Winter 1971; contribution in *Perspecta 13/14* (New Haven, Connecticut), 1971; "Art: An Interview with Ed Ruscha," with Robert Colaciello, in *Inter/View* (New York), March 1972; " . . . a Kind of a Huh?," interview with Willoughby Sharp, in *Avalanche* (New York), Winter/Spring 1973; "Swollen Eye, 1973" in *Flash Art* (Milan), February/March 1975; "Interview with Ed Ruscha," with Barbara Radice, in *Flash Art* (Milan), May 1975; "The Information Man" in *Journal* (Los Angeles), June/July 1975; "Bless You" in *Vision* (Oakland, California), September 1975; "Devil or Angel" in *Art-Rite* (New York), Winter/Spring 1975–76; "Home Q & A: Edward Ruscha," with Marshall Berges in *Home Magazine: Los Angeles Times*, 28 March 1976; "They Shoot Corners, Don't They?" in *Esquire* (New York), January 1977; "Feature Interview: Edward Ruscha," with Diane Spodarek, in *Detroit Artists Monthly*, April 1977; "A Conversation with Ed Rusacha," with Trina Mitchum, in *LAICA Journal* (Los Angeles), June/July 1979; "Ed Ruscha on V-Various S-Subjects" in *Stuff Magazine* (Los Angeles), No. 24, 1980; "Ed Ruscha: An Interview," with Henri Man Barendse, in *Afterimage* (Rochester, New York), February 1981; fims—*Premium*, 1972; *Miracle*, 1974.

On RUSCHA: books—*Changing: Essays in Art Criticism* by Lucy R. Lippard, New York 1971; *14 Big Prints* by Bernard Jacobson, London 1972; *Edward Ruscha: Prints and Publications 1962–1974*, exhibition catalogue, by Reyner Banham, London 1975; *Paintings, Drawings and Other Works by Edward Ruscha*, exhibition catalogue, by Linda L. Cathcart, Buffalo, New York 1976; *Painting and Sculpture in California: The Modern Era*, exhibition catalogue, by Henry T. Hopkins, San Francisco 1977; *Cities* by Joseph A. Gatto, Worcester, Massachusetts, 1977; *Graphic Words by Edward Ruscha*, exhibition catalogue, by Andrew Boyle, Auckland 1978; *The 73rd American Exhibition*, exhibition catalogue, by Anne Rorimer and James Speyer, Chicago 1979; *Fifty West Coast Artists* by Henry Hopkins abd Mimi Jacobs, San Francisco 1981; *The Works of Ed Ruscha*, exhibition catalogue with texts by Dave Hickey and Peter Plagens, San Francisco 1982; *Photography and Art 1946–86* by Andy Grundberg and Kathleen M. Gauss, Los Angeles 1987.

According to his own record, Edward Ruscha has been in and out of painting and then back in again. Indisputably, this American is an organized and effective academic artist. For a large and not always sympathetic public he certainly can draw and paint naturalistic imagery of hyper-realist faultlessness. He spent some time—between 1956 and 1960—at the Chouinard Art Institute, but on the whole he is a *natural* artist with automatic talent. Much of his screenprint and lithographic work together with a number of *the books* he has published served to introduce him to the British, a result of the interest and enthusiasm of Nigel Greenwood.

What does Ruscha actually do?

He records the contemporary scene and its flavours.

But not just as a topographer. Ruscha selects, often the most ordinary details of modern life—as in his series of "Twentysix Gasoline Stations" (1962). Somehow, somewhere, and definitely not just round the corner, Ruscha found garages and gave to each a character no passerby would ever have imagined; he gave these petrol stations *identity* without in any way altering their actual appearance.

A sort of magic!

It is difficult to tell; still more awkward to explain. Ruscha paints (lifts!) the gargantuan neon sign that says "Hollywood" at hillcrest height. Never mind if its natural site is half-way down the slope. For him it is a beacon, and blazing signs like that need to be seen from far, far away. So that is how he makes the picture.

Is this what contemporary art is about?

Ed Ruscha has made his mark. The choice lies with his viewers. How many of them want to know "Every Building on the Sunset Strip"?

                      —Sheldon Williams

RUTHENBECK, Reiner.

German. Born in Velbert, 30 June 1937. Studied art, under Joseph Beuys, at the Staatliche Kunstakademie, Dusseldorf, 1962–68. Married Erika Schussler in 1962. Worked as photographer, in Velbert, West Berlin and Dusseldorf, until 1962; Sculptor, Dusseldorf, since 1967: began transcendental meditation 1972. Instructor, Hochschule für Bildende Künste, Hamburg, 1975–76, and Staatliche Kunstakademie, Dusseldorf, since 1980. Recipient: Kunstpreis der Stadt, Krefeld, 1973; Konrad-von-Soest Preis, Munster, 1982. Address: Frankenstrasse 23—Hof, 4000 Dusseldorf 30, West Germany.

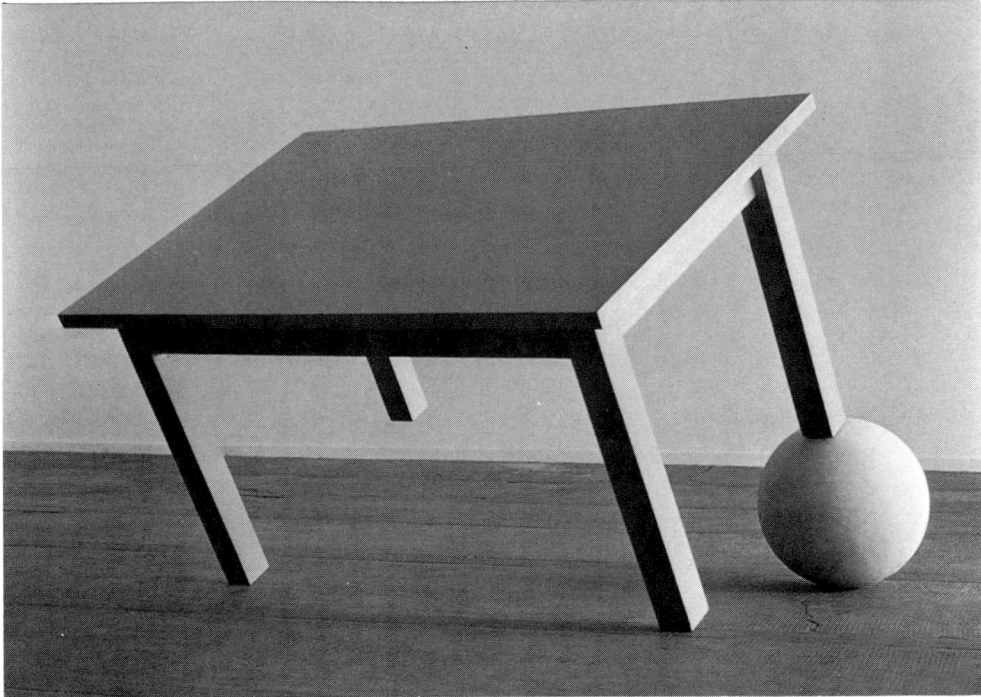

Reiner Ruthenbeck: *Tisch auf gelber Kugel*, 1984

Individual Exhibitions:

1967   Galleri Charlottenburg, Copenhagen
1968   Galerie Konrad Fischer, Dusseldorf
        Wide White Space Gallery, Antwerp
1969   Galerie Konrad Fischer, Dusseldorf
        Galerie René Block, West Berlin
        Galerie Heiner Friedrich, Munich
1970   Galerie Konrad Fischer, Dusseldorf
1971   Galerie Heiner Friedrich, Munich
        Kabinett für Aktuelle Kunst, Bremerhaven, West
            Germany
        Westfälischer Kunstverein, Münster, West Germany
1972   Städtisches Museum, Mönchengladbach, West Ger-
            many
        Galerie Konrad Fischer, Dusseldorf
1973   Kunstverein, Krefeld, West Germany
        Kunsthalle, Kiel, West Germany
1974   Städtisches Kunsthalle, Dusseldorf
        Galerie Rolf Preisig, Basle
        Kabinett für Aktuelle Kunst, Bremerhaven, West
            Germany
        Galerie Müller, Stuttgart
        Galerie René Block, West Berlin
1975   Galerie Klein, Bonn
        René Block Gallery, New York
1976   Kabinett für Aktuelle Kunst, Bremerhaven, West
            Germany
        Galerie Durand-Dessert, Paris
1977   Centre Culturel du Marais, Paris
        Galleria Peccolo, Livorno, Italy
1978   *Handzeichnungen*, Museum Haus Lange, Krefeld,
            West Germany
        Samangalleria, Genoa
        Galerie Klein, Bonn
1979   Samangalleria, Genoa
        Galerie Maier-Hahn, Dusseldorf
1980   Galerie Erika und Otto Friedrich, Berne
1981   Galerie Klein, Bonn
1982   Galerie Konrad Fischer, Dusseldorf
        Forum Kunst, Rottweil, West Germany
1983   Kunstverein, Braunschweig, West Germany
1986   Musée d'Art Moderne de la Ville, Paris
        Galerie Muller-Roth, Stuttgart
        Galerie Akumulatory II, Poznan, Poland
1987   Slalom, Salon am Burgplatz, Dusseldorf

Selected Group Exhibitions:

1969   *When Attitudes Become Form*, Kunsthalle, Berne
            (toured Europe)

1972   *Documenta 5*, Museum Fridericianum, Kassel, West
            Germany (and *Documenta 6*, 1977; *Documenta 7*,
            1982)
1976   *Biennale*, Venice
1978   *Focus '78*, Centre Culturel de Marais, Paris
1979   *Wahrnehmungen, Aufzeichnungen, Mitteilungen*,
            Museum Haus Lange, Krefeld, West Germany
            (travelled to the Nationalgalerie, West Berlin)
1980   *Pier and Ocean*, Hayward Gallery, London (trav-
            elled to Rijksmuseum Kröller-Müller, Otterlo,
            Netherlands)
1981   *Art Allemand Aujourd'hui*, Musée d'Art Moderne,
            Paris
1982   *Kunst wird Material*, Nationalgalerie, West Berlin
1986   *Von Zwei Quadraten*, Wilhelm-Hack-Museum, Lud-
            wigshafen, West Germany
1987   *Das Andere Medium*, Museum am Ostwall, Dort-
            mund, West Germany

Collections:

Kunstmuseum, Dusseldorf; Museum Ludwig, Cologne;
Kunsthalle, Hamburg; Staatsgalerie, Stuutgart; Kaiser Wil-
helm Museum, Krefeld, West Germany; Hessiches Landes-
museum, Darmstadt; Von der Heydt Museum, Wuppertal,
West Germany; Städtisches Museum, Bonn; Centre Georges
Pompidou, Paris; Museum of Modern Art, New York.

Publications:

By RUTHENBECK: book—*Dach Skulptur*, Mönchengladbach, West Germany 1972; article—"Ruthenbeck" in *Interfunktionen* (Cologne), no. 10, 1973; videos—*Papier*, 1970;
Object to Partially Conceal a Video Screen, 1972.

On RUTHENBECK: books—*Deutsche Kunst: Eine neue
Generation* by Rolf-Günter Dienst, Cologne 1970; *Bis Heute*
by Karin Thomas, Cologne 1972; *Kunstpraxis Heute* by
Karin Thomas, Cologne 1972; *Handzeichnungen*, exhibition
catalogue, with text by Gerhard Storck, Krefeld, West Germany 1978; *Art Allemand Aujourd'hui*, exhibition catalogue,
Paris 1981; *Gesprache mit Kunstlern* by A. Haase, Cologne
1981; *Reiner Ruthenbeck: Arbeiten 1965–1983*, exhibition
catalogue, Braunschweig 1983; *Reiner Ruthenbeck: entre
chien et loup*, exhibition catalogue, Paris 1986; *Reiner
Ruthenbeck*, exhibition catalogue, Stuttgart and Nuremberg
1986.

In my work I have tried, among other things, to bring
polarities, contrasts and tensions to a formal unity.
    By a reduction to simple lucid structures which ap-

pear to offer little nourishment to the intellect, I
would like to lead the spectator to an entirely contemplative view of my art.

                                    —Reiner Ruthenbeck

Before Reiner Ruthenbeck went to the Kunstakademie
of Dusseldorf as a pupil of Joseph Beuys, he was a
photographer. Certainly, the fact that he had been a
photographer exercised no immediate influence on his
plastic works, and yet certain motifs in his photographs remind one of those which are characteristic
of his sculptures. That almost oppressive taciturnity
and that atmosphere of tension which distinguish his
works over and above any artistic virtuosity were already evident in his photographs. Empty streets and
half-demolished house fronts are depicted; a climate
of tangible desolation is built up. Or a window in
which a curtain is gently blown by the wind. Peace—
silence. Every movement appears literally frozen.
The scenery is in a state of suspended animation; the
stillness is ghostlike and oppressive. In familiar objects Ruthenbeck reveals the strangeness which will
not be bound by the conventions of normal experience.
    At the beginning of his artistic career, Ruthenbeck
always made use of a single material for the production of an object. Iron, for example, or wood. He
fashioned sculptures from these, which mirror the
forms of simple objects from everyday life. With distortions, of course. Giant spoons are created, two and
a half metres high; giant umbrellas, a metre higher
than that; tiny cupboards on one-dimensional legs—
and ladders whose rungs are so closely spaced that
they are impossible to climb. Although Ruthenbeck
was more concerned with the forms of objects that
their function, for example the rounding of the
spoons, the cool stereometry of the cupboards, the
uniform rhythmicality of the steps of the ladder, nonetheless there is at the same time an unmistakeable
attempt to make would-be useful objects unusable.
Without, however, annihilating them. Unusable solely
as a result of placing undue emphasis on their formal
qualities and peculiarities.
    On the other hand one can not overlook the point
that Ruthenbeck is trying to protect the objects from
total use and, consequently, their gradual destruction.
The concave inner surfaces of the spoons are wrapped
in thin bands of iron, as if they required protection
from some external threat, just as an umbrella guarantees protection to the space beneath it when it
rains. Strips of material cut in oblongs hang in a wire
cage, beyond the reach of grasping hands. And finally, a large heap of ashes is provided with a mesh of
wire and iron bars, like a hedgehog that has curled
itself up into a ball before an aggressor.
    Later Ruthenbeck proceeded to eradicate the
former "literary" dimensions in his works in favour
of a subtle development of materials. He combined
differing materials which evoke contrary responses in
the observer; dark red widths of cloth, often cut in
rectangles and sewn together, stretched taut by means
of iron and glass plates which Ruthenbeck inserts into
them, or else hung down limply from cords fastened
diagonally across the exhibition space and thrown
over iron poles. Ruthenbeck tracks down hidden tensions, indeed he provokes them. As a result of this,
cloth, to which the observer attributes the quality of
softness, is unexpectedly revealed as a "hard" material. Convention is broken down; things learnt from
experience turn upside-down.
    Above all, he affords things, dispassionately,
whether it is a question of the purely artistic or the
unequivocally practical, a personal dignity and autonomy, values which are commonly reserved for things
seen as art, but denied to the practical.
    This dignity is also to be found in the architectural
spaces to which the sculptor has in recent years
turned his attention. His contribution to the 1976
Biennale in Venice consisted of a project called
"Doorway" which was quite simply a doorway.
Ruthenbeck stretched rubber cables through two
inner-connecting rooms. The rubber cables were fastened to and covered the whole surface area of the

opposing walls. In the doorway they bunched up, and created there a kind of energy centre. Reiner Ruthenbeck turned an ordinarily accessible room into a seeing room. Its structural identity and identity as object became more important than his own purposes.

—Klaus Honnef

RYMAN, Robert

American. Born in Nashville, Tennessee, 30 May 1930. Educated at Tennessee Polytechnic, Cookville, 1948–49; George Peabody College for Teachers, 1949–50. Worked as a guard, Museum of Modern Art, New York, in the 1950s. Independent artist, New York, since 1966. Member, Art Commission of New York, 1982–85. Agent: Galerie Maeght Lelong, 9 West 57th Street, New York, New York 10019. Address: 17 West 16th Street, New York, New York 10011, U.S.A.

Individual Exhibitions:

1967	Paul Bianchini Gallery, New York
1968	Konrad Fischer Gallery, Dusseldorf
	Heiner Friedrich Gallery, Munich
1969	Konrad Fischer Gallery, Dusseldorf
	Heiner Friedrich Gallery, Munich
	Fischbach Gallery, New York
	Francoise Lambert Galleria, Milan
	Galerie Yvon Lambert, Paris
	Ace Gallery, Los Angeles
1970	Fischbach Gallery, New York
1971	Fischbach Gallery, New York
	Current Editions, Seattle
	Dwan Gallery, New York
	Heiner Friedrich Gallery, Cologne
1972	Heiner Friedrich Gallery, Cologne
	Current Editions, Seattle
	John Weber Gallery, New York
	Guggenheim Museum, New York
	Galerie Annemarie Verna, Zurich
	Galleria del Cortile, Rome
	Lisson Gallery, London
1973	Galleria San Fedele, Milan
	John Weber Gallery, New York
	Konrad Fischer Gallery, Dusseldorf
	Art and Project, Amsterdam
1974	Stedelijk Museum, Amsterdam
	Westfalischer Kunstverein, Munster, West Germany
	Palais des Beaux-Arts, Brussels
	John Weber Gallery, New York
1975	John Weber Gallery, New York
	Kunsthalle, Basle
1977	Public School #1, Long Island City, New York
	Gian Enzo Sperone Galeria, Rome
	Galerie Annemarie Verna, Zurich
	Galerie Charles Kriwin, Brussels
	Whitechapel Art Gallery, London
1978	Galerie Inc., Zurich
1979	Galerie Inc., Zurich
	Sidney Janis Gallery, New York
1980	Konrad Fischer Galerie, Dusseldorf
	Paintings 1958-1980, Galerie Inc., Zurich
	Kunstraum, Munich
1981	Sidney Janis Gallery, New York
1982	Young Hoffman Gallery, Chicago
	James Mayor Gallery, London
	Kunsthalle, Dusseldorf
1983	Bonnier Gallery, New York
	Daniel Weinberg Gallery, Los Angeles
1984	Galerie Maeght Lelong, New York
	Galerie Maeght Lelong, Paris
1987	Art Institute of Chicago
1988	San Francisco Museum of Modern Art

Selected Group Exhibitions:

1968	*Gordon/Lonzano/Ryman/Stanley*, Contemporary Arts Center, Cincinnati, Ohio
1977	*Documenta 6*, Museum Fridericianum, Kassel, West Germany (and *Documenta 7*, 1982)
1978	*American Post-War Painting from the Guggenheim Collection*, Guggenheim Museum, New York
1979	*73rd American Exhibition*, Art Institute of Chicago
1980	*Printed Art: A View of 2 Decades*, Museum of Modern Art, New York
1981	*A New Spirit in Painting*, Royal Academy of Arts, London
1982	*The New York School*, Guggenheim Museum, New York
1983	*Abstract Painting 1960-69*, Project Studio One, New York
1984	*The Meditative Surface*, Renaissance Society, Chicago

Collections:

Museum of Modern Art, New York; Guggenheim Museum, New York; Sidney Janis Gallery Collection, New York; Dayton Art Museum, Ohio; Minneapolis Art Institute; San Francisco Museum of Modern Art; Stedelijk Museum, Amsterdam.

Publications:

By RYMAN: articles—statement in *Art in Process IV* (New York), December 1970; "An Interview with Robert Ryman," with Phyllis Tuchman, in *Artforum* (New York), May 1971; statement in *Art Now: New York*, September 1971; "An Interview with Robert Ryman," with Achille Bonito Oliva, in *Domus* (Milan), February 1973; "Robert Ryman, Le Geste" in *Revue d'Art Contemporain* (Paris), November 1974; statement in *Fundamental Painting*, exhibition catalogue, Amsterdam 1975; statement in *Prints: Bochner/LeWitt/Mangold/Marden/Martin/Renouf/Rockburne/Ryman*, exhibition catalogue, Toronto 1975; interview with Barbaralee Diamondstein, in *Inside New York's Art World*, New York 1979; statement in *Wall Painting: Hafif/Jackson/Pozzi/Ryman/Yasuda*, exhibition catalogue, Chicago 1979; "Robert Ryman," interview with Peter Blum, in *Du* (Zurich), Summer 1980; videotape—interview for *Video Data Bank*, School of the Art Institute of Chicago, Spring 1979; film—interview for *Art Report*, television program, by Hideo Kinoshita, for Art Agency, Tokyo 1979.

On RYMAN: books—*Changing: Essays in Art Criticism* by Lucy R. Lippard, New York 1971; *Robert Ryman*, exhibition catalogue, with an introduction by Diane Waldman, New York 1972; *Robert Ryman*, exhibition catalogue, with an introduction by Naomi Spector, Amsterdam 1974; *Robert Ryman*, exhibition catalogue, with an introduction by Carlo Huber, Basle 1975; *Drawing Now*, exhibition catalogue, with an introduction by Bernice Rose, New York 1976; *Yesterday, Today, Tomorrow*, exhibition catalogue, with an introduction by Paul E. Thompson, Miami 1976; *Robert Ryman*, exhibition catalogue, introduction by Naomi Spector, London 1977; *73rd American Exhibition*, exhibition catalogue, with an introduction by Anne Rorimer, Chicago 1979; *Inside New York's Art World* by Barbaralee Diamondstein, New York 1979; *Robert Ryman: Paintings 1958-1980*, exhibition catalogue, with an introduction by Christel Sauer, Zurich 1980; *Appreciating Ryman*, by Jeremy Gilbert-Rolfe 1980; *Printed Art: A View of 2 Decades*, exhibition catalogue, New York 1980; *Art of the 70's*, exhibition catalogue, Venice 1980; *A New Spirit in Painting*, exhibition catalogue, London 1980; *Minimal Art from Crex Collection*, exhibition catalogue, Madrid 1981; *Robert Ryman: reperes*, exhibition catalogue with preface by Jean Fremon, Paris 1984; *Robert Ryman: The Charter Series*, exhibition catalogue with text by Neal Benezra, Chicago 1987.

*   *   *

"Before a picture represents a battlefield, a nude or some other anecdote, it is first of all a surface covered with paints applied in a special way." These famous words of Maurice Denis are rightly put at the head of any experiment in "pure painting." The great majority of Robert Ryman's pictures are rectangular in shape and painted in white. They refer to nothing beyond themselves; they are simply "surfaces covered with paint." Thus what comes clearly to the fore is the language, or rather the various languages, of the material, released from any obligation to depict actual existing phenomena.

The painting is an existing phenomenon in itself, an object among other objects. Ryman does not paint entirely in monochrome; since his white is totally and definitely empirical, concrete, phenomenal, it is as if it had broken down into a number of "whites." It is thus a pure relationship—but a relationship with what? With what other factors? Ryman takes into account everything involved in painting; he works them and manipulates them so as to explore the depths of their formal significance. Cotton, canvas, steel, cardboard, wood, fibreglass—all these are materials which have their own specific languages, which form relationships producing new interactions and novel perceptions with oils, tempera, acrylics and so on. Many different levels of brightness, of softness, of dark or light tone, of shade, and refractions arise from this treatment. And then the format (Ryman often works on a number of paintings in series) is always determined in relation to the size of the wall, the height at which the painting is to be hung and so on, thus creating a complex network of interactions which almost make a "story" in themselves, even though nothing is represented or portrayed by them.

It is the actual story of the material—which obviously has its own mental, even conceptual, significance—that is diversified by itself, empirically: "to make" is in fact perhaps Ryman's favorite word. And he identifies "making" with knowing the languages of the materials and what can be deduced and produced from them. This has always been the prime skill of the painter; and this is Ryman's skill.

—Massimo Carboni

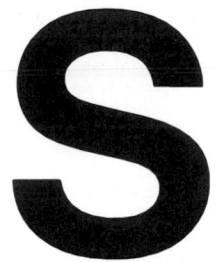

SAINT-PHALLE, Niki de.

French. Born Neuilly-sur-Seine, Paris, 29 October 1930. Educated at Convent of Sacre Coeur, New York, 1936–45; self-taught in art, but influenced by work of Antoni Gaudi and Le Facteur Cheval. Married the writer Harry Mathews in 1948 (separated, 1960); children: Laure and Philippe; lived with the artist Jean Tinguely from 1960. Independent artist, since 1952, in Paris, subsequently in Soisy-sur-Ecole, France: first painting, 1952; first object-reliefs and assemblages, 1956; first experimental rifle-shot paintings, 1960; happenings and manifestations, with Jean Tinguely, from 1961; first "Nana" sculptures, with daughter Laure, 1965; first theatre decors, with Martial Raysse and Jean Tinguely, 1966; first films, 1973; worked on Tarot Garden outdoor sculptures project, in Tuscany, Italy, from 1979. Agents: Gimpel Fils, 30 Davies Street, London WIY ILG, England: Marisa del Re Gallery, 41 East 57th Street, New York, New York 10022, U.S.A. Address: I'Auberge du Cheval-Blanc, 91840 Soisy-sur-Ecole, Essones, France.

Individual Exhibitions:

1961	Galerie J. Paris
	Galerie Koepcke, Copenhagen
	Moderna Museet, Stockholm
1962	Dwan Gallery, Los Angeles
	Galerie Rive Droite. Paris
	Alexandre Jolas Gallery, New York
1963	Dwan Gallery, Los Angeles
1964	Hanover Gallery, London
	Palais des Beaux-Arts, Brussels
	Galrie Iolas, Geneva
1965	Alexandre Iolas Gallery, New York
	Galrie Alexandre Iolas, Paris
1966	Alexandre Iolas Gallery, New York
1967	Stedelijk Museum. Amsterdam
	Galerie Espace. Amsterdam
	Fondation Maeght, St. Paul-de-Vence, France
1968	Gimpel und Hanover Galerie, Zurich
	Hanover Gallery, London
	Kunstverein, Dusseldorf (retrospective)
	Stadttheater, Kassel, West Germany (decors for *Ich*, with Rainer von Diez)
1969	Kunstverein. Hannover (retrospective)
	Galerie Stangl, Munich
	Kunstmuseum, Lucerne (retrospective)
	Galerie Iolas. Geneva
	Galerie Seriaal, Amsterdam
	Galerie Ad Libitum. Antwerp (with Jean Tinguely)
1970	Galerie Alexandre Iolas, Paris
	Les Halles, Paris
	Galerie Der Spiegel, Cologne
	Please Give Me a Few Seconds of Your Eternity. Galleria Iolas, Milan
	Gimpel und Hanover Galerie. Zurich
	Musée des Beaux-Arts, Lille, France
1971	Galerie Espace. Amsterdam
	Galerie Runquist, Stockholm
	Galleria Carmine, Rome
	Gimpel and Weitzenhoffer, New York
1972	Galerie Rive Gauche, Brussels
	Galerie Alexandre Iolas, Paris
	Galerie Bonnier, Geneva
	Gimpel Fils, London
	Galerie Stangl, Munich
1973	Gimpel and Weitzenhoffer, New York
1974	Galerie Alexandre Iolas, Paris
1975	Musée d'Art et d'Industrie, Arles, France
	Galerie Le Point, Beirut
1976	Nordijyllands Konstmusemum, Aalborg. Denmark
1977	Fondation Veianneman, Kruishoutem, Belgium
1978	Gimpel and Weitzenhoffer, New York
	Banque Lambert, Brussels
1979	Watari Gallery, Tokyo
	Gallery Iolas, Athens
	Gimpel and Weitzenhoffer, New York
1980	Galerie Bischofberger, Zurich
	Bawag Foundation, Vienna
	Ulmer Musemum, Ulm, West Germany
	Museum of Fine Arts, Columbus, Ohio (toured the United States)
	Centre Georges Pompidou, Paris (retrospective; toured Germany, Austria, Britain, Sweden and Israel)
1981	Galerie Bonnier, Geneva
1982	Gimpel and Weitzenhoffer, New York
	Gimpel Fils, London
1983	Gallery Esperanze, Montreal
1985	Casino Knokke, Belgium
	Gimpel Fils, London
	Gimpel and Weitzenhoffer, New York
	Galerie Klaus Littmann, Basle
1987	Space Niki/Sagacho Exhibit Space, Tokyo
	Kunsthalle der Hypo-Kulturstiftung, Munich
	Galerie Bonnier, Geneva
	Nassau County Museum of Fine Art, Roslyn, New York

Selected Group Exhibitions:

1961	*The Art of Assemblage*, Museum of Modern Art, New York
1963	*Biennale de Paris*, Musée d'Art Moderne. Paris
1966	*4 European Artisis and the Figure*, Art Institute of Chicago
1968	*Dada, Surrealism and Their Heritage*, Museum of Modern Art, New York
1970	*Pop Art, Nouveau Realisme*, Casino Communal, Knokke, Belgium
1972	*12 Ans d'Art Contemporain en France*, Grand Palais, Paris
1978	*Collection Hammer*, Kunstmuseum, Basle
1980	*The Figurative Tradition*, Whitney Museum, New York
1985	*Nouveau Realisme and Pop*, Museum of Contemporary Art, Chicago
1987	*Sacred Spaces*, Everson Museum of Art, Syracuse, New York

Collections:

Centre Georges Pompidou, Paris; Stedelijk Museum, Amsterdam; Museum Boymans-Van Beuningen, Rotterdam; Nellens Collection, Knokke-le-Zoute, Belgium (sculpture/environment commission); Moderna Museet, Stockholm; University of Ulm, West Germany; Rabinowitsch Park, Jerusalem (sculpture/environment commission); Whitney Museum, New York.

Publications

By SAINT-PHALLE: books—*Niki de Saint Phalle*, London and Milan 1968; *Niki de Saint Phalle: My Love*, Stockholm 1971; *The Devouring Mothers*, London 1972; *Tarot Cards in Sculpture by Niki de Saint Phalle*, with Fausta Squatriti, London and Milan 1985; *AIDS: You Can't Catch It Holding Hands*, with Silvio Barandun, Munich and Lucerne 1986, Paris, Milan and San Francisco 1987; films—*Daddy*, with Peter Whitehead, 1973; *Une reve plus long que la nuit*, with Laura and Laurent Condominas, 1975.

On SAINT-PHALLE:books—*Niki de Saint-Phalle*, exhibition catalogue, with texts by Pierre Restany and John Ashbery, Paris 1962; *Niki de Saint-Phalle*, exhibition catalogue, with text by Pierre Descargues, Paris 1965; *Niki de Saint-Phalle: Les Nana au Pouvoir*, exhibition catalogue, with text by Pierre Descargues, Amsterdam 1967; *Niki de Saint-Phalle:Please Give Me a Few Seconds of Your Eternity*, exhibition catalogue, Milan 1970; *Niki de Saint-Phalle*, exhibition catalogue, with text by Yoshiaki Tono, Tokyo 1979; *Niki de Saint-Phalle*, exhibition catalogue, with text by K. G. Pontus Hulten, Pierre Restany, John Ashbery, Larry Rivers and Jean-Yves Mock, Paris 1980; *Niki at Nassau*, exhibition catalogue with texts by David Bourdon, John Cage and Harry Mathews, Roslyn, New York 1987.

"I come from a respectable family and religious institution," said Niki de Saint-Phalle. What she has made of life after such staid beginnings might be the starting point for an interesting psychological investigation.

"HON" is the Swedish for SHE. This was an enormous construction, the joint creation of Niki de Saint-Phalle, Jean Tinguely and Per Olof Ultvedt. A great sprawling giantess, lying on her back, stretched out on the floor of Stockholm's Moderna Museet. The Year was 1963. Those entering HON, for she was also a house of many mansions with bar, music rooms, and cinema, did so by mounting the ramp leading to the doorway between her legs, a typical example of what this artist would regard as apposite not only as a philosophic point but also *epater-la-bourgeoisie*. HON was mostly black inside but her outer skin was decorated in bright colours painted on white.

Described by her makers as 82 feet long, 20 feet high and 30 feet large(?). Layout contained "lovers' nest" with built-in microphone to relay love-talk to the bar, a gallery of fake paintings, an aquarium, a telephone, the bar with coca-cola automat, a cinema for Greta Garbo movies, a planetarium, a mill for grinding empty bottles when they were thrown down the chute and viewing platform from HON's head. The head also contained an infernal machine. Her heart and lungs were constructed to expand and contract to simulate breathing.

And all this was the inspiration of Niki de Saint-Phalle who a few years previously had been demonstrating the absurdity of the permanent by raking a wall hung with hotwater bottles with rifle fire.

The *nanas* which are, in the modern sense of the term, Niki de Saint-Phalle's stock-in-trade today, are

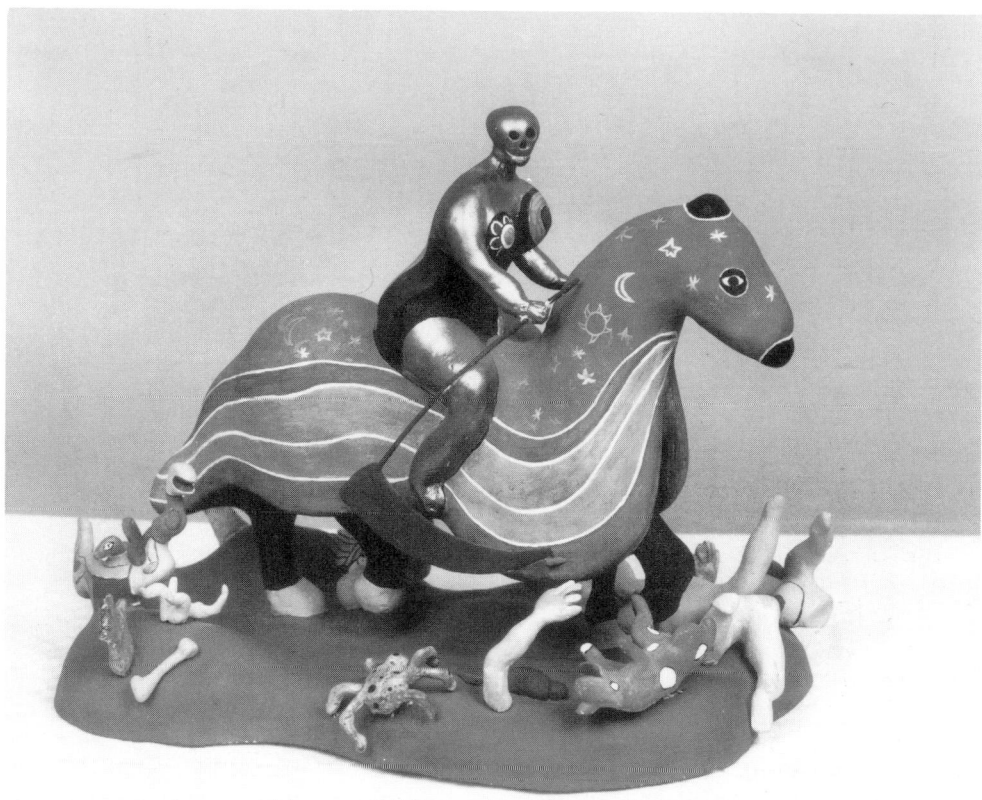

Niki de Saint-Phalle: *Death*, 1985 Courtesy Gimpel Fils, London

Collections:

Museum of Modern Art, Kamakura, Japan; National Museum of Modern Art, Tokyo; Museum of Contemporary Arts, Nagaoka, Japan; Rockefeller Collection, New York; Museum of Fine Arts, Houston; Rijksmuseum Kroller-Muller, Otterlo, Netherlands; Tochigi Prefectural Museum of Fine Arts, Japan; Nagaoka Museum of Contemporary Art, Japan; Metropolitan Art Museum, Tokyo.

Publications:

By SAITO: books—*Yoshishige Saito*, Tokyo 1964; *Yoshishige Saito*, Tokyo 1973.

On SAITO: books—*Modern Art in Japan* by Teichi Hijikata, Tokyo 1966; *Avant-Garde in Japan* by Masayoshi Honma, Tokyo 1971; *Japan: Tradition und Gegenwart*, exhibition catalogue, with texts by Jurgen Harten, Joseph Love and others, Dusseldorf 1974; *Yoshishige Saito*, exhibition catalogue, Tokyo 1979; *Yoshishige Saito: Disproportion*, exhibition catalogue, with text by Shigeo Chiba, Tokyo 1980; *Yoshishige Saito: Sculpture and Installations*, exhibition catalogue, London 1988.

*

the total expression of arch-femininity. They were even present, albeit in gestatory stage, in the early reliefs encrusted with all kinds of trinkets (usually of plastic), even dolls' kitchenware, along with knitting needles and crochet hooks—a splendid bullseye material for the rifle brigade who could commit a sacrilege that incurred no penance when they destroyed the *altars* made by Niki de Saint-Phalle. But nobody shoots *nanas*. If anybody indulges in target-practice, it is they who will be the practitioners when they thrust their gaudy primary characteristics at goggle-eyed hermits. St. Anthony is lucky to be beyond their clutches.

HON was more like the Niki de Saint-Phalle of the 1960's and 1970's. This enormous pregnant lady of Stockholm was an early version of Niki de Saint Phalle's *nanas*, the hefty ladies whose ornamented bodies look as if they have renounced centuries of sophistication and civilization to go back to a time when peasant-style decoration was the natural way to express personality and seek to attract the opposite sex. The casual traditionalism of their swollen bodies and the patterns painted on them propose a sort of archetypal verity they were never perhaps in the first place intended to have.

—Sheldon Williams

SAITO, Yoshishige.

Japanese. Born in Tokyo, 4 May 1904. Educated at Nihon Middle School, Tokyo, 1918–24; at Waseda Kotogakuin, Tokyo, 1924. Married Tomoko Sato in 1961; children: Wado and Shimon. Independent painter and sculptor, Tokyo, since 1925: founder-member, Art Culture Association, Tokyo, 1939–53. Professor of Art, Tama Art University, Tokyo, 1964–73. Recipient: Mr. K. Prize, 1957, National Museum Prize, 1959, Grand Prize, 1960, *International Art Exhibition*, Tokyo; Major Prize, 1958, Ohara Museum Prize, 1971, *Contemporary Art Exhibition*, To-

kyo; International Federation of Art Critics Award, 1959; Major Prize, *Guggenheim International Art Exhibition*, New York, 1960; Painting Prize, *6th Bienal de Sao Paulo*, Brazil, 1961; Asahi Prize, Tokyo, 1984. Agent: Tokyo Gallery, 8-6-18 Ginza, Chuo-ku, Tokyo 194. Address: 2-79 Mutsukawa, Minami-ku, Yokohama 232, Japan.

Individual Exhibitions:

Selected Group Exhibitions:

Born in 1904, Yoshishige Saito has been earning his fame as one of the most challenging artists in Japan for a long time. Inspired by the paintings of Russian Futurist David Davidovich Burliuk, who organized the Russian painting exhibition in Tokyo in 1920, 16-year-old Saito made up his mind to enter upon an artist's career. During the following years in his early twenties, he was constantly exposed to the modernist movements, especially Constructivism and Dada, which were introduced by Japanese pioneer avant-garde artists who had studied in Europe and came back to Japan with the exciting new ideas.

Constructivism and Dada made young Saito somewhat suspicious of the possibility of painting, so that he began to make Constructivistic sculptures. In 1936 he met Haruyoshi Yoshihara, the leader of Gutai group which was to be known as one the most experimental avant-garde groups in Japan. Being encouraged by Yoshihara, Saito made his first comemorative sculpture *Kara Kara*, which had great affinity with the work by Naum Gabo.

During the World War 11, the difficulty in obtaining the supplies of material compelled the artist to make black reliefs in simple plywood, and the experience was to affect his later work a great deal. He lost all his work in a fire in the year the war ended.

The new abstract movement in painting in Europe and the United States in the post-war period influenced the artist, and he devoted himself to abstract-expressionistic painting in parallel with his plywood relief making. He was 54 when he gave his first one-person show at the Tokyo Gallery in 1958, and the show included *Painting E* which was awarded the prize of the International Association of Art Critics in the following year.

In the middle of 1960's he came to concentrate most of his energy to plywood reliefs rather than oil painting. Those reliefs had roundish cut-out polygons juxtaposed on rectangle supports in witty equilibrium.

He was offered the post as a professor in Tama College of Art in 1964, and had taught there until he retired in 1973. But he never retired from art-making. He had great energy to renovate his style with more open and lighter structure by utilizing straight boards in his reliefs. His major retrospective was held at the National Museum of Modern Art in Tokyo in 1979. For that show, he made his first three-dimensional floor pieces by composing plain boards into geometri-

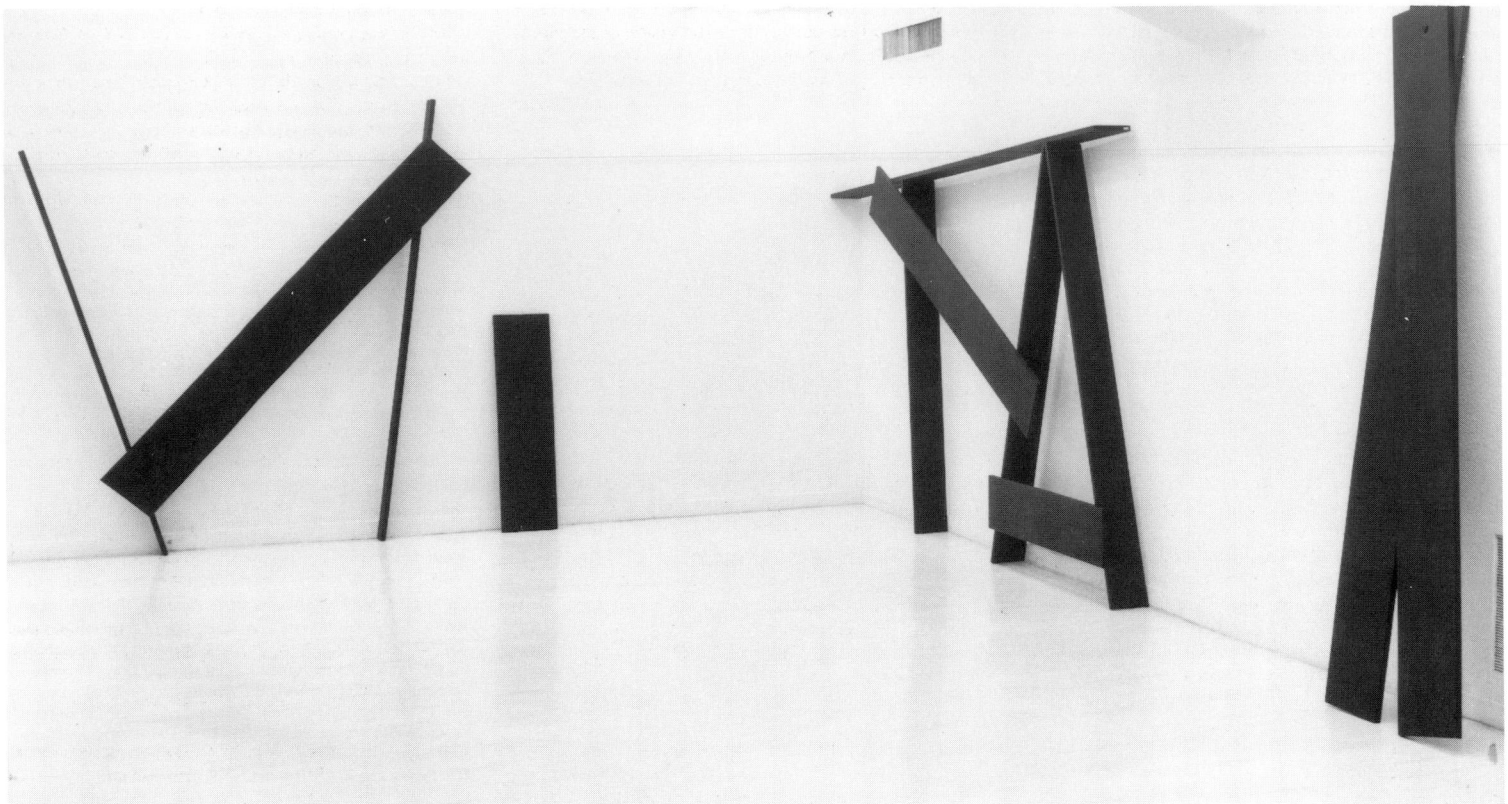

Yoshishige Saito: *Disproportion* sculptures at the Tokyo Gallery, 1980

cal forms. His second retrospective was organized successfully in 1984 with the cooperative sponsorship of five major Japanese museums. He exhibited his work in the 18th Sao Paolo Bienniale and *"The Reconstruction: Avant-Garde Art in Japan 1945–1965"* held at the Oxford Gallery of Modern Art in England in 1985. Since 1984 he has developed more original open-structured 3-D installations by black-painted boards. Those remarkable installations including works with graffiti-scribbled blackboards were shown at Yurakucho Asahi Gallery in Tokyo in 1986. One of his old works was exhibited in *"Japon des Avant Gardes: 1910–1970"* at the Centre de Georges Pompidou in Paris in 1986.

—Tazmi Shinoda

SALLE, David.

American. Born in Norman, Oklahoma, 28 September 1952. Studied at the California Institute of Arts, Valencia, 1971–75, BFA 1973, MFA 1975. Independent painter, New York, since 1975. Recipient: Creative Artists Public Service Grant, New York, 1979. Agent: Mary Boone Gallery, New York. Address: c/o Mary Boone Gallery, 420 West Broadway, New York, New York 10012, U.S.A.

Individual Exhibitions:

1976	Artists' Space, New York
1977	Fondation de Appel, Amsterdam
	The Kitchen, New York
1979	The Kitchen, New York
1980	Annina Nosei Gallery, New York
	Galerie Bischofberger, Zurich
1981	Mary Boone Gallery, New York
	Larry Gagosian Gallery, Los Angeles
	Galleria Lucio Amelio, Naples
1982	Galleria Mario Diacono, Rome
	Mary Boone/Leo Castelli Gallery, New York
	Galerie Bischofberger, Zurich
1983	Akira Ikeda Gallery, Tokyo
	Museum Boymans-van Beuningen, Rotterdam
	Mary Boone Gallery, New York
	Larry Gagosian Gallery, Los Angeles
	Galerie Schellmann und Kluser, Munich
1984	Leo Castelli Gallery, New York
	Galerie Bischofberger, Zurich
	Galerie Gillespie-Laage-Salomon, Paris
1985	Texas Gallery, Houston
	Galerie Daniel Templon, Paris
	Mary Boone Gallery, New York
	Galerie Michael Werner, Cologne
	Donald Young Gallery, Chicago
1986	Leo Castelli Galery, New York
	Mario Diacono Gallery, Boston
	Institute of Contemporary Art, Philadelphia
	Institute of Contemporary Art, Boston
	Galerie Sabine Knust, Munich
1987	Whitney Museum, New York
	Museum of Contemporary Art, Los Angeles
	Art Gallery of Ontario, Toronto
	Museum of Contemporary Art, Chicago
	Mary Boone Gallery, New York

Selected Group Exhibitions:

1979	*Imitation of Life*, Hartford Art School, Connecticut
1980	*Apres le Classicisme*, Musée d'Art et d'Industrie, St. Etienne, France
1981	*Young Americans*, Allen Memorial Art Museum, Oberlin, Ohio
1982	*Documenta 7*, Museum Fridericianum, Kassel, West Germany
1983	*New Art*, Tate Gallery, London
1984	*The Restoration of Painterly Figuration*, Kitakyushu Municipal Art Museum, Tokyo
1985	*Biennale de Paris*, Grand Halle du Parc de la Villette, Paris
1987	*Avant-Garde in the Eighties*, Los Angeles County Museum of Art
1988	*Contemporary American Art*, Sara Hilden Art Museum, Tampere, Finland (travelled to Oslo)

Collections:

Whitney Museum, New York; Museum Boymans-van Beuningen, Rotterdam; Kunstmuseum, Basle; New York Public Library.

Publications:

By SALLE: articles—"David Salle Interview", with Peter Schjeldahl, in *Journal* (New York), September/October 1981; "An Interview with David Salle", with John Roberts, in *Art Monthly* (London), March 1983; "Interview with David Salle", with Robert Picnus-Witten, in *Arts Magazine* (New York), November 1985.

On SALLE: books—*David Salle*, exhibition catalogue, Rotterdam 1983; *David Salle Paintings*, exhibition catalogue, Philadelphia 1986; *Contemporary American Art*, exhibition catalogue with foreword by Peter Schjeldahl, Tampere 1988.

The paintings of David Salle, like those of Picabia, have a particular 'transparency'. The figures are outlined across the surface of the picture against a background of colour. Everything is provisional and insubstantial as though about to disappear in the volubility of this transparent arena, as in *Hundreds of Tons* (1980), and *Rational Censor* (1981). The visual situation with its ephemeral aura hovering between sign and material constitutes a complete harmony. The programmed shifts in imagery share something with advertisement signs.

Salle, however, takes nothing from Pop Art, nor from Hyperrealism. His mode of narrative is the result of psychic impulses that reflect a humorous fantasy. In this respect, his vision of daily life is individual and introspective, an opaque mirror of a fascinating world full of the intriguing expression of his imagination and expressive imagery. The subject appears as a mutation of the moment and of voluptuous desire. It offers an infinite combination of iconographic visions, and it is not important that these icons have been seen and gathered from other sources. They appear afresh, signifying their essential modernity.

For Salle, it is not a style nor a deception which

promotes the fantasy; rather, it is the fixing of the moment of maximum intensity. A visual contest is established, in which indeterminate visual sensations are ensnared. It is no accident that most of his works are untitled. The picture is frequently highly energized, and it is not without discernment that Salle arrives at these visual effects—an intriguing superimposition of transparent layers. The expression is adroitly handled, the effervescent surface sheltering barely perceptible images. Not everything has coherence or stylistic harmony; things and events often appear separately. The skill of the artist lies in his consistent manipulation of a ravenous media.

Salle's images are also the stuff of dreams, and the means of reaching them almost scandalous—like Narcissus with his reflection. The melancholy and arrogant creative spirit which mobilizes the raw material of the surface establishes a certain excitement born of subconscious desires.

Perhaps Salle seeks a disarming effect in the near-imperceptible presence of his secretly assembled iconography. The areas into which the picture plane is sub-divided have their own autonomy in spite of their close juxtaposition. This is clearly visible in the fine work from 1982 onwards, exhibited at the *Zeit Geist* show in Berlin—notably in *Was My Husband A Doctor Or A Patient*(1982). Here, as in other works, the various combinations of colour and sign form a kind of creative and expansive connivance between figuration and abstraction. The hyperbole of transparency prompts a sense of arrested flight.

Salle as an artist is more European than American. His images are drawn more in the manner of Picabia than of the urban graffitist. Moreover, we see in him a concern for the metaphysical mysteries of art that is peculiar to European culture. The vision of the real is always an interior Conceptualisation. Video for Salle is a pretext, just as the libretto is for a musician.

—Italo Mussa

SAMARAS, Lucas.

American. Born in Kastoria, Macedonia. Greece, 14 September 1936; emigrated to the United States, 1948: naturalized, 1955. Educated at Memorial High School, West New York, New Jersey, 1951–55; studied, under Allan Kaprow, at Rutgers University, New Brunswick, New Jersey, 1955–59, B.A. 1959; Columbia University, New York (Woodrow Wilson Fellow), 1959–62. Artist and photographer, New York, since 1964: first "autopolaroid" photographs, 1970; first "photo-transformations," 1973. Visiting Instructor in Sculpture, Yale University, New Haven, Connecticut, 1969; Instructor, Brooklyn College, New York, 1971–72. Agent: Pace Gallery, 32 East 57th Street, New York, New York 10022. Address: 52 West 71st Street, New York, New York 10023, U.S.A.

Individual Exhibitions:

1955 Rutgers University, New Brunswick, New Jersey

1959 Reuben Gallery, New York
1961 *Dinners, Liquid Aluminum, Pastels and Plasters,* Green Gallery, New York
1962 *Pastels,* Sun Gallery, Provincetown, Massachusetts
1964 *Boxes, Constructions,* Dwan Gallery, Los Angeles
Bedroom, Boxes, Plastics, Green Gallery, New York
1966 *Samaras: Mirror Room: Selected Works 1960–66,* Pace Gallery, New York
1968 *Transformations, Mirror Stairs. Paintings and Drawings,* Pace Gallery, New York
1969 *Book,* Museum of Modern Art, New York
Mirror Room 3, Boxes and Drawings, Galerie der Spiegel, Cologne
1970 *Chair Transformations,* Pace Gallery, New York
Mirror Room 3, Kunstverein, Hannover
1971 *Stiff Boxes and Autopolaroids,* Pace Gallery, New York
Acrylics, Pastels, Inks, Phyllis Kind Gallery, Chicago
Lucas Samaras' Boxes, Museum of Contemporary Art, Chicago
1972 *Chicken Wire Boxes,* Pace Gallery, New York
Whitney Museum, New York (retrospective)
1974 *Photo-Transformations,* Pace Gallery, New York
1975 *Pastels,* Museum of Modern Art, New York
Makler Gallery, Philadelphia
Samaras and Some Others, Pace Gallery, New York
Photo-Transformations California State University at Long Beach
1976 University of North Dakota Art Gallery, Grand Forks
Wright State University Art Gallery, Dayton, Ohio
Institute of Contemporary Art, Boston
Seattle Art Museum

David Salle: *Coming and Going*, 1987 Courtesy Mary Boone Gallery, New York

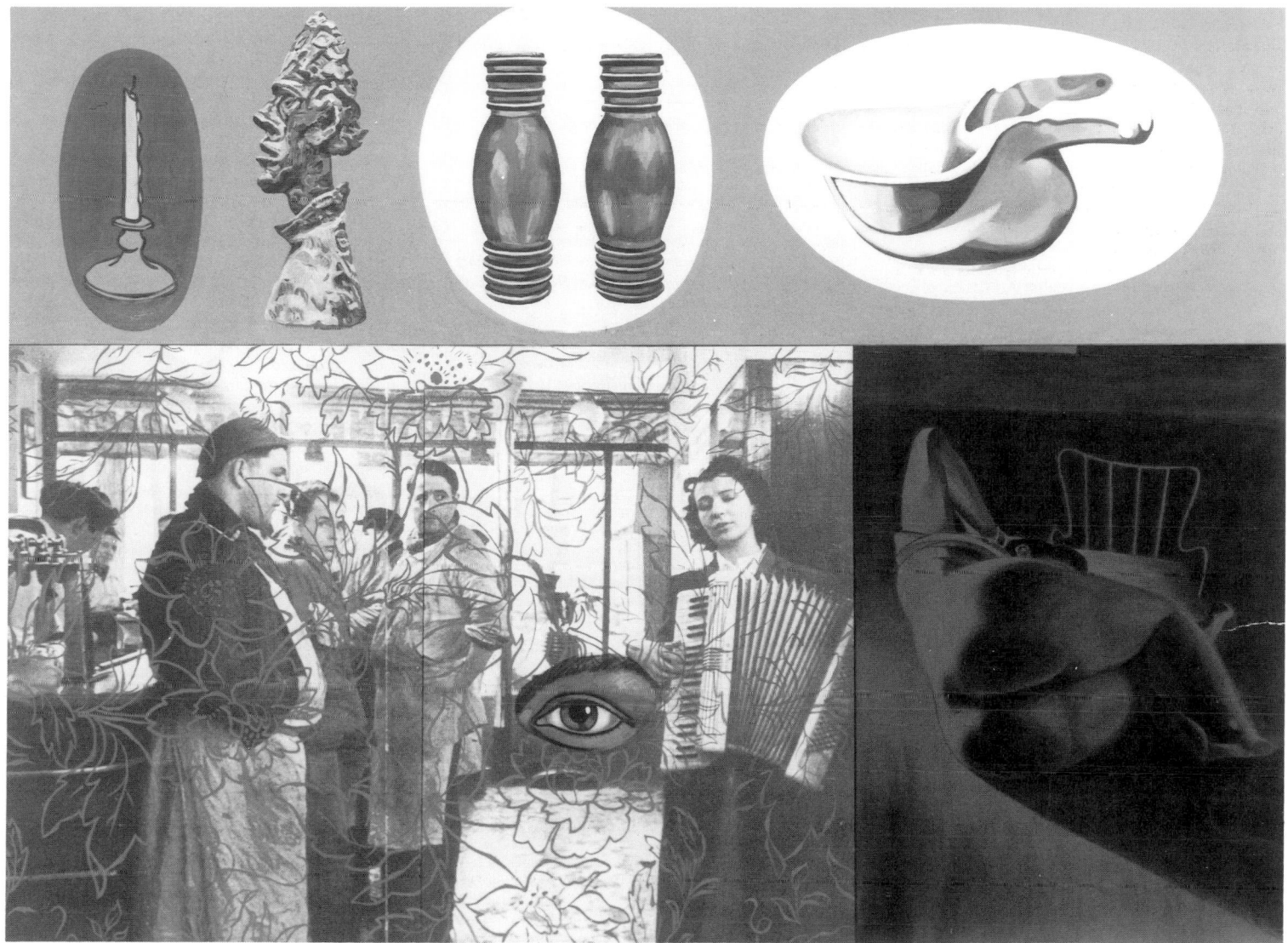

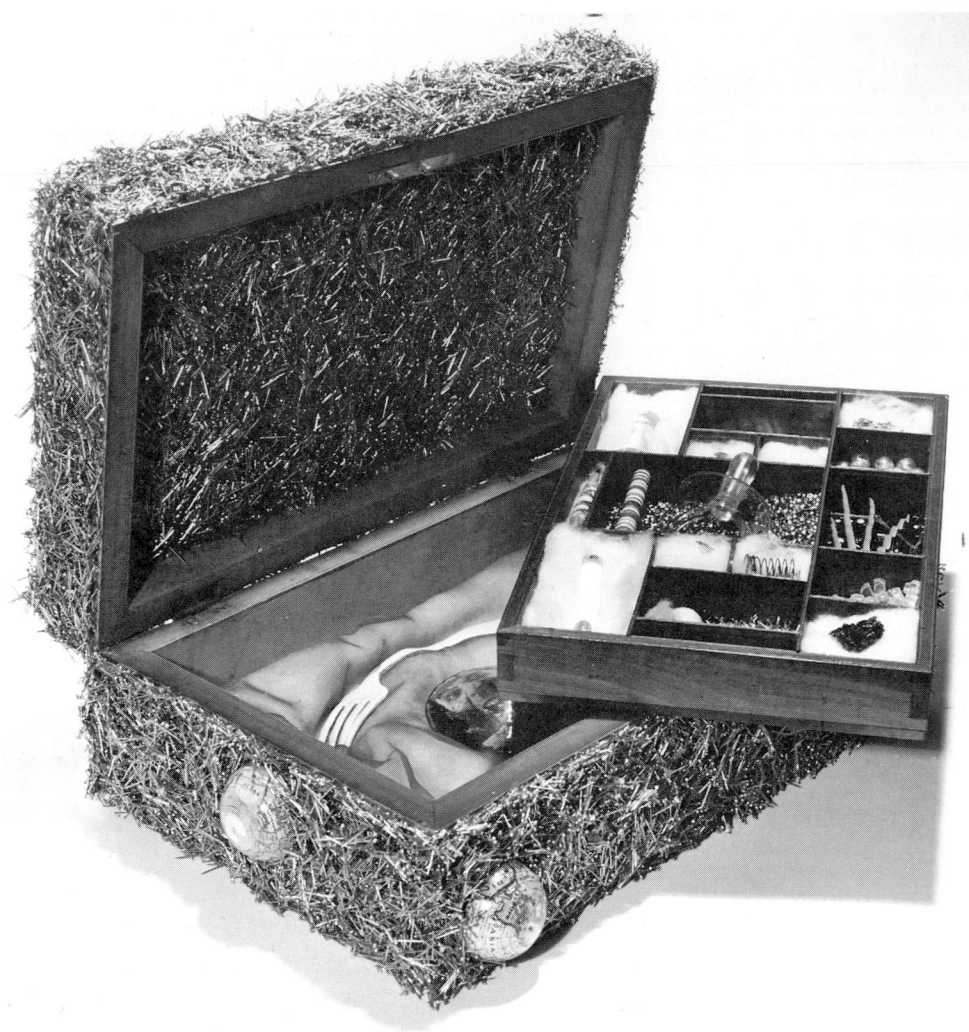

Lucas Samaras: *Box No. 92*, 1974

A.C.A. Gallery, Alberta College of Art, Calgary
Phantasmata, Pace Gallery, New York
Margo Leavin Gallery, Los Angeles
1977 *Photo-Transformations*, Galerie Zabriskie, Paris
Photo-Transformations, Walker Art Center, Minneapolis
1978 *Reconstructions*, Pace Gallery, New York
Mayor Gallery, London
Reconstructions and Photo-Transformations, Akron Art Institute, Ohio
1979 Richard Gray Gallery, Chicago
1980 *Reconstructions*, Pace Gallery, New York
Reconstructions, Photo-Transformations and Word Drawings, Pace Gallery, Columbus, Ohio
Polaroid Photographs, Pace Gallery, New York
1981 Galerie Watari, Tokyo
1982 *Pastels, Lowe Art* Museum, University of Miami
1983 *Photographs 1969-83*, Centre Georges Pompidou, Paris
Kunstverein, Frankfurt
1984 *Polaroid Photographs 1969-83*, International Center of Photography, New York
Chairs, Heads, Panoramas, Pace Gallery, New York
1985 Madison Art Center, Wisconsin
Pace Gallery, New York
1986 *Polaroid Photographs*, Serpentine Gallery, London
Mayor Gallery, London

Selected Group Exhibitions:

1961 *The Art of Assemblage*, Museum of Modern Art, New York
1967 *American Sculpture of the 60's*, Los Angeles County Museum of Art
1968 *The Obsessive Image*, Institute of Contemporary Arts, London

1974 *Photography in America*, Whitney Museum, New York
1977 *Documenta* 6, Kassel, West Germany
1978 *Mirrors and Windows: American Photography since 1960*, Museum of Modern Art, New York (toured the United States, 1978-80)
1979 *One of a Kind: Polaroid Color*, Corcoran Gallery, Washington, D.C. (toured the United States)
1980 *La Photo Polaroid*, Musée d'Art Moderne, Paris
1983 *Arranged Image Photography*, Boise Gallery, Idaho
1986 *Photography as Performance*, The Photographers' Gallery, London

Collections:

Metropolitan Museum of Art, New York; Museum of Modern Art, New York; Whitney Museum, New York; Guggenheim Museum, New York; Albright-Knox Art Gallery, Buffalo, New York; Larry Aldrich Museum, Ridgefield, Connecticut; Wadsworth Atheneum, Hartford, Connecticut; Art Institute of Chicago; Walker Art Center, Minneapolis; Los Angeles County Museum of Art.

Publications:

By SAMARAS: books—*Samaras Album, Autobiography, Autointerview, Autopolaroids*, New York 1971; *Lucas Samaras: Photo-Transformations*, with text by Arnold B. Glimcher, New York 1975; *Lucas Samaras*, with text by Kim Levin, New York 1975; *Photos, Polaroid Photographs 1969-1983*, exhibition catalogue, New York 1984; articles—"An Exploratory Dissection of Seeing" in *Artforum* (New York), December 1967; "Greece 1967; A Reconstituted Diary" in *Artforum* (New York), October 1968; "Autopolaroids and Autointerview" in *Art in America* (New York), November December 1970; "The Art of Portraiture, in the Words of Four New York Artists" in the *New York Times*, 31 October

1976; interview, with Barbara Rose, in *Samaras: Reconstructions*, exhibition catalogue, New York 1978; interview in *Artists in Their Own Words* by Paul Cummings, New York 1979. film—*Self*, 1969.

On SAMARAS: books—*Samaras: Selected Works 1960-66*, exhibition catalogue, with text by Lawrence Alloway, New York 1966; *Chair Transformations*, exhibition catalogue, New York 1970; *Samaras: Selected Works 1960-1969*, exhibition catalogue, with text by Joan Siegfried and Lawrence Alloway, Chicago 1971; *Lucas Samaras' Boxes*, exhibition catalogue, with text by Joan Siegfried, Chicago 1971; *American Art in the 20th Century* by Sam Hunter, New York 1973; *Photography in America*, edited by Robert Doty, with an introduction by Minor White, New York and London 1974; *Art in Boxes* by Alex Mogelon and Norman Laliberte, New York 1974; *Lucas Samaras* by Kim Levin, New York 1975; *Mirrors and Windows: American Photography since 1960* by John Szarkowski, New York 1978; *Lucas Samaras: Photographs 1969-1983*, exhibition catalogue with essays by Roger Marcel Mayon and William A. Ewing, Paris 1983; *Lucas Samaras: Chairs, Heads, Panoramas*, exhibition catalogue with text by Douglas Blau, New York 1984.

Lucas Samaras is one of the most brilliant and respected of the American artists to have come to prominence during the post-abstract reaction of the 1960's. His work was in the forefront of that art which kept alive the possibilities of an expressionist-surrealist idiom; while incorporating some of the radical attitudes of that time—about personal revelation, common object reference, environmental art, bodily performance, serial production—his art nonetheless remained a traditional visual art product. And it may be this perennial confidence in the object and its existential power—the anxiety within his work is always immediate—that is a prime source of the satisfaction which his art often inspires.

Samaras' work originates from the strong Surrealist milieu omnipresent in New York City. Most influential was his personal acquaintance with the group of artists who would form the Pop Art movement, and others with equally strong object orientation such as Rauschenberg and Johns. As Samaras left behind the coarse materials of his earliest works—plaster, tin foil, rags—to assume the fragile and meticulous elegance of his mature works as in the "Boxes" series from the mid-60's on, the influence of Joseph Cornell was clearly felt.

It is no doubt meaningful to ascribe some important part of the bizarre intensity and glee in both self-examination and object-obsession that pervade his work to Samaras' fantastic early boyhood experiences in his native Greece which he left in 1948 to come to the U.S. at the age of 12. He clearly recalls—his *Autobiography* is in continual progress and he has constantly produced stories whose characters and attitudes can be felt in his visual work—his home town where there were 72 churches for 10,000 people; where the dead were unburied after three years and their bones, with which he played, placed in black boxes along the church walls; where the Greek Civil War raged and shots and executions were frequent. He is himself elusive and secretive, and it might be said that his production is an effort both to retain and yet transmute the sense of life's intensity and fragility learned in his early years.

Although much of his major work in the 1960's was done with assemblage materials, the objects were rarely themselves exotic, becoming so only through the artist's manipulations. Critical attention has rightly been focused on the hurtful, inherently destructive objects—the knives, pins, tacks, razor blades—which proliferate in the "Boxes" series; yet an older Surrealist romance also accompanies these in the shells, jewel-like glitter, stuffed birds, and the pervasive sense of obscene treasure. But the eclectic nature of Samaras' imagination can also invest American Pop art-like objects—hardware, pencils, X-Rays—with a personal and perverse magic.

The "Boxes," which accumulated to about 80, were the microworlds, with dimensions not larger than 20 inches, which allowed him at that time to develop his passion for personal expression via the older European surreal traditions of fetishism and the elusive literal. But equally a trademark and an almost ironic foil for these emblems of illness and maso-sadistic urgings, was Samaras' assumption of the Pop Art use of the rainbow spectrum and its perhaps universal sense of magic and good cheer. It often appeared on the boxes as a tight banding of yarns. Samaras' uncanny ability to manipulate the literal and produce a heart-felt yet ironic wit—his work is never sentimental—is also clearly felt in his "Transformations" series: knives, chair, eyeglasses, utensils, etc., are all subjected in the later 60's to both stylistic and its concomitant expressive alterations.

Aside from the drawings and small, icon-like acrylic paintings which he has continuously produced, some other important work of the 1960's may seem, at first, unrelated to the spirit of the assemblages. In 1964, Samaras produced a full-sized *Room* for a gallery exhibition. Related of course to his Happenings experience and his on-going personal sense of the necessity to incorporate all of his life in his work, this first room—never reassembled for exhibition—was a replica of his life-stage and filled with actual objects. Much better known are the "Mirror" room works of 1966-68 where all the surfaces both inside and out, including the furniture, were made of mirrors. If the on-going metaphor of Samaras' art is the transformation available in the juxtaposition of pathos and elegance, of mundaneness and glamour, it is here, as elsewhere in his art, kept in delicate balance.

The "Cut-Paper Drawings," a long series in 1968—a format returned to in 1975 in the similarly flat, cut, and now painted aluminum works—are cut white papers placed against dark backgrounds to create images from the silhouetted white papers. In this fragile and virtuoso contrivance, perhaps also in their reference to an older folk art tradition, these works are all the more perverse as the cutting process which naturally produced them in the first place, and may be read as a pun upon their frequently threatening subject matter.

From both his life-long involvement with theatre (Samaras has been a drama student sporadically) and his penchant for self-revelation has come his commitment to the visual arts as a field for literal self-presentation. In his use of his body, Samaras thus parallels and anticipates the recent phenomenon of Body and Performance Art. And in contrast to other recent erotic art, for instance Oldenburg's sexual similes with their peculiarly American phallic innocence, Samaras' subtlety and fantasy make the viewer seem truly a voyeur, and his art has thrived on a wide array of androgynous display—especially in the 1970's with his photograph series unrelentingly featuring his body.

Samaras' preoccupation with photography so that it has become his leading medium began after the completion of the movie *Self* in 1969. This major body of work, entirely based upon the instant image-making inherent in the Polaroid photographic print, is available only on the miniature stage of the 2 by 3 inch format of the photograph. Yet through the sense of "actuality" which we tend to associate with a photograph, Samaras is able to reiterate that sense of the immediate literal present, so much a part of the attraction of his earlier work; and even more compelling, he has extended and intensified his opportunities and skills in presenting "transformations."

In a fascinating and characteristic exhaustive display of invention, Samaras at first ("Autopolaroids" 1970-71) showed multiple exposures and color changes within the camera itself, together at times with further painting and drawing upon the finished photographic print surface; then in the "Phototransformations," 1973-74, using the recently available Polaroid transfer-dye print process (SX-70), he reworked the actual color chemistry of the print surface. In the traditional two-dimensional pictorial format, Samaras has been able, as he did in his earlier sculptural work, to enliven an existent modernist tradition—but here significantly by his intuitive use of a technological instrument. Few have done better.

His recent bodies of work include the series of varied fabric fragments sewn into often very large flat

patterns, "Reconstructions"—which he has called homage to his mother's vision. In 1977, Samaras continued his "body art" "Phototransformations" as "Phantasmata": the already familiar/self images in his living quarters altered by surface manipulation on the polaroid print itself, and here extended by the use of colored lights, slide projectors, and fabrics all involving the artist's body. In 1981, he returned to this format, but now in the large polaroids—20 by 24 inches—and produced the series "Sittings" where Samaras' head appeared at the margin of images of art world personalities in the nude and surrounded by the paraphernalia which heretofore he had lavished only upon himself. There was no surface alteration of the literal print itself.

The *Panoramas* in 1983 were horizontal images composed of narrow vertically cut strips of Polaroid prints, reassembled to produce a strobe-like picture with staccato, multiple appearances of figures. As usual in his work, whatever formalist references were felt—here Cubo-Futurist—were rendered irrelevant by Samaras' rolling anxiety and energy. His early 1980s works also include pastel drawings of heads, and casts of complex modeled clay figures, all with a gruff expressionist style and compounded bodies and body parts.

Similarly grotesque and mocking, a group of Giacometti-like heads of art world representatives shown as rotting death's heads, were his first return to painting in 16 years (1985). Just so, the artist returned to youthful techniques in the 1987 *Chair Transformations*. The wire hanger-based forms were filled with an irrational assemblage of tasteless mundane objects manipulated towards a Surreal decadence.

While bodies of work so clearly predicated upon "self" have often been exhausted and become mannered upon the artist's psychic exhaustion, Samaras' wit, candor and formalist sense allow him to carry his art forward.

—Joshua Kind

SANDBACK, Fred.

American. Born in Bronxville, New York, 29 August 1943. Educated at Williston Academy, Easthampton, Massachusetts, 1957-61, and Theodor Heuss Gymnasium, Heilbronn, West Germany, 1961-62; studied at Yale University, New Haven, Connecticut, 1962-66, B.A. 1966: and Yale School of Art and Architecture, 1966-69, B.F.A. 1967; M.F.A. 1969. Recipient: Creative Artists Program Service Grant, New York, 1972. Agent: John Weber Gallery, 142 Greene Street. New York, New York 10012. Address: 561 Broadway, New York, New York 10012, U.S.A.

Individual Exhibitions:

1968	Galerie Konrad Fischer, Dusseldorf
	Galerie Heiner Friedrich, Munich
1969	Dwan Gallery, New York
	Ace Gallery, Los Angeles
	Museum Haus Lange, Krefeld, West Germany
1970	Galleria Francoise Lambert, Milan
	Galerie Yvon Lambert, Paris
	Dwan Gallery, New York
	Galerie Reckermann, Cologne
	Galerie Heiner Friedrich, Munich
1971	Galerie Annemarie Verna, Zurich
1972	John Weber Gallery, New York
	Galerie Annemarie Verna, New York
	Galerie Reckermann, Cologne
	Galerie Heiner Friedrich, Munich
	Galerie Diogenes, Berlin
1973	Galerie Nachst St. Stephan, Vienna
	Galerie Heiner Friedrich, Munich
	Galerie im Taxispalais, Innsbruck
	Kunsthalle, Berne
1974	John Weber Gallery, New York
	Galleria Martano, Turin
	Galleria Milano, Milan
	Galleria Primo Piano, Rome
	Galerie Heiner Friedrich, Munich
	Studio Schloss Morsbroich, Leverkusen, West Germany
	Clocktower, New York
	Folkwang Museum, Essen
1975	Galerie Heiner Friedrich, Munich
	Kunstraum, Munich
	Galerie Müller-Roth, Stuttgart
	Galerie Dorothea Loehr, Frankfurt
1976	Brooke Alexander Inc., New York
	Galerie Heiner Friedrich, Munich
	John Weber Gallery, New York
	Galerie Annemarie Verna, Zurich
	Galleria Primo Piano, Rome
	Galerie Durand-Dessert, Paris
1977	Lisson Gallery, London
	Hester Van Royen Gallery, London
1978	Galerie Heiner Friedrich, Munich
	Heiner Friedrich Gallery, New York
	P.S.1. Long Island City, New York
	Museum of Modern Art, New York
1981	Galerie Annemarie Verna, Zurich
	Fred Sandback Museum, Winchendon, Massachusetts
	Galerie Durand-Dessert, Paris
1982	Galerie Editions Media, Neuchatel, Switzerland
1983	Marian Goodman Gallery, New York
	Fred Sandback Museum, Winchendon, Massachusetts
	Galerie Fred Jahn, Munich
	University of Massachusetts, Amherst
1984	Galerie Le Consortium, Dijon, France
1985	University of Illinois, Champaign
	Kunsthaus, Zurich
	Galerie Durand-Dessert, Paris
	Marian Goodman Gallery, New York
1986	Kunsthalle, Mannheim, West Germany
1987	Westfalischer Kunstverein, Munster, West Germany
1988	Galerie Fred Jahn, Munich

Selected Group Exhibitions:

1968	*Artists Under 40*, Whitney Museum, New York
1969	*New Media/New Methods*, Museum of Modern Art, New York
	When Attitudes Become Form, Kunsthalle, Berne (toured West Germany and the U.K.)
1971	*Sonsbeek 1971*, Arnhem, Netherlands
1974	*Multiples*, Kunstverein, Berlin
1976	*Drawing Now*, Museum of Modern Art, New York
1980	*Pier and Ocean*, Hayward Gallery, London
1981	*Construction in Process*, Muzeum Sztuki, Lodz, Poland
1983	*Presence Discrete*, Musee des Beaux-Arts, Dijon, France
1985	*Vom Zeichen*, Kunstverein, Frankfurt

Collections:

Museum of Modern Art, New York; Whitney Museum, New York; Rhode Island School of Design, Providence; Kaiser-Wilhelm Museum, Krefeld, West Germany.

Publications:

On SANDBACK: books—*Fred Sandback* by Hermann Kern, Munich 1975; *Fred Sandback: Sculpture 1966-86*, exhibition catalogue with texts by Manfred Fath and Fred Jahn, Mannheim 1986; articles—"Fred Sandback at Dwan" in *Arts Magazine* (New York), May 1970; "Lettre de New York" by J. Patrice Marendel in *Art International* (Lugano, Switzerland), Summer 1970; "Sculpture at Sonsbeek" by Carel Blotkamp in *Studio International* (London), September 1971; "Fred Sandback" by Ellen Lubell in *Arts Magazine* (New York), May 1974; "Reviews" by Lawrence Alloway in *Artforum* (New York), May 1974; "Question: How Do You Buy a Work of Art Like This?" by Roy Bongartz in the *New York Times*, 11 August 1974.

From around 1967-68, Fred Sandback has persistently continued in his singular development consisting of extremely spare, geometrically based, linear constructions in space made out of colored yarn or elastic or painted rope. Sandback's work relates closely to the prominent development in the 1960s of Minimal/Conceptual sculptural forms which use little materials to define large spaces. Sandback's work is closest in its conceptual underpinnings to the oeuvre of Sol LeWitt and Barry Le Va, the difference being that Sandback pushes his visualizations even closer to the edge of the invisible, hovering on the extreme point wherein dematerialization is about to occur.

In Sandback's constructions of the late 1960s, placement was at first against the wall, using geometrical shapes in repetition and then moving to singular and larger shapes. Sandback next began stretching his linear materials across rooms which became his "framing" environments of three dimensional space, defining shapes less specific than before. He moved into creation of combinations of both these types of configurations, using simpler configurations and more expansive spaces. Sandback has also made serial pieces, installed in the gallery at different times over the interval of the exhibition. In "Sixteen Two-Part Pieces" (1974), for example, two lengths of dark yarn crossing the small room were changed sixteen times to produce variations on the theme which he had systematically worked out through a diagrammatic drawing. For a 1978 installation, Sandback made three separate "Constructions," which were shown variously over a period of several weeks. In many ways, the initial diagrams/drawings for the works convey enough information in themselves to perceive the constructions' possible implications, yet their physical makeup achieves an illusionistic inference and spatial experience not possible through the concept alone nor through the two dimensional plan. Depending on the viewer's placement of self in just the right spot, the linear is transformed into an inference of the volumetric; the fragile, thin threads appear to become the edges of planes and/or geometrical shapes. The illusion of volume is hypothetical yet made visible tenuously, dependent on physical placement and mental involvement. This tension between what is really there and what seems to be there infers the tenuous nature of relationships between premises and the visualizations which follow them. It is not unlike the juxtapositions of drawings and written theorems found in geometrical texts.

One problem in Sandback's work is whether the geometrical basis is transformed adequately enough to warrant its being called art. The major problem, though, rests on the question of whether Sandback's longtime repetition of such strict limitations can retain any real significance, either conceptually or visually.

—Barbara Cavaliere

SANDLE, Michael.

British. Born in Weymouth, Dorset, 18 May 1936. Educated in Douglas, Isle of Man: studied drawing, painting and lithography at Douglas School of Art and Technology, Isle of Man, 1954-56; Slade School of Fine Art, London, 1956-59. Married Cynthia Dora Koppel in 1972 (divorced, 1974). Graphic artist and sculptor: worked as a lithographer. Paris, 1959-60; Founder-Member, with Cristina Bertoni, Laurence Brut, Michael Chilton and others, Leicester Group, 1961-63; associated with members of Art and Language group while living in Coventry, 1964-68. Part-time Assistant Lecturer, Foundation Studies Department, Leicester College of Art, 1961-63; Lecturer Coventry College of Art, 1964-68; Visiting Professor, University of Calgary, Alberta, 1970-71; Visiting Associate Professor, University of Victoria, British Columbia, 1971-72; Lecturer, 1973, and Professor in Sculpture, 1977, Fachhochschule für Gestaltung, Pforzheim, West Germany. Professor in Sculpture, Akademie der Bildenden Künste, Karlsruhe, West Germany, since 1980. Recipient: Abbey Minor Travelling Scholarship, 1959; French Government Scholarship, 1960; Nobutaka Shikanai Prize, *Rodin International Exhibition*, Hakone Open-Air Museum, Japan, 1986; Chantrey Bequest Award, 1987. Agent: Fischer Fine Art. King Street, London SWI, England. Address: c/o Kunststoff Institut, Schloss Scheibenhardt, 7500 Karlsruhe, West Germany.

Individual Exhibitions:

1963	Drian Galleries. London
1966	Grabowski Gallery. London (with Ivor Abrahams and Michael Chilton)
1975	*Drawing Exhibition*, Haus am Lützow Platz. West Berlin
	Galerie der Spiegel, Cologne
	Drawing Exhibition, Galerie Suzanne Fischer, Baden-Baden, West Germany
1976	Galerie Hecate, Paris
	Bernard Jacobson Gallery, New York
	Felicity Samuel Gallery, London
1977	Galerie 2, Stuttgart
1981	Fischer Fine Art, London
1983	Kunstverein, Mannheim, West Germany
1984	Wilhelm Lehmbruck Museum, Duisburg, West Germany
1985	Fischer Fine Art, London

Selected Group Exhibitions:

1965	*Inner Image*, Grabowski Gallery, London
1967	*Biennale*, Paris
1968	*Documenta*, Kassel, West Germany
1972	*British Sculptors*, Royal Academy of Arts, London
1975	*DAAD Ausstellung*, Haus am Lützow Platz, West Berlin
1977	*Le Dessin*, Musée d'Art Moderne de la Ville, Paris
1978	*Hayward Annual*, Hayward Gallery, London
1982	*British Sculpture in the 20th Century*, Whitechapel Art Gallery, London
1984	*The Geometry of Rage*, Arnolfini Gallery, Bristol
1986	*Das Andere Land*, Nationalgalerie, West Berlin (toured West Germany and Luxembourg)

Collections:

British Museum, London; Imperial War Museum, London; Victoria and Albert Museum, London; Museum of Modern Art, New York: Metropolitan Museum of Art, New York; Museum of Fine Arts, Dallas: Wilhelm Lehmbruck Museum, Duisburg, West Germany; Kunsthalle, Stuttgart; National Gallery, Warsaw; Museum of Fine Arts, Lodz, Poland.

Publications:

By SANDLE: statements—in *Inner Image*, exhibition catalogue, London 1965: in *Abrahams, Chilton, Sandle*, exhibition catalogue, London 1966: in *Michael Sandle Drawing Exhibition*. exhibition catalogue. Baden-Baden, West Germany 1975; in *Michael Sandle Drawing Exhibition*, catalogue, Berlin 1975; in *Hayward Annual*, exhibition catalogue, 1978; "In eigener Sache" in *Michael Sandle 1984*, exhibition catalogue, Duisburg 1984; in *Celtic Vision*, exhibition catalogue, Madrid 1986.

On SANDLE: books—*Art in Britain* by Edward LucieSmith and Patricia White, London 1969; *6 at the Hayward*, exhibition catalogue, by Michael Compton, London 1969; *British Sculptors*, exhibition catalogue, by Bryan Robertson, London 1972; *Michael Sandle Drawing Exhibition*, exhibition catalogue, by Karl Ruhrberg, Berlin 1975; *Michael Sandle*, exhibition catalogue, by John McEwen, London 1981; *Michael Sandle*, exhibition catalogue with essay by Kurt Lankheit, Mannheim 1983; *Michael Sandle 1984*, exhibition catalogue with text by Karl-Egon Vester, Duisburg 1984; *The Geometry of Rage*, exhibition catalogue with texts by Sarah Kent, Lewis Biggs and James Stevens Curl, Bristol 1984; *Visages Contemporains de la Sculpture en Europe*, exhibition catalogue by Gerhard Fries, Maubeuge 1985.

I have always worked towards the goal of achieving a synthesis of my disparate or seemingly irreconcilable notions of content, form and intention. Objectively, I know this to be almost impossible but it is my bad luck to be programmed to keep trying and, what is worse, care about it when I fail.

It is my misfortune to see art (read life) as a conflict, as an enervating struggle against mediocrity; in the first instance my own. We do, however, live in times of stupendous, quite heroic mediocrity. It is more than depressing to see the visual arts contaminated with the "New Spirit" of cynicism, or, what is even worse, through benign "democratic" agencies, being turned into a meaningless pap.

Bad art serves one good purpose, I find. However sharp the feelings of anguish and despair at my own shortcomings may be, I believe that there are hundreds who should shoot themselves first.

—Michael Sandle

Michael Sandle is one of the most gifted and enigmatic British artists of his generation. His drawings and sculptures are unlike those of any of his contemporaries, and, indeed, one must go back to Victorian comic draughtsmen and fantasists to establish any likely lineage.

He works extremely slowly, so that whilst he has often been included in group shows, he has never, in fact, held a one-man exhibition of any dimension. He describes himself as an "expressionist," and says that his work is compounded of nostalgia, dreams and perception. Sandle is a deeply personal, introverted artist, concerned, as he has stated, with magic and wonder, the very opposite of detached intellectualism. This romantic, poetic stance is clearly not pretentious, but rather the outcome of a very special kind of personality.

It would, however, be wrong and misleading to suggest that Sandle's rare, but impressive, work is in any way twee or indulgent. Both in his drawings and sculpture it is clear that his method is based on selection and isolation, so that whilst separate images or elements can be directly traced to known reality, in their assembling they take on a life of their own. Equally confusing is the remarkable range of source-inspiration called upon by Sandle: nature, animal forms, architecture and design, as well as the diverse materials used in his sculptures, polyester resin, glass fibre and brass.

Basically he is a "black and white" artist, and in this sense, as well as in a more subtle and deeper connotation, he bears a definite relationship to the important tradition of English illustrators, including Aubry Beardsley. Sandle is a fantastist and surrealistic, his large, hieratic, heraldic sculptures emerging as almost Disneyish illustrations for *Alice in Wonderland*, but, although compounded of a strange wit and remarkable invention, they are in no sense coy or merely humorous. Neither are they violent or aggressive. They are, indeed, within his own terms, dreamlike, strange beings almost natural, yet at the same time invented.

Charles Spencer

SANEJOUAND, Jean-Michel.

French. Born in Lyon, 18 July 1934. Studied law, then politics, Lyon, 1951-55; self-taught in art, from 1955. Married Michelle Bourgeois in 1957; sons: Yves-Henri and Ludovic. Independent artist, Lyon, 1955-59, and in Paris since 1959: abstract paintings,

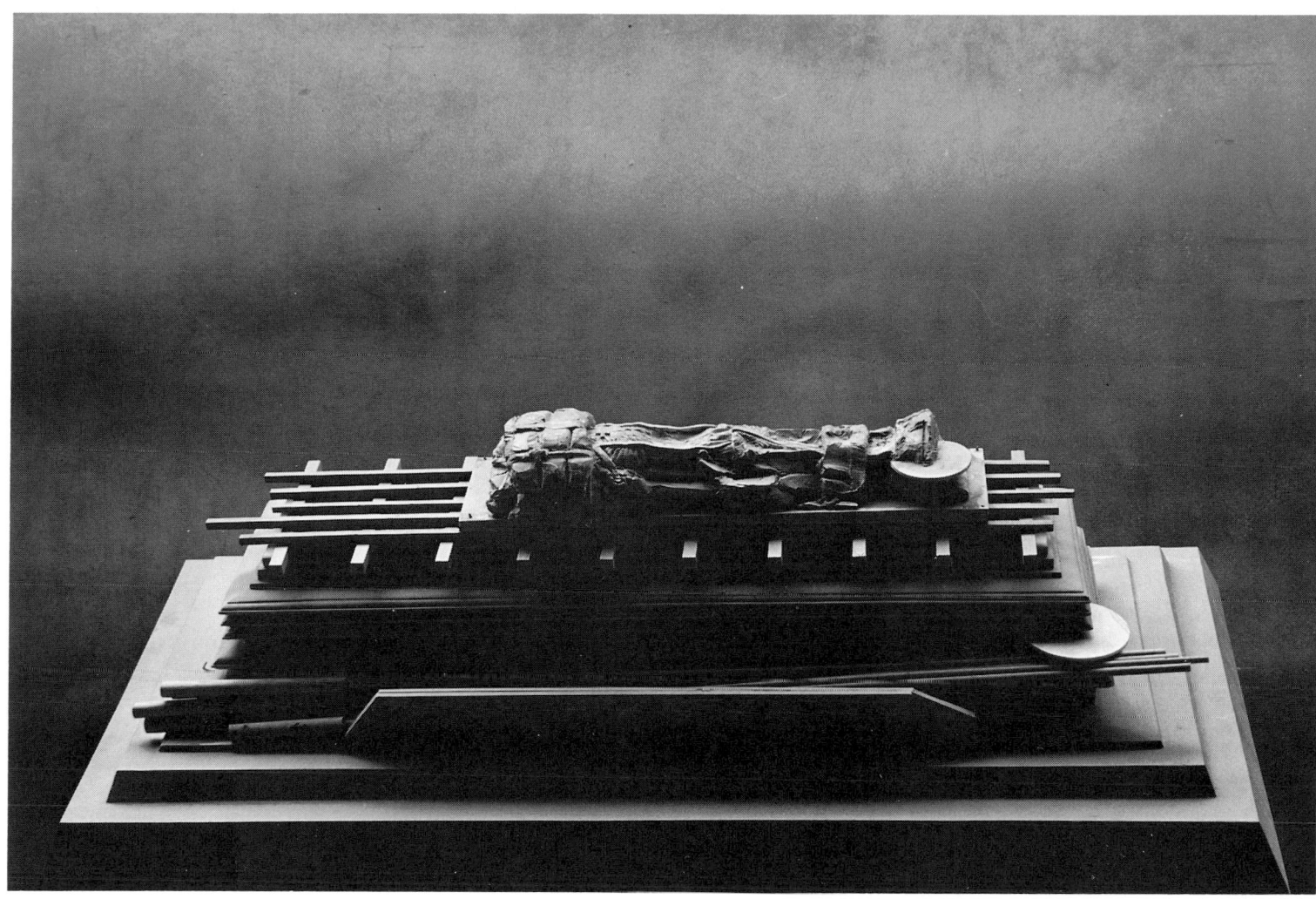

Michael Sandle: *Catafalque for Anton Bruckner*, 1981

1955–62; "object-load" assemblage and environmental works, 1963–75; calligraphic works on canvas, 1969–78; painted and drawn works since 1978. Address: 27 rue Jasmin, 75016 Paris, France.

Individual Exhibitions:

1964	Galerie Yvette Morin, Paris (with Smerck and Chabaut)
1965	Salon Regain, Lyon (with Smerck and Jacquet)
1967	Ecole Polytechnique, Paris
1968	Galerie Yvon Lambert, Paris
1970	Galerie Mathias Fels, Paris
1973	Centre National d'Art Contemporain, Paris
	Palais des Beaux-Arts, Brussels
1974	Internationaal Cultureel Centrum, Antwerp
	Galerie Germain, Paris
1975	Galerie Germain, Paris
1979	The Antwerpen Gallery, at *FIAC 79*, Grand Palais, Paris
1982	Galerie de France, Paris
	Lens Fine Art, Antwerp
1986	Espace Claudine Breguet, Paris
	Palais des Beaux Arts, Lyon, France

Selected Group Exhibitions:

1964	*La Leçon des Choses*, Galerie du Ranelagh, Paris
1967	*Superlund*, Lunds Konsthall, Sweden
1969	*Le Décor Quotidien de la Vie en 1968*, Musée Galliera, Paris
1970	*Information*, Museum of Modern Art, New York
1971	*Peintures et Objets*, Musée Galliera, Paris
1972	*Amsterdam-Paris-Dusseldorf*, Guggenheim Museum, New York
1976	*Biennale*, Venice
1982	*Actuele Franse Kunst*, Internationaal Cultureel Centrum, Antwerp
1983	*Zwanzig Jahre Kunst in Frankreich 1960–80*, Kunstmuseum, Mainz, West Germany (travelled to Tubingen and West Berlin)
1986	*Qu'est ce que l'art francais?*, Centre Régionale d'Art Contemporain, Labège, France (travelled to Innopole and Toulouse)

Collections:

Fonds National d'Art Contemporain, Paris; Musée National d'Art Moderne/Centre Georges Pompidou, Paris; Musée d'Art Moderne de la Ville de Paris; Musée St. Pierre d'Art Contemporain, Lyon; Collection Mobilier National, Gobelins.

Publications:

By SANEJOUAND: books—*Introduction aux espaces concrets*, Paris 1970; *Plans d'organisations d'espaces*, Paris 1970; interviews—with Pierre Cabanne, in *Matinees de France Culture*(Paris), April 1968; with Daniel Abadie, in *Archives du CNAC*(Paris), September 1971; with Catherine Millet, in *Art Press*(Paris), no. 3, 1973; with Jacques Bertoin, in *Arte Factum*(Antwerp), no. 1, 1983; with Alain Avila and Valere Bertrand, in *France Culture*(Paris), 21 April 1986; films—*Soda*, 1965; *Trente-Trois Minutes, Neuf Secondes*, 1967; *L'Espace de la Tour Nord Est du Grand Palais*, 1972; *Quelques Espaces*, 1973.

On SANEJOUAND: books—*Neue Dimensionen der Plastik* by Udo Kultermann, Tubingen 1967; *Jean-Michel Sanejouand: Deux Organisations d'Espaces*, exhibition catalogue with essay by Gregoire Muller, Paris 1968; *Jean Michel Sanejouand: Plans d'Organisations d'Espaces*, exhibition catalogue with text by Pierre Restany, Paris 1970; *Sanejouand Ruimtelijke organisatie in het Koniklijk paleis (ICC) te Antwerpen* exhibition catalogue with text by Claude Devos, Antwerp 1974; *Actuele Franse Kunst*, exhibition catalogue with text by Florent Bex, Antwerp 1982; *Zwanzig Jahre Kunst in Frankreich 1960–1980*, exhibition catalogue with essay by Marcelin Pleynet, Mainz 1983; *Jean-Michel Sanejouand*, exhibition catalogue with text by Bernard Lamarche-Vadel, Paris 1986.

When I stopped painting at the end of 1962 I was convinced that it was the final break. For the previous few years I had painted abstracts as now on white backgrounds. To a very superficial observer today they might appear quite similar to my current work. My panting was confined to a fairly naive, purely imaginary space. The "object-loads", ("charges-objects"), my arrangements of pieces of striped tarpaulin, metal grating, strips of printed linoleum and so on which replaced the paintings reflected a suddenly compelling need to experiment with real space, a tremendous urge to confront this space. They were also an acknowledgement of the ludicrous. After 1967 there was a logical progression with these arrangements making way for my work directly on concrete space in what I called my organizations of spaces. The space of various places: a courtyard, a building site, an exhibition hall, became my raw material. Everything seemed to be going fine.

Yet in 1969 I began to conceptualize my work with space more by drawing plans and I felt an urge to hold a paintbrush again, to dip it in the ink and draw figures, generally grotesque and aggressive ones. For nine years I had to struggle on with both activities: my work with actual space and then these calligraphies of mood, as I call them, which in a way were my painting resurfacing. Of course, they were not only and not entirely that—far from it! My distrust of painting still ran very deep. I would take a canvas that was ready to be painted on and would just draw a few

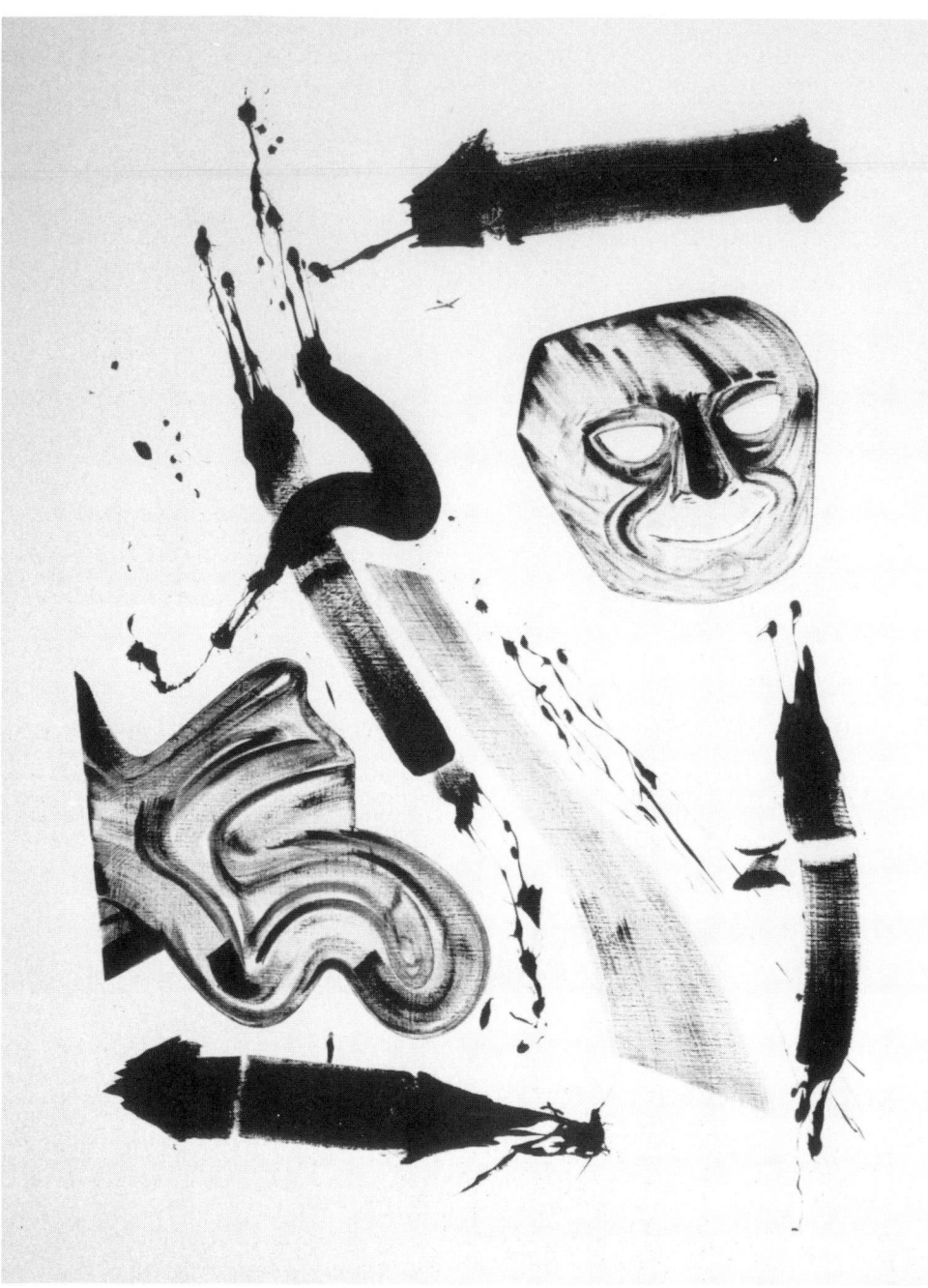

Jean-Michel Sanejouand: *Untitled*, 1987

1967–68. Travelled in Mexico, Europe and North Africa; lived in India, 1971–73; now lives and works in New York. Visiting Artist in Sculpture, University of California at Irvine, 1979. Recipient: Guggenheim Fellowship, 1969; National Endowment for the Arts Grant, 1975; Creative Artists Program Service Grant, New York, 1976. Agent: Margo Leavin Gallery, 812 North Robertson Boulevard, Los Angeles, California 90069. Address: 65 South 11th Street, New York, New York 11211, U.S.A.

Individual Exhibitions:

1968	Bykert Gallery, New York
	3 Young Americans: Krueger, Nauman, Saret, Allen Memorial Art Museum, Oberlin, Ohio
1970	Bykert Gallery, New York
1971	Katonah Gallery, Katonah, New York
1973	Clocktower, New York
1975	597 West Broadway, New York
1977	Seattle Art Museum
	And/Or, Seattle
1978	University of California, Berkeley
1979	SITE, San Francisco
	Weinberg Gallery, San Francisco
1980	Charles Cowles Gallery, New York
1981	University of Rhode Island, Kingston
	Galerie Rudolf Zwirner, Cologne
1982	Charles Cowles Gallery, New York
	Newport Harbor Art Museum, Newport Beach, California
1983	Albright-Knox Art Gallery, Buffalo, New York
	Hallwalls, Buffalo, New York

Selected Group Exhibitions:

1968	*Whitney Annual*, Whitney Museum, New York
1969	*When Attitudes Become Form*, Kunsthalle, Berne (toured Europe)
1971	*6 Sculptors: Extended Structures*, Museum of Contemporary Art, Chicago
1976	*American Art of the 20th Century*, Allen Memorial Art Museum, Oberlin, Ohio
1977	*Open to New Ideas*, University of Georgia, Athens
1980	*Biennale*, Venice
	Drawing/Structures, Institute of Contemporary Art, Boston
1981	*Developments in Recent Sculpture*, Whitney Museum, New York
1982	*Kunst Wird Material*, Nationalgalerie, West Berlin

Collections:

Whitney Museum, New York; Museum of Modern Art, New York; University of Georgia, Athens; Detroit Institute of Arts; Museum of Contemporary Art, Chicago; Dallas Museum of Fine Arts; Art Museum of South Texas, Corpus Christi; Los Angeles County Museum of Art; San Francisco Museum of Modern Art; Society of the Four Arts, Toronto.

Publications:

By SARET: article—"An Interview with Alan Saret and Jeffrey Caw" in *Avalanche* (New York), Winter 1971.

On SARET: articles—"3 Young Americans: Krueger, Nauman, Saret" by Ellen H. Johnson and Athena Spear in the *Allen Memorial Art Museum Bulletin* (Oberlin, Ohio), Spring 1968; "New York: Alan Saret, Bykert Gallery" by Emily Wasserman in *Artforum* (New York), January 1969; "9 Men in a Warehouse" by Max Kozloff in *Artforum* (New York), February 1969; "Alan Saret's Studio Exhibition" by Emily Wasserman in *Artforum* (New York), March 1970; "Methods and Materials New and Old" by B. Schwartz in *Craft Horizons* (New York), December 1975; "Alan Saret" by Jonathan Crary in *Arts Magazine* (New York), September 1977; "Alan Saret: Skulpturen und Zeichnungen" by A. Pohlen in *Kunstforum International*(Mainz), no. 1, 1981.

lines in ink. It was a difficult, even a painful experience, but I truly had no choice. I did not then understand that I only needed these calligraphies because they gave me an opportunity to work with imaginary space. The sense of the ludicrous, inaugurated in my "object-loads", was very apparent in these 'figurative' drawings, but also in my carefully elaborated plans with their undertones of a contained frenzy and in my organization of the planet Earth using "orientation tables" that I worked on from 1974 to 1977. In any event it was in 1977 that both my calligraphies of mood and my orientation tables became pictorialized.

What had happened? Quite simply, I had never stopped looking at painting all those years. Gradually the conviction that I had underestimated it took hold of me. Of course, I do not mean just any painting! Painting in general seemed to me then—and still does today—to be a rather pointless exercise. All those surfaces covered in what is often just filling bore me and even irritate me most of the time. However, I began to realize that painting, if handled with stringent discipline, could be a gateway leading on towards a different consciousness. It was also a way of not skirting the fundamental issue of transposition which is the nobility of Art.

Anyway, since 1978 which was when I accepted that I would start painting again, I have felt a lot happier, relieved, as though freed from the wearying, two-fold course which I had had to pursue.

However, I was unable to apply the analytical discipline I mentioned to my own use of the brush immediately. Not for technical reasons alone—that wasn't much of a problem—but because I could not shake off my distrust all at once. I had an absolute need to wipe my brush regularly over the canvas. It is only over the last two or three years that I have dismissed my last reservations on the subject and that I have at last been able to rise above the ludicrous smilingly.

—Jean-Michel Sanejouand

SARET, Alan (Daniel).

American. Born in New York City, 25 December 1944. Studied at Cornell University, Ithaca, New York, 1961–66, B.Arch.; Hunter College, New York,

SARKIS.

French. Born Sarkis Zabunyan, in Istanbul, Turkey, 26 September 1938; emigrated to France, 1964: naturalized, 1985. Studied at the Academy of Fine Arts, Istanbul, 1957–60. Served in the Turkish Army, Ministry of Defence, Istanbul, 1961–63: Lieutenant. Married Isil Akyuz in 1963; sons: Elvan and Dork. Worked as a part-time draughtsman in an architect's office, Istanbul, 1961–63; first paintings, 1961; full time artist, in Istanbul, 1963–64, in Paris since 1964. Professor, Ecole des Arts Decoratifs, Strasbourg, since 1980. Recipient: First Prize for Painting, *Biennale de Paris,* 1967. Chévalier, Ordre des Arts et des Lettres, Paris, 1985. Agent: Galerie Sonnabend, 12 rue Mazarine, 75006 Paris. Address: 67 rue Vergniaud, 75013 Paris, France.

Individual Exhibitions:

1967	Galerie Blumenthal, Paris
1968	Galleri Klipans, Gothenburg, Sweden
1970	Galerie Sonnabend, Paris
	Musée d'Art Moderne, Paris
1971	Galerie Sonnabend, Paris
	Galerie Handschin, Basle
1972	Kunsthalle, Dusseldorf
	Galerie Sonnabend, Paris
	Galerie Ben Doute de Tout, Nice
	Galerie Handschin, Basle
1973	Musée Galliera, Paris
	Institut Pasteur, Paris
1974	Musée d'Art et d'Industrie, Saint Etienne, France
	Galleria La Salita, Rome
	Modern Art Agency, Naples
	Galerie Sonnabend, Paris
	Galerie Handschin, Basle

1975	Galleria Cenobio-Visualita, Milan
	Galerie Le Metronome, Paris
	Galerie Sonnabend, Paris
	Galerie Handschin, Basle
	Salle d'Art Contemporain. Geneva
	Galerie Folker Skulima, West Berlin
1976	Galerie Sonnabend, Paris
	Galleria Cenobio-Visualita, Milan
1978	Westfälischer Kunstverein, Munster, West Germany
1979	Neue Galerie, Aachen, West Germany
1980	Centre des Arts Plastiques Contemporain. Bordeaux
	Galerie Sonnabend, Paris
	Galerie Attitude, Strasbourg, France
1981	Centre d'Art Contemporain, Geneva
	Galerie Baronian, Brussels
1982	Galerie J. J. Donguy, Paris
	Galerie Catherine Issert, St. Paul de Vence, France
	Galerie Eric Fabre, Paris
1983	Grand Garage, Strasbourg, France
	Tartar Gallery, Edinburgh
	Macka Sanat Galerisi, Istanbul
1984	ARC/Musée d'Art Moderne, Paris
	Galerie Eric Fabre, Paris
	DAAD-Galerie, West Berlin
1985	Chapelle Sainte Marie, Nevers, France
	Galerie Eric Fabre, Paris
	Centre D'Art Contemporain, Chateauroux, France
	Kunsthalle, Berne
	Centre d'Art Contemporain, Geneva
	Le Nouveau Musée, Villeurbanne, France
1986	Ecole Nationale d'Art Décoratif, Limoges,France
	Macka Sanat Galerisi, Istanbul
	Placard d'Eric Satie, Paris
	Galerie de Paris, Paris
1987	Maison de la Culture, La Rochelle, France
	Chateau Lynch-Bages, Bordeaux, France
	't Kromhout Museum, Amsterdam

Selected Group Exhibitions:

1967	*Biennale de Paris,* Musée d'Art Moderne, Paris (and 1969, 1971)
1969	*When Attitudes Become Form,* Kunsthalle, Berne (toured Europe)
1970	*6 Propositions,* Centre Culturel Americain, Paris
1972	*Intervention à la Galerie Duncan,* Galerie Raymond Duncan, Paris
1974	*Ars 74,* Museum Ateneum, Helsinki
1975	*Photographie dans l'Art,* Musée des Beaux-Arts, Rennes, France
1976	*Identité-Identifications.* Centre des Arts Plastiques Contemporains, Bordeaux
1982	*Documenta,* Kassel, West Germany
1985	*L'Oeil Musicien,* Palais des Beaux-Arts, Charleroi, Belgium
1987	*Maintenant,* Palais de Rohan, Strasbourg, France

Collections:

Centre Georges Pompidou, Paris; Kaiser-Wilhelm-Museum, Krefeld, West Germany; Kunstmuseum, Basle; Konstmuseum, Gothenburg, Sweden; Art Gallery of New South Wales, Sydney; Musée Saint-Pierre, Lyon; Le Nouveau Musée, Villeurbanne; Musée Cantini, Marseille; Musée de Strasbourg.

Publications:

By SARKIS: books—*La Drama of the Tempest,* St Etienne, France 1974; *Blackout,* Geneva 1975; *Der Blackout ist voller schwarzer weisser blauer roter goldener Farbe so wie der Anstreicher,* with Wolfgang Becker, Aachen, West Germany 1979; *Kriegsschatz-Klassenkrieg,* with Herbert Molderings, Münster, West Germany 1978; *Reserves sans Retour,* Bor-

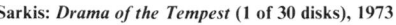

Sarkis: *Drama of the Tempest* (1 of 30 disks), 1973

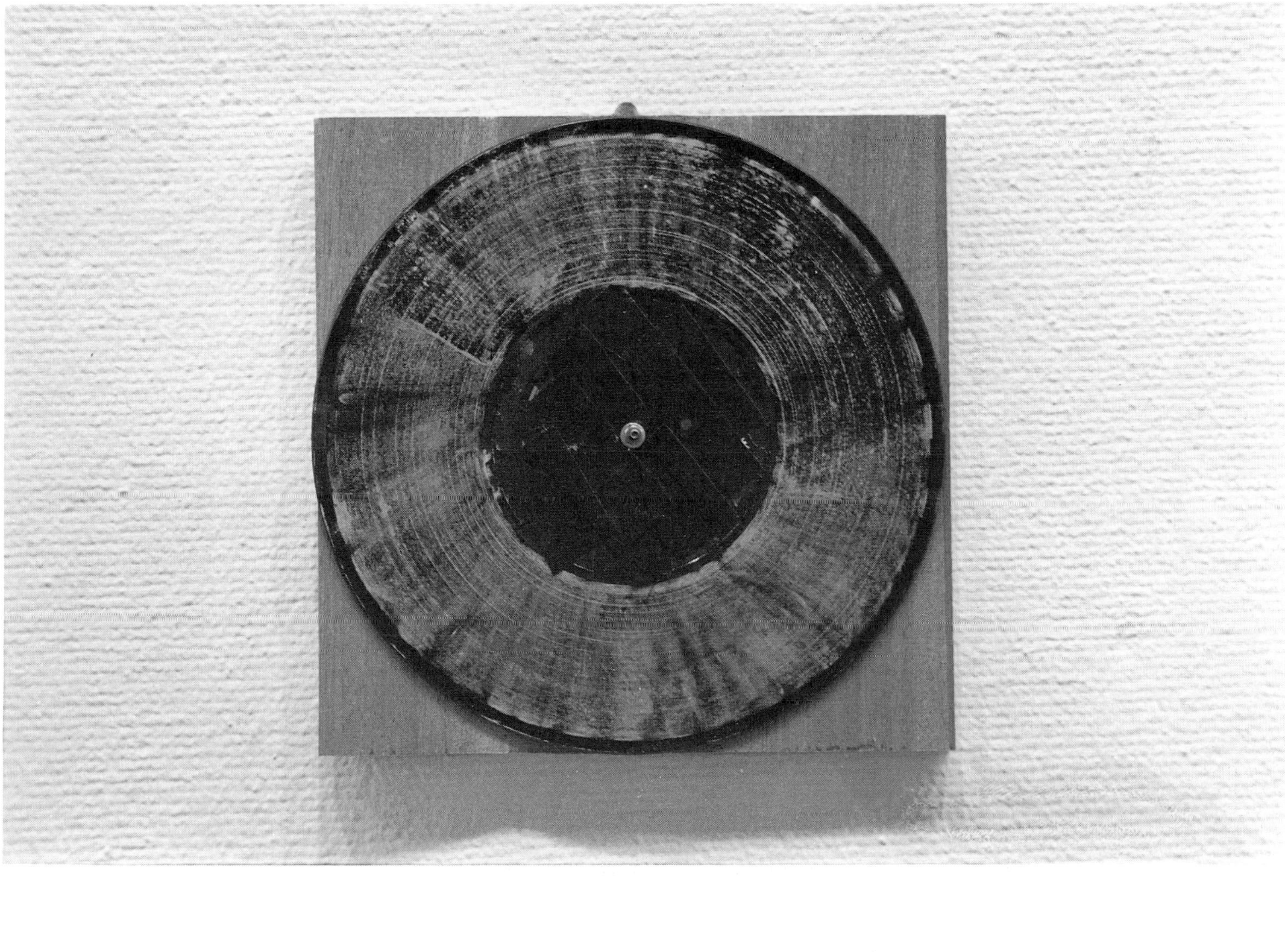

deaux 1980; discs—*Litho Disc*, Rome 1974; *La Drama of the Tempest*, Rome 1974; *Enquete . . .* , Geneva 1975.

On SARKIS: books—*Sarkis: Le Troisieme Reich. des Origines á la Chute.* exhibition catalogue, Paris 1971; *Sarkis Zabunyan*, exhibition catalogue, with an introduction by Jürgen Harten, Dusseldorf 1972; *Art en France: une nouvelle generation* by Jean Clair, Paris 1973; *Sarkis*, exhibition catalogue, with an introduction by Bernard Ceysson, St. Etienne, France 1974; *Art Actuel en France* by Anne Tronche and Hervé Gloaguen, Paris 1974: *Documenta 7* exhibition catalogue, 2 vols., edited by Rudi H. Fuchs, Kassel, West Germany 1982; *Sarkis: Der Anfang der Jahrhunderts*, exhibition catalogue with text by Claude Gintz, West Berlin 1984; *Trois Mises en Scene de Sarkis*, exhibition catalogue with text by Jean-Hubert Martin, Berne 1985; *Vie et Legende du Captain Sarkis* by Jean-Marie Touratier, Paris 1986; *Sarkis: It's Time, Time, Time,* exhibition catalogue with text by Elvan Zabunyan, La Rochelle 1987.

SARKISIAN, Paul.

American. Born in Chicago, Illinois, 18 August 1928.Studied at the School of the Art Institute of Chicago, 1945–48; Otis Art Institute, Los Angeles, 1953–54; Mexico City College, 1955–56. Independent painter, in California and New Mexico, since 1956. Taught at the Pasadena Art Museum, California, 1965–69; University of Southern California, Los Angeles, and the Art Center, Los Angeles, 1969; University of California, Berkeley, 1970; University of Oregon, Eugene, 1971; and University of South Florida, Tampa, 1972. Agent: Nancy Hoffman Gallery, New York. Address: c/o Nancy Hoffman Gallery, 429 West Broadway, New York, New York 10012, U.S.A.

Individual Exhibitions:

1958	Nova Gallery, Boston
1962	Aura Gallery, Pasadena, California
1963	La Jolla Art Center, California
1968	Pasadena Art Museum, California
1969	Corcoran Gallery, Washington, D.C.
1970	Michael Walls Gallery, San Francisco
	Santa Barbara Museum of Art, California
1972	Museum of Contemporary Art, Chicago
1973	Michael Walls Gallery, Los Angeles
1975	*Featured Painting*, Museum of Contemporary Arts, Houston
1977	Museum of Contemporary Arts, Houston
1978	Nancy Hoffman Gallery, New York
1979	Arts Club of Chicago
1980	Wright State University, Dayton, Ohio (travelled to the Herron Gallery, Indianapolis, and Ohio State University, Columbus)
	Nancy Hoffman Gallery, New York
1981	Arco Center for Visual Arts, Los Angeles
1982	Aspen Center for the Visual Arts, Colorado

Selected Group Exhibitions:

1977	*A View of the Decade*, Museum of Contemporary Art, Chicago
	Illusions of Reality, Australian National Gallery, Canberra (travelled to the Western Australia National Gallery, Perth)
1979	*Prospectus: The 70's*, Aldrich Museum, Ridgefield, Connecticut
	Reality of Illusion, Denver Art Museum (travelled to the Honolulu Academy of Art; Oakland Museum of Art, California; University of Texas Art Museum, Austin: and Johnson Museum of Art, Cornell University, Ithaca, New York. 1979–80)
1980	*American Art since 1950*, Santa Barbara Museum of Art, California
	Contemporary Art from New Mexico, Scottish Arts Council, Edinburgh
1981	*Real, Really Real and Super Real*, San Antonio Museum Association, Texas
1985	*American Realism*, San Francisco Museum of Modern Art (toured the United States, 1986–87)

Collections:

Corcoran Gallery, Washington, D.C.; Hirshhorn Museum and Sculpture Garden, Washington, D.C.; Art Institute of Chicago; Indianapolis Museum of Art; Des Moines Art Center, Iowa; Milwaukee Art Center; Oakland Museum of Art, California; Norton Simon Museum of Art, Pasadena, California; Santa Barbara Museum of Art, California; Aachen Museum, West Germany.

Publications:

On SARKISIAN: book—*Paul Sarkisian*, exhibition leaflet, with an essay by Philip Yenawine, Aspen, Colorado 1982.

This foremost American ultra-illusionist is often spoken of in the lineage of the 19th century Americans such as Peale, Harnett, and Peto who similarly practiced trompe l'oeil, all thus touching the American literalist nerve. Sarkisian began during the 1960s to assert that he had gained a sense of the present by a past-glance, in a series of satirical Pop-academic paintings. However he then gained wide recognition with vernacular subjects—store fronts—in spectacular life-scale monochromatic paintings of the earlier 1970s. From that time, has come the almost two-decade-long drive — coinciding with a greatly strengthened grasp both technical and ideational— towards what has been called an illusionist transcendental collage (V.B. Price). These oft large works have featured mundane objects, such as printed commercial packaging, newspapers, letters, et al, most often seen flattened against a milky light background. Compositions were usually unbalanced, as if relationality and thus "art-fulness" were de-emphasized. The surface of these works become breathless, and so achieved with both air brush and subtle silkscreen techniques, an immaculate hologram-like three-dimensional phenomenom. (Shadows, for instance, were air-brushed adjacent to the represented objects to lift them from the canvas surface.)

Perhaps such delving into the apparitional quality of the light-lit object, is enhanced and supported by the artist's 25-year-long residence in New Mexico; his illusionist work also coincides with, albeit in art far more abstracted, the work of other far-western artists likewise infatuated with the mysterious revelations of light—Irwin, Bell, Valentine, Turrell. Within

Paul Sarkisian: *Untitled (Has Beautiful Display)*, 1980

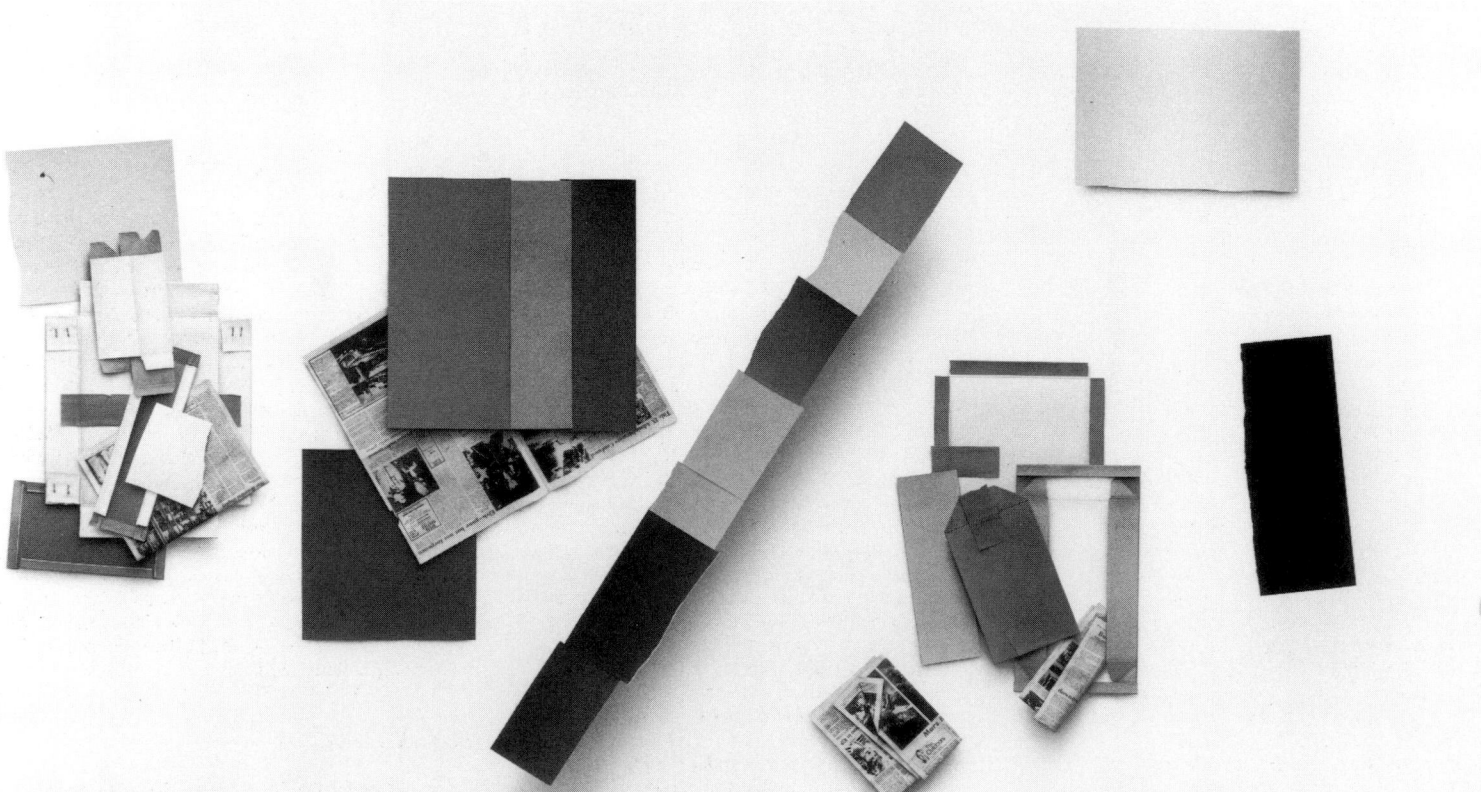

the last half-decade, as almost a logical progress, Sarkisian eliminated more-and-more the printed sections and other specifically referential qualities of his collage groupings, so that he seemingly intended a material purity which might be read as shape and color alone. Although still trompe l'oeil, the images appear as hardedge geometric art with at times a postmodernist reference to old master modernist work of Max Weber, Malevich, and as well the illusionism of Harnett.

It would seem that Sarkisian has attempted to make the non-modern illusionist tradition appropriate to a post modern environment with allusions both general and specific to the abstract art which discarded that illusionism.

—Joshua Kind

SAUL, Peter.

American. Born in San Francisco, California, 16 August 1926. Studied at Stanford University School of Fine Arts, California, 1949–50; California School of Fine Arts, San Francisco, 1950–52; Washington University School of Fine Arts, St. Louis. with Fred Conway, 1952–56, B.F.A. 1956. Painter: lived in the Netherlands, 1956–58; Paris, 1958–62; Rome, 1962–64; and in California, since 1965. Recipient: Copley Foundation Award. 1961; *Art in America* New Talent Award, 1962; National Endowment for the Arts grant, Washington, D.C., 1980. Agents: Allan Frumkin Gallery, 50 West 57th Street, New York, New York 10019; Frumkin and Struve Gallery, 309 West Superior Street, Chicago, Illinois 60610; and Landfall Press, Chicago. Address: c/o Landfall Press, 5863 North Kenmore, Chicago, Illinois 60660, U.S.A.

Individual Exhibitions:

1961	Allan Frumkin Gallery, Chicago
1962	Allan Frumkin Gallery, New York
	Galerie Breteau, Paris
1963	Allan Frumkin Gallery, New York
	Rolf Nelson Gallery, Los Angeles
	Galleria Tartaruga, Rome
1964	Rolf Nelson Gallery, Los Angeles
	Galleria Notizie, Turin
	Galerie Breteau, Paris
1965	Galerie Anne Aebels, Cologne
1966	Allan Frumkin Gallery, New York
	Allan Frumkin Gallery, Chicago
1967	Galerie Breteau, Paris
	Contemporary Gallery, Kansas City
	Wanamaker's, Philadelphia
1968	San Francisco Art Institute
	California College of Arts and Crafts Gallery, Oakland
	Reed College, Portland, Oregon
	Allan Frumkin Gallery, New York
1969	Allan Frumkin Gallery, Chicago
	Allan Frumkin Gallery, New York
	Galerie Darthea Speyer, Paris
1971	Allan Frumkin Gallery, New York
	Musée d'Art et d'Industrie. Saint-Etienne, France
1972	Allan Frumkin Gallery, Chicago
	Galerie Darthea Speyer, Paris
1973	California State University at Sacramento
	Allan Frumkin Gallery, New York
	Galerie Klang, Cologne
1974	Allan Frumkin Gallery, Chicago
1975	Allan Frumkin Gallery, New York
1976	Housatonic Museum of Art, Bridgeport, Connecticut
1977	Allan Frumkin Gallery, Chicago
1978	Allan Frumkin Gallery, New York
1980	University of Northern Illinois, DeKalb (retrospective)
	Madison Art Center, Wisconsin (retrospective)
1981	Allan Frumkin Gallery, New York

Selected Group Exhibitions:

1970	*Drawings 1970*, University of California at Santa Barbara (toured the United States)
1972	*American Exhibition*, Art Institute of Chicago (and 1976)
1973	*Voices of Alarm*, Lerner-Heller Gallery. New York
1974	*Painting and Sculpture Today 74*, Indianapolis Museum of Art (travelled to the Taft Museum, Cincinnati, Ohio)
1977	*The Modern Era: Bay Area*, Huntsville Museum of Art, Alabama
1978	*Art About Art*, Whitney Museum, New York
1979	*Painting, Drawing and Sculpture*, University of Virginia Art Museum. Charlottesville
1980	*The Figurative Tradition and the Whitney Museum*, Whitney Museum, New York
1981	*Crimes of Compassion*, Chrysler Museum, Norfolk, Virginia
1984	*The Human Condition*, San Francisco Museum of Modern Art

Collections:

Museum of Modern Art, New York; Whitney Museum, New York; University of Massachusetts, Amherst; Allen Art Museum, Oberlin, Ohio; Krannert Art Museum, University of Illinois, Champaign; Art Institute of Chicago; Elvehjem Art Center, Madison, Wisconsin.

Publications:

On SAUL: books—*Peter Saul*, exhibition catalogue, Los Angeles 1963; *Peter Saul*. exhibition catalogue, with text by Cesare Vivaldi, Rome 1963; *Peter Saul*, exhibition catalogue, text by Cesare Vivaldi. Turin 1964; *Human Concern? Personal Torment*, exhibition catalogue. by Robert Doty, New York 1969; *Peter Saul*, exhibition catalogue, text by J. Beauffet, Saint-Etienne, France 1971; articles—"That's Saul Folks" by David Zack in *Artnews* (New York), November 1969; "Peter Saul" in *Mizue* (Tokyo), no. 788, 1970; "Saul ou la Mauvaise Conscience" by C. Bouyeure in *Opus International* (Paris), December 1972; "Peter Saul, Allan Frumkin Gallery" by J. Masheck in *Artforum* (New York), January 1972; "Peter Saul, Galerie Klang" by B. Catoir in *Das Kunstwerk* (Baden-Baden, West Germany), November 1973; "Art People" by Grace Glueck in the *New York Times*, 2 January 1981; "Cartoons Are No Longer Funny" by Elizabeth Hess in the *Village Voice* (New York). 14 January 1981; "Art View" by Hilton Kramer in the *New York Times*, 18 January 1981.

Peter Saul, his name itself—with its instant yet chronologically backwards juxtaposition of the Christian New and the Judaic Old Testaments—is appropriate for the fierce and perverse moralist that the artist has been all his working life. In his European works of the early 60's, although he is still absorbed by the painterliness of abstract-expressionism, mundane objects appear, rendered in a soft, fat cartoon style, like late-Guston; absurdity and surrealism are suggested by obscure actions and space, and by titles such as "Icebox," "Bathroom Sex Murder," and "Super Crime Team." In the later 1960's, Saul moved to images of clear political dissent with Viet Nam and Civil Rights themes dominating; his technique also became less painterly and more strident in its continuing cartoon-qualities, and in its thin and harsh coloration and drawing. If these works might be considered in the tradition of American interwar Social Realism, Saul's career is clear example of the alienation that a social-political art has undergone from the culture of high art.

To the present time, even though Saul returned to more generalized social satire in the 1970's, his works (called "splatter-film violence", R. Storr) appear "difficult" in an art gallery. Such feeling may arise from the tension that they exude between their political-moral intensity, apparently much intended by the artist, and an equally desired aestheticism. He is haunted by the need to be "public": "My idea is to make my paintings interesting enough that all kinds of people can look at them without inducement from expert opinion." And yet Saul is much like his formalist predecessors in the 1950's—exuberantly inventive in shape and pattern, and his comic-like characters move with a vividly personal dreamy flow.

Saul appears constantly embarrassed by his involvement in high culture, and so it seems logical that in a long series of works "Artfront," in the early 1970's his attacks were directed against members of the art world. The pornographic virulence of these often scatological works also extended over to subjects such as ethnic prejudice, governmental structure, and the police. During this decade, Saul developed a pristine acrylic technique which featured brilliant color, including the shrill bad taste of Day-Glo pigments, applied to long stretched-out forms—his figures seemed made of extruded plastic; he also continued his art world antagonism with parodies of major works of art—"The Night Watch" of Rembrandt; DeKooning's "Woman"; "The Death of Sardanapalus" of Delacroix, and many more.

Like Shahn and Guston in the early 1940's, Saul may have experienced a time of strain, as if constant attention to social and political matters of the moment was creatively exhausting. And yet in his recent exhibitions, with works such as "The Arsonist," "The Rapist," and "Three Mile Island," constructed in a Picassoid-plastic style, Saul returns to the rage and motifs of violence that characterized his earlier works. The monstrous exaggerations and dissolutions of the body parts achieve a hovering sadism and perhaps hypnotic disgust, and yet usually to the end of moral outrage. If his works were considered adversary political images, then his creative mechanisms may be analogous to those of fiction writers with political subjects. Since his vituperation is easy to follow, and because satirical force but no satirical narrative exists, Saul's paintings have long resembled the apocalyptic atmosphere of such books as *The Public Burning* of Robert Coover and E. L. Doctorow's *The Book of Daniel*. The shrill satire misleads us to feel that Saul's anarchic despair is only about his subjects; perhaps he revives the continuing despair about the art act itself.

—Joshua Kind

SAURA, Antonio.

Spanish. Born in Huesca, 22 September 1930. Educated in Madrid, Valencia and Barcelona, 1936–48; self-taught in art, from 1947. Painter: has lived and worked in Madrid, 1947–53, Paris, 1953–55, again in Madrid 1955–78, and in Cuenca since 1978: associated with group of surrealist artists and writers, Paris, 1953–55; founder-member and director of activities, El Paso group of painters, Madrid, 1957–60; first lithographs, Madrid 1958; collaborated with "Estampa Popular" group, Madrid, 1960; first welded metal sculptures, Madrid, 1961; abandoned painting on canvas for works on paper, Madrid, 1971–73. Recipient: Guggenheim Award, 1960; Carnegie Prize, Pittsburg with Chillida and Soulages, 1964; Grand Prize, *Biennale Biancoe Nero*, Lugano, Switzerland, 1966; First Prize, *Print Biennale*, Heidelberg, 1979; Gold Medal for Fine Arts, Madrid, 1982. Agents: Galerie Stadler, 51 rue de Seine, 75006 Paris, France; Pierre Matisse Gallery, 41 East 57th Street, New York, New York 10022, U.S.A. Address: 17 rue du Javelot, 75013 Paris, France; or San Pedro 27, Cuenca, Spain.

Individual Exhibitions:

1950	Liberia Libros de Zaragoza, Saragossa, Spain
1951	Galeria Buchholz, Madrid

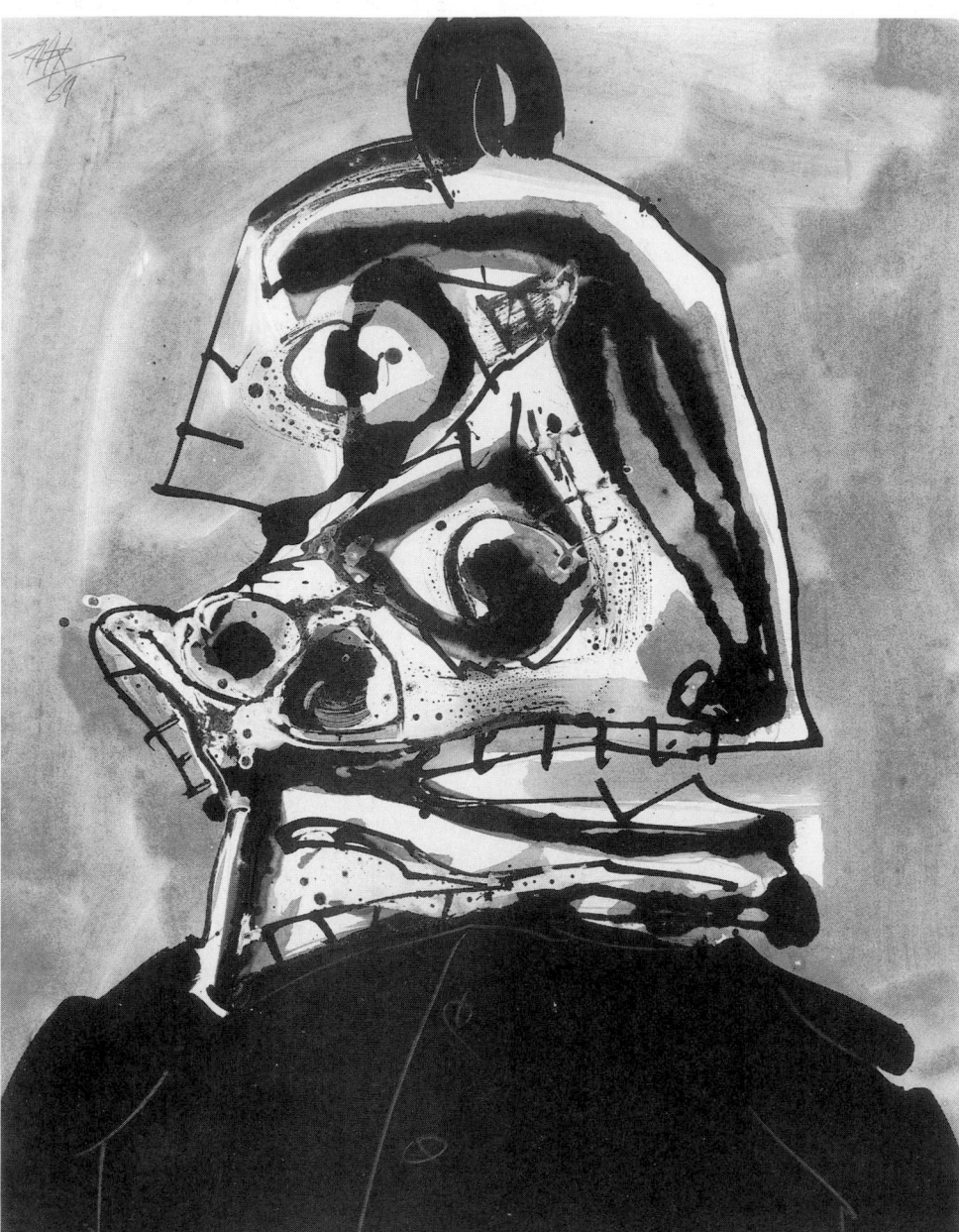

Antonio Saura: *Retrato Imaginario de Felipe II,* 1969

1953	Liberia Clan, Madrid	1975	Galerie Nouvelles Images, The Hague

1975   Galerie Nouvelles Images, The Hague
      Galeria Juan Martin, Mexico City
      Galerie Van de Loo, Munich
      Galleri Blanche, Stockholm
      Galerie Henry Meyer, Lausanne
      At *Art 6 75,* Basle
      Tres pintores del Paso, Galeria Juana Mordo, Madrid
      Papers, Galeria Maeght, Barcelona
1976   Galerie Benador, Geneva
      Galleria Grafica Club. Milan
      Galerie Mailliard. St. Paul-de-Vence, France
      Galeria Edurne. Madrid
      Libreria Popular, Albacete, Spain
1977   Galeria 42, Barcelona
      Galerie Nouvelles Images, The Hague
      Galeria Juana Mordo. Madrid (travelled to Galerie Stadler, Paris, and the *Festival Cinematografico,* Pontarlier)
      Galerie Stadler, at *FIAC 77,* Paris
      Musée des Beaux-Arts, Besanson, France
1978   Fondation Nationale des Arts Graphiques et Plastiques. Paris
      Galeria Torques, Santiago de Compostela, Spain
      Galeria Punto, Valencia
      Galeria Rebollo. Zaragoza
      Caja de Ahorros Municipal, Vigo. Spain
1979   *Peintures 1978–1979,* Galerie Stadler, Paris
      Galerie Lauter. Mannheim
      Union des Arts Plastiques, St. Etienne de Rouvray, France
      Galerie Nouvelles Images, The Hague
      Galeria Carmen Durgano, Valladolid, Spain
      Galeria 4 Gats. Palma de Mallorca, Spain
      Maison de la Culture de Belleville, Paris (toured France)
      Stedelijk Museum. Amsterdam (retrospective; travelled to the Kunsthalle, Dusseldorf)
      Galerie Jack Visser, Amsterdam
1980   Casa de Alhajas, Madrid
      National Gallery. Reykjavik
      Exposición Antologica 1948–1980. Fundacion Joan Miro. Barcelona
      Centre d'Action Culturelle. Montbeliard, France
      Centre Gerard Philippe, Venissieux, France
      Lens Fine Art, Antwerp
      Galeria Benedet, Oviedo, Spain
      Galeria Juan Martin, Mexico City
1981   Sala Luzan. Zaragoza
      Galerie Moderne, Silkeborg. Denmark
      Galerie Nouvelles Images, The Hague
      Sa Pieta Freda, Majorca, Spain
      Portraits Raisonnes, Galerie Stadler, Paris
      Galerie Jack Visser, Amsterdam
      Museo de Arte Contemporaneo de Altoaragon, Huesca, Spain
1982   Galeria Diart, Madrid
1983   Maison de Goya, Bordeaux, France
      Casa de Espana, Paris
      Galerie Antonio Machon, Madrid
1984   Galerie Wewerka, West Berlin
      Galerie Van de Loo, Munich
      Galeria Maeght, Barcelona
1985   Galerie Lauter, Mannheim, West Germany
      Musée Bonnat, Bayonne, France
      Kunstamt Wedding, West Berlin
      Galleri Kaj Forsblom, Helsinki
1986   Galerie XPO, Hamburg
      Neue Galerie/Sammlung Ludwig, Aachen, West Germany
      Galeria del Palau, Valencia, Spain
1987   Galerie P. J. Meurisse, Toulouse, France
      Galerie Stadler, Paris

1953   Liberia Clan, Madrid
1956   Palacio de Bibliotecas y Museos, Madrid
1957   Galerie Stadler, Paris
1959   Galerie Stadler, Paris
      Galerie Van de Loo, Munich (with Antoni Tapies)
      Galeria Machetti, Cuenca, Spain
1960   Galerie Stadler, Paris
      Galleri Blanche, Stockholm
      Galleria Odyssia, Rome
1961   Pierre Matisse Gallery, New York
      Galerie Van de Loo, Munich
      Galleria Dell'Ariete, Milan
1962   Galria Biosca, Madrid
1963   Galerie Stadler, Paris
      Stedelijk Van Abbemuseum, Eindhoven, Netherlands (travelled to the Kunstkring, Rotterdam)
      Museo de Arte Moderno, Buenos Aires (travelled to Museo de Arte Moderno, Rio de Janeiro
      Palais des Beaux-Arts, Bussels
1964   *Recent Paintings,* Pierre Matisse Gallery, New York
      Stedelijk Museum, Amsterdam (travelled to the Kunsthalle. Baden-Baden, West Germany, and the Konsthall, Gothenburg, Sweden)
1965   Galerie Stadler, Paris
      Galeria Juana Mordo, Madrid (travelled to the Galerie Liceo, Cordoba; La Pasarela, Seville; Galerie Krikhaar, Amsterdam)

1966   Casa de las Americas, Havana, Cuba
      Institute of Contemporary Arts, London
      Galeria Grises, Bilbao, Spain
1967   Galerie Stadler, Paris
      Galerie Buchholz, Munich
1968   Galerie Van de Loo, Munich
      Frankfurter Kunstkabinett, Frankfurt
1969   *Peintures sur papier,* Galerie Stadler, Paris
      Galeria René Metras, Barcelona
1971   Galerie Stadler, Paris
      Pierre Matisse Gallery, New York
1972   *Trois Visions, and Retratos Imaginarios,* Galeria Juana Mordo, Madrid (2 shows)
1973   Colegio de Arquitectos, Santa Cruz de Tenerife, Canary Islands
      Galeria 42, Barcelona
      Caja de Ahorros de Navarra, Pamplona. Spain
      Galeria Carl van der Voort. Ibiza, Spain
      Galeria Fort, Tarragona, Spain
      Galeria Moira, Madrid
      Galeria Trece, Barcelona
1974   Centro M-II, Seville
      Galerie Stadler. Paris
      Sala Pelaires, Palma de Mallorca, Spain
      Galeria Zarte, Bilbao, Spain
      Grupo 15, Madrid
      Sala Conca, La Palmas, Spain

Selected Group Exhibitions:

1952   *Tendencias I. Casa* Americana, Madrid
1964   *Documenta,* Kassel, West Germany (and 1977, 1982)
1969   *Contemporary Portraits,* Museum of Modern Art, New York
1972   *Estampa Popular,* Libreria Antonio Machado, Madrid

1976	*Biennale*, Venice
1978	*Arte Iberoamericano de Hoy*, Museo de Arte Contemporaneo, Caracas
1979	*L'Homme dans l'Art Europeen apres 1945*, Fundatie Kunsthuis, Amsterdam
1980	*Recent European Drawings*, Art Gallery of New South Wales, Sydney
1981	*Westkunst*, Rheinhallen, Cologne
1982	*Quatre Images Seditieuses*, Fondation du Chateau de Jau, France

Collections:

Museo Espanol de Arte Contemporaneo, Madrid; Fundacion Juan March, Madrid; Neue Pinakothek, Munich; Museum des 20. Jahrhunderts, Vienna; Musée d'Art or d'Histoire, Geneva; Moderna Museet, Stockholm; Stedelijk Museum, Amsterdam; Centre National d'Art Contemporain, Paris; Tate Gallery, London; Museum of Modern Art, New York.

Publications:

By SAURA: books—*Programie*, Madrid 1951; *Arte Fantastico*, with Carlos Saura, Madrid 1953; *Carta al espectador*, Madrid 1953; *Cartas de El Paso: Manifiestos*, with others, Madrid 1957; *Carta Abietta a Antonio Pericas*, Madrid 1961; *Antonio Saura: Superpositions*, Paris 1974; *Contra el Guernica*, Madrid 1982; *Antonio Saura: Notebook 1958–1980*, Madrid 1982; also articles in numerous catalogues and periodicals since 1951; also numerous limited edition print portfolios, from 1959.

On SAURA: books—*Saura* by Erik Borman, Madrid, 1956; *La Obra de Saura* by Juan Eduardo Cirlot, Barcelona 1960; *Antonio Saura*, exhibition catalogue, with text by Michel Tapie, Rome 1960; *Saura-Crucifixion* by Enrico Crispolti, Rome 1961; *Antonio Saura*, exhibition catalogue, with texts by Michel Tapie and José Ayllon, New York 1961; *Antonio Saura*, exhibition catalogue, with text by Vincente Aguilera Cerni, Munich 1961; *Saura*, exhibition catalogue, with text by José Ayllon, Eindhoven, Netherlands 1963; *Saura: Recent Paintings*, exhibition catalogue, with text by Yvon Taillandier, New York 1964; *Antonio Saura*, exhibition catalogue, with text by José Ayllon, Amsterdam 1964; *Saura* by Georges Boudaille, Paris 1967; *Peintures sur papier de Saura*, exhibition catalogue, with text by Fernando Arrabal, Paris 1969; *Antonio Saura* by José Ayllon, Barcelona 1969; *Trois Visions: Antonio Saura*, exhibition catalogue, with text by Claude Roy, Madrid 1972; *Antonio Saura: Retratos Imaginarios*, exhibition catalogue, with texts by Waldemar George and Jean-Clarence Lambert, Madrid 1972; *Saura: Obra Grafica* by Eduardo Westerdahl and José Maria Moreno Galvan, Santa Cruz de Tenerife 1973; *Antonio Saura*, exhibition catalogue, with texts by Jean Manuel Bonet and others, Seville 1974; *Antonio Saura: Papers*, exhibition catalogue, with texts by Oscar Collazos, Alexandre Cirici-Pellicer, Roland Penrose and others, Barcelona 1975; *Saura: un message pour l'homme d'aujourd'hui* by Paul Gauthier, Paris 1977; *Saura: Peintures 1978–1979*, exhibition catalogue, with text by Marcel Cohen, Paris 1979; *Antonio Saura*, exhibition catalogue, with texts by Bert Schierbeek, Lucebert and Ad Petersen, Amsterdam 1979; *Antonio Saura*, exhibition catalogue, with text by Jürgen Partenheimer, Dusseldorf 1979; *Saura* by Gerard Xuriguera, Paris 1979; *Antonio Saura* by Alexandre Cirici-Pellicer, Madrid and Paris 1980; *Periodico de Exposiciones 1: Antonio Saura*, Madrid 1980; *Antonio Saura: Exposición Antologica 1948–1980*, exhibition catalogue, with texts by Javier Tusell Gomez, Ad Petersen, Alexandre Cirici-Pellicer and others, Barcelona 1980; *Antonio Saura: antologia de obras en papel* by Federico Torralba and others, Zaragoza 1981; *Saura: portraits raisonnes*, exhibition catalogue, with text by Severo Sarduy, Paris 1981; *Espiral-Figuras: Saura* texts by several authors, Madrid 1982; *Saura*, exhibition catalogue with text by Edmond Jabes, Paris 1987.

The stranglehold of the bourgeoisie over the visual arts is revealed most clearly by the history of immediately post-war art in Europe. When one sees the bland prettiness of most French artists of the 1950's adherents of "Tachism," one finds nothing to indicate that the whole of northern Europe had been fought across, bombed, burned and then held in the grip of Fascism for five years. French art took up its brushes exactly where it had been left off; there is a gap, that's all.

This was not the case in literature or philosophy, Sartre, Genet, Camus, Barthes wrote and thought about an unmistakably post-war world, one in which the traditional values of the bourgeoisie were rejected and full consciousness of the corruptibility of man was taken into account. For writers such as these the war was liberating, a fire storm that sucked the old stratified and inhabited way of life into its centre and spat out the bare bones of existence. It was a confirmation of the thought of Husserl and Heidegger, a chance to start again with no illusions.

But painting, which is in the hands of a small and wealthy minority, was not so affected. The economics of literature allow ideas to spread with comparative ease; those of painting restrict the movement of ideas. Instead of a visual equivalent of existentialism we were offered the bland mush of *L'Art Informel* between the twin poles of the circus tricks of Mathieu and the high catholicism of Manessier.

Liberation of the painting in Europe came from a country that had not suffered the war, Spain. Instead it had known something far worse, a civil war which tore the country to shreds and left gaping wounds of injustice which still are not healed. The bourgeoisie in Spain had not taken over painting, as there had been no painting to take over. Artists simply fled because Franco's Fascism, in the early stage, was repressive of any manifestation of independent thought. Those that did stay worked secretly, without hope.

By the mid 50's, however, Franco found himself isolated, the only Fascist dictator left. American money kept him firmly in power, but in return he had to make a few gestures towards a token liberalism. As a result the visual arts came out of hiding and were allowed to pursue a very restricted course of experiment. Direct political comment was, of course, not allowed, but abstraction, well that could hurt nobody.

The result of policy was the Spanish school of tachism, led by Tapies and including Antonio Saura. Although it was mild, in terms of political comment, it revitalised European painting. The Spanish school had no time for prettiness; the dominant texture was thick and viscous, often using sand mixed in the paint. Compared with French painting it was serious, mature and painful.

Saura's contribution was the most violent. The dominant colours of his art are black and red. Unlike most of the other Spanish painters he introduced the human figure into his canvases, but the figure distorted, wild, in extremity. Huge eyes stare, jaws gape like the painting of a child living in a nightmare, The paintings seem to have been made in a frenzy; paint drips like blood from an open wound and the surface is ripped open to reveal the lacerated canvas beneath.

In the 1980's such painting can seem naive; Saura himself has moved away from it towards a more cartoon-like drawing, more overtly political. But at the time it was brave painting that avoided for a long time the self-satisfied embrace of the middle-class public and did a great deal towards restoring a dignity and seriousness of purpose to European art.

—Alastair Mackintosh

SAVELLI, Angelo.

Italian. Born in Pizzo, Calabria, 30 October 1911. Studied at the Liceo Artistico, Rome, 1930–32, and the Accademia di Belle Arti, Rome, under Ferruccio Ferrazzi, 1932–36, Diploma di Decorazione 1936. Married Elizabeth Fisher Friedman in 1953. Artist, in Rome, 1936–54, and in New York, since 1954; Founder Member, with Severini, Prampolini, Fazzini and others, Art Club, Rome, 1944. Instructor in Art, Collegio Nazionale, Rome, 1939–40; Professor, Liceo Artistico, Rome, 1940, 1943, 1948, 1954; Instructor, Scarsdale, New York Art Workshop, 1957–61, and New School for Social Research, New York, 1959–65; Associate Professor of Fine Art, University of Pennsylvania, Philadelphia, 1960–69; Art Instructor, Columbia University, New York, 1966, and Hunter College, New York, 1968; Guest Artist, Wisconsin State University at Menomonie, 1972, and University of Minnesota, Duluth, 1974; Visiting Artist, Cornell University, Ithaca, New York, 1974; Guest Artist, Pennsylvania Academy of Fine Art, Philadelphia, 1975; Visiting Artist, University of Arkansas, Little Rock, 1975, and University of Texas at Arlington, 1978, 1979. Recipient: Italian Ministry of Education Study Fellowship, 1948; Grand Prize, *Biennale*, Venice, 1964; Purchase Prize for Graphics, State University of New York at Potsdam, 1965; Purchase Prize, Vancouver Art Gallery, 1968; Tiffany Grant, 1975; Guggenheim Fellowship, 1979. Agent: Leo Castelli Gallery, New York. Address: c/o Leo Castelli Gallery, 420 West Broadway, New York, New York 10012, U.S.A.

Individual Exhibitions:

1941	Galleria Roma
1942	Galleria Cairola, Genoa
1947	Galleria dell'Obelisco, Rome
	Galleria del Naviglio, Milan
1952	Centre d'Art Italienne, Paris
1954	Galleria del Naviglio, Milan
1955	The Contemporaries, New York
1958	Leo Castelli Gallery, New York
	Galleria del Cavallino, Venice
1960	University of Minnesota, Duluth
1961	Galleria del Naviglio, Milan
1962	Peter Deitsch Gallery, New York
1963	Art Alliance, Philadelphia
	D'Arcy Galleries, New York
1969	Henri Gallery, Washington, D.C.
	Peale Galleries, Philadelphia
1972	Everson Museum, Syracuse, New York
1973	University of Wisconsin Art Gallery, Menomonie
1974	University of Minnesota, Duluth
1975	Pennsylvania State University, University Park
1976	Pennslvania State University, University Park
1978	Max Hutchinson Gallery, New York
	Sculpture Now, New York
	Parsons-Dreyfus Gallery, New York
1981	Lorenzelli Arte, Milan
	Gimpel-Hanover/André Emmerich Gallery, Zurich

Selected Group Exhibitions:

1943	*Quadriennale*, Rome
1950	*Biennale*, Venice
1956	*International Collage Exhibition*, Rose Fried Gallery, New York
1957	*Collage in America*, American Federation of Arts, New York (toured the United States)
1958	*Group Exhibition*, Leo Castelli Gallery, New York
1964	*International Print Biennale*, Gallery of Modern Art, Ljubljana, Yugoslavia
1966	*Annual Exhibition*, Whitney Museum, New York
1969	*Salon du Mai*, Paris
1971	*White on White*, Museum of Contemporary Art, Chicago
1978	*Festival of Two Worlds*, Charleston, North Carolina

Collections:

Rockefeller Collection, New York; New York Public Library; Brooklyn Museum, New York; Everson Art Museum, Syracuse, New York; Chrysler Museum, Provincetown, Massachusetts; Museum of Modern Art, Cincinnati, Ohio; Museum of Art, Phoenix, Arizona; Vancouver Art Gallery; Victoria and Albert Museum, London; National Museum of Art, Helsinki.

Publications:

On SAVELLI: article—"The Embossed Lithographs of Angelo Savelli" in *Artist's Proof* (New York), no 8, 1971.

In the space which is the result of thinking and seeing, there is no creativity—this space gives no sublimation to the viewer. Rather, it puts him in a conflict of life-mirror and leaves him in routine-thinking, of everyday life and common behavior, because thought is circling around a limited space.

For that is what the mind knows, by identifying itself in that area of thinking. And the narrow restrictions for resistance to the uncommon are born just in that space. Giving him nothing of what expectation of unknown form is. But there's another space which does not come from seeing and imitating but from transformation of the real and, most of all, from nothing . . . .

—Angelo Savelli

If the function of art is to inspire new art, then all artists worth a second glance must have at least a rudimentary knowledge of the creative insights standing behind them in history. The themes of the great poets and painters, sculptors and philosophers, who, like photographers, managed to capture the human spirit in stop-motion, recur in their work. Angelo Savelli, surely one of the major American artists of the 20th century, expands traditional themes to fit the context of modern society. His work is essentially religious, representing an incessantly poetic and unique search for truth.

Savelli's career has been disciplined by years of dedicated painting, including sculpture, print-making, conceptual and architectural projects. An Italian immigrant to the United States in the early 1950s, his art was naturally influenced by the harsh, abstract-expressionism coming out of his country during that period. His early collages are often a metaphor for the unconcious, smothered by the dense texture of abstract element which the modern world represents. At once we see images of the Jungian Id.

His subsequent work evolved to simple but profound minimalization of surface elements—partially achieved through the exclusive use of the colour white and of an essential geometry. Perhaps unconciously, Savelli reaches to the geometry of the Ancient Greeks to polish his art. During the late 50s his compositions were enhanced with pieces of rope, a central image for his work thereafter. Again, Savelli is drawn under the influence of another great thinker, W. B. Yeats. The rope, metaphorical in effect, embodies the Yeatsian concept of the spiral, whose vibrating impulse upwards relates to that special movement in the soul which occurs when inspiration becomes reality. Twice more during that period he was honored for his innovations. First, he pioneered in the development of lithography, and later he contributed to the development of the shaped canvas.

In 1964 Savelli introduced a series of white, box-like sculptures which hosted a heavy, taut, white rope, its most important symbol. They were the forerunners to a similar series entitled *Dante's Inferno,* whose effects remain consistent with the purpose of Dante's imaginary reality. The composition entitled *Paradise* evolved out of the small boxes of the *Inferno.* A series of rectangular and triangular white spaces, they block a spectator's view from the white paintings contained within them. Their symmetry gives them a quality of serenity; the light permeating is almost ethereal. They are meant to be contemplated, and symbolize the path to metaphysical tranquility purported in *The Divine Comedy.* The immediate goal of these works is to blend the extraordinary use of lighting effects and geometric space into "the viewers' aura in order to reach an aesthetic, ideal purity." Further, they are the author's interpretation of the universal theme portraying the process of damnation to paradisical happiness, through the media of modern techniques and symbols.

Savelli's career has been a synthesis of traditional and unique ideas. His work echoes the development which includes Brancusi, and Arp, Malevich and the Constructionists, the neo-classical expressions of the Bauhaus, and the Italian trend typified by Lucio Fontana. Yet his new and complex uses of the rope, coupled with the use of white as a means of intensifying light, unifies and emphasizes the originality of his work.

—Carrie Barker

SAXE, Henry.

Canadian. Born in Montreal, Quebec, 24 September 1937. Studied at Sir George Williams University, Montreal. 1955–56; Ecole des Beaux-Arts, Montreal, under Albert Dumouchal, 1956–62, B.A. 1960; also studied in London, England, 1968. Independent sculptor, since 1962: lives and works in Tamworth, Ontario. Agent: Olga Korper Gallery, Toronto. Address: Tamworth, Ontario K0K 3G0, Canada.

Individual Exhibitions:

1962	Galerie Libre, Montreal
1963	Galerie Camille Hebert, Montreal
1966	Galerie du Siècle, Montreal
1968	Dunkelman Gallery, Toronto
1969	20/20 Gallery, London, Ontario
1970	Carmen Lamanna Gallery, Toronto
1972	Musée d'Art Contemporain, Montreal
1973	*Henry Saxe/Milly Ristvedt,* Musée d'Art Contemporain, Montreal
	National Gallery of Canada, Ottawa
1975	Agnes Etherington Art Gallery, Queens University, Kingston, Ontario
1976	Mt. Allison University Art Gallery, Sackville, New Brunswick
	Dunlop Art Gallery, Saskatoon
1977	Galerie Gilles Gheerbrant, Montreal
1978	Center of Inter-American Relations, New York
1979	Canadian Culture Centre, Paris
	Harbourfront Art Gallery, Toronto
1981	Galerie Gilles Gheerbrant, Montreal
1982	Galerie Gilles Gheerbrant, Montreal
1983	Agnes Etherington Art Centre, Kingston, Ontario
1985	Olga Korper Gallery, Toronto
1987	Olga Korper Gallery, Toronto

Selected Group Exhibitions:

1968	*Artists under 35,* at the *Biennale,* Paris
1973	*Boucherville, Montreal, Toronto, London,* National Gallery of Canada, Ottawa
1978	*Biennale,* Venice
1982	*Contemporary Sculpture at the Guild,* Toronto
1983	*Drawing Show,* Sadie Bronfman Centre, Montreal

Collections:

National Gallery of Canada, Ottawa; Museum of Fine Arts, Montreal; Musée d'Art Contemporain, Montreal; Musée de Quebec; Art Gallery of Ontario, Toronto; Agnes Etherington Art Centre, Queen's University, Kingston, Ontario; Canada Council Art Bank, Ottawa; Department of External Affairs, Ottawa; Nickle Arts Museum, Calgary.

Publications:

By SAXE: articles—"Address to the General Assembly of the Nihilist Party of Canada" in *20 Cents Magazine* (London, Ontario), October 1969; "Deux Ans en 25 Nouvelles" in *La Presse* (Montreal), January 1970.

On SAXE: books—*Boucherville, Montreal, Toronto, London, 1973,* exhibition catalogue by B. Smith and P. Theberge, Ottawa 1973; *Henry Saxe: Two Works,* with text by P. Fry, Regina 1975; *Venice Biennial 1978: Canada—Ron Martin, Henry Saxe* by P. Theberge, Ottawa 1977; articles— "Henry Saxe, avant tour un graveur" by J. Sarrazin in *Le Nouveau Journal* (Montreal). January 1962; "Henry Saxe à la Galerie Libre" by L. Lamy in *Le Devoire* (Montreal), January 1962; "Saxe: Recherche d'un Langage" by C. Jasmin in *La Presse* (Montreal). January 1962; "Les Objects Inaltendus de Saxe" by Y. Ribillard in *La Presse.* (Montreal), April 1966; "Canada Didn't Lose This One Anyway" by B. Lord in *Toronto Daily Star,* January 1970; "In the Galleries: Toronto" by G. M. Dault in *ArtsCanada* (Toronto), February 1971; "Montrer All" by Myra and Irwin Gophik in *Artscanda.* (Toronto). Spring 1972; "Art: Work That's Debatable" by C. Bates in the *Montreal Star,* April 1973.

SCANAVINO, Emilio.

Italian. Born in Genoa, 28 February 1922. Educated in schools in Genoa; studied at the Nicolo Barabino Art School, Genoa, 1938–41; studied architecture at the University of Milan, 1942–43. Served in the Italian Army, 1943. Married Georgina Graglia in 1946; children: Sebastiano and Paola. Draughtsman in local government offices, Genoa, 1945–50; full-time painter from 1950; worked for Mazzotti ceramic factory, Albisola, Italy, 1951–52; co-signed, with Lucio Fontana, Giuseppe Capogrossi, Roberto Crippa and others, *III Manifesto dello Spazialismo,* Milan, 1952; settled in Milan, 1960; transferred his studio to Calice Ligure, 1962; lived in Varese, 1965–67, and moved to Calice Ligure, 1968. Lecturer, Liceo Artistico, Genoa, 1952. Recipient: Premio Graziano, 1955; Premio Lissone, 1958; Premio Prampolini, *Biennale,* Venice, 1958; Premio Spoleto, 1960; Premio Sassari, 1960; Premio Valsesia, 1960; Premio Lignano, 1960; Premio La Spezia, 1963; Grand Prix, *Biennale,* Menton, France, 1970. *Died* (in Calice Ligure) *28 November 1986.*

Individual Exhibitions:

1948	Galleria Isola, Genoa
1951	Apollinaire Gallery, London

Henry Saxe: *Sight Site*

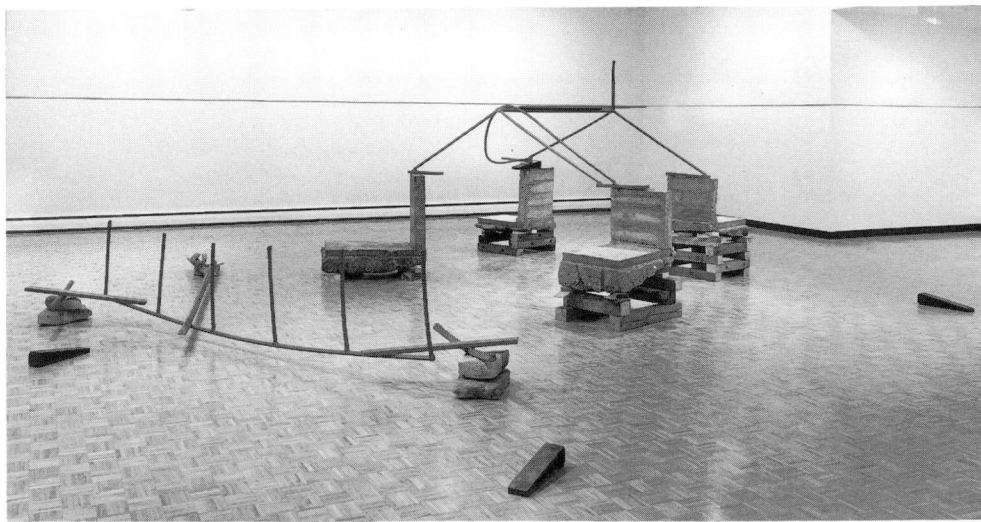

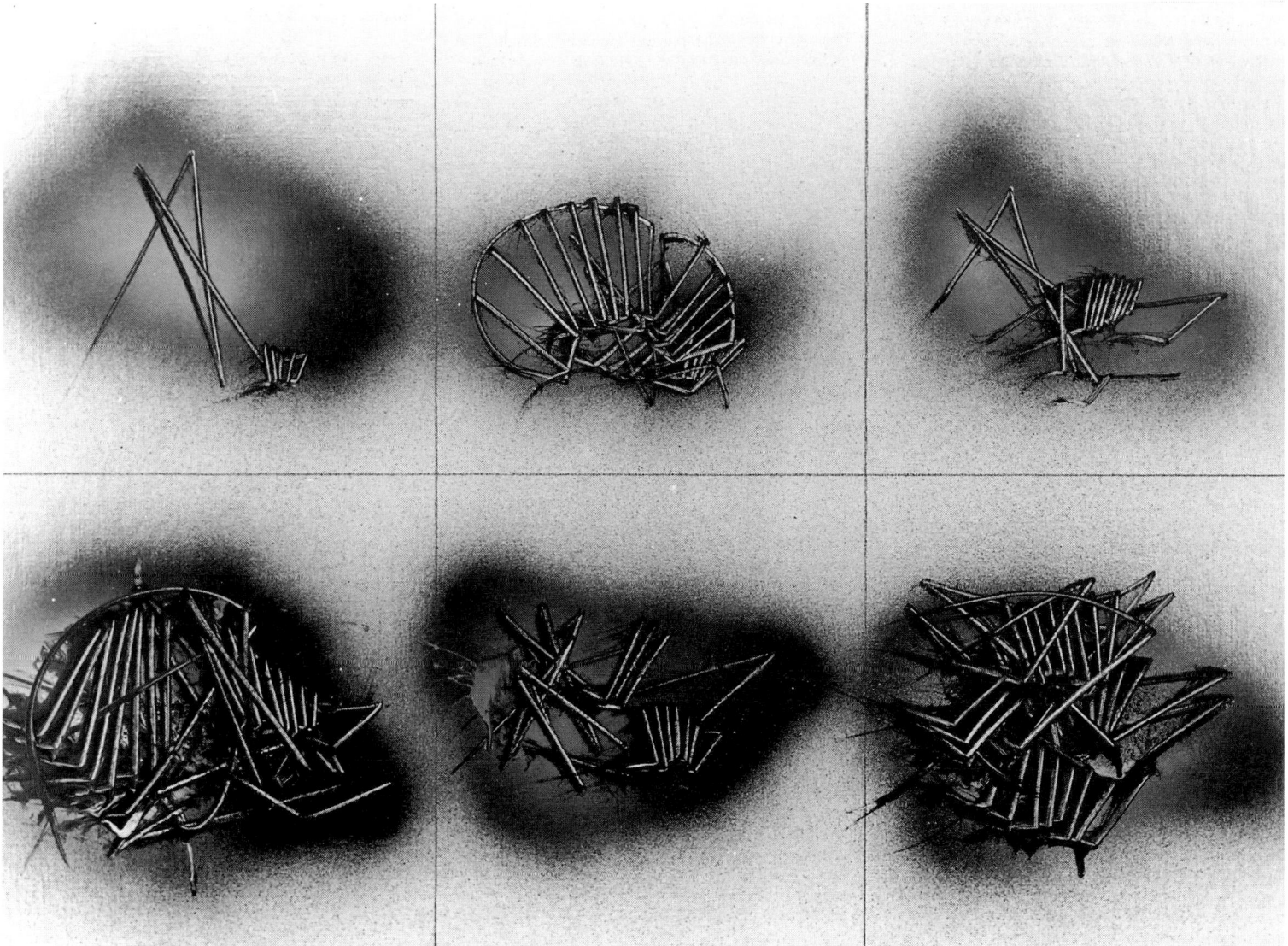

Emilio Scanavino: *Bestiario*, 1986

1953	Galleria del Cavallino, Venice	1972	Galleria Gissi, Turin	1984	Galleria Civica, Valdagno, Italy
1955	Galleria del Naviglio, Milan	1973	Galleria del Naviglio, Milan		Galleria L'Angolo, Bra, Italy
1956	Galleria Apollo, Brussels		*Malerei/Zeichnung/Graphik,* Kunsthalle, Darmstadt		Galleria Omar Ronda Aprile, Biella, Italy
1957	Galleria Selecta, Rome		Palazzo Grassi, Venice		Galleria Morone 6, Milan
1959	Galleria del Naviglio, Milan	1974	Palazzo Reale, Milan		Galleria Blu Art, Varese
1960	Palais des Beaux-Arts, Brussels	1975	Galleria Thomas Levy, Hamburg		Galleria La Loggia, Bologna
	Biennale, Venice	1976	Galleria Il Canale, Venice	1985	Studio Ganzerli, Naples
1961	Galleria del Naviglio, Milan		Galleria Plurima, Udine, Italy		Galleria F22, Palazzolo, Italy
	Galleria del Cavallino, Venice		Galleria Qui Arte Contemporanea, Rome		Galleria Barrel, Genoa
1962	Galerie International d'Art Contemporain, Paris		Galleria 4M, Florence		Studio Albanese, Vicenza
	Galleria del Cavallino, Venice		Studio Marconi, Milan		Limonaia Palazzo dei Congressi, Florence
	Galleria l'Attico, Rome		Galleria Marin, Turin	1986	Valente Arte Contemporanea, Finale Ligure, Italy
	Joachim Gallery, Chicago (with Giuseppe Capo-		Galleria La Chiocciola, Padua		Galleria Gastaldelli, Milan
	grossi)		Galleria Civica d'Arte Moderna, Portofino, Italy	1987	Galleria Giuli, Lecco, Italy
1963	Galleria del Naviglio, Milan	1977	Galleria Rotta, Genoa		Qui Arte Contemporanea, Rome
	Galleria Hausmann, Cortina d'Ampezzo, Italy	1978	Centro Olivetti, Ivrea, Italy		Galleria XX Settembre, Genoa
	Galerie Smith, Brussels	1979	Galerie Mathias Gels, Paris		Museo d'Arte Contemporanea di Villa Croce,
	Galleria Birch, Copenhagen		Galleria Zaratustra, Milan		Genoa
	Galleria Rotta, Genoa		Galleria Cesarea, Genoa		
1964	Galleria la Bussola, Turin	1980	Galleria Giuli, Lecco, Italy		
	Galleria del Cavallino, Venice		Padiglione d'Arte Contemporanea, Parco Massari,		
1965	Galleria 'Argentario, Trento, Italy		Ferrara, Italy		
	Galleria Ferrari, Verona		Mercato del Sale, Milan		**Selected Group Exhibitions:**
1966	Galleria de Foscherari, Bologna	1981	Galleria Gastaldelli, Milan		
	Biennale, Venice		Galleria Cesarea, Genoa	1950	*Biennale,* Venice
1967	Philadelphia Art Alliance		Galleria Il Narciso, Rome	1959	*Documenta,* Kassel, West Germany
	Galleria del Naviglio, Milan		Galleria Planetario, Trieste	1961	*Italian Art Today,* Kunstnernes Hus, Oslo
1969	Studio S. Andrea, Milan	1982	Galleria Planetario, Trieste	1964	*Pittsburgh International,* Carnegie Institute, Pitts-
	Galleria del Naviglio, Milan		Galleria Lo Spazio, Naples		burgh
1970	Galerie Smith, Brussels		Castello Aragonese, Ischia, Italy	1966	*Prospekt,* Dusseldorf
	Galleria Poliantea, Terni, Italy		Galleria Pagani, Legnano, Italy	1967	*Omaggio allo Spazialismo,* Villa Reale, Milan
	Galleria Cantini, Rome	1983	Azienda Turismo, Marina di Massa, Italy	1969	*Maitres de la Peinture Italienne,* Cagnes-sur-Mer,
	Galleria 3B, Bolzano, Italy		Arte Studio, Modena		France
	Biennale, Menton, France		Galleria Santo Stefano, Iarnico, Italy	1971	*20 Artistas Italianos,* Museo de Arte Moderno,
					Mexico City

1977   *La Traccia del Racconto,* Villa Comunale Ormand,
        San Remo, Italy
1981   *Aspetti dell'Informale,* Palazzo Reale, Genoa

Publications:

On SCANAVINO: books—l *Simboli trovati di Scanavino* by
Eligio Cesana, Lecco, Italy 1969; *20 Artistas Italianos,* exhi-
bition catalogue, by Roberto Sanesi, Mexico City 1971;
Scanavino io mani by Alain Jouffroy and Enrico Crispolti,
Milan 1971; *Il Progetto dell'Irrazionale di Scanavino* by
Francesco de Bartolomis, Milan 1972; *Emilio Scanavino,* ex-
hibition catalogue, by Aldo Passoni, Turin 1972; *Scanavino*
by Alain Jouffroy, Paris 1973; *Scanavino: Malerei/
Zeichnung/Graphik,* exhibition catalogue, by Bernd Krim-
mel, Darmstadt 1973; *Scanavino,* exhibition catalogue, by
Guido Ballo, Trieste 1982 *Le Ceramiche di Scanavino* by
Roberto Sanesi, Milan 1981; *Scanavino,* exhibition catalogue
by Guido Ballo, Trieste 1982; *Scanavino: La Memoria del
Tempo,* with texts by Flavio Vangeli, Umbro Apollonio, Gillo
Dorfles and others, Milan 1986.

It has been said that the work of Emilio Scanavino
typifies in its sombre arrogance something of the
character of his native city—Genoa. Certainly there is
much more in his paintings than stylistic search for
effect *per se.* In fact the impression is readily received that the picture frame is the proscenium within
which a drama is presented in quasi-abstract terms
that hints at tragic impending events. It is evident too
that the import of those dark compositions is more
than formal.

There is however a certain squared-up structure to
most of his paintings that bears certain allusive properties one might identify with a stage or a judicial
bench or even the nave of a cathedral. The allusions
are not overtly emphasised; what they are is hinted at
rather than elaborated, yet in a large painting such as
"In prossimita di un evento" (1964) there is under a
central swirling orb the tangled silhouette of something that might be a stricken village or the wreck of
an aircraft. The detail is unimportant, but the atmosphere is one of menace and threat, a shadow of contemporary history. It is also present in his "Tempo
presente," an upright canvas composed around a central blank light rectangle. The two figures in the foreground might represent two viewers of a TV screen,
while in the upper section a disregarded holocaust is
occurring.

This ambiguity accounts for Scanavino's inclusion
among the ranks of the surrealists of our epoch,
though his imagery is largely abstract as opposed to
that of Genoves, for example. In spite of the appearance of his works, which bear the calligraphic knot-
ting and rhythms of central spherical motives
counterpoised against dark and blurred rectangles,
Scanavino works relatively slowly, the execution
awaiting the decision of the appropriate symbol to express his mood. For in his colours and tones the setting is analogous to music in which the movement of
its abstract players responds to his poetic choreography. There is a certain analogy of style with Georges
Mathieu but this is merely a superficiality in the relief
of the raised brush strokes linked and cursive in their
notation of the symbols.

Scanavino has also a deeper sense of occasion, of
compelling an appreciation of the presence of his picture such as "I Loculi" (The Tombs) in which the
present and the past are represented by an upper
frieze of free gyrating forms, obviously implying the
abandon and frenzy of life, and below it two black
boxes seem to symbolise the shrunken immobility of
death, reminiscent of cadavers in the catacombs. This
ambivalence between the figurative and the abstract is
probably less difficult to understand when the artist's
intentions are clarified as they are by his choice of
titles; they give unequivocal directions of the import
of his message; the language is personal and symbolic, and the handling of the medium is traditionally
respectful of its capacity for underlying mood by colour and comprehension in an easily understood code
for joyous and moribund, moving and static. Beyond
the meaning of the paintings they stand witness to the

superlative quality of the artist to create a painted
object that by itself stands unique in evidence of vital
and essential command of expressive form in paint.
                                        —G. S. Whittet

SCANGA, Italo.

American. Born in Lago, Calabria. Italy, 6 June
1932; moved to the United States in 1947. Educated
in Italian public schools; studied sculpture at Michigan State University, East Lansing, under Lindsey
Decker and Charles Pollack, 1955-61. B.A. 1959,
M.A. 1961. Served in the United States Army, in
Austria, 1953-55. Sculptor: now lives and works in
Southern California. Instructor, University of Wisconsin, Madison, 1961-64; Assistant Professor,
Rhode Island School of Design, Providence, 1964-
66; Assistant Professor, Pennsylvania State Univer-
sity, University Park, 1966-67; Associate Professor
of Sculpture, Tyler School of Art, Elkins Park, Penn-
sylvania, 1967-78; Visiting Associate Professor,
1976-77, and since 1978 Professor of Visual Arts,
University of California at San Diego. Recipient: Lou
Tendler Memorial Prize, Detroit Institute of Arts,
1960; Sculpture Prize. *Annual Wisconsin Salon of
Art,* Milwaukee, 1961: Howard Foundation Grant,
Brown University. Providence, Rhode Island, 1970;
Cassandra Grant, Chicago, 1972; National Endow-
ment for the Arts Grant, 1973. Agents: Daniel Wein-
berg Gallery, 2140 Bush Street. San Francisco,
California 94115; Charles Cowles Gallery, 429 West
Broadway, New York, New York 10012. Address:
6717 Vista Del Mar, La Jolla, California 92037,
U.S.A.

Individual Exhibitions:

1959   Valparaiso University, Indiana
1960   Kresge Art Center, Michigan State University, East
        Lansing
1962   Lawrence College, Appleton, Wisconsin
        Memorial Union Gallery, University of Wisconsin,
        Madison
1964   Milwaukee Art Center
        Art Unlimited, Providence, Rhode Island
1970   Rhode Island School of Design, Providence
        Chapman-Kelly Gallery, Dallas
1971   Henri Gallery, Washington. D.C.
        Depth in Presence, Corcoran Gallery (with Robert
           Rauschenberg and Joseph Cornell)
        93 Grand Street, New York
        University of Rochester, New York
        University of Massachusetts, Amherst
1972   Tyler School of Art. Rome
        Water, Everson Museum, Syracuse, New York (with
           Yoko Ono)
        Whitney Museum, New York
        Pennsylvania Academy of Fine Arts, Philadelphia
        Museum of Contemporary Art, Chicago
1973   University of Rhode Island, Providence
1974   112 Greene Street, New York
1975   Henri Gallery, Washington, D.C.
        Brown University, Providence, Rhode Island
1979   Palomar College, San Maracos, California
        San Jose State University, California
1980   Frank Kolbert Gallery, New York
1981   Crown Point Gallery, Oakland, California
        Daniel Weinberg Gallery, San Francisco
1982   Charles Cowles Gallery, New York
        State University of New York at Purchase
1983   La Jolla Museum of Contemporary Art, California
        Los Angeles County Museum of Art
1984   Delahunty Gallery, Dallas
        Rhona Hoffman Gallery, Chicago
1985   Quint Gallery, Dallas
        Burnett Miller Gallery, Los Angeles
        Indianapolis Center for Contemporary Art, Indiana
1986   Oakland Museum, California

Selected Group Exhibitions:

1957   *Michigan Artists.* Detroit Institute of Arts
1961   *Photographs and Drawings,* Antioch College, Yel-
        low Springs, Ohio
1966   *Mutiplicity,* Institute of Contemporary Art, Boston
        (with Nancy Graves, Eva Hesse, and Robert Mor-
        ris)
1970   *Whitney Sculpture Annual,* Whitney Museum, New
        York
1972   *Drawings and Sculpture,* Philadelphia Museum of
        Art
1974   *Questions Answered,* Sarah Lawrence College,
        Bronxville, New York
1977   *A View of a Decade,* Museum of Contemporary Art,
        Chicago
1981   *Figuratively Sculpting,* Project Studio One, New
        York
1983   *New Epiphanies,* University of Colorado, Colorado
        Springs
1985   *Manifestations of the Figure,* Tibor de Nagy Gallery,
        New York

Collections:

Metropolitan Museum of Art, New York; Rhode Island
School of Design Museum of Art, Providence, Rhode Island;
Fogg Museum, Harvard University, Cambridge, Massachu-
setts; Philadelphia Museum of Art; Pennsylvania Academy of
Fine Arts, Philadelphia; University of Wisconsin, Madison;
Wright Art Center, Beloit, Wisconsin; Milwaukee Art Center.

Publications:

By SCANGA: book—*Pilchuck Projects,* Philadelphia 1973.

On SCANGA: books—*Arts Yearbook of Contemporary
Sculpture,* New York 1965; *Rhode Island School of Design
Alumni Bulletin,* Providence, Rhode Island 1966; *Direct
Metal Sculpture,* New York 1966; *Restoration Pieces,* exhibi-
tion catalogue, by Alan Moore, New York 1974; *Societa per
Azzione* by Tullio Catalono, Milan 1975; *Italo Scanga:
Heads,* exhibition catalogue with text by Maurice Tuchman,
Los Angeles 1983; *Italo Scanga 1972-85,* exhibition cata-
logue with text by Paul Tomidy, Oakland 1986.

On two facing walls Italo Scanga hangs handsomely
framed reproductions of kitschy religious paintings
spattered with red paint. Before these, he places urns
containing spices or grains, and occasionally leans
farming implements, a rake or a hoe, against the
wall. At the rear of the room, he hangs large bunches
of dried herbs. Scanga constructs a kind of ritual
space which resembles a series of ambulatory chapels
in a cathedral, each with its own devotional image.

One has to kneel to examine the paintings closely,
since they are hung so low to the ground, and from
there it's a natural step to smell or taste the foodstuffs
in the urns. The reproductions Scanga appropriates
are the kind of sweet versions of gruesome imagery—
bleeding martyrs and sacred hearts—found in poorer
Italian homes. The spots and streaks of the thin red
paint have been applied helter skelter, almost as if he
had opened a vein before the images. Scanga's allusion to desecration (or perhaps it is an extreme form
of veneration) speaks directly to the devotional function of these images.

So do the tools leaning against the wall. Many a
Catholic saint was martyred by common people who
used just such pedestrian implemens. In medieval
times, peasants used their tools as weapons since only
gentry were allowed to use swords. Yet these implements are muffled. The tines of the rake, for example, are braided with straw, which indicates and
mutes the tool's deadly function. Thinking about why
those tools are there, kneeling and realizing just what
Scanga has done to his images, together with smelling
and tasting the urns' contents draws the spectator into
a kind of kinesthetic parody of Holy Communion.

Scanga appears to be forcing a familiar religious
issue here, pointing up the discontinuity between the
painful violence the martyrs underwent and the devo-

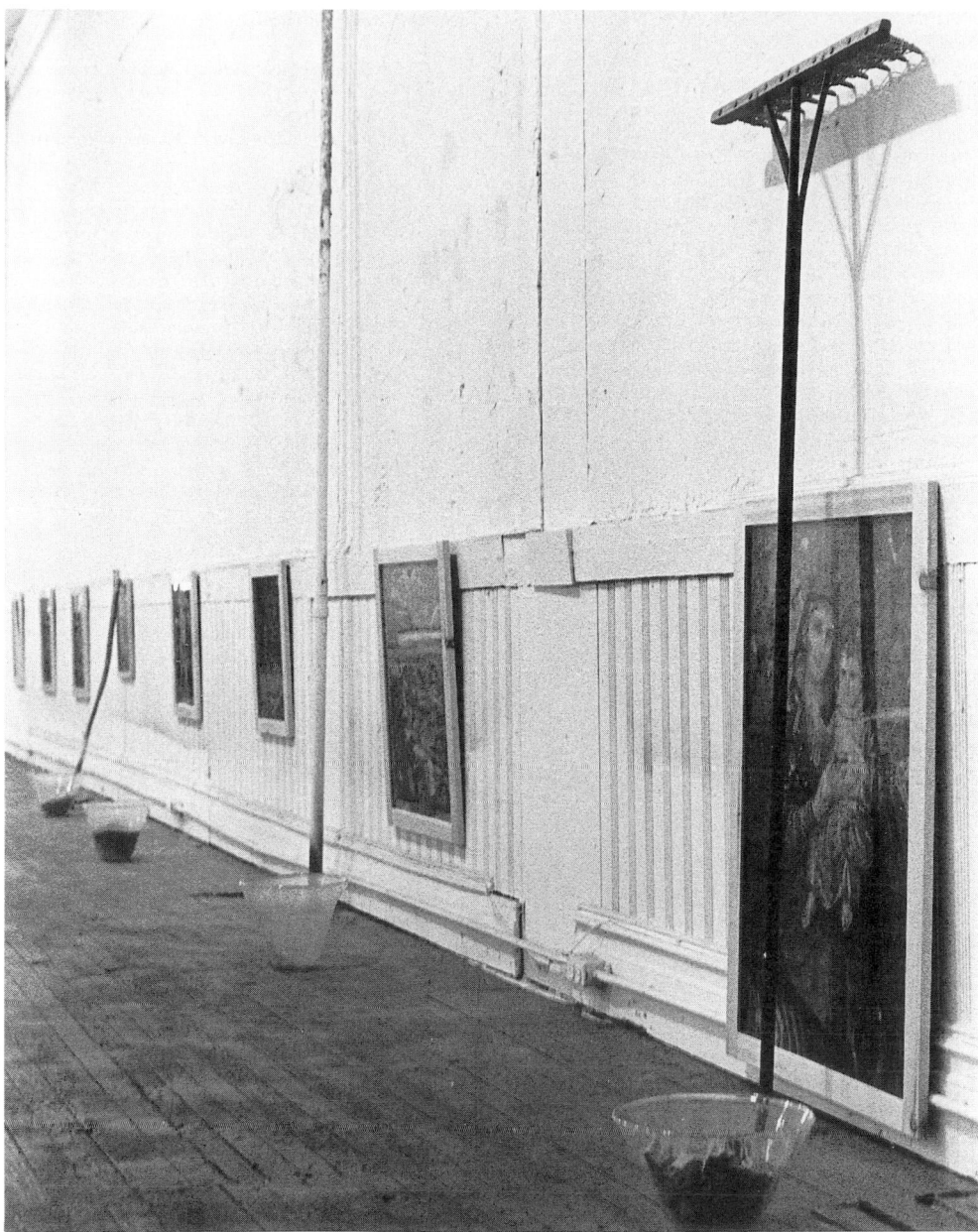

Italo Scanga: Installation at 112 Greene Street, New York, 1974

tional images that abstract sweet sanctity from suffering. Scanga places an urn brimming with chili powder before the bespattered images of the Christ child as Salvator mundi, so that the tasting becomes almost like one of St. Ignatius of Loyola's spiritual exercises, an encouragement for us to empathize with His suffering for us. But Scanga's iconography is a bit more complex than this. The Baroque era during which St. Ignatius wrote his Exercises also saw the culmination of a particular tradition of natural magic. This humanist systematization of the natural world was no more or less respectable in the eyes of the church than the then-emerging scientific attitude. Two of the leading philosophers and practitioners of this tradition of magic, Giordano Bruno (who was burned for his views) and the dominican friar Tommasco Campanella, were born in Calabria, Italy, as was Scanga himself. Campanella was frequently jailed during his lifetime, once for defending Galileo. But his development of a powerful astrological magic won him the support of Pope Urban VII, who in 1628 called upon Campanella to use his magic to ward off the planetary influences threatening the pontiff's life. In performing the embarrassingly pagan ritual derived from Bruno and earlier magicians, the Pope and the friar sang, lit candles to stimulate the planets in a safe arrangement, drank specially distilled liquors, and sprinkled and burned selected herbs. In return for this service, Campanella gained the Pope's support

for the establishment of a short-lived order to proselytise a syncretistic brand of millennial Catholicism and sun worship.

Scanga's art is informed by an awareness of 17th century Calabrian magical tradition, which was by no means a populist shamanism. Campanella, among others, thought of Catholicism as contiguous with the natural magic they had wrought out of Humanist philosophy. Similarly, Scanga's art infers a kind of community between cooking and religion and magic; it is not a new attempt at an orthodox Christian art. There is some way in which the effort to reduce and control the elements in an artwork becomes an effort to control the spectator's reaction to it. This effort, particularly in sculpture, can in turn become an attempt to seize and marshal the spectator's sensibilities.

—Alan Moore

SCARPITTA, Salvatore.
American. Born in New York City in 1919; grew up in Los Angeles; lived in Italy, 1936–59. Studied at the Italian Academy of Fine Art, and the American Academy of Fine Art, and the American Academy,

Rome. Served with the United States Marines in Italy during World War II. Has lived and worked in New York since 1959. Visiting Critic, Maryland Institute College of Art, Baltimore, since 1965. Agent: Leo Castelli Gallery, 420 West Broadway, New York, New York 10012. Address: 307 East 84th Street, New York, New York 10028, U.S.A.

Individual Exhibitions:

1949	Galleria Chiurazzi, Rome
1951	Galleria Il Pincio, Rome
1955	Galleria La Tartaruga. Rome
1956	Galleria del Naviglio, Milan
1957	Galleria La Tartaruga. Rome
1958	Galleria del Naviglio, Milan
	Galleria La Tartaruga, Rome
1959	Leo Castelli Gallery, New York
1960	Leo Castelli Gallery, New York
1961	Dwan Gallery, Los Angeles
1963	Galerie Schmela, Dusseldorf
	Galleria dell'Ariete, Milan
	Musée des Beaux-Arts, Brussels
	Leo Castelli, Gallery, New York
1965	Leo Castelli Gallery, New York
1968	Galleria La Tartaruga, Rome
1969	Leo Castelli Warehouse, New York
1972	Galleria Notizie, Turin
	Studio C, Brescia, Italy
1973	Galerie Jacques Benador, Geneva
1974	L'Uomo e L'Arte, Milan
1975	Leo Castelli Gallery, New York
1976	Galleria La Tartaruga, Rome
1977	Contemporary Arts Museum, Houston (retrospective)
1978	Robinson Galleries, Houston
	Portland Center for the Visual Arts, Oregon
1980	Leo Castelli Gallery, New York
1982	Leo Castelli Gallery, New York
1986	Leonarda Di Mauro Gallery, New York

Selected Group Exhibitions:

1959	*Work in 3 Dimensions*, Leo Castelli Gallery, New York
1961	*Corcoran Biennial*, Corcoran Gallery, Washington, D.C.
1963	*Salon International de Galeries Pilotes*. Musée Cantonal des Beaux-Arts, Lausanne, Switzerland
1970	*Highway*, Institute of Contemporary Art, Philadelphia
1971	*Art Around the Automobile*, Hofstra University, Hempstead, New York
1976	*Personal Mythologies*, Fine Arts Building, New York
1979	*Sustained Vision*, New Museum, New York
1984	*Content: A Contemporary Focus 1974–84*, Hirshhorn Museum, Washington, D.C.
1986	*Drawings by Sculptors*, Nohra Haime Gallery, New York

Collections:

Museum of Modern Art, New York; Albright-Knox Art Gallery, Buffalo, New York; Los Angeles County Museum of Art; Stedelijk Museum, Amsterdam; Gallery of Modern Art, Tel Aviv.

Publications:

On SCARPITTA: books—*Collage* by Harriet Janis and Rudi Blesh, New York 1962; *The Joys and Sorrows of Recent American Art* by Allen S. Weller, Chicago 1968; *Attributi dell'Arte Odierna 1947-1969* by Emilio Villa, Milan 1970; article—"The Ivory Tower" by B. H. Friedman in *Art News* (New York), april 1969.

Salvatore Scarpitta, as much as Rauschenberg and Johns (with him at the Castelli Gallery since its founding), presents the contained energy of *things*. For some 25 years now Scarpitta has been making *things*—the "shaped canvases" of the late 1950's (before the term was invented); the kite, rollbar, and halter or harness works of the early 60's; the racing cars of the late 60's; the armored cars, sleds, and bins of the 70's. Consistently, all of this work is at once open and closed, visible and wrapped, sculptural and painterly, energetic and quiet. Even in his early work, beginning in 1936 at the Royal Academy in Rome, though he was attracted to a sort of neo-Futurism, he was more interested in the subject itself, its *presence*, than in its dynamics and was closer in spirit to the metaphysical quietism of Morandi than to the extrovert emphasis of Futurism.

As a boy in Los Angeles Scarpitta saw a lot of dirt-track car racing, participated in its violence and glory, perhaps romanticized the rugged beauty of homemade cars. During World War II his vision matured. He saw the vehicles of war as simultaneously protective and aggressive, contained and explosive. The two-dimensional canvas must have seemed inadequate to express what he felt, what he had seen in the "bull-ring" tracks of California and more recently, more profoundly, on the battlefields of Europe. Emotions are difficult to particularize, espcially within the tradition of Italian painting where expressionism hardly existed. But so, again, are *things*—hurt, bent, tortured, broken things. Scarpitta began to cut up his canvases, to bandage stretchers with these strips, to pierce his work in order to let it breathe. In effect, he hid his pain to make it visible. From the late 50's on, his canvases bled.

In the catalogue introduction for a 1958 exhibition in Rome, Cesare Vivaldi used images that both describe and anticipate the direction in which Scarpitta was moving: "Canvas: twisted, stretched, slashed, ripped, taut as the roof of an ancient touring car . . . ." And: " . . . this canvas of his [*Moby Dick*] is composed into planes, it spreads out into wings, it bristles and bulges, it is articulated into hood-like shapes . . . . "

By the early 60's Scarpitta was incorporating in new work not only his own previous work but also salvaged parts of racing cars, safety belts and their hardware, more modern shoulder harnesses . . . . Then he began building cars—as sought rather than found objects, as reconstructed history. The fragments of these dreams came partly from the drivers Scarpitta knew as a boy—a steering wheel from one, a radio cap from another, a chassis from a third. Other parts were cut, forged, welded as needed. As in "Rajo Jack," sometimes, because a shape seemed right, an axe was used as a tie-rod; sometimes, because that's the way it was done then, a circular saw blade was made into a steering wheel.

Scarpitta's work is not an exercise in restoration but re-creation. In all of it—the early kites as well as the recent sleds and bins—he is a sort of Robinson Crusoe, involved with re-invention rather than research. Primitive wheel-less vehicles and carriers move within their own rhythm of criss-crossed and bound laces and tape. Tents, sails, obstetrical shrouds, stand still, permit the flow of air through them, move in place, creating an environment as expansive as those of Rothko and Pollock, as specific as those Fords and dogsleds.

—B. H. Friedman

SCHAD, Christian.

German. Born in Miesbach, Upper Bavaria, 21 August 1894. Educated in Munich, Germany, until 1913; studied painting, under Heinrich von Zügel, Akademie der Bildenden Künste, Munich, 1913–14. Served briefly in German Army, Munich, 1915. Married Marcella Arcangeli in 1923 (separated, 1927);

son: Nikolaus; married Bettina Mittelstädt in 1947. Independent painter, working for Walter Serner's *Sirius* magazine, Zurich, 1915–16, and with other Dadaist artists and writers Hans Arp, Hugo Ball, Emmy Hennings, Tristan Tzara, etc., in Geneva, 1916–20; experimentation with photographic processes, first "Schadograph" photograms, Geneva, 1918; independent painter, associating with Jules Evola, Enrico Prampolini and the Casa d'Arte Bragaglia avant-garde artists group, in Rome, 1920, travelling with Walter Serner throughout Italy; in Naples and Rome, 1920–25; in Vienna, 1925–27; in Berlin, establishing own studio, 1927–43 (destroyed, 1943): worked at various professions including picture-restorer, theatre critic, teacher, etc., and as manager of a brewery office, 1935–42; lived and worked in or near Aschaffenburg, Germany, 1943–82: concentrated on painting, from 1951, and on new "Schadographs," from 1960. Recipient: Cross of Merit First Class, Republic of West Germany, 1979; Honorary Professor Award, Bürgermeister of West Berlin, 1980. Agent: Kunstkabinett G. A. Richter, Königstrasse 33, Haus Englisch, 7000 Stuttgart 1. West Germany. *Died 25 February 1982.*

Individual Exhibitions:

1921	Galerie Goldschmidt, Frankfurt
	Galerie Gurlitt, Berlin
1927	Galerie Wurthle, Vienna
1928	Galerie Neumann-Nierendorf, Berlin
1929	Galerie Gurlitt, Berlin
1930	Haus der Juryfreien, Berlin
1956	Kunstverein, Frankfurt
1959	Museum der Stadt Aschaffenburg, West Germany
	Kunstverein, Frankfurt
1960	Stadtische Museum, Braunschweig, West Germany
	Roemer Pelizaeus Museum, Hildesheim, West Germany
1961	Stadtisches Kulturamt, Remscheid, West Germany
	Haus am Waldsee, West Berlin
1962	Stadtische Galerie, Wurzburg, West Germany
1964	*Präsenation zum 70. Geburtstag.* Galerie Dorothea Loehr and Hessischer Rundfunk. Frankfurt
1969	*Bilder und Graphik nach 1945,* Neue Münchner Galerie. Munich
1970	*Schad/Dada,* Galleria Schwarz, Milan
1971	Städisches Museum, Trier, West Germany (retrospective)
	Galerie Loehr, Frankfurt (with Boris Keint)
1972	Palazzo Reale, Milan (retrospective)
1973	Galleria Stivani, Bologna
	Galleria Fant Cagni, Brescia, Italy
	Schadographien, Galleria del Levante, Munich
1974	Galerie G. A. Richter, Stuttgart
1975	*Schadographien 1918–1975,* Von der Heydt-Museum, Wuppertal, West Germany
1976	*Christian Schad,* Kunstkabinett G. A. Richter display, *Art 7,* Basle
	Christian Schad, Kunstkabinett G. A. Richter display, at the *Internationaler Kunstmarkt,* Dusseldorf
	Galerie Hilger, Vienna
	Galerie Piro, Frankfurt
1977	*Schadographien,* Kunstkabinett G. A. Richter display, at *Art 8,* Basle
	Kunstkabinett G. A. Richter, Stuttgart (2 exhibitions)
	Galerie Karin Brass, Aschaffenburg, West Germany
1978	*Das Graphische Werk und Schadographien,* Museum des 20. Jahrhunderts, Vienna (travelled to Kulturhaus der Stadt Graz, Austria)
	40 Schadographien von Christian Schad, Stadtmuseum Linz/Donau, Austria
	Goethe Institut, Munich (and world tour)
1979	Museum Stadt Miesbach, West Germany
	Vom Expressionismus bis zum Magischen Realismus, Kunstkabinett G. A. Richter, Stuttgart
1980	*Schadographien,* Galerie Beck, Augsburg. West Germany
	Staatliche Kunsthalle, West Berlin (retrospective)
1981	*Etchings, Woodcuts, Schadographs,* Leinster Fine Art, London
1984	Galleria Civica d'Arte Moderna, Palermo, Sicily

Selected Group Exhibitions:

1929	*Neue Sachlichkeit,* Stedelijk Museum, Amsterdam
1936	*Fantastic Art, Dada and Surrealism,* Museum of Modern Art, New York
1951	*Abstraction in Photography,* Museum of Modern Art New York
1958	*Dada: Dokumente einer Bewegung,* Kunstverein, Düsseldorf
1966	*Dada, 1916–66,* Kunsthaus, Zurich (travelled to Musée d'Art Moderne, Paris)
1968	*Dada, Surrealism and Their Heritage,* Museum of Modern Art, New York (toured the United States)
1970	*Photo Eye of the 20's,* Museum of Modern Art, New York (toured the United states)
1977	*Tendenzen der 20er Jahre,* Europäische Kunstausstellung, West Berlin
1978	*Dada and Surrealism Reviewed,* Hayward Gallery, London
1983	*Fotogramme: Die lichtreichen Schatten,* Fotomuseum in Stadtmuseum, Munich

Collections:

Württembergische Staatsgalerie, Stuttgart; Museum Ludwig, Cologne; Kunsthalle, Basle; Kunsthaus, Zurich; Museum of Modern Art, New York; Gernsheim Collection, University of Texas at Austin.

Publications:

By SCHAD: books—*Christian Schad: 10 Woodcut Prints,* portfolio, Zurich 1915; *Christian Schad: Hommage à Dada 1916–1976,* portfolio of 10 schadographs, Stuttgart 1976; *Christian Schad: Gaspard de la nuit oder Die Hochzeit der Romantik mit dem Geist Dadas,* portfolio of 20 schadographs, Stuttgart 1978; *Gauguins und Seidenstrümpfe,* Stuttgart 1981; articles—"Köpfe" in *Sirius* (Zurich), December 1915; "Graphik" in *Sirius* (Zurich), January 1916; "Mein Legensweg" in *Christian Schad,* exhibition catalogue, Vienna 1927; "Grünewald-Kopie in der Stiftskirche zu Aschaffenburg" in *Maltechnik* (Munich), vol. 2, 1961; "Zürich/Genf: Dada" in *Imprimatur III,* Frankfurt 1962; "Appunti Autobiografici" in *Schad/Dada,* exhibition catalogue, edited by Arturo Schwartz, Milan 1970; "Relative Realitäten: Erinnerungen um Walter Serner" in *Die Tigerin* by Walter Serner, Munich 1971; "Dada, Surrealism et Autre Chose" in *Gradiva* (Brussels), May 1971; "Arte 80 intervista Christian Schad" in *Arte 80* (Rome), Autumn 1973.

On SCHAD: books—*Der Maler Christian Schad* by Max Osborn, Berlin 1927; *Fantastic Art, Dada and Surrealism* by Alfred H. Barr Jr., New York 1936, 1937; *Photography: A Short Critical History* by Beaumont Newhall, New York 1938; *Histoire de la Photographie* by Raymond Lecuyer, Paris 1945; *The History of Photography* by Beaumont Newhall, New York 1949, 1964; *Dada: Monographie einer Bewegung* by Willy Verkauf, Teufen, Switzerland 1957, New York and London 1973; *Creative Photography* by Helmut Gernsheim, London 1962; *The Painter and the Photograph* by Van Deren Coke, Albuquerque, New Mexico 1964, 1972; *Dada à Paris* by Michel Sanouillet, Paris 1965; *A Concise History of Photography* by Helmut and Alison Gernsheim, London 1965; *Le Futurisme et le Dadaisme* by José Pierre, Lausanne 1966; *Kunst und Photographie* by Otto Stelzer, Munich 1966; *Art and Photography* by Aaron Scharf, London 1968; *Die Collage* by Herta Wescher, Cologne 1968; *Designing with Light on Paper and Film* by Robert W. Cooke, Worcester, Massachusetts 1969; *Pioneers of Modern Typography* by Herbert Spencer, New York 1969; *The Picture History of Photography* by Peter Pollack, New York 1970; *Christian Schad,* exhibition catalogue, by Giovanni Testori. Milan 1970; *Photography Without a Camera* by Patra Holter, New York 1972; *Schadographien,* exhibition catalogue, by Daniela Palazzoli, Munich 1973; *Photographie als Künstlerisches Experiment* by Willy Rotzler, Lucerne and Frankfurt 1974; *Schadographien 1918–75,* exhibition catalogue, with text by Kah Jagals, Wuppertal, West Germany 1975; *Photomontage* by Dawn Ades, London 1976; *Dictionnaire du Dadaisme 1916–1922* by Georges Hugnet, Paris 1976; *Almanacco Dada,* edited by Arturo Schwarz, Milan 1976; *Geschichte der Fotografie im 20. Jahrhundert/Photography in the 20th Century* by Petr Tausk, Cologne 1977, London 1980; *Malerei und Photographie im Dialog,* exhibition catalogue, by Erika Billeter. Berne 1977; *Das Experimentelle Photo in Deutschland 1918–1940* by Emilio Bertonati, Munich 1978; *Dada und Surrealism Reviewed,* exhibition catalogue, by Dawn Ades, London 1978; *40 Schado-*

graphien von Christian Schad, exhibition catalogue, with text by Arnulf Rohsmann, Linz, Austria 1978; *Photographie als Kunst 1879–1979/Kunst als Photographie 1949–1979*, exhibition catalogue, 2 vols., by Peter Weiermair, Innsbruck, Austria 1979; *Christian Schad: Gaspard de la Nuit*, exhibition catalogue, with text by Kurt Leonhard, Stuttgart 1979; *Avant-Garde Photography in Germany 1919–1939*, exhibition catalogue, by Van Deren Coke, Ute Eskildsen and Bernd Lohse, San Francisco 1980; *Das imaginäre Photo-Museum*, by Renate and L. Fritz Gruber, Cologne 1981; *Monographie Christian Schad*, edited by G. A. Richter, Stuttgart 1981.

In retrospect, longevity is mostly a disadvantage to an artist; a spark of genius appearing at an early age could burn out or cease to develop. There can be no easing off—it has to be worked on. The work of Leonardo, Michelangelo, Picasso—great artists whose active lives spanned six decades or more—never stopped evolving; they had to be prepared to change with the development of the life around them often becoming controversial on the way.

Christian Schad, a masterly painter throughout his long life, managed to absorb the ideas of the moment, but never became so obsessed that he was unable to withdraw and go on to the next thing. He more than flirted with various movements, but was always on the periphery—"I was always a little bit on the outside of things" enjoying the formation of a movement and soon tiring of it. With the new wave of interest and enthusiasm in German art during the Weimar Republic, Schad's place as an important figure in the *Neue Sachlichkeit* movement is now firm despite the fact that he was not living in his native country from 1915–27. Critics of the numerous exhibitions that have taken place since the 70s in Europe and the United States consider him to be one of the more sober members, presenting the same political message, but in a more subtle, less aggressive manner.

At 24, exprimenting with photography, he produced his photograms; returning to this field in 1919, he developed what Tristan Tzara termed 'Schadographs' for which he is most well known—a method without the use of a camera, the individuality supplied by arbitrary interference with the development process. His observance always supplied him with material—searching out objects in the most unlikely places.

His early woodcuts were sufficiently dynamic to be published already in 1913 and he continued to work in this medium until 1921.

His determination not to get drafted into the German Army made him decide to leave Germany and, with the help of spurious medical documents from doctor friends, he moved to Zurich where, at first, he worked for *Die Aktion*, the avant-garde magazine published in Berlin. He soon teamed up with Walter Serner and produced *Sirius*, which ran for about a year. Dada was then about to burst on Zurich. Schad considered the movement "really more of a reaction against a banal intellectualism that functioned on memory rather than intelligence . . . and had to act in an illogical way so as to keep it from being absorbed by intellectual common places." He was never totally convinced by Dadaism and cared little for the more flamboyant side of the movement. However, his portraits of around 1918 had backgrounds littered with Dada flotsam which later became even more circus-like. Whatever influences were present in Schad's work, his own individuality was always present. It was during these years that his paintings, though cubist in concept, showed his sensitivity to classical composition which, through all his varying phases, never left him.

From Zurich Schad moved to Geneva 'for a change of air and French surroundings probably as a reaction to German chauvinism and militarism'.

He said that he had no time for academics, but influences there were and they ranged from the most avant garde to the old masters, his particular idols being Botticelli, Carpaccio, Raphael and Leonardo. His *Lady from Pozzuoli* (1925) sits to the left of the picture, a few tulips beside her—the rest of the painting lies outside, seen from the window as in a Renaissance painting of a madonna. Schad shows an industrial townscape with the chimneys rising, replacing the cypresses of the 15th Century Tuscan countryside: a butterfly, with wings closed, clings to the frame of the window to break the perpendicular line; the meadow grass covers the base of the stone buildings showing how industry quickly takes over from nature. If ever a painting illustrated the mood of the moment, but incorporates and preserves the culture and the influences of the past, this is it.

Schad himself was a very distinguished figure, with long slender hands and gentle features. He worked in myriad styles and occasionally briefly abandoned art for more mundane pastimes. His sensitivity became more acute as he grew older and in the last phases of his artistic life, his drawings and paintings of children and young adults, though soft and sensitive, show great human feelings and strength of portrayal. His ability to characterise remained with him to the end.

—Muriel Emanuel

SCHAPIRO, Miriam.

American. Born in Toronto, Ontario, Canada, 15 November 1923. Educated at Erasmus Hall High School, Brooklyn; studied at the Museum of Modern Art, New York, 1937–41; Hunter College, New York, 1941–43; State University of Iowa, Iowa City, 1943–49. B.A. 1945, M.A. 1946, M.F.A. 1949. Married Paul Brach in 1946; son: Peter. Worked as teacher and secretary, Columbia, Missouri, 1950–52; children's art teacher, real estate secretary and bookshop assistant, New York, 1952–55. Full-time artist since 1955. Visiting Lecturer, Connecticut College for Women, New London, 1966–67; Lecturer, later Acting Assistant Professor, University of California at San Diego Art Department, La Jolla, 1967–69; produced series of computer painting and drawings, with David Nalibof, La Jolla, 1969; Faculty Member, California Institute of the Arts, Valencia, 1970–71; met Judy Chicago, Fresno State College, and together they co-founded and co-directed Feminist Art Program, 1973; co-directed Womanhouse Environment, Los Angeles Institute of Contemporary Art, 1974. Recipient: Ford Foundation Grant for printmaking, with Paul Brach, Tamarind Lithography Workshop, 1964. Agent: Barbara Gladstone Gallery, 152 Wooster Street, New York, New York 10012. Address: 393 West Broadway, New York, New York 10012, U.S.A.

Individual Exhibitions:

1951	University of Missouri, Columbia
	Illinois Wesleyan University, Bloomington
1958	André Emmerich Gallery, New York
1960	André Emmerich Gallery, New York
1961	André Emmerich Gallery, New York
1963	André Emmerich Gallery, New York
1964	Skidmore College, Saratoga Springs, New York
1966	Franklin Siden Gallery, Detroit
	The Lyman Allyn Museum, New London, Connecticut
1967	André Emmerich Gallery, New York
1969	André Emmerich Gallery, New York
1971	André Emmerich Gallery, New York
1973	André Emmerich Gallery, New York
1974	The Comsky Gallery, Los Angeles
1975	The Comsky Gallery, Los Angeles
	Mandeville Art Gallery, University of California at San Diego
	Benson Gallery, Bridgehampton, New York
	Mills College, Oakland, California
1976	Mabel Smith Doglass College Library, New Brunswick, New Jersey
	Mitzi Landau Gallery, Los Angeles
	André Emmerich Gallery, New York
	Douglas Drake Gallery, Kansas City
	A.R.C. Gallery, Chicago
	University of Wisconsin at LaCrosse
1977	Fairbanks Gallery, University of Oregon, Eugene
	Oberlin College, Ohio
	Reed College, Portland. Oregon
1979	Davenport Municipal Art Gallery. Iowa
	Gladstone-Villani Gallery, New York
	Lerner-Heller Gallery, New York
	Galerie Liatowitsch, Basel
	Douglass Drake Gallery, Kansas City
	Center Gallery, Madison, Wisconsin
1980	Dart Gallery, Chicago
	Barbara Gladstone Gallery. New York
	Lerner-Heller Gallery, New York
	Muse Gallery, Philadelphia
	Miriam Schapiro, A Retrospective: 1953–1980, College of Wooster Art Museum, Ohio (touring exhibition)
1981	Barbara Gladstone Gallery, New York
	Galerie Rudolf Zwirner, Cologne

Selected Group Exhibitions:

1963	*Toward a New Abstraction*, Jewish Museum, New York
1973	*21 Artists—Invisible/Visible*, Long Beach Museum of Art, California
1977	*10 Approaches to the Decorative*, Allesandra Gallery, New York
1979	*Feministische Kunst International*, Gemeentemuseum, The Hague (toured the Netherlands)
	Pattern Painting, Palais des Beaux-Arts, Brussels
	The Decorative Impulse, Institute of Contemporary Art, University of Philadelphia
1980	*Les Nouveaux Fauves di Neuen Wilden*, Ludwig Museum, Aachen
1981	*Retrospective Show—Women Artists' Series*, Douglass College, Rutgers State University, New Brunswick, New Jersey
1983	*Women Artists of the 1970s*, State University of New York, Cortland
1986	*I'm Dancing As Fast As I Can*, Bernice Steinbaum Gallery, New York

Collections:

Museum of Modern Art, New York; Whitney Museum, New York; New York University; Hirshhorn Museum, Washington, D.C.; St. Louis Art Museum, Missouri; Indianapolis Museum; Minneapolis Institute of Art; La Jolla Museum of Art, California: Newport Harbor Art Museum, Newport Beach. California; University of California Art Museum, Berkeley.

Publications:

By SCHAPIRO: book—*Anonymous Was a Woman*, editor, Valencia, California 1974; articles—"Artists on Their Art" in *Art International* (Lugano), February 1968; "Introduction" and "Out of Isolation" in *Every Woman* (Los Angeles). May 1971; "Dollhouse Room," statement with Judy Chicago, in *Womanhouse*, exhibition catalogue, Los Angeles 1972; statement, with Judy Chicago, in *21 Artists—Invisible/Visible*, exhibition catalogue, Long Beach, California 1972; statements in "Feminine Sensibility: An Analysis" by Patricia Mainardi in *The Feminists Art Journal* (New York). Autumn 1972; "Our Beginning" in *Womanhouse Journal* (Los Angeles), February 1973; "Female Imagery," with Judy Chicago, in *Womanspace Journal* (Los Angeles), June 1973; "Woman and the Creative Process: A Discussion" in *Mosaic* (Winnepeg), Autumn 1974; "More on women's Art: An Exchange." with others, in *Art in America* (New York), November/December 1976; "Interview with Miriam Schapiro," with Donald Kuspit, in *Art in America* (New York). September 1977; essay in *Reed College Exhibition: Anatomy of a Kimono*, exhibition catalogue, Portland, Oregon 1978; "Femmage" in *Helicon Nine* (New York), Spring 1981.

On SCHAPIRO: books—*Toward a New Abstraction*, exhibition catalogue, with an essay by Dore Ashton, New York 1963; *Womanhouse*, exhibition catalogue, Valencia, California 1972; *21 Artists—Invisible/Visible*, exhibition catalogue, Long Beach, California 1972; *Sunshine Muse: Contemporary Art on the West Coast* by Peter Plagens, New York and Washington, D.C. 1974; *The Shrine, the Computer and the Dollhouse: Miriam Schapiro*, edited by Moira Roth, La Jolla, California 1975: *Working It Out: 25 Women Writers, Artists,*

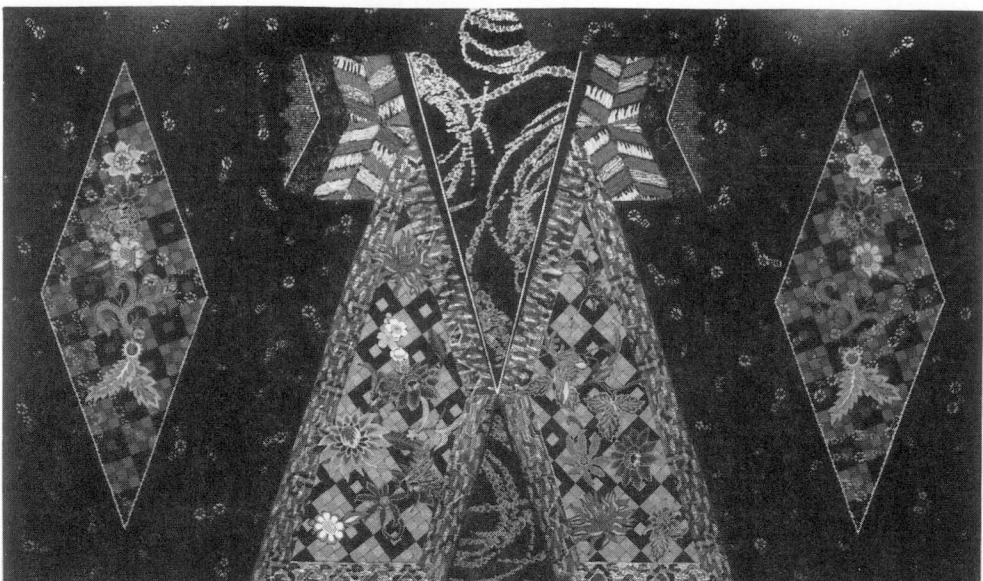

Miriam Schapiro: *Josephine B*, 1981

Scientists and Scholars Talk about Their Lives and Work, edited by Sara Ruddick and Pamela Daniels, New York 1977; *Feminist Collage: Educating Women in the Visual Arts,* edited by Judy Loeb, New York 1979; *The Originals* by Eleanor Munro, New York 1979; *Pattern Painting,* exhibition catalogue, by John Perreault, with an introduction by K. J. Geirlandt, Brussels 1979; *The Decorative Impulse,* exhibition catalogue, by Janet Kardon, Philadelphia 1979; *Feministische Kunst International,* exhibition catalogue, edited by Rosa Lindenburg, The Hague 1979; *Miriam Schapiro, A Retrospective: 1953-1980,* exhibition catalogue, edited by Thalia Gouma-Peterson Wooster, Ohio 1980; *Les Nouveaux Fauves de Neuen Wilden,* exhibition catalogue, 2 volumes, Aachen, West Germany, 1980; *Miriam Schapiro,* exhibition catalogue, by Max Kozloff, Cologne 1981; *Women and Art,* exhibition catalogue, with an essay by Erma Bombeck, Scottsdale, Arizona 1981; articles—"Miriam Schapiro" by Mary Stofflet in *Arts Magazine* (New York). May 1977; "Miriam Schapiro's Collection" by Mike Walsh in *Artweek* (Oakland, California), 19 February 1978; "Placing Women in History: Miriam Schapiro's Fan and Vestiture Series" by Paula Bradley in *Arts Magazine* (New York), February 1979; "Decoration, Ornament, Pattern and Utility" by Carrie Rickey in *Flash Art* (Milan), June/July 1979; "The Heart of the Matter" by John Perreault in the *Soho Weekly News* (New York), 13 February 1980; "Women Artists 80" by Grace Glueck and "A Decade of Progress" by Avis Berman in *Art News* (New York), October 1980; "Women and Art" by Carol Donnellkj-Kotrozo in *Arts Magazine* (New York). March 1981.

Process and Ideology in an Opulent, Multi-layered, Eccentric, and Hopeful Abstract Art:

1. The need for order and stability.
2. The need to destroy order and stability in order to find something else.
3. Finding something else.

Pattern, itself an architectural species, reflects order and stability. Then a need to create chaos as though life itself were taking place. Finally the bonding (layer by layer), the interpenetration of paint, fabric, photograph, tea towel, ribbon, lace and glue. a collage: a simultaneity; a visual dazzlement, a multilayering, a final message for the senses. And the ideology which inspires the work itself? That is feminism, the wish to have the art speak as a woman speaks. To be sensitive to the material used as though there were a responsibility to history to repair the sense of omission and to have each substance in the collage to be a reminder of a woman's dreams.

—Miriam Schapiro

Miriam Schapiro emerged as an ardent feminist in the late 1960's when she began to bring her life as a woman and an artist together. She felt she had to become one woman, one identity, and began by re-evaluating notions of the (male) public and the (female) private in hopes of repairing her own sense of self. After taking inventory of her separate roles, she looked into her specific experience as a female to find sources of making art that would be more personally relevant and expressive. A decade of personal and political struggle with feminist issues crystallized in her pioneering and collaborative involvement in Womanhouse. Co-directing the Feminist Art Program with Judy Chicago at the time (1970), they started off the school year by involving their students in a project which would allow them to project all their dreams and fantasies by creating an exclusively female environment in an old house. After renovating the house, they transformed it with performance and art works which dealt with specifically feminist issues. They used this explorative process as a means of restructuring their identities as women artists in a patriarchal (art) world.

Miriam Schapiro began her professional career in the 1950's as an abstract expressionist. In her early work one can often find vague images of the human figure and semi-submerged female symbols. In the 1960's she worked in a hard-edged, minimalist but illusionistic style. Some of the recurring female symbols become more obvious. Moody opulent color characterizes all of her work. It was during this time that Schapiro faced tumultuous confusion about her relationship to (art) history. Though working abstractly, a number of these paintings contain allusive messages about women in diverse roles (see for examples: "The Law," 1961; "Shrine for Two Paint Tubes," 1962; and "Shrine: Homage to M.L.," 1963). By 1965 she had almost completely suppressed all references to her personal self. Persevering with personal/artistic struggles led her to a resolution of proud feminist commitment. The major battles ending in 1970, Schapiro had travelled (like many others at the time) the dangerous journey through emotional, psychological, and spiritual darkness. The abyss closed. She emerged powerful and fresh.

Since then, Miriam Schapiro has been giving the history of women's "covert" art a brightly lit showcase. The once-tabooed scraps: sequins, buttons, threads, rickrack, spangles, yarn, silk, taffeta, cotton, burlap, and wool, were excavated from the musty attics and dredged from the dark closets of art history. Now, they are assembled and coordinated with emotional and creative thought into "femmages." From Schapiro's collaborative efforts with other feminist artists, particularly Melissa Meyer, she invented this word to describe art made in the techniques traditionally ascribed to women (i.e. sewing, embroidery, piece work, appliqué, etc.). It is a potpourri of collage, costume design, assemblage, decoupage, and photomontage seasoned with spiritual symbols, decorative motifs, and personal, anecdotal information.

A protector and preserver of women's heritage, her art is for everyone, as is feminism itself. She often incorporates motifs and imagery derived from women artists who worked anonymously or have been submerged by history (see for examples: "Lady Gengi's Maze," 1972; "Collaboration Series: Mary Cassatt and Me," 1975; "Anonymous Was a Woman," 1977). Her femmages are externalized projections of her interior world as well as information gathered from her daily life.

Before the patriarchal mind-body dichotomy came to reign and analytical, linear thinking (known as "intellectual") came to be hallowed as superior to non-rational (not necessarily irrational!) and creative thought/experience, there was no split, no compartmentalizations. Miriam Schapiro reunites all of these aspects in her work, protesting against society's unnatural and oppressive programming of our thinking.

Organized with geometrical unity, Schapiro's own language of flowers and decorative motifs speaks to the viewers. Her work makes us think and feel simultaneously by monumentalizing such (female) symbols as the home, the kitchen, the shrine, the theatre, the egg, hearts, handkerchiefs, and kimonos. Since ideas and things related to the realm of women had been rendered inconsequential and unintelligent by history, and "insignificant" things have been tabooed by a male-dominated art world, Schapiro restores these metaphors' many meanings. The patterned picture planes flow with human and organic rhythm. In the presence of her work, one can imagine being crooned to a state of peacefulness. Her use of color and her sense of discipline and order, also derived from deep awareness of her physical life and cycles, is passionately saturating and evocative of moody atmospheres. Schapiro's strong sense of nostalgia and proud sentimentality is often heightened by attachments of mementos from her personal and/or collective past. All of these naughty "no-no's" become subjects of spiritual devotions and gems to behold. But, then, the original etymological meaning of the word "taboo" is restored: something to be revered, respected, and preserved as sacred.

Both explosively commanding and dramatic and yet lyrical and poignant, Miriam Schapiro wields power and gives nurturance at the same time. As she said recently: "I see that all mental issues really come from a very deep perception of one's own body; how it is different from a man's. You look into yourself, and from that intimate view grows a view of the world."

Through the many layers of geometry and rich hues her work stimulates us to explore and feed our souls and from that base develop an understanding of the parallels and messages in the world around us. Having taken embroidered upholstery out of the parlor, quilts off beds, clothing off hangers, scrapbooks out of trunks, and tapestries from beneath our feet, Schapiro reeducates us about a history of buried art, women's art. As children we are stimulated and fed on all levels (creatively/emotionally/intuitively/perceptually/intellectually) and physically protected and spoiled by the art of female guides in our own families. We grow up taking these luxurious environments for granted, as society encourages. Ecologist of women, and therefore all of humanity, Miriam Schapiro encourages us to take heed and give gratitude to these traditions, in hopes of motivating us to make our culture whole again.

—Elise LaRose

SCHIFANO, Mario.
Italian. Born in Homs, Libya, in 1934. Painter: lives and works in Rome. Recipient: Premio Lissone,

1961. Agent: Studio Marconi, via Tadino 15. 20124 Milan. Address: via del Babuino 51, Rome, Italy.

Individual Exhibitions:

1959	Galleria Appia Antica. Rome
1961	Galleria La Tartaruga, Rome
1963	Galleria dell'Ariete, Milan
	Galerie Ileana Sonnabend, Paris
	Galleria Odyssia, Rome
1964	Galleria dell'Ariete, Milan
	Odyssia Gallery, New York
	Galleria Odyssia, Rome
	Galleria II Punto, Turin
1965	Studio Maraconi, Milan
	Galleria La Tartaruga, Rome
1966	Galleria Il Canale, Venice
	Galleria Il Punto, Turin
	Studio Maraconi, Milan
	Galleria Stein, Turin
1967	Galleria La Tartaruga, Rome
	Galleria Stein, Turin
	Galleria La Bertesca, Genoa
	Galleria Stefanoni, Lecco, Italy
	Studio Marconi, Milan
1968	Galleria del Minotauro, Brescia, Italy
	Studio Marconi, Milan
1969	Galleria della Chiocciola, Padua
1970	Studio Marconi, Milan
	Galleria La Città, Verona
1972	Galleria L'Uomo e L'Arte, Milan
	Galleria Soligo, Rome
1973	Galleria Il Gabbiano, Rome
	Galleria della Steccata, Rome
	Galleria II Punto Turin
1974	Galleria Lia Rumma, Naples
	Istituto di Storia dell'Arte, University of Parma
	Studio Marconi, Milan
1975	Galleria dei Mille, Bergamo, Italy
1984	Palazzo delle Prigioni Vecchie, Venice
	Galleria Bergamini, Milan
	Galleria Ravagnan, Venice
1985	Galerie Reckermann, Cologne
	Italienische Institut, Cologne

Selected Group Exhibitions:

1960	*5 Giovani Pittori Romani*, Galleria II Cancello, Bologna (travelled to Galleria La Salita, Rome)
1962	*The New Realists*, Sidney Janis Gallery, New York
1964	*Carnegie International*, Carnegie Institute. Pittsburgh
1966	*Contemporary Italian Art*, Museum am Ostwall, Dortmund, West Germany (travelled to Moderna Museet. Stockholm)
1969	*Aspekte aus Italien*, Galerie im Taxispalais. Innsbruck (travelled to the Galerie Nächst St. Stephan, Vienna)
1973	*Combattimento per un'Immagine*, Galleria Civica d'Arte Moderna, Turin
1977	*La Traccia del Racconto*, Villa Comunale Ormand, San Remo, Italy
1980	*Arte e Critica*, Galleria Nazionale d'Arte Moderna, Rome
1982	*Arte Italiana 1960–1982*, Hayward Gallery, London
1986	*Aspects of Italian Art 1960–85*, Kunstverein, Frankfurt

Collections:

Galleria Nazionale d'Art; Moderna, Rome: Museu de Arte Moderna, Sao Paolo; Museum of Modern Art, Tokyo.

Publications:

On SCHIFANO: books—*Schifano*. exhibition catalogue, by Maurizio Calvesi. Milan 1964: *Schifano*, exhibition catalogue, by Frank O'Hara, New York 1964: *Schifano*, exhibition catalogue, by Maurizio Fagiolo, Venice 1966: *Le Due Avanguardie* by Maurizio Calvesi, Milan 1966; *Mario Schifano*, exhibition catalogue, by Arturo C. Quintavalle, Vittorio

Fagone, and Maurizio Calvesi, Milan 1974 *Mario Schifano: Naturale Sconosciuto*, exhibition catalogue, Venice 1984; *Mario Schifano: Bilder und Gouachen 1962-1983*, exhibition catalogue, Cologne 1985.

Perceptive observation has always been at the base of Mario Schifano's work. While he is a realistic painter, he has produced pictures that have become known in the range established by the system of theoretical-ideological syntheses or of simplifications (or elaborations) on logical lines. The artist, that is, has not wanted to use his works to give solutions to the problems of real life, nor even to report on its conditions, so much as to counter painting in its density, in the complex web of relationships between the methods of interpreting a picture and its "use" for communication. That is why his pictures when completed are deliberately imperfect, with no conclusions and no emphasis on subject matter. Everything in them has to be clearly visible, so that nothing in them has to be explained. They show what is to be seen, and in so doing lead to that logic of communication which—as Wittgenstein emphasizes—allows us to cross the street without being knocked down. Schifano paints what he has observed, and since the world is changing, his art changes with it. It has not been adapted to the times; it is part of time.

In Mario Schifano's pictures everything is reduced to a self-explanatory image, even the captions, which are no more than a picture within a picture, decodified fragments with an autonomous life of their own. The picture is a photograph made by hand, a photogram fixed, filtered and flattened, using a mechanical eye to put distance between man and objects, between the objects and the pictures of them.

An art so carried out takes on a marked objectifying character; the edges of the canvas become the limits of the visible field and the picture the mirror of a fragment of reality in which the presence of the whole is manifested.

The artist represents the diversity of things by means of a realism filtered by the ordinary use of the language of advertising. That is not, of course, to say that his pictures are like advertisements—far from it; they are born of the need to manifest a plurality of aspects within the object represented, which is manipulated by the artist in order to have a relationship with it. In the end the painted canvas acquires an

essence, a sort of internal spirit of the objects. It is this desire to get to the bottom of things that lies at the base of the serial and repetitive procedure employed by Schifano, a procedure that has enabled him to give substance to his pictures swiftly, putting them in a state of precarious equilibrium that makes them "alive" even before they are finished.

—Demetrio Paparoni

SCHMIDT, Julius.

American. Born in Stamford, Connecticut, 6 February 1923. Studied at Oklahoma A and M University, Stillwater, 1950-51; Cranbrook Academy of Art, Bloomfield Hills, Michigan, 1951-55, B.F.A. 1952, M.F.A. 1955; studied with Ossip Zadkine, in Paris, 1953, and at the Accademia di Belle Arti, Florence, 1954. Served with the United States Army, in the Pacific, during World War II. Independent sculptor, since 1955: lives and works in Iowa City. Chairman of Sculpture, Kansas City Art Institute, Missouri, 1955-59; taught at Rhode Island School of Design, Providence, 1959-60, and University of California, Berkeley, 1961-62; Head of the Department of Sculpture, Cranbrook Academy of Art, 1962-69. Since 1970, Head of the Department of Sculpture, University of Iowa, Iowa City. Recipient: Guggenheim Fellowship, 1963. Agent: Gallery K, R Street N W, Washinton, D.C. 20036. Addresses: 5 Highview Knoll, Iowa City, Iowa 52240, U.S.A.; Department of Art, University of Iowa, Iowa City, Iowa 52240, U.S.A.

Individual Exhibitions:

1953	Silvermine Guild of Artists, New Canaan, Connecticut
1957	Kansas City Art Institute, Missouri
1958	Nelson Gallery, Kansas City, Missouri
1961	Santa Barbara Musuem of Art, California
	Otto Gerson Gallery, New York
1962	University of California. Berkeley

Mario Schifano: *Ultimo Programma*, 1972

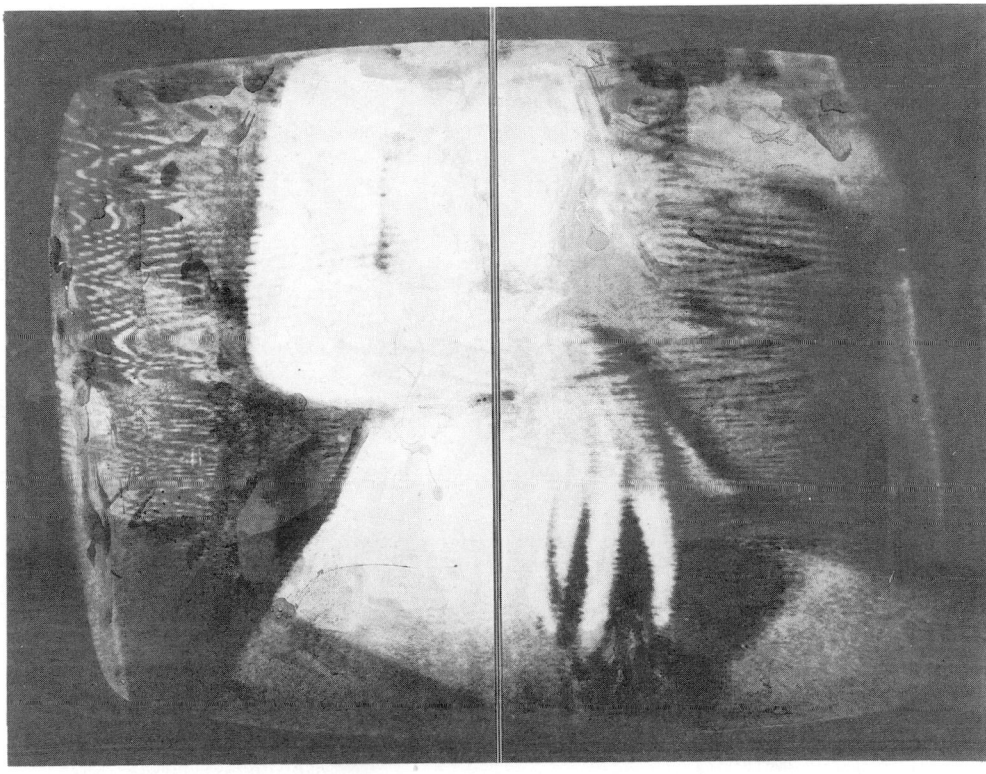

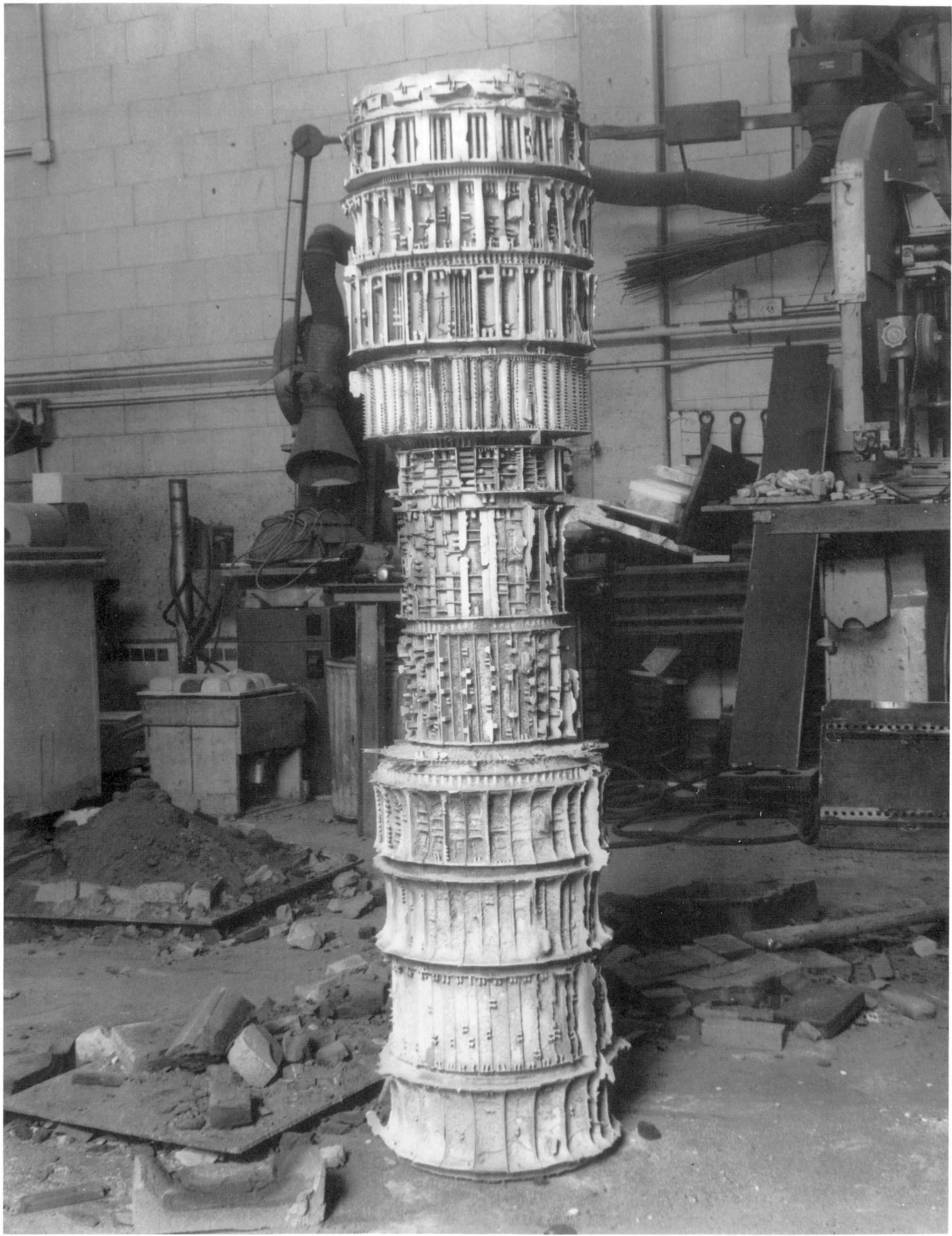

Julius Schmidt: *Cast Bronze*, 1985

1963	Otto Gerson Gallery, New York
1964	Franklin Siden Gallery. Detroit
1966	Marlborough-Gerson Gallery, New York
	Kansas City Art Institute, Missouri
	Taudega College, Alabama
1967	Gertrude Kasle Gallery, Detroit
1969	Cranbrook Academy of Art, Bloomfield Hills, Michigan
1971	Marlborough Gallery, New York
	Madison College, Virginia
1972	Gertrude Kasle Gallery, Detroit
1974	University of Iowa Museum of Art, Iowa City (retrospective)
	Gertrude Kasle Gallery, Detroit
	Rockford College, Illinois
1980	Swope Art Gallery, Terre Haute, Indiana
1981	Augusta College, Georgia
1984	Monmouth College, Illinois
1985	Sheldon Swope Art Gallery, Terre Haute, Indiana
1987	University Hospital, Iowa City

Selected Group Exhibitions:

1958	*6 American Sculptors*, Arts Club of Chicago
1959	*16 Americans*, Museum of Modern Art, New York
1960	*Aspects of American Sculpture*, Galerie Claude Bernard. Paris
1962	*The Hirshhorn Collection*, Guggenheim Musuem, New York
1963	*Bienal*, Sao Paulo
	Sculpture in the Open Air, Battersea Park, London
1964	*American Vision*, Marlborough-Gerson Gallery, New York
1966	*Lipman Collection*, Whitney Museum, New York
1973	*Biennial*, Middelheim Park, Antwerp

1983	*Iron Cast/Cast Iron*, Pratt Gallery, New York (travelled to Washington, D.C.)

Collections:

Museum of Modern Art, New York; Whitney Museum, New York; Albright-Knox Art Gallery, Buffalo, New York; Detroit Institute of Arts; Art Institute of Chicago; Walker Art Center, Minneapolis; Nelson Gallery, Kansas City, Missouri; Hirshhorn Museum, Washington, D.C.; Princeton Museum of Art, New Jersey; Santa Barbara Museum of Art, California.

Publications:

On SCHMIDT: books—*16 Americans,* exhibition catalogue. New York 1959; *Concise History of Modern Sculpture* by Herbert Read. London 1964; *Art in Architecture* by Redstone, New York 1968; *American Sculpture in Process 1930-1970,* New York 1975; *The Metaphorical Imagery of Julius Schmidt* by Robert D. Kinsman, New York 1985.

On the Machine Form: Images that involve the insoluble problem of technology/humanity—concerns with the measure of civilized society and the pursuit of technology.

On Cast Iron: The reasons for working with cast iron are numerous and complex. Conscious, subconscious, atavistic, inherited—one does not always know what directs one's efforts. However, there remains the strong, persistent desire to use the material—to engage in the ritual aspects of melting and pouring, events that evoke countless associations linked deep in the mind of man.

—Julius Schmidt

SCHNABEL, Julian.

American. Born in Brooklyn, New York in 1951; raised partly in Brownsville, Texas. Studied at the University of Houston, 1969–72. B.F.A. 1972; Whitney Museum Independent Study Program, New York, 1973. Married. Did odd jobs and worked as a cab driver in New York in the mid-1970's; returned to Texas for a year, then travelled to Europe and back to New York; worked as a cook in Locale Restaurant, Greenwich Village; travelled in France and Italy, 1976, and in Spain, Italy and Germany, 1978. Agent: Mary Boone Gallery, New York. Address: c/o Mary Boone Gallery, 417 West Broadway, New York, New York 10012, U.S.A.

Individual Exhibitions:

1976	Contemporary Arts Museum, Houston
1978	Galerie December, Dusseldorf
1979	Mary Boone Gallery, New York (2 exhibitions)
	Daniel Weinberg Gallery, San Francisco
1980	Bruno Bischofberger, Zurich
	Young-Hoffman Gallery, Chicago
1981	Mary Boone and Leo Castelli Galleries, New York (joint exhibition)
	Margo Leavin Gallery, Los Angeles
	Schnabel/Rothenberg/Moskowitz. Kunsthalle, Basle (travelled to the Kunstverein, Frankfurt, and the Louisiana Museum, Humlebaek, Denmark)
1982	Stedelijk Museum, Amsterdam (retrospective)
	Mary Boone Gallery, New York
	Tate Gallery, London
1983	Galerie Bischofberger, Zurich
	Castelli Graphics, New York
	Akron Art Museum, Ohio
	Galerie Daniel Templon, Paris

Julian Schnabel: *Hope,* **1982** Courtesy Whitney Museum, New York

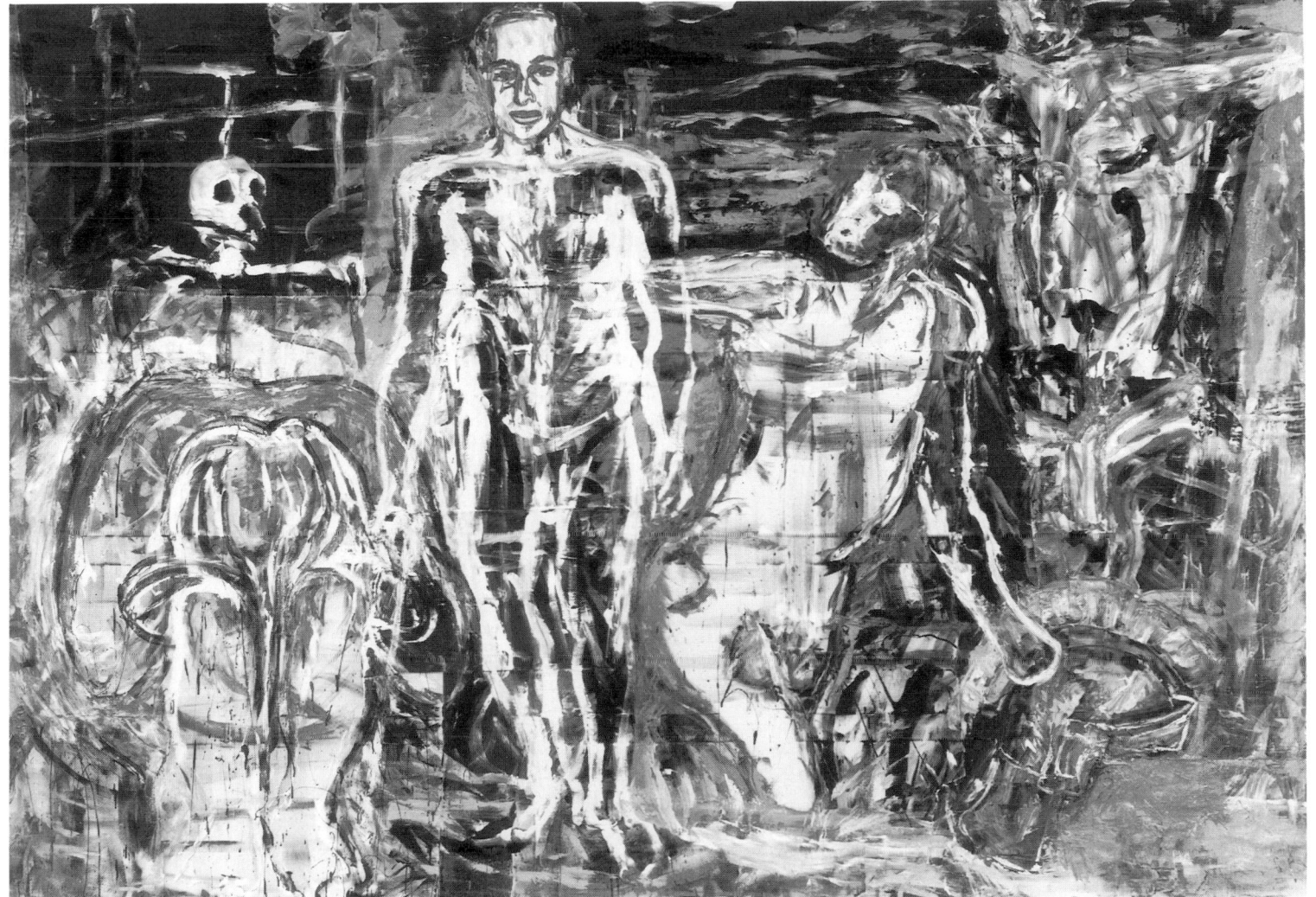

	Galleria Mario Diacono, Rome
	Waddington Galleries, London
1984	Akira Ikeda Gallery, Tokyo
	Galerie Bischofberger, Zurich
	Pace Gallery, New York
1985	Galerie Bischofberger, Zurich
	Galleria Sperone, Rome
	Waddington Galleries, London
1986	Whitechapel Art Gallery, London (travelled to Paris; toured the United States, 1987–88)
	Pace Gallery, New York

Selected Group Exhibitions:

1977	*Surrogate/Self Portraits.* Holly Solomon Gallery, New York
1980	*L'Amerique aux Independants*, Grand Palais, Paris
	Painting and Sculpture Today, Indianapolis Museum of Art
1981	*Whitney Biennial*, Whitney Museum, New York
	A New Spirit in Painting. Royal Academy, London
	Figurative Aspects of Recent Art, Massachusetts Institute of Technology. Cambridge
1982	*Focus on the Figure*, Whitney Museum, New York
1984	*Legendes*, Musée d'Art Contemporain, Bordeaux, France
1986	*Carnegie International*, Carnegie Institute, Pittsburgh

Publications:

On SCHNABEL: books—*Julian Schnabel*, exhibition catalogue with text by Wilfried Dickhoff, New York 1986; *Julian Schnabel: Paintings 1975–1986*, exhibition catalogue with essay by Thomas McEvilley, London 1986; articles—"2 Painters Explore New Wave" by Hilton Kramer in the *New York Times*, 17 April 1981; "Is Julian Schnabel That Good" by John Perreault in the *Soho News* (New York), 22 April 1981; "The Ardor of Ambition" by Peter Schjeldahl in the *Village Voice* (New York). 23 February 1982; "Julian Schnabel" by Cathleen McGuigan in *Artnews* (New York). Summer 1982.

Julian Schnabel's rapid and controversial rise to critical focus—if not acclaim—has been taken as an emblem of the art world's present search for new form-givers, the equal of those who arose in earlier decades. so that both his appearance and the nature of his work itself may be taken as emblem of the unstable nature of avant-gardist visual culture—subject to media exploitation, and itself quite willing to manipulate its image for the purposes of commerce under the guise of the promulgation of an authentic aesthetic discovery or extension.

Schnabel's collage mode, both in its literal materiality and in its multi-style references and clear homage to artists of the recent past, is a characteristic mark of the eclectic drift of the early 1980's. His special contribution to such style uneasiness, and the general primitivizing and nervously mannered neo-expressionistic mode, may be his clearly kitsch approach—his appropriation of cliché seemingly without an ironic or distancing stance. Although the latter and traditional modernist attitude toward such material may be implicit in his usual ambitiously bombastic images—best known have been the work with shards of china imbedded in the impasto ground and his use of velvet as ground—nonetheless, Schnabel's intense and deliberate mindless presentation, as well as his religious and sexual aura, does not lend itself to such objectivity. (" . . . the emotive effect arises less from the image, which is not immediately decipherable, than from an audacious stylistic performance . . . evoking the conflicted drama of delusionary omnipotence undermined by self-protective ambivalence."—D. Wheeler).

The fear and wariness of many critics has been apparently the clear index in such works to the weakening of the older avant-gardist distinction of high and low culture; and thus if such work as Schnabel's is the further triumph of a Pop Art, it is now cynically and exhaustedly stripped of both the optimism and the clear striving for personal expressiveness within older recent art.

In recent exhibitions, the artist's longtime extravagance in scale, subject, and hyper-elaborate titling, and as well in a bravura handling of material, but there has been a dampening of the horror vacui which led to the earlier surface encrustation, and the mid-1980s works have a more resolved appearance. Also, Schnabel's celebration of his own celebrity and his seeming exultation of the banal culminated, for the time being, in the publication of a memoir *C.V.J.: Nicknames of Maitre D's and Other Excerpts from Life*. There is now a greater confidence in pictorial invention, and so line and shape appear openly and are stamped with authority. Still, his work continues to be read as if it were a body of sophisticated juvenalia, somehow trivializing both theme and performance through lack of justification for either.

Critical focus has been constant upon this psycho-social aspect of his career for some time: his self-conscious attempt to present his art and persona as mythic and thus create at only the extremities. If his neo-expressionist paintings from the later 1970s on were thereby bathetic and anxiety-ridden, their more current dependence upon an easier decorative command may yield an oeuvre less temporal in its appeal.

—Joshua Kind

SCHNEEMANN, Carolee.

American. Born in Fox Chase, Pennsylvania, 12 October 1939. Studied at the University of Illinois, Urbana; Bard College, Annandale-on-Hudson, New York; Columbia University School of Painting and Sculpture, New York; New School for Social Research, New York; Universidad de Puebla, Mexico. Married the artist Anthony McCall in 1972. Independent artist, New York, since 1962: founder-director, Kinetic Theater movement and design workshops, New York, 1963–68; founder-member, with Joseph Kosuth, Anthony McCall and others, International-Local group, New York, 1976. Art instructor, University of Illinois, Urbana, 1961–62; Artist-in-Residence, Colby College, Maine, 1968, and Dartington College, Totnes, Devon, 1972. Recipient: Performance Grant, Benedict Arnold Foundation, New York, 1964; Writers grant, Croton Press, New York, 1968; New York State Council on the Arts Grant, 1968, 1974, 1975, 1976, 1977; Cassandra Foundation Grant, New York, 1970; National Endowment for the Arts Grant, Washington, D.C., 1974, 1977, 1978, 1983, 1985; New York Foundation for the Arts Grant, 1974, 1977, 1978, 1987; Creative Artists Public Service Grant, New York, 1978; Art Matters Inc. Grant, New York, 1986. Address: 114 West 29th Street, New York, New York 10001, U.S.A.

Individual Exhibitions:

1962	*Mink Paws Turret*, Artist's Studio, New York
1963	*Eye Body*, Artist's Studio, New York
1964	*Environment*, Artist's Studio, New York
1969	*Performance Drawings and Photo/Collage*, Chelsea School of Art, London
1973	*Performance Drawings and Photo/Collage*, Camden Arts Centre, London
1974	*Up to and Including Her Limits*, University of California, Berkeley
1976	*Up to and Including Her Limits*, Studiogalerie, West Berlin
	Up to and Including Her Limits, The Kitchen, New York
1977	Galerie De Appel, Amsterdam
	Multiples, Archives Francesco Conz, Italy
1979	*ABC:We Print Anything/In the Cards*, Galerie De Appel, Amsterdam

	Forbidden Actions, C. Space, New York
	Bard College, Annandale-on-Hudson, New York
1980	*Dirty Pictures*, A.I.R. Galery, New York
1981	*Image/Texts*, Washington Project for the Arts, Washington, D.C.
	Images/Texts and Debris Grid, Real Artways, Hartford, Connecticut
1982	*Early Work*, Max Hutchinson Gallery, New York
1983	*Works on Paper*, Rutgers University, New Brunswick, New Jersey
	Image/Text, Colby-Sawyer College, New London, New Hampshire
	Recent Work, Max Hutchinson Gallery, New York
1984	*Performed Paintings and Works on Paper*, Kleinert Gallery, Woodstock, New York
	Cycles-Re-Cycles, Kent State University, Ohio
1985	*Recent Work*, Max Hutchinson Gallery, New York
1986	*Performance Notebooks and Scores*, University of California at Los Angeles
	Recent and Early Work, Henri Gallery, Washington, D.C.
1988	*Self-Shot*, Emily Harvey Gallery, New York
	New Rituals, Boston Museum School of Fine Arts, Massachusetts

Happenings and Performances include: *Labyrinths*, Sidney, Illinois, 1960; *Glass Environment for Sound and Motion*, Living Theater, New York, 1962; *Chromelodeon*, Judson Dance Theater, New York, 1963; *Meat Joy*, at *Festival de la Libre Expression*, Paris, Dennison Hall, London, and Judson Church, New York, 1964; *Water Light/Water Needle*, St. Mark's Church, New York, 1966; *Snows*, Martinique Theatre, New York, 1967; *Object in Process*, Something Else Gallery, New York, 1968; *Expansions*, Round House, London, 1969; *Film/Action Theatre*, Paradiso Theatre, Amsterdam, 1971; *Interior Scroll*, East Hampton, Long Island, New York 1975; *Fresh Blood: A Dream Morphology*, Real Artways, Hartford, Connecticut, 1981.

Selected Group Exhibitions:

1967	*Avant-Garde Festival*, Staten Island Ferry, New York
1971	*Happening und Fluxus*, Kunstverein, Cologne
1975	*Artists and Post Cards*, Loeb Student Center, New York University
1977	*La Boutique Aberrante*, Centre Georges Pompidou, Paris
1980	*A Decade of Women's Performance Art*, Contemporary Art Center, New Orleans
1982	*Labyrinth of Self-Consciousness*, Narodowe, Warsaw (travelled to Lodz and Wroclaw)
1984	*Blam! Pop, Minimalism and Performance 1958–64*, Whitney Museum, New York
1986	*The Heroic Female*, Ceres Gallery, New York
1988	*Apollo, Dionysius and Job*, Alternative Museum, New York

Collections:

Philadelphia Museum of Art, Pennsylvania; Detroit Institute of Art, Michigan; Institute of Contemporary Art, Chicago; Los Angeles Institute of Contemporary Art; Cincinnati Museum of Art, Ohio; Contemporary Archives, University of Massachusetts, Amherst; Krannert Art Gallery, University of Illinois, Urbana; Institute of Contemporary Arts, London; Kunsthaus, Zurich; Archives of Modern Art, Zagreb, Yugoslavia.

Publications:

By SCHNEEMANN:books—*Parts of a Body House Book*, Cullompton, Devon 1972; *Cezanne, She Was A Great Painter*, New York 1974, 1976; *ABC: We Print Anything—In the Cards*, Beuningen, Netherlands 1977; *More Than Meat Joy: Complete Performace Works and Selected Writing*, New York 1979; *Early and Recent Work*, with texts by J. Ballerini and Ted Castle, New York 1983.

On SCHNEEMANN: books—*A Primer of Happenings and Time/Space Art* by Al Hansen, New York 1966; *Technicians of the Sacred*, edited by Jerome Rothenberg, Garden City, New York 1967; *Happening und Fluxus* by Harald Szemann and Hanns Sohm, Cologne 1970; *Environments, Happen-*

ings, *Performance* by Adrian Henri, London 1974; *Performance Art* by Roselee Goldberg, London 1978; *Judson Dance Theater: 1962-1966*, edited by Wendy Perron and Daniel Cameron, Benninton, Vermont 1981; *The Amazing Decade: Women and Performace Art 1970-1980*, edited by Moira Roth, Los Angeles 1982; *The Object of Performance: The American Avant-Garde Since 1970* by Henry Sayre, Chicago 1987.

Performance art found its culmination in its early phase of development, in the works of Carolee Schneemann. Her early performances were documentations of a new view of art in general, continuing the traditionally separated disciplines of painting, sculpture, film and real life events. Merging these disciplines new modalities were explored which resulted in a new autonomous medium. Female sensibility which had never been articulated with radical clarity is related to the inauguration and establishment of this medium. In addition to her creative work Carolee Schneemann is also one of the most intelligent and perceptive critics of the art of our time.

Born in 1939 in Fox Chase, Pennsylvania, Carolee Schneemann studied painting in Urbana, Illinois, New York and Puebla, Mexico. She also worked with dancers like Trisha Brown, Deborah Hay and Yvonne Rainer, film makers like Stan Brankhage and artists like Robert Morris and Claes Oldenburg. Her early work *Eye Body* of 1963 grew out of the artistic climate in New York, and with it she established her own independent contribution to contemporary art. It is the artist herself which is made part of the environment, and the interaction of materials, living snakes, human bodies and a feminist strategy constitutes something which in this combination did not exist before.

One year after this important event a fundamental breakthrough took place in Schneemann's *Meat Joy*, performed in May 1964 in Paris, then in London and in New York. With this work the course of performance art took a different direction. *Meat Joy* was based on a dream-like sequence of movements of the participants, who were not actors or dancers in the traditional sense, but participants of a new medium. A choreography of a different kind was established which encompassed psychological and physical relationships, resulting in an erotic ritual in which the newly achieved structures of freedom, orgiastic exuberance and vitality were manifest.

Since 1964 Carolee Schneemann has expanded her work into several directions: the film *Fuses* of 1964 in which the artist is both film-maker and participant is an artistic celebration of the sexual act. Gene Youngblood described it: "A film which breaks the barriers between the private and public subject-matter. From her background as a painter, Schneemann was free to explore the physical-visual contexts of sexuality in rhythmic layers of collaged imagery."

In 1966 the event *Water Light/Water Needle* explored the human body in the context of natural forces; *Kitch's Last Meal* of 1973-1978 was a celebration of a relationship between the artist and her cat; *Thames Crawling* of 1970 is a vital choreography of bodies in movement.

Around 1973/1974 Carolee Schneemann entered yet another phase of her development which went even further in directly relating the personal life of the artist to her work. *Up To And Including Her Limits* of 1973 is a typical example: the artist hangs from a rope for extended durations swinging in limited directions as she marks the floor and walls with chalk. The work is a brilliant document of artistic activity itself, but at the same time it exemplifies the state of the life of the artist. *Interior Scroll* of 1975 continues these tendencies to its most radical consequences; it creates a powerful symbol in which the body of the artist and literary tradition of knowledge are united. Standing on a stage the artist reads from a scroll which she slowly pulls out of her vagina. The artist wrote about this work: "I saw the vagina as a translucent chamber of which the serpent was an outmoded model: enlivened by its passage from the visible to

the invisible, a spiraled coil ringed with the shape of desire and generative mysteries, attribute of both female and male sexual powers."

Carolee Schneemann's recent actions and performances, which are parallel—as in all the phases of her work—to her paintings, sculptures, collages and environments, continue to explore more complex idiosyncrasies of life and art, the rational and the emotional, male and female sensibilities. In her *Venus Vectors-Abstract*, first installed in the Everson Museum of Art in Syracuse in 1987, the artist built an environmental sculpture encompassing her 1983 performance *Fresh Blood–A Dream Morphology*, combining visual, acoustical, electronic as well as action and viewer participation into a universal work of art, all elements merging into a symbolic language of high intensity. In regard to her stature as an artist and her unique achievements since 1963 Carolee Schneemann can be seen on the level of other pioneering artists such as Stan Brakhage, Nam June Paik, Pina Bausch and Phil Glass, each inaugurating and perfecting a newly created medium of contemporary artistic activity.

—Udo Kultermann

SCHÖFFER, Nicolas.

French. Born in Kalocsa, Hungary, 6 September, 1912; emigrated to France, 1936: naturalized, 1948. Studied at the School of Fine Arts, Budapest, 1932–35; Ecole des Beaux-Arts, Paris, 1936–39. Married Marguerite Orlhac in 1945 (died, 1970); married Eleonore de Lavandeyra in 1971. Agricultural worker, Auvergne 1941–42, 1944–45; foundry-worker, Saint-Etienne 1943; hotel night-porter, Paris 1946–47; doll factory-worker, Paris 1949–51. Independent artist, Paris, since 1948: first "spatiodynamic" sculptures. 1948: first cybernetic sculptures, 1955; "luminodynamic" works, from 1957; "chronodynamic" works, from 1959; video-art works, from 1961; musical researches, from 1977. Instructor in Art and Programming, Ecole Nationale Supérieure des Beaux-Arts, Paris, 1966–71; Visiting Lecturer, McGill University, Montreal 1971; Université de Bruxelles, 1971; Cité Universitaire, Neuchatel, Switzerland, 1972; Sorbonne, Paris 1972, 1977; French Institute, Athens 1974; Ecole des Beaux-Arts, Orleans, 1975; and the Kunstakademic, Stuttgart, 1977. Nicolas Schöffer Museum, Kalocsa, Hungary, established 1980. Recipient: Grand Prix, *Biennale*, Venice, 1968; First Prize, *Henry Moore Exhibition*, Hakone Museum, Japan, 1980; Frank J. Malina/Leonardo Prize, San Francisco, 1986. Member of the Institut, Académie des Beaux-Arts, Paris, 1982; Officier, Ordre des Arte et des Lettres; Officier, Légion d'Honneur; Ordre du Drapeau, Budapest. Agent: Artcurial, 9 Avenue Matignon, 75008 Paris. Address: 15 rue Hegesippe Moreau, 75018 Paris, France.

Individual Exhibitions:

1950	Galerie des Deux-Iles, Paris
1952	Galerie Mai, Paris
1957	Theatre d'Evreux, France (spatiodynamic spectacle)
	Grand Central Station, New York (spatiodynamic spectacle)
1958	Galerie Denise René, Paris
1960	Institute of Contemporary Arts, London
1961	Palais des Beaux-Arts, Brussels
1963	Musée des Arts Décoratifs, Paris (retrospective)
	Theatre de la Cité, Lyon-Villeurbanne, France (with Roger Planchot)
1964	*Ruimte/Licht/Tijd*, Stedelijk Museum, Amsterdam
	Stedelijk Van Abbemuseum, Eindhoven, Netherlands
1965	Jewish Museum, New York (with Jean Tinguely; travelled to the Washington Gallery of Modern Art; and the Carnegie Institute, Pittsburgh)
1966	Galerie Denise René, Paris
1968	Waddell Gallery, New York
	Kinetische Plastiakk/Licht/Raum/Bewegung, Kunsthalle, Dusseldorf
	Hamburg Oper (luminodynamic spectacle at Menotti/Nikolais ballet)
1969	Galerie Denise René, Paris
	Henie-Onstad Kunstsenter, Oslo
	Musée d'Art Moderne, Paris (audio-visual spectacle)
1970	Fundacion Mendoza, Caracas
	Spanodynamisme/Luminodynamisme/Chronodynamismee/Cybernetique: Recherches de 1948 à 1970, Galerie Denise René, Paris
1971	Cercle Noroit, Arras, France
1972	Denise René Gallery, New York
	Cité Universitaire, Neuchatel, Switzerland
1973	Kunstmuseum, Aarau, Switzerland
	Hamburg Oper (cybernetic spectacle; with Pierre Henry and Alwin Nikolais)
	Maison de la Culture, Chalon-sur-Saône, France
	Centro Industria Montedison, Milan
1974	Galeria Arte/Contacto, Caracas
	Musée d'Art Moderne de la Ville, Paris
1975	Galerie Denise René, Paris
	Galerie Denise René/ Hans Mayer, Dusseldorf
	Artcurial, Paris
1977	Kunstmuseum, Bonn
1978	Maison de la Culture, Chatou, France
1979	Centre Culturel Suedois, Paris (concert performance)
1980	Nicolas Schöffer Museum, Kalocsa, Hungary (inaugural exhibition)
1982	Artcurial, Paris
	Mucsarnok/Museum of Modern Art, Budapest
1984	Cathedral of Kalocsa, Hungary
	IRCAM, Paris

Selected Group Exhibitions:

1956	*Festival d'Art Avant-Garde*, Habitation Le Corbusier, Marseilles
1965	*Kinetic and Optic Art Today*, Albright-Knox Art Gallery, Buffalo, New York
1968	*Biennale*, Venice
1970	*Expo 70*, Osaka, Japan
1971	*Biennale de Paris*, Parc Floral, Paris
1975	*Festival d'Automme*, Chapelle de la Sorbonne, Paris
1977	*Biennale de la Tapisserie*, Lausanne
1981	*Paris-Paris*, Centre Georges Pompidou, Paris
1983	*Electra*, Musee d'Art Moderne, Paris
1987	*Digital Visions: Computers and Art*, Everson Art Museum, Syracuse, New York

Collections:

Nicolas Schöffer Museum, Kalocsa, Hungary; Centre Georges Pompidou, Paris; Musée de Plein air, Paris; Musée de la Tapisserie, Beauvais, France; Museum of Modern Art, Tel-Aviv; Galleria Nazionale d'Arte Moderna, Rome; Office Européen des Brevets, Munich; City Administration Centre, Bonn; Embarcadero Center, San Francisco; Hakone Open-Air Museum, Tokyo.

Publications:

By SCHÖFFER: books—*Le Spatiodynamisme*, Boulogne-sur-Seine 1955; *La Ville Cybernetique*, Paris 1969; *Le Nouvel Esprit Artistique*, Paris 1970; *Entretiens avec Nicolas Schöffer*, with Philippe Sers, Paris 1971; *La Tour Lumiére Cybernetique*, Paris 1973; *La Nouvelle Charte de la Ville*, Paris 1974; *Art et société*, portfolio, with text by Jean Louis Ferrier, Paris 1976; *Perturbation et Chronocratie*, Paris 1978; *Sur l'Amenagement du Temps—essai de chronogenie*, with others, Paris 1981; *La Theorie des Miroirs*, Paris 1981; *Discours d'Election a l'Académie des Beaux-Arts*, Paris 1984; *Temps et Programmation, Temps libre*, Paris 1985; films—*Fer Chaud*, with Jacques Brissot, 1957; *Spatiodynamisme*, with Langlois, 1958; *Mayola*, with Gruel, 1958; *Variations Luminodynamiques l*, with Jean Kerchbron, 1961;

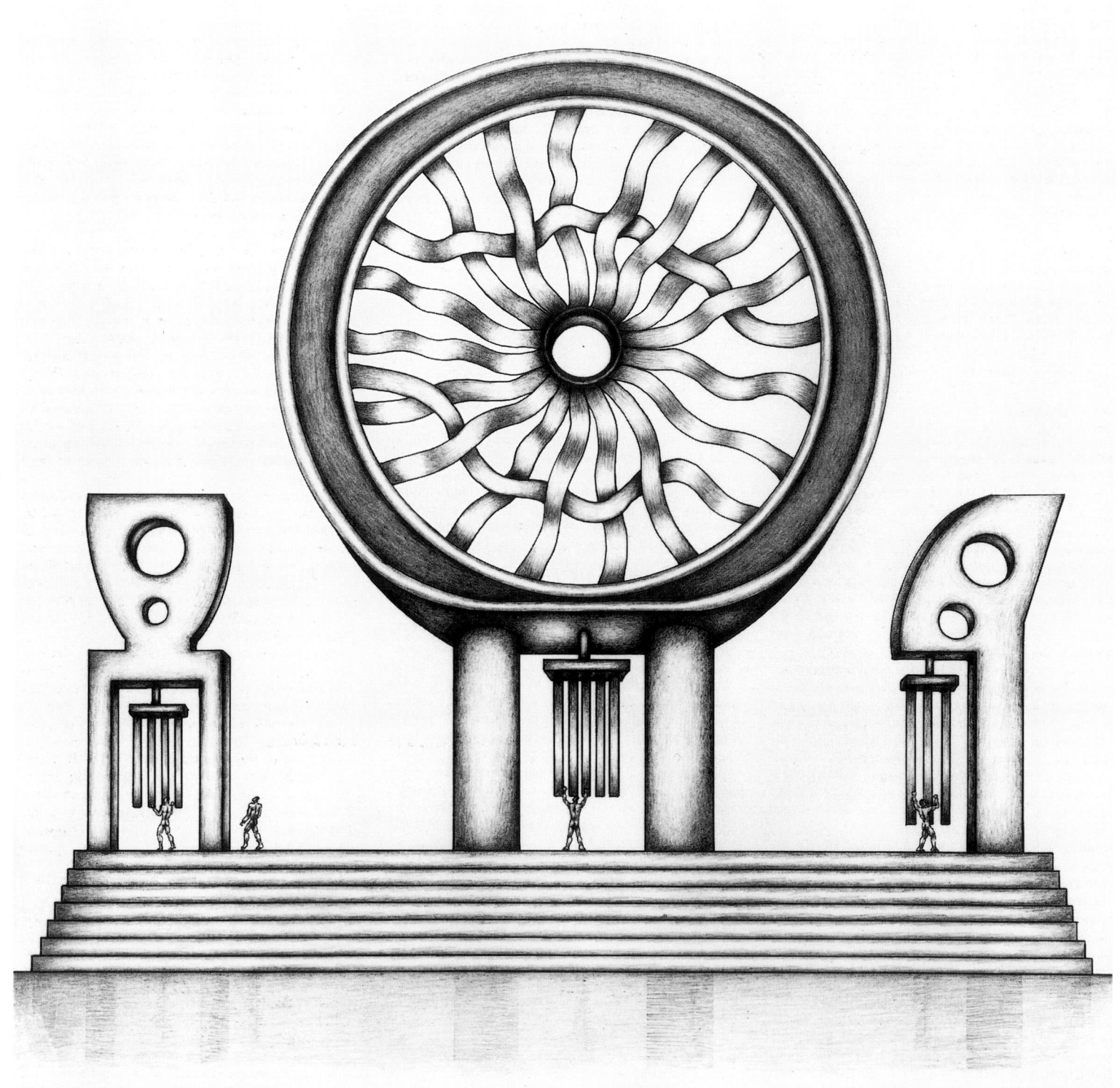

Nicolas Schöffer: *Soleison*, 1987

Astronomie, with Guy Job, 1969; *Klydex I*, with Klaus Lindemann, 1973; *Variations Luminodynamiques 2*, with Hermann, 1974; *Variations Luminodynamiques 3*, with Rainai, 1981; record—*Hommage à Bartok*, Budapest 1979.

On SCHÖFFER: books—*Nicolas Schöffer*, exhibition catalogue, with text by Raymond Bayer, Paris 1950; *Schöffer*, exhibition catalogue, with text by Michel Seuphor, Paris 1952; *Schöffer*, exhibition catalogue, with text by Marcel Brion, Paris 1958; *The Sculpture of This Century by* Michel Seuphor, New York 1959; *Schöffer*, exhibition catalogue, with texts by Jean Cassou and Guy Habasque, London 1960 *Nicolas Schöffer* by Guy Habasque and Jacques Menetrier, Neuchâtel, Switzerland 1963; *Schöffer*, exhibition cataogue, with texts by Jean Cassou and Guy Habasque, Amsterdam 1964; *The Nature and Art of Motion* by Gyorgy Kepes, New York 1965; 4 *Essays in Kinetic Art* by Frank Popper, Reg Gadney, Stephen Bann and Philip Steadman, London 1966; *Naissance de l'Art Cinetique* by Frank Popper, Reg Gadney, Stephen Bann and Philip Steadman, London 1966; *Naissance de l'Art Cinetique* by Frank Popper, Paris 1967; *Nicolas Schöffer: kinetische Plastik/Licht/Raum/Bewegung*, exhibition catalogue, with texts by Karl Ruhrberg and Frank Popper, Dusseldorf 1968; *Man and His Images—A Way of Seeing* by Georgina Oeri, New York 1968; *Nicolas Schöffer: Spatiodynamisme/Luoninodynamisme/Chronodynamisme/ Cybernetique: recherches de 1948 à 1970*, exhibition catalogue, with text by Philippe Sers, Paris 1970; *La Tour Lumiére Cybernetique de Nicolas Schöffer* by Jacky Mandin, Paris 1972; *Nicolas Schöffer*, exhibition catalogue, with text by Frank Passoni, Milan 1973; *Nicolas Schöffer*, exhibition catalogue, with texts by Eleanore de Lavandeyra and Bernadette Contensou, Paris 1974; *The Tradition of Constructivism* by Stephen Bann, New York 1974; *Nicolas Schöffer by* Pedro Fiori, Madrid 1974; *Nicolas Schöffer: l'aventure de l'art moderne* by André Parinaud, Paris 1975; *L'Univers Trame de Nicolas Schöffer* by Claude Heyligers, Paris 1975; *Nicolas Schöffer: un immense massage visuel* by Pierre Cabanne, Paris 1975; *Schöffer: pour un art tonique* by J. Warnod, Paris 1982; *Nicolas Schöffer* by Istvan Porkony, Budapest 1985; films—*Sculptures, Projections, Peintures* by Jacques Brissot, 1956; *Tour de Liége by Gruel, 1961; Tout Voir: Nicolas SChöffer* by Charles Chaboud, 1966; *Portrait: Nicolas Schöffer* by Charles Chaboud, 1966; *Portrait: Nicolas Schöffer* by Gerd Kairath, 1970; *L'Invite du Dimanche* by Anne Beranger, 1971; *La Tour Lumiére Cybernetique* by Adam Saulnier, 1971; *La Tour Cybernetique de La Défense* by Adam Saulnier, 1973; *Nicolas Schöffer* by Angeliki Haas, 1973; *Le Grand Prisme de la Sorbonne* by Jean Deveze, 1975; *Le Grande 'isme de la Sorbonne* by Angeliki Haas, 1975; *Nicolas Schöffer* by Egri, 1982; *Nicolas Schöffer* by Gabor Takacs, 1983; *Le Graphilux* by Laszlo Kovacs, 1984.

The only possible action for an artist worthy of the name is to create the new, to discover the unknown, to begin the foundations of real progress, for Art is the product of the richness of the free and liberated imagination of a few creators who have worked for society with a view to overcoming the prevailing mediocrity. Man owes to these artists who have left the beaten paths the clarification of his finalities, which are above all ethical and aesthetic and give him his real reason for living.

The artist owes it to himself to proclaim his own truth in his works with complete freedom. His cries, often ineffective at the actual moment, finally penetrate the collective conscience.

Great revolutions are never bloody; they are provoked by ideas and occur above all at the level of ideas. Now an artistic effect develops from an artistic idea through an artistic object or programme. (It is the same with commercial, scientific, technological ideas) The artist does not create only for himself. The effect of his idea must therefore reverberate as widely as possible, without compromise, censorship or self-criticism, in order to prepare the stages of our evolution at all levels including those that concern fundamental spiritual, cultural, ethical and aesthetic values.

My definition of art: "Art is the creation, invention, at the level of the mechanism of thought and imagination, of an original idea with aesthetic content translatable into perceptible effects. The development and arrangement of these effects are drawn up in a programme in time or space, or in both, a programme whose composition and proportional relationships are most favourable, new and aesthetic. These effects are transmitted by the use of visual, auditory or audio-visual signals to all those who accidentally or voluntarily become temporary or permanent spectators or listeners. A process of fascination results, provoking a more or less profound modification of their psychological field according to the degree of the creation's aesthetic value. This modification has to go in the direction of transcendence, sublimation and spiritual enrichment though the complex play of sensibility and human intellect. In this way, thanks to the creator's ability, striking aesthetic products penetrate social reality through multiple channels of communication. In order to achieve this goal, the creator must use a language and techniques which correspond to the true level of development of his era."

My research clearly reflects this tendency to contemporaneity. For the artist who agrees to relinquish the iron chisel, there is the electric or electronic chisel and even the computer, but access to them is not easy. One has to fight and make it understood that new tools have to be available to artistic research and creation as much as if not more than to all kinds of industry including that of armaments. I am working at this. But as soon as an artist resorts to contemporary technology and develops his ideas and his works in relation to socio-cultural needs arising from situations provoked by new technology, cybernetics inevitably becomes part of his preoccupations, for the galloping technicoscientific development which introduces in increasing doses dynamic factors in every sector of daily life (transport, information), accompanying an extra ordinary growth in channels of communication and exchange, modifies completely the programmes of human life.

My definition of cybernetics: "Cybernetics is the recognition of the vital process which keeps all phenomena in equilbrium. It is the science of effectiveness and of government by the organized control of all information including that which concerns perturbations of any kind, with a view to their treatment in order to achieve optimum regulation of all organic, physical or aesthetic phenomena. As a result there is a fluid permanence in supple equilibrium where each appearance of a tendency to periodicity or to stagnation provokes the intervention of perturbations or of adequate modifications to preserve the opening and aleatory character of every evolutionary process."

As regards perturbation: "It is the unexpected, brusque or progressive appearance of news, events, ideas or objects which modify, bend, distort or annul a programme, whether it is a question of a localised or generalised, physical or organic, individual or collective, natural phenomenon, or whether it is a question of a programming of human origin, fixed or aleatory, limited or not in time and space with social, economic, political, philosophical, spiritual, aesthetic, scientific, technological or other tendency. According to the strength of its impact, the perturbation provokes more or less profound repercussions on the very structures of the programmed system going as far as their immediate or progressive disappearance and, on the contrary hypothesis, towards their optimisation, transformation or diversification."

This definition evokes the no less important phenomenon of rupture: "In the evolution of each phenomenon there is a point at which saturation, exhaustion, lead to inertia. The opportune intervention of a force or a formulated energy, however small it may be, can provoke rupture on condition that it is communicable and diffusible. That is to say that energy formulated by concrete propositions in a new language and by means of a new technique enters straight away into the circuit of the human complex, rapidly eliminating the traces of the previous phenomenon."

These definitions also fundamentally concern the problem of art. In the history of art the perturbations provoked by perturbatory artists, the ruptures generated by these perturbations and the re-equilibrations resulting from the omnipresent cybernetic function are numerous. Art emphasizes the salutory and nourishing contribution of perturbations and ruptures, significant and indispensable factors of change and progress.

This quip could really be a complete programme: "An artist has to expose, most certainly, but he has also to expose himself in order to impose himself and, if necessary, to explode."

—Nicolas Schöffer

In the late 1950's there grew up a loose confederation of artists grouped round the Denise René gallery in Paris who for want of a better term were labelled Kinetic. They shared a belief that modern industrial methods and materials could be harnessed for use in art. They thought that in this way the science/art dichotomy could be resolved and a new fusion be created. They were wrong, of course, but the blame for their failure cannot be laid at their door.

Most art of the period was based on the human figure, and the most pervasive mood was "angst". "Angst," redolent with existentialist hopelessness, was the perfect image for the industrialists who became the new patrons of art. It enabled them to continue exploiting everything and everybody while pointing to the tragic inevitability of it all. After all if artists thought the whole thing was a pointless farce, who were they to disagree?

The Kinetic artists disagreed,though. They refused to join in the mourning. It was clear to them that glass, plastic, stainless steel and so on were beautiful materials if used properly, and that the techniques of cybernetics could be used to add complexity to their works. In their hands art became machine, machine turned to art. Pity that no one else went along.

Nicolas Schöffer is the Grand Old Man of this tradition, and unlike many of them has survived. He has even managed to convince his own government to build some of his works on a scale which would be beyond the purse of an individual. He remains a voice crying in the wilderness, though, and his optimism has once again been superseded. We are back to angst these days.

Like many of the kinetic artists Schöffer evolved a particular technique and stuck to it. Pieces by Schöffer are in two parts: a solid sculptural core and its reflection cast upon a suitable surface. The sculptural half usually moves and is made of many small pieces of reflective steel, put together in a constructivist manner. The whole edifice turns, and within this principal movement there is often other movement, creating a positive waterfall of light.

Aimed at this are spotlights, often of different colours which cast a huge shadow onto a screen. Sometimes the whole piece is viewed at once, sometimes just the shadows are visible, sometimes the image is repeated ad infinitum by the use of mirrors. The general effect is one of considerable abstract beauty.

Frequently these pieces are equipped with cybernetic systems that react to environmental influences. The largest outdoor pieces are often huge weather vanes, reacting to wind speed, atmospheric pressure, sunlight and so on. They are ikons for a technological society, with no reference to the past or to the human figure.

Visionaries—one thinks of Sant'Elia or Tatlin—who conceive societies in which art can play an everyday and functional role are rarely given more than short shrift. Perhaps it is for the best; a few works by Schöffer are stimulating and beautiful; a whole world filled with them might be an inhuman place to live.

The technologists and the kineticists tend to forget that Man is a messy creature, one that enjoys picking at the scabs of his unconscious and living in the refuse of his dreams. Let us be thankful that we cannot be controlled to be sane, but also sorry that sanity, when it appears, is given so little chance.

Schöffer will probably never be able to realize his grandest plans; we will have to make do with his sketches.

—Alastair Mackintosh

SCHOONHOVEN, Jan J.

Dutch. Born Johannes Jacobus Schoonhoven, in Delft, 26 June 1914. Studied art at the Koninkiijke Academie voor Beeldende Kunsten, The Hague, 1932–36. Married Anita de Geus in 1939; son: Jaap. Independent painter, The Hague, subsequently in Delft, from 1938: gouaches and colour drawings, 1948–58; first reliefs and papier-maché works, 1957; all-white works, 1960–65. Member, Nederlandse Informele Groep, 1957–59: Founder-Member, with Armando, Hendrikse and Henk Peeters, Nul Groep, 1960–65. Also worked for the Dutch Post Office, The Hague, 1946–79. Recipient: Second Prize, *Bienal,* Sao Paulo, 1967; David-Roell Prize, Amsterdam, 1984. Agent: Galerie Orez Mobiel, Paviljoensgrancht 68/70, 2512 BR The Hague. Address: Vrouw Juttenland 19, 2611 LB Delft, Netherlands.

Individual Exhibitions:

1950	't Venster, Rotterdam
1965	Galerie Wulfengasse 14. Klagenfurt. Austria
	Galerie Delta, Rotterdam
1967	Haags Gemeentemuseum, The Hague
1968	Stedelijk Van Abbemuseum, Eindhoven, Netherlands
1969	Galerie Ursula Lichter, Frankfurt
	Galerie Loehr, Dusseldorf
	Galerie M, Bochum, West Germany
	Utrechtse Kring, Neudeflat, Utrecht
1970	Galerie Orez. The Hague
	Galleria Vismara, Milan
	Galerie M, Bochum, West Germany (2 shows)
1971	Galleria Ferrari, Verona
	Lucy Milton Gallery, London
	Galleria Vismara, Milan
	Tekeningen, Stedelijk Museum, Amsterdam
1972	Stadtisches Museum, Monchengladbach, West Germany
	Museum Van Bommel-van Dam, Venlo, Netherlands
	Badischer Kunstverein, Karlsruhe
	Galerie Annemarie Verna, Zurich
1973	Galerie Plus-Kern, Ghent
	Lens Fine Art, Antwerp
	Galerie Muller-Roth. Stuttgart
	Retrospectief, Stedelijk Museum, Amsterdam
1974	Galerie Collection d'Art. Amsterdam
1975	Salone Annunciata. Milan
	Zeichnungen, Tekeningen 1940–1975, Stadtische Kunsthalle. Dusseldorf
	Museum Boymans-van Beuningen. Rotterdam
1976	Ulmer Museum. Ulm. West Germany
	Galerie Elke Droscher, Hamburg
1977	Museum 't Coopmanshus, Franeker, Netherlands
	Annely Juda Fine Art, London
	Galerie Hildebrand, Klagenfurt, Austria
1978	Lens Fine Art, Antwerp (with A. Calderara)
	Galerie De Vries en Roeloff, Rotterdam
	Stedelijk Museum, Alkmaar, Netherlands
1979	Galerie Delta, Rotterdam
	Kunsthaus, Zurich
	Stadtische Galerie, Nordhorn, West Germany (with C. Visser)
	Lens Fine Art, Antwerp
1980	Galerie Nouvelles Images, Amsterdam
	Galerie M, Bochum, West Germany
1981	Stadtisches Museum, Leverkusen, West Germany
	Galrie Orez-Mobiel, The Hague (with A. Berkulin)
	Galerie Blanche, Stockholm
1982	Galerie De Vries en Roeloff, Rotterdam
	Galrie Brinkman, Amsterdam
	Galerie Vecu, Antwerp (with A. Dekkers)
1983	Kunstcentrum, Enschede, Netherlands
1984	Museum Boymans-van Beuningen, Rotterdam
	Haags Gemeentemuseum, The Hague
1985	Badischer Kunstverein, Karlsruhe, West Germany
	Louisiana Museum, Humlebaek, Denmark
	Kunsthalle, Nuremberg, West Germany
	Galerie M, Bochum, West Germany
1987	Florida Atlantic University, Boca Raton
	University of South Florida, Tampa
	Rice University, Houston
	University of Texas, Arlington

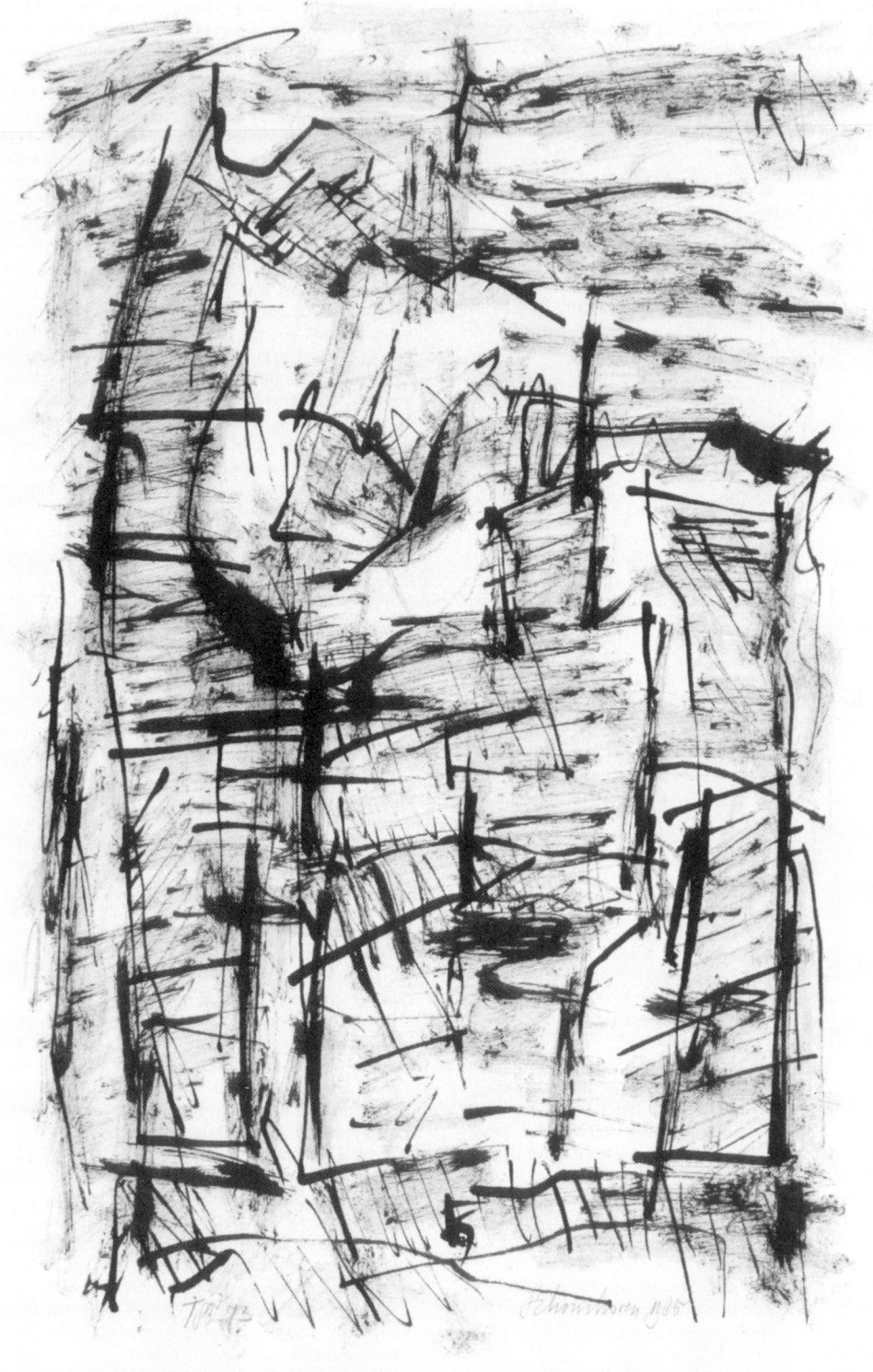

Jan J. Schoonhoven: *T 85–73,* 1985

Centre National d'Art Conemporain, Grenoble, France
1988   Galerie Lüpke, Frankfurt

Selected Group Exhibitions:

1938	*De Onafhankelijken Holland-Frankrijk,* Stedelijk Museum, Amsterdam
1952	*Vrij Beelden,* Museum Fodor, Amsterdam
1962	*Nul,* Stedelijk Museum, Amsterdam
1968	*Documenta 6,* Museum Fridericianum, Kassel, West Germany
1971	*Europalia '71,* Musee des Beaux-Arts, Liege, Belgium
1975	*Elementarformen,* Rheinisches Landesmuseum, Bonn

1981	*Westkunst: Zeitgenossische Kunst seit 1939,* Messehallen, cologne
1982	*Contemporary Art from the Netherlands,* Museum of Contemporary Art, Chicago
1984	*Twenty Years of Collecting,* Stedelijk Museum, Amsterdam
1987	*Hollands Landschap,* Museum Overholland, Amsterdam (travelled to the Grand Palais, Paris)

Collections:

Stedelijk Museum, Amsterdam: Stedelijk Van Abbemuseum, Eindhoven, Netherlands; Tate Gallery, London: Städtisches Museum, Mönchengladbach, West Germany; Städtisches Kunsthalle, Dusseldorf; Atheneum Museum, Helsinki; Museu de Arte Moderna, Sao Paulo; Guggenheim Museum,

New York; Museum of Modern Art, New York; Centre Georges Pompidou, Paris.

Publications:

By SCHOONHOVEN: articles—"Zero" in *Facetten van de Hedendaagse Kunst*, exhibition catalogue, Twenthe 1958; "Zero", in *Hollandische Informelle Gruppe*, exhibition catalogue, Kassel, West Germany 1960; "Dynamo Schoonhoven" in *Zero* (Dusseldorf), no. 3, 1961; "Zero" in *De Nieuwe Stijl* (Amsterdam). no.1. 1965; "Jan Schoonhoven: Brief aan Hank Peeters" in *Zero*, exhibition catalogue, Amsterdam 1970; "Schoonhoven" in *Flash Art* (Milan), May 1971; "Inleiding" in *Mededelingen Centraal Museum Utrecht* (Utrecht), no. 6, 1974.

On SCHOONHOVEN: books—*Een Cheque voor de Tandarts* by K. Schippes and J. Bernlef, Amsterdam 1967; *Schoonhoven*, exhibition catalogue, with text by R. H. Fuchs, Eindhoven, Netherlands 1968; *ROSC 71: The Poetry of Vision*, exhibition catalogue, with texts by Werner Schmalenbach, K. G. Pontus Hulten and James Johnson Sweeney, Dublin 1971; *J. J. Schoonhoven: Tekeningen*, exhibition catalogue, with text by R. H. Fuchs, Amsterdam 1971; *Jan Schoonhoven: Retrospectief*, exhibition catalogue, with text by W.A.L. Beeren, Amsterdam 1973; *Basically White* exhibition catalogue, with texts by Carel Blotkamp and Lucy Milton. London 1974; *J. J. Schoonhaven: Zeichnungen, Tekeningen 1940-1975*, exhibition catalogue, with texts by Jürgen Harten, J. C. Ebbinge Wubben and Antje van Graenenitz. Dusseldorf 1975; *Jan Schoonhoven: Zeichnungen, Reliefs/Carel Visser: Plastiken*, exhibition catalogue by Henk Peeters, Nordhorn 1979; *Nederlandse Musea IV: Stedelijk Van Abbemuseum Eindhoven* by Jaap Bremer, Haarlem 1982. films—*Schoonhoven* by Heiner Hepper, 1969; *Schoonhoven* by Heiner Hepper, 1974.

If there is a Dutch artist whose work deserves the epithets "consistent" and "unassuming," it is surely Jan Schoonhoven. After having worked primarily under the influence of Paul Klee until about 1957, Schoonhoven began making his white *papier-maché* reliefs, many of which seemed to represent, in abstract terms, the processes of organic growth ("Vegetation," for example, from 1959). At this time Schoonhoven, like Armando and Kees van Bohemen, was a member of the "Netherlands Informal Group," while from 1960 to 1965 he was a member of the NUL or "Zero" group (other members included, Armando, Jan Hendrikse and Henk Peeters). The founding of this group took place at an important moment in the art world of the Netherlands. The museums and galleries were dominated by *tachisme* and abstract expressionism, which had been imported from America and attracted many followers who seemed to be interested in painting only as a personal, emotional gesture. NUL was in rebellion against all this, an attack on *tachisme*, Cobra and abstract expressionism which was designed as a way of radically purifying the means which the artist employs in his work. Appreciation of NUL's aims came quickly, especially from official institutions. NUL's second exhibition, held in Amsterdam in 1965, was actually a retrospective show of the work of Lucio Fontana, Hans Haacke and Gianni Colombo (but not of Hendrikse).

Schoonhoven is one of the few artists who have remained faithful to the radical aims of NUL. It is impossible to talk about his white reliefs in terms of "composition." The elements of his work are always the same, as are their arrangements. Schoonhoven *builds* his reliefs, using extremely simple modes of organization: the parts of the whole are then brought to life by the play of light which touches them. His reliefs, like his drawings, always maintain a degree of intimacy, while at the heart of his work there is a deliberate refusal to dominate the viewer or force him to make a certain kind of interpretation. Schoonhoven himself speaks as softly as possible: the works are simply there as objects for meditation.

—A. F. Wagemans

SCHULT, HA (Hans-Jurgen).

German. Born in Parchim/Mecklenburg, 24 June 1939. Studied art, under K. O. Gotz, at the Staatliche Kunstakademie, Dusseldorf, 1959-61; influenced by work of Yves Klein, Nam June Paik and Jackson Pollock, from 1958. Has lived with the actress Elke Koska since 1967. Worked occasionally as railwayman, building labourer, factory worker, driver, and advertising art director, from 1959; as independent artist, Dusseldorf, Munich and Cologne, 1959-82, in New York, since 1982: first organic-kinetic works, 1960; biokinetic and environmental actions, from 1968. Guest-Instructor, Kasseler Kunstakademie, Kassel, West Germany, 1971. Address: 203 West Houston Street, New York, New York 10014, U.S.A.

Individual Exhibitions:

1968	Galerie Ekto, Munich
1969	Galerie Nachst St. Stephan, Vienna
	Städtisches Museum Schloss Morsbroich, Leverkusen, West Germany
	Galerie Klaus Lupke, Frankfurt
	Galerie Ingo Kummel, Cologne
1970	Kunstverein, Munich
	Galerie Rudolf Zwirner, Cologne
1971	Galerie Rudolf Zwirner, Cologne
	Kunstverein, Heidelberg
	Spot Galerie, Kiel University
	Neue Galerie, Aachen, West Germany
	Kunsthalle, Cologne
1972	Galerie Van de Loo, Munich
	Galerie Rochus Kowallek, Frankfurt
	Galerie Klaus Lupke, Frankfurt
1973	Galerie Inge Baecker, Bochum, West Germany
	Galerie Falazik, Neuenkirchen, West Germany
	Museum Wiesbaden, West Germany
	Galerie Inge Baecker, at the *IKI Art Fair*, Dusseldorf
	Galerie Edith Seuss, Buchschlag, West Germany
1974	Museum Folkwang, Essen
	Kunsthalle, Kiel
	Kunstverein, Stuttgart
	Stadtische Galerie im Lenbachhaus, Munich
	Junior-Galerie, Hannover
	Galerie Inge Baecker, Bochum, West Germany
	Bundesministerium für Stadtebau, Bonn
	Württembergischer Kunstverein, Stuttgart
	Galerie Ubu, Karlsruhe
	Junior-Galerie, Cologne
	Galerie Thomas, Munich
1975	Stadtische Galerie Altes Theater, Ravensburg, West Germany
	Galerie Edith Seuss, Buchschlag, West Germany
1976	Galerie Lauter, Mannheim
1977	Galerie Camomille. Brussels
	Palazzo Spaletti, Naples
	Palazzo Odescalchi, Rome
1978	Museum Mulheim, West Germany
	Galerie Bergkamen, West Germany
	Museum am Ostwall, Dortmund, West Germany
1980	Museum Ludwig, Cologne
1982	Galerie Hans Strelow, Dusseldorf

Schult has also created many individual "Actions," both outdoor and indoor, throughout Germany and Italy, since 1968

Selected Group Exhibitions:

1968	*Sub-Art*, U-Bahnhof Giselastrasse, Munich
1970	*Jetzt. Kunste in Deutschland Heute*, Kunsthalle, Cologne
1972	*Documenta, Kassel*, West Germany
1974	*Projekt 74*, Kunsthalle, Cologne
1975	*Der ausgesparte Mensch*, Kunsthalle, Mannheim
1976	*Schuh-Werke*, Kunsthalle, Nuremberg
1979	*The Image of Man since 1945*, Funatie Kunsthuis, Amsterdam
	Im Namen des Volkes, Wilhelm-Lehmbruck-Museum, Duisburg, West Germany (travelled to Kunstlerhaus Wien, Vienna)
1982	*L'Art Sociologique*, Musée de la Ville, Nice
	Kunst wird Material, Nationalgalerie, West Berlin

Collections:

Wilhelm-Lehmbruck-Museum, Duisburg, West Germany; Kunsthalle, Kiel; Museum Wiesbaden, West Germany; Museum am Ostwall, Dortmund, West Germany; Museum Lübeck; Kunsthalle, Nuremberg; Kunsthalle, Recklinghausen, West Germany; Leopold-Hoesch-Museum, Duren, West Germany; Kunsthalle, Mannheim; Sammlung Bundesrepublik Deutschland, Bonn.

Publications:

By SCHULT: books and leaflets—*Situation Schackstrasse*, manifesto, Munich 1969; *Aktion 20,000 km*, action-text, Munich 1970; *Die Schultfrage*, Cologne 1971; *Actif au Maroc*, Munich and Casablanca 1971: *Der Schlussel steckt*, action-text, Munich 1971; *Biokinetische Landschaft und Soldat*, flysheet, Munich 1972; *Brief an Georg Jappe (1)*, Munich 1973; *Brief von Georg Jappe an HA Schult/Brief von HA Schult an Georg Jappe (2)*, Munich 1973; *Die zum Stillstand gebrachte Zeit*, flysheet, Munich 1974; *Venezia Vive*, action-flysheet, Munich 1976; *Crash!*, action-flysheet, Munich 1977; *Venezia Vive*, magazine, Munich 1977; *Ruhr-Tour*, magazine, Cologne 1978; *HA Schult: Der Macher*, Cologne 1978; *Trash*, manifesto, Cologne 1979; *Der Alltag* flysheet, Cologne 1980; *Jetzi! Zeit . . .*, flysheet, Cologne 1980; *Jetzi! Zeit . . .*, exhibition catalogue, Cologne 1980.

On SCHULT: books—*H A Schult: Biokinetische Situationen*, with text by Rolf Wedewer, Leverkusen, West Germany 1969; *Expansion der Kunst* by Jürgen Claus, Reinbeck, West Germany and Mexico City 1970; *Deutsche Kunst:eine neue Generation* by Rolf-Günter Dienst, Cologne 1970; *Leben und Kunst* by Udo Kultermann, Tübingen 1970; *Science and Fiction* by Walter Aue, Frankfurt 1971; *Bis Heute: Stilgeschichte der Bildenden Kunst im 20. Jahrhundert* by Karin Thomas, Cologne 1971; *Jam* by James Burns, Cologne and New York 1971; *Kunst ist Utopie* by Heinz Ohff, Gutersloh 1972; *Verkehrskultur* by Klaus Honnef, Recklinghausen, West Germany 1972; *Art Now: The New Age* by Ichiro Haryu, Tokyo 1972; *Funktionen der Bildenden Kunst im Spatkapitalismus* by Martin Damus, Frankfurt 1973; *Der ausgesparte Mensch*, exhibition catalogue, with text by Heinz Fuchs, Mannheim 1975; *Landscape: A New Aspect* by Dietrich Mahlow, Stuttgart 1976; *Dumont Kunstlerlexikon* by Karin Thomas and Gerd de Vries, Cologne 1977; *De-architecture* by the SITE group, New York 1978; *Landschaftsmalerei* by Rolf Wedewer, Cologne 1978; *Art in the 70's* by Edward Lucie Smith, Oxford 1980; *Gesprache mit Kunstlern* by Amine Haase, Cologne 1981; *Kunst wird Material*, exhibition catalogue, with text by Dieter Honisch and Michael Pauseback, West Berlin 1982.

H. A. Schult, born in Parchim/Mecklenburg in 1939, calls himself quite simply "The Maker". This epithet is not merely a circumlocution for something unclassifiable, it is also programmatic; it designates the unity, as actually experienced, between life and art, but also points to the multiplicity of the artist's work. From the start it was impossible to associate him with a particular genre, let alone an artistic trend or style. Schult made a name for himself via objects, but he has since concentrated on action art, making extensive use of the media and gaining worldwide recognition. The spectacular is his metier, in which, as an accomplished self-publicist, he exercises perfect control. And yet Schult is far more than just a showman; he is no mere exhibitionist, but rather a missionary earnestly seeking, if with a great deal of wit, to alter public awareness and to make people think.

Schult's art is always above all a criticism of society. After studying at the Academy of Art in Düsseldorf under K. O. Goetz, he was influenced by action-painting artist Jackson Pollock and increasingly by Yves Klein and the action musician Nam June Paik. He subsequently worked as Director of Art for Industry and in numerous other occupations—more than fifty, according to Schult himself. He was the first artist to recognise the potential of the environment as a theme for artistic processes. He coined the term biokinetics and using bacterial cultures demonstrated the kinetic principle of constant change and decomposition. What he created was of necessity not a lasting work of art for a museum. He was thereby also seeking to demonstrate that there are no lasting works of art, since every work of art disintegrates, becoming something else. The public was given the

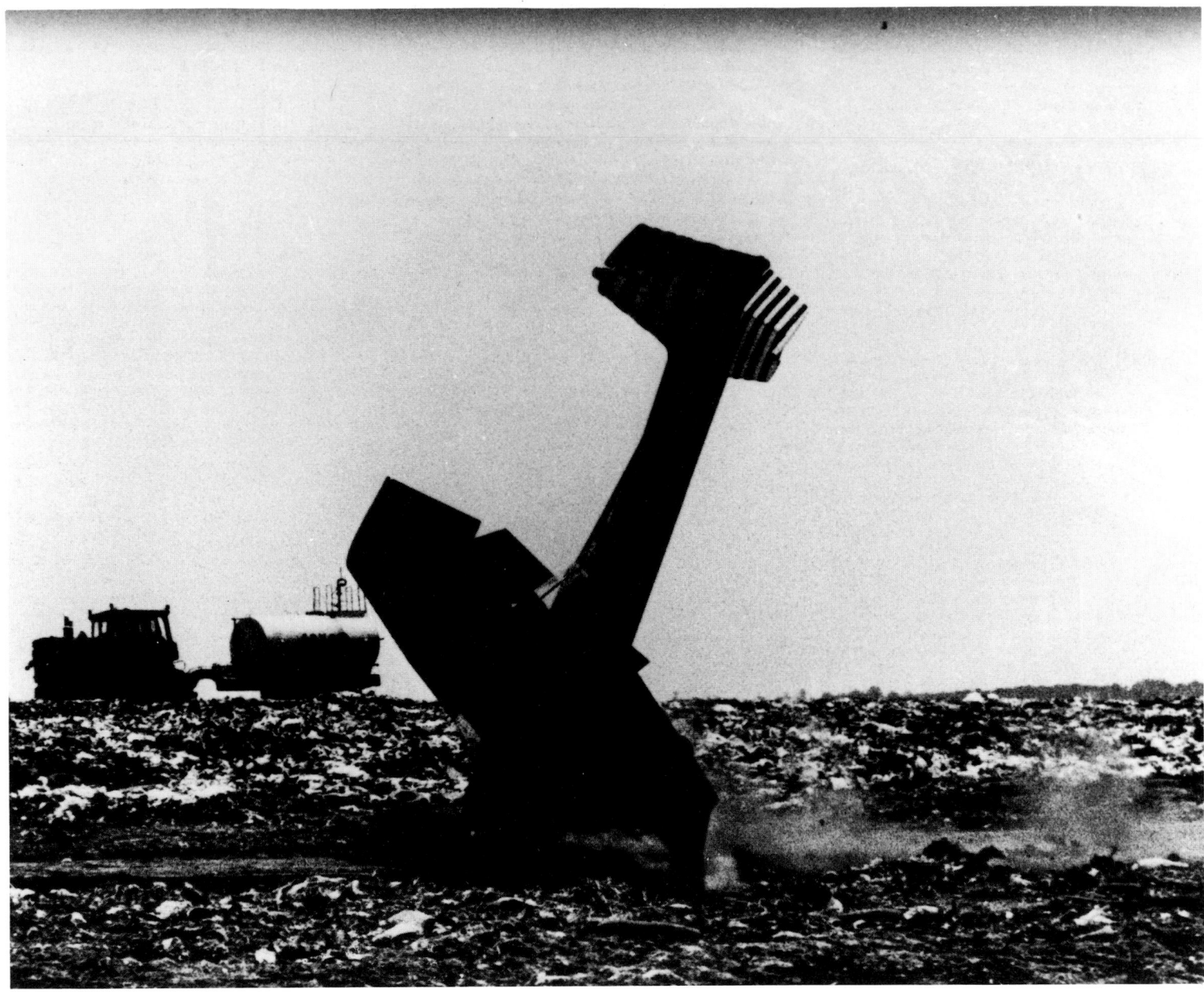

HA Schult: *The Crash*, at Kassel, 1977

opportunity to intervene in the process, to regulate the change that was taking place: change as a possibility to be experienced. Later Schult demonstrated in object-boxes how technology and civilisation increasingly violate nature, how nature and culture are dying, idylls are wearing out.

Alongside these slight works Schult was already producing his happening-actions at the end of the sixties. In Munich he piled up a gigantic paper mountain in a street, set up refuse actions, made a collection of the football star Franz Beckenbauer's left-overs and rubbish, launched a 20,000-kilometre rally and organised an archaeological journey through the present as well as a "Rühr Tour" into the "District's Here and Now". When the *Documenta 6* exhibition opened in Kassel in 1977 he crashed a plane into a rubbish dump in New York, an incident which was relayed on television.

The most expensive happening was the *Berlin—New York* one, where identical events were organised to occur simultaneously in both cities.

There are plans afoot for a happening in Peking, and also for the foundation of an "HA Schult Museum for Action Art" in Essen, intended to document the history of this art form and to provide the opportunity to experience past happenings through a series of different scenarios.

—Werner Schulze-Reimpell

SCHULTZE, Bernard.

German. Born in Schneidemühl, West Prussia, now Pila, Poland, 31 May 1915. Educated at Prinz Heinrichs-Gymnasium, Berlin, 1925–34; studied art at the Kunsthochschule, Berlin, 1934 and at the Kunst Akademie, Dusseldorf, 1939. Served in the German Army, in Russia and Africa, 1939–45. Married Ursula Bluhm in 1955. Painter: has lived and worked in Flensburg, 1945–47; Frankfurt-am-Main 1947–68; in Paris, 1950–64; and in Cologne, since 1968: first "tachiste" paintings, influenced by Lanskoy and Riopelle, 1951; first reliefs, 1956; first "tabuskris" and free-standing reliefs, 1959; first "migofs," 1961; first grisaille works, 1972; Member, with K. O. Gotz, Otto Greis and Heinz Kreutz, "Quadriga" group, Frankfurt, 1952; designed stage decor for Deutsche Oper am Rhein, Dusseldorf,1970. Recipient: Kunstpreis, Darmstadt, 1967; Kunstpreis der Stadt, Cologne, 1969; Kunstpreis Wormland, Munich, 1983; Grosser Hessischer Kulturpreis, 1984; Golden Laurel Award, Gesellschaft Bildender Kunstler, Vienna, 1985; Lovis-Corinth-Preis, 1986. Honorary Member, Akademie der Künste, West Berlin, 1972; Honorary Professor, Landgovernment of Nordrhein-Westfalen, 1981. Address: Riehlerstrasse 53, 5000 Cologne 1, West Germany.

Individual Exhibitions:

1947	Galerie Junge Kunst, Hamburg
1948	Moderne Galerie Egon Günther, Mannheim (and regularly until 1951)
1949	Zimmergalerie Franck, Frankfurt (and regularly until 1958)
1956	Galerie Parnass, Wuppertal, West Germany
	Studio Paul Facchetti, Paris
	Wittenborn Gallery, New York
1957	Galerie Schuler, West Berlin
	Galerie 22, Dusseldorf
1958	Galerie Inge Ahlers, Mannheim
	Die Insel, Hamburg
	Galerie Daniel Cordier, Paris
	Galerie Nohl, Siegen, West Germany
	Städtische Kunstmuseum, Duisburg, West Germany
1959	Galleria Montenapoleone 6A, Milan
1960	*Plastikbilder, Tabuskris, Zeichnungen*, Galerie Daniel Cordier, Frankfurt
	Galerie Schuler, West Berlin
1961	Kunsthalle, Baden-Baden, West Germany
1962	*Peintures et Reliefs*, Musée des Beaux-Arts, La Chaux de Fonds, Switzerland
	Städtische Museum, Wiesbaden, West Germany
	Kunstverein, Wuppertal, West Germany
	Reliefs et Dessins, Galerie Daniel Cordier, Paris
1963	Galerie Schuler, West Berlin

1964	Galerie Schmela, Dusseldorf	1975	*Die Welt der Migofs: Bilde und Objekie aus 25 Jahren*, Galerie Brusberg, Hannover		Ostdeutsche Galerie, Regensburg, West Germany	

1964 Galerie Schmela, Dusseldorf
Galleria L'Attico. Rome
Galerie der Edition Rothe, Heidelberg
1965 Howard Wise Gallery, New York
1966 Kestner-Gesellschaft. Hannover
Stüdtische Museum. Leverkusen, West Germany
Badischer Kunstverein, Karlsruhe
Galleria Senior, Rome
San Francisco Museum of Art
Wide White Space, Antwerp
Studio B, Bamberg, West Germany
1967 London Arts Gallery. Detroit
1968 *Alte und Neue Arbeiten*, Kölnischer Kunstverein, Cologne
Kunstverein, Braunschweig, West Germany
Kunstverein, Darmstadt
Galerie Rudolf Zwirner, Cologne (with Robert Graham)
1969 Haus am Waldsee, West Berlin
Palais des Beaux-Arts, Brussels
Galerie Felix Handschin, Basle
1970 Galerie Brusberg, Hannover
Bernard Schultze 1960–1970, Museum Bochum, West Germany
1971 Centre National d'Art Contemporain, Paris
Pfalzgalerie, Kaiserslautern, West Germany
Galerie Arcanes, Brussels
Galerie MARC, Washington, D.C.
1972 Galerie der Spiegel, Cologne
1973 *Die Migofs 1958 bis 1973*, Baukunst, Cologne
1974 Museum Boymans-van Beuningen, Rotterdam
Galerie Nova, Hagen, West Germany
Galerie Defet, Nuremberg
Galerie B, Paris
Die Welt der Migofs, Staatliche Kunsthalle, Baden-Baden, West Germany

1975 *Die Welt der Migofs: Bilde und Objekie aus 25 Jahren*, Galerie Brusberg, Hannover
Aus-und Fortbildungsstatte, Bonn
Galerie Schuler, West Berlin
1976 Galerie Rothe, Heidelberg
Galerie der Spiegel, Cologne
1977 Deutsche Aktiengesellschaft, Clubheim-Hamburg
Kunstverein, Salzgitter, West Germany
1978 Galerie Rothe, Heidelberg
Kulturabteilung Bayer, Erholungshaus-Leverkusen, West Germany
1979 Galerie Jean Leroy, Paris
Kunstlerhaus Wien, Vienna (with Ursula Schultze)
Städtische Museum, Leverkusen, West Germany
1980 *Zerbrochene Verstecke*, Kunsthalle, Hamburg
Städtische Kunsthalle, Dusseldorf
1981 Akademie der Künste, West Berlin
Kunstverein, Frankfurt
Saarland Museum, Saarbrucken
Galerie R. Haftmann, Zurich
Galerie der Spiegel, Cologne
1982 Graphische Sammlung Albertina, Vienna
Galerie Gunzenhauser, Munich
1983 Galerie Schueler, West Berlin
1984 Albertina, Vienna
Rheinisches Landesmuseum, Bonn
Kunsthalle, Tubingen, West Germany
Wilhelm-Hack-Museum, Ludwigshafen, West Germany
Kunsthalle, Nuremberg, West Germany
Galerie Rothe, Heidelberg, West Germany
Wallraf-Richartz-Museum, Cologne
Galerie Hans Strelow, Dusseldorf
1985 Galerie Hans Strelow, Dusseldorf
Baukunst-Galerie, Cologne
Galerie Brusberg, West Berlin

Ostdeutsche Galerie, Regensburg, West Germany
Galerie Schueler, West Berlin
Galerie Gunzenhauser, Munich
1986 Kunstverein, Dortmund, West Germany
Galerie Der Spiegel, Cologne
Ostdeutsche Galerie, Regensburg, West Germany
1987 Galerie Pro Arte, Freiburg, West Germany
Galerie Hans Strelow, Dusseldorf
Galerie Timm Gierig, Frankfurt
1988 Galerie Dieter Wilbrand, Cologne

Selected Group Exhibitions:

1948 *Vision und Magie*, Moderne Galerie Egon Günther, Mannheim
1954 *3rd International Biennale of Color Lithography*, Cincinnati Art Museum, Ohio
1960 *Guggenheim International*, Guggenheim Museum, New York
1963 *Schrift und Bild*, Kunsthalle, Baden-Baden, West Germany
1966 *Labyrinthe*, Akademie der Künste, West Berlin (travelled to the Kunsthalle, Baden-Baden, West Germany and the Kunsthalle, Nuremberg)
1968 *Dada, Surrealism and Their Heritage*, Museum of Modern Art, New York (travelled to Los Angeles County Museum of Art, and the Art Institute of Chicago)
1975 *Surrealitat-Bildrealitat 1924–1974*, Kunsthalle, Dusseldorf
1977 *Documenta*, Kassel, West Germany
1978 *Museum des Geldes*, Kunsthalle, Dusseldorf
1979 *Weich und Plastisch/Soft Art*, Kunsthaus, Zurich

Bernhard Schultze: *Duell der Migofs*, 1981

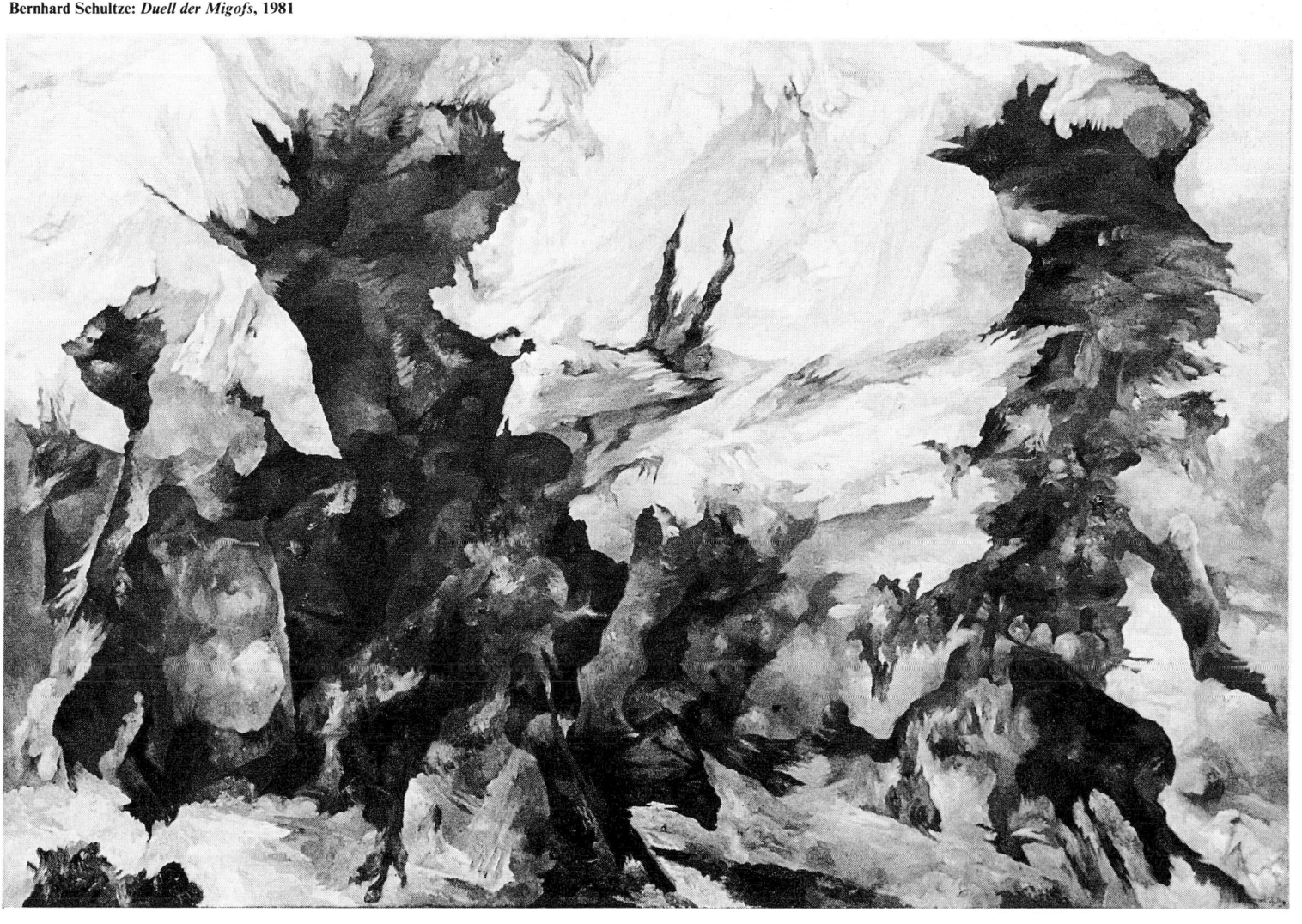

Collections:

Kunsthalle, Mannheim; Museum Ludwig, Cologne; Pfalz-Galerie, Kaiserslautern, West Germany; Museum Bochum, West Germany; Hessisches Landesmuseum, Darmstadt; Wilhelm-Lehmbruck Museum, Duisburg, West Germany; Stiftung Preussischer Kulturbesitz, West Berlin; Wallraf-Richartz Museum, Cologne; Centre Georges Pompidou, Paris; Museum Boymans-van Beuningen, Rotterdam.

Publications:

By SCHULTZE: books—*Migof-Reden Texte und zeichnungen*, Stierstadt im Taunus, West Germany 1971; *Im Sieb die gelbroten Korner*, portfolio, Hamburg 1972; *Sperriger Zaun aus Zeit: Neue Migof-Reden und Offsetlithographien*, Dusseldorf 1976.

On SCHULTZE: books—*Bernard Schultze*, exhibition catalogue, with text by Will Grohmann, Paris 1956; *Bernard Schultze*, exhibition catalogue, with text by Edouard Jager, Mannheim 1958; *Bernard Schultze*, exhibition catalogue, with text by Hanns Theodor Flemming, Hamburg 1958; *Bernard Schultze: Plastikbilder, Tabuskris, Zeichnungen*, exhibition catalogue with text by Wolfgang Grozinger, Frankfurt 1960; *Bernard Schultze: Reliefs et Dessins*, exhibition catalogue, with text by Julien Alvard, Paris 1962; *Bernard Schultze: Peintures et reliefs*, exhibition catalogue, with a foreword by Paul Seylaz, La Chaux de Fonds, Switzerland 1962; *Schultze*, exhibition catalogue, with text by Enrico Crispolti and Alain Jouffroy, Rome 1964; *Bernard Schultze*, exhibition catalogue, with text by Filiberto Menna, Rome 1966; *Bernard Schultze*, exhibition catalogue, with text by Manfred de la Motte, Bamberg, West Germany 1966; *Bernard Schultze*, exhibition catalogue, with texts by Rolf Wedewer and Peter W. Jansen, Leverkusen, West Germany 1966; *Bernard Schultze: Alte und Neue Arbeiten*, exhibition catalogue, with text by Heinz Ohff, Cologne 1968; *Bernard Schultze 1960–1970*, exhibition catalogue, with text by Peter Leo and José Pierre, Bochum, West Germany 1970: *Bernard Schultze*, exhibition catalogue/book, with texts by Alain Jouffroy, Will Grohmann, Peter Selz and José Pierre, Paris 1971; *Bernard Schultze: Die Migofs 1958 bis 1973*, exhibition catalogue, with text by Wieland Schmied, Cologne 1973; *Bernard Schultze—Die Welt der Migofs*, exhibition catalogue, with texts by Hans-Albert Peters and Eberhard Roters, and an interview by Barbara Catoir and Hans-Albert Peters, Baden-Baden, West Germany 1974; *Bernard Schultze—Het Woud der Migofs/Ursula—Dromen in veren en bont*, exhibition catalogue, with text by Eberhard Roters, Rotterdam 1974; *Bernard Schultze Die Welt der Migofs—bilde und objekte aus 25 jahren*, exhibition catalogue, with text by Jean Dypreau, Eberhard Roters and Bruno Schulz, Hannover 1975: *Bernard Schultze/Ursula*, exhibition catalogue, with text by Eberhard Roters, Vienna 1979; *Bernard Schultze*, exhibition catalogue, with text by Rolf Wedewer, Leverkusen, West Germany 1979; *Bernard Schultze: Zerbrochene Verstecke*, exhibition catalogue, with an introduction by Werner Hofmann and Helmut Leppien, Hamburg 1980.

Until 1940 I worked in accordance with Menzel's motto: "It is good to draw anything, it is better to draw everything". So I tried to draw everything around me, first as precisely as possible and then again in sketchy loose strokes. I rigorously repressed, as though a bad conscience, my even then narcissistic wandering dreamlike images, influenced by Kubin's chimaera, in order to learn once and for all the ABC's and do homage to a certain realism which at the time of the beginnings of National Socialism was in any case taught at the Academy. When I completed my studies I became a soldier and limited myself to a strictly recorded representation of life in both drawing and painting, certainly as a protection of my interior monologue. Now and again I allowed myself, regarding it almost as an offence, to wander in my realms of fantasy; something of this is seen in the work "The Temptation of Saint Antony." I let myself drift in the sudden flood of pictures which appeared to me: the corner of the room at evening secure in the lamplight, bursting out into savage vegetation: tree trunk, distant landscape with Russian cathedrals and buried in sand the ugly enticing whore's face. This was perhaps a prophetic pointer, for the Russian campaign soon began, and in the gruesome drawing of corpses, the executed, ruined churches and burning villages I again with Kubin and Ensor kept joy-dispelling company. Towards the end of the war, in short days of holiday, I painted, on a bed sheet on which a German fighter pilot had died of his burns, a pale gloomy picture of drifting dead on black water, of mountains which consisted of pallid white monsters beneath a thundery sky in a kind of El Greco style, and subsequently a picture of my dead grandmother, the lace of the bed linen and pillows around her yellow as wax face. I showed the picture to my former teacher Willy Jäckel whose careful appreciation gave me the courage to continue with this preoccupation only with oneself.

Then came the great conflagration, the hail of bombs, in which everything that I had previously painted and drawn disappeared in the golden glow. A turning point in my life. The fetters were broken. On the poorest scraps of paper with coloured pencil and with self-made water colours on black-out paper I now began to revel in my spendidly gruesome fairy tales. As a refugee in Flensburg I was able to show Nolde some of these. The coloured pencil scenes in shrill descant tones particularly pleased him. The labyrinthine way allowed me to stumble into the unconscious, encouraged by a psychotherapist: "The doors to your unconscious must always stand wide open," as she later confirmed similarly in front of my wife's works. At that time I was already working to the "dictates of the unconscious" without having heard anything at all of Breton. And just at that time, towards the end of the 1940's, I also came across Prinzhorn's book *The Plastic Arts of the Mentally Ill*. In 1947 I had my first exhibition in a gallery of little significance in Hamburg. Hanns Theodor Flemming reviewed it and gave me just the acknowledgment I needed at that moment.

Then in Frankfurt, no longer cut off from the unrestrained development of artistic life in Berlin above all and in the Rheinland, it was the Egon Günther Mannheim Gallery, the only one at that time that was interested in surreal art, that showed some of my works along with those of Max Ernst, Viktor Brauner and Miró. In great haste I passed through the stations of this wonderful dream world and began even more resolutely to delve into myself, producing for example "Circus," a picture carried out almost in a state of trance. The gate was pushed open: in 1951 I made my first visit to Paris where Wols' drawings, but above all Riopelle's spatula executed colour-field orgies, overwhelmed me like new earthquake pictures. My Friends Götz, Greis and Kreuz were similarly affected, and the great fever attacked us.

Each of us now in his own way painted this as it were shock to the soul. Parisian colleagues, writers on art supported us. We were called the new German romantics. It was Edouard Jaguer who with René Drouin proclaimed the four of us the Frankfurt Quadriga, as the first independent German variants of tachism, as were Vedova in Venice and Burri in Rome. 1952 was our comet year. And yet each of us was so utterly occupied with himself that our paths soon diverged. At that time I had a children's painting class in Frankfurt's America House. Once again, but on a different level of the secret spiral, I was led back to the source as I had been in Flensburg when reading and contemplating the Prinzhorn book. At the same time my wife began quite abruptly to paint, in an equally original manner, untamed, not yet expelled from Paradise. COBRA friends visited us; it was a marriage of regal and yet dogged work.

Like children on the beach, crouching in the slimy sand and playing with buckets full of sea water, I did likewise with self-mixed, thickened colour brews and coloured water, masses of colour dissolved in turpentine. With pieces of wood, my hands, the brush, I let myself drift over the horizontal painting ground, fell into a panic at the horror of the vacuum, tried to rescue myself by throwing the coloured turpentine over it. Pools, hills, valleys, crevasses, scabby exuberant growths formed themselves, the crumbling walls, the delta landscapes, the desolate steppes and expanses of Russia emerged, the dark green forests of my childhood on the Polish border.

Such pictures precipitating in me shreds of memory, I let myself be washed away by them in a chain of associations and simultaneously tried to see over my own shoulder. The exciting game of inspiration and control in rapid succession had begun. That was the stimulant, for that reason painting was a substitute for living. I have never been able to establish a connection as in the dogma of the young today. On the contrary I lived my outward life day in day out soberly and inconspicuously and with it screened off so as to live my real life—yes, really—in the ivory tower.

At the end of the 1950's, beginning of the 1960's, my wife, whose pictures had been acquired by Dubuffet for his famous art-brut collection, and I entered the circle of the Daniel Cordier Gallery, the most individual gallery in Paris at that time—a circle of outsiders commanded as it were by Dubuffet. His method, his inward construction of discovery, of pressing on to the summit and then already taking the next step into fresh and unknown realms, was a model for us. Those of us coming from Sweden, Yugoslavia, Italy, USA and Germany understood this mixture of latin-celtic harmony of spirit given perhaps only to the French: vitality, laying oneself open to the unconscious and yet objectifying in an organized manner everything contradictory. Such a stormily creative climate gave me sufficient courage to risk a step into the third dimension, to create the coloured "Unnameable," later called "Migof" structures, at the junction between painting and sculpture. There were also the groups, the "Environments:" my first "Migofs" 1959, my first "Environment" 1961 for Mahlow's exhibition in the Baden Baden Art Museum: *Fantasy Architecture*.

For the first time I then tried to let myself be led into relief pictures carried out in accordance with the rules of drawing, and to coloured sculpture in a transition, a metamorphosis from the one to the other. The joy of such confused games, of such adventures as it were behind the thorny hedge of the fairy tales in ever more brilliant labyrinths, had reached a summit when I saw in the circle around Cordier and Eckstrom in New York the first pictures of Richard Lindner, also a dream-painter, but letting himself be slowly drawn in, so infinitely slowly that I thought of the torments of the dying and said as much to him when we were able to see him at work. I tried to provide him with a solution from my labyrinth, a very difficult undertaking to draw his slowness into my nervous and at the same time baroque net. Combinations were generated and new dense complex Environments. The manneristic impulse, belonging it is true to my basic structure, and emerging here and there at the end of the 1940's, fulfilled me and drove me on. At this point my "life-long interior monologue" now began for the first time to be conclusively settled. An Environment hanging from the ceiling, branching out, on the ground as a complete optical work of art spreading out, surrounded by four Migof guardians. Such crowding, such possession and encroachment of space changed, almost imperceptibly, into the "grisailles," stormily baroque and simultaneously ghostly silent cold pictures, which thereafter, and that is my present position, led quite contrarily to the very large vibrant water colours shot through with paths of light where early memories of Ensor and Turner emerge.

In thick over-ripe oil colours bearing a certain relationship perhaps to the colour brew informal picture of the 1950's, there are now bright dream scenes, tumbling Migof structures sretching themselves, changing and on the other hand not decipherable in terms of the figurative, of cliff faces, ravishing glimpses of landscape in waterfalls and tumbling clouds, associations as they catch me when in front of the white canvas I begin bit by bit to string together the colour tones, like picture and word fragments, gradually covering and weaving the surface.

—Bernard Schultze

More than seventy years of age, born in 1915 in Schneidemühl near the Polish border, Bernard Schultze is still one of the really young painters. He is now, as always, in search of mysteries in the labyrinthine depths of his sub-conscious. There the apparently inexhaustible springs of his scurrilous imagination bubble forth, regularly brought into harmony, however, by his "Prussian-like" sober and realistic intelligence, with the social reality of the present time to which his avant garde work responds in all its transformations and in its constantly new approaches.

Nevertheless, Bernard Schultze is a painter in the continuity of tradition. His work always stood in relation to admired painters of other generations who served him as fixed stars for orientation. In the beginning he tried, following Menzel's example, to draw as precisely as possible whatever was in front of him—true to nature, of course. But the affinity to Kubin continually haunted his work like a hobgoblin. Later on, in Belgium during the war, he happened to come across a book with pictures by Ensor, who became his guiding star for a long time. Ensor was displaced by Wols, Riopelle and Pollock—Schultze became co-creator of the German version of the informal, a tachist, and in 1952 had his breakthrough. Increasingly he developed sculptural images which, around 1957, protruded from the picture surface and finally became independent as "soft sculptures" on the dividing line between painting and sculpture. These mysterious creations called "Migofs," garishly coloured and bizarre in form, make palpable for the first time a formative reference point in his work: a spiritual connection with Surrealism. These Migofs soon united to form groups, atavistic Migof environments, frightful images of a society after the end of civilization.

While he was producing the Migofs (until far into the 1970's) Bernard Schultze also returned to canvas. As "Tabuskri" he showed delicate oil paintings which change into pen and ink drawings. He also worked on a series of water-colours and grey toned grisailles. Thereafter his palette quickly lightened again with homages to Impressionism: entirely fresh nuances in the painter's work appear in the latest extremely poetic pastel toned pictures which suggest unidentifiable plants and in no way conceal a reference to Corinth and Kokoschka. Even Schultze himself draws attention to such references which are related to the spiritual rather than the stylistic: it is more than obvious that in this case one original artist is saluting the other and that no one could suppose epigonal dependence.

This oeuvre is stamped with unmistakeable individuality; it is difficult to classify. It would certainly not be wrong to describe Bernard Schultze as a painter of secret landscapes who found his place between abstraction and surrealism. His continually restrained pleasure in rampant fantasy is in harmony with the tendency to harmony and order which aims at beauty and perfection. Yet Schultze is of his age and proffers an image of the present. Its reality, however, is shown in the caricature of the fragmentary and incessant destruction of the beautiful. The Migofs are significantly appropriate. His later mature work has employed more intense colours, and his pictures have gained an increased luminosity.

—Werner Schulze-Reimpell

SCHUMACHER, Emil

German. Born in Hagen, 29 August 1912. Studied art, Kunstgewerbeschule, Dortmund, 1932-35. Served as conscripted armaments factory worker, Hagen, 1939-45. Married Ursula Klapprott in 1940; son: Ulrich. Independent painter, Hagen, 1935-39, and since 1945: Co-Founder, Junger Westen artists association, Recklinghausen, 1947. Professor, Hochschule für Bildende Künste, Hamburg, 1958-60, and Staatliche Akademie der Bildenden Künste, Karlsruhe, 1966-77; Guest Professor/Visiting Artist, Minneapolis School of Art, 1967-68. Recipient: Kunstpreis "Junger Westen," Recklinghausen, West

Germany, 1948; Kunstpreis, Stadt Iserlohn, 1955; Conrad-von-Soest-Preis, Münster, 1956; Karl-Ernst-Osthaus-Preis, Hagen, 1958; Guggenheim Award, 1958; Japanese Ministry of Culture Prize, *International Art Exhibition,* Tokyo, 1959; Premio Cardazzo, *Biennale,* Venice, 1962; First Prize/Silver Medal, Bang Danh-Du Award, *International Arts Exhibition,* Saigon, 1962; Grosser Kunstpreis des Landes Nordrhein-Westfalen, Dusseldorf, 1963; Governor's Prize, Tokyo, 1966; Cross of Honour First Class, 1968, and Grand Cross of Honour with Star, 1983, Federal Republic of Germany; City of Ibiza Prize, *Graphics Biennale,* Ibiza, 1974; August Macke Prize, City of Menschede, 1978; Rubens Prize, City of Siegen, 1982; Ehrenring Award, 1982, and Honoured Citizen, 1987, Stadt Hagen; Jorg Ratgeb Pries, Reutlingen, 1987. Member, Akademie der Künste, West Berlin, 1968. Member, Order of Merit, für Wissenschaften und Künste, West Germany, 1982. Agent: Galerie Strelow, Luegplatz 3, 4000 Dusseldorf 11. Address: Bleichstrasse 11, 5800 Hagen, West Germany.

Individual Exhibitions:

1947	Studio für Neue Kunst, Wuppertal, West Germany
1956	Freie Kunstlergemeinschaft Schanze, Münster, West Germany
	Galerie Parnass, Wuppertal, West Germany
1957	Galerie Parnass, Wuppertal, West Germany
	Galerie 22, Dusseldorf
	Galerie Il Milione, Milan
1958	Galerie Schuler, West Berlin
	Galerie Van de Loo, Munich
	Galerie Brockstedt, Hannover
	Galerie Stadler, Paris
	Karl-Ernst-Osthaus Museum, Hagen, West Germany
1959	Galleria dell'Ariete, Milan
	Samuel L. Kootz Gallery, New York
	Galleria La Medusa, Rome
	Galerie Schuler, West Berlin
	Galerie Muller, Stuttgart
	Galerie Van de Loo, Munich
1960	Kootz Gallery, New York
	Galerie Van de Loo, Munich
1961	Kestner-Gesellschaft, Hannover
	Galerie Schuler, West Berlin
	Galerie Art, Bremen, West Germany
1962	Westfälischer Kunstverein, Münster, West Germany
	Kunstverein, Hamburg
	Stadtische Kunstmuseum, Duisburg, West Germany
	Kunstverein, Freiburg
	Opere Recenti, Galleria La Medusa, Rome
	Galleria Blu, Milan
	Oldbilder und Gouachen 1962, Galerie Van de Loo, Munich
	Galerie Baier, Mainz, West Germany
1963	German Pavilion, at the *Bienale,* Sao Paulo
	Galleria L'Indiano, Florence
	Galerie Nachst St. Stephan, Vienna
	Galerie Schmucking, Braunschweig, West Germany
1964	Galleria L'Indiano, Florence
	Galerie Brechbuhl, Grenchen, Switzerland
	Azienda Autonoma Soggiorno e Cura, Meran, Italy
1965	*Oldbilder, Gouachen, Grafik 1964-65,* Galerie Van de Loo, Munich
	Galerie Alice Pauli, Lausanne, Switzerland
	Galerie Gerber, Berne
	Galerie Nohl, Siegen, West Germany
1966	Kleine Graphik Galerie, Bremen, West Germany
	Galerie Brusberg, Hannover
	Galleri Haaken, Oslo
	Galerie Schuler, West Berlin
1967	Galerie Ariel, Paris
	Salle d'Honneur, *International Graphics Exhibition,* Ljubljana, Yugoslavia
	Narodni Galerie, Prague
	Galerie Rothe, Heidelberg
1968	*The Minnesota Suite,* Lefebre Gallery, New York
1969	Galerie de Montreal
	Galerie Defet, Nuremberg
	Galerie Rothenstein, Bremen, West Germany
	Galerie Kuhn, Aachen, West Germany

1970	Galleria L'Indiano, Florence
	Galleria Morone, Milan
1971	Kunstmuseum für Rheinlande und Westfalen, Dusseldorf
1972	Badischer Kunstverein, Karlsruhe
	Galerie Schottenring, Vienna
	Haus am Waldsee, West Berlin
	Galerie Nowa, Hagen, West Germany
	Galerie Rothenstein, Bremen, West Germany
1973	Galerie Rothenstein, Bremen, West Germany
	Galerie Rothe, Heidelberg
1975	*Arbeiten 1957 bis 1975,* Karl-Ernst-Osthaus Museum, Hagen, West Germany
	Forum Kunst, Rottweil, West Germany
	Galleria Falchi, Milan
	Galerie Nothelfer, West Berlin
	Galeria Van de Voort, Ibiza, Spain
	Galeria Internacional de Art, Madrid
	Galerie Hilbur, Karlsruhe
1976	Galerie Ostertag, Frankfurt
	Galerie Werner, Bremen, West Germany
	Palazzo delle Prigioni Vecchie, Venice
	Neue Galerie am Wolfgang Gurlitt Museum, Linz, Austria
	Galerie Veith Turske, Cologen
1977	Karl-Ernst-Osthaus Museum, Hagen, West Germany
	Galerie Rothe, Heidelberg
	Galerie Van de Loo, Munich
	Galerie Oben, Hagen, West Germany
1978	Galerie Elke und Werner Zimmer, Dusseldorf
	Galerie Falchi, Milan
	Modern Art Galerie, Vienna
	Galerie Ferdinand Meier, Kitzbuhl, Austria
	Kunstverein, Braunschweig, West Germany
1979	Stadtische Museum, Meschede, West Germany
	Fritz-Winter-Haus, Ahlen, West Germany
1980	Galerie Merten Slominsky, Mulheim, West Germany
	Galerie Van de Loo, Munich
	Galerie Alice Pauli, Lausanne, Switzerland
	Galerie Schlegl, Zurich
	Galerie Oben, Hagen, West Germany
1981	Galerie Gunzenhauser, Munich
	Galerie Dr. Krohn, Badenweiler, West Germany
	Galerie Rothe, Heidelberg
	Galerie Strelow, Dusseldorf
	Overbeck-Gesellschaft, Hannover
1982	*Rubenspreis—Siegen '82,* Haus Seel, Siegen, West Germany
	Galerie Strelow, Dusseldorf
	Kunstmuseum, Hannover
1983	Kunsthalle, Darmstadt, West Germany
	Wilhelm-Hack-Museum, Ludwigshafen, West Germany
	Westfälisches Landesmuseum, Münster, West Germany
	Galerie Strelow, Dusseldorf
	Galerie Skulima, West Berlin
1984	Galerie Rothe, Heidelberg, West Germany
	Galerie Strelow, Dusseldorf
	Kunsthalle, Bremen, West Germany
1985	Badischer Kunstverein, Karlsruhe, West Germany
	Kunstverein, Augsburg, West Germany
	Galerie Strelow, Dusseldorf
	Galerie Marghescu, Hannover
1986	Herstand Gallery, New York
	Galerie Pro Arte, Freiburg, West Germany
	Städtische Galerie, Quakenbrück, West Germany
	Städtisches Museum, Mulheim, West Germany
	Galerie Strelow, Dusseldorf
1987	Städtische Galerie, Lüdenscheid, West Germany
	Städtische Galerie, Rosenheim, West Germany
	Galerie Meyer-Ellinger, Frankfurt
	Städtisches Museum, Gelsenkirchen, West Germany
	Institut für moderne Kunst, Nuremberg, West Germany
	Städtische Galerie, Reutlingen, West Germany
	Kunsthalle, Kiel, West Germany
	Karl Ernst Osthaus Museum, Hagen, West Germany

Selected Group Exhibitions:

1951	*Kunder unseres Jahrhunderts,* Ruhrfestspiele, Recklinghausen, West Germany

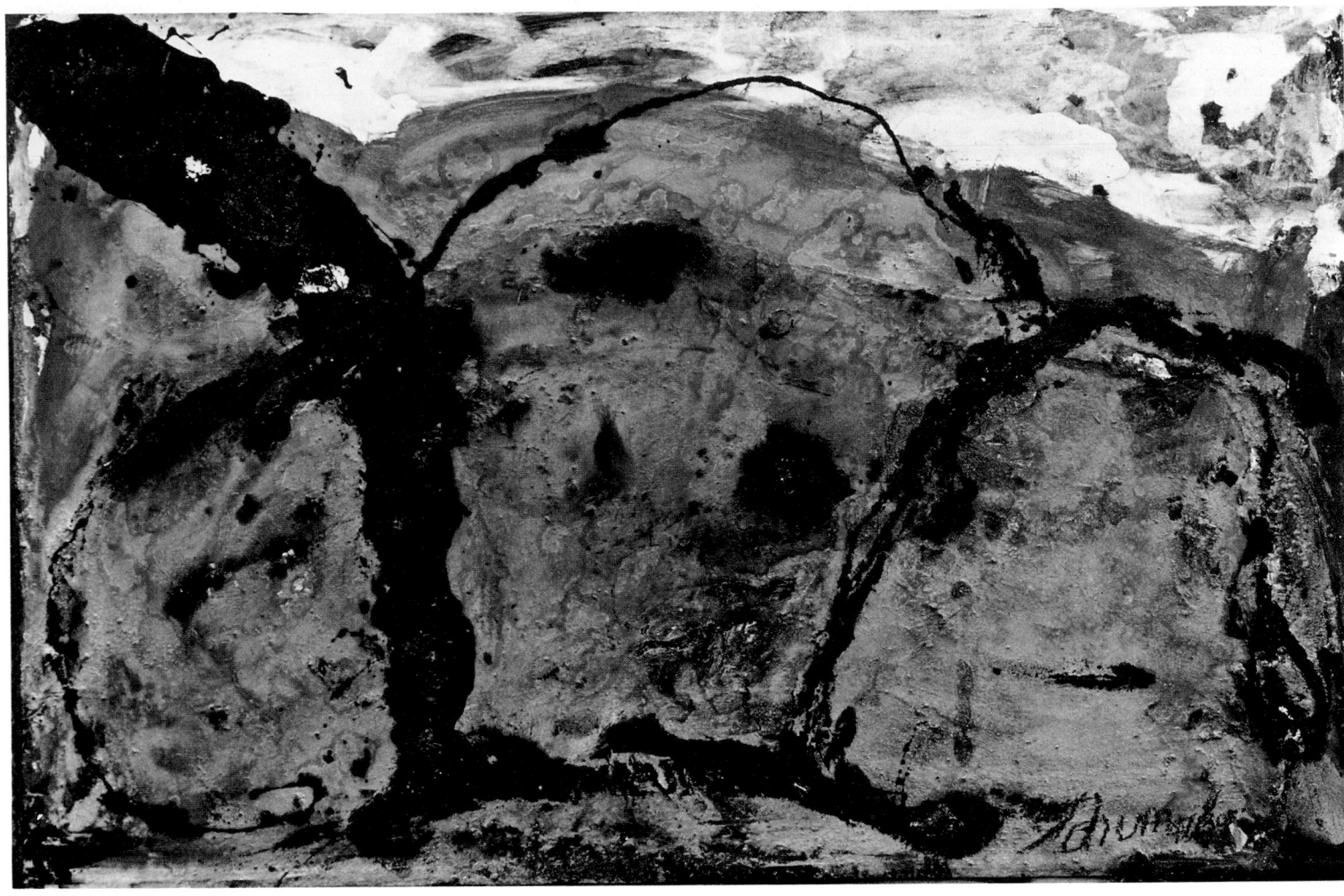

Emil Schumacher: *Mesa*, 1986

Collections:

Nationalgalerie, West Berlin; Städtisches Kunstmuseum, Bonn; Karl-Ernst-Osthaus Museum, Hagen, West Germany; Museum of Modern Art, Belgrade; Muzeum Nradowe w Karkowie, Cracow, Poland; Musée Cantonal des Beaux-Arts, Lausanne, Switzerland; Neue Galerie der Stadt, Linz, Austria; Moderna Galerija, Ljubljana, Yugoslavia; Albright-Knox Art Gallery, Buffalo, New York; Art Institute of Chicago.

Publications:

By SCHUMACHER: articles—"Farben und Einfalle" in *Blatter und Bilder* (Wurzburg), March/April 1959; "Neue Kunst in Deutschland" in *The Geijutsu-Shino* (Tokyo), October 1960; "Wegzeichen im Unbekannten" in *Neunzehn deutsche Maler zu Fragen der zeitgenossische Kunst*, edited by Wolfgang Rothe, Heidelberg 1962; "Aphorismen" in *Ein Buch mit Sieben Siegeln*, Heidelberg 1972.

On SCHUMACHER: books—*Emil Schumacher* by Erwin Sylvanus, Recklinghausen, West Germany 1959; *Emil Schumacher*, exhibition catalogue, with text by Werner Schmalenbach, Hannover 1961; *Emil Schumacher: Olbilder und Gouachen 1962*, exhibition catalogue, with text by Michel Tapie, Munich 1962; *Emil Schumacher*, exhibition catalogue, with text by Werner Schmalenbach, Milan 1962; *Opere Recenti di Emil Schumacher*, exhibition catalogue, with text by Werner Schmalenbach, Rome 1962; *VII Bienal de Sao Paulo: Emil Schumacher*, exhibition catalogue, with text by Werner Schmalenbach, Dusseldorf 1963; *Emil Schumacher: Olbilder, Gouachen, Grafik 1964/65*, exhibition folder, Munich 1965; *Emil Schumacher*, exhibition catalogue, with text by Werner Schmalenbach, Lausanne, Switzerland 1965; *Der doppelte Masstab, Kunstkritik 1955-1966* by John Anthony Thwaites, Frankfurt 1967; *The Minnesota Suite* by Emil Schumacher, exhibition catalogue, with text by Werner Schmalenbach, New York 1968; *Emil Schumacher*, exhibition catalogue, with text by Werner Schmalenbach, Dusseldorf 1971; *Emil Schumacher: Neue Bilder und Gouachen*, exhibition catalogue, with text by Dr. Hesse and Rolf-Günter Dienst, Hagen, West Germany 1975; *Emil Schumacher*, exhibition catalogue, with text by Bernard Holeczek, Braunschewig, West Germany 1978; *Emil Schumacher*, exhibition catalogue, with text by Jürgen Wissmann, Mulheim, Lausanne and Zurich 1980; *Emil Schumacher* by Werner Schmalenbach, Cologne 1981; *Emil Schumacher: Rubenspreis: Siegen '82*, exhibition catalogue, with text by Werner Schmalenbach, Siegen, West Germany 1982; *Emil Schumacher: Arbeiten auf Papier 1957-1982*, exhibition catalogue with texts by Joachim Buchner and Bernhard Holeczek, Hannover 1982; *Emil Schumacher: Djerba*, with text by Ernst-Gerhard Guse, Stuttgart 1983; *Emil Schumacher*, exhibition catalogue with texts by Gunter Busch, Annette Meyer zu Eissen and Andreas Vohwinkel, Bremen 1984; *Emil Schumacher: Maroc*, with text by Jens Christian Jensen, Stuttgart 1987.

Form: Everything that exists has its appropriate form or tends to assume form: island formations after flood, remnants of snow after thaw, cinders after fire. Form that presupposes life—form that comprises life—is "formless" and yet form.

Line: "The shortest connection between two points is the straight line" according to geometry. Within the picture the shortest connection between two points can be curved, winding, even discontinuous, but also straight. For the measure of the picture is the force which dictates the path of the line.

Colour: It is not enough to say: this colour is red, this colour is also red matter, palpable, tangible matter. Its flexibility has to be overcome. Only then does it assume character.

Matter: Picture material and picture matter: the one stands at the beginning, the other at the end. Material stands for both inspiration and resistance. The picture is formed from the essence but also the resistance of the material. The character of the picture cannot only be that of its materials.

Destruction: The most extreme form for crushing resistance is destruction: a primitive gesture of despair and desire. The answer is not sanctify, but: exorcise; not: restore, but incorporate the act of destruction in the picture—as expression and as form.

Space: Depth: not only the depth dimension of the picture but palpable tangible nearness: the picture space is closed in the background, presses forward. Width: line which describes the space. Curves which span it, contours which define it. Defined finitely measurable—and yet not measurable again—space.

Nature: In any case the earth closer than the stars. So thought turns to landscape: above and below the horizon line. They are not landscapes; but how could I elude nature?

—Emil Schumacher

Emil Schumacher belongs to that generation of German artists who spent their youth separated from the artistic developments beyond the German frontiers. In his birthplace of Hagen the memory of the early years of modernism remained alive in the survival of Karl

Ernst Osthaus' activities and in the Folkwang Museum which he founded, and finally through the painter Christian Rholfs who had accomplished in his work the development from realism to an expressionism which used colour as an independent value. Schumacher's early gouaches, woodcuts and paintings follow, with perceptible modification to colour and drawing, the late works of Rholfs. His most important themes are still-lifes with the simplest every day objects, whose poetry Schumacher makes visible with variations of tone or luminous colours. The tendency to experiment with unconventional materials is seen in his graphic prints during this period.

In 1950 Schumacher, influenced by developments in France, turned to abstract painting which through him gains a content which is difficult to express in words. After the mid 1950's the initial solid closed forms become more open, more relaxed, more defined by the colour structure. Between 1955 and 1958 the "Test Objects" which, without constricting frames, are conceived as independent sculptural reliefs, led to the mature period of his oeuvre. Schumacher's creative ideas are based on the material beauty of substance and colour which he condenses to independent paraphrastic signs. The creative constellations and picture titles awaken associations with objective realms without restricting the spectator, yet marking his perception as if with a poetry without words. Schumacher's art lives in the controlled spontaneity of the production process and in a subject related freedom both for himself and for the spectator. Without following in an historic manner tendencies imitative of Japanese art, he employs suggestions of it in oriental calligraphy.

In Western art of the last decades there are few examples which approach so closely the Far Eastern concept of painting as Schumacher's pictures, not because of formal parallels to calligraphy but above all because of the poetic subjectivity which for a Far Eastern viewer is central to his conceptions of art. For this reason distinctions in Tokyo and Saigon were among the earliest appreciations of Schumacher at an international level. From the late 1950's on, the artist numbered among the leading representatives of an informal painting whose fashionable period he survived by virtue of the subtlety and strength of his pictures.

A picture by Schumacher results as a rule from a process in which tempo of painting and lengthy periods of waiting, leading to a finished article, its destruction and renewed completion, succeed one another. His painting could be described as a dialectical process on the level of purely material experience if such a formulation did not hide the risk of it being understood as calculated intellectual aestheticism. Schumacher who, as his picture titles demonstrate, has a thorough command of words, declines to deliver rational, analytic explanations of his activity. This also makes him into a European kindred spirit of the Zen Master.

—Heinz Spielmann

SCOTT, Tim.

British. Born in Richmond, Surrey, 18 April 1937. Educated in Lausanne, Switzerland; studied at Tunbridge Wells School of Art, Kent, 1954, Architectural Association, London, 1954–59, and, under Anthony Caro, at St. Martin's School of Art, London, 1955–59. Married Malkanthi Wirekoon in 1958; children: Paloma, Roman, Maya, Chantal, and Anil. Independent sculptor, since 1960. Worked in the Atelier Le Corbusier/Wogenscky architectural office, Paris, 1959–61; and as an architect for Fry, Drew and Partners, London, 1962. Lecturer since 1962, and currently, Head of the Department of Sculpture, St. Martin's School of Art, London. Recipient: Peter Stuyvesant Bursary, 1965. Agent: Galerie Wentzel,

St. Apernstrasse 26, 5000 Cologne 1, West Germany. Address: 7 Prideaux Place, London, WCIX 9PP, England.

Individual Exhibitions:

1966	Waddington Galleries, London
1967	Whitechapel Art Gallery, London
1969	*New Sculpture*, Museum of Modern Art, Oxford
	Lawrence Rubin Gallery, New York
	Waddington Galleries, London
1971	Lawrence Rubin Gallery, New York
	Waddington Galleries, London
	Tate Gallery, London
1972	Museum of Fine Arts, Boston
1973	Corcoran Gallery of Art, Washington, D.C.
	Waddington Galleries, London
1974	André Emmerich Gallery, New York
1975	Waddington and Tooth Galleries, London
1976	Edmonton Art Gallery, Alberta
	Norman McKenzie Art Gallery, Regina, Saskatchewan
	Art Gallery of Windsor, Ontario
	David Mirvish Gallery, Toronto
1977	Tibor de Nagy Gallery, New York
	Waddington and Tooth Galleries, New York
	Galerie Wentzel, Hamburg
1979	Knoedler Gallery, London
	Tiergarten 105, Hannover
	Kunsthalle, Bielefeld, West Germany
1980	Knoedler Gallery, London
	Kettle's Yard Gallery, Cambridge (retrospective)
	Galerie Ziegler, Zurich
1981	Kunsthalle, Hamburg
1982	Galerie Wentzel, Cologne
1983	Atrium der Stadt Aachen, West Germany
	Klonaridis Inc., Toronto
1984	Galerie Wentzel, Cologne
1986	Kunsthandel Grill, Vienna
1987	Galerie Wentzel, Cologne
	Galerie Appel und Fertsch, Frankfurt

Selected Group Exhibitions:

1958	*Young Contempories*, RBA Gallery, London (and 1959)
1961	*26 Young Sculptors*, Institute of Contemporary Arts, London
1965	*New Generation*, Whitechapel Art Gallery, London
1966	*Primary Structures*, Jewish Museum, New York
1967	*Young British Sculptors*, Kunsthalle, Berne
1968	*Junge Generation Grossbritannein*, Akademie der Bildenden Kunst, Berlin
1970	*Contemporary British Art*, National Museum of Modern Art, Tokyo
1974	*Sculpture in Steel*, Edmonton Art Gallery, Alberta
1976	*Arte Inglesi Oggi 1960–1976*, Palazzo Reale, Milan
1981	*20th Century British Sculpture*, Whitechapel Art Gallery, London

Collections:

Tate Gallery, London; Arts Council of Great Britain, London; Gulbenkian Foundation, Lisbon; Museum of Modern Art, New York; Museum of Fine Arts, Boston; Hirshhorn Museum and Sculpture Garden, Smithsonian Institution, Washington, D.C.; National Gallery of Victoria, Melbourne.

Publications:

By SCOTT: articles—"Tim Scott, Sculptor," interview, in *Journal of the Architectural Association* (London), May 1967; "Reflections on Sculpture: A Commentary on Notes by William Tucker" in *Tim Scott*, exhibition catalogue, London 1967, reprinted in *I.C.A. Magazine* (London), April 1968; "Colour in Sculpture," with Phillip King, David Annesley, and William Turnbull, in *Studio International* (London), January 1969, reprinted in *Tim Scott: New Sculpture*, exhibition catalogue, Oxford, 1969; "Extracts from Tim Scott's Personal Notebooks (1958–9, 1961, 1965)" in *Potlatch* (London), May 1969; "Gone Too Far", with Alan Gour, in *Artscribe* (London), Summer 1983.

On SCOTT: books—*New Generation*, exhibition catalogue, by Bryan Robertson, London 1965; *Tim Scott: Sculpture 1961–67*, London 1967; *Tim Scott*, exhibition catalogue, London 1969; *Tim Scott*, exhibition catalogue, by Karen Wilkin, Edmonton, Alberta 1976; *Sculpture in Great Britain 1960–66 by the St. Martin's Group* by R. C. Rossi, Ph.D. thesis, New York University 1978; *Tim Scott*, exhibition catalogue, Bielefeld, West Germany 1979.

*   *   *

Tim Scott is probably the best of his generation of post-Caro English sculptors. Although he was a student of Caro's, he managed to avoid the pervasive influence of the older artist and stake out territory of his own. The clear articulation in space which is typical of Scott's work may owe something to Caro, but its bulk and mass do not. If anything, it seems closer to the tradition of the solid figurative monolith than to modernist construction. This sounds less far fetched in relation to work which had been abstract and usually made by collaging, if we consider the history of Scott's development.

His early work was a response to Brancusi, the only modernist sculptor whose work he knew first hand who seemed to offer a way into abstraction. At the time, Scott knew of David Smith only through photographs seen by chance at a U.S. Information Service library, when he was living in Paris, and his studies with Caro pre-dated Caro's use of steel. Scott liked the simplicity and solidity of Brancusi's forms, and says that his work of the early 60's was an attempt to get past Brancusi, not through open construction (which he knew little about) but by using materials and technology which allowed him to assemble volumetric, large scale forms in unconventional ways. Scott's works of the 60's are made of such diverse materials as fiberglass, sheet acrylic, glass and metal tubing, employed equally for their unique properties and for the contrasts their combination afforded.

The sculptures are both delicate and remarkably generous in scale. They are the equivalent of drawing with sweeps of the entire arm, rather than with controlled hand movements. Large geometric solids are played against thin acrylic sheets; flat shiny sheets are played, in turn, against metal tubing. Tubing outlines structures which echo solid forms, and flat cut-out shapes translate these outlines into yet another dimension. If there is any overt connection with Brancusi, it is in this counterpoint of like and unlike forms, which could be related to the way the Rumanian artist set his referential organic sculptures on severe and generalized bases; the stacking of wood, stone and metal in these assemblies must also have interested Scott. But even if Brancusi was a chosen ancestor, Scott's work never looked like anyone else's. His use of color in the 60's pieces is especially personal. The sculptures are widely polychromatic, sometimes incorporating as many as six or eight different hues. But color is always a function of materials, a way of differentiating forms—or, as in the "Bird in Arras" series of 1967–70, a way of generating forms. It never serves as a unifying skin.

As if in response to these extraordinary, fragile, colored sculptures, Scott began using thick acrylic slabs and correspondingly thick unpainted steel bars, in his works of the early 70's. This uncanny series depends upon seemingly contradictory qualities of transparency and brutal bulk. Gradually, the steel elements of these works began to dominate the plastic slabs, and by 1975 Scott was working exclusively in steel.

He had been dissatisfied for some time with the indirectness of his earlier working methods, and relished the new immediacy of welded construction, but the essential qualities of his mixed media work remained in the steel pieces. Like the earlier sculptures, they are generous in scale, no matter what their size, and, despite the uniformity of their material, they still depend upon dramatic contrasts of like and unlike forms. The piled steel and iron components of a single sculpture may be related by virtue of similar density and mass, but they are often completely unlike in other respects. Ragged flame-cut edges are juxtaposed with smooth geometric solids; thick sheets are

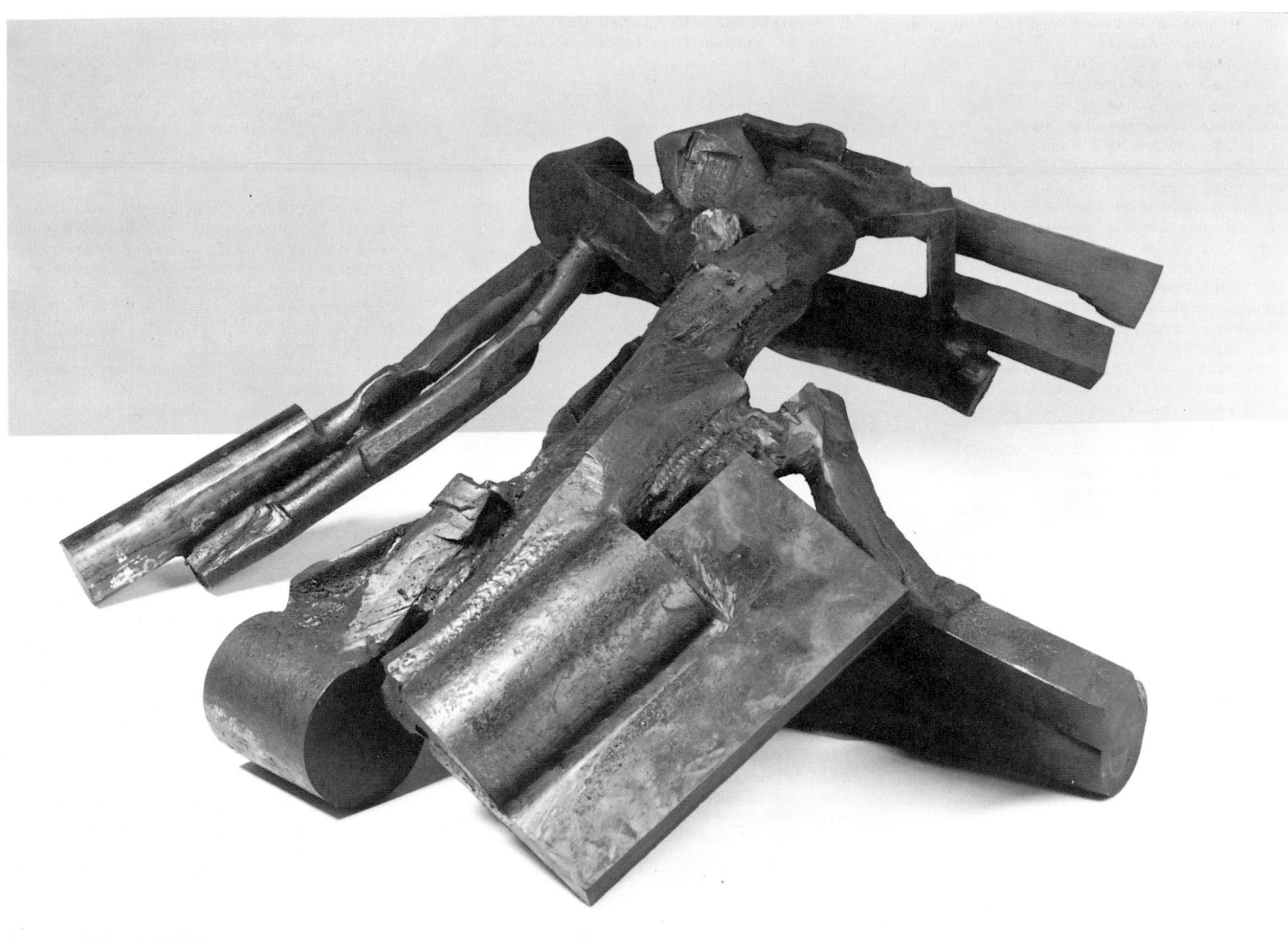

Tim Scott: *Feminine for Structure VII*, 1986

contrasted with chunky bars and discs. And no matter how massive their components, Scott's sculptures in steel retain the vigorous, expansive drawing of his early works.

Since about 1980, Scott has intensified his pursuit of directness. Reflecting on what characterized the sculpture he admired most, he concluded that a sense of tension and stress analagous to that of the body in motion was critical. He also became convinced that steel that had already been processed, turned into channel, plate, or angle, for example, was too inexpressive for his purposes. He wished to shape the metal himself and began a series made by the laborious process of forging. Because of inevitable limitations inherent in this method of working steel, the forged sculptures tend to be small in size—they can be monumental in scale—but extraordinarily complex and powerful.

Scott's typical generous drawing is translated into inflections and bends in massive lengths of metal. We are acutely aware of the physical effort expended in shaping these members, but they move so effortlessly through space, play so eloquently off less worked blocks of steel, that our perception of Scott's initial labor seems irrelevant. Paradoxically, despite their intense physicality, Scott's forged pieces are so much about the material itself, its ability to change shape when heated and pounded, that his sculptures have a curious kinship with abstract paintings by those of his colleagues, such as Jules Olitski or Lawrence Poons, or their common ancestor, Jackson Pollock, who "find" their images by paying close attention to how their materials behave.

Recently, Scott has experimented with still other materials and other processes, but his sculpture has remained generous, expansive, and richly articulated. By rethinking the properties of abstract constructed sculpture, Scott has expanded possibilities, and a group of young British sculptors, mostly former students at St. Martin's School of Art when Scott was head of the sculpture department, are currently attempting to expand them still further. Scott's work continues to criticize theirs. His apparently unyielding, dense, worked elements are used aggressively to embrace and activate large areas of space. They are sculptures that cannot be ignored, but they refuse to be ingratiating. Like his earlier works, the best of Scott's forged sculptures are at once powerful, lyrical, and brutal.

—Karen Wilkin

SCOTT, William.

British. Born in Greenock, Renfrewshire, Scotland, 15 February 1913; moved with his family to Enniskillen, Northern Ireland, 1922. Studied privately with Kathleen Birdie, Enniskillen, Northern Ireland, c. 1926; Belfast College of Art, 1928–30; studied sculpture, 1931–33, and painting, 1934–35, at the Royal Academy Schools, London, Military service, 1942–46. Married Mary Lucas in 1937; sons: Robert and James. Painter: worked in Cornwall for six months, 1936; visited France and settled in Pont Aven, Brittany, 1937; Founder, with Mary Scott and Geoffrey Nelson, Summer Painting School, Pont Aven, France, 1938; Member, Société du Salon d'Automne, Paris, 1938; lived in St. Tropez, France, 1938–39, but fled at outbreak of war, via Dublin, to London, where he settled in Chelsea; moved to Hallatrow, Somerset, 1941; Member, *Festival of Britain* Commission, London 1951; visited the United States, 1953 and 1959; settled in Edinburgh. Part-time Lecturer, 1941, and Senior Painting Master, 1946–56, Bath Academy of Art, Corsham, Wiltshire; Artist-in-Residence, Ford Foundation, Berlin, 1963. Recipient: Silver Medal for Sculpture, Royal Academy of Arts, London, 1933; Landseer Scholarship in Painting, London, 1934; Leverhulme Travel Scholarship, 1935. Associate of the Royal Academy of Arts, 1977. Agent: Waddington Galleries, 34 Cork Street, London, W.1, England. Address: 6 Stevenson Road, Edinburgh 11, Scotland.

Individual Exhibitions:

1942	Leger Galleries, London
	Leger Galleries, London
	Leger Galleries, London (with Mary Scott)
1950	Whitechapel Art Gallery, London
1953	Hanover Gallery, London
1954	Hanover Gallery, London
	Martha Jackson Gallery, New York (with Barbara Hepworth and Francis Bacon)

1955	Hanover Gallery, London (with Francis Bacon and Graham Sutherland)	1975	Martha Jackson Gallery, New York

1955   Hanover Gallery, London (with Francis Bacon and Graham Sutherland)

1956   Hanover Gallery, London
Martha Jackson Gallery, New York

1958   *Biennale*, Venice (toured Europe)

1959   Martha Jackson Gallery, New York
Galleria Galatea, Turin
Galleria Blu, Milan
Galerie Charles Lienhard, Zurich
Galleria dell'Ariete, Milan

1960   Kestner Gesellschaft, Hannover (toured West Germany)

1961   Esther Robles Gallery, Los Angeles
Hanover Gallery, London
Galerie Schmela, Dusseldorf

1962   Hanover Gallery, London
Museu de Arte Moderna, Rio de Janeiro (travelled to the Museo Nacional de Bellas Artes, Buenos Aires)
Martha Jackson Gallery, New York

1963   Kunsthalle, Berne
Hanover Gallery, London
Ulster Museum, Belfast
Galerie Anderson-Mayer, Paris

1966   Galerie Gimpel-Hanover, Zurich

1967   Dawson Gallery, Dublin
Bear Lane Gallery, Oxford
Hanover Gallery, London

1968   Hanover Gallery, London
Dawson Gallery, Dublin

1969   Richard Demarco Gallery, Edinburgh
Hanover Gallery, Lodnon

1971   Hanover Gallery, London
Scottish National Gallery of Modern Art, Edinburgh (travelled to the Aberdeen Art Gallery, Scotland)

1972   *Paintings, Drawings, Gouaches 1938–1971*, Tate Gallery, London

1973   Martha Jackson Gallery, New York
Gallery Moos, Toronto

1974   Gimpel Fils Gallery, London
Arnolfini Gallery, Bristol
Galerie Gimpel-Hanover, Zurich

1975   Martha Jackson Gallery, New York
Albright-Knox Art Gallery, Buffalo, New York
Santa Barabara Museum of Art, California
Gallery Moos, Toronto

1976   Gimpel Fils Gallery, London
Kasahara Gallery, Tokyo
Martha Jackson Gallery, New York

1979   Fermanagh County Museum, Orchard Gallery, Londonderry (travelled to Norther Ireland Arts Council Gallery, Belfast)

1981   Imperial War Museum, London

1985   Gimpel Fils, London

1986   Ulster Museum, Belfast
Guinness Hop Store, Dublin
Scottish National Gallery of Modern Art, Edinburgh

Selected Group Exhibitions:

1950   *Painter's Progress*, Whitechapel Art Gallery, London

1953   *Bienal*, Sao Paulo

1955   *Carnegie International*, Carnegie Institute, Pittsburgh

1963   *Some Aspects of Contemporary British Painting*, Art Gallery of Ontario, Toronto

1964   *Documenta*, Kassel, West Germany

1977   *British Painting 1952–1977*, Royal Academy of Arts, London

1983   *Aspects of British Art*, Guggenheim Museum, New York

1985   *The Irresistible Object: Still Life 1600–1985*, Leeds City Art Gallery, Yorkshire

Collections:

Tate Gallery, London; Victoria and Albert Museum, London; Scottish National Gallery of Modern Art, Edinburgh; Nationalgalerie, West Berlin; Kunsthalle, Hamburg; Museum des 20. Jahrhunderts, Vienna; Centre Georges Pompidou, Paris; Konstmuseum, Gothenburg, Sweden; National Gallery of Victoria, Melbourne; Brooklyn Museum, New York.

Publications:

By SCOTT: books—*A Girl Surveyed*, with poems by Edward Lucie-Smith, London 1971; articles—statement in *The New Decade*, exhibition catalogue, New York 1955; "Mr. William Scott Talks of Developments in Abstract Art" in *The Times* (London), January 1960; "William Scott in Conversation with Tony Rothon" in *Studio International* (London), December 1974.

On SCOTT: books—*9 Abstract Artists: Their Work and Theory* by Lawrence Alloway, London 1954; *William Scott* by Ronald Alley, London 1963; *William Scott: Paintings* by Alan Bowness and others, London 1964; *William Scott: Paintings, Drawings and Gouaches 1938–1971*, by Alan Bowness, London 1972; *William Scott: Drawings*, edited by Lou Klepac, New York 1975; *William Scott*, exhibition catalogue with texts by Ronald Alley and T. P. Flanagan, Belfast 1986.

William Scott is a member of the generation of English artists who were still dominated and influenced by Europe, notably Paris, a situation radically changed by the decline of the modern art situation in France, and the virtual termination of its power to attract and stimulate, which dates from the outbreak of the 1939 war. His Scottish/Irish origins are, in this context, important since Scottish art has always had a stronger relationship to French than to English painting, and, indeed, the Scots produced a far more successful brand of both Impressionism and post-Impressionism than their fellow-islanders. Where Scott is exceptional is that, unlike his compatriots, he progressed to the possibilities of post Cubism, so that whilst retaining the native love for rich colour and the Scottish instinct for controlled design, he was able to develop a neo-cubist formula for the heightened, dramatic presentation of everyday objects.

It is precisely in this mixture of unpretentious simplicity and dramatic, decorative creativity, that Scott emerges as an artist of individuality. He spent a number of years before the outbreak of the war travelling

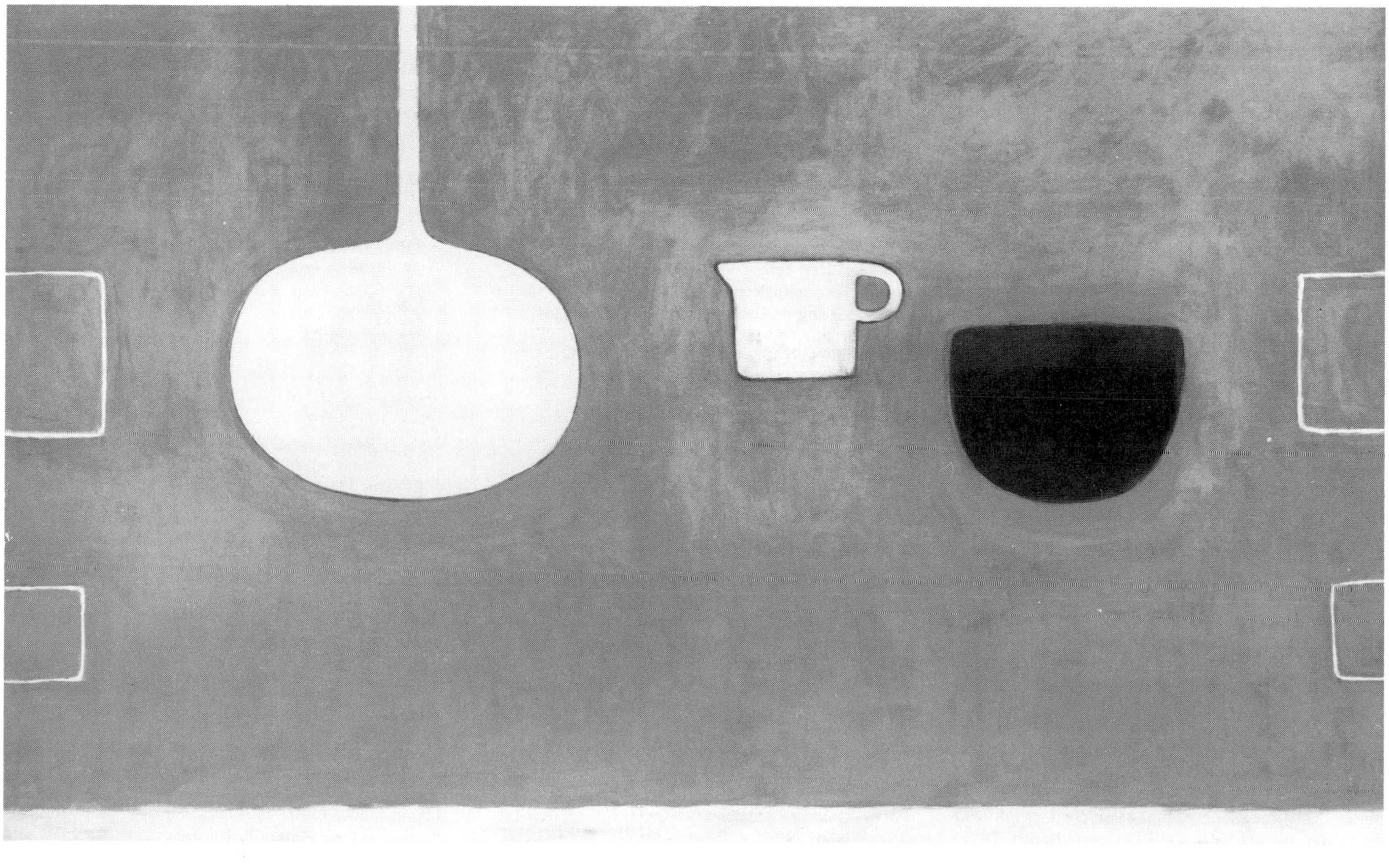

William Scott: *Blues*, 1981 Courtesy Gimpel Fils, London

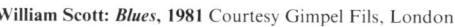

and working in Italy and France, copying the work of Italian masters, including Piero della Francesca—a good foundation for disciplined, neo-geometric composition—and in France was attracted by the sensuous colourists, Corot, Manet, Gauguin, Bonnard, Matisse. His increasing involvement with still-life resulted in a desire, in his own words, "to look at Cézanne not through cubist eyes, but rather through the eyes of Chardin."

This phrase is an important clue: Scott has never worked clinically, analyzing space and form, but rather as a relaxed humanist, finding in everyday domestic objects sufficient variations, combinations, reflections of the human situation. His early works in the genre are sombre, disciplined, tonally dry compositions, very much in the social-realist style of the Euston Road School. An early visit to Cornwall affected both his colour, the use of light, and the growing abstract formalism in his work. He resisted the immense impact of surrealism, and the introverted fantasy worlds of Klee or Kandinsky, which affected his generation. After a slight involvement in the romantic landscape movement, and a series of monumental, Gauguinesque portrait studies, in the post-war period Scott found his true subject, still-life, and as a result of living in Cornwall, a stylized, symbolic composition related to the formula of Ben Nicholson.

From the end of the 1940's Scott produced a fine series of still-life paintings, imbuing innocent objects with both sexual and metaphysical connotations, as have the best painters in the genre, from Chardin to Morandi. Realistic details were increasingly eliminated, so that the painting area becomes an isolated table-top, on which the chosen objects are carefully arranged, and painted with elegant, abstract discrimination. In time these compositions took on architectonic, linear mannerisms, ending in complete abstraction; but by the end of the 1950's Scott returned to realistic commitment, although now adopting a more complex plastic method. By the turn of the decade yet another switch to decorative abstraction had taken place, culminating in series of public murals.

This long period of uncertainty and searching resolved itself by a return to still-life, no longer descriptive, now extenuated with almost oriental elegance into carefully placed formalized objects in seas of brilliant colour. In the intervening period Scott had spent periods teaching in Canada and visiting the United States, the first European painter to visit Pollock, meeting Rothko and Kline. Scott was bewildered and impressed by the scale and self-confidence of their work; the effect, he says, was the discontinuance of abstraction in order to develop his own brand of symbolic realism on a larger scale.

—Charles Spencer

SEDGLEY, Peter.

British. Born in London, 19 March 1930. Studied building and architecture at Brixton Technical College, 1944–46; mainly self-taught in art, from 1959. Served in the Royal Army Ordinance Corps, Egypt, 1948–50, and in the Royal Air Force, 1959. Married Marguerite Wiltshire in 1951; children: Richard and Laura. Architectural assistant, R. Ward and Partners, London, 1946–48 and 1950–52, Gollins, Melvin, Ward, London, 1953–54, Clifford Culpin, London, 1955–56, and Architects Co-Partnership, London, 1956–59. Independent artist since 1966. Founded Building Technicians Co-operative, making prototype dwellings and furniture, 1957–58, and Art Information Registry (AIR) and Space Provision Artists Cultural and Education (SPACE), London 1968. Lives and works in West Berlin, and in Worthing, Sussex, since 1971. Recipient: Prize, *Mainichi International Biennale*, Tokyo, 1966; DAAD Grant, Berlin, 1971.

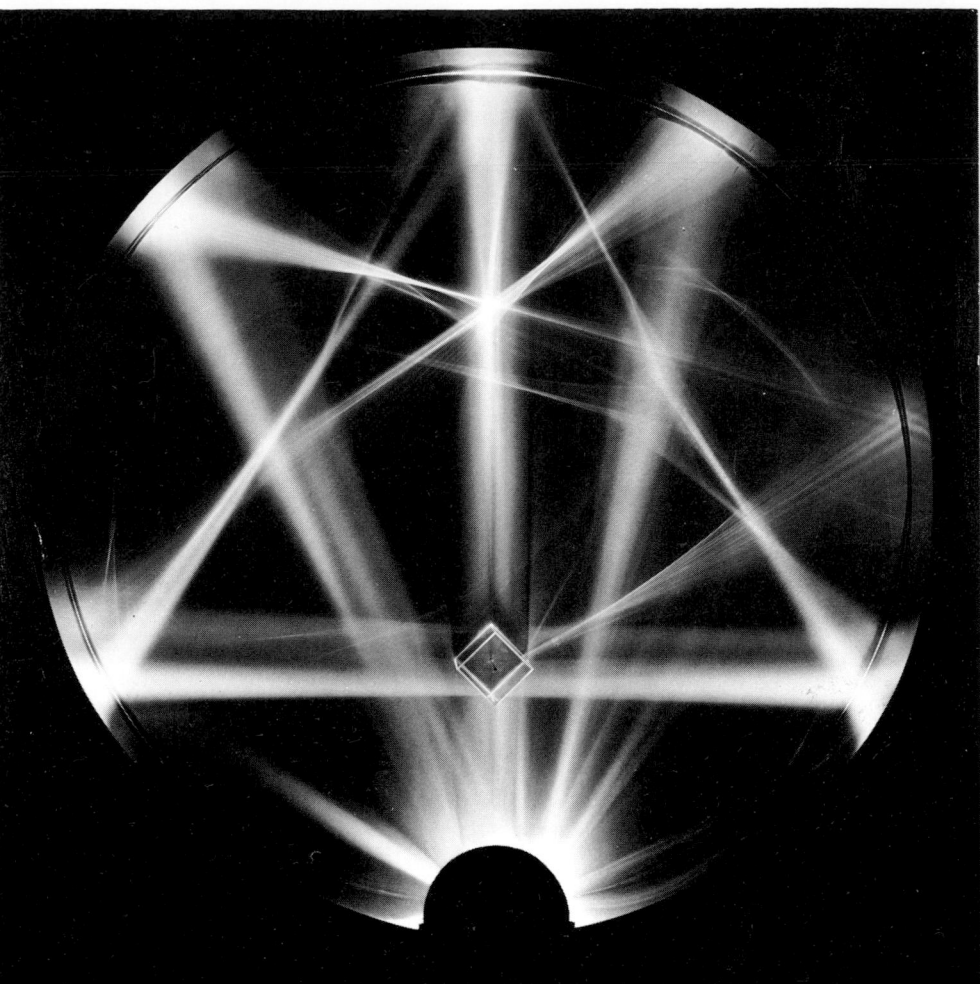

Peter Sedgley: *Spin*, 1981

Agent: Galerie Blanche, Stockholm. Address: Lindenallee 20, 1000 Berlin 19, West Germany.

Individual Exhibitions:

1965	McRoberts and Tunnard Gallery, London
	Howard Wise Gallery, New York
1966	McRoberts and Tunnard Gallery, London
	Howard Wise Gallery, New York
	Richard Feigen Gallery, Chicago
1968	Galerie Neuendorf, Hamburg
	Redfern Gallery, London
	Galerie Reckermann, Kassel, West Germany
1970	Trintiy College, Dublin
1971	St. Paul's School, London
	Haus am Waldsee, Berlin
1972	Forum Kunst, Rottweil, West Germany
1973	Ikon Gallery, Birmingham
	DLI Museum, Durham
	Midland Group Gallery, Nottingham
	Arnolfini Gallery, Bristol
1977	Redfern Gallery, London
1978	Akademie der Kunst, Berlin
1979	Overbeck-Gesellschaft, Lübeck
1980	Redfern Gallery, London
1981	Hendriks Gallery, Dublin
	Project Gallery, Dublin
	Galerie im Zentrum, Berlin
1982	Galerie Ferme, Malmo, Sweden
1983	Redfern Gallery, London
1984	Galerie Seestrasse, Steckborn, Switzerland
1985	Bede Gallery, Jarrow, County Durham
	Galerie Ferme, Malmo, Sweden
1986	Galerie Ferme, Malmo, Sweden
	Galerie Blanche, Stockholm
1987	Groninger Museum, Groningen, Ntherlands
	Norrkoping Art Museum, Sweden

Selected Group Exhibitions:

1965	*The Responsive Eye*, Museum of Modern Art, New York
1966	*Mainichi International Biennale*, Tokyo
1970	*Contemporary British Art*, National Museum of Art, Tokyo
1977	*Silver Jubilee*, Tate Gallery and Royal Academy of Arts, London
1978	*Constructive Tendencies*, Galerie Christl, Stockholm
1980	*Kelpra Studio Collection*, Tate Gallery, London
1981	*Distinct Form*, Konsthallen, Skövde, Sweden
1982	*Konsekvens: A Tribute to Olle Baertling*, Liljevalchs, Stockholm
1986	*Art and Science*, at the *Biennale*, Venice

Collections:

Tate Gallery, London; Arts Council of Great Britain, London; Victoria and Albert Museum, London; Art Museum of Ateneum, Finland; Museum of Sketches, Lund, Sweden; Albright-Knox Art Gallery, Buffalo, New York; Walker Art Center, Minneapolis; St. Louis Art Museum; Museum of Modern Art, Rio de Janciro.

Publications:

By SEDGLEY: articles—"Peter Sedgley", interview with Maurice de Sausmarez, in *Leonardo* (Oxford), vol. 4, 1971; "My Kinetic Art Works and Paintings 1971–1982," with Heinz Ohff, in *Leonardo* (London), vol. 15, 1982.

On SEDGLEY: books—*Constructivism: Orgins and Evolution* by George Rickey, New York 1967; *Movements in Art since 1945* by Edward Lucie-Smith, Lodnon 1969; *Op Art* by Frank Popper, Paris 1968; *Peter Sedgley*, exhibition catalogue, by Cyril Barrett, Birmingham 1973; *Lights and Pig-*

ments by Roy Osborne, London 1980; *Sedgley: Paintings, Objects and Installations 1963-1980* by Cyril Barrett, London, 1980; *100 Years of Metal Sculpture* by Dietrich Mahlow, Frankfurt, 1982.

In the way that philosophy belongs to the metaphysics of thought, colour occupies a similar position in the metaphysics of vision, namely art. Tracing the evolution (if that is the right word) of colour, it is impossible to isolate it from the development of art, which bears the codescript of successive stages of human sociological adaptation, giving colour a definitive role.

But colour, like water, depends on factors outside itself to give it form, identifying it with something more tangible than pure abstraction. We may speak of colour quite freely, but when one needs to illustrate it in our "mindseye" it involves a conscious effort to rehearse the sensation of colour without reference to a shape or context.

In pursuit of translating these sensations in painting, I respect an intrinsic geometry in the eye through which the transmission of colour may be facilitated.

By using simple geometric elements, I have tended to neutralize form in the spatial sense, i.e. shape, while placing greater emphasis on colour in the sequential form, relationships and displacement in time and in this way the visual arts are brought into proximity to the audio arts with the common parameter of time.

This combination of disciplines I have explored in different ways during the past years and several works have been realized. My interest in painting and kinetic object making, however, remains as intense as ever.

—Peter Sedgley

Peter Sedgley first made use of the startling two dimensional visual effects of op art, giving the impression of movement, before going on to explore actual movement in three-dimensional kinetic works. But unlike Bridget Riley, a close friend who originally confined her work in the early 1960's to producing optical effects using only black and white, Sedgley from the first made use of the optical interaction of colour and form, in severely geometric canvases, making great use of the recurrent theme of concentric circles as well as horizontal lines and intersecting rectangles.

Although he does not use mathematical systems like Jeffrey Steele, the idea of building up a strict colour scale is crucial to his work. This colour keyboard is based on the spectral colours taken strictly in order—violet, blue, green, yellow, red. White he uses as a sort of pause in the sequence, enabling him to repeat a colour without interrupting the series. However, he restricts himself to three colours within any one composition. And from the first he was interested in the interaction to form with colour, and the way the colours seem to change accordingly to their juxtapositions, so that in pictures like the Tate Gallery's "Yellow Attenuation" it is difficult to believe that the same yellow is being used throughout. Similarly with works such as "Trace 7," where concentric yellow circles on a green ground are intersected by white right angles growing bigger across the canvas, to give not only colour changes but also a moire pattern as a sort of added bonus.

Sedgley has always preferred circular forms, since because they don't vary in outline they allow concentrations on colour. His earlier target paintings have precise, hard contours which when painted on a black ground seem to revolve and pulsate with a striking hypnotic effect. The hypnotic effects of recession draw the spectator into a dark tunnel of endlessness, or else seem to float towards him in a vision of brightness. Either way he is almost physically involved with the painting, disoriented or made dizzy (achieving by another path the unfocussing recommended by Cage). These effects were most powerfully achieved when Sedgley softened and blurred the edges of his first

"hard edge" target paintings, which pulsated out from his black backgrounds.

While arranging his studio for evening showings, he became interested in the varying effects of different coloured lights on his targets, experimenting with red, yellow and blue filters. The effect of colour light is not merely to transform the hue, but to turn some colours black and make others disappear, and by programming the colour light he could control these transformations, and thus the rate at which the targets pulsate, expand, and contract. From these gyrating circles of light and colour Sedgley then took the short but logical step into the actual movement of kinetic art by developing his "Video Rotors." These are moving target pictures covered with small patches of fluorescent paint, which coalesce and change colour as the movement increases. They show clearly that Sedgley is more concerned with visual experience than with the painting as an object—with such effects as the way green and yellow at a certain speed appear white; some rows move rapidly, others slowly; some seem to move in opposite directions to the rest, others to stand still. The result is a complex dance of movement and colour changes.

Apart from his own artistic work, Peter Sedgley has also been very active in such ventures as the Artist's Registry, and with Bridget Riley as the leader of SPACE, which sought out such places as St. Catherine's Dock for young artists involved with new expressive media on a large scale.

—Lavinia Learmont

SEGAL, George.

American. Born in New York City, 26 November 1924. Studied at the Cooper Union, New York, 1941-42; Rutgers University, New Brunswick, New Jersey, 1942-46, 1961-63, M.F.A. 1963; Pratt Institute, Brooklyn, New York, 1947-48; State University of New York at Purchase, B.S. 1949, B.A. 1950. Married Helen Steinberg in 1946; has 2 children. Chicken farmer, North Brunswick, New Jersey, 1949-58; began painting, North Brunswick, 1950; and subsequently created first plaster sculptures; also taught in New Jersey high schools, 1957-64; participated in "happenings," with Oldenburg, Kaprow and others, in New York and New Jersey, 1956. Full-time artist in 1964. Lecturer, Princeton University, New Jersey, 1968-69. Recipient: Walter K. Gutman Foundation grant, 1962; Sculpture Prize, Art Institute of Chicago, 1966. Honorary doctorate: Rutgers University, 1970. Agent: Sidney Janis Gallery, 6 West 57th Street, New York, New York 10019. Address: R.F.D. 4 Box 323, North Brunswick, New Jersey 08902, U.S.A.

Individual Exhibitions:

1956	Hansa Gallery, New York
1957	Hansa Gallery, New York
1958	Hansa Gallery, New York
	Rutgers University, New Brunswick, New Jersey
1959	Hansa Gallery, New York
1960	Green Gallery, New York
1962	Green Gallery, New York
1963	Galerie Sonnabend, Paris
	Schmela Gallery, Dusseldorf
	Douglass College, New Brunswick, New Jersey
1964	Green Gallery, New York
1965	Sidney Janis Gallery, New York
1967	Sidney Janis Gallery, New York
	Dine/Oldenburg/Segal, Art Gallery of Ontario, Toronto (travelled to the Albright-Knox Art Gallery, Buffalo, New York)
1968	Sidney Janis Gallery, New York
	12 Human Situations, Museum of Contemporary Art, Chicago
1969	Galerie Dorthea Speyer, Paris
	Princeton University, New Jersey
1970	Western Gallery, Western Washington State College, Bellingham
	Sidney Janis Gallery, New York
1971	Sidney Janis Gallery, New York
	New Jersey State Museum, Trenton (with Richard Anuskiewicz)
	Onnasch Galerie, Cologne
	Galerie Dorthea Speyer, Paris
	Kunsthaus, Zurich (toured Europe)
1972	Centre National d'Art Contemporain, Paris
1973	Sidney Janis Gallery, New York
	The Private World of George Segal, University of Wisconsin, Madison (travelled to the Museum of Art, Indianapolis)
1974	*Basel Art Fair*
	Sidney Janis Gallery, New York
1975	André Emmerich Gallery, Zurich
	Hopkins Center Art Galleries, Dartmouth College, Hanover, New Hampshire
1976	*Environments*, Institute of Contemporary Art, Philadelhia
	Baltimore Museum of Art
	Nina Freudenheim Gallery, Buffalo, New York
	Art Association of Newport, Rhode Island
	Suzette Schochet Gallery, Newport, Rhode Island
	Santa Barbara Museum of Art, California
1977	Sidney Janis Gallery, New York
	Pastels 1957-1965, Art Gallery, State University of California at Long Beach
1978	*Blue Jean Series*, Staten Island Museum, New York
	Sculptures, Walker Art Center, Minneapolis (retrospective)
	San Francisco Museum of Art (retrospective)
	Whitney Museum, New York (retrospective)
1979	Hope Makler Gallery, Philadelphia
	Serge DeBloe, Brussels
1980	Gloria Luria Gallery, Bay Harbour, Florida
	Akron Art Institute, Ohio
	New Brunswick Tercentennial Committee, New Jersey
	Gatoda Gallery, Tokyo
	Fay Gold Gallery, Atlanta
	Sidney Janis Gallery, New York
1982	Sidney Janis Gallery, New York
1983	National Museum of Art, Osaka, Japan
1984	Galerie Reinhard Onnasch, West Berlin
	Sidney Janis Gallery, New York
1985	Galerie Maeght Lelong, Paris
	Israel Museum, Jerusalem
1986	Galerie Brusberg, West Berlin
	Sidney Janis Gallery, New York
	Galerie Joan Prats, Barcelona

Selected Group Exhibitions:

1957	*New York School Second Generation*, Jewish Museum, New York
1963	*VII Bienal de Sao Paulo*, Brazil
1965	*A Decade of American Drawings 1955-65*, Whitney Museum, New York
1967	*American Sculpture of the 60s*, Los Angeles County Museum of Art
1969	*Pop Art*, Hayward Gallery, London
1971	*White on White*, Museum of Contemporary Art, Chicago
1973	*Art in Space*, Detroit Institute of Arts, Michigan
1979	*American Portraits of the 60s and 70s*, Aspen Center for the Visual Arts, Colorado
1980	*Mysterious and Magical Realism*, Aldrich Museum of Contemporary Art, Ridgefield, Connecticut

Collections:

Museum of Modern Art, New York; Whitney Museum, New York; Neuberger Museum, Purchase, New York; Albright-Knox Gallery, Buffalo, New York; Art Institute of Chicago; Walker Art Center, Minneapolis; San Francisco Museum of Modern Art; Centre Nationale d'Arte Contemporain, Paris; Stedelijk Museum, Amsterdam; Moderna Museet, Stockholm.

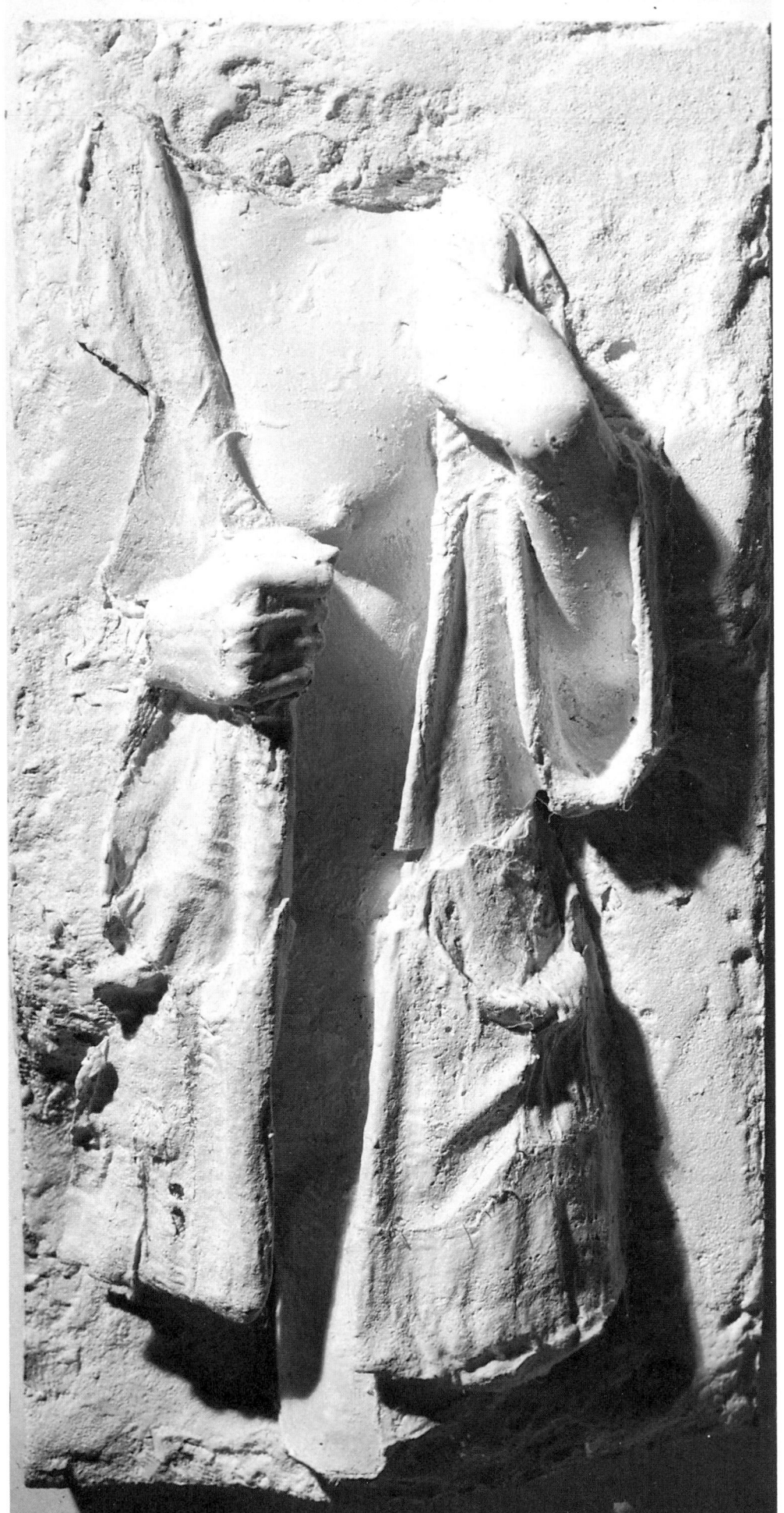

George Segal: *Girl in Robe III*, 1974

Publications:

By SEGAL: books—*Sculpture, Painting, Pastels: A Discussion of My Recent Work*, M.F.A. Thesis, New Brunswick, New Jersey 1963; *Girl on a Chair: Excerpts from a Conversation between Richard Bellamy and George Segal*, New York 1970; articles—"An Interview with George Segal," with Henry Geldzahler, in *Artforum* (New York), November 1964; "George Segal on the New York School" in *Albright-Knox Art Gallery Notes* (Buffalo, New York), Autumn 1966; "Segal's Explique" in *Aujourd'hui* (Paris), January 1967; "Sensibility of the 60's" in *Art in America* (New York), January/February 1967; "Jackson Pollock: An Artists' Symposium—Part II" in *Art News* (New York), May 1967; "The Sense of 'Why Not?': George Segal on His Art" in *Studio International* (London), October 1967; statement in *Sao Paulo 9*, exhibition catalogue, Sao Paulo 1960; statement in *Art Now: New York*, June 1970; "Interview with George Segal," with Phyllis Tuchman, in *Art in America* (New York), May/June 1972; "Pop" in *Art News* (New York), May 1974; "A Conversation with the Artist," with Constance W. Glenn, in *George Segal: Pastels 1957–1965*, exhibition catalogue, Long Beach, California 1977; comments in *George Segal: Sculpture*, exhibition catalogue, Minneapolis 1978.

On SEGAL: books—*Recent American Sculpture*, exhibition catalogue, with an essay by Henry Geldzahler, New York 1964; *Amerikanst Pop-konst*, exhibition catalogue, Stockholm 1964; *8 Sculptors: The Ambiguous Image*, exhibition catalogue, with an essay by Jan van der Marck, Minneapolis 1966; *Dine/Oldenburg/Segal*, exhibition catalogue, with an essay by Robert Pincus-Witten, Toronto 1967; *George Segal: 12 Human Situations*, exhibition catalogue, with a preface and introduction by Jan van der Marck, Chicago 1968; *George Segal*, exhibition catalogue, by Martin Friedman, Paris 1969; *George Segal*, exhibition catalogue, with texts by P. Kelleher and Hedy Backlin-Landman, Princeton, New Jersey 1969; *George Segal: Ruth in Her Kitchen* by Gert Kreytenberg, Stuttgart 1970; *George Segal*, exhibition catalogue, Zurich 1971; *George Segal*, exhibition catalogue, Cologne 1971; *Anuskiewicz/Segal*, exhibition catalogue, with text by Zoltan Buki, Trenton, New Jersey 1971; *George Segal* by William C. Seitz, Stuttgart and New York 1972; *George Segal*, exhibition catalogue, Paris 1972; *The Private World of George Segal*, exhibition catalogue, with text by José L. Bario-Garay and John Lloyd Taylor, Milwaukee 1973; *George Segal* by Jan van der Marck, New York 1975; *George Segal: Environments*, exhibition catalogue, by José L. Bario-Garay and Suzanne Delahanty, Philadelphia 1976; *George Segal Pastels 1957–1965*, exhibition catalogue, Long Beach, California 1977; *George Segal: Sculpture*, exhibition catalogue, by Martin Friedman and Graham W. Beal, Minneapolis 1978; *George Segal: Blue Jean Series*, exhibition catalogue, Staten Island, New York 1978; *George Segal* by José L. Bario-Garay, Barcelona 1979; *George Segal*, exhibition catalogue, New York 1980; *George Segal: reperes*, exhibition catalogue with preface by Pierre Restany, Paris 1985; *George Segal*, exhibition catalogue with texts by Sam Hunter and Donald Hawthorne, Jerusalem 1985.

For all its varied techniques, vast scale, day-glow colours, and advertising strategies, American art in recent years has failed to capture the particular insanity that characterizes the state of Western society in postwar years. With the honourable exception of Kienholz, there is no rage in contemporary American art, no fierce questioning or rejection. There is either bland acceptance, or sadness, emptiness, void. George Segal is the master of sadness.

There was a time, not so long ago, when a representative exhibition of American Art would have automatically included Segal; but not any longer. The bright light of critical acclaim has passed beyond him; his newness has been digested, the content ignored, and he must join the growing band of middle-aged old masters wondering where all the champagne and earnest interviewers from *Artforum* have gone. And unlike many of them, he doesn't even have the comfort of seeing his work change hands for ever increasing prices in the saleroom. His work, you see, is virtually unsellable.

An image by Segal is instantly recognizable. Figures cast from living models in plaster of paris inhabit environments typical of an affluent age. They never communicate to each other; each is locked inside himself. The impression is helped by the fact that Segal does not cast from the internal impression of the plaster, which would give a totally lifelike rendering, but simply cuts the mold open to allow the sitter to escape and then joins it back together again. The surface, then, is irregular, impressionistic. The figures look as if there might still be a body inside them, abandoned by the artist to eternal incarceration.

The only communication in a piece by Segal is between the "furniture" of the settings. These are real: beds, petrol pumps, Coke dispensing machines and beside them the figures look like ghosts. Kienholz also uses real objects as furniture, but he transforms them, so that they become menacing and hostile. In Segal's work, they are left exactly the way they were made, masters of the human wraiths that use them, bland, without intelligence, empty.

The process of making the work contrasts with the final effect. Segal has himself noted that there is something sadistic and fetishistic is encasing people in slowly hardening plaster. Some sit stolidly, enduring the discomfort for the sake of Art, some panic and scream, others actually enjoy the experience. Segal's studio is obviously a place of secret emotion, where regularly a human is turned, albeit temporarily, into a thing, a process that is near to the hidden mainspring of our sexual and political fantasies. Yet little of this process escapes into the final work; only its desolation survives.

Segal was never as successful as those Pop artists who offered a happier view of the American Dream. And when conceptualism made complexity and subtlety the prime virtues, Segal's work was too obvious, its melancholy poetry too direct. Slowly his work is being removed from the exhibition rooms in the museums to the storage areas, to be replaced by safer, more arty, work.

Like almost all American artists, Segal has been unadventurous in matters of style; he found his formula and stuck to it, and there is a limit to how much any single style can reveal. There is never much variation of mood in his sculpture; although the furniture may change, the loneliness is always present. And the buyers and museum directors apparently don't want to hear about loneliness anymore.

Probably they know it too well already.

—Alastair Mackintosh

SEKINE, Nobuo.

Japanese. Born in Imiya City, Saitama Prefecture, in 1942. Studied painting at the Tama College of Art, Tokyo, 1964-68. Sculptor, Tokyo, since 1967. Recipient: Sculpture Prize, Nagaoka Art Museum, 1968; Sculpture Prize, Hakone Open-Air Museum, 1969. Agent: Tokyo Gallery, Chuo-ku, Ginza 8-6-18, Tokyo. Address: Otaku, Minami-Yuigaya 2-14-2, Tokyo, Japan.

Individual Exhibitions:

1965	Tokyo Gallery
1969	Tokyo Gallery
1973	Tokyo Gallery
1977	Tokyo Gallery
	Sakura Gallery, Nagoya, Japan
1978	Louisiana Museum, Humlebaek, Denmark
1979	Henie-Onstad Kunstsenter, Oslo

Selected Group Exhibitions:

1968	Contemporary Art Exhibition of Japan, Tokyo
	Modern Japanese Art, Institute of Contemporary Arts, London
	Outdoor Sculpture Exhibition, Kobe, Japan
	Annual Sculpture Exhibition, Nagaoka Art Museum, Japan
1969	Biennale des Jeunes, Musée d'Art Moderne, Paris
	International Sculpture Exhibition, Hakone Open-Air Museum, Tokyo
1970	Biennale, Venice
1974	Japan: Tradition und Gegenwart, Städtische Kunsthalle, Dusseldorf
	Tokyo Biennial

Collections:

Nagaoka Art Museum, Japan; Hakone Open-Air Museum, Tokyo; Louisiana Museum, Humlebaek, Denmark.

Publications:

On SEKINE: books—Art in Japan Today, edited by S. Takashina, Yoshiaki Tono and Yusuke Nakahara, Tokyo 1974; Japan: Tradition und Gegenwart, exhibition catalogue, by Jürgen Harten, Joseph Love and others, Dusseldorf 1974.

Nobuo Sekine is one of the most noteworthy young artists of recent years. He graduated from the oil painting department of Tama College of Art in 1968, but showed his work in group exhibitions even while a student. "Phase," a work made soon after graduation, in which Sekine used tubular materials, demonstrated the artist's interest in topology, and earned for him a prize at the 1968 Contemporary Art Exhibition of Japan. This work was also shown at the modern Japanese art exhibition in London's I.C.A. For the Kobe outdoor sculpture show, Sekine excavated a round pit in the ground and piled the earth around it to make "Phase Mother Earth," which won a prize and considerable attention for the artist. The hole and excavated earth had a complementary relationship.

Transporting the earth from the ground to the surface without changing its shape was to show the relationship between the convex and the concave of the "Phase—Nothingness." In the same year, Sekine won a prize at the Nagaoka Art Museum prize exhibition for another work also entitled "Phase," which consisted of a cylindrical sponge on top of which Sekine placed a heavy steel plate. It was interesting because it stressed the complementary relationship between the sponge and the steel, rather than just showing the sponge's shape being altered by the weight of the steel.

It is characteristic of Sekine to indicate conditions of existence rather than to form things. For his one-man show at Tokyo Gallery in 1969, Sekine brought in huge heaps of clay and directed that gallery visitors were to move them about as they pleased. He filled round and square steel tubs with water to make a "Phase of Nothngness" for the Contemporary Art Exhibition of Japan, and this was included in a group exhibition at the International Young Artist Exhibition at Hakone Open-Air Museum; he won a prize for another "Phase" work, this time by elevating a huge volcanic rock on a large pole of stainless steel which he had polished to mirror like brightness. The mirror surfaces reflected the sky and surrounding countryside, and created a sense of unease in relation to the huge elevated stone.

Sekine made a similar work for the Venice Biennale in 1970. In 1972 he was commissioned to make a sculpture for the Shigi City Hall in Saitama Prefecture. In 1976, he was commissioned by the Louisiana Museum, Humlebaek, Denmark, to construct works in the sculpture garden of the museum.

In the early part of the 1980s, Sekine set out to express his ideas in relief sculptures in steel plates, and these developed into his unique sculpture/painting series of 1987, entitled Phase Conception. Thick, multi-layered Japanese paper was used for the supports, with gold or silver foil pressed onto them, revealing excavated holes and scratches which had the appearance of scars or traumas.

—Yoshiaki Tono

SELF, Colin.

British. Born in Norwich, Norfolk, 17 July 1941. Studied at the Norwich School of Art, Norfolk, and the Slade School of Fine Art, London. Travelled extensively in the United States and Canada, 1962 and 1965. Lecturer, Norwich School of Art, Norfolk. Recipient: Drawing Prize, Biennale, Paris, 1967; Giles Bequest Prize, British Print Biennale, Bradford, Yorkshire, 1968; Etching Prize, International Print Biennale, Bradford, Yorkshire, 1969. Address: 31 St. Andrews Avenue, Thorpe, Norwich, Norfolk NR7 0RG. England.

Individual Exhibitions:

1965	Piccadilly Gallery, London
1966	Galerie Yvon Lambert, Paris
	Robert Fraser Gallery, London
1968	Galerie Neuendorf, Hamburg
	Galerie Rudolf Zwirner, Cologne
	Alecto Gallery, London
1969	Prints and Drawings, DLI Museum and Arts Centre, Durham
1976	Playhouse Gallery, Harlow, Essex (with John Riches)

Selected Group Exhibitions:

1964	Summer Show, Kasmin Gallery, London
1965	London under 40, Galleria Milano, Milan
1967	Salon de la Jeune Peinture, Musée d'Art Moderne de la Ville, Paris
	Englische Kunst, Galerie Bischofberger, Zurich
	British Drawing: New Generation, Museum of Modern Art, New York
1968	The Obsessive Image, Institute of Contemporary Arts, London
1969	Israel: The Reality, Jewish Museum, New York (toured the United States)
1970	Kunst und Politik, Badischer Kunstverine, Karlsruhe, West Germany
1971	Bienal, Sao Paulo
1973	11 Englischer Zeichner, Kunsthalle, Baden-Baden, West Germany (toured West Germany)

Collections:

Arts Council of Great Britain, London; Victoria and Albert Museum, London; Museum of Modern Art, New York

Publications:

By SELF: books—Power and Beauty, New York 1968; Out of Focus, New York 1968; Colin Self's Prelude to a 1000 Objects, New York 1971; articles—"Drawings" in London Magazine, May 1969; statement, in Colin Self: Prints and Drawings, exhibition catalogue, Durham 1969.

On SELF: books—Colin Self: Prints and Drawings, exhibition catalogue, Durham, 1969; A Decade of Printmaking, London 1973; 11 Englische Zeichner, exhibition catalogue, Baden-Baden, West Germany 1973; article—"Graphics: Colin Self" by Pat Gilmour in Arts Review (London), December 1971.

The period when British contemporary art had yet another reawakening—during the 1950s and 60s—could claim to have witnessed the emergence of a number of outstanding new talents as various and individual as a greedy world could wish; names like Davie, Paolozzi, Allen Jones, Hodgkin and Caulfield . . . and there were many many more, nearly all of which have earned themselves a national and often global reputation.

Amongst them was the precise and bijou-brilliant Colin Self who originally made his impact in the art world with a number of surprise drawings of heavily upholstered and outmoded couches. In works like these, the pencil (the ordinary everyday people's pencil) was allowed to dig deeply into the paper. The graphite was encouraged to cover areas with a dense shiny opacity as well to fill in fundamental outlines. With the same emphasis, equally plebean coloured-pencils were employed to add the coloration (which was generally auxiliary).

These early drawings combined an expert refinement with a paradoxical bluntness. The reaction they evoked in the eye of the viewer was of seeing something conjured up by a precocious student draughtsman, free from the sophistication his work might encounter in later years, but already in mid-flight.

Having said that, it is necessary to point out that the suggestion of pre-professional ability in these early drawings by Self has no sort of parallel with "sophisticated" naivety to be found in the drawings and graphics by his contemporary David Hockney in his middle period.

Self is essentially a man for paper. He is a deserving award winner and a participator in international graphics contests. His control of photographic elements in his delicate handling of etching and the screenprint medium must be the envy of many other artists.

Still staying in the context of "absolute" reality, he has been able to make a wonderland of the faded transparency of pressed flowers with the same aplomb, albeit in a rather different atmosphere, as he was able to bring to his famous automobile etching "Car."

Works like these have none of the direct sugariness or brutality that has marked seriograph series by so many other artists of today. Colin Self is like an al-chemist, clearly within sight of the eventual change from base metal into gold. Glimpses of his experiments with graphic media on the way to this goal are the public's reward.

No doubt his admirers fall into three (not always distinct) categories; those who are impressed by his imagery and his adept composition, the media-aparatchiks who are fascinated by his investigation of novel techniques, and the fanatical amateurs of prints. All three can expect relatively few disappointments.

—Sheldon Williams

SERRA, Richard.

American. Born in San Francisco, California, 2 November 1939. Studied at the University of California, Berkeley and Santa Barbara, 1957–61, B.A., M.A.; Yale University, New Haven, Connecticut, 1961–64, B.A., M.F.A.; study-travels in Paris and Italy, 1964–66. Independent sculptor, New York, since 1966: rubber and neon works, 1966–67; molten and cast lead works, 1968–69; cut and torn works, 1968–70; weighted leaning pieces, 1968–71; films and video-tapes, 1968–77; large interior and exterior landscape pieces in steel, since 1970. Recipient: Yale Travel Fellowship, 1964; Fulbright Study Grant, 1965; Skowhegan Sculpture Award, Maine, 1975; Honorary Fellowship, Bezalel Academy of Arts and Design, Jerusalem, 1983. Agent: Leo Castelli Gallery, 420 West Broadway, New York, New York 10012. Address: Post Office Box 645, Canal Street Station, New York, New York 10013, U.S.A.

Individual Exhibitions:

1966	Galleria La Salita, Rome
1968	Galerie Ricke, Cologne
1969	Galleria Lambert, Milan
	Leo Castelli Gallery, New York
1970	Joseph Helman Gallery, St. Louis
	Ace Gallery, Los Angeles
	University of California at San Diego
	Pasadena Museum of Art, California
1972	Ace Gallery, Los Angeles
	Castelli Graphis, New York

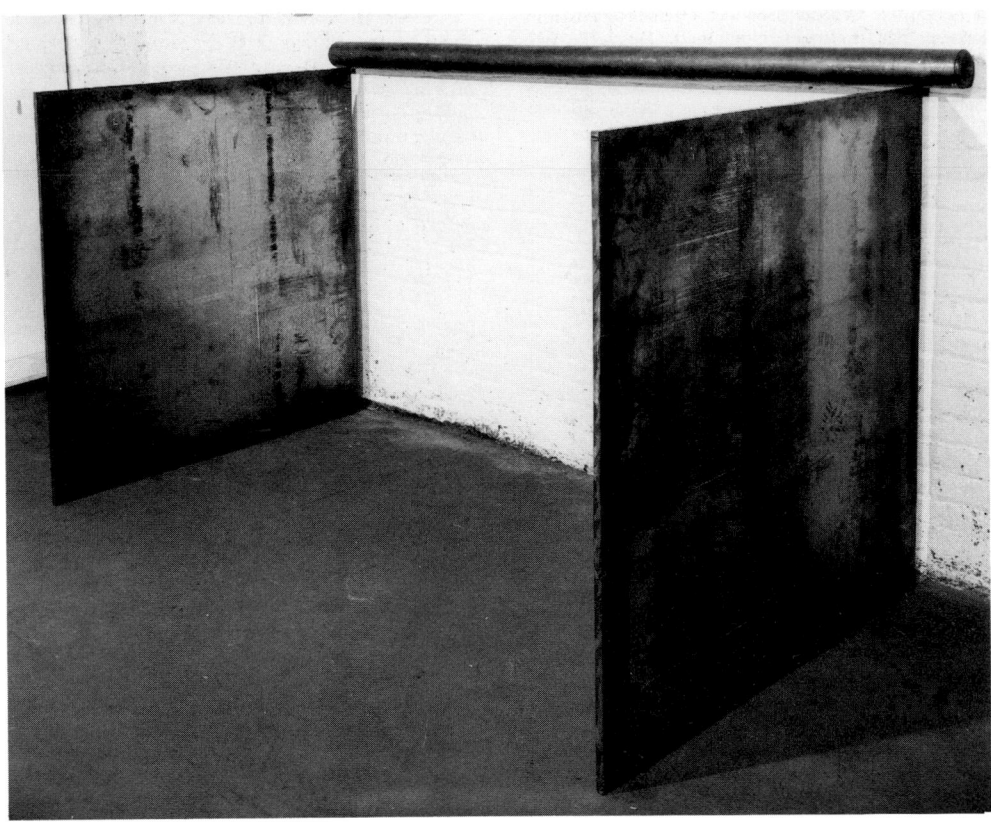

Richard Serra: *Number 5*, 1969

1973	Galerie Ricke, Cologne
	Ace Gallery, Los Angeles
1974	School of Visual Arts, New York
1976	Ace Gallery, Los Angeles
	Blum Helman Gallery, New York
1977	Galerie Daniel Templon, Paris
	Galerie Bochum-Weitmar, West Germany
	Stedelijk Museum, Amsterdam
1978	Ace Gallery, Venice, California
	Blum Helman Gallery, New York
	Museum of Modern Art, Oxford
1979	Richard Hines Gallery, Seattle
	University of California, Berkeley
	KOH Gallery, Tokyo
	Galeria Schmela, Dusseldorf
1980	Hudson River Museum, Yonkers, New York
	Museum Boymans-van Beuningen, Rotterdam
1981	Blum Helman Gallery, New York
	KOH Gallery, Tokyo
	Castelli Gallery at 142 Greene Street, New York
	Monchehausmuseum, Goslar, West Germany
	Castelli Graphics, New York
1982	Gemini G.E.L., Los Angeles
	Leo Castelli Gallery, New York
	Castelli Gallery at 142 Greene Street, New York
	St. Louis Art Museum, Missouri
	Carol Taylor Art Museum, Missouri
1983	Centre Georges Pompidou, Paris
	Larry Gagosian Gallery, Los Angeles
	Musée d'Art Moderne, Paris
	Akira Ikeda Gallery, Tokyo
	Blum Helman Gallery, New York
	Reinhard Onnasch Ausstellungen, West Berlin
	Galerie Nordenhake, Malmo, Sweden
1984	Leo Castelli Gallery, New York
	Galerie Nordenhake, Malmo, Sweden
	Galerie Daniel Templon, Paris
	Larry Gagosian Gallery, Los Angeles
1985	Galerie Maeght-Lelong, New York
	Museum Haus Lange, Krefeld, West Germany
	Gemini G.E.L., Los Angeles
	Akira Ikeda Gallery, Tokyo
	Galleria Christian Stein, Milan
1986	Museum of Modern Art, New York (retrospective)
	Castelli Gallery at 142 Greene Street, New York
	Larry Gagosian Gallery, Los Angeles

	Galerie Maeght-Lelong, New York
	New City Editions, Venice, California
	Galerie Jean Bernier, Athens
1987	Hoffman Borman Gallery, Santa Monica, California
	Harcus Gallery, Boston
1988	Kunsthalle, Basle
	Galerie Littmann, Basle
	Stadtische Galerie im Lenbachhaus, Munich

Selected Group Exhibitions:

1966	*From Arp to Artschwager I*, Bellamy/Goldowsky Gallery, New York
1970	*Identifications*, Kunstverein, Hannover
1974	*The Condition of Sculpture*, Hayward Gallery, London
1976	*200 Years of American Sculpture*, Whitney Museum, New York
1977	*Documenta*, Kassel, West Germany
1978	*Between Sculpture and Painting*, Worcester Art Museum, Massachusetts
1981	*Biennale*, Venice
1983	*Sculpture: The Tradition in Steel*, Nassau County Museum of Art, Roslyn, New York
1985	*Maximal Implications of the Minimal Line*, Bard College, Annandale-on-Hudson, New York
1987	*The Great Drawing Show 1587–1987*, Michael Kohn Gallery, Los Angeles

Collections:

Museum of Modern Art, New York; Whitney Museum, New York; Guggenheim Museum, New York; Los Angeles County Museum of Art; Norton Simon Museum of Art, Pasadena, California; Art Gallery of Ontario, Toronto; National Gallery of Canada, Ottawa; Tate Gallery, London; Stedelijk Museum, Amsterdam; Moderna Museet, Stockholm.

Publications:

By SERRA: articles—"Statements" in *Artforum* (New York), September 1971; "Paul Revere," with Joan Jonas, in *Artforum*, (New York), September 1971; "Richard Serra: Shift," edited by Roaslind Krauss, in *Studio International* (London),

October 1973; "Richard Serra and Robert Bell: Prisoner's Dilemma" in *Avalanche* (New York), May/June 1974; films—*Hand Catching Lead,* 1968; *Tied,* 1968.

On SERRA: articles—"Slow Information: Richard Serra" by Robert Pincus-Witten in *Artforum* (New York), September 1969; "Richard Serra, Castelli Warehouse" by P. Leider in *Artforum* (New York), February 1970; "Critic's Choice: Serra" by E. C. Baker in *Artnews* (New York), February 1970; "Los Angeles: Craig Kauffman and Richard Serra, Pasadena Art Museum" by Peter Plagens in *Artforum* (New York), April 1970; "Los Angeles: Richard Serra Films, Ace Gallery" by J. E. Young in *Art International* (Lugano, Switzerland), October 1970; Toronto: Serra's Visit and After" by Mario Amaya in *Art in America* (New York), May/June 1971; "Richard Serra: Sculpture Redrawn" by Rosalind Krauss in *Artforum* (New York), May 1972; "Richard Serra" by Otto Hahn in *Art Press* (Paris), February 1974; "Working Out: The Work of Richard Serra" by John Anthony Thwaites in *Art and Artists* (London), March 1974; review by Elizabeth Frank in *Art in America* (New York), Summer 1981.

Acutely aware of the interrelationship of recent investigations in the plastic and temporal arts, the sculptor Richard Serra produced a series of films in the late 1960's that are paradigmatic of much of his work. The films, in their austere and repetitive meditation on the performance of simple, generally absurd tasks, transcend traditional narrative associations. In *Hand Catching Lead* (1968), for example, Serra focuses on his own hand as it attempts to catch a sequence of falling strips of metal, while *Hands Tied* (1968) is centered on the unshackling of the artist's bound hands. Unfolding in real, operational time, these films depict self-referential states where "meaning" is external and inextricably woven into the formal conditions of the act itself. Concomitantly, these acts project the kind of compulsion that governs human behavior without asserting the underlying logic of such behavior; the viewer is not made cognizant of the circumstances that precipitate the artist's Sisyphean goal. In the space-time continuum of Serra's films, a task is simply a task.

Stemming from the interest in process inherent in his films, Serra's minimalist and site-specific pieces challenge traditional notions of sculpture. From 1968–69, the artist made nearly 100 works centered on the manipulation of lead and generated by his "Verb List" (1967), a series of transitive verbs (to roll, to crease, to fold . . .) that served as a simple program for the artist's task-performance. Disrupting the tradition of the closed sculptural object, a tradition that continued throughout the modernist epoch, Serra produced pieces such as "Splash Piece" (1968) and "Casting" (1969), both involving the tossing of molten lead into the juncture of wall and floor. Rather than conflating time into a single, conceptualized moment, the works, as the residue of self-evident processes, submit to the ebb and flow of real time. It is in their obsession with the performance of tasks in a real space-time continuum that Serra's films can be seen to co-opt these new sculptural concerns. While Serra has said that "sculpture can not be similar to or influenced by the illusion in film," the process pieces of the late 1960's clearly assume the compulsive strategies of his films.

In the 1970's Serra's work was increasingly directed toward one central issue: contingency. By utilizing mass-produced industrial materials (e.g., lead and steel plates), Serra could ultimately divest the art object of the aura of uniqueness and timelessness. This retreat from the reverential resulted in a much less passive relationship between object and viewer, launching, as the critic Douglas Crimp has suggested, "an all-out attack on the prestige of the artist, granting that prestige instead to the spectator." Site-specific pieces such as "Shift" (1970–72), six rectangular cement sections embedded on a snowy slope in King City, Canada, expand the closed sculptural vocabulary to include the possibilities of architecture and landscape. Serra's opening-up of sculpture to the conditions of time and place once again parallels the space-time continuum of his films. "One Ton Prop (House of Cards)" (1969), an arrangement of four 500 lb. plates of lead propped up to form a cube, sustains itself by virtue of a continual reassertion of its balance, a situation wholly contingent on gravity and time. Perhaps the ultimate minimalist object, "One Ton Prop" maintains an active relationship to the world even without the presence of a spectator; it makes its point simply by being.

—Maurice Berger

SERRANO, Pablo.

Spanish. Born in Crivillen, Teruel, 10 February 1910. Studied at Colegio de los Escolapios, Zaragoza, 1917–20, and Colegio de los Jesuitas, Zaragoza, 1920–24; studied painting and sculpture at the Colegio Salesianos, Barcelona, 1925–28. Married the artist Juana Frances in 1974. Sculptor, in Zaragoza, 1928–30, Montevideo, Uruguay 1930–54, and in Madrid, 1954 until his death in 1985: academic sculptures, 1928–40; first experiments in abstract sculpture, in association with the artist Joaquin Torres Garcia, 1946; influenced by work of sculptor Julio Gonzalez, 1956; Founder-Member, El Paso group of artists, Madrid, 1957–60; Member, Société Européene de Culture, 1968. Instructor in Sculpture and Composition, Escuela de Arte, Montevideo, 1930–33. Recipient: Gran Premio de Escultura, *Bienal Hispanoamericana,* Barcelona, 1954; Premio Julio Gonzalez, *Salon de Mayo,* Barcelona, 1961; Premio San Jorge, Zaragoza, 1967; Grand Prize, *International Sculpture Exhibition,* Budapest, 1971; El Batallador Prize, Zaragoza, 1975; El Dragon de la Seguarida Prize, Madrid, 1975. *Died* (in Madrid) *26 November 1985.*

Individual Exhibitions:

1957	Sala Santa Catalina, Madrid
	Galeriea Syra, Barcelona
1958	Galerie Edouard Loeb, Paris
1959	Galeria Nebli, Madrid
	Galeria San Jorge, Madrid
	Stedelijk Museum, Amsterdam
	Galerie 59, Aschaffenburg, West Germany

1961	Galleria L'Attico, Rome
1963	Galleria L'Annunciata, Milan
	Galleria L'Attico, Rome
	Galeria René Metras, Barcelona
1967	Galeria Juana Mordo, Madrid
	Städtisches Museum, Bochum, West Germany (toured Germany and Denmark)
1971	Galeria Rayuela, Madrid
1973	Museo Espanol de Arte Contemporaneo, Madrid
	Musée d'Art Moderne de la Ville, Paris
	Middelheim Museum, Antwerp
	Galeria Ynguanzao, Madrid
	Galeria Antonio Machado, Madrid
	Galeria Prima, Zaragoza
	Galeria Zodiaco, Madrid
	Galeria Studium, Valladolid, Spain
1974	Convent of Santo Domingo, Valencia
1975	Galeria Doble Ele, Valencia
	Fundación Juan March, Madrid
	Galeria Avinon, Madrid
1978	Roswitha Haftmann Modern Art, Zurich

Selected Group Exhibitions:

1957	*Grupo El Paso,* Libreria Buchholz, Madrid
1958	*Art du 21. Siècle,* Musée des Beaux-Arts, Charleroi, Belgium
1960	*Spanish Painting and Sculpture,* Museum of Modern Art, New York (toured the United States)
1961	*Carnegie International,* Carnegie Institute, Pittsburgh
1962	*Biennale,* Venice
1965	*Internazionale del Bronzetto,* Sala della Ragione, Padua
1967	*International Sculpture Exhibition,* Guggenheim Museum, New York (toured the United States)
1968	*Hedendaagse Spaanse Kunst,* Museum Boymans-van Beuningen, Rotterdam (toured Europe)
1969	*Sculpture Biennale,* Middelheim Park, Antwerp
1973	*Miró 80,* Colegio de Arquitectos, Palma, Majorca, Spain

Collections:

Museo Nacional de Art Moderno, Madrid; Museo de Villafames, Valencia; Galleria Nazionale d'Arte Moderna, Rome; Middelheim Museum, Antwerp; Musée National d'Art Moderne, Paris; Museum of Modern Art, New York; Guggenheim Museum, New York; Universidad de Rio Piedras, Puerto Rico; Museo Nacional de Bellas Artes, Montevideo.

Pablo Serrano: *Bronze,* 1962

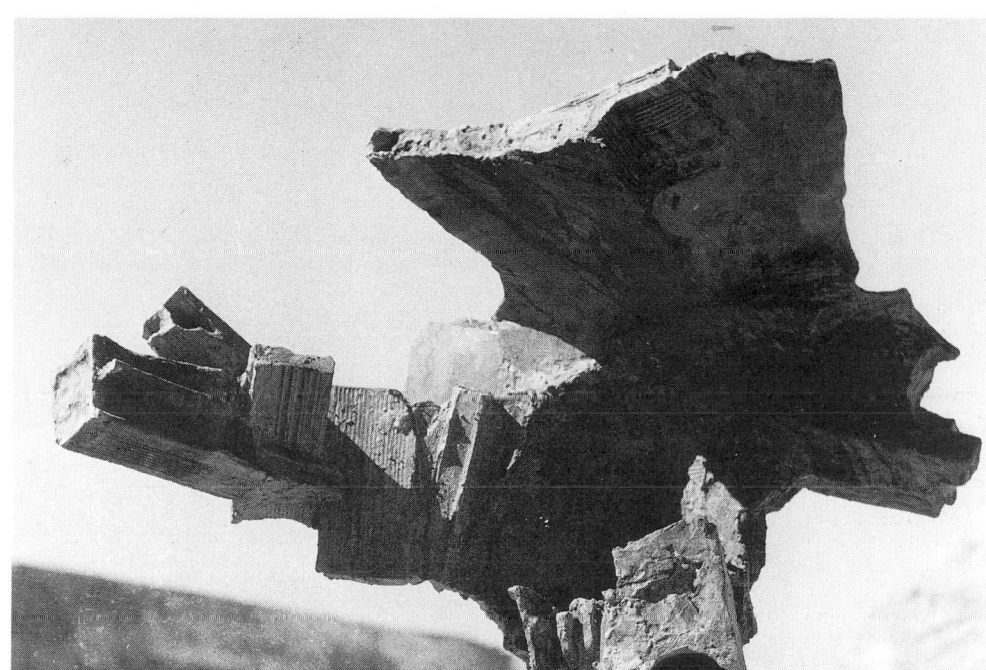

Publications:

On SERRANO: books—*Pablo Serrano* by Juan Eduardo Cirlot, Madrid 1957; *Serrano*, exhibition catalogue, with text by Giuseppe Marchiori, Rome 1961; *Serrano*, exhibition catalogue, with text by Giuseppe Marchiori, Milan 1963; *Pablo Serrano*, exhibition catalogue, with text by Jesus Lopez Paheco, Madrid 1967; *Pablo Serrano*, exhibition catalogue, with texts by Jacques Lassaigne, Michel Tapie, José Camon Aznar and others, Paris 1973; articles—"Pablo Serrano" by Luis Paccusse in *Revista de La Plata* (Argentina), March 1938; "Pablo Serrano: el escultor Aragones que tiunfo en Montevideo" by Manuel Zuasti in *Diario Madrid*, August 1955; "Escultura Sintetica de Pablo Serrano" by Luis Figuerola Ferretti in *Arriba* (Madrid), January 1957; "Ritmos en el Espacio de Pablo Serrano" by Miguel Fisac in *Revista Arquitectura* (Madrid), February 1960, "Pablo Serrano" by José Maria Moreno Galvan in *Contemporary Sculpture* (New York), April 1964; "Expressive Sculptor Pablo Serrano Plans Major Work Here" by Ann Holmes in the *Houston Chronicle*, December 1974.

I want to say that the first idea in my mind is between clouds; not pinned down, not grasped completely.

When I wish to make something in words or forms or colour, I pursue that doubt between the clouds; it is exactly this (the doubt) that can make form and words concrete.

Raising this doubt to the level of "communication;" "communication between men," the "caves of refuge," the "men with gateways," the "united-pair," concrete stages in forms, in materials, brass or stone. Do these forms speak to us of this preoccupation?

I think that the spectator submerges himself, must submerge himself, in the most profound darkness.

And if there is no initiation (participation), some experience that has spoken to us of this primary idea—the intent and communication of the creator—then it is better that there be nothing but a void between the work of art and the observer.

When there is inexperience in interpreting or lack of feeling to read the form. When there is failure to understand the form and content, the lack of understanding is far more profound.

The object thus isolated, alone, face to face with the world, I ask myself, does it really communicate the intent of the creator? The object is there and it must speak for itself. And thus it does. But not to everyone.

As I said before, for those who understand the "language," does the intent of the object link up with the humanistic problems put forth by its creator?

If the creator's fundamental idea takes this human, concerned point of departure, that of human communication aimed towards mutual understanding, and if his expression is searched for through the complete object, it shines in the dark inner spaces. The object, does it constitute a clear language for those who try to read and understand it? Does it transmit to us this concern with communication?

If each one of those who believes puts himself in his work and defends his idea as far as it may go, that is a sufficient achievement.

As for me, I try to defend the qualities of a humanity that is rational, intelligent and creative. Man is rational, intelligent in that he relates to others. These ideas which can bring us to other roads, derived and diverse, but which form the embryo of other beginnings.

I am a pessimist regarding the manner in which men actually understand each other; reason is destructive while emotion is creative. However, I am an optimist with regard to man's creative capacity and with regard to this transmitting and generative path.

The most difficult thing is, to know how to combine reason and emotion into something expressive, in order that its language will not lack any of those essential values.

The doubt as to whether one has created an object which realizes all its capacities will always exist. The fear that we will not see its capacities of resistance, assimilation and actuation in the face of difficulties and enemies.

Everything in life requires effort and as José Luis Lopez Aranguren says, "This, in effect, man searches for *in recto* and *in obliquo*, extracted laboriously and with titantic effort from its remotest origins, or refracting it ludicrously in a respectful parody."

—Pablo Serrano (1983)

SEUPHOR, Michel.

French. Born Fernand-Louis Berckelaers in Antwerp, Belgium, 10 March 1901; adopted the pseudonym "Seuphor" (anagram of Orpheus) in 1918; emigrated to France, 1925: naturalized, 1965. Studied Latin and Greek at the College of Antwerp, 1909–17; self-taught in art. Served in the Belgian Resistance in Grenoble, France, 1943–44. Married Suzanne Plasse in 1934; sons: Clement (died, 1935) and Regis. Poet and writer on art, Antwerp, 1921–22, and in Berlin, Paris, Amsterdam and Tunis, 1922–25; writer, painter, graphic artist and exhibition organizer, Paris, 1925–34, Anduze, France, 1934–45, Bagnols-sur-Ceze, France, 1945–48, and again in Paris since 1948: associated with the De Stijl artists, Antwerp, 1921, Der Sturm artists, Berlin, 1922, Dadaists, Berlin and Paris, 1923–24, and the Futurist artists in Italy, 1926; Founder, with Arp, Schwitters, Mondrian, Kandinsky, Léger, Stazewski, etc., Cercle et Carre group, Paris, 1930 (disbanded, 1931; formed Abstraction-Creation group). Founder and Editor, with Jozef Peeters. *Het Overzicht*, Antwerp, 1921–25, and, with Paul Dermée, only issue of *Documents Internationaux de l'Esprit Nouveau*, Paris, 1927; Editor, 3 issues of *Cercle et Carre*, Paris, 1930; Contributor, *Esprit*, Paris, 1933, *Sept* and *L'Aube*, Paris, 1934–45, and *Art d'Aujourd'hui*, Paris, 1951; Paris Correspondent, *Art Digest*, New York, 1952–53. Recipient: Premio Internazionale Diano Marina, Italy, 1978; Special Award of Honour, Biennale of Ljubljana, 1987. Chevalier, 1962, and Commandeur, 1977, Ordre des Arts et Lettres, Paris. Seuphor Medal struck by la Monnaie de Paris, 1980. Agent: Galerie Convergence, 39 rue des Archives, Paris. Address: 83 avenue Emile-Zola, 75015 Paris, France.

Individual Exhibitions:

1933	Galerie Manassero, Lausanne, Switzerland
1954	Galerie Berggruen, Paris
	Modern Art Galerie, Basle
1955	Rose Fried Gallery, New York (with Alcopley and Hassegawa)
1956	Galerie Saint-Laurent, Brussels
	Galerie Accent, Antwerp
1957	Galerie St. Stephan, Vienna (with Hans Arp and Sophie Taeuber Arp)
1958	Galerie der Spiegel, Cologne (with Hans Arp and Sophie Taeuber Arp)
1959	Galerie Denise René, Paris
	Galleria Grattacielo, Milan
1960	Galeria Libertad, Buenos Aires
	Esther Robles Gallery, Los Angeles
1961	Galerie Hybler, Copenhagen
	Galerie Raaklijn, Bruges, Belgium
1962	Galerie Würthle, Vienna
	Galleria Lorenzelli, Milan
1963	Galerie Denise René, Paris
	Esther Robles Gallery, Los Angeles
	Abbaye Saint-Pierre, Ghent
1965	Galleria Lorenzelli, Milan
	Galerie Renée Ziegler, Zurich
	Fresno State College, California
1966	Musée des Beaux-Arts, Nantes, France (retrospective)
	Librairie-Galerie La Hune, Paris
1967	Galerie L'Oeil Ecoute, Lyons
	Galerie Schutze, Bad Godesburg, West Germany
	Galleria Martano, Turin
	Muzeum Sztuki, Lodz, Poland
	Galerie Hybler, Copenhagen (with Sonia Delaunay and Serge Poliakoff)
1968	Musée des Beaux-Arts, La Chaux de Fonds, Switzerland
	Galleria Laboratorio II Parametro, Milan
1969	Inter Gallery, Brussels (with Arturo Bonfanti and Kurt Lewi)
	Galleria Rizzoli, Rome
	Centre CO-MO, Paris
	Galerie Argos, Nantes, France
	Maison du Tourisme, Auxerre, France (with Alicia Penalba)
1970	Galleria Martano, Turin
	Musée de Deurle, Belgium
1971	Musée d'Art et d'Industrie, Saint-Etienne, France (retrospective)
	White Gallery, Lausanne, Switzerland
1972	Galleria Borgonuovo, Milan
	Galleria La Polena, Genoa
	Centre Marcel Peeters, Antwerp (retrospective)
1973	Galleria Peccolo, Livorno, Italy
	Galleria Lorenzelli, Milan (with Henri Michaux)
	Galeri La Tortue, Paris
	Centre Leonard de Vinci, Toulouse
	Galerie Memling-Galerie Orangerie, Ostend, Belgium
	Galerie Nouvelles Images, The Hague (with Jean Ricardon)
	Galleria Vismara, Milan
	Galleria Pictogramme, Rome
1974	Palais de l'Athenée, Geneva
	Galerie Govaerts, Brussels
1975	Galerie Attali, Paris
	Galleria Beniamino, Sanremo, Italy
	Galerie De Greyse, Tielt, Belgium
1976	Palais Granvelle, Besancon, France
	Galerie Carmen Martinez, Paris
	Gemeentemuseum, The Hague
	Galerie Nouvelles Images, The Hague (with Hans Arp and Sophie Taeuber Arp)
	Galerie Synthese, Antwerp
	Galerie Günter und Schwan, Essen
1977	Centre Georges Pompidou, Paris
	Galerie Attali, Paris
	Librairie-Galerie J.- M. Place, Paris
	Galerie V.E.C.U., Antwerp
	Galerie Convergences, Nantes, France
	Galerie 2016, Hauterive/Neuchâtel, Switzerland
	Galerie L'Orangerie, Ostend, Belgium
1978	Treffpunkt Kunst, Saarlouis, West Germany
	Galleria della Piazza, Varese, Italy
1979	Galerie Abras-Mont-Des-Arts, Brussels
	Galerie Nouvelles Images, The Hague
	Galerie Modern Art International, Munich
	Saarland Museum, Saarbrucken
	Galerie Schindler, Berne
	Azienda del Turismo, Diano-Marina, Italy
1980	Mathys Galerie, Herstal, Belgium
	Galerie Jacques Visser, Amsterdam
1981	Musée de la Boverie, Liège, Belgium
	Mathys Galerie, Herstal, Belgium
	Galerie Nouvelles Images, The Hague
	Galerie Traces, Rouen
	Galerie Convergences, Nantes, France
	Centre Provincial Arenberg, Antwerp
1982	Kunstverein, Bamberg, West Germany
1983	Moris Gallery, Tokyo
1984	Palazzo dei Diamanti, Ferrara, Italy
1985	Musée des Beaux-Arts, Nantes, France
	Club 44, La Chaux-de-Fonds, Switzerland
	Museo d'Arte Moderno, Ciudad Bolivar, Venezuela
	Urania Galerie, Zurich
	Edwynn Houk Gallery, Chicago
1986	Musée de Grenchen, Switzerland
	Galerie Convergence, Paris
	Treffpunkt Kunt, Saarlouis, West Germany
	VTB Antwerpen, Antwerp
1987	Centro Culturale, Pordenone, Italy
	Galerie Sacre du Printemps, Brussels

Selected Group Exhibitions:

1930	*Cercle et Carre*, Galerie 23 rue La Boetie, Paris

Michel Seuphor: *Carré Allège*, 1984

1955   *Salon des Réalités Nouvelles*, Paris
1959   *Documenta*, Kassel, West Germany
1960   *Construction and Geometry in Painting*, Galerie Chalette, New York (toured the United States)
1963   *Schrift und Bild*, Kunsthalle, Baden-Baden, West Germany
1964   *50 Ans de Collage*, Musée d'Art et d'Industrie, Saint-Etienne, France
1972   *De Stijl, Cercle et Carre*, Galerie Gmurzynska, Cologne
1980   *Konstruktion, Struktur . . .* , Galerie Tempel, Cologne
1982   *Hommages*, Musée du Havre, France
1987   *Biennale of Graphic Art*, Ljubljana, Yugoslavia

Collections:

Centre Georges Pompidou, Paris; Musée d'Art Moderne de la Ville, Paris; Musée des Beaux Arts, Antwerp; Musée des Beaux Arts, Ghent; Museum Boymans-van Beuningen, Rotterdam; Gemeentemuseum, The Hague; Muzeum Sztuki, Lodz, Poland; Museo d'Arte Moderna, Turin; Albright-Knox Art Gallery, Buffalo, New York; Los Angeles County Museum of Art.

Publications:

By SEUPHOR: books—*Mariage Filme*, Antwerp 1924; *Diaphragme Interieur*, Paris 1926; *Lecture Elementaire*, Paris 1928; *Un Renouveau de la Peinture en Belgique Flamande*, Paris 1932; *Les Evasions d'Olivier Trickmansholm*, Paris 1939; *La Maison Claire*, Lyons 1943; *Informations*, Paris 1944; *Tout Dire*, Paris 1945; *Itineraire Spirituel de Michel Seuphor*, edited by Francis Bernard, Tornac, France 1946; *Le Visage de Senlis*, Paris 1947; *L'Art Abstrait, ses Origines, ses Premieres Maitres*, Paris 1949; *Piet Mondriaan*, Paris, Cologne and New York 1956; *Dictionnaire de la Peinture Abstraite*, Paris and London 1957; *La Peinture Abstraite en Flandre*, Brussels 1963; *Le Style et le Cri*, Paris 1965; *Le commerce de l'art*, Paris 1966; *La Vocation des Mots*, Lausanne, Switzerland 1966; *Le Monde est Plein d'Oiseaux*, Lausanne, Switzerland 1968; *Le Chantier*, Turin 1970; *Le Don de la Parole*, Paris 1970; *L'Ephèmére est éternel*, Turin 1972; *Les Dimensions de la Liberté*, Paris 1972; *Le Jardin Privé au Geometrie*, Zurich 1974; *Onze essais de voix pour un chant du soir*, The Hague 1976; *Tout homme*, Paris 1978; *Les Innocents*, Paris 1979; *Contes Batabraf*, Milan 1981; *C'est l'evidence meme*, Paris 1982; *Chronique de Barbebasse*, Nantes 1983; *La cinquième roue*, Nantes 1986; *Solfege*, Nantes 1987.

On SEUPHOR: books—*Zeichen des 20. Jahrhunderts*, West Berlin 1956; *Encycopedie de l'Architecture Nouvelle*, vol. 2, by Alberto Sartoris, Milan 1957; *Geocultura de la Europa de hoy* by Gyula Kosice, Buenos Aires 1959; *Michel Seuphor: Exposition Retrospecitve*, exhibition catalogue, with a preface by Maurice Allemand, Nantes, France 1966; *10 Huize van . . .* , vol. 4, by Joos Florquin, Louvain 1968; *L'Esprit Dada en Belgique* by Rik Sauwen, Leuven 1969; *An Artist's Workbook* by Natalie d'Arbeloff, London 1969; *Michel Seuphor*, exhibition catalogue, with texts by Jan Martens and Maurits Bilcke, Antwerp 1972; *Michel Seuphor*, exhibition catalogue, with prefaces by Bernard Ceysson and Maurice Allemand, Saint-Etienne, France 1971; *Seuphor* by Herbert Henkels, Paris and Antwerp 1976; *Seuphor: Monographe*, edited by Carmen Martinez, with texts by several authors, Paris 1976; *Michel Seuphor*, exhibition catalogue, with pref-ace by Georg W. Keltzsch, Saarbrucken 1979; *Michel Seuphor*, exhibition catalogue, with a foreword by Georges Goldine, Liége, Belgium 1981; *Les Yi-King vus par Seuphor*, 64 serigraphs with preface by J. Vercruysse, Brussels 1983; *Structures et Modulations: Oeuvres de Seuphor de 1926 a 1984*, Milan 1984; *Entretiens sur Michel Seuphor*, Paris 1986.

I have never really known what I am doing nor why I am doing it. I draw a lot, I write a lot. Something within me calls me, and I obey. I don't know at all whether it has any value or not. In front of what I have just completed, my opinion is undecided. Sometimes a drawing or a collage that I have never liked, and which by some miracle I have not myself destroyed, suddenly becomes a work that I find good. But I wouldn't know what to think of such inconstant feelings. The only value is that given by the spectator to a man's work: without him there is no work of art at all. The real creator is found hidden in the gaze of the amateur.

The artist must ask nothing more from society than independence, but this has to be absolute. Its greatest reward is not glory or renown; it is the liberty it brings.

—Michel Seuphor

This Fleming has two claims to fame. Michel Seuphor is a renowned literary commentator on the visual arts (particularly non-figurative visual art) and he is an eminent artist in his own right (something that has rebounded to his credit ever since Arp recommended him to Berggruen).

Seuphor has not stopped writing, but he once observed "When a writer sets himself to painting or drawing, it probably means that he has found words to be no longer sufficient, that he imagines other poetic joys than those of speech . . . . "

During the decade 1923/33, he saw a great deal of Mondrian with whom he formed a close association and, although the work of the two artists bears only a superficial resemblance, in a way Seuphor was able to advance many of the ideas of the Dutch painter by exploring their potentialities in graphic works. A diligent researcher, in 1946 Seuphor produced 96 drawings, all of them variants on a single theme.

After 1954 he turned his attention to making collage-drawings, and it is worth noting that Arp actually used many of the Belgian's torn drawings to make collages of his own.

A further extension of his work subsequently took place when he made photographic enlargements of drawings which were then used as the designs for tapestries.

Seuphor lurks in the couloirs of contemporary art. Recognized as an inspired theoretician, capable of all sorts of extensions of the purposes of non-figurative art, he has been too easily relegated to the *rôle* of pundit. It should be more readily realized that he is also a fine exponent.

—Sheldon Williams

SHAHN, Ben.

American. Born in Kovno, Lithuania, 12 September 1898; emigrated to the United States in 1906 and subsequently naturalized. Apprenticed to lithographer Heisenberg while completing high school education in evening classes, New York, 1913–17; studied briefly at Art Students League, New York, 1916; New York University, 1919; studied biology, City College of New York, 1919–22; painting, National Academy of Design, New York, 1917–22; biology, Marine Biological Laboratory, Woods Hole, Massachusetts, 1920, 1921, and 1922; painting, Académie de la Grande Chaumière, Paris, 1925; fresco painting, under Jean Charlot, Art Students League, New York, 1940. Married Tilly Goldstein in 1922 (separated, 1932); children: Judith and Ezra; married Bernarda Bryson in 1935; children: Susanna, Jonathan, and Abigail. Painter and photographer: lived in New York, with summers in Truro, 1926–30; shared studio with photographer Walker Evans, 1928; assisted Diego Rivera on mural for Rockefeller Center, New York, 1933; worked on commission (later abandoned) for Public Works of Art Project, Central Park Casino, New York, 1934; worked with Lou Block on mural (rejected) commissioned by Federal Emergency Relief Administration for Rikers Island Penitentiary, New York, 1935–35; worked as photographer and designer, Farm Security Administration, Washington, D.C., 1935–38; settled in Jersey Homesteads (later Roosevelt, New Jersey), 1939; worked on murals (rejected) for Post Office, St. Louis, Missouri; designed posters for Graphic Arts Section, War Information Office, 1942–44; worked as commercial artist and illustrator, New York, from 1944; produced *Sweet Was the Song,* for the Museum of Modern Art, New York, 1956; designed sets and poster for *New York Expert—Opus Jazz* ballet by Jerome Robbins, Spoleto, Italy, 1958; designed sets for e. e. cummings' play *Him* and for *Events* ballet by Jerome Robbins, Spoleto, 1960; involved in creation of Roosevelt Memorial Park, New Jersey, 1962; worked with Henri Deschamps on lithographs, Paris, 1968–69. Lecturer, Boston Museum of Fine Arts Summer School, Pittsfield, Massachusetts, 1947; University of Colorado Summer Session, Boulder, 1950; and Brooklyn Museum Art School, New York, 1951; Visiting Artist, Black Mountain College Summer Session, Beria, North Carolina, 1951; Charles Eliot Norton Professor of Poetry, Harvard University, Cambridge, Massachusetts, 1956. Recipient: Joseph Pennell Memorial Medal, Pennsylvania Academy of the Fine Arts, Philadelphia, 1931; President's Medal, Art Directors Club of New York, 1949; Gold Medal Philadelphia Watercolor Society, 1952; Gold Medal, American Institute of Graphic Arts, New York, 1958; Gold Medal, National Institute of Arts and Letters, New York, 1964; Gold Medal, American Institute of Architects, New York, 1966. Honorary doctorate: Princeton University, New Jersey, 1962; Hebrew Union College, Cincinnati, Ohio, 1964; Rutgers University, New Brunswick, New Jersey, 1964; Pratt Institute, New York, 1966; Harvard University, Cambridge, Massachusetts, 1967. Honorary Member: Signet Society, Harvard University, 1956; Academia de Artes y Cinecias, Puerto Rico, 1967. Fellow, American Academy of Arts and Sciences, 1959. *Died* (in New York) *14 March 1969.*

Individual Exhibitions:

1930	Downtown Gallery, New York
1932	Harvard Society of Contemporary Art, Cambridge, Massachusetts
	Downtown Gallery, New York
1933	Downtown Gallery, New York
1940	Julien Levy Gallery, New York
1944	Downtown Gallery, New York
1945	Art Institute of Chicago
1947	Museum of Modern Art, New York
	Mayor Gallery, London (toured the U.K.)
	Downtown Gallery, New York
1949	Downtown Gallery, New York
1950	Albright-Knox Art Gallery, Buffalo, New York
	Frank Perls Gallery, Los Angeles
	Phillips Gallery, Washington, D.C.
1951	Arts Club of Chicago (with Willem de Kooning and Jackson Pollock)
	Boris Mirsky Gallery, Boston
	Downtown Gallery, New York
1952	Santa Barbara Museum of Art, California (with Lee Gatch and Karl Knaths; travelled to the Palace of the Legion of Honor, San Francisco, and the Los Angeles County Museum of Art)
	Downtown Gallery, New York
1953	Minneapolis Institute of Arts
1954	*Biennale,* Venice (with Willem de Kooning)
	Detroit Institute of Art (with Charles Sheeler and Joe Jones)
	Allyn Art Gallery, Southern Illinois University, Carbondale
	Renaissance Society, University of Chicago
1955	Downtown Gallery, New York
	Galleria Tartaruga, Rome
1956	Fogg Art Museum, Harvard University, Cambridge, Massachusetts
1957	Institute of Contemporary Art, Boston
	American Institute of Graphic Arts, New York
1959	Downtown Gallery, New York
	Katonah Gallery, New York
	Galleria del'Obelisco, Rome
	Leicester Galleries, London
1960	Jewish Community Center, Milwaukee (with Jack Levine and Abraham Rattner)
	Galleria del'Obelisco, Rome
	Downtown Gallery, New York
	University of Louisville, Kentucky
	University of Utah, Salt Lake City
1961	Downtown Gallery, New York
	Jewish Community Center, New Haven, Connecticut
	Stedelijk Museum, Amsterdam (toured Europe)
1962	Staatliche Kunsthalle, Baden-Baden, West Germany (toured Europe, Israel and Japan)
	Armand Gallery, Sarasota, Florida
1963	Dartmouth College, Hanover, New Hampshire
1964	Leicester Galleries, London
1966	St. Paul Art Center, Minnesota
	Randolph-Macon Woman's College, Lynchburg, Virginia
	Galleria Ciranna, Milan
1967	*The Collected Prints,* Philadelphia Museum of Art
	Santa Barbara Museum of Art, California (travelled to the LaJolla Museum of Art, California, and the Herron Gallery of Art, Indianapolis)
1968	Museum of African Art, Washington, D.C.
	Orland Gallery, Encino, California
	Kennedy Galleries, New York
1969	Kennedy Galleries, New York
	Museum of Modern Art, New York
	New Jersey State Museum, Trenton
	Fogg Art Museum, Harvard University, Cambridge, Massachusetts
	Andrum Gallery, Los Angeles
1970	Kennedy Galleries, New York
	National Museum of Modern Art, Tokyo (toured Japan)
	Nantenshi Gallery, Tokyo
1971	Kennedy Galleries, New York
	Joseph Devernay-Behren and Co., New York
1973	Kennedy Galleries, New York
	Joseph Dernay/Esther Begell Gallery, Washington, D.C.
1974	Joseph Devernay Schloss Remseck, Basle
1975	Allentown Art Museum, Pennsylvania
	Galerie Schloss Remseck, Stuttgart
1976	Kennedy Galleries, New York
	Joseph Dernay/Esther Begell Gallery, Washington, D.C.
	Jewish Museum, New York (toured the United States, 1976–78)
1977	*The Mural Art,* Lowe Art Museum, Syracuse University, New York
1979	Nardin Galleries, New York
1980	Musée de l'Art et d'Histoire, Chambéry, France
1981	Santa Fe East Gallery, New Mexico
1984	Leinster Fine Art, London
1986	Pembroke Gallery, Houston, Texas

Selected Group Exhibitions:

1930	*33 Moderns,* Downtown Gallery, New York
1932	*Murals by American Painters and Photographers,* Museum of Modern Art, New York
1940	*Mural Designs for Federal Buildings,* Whitney Museum, New York
1946	*Survey of American Painting,* Tate Gallery, London
1950	*100 American Paintings of the 20th Century,* Metropolitan Museum of Art, New York
1958	*50 Ans d'Art Moderne,* Palais de Beaux-Arts, Brussels
1961	*Oposizione al Nazismo,* Galleria dell'Obelisco, Rome
1974	*Photography in America,* Whitney Museum, New York
1977	*Documenta 6,* Museum Fridericianum, Kassel, West Germany
1980	*Les Années Amères de l'Amerique en Crise,* Galerie Municipale du Chateau d'Eau, Toulouse, France

Collections:

Museum of Modern Art, New York; Metropolitan Museum of Art, New York; Brooklyn Museum, New York; Syracuse University, Syracuse, New York; Brandeis University, Waltham, Massachusetts; Art Institute of Chicago; Tate Gallery, London.

Publications:

By SHAHN: books—*Partridge in a Pear Tree,* New York 1947; *Symposium: The Relation of Painting and Sculpture in Architecture,* New York 1951; *Paragraphs on Art,* New York 1952; *The Alphabet of Creation,* New York, 1954; *The Biography of a Painting,* Cambridge, Massachusetts 1956; *The Shape of Content,* Cambridge, Massachusetts 1957; *Love and Joy about Letters,* New York 1963; *The Cherry Tree Legend,* New York 1967; books illustrated—*The Sorrows of Priapus,* New York 1957; *Ounce Dice Trice,* New York 1958; *Love Sonnets,* New York 1963; *Ecclesiastes; or, The Preacher,* New York 1964; *Kuboyama and the Saga of the Lucky Dragon* by Richard Hudson, New York 1965; *Notebooks of Malte Laurids Brigge,* with others, by Rainer Maria Rilke, New York 1968; articles—statement in *American Realists and*

Politicians" in *Artnews* (New York), October 1954; "Shahn in Amsterdam" in *Art in America* (New York), no. 3, 1961; "Imagination and Intention" in *Review of Existential Psychology* (New York), Winter 1967.

On SHAHN: books—*Ben Shahn* by James Thrall Soby, New York 1947; *Portrait of the Artist as an American: Ben Shahn* by Selden Rodman, New York 1951; *Ben Shahn: Graphic Work* by James Thrall Soby, New York 1957; *Ben Shahn: Paintings* by James Thrall Soby, New York 1963; *The Collected Prints of Ben Shahn*, exhibition catalogue, Philadelphia 1967; *Ben Shahn: The Passion of Sacco-Vanzetti* by Martin Bush, Syracuse, New York 1968; *Ben Shahn, Photographer: An Album from the Thirties*, edited by Margaret R. Weiss, New York 1973; *The Complete Graphic Works of Ben Shahn* by Kenneth W. Prescott, New York 1973; *Ben Shahn* by Bernarda Bryson Shahn, New York 1975; *The Photographic Eye of Ben Shahn*, edited by David Pratt, Cambridge, Massachusetts 1975; *Ben Shahn*, exhibition catalogue, by Kenneth W. Prescott, New York 1976; *The Mural Art of Ben Shahn*, exhibition catalogue, by Mary Takach, Syracuse, New York 1977; *Ben Shahn*, exhibition catalogue, by A. S. King, Santa Fe, New Mexico 1981.

Ben Shahn is probably the leading painter of the American movement known as "Social Content," which emerged as a definite school during the depression of the 1930's. He was also one of the most versatile and gifted artists in 20th century American art, excelling as a photographer, draughtsman, illustrator, designer, painter, polemicist and writer, and a teacher of distinction. The terrible depression of the '30's had two important, and interrelated, effects; it produced a subject matter which insisted itself onto the American creative consciousness, not only in painting, but most effectively in writing, the theatre and the cinema; and through the Government art programmes, provided work for thousands of professional artists. Shahn worked as a muralist on Government projects, an experience which in turn affected the scale and style of his easel paintings. A special quality to his social-realistic works is a refusal to preach; in this sense he possessed the finest qualities of the great journalist, who feels impelled to tell the story, to draw the picture, but to leave conclusions to others.

His most memorable images belong to the Vanzetti and Sacco series, painted after the infamous trial and imprisonment of the two anarchists. Never again was Shahn to be so impassioned and moved by human cruelty and indignity, although throughout his life he outspokenly drew attention to social evils. In the earliest period of his artistic career, Shahn, as most of his generation, came under the spell of French post-Impressionist painting, particularly in a series of nude bathers. He once wrote that despite the admiration these works evoked, he found himself asking "Is that enough? Is That All?" He decided that they contained little of his life or personality, none of his views on social and political matters.

First the Dreyfus case and then the contemporary fate of Sacco and Vanzetti provided the route for a more socially-conscious art; and in the process Shahn developed a sharper, almost satiric draughtsmanship, and, in tempera painting, a dry, impersonal technique, which, however, retained some of the influence of Impressionism. When devoid of immediate social content, it is fascinating to realize the resemblance between Shahn's manner and that of the great American realist Andrew Wyeth, and even, more curiously, the intimate abstraction of Mark Tobey. As a draughtsman and illustrator Shahn has few equals in modern American, or world, art, but the lasting impression is of a good man using his brilliant gifts as a communicable force.

—Charles Spencer

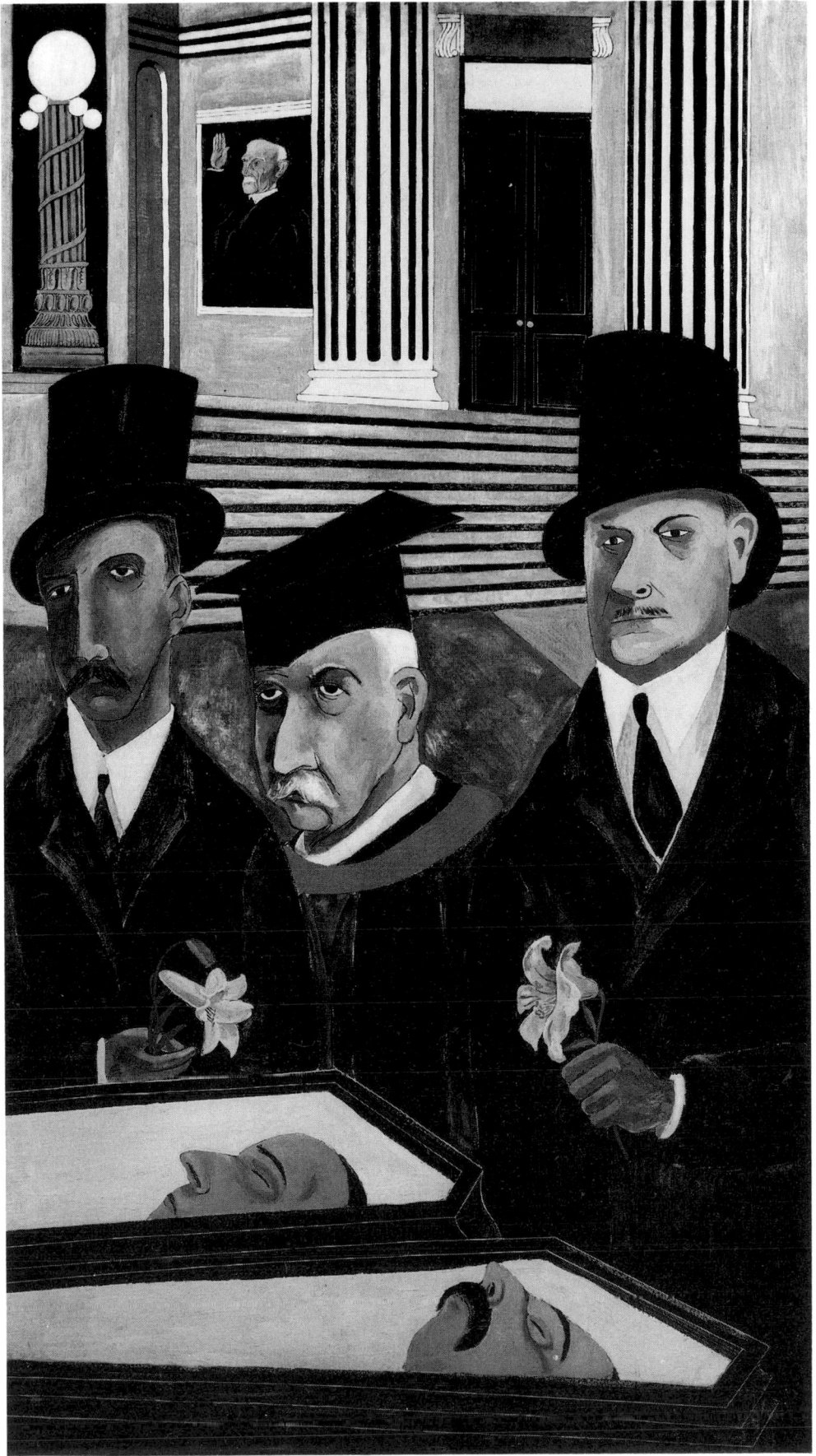

Ben Shahn: *The Passion of Sacco and Vanzetti*, 1931/32 Courtesy Whitney Museum, New York

Magic Realists, exhibition catalogue, by Dorothy C. Miller and Alfred H. Barr, New York 1943; "Ben Shahn: An Interview," with John D. Morse in *Magazine of Art* (New York), April 1944; "Photos for Art" in *U.S. Camera* (New York), May 1946; "An Artist's Credo" in the *College Art Journal* (Menasha, New York), Autumn 1949; "The Artist's Point of View" in *Magazine of Art* (New York), November 1949, "Aspects of the Art of Paul Klee" in *Museum of Modern Art Bulletin* (New York), Summer 1950; "The Future of the Creative arts: A Symposium" in *University of Buffalo Bulletin* (Buffalo, New York), February 1952; "What Is Realism in Art" in *Look* (New York), January 1953, "How an Artist Looks at Aesthetics" in *Journal of Aesthetics and Art Criticism* (Philadelphia), September 1954; "The Artist and the

SHAPIRO, Joel.
American. Born in New York, 27 September 1941. Educated at New York University, 1961–69, B.A. 1964, M.A. 1969. Independent sculptor, New York,

since 1969. Instructor, Princeton University, New Jersey 1974–76. Instructor, School of Visual Arts, New York, since 1977. Recipient: National Endowment for the Arts Grant, 1975; Brandeis Award, Waltham, Massachusetts, 1984; Skowhegan Medal for Sculpture, Maine, 1986. Agent: Paula Cooper Gallery, 155 Wooster Street, New York, New York 10012. Address: 54 Leonard Street, New York, New York 10013, U.S.A.

Individual Exhibitions:

1970	Paula Cooper Gallery, New York
1972	Paula Cooper Gallery, New York
1973	The Clocktower, New York
1974	Salvatore Ala Galleria, Milan
	Paula Cooper Gallery, New York
1975	Paula Cooper Gallery, New York
	The Garage, London (with Jennifer Bartlett)
	Walter Kelly Gallery, Chicago
1976	Paula Cooper Gallery, Los Angeles
	Museum of Contemporary Art, Chicago
1977	Max Protetch Gallery, Washington, D.C.
	Albright-Knox Art Gallery, Buffalo
	Suzanne Hilberry Gallery, Detroit
	Paula Cooper Gallery, New York
	Galerie Nancy Gillespie-Elisabeth de Laage, Paris
	Galerie Aronowitsch, Stockholm
1978	Greenberg Gallery, St. Louis
	Galerie M, Bochum, West Germany
1979	Akron Art Institute, Ohio
	Galerie Nancy Gillespie-Elisabeth de Laage, Paris
	Paula Cooper Gallery, New York
	Ohio State University, Columbus
1980	Paula Cooper Gallery, New York
	Sculpture and Drawing, Whitechapel Art Gallery, London
	Museum Haus Lange, Krefeld, West Germany
	Galerie Mukai, Tokyo
	Asher-Faure Gallery, Los Angeles
	Brooke Alexander Gallery, New York
	Delahunty Gallery, Dallas
	Moderna Museet, Stockholm
	Galerie Aronowitsch, Stockholm
	Bell Gallery, Brown University, Providence, Rhode Island
1981	Ackland Art Museum, University of North Carolina, Chapel Hill
	Georgia State University, Atlanta
	Contemporary Arts Center, Cincinnati
	John Stoller Gallery, Minneapolis
	Daniel Weinberg Gallery, San Francisco
	Israel Museum, Jerusalem
	Gallery Mukai, Tokyo
	Young-Hoffman Gallery, Chicago
1982	Paula Cooper Gallery, New York
	Portland Center for the Visual Arts, Oregon
	Susanne Hilberry Gallery, Birmingham, Michigan
	Yarlow/Salzman Gallery, Toronto
	Whitney Museum, New York (travelled to Dallas; Toronto; La Jolla, California)
1983	Galerie Aronowitsch, Stockholm
	Paula Cooper Gallery, New York
	Asher/Faure, Los Angeles
1984	Paula Cooper Gallery, New York (twice)
	Galerie Aronowitsch, Stockholm
1985	Knoedler/Kasmin, London
	Stedelijk Museum, Amsterdam (travelled to Dusseldorf and Baden-Baden)
1986	Seattle Art Museum, Washington
	Galerie Daniel Templon, Paris
	Ringling Museum of Art, Sarasota, Florida
	Paula Cooper Gallery, New York
	Asher/Faure, Los Angeles
1987	Donald Young Gallery, Chicago

Selected Group Exhibitions:

1969	Anti-Illusion: Procedure/Material, Whitney Museum, New York
1973	New American Graphic Art, Fogg Art Museum, Cambridge, MAssachusetts
1977	Foire Internationale d'Art Contemporain, Grand Palais, Paris
1978	Made by Sculptors, Stedelijk Museum, Amsterdam
1979	Contemporary: Sculpture: Selections from the Collection of the Museum of Modern Art, Museum of Modern Art, New York
1980	Pier + Ocean, Hayward Gallery, London (travelled to the Rijksmuseum Kroller-Muller, Otterlo, Netherlands)
1981	Biennial, Whitney Museum, New York
1983	Back to the USA, Rheinisches Landesmuseum, Bonn (travelled to Lucerne and Stuttgart)
1985	Transformations in Sculpture, Guggenheim Museum, New York
1987	Cast in Bronze, Kansas City Gallery of Art, Missouri

Collections:

Whitney Museum, New York; Museum of Modern Art, New York; Picker Art Gallery, Colgate University, Hamilton, New York; University of Massachusetts, Amherst; Fogg Art Museum, Harvard University, Cambridge, Massachusetts; Weatherspoon Art Gallery, University of North Carolina, Greensboro; Lannan Foundation, Palm Beach, Florida; National Gallery of Australia, Canberra.

Publications:

By SHAPIRO: articles—"Joel Shapiro Torquing: A Dialogue with Liza Bear" in *Avalanche* (New York), Summer 1975; interview, with Susan Logan, in *Early Work by 5 Contemporary Artists,* exhibition catalogue, New York 1977; "Joel Shapiro: An Interview," with John Coplans, in *Dialogue* (Akron, Ohio), January/February 1979.

On SHAPIRO: books—*Critical Perspectives in American Art,* exhibition catalogue, with an essay by Rosalind Krauss, Amherst, Massachusetts 1976; *Joel Shapiro,* exhibition catalogue, by Linda Cathcart, Buffalo, New York 1977; *Pictures,* exhibition catalogue, by Douglas Crimp, New York 1977; *Ideas in Sculpture 1965-1977,* exhibition catalogue, with an essay by Anne Rorimer, Chicago 1977; *Early Works by 5 Contemporary Artists,* exhibition catalogue, by Marcia Tucker, New York 1977; *The Minimal Tradition,* exhibition catalogue, Ridgefield, Connecticut 1979; *Drawings: The Pluralist Decade,* exhibition catalogue, with an introduction by Janet Karden, Philadelphia 1980; *Skulptur im 20. Jahrhundert,* exhibition catalogue, Basel 1980; *Joel Shapiro: Sculpture and Drawings,* exhibition catalogue, by Roberta Smith, London 1980; *Joel Shapiro,* exhibition catalogue with essays by Richard Marshall and Roberta Smith, New York 1982; *Joel Shapiro,* exhibition catalogue with texts by Marja Bloem and Karel Schampers, Amsterdam 1985; *Joel Shapiro: Sculpture and Drawings 1981-85,* exhibition catalogue with essay by Mark Ormond, Sarasota 1986.

*   *   *

In contrast to minimalism's concentration on self-referentiality, Joel Shapiro, in the early 1970's, contributed to a new direction in sculpture by reexamining the possibilities of memory association and psychological content. Following an interest in Process Art (in which "raw" materials were explored for their innate properties or metals were pounded or forged to accept new forms), Shapiro began to explore figurative content: miniaturist houses, chairs, human figures, coffins, bridges, and horses became a part of his sculptural lexicon. By investing his blocky cast bronze and iron forms with allusions to common objects, Shapiro permitted his work to provoke associations beyond their basic external values.

Aside from their psychological content, these objects exist correlatively, to be experienced apart from *a priori* meaning: "if you see the work as some locater of experience," Shapiro has said, " . . . the work has an internal reference to some metaphoric thought. The analogy would be to use language to describe an experience. The language is never commensurate with experience." The external, formal properties of Shapiro's sculptural language constitute a barrier to association. While his chairs and houses may evoke certain memories, they also function self-referentially: "you can't just say that's just a chair," Shapiro has observed in reference to memory, "you

have to deal with what it's doing in space . . . . It's an image that's referential, unless the piece is functioning so dynamically and on such a specific level that maybe then you could overcome associations." Corresponding to this earlier interest in "process," which centered on the passage from nature to culture, Shapiro's sculptures are simple shapes at the verge of signification; they are neither "empty signs" nor fully realized cultural icons.

The balance between evocation and objecthood extends to Shapiro's extraordinary drawings. Composed of simple geometric outlines or silhouettes that recall both architectural and sculptural forms, the drawings play on the dynamics of scale and shape. Shapiro's images are engaged in a visual dialectic, setting spatial illusionism against the nuances of their own surfaces. While the contrast of dark charcoal bands with their resonant "ghosts" suggest a conceptual penetration into space, the fingerprints, smudges, and erasures on the surface of Shapiro's drawings serve as a record of process, continually redirecting the eye to the drawing's surface. By injecting figurative imagery into his drawings (houses or more recently simplified figures disposed in animated groups), Shapiro revives the modernist strategy of questioning representation's reliance on the condition of absence. These drawings subvert the idea that a sign serve as a proxy for an absent object, for in their formal, architectonic integrity and voluptuous exposition of process, they never entirely submit to a representational status. Like his sculptures, the external *presence* of Shapiro's drawings are as significant as the absent forms or spaces they purport to represent.

Another important aspect of Shapiro's activity, small wall "reliefs" in wood or plaster, challenges the rationalist ideal of experience in sculpture: rather than offering multiple views of the same object in one synoptic view (in an effort to "grasp" it by revealing simultaneously its concomitant physical situations), the literal contours of these constructions cannot be apprehended without *experiencing* them in a full 180° viewing range. Similarly, Shapiro's miniaturist houses and bridges, deployed throughout the gallery space, situate the viewer in a special relationship to the work. Within such a spatial context, these apparently absurd relationships command a re-ordering of the viewer's sense of scale. The sculptures' persistent occupancy of the public gallery space thrust that space into unconventional roles, charging it with ironic associations to landscape an architecture that are as fleeting as the mythologized memories that initially activate Shapiro's simple forms. Absence yields to presence, memory to experience, as the viewer apprehends the external realities of his unique situation.

—Maurice Berger

SHAW, Jeffrey.
Australian. Born in Melbourne, Victoria, 23 October 1944. Educated at Melbourne High School, 1958–62; studied architecture and humanities at the University of Melbourne, 1963–64; studied sculpture at the Accademia di Brera, Milan, 1965 and at St. Martin's School of Art, London, 1966. Independent artist, London, 1966, in Amsterdam since 1967; Founder, with Theo Botschuyver, Eventstructure Research Group, Amsterdam, 1967–82, with participation from Sean Wellesley-Miller, 1967–69; Founder, with Marga Adama and John Munsey, Javaphile Group, Amsterdam, 1977–81. Recipient: First Prize, *Young Minds Exhibition,* Victoria, 1963; Commonwealth Scholarship, 1963; Arts Council of Great Britain grant, 1969, 1973; Dutch Ministry of Culture grant, 1970–75, 1981–82. Address: Javastraat 126, Amsterdam 1094 HP, Netherlands.

Individual Exhibitions:

1966	Kingly Street Gallery, London (with T. van Tijen)

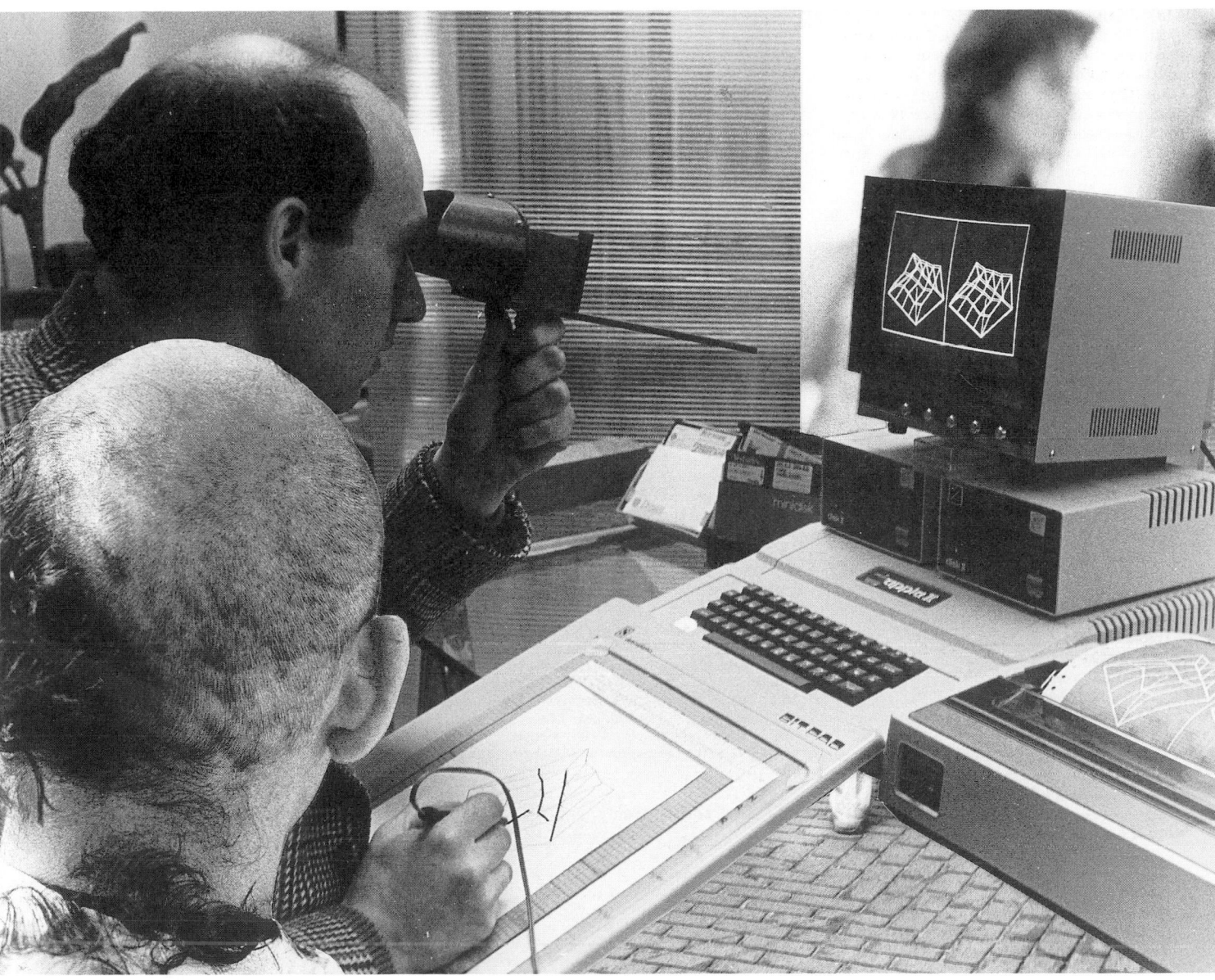

Jeffrey Shaw: *Collage,* **1982**

Better Books, London (with John Latham)
1967   Sigma Projects, Amsterdam (with Eventstructure Research Group)
Sigma Projects, Rotterdam (with E.R.G.)
Casino Communal, Knokke, Belgium (with E.R.G.)
1968   Museum of Modern Art, Oxford (with E.R.G.)
Open-Air display, *Brighton Festival,* Sussex (with E.R.G.)
Open-Air display, *City of London Festival* (with E.R.G.)
1969   Institute of Contemporary Arts, London (with E.R.G.)
Six Events display, Amsterdam (with E.R.G.)
Six Events display, Rotterdam (with E.R.G.)
St. George's Art Centre, Liverpool (with E.R.G. and John Latham)
1970   Stedelijk Museum, Amsterdam (with E.R.G.)
1972   National Gallery of Victoria, Melbourne (with E.R.G.)
1973   Pinacotheca Gallery, Melbourne (with E.R.G.)
Tolarno Gallery, Melbourne (with E.R.G.)
1974   Stedelijk Museum, Amsterdam (with E.R.G.)
De Lantarn, Rotterdam (with E.R.G.)
Drama Institute Theatre, Amsterdam (with E.R.G.)
1975   National Bus Company, London (with E.R.G. and Artist Placement Group)
1976   Genesis World Tour (with Genesis rock group and E.R.G.)
1978   Stichting de Appel, Amsterdam (with E.R.G.)
1979   Koopwaarders Plantsoen, Amsterdam Noord (permanent installation; with E.R.G.)

1980   De Hoogeberg, Belsen, Netherlands (permanent installation; with E.R.G.)
1981   Frascati Theatre, Amsterdam (permanent installation; with E.R.G.)
1982   Scholengemeenschap Quirijn, Tilburg, Netherlands (permanent installlation; with E.R.G.)

Selected Group Exhibitions:

1968   *Structures Gonflables,* Musée d'Art Moderne, Paris
1969   *Art after Plans,* Kunsthalle, Berne
1970   *Street Art Program,* Hannover
1971   *Inno '70,* Hayward Gallery, London
1972   *British Avant Garde,* Gallery House, London
1974   *Tabarka Festival,* Tunisia
1976   *Biennale,* Paris
1977   *Ongellukkige Liefde Festival,* De Lantarn Theatre, Rotterdam
1978   *Lucht,* Stedelijk Museum Schiedam, Netherlands
1979   *One World Poetry Festival,* Melkweg, Amsterdam

Collections:

City Collection, Amsterdam; Dutch National Collection, The Hague; City Collection, Haarlem, Netherlands.

Publications:

By SHAW: books—*Evenstructures,* with E.R.G., Delft 1972;

Prospectus for the Strombeeld Foundation, with E.R.G., Amsterdam 1980; articles—"Inflatable Structures and Participation," with E.R.G., in *Robho* (Paris), Spring 1968; "Concepts for an Operational Art," with E.R.G., in *Art and Artists* (London), January 1969.

On SHAW: books—*Arthropods* by Jim Burns, New York 1971; *Kunst van Nu,* Amsterdam 1971; *Sonsbeek '71 Report,* Arnhem 1972; *9th Biennale de Paris,* exhibition catalogue, Paris 1975; articles—"Evenstructures" by Albrecht Kwast in *Pneutube,* exhibition catalogue, London 1969; "Evenstructure Research Group" by Ruud Englander in *Mickery Mouth* (Amsterdam), no. 11, 1971; "ERG in Australia" by Terry Smith in *Studio International* (London), October 1972; "Diadrama" by Max Adrian in *Toneel Teatral* (Amsterdam), no. 1, 1974.

Working inside the frameworks of contemporary art, bound to its matrix of expectancy—if information is a function of interference, then where is the surprise?

"Roll away the reel world, the reel world, the reel world! Cherchons La Flamme!"

No doubt in whose interests the new technologies such as computers are being developed. But at the same time these technologies make possible the creation of "interactive" art works which have an on-going dialogue with their audience and/or surroundings. Thus the form of such an art work expands to include the nature and quality of its interactivity in time.

—Jeffrey Shaw

SHIELDS, Alan J.

American. Born in Harrington, Kansas, 4 February
1944. Educated at Kansas State University, Manhattan, 1963–66; spent two summers with the Theatre
Workshop, University of Maine, 1966–67. Independent painter and sculptor, New York, since 1968. Recipient: Guggenheim Fellowship, 1973. Agent: Paula
Cooper Gallery, 155 Wooster Street, New York
10012. Address: Post Office Box 1554, Shelter Island, New York 11964, U.S.A.

Individual Exhibitions:

1969	Paula Cooper Gallery, New York
1970	Paula Cooper Gallery, New York
	Janie C. Lee Gallery, Dallas
1971	Janie C. Lee Gallery, Dallas
	The New Gallery, Cleveland
	Galerie Ileana Sonnabend, Paris
1972	Galleria dell'Ariete, Milan
	Paula Cooper Gallery, New York
1973	Hansen-Fuller Gallery, San Francisco
	Museum of Contemporary Art, Chicago
	University of Rhode Island, Kingston
	Contemporary Arts Museum, Houston
	Madison Art Center, Wisconsin
	Galerie Aronowitsch, Stockholm
1974	Richard Gray Gallery, Chicago
	Phoenix Gallery, San Francisco
	Paula Cooper Gallery, New York (twice)
	Barbara Okun Gallery, St. Louis
	Texas Gallery, Houston
1975	Galleria dell'Ariete, Milan
	Dootson-Calderhead Gallery, Seattle
	Museum of Art, University of Kansas, Lawrence
	E. G. Gallery, Kansas City
	Galerie Daniel Templon, Paris
1976	Richard Gray Gallery, Chicago
	Musée de Saint-Etienne, France
	Portland Center for the Visual Arts, Oregon
	Paula Cooper Gallery, New York
	Paula Cooper Gallery, Los Angeles
	Museu de Arte Moderna, Rio de Janeiro
	Galerie Simone Stern, New Orleans
1977	Moore College of Art, Philadelphia
	Nina Freudenheim Gallery, Buffalo
	Musée d'Art Moderne, Strasbourg
1978	Paula Cooper Gallery, New York
	Galerie Daniel Templon, Paris
	Galerie Munro, Hamburg
	Public School N1, Long Island City, New York
	Galeria Luisa Strina, Sao Paulo
	Barbara Okun Gallery, St. Louis
	Thomas Segal Gallery, Boston
	Gimpel-Hanover Galerie, Zurich
	André Emmerich Galerie, Zurich
	Williams College Museum of Art, Williamstown, Massachusetts
1980	Paula Cooper, New York
	Dorry Gates Gallery, Kansas City
1981	Bowdoin College, Brunswick, Maine
	Heath Gallery, Atlanta, Georgia
1982	Fine Arts Museum of the South, Mobile, Alabama
	Middlebury College, Vermont
	Paula Cooper Gallery, New York
	State University of New York, Stony Brook
	State University of New York, Purchase
1983	Gallery Uoda, Tokyo
	Paula Cooper Gallery, New York
	Thomas Segal Gallery, Boston
	Brooks Memorial Art Gallery, Memphis, Tennessee (travelled to Coral Gables, Florida; Kansas City, Missouri)
1984	Paula Cooper Gallery, New York
	Galerie Andre Emmerich, Zurich
1985	University of Massachusetts, Amherst
	Paula Cooper Gallery, New York
1986	Paula Cooper Gallery, New York
	Cleveland Center for Contemporary Art, Ohio (travelled to Standard Oil Headquarters, Cleveland)
1987	Dorry Gates Gallery, Kansas City, Missouri
	State University of New York, Purchase

Selected Group Exhibitions:

1969	Soft Art, New Jersey State Museum, Trenton
1974	Printed, Cut, Folded and Torn, Museum of Modern Art, New York
1977	Drawings of the 70's, Art Institute of Chicago
1978	Recent Drawings by Younger Artists, Whitney Museum, New York
1979	Oeuvres Contemporaines des Collections Nationales: Accrochage 2, Centre Georges Pompidou, Paris
1980	Perceiving Modern Sculpture, Grey Art Gallery, New York University
1982	The Americans: Collage 1950–82, Contemporary Arts Museum, Houston
1984	Maximal Implication of the Minimal Line, Bard College, Annandale-on-Hudson, New York
1986	Paper as Subject, Circulo de Bellas Artes, Madrid

Collections:

Museum of Modern Art, New York; Metropolitan Museum
of Art, New York; Whitney Museum, New York; Guggenheim Museum, New York; Hirshhorn Museum and Sculpture
Garden, Washington, D.C.; Allen Memorial Art Museum,
Oberlin, Ohio; Akron Art Institute, Ohio; Fort Worth Art
Center, Texas.

Publications:

By SHIELDS: articles—"A Talk with Alan Shields," with
Emily Wasserman, in Artforum (New York), February 1971;
"Tales of Brave Ulysses: Alan Shields Interviewed by Howardena Pindell" in The Print Collector's Newsletter (New
York), January/February 1975; interview in Alan Shields, exhibition catalogue, Milan 1975; notes in Alan Shields, exhibition catalogue, Philadelphia 1977; interview, with Kathy
Halbreich, in Paper Forms Handmade Paper Projects, exhibition catalogue, Cambridge, Massachusetts 1977; "Interview:
Alan Shields", with Jan Avgikos, in Art Papers (Atlanta),
May-June 1982.

On SHIELDS: books—Painting Annual, exhibition catalogue, with an essay by John I. H. Baur, New York 1969;
Highlights of the Season, exhibition catalogue, Ridgefield,
Connecticut 1971; Grids, exhibition catalogue, with an essay
by Lucy Lippard, Philadelphia 1972; Alan Shields, Artist,
exhibition catalogue, Milan 1972; Documenta 5, exhibition catalogue, by Harald
Szeeman and Jean-Christophe Ammann, Kassel, West Germany 1972; 12 Statements Beyond the 60's, exhibition catalogue, with an essay by Frank Kolbert, Detroit 1972; Painting
Annual, exhibition catalogue, New York 1972; Alan Shields,
exhibition catalogue, with an essay by Carter Ratcliff, Chicago 1973; Alan Shields, exhibition catalogue, Houston
1973; Alan Shields, exhibition catalogue, Houston 1973; The
Book as Art, exhibition catalogue, Washington, D.C. 1976;
30 Years of American Printmaking, exhibition catalogue, with
an essay by Patterson Sims, Philadelphia 1977; Painting
1975-76-77, exhibition catalogue, Bronxville, New York
1977; Alan Shields, exhibition catalogue, with an essay by
Daniel Abadie, Strasbourg 1977; American Painting of the
1970's, exhibition catalogue, with an essay by Linda Cathcart, Buffalo, New York 1978; Disseminazione, exhibition
catalogue, Varese, Italy 1978; Drawings About Drawing Today, exhibition catalogue, by Innis Shoemaker, Chapel Hill,
North Carolina 1979; Soft Art, exhibition catalogue, by Erika
Billeter Zurich 1979; La Peinture Americaine by Madeleine
Deschamps, Paris 1981; Alan Shields, exhibition catalogue
with introduction by Deborah Emont, essay by Shigeo Chiba,
Tokyo 1983; Alan Shields, exhibition catalogue with essay by
Deborah Emont-Scott, Memphis 1983; American Art Now by
Edward Lucie-Smith, New York 1985.

Alan J. Shields is identified with an exuberant "pictorial sculpture"—that is, color stained and whimsical,
craft-decorated canvas often constructed as both
opened and enclosed three-dimensional forms. His
career-long fascination has been with an eclectic pat-

Alan Shields: Mat Me, 1986

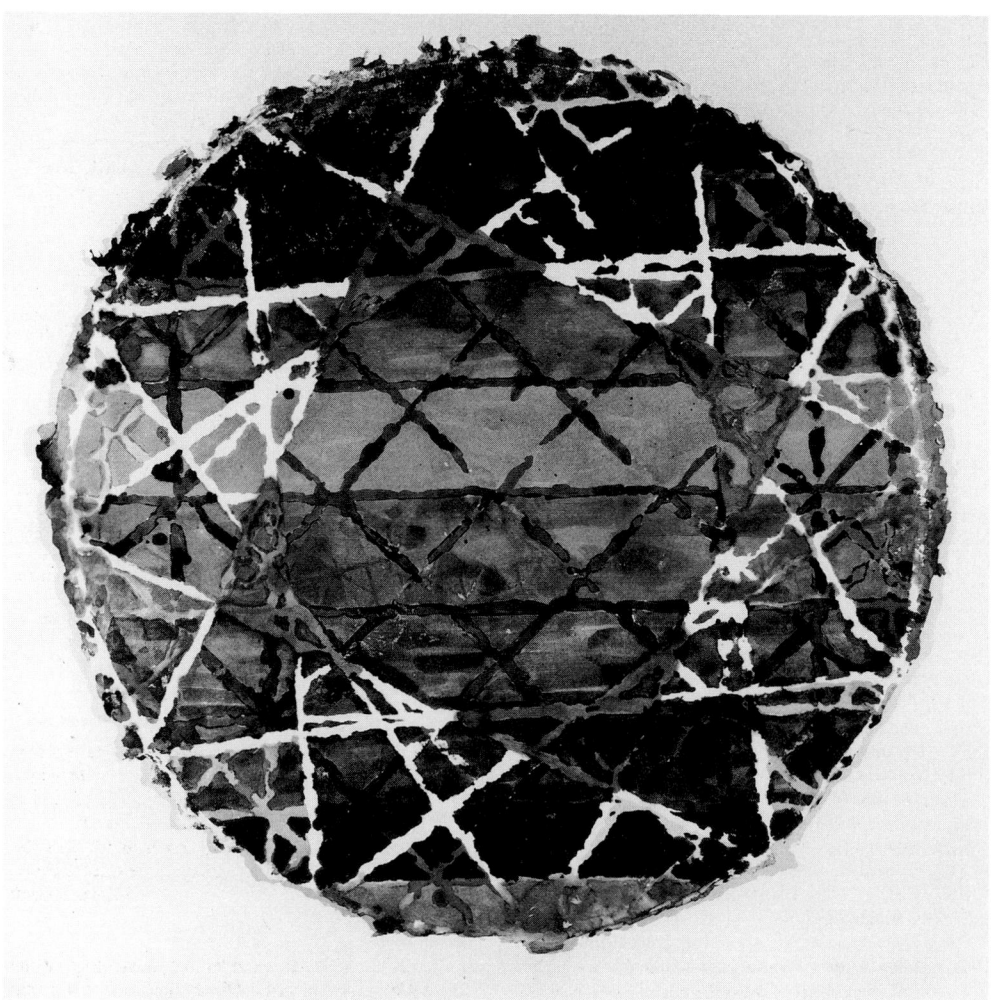

terning generally set upon a base of stained hues; his work has then been a variant of the later 1960's return to confidence in the possibilities of large scale abstraction. In his earliest exhibitions at that time, he already showed two-sided paintings. His desire for viewer involvement and movement, felt throughout his work by its charm, as well in its often meandering and pointed titles, is perhaps ascribable to his youthful fondness for the travelling carnivals in his hometown.

This tendency is easily seen in what may still be Shields' most oft-referred to works: a cylindrical and drum-like painting, 8 feet in height with a 16 foot diameter; and his free-hanging rectangular, open-grids of sewn, collaged, and stained strips of cotton belting. To these works, Shields would add stitching, crochet, beads, twigs, and other attachments. His strength of feeling for craft materials and processes traditionally held peripheral to the painter's art has carried over to his elaborated silk screen prints and his use of paper pulp. The many forms in which Shields has manipulated his essentially joyous color art include cylinders, pyramids, ladders, ropes, and banners.

While the critical literature contains affirmative statements referring to the inventive and sensual atmosphere of his individual works and exhibitions, the counter to such attitude is the sense that the primarily pleasureful or "decorative" aspect of his art is self-indulgent and without the focus of what has been conceived of, even within late-modernism, as "high" art. Yet precisely because of this approach to surface and form-shape, Shields must number among the important influences in the formation of the Pattern and Decoration movement of the later 1970s.

He has continued his multi-faceted work unabated into the decade of the 1980s, with perhaps greater emphasis upon personalized Multiples. He is now in the poignant position of continuing in a decorative mode—albeit wide-ranging—akin to that of the Pattern and Decoration movement which he foreshadowed and is now essentially static if not in decline. Shields' art has been surely marked by the greatly expanded sense of possibility in visual art activities that came into being during the 1960's. Yet he has transferred this freedom to the smaller field essentially known as easel painting and printmaking; and there, despite the outward glamour of his at times large and eccentric-seeming forms, Shields has produced work as if to expand the traditional painter's art not so much conceptually as emotionally.

—Joshua Kind

SHIOMI, Mieko.

Japanese. Born in Okayama, Japan, 13 December 1938. Educated in Musicology at Tokyo University of Music and Fine Art, 1957–61, B. Music 1961. Married Akira Sakaguchi in 1971; children: Tohru and Taku. Independent musician and performance artist, since 1961. Founded Group-Ongaku with Takehisa Kosugi and others, 1961; participated in Fluxus activities, New York, 1964–65. Member, Japanese Federation of Composers, 1972. Agents: Jaap Rietman, 157 Spring Street, New York, New York 10012; Parachute, C.P. 730 Succorsale, North Montreal, Quebec H2X 3N4, Canada; Büchhandlung Walther König, Breite Strasse 93, 5 Cologne 1, West Germany; Ecart Gallery, 6 rue Plantamour, 1201 Geneva, Switzerland. Address: c/o Sakaguchi, 1-24-38 Sakurai, Minoo, Osaka, Japan.

Individual Exhibitions:

1963   7 *Performances*, Okayama Cultural Centre, Japan
        (with members of Sanyo Broadcasting Company)

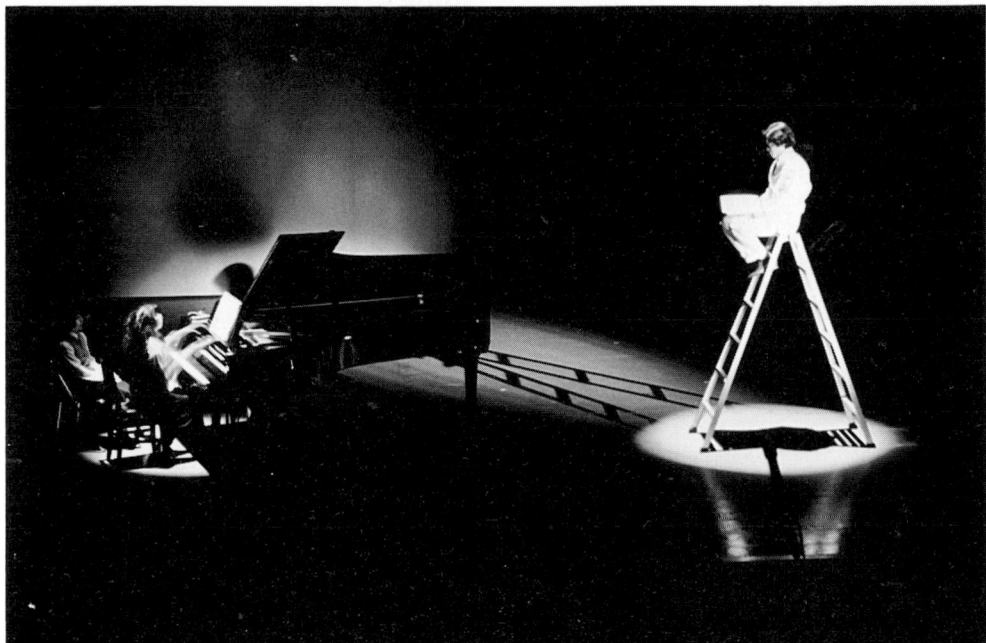

Mieko Shiomi: *In the Afternoon of Structure of the Dream*, 1982

1964   *Flux Concert: Mieko Shiomi*, Washington Square
        Gallery, New York
1965   *Water Music, Air Event, Music for 2 Players IV*,
        Crystal Gallery, Tokyo

Selected Group Exhibitions:

1961   *Group-Ongaku Concert*, Sogestu Hall, Tokyo
1966   *From Space to Environment*, Sogestu Hall, Tokyo
1969   *Intermedia Art Festival*, Killer Joe Discotheque,
        Ginza and Nikkei Hall, Tokyo
1975   *Luna Festival*, Ashiya, Japan
1979   *Japanese Composers*, Iino Hall, Tokyo
1980   *Movements & Music*, Goethe Institute, Osaka
1981   *German-Japanese Contemporary Music Series*, Piccolo Theatre, Amagasaki, Japan
1982   *Live Art Theatre*, Modern Art Museum, Kobe, Japan
1986   *Koto Recital*, Rohdoh Center Hall, Osaka, Japan
1987   *Second Annual Exhibition of Miniature Art*, De Bello Gallery, Toronto

Collections:

Archiv Sohm, Markgroeningen, West Germany; Jean Brown Archive, Tyringham, Massachusetts.

Publications:

By SHIOMI: books—*Event Pieces*, New York 1963; *Spatial Poem* (complete edition, no. 1–9), New York 1976; articles—"Media-Technology-Art" in *Ongaku Geijutsu* (Tokyo), April 1969; "Mieko Shiomi" in *Art and Artists* (London), October 1973; "Products of Musical Thoughts Wandering Beyond the Sound" in *Geijutsu Club* (Tokyo), April 1974; "Score (on the 3 rings)" in *Transonic* (Tokyo), winter 1974; music scores—*As It Were Floating Granules*, 1976; *The Bird Dictionary*, 1979; *If We Were a Pentagonal Memory Device*, 1981, recording 1982; *Spring*, 1982; *The Waltz in the Shape of a Star* (piano suite), 1987.

These past ten years or so I have been engaged in composing vocal music, with words, instruments, lights and simple apparatuses, which could be said to have a style between opera and theatre pieces.

My concern is how to develop an art work of cross-media out of simple words, objects, or even concepts.

—Mieko Shiomi

In the early 1960s, as a student of musicology at the Tokyo University of Arts, Mieko Shiomi and a group

of musicians founded Group Ongaku and presented improvised performances at weekly meetings. From 1961 to 1963 the group sought to redefine music and find new sound producing materials, using, at times, ordinary objects such as tables, and chairs, ash trays, and bunches of keys. Shiomi, interested in the juxtaposition of sounds and silence, created "Boundary Music," 1963, and "Music for Two Players," 1963.

Shiomi described "Boundary Music" as follows: "Make the faintest possible sounds of a boundary condition whether the sounds are given birth to as sounds or not. At the performance, instruments, human bodies, electronic apparatuses or anything else may be used."

"Endless Box," done during the same period, required the viewer to remove successive paper box coverings, thereby establishing a pattern of activity similar to that of the sound pieces. Inspired to connect with the Fluxus group after seeing a Fluxus work by George Brecht at T. Ichiyanagi's, Shiomi traveled to New York in 1964 where she met George Maciunas, Dick Higgins, Alison Knowles, Nam June Paik, and Ay-O. As a participant in some performances and viewer of others, Shiomi felt that she was too restricted by being in only one place at one time. She writes, "I felt that art should be alive everywhere all the time, and at any time anybody wanted it and so I came up with the idea of the *Spatial Poem*."

Spatial Poem, a prolonged correspondence art activity eventually became an artist's book which documents nine events orchestrated by Shiomi between 1965 and 1975. Instructions were sent to each participant, for example: word event "write a word or words on the enclosed card and place it somewhere," or disappearing event, "observe the natural phenomenon that something is going to disappear." The response was international. Daniel Spoerri placed the word "merde" in a hotel room in Paris; Geoff Hendricks placed "ritual meaning" in the Prado; and Michael Kirby placed "continuation" at the bottom of lower New York Bay. As a 70-page book filled with statements, photographs, and drawings done in response to Shiomi's instructions, *Spatial Poem* is a significant contribution to, and compendium of, activity in the correspondence art network. As a manifestation of Shiomi's idea, to have simultaneous performances at different places all over the world, it is a carefully-designed documentation which includes world maps and time clocks as a background for the responses which are printed on small flags. Thus the artist captures the concept of intermittent simultaneity over the duration of time.

—Mary Stofflet

SIEVERDING, Katharina.

German. Born in Prague, Czechoslovakia, in 1944. Educated in Castrop-Rauxel, and at the Kathe-Kollwitz-Gymnasium, Dortmund, 1949-62; studied art, Hochschule für Bildende Kunste, Hamburg, 1962-63; studied stage design under Teo Otto, 1964-67, painting under Joseph Beuys, 1967-72, and film under Ole John, 1972-74, Staatliche Kunstakademie, Dusseldorf; also independent studies, on the Whitney Museum Program, and at the New School for Social Research, New York, 1976-77. Worked as a stage designer for theatre productions in Hamburg, Vienna, Dusseldorf, Berlin and Salzburg, 1963-67. Artist-photographer and filmmaker, Dusseldorf, since 1969. Recipient: Forderungspreis des Landes Nordrhein-Westfalen, 1975; DAAD-Fellowship, to New York, 1976; Forderpreis, Kulturkreis Bund Deutscher Industrie, 1979; Karl Schmidt-Rottluff Stipend, West Germany, 1980; Kunstfonds Award, West Germany, 1981; Berkenhoff Award, 1984. Address: Nordstrasse 111A, 4000 Dusseldorf 30, West Germany.

Individual Exhibitions:

1972	Galleria L'Attico, Rome
1973	Galerie Oppenheim, Cologne
	Galerie Oppenheim, Brussels
1975	Galerie Klein, Bonn
	Galleria Francoise Lambert, Milan
	Galerie Konrad Fischer, Dusseldorf
1977	Museum Folkwang, Essen, West Germany
1978	Rheinisches Landesmuseum, Bonn
	Galerie Klein, Bonn
	Stichting de Appel, Amsterdam
1979	Van Abbemuseum, Eindhoven, Netherlands
1980	Kunsthalle, Dusseldorf
1980	Galerie Klein, Bonn
1984	Moltkerei, Colonge
	Museum Abteiberg, Mönchengladbach, West Germany
1985	Galerija Studentskog Centra, Zagreb, Yugoslavia
	MM Centar SC, Zagreb, Yugoslavia
1987	Badischer Kunstverein, Karlsruhe, West Germany
	Kunstverein, Kassel, West Germany

Selected Group Exhibitions:

1965	*4. Biennale de Paris*, Musée d'Art Moderne, Paris
1969	*Beuysklasse*, Stadtisches Museum, Trier, West Germany
1971	*Film-Kritisch*, Kunsthalle, Dusseldorf
1973	*Medium Fotografie 1910-73*, Stadtisches Museum, Leverkusen, West Germany
1975	*Selbstportrat als Selbstdarstellung*, Galerie im Taxispalais, Innsbruck, Austria
1977	*Documenta 6*, Museum Fridericianum, Kassel, West Germany
1980	*Kunst der 70er Jahre*, at the *Biennale*, Venice
1982	*Videokunst in Deutschland*, Kunstverein, Cologne
1985	*Kunst in der Bundesrepublik 1945-85*, Nationalgalerie, West Berlin
1987	*Blow Up*, Kunstverein, Hamburg (travelled to Hannover)

Publications:

By SIEVERDING: books—*Grossfotos I-X/1975-1977*, exhibition catalogue edited by Zdenek Felix, Essen 1977; *Norad XVIII-XXIII/1980*, West Berlin 1983; *Die Sonne um Mitternacht Schauen I/I-VII/196/1973*, exhibition catalogue, Monchengladbach 1984; *Du Sollst nicht gegen die Sonne Reden*, exhibition catalogue, Karlsruhe 1987.

On SIEVERDING: books—*Medium Fotografie*, exhibition catalogue with texts by Rolf Wedewer and Lothar Romain, Leverkusen 1973; *Transformer: Aspekte der Travestie*, exhibition catalogue edited by Jean-Christophe Ammann, Lucerne 1974; *Korpersprache*, exhibition catalogue with texts by Georg Bussmann, Thomas Kempas, Bazon Brock and others, West Berlin 1975; *Buren/Burgin/Dimitrijevic/Haacke/Herring/Sieverding*, exhibition catalogue edited by Clara Weyergraf, Bochum 1978; *Documenta 7*, exhibition catalogue, 2 vols., edited by Rudi H. Fuchs, Kassel 1982.

SIMONDS, Charles.

American. Born in New York City, 14 November 1945. Studied at the University of California, Berkeley, 1963-67, B.A. 1967; Rutgers University, New Brunswick, New Jersey, 1967-69, M.F.A. 1969. Lives and works in New York. Instructor, Newark State College, New Jersey, 1969-71. First concentrated on working in streets, constructing places for imaging civilizations, 1970. Member of the Board, Lower East Side Coalition for Human Housing, New York, since 1973. Recipient: National Endowment for the Arts grant, 1974; New York State Council for the Arts grant, 1974. Address: 26 East 22nd Street, New York, New York 10010, U.S.A.

Individual Exhibitions:

1975	Centre National d'Art Contemporain, Paris
	Demeures et Mythologies, Samangallery, Genoa
1976	*Projects: Charles Simonds: Picaresque Landscape*, Museum of Modern Art, New York (travelled to the New York Public Library, Tompkins Square)
1977	*Temenos*, Albright-Knox Art Gallery, Buffalo, New York
1978	*Floating Cities and Other Architectures*, Westfälischer Kunstverein, Münster, West Germany (travelled to the Kunstverein, Bonn)
1979	*Circles and Towers Growing*, Wallraf-Richartz Museum, Museum Ludwig, Cologne (travelled to the Nationalgalerie, Berlin; Musee de l'Abbaye Sainte-Croix, Les Sables-d'Olonne, France, and the Galerie Baudoin Lebon, Paris)
	Floating Cities, Centre d'Art Contemporain, Geneva (travelled to the Samangallery, Genoa)
1980	Beaumont May Gallery, Dartmouth College, Hanover, New Hampshire
	California State University at Los Angeles
1981	*Circles and Towers Growing*, organized by the Museum of Contemporary Art, Chicago (toured the United States)
1984	*House Plants and Rocks*, Leo Castelli Gallery, New York
1985	*Three Trees*, Architekturmuseum, Basle
1986	Galerie Maeght Lelong, Paris
1987	Galerie Baudoin Lebon, Paris

Selected Group Exhibitions:

1971	*112 Green Street Group*, 112 Greene Street, New York
1974	*Interventions in Landscape*, Massachusetts Institute of Technology, Cambridge
1975	*Primitive Presence in the 70's*, Vassar College, Poughkeepsie, New York
1976	*Biennale*, Venice
1977	*Contemporary American Art*, Whitney Museum, New York
1978	*Made by Sculptors*, Stedelijk Museum, Amsterdam
1981	*Architecture by Artists*, Rosa Esman Gallery, New York
1983	*New Art*, Tate Gallery, London
1985	*Transformations in Sculpture*, Guggenheim Museum, New York
1986	*An American Renaissance*, Fort Lauderdale Museum of Art, Florida

Collections:

Museum of Modern Art, New York; Whitney Museum, New York; Massachusetts Institute of Technology, Cambridge; Allen Memorial Art Museum, Oberlin College, Ohio; Museum of Contemporary Art, Chicago; Centre Georges Pompidou, Paris; Kunsthaus, Zurich; Museum Ludwig, Cologne; Walker Art Center, Minneapolis; Guggenheim Museum, New York.

Publications:

By SIMONDS: books—*3 Peoples*, Genoa 1975; *Art/Cahier 2: Charles Simonds*, Paris 1975; article—"Microcosm to Macrocosm: Fantasy World to Real World" in *Artforum* (New York), February 1974; "Entretien avec Charles Simonds", with Didier Semin, in *Beaux-Arts* (Paris), no. 39, 1986; films—*Birth*, 1971; *Dwellings*, with David Troy, 1972; *Body Earth*, with Rudy Burckhardt, 1974; *Dwellings Winter*, with Rudy Burckhardt, 1974; *Niagara Gorge 1974*, with Emil Antonucci, 1974.

On SIMONDS: books—*Charles Simonds: Demeures et Mythologies*, exhibition catalogue, Genoa 1975; *Charles Simonds: Temenos*, exhibition catalogue, Münster and Bonn 1978; *Circles and Towers Growing*, exhibition catalogue, Cologne 1979; *Charles Simonds*, exhibition catalogue with essays by John Hallmark-Neff, Daniel Abadie and John Beardsley, Chicago 1982; *Charles Simonds*, exhibition catalogue, Paris 1986.

*   *   *

During the past 12 years I have worked on the streets of New York building tiny landscapes, dwellings, ruins and ritual places for an imaginary civilization of "Little People" who are migrating through the city. Each "place" is made of raw clay and tiny bricks. On the Lower East Side, where I have worked for the past 10 years in walls, vacant lots, gutters, etc., I am in constant dialogue with passersby, many of whom see this fragile fantasy world as a microcosm of their own lives and view its destruction as emblematic of their own attempts to improve their neighborhood. Through this activity I became involved in designing with the community a park/playlot/sculpture—a hilly landscape in the midst of the city: as a member of the Lower East Side Coalition for Human Housing, I have since helped administer other community programs.

Some other works: "The Growth House" is a seasonally renewable dwelling constructed of earth bricks with seeds inside. As the seeds sprout, growth transforms the built structure; the dwelling is converted from shelter to food, and is harvested and eaten (constructed at Artpark, Lewiston, New York, 1975). "Niagara Gorge" is a full-scale dwelling and ritual place—the excavation and inhabitation of the remains of a 19th century railroad tunnel (constructed at Artpark, 1974). "Birth," "Body—Earth," and "Landscape—Body—Dwelling" are rituals documented by 16mm film.

—Charles Simonds

*   *   *

Since 1970, Charles Simonds has been making miniature clay architectural "dwellings," the remains left behind by an imaginary civilization of nomadic "Little People." The first 200 or so were built on various sites among the streets and buildings on the Lower East Side of Manhattan, and, since then, others have appeared in Paris, Berlin, Shanghai and a variety of locations including museum sites.

As Simonds' tiny dwellings have accumulated, they have created a history for his migrant minigroup who continually move onward in their patterns of flux, building, decaying and rebuilding their ritualistic living places, always staying one or many steps ahead of the game as portrayed by Simonds' organic/architectural landscapes which memorialize their former presence and lifestyle.

Simonds' "Little People" are generally of three types: people who live in a line, people who live in a circle, and people who live in a spiral. In each case, danger seems implicit in their states of change in time and in space alike. Psychological and sociological mores are revealed through patterns of structure and growth. For example, as the "Spiral People" move forward and inward along their route, burying their past and building on top of it, they leave less and less room for people, narrowing through each cycle and ultimately constricting themselves toward imminent extinction. In the twelve part series titled "Circles and Towers Growing" (1978), Simonds brings his Tom Thumb people full cycle, from beginnings in the dry, cracked earth, through a process of organic, architectural buildup and synthesis, passing through subsequent levels of decay, and ending up in a landscape which verges on the nothingness out of which it all started.

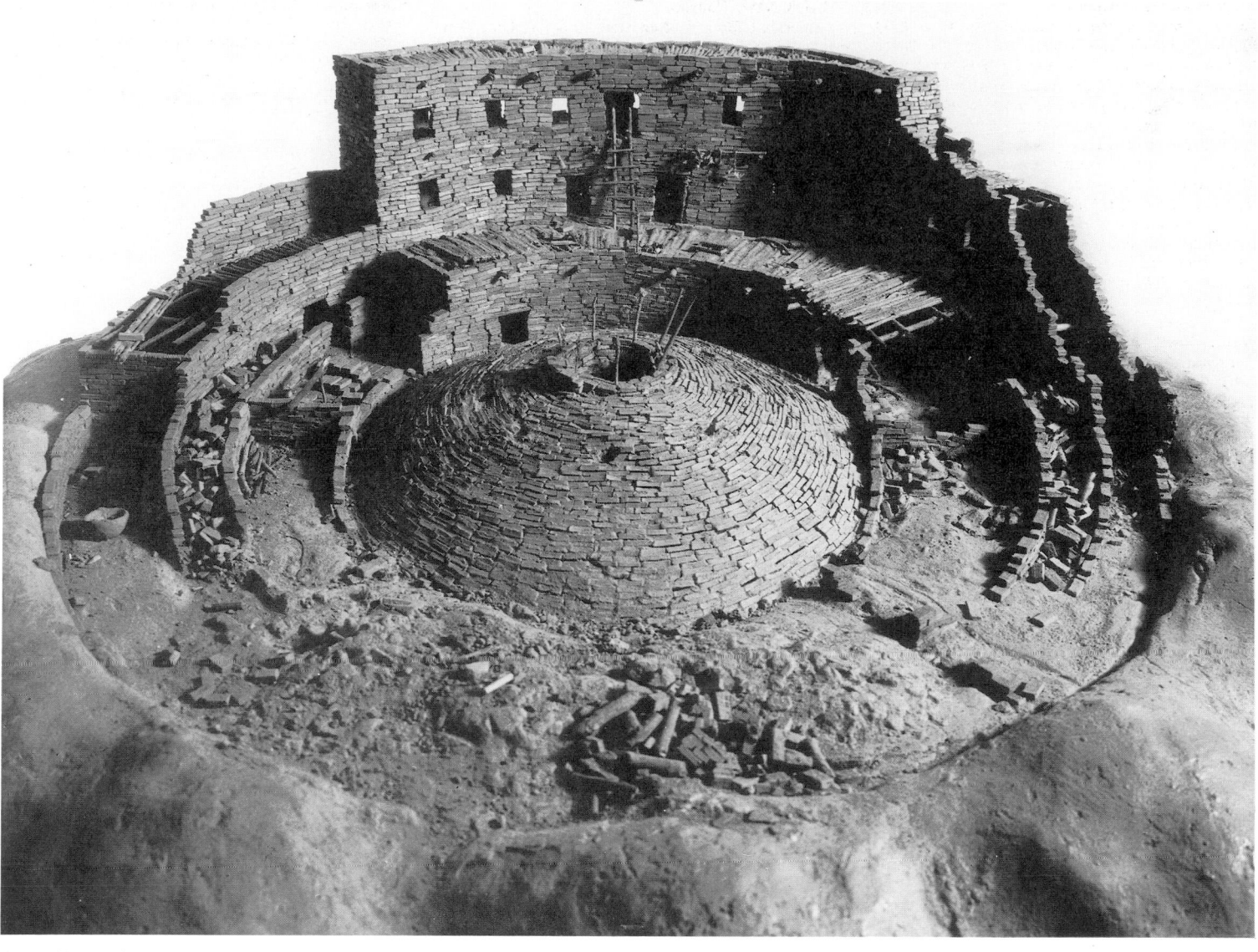

Charles Simonds: *People Who Live in a Circle*, 1972

Simonds' diminutive works are accompanied by written narratives in which he explicates the outer patterns and inner implications underlying the structures in a manner very like that of Borges in his labyrinthean journeys. In three short films, made in collaboration with Rudy Burkhardt (photographer and filmmaker), Simonds himself appears in various states of transformation in concert with the earth. In the first, his body is literally emerging from an earth mound; in the second, he is writhing in the actions of sexual procreation with the clay earth; in the third, he gives birth, as it were, to tiny clay architectural forms which are growing directly on his body. Besides lending additional fantastic levels to his sculptural landscapes, the writing and films seem to indicate Simonds' felt relationships with his mythic peoples, they are his creations out of self, symbolic of the artist's godlike role as maker who, in *Genesis*, scoops up a handful of clay and forms it into something breathing, intelligent and mysteriously possessing a free-will life of its own.

In many ways, Simonds is in tune with the sensibility of Robert Smithson who, in the late 1960's, noted that our future tends to be primitive. Of course, unlike Smithson's monumental Earthworks in which we are the Lilliputians, in relation with Simonds' dwarfed environments we are the Gullivers. This difference in feeling as well as in scale helps save Simonds' works from lapsing too deeply into the primitive past. In contemporary life, it is we who tend to crush the environment, having become too big for our own good.

In developing his mythical archaeology of "Little

People," Simonds has given us a ritualistic emblem for life/art processes which point up our ongoing game-playing, childlike, sexual and mystical, which we continue in the midst of "progress" and "decay." As of the moment, there seem to be two problematic elements in his future development. How long can Simonds' singular approach retain its fascination and its possibilities? And does his recent making of tabletop models, by lessening our sense of discovery, lose some of the lifegiving element in his site-specific dwellings?

—Barbara Cavaliere

SMITH, David (Roland).
American. Born in Decatur, Indiana, 9 March 1906. Educated at Paulding, Ohio; studied drawing, via a correspondence course, from the Cleveland Art School, 1923; studied woodcutting, Ohio University,

Athens, 1924–25; spent one term at Notre Dame University, Indiana, 1925; studied, under Richard Lahey, John Sloan, Jan Matulka and Kimon Nicolaides, at the Art Students League, New York, 1927–32. Married Dorothy Dehner in 1927 (divorced, 1952); married Jean Freas in 1952 (divorced, 1961); daughters: Rebecca and Candida. Sculptor: lived and worked in New York from 1926; also lived on his farm at Bolton Landing, New York, from 1933; Art Editor, *Tennis*, New York, 1930; established studio at Terminal Iron Works, Brooklyn, New York, 1934; worked for the Fine Arts Section, Treasury Relief Project, 1934; travelled extensively in Europe and Russia, 1935–36; worked for the Works Progress Administration Federal Art Project, New York, 1937; worked as a machinist in Glens Falls, New York, 1940; designed medals for the Chinese Army, commissioned by T. V. Soong, 1942; worked as a welder on war vehicles for the Americna Locomotive Company, Schenectady, New York, 1942–44; close friendship with Kenneth Noland from 1951; American Delegate, Unesco First International Conference on Plastic Arts, Venice, 1954; close friendships with James Rosati from 1955 and Robert Motherwell from 1957; commissioned by the Art Institute of Chicago to design medal for the Logan Prize, 1957; spent several months in Spoleto and Voltri, Italy, working on sculptures for the Italian Government and for Gian Carlo Menotti's *Festival of Two Worlds*, Spoleto, 1962. Lecturer, Sarah Lawrence College, Bronxville, New York, 1948–50; Guest Lecturer, University of Arkansas, Fayetteville, 1953, and University of Indiana, Bloomington, 1954; Lecturer, University of Mississippi, Oxford, 1955.

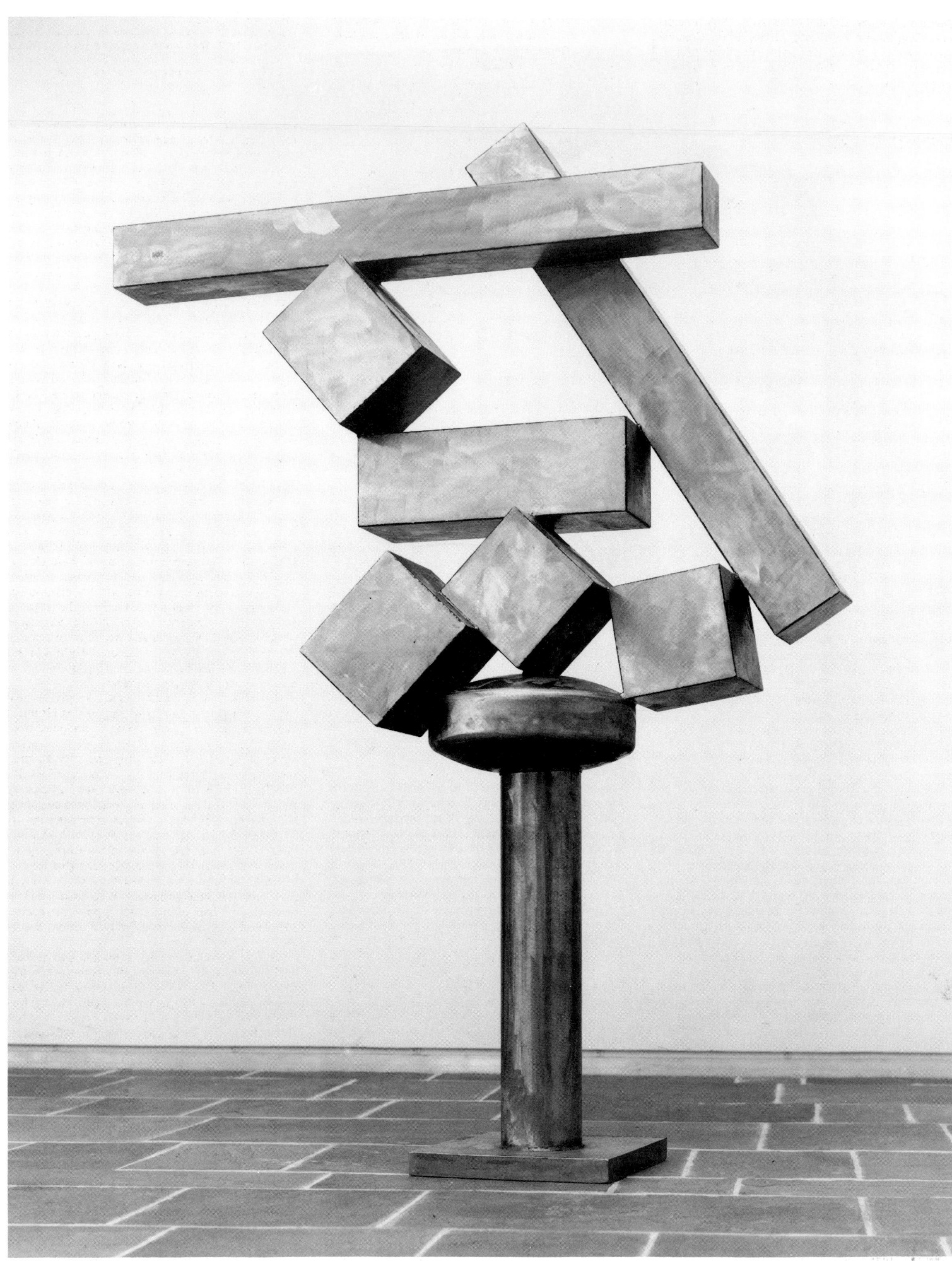

David Smith: *Cubi XVIII*, 1960

Member, National Council of the Arts, 1965. Recipient: Guggenheim Fellowship, 1950, 1951; Creative Arts Award, Brandeis University, Waltham, Massachusetts, 1964. *Died* (in motor accident, in Bennington, Vermont) *23 May 1965.*

Individual Exhibitions:

1938	Willard Gallery, New York
1940	Neumann-Willard Gallery, New York
	Willard Gallery, New York
1941	Kalamazoo Institute of Art, Michigan
	St. Paul Gallery and School of Art, Minnesota
1942	Walker Art Center, Minneapolis
1943	Albany Institute and School of Art, New York (with Dorothy Dehner)
	Willard Gallery, New York
	Skidmore College, Saratoga Springs, New York
1946	Buchholz Gallery, New York
	Skidmore College, Saratoga Springs, New York
1947	East Central State College, Ada, Oklahoma (toured the United States)
	Willard Gallery, New York
	Skidmore College, Saratoga Springs, New York
	Munson-Williams-Proctor Institute, Utica, New York
1948	Allen R. Hite Institute, University of Louisville, Kentucky
1950	Willard Gallery, New York
1951	Bennington College, Vermont
	Junior Gallery, Louisville, Kentucky (toured the United States)
	Willard Gallery, New York
1952	Willard Gallery, New York
	Walker Art Center, Minneapolis
	Williams College, Williamstown, Massachusetts
1953	Willard Gallery, New York
	Kootz Gallery, New York
	University of Arkansas, Fayetteville
	Philbrook Art Center, Tulsa, Oklahoma
	Portland Art Museum, Oregon
	Catholic University of America, Washington, D.C.
1954	Willard Gallery, New York
	Cincinnati Art Museum, Ohio
1956	Museum of Modern Art, New York
	Fine Arts Associates, New York
	Widdifield Gallery, New York
1959	Bennington College, Vermont
	French and Company, New York
1960	Everett Ellin Gallery, Los Angeles
	French and Company, New York
1961	Otto Gerson Gallery, New York (toured the United States and Canada)
1963	Balin-Traube Gallery, New York
	Museum of Modern Art, New York (toured the United States)
1964	Institute of Contemporary Art, Philadelphia
	Hyde Collection, Glens Falls, New York
	Marlborough-Gerson Gallery, New York
1965	Hyde Collection, Glens Falls, New York
	Los Angeles County Museum of Art
1966	Fogg Art Museum, Harvard University, Cambridge, Massachusetts (travelled to the Gallery of Modern Art, Washington, D.C.)
	Guggenheim Museum, New York
	Rijksmuseum Kröller-Müller, Otterlo, Netherlands (toured Europe)
1967	Marlborough-Gerson Gallery, New York
1968	Marlborough-Gerson Gallery, New York
1969	Guggenheim Museum, New York (travelled to the Museum of Fine Arts, Dallas, and the Corcoran Gallery of Art, Washington, D.C.)
1970	Indiana University Art Museum, Bloomington (with George Rickey and Isamu Noguchi)
1972	Fuji TV Company Gallery, Tokyo (with Alexander Calder and Louise Nevelson; travelled to the Galerie Beyeler, Basle)
1973	Whitney Museum, New York (with Alexander Calder and Louise Nevelson)
1974	Knoedler Contemporary Art, New York
1976	Storm King Art Center, Mountainville, New York

	Staatsgalerie, Stuttgart (travelled to the Nationalgalerie, West Berlin, and the Museum der Stadt, Duisburg, West Germany)
1978	Knoedler and Company, New York
1979	Hirshhorn Museum and Sculpture Garden, Smithsonian Institution, Washington, D.C.
	Museo de Arte Contemporaneo, Caracas (with Robert Motherwell)
	Whitney Museum, New York
1980	Serpentine Gallery, London
	Knoedler Gallery, New York
1981	Edmonton Art Gallery, Alberta (toured Canada)
1982	Janie C. Lee Gallery, Houston, Texas
	Storm King Art Center, Mountainville, New York
	Smithsonian Institution, Washington, D.C.
	National Gallery of Art, Washington, D.C.
1983	M. Knoedler and Company, New York
	Arts Club of Chicago
	Washburn Gallery, New York
1985	Anthony D'Offay Gallery, London
	Oklahoma Museum of Art, Oklahoma City
	International Exhibition Foundation, Washington, D.C.
1986	Kunstsammlungen Nordrhein-Westfalen, Dusseldorf
	Stadtische Galerie im Stadelschen Kunstinstitut, Frankfurt
1987	Whitechapel Art Gallery, London
	Washburn Gallery, New York

Selected Group Exhibitions:

1930	*Annual Exhibition of American Block Prints*, Print Club of Philadelphia
1938	*American Abstract Artists*, Fine Arts Galleries, New York
1942	*Artists for Victory*, Metropolitan Museum of Art, New York
1944	*Art in Progress*, Museum of Modern Art, New York
1954	*Biennale*, Venice
1963	*Painting and Sculpture of a Decade 1954–1964*, Tate Gallery, London
1977	*American Drawing 1927–77*, Minnesota Museum of Art, St. Paul
1981	*Sculpture du XXe, Siecle 1900–45*, Fondation Maeght, St. Paul de Vence, France
1985	*Transformations in Sculpture*, Guggenheim Museum, New York

Collections:

Museum of Modern Art, New York; Guggenheim Museum, New York; Hirshhorn Museum and Sculpture Garden, Smithsonian Institution, Washington, D.C.; Art Institute of Chicago; Los Angeles County Museum of Art; Wilhelm Lehmbruck Museum, Duisburg, West Germany.

Publications:

By SMITH: book—*David Smith by David Smith*, edited by Cleve Gray, London 1968; New York 1969; articles—"Sculpture: Art Forms in Architecture, New Techniques Affect Both" in *Architectural Record* (New York), October 1940; "I Never Looked at Landscape . . . . Sculpture Is . . . . " in *Possibilities* (New York), Winter 1947/48; "The Golden Eagle: A Recital" in *Tiger's Eye* (New York), June 1948; "Language Is Image" in *Arts and Architecture* (New York), February 1952, "Who Is the Artist? How Does He Act?" in *Numero* (Florence), May/June 1953; "Gonzalez: First Master of the Torch" in *Artnews* (New York), February 1956; "Sculpture and Architecture" in *Arts Magazine* (New York), May 1957; "Notes on My Work" in *Arts Magazine* (New York), February 1960; "David Smith: Interview," with David Sylvester, in *Living Arts* (New York), April 1964; "The Secret Letter" in *David Smith*, exhibition catalogue, by Thomas B. Hess, New York 1964; "Some Late Words from David Smith" in *Art International* (Lugano, Switzerland), October 1965; "Words by David Smith" in *Artforum* (New York), December 1979.

On SMITH: books—*David Smith*, exhibition catalogue, by Jane Harrison Cone, New York 1966; *David Smith*, exhibition catalogue, by Edward E. Fry, New York 1969; *Terminal Iron Works: The Sculpture of David Smith*, by Rosalind Krauss, Cambridge, Massachusetts 1971; *David Smith*,

edited by C.Garnett McCoy, London 1973; *The Sculpture of David Smith: A Catalogue Raisonné* by Rosalind Krauss, New York 1977; *The Drawings of David Smith* by Trinkett Clark, Washington, D.C. 1985; *David Smith: Sculpture and Drawings*, edited by Joern Merkert, Munich 1986.

*

A pioneer of welded metal sculpture and a forceful individualist, David Smith created a great variety of work which though highly influential is also intensely personal. He is generally acknowledged to have been the most powerfully inventive sculptor of his generation, and is considered by many to have been "America's greatest sculptor." His enormous and intense productivity made him a Balzacian artist, so copious and energetic in his pursuit of new ideas and images that his production was at times too indiscriminate, especially as he showed everything he finished, even the failures.

A development of Smith's sculpture parallels the changes that were taking place in contemporary American painting, moving from a position roughly equivalent to Abstract Expressionism to one related to post-painterly abstraction. It is a change from a highly personal art strongly influenced by surrealism, when Smith occupies almost the same position in the history of post-war sculpture as Pollock does in that of post-war painting, to the later works of the 1960's with strong, simple monumental forms which are classic in their lucidity, like those of the colour-field abstractionists in painting.

And like the Abstract Expressionist painters, he first assimilated and then transformed European modernism by extending its principles as far as possible. It is therefore crucial to the understanding of his work to realize not only that he was profoundly influenced by the Cubist sculpture of Picasso and Julio Gonzalez, but also that he was himself very much the product of American technological civilization. Descended from a pioneer blacksmith, he acquired his intimate knowledge of metalwork techniques while working in his youth as a riveter in an automobile factory, and during the Second World War his sculpture was drastically curtailed by his return to heavy industry to work as a welder.

This skill was originally gained simply so that Smith could support himself while pursuing his initial interest in painting. His transition to sculpture from 1931–1933 came through collage, in which the painting gradually thickened into sculpture: "The painting was a sculpture." And his early sculptures of welded iron, fashioned from parts of agricultural machinery and "found" objects, are an unprecedented attempt at a kind of sculptural collage which anticipates the assemblages Stankiewicz was later to make from scrap metal. Smith said that the aim of his work was the creation of contemporary symbols, and that he preferred to work in iron or steel because "the metal itself possesses little art history. What associations it possesses are those of this century, power, structure, movement, progress, suspension, destruction, brutality."

But he never allowed his compositions to become totally abstract, for even the last apparently severely geometrically abstract works still contain human references. In fact, though Smith's sculptural method stems from technology, his art is conceptual, and has always been seen as having a strong moral content, consistently concerned with the universal themes of human violence and greed, and expressing his deep ambivalence about sexuality because of the potential for violence latent in it. These recurring motifs are particularly clearly seen in the "Medals for Dishonor" he made from 1937 to 1940, bronze plaques which use surrealistic imagery sometimes derived from Picasso's "Guernica" to produce a searing indictment of war, fascism and the hypocritsies and injustices of American society—though he himself later realized that these were among his weakest works, because too directly propagandistic.

When he was able to resume sculpture again after the war, he went on to the exploration of his own identity and the discovery of his own imagery, moving freely in and out of figurative and non-figurative modes, producing heads, figures, landscapes, mythical and surrealist fantasies, but with the theme of human violence and greed still expressed metaphorically in the gaunt skeletal, tortured configurations of such works as "Pillar of Sunday" (1945) or "The Royal Bird" (1947-8). But his themes are also pastoral and lyrical landscapes, and in expressing such themes he went through a linear phase in the late 1940's and early 1950's, a kind of two-dimensional Constructivist calligraphy, in which his works become like open drawings in space, as in the well-known "Hudson River Landscape" (1951).

In the mid-50's Smith's works became larger and larger in scale, and he began to conceive them no longer as individual pieces but in series, in which a single idea could be put through many different permutations. The earlier ones such as the "Agricola" and "Tank Totem" series are still clearly based on the human figure, and incorporate many "found" objects which were usually standard industrial units which could be recombined within the series in different ways. Smith's immense energy is well seen in the "Voltri" series made in 1962 at the *Spoleto Festival* in Italy, when he made 26 huge sculptures in 30 days. This is the last series based on human figure. In the final flowering of his creativity, before his life was abruptly cut short in an automobile crash, he produced two more series, "Zig" and "Cubi." These show his sculptures growing still larger, more monumental, increasingly abstract, with strong, simple geometrical forms completely ousting the organic romanticism of his earlier works. He was now using stainless steel, polished to a reflective sheen, so that light became a major ingredient. These later pieces were in fact very specifically designed to be seen out of doors, as they were erected in the grounds of Smith's own farm at Bolton Landing.

David Smith was in many ways a revolutionary sculptor. He completely accepted the machine age, and his ambition was to produce sculpture whose forms were as impressive, monumental and contemporary as a locomotive. He often painted his works, and this and his technical directness and imaginative exploration of industrial steel shapes all influenced younger sculptors like Caro, who has often been regarded as David Smith's heir. But though these and other elements in his work were enormously influential, he created such an intensely personal style that in its totality it was finally inimitable.

—Konstantin Bazarov

SMITH, Richard.

British. Born in Letchworth, Hertfordshire, 27 October 1931. Studied at the Luton School of Art, Bedfordshire, 1948-50; St. Albans School of Art, Hertfordshire, 1952-54; Royal College of Art, London, 1954-57. Served in the Royal Air Force, in Hong Kong, 1950-52. Married Betsy Scherman in 1964; sons: Edward and Harry. Painter and graphic artist: lived in London until 1976; visited New York frequently, from 1957; settled there in 1976. Lecturer in Mural Decoration, Hammersmith College of Art, London, 1957-58; Lecturer, St. Martin's School of Art, London, 1961-63; Artist-in-Residence, University of Virginia, Charlottesville, 1967; University of California at Irvine, 1968; University of California at Davis, 1976. Recipient: Travelling Scholarship, Royal College of Art, London, 1957; Harkness Travelling Fellowship, 1959; Robert C. Scull Prize, *Biennale*, Venice, 1966; Grand Prix, *Bienal*, Sao Paulo, 1967. C.B.E. (Commander, Order of the British Empire), 1972. Agent: Knoedler Gallery, London. Address: c/o Knoedler Gallery, 22 Cork Street, London W1X 1HB, England.

Individual Exhibitions:

1961	Green Gallery, New York
1962	Richard Smith Studio, Bath Street, London
	Institute of Contemporary Arts, London
1963	Kasmin Gallery, London
	Green Gallery, New York
1965	Green Gallery, New York
1966	Whitechapel Art Gallery, London
	Richard Feigen Gallery, New York
	Editions Alecto, London
1967	Kasmin Gallery, London
	Bienal, Sao Paulo
	University of Virginia, Charlottesville
	Galerie Denise René Hans Mayer, Krefeld, West Germany
1968	Richard Feigen Gallery, New York
1969	Galleria dell'Ariete, Milan
	Kasmin Gallery, London
1970	Arnolfini Gallery Bristol
	Biennale, Venice
1971	Richard Feigen Gallery, Chicago
	Kasmin Gallery, London
1972	Galleria dell'Ariete, Milan
	Museum of Modern Art, Oxford
	Bear Lane Gallery, Oxford
	Kasmin Gallery, London
1973	Ruth S. Schaffner Gallery, Los Angeles
	Garage Art, London
	Waddington Graphics, London
	Galerie Schottenring, Vienna
	Hayward Gallery, London
1974	O. K. Harris Gallery, New York
	Galerie Swart, Amsterdam
	Neue Galerie der Stadt, Linz, Austria
	Galerie Schottenring, Vienna
	D.M. Gallery, London
	Bernard Jacobson Ltd., London
1975	Museo de Arte Contemporaneo, Caracas
	Kettle Yard, Cambridge (travelled to the Ashmolean Museum, Oxford)
	Tate Gallery, London
	Gimpel Fils Gallery, London
	Museu de Arte Moderna, Rio de Janeiro
1976	Galleria Vinciana, Milan
	Gimpel Fils Gallery, London
	Galleria La Polena, Genoa
	Galleria del Cavallino, Venice
	Kasahara Gallery, Osaka
	Museo de Arte Moderna, Bogota
1977	Arte Contacto, Caracas
	Recent Work 1972-1977: Paintings, Drawings and Graphics, Massachusetts Institute of Technology, Cambridge, Massachusetts (toured the United States)
	Galerie Daniel Templon, Paris
	Studio La Città, Verona
	Galleria La Piramide, Florence
	Studio Arco d'Alibert, Rome
	Galerie Orny, Munich
	Galerie Gimpel und Hanover, Zurich
	Modulo, Porto, Portugal
1978	Galerie Artline, The Hague
	Hayden Gallery, Massachusetts Institute of Technology, Cambridge (travelled to the Chrysler Museum, Norfolk, Virginia, and Walker Art Center, Minneapolis)
	Anthony Stokes Gallery, London
	Studio G7, Bologna
	Padiglione d'Arte Contemporanea, Parco Massari, Ferrara, Italy
	Galleria La Polena, Genoa
	Studio Rotelli, Finale Ligure, Italy
	Young Hoffman Gallery, Chicago
	Galleria dell'Ariete, Milan
	Galeria San Diego, Bogota
	Hudson River Museum, New York
	Kornblee Gallery, New York
1979	Hedendaagse Kunst Museum, Utrecht (travelled to Museum Het Bruggenbouw, Emmen, Netherlands)
	Galerie Artline, The Hague
	Galleria Il Sole, Bolzano, Italy
	Saskatoon Gallery, Saskatchewan
	Fort Worth Art Museum, Texas
1980	Knoedler Gallery, London
	Bernard Jacobson Ltd., New York
	Cartouche Series, Norman Mackenzie Art Gallery, Regina, Saskatchewan
	Arco Center for the Visual Arts, Los Angeles
	Studio La Città, Verona
	Galleria La Polena, Genoa
	Neue Arbeiten, Stadtsmuseum, Ulm, West Germany
	Hansen-Fuller-Goldeen Gallery, San Francisco
1982	Knoedler Gallery, London

Selected Group Exhibitions:

1954	*Young Contemporaries*, RBA Galleries, London
1957	*New Trends in British Art*, New York Art Foundation, Rome
1961	*Carnegie International*, Carnegie Institute, Pittsburgh
1964	*The Shaped Canvas*, Guggenheim Museum, New York
1967	*New Shapes of Colour*, Stedelijk Museum, Amsterdam
1970	*Contemporary British Art*, Museum of Modern Art, Tokyo
1973	*La Peinture Anglaise Aujourd'hui*, Musée d'Art Moderne de la Ville, Paris
1974	*British Painting '74*, Hayward Gallery, London
1976	*Arte Inglese Oggi 1960-1976*, Palazzo Reale, Milan
1983	*Aspects of British Art*, Guggenheim Museum, New York

Collections:

Tate Gallery, London; Victoria and Albert Museum, London; Galleria Nazionale d'Arte Moderna, Rome; Staatliche Graphische Sammlung, Munich; Kaiser Wilhelm Museum, Krefeld, West Germany; Art Gallery of Western Australia, Perth; Hirshhorn Museum and Sculpture Garden, Smithsonian Institution, Washington, D.C.; Walker Art Center, Minneapolis.

Publications:

By SMITH: book—*Paginas Amarillas*, exhibition catalogue, Caracas 1975; articles—"Ideograms" in *Ark* (London), no. 16, 1956; "Film Backgrounds: Two Sitting in the Middle of Today" in *Ark* (London), no. 19, 1957; "That Pink" in *Gazette* (London), no. 2, 1961; "Brief Statement" in *Metro* (Milan), no. 6, 1962; "Trailer: Notes Additional to a Film" in *Living Arts* (London), no. 1, 1963; "Pre-Occupations: Richard Smith Talks to Anne Seymour" in *Art and Artists* (London), June 1970; statement in *Richard Smith: Cartouche Series*, exhibition catalogue, Regina, Saskatchewan 1980.

On SMITH: books—*Richard Smith: Seven Exhibitions*, with text by Barbara Rose, London 1975; *Richard Smith: Recent Work 1972-1977: Paintings, Drawings and Graphics*, exhibition catalogue, by Wayne Anderson, Cambridge, Massachusetts 1978; *Richard Smith: Neue Arbeiten*, exhibition catalogue, by Norbert Nobis, Ulm, West Germany 1980; articles—"Richard Smith, Sculptor or Painter?" by Cyril Barrett in *Art International* (Lugano, Switzerland), October 1967; "A Double Reality: The Work and Career of Richard Smith" by Bernard Denvir in *Art International* (Lugano, Switzerland), Summer 1970; "Richard Smith in New York" by T. Castle in *Art Monthly* (London), September 1979.

At first Richard Smith just jumped out at us. His early, exuberant, abstracted-Pop subjects literally jutted out from the wall like large, formal pages from some pop-up book of abstractions. It was clear from the beginning that this English painter was enamored of American advertising, its imagery and ideas. So much so, that he travelled to New York and exhibited big, brash canvases which directly referred to commercial products. There were cigarette-package-like shapes and titles incorporating things like shampoo.

This love affair with Pop never wholly conquered Smith's deepest interests, which had to do with the formal properties of painting—with color, with structure, with form—and he soon left behind the world of commonplace images to paint several series of minimal-like, shaped canvases. A number of these had to do with time and sequence. One set evolved from the idea of pages turned down and removed from a calendar: canvases "turned down" at one corner until the last rectangle was reduced to a triangle and the sequence of color changes brought to a halt.

The surfaces of these paintings were most often painted one color with a second acting as an accent. Later, thin, watercolor-like treatment emerged and there began references to nature—to woods, fields, and rivers. Nothing figurative though.

In turn this has given way to other series and sequences, but now off the stretcher and held firm by rods and sticks and rings and string or rope. Things are tied and sometimes the knots act as color comments. The over-all effect is like that of kites or sails on a Chinese junk, the canvas shaped into squares, rectangles or polygons and suspended in sequences fanned out along a wall like some huge hand of cards or from the ceiling like a chain of banners.

Smith's work has developed from a loud, aggressiveness to an almost oriental delicacy and subtleness. Now his color is more beautiful than ever and his "message" almost serene.

—Ralph Pomeroy

SMITH, Tony.

American. Born in South Orange, New Jersey, in 1912. Attended night classes at the Art Students League, New York, 1933-36; studied architecture, New Bauhaus, Chicago, 1937-38; architectural apprentice to Frank Lloyd Wright, 1938-40. Married: had 3 daughters. Worked as tool-maker and draftsman, New York, 1933-36; practicing architect, 1940-60; full-time sculptor and painter from 1960. Taught at New York University School of Education, 1946-50; Cooper Union and Pratt Institute, New York, 1950-53; Pratt Institute, Brooklyn, New York, 1957-58; Bennington College, Vermont, 1958-61; Hunter College, New York, 1962-74. Recipient: Longview Art Award, 1966; National Council for the Arts Award, 1966; Guggenheim Award, 1968; Fine Arts Medal, American Institute of Architects, New York, 1971; College Art Association Distinguished Teacher of Art Award, 1974; Creative Arts Award for Sculpture, Brandeis University, Waltham, Massachusetts, 1974. Agent: Pace Gallery, 32 East 57th Street, New York, New York 10022, U.S.A. *Died* (in Orange, New Jersey), *26 December 1980.*

Individual Exhibitions:

1966	*Two Exhibitions of Sculpture,* Wadsworth Atheneum, Hartford, Connecticut
	Institute of Contemporary Art, Philadelphia
1967	Walker Art Center, Minneapolis
	Galerie Müller, Stuttgart
	Bryant Park, New York
1968	Galerie René Ziegler. Zurich
	Galerie Yvon Lambert, Zurich
	Donald Morris Gallery, Detroit
	Fischbach Gallery, New York
	Museum of Modern Art, New York (travelling exhibition)
1969	University of Hawaii, Honolulu
1970	Newark Museum, New Jersey
	Montclair Art Museum, New Jersey
	Art Museum, Princeton University, New Jersey
1971	*9 Sculptures,* New Jersey State Museum, Trenton (toured New Jersey)
	Recent Sculpture, Knoedler Gallery, New York
	Museum of Modern Art, New York
	Painting and Sculpture, University of Maryland Art Gallery, College Park
1976	Fourcade/Droll Gallery, New York
1977	Susanne Hilberry Gallery, Birmingham, Michigan

1978	*Models and Drawings,* Montclair College, New Jersey
1979	*10 Elements and Throwback,* Pace Gallery, New York
1980	Richard Gray Gallery, Chicago
1981	Richard Gray Gallery, Chicago
1983	Pace Gallery, New York
1985	Paula Cooper Gallery, New York
	Margo Leavin Gallery, Los Angeles
	Xavier Fourcade Inc., New York

Selected Group Exhibitions:

1968	*Biennale,* Venice
	Plus by Minus: Today's Half Century, Albright-Knox Art Gallery, Buffalo, New York
	Minimal Art, Gemeentemuseum, The Hague
1969	*New York Painting and Sculpture 1940-1970,* Metropolitan Museum of Art, New York
1970	*Expo '70,* Osaka, Japan
1971	*L'Art Vivant Américain,* Fondation Maeght, St. Paul-de-Vence, France
	Biennale of Outdoor Sculpture, Antwerp
1976	*200 Years of American Sculpture,* Whitney Museum, New York
1977	*New York: The State of the Art,* New York State Museum, New York
1980	*10 American Artists,* Wildenstein Gallery, London

Collections:

Museum of Modern Art, New York; Albright Knox Art Gallery, Buffalo, New York; Memorial Art Gallery, University of Rochester, New York; Wadsworth Antheneum, Hartford, Connecticut; Princeton University, New Jersey; Corcoran Gallery of Art, Washington, D.C.; Detroit Institute of Art; Walker Art Center, Minneapolis; Institute of the Arts, Rice University, Houston; National Gallery of Canada, Ottawa.

Publications:

By SMITH: articles "Talking with Tony Smith," interview, with Samuel Wagstaff, Jr., in *Artforum* (New York), December 1966; statement, in "Homage to the Square" in *Art in America* (New York), July 1967; "The Maze" in *Aspen* (New York), nos. 5-7, 1967; "Die" in *Art Now: New York,* November 1969; statement, in *Design Quarterly* (Minneapolis), nos. 78, 79, 1970; statement, in *Tony Smith: Two Exhibitions of Sculpture,* exhibition catalogue, Hartford, Connecticut 1966.

On SMITH: books—*Tony Smith: Two Exhibitions of Sculpture,* exhibition catalogue, by Samuel Wagstaff, Jr., Hartford, Connecticut 1966; *Tony Smith,* exhibition catalogue, by Renée Sabatello, New York 1968; *9 Sculptures by Tony Smith,* exhibition catalogue, with text by Eugene Goossen, Newark, New Jersey 1971; *Tony Smith: Recent Sculpture,* exhibition catalogue, by Martin Friedman and Lucy R. Lippard, New York 1971; *Tony Smith* by Lucy R. Lippard, London and Stuttgart, 1972; *Tony Smith: Painting and Sculpture,* exhibition catalogue, with a foreword by Eleanor Green, Baltimore 1974; *Tony Smith: 10 Elements and Throwback,* exhibition catalogue, with text by Sam Hunter, New York 1979; *Tony Smith: Paintings and Sculpture,* exhibition catalogue with text by Robert Hobbs, New York 1982.

Probably the most important sculptor to emerge from the minimal movement that surfaced in the 60's, Tony Smith seemed at the time to come from nowhere. Certainly his name was not known to any but a few fellow artists, and any "outsider" who had heard of him associated him with his work as an architect. Then he became famous, even being featured on the cover of *Time* magazine.

The reason for this, I think, is obvious. His sculpture was just too powerful not to demand immediate attention. Timing was also an important factor: when the world (or New York anyway) was ready for minimalism, Smith was ready for the world. His background as an architect gave him a mastery of the scale and placement so that his huge black forms—three-dimensional geometries—seemed powerful and elegant at the same time. This, even though his material

was purposely "ugly." His sculptures were relatively inexpensive metaphors for steel and bronze made of ordinary plywood daubed with thick, irregular, greasy-looking black. Their surfaces suggested density, solidity, strength, and weight—at their scale, tons.

And yet there was also a freedom implied. Certain works got off the ground and even allowed us to walk under as well as between, within, and around them. Smith's stunning debut included a whole park full of black blocks, columns and pyramids especially thrilling covered partly by a fresh fall of snow. As a matter of fact the sculptures' curiously oriental quality was greatly underlined by the marvelous contrast of black, hard-edged, man-made forms with white, soft, rounded drifts and mounds—minimal coupled with minimal, so to speak. Ying and yang.

Later, in a series of small-scale, closely related pieces, Smith proved he could produce poetry in a non-natural way as truly as that produced by the arrangement of rocks in dry gardens by the Japanese. A further example of the paradoxes inherent in so reductive and abstract an art.

—Ralph Pomeroy

SMITHSON, Robert (Irving).

American. Born in Rutherford, New Jersey, 2 January 1938. Educated in New Jersey primary schools; attended evening classes while in high school, the Art Students League, New York, 1953; studied at Brooklyn Museum, New York, 1956. Served in the Army Reserve Forces, Special Services, Fort Knox, Kentucky, 1956. Married the artist Nancy Holt, q.v., in 1963. Earth sculptor: settled in New York, 1956; visited Rome, 1961; experimented with drugs in 1961 and 1962, and withdrew temporarily from art; started to write, 1964; visited quarries frequently in the United States and Canada from 1965; Artist-Consultant, Tippetts-Abbett-McCarthy and Stratton, architects and engineers, 1966-1967; visited the Yucatan, Mexico, 1969; travelled in England and Wales, visiting Stonehenge and other ruins, 1969; spent years searching for island sites to buy: purchased island in Maine and site in Utah, 1971-72; proposed various schemes to interested mining companies: plans never fulfilled. Lecturer in Painting, Police Athletic League, New York, 1959; Visiting Lecturer, University of New Mexico, Albuquerque, 1973. Recipient: Art Institute of Chicago Award, 1972. *Died* (in airplane crash, in Amarillo, Texas) *20 July 1973.*

Individual Exhibitions:

1958	Artists Gallery, New York
1960	Richard Castelline Gallery, New York
1961	Galleria George Lester, Rome
1966	Dwan Gallery, New York (with Sol Lewitt and Leo Valledor)
1968	Galerie Konrad Fischer, Dusseldorf
	Dwan Gallery, New York
1969	Galleria L'Attico, Rome
	Dwan Gallery, New York
1970	Dwan Gallery, New York
	Ace Gallery, Los Angeles (travelled to the Ace Gallery, Vancouver)
1974	*Drawings,* New York Cultural Center (toured the United States)
1976	John Weber Gallery, New York
1980	Galerie Ricke, Cologne
	Sculpture, Herbert F. Johnson Museum of Art, Cornell University, Ithaca, New York (toured the United States, 1980-82)

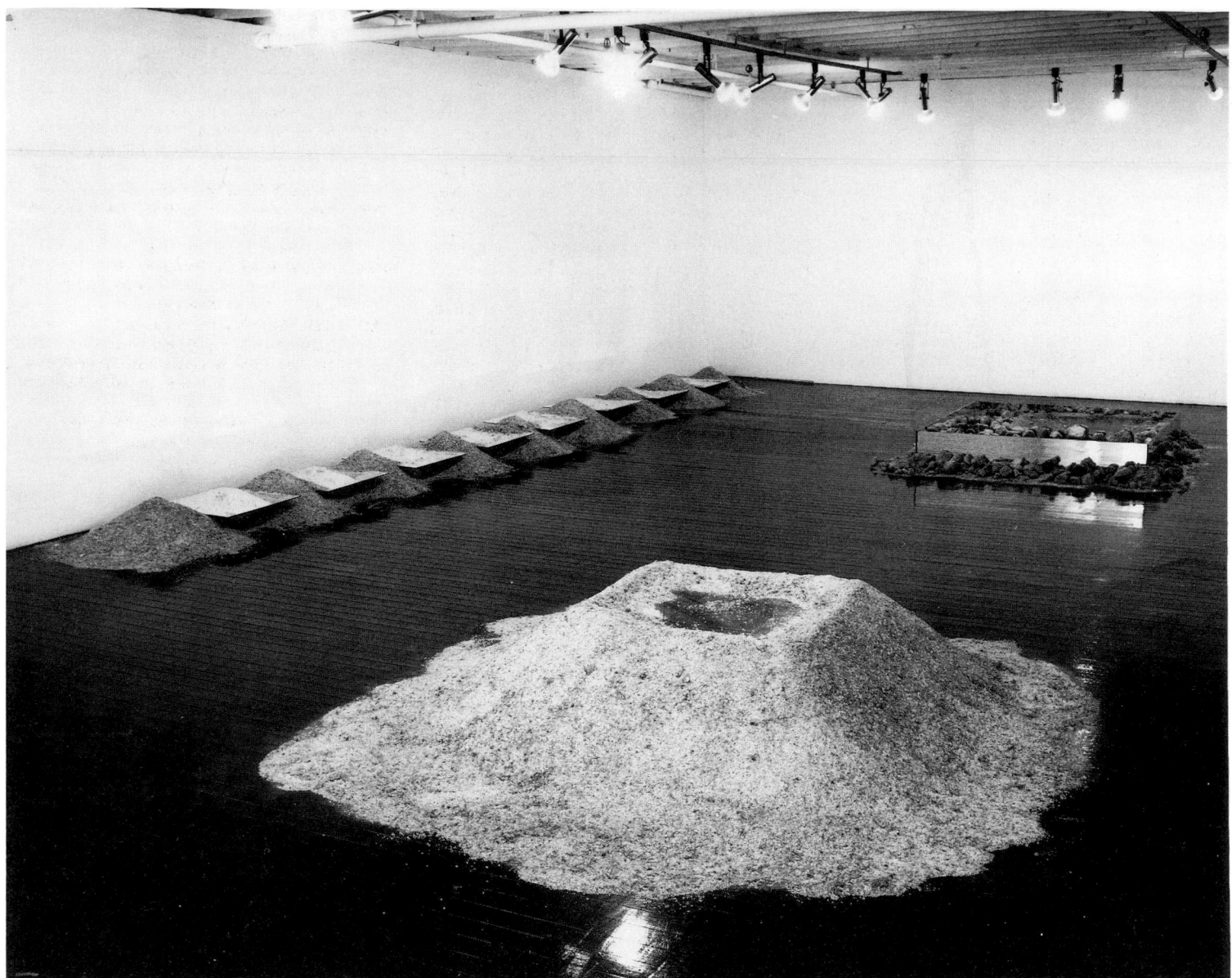

Robert Smithson: *Mirror/Salt Pieces*, 1969

Selected Group Exhibitions:

1965	*Current Art,* Institute of Contemporary Art, Philadelphia
1966	*Primary Structures,* Jewish Museum, New York
1967	*Color, Image and Form,* Detroit Institute of Arts
1968	*Minimal Art,* Gemeentemuseum, The Hague
1969	*When Attitude Becomes Form,* Kunsthalle, Berne (travelled to Museum Haus Lange, Krefeld, West Germany, and the Institute of Contemporary Arts, London)
1970	*Information,* Museum of Modern Art, New York
1971	*Elements of Art,* Museum of Fine Art, Boston
1972	*Documenta,* Kassel, West Germany
1973	*Contemporary Drawing,* Whitney Museum, New York

Collections:

Whitney Museum, New York; Museum of Modern Art, New York; Milwaukee Art Institute; Neue Galerie, Aachen, West Germany.

Publications:

By SMITHSON: book—*The Writings of Robert Smithson,* edited by Nancy Holt, New York 1979; articles—"Donald Judd" in *7 Sculptors,* exhibition catalogue, Philadelphia 1965; "The Crystal Land" in *Harper's Bazaar* (New York),

May 1966; "Entropy and the New Monuments" in *Artforum* (New York), June 1966; "The Domain of the Great Bear," with Mel Bochner, in *Art Voices* (New York), Fall 1966; "Quasi-Infinities and the Waning of Space" in *Arts Magazine* (New York), November 1966; "Toward the Development of an Air Terminal" in *Artforum* (New York), June 1967; "Ultra-Moderne" in *Arts Magazine* (New York), September/October 1967; "Some Voice Thoughts on Museums" in *Arts Magazine* (New York), November 1967; "The Monuments of Passaic" in *Artforum* (New York), December 1967; "Dialogue with Allan Kaprow: What is a Museum?" in *Arts Yearbook,* New York 1967; "Strata: A Geophotographic Fiction" in *Aspen* (Colorado), no. 8, 1967; "A Museum of Language in the Vicinity of Art" in *Art International* (Lugano, Switzerland), March 1968; "The Establishment" in *Metro* (Venice), June 1968; "Minus Twelve" in *Minimal Art,* edited by Gregory Battcock, New York 1968; "A Sedimentation of the Mind: Earth Projects" in *Artforum* (New York), September 1968; "Aerial Art" in *Studio International* (London), February/April 1969; "Incidents of Mirror Travel in the Yucatan" in *Artforum* (New York), September 1969; "Tempo Concreto: Robert Smithson Has Been Interviewed in Rome" by Achille Bonito Oliva in *Domus* (Milan), December 1969; "Discussions with Heizer, Oppenheimer, Smithson" in *Avalanche* (New York), Fall 1970; "Symposium" in *Earth Art,* exhibition catalogue, Ithaca, New York 1970; "A Cinematic Atopia" in *Artforum* (New York), September 1971; "The Spiral Jetty" in *Arts of the Environment,* edited by G. Kepes, New York 1972; "Frederick Law Olmsted and the Dialectical Landscape" in *Artforum* (New York), February 1973; "Robert Smithson on Duchamp: An Interview" by M. Roth in *Artforum* (New York), October 1973; films—*The Spiral Jetty,* with Bob Fiore and Barbara Jarvis, 1970; *Swamp,* with Nancy Holt, 1971; videotape—*East Coast/West Coast,* with Nancy Holt, New York 1969.

On SMITHSON: books—*Arte Povera* by Germano Celant, Milan 1969; *The New Avant-Garde* by Gregoire Muller, Venice and London 1972; *Robert Smithson: Drawings,* exhibition catalogue, by Susan Ginsburg, New York 1974 (includes bibliography); *Robert Smithson: Sculpture,* exhibition catalogue, by Robert Hobbs, Ithaca, New York 1982; articles—"American Sculpture: The New Scene" by Gene Baro in *Studio International* (London), January 1968; "The Spiral Jetty is a Verb!" by D. Wheeler in *Artscanada* (Toronto), April/May 1971; "Robert Smithson's Development" by Lawrence Alloway in *Artforum* (New York), November 1972; "Amarillo Ramp" by Nancy Holt and Liza Bear in *Avalanche* (New York), Fall 1973; "For Robert Smithson" by Philip Leiden in *Art in America* (New York), November/December 1973; "Robert Smithson: Amarillo Ramp" by John Coplans in *Artforum* (New York), April 1974.

Simultaneous with DeMaria and Heizer, Robert Smithson formulated the art movement utilizing earth as sculptural material. "Spiral Jetty," the spiral ridge protrusion of earth and rocks dumped and sculptured in the Great Salt Lake, on last counts partially submerged, has been Smithson's most observed work. Another semi-submerged work, "Partially Buried Woodshed," at Kent State, Ohio, consists of a shed with earth and dirt encroaching upon the sagging structure. Smithson described the work as an experiment in "buried architecture."

Smithson's earthworks have always referred to the history of earth rituals. Particularly after his death, the works began to have a sense of the future as they wore away. To arrive at "Amarillo Ramp" is an individuated, long drive from main roads, and, without a knowledgeable guide, is a barely detectable structure, especially with the overgrowth of weeds and flowers and the weathering of the earth. Sculpture has recently gained such a quality of "found-ness," a sense that *physical detection,* through a process of discovery or categorization, is as important as sculptural *form.* Such sculptures are the Duchampian "found objects" of the 1970's and 1980's. Clearly Smithson's earthworks are not part of the later European art historical tradition, which tended to base sculpture on imagery from painting, rather than basing sculpture on physical relations and physical objects. Sculpture has now regained a physicality, which is always apparent in Smithson's work.

Smithson's "Amarillo Ramp," in Tecovas Lake, is located outside of the city of Amarillo. Amarillo houses the final assembly plant for American nuclear warheads. These two facts parallel each other in their respective fields of art and science. In science, the progress of metallurgy and the development of craft have led to the development of nuclear warheads. Concurrently, the development of art reaches an apex in Smithson's curved mound of earth and rocks. These two products are close in geographical proximity, yet exhibit hundreds of years of disagreement between the disciplines of science and art, and therefore possess the real secret between craft and artifice. Historically, science and art have exhibited characteristics now incorporated into the opposing discipline. Science historically included observations by way of outdoor mounds of earth, while art was a progress of formation of minerals, casting and bronzing. Herein lies the evident advancement of both fields.

—John Robinson

SNELSON, Kenneth.

American. Born in Pendleton, Oregon, 29 June 1927. Studied at the University of Oregon, Eugene, 1946–47; Black Mountain College, North Carolina, under Josef Albers, Buckminster Fuller, and Willem de Kooning, 1947–48; and Académie Montmartre, Paris, under Fernand Léger, 1949. Served in the United States Navy, 1945. Married Katherine Kaufmann in 1972; daughters: Andrea and Nicole. Independent sculptor, since 1960: lives and works in New York. Has taught at Cooper Union, New York; Pratt Institute, Brooklyn, New York; School of Visual Arts, New York; Southern Illinois University, Carbondale; and Yale University, New Haven, Connecticut. Member, Advisory Board, Public Arts Council, New York, since 1974. Recipient: Sculpture Award, New York State Council on the Arts, 1971; Reynolds Metals Sculpture Award, 1974; National Endowment for the Arts Grant, 1974; Prize, Iowa City Sculpture Competition, 1974; DAAD Fellowship, Berlin, 1975; National Endowment for the Arts Grant, 1975; American Institute of Architects Medal, 1981; American Institute of Arts and Letters Award, 1987. DHL: Rensselaer Polytechnic Institute, 1985. Agent: Zabriskie Gallery, 724 Fifth Avenue, New York, New York 10019; and 376 rue Quincampoix, 75004 Paris, France. Address: 140 Sullivan Street, New York, New York 10012, U.S.A.

Individual Exhibitions:

1962	Pratt Institute, Brooklyn, New York
1966	Dwan Gallery, New York
1967	Dwan Gallery, New York
1968	Dwan Gallery, New York
	Bryant Park, New York
1969	Fort Worth Museum of Art, Texas
	Rijksmuseum Kröller-Müller, Otterlo, Netherlands
1970	Kunsthalle, Dusseldorf
1971	Kunstverein, Hannover
1972	John Weber Gallery, New York
	Galerie van der Voort, Ibiza, Spain
1974	Waterside Plaza, New York
1975	Galerie Buchholz, Munich
1977	Nationalgalerie, Berlin
	Wilhelm-Lembruck-Museum, Duisburg, West Germany
	Galerie de Gestlo, Hamburg
1978	*Portrait of an Atom,* Maryland Academy of Science, Baltimore
	Sonnabend Gallery, New York
1981	Hirshhorn Museum, Washington, D.C.
	Albright-Knox Art Gallery, Buffalo, New York
	Zabriskie Gallery, New York
1982	University of Houston, Texas
	University of Pittsburgh, Pennsylvania
	Museum of Science and Industry, Tampa, Florida
	North Carolina Museum of Life and Science, Durham
1983	Impression 5 Museum, Lansing, Michigan
	Schenectady Museum, New York
1984	Zabriskie Gallery, New York
	Columbus Museum of Art, Ohio
	Galerie Zabriskie, Paris
	De Cordova Museum, Lincoln, Massachusetts
1986	Zabriskie Gallery, New York
	Galerie Zabriskie, Paris

Selected Group Exhibitions:

1964	*20th Century Engineering,* Museum of Modern Art, New York
1966	*Whitney Sculpture Annual,* Whitney Museum, New York
1967	*Sculpture of the 60's,* Los Angeles County Museum of Art

Kenneth Snelson: *Mozart,* 1982

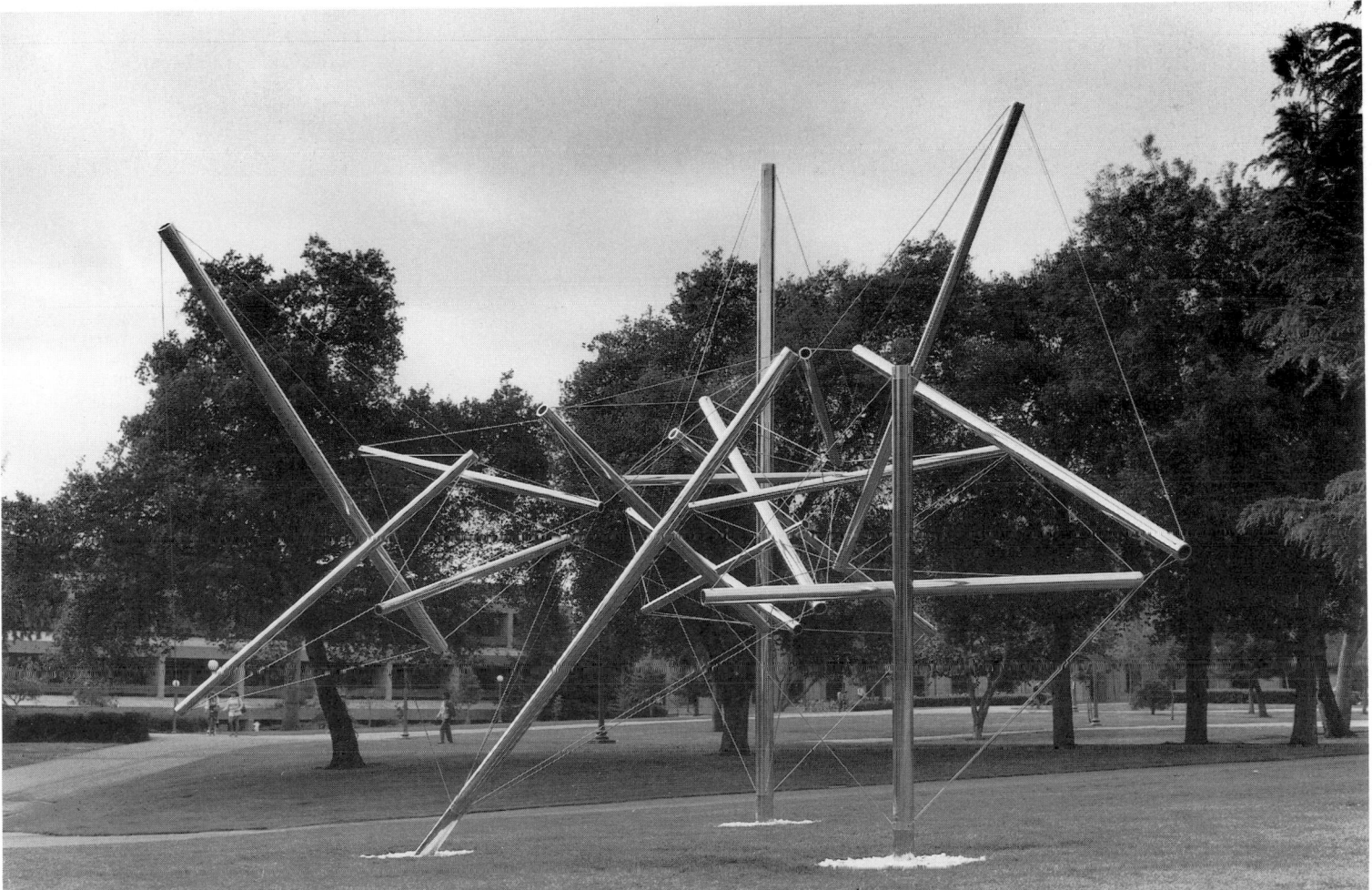

Collections:

Museum of Modern Art, New York; Whitney Museum, New York; Hirshhorn Museum, Washington, D.C.; Hunter Museum of Art, Chattanooga, Tennessee; Art Institute of Chicago; Milwaukee Art Center; Rijksmuseum Kröller-Müller, Otterlo, Netherlands; Stedelijk Museum, Amsterdam.

Publications:

By SNELSON: articles—"A Design for the Atom" in *Industrial Design* (New York), February 1963; "Proprietary Protection" in *Progressive Architect* (New York), June 1964; "How Primary is Structure" in *Art Voices* (New York), Summer 1966; "An Interview with Kenneth Snelson," with John Coplans, in *Artforum* (New York), vol. V, no. 7, 1967.

On SNELSON: books—*Struktur und Spannung*, exhibition catalogue by Laszlo Glozer, Hannover 1971; *Kenneth Snelson*, exhibition catalogue with essay by Howard Fox, Washington, D.C. 1981; articles—"Kenneth Snelson: Dialogue Between Stress and Tension" by Gregory Battcock in *Arts Magazine* (New York), February 1968; "Kenneth Snelson: The Elegant Solution" by Stephen Kurtz in *Artnews* (New York), October 1968; "Snelson and Structure" by Deborah Perlberg in *Artforum* (New York), May 1975; "Kenneth Snelson: Straddling the Abyss Between Art and Science" by Richard Whelan in *Art News* (New York), February 1981; "Full Circle" by Charles Hagen in *Camera Arts* (New York), January/February 1982.

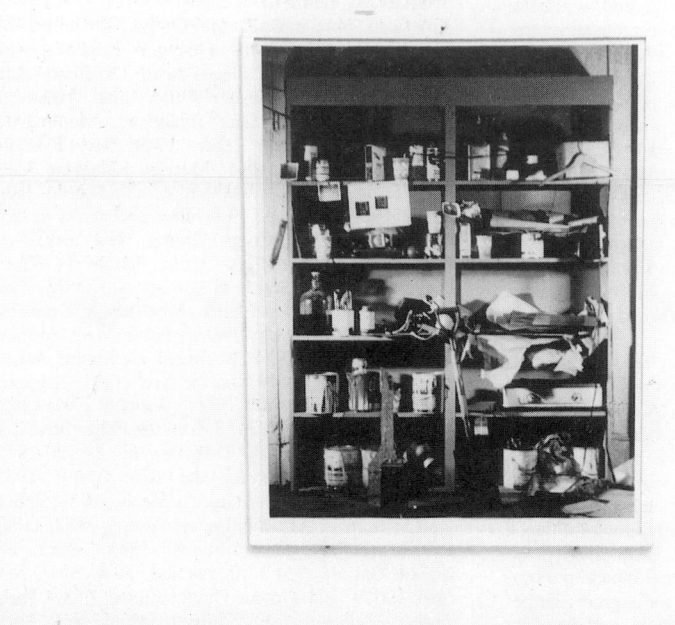

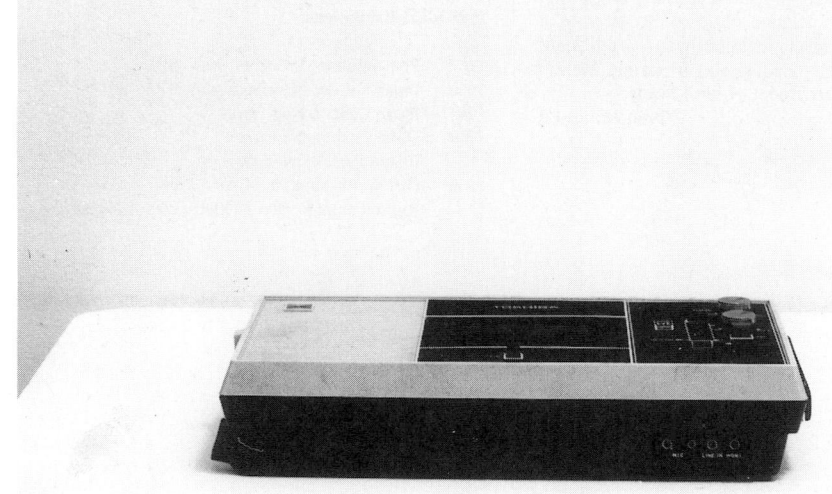

Michael Snow: *A Casing Shelved*, 1970

SNOW, Michael (James Aleck).
Canadian. Born in Toronto, Ontario, 10 December 1929. Educated at Upper Canada College, Toronto, 1946–51; studied at Ontario College of Art, Toronto, 1951–55. Married the artist and filmmaker Joyce Wieland, *q.v.* in 1959. Independent artist, musician, filmmaker and photographer, Toronto, since 1955. Professor of Advanced Film, Yale University, New Haven, Connecticut, 1970; Visiting Artist, Nova Scotia College of Art and Design, Halifax, 1970, 1974, and Ontario College of Art, Toronto, 1973, 1974, 1976. Also, a musician: member of the CCMC, Toronto, since 1974. Recipient: Purchase Award, *Winnipeg Exhibition*, 1958; Canada Council Arts Grant, 1959, and Senior Arts Grant, 1966, 1973, 1980; Henry Street Settlement Exhibition Award, New York, 1964; Guggenheim Fellowship, 1972; Independent Experimental Film Award, Los Angeles Film Critics Association, 1983. LL.D.: Brock University, St. Catherines, Ontario, 1975. Order of Canada, 1981. Agent: The Isaacs Gallery, Toronto. Address: c/o The Isaacs Gallery, 179 John Street, Toronto, Ontario M5T 1X3, Canada.

Individual Exhibitions:

Individual Film Screenings: Filmmakers Cinematique, New York, 1967, 1968, 1969; Gallery of Modern Art, New York, 1969; Whitney Museum, New York, 1969; Museum of Modern Art, New York, 1969, 1970; Edinburgh Film Festival, 1969, 1975; The Jewish Film Museum, New York, 1970; Pesaro Film Festival, Italy, 1973; *Rameau's Nephew*, world premiere, National Gallery, Ottawa, 1974; Cinematique Quebecoise, Montreal, retrospective, 1975; Museum of Modern Art, New York, retrospective, 1976; Anthology of Film Archives, New York 1975, 1976; Art Gallery of Ontario, Toronto, 1981; Osterreichisches Filmmuseum, Vienna, 1981; Canada House, London, 1983; University of California, Los Angeles, 1983.

Selected Group Exhibitions:

1962	*Canadian Painting Today*, J. B. Speed Museum, Louisville, Kentucky
1966	*The Satirical in Art*, York University, Toronto
1969	*Anti-Illusion: Procedures and Materials*, Whitney Museum, New York
1971	*Prospect 71*, Kunsthalle, Dusseldorf
1973	*Options and Alternatives*, Yale University, New Haven, Connecticut
1977	*Documenta 6*, Museum Fridericianum, Kassel, West Germany
1979	*Re-Visions*, Whitney Museum, New York
1985	*Aurora Borealis*, Centre d'Art Contemporain, Montreal

Collections:

National Gallery of Canada, Ottawa; Canada Council Art Bank, Ottawa; Art Gallery of Ontario, Toronto; Montreal Museum of Fine Arts; Winnipeg Art Gallery; Museum of Modern Art, New York; Philadelphia Museum of Art; Milwaukee Art Center, Wisconsin.

Publications:

By SNOW: books—*Place of Meeting*, with text by Ray Souster, Toronto 1962; *Michael Snow: A Survey*, with text by P. Adam Sitney, Toronto 1970; *Cover to Cover*, Halifax, Nova Scotia 1975; *High School*, Toronto 1980; article—"Passage" in *Artforum* (New York), September 1971; films—*A to Z*, 1956; *New York Eye and Ear Control (A Walking Woman Work)*, 1964; *Short Shave*, 1965; *Wavelength*, 1967; *Standard Time*, 1967; *Back and Forth*, 1969; *One Second in Montreal*, 1969; *Dripping Water*, 1969; *Side Seat Paintings Slides Sound Films*, 1970; *La Region Centrale*, 1970–71; *Table Top Dolly*, 1972; *Rameau's Nephew by Diderot (Thanks to Dennis Young) by Wilma Schoen*, 1974; *Presents*, 1980; sound recordings—*The Artists Jazz Band*, 1974; *CCMC*, 5 vols., 1974–80; *Michael Snow: Music for Whistling, Piano, Microphone, and Tape Recorder*, 1975; *The Artists Jazz Band: Live at the Edge*, 1977.

On SNOW: books—*Expanded Cinema* by Gene Youngblood, New York, 1970; *Negative Space* by Manny Farber, New York 1971; *Experimental Cinema* by David Curtis London 1971; *Visionary Film* by P. Adams Sitney, New York 1974; *Une Histoire du Cinema* by Peter Kubelka and others, Paris 1976; *Documenta 6/Band 2*, exhibition catalogue, by Klaus Honnef and Evelyn Weiss, Cologne 1977; *Michael Snow*, exhibition catalogue, Lucerne 1979; *Snow Seen* by Regina Cornwell, Toronto 1980; *Michael Snow: Selected Photographic Works*, exhibition catalogue with essays by Pierre Theberge and Christopher Dewdney, Los Angeles 1983; *Walking Woman Works: Michael Snow 1961–67*, exhibition catalogue with text by Louise Dompierre, Kingston 1983.

A supremely cerebral artist, Michael Snow has produced an oeuvre marked by an almost philosophical examination of perception. Over the course of some thirty years—as painter, sculptor, filmmaker, musician, holographer and bookmaker—Snow has continually experimented in order to perceive the world without regard to convention and tradition. His artistic enterprise differs profoundly from other protean efforts in modern art; within his Renaissance scope of activities Snow, like Leonardo himself, is a skeptic—one who believes that increased knowledge only illuminates a vaster abyss. From his well-known, ubiquitous *Walking Woman* series (1961–67), in which a singular, virtually identical silhouette of a walking woman adorned some 200 works in assorted media, Snow has developed an art that, in its stylistic and technological diversity, questions the function of culture today.

Snow's film *Wavelength* (1967)—an obsessive 45-minute zoom across a loft space to a photograph of the sea—defined the artist's commitment to a "new cinema of structure." Eschewing the human subject and its intrinsic gaze, the artist was freer to examine the pure optical conditions of seeing—all the subliminal physiological experience hitherto subsumed by narrative.

Within this objective perceptual field, Snow began isolating certain characteristics specific to film (e.g., the contrast of stillness and movement), an activity

that paralleled the kind of purity of medium espoused by Greenbergian late-modernism. For Snow, however, such formalism was neither exclusive nor to be experienced autonomously, unrelated to reality and to a developing critical, theoretical discourse. Works like *Wavelength* or *La Région Centrale* (1971)—a three-hour film consisting entirely of images shot in the bush in Quebec in which the main character is the camera itself—are as much about film as they are about narrative or representation. The artist's equation of *perception* with film allows a different type of psychology or subconscious to emerge. Of central importance, therefore, is the artist's device of framing, of asserting a disturbingly intractable perspective. In his video installation *De La* (1969–71), for example, a rotating mechanical sculpture—actually an elaborately engineered camera designed by the artist—projected images on four circumscribing video screens. The spectator's perceptual field was constantly challenged and exceeded by the swirling projection of images around him.

Snow's use of cinematic repetition, which parallels his 1960s collaborations with New Music composers Philip Glass and Steve Reich, elicits a hyperacute sensitivity from the viewer. Snow, in fact, has carried his photographic and film techniques to his own musical compositions. In the tradition of Duchamp and Cage, the artist's inclusion of chance and the "raw process" of art-making became part of the finished composition. His liner notes to his solo album *Music For Piano, Whistling, Microphone and Tape Recorder* (1975), for example, indicates that he placed a microphone on top of his piano and turned up the recording volume in order to make "a part of the recording process a part of the music" by allowing ambient sounds (such as a ringing telephone) to register on the master tape.

Sythesizing his earlier multiplicity of techniques, Snow has recently worked in holography. His installation at Vancouver's Expo 86—*The Spectral Image*—was seen in a vast cathedral-like hall illuminated by colored filters, a work that continues his implementation of the most advanced technology into his art. Snow's work in the recent exhibition *Visionary Apparatus* at the Massachusetts Institute of Technology's Hayden Gallery, like *The Spectral Image*, resounds with the added dimension of laser-pulse holographic illusionism, a sophisticated technology that once again attests to the artist's conviction in the mutually redemptive relationship between art and science.

—Mason Klein

SONDERBORG, K. R. H.

Danish. Born Karl Richard Horst Hofmann in Sonderborg, 5 April 1923; later adopted his name "Sonderborg." Studied painting, under Ewald Becker-Carus, in Hamburg, 1946, and at the Landeskunstschule, Hamburg, 1947–49; studied printmaking, under S. W. Hayter, at Atelier 17, Paris, 1953. Imprisoned by the Gestapo, Hamburg-Fuhlsbuttel, 1941–42; escaped, working as a sales man for an export company, Hamburg, 1942–45; full-time artist since 1949, in Hamburg, subsequently in New York and Copenhagen: Member, "Zen 49" artists group, 1953. Recipient: Lichtwark Preis, Hamburg, 1955; Karl-Ernst-Osthaus Preis, Hagen, West Germany, 1955. Agent: Galerie Karl Flinker, 25 rue de Tournon, 75006 Paris, France. Address: Kongens Nytorv 1, 1050 Copenhagen, Denmark.

Individual Exhibitions:

1956	Kestner-Gesellschaft, Hannover
	Galleri Samlaren, Stockholm
1957	Kunstverein, Cologne
	Galerie Springer, West Berlin
	Galerie René Drouin, Paris
	Galerie Van de Loo, Munich
1959	*Neue Bilder*, Galerie Van de Loo, Essen
1960	*Peintures, Dessins*, Galerie Karl Flinker, Paris
1961	Lefebre Gallery, New York
1962	Galerie Handschin, Basle
	Galerie Schmela, Dusseldorf
	Kunstverein, Freiburg
	Galerie Müller, Stuttgart
	Galerie Karl Flinker, Paris
1963	Galleri Blanche, Stockholm
1964	Tokyo Gallery
1965	Galerie Karl Flinker, Paris
	Lefebre Gallery, New York
	Gemalde, Zeichnungen, Kunstverein, Cologne
	Stedelijk Museum, Amsterdam
	Schilderijen, Tekeningen, Stedelijk Van Abbemuseum, Eindhoven, Netherlands
	Tuschen, Gimpel und Hanover Galerie, Zurich
	First British Exhibition, Stone Gallery, Newcastle upon Tyne
1966	Louisiana Museum, Humlebaek, Denmark
	Galleria Stendhal, Milan
	Hammerlunds Kunsthandel, Oslo
1967	Guggenheim Museum, New York
	Carnegie Institute, Pittsburgh
1968	Galerie de France, Paris
	Galerie Daniel Gervis, Paris
	Manus-Presse, Stuttgart
1971	Galerie Daniel Gervis, Paris
1976	Galerie Daniel Gervis, Paris
1978	Kunstverein, Sonderborg, Denmark
1979	Galerie im Haus Behr, Stuttgart
	Galerie am Markt, Schwabisch Hall, West Germany
1983	Galerie Hubert Winter, Vienna
1985	Kunstverein, Augsburg, West Germany
	Galerie Nothhelfer, West Berlin
	XPO Galerie, Hamburg
	Staatsgalerie, Stuttgart
1986	Graphische Sammlung, Stuttgart

Selected Group Exhibitions:

1952	*Zen 49*, Galerie Bohler, Munich
1954	*Art After 1945*, Stedelijk Museum, Amsterdam
1958	*Biennale*, Venice
1959	*Documenta*, Kassel, West Germany
1960	*Guggenheim International*, Guggenheim Museum, New York
1963	*Bienal*, Sao Paulo
1965	*Painting Without a Brush*, Institute of Contemporary Art, Boston
1973	*Kunst In Deutschland 1898–1973*, Kunsthalle, Hamburg (travelled) to the Stadtische Galerie im Lenbachhaus, Munich)
1981	*Westkunst*, Messehallen, Cologne
1983	*Informel 1953–83*, Kunstverein, Lingen, West Germany

Collections:

Kunsthalle, Hamburg; Nationalgalerie, West Berlin; Wallraf-Richartz Museum, Cologne; Stedelijk Van Abbemuseum, Eindhoven, Netherlands; Louisiana Museum, Humlebaek, Denmark; Guggenheim Museum, New York.

Publications:

On SONDERBORG: books—*Sonderborg: Neue Bilder*, exhibition catalogue, with text by Carl Laszlo, Essen 1959; *Sonderborg: Peintures, Dessins*, exhibition catalogue, with text by Will Grohman, Paris 1960; *Sonderborg*, exhibition catalogue, with text by Annette Michelson, Paris 1962; *K. R. H. Sonderborg: VII Bienal de Sao Paulo 1963*, exhibition catalogue, with text by Werner Schmalenbach, Dusseldorf 1963; *Sonderborg*, exhibition catalogue, with text by Otto Hahn, New York 1965; *K. R. H. Sonderborg: Gemalde, Zeichnungen*, exhibition catalogue, with text by Werner Haftmann, Cologne 1965; *Sonderborg: Schilderijen, Tekeningen*, exhibition catalogue, with text by Werner Haftmann, Eindhoven, Netherlands; *K. R. H. Sonderborg: First British Exhibition*, exhibition catalogue, with text by Friedrich Bayl, Otto Hahn and Thomas T. Ichinose, Newcastle upon Tyne 1965; *K. R. H. Sonderborg: Tuschen*, exhibition catalogue, Zurich

1965; *K. R. H. Sonderborg*, exhibition catalogue, with text by Willem Sandberg, Paris 1968; *Kunst in Deutschland 1898–1973*, exhibition catalogue, with text by Werner Hofmann, Hamburg 1973; *K. R. H. Sonderborg: Arbeiten auf Papier*, exhibition catalogue, with text by Hans Platschek, Kurt Leonhard and others, Stuttgart 1985.

The earliest painting by K. R. H. Sonderborg—on a canvas given to him by his father when he was 15 years old—was destroyed in an air raid over Hamburg. It probably has little bearing upon the subsequent development of this Danish-born artist but it does imply that Sonderborg's talent even from the start had a habit of cropping up in a variety of unlikely addresses. In a relatively short time he was able to install himself and his art in Cornwall, the Hebrides, Orkneys, Shetlands, Scotland, Paris and the United States. Perhaps something of this hither and thither existence is reflected in his pictures. They certainly have a staccato beat, a rhythm not unlike the clatter of a typewriter under the fingers of a fastmoving stenographer.

Sonderborg's nearest parallel in contemporary art is Erwin Bechthold, but even here there is no more than a superficial resemblance. Their approach is different. Only the end result shows some degree of kinship.

Three clues point to the sources of inspiration in Sonderborg's pictures—especially since his time in the United States. First there is his absorption in machinery and its operation. Then there is his hand-camera pressed into service whenever he sees a detail or element of the contemporary world that he believes to be visually worth recording (parts of machinery and angle shots of the industrial and urban scenes). And finally there are the scraps, clippings and cutouts he can harvest from the media.

The salad he mixes out of all three is frequently the raw meat of his pictures, although all such ingredients undergo a Sonderborg change before they are finalised in pictorial form. Much of his work is basically black and white, but when colours are involved, these tend to cleave to the characteristics of a technical universe.

Not that they are always the portrait of technical imagery. It is just that the final Sonderborg transformation makes them appear so. A specific example of the stages through which this alchemic process can go is provided by four pictures based upon a newsprint photo of President Kennedy's golf kit. The first of these was painted in 1962, but execution of the entire series continued over four years. To give some idea of a Sonderborg synthesis it should be mentioned that in the second picture the JFK golf bag somehow became involved in and absorbed by the controls room of Karlsruhe's atomic energy plant.

Sonderborg is an inspired collector. He has gathered together many of the simplest mechanical statements—a metal coil, a spark, a cog—and set them up in contrast with some of the most complex contemporary mechanisms.

—Sheldon Williams

SONFIST, Alan.

American. Born in New York, 26 May 1946. Studied at the Art Students League, New York, 1963; studied painting and art education, Western Illinois University, Macomb, 1964–67, B.A. 1967; also studied at the Pratt Institute, New York, summers 1965, 1966, Ohio State University, Columbus, 1967–68, and painting and sculpture at Hunter College, New York, 1968–69, M.F.A. 1969. Independent artist, since 1970. Instructor at numerous universities and colleges, throughout the United States, since 1967. Recipient: Graham Foundation grants, 1971, 1972; Chase Manhattan Foundation for Environmental and Fine Arts Grant, 1975; National Endowment for the Arts grant, 1975, 1978, 1979, 1981; Creative Artists

Public Service Grant, New York, 1977; United States Information Service Grant, to Paris, 1977; Con Edison Foundation Grant, New York, 1978; Citibank Foundation Grant, New York, 1978; Australian Arts Council Travel Grant, 1981; New Zealand Travel Grant, 1984. Address: 205 Mulberry Street, New York, New York 10012, U.S.A.

Individual Exhibitions:

1970	Reese Palley Gallery, New York
	The Nature of Things, Harcus-Krakow Gallery, Boston
	Star Chartings and Others, Deson-Zaks Gallery, Chicago
	Outdoor Crystal Sculpture, Finch College Museum of Art, New York
	Diagramma, Milan
1972	Institute of Contemporary Arts, London
	Army Ants: Patterns and Structures, Automation House, New York
	Sonfist Art, Akron Institute, Ohio
	Lanscapes, Paley and Lowe Gallery, New York
1964	Carl Solway Gallery, Cincinnati, Ohio
	Galerie Thelen, Cologne
1975	*Running Dead Animal*, Stefanotty Gallery, New York
	Time-Landscape, Finch College Museum of Art, New York
	Autobiography of Alan Sonfist, Herbert F. Johnson Museum of Art, Cornell University, Ithaca, New York
	Autobiography of an Abandoned Animal Hole, Adiene Gallery, New York
1976	*Autobiography of Hemlock Forest*, Galerie Massimo Valsecchi, Milan
	Galleria Cavallino, Venice
	Adiene Gallery, New York
	Autobiography of Time Landscape, 112 Greene Street Workshop, New York
	Autobiography of Time Landscape, Centre Cultural Americain, Paris
1977	Carl Solway Gallery, Cincinnati, Ohio
	Neue Galerie Sammlung Ludwig, Aachen, West Germany
	Light Gallery, New York
	Museum of Fine Arts, Boston
	Galerie Bama, Paris
1978	*Public Monuments*, Neuberger Museum, Purchase, New York
	Leo Castelli Gallery, New York
	National Collection of Fine Arts, Smithsonian Institution, Washington, D.C.
1979	Multiples Gallery, New York
	Monument to Atlanta, High Museum of Art, Atlanta
	State University of New York, Stony Brook
1980	Albright-Knox Art Gallery, Buffalo, New York
1981	J. B. Speed Art Museum, Louisville, Kentucky
	National Gallery of Art, Melbourne, Victoria
	Marion Goodman Gallery, New York
1982	Carl Solway Gallery, Cincinnati
	Lowe Art Museum, Coral Gables, Florida
1984	Corcoran Gallery of Art, Washington, D.C.
	Galleria del Cavallino, Venice
1986	Diane Brown Gallery, New York
	Nelson Museum, Kansas City, Missouri

Selected Group Exhibitions:

1969	*Invisible Image*, School of Visual Arts, New York
1971	*The Nature of Things*, Harcus-Krakow Gallery, Boston
1973	*Trees of Manhattan*, Finch College Museum of Art, New York
1974	*Projekt '74*, Wallraf-Richartz Museum, Cologne
1975	*Biennale*, Paris
1977	*Documenta*, Kassel, West Germany
1979	*Views of America*, Penthouse, Museum of Modern Art, New York
1981	*Natur-Skulptur*, Kunstverein, Stuttgart
1982	*Mapped Art*, Toledo Museum of Art, Ohio
1985	*The Artist as Social Designer*, Los Angeles County Museum of Art

Collections:

Museum of Modern Art, New York; Everson Museum, Syracuse, New York; Museum of Fine Arts, Boston; Akron Art Institute, Ohio; Allen Museum of Fine Arts, Oberlin College, Ohio; Museum of Contemporary Art, Chicago; High Museum, Atlanta; Museum of Fine Art, Dallas; Wallraf-Richartz Museum, Cologne; Power Institute of Fine Arts, Sydney.

Publications:

By SONFIST: videotapes—*Tiger-Chance-Kill*, 1976; *Nature's Time, Artificial Time*, 1976.

On SONFIST: books—*Science and Technology in Art Today* by Jonathan Benthall, New York 1972; *Art and the Future* by Douglas Davis, New York 1973; *Autobiography of Alan Sonfist*, exhibition catalogue, by Lawrence Alloway, Ithaca, New York 1975; *Unbuilt America*, edited by Carson and Sky, New York 1976; *The American Land* by Joshua C. Taylor, New York 1979; *Art of the Seventies* by Edward Lucie Smith, London 1980; *Overlay* by Lucy Lippard, New York 1983; *Artforms: An Introduction to the Visual Arts* by Duane and Sarah Preble, New York 1985.

My body is my museum; it's my history. It collects and absorbs observations-interactions. It is the deciphering of these recordings that I project into the outside world. My boundaries define the world of Art. I clarify my own common boundaries in relationship to the outside whether it be the room I exist in, the country I exist in, the universe I exist in. By adding other awareness, I am constantly redefining my boundaries and projecting these awarenesses into my art.

My work deals with the idea that the world is always in a state of flux. My art deals with the rhythm of the universe. The pieces are part of the rhythm. A plant grows in cycles—a man moves in cycles—my work tries to bring about awareness of these movements. My works are transitions—they provoke associations. One has to mediate with my work to gain understanding. It is not the beginning or the end that I am concerned with, but the energy that is given or received through communication with my art.

—Alan Sonfist

The links between nature and Alan Sonfist's art are varied and numerous. They include wet canvases in which mildew takes gradual possession of the linen surface and containers of micro-organisms, in which fungoid and bacterial growth generate changing displays. These are usually enclosed in sealed boxes, a form of containment extended into plexiglass columns with crystalline structures reactive to light, heat, and the spectator's presence. To quote the artist: "the growth of the work is characterized by patterns of indeterminacy, since a multiplicity of natural variables creates unforeseen occurrences." The technology involved and the neat craft should not obscure the fact that Sonfist's basic interest is in nature and not in the artifacts by which it is contained.

Another nature-based piece is the celebrated colony of army ants (1972) whose movements in search patterns for food revealed the graphic shape of a society. This notion recurs, in an extraordinary metamorphosis, in Sonfist's later work, "Abandoned Animal Hole," a cast of the warren of tunnels built by muskrats. The cement, pushed a section at a time into the burrows, converts hidden space into solid form in a way that constitutes a monument to the morphology of branching structure. It is an underground "tree." In these works Sonfist initiated processes and made them visible within a limited zone, such as a box, or a room, or a joined casting. In addition to the enactment of organic process he makes works that consist of objects removed from the unbounded field of the world. Here he subtracts from an existing endless process rather than beginning new ones, as in "Collection Bags," rows of soft containers for found objects. These consisted of things taken from the

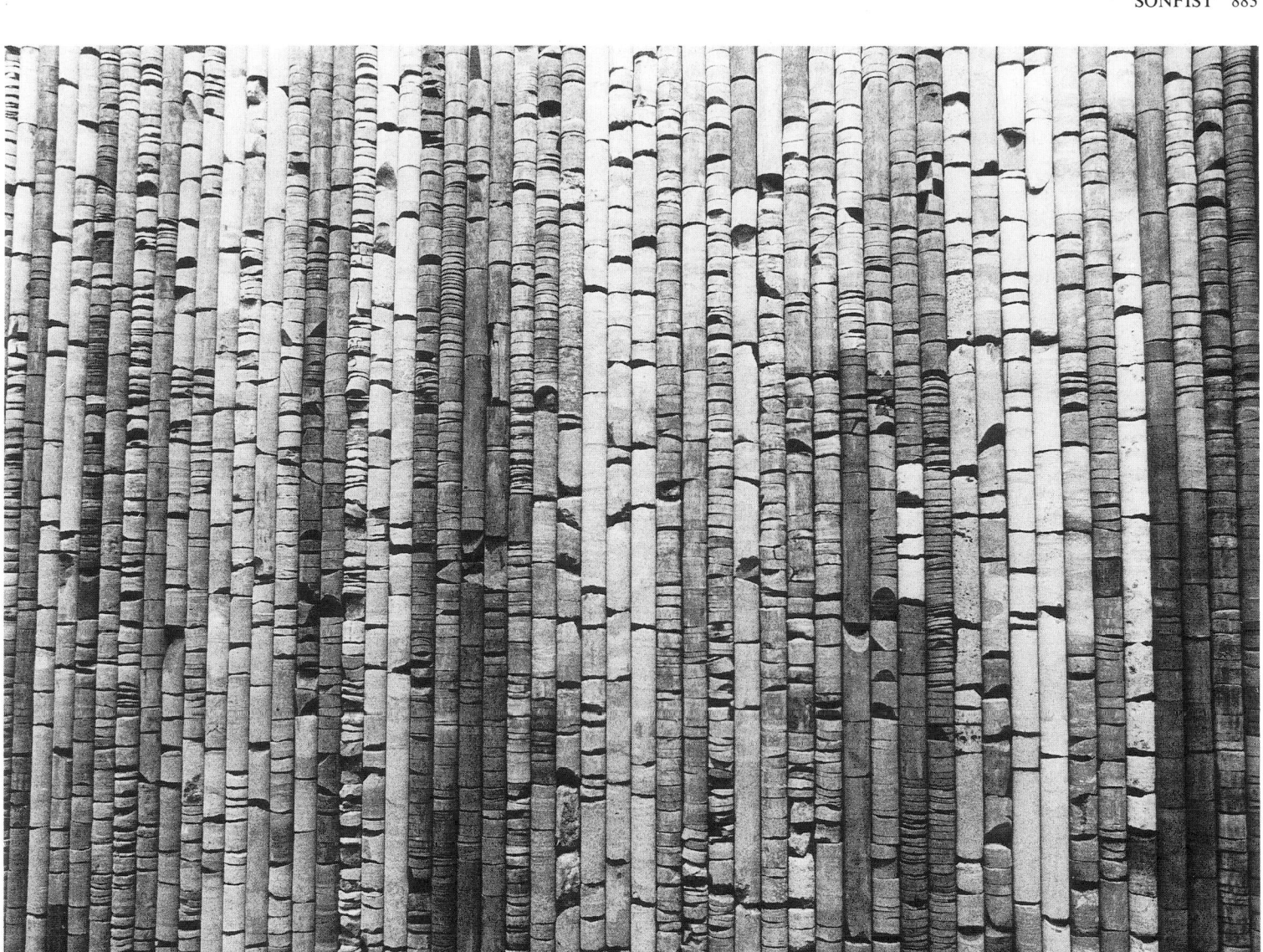

Alan Sonfist: *Wall of Earth*, 1978

ground: twigs from the forest floor, for example, not parts broken off growing trees, a restraint that is characteristic of Sonfist's approach to nature. These finds are sometimes accompanied by texts:

I could feel the lines on my skin. The cold wind passed. The twigs formed their own lines moving back and forth from the rock.

He has also expressed a great kinship with Asher B. Durand, the Hudson River School painter. What touched Sonfist, leading him to visit the site in Troy of one of Durand's paintings, was a letter of 1881:

All the license that the artist can claim or desire is to choose the time and place were Nature displays her chief perfections, whether of beauty or majesty, repose or action.

The interaction of artist and nature is the basis of Sonfist's interest in Durand. On sites similar to Durand's Sonfist collects small objects that are an equivalent of the plentitude of details in the landscape paintings of Durand.

In the works in which he uses material collected at the site Sonfist lovingly turns random samples into precious quotations. Nature is evoked as a limitless field, the found parts of which, the details, transported from the site by Sonfist are not restructured in ways that suggest their solidification. On the contrary, the "non-site," to use a term of Robert Smithson's, preserve a kind of serious nonchalance, as if the relics meant too much to change after the crucial acts of removal and storage. Placing the twigs, the stones, the feathers, is equivalent to preservation rather than to designing.

Sonfist's ability to reveal the forms of communities and processes and his participation in limitless nature have been recognized and well-discussed, but another aspect of his work is less familiar. To work with natural processes as media is of course to work in time, but the definition of time in his art is not restricted to this sense. There is also time as it relates the artist himself to his work, which is the central theme of the exhibition *The Autobiography of Alan Sonfist*. To understand the implication of this it helps to know that in 1970 he wanted to call his first exhibition *Retrospective*, but the gallery objected. The reason for using the word, which usually refers to an exhibition that summarizes a working life by looking backwards, is that this show represented, to quote the artist, "pieces of my past" and was thus the projection into the present of experiences that preceded the exhibition.

The extension of Sonfist's work in time is a central fact of his esthetic. To the extent that any work of art survives it is a projection of the past into what I shall call the unknown present. Sonfist is concerned with time beyond this and, in effect, dissolves the possibility of dating art at all, or at least reduces dating to an arbitrary convention. He does not use dates to indicate the time of production, but to indicate sequence. All his works can be viewed as 1946 *et seq.;* "my first experience was air." Sonfist considers that the materialization of a work of art, though obviously a crucial step if the work process is to be legible to others, has been over-emphasized. In his work he is "bringing back images of my past" and, therefore, "each piece will have its autobiography." His art is authenticated by its place in a continuum that includes all phases of the artist's life. Thus the act of dating has the effect of isolating art from the full range of genetic elements.

There is a sense in which genetic dating is applicable to all artists, on the principle of Whistler's incisive answer to the question of how long it took to do one of his paintings: "all my life." There is more to it than this, however, because the content of Sonfist's art is oriented, to a remarkable extent, toward memory and memories. Hence his anti-periodization protects his life as a continuum in which early experiences occur as survivals, reconstructions, and fantasies. Sonfist would not differentiate between these states: all are means to bind his experiences of life into unity. He writes: "My body is my museum, it's my history," and as such it is subject to the same changes in time as his work. Sonfist's offer of his body after death to the Museum of Modern Art to be preserved in the collection is a logical extension of the fusion of the ideas of process and time. Supporting this view of the self as subject-matter is his temperamental inclination towards recollection, activated by surviving drawings, early diaries and scrap books, and what Sonfist calls "vague experiences" of growth and discovery as a child. Typically his tree pieces, which consist of flattened tracings of the trunks, were initiated by the rediscovery of a tree in the Bronx Park that he had climbed in childhood:

> The distances of my hand had changed and the surface of the tree had also. I can remember the feel—the smell—and the taste of the tree as I once had.

Art is not presumed to be complete when it is done: both the work's prior and subsequent history force us to a perpetual recontextualization. In the chronology of "Running Dead Animal," for example, Sonfist proposes such events as: "1953: upon tight-roping on a waterfall I woke up in a hospital with my face bandaged" and the period 1954–59 included monthly visits to the Museum of Natural History "to observe the stuffed animals." "1959: sat with an antelope in its cage. 1961: my brother shot a bird and I cried." Some of these events are repeated in genetic chronology of other works, some not. Thus the concept of art as the product of potent cause is diffused over the life of the artist. The only analogy to this historical layering of the work becoming the form of the work that I can think of is René Char's *Arrière-Histoire de Poème Pulverise*, in which annotations by the poet in a copy of a book become a book added to the original. Char records his hesitation about regarding the manuscript notes on equal terms with the poems, but he is wrong to feel that it was necessary to defend the primacy of the poems. What we get from the notes is a relationship, a connection between poetry and what Char calls "the awkward and untenable world that served in its making." "Each poem is accompanied by its confidential marginalia, like a whispering stream."

If we estimate Sonfist's art as beginning in 1946 we should not expect the chronologies to end with the production of the work and in fact the "autobiographies" that accompany each work must be revised, like the provenance of paintings, to bring them up to date. The work's meaning therefore is not something that emerges on its completion and exists thereafter in absolute form. On the contrary art demonstrates a principle of delayed coherence: it is a structure that can change and our knowledge of it changes also. Thus the "autobiographies" will gradually extend as they become a history of spectator-responses (interpretations) and itinerary (socially-conditioned distribution) attached to the work. In the earlier pieces the presence of the spectator initiated physical changes in Sonfist's work (crystal formation, movement of a school of fish), changes that occurred unpredictably but logically within the limits of the system prepared by the artist. The extension of the autobiography of the work incorporates the viewer in another way, drawing on our cognitive and social interaction with the artist via the work of art.

—Lawrence Alloway

SONNIER, Keith.

American. Born in Mamou, Louisiana, in 1941. Educated at the University of Southwestern Louisiana, Lafayette, 1959–63, B.A. 1963; travelled and studied in France, 1963–64; studied at Rutgers University, New Brunswick, New Jersey, 1965–66, M.F.A. 1966. Full-time artist: now lives and works in New York. Recipient: Guggenheim Fellowship, 1974; First Prize, *Tokyo Prints Biennale*, 1974. Agent: Leo Castelli Gallery, New York. Address: c/o Leo Castelli Gallery, 420 West Broadway, New York, New York 10012, U.S.A.

Individual Exhibitions:

1966   Douglass College, New Brunswick, New Jersey
1968   Galerie Ricke, Cologne
1970   Leo Castelli Gallery, New York
        Ace Gallery, Los Angeles
        Stedelijk Van Abbemuseum, Eindhoven, Netherlands
1971   *Projects*, Museum of Modern Art, New York
        Galerie Ricke, Cologne
1972   Leo Castelli Gallery, New York
        Galerie Ricke, Cologne
1974   *Radio Mix*, Leo Castelli Gallery, New York
        Seder-Creigh Gallery, Coronado, California
1975   Leo Castelli Gallery, New York
        Galerie Ricke, Cologne
        Ace Gallery, Los Angeles
1976   *ABACA Code*, Leo Castelli Gallery, New York
        ABACA Code, Hand Cast Paper Sculpture and Other Work 1969–76, Seder/Creigh Gallery, Coronado, California
1977   Ace Gallery, Los Angeles
1978   Leo Castelli Gallery, New York (drawings)
        Castelli Graphics, New York (lithographs)
        Galerie Ricke, Cologne
        Simultaneous Regional Editions, Rosamund Felsen Gallery, Los Angeles
        Porte-Voix Audio Installation, The Clocktower, New York
1979   *BA-O-BA SEL Series*, Museum Haus Lange, Krefeld, West Germany
        Expanded SEL Series, Leo Castelli Gallery, New York
        AM/FM Radio Installation, Galerie Michele Lachowsky, Brussels
        Porte-Voix, Eric Fabre Gallery, Paris
        Porte-Vue, Centre Georges Pompidou, Paris
1980   *Pictographs*, Tony Shafrazi Gallery, New York
        Galerie France Morin, Montreal
1981   *Runic Series 1980*, Galerie Ricke, Cologne
        Dom Basor Series: India 1981, David Bellman Gallery, Toronto
        Michele Lachowsky Gallery, Antwerp
        Portland Center for the Visual Arts, Oregon
1982   *Rangoli: Aluminum Works Made in India 1981*, Rosamund Felsen Gallery, Los Angeles
        Leo Castelli Gallery, New York
        Galerie Eric Fabre, Paris
1983   Project Studio One, Long Island City, New York
1984   Galleria Schema, Florence (twice)
        Carol Taylor Art, Dallas, Texas
        Galerie Rolf Ricke, Cologne
        Hara Museum of Contemporary Art, Tokyo (travelled to Nagoya and Osaka)
        Leo Castelli Gallery, Greene Street, New York
        Virginia Polytechnic Institute, Blacksburg
1985   Rosamund Felsen Gallery, Los Angeles
        Susanna Hillberry Gallery, Birmingham, Michigan
        Leo Castelli Gallery, Greene Street, New York
1986   Galerie Montenay Delsol, Paris
        Tilden Foley Gallery, New Orleans
1987   Galerie Nature Morte, New York
        Domaine de Kerguehennec, Rennes, France

Selected Group Exhibitions:

1970   *Information*, Museum of Modern Art, New York
1972   *Biennale*, Venice
1973   *Options and Alternatives: Some Directions in Recent Art*, Yale University Art Gallery, New Haven, Connecticut
1975   *Sculpture: American Directions 1945–1975*, National Collection of Fine Arts, Smithsonian Institution, Washington, D.C.
1978   *20th Century American Drawings: 5 Years of Acquisitions*, Whitney Museum, New York
1980   *Yesterday and After*, Museum of Fine Arts, Montreal
1982   *Americanische Zeichnungen der 70er Jahre*, Städtische Galerie, Munich
1984   *Neon, Fluorescent et Cie*, Institut Superieur d'Etude du Langue Plastique, Brussels
1986   *Temporary Contemporary*, Museum of Contemporary Art, Los Angeles

1987   *Tribute to Leo Castelli and His Artists*, Museo de Arte Contemporaneo, Mexico City

Collections:

Museum of Modern Art, New York; Whitney Museum, New York; Fogg Art Museum, Harvard University, Cambridge, Massachusetts; University of North Carolina, Greensboro; Moderna Museet, Stockholm; Ludwig Collection, Aachen, West Germany; Museum of Contemporary Art, Tehran; Australian National Gallery, Canberra.

Publications:

By SONNIER: books—*Object—Situation—Object 1969–70*, Cologne 1972; films—*Untitlted*, 1969; *Untitled II*, 1969; *Negative-Positive*, 1970; *Rub Down*, 1970; *Untitled III*, 1970; *Painting Foot*, 1970; articles—"Keith Sonnier," interview with Liza Bear, in *Avalanche* (New York), May/June 1974; "An Interview with Keith Sonnier," with Calvin Harlan, in *Parachute* (Montreal), Spring 1977; "Keith Sonnier Interview," with Craig Gohlson, in *Interview* (New York), November 1977; "Interview with Keith Sonnier," with Bernard Lamarche-Vadel, in *Artiste* (Paris), October/November 1979.

On SONNIER: books—*Documenta 5*, exhibition catalogue by Harald Szeeman, Jean-Christophe Ammann and others, Kassel 1972; *Some Recent American Art*, exhibition catalogue by Jennifer Licht, New Haven 1973; *Keith Sonnier: Argon-und-Neon-Arbeiten*, exhibition catalogue, Krefeld 1979; *Keith Sonnier: Runic Serie 1980*, exhibition catalogue, Cologne 1981; *Keith Sonnier*, exhibition catalogue by Alanna Heiss, Long Island City 1983; articles—"Eccentric Abstraction" by David Antin in *Artforum* (New York), November 1966; "On Erotic Art" by Lucy Lippard in *Hudson Review* (New York), Spring 1967; "Primary Energy and the Microemotive Artists" by Piero Gilardi in *Arts Magazine* (New York), September 1968; "New York: Moving Out" by Ralph Pomeroy in *Art and Artists* (London), January 1969; "Le Neon dans l'Art Contemporain" by Beatrice Parent in *L'Art Vivant* (Paris), May 1971; review in *Flash Art* (Milan), December 1971; "Keith Sonnier: Video and Film as Color Field" by Robert Pincus-Witten in *Artforum* (New York), May 1972; "Keith Sonnier" by Jon Meyer in *Arts Magazine* (New York), September 1982; "Keith Sonnier at Nature Morte" by Stephen Ellis in *Art in America* (New York), June 1987.

A study of Keith Sonnier's 1982 sculpture *Aesthesipol* resurrects the themes and concerns of his career. The word itself seems on the verge of signifying something, though it never quite resolves in specific meaning—for the artist invented it. *Aesthesipol* provides a summary of Sonnier's work: sculpture aimed at the process of language making. His primary concern, like that of many graffiti artists, is of inventing new ways to propel writing (and the meaning of writing) into vision. His favoured medium: technology. *Aesthesipol* is exemplary, a rambling glyph of extruded aluminium with a working pay phone attached to one of its three vertical members and a portable television attached to another. The sculpture assails the viewer with interacting and interchangeable waves of the aural, the visual, and the tactile. This type of pictured, rather than merely phonetic writing, is symptomatic in his work, and suggests a return to and reinvention of the moment when picturing and writing were one.

Pictured writing is grounded in touch, and establishing space and place for his sense of touch became Sonnier's first goal when he arrived in New York in 1966. His previous endeavours were limited by the isolating experiences in rural Louisiana where he lived in the unassimilated French community of the Cajuns until early adulthood. His early works stressed perfect symmetry and order. After studying in France for a year in 1963 he moved to New York where he abandoned the conventional techniques of figurative paintings of his student days in favour of a direct manipulation and exploration of a variety of materials ranging from satin to satellite.

From 1967 to 1969 Sonnier's work became a revelation—and invitation—to the pleasures of touch. Shreds of flesh-toned silk and satin, frequently combined with pleated dacron screening, drape and drip off the wall and floor in soft sublimations of lingerie experience. He applies planes of latex to the wall which he either peels up and leaves hanging or peels down, attaching it to the floor with strings. The effect of the different planes comments on the nature of touch.

In 1969 Neon became Sonnier's primary medium. His first neon pieces are configured in gestural loops and curls that look like semi-conscious writing of doodles. He wraps neon around neon or incandescent light bulbs in a loose mirrored symmetry that creates the illusion of light reflecting itself. In these sculptures the light itself becomes the architecture. The gaseous flush of the neon thereafter thickens the surrounding atmosphere to the edge of tangibility.

The performance nature of much of Sonnier's work, his interest in dance, and his attraction to tactile light coupled with the new availability and portability of video hardware made television the next logical medium for him. During the '70s he introduced video tapes into his work. Like the neons, the tapes represented a distanced restraint that let the medium play with and against itself. In 1971 Sonnier isolated sound. *New Delhi Sound Piece* consisted of two speakers, one with a microphone attached to it causing feedback, another amplifying the sounds of passers by. These three new mediums incorporated the notion of feedback in Sonnier's subsequent work.

From 1977 to 1979 he intensified his pursuit of public communications. His efforts were almost solely devoted to researching and commandeering a satellite system, which resulted in his piece *Send-Receive* in 1979, a complex visual and verbal dialogue and feedback made possible by satellite technology. The piece consisted of a group of artists and performers in a San Francisco studio making a simultaneous exchange with a corresponding group in New York. San Francisco to New York, New York to San Francisco, dancer to dancer, musician to musician, speaker to speaker—layers of duets of visual and verbal cues, commands, and feedback mixed in material metaphor.

Sonnier, as much a writer as a sculptor, is in constant search of new mediums and new meanings. His pictured language, which thrives on technology, dares to expand past artistic conventions. His art speaks for itself; Sonnier's innovations of the '80s have continued to open new channels of communication.

—Carrie Baker

SORGE, Peter.

German. Born in Berlin, 14 April 1937. Educated in Mecklenburg, 1941–50, and in Dortmund, 1950–58; studied art-teaching at the Hochschule für Bildende Künste, West Berlin, 1958–64; studied painting, under Fred Thieler and Mac Zimmerman, in West Berlin, 1964–65. Married Maina-Miriam Munsky in 1970; son: Daniel. Independent "realist" painter, West Berlin, since 1964: Co-Founder, Ausstellungsgemeinschaft "Grossgorschen 35," West Berlin, 1964–69; Zehn Neun art association, 1969; Aspekt artists' group, 1972. Recipient: Second Burda-Preis, for graphics, Munich, 1968; Graphik-Preis der Stadt Wolfsburg, West Germany, 1969. Agent: Galerie Poll, Lutzowplatz 7, 1000 Berlin 30. Address: Clausewitzstrasse 7, 1000 Berlin 12, West Germany.

Individual Exhibitions:

1965	Grossgorschen 35, West Berlin
	Galerie für Grafikfreunde, Frankfurt
	Galerie Falazik, Bochum, West Germany
1966	Galerie Tobies und Silex, Cologne
	Grossgorschen 35, West Berlin
1967	Galerie Ketterer, Kiel
1968	Galerie Klaus Groh, Oldenburg, West Germany
	Galerie D. und R. Rothe, Wolfsburg, West Germany
	Galerie Ostentor, Dortmund, West Germany
	Galerie Poertner, Sennestadt, West Germany
	Galerie Poll, West Berlin
1969	Galerie Schmucking, Braunschweig, West Germany
	James-Bond-Oratorium, Akademie der Künste, West Berlin (with W. D. Siebert)
	Galerie Klaus Groh, Oldenburg, West Germany
	Diehl/Petrick/Sorge: Malerei, Graphik, Material, Haus am Waldsee, West Berlin (with Hans-Jürgen Diehl and Wolfgang Petrick; travelled to the Badischer Kunstverein, Karlsruhe)
1970	Kunstverein, Mannheim
	Galerie Poll, West Germany
	Galerie Kerlikowsky und Kneiding, Munich (with Hans-Jürgen Diehl and Wolfgang Petrick; toured Germany)
	Galerie Ostentor, Dortmund, West Germany (with Munsky)
1971	Kunsthistorisches Institut, Groningen, Netherlands
	Institut voor Industrielevoorngeving, Delft
	Youth Center, Utrecht
	Galerie de Tor, Amsterdam
	Galerie Wentdorf und Swetec, Dusseldorf
	Galerie im Espresso, Trier, West Germany
	Galerie Kafseck, Paderborn, West Germany
	Galerie Bauer und Pietschner, Bochum, West Germany
	Kunstverein, Kassel, West Germany
1972	Kunstkreis, Gelsenkirchen, West Germany
	Galerie Poll, West Berlin
	Galleria Vinciana, Milan (with Hans-Jürgen Diehl and Wolfgang Petrick)
	Galleria San Michele, Brescia, Italy (with Hans-Jürgen Diehl and Wolfgang Petrick)
1975	Kunsthalle, Nuremberg, West Germany
1976	Galerie Poll, West Berlin
1978	Galerie Art Moderna, Freiburg, West Germany
	Goethe-Institut, Paris
1979	Galerie Zoellner, Bremen, West Germany
	Galerie Poll, West Berlin
	Kunstverein, Frechen, West Germany
1980	Kunstverein, Ludwigshafen, West Germany
1981	Galerie Peterson, Flensburg, West Germany
1982	Galerie im Judenturm, Coburg, West Germany
1984	Galerie Apex, Gottingen, West Germany
1985	Galerie Poll, West Berlin

Selected Group Exhibitions:

1961	*Junge Stadt sieht junge Kunst*, Städtische Museum, Wolfsburg, West Germany
1966	*Junge Berliner Kunstler*, Kunsthalle, Basle
1967	*Neue Realismus*, Haus am Waldsee, West Berlin
1968	*International Print Biennale*, City Museum and Art Gallery, Bradford, Yorkshire
1970	*Pop-Sammlung Beck*, Kunsthalle, Bonn (travelled to Darmstadt and Dortmund)
1971	*Biennale de Paris*, Parc Floral, Paris
1972	*Prinzip Realismus*, DAAD-Galerie, West Berlin
1978	*Funf Berliner Realisten*, Museum am Dom, Lubeck, West Germany
1980	*Berlin Realistisch 1890–1980*, Berlinische Galerie, West Berlin
1983	*Realistische Zeichnungen*, Nationalgalerie, West Berlin

Collections:

Kunstverein, Kassel, West Germany; Kunstverein, Mannheim; Berlinische Galerie, West Berlin; Nationalgalerie, West Berlin; Nationalgalerie/Kupferstichkabinett, East Berlin; Institut fur Auslandsbeziehungen, Stuttgart; Herzog Anton Ulrich-Museum, Braunschweig; Stadtische Kunstsammlungen, Bonn; Kunstverein fur die Rheinlande und Westfalen, Dusseldorf.

Publications:

By SORGE: books—*Zitate zur StVO*, Burgdorf, West Germany 1970; *Varspiele*, West Berlin 1972.

Keith Sonnier: *Expanded Sel III*, 1979

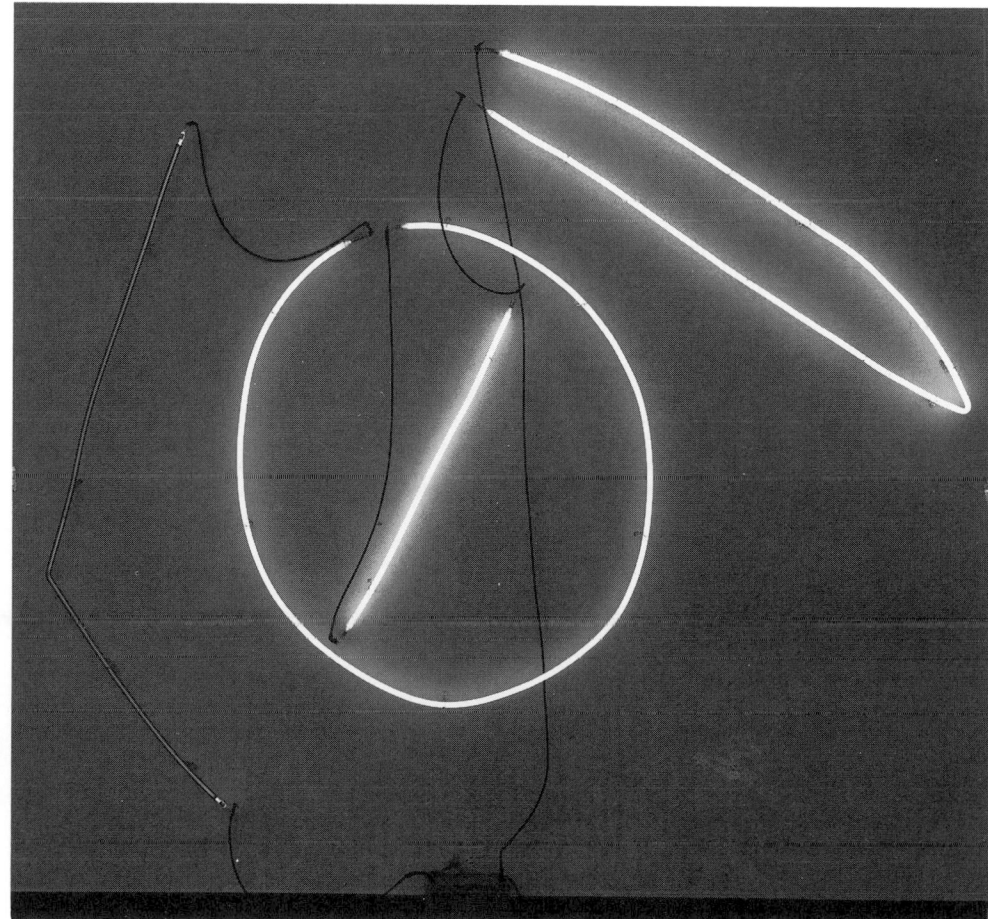

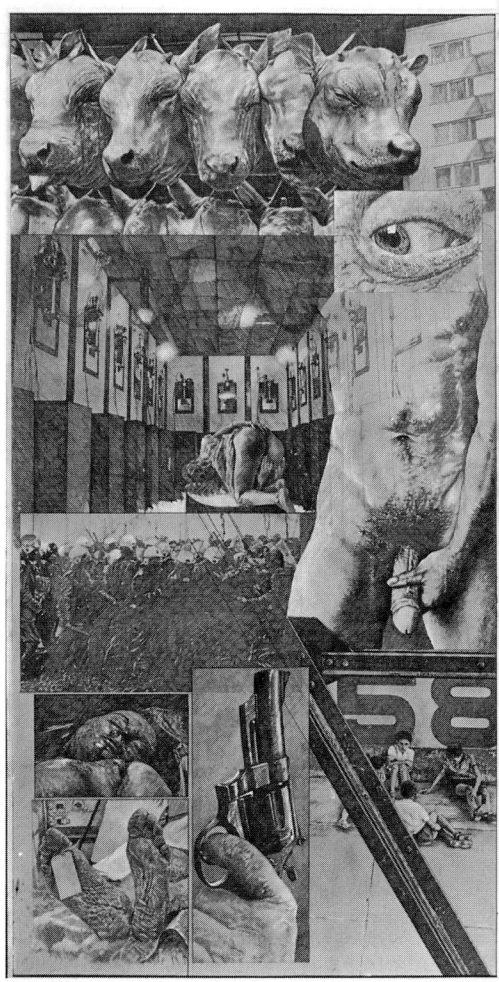
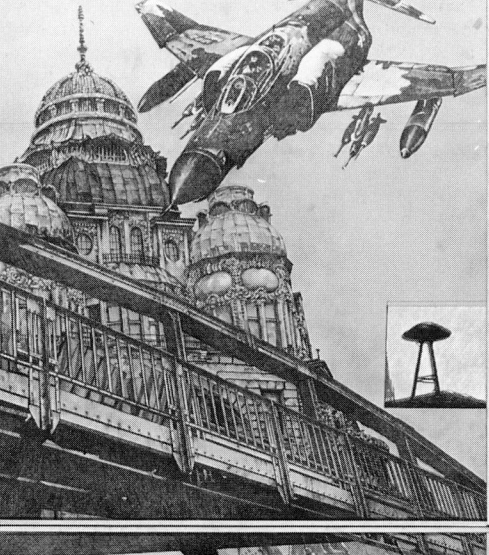
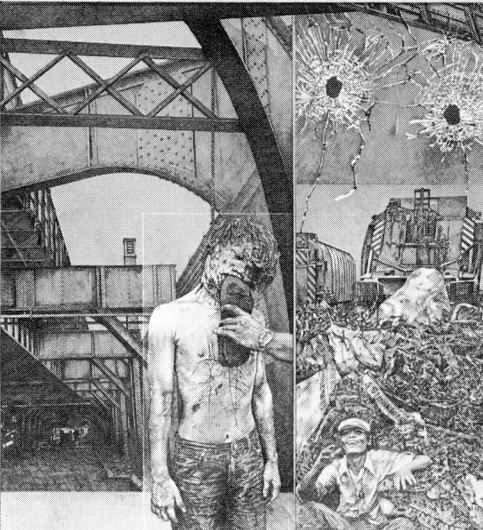
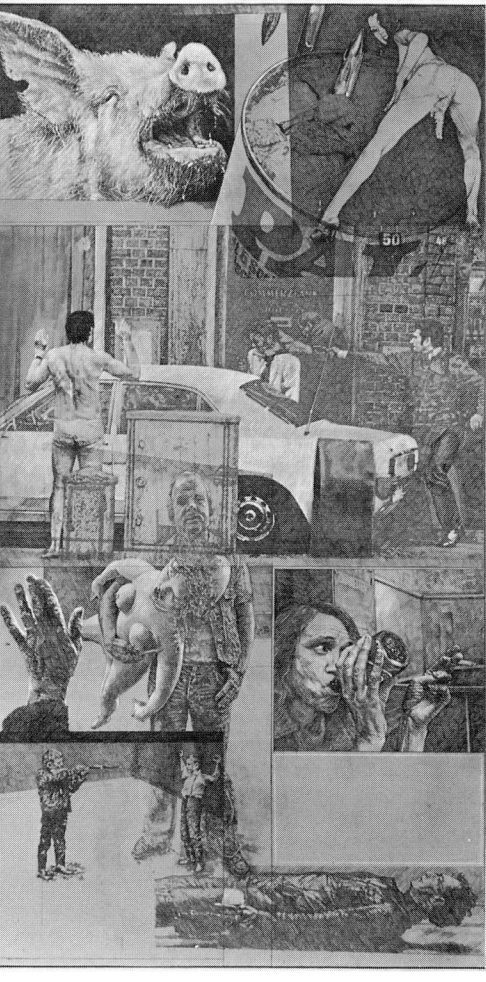

Peter Sorge: *Versuche uber die Grossstadt,* 1977

On SORGE: books—*Diehl/Petrick/Sorge: Malerei, Graphik, Material,* exhibition catalogue, West Berlin 1969; *Peter Sorge: Werkverzeichnis der Druckgraphik und Handzeichnungen 1963-70,* West Berlin 1970, rev. ed. 1972; *Deutsche Kunst der 60er Jahre: Malerei, Collage, Op-Art, Graphik* by Juliane Roh, Munich 1971; *Prinzip Realismus,* exhibition catalogue, West Berlin 1972; *Westberliner Realisten* by G. Strathmann, West Berlin 1979; *Peter Sorge,* exhibition catalogue with text by Lucius Grisebach, West Berlin 1985.

The terrors of engagierter Kunst receive their fullest freedom at the hands of Peter Sorge. His devastating (the correct word in this instance) realist style makes the most savage political and sociological cartoon look anaemic by comparison. It is not so much his expert control of narrative art that makes his works compelling and outstanding as the acid sense of drama which he is able to inject into them. The girl the soldiers picked up was the romantic figure in the first frame, but after they had taken her apart she features in the second half of the diptych-print as a broken disposable. Her two comrades (assailants) may not look so engaging in chapter two, but they at least are not smashed up like their poor victim.

Sorge makes the gun mean. No pistol in his prints could be less than villainous. Sorge firearms are not instruments for protective use; they are not even elements of martial equipment, a part of uniform. They are extensions of cruelty that will be brought into play if brute force fails to achieve objectives.

It is difficult to believe that this Berlin artist is just past 50 years of age. His technique and imagery suggest that he should either be much older (!), leaning back upon experience of a cruder past or at least re-flecting or revivifying visions culled from the memoirs of a generation before—or, at the other extreme, he ought to be a "young" artist, gifted beyond his years, seeking to exhume the cruelties of a past era which he mercifully avoided.

The etchings and lithographs he makes of these nightmares are visually magnetic because of his inspired and accurate talent. His system of building up a graphic in compartments which often present a storyline need not always be the work pattern for horror, but it is significant that this artist will never sacrifice acid for saccharine. "How to achieve work and loveliness," for instance, is divided into three sections: top left—the rippling torso of a muscle man; top right—a faucet out of which descends a flow of water (like a single frame from a carefully made movie); bottom half—the flanks of a man and a woman; he hesitant, she inclining her pelvis toward his hip . . . a joint gesture of natural naked affection, except the half-lemon he is holding behind his back injects an acrid note.

—Sheldon Williams

SOTO, Jesus Rafael.
Venezuelan. Born in Ciudad Bolivar in 1923. Studied at the Academia de Bellas Artes, Caracas, 1942–47. Married in 1952. Painter: Director, Maracaibo School of Fine Arts, Venezuela, 1947–50; has lived and worked in Paris since 1950; also a musician. Recipient: Hatch Prize for Abstract Painting, Caracas, 1957; National Prize, Venezuela, 1960; Virgilio Cordo Prize, Caracas, 1960; Wolf Prize, *Bienal,* Sao Paulo, 1963; Premio David Bright, *Biennale,* Venice, 1964; First Prize, *Bienal America,* Cordova, Peru, 1964; Prize of the City of Cordova, 1964; First Prize, *Salon of Pan-American Painting,* Cali, Colombia, 1965; Medaglia d'Oro, Convegno Internazionale Studiosi d'Arte, Rimini, Italy, 1967. Agent: Galleria Naviglio, Milan. Address: c/o Galleria del Naviglio, Via Manzoni 45, 20121 Milan, Italy.

Individual Exhibitions:

1949 Atelier Libre de Arte, Caracas
1956 Galerie Denise René, Paris
1957 Galerie Aujourd'hui, Palais des Beaux-Arts, Brussels
     Museum of Modern Art, Caracas
1959 Galerie Iris Clert, Paris
1961 Museum of Modern Art, Caracas
     Galerie Rudolf, Zwirner, Essen
     Galerie Brusberg, Hannover
1962 Galerie Ad Libitum, Antwerp
     Galerie Edouard Loeb, Paris
1963 Museum Haus Lange, Krefeld, West Germany
1964 Galerie Müller, Stuttgart
1965 Galerie Edouard Loeb, Paris
     Kootz Gallery, New York
     Signals Gallery, London
1966 Galerie Schmela, Dusseldorf

Galleria del Naviglio, Milan
Galleria del Deposito, Genoa
Centre de l'Art Vivant, Trieste
Pfalzgalerie, Kaiserlautern, West Germany
1967 Galerie Denise René, Paris
1968 Galerie Francoise Mayer, Brussels
Kunsthalle, Berne
Stedelijk Museum, Amsterdam
Marlborough Galleria d'Arte, Rome
1969 Palais des Beaux-Arts, Brussels
Galleria Lorenzelli, Bergamo, Italy
Galleria Notizie, Turin
Galleria del Naviglio, Milan
Galleria Flori, Florence
Galleria Giraldi, Livorno
Galeria Estudio Actual, Caracas
Musée d'Art Moderne de la Ville, Paris
Svensk-Franska Kunstgalleriet, Stockholm
1970 Galerie Denise René, Paris
Galerie Godart Lefort, Montreal
Galerie Suvremene, Zagreb
Galleria de la Nova Loggia, Bologna
Galerie Semiha Huber, Zurich
Kunstverein, Mannheim
Marlborough Gallery, New York
Galerie Buchholz, Munich
Ulm Museum, West Germany
1971 Museum of Contemporary Art, Chicago
Galleria Rotta, Milan
Martha Jackson Gallery, New York
Galerie Denise Reneé-Hans Meyer, Dusseldorf
Kunstverein, Kaiserlautern, West Germany
Museo de Bellas Artes, Caracas
1972 Galerie Pauli, Lausanne, Switzerland
Galerie Beyeler, Basle
Galleria Levi, Milan
Museo de Arte Moderno, Bogota
1973 Galeria Tempora Calle, Bogota
Galleria Corsini, Rome
Universidad Central de Venezuela, Caracas
Estudio Dos, Valencia, Venezuela
Arte Contacto, Caracas
Galleria Godel, Rome
1974 Guggenheim Museum, New York (retrospective)
Denise René Gallery, New York
1975 Denise René Gallery, New York
1979 Museo de Arte Contemporaneo, Caracas
Centre Georges Pompidou, Paris
1981 Galeria Tempora Calle, Bogota
Galeria Theo, Madrid
Sala Celini, Madrid
1983 Museo de Arte de Caracas, Venzuela

Selected Group Exhibitions:

1943 *Annual Art Exhibition*, Caracas
1955 *Le Mouvement*, Galerie Denise René, Paris
1957 *Bienal*, Sao Paulo
1958 *World's Fair*, Brussels
Bienal, Sao Paulo
Biennale, Venice
1962 *Biennale*, Venice
1967 *International Exhibition*, Carnegie Institute, Pittsburgh
1969 *Middelheim Biennale*, Antwerp
1974 *Neuve Artistas Venezolanos*, Museo de Arte Contemporaneo, Caracas

Collections:

Cali Institute of Fine Arts, Colombia; University City, Caracas, Albright-Knox Art Gallery, Buffalo, New York; Stedelijk Museum, Amsterdam; Palais des Beaux-Arts, Brussels; Centre Georges Pompidou, Paris; Kunsthaus, Zurich; Moderna Museet, Stockholm; Louisiana Museum, Humlebaek, Denmark; National Gallery of Victoria, Melbourne.

Publications:

By SOTO: article "Dialogue: Jesus Rafael Soto and Guy Brett" in *Museumjournaal* (Amsterdam), February 1969.

On SOTO: books—*Soto*, exhibition catalogue, by Jean Clay, Paris 1969; *Soto*, exhibition catalogue, by Guy Brett, New York 1970; *Soto* by Alfredo Boulton, Caracas 1973; *Soto*, exhibition catalogue, Caracas 1983; articles—"J. R. Soto" by Jean Clay in *Signals* (London), 1/10, 1965; "Soto" by Jean Clay in *Connaissance des Arts* (Paris), June 1969; "Soto dans le Labyrinthe" by Philippe Comte in *Opus International* (Paris), June 1969; "Soto's X Penetrables" by Jean Clay in *Studio International* (London), September 1969; "Soto's Logic" by Patrick d'Elme in *Cimaise* (Paris), May/August 1970; "Soto" by E. L. L. de Wilde in *Museumjournaal* (Amsterdam), October 1973.

*   *   *

Jesus Rafael Soto began as a painter and out of painting developed kinetic relief constructions which gradually grew into autonomous environments. In these, the spectator-turned-participant assumes a position so central that he is no longer divorceable from the work of art which without him remains incomplete. This process, traceable from phase to phase, took close to three decades of the artist's diligent and inventive life and gained for him an important place in post-war art.

As a student painter in Venezuela, where Soto was born, his first serious creative impetus came to him from a Cubist Braque still-life in a thrilling moment of comprehension, and his subsequent early work is an academic effort to learn from Cubism and from Cézanne the lessons of geometric simplification. When, as a youth of 27, Soto arrived in Paris, his avowed purpose was to find out what had happened in world art since Braque painted the still-life that had so moved him. Proceeding from a sense of stylistic continuity, he shortly thereafter determined to put his own shoulder to the wheel at the point at which the art-historical carriage seemed to him to be struck. Soto saw this point not in the prevalent area of tachist expression (which he dismissed as irrelevant) but, rather, within an investigative tradition concerned with the object's position in time and space. He correctly traced the modern origins of this issue to Picasso's constructions, the researches of Gabo and Moholy-Nagy, the spatially suggestive paintings of Mondrian and Malevich and, more immediately, to the kinetic mobile art of Alexander Calder.

The young Venezuelan showed implicit faith in the logical progression of art. As a young investigator, but no longer student, he found himself attracted, together with Agam and Tinguely, to the orbit of the Salon des Réalités Nouvelles, established in Paris in 1946, and to the Galerie Denise René, which had opened its doors two years earlier. The group's patron-saint was Vasarely, and each of the young men in his own way embarked upon research having as its objective the visual representation of movement. By the mid-50's, Soto and his friends had articulated their position and invented visual instruments for the expression of their principles.

Calder, as already mentioned, was the point of departure, but Soto's movement from the outset was different from that of the North American mobile maker. For Calder—the man who made sculpture move—did so mostly by letting carefully weighted, painted objects swing in the breeze, while Soto reduced physical motion to sensory vibration. The vibrating effect was either entirely based on optical responses to a physically static surface or further aided by the gentle movement of optically energetic suspended bodies as these came to act against similarly active optical surfaces. Leaving aside more distant antecedents, it may therefore be said that Soto related Calder's physical to Vasarely's optical kineticism, thereby combining palpable and visual kinetic elements into a new form language.

The environments that Soto created, at the outset in experimental modesty, developed their own momentum and eventually spilled over from his visual laboratory into the world at large. His planes, initially created to reflect vibrations, gradually grew into a striated cube large enough to accommodate the traffic of crowds, and eventually came to dwarf and submerge man as he literally made his way through resisting but penetrable mazes. The prime experience in Soto's later works is no longer optical, but tactile and

sonorous as the human participant, through his act of penetration, agitates not only the real space before him but also our aural ambience. Quite logically, Soto's recent works are architectural. In his monumental factory interior for Renault in Paris, the decorative and the structural elements of his kinetic idiom merge.

Soto's art, then, gradually develops from a sensory and contemplative to a physical, and, in the case of the penetrable, to an athletic dimension: from the small laboratory experiment to monumental architectural scale: and from a self-contained aesthetic unity to one complementary to participatory activity by the viewer. Together with others, Soto has thus blurred the dividing line between the plastic and the performing arts: he has transformed the spectator outside the object to a central agent within the work itself; and reduced or radically altered the distance between art produced and consumed. Through these combined measures, for better or worse, Soto has greatly contributed to a perceptible shift away from art and toward life.

—Thomas Messer

SOULAGES, Pierre.
French. Born in Rodez, Aveyron, 24 December 1919. Educated at the Lycée Rodez until 1938; studied art at the Ecole des Beaux-Arts, Montpellier, 1941. Served in French Army, in Bordeaux and Nyons, 1939–41. Worked as a vineyard labourer, Montpellier, 1943–45; independent painter, Courbevoie, 1946, and in Paris, since 1947. Recipient: Painting Prize, *Bienal*, Sao Paulo, 1953; Grand Prize, *International Exhibition*, Tokyo, 1957; Grand Prize, *Graphics Biennale*, Ljubljana, Yugoslavia, 1959; Carnegie International Prize, Pittsburgh, 1964; Palette d'Or, *Festival International de Peinture*, Cagnes, 1972; Grand Prize des Arts de la Ville de Paris, 1975; Rembrandt Prize, Goethe-Institut, Basle, 1976; Grand Prix National des Arts, Paris, 1987. Agent: Galerie de France, 52 rue de la Verrerie, 75004 Paris. Address: 18 rue des Trois-Portes, 75005 Paris, France.

Individual Exhibitions:

1949 Galerie Lydia Conti, Paris
1951 Galleri Birch, Copenhagen
1952 Galerie Stangl, Munich
1954 Kootz Gallery, New York
1955 *Paintings*, Gimpel Fils, London
Arts Club of Chicago
Kootz Gallery, New York
1956 Galerie de France, Paris
Kootz Gallery, New York
1957 Galerie Berggruen, Paris
Kootz Gallery, New York
1958 Galerie Rosen, West Berlin
Kunstverein, Braunschweig, West Germany
Gimpel Fils, London
Howard Wise Gallery, Cleveland
1959 Kootz Gallery, New York
1960 Kestner-Gesellschaft, Hannover (retrospective)
Galerie de France, Paris
1961 Museum Folkwang, Essen (retrospective; travelled to the Hague and Zurich)
Museum of Modern Art, Ljubljana, Yugoslavia (graphics retrospective)
Kootz Gallery, New York
1962 Massachusetts Institute of Technology, Cambridge (retrospective)
Museum of Zagreb (graphics retrospective; toured Yugoslavia and Austria)
1963 *Malerier og Raderinger*, Ny Carlsberg Glyptotek, Copenhagen (retrospective)
Peintures sur Papier 1946–1963, Galerie de France, Paris

Pierre Soulages: *Peinture,* **1977**

1964	Kootz Gallery, New York		Gentofte Radhus, Denmark
1965	Kootz Gallery, New York		Gimpel und Hanover Galerie, Zurich
1966	Museum of Fine Arts, Houston (retrospective)		Musée d'Art et d'Histoire, Neuchâtel, Switzerland
1967	Musée d'Art Moderne, Paris (retrospective)	1974	Musée Dynamique, Dakar, West Africa (retrospective)
	Gimpel und Hanover Galerie, Zurich		Maison des Arts et Loisirs, Montbeliard, France (graphics retrospective)
	Gimpel Fils, London		
	Galerie de France, Paris		Galerie de France, Paris (graphics retrospective)
1968	Museum of Art, Pittsburgh (retrospective; toured the United States and Canada)		Galerie-Librairie La Hune, Paris
		1975	Fundacao Gulbenkian, Lisbon (retrospective; travelled to Madrid and Montpellier)
	Paintings since 1963, M. Knoedler Inc., New York		
	Comité d'Enterprise Credit Lyonnais, Paris		Museo de Arte Moderno, Mexico City (retrospective)
1971	Galerie Jobbe-Duval, Rennes, France		
1972	University of Maryland, College Park (retrospective)	1976	Museo de Bellas Artes, Caracas (retrospective; toured Brazil and Venezuela)
	Galerie de France, Paris		Musée d'Art et d'Industrie, St. Etienne, France (retrospective)
	Gimpel Fils, London		
	Galerie Protée, Toulouse		
	Galerie-Librairie La Hune, Paris	1977	Grand Palais, Paris (at *Foire International d'Art Contemporain*)
1973	Henie-Onstad Kunstsenter, Oslo		
	Nordyllands Kunstmuseum, Aalborg, Denmark		Galerie de France, Paris

1978	Galerie Ulysses, Vienna
	Galerie Madoura, Vallauris, France
	Institut Francais, Athens
1979	Galleri Birch, Copenhagen
	Fondation Veranneman, Kruishoutem, Belgium
	Peintures Récentes, Centre Georges Pompidou, Paris
1980	Musée de la Boverie, Liege, Belgium
	Kunstlerhaus, Salzburg, Austria
1982	Galerie Ostertag, Frankfurt
	Altes Schloss Museum, Giessen, West Germany
	Galerie Ponce, Mexico City
	Musee Charlottenburg, Copenhagen (retrospective; toured Denmark)
1983	Musée d'Unterlinden, Colmar, France
1984	Seibu Museum, Tokyo
1985	Pulchri Studio, The Hague
1986	Galerie de France, Paris
1987	Musée St. Pierre, Lyon, Frances
	H.-Thoma Gesellschaft, Reutlingen, West Germany
	Galerie E. Rieber, Munich

Selected Group Exhibitions:

1948	*Franzosisher Abstrakter Malerei,* Kunsthalle, Stuttgart (toured Germany)
1953	*Younger European Artists,* Guggenheim Museum, New York
1955	*The New Decade,* Museum of Modern Art, New York
1964	*Painting in France 1900–67,* National Gallery, Washington, D.C. (toured the United States)
1973	*Aspects of Contemporary Art,* South African National Gallery, Cape Town (toured South Africa)
1978	*Points de Reperes,* Palazzo Reale, Milan (travelled to Naples, Florence, Wroclaw, Poznan, Warsaw, Madrid, and Lisbon)
1981	*Westkunst,* Messehallen, Cologne
1986	*The Spiritual in Art,* Los Angeles County Museum of Art
1987	*Lumière de la Mediterranée,* Israel Museum, Jerusalem

Collections:

Centre Georges Pompidou, Paris; Nationalgalerie, West Berlin; Museum des 20. Jahrhundert, Vienna; Museum Boymans-van Beuningen, Rotterdam, Netherlands; Kunsthaus, Zurich; Galleria Civica d'Arte Moderna, Turin; Tate Gallery, London; Museum of Fine Arts, Montreal; Art Institute of Chicago; Museum of Modern Art, New York.

Publications:

On SOULAGES: books—*Abstrakte Franzosischer Malerei* by René Massat, Stuttgart 1948; *The Changing Forms of Art* by Patrick Heron, London 1955; *Pierre Soulages: Paintings,* exhibition catalogue, with text by Bernard Dorival, London 1955; *L'Art Abstrait* by Marcel Brion, Paris 1956; *Soulages* by R. van Gindertael, Paris 1957; *Musée de Poche: Pierre Soulages* by Hubert Juin, Paris 1958, as *Soulages,* New York 1959; *Pierre Soulages,* exhibition catalogue, with text by Werner Schmalenbach, Hannover 1960; *Soulages,* exhibition catalogue, with photo-reportage by Izis, Paris 1960; *Pierre Soulages,* exhibition catalogue, with text by Eduard Huttinger, Zurich 1961; *Les Peintures sur Papier de Soulages* by Michel Ragon, Paris 1962; *Soulages: Peintures sur Papier 1946–1963,* exhibition catalogue, Paris 1963; *Soulages: Malerier og Raderinger,* exhibition catalogue, with text by Haavard Rostrup, Copenhagen 1963; *Pierre Soulages,* exhibition catalogue, with text by Bernard Dorival, James Fitzsimmons and Werner Schmalenbach, Zurich 1967; *Soulages,* exhibition catalogue, with text by Bernard Dorival, Paris 1967; *Soulages: Paintings since 1963,* exhibition catalogue, with text by James Johnson Sweeney, New York 1968; *Soulages 1970–72,* exhibition catalogue, Paris 1972; *Pierre Soulages* by James Johnson Sweeney, Neuchâtel, Switzerland 1972, New York, London and Stuttgart 1973; *Pierre Soulages* by Michel Ragon, Paris 1974; *Soulages: Eaux-Fortes, Lithographies* by G. Duby and C. Labbaye, Paris 1974; *Pierre Soulages,* exhibition catalogue, with an interview by Bernard Ceysson, St. Etienne, France 1976; *Soulages: Peintres Récentes,* exhibition catalogue, with text by Alfred Pacquement, Paris 1979; *Soulages* by Bernard Ceysson, Nafels 1979; *Pierre Soulages,* exhibition catalogue with texts by Alfred Pacquement and Ashido Okada, Tokyo 1984; *Pierre Soulages,* exhibition catalogue with texts by George Duby, Clement Rosset and others, Lyon 1987.

Prominent among the abstract painters of the School of Paris who won celebrity after 1945, Pierre Soulages has been consistent in his strength of expression, though the resources of his work have been restricted both in format and in palette. Colour as such is eliminated almost entirely, except where it is mixed with black. Black with brown, grey, green and blue dictates the mood of each painting. Handling of the oil pigment in varied thicknesses from quite high impasto to a transparent solution is always sensuous. By subtracting colour and mixing the pigment only in primarily tonal effectiveness, the imposition of the formal structure is emphasized.

Reflection is of the utmost importance in Soulages' paintings, not merely the reflection from the paint surface itself but in the diffusion of light in the chiaroscuro. Broad pathways of paint indicate the passages of intent, so that each canvas is a plan of tactile directions in which the reflections illuminate the plastic configuration of the paint. This plastic topography is, at first glance, strong in its negative saturation of the light, then grows in assertiveness as the subtle graduations of the shadowy reliefs are traversed. Activation of the picture space and an imaginary depth beyond it, implied by the lighter tones, expands the superficial limits of the non-objective image.

Soulages' contributions to theatre design in the 1949 sets for Graham Greene's *Heloise et Abelard* in Paris and in the 1952 ballet *Geste pour un genie* in honour of Leonardo's 500th anniversary demonstrate that his association with light and dark translate effectively in the proscenium frame. Those broad black bands, meeting and diagonally separating, construct dark and monolithic shapes that have their prototypes in memories of the ancient menhirs and the numinous sculptures of the old Romanesque churches abounding around Soulages' childhood home in the Massif Central. This solemn aura that broods over all of Soulages' work, either in paint or in prints, removed it from the context of ephemeral art styles and identifies it closely and specially with the rich and sensuous empathy of gesture, and the secret impulses of movements in the world of nature by night.

It is a magic and mysterious atmosphere that Soulages can conjure up, with no more than a personal Braille system of signs and reliefs in which the eye searches vainly for explicit directions and data. "Out of darkness came forth light," in the physical no less than the spiritual sense, is the import of Soulages' message. It also has the ambiguous paraphrase of the light that, dispelling our fears of the unknown, may also make clear the horrors the darkness has mercifully shrouded.

—G. S. Whittet

SPADARI, Giangiacomo.

Italian. Born in the Republic of San Marino, 4 April 1938. Lives and works in Milan. Address: viale Tunisia 23, 20124 Milan, Italy.

Individual Exhibitions:

1961	Galleria Spotorno, Milan
1965	Galleria Stefanoni, Lecco, Italy
	Galleria Gianferrari, Milan
1966	Libreria Einaudi, Milan
1968	Galleria Bergamini, Milan
1969	Galleria Il Minotaura, Brescia, Italy
	Fondacion Mendoza, Caracas
	Galleria Il Punto, Turin
1970	Galleria Schwarz, Milan
	Galerie Richard Foncke, Ghent

1971	Galleria Ciak, Rome
1972	Galleria Schwarz, Milan
	Museo Civico, Modena, Italy
1973	Galerie Poll, Berlin
1974	Galleria Bocchi, Parma
1975	*Garibaldi e il Compromesso Storico,* Galleria Borgogna, Milan
1979	*1968: Tra Cronaca e Storia,* Centro Attività Visive, Palazzo dei Diamanti, Ferrara, Italy

Selected Group Exhibitions:

1968	*Biennale de l'Estampe,* Musée d'Art Moderne de la Ville, Paris
1969	*Salle Rouge pour le Vietnam,* Musée d'Art Moderne de la Ville, Paris
	Kunst und Politik, Kunstverein, Karlsruhe, West Germany
1972	*Quadriennale,* Rome
1973	*Quattro Pittori: Una Città,* Palais des Beaux-Arts, Brussels (travelled to the Musée d'Art Moderne de la Ville, Paris)
1974	*Arts '74,* Helsinki

Publications:

By SPADARI: articles—"Giangiacomo Spadari" in *d'Ars* (Milan), December 1978; statement in *Giangiacomo Spadari: 1968: Tra Cronaca e Storia,* exhibition catalogue, Ferrara, Italy 1979.

On SPADARI: books—*Richerchi dopo l'Informale* by Enrico Crispolti, Rome 1968; *Giangiacomo Spadari: Garibaldi e il Compromesso Storico,* exhibition catalogue, by Mario Perazzi, Milan 1975; *Giangiacomo Spadari: 1968: Tra Cronaca e Storia,* exhibition catalogue, by Alik Cavaliere, Ferrara, Italy 1979; article—"Spadari: de la Chronique a l'Histoire" in *Opus International* (Paris), Spring 1978.

SPAGNULO, Giuseppe.

Italian. Born in Grottaglie, Tarnato, 28 December 1936. Educated in Grottaglie primary and secondary schools; studied ceramic technology in father's worshop, Grottaglie, 1948–49; at the Scuola d'Arte, Faenza, Italy, 1953–55 and 1956–57; studied sculpture, under Marino Marini, at the Brera Accademia di Belle Arti, Milan, 1959–60. Served in the Italian Army Infantry, in Bari, Maddaloni and Milan, 1961–63. Married Clara Dalla Chiara in 1966; sons: Frederico and Andrea. Sculptor: worked as an assistant in sculpture, studio of Lucio Fontana, and of Gio and Arnaldo Pomodoro, Milan, 1959–60; produced first stone works, 1960–65; first wood and iron works, 1965–76; designed first stage sets, Bologna, 1975; has worked with cardboard, landscape, and archaeological themes, since 1976; spent year in Berlin, 1980. Lecturer in Sculpture, Istituto d'Arte, Monza, Italy, 1968–69. Recipient: Purchase Prize, *Mostra del Disegno,* Appiano Gentile, 1968; Purchase Prize for Drawing, Galleria delle Ore, Milan 1969; First Sculpture Prize, Seregno-Brianza, Italy, 1974. Agent: Studio Carlo Grossetti, via dei Piatti 9, 20123 Milan. Address: Viale Col de Lana 9, 20100 Milan, Italy.

Individual Exhibitions:

1965	Salone Annunciata, Milan
1968	Salone Annunciata, Milan
1969	Galleria Ferrari, Verona
	Galleria Martano Due, Turin
1970	*Une Scultura nella Strada: Black Panther,* via Borgospesso, Milan
1971	Salone Annunciata, Milan
	Studio Marconi, Milan
1972	*Ferri Spezzati,* Salone Annunciata, Milan
1973	*Scultura nella Città,* Nova Arte Moderna, Prato, Italy

Giangiacomo Spadari: *Congresso,* 1969

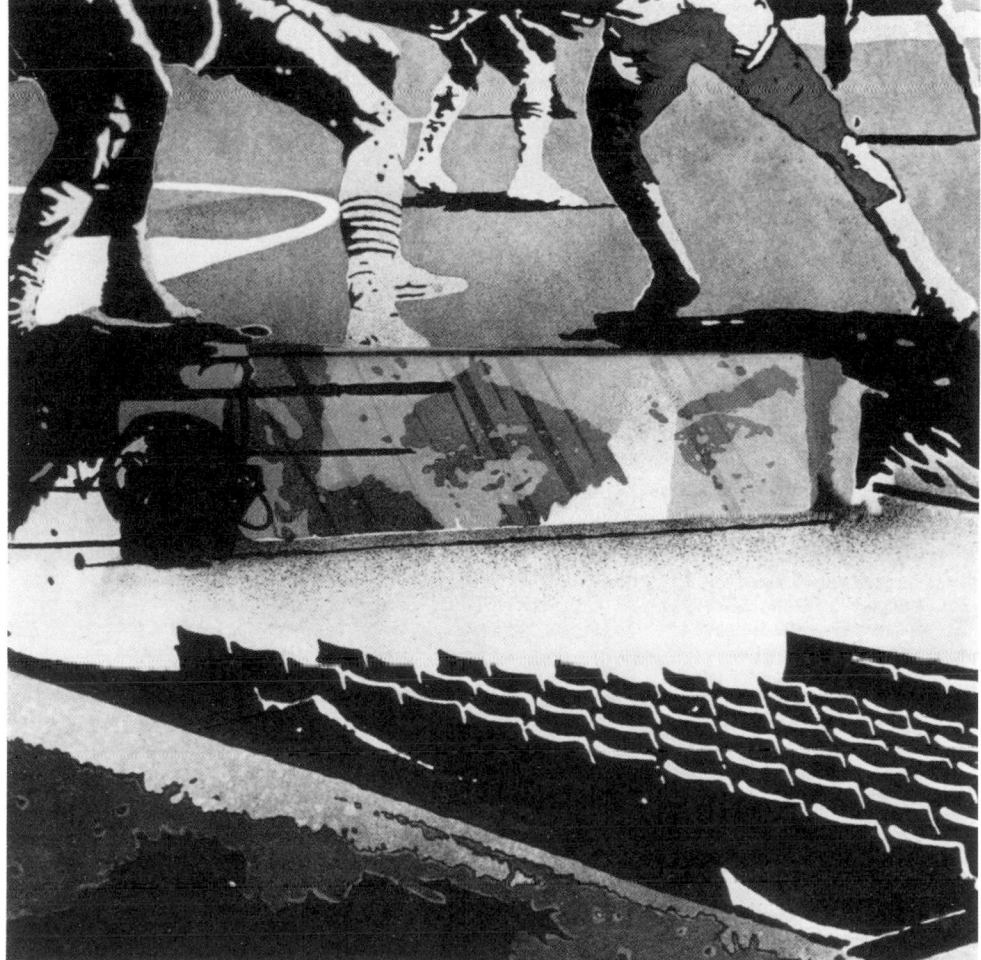

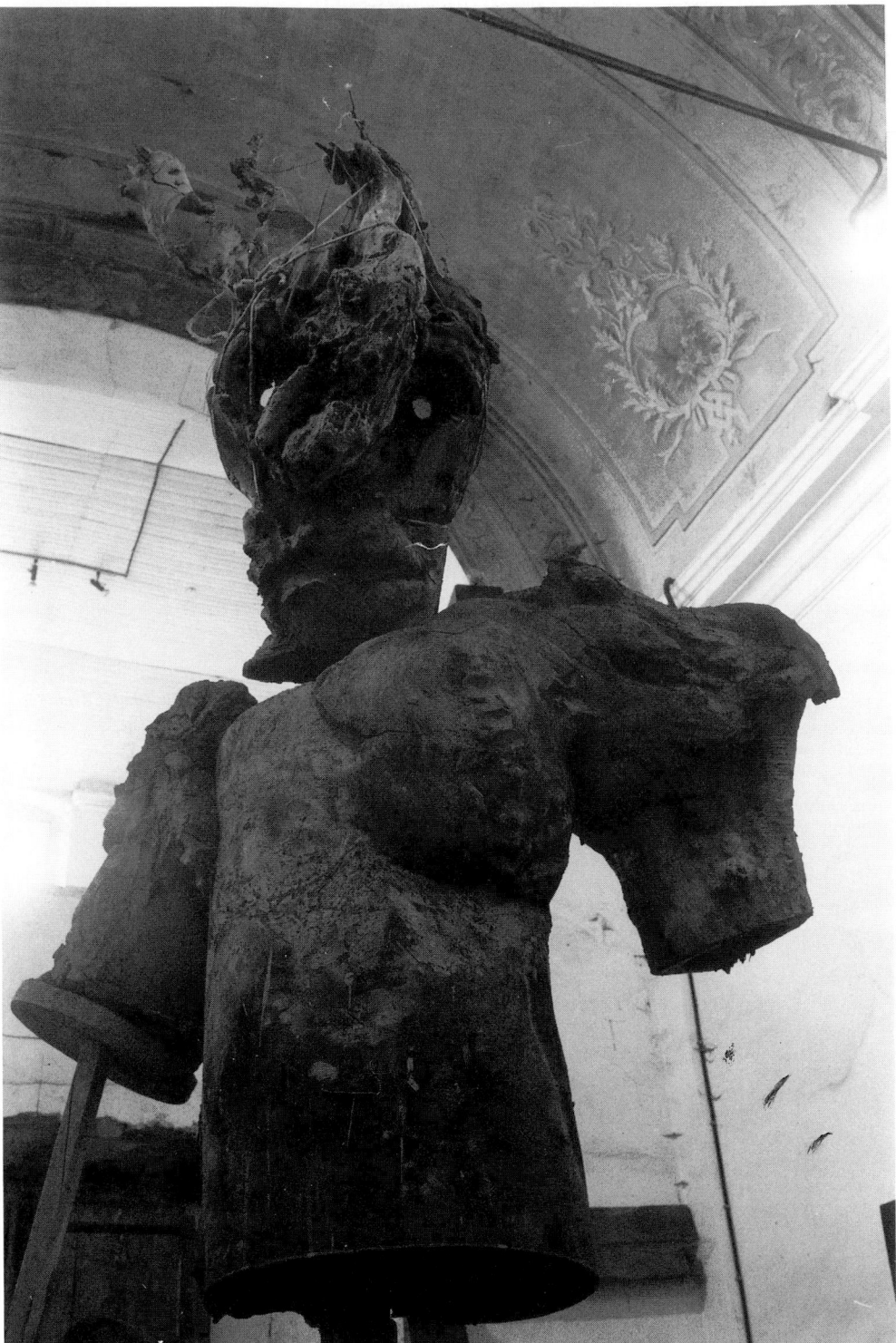

Giuseppe Spagnulo: *Il Perseo* (detail), 1986

1974	Galerie Semiha Huber, Zurich	1978	Kunsthalle, Bielefeld, West Germany
	Galerie M, Bochum, West Germany		Galleria Il Tritone, Biella, Italy
	Studio Casati, Merate, Italy		Studio Carlo Grossetti, Milan
1975	Galleria Schwarz, Milan		Galerie D + C Müller-Roth, Stuttgart
	Salone Annunciata, Milan		Studio Casati, Merate, Italy
1976	Galleria Il Sole, Bolzano, Italy		Galerie Walter Storms, Munich
	Galerie M, Bochum, West Germany	1979	Galleria E Tre, Rome
	Galerie M, The Hague		Galerie Appel und Fertsch, Frankfurt
	Centro Sant'Elmo, Salò, Italy	1980	Galerie Munro, Hamburg
	Galleria 72, Bergamo, Italy		Galerie Walter Storms, Munich (with Marco Gastini
	Galleria Il Segnappasi, Pesaro, Italy		and Gilberto Zorio)
	Salone Annunciata, Milan (with Marco Gastini)		Studio Carlo Grossetti, Milan
1977	Galleria Civica d'Arte Moderna, Turin		Galerie Walter Storms, Villigen, West Germany
	Salone Annunciata, Milan	1981	Studio G 7, Bologna
	Galerie Walter Storms, Munich		*Erotish, Rhetorisch, Heroisch,* Nationgalerie, West
	Newport Harbor Art Museum, Newport Beach, Cal-		Berlin
	ifornia		Kunstverein, Braunschweig, West Germany

1982 *L'Istinto e Sempre in Cerca di Anima,* Städtische Ga-
 lerie im Lenbachhaus, Munich
1983 Studio Carlo Grossetti, Milan
 Galerie Susanna Kulli, St. Gallen, Switzerland
 Salone Villa Romana, Florence
1984 Galleria Civica, Modena, Italy
 Galleria L'Isola, Rome
1985 Galleria Martano, Turin
 Galleria Piero Cavellini, Milan
 Wilhelm-Lehmbruck-Museum, Duisburg, West Ger-
 many
 Kunstverein, Hamburg
 Lunds Konsthall, Lund, Sweden
1986 Galerie Susanna Kulli, St. Gallen, Switzerland
 Galerie Walter Storms, Munich
 Spagnulo, at the *XLII Biennale,* Venice
 Spagnulo, at the *XIX Biennale di Gubbio,* Italy
 Galerie Hans Barlach, Cologne
1987 Galerie Hans Barlach, Hamburg
 Galleri Nordenhake, Stockholm
 Studio Carlo Grossetti, Milan

Selected Group Exhibitions:

1972 *Progetto/Intervento/Verifica,* Palazzo Reale, Milan
1975 *Empirica: L'Arte tra Addizione e Sottrazione,* Museo
 di Castelvecchio, Rimini
1977 *Arte in Italia 1969–1977,* Galleria Civica d'Arte
 Moderna, Turin
1979 *Le Stangze del Gioco,* Loggetta Lombardesca, Pinacoteca, Ravenna
1980 *Skulptur im 20. Jahrundert,* Wenkenpark, Riehen,
 near Basle
1981 *Linea della Ricerca Artistica in Italia 1960–1980,*
 Palazzo dell Esposizioni, Rome
1982 *Arte Italiana 1960–1982,* Hayward Gallery, London
1983 *L'Informale in Italia,* Galleria Comunale d'Arte Moderna, Bologna
1985 *A Generation of Italian Art,* Alvar Aalto Museum,
 Jyvaskyla, Finland (travelled to Pori, Finland)
1987 *Kunst RAI 87,* Amsterdam

Collections:

Galleria Civica d'Arte Moderna, Turin; Museo de Gibellina,
Italy; Galleria Comunale d'Arte Moderna, Cagmiari, Italy;
University of Parma; Nationalgalerie, West Berlin; Kuns-
thalle, Bielefeld, West Germany; Städtische Galerie im Len-
bachhaus, Munich; Museum am Ostwall, Dortmund, West
Germany; Bochum University, West Germany.

Publications:

On SPAGNULO: book—*Spagnulo e la Pratica Sociale della
Scultura* by Tommaso Trini, Milan 1975; *Giuseppe
Spagnulo: Erotisch, Rhetorisch, Heroisch,* exhibition cata-
logue, West Berlin 1981; *Giuseppe Spagnulo: L'Istinto e
Sempre in Cerca di Anima,* exhibition catalogue, by Helmut
Friedel, Munich 1982; articles—"Giuseppe Spagnulo" by
Robert Sanesi in *Marcatre* (Milan), December 1966;
"Spagnulo" by Zeno Birolli in *Nac* (Milan), June 1970.

One of the greatest stimuli to the work of Giuseppe
Spagnulo at the start of his creative activity seems to
have been the urge to overcome the weight of an inert
material, to create a form that contradicts the true
nature of the material used. This became evident
when gigantic metal shapes (or even minute blocks of
the same material) were bent in unlikely directions
and fixed in a state of perpetual tension which made
them dynamic. Later on, the evolution of Spagnulo's
art was to become clearer with his approach to various materials, which made his aim more explicit. It
can be recognized in his numerous series of *Cartoni:*
raw cardboard, left in the natural state or just stained
with lampblack, which can be folded and then
pressed so as to achieve the desired form.

In the wake of the *Cartoni* came another interesting
period, that of the series of works in clay (which
Spagnulo christened "Landscapes"), in which another principle can be perceived, very much in keep-

ing with the moment in history through which we are passing today; that of extemporaneousness. These are works that the artist carries out with very simple, spare means: a surface of clay with pieces of tile or sheets of glass superimposed on them, on which he simply walks so as to give a wavy effect to the surface; this may even break the glass or drive the pieces of tile or stone into the clay. From these extempore works Spagnulo moved on most recently (1975–81) to another fascinating series, which he describes as "Archaeology." In these he works with solid iron plates with a deep groove in them; these are pressed on to similar iron plates which have been softened by heating, so as to obtain on the half-melted plate the impression of the groove in the first plate in relief. In this way it is possible to obtain works, always matched, which are presented as "traces of memory" (to use the sculptor's own well chosen expression). One plate is actually the "memory" of the other. The first is the matrix of the second, so that, rather than a "negative," what we have here is a sort of "twinning"—a double organism obtained from the interaction of the two aspects, one subordinate to and dependent on the other, a repeated record of what has its own form and yet is a mirror image of the other.

—Gillo Dorfles

SPERO, Nancy.

American. Born in Cleveland, Ohio, 24 August 1926. Studied at the Art Institute of Chicago, 1945–49, B.F.A. 1949; Atelier André Lhote, and Ecole des Beaux-Arts, Paris, 1950–51. Married the artist Leon Golub, *q.v.*, in 1951; children: Stephen, Phillip, and Paul. Independent artist, since 1949: lived and worked in Ischia and Florence, 1956–57, and in Paris, 1959–64; now lives and works in New York. Co-Editor, *Rip-Off* magazine, ad hoc committee of women artists, since 1972. Guest Artist, Sacramento State University, California, 1974; Visiting Artist, School of the Art Institute of Chicago, 1974; and St. Lawrence University, Canton, New York, 1975. Recipient: Creative Artists Public Service Fellowship, New York State Council on the Arts, 1976; National Endowment for the Arts Grant, Washington, D.C., 1977. Agent: Josh Baer Gallery, 270 Lafayette Street, New York, New York 10012. Address: 530 La Guardia Place, New York, New York 10012, U.S.A.

Individual Exhibitions:

1962   Galerie Breteau, Paris
1965   Galerie Breteau, Paris
1968   Galerie Breteau, Paris
1971   University of California at San Diego
       Mombaccus Art Center, New Paltz, New York
1973   A.I.R. Gallery, New York
1974   Women's Center, Williams College, Williamstown, Massachusetts
       Douglass College Library, Rutgers University, New Brunswick, New Jersey
       A.I.R. Gallery, New York
1977   Marianne Deson Gallery, Chicago
1978   Art Library, Queens College, New York
       Herter Gallery, University of Massachusetts, Amsterdam
       The Woman's Building, Los Angeles
1979   Peachtree Center Gallery, Atlanta
       Hampshire College Art Center, Amherst, Massachusetts
       Real Art Ways, Hartford, Connecticut
       Picker Art Gallery, Colgate University, Hamilton, New York
       A.I.R. Gallery, New York
1980   Livingston Gallery, Rutgers University, New Brunswick, New Jersey

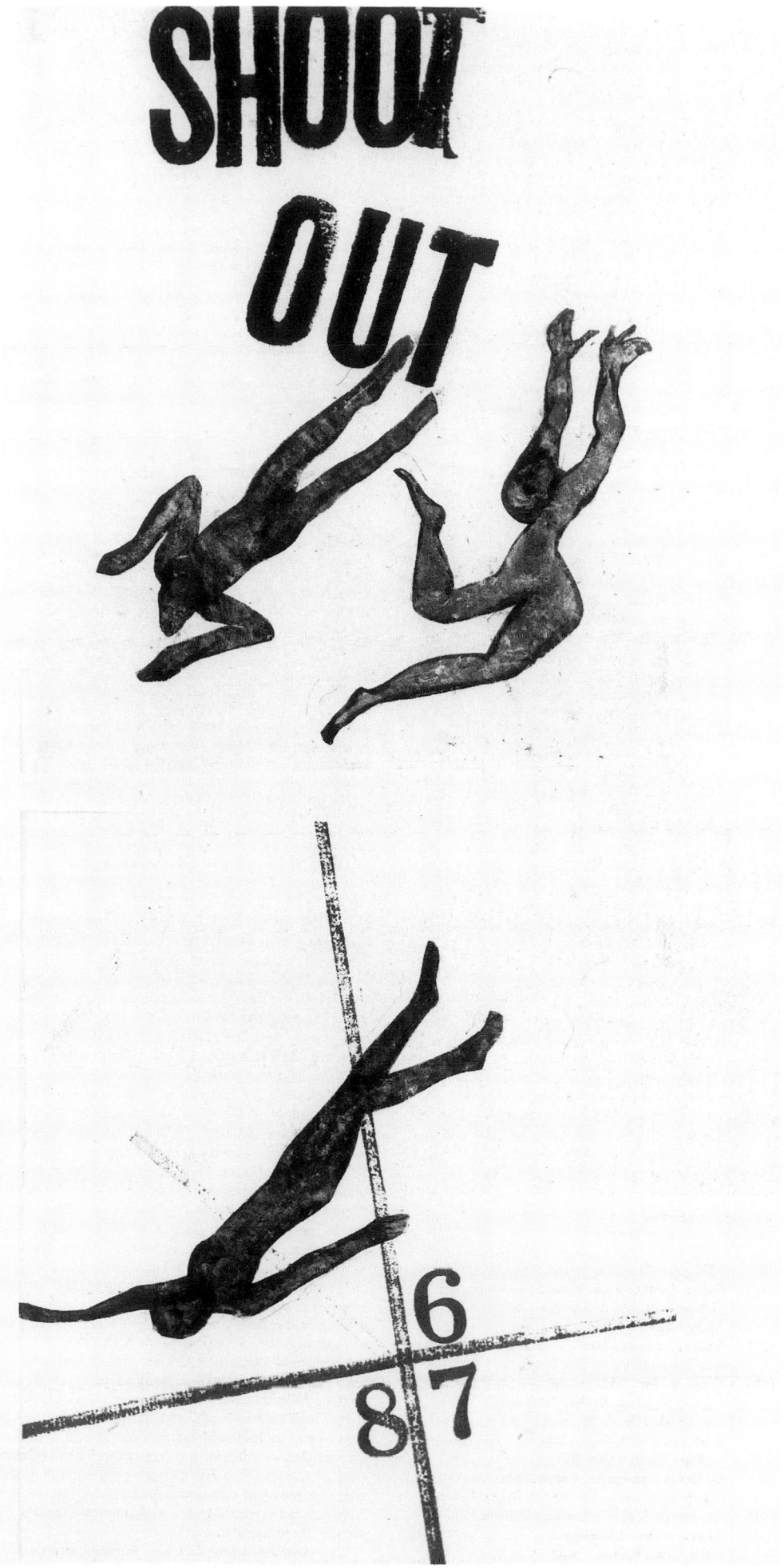

Nancy Spero: *Shoot Out*, 1974

1981	The Sarah Institute, New York
	Ben Shahn Gallery, William Patterson College, Wayne, New Jersey
	Herter Gallery, University of Massachusetts, Amherst
	A.I.R. Gallery, New York
1982	*Nancy Spero/Leon Golub*, Florence Wilcox Gallery, Swarthmore College, Pennsylvania
	Rockwell Kent Gallery, State University of New York at Plattsburgh
	Francis Colburn Gallery, University of Vermont, Burlington
	Vietnam War, Tweed Arts Group, Plainfield, New Jersey (with Leon Golub)
	Galerie France Morin, Montreal
	Matrix Gallery, Wadsworth Atheneum, Hartford, Connecticut
1983	University of New Mexico, Albuquerque (with Leon Golub)
	Fire Station Gallery, Houston
	Project Studio One, Long Island City, New York (with Leon Golub)
	Art Galaxy, New York
	A.I.R. Gallery, New York
	Art for Social Change, New York
	Brucknerhaus, Linz, Austria
	Center for Creative Studies, Detroit (with Leon Golub)
	Rhona Hoffman Gallery, Chicago
	Willard Galleries, New York
1984	University of California, Berkeley
	Riverside Studios, London
	Cash Gallery, New York (with David Reynolds; travelled to A.R.C., Toronto)
	Reed College, Portland, Oregon
	University of Chicago, Champaign
1985	Lawrence Oliver Gallery, Philadelphia
	Carnegie-Mellon University, Pittsburgh
	University of Iowa, Iowa City
	Powerhouse Gallery, Montreal
	S. L. Simpson Gallery, Toronto
	Coca Space, Seattle, Washington
	Burnett Miller Gallery, Los Angeles
	University of Connecticut, Storrs
1986	Hobart and William Smith Colleges, Geneva, New York (with Nicole Jolicoeur)
	Museum Villa Stuck, Munich
	Center Gallery, Carrboro, North Carolina
	Greenville County Museum of Art, South Carolina (with Leon Golub)
	Josh Baer Gallery, New York
	Rhona Hoffman Gallery, Chicago
1987	Orchard Gallery, Derry, North Ireland
	Fruit Market Gallery, Edinburgh
	Institute of Contemporary Art, London
	S. L. Simpson Gallery, Toronto
	Washington Project for the Arts, Washington, D.C.
	Josh Baer Gallery, New York
	Lawrence Oliver Gallery, Philadelphia
	Everson Museum of Art, Syracuse, New York (retrospective; travelled to New York City and Saskatoon, Canada)

Selected Group Exhibitions:

1963	*Salon International de Galeries Pilotes*, Musée Cantonal des Beaux-Arts, Lausanne, Switzerland
1972	*American Woman Artist Show*, Gedok-Kunsthaus, Hamburg
1977	*Words at Liberty*, Museum of Contemporary Art, Chicago
1979	*Feministische Kunst Internationaal*, Gemeentemuseum, The Hague (toured Holland)
1980	*Art of Conscience: The Art of the Last Decade*, Wright State University, Dayton, Ohio (toured the United States, 1981–82)
1981	*Crimes of Compassion*, Chrysler Museum, Norfolk, Virginia
1982	*Atomic Salon*, Ronald Feldman Gallery, New York
1984	*Content: A Contemporary Focus 1974–84*, Hirshhorn Museum, Washington, D.C.
1985	*Nude, Naked, Stripped*, Massachusetts Institute of Technology, Cambridge

1987	*Stations*, Centre International d'Art Contemporain, Montreal

Collections:

Judson Memorial Church, New York; Ramapo College, New Jersey; Institute of Technology, Boston.

Publications:

By SPERO: articles—"The Whitney Museum and Women" in *Art Gallery* (Ivoryton, Connecticut), January 1971; "Women's Speakout" in *New York Element*, February/March 1972; "Art: A Woman's Sensibility" in *California Institute of the Arts*, Valencia, California 1975; "Art Politics and Ethics: Interview with Leon Golub and Nancy Spero," with Derek Guthrie, in *New Art Examiner* (Chicago), April 1977; "Interview with Nancy Spero," with Donald Kuspit, in *Art in America* (New York), September/October 1977; "Ende" in *Women's Studies* (London), vol. 6, 1978; interview, with Nicole Jolicoeur and Nell Tenhaaf, in *Parachute* (Montreal), June/August 1985.

On SPERO: books—*American Sculpture in Process 1930–1970* by Wayne Andersen, Boston 1975; *From the Center* by Lucy Lippard, New York 1976; *Nancy Spero: The Black Paris Paintings*, exhibition catalogue with essay by Elaine King, Pittsburgh 1985; *Nancy Spero*, exhibition brochure with text by Rosetta Brooks, Philadelphia 1987; *Nancy Spero: Retrospective*, exhibition catalogue with essay by Jon Bird, London 1987; articles—"Bombs and Helicopters: The Art of Nancy Spero" by Leon Golub in *Caterpillar I* (New York), 1967; "Women Choose Women" by April Kingsley in *Artforum* (New York), March 1973; "Nancy Spero" by Donald Kuspit in *Art in America* (New York), July/August 1975; "Nancy Spero" by Lawrence Alloway in *Artforum* (New York), May 1976; "Women Ain't Losers" by John Perreault in the *Soho Weekly News* (New York), 23 September 1976; "Nancy Spero" by Corinne Robins in *Arts Magazine* (New York), November 1976; "Caring: 5 Political Artists" by Lucy Lippard in *Studio International* (London), vol. 193, no. 987, 1977; "Words and Images Through Time: The Art of Nancy Spero" by Corinne Robins in *Arts Magazine* (New York), December 1979; "Spero's Apocalypse" by Donald Kuspit in *Artforum* (New York), April 1980; "Nancy Spero" by Michael Newman in *Art Monthly* (London), September 1984; "Nancy Spero: Woman as Protagonist" by Jeanne Siegel in *Arts Magazine* (New York), September 1987.

From 1951 until 1965 I worked in oils on canvas. This group of existential works included lovers, prostitutes, mythological great mothers, etc.

From 1966 on I have worked exclusively on paper. 1966 to 1970: I made a series of over 100 war paintings. The paintings have messages, inscriptions, graffiti, i.e., S.E.A.R.C.H. and D.E.S.T.R.O.Y., L.O.V.E. TO H.A.N.O.I., etc. Victims are thrown from planes, the helicopter consumes its victims. "The Bomb," a human torso with obscene phallic heads spitting blood or fire—technological war.

"The Codex Artaud," 1971–72, have a cinematic quality—through extension (2 feet high and from 8 to 15 feet in length)—a fragmented and staccato positioning of the images of quotations. One has to change location, move in or distance oneself according to the scale of the images to follow the action. The rhythm of the whole is seemingly discordant and incomplete, relating to fractured time.

"Tortured in Chile," 1974, documents the torture of women political prisoners. From this work on I decided to represent "man" only through images of women.

"Torture of Women," 1976, extends in a continuous linear band, 20 inches high by 125 feet in length and contains case histories of women political prisoners from Latin American, Turkey, Iran, etc. (information from Amnesty International, etc.) combined with major references of mythological examples of the repression of women. The text is hand-painted with wood type alphabets and collaged bulletin style. Figures are collaged in to document and transcend the horror of immediate external realities.

"Notes on Women Part II—Women: Appraisals, Dance and Active Histories," 1979, is 20 inches high by 225 feet in length. A range of variously scaled hand-painted and collaged painted images weave through and interact with the 96 quotations and references, assembled from many cultures up to the present, defining aspects of existence with woman as the protagonist, an independent and positive force in a male-controlled world.

"The First Language," 1981, 20 inches high by 190 feet long, moves from war and rape to women's power, sexuality, grace and strength. There is no text in this piece, since gesture and movement are the earliest forms of human communication.

I use only images of women, to represent woman as protagonist and hero. This is a reversal of the typical art practice of portraying men as heroes and protagonists. I articulate women's situation and actions from repressed, victimized states to buoyant, self-confident stances.

These works are distanced from the Westernized notions of the personal subjective portrayal of individuality. The works deal with rhythm, stylization, contrast of body types, the juxtaposition of images past and present, varied historical references from disparate cultures, political information, etc.

I am not interested in individual physiognomies or personifications. The figures become generic in a somewhat similar way to, for example, the stylizations of Australian aboriginal art, early Greek vase painting, prehistoric art, etc. I combine in one work figures derived from various cultures whose extremely diverse and often disproportionate body sizes and types coexist in simultaneous time.

I use photographs informationally to derive images of contemporary women, for example, older Vietnamese women, a range of war and rape victims, youthful celebratory figures, who are depicted in stressed actions and symbolic representations. This is often emphasized by repeating the same figures but printed differently so that change between images is based on characteristics of tempo and time spans creating movement across the page. The repetition de-individualizes Western "subjectivity" in a non-hierarchical continuous presence.

—Nancy Spero

Nancy Spero's art/politics needs neither soap boxes nor labyrinthine rhetoric camouflaged in political jargon, to take control. Spero's images are ideographs montaged in staccato with verbal texts on long paper scrolls which become like personal holy scriptures. Since she knows all too well the effectiveness of hypnotic banality and subliminal ploys of the media, she rebukes them by using blunt dramatic symbols to confront the viewers. Traditional iconography would be inappropriate for her unconventional and sometimes harrowing messages about rape, murder, and political atrocities. Instead, she compresses information bits from hidden documents and the media, past and present, into verbal fragments. These are juxtaposed with figural analogies from the events. Spero demonstrates the persistence of these nightmarish occurrences throughout history. Beyond journalistic reportage, these collages grab the viewers in the way only art can.

More specifically, the history of torture, especially of women, is older than, but blasphemously aided by the *Bible*, the *Koran*, and all other generally respected sacred texts. Spero displays all kinds of tools of victimization with haunting beauty, with exquisite compassion and creative perspicacity.

A perfect example of this humanity is found in her work, "Codex Artaud." While Artaud had serious misogynistic tendencies, she empathized with his struggle to give birth to himself. She recognized in his struggles, his madness and spiritual anguish, a similarity to the history of women. The "Codex Artaud" had grown out of a preceding decade of work centering on anti-war responses to the Vietnam trauma. Phallic, tongue, and insectlike bombs spit death. The victims are seen licking the oppressor and vice-versa. Screeching slogans are scrawled on the paper as though in great desperation.

By 1974, Spero had come to the conclusion that the culprit of all the sado-sexual oppression grew out of the Patriarchy and, thus, has devoted herself exclusively to themes of women and feminism ever since. It was also at this time that her unique usage of the collage medium was honed. Ways of seeing and methods of communication become synonymous in intensely compressed collages of figure fragments and label-printed type-scripts of personally and quoted texts. Exaggeratedly posed goddesses, classical figures, and monsters run, dance, kneel, and tumble as they stutter and shout the cacophony of horrific realities that compromise the "news." Since 1974 she has done works—"The Torture of Women" and "Notes on Women Part II: Women: Appraisals, Dance, and Active Histories"—which run rapid-fire through a gamut of themes: childbirth, girlhood, menstruation, and divorce. These are often spliced with themes of collective import such as: women's survival, male appraisals, racism, women's role in revolution, etc. New works evolve from unresolved ideas from past pieces and are expanded by the addition of more recent and profound insights.

While Spero's focus has widened over the years, there is a consistency and high-pitched concentration in her work that remains throughout. Though the visual and the verbal are interwoven in what seems like an erratic grouping of various sizes and scales, it is far from unplanned, and creates a sense of the rhythms of abuses. Snaps and snatches, jagged slashes of the stiletto, jolts of punctures and ballistic torment, all leave the viewers in a paralyzed free-fall through an angst-ridden existential abyss. And there is no sweet calm genesis after apocalypse; no consolation of death; no salvation. Instead, her "heretical" collages make it clear that any one of us is a potential victim of similarly gruesome offenses.

—Elise LaRose

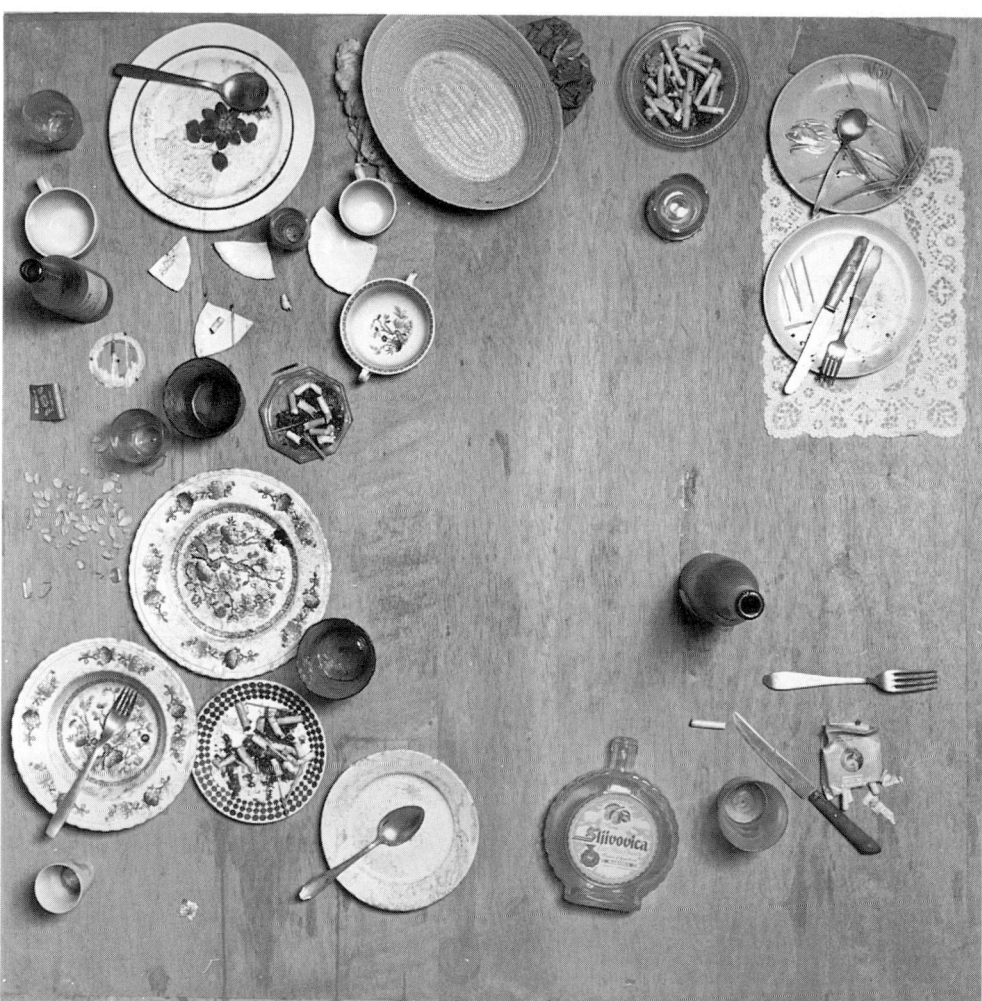

Daniel Spoerri: *Table Sculpture*, 1964

SPOERRI, Daniel.

Swiss. Born Daniel Isaac Feinstein in Galati, Rumania, 27 March 1930; emigrated to Switzerland, and adopted by his uncle Theophile Spoerri, Zurich, 1942. Educated in Zurich schools; studied at the Ecole des Hautes Etudes Commercials, Basle, 1947–48; studied ballet at the School of Dance, Opera de Zurich, 1950–52; studied classical ballet, under Preobrajenska and Kniaseff, and mime, under Decroux and Marceau, Paris, 1952–53. Worked for Wacker Dance Studios, Paris, 1952–54; Principal Dancer, Berne Opera, 1953–57; assistant to Gustav-Rudolf Sellner, Landestheater, Darmstadt, 1957–59. Independent plastic artist, Paris, 1959–66, Symi, Greece, 1966–68, Dusseldorf, 1968–71, Cavigliano, Italy and Zurich, 1972–3, and in La Selle sur le Bied, France, since 1973. Founder-Member, with Pierre Restany, Yves Klein, Jean Tinguely, Martial Raysse, Arman and others, New Realists group, Paris, 1960; Organizer, with K. G. Pontus Hulten, *Bewogen Beweging* exhibition, Stedelijk Museum, Amsterdam, 1961; produced first tableau-pieds, 1961; first happenings and events, from 1962; "objets de magie à la noix" and exchanged objects according to emotional value ("feilschmarkt" works), from 1966; first eat-art events, from 1968. Also a poet, and choreographer and producer of "Autotheatre" works, mainly with Jean Tinguely, from 1953. Founder-Editor, *Material,* concrete poetry review, 5 issues, Darmstadt, 1957–59, Editions Mat (Multiplication d'Art Transformable), Paris, from 1959, and *Le Petit Colosse de Symi*, Greece, 1967–68; proprietor, with Carlo Schroter, Eat-Art Restaurant, 1968–71, and Eat Art Galerie, Dusseldorf, 1970–71. Professor of Multimedia, Fachhochscule für Kunst und Design, Cologne, 1977; Guest Lecturer, San Francisco Art Institute, 1975; Lecturer, Hochscule für Bildende Künste, Hamburg, 1980. Recipient: DAAD Artist's Fellowship, West Berlin, 1978. Agent: Galerie Bonnier, 4 rue Saint Laurent, 1207 Geneva, Switzerland. Address: Moulin Boyard, 45210 La Selle sur le Bied, France.

Indiviual Exhibitions:

1961 *I Quadri a Trappola* Galleria Schwarz, Milan
Galleri Koepcke, Copenhagen
1962 Galerie Laurence, Paris
Galerie Lauhaus, Cologne
Studio F, Ulm, West Germany
1963 Galerie J, Paris
Galleria Schwarz, Milan
Galerie Rudolf Zwirner, Cologne
Galerie Dorothea Loehr, Frankfurt
Galerie Gerstner und Kutter, Basle
1964 Allan Stone Gallery, New York
Haus am Lutzowplatz, West Berlin
Galerie Rudolf Zwirner, Cologne
Galerie J, Paris
1965 Green Gallery, New York
Allan Stone Gallery, New York
Galleria Schwarz, Milan
Galerie Ad Libitum, Antwerp
City-Galerie, Zurich
Galerie Nachst St. Stephan, Vienna
1966 Galerie J, Paris (with Arman)
City Galerie, Zurich
1967 Spoerri House, Symi, Greece
1968 Galerie Gunar, Dusseldorf
Eat-Art Restaurant, Dusseldorf (opening event)
1969 Gegenverkehr, Aachen, West Germany
Galerie Handschin, Basle
1970 Eat-Art Galerie, Dusseldorf
Galleria al Vecchio Pastificio, Cavigliano, Italy
1971 Galerie Denise René-Hans Mayer, Dusseldorf
Eat-Art Gallery, Dusseldorf
Stedelijk Museum, Amsterdam (retrospective)
Galerie Seriaal, Amsterdam
Galerie Bischofberger, Zurich
Kunsthalle, Hamburg
1972 Centre National d'Art Contemporain, Paris
Helmhaus, Zurich

1974 Galerie Ben, Nice (with Claude Torey)
Galerie Germain, Paris
Kunsthalle, Dusseldorf
Galerie Günther Sachs, Hamburg
Schauspeilhaus, Bochum, West Germany (theatre decor for *Blue Angel*)
1975 Kunsthandel Brinkman, Amsterdam
Galerie Loeb, Berne
Galerie Bama, Paris
Galleria Multiphla, Milan
Galerie Bischofberger, Zurich
European Gallery, San Francisco
La Galerie Aberante, Plateau Beaubourg, Paris
1976 Spoerri Room, at *Dodspringet*, Charlottenborg, Copenhagen
1978 Galerie Levy, Hamburg
Spoerri Room, *Hammerausstellung*, Kunsthalle, Basle
Deutsches Schauspielhaus, Hamburg (theatre decor for *A Winter's Tale*)
1979 Kölnischer Kunstverein, Cologne (for *Musée Sentimental*, with M. L. Plessen)
1981 Galerie Bonnier, Geneva
1987 Galerie Littman, Basle

Spoerri has also presented numerous banquets and Eat-Art events throughout Europe since 1970.

Selected Group Exhibitions:

1959 *Dynamo-Mouvement*, Hessenhuis, Antwerp
1960 *Festival d'Avant-Garde*, Musée d'Art Moderne, Paris
1961 *The Art of Assemblage*, Museum of Modern Art, New York
1962 *Dylaby*, Stedelijk Museum, Amsterdam
The New Realists, Sidney Janis Gallery, New York
1965 *MAT und MAT MOT*, Galerie der Spiegel, Cologne

1970 *Nouveau Realisme 1960–70*, Rotonda della Besana, Milan
1975 *Biennale*, Venice
1977 *Sucre d'Art*, Musée des Arts Décoratifs, Paris
1980 *Art Zanders '80*, Zanders Feinpapiere AG, Bergisch Gladbach, West Germany

Collections:

Sammlung Hahn, Museum für Moderne Kunst, Vienna; Kunstmuseum, Dusseldorf; Kaiser-Wilhelm Museum, Krefeld, West Germany; Centre Georges Pompidou, Paris; Stedelijk Museum, Amsterdam; Kunsthaus, Zurich.

Publications:

By SPOERRI: books—*Topographie Anecdote du Hasard: An Anecdoted Topography of Chance*, with Robert Filliou, Paris 1961, new edition, with notes by Emmett Williams, New York 1966, with additional notes, by Dieter Rot, Neuwied 1968; *L'Optique Moderne*, with Francois Dufrene, edited by George Maciunas, New York 1962; *Gastronomisches Tagebuch*, Neuwied/West Berlin 1970; *My Mythological Travels*, New York 1970; *Sur les Keftedes*, Paris 1970; *Hommage à Isaac Feinstin—Motto: Daniel, du Apfel, falle weit vom Stamm*, exhibition catalogue, with an introduction by E. de Wilde, documents by Spoerri and others, Amsterdam 1971; *Krims Krams Magie*, Hamburg 1971; *Daniel Spoerri*, exhibition catalogue with Francois Dufrene, Paris 1972; *Die Bretonische Hausapotheke*, with M. L. Plessen, Cologne 1976; *Bretonische Heilquellen*, Cologne 1980; *Daniel Spoerri: Catalogue anecdote de seize oeuvres de l'Artiste de 1960 à 1964*, exhibition catalogue, Geneva 1981; film—*Resurrection*, with Tony Morgan, 1968.

On SPOERRI: books—*I Quadri a Trappola di Daniel Spoerri*, exhibition catalogue, with text by Alain Jouffroy, Milan 1961; *Daniel Spoerri*, exhibition catalogue, with text by Pierre Restany, Milan 1963; *Encyclopedie des Fraces, Attrapes et Mystifications* by N. Arnaud, Paris 1964; *Pop Art* by Lucy R. Lippard, New York and London 1966; *FOEW & ONBWHNW* by Dick Higgins, New York 1969; *Architektur, Concept Art* by Dick Higgins and Wolf Vostell, Dusseldorf 1969; *Pop Art et Cie* by Francois Pluchart, Paris 1971; *Daniel Spoerri*, exhibition catalogue, with texts by Claus Bremer and Marja Bloem, Zurich 1972; *Daniel Spoerri*, exhibition catalogue, Paris 1972.

Daniel Spoerri, who acted and danced when he was a youth, has a strong sense of theater, whether visual or in the actual performance.

His personal motto is: "Daniel, du Apfel falle weit vom Stamm."

In the mid 1950's he moved on from an appearance in the everlasting *Count of Luxembourg* to join the cast of the Berne Stadttheater's production of *Peter and the Wolf* (1956) and later produced and created the choreography for Tschumi ("Colour Ballet" in which he also danced).

Then he and Dieter Rot, with Pol Bury, Emmett Williams, Luca and Bremer published a review of concrete and ideogrammatic poetry called *Material*.

By 1960 this indefatigable and inventive Rumanian was staging exhibitions of his own works, having made contact with an assortment of other artists, including Duchamp, Albers, Soto and Agam. Later in Paris he joined forces with Gerstner, Man Ray, Tinguely and Vasarely. At this time he was deep into his MAT experiments (Multiplication/Art/Transformation).

Spoerri seems to have been at the centre of so many co-operative performances by contemporary artists (Luginbuhl, Ultvedt, Niki de Saint-Phalle, Rauschenberg and Raysse). What is so extraordinary about him and his *gauchiste* activities?

In 1962 it was typical of him and his works that he should have starred in Victor Musgrave's *Festival of Misfits* at London's Gallery One where the windows of 6 North Audley Street were covered with white sheets behind which the visual carnage was running riot. The other eight participants included Ben Vautier and Olof Ultvedt, but Spoerri's messy unfinished meals, dirty glasses and cigarette stubs attached to their uncleared tables made the deepest impression. Here was a terrible paradox—immediacy frozen into permanence. Litter and corruption were suddenly given art status. "The Bones of Szekely Gulyas—with the cooperation of rats" was offered as proof that actuality, even if it suffers the onslaught of time, *still matters*.

What happened to all this poignant disarray?

As usual with this artist, he operated on several levels simultaneously. The tables might be tidied up a bit and then "hung" like pictures on the wall, their bottles, plates, cutlery and napkins all firmly glued into place and perpetuity for the benefit of those who came to see them at the CNAC in Paris, or his admirers could join in a culinary frolic at Dusseldorf's Eat Art gallery where a special Spoerri triple-tiara cake presented to Pierre Restany amid art-debris like the *appetisers* he cooked in the manner of Arman and other artists, but for Seerials, the multiple-shop in Amsterdam, he had other aspects of anti-gravity and inverse-sociology to provide: "Le Pourboire de Madeleine" (a round tin tray with coins stuck to it so that it could be suspended picture-style from the wall) or his experiments with pairs of children's shoes (one lot suffering from rat urination, another showing how it had been deftly chewed, and in one case the calamity of the shoe caught in the mouse trap—all of them presented on trays of gravel). Spoerri's imagination is always heretical. His "Homage to an Unknown Soldier" is an erect penis with a crown like a stahlhelm, the whole trophy mounted like a big game hunter's prize on a wooden shield.

The artist is like the clown of contemporary art. All great clowns are artists.

—Sheldon Williams

STAECK, Klaus.

German. Born in Pulsnitz, Dresden, 28 February 1938. Educated in Bitterfeld, near Halle/Saale, 1944–56; studied law in Heidelberg, Hamburg, and West Berlin, 1957–64; self-taught in art. Independent artist, Heidelberg, since 1964: first prints and posters, 1960; first wood-prints, 1964–67; Founder, Edition Tangente, now Edition Staeck press, Heidelberg, 1965; Founder-Editor, with Peter Knorr and Siegfried Mahnert, *Tangente-Report* magazine, Heidelberg, 1965; worked with the artists Jochen Gerz, 1967, and Gerhard Steidl, 1970. Founder, Politischer Arbeitskreises, Student Association, Klausenpfad, Heidelberg, 1961; Candidate, Social Democratic Party (SPD) 1967; Chairman, Lawyer and Graphics Editor, Freie Hochschule für Kreativitat und Interdisziplinaire Forschung, Dusseldorf, 1973. Art tutor, Studenthochhausen, Klausenpfad, Heidelberg, 1967–69; Guest Instructor, Gesamthochschule, Kassel, West Germany, 1971; Professor, Gesamthochschule, Universitat Essen, 1981; Professor, Kunstakademie, Dusseldorf, 1986–88. Recipient: Zille-Preis, *Exhibition of Socio-Critical Art*, West Berlin, 1970; Pratt Center Prize, New York, 1968; Verkehrsburos prize, *Grafikbiennale*, Vienna, 1972; Forderpreis, *Intergrafik*, East Berlin, 1976; Kritikerpreis, West Berlin, 1979; Gold Medal, *Biennale für Fotomontage*, Gridziadz, Poland, 1979. Address: Ingrimstrasse 3/Postfach 102063, 69 Heidelberg, West Germany.

Individual Exhibitions:

Staeck has had more than 3,00 one-man exhibitions at galleries, universities and institutes throughout Germany and Europe since 1960, including:

1965 Viola Gallery, Prague
1975 *Politick Affiches*, Stedelijk Van Abbemuseum, Eindhoven, Netherlands
1978 *Ruckblick in Sachen Kunst und Politik*, Kunstverein, Frankfurt (travelled to Heidelberg, Graz, West Berlin, Vienna, Aarhus, Russelheim and Hannover)
1979 Wilhelm-Lehmbruck-Museum, Duisburg, West Germany
1983 Henie-Onstad Kunstsenter, Hovikodden, Norway
1985 Konsthall, Malmo, Sweden
1986 Kunsthalle, Darmstadt, West Germany

Selected Group Exhibitions:

1967 *International Graphics Biennale*, Ljubljana, Yugoslavia
1969 *Intermedia 69*, Heidelberg
1970 *Kunst und Politik*, Badischer Kunstverein, Karlsruhe (toured Europe)
1971 *Biennale de Paris*, Parc Floral, Paris

Klaus Staeck: *Die Kunst ist Frei*, 1987

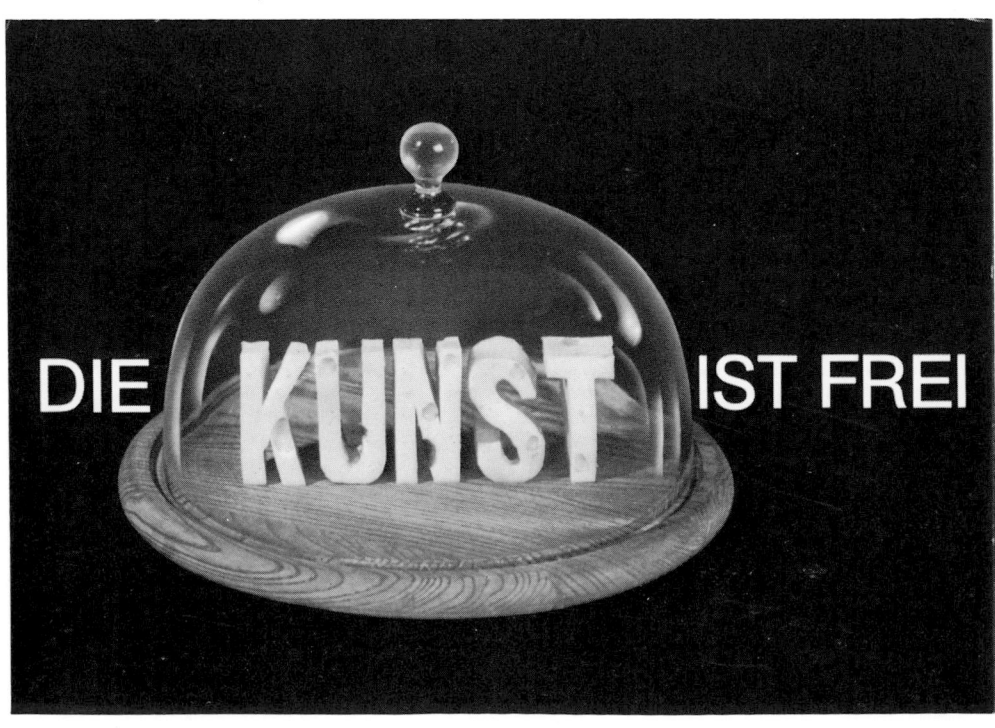

1972	*Documenta*, Kassel, West Germany
1973	*Kunst im Politischen Kampf*, Kunstverein, Hannover
1974	*Projekt 74*, Kunstverein, Cologne
1977	*Documenta 6*, Museum Fridericianum, Kassel, West Germany (and *Documenta 7*, 1982; *Documenta 8*, 1987)
1985	*Kunst in der Bundesrepublik 1945-85*, Nationalgalerie, West Berlin
1986	*Beuys zu Ehren*, Lenbachhaus, Munich

Collections:

Kunstverein, Heidelberg; Kunstverein, Dusseldorf; Kunsthalle, Cologne; Kaiser-Wilhelm-Museum, Krefeld, West Germany; Nationalgalerie, East Berlin; Kunstmuseum, Basle; Museum des 20. Jahrhunderts, Vienna; Stedelijk Van Abbemuseum, Eindhoven, Netherlands; Mahnsche Galerie, Brno, Czechoslovakia; Kulturhuset, Stockholm.

Publications:

By STAECK: books—*Intermedia 69*, exhibition catalogue, with Jochen Goetze, Heidelberg 1969; *Pornografie*, with Peter Gorsen, Giessen and Göttingen 1971; *Befragung der Documenta*, Göttingen, 1972; *Plakate Abreissen Verboten*, with Ingeborg Karst, Göttingen 1973; *Die Reichen mussen noch Reicher Werden*, with Ingeborg Karst, Reinbeck 1973; *Der Fall Staeck*, Göttingen 1975; *Die Kunst findet nicht im Saale statt*, with Dieter Adelmann, Reinbek 1976; *Eine Zensur findet gelegentlich statt*, with Dieter Adelmann, Göttingen 1977; *Gedichte/Collagen*, with Heinrich Boll, Göttingen 1979; *Die Gedanken sind frei*, East Berlin 1982; *Staeck's Umwelt*, Göttingen 1984.

On STAECK: books—*Kunst und Politik*, exhibition catalogue, with texts by G. Bussmann, Robert Kudielka, Herbert Marcuse and Gérald Gassiot-Talabot, Karlsruhe 1970; *Mail Art: Communications à Distance, Concept* by Jean-Marc Poinsot, with a preface by Jean Clair, Paris 1971; *Kunstjahrbuch 2*, edited by Jürgen Harten, Horst Richter, Karl Ruhrberg and Wieland Schmied, Hannover 1972; *Deutsch Kunst der 70er Jahre: Plastik, Objekte, Aktionen* by Jürgen Morschel, Munich 1972; *Projekt 74: Aspekte internationaler Kunst am Anfang der 70er Jahre*, exhibition catalogue, with texts by Dieter Ronte, Evelyn Weiss, Manfred Schneckenburger and others, Cologne 1974; *Klaus Staeck: Politik Affiches*, exhibition catalogue, Eindhoven, Netherlands, 1975; *Klaus Staeck: Ruckblick in Sachen Kunst und Politik*, exhibition catalogue, with texts by G. Bussmann, Dieter Adelmann, Bazon Brock and others, Frankfurt 1978; *Documenta*, exhibition catalogue, 2 vols., edited by Rudi H. Fuchs, Kassel, West Germany 1982; *Documenta 8*, exhibition catalogue edited by Manfred Schneckenburger, Kassel, West Germany 1987.

With my work I would like to contribute towards exposing the untruthfulness of the excess of pictures surrounding us—I should like not to present what has been exposed, but to expose what has been presented.

As method I have chosen irony because to me the acridity and dullness that characterize most political discussions arouse fear. Dogmatism and oppression are often not far apart. To create a lasting alteration of consciousness in the direction of democratic socialism in the minds of those who hold differing political opinions, it is necessary to be inventive. Against an inert mass, cunning offers the only chance. I want to bring about necessary discussions on important political problems. I should like to place questions in such a way that they are hard to avoid. Irony helps me in this and is usually more effective than ponderous appeals or threats.

For me the attempt to reflect reality with pictorial means and to effect something in it represents rising above traditional art. An intensive study of the media is essential to any serious attempt at departure from the restrictions imposed by the encrusted art concept. In my case this led to posters, stickers, postcards and leaflets. It is with these media that I obtain access to the public, without which my work would be pointless. I convey my political ideas through posters which are made for the streets. Thus I reach everyone participating in daily life on the streets, in contrast to the past, when I had to rely on a small, elite circle of addresses.

The breakthrough out of boredom of the art ghettos, where paintings have stagnated to become pure decor, brought with it, though, along with problems of content, also new distributional and financial problems. Since then my work has largely drawn away from the business of art. It is mainly young people who employ my posters politically, but several hundred thousand posters and stickers have, for instance, been acquired by workers: those same workers that so many would like to get through to, but actually cannot. I know from representative inquiries which population groups I reach with my work: all groups feel themselves to be approached, though some more than others.

At present I am in the process of intensifying my contacts with the trade unions: numerous exhibitions in union headquarters, contributions to union newspapers and discussions with workers. At the same time I am increasingly engaged in collaboration with youth groups (e.g. exhibitions in youth centres and schools).

—Klaus Staeck

STAMOS, Theodoros.

American. Born in New York City, 31 December 1922. Educated in public schools, New York; studied sculpture, under Simon Kennedy and Joseph Kouzal, at the American Artist School, New York, 1936 (on scholarship). Painter: worked as hatblocker, florist, printer, and frame-maker, 1939-43; commission for work on *SS Argentina*, Moore McCormack Lines, New York, 1946; toured Western America, 1947; travelled to France, Italy, and Greece, 1948. Taught at Hartley Settlement House and Black Mountain College, North Carolina, 1950-54; Instructor, Art Students League, 1955; Lecturer, School of Fine Arts, Columbia University, New York, 1966; Professor, Brandeis University, Waltham, Massachusetts, 1967-68. Recipient: Tiffany Foundation Fellowship, 1951; National Institute of Arts and Letters Award, New York, 1956; Brandeis University Creative Arts Award, Waltham, Massachusetts, 1959; Mainichi Newspaper Prize, *Tokyo International*, 1967; National Arts Foundation Award, Washington, D.C., 1967. Agent: Louis K. Meisel Gallery, 141 Prince Street, New York, New York 10012. Address: 37 West 83rd Street, New York, New York 10024, U.S.A.

Individual Exhibitions:

1943	Wakefield Gallery, New York
1945	Mortimer Brandt Gallery, New York
1947	Betty Parsons Gallery, New York
1948	Betty Parsons Gallery, New York
1949	Betty Parsons Gallery, New York
1950	Phillips Memorial Gallery, Washington, D.C.
1951	Betty Parsons Gallery, New York
1953	Betty Parsons Gallery, New York
1954	Phillips Memorial Gallery, Washington, D.C.
1956	Betty Parsons Gallery, New York
1957	Philadelphia Art Alliance
	Gump's Gallery, San Francisco
	André Emmerich Gallery, New York
1958	Corcoran Gallery of Art, Washington, D.C. (retrospective)
1960	André Emmerich Gallery, New York
	Gimpel Fils Gallery, London
	McNay Art Institute, San Antonio, Texas
1961	André Emmerich Gallery, New York
	Galleria del Naviglio, Milan
1962	André Emmerich Gallery, New York
1963	André Emmerich Gallery, New York
1964	André Emmerich Gallery, New York
1966	André Emmerich Gallery, New York
1967	Spingold Theater Arts Center Gallery, Waltham, Massachusetts

1968	André Emmerich Gallery, New York
1969	Waddington Fine Arts Gallery, Montreal
1970	André Emmerich Gallery, New York
1972	Marlborough-Gerson Gallery, New York
1973	Joslyn Art Museum, Omaha, Nebraska
1974	Athens Gallery
1977	Louis K. Meisel Gallery, New York
	Galerie Le Portail, Heidelberg
	Morgan Art Gallery, Shawnee Mission, Kansas
1978	Hokin Gallery, Palm Beach, Florida
	Union College, Schenectady, New York
1979	Wichita State University, Kansas
1980	Munson-Williams-Proctor Institute, Utica, New York
	State University of New York at New Paltz (retrospective)
1981	Martha White Gallery, Louisville, Kentucky
	Louis K. Meisel Gallery, New York
1982	Karen and Jean Bernier Gallery, Athens
1984	Knoedler Gallery, Zurich
1985	Galerie Wurthle, Vienna
	Kouros Gallery, New York
	Ericson Gallery, New York

Selected Group Exhibitions:

1945	*Whitney Annual*, New York (and 1946)
1948	*Biennale*, Venice
1950	*Contemporary American Painting*, University of Illinois, Urbana
1952	*Carnegie International*, Carnegie Institute, Pittsburgh
1959	*Documenta*, Kassel, West Germany
1961	*Biennale*, Tokyo
1968	*Dada, Surrealism, and Their Heritage*, Museum of Modern Art (toured the United States)
1978	*Abstract Expressionism: The Formative Years*, Cornell University, Ithaca, New York
1980	*American Drawings*, Du Bose Gallery, Houston
1982	*A Curator's Choice 1942-63*, Rose Esman Gallery, New York

Collections:

Museum of Modern Art, New York; Whitney Museum, New York; Metropolitan Museum of Art, New York; Albright-Knox Art Gallery, Buffalo, New York; Hirshhorn Museum and Sculpture Garden, Smithsonian Institution, Washington, D.C.; Corcoran Gallery of Art, Washington, D.C., Walker Art Center, Minneapolis; Art Institute of Chicago; California Palace of the Legion of Honor, San Francisco; Tel Aviv Museum.

Publications:

On STAMOS: books—*Stamos*, exhibition catalogue, by B. B. Newman, New York 1947; *Theodoros Stamos* by Kenneth Sawyer, Paris 1960; *Stamos* by Ralph Pomeroy, New York 1971; *Theodoros Stamos* by Ralph Pomeroy, New York 1973; *Theodoros Stamos: Works from 1945 to 1984*, exhibition catalogue with essays by Barbara Cavaliere and Theodore F. Wolff, Zurich 1984; *Stamos*, exhibition catalogue with essay by Dore Ashton, New York 1985.

Younger by many years, but professionally their contemporary, Stamos (as he prefers being called) shared the explorations and discoveries of the American abstract painters who found their profound footing after the Second World War. Along with such painters as Baziotes and Rothko he depicted biomorphic subject matter in thin washes of pigment—in his case the sea and its creatures, rocks, plants and leaves. Which led to the abstraction of cultivated fields on Long Island and a series of works influenced by the Orient having mostly to do with the effect of light falling through semi-transparent screens: imaginary, non-literal tea houses. Fire and snow played their parts too along with the over-head viewpoint, turned toward river-bed-like channels of thick, rich paint—"landscapes" without any horizons--that occupied him in the 50s.

A long series of "sun boxes" followed. Paintings in which two rectangles suspended like reflections of one another balanced in fields of radiant color. During this same period a group of wall hangings were produced after "cartoons" fashioned from the cut and torn paper, along with works on paper and a series of prints.

A trip to Greece resulted in a shift from the sunbox format—the "boxes" giving way to larger, more open rectangles with washes of paint sweeping into various parts of the canvas much like shallow waves. These paintings were an extension of an "Infinity Series" begun in the late 60s where an effort to push forms nearer and nearer to the periphery of the actual canvas led to emptier and emptier expanses of color. More or less in reaction to this, there then evolved paintings full of small, highly active forms, intricately composed, which are a little like the shapes found in the work of Arthur Dove (an artist much admired by Stamos).

A subtle, complex and powerful colorist, Stamos continues to probe the limits of abstraction in the last quarter of this century, firmly committed to the tradition of the easel picture and the painterly concerns which it has produced.

—Ralph Pomeroy

STÄMPFLI, Peter.

Swiss. Born in Deisswil, Switzerland, 3 July 1937. Educated at Ecole des Arts et Métiers, Bienne, Switzerland, 1954–55; studied painting with Max von Muhlenen, Berne, 1954–59. Married Ana Maria Torello in 1961. Independent painter, Paris, since 1960: images of human body and food details, 1963–65; automobile and tyre details, 1966–70; tyre-track images, from 1970; first sculptures, 1985. Agent: Galerie Lelong, 13 rue de Teheran, 75008 Paris. Address: 54 rue Notre Dame de Lorette, 75009 Paris, France.

Individual Exhibitions:

1966	Galerie Bischofberger, Zurich
	Galerie Rive Droite, Paris
1967	Galerie Tobies et Silex, Cologne
1968	Instituto Torcuato di Tella, Buenos Aires
1969	Galerie Rive Droite, Paris
	Galerie Bischofberger, Zurich
1970	Galerie Rive Droite, Paris
1971	Galerie Rive Droite, Paris
	Galerie Richard Foncke, Ghent
	Galleria Christian Stein, Turin
1972	Palais des Beaux-Arts, Brussels
1974	Musée Galliera, Paris
1976	Galerie Jean Larcade, Paris
	Musée de l'Abbaye Sainte Croix, Les Sables-d'Olonne, France
1978	Galerie Jean Larcade, Paris
1979	Galerie Maeght, Zurich
	Musée d'Art et d'Industrie, St. Etienne, France
1980	Centre Georges Pompidou, Paris
	Galerie Maeght, Paris
1982	Galerie Maeght, Zurich
	Kunsthaus, Aarau, Switzerland
	Galerie Sapone, Nice, France
1987	Palais Municipal, Lyon, France
1988	Galerie Lelong, Paris

Selected Group Exhibitions:

1960	*42 Jung Schweizer,* Kunstmuseum, Leverkusen, West Germany
1963	*Biennale,* Paris
1967	*Bienal,* Sao Paulo
1969	*22 Jonge Zwitsers,* Stedelijk Museum, Amsterdam
1970	*Biennale,* Venice
1973	*Contemporary Swiss Art,* Tel Aviv Museum

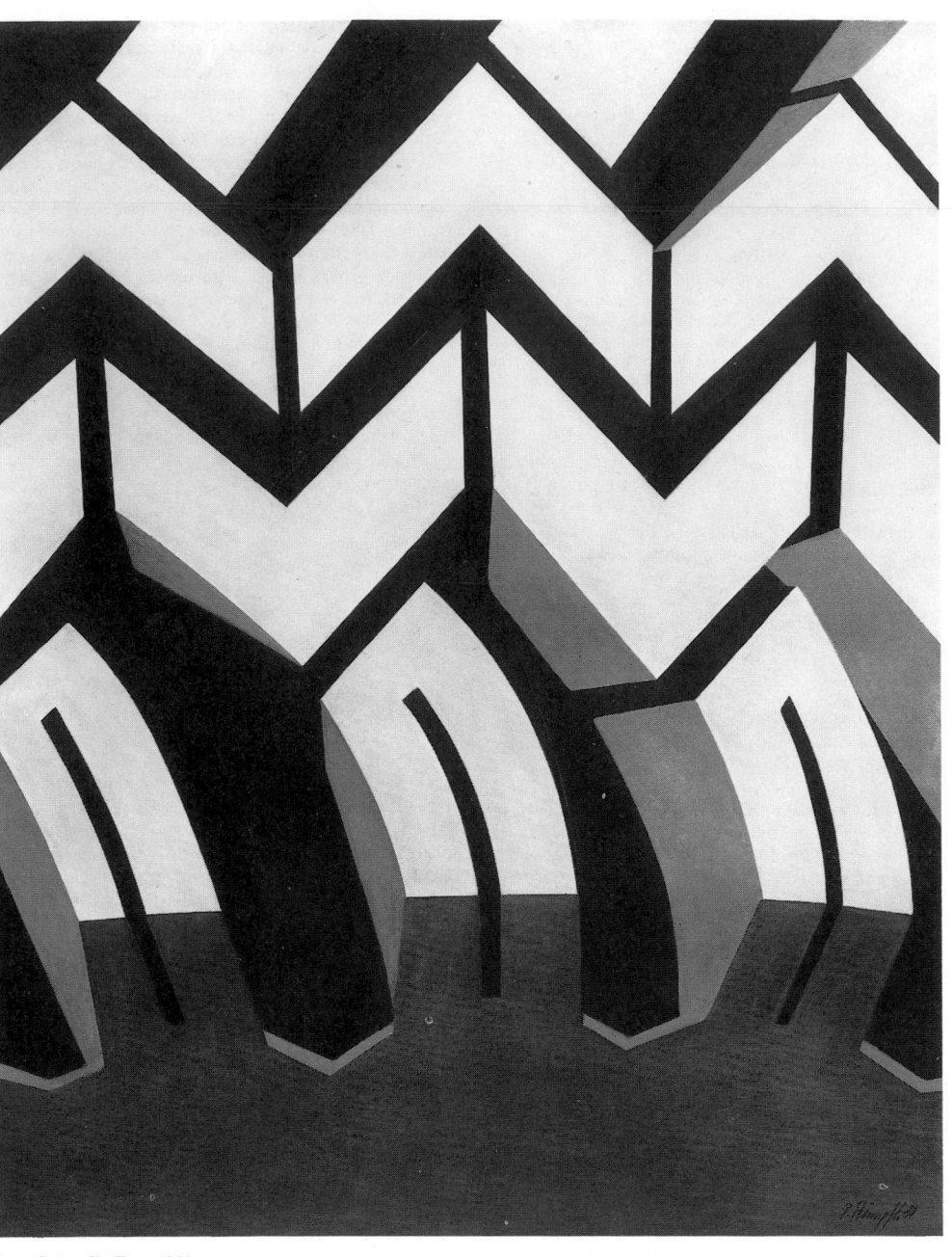

Peter Stämpfli: *Zeus,* 1980

1974	*Hyperrealistes Americains/Realistes Europeens,* Centre National d'Art Contemporain, Paris (travelled to Hannover; Rotterdam; Milan)
1976	*Aspects of Realism,* Rothmans Gallery, Stratford, Ontario (toured Canada)
1978	*Art Contemporain Suisse,* Helmhaus, Zurich
1985	*Dinge des Menschen,* Stadtische Kunsthalle, Recklinghausen, West Germany

Collections:

Kunsthaus, Zurich; Collection de la Peau de Lion, Zurich; Fonds National d'Art Contemporain, Paris; Centre Georges Pompidou, Paris; Kunstmuseum, Berne; Kunsthaus, Aarau; Fonds Regional d'Art Contemporain, Picardy; Musée d'Art et d'Industrie, St. Etienne; Musée de Dunquerque; Musée des Sables d'Olonne.

Publications:

On STÄMPFLI: books—*Le Peinture de Stämpfli* by Alain Jouffroy, Turin 1970: *Art in France* by Jean Clair, Paris 1972; *Peter Stampfli,* exhibition catalogue with essay by Bernard Ceysson, Aarau 1982; *Peter Stampfli: Vom Objektportrat zur geometrischen Struktur,* exhibition catalogue with preface by Fritz Billeter, Zurich 1982; *Le Pastel* by Genevieve Monnier, Geneva 1985; *25 Ans d'Art en France* by Jean Louis Pradel, Paris 1986.

All my work consists of seizing the image, the gesture, the objects which surround us, living what is going on around us, being sensitive to present events and translating them into painting.

I have taken a more particular interest in cars: I was dazzled by the object in its new, intact, self-advertising state, never by the used object. There was never the red print of lipstick on my glasses, never a trace of dirt on the wing of a car. I painted chrome bumpers, headlights, radiators, and then my attention fixed itself on the wheels. From the wheels I passed to the tyre, then to the tyre-mark . . . . The city is a part of all our lives. There was a period when painters depicted hunting scenes, portraits of kings. Today, the artist can only paint what he sees. I am not making an ironic proposal, I am simply seeking to draw up a report of a period. My images are in no instance reproductions; they are interpretations. The photograph is a starting-point, which I then translate into paint. It is very probable that one day I shall paint something other than tyres; it would take more than that to stop me from painting. The development of my plastic itinerary can appear extremely linear and logical: wheels-tyres-tyremarks-structures. But if someone had told it to me ten years ago I wouldn't have believed them.

—Peter Stämpfli

What immediately holds one's attention in Stämpfli's work is the imperious and absolute character of its forward progression. Nothing to cling to, to stop and take pleasure in: just series of pictures carried so implacably to their extreme consequences that, exclusively retaining the attention, they displace it from the preceding work, making of the oeuvre as a whole a phenomenon of perpetual actuality. What is more, the current language of the art world translates this state of fact perfectly: Stämpfli has been by turns, without anybody having emphasised these successive shifts, the painter of cars, the painter of wheels, the painter of tyres. He is , today, the painter of tyre-marks.

Between Stämpfli and James Rosenquist exists the same relationship as between Yves Klein and Mondrian: there has, indeed, been no lack of comparisons between Stämpfli's first pictures, painted at the same time as those of the initial generation of pop artists, and the works of Rosenquist. It was a way for critics to confine themselves to a thematic reading without noting the specificness of Stämpfli's work. Renouncing all montage of images, all relationships of an intellectual or emotional nature, isolating, on the contrary, the object on the white background of the canvas, he situates the object in an abstract space, depersonalises it. This dwindling of the context was given material form by Stämpfli when in 1966, in "Rouge Baiser" (Red Kiss), he cut out the picture following the exact shape of the lips. With "SS 396, No. 2" (1969) Stampfli's procedure marks a decisive step. The picture, in the shape of a wheel, is at once object and painting: the subject can be read simultaneously as realist painting, image of industrial civilization, and as concentric zones of colour, close to the works of Kenneth Noland, for example.

The reductive character which is clearly marked in Stämpfli's work, in his circumscribing his field of investigation from the wheel to the tyre alone, pushed this ambiguity of reading even further: the sculpted motif is at once both something real, everyday, identifiable in the repertoire of trademarks and industrial firms, and a structure which is abstract, repetitive, serial. The surface of the canvas assuming the precise form of the object, the identity is—except for volume—total. Perhaps it is in this slight distance—the perspectival crushing of an object reduced to the two-dimensional surface of the canvas—that the reason for the following stage should be sought.

The tyre-mark, the negative of the schema of the tyre, first combined with the picture, then independent, is a questioning of the classical structure of the picture: canvas of rectangular, square, or round format covered with paint. Through his personal language, Stämpfli joins up with the questions posed by an artist such as Frank Stella. He gives them, however, a more conceptual continuation as a result of the dialectic shift of the content of the work, in the absence of gratuitousness of the realist mode of writing finding its elements outside all formalism. The recent continuations of Stämpfli's work, all questioning of visual reality by means of perspective, the conflict with pictorial reality, place these apparently so specific paintings among those which are entering in the most penetrating fashion the debate being carried on by contemporary artists, that of the nature of art itself

—Daniel Abadie

STANKIEWICZ, Richard (Peter).

American. Born in Philadelphia, Pennsylvania, 18 October 1922; moved with his family to Detroit, 1929. Educated at Cass Technical School, Detroit, M.I. 1940; studied at the Hans Hofmann School of Fine Arts, New York, 1948–50, and under Fernand Léger, 1950, and under Ossip Zadkine, 1950–51, in Paris. Served in the United States Navy, 1941–45. Married Patricia M. Doyle in 1961; children: Peter and Anthony. Sculptor: lived in Paris, 1950–51; settled in New York, 1952; Co-Founder, Hansa Gallery Cooperative, New York, 1952–58; lived in Worthington, Massachusetts, 1959 until his death in 1983. Artist-in-Residence, Tampa Art Institute, Florida, 1965; Lecturer, University of Miami, 1966. Professor of Art, State University of New York at Albany, 1967–82. Artist-in-Residence, Amherst College, Massachusetts, 1970–71; Salzman Visiting Artist, Brandeis University, Waltham, Massachusetts, 1973. Recipient: Brandeis University Creative Arts Award; National Arts Council Grant; Ford Foundation Grant. Agent: Zabriskie Gallery, 29 West 57th Street, New York, New York 10019. *Died* (Worthington, Massachusetts) *27 March 1983.*

Individual Exhibitions:

1953	Hansa Gallery, New York
1954	Hansa Gallery, New York
1955	Hansa Gallery, New York
1956	Hansa Gallery, New York
1957	Hansa Gallery, New York
1958	Hansa Gallery, New York
	Frumkin Gallery, New York
	Landau Gallery, Los Angeles
1959	Stable Gallery, New York
1960	Stable Gallery, New York
	Galerie Neufville, Paris
1963	Robert Fraser Gallery, London
1965	Stable Gallery, New York
	Tampa Art Institute, Florida
1969	Frank Walters Gallery, Sydney
	National Gallery of Victoria, Melbourne
1971	Zabriskie Gallery, New York
1972	Zabriskie Gallery, New York
1973	Zabriskie Gallery, New York
1975	Zabriskie Gallery, New York
1977	Zabriskie Gallery, New York
1979	State University of New York at Albany (retrospective)
1981	Zabriskie Gallery, New York
1984	Zabriskie Gallery, New York
1987	Zabriskie Gallery, New York

Selected Group Exhibitions:

1958	*Biennale*, Venice
	Carnegie Insternational, Carnegie Institute, Pittsburgh
1961	*Bienal*, Sao Paulo
	Bewogene Beweging, Stedelijk Museum, Amsterdam
	4 Amerikanare, Moderna Museet, Stockholm (travelled to the Kunsthalle, Berne)
1963	*International Sculpture Exhibition*, Battersea Park, London
1964	*Recent American Sculptors*, Jewish Museum, New York
1968	*The Machine*, Museum of Modern Art, New York
1982	*3 Sculptors/3 Photographers*, Zabriskie Gallery, New York

Collections:

Guggenheim Museum, New York; Museum of Modern Art, New York; Whitney Museum, New York; Albright-Knox Art Gallery, Buffalo, New York; Philadelphia Museum of Art; Hirshhorn Museum and Sculpture Garden, Smithsonian Institution, Washington, D.C.; Dayton Art Institute, Ohio; Art Institute of Chicago; Centre Georges Pompidou, Paris; Moderna Museet, Stockholm.

Publications:

By STANKIEWICZ: articles—"Untitled" in *Art Now* (New York), no. 4, 1972.

On STANKIEWICZ: books—*Theories of Modern Art: A Source Book by Artists and Critics*, edited by Herschel B. Chipp, Berkeley, California 1970; *Icons and Images of the 60's*, edited by Nicolas and Elena Calas, New York 1971; *Richard Stankiewicz*, exhibition catalogue with essay by Fairfield Porter, New York 1987; articles—"2 New York Sculptors in Sydney" by Daniel Thomas in *Art in Australia* (Sydney), September 1969; "Letter from Australia" by Elwyn Lynn in *Art International* (Lugano, Switzerland), November 1969; "New York Letter" by A. Smith in *Art International* (Lugano, Switzerland), Summer 1972.

*

Richard Stankiewicz was born in Philadelphia in 1922 to a Polish emigrant family. In accordance with his family's wishes he studied engineering and worked in the tool industry in Detroit. Then, at the outbreak of the Second World War, he joined the U.S. Navy. So it was not until the age of 26 that he actually began his vocation: he enrolled at Hans Hofmann's school of painting in New York. On graduating in 1950 he lived for a while in Paris, where he studied with Léger and spent some time in Zadkine's workshop. He returned to New York and made his debut in 1953 at the Hansa Gallery, exhibiting spatial constructions made from welded scraps of industrial origin—pieces of pipe, wire, cable, chain, cogs, boilers, pistons, drums or unidentified pieces of used metal. The critics read meanings into these objects, conjecturing that the author was criticizing society's mechanical civilization and making fun of its technical arrogance. But the idea of using junk as a valuable artistic medium could also be said to involve the artist's memories of childhood, games on foundry slag heaps and refuse dumps. On an aesthetic level, the idea has precedence in Duchamp's *objets trouvés*, the "ready-mades" of Schwitters' "Merz" series, and from the use of chance as the antithesis of order—the mode of the avantgarde of the 1970's. It is easy to see the link between Stankiewicz and Dada. A kind of nonsense and a mockery of common sense and all logic appear in his work, similar to the collages and assemblages of Dada. On this basis, Stankiewicz's work is often considered a part of the neo-Dada movement that appeared in Europe and America at the end of the 1950's—for example, in the work of David Smith, John Chamberlain, or Mark di Suvero. Some critics have also pointed out all the similarity with abstract expressionism, since a reliance on the physical nature of materials, a spontaneity of gesture and a loosening of order and structure can all be seen in Stankiewicz's work.

By the 1960's Stankiewicz was already one of those sculptors whose formal ideas were of great interest; he was making a name for himself. The irony and element of subtle humor in his sculptures were particularly of note. For example: "Kabuki Dancer," 1954; "The Secretary," 1955; "Bird Lover," 1957; "The Candidate," 1960. This chapter in Stankiewicz's artistic biography was closed when he took part in the American Section of the 1958 Venice *Biennale* and gave his first one-man show in Paris in 1960. Few Americans abroad at that time succeeded in calling forth such a reaction. No one had displayed "junk" materials there before, and certainly not in such a way. It is likely that Tinguely, the creator of the "anti machines" from junk, owes the impetus of many of his investigations in sculpture to Stankiewicz.

A break followed, filled with reflections and teaching. In 1969, Stankiewicz went on a journey to Australia. It made a great impression on his development and inaugurated changes in his workshop. The critic James R. Mellow has called these changes the road "from the comic to the classic." He was thinking about change from objects composed in an unconstrained manner, with a social message in the subtext, to rigorously abstract sculptured solids. The constructions were modelled from beams and plates of sectioned steel, from steel cylinders of varying size and diameter. Everything is compact, massive, credible in its reserved geometric silhouette. Objects arise, exhibiting geometry. Their basic element is a short, stumpy cylinder, wedged into its neighbor, hanging from it, placed at an angle to it. It can be seen that the artist is in some way verifying the physical laws governing solids—the balance and disturbance when a mass is displaced and the powers of gravity are negated. A fascination with matter, and anti-matter, the wedging of edges and levitation of solid figures, pulls the viewer into the play of pure form. This backing out of an outdated, restrained way of thinking and creating, without regard to the mainstream, is proof of this artist's courage and self-hood.

A surprise and a shock—the works of the second half of the 70's. They deny some of the axioms of sculpture—volume, mass, space—in the interests of linear form. Bas relief, contour, outline, open work instead of heavy, totemic masses—all of these works suggested new possibilities.

At the beginning of the 1980's the artist finds pleasure in placing contrasting materials next to one another—the flat with the 3-dimensional, the regular with the irregular, the smooth with the rough, new material with pieces of junk, natural rust with a treated surface. This expressively contrasted world of forms is seen across a frame forming a load-bearing construction. Square or rectangular frames here symbolize the aesthetic order so sought after in the "uncalm" art of our period.

The controversy accompanying all Stankiewicz's artistic work shows a link between his work and the traits of his personality, which tries to combine polarities of character. Perhaps this is why he needed to live outside noisy New York City in an area that is squeezed in between forested massifs that are scarcely populated.

—Szymon Bojko

STANLEY, Robert.

American. Born in Yonkers, New York, 3 January 1932. Studied at Oglethorpe University, Atlanta, 1949-53, B.A. 1953; High Museum of Art, Atlanta, 1952; Columbia University, New York, 1953; Art Students League, New York, 1953; Brooklyn Museum of Art School, New York (Max Beckman Scholarship), 1954-56. Married Jane Hutchinson in 1961 (divorced, 1968); married Marilyn Herzka in 1970. Independent artist known for very large figurative paintings: lives and works in New York. Instructor of Drawing and Painting, School of Visual Arts, New York, 1970-72; Visiting Artist, Louisiana State University, Baton Rouge, 1976; Visiting Lecturer, St. Lawrence University, Canton, New York, 1978; Visiting Artist, Syracuse University, New York, 1978; and Princeton University, New Jersey, 1979-80. Recipient: Cassandra Foundation Award, 1969; Igor Foundation Award for Painting, 1987. Agents: John Davis Gallery, 568 Broadway, New York, New York 10012; Bo Alveryd, 71 Avenue du Lac, 2028 Vaumarcus, Switzerland. Address: 3 Crosby Street, New York, New York 10013, U.S.A.

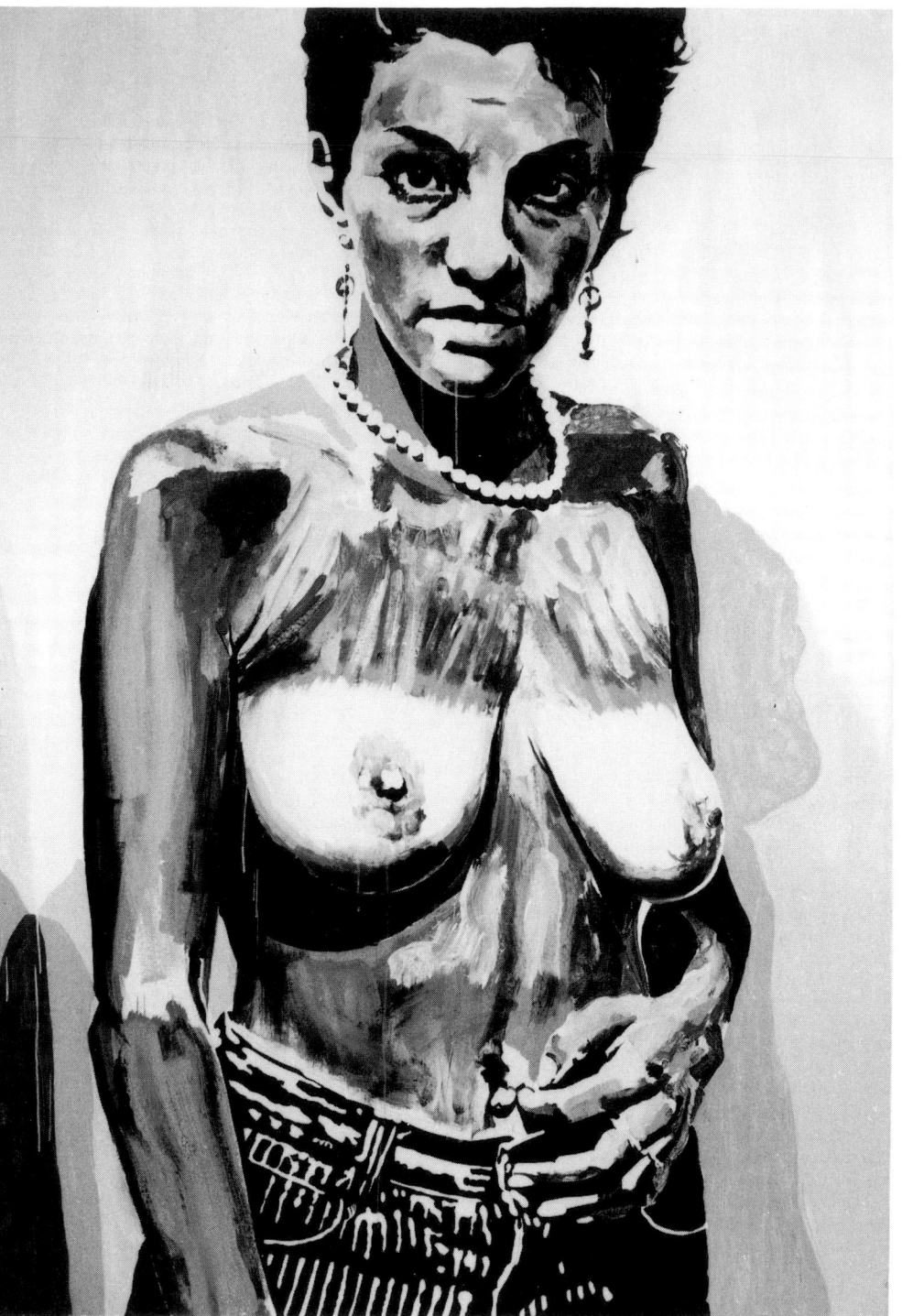

Robert Stanley: *Elena*, 1986

Individual Exhibitions:

1965 Bianchini Gallery, New York
1966 Bianchini Gallery, New York
Galerie Orez, The Hague
Contemporary Arts Center, Cincinnati, Ohio
Galerie Ricke, Kassel, West Germany
1967 Galerie Ricke, Kassel, West Germany
Galerie Kuckels, Bochum, West Germany
1968 Kleine Galerie, Frankfurt
1969 Gegenverkehr, Aachen, West Germany
On 1st, New York
1972 Warren Benedek Gallery, New York
1974 New York Cultural Center
1976 Union Gallery, Louisiana University, Baton Rougue
1977 P.S. 1, Long Island City, New York
1978 Hal Bromm Gallery, New York (photographs)
St. Thomas Aquinas College, Sparkill, New York
E. Weiner Gallery, New York

1980 E. Weiner Gallery, New York
Holly Keenberg Contemporary Art, Winnipeg, Manitoba (retrospective)
1983 Bucklew-Goehring Gallery, Tampa, Florida
1986 Le Consortium Centre d'Art Contemporain, Dijon, France
John Davis Gallery, New York
1987 Galerie Lavrov, Paris
New Arts Program, Kutztown, Pennsylvania
John Davis Gallery, New York

Selected Group Exhibitions:

1968 *Documenta 4*, Kassel, West Germany
1970 *Monumental Art*, Contemporary Arts Center, Cincinnati, Ohio
1973 *Biennial*, Whitney Museum, New York
1975 *The Nude in American Art*, New York Cultural Center

1977 *Outside the City Limits: Landscapes by New York City Artists*, Thorpe Intermedia Gallery, Sparkill, New York
1980 *The Director's Choice*, Fine Arts Gallery, University of Wisconsin at Milwaukee
1981 *Illusions of Light*, Worcester Art Museum, Massachusetts
1983 *Rutgers Archives for Printmaking*, Jane Voorhees Zimmerli Art Museum, Rutgers, New Jersey
1985 *A Decade of Visual Arts at Princeton*, Princeton Art Museum, New Jersey
1987 *Overtalk*, White Columns, New York

Collections:

Whitney Museum, New York; Metropolitan Museum of Art, New York; Housatonic Community College, Stratford, Connecticut; Fogg Art Museum, Cambridge, Massachusetts; Contemporary Art Center, Milwaukee, Wisconsin; Washington University, St. Louis, Missouri; Ludwig Collection, Aachen, West Germany.

Publications:

By STANLEY: books—*Tracks*, New York 1982; article—"Big Paintings: Bob Stanley," interview, with Robert Christgau, in *Cheetah* (New York), May 1968.

On STANLEY: books—*Erotic Art* by Phyllis and Eberhard Kronhausen, 2 vols., New York 1968, 1970; *Gordon/Lozano/Ryman/Stanley*, by Robert Christgau, Cincinnati, Ohio 1968; *Directions 2: Aspects of a New Realism*, by William Wilson, Milwaukee, Wisconsin 1969; *Robert Stanley*, exhibition catalogue, by Klaus Honnef, Aachen, West Germany 1969; *Bob Stanley's Louisiana Sweet* by Mario Amaya and Naomi Spector, New York 1978; articles—"The Flip Side" by David Bourdon in the *Village Voice* (New York), 17 June 1965; "The New Eroticism" by Douglas Davis in *Evergreen* (New York), September 1968; "Eros erinnert an Dharma" by John Anthony Thwaites in *Christ und Welt*, Dusseldorf 1969; "The Spectrum of Monochrome" by Lawrence Alloway in *Arts Magazine* (New York), December/January 1971; "Robert Stanley" by G. Gassiot-Talbot in *Opus International* (Paris), December 1971; "Bob Stanley" by John Lloyd Taylor in *Art International* (Lugano, Switzerland), September 1974; "Bob Stanley and Bart Wasserman at P.S. 1" by Carter Ratcliff in *Art in America* (New York), January/February 1978; "Paint Misbehavin' " by Peter Frank in the *Village Voice* (New York), 16 October 1978; "Bob Stanley" by William Zimmer in the *Soho Weekly News* (New York), 8 October 1980; "Bob Stanley" by Michael Florescu in *Arts Magazine* (New York), November 1980; "Parade in the Face of Death: the work of Robert Stanley" by Richard Artschwager in *Galeries* (Paris), Summer 1987

*

Michael Florescu has said the following about my work:

"The work of Bob Stanley, it seems to me, is imbued with an old-fashioned morality, if not didacticism—a strange response, perhaps, to an artist whom Mario Amaya has dubbed 'that pirate of the Pop Art movement.' But in a time of pluralism in the visual arts, a phrase that has come to mean a time of multiple warring assertions, Stanley stands out as a questioner. His work is interrogative of the contemporary conventional wisdom rather than declarative. Uncharacteristically for a questioner, there is little humility about his paintings: they are big (not to mince works, they are enormous), and to quote Amaya again, they are 'as cyclical and all encompassing as the walls of an early Renaissance chapel.' "

—Robert Stanley

STAZEWSKI, Henryk.

Polish. Born in Warsaw, 9 January 1894. Educated at Kowalski's Secondary School, Warsaw; studied at the School of Fine Arts, Warsaw, under Stanislaw Lent, 1913-19. Painter: lived and worked in Warsaw from 1920; produced paintings and reliefs from 1920, neoplastic house interiors, 1923-32; Founder-Member, with Wladyslaw Strzeminski, Mieczyslaw Szulc, Henryk Berlewi and others, Blok artists group, Wilno, 1923-36; Editor, *Blok* magazine, nos. 1-5, 1924; Founder-Member, Praesens painters and architects group, Warsaw, 1926-29; Founder-Member, with Wladyslaw Strzeminski, Katarzyna Kobro, Julian Przybos and others, a.r. group, Lodz, 1929; Member, Michel Seuphor's Cercle et Carre group, Paris, 1930-31; and Abstraction-Creation group, Paris, 1931; Founder-Member, KAGR publicity graphic artists group, Warsaw, 1933; Member, Editorial Board, *Glos Plastykow* magazine, Warsaw, 1933; Founder-Member, Trade Union of Plastic Artists, Warsaw, 1935. Recipient: Ministry of Culture Prize, Warsaw, 1965; J. G. Herder Prize, University of Vienna. 1972. Member, Association Internationale des Arts Plastiques (A.I.A.P.), Paris, 1962. Golden Cross of Merit, 1955; Officer, Cross of the Order Polonia Restituta, Warsaw. Agents: Galerie Schlegel, Minervastrasse 119, 8000 Zurich, Switzerland; Crane Arts, 321 Kings Road, London S.W.3, England. *Died* (in Warsaw) *June 1988.*

Individual Exhibitions:

1921	Polonia Artists Club, Warsaw (with E. Miller and M. Szczuka)
1933	Art Propaganda Institute, Warsaw (with Karol Krynski)
1934	Art Propaganda Institute, Warsaw (with Wladyslaw Strzeminski)
1955	Polish Union of Writers Club, Warsaw
1956	Galleria Incontro, Rome (with Aleksander Winnicki)
1959	Kordegada, Warsaw
1960	Krzywekolo Gallery, Warsaw
1961	Castle of Lublin, Poland
	Krzywekolo Gallery, Warsaw
1962	Krzywekolo Gallery, Warsaw
1963	*Reliefs and Collages*, Grabowski Gallery, London
1965	Galeria Zacheta, Warsaw
1966	Kazimir Gallery, Chicago
1967	Galerija Foksal, Warsaw
1969	Galerija Foksal, Warsaw
	Museum of Fine Arts, Lodz, Poland
1970	Narodna Gallery, Prague
	Galerija Foksal, Warsaw
	Galerija Krzystofory, Cracow
1972	Mecatorhalle, Duisburg, West Germany
1974	Galerie 16, Paris
	Wide White Space Gallery, Brussels
	Galerie Polart, Dusseldorf
	Biuro Wystawy Artystycznych, Lodz, Poland
	Pape Ruddy Gallery, Los Angeles
	Museum of Fine Arts, Lodz, Poland
1975	Galerie Schlegl, Zurich
1976	Galerija Wspolczesna, Warsaw
	Galerija 72, Chelm, Poland
1977	Galerie Teufel, Cologne
1978	Galerija Zacheta, Warsaw
1979	Palazzo delle Esposizione, Rome (travelled to the Teatro del Falcone, Genoa, and the Museo d'Arte Moderna Ca Pesaro, Venice)
	Recent Paintings, Fruit Market Gallery, Edinburgh (travelled to the Third Eye Centre, Glasgow)
	Galerija Zapiecek, Warsaw
1980	Galerija Krytykow, Warsaw
	Biuro Wystaw Artystycznych, Torun, Poland (retrospective)
	Biuro Wystaw Artystycznych, Bydgoszcz, Poland
	Galerie Quadrat, Bottrop, West Germany
1982	Galerie Denise René, Paris

Selected Group Exhibitions:

1922	*F9 Formist Artists Group: 3rd Exhibition*, Salon-Garlinski, Warsaw
1926	*Praesens Group*, Galerija Zacheta, Warsaw
1947	*1st Salon of ZPAP*, National Museum, Warsaw
1957	*Precurseurs d'Art Abstrait en Pologne*, Galerie Denise René, Paris
1961	*15 Polish Artists*, Museum of Modern Art, New York
1966	*Biennale*, Venice
1972	*The Non-Objective World 1939-55*, Annely Juda Fine Art, London (travelled to the Galerie Liatowisch, Basle, and the Galleria Milano, Milan)
1977	*Constructivisme Polonais 1923-36*, Musée d'Art Contemporain, Montreal
1978	*Abstraction-Creation 1931-36*, Westfälischer Landesmuseum, Münster, West Germany (travelled to the Musée d'Art Moderne de la Ville, Paris)
1980	*Polnische Kunst aus 3 Jahrzehnten*, Staatliche Kunstsammlungen, Dresden

Collections:

Museum of Fine Arts, Lodz, Poland; National Museum, Warsaw; National Museum, Cracow; Tate Gallery, London; Museum der Stadt, St. Gallen, Switzerland; Rijksmuseum Kröller-Müller, Otterlo, Netherlands, Stedelijk Museum, Amsterdam; Städtische Kunstgalerie, Bochum, West Germany; Museum of Modern Art, New York; Guggenheim Museum, New York.

Publications:

By STAZEWSKI: books illustrated—*Praesens Library no. 2: The Human Creative Mission in the Fine Arts* by Albert Gleizes, Warsaw 1927; *Praesens Library no. 3: Unism in Painting* by Wladyslaw Strzeminski, Warsaw 1928; *The Angelic Ruffian* by Anatol Stern, Warsaw 1928.

On STAZEWSKI: books—*Reliefs and Collages by Henryk Stazewski*, exhibition catalogue, with texts by Alan Bowness and Wieslaw Borowski, London 1963; *Contemporary Polish Painting: Henryk Stazewski* by Hanna Ptaskowska, Warsaw 1965; *Stazewski*, exhibition catalogue, with texts by Ryszard Stanislawski, Hanna Ptaszkowska and Wieslaw Borowski, Lodz, Poland 1969; *The Non-Objective World 1939-55*, exhibition catalogue, with text by George Rickey, London 1972; *Geometric Abstraction 1926-1942*, exhibition catalogue, with texts by Michel Seuphor and John Elderfield, Dallas 1972; *Henryk Stazewski: Malarstwo z lat 1923-1974*, exhibition catalogue Lodz, Poland 1974; *Henryk Stazewski*, exhibition catalogue, Brussels 1974; *Henryk Stazewski*, exhibition catalogue, Paris 1974; *Henryk Stazewski: Recent Paintings*, exhibition catalogue, with texts by Richard Demarco and Janina Ladnowska, Edinburgh 1979; *Henryk Stazewski*, exhibition catalogue, with texts by Ulrich Schumacher, Ryszard Stanislawski and Janina Ladnowska, Bottrop, West Germany 1980; *Stazewski*, exhibition catalogue, with text by Anka Ptaszkowska, Paris 1982.

*

Henryk Stazewski, a survivor of the heroic period of the Polish avant garde, and one of the promoters of abstraction (he was a member of Cercle et Carre), began his work as a painter and art theoretician in the 1920's. He was then in favor of the constituent elements of form—the independent roles of line and color, chiaroscuro and fracture: in his pictures the artist linked these elements equally. He wished to create an objectless world that would make the eye sensitive to only that which was universal—above all, to geometric form and to color.

Stazewski continued his pursuit of this problem after the war, in the 1950's. The idea of movement also concerned him at this time. Originally this was provoked by the structure of form which then developed in the sphere of "open structures."

In 1957 a new problem arose. The artist stopped painting pictures and turned to the construction of reliefs from flat smooth forms. He simultaneously executed radical simplifications, reducing form to a single element the module; and color to black, white and grey. Stazewski then moved on to reliefs from smooth, polished metal. An artist whose creativity had drawn from the sources of abstraction—e.g., Mondrian—now developed a completely new kind of abstraction. In Mondrian's time the fixed relationships between the various respective elements were described in abstract pictures. In his reliefs, however, Stazewski introduced identical forms—modules (e.g., the square with concave sides, the ellipse with two ends cut off). Repeating these many times within the framework of a single picture, the artist removed their stamp of individuality; he "neutralized" them. Also, by repeating the same form-module, he focused attention not on form but on the various ways that it could be arranged.

The picture is thus constructed in an open manner which conceals potential changes of shape. As a result, the mid-1960s saw a sudden increase in interest in Stazewski's work. The possibilities of change inherent in his work prompted several critics to search for precursive elements with respect to the worldwide movement of visual art and the concepts of a neutral, anonymous art. Stazewski's work was thus suddenly regarded as of general importance; it could be re-created and given the greatest possible circulation.

In 1968 Strazewski returned to the problem of color. In a series of paintings from this period he analyzed color phenomena and the laws of visual perception. He based his research on scientific foundations. Using squares marked on his canvases, he carried out a graduation of chromatic color of a section of the spectrum, achieving shades that differ so minimally that it is almost impossible to perceive the delineation.

In 1973 Stazewski created a series of white pictures the surfaces of which are divided simultaneously in rhythmical and unsettled sections with the help of parallel lines. The rhythms of the lines converge or diverge, change their course, undergo short jumps. In spite of these dynamizing moments, the artist achieves homogeneous surfaces by using one kind of method, the minimal mutations always taking place within the framework of one basic module.

A phenomenon of Stazewski's artistic personality is the fact that, although he was one of the pioneers of geometric abstraction, he was still very sensitive to the ephemera of nature. But he always sought a permanent form for that which is only transitory. An example of this is the cycle of work begun in 1975, inspired by the wintry landscape of a small town. In these works the artist uses only geometric designs of black lines on a white ground. At the same time he writes: "The artist ought to beware the ephemeral, but he can in art give certain observed ephemeral phenomena a permanence and an extension of their existence." He continues: "Creating art, one has no understanding of the transitoriness of that which one is doing. One is led by a false feeling of permanence without being aware of the withering of a rose." In other words, Stazewski, who always wanted to commemorate the world in universal and permanent forms, also had strong feelings about the impermanence of all that exists. The tension between that which is universal and that which is individual, between intellectual reflection and the sphere of emotion, protects his art from a dry one-sidedness and marks it with strong personal sensitivity.

—Alicja Kepinska

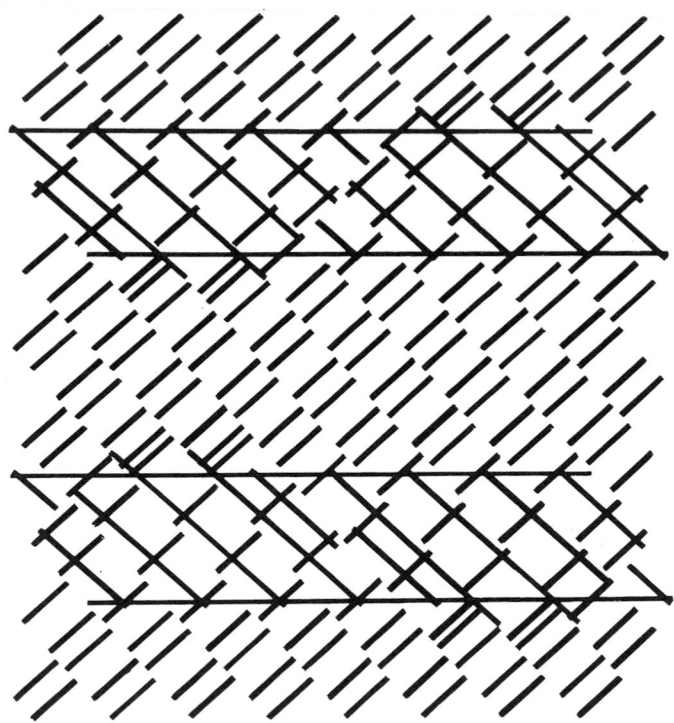

Jeffrey Steele: *Sg III. 45*, 1985

STEELE, Jeffrey.

British. Born in Cardiff, South Wales, 3 July 1931. Studied at Cardiff College of Art, 1948–50; studied painting at Newport College of Art, South Wales, 1950–52; also studied at the Ecole des Beaux Arts, Paris, 1959–60. Married Glenda Reynolds in 1958 (divorced, 1966); children: Simon and Tamara; married Arja Nenonen in 1966 (divorced, 1976); daughter: Clara. Independent painter, since 1952. Worked as hospital porter, Cardiff, 1953–55; as cellarman, London, 1955–57; as radio operator, Cardiff, 1957–59. Co-Founder, Systems Group of Artists, London 1969 (dissolved, 1976). Lecturer, Barry Summer School, Glamorgan, South Wales, 1962–73; Lecturer in Painting, Newport College of Art, South Wales, 1965–68; Principal Lecturer, Portsmouth Polytechnic, since 1969. Recipient: French Government Scholarship, 1959; Welsh Arts Council Bursary, 1963; Painting Prize, Northern Ireland Arts Council, 1968; Painting Prize, *Welsh Arts Council Open Painting Exhibition*, Barry, Wales, 1968. Agents: Galerie Schoeller, Poststrasse 2, 4000 Dusseldorf 1, West Germany; Patricia Knight Fine Art, 21 Phipp Street, London EC2A 4NP, England; Galerie Media, rue des Moulines, 29, Neuchâtel, Switzerland. Address: 11a Eastern Villas Road, Portsmouth, Hampshire PO4 OSU, England.

Individual Exhibitions:

1961 Institute of Contemporary Arts, London
1963 Dillwyn Gallery, Swansea, South Wales
1964 Grabowski Gallery, London
     Regional College of Art, Manchester
1966 McRoberts and Tunnard Gallery, London
1967 Sheffield University Arts Tower
     City Art Gallery, Manchester (with Benjamin and Tyzack)

1974 *Current Work*, Lucy Milton Gallery, London
     Galerie Media, Neuchâtel, Switzerland
1975 Galerie Jacomo-Santiveri, Paris (with Dilworth and Kidner)
1976 Le Disque Rouge, Brussels
1977 Galerie Gilles Gheerbrant, Montreal
     Galerie Swart, Amsterdam
1978 Galerie Swart, Amsterdam
1979 Galerie Lydia Megert, Berne
1985 Kunsthaus, Nuremberg, West Germany

Selected Group Exhibitions:

1962 *The Geometric Environment*, Artist's International Association Gallery, London
1965 *The Responsive Eye*, Museum of Modern Art, New York (toured the United States)
1967 *Pittsburgh International*, Carnegie Institute, Pittsburgh
1968 *Cybernetic Serendipity*, Institute of Contemporary Arts, London
1969 *Systeemi*, Amos Andersonin Taidemuseo, Helsinki
1973 *Illusion in 20th Century Art*, University of Stirling, Scotland
1976 *System and Programme*, Palac Kultury i Nauki, Warsaw
1977 *Sul Concetto di Serie*, Museo Civico, Varese, Italy
1983 *Arte Programmata e Cinetica 1953–63*, Palazzo Reale, Milan
1986 *Arte e Scienza*, at the *42nd Biennale*, Venice

Collections:

Arts Council of Great Britain, London; British Council, London; Victoria and Albert Museum, London; Museum Boymans-van Beuningen, Rotterdam; Cabinet des Estampes, Geneva; Kunsthaus, Aarau, Switzerland; National Museum of Wales, Cardiff; Ateneum Art Museum, Helsinki; Museum Sztuki, Lodz, Poland.

Publications:

By STEELE: articles—"Towards a Non-Egocentric Art" in *ICA bulletin* (London), December 1966; "Statement of Kinetics" in *Studio International* (London), February 1967; "Cicerone" in *Anglo-Welsh Review* (Caerlean), Winter 1967; "Syntactic Art" in *Systeemi*, exhibition catalogue, Helsinki 1969; "Systems Theory and Syntactic Art" in *Systems*, exhibition catalogue, London 1972; "Structural Analysis of My Painting" in *Review Integration* (Eschenau, West Germany), October 1972; "Note on My Current Work" in *Jeffrey Steele: Current Work*, exhibition catalogue, London 1974; "Note on the Relationship of Systematic-Constructivist Art to Architecture" in *Beispiele aus dem Grenzbereich Kunst-Architektur*, Berne 1975; "Portsmouth Fine Art Music" in *Experimental Music*, exhibition catalogue, by Gavin Bryars and Michael Nyman, London 1975; "Notes sur le Travail do Trevor Clarke" in *Media* (Neuchâtel, Switzerland), May 1976; "General Notes on Sg 1 . . . Drawings" in *Engelse en Nederlandse Rationele Tekeningen*, exhibition catalogue, Delft 1976; "Collaborative Work at Portsmouth" in *Studio International* (London), November/December 1976; "Core Conditions and Boundary Conditions" in *Artscribe* (London), July 1977; "The Identity Concept in the Constructive Context" in *Constructive Context* (London), 1978; "Notes Towards Some Theses Against the New Kitsch" in *Art Monthly* (London), July/August 1978; "Closing the Dossier on 'Pier and Ocean' " in *Art Monthly* (London), October 1980; "Vilification of Constructive Art" in *Art Monthly* (London), November 1982; "Die Kunstpraxis als Teil des grosseren Bereiches von linguistischer Praxis" in *Jeffrey Steele: Konkret Funf*, exhibition catalogue, Nuremberg 1985.

On STEELE: books—*Jeffrey Steele*, exhibition catalogue, by Sir Herbert Read, London 1964; *Jeffrey Steele*, exhibition catalogue, by Cyril Barrett, London 1966; *Optical Illusions and the Visual Arts* by Ronald G. Carracher and Jacqueline B. Thurston, New York and London 1966; *Constructivism* by

George Rickey, London 1967; *Op-Art* by Cyril Barrett, London 1969; *An Introduction to Optical Art* by Cyril Barrett, London 1971; *Introducing Op-Art* by John Lancaster, New York and London 1973; *Art since Pop* by John A. Walker, London 1975; *The Modern* by Terry Measham, Oxford 1976; *L'Ultima Avanguardia*, edited by Lea Vergine, Milan 1983; *Art & Science* by Ans van Berkum and Tom Blekkenhorst, Vlissingen 1986.

Since the year 1960 my general policy as an artist has been to attempt to instill a principle of necessity, to replace the subjective, contingent and random factors more normally associated with artistic production. This attempt has led to the elaboration of an appropriate formal system which, in conformity with the terminology used with the disciplines of semiology and linguistics, I call the *system* and designate "System Sy." Material works have the status of *representations* of this formal system in discrete states of its syntactic transformation, they stand in syntagmatic relation to it, and so I call them "Syntagms Sg" and number them in bureaucratic style: Sg I 1, Sg I 2, . . . Sg II 1, Sg III 1, 2, 3 and so forth.

Any given syntagm-figure is analysable into the momentary states of its component variables and each state of each variable is also given, as it is realized, an identifying number. I have found that this step-by-step method of research generates interesting data in the field of morphology, of topological connectivity, of serial and symmetry relations, etc.

Presentation of a sub-series of one or more of these syntagm-objects in a particular social context becomes a focus for cultural transactions; interaction amongst the sets of internal and external relations proper to the four different kinds of entity involved: the formal system, the material syntax, the percipient subject and the ideological state apparatus. A collective theoretical practice attempts to locate the content of these cultural transactions within a wider epistemological field.

—Jeffrey Steele

Jeffrey Steele is associated with a form of painting described as Systems. This, as its name implies, involves the use of some system in the construction of a picture.

There are two ways of using a system. One is to use it to generate some interesting visual image, but alter it in mid-stream, if it is not aesthetically satisfactory. The other, which is the course Steele follows, is to carry the system right through, and, if the result is aesthetically uninteresting, scrap it. Artistic control, thus, operates at the two ends, but not in the middle. There is a choice of system, and a verdict on the outcome of its use, but no tampering.

It may have been a coincidence, but Steele's early work had an optical-kinetic quality. He had been impressed by the work of Vasarely, though he felt that he had betrayed his original principles when, in the 1950's, he turned from black and white and from art with optical pulsations to his more characteristic ambiguous figures, a kind of abstract Cubism.

Steele's own work in the 60's had great optical vibrancy. He, as so many other so-called Op artists, discovered to his surprise that by a regular repetition of forms he obtained this vibrancy unsolicited. What had motivated him in the late 50's was a desire to break with *tachisme*, "the individual artist's 'touch' or handwriting." He had been attracted to Neo-Plasticism and Constructivism, but was most impressed, while in Paris, with the work of Albers, Bill, Soto and Vasarely. But it was only on his return home that he hit on his own brand of optical effect.

The characteristic of his work in the 1960's was the intensification and movement of light which his structures induce. During this period he worked exclusively in black and white. The stark contrast of tones helped to enhance the luminous effect of his work. At times his pictures are rectilinear, as in "Divertissement" or "Lavolta." The first builds up to a great intensity of light in the centre; the second disperses light along its axes, and the light pulsates, and even rotates. But he was also producing curvilinear structures, such as "Baroque Experiment," a sort of limitless series of reflecting mirrors, slightly out of kilter, whose divergencies from the norm set up optical vibrations, of "Sub Rosa" which suggests the luminous flow of water.

Basically, however, Steele is concerned with structures. Even in those early paintings, such as "Divertissement" and "Lavolta," the structural element dominates: the hidden squares, the crossing axes, the undulations swimming against the current. In some cases these counter-structures are evident; in others they are so subtle as to escape the notice of the unperceptive.

In 1965 some of his paintings were used in fabric design, in particular a design for a bikini based on "Baroque Experiment." This was both flattering and embarrassing to Steele, particularly as a year later that same bikini was shown with the caption: "Take it off (this is last year's swimsuit)." This proves, if it proves anything, not that Steele's work at the time was ephemeral, but that fashion is fickle. The only ephemeral aspect of his work—the aspect which did not persist—is the optical effect, which was incidental anyway, even though it gave him public recognition. It was always his aim to counterbalance the optical effect.

In the late 60's Steele turned to colour and reverted entirely to his original interest in formal, as opposed to informal, structures. He developed an elaborate terminology to describe his systematic method of working, too elaborate to expound here. Each work is designated by a symbol (Sg) and a number: Sg I 1, I 2, etc. At present the symbol is Sg VI, but there is no reason why Steele should not revert to Sg I or Sg II which date from the early 1970's, and develop their possibilities further. An Sg (syntagm) is a material realization of a system (Sy) governed by operations, mappings, distributions, networks, syntaxes, etc. The terminology is drawn from linguistics. Steele believes that his systematic approach is a contribution to research in the field of morphology, topology, serial relations.

The earlier works put strong emphasis on the diagonal, and are very dynamic. The more recent works (Sg VI) consist of horizontal bands of rectangular areas of colour arranged on either side of a central axis, reminiscent of certain works of Lohse, for whom Steele has an undying admiration. They are imposing, even if they lack the dynamism and the over-lying structures of earlier works.

However interesting it may be to know the methods by which Steele arrives at his images, it is the images themselves which ultimately matter. Nevertheless the presence of an underlying structure based on a system makes itself felt if scarcely perceptibly: the visual stimulation is underwritten by a hidden order.

—D. C. Barrett

STEINBERG, Saul.

American. Born in Ramnicul-Sarat, near Bucharest, Rumania, 15 June 1914; emigrated to the United States, 1941; naturalised, 1943. Studied sociology and psychology at the University of Bucharest, 1932; studied architecture at the University of Milan, 1932. Served in the United States Navy, 1943-46. Cartoonist for *The New Yorker* since 1941; cartoons contributed to numerous other U.S. periodicals: his objects and drawings satirize contemporary society and the activity of making art. Artist-in-Residence, Smithsonian Institution, Washington, D.C., 1967. Agent: The Pace Gallery, New York. Address: c/o The Pace Gallery, 32 East 57th Street, New York, New York 10022, U.S.A.

Individual Exhibitions:

1943	Wakefield Gallery, New York
1945	Young Books Inc., New York
1948	Institute of Design, Chicago
1950	Rhode Island School of Design, Providence
	Betty Parsons Gallery, New York
1951	Galleria l'Obelisco, Rome
1952	Galeria de Arte, São Paulo
	Museu de Arte, São Paulo
	Gump's Gallery, San Francisco
	Institute of Contemporary Arts, London
	Sidney Janis Gallery, New York
	Kunsthalle, Wuppertal-Barmen, West Germany
	Leopold-Hoesch-Museum, Düren, West Germany
	Galleria l'Obelisco, Rome
	Betty Parsons Gallery, New York
	Frank Perls Gallery, Beverly Hills, California
1953	*Steinberg Drawings*, Arts Club of Chicago
	Galerie Blanche, Stockholm
	Galerie Maeght, Paris
	Stedelijk Museum, Amsterdam
	Virginia Museum of Fine Arts, Richmond
1954	Corcoran Gallery of Art, Washington, D.C.
	Dallas Museum of Fine Arts
	Museum am Ostwall, Dortmund, West Germany
	Kunstkabinett, Frankfurt
	Kestner-Gesellschaft, Hannover
	Kunstmuseum, Basel
	Santa Barbara Museum, California
1955	Harvard School of Design, Cambridge, Massachusetts
1956	Allan Frumkin Gallery, Chicago
1957	Institute of Contemporary Arts, London
1959	Musée d'Art Moderne, Brussels
1962	University of California at Santa Barbara
1965	Davison Art Center, Wesleyan University, Middletown, Connecticut
1966	Sidney Janis Gallery, New York
	Galerie Maeght, Paris
	Betty Parsons Gallery, New York
	Wallraf-Richartz-Museum, Cologne
1967	B. C. Holland Gallery, Chicago
	Museum Boymans-van Beuningen, Rotterdam
	Obelisk Gallery, Boston
	Aquarelles, Dessins et Collages 1955-1967, Musées Royaux des Beaux-Arts, Brussels
1968	Museo de Bellas Artes, Caracas
	Zeichnungen und Collagen, Kunsthalle, Hamburg
	Irving Galleries, Milwaukee
	Louisiana Museum, Humlebaek, Denmark
	Moderna Museet, Stockholm
1969	J. L. Hudson Gallery, Detroit
	Sidney Janis Gallery, New York
	Betty Parsons Gallery, New York
1970	Felix Landau Gallery, Los Angeles
1971	Richard Gray Gallery, Chicago
	Ölbilder, Gouachen, Zeichnungen, Galerie Maeght, Zurich
1973	Galleria Galatea, Milan
	Sidney Janis Gallery, New York
	Galerie Maeght, Paris
	Betty Parsons Gallery, New York
	Steinberg at the Smithsonian, National Collection of Fine Arts, Smithsonian Institution, Washington, D.C.
1974	Institute of Contemporary Art, Boston
	Galerie Maeght, Paris
	Zeichnungen, Aquarelle, Collagen, Gemälde, Reliefs 1963-74, Kölnischer Kunstverein, Cologne (exhibition travelled throughout Germany and to Vienna)
1976	Sidney Janis Gallery, New York
	Betty Parsons Gallery, New York
1977	Galerie Maeght, Paris and Zurich
1978	Whitney Museum, New York (retrospective; travelled to the Hirshhorn Museum, Smithsonian Institution, Washington, D.C.; Serpentine Gallery, London; and Fondation Maeght, St.-Paul-de-Vence, France)
1982	The Pace Gallery, New York
1983	Waddington Galleries, London
1986	Galerie Maeght Lelong, Paris
1987	Pace Gallery, New York

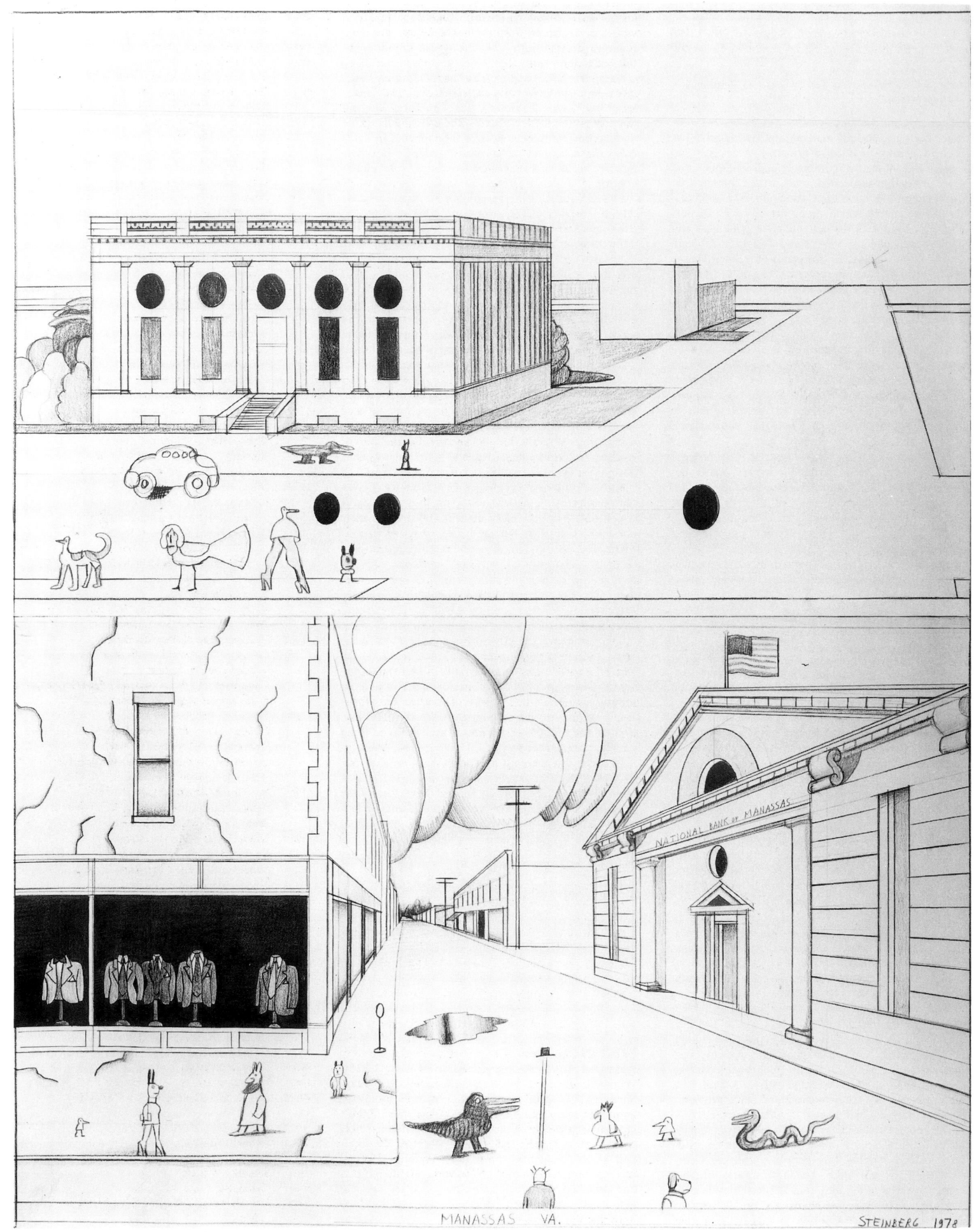

Saul Steinberg: *Main Street, Manassas, Virginia,* 1978

Selected Group Exhibitions:

Collections:

Museum of Modern Art, New York; Metropolitan Museum of Art, New York; Albright-Knox Art Gallery, Buffalo, New York; Fogg Museum, Harvard University, Cambridge, Massachusetts,; Detroit Institute of Arts; Victoria and Albert Museum, London.

Publications:

By STEINBERG: books—*All in Line*, New York 1945; *The Art of Living*, New York 1949; *The Passport*, New York 1954; *Steinberg's Umgang mit Menschen*, Hamburg 1954; *Dessins*, Paris 1956; *The Labyrinth*, New York 1960; *The Catalogue*, Cleveland 1962; *Steinberg's Paperback*, Hamburg 1964; *The New World*, New York 1965; *Le Masque*, with texts by Michel Butor and Harold Rosenberg, Paris 1966; *The Inspector*, New York 1973; articles—"Life in the Guatavir Line" in *Life* (New York), May 1940; "Mottocs Illustrated" in *Harper's* (New York), August 1946; "Recapitulation" in *Architectural Review* (London), December 1950; "Italy: Drawings" in *Harper's* (New York), February 1952; "Built in U.S.A.: Postwar Architecture, 1945-52" in *Artnews* (New York), February 1953; "Steinberg at the Bat" in *Life* (New York), 11 June 1955; "Drawings of Athens" in *Harper's* (New York), February 1956; "Steinberg U.S.A." in *Harper's* (New York), September 1960; "Statements and Documents" in *Daedalus* (New York), Winter 1960; "The Nose Problem" in *Location* (New York), Spring 1963; "Our False-Front Culture" in *Look* (New York), 9 January 1968.

On STEINBERG: books—*14 Americans*, exhibition catalogue, edited by Dorothy Miller, New York 1946; *Saul Steinberg*, exhibition catalogue, London 1952; *Saul Steinberg*, exhibition catalogue, Amsterdam 1953; *The Roy and Marie Neuberger Collection*, exhibition catalogue, New York 1954; *Steinberg*, exhibition catalogue, by Alfred Hentzen, Hannover 1954; *Conversations with Artists*, introduced by Alexander Eliot, New York 1961; *Steinberg Aquarelles, Dessins et Collages 1955-1967*, exhibition catalogue, Brussels 1967; *Steinberg*, exhibition catalogue, by Pierre Baudson, Rotterdam 1967; *Steinberg: Zeichnungen und Collagen*, exhibition catalogue, by Helmut Leppien, Pierre Baudson and Manuel Gasser, with an interview by André Parinaud, Hamburg 1968; *Saul Steinberg oder Philosophie der Zeichnung* by Franz Wittkamp, Mainz 1971; *Steinberg: Ölbilder, Gouachen, Zeichnungen*, exhibition catalogue, by Manuel Gasser, Zurich 1971; *Steinberg at the Smithsonian*, exhibition catalogue, by John Hollander, Washington, D.C. 1973; *Saul Steinberg: Zeichnungen, Aquarelle, Collagen, Gemälde, Reliefs 1963-74*, exhibition catalogue, Cologne 1974; *Here at the New Yorker* by Brendan Gill, New York 1975; *The New Yorker Album of Drawings 1925-1975*, New York 1975; *American Drawings 1927-1977*, exhibition catalogue, by Paul Cummings, St. Paul, Minnesota 1977; *Saul Steinberg*, exhibition catalogue, by Harold Rosenberg, New York 1978; *Saul Steinberg: repères*, exhibition catalogue with introduction by Jean Fremon, Paris 1986; *Saul Steinberg's Gift*, exhibition catalogue with text by Adam Gopnik, New York 1987.

*   *   *

For many years Saul Steinberg has been placed in limbo by critics and the public, but the retrospective held at the Whitney Museum in 1978 must finally have confirmed him to be an artist rather than a cartoonist.

Steinberg's style is completely original. Noises, jokes, puns pervade his work. American society is made up of robots, mickey mouse ladies, growling dogs, majorettes and eagles. New York seems to envelop the world in the famous *New York* poster; Siberia appears only a few inches away. Buildings and monuments tower above the "little men." This recurrent figure reminds one of Chaplin in *Modern Times* and Meursault in *L'étranger*. Somehow things happen to these men; they do not have the power to form their own destiny. In "Graph Paper Building" the skyscraper dwarfs the tiny stick figures and the stucco buildings—it is an ugly, unnecessary intrusion. However, in "Piazza San Marco, Venice" the Italians inhabiting the pen and ink square scream and fight one another, while the tourists merely look at the architecture, never at each other.

From the paintings bursting with characters, Steinberg also goes on to draw individuals. The army man sits at a table and casually removes his nose. Simple immaculate lines convey this action; they are stamped with Steinberg's seal of officialdom. A minute horseman is chased by a massive boulder, which in turn is hounded by a crocodile down a steep hill. An outrageous situation—but one still hopes that the lone horseman will survive. One of my favourite and equally "crazy" paintings is "March-April 1966." Specific segments of land represent one month, and the cat/man bicycles across the bridge from March to April. The concept is witty and charming. Steinberg's vision of a taxi cab made up of crooked lines cannot help but give delight.

Among the most sombre but at the same time most exquisite paintings are "Anatolia" (1973) and "Camp II" (1960). In the former miniscule figures stare out at the horizon whose blue sky is interrupted by few clouds. Although the setting is perfect, there is a sense of doom, just as in *Waiting for Godot* one expects an explosion. In the latter the Camp is reminiscent of concentration camps, solid black towers dwarfing helpless people. "Kisumu", "Kunming", "Eastern Sunsets" and "African Postcards" have similar atmosphere and quality because of the free flowing watercolour technique.

Steinberg can paint with the eye of a child, producing simple yet ingenious pen and ink riddles, then in another moment paint landscapes that possess the beauty of Turner inhabited by the figures of Dali. He is a talented and deeply human painter.

—Carine Maurice

STELLA, Frank.

American. Born in Malden, Massachusetts, 12 May 1936. Studied painting, under Patrick Morgan, Phillips Academy, Andover, Massachusetts; under William Seitz and Stephen Greene, Princeton University, New Jersey. Married Barbara Rose in London, 1960 (divorced); children: Rachel and Michael. Painter: has lived and worked in New York since 1958. Artist-in-Residence, Dartmouth College, Hanover, New Hampshire, 1963; rejected Artist in Residence position, University of California at Irvine, by refusing to sign State's Loyalty Oath, 1965; Lecturer, Yale University, New Haven, Connecticut, 1965; Visiting Critic, Cornell University, Ithaca, New York, 1965; Art instructor, University of Saskatchewan, Saskatoon, Summer 1967, and Brandeis University, Waltham, Massachusetts, 1968. Recipient: First Prize, *International Biennial Exhibition of Paintings*, Tokyo, 1967. Agent: M. Knoedler and Company, 19 East 70th Street, New York, New York 10021. Address: 17 Jones Street, New York, New York 10013, U.S.A.

Individual Exhibitions:

Selected Group Exhibitions:

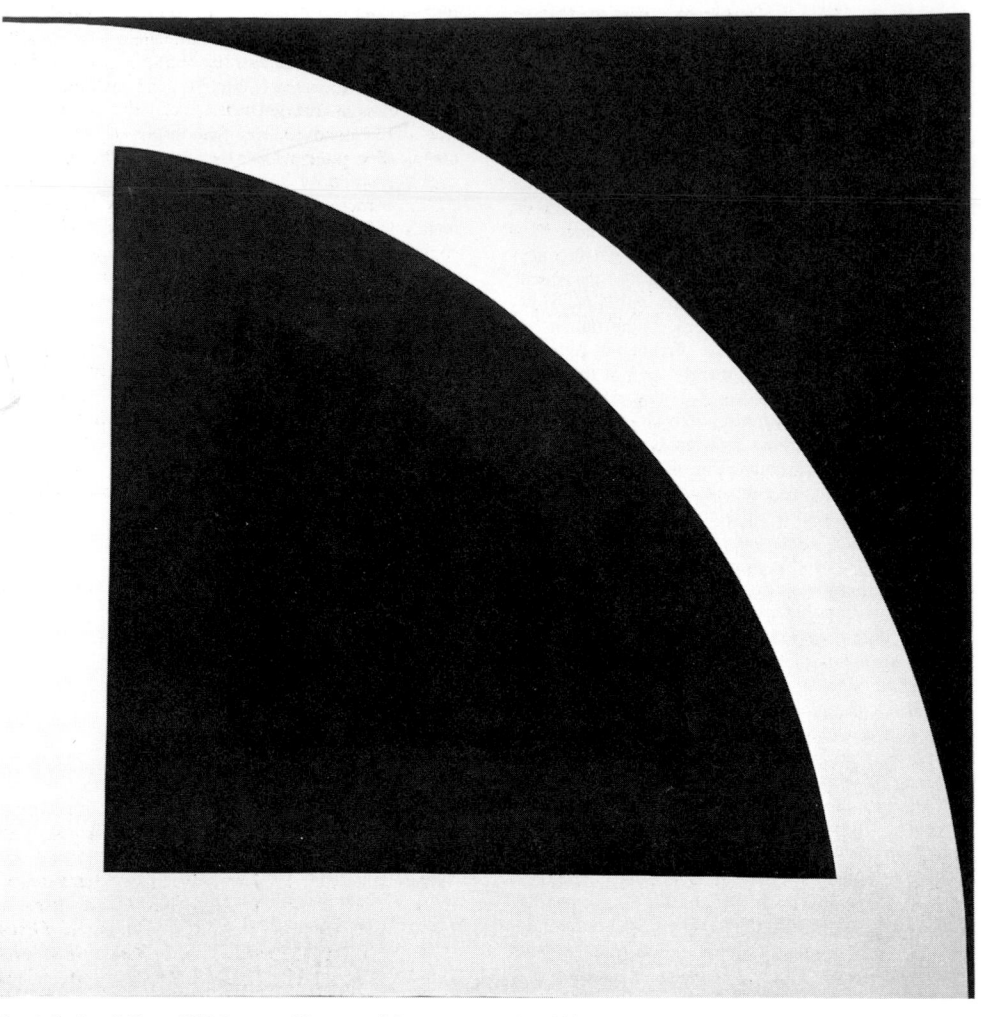

Frank Stella: *C-Type*, **1984** Courtesy Museum of Contemporary Art, Chicago

contrapuntal effect on the wall against which they hung. The inverted V's and diagonally based triangles, cutting into a square as an off-centre Z, had the fragmenting dislocation of the plane to contend with, though here (as in all Stella's works) the flatness of the synthetic hues, together with the occasional use of fluorescent paint, preserves the integrity of surface in a bland non-reflective total.

By the early 1970's Stella had won an assured command of his means, often within both tall and wide formats of rectangular plan on which circles and hemispheres and wide band arcs performed progressive ballets on the one plane. Colours switched values as the eyes moved across the composition, and one colour area would merge irrevocably into its neighbour.

Interrelationships of parallel forms and complementary colours are conditions at the heart of Stella's statement, moving yet seeming static, monumental though momentarily in flux.

G. S. Whittet

STEPHENSON, Ian.
British. Born in Browney, near Meadowfield, County Durham, 11 January 1934. Early education in Blyth, Northumberland; studied, under Lawrence Gowing, King Edward VII School of Art, King's College, University of Durham, Newcastle upon Tyne, 1951–56, B.A. 1956 (Hatton Scholar, 1955–56; Art Editor, *Northerner* student magazine, 1955–57); Lecturer and Studio Demonstrator, King's College, 1956–58; designed, with Victor Pasmore, *The Developing Process,* a basic pedagogic course dedicated to a new creativity in art; Boise Scholar (University of London), in Italy, 1958–59. Married Kate Brown in 1959; children: Stephen and Stella. Painter: shared studio with Richard Hamilton, Newcastle upon Tyne, 1956–58; lived in London, 1959–66; participated in the film *Cubism and After,* BBC, London, 1962; contributed to the film, *Blow-Up,* by Michelangelo Antonioni, Metro-Goldwyn-Mayer, 1966; lived in Newcastle upon Tyne, 1966–70; abandoned easel painting for mural-scale abstracts on sectional canvases, 1966–70; returned London, 1970. Visiting Lecturer in Extempore Studies, London Polytechnic School of Art, 1959–62; Visiting Lecturer in Basic Design, and later in Painting, Chelsea School of Art, London, 1959–66; Director of Foundation Studies, Department of Fine Art, University of Newcastle, 1966–70. Director of Master's Degree Postgraduate Painting, Chelsea School of Art, since 1970. International Course Leader, Voss Summer School of Fine Arts, Norway, 1979. Member: Visual Arts Panel, Northern Arts Association, Newcastle upon Tyne, 1967–70; Fine Art Panel, National Council for Diplomas in Art and Design, London, 1972–74; Permanent Committee, New Contemporaries Association, London, 1973–75; Fine Art Board and Specialist Adviser, Council for National Academic Awards, London, 1974–75, 1980–83; Selection Juror, *British Painting Exhibition,* Hayward Gallery, London, 1974; Advisory Committee, *National Exhibition of Children's Art,* Manchester, since 1975; Working Party, *Jubilee Exhibition,* Royal Academy of Art, London, 1976–77; Selection Committee, Arts Council Awards, London, 1977. Recipient: Junior Section Prize, *John Moore's Exhibition,* Liverpool, 1957; Gulbenkian Foundation Purchase Award, London, 1960; Marzotto International Selection Prize, 1964; First Prize, *Northern Painters Exhibition,* Newcastle upon Tyne, 1966; Gold Medal and Diploma of Merit, Accademia Italia and Universita delle Arti, Parma, Italy, 1980–81. Honorary Member: Mark Twain Society, Missouri, 1978; Painting Faculty, British School, Rome, 1978; Contemporary Art Society, London, 1980; Accademia Italia delle Arti, Parma, Italy, 1980. Associate, 1975, Royal Academician, 1986, Royal Academy of Arts, London. Address: 49 Elm Park Gardens, London SW10 9PA, England.

1974   *Prints from Gemini G.E.L.,* Walker Art Center, Minneapolis (toured the United States)
1976   *20th Century American Drawing,* Guggenheim Museum, New York
1978   *Art about Art,* Whitney Museum, New York
1985   *Painterly Visions 1940–84,* Guggenheim Museum, New York
1988   *Contemporary American Art,* Sara Hilden Art Museum, Tampere, Finland (travelled to Oslo)

Collections:

Museum of Modern Art, New York; Whitney Museum, New York; Albright-Knox Art Gallery, Buffalo, New York; Walker Art Center,Minneapolis; Art Institute of Chicago; San Francisco Museum of Modern Art; Centre Georges Pompidou, Paris; Kaiser Wilhelm Museum, Krefeld, West Germany; Stedelijk Museum, Amsterdam; Stedelijk van Abbemuseum, Eindhoven, Netherlands.

Publications:

On STELLA: books—*3 American Painters,* exhibition catalogue, by Michael Fried, Cambridge, Massachusetts, April 1965; *Recent Paintings by Frank Stella,* exhibition catalogue, by William Seitz, Waltham, Massachusetts 1969; *Frank Stella,* exhibition catalogue, Amsterdam 1979; *Frank Stella,* exhibition catalogue, by William S. Rubin, New York 1970; *Frank Stella* by Robert Rosenblum, London 1971: *Frank Stella Prints 1967–1982,* catalogue raisonne by Richard H. Axsom, Ann Arbor 1982; *Frank Stella: Working Space,* Cambridge, Massachusetts 1986; *Frank Stella 1970–1987,* exhibition ctalogue with text by William Rubin, New York 1987.

When he had his first one-man show in New York in 1960, Frank Stella at 24 was not yet committed to a programme of irreversible iconoclasm. From his "Island" paintings of 1958 it was possible to detect some of the polarisation that had been effected by Jasper Johns in the large striped canvases and their enclosed square of pure colour. This welcome move away from the random impulses of Abstract Expressionism seen in de Kooning and Kline decided the subsequent moves on the board for Stella. Of the 1960 "Black Paintings," the emphasis was linear; metallic paints tracing enclosures of geometric shapes in large formats. The to-and-froing of the lines in parallel was given some rapid change of pace by stepping and switching through right angles to which the canvas stretcher was trimmed. These massive plans, hung vertically, had their strong two-dimensional presences as much by their rejection of the conventional shape of the support as their integration with mural space, using and adjusting to it as complementary to each work's internal proportions.

About 1962 the relative reticence of the stripes expanded so they became bands of pure and semi-transparent colour edged in white. Recession was accomplished by slightly varying the apex height of adjacent pyramids each formed by four triangles laid side by side. This contrast in colour none the less maintained the integrity of the plane. Other hexagonal motives divided by bands of colour retained their adhesion to the surface level.

Stella's arrowhead paintings of 1964, though large in scale, sacrifice something of their architectural integration in their green grounds hatched by light-toned metallic lines.

Up to 1965, the overall shape of the stretcher had decided the parallel of the design within it, but from here Stella alternated the important elements of the picture against a pure ground with a negative profile created from the shaping of the ground itself.

This return to the internal stresses of abstract cut-out shapes placed a greater strain on the applied colour weights, not only for themselves but for their

Individual Exhibitions:

Selected Group Exhibitions:

Collections:

Tate Gallery, London; Victoria and Albert Museum, London; Arts Council of Great Britain, London; Hatton Gallery, Newcastle upon Tyne; Whitworth Art Gallery, Manchester; Hunterian Museum and Art Gallery, University of Glasgow; National Museum of Wales, Cardiff; National Gallery of Victoria, Melbourne; Madison Art Center, Wisconsin.

Publications:

By STEPHENSON: articles—"Statements" in *Studio International* (London), September 1967; "Explanatory Note: Paintings 1968–79" in *Ian Stephenson,* exhibition catalogue, Newcastle upon Tyne 1970; "Remarks" in *One Magazine* (London), April 1974; "Correspondence: Without Recourse" in *Art Monthly* (London), November 1981.

On STEPHENSON: books—*Contemporary British Art* by Herbert Read, London 1964; *Private View* by John Russell, Bryan Robertson and Lord Snowdon, London 1965; *Adventure in Art,* edited by Hendrik Scheepmaker, New York 1969; *Ian Stephenson,* exhibition catalogue, by Andrew Forge, Newcastle upon Tyne 1970; *Ian Stephenson: Paintings 1955–56 and 1966–77,* exhibition catalogue, by William Feaver, London 1977; *Ian Stephenson: Ionic Variation Paintings on Paper 1961–1977* by Andrea Rose, Birmingham 1978; *Tendenze e Testimonianze dell'Arte Contemporanea,* edited by Nicolo Panepinto, Parma 1983.

*   *   *

Ian Stephenson, it seems, is hardly capable of laying paint on flat. Everything that he has done, from his earliest tentative studies to the 12 foot canvases, has in common a stippled surface. It is an obsession, and as such it is rooted at a far deeper level than the specialized preoccupations of a particular year. It is not, one might guess, just the consequence of a stylistic decision but the reflection of some ancient relationship, essential not only to his view of painting but of the world itself.

There are areas in his paintings—particularly the latest—where the numberless particles of paint are massed at random. The canvas is covered with layer upon layer of dots; individual colour differences are absorbed in the tonality of the mass. One is confronted by a cloud, spongy, shifting. We recognize sensations of distance—and its opposite as when with closed lids we contemplate the warm veiled greys and shifting points and sparks that are all one can see with one's eyes shut. There are no stepping stones in these last pictures, no anchorages with spaces in between. All is filled. All is void.

There is an analogy here with the filmy fields of Rothko. But the differences are extremely significant. When in front of a Rothko and one moves in close, the colour wraps round more closely. The expreience is heightened. The surface of the picture is a surface of semi-transparent colour, closer, more enveloping. Here, though, with Stephenson, the surface is not the same. The picture changes scale as one draws into it. The surface resolves itself into thousands and thousands of dots which one is far more clearly aware of outside oneself—at a distance—than before. To the oceanic sensations of the whole is added an awareness of multitude, sharpness, and the minute structure that the eye unravels in each inch of paint. The transitions from "cloud" to "myriad" and back again is available at will. There is no "correct" view of it.

Compare these paintings with the images on a TV screen, a newsprint photograph or a mezzotint. In all these cases the lines or dots are functional; in moving "in" to examine the system or "out" to read the image, we are crossing a distinct threshold in the quality of our attention. This journey does not span either/or alternatives: the work is a totality and each movement we make is an enlargement of our relationship to it, and indeed uncovers new dimensions of the subject-matter. The point is that the image is the upshot of how it is made.

This complexity is typical of the way Stephenson relates to painting himself: painting, one feels, encompasses a multiplicity of experience, widely contrasting sensations stemming from the same source, untrammelled choice. His pictures are the opposite of one-shot. They are difficult, demanding close and varied attention. There is much of the pedagogue in him, a tendency towards extreme conceptualization which shows particularly in some of the "Spray Studies," which are like laboratory demonstrations. At the same time doubt is always present, and the techniques and programmes he devises for himself are invariably open, wayward and humorous even, with room for endless speculation and revision. His ideas are rigorous; the processes they set in motion are subject to infinite nuance.

—Andrew Forge

STEVENSON, Harold.

American. Born in Idabel, Oklahoma, 11 March 1929. Studied at the University of Oklahoma, Norman; University of Mexico, Mexico City; and Art Students League, New York. Established residence in Paris, 1959; studio in Idabel, 1965; now lives in Long Island City, New York. Agent: Keith Green Gallery, 500 Park Avenue, New York, New York 10022. Address: 21-14 45th Avenue, Long Island City, New York 11101, U.S.A.

Individual Exhibitions:

Ian Stephenson: *Ceolfrith Caper,* **1984**

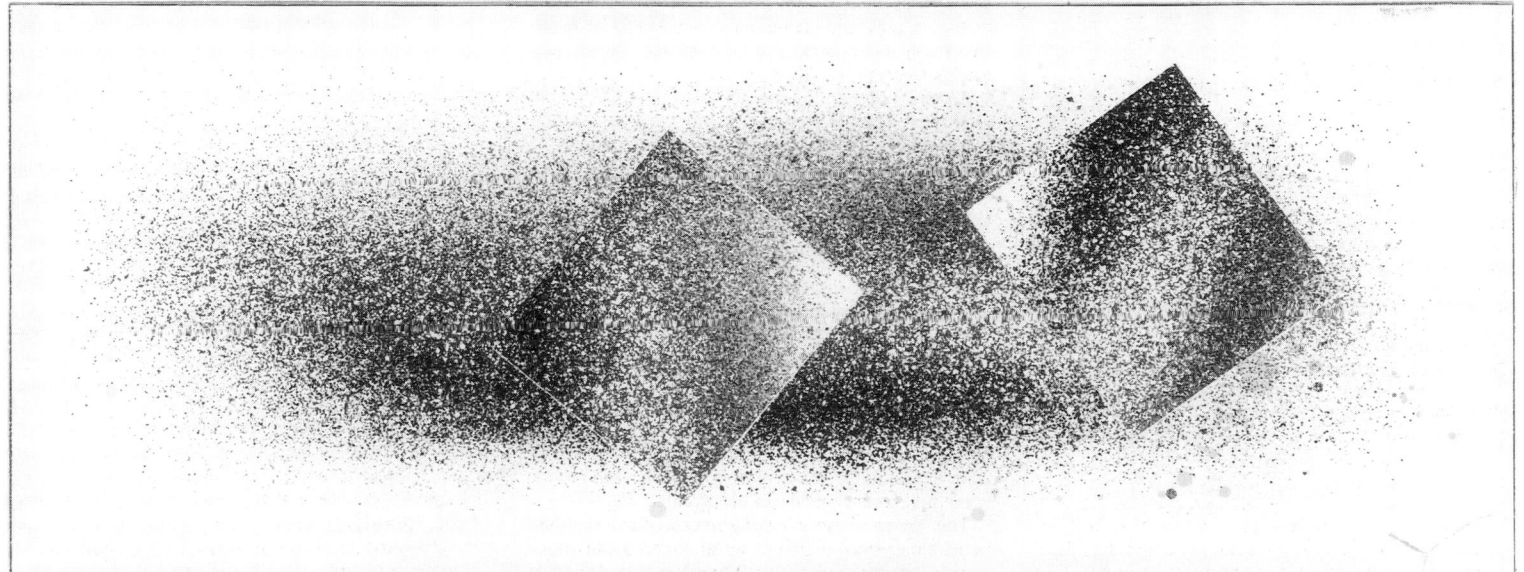

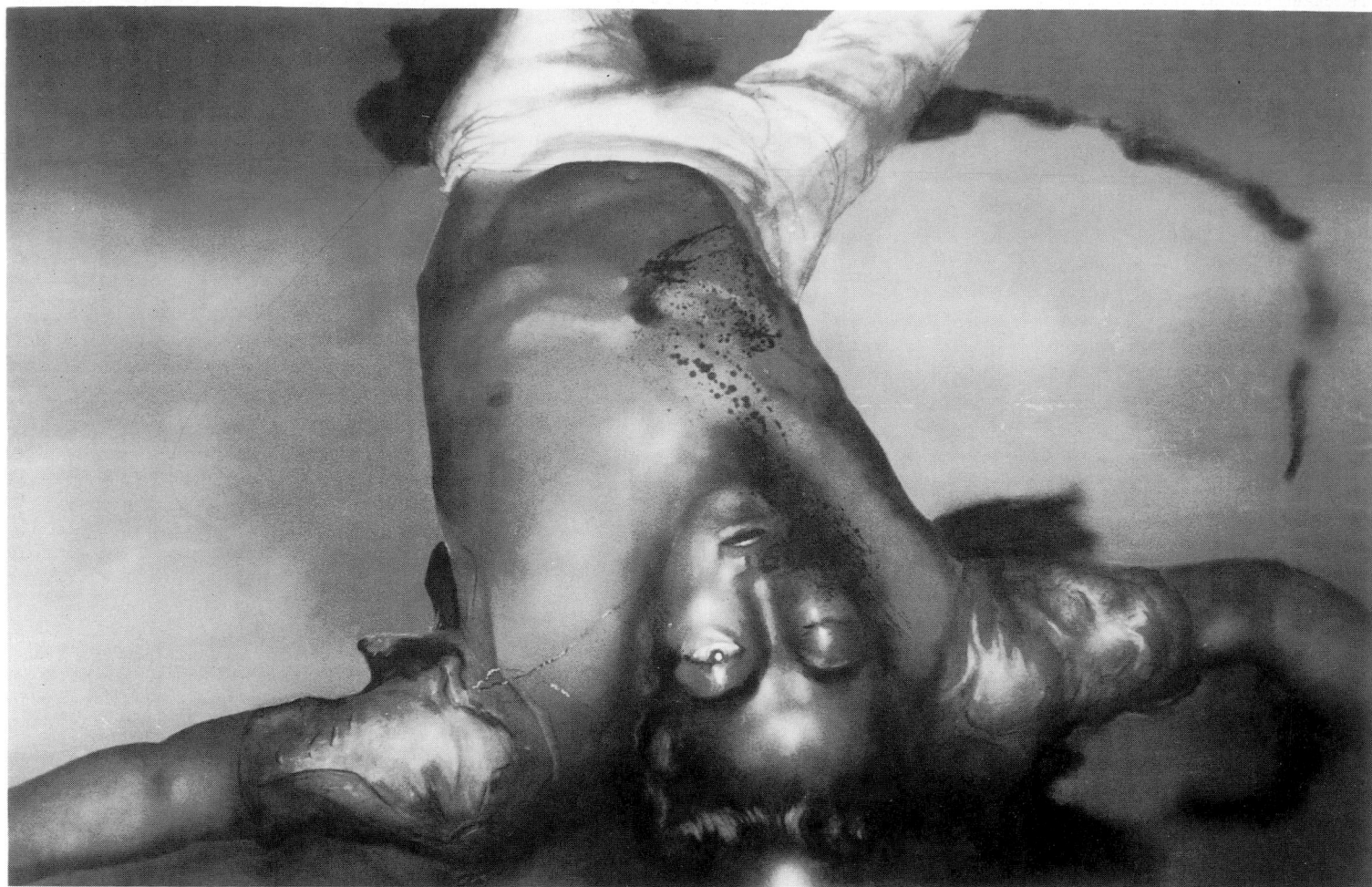

Harold Stevenson: *Death at Tom (Memorial to Lightning Billy)*, 1977

1965	*The Idabel Paintings,* Alexander Iolas Gallery, New York
1968	*The Great Society,* Galerie Iris Clert, Paris
	La Chasse, Galerie Iris Clert, Paris
1969	Galerie Hake, Kolo, West Germany
1970	Galleria La Medusa, Rome
1972	Alexander Iolas Gallery, New York
1973	Alexander Iolas Gallery, New York
	Galleria La Medusa, Rome
	ARA Pacis, Galerie Alexandre Iolas, Paris
	Zoumboulakis Gallery, Athens
1974	*Black Fates,* Alexander Iolas Gallery, New York
1975	*Votives and Greek Themes,* Brooks Jackson-Iolas Gallery, New York
1976	*La Victoire and Death of the American Dream,* Brooks Brooks-Iolas Gallery, New York
1979	Galerie Iris Clert, Paris

Selected Group Exhibitions:

1962	*Piccola Biennale,* Venice
	Annual Exhibition, Whitney Museum, New York
1965	*Pop Art,* Palais des Beaux-Arts, Brussels
1966	*Erotic Art '66,* Sidney Janis Gallery, New York
1968	*The Obsessive Image,* Institute of Contemporary Arts, London
	Prospect '68, Dusseldorf
1972	*Pop Art,* Alexander Iolas Gallery, New York
1979	*Americans in Paris,* Centre Georges Pompidou, Paris
	La Famille des Portraits, Musée du Louvre, Paris

Collections:

Whitney Museum, New York; Musée Nationale d'Art Moderne/Centre Georges Pompidou, Paris.

Publications:

On STEVENSON: books—*Pop Art* by Lucy Lippard, New York 1966; *Iris-Time* by Iris Clert, Paris 1978; *Le Milieu de l'Art,* with photographs by André Morain, Paris 1978; film—*Harold* by Andy Warhol, 1964.

My particular search for the spirit of Alexander began in Paris about 20 years ago, and by the late 1960's I had made several Alexander paintings. Iris Clert showed some of them, the Empress Farah Diba bought one, and after those first pictures dealing with the known historic images but making them monumental in scale and giving the stone likenessess flesh-like qualities, I found the problem got bigger and more evasive.

Brooks Jackson, Alexander Iolas, Iris Clert, and Bruni and Allen in Rome all asked for more Alexander pictures. They would be a long time coming. I had scratched the surface out of love and devotion, and to probe deeper meant a far more extensive involvement than I had ever anticipated.

In thinking back, I realize that I may have always been in love with the legend of Alexander the Great. The antique Greek world was dear to me even in my childhood; I knew instinctively what inspired Isadora Duncan; the ideal beauty of man seemed the most natural demand one should make; I dreamt of those ideals of beauty, freedom, democracy, diplomacy, fraternal passions, fidelity of the spirit . . . and all those gestures that inspired love in soldiers, jealousy in statesmen, fear in kings, insanity in the inner circle. Everyone I have ever loved personally has had for me some touch of Alexandrian beauty.

The personal search (in art) is such a time-consuming, over-all passion that there is not much energy left for explanations. I wouldn't be trying to say words now except out of a kind of frustration . . . I couldn't find anyone to capsule these many years.

How awkward it seems now after years of close association to place Alexander back into history. He is still so avant-garde, so modern, so untouched by the neurosis of our Judeo-Christian system (our system still wants to make him out to have been an alcoholic in need of a psychiatrist . . . how ludicrous!). It would appear to me that he is the model for men of the future; a man who dared to live his own singular destiny. What are all our worthless lives today amounting to? We conform, consume, take vitamins, get passports, vote, end up in nursing homes, die with social security numbers around our necks. The god-like quality of men is somehow lost in this conformist existence. Aristotle did not teach Alexander how to conquer the world; he taught him how to think.

I am a non-decorative painter; I do not paint to decorate anyone's existence, much less his "living room," nor do I paint for museums. My work is a matter of passion, and to live with my pictures means you have to live with my passion (in front of you). I am an old lover of Alexander, and what I don't understand about him does not make me love him less. Maybe I will understand him more in the future. Or, as one dear friend said shortly before he died, "I have loved you in this life, and I will love you in the next."

—Harold Stevenson

Alone, adrift, he rides across the vast plain in anarchic pursuit of the world's exploiters: moneylenders, shopkeepers, lawyers, bankers, businessmen, criminals. He stands outside of the law, feet apart, dressed to pronounce his virility, trigger-finger hungrily grazing the cold metal shaft of the pistol at his side. He is the self-appointed nemesis to the injustices hiding in the legal system. He is Outlaw, he is Hero, he is a killer who enters battles to affirm his manhood through symbolic sexual rituals. Death and violence alone satisfy him. He is the Cowboy. He is a myth.

The Cowboy, a palpably sexual image—more accurately homosexual, derived as a response to the increasing confusion in sexual roles and male identity produced by industrialization and urbanization in America during the first decades of this century. Sensing his control over his own life weakening—indeed his masculine mastery and command, the American male created the Cowboy—a figure of super-masculinity and individual power—to combat his feelings of alienation. Harold Stevenson is one of the few American artists to recognize the myth's tenacious grip over the American imagination. His paintings comment on the continuing inability in the American male to reconcile what he would like to be with what he really is. Under the weight of his own inadequacies he is crushed, crushed by the compensatory myth of the Cowboy. Since the '50s Stevenson has been analysing and translating the physical and psychological consequence onto canvas, delivering a shocking, pornographic, sometimes unrecognizable portrait of the human condition as it really is.

Stevenson was born in a part of America that less than a century ago was populated by Indians until pioneers—among them an older generation of Stevenson's family—slaughtered and drove them from the land with fierce weapons. To this day his small home town, Idabel, Oklahoma remains a vacant, lonely region haunted by the memory of racial murder. Furthermore, for the few whites who live there, it is a land of alienation, one with no native history, for the rich oral culture of the Indians was forever lost through racial indifference and contempt. Consequentially, Stevenson relied on various foreign sources to provide the settings for his paintings. Of these he favoured the Roman or Greece warrior in classical form, for he could imbue it with all the sexual longing and the violence endemic to the Southwest of his boyhood.

Idabel, Oklahoma was the topic of his 1967 painting *The Great Society* which consisted of one hundred faces of various townspeople. The faces are a metaphor for the human race, the faces alienated from their bodies as Americans are from the land they possess. The artist blatantly avoids the townspeople's sexuality, seeing them rather as he did as a boy. For growing up in Idabel his own sexuality was denied, repressed, something sinful, which, because of this repression, is why sensuality is the exuberant force behind the majority of his work. *The Great Society,* however, invites no sexual fantasy, the bodies covered and their sexual energy passed forever like dead men. These are his people: once filled with the drive and excitement of violence, now repressed, anti-sexual, unfeeling, defeated.

Nearly all of Stevenson's paintings celebrate the relationship between male sexuality, violence and death. Part of the early romanticization of the male involved an intimacy between the three. And since the Cowboy is the preeminent symbol of masculinity in American culture, violence and death itself took on sexual attributes. His heroes thus become naked warriors pitted against death. This American idiom illustrates Stevenson's understanding of the darker aspects of American history; specifically, the anguish of disfigured manhood and the way in which it requires the romanticizing of violence. Equally, this illustrates his understanding of why Vietnam occurred, and why there might be more Vietnams.

The Altar of Peace (1973), probably Stevenson's best work to date, is a bitter and ironic commentary on the nature of war and throbs with references to Vietnam. Stevenson sets the piece in a pagan mode, appealing to a pre-Christian age to find his metaphor for the evil of Vietnam, an age without hope of redemption, a time before salvation. The stage is deliberately set outside of American history wherein he introduced American themes and images. The individual figures were taken from earlier works, then further developed and were finally collected on one

canvas. Among them include a young boy embracing a black statue which has been mutilated, recalling a theme of the living male idealizing a hero. Right centre stands a warrior with a winged helmet passively watching the weeping youth whilst pressing his hands upon the buttocks of another warrior who is raping a woman. The gesture is ambiguous: he is either applauding the warrior or initiating his own sexual act upon his fellow. The scene rings with homosexuality as the warrior's attention is caught by the youth's grief—or his beauty. In the lower lefthand corner are two warriors, one of whom is sexually assaulting the other anally while his hand grips the base of a broken phallic monument. The monument is symbol of the defeated, as is the warrior being raped. A third warrior crouches behind a stone fragment watching the scene. Ironically his body seems to be becoming stone. The skin is ashen. His hair alone appears alive. He is the conquering warrior becoming Hero.

Altar of Peace suggests that war is mutilated male sexuality. It is violence without responsibility. It is the result of sexual confusion and inadequacy. Stevenson so adeptly summarizes this idea by castrating the defeated male; the Hero Death indifferently waves a broken arm or phallus. Winning is manhood; defeat is emasculation. War is the result of the inability to establish manhood and sexual competence nonviolently. It is the nature of Man in general and of the perversions and fantasies of the American male in specific Stevenson has recorded with such accuracy, an accuracy many viewers resist knowing.

—Carrie Barker

STEZAKER, John.

British. Born in Worcester in 1949. Studied at Nottingham School of Art; Slade School of Fine Art, London, 1967–73. Founder and Co-Editor, *Frameworks Magazine,* London. Former Lecturer, Chelsea School of Art, London. Lecturer, St. Martin's School of Art, London, since 1975. Agent: Nigel Greenwood Inc., 4 New Burlington Street, London W1. Address: 61 Praed Street, London W.10, England.

Individual Exhibitions:

1970	Sigi Krauss Gallery, London
	Forum Stadtpark, Graz, Austria
1972	Nigel Greenwood Gallery, London
	King's College, Cambridge
1973	Nigel Greenwood Gallery, London
	Museum of Modern Art, Oxford
1974	Galerie December, Münster, West Germany
1975	Nigel Greenwood Gallery, London
	Galleria Lia Rumma, Rome (travelled to Galleria Lia Rumma, Naples)
1976	Nigel Greenwood Gallery, London
	Galerie Eric Fabre, Paris
1977	Nigel Greenwood Gallery, London
	Spectro Arts, Newcastle upon Tyne
	Galleria Schema, Florence
1978	The Photographers' Gallery, London
	Ikon Gallery, Birmingham
	City Museum, Southampton
1979	*Works 1973–1978,* Kunstmuseum, Lucerne
	New '57 Gallery, Edinburgh

Selected Group Exhibitions:

1970	*Young Contemporaries,* London
	3 Schools Exhibition, Royal Academy of Arts, London
1971	*Wall Show,* Lisson Gallery, London
1972	*The New Art,* Hayward Gallery, London
1973	*Critics' Choice,* Tooth's Gallery, London
1974	*Projekt '74,* Kunsthalle, Cologne
1975	*Structures and Codes,* Royal College of Art, London

1976	*Arte Inglese Oggi 1960–1976,* Palazzo Reale, Milan
1979	*Un Certain Art Anglais,* Musée d'Art Moderne de le Ville, Paris
1982	*Hayward Annual: British Drawing,* Hayward Gallery, London

Collections:

Victoria and Albert Museum, London; Tate Gallery, London

Publications:

By STEZAKER: book—*Beyond Art for Art's Sake: A Propos Mundas,* London 1973; articles—"3 Paradoxes and a Resolution" in *Studio International* (London), May 1972; "Conceptual Art" in *Studio International* (London), June 1972; interview, with Anne Seymour, in *The New Art,* exhibition catalogue, London 1972; "2 Instances of Institutional Determinancy of Art" in *Control Magazine* (London), no. 7, 1973; "Premises" in *Flash Art* (Milan), March/May 1973; "Post-Duchamp Reversal" in *Art and Artists* (London), December 1973; "Priorities I, II and III" in *Frameworks Journal* (London), vol. 1, nos. 1–3, 1974; "Ideal Types and Utopias" in *Control Magazine* (London), no. 8, 1974; "Conversation with Peter Smith" in *Studio International* (London), March/April 1975; "Social Expression: Social Reality" in *Meantime,* no. 1, 1977; interview in *Artlog* (London), January 1979.

On STEZAKER: books—*5 Collages by John Stezaker,* with text by John W. Walker, Birmingham 1978; *John Stezaker: Works 1973–1978,* exhibition catalogue, by B. Hatten and M. Kunz, Lucerne 1979; articles—"Problem Solving and Question Begging: The Works of Art-Language and John Stezaker" by Rosetta Brooks in *Studio International* (London), December 1973.

STILL, Clyfford.

American. Born in Grandin, North Dakota, 30 November 1904; moved with his family to Spokane, Washington, 1905. Educated in Spokane; enrolled at the Art Students League, New York, but withdrew after the first day, 1926; studied at Spokane University, Washington, 1926–27 and 1931–33, B.A. 1933; Fellow, Trask Foundation, Saratoga Springs, New York, 1934–35; studied art, philosophy and literary criticism, under Murray Bundy, Washington State University, Pullman, M.A. 1935 (Teaching Fellow). Married: daughters: Sandra and Diane. Painter: lived in Canada, 1927–31, then returned to Washington; worked in shipbuilding and aircraft industries, Oakland and San Francisco, 1941–45; settled in New York, 1945; Founder, with Mark Rothko, Robert Motherwell and others, Subjects of the Artist teaching group, New York, 1948–49; settled in Carroll County, near Westminster, and purchased a house in New Windsor, Maryland, 1966. Lecturer, 1935–40, and Assistant Professor of Fine Arts, 1940–41, Washington State University, Pullman; Professor, Richmond Professional Institute, Virginia, 1943–45; Lecturer, California School of Fine Arts, San Francisco, 1946–50; Summer School, Hunter College, City University of New York, 1951; and Brooklyn College, New York 1952–53; Visiting Artist and Lecturer, University of Colorado, Boulder, 1960. Recipient: Award of Merit Medal, American Academy of Arts and Letters, New York, 1972; Skowhegan Medal for Painting, Skowhegan School of Painting and Sculpture, Maine, 1974; Alumni Achievement Award, Washington State University, Pullman, 1975. D.F.A.: Maryland Institute, Baltimore, 1967; North Dakota State University, Fargo, 1972; San Francisco Art Institute, 1976. Honorary Member, Buffalo Fine Arts Academy, New York, 1962. Member, American Academy of Arts and Letters, New York, 1978. *Died* (in Baltimore, Maryland) *23 June 1980.*

Clyfford Still: *Untitled*, **1957** Courtesy Whitney Museum, New York

Individual Exhibitions:

1943　San Francisco Museum of Art
1946　Art of This Century, New York
1947　Betty Parsons Gallery, New York
　　　California Palace of the Legion of Honor, San Francisco
1950　Metart Gallery, San Francisco
　　　Betty Parsons Gallery, New York
1951　Betty Parsons Gallery, New York
1959　Albright-Knox Art Gallery, Buffalo, New York
1963　Institute of Contemporary Art, University of Pennsylvania, Philadelphia
1966　*33 Paintings for the Albright-Knox Art Gallery,* Albright-Knox Art Gallery, Buffalo, New York
1969　Marlborough-Gerson Gallery, New York
1970　Marlborough-Gerson Gallery, New York
1976　San Francisco Museum of Modern Art
1979　Metropolitan Museum of Art, New York

Selected Group Exhibitions:

1935　*Annual Exhibition,* National Academy of Design, New York
1945　*Autumn Salon,* Art of This Century, New York
1952　*15 Americans,* Museum of Modern Art, New York
1956　*Modern Art in the United States,* Tate Gallery, London
1958　*The New American Painting,* travelling exhibition (toured Europe)
1959　*Documenta,* Kassel, West Germany
1965　*The New York School: The First Generation,* Los Angeles County Museum of Art

1969　*The New American Painting and Sculpture,* Museum of Modern Art, New York
1972　*Color Forum,* University Art Museum, Austin, Texas
1987　*American Painting: Abstract Expressionism and After,* San Francisco Museum of Modern Art

Collections:

Museum of Modern Art, New York; Whitney Museum, New York; Albright-Knox Art Gallery, Buffalo, New York; Hirshhorn Museum and Sculpture Garden, Smithsonian Institution, Washington, D.C.; Art Institute of Chicago; Museum of Fine Arts, Houston; San Francisco Museum of Modern Art; Tate Gallery, London; Kunsthalle, Basle.

Publications:

By STILL: articles—statement in *Americans,* exhibition catalogue, New York 1952; letter in *Paintings by Clyfford Still,* exhibition catalogue, Buffalo, New York 1959; "Comment" in *Albright-Knox Gallery Notes* (Buffalo, New York), Summer 1960; statement in *Clyfford Still,* exhibition catalogue, Philadelphia 1963; "An Open Letter to an Art Critic" in *Artforum* (San Francisco), December 1963; letter in *Artforum* (San Francisco), February 1964; statement in *33 Paintings for the Albright-Knox Art Gallery,* exhibition catalogue, by Katherine Kuh, Buffalo, New York 1966; "Notes by Clyfford Still" in *Clyfford Still,* exhibition catalogue, San Francisco 1976; "A Conversation with Clyfford Still" by Thomas Albright in *Artnews* (New York), March 1976; "Diary Notes and Letters" in *Clyfford Still,* exhibition catalogue, New York 1979.

On STILL: books—*Clyfford Still,* exhibition catalogue, by Ti-Grace Sharpless, Philadelphia 1963; *Clyfford Still,* exhibition catalogue, New York 1970; *Clyfford Still,* exhibition catalogue, by Katherine Kuh, New York 1979; articles— "Clyfford Still" by Hubert Crehan in the *San Francisco Chronicle,* July 1950; "U.S. Painters Today: Clyfford Still" by Kenneth Sawyer in *Portfolio and Art News Annual No. 2,* New York 1960; "The Outsider" by Thomas B. Hess in *Artnews* (New York), December 1969; "Still: The Enigma" by Katherine Kuh in *Vogue* (New York), February 1970; "Clyfford Still's Gift to the San Francisco Museum of Modern Art" by Henry T. Hopkins in *American Art Review,* January/February 1976; "Clyfford Still" by Clement Greenberg in *Arts Magazine* (New York), October 1980; "Regression and Color in Abstract Expressionism: Barnett Newman, Mark Rothko, Clyfford Still" by A. Gibson in *Arts Magazine* (New York), March 1981.

*

Though invariably linked with Newman and Rothko among the Founding Fathers of New York Abstract Expressionism, as early as 1944, Clyfford Still was capable of arriving at a sufficiently differentiated image to leave him identifiable from his colleagues while at the same time escaping a systematic formula of composition.

In these early pictures he maintained a contrast between those dark cloud-like outlines and the light tone of the ground on which they disported themselves. His common forms were of an organic base placed in an atmosphere of two-dimensional space on which they loomed. Then began the overloading of surface with pigment in dark weights of black and purples through which the light glinted as of a rosy dawn waking against an almost impenetrable night.

Despite an uncompromising commitment to colour

areas of unallusive significance, there came through in Still's works, especially those of mural scale, the inevitable visual comparisons with the massive backdrops of nature in mountain scenery. Yet in this giant environmental ambiance the paintings assumed elemental presences of their own on a positive and physically active spirit.

In consummation of paint worked and spread and played against its neighbour Still remained faithful to the concept of Action Painting in its crude evidence of sensual involvement. Refinement came in the choice of a limited palette that was flavoured of the fire-hot reds and yellows and sooty blacks and blues; Still's colours emerged not to rest but as alive in high impasto reliefs of chromatic textures akin to the molten debris of a furnace.

Realizing his own vision is Still's admitted assessment of the function of the artist; its apotheosis is reached in his many examples of total commitment to the evolution of a picture not from a process of rational addition but the superimposed stages of growth into a seemingly natural climax. This culmination of glowing and maturing areas until final abandonment epitomises the unique quality of Still; it is as though by the alchemy of prime selection of colours, few as they may be, and their spread on the support, each painting takes control of its own destiny, and the result is as much a fusion of conflicting impulses and forces as a pre-ordained exegesis of the artist's preformed image in his mind.

One was never under any illusion that for Clyfford Still painting was a succession of gestures applied in blanket saturation of the white ground, each laying on top of the previous coat in a woven chromatic depth of tactile subtle strength. Eye and finger-tip came together in appreciating Still in his joint impact where size too had its vital ingredient. Still's influence and effect were strong enough to persuade younger followers towards a greater self-confidence in the ability of a surface area to bear its own potentials of expansion outwards towards the spectator rather than away towards an imaginary horizon.

His paintings typically bore no names, merely being described as "Painting" or numbered. One catalogued as "Untitled" 1957 in the Whitney, New York, sums it up. It is a riven banner of blood stains and blob-splattered fabric, historic standard of a battle fought by American artists against the past and suffering defeat only when they themselves were overtaken by time.

—G. S. Whittet

STUART, Michelle.

American. Born in Los Angeles, California, 10 February 1938. Studied at Chouinard Art Institute, Los Angeles, 1954–55; Instituto de Bellas Artes, Mexico City, under Diego Rivera, 1955–56; and New School for Social Research, New York, 1958–60. Married Jose Barton in 1950 (divorced, 1974). Worked as a topographical draftswoman, Los Angeles, 1955; lived in Mexico, 1955–56, and in Paris, 1956–58; now a full-time artist, living and working in New York, since 1958. Adjunct Instructor, Pratt Institute School of Art and Design, New York, 1975–76, Parsons School of Design, New York, 1976–78, and Fordham University, New York, 1976–79. Recipient: MacDowell Fellowship, Peterborough, New Hampshire, 1974; National Endowment for the Arts Grant for Individual Artists, 1974–1977, 1980; Tamarind Institute Grant, 1974; New York Creative Artists Public Service Grant in Painting, 1974; Guggenheim Fellowship, 1975; Finnish Art Association Fellowship, Helsinki, 1985; Artists' Fellowship, New York Foundation for the Arts, 1987. Agents: Max Protetch Gallery, 560 Broadway, New York, New York 10012; Saxon/Lee Gallery, 7525 Beverly, Los Angeles, Cali-

fornia 90036; Galerie Veda, Ginza Asahi Building, 6–6-7 Ginza, Chuo-ku, Tokyo 104, Japan; and Galerie Alfred Schmela, Mutter-Ey-Strasse 3, 4 Dusseldorf, West Germany. Address: 152 Wooster Street, New York, New York 10012, U.S.A.

Individual Exhibitions:

1973 Douglass College, Rutgers University, New Brunswick, New Jersey
      Windham College, Putney, Vermont
1974 Max Hutchinson Gallery, New York
      Galerie Alfred Schmela, Dusseldorf
1975 Max Hutchinson Gallery, New York
      Fine Arts Center Gallery, State University at Oneonta, New York
      Niagara Gorge Path Relocated, Lewiston, New York (site work)
1976 Galerie Alfred Schmela, Dusseldorf
      Gallery of Fine Arts, State University of New York at Stony Brook
      Galerie Farideh Cadot, Paris
      Max Hutchinson Gallery, New York
      Zolla/Lieberman Gallery, Chicago
      East/West Wall Memory Relocated, P.S. 1, Institute for Art and Urban Resources, New York (site work)
1977 Massachusetts Institute of Technology, Cambridge
      Williams College Museum of Art, Williamstown, Massachusetts
      Galerie Munro, Hamburg
      Strata: Graves/Hesse/Stuart/Winsor,, Vancouver Art Gallery
      Galerie Alfred Schmela, Dusseldorf
      Color/Time/Landform/Transformation, Tomkins Cove Quarry, Tomkins Cove, New York (site work and video project)
      Incidents of Travel in Nature: A Space/Time Book and Video Project, Moore College of Art, Philadelphia
1978 University of New Mexico Art Gallery, Albuquerque
      Incidents of Travel in Nature: A Space/Time Book and Video Project, Art Gallery, University of California at Long Beach (site work)
      Fine Arts Gallery, Wright State University, Dayton, Ohio
      Galerie Farideh Cadot, Paris
      Centre d'Arts Plastiques Contemporains, Bordeaux
      Zand Gallery, Teheran
      Tanit Galerie, Munich
      Zolla/Lieberman Gallery, Chicago
1979 Ehrensberger Gallery, Zurich
      Droll/Kolbert Gallery, New York
      Foster White Gallery, Seattle
      Stone Alignments/Solstice Cairns, Portland Center for the Visual Arts, Oregon (permanent sculpture site work)
      Galerie Schmela, Dusseldorf
      Paperwork, Institute of Contemporary Arts, London
      Janus Gallery, Venice, California
1980 Galerie Munro, Hamburg
      Galerie Ahlner, Stockholm
      Galleriet, Lund, Sweden
      Galerie Aronowitsch, Stockholm
1981 *Correspondences*, Joslyn Art Museum, Omaha, Nebraska (audio visual room installation)
      Galerie Tanit, Munich
      Correspondences, P.S. 1, Institute for Art and Urban Resources, New York (audio visual room installation)
1982 *Correspondences*, St. Louis Art Museum (audio visual room installation)
      Susan Caldwell Gallery, New York
      Galerie Schmela, Dusseldorf
1983 Walker Art Center, Minneapolis
      Janus Gallery, Los Angeles
      Haags Gemeentemuseum, The Hague
      Galleriet Anders Tornberg, Lund, Sweden
      Galerie Ahlner, Stockholm
1984 *Sacred Precincts*, State University of New York, Purchase
      Galerie Krista Mikkola, Helsinki
      Gallery Ueda Warehouse and Ginza, Tokyo

1985 Long Island University, Greenvale, New York (travelled to Syracuse, New York; Boulder, Colorado; Binghamton, New York)
1986 Saxon/Lee Gallery, Los Angeles
      Paradisi, Brooklyn Museum, New York
      Arts Club of Chicago
      Max Protetch Gallery, New York
1987 Thorden Wetterling Gallery, Goteborg, Sweden
      Toni Birckhead Gallery, Cincinnati
      Paintings and Prints, Anders Tornberg Gallery, Lund, Sweden
      Malningar, Galerie Aronowitsch, Stockholm
      Pfizer Inc., New York

Selected Group Exhibitions:

1972 *Outsize Drawings*, Loeb Art Center, New York University
1976 *Handmade Paper: Prints and Unique Work*, Museum of Modern Art, New York
1977 *Documenta*, Kassel, West Germany
1978 *Paper as Medium*, Smithsonian Institution, Washington, D.C.
1979 *The Presence of Nature*, Whitney Museum, New York
1980 *With Paper, About Paper*, Albright-Knox Art Gallery, Buffalo, New York
1981 *Le Moderna Museet de Stockholm à Bruxelles*, Palais des Beaux-Arts, Brussels
1982 *Sans Titre: 4 Années d'Acquisition au Musée de Toulon*, Musée d'Art, Toulon, France
1985 *Livres d'Artistes*, Centre Georges Pompidou, Paris
1987 *Sacred Spaces*, Everson Museum of Art, Syracuse, New York

Collections:

Museum of Modern Art, New York; Brooklyn Museum, New York; Albright-Knox Art Gallery, Buffalo, New York; Museum of Contemporary Art, Chicago; Walker Art Center, Minneapolis; Cincinnati Art Museum, Ohio; Kaiser-Wilhelm Museum, Krefeld, West Germany; Moderna Museet, Stockholm; Stadtisches Museum, Monchengladbach, West Germany; National Collection of Australia, Canberra.

Publications:

By STUART: books—*The Fall*, New York 1976; *A Complete Folk History of the United States at the Edge of the Century*, Dayton, Ohio and New York 1978; *From the Silent Garden*, Williamstown, Massachusetts 1979; *I-80 Series: Michelle Stuart*, exhibition catalogue, Omaha 1981; *Sacred Precincts: From Dreamtime to the South China Sea . . .*, New York 1984; aritcles—"Project, Then/Now" in *Artforum* (New York), February 1980; "American Frontiers: The Photographs of Timothy O'Sullivan 1867–1874" in *The Print Collector's Newsletter* (New York), July/August 1982.

On STUART: books—*Michelle Stuart*, exhibition catalogue, with an essay by Lawrence Alloway, Oneonta, New York 1975; *From the Center* by Lucy Lippard, New York 1976; *Michelle Stuart*, exhibition catalogue, with an essay by Robert Hobbs, Cambridge, Massachusetts 1977; *Strata: Graves/Hesse/Stuart/Winsor*, exhibition catalogue, with an essay by Lucy Lippard, Vancouver 1977; *Michelle Stuart*, exhibition catalogue, with an essay by Jean-Pierre Sanchez, Bordeaux 1978; *Originals: American Women Artists* by Eleanor Munro, New York 1979; *Michelle Stuart: Paperwork*, exhibition catalogue, with text by Sarah Kent, London 1979; *With Paper, About Paper*, exhibition catalogue, with an essay by Carlotta Kotik, Buffalo, New York 1980; *La Peinture Américaine: Le Mythes et al Matière* by Madeleine Deschamps, Paris 1981; *Michelle Stuart: Place and Time*, exhibition catalogue, with text by Graham Beal, Minneapolis 1983; *The Pluralist Era: American Art 1968–81* by Corinne Robins, New York 1984; *Michelle Stuart: Voyages*, exhibition catalogue, with texts by Ted Castle and Judith Van Wagner, Greenvale, New York 1985; *Michelle Stuart*, exhibition catalogue, with text by Esther Sparks, Chicago 1986.

For some years I have been making large scale works concerned with the visual and conceptual experience in nature. The earlier ones were topographical renderings of cratered surfaces, sometimes with ele-

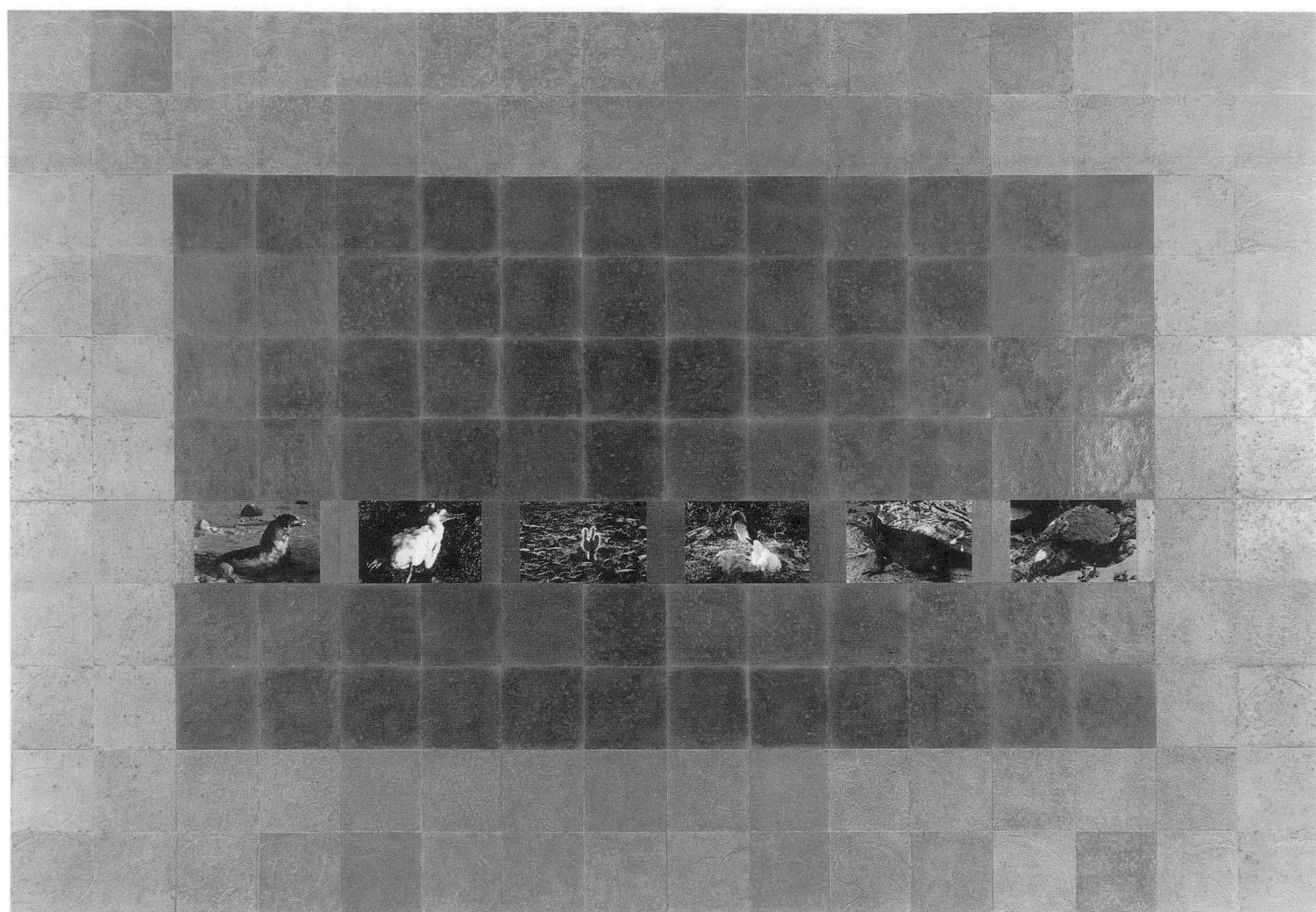

Michelle Stuart: *Islas Encantadas, Seymour Island Cycle,* 1982

ments suggesting waves and currents. The pieces that followed were multi-unit drawings in series that documented changes in nature using real geological surfaces. The marks were made with graphite on paper. The viewer moved physically with the piece. The units were two feet square with two inch intervals extending horizontally on the wall for as long as 12 feet. Parallel to the physical movement, passage of time was demonstrated in the sequence. It formed an open-ended continuum that described change.

During the last 8 years I have used rocks and earth as well as graphite, on muslin mounted rag paper. The height of the work is usually 9 to 12 feet by 5 feet wide. Most of the work is three-dimensional to some degree and some pieces move into the floor space. These pieces are a continuation of both the continuum and geological concepts, but deal directly with specific sites. They are made by violently indenting or impressing the paper repreatedly with rocks and layering and polishing the surface with earth from locations in which I feel strong sentient associations. The pulverized earth or mineral deposits color the paper and the rock marks become random events locked into the surface of the work. The process entails a continuous repetition of body movement. Each gesture varies from the preceding one and thus describes distinct patterns in time. Each repeated rock impression is configurationally infinite.

In special projects such as *Niagara Gorge Path Relocated,* executed at Artpark in Lewiston, New York, I worked in the same way, but the gorge was part of the piece. By relocating topographically the Niagara cascade to its original site I sought to evoke the perception of time and the flow of nature's processes. This piece included some public participation in the process.

In Project Studio 1 (an abandoned school now used for art projects) I made *East/West Wall Memory Relocated.* In this particular piece I sought to record the way in which memory shifts in time and space and a displacement occurs that re-forms our perceptions. In the two-part piece the texture of the wall's aging surface was rendered visible with graphite on paper and the parallel but opposite 13 foot by 5 foot wall units were interchanged.

Since the beginning of 1975 I have also been making intimate paper objects that I call "rock books." They are 'histories' of a place. 'Notebooks' relating to strata forms and time duration in nature. They are quiet, tactile explorations of the earth in specific geological sites. Some of them are handmade paper that in the process of making, I color with earth pigment. Some, tied with woven string, cannot be opened while others upon opening reveal the sequence of geologic processes that exist when the strata layers of an area are unveiled.

From 1977 to 1982 my work has continued to be involved with nature, but with the additional dimension of nature as a setting for man. This correspondence between the two, man and nature, inspired the passage work *Stone Alignments/Solstice Cairns,* a permanent outdoor sculpture made of boulders and stone that lies on a plateau overlooking the Columbia River Gorge in Oregon. The piece is 1000' x 600'. Also, the historical aspect was the idea behind a large audio-visual room installation called *Correspondences,* dealing with the perceptual relationship and marriage of two cultures, the Spanish and Maya in the Yucatan area of Mexico.

In addition the work during this period has included photographs, both black and white and color taken on the site by the artist. These photographs ren-

der narrative sequence both to nature cycles, such as "Islas Encantadas: Seymour Island Cycle" (The Galapagos Islands), and demonstrate symbolically or metaphorically man's inspiration from and use of natural resources such as stone and earth, and how, particularly with architecture, this influences his reality.

Recently, I have been doing large-scale paintings, installations and commissions in encaustic (wax) process with plants, earth and archaeological shards. I have also worked on large bronze site-specific commissions.

—Michelle Stuart

SUGA, Kishio.
Japanese. Born in Morioka, 19 February 1944. Studied at Tama Art College, Tokyo, 1964–68. Married Taeko Tomioka in 1969. Lives and works in Kawasaki. Travelled in Europe and the United States, 1970, in France, 1973. Recipient: First Prize, *Shell Art Exhibition,* Tokyo, 1967; Second Prize, Art Critics Competition, *Bijutsu-Techo* magazine, Tokyo, 1969; Grand Prize, *Japan Art Festival,* Tokyo, 1970. Agent: Tokyo Gallery, Japan. Address: c/o Tokyo Gallery, 8–16–18 Ginza, Chuo-ku, Tokyo, Japan.

Individual Exhibitions:

1968   Tsubaki Kindai Gallery, Tokyo
1969   Tamura Gallery, Tokyo

1970	Tamura Gallery, Tokyo
1971	Sato Gallery, Tokyo
1972	Tamura Gallery, Tokyo
	Kinokuniya Gallery, Tokyo
	Roppongi Building, Tokyo
1973	Tamura Gallery, Tokyo
	Sato Gallery, Tokyo
	City Hall, Morioka City, Japan
1974	Tamaru Gallery, Tokyo
	Gallery 16, Kyoto
1975	Tokiwa Gallery, Tokyo
	Maki Gallery, Tokyo (2 exhibitions)
	Kaneko Art Gallery, Tokyo (2 exhibitions)
1976	Maki Gallery, Tokyo
	Tokyo Gallery
	International Christian University, Tokyo
1979	Tokyo Gallery

Selected Group Exhibitions:

1966	*International Young Artists Exhibition*, Tokyo
1967	*Shell Art Exhibition*, Shirokiya Department Store, Tokyo
1970	*Japan Art Festival, Tokyo*
	Aspects of New Japanese Art, National Museum of Modern Art, Kyoto
1972	*Contemporary Japanese Graphics Exhibition*, Institute of Contemporary Arts, London
1973	*Biennale de Paris*
1974	*Japan: Tradition und Gegenwart*, Städtisches Kunsthalle, Dusseldorf
1975	*Materials Exhibition*, Stedelijk van Abbemuseum, Eindhoven, Netherlands
1976	*Kyoto Biennale*
	International Open Encounter on Video, Museo de Arte Contemporaneo, Caracas

Publications:

By SUGA: articles—"Invisible Words in an Invisible World" in *Space Design* (Tokyo), October 1969; "The Starting Point of Disappearance" in *Space Design* (Tokyo), December 1969; "To Exist Beyond the Situation" in *Bijutsu-Techo* (Tokyo), February 1970; "Unnamable" in *Bijutsu-Techo* (Tokyo), May 1972.

On SUGA: articles "Suga," special issue of *Kirokutai* (Tokyo), November 1972; "Current Critic" by Toshiaki Minemura in *Bijutsu-Techo* (Tokyo), June 1973; "In the Case of Suga's Work" by Toshiaki Minemura in *Sogetsu* (Tokyo),

June 1973; "Thing's School" by Ichiro Haryu in *Asahi Journal* (Tokyo), no. 33, 1974; "Suga" by Toshikuni Maeno in *L'Art Vivant* (Paris), no. 45, 1974; "The Works of Kishio Suga" by Toshikuni Maeno in *Obararyusoka* (Tokyo), 1974; "Suga's Work with Natural Things" by Yusuke Nakahara in *Space Design* (Tokyo), March 1975; "Suga's Event in Tokiwa Gallery" by Yoshiaki Tono in *Obararyusoka* (Tokyo), June 1975; "Current Critic" by Toshiaki Minemura in *Obararyusoka* (Tokyo), October 1976.

I never intended to create "Art" in my work. "Art" or non-"Art" is just the result, and it is decided by other people, not by myself. I think about "Thing" and about the situation of an existing "Thing." I want to recognize the reality of "Thing" and its system. And, as "Thing" does not exist in isolation, I want to achieve its reality in Nature.

To achieve the situation of "Thing," I have to recognize "dependence" or being "dependent." this is one of my important concerns in deciding my position as regards the external world. I wish I had a window looking into my consciousness, just like the window of my room. I suppose a place in which to reflect my consciousness, which in this case, in my case, is Nature.

I am interested in each thing that is involved in the construction of nature. Each thing has an existence by itself, one by one, but nature has no center. Each thing is not a part of nature so much as it is a whole unto itself.

Various things are gathered together in nature, yet it seems that they have no relation to each other—but they are related: sometimes we can see it, sometimes we cannot.

I think that "relation" and "system" in nature are on the same level: seemingly separate relations have to be dependent on each other in order to be whole. That is to say, "system" in nature is a system of dependence, and it must be considered as a fact of "Thing." There is the absolute position of "Thing," which cannot be conveyed by fabricated rhetoric.

—Kishio Suga

In one of Kishio Suga's experiments can be seen the following work. A board is set across two walls horizontally in a corner, and a piece of cloth is folded and set upon it. The board is cut across to join the two walls, and the cloth is folded to make creases at the point where it touches the walls. What is interesting about the work is the feeling one has of the reversal of

composition and external appearance. There is something wilful about setting the board across the corner and putting the cloth on top, but the folding of the cloth as it hits the wall at both ends seems to depend on something beyond this. From the middle upwards, it seems to depend on the state of physical contact with the wall as something exterior. But this folded part seems to be very artificial in physical appearance, while the upper cloth area seems to have been accomplished without this artificiality. This undoubtedly is because folding is the means employed, but this is accomplished forcibly as it were by the walls. Now if that be the case, this work of Suga shows the possibility of revealing how the act of making is regulated by means of the act being made. The corner is a space Suga is particularly fond of, and this work is characterized by the insertion into the work of a conversion power as against the act of that corner.

Obviously in whatever work of art the act of making can not overstep the physical conditions. And yet it is difficult to say that this fact is the same as determining a work through the conscious introduction of that area of letting something be made. Yet if we exaggerate this one point of letting something be made, we will inevitably end up with the result of bringing the material's physical qualities into prominence. It seems to me that the delicate balance between both poles is recovered in this cloth-corner work.

We can only wait in expectation to see how this kind of quality will appear in the other works, but it will be of deep interest to see how Suga suggests the work's possible expanse as the product that results from reversing the action of determining the work in a dislocation of the condition of this space.

—Yusuke Nakahara

SUGAI, Kumi.

Japanese. Born in Kobe, Japan, 13 March 1919; has maintained residence in Paris since 1952. Educated at the School of Fine Arts, Osaka. Married to Mitsuko Sugai. Independent artist now practicing a spare, non-personal style of abstraction. Recipient: Grand Prize, *Triennal International de Gravure*, Grenchen, Switzerland, 1961; Grand Prize, *Biennal International de Gravure*, Cracow, 1966. Address: 91 rue de l'Amiral Mouchez, Pavillon 6, 75013 Paris, France.

Individual Exhibitions:

1954	Galerie Craven, Paris
	Palais des Beaux-Arts, Brussels
1957	Galerie H. Le Grendre, Paris
1958	Galerie Creuzevaut, Paris
1959	Kootz Gallery, New York
1960	Städtisches Museum, Leverkusen, West Germany (retrospective)
1961	Kootz Gallery, New York
1962	Kootz Gallery, New York
1963	Galerie Creuzevaut, Paris
	Kestner-Gesellschaft, Hannover (retrospective)
1964	Kootz Gallery, New York
	Galerie Toni Brechbuhl, Grenchen, Switzerland
	Die Insel, Hamburg (retrospective)
1965	American Art Gallery, Copenhagen
	Galerie Bleu, Stockholm
	Sundsvall Museum, Sweden
	Kunsthallen, Gothenburg, Sweden
1967	Lefebre Gallery, New York
	Kunstnernes Hus, Oslo (retrospective)
	Galerie Brusberg, Hannover
1968	Galerie Defet, Nuremberg
	Galerie Hilt, Basel
1969	Court Gallery, Copenhagen
	Kunsthallen, Gothenburg, Sweden
	Galerie Klipan, Stockholm
	Tokyo Gallery, Tokyo

Kishio Suga: *Extending Existence*, installation at the Maki Gallery, Tokyo, 1976

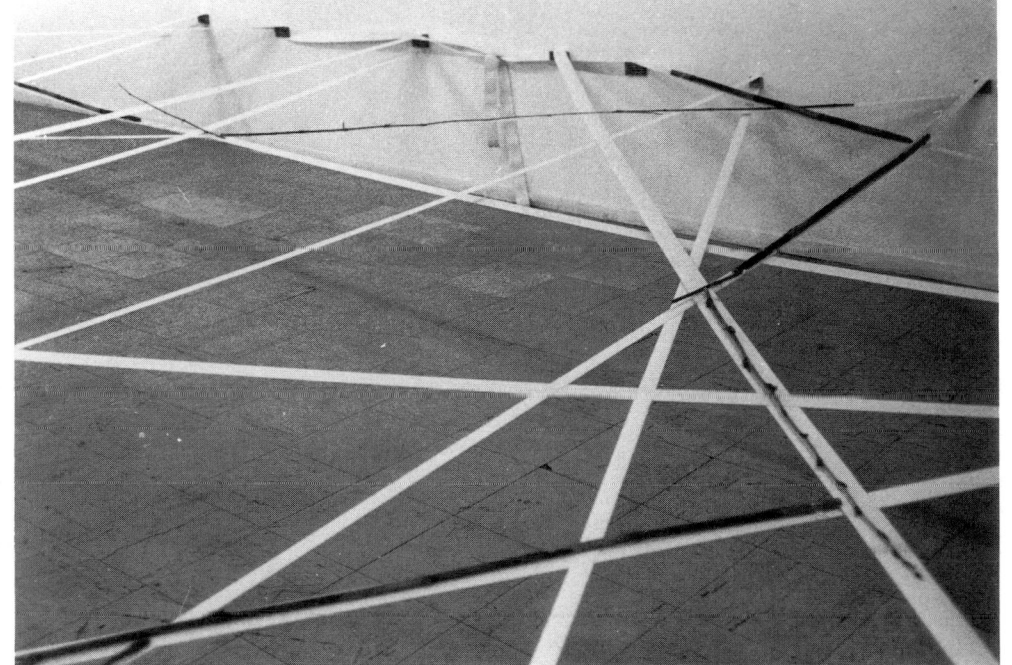

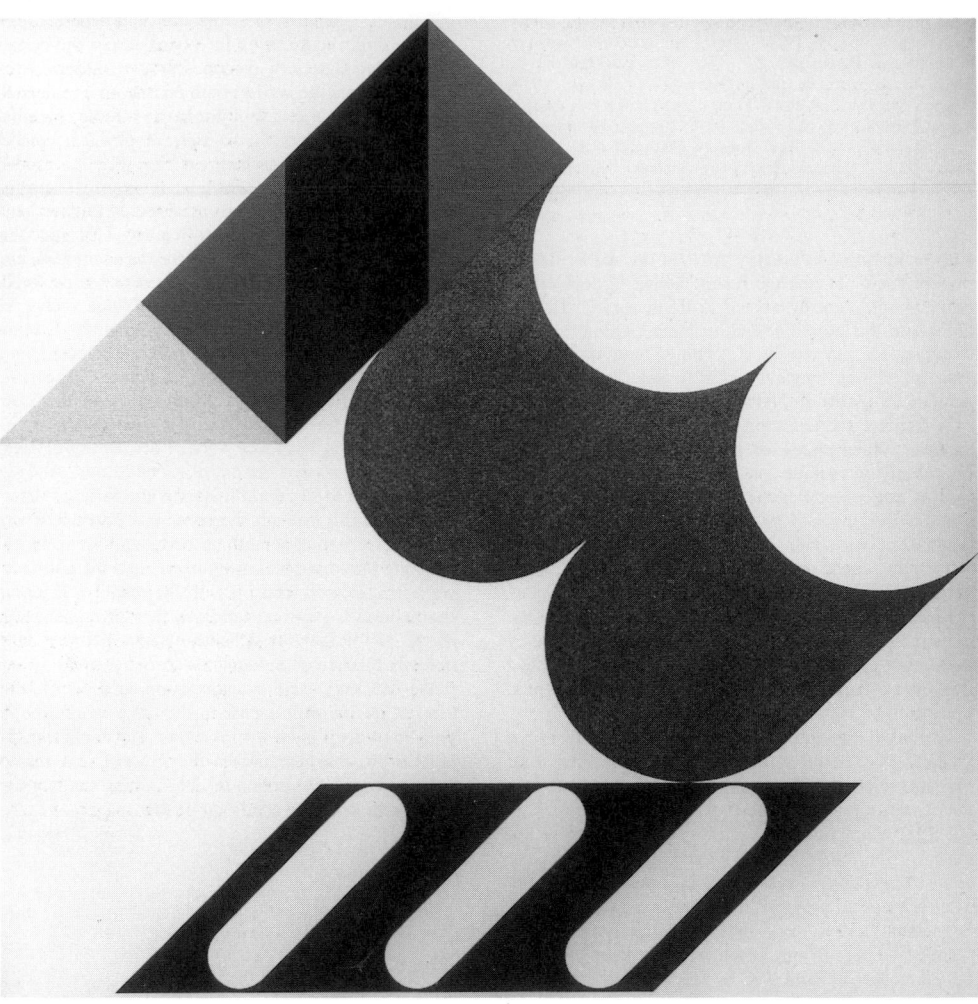

Kumi Sugai: *Femme et Homme B*, 1982

color came to dominate his work during the 1960's, infusing his paintings with freshness and dynamism. In addition to painting, Sugai is a printmaker who has won numerous prizes.

In 1969, at the age of 40, he returned from Paris and executed paintings for the walls of the new building of the National Museum of Modern Art, Tokyo. In this work Sugai demonstrated his excellent technique in composition by combining manifold elements covering an expansive area into a unified composite view.

Sugai's one-man show in 1976 (Minami Gallery, Tokyo) marked a new development for the ex-Ecole de Paris painter from Japan. A huge canvas in the show depicted an icon on a shiny Italian sportscar interlaced with bright-colored geometrical patterns. Sugai is now essentially uninterested in emotional hand-painted works and tends to hide his handtraces by mechanical non-personal expression.

In the 1980s, his geometric compositions began to break loose, and spread diagonally, leaving more vacant space in white. Clear-cut grey and black forms now dominated the canvases, with accentuated red shapes impressing themselves onto and integrating themselves into the formerly monochrome compositions.

—Yoshiaki Tono

Minami Gallery, Tokyo
National Museum of Modern Art, Kyoto (retrospective)
1970   Galerie d'Eent N.V., Amsterdam
1971   Circle Gallery, London
       Court Gallery, Copenhagen
       Galerie Schottenring, Vienna
1972   Galerie Defet, Nuremberg
       Galerie Hakken, Oslo
       Galerie Christael, Helsinki
       Galerie Hilt, Basel
1974   Galleria Annunciata, Milan
       La Galerie Esplanade de la Défense, Paris
1976   Minami Gallery, Tokyo
1981   Satani Gallery, Tokyo
1983   Nantenshi Gallery, Tokyo
       Seibu Museum of Art, Tokyo
1984   Seibu Hall, Ohtsu, Japan
       Ohara Museum of Art, Kurashiki, Japan
1985   Nantenshi Gallery, Tokyo
1987   Nantenshi Gallery, Tokyo

Selected Group Exhibitions:

1956   *Salon Réalités Nouvelles*, Paris (and annually through 1982)
1957   *Salon de Mai*, Paris (and annually through 1982)
1959   *Biennal International de Gravure*, I jubljana, Yugoslavia (and annually through 1981)
       Documenta, Kassel, West Germany
1961   *Trienal International de Gravure*, Grenchen, Switzerland
1962   *Biennale*, Venice
1964   *Painting and Sculpture of a Decade*, London
1966   *Salon Grands et Jeunes d'Aujourd'hui*, Paris (and annually through 1981)
1969   *Exposition Ars '69*, Helsinki
1972   *Biennal International de Gravure*, Norway

Collections:

Nationalgalerie, Berlin; Landesmuseum, Hannover; Centre Georges Pompidou, Paris; Galleria Nazionale d'Arte Moderna, Rome; Moderna Muséet, Stockholm; National Museum of Modern Art, Tokyo; National Museum of Modern Art, Kyoto; Museum of Modern Art, Toyama, Japan; Museum of Modern Art, New York; Art Institute of Chicago.

Publications:

By SUGAI: book of drawings—*Albam*, with poems by André Pieyre de Mandiargues, Paris 1960; books of prints—*La quête sans fin*, Paris 1957; *Repos goûte*, Paris 1964; *Sugai, ou la tension maxima*, Milan 1966; *Octobre*, Milan 1969; *Sugai*, Chikuma, Japan 1970; *Alea*, Paris n.d.; *Sugai gravure*, Tokyo n.d.

On SUGAI: books—*L'Aventure de l'art abstrait* by Michel Ragon, Paris 1956; *Kumi Sugai*, exhibition catalogue, Leverkusen, West Germany 1960; *Sugai* by André Pieyre de Mandiargues, Paris 1960; *Le voir dit* by Jean-Clarence Lambert, Paris 1962; *Kumi Sugai*, exhibition catalogue, by Wieland Schmidt and Irmtraud Schaarchmidt-Richter, Hannover 1963; *Kumi Sugai*, exhibition catalogue, by Hanns Theodor Flaemming, Hamburg 1964; *Kumi Sugai*, exhibition catalogue, by Fredrik Matheson and Oistein Parmann, Oslo 1967; *Japan: Tradition und Gegenwart*, exhibition catalogue, by J. Harten and others, Dusseldorf 1974; *Sugai*, Tokyo 1975; articles—"Sugai" by Jean-Clarence Lambert in *La jeune école de Paris*, Paris 1956; review by J. S. Byrd in *Art International* (Lugano, Switzerland), September 1965; "Kumi Sugai, Circle Gallery" by Peter Fuller in *Arts Review* (London), April 1971; "Sun King" in *Design* (London), June 1971; "Kumi Sugai" by A. P. de Mandiargues in *Le Arti* (Milan), May 1974.

Kumi Sugai's early abstract paintings were characterized by gloomy images suggestive of Japanese folklore, but clarity of composition and brightness of

---

SUGARMAN, George.

American. Born in New York City, 11 May 1912. Studied at City College of New York, 1934–38, B.A. 1938; Zadkine School of Sculpture, Paris, 1955–56. Served in the United States Navy, 1941–45. Sculptor: lives and works in New York: travelled in Europe and lived in Paris, 1951–55. Instructor, Hunter College Graduate School, New York, since 1960. Instructor, Yale University Graduate School of Art, New Haven, Connecticut, 1967–68. Recipient: Second Prize, *Carnegie International*, Pittsburgh, 1961; Longview Foundation Grant, 1961, 1962, 1963; National Endowment for the Humanities grant, 1966; Art Award, American Academy and Institute of Arts and Letters, 1985. Agent: Robert Miller Gallery, 41 East 57th Street, New York, New York 10022. Address: 21 Bond Street, New York, New York 10012, U.S.A.

Individual Exhibitions:

1958   Widdifield Gallery, New York
1961   Stephen Radich Gallery, New York
1964   Stephen Radich Gallery, New York
1965   Philadelphia Art Alliance
       Stephen Radich Gallery, New York
1966   Dayton's Gallery, Minneapolis
       Stephen Radich Gallery, New York
1967   Galerie Schmela, Dusseldorf
       Galerie Ziegler, Zurich
       Fischbach Gallery, New York
1969   *Plastiken, Collagen, Zeichnungen*, Kunsthalle, Basel (retrospective: travelled to Leverkusen, Berlin, and Amsterdam, 1969–70)
1970   Galerie Ziegler, Zurich
1971   Gallery 118, Minneapolis
1974   Zabriskie Gallery, New York
       Dag Hammarskjold Plaza, New York
1977   Robert Miller Gallery, New York
1978   Robert Miller Gallery, New York
1979   Galerie Liatowitsch, Basel
1980   Robert Miller Gallery, New York
       Galerie Rudolf Zwirner, Cologne
1981   Smith Gallery, Palo Alto, California
       Galerie Ziegler, Zurich
1982   Robert Miller Gallery, New York
1984   Fuller Goldeen Gallery, San Francisco
1985   Robert Miller Gallery, New York
       780 Third Avenue, New York (installation)
       Whitney Museum, New York

Doris Freedman Plaza, Central Park, New York (installation)
1986 Whitney Museum, New York
1987 Todd Capp Gallery, New York
       Helander Gallery, Palm Beach, Florida

Selected Group Exhibitions:

1952 *IV Salon de la Jeune Sculpture,* Musée Rodin, Paris
1956 *Sculptors Selected by Painters,* Tanager Gallery, New York
1963 *Bienal,* Sao Paulo
1967 *Sculpture of the 60's* Los Angeles County Museum of Art
1970 *Monumental Art,* Contemporary Arts Center, Cincinnati, Ohio
1975 *Sculpture: American Directions,* National Collection of Fine Arts, Washington, D.C.
1979 *The Decorative Impulse,* Institute of Contemporary Art, Philadelphia (travelled to San Diego, California; Minneapolis; Chicago)
1982 *Postminimalism,* Aldrich Museum of Contemporary Art, Ridgefield, Connecticut
1985 *Forms in Wood: American Sculpture of the 1950s,* Philadelphia Art Alliance, Pennsylvania
1987 *Sculpture: Exploration of Space,* Anchorage Museum of History and Art, Alaska

Publications:

By SUGARMAN. article—"Square Spiral" in *Art Now: New York,* January 1969.

On SUGARMAN: books—*Collage: Personalities, Concepts, Techniques* by Harriet Janis and Rudi Blesh. Philadelphia and New York 1962: *New York School. The First Generation: Paintings of the 1940s's and 1950's.* edited by Maurice Tuchman, Los Angeles 1965: *Constructivism: Origins and Evolution* by George Rickey, New York 1967; *Minimal Art: A Critical Anthology,* edited by Gregory Battcock, New York 1968; *George Sugarman: Plastiken, Collagen, Zeichnungen,* exhibition catalogue, by Amy Goldin and Peter F. Althaus, Basle 1969: *George Sugarman* exhibition catalogue, by Irving H. Sandler, Amsterdam 1970; *Icons and Images of the 60's* by Nicolas and Elena Calas, New York 1971: *Shape of Space: The Sculpture of George Sugarman* by Holliday T. Day, New York, 1981: *George Sugarman: Painted Wood Sculpture,* exhibition catalogue, New York 1985.

*

I believe that sculptural space is different from ordinary space, and each of my sculptures is an attempt to create, to define and to articulate an aesthetically significant space. And so, early on, I became interested in floor space, as in "Inscape" and horizontal extensions as in "Two in One." I have always avoided industrially available forms because I believe that they blur the particularity of the statement, so I have used as many different forms as I have been capable of imagining often within the same sculpture to create a rich and complex experience. These works ask such questions as "What is sculptural unity?" and "What are artistic relationships, not only within the work itself but also to the space it creates around it?"

Although most people respond to my use of color on a purely emotional basis and although it has been said that my work forms a bridge between painting and sculpture, my own reason for using the full range of color is purely formal, i.e. to help articulate the formal problem set in each sculpture.

Now that I am more concerned with outdoor, public sculpture, I have asked myself "What does *public* sculpture mean?" Certainly it has a different function than a gallery or museum-oriented work. Equally certain, it should be something more readily accessible to the general public. I think it is possible to do this and not only retain but even heighten all the aesthetic "high-art" values one believes in. My sculpture for the Federal Building in Baltimore shows my interest in the creation of a particularized, extended space, in interior volumes, in relationships between different forms, and it does it in ways appropriate only to outdoor sculpture: by its relation to the building it is placed in front of and by its function as a possible symbol of community.

—George Sugarman

George Sugarman has brought strong pictorial sensibility to contemporary sculpture. A student of Ossip Zadkine in Paris, Sugarman made sculptures in the early 1950's that had the deliberate, weighty and solid properties associated with his teacher's strong grounding in Cubism. By the late 1950's, however, Sugarman began to break away from the Cubist cube and to elaborate a more open and distinctively colorful approach to sculpture. As head of the New York-based New Sculpture Group, he was at the forefront of both the discussions and the practical investigations of new treatments of abstract sculpture, based on non-relational structures. In the sculptures of the late 1950's and early 1960's, he started to shape space

George Sugarman: *Baltimore Federal,* 1977

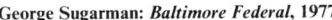

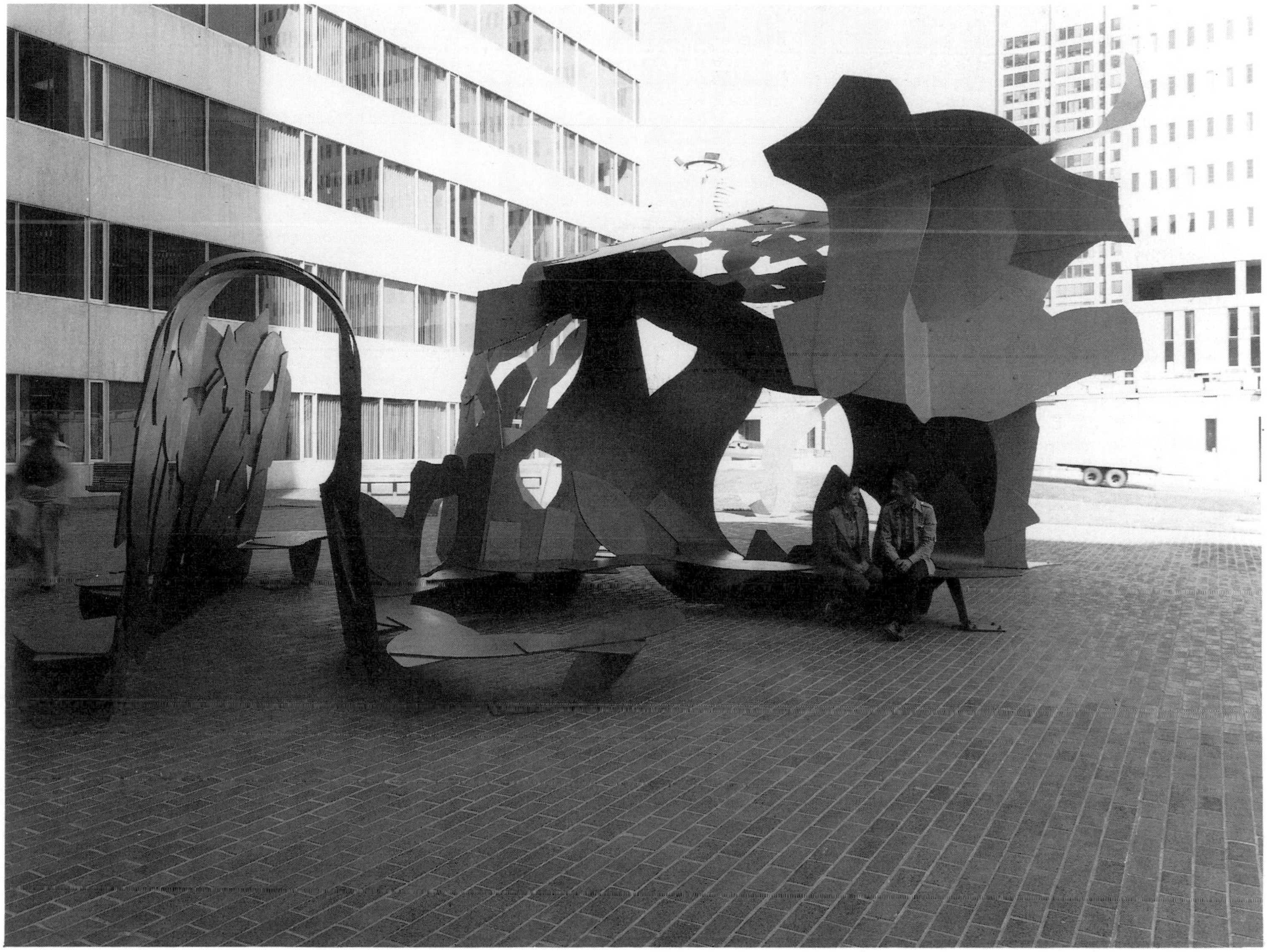

into a bold intrastructure of solids and voids, using juxtaposed arrangements of curved and straight edged forms as the means. For example, in *Yellow Top* (1960) a polychrome wood sculpture, different colors are used to articulate each separate element, drawing attention simultaneously, to the linear contours of the piece and its definition of space. It is during this period, also, that the sculptures begin to spill directly onto the floor and, even more forcefully, they stress the relationships of parts to parts in the bold but jungle-like compositions that Sugarman has continued to favor. In addition to the base and the floor, the wall has also occupied his attention. Strongly colored, his wall reliefs are volumetric and specifically structured forms that challenge cliché notions about the relationship of painting and sculpture.

In the late 1960's Sugarman began to interest himself in the demanding area of public art. Changing his materials from wood to metal, he has designed large-scaled and outdoor polychromed pieces, whose brightly colored, cut-out parts give a rich and varied experience of structure and space, wondrously accessible to the average user of the public places in which they stand. *Kite Castle* (1974), shown at the Hammarskjold Plaza in New York City, is revealing of the role of constructive animator which color—here the dominant tonal combination is red and blue—has in encouraging a positive reception to the piece. In his public art works, Sugarman aims to delight the viewer/stroller and to enhance the environment without overwhelming either one.

The exuberant qualities of his sculptures continued developing in the 1980s. *Big Ride* (1981), a relief collage with a dynamically angled multipart structure, shows increasing interest in heightening the illusion of movement through the juxtapositions of different shapes, colors and textured surfaces. In *Ariel* (1984), that illusion is so striking as to make the complex cut-out structure of this painted aluminum sculpture seem to rise up on the energy generated from the tensions within its various parts from the ground. In *Waltz* (1985), the organic flow to the rhythmical structure of this multipart piece brings to mind the swaying configurations of flowers. References to nature serve to enhance the impact of much of Sugarman's recent work.

—Ronny Cohen

SUTHERLAND, Graham (Vivian).

British. Born in London, 24 August 1903; Educated in Sutton, and at Epsom College, Surrey; studied mathematics, Battersea Polytechnic, London, and apprenticed to Midland Railway Engineering Works, Derby, 1919–20; studied engraving techniques, under Stanley Anderson and Malcolm Osborn, Goldsmiths' College of Art. London, 1921–26. Served as Official War Artist, In England and France, 1941–44. Married Kathleen Frances Barry in 1927. Painter and designer: worked, with Clive Gardiner, on *Wembley International Exhibition* decorations, 1924; moved to Farningham, Kent, 1928, and to Eynsford, Kent, 1930; designed posters for Shell-Mex, London Passenger Transport Board, and the London Post Office, from 1930; moved to Sutton-at-Hone, and made first of several visits to Pembrokeshire, Wales, 1934; worked on china and glass designs, from 1935; moved to Trottiscliffe, 1936, and to Tetbury, Gloucestershire, 1939; designed sets and costumes for *The Wanderer* ballet by Frederick Ashton, Sadlers Wells Theatre, London, 1941; spent several months of each year in Southern France, from 1947; worked on designs for Coventry Cathedral tapestry, "Christ in Glory," 1954–57, woven in Felletin, 1958–62; purchased a house and settled in Menton, Southern France, but made frequent visits to England and Wales, from 1955: commissioned by Queen Elizabeth to paint composition for the President of Portugal on

"the Common Interest of Portugal and England," 1957; visited New York, 1964; commissioned by Queen Elizabeth to paint picture for President Pompidou of France, 1972; inaugurated Graham Sutherland Gallery (now Graham and Kathleen Sutherland Foundation), under Picton Castle Trust, Haverfordwest, Wales, 1976. Lecturer in Engraving, 1928–32, and in Composition and Book Illustration, 1932–39, Chelsea School of Art, London; Lecturer in Painting, Goldsmiths' College of Art, London, 1946–47. Recipient: Acquisition Prize, Museum of Modern Art, Sao Paulo; Prize, *Biennale*, Venice, 1952; Foreign Minister's Prize, Tokyo, 1957; First Prize, *Biennale International d'Art*, Menton, 1972; Shakespeare Prize, Hamburg, 1974. D. Litt.: Oxford University, 1962; University of Leicester, 1965; University of Cardiff, 1979. Honorary Member, American Academy of Arts and Letters, 1972: Honorary Fellow, Accademia de San Luca, Rome, 1973; Commandeur des Arts et des Lettres, France, 1973; Honorary President, *Biennale Internationale d'Art*, Menton, 1974. Associate, Royal Society of Painters, Etchers and Engravers, 1925 (expelled, 1933); Trustee, Tate Gallery, London, 1949 (resigned, 1954). Order of Merit, 1960. *Died* (in London) *17 February 1980.*

Individual Exhibitions:

1925	XXI Gallery, London
1928	XXI Gallery, London
1938	Rosenberg and Helft Gallery, London
1940	Leicester Galleries, London (with Walter Goetz)
1941	Temple Newsom, Leeds (with Henry Moore and John Piper)
1946	Buchholz Gallery, New York
1947	Lefevre Gallery, London
	Roland Browse and Delbanco, London
1948	Hanover Gallery, London
	Buchholz Gallery, New York
1949	Stedelijk Museum, Amsterdam
1951	Institute of Contemporary Arts, London
	Hanover Gallery, London
1952	Hanover Gallery, London
	Redfern Gallery, London
	Biennale, Venice (travelled to the Musée National d'Art Moderne, Paris)
1953	Kunsthaus, Zurich
	Curt Valentin Gallery, New York
	Tate Gallery, London
	Stedelijk Museum, Amsterdam
1954	Akademie der Bildenden Künste, Vienna (toured Austria and West Germany)
1955	*Bienal*, Sao Paulo
1956	Roland Browse and Delbanco, London
1957	Kunstkabinett, Frankfurt
	Hoffman Galerie, Hamburg
1958	Redfern Gallery, London
1959	Redfern Gallery, London
	Arthur Jefress Gallery, London
	Belfast Museum and Art Gallery
	Paul Rosenberg Gallery, New York
1960	Roland Browse and Delbanco, London
1961	Arts Council Gallery, London (with Stanley Spencer and Ivon Hitchens)
	Galleria Galatea, Turin (travelled to the Galleria Galatea, Milan)
1962	Marlborough Fine Art, London
1963	Galleria Fanti di Spade, Rome
	Galleria Gallatea, Turin
	Galleria Il Centro, Naples (with Francis Bacon)
	Prebendal House, Llandaff Cathedral, Cardiff
1964	Redfern Gallery, London
	Paul Rosenberg Gallery, New York
1965	Galleria Civica d'Arte Moderna, Turin
	Haus der Kunst, Munich
	Gemeentemuseum, The Hague
	Haus am Waldsee, West Berlin
	Wallraf-Richartz Museum, Cologne
1966	Marlborough Fine Art, London
	Kunsthalle, Basle
1967	Haus der Kunst, Munich (toured the Netherlands and West German)
1968	Marlborough Fine Art, London
1969	Kestner Gesellschaft, Hannover
	Galleria Il Fauno, Turin
	Palais de l'Europe, Menton, France
	Druikgraphik und Zeichnungen, Albrecht Dürer Gesellschaft, Nuremberg
1970	Marlborough Fine Art, London (with Pablo Picasso and Henry Moore)
1971	William West Gallery, London
1972	Galleria Il Fauno, Turin
	Galleria Narciso, Turin
	Galleria Bergamini, Milan
1973	Marlborough Galerie, Zurich (travelled to Marlborough Fine Art, London)
1974	Marlborough Fine Art, London
	Galleria d'Arte Sant'Ambrogio, Milan
1975	Lefevre Gallery, London
	Alexander Postan Fine Art, London
1976	Redfern Gallery, London
	Galleria dei Foscherari, Bologna
	Palazzo Liceo Saracco, Acqui Terme, Italy
1977	Marlborough Fine Art, London
	Portraits, National Portrait Gallery, London (retrospective)
1978	Graham Sutherland Gallery, Picton Castle Haverfordwest, Wales
1979	Marlborough Fine Art, London
	Disegni di Guerra, Palazzo Reale, Milan
1980	Gawthorpe Hall, Padiham, Lancashire (with Oskar Kokoschka)
	Le Point, Rome
1981	Palazzo delle Albere, Trento, Italy
	Galleria Bergamini, Milan
1982	Tate Gallery, London
	Imperial War Museum, London
	Redfern Gallery, London
1986	Goldsmith's Gallery, London
1987	Galleria del Cavallino, Venice
	Christopher Hall Gallery, London
1988	Galerie Patrice Trigano, Paris

Selected Group Exhibitions:

1935	*Exhibition of British Art*, Royal Academy of Arts, London
1936	*International Surrealist Exhibition*, New Burlington Galleries, London
1939	*Contemporary British Art*, at the *World's Fair*, New York
1941	*Britain at War*, Museum of Modern Art, New York
1955	*Documenta*, Kassel, West Germany
1960	*British Painting 1700–1960*, Pushkin Museum, Moscow (travelled to the Hermitage Museum, Leningrad)
1962	*British Art Today*, San Francisco Museum of Art (toured the United States)
1969	*British Drawings 1939–1949*, Scottish National Gallery, Edinburgh
1977	*British Painting 1952–1977*, Royal Academy of Arts, London

Collections:

Tate Gallery, London; Arts Council of Great Britain, London; Imperial War Museum, London; British Museum, London; Victoria and Albert Museum, London; Albertina Academy, Vienna; Centre Georges Pompidou, Paris; Kunstmuseum, Basle; National Gallery of Victoria, Melbourne; Art Gallery of Ontario, Toronto.

Publications:

By SUTHERLAND: book—*Graham Sutherland; Parafrasi della Natura e altre Corrispondenze*, edited by Roberto Tassi, Parma, Italy 1979; articles—"A Trend in English Draughtsmanship" in *Signature*, July 1936, "Graven Images; Line Engraving and the Illustrated Book" in *Signature* July 1937; "The Living Image; Art and Life" in the *Listener* (London), 13 November 1941; "Welsh Sketch Book" in *Horizon* (London), April 1942; "American Art Explained by American Artists, Part I" in *The Artist*, March 1944; letter, to H. P. Juda, in "thoughts on Painting" in *The Listener* (London), 6 September 1951; statement in *8 European Artists*, edited by

Felix H. Man, London, 1954; statement in *Conversations with Painters* by Noel Barber, London 1964; "Interview with Graham Sutherland" in *Druckgraphik und Zeichnungen mit dem Vollständigen Bestiarium*, exhibition catalogue, Nuremberg 1969; letter in the *Sunday Telegraph Magazine* (London), 10 September 1971; introduction to *The English Vision*, exhibition catalogue, London 1973; "Conversation with Paul Nicolls" in *Graham Sutherland*, exhibition catalogue, Turin 1976; "Conversation with Graham Sutherland" in *Portraits by Graham Sutherland*, exhibition catalogue, by John Hayes, London 1977; "The Nature of Poetry and Painting" in *The Sutherland Gift to the Nations*, exhibition catalogue, London 1979; statement in *Sutherland— Disegni di Guerra*, exhibition catalogue, Milan 1979; books illustrated—*Henry IV: Part I* by Shakespeare, New York 1940; *Le Bestiare ou Cortege d'Orphée* by Guillaume Apollinaire, London 1979.

On SUTHERLAND: books—*Graham Sutherland* by Edward Scakville-West, London 1943, 1953; *The Imagery of Graham Sutherland* by Robert Melville, London 1950; *The Work of Graham Sutherland* by Douglas Cooper, London 1961; *Graham Sutherland: Das Graphische Werk 1922–1970* by Felix H. Man, Munich 1970; *Graham Sutherland* by Francesco Arcangeli, Milan 1973, New York 1975; *Sutherland Sketchbook*, London 1974; *Portraits by Graham Sutherland*, exhibition catalogue, by John Hayes, London 1977; *Graham Sutherland: Complete Graphic Work* by Roberto Tassi, London 1978; *Sutherland: Wartime Drawings* by Roberto Tassi, Milan 1979, London 1980; *The Art of Graham Sutherland* by John Hayes, Oxford 1980; *Graham Sutherland*, exhibition catalogue, by Ronald Alley, London 1982; *Graham Sutherland: The Early Years 1921–40*, exhibition catalogue with essay by Nannette Aldred, London 1986; *Graham Sutherland: Aquarelles et Dessins*, exhibition catalogue with text by Pierre Cabanne, Paris 1988; films—*Graham Sutherland* by John Read, BBC-TV, London 1954; *Graham Sutherland* by Margaret McCall, BBC-TV, London 1968; *Graham Sutherland: Lo Specchio e il Miraggio* by Pierpaolo Ruggerini, RAI-TV, Rome 1969; *Sutherland in Wales* by John Ormand, BBC-TV, London 1977; *Graham Sutherland* by Adriano Viale, 1977.

*

Although Graham Sutherland is usually thought of in terms of the neo-romantic naturalism that dominated the British art scene in the 1930's and 1940's, he was always a painter both firmly rooted in the native English tradition and fully aware of the complex development of modern European art. Yet the core of his own art is an attempt to express an essence which lies beyond sensible form, whether in the surrealistic appreciation of natural forms, or the imaginative symbolism of the Coventry Cathedral tapestry.

This was already apparent in his early etchings, which are in the tradition of the mystical Romanticism of Blake, or of Samuel Palmer's intense visionary landscapes. In the early 1930's he turned from engraving to oil and watercolour painting, and in the years up to the war worked chiefly on a series of Welsh landscapes which he described as imaginative paraphrases of the landscape of Pembrokeshire: "I felt I could express what I felt only by paraphrasing what I saw." These merge the English Romantic feeling for landscape with an imaginative freedom influenced by Surrealism, so could appropriately be exhibited in the 1936 *International Surrealist Exhibition*. They reveal Sutherland's fascination with the way in which organic forms undergo disturbing and sinister transformations, taking on an uncanny presence, which he also discovered in found objects: "Their sap may have gone out of them but their form remains . . . I am fascinated by the whole problem of the tensions produced by the power of growth."

He was therefore well-placed as an official war artist from 1941 to 1944 to capture the poignancy of the weird effects of destruction caused by bombing, with twisted iron and shattered masonry. This more cruel and violent vision he carried over into his spiky nature studies, which bring out the emotional meaning he found in the tortured forms of thistles, the gnarled branches of a tree, the spikes of a thorn bush, the jumbled masses of fallen rocks. The "Thorn Tree" paintings of 1946-7 and the "Standing" or "Hanging Forms" of the early 1950s contain all kinds of painterly ambiguity which make them seem charged with mysterious enigmatic presences, as though ghostly semi-human forms or monsters are about to emerge

from them, paralleling Henry Moore's identification of the human figure with landscape.

In the 1960's Sutherland's particularly English blend of Surrealism and Romanticism made him the father-figure of a group of younger painters such as Keith Vaughan and John Minton. The sense of strangeness remained a constant factor in his own work, though after the war this greatly increased in diversity and variety, not only incorporating machine forms and depicting animals, birds and insects, but showing a new interest in the human figure both in his portraits and his series of religious pictures. The earliest of these, the 1944 "Crucifixion" for St. Matthew's Church, Northampton, is a tortured expressionistic work which fuses a modern idiom with the inspiration of old masters, especially Grünwald, combined with savage modern sufferings typified by Belsen. But the immense tapestry of "Christ in Glory" that he designed between 1954 and 1957 to occupy the entire east wall of the new Coventry Cathedral so that the whole vista leads up to this intentionally awe-inspiring creation, is a more Byzantine work, and its icon-like flattened space and compartmentalized composition recur in many of his later works.

As a portrait painter he showed a sharp eye for revealing detail which catches the essence of his sitters, as in the earliest in 1949, in which the folds and wrinkles of Somerset Maugham's face are emphasized almost to suggest the fibrous leaves of some tropical plant. The later highly dramatized portraits of Churchill (1955), Beaverbrook (1957) and Helena Rubinstein (1957) show similar symbolic transformations taking place, though carefully controlled by the demands of getting a reasonable external likeness as well as what Sutherland calls "pinning down a person's essence."

But landscape remained a continuing preoccupation, though Sutherland's move to the south of France seemed to mark a move towards a more "international" approach. However, he came to think that he was mistaken in making a prolonged break from renewing himself from the Welsh landscape which once so obsessed him, and from the late 60's he returned there at least two or three times a year to work in this "curiously charged atmosphere—at once calm and exciting." The relationship between artist and landscape finally reached what now seems the inevitable and logical conclusion with his donation of an important collection of his oils, watercolours and lithographs to form the new Graham Sutherland Gallery at Picton Castle near Haverford-west, within walking distance of the actual landscapes which were such a potent source of inspiration to him. Sutherland himself expressed his intentions exactly by saying "I believe that work done in a certain area is to be seen in that area."

—Lavinia Learmont

SUTTON, Philip.

British. Born in Poole, Dorset, 20 October 1928. Studied painting, under William Coldstream, at the Slade School of Fine Art, London, 1950–54. Served in the British Army, 1947–49. Married Heather Minifie Ellis Cooke in 1953; children: Jacob, Imogen, Saskia and Rebekah. Independent painter, in Snape, Suffolk, 1955–58, and in London since 1958; Member, London Group, 1956. Instructor, Slade School of Fine Art, London, 1956–75. Royal Academician, 1977. Agent: Browse and Darby Ltd., 19 Cork Street, London W1. Addresses: (studio) 7 Melbourne Grove, London SE22; (home) 10 Soudan Road, London SW11 4HH, England.

Individual Exhibitions:

1956	Roland, Browse and Delbanco, London
1958	Roland, Browse and Delbanco, London
1959	Geffrye Museum, London
1960	City Art Gallery, Leeds, Yorkshire
	Roland, Browse and Delbanco, London
1962	Stone Gallery, Newcastle upon Tyne
	Lane Gallery, Bradford, Yorkshire
	57 Gallery, Edinburgh
	Roland, Browse and Delbanco, London
1963	David Jones Gallery, Sydney
	Gallery A, Melbourne
	Rose Skinner Gallery, Perth, Western Australia
	Roland, Browse and Delbanco, London
	Battersea District Library, London
1965	*Paintings from Fiji*, Roland, Browse and Delbanco, London
1966	Curwen Gallery, London
	David Jones Gallery, Sydney
1967	*Recent Paintings*, Roland, Browse and Delbanco, London
	London Arts Gallery, Detroit
	David Jones Gallery, Sydney
	Arnolfini Gallery, Bristol
	Arts Centre, Folkestone, Kent
1969	Roland, Browse and Delbanco, London
	Hambledon Gallery, Blandford Forum, Dorset, England
1970	Park Square Gallery, Leeds
	Paintings/Drawings/Prints, Arnolfini Gallery, Bristol
	Paintings, Drawings, Prints and Sculptures, Arts Centre, Folkestone, Kent
	David Jones Gallery, Sydney
1971	Graves Art Gallery, Sheffield
	Roland, Browse and Delbanco, London
	Battersea District Library, London
	Oxford Gallery
	Park Square Gallery, Leeds
1972	Battersea District Library, London
	Studio Prints, London
	Compendium Galleries, Birmingham
1973	Roland, Browse and Delbanco, London
	David Jones Gallery, Sydney
	Peterloo Gallery, Manchester
1974	J. P. Lehmans Gallery, London
1975	Roland, Browse and Delbanco, London
1976	Orde Levinson, Johannesburg (travelled to Durban and Cape Town)
1977	Falmouth School of Art, Cornwall
	Royal Academy of Art, London
1979	Annex Gallery, Wimbledon, London
	Browse and Darby, London
	David Jones Gallery, Sydney
1980	Holsworthy Gallery, London
	Margaret Fisher Gallery, London
1981	Browse and Darby, London
	Minden Gallery, Jersey, Channel Islands
1982	Christopher Hall Gallery, London
	Browse and Darby, London
1983	John Brinkley Fellowship Exhibition, Norwich, Norfolk
	Beaux Art Gallery, Bath, Avon
1984	Shell Headquarters Gallery, London
	Browse and Darby, London
	Manor House Society, London
	Beaux Arts Gallery, Bath, Avon
	Bermondsey Gallery, London
1985	Lichfield Arts, Lichfield, Staffordshire
	Beaux Arts Gallery, Bath, Avon
	Dulwich Art Gallery, London
1986	Cambridge Art Gallery, Cambridge
	Municipal Gallery, Stoke-on-Trent, Staffordshire
	Poole Gallery, Dorset
	Newport Gallery, Isle of Wight
1987	Odette Gilbert Gallery, London
	Beaux Arts Gallery, Bath, Avon

Selected Group Exhibitions:

1952	*London Group*, Beaux-Arts Gallery, London
1955	*Critic's Choice*, Arthur Tooth and Sons, London
1956	*Contemporary British Painters*, Parsons Gallery, London
	6 Young Painters, Tate Gallery, London
1957	*Guggenheim International*, New York

Collections:

Arts Council of Great Britain. London: Tate Gallery, London; Ministry of Works, London; City Art Gallery, Birmingham; Cecil Higgins Museum and Gallery, Bedford; City Art Gallery, Leeds; Durban Museum, South Africa; National Gallery of South Australia, Adelaide; National Gallery of Victoria, Melbourne; Perth Art Gallery, Western Australia.

Publications:

On SUTTON: books—*Philip Sutton*, exhibition catalogue, London 1958; *Philip Sutton: Paintings from Fiji*, exhibition catalogue. London 1965; *Recent Paintings by Philip Sutton*, exhibition catalogue, with text by David Storey, London 1967; *Philip Sutton: Paintings/Drawings/Prints*, exhibition cards, with text by David Storey, Bristol 1970; *Philip Sutton: paintings, drawings, prints and sculptures*, exhibition catalogue, with text by David Storey, Folkestone 1970; *Philip Sutton*, exhibition catalogue, with texts by Frank Constantine and David Storey, Sheffield 1971; *Israel Observed*, exhibition catalogue, with text by Helene Marks, Jerusalem 1980.

Self-activation has always operated on Philip Sutton.

After a spell in the R.A.F. he went to the Slade and became hooked on a lively figurative style without hang-ups on subject. He was exhibiting by 1952 and had his first one-man show in 1956. He was then 28 years old. Since that time he has worked in a progress of refinement and freshness of concentration on mood and colour. The early paintings were concerned with the use of medium, how to apply the paint so that it built up in an overall system of chords somewhat in the manner of an expressionist Cézanne. Colour was strong on key, the primaries especially the reds taking a predominant share. Generally the motives triggered off the painting, and sometimes in the landscapes there was a suspicion of the scene dictating too much in the organization of the composition. Exceptions were the interiors and the still life subjects where less complicated systems of pattern and colour became enriched by the freedom from detail. This conflict between truth to motive and unity of picture structure was to be resolved gradually in the flower pieces of 1957 and later when the ever-smiling ghost of Matisse encouraged the young Englishman.

After having lived in the Suffolk countryside for years, Sutton came to live in Battersea, a densely populated quarter of south London. Nature in its green growth was no longer pressing its vegetable lushness upon him, and he painted many interiors with his family of four and his wife as models. They took their places as broadly brushed passages centrally on the canvas, blues, pinks, deep cadmium reds and bright yellows all singing in euphoric harmony.

This was a realism no less credible for its chromatic abandon. The colours were genuinely faithful to each other if not to local visual fact, and the drawing of the figures was portrayal of his offspring recognizably and unsentimentally abstracted in their outlines and broad summaries of their features and tonality.

For an artist who responds to the stimulus of his surroundings, Battersea seemed to lose even its intimate satisfactions, and in 1963 Sutton set off with his wife and four children to indulge what could be called a Gauguinesque dream. They ended up on one of the Fijian islands in the blue Pacific, and Sutton happily began painting; he made hundreds of oils, filled 30 sketchbooks and made many woodcuts.

The result, shown on his return to London, was an uncomplicated reflection of a peaceful locality where sun, sea and lush vegetation set up varied motives for pictures of a relaxed and pleasantly unpolluted atmosphere. This mood of relaxation is one that prevails in Sutton's paintings where only in the nudes is there any hint of tension, and this is implied by muscular pose rather than in any contrived conflict of tones or rhythms.

Sutton has the contemporary painter's engagement with the flat area of his surface totally; whether the central space defines a nude woman or a bunch of gladioli is important only for its contribution of colour and its form to the total experience. In this he is at one with both Bonnard and Matisse in the continued mood of optimism.

—G. S. Whittet

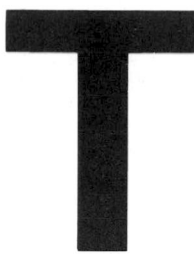

TADINI, Emilio.

Italian. Born in Milan, 5 June 1927. Studied art: received degree. Married Antonia Perazzoli in 1959; children: Francesco and Michele. Independent artist, Milan, since 1960. Art Instructor, Nuova Accademia Di Belle Arti, Milan, 1980–82. Agent: Studio Marconi, via Tadino 15, 20124 Milan. Address: via Jommelli 24, 20131 Milan, Italy.

Individual Exhibitions:

1961	Galleria del Cavallino, Venice
1966	Galleria II Punto, Turin
1967	Galleria del Minotaura, Brescia, Italy
	Vita di Voltaire, Studio Marconi, Milan
1968	Galleria La Chiocciola, Padua
	Gallerie Richard Foncke, Ghent
1969	Galleria Tempo, Bologna
	Studio Condotti, Rome
1970	Studio Marconi, Milan
	Gallerie Richard Foncke, Ghent
1971	*Viaggio in Italia*, Studio Marconi, Milan
	Galleria San Michele, Brescia, Italy
1972	Studio Condotti, Rome
	Galleria Quattro Venti, Palermo, Sicily
	Galleria la Chiocciola, Padua
	Gallerie Richard Foncke, Ghent
1973	Galleri A. H. Stockholm
1974	Galleria Europa, Bolzano, Italy
	Estudio Actual, Caracas
	La Struttura della Condensazione e dello Spostamento, Studio Marconi, Milan
1975	Galleria Torbandena, Treiste
	Galleria II Triangolo, Pescara, Italy
	Gallerie Rencontres, Paris
	Galleria Quarta Dimensione, Arezzo, Italy
	Università di Parma, Italy
	Studio G7, Bologna
	Gallerie Micha, Brussels
1976	Galleria Rizzardi, Milan
	Galleria Cesarea, Genoa
	Galleria Rondanini, Rome
	Galleria Solferino, Milan
1977	Galleria Mercato del Sale, Milan
	Museo Civico, Alessandria, Italy
	Galleria d'Arte Contemporanea, Suzzara, Italy
1978	Galleria 72n, Bergamo, Italy
	Studio Baleri, Bergamo, Italy
	Studio Marconi, Milan
	Gallerie C., Paris
1979	Galleria Torbandena, Trieste
	Galleria 4M, Florence
	Galleria Marin, Turin
	Galleria Le Feu Vert, Cagliari, Italy
	Centro Culturale Olivetti, Ivrea, Turin
	Galleria La Chiocciola, Padua
	D'Ars Agency, Milan
	Galleria Greminger, Genoa
1980	Banca Popolare di Milano, Rome
	Galleria II Disegno, Rome
	Galleria II Triagono, Nola, Italy
	Galerie Pieter van Coecke, Aalst, Belgium
	Galerie Atmosphere, Brussels
	Arte Incontri, Fara d'Adda, Italy
1981	Galleria La Bottega,, Parma
1982	Galerie J. L., Ostend, Belgium
	Galleria Civica d'Arte Moderna, Suzzara, Italy

Selected Group Exhibitions:

1965	*Operazione Goldfinger*, Galleria Levi, Milan
1967	*Contemporary Italian Art*, Gemeentemuseum, The Hague
1970	*Studio Marconi at Felix Landau*, Felix Landau Gallery, Los Angeles
1971	*New Italian Art 1953-1971*. Walker Art Gallery, Liverpool
1973	*Pittura in Lombardia 1945-70*, Villa Reale, Monza, Italy
1977	*Quotidien, Histoire et Utopie*, Maison de la Culture, Grenoble, France
1978	*Biennale*, Venice (and 1982)
1979	*Testuale: Le Parole, le Immagini*, Rotonda di via Besana, Milan
1982	*L'Opera Dipinta*, Galleria La Pilotta, Parma, Italy (travelled to Rotonda di via Besana, Milan)
1986	*Aspects of Italian Art 1960-85*, Kunstverein, Frankfurt

Publications:

By TADINI: books—*Le Armi, l'Armore*, Milan 1963; *L'Opera*, Milan 1980.

On TADINI: books—*Emilio Tadini*, exhibition catalogue, with text by A. Martini, Venice 1961; *Emilio Tadini*, exhibition catalogue, with text by Guido Ballo, Turin 1966; *Tadini*, exhibition catalogue, with text by Roberto Sanesi, Brescia, Italy 1967; *Emilio Tadini: Vita di Voltaire*, exhibition catalogue, with texts by Henry Martin, Roberto Sanesi and Guido Ballo, Milan 1967; *Ricerche dopo l'Informale* by Enrico Crispolti, Rome 1968, *Emilio Tadini*, exhibition catalogue, with text by J. L. Schefer, Milan 1970; *Emilio Tadini: Viaggio in Italia*, exhibition catalogue, edited by Giorgio Marconi, Milan 1971; *New Italian Art 1953-1971*, exhibition catalogue, with text by Giovanni Carandente, Liverpool 1971; *Emilio Tadini: La Struttura della Condensazione e dello Spostamento*, exhibition catalogue, with text by Arturo Carlo Quintavalle, Milan 1974; *Emilio Tadini*, exhibition catalogue, with text by J. L. Schefer, Paris 1975; *Testuale: Le Parole, le Immagini*, exhibition catalogue, with texts by Flavio Caroli and Luciano Caramel, Milan 1979; *Emilio Tadini: Aquarelli*, exhibition catalogue, with texts by F. Vincitorio and others, Rome 1980.

*   *   *

Emilio Tadini took up painting during the 1960's, after having worked for years as a writer, critic and theorist of art, and as a novelist. His writing experience and literary acumen are in fact an important element in his painting. The 60's, characterized by the explosion of Pop Art, gave Tadini a feeling for flat colour, precise drawing, a vaguely advertisement-style of picture—generally, of a super-finished work. Where Pop Art was concerned to glorify consumer goods (Campbell's Soup), Tadini offers us literary goods (the Gate, The Cloth Column); where Pop Art chooses the film star (Marilyn Monroe), for subject, Tadini chooses the literary star (Voltaire, Goethe); where Pop Art illustrates the environment as a great supermarket, Tadini presents it as the place of nostalgically well educated babies.

There is a picture of his from 1975, called "Magasins Réunis," in which he tackles the theme of the supermarket, a subject that does suggest Pop Art themes; but it is a pretext for literature. From the godlike body of Superman there grows the head of a metaphysical manikin, Nembo Kid; surprised by this head, one asks about the present through the unrealized hopes of the past; a German helmet at the side reinterprets the tragedy of a recent past.

The past is injected into the present, as the historical symbols live together with the symbols of the present day. History and news coexist in a picture written on the canvas with the same sort of pleasure with which tin soldiers are paraded by children on the floor of a nursery.

The figures in Tadini's works, so definitely outlined as to look like coloured silhouettes, are combined with texts which do not name things but illustrate a kind of vocabulary where words and things each go their own way. Like a cosmos in miniature, a syllabary never completed, where words and pictures live only for the euphoria of a text meant only for looking at.

While we normally look at the pictures and read the words, Tadini shows us how it is possible to look at the alphabet too: an alphabet for the eyes which releases the letters from specific meaning and throws them on the table for visual feast.

Tadini's painting is a sort of Luna Park of words and pictures: a question mark makes a column ask a question: the word "house" is inscribed between, among other things, a table, a tricycle and a revolver. Pictures and words are used to portray an impossible literature, a literature that cannot exist in writing, a text that cannot be read, a writing that cannot be spoken but only looked at: it is the pleasure of painting.

Painting is presented, then, as an ever-open syllabary, a syllabary made from intimacy, archaeology, comments, travel, from cold gardens, from troubled holidays—a syllabary made to delight the eye. An eye which lingers equally on the particular and the universal, on words and on pictures, on history and on everyday life, but above all an eye that can never cease to narrate.

—Loredana Parmesani

TAJIRI, Shinkichi.

American. Born in Los Angeles, 7 December 1923. Studied at the Art Institute of Chicago, 1947–48, and with Ossip Zadkine and with Fernand Léger, Paris, 1948–50, and at the Académie de la Grande Chaumière, Paris, 1950–51. Served as volunteer in United States Armed Forces, 1943–46; awarded Purple Heart Medal. Married Denise Martin in 1951 (divorced, 1955); married Ferdina Jansen in 1957 (died, 1969); children: Giotta Fuyo and Ryu Vinci; married Suzanne van der Capellen in 1976. Worked as re-

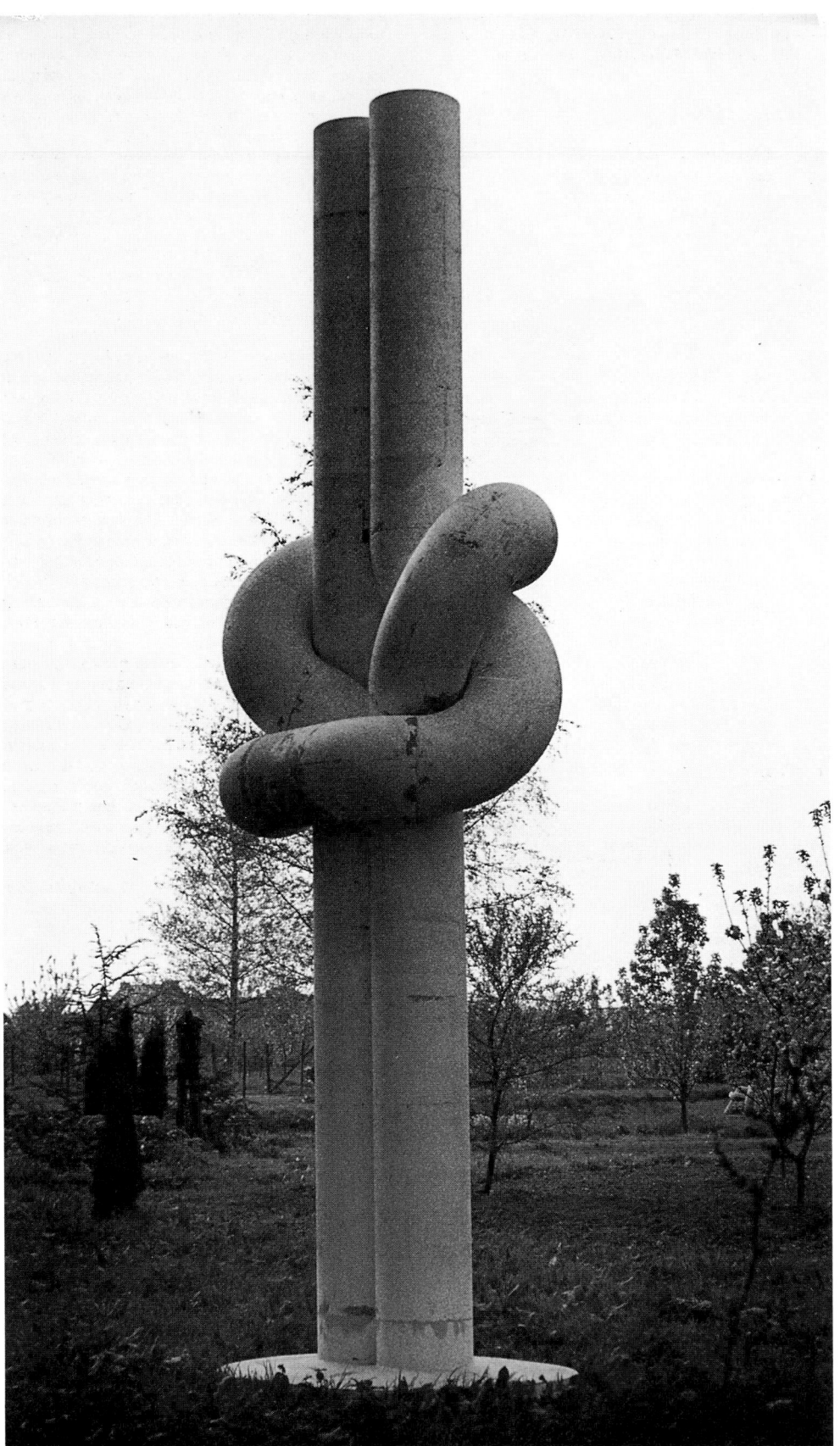

Shinkichi Tajiri: *Square Knot,* 1973

storer of antiques, Chicago, 1946. Independent artist, since 1949: associated with *Cobra* group, 1949–1950; Co-Founder of Galerie 8, Paris, Paris. 1950; designer at Rasch Wallpaper, Bramsche, West Germany, 1952. Guest Lecturer Werkkunstschule, Wuppertal, West Germany, 1951–53; Visiting Professor, College of Art and Design, Minneapolis, 1964–65 and 1972. Professor of Fine Art, Hochschule der Künste, Berlin, since 1969. Recipient: First Prize,

International Wallpaper Exhibition. Darmstadt, 1953; Golden Lion, *8th Amateur Film Festival,* Cannes, 1955; Copley Foundation Grant, 1959; Whitney Foundation Fellowship for Sculpture, 1960; Mainichi Shinbun Prize for Sculpture, Tokyo, 1963. Agent: Court Gallery, Ostergade 24, Copenhagen, Denmark. Address: Castle Scheres. 5991 NC Baarlo (Limburg), Netherlands.

Individual Exhibitions:

1951	Galerie Parnass, Wuppertal, West Germany
1953	Kunsthandel Martinet, Amsterdam (with Pierce Alechinsky)
1954	Galerie d'Aujourd'hui, Brussels
1955	Galerie Colette Allendy, Paris
1957	Galerie Parnass, Wuppertal, West Germany
1958	Kunstring, Rotterdam
	Galerie Lucien Durand, Paris
1959	de Jong & Co., Hilversum, Netherlands
1960	Stedelijk Museum, Amsterdam
	American Cultural Center, Paris
1961	Gemeentemuseum, Arnhem, Netherlands
1962	Galleria Odyssia, Rome
	Galerie Parnass, Wuppertal, West Germany
1963	Tokyo Gallery
1964	Hamilton Gallery, London
	American Art Gallery, Copenhagen
	Galerie 20, Amsterdam
1965	Minneapolis Institute of Art
	André Emmerich Gallery, New York
1966	Court Gallery, Copenhagen
1967	Stedelijk Museum, Amsterdam
1968	Palais des Beaux-Arts, Brussels
	University of Economics, Tilburg, Netherlands
	Von der Heydt Museum, Wuppertal, West Germany
1969	Kunsthalle, Basle
	Galerie d'Espace, Amsterdam
1970	City Hall, Heerlen, Netherlands
1971	Konsthall Lund, Sweden
	Norrkoping Museum, Sweden
1972	Sodertalie Konsthall, Sweden
	Amos Andersons Taidemuseum, Helsinki
	Vasterbotten Museum, Umea, Sweden
	Kunstnernes Hus, Oslo
	Aarhus Museum, Denmark
	Galerie Judith Weingarten, Amsterdam
1974	Boymans Van Beunigen Museum, Rotterdam
	Bonnefanten Museum, Maastricht, Netherlands
1976	*Tajiri's Daguerrotypes,* Stedelijk Museum, Amsterdam
	Tajiri's Rediscovery of the Daguerrotype, Künstlerhaus Bethanien, Berlin
1977	Rheinisches Landersmuseum, Bonn
	Van Abbemuseum, Eindhoven, Netherlands
	Stadtisches Kunstahalle, Dusseldorf
	Münchener Stadtmuseum, Munich
	Kunstchau Böttcherstrasse, Bremen, West Germany
	Rijksmuseum Kröller-Müller, Otterlo, Netherlands
1979	*Stereoscopic Views by Tajiri,* Stedelijk Museum. Amsterdam
	Galerie Fiolet, Amsterdam
1980	Rijksmuseum Kröller-Müller, Otterlo, Netherlands
	Kunstlerhaus Bethanien, Berlin
1981	Gemeentemuseum, Vlissingen, Netherlands
1982	Galerie Kunstbezit, Heerlen, Netherlands
1983	Collection d'Art, Amsterdam
1984	Galerie Wansink, Roermond, Netherlands
1985	Bonnefantenmuseum, Maastricht, Netherlands
.1986	Galerij Paule Pia, Antwerp, Belgium
1987	Galerie Artline, The Hague

Selected Group Exhibitions:

1949	*International Exhibition of Experimental Art (COBRA),* Stedelijk Museum, Amsterdam
1951	*COBRA,* Palais des Beaux-Arts, Liège, Belgium
1957	*Phases,* Stedelijk Museum, Amsterdam
1959	*Documenta 2,* Kassel, West Germany
1961	*Art of Assemblage,* Museum of Modern Art, New York
1968	*Science Fiction,* Kunstverein, Dusseldorf
1973	*Video,* Rotterdamsche Kunststichting, Rotterdam
1982	*Cobra,* Musée d'Art Moderne, Paris
1984	*L'Art a Paris 1945–66,* Centre National des Arts Plastiques, Paris
1987	*Paper as Medium,* Galerie Horst Dietrich, West Berlin

Publications:

By TAJIRI: books—*Ferdi*, Baarlo, Netherlands 1969; *May-day I* and *II*, Baarlo, Netherlands 1970; *The Wall, Die Mauer, La Mur*, Berlin 1971; *Portrait, Self-Portrait and Measurements*. Berlin 1972; article—"Beyond Pornography" in *Suck* (Amsterdam), 1973; films-*The Vipers*, Paris 1955; *Ferdi*, 1955; *The Birth of Giotta Fuyo Tajiri, 6 June 1957*, 1957; *Bodil Joensen, A Summer Day*, Copenhagen 1970.

On TAJIRI: books—*Shinkichi Tajiri*, exhibition catalogue, by Aldo van Eyck, Amsterdam 1969; *Shinkichi Tajiri*, exhibition catalogue, by Dick Hillenius, Rotterdam 1974; *Tajiri's Daguerrotypes*, exhibition catalogue, by Ed van der Elsken, Amsterdam 1976; *Tajiri's Rediscovery of the Daguerrotype*, exhibition catalogue, by Michael Haerdter, Berlin 1976; *Stereoscopic Views by Tajiri*, exhibition catalogue, by Els Barent, Amsterdam 1979; *Tajiri*, exhibition catalogue by Nicole Gast, Maastricht 1985, film—*The World of Tajiri* by Ben Berbong, 1973.

My works are resumés of explorations into inner space.

—Shinkichi Tajiri

The strange mixture of cultural sources and influences in Shinkichi Tajiri's life seems to have given him great freedom of expression. Born in the United States of Japanese parents, his father a former member of the Samurai caste, Tajiri left his native country as a protest against the treatment of American Japanese during the war. He had previously studied with the famous sculptor Noguchi, who shares his mixed background, and in Paris became a pupil of both Léger and Zadkine. In Paris he was one of the pioneers of the junk-art school, his first impressive group of sculptures being based on bronze foundry droppings, welded into delicate, feathery torsos of vegetable forms.

The instinctive, elegant, oriental seductiveness is something Tajiri immediately rejects once it becomes dominant. A more acceptable inheritance is his fascination with technology and machinery; he is intrigued by the way anything is made, and to some extent his career has been a move away from junk-assemblage, to the re-assembling of natural and man-made shapes. His mature work is a personal mixture of sexual and erotic forms, organised with mechanistic formality. Nature, sex and machines come together in monumental, hieratic sculptures, in which human and plant verticality is conditioned by symbols of growth and procreation. They contain endless echoes and suggestions—the spiky aggression of armoured Samurai, the thrusting determination of natural growth, the urgent confrontation of male and female.

In recent years Tajiri has combined these sculptural forms with informal artistic presentations, happenings which include dance, live nude models, or photographic backgrounds.

—Charles Spencer

TAKAMATSU, Jiro.

Japanese, Born Shinpachiro Takamatsu in Tokyo in February 1936. Studied at Tokyo University of Art, 1954–58. Married Yasuko Takamatsu in 1963; child: Kei. Painter: lives and works in Tokyo. Color Designer, Tohei Animation Company, 1958–59; Industrial Designer, Silver Seikoh Company, 1960–66. Full-time Lecturer, Tokyo University of Art, 1972–75. Recipient: First Prize, *Shell Exhibition*, Tokyo, 1965; First Prize, Museum of Contemporary Art, Nagaoka, Japan, 1965; Theodoron Foundation Prize, *Biennale de Paris*, 1967; Prize, *Tokyo Biennale*, 1967; DeCarlo Cardazzo Prize, *Biennale*, Venice, 1968; Prize, *Contemporary Art Exhibition*, Museum of Ohara, Kurashiki, Japan, 1969; First Prize, *Exhi-*

bition of Prints, Tokyo, 1972. Agent: Tokyo Gallery, 8-6-18 Ginza, Chuo-ku, Tokyo 104. Address: 2-2-27 Shimorenjaku, Mitaka, Tokyo 181, Japan.

Individual Exhibitions:

1966   Tokyo Gallery
1967   Galleria d'Arte del Naviglio, Milan
        New Smith Gallery, Brussels
1969   Tokyo Gallery
1971   Tokyo Gallery
1978   Tokyo Gallery

Selected Group Exhibitions:

1967   *Biennale*, Paris
        Object '67, Galerie Mathias Fels, Paris
1968   *Biennale*, Venice
1971   *International Sculpture Exhibition*, Guggenheim Museum, New York
1973   *The Art of Surface*, Art Gallery of New South Wales, Sydney
1974   *Japan: Tradition und Gegenwart*, Kunsthalle, Dusseldorf
        Japanese Art in Scandinavia, Gothenburg Museum, Sweden (travelled to the Henie-Onstad Art Center, Oslo)
        Japan Pa Louisiana, Louisiana Museum, Humlebaek, Denmark
1975   *A View of Japanese Contemporary Art*, Seibu Museum of Art, Tokyo
1977   *Painting in the Age of Photography*, Kunsthaus, Zurich

Collections:

Museum of Contemporary Art, Nagaoka, Japan; National Museum of Modern Art, Tokyo; Museum of Modern Art, Kanagawa, Japan; Ohara Museum of Art, Kurashiki, Japan; Australian National Gallery, Canberra.

Publications:

On TAKAMATSU: books—*Guggenheim International Exhibition*, exhibition catalogue, New York 1971; *Japan: Tradition und Gegenwart*, exhibition catalogue, by J. Harten and J. P. Love, Dusseldorf 1974; articles—"Jiro Takamatsu" in *Mizue* (Tokyo), no. 2, 1971; "Tokyo Letter" by J. P. Love in *Art International* (Lugano, Switzerland), February 1972.

In his first public showing, Jiro Takamatsu stretched twine out of the museum, stuffed twine into glass bottles, and even wound other twine around his body much like a silkworm spinning a cocoon. This "String" series was his contribution to the *Yomiuri Independent Exhibition* in 1961. It was three years after he had graduated from the faculty of oil painting at the Tokyo University of Fine Arts. Then only 25, Takamatsu has sought to materially express, at the exhibition, the concepts of line and distance. He bottled, in effect, a hundred meters "distance."

He soon teamed with Gemei Akasegawa and Natsuyuki Nakanishi to form the High Red Center, which created happenings in such places as Ginza streets. It was not until 1964, however, that he began to attract serious attention in art circles, by means of a series "Shadows." In these works, he deliberately outlined, on white canvas, the shadows of every-day objects such as jars and clothing brushes, and people in various positions. If painting since the discovery of perspective, born of the camera obscura of even longer ago, has been depicting "shadows" on two dimensional canvas to show the three-dimensional outer world, then to merely paint shadows was to be true to that principle—moreover, it had significance as a denial of the reality. Doubt about the existence of the real world was what Takamatsu showed by painting shadows, and it was, further, a lyrical expression.

The "Perspective" series which followed was Takamatsu's essay in solidifying for our view the decep-

tion in the relationship between the real world and human beings. As the laws of perspective have it, the further an object is from the viewer the smaller it appears, but in Takamatsu's tables, in this series, the diminution is real, not merely apparent, and exaggerated beyond what the eye has been trained to perceive. Chairs too, and entire interiors, rush away from the viewer toward distant vanishing points. A culmination of this work was "Perspective Dimension—Sky" which earned Takamatsu a prize at the Venice *Biennale* in 1968. Then, in 1970, at the Festival Plaza at the *World's Fair* in Osaka, his "Perspective Construction," with its mirror surfaces which reflected the sky and created strange illusions also attracted considerable critical attention.

Having brought out the fiction of our habitual perception of the real world by means of his Shadow and Perspective works, Takamatsu since 1969 has come to be interested in how to perceive things under conditions of absolutely minimal participation by the person involved. He painted numbers on rounded river stones, and attempted other experiments in this quest. More recently, he has been cutting tree trunks in great slices and then stacking them as they had been before, or breaking a block of concrete into fragments which he would then fit into a box. One such reassembled box was included in the *International Sculpture Exhibition* at the Guggenheim in 1971, where it was praised as a fine example of conceptual art. In 1972 he received the grand prize for his arrangement of alphabetical letters at the Eighth *International Prints Biennale* in Tokyo.

In the 1980s, Takamatsu resumed painting with a completely abstract style. He was exploring the narrow possibilities of pictorial diversification via grids of entangled wavy lines overlaid with washes of vivid colors to promote and illusion of depth. The pictures sometimes have the appearance of seaweed dancing in water and reflecting the varying moods of light throughout the day; at other times, they appear as a retinal fantasy that can only be experienced deep in a forest or in the brilliance on sunlight on a white beach.

—Yoshiaki Tono

TAKIS.

Greek. Born Panayotis Vassilakis in Athens, 29 October 1925. Self-taught in art, from 1946. Married the artist, Liliane Lijn, q.v., in 1961 (divorced, 1967); son: Athanasios Thanos; married Do Koenig in 1971. Sculptor, Athens, 1945–46, in Paris and London, 1954–59, in Paris and Athens, since 1959; produced first "Signals," 1954–58; first telemagnetic sculptures, 1958; first electro-magnetic musical works, 1973. Recipient: Fellowship in Advanced Visual Studies, Massachusetts Institute of Technology, Cambridge, 1968–70; Prix de la Biennale, *Biennale de Paris*, 1985. Agents: Galerie Lelong, 13 rue de Teheran, 75008 Paris, France; Alexandre Iolas Gallery, 15 East 55th Street, New York, New York 10022. U.S.A. Addresses: 22 rue Liancourt, 75014 Paris, France; and Odos Dervenakious, Gero Vounos, Aharne, Attikis, Athens, Greece.

Individual Exhibitions:

1955   Hanover Gallery, London
        Galarie Furstenberg, Paris
1958   Hanover Gallery, London
1959   Galerie Iris Clert, Paris
        Alexandre Iolas Gallery, New York
1960   *L'Impossible, un homme dans l'espace*, Galerie Iris Clert, Paris
1961   Alexandre Iolas Gallery, New York
1962   *Signals and Telesculptures*, Galleria Schwarz, Milan
1963   Alexandre Iolas Gallery, New York

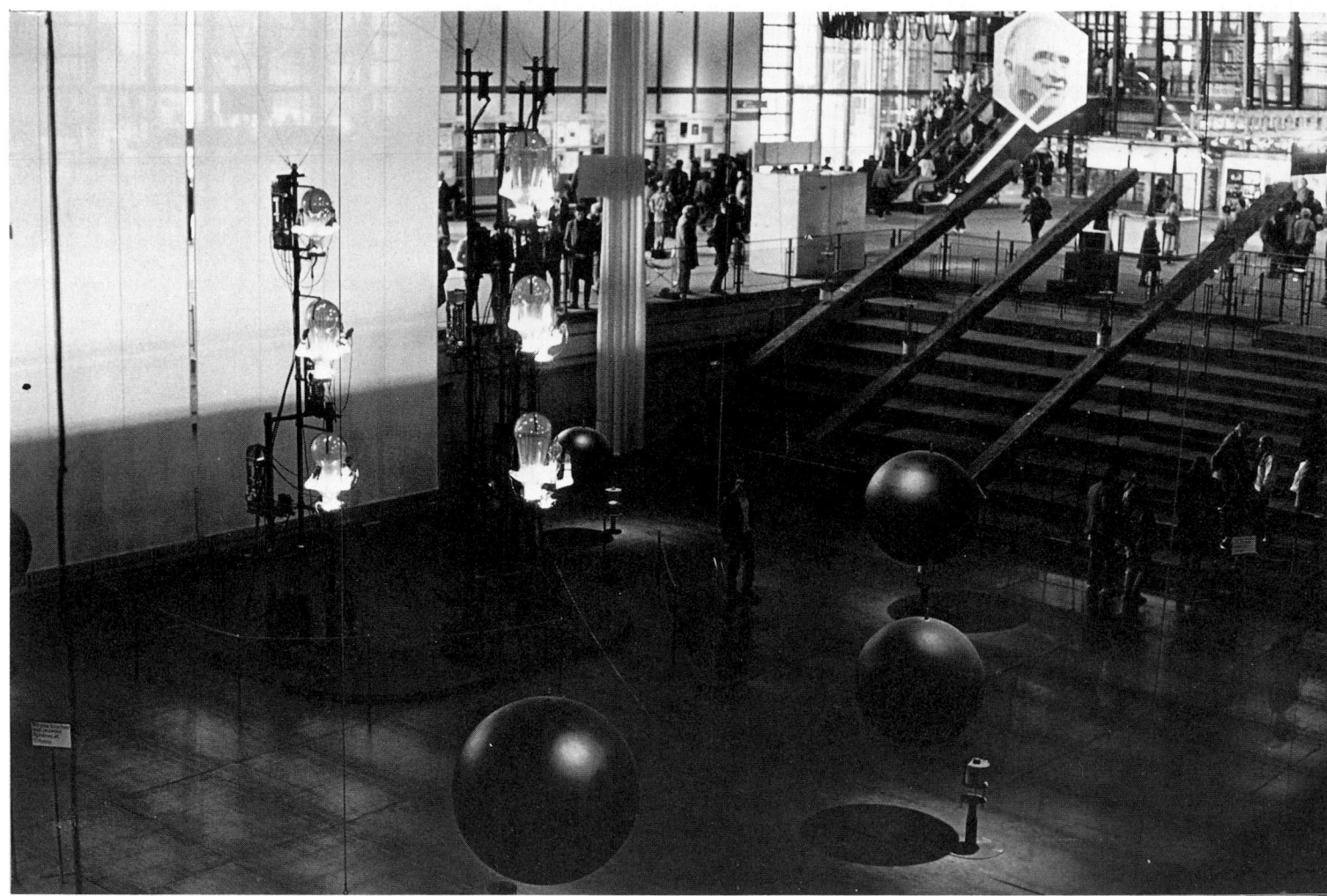

Takis: *Three Totems/Espace Musical*, 1981

1964	Galerie Alexandre Iolas, Paris		1981	Centre Georges Pompidou, Paris

1964   Galerie Alexandre Iolas, Paris
     Signals Gallery, London
1965   Galerie Alexandre Iolas, Geneva
1966   Galerie Alexandre Iolas, Paris
     Hanover Gallery, London
     Indica Gallery, London
1967   Howard Wise Gallery, New York
     Galerie Krikhaar, Amsterdam
     Galerie Claude Givaudan, Paris
1968   Galleria Schwarz, Milan
     Arts Laboratory, London
     Widcombe Manor, Bath, England
1969   Howard Wise Gallery, New York
     Massachusetts Institute of Technology, Cambridge (retrospective)
1970   Städtisches Museum Schloss Morsbroich, Leverkusen, West Germany (retrospective)
     Howard Wise Gallery, New York
1971   Galerie Alexandre Iolas, Paris
     Galerie Bama, Paris
1972   Galleria Iolas, Milan
     Centre National d'Art Contemporain, Paris (retrospective)
1973   Nederlands Dans Theater, Amsterdam (decors for ballet *Elkesis*)
1974   Zoumboulakis Gallery, Athens
     Musikalische Raume, Kunstverein, Hannover
     Espace Cardin, Paris
1975   Galerie Fred Lanzenberg, Brussels
1976   Galerie Alexandre Iolas, Paris
1977   Galerie Artcurial, Paris
     New Smith Gallery, Brussels
     Trito Mati Gallery, Athens
1978   Musée d'Art Moderne de la Ville, Paris
1979   Kölnischer Kunstverein, Cologne
     Galarie Reckermann, Cologne
     Musée de la Ville, Calais

1981   Centre Georges Pompidou, Paris
     Galerie Maeght, Paris
1983   Galerie Maeght Lelong, Paris
1985   Centre Georges Pompidou, Paris
     Ecole Régionale des Beaux Arts, St. Etienne, France
1986   Musée Rath, Geneva
     Galarie Hotel de ville, Villeurbanne, France

Selected Group Exhibitions:

1952   *Exposition Internationale*, Delphi, Greece
1959   *14 European Sculptors*, Staempfli Gallery, New York
1961   *Bewogen Beweging*, Stedlijk Museum, Amsterdam (toured Scandinavia)
1965   *Lumière et Mouvement*, Kunsthalle, Berne (toured Belgium and Germany)
1967   *The Machine*, Museum of Modern Art, New York
1974   *Art of the 20th Century*, Fondazione Peggy Guggenheim, Venice (toured Europe)
1977   *Documenta*, Kassel, West Germany
1981   *Machins-Machines*, Centre Culturel, Bretigny, France
1983   *Electra*, Musée d'Art Moderne de la Ville, Paris
1985   *Biennale de Paris*, Musé d'Art Moderne, Paris

Collections:

Centre Georges Pompidou, Paris; Centre National d'Art Contemporain, Paris; Städtisches Museum Schloss Morsbroich, Leverkusen, West Germany: Arts Council of Great Britain, London; Tate Gallery, London; Museum of Tel Aviv; Museum of Modern Art, New York; Guggenheim Museum, New York; Art Institute of Chicago; Art Gallery of Ontario, Toronto.

Publications:

By TAKIS: books—*Estafilades*, Paris 1961; *Poems 1942–46*, Paris 1972; *Elkesis*, Rotterdam 1973; *Musique Magnetique*, Paris 1975; articles—"Conversation dans l'Atelier," interview, with Luce Hoctin in *L'Oeil* (Paris), November 1964, "Statements by Kinetic Artists" in *Studio International* (London), February 1967; "Revelations: Interview de Takis," with Jean Clay, in *Rhobo* (Paris), Spring 1968; "Technology Against Technology = Anti-technology" in *Radical Software* (New York). no. 2, 1970; "Lignes Paralleles" in *Takis*, exhibition catalogue, Paris 1971; "Interview de Takis," with Catherine Millet, in *Chroniques de l'Art Vivani* (Paris), May 1971.

On TAKIS: books—*La Sculpture de ce Siècle* by Michel Seuphor, Paris 1959; *Takis: l'Impossible un homme dans l'espace*, exhibition catalogue, with texts by Alain Jouffroy, Gregory Corso, William Burroughs, Bryon Gysin and others, Paris 1960; *Icons and Images of the 60's* by Nicolas and Elena Calas, Paris 1961; *Takis: Signals and Telesculptures*, exhibition catalogue, with texts by William Burroughs, Alain Jouffroy, Nicolas Calas and others, Milan 1962; *Une Révolution du Regard* by Alain Jouffroy, Paris 1964; *Naissance de l'Art Cinétique* by Frank Popper, Paris 1967; *Nature and the Art of Movement* by Gyorgy Kepes, Paris 1968; *Kinetic Art: The Language of Movement* by Guy Brett, London 1968; *25 Ans d'Art Vivant* by Michel Ragon, Paris 1969; *L'Avant Garde au 20eme Siècle* by Pierre Cabanne and Pierre Restany, 1969; *L'Art Present dans la Cité* by Adam Saulnier, Paris 1969; *Focus* by Pierre Cabanne, Paris 1971; *Takis*, exhibition catalogue, with text by J. J. Lebel, Nicolas Calas, Alain Jouffroy and others, Paris 1972; *Takis: Musikalische Raume*, exhibition catalogue, with texts by Helmut R. Leppien and Christos M. Jachimides, Hannover 1974; films—*Takis* by Jean-Marie Drot, 1960; *10 Artists de Paris*, French television film, 1965; *Meet the Artist* by Colette Robert, 1967; *Takis Unlimited* by Mahmoud K. Khosrowshaki, 1967; *Takis, Chant of the Magnetic Minstre* by Richard Edelman, 1968; *Takis* by Wayne Anderson, 1969; *Takis* by ARC-New Film, 1969; *CBS-TV: 21st Century* by Keeper Poor, 1969.

I will try to put down on paper something about magnets. I have been intrigued by radar systems, and tried to find out how they function. I was told that they depend on a magnet which swings around through the full 360 degrees of the compass. The signal reported to the observer tells him of the presence of some other metallic object in space. I bought my first magnet and dreamt of using it in some way to bring about a perpetual movement by using the force of the magnet. I hoped to make some metallic object move forever. And I saw that the magnet gave me the use of a new fantastic element which I could apply to the iron-work which I had done before. (The "tiges" which I had been making were antennae to capture the force of nature in the clouds . . . electricity. In other works they had been receivers all along. This struck me as being incomplete.) Magnets, however, are not "receivers" but "senders". Yet, like radar itself a magnet "feels" out towards any passing metallic object facing the magnet. What I had been doing up until the moment I started with the magnets was making signals which merely received the electricity from the sky. Even though they moved, my sculptures seemed to me to still be static.

Up until now those who made metal sculptures had been trying to create tension by twisting iron bars. Many sculptors had been making twisted and pointed forms which were intended to create a sort of vibration between two points; the unreal made to seem real through the talent of the sculptor himself, if you like. What I wanted was to make what I felt to be really REAL. A magnet is not an idea—it is something so real that I was led to dream of making a Perpetual Motion machine with magnets. Very soon I realised that this was not really my intention. What interested me was, rather, the way in which magnetism creates a connection between two metallic objects through the magnetic waves which are a communication. When Gonzales twisted iron objects he produced only a graphic achievement such as the painters had been interested in. Many painters like Matta and Lam have worked along that line as have others who were more interested in creating an illusion of space rather than an action in space which I feel is the role of the sculpture.

When I wished to express the space-communication between an object and a magnet I was obliged to tie up the object. When I did this in order to keep an object at a distance from a magnet, I realized that I had "floated" the object. My metallic object floated in the air and vibrated. This was even further from my original intention. I had wished to communicate the two metals only symbolically but, now, they communicated realistically through the magnetic field. Immediately they gave the sensation of being alive. A new and very real force was working between the two objects which I had approached one to the other. When I attached an object by a string and floated it towards the magnet, even a breath of air started a visible vibration. In actual fact the vibration is continuous whether one sees it or not through the wave-motion of the magnetic field, working alternatively but continuously. The vibration is perpetual. What interested me was to put into iron sculpture a new, continuous, and live force. The result was in no way a graphic representation of a force but the force itself which had to be handled as one would handle any other force in nature—even an animal force. The perpetual movement aspect of it became obviously of secondary interest and I put myself to treating, guiding and dominating magnetic force itself in its aspects of real communication . . . the space communication of objects on this planet. More than that, I have wanted to bring off what the Egyptians tried to communicate through the human form in which muscles were represented in a state of tension or slack. The ancient Cycladic sculptors, too, tried to represent these forces through the action of the muscles and forms. In what I do I intend that the tension of forces shall be as visible as the nylon cord which floats an object in front of the magnet whose live force and vibration gives life to what has seemed to be dead material.

—Takis

Takis is a pioneering kinetic sculptor who has effectively fulfilled his intention of bridging the barriers between art and science by making his own art one which used or unleashes the natural forces of gravity, magnetism and electromagnetism, the movement of the tides, or light. He is an elemental sculptor in much the same sense as Turner was an elemental painter, concerned not so much with the visible surface of the world but with the underlying natural forces, which can be enormously destructive and yet have been harnessed by man to drive the Industrial Revolution, a revolution which depended on the new scientific concept of nature as the carrier of energy.

The progress of Takis' work can be seen as a constant attempt to intensify the presence of energy, to make these powerful natural forces the living core and essence of his sculpture, which with his electromagnetic works he triumphantly has done. He has told how he was fascinated as a child by the way Greek children cut vegetable roots into dolls and hang them on a string to float in the wind. But he came to kinetics only gradually, starting as a self-taught sculptor who at the age of 21 made objects in clay, then for several years from 1948-1953, carved in wood. These wooden sculptures were of the human figure, more or less in the Giacometti tradition, though from 1953-1955 they became more and more abstract, and Takis came to regard abstraction as inseparable from an objective view of the modern world of science and technology.

Since 1974 he has lived mainly in Paris, though with prolonged stays in London. Here his work crystallized, and from making bronze "idols" with flexible wire necks, or arrow-and piston-headed flower sculptures, he moved decisively into the kinetic sphere with the series of works he called "Signals". He has described how the idea germinated while he was waiting three of four hours for a train in Calais, and became fascinated by the signalization of the railways: "I drew some sketches, thinking how dramatic this signalization was, and how necessary a part of our century this was. When I came back to Paris I started making a sort of imitation of those signals, and as I used thin wires as bodies to hold the signals, accidentally they started moving, and I thought it was very fascinating." These Signals consist of modelled forms on the end of long rods of steel, an extremely pliable and light material which allows them to remain in constant vibration when set in motion. They contain suggestions not only of railway signals, but also of road signs, antennae, and all sorts of other aspects of our technological environment.

His next step of using magnetic and electrical forces instead of gravity was inspired by seeing "radar scanners moving as if directed by an invisible power." He was trying to build his own radar machine, which included piano wires in the hope that it would also make mysterious music, when one day these wires broke because of their tension and floated towards a magnet which was next to the machine. This led him to focus his attention on forces rather than on objects, trying to make visible in his sculptures the invisibly energy of magnetism. The magnetic and telemagnetic sculptures he began making in 1959, in which balls, cones or needles are suspended in a magnetic or electromagnetic field, do not exist as forms, like traditional sculptures, but an invisible energy which makes them move and change.

The idea that the locally more powerful force of magnetism could liberate objects from the earth's gravity excited him, and in November 1960 Takis put a man in space by suspending the poet Sinclair Beiles in a magnetic field. The following year he was producing his "Magnetic Ballets," which depend on combining and controlling two different forces, electromagnetism and gravity, by suspending balls over upturned electromagnets and making them swing and gyrate in a cosmic dance which makes perceptible the energy that is all around us and the forces that dominate the natural world.

An extension of this is to increase the tension at the centre of this moving kinetic energy sculpture by revealing the source of energy of the electromagnet, which is operated by a blue mercury vapour lamp.

This not only used light in the sculpture, but shows that light itself is just another form of electromagnetic energy. Yet the constantly flickering mercury vapour lamp is also poetic in character, so that Takis can think of it as "cosmic flower" emitting its energy. Takis has shown constant inventiveness in finding fresh sources such as signal-lamps, aircraft instruments and fireworks for revealing the energy which is always the core of his recent sculptures. At MIT's Center for Visual Studies in 1968 he turned to yet another natural source of energy in his "Hommage a Marcel Duchamp." The original bicycle wheel exhibited by Duchamp was mounted so that it could be turned by hand, but Takis floated a similar bicycle wheel in the sea so that it was perpetual motion, driven by the motion of the tides.

Takis also offers homage to Thales of Miletus, for it was the pioneering Greek scientist who first described magnetism and electricity 2,500 years ago. And though modern science has learnt how to harness such forces, and that they are interchangable with light, heat and even matter, their ultimate nature remains as mysterious as it was when Thales first described them. Schlegel's prediction that the response to a scientifically explored universe ought to be that it is a still intractable mystery has proved true with a vengeance, and the fascination of Takis' kinetic sculptures is that they are not parodies of technological instruments but highly poetic creations which bring us into direct contact with the fundamental and still mysterious forces which power nature and life. No wonder that Takis in his own statements often seems to verge on animism when he talks about his works as cosmic flowers.

—Konstantin Bazarov

TAL-COAT, Pierre.

French. Born Pierre Jacob in Clohars-Carnoet, Finistere, 12 December 1905; adopted pseudonym "Tal-Coat" in 1926. Educated in Quimperle, 1912-18; studied at Ecole Supérieure, Quimperle, 1919-22; studied casting, Académie de la Grand Chaumière, Paris, 1924-26, and pottery moulding at a manufacturer in Sevres, 1926. Served in French Army, 1925-26, 1939-40. Married Bronislawa Lewandowska in 1927; daughter: Pierette; married Xaviere Angeli in 1950 (died, 1970). Independent artist, Paris, 1924, Brittany, 1927-39, Paris, 1931-40, Aix-en-Provence, 1940-56, and St. Pierre de Baileul, L'Eure, 1956 until his death in 1985: Founder-Member, with R. Humblot, H. Jannot, J. Lasne, A. Pellan and G. Rohner, "Forces Nouvelles," Paris, 1932-39. Recipient: Prix Paul Guillaume, 1936; Grand Prix National des Arts, 1968. Commandeur, Ordre des Arts et Lettres, 1976. Agents: Galerie Maeght, 13 rue de Teheran, 75008 Paris; Galerie Benador, rue Hotel de Ville 7, Place Saconnerie 10, Geneva 1200; and Galerie Clivages, 46 rue de l'Université, 75007 Paris. *Died* (in Saint-Pierre de Baileul) *11 June 1985.*

Individual Exhibitions:

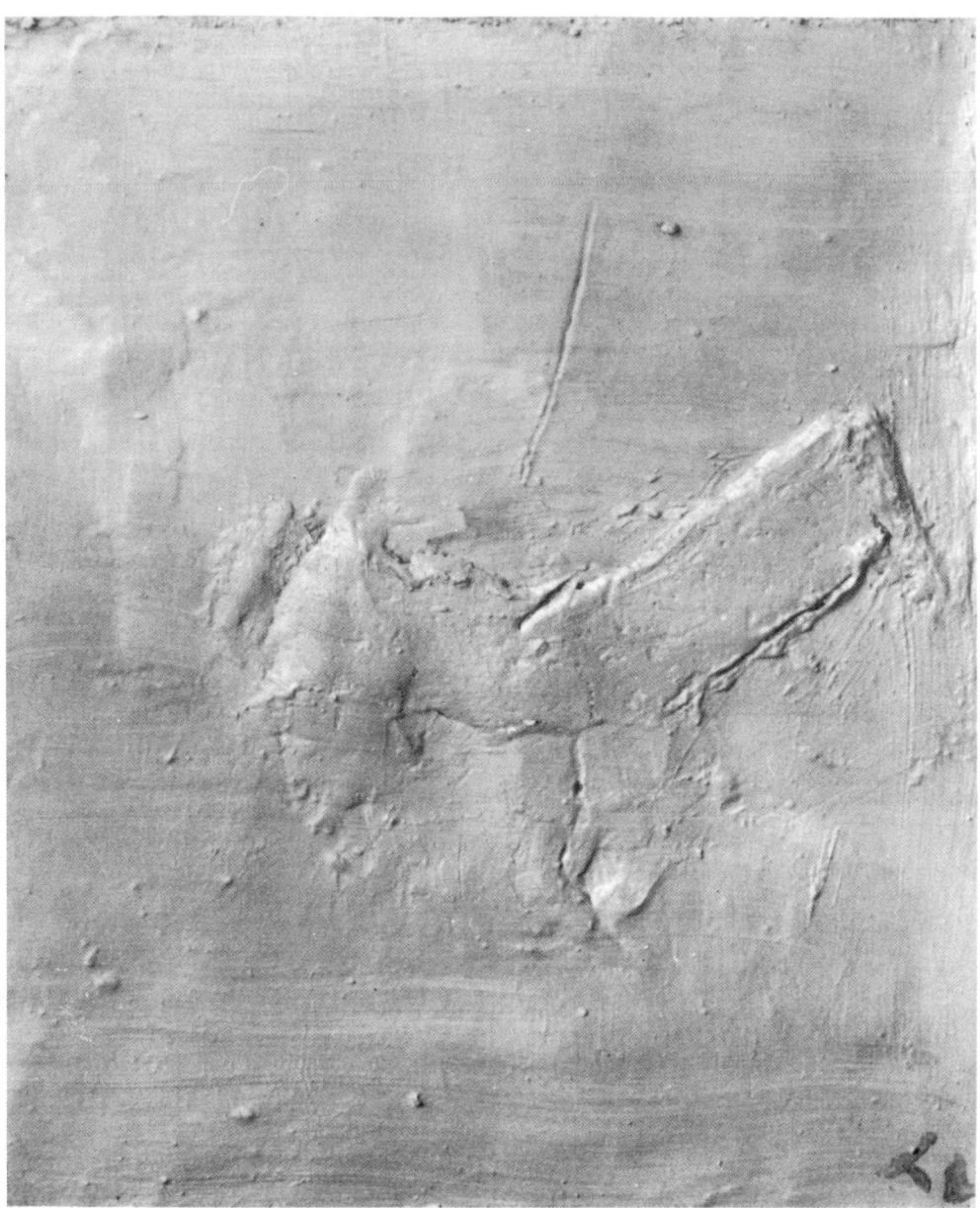

Pierre Tal-Coat: *Passage Gris*

1965	Galerie Beno d'Incelli, Paris	1980	Galerie Benador, at *F.I.A.C.*, Paris
1968	Galerie Henri Benezit, Paris	1981	Galerie Clivages, Paris
	Galerie André Schoeller, Paris		Chapelle de Locronan, Brittany, France
	Galerie Beno d'Incelli, Paris		Centre d'Art Contemporain, Jouy-sur-Eure, France
1969	Palais de l'Europe, Menton, France		Galerie Clivages, at *F.I.A.C.*, Paris
	Maison de la Culture, Le Havre, France	1982	Galerie Clivages, Paris
	Maison de la Culture, Amiens, France		Grand Palais, Paris
1970	*Ocuvres Récentes,* Galerie Benador, Geneva	1983	Galerie Clivages, Paris
1972	*Almanach de Tal-Coat,* Galerie Benador, Geneva		Galerie Michel Cachoux, Paris
1973	Galerie L'Entracte, Lausanne, Switzerland		Galerie Patrice Trigano, Paris
1974	Galerie Maeght, Zurich	1984	Centre Noiroit, Arras, France
	Museée des Beaux-Arts, Metz, France		Galerie Clivages, Paris
1975	Galerie Benador, Geneva		Galerie Sapone, Nice, France
	Ueno Royal Museum, Tokyo (travelled to the Hakone Open-Air Museum, Ninotaira).	1985	Galerie Clivages, Paris
			New Museum of Contemporary Art, New York
1976	Grand Palais, Paris		Cabinet des Estampes, Geneva
	Musée d'Art Moderne, Paris	1986	Gallery Art Point, Tokyo
	Galerie Eveil, Marlenheim, West Germany		Galerie Clivages, Paris
	Galerie Shapiro, Paris		Galerie L'Entract, Lausanne
	Galerie de France, Paris		Centre Gerard Philippe, Bretigny-sur-Orge, France
	Galerie du Benelux, Brussels	1987	Maison de la Culture, Bourges, France
1978	Galerie Biren, Paris		Musée de Valence, France
	Galerie de l'Entracte, Lausanne, Switzerland		Galerie Clivages, Paris
1979	Galerie Benador, Geneva (travelled to the Galerie Karsten-Greve, Cologne)		
	Chateau de Ratilly, Yonne, France (with André du Bouchet)		
	Galerie Ditesheim, Neuchâtel, Switzerland		
	Bibliotenque de Lyons, France		

Selected Group Exhibitions:

1934   *Bateaux et Marin,* Galerie Billiet Pierre Vorms, Paris

1935   *Forces Nouvelles,* Galerie Billiet Pierre Vorms, Paris

1949   *La Jeune Peinture Francaise,* Leicester Galleries, London

1955   *Documenta 1,* Kassel, West Germany (and *Documenta 2,* 1959)

1968   *Painting in France 1900–1967,* National Gallery of Art, Washington, D.C. (toured the United States)

1973   *Collections Genevoises: Art du 20e. Siècle,* Musée Rath, Geneva

1976   *Front Populaire,* Ancienne Gare de la Bastille, Paris

1980   *Forces Nouvelles 1935–39,* Musée d'Art Moderne de la Ville, Paris

1981   *Paris-Paris,* Centre George Pompidou, Paris

1982   *Bretons à Paris,* Grand Palais, Paris

Collections:

Centre Georges Pompidou, Paris: Musée de Grenoble, France; Fondation Maeght, Saint-Paul-de-Vence, France.

Publications:

By TAL-COAT: books illustrated—*Honore de Balzac,* Geneva 1946; *Elements de Nature,* Paris 1949; *Colle Surface,* with text by André du Bouchet, Paris 1956; *Sur le Pas,* with text by André du Bouchet, Paris 1959; *Traverse d'un Plateau,* Paris 1963; *Laisses,* with text by André du Bouchet, Lausanne 1975; *Espace Delute,* with text by Pierre Torreilles, Paris 1976; *Sous le Linteau en Forme de Joug,* with text by André du Bouchet, Lausanne 1978; *Surface d'eceuil,* with text by Philippe Denis, Paris 1980.

On TAL-COAT: books—*Pierre Tal-Coat: Peintures,* exhibition catalogue, with text by Michel Florisoone, Paris 1945; *Tal-Coat,* exhibition catalogue, with text Jacques Lassaigne, Paris 1950; *Tal-Coat,* exhibition catalogue, with text by F. Meyer, Berne 1957; *Peintres Contemporains* by Georges Duthuit and others, Paris 1964; *Tal-Coat,* exhibition catalogue, with texts by Francis Palermo and E. Marze, Menton, France 1969; *Tal-Coat: Oeuvres Récentes,* exhibition catalogue, with text by Henri Maldiney, Geneva 1970; *Almanach de Tal-Coat,* exhibition catalogue, with text by Pietro Sarto, Geneva 1971; *Pierre Tal-Coat,* exhibition catalogue, with text by Raoul-Jean Moulin, Zurich 1974; *Forces Nourvelles 1935–1939,* exhibition catalogue, with text by Pierre Vorms, Paris 1980; *Tal Coat,* exhibition catalogue, with text by Jean Pascal Leger, Valence 1987.

Prior to the naming of things invisible wave sweeping us out of our cell of insistent visitation. Seized by such an awareness, beyond the dull means of pastures old, I had to proceed towards that which, from the curves, from even our stammerings, can attempt to express what otherwise escapes fair reason. I mean that which cannot be partitioned off by fluctuating edges and escapes from the filed frame, from the established patterns. And that it was the extreme precariousness of the enterprise at which every extremity gleamed a possibility of freedom which is beyond tensions.

Here, accosted by the world, overrun on all ideas, unable to claim I observe it, which always implies perception lagging behind for excess of reference. This said to explain my attempt to raise myself to the level of the experienced without the convention of the known. And the necessity to proceed forbids recapitulation, for all that belongs to the moment is its one guarantee in the ineffable of its presence.

And to yield to one's wonderment requires a necessary precariousness. But no less precarious the continuing awakening to preserve expressive harmony. To thus proceed suits me, demanding neither courage nor special gift: that which is given to each in its emerging necessity.

Thus the arid path common to all has always given out into more distance from the mirage of proximity, for always is the shackle. But also proceeding likewise, in the grip of the ungraspable.

—Pierre Tal-Coat (1983)

Son of a Breton fisherman, Pierre Tal-Coat was largely self-taught as a painter. His first stay in Paris lasted only two years but by 1931 he was back in the French capital where he quickly became popular with liberal collectors and fellow-artists. He was figurative in his approach, and his portrait of Gertrude Stein was hailed as a fine example of his work that reflected a kind of primitive monumentality. He mixed with the avant-garde painters of his time and his experiences in the Spanish Civil War became the subject of a series "Massacres" that has been compared with Picasso's "Guernica," though Tal-Coat's treatment was more emotional and directly figurative. By about 1945 he in fact came under the influence of Picasso and then two years later André Masson introduced him to the lyrical interpretation of landscape by Chinese artists. This phase continued into the 1960's.

These landscapes represent perhaps the peak of Tal-Coat's art, for in them he aimed at a synthesis of nature that came close to a perfect analogy in its choice of motives more or less echoing reality. The pale grounds of pure tone bore patches of colour that might be held to represent clouds in the sky or boats at anchor on a sunlit bay. This Funambuliste equivocation in his compositions was invariably handled with a sensitive and delicate control of mass and spatial relationship that gave the works a great feeling of atmosphere: the transparency of air and the quivering essence of light were understated in soft-edged outlines. In other works the colours were more violently contrasted in intensity and weight with central motives taking stronger emphasis often in themes redolent of country-side. It is this lack of precision in identification of the objects suggested in his landscapes that gives Tal Coat's work its edge of interest, for though the associations are less than exact their massing and placing on the canvas have a direct and powerful dynamic operating over the surface of the canvas. By 1974 he was still capable of painting some huge monochrome pictures such as "Bleu surgi" that seemed derivative of earlier works by Yves Klein.

His later work shows a rough and vital animation of pigment, scarring its own surface in the relief contour of a lunar landscape, certainly devoid of human habitation and having in its mineral colour something hinting at volcanic origins. "Depot 2" (1974) is a painting of this geological metaphor where a dark gesture raises its facets to reflect the light in an aerial panorama shading into the void of outer space itself. In their own terms the paintings indicate their process of maturing through periods of time in which the surface is moulded, melted, suffering fission and enduring heat and eruption. Tal-Coat has described his motivation. "As though beyond me a vision, a hand has overruled my blindness, conducting me I know not where nor cannot see."

—G. S. Whittet

TAMAYO, Rufino.

Mexican. Born in Oaxaca in 1899; moved to Mexico City, 1911. Studied at the Academia de Bellas Artes, Mexico City, 1917 20. Married Olga Flores Rivas in 1934. Painter: travelled frequently from Mexico City to New York, 1926–36; lived in New York, 1936–1954, and in Paris, 1954 until his return to Mexico, 1964; donated museum for permanent display of his Mexican Pre-Columbian art collection of more than 1000 works, Oaxaca, 1974; donated his international collection of contemporary art to the Mexican People: Museo Rufino Tamayo Arte Contemporaneo International officially opened in Chapultepec Park, Mexico City, May 1981. Chairman, Department of Ethno graphic Drawing, Museo Nacional de Arqueologia, Mexico City, 1921–23. Recipient: First Prize, *Carnegie International*, Pittsburgh, 1952; First Prize for Painting, *Bienal*, Sao Paulo, 1953; Guggenheim International Foundation Award, 1960; National Award for Artistic Merit, Mexico City, 1964; Calouste Gulbenkian Prize, Institut Francais, Paris, 1969; First Prize, 10th Triennale of Colour Graphics, Gren-

chen, Switzerland, 1985. Street named in his honor, Oaxaca, 1972. Member: Argentinian Academy of Art; Accademia Disegno, Florence; Academy of Arts, Buenos Aires, 1959; American Institute and Academy of Arts and Letters, 1961. Chevalier, 1957, Officier, 1970, and Commandeur, 1975, Légion d'Honneur, France; Comendador of the Italian Republic, 1971. Agent: Marlborough Gallery, Inc., 40 West 57th Street, New York, New York 10019, U.S.A. Address: Callejon del Santisimo 12, San Angel, Mexico D.F., Mexico.

Individual Exhibitions:

1926 Weyhe Gallery, New York
1929 Palacio de Belles Arts, Mexico City
1931 Julien Levy Gallery, New York
1937 Julien Levy Gallery, New York
1938 Galeria de Arte Mexicano, Mexico City
     Catherine Kuh Gallery, Chicago
1939 Valentine Gallery, New York
1940 Valentine Gallery, New York
1942 Valentine Gallery, New York
1945 Arts Club of Chicago
1946 Valentine Gallery, New York
1947 Cincinnati Art Museum, Ohio
     Pierre Matisse Gallery, New York
1948 *Retrospective of 25 Years of Painting*, Palacio de Bellas Artes, Mexico City
1950 *16 Paintings*, at the *Biennale*, Venice
     Galerie des Beaux-Arts, Paris
     Palais des Beaux-Arts, Brussels
     Knoedler Gallery, New York
1951 Instituto de Arte Moderno, Buenos Aires
     Salon de la Plastica Mexicana, Mexico City
     Frank Peris Gallery, Los Angeles
     Knoedler Gallery, New York
1952 individual exhibition, at the *Arte Mexicain du Pre-Columbien à nos Jours*, Musée d'Art Moderne, Paris
     Fort Worth Art Museum, Texas
     Pan American Union, Washington, D.C.
1953 Knoedler Gallery, New York
     Frank Perls Gallery, Los Angeles
     Santa Barbara Museum of Art, California
     San Francisco Museum of Art
1956 Museum of Fine Arts, Houston
     Knoedler Gallery, New York
1959 Kunstnernes Hus, Oslo
     Felix Landau Gallery, Los Angeles
     Knoedler Gallery, New York
1960 Galerie de France, Paris
1961 Gallery One, London
1962 Galeria Misrachi, Mexico City
     Knoedler Gallery, New York
1963 Mainichi Newspaper, Tokyo (retrospective)
     Association of Museum of Israel (travelling exhibition)
1965 Galerie Semiha Huber, Zurich
1968 Palacio de Bellas Artes, Mexico City (retrospective of 103 works)
     Exhibition of 124 Works from American Collections, Phoenix Art Museum, Arizona
     Biennale, Venice (retrospective of 100 works)
1971 Perls Gallery, New York
1973 Galeria Misrachi, Mexico City
     Perls Gallery, New York
1974 Museo de Arte Moderno, Mexico City
     Musée d'Art Moderne, Paris
1975 Palazzo Strozzi, Florence
1976 Museo de Arte Moderno, Mexico City
     National Museum of Modern Art, Tokyo
1977 *Bienal*, Sao Paulo (retrospective of 134 paintings)
     Marlborough Galery, New York
1978 Phillips Collection, Washington, D.C.
1979 Marion Koogler McNay Art Institute, San Antonio, Texas
     Myth and Magic, Guggenheim Museum, New York
     Marlborough Fine Art, London
1981 Brenner Gallery, Boca Raton, Florida
     Marlborough Gallery, New York
1982 Marlborough Fine Art, London
1983 Graphische Sammlung Albertina, Vienna
1984 Marlborough Fine Art, Tokyo
1985 Marlborough Gallery, New York
1986 Marisa Del Re Gallery, New York

Collections:

Museo de Arte Moderno, Mexico City; Centre Georges Pompidou, Paris; Musée Royal, Brussels, Galleria Nazionale de Arte Moderna, Rome; Museum of Modern Art, Tokyo; Nasjonalgalleriet, Oslo; Museum of Modern Art, New York; Guggenheim Museum, New York; Albright-Knox Art Gallery, Buffalo, New York; Art Institute of Chicago.

Publications:

By TAMAYO: book—*Drawings by Tamayo*, Mexico City 1950.

On TAMAYO: books—*Tamayo* by Robert Goldwater, Mexico City 1947; *Rufino Tamayo* by Enrique Gual, Mexico City 1947; *Tamayo* by Paul Westheim, Mexico City 1957; *Tamayo en la Pintura Mexicana* by Octavio Paz, Mexico City 1959; *Tamayo* by Juan Garcia Ponce, Mexico City 1967; *Tamayo* by Octavio Paz, Mexico City 1967; *Rufino Tamayo* by Emily Genauer, New York 1974; *Rufino Tamayo: 50 Years of His Painting*, with an introduction by James G. Lynch, Jr., Washington, D.C. 1979; *Rufino Tamayo: Recent Paintings 1980–85*, exhibition catalogue, New York 1985; films—*Birth of a Mural*, Universidad Nacional de Mexico, 1965; *Rufino Tamayo*, BBC, London, 1966; *Tamayo*, directed by Max Pol Fouchet, Paris, 1970; *The Artistic Life of Rufino Tamayo*, directed by Gary Conklin, 1973.

Although it was not until 1972 that a street was named Calle Rufino Tamayo in Oaxaca City (his birthplace), like so many others, worldwide, I was already familiar with Tamayo works from the 1-man exhibition of his paintings mounted by Victor Musgrave at London's Gallery One (1961), the first showing of his work to reach British shores, but by no means his first personal exhibition. That had been at the Weyhe Gallery, New York, in 1926 and he had held at least 25 Tamayo exhibitions in Mexico, the United States, Paris, Brussels and Buenos Aires in that interim.

Tamayo, with some reservations, may be described as a kind of Expressionist (although probably not easily recognisable as such to those who have clear title to that description)—there is plenty of latent Thunder in some of his paintings, but on the whole expressionist Lightning stays muted by his personal colouration and the diminution of the flash. This in no way reduces hints of manic/magical violence when he decides such drama should enter his pictures. In its anti-hysterical manner this cool portrayal of vibrant passions is an inheritance (over the heads of North American and European modernisms) to the cultures and art products of the Ancient Mexicans—Aztec, Toltec, Mayan. Their quiet fierceness, and their placid monumentality as well, would seem naturally handed down to a *modern* artist familiar—as he is—with the ethnical ties of his country's *ur-alt* past. And it should be remembered that, not without good reason, Tamayo was appointed in 1921 for three years as Head of the Department of Ethnographic Drawing by the Museo Nacional de Arqueologia in Mexico City.

Along with all the contacts he had with contemporary art—his early years (1926–49) were frequently spent in New York interspersed with return visits to Mexico and during the succeeding ten years he was domiciled in Paris—and his special knowledge of the traditions of ancient Mexican art and their esoteric meanings, he was able to build up an important reputation as an exceptional artist.

Tamayo's painting is essentially constructed upon three foundations: a vagrant and beguiling figuration, sometimes departing from exact imagery, at others plotted with unerring potency that leaves no bewilderment—techniques of paintwork which include very careful preparations of surfaces from which a picture is to emerge coupled with elaborate mixing of tints, colours and numerous variations beautifully subtly wrought—both these fundamental aspects are inbued with the pervading character of mystery to be expected from one steeped in occult knowledge and feeling. As can be observed, this is not an artistic talent and its attendant attributes that can be summed up in some sort of art-critical shorthand.

Rufino Tamayo has always had a strong sense of monumentality, borne out by his close attachment (in itself a particularly Mexican enthusiasm) for the opportunities to hand for mural painting (one recalls the politico-historical huge wall paintings by Siquieros—some of which led to his imprisonment as a dissident at one stage—the equally violent enormous pictorial statements produced by the—more fortunate—Orozco, and the many, many examples in his murals output by the politically unassailable Diego Rivera) but based upon (in spirit, not in copyist content) art which proceeded from the great Mexican Empires in the years before the coming of the Europeans. Not for him the towering political propaganda wall paintings from the Mexican artists of a generation before his own, busy celebrating revolution and less or more Marxist supremacy of a new-born republic. With a long look over his shoulder, he always thought back to the wall masterpieces of Pre-Columbian days and has sought to inject into his own commissioned murals (*and* his paintings) echoes of that greatness. Amongst the many Tamayo-made monuments of this kind, his work for the UNESCO Building in Paris is particularly memorable.

It can be seen that this unique artist has many ingredients with which to attract, but it should not be overlooked that there is a certain duality in much of his work so that monumentality is never supremely overwhelming because the way these works of art are fashioned besides seeking their goal of greatness reserves a direct personal approach of equal veracity for the lone viewer, admirer and collector alike.

—Sheldon Williams

TAPIÈS, Antoni.

Spanish. Born in Barcelona, 13 December 1923. Educated at the College of the Sisters of Loreto, Barcelona, 1926–29; Escuela Alemana, Barcelona, 1928–31; Colegio Balmes, Order of Christian Schools, Barcelona, 1931, 1940; Liceo Pratico, Barcelona, 1934–36; and at the Instituto Menendez y Pelayo, Barcelona, 1939; studied law at the University of Barcelona, 1943, 1945–46; studied drawing at the Academia Valls, Barcelona, 1944. Married Teresa Barba in 1954; children: Antoni, Clara and Miguel. Concentrated on painting and established his first studio, Barcelona, 1943; as independent artist, Barcelona, since 1946; Member, "Dau al Set" group of artists and writers, Barcelona, 1948–51, and Founder, with others, *Dau al Set* review, Barcelona, 1948. Recipient: French Government Scholarship, Paris, 1950; Academia Breve prize, Madrid, 1950, 1951: Acquisition Prize, Bienal, Sao Paulo, 1953; First Prize, Salon del Jazz, Barcelona, 1954; Republic of Colombia Prize, *Bienal Hispano-Americana*, Barcelona, 1955; Premio Lissone, Milan, 1957; Unesco Prize, 1958; David Bright Foundation Prize, Los Angeles, 1958; First Prize, *Carnegie International*, Pittsburgh, 1958; Ministry of Foreign Affairs Prize. *International Biennale of Graphics*, Tokyo, 1960; Providence Art Club Prize, Rhode Island, 1963; Guggenheim Foundation Award, 1964; Grand Prix, *Biennale de Menton*, France, 1966; Gold Medal, 15th Congress of Art Critics, Historians and Artists, Rimini, Italy, 1966; Grand Prize, *7th International Biennale of Graphics*, Ljubljana, Yugoslavia, 1967; Rubens Prize, City of Siegen, West Germany, 1972; British Arts Council Prize, *German International Graphics Exhibition*, 1974; Stephan-Locher Medal, Cologne, 1974; Plastic Arts Prize, City of Barcelona, 1979; Gold Medal for Fine Arts,

Ministry of Culture, Madrid, 1981; Wolf Foundation Prize, with Marc Chagall, Israel, 1982. Honorary doctorate: Royal College of Art, London, 1981. Honorary Member, Akademie der Künste, West Berlin, 1979. Agent: Galeria Maeght, Calle Montcada 25, Barcelona-3, Spain. Address: Saragossa 57, Barcelona-6, Spain.

Individual Exhibitions:

1950	Galerias Layetanas, Barcelona
	Museo Municipal, Barcelona
1952	Galerias Layetanas, Barcelona
1953	Marshall Field Art Gallery, Chicago
	Galeria Biosca, Madrid
	Martha Jackson Gallery, New York
1954	Galerias Layetanas, Barcelona
1955	Club 49, Sala Gaspar, Barcelona
1956	*Tapies et l'Oeuvre Complete*, Galerie Stadler, Paris
	Club 49, Sala Gaspar, Barcelona
1957	Galerie Schmela, Dusseldorf
	Martha Jackson Gallery, New York
	Galerie Stadler, Paris
1958	Galleria dell'Ariete, Milan
	Spanish Pavilion, at the *Biennale,* Venice
1959	Martha Jackson Gallery, New York
	Galerie Stadler, Paris
1960	Sala Gaspar, Barcelona
	Museo de Arte, Bilbao, Spain
	Martha Jackson Gallery, New York
1961	Martha Jackson Gallery, New York
	David Anderson Gallery, New York
	Galerie Stadler, Paris
	Instituto Torcuato di Tella-Museo Nacional, Buenos Aires
	Galleri Blanche, Stockholm
	Galerie Rudolf Zwirner, Essen
1962	Kestner-Gesellschaft, hannover (retrospective)
	Guggenheim Museum, New York (retrospective)
	Kunsthaus, Zurich
	Museo Nacional de Bellas Artes, Caracas
	Galleria II Segno, Rome
	Galleri Pierre, Stockholm
1963	Pasadena Art Museum, California
	Galerie Berggruen, Paris
	Galerie Im Erker, St. Gallen, Switzerland
	International Center of Aesthetic Research, Turin
	Galleria Notizie, Turin
	Martha Jackson Gallery, New York
1964	Galleria La Tartaruga, Rome
	Galerie Rudolf Zwirner, Cologne
	Galerie Stadler, Paris
	Galleri Buren, Stockholm
	Moss Gallery, Toronto
	Galerie Agnes Lefort, Montreal
	Sala Gaspar, Barcelona
1965	Galerie Rudolf Awirner, Cologne
	Galerie Van de Loo, Munich
	Institute of Contemporary Arts, London
	Galerie Im Erker, St. Gallen, Switzerland
	Sala Gaspar, Barcelona
1966	Cercle Artistic, Manresa, Barcelona
	Galeria Biosca, Madrid
	Galerie Stadler, Paris
	Galerie Jacques Verrière, Cannes
	Galleri Buren, Stockholm
1967	Martha Jackson Gallery, New York
	Kunstmuseum, St. Gallen, Switzerland (graphics retrospective)
	Galerie Maeght, Paris
	Sala Gaspar, Barcelona
1968	Museum des 20, Jahrhunderts, Vienna (retrospective)
	Galerie Im Erker, St. Gallen, Switzerland
	Librairie-Galerie La Hune, paris
	Kunstverein, Hamburg (retrospective)
	Kunstverein, Cologne (retrospective)
	Martha Jackson Gallery, New York
	Galerie Maeght, Paris
	Galerie Schmela, Dusseldorf
1969	Galerie Maeght, Paris
	Sala Gaspar, Barcelona
	Galerie Stadler, Paris

	Tapies Room, At *Biennale of Prints*, Ljubljana, Yugoslavia
	Museum of Modern Art, Belgrade
	Kunstverein, Kassel, West German (graphics retrospective)
1970	Galleria dell'Ariete, Milan
	Galleri Blue, Stockholm
	Martha Jackson Gallery, New York
	Neue Galerie, Baden-Baden, West German
1971	Galleria San Luca, Bologna
	Galerie Hachette, London
	Galerie Maeght, Zurich
	Sala Pelaires, Palma de Mallorca, Spain
	Galleri Borjeson, Malmo, Sweden
	Sala Gaspar, Bracelona
	Galleria II Collezionista, Rome
1972	Galerie Hans Seel, Siegen, West German
	Galerie Maeght, Paris
	Museo de Mataro, Spain
1973	Galleri Borjeson, Malmo, Sweden
	Galerie Wünsche, Hamburg
	Musée d'Art Modern, paris (retrospective)
	Musee Rath, Geneva (retrospective)
	Galeria As, Barcelona
	Jodo Seully Gallery, Los Angeles
	Galeria 42, Barcelona
	Sala Gaspar, Barcelona
	Daual Set-Galeria d'Art, Barcelona (retrospective)
	Galeria Juana Mordo, Madrid (retrospective)
1974	Nationalgalerie, West Berlin (retrospective)
	Galerie Schmela, Dusseldorf
	Glynn Vivian Gallery, Swansea, Wales
	Martha Jackson Gallery, New York
	Galerie Maeght, Paris
	Hayward Gallery, London (retrospective)
	Galerie Carl Van der Voort, Ibiza, Spain
	Galeria Jaun Martin, Mexico City
	Louisiana Museum, Humlebaek, Denmark (retrospective)
1975	Galeria Maeght, Barcelona
	Galerie Jeanne Castel, Paris
	Galeria Ruiz Castillo, Madrid
	Galeria La Mulassa, Barcelona
	Galeria Juana de Aizpuru, Seville
	Sala Pelaires, Palma de Mallorca, Spain
	Galeria La Kabala, Madrid
	Galerie Maeght, Zurich
	Erker-Galerie, at *Art 6 75*, Kunstmesse, Basle
	Galeria Kreisler 2, Madrid
	Galerie Beyeler, Basle (retrospective)
	Galeria Ciento, Barcelona
	Martha Jackson Gallery, New York
	Galerie Le Scriptorium, Paris
1976	Galeria Carmen Durango, Valladolid, Spain
	Galeria d'Art 3 i 5, Gerona, Spain
	Galeria Rayuela 19, Madrid
	Galerie Maeght, Paris
	Galeria Joan Prats, Barcelona
	Edit Art, Geneva
	Fondation Maeght, St. Paul-de-Vence, France (retrospective)
	Seibu Museum of Art, Tokyo (retrospective)
	Fundacio Joan Miró, Barcelona (retrospective)
	Galeria Maeght, Barcelona
1977	Albright-Knox Art Gallery, Buffalo, New York (retrospective)
	Galeria del Banco de Granda, Spain
	Galeria Yerba, Murcia, Spain
	Museum of Contemporary Art, Chicago (retrospective)
	Biblioteca de la Caixa de Pensions, Sant Celoni, Barcelona
	Marion Koogler McNay Art Institute, San Antonio, Texas (retrospective)
	Sala Celini, Madrid
	Des Moines Art Center, Iowa (retrospective)
	Kunsthalle, Bremen, West Germany (retrospective: works on paper)
	Galeria Terra, Catellon, Spain
	Galeria Cop d'Ull, Lerida, Spain
	Musée d'Art Contemporain, Montreal (retrospective)
	Staatliche Kunsthalle, Baden-Baden, West Germany (retrospective: works on paper)

1978 Kunstmuseum, Winterthur, Switzerland (retrospective: works of paper)
Galeria Lucas, Gandia, Spain
Martha Jackson Gallery, New York
Musée Municpal de l'Abbaye Sainte-Croix, Les Sables d'Olonne, France
Galeria Juana Mordo, madrid
Centre d'Etudes Catalans, Paris
Galeria Sen, Madrid
Galeria A, Vilafranca del Penedes, Barcelona
Galerie Amstutz, Zurich
Caixa d'Estalvis Laietana, Mataro, Barcelona
Galeria Artema, Barcelona (retrospective, 1945–54)
Galeria Im Erker, St. Gallen, Switzerland
Munro Galerie, Hamburg
Galeria Isernhagen, Burgdorf, West Germany
Galeria Maeght, Barcelona
Hating Gallery-Spanish Institute, New York
1979 Galeria Torques, Santiago de Compostela, Spain
Galeria A i B, Granollers, Barcelona
Galerie Maeght, Paris
Badischer Kunstverein, Karlsruhe (retrospective)
Galeria Atelier Hilbur, Karlsruhe
Caja de Ahorros Municipal, Pamplona, Spain
Galeria Joan Prats, Barcelona
Sala Esplai, Gerona, Spain
1980 Kunsthalle, Kiel, West Germany (retrospective)
Caja Insular de Ahorros, Las Palmas, Canary Islands
Escola Taller d'Art, Reus, Tarragona, Spain
Neue Galerie am Wolfgang Gurlitt Museum, Linz, Austria (retrospective)
Galeria de la Caixa d'Estalvis, Manresa, Barcelona
Estudio Palmo, Malaga, Spain
Studio Dueci, Rome
Museo Espanol de Arte Contemporano, Madrid (retrospective)
Stdelijk Museum Amsterdam (retrospective)
Galeria Brinkman, Amsterdam
Sala d'Art La Tralla, Vich, Barcelona
Galeria Carmen Durango, Valladolid, Spain
Galeria Maeght, Zurich
1981 *Antoni Tapiès o lárt del mon no dit*, Galerie Maeght, Barcelona
Galeria Cuatro, Valencia
Galeria Punto, Valencia
Galeria Yerba, Murcia, Spain
Ueda Gallery, Tokyo
Kasamara Gallery, Osaka
Galeria Rayuela 19, Madrid
Galeria de la Mota, Madrid
Satany Gallery, Tokyo
Fondation du Chateau de Jau, France (retrospective)
M. Knoedler Gallery, New York
Stephan Wirtz Gallery, Los Angeles
Galerie Maeght, Zurich
Galeria Ponce, Mexico City
1982 Palacio do la Lonja, Saragossa, Spain (retrospective)
Galerie Art in Progress, Munich
Escola Massana, Barcelona
Galeria Art-3, Figueres, Gerona, Spain
Marisa del Re Gallery, New York
Union des Arts Plastiques, St Etienne du Rouvray, France
Galerie Maeght, Paris
Scuola Grande San Giovanni Evangelista, at the *Biennale*, Venice
Galeria Academia, Salzburg
1983 Stadtische Galerie im Prinz-Max-Palais, Karlsruhe, West Germany
Galeria Maeght Lelong, Paris
1984 Galerie Maeght Lelong, Zurich
Fundacio Joan Miro, Barcelona
Galeria Maeght, Barcelona
1985 Musee d'Art Moderne, Brussels
Galleria Gabriele Mazzotta, Milan
1986 Kunstlerhaus, Vienna
Van Abbemuseum, Eindhoven, Netherland
Galeria Theo, Madrid
Galerie Maeght Lelong, New York
1987 Galeria Maeght, Barcelona
1988 Annely Juda Fine Art, London

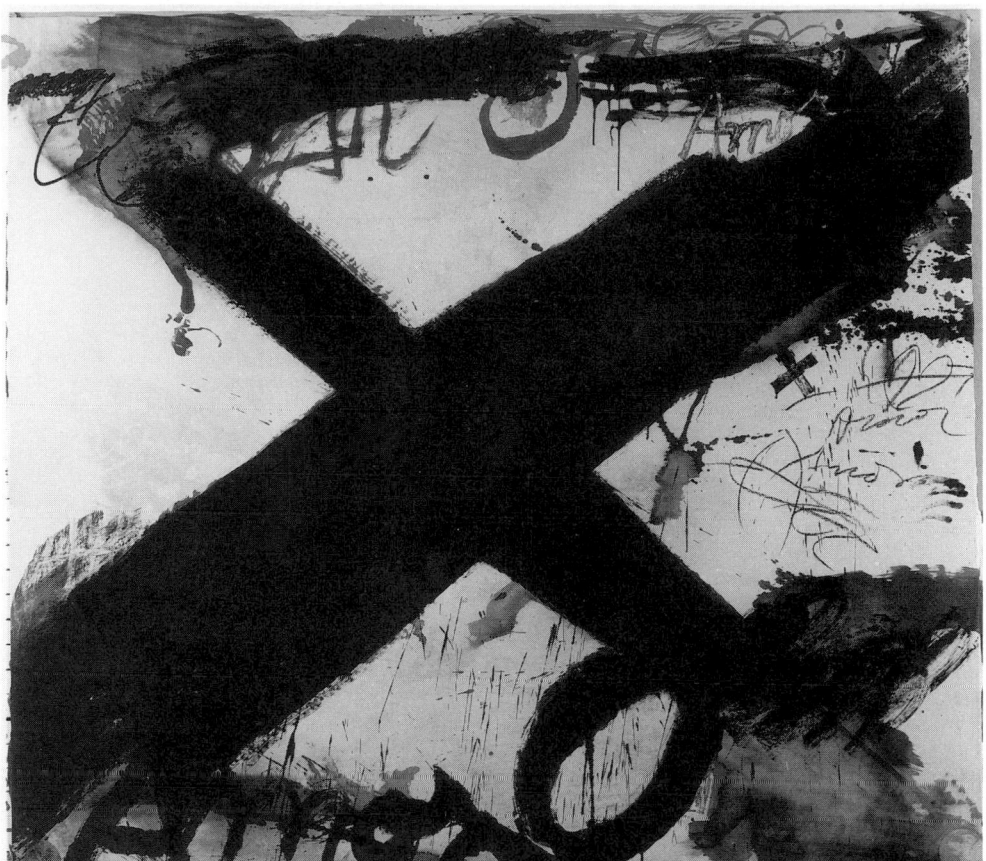

Antoni Tapiès: *Gran X con Grafismo*, 1979

Selected Group Exhibitions;

1948 *1st Salon de Octubre*, Barcelona
1949 *Un Aspecto de la Pintura Catalana*, Instituto Frances, Barcelona
1950 *Carnegie International*, Pittsburgh
1951 *Dau al Set*, Sala Caralt, Barcelona
1952 *Biennale*, Venice
1953 *Bienal*, Sao Paulo
1960 *Before Picasso, after Miró*, Guggenheim Museum, New York
1964 *Documenta*, Kassel, West German
1978 *Foire Internationald'Art Contemporain/FIAC*, Paris
1985 *Painterly Visions 1940–84*, Guggenheim Museum, New York

Collections

Museo Espanol de Arte contemporaneo, Madrid; Museo de Arte Moderno, Barcelona; Centre Georges Pompidou, Paris; Tate Gallery, London; Nationalgalerie, West Berlin; Stedelijk Museum, Amsterdam; Kunsthaus, Zurich; National Gallery of Victoria, Melbourne; Musée d'Art Contemporain, Montreal; Museum of Modern Art, New York.

Publications:

By TAPIÈS: books—*El pa a la Braca*, with poems by J. Brossa, Barcelona 1963; *Album Saint-Gallen*, with J. Brossa, Barcelona 1965; *Novella*, with J. Brossa, Barcelona 1965; *La Nuit Grandissante*, with text by Jacques Duplin, Paris 1967, *Fregoli*, with J. Brossa, Barcelona 1969; *Nocturn Matinal*, with J. Brossa, Barcelona 1970; *Air*, with text by André du Bouchet, Paris 1970; *La Practica de l'Art*, Barcelona 1970; *La Clau del Foc*, with text by Gimferrer, Barcelona 1973; *Suite Catalana: Poems from de Catalan*, with poems by J. Brossa, introductory text by Arthur Terry and Roland Penrose, Barcelona 1973l *Cartes per a la Teresa*, Barcelona 1974; *L'Art contre L'Estetica*, Barcelona 1974; *Llamberec Material*, with poems by Takiguchi, Paris 1975; *Ca suit son cours*, with poems by Jean Daive, Paris 1975; *Oda a Xirinachs*, with poems by J. Brossa, Barcelona 1975; *Dialogo sobre arte, cultura y sociedad*, with Imma Julian, Barcelona 1977; *Memorial Personal*, autobiography, Barce-

lona 1978; *Retorno de lo vivo lejano*, with poems by Rafael Alberti, Madrid 1978; *Sinnieren über Schmutz*, with text by Alexander Mitscherlich, St. Gallen, Switzerland 1978; *U no es ningu*, with poems by Jorge Guillen, Valladolid, Spain 1980; *Conversaciones con Tapies*, with Miguel Fernandez-Brasso, Madrid 1981.

On TAPIÈS: books—*Antoni Tapiès* by Enric Jardi, Barcelona 1950. *Antoni Tapiès o el Dau Modern de Versailles* by Joan Josep Tharrass, Barcelona 1950; *Tapiès et l'Oeuvre Complete* exhibition catalogue, with text by Michel Tapie, Paris 1956; *Antoni Tapiès* by Michel Tapie, Barcelona 1959; *Tapiès* by Juan Eduardo Cirlot, Barcelona 1960; *Antonio Tapiès*, exhibition catalogue, with text by Lawrence Alloway, New York 1962; *Significacion de la Pintura de Tapiès*, Barcelona 1962; *Tapiès* by Blai Bonet, Barcelona 1964; *Antoni Tapiès: Fustas, papers, cartons i collages* by Joan Teixidor, Barcelona 1964; *Tapiès* by Joan Brossa and Francesco Vicens, Barcelona 1967; *Antoni Tapiès*, with texts by Guisepppe Gatt, Guilio Carlo Argan, Renato Barilli and others, Bologna 1967; *Grandi Monografie Pittorie Scultori d Oggi: Antoni Tapiès* by Michel Tapie, Milan 1969, *Tapiès: Testimino del silenci* by Alexandre Circi, Barcelona 1970; *Tapiès*, exhibition catalogue, with texts by Nello Ponenete and Guiseppe Gatt, Rome 1971; *Antoni Tapiès* by Vera Linhartova, Stuttgart and Barcelona 1972; *Tapiès: Obra Grafica 1947–1972* by Carl Vogel, Barcelona 1973; *Antoni Tapiès: Zeichen und Strukturen* by Werner Schmalerbach, West Berlin 1974; *Antoni Tapiès* 1975; *Antoni Tapiès*, exhibition catalogue, with text by Tomas Llorens, Barcelona 1976; *Tapiès: Meditaciones 1976* by José Medina, Madrid 1976; *Tapiès* by Georges Raillard, Paris 1976; *Tapiès* by Roland Penrose, Barcelona 1977; *Antoni Tapiès: Kunstlerische Herkunft und Entwicklung* by Andreas Franzke, Stuttgart 1979; *Antoni Tapiès*, exhibition catalogue, with texts by Lluis Permanyer and Jose Maria Valverde, Madrid 1980; *Antoni Tapiès o l'Art del mon no dit*, exhibition catalogue, with text by Alexander Circi, Barcelona 1981; *Tapiès* by Carmine Beninasa, Rome 1982; *Antoni Tapiès: Dipinti, Sculpture, Opere su Carta, Grafiche*, exhibition catalogue with text by Guido Ballo, Milan 1985; *Tapiès*, exhibition catalogue with text by Francesc Farreras, Barcelona 1987.

When silence manifests itself in quiet waves of meditative hues crisscrossed with deeply etched scarifica tions, its evocation can be spellbinding. But when energy and matter brood in contained dynamic markings spread over contemplative fields of subdued color that expand into new forms, the experience is often overwhelming. Antoni Tapiès, whose aesthetic is deeply rooted in the "matter painting" idiom of Europe's "art informel," uses silence as a symbol—a key to a private mythology in which raw materials (earth, sand, X-ray film, labels, rags, and paint in various degrees of thickness and consistency) transcend their physicality to become mute metaphors of a world in which existential passions have given way to the serenity of resignation and acquiescence. In the limelight since the early 1950's, Tapiès is one of a number of post World War II European artists who, in their attempt at breaking through the constraints of cubism and geometric abstraction, came out with revolutionary seminal styles that roughly paralleled the development of Abstract Expressionism in the United States. Although he grew up in a time of political ferment, when much of Western art focused on rebellion, struggle, and isolation, and although he was, in politics, a liberal, his forms were never totally circumscribed by radical dictates. For him, for instance, geometry was never the anathema that it was for many of his contemporaries. In fact, an intuitive, spontaneous approach tempered through geometric organization is the one factor that served as a distinguishing mark of his early works—a mark which, over the years, proved to be the fundamental variable that spurred a pattern of growth and gradual change without compromise to the integrity of his forms. Thus, what in the 50's were crude expressions of the artist's fascination with the effect of timeworn surface texturized by several generations of the clandestine graffiti of Catalonian walls, was tranformed, in the 1960's and 70's, into poetically charged statements about cosmic intelligence and the unification of all matter into infinity. And, when such words as "essence," "purity," and "reduction" were, once again, part and parcel of the artistic vocabulary of the Western world, Tapiès was able to make the transition—to accommodate his vision to the new order while, at the same time, gaining a new stature.

. . . Everything joined together in a uniform mass. What was ardent ebullition was transformed into static silence. It was a great lesson in humility received by the haughtiness of violent passion. And one day I tried to arrive directly at silence with more resignation, giving into the fatality that governs all profound struggle. The millions of furious stabs were transformed into millions of grains of dust, of sand . . . suddenly before me a new landscape was opened, the same as the one in the story about crossing through the mirror, as if to communicate to me the most secret interior parts of all things . . .

These words, written by Antoni Tapiès, summarize the metamorphosis—describe what he calls his "qualitative jump." Underlining a lifetime of sustained creativity, they explain the poetry, the profundity of his vision, as the paintings resonate over two continents with a sense of total resolution—a feeling of attainment and completion.

—Andrée Maréchal-Workman

TATAFIORE, Ernesto.

Italian. Born in Marigliano, near Naples, in 1943. Educated at Giambattista Vico High School, Naples, 1956–60; mainly self-taught in art. Married Simonetta; son: Marco. Painter: lives and works in Naples, Address: Piazza Medaglie d'Oro 51, 80129 Naples, Italy.

Individual Exhibitions:

1969	Galleria Lucio Amelio, Naples
1970	Galleria Lucio Amelio, Naples
1972	Galerie Stampa, Basle
1973	Galleria La Salita, Rome
1974	Galleria Lucio Amelio, Naples
	Studio Carla Ortelli, Milan
1975	Galleria Lucio Amelio, Naples
	Galleria Lucio Amelio, at *Expo Arte Fiera*, Bari, Italy
1976	Galleria La Salita, Rome
1977	Galleria Lucio Amelio, Naples
1978	Galerie Stampa, Basle
	Galleria Lucio Amelio, Naples
	Galerie Paul Maenz, Cologne
1979	Studio Memini, Naples
	Arte 10 79, Kunstmesse, Basle
	Galerie Stampa, Basle
	Galleria Fabjbasaglia, Bologna
1980	Galerie Stampa, Basle
	Galerie 't Venster, Rotterdam
	Incontri 1980, Spoleto, Italy
	Kunsthalle, Basle
	Biennale, Venice
	Museum Folkwang, Essen
	Stedelijk Museum, Amsterdam
1981	Annina Nosei Gallery, New York
	Lisson Gallery, London
	Galleria Lucio Amelio, Naples
1982	Galerie Jossevel, Zurich
	Galleria Lucio Amelio, Naples
	Istituto Italiano di Cultura, Madrid
	Galeria Ehrhardt, Madrid
	Aetatis Suae, Kunstmuseum, Lucerne
1983	Andre Emmerich Gallery, New York
	Gimpel-Hanover/Andre Emmerich Galeries, Zurich
1984	Galleria Lucio Amelio, Naples
1985	Il Ponte Editrice d'Arte, Rome
	Mezzanine Gallery, New York
	Metropolitan Museum of Art, New York

Seclected Group Exhibitions:

1966	*Quadriennale d'Arte*, Palazzo dell'Exposizione, Rome
1967	*Arte Grafica Oggi*, Palazzo Reale, Naples
1970	*Italy II: Art Aournd 70*, Philadelphia Museum of Art
1973	*Biennale*, Paris
1978	*Der Kulturelle Unterschied*, Stuttgart
1979	*Arte Cifra*, Galerie Paul Maenz, Cologne
1980	*Kunstforum*, Städtische Galerie im Lenbachhaus, Munich
1981	*Linee della Ricerca Artistica in Italia 1960–1980*, Palazzo delle Esposizioni, Rome
1983	*Tema Celeste*, Museo di Gibellina, Sicily
1984	*Painting and Sculpture Today*, Indianapolis Museum of Art, Indiana

Publications:

On TATAFIORE: books—*Arte Cifra*, exhibition catalogue, with an introduction by Wolfgang Max Faust, Cologne 1979; *7 Junge Künstler aus Italien*, exhibition catalogue, with text by Zdenek Felix, Essen 1980; *Ernesto Tatafiore: Aetatis Suae*, exhibition catalogue, with texts by Marlis Gruterich, Michael Newman and Harald Szeeman, and an interview by Martin Kunz, Lucerne 1982; *Ernesto Tatafiore: New Work*, exhibition catalogue, with text by Martin Kunz, New York 1983; *Ernesto Tatafiore*, exhibition catalogue with introduction by Ronny Cohen, New York 1985.

I was born at Marigliano, near Naples, my mother's name was Ida and my father's Enrico.
When I was a child I played with the sea, the sand and the stones then I enjoyed painting "from life" beside my father.
When I was about ten years old my mother took my sister Maria Antonietta and me to see Rome and Florence, Giotto's tall bell-tower, thousands and thousands of steps.
Classical high school at the «Giambattista Vico».
Literature, poets, philosophy and then politics, strikes.
Medicine and art as mystery and discovery.
Meeting Simonetta and the journeys in Africa: Morocco, Tunisia, Algeria, then Turkey and Istanbul, London and Paris.
Marco is born.
Psychoanalysis tripping up the system of logic.
Painting as a game without end or purpose.

—Ernesto Tatafiore

Ernesto Tatafiore prepares free associations between selected episodes, episodes that revolve round the themes of the French Revolution and the *Titanic* disaster. Using these as an interpretative grid and as a track on which a journey is still only partly and temporarily completed, Tatafiore makes psychological use of pretexts borrowed from the reservoir of history; the mind is left free to float up and down within the area affected by the subject, an area chosen as a limiting field of associative-metaphorical forces which of course can be aroused in confrontation with the pretext.

Robespierre, Marie Antionette, Louis XVI, Charlotte Corday, Marat, the *Titanic*—all take on an emblematic quality. Robespierre presides over a dinner of dead men; the *Titanic* becomes the hopeless shipwreck following the "crisis" of scientific "presumption" (ships built with watertight compartments do sink; the iceberg does remain in its rough shape with its tip above the surface; the absence of lifeboats is further evidence of lack of precaution). The event is still, as ever, in the hands of fate, and history as such continues in its meretricious oscillation of permanent instability: illusion and madness.

The features of the cherubic faces of the actors in the scene that Tatafiore depicts hide the images of the guillotine. The venom is concealed by the grace and sensuality of the drawing; it is deliberately given to fragile, delicate figures and to such symbols as caresses; the saliva passed from mouth to mouth with a kiss starts up deadly mechanisms; the poison may even have a taste of honey. The solidity of the outlines of the historical figures evoked is turned back into a cloud of memory, and history is focussed on events that can be selected at will and used on associationistically. The correspondence between "sign-picture" and "truth of the conclusion" is then played upon by the view in his own way; only he can read the word of history as an individual story as he sees it himself. Vision will condition choice.

—Demetrio Paparoni

TÉLÉMAQUE, Hervé.

Haitian. Born in Port-au-Prince, 5 November 1937. Studied art, under Julien Levy, at the Art Students League, New York, 1957–60. Painter and graphic artist, Paris, 1961–81; in Villejuif, France, since 1982. Recipient: Ingram Merrill grant, 1972; Art Grant, Regie Renault, Paris, 1980. Agents: Gianni Schubert, Galleria Arte Borgogna, Via Borgogna 7, 20121 Milan, Italy; G. de Muga, Galeria Joan Prats, Rambla de Catalunya 54, Barcelona 7, Spain. Address: 52 Avenue de Paris (10–12 impasse Ernest Renan), 94800 Villejuif, France.

Individual Exhibitions:

1964	Galerie Mathias Fels, Paris
	Hanover Gallery, London (with Gessler)
1965	Galleria L'Attico, Rome
1966	Galleria Il Punto, Turin
1967	Galerie Mathias Fels, Paris
	Studio Marconi, Milan
1968	Galleria del Minotaura, Brescia, Italy
	Galleria de'Foscherari, Bologna
1969	Galerie Brusberg, Hannover
	Ulmer Museum, Ulm, West Germany
1970	Galerie Mathias Fels, Paris

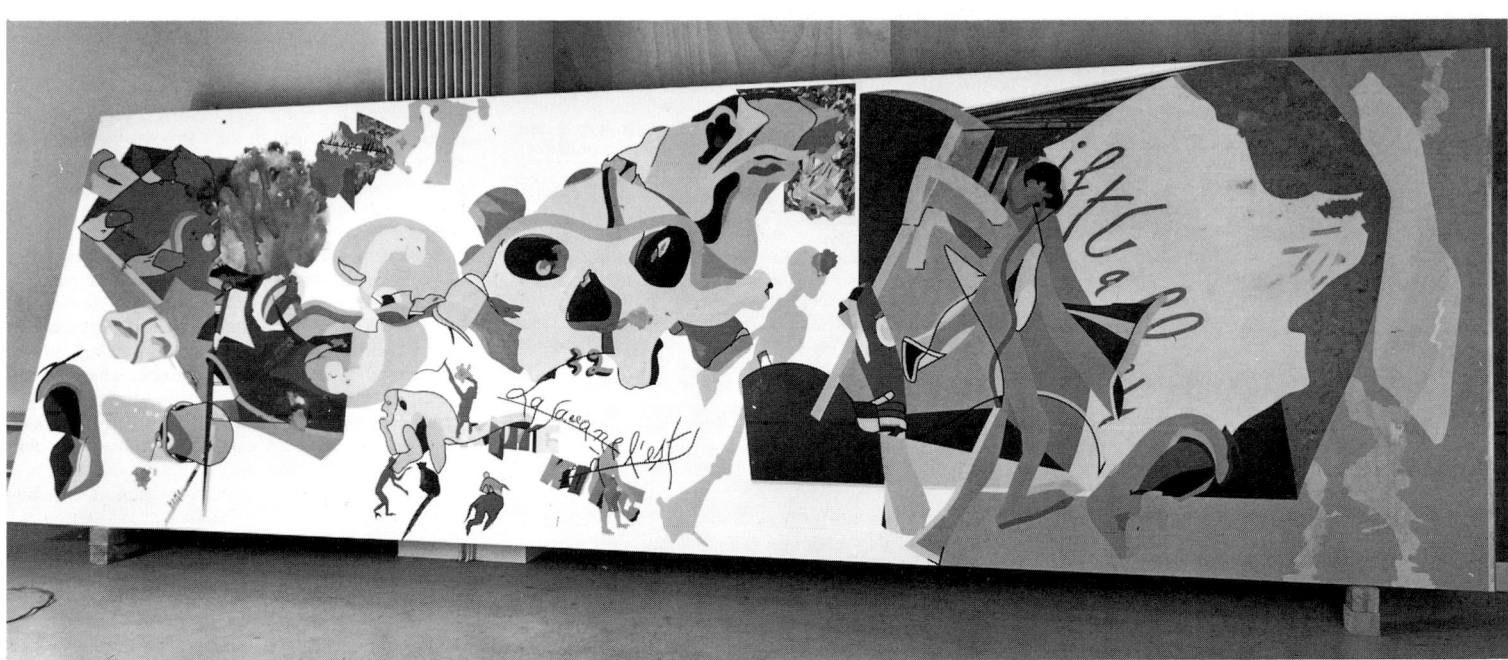

Hervé Télémaque: *Vallie de l'Ohio*, 1986

Selected Group Exhibitions:

Collections:

Fond National d'Art Contemporain, Paris; Bibliothèque Nationale, Paris; Musée d'Art Moderne de la Ville, Paris; Goteborgs Kunstmuseum, Gothenburg, Sweden; Moderna Museet, Stockholm; Hunterian Museum and Art Gallery, Glasgow; Musée d'Art Haitien, Port-au-Prince; Casa de las Americas, Havana; Museo de Bellas Artes, Caracas; University of California, Berkeley.

Publications:

On TÉLÉMAQUE: books-*Télémaque-Geissler,* exhibition catalogue, with text by John Ashbery, London 1964; *Hervé Télémaque,* exhibition catalogue, with text by Albert Boatto and José Pierre, Rome 1965; *L'Avant-Garde Internationale de Paris* by Alain Jouffroy and others, Cologne 1966; *Hervé Télémaque,* exhibition catalogue, with texts by Christopher Finch and José Pierre, Paris 1967; *Pop Art* by Lucy R. Lippard, New York 1968; *Télémaque,* exhibition catalogue, with text by Jean-Patrice Marandel, Paris 1970; *Reperes: La Peinture en France debut et fin d'un systeme visuel 1870–1970* by Dora Vallier, Paris 1976; *Depuis 1945* by Gerald Gassiot-Talabot and others, vol. 2, Brussels 1971; *Le Surréalisme* by José Pierre, Lausanne 1971, Paris 1972; *Art en France; Une nouvelle generation* by Jean Clair, Paris 1972; *Hervé Télémaque,* exhibition catalogue, with text by Gerald Gassiot-Talabot, Milan 1973; *L'Art Actuel* by Anne Tronche, Paris 1973; *Le Pop Art* by José Pierre, Paris 1975; *Hervé Télémaque,* exhibition catalogue, with text by Bernard Noel, Paris 1976; *Dictionnaire Universel de la Peinture* by R. Mayard, vol. 4, Paris 1976; *Télémaque,* exhibition catalogue, with a preface by Carlos Franqui, Barcelona 1977; *Figures d l'Art Contemporain* by M. Le Bot, Paris 1977; *Hervé Télémaque,* exhibition catalogue, with texts by Bernard Noel and Catherine Thieck, Paris 1981.

*

An artist is not a machine producing and immediately recuperating fine feelings. I accept objects as they are—they make up a kind of landscape of our life in the midst of a consumer society. It is interesting to see how these objects speak to us at the unconscious level. This is the reason why I have called upon familiar everyday objects—a walking stick (difficulty of locomotion)—a corset (the idea of desire)—a whistle (a scream).

My purpose is not to blame the consumer society— this invasion certainly causes me a great deal of anguish, but a certain history of human activity is contained in it. I think that the unconscious can begin to function using this collection of forms as a starting point. But it was an easy temptation to represent the objects. It is a question of relating this object to others by allusion, by a suppression of the pictorial illusion.

In the past the spectator plunged into the spatial illusion of the painting. Van Gogh's chair is very close to us. Today it is better to keep to a minimum any illusion, any manipulation of fictional space, any balancing of all these objects towards the spectator. I want to be concrete.

—Hervé Télémaque

Hervé Télémaque's work is a constant interrogation of the world of man-made objects that surround him, and he seems constantly to be asking himself about the way these objects correspond to his own intimate needs. Do they or don't they, and to what degree, and to precisely what kind of need? He looks at a shoe or a saddle or a house and asks himself how he feels about it, he asks himself how he feels about the very idea of a shoe or a saddle or a house, he asks himself how he feels about depicting the idea of a shoe or a saddle or a house. He is not a social critic since he is gifted or burdened with a penchant for a kind of emotional skepticism that goes much farther than that. He asks himself not why these things exist in society, but rather why they exist in his universe. He seems not quite sure that he should have any need of needs at all.

Télémaque works as much with collages of cutouts of colored paper as he does with paint and brush, and when he does work with paint and brush the result can easily look like collages of cut-out paper. His earlier work often created a whole community of images where real objects (ropes, or a cane or a shopping net stuffed with a ball of newspaper) existed on an entirely equal footing with painted representations of other objects (a weight, a tent, a cup of coffee, a facade). His forms are always flat and very simple, geometrically clear but never harsh: there are curves in his collages and painted images that are difficult to imagine as belonging originally to their subjects. His colors are always uniform, muted, and highly saturated with grey, even though the range of his palette runs all the way from one end of the spectrum to the other. The world, as Télémaque wants to show it to us, is a little less real, a little less up front, than we ordinarily imagine it to be, and as it recedes a step or so away from us, there is a little more room in which to think about it. Télémaque is also an excellent draughtsman, and in some of the works he has been doing since 1978, collage versions of a subject are juxtaposed to drawings of precisely the same view, but with the difference that what reads from right to left in the drawing will read from left to right in the collage; and when the subject permits (which is to say with subjects that have no clear right-side-up and upside-down) the axis of symmetry, rather than horizontal, is vertical. These drawings are in fact the transparent stencils on the basis of which the collage cut-outs were made, and the works of which they form a 'second' part can also be completed by still a third panel in which some of the individual collage elements that go to form the image (or scraps that fell away from the forming of the image) are presented as though free-floating and out of context. Télémaque shows us various stages in giving concreteness to an image as though to imply that the real world of humanly made objects is itself but another stage in the very same process.

—Henry Martin

THEK, Paul.

American. Born in Brooklyn, New York, 2 November 1933. Studied at Cooper Union, New York; Art Students League, New York; and Pratt Institute, New York, 1951–54. Lived in Florida, 1955–57, and Italy, 1957–62; lived in New York, 1962–68, then returned to Europe; designed sets and costumes for *Arena*, ballet, Nederlands Dance Theatre, 1969; sets for Louis Falco Dance Company, New York, 1978. Recipient: Fulbright Fellowship, 1967; National Endowment for the Arts Award, 1977. Agents: Galerie M. E. Thelen, Cologne, West Germany; and Iolas-Jackson Gallery, New York. Address: 58 East Third Street, New York, New York 10003, U.S.A.

Individual Exhibitions:

1957	Mirrell Gallery, Miami
1963	Galleria 88, Rome
1964	Stable Gallery, New York
1966	Pace Gallery, New York
1968	Institute of Contemporary Arts, London
	Galerie M. E. Thelen, Cologne
1969	Stable Gallery, New York
	Stedelijk Museum, Amsterdam
	Moderna Museet, Stockholm
1972	Moderna Museet, Stockholm
1973	Kunstmuseum, Lucerne
	Galerie Stahli, Lucerne
	Wilhelm Luhmbruck Museum, Duisburg, West Germany
1975	Alexandre Iolas Gallery, New York
1976	Galerie Alexandre Iolas, Paris
1977	Il Fante di Spade, Rome
	Iolas-Jackson Gallery, New York
1980	Iolas-Jackson Gallery, New York
1981	Iolas-Jackson Gallery, New York

Selected Group Exhibitions:

1967	*Carnegie International*, Carnegie Institute, Pittsburgh
1968	*The Obsessive Image*, Institute of Contemporary Arts, London
	Documenta, Kassel, West Germany
1969	*Kunst der Sechziger Jahre*, Wallraf-Richartz Museum, Cologne
1972	*Documenta*, Kassel, West Germany
1976	*Biennale*, Venice
1977	*Processions*, Institute of Contemporary Art, University of Pennsylvania
1980	*Biennale*, Venice

Collections:

Stedelijk Museum, Amsterdam; Moderna Museet, Stockholm; Centre National d'Art Contemporain, Paris; Wallraf-Richartz Museum, Cologne; Smithsonian Institution, Washington, D.C.

Publications:

By THEK: book—*A Document Made by Paul Thek and Edwin Klein*, Amsterdam and Stockholm 1969; articles—"An Interview with Paul Thek," with G. R. Swenson, in *Artnews* (New York), April 1966; "Paul Thek: Entretien avec Harald Szeeman" in *Chroniques de l'Art Vivant* (Paris), April 1974.

On THEK: articles—"The New School of New York" by Lil Picard in *Das Kunstwerk* (Baden-Baden, West Germany) December 1964; "Beneath the Skin" by G. R. Swenson in *Artnews* (New York), April 1966; "In the Galleries: Paul Thek" by William Berkson in *Arts Magazine* (New York), June 1966; "In the Galleries: Paul Thek" by Mary Stewart in *Arts Magazine* (New York), November 1967; "Paul Thek: Love-Death" by William Wilson in *Art and Artists* (London), April 1968; "Before Nature Disappears, Let Us Return" by B. Sydgoff in *Domus* (Milan), March 1972; "Individuelle Mythologien" by B. Catoir in *Das Kunstwerk* (Baden-Baden, West Germany), March 1974; review by Elizabeth Frank in *Art in America* (New York), Summer 1981.

*

Paul Thek's works from 1964 to 1967 consisted mainly of wax facsimiles of raw, fleshy meat incased in plexiglass boxes which became more and more elegant and ornamental. These chunks of tormented fleshiness in their pristine enclosures, which look very like the artifacts we see in museums of natural history, are provocative symbols for humanity's entrapment in technologically caused boxes, sealed off artificially from the life of the spirit. Thek's "Meat Piece with Warhol Brillo Box" (1965) suggests his opinion that Pop Art, among other things, had done nothing to change or help alleviate this human condition.

In his 1967 environmental sculpture titled "The Tomb—Death of a Hippie", Thek further developed his allegorical and ritualistic intentions involving themes of survival in the secularized world of life and art. Placed within a hazy atmosphere of rosy light and incense is a large three-tiered ziggurat which houses the artist's tomb, complete with realistically detailed wax-cast effigy of Thek accompanied by the accoutrements of his past life and symbolic objects of use for his future life. Among the many things surrounding the artist's wax duplicate are the fingers missing from it, severed parts being one of Thek's recurrent images suggestive of the individual's frustrations at feeling fragmented both physically and spiritually. Accompanying "The Tomb" are a series of "offerings," boxes containing arms, hands, legs and artificial limbs and supports, all altered to evoke various states of mutilation or decay. After this surreal, fetishistic use of self in portrayal of the artist/individual's feelings of separateness from the world at large, Thek left New York for Europe in 1968.

Since then he has continually traveled throughout Europe together with a small group of collaborators, creating a series of complex, transitory environments with multifarious elements including ordinary objects and also paintings and sculptures of his own in various states of transformation and overlap. With his characteristic flair for irreverent reverence, Thek calls these works 'Processions,' a title which acts both as an allusion to the spiritualizing nature of the pieces and as a reference to process art.

Thek's major work of the next decade is this unfolding series of "Processions," loaded with signs and symbols from various historical periods of high and low culture which are combined, re-used, altered to convey mythic and religious levels. As the works move from place to place, presented when possible in correspondence with religious holidays, objects from Thek's own past work and elsewhere re-enter along with things accumulated along the "processional" route. A partial listing of the elements included in "Pyramid/A Work In Progress" (1971–72) amply communicates the extremely fetishistic complexity of Thek's works. In this work were parts from Thek's "The Artist's Co-op" (1969) such as the Coop, the worktable-bridge which carried Thek's "Fishman" (1968) and "The Tomb" (1967), the crates in which these works had been shipped, a fishing boat, old bathtubs, park benches, a piano, tissues, paint, drawings, letters, seashells, and many more. Moving

through such a fantastic conglomerate of stuff, the viewer is stimulated to see these things as out-of-the-ordinary, strange indications of the mystical life-quality each component seems to possess. Thek is not nihilistic in his cryptic and theatrical narratives. His continual commitment to the "Processions" is linked to his desire to convey a spiritual life by making the ordinary and his own past work as well vehicles to insert the mystical element back into our secularized society.

It is this positive spirit, accompanied by a touch of humor, which also informs Thek's small paintings such as "Periscope" and "Hot Potatoes" (both 1979–80), which seem, at least in part, a hommage to Philip Guston's moving late pictures. Thek has received most of his attention in Europe, where he continues to spend most of his time perhaps largely because he feels the need to be "in the regions", away from the New York art world and closer to the older mystical history of Europe.

—Barbara Cavaliere

THIEBAUD, Wayne.

Born in Mesa, Arizona, 15 November 1920. Educated in California public schools; studied at San Jose State College, California, and Sacramento State College, California, B.A. 1951, M.A. 1952. Served in the United States Air Force, at Mather Army Air Field, Sacramento, and in Culver City, California, 1942–45. Married Patricia Patterson in 1943 (divorced, 1959); daughters: Twinka and Mallary Ann; married Betty Jean Carr in 1959; sons: Paul Le Baron and (adopted) Matthew Bult Carr. Painter, in Sacramento, California, from 1950, and in San Francisco from 1972: worked as sign painter, cartoonist, commercial artist, illustrator, designer and advertising art director, 1938–49; Design and Art Consultant, *California State Fair*, 1950–57; designed sets for music festivals, Sacramento City schools, 1953–55; producer of educational films, Patrician Films, Hollywood, 1954–59; co-founder, Artists' Cooperative Gallery (now Artists Contemporary Gallery), Sacramento, 1958. Instructor in Art, 1951–59, and Chairman of the Department of Art, 1954–57, Sacramento City College; Assistant Professor, 1960–63, Associate Professor, 1963–67, and Professor since 1967, University of California, Davis; Visiting Professor at numerous colleges and universities in the United States, since 1967. National Juror, National Endowment for the Arts, Washington, D.C., 1972. Recipient: Golden Reel, *American Film Festival*, Chicago, 1956; First Prize, *Art Film Festival*, at the California State Fair, 1956; Columbia Records Award, 1959; Creative Research Foundation Grant, 1961; Scholastic Art Award, for film, *Space and Design*, 1961; Creative Research Grant, 1964, Golden Apple Award, 1972, and Faculty Research Lecture Medal, 1984, University of California, Davis; Distinguished Studio Teacher Award, College Art Association of America, 1981; Award of Distinction, National Art Schools Association, 1984; Special Citation, National Association of Schools of Art and Design, 1984; Cyril Magnin Award, San Francisco Chamber of Commerce, 1987. Honorary Doctorate: California College of Arts and Crafts, Oakland, 1972; Dickinson College, Carlisle, Pennsylvania, 1983. Member, American Academy and Institute of Arts and Letters, 1985; Associate, 1986, and Academician, 1987, National Academy of Design, New York. Agent: Allan Stone Gallery, 48 East 86th Street, New York, New York 10028. Address: c/o Paul Thiebaud, 1617 Seventh Avenue, Sacramento, California 95818, U.S.A.

Individual Exhibitions:

1951	Crocker Art Gallery, Sacramento, California
1957	Artists Co-Op Gallery, Sacramento, California

Selected Group Exhibitions:

Collections:

Museum of Modern Art, New York; Metropolitan Museum of Art, New York; Whitney Museum, New York; Albright-Knox Art Gallery, Buffalo, New York; Wadsworth Atheneum, Hartford, Connecticut; Philadelphia Museum of Art; Hirshhorn Museum, Washington, D.C.; Art Institute of Chicago; Museum of Fine Arts, Salt Lake City; San Francisco Museum of Modern Art.

Publications:

By THIEBAUD: book—America Rediscovered, 1963.

On THIEBAUD: books—Documenta 5, exhibition catalogue, Kassel, 1972; 25 Years of American Painting 1948-73, exhibition catalogue, by Max Kozloff, Des Moines, Iowa 1973; Separate Realities: Developments in California Representational Painting and Sculpture, exhibition catalogue, by Laurence Dreiband, Los Angeles 1973; Wayne Thiebaud, exhibition catalogue with essay by Karen Tsujimoto, San Francisco and Seattle 1985; articles—"Slice of Cake School" in Time (New York), May 1962; review by Thomas B. Hess in Artnews (New York), May 1962; "Something's Cooking" in Life (New York), June 1962; article in Life (New York), September 1963; article in Time (New York), April 1963; "Eros in the Cafeteria" by Diane Waldman in Artnews (New York), March 1966.

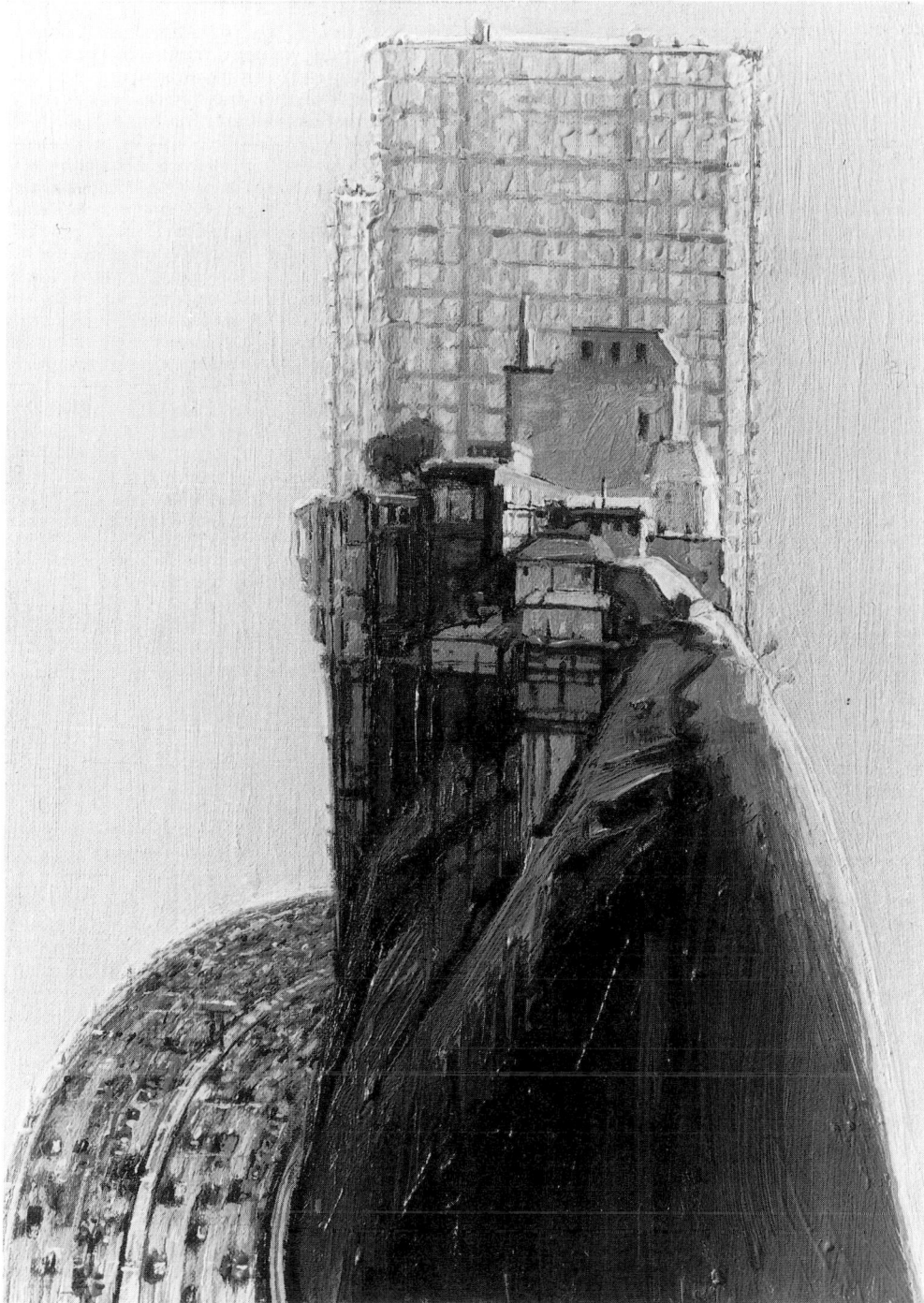

Wayne Thiebaud: *Study for Apartment Hill*, 1980

When Wayne Thiebaud showed his urban landscapes for the first time at the San Francisco Museum of Modern Art in 1978, the question of an essentialization ultimately leading to non-objectivity came to mind. Viewed in the context of both the prevalent trends in California art and the artist's candid acknowledgement of the influence of Richard Diebenkorn's landscapes of the 1960's, the cubes, the columns, the simplified architectonic compositions, the flat crosses, the patterns carried out in rhythmic repetitions of color seemed prophetic of a direction toward absolute abstraction. But Thiebaud's strong realist orientation proved too emphatic an impulse, and it is now obvious that the simplified forms were not indicative of a reductive sensibility, but instruments of exploration into the realist idiom. "Reduction in a realist painting is the same as reducing a sauce," he explains. "You take away by simplification, by leaving out details. But you also put in selective bits of other experiences, or perceptual nuances which enforce it, giving it more of a multi-dimension than if it were done directly as a visual recording."

Thiebaud emerged on the New York art scene in the early 60's, when the Pop movement was beginning to be recognized as the new acceptable form of American art. He did not participate in the movement, but, because of his predilection for mundane subject matter (pinball machines, dimestore lipsticks, bakery and delicatessen foodstuff), he has, at times, been identified as a Pop artist. The association was fortuitous, however, for Thiebaud's choice of imagery was then, as it is today, predicated upon formal concerns rather than identification with specific objects. An avowed realist whose roots are steeped in tradition, he is best characterized as heir to such masters as Vermeer, Chardin, and Thomas Eakins for whom the creation of a painting involved hours of scrutinizing an object in order to arrive at stylistic individualization. "For me, realist painting is an alive confrontation," he says. "If you stare at an object, as you do when you paint, there is no point at which you can stop learning things about it. You can just look and look, and, if you really are a realist painter, you finally realize that what you are doing is a tremendous amount of adoption, adaptation, and change."

"Adopting, adapting, and changing"—his subjects according to the tenets of 20th Century modernism—is precisely what Thiebaud has been doing for almost 30 years. With the sure eye of a modernist, he has transformed cakes into circles, still-lifes and figures into arrangements of spheres, triangles, and cylinders with the same alacrity that he is, today, translating street panoramas into compositions in which arcs, cubes, and complex networks of diagonal and rectangular lines play a sophisticated game of dialectic between geometry and realism.

With the urban landscapes, however, Wayne Thiebaud has reached a new zenith. In many respects, they build on earlier Thiebaud forms and concepts, but they also bring to his vocabulary a new dramatic dimension—a feeling of pressure, a compaction, of vertigo that affect the framework of his pictorial space. In this sense, they come to the forefront of his oeuvre, and represent the upmost in the resolution of that special tension between modernism and tradition that has been his trademark since the very beginning of his career.

The retrospective that premiered at the San Francisco Museum of Modern Art in September 1985 confirmed Thiebaud's unflagging commitment to a modern traditionalist aesthetic. When asked to explain what motivated such new "dark paintings" as *Black Shoes* and *Dark Lipstick,* (1983), he replied that they were prompted by "looking at dark paintings done by a great many artists." Rembrandt, Goya, Whistler, Balthus were among those from whom he sought counsel, and if the results prove that the lessons were well learned, they also unveil an energized pictorial repertoire—reinforcing Thiebaud's often acknowledged opinion that art can never be re-invented, only refreshed through constant practise and experimentation.

Sometimes the experimentation is of a technical nature, such as the manipulation of acrylic and oil paints to create new surface characters and formulations. "If you wash into oil," he explains, "the surface of the paint is being dissolved all the time. On the other hand, the acrylic dries and creates those terrific washes which you can rework with oil, and then use the underpainting combined with oil paint later on." Such manipulations strengthened the artist's landscape idiom by changing what he feels were "pictorially dominant" compositions into visual reconstructions of such forces of nature as feelings of light, texture, rutting—thus adding structural factors to the framework of Thiebaud's dramatic vocabulary.

But the significance of the retrospective overrides considerations of style and content. A California painter of major standing, Thiebaud has been channeled into as many movements, modes, and characterizations as there are essays written about his work by critics and art historians. Pop Art, New Realism, American Realism have been cited as peer groups, and a rich, complex interpretative menu of his aesthetic has been offerred as possible identifications of his oeuvre. What the perspective of some 23 years suggested, however, is a novel interpretation which, based upon the artist's repeatedly stated views of his forms, brings into focus the theme of *abstraction* as the one consistent thread that unifies, and thus gives identity, to the entire body of his work. To be sure, it is evident that realism is a dominant element; but the picture that emerged out of the Retrospective is one in which the term "realism" is translated into "abstraction": Abstraction as reduction or essentialization; abstraction as an alteration of reality; abstraction as a conceptualized force of realism; abstraction as one source of illusionism. In short, "abstraction" in all but the non-objective sense of the word.

—Andree Marechal-Workman

TILLERS, Imants.

Australian. Born in Sydney, New South Wales, in August 1950. Studied architecture, Sydney University, 1969–72. Married Jennifer Slayter in 1972; son: Isidore. Independent painter, Sydney, since 1973. Recipient: University Architecture Medal, Sydney University, 1973. Agents: Bess Cutler Gallery, 164 Mercer Street, New York, New York 10012; Yuill/Crowley Gallery, 270 Devonshire Street, Surry Hills 2010, Sydney, New South Wales. Address: 66 Raglan Street, Sydney, New South Wales 2088, Australia.

Individual Exhibitions:

1983	Yuill/Crowley Gallery, Sydney
	Matt's Gallery, London
1984	Yuill/Crowley Gallery, Sydney
	Bess Cutler Gallery, New York
1985	Yuill/Crowley Gallery, Sydney
	Bess Cutler Gallery, New York
1986	Yuill/Crowley Gallery, Sydney
	Australian Pavilion, *Biennale,* Venice
1987	Queensland Art Gallery, Brisbane
	Australian Centre for Contemporary Art, Melbourne
	Art Gallery of South Australia, Adelaide
	Reed College, Portland, Oregon
	Bess Cutler Gallery, New York
	Galerie Susan Wyss, Zurich
	Yuill/Crowley Gallery, Sydney
1988	Institute of Contemporary Arts, London
	Bess Cutler Gallery, New York
	Yuill/Crowley Gallery, Sydney
	National Gallery of Victoria, Melbourne
	Wellington Art Gallery, New Zealand

Selected Group Exhibitions:

1982	*Documenta 7,* Museum Fridericianum, Kassel, West Germany
1984	*An Australian Accent,* Project Studio One, New York (travelled to Washington, D.C.; Perth; Sydney)
1985	*Two Words Collide,* Artspace, Sydney
1986	*Contemporary Issues III,* Trenton State College, New Jersey
1987	*Avant Garde in the Eighties,* Los Angeles County Museum of Art
1988	*Contemporary Australian Painting,* Auckland City Art Gallery, New Zealand (travelled to Wellington)

Collections:

Australian National Gallery, Canberra; Art Gallery of New South Wales, Sydney; Art Gallery of South Australia, Adelaide; Art Gallery of Western Australia, Perth; Queensland Art Gallery, South Brisbane; National Gallery of Victoria, Melbourne.

Imants Tillers: *Opus Pataphysicum,* 1986

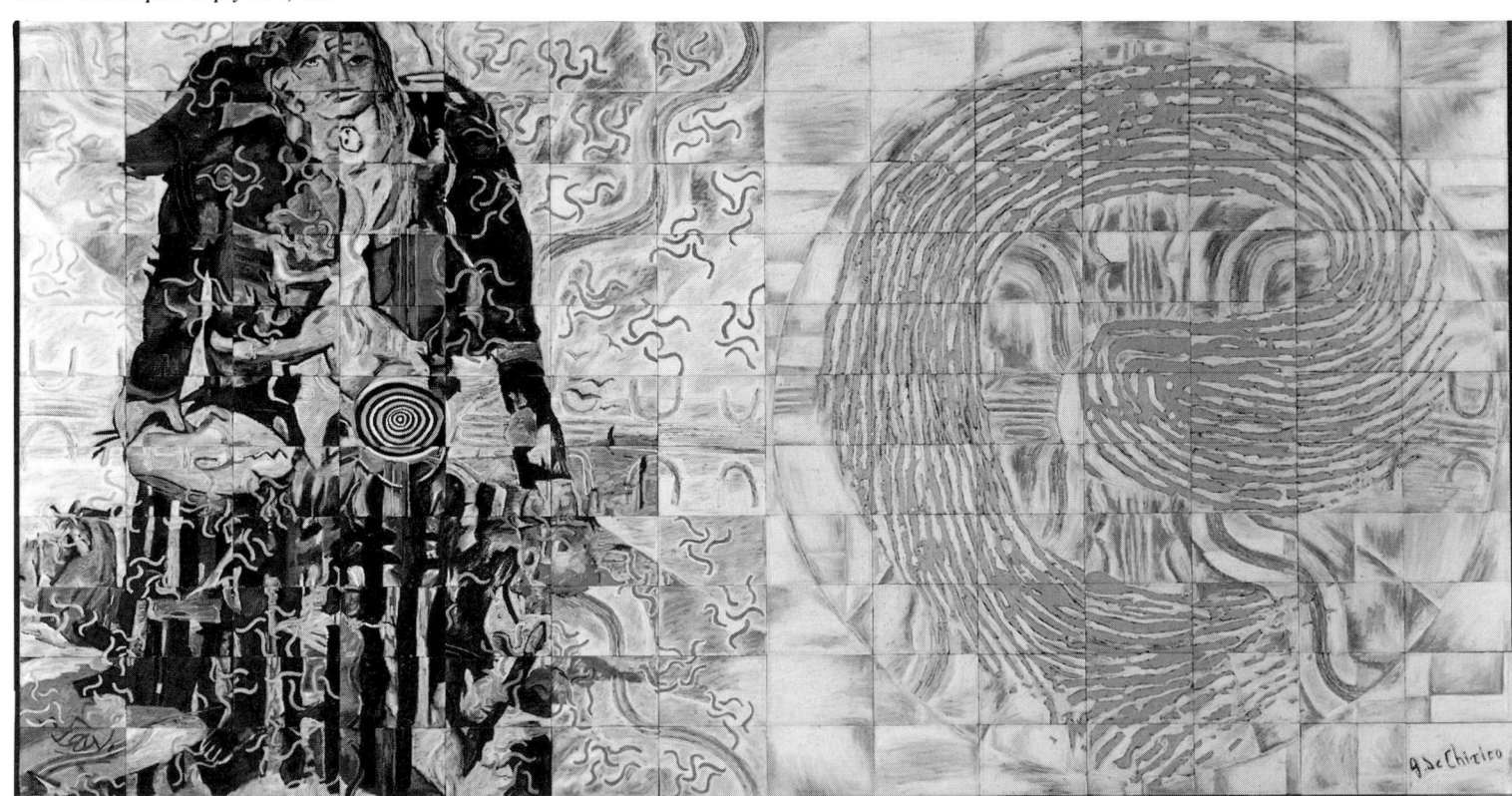

Publications:

On TILLERS: books—*Imants Tillers: White Aborigines*, exhibition catalogue with text by Paul Taylor, London 1983; *Imants Tillers: Venice Biennale 1986, Australia*, exhibition catalogue edited by Kerry Crowley, Sydney 1986; *Australian Appropriations: Recent Paintings of Imants Tillers*, exhibition catalogue with essay by John S. Wber, Portland 1987; *State of Art: Ideas and Images in the 1980s* by Sandy Nairne, London 1987; *Imants Tillers*, exhibition catalogue with text by Stuart Morgan, London 1988.

TILLIM, Sidney.

American. Born in Brooklyn, New York, 16 June 1925. Studied at the College of Fine Arts, Syracuse University, New York, 1946–50, B.F.A. 1950. Served in Engineer Corps, United States Army, 1943–46. Married Muriel Sharon in 1956. Independent artist since 1950, known for historical, narrative paintings, and, more recently, abstract works: lives and works in New York. Contributing Editor, *Arts Magazine*, New York, 1959–65; Contributing Editor, *Artforum*, New York, 1965–69. Instructor, Parsons School of Design, New York, 1961–63; Instructor, Pratt Institute, Brooklyn, New York, 1964–68. Instructor, Bennington College, Vermont, since 1966. Recipient: Yaddo Fellowship, Saratoga Springs, New York, 1963; National Endowment for the Arts Grant, 1975; Painting Grant, Ingram-Merrill Foundation, 1976. Address: 17 Bleecker Street, New York, New York 10012, U.S.A.

Individual Exhibitions:

1960	Cober Gallery, New York
1965	Robert Schoelkopf Gallery, New York
1967	Robert Schoelkopf Gallery, New York
1969	Georgia State College, Atlanta
	Noah Goldowsky Gallery, New York
1970	Benson Gallery, Bridgehampton, New York
1973	Edmonton Art Gallery, Alberta
1974	Noah Goldowsky Gallery, New York
1976	Edmonton Art Gallery, Alberta
1977	Tibor de Nagy Gallery, New York
1979	Meredith Long Gallery, New York
1986	Bennington College, Vermont

Selected Group Exhibitions:

1964	*Contemporary Realism in Figure and Landscape*, Wadsworth Atheneum, Hartford, Connecticut
1966	*Recent Still Life*, Museum of Art, Rhode Island School of Design, Providence
1968	*Realism Now*, Vassar College, Poughkeepsie, New York
1970	*Aspects of a New Realism*, Milwaukee Art Center
1972	*Whitney Annual*, Whitney Museum, New York
1975	*Modern Views of George Washington*, New Jersey State Museum, Trenton
1980	*Realism and Metaphor*, University of South Florida, Tampa
1981	*Contemporary American Realism since 1961*, Pennsylvania Academy of Design, Philadelphia
1984	*American Still Life 1945–83*, Contemporary Arts Museum, Houton
1986	*Artists Choose Artists*, CDS Gallery, New York

Collections:

Dana Art Center, Colgate University, Hamilton, New York; New Jersey State Museum, Trenton; Hirshhorn Museum, Washington, D.C.; City Art Museum, St. Louis; Weatherspoon Art Gallery, University of North Carolina, Greensboro; University of New Hampshire; Edmonton Art Gallery, Alberta; Alten Kurhaus, Aachen, West Germany.

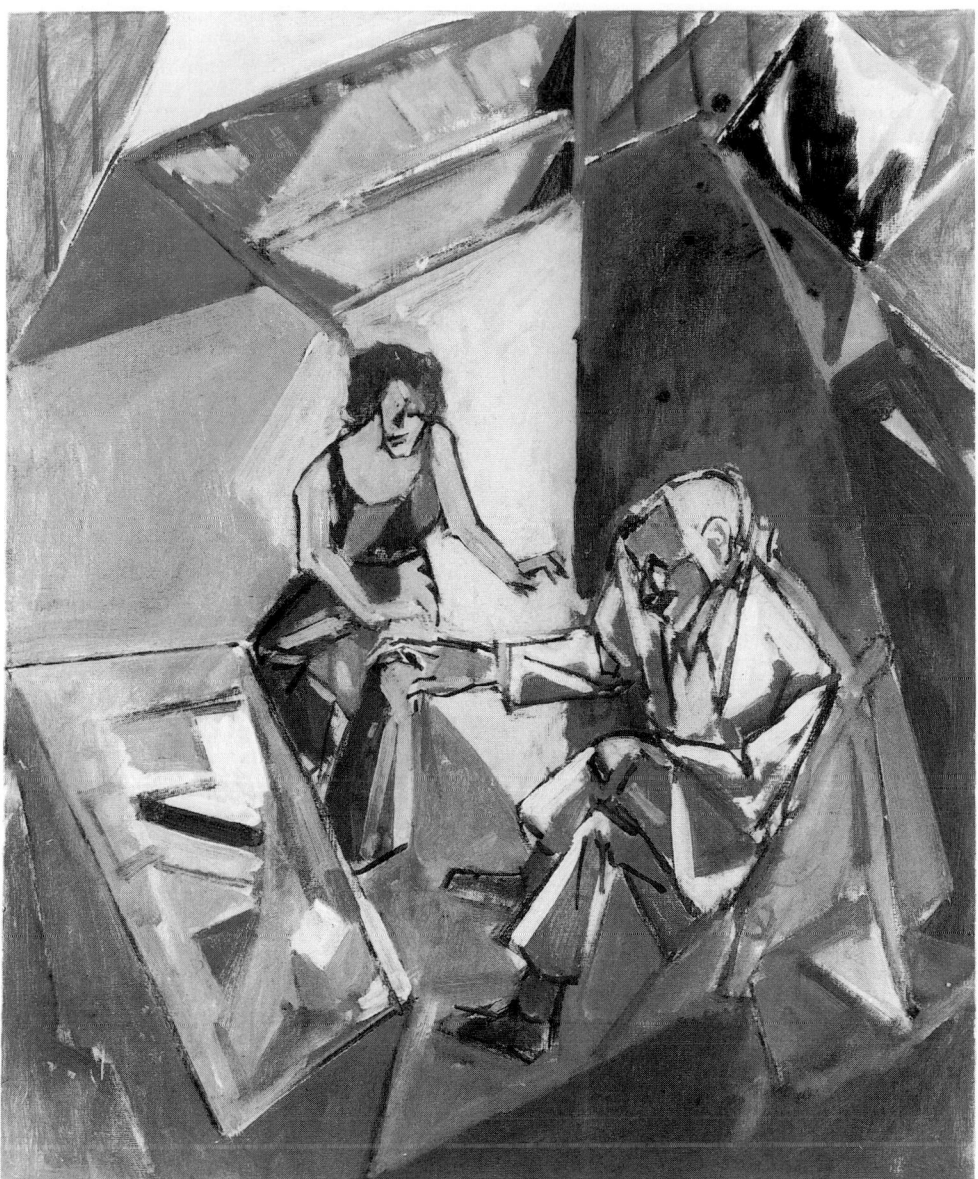

Sidney Tillim: *Reassurance*, 1979

Publications:

By TILLIM: book—*Richard Lindner*, Chicago 1960; articles—"Notes on Narrative and History Painting" in *Sidney Tillim*, exhibition catalogue, Hamilton, New York 1973, revised version in *Artforum* (New York), May 1977; "The Ideal and the Literal Sublime" in *Artforum* (New York), May 1976; "Benjamin Reconsidered: The Work of Art After the Age of Mechanical Reproduction" in *Artforum* (New York), May 1983; "The Modest Greatness of Julio Gonzalez" in *Art in America* (New York), October 1983; "The View from Past 50" in *Artforum* (New York), May 1984; "Abstraction Revisited" in *Art in America* (New York), April 1986; "Criticism and Culture, or Greenberg's Doubt" in *Art in America* (New York), May 1987.

On TILLIM: books—*Neue Formen des Realismus* by Peter Sager, Cologne 1973; *Sidney Tillim*, exhibition catalogue, by Terry Fenton, Edmonton, Alberta 1973; *Artists Choose Artists*, exhibition catalogue with essay by Max Kozloff, New York 1986; articles—review by Donald Judd in *Arts Magazine* (New York), November 1960; review by Dennis Adrian in *Artforum* (New York), September 1967; "Unconventional Realists" by Gabriel Laderman in *Artforum* (New York), November 1967; "22 Realists at the Whitney Museum" by Douglas Davis in *Newsweek* (New York), February 1970; "Neuer Realismus" in *Der Spiegel* (Hamburg), August 1970; review by Jed Perl and Deborah Rosenthal in *Arts Magazine* (New York), January 1980; review by Gerrit Henry in *Art in America* (New York), January 1980; "The Representational Impulse" by Jed Perl in *The New Criterion* (New York), April 1985.

*

Between 1958 and 1978 I painted in a representational and ultimately narrative style. In 1979 my work became more expressionist and semi-abstract. And in 1980 it became entirely abstract. In short, I resumed the modernist style I had abandoned in 1957. There were no profoundly ideological reasons for making this change. Perhaps I had begun to feel too ideologically constrained by the ambitious history paintings I had been painting since the mid-60's. In any event, assumptions about the demise of modernism, and by extension abstract art, are now virtually commonplace, so that any abstract art has a certain ideological function imposed on it. For me, resuming an abstract style marks some sort of *return*, and in this sense I have not abandoned the nostalgic impulses that informed that aspect of my representational work that was dominated, perhaps even distorted, by ideological demands. I feel my nostalgia—which I do not feel *as* nostalgia—is more organic now and is thus a more complete embrace of art and tradition. I never consciously attempted to create something new, just something that was my own. For artists like myself, the search for a style is largely a search for something upon which to build. "We are all going to heaven," said Gainsborough on his deathbed, "and Van Dyke is of that company." On the other hand, as Marie Bashkirtseff noted in her journal, "What I require is all the recognition that has been denied me since the beginning of time."

—Sidney Tillim

After abandoning his beginnings as a geometric abstract painter more than 15 years ago, Sidney Tillim proceeded to develop a kind of stylized representationalism. In his still-lifes of the 1960's, Tillim painted random arrangements in close-up, cropped compositions which reveal connections with the photographic as antecedent. Like Lowell Nesbitt, Tillim opted for firm, unbroken contours and cooly descriptive surfaces. Next came a range of figure pictures dealing with the artist's childhood and family life. In "A Dream of Being" (1968-69), crisp, simplified, caricaturized figures are arranged in a highly formalized composition, caught in a moment of frozen activity which suggests a modern-day allegorical theme about the passage of time and life. Next, Tillim began making paintings of more generally historical themes, his subjects including the early history of the United States, the Jews and the Bible. He underwent a campaign to help revive the genre of epic history painting and became known as a "social historian" during the 1970's. Often compared with Puvis de Chavannes and Nicolas Poussin, Tillim rejected modernist canons of picture making, emphasizing communication of the narrative by negating the painterly handwriting of the expressionist artist. He created complex compositions filled with arrested action aimed at heightening the drama of an often violent moment from past history of historic myth. Of his intentions in such pictures Tillim has noted, "History painting gambles more recklessly than most on the problem of converting tastes to its own point of view." His choices of particular themes were, according to his own statements, predicated on their relevance for the present moment, and it is this symbolic and psychological connection which he wants to convey without using methods of contemporary art. Considering this desire for subjects analogous with the present, it is not surprising to find Tillim also painting themes taken from the movies and from media accounts of current events.

What is surprising is Tillim's switch in 1978-79 from anti-modernist representation to a more abstracted stylization which resembles Cubism and Vorticism. In this new work, Tillim continues to deal with social themes, now depicting them in an angular, jagged planar structuring with openly agitated brushstrokes. It is a turnaround which seems well suited for subjects such as "The Capture of Patti Hearst," "An American Tragedy" (Norman Mailer's knife attack on his wife at a party), and "Murder Hollywood Style" (scene from the movie *The Big Sleep*). In many of the pictures from this group, the vantage point is downward on an angle to view a series of overlapping triangular planes. The sharpness and frenetic energy of the rather summary stylization works well to enhance the frenetic emotiveness of the subject matter, and Tillim's confrontation with modernism in such a personal form has brought with it a rewarding effectiveness.

Among the qualities which persist throughout Tillim's development are stylization for dramatic effect and satirical edge. In these and other ways, Tillim can be compared with the American magic and Social Realists who developed during the 1930's and 1940's. Tillim's earlier works resemble the figural stylizations of George Tooker or Peter Cadmus, and it is not unenlightening to see his newer pictures in comparison with a painter such as Ben Shahn, or even with the painter of an earlier "American Tragedy," Phillip Evergood.

—Barbara Cavaliere

TILSON, Joe.
British. Born in London, 24 August 1928. Studied, with Frank Auerbach and Leon Kossoff, St. Martin's School of Art, London, 1949-52; also studied at the Royal College of Art, London, 1952-55, A.R.C.A. 1955. Served in the Royal Air Force, 1946-49. Married Joslyn Morton in 1956; children: Jake, Anna and Sophy. Worked as carpenter and joiner, London, 1944-46. Independent artist: in Italy and Spain, 1955-57; in London, 1958-72; and in Christian Malford, Wiltshire, and Italy, since 1972. Instructor, St. Martin's School of Art, London, 1958-63; Visiting Lecturer, University of Durham, Newcastle upon Tyne, 1962-63; Instructor, School of Visual Arts, New York, 1966; Visiting Lecturer, Staatliche Hochschule für Bildende Künste, Hamburg, 1971-72. Recipient: Knapping Foundation Prize, London, 1955; Rome Prize, 1955; Painting Prize, *John Moores Exhibition*, Liverpool, 1957, 1967; Painting Prize, *Gulbenkian Foundation Exhibition*, London, 1960; Gold Medal, *Biennale*, San Marino, 1963; Print Prize, *Exposition Internationale de Gravure*, Ljubljana, 1965, 1967, 1975, 1977, 1979, 1983; Grand Prize, *Graphics Biennale*, Krakow, 1974; First Prize, Bradford Print Biennale, 1984; Grand Prix d'Honneur, *16th Biennale de la Gravure*, Liubliana, 1985. Agent: Waddington Galleries, 11 Cork Street, London W1 XPD. Address: The Old Rectory, Christian Malford, Wiltshire SN15 4BW, England.

Individual Exhibitions:

1962	Marlborough New London Gallery
1963	Hatton Gallery, Newcastle upon Tyne
	Ferens Art Gallery, Hull
	Walker Art Gallery, Liverpool
	University of Nottingham
1964	Marlborough New London Gallery
1966	Marlborough Graphics, New York
	Marlborough New London Gallery
1967	Galleria del Naviglio, Milan
	Galleria del Deposito, Genoa
	Galleria Fiori, Montecatini, Italy
	Marlborough-Gerson Gallery, New York
	Galleria Marlborough, Rome
1968	Galleria Ferrari, Verona
	Galleria de'Foscherari, Bologna
	Galerie Brusberg, Hannover
1970	Marlborough New London Gallery
	Hausam Waldsee, West Berlin (with Gerd Winner)
1971	CAYC: Centro de Arte y Comunicacion, Buenos Aires
	Waddington Galleries, London
1972	Abrams Gallery, Amsterdam (with Juan Genoves)
	Galerie René Block, West Berlin
1973	Museum Boymans-van Beuningen, Rotterdam (retrospective)
1974	Musée Royal des Beaux-Arts, Antwerp
	Galerie von Loeper, Hamburg
	University of Parma, Italy (retrospective)
1975	Studio Marconi, Milan
	Galleria Marlborough, Rome
	Galleria del Cavallino, Venice
1976	Galerie Espace, Amsterdam
	Galleria Il Chiodo, Mantua, Italy
	Galleria Il Tritone, Biella, Italy
	Marlborough Fine Art, London
	Galerija Krzysztofory, Cracow, Poland
	Galleria Corsini, Intra, Italy
1977	Galleria Rizzardi, Milan
	Galleria La Chiocciola, Padua
	Galleria A, Parma, Italy
1978	Waddington-Tooth Galleries, London
	Tate Gallery, London
	Peterloo Gallery, Manchester
	Galleria Giuli, Lecco, Italy
1979	Waddington Galleries, London
	Van Straaten Gallery, Chicago
	Clark Gallery, Boston
	Aronson Gallery, Atlanta
	Edward Tohta Gallery, London
	Graphics, Vancouver Art Gallery (graphics retrospective)
1980	Galerie Espace, Amsterdam
	De Vries ond Roeloff, Rotterdam
	Erica Williams-Ann Johnson Gallery, Seattle
	Horwitch Gallery, Scottsdale, Arizona
	Galleri 22, Aarhus, Denmark
	Gumps Gallery, San Francisco
	Hokin Gallery, Miami
1981	Fitterman Gallery, Minneapolis
	Meridan House, Washington, D.C.
	University of Maryland, College Park
	Schneebach Gallery, Cincinnati, Ohio
	Galerie Mira Godard, Toronto (travelled to Mira Godard Gallery, Calgary)
	Galleria Il Chiodo, Mantua, Italy
	Galleria Il Sole, Bolzano, Italy
1982	Galleria Meta, Florence
	Galleria Adelfi, Padua
	University of Pittsburgh
	Joseph Wolpe Gallery, Cape Town
	Natalie Knight Gallery, Johannesburg
	Galerie Kammer, Hamburg
1983	Galleria d'Arte, Volterra, Italy
	Thorden Wetterling Gallery, Goteborg, Sweden
	Galleria Dabbeni, Lugano, Switzerland
	Galleria Menghelli, Florence
	Galleria Rotta, Genoa, Italy
1984	Galleria Nazzari, Parma, Italy
	Arnolfini Gallery, Bristol, Avon
1985	Galleria del Cavallino, Venice
1987	Art Museum of Liubliana, Yugoslavia (retrospective)
	Thorden Gallery, Goteborg, Sweden

Selected Group Exhibitions:

1961	*Biennale*, Paris
1964	*Biennale*, Venice
1965	*Op and Pop*, Moderna Museet, Stockholm
1969	*Pop Art*, Hayward Gallery, London
1976	*Pop Art in England*, Kunstverein, Hamburg
1979	*Photography in Printmaking*, Victoria and Albert Museum, London
1981	*Landscape*, Tate Gallery, London
1983	*Pintura Britanica Contemporanea*, Museo Municipal, Madrid
1985	*Modern Artists' Books*, Victoria and Albert Museum, London
1987	*Pop Art USA/UK*, Metropolitan Museum, Tokyo (travelled to Osaka, Funabashi and Yokohama)

Collections:

Tate Gallery, London: Victoria and Albert Museum, London; Stedelijk Museum, Amsterdam; Museum Boymans-van Beuningen, Rotterdam; Musée Royal des Beaux-Arts, Antwerp; Kunstmuseum, Hannover; Galleria Nazionale d'Art Moderna, Rome; National Gallery of South Africa, Johannesburg; National Gallery of Australia, Canberra; Museum of Modern Art, New York.

Publications:

By TILSON: books—*A-Z Box, Fragments of an Oneiric Alphabet*, London 1970; *Alchera . . . notes for Country Works*, London 1976; *Alchera: 1970-76*, Pollenza, Italy 1977; *Wessex*, Pollenza, Italy 1977; *Alchera—Joe Tilson*, exhibition catalogue, London 1978; *Joe Tilson: Proscinemi, Oracles*, exhibition catalogue, London 1978; *Hesiod's Crown*, London 1984; *Joe Tilson: Festivals*, London 1987.

On TILSON: books—*Collage* by Harriet Janis and Rudi Blesh, New York 1962; *Contemporary = British Art* by Herbert Read, London 1964; *The Painter and the Photograph: From Delacroix to Warhol* by Van Deren Coke, Alburquerque, New Mexico 1964, 1972; *Pop as Art* by Mario Amaya, London 1965; *Pop Art* by Lawrence Alloway and Lucy Lippard, London 1966; *Pop Art Redefined* by John Russell and Suzi Gablik, London 1969; *Pop Art* by Michael Compton, London, New York, Sydney and Toronto 1970; *Tilson—Winner*, exhibition catalogue, with text by Thomas Kempas, West Berlin 1970; *Eroticism in Contemporary Art* by Volker Kahmen, London 1970; *The Moderns* by Terry Measham, London 1976; *Pop Art in England*, exhibition catalogue, with text by Uwe M. Schneede, Hamburg 1976; *Arte Inglese Oggi 1960-1976*, exhibition catalogue, by Norbert Lynton, 2 vols., London and Milan 1976; *Tilson* by Arturo C. Quintavalle, with a preface by Pierre Restany, Milan 1977; *Understanding Prints* by Pat Gilmour, London 1979; *Photography in Printmaking* by Charles Newton, London 1979; *Joe Tilson: Graphics*, exhibition catalogue, with text by Pat Gilmour, Vancouver 1979; *Maestri Contemporanei: Tilson* by Gillo Dorfles and Michael Compton, Milan 1982.

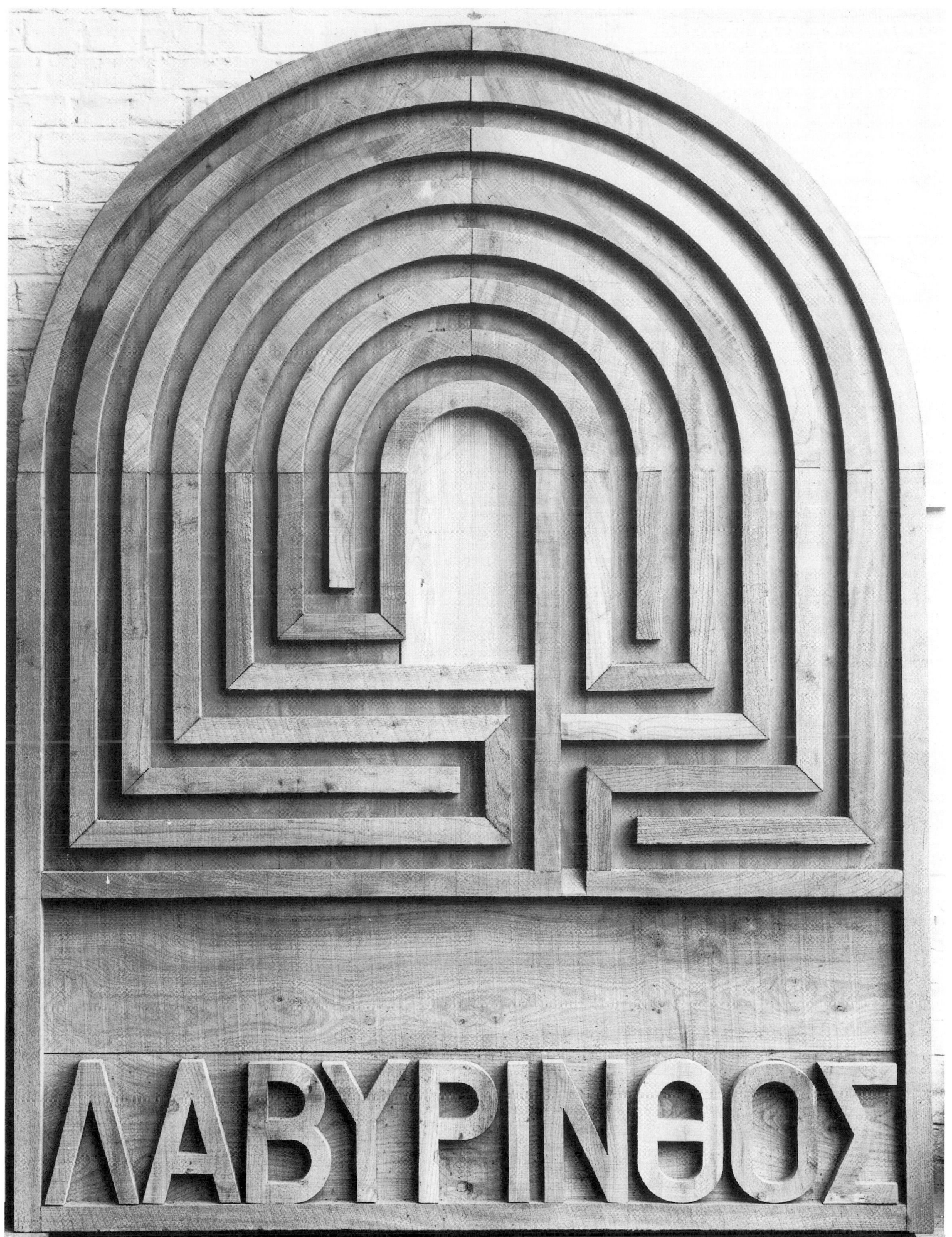

Joe Tilson: *Trojan Door*, 1974

Joe Tilson is a rare example, among British artists, of a multi-media creator, not tied to technique or material, yet always able to stamp the mark of his personality and inventive constructivist manner on all his work.

In general terms it is probably easiest to label him a Pop-artist, since it is clear that what motivates his creative juices is the stimulation of every-day, urban, industrial society. On the other hand, he could be labelled a "land-scapist," with the proviso that what arrests his attention and inspires his art is the landscape of the modern city and its decorative addenda. In essence this is a non-analytical or non-critical stance; Tilson does not judge modern society and the physical or moral forms of life it produces. He is a traditionalist in the sense that the English landscape poets or painters looked at nature, analyzed its forms, produced and perfected the means of producing images based on this phenomena, and thereby expressed their relationship with nature. There was no question of "criticising" nature, since it is a non-criticisable force. Modern industrial society is, however, open to criticism or disapproval, but it is also there to be observed, to be analysed formally, to be used as the basis of design and art.

Pop-artists are not critics or philosophers; they are poets. Tilson, in fact, can be compared with the Italian Metaphysical painters, with de Chirico in particular, sharing their detachment from the symbols they chose in order to express a state of mind or spirit. Thus when Tilson builds a column of wooden blocks, whose four sides all bear the word "Yes," he is both creating a plastic form, a sculpture, and also a combination of fact and abstraction which is concerned with everyday life, yet which mysteriously, even perhaps mystically, stands apart from it. Tilson, in fact, spent two years in Italy, in the late 50's and has maintained connections with the country.

Tilson is a member of a remarkable generation of English artists who were connected with the Institute of Contemporary Arts in London when the critic Lawrence Alloway, and artists such as Richard Hamilton and Eduardo Paolozzi were attempting to work out the relationship of art to life and the public. These artists included Peter Blake, Ron Kitaj, Peter Phillips and David Hockney. The intellectual and stylistic example of Hamilton, and the brilliant inventiveness of Paolozzi, led to the special English branch of Pop-art, long before the emergence of the American brand; the younger artists, many of whom visited the United States as students and teachers, created a bridge between the continents.

Tilson, as indeed his English contemporaries, whilst impressed and affected by the remarkable American generation of Pop-artists, retained his own individuality. This is compounded by a love and use of words as symbols equally useful and powerful as images, as well as the incorporation of geometrical and three-dimensional forms as extensions of flat surfaces. He is catholic in the use of materials, used uniquely or in combination—wood, plastics, painted surfaces, photographic images, collage, screen printing, etc. As well as the abstract insertion of single words, or the serialised image of an eye, Tilson reproduces newspaper photographs, pages from magazines, references to contemporary events, as well as details of famous works of art. None of this is erratic or chance; Tilson is careful and positive in his choice and juxtaposition of conponents, even if, to the viewer, it is a total effect, either of forms, images, or even verbal messages, rather than an immediately understood philosophy, which makes its impact. Probably Tilson's finest gift is for public communication, evident in the murals he has constructed in different parts of the world.

—Charles Spencer

TINDLE, David.

British. Born in Huddersfield, Yorkshire, 29 April 1932. Educated in Coventry, Warwickshire public schools; studied at the Coventry School of Art, 1945-46. Married Janet F. Trollope in 1969; children: Saskia, Charlotte and Nathan. Painter: in London, 1951-56; in Arbroath and Wantage, 1956-58; in London, 1959-64; in Brome, Suffolk, 1964-66; in London, 1966-69; in East Hadden, Northamptonshire, 1969-80; in Clipston, Leicestershire, 1980-86; in Leamington Spa, Warwickshire, since 1986. Lecturer, Hornsey College of Art and Byam Shaw School of Painting, London, 1959-74. Part-time Lecturer, Royal College of Art, London, since 1972. Recipient: Painting Prize, *Chichester National Art Exhibition*, Sussex, 1975. Associate, 1973, Royal Academician, 1979, Royal Academy of Art, London; Associate, 1973, Fellow, 1981, and Honorary Fellow, 1984, Royal College of Art, London; Ruskin Master of Drawing and Fine Art, Oxford University, 1985. Honorary MA: St. Edmund Hall, Oxford, 1985. Agent: Fischer Fine Art, London. Address: c/o Fischer Fine Art, 30 King Street, London SW1, England.

Individual Exhibitions:

1954	Piccadilly Gallery, London (and regularly 1954-83)
	Crane Gallery, Manchester, England
1957	City Art Gallery, Coventry, England
	57 Gallery, Edinburgh
1958	Stone Gallery, Newcastle upon Tyne, England
1961	*New Painting*, Bear Lane Gallery, Oxford
1963	Metropole Gallery, Folkestone, England
1964	Galerie du Tours, San Francisco (travelled to Galerie du Tours, Los Angeles)
1965	Metropole Gallery, Folkestone, Kent
1968	Galleria Carbonesi, Bologna
	Galleria Vinciana, Milan
1970	27 Gallery, Northampton
1972	City Art Gallery, Northampton (retrospective)
1974	Galerie XX, Hamburg
1977	Galerie XX, Hamburg
1980	Galerie XX, Hamburg
1985	Fischer Fine Art, London

Selected Group Exhibitions:

1958	*International Biennale of Realist Art*, Bruges, Belguim
1959	*John Moore's Exhibition*, Liverpool (and 1961)
1967	*Mostra Mercate d'Arte Contemporanea*, Florence
1974	*British Painting 74*, Hayward Gallery, London
1975	*Art 6 '75*, Kunstmesse, Basle
1977	*British Painting 1952-77*, Royal Academy of Art, London
1978	*English Realism*, Waddington Galleries, Montreal
1979	*The British Art Show*, toured Britain

Collections:

Tate Gallery, London; Arts Council of Great Britain, London; Department of the Environment, London; London Museum; Contemporary Art Society, London; Walker Art Gallery, Liverpool; Whitworth Art Gallery, Manchester; Wakefield Art Gallery, Yorkshire; Arts Council of Northern Ireland, Belfast.

Publications:

On TINDLE: *David Tindle*, exhibition catalogues, edited by Piccadilly Gallery, London 1957, 1963, 1965, 1966, 1968, 1971, 1973, 1976, 1979; *David Tindle: New Paintings*, exhibition catalogue, Oxford 1961; *David Tindle: Paintings 1962*, exhibition catalogue, with text by Neville Wallis, London 1962; *Exhibition of Works by David Tindle*, exhibition catalogue, Northampton 1972; *David Tindle*, exhibition catalogue with text by Marina Vaizey, London 1985.

*

The images I paint are of things I know best or can remember most. I try to place them in an order that expresses the feelings I have about them. It is not a question of painting them as realistically as I can, but to get the right tonality, so that memory and presence are very close.

—David Tindle

*

"20th-century art, now free from the intolerable burden of representation . . . "—how often has one heard that phrase! Yet, if one casts around for contemporary artists whose work asserts the enduring value of representation as a way of finding oneself in the universe, there are very few who offer visible, incontrovertible evidence. David Tindle is one of them.

Why is he so much less acclaimed than, say, Wyeth in the United States? He has been the victim of a special situation in Britain: art, and especially "modern" and abstract art, has had such an uphill task to win recognition, interest and respectability in the first half of the 20th century that sitting in front of an easel and nature, and *learning* from it by making marks and looking again, has been made to seem like a reactionary gesture. And the fact that the brightest talents of those decades chose more immediate forms of self-expression weighed the public scales even more against it.

Tindle moved from vigorous, gestural paintings of such subjects as high seas breaking on the shore, towards "every-blade-of-grass" scenes of landscape seen out of windows, or evocative still-lifes of straw hats on chairs, done in traditional tempera and much like old Roman murals in their effect; but not with that obsessional deadness that high detail so often carries, but a fine, refined, luminescent and atmospheric stillness, full of lively details of observed light, direct and reflected, as in Vermeer or de Hoogh; they have manifest presence. These are paintings which "are what they do"; some find a melancholy in them, others, the timeless repose of the suspended moment, complete in itself. In them, "representation" catches our remembering that "that is how it is"—but "how it is" includes the recognition or memory of mental and spiritual worlds beyond the physical and manifest.

From time to time, Tindle has painted very straightforward portraits of young art students; these in their directness deserve to be seen more publicly. Tindle's is a major, little-recognized contribution to 20th-century factual realism, and to art itself, as a method and also a gift of self-realization.

—Michael Shepherd

TINGUELY, Jean.

Swiss. Born in Fribourg, 22 May 1925. Educated at primary and secondary schools, in Basle, 1930-39; apprentice decorator, Globus Department Store, Basle, 1941-45; studied art at the Kunstgewerbeschule, Basle, 1941-45. Married the artist Eva Aeppli in 1951 (separated, 1958). Independent artist, in Basle, 1945-52; subsequently in Paris, Basle, and in Soisy-sur-Ecole, France; abstract paintings and kinetic assemblage-sculptures, 1945-52; first "Metamecanisms," 1952; first "Metamatics," 1959; collaborative works with artists Yves Klein, 1958-62, Niki de Saint-Phalle, from 1960, and with Bernard Luginbuhl, 1968-72. Member, Pierre Restany's "Nouveaux Réalistes" group of artists, Paris, 1960-70. Address: L'Auberge du Chéval-Blanc, 91840 Soisy-sur-Ecole, Essones, France.

Individual Exhibitions:

1954	Galerie Arnaud, Paris
	Studio d'Architettura, Milan
1955	Galleri Samlaren, Stockholm

David Tindle: *Room*, 1985

1956	Galerie Denise René, Paris
1957	Galerie Edouard Loeb, Paris
	Galerie Denise René, Paris
1958	Galerie Iris Clert, Paris
1959	Galerie Schmela, Dusseldorf
	Kaplan Gallery, London
	Galerie Iris Clert, Paris
	Institute of Contemporary Arts, London (happening-event)
1960	Staempfli Gallery, New York
	Museum of Modern Art sculpture garden, New York (outdoor event)
	Galerie des Quatres Saisons, Paris
	Museum Haus Lange, Krefeld, West Germany
	Kunsthalle, Berne, Switzerland (with Bernard Luginbuhl and Norbert Kricke)
1961	Moderna Museet, Stockholm
	Louisiana Museum, Humlebaek, Denmark
	Staempfli Gallery, New York
	Galerie Rive Droite, Paris
	Galleria Schwarz, Milan
1962	Galerie Handschin, Basle
	Everett Ellin Gallery, Los Angeles
	Alexandre Iolas Gallery, New York
1963	Minami Gallery, Tokyo
	Dwan Gallery, Los Angeles
1964	Galerie Alexandre Iolas, Geneva
	Kunsthalle, Baden-Baden, West Germany
	Galerie Rudolf Zwirner, Cologne
1965	*Sculpture*, Museum of Fine Arts, Houston
	Palais des Beaux-Arts, Brussels

	3 Sculpteurs: Cesar, Roel d'Haese, Tinguely, Musée des Arts Décoratifs, Paris
	2 Kinetic Sculptors: Nicolas Schoffer and Jean Tinguely, Jewish Museum, New York (toured the United States)
	Alexandre Iolas Gallery, New York
	Kunsthalle, Berne
1966	Ohio State University, Columbus
	Gimpel und Hanover Galerie, Zurich
	Hon-en Katedral, Moderna Museet, Stockholm (with Niki de Saint-Phalle and Per Olof Ultveldt)
1967	Galerie Alexandre Iolas, Paris
	Galleria Iolas, Milan
	Rijksmuseum Kröller-Müller, Otterlo, Netherlands (with Bernard Luginbuhl)
	Galleri Buren, Stockholm
1968	Hanover Gallery, London
	Tekeningen, Stedeijk Museum, Amsterdam
	Museum of Contemporary Art, Chicago
1969	Gimpel und Hanover Galerie, Zurich
	Victor Loeb Department Store, Berne
1970	Galleria Iolas, Milan
	Galerie Alexandre Iolas, Geneva
	Galleria L'Attico, Rome
1971	*Machines de Tinguely*, Centre National d'Art Contemporain, Paris (toured Europe, 1971–72)
1974	*Debricollages*, Galerie Bischofberger, Zurich
1975	*Reliefs et Sculptures 1954–1965*, Galerie Bonnier, Geneva
1976	*Dessins et Gravures pour les Sculptures*, Musée d'Art et d'Histoire, Geneva

	Tinguely in Kunstmuseum Basle, Kunstmuseum, Basle
	Galerie Bischofberger, Zurich
1978	Wilhelm-Lehmbruck-Museum, Duisburg, West Germany (retrospective)
1979	*Jean Tinguely im Stadel*, Städtische Galerie, Frankfurt
1981	Galerie Bischofberger, Zurich
	Abbaye de Senanque, Vaucluse, France
1982	Kunsthaus, Zurich (travelled to the Tate Gallery, London, Palais des Beaux-Arts, Brussels, and the Musée d'Art et d'Histoire, Geneva)
1983	Centre Georges Pompidou, Paris
1984	Stedelijk Museum, Amsterdam
1985	Kunsthalle der Hypo-Stiftung, Munich
1986	Louisiana Museum, Humlebaek, Denmark
	Kunsthalle der Hypo-Stiftung, Munich
1987	Galerie Beyeler, Basle
	Palazzo Grassi, Venice

Selected Group Exhibitions:

1955	*Le Mouvement*, Galerie Denise René, Paris
1959	*Biennale*, Paris
1961	*Le Mouvement dans l'Art*, Stedelijk Museum, Amsterdam (travelled to the Moderna Museet, Stockholm, and the Louisiana Museum, Humlebaek, Denmark)
1964	*Biennale*, Venice
1967	*French Art Today*, at *Expo 67*, Montreal

1968 *The Machine*, Museum of Modern Art, New York
1977 *Paris-New York*, Centre Georges Pompidou, Paris
1980 *Paris-Paris 1937-57*, Centre Georges Pompidou, Paris
1982 *60-80: Attitudes, Concepts, Images*, Stedelijk Museum, Amsterdam
1984 *Salvaged: Altered Everyday Objects*, Project Studio One, Long Island City, New York

Collections:

Centre Georges Pompidou, Paris; Kunsthaus, Zurich; Kunstmuseum, Dusseldorf; Kaiser-Wilhelm-Museum, Krefeld, West Germany; Stedelijk Museum, Amsterdam; Stedelijk Van Abbemuseum, Eindhoven, Netherlands; Museum of Modern Art, New York; Museum of Fine Arts, Houston.

Publications:

By TINGUELY: book—*Für Statik*, manifesto, Dusseldorf 1959.

On TINGUELY: books—*Tinguely*, exhibition leaflet, with text by Pontus Hulten, Paris 1957; *3 Sculpteurs: Cesar, Roel d'Haese, Tinguely*, exhibition catalogue, with texts by Francois Mathey, Chris Yperman and James Johnson Sweeney, Paris 1965; *Jean Tinguely: Sculpture*, exhibition catalogue, with text by James Johnson Sweeney, Houston 1965; *2 Kinetic Sculptors: Nicolas Schoffer and Jean Tinguely*, exhibition catalogue, with texts by Sam Hunter and K. G. Pontus Hulten, New York, 1965; *Jean Tinguely*, exhibition catalogue, with text by Jean-Christophe Ammann, Zurich 1966; *Jean Tinguely: Tekeningen*, exhibition folder, Amsterdam 1968; *Tinguely*, exhibition catalogue, with texts by Peter F. Althaus, and others, Basle 1972; *Jean Tinguely*, exhibition catalogue, with texts by Wieland Schmied, Peter F. Althaus and others, Hannover 1972; *Jean Tinguely: 166 Fotos von Leonardo Bezzola*, with texts by Eva Aeppli, Bernard Luginbuhl, Niki de Saint-Phalle and others, Zurich 1974; *Jean Tinguely: Debricollages*, exhibition catalogue, with text by Gerald Minkoff, Zurich 1974; *Mesa* by Pontus Hulten, London 1975; *Jean Tinguely: Reliefs et Sculptures 1954-1965*, exhibition catalogue, Geneva 1975; *Jean Tinguely: dessins et gravures pour les sculptures*, exhibition catalogue, with an interview by Charles Georg and Rainer Michael Mason, Geneva 1976; *Tinguely in Kunstmuseum, Basle*, exhibition catalogue, with text by Franz Meyer, Basle 1976; *Jean Tinguely im Stadel*, exhibition catalogue, with texts by Klaus Gallwitz and Willy Rotzler, Frankfurt 1979; *Der Tinguely-Brunnen in Basle* by Annemarie Monteil, Basle 1980; *Tinguely*, exhibition catalogue, with texts by Felix Baumann, and Richard Calvocoressi, Zurich 1982; *Jean Tinguely: catalogue raissone 1954-1968*, compiled by Christina Bischofberger, Zurich 1982; *Jean Tinguely*, exhibition catalogue with texts by Carla Schulz-Hoffmann and Stephanie Poley, Munich 1985; *Jean Tinguely*, exhibition catalogue with text by Gert Kaiser, Basle 1987.

Tinguely's formal artistic training was at the School of Art and Crafts in Basel from 1941-45, though his attendance was irregular. By 1945 he was painting abstract pictures and making constructions from wire, metal and other materials, influenced by the work of Kurt Schwitters. It was also at this time that he expressed interest in movement as an artistic medium.

Between 1945-53, Tinguely worked at various jobs in Basel and was attracted to the work of Paul Klee and the Bauhaus, Tanguy, Dali and Miro. He was living in Paris in 1953 and worked with Daniel Spoerri in Jean Lurcat's studio on a project for 'autotheatre', which was intended to bring action to the stage with or without actors. Tinguely spent most of the 1950's working on various series of reliefs: 1954—reliefs made up of layers of moving rods; 1954-56 "meta-mechanical" reliefs and free-standing sculptures; 1956-59 reliefs with rotating metal elements. The late 1950's to early 1960's saw the advent of Tinguely's first 'painting machines' and his involvement with *Nouveaux Realisme*, which rejected the ivory tower world of abstract painting (then the major international trend in painting), and advocated the use of real materials and found objects; all of which was a harkening back to *Dada*. Indeed, Tin-

guely's own constructions owed a great deal to Picabia's work of 1917-19.

In 1960 one of Tinguely's most famous series was inaugurated with the *Hommage à New York*, a sculpture which self-destructed in the garden of New York's Museum of Modern Art. By the mid-1960's the sculptures were becoming huge and were major media events, especially if they were of the self-destructing variety.

Tinguely's machines usually worked in some way, even if only just. The irony inherent in his early work, particularly the painting machines, receded though never entirely disappeared. He brought together a combination of a dadaist tradition with the fascination for humourous and outlandish machines as seen by artists such as Paul Klee and the Surrealists, adding to all this a concern for the use of cast off materials and an overwhelming interest in movement.

—Victoria Keller

TITUS-CARMEL, Gerard.

French. Born in Paris, 10 October 1941. Studied engraving at the Ecole Boulle, Paris, 1958-62. Served in the French Air Force, 1962-64. Married Joan C. Robinson in 1971; children: Jeanne and Guillaume. Independent artist, Paris, 1964-82, and in Oulchy-le-Château, Aisne, since 1982; also, filmmaker, since 1972. Recipient: First Prize, *Drawing Biennale*, Rijeka, 1970; International Art Critics Association Prize, *Biennale de Paris*, 1971; First Prize, *Biennale of Alexandria*, 1971. Agent: Galerie Lelong, Paris. Address: c/o Galerie Lelong, 13 rue de Teheran, 75008 Paris, France.

Individual Exhibitions:

1967 Galerie du Fleuve, Paris
1968 Galerie du Fleuve, Paris
1969 Galerija 212, Belgrade
1970 Galerie Daniel Templon, Paris
     Galerie A.P.I.A.W., Liège, Belgium
1971 Musée d'Art Moderne de la Ville, Paris
     Galerie Bama, Paris
     Galleria La Salita, Rome
1972 Neue Galerie, Aachen, West Germany (retrospective)
     Galerie Daniel Templon, Paris
     Muzeum Sztuki, Lodz, Poland
     French Pavilion, at the *Biennale*, Venice
     Galerie du Fleuve, Bordeaux
     Royal College of Art, London
     Galleria Diagramma, Milan
1973 Galerie Godula Buchholz, Munich
     Stedelijk Museum, Amsterdam
     La Strategia del Disegno, Galleria Schwarz, Milan
     Galerie Jalmar, Amsterdam
1974 Galerie Daniel Templon, Paris
     Le Grifforme, Galerie La Hune, Paris
     Galerie La Touriale, Marseilles
     Galerie Birger Arnesen, Copenhagen
     Galerie Vega, Liège, Belgium
1975 Galerie Graphikhuset Futura, Stockholm
     Galerie Daniel Templon, Paris
     Galerie Hecate, Paris
     Palais des Beaux-Arts, Brussels
1976 Galerie La Hune, Paris
     Galerie Therese Roussel, Perpignan, France
     Galerie Baudoin Lebon, Paris
1977 Gimpel und Hanover Galerie, Zurich
     Gimpel Fils, London
     Kunstbandel Brinkman, Amsterdam
     Galerie Art Actuel, Nancy, France
1978 Centre Georges Pompidou, Paris
     Galerija Krzysztofory, Cracow
     Galerie Maeght, Paris

1979 Kunstverein für die Rheinlande und Westfalen, Dusseldorf
     Galerie Maeght, Zurich
     Galerie Charles Kriwin, Brussels
1980 Kunsthalle, Bielefeld, West Germany
     Stadia Graphics Gallery, Sydney
     Kunstverein, Kassel, West Germany
     Nishimura Gallery, Tokyo
1981 Oberbeck-Gesellschaft-St. Annen Museum, Lübeck
     Galerie Maeght, Paris
     Kunsthalle, Nuremberg
     Musée de l'Abbaye Sainte-Croix, Les Sables-d'Olonne, France
     Nishimura Gallery, Tokyo
     Henie-Onstad Kunstsenter, Oslo
1982 Xavier Fourcade Inc., New York
     Galerie Chappe-Lautier, Toulouse
     Galerie Maeght, Zurich
     Galerie Maeght, Paris
1983 Galerie Elisabeth Franck, Knokke-le-Zoute, Belgium
     Studio Marconi, Milan
1984 Galerie de la Cite, Luxembourg
     Galerie de l'Ancienne Poste, Calais, France
     Galerie Maeght Lelong, Paris
1985 Galerie des Ponchettes, Nice, France
     Spaightwood Galleries, Madison, Wisconsin
     Tours Narbonnaises, Carcassonne, France
     Institute Francais, Stuttgart (travelled to Hamburg, Munich and Bonn)
     Musee d'Art Moderne, Villeneuve d'Ascq, France
1986 Galerie Maeght Lelong, Paris
     Galerie Graff, Montreal
     Galerie Brinkman, Amsterdam
     Galerie du Musee du Quebec, Canada
     Spaightwood Galleries, Madison, Wisconsin
1987 Mucsarnok, Budapest
     Fuji Television Gallery, Tokyo
     Galleri Asbaeck, Copenhagen
     Abbaye des Cordeliers, Chateauroux, France
     Galerie La Hune, Paris
     Denise Cade Gallery/Art Prospect Inc., New York
     Lelong Gallery, New York

Selected Group Exhibitions:

1965 *Biennale*, Musée Municipal d'Art Moderne, Paris
1972 *Amsterdam-Paris-Dusseldorf*, Guggenheim Museum, New York (travelled to the Pasadena Art Museum, California, and Dallas Museum of Fine Arts)
1974 *Hyperréalistes Americains, Réalistes Européens*, Centre National d'Art Contemporain, Paris (travelled to the Museum Boymans-Van Beuningen, Rotterdam, and the Rotonda Besana, Milan)
1975 *Junggesellenmachinen*, Kunsthalle, Berne (travelled to the *Biennale*, Venice, and the Palais des Beaux-Arts, Brussels)
1976 *International Print Biennale*, National Museum of Modern Art, Tokyo (travelled to the National Museum, Kyoto)
1977 *Trois Villes, Tois Collections*, Musée Cantini, Marseilles (travelled to the Musée de Peinture, Grenoble; Musée d'Art et d'Industrie, St. Etienne; and the Centre Georges Pompidou, Paris)
1979 *European Dialogue*, at the *Biennale*, Art Gallery of New South Wales, Sydney (toured Australia)
1980 *Printed Art: A View of 2 Decades*, Museum of Modern Art, New York
1981 *Biennale der Europaischen Grafik*, Pavillon des Olympischen Kongress, Baden-Baden, West Germany
1982 *Statements: Leading Contemporary Artists from France*, Delahunty and Carol Taylor Gallery, Dallas (travelled to Hansen-Fuller-Golden Gallery, Dallas; Hansen-Fuller-Golden Gallery, San Francisco; and the Richard Hines Gallery, Seattle)

Collections:

Centre Georges Pompidou, Paris; Victoria and Albert Museum, London; Stedelijk Museum, Amsterdam; Musées Royaux des Beaux-Arts, Brussels; Kobbersticksamlingen ved

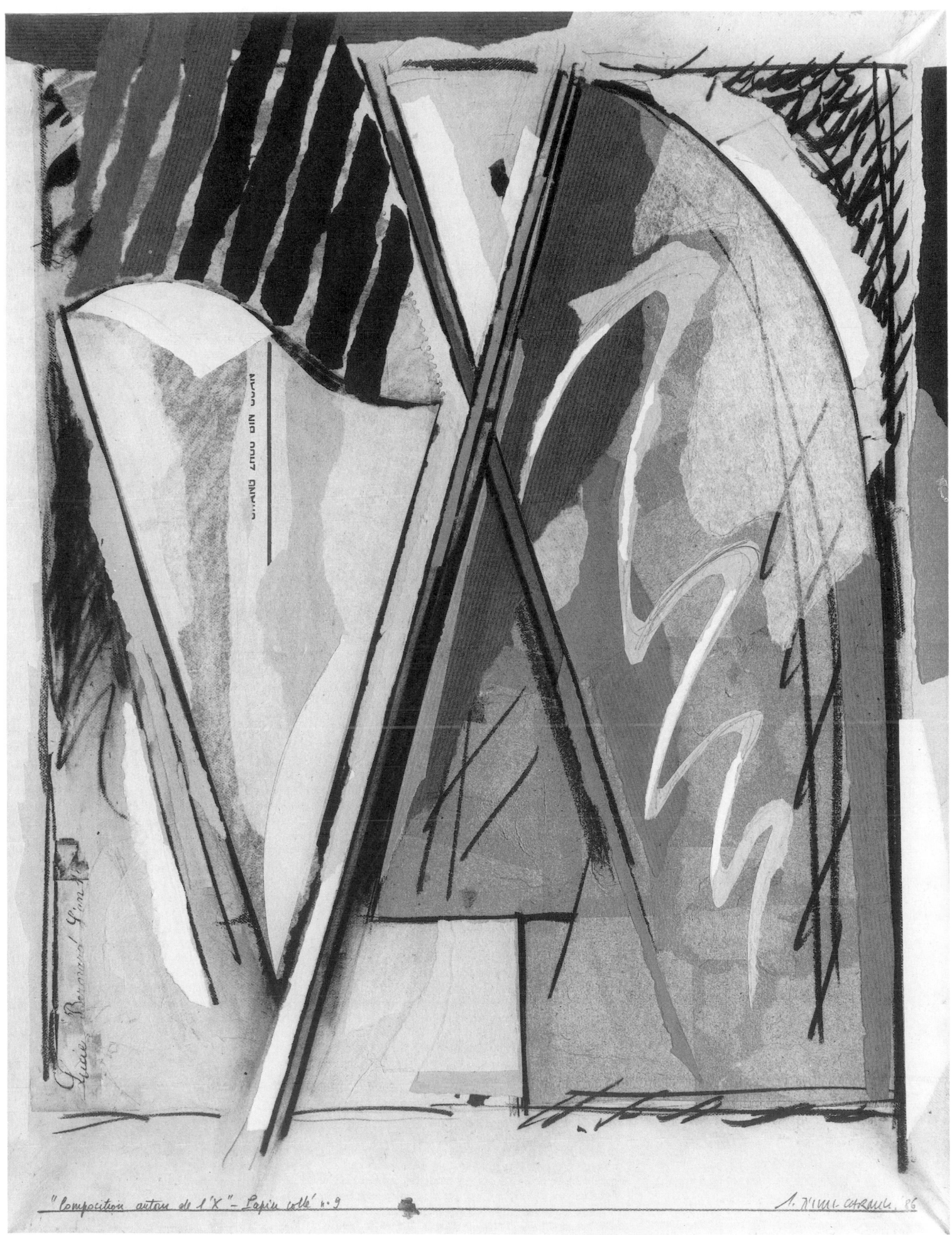

Gerard Titus-Carmel: *Papier Collé No. 9,* 1986

Statens Museum for Kunst, Copenhagen; Staatliche Graphische Sammlung, Munich; Kunsthaus, Zurich; Fundacio Joan Miró, Barcelona; Australian National Gallery, Canberra; Museum of Modern Art, New York.

Publications:

By TITUS-CARMEL: books—*Joaquin's Love Affair,* Paris 1971; *The Pocket Size Tlingit Coffin,* Paris 1976; books illustrated: *Pour Bramm* by Mathieu Benezet, Paris 1965; *La Porte de Nuit* by Dusan Matic, Montpellier, France 1972; *L'Humus l'Hymen* by Jean-Marc Tisserant, Montpellier, France 1973; *Matière Première* by Denis Roche, Paris 1976; *Verres* by Jean-Pierre Faye, Paris 1977; *Sarx* by Pascal Quignard, Paris 1977; *Noeud* by Jean Fremon, Paris 1978; film—*Joaquin's Love Affair,* 1972.

On TITUS-CARMEL: books—*Gerard Titus-Carmel,* exhibition catalogue, with text by Jean Marc Tisserant, Liège, Belgium 1970; *Titus-Carmel,* exhibition catalogue, with texts by Mathieu Benezet, Jean-Pierre Faye, and an interview by Maurice Maurin, Paris 1971; *Gerard Titus-Carmel,* exhibition catalogue, with a preface by Wolfgang Becker, texts by others, Aachen, West Germany 1972; *Art en France: Une nouvelle generation* by Jean Clair, Paris 1972; *L'Art Actuel en France* by Anne Tronche, Paris 1973; *Gerard Titus-Carmel of het Juk van de Weegschaal,* exhibition catalogue, with text by Irmeline Lebeer, Amsterdam 1973; *La Strategia del Disegno: Gerard Titus-Carmel,* exhibition catalogue, with text by Tommaso Trini, Milan 1973; *Gerard Titus-Carmel ou le Procès du Modele* by Jean-Marc Tisserant, Paris 1974; *Gerard Titus-Carmel: Le Grifforme,* exhibition catalogue, with text by Jean-Pierre Faye, Paris 1974; *Dictionnaire Universel de la Peinture,* edited by Robert Maillard, Paris 1975; *Reperes, La Peinture en France: Debut et fin d'un systeme visuel 1870–1970* by Dora Vellier, Paris 1976; *Gerard Titus-Carmel,* exhibition catalogue, with an introduction by Willy Rotzler, London 1977; *Le Verité en Peinture* by Jacques Derrida, Paris 1978; *Gerard Titus-Carmel,* exhibition catalogue, with texts by Jacques Derrida and Gilbert Lascault, Paris 1978; *Ecrits Timides sur le Visible* by Gilbert Lascault, Paris 1979; *Petit Larousse de la Peinture,* edited by Michel Laclotte, Paris 1979; *Dictionnaire International des Beaux-Arts,* edited by Pierre Cabanne, Paris 1979; *Gerard Titus-Carmel,* exhibition catalogue, with preface by Günter Metken, and an introduction by Karl-Heinz Hering, Dusseldorf 1979; *Great Drawings of All Times* by Genevieve Monnier and others, Tokyo 1979, New York 1980; *Titus-Carmel,* exhibition catalogue, with an introduction by Erich Franz, texts by others, Bielefeld, West Germany 1980; *Gerard Titus-Carmel,* exhibition catalogue, with a preface by Yoshiaki Tono, Tokyo 1981; *Gerard Titus-Carmel,* exhibition catalogue with preface by Jean Fremon, Chateauroux 1987; films—*Gerard Titus-Carmel* by Jacques Scandelari, 1973; *Titus-Carmel* by Angeliki Haas, 1975; *Gerard Titus-Carmel ou l'Aventure du trait* by Teri Wehn-Damisch, 1977; *Gerard Titus-Carmel* by Alain Sayag, 1978; *Gerard Titus-Carmel, un Artiste trait pour trait* by Carlos Vilardebo, 1982.

DRAWING

1. To draw: to deposit. To engrave: to remove. (idea of a work situated halfway between these two mutilations of the support: the significant maculation of the paper, the matricial groove of the metal).
2. To draw, to encroach: to cover. (Would the *image* be the *mask* of the paper?).
3. Drawing is, above all, a work on a double loss: loss of white (loss of consciousness), loss of materiality (diversion).
4. "Carta Tina." Drawing the shadows, lighting the lights: between the deaf *sanguine* and the chalky luminosity, the tinted paper is SIGNIFICANT MATTER.
5. On white paper, the brightness (the light) is the absence of drawing—the *lack;* to cease shading is to *enter into light.* On a tinted background, at the end of a stump, there is a rediscovery of the paper's matter as a designated element of form, the *interstatement,* just before the hollow shading, the countertype: the drawing of the luminosities with a white pencil.
6. Praxis of drawing, alluvia of the graphite.
7. Drawing as the practice of *outrage: to mark* the paper, to leave (plumbaginous traces).
8. Before the mark: *the image* of the mark, defined simultaneously as the striation of the void and the stigma (blemish) of its model.

—Gerard Titus-Carmel

Although he did not have his first exhibition until 1964, this artist, having completed his studies at the École Boulle in Paris, has mounted 81 one-man shows in many parts of the world during the intervening years (including 48 + prints at the Abbaye des Cordeliers, Châteauroux, 1987).

Essentially, that early training at the École Boulle has stood him in good stead largely because he has proved himself a master of linear craft with a particular understanding of the extra fulfilment he can acquire from the promise that the paper has to offer depending upon its 'character'. Evidence of this special gift has been attested on a global scale. (In point of fact, Titus-Carmel ceased to paint pictures in oils after 1969, and did not employ oil again as a medium until the huge *IX Ombres pour STC* series of 1984.)

Important enough; but this is only half of the story. From his well-established basis as an exceptional draughtsman, he has gone to the heart of 'figuration' and linked it with a controlling—in Willy Rotzler's words—conviction "of the *reflection* of the *functioning*" of subject and technique combined. What this means becomes clear and apparent in actual contact with his works. Then it can be seen that the 'figuration' is still realised even when it is clothed and engulfed by the creator's graphic and detailed techniques.

These descriptions refer to the artistic production of the 1970s when Titus-Carmel sought to swathe and tightly bandage his subjects with taut accuracy. More recently, and increasingly at the present time, his work in style and its current huge dimensions has undergone a number of fundamental changes. The devastating 'neatness' of the earlier pictures has given way to a calculated flamboyance decked out for the most part in washes of pulsating darknesses with rare flashes of brightness almost like accents in the course of some heroic oratory.

Typical instances of this transformation occur in the two collections: *Eclats* and *Caparaçons.* These began in 1980, lasting for two more years before going on show at the Galerie Maeght, Paris. All the works shown then, although they were emphasised with rich stretches of watercolour/sometimes browns or greys, sometimes a combination of both/in certain cases more varied with a colour scale ranging through blues, greens, yellows and reds/together with their colour fabrics/continued to be supported by his deft ability—even in this new approach—as a supreme draughtsman. His work now avoided his erstwhile strict linear sharpenss. The images, including their outline edges, possessed the rolling rhythm of waves—especially in the *Éclats.* They created a theatre-in-the-round (even when they gave sweeping glimpses of the half-filled glass at the Circle Bar) which could flow from stage to amphitheatre and back, whereas the *Caparaçons* concentrated on the curtain concealing the stage, or upon the stage itself alive with decor-scaffolding bric-a-brac. Swish curtains or unwriggled forefront of rich opacity, both these kinds of imagery evoke a magic of the playhouse never previously present in works of art.

After the *Éclats* and the *Caparaçons,* he became busy with work on other themes: the *Suite Chancay,* his *Boréales,* the *Compositions autour de l'X* and this year's *Interieurs.* Something of the meaning of this artist's raison-d'être development—not always easy to perceive—has yielded a part of its secrets during the past two years.

Possibly Jacques Henric who knows Titus-Carmel well has put his finger on the pulse when he looks into T-C's means and motives. Most of all he asserts that here is a creator who understands that the finest perfume always requires a fly-in-the-ointment. This does not mean that for Titus-Carmel *Perfection* is a dirty word, but rather to draw near to unsullied beauty it is necessary to introduce a soupçon of *valde malum* to offset a pervading atmosphere of *valde bonum*! More than that. As this hardening process has continued in the artist's works, so a stripping and scalping, a ripping off of some of the epidermis element has had to be introduced. It is almost as if *id quod visum placet* has needed to be debunked because under the skin real beauty lies hidden. Not that such a painful operation should be brought about in one fell swoop. Such a revealing has to be accomplished only a tiny bit at a time.

Paradoxically a suggestion of the same result can be obtained (and is obtained by Titus-Carmel) by his concern with what he modestly dubs Papiers-Collés, only in such instances (especially the most recent) these additives obscure parts and surfaces of the original washes and linear structures of his huge pictures—a sort of agreeable torture inflicted upon ideas. His is not, however, a destructive intention. On the contrary, he is seeking to find hidden realities of what his pictures have in their innermost recesses by use of a continuing subtraction of surplus avoir-du-poids until deepseated (and eternal, past and future) truths within the essence of subjects and matter come to the surface. Put another way, this artist is in a sense riding off at a tangent in the belief that the cruder aspect of original picture painting ought not to be allowed to stay in situ. Rather they should be opening doors, windows, even secret trap-doors to divulge what lies within.

Grand displays of this latest period in the artist's career have been organised by Louis-François Larnaud for Montpellier, Carcassone and the Narbonnaise area, as well as by Daniel Lelong at the Galerie Maeght Lelong in Paris, and now by the Service de la Ville de Châteauroux in the Abbaye des Cordelliers.

—Sheldon Williams

TOBEY, Mark.

American. Born in Centerville, Wisconsin, 11 December 1890. Educated in Trempealeau, Wisconsin and Hammond, Indiana; attended Saturday classes at the Art Institute of Chicago, 1906, then studied under Frank Zimmerman and Professor Reynolds at Art Institute of Chicago, 1906–08; studied calligraphy and composition under Teng Kwei, University of Washington, Seattle, 1922–25, and Chinese calligraphy, privately, under Teng Kwei, Shanghai, 1934–35. Painter: occasional illustrator for a fashion design studio, Chicago, 1909–10; lived in Chicago and New York, 1912–17; interior designer, New York, 1918–22; joined Bahai movement, c. 1918; moved to Seattle, 1922; travelled in Europe, 1925–26; visited Mexico, 1931; lived in England, 1931–38; spent a month in a Zen monastery in Kyoto and travelled in Japan, 1934; visited Ceylon, Hong Kong, and Shanghai, 1934–35; Easel Painter, Works Progress Administration, Federal Art Project, Seattle, 1938; travelled in Sweden where he associated with Pehr Hallsten, 1954; settled in Basle, in Paul Klee's former house, 1960. Lecturer, Cornish School, Seattle, 1923–29; Lecturer in Art, 1930, and Artist in Residence, 1931–38, Dartington Hall, Devon, England. Recipient: Katherine Baker Memorial Award, Seattle Art Museum, 1940; Artists for Victory Prize, 1942; Guggenheim International Award, 1956; Fine Arts Medal, American Institute of Architects, 1957; First Prize for Painting, *Biennale,* Venice, 1958; First Prize for Painting, *Carnegie International,* Pittsburgh, 1961. Honorary Member, National Institute of Arts and Letters. 1956. Commandeur de l'Ordre des Arts et des Lettres, Paris, 1968. *Died* (in Basle), *24 April 1976.*

Individual Exhibitions:

1917	M. Knoedler Gallery, New York
1928	Arts Club of Chicago
1929	Romany Marie Café Gallery, New York
1930	Cornish School, Seattle
1931	Contemporary Arts Gallery, New York
	Harry Hartman Bookstore Gallery, Seattle
	Beaux-Arts Gallery, London
1934	Paul Elder Gallery, San Francisco

1935	Stanley Rose Gallery, Hollywood
	Seattle Art Museum
1940	Arts Club of Chicago
1942	Seattle Art Museum
1944	Willard Gallery, New York
1945	Arts Club of Chicago
	Willard Gallery, New York
	Portland Art Museum, Oregon
	San Francisco Museum of Art
1946	Arts Club of Chicago
	Detroit Institute of Arts
1947	Willard Gallery, New York
1949	Margret Brown Gallery, Boston
	Willard Gallery, New York
1950	Willard Gallery, New York
1951	Margret Brown Gallery, Boston
	California Palace of the Legion of Honor, San Francisco
	Henry Gallery, Seattle
	Santa Barbara Museum of Art, California
	Whitney Museum, New York
	Willard Gallery, New York
1952	University of Chicago
	Zoe Dusanne Gallery, Seattle
1954	Willard Gallery, New York
	Otto Seligman Gallery, Seattle
	Margret Brown Gallery, Boston
1955	Arts Club of Chicago
	Gump's Gallery, San Francisco
	Gallery of Art Interpretation, Chicago
	Galerie Jeanne Bucher, Paris
	Paul Kantor Gallery, Los Angeles
	Institute of Contemporary Arts, London
1956	Margret Brown Gallery, Boston
	Contemporary Art Museum, Houston (with John Marin and Morris Graves)
1957	Willard Gallery, New York
	Margret Brown Gallery, Boston
	Otto Seligman Gallery, Seattle
	Art Gallery of Greater Victoria, British Columbia
1958	Galerie Stadler, Paris
1959	Galerie Jeanne Bucher, Paris
	St. Albans School, Washington, D.C.
	Seattle Art Museum (toured the United States)
	Portland Art Museum, Oregon
	Fine Arts Center, Colorado Springs
	Pasadena Art Center, California
	M. H. de Young Memorial Museum, San Francisco
1960	Frederic Hobbs Fine Art, San Francisco
	Associazione Arti Figurative, Turin
	Kunsthalle, Mannheim, West Germany
1961	Musée des Arts Décoratifs, Paris (travelled to the Whitechapel Art Gallery, London)
	Galerie Beyeler, Basle
	Royal Marks Gallery, New York
1962	Otto Seligman Gallery, Seattle
	Willard Gallery, New York
	Phillips Gallery, Washington, D.C.
	Museum of Modern Art, New York (travelled to the Cleveland Museum of Art and the Art Institute of Chicago)
	Konstsalongen Samlaren, Stockholm (travelled to the Konstmuseum, Gothenburg, Sweden)
1963	Seattle Art Museum
	Galerie Beyeler, Basle
1965	Willard Gallery, New York
	Otto Seligman Gallery, Seattle
	Galerie Jeanne Bucher, Paris
	Galerie Alice Pauli, Lausanne, Switzerland
1966	Galerie Beyeler, Basle
	Stedelijk Museum, Amsterdam
	Kestner-Gesellschaft, Hannover
	Kunsthalle, Berne
	Kunstverein, Dusseldorf
1967	Willard Gallery, New York
	Stanford University Art Gallery, California
1968	Galerie Jeanne Bucher, Paris
	Museum of Fine Arts, Dallas
	Hanover Gallery, London
1969	Bon Marché, Seattle
1970	*Tobey's 80: A Retrospective*, Seattle Art Museum
	Galerie Beyeler, Basle
1971	Galerie Alice Pauli, Lausanne, Switzerland
	Willard Gallery, New York

Mark Tobey: *Interspersed*, 1970

	Baukunst Galerie, Cologne
	Galleria dell-Ariete, Milan
	Kunstkabinett, Frankfurt
	Galleria Il Fauno, Turin
	National Academy of Design, New York
	Galerie Marbach, Paris
	Whitney Museum, New York
	Galerie Ursus Presse, Dusseldorf
1972	Galerie Beyeler, Basle
	Willard Gallery, New York
	Martha Jackson Gallery, New York
	Cincinnati Art Museum, Ohio
	Martha Jackson Gallery, New York
1973	Willard Gallery, New York
	Martha Jackson Gallery, New York
	Foster-White Gallery, Seattle
	Galerie Ursus Presse, Dusseldorf
1974	*Tribute to Mark Tobey*, National Collection of Fine Arts, Smithsonian Institution, Washington, D.C. (travelled to the Seattle Art Museum and the St. Louis Art Museum)

1975	Museum Haus Lange, Krefeld, West Germany
	Galerie Darthea Speyer, Paris
1978	Galleria del Naviglio, Venice
	Galleria del Naviglio, Milan
1982	Galerie Jacqueline Schotland, Basle
1983	Galerie Vomel, Dusseldorf
1984	National Gallery of Art, Washington, D.C.
1986	Erker-Galerie, St. Gallen, Switzerland
1987	Baukunst Galerie, Cologne

Selected Group Exhibitions:

1929	*Paintings by 19 Living Americans*, Museum of Modern Art, New York
1939	*World's Fair*, New York
1943	*Romantic Painting in America*, Museum of Modern Art, New York
1948	*Biennale*, Venice
1950	*American Painting Today*, Metropolitan Museum of Art, New York

1956 *50 Ans d'Art aux Etats-Unis*, Musée National d'Art Moderne, Paris
1957 *International Contemporary Art Exhibition*, New Delhi, India
1958 *Nature in Abstraction*, Whitney Museum, New York
1966 *Two Decades of American Painting*, National Museum of Modern Art, Tokyo
1973 *Futurism: A Modern Focus*, Guggenheim Museum, New York

Collections:

Museum of Modern Art, New York; Metropolitan Museum of Art, New York; Whitney Museum, New York; Albright-Knox Art Gallery, Buffalo, New York; Seattle Art Museum; Portland Museum of Art, Oregon; Tate Gallery, London; Kunstmuseum, Basle; Kunsthalle, Bremen, West Germany; Staatsgalerie, Stuttgart.

Publications:

By TOBEY: book—*Mark Tobey: The World of a Market*, Seattle 1964; articles—"Reminiscence and Reverie" in *Magazine of Art* (New York), October 1951; "Japanese Traditions and American Art" in *College Art Journal* (New York), Fall 1958; "The Painter Meets the Critic," interview with Katherine Kuh, in the *Saturday Review* (New York), July 1960; "Mark Tobey," interview, in *The Artist's Voice: Talks with 17 Artists* by Katherine Kuh, New York 1960; "Une Journée avec Mark Tobey," interview, with Denys Chevalier, in *Aujourd'hui* (Paris), October, film—*Mark Tobey, Artist*, with Robert Gardner, Seattle 1952.

On TOBEY: books—*Mark Tobey* by Colette Roberts, New York 1959; *Mark Tobey*, exhibition catalogue, by Edward B. Thomas, Seattle 1959; *Mark Tobey* by Francoise Choay, Paris 1961; *Mark Tobey*, exhibition catalogue, by Julien Alvard, Paris 1961; *Mark Tobey*, exhibition catalogue, by William C. Seitz, New York 1962; *Mark Tobey* by Wieland Schmied, London and Stuttgart 1966; *Tobey's 80: A Retorspective*, exhibition catalogue, Seattle 1970; *Tobey* by John Russel, New York 1971; *Tobey* by Wieland Schmied, New York 1972; *Tribute to Mark Tobey*, exhibition catalogue, by Joshua C. Taylor, Washington, D.C. 1974; *Mark Tobey: City Paintings*, exhibition catalogue with essay by Eliza E. Rathbone, Washington, D.C. 1984; *Mark Tobey: Graphische Arbeiten*, exhibition catalogue with introduction by Gunter Ott, Cologne 1987.

*

The calligraphic "white writing" of Mark Tobey (1890-1976) stands as his major contribution to modernism. Secondarily, his formulation of a spatially ambiguous, overall composition of repetitious and undifferentiated line heralds the "drip" paintings of Pollock. Yet his breakthrough developed not from the secular *angst* of the American Abstract Expressionists and the School of Paris painters (to whom Tobey was regarded as the foremost American painter of those post-war years). Tobey's development of an abstract mode derived from his intense beliefs in the Bahai'i faith. In that regard, he belongs to a fellowship of stylistic pioneers in modern art (Kandinsky, Malevich, Mondrian) whose adoption of pure abstraction was spiritually or metaphysically motivated.

The Bahai'i tenets of unity, humanity and "progressive revelation" are first seen in Tobey's use of its cosmological symbolism, lending to his early work a stilted romanticism and profundity. Tobey manifested his fascination with Oriental religion, art and philosophy after visiting Asia in 1934, to study calligraphy and meditate at a Zen monastary. He abandoned a pseudo-Cubistic modeling of form for a linear description applied to representational elements in concert with purely abstract and spatial motifs. The small abstract tempera painting "Broadway Norm" (1935) announced this change with its matrix of coiling white line. The encroachment of Eastern pictorial modes propelled Tobey's art into its most genuinely individualistic and diverse phase—an inner expression of spiritual man and the city manifested as light, noise and energy.

Returning to Seattle at the eve of World War II, Tobey further developed his "white writing," which took the form of angular and curvilinear networks of line over a tonally dark and modulated ground. Figurative elements and intimations of architectural form (Gothic vaults and spires, city lights, vertically thrusting skyscrapers) were compressed and distributed across the picture plane. This formula eventually transfigured into non-hierarchial, non-objective abstract compositions: dense patterns of line expanding out to the picture edge, seeming to palpitate with a shifting focus and depth. Tobey's modified late style stemmed from experiments with *sumi* painting in the late 1950's. A broader stroke and more dabbled gesture took its place alongside his *repertoire* of anastomotic inscriptions; the "white writing" gave way to polychrome and black. Surface pattering became more chromatic and decorative, even serene. Controlled gestural surfaces superseded the spontaneous and energized calligraphy.

Tobey accepted the organic and dynamic Romantic conception of artistic creation as the proper analogue to a universal and religious interpretation of Creation. His deeply felt faith leads to the regard of his diverse art as emotionally and spiritually authentic despite stylistic and thematic fluctations and inconsistencies. "The dimension that counts for the creative person is the Space he creates within himself," Tobey once wrote. "This inner space is closer to the infinite . . ." What William Seitz has called his "world view" is Tobey's dynamic and dualistic encompassing of the inner and outer self, of internal and external space, and the synthesis of Eastern and Western thought. "At a time when experimentation expresses itself in all forms of life, search becomes the only valid expression of the spirit . . . "

—Ron Glowen

TOMASZEWSKI, Henryk.

Polish. Born in Warsaw, 10 June 1914. Studied graphics, under Mieczyslaw Kotarbinski, at the Art Academy, Warsaw, 1934-39. Graphic artist and poster designer, Warsaw, from 1946: Co-Founder, Poster Museum, Warsaw, 1968. Professor of graphic design, Art Academy, Warsaw, since 1952. Recipient: First Prize, *Polish Posters Exhibition*, Wieden, 1956; First Prize, *Bienal*, Sao Paulo, 1963; Medal, *Internationale Buchkunst Ausstellung*, Leipzig, 1965; Gold Medal, *Poster Biennale*, Warsaw, 1970; First Prize, *3rd Poster Biennale*, Lahti, Finland, 1979; First Prize, *Colorado International Poster Exhibition*, 1981; ICOGRADA Excellence Award, 1986. Honorary Royal Designer to Industry (U.K.), 1976. Address: Jazgarzewska Street 13, 00-730 Warsaw, Poland.

Individual Exhibitions:

1969 Kunstverein/Kongresshaus, Biel-Bienne, Switzerland
1972 Poster Museum, Wilanow, Poland
1984 Gallery A. and B. Wahl, Warsaw

Selected Group Exhibitions:

1948 *Miedzynarodowa Wystawa Plakatu*, Wieden, Poland
1963 *Bienal*, Sao Paulo (and 1979)
1966 *International Poster Biennale*, Warsaw (and regularly, 1968-86)
1971 *Polske Plakater*, Louisiana Museum, Humlebaek, Denmark
1978 *International Biennale of Design*, Wroclaw, Poland
1980 *Das Polnische Plakat von 1892 bis Heute*, Hochschule der Kunste, West Berlin
1981 *Colorado International Invitational Poster Exhibition*
1982 *Biennale of Graphic Arts*, Brno, Czechoslovakia
1985 *First International Poster Triennial*, Toyama, Japan
1986 *International Poster Salon*, Paris (and 1987)

Collections:

National Museum, Warsaw; Deutsches Plakat-Museum, Essen, West Germany; Kunstgewerbemuseum, Stockholm; Stedelijk Museum, Amsterdam; Kamakura Museum of Modern Art, Kamakura, Japan; Museum of Modern Art, New York; Museu de Arte Moderno, Sao Paulo.

Publications:

By TOMASZEWSKI: book—*Book of Complaints*, Warsaw 1961.

On TOMASZEWSKI: books—*Henryk Tomaszewski* by Barbara Kwiatkowska, Warsaw 1959; *International Poster Biennale*, exhibition catalogue, with text by J. Fijalkowska, Warsaw 1966; *Polski Plakat Filmowy 1947-1967*, exhibition catalogue, with text by Z. Schubert, Poznan 1969; *Polska Sztuka Plakatu* by Szymon Bojko, Warsaw 1971; *Das Polnische Plakat von 1892 bis Heute*, exhibition catalogue, West Berlin 1980; articles—"Polish Film and Theatre Posters" by Charles Robonyi in *Graphis* (Zurich), no. 63, 1956; "3rd Internationale Plakat-Biennale in Warschau 1970" by J. Spohn in *Gebrauchsgraphik* (Munich), no. 11, 1970; "Graphic Design in Poland" by Szymon Bojko in *The Penrose Annual*, London 1973; "Universal Dimensions" by Szymon Bojko in *Art and Artists* (London), September 1976; "Henryk Tomaszewski" by Jan Zielecki in *Projekt* (Warsaw), no. 4, 1985.

*

Thanking you, Henryk: read the eulogizing title of an exhibition held in Warsaw in 1975 by an international group of post-graduate students connected with Professor Tomaszewski's studio. In exhibiting their own works, the young graphic artists paid homage to the teacher who fascinated them by his personality. One of them wrote: "Since I have met Professor Henryk Tomaszewski, I know that the art of the poster is a moral discipline." Another student tried to sketch the Professor's stimulating way of mediating and making non-verbal comment: "With one hand, Henryk lights his 87th cigarette from the end of the 86th one, while with his other hand he puts on his spectacles No. 5; with his third hand he cuts a rectangular piece of glossy red paper which will 'play' on crumpled grey backing paper, pinned up with his fourth hand. For the 29th time he moved the edge of this paper, cuts another red rectangle, changes his spectacles to No. 2, paces back, returns, softens up a bright light, again steps back, and says 'This must sing . . . ' "

This lengthy quotation was necessary. Rare as it happens, a characteristic portrait of the artist in question is a mirror of his creative and teaching activity. Young people from various continents, desirous of moral and ethical wisdom, move to Tomaszewski's post-graduate studies, which brings to mind similar treks to Grotowski's Laboratory Institute. They rarely meet with disappointment. In Warsaw they find an impulse for spontaneous action. Freeing themselves from memorized rules and methods, they return to a happy land of free imagination. The 61-year-old dean of the Polish school of the poster is now surrounded by the legend of a man sensitive to deceit and hypocrisy. He is merciless to appearances and to sullen solemnity. With his stand and his graphic work he immunizes his fellow-countrymen to empty bureaucratic language, phraseology, and pretentiousness. He is credited with many sayings and ironic maxims, maybe once heard in the street, passed on from slang into the literary language. Resentful towards dogmas and pseudo-rationalist doctrines, intellectually independent and contrary, he has greatly influenced the artistic consciousness of a few generations of graphic artists, illustrators, and cartoonists.

Tomaszewski has originated a style of mass graphic art, demanding of the viewer some mental effort, as well as an ability to grasp rapidly the sense of abbreviations, associations, understatements, and paradoxes. Nothing should be taken seriously, verbatim, or without detachment. This work has incorporated the play element, and from child's sensitivity a kind of sophisticated infantilism. At the same time, it is opulent in subtle nuances, possessing neither cruelty, nor black humour, nor riddle. Rather irony and self-

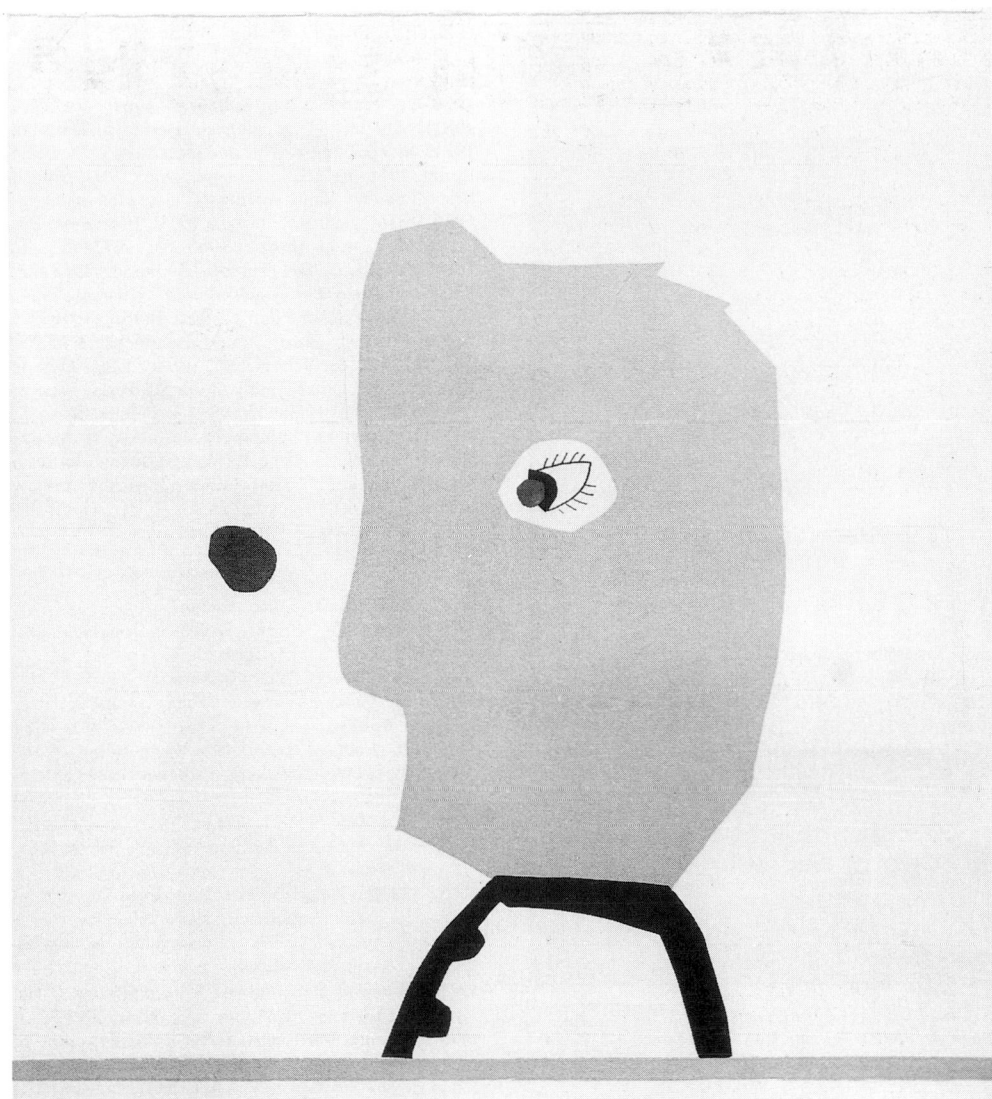

Henryk Tomaszewski: *Poster Design*, 1969

TORONI, Niele.
Swiss. Born in Locarno-Muralto, 15 March 1937.
Educated in Locarno. Independent artist, Locarno,
subsequently in Paris; Member, with Buren, Mosset
and Parmentier, Groupe BMPT, Paris 1966-68.
Agent: Galerie Yvon Lambert, 5 rue Grenier Saint
Lazare, 75003 Paris. Address: 73 rue Damremont,
75018 Paris, France.

Individual Exhibitions:

1969	16 rue Castagnary, Paris
1970	Galerie Yvon Lambert, Paris
	Galerie MTL, Brussels
1971	Galerie Michael Werner, Cologne
1972	Galerie Yvon Lambert, Paris
	Jack Wendler Gallery, London
	Galerie Michael Werner, Cologne
1973	Galleria Francoise Lambert, Milan
	Wide White Space Gallery, Antwerp
1974	John Gibson Gallery, New York
	Galleria Forma, Genoa
	Galleria d'Alessandro Ferranti, Rome
1975	Wide White Space Gallery, Antwerp
	Palais des Beaux-Arts, Brussels
	Galerie MTL, Brussels
	Galleria Francoise Lambert, Milan
	Galerie Yvon Lambert, Paris
1976	Galerie Paul Maenz, Cologne
	Robert Self Gallery, London
	Galerie Maier-Hahn, Dusseldorf
	Galleria Banco, Brescia, Italy
1977	Galleria Ferranti, Rome
	Galerie Yvon Lambert, Paris
	Museum Haus Kemnade, Bochum, West Germany
	Galerie MTL, Brussels
	Van Abbemuseum, Eindhoven, Netherlands
1978	Galleria Francoise Lambert, Milan
	Samngallery, Genoa, Italy
	Kunsthalle, Berne
1979	Galerie Yvon Lambert, Paris
	Galleria Ferranti, Rome
	Galerie Paul Maenz, Cologne
1980	Centre d'Art Contemporain, Geneva
	Hotel Wolfers, Brussels
1981	Galleria Banco, Brescia, Italy
	Samangallery, Genoa, Italy
	Galleria Francoise Lambert, Milan
1982	Museum van Hedendaagse Kunst, Ghent, Belgium
	Galerie M. Szwajcer, Antwerp, Belgium
	Galerie Media, Neuchatel, Switzerland

Selected Group Exhibitions:

1967	*Biennale*, Musée d'Art Moderne, Paris
1969	*Prospect 69*, Kunsthalle, Dusseldorf
1970	*18 Paris IV 70*, 66 rue Mouffetard, Paris
1972	*Actualités d'un Bilan*, Galerie Yvon Lambert, Paris
1973	*La Peinture en Question*, 16 Place Vendôme, Paris (travelled to Mönchengladbach and Antwerp)
1975	*Pour—Le/Nous*, Mesée d'Ixelles, Brussels
1977	*Europe in the Seventies*, Art Institute of Chicago
1981	*Mise en Pieces . . .* , Maison de la Culture, Chalon-sur-Saône, France (travelled to Le Coin du Miroir, Dijon)
1982	*Documenta*, Kassel, West Germany

Collections:

Musée National d'Art Moderne/Centre Georges Pompidou,
Paris; Musée de Toulon; Musée des Beaux-Arts, Ghent; Van
Abbemuseum, Eindhoven; Stadtisches Museum, Mon-
chengladbach.

Publications:

By TORONI: books—*11 Documents photographiques reunis
par Niele Toroni*, Brussels 1975; *Galleria Allegria*, Paris
1981.

---

irony. Its aesthetic origin is eminently Polish and is
situated in the same development line as the prose and
drama of Witkiewicz, Schulz, Gombrowicz, and
Mrozek, and the poetry of Tuwim and Galczynski, as
well as the literary and student revues of the 1960's
and earlier, headed by the Bim-Bom, crammed with
grotesquerie, parody, and sneer. One may say that the
posters and drawings by Tomaszewski are a mirror of
popular Polish mentality. They always create an impression of handwriting, thus attaining the value of an
intimate notebook, not intended for strange eyes. The
line, drawn as if by a maladroit child's hand, breaks
off, looses the trend on the way, and keeps scrawling.
The colour plane is simultaneously undecided, and it
rarely runs along the outline. It has the charm of an
improvisation, and of an unconcerned scrawl. In fact,
the artist prepares every line and colour patch with
the greatest of care. He even brings a complicated
thought or idea down to a synthesis or to a sign deriving from the drawing devoid of embellishments.

Tomaszewski has had a great moral influence in the
country. Each one of his new works elicits aesthetic

and social comments. In a recent interview he said
that most important for him is the motive of the communication and its range of meaning: "Often on my
piece of paper, there is as if nothing to be looked at,
nothing beautiful. These are things unable to caress
the eye." And somewhere else, in the same spirit: "I
prefer a foolish proposition to mastered perfection."

The artist's poster achievement is generally known
from exhibitions and publications. Many of his works
have a permanent place in 20th century art, including
posters for the film *La Beaute du diable* (1954), for
an exhibition of sculpture by Henry Moore (1959),
for the theatrical performances of *Hamlet* (1970),
Slub (The Marriage) by Gombrowicz (1974), and
Witkacy—a stage collage of plays by Witkiewicz
(1974), and for the Theatre of the Nations session in
Warsaw (1976). His drawings are dispersed among
various periodicals and, apart from the album
Ksiazka zazalen (The Book of Complaints), 1961,
have not been the subject of a monograph so far.

—Szymon Bojko

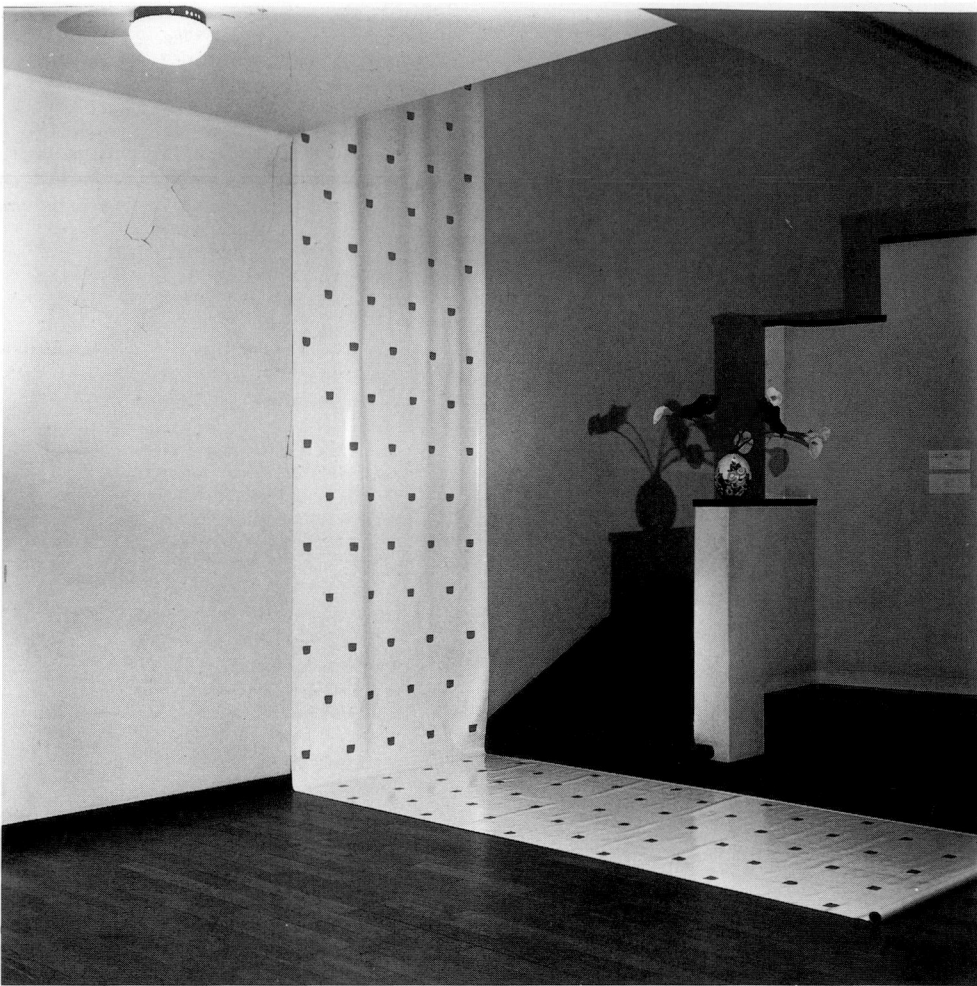

Niele Toroni: *Rouleau—toile cirée,* 1968

On TORONI: books—*18 Paris IV 70,* exhibition catalogue/book/with text by Michel Claura, Paris and New York 1970; *Actualité d'un Bilan,* exhibition catalogue, edited by Yvon Lambert, Paris 1972; *La Peinture en Question,* exhibition catalogue, with texts by Michel Claura and René Denizot, Paris 1973; *Un Empreinte n'est jamais seule* by René Denizot, Paris 1975; *Niele Toroni,* exhibition catalogue, with text by René Denizot, Eindhoven, Netherlands 1977; *Niele Toroni: 52 pages, 52 pagine, 52 seite,* exhibition catalogue, with text by Johannes Gachnang, Berne 1978; *Mise en Pieces, Mise en Place, Mise au Point,* exhibition catalogue, with an introduction by Xavier Douroux and Christian Besson, Chalon-sur-Saône, France 1981; *Documenta 7,* exhibition catalogue, 2 vols., edited by Rudi H. Fuchs, Kassel, West Germany 1982; *Formalité et Historicité* by Benjamin Buchloh, Paris 1982.

Why is it that someone who *does something* (and I underline this because there are so many very active people who never do anything at all) is continually asked "why", for a justification? Is it for reassurance?

In this instance is it because you don't have the courage to accept your reaction in front of this work? Whether negative or positive, that's not the point. The problem is this need for a "debate on", which pretends parasitically to exist in the place of that which stimulates it; this need for intermediaries; it's true that it maintains quite a lot of people, in fish, in vegetables, in art.

It's again the problem of conditioning. (There are) those who don't even dare to say "I'm fine", "I feel bad"; first they want explanations (the famous why), to know if perhaps they are unhappy because they haven't understood that they should be happy, bravo, the brave face. When you feel bad, say so, bawl it out.

To return to our story, in front of a work begin by accepting what goes through your mind (if something does, it is not an absolute necessity!). No explanation can take its place or then lots of explanations will make you admit anything. Marcel Proust wrote: "As soon as reasoning intelligence wants to judge works of art, nothing is any longer definite or indisputable: one can prove whatever one wants to". That's true enough, especially these days with the swarms of "intelligent debaters". Whoever doesn't know what to do talks painting, writes painting, understands painting . . . . but take care not to touch a brush, you could dirty your little hands or other things! It's a pity that one still doesn't know where a work of art begins and where it ends . . . . .

All this to let you know that my work/painting cannot, must not be of more or less interest depending on what I could say to you or what others might say to you about it.

It's painting and that's all.

Visible marks of a no.50 brush (typically pictural work tool), for the brush, so that it can leave its mark, is saturated with paint, paint which is colour, colour that one doesn't see as a rule because it's in a tin and is revealed by application of the brush. No. 50 brushmarks, "spots" of paint if you like, (the surface covered with colour being determined by the dimension of the hairy part of the brush, that part which is used for painting) repeated at regular intervals (30cm), occupying the chosen support while leaving it visible, legible.

Read a wall. Why not? It's up to you to see.

—Niele Toroni

TOT, Endre.

Hungarian. Born Endre Toth in Sumeg, 5 November 1937; adopted the name "Tot" in 1965. Studied at the Hungarian Academy of Applied Arts, Budapest, 1959–65. Married Teri Simon in 1969 (divorced, 1981); daughter: Bea; married Herta Paraschin in 1981. Independent artist, Budapest, 1965–78, West Berlin, 1978–79, and in Cologne, since 1980: painted first Zero and Rain works, 1971; ceased painting, 1971; first "gladness" works, 1971. Instructor, Budapest elementary school, 1965–68, 1972–75, and Technical School for Printing, Budapest, 1968–72. Recipient: Prize, *Drawing Triennale,* Wroclaw, 1974, 1977; DAAD Scholarship to West Berlin, 1978–79. Agents: Galerie Orez Mobiel, Paviljoensgracht 68/70, NL-2512 BR The Hague, Netherlands; Galerie Bama, 40 rue Quincampoix, F-75004 Paris, France; Galerie Magers, Handelstrasse 13, D-5300 Bonn 1, West Germany; and Edition Hundertmark, Brusselerstrasse 29, 5000 Cologne 1, West Germany. Address: Engelbertstrasse 55, 5000 Cologne 1, West Germany.

Individual Exhibitions:

Tot has also presented numerous performances and actions throughout Europe since 1972.

Selected Group Exhibitions:

1984   *International Kunstler Gremium Ausstellung*, Museum Fridericianum, Kassel, West Germany

1985   *Livres d'Artistes*, Centre Georges Pompidou, Paris

Collections:

Kulturministerium Nordrhein-Westfalen, Dusseldorf; Lambert Collection, Paris; Bibliothèque Nationale, Paris; Centre National d'Art Contemporain, Paris; Cabinet des Estampes, Geneva; Gemeentemuseum, The Hague; National Museum, Warsaw; Israel Museum, Jerusalem; Kunsthalle, Hamburg; Nationalgalerie, West Berlin.

Publications:

By TOT: books and cards—*My Unpainted Canvases*, Budapest 1971; *The States of Zeros*, Budapest 1971; *Incomplete Information (Verbal and Visual)*, Oldenburg, West Germany 1972; *Possessive Adjective*, Budapest 1972; *I Am Glad If I Can Write Sentences, One After the Other*, Budapest 1973; *One Dozen Rain Postcards (1971-73)*, Budapest 1973; *On the Next Page I Shall Say Something*, Budapest 1973; *Zero-Texts (1971-72)*, Graz, Austria 1974; *Night Visit to the National Gallery*, Cullompton, Devon 1974; *Zeropost*, Hinwil 1974; *Nullified Dialogue*, Hinwil 1974; *Correspondance avec John Armleder*, Geneva 1974; *TOTal Questions by TOT*, West Berlin 1974; *1/2 Dozen Incomplete Visual Informations (1971-74)*, Budapest 1974; *One Dozen Rain Postcards (1971-73)*, Stuttgart 1974; *Rainproof Ideas (1971-74)*, Jerusalem 1975; *TOTalJOYS (1971-75)*, Geneva 1976; *Zeropost*, Geneva 1976; *Gladness Writings (1973-76)*, Liège, Belgium 1977; *TOTal Zeros (1973-77)*, Budapest 1977; *1/2 Dozen Berliner Gladness Postcards (1973-78)*, West Berlin 1979; *Ich freue mich, wenn ich auf Plakaten werben kann*, West Berlin 1979; *TOTalJOYS*, West Berlin 1979; *Dirty Rains*, Lund, Sweden 1979; *Some Nullified Questions*, Amsterdam 1979; *Ten Documents (1973-80)*, Amsterdam 1980; *Very Special Drawings*, West Berlin 1981; *Book of an Extremely Glad Artist*, West Berlin 1981; *From Cologne some Jecke Dinge to you, everybody and nobody*, Cremlingen 1983; *Stamps 1971- 83*, Cremlingen 1983; *Special Drawings—Private Space*, Kassel 1984. films—*One Step*, 1972; *I Am Glad If . . .* , 1974; *TOTalJOYS*, 1976; video—*I'm Glad if I Can Say Sentences, One After the Other*, 1979; *TOTalJOYS*, 1979.

On TOT: books—*Mail Art: Communication: A Distance-Concept*, edited by Jean-Marc Poinsot, Paris 1971; *Aktuelle Kunst in Osteuropa*, edited by Klaus Groh, Cologne 1972; *Stamp Activity* by Jiri H. Kocman, Brno, Czechoslovakia 1972; *An Annual of New Art and Artists 1973-74*, edited by W. Sandberg, Cologne 1974; *Art et Communications Marginale* by Hervé Fischer, Paris 1974; *Funf Osteuropaische Kunstler*, edited by Klaus Groh, Nuremberg 1975; *Visual Poetry Anthology*, edited by G. J. de Rook, Utrecht 1975; *Europe/America: The Different Avant Gardes* by Achille Bonito Oliva, Milan 1976; *The Museum of Drawers*, edited by Herbert Distel, Berne 1978; *Fotografie als Kunst/Kunst als Fotografie* by Floris M. Neusüss, Cologne 1979; *Testuale: Le Parole e le Immagini*, exhibition catalogue, edited by F. Caroli and L. Caramel, Milan 1979; *Kunst in Sozialistischen Staaten* by J. Weichart, Oldenburg, West Germany 1980; *Books by Artists* by T. Guest and Germano Celant, Toronto 1981; *Correspondence Art*, edited by M. Cramer and M. Stofflet, San Francisco 1984; *International Artists' Postage Stamps*, edited by B. Lobach, Cremlingen 1985; *Livres d'Artistes*, edited by A. Moeglin-Delcroix, Paris 1985; *Wer hat Augst von Moholy-Nagy?*, edited by T. Straus, Cologne 1987.

I am always glad of those days, when nothing happens to me except that I wake up in the morning and go to bed in the evening.

—Endre Tot

TOUSIGNANT, Claude.

Canadian. Born in Montreal, Quebec, 23 December 1932. Studied at the School of Art and Design, Montreal Museum of Fine Arts, 1948–51; Académie Ranson, Paris, 1952. Has lived with Judith Terry since 1968; daughters: Isa and Zoe. Worked as surveyor, window-dresser, fireman and show salesman at various times; currently, independent artist. Instructor, School of Art and Design, Montreal Museum of Fine Arts, 1961–63; Instructor, École des Beaux-Arts, University of Quebec, Montreal, 1970. Recipient: First Prize (Painting), *Salon de la Jeune Peinture*, Paris 1962; First Prize (Painting), *Perspective '67*, Toronto, 1967; Italian Government Rome Prize, 1973. Addresses: (office) 3684 St. Lawrence Boulevard, Montreal, Quebec H2X 2V4; (home) 4678 St. Andre, Montreal, Quebec H2J 3A1, Canada.

Individual Exhibitions:

1955   L'Echouerie, Montreal
1956   L'Actuelle, Montreal
1957   L'Actuelle, Montreal
1961   Museum of Fine Arts, Montreal
1962   Galerie Denise Delrue, Montreal
1963   Dorothy Cameron Gallery, Toronto
1964   Galerie du Siècle, Montreal
1965   East Hampton Gallery, New York
1966   East Hampton Gallery, New York
        Galerie du Siècle, Montreal
1968   Galerie du Siècle, Montreal
        Gallery Moos, Toronto
1969   Galerie Sherbrooke, Montreal
1970   Galerie Jolliet, Quebec

Endre Tot: *Zero-Demonstration*, 1972

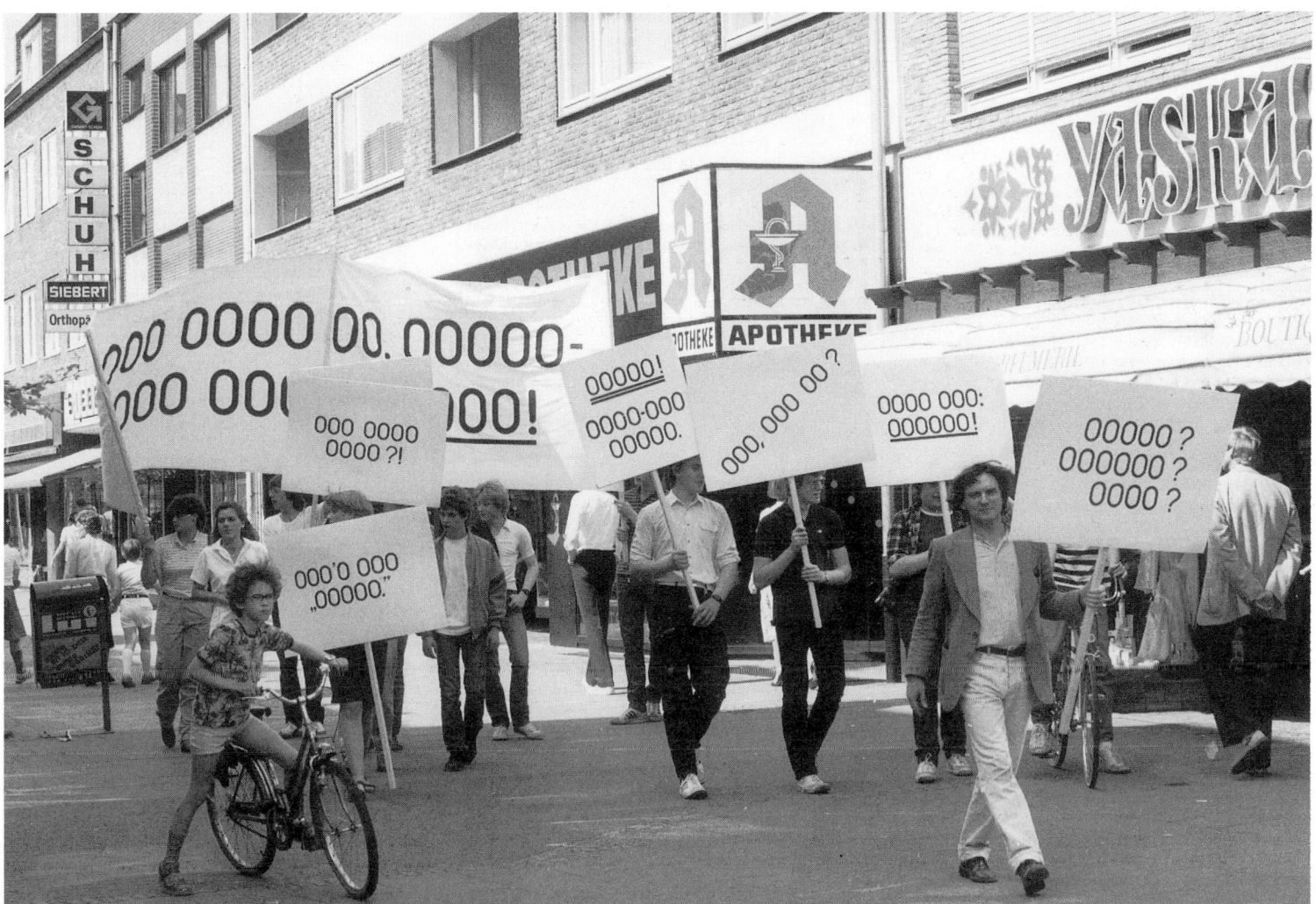

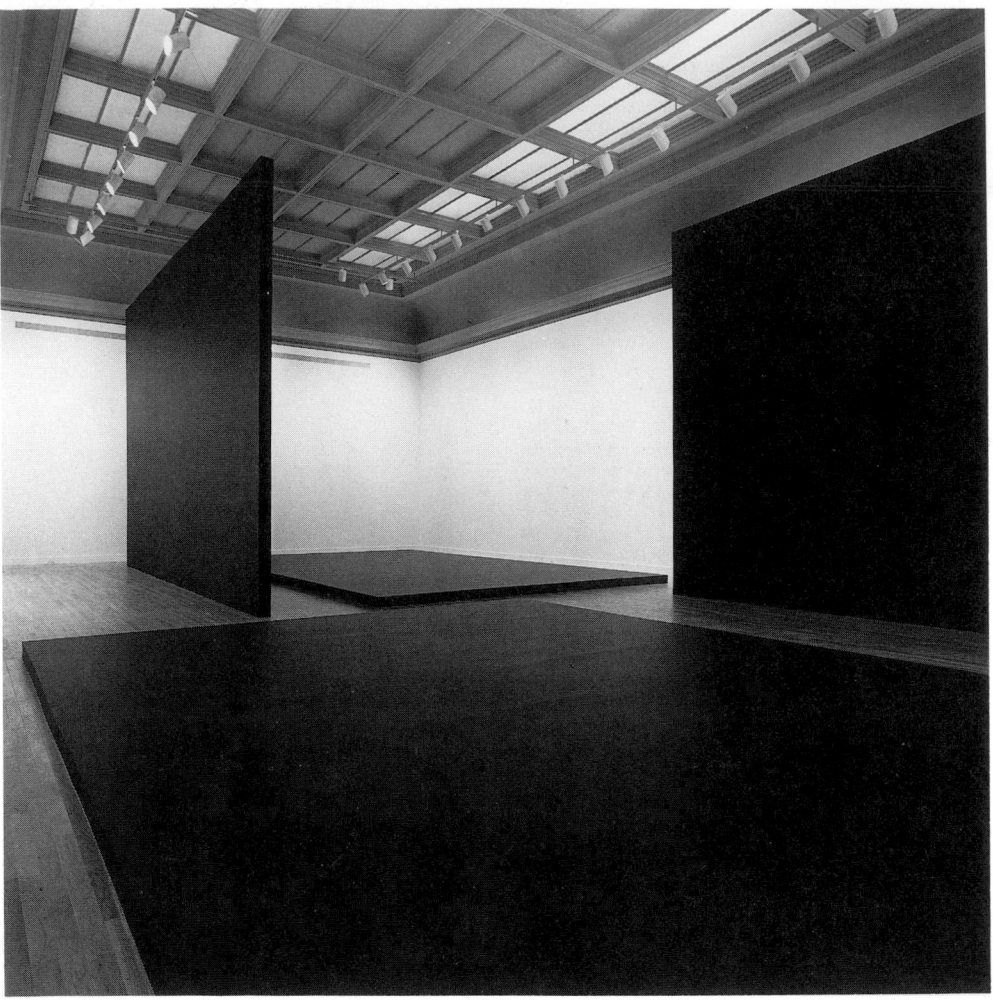

Claude Tousignant: *420*, 1982

bring it back to its source—where only painting remains, emptied of all extraneous matter—to the point at which painting is pure sensation.

—Claude Tousignant

Claude Tousignant has been painting since 1948, "and is still in transformation," he says. He admires greatly the American painter, Barnett Newman—for him the most radical of the New York school. The initial works through which he became known on the Canadian scene were, like those of other painters in Montreal, hard edged and sharp, with bright colours. In his circular paintings in particular, he used a series of rings of colour. "The hard edge was there for functional reasons."

Today Tousignant is more of a sculptor—in the sense that sculpture deals with material—"and if he paints a surface it is as a material." His large works (some are 14 feet by 8 feet), often in a series, are monochrome, flat, and in primary colours. Study of Matisse's "Dance" from the Mellon Collection in London, England, in 1968, along with a stay in Italy in 1973, led to Tousignant's later works with arches (from 1973-74 on).

The source for his more recent sculptures is a monochrome painting, *Monochrome Rangé* (Montreal Museum of Fine Arts), he painted flat, with shiny orange enamel, in 1956. (Previously his paintings had two or three divisions, horizontal or vertical). The work hung on the wall of his apartment: "I started to see it as an object in the environment." "It acted like a sculpture." Tousignant says: "If there is no image, and the object is not about something else, the viewer feels the actuality of the material, dimension, surface, colour, etc., and is physically implicated by the work."

Tousignant continues to preceive his work as non-anecdotal and non-symbolic. He is still exploring the "painting as an object", manipulating existential rather than aesthetic space.

—Joan Murray

1972	Gallery Moos, Toronto
2973	National Gallery of Canada, Ottawa (retrospective)
1974	Art Gallery of Ontario, Toronto (retrospective)
1976	Winnipeg Art Gallery
	Waddington Gallery, Montreal
1977	Windsor Art Gallery, Ontario
1979	Graff Gallery, Montreal (prints)
1980	Musée d'Art Contemporain, Montreal
1982	Musée des Beaux-Arts, Montreal (sculptures)

Selected Group Exhibitions:

1962	*Modern Canadian Painting*, Palazzo Collicola, Spoleto, Italy
1965	*The Responsive Eye*, Museum of Modern Art, New York (toured the United States)
1968	*Canada: Art d'Aujourd'hui*, Musée National d'Art Moderne, Paris (toured Italy, Switzerland and Belgium)
	7 Montreal Artists, Hayden Gallery, Massachusetts Institute of Technology, Cambridge
1969	*Form-Colour*, National Gallery of Canada, Ottawa (toured Canada)
1970	*Panorama de la Sculpture au Quebec 1945-1970*, Musée d'Art Contemporain, Montreal (travelled to the Musée Rodin, Paris)
1971	*49th Parallels: New Canadian Art*, Ringling Museum, Sarasota, Florida
1974	*Recent Canadian Painting*, Art Gallery of Ontario, Toronto
1975	*Time Canada*, Musée d'Art Contemporain, Montreal (toured Canada)
1976	*Trois Generations d'Art Quebecois*, Musée d'Art Contemporain, Montreal

Collections:

Art Gallery of Ontario, Toronto; York University, Toronto; Canada Arts Council, Ottawa; National Gallery of Canada, Ottawa; Museum of Fine Arts, Montreal; Musée d'Art Contemporain, Montreal; Musée du Quebec, Quebec City; Vancouver Art Gallery; Larry Aldrich Museum, Ridgefield, Connecticut; Phoenix Museum of Art, Arizona.

Publications:

By TOUSIGNANT: articles—"Pour une peinture evidentille" in *Art Abstract*, exhibition catalogue, Montreal 1959; "Quelques precisions essentielles" in *Peinture Canadienne Française*, Montreal 1971.

On TOUSIGNANT: books—*Modern Canadian Painting*, exhibition catalogue, by Charles Delloye, Spoleto, Italy 1962; *7 Montreal Artists*, exhibition catalogue, by Bernard Teyssedre, Cambridge, Massachusetts 1968; *Claude Tousignant*, exhibition catalogue, by Danielle Corbeil, Ottawa 1973; *Claude Tousignant: Sculptures*, exhibition catalogue with essay by Normand Theriault, Montreal 1982; articles—"La jeune peinture au Quebec" by Francois Gagnon in *Revue d'Esthetique No. 3: Art au Quebec*, Quebec 1963; "L'Illusion optique de l'Op Art" by Fernande Saint-Martin in *Vie des Arts* (Montreal), no. 39, 1965; "Le dynamisme des plasticiens de Montreal" by Fernande Saint-Martin in *Vie des Arts* (Montreal), no. 44, 1966; "Structure de l'espace pictural" by Fernande Saint-Martin in *Constantes* (Montreal), no. 17, 1968; "Claude Tousignant" by Pierre Theberge in *Canada: Art d'Aujourd'hui*, exhibition catalogue, Paris 1968; "Les Plasticiens" by Pierre Theberge in *Studio International* (London), 1970.

What I wish to do is to make painting objective, to

TRBULJAK, Goran.

Yugoslav. Born in Varazdin, Croatia, 21 April 1948. Studied photography at the School of Applied Arts, Zagreb, 1963-68; studied graphics at the Academy of Fine Arts, Zagreb, 1968-72; Ecole National Supérieure des Beaux-Arts, Paris, 1974-75. Independent artist, since 1970: lives and works in Zagreb. Director of the Photography Department, Academy of Theatrical and Film Arts, Zagreb, from 1980. Recipient: Sedam Sekretara Skoja, 1972, 1979; Kodak nagrada za kameru, 1980; National Film Festival Award, Pula, 1984, 1986. Address: Djalskog 39, 41000 Zagreb, Yugoslavia.

Individual Exhibitions:

1970	Ilica 85, Zagreb
1971	Likovni Salon tribine mladih, Novi Sad, Yugoslavia
	Galerie S.C., Zagreb
1972	Galerie des Locataires, Paris
	Galerie S.K.C., Belgrade
1973	Likovni Salon Tibine Mladih, Novi Sad, Yugoslavia
	Gallery of Contemporary Art, Zagreb
1974	Galery Remont, Warsaw
1975	Galerie 28, Paris
1976	Galery Znak, Bialystok, Poland
	Atelier Milch Strasse, Freiburg, West Germany
	Galerie S.K.C., Belgrade
	Medvescak Library, Zagreb
1977	Galleria del Cavallino, Venice
	Galleria Civica d'Arte Moderna, Moderna, Italy
	Studio 16E, Turin
	Gallery Nova, Zagreb
	Gallery S.K.C., Belgrade

1979	Gallery of Contemporary Art, Zagreb
	Hotel Dubrovnik, Zagreb
1981	Salon Muzeja savrement Umjetnosti, Belgrade
	Galerija studentskog centra, Zagreb
	Gallery PM, Zagreb
1986	Gallery PM, Zagreb

Selected Group Exhibitions:

1971	*Conceptual Art in Yugoslavia,* Museum of Modern Art, Belgrade
1972	*Internationale Malewochen,* Graz, Austria
1973	*Biennale de Paris*
1975	*Kunst aus Jugoslawien,* Akademie der Bildenden Künste, Vienna
1976	*Video,* Kunstmuseum, Aarhus, Denmark
1977	*Moderne Kunst in Kroatien,* Rathaus, Mainz, West Germany
1978	*Analytical Works,* Gallery S.K.C., Belgrade
1982	*Internationale Jugendtriennale,* Kunsthalle, Nuremberg
1983	*Triennale of Drawing,* Warsaw
1986	*Art and Criticism in the mid-eighties,* Sarajevo, Yugoslavia

Collections;

Gallery of Contemporary Art, Zagreb; Muzej Savremene Umjetnosti, Belgrade; Museum of Modern Art, Zagreb.

Publications:

By TRBULJAK: books—*Artiste Anonyme,* Zagreb and Belgrade 1976; *Ecrits d'un Artiste,* Zagreb 1980; *Les Pages Non-Publiés des Ecrits d'un Artiste,* Zagreb 1980; article—"Artiste Anonyme" in *Flash Art* (Milan), June 1974.

On TRBULJAK: books—*Aktuelle Kunst in Osteuropa,* edited by Klaus Groh, Cologne 1972; *Goran Trbuljak,* exhibition catalogue, with text by Jesa Denegri, Zagreb 1973; *8th Biennale de Paris,* exhibition catalogue, with texts by J. Cahen-Salvador, G. Boudaille, J-M Poinsot and others, Paris 1973.

Under the slogan, "An artist is anyone who is given the opportunity to be one", the first referendum was held on the 1st July 1972, in which ordinary citizens had to decide whether or not someone is an artist. With their choice, people were to proclaim as an artist some person whose name was previously unknown to them (the name actually printed on the ballot forms was of a person who had attended art school—and was herself passing out the ballot papers—so, for the purposes of the exercise, it was irrelevant for the recipient of votes to deal in any kind of creative activity, or even to exist at all). Out of 500 ballots, there were 259 positive decisions and 204 negative ones, the person selected as an artist being totally unknown to the voters.

—Goran Trbuljak

TREMLETT, David.

British. Born in St. Austell, Cornwall, 13 February 1945. Studied under Terry Pascoe, Falmouth School of Art, Cornwall, 1962–63; Birmingham College of Art, 1963–66; Royal College of Art, London, 1966–69. Full-time artist since 1969: travelled in Spain, Netherlands and Australia, 1969; in Malawi, Tanzania, Botswana, Mozambique, Middle East and Far East, 1970–79; in Alaska, Canada, India, Mexico and Australia, 1980–87. Agent: Hester Van Royen, Flat 3, 53 Drayton Gardens, London SW10. Address: "Broadlawns", Chipperfield Road, Bovingdon, Hertfordshire HP3 OJR, England.

Individual Exhibitions:

1969	Grabowski Gallery, London
1970	Nigel Greenwood Gallery, London
1971	Nigel Greenwood Gallery, London
	Galerie Ernst, Hannover
	Folker Skulima Galerie, West Berlin
1972	Nigel Greenwood Gallery, London
	Tate Gallery, London
	Galerie Konrad Fischer, Dusseldorf
1973	Museum of Modern Art, New York
	Harold Rivkin Gallery, Washington, D.C.
	Nigel Greenwood Gallery, London
1974	Nigel Greenwood Gallery, London
	Museum of Modern Art, Oxford
1975	Galleria Marilena Bonomo, Bari, Italy

Goran Trbuljak: *Artiste en Crise,* 1987

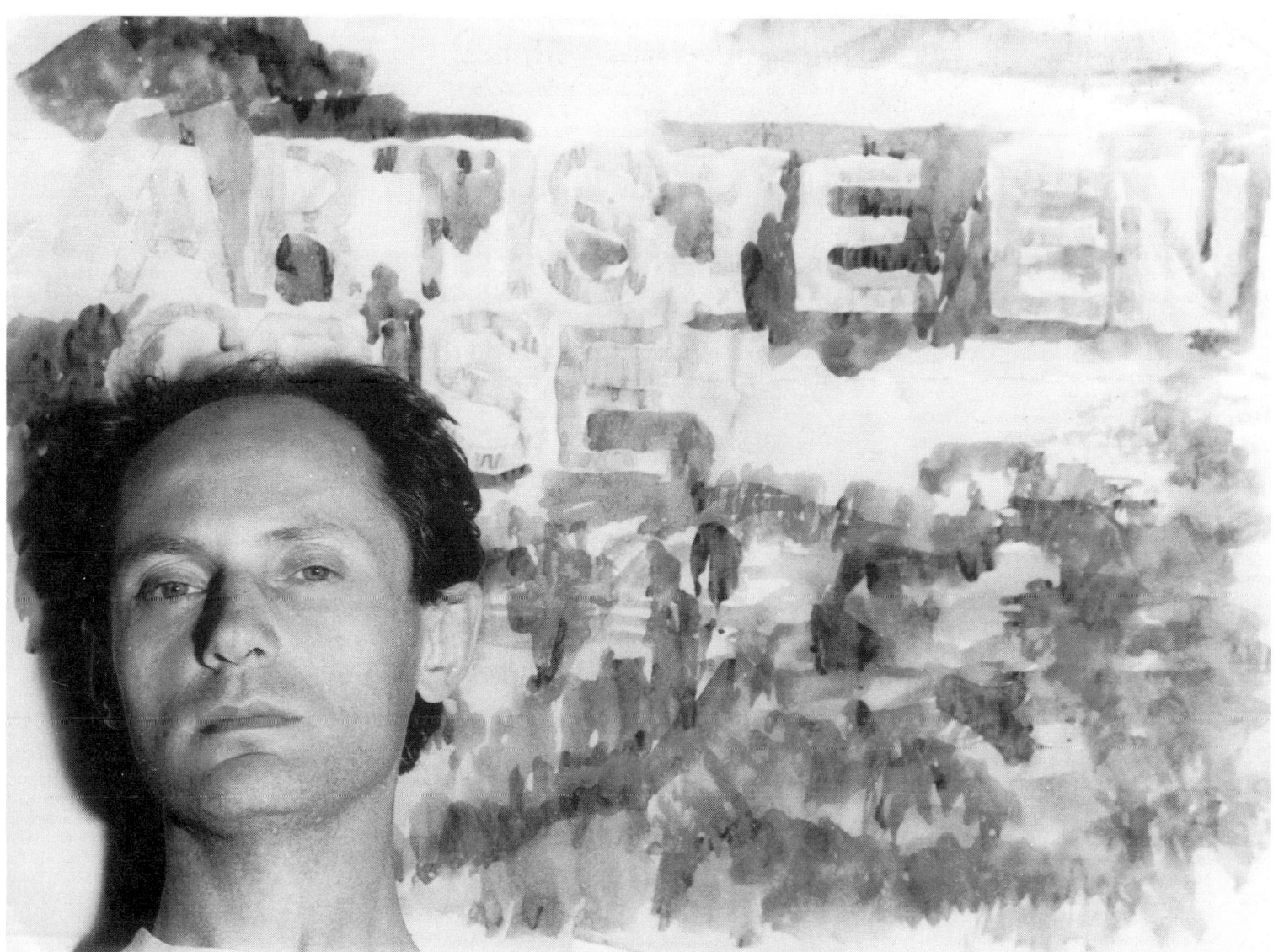

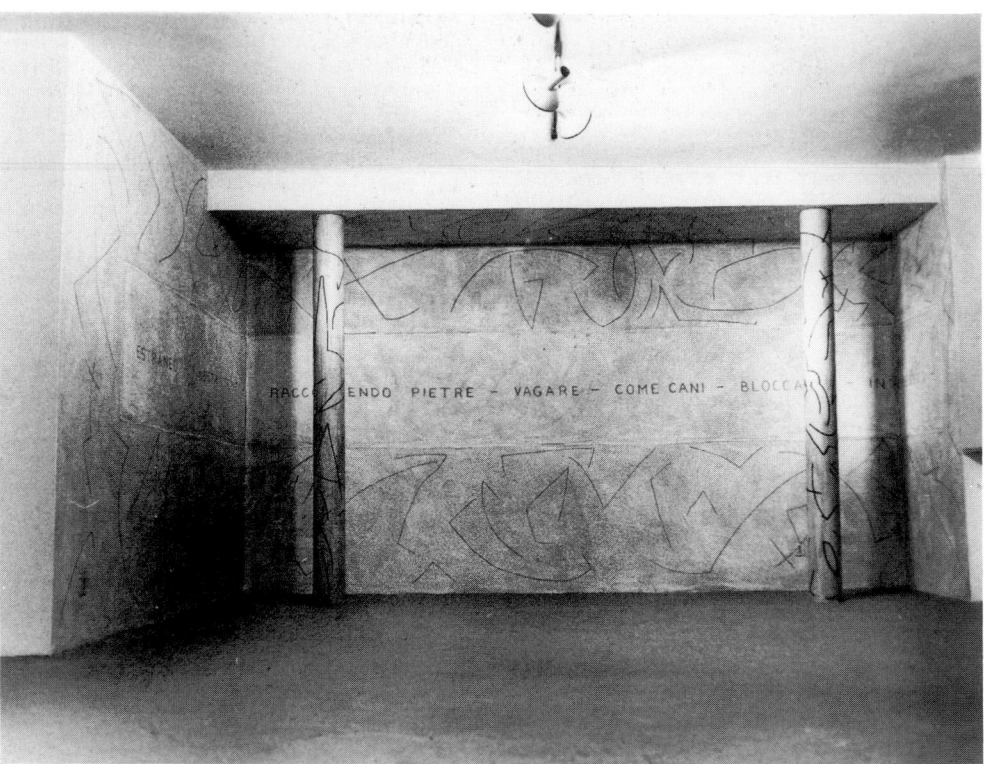

David Tremlett: *Come Cani*, 1985

1976   Galerie Rolf Preisig, Basle
      Nigel Greenwood Gallery, London
      Art and Project, Amsterdam
      Robert Self Gallery, Newcastle-on-Tyne
      Galleria Marilena Bonomo, Bari, Italy
      Galerie Durand-Dessert, Paris
      Institute of Contemporary Arts, London
1977   Galerie Durand-Dessert, Paris
1978   Plymouth Arts Centre, Devon
      Galleria Massimo Valsecchi, Milan
      Zomba Road, Malawi, Africa
      Art and Project, Amsterdam
1979   Galleria Marilena Bonomo, Bari, Italy
      Librairie Post Scriptum, Brussels
      Galleria Massimo Valsecchi, Milan
      Stedelijk Museum, Amsterdam
1980   Galerie Durand-Dessert, Paris
      Gordon Jetty, Tasmania
1981   John Hansard Gallery, Southampton, Hampshire
      Galleria Massimo Valsecchi, Milan
      Art and Project, Amsterdam
      Waddington Galleries, London
      Galleria Marilena Bonomo, Bari, Italy
1982   Riverside Studios, London
      Galerie Durand-Dessert, Paris
1983   Galerie Durand-Dessert, Paris
      Galleria Massimo Valsecchi, Milan
      Galleria Marilena Bonomo, Bari, Italy
      Raum fur Kunst, Hamburg
      Waddington Galleries, London
1984   Waddington Galleries, London
      Art and Project, Amsterdam
1985   Centre Georges Pompidou, Paris
      Leicester Polytechnic, Leicestershire
      Gallery 865, Aalst, Belgium
      Le Crystal, Paris
      Galleria Marilena Bonomo, Bari, Italy
1986   Orchard Gallery, Londonderry, Northern Ireland
      (with Hamish Fulton)
      Waddington Galleries, London
      Institute of Contemporary Arts, London
      Museum Van Hedendaagse Kunst, Ghent, Belgium
1987   22 All Saints Road, London
      Galerie Durand-Dessert, Paris
      Galleria Massimo Valsecchi, Milan
      Artek Gallery, Helsinki

Selected Group Exhibitions:

1970   *British Sculpture of the Sixties*, Institute of Contemporary Arts, London
1971   *The British Avant Garde*, New York Cultural Center
1972   *Documenta 5*, Museum Fridericianum, Kassel, West Germany
1974   *An Element of Landscape*, Mappin Art Gallery, Sheffield, Yorkshire (toured Britain)
1975   *New Media I*, Konsthall, Malmo, Sweden
1977   *03-23-03*, Institute of Contemporary Art, Montreal
1979   *Un Certain Art Anglais*, Musee d'Art Moderne de la Ville, Paris (travelled to Brussels)
1981   *British Sculpture in the Twentieth Century*, Whitechapel Art Gallery, London
1984   *The Critical Eye/1*, Yale Center for British Art, New Haven, Connecticut
1987   *L'Exotisme au Quotidien*, Musee des Beaux-Arts, Charleroi, Belgium

Collections:

Tate Gallery, London; Victoria and Albert Museum, London; Arts Council of Great Britian, London; Stedelijk Museum, Amsterdam; Museum Boymans-van Beuningen, Rotterdam; Centre Georges Pompidou/Musee National d'Art Moderne, Paris; Musee d'Art et d'Industrie, St. Etienne, France; Philadelphia Museum of Art.

Publications:

By TREMLETT: books—*Some Places to Visit*, London 1975; *On the Waterfront*, Newlyn, Cornwall 1978; *Scrub*, Bari and Paris 1978; *On the Border*, Amsterdam 1979; *Restless*, London 1983; *Old Tom and Hotel Room*, New Haven, Connecticut 1984; *Rough Ride*, Paris and London 1985; *Ruin*, Amsterdam 1987.

On TREMLETT: books—*David Tremlett: 4 Sculptures*, catalogue poster with essay by Peter Atkins, London 1969; *The British Avant-Garde*, exhibition catalogue by Charles Harrison and Donald Karshan, New York 1971; *Documenta 5: Befragung der Realitat*, exhibition catalogue edited by Harald Szeemann and others, Kassel 1972; *An Element of Landscape*, exhibition catalogue with text by Jeremy Rees, London 1974; *British Sculpture in the Twentieth Century*, exhibition catalogue by Sandy Nairne and Nicholas Serota, London 1981; *The Critical Eye*, exhibition catalogue with essay by S. Paoletti, New Haven, Connecticut 1984.

In common with Richard Long, Hamish Fulton or Lothar Baumgarten, the artist David Tremlett takes his inspiration from traditions totally outside his own. For Tremlett, it is the journey, with its transitory locations, temporary resting places and defined cultural identities, which is his stimulus. This does not mean that his language is simply 'cosmopolitan' or more international, but rather that his subject is atopical. He does not renounce that which is conventionally understood as a 'work of art', but he disrupts its traditional modes of expression and the gulf which, in our world, distinguishes the practice of the artist from that of daily life.

He has made frequent trips through Africa and Mexico where he has assimilated ideas and forms belonging to different systems of thought, in order to formulate a vocabulary which vitalizes that formal repertory inherited from Western culture. Very simplified images, latently symbolic and vaguely totemic but stripped of every connotation, become the synthetic schema which are the style of this artist.

It is not without significance that the creative process is instinctive and immediate, employing a direct physical involvement of the artist himself with his materials. Tremlett chooses media such as coloured pastels reminiscent of the organic and allusive elements of the earth, or even extracts his own pigments directly from the earth. At times, he limits himself to elementary black and white, to primary tonalities. Often, the actual wall of the gallery accommodates his images. Spreading the colour directly onto the wall with his hands, Tremlett allows a certain degree of chance in the execution of the work. The wall reveals its unpredictable qualities, its porous and pitted surface reacting in unforeseen ways with the pigment. This unpredictability does not disrupt but actually qualifies the work.

In his works on paper, the drawing signifies the concentration of the mind in the act of governing internal processes. In most cases, the act of drawing determines the dimensions of the project. The environment of the picture plane is scrupulously constructed as a rigorously two-dimensional space, while the titles of the works make reference to architectural space. The images that Tremlett adopts open a discourse on the ambiguity of traditional definitions. Each work, whilst maintaining internal references to its own fulfilment, gestures towards the work which will follow. The pigmentation reclaimed from the earth is the essential material of building and sculpting. The physical work, the action, moulding and consolidation done with the hands, result in the very material of the work.

—Giorgio Verzotti

TREVELYAN, Julian (Otto).
British. Born in Dorking, Surrey, 20 February 1910. Educated at Bedales School, Hampshire, 1922-27; studied at Trinity College, Cambridge, 1928-30; studied printmaking under S. W. Hayter at Atelier 17, Paris, 1931-34. Served as camouflage officer, Royal Engineers, British Army, 1940-43. Married Ursula Darwin in 1934 (divorced, 1950); married Mary Fedden in 1951; son: Philip. Painter and graphic artist, Hammersmith, London, from 1935; Member, London Group of painters, 1948-63. Tutor in Etching, Royal College of Art, London, 1955-63. Agent: New Grafton Gallery, 49 Church Road, Barnes, London SW13. *Died* (in London) *12 July 1988.*

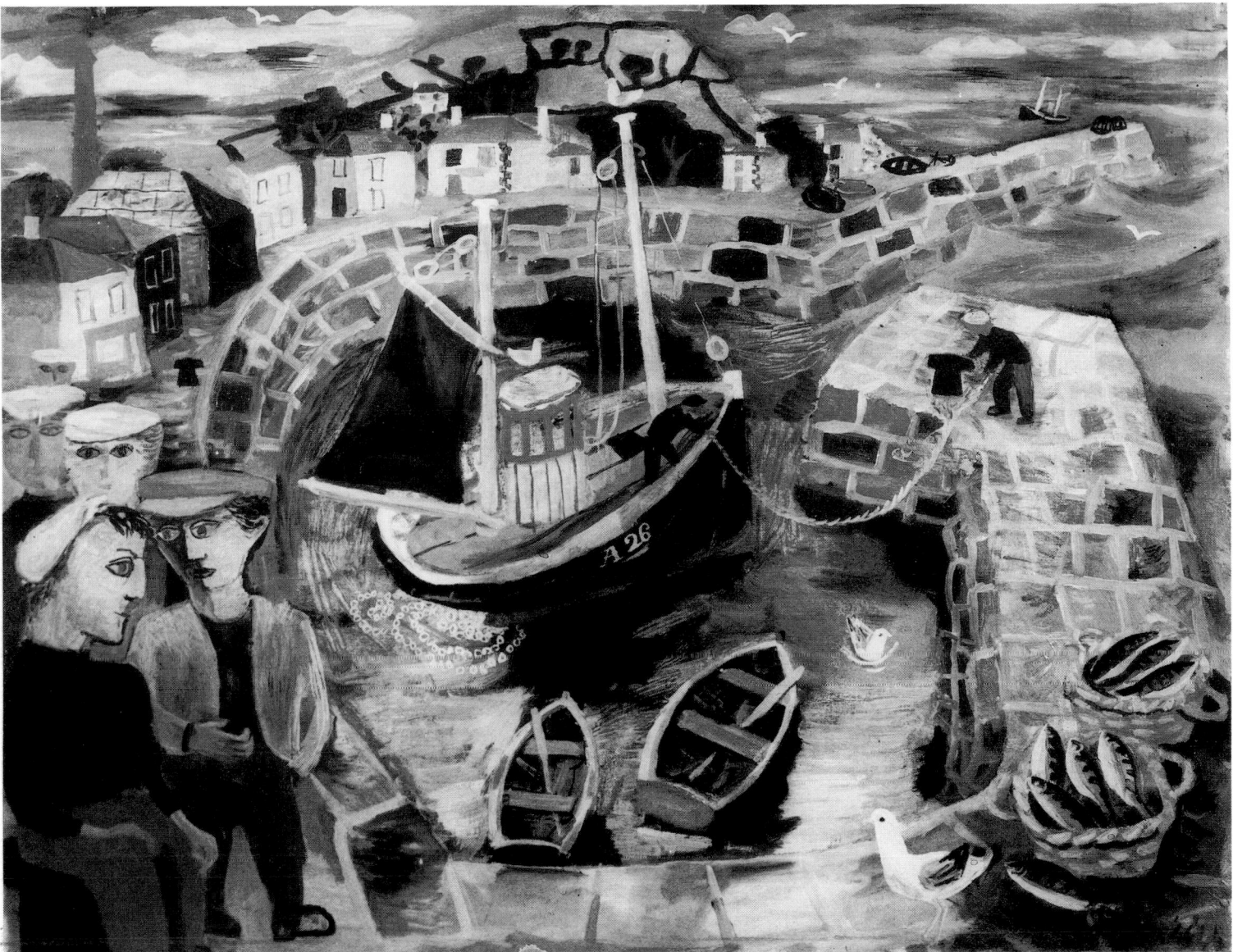

Julian Trevelyan: *Harbour*, 1944

Individual Exhibitions:

1932	Bloomsbury Gallery, London (with Robin Darwin)
1934	Bloomsbury Gallery, London (with Robin Darwin)
1935	Tate Gallery, London
1936	Lefevre Gallery, London
1939	Guggenheim Gallery, London
1942	Lefevre Gallery, London
1944	Lefevre Gallery, London
1946	Lefevre Gallery, London
1948	Lefevre Gallery, London
	Galerie de France, Paris
	Konsthall, Gothenburg, Sweden
	Galleri Fargi Form, Stockholm
1950	Gimpel Fils Gallery, London
1952	Redfern Gallery, London
1955	Zwemmer Gallery, London (with K. Allen)
1958	Zwemmer Gallery, London
1959	St. George's Gallery, London
1960	Zwemmer Gallery, London
1961	Arnolfini Gallery, Bristol
1963	Zwemmer Gallery, London
	Aldgate Gallery, Farnham, Surrey
1964	Thames Gallery, Eton, Buckinghamshire
1965	Zwemmer Gallery, London
	Ashgate Gallery, Farnham, Surrey
1966	Thames Gallery, Eton, Buckinghamshire
	Zwemmer Gallery, London
1968	Ashgate Gallery, Farnham, Surrey
1970	Hambledon Gallery, Blandford Forum, Dorset
1973	Alexander Postan Fine Art, London
1974	Printmakers Council/Oxford Press, London

1977	Tate Gallery, London
1978	New Grafton Gallery, London
1981	Holsworthy Gallery, London
1983	Bohun Gallery, Henley-on-Thames, Oxfordshire
1985	Waterman's Arts Centre, Brentford, Middlesex
1986	Norwich School of Art, Norfolk
	Bolton Museum and Art Gallery, Lancashire
	Waterman's Arts Centre, Brentford, Middlesex
1987	New Grafton Gallery, London

Selected Group Exhibitions:

1936	*International Surrealist Exhibition*, New Burlington Galleries, London
1945	*A.I.A. Exhibition*, Whitechapel Art Gallery, London
1947	*English Art*, Galleri Farg i Form, Stockholm
	English Art, Galerie de France, Paris
1955	*Figures in a Setting*, Tate Gallery, London
1958	*London Group*, Whitechapel Art Gallery, London
1964	*London Group: Retrospective*, Tate Gallery, London
1971	*Britain's Contribution to Surrealism of the 30's and 40's*, Hamet Gallery, London
1980	*Atelier 17*, Brooklyn Museum, New York
1982	*Peinture Surréaliste en Angleterre 1930–1960*, Galerie 1900–2000, rue Bonaporte, Paris

Collections:

Tate Gallery, London; Contemporary Art Society, London; Arts Council of Great Britain, London; City Art Gallery, Southampton, Hampshire; City Art Gallery, Aberdeen; Museum of Modern Art, New York; Brooklyn Museum, New York; Library of Congress, Washington, D.C.; Seattle Museum of Art.

Publications:

By TREVELYAN: books—*Indigo Days* (autobiography), London 1957; *The Artist and His World*, London 1960; *Etching*, London 1963; *A Place, A State*, with Kathleen Rhine, London 1974.

On TREVELYAN: books—*The Painter's Object*, edited by Myfanwy Evans, London 1937, New York 1970; *Britain's Contribution to Surealism of the 30's and 40's*, exhibition catalogue, London 1971; *Julian Trevelyan: First Retrospective*, exhibition catalogue with text by Nicholas Usherwood, Brentford 1986.

*

To start young with an eccentric vision of urban sky lines and streets and riverbanks plus a sky hospitable to both heavenly bodies and balloons and aircraft—a sort of British Paul Klee, but one riveted in a single channel of inspiration—this can make an overnight reputation, especially if the author is capable of producing both paintings and graphics to support such a quasi-original style. It was pictures of this nature that made Julian Trevelyan's name for him, and which ensured that at the time (during the 1930's) he would be included in every up-to-date anthology of the visual arts.

What happened? Like John Piper, only not quite so decisively, he abandoned the way he had chosen and turned to something which, even if it was well made, had nothing of the bite of his initial work. Piper, following the Brighton aquatints and the commission he received from Queen Mary to do much the same for Windsor, ceased to be an abstract artist. With an ironic touch of irony the change took place just around the time when the avantgarde magazine *Transition* illustrated one of his abstract pictures. The alteration in the style of Julian Trevelyan's work was not quite so cataclysmic, but at one stage it had a terminal ring about it. He went bucolic. Bullocks replaced boats. Seagulls took over from skyscrapers.

What had once been finely executed: cobweb lines to match the skeletons of leaves pressed into service upon the paint or paper: all this was replaced by firm didactic paint, or, in the case of the graphics, by an unyielding line that framed carefully chosen areas of colour.

Was this about-face a bid for broader popularity? Maybe. Certainly with the years Trevelyan's control over his new imagery and the way in which he painted it became steadily more accomplished and resolute.

But this is not the end of the story. Late in his career, and obviously with the intention of continuing in yet another departure from what has come to be recognized as his style, the artist set about making some interesting assemblages, marine flotsam that are closer to what he was doing before the War than to what he had done since. These constructions are well finished and despite the age or nature of their component parts they have a weatherworn appearance that recalls the lichenous patina of some of the early works.

—Sheldon Williams

TROCKEL, Rosemarie.

German. Born in Schwerte, 13 November 1952. Studied at the Werkkunstschule, Cologne, 1974–78. Independent artist, Cologne, since 1979. Agent: Galerie Monika Spruth, Maria-Hilf-Strasse 17, 5000 Cologne 1. Address: Reinoldstrasse 6, 5000 Cologne 1, West Germany.

Individual Exhibitions:

1983	Galerie Monika Spruth, Cologne
	Galerie Philomene Magers, Bonn
1984	Galerie Monika Spruth, Cologne
	Galerie Ascan Crone, Hamburg
	Gallerie Stampa, Basle
1985	Galerie Monika Spruth, Cologne
1986	Galleria Stampa, Basle (with Tatafiore and Stumpf)
	Galerie Monika Spruth, Cologne
1987	Galerie Tanit, Munich
1988	Kunsthalle, Basle
	Museum of Modern Art, New York

Selected Group Exhibitions:

1982	*Licht bricht sich in der oberen Fenstern*, Klapperhof 33, Cologne
1984	*Kunstlandschaft BRD*, Kunstverein, Lubeck, West Germany
	Bella Figura, Wilhelm-Lehmbruck-Museum, Duisburg, West Germany
1986	*Sculptures*, Galleria Stampa, Basle
1987	*Een Keuze/A Choice*, Kunst RAI, Amsterdam
	Art from Europe, Tate Gallery, London

Publications:

On TROCKEL: books—*Rosemarie Trockel: Plastiken 1982-*

83, exhibition catalogue with text by Wilfried Dickhoff, Bonn and Cologne 1983; *Kunstlandschaft BRD*, exhibition catalogue with essay by Wulf Schadendorf, Lubeck 1984; *Rosemarie Trockel: Skulpturen und Bilder*, exhibition catalogue with texts by A. R. Penck and Reiner Speck, Hamburg 1984; *Bella Figura*, exhibition catalogue with essay by Karl-Egon Vester, Duisburg 1984; *Rosemarie Trockel: Bilder, Skulpturen, Zeichnungen*, with text by Wilfried Dickhoff, Cologne 1985; *Rosemarie Trockel: Arbeiten 1980-1985*, Bonn and Cologne 1986.

Interest in Rosemarie Trockel's work has grown over the last few years due to recent abstract-geometric tendencies in painting. In fact, it could be argued that the decade of the 1980s is characterized by a predilection for cool analytical work, supplanting the earlier vogue for figurative and neo-expressionist passion. This current abstraction establishes a critical and ironic distance vis-a-vis the great tradition of abstract painting—i.e., of Malevich and Reinhardt. According to these new tendencies, the epic attempt to re-establish perspectival space falls apart, as does the attempt to achieve ultimate or 'supreme' forms.

Rosemarie Trockel aligns herself with this critical reappraisal of historical abstraction: as Klaus Ottmann has rightly pointed out, her intention is to deconstruct the aesthetic categories of modern rationalism as much as the hedonism of the Postmodernist age. She does not aim at re-establishing an up-to-date aesthetic, as Peter Halley does, neither does she intend to parody the 'fifties in the manner of John Armleder. Trockel elaborates a visual repertoire that focuses on what has been 'removed' from the realm of art by reintroducing a discussion of the categories of creativity: in doing so, she aims at positing a definition of 'feminine'.

She sees the 'feminine' as a historical dimension and an essential component of art. Typically, she expresses this idea by the device of stretching a length of knitted material onto a frame (like a painting on canvas), the material patterned with motifs akin to those in contemporary clothing. These decorative motifs, typical of feminine creativity within the domestic realm, are now presented as autonomous and formal. The result is a surprising 'pattern-painting', genetically transformed in its function and component parts. Trockel thus promotes a critique of the grand theories of abstraction by suggesting that the mundane is fundamental to all great discourses. This dimension of the mundane can be defined as 'the feminine'—a concept that the artist uses as a provocative device.

In addition to geometrical motifs, often employed as parody, Trockel has used woven wool and, more recently, fabrics printed with the most common visual stereotypes of consumerism: the Cowboy, the Hammer and Sickle, the advertising logo 'Made in West Germany'—banal or trivialized insignia of common currency which have lost any (assuming they ever possessed) original meaning.

Trockel's visual repertoire is based on ambiguity; her images are suspended between abstraction and figuration, abandoning their original meaning to appear empty. The serial form of presentation weakens their connotative power, while the elementary manner (based on pure contiguity) in which they are inserted into the visual field prevents their becoming proper structural elements. The artist explicitly talks about the 'depreciation' she intends to inflict upon the visual elements she has selected. The hammer and sickle lose their ideological significance of which they were a symbol as they become 'purified' into a geometrical motif.

This negation of the values of signs is a critique of ideologies as totalitarian world-views with their need to legitimize themselves by censoring anything that does not conform. Trockel works at what is considered to be 'insignificant' and ineffective against totalitarian ideologies. In this 'irrelevance' resides the definition of difference, and in its consecration as art lies its power to change the world.

—Giorgio Verzotti

TROOSTWYK, David.

British. Born in London. 5 August 1929. Studied at St. Albans School of Art, Hertfordshire, 1950–53; Royal College of Art, London, 1953–56, A.R.C.A. 1956. Served in the Royal Air Force, 1947–49. Married Ursula Janet Freer in 1953 (divorced, 1963); married Yvette Jean-Marie Bouzigues in 1963 (divorced, 1972); daughter: Lois. Worked as a display artist, London Display Company, 1949–50. Independent painter, London, since 1956. Visiting Lecturer, Camberwell School of Art, London, 1966–70; Chelsea School of Art, London, 1970–71; Sydney College of the Arts, 1978–79. Recipient: Painting Prize, *John Moores Exhibition*, Liverpool, 1969; First Prize, *British International Drawing Biennale*, Teesside, England, 1973. Agent: Matt's Gallery, London. Address: c/o Matt's Gallery, 10 Martello Street, London E8, England.

Individual Exhibitions:

1964	Southampton University, Hampshire
1969	R.C.A. Galleries, London
1970	Angela Flowers Gallery, London (with Alan Davie)
	Axiom Gallery, London (with Ivor Abrahams)
1971	Kasmin Gallery, London
1974	Institute of Contemporary Arts, London
1977	Felicity Samuel Gallery, London
1979	Institute of Modern Art, Brisbane
	Matt's Gallery, London
1980	Galerija Akumulatory, Poznan, Poland
1981	Matt's Gallery, London
1983	Holland Festival Gallery, Amsterdam
1985	Matt's Gallery, London

Selected Group Exhibitions:

1967	*4 Abstract Painters*, Institute of Contemporary Arts, London
1969	*John Moores Exhibition*, Walker Art Gallery, Liverpool
1973	*British International Drawing Biennale*, Teesside, England
1974	*International Poezie*, Rotterdam
1975	*Art 75*, Basle
1976	*Biennale*, Art Gallery of New South Wales, Sydney (and 1982)

Collections:

Tate Gallery, London; Arts Council of Great Britain, London.

Publications:

By TROOSTWYK: books and leaflets—*Imitation*, London 1977; *20 Broadsheets*, London 1979; *National Day*, London 1981; *Holiday Island*, London 1985; article—"Euan Uglow's Diagonal" in *Studio International* (London), May 1974; recording—*Advertisement of an Idea*, Audio Arts tape cassette, London 1976; *Live to Air*, Audio Arts tape cassette, London 1982.

This artist has found himself a niche amongst the painters accepted in Britain, a prizewinner and joining the elect included in the permanent collection of the Tate Gallery. But such honours do little or nothing to explain the talents of this artistic Banquo. Absent from the feast, but present in absentia. 'To make what I like and when I like may not always be easy, but what it is is what I *should do.*'

Selling antique photographs culled from sales and auction rooms to be resold in the Portobello Market reduces the financial strain on David Troostwyk, and the small profits he acquires in this way pay for canvas, stretchers and paints; but above all these monies ensure a large measure of artistic freedom so that he can pursue his ambitions as a painter relying solely upon the understanding of his works and the impact upon a public whose predilections need no cajoling of

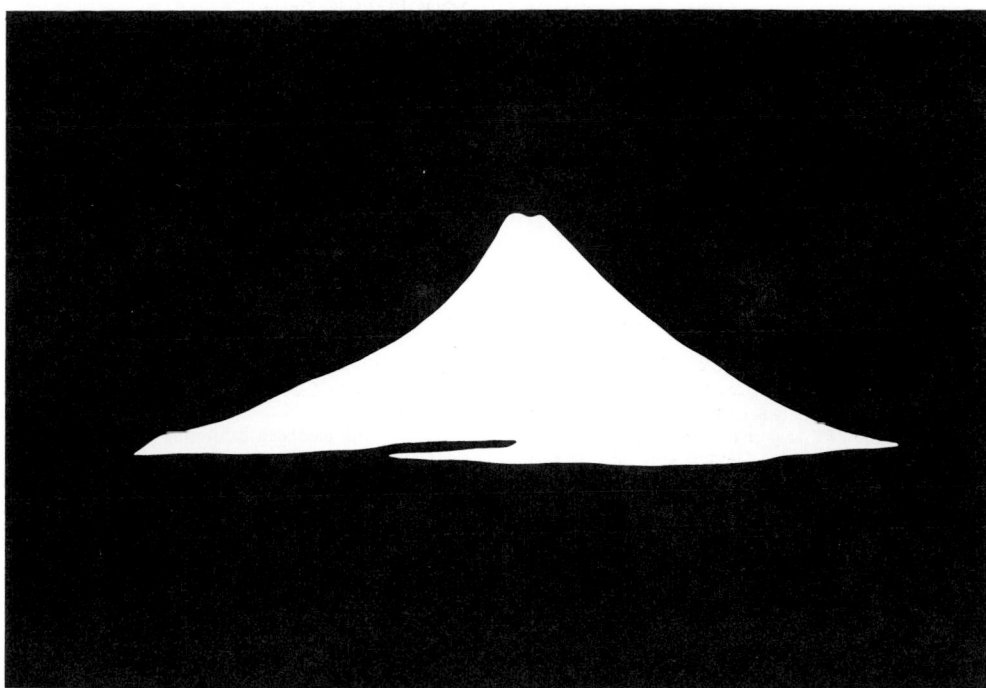

David Troostwyk: *Mount Fuji*, 1987

At no time can he assemble a great number of pictures in his studio. Short of the offer of a forthcoming exhibition he accepts no pressures from the outside world to perform extra feats of uncomplicated (yet haunting) painting unless suddenly inspired by a to him attractive form or feature to place in a chosen position on one of his vast canvases. The 'sections' of architecture which appear in rigid whiteness against the black background of *Heliopolis*—totalities, never randomly positioned, are a fragment of a *loge* which have not only strayed to one side (the left side of the picutre) but are quietly defying gravity.

Perhaps David Troostwyk should have the last word. He declares "Whatever sensations you receive from looking at one of my pictures are certainly enriched *after* you leave the studio with the painting still imprinted on your mind's eye"

—Sheldon Williams

any kind insofar as his coolly detached stance as an artist is concerned.

The process of artistic creation for him has been both natural and artificially encouraged. As soon as he was able to claim a pencil as his friend and companion, carefully nurtured—as he came to realise—as a child, but spiritually *relegated* by respectable parents, he filled this social gap sitting sketching on his own in a corner.

Today, this obsession to enter life through making pictures has been carefully tailored. Images, very thoughtfully selected—visual platitudes for the most part—are placed in a monochrome setting, often a black one, the white 'object' or 'statement' asserting its message against a field of black opacity. Troostwyk, who regards paint as only a *medium* (practical and necessary), steers clear of anything approaching a nuance; this is one of the reasons why he eschews the description of 'painter', preferring the title of 'artist'.

He sums up the Why and Wherefore of his creations as 'Communication'. For him, the eye of the beholder can indulge in any interpretive assessment it chooses; his wish as artist is entirely focused on telling a direct truth in absolute terms. So, the 'Empire State Building', white of course, poses with casual tilt in a stygian background or, in less audacious mood, two apples lurk in happy white purity in the midst of a black square. Painting in his Kennington studio in St. Anselm's Church Hall, he is supremely indifferent to critical reaction. These pictures are his remote exploration of finite verities into which those with a desire to investigate may delve but need never feel beholden so to do.

Troostwyk devises paper or card templates. He might make preliminary plans on paper, sketching out his eventual intentions, but he establishes these cutouts as basic aids to be placed—in scale—on his vast canvases. They are, or try to be, the exact guts of the imagery appearing in his picutres. Each of these emplacements—generally one to each picture—is a vital beginning for what will be the finalised pictorial meaning, however frequently readjusted. This is an artist who finds it difficult to persuade himself that any of his works has reached its clinching fulfilment. Many of them stand around the studio awaiting the final coup-de-grace—waiting—they may wait until their place is required in an exhibition, and only then will they receive the last coat of paint and the fine-edge finish that will gain them his personal decision that they should be allowed to go before a public.

Just to give examples of the works of this artist, who makes it a solemn contract with himself never to desert supreme symbols (immediately recognisable to the *hoi polloi*, even though the soul of such simplicity could be described as a 'slow burn' only making itself clear to the majority after long / and often returning to / contemplation) is no easy task. One needs to mentally take a stroll through the familiar in order to cross a barrier separating the obvious from the *extra* experience. A large composition like *Fuji*, a white mountain at ease (or not, depending upon mood), solid in its solitude in a surrounding total blackness is what Troostwyk calls one of my 'negatives' (in the photographic sense). Another 'negative' (and one wonders if the flavour is sardonic) is the happy-cum-alone signature of Ronald Reagan, clean and white, sprawling across the anonymous black of another work of massive dimensions. (Except in one little canvas, this painter has found it extremely difficult to extract satisfaction from painting on a small scale).

A departure from black/white occurs in his picture of the 'Ring'. The usual containing background in this case is a warm and pale brown madder broken up at casual intervals by unobtrusive glitter-spots. The Ring itself is set in innocent and not very complex curves, but if it is looked at with the aid of a simple optical appliance this unalluring sample of jewellery thrusts itself into a third-dimensional advance out of the canvas. David Troostwyk is pleased about this interference with routine vision but, at the same time, is slightly appalled that he could so easily be accused of indulging in gimmickry—the last thing such a purist should have to fear.

A more uncanny—yet typical—canvas, and one of Troostwyk's finest, is the picture he calls *The Russian Chair* (for which he made several studies and a smaller version). This is not one of his 'negative' paintings. It portrays in a strange twisted version a variety of perspectives to form a *portrait* of a famous chair from the experimental period of the great Russian sculptor and designer Vladimir Tatlin. In a strange way the character of Tatlin's chair, despite its curious figuration typifying the acceptance of *new ideas* of the Russian Revolutionary 'Acceptance' of every break with tradition, complies with Troostwyk's determination to communicate with the public through easily digested pictorial statements (in several steps ranging from symbols to absolute realism).

It is worth mentioning here that Troostwyk is an artist who works slowly and with great deliberation.

TROTTA, Antonio A.

Argentinian. Born in Stio, Italy, 21 December 1937; lived in Argentina until 1968. Educated in architecture at the University of La Plata, Argentina. Independent painter and sculptor, in Buenos Aires, 1960–68, and in Milan since 1968. Recipient: Painting Prize, Mar del Plata Salon, 1966; Prize, Museum of Fine Arts, Buenos Aires, 1966; Sash of Honour, Ver y Estimar Prize, Buenos Aires, 1966 and 1967. Address: via Lamarmora 15, 20122 Milan, Italy.

Individual Exhibitions:

1965	Galeria Lirolay, Buenos Aires
1970	Galleria Lambert, Milan
1971	Galleria Christian Stein, Turin
1972	Galleria Marilena Bonomo, Bari, Italy
	Studio Maddilena Carioni, Milan
1974	Galleria Christian Stein, Turin
	Qui Arte Contemporanea, Rome
1976	Galleria Borgogna, Milan
1977	Galleria Christian Stein, Turin
1978	t'Venster, Rotterdam
1981	Galleria Piero Cavellini, Brescia, Italy
1982	Più due Cannaviello, Milan

Selected Group Exhibitions:

1961	*Gruppo SI*, Museo de Artas Plasticas, La Plata (travelled to Museo de Arte Moderno, Buenos Aires and Museo de Bellas Artes, Lima)
1967	*Più in là della geometria*, Istituto de Tella, Buenos Aires
1971	*Arte de Sistemas*, Museo de Arte Moderno, Buenos Aires
	Understatement, Qui Arte Contemporanea, Rome
1974	*Della Falsità*, Palazzo della Pilotta, Parma
1977	*Senza Relazione: Il verosimile critico*, Palazzo Comunale, Acireale, Italy
1978	*Biennale*, Venice
1979	*L'Annunciazione di Antonello*, Museo Nazionale, Siracusa
1980	*Arte e critica 1980*, Galleria Nazionale d'Arte Moderna, Rome
1982	*La Sovrana Inattualita*, P.A.C., Milan

Publications:

By TROTTA: books—*Divagaciones*, Buenos Aires 1967; *Lo Spazio fra Me e l'Opera*, Milan 1972; *La Cruz del Sur*, Milan 1974; *Rose, Rose, Rose*, Milan 1974; *Le Finzioni Popolari*, Turin 1976; videotapes—*Punto*, Milan 1969; *Il Sogno di Coleridge*, Milan 1972; *Silbando*, Milan 1972; *Unacita*, Milan 1973.

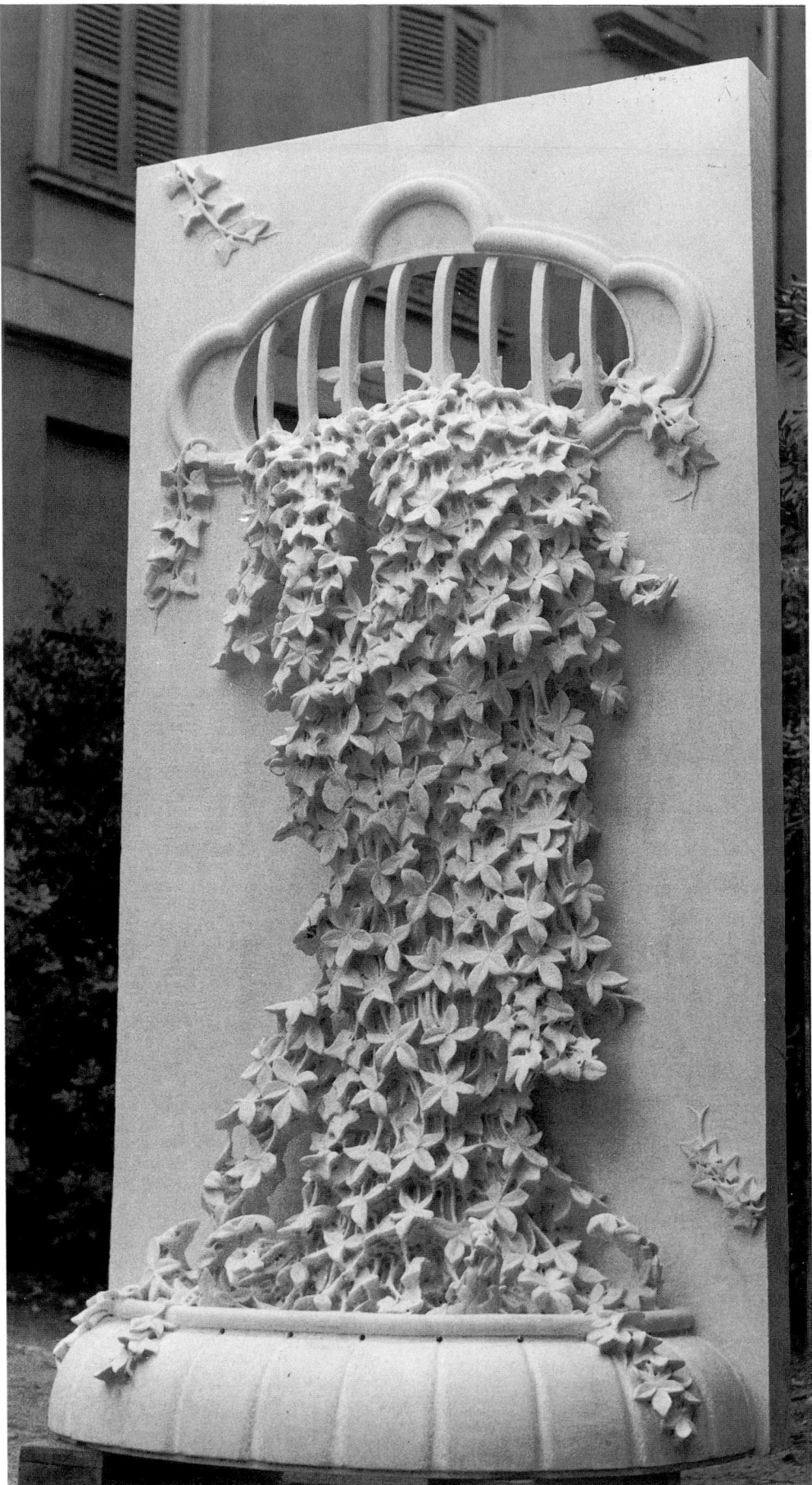

Antonio Trotta: *La Cascata*, 1981

On TROTTA: books—*Antonio Trotta* by Romero Brest, Buenos Aires 1967; *Il corpo come linguaggio* by Lea Vergine, Milan 1974; *Antonia Trotta*, exhibition catalogue, Rome 1974; *Extra Media* by E. Crispolti, Turin 1978; *Art in Argentina* by Jorge Glusberg, Milan 1986; articles—"Letter from Buenos Aires" by G. Whitelow in *Art International* (Lugano, Switzerland), May 1969; "Antonio Trotta" by J. R. Brest in *Flash Art* (Milan), February/April 1972; "Antonio Trotta" by L. Haller in *Flash Art* (Milan), January 1973; "Antonio Trotta" in *Utopia Rivisitata*, Milan 1974; "Miracolo a Milano" by Tommaso Trini in *Data* (Milan), Spring 1975; "Antonio Trotta" in *Art Magazine Bijutsu Techo* (Tokyo), February 1975; "La Pop Art" by M. Volpi Orlandini in *L'Arte Moderna*, Milan 1975; "Antonio Trotta, lo scultore si scolpisce" in *Data* (Milan), January February 1978; "La découverte des origines" in *Art Aktuel: Skira Annual*, Geneva 1979.

Antonio Trotta has been exhibiting his work in Italy since 1970, after an extended stay in Argentina. His work is directed towards an enquiry into the rapport between the artist and the work of art—and the space that separates them. In 1972 the Toselli Gallery in Milan published a catalogue of works by Nagasawa, Salvadori and Trotta. Trotta's own preface was titled *Images Relating to the Period of the Disappearance of Giovanni Bellini's Saint Sebastian*, a title which may be understood as Trotta's declaration of an analytical view of the work of art which is internal to his own tradition. In the works which followed, Trotta revealed the ideas central to his concern with images of reality and, above all, with the superimposition of the artist's view onto the work of art. *Ricamandosi* (1974–75) is a portrait, perhaps even a self-portrait, made in embroidery. This work forms a direct link with *L'Artifice* (1977), a piece sculpted out of several different slabs of marble, and representing the sculptor at work—"a sculpture of the sculptor sculpting". This simple but effective idea demonstrates the rapport between illusion and reality which is the basis of everything.

A declaration of 1972, entitled *The Space Between Me and the Work*, indicates unequivocally where Trotta's interest lies. "The space between me and the work begins to be dissolved in that moment when it is possible to see that everything surrounding me has already been painted or sculpted. These objects are in a state of petrification, ensnared by those sensations of doubt that form our existence. In them, we observe the unreality which exists in the reality of the work."

L'Artifice reveals the artist observing his own work from the inside, the sculpture itself reflecting like a mirror the illusion of reality—a concept central to the philosophy of Borges, and perhaps developed during Trotta's time in Argentina. This work is expressed in a variety of different marbles employing quite sophisticated techniques, sometimes smooth or inlaid with a counterpoint of variously toned pieces. This sort of craftsmanship represents another aspect of Trotta, in which he participates in the tradition of the artisan, directing it towards a dialogue of invention and technique.

In June of 1976, the Turin gallery of Christian Stein published one of Trotta's works in book form under the title *Le Finzioni Popolare* (The Popular Illusion). Written the previous summer, the first part is dedicated to the window. The Window is seen from a variety of viewpoints as a screen which divides inside from outside, in a poetic sense. Thus each segment is prefaced by quotations from Mallarmé's poem *La Fenêtre*, and from Miguel Hernandez' *The Farewell is Muffled Behind the Window Pane*. The sequence comprises *La Finestra sul Vetro* (urban images superimposed onto the structure of the window), and *Dietro la Finestra sul Vetro* (external and internal images of life). The same attention, both literary and actual, is focussed onto a balcony, with a quotation from Baudelaire's *Le Balcon*. Trotta subsequently went on to make a number of works and installations on these themes.

La Trilogia: Balcone, Grata, Lampione is a work dated 1974–76 in which objects are reproduced from photographic images, but installed and illuminated in a manner that perfectly simulates that photographic reality. Here again is one of the dominant motifs of Trotta's work—that is, the rapport between reality and appearance which exists between the artist and the work of art. The preoccupation continues to be characteristic.

—Roberto Lambarelli

TROUILLE, (Camile) Clovis.

French. Born in La Fère, Aisne, 24 October 1889. Studied painting, drawing and modelling at the Ecole des Beaux-Arts, Amiens, 1905–10. Served in the Dragoons, French Army, in Lunéville and Paris, 1910–12; active service in Champagne and Picardy, 1914–19; Gendarmerie, Picardy War Front, 1939–40. Married Jeanne Vailland in 1920 (divorced, 1922). Painter, since 1930: associated with André Breton, Salvador Dali, Louis Aragon, Paul Eluard, and other Surrealist artists and writers, Paris. Fashion design illustrator, Draeger Frères, Paris, 1912–14; wax mannequin modeller and decorator, Fabrique Pierre Imans, Paris, 1920–60. Recipient: First Prize, Collection Beaux-Arts, Amiens, 1907; Medaille d'Honneur du Travail, 19th Arrondissement, Paris, 1960. Agent: Editions Jean-Jacques Pauvert, 8 rue de Nesle, 75006 Paris. Address: 57 avenue Mathurin Moreau, Paris, France.

Individual Exhibitions:

1963 Galerie Raymond Cordier, Paris

Selected Group Exhibitions:

1930 *Salon des Artistes et Ecrivains Révolutionnaires*, Parc des Expositions, Paris
1934 *Salon des Surindépendants*, Paris
1941 *Salon des Indépendants*, Paris
1944 *Groupe Surréaliste*, at Salon d'Automne, Paris
1947 *Exposition Surréaliste*, Galerie Maeght, Paris
1959 *Exposition Internationale Surréaliste*, Galerie Daniel Cordier, Paris
1960 *Surrealist Intrusion*, D'Arcy Galleries, New York
1963 *L'An 2104*, Galerie Iris Clert, Paris
1964 *Le Surréalisme: Sources, Histoire, Affinités*, Galerie Charpentier, Paris
1965 *Salon de Mai*, Paris

Collections:

Centre Georges Pompidou, Paris.

Publications:

By TROUILLE: book illustrated—cover design for *La Clé des Songes* by Artemidore d'Ephese, Paris 1953; article—"Tout Ma Vie" in *Clovis Trouille*, Paris 1972.

On TROUILLE: books—*The History of Surrealist Painting* by Marcel Jean, Paris 1959; *Le Surréalisme: Sources, Histoire, Affinités*, exhibition catalogue, edited by Patrick Waldberg, Paris 1964; *Clovis Trouille* by Jean-Marc Campagne, Paris 1969; *Clovis Trouille* by Raymond Charmet, Paris 1972; *Antologia Grafica del surrealismo* by Maurice Henry, Milan 1972; articles—"Clovis Trouille" in *Le Surréalisme A.S.D.L.R.* (Paris), December 1931; "Chronicles of Clovis" by John Lyle in *Art and Artists* (London), February 1973; "Religion, Sex och Dod" by F. Kusan in *Paletten* (Gothenburg, Sweden), no. 1, 1978.

*

My parents were horticulturists in Amiens. I developed a taste for painting very early. It happened to me in a very odd way. As a child I saw a picturesque man describing his journey around the world in the bistros; he used to give away painted plates in a raffle which he organized. It was on these plates that I admired the sea, the waves "laid on thick." I saw real waves sparkling in the window of the grocer's shop-bistro where these plates ran around. There was also in Amiens Merovac, the cathedral man: wherever there were cathedrals he did drawings of them. He was dressed in a large cloak and sported a large Lavaliere cravat as well as a hat à la Rubens. His exhibition hall was the shop of the local photographer where I myself displayed caricatures of local characters.

I did my studies at the regional school in Amiens with marvellous teachers. The teachers paid a lot of attention to us. The feminine element (young ladies of good background) formed the majority of the pupils. I executed landscapes, but above all portraits. The *Child in Straw Hat* gained the admiration of my teacher: "Trouille," he said to me one day, "I shall not retouch your work. You equal the greatest." I often went off into the Picardy countryside with my fellow-students. I had two favourite artistic high-spots: Amiens Cathedral and the Picardy Museum where I did copies of 17th and 18th century works. I did caricatures for the paper *Notre Picardie*. It was thanks to this paper that I was put in touch with their Paris photographer who recommended me to a fellow who specialized in fashion drawings: Berthold Mann, my first patron. I had first met him during my studies at the Académie in Amiens: he was taking advantage of his four weeks training for the military reserve to come there and draw nudes. Then I went on to become a designer for Draeger. Then came the 1914–18 war. I was a soldier for seven years. This period is very important to my work. On my return from war I went to work for the firm of Imans which made mannequins. I started by modelling faces and I placed glass eyes and sets of teeth for the "smilers." The heads were made of wax. One day, the artists of this firm held an exhibition. The management took notice then that I was a painter. They put me on to makeup (eyebrows, lips). You can't imagine the importance of makeup. How one can transform a face. For me it was of capital importance. A unique experience. This work was routine, I could think of my painting. I remained with Imans forty years. I have a long service medal for it.

Before the war my subjects were still-lifes, countrysides, portraits. A discreet type of painting. After the war, after reading Rimbaud, Sade, Lautreamont, I became an anarchist. I didn't forgive it, the war. You think it's beautiful, war? I was completely traumatised. It made me join the surrealists. Something important happened to me: the exhibition of revolutionary artists and writers at the Porte de Versailles with Aragon, Vaillant-Couturier. I exhibited there a picture which caused a sensation: "Remembrance." An anti-clerical, anti-militarist work. A German soldier and a French soldier ask what they've come to do in the war (for them it's the cross . . . the military cross); the Republic distributes decorations; the bishop blesses the shirkers and the soldiers; white rabbits symbolise the sacrifices of soldiers. I have always been against the imposture of religions. Was it in painting Amiens Cathedral that I became aware of all this "music-hall"? I remember in Amiens, a lorry passing which was distributing *Les Corbeaux*, an anti-religious humorous paper. I found it very funny. How did I become anti-religious? I don't remember. Priests have become priests because they don't feel up to working; for them, it's a sinecure. The surrealist group stopped in front of "Remembrance." Breton came to look for me outside Imans and he took me to Cyrano's, a café near the Moulin-Rouge. And Breton presented me to Eluard. Breton gave us the obligation of excluding people. It was a pain in the arse.

What interests me the most in my work is its intrinsic value: colour, the subject. Which didn't interest Breton at all; he wasn't retinal; he saw only history. What counts is composition, the subject: what I studied at the Picardy Museum in the presence of Velasquez. I place myself in a very independent way. I have never admitted cubism. It didn't move me. I like to paint feminine beauty. All my life I have looked for what was most beautiful in nature so I could express it in my pictures. I have found nothing more beautiful than the nude body of a young girl. For men who are men it is a moving spectacle. In the woman's sex, God reveals himself. I am not so attached to painting men in my pictures. You see, with men, it's no fun.

—Clovis Trouille

*

Who better than Clovis Trouille to paint the picture which became the design for the original poster for Kenneth Tynan's *Oh Quel cul t'as (Oh Calcutta!)*! Trouille specializes in erotic images with posteriors high on his list. Referring to him in *Eros and Surrealism*, Robert Stuart Short says "In an orgy of combative black humour, Clovis Trouille painted a whole series of lecherous festivals for pantied priests and rampant nuns, exploiting all the clichés of commercial sex mixed up with the panoply of organized religion. In 'Mes Funerailles' the fleshy buttocks of the officiants affirm the triumph of desire over death itself". This is a relatively cool assessment of the outrageous imagery of which this artist is capable. Not surprisingly he has been featured in the French magazine *Plexus* with pullouts that make anything approaching a sexy ploy by *Playboy* look demure.

Trouille works with dainty, albeit devastating, detail all carried out in bright "illustration" colours, to suggest that life, and particularly its most serious and calvanist moments, is a carnal romp. His "church" and "nunnery" pictures make "The Devils of Loudun" the rule rather than the exception.

Trouille is the most erotic of all the painters who make up the pattern of contemporary art (only Hans Bellmer comes near to him when it is a matter of *épater la bourgeoisie*). His audacity and indifference to establishment beliefs (however hypocritical they may be) have hardly been matched by any of the artists of antiquity, including the works of those kept under lock and key in the restricted collection departments of the British Museum and the Victoria and Albert Museum.

—Sheldon Williams

TRUITT, Anne.

American. Born Anne Dean in Baltimore, Maryland, 16 March 1921. Studied psychology at Bryn Mawr College, Pennsylvania, 1939–43, B.A. 1943; studied at the Institute of Contemporary Art, Washington, D.C., 1948–50. Married James McConnell Truitt in 1947 (divorced, 1971); children: Alexandra, Mary, and Samuel. Worked as a psychologist at Massachusetts General Hospital, Boston, 1943–46; full-time artist since 1950; lived in Japan, 1964–67. Lecturer, 1975–80, and since 1980 Professor in Art, University of Maryland, College Park. Recipient: Guggenheim Fellowship, 1970; National Endowment for the Arts Fellowship, 1971, 1977; Stern Foundation Grant, 1972; Australian Arts Council Fellowship, 1981. DHL: Corcoran School of Art, Washington, D.C., 1985; DFA: Kansas City Art Institute, Missouri, 1987. Agents: André Emmerich Gallery, 41 East 57th Street, New York, New York 10022; Osuna Gallery, 407 6th Street N.W., Washington, D.C. 20004. Address: 3506 35th Street N.W., Washington, D.C. 20016, U.S.A.

Individual Exhibitions:

1963 André Emmerich Gallery, New York
1964 Minami Gallery, Tokyo
1965 André Emmerich Gallery, New York
1967 Minami Gallery, Tokyo
1969 André Emmerich Gallery, New York
     Baltimore Museum of Fine Arts
1971 Pyramid Galleries, Washington, D.C.

1973	Whitney Museum, New York
	Pyramid Galleries, Washington, D.C.
1974	Corcoran Gallery, Washington, D.C.
	Baltimore Museum of Art
1975	André Emmerich Gallery, New York
	Pyramid Galleries, Washington, D.C.
1976	University of Virginia Museum of Art, Charlottesville
1977	Pyramid Galleries, Washington, D.C.
1979	Osuna Gallery, Washington, D.C.
1980	André Emmerich Gallery, New York
1981	Osuna Gallery, Washington, D.C.
1983	James Madison University, Harrisonburg, Virginia
	Artemisia Gallery, Chicago
1986	Neuberger Museum, Purchase, New York
	Andre Emmerich Gallery, New York
	Osuna Gallery, Washington, D.C.

Selected Group Exhibitions:

1953	*8th Corcoran Annual,* Corcoran Gallery, Washington, D.C. (and 1954, 1975)
1964	*Black, White, and Grey,* Wadsworth Atheneum, Hartford, Connecticut
1966	*Color and Space,* Minami Gallery, Tokyo
	Primary Structures: Younger American and British Sculptors, Jewish Museum, New York
1968	*Annual Exhibition: Contemporary American Sculpture,* Whitney Museum, New York (and 1972)
1975	*Sculpture: American Directions 1945-1975,* National Collection of Fine Arts, Washington, D.C.
1982	*Grace Hartigan/Morris Louis/Clyfford Still/Anne Truitt,* Baltimore Museum of Art
1985	*Amerikanische Zeichnungen 1930-80,* Stadtische Galerie, Frankfurt
1987	*The Hard Edge—Part I: the 60s,* Andre Emmerich Gallery, New York

Collections:

Whitney Museum, New York; Metropolitan Museum of Art, New York; Museum of Modern Art, New York; Albright-Knox Art Museum, Buffalo, New York; Hirshhorn Museum and Sculpture Garden, Washington, D.C.; National Gallery, Washington, D.C.; Museum of American Art, Washington, D.C.; St. Louis Museum of Art; Walker Art Center, Minneapolis; Museum of Fine Arts, Houston.

Publications:

By TRUITT: books—*Marcel Proust and Deliverance from Time* by Germaine Bree, translator with C. J. Hill, New Brunswick, New Jersey 1955; *Daybook: The Journal of an Artist,* New York 1982, 1984: *Turn: The Journal of an Artist,* New York 1986, 1987; article—"Interview with Anne Truitt" in *Asahi Shimbum* (Tokyo), March 1964.

On TRUITT: books—*Minimal Art: A Critical Anthology,* edited by Gregory Battcock, New York 1968; *Anne Truitt,* exhibition catalogue with essay by Walter Hopps, Washington, D.C. 1974; *Anne Truitt,* exhibition catalogue with text by E. A. Carmean, Charlottesville, Virginia 1976; *Originals: American Women Artists* by Eleanor Munro, New York 1979; articles—"Black, White and Grey" by Donn Judd in *Arts Magazine* (New York), March 1964; "Changer: Anne Truitt, American Artist Whose Painted Structures Helped to Change the Course of American Sculpture" by Clement Greenberg in *Vogue* (New York), May 1968; "Vicissitudes of Sculpture" by Peter Schjeldahl in the *New York Times,* February 1969; "Truitt's Box-Sculptures: Now You See Them" by Paul Richard in the *Washington Post,* April 1971; "Anne Truitt: The Whitney Museum" by Jeremy Gilbert-Rolfe in *Artforum* (New York), March 1974; "Anne Truitt at the Corcoran" by Gene Baro in *Art in America* (New York), July/August 1974; "New Sculptures by Anne Truitt" by John Russell in the *New York Times,* 7 March 1980; "Daybook: The Journal of an Artist" by Sara Mandelbaum in *Ms.* (New York), February 1983; "Anne Truitt" by Mary Swift in *Washington Review,* April-May 1986; "Anne Truitt at Andre Emmerich Gallery" by Nancy Princenthal in *Art in America* (New York), 1987.

Since 1961, Washington, D.C. sculptor Anne Truitt has been making austerely reductive structures of wood painted with variously hued bands of color. Truitt's simple, abstract forms resemble Minimalism's "primary structures," but her personal and intiutive application of shape and color communicate ideas associative with significative meanings beyond strictly formal ones, suggesting Truitt's connections with Abstract Expressionism, specifically with the work of Barnett Newman.

It was after Truitt saw the work of Newman during a trip to New York in 1961 that she began working in the form which was to characterize her work over the next two decades to the present. Truitt's ideological foundations had been formed through long-time friendship with Kenneth Noland, whom she had known since 1948. She had developed through the 1950's from a kind of stylized figure and landscape sculpture to geometrical works in clay which suggested primitive architectural forms. In 1961, she made a generative work titled *First,* a vertical sculptural construct resembling three sections of a picket fence. In 1962, she made a number of drawings and 32 sculptures, her first mature work. *Insurrection* (1962) consists of a vertical rectangular form rising from a small base. The column is painted in two vertical sections, half red, half maroon, in a composition very like Newman's symmetrical pictures in a color combination favored by Newman from 1949 to the early 1950's, and in a vertical configuration directly related with Newman's extremely narrow and tall series of Untitled canvases (Numbers 1 through 5) of 1950.

Like her Abstract Expressionist precursors, Truitt is an artist who finds her preferred form and proceeds consistently to find possible variations within her chosen limitations. Hers is a transposition out of painterly precedents into the more three dimensional realm. All traces of process are obliterated in her sleek, unabashedly lovely columns, sometimes leaning against the wall, mostly standing straight and tall with an aura of silent stateliness which invokes memories of the continuities and subtle changes which unfold through time and space. Truitt uses her skills as a subtly strong colorist to create a tense ambiguity between the planar and the three dimensional. In various combinations from one work to the next, vertical bands of color divide the surfaces, wrap around the corners and coexist with horizontal bands on the tops of the columns and on the thin bases. Harmonizing pastels or contrasting hues work with her diverse compositional formats to create a space which is simultaneously continuous and changing. A tense balance between gravity and weightlessness is amplified by the use of horizontal bands of color on the narrow, recessed bases. Titles, usually given when the work is nearly or totally completed, often refer to persons, places and events from Truitt's experience, reiterating her intentions for conveying associative meanings.

Truitt's sculptures are neither heroic nor monumental in scale or attitude. She developed her vocabulary alone, unusually separate from most of her contemporaries, and it is this sense of mysterious aloofness which animates her basically unitary and reductive forms. She has created a sincere and personally felt body of work which is firmly rooted in a long established line of modernist abstraction that was nearing its end by the 1950's.

—Barbara Cavaliere

TSOCLIS, Costas.
Greek. Born in Athens, 24 May 1930. Studied at the School of Fine Arts, Athens, 1948-54; University of Rome, 1957-60. Served in the Greek Army, 1954-56. Married Helen Caplanidou in 1975; daughter: Maya. Painter, Athens, 1954-57; painter and sculptor, Paris, 1960-70; in West Berlin, 1971-72; in Athens and Paris, since 1973. Recipient: Greek State Scholarship to Rome, 1957; D.A.A.D. Fellowship to West Berlin, 1971. Agent: Zomboulakis Gallery, Kriezotu 7, Athens. Address: Axiou 15, 13671 Aharnes, Greece.

Individual Exhibitions:

1965	Hilton Gallery, Athens
1969	Galerie Richard Foncke, Ghent
	Galerie Michael Werner, Cologne
1970	Galerie Sonnabend, Paris
	Studio Santandrea, Milan
	Galerie Richard Foncke, Ghent
	Galerie Defacqz, Brussels
1971	Palais des Beaux-Arts, Brussels
	Goethe Institut, Athens
	Galerie Springer, West Berlin
	Galerie Lichter, Frankfurt
	Galerie Reckermann, Cologne
1972	Galerie Richard Foncke, Ghent
	Ehemalige Galerie des 20 Jahrhunderts, West Berlin
	Kunsthalle, Dusseldorf
1973	Galerie Iolas-Zouboulakis, Athens
	Galerie Alexandre Iolas, Paris
1974	Galerie Marzona, Bielefeld, West Germany
	Galerie Alexandre Iolas, Paris
1976	Studio Santandrea, Milan
	Galerie New Smith, Brussels
	Galerie Alexandre Iolas, Paris
	Galerie Iolas-Zoumboulakis, Athems
1977	Galerie Desmos, Athens
	Alexandre Iolas Gallery, New York
	Galerie der Spiegel, Cologne
1978	Galerie Miranda, Hydra, Greece
	Palais des Beaux-Arts, Brussels
	Galerie Nothelfer, West Berlin
	Axionsgalerie, West Berlin
1979	Studio Santandrea, Milan
	Galerie Desmos, Athens
1980	Sala Communale d'Arte Contemporanea, Alessandria, Italy
	Galerie Miranda, Athens
1981	Galerie Z.M., Thessaloniki, Greece
	Galerie Oraisma, Athens
1982	Galleria Dossi, Bergamo, Italy
1983	Gallery 3, Athens
	Iolas Gallery, New York
	Pinacotheque Pierides, Athens
1984	Plaka Intervention, Athens
	Macedonian Center of Contemporary Art, Salonika, Greece
1985	Zomboulakis Gallery, Athens
1986	Greek Pavilion, *Biennale,* Venice
1987	Castello di Rodi, Rhodes, Greece

Selected Group Exhibitions:

1963	*Biennale de Paris*
1965	*Bienal,* Sao Paulo
1969	*Avantgarde Grechenland,* Kunstverein, Stuttgart (travelled to the Haus am Lutzowplatz, West Berlin)
1970	*Surrealisme,* Moderna Museet, Stockholm
1972	*Zehn Berlin,* Kunstverein, Stuttgart
1975	*8 Artists/8 Attitudes/8 Greeks,* Institute of Contemporary Arts, London
1977	*Documenta,* Kassel, West Germany
1982	*Europalia Greece,* Palais des Beaux-Arts, Brussels
1987	*Artware,* Kunstmuseum, Hannover (travelled to Dusseldorf)

Collections:

Centre National d'Art Contemporain, Paris; Museum van Hedendaages Kunst, Ghent; Museum of Contemporary Art, Utrecht; Museum Boymans-van Beuningen, Rotterdam; Musée d'Ixelles, Brussels; Museo de Bellas Artes, Caracas; Musée d'Art Contemporain, Brussels; Fattoria di Celle, Pistoia, Italy; Pinacotheque Pierides, Athens; Vorres Museum of Modern Art, Athens.

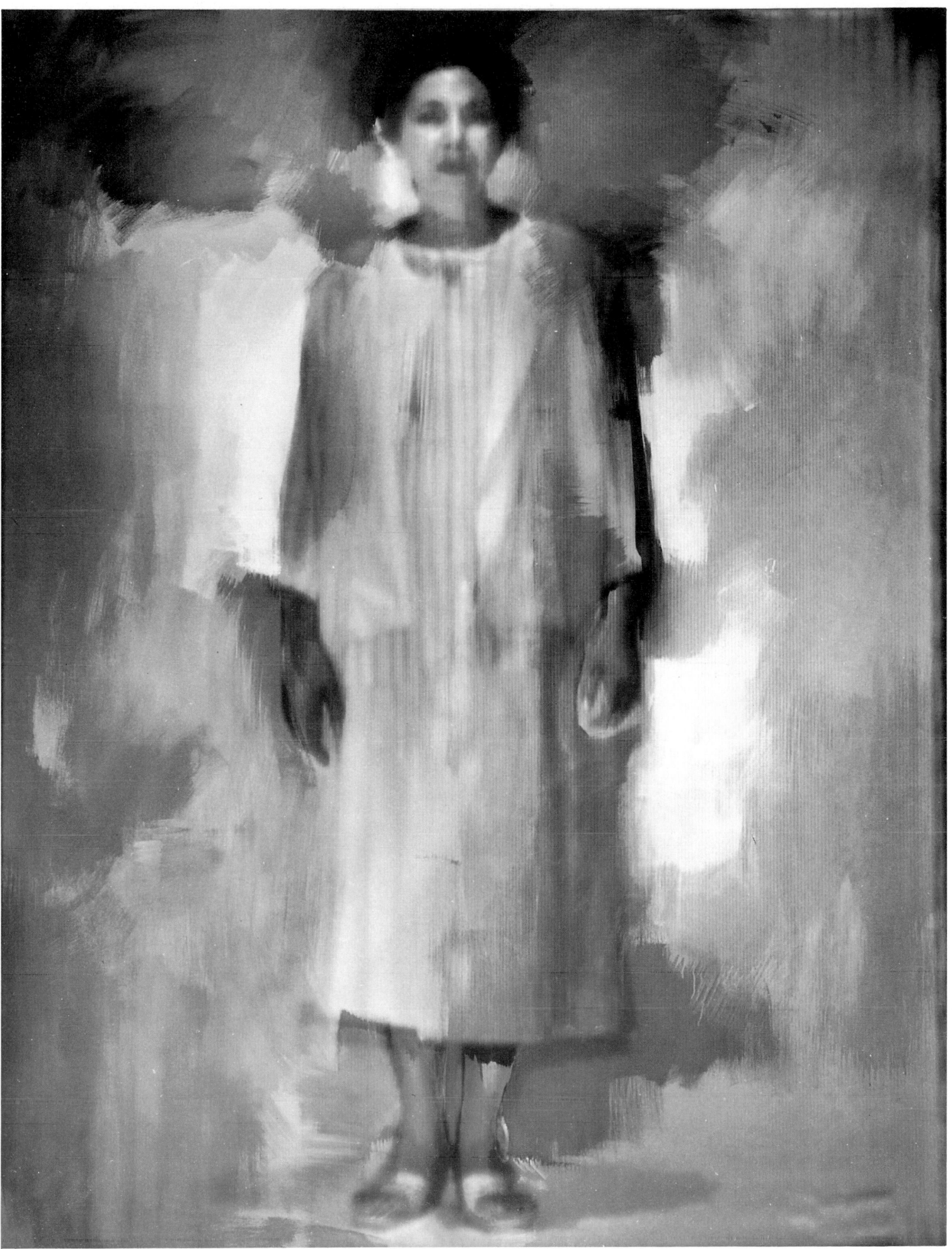

Costas Tsoclis: *Eleni Tsoclis*, 1986

Publications:

By TSOCLIS: books—*Rue des Ecouffes*, portfolio of 8 lithos, with text by D. Analis, Paris 1973; *Anamnissis 1971-73*, portfolio of 30 lithos, Paris 1974; *Arbre, Tree, Albero, Aentpo*, book-object, Milan 1980; *Arbre*, portfolio of 8 lithos, with texts by José Pierre, C. Cafopoulos, J. P. Van Teighem and others, Paris 1982.

On TSOCLIS: books—*Art of our Time* by D. Fatouros, London and Cologne 1966; *Costas Tsoclis*, exhibition catalogue, with texts by José Pierre, Paris 1970; *Costas Tsoclis*, exhibition catalogue, with texts by Karl Geirlandt and Jean Dypreau, Brussels 1971; *Costas Tsoclis*, exhibition catalogue, with text by G. Vlachos, Ghent 1972; *Costas Tsoclis*, exhibition catalogue, with texts by Karl Ruhrberg and Peter Nestler, West Berlin 1972; *Tsoclis*, with texts by Jean Dypreau, Karl Geirlandt, José Pierre, Tony Spiteris and others, Athens 1975; *Costas Tsoclis*, exhibition catalogue, with text by M. Mauzommatis, Alessandria, Italy 1980; *An Aspect of Postwar Art in Greece* by E. Vakalo, Athens 1981; *Artware, Kunst und Electronic*, with text by N. Missirlis, Dusseldorf, Vienna and New York 1987.

As an artist, I have never selected my means of expression—no more than, as a child, I have ever devised my playthings—outside a range of "situations-objects" to which I was linked by a bond of love or necessity.

An offspring of the capital, not expecting or caring to discover my roots, I fed on facts, not myths, on things whose prior stages I was not aware of. The myths—I made them up myself from such things and facts.

It took me a long time to see the Acropolis as a vestige of a period gone for ever and not as a set of abstract and unserviceable structures, playing nevertheless a determining role in the aesthetic character of the city, and therefore in the psychology of its inhabitants.

The basements of the small houses that used to shelter my family, I considered, with no bitterness whatever, as my home, in no way inferior to the big houses, those of the rich, which I merely looked upon as the big houses of "my" neighbourhood.

Then, I was not yet trying to find out the how, or the why.

My first works recognizable as such are "objects-fragments" of that environment, both forced upon me and taken for granted, reconstructed, however, so that they should remain faithful to their inner truth, and bear the indelible mark of my own vision.

(Now, after looking for and finding that literary definition of my quest during that long period of my life, I rejoice and consider I have not worked in a barren field.)

Yet, in order to reconstruct my objects, I had to handle patiently the materials with which such objects were made. Gradually, I became familiar with a new world, the world of virgin matter and with it I began to develop bonds, memories and even secret correspondences. Thus, for a few years, the new object of my work had become the very matter of my former objects. A long series of works scattered here and there, whose theme-object is merely wood, paper, steel, colour, water, cement, testify to that boundless love for matter which has certainly not palled so far.

Now, if "love" means endeavouring to probe into the truth of the beloved object, possess oneself of its charms, finally identify oneself with it for mutual pleasure and fulfilment, then that is what I did.

And if "art" means offering a new way, a new transitory and, no doubt, incomplete code to organize, conceive and interpret facts and environments so as to attain new emotions and balances, then that is what I felt.

One day, a small revelation became the new guide of my sensibility. A tree whose fitful and phantasmal image had been imparting a touch of beauty to my life was broken by the wind and revealed to me its concrete and enduring truth: the wood, so long hidden under its transient image; and I took a fancy to that glorious wound, and I perceived an inverted continuity between the object, matter and nature and in my recent work I have endeavoured to fuse into one artistic fact the image, the source of that image and the use of that source.

As if one painted the portrait of a man not with colour but with human flesh.

—Costas Tsoclis

TUCKER, Albert.

Australian. Born in Melbourne, Victoria, 29 December 1914. Self-taught in art. Served in the Australian Army, 1942. Married Barbara Anne Bilcock in 1964. Painter: influential, with Sidney Nolan, in forging an Australian modernism; produced "Images of Modern Evil" series, 1943-47, before self-inflicted exile from Australia; lived in London, where he produced a "Thames Waterfront" series, 1947-48; travelled to Paris, with critic Lawrence Alloway, and became fascinated by the work of Jean Dubuffet, then yet unknown, in early 1948; returned shortly thereafter to Paris to live, met Alberto Giacometti and Rufino Tamayo, and made frequent trips to London, Germany, Holland, Belgium, and Italy: influenced by the work of Max Beckmann, Otto Dix, Dubuffet, and the German modernists; moved to Neu Isenburg, near Frankfurt, West Germany, 1951; returned to Paris, 1952, then travelled south, to Noli, Italy, where he lived until mid-1953; lived in Rome and Grottaferrata, 1953-56: met, and was influenced by, Alberto Burri, de Chirico, Capogrossi, and Campigli; also renewed contact with Australian compatriot Sidney Nolan, who initiated his return to interest in Australian subjects; worked on "Pan in Armour" series to parody Nolan's "Kelly" series, 1955-59; returned to London, where he met Eduardo Paolozzi and Richard Smith, 1956-57; lived in New York, where he met abstract painters of the New York School, 1958-60; his work began to receive recognition in Australia, and he returned to his native country after a 13 year absence, 1960. Recipient: Kurt Geiger Award, Australian Museum of Art, 1960; Order of Australia, 1984. Agent: Tolarno Galleries, 98 River Street, South Yarra, Victoria 3141. Address: 55 Blessington Street, St. Kilda, Victoria 3182, Australia.

Individual Exhibitions:

1951 Kunstzaal van Lier, Amsterdam
1952 Galerie Huit, Paris
1953 Galleria ai Quattro Venti, Rome
1954 Associazione della Estampa Estera, Rome (with Sidney Nolan)
1957 Imperial Institute, London
1960 Waddington Galleries, London
     Hirschl and Adler Galleries, New York
1961 Australian Museum of Modern Art, Melbourne (toured the capitals of Australia, 1961-62)
1969 Poindexter Gallery, New York
     Instituto Nacional de Bellas Artes, Mexico City
     Galeria de Antonia Souza, Mexico City
1971 Australian National Gallery, Canberra (Australian Government travelling exhibition; toured Japan, Phillipines, Korea and Formosa)
1982 *Paintings 1945-60*, Tolarno Galleries, South Yarra, Victoria
     Night Images (Images of Modern Evil) 1943-1947, Sweeney Reed Galleries, Fitzroy, Victoria
1985 *Faces I Have Met*, Tolarno Galleries, Melbourne

Selected Group Exhibitions:

1956 *Biennale*, Venice
1959 *Transferences in Art*, Smithsonian Institution, Washington, D.C. (toured the United States)
     Experiences in Art, Hirschl and Adler Galleries, New York

     Recent Acquisitions, Museum of Modern Art, New York
1963 *Bienal*, Sao Paulo
1964 *Australian Painting Today*, toured Europe

Collections:

Australian National Gallery, Canberra; Australian Museum of Modern Art, Melbourne; Dunedin Art Gallery, New Zealand; Museum of Modern Art, New York; Guggenheim Museum, New York; Instituto Nacional de Bellas Artes, Mexico City.

Publications:

By TUCKER: book designed and compiled—*Albert Tucker: Paintings 1945-1960*, exhibition catalogue, with William Mora, with an introduction by Richard Haese, South Yarra, Victoria 1982.

On TUCKER: books—*Albert Tucker* by Christopher Uhl, 1969; *Modern Painters 1931-1970* by James Gleeson, Melbourne 1971; *Albert Tucker* by James Mollison and Nicholas Bonham, 1982; *Albert Tucker: Night Images (Images of Modern Evil) 1943-1947*, exhibition catalogue, with text by John Henshaw, Fitzroy, Victoria 1982.

Australia during World War II felt peculiarly isolated from its cultural sources in Europe, yet it was a time which saw a most extraordinary collective achievement by certain painters working in Melbourne. Extreme individualists, Albert Tucker, Sidney Nolan and Arthur Boyd nevertheless shared both a humanist attitude and stylistic sources in Surrealism and Expressionism.

Tucker in 1950 wrote: " . . . for me the drama and tragedy of life—my feeling is quite Websterian—this 'shadow or deep pit of darkness where mankind lives.' To sing of death or disaster does not make for popularity, I'm afraid. But it's my song and I've got to sing it."

His art is the hardest from that time. It received no public praise. Its haptic forms have primitive, rock-like firmness; and after Alberto Burri introduced him to the polyvinyl acetate medium in 1954, Tucker's paintings quickly acquired a hard flinty surface, often in considerable relief. Tucker's is also an art of clear intelligence and hard statements.

As a young man on the edge of poverty in the 1930's economic depression, from a family struggling to maintain middle-class values, he had good reason to feel oppressed and humiliated by society in general. As a radical artist he soon felt oppressed by the required subservience to a common political cause. Most of all as an army conscript in 1942 he was oppressed by military authority. However, work amongst the mad and the maimed in a military hospital, drawing illustrations of wounds for plastic surgery, was an experience which supplied images to energize his art for years to come—the gaping holes below a sliced-off nose, limbless torsoes, blood-stained mouths. The following year, 1943, his extensive series of "Images of Modern Evil" began.

Apparently an indictment of social decay caused by soldiers and their mostly amateur prostitutes in wartime Melbourne, the paintings show momentarily spotlit lumps of pale naked flesh, attached to red crescent mouths, floating in the night darkness of streets and cinemas. But the vulnerability and the uninhibited freedom implied by these fleshly images might also be presented for envious admiration by a conventionally constrained society. By the way of contrast, a series of portraits, "Faces 1946," at first sight straightforward sympathetic likenesses become on second sight hauntingly ravaged souls.

Tucker left Australia in 1947 for thirteen years of expatriation in Paris, Frankfurt, Rome, New York and London. Picasso, Beckmann and Dubuffet (a new discovery in 1948) were the modern masters who most enthralled him; the exposure to old masters produced biblical subjects, Job, Judas, Lazarus. Night in the European cities was presented less hysterically than in Melbourne.

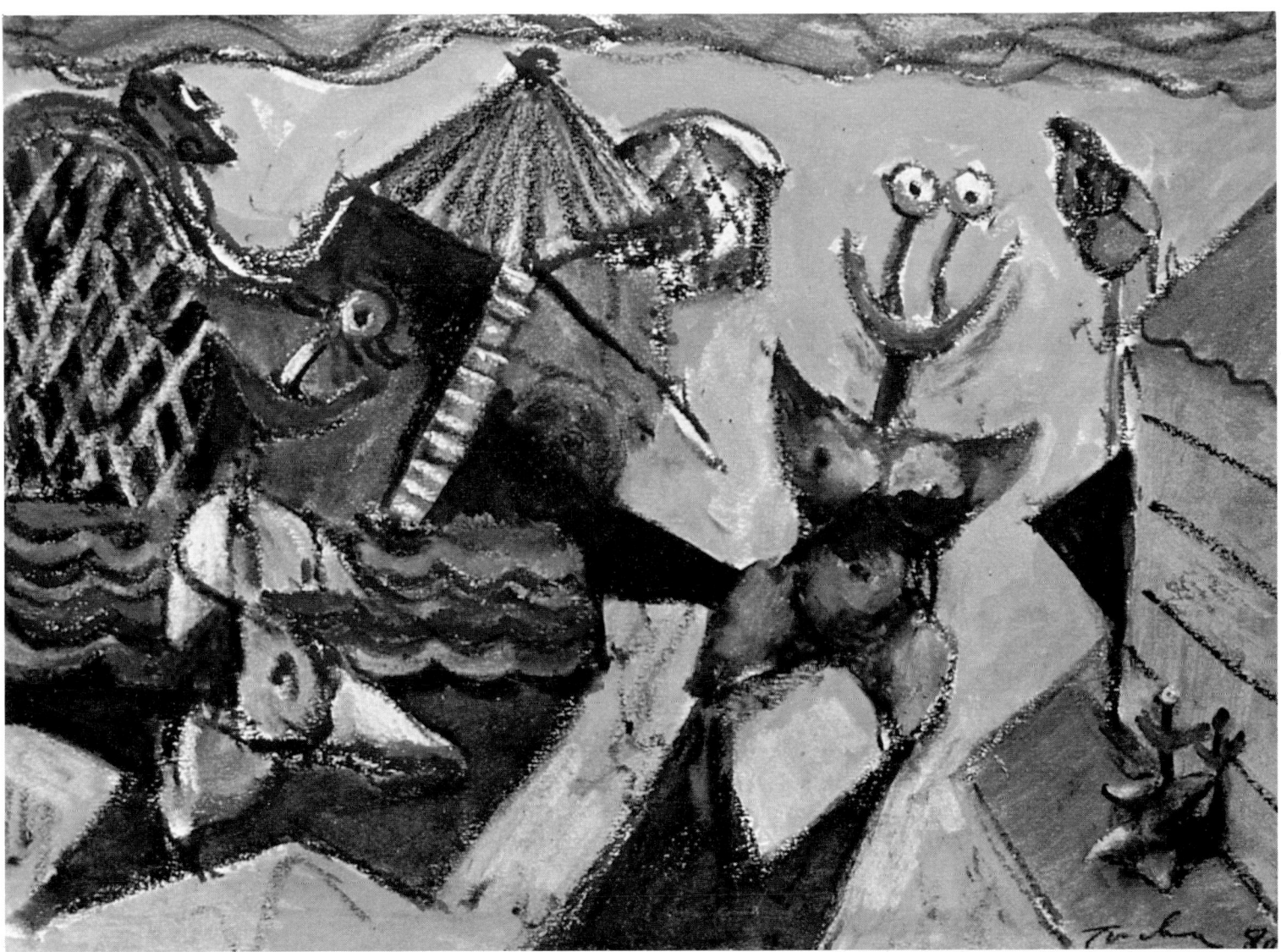

Albert Tucker: *Luna Park*, 1980

Paradoxically but not surprisingly, Tucker became an Australian artist in Rome, in 1955. Direct confrontation with Europe always makes those from transplanted European cultures intensely aware of their own non-European character. Tucker began to paint explorers and bandits from Australian history, their features ambiguously treated as Australian desert landscape, and both the figures and landscapes treated with scars, boils and wounds.

Such themes still continue in his art. They can be interpreted as an attempt to equip the Australian landscape with mythology-figures and as a comment on European disruption of the well-balanced Aboriginal ecology. But they are primarily an expression of Tucker's personal relish for flouted authority, for large-scale failures and for marks of retribution. Tragedy is a relatively uncommon mode in contemporary painting, and Tucker is one of its few masters.

—Daniel Thomas

TUCKER, William.

British. Born, of English parents, in Cairo, Egypt, in 1935. Studied history at Oxford University, 1955–58; studied sculpture at the Central School of Art and Design and St. Martin's School of Art, London, 1959–60. Worked at the Victoria and Albert Museum, London, 1961. Sculptor, working in steel, fi-

breglass, plastics and wood, London, since 1962. Instructor, Goldsmith's College and St. Martin's School of Art, London, 1961–62; University of Western Ontario, London, 1976; and Columbia University and New York School of Painting and Sculpture, New York, 1978. Recipient: Sainsbury Scholarship, London, 1961; Peter Stuyvesant Foundation Travel Bursary, London, 1965; Gregory Fellowship in Sculpture, University of Leeds, 1968–70; Guggenheim Fellowship, 1980. Agent: Waddington Galleries, 2 Cork Street, London W1X 1PA. Address: 102 Greencroft Gardens, London NW6, England.

Individual Exhibitions:

1962	Grabowski Gallery, London (with Michael Kidner)
1963	Rowan Gallery, London
1965	Richard Feigen Gallery, New York
1966	Rowan Gallery, London
1967	Kasmin Gallery, London
1968	Elkon Gallery, New York
1969	Leslie Waddington Prints, London
	Kasmin Gallery, London
	City Art Gallery, Leeds
1970	Kasmin Gallery, London
1972	British Pavilion, at the *Biennale*, Venice
1973	Kunstverein, Hamburg
	Kunstmuseum, Bochum, West Germany
	Galerie Müller-Wintersberger, Cologne
	Serpentine Gallery, London
	Waddington Galleries II, London
1974	*Drawings*, Hester van Royen Gallery, London
1976	Galerie Wintersberger, Cologne

1977	Elkon Gallery, New York
	Kasmin Gallery, London
1978	Fruit Market Gallery, Edinburgh
	Sable-Castelli Gallery, Toronto
1979	Elkon Gallery, New York
1980	David Reid Gallery, Sydney
	Powell Street Gallery, Melbourne
	Elkon Gallery, New York
1981	Galleria L'Isola, Rome
1982	Bernard Jacobson Gallery, Los Angeles
	Sculpture and Drawings, Elkon Gallery, New York
1984	David McKee Gallery, New York
	Galleria L'Isola, Rome
1985	Pamela Auchincloss Gallery, Santa Barbara, California
	David McKee Gallery, New York
	Neuberger Museum, Purchase, New York
1987	Pamela Auchincloss Gallery, Santa Barbara, California
	Tate Gallery, London
	David McKee Gallery, New York
	Annely Juda Fine Art, London
	Padiglione d'Arte Contemporanea, Milan
	Galleria L'Isola, Rome

Selected Group Exhibitions:

1961	*Biennale*, Paris
1965	*London: The New Scene*, Walker Art Center, Minneapolis
1966	*Primary Structures*, Museum of Modern Art, New York
1968	*Documenta*, Kassel, West Germany

1970   *Contemporary British Painting and Sculpture,* National Museum of Modern Art, Tokyo

1975   *The Condition of Sculpture,* Hayward Gallery, London

1979   *Contemporary Sculpture,* Museum of Modern Art, New York

1981   *Il Luogo della Forma,* Museo di Castelvecchio, Verona

1983   *Monumental Drawings by Sculptors,* Long Island University, New York

1985   *Working in Brooklyn: Sculpture,* Brooklyn Museum, New York

Collections:

Arts Council of Great Britain, London: British Council, London; Tate Gallery, London; Victoria and Albert Museum, London; Rijksmuseum Kroller-Muller, Otterlo, Netherlands; Louisiana Museum, Humlebaek, Denmark; Museum of Modern Art, New York; Guggenheim Museum, New York; Walker Art Center, Minneapolis.

Publications:

By TUCKER: book—*The Language of Sculpture,* London 1974; articles—"Reflections on Sculpture" in *Tim Scott,* exhibition catalogue, London 1967; "Moore at the Tate" in *Studio International* (London), October 1968; "Anthony Caro's Work: A Symposium," with others, in *Studio International* (London), January 1969; "An Essay on Sculpture" in *Studio International* (London), January 1969; "Sidney Nolan and William Tucker Discuss Their Recent Work" in *Studio International* (London), June 1969; "The Sculptures of Matisse" in *Studio International* (London), July 1969; "4 Sculptors: Brancusi, Picasso, Matisse, David Smith" in *Studio International* (London), April, May and September 1970 and January 1971; "Notes on Sculpture, Public Sculpture and Patronage" in *Studio International* (London), January 1972; "Sculpture and Architecture: An Introduction to My Recent Work" in *Studio International* (London), June 1972; "What Sculpture Is" in *Studio International* (London), December 1974 and March/April 1975; statement in *William Tucker: Horses,* exhibition catalogue, Rome 1987.

On TUCKER: books—*William Tucker: Sculpture,* exhibition catalogue, with text by Christopher Salveson, London 1963; *36th Biennale di Venezia: British Pavilion: William Tucker,* exhibition catalogue, with text by Andrew Forge, London 1972; *William Tucker: Sculpture 1970-73,* exhibition catalogue, with text by Andrew Forge, London 1973; *William Tucker: Drawings,* exhibition catalogue, with text by Barry Martin, London 1974; *William Tucker,* exhibition catalogue, Rome 1981; *William Tucker: Sculpture and Drawings,* exhibition catalogue, with text by Andrew Forge, New York 1982; *William Tucker—Gods" Five Recent Sculptures,* exhibition ctalogue with text by Dore Ashton, London 1986.

In that group of sculptors who emerged from St. Martin's School of Art in London in the mid-60's, a group which included Phillip King, Isaac Witkin and Tim Scott, William Tucker was noted for the strongly theoretical nature of his approach to sculpture. A concern with certain qualities which he considered fundamental to sculpture—its objecthood, its literalness—has consequently informed all his works. In sculptures like "Meru I & II" he explored some of the variety of ways in which an object may be apprehended: how presence is conveyed, together with weight, mass, volume, stability and so on. Though occasionally he used unconventional materials, like resins, Tucker's aims were not iconoclastic: on the contrary, he sought to re-examine many of the crucial questions that sculptors have always faced. The rigor of his approach, however, meant that his works generally lacked the witty or playful aura found in the sculpture of many of his contemporaries.

In the late 60's Tucker turned to more attenuated forms, more nakedly structural and expressive in character, as found in the "Beulahs" and "Cat's Cradles." Still human in scale and still related to the activity of the body, these works were strictly abstract in character although individual components often had architectural associations. As Tucker explained: "the 'architectural' experience of the sculpture, that is the way in which it could be experienced with the spectator's whole body by analogy with his experience of traversing and using space, replaced the specifically 'tactile,' the experience, real or imagined, or the spectator's hands in previous sculpture."

In the 70's an increased scale, together with a greater emphasis on the mass and texture of materials, made works like "Tunnel" not only more monumental but also more architectonic than hitherto. At the same time, or perhaps as a result, they took on connotations which formerly would have been eschewed. Although not totemic objects, they are more than just structures in space, they have a new resonance or "character."

In his recent large charcoal drawings these concerns are paralleled in handsome fashion. These are not sculptor's drawings in the usual sense, for they do not simply depict a solid object in three-dimensional space; Tucker always carefully aligns the image to the format and to the surface in which it lies. Once again, that rigorous questioning which informs all his activity is apparent.

—Lynne Cooke

TURCATO, Giulio.
Italian. Born in Mantua, 16 March 1912. Studied at the Scuola d'Arte dei Carmine, Venice, 1928-31, Liceo Artistico, Venice, 1932-33, and Scuola Libera del Nudo, Venice, 1933-35. Served in the Italian Army, in Sicily, 1935-36. Married Vana Caruso in 1964. Assistant draughtsman to the architect Muzio, Milan, 1937-39. Painter and graphic artist in Milan, 1939-42, and in Rome, since 1943: Member, Corrente Group of artists, Milan, 1939; Founder Member, International Independent Artists Art Club, Rome, 1945, and, with Consagra, San Filippo, Dorazio, Guerrini and Perilli, Gruppo Arte Sociale, Rome, 1946; Co-Editor, *Forma 1* formalist art manifesto, Rome, 1947; Member, Nuovo Fronte delle Arti, Rome, 1949, Gruppo degli Otto, Rome, 1950, and, with Novelli, Perilli, Dorazio, Consagra, and Gio and Arnaldo Pomodoro, Gruppo Continuità, Rome, 1960-62. Instructor in Drawing and Design, Vocational School, Portogruaro, Italy, 1942-43. Professor, Liceo Artistico, Rome, 1953-82. Recipient: National Prize, *Biennale,* Venice, 1958; Fiorino Prize, Florence, 1962; Esso Prize, Rome, 1962; Painting Prize, *Review of Figurative Art,* Rome, 1963; Painting Prize, Termoli, 1963; First prize, *Quadriennale,* Rome, 1966; San Sofia prize, 1971; Painting Prize, Volleverede, 1972. Address: via del Pozzetto 117, 00187 Rome, Italy.

Individual Exhibitions:

1949   Galleria La Giostra, Asti, Italy
1950   Galleria del Secolo, Rome
1951   Galleria del Naviglio, Milan
1952   Galleria La Cassapanca, Rome
1953   Galleria del Naviglio, Milan
1955   Galleria La Tartaruga, Rome
      Galleria del Grattacielo, Milan
1956   Galleria L'Indiano, Florence
      Galleria del Grattacielo, Milan
1957   Galleria La Tartaruga, Rome
1960   Galleria del Grattacielo, Milan
1961   New Vision Centre, London
      Galleria Il Canale, Venice
1962   Galerie Burdeke, Zurich
      Galleria La Tartaruga, Rome
1963   Galleria Il Quadrante, Florence
1964   Galleria La Scaletta, Catania, Italy
      Galleria Il Segno, Rome
      Galleria La Polena, Genoa
1965   Galleria Marlborough, Rome
      Galleria del Naviglio, Milan
      Galleria Il Segno, Rome

1967   Galleria Arte Oggi, Pescara, Italy
      Galleria Le Muse, Bologna
      Galleria L'Indiano, Florence
      Galleria Arco d'Alibert, Rome
1968   Galleria del Naviglio, Milan
      Galleria Il Punto, Turin
      Studio G30, Paris
      Galleria Alfieri, Venice
      Galleria L'Oca, Rome
      Galleria Regis, Cadice Ligure, Italy
      Galleria Ferro di Cavallo, Rome
1969   Galerie D.I.V., Frankfurt
      Galleria L'Indiano, Florence
      Galleria La Barcaccia, Montecatini, Italy
      Galleria Il Capitello, Rome
      Studio Santandrea, Milan
1970   Galleria Boni-Schubert, Lugano, Switzerland
      Galleria del Foglio, Rome
      Galleria Il Segno, Turin
      Galleria La Sfera, Milan
      Galleria Giovio, Lake Como, Italy
      Galleria Schubert, Milan
      Grafica Romero, Rome
1971   Galleria Il Segnapassi, Pesaro, Italy
      Galleria La Cornice, Latina, Italy
      Galleria Il Nettuno, Bologna
      Galleria Barozzi, Venice
      Studio Barozzi, Milan
      Galleria La Bussola, Cosenza, Italy
      Galleria Sinibaldi, Cagliari, Italy
      Galleria Martano Due, Turin
      Studio Santandrea, Milan
      Galleria La Seggiola, Salerno, Italy
      Galleria Duomo, Piacenza, Italy
1972   Galleria La Gradiva, Florence
      Galleria Il Salotto, Como, Italy
      Studio Cortina, Pescara, Italy
      Galleria Editalia, Rome
      Galleria Il Pozzo, Citt;a di Castello, Italy
      Galleria Il Segno, Rome
      Galleria Il Capricorno, Venice
      Galleria Piero della Francesca, Arezzo, Italy
      Square Gallery, Milan
      Galleria La Sirenella, Sorrento, Italy
      Galleria Nuovo Carpine, Porto Cervo, Italy
      Studio d'Arte Hermes, Rome
      Galleria Rotta, Milan
1973   Galleria Il Giorno, Milan
      Grafica Romero, Rome
      Palazzo Ancaini, Spoleto, Italy (retrospective)
1974   Galleria Editalia, Rome
      Galleria i Diamante, Pescara, Italy
      Palazzo delle Prigioni Vecchie, Venice
      Galleria Ravagnan, Venice
      Palazzo delle Esposizione, Rome (retrospective)
1975   Studio Latronica, Todi, Italy
      Galleria Nuovo Saggitario, Milan
      Galleria Editalia, Rome
      Galleria La Gradiva, Florence
1976   Galleria Colasanti, Rome
      Galleria Nuove Colonne, Trieste, Italy
1977   Galleria Il Pilastro, Rome
      Galleria Lo Spazio, Naples
      Galleria Ferretti, Viareggio, Italy
      Galleria Pancheri, Rovereto, Italy
      Galleria Ravagnan, Venice
      Galleria Linea Settanta, Verona
      Galleria Borghese 31, Rome
      Istituto Italiano di Cultura, Cairo
1978   Istituto Italiano di Cultura, New York
      Westend Galerie, Frankfurt
1979   Galleria Numerosette, Naples
      Museum of Modern Art, Bucharest
      Galleria del Falconiere, Ancona, Italy
1980   Agenzia d'Arte Moderna, Rome
      Musee de l'Athenee, Geneva
      Galleria del Milione, Milan
1981   Galleria Mazzoli, Modena, Italy
      Galleria Cesarea, Genoa
      Galleria Planetario, Trieste, Italy
      Castello di San Giusto, Trieste, Italy
      Auditorium San Lorenzo, Cento, Italy
      Studio Solige C.V. 79, Rome
1982   Pinacoteca, Ravenna, Italy

Galleria De Amicis, Florence
Galleria De Crescenzo, Rome
Galleria Linea 70, Verona
Iterarte Circolo Artistico, Bologna
Galleria Pantha Arte, Como, Italy
Galleria Il Luogo, Rome
Galleria Adriano Villata, Cerrina Monferrato, Italy
1983   Galleria Nazionale d'Arte Moderna, Rome
1984   Padiglione d'Arte Contemporanea, Milan
1985   Staatsgalerie Moderner Kunst, Munich
Kunstverein, Frankfurt
1986   Galleria Nazionale d'Arte Moderna, Rome

Selected Group Exhibitions:

1945   *Associazione Artistica Internazionale Indipendente
"Art Club",* Galleria San Marco, Rome
1948   *Biennale,* Venice (and 1950, 1952)
1957   *Painting in Postwar Italy,* Columbia University, New
York
1959   *Documenta,* Kassel, West Germany
1963   *6 Italienska Malare,* Moderna Museet, Stockholm
1968   *Arte Italiana dal Futurismo ad Oggi,* Galleria Nazionale d'Arte Moderna, Rome
1971   *New Italian Art 1953-71,* Walker Art Gallery, Liverpool
1973   *Bienal,* Sao Paulo
1980   *Arte Astratta Italiana 1909-59,* Galleria Nazionale
d'Arte Moderna, Rome
1982   *L'Immagine del Socialismo,* Palazzo delle Esposizioni, Rome

Collections:

Galleria Nazionale d'Arte Moderna, Rome; Musée d'Art
Moderne de la Ville, Paris; Kunsthalle, Lund, Sweden;
Konsthall, Gothenberg, Sweden; Museum of Modern Art,
New York; Brooklyn Museum, New York; Museu de Arte
Moderna, Sao Paulo; Galleria Civica d'Arte Moderna, Turin;
Bayerische Staatsgemaldesammlungen, Munich.

Publications:

By TURCATO: articles—"Crisi della Pittura" in *Forma 1*
(Rome), March 1947; "Tre Biscotti" in *Pittori che Scrivono,*
Milan 1954; "Tempi di Riscatto" in *Realismo* (Milan),
March 1955; "Pensiero sul Disegno" in *Civiltà delle Machine,* Rome 1956; "Declaration" in *Pittura Italiana del Dopoguerra,* edited by T. Sauvage, Milan 1957; "Le Correnti
dell'Astrattismo" in *Il Punto* (Rome), April 1957; "Confor-
mismo: Pigrizia Intellettuale" in *Arte Oggi,* Rome 1959;
"Considerazione" in *Alfabeto* (Rome), February 1963; "Un
Pelo dal Naso" in *Carte Segrete* (Rome), no. 3. 1967; interview, with Gerardo de Simone, in *Turcato,* exhibition catalogue, Naples 1981.

On TURCATO: books—*Giulio Turcato,* exhibition catalogue,
with an introduction by Palma Bucarelli, Rome 1950; *Otto
Pittori Italiani* by Luca Venturi, Rome 1952; *Dictionnaire de
la Peinture Abstraite* by Michel Seuphor, Paris 1957; *Arte e
Artisti d'Avanguardia in Italia 1910-1950* by Giuseppe Marchiori, Milan 1960; *Ultime Tendenze nell' Arte d'Oggi* by
Gillo Doriles, Milan 1961; *Giulio Turcato,* exhibition catalogue, with an introduction by Giulio Carlo Argan, London
1961; *Turcato,* exhibition catalogue, with text by Carla
Lonzi, Rome 1965; *Turcato* by Mercuri, Rome 1968; *L'Arte
del XX. Secolo* by H.L. Jaffe, Florence 1970; *Turcato* by
Giorgio de Marchis, Milan 1971; *New Italian Art 1953-
1971,* exhibition catalogue, with text by Giovanni Carandente, Liverpool 1971; *Giulio Turcato* by Giovanna dalla
Chiesa and Italo Mussa, Rome 1974; *Turcato,* exhibition
catalogue, with text by Giovanni Caradente, Naples 1981; *Turcato* by Flaminio Gualdoni, Ravenna 1982, *Giulio Turcato,*
exhibition catalogue with texts by Thomas Messer, Carlo
Proietti and others, Rome 1986.

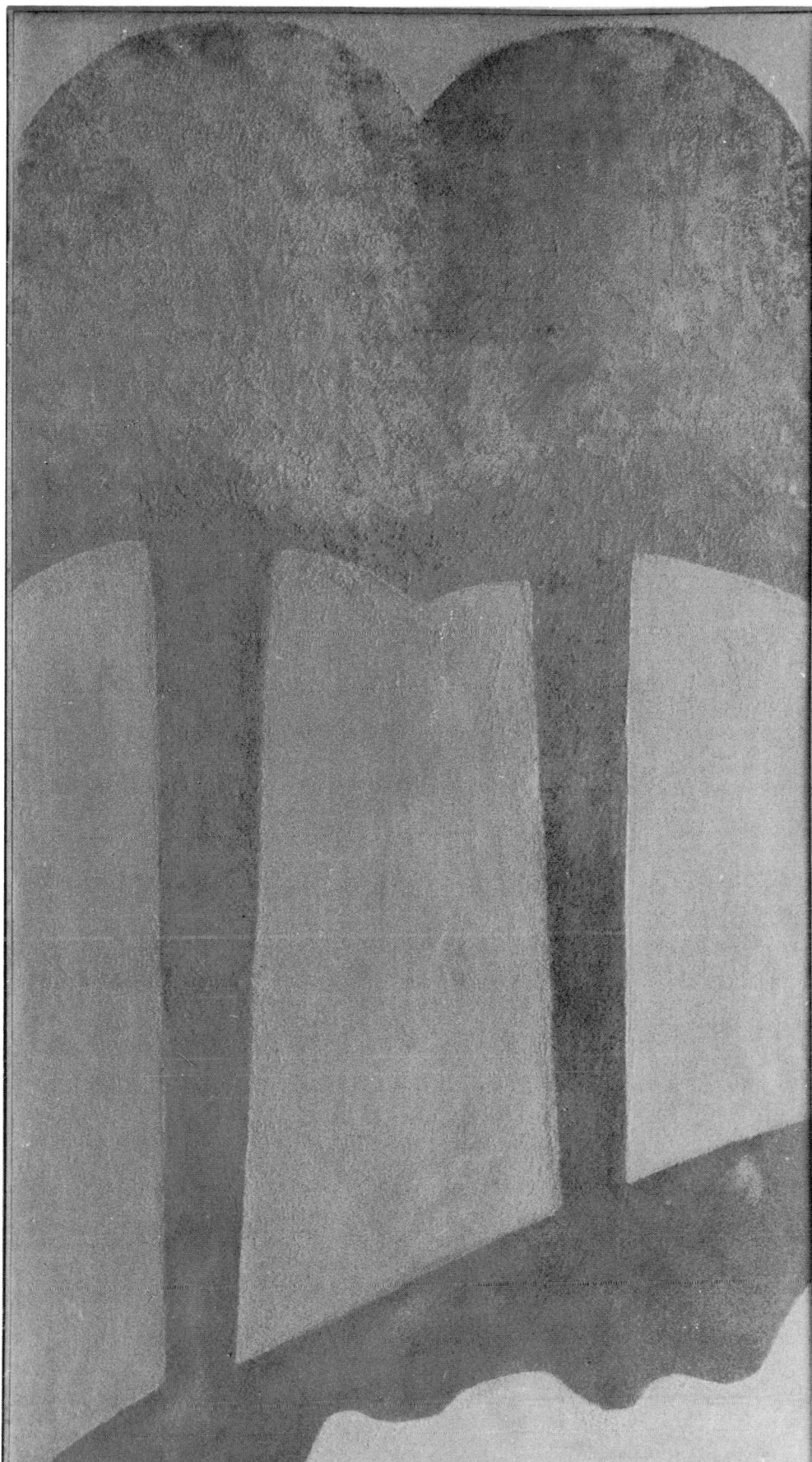

Giulio Turcato: *Florescenza Nucleare,* 1982

Although my works for the last 30 years can be seen
as unified within the same basic aesthetical principles, their contents have differed depending upon the
ideas and poetic allusions I've sought to convey. My
paintings quickly developed from geometric abstractions to a more personal and dynamic form, pictori-
cally closer to the original futurist breakthroughs of
Boccioni and Balla but with contents inspired by the
revolutionary enthusiasm that followed Europe's liberation from Fascism. (For example, such works as
"Comizi" (Demonstration), 1948; "Rivolta" (Revolt), 1949; "Le Rovine di Varsavia" (The Ruins of
Warsaw) 1949; "Fabbrica" (Factory), 1949; "Min-
niere" (Mines), 1950; "1 Maggio '45, a Mosca"
(May 1, 1945 in Moscow), 1950.

Then, in the early 50's, I began a series of paintings whose primary concern was pure line and
color—"Composizione;" "Reticolo" (Net); "La-

birinto" (Labyrinth); and a series inspired by ecological concerns—"Il Giardino de Miciurin", (The Garden of Miciurin), 1952; "Paesaggio Cosmico" (Cosmic Landscape), 1953. These concerns for pure line, color and form have remained and can be seen continuing in a series of works entitled, "Mosche Cinese" (Chinese Flies), 1957; "Arcipelago" (Archipelago), 1958; "Subacqueo", (Underwater), 1961; "Floreale" (Floral), 1961.

Two important works, "Il Deserto dei Tartari" and "Desertico" were painted after a trip in 1956 to China by plane across the vast continent of Russia and Central Asia. At about the same time I began with "Le Cavallette" (Grasshoppers) a more informal technique using colored sand surfaces that visually changed as the viewer moved his physical point of view, works such as "La Bava" (Drivel), 1960; "Astronomical", 1959; "Via Lattea" (Milky Way) 1959; "Itinerari" (Traces), 1960. Later, I would pursue this theme by using fine powdered glass that glistens or disappears depending upon the viewer's own movement in front of the painting.

Continuing this search beyond the normal confines of oil on canvas, I began in the early 60's a series of collages on surfaces of sand and asphalt and using the dollar, the lire and a carbon paper whose trade-mark was the image of the Acropolis—these images of money and the Acropolis were for me polemic symbols of power. In a related manner, on the same surfaces of sand and asphalt I placed real sedatives and tranquilizers as symbols of contemporary neurosis. These collages were actually only enlargements of a painting I did in 1953 in which I painted in oil the repeated image of the lire (being much too poor to even imagine placing real money on canvas in those days). This painting, "Ricordo di S. Rocco" (Memory of Saint Rocco), shown in the Venice Biennale of 1954, was inspired by my seeing the poor immigrants of the village of Pisticci as they attached lire to the religious statue of Saint Rocco.

Breaking completely from canvas, in 1963, I began to work directly on rough pockmarked sheets of foam rubber that gave to me the sense of the surface of the moon, painting them in white, silver, and dark metallic browns and violet-blues with occasional dots of fluorescent and phosphorescent pigment because I believe a painting can change light within itself. Above all, with the use of phosphorescent pigment I was searching to make painting visible in the dark because, for me, it is absurd that one cannot see a painting or a wall in the dark.

Another group of paintings, interesting and for me fundamental, are those entitled "Fuori dello Spettro" (Outside of the Spectrum) since they were made to isolate colors scientifically considered not within the classified color spectrum: maroon and amaranth. I made many experiments (anticipated by a painting of the same title in 1963), and then in 1972 I showed seven paintings based purely on the color spectrum. From a quick glance around the room there remained a fleeting visual impression of maroon and amaranth. From this experiment were born other paints of monochromatic surfaces, each of a different color; each an evidence of the strength within a restraint of using only a single color on canvas.

From a desire to change the square dimensions of painting, I at first painted circular forms, later truncated triangles, until in the early 70's I created shapes in canvas and then in wood entitled "Oceanica" for their similarity to the primitive oval forms of the island civilizations of the Pacific or perhaps to the surf boards originally used by the Maori. I wanted to structuralize existing forms since I don't believe much in sculpture in its classical sense. From this came also the works entitled, "Libreria Incatenata" (Chained Library), tall wooden structures, tied in their final narrowing height by iron ropes, and painted in vivid fluorescent colors with some sections of phosphorescent pigment that can be seen in the dark. These and other objects such as the "Sarcofaghi" were intentionally painted with transparent material that gives off an illumination from inside as if by neon signs. They are the continuation of my interest in collage, but within space; adaptable to any

space available—in a small space there can be one, in museum spaces I've shown 10 or 15; they can hang from the ceiling or lean on a wall or block a corridor. By being independent of any particular space, their presence underlines the very existence of free space and the artist's fundamental act of changing a previously defined ambience.

—Giulio Turcato

Everyone knows that Giulio Turcato is a born painter who lives to paint, and since early youth has done nothing else but paint. Around 1942–43 he taught drawing and design in a vocational school at Portogruaro, and from 1953 has taught figure drawing in the Liceo of Fine Arts in Rome. On the other hand, he has always found someone to buy one of his paintings. Like this, he lives. His official position and fame are much below his value because he is timid and indifferent to any public recognition, and in spite of having some difficult moments he is content in his bohemian life, the only one he considers worthy of an artist, because more than free it is anarchic. But the anarchy of Turcato is extemely gentle. It has a Venetian mood, wouldn't hurt a fly and is so disinterested that it becomes itself a work of art. If one adds that he is capable of intense work, but is desultory sometimes for great intervals, we can understand how he owes to himself the limits of his fame and of the value given to some of the great periods of his work. The last few years have been a recovery and ones of intense and happy activity. It's just the moment to speak of him.

An essential quality of Turcato, which is acknowledged by his colleagues, is his sense of the limits and an absolute lack of rhetoric. When Turcato dedicated himself to pure abstractionism, he didn't fall into it as an experiment or a joke or just for the spontaneous engagement of his painting. It never came into his mind to place a line or colour to show his ability, but only to express a feeling or to indicate an idea or to make poetic allusion. Turcato's strength often consists in his refusal to "do the painting" so that he can express a moment of his fantastic vision. Therefore, his paintings appear, and often seem to be, unfinished in spite of their authentic artistic worth. But few artists today, as in the past, are able to escape a bias to finish.

I think I have indicated here many reasons why Turcato's fame is below his value: shyness, indifference to public acknowledgement, a bohemian life, intermittent work, a sense of bounds, delicateness, and also a tenuous inspiration. He considers his art as being completely abstract. He distinguishes three types of abstraction: the American, represented by Pollock, the French and the European trend, in which he prefers Hartung. Poliakoff is too romantic for him. Matta is too surrealistic, and Manessier too tied up with impressionism. Among Italian painters he feels sympathy for Corpora, Vedova and Afro, and the young Dova and Perilli. He does not take an interest in Mondrian's constructivism because to Turcato a painting is a space charged with emotion, without a center,and without the doors of a triptych. He finds that surrealism was useful because it allowed thought to untie itself from literary tradition. What he asks of painting is for it to have an emotion that exceeds the painting, a surrealistic impulse without the need of an unconscious mind, able not to create romantic drama but colour-form. According to him, painting creates a space in eternal movement, free from any theory, that attempts to transform and modify the life of feeling.

In Forma 1 review (April 1947) he published an article entitled "Crisis of Painting . . . " I would like readers to reflect on the fact that this text was written in 1947, and that it has prophetic value in regard to the following development of Italian painting: "Those who kept a tie with the 19th century style, or wanted to use a realistic style, or gave a small touch of Lombardic feeling to their imitative forms of Picasso, all failed . . ." Already in 1947 Turcato understood the historical condition of painting in Italy and abroad better than many eminent persons who were supposedly more learned than he. To understand the history of painting, you must understand painting. And Tur-

cato is a born painter. Afte a show with the "Fronte Nuovo" at the Venice Biennale of 1948, Turcato found himself the foremost target in the condemnation of abstractionism by the Communist Party—and he was a Communist. This obstacle, arising directly in the midst of his natural development, did not leave him unaffected. On the contrary, he tried in various ways to find an accord between his convictions as a man and as an artist: he attempted figuration, symbolism, and even surrealism. But his artistic nature prevailed. Besides, he was enough of an anarchist to disregard superior orders. In facing Cagli and Guttuso, moreover, he defended his freedom with his fists. Not that Turcato refused to deal with social problems in which he believed, like in the works "Meeting," "Revolt" and "Warsaw Ruins," but he represented them in an abstract form, thereby destroying their effectiveness as propaganda in a heretical way. In the meantime, he gained a scholarship in 1950 to stay in Paris and has returned there many times. He also made other travels to Germany and as far from home as China. So, in his own way, he dominates the panorama of international art.

—Luca Venturi

TURNBULL, William.

British. Born in Dundee, Scotland, 11 January 1922. Studied at Slade School of Fine Art, London, 1946–48. Served in Royal Air Force in Canada, India, and Ceylon, 1941–46. Married Kim Lim in 1960; sons; Alexander and Jonathan. Painter and sculptor, in illustration department of D. C. Thompson magazine publishing company, Dundee, 1939–41; moved to Paris, 1948, and to London, 1950. Instructor in experimental design, 1952–61, and in sculpture, 1964–72, Central School of Arts and Crafts, London. Agent: Waddington Galleries, 11 Cork Street, London W1X, 1PD. Address: 40 Camden Square, London NW1 9XA, England.

Individual Exhibitions:

1950	Hanover Gallery, London (with Eduardo Paolozzi and Phillip King)
1952	Hanover Gallery, London
1957	Institute of Contemporary Art, London
1960	Paintings, Molton Gallery, London
1961	Molton Gallery, London
1963	Marlborough-Gerson Gallery, New York
	Detroit Institute of Arts
1965	Bennington College, Vermont
	Galerie Müller, Stuttgart
1966	Sculpture and Paintings, Pavilion Gallery, Balboa, California
1967	Bienal, Sao Paulo (toured South America)
	Waddington Galleries, London
1968	Hayward Gallery, London
	Museo de Arte Moderna, Rio de Janeiro
	Museo Nacional de Bellas Artes, Buenos Aires
	Instituto de Artes Plasticas, Santiago, Chile
1969	Waddington Galleries, London
1970	Waddington Galleries, London
1973	Sculpture and Paintings, Tate Gallery, London (retrospective)
1974	Scottish Arts Council Gallery, Edinburgh
	Galerie Müller, Stuttgart
1976	Waddington Galleries, London
1978	Waddington Galleries, London
1981	Waddington Galleries, London
1982	Waddington Galleries, New York
	Waddington Galleries, Toronto
1983	Galerie Kutter, Luxembourg
1984	National Museum Art Gallery, Singapore
1985	Waddington Galleries, London
1986	Terry Dintenfass Gallery, New York
1987	Galerie Folker Skulima, West Berlin
	Waddington Galleries, London
1988	Terry Dintenfass Gallery, New York

Selected Group Exhibitions:

1952 *Biennale*, Venice (and 1957)
1958 *Carnegie International*, Pittsburgh (and 1961)
1960 *Situation*, R.B.A. Galleries, London
1964 *Guggenheim International*, Guggenheim Museum, New York
1966 *New Shapes and Forms of Colour*, Stedelijk Museum, Amsterdam
1968 *Documenta*, Kassel, West Germany
1976 *Arte Inglese Oggi*, Palazzo Reale, Milan
1982 *British Sculpture in the Twentieth Century: II*, Whitechapel Art Gallery, London
1985 *Sculptors' Drawings*, Scottish Arts Council Gallery, Edinburgh (toured Britain)
1987 *British Art in the Twentieth Century*, Royal Academy, London (travelled to Stuttgart)

Collections:

Tate Gallery, London; Victoria and Albert Museum, London; Dundee Art Gallery, Scotland; Scottish National Gallery of Modern Art, Edinburgh; Candiff Museum, Wales; Albright-Knox Art Gallery, Buffalo, New York; Hirshhorn Museum & Sculpture Garden, Smithsonian Institution, Washington D.C.; Städtisches Museum Schloss Morsbroich, Leverkusen, West Germany; Westfälischer Landesmuseum, Münster, West Germany; Teheran Museum of Contemporary Art.

Publications:

By TURNBULL: books illustrated—*Basho: The Records of a Weather Exposed Skeleton* (book/object). London 1969; *The Garden of Caresses*, translated from Arabic by Franz Toussaint, London 1970; *Der Wassermaier* by Helmut Heissenbuttel, Zurich 1976; articles—"White Text on Black Ground," with Theo Crosby, Germano Facetti, and Edward Wright, in *This is Tomorrow*, exhibition catalogue, London 1956; "William Turnbull 1949–60" in *Uppercase* (London), no. 4, 1960; "The Joining Edge" in *Gazette* (London), no. 1, 1961; "Images without Temples" in *Living Arts* (London), no. 1, 1963; "Notes on Sculpture," with others in *Studio International* (London), November 1968; "Colour in Sculpture, with Phillip King, Tim Scott and David Annesley, in *Studio International* (London), January 1969; "Statement on Sculpture," with others, in *Studio International* (London), July/August 1972; film—*83 B*, with Alan Forbes, 1953.

On TURNBULL: books—*William Turnbull*, exhibition catalogue, with text by David Sylvester, London 1950; *Sculpture of the 20th Century* by Andrew C. Ritchie, New York 1952; *William Turnbull*, exhibition catalogue, with text by Lawrence Alloway, London 1957; *The Sculpture of This Century* by Michel Seuphor, New York 1960; *Contemporary Sculpture* by Carola Giedion-Weckler, New York 1960; *Situation*, exhibition catalogue, with introduction by Roger Coleman, London 1960; *William Turnbull: Paintings*, exhibition catalogue, with text by Lawrence Alloway, London 1960; *Modern Sculpture in the Joseph H. Hirshhorn Collection*, exhibition catalogue, with introduction by H. H. Arnason, New York 1962; *A Concise History of Modern Sculpture* by Herbert Read, London 1964; *William Turnbull: Sculpture and Paintings* exhibition catalogue, with introduction by Jules Langsner, Balboa, California 1966; *IX Bienal de Sao Paulo: British Section—William Turnbull*, exhibition catalogue, with text by Alan Bowness. London 1967; *William Turnbull: Sculpture and Painting*, exhibition catalogue, with introduction by Richard Morphet, London 1973; *Turnbull*, exhibition catalogue, with introduction by Robert Kudielka. Stuttgart 1974; *The Potent Image* by Frederick S. Wight, New York 1976; *British Art* by Simon Wilson, London, 1979; *William Turnbull*, exhibition catalogue with introduction by Roger Bevan, London 1987; article—"William Turnbull—Sculptor and Painter" by Bernard Cohen in *Studio International* (London), July/August 1973.

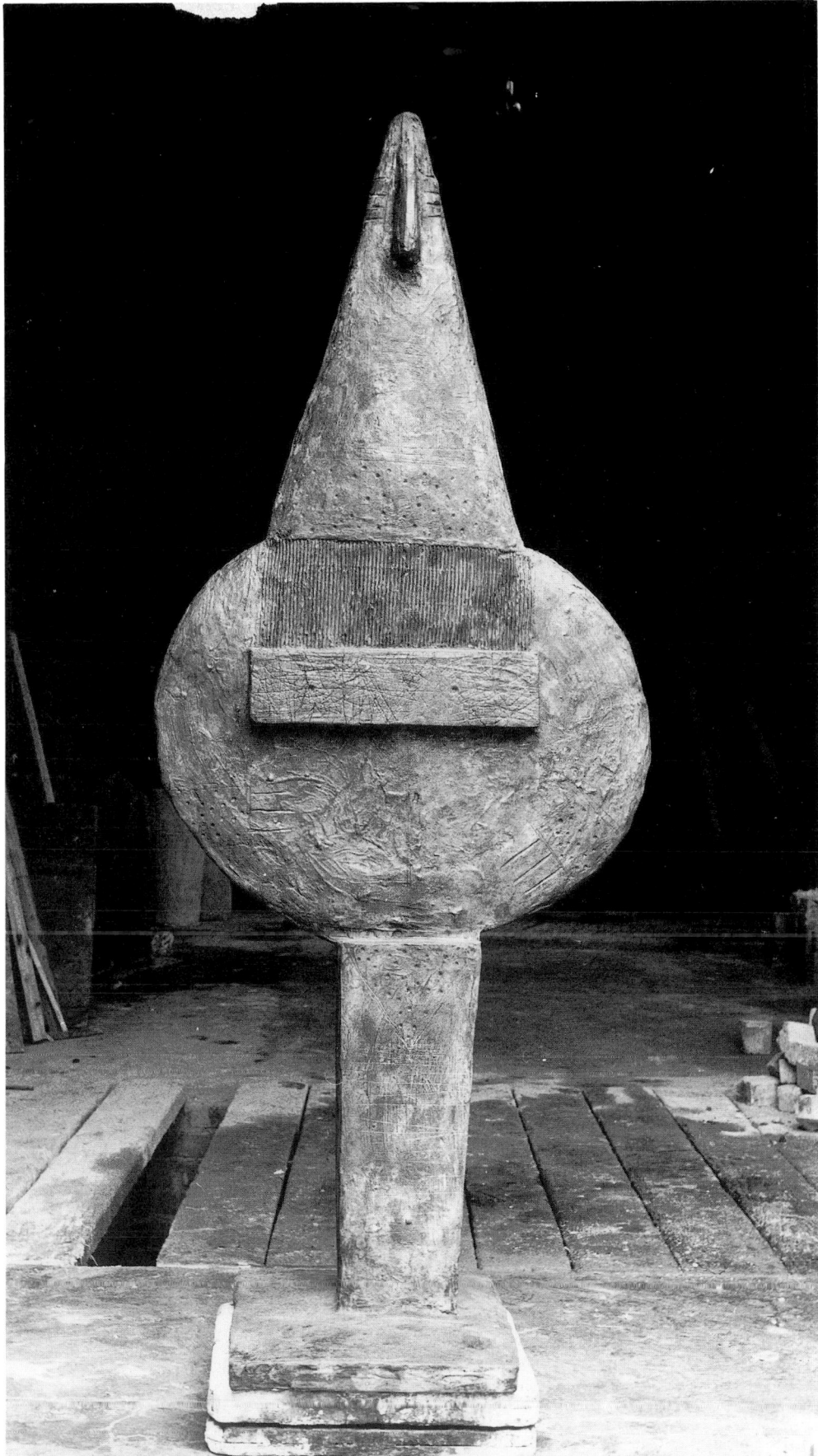

William Turnbull: *Idol No. 5*, 1957

Although British, William Turnbull has more in common with his colleagues on the Continent than with his fellow islanders. For one thing he is equally committed to the major arts of painting and sculpture—activities typical of such continental artists as Picasso and Matisse. For another, his kinship seems closer to a sculptor like Brancusi, a painter like Albers, a draughtsman like Matisse, than to any Briton.

At the same time, his painting as it has evolved, would be hard to imagine without the precedent of the break-through Americans of the post World War II era. Rothko pre-eminently. This is not to suggest that Turnbull is merely a derivative artist—rather that he has been released into his own sensibility through an emotional tie to certain artists' work. In the formal sense, he is one of the most "serious" artists in England, producing works in wood and metal in a minimal vein which have haunting overtones of primitive art as well as an elegance which could be called oriental. His large format paintings have been "about" fields of color in which the paint surface is handled with wonderful virtuosity being lively and rich instead of merely a flat expanse.

In recent work color-saturated, brush-inflected canvases are bordered by closely related color the hue and value of which sets up a tension between the field and its boundary, both in turn related to the actual stretcher edge. This concern with the edge/field has become a major interest to painters in the later part of our century. The "compositional" material of such paintings is often the character of the paint application itself together with whatever optical contrasts the colors provide. It is one of the extremely pure developments in modernist art and demands from the viewer a high degree of aesthetic response. As it is about the art of painting as such, it is necessary for the viewer to acquaint himself with the elements that comprise art. Except for the fact that its three-dimensionality causes it to exist in "real" space and cast "real" shadows in "real" light, thus giving us information outside of itself, much the same necessity to know its nature can be demanded by minimal sculpture as well.

Such purism can be mis-read by the impatient or lazy. A danger artists like Turnbull risk.

—Ralph Pomeroy

TURRELL, James (Archie).

American. Born in Los Angeles, California, 6 May 1943. Educated at Pasadena High School, California, 1957–61; studied at Pomona College, Claremont, California, 1961–65, B.A. in psychology 1965; University of California at Irvine, 1967; Claremont Graduate School, M.A. in Art 1973. Married Elizabeth Bartlett Elgin in 1965; children: Shana and Jennifer. Independent artist since 1967. Lecturer, University of California at Los Angeles, Summer 1968, and University of California at Riverside, 1971; Visiting Artist, Pomona College, 1971–73; Lecturer, University of California at Irvine, 1974. Recipient: National Endowment for the Arts grant, 1968; Guggenheim Fellowship, 1974; National Endowment for the Arts Matching Grant, 1975. Agent: Blum Helman Gallery, 20 West 57th Street, New York, New York 10019. Address: Box 725, Flagstaff, Arizona 86002, U.S.A.

Individual Exhibitions:

1967 Pasadena Art Museum, California
1976 Stedelijk Museum, Amsterdam
1981 Portland Center for the Visual Arts, Oregon
1982 Center for Contemporary Art, Seattle, Washington
Israel Museum, Jerusalem
1983 ARC/Musée d'Art Moderne de la Ville, Paris
1987 Kunsthalle, Basle

Selected Group Exhibitions:

1969 *Light Spaces*, Main and Hill Studio, Los Angeles
1973 *3D into 2D*, New York Cultural Center
1976 *Light Space*, Arco Center for the Visual Arts, Los Angeles
1980 *Light and Space*, Whitney Museum, New York
1982 *American Exhibition*, Art Institute of Chicago

Collections:

Stedelijk Museum, Amsterdam

Publications:

On TURRELL: books—*James Turrell*, exhibition catalogue with essay by Claude Gintz, Paris 1983; *James Turrell: Mapping Spaces/Kartographie des Raumes*, exhibition catalogue

James Turrell: *Crater Site Plan with Survey Net,* **1986** Courtesy Guggenheim Museum, New York

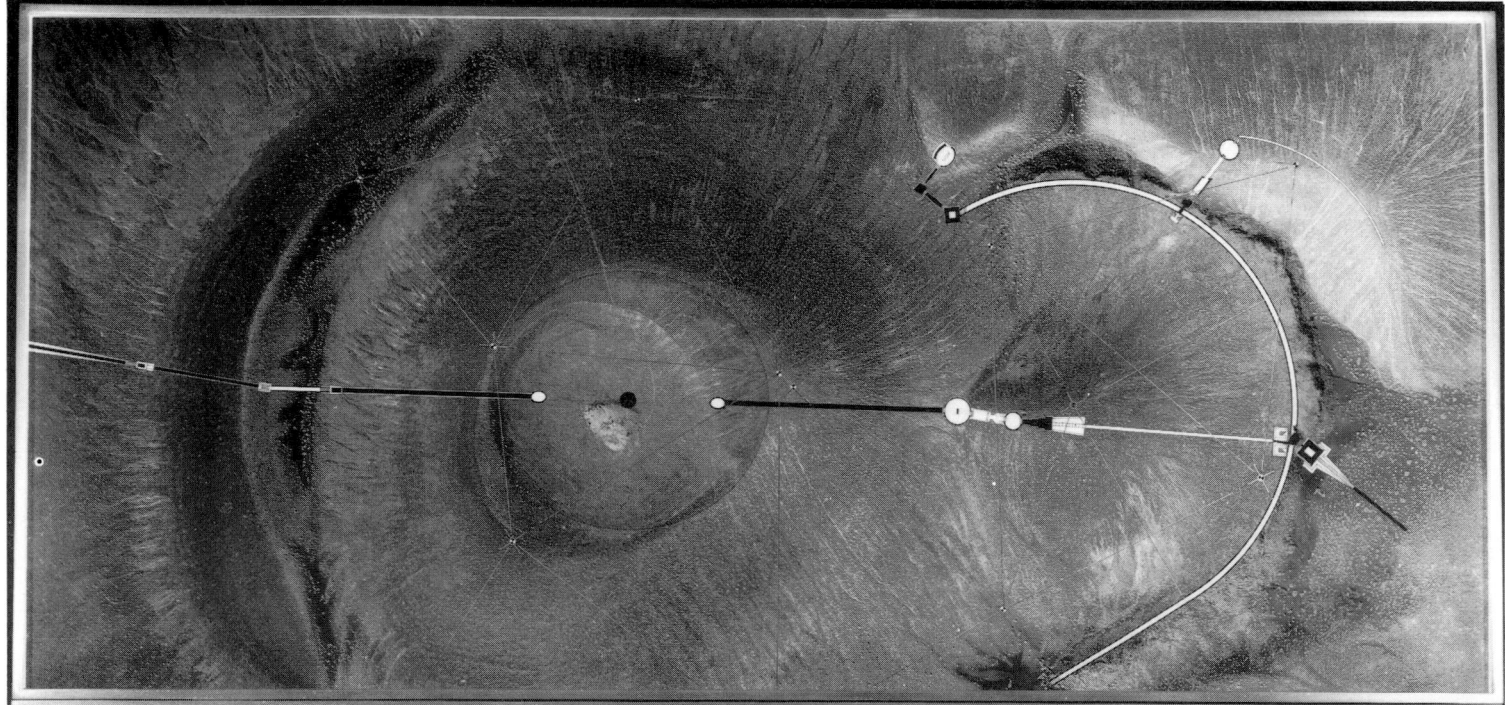

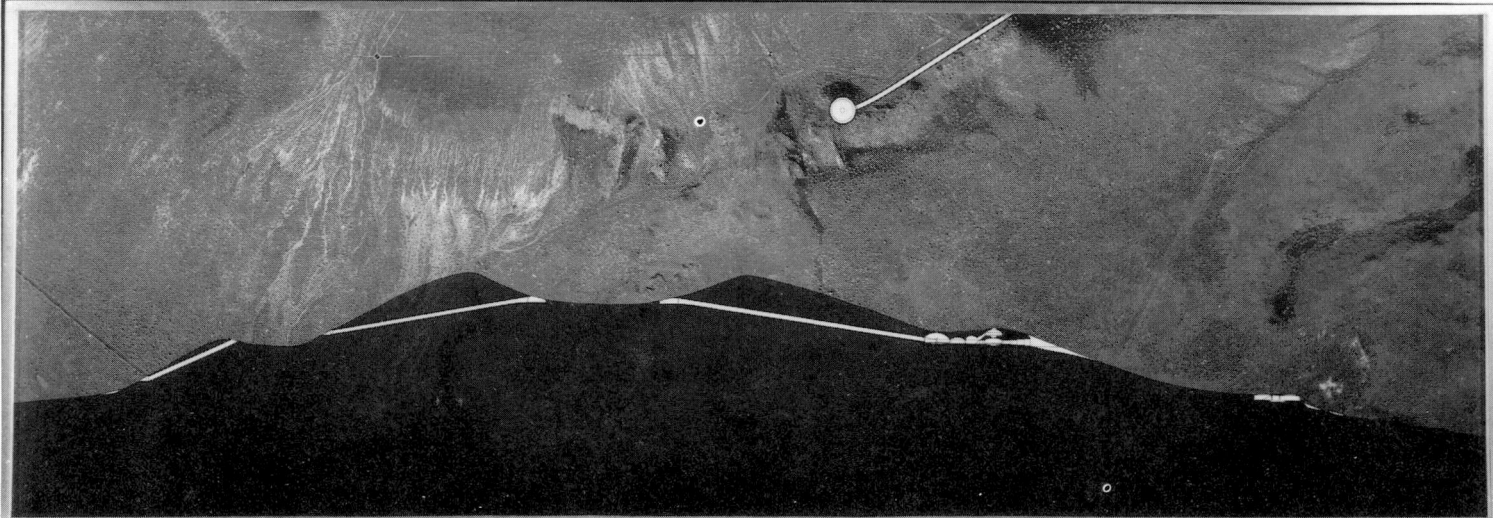

with texts by Craig Adcock, Jean-Christophe Ammann and others, New York and Basle 1987; articles—"James Turrell: Projected Light Images" by John Coplans in *Artforum* (New York), October 1967; "A Gallery Without Walls" by Barbara Rose in *Art in America* (New York), March/April 1968; "New Directions in Southern California Sculpture" in *Arts Magazine* (New York), Summer 1970; "The Talk of the Town—Light" by Calvin Tomkins in the *New Yorker,* 15 December 1980; "Poetry Out of Emptiness" by Robert Hughes in *Time* (New York), 5 January 1981; "The Art of Deception" by Nancy Marmer in *Art in America* (New York), May 1981.

TUTTLE, Richard.

American. Born in Rahway, New Jersey, in 1941. Educated at Trinity College, Hartford, Connecticut, B.A. 1963; Cooper Union, New York, 1963-64. Painter: lives and works in New York. Agent: Blum Helman Gallery, 20 West 57th Street, New York, New York 10019. Address: 734 11th Avenue, New York, New York 10019, U.S.A.

Individual Exhibitions:

1965	Betty Parsons Gallery, New York
1967	Betty Parsons Gallery, New York
1968	Betty Parsons Gallery, New York
	Galerie Schmela, Dusseldorf
1969	Nicholas Wilder Gallery, Los Angeles
1970	Betty Parsons Gallery, New York
	Galerie Rudolf Zwirner, Cologne
	Albright-Knox Art Gallery, Buffalo, New York
1971	Museum of Fine Arts, Dallas
1972	Museum of Modern Art, New York
	Galerie Yvon Lambert, Paris
	Betty Parsons Gallery, New York
	Galerie Rudolf Zwirner, Cologne
1973	Clocktower, Institute for Art and Urban Resources, New York
	Kunstraum, Munich
	Galerie Heiner-Friedrich, Munich
	Daniel Weinberg Gallery, San Francisco
	Galerie Annemarie Verna, Zurich
	Konrad Fischer Gallery, Dusseldorf
1974	Betty Parsons Gallery, New York
	Galerie Lambert, Paris
	Galleria Toselli, Milan
	Galleria Marilena Bonomo, Bari, Italy
	Cusack Gallery, Houston
	Nigel Greenwood Gallery, London
1975	Whitney Museum, New York (retrospective)
	Cusack Gallery, Houston
	Parsons-Truman Gallery, New York
	d'Alessandro Ferranti Gallery, Rome
	Wadsworth Atheneum, Hartford, Connecticut
1976	Galerie Lambert, Paris
	Otis Art Institute, Los Angeles
	Brooke Alexander Gallery, New York
	Northwest Artists Workshop, Portland, Oregon
	Fine Arts Building Gallery, New York
	University of Western Ontario, London
	Graeme Murray Gallery, Edinburgh
1977	Ohio State University, Columbus
	Galleria Ugo Ferranti, Rome
	Kunsthalle, Basle
	Kunstraum, Munich
	Galerie Heiner-Friedrich, Munich
	Yale University, New Haven, Connecticut (with Long and Hewitt)
1978	Betty Parsons Gallery, New York
	Galerie Lambert, Paris
	Ugo Ferranti Gallery, Rome
	Young-Hoffman Gallery, Chicago
	Brown University, Providence, Rhode Island
	Daniel Weinberg Gallery, San Francisco
	Galleria Francoise Lambert, Milan
	Musée d'Art Moderne, Ghent, Belgium
	Galerie Schmela, Dusseldorf

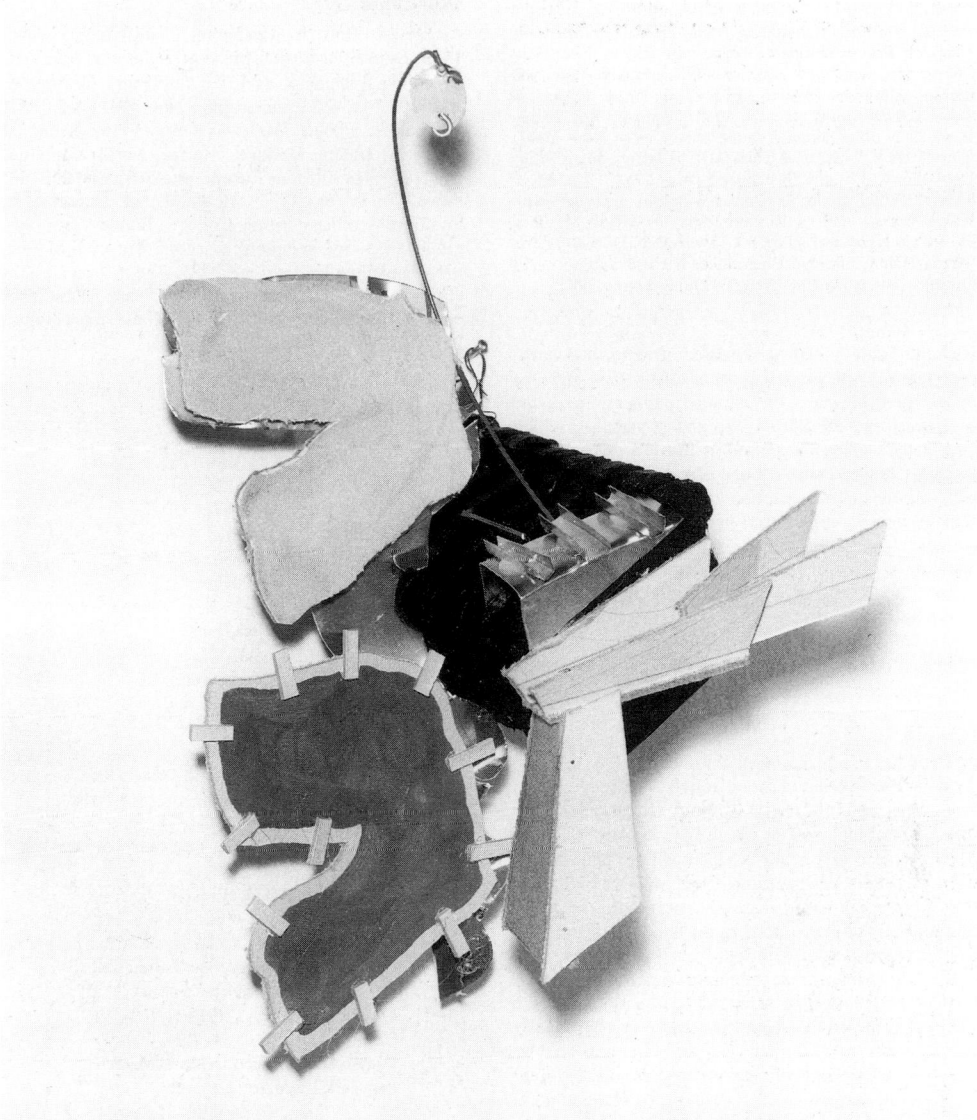

Richard Tuttle: *Silver Mercury*, **1986** Courtesy Whitney Museum, New York

1979	Galerie Annemarie Verna, Zurich
	Galleria Marilena Bonomo, Bari, Italy
	Brooke Alexander Gallery, New York
	Galleria Ugo Ferranti, Rome
	Stedelijk Museum, Amsterdam
	Truman Gallery, New York
	University of California at Santa Barbara
	Centre d'Arts Plastiques Contemporains, Bordeaux
1980	Centre d'Art Contemporain, Geneva
	California institute of Technology, Pasadena
1982	Blum Helman Gallery, New York (with Robert Ryman and Cy Twombly)
1983	Galerie Hubert Winter, Vienna
	Blum Helman Gallery, New York
1984	Studio La Citta, Verona, italy
	Galerie Yvon Lambert, Paris
	Galerie Schmela, Dusseldorf
	Galerie Annemarie Verna, Zurich
1985	Galerie Schmela, Dusseldorf
	Galleria Toselli, Milan
	Institute of Contemporary Arts, London
	Galerie Yvon Lambert, Paris
1986	Victoria Miro Gallery, London
	Galerie Reinhard Onnasch, West Berlin
	CAPC/Musée d'Art Contemporain, Bordeaux, France
	ARC/Musée d'Art Moderne de la Ville, Paris

Selected Group Exhibitions:

1968	*Other Ideas*, Detroit Institute of Arts
1970	*Using Walls*, Jewish Museum, New York
1971	*Painting Without Supports*, Bennington College, Vermont
1972	*Documenta 5*, Museum Fridericianum, Kassel, West Germany (and *Documenta 6*, 1977; *Documenta 7*, 1982)
1973	*Young American Artists*, Kunsthalle, Hamburg (travelled to the Moderna Museet, Stockholm)
1975	*14 Artists*, Baltimore Museum of Art
1976	*Drawing Now*, Museum of Modern Art, New York
1983	*Abstract Painting 1960–69*, Project Studio One, New York
1985	*New Dialogues*, Dracos Art Centre, Athens
1988	*Contemporary American Art*, Sara Hilden Museum, Tampere, Finland (travelled to Oslo)

Collections:

Museum of Modern Art, New York; Whitney Museum, New York; Albright-Knox Art Gallery, Buffalo, New York; Corcoran Gallery of Art, Washington, D.C.; St. Louis Art Museum; National Gallery of Canada, Ottawa; Stedelijk Museum, Amsterdam; Waliraf-Richartz Museum, Cologne; Kaiser-Wilhelm Museum, Krefeld, West Germany; Kunsthaus, Zurich.

Publications:

By TUTTLE: article statement in *Richard Tuttle*, exhibition catalogue, Paris 1986.

On TUTTLE: books—*Richard Tuttle*, exhibition catalogue with text by Robert Murdock, Dallas 1971; *Contemporary American Art*, exhibition catalogue with text by Peter Schjeldahl, Tampere 1988; articles—"Reviews and Previews: Richard Tuttle at Parsons Gallery" by Scott Burton in *Artnews* (New York), January 1968; "Simple, Not Simple Minded" by John Perreault in the *Village Voice* (New York), January 1968; "Artists on Their Art" by Jeffrey Smart in *Art International* (Lugano, Switzerland), May 1968; "The Art of Richard Tuttle" by Robert Pincus-Witten in *Artforum* (New York), February 1970; "Richard Tuttle" by Robert Murdock in *Art International* (Lugano, Switzerland), May 1971; "Wire, Pencil, Shadow: Elements of Richard Tuttle" by E. Lubeel in *Arts magazine* (New York), November 1972.

Richard Tuttle's intimately scaled, fragile, awkward, eccentrically shaped works seem to question both the boundaries between the graphic/painterly and the sculptural and the heroic size and physicality which dominated during the period of Tuttle's development in the 1960's. Tuttle's work, from his ideographic wall reliefs to those composed of various combinations of pencil, wire, cloth, paper, metal and wood, is usually classified under the Postminimalist heading, and his is a particularly quirky and subtly effective variant in the range of work made by the diverse group so clustered.

In 1963–65, Tuttle was making small, paper, box constructions such as his three-inch cube *Box* (1964), using geometric shape to emphasize individual personality and also the making process. "Toy like" qualitites along with folds, slits and cuts tend toward an Arp-like anthropomorphism which carries into Tuttle's 1965 series of wood reliefs, rounded shapes painted in one color with abstract references to nature, landscape and symbolically cryptic writing. These were either hung on the wall or lain on the floor in a kind of scattering effect which heightened their personally based, intuitive nature. In 1967 Tuttle made a group of shaped canvases, shaped in irregular octagonal configurations, dyed in Tintex in a range of washy tones, hemmed and either pinned loosely on the wall or arranged on the floor. As the series progressed the shapes became more personally warped versions of the octagon, an effect achieved by Tuttle's cutting out of interior angles on different sides of the canvas. In their fusion of soaked-in paint and fragile three dimensionality, these works invoked a fusion of painting and sculpture into a tense but material coupling. In his push to achieve new levels of delicate subtlety, Tuttle made his 1972 series of wire and graphite wall works, combining illusion and allusion through the juxtapositioning of wavey, twisting lengths of wire with nervous, straggley graphite lines. The shadows created by the wire lengths adds the third dimension, while the whole acting in concert activates the metaphorical fourth dimensional, suggesting rhythms beyond those seen with the eyes.

Throughout the past decade, Tuttle has continued to experiment with the possibilities inherent in the basic methodologies he had established during the previous decade. He has managed to achieve considerable variety and freshness by diversely combining small, simple shapes in low relief with either painted or linear elements which extend these shapes onto the wall. The works are both objects and references to drawings or paintings of objects. Their qualities of tentative whimsy and miniaturization use dephysicalized presence to intensify the personal. Because they are so odd, so attenuated and so close to becoming invisible, they draw the viewer closer to contemplate the delicate interplays between the solid and the ephemeral. Tuttle's mini-world of shadowy, elusive, and deceptively simple form offers hopeful proof that art need not be huge and heavy to achieve the strong effect.

—Barbara Cavaliere

TWOMBLY, Cy.

American. Born in Lexington, Virginia, 25 April 1929. Studied at Boston Museum School of Fine Art, 1948–49; Washington and Lee University, Lexington, 1949–50; Art Students League, New York, 1950–51; and, under Robert Motherwell and Franz Kline, at Black Mountain College, Beria, North Carolina, 1951–52. Travelled in Europe and Africa, 1952–53; moved to Rome, 1957. Head of Art Department, Southern Seminary Junior College, Buena Vista, Virginia, 1955–56. Recipient: Virginia Museum of Fine Arts Travelling Fellowship, 1952. Agent: Leo Castelli Gallery, 420 West Broadway, New York, New York 10021, U.S.A. Address: 149 via Monserrato, Rome, Italy.

Individual Exhibitions:

1951	Kootz Gallery, New York
	Seven Stairs Gallery, Chicago
1953	Stable Gallery, New York
	Galleria Contemporanea, Florence
	Little Gallery, Princeton, New Jersey
1955	Stable Gallery, New York
1957	Stable Gallery, New York
1958	Galleria La Tartaruga, Rome
	Galleria del Naviglio, Milan
	Galleria del Cavallino, Venice
1960	Leo Castelli Gallery, New York
	Galleria La Tartaruga, Rome
	Galleria del Naviglio, Milan
	Galerie 22, Dusseldorf (with Robert Rauschenberg)
1961	Galleria La Tartaruga, Rome
	Galleria del Naviglio, Milan
	Galerie Zwirner, Essen, West Germany
	Galerie J, Paris
1962	Galerie Aujourd'hui, Brussels
	Galleria del Leone, Venice
1963	Galerie Anne Abels, Cologne
	Galerie Bonnier, Lausanne, Switzerland
	Galerie Jacques Benador, Geneva
	Galleria La Tartaruga, Rome
1964	Galerie Handschin, Basle
	Galerie Friedrich und Dahlem, Munich
	Leo Castelli Gallery, New York

1965	Museum Haus Lange, Krefeld, West Germany
	Palais des Beaux-Arts, Brussels
	Galleria Notizie, Turin
	Galleria La Tartaruga, Rome
1966	Stedelijk Museum Amsterdam
	Kunstverein, Freiburg, West Germany
	Leo Castelli Gallery, New York
1967	Leo Castelli Gallery, New York
	Galleria La Tartaruga, Rome
	Galleria Notizie, Turin
1968	Galleria La Tartaruga, Rome
	Milwaukee Art Center
	Leo Castelli Gallery, New York
1969	Galerie Zwirner, Cologne
	Nicholas Wilder Gallery, Los Angeles
1970	Galerie Neurendorf, Cologne
	Modern Art Agency, Naples
	Svensk-Frenska Konstgalleriet, Stockholm
	Gallerie Bonnier, Geneva
1971	Galleria Sperone, Turin
	Galerie Mollenhoff, Cologne
	Galerie Yvon Lambert, Paris
	Galleria dell'Ariete, Milan
	Galerie Denise René-Hans Meyer, Dusseldorf
1972	Modern Art Agency, Naples
	Dunkelman Gallery, Toronto
	Locksley Shea Gallery, Minneapolis
	Janie C. Lee Gallery, Dallas
	Leo Castelli Gallery, New York
1973	School for Visual Arts, New York
	Art in Progress, Zurich
	Kunstmuseum, Basle
	Kunsthalle, Berne
	Städtische Galerie im Lenbachhaus, Munich
	Mavor Gallery, London
	Galleria Sperone, Turin
1974	Galerie Oppenheim, Brussels
	Leo Castelli Gallery, New York
	Modern Art Agency, Naples
1975	Modern Art Agency, Naples
	Art in Progress, Munich
	Galerie Karsten Greve, Cologne
	Paintings, Drawings, Constructions 1951–74, Institute of Contemporary Art, Philadelphia
	Galerie Jacques Benador, Geneva
	Galleria Bertesca, Genoa

Cy Twombly: *Roman Note 10*, 1970 Courtesy Anthony D'Offay Gallery, London

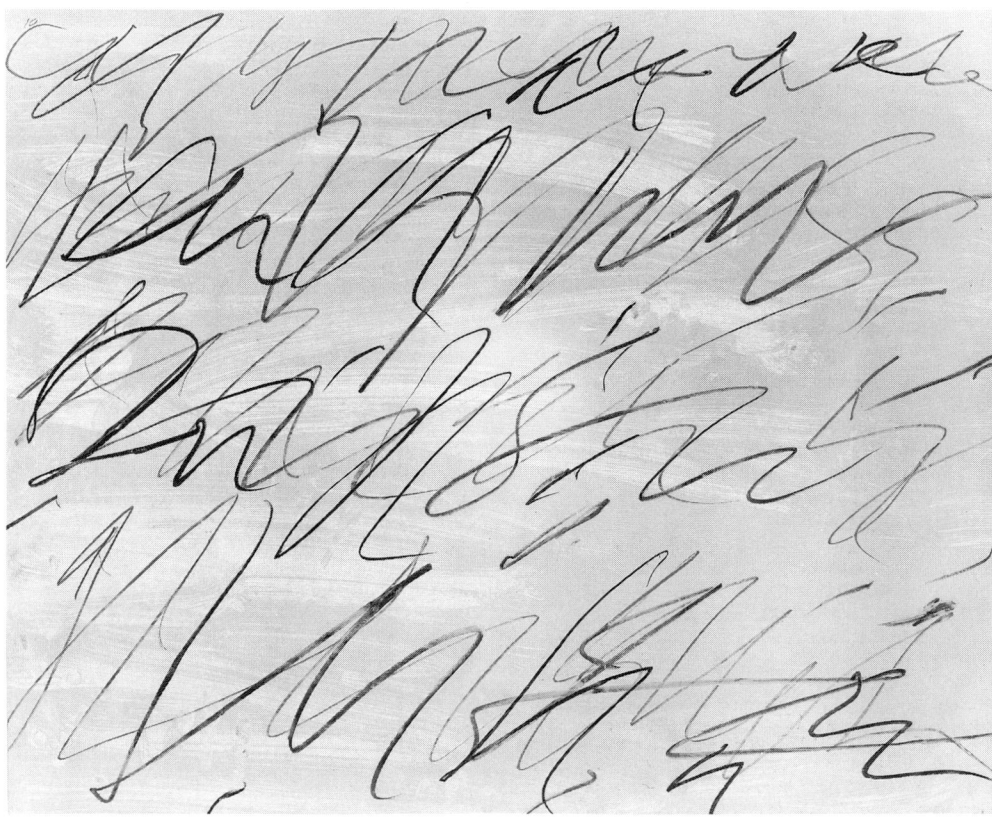

San Francisco Museum of Modern Art
1976 Art in Progress, Dusseldorf
Kestner-Gesellschaft, Hannover
Leo Castelli Gallery, New York
Musée d'Art Moderne, Paris
Galerie Jacques Brosser, Paris
Galleria Gian Enzo Sperone, Rome
1977 Galerie Yvon Lamberg, Paris
School of Visual Arts, New York
1978 Heiner-Friedrich Gallery, New York
Galerie Klewan, Munich
1979 Whitney Museum, New York (retrospective)
Galleria Lucio Amelio, Naples
Galleriet, Lund, Sweden
Galerie Karsten Greve, Cologne
1981 Castelli Graphics, New York
Museum Haus Lange, Krefeld, West Germany
Newport Harbor Art Museum, Newport Beach, California (travelled to Madison, Wisconsin; Richmond, Virginia; Toronto)
1982 Blum-Helman Gallery, New York (with Robert Ryman and Richard Tuttle)
Sperone Westwater Fischer, New York
Mayor Gallery, London
Galerie Karsten Greve, Cologne
Galerie Yvon Lambert, Paris
1983 Stephen Mazoh Gallery, New York
1984 Galerie Karsten Greve, Cologne
Mayor Gallery, London
Galleria Lucio Amelio, Naples
Hirschle and Adler Modern, New York
Galerie Ulysses, Vienna
CAPC/Musee d'Art Contemporain, Bordeaux, France
Kunsthalle, Baden-Baden, West Germany
Galleria Gian Enzo Sperone, Rome
Santa Barbara Contemporary Arts Center, California
1986 Larry Gagosian Gallery, New York
Hirschl and Adler Modern, New York
Dia Art Foundation, New York
Galerie Yvon Lambert, Paris
1987 Kunsthaus, Zurich
Stadtisches Kunstmuseum, Bonn
Palacio de Velazquez, Madrid
Whitechapel Art Gallery, London
Anthony D'Offay Gallery, London
Kunsthalle, Dusseldorf
1988 Centre Georges Pompidou, Paris
Galerie Klewan, Munich
Pace Gallery, New York
Anthony D'Offay Gallery, London

Selected Group Exhibitions:

1958 *Gutai 9: International Festival*, Osaka, Japan
1964 *XXXIII Biennale*, Venice
1969 *Painting and Sculpture Today*, Indianapolis Museum of Art, Indiana
1971 *The Structure of Color*, Whitney Museum, New York
1973 *Contemporanea*, Parcheggio di Villa Borghese, Rome
1976 *Drawing Now*, Museum of Modern Art, New York
1981 *A New Spirit in Painting*, Royal Academy of Arts, London
1983 *American Accents*, The Gallery, Stratford, Ontario (travelled to Toronto, Quebec City, Halifax, Windsor, Edmonton, Vancouver, Calgary and Montreal)
1986 *Hommage a Beuys*, Stadtische Galerie im Lenbachhaus, Munich
1988 *Contemporary American Art*, Sara Hilden Art Museum Tampere, Finland (travelled to Oslo)

Collections:

Museum of Modern Art, New York; Whitney Museum, New York; Rhode Island School of Design, Providence; Milwaukee Art Center; First National City Bank, Houston; Wallraf-Richartz Museum, Cologne; Hessisches Landesmuseum, Darmstadt; Neue Galerie-Sammlung Ludwig, Aachen, West Germany; Galleria Nazionale d'Arte Moderna, Rome.

Publications:

On TWOMBLY: books—*Cy Twombly,* exhibition catalogue, with notes by Robert Motherwell, Chicago 1951; *Cy Twombly: Paintings, Drawings, Constructions 1951–74,* exhibition catalogue, by Suzanne Delehanty and Heiner Bastian, Philadelphia 1975; *Drawing Now,* exhibition catalogue, by Bernice Rose, New York 1976; *Cy Twombly: Bilder/Paintings 1952–1976,* with text by Heiner Bastian, West Berlin 1978; *Cy Twombly: catalogue raisonne des oeuvres sur papier, 1973–1976,* edited by Yvon Lambert, Milan 1979; *Cy Twombly: Works on Paper 1954-1976,* exhibition catalogue with text by Susan C. Larsen, Newport Beach 1981; *Cy Twombly: Skulpturen,* exhibition catalogue with introduction by Gerhard Storck, Krefeld 1981; *Cy Twombly: retrospective,* exhibition catalogue with essay by Katharina Schmidt, Baden-Baden 1984; *Cy Twombly: A catalogue raisonne of the printed graphic work 1983–84,* with introduction by Heiner Bastian, Munich and New York 1985; *Cy Twombly,* exhibition catalogue edited by Harald Szemann, Zurich 1987.

*   *   *

Since the 1960's the painting/poetry of Cy Twombly has, by way of a variety of signs, fed on his own research, made prevalently of interruptions or annotations, only apparently but actually brilliantly thought out. The painting traces the poetry, while the poetry retraces the painting and defines evasive paths. Thus those different signs tell the legend, and in it stray to the infinite. It is not true, therefore, that they are something impersonal. Art is always the forbidden fruit of the imagination, and the "Roman" artist with his visual paradigms sets it out in an inestimable spatiality (that of the surface of the canvas or the sheet of paper), where there is a collection of graphic crossings and groupings so complex as to be almost impossible to follow. In Cy Twombly's works classical quotation seems more like metaphor than literary erudition. In "Empire of Flora," "School of Athens" and "Leda and the Swan" (all works of 1961) the mythological metaphor is something secretly indestructible that memory re-echoes in shapes and colours, in memory of a past splendour.

Cy Twombly evokes in his works antique myths perhaps inexplicable to contemporary sensibility. And yet, without the memory of them, the hide-and-seek of those different signs would remain as if suspended, lacking the true secrecy of that search for beauty that evokes rapture. Like marble or paint, Cy Twombly's different signs possess an immortality of their own, transforming the inexpressible into a living manifestation; the apparent chaos releases the silence, introducing incisive light and shade where there have been rare spaces in the handwriting. The beauty flows most subtly, imperceptibly; it always follows the handwriting, when it slows down or breaks off. The artist has before him, not the whirlpool, but the silence of the past which unexpectedly becomes articulate sound, dancing movement, a dream, a memory of happenings of long ago.

In Cy Twombly's painting the secret of art reveals its true mythical origin in this way; its beauty lies in the disorder, not in the polished form. Unexpectedly, those different signs appear as veiled shadows in new dress, so classical is their poetic manifestation. Hence they are not writing (unless perhaps an automatic writing); what Cy Twombly puts down on the canvas or the paper is a sort of poetically conceived composition, as in Hölderlin or Novalis. The abstraction formed by the signs may perhaps be a discourse, as we can see from the work called "Nine Discourses on Commodus" (1963). But, following Plato, it is clear that Cy Twombly knows how not to be wiser but to love wisdom; since it is only in that that the revelation of the new writing exists. Thus his work of the past 20 years is nothing less than a revelation and a concealment of a lost classical integrity.

—Italo Mussa

TWORKOV, Jack.
American. Born in Biala, Poland, 15 August 1900; emigrated to the United States, 1913: naturalized, 1928. Educated in New York City public schools; studied at Columbia University, New York (majored in English), 1920–23, and at the Art Students League, New York, 1923–26. Married Rachel Wolodarsky in 1935; daughters: Hermine and Helen. Painter: lived and worked in New York and Provincetown, Massachusetts. Teacher at the Fieldston School, New York, 1931; American University, Washington, D.C., 1948–51; Queens College, Flushing, New York, 1948–55; and Pratt Institute, Brooklyn, New York, 1955–58; Professor of Art, 1958–69, Chairman of the Art Department, 1963–69, and William C. Leffingwell Professor of Painting Emeritus, 1969–82, Yale University, New Haven, Connecticut. Visiting Professor of Painting, Cooper Union, New York 1970–72; Artist-in-Residence, American Academy in Rome, 1972; Visiting Critic, Columbia University, 1973; Artist-in-Residence, Hopkins Center, Dartmouth College, Hanover, New Hampshire, 1973; Visiting Critic, Royal College of Art, London, 1974. Recipient: William A. Clark Prize and Gold Medal, Corcoran Gallery of Art, Washington, D.C., 1963; Guggenheim Fellowship, 1971; Painter of the Year Award, Skowhegan School of Art, Maine, 1971. M.F.A.: Yale University, 1963; D.F.A.: Maryland Institute of Art, Baltimore, 1971; D.H.L.: Columbia University, 1972. Member, American Academy and Institute of Arts and Letters, 1981. Agent: Nancy Hoffman Gallery, 429 West Broadway, New York, New York 10012, U.S.A. *Died* (in Provincetown, Massachusetts) 4 September 1982.

Individual Exhibitions:

1940 ACA Gallery, New York
1947 Egan Gallery, New York
1948 Egan Gallery, New York
Baltimore Museum of Art
1949 Egan Gallery, New York
1950 Egan Gallery, New York
1951 Egan Gallery, New York
1952 Egan Gallery, New York
1953 Egan Gallery, New York
1954 Egan Gallery, New York
University of Mississippi
Stable Gallery, New York
1955 Stable Gallery, New York
1956 Stable Gallery, New York
1957 Stable Gallery, New York
Walker Art Center, Minneapolis
1960 Holland-Goldowsky Gallery, Chicago
1962 Holland-Goldowsky Gallery, Chicago
1963 Holland-Goldowsky Gallery, Chicago
Yale University Art Gallery, New Haven, Connecticut
1965 Castelli Gallery, New York
Whitney Museum, New York (toured the United States)
1966 Castelli Gallery, New York
Gertrude Kasle Gallery, Detroit
1967 Castelli Gallery, New York
1968 Castelli Gallery, New York
1969 Gertrude Kasle Gallery, Detroit
1971 Gertrude Kasle Gallery, Detroit
Whitney Museum, New York
Toledo Museum of Art, Ohio
1972 French and Company Gallery, New York
1973 Jaffe-Friede Gallery, Dartmouth College, Hannover, New Hampshire
Gertrude Kasle Gallery, Detroit
Jack Glenn Gallery, Corona del Mar, California
Jacobs Ladder Gallery, Washington, D.C.
1974 Nancy Hoffman Gallery, New York
Denver Art Museum
Portland Center for the Visual Arts, Oregon
Reed College, Portland, Oregon
Harcus-Krakow Rosen Sonnabend Gallery, Boston
1975 Nancy Hoffman Gallery, New York
New Gallery, Cleveland (travelled to the Contemporary Arts Center, Cincinnati, Ohio)

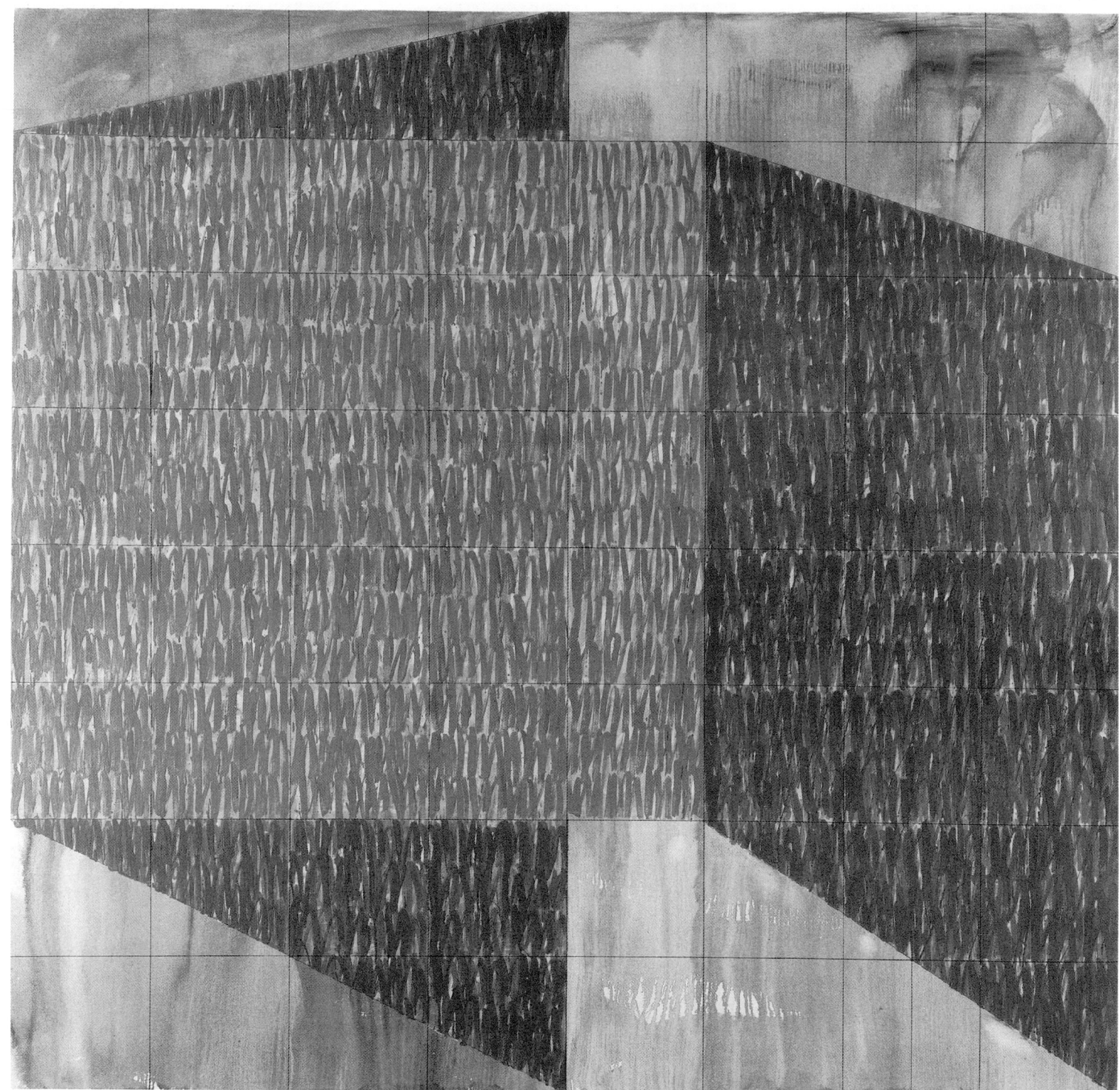

Jack Tworkov: *Q1–75–No. 6,* 1975

1982   *15 Year Retrospective Exhibition,* Guggenheim Museum, New York

Selected Group Exhibitions:

1958   *New American Painting,* Museum of Modern Art, New York (toured Europe, 1958–60)
1973   *Biennial Exhibition of Contemporary Art,* Whitney Museum, New York
1974   *12 American Artists,* Virginia Museum of Fine Arts, Richmond
        5 American Painters, University of California at Santa Barbara
        Painting and Sculpture Today, Indianapolis Museum of Contemporary Art

Contemporary American Painting and Sculpture, Krannert Center, University of Illinois, Urbana
Contemporary American Painters, Cleveland Museum of Art
1975   *Corcoran Biennial,* Corcoran Gallery of Art, Washington, D.C.
1976   *Bicentennial Exhibition,* Hirshhorn Museum, Washington, D.C.

Collections:

Whitney Museum, New York; Guggenheim Museum, New York; Museum of Modern Art, New York; Metropolitan Museum of Art, New York; Yale University, New Haven, Connecticut; Baltimore Museum of Art; National Collection, Washington, D.C.; Cleveland Museum of Art; Detroit Institute of Arts; Indianapolis Museum of Art.

Publications:

By TWORKOV: articles—"Wandering Soutine" in *Artnews* (New York), November 1950; "Flowers and Realism" in *Artnews* (New York), May 1954; "Tworkov's Journal," excerpts, in *It Is* (New York), Spring 1958, Autumn 1958, Autumn 1959, Spring 1960; "Jack Tworkov," interview, with Phyllis Tuchman, in *Artforum* (New York), January 1971; "Notes on My Painting" in *Art in America* (New York), September 1973; "On My Outlook as a Painter" in *Leonardo* (Oxford), Spring 1974.

On TWORKOV: books—*Jack Tworkov,* exhibition catalogue, by Edward Bryant, New York 1964; *Jack Tworkov,* exhibition catalogue, with an introduction by Marcia Tucker, New York 1971; articles—"Quartered and Drawn" by Douglas Crimp in *Artnews* (New York), March 1972; "Jack Tworkov" by Kasha Linville Gula in *Art in America* (New York), September 1973.

Tworkov and his family emigrated to New York in 1913. As an undergraduate, studying English, at Columbia University (1920–23), he first saw paintings by Cezanne and Matisse. From 1923–25 he studied at the National Academy of Design and then at the Art Students' League under Guy Pené du Bois and Boardman Robinson.

During the Depression of the 1930s Tworkov was involved with the Public Works of Art Project (1934) and the Federal Art Project of the W.P.A., (1935–41). The pictures and murals of this time were mainly still-lifes, portraits and landscapes, which showed strong links with European art. He came to dismiss the work of this period as being necessary to the time but bearing little relevance to his later painting. However, during the 1930s he met William de Kooning, a friendship which was to prove very important to his mature work.

WWII proved a decisive period for Tworkov's artistic development. From 1942–45 he worked as a tool designer, cut off from the art world, except for his contact with de Kooning, and he didn't paint at all. The later 1940s was witnessing the development in New York of a strong school of abstract painting and by 1947 Tworkov was a fully committed 'Abstract Expressionist'.

Tworkov was teaching by 1948 (American University in Washington D.C.), and he was a visiting artist at Black Mountain College in North Carolina in 1952. Through the years 1948–53 de Kooning had remained an important influence as the two artists had adjoining studios. By 1949 Tworkov's painting was becoming concerned with the figure, employing a very free and energetic method.

From 1963–69 Tworkov was Chairman of the Art Department at Yale University. With the 1960's he had begun to study elementary geometry and the theories of number systems and by the 1970's his painting was moving away from Abstract Expressionism to a more disciplined and contemplative form—less gestural, more geometric and static, though by no means hardedged, as it retained its strong 'painterly' inclinations.

—Victoria Keller

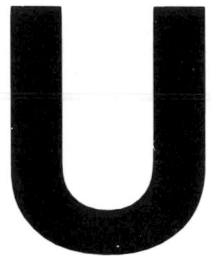

UECKER, Günther.

German. Born in Wentdorf/Mecklenburg. 13 March 1930. Educated in Wismar; studied art at the Akademie der Künst, Berlin-Weissensee, and at the Staatliche Kunstakademie, Dusseldorf. Independent artist, Dusseldorf, since 1955: colour-structure paintings, 1955–56; first white structural objects and nail-paintings, 1957; mathematical computable structure series, 1958–59; kinetic structural discs, 1960; Member, Zero Group, with Otto Piene and Heinz Mack, 1961–66. Professor, Staatliche Kunstakademie, Dusseldorf, 1974. Recipient: Prize, *Biennale di San Marino*, 1963; Talent Prize, Landes Nordrhein-Westfalen, 1964; Prize, *Bienal*, Sao Paulo, 1971. Agent: Galerie M, Haus Weitmar, 4630 Bochum, West Germany. Address: Dusseldorferstrasse 29A, 4000 Dusseldorf II, West Germany.

Individual Exhibitions:

1959	Galleria Azimuth, Milan
1960	Galerie Schmela, Dusseldorf
1961	Galleria La Salita, Rome
1962	Galerie Ad Libitum, Antwerp
1963	*Mack/Piene/Uecker*, Museum Haus Lange, Krefeld, West Germany
1964	Howard Wise Gallery, New York
1965	Galerie Orez, The Hague
	Kestner-Gesellschaft, Hanover
1967	*Flemish Landscape*, Mullen, Belgium (with Jef Verheyen)
1968	Kunsthalle, Baden-Baden, West Germany
1969	Kunsthalle, Dusseldorf
1970	Kunsthalle, Bremerhaven, West Germany
1971	*Bildobjekie 1957–1970*. Moderna Museet, Stockholm
	Museum Folkwang, Essen
	Galerie Zachea, Warsaw
	Nationalgalerie, West Berlin
1972	Kestner-Gesellschaft, Hanover
1974	Muzeum Sztuki, Lodz, Poland
	Galerie Rothe, Heidelberg
	Kolnischer Kunstverein, Cologne
	Kunsthalle, Cologne
1975	Museum Folkwang, Essen
	Galerie im Erker, St. Galen, Switzerland
	Galerie Denise René/Hans Mayer, Dusseldorf
	Galerie M, Bochum, West Germany
	Galerie St. Johann, Saarbrucken
	Kunstmuseum, Dusseldorf (2 shows)
	Wüttembergische Staatsgalerie, Stuttgart
	Württembergisches Staatstheater, Stuttgart (decors for Wagner's *Parsifal*)
	Antwerp Gallery
	Galerie Denise René/Hans Mayer, Dusseldorf (with Heinz Mack)
1977	Forum Metall, Linz, Austria
1978	Galerie Reckermann, Cologna (travelled to Detmold, Dublin and Munich)
1979	*Bilder und Zeichnungen*, Kunstverein. Braunschweig, West Germany
	Erker-Galerie, St. Gallen, Switzerland
	Stüdtisches Museum Schloss Morsbroich, Leverkusen, West Germany
1981	Erker-Galerie, St. Gallen, Switzerland
1982	Galerie Walter Storms, Munich
	Raumberkeilung—Bilder den Wanden zugekeht, Galerie Lohrl, Mönchengladbach, West Germany
	Nationalgalerie, West Berlin
1983	Kunsthalle, Dusseldorf
	Galerie Schmela, Dusseldorf
	Galerie Loehrl, Monchengladbach, West Germany
	Galerie Wallstrasse, Moers, West Germany
1984	Galerie Brusten, Wuppertal, West Germany
	Villa Merkel, Esslingen, West Germany
	Kamakura Gallery, Tokyo
	Galerie im Gauserhaus, Wasserburg, West Germany
	Yares Gallery, Scotsdale, Arizona
1985	Moderner Galerie, Bottrop, West Germany
	Museum of Modern Art, Istanbul
	Josef Albers Museum, Bottrop, West Germany
1986	Galerie Lupke, Frankfurt
1987	Vasarely Museum, Pecs, Hungary
	Galerie Ronny Van de Velde, Knokke, Belgium
1988	Galerie Reckermann, Cologne

Selected Group Exhibitions:

1965	*Licht und Bewegung*, Kunsthalle, Berne
1968	*Documenta, Kassel*, West Germany (and 1977)
1972	*Amsterdam-Paris-Dusseldorf*, Guggenheim Museum, New York
1974	*Basically White*, Institute of Contemporary Arts, London
1976	*Europa/America*, Galleria d'Arte Moderna, Bologna
1978	*Elements of Drawing*, Galerie Studio, Warsaw
1979	*Zero International*, Koninklijk Museum voor Schone Kunsten, Antwerp
1981	*Schwarz*, Kunsthalle, Dusseldorf
1982	*60–80: Attitudes, Concepts, Images*, Stedelijk Museum, Amsterdam
1985	*Hundert Jahre Kunst in Deutschland 1885–1985*, Kunsthalle, Ingeleheim, West Germany

Collections:

Städtisches Kunstmuseum, Dusseldorf; Wallraf-Richartz Museum. Cologne: Kaiser-Wilhelm Museum, Krefeld, West Germany; Museum Folkwang, Essen; Stedelijk Van Abbemuseum, Eindhoven, Netherlands; Museum des 20 Jahrhunderts, Vienna; Muzeum Sztuki, Lodz Poland; Galleria Nazionale d'Arte Moderna, Rome; Tate Gallery, London; Museum of Modern Art, New York.

Publications:

By UECKER: books and pamphlets—*Projektionen von Heute*, with Otto Piene and Heinz Mack, Dusseldorf 1961; *Uecker-Zeitung*, vols. 0–9, editor, Dusseldorf 1968–82: *Der heutige kunstler . . .*pamphlet, Dusseldorf 1969; *Uber Steine: zu Skulppuren von Rolf Jorres*, pamphlet, Dusseldorf 1969; *Uecker*, portfolio of 5 lithos, with text by Lothar Wolleh, Cologne 1970; *Flamische Landschaft*, with Jef Verheyen, Dusseldorf 1970; *Einsam Gemeinsam*, book with 5 prints, text by Eugen Gomringer, Dusseldorf 1971; *Vom Licht*, with prints by Uecker and others, and an introduction by Gerhard Storck, Heidelberg 1973; *Manuelle Strukturen*, casette with 10 lithos, St. Gallen, Switzerland 1975; *Anonym*, casette with objects and 6 silkscreens, Dusseldorf 1976; *Zum Schweigen der Schrift oder die Sprachlosigkeit*, 17 silk-screens, with text by Eugen Gomringer, St. Gallen, Switzerland 1976; *Uecker: Ludwig von Beethovens Leonore*, with text by Gerhard Storck, photos by Lothar Wolleh, Stuttgart and Zurich 1978; *Schrifien, Gedichte—Projekiebeschreibungen—Reflexionen*, St. Gallen, Switzerland 1980; *Littenheid—Eine Studie . . .mit Studenien der Klasse Uecker*, with Hans Geigenmuller, St. Gallen, Switzerland 1980; *Buhnenskulpturen für Lohengrin*, with text by Guido de Werd, photos by Lothar Wolleh, Kleve and Dusseldorf 1981; films—*Eckenfilm*, 1969; *Nagelfeldzug*, 1969; *Bauchfilm*, 1970.

On UECKER: books—*Mack/Piene/Uecker*, exhibition catalogue, with foreword by Paul Wember, Krefeld, West Germany 1963; *Günther Uecker: Ten Years of a Kineticist's Work* by Willoughby Sharp, New York 1966; *Gunther Uecker* by Dietrich Helmz, Recklinghausen, West Germany 1970; *Günther Uecker: Bildobjekte 1957–1970*, exhibition catalogue, with text by K. G. Pontus Hulten, Stockholm 1971; *Günther Uecker*, exhibition catalogue/book, with texts by Wieland Schmied, Hans Strelow, Rolf-Günther Dienst and others, Hanover and St. Gallen, Switzerland 1972; *Günther Uecker*, exhibition catalogue with text by Dieter Honisch, Lodz Poland 1974; *Uecker: Bilder und Zeichnungen*, exhibition catalogue. Braunschweig, West Germany 1979; *Uecker: Raumverkeilung—Bilder den Wanden zugekehrt*, exhibition catalogue, with text by Sabine Kimpel-Fehlemann, Mönchengladbach, West Germany 1982; *Uecker* by Dieter Honisch and Marion Haedecke, Stuttgart 1983; *Gunther Uecker*, exhibition catalogue with text by Friedrich W. Heckmanns, Bottrop 1985.

The present-day artist produces and realizes ideas which could serve as examples for a new environment. The idea will come into being as a product. These real objects are clarifications of a new way of looking at things. These objects have no objective value; they have served their purpose in the instant that they are taken into consciousness. These objects can be understood as tools for thought processes.

An artist is an inventor, an inventory of ideas. Which can be realized visually. Which can serve as parables for spiritual development.

—Günther Uecker

The Zero Group was formed in 1961. For five years Otto Piene, Heinz Mack and Günther Uecker exhibited jointly as a trio the wax/soot fire-works of Piene, the silver reflections of Mack and the nail constructions and light experiments of Uecker.

Of the three Uecker was the most international in the character of his work. However different in realization and intention, his nail works use the same raw materials as those of the Canadian David Partridge, and, in their way, they imply some of the same effects of light and shade to be found in the stunted peg reliefs of the Brazilian Sergio de Camargo. But there the relationships terminate.

Uecker's use of *white* is wholly different from that of Camargo, and his understanding of the character of upstanding nails and how they can play games with chiaroscuro has nothing to do with Partridge's gleaming carpets of nail-heads. The German artist keeps sternly aloof from the decorative dangers that sometimes beset the works of both of the others. He also has a non-architectural attitude towards the transformation games he plays with "objects" like a chair or

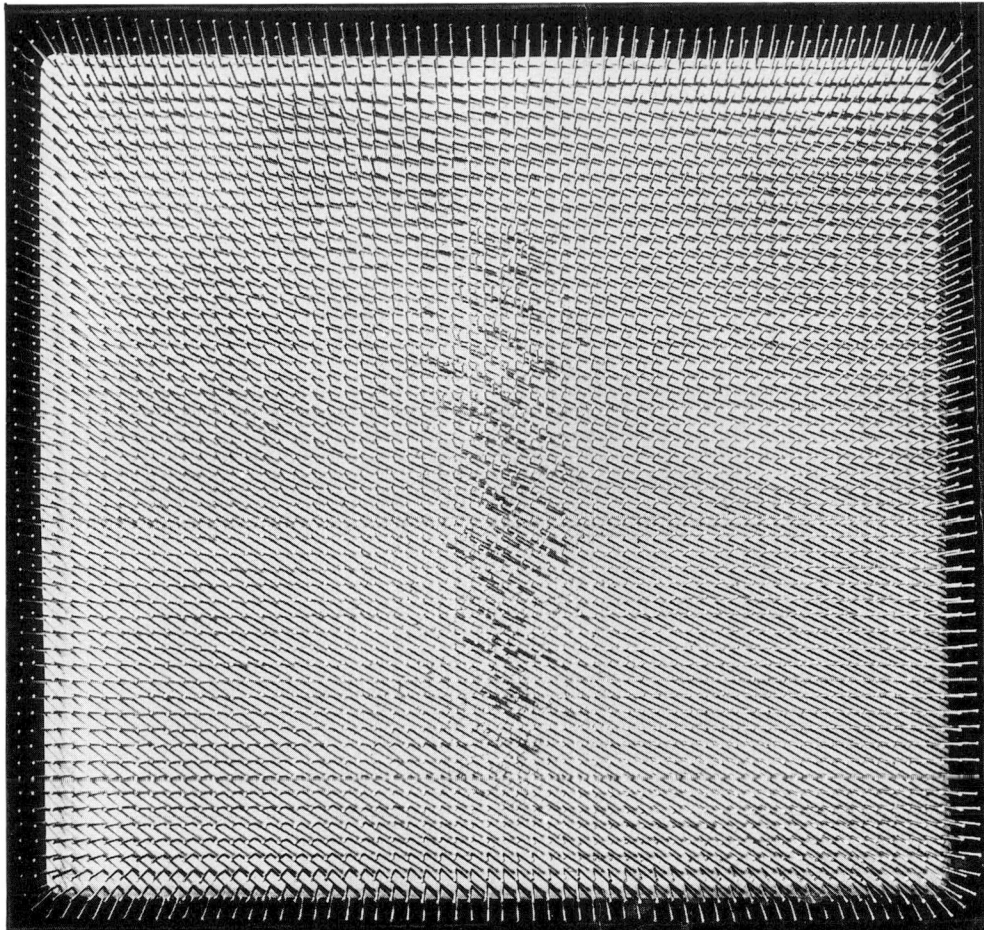

Günther Uecker: *White Work*, 1959

a picture frame. In such a mood he is demonstrating that he has the same European elan as Jean-Pierre Raynaud or Pol Bury.

Artists like Uecker are revitalising the Old World, not doing a raw survey of artistic potentialities of the New. The aggressive defiance of the Americas is not their style, and their works have no American accent, not even a mid-Atlantic one.

—Sheldon Williams

ULRICHS, Timm.

German. Born in Berlin, 31 March 1940. Educated at primary school in Bremen, 1954–59; studied architecture at the Technische Hochschule, Hannover, 1959–66; mainly self-taught in art, from 1959. Independent artist, Hannover, since 1959. Guest Professor, Hochschule für Bildende Künste, Braunschweig, 1969–70. Professor, Institut für Kunstlerzieher Münster der Staatlichen Kunstakademie. Dusseldorf, since 1972. Recipient: Literatur-Forderpreis des Niedersachsischen Kunstpresses, 1968; Kritikerpreis fur Bildende Kunst, West Berlin, 1977; Niedersachsisches Kunstlerstipendium, Hannover, 1979; Kunstpreis der Stadt Nordhorn, 1980. Address: Sodenstrasse 6, Postfach 6043, 3000 Hannover 1, West Germany.

Individual Exhibitions:

1961	Totalkunst-Zimmergalerie Ulrichs. Hannover
1964	Haus am Lutzowplatz, West Berlin
1966	Galerie Patio, Frankfurt
	Bauhutte, Hannover
1967	Galleria Alpha, Modena, Italy
	Galleria Il Portico, Reggio Emilia, Italy
1968	Studio di Informazione Estetica, Turin
	Institut für Visuelle Kommunikation, West Berlin
	Institut Autoretique, Kiel
	Galerie Daedalus, West Berlin
	Top-Shop, West Berlin
1969	Edition H, Hannover
	Galerie Patio, Frankfurt
	Galerie Kummel, Cologne
	Kunstraum, Hannover
	Galerie Reckermann, Cologne
1970	Kunstverein, Göttingen, West Germany
	Galerie Nachst St. Stephan, Vienna
	Neue Galerie, Aachen, West Germany
	Kabinett für Aktuelle Kunst, Bremerhaven, West Germany
	Museum Haus Lange, Krefeld, West Germany (retrospective)
	Galerie Wildeshausen, Wildeshausen, West Germany
	Christian-Albrechts-Universitat, Kiel
1971	Zimmertheater, Tübingen, (with Klaus Hoffmann)
	Kunsthaus, Hamburg
	Städtisches Museum, Wiesbaden
1972	Atelier NW8. Beindersheim, West Germany
	Galerie Kummel, Cologne
	Galerie Wildeshauen, Wildeshausen, West Germany
	Kulturzentrum Ulrichs, Hannover
1973	Galerie Ernst, Hannover
	Galerie Langer, Braunschweig, West Germany
	Kunsthalle, Bielefeld, West Germany
	Kunstverein, Celle, West Germany
1974	Galerie Magers, Bonn
	Kunsthalle, Bremen, West Germany
	Galerie Apex, Göttingen, West Germany
	Stadtische Galerie, Bergkamen, West Germany
	Galerie, Defet, in the Kunsthalle, Nuremberg
1975	Werkstatt Breitenbrunn, Breitennbrunn, West Germany
	Kunstverein, Hannover

	Westfälischer Landesmuseum, Münster, West Germany
	Kunstverein, Freiburg
	Konzert-Aula, Kamen, West Germany
	Mobile Galerie, Frankfurt
	Dierks Galleri, Aarhus, Denmark
	Kunstkontor Blank, Marburg Lahn, West Germany
	Restrospective 1960–1975. Kunstverein, Braunschweig, West Germany (travelled to the Karl-Ernst-Osthaus Museum, Hagen, West Germany; Kunstverein, Heidelberg; and Kunstverein, Hannover)
1976	Galleria Giurca, Modena, Italy
	Galerie Wildeshauen, Wildeshauen, West Germany
	Studio Kausch, Kassel, West Germany
1977	Galerie Space, Wiesbaden
	Galerie und Versmolder Kunstkreis, Versmold, West Germany
	Forum Kunst, Rottweil, West Germany
	Galerie Gamma, Utrecht
1978	Paula Becker Modersohn Haus, Bremen, West Germany
1979	Galerie Studio M, Bamberg, West Germany
	Galerie Petersen, West Berlin
	Kunstmuseum, Hannover
1980	*Totalkunst,* Städisches Galerie, Ludenscheid, West Germany
	Druckgraphik, Zeichnungen, Objekte. Deutsche BP Aktiengesellschaft-Clubheim, Hamburg
	Städtisches Galerie, Nordhorn, West Germany
1981	Kunstraum Fuhrwerkswaage, Cologne
1982	Galerie H.C. Scheerer, Tuttlingen, West Germany
	Galerie im Orangerie-Cafe, Kassel, West Germany
1984	Wilhelm-Hack-Museum, Ludwigshafen am Rhein, West Germany

Selected Group Exhibitions:

1969	*Konzeption-Conception,* Stadisches Museum, Lverkusen, West Germany
1970	*Konkrete Poesie/Visuelle Texte,* Stedelijk Museum, Amsterdam (toured Europe)
1974	*Multiples,* Neuer Berliner Kunstverein, West Berlin
1975	*Korpersprache-Bodylanguage,* Kunstverein, Hamburg (travelled to West Berlin and Frankfurt)
1977	*Documenta 6,* Neue Galerie, Kassel, West Germany
1978	*Art—Museum des Geldes,* Stadtische Kunsthalle, Dusseldorf (travelled to Eindhoven and Paris)
1980	*Monuments-Denkmal,* Kunstverein, Cologne (travelled to Karlsruhe)
1981	*Dimensionen der Plastischen,* Neuer Berliner Kunstverein, West Berlin
1982	*Momentbild: Kunstlerphotographien,* Kestner-Gesellschaft, Hannover

Collections:

Kaiser-Wilhelm-Museum, Krefeld, West Germany; Museum, Wiesbaden; Städtische Galerie, Wolfsburg, West Germany; Stadt Bergkamen, West Germany; Kunstverein, Braunschweig, West Germany; Kunstverein, Gelsenkirchen, West Germany; Kunsthalle, Hamburg; Kunstmuseum, Hannover; Städtische Galerie, Ludenscheid, West Germany.

Publications:

By ULRICHS: books—*Totalkunst: Das neue Mass aller Dinge,* Hannover 1961; *Fragment,* West Berlin 1964; *Klartecte,* Hannover 1966; *Spiel plane,* Hannover and Moderna 1967; *Beschriebone Blatter,* Hannover and Göttingen 1967; *Schriftstucke,* Munich 1967; *Ich Bin ein Gedicht,* Vienna 1968; *Lesarien und Schriebweisen,* Stuttgart 1968; *Interferenzen I,* Cologne 1968; *Interferenzen II,* Basle 1968; *Des Grossen Erfolges Wegen,* Hannover 1968; *Owertzuoipu.* Hannover 1968; *ich als Kunstfigur,* Vienna 1969; *Weiter im Text.* Hannover 1969; *Bild-Band,* West Berlin 1970; *Fernsehen in Nahsicht,* Göttingen 1970; *Kanaldeckel 1962/64,* Göttingen 1970; *Einweg-Buch,* Hannover 1972; *Die Zeitungsannonce ais Kunstwerk 1964/74* exhibition catalogue, Bonn 1974, *Utersetzung-Translation-Traduction,* Hannover 1974; *Die Photokopie der Photokopie der Photokopie,* Hannover 1975; *1984 (Spionbuch),* Hannover 1975; *Bilder, auf den Leib geschrieben,* Hannover 1975; *Dem Leser den Rucken zukehrend,*

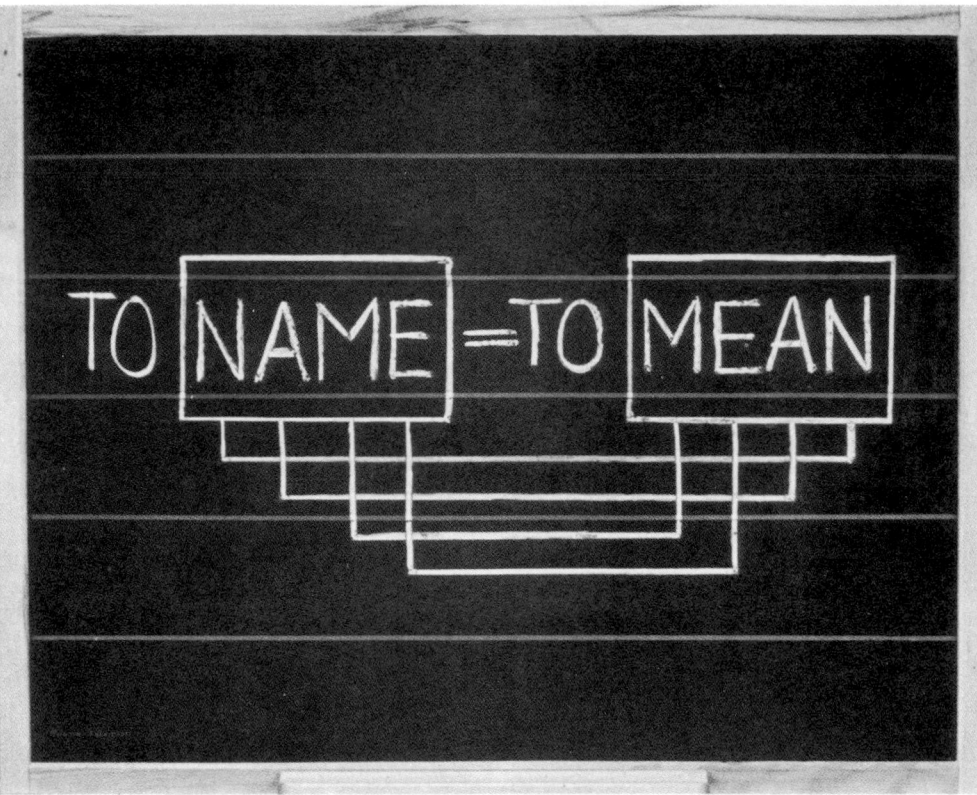

Timm Ulrichs: *To Name = To Mean*, 1968

Hannover 1976; *Ich mache (diese) Schlagzeilen*, Hannover 1977; *Ich, Gott und die Welt*, Hannover 1978; *The Infinite Book*, Hannover 1978; *Kunst: im Schweisse des Angesichts*, Hannover 1978; *Buch-(EHE)-Paar*, Hannover 1979; *Lektionen*, Frankfurt 1979; *Die Kunst des schonen Schreibens*, 2 vols., Hannover 1979.

On ULRICHS: book—*Pop und die Folgen* by Heinz Ohff, Dusseldorf 1967; *Deutsche Kunst: eine neue generation* by Rolf-Günter Dienst, Cologne 1970; *Galerie der neuen Künste* by Heinz Ohff, Gutersloh 1971; *Bis Heute* by Karin Thomas, Cologne 1971; *Konkrete Poesie* by Eugen Gomringer, Stuttgart 1972; *Kunst-im-Kopf: Aspekte der Real-Kunst* by Klaus Hoffmann, Cologne 1972; *Deutsche Kunst der 60er Jahre* by Jürgen Morschel, Munich 1972; *Il Territorio Magico* by Achille Bonito Oliva, Florence 1972; *Objekt Kunst:von Duchamp bis Kienhol:* by Willy Rotzler, Cologne 1972; *Visuelle Poesie International* by Klaus-Peter Dencker, Cologne 1973; *Selbstdarstellung*, edited by Wulf Herzogenrath, Dusseldorf 1973; *Kunst in Krefeld* by Paul Wember, Cologne 1973; *Timm Ulrichs: Retrospektive 1960-1975*, exhibition catalogue, with texts by Margarethe Jochimsen, S.J. Schmidt and Klaus Hoffmann, Braunschweig, West Germany 1975; *Timm Ulrichs: Druckgraphik, Zeichnungen, Objekte*, exhibition catalogue, with text by Carl Vogel, Hamburg 1980; *Timm Ulrichs: Total-kunst*, exhibition catalogue, with texts by Uwe Obier, and Helmut R. Leppien, Ludenscheid, West Germany, 1980; *Vergangenheit-Gegenwart-Zukunft*, exhibition catalogue, with an introduction by Tilman Osterwold, Stuttgart 1982; *Timm Ulrichs* by Bernhard Holeczek, Bruanschweig 1982; *Timm Ulrichs: Totalkunst—Angesammelte Werke*, exhibition catalogue with text by Bernhard Holeczek, Ludwigshafen 1984.

UNCINI, Giuseppe.

Italian. Born in Fabriano, 31 January 1929. Attended Aldo Calo's lectures, Istituto Statale d'Arte, Rome, 1959; mainly self-taught in art. Served in the Italian Army, 1950. Married Marioline Delicati in 1963; son: Marzio. Worked as graphic artist and lithographer, Cartotechnica Fratelli Carmenati, Fabriano, Italy, 1948-51, and Tipolitografia Sabatini, Falconora

Marittima, Ancona, 1951-53; settled in Rome where he associated with Edgardo Mannucci, Ettore Colla, Achille Perilli, and Gastone Novelli; travelled in Europe, 1956; produced jewelry for Gioiellieri Masenza from 1960; Founder, with Gastone Biggi, Nicola Carrino, Nato Frasca, Achille Pace, and Pasquale Santoro, Gruppo Uno, Rome, 1962-67. Lecturer in Mosaics, 1960-67, and since 1967 Director of the Department of Metalwork, Istituto Statale d'Arte II, Rome. Recipient: First Prize, *Mostra Concorso Ministero Pubblica Istruzione*, Rome, 1957 and 1963; First Prize, *X Premio Spoleto*, 1962; First Prize, *Premio G. B. Salvi*, Sassoferrato, 1967. Agent: Studio Marconi, via Tadino 15, 20124 Milan. Address: via Felice Cavalotti 57, 00152 Rome, Italy.

Individual Exhibitions:

1958   Chiostro Quattrocento, Fabriano, Italy
1959   Galleria La Salita, Rome (with Tano Festa and Franco Angeli)
       Contemporaries Art Gallery, New York (with L. Brown)
1961   Galleria L'Attico, Rome
1963   Auditorium, l'Aquila, Italy
1967   Galleria Posto, San Remo, Italy
1968   Galleria Christian Stein, Turin
1969   Salone Annunciata, Milan
1970   Qui Arte Contemporanea, Rome
1971   Galleria Christian Stein, Turin
1973   Galleria 3B, Bolzano, Italy
       Studio Marconi, Milan
1974   Galleria Godel, Rome
       Galleria Ferrari, Verona
1975   Galleria La Chiocciola, Padua
       Galleria Christian Stein, Turin
       Galleria Seconda Scala, Rome
       Galleria dei Mille, Bergamo, Italy
1976   Galleria Peccolo, Livorno
       Studio Marconi, Milan
       Galleria Rondanini, Rome
       Galleria La Piramide, Florence
1979   Palazzo dei Consoli, Gubbio, Italy
1980   Studio Marconi, Milan
1983   Pinacoteca e Musei Conunali, Macerata, Italy

Selected Group Exhibitions:

1955   *Quadriennale*, Rome
1960   *Rome '60: 5 Pittori a Rome*, Galleria La Salita, Rome
1963   *Gruppo Uno*, Galleria Medusa, Rome
1966   *20th Century Italian Art*, Baltimore Museum of Art
1971   *Vitalità del Negativo*, Palazzo Esposizione, Rome
1972   *Progetto: Intervento: Verifica*, Palazzo Reale, Milan
1975   *Didattica*, Pinacoteca Civica, Modigliana, Italy
1977   *16 Italianse Kunstenaars*, Museum Boymans-van Beuningen, Rotterdam
1980   *Arte e Critica*, Galleria Nazionale d'Arte Moderna, Rome
1982   *Arte Italiana 1960-1982*, Hayward Gallery, London

Collections:

Galleria Nazionale d'Arte Moderna, Rome; Museo Civico, Turin; Museo d'Arte Progressiva, Livorno; Pinacoteca Civica, Termoli, Italy; Museum Boymans-van-Beuningen, Rotterdam; Nijgata Art Museum, Japan.

Publications:

By UNCINI: book—*Gruppo I*, with Nicola Carrino and Nato Frasca, Venice 1966; articles—"Dichiarazione de Poetica" in *Gruppo Uno*, exhibition catalogue, Rome 1963; "La Poetica della Percezione" in *Gruppo Uno*, exhibition catalogue, Venice 1964; "Techniche e Materiali," interview with Marisa Volpi, in *Marcatre*, (Genoa), May 1968; "Lettera a Maurizio Fagiolo" in *Didattica*, exhibition catalogue, Rome 1975.

On UNCINI: books—*Gruppo Uno* by Giulio Carlo Argan and others, Rome 1963; *Dall'Occhio al Cervello* by F. Sossi, Taranto, Italy 1965; *Gruppo Uno* by E. Marsili and Giulio Carlo Argan, Rome 1965; *Calderara e Gruppo Uno* by Giulio Carlo Argan, Milan 1966; *Le Correnti Pittoriche non Oggettive degli Anni Sessanta* by Filberto Menna, Milan 1967; *Ricerche dopo l'Informale* by Enrico Crispolti, Rome 1968; *Luce: Spazio: Strutture* by F. Sossi, Taranto, Italy 1968; *Erotismo nell'Arte Astratta* by Enrico Crispolti, Trapani, Italy 1976; *Il Artisti Italiani* by Antonio del Guercio, Verona 1976; *Uncini: La logica Fantastica*, exhibition catalogue with text by Luciano Marziano, Macerata 1983.

In Roman artistic circles in the 1960's Giuseppe Uncini (with Lo Savio, Schifano and Festa) had already progressed beyond informal painting. His first *Cementarmato* (reinforced concrete—concrete with an iron framework) has an early date—1959. It is a monochrome surface intended as an "object"—that is to say, no longer as a field of colour thick with emotive tensions—in which the grouping of the materials side by side gives the "construction" of a new dimension, more realistic than cerebral. But, in giving up spatial connexions, partly brought about by the interaction of the iron element and the monochromatic spread of the cement, the construction does not describe the period of work. It has its strong concrete presence, the presence of one who thinks with his hands, so that the cerebral dimension is absorbed by the realistic.

Undoubtedly constructive methods and mental periods are one and the same to Uncini; in practice, in the joining or dismantling, the assembling or opening/closing of the structure, which is a model on its own and not a vehicle for repetitions (visual or intellectual) with the viewer. An extreme strictness, then, which of course does not in itself exclude the unforseen manual event, the nature of which is certainly not existential. Uncini always leaves the structure of his work open; then, when the manual element does occur, its presence is immediately visible. Above all a craftsman (in the lay sense indicated by Alain), Uncini believes that thought is work and work thought—with the forthrightness of *homo faber*. Thus his works in reinforced concrete and in brick have their own meaning, leaving no margin for subjective interpretation. When that is there, it is to be found in the structure itself, with its two-dimensional or three-dimensional orders that concrete and bricks stabilize in an open space. A typical feature of Uncini's works,

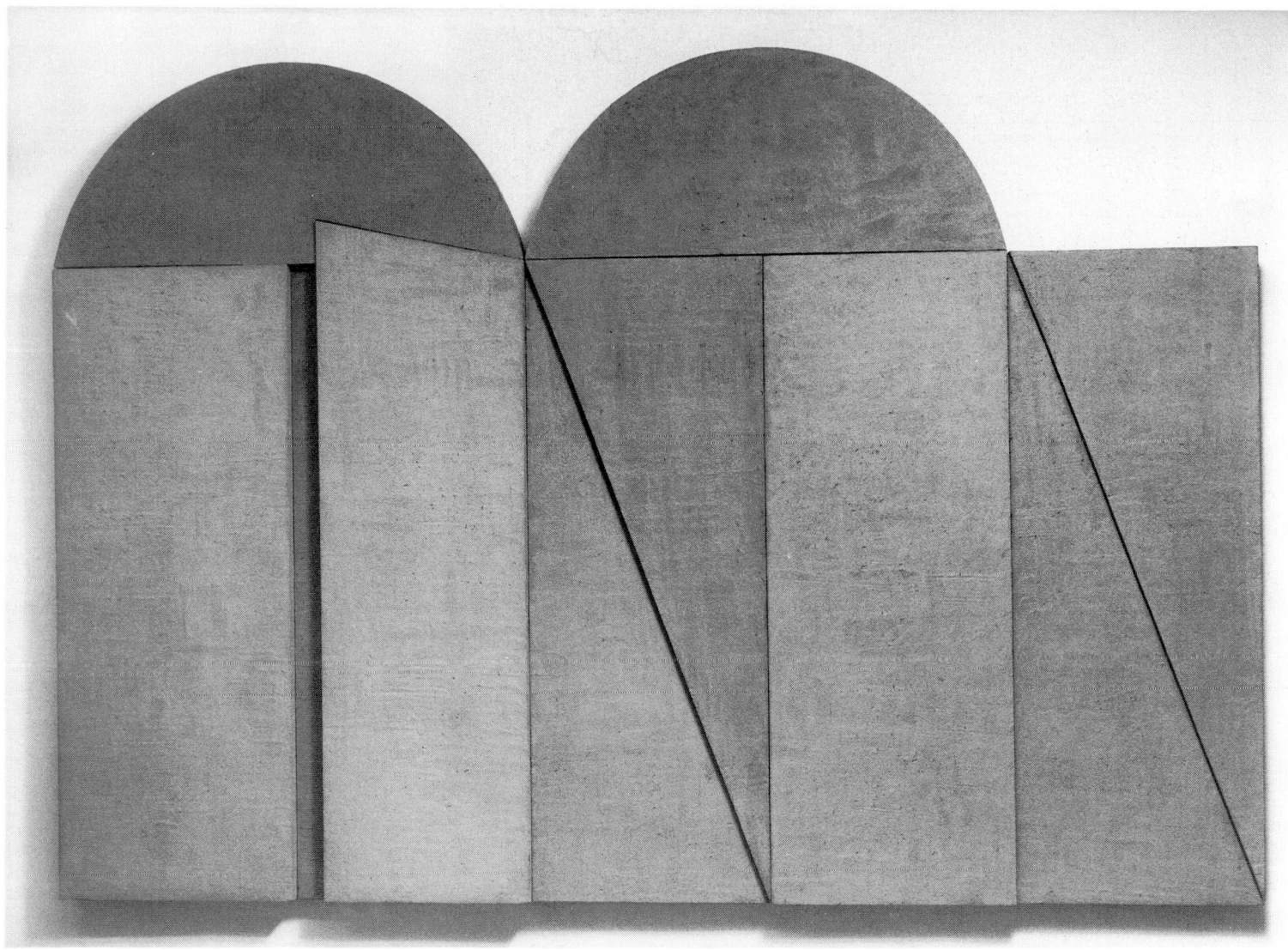

Giuseppe Uncini: *Dimore No. 12,* 1982

in fact, is the spatial opening, based on constructive theories not wholly defined. His reinforced concrete and brick works are extraordinarily different forms.

With his "Room" and "Door Wall and Shadow" the spatiality, accompanied now by its shadows, becomes a symbolic structure, linked between the full and the empty (of light and shade), continually changing and unforeseeable. The spatial structure, standing by itself, is worked out in an environment whose perspectives look broken up in some way, not by creating an illusory effect but by the direct intervention of the viewer. In fact the environment is always present, insofar as the light and shade fall on the spatial construction to an equal extent. A full light framed by shadow, by means of concrete observations of the space, can be achieved in a variety of materials. A reflection that Uncini extends to the "everyday landscape" within which his works, from the 1960's to the present, have been born. In the everyday landscape he works out one of his "Theories of visibility," even seeing the possibility of a revival of classical typological forms. But he is not giving up his constructional methods; indeed he is broadening them, still in constructional style. "Vertical-Horizontal," "Columns," the "Arch," "Buttressed Wall" and the "Cloaca Maxima" are examples of works in which the classical typological form prevails, carried out in both concrete and brick together. But the artist himself declares: "They may be concrete materials and at the same time strike our cognitive consciousness as new concepts." Being in fact positive calks of what we see in negative, those historical forms show once again how light-shade-space are in real terms assumed by visibility to be actual reality, without meta-

physical projection, and by iconographic recovery to be mental analysis beyond didactic proof.

Even in this last constructive fantasy Uncini remains faithful to the fact that the object must "mean" only itself—he displays the consistency of one who believes that, if visibility varies, there is only one way of representing it. The work is therefore never out of its element; everything goes back into place without ever leaving behind existential doubts.

—Italo Mussa

UNSWORTH, Ken.

Australian. Born in Richmond, Victoria, 28 May 1931. Educated at the University of Melbourne and Melbourne Teachers' College, 1952–54; studied at the National Art School, Sydney; influenced by John Passmore and Godfrey Miller, 1962–63. Married Elisabeth Crouch in 1954. Independent painter, Melbourne and Sydney, 1954–66; sculptor, Sydney, since 1966; also, performance artist since 1975. Art teacher, Victoria and New South Wales high schools, 1955–65; Lecturer in Art, Bathurst Teachers' College, New South Wales, 1966–68; Chairman, Art Teacher Education, Tasmanian School of Art, Ho-

bart, 1969–71. Lecturer in Sculpture, Sydney College of Advanced Education, since 1972. Executive Member, Contemporary Art Society of Australia, New South Wales, since 1972. Recipient: Captain Cook Bicentenary Sculpture Prize, Sydney, 1970; Australian-American Education Foundation Grant, to the United States, 1971; Residency, Power Studio, Cité des Arts, Paris, 1979–1980; Residency, Kunstlerhaus Bethanien, West Berlin, 1980; DAAD Artist Fellowship, West Berlin, 1987. Agent: Roslyn Oxley 9 Gallery, 13 Macdonald Street, Paddington, New South Wales. Address: 86 Paddington Street, Paddington, New South Wales 2021, Australia.

Individual Exhibitions:

1975   Institute of Contemporary Art, Sydney
1977   Institute of Contemporary Art, Sydney
1978   *Project 28,* Art Gallery of New South Wales, Sydney
        Australian Pavilion, at the *Biennale,* Venice (with Robert Owen and John Davis)
1979   Institute of Contemporary Art, Sydney
        Australian Embassy, Paris
1980   Kunstlerhaus Bethanien, Berlin
1981   Institute of Contemporary Art, Sydney
1982   Ivan Dougherty Gallery, Sydney
1983   Kobayashi Gallery, Tokyo
        National Gallery of New Zealand, Wellington
1984   Roslyn Oxley 9 Gallery, Sydney
        Art Gallery of New South Wales, Sydney
1985   Roslyn Oxley 9 Gallery, Sydney
1987   DAAD-Galerie, West Berlin
        Roslyn Oxley 9 Gallery, Sydney

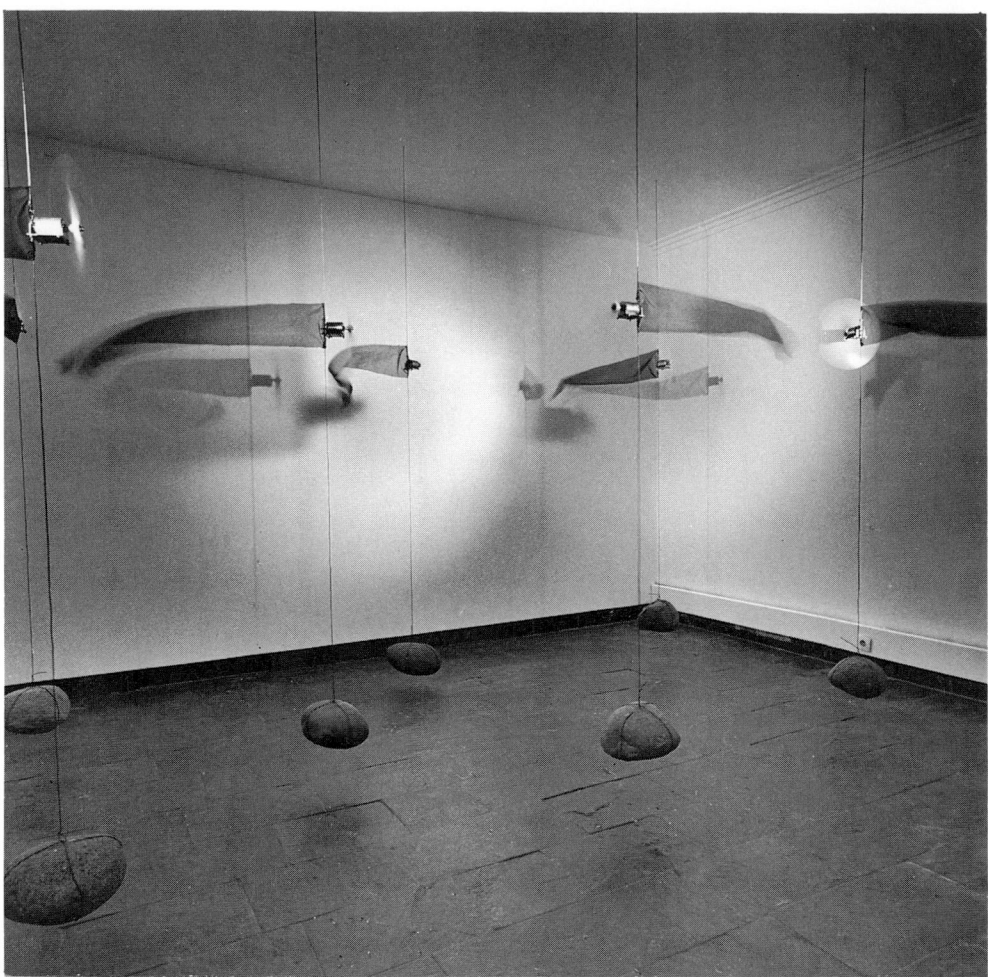

Ken Unsworth: *Zone of Wistful Thoughts*, 1985

Selected Group Exhibitions:

1967   *Alcorso-Sekers Sculpture Competition*, Art Gallery of New South Wales, Sydney

1968   *Flotta Lauro Sculpture Competition*, National Gallery of Victoria, Melbourne

1970   *14th Tasmanian Art Gallery Exhibition*, Hobart

1973   *Sculpturescape Triennale*, Mildura, Victoria (and 1975, 1978)

1976   *Biennale of Sydney*, Art Gallery of New South Wales, Sydney

1981   *1st Australian Sculpture Triennale*, Latrobe University, Melbourne

1982   *Biennale of Sydney*, Art Gallery of New South Wales, Sydney

1983   *Presence and Absence*, Art Gallery of Western Australia, Perth

1985   *Funf vom Funften*, DAAD-Galerie, West Berlin

1987   *ZeitBerliner*, I.F.A. Galerie, Stuttgart

Collections:

Art Gallery of New South Wales, Sydney; National Gallery of Australia, Canberra; National Capital Development Commission, Canberra; Australian National University, Canberra; National Gallery of Victoria, Melbourne; Flinders University, Adelaide, South Australia; City Art Gallery, Wollongong, New South Wales; Rijksmuseum Kröller-Müller, Otterlo, Netherlands; Museum Sztuki, Lodz, Poland.

Publications:

On UNSWORTH: books—*The Development of Australian Sculpture* by Graeme Sturgeon, London 1978; *Ken Unsworth: Project 28*, exhibition catalogue with text by Paul McGilliek, Sydney 1978; *Australian Sculptors* by Ken Scarlett, Sydney 1980; *Presence and Absence*, exhibition catalogue with essay by Jonathan Watkins, Perth 1983; articles—"The Performance Works of Ken Unsworth" by Paul McGillick in *ICA Magazine* (Sydney), January/March 1978; "The Venice Biennale: Back to Nature" by Henry Martin in *Art International* (Zurich), no. 6, 1978; "Art and Nature at the Biennale" by Milton Gendel in *Art in America* (New York), September 1978; "Australia: A Multiple Reality" by Pierre Restany in *Domus* (Milan), July 1979; "Ken Unsworth: Some Recent Works" by Paul McGillick in *Aspect* (Sydney), no. 4, 1981.

*

My use of technology, electronic and biomechanical, is to explore neither the dimensions of its own possibilities nor its poetic potential, but rather a subliminal, low-profile, low-key, low-technology application and adaptation in order to realise the dream—never to lose in my work the feeling of being, rather to pluck the strings of forgotten memories and emotions to invoke the sensations of the other life.

My intention is to create strange, ritualistic provocations whose outward forms and appearances implant themselves in the mind, and assert their essential inwardness by resonating with the viewer's own footsteps—sounds surrounded by sound, light caught in light, and movement in motionless movement. These visual manifestations don't happen in the real world; they are not experienced in the real world, yet happen constantly, endlessly recurring, but we only see them in that split-second of a blink of an eye, in the moment of a dream or in the sound of a door slamming.

The zone of wistful thoughts is a dimension-less space in which thought, like soft-teased skeins of solar winds, eternally streams, half-felt, half-heard, half-remembered, though the void.

The formal appearance of the installation itself perpetuates the inherent structural and perceptual ambiguities. Seemingly self-supporting, self-generating electric motors driving propellers, in whose slipstream black silken pennants constantly flutter, are held in tension in the mist of their own shadows by river stones floating several inches off the floor.

Gravity is suspended, time is motionless, and the soundless sounds of energy prevail.

—Ken Unsworth

*

Ken Unsworth came late to his art. Not till he was about 40 did he discover that sculpture was best able to embody his feelings. In an Australian art world which especially prized subtle observation of landscape, he instead felt a need to express great human emotions, with simple directness. In 1967 his earliest venture away from painting was biomorphic soft sculpture; sensuous, even erotic, but too complicated. By 1971 he had found his personal language of forms. Surface manipulation and detail were eliminated, and at first glance purely sculptural experiences were readily apprehended: they were usually extreme states of tension, compression or balance. Although these first mature works were welded metal constructions and concrete slab constructions, they were not formalist drawing-in-space but instead had the abstract energy of a human body testing its limits.

Thus in 1975 it was perhaps inevitable that the breakthrough into art of considerable quality was Unsworth's first essay at performance art. "Five Secular Settings for Sculpture as Ritual and Burial Piece" was a series of five briefly-held static body-sculptures, in which Unsworth was suspended from various supports; followed by burial alive under shovelsful of sand while standing in an upright glass "coffin" from which he was released by a bystander smashing the glass and allowing the dry sand to drain away. In the same year the static sculptures turned to sensuous though plain materials such as worn river-stones floating from wires, or caked and sliced earth.

Music accompanied the "Five Secular Settings".., and music or other sounds—babies crying, gun fire, night birds and wind—have been integral to subsequent performance pieces or installations. "Face to Face", 1977, was another physically demanding seven-part brief performance in which the artist, suspended upside-down, first knifed his way out of a sack, and ended lying propped on sticks.

Since then the artist has more often been a background element, endlessly replacing a mechanical crawling doll-child on a plank from which it endlessly falls, to the accompaniment of the staccato beat of a mechanical doll drummer, or sitting immobile by a doll-child and an endlessly bouncing ball.

Such pieces, contributed to *Biennales* of Sydney at the Art Gallery of New South Wales, were maintained for many weeks and (like Gilbert and George's five-day living sculpture and Marina and Ulay's 16 day static performance at the same museum in 1973 and 1981 respectively) were remarkably successful assertions of performance art as primarily a visual art properly shown in the context of a visual-arts museum. Their non-narrative character, or else their endlessly repeated brief narrative, ensured that they were not experienced as out-of-context theatre.

Unsworth's work has gained him invitations from the museum at Lodz, Poland, and the experience of a society under such stress as Poland's in turn influenced a 1982 installation, of two rooms from which humans had fled, leaving only the sense of fear and desperation, and implicit cries for help.

In his various ways—object sculpture, body sculpture, performance art, installation—Unsworth has shown that contemporary art can address itself plainly and with seriousness to the universal mysteries of birth, life, survival, death and resurrection. A body can float, stones hold themselves gracefully in the air: souls therefore may leap across voids, and meet.

—Daniel Thomas

URBAN, Janos.
Swiss. Born in Szeged, Hungary, 5 November 1934; emigrated to Switzerland, 1956: naturalized, 1976;

educated at Secondary Arts and Crafts School, Budapest, until 1953; studied art history and philosophy at Eotovos Lorand University, Budapest, 1953–56 and art at the Ecole Cantonale des Beaux-Arts, Lausanne, Switzerland, 1957–61. Married Jacqueline Nicod in 1963; son: Matthias. Independent artist, Lausanne, since 1961; mixed media work with phosphorus, UV light and radio waves, from 1967; "Memorandum Ancona" and "Lived-in Places," scripto-visual works, from 1970. Professor, Ecole des Beaux-Arts, Lausanne, since 1963. Recipient: City of Geneva Prize, *Salon de la Jeune Gravure Suisse,* 1970; Landis and Gyr-Forderungspreis, Zug, 1974. Address: 4 Chemin de Pre-Fleuri, 1006 Lausanne, Switzerland.

Individual Exhibitions:

1961	Galerie L'Entracte, Lausanne
1963	Galerie L'Entracte, Lausanne
1966	Galerie L'Entracte, Lausanne
1970	Galerie Palette, Zurich
	Galerie Impact, Lausanne
	Bischofsmuhle, Hildesheim, West Germany
1971	Galleria Sincron, Brescia, Italy

1973	Galerie la Fenetre, Nice
	Galerie Akumulatory, Poznan, Poland
1974	Salle Patino, Geneva
	Galerie der Reflektion Press, Stuttgart
1976	Galleria Civica d'Arte Moderna, Modena, Italy
1977	Galerie R + B, Fribourg, Switzerland
1980	Stempelplaats, Amsterdam
	Bazillus Arts Space, Wurzburg, West Germany

Selected Group Exhibitions:

1969	22 *Jonge Switzers,* Stedelijk Museum, Amsterdam
1972	*Art Systems* 2, Museo de Arte Moderna, Buenos Aires
1973	*Biennale de l'Art Suisse,* Kunsthaus, Zurich
1978	*Sammlung der Gotthard-Bank,* Helmhaus, Zurich
1979	*International Print Biennale,* City Art Museum, Bradford, England
	Art Documentation 79, California State University at San Jose
1980	*Videowochen Essen,* Museum Folkwang, Essen
	22 Artistas Suicos, Galeria Nacional Belem, Lisbon
1981	*Videoarte Suizo,* Centro de Arte y Communicacion, Buenos Aires

Janos Urban: *Diapositive* sound and light installation

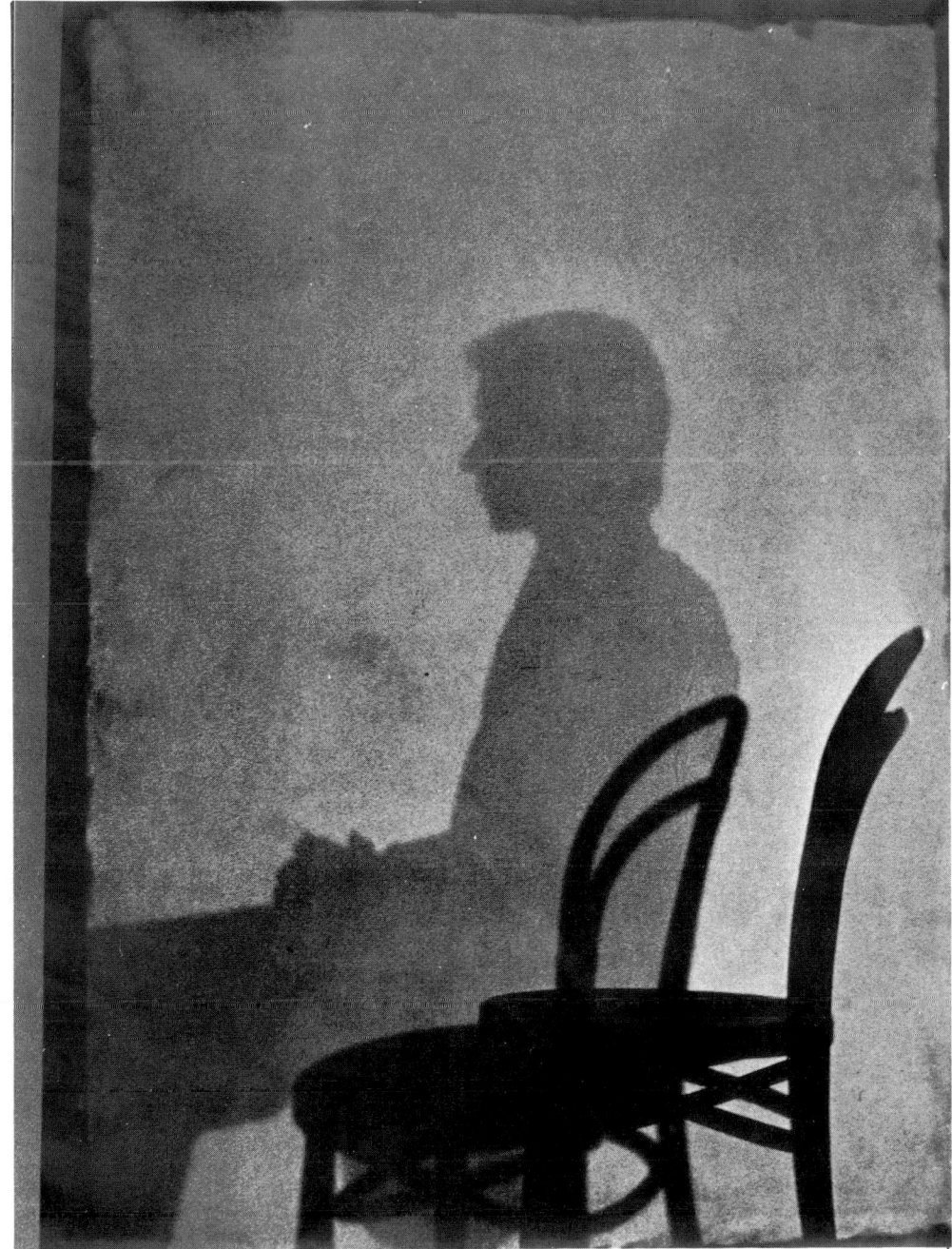

1982   *Documenta 7,* Museum Fridericianum, Kassel, West Germany

Collections:

Musé Cantonal des Beaux-Arts, Lausanne; Cabinet des Estampes, Geneva; Kunsthaus, Zurich; City of Berne.

Publications:

By URBAN: books—*Approche des Iles—a scripto-visual work,* with others, Lausanne 1972; *Le Bateau de 13 h. 15,* with J. Monnier and L. Prebandier, Lausanne 1973; *Erlebte Erdteile,* Geneva 1974; *Praxis,* Lausanne 1978; *Poiesis,* Lausanne 1979; films—*Again . . . and Again,* 1973; *The Skating Rink,* 1973; *Cross-Talkas,* with L. Prebandier and Hans-Werner Kalkmann, 1973.

On URBAN: books—*If I Had a Mind . . . ,* edited by Klaus Groh, Cologne 1971; *Il Corpo come Linguaggio* by Lea Vergine, Milan 1974; *Cine-Graphia: 10th Festival Videoart, Locarno,* exhibition catalogue, Locarno 1980; *Schweizer Kunst 70–80,* exhibition catalogue, Lucerne 1981; *Fri-Art 81,* exhibition catalogue, Fribourg 1981; *Love/Hate/Fear/ Suicide: Mail Art,* exhibition catalogue, Brussels 1981; *Bodies of Artists,* exhibition catalogue, by Carsten Schmidt-Olsen, Aalborg 1981; *A Mail Art Show,* exhibition catalogue, Detroit 1981; *Stalin: Centenaire de Joseph Djougachvili,* exhibition catalogue, Nice 1981.

URIBURU, Nicolas (Garcia).

Argentinian. Born in Buenos Aires in 1937. Studied architecture in Buenos Aires. First Colouring project, Grand Canal, Venice, 1968; has worked on colouring natural phenomena since 1968. Lives and works in Paris. Recipient: Prix Braque, 1964; Prix Lefranc, 1967; Grand Premio Nacional, Buenos Aires, 1968; First Prize, *Biennale,* Tokyo, 1975. Address: 67 rue St. Dominique, Paris 7, France.

Individual Exhibitions:

1954	Galeria Muller, Buenos Aires
1960	Galeria Lirolay, Buenos Aires
1962	Galeria Antonio Souza, Mexico City
1963	Galeria Rubbers, Buenos Aires
1965	Galeria Guernica, Buenos Aires
1967	Galerie Iris Clert, Paris
1968	General Electric Institute, Montevideo
1972	Galerie Spectrum, Antwerp
1973	Centro de Arte y Communicacion, Buenos Aires work
	Musé d'Art Moderne, Paris
1974	Leo Castelli Graphics, New York
	Musée Galliera, Paris
1978	Museum of American Art, Maldonado, Uruguay
1979	Salas Nacionales de Exposicion, Buenos Aires
1982	Hara Museum, Tokyo

Selected Group Exhibitions:

1967	*Salon de Mai,* Paris
1968	*Graphics Biennale,* Paris
1971	*Air, Fire, Earth and Water,* Museum of Fine Arts, Boston
	Biennale, Paris
1972	*Bienal,* Medellin, Colombia
1974	*International Graphics Biennale,* Tokyo
	Art and Culture in the Third World, Institute of Contemporary Arts, London
	Contraste Simultane des Couleurs, Faculty of Medicine, Paris
1980	*Biennale,* Tokyo
1982	*Documenia,* Kassel, West Germany

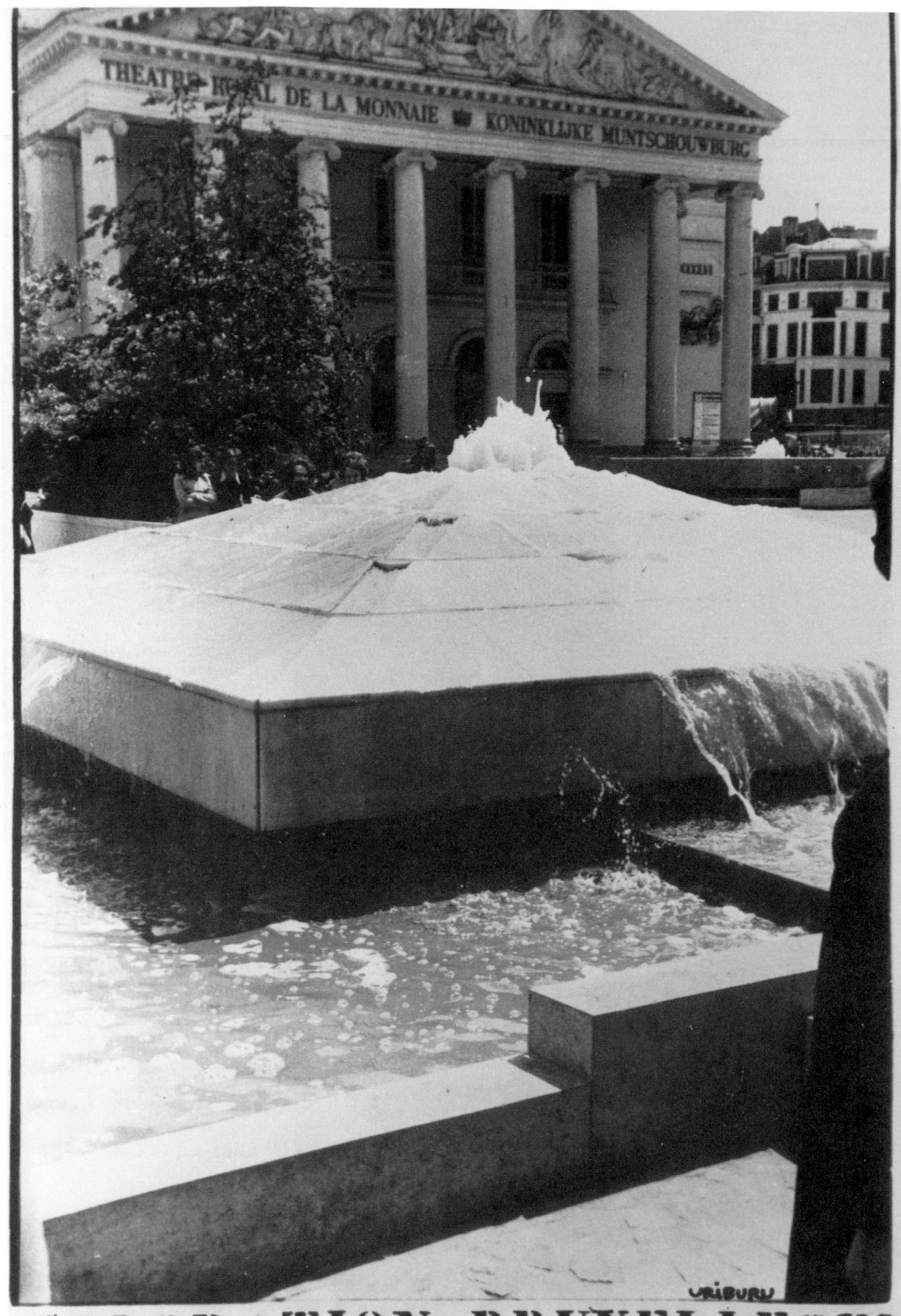

Nicolas Uriburu: *Collage,* 1974

Publications:

On URIBURU: book—*Art in Argentina* by Jorge Glusberg, Milan 1986; articles—"Nicolas Uriburu" by John Perreault in the *Village Voice* (New York), 4 June 1970: "Art Concepts from Europe" by Pierre Restany in *Domus* (Milan). June 1970; "Nicolas Garcia Uriburu" by Jorge Glusberg in *Art and Artists* (London), January 1971: "Le marche aux Puces de l'art moderne" by Otto Hahn in *L'Express* (Paris). October 1971; "Uriburu: Coloration" by C. Bovyeure in *Lettres Francaises* (Paris), June 1972; "The World All in Green" by Pierre Restany in *Domus* (Milan), April 1973; "Une Perception Autre" by P. Borgeaud in *Pariscope*, December 1973; "Uriburu: La Vie en Vert" in *Connaissance des Arts* (Paris), February 1974; "Dix Questions sur l'Art et Les Nouveaux Media" in *Artitudes* (St. Jeannet, France), July 1974; article by Pierre Restany in *Domus* (Milan), October 1981.

*   *   *

My work is about ecology. I began by painting a series of trees in Argentina in 1960. In 1964 I won the Prix Braque, a scholarship to Paris. In 1968 during the Venice *Biennale* I coloured the waters of the Grand Canal in fluorescent green (about 3 kilometers): that was the beginning of a series of colourings in different waters all over the world: the East River, New York: the Seine, Paris; the Rio de la Plata, Buenos Aires—and fountains, lakes, ports, etc., always in a fluorescent green, showing my alarm about pollution. In New York in 1970 I began a series in green colours, "Antagonism Between Nature and Civilization." I have also done some body art, colouring my sexual organs, face and hair in green. In 1971 I began a defence of the trees of a park that the authorities wanted to cut; next I planted some trees in the city of Buenos Aires and also in a museum in Uruguay. I've coloured the waters of the Rhine in collaboration with the German artist Joseph Beuys and planted with him the first 7 trees (of what will eventually be about 7,000) at Documenta 7 in Kassel. Now I am working on a series about animals that are disappearing from the world. My art defines the struggle between nature and civilization. That's why I colour my body, my genitals, and the great waters of the world. The more developed countries are destroying water, land and air, resources for the future in Latin American countries.

—Nicolas Uriburu

*   *   *

The relation between man and his environment has always been a matter of concern for all societies. Ecology, a discipline that began to develop at the beginning of the 20th century, is a branch of biology that deals with the relation between living things and their environment. Organisms, plants, animals, all of them perform certain activities which tend mainly to their adaptation to the surrounding medium. The three large constituent areas of ecology—vegetable, animal and human—roused successively the interest of botanists, zoologists, and lastly, of sociologists. The term "human ecology" appeared in 1921, and since then, that region has been part of the region of social sciences. Its problems are not only limited to pointing out the mutual connections between man and his environment, but emphasize the social aspects of his adaptation. If by the term eco-system is meant the universe of the elements which surround the subject as they become signs, that is to say, when man supplies them with a meaning—a topological semantics would explain the large number of forms in which man articulates space and establishes semantic relations with it. One of the manifestations of this production of meaning, born from man's relations with his environment, is the "artistic discourse," particularly that which is called "ecological art." The ecological artist develops his language in connection with two types of elements of the eco-system: the natural ones (rivers, mountains, etc.) and the artificial ones (buildings, urbanistic complexes, highways). The intersection between the artistic and what the ecologists call "natural areas" (territorial unities created and/or conditioned or not by human activity) constitutes a new phenomenon, which compels us to adopt a critical point of view in an entirely different way. Nicolas Uriburu coloured the waters of Venice Canals with green aniline in 1968, during the year's Biennial. In May and June, 1970, he coloured the East River in New York, the River Seine in Paris, once again the Grand Canal in Venice and the River Plata in Buenos Aires. In 1971, when the Paris Biennial took place, he coloured the Vincennes Lake, and he coloured himself, as a participant at a meeting (colour body work); in June, 1972, he coloured fourteen fountains at Kassel, in 1973 the Riachuelo in Buenos Aires; in 1974 the fountains in Brussels. The ecological proposals of Uriburu extend to future projects: the colouring of the fountains of Versailles, that of the snows of Mont Blanc, and of Iguazu and Niagara Falls. The project called "Cono Sur" consists of the simultaneous colouring of every river in the different countries of the southern hemisphere, by an artist from each country; through the project "Agua Nuestra" he will colour every Latin American place (Uriburu is an Argentinian architect) where water represents conflict: Panama, Iquitos, Titicaca, Puna Arenas. Uriburu's work fuses with nature and at the same time it complements her. We are, thus, in front of a different event: the artist's language inscribes itself in the space transformed by man, the signs spread over large extensions, and thus man gets himself, literally speaking, "to pervade nature with humanity." Uriburu's art refuses to adapt itself to the rules imposed by the important museums or the international galleries, but intends to take the Trojan horse out of its walls, in order to see whether the works done in the 60's are able to endure living in the open air of daily life. The protecting confinement is no longer an attraction for the vanguard, who want to operate in the reality of the profane ambits. The artist who lives in the second half of his century no longer creates new works, but new channels of sensibility, new discoveries which propose different fields of exploration of the spirit. Instead of undertaking the recreation of reality by means of imitative or decorative objects, the artist makes use of representations which do not exist as separate entities, but as elements which supply the sites where they are placed with a new definition or a new point of view. The traditional work of art has begun to be sustained by an artistic situation composed by happenings which correspond to social and ideological function, and to function related to creativeness and play, all of them belonging to the field of probability, to the world of free relation. In order to convey his sensible message, the traditional artist repeats the act of creation in a God-like manner, resorting to those tricks painters and sculptors have made use of for centuries. The ecological artists carry on with their researches in different operation levels. They are no longer interested in the space that must be filled, nor in the academic discussions about the limits between poetry and painting, nor between fullness and void, because the matter has become a situation; and this situation is communicating, is a creator of signs, and it comprises forms, ideas and being; it probably does not turn out faultless products of "good art"; it deals with the artistic event as a cultural phenomenon, as a sociological experience, as a practical work in psychology, an urbanistic project, a sort of theoretical and experimental illustration of human behaviour.

—Jorge Glusberg

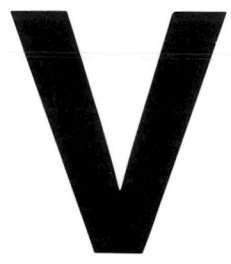

VALENTINE, DeWain.

American. Born in Fort Collins, Colorado, 27 August
1936. Educated at University of Colorado, Boulder,
1954–60, B.F.A. 1958, M.F.A. 1960. Independent
sculptor, in Colorado, 1960–65, and in Venice, California since 1965: cast polyester works, 1967–75;
laminated glass works from 1976. Instructor, University of Colorado, Boulder, 1959–61; Instructor, University of California at Los Angeles, 1965–67.
Recipient: Yale-Norfolk Art School Fellowship, New
Haven, Connecticut, 1958; Guggenheim Fellowship,
1980; National Endowment for the Arts Fellowship,
1981. Address: 69 Market Street, Venice, California
90291, U.S.A.

Individual Exhibitions:

1958	University of Colorado, Boulder
1960	University of Colorado, Boulder
1964	The Gallery, Denver
1968	Douglas Gallery, Vancouver
	Ace Gallery, Los Angeles
1969	University of British Columbia, Vancouver
	Galerie Bischofberger, Zurich
	University of Washington, Seattle
1970	Pasadena Museum of Art, California
1973	Denise René Gallery, New York
	Walter Kelly Gallery, Chicago
1974	San Jose Museum of Art, California
	Edward Thorp Gallery, Santa Barbara, California
	Betty Gold Gallery, Los Angeles
1975	La Jolla Museum of Contemporary art, California
	California State University at Northridge
	Long Beach Museum of Art, California
1977	Santa Barbara Museum of Art, California
1979	Los Angeles County Museum of Art
1980	Malinda Wyatt Gallery, Venice, California
1981	Projects Studio One, Institute for Art and Urban Re-sources, New York
1982	Thomas Babeor Gallery, La Jolla, California
	Malinda Wyatt Gallery, Venice, California
	Missouri Botanical Garden, St. Louis
	Laumeier Sculpture Park, St. Louis
1983	Madison Art Center, Wisconsin
1984	Thomas Babeor Gallery, La Jolla, California
1985	Honolulu Academy of Arts, Hawaii
	Contemporary Arts Center, Honolulu, Hawaii

Selected Group Exhibitions:

1966	*Whitney Annual Sculpture Exhibition*, Whitney Mu-seum, New York
1969	*The Industrial Edge*, Walker Art Center, Minneapo-lis
1973	*American Art 1948–1973*, Seattle Art Museum, Washington
1976	*Contemporary Masters*, Libra Gallery, The Clare-mont Colleges, California
1979	*Change, Inc. West*, Newport Harbor Art Museum, California
1980	*Sculpture in California 1975–1980*, San Diego Mu-seum of Art
1981	*California Light and Space*, Lonny Gans and Asso-ciates, Venice, California

1983	*Urban Sculpture/Architectural Concerns*, Security Pacific National Bank Gallery, Los Angeles
1985	*California Sculpture Show*, Yorkshire Sculpture Park, Bretton Hall College
1987	*Sculpture of the Sixties*, Margo Leavin Gallery, Los Angeles

Collections:

Whitney Museum, New York: Art Institute of Chicago; Milwaukee Art Center; Los Angeles County Museum of Art;
Norton Simon Museum, Pasadena, California: La Jolla Museum of Contemporary Art, California; Palm Springs Desert
Museum, California; Aldrich Museum of Contemporary Art,
Ridgefield, Connecticut; Contemporary Arts Center, Honolulu, Hawaii; Vancouver Art Gallery, British Columbia.

Publications:

By VALENTINE: articles—"An Interview with DeWain Valentine." with Kurt Von Meier, in *Artforum* (New York). May
1969; "DeWain Valentine: An Interview," with Melinda
Wortz in *Journal* (Los Angeles), June 1974.

On VALENTINE: books—*Neue Dimensionen der Plastik* by
Udo Kultermann, Tübingen. West Germany 1967; *Plastics in
Arts* by Pierre Restany, Paris 1974; *A Decade of Sculpture:
The 1960's* by Julia Busch. Philadelphia 1974; *Sunshine
Muse* by Peter Plagens. New York 1974; *Art and Plastics* by
Franco Passoni, Milan 1975: *50 West Coast Artists* by Henry
Hopkins, San Francisco 1982; *Living Materials: A Sculptor's
Handbook* by Oliver Andrews, Berkeley 1983; *DeWain Val-
entine: Recent Works* exhibition catalogue with essay by Me-
linda Wortz, Honolulu 1985.

Sculptor DeWain Valentine, who moved to Southern
California from Colorado in 1965, has been closely
identified with the so-called "L.A. Look," which
during the 1960's began to attract international attention to contemporary art activity in Los Angeles. A
"cool" minimalism and preoccupation with elegant

DeWain Valentine: *Triangle Gray*, 1982

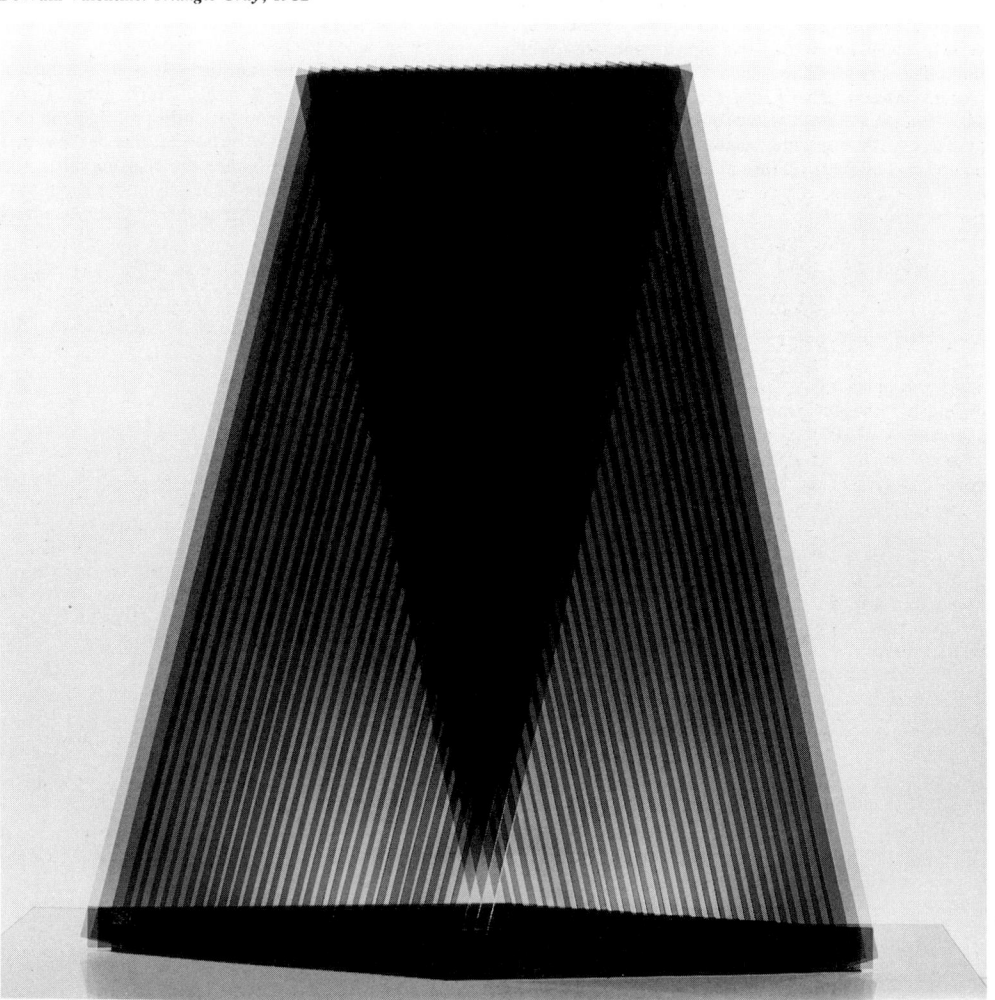

surfaces was indeed characteristic of the work of artists such as Valentine, Larry Bell, Craig Kauffman, and Robert Irwin. However, despite certain mutual interests (for example, the aesthetic potential of industrial materials), neither these arts nor their works participated in a cohesive "movement." The most prominent figures associated with the emergence of contemporary Los Angeles art in fact displayed a wide variety of interests as represented by the quasi-POP imagery of Ed Ruscha and Billy Al Bengston, the tableaux assemblages of Ed Keinholz, or Irwin's optical experimentation. Nonetheless, fascination with technology, industrial materials, crafted surfaces, and visual sensuality were characteristic of one notable aspect of the creative milieu in which Valentine worked in the late 1960's. With his elegantly seductive cast-resin sculptures, Valentine played an important role in the development of what became widely regarded as the prevailing Southern California aesthetic. Furthermore, in his subsequent work he has continued to pursue the same basic concerns—mainly the exploration of light—which motivated his earlier work. Valentine's unparalleled technical virtuosity in resin casting on a monumental scale and the undeniable beauty of his work has, unfortunately, tended to obscure his important goals. Over the years Valentine has consistently developed a body of sculptural work based on geometric forms infused with subtle gradations of transparent or transluscent color "activated" (and modified) by ambient light. Consisting of polyester resin or acrylic plastic discs, wedges, rings, slabs and related shapes, Valentine's art achieves a remarkably effective fusion of physical substance and light. The installations done in the early 1970s mark an important and logical progression from these individual objects to the light environments and related work of the past decade. Throughout, his basic goal has remained the figurative and literal "illumination" of a fundamental duality: matter and phenomenon ("tonnage and ethereality," to use the artist's words) manipulated into visual harmony by technical means. Despite his use of industrial materials and techniques, these concerns place Valentine firmly within a naturalist tradition. The prismatic lenses of the late 1960's, the camera obscura pieces and photomontages of the mid 1970's, and even the concurrent planes and spectrums (cantilevered, suspended, curved), all depend upon natural phenomena to reveal their true content. In every case, there is present a view of the world that is firmly rooted in landscape. Even the delicate suspended-rod installations (such as *Catenary Light*), by introducing a curved shaft of exterior light into a dark room, deal with the experience of natural light as it responds to weather, season and time of day. The same basic perceptual concerns and interest in transparency of form underlie Valentine's recent large-scale laminated glass constructions. As always, an undeniable physical beauty and technical mastery are subservient to ideas based on nature and the almost mystical quality of light. Valentine's philosophical goals clearly separate his art from minimalist refinement and decorative formalism. His accomplishment has been the dematerialization of physicality in a way that asserts the primacy of light. Viewed in perceptual terms, Valentine's interest would appear to have more in common with French Impressionist ideas than with recent formalist theory. Nonetheless, his work does relate to that of the "environmentalists" (Irwin, Michael Asher, James Turrell) whose non-object investigations of light and perception constitute one of Southern California's significant contributions to contemporary art.

—Paul J. Karlstrom

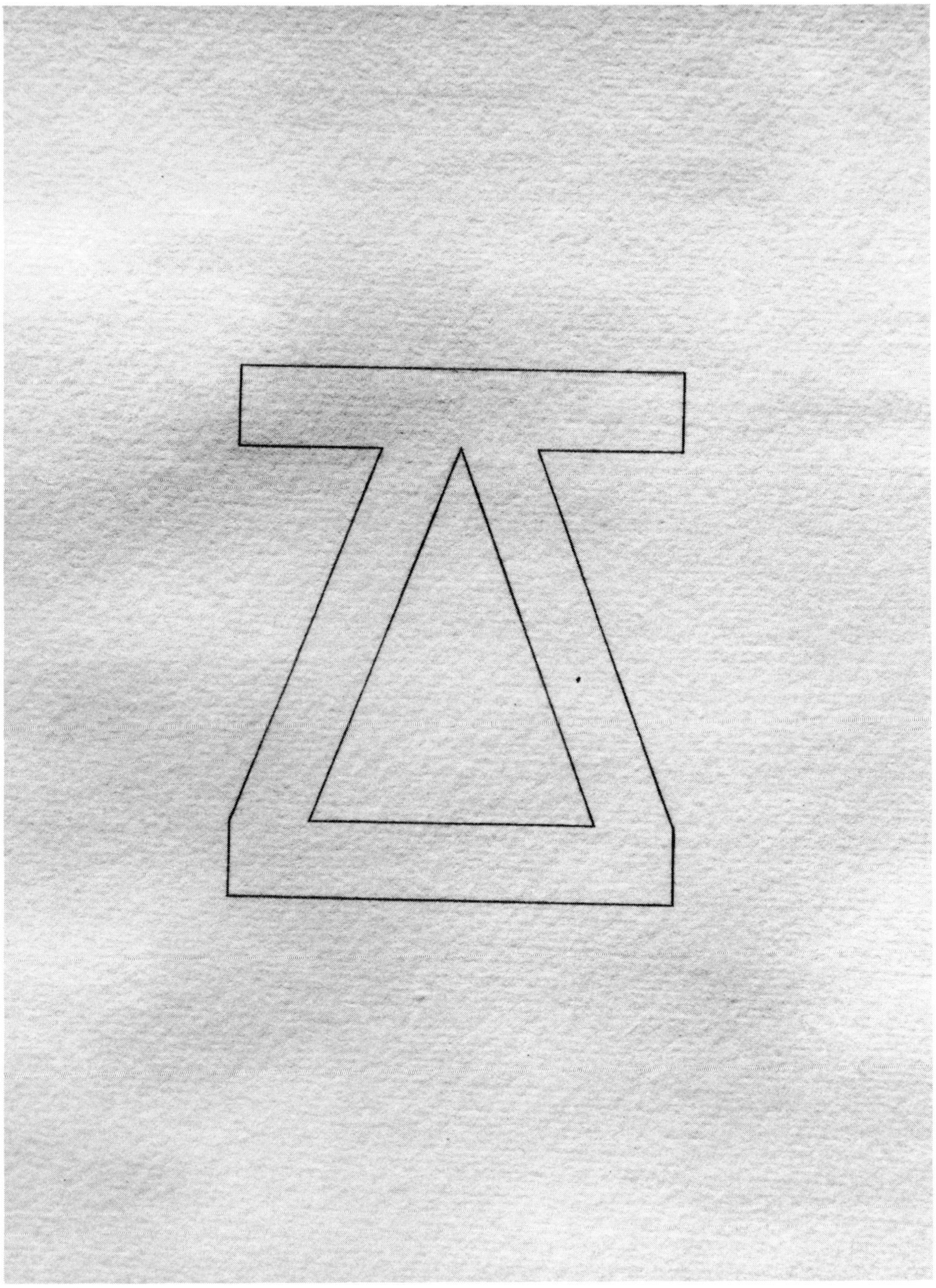

VALOCH, Jiri.

Czechoslovakian. Born in Brno, 6 September 1946. Studied Bohemistics, Germanistics and aesthetics,

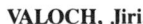

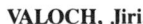

Jiri Valoch: *Sign 2 × Z*, 1987

J. E. Purkyně University, Brno, 1965-70. Married Mirka Antonova in 1971 (divorced, 1972). Produced first visual poems and typestracts, 1964; first photographic works, 1969; first conceptual poetry, 1970. Artist and art theoretician, House of Arts, Brno, since 1972: has organized exhibitions and written articles on numberous Czech artists. Address: Jugoslavska 46a, 61300 Brno, Czechoslovakia.

Individual Exhibitions:

1966   Music Theatre, Ústi and Labem, Czechoslovakia
1969   Museum, Krnov, Czechoslovakia
1970   House of the Young, Jindřichuv Hradec, Czechoslovakia
1971   Regional Gallery, Jihlava, Czechoslovakia
1972   Information Centre for Events, Bielefeld, West Germany
1974   *Sculptures*, Gallery Akumulatory, Poznan, Poland
1977   *Relations*, Galleria Mercato del Sale, Milan
1978   *Relations and Haiku*, Municipal Library, Wroclaw, Poland
1979   *In, Oltre*, Centro Culturale, Monza, Italy

1984   *Werken uit 1964–82*, Het Apollohuis, Eindhoven, Netherlands
1985   *Vizuální poezie*, Kulturní středisko města Blanska, Czechoslovakia

Selected Group Exhibitions:

1966   *Umĕni pisma—Poezie pisma—Visudiní poezie*, Moravian Museum, Brno
1970   *Konkrete Poezie?*. Stedelijk Museum. Amsterdam
1971   *Arte de Sistemas I*, Centro de Arte y Communicacion, Buenos Aires
1973   *Texts*, Balatonboglár, Hungary
1977   *Texty Wisualne*, Gallery Labyrint, Lublin, Poland (travelled to Lodz, 1978)
1979   *Sprachen jenseits von Dichtung*. Kunstverein, Münster, West Germany
1980   *Drawing '80*, Pécz Gallery, Hungary
1981   *Kunstlerbücher*, Kunstverein, Frankfurt
1984   *Am Anfang war das Wort*, Städtisches Galerie, Lüdenscheid, West Germany
1985   *Salut Chlebnikow*, Staatliches Lindenaumuseum, Altenburg, East Germany

Collections:

Archief voor Visuele, Concrete en Experimentele Poezie, Dutch Literary Museum. The Hague; Muzeum Sztuki, Lodz, Poland; Muzeum Narodowe, Wroclaw, Poland; Regional Gallery, Jihlava, Czechoslovakia; Moravian Gallery, Brno; Kupferstichkabinett der Staatlichen Kunstsammlungen, Dresden; Archive Hanns Sohm, Markgronimgen, West Germany; Stedelijk Museum, Amsterdam; Schlubladenmuseum Herbert Disel, Berne; Museo Laboratorio Casabianca, Malo, Italy.

Publications:

By VALOCH: books and phamphlets—*HLAS/VOICE/VOIX/STIMME*, London 1966; *9 Optical Poems*, London 1967; *Unlucky Number—13 mimeoenphamphs*, Toronto 1968; *An Interrupted Poem*, Toronto 1969; *Optical Book*, Brescia, Italy 1970; *Ga: The First and Last Collection of Sound Poems by Jiri Valoch*, London 1971; *A Minimal Monument*, Welling, Kent 1971; *Poem for Ad Reinhardt*, London 1971; *Landscapes I*, Utrecht 1972; *See Page 13*, Friedrichfehn 1973; *Hommage á Valoch*, West Berlin 1975; *12 Excercises*, West Berlin 1976; *Mobile-Two Structures-Piece III*, London 1980; *20 Works: Kunstinformatie 35*, Gorinchem 1981; *Haiku*, Toronto 1983; *Pozorování—kniha pro přátele*, Brno 1983; *Word Works*, West Berlin 1984; *Five Parts of One Piece*, Eschenau 1984; *Three Sheets*, Eschenau 1984; *Werken uit 1964–1982: Collection Herman de Vries*, Eindhoven 1984; *8 x 2 Portfolio: Czech Visual Texts*, editor, Dresden 1986; *Semantic Study*, Munich 1986.

On VALOCH: books—*Experimentalni poezie*, edited by J. Hirsal and B. Grogerova, Prague 1966; *Once Again* by Jean-Francois Bory, New York 1967; *Verso la Poesia Totale*, edited by A. Spatola, Milan 1967; *Poezie in Fuzie*, edited by Paul de Vree, Antwerp 1967; *Concrete Poetry: A World View*, edited by M. E. Solt, Bloomington, Indiana 1968; *Aktuelle Kunst in Ost Europa*, edited by Klaus Groh, Cologne 1970; *Exempla: Documents of Concrete and Visual Poetry*, edited by Maurizio Nannucci, Florence 1970; *Konkretedichtung*, edited by S. J. Schmidt, Munich 1972; *Poesia Visiva Internazionale*, edited by Galleria ll Canale, Venice 1974; *Concrete, Visual and Signalist Poetry*, edited by M. Todorovic, Belgrade 1975; *La Escritura en Liberiad*, edited by F. Millan and R. Sanchez, Madrid 1975; *Von für über—Heinz Gappmayr*, edited by Peter Weiermair, Frankfurt 1985; *Zwanzig Jahre Rainer Verlag: Eine Anthologie, Ein Almanach*, edited by R. Pretzell and T. Milch, West Berlin 1986; *Artists' Statements*, edited by Richard Kriesche, Graz 1987; *Geschichte des Fotogramms*, edited by Floris M. Neususs, Cologne 1987.

All my work has been and is motivated language—in the sixties by the possibility to isolate its elements and to create from them a purely aesthetic structure, since the break of the sixties and seventies by seeking limitations and relations that the extremely reduced language can form, either in non-verbal context/phototexts, verbal interventions in nature/or in itself. The starting point is the annihilation or at least the maximal suppression of the signifier/signified relationship. When language is released from these bonds, it is possible to work with it in another way. I am interested in semantic complications, giving evidence of the language as such, and in autonomous language structures formed by isolating the meaning or by repeating identical isolated elements. I am interested in the metamorphosis of the sign into a quasi-sign which cannot be drawn into a conventional communication system.

—Jiří Valoch

van AMEN, Woody.

Dutch. Born in Eindhoven, 26 August 1936. Studied art at the Akademie van Beeldende Kunsten, Rotterdam, 1956–58; mainly self-taught in painting. Served in Geneeskundige Troepen, Dutch Army, Amersfoort, 1956. Married Cocky Voermans in 1961; daughters: Cybele and Claudia-Nathalie. Worked as window-dresser, gardener, sailor, housepainter, docker, wood-finisher, etc., in Rotterdam, 1958–60. Independent artist, in Rotterdam, since 1960 (worked in New York City, 1961–63). Worked with Scarabee Experimental Theatre Group, Haarlem, 1967; Academie van Beeldende Kunsten, Rotterdam, 1973. Recipient: Dutch Ministry of Culture Stipend, 1967–69; Rotterdam Arts Foundation Stipend, 1969. Address: Benedenstraat 87, 3077 BA Rotterdam, Netherlands.

Individual Exhibitions:

1962	Cottage Club on the Lake, New York
1963	Galerie Delta, Rotterdam
1965	Galerie 't Venster, Rotterdam
	Stedelijk Museum, Amsterdam
1966	Galerie Delta, Rotterdam
1967	Galerie 20, Amsterdam
1968	Galerie Waalkens, Finsterwolde. Netherlands
	Markt 17, Enschede, Netherlands
1969	Galerie 't Venster, Rotterdam
	Galerie 20, Amsterdam
	Galerie Jalmar, Amsterdam
1970	Galerie De Doelen, Rotterdam (with Wim Gijzen)
	Galerie Defacqz, Brussels
	Galerie 't Venster, Rotterdam
1971	Galerie 20, Amsterdam
1973	Galerie Yaki Kornblit, Amsterdam
	Galerie Richard Foncke, Ghent
1974	Galerie Yaki Kornblit, Amsterdam
1975	Pander Kunstcentrum, The Hague
	Galerie Yaki Kornblit, Amsterdam

1978	*Moderne Kunstvoorwerpen*, Museum Boymans-van Beuningen, Rotterdam
	Musée d'Art et d'Histoire, Geneva
	Museum Het Prinsenhof, Delft, Netherlands
	Galerie Brinkman, Amsterdam
1980	Galerie Lara Vincy, Paris
	Galerie Brinkman, Amsterdam
1981	Kunstcentrum De Vaart, Hilversum, Netherlands
	Buchmann Art Gallery, Antwerp
1982	Stichting Kasteel van Rhoon, Netherlands
	National Museum, Singapore
	Centre International d'Art Plastique, Hasselt, Belgium
	Gemeentemuseum, The Hague
1983	Gallery Black Cat, Rotterdam
	Centre International d'Art Plastique, Hasselt, Belgium
1984	Galerie J.L., Ostende, Belgium
1985	Van Abbemuseum, Eindhoven, Netherlands
1986	Gallery Art Action, Singapore
	Le Cadre Gallery, Hong Kong
	Oets Fine Art Gallery, Djakarta, Indonesia

Selected Group Exhibitions:

1964	*Neue Realisten and Pop Art*, Akademie der Künste, West Berlin
1968	*European Painters Today*. Musée des Arts Décoratifs, Paris (toured the United States)
1970	*De Metamorfose van het Objekt*, Museum Boymans-van Beuningen, Rotterdam (toured Switzerland. Germany and Italy)

Woody Van Amen: *Steenrandsel Spel*, 1972

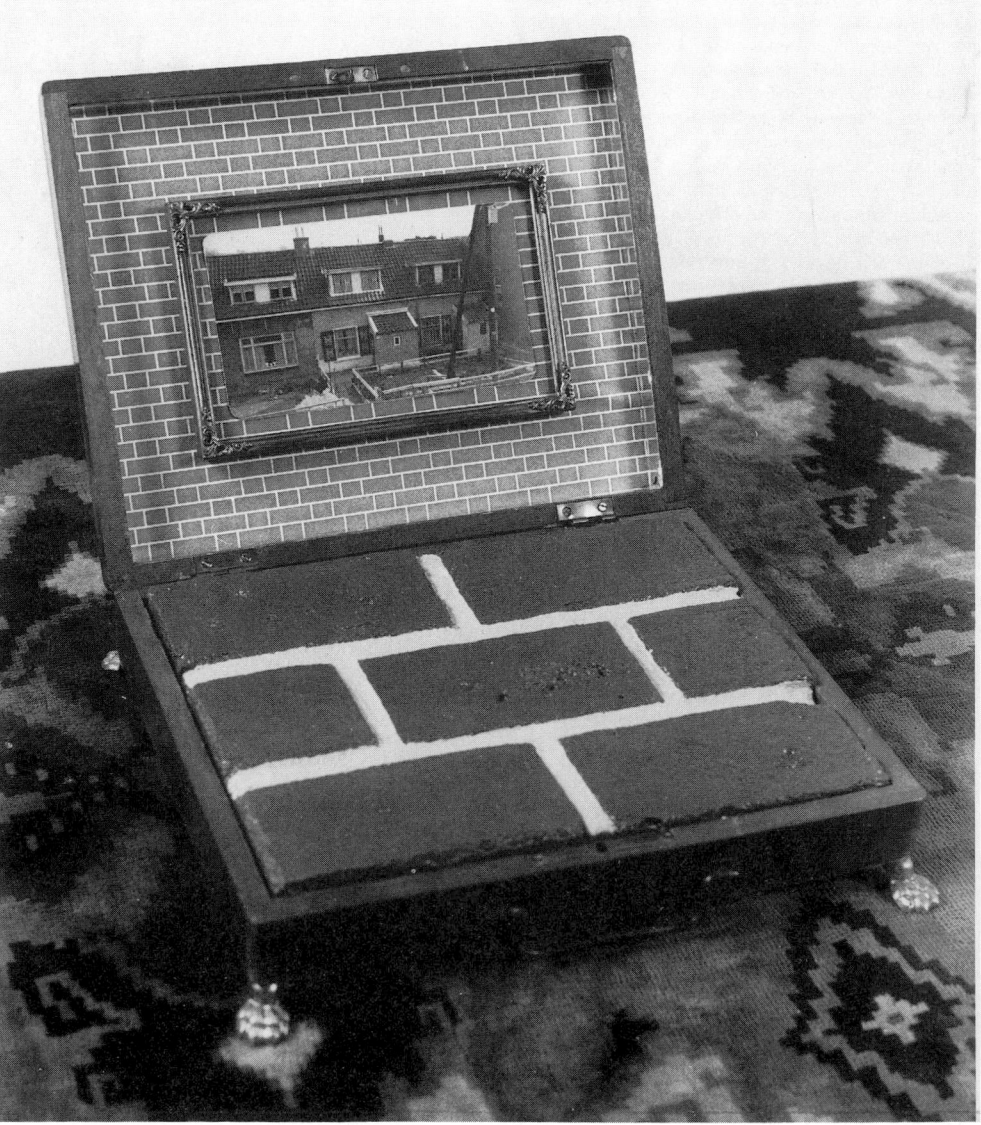

1975 *Art Information Festival*, Middelburg, Netherlands
1976 *Biennale*, Venice
1977 *Beethoven, Music for the Millions*, Gemeentemuseum, Arnhem, Netherlands
1979 *De Jaren Zestig*, Galerie De Vries en Roeloff, Rotterdam
1981 *Not Waving*, Palais des Beaux-Arts, Brussels
1985 *Mens en Omgeving*, De Beyerd Centrum, Breda, Netherlands
1987 *Line and Image*, Muhlenberg College, Allentown, Pennsylvania (toured the United States 1988–89)

Collections:

Stedelijk Museum, Amsterdam: Peter Stuyvesant Foundation. Amsterdam; Museum Boymans-van Beuningen, Rotterdam; Centraal Museum, Utrecht; Frans Halsmuseum, Haarlém, Netherlands; Palais des Beaux-Arts, Brussels.

Publications:

By van AMEN: books and pamphlets—*Filosofie van de Nieuwe Romantiek*, Rotterdam 1973; *Book of Stamps*, with others, Amsterdam 1976; *Transit 3: Translation-Transformation*, Amsterdam 1977; *240 Days/Dagen/Jours/Tage*, with foreword by R. H. Fuchs, Amsterdam 1985; disc—*Het leven van Woody*, sound recording with Jan Donia, 1966.

On van AMEN: books—*Art Around the World* by R. W. D. Oxenaar, New York 1966; *Le Livre Rouge de la Revolution Picturale* by Pierre Restany, Milan 1968; *De Eksplosie van het Intellekt* by Jan Donia, Hilversum 1968; *Le Livre Blanc* by Pierre Restany, Milan 1969; *Le Pop Art* by Jose Pierre, Paris 1975; *Woody van Amen: Moderne Kunstvoorwerpen 1963-1977*, exhibition catalogue, with texts by R. Hammacher-van den Brande, Jan Donia, Pierre Restany, Goose Oosterhof and Peter Bulthuis, Rotterdam 1978; *Nieuwe Romantiek van Woody van Amen*, exhibition catalogue with texts by Rein-Arend Leeuw and Peter Bulthuis, Delft 1978; *Woody van Amen: objecten, tekeningen, grafiek*, exhibition catalogue with text by Kees Broos, The Hague 1982; *Beeldende kunst uit de verzameling van Agnes en Frits Becht*, with texts by R. H. Fuchs and Saskia Bos, Utrecht 1984.

* * *

New Romanticism

1. "New Romanticism" aims at enriching contemporary art by assigning a major role to feeling and imagination.
2. In a cool society which produces "cool art," "new romanticism" presents a form of art which meets the longings of people today for warmth, happiness and recognizable contents.
3. The need for romance has been clearly recognized in the world of films, fashion and theatre, but the plastic arts are lagging behind in this respect. New romanticism has made it its task to re-activate romanticism in the plastic arts.
4. The chief motive of "new romanticism" is to make—and make recognizable again—the ordinary things which people tend to think of as nice.
5. Socially this point of departure could prove to be of great value: it will restore the basic function of art as a means of communication intelligible to all.
6. The views of "new romanticism" will restore some balance in the chaotic and confusing multitude of art expressions of today.
7. The emphasis on feeling and imagination and the use of ordinary and familiar means of portrayal will set free the personal creativity of the "consumer." This will once again stimulate spontaneity in making and experiencing art.
8. "New romanticism" is improving the image of art.

—Woody van Amen

Camesi in Switzerland concentrates upon making art (pictures, etc.) the servant of a kind of aesthetic architecture. Pictures, like bricks, can, he has been able to show, build walls, fireplaces, houses even. At the Sao Paulo *Bienal* of 1973 he constructed a wall of self-portraits. Woody van Amen does the opposite. His *new realism* quite frequently demonstrates that architecture (and furniture), with only slight interpolations, can become pictures or *objects*. What he seeks to make clear, often with many humorous interjections, is that the world we know—from ice-block to pavingstone, from *Grande-armoire* to kitchen sink—is a natural-cum-manmade world, ripe for plunder by an artist if he knows what to do with so much valuable raw material. Not that he is suggesting a scratch round for easy-to-come-by readymades. The contrary. Whatever takes his fancy also inspires him to give it an artistic facelift. Bright colours. Aesthetic machinery. Unexpected conjunctions. Van Amen implies that the spade work performed in this field by Dada and Surrealism is already dated, and that it is time to start creating anew with materials which even if they are not raw can still be coaxed by inventive processes into the furniture and fittings of an unexplored demi-paradise.

—Sheldon Williams

VAN BUREN, Richard.

American. Born in Syracuse, New York, in 1937. Educated at San Francisco State College, the University of Mexico, and Mexico City College. Taught at the School of Visual Arts, New York. Agent: Paula Cooper Gallery, New York. Address: c/o Paula Cooper Inc., 155 Wooster Street, New York, New York 10012, U.S.A.

Individual Exhibitions:

1961 New Mission Gallery, San Francisco
1962 San Francisco Museum of Art
1964 Dilexi Gallery, San Francisco
1967 Bykert Gallery, New York
1968 Bykert Gallery, New York
1969 Bykert Gallery, New York
1970 Bennington College, Vermont
     Ithaca College, Museum of Art, New York (with Benglis and Sanderson)
1972 Paula Cooper Gallery, New York
1973 112 Greene Street, New York
1974 Texas Gallery, Houston
     Rice University. Houston
1975 Paula Cooper Gallery, New York
     Graduate Center, City University of New York
1977 Paula Cooper Gallery, New York

Selected Group Exhibitions:

1964 *Bay Area Artists*, San Francisco Museum of Art
1967 *A Romantic Minimalism*, Institute of Contemporary Art, Philadelphia
1968 *Whitney Annual*, Whitney Museum, New York (and 1970)
1969 *Art and Process IV*, Finch College Museum of Art, New York
     American Exhibition, Art Institute of Chicago (and 1972)
1970 *L'Art Vivant aux Etats-Unis*, Fondation Maeght, Vence, France
     The Larry Aldrich Collection, Museum of Modern Art, New York
1972 *Eight*, Contemporary Art Museum, Houston
1973 *New American Graphic Art*, Fogg Art Museum, Cambridge, Massachusetts
1974 *Choice Dealers/Dealers' Choice*, New York Cultural Center

Collections:

Museum of Modern Art, New York; Walker Art Center, Minneapolis: Southern Texas Art Museum, Corpus Christi; National Gallery of Australia, Canberra.

Publications:

By VAN BUREN: article—"An Interview with Richard Van Buren," with Phylis Tuchman, in *Artforum* (New York), September 1969.

On VAN BUREN: articles—"In the Galleries" in *Arts Magazine* (New York), May 1967; "Reviews and Previews" by Harris Rosenstein in *Artnews* (New York), Summer 1967; "Reviews and Previews" by Harris Rosenstein in *Artnews* (New York), April 1968; "New York Commentary" by Dore Ashton in *Studio International* (London), June 1968; "In the Galleries" in *Arts Magazine* (New York), Summer 1969; "Reviews and Previews" by Stephen A. Kurtz in *Artnews* (New York), Summer 1969; "New York Letter" by Peter Schjeldahl in *Art International* (Lugano, Switzerland), September 1969; "New York" by Emily Wasserman in *Artforum* (New York), September 1969; "Reviews and Previews" by Stephen A.Kurtz in *Artnews* (New York), January 1970; "New York Letter" by Carter Ratcliff in *Art International* (Lugano, Switzerland), January 1970; "New York Commentary" by Dore Ashton in *Studio International* (London), March 1970; "New York Letter" by Carter Ratcliff in *Art International* (Lugano, Switzerland), May 1970; "New York" by Robert Pincus-Witten in *Artforum* (New York), September 1970; "Reviews and Previews" by Harris Rosenstein in *Artnews* (New York), October 1970; "Galleries" by Willis Domingo in *Arts Magazine* (New York), November 1970; "New York" by Robert Pincus-Witten in *Artforum* (New York), December 1970; "New York Letter" by Carter Ratcliff in *Art International* (Lugano. Switzerland), December 1970; "Reviews and Previews" by Bruce Wolmer in *Artnews* (New York), February 1971; "Richard Van Buren" by Susan Heineman in *Artforum* (New York), April 1975.

* * *

Richard Van Buren's eccentric abstractions are exemplary of the move to hybridize painting and sculpture which became prominent during the late 1960's and came to be placed under the heading of "Postminimalism." After a period around 1968 when he made fiberglass-covered wood beam works which resembled Minimalism's "primary structures," Van Buren shifted toward using fiberglass as his basic medium and toward making forms of a more irregular, idiosyncratic nature. In his colorfield and scatter wall reliefs of the early 1970's, Van Buren built layers of varied density, using combinations of additives in his fiberglass resin base such as charcoal, ground glass, plaster and chalk to achieve textural and chromatic effects. He made these works by a slow process in which he poured plastic on the ground, let additional materials float on or sink into the materials, and allowed the whole to congeal before hanging. There are connections with second generation color field painters, especially with Jules Olitski, in these wall reliefs, but Van Buren places deeper emphasis on the materiality of his process and materials and on the incongruity of the resulting shapes. Color becomes part of the physical properties of the material itself, its hue and intensity determined by the density of the resin in which it resides. The quirky, oddball shapes avoid notions of formal composition, stressing rather a non-hierarchical, non-ordering, emphasizing simply its physical presence, made possible by fragile looking yet solid material and process. In 1973 Van Buren began making free-standing, three-dimensional sculptures which further stretch the possibilities of his chosen medium of fiberglass and polyester resin. Strange, frail looking, skeletal structures seem in tense balance, poised precariously on fiberglass legs which jauntily support tube-like lengths. Many of these works take on anthropomorphic correspondences similar to the works from the same period by Rosemary Castoro. Van Buren's long and linear constructs seem also to allude to industrial structures gone whimsical, suggesting tough, handmade bridges or pipelines made by some knowing child. Van Buren pours polyester resin into troughs and lays fiberglass rope at regular intervals. The technical process is purposefully allowed to remain a visible element in the finished work, acting as an integral part of the whole. Whereas in the wall pieces, colored light is often blurred by the proximity to the opaque wall, in these free-standing sculptures it is permitted to pass through translucent materials openly to achieve a glow of unhampered radiance. It is this quality of pale, watery translucence which allows Van Buren his most personal touches in a body of work which might otherwise seem simply one of many which have followed the Postminimal direction.

—Barbara Cavaliere

VAN DER HEYDEN, J(acob) C(ornelis) J(ohan).

Dutch. Born in Den Bosch, 23 June 1928. Studied at the Koninklijke Akademie, Den Bosch, 1946–49; Rijksakademie, Amsterdam, 1952–53; Art School, Tilburg, 1954–55; and Jan Van Eyck Academie, Maastricht, 1955–57. Served in the Dutch Army, 1949–51. Married Johanna van Rysewyk in 1962; children: Paul, Jan and Maria. Worked at Philips Electronics, Eindhoven, 1951; drawing master in colleges at Roermond and Nijmegen, 1954–56; independent artist, Den Bosch, since 1958; paintings and prints, 1958–66; films, since 1967; computer compositions, 1968; sound and television works, 1969; calendar and time-related works, from 1973: has worked in open-air studio since 1975. Guest instructor. Jan Van Eyck Academie, Maastricht. 1971–73; Professor, State Academy, Amsterdam, since 1986. Agent: Galerie Van Gelder, Plancius Straat 9A, Amsterdam. Address: Louwse Poort 83, 5211 NE Den Bosch, Netherlands.

Individual Exhibitions:

1964 Gemeentemuseum, The Hague
1965 Galerie Swart, Amsterdam
1966 Kunststichting, Rotterdam
       Prentenkabinet, Gemeentemuseum, The Hague
1967 Stedelijk Van Abbemuseum, Eindhoven, Netherlands
1971 Galerie Collection d'Art, Amsterdam
       Stedelijk Van Abbemuseum, Eindhoven, Netherlands (with Kees Buurman and Carel Visser)
1977 Gemeentemuseum, The Hague (retrospective; travelled to the Van Abbemuseum Eindhoven, Netherlands)
1981 Stedelijk Van Abbemuseum, Eindhoven, Netherlands
1983 Van Abbemuseum, Eindhoven, Netherlands (retrospective)
1986 Galerie Van Gelder, Amsterdam

Selected Exhibitions:

1970 *Kontrasten,* Gemeentemuseum, The Hague
1973 *Varianten, Ministry* of Cultural Affairs, The Hague (toured the Netherlands)
1981 *Instant Fotografie,* Stedelijk Museum, Amsterdam
1982 *Contemporary Art from the Netherlands,* Museum of Contemporary Art, Chicago (travelled to Toronto and New York)
       Documenta, Kassel, West Germany
1986 *Les Abstraits,* Galerie Le Consortium, Dijon, France (travelled to Nice)
1987 *Contour,* Prinsenhof, Delft, Netherlands

Collections:

Haags Gemeentemuseum, The Hague, Netherlands; Stedelijk Van Abbemuseum, Eindhoven, Netherlands; Rijksmuseum Kröller-Müller, Otterlo, Netherlands; Museum Boymans-van Beuningen, Rotterdam.

Publications:

By VAN DER HEYDEN: books—*J. C. J. Van der Heyden,* with texts by J. L. Locher and C. Blok, The Hague 1977; *Himalaya-Chomolungma,* Utrecht 1981; articles—"Child of His time" in *Konstrasten,* exhibition catalogue, The Hague 1970; "J. C. J. Van der Heyden: Essay" in *Elementary Forms,* exhibition catalogue, Amsterdam 1976; films—*Art Is Only for Beginners,* with Richard Menken and Henk van de Rijdt, 1969.

On VAN DER HEYDEN: books—*J. C. J. Van der Heyden* exhibition catalogue, with text by J. L. Locher, The Hague 1966; *Van der Heyden,* exhibition catalogue, with text by Lambert Tegenbosch, Eindhoven, Netherlands 1967; *Warning Against the Work of J. C. J. Van der Heydan* by Cor Blok, Amsterdam 1971; *Kees Buurman/Carel Visser/J. C. J. Van der Heyden,* exhibition catalogue, with text by Jaap Bremer and Hein Reedijk, Eindhoven, Netherlands 1971; *J. C. J. Van der Heyden,* exhibition catalogue, Eindhoven, Netherlands 1977; *Instant Fotografie,* exhibition catalogue, with text by Els Barents, Amsterdam 1981; *Contemporary Art from the Netherlands,* exhibition catalogue, with texts by Marianne Brouweer and others, Amsterdam 1982; *J. C. J. van der Heyden: retrospective,* exhibition catalogue, Eindhoven, Netherlands 1983; articles—"7 Dutch Artists" by R. Fuchs, B. Reise and C. Broos, in *Studio International* (London), May 1973; "J. C. J. van der Heyden" by Kees van Gelder in *Code* (Amsterdam), June 1986.

Painting before 1967 had as subject amongst others: the painting as screen and wall, appearing as image or

J. C. J. Van der Heyden: *Six Times Four,* 1987

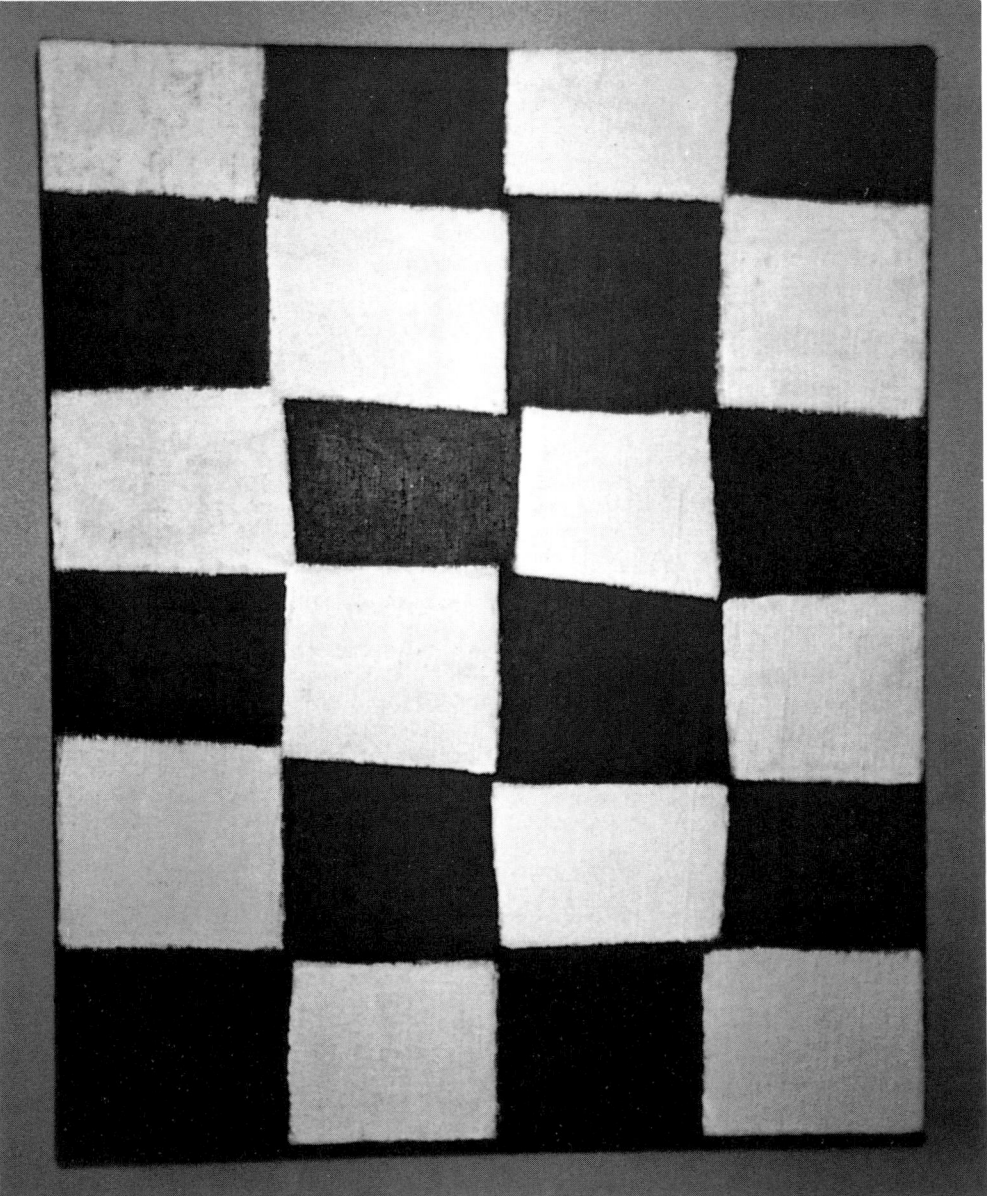

sign (2 to 3 meters high). I had a preference for observing them together with other paintings and all of the space of the vicinity. I also made accumulations, on a smaller scale, bringing some paintings or/and prints together, as one thing. After 1966 I stopped painting. Painting had become its own subject, and by degrees I have increasingly become my own subject. I saw myself painting the painting as an artist. In 1970: "I wonder if I can go on pretending to be an artist. What I am now is an open question, not too quickly to be filled with an answer. If artists are not artists any more, they still belong to that kind of people who realize today what will be possible tomorrow. With pretentions or without, with effects or without". After 1970, I preferred a certain silence. Relationship outside/inside has become the subject in an open air studio, working with visual and non-visual things, without a direct specialization. I have, however, maintained the role of a painter. You don't have to do very much in your life, only a few things which keep on recurring.

—J. C. J. van der Heyden

J. C. J. van der Heyden's place in Dutch painting is a special one. For more than twenty years he has lived and worked in the provincial town of Den Bosch, outside the centre of artistic life. At appropriate times, he shows his works and causes a stir—in recent years, even some general appreciation. In 1968 the young art historian Rudi Fuchs wrote an article on van der Heyden's work in the serious art-historical periodical *Simiolus*. Fuchs discussed the painting *Blue Cross* (1965/66) in the light of some formal aspects of Mondrian's work. He called attention to the importance of the edges of the canvas that, in Mondrian, still belong to the realm of illusionism, but in *Blue Cross* are of a literal character. Throughout the 1970s, van der Heyden enjoyed considerable attention from the Municipal Museum in The Hague, an institution that now owns a substantial part of his early works. According to van der Heyden, the year 1970 was a turning-point. From then on, he rigorously separated himself from the outside world, including the art-world. Painting itself was not to be considered as a necessary activity. A symptom of this attitude is the manipulation of his own signature. His first name (Jacob) disappears in favour of the neutral J. C. J. that creates a distance between the painter/producer and the observer. This procedure becomes understandable if one realizes that a considerable part of van der Heyden's oeuvre consists of a re-use of his own, already executed and finished, paintings. His routine is manifold. In his studio he continuously arranges new situations with the finished canvases he has at his disposal. He observes his own paintings in various situations that he records photographically. He also uses finished compositions, usually repainted in much smaller dimensions, as part of his new paintings. Between 1967 and 1975 he made no paintings at all, only studio photos. New versions of older paintings date from after 1975. Of great importance was a trip by airplane to India in 1977. The photos taken from the inside of the plane, showing pure blue air above the white woolly clouds, have given rise to a series of convincing paintings. Van der Heyden's use of colour is very reduced and elementary (blue, yellow, black and white, and, very rarely, red). Of interest is the project *Two Cabins,* from 1972. One is dark; from the outside one sees into a closed inner space where various objects of van der Heyden's vocabulary are barely discernible. The other one, the lighter cabin, is an outdoors piece that has a roof covered in transparent plexiglass. Here, the sky is the object of meditation.

—A. F. Wagemans

VAN ELK, Ger(ard Pieter).

Dutch. Born in Amsterdam, 9 March 1941. Studied art at the Kunstnijverheidesschool, Amsterdam, 1959–61; studied art and history at Immaculate Heart College, Los Angeles, 1961–63, and art history at the Rijksuniversiteit, Groningen, Netherlands, 1965–66. Independent artist, Amsterdam, since 1961; Founder with Wim T. Schippers, Adynamic group, Amsterdam, 1961–62; with Reinier Lucassen and Jan Dibbets, International Institute for Re-Education of Artists, Amsterdam, 1968. Instructor, Ateliers 63, Haarlem, since 1972. Agent: Art and Project, Prinsengracht 785, Amsterdam. Address: Oude Zijds Achterburgwal 198, Amsterdam, Netherlands.

Individual Exhibitions:

1962	Museum Fodor, Amsterdam (with Wim T. Schippers)
	Dilexi Gallery, Los Angeles
1965	Instituut voor Kunstgeschiednis, Groningen, Netherlands
1966	Galerie Swart, Amsterdam
1967	Galerie de Mangelgang, Amsterdam
	Galerie Espace, Amsterdam
1968	Galleria La Nuova Loggia, Bologna (with Marinus Boezem)
	Galerie Swart, Amsterdam (with Marinus Boezem and Jan Dibbets)
1969	Koninklijke Academie voor Beeldenden Kunste's, Hertogenbosch, Netherlands
	Galerie Walenkamp, Leiden
	Kunstkring, Rotterdam
1970	Art and Project, Amsterdam
1971	Mount San Antonio College, Walnut, California
	Art and Project, Amsterdam (2 exhibitions)
	De Utrechtse Kring, Neudeflat, Utrecht
	Pomona Art Gallery, Los Angeles (with Ader and Leavitt)
1972	Montgomery Art Center, Claremont, California
	Nova Scotia College of Art and Design, Halifax
	Art and Project, Amsterdam
	Kabinett Für Aktuelle Kunst, Bremerhaven, West Germany
	Utrechten Ring, Utrecht
1973	Stedelijk Van Abbemuseum, Eindhoven, Netherlands
	Galerie Ernst, Hannover
	Wide White Space Gallery, Antwerp
	Wide White Space Gallery, Brussels
	Galerie Waalkens, Finsterwolde, Netherlands
	Grafiek 50 VZW, Wakken, Belgium
	Claire Copley Gallery, Los Angeles
1974	Art and Project, Amsterdam (2 exhibitions)
	Nigel Greenwood Gallery, London
	Stedelijk Museum, Amsterdam
	Palais des Beaux-Arts, Brussels
1975	Museum of Modern Art, New York
	Stedelijk Museum de Lakenhal, Leiden
	Palais des Beaux-Arts, Brussels
	Nigel Greenwood Gallery, London
	Kabinett für Aktuelle Kunst, Bremerhaven, West Germany
1976	Nigel Greenwood Gallery, London
1977	Art and Project, Amsterdam
	Arbeiten von 1969–1977, Badischer Kunstverein, Karlsruhe, West Germany
	Rheinisches Landesmuseum, Bonn
	Kunstverein, Braunschweig, West Germany
1978	Marian Goodman Gallery, New York
	Hansen-Fuller Gallery, San Francisco
1979	Marian Goodman Gallery, New York
	Art and Project, Amsterdam
	Nigel Greenwood Gallery, London
1980	Galleria Lucio Amelio, Naples
	Biennale, Venice
	Kunsthalle, Basle
	Musée d'Art Moderne de la Ville, Paris
	Museum Boymans-van Beuningen, Rotterdam
1981	*Recent Painting and Sculpture and a Selection of Earlier Work,* Fruit Market Gallery, Edinburgh (travelled to Serpentine Gallery, London, and Arnolfini Gallery, Bristol)
1984	Art Institute of Chicago

Selected Group Exhibitions:

1967	*Beelden en Bouwen,* Plan International, Doortwerth, Netherlands
1969	*When Attitudes Become Form,* Kunsthalle, Berne (toured Europe)
1970	*Biennale,* Tokyo
1971	*Prospekt 17,* Kunsthalle, Dusseldorf
1972	*Documenta,* Kassel, West Germany (and 1977)
1976	*Reflektie en Realiteit,* Palais des Beaux-Arts, Brussels (toured Europe)
1977	*Europe in the 70s,* Art Institute of Chicago (toured the United States)
1978	*Fotografie in Nederland 1940–75,* Stedelijk Museum, Amsterdam
1979	*European Dialogue,* at the *Biennale,* Sydney
1980	*Artist and Camera,* Mappin Art Gallery, Sheffield (toured the U.K.)

Collections:

Stedelijk Museum, The Hague; Gemeentemuseum, The Hague; Museum Boymans-van Beuningen, Rotterdam; Stedelijk Van Abbemuseum, Eindhoven, Netherlands; Frans Halsmuseum, Haarlem, Netherlands; Palais des Beaux-Arts, Brussels; Museum van Hedendaagse Kunst, Ghent; Centre Georges Pompidou, Paris; Museum of Modern Art, New York; Tate Gallery, London.

Publications:

By VAN ELK: articles—"Het Eerste (Voorlopige) A-Dynamische Manifest" in *Vrif Nederland* (Amsterdam), December 1961; "Trips voor Verzamelaars" and "Vele Landen Maken Licht Werk" in *Museumjournaal* (Amsterdam), no. 2. 1968; "The Haircut, Big Cut—Big Savings" in *Museumjournaal* (Amsterdam), July 1971; interview, with Ron Kaal, in *Ger Van Elk,* exhibition catalogue, Eindhoven, Netherlands, 1973; interview, with Antje von Graevenitz, in *Ger Van Elk: Arbeiten von 1969–1977,* exhibition catalogue, Karlsruhe, West Germany 1977; films—*The Absorption of a Shadow,* 1969; *The Fluttering Pennon,* 1969; *How Van Elk Inflates His Left Foot with His Right One,* 1969; *Self-Portrait Behind a Wooden Fence,* 1969; *Some Natural Aspects of Painting and Sculpture,* 1971; *La Pièce,* 1971; *The Well-Shaven Cactus in Identifications,* edited by Gerry Schum, 1971; *Videopiece,* 1971; *Short Play with Morandi, Klee and Kandinsky,* 1972.

On VAN ELK: books—*Arte Povera* by Germano Celant, Milan 1969; *Ger Van Elk,* exhibition catalogue, with texts by Jan Leering and Rudi H. Fuchs, Eindhoven, Netherlands, 1973; *Ger Van Elk,* exhibition catalogue, with text by Rudi H. Fuchs, Amsterdam 1974; *The Magic Image: The Genius of Photography from 1839 to the Present Day* by Cecil Beaton and Gail Buckland, London and Boston 1975; *Ger Van Elk: Arbeiten von 1969–1977,* exhibition catalogue, with texts by Rudi H. Fuchs and Michael Schwarz, Karlsruhe, West Germany, 1977; *Fotografie in Nederland 1940–1975,* exhibition catalogue, by Els Barents, Amsterdam 1977; *Ger Van Elk; La Biennale di Venezia 1980,* exhibition catalogue, with texts by Gijs Van Tuyland Wim Beeren, Amsterdam 1980; *Ger Van Elk,* exhibition catalogue, with texts by Suzanne Pagé, Jean-Christophe Ammann, and Wim Beeren, Rotterdam 1980; *Ger Van Elk: Recent Paintings and Sculpture and a Selection of Earlier Work,* exhibition catalogue, with texts by Jean Fisher and others, Edinburgh 1981.

*

In Ger Van Elk's work, perception is arbitrary; he manipulates facts that common sense tells us are self-evident to the perceiver. Fitting the image to an idea, he presents the image and the idea simultaneously, as a dialectical whole no longer divisible. In this way he constructs a representation played on the complexity of individual psychic activity; reality is defined as a dimension internal to the object which can be manifested only through individual subjectivity. Van Elk uses photographic pictures; he manipulates them, paints over them, distorts the dimensions, alters the perspective by shifting the vanishing point of the picture according to mental demands, removes or adds, associates the idea with the shape, deriving a representation which, while it uses techniques characteristic of surrealism (extrapolation of detail, substitutions, removal of elements, presentation of the image out of context), results in an art that is not surrealist, in that the unconscious component is associated with a definite mental planning, full of conscious, often autobiographical, references, which is legitimized through the awareness acquired from the "pre-pictorial" art of the 70's. By means of a "monumental" figuration using "exaggerated" dimensions, which brings out the tension between the opposed elements, the trick of separatism-dualism is presented as a dialectical whole. In this way the photographic image is also reintroduced into the painted picture and amplifies its evocative and allusive capacity. By forcing the lines of reality into a geometrizing figuration, the artist paradoxically geometrizes reality itself to its extreme formal effects. That leads to a situation of friction between sense and nonsense, giving rise to a suggestion of interpretation oriented in the direction of the forces internal to the field taken as the area of operative intervention; just as the artist dismantles the rules of perspective, so the viewer of the work is obliged to dismantle the rules of normal everyday interpretation. Thus we find here, in a behavior pattern area of a reality that he has adopted as internal to his own constitution, new "necessary" aspects that make of his actual "structure" a "polylegible" whole.

—Demetrio Paparoni

VAN KONINGSBRUGGEN, Rob.

Dutch. Born Rudolphus Johannes Philippus van Koningsbruggen, in The Hague, 23 September 1948. Studied at the Koninklijke Academie voor Beeldende Kunsten, The Hague, 1968; Vrije Akademie, The Hague, 1969–70; Ateliers 63, Haarlem, 1970–72. Painter, living and working in Amsterdam, since 1973. Agent: Galerie van Krimpen, Prinsengracht 629, Amsterdam. Address: Louriergracht 166, Amsterdam, Netherlands.

Individual Exhibitions:

1970	Galerie Nouvelles Images, The Hague
1971	Galerie de Mangelgang, Groningen, Netherlands
	Galerie Orez, The Hague
1972	Galerie Swart, Amsterdam
	Haags Gemeentemuseum, The Hague
1973	Galerie Swart, Amsterdam
1974	Galerie Waalkens, Finsterwolde, Netherlands
	Galerie t'Venster, Rotterdam
	Van Abbemuseum, Eindhoven, Netherlands
1975	Galerie Swart, Amsterdam
1976	Galerie Swart, Amsterdam
1977	Galerie Swart, Amsterdam
	Galerie Swart, Amsterdam (with Peter Struycken)
	Galerie Swart, Amsterdam (with John Duff)
1978	Galerie Swart, Amsterdam
1979	Verfindustrie Jac Eyck BV, Heerlen, Netherlands
	Schilderijen/Paintings 1971–78, Stedelijk Museum, Amsterdam
1980	Galerie M, Bochum, West Germany
	Galerie Swart, Amsterdam
1981	Galerie van Krimpen, Amsterdam
1982	Museum Fodor, Amsterdam
	Galerie van Krimpen, Amsterdam
1983	Galerie van Krimpen, Amsterdam
1984	Galerie van Krimpen, Amsterdam
1985	Rijkschuur Acquoy, Amsterdam
	Galerie van Krimpen, Amsterdam
1986	Galerie van Krimpen, Amsterdam
1987	Museum Boymans-van Beuningen, Rotterdam
	Rembrandthuis, Amsterdam

Selected Group Exhibitions:

1973	*Lof der Tekenkunst,* Van Abbemuseum, Eindhoven, Netherlands
1974	*11 Dutch Artists,* Fruit Market Gallery, Edinburgh (travelled to the Aberdeen Art Gallery)
1975	*Dutch Modern Art,* Museum of Modern Art, Ghent
1976	*7 Hollandische Kunstler,* Kunstmuseum, Lucerne
1979	*Gallery Artists,* Galerie Swart, Amsterdam
1980	*Neue Malerei aus den Nederlanden,* Neue Galerie am Landesmuseum Graz, Austria
1983	*Modern Dutch Painting,* National Gallery, Athens
1985	*De Nederlandse Indentiteit in de Kunst na 1945,* Rijksmuseum Vincent Van Gogh, Amsterdam
1987	*Bienal,* Sao Paulo, Brazil

Collections:

Stedelijk Museum, Amsterdam; Haags Gemeentemuseum, The Hague; Museum Boymans-van Beuningen, Rotterdam; Groninger Museum, Groningen, Netherlands; Stedelijk Museum, Schiedam, Netherlands.

Publications:

On VAN KONINGSBRUGGEN: books—*Rob van Koningsbruggen,* exhibition catalogue, The Hague 1972; *Konstruktive Konzepte* by Willy Rotzler, Zurich 1977; *Rob van Koningsbruggen: schilderijen/Painttings 1971–78,* exhibition catalogue, with text by Rini Dippel, Amsterdam 1979; *Rob van Koningsbruggen: Schilderijen en tekening 1979-1987,* exhibition catalogue with text by Erik Beerken, Rotterdam 1987; articles—"Van Koningsbruggen schrift en breit" by Carel Blotkamp in *Vrije Nederland* (Amsterdam), 27 March 1971; "Signalement van Rob van Koningsbruggen" by T. Cruls in *Museumjournaal,* (Amsterdam), vol. 16, no. 4, 1971; "Rob van Koningsbruggen breit zeroistische avon-

turen" by K. Schipper in *Haagse Post* (The Hague), 21 April 1971; "Waarom Rob van Koningsburggen strafregels schreef" by Dolf Welling in *Haagsche Courant* (The Hague), 30 October 1972; "Van Koningsbruggen's debuut als schilder" by Carel Blotkamp in *Vrije Nederland* (Amsterdam), 11 November 1972; "Twee Schilders: Rob van Koningsbruggen, Toon Berhoef" by Carel Blotkamp in *Museumjournaal* (Amsterdam), vol. 24, no. 2 1979; "De modelfunctie van Rob van Koningsbruggen" by Carel Blotkamp in *Museumjournaal* (Amsterdam), no. 6, 1985.

*

Everything can become a mannerism, including my "shoved" paintings. When it has reached a certain point, I stop. I began making "shoved" paintings because the brushwork (in larger and larger works also became mannered. By coincidence, I noticed that my brush itself became a painting, for on the brush was reflected the same features as appeared in the painting—so it was only a small step to use my painting as a brush. Now I have abandoned also those principles. Many of my "shoved" paintings consisted of three parts: yellow, red and blue—and I discovered, that these three primary colours could produce a deep black. Making art is making discoveries—and art in itself must be renewable. So now I am using mixtures of colours—orange, purple and green, and tonal extremes—and allow them to end in black.

—Rob van Koningsbruggen

*

The work of the 23-year old painter Rob Van Koningsbruggen—and the motives behind it—caused something of a sensation in the Netherlands in 1971. Established critics such as Schippers and Blotkamp used his drawings and knitted objects as the point of departure for a debate about the "credibility" of the artist, although that issue had really been in the air for more than twenty years. What matters in Van Koningsbruggen's work is the action involved in painting and not the work as a finished object. The painting itself is simply the residue of an action which is a concentrated and intense as possible. Van Koningsbruggen's paintings from 1972, for example, are composed of raised horizontal streaks of paint as broad as the brush which produced them. There is no room for interpretation here: we are confronted with a simple fact (and in this respect Van Koningsbruggen's work can be compared to that of the Zero-artist, Jan Schoonhoven). Success or failure in the usual

sense of those terms is irrelevant. The artist has no knowledge in advance of how his work will finally look. This tendency is emphasized even more strongly in Van Koningsbruggen's paintings after 1974. Here he uses the stretched canvas itself as a "brush." He applies paint on two canvases, on their sides or in simple geometric figures, such as circles and rectangles, painted on the surfaces; then he rubs the two canvases together for a few seconds. The results are unexpected for the painter himself, who is really no more than a machine which lets the painting create itself. There is a traditional element in Van Koningsbruggen's work, in his use of color. Because he uses only red, yellow, blue and black, he invites comparison with other painters in the mainstream of 20th century Dutch artists. His work demonstrates that pictorial quality involves more than painterly skills; for him what matters is the intelligence of the artist. Even in complex works, the presence—or absence—of this intelligence is something which the viewer can sense immediately.

Van Koningsbruggen's paintings from 1981 onwards differ considerably. He has chosen to work in small scale size, the paintings themselves usually resulting from a series of long work processes. These abstract pieces are, above all, experiments in colorism. In an unconventional (and in no respect systematic) way, verging on the naive, Van Koningsbruggen's goal each time is to achieve harmony anew.

—A. F. Wagemans

van MUNSTER, Jan.

Dutch. Born in Gorinchem, 3 July 1939. Studied at the Academie voor Beeldende Kunsten, Rotterdam, 1955–57; Instituut voor Kunstnijverheid, Amsterdam, 1957–59. Married Geertje de Stigter in 1962; daughter: Anna-Lorene. Independent artist, working with light and sound environments, in Gorinchem, 1960–66, in Rotterdam, 1967–85, and in Renesse, since 1985. Art Instructor, Ateliers 63, Haarlem, 1970–72; Academie voor Beeldende Kunsten, Rotterdam, 1973–74; Koninklijke Academie voor Kunst en

Rob Van Koningsbruggen: *Untitled,* 1987

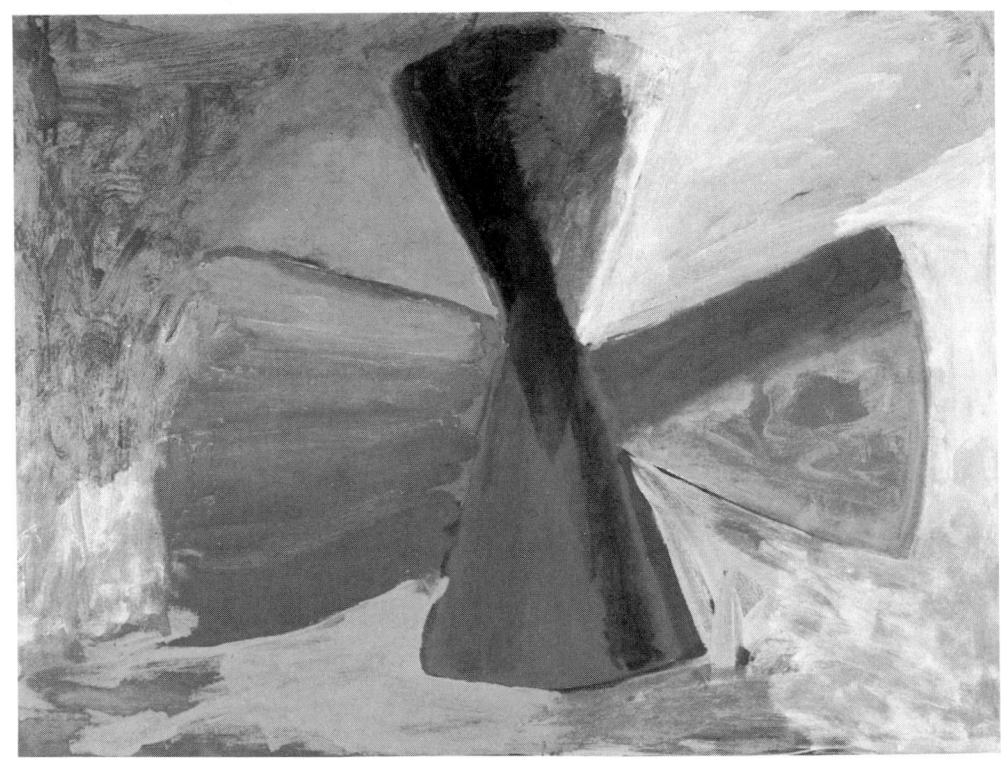

Voormgeving, 's-Hertogenbosch, since 1978. Recipient: A. Schwarz Prize for Sculpture. 1966; Travel Scholarship to London, 1967, Grant, 1969, and Film Bursary, 1973, Ministrie van Cultuur, Recreatie en Mattschappelijk, 1967; Object Prize. Salon van de Maassteden, Schiedam, 1969; Chabot-Prize, Rotterdamse Anjerfonds, 1971. Agents: Galerie Fenna de Vries, Eendrachtplein 18, Rotterdam; and Galerie Orez, Paviljoensgracht 68-70, The Hague. Address: Rampweg 24, 4326 LK Noordwelle (Renesse), Netherlands.

Individual Exhibitions:

1962 't Venster. Rotterdam (with Ad Dekkers)
1963 Galerie de Drie Hendricken, Amsterdam (with Ad Dekkers)
1964 Galerie Punt 31, Dordrecht, Netherlands (with Marinus Boezem)
      Rotterdamse Kunststichting, Rotterdam (with Ad Dekkers)
1965 Galerie C. C. C., Schiedam, Netherlands
      Galerie Garage, Gorcum, Netherlands
      Galerie 845, Amsterdam (with Marinus Boezem)
      Dromedaris, Enkhuizen, Netherlands (with Marinus Boezem)
1966 Rotterdamse Kunstkring, Rotterdam (with Nans Verweij)
      De Jong-Bergers, Maastricht, Netherlands
1967 Galerie Espace, Amsterdam
      Galerie Waalkens, Finsterwolde, Netherlands
      Galerie C. C. C., Vlaardingen, Netherlands
1968 Market 17, Enschede, Netherlands
      Galerie Julicher, Gutzenrather, West Germany
      Galerie Ad Libitum, Antwerp
1969 Galerie C. C. C., Vlaardingen, Netherlands (with Mathieu Ficheroux)
      Galerie Mickery, Loenersloot, Netherlands
      Stedelijk Museum, Amsterdam
      Internationale Galerie Orez, The Hague
1970 Dordrechts Museum, Dordrecht, Netherlands
      Van Abbemuseum, Eindhoven, Netherlands
      Centraal Museum, Utrecht
1971 Galerie Design, Rotterdam
      Galerie Design, Rotterdam (Chabot-Prize exhibition)
1972 Museum Boymans-van Beuningen, Rotterdam (retrospective)
      Galerie Fenna de Vries, Rotterdam
1973 Henie-Onstad Kunstsenter, Hovikodden, Norway (with Pieter Engels and Wim Gijzen)
      Galerie Yaki Kornblit, Amsterdam
1974 Electric Gallery, Toronto
1975 Galerie Fenna de Vries, Rotterdam
1977 Galerie Orez, The Hague
1978 *Jan van Munster/David van de Kop/Wim Gijzen; Recent Werk,* Rijksmuseum Kröller-Muller, Otterlo, Netherlands
1980 Galerie Orez, The Hague
1981 Kunstcentrum Radhuis, Gorinchem, Netherlands
1982 Galerie Orez, The Hague
      Kruithuis, Den Bosch, Netherlands
1983 Galerie Pictura, Dordrecht, Netherlands
1984 Galerie Orez Mobiel, The Hague
1986 Grote Kerk, Goes, Netherlands (installation)
1987 Suzanne Niederberg Galerie, Amsterdam
      Galerie A. Hoffman, Friedberg, West Germany
      Wilhelm-Hack-Museum, Ludwigshafen, West Germany
1988 Galerie A. Hoffmann, Friedberg, West Germany
      Rijksmuseum Kroller-Muller, Otterlo, Netherlands
      Museum Boymans-van Beuningen, Rotterdam

Selected Group Exhibitions:

1963 *Gorkum '63,* Nieuwe Doelen, Gorinchem, Netherlands
1964 *Stichting Nieuw Beelden,* Stedelijk Museum, Amsterdam
1965 *4th Biennale de Paris,* Musée d'Art Moderne de la Ville, Paris (and *8th Biennale,* 1973)
1967 *Science Fiction,* Kunsthalle, Berne

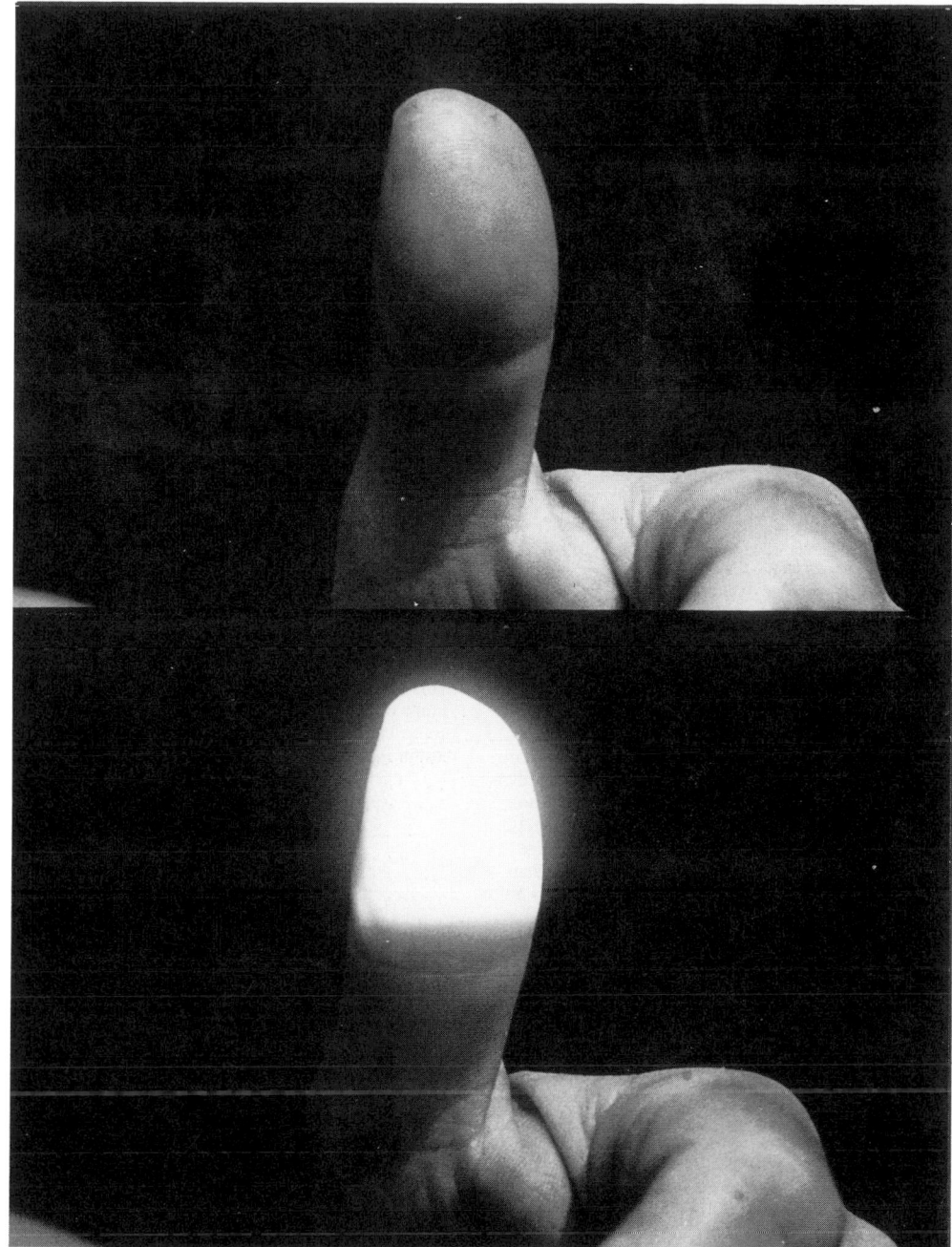

Jan Van Munster: Still from the film *Projection*, 1972

1970 *7 Rotterdam Kunstenaars,* Museum Boymans-van Beuningen Rotterdam
1972 *Van Medicijnman tot Medicus,* Frans Halsmuseum, Haarlem
1978 *Paper for Space,* Stedelijk Museum, Amsterdam
1982 *Beelden op de Berg,* Wageningen Museum, Netherlands
1984 *Kunst aus Rotterdam,* Museum Boymans-van Beuningen, Rotterdam
1986 *Von zwei Quadraten,* Wilhelm-Hack-Museum, Ludwigshafen, West Germany

Collections:

Museum Boymans-van Beuningen, Rotterdam; Stedelijk van Abbemuseum, Eindhoven, Netherlands; Stedelijk Museum, Schiedam, Netherlands; Dordrecht Museum, Dordrecht, Netherlands; Kröller-Müller, Otterlo, Netherlands; Rijks Collectie, The Hague; Stedelijk Museum, Amsterdam; Centre Georges Pompidou, Paris; Caracao Museum, Dutch Antilles.

Publications:

By van MUNSTER: articles—"Kunst Kijkt naar 2000" in *Revue*(Rotterdam), no 6, 1968; "Mijn Mechanische Mens" in *Vrije Geluiden* (Amsterdam), no 17, 1969.

On van MUNSTER: books—*De Exploisive van het Intellect* by Jan Donia, Hilversum, Netherlands 1968; *Jan van Munster,* exhibition catalogue, with text by Liesbeth Brandt-Cortius, Rotterdam 1972; *Jan van Munster,* exhibition catalogue with text by Jo-Anne Birnie Dantzker, Toronto 1974; *Paper for Space,* exhibition catalogue, with text by Gijs van Tuyl, Amsterdam 1978; *Jan van Munster, David van de Kop, Wim Gijzen: Recent Werk,* exhibition catalogue, with text by Paul Hefting, Otterlo, Netherlands 1978; *Kunst aus Rotterdam,* exhibition catalogue by Wim Beeren, Rotterdam 1984; *De eigen ruimte—Beeldhouwkunst in Nederland na 1945* by Paul Hefting, Amsterdam 1986; *Jan Van Munster: Energie Objecten, Zeichnungen, Tekeningen,* exhibition catalogue with essay by Kees Broos, Friedberg 1987; *Jan Van Munster,* 2 vols., with texts by Kees de Boer and Paul Hefting, Utrecht 1988.

I am not concerned just with the visual impression of light, but especially with the fact that it is charged with invisible energy. This involves the mystical side of the object, characterized by a kind of enclosedness. What is enclosed is brought out by a particular way of arranging the elements. This produces a tension, a radiation into space, the light seeming to burst forth. . . . The light must be on, even in the black lights: that is, compressed energy, the charge there is in me, in everyone. The light is there, even if it is not visible, just as lots of things are invisible. My work is not abstract. It is concerned with emotions, with attraction and repulsion. I want to make the tension between me and others visible in the space I am working in.

—Jan van Munster

In the catalogue of Jan van Munster's retrospective exhibition at the Boymans van Beuningen Museum, Rotterdam (1972), Liesbeth Brandt-Cortius described as follows the ways in which van Munster worked with light to produce form and specify space: "In 1972, the objects became visually less important than the shape that, from the object, via the light, is projected onto the ceiling wall and floor. The tangible objects are concentrated into small closed cubes or square poles out of which a single, very simple shape is sawn: the outline of a square with an opening on one side, a zig-zag line or a straight or dotted line. The poles or cubes stand on the floor or hang from the ceiling, and the strong bulb inside projects the sawn-out shapes, much magnified, onto the wall, floor or ceiling. In a dark room one sees first of all the light lines, and only afterwards one sees the source of light and finds the small object. The whole area seems to be dominated by insignificant objects. Each object, with its projection, forms the image." These light projections induced the Algemene Bank Nederland to give Jan van Munster a commission for its new head office building in Amsterdam, located in the Vijzelstraat between Keizersgracht and Prinsengracht. Here he was able to apply light in this form to architecture. The pavement is covered over the whole length of the building. Van Munster has applied his lightlines in this arcade, in the floors, ceiling and along the walls. As a result, some parts are concentrated, others "disappear." New space is created.

The lightlines, arranged in simple geometric patterns, definitely change the actual area in one's perception and experience of it, van Munster says: "I can make crosses, rooms and doorways from lightlines." And in this way he has given the passage under the building a new spatial function with inbuilt lightshapes in the pavement and correspondingly in the ceiling.

The shapes are: an open square, consisting of three self-expanding right angled corners—obstruction; line and dotted line—movement; parallel lines—zebra crossing; steps, seen from the side or tipped-up steps—escort (to an important point, e.g. entrance); square with openings on all sides—room or base; the same as above but in the corner of a passage—doorway; square with openings on two sides—lock; cross with double lines, signals for guiding traffic in different directions; metal benches, split in the middle, from where light shines—lighting. In these neutral geometrical shapes, van Munster has conjured up a form of "environmental design," through which this small area of a city undergoes a real, palpable experience.

Both the formal means and the materials used—the intangible light—guarantee that this experience is not forced upon one. The light suggests space and plasticity: one can follow the suggestion, one can just as easilty ignore it or put it aside, van Munster says: "It remains as a guide; it is like hopscotch, whoever want to . . . plays the game those who don't walk through it."

It is a sort of example—a guide—to a conscious experience of the environment. Nothing is enforced, as so often is the case in mental designs which compelling instruct the users how they must act, by an emphatic use of form, colour and structure.

"Too imposed," says van Munster. He limits himself; he even willingly accepts the effect to the difference between day and night. His shapes are indications; for those who want to see, they change the space from the endlessly long to a series of short distances; the light offers instruction, suggesting a narrowing or widening of the space; it helps to span distances, and helps one to experience part of the space as a room, base, lock, etc. The effect of familiarization—which is already accomplished by the use of light as a spatial and plastic element—is further emphasized by the placing of the lightlines at the same distances from each other as traffic lines on the road (to which everyone is accustomed). The idea is to call to mind plasticity by means of directed light. What van Munster made previously as a sculptor, in wood, stone and plastic, with mass and volume, it now realized with light in an exactly stipulated shape or form.

What he wants to achieve with light is clear in his object "Pressed Light" (1971). This object is of two metal sheets, clamped together, with a source of light between them. The object itself, depending on the space in which it stands, becomes relatively less important, because through the radiated beams of light on the walls the whole area is "influenced." Light as a definer of space in a controlled (dark) area—a distinct sculptor's concept, involving as it does the relationship between interior and exterior form—appears to work excellently in the arcade. In the space of 24 hours the suggested spatial differences are alternately strong or hardly noticed at all. An interaction between natural and artificial concepts maintains the tension in the experience.

—H. J. A. M. van Haaren

VAN VELDE, Bram.

Dutch. Born in Zoeterwoude, near Leiden, 19 October 1895. Apprenticed to Kramer painting and decorating company, The Hague, 1907–14; mainly self-taught in painting, under Kramer's sponsorship, in Munich, 1922–23, and in Worspwede, West Germany, 1923–25. After wife died, lived with Marthe Arnaud (died 1959), 1936–59, and with Madeleine Spierer, 1960–81. Painter: lived in Worpswede, West Germany, 1923–25, where he associated with Lokemar, Vogeler, Modersohn-Becker and other expressionist painters; in Paris, 1925–30; in Corsica, 1930–31; in Paris, 1931–32; in Majorca, 1932–36; in Paris, 1936–58 (ceased painting, 1940–44); in Fox, Haute-Provence, 1958–59; and in Grimaud, near Geneva, 1959–81. Recipient; Painting Prize, Heerlen, 1969; Prix National des Arts et Lettres. Paris, 1973; Prix des Belles Lettres, Geneva, 1975. *Died* (in Grimaud) *28 December 1981.*

Individual Exhibitions:

1945	Galerie Mai, Paris
1948	*Derrière Le Miroir,* Galerie Maeght, Paris
	Kootz Gallery, New York
1952	Galerie Maeght, Paris
1955	Galerie Michael Warren, Paris
1957	Galerie Michael Warren, Paris
1958	Kunsthalle, Berne
1959	Stedelijk Museum, Amsterdam
1960	Galleria Notizie, Turin
1961	Galleria l'Obelisco, Rome
	Galerie Knoedler, Paris
1962	Knoedler Gallery, New York
	Galerie Krugier, Geneva
	Walker Art Center, Minneapolis
	Galleria l'Obelisco, Rome
1964	Knoedler Gallery, New York
1965	San Francisco Museum of Art
	Colorado Springs Fine Art Center

1966	Wallraf-Richartz Museum, Cologne
	Galerie Leonhart, Munich
	Galleri Birch, Copenhagen
	Galerie La Balance/Galerie Stephane Janssen, Brussels
	Museo Civico d'Arte Moderna, Turin
1967	Kunstnernes Hus, Oslo
1968	Galerie Knoedler, Paris
	Paintings 1957–1967. Knoedler Gallery, New York
	Albright-Knox Art Gallery, Buffalo, New York
1969	Galerie Benador, Geneva
	Das Graphische Werk, Kunsthalle, Worpswede, West Germany (toured Europe)
1970	Galerie Stephane Janssen, Brussels
	Musée d'Art Moderne, Paris
1971	Musée Rath, Geneva
	Stedelijk Van Abbemuseum, Eindhoven, Netherlands
	Kunsthalle, Basle
1972	Galerie Stephane Janssen, Brussels
1973	Galerie Collection d'Art, Amsterdam
	Fondation Maeght, St. Paul-de-Vence, France
1974	*Oeuvre Lithographie 1923–1973,* Musée d'Art et d'Histoire, Geneva (toured Switzerland)
1975	Galerie Maeght, Paris
1976	Galerie Maeght, Zurich
1977	Galerie Collection d'art, Amsterdam
	Museum de Lakenhal, Leiden, Netherlands
	Apeldoorn Museum, Netherlands
	Bonnefantenmuseum, Maastricht, Netherlands
	Kunst Forum, Schelderode, Belgium
1978	*Retrospectiva 1908–1978,* Galeria Maeght, Barcelona
	Chapelle de la Charité, Arles, France (travelled to Dordrecht, Netherlands; Randers, Denmark; Bremen and Worpswede, West Germany)
	Galerie Maeght, Paris
1979	Musée Rath, Geneva
1980	Galerie Collection d'Art, Amsterdam
	Galerie Maeght, Paris
1982	*Bram Van Velde: 1895–1981,* Lefebre Gallery, New York
	Lithographies, Galerie de la Seita, Paris
1984	Galerie Maeght Lelong, Paris

Selected Group Exhibitions:

1926	*Salon des Indépendants,* Paris (and regularly thereafter)
1968	*Painting in France 1900–67,* National Gallery of Art, Washington, C.C. (toured the United States)
1953	*Elf Tijdenoten uit Parijs,* Stedelijk Museum, Amsterdam

Collections:

Stedelijk Museum, Amsterdam; Stedelijk Van Abbemuseum, Eindhoven, Netherlands; Centre Georges Pompidou, Paris; Centre National d'Art Contemporain, Paris; Musée d'Art et d'Industrie, St. Etienne, France; Fondation Maeght, St.-Paul-de-Vence, France; Musée Rath, Geneva; Musée d'Art et d'Histoire, Geneva.

Publications:

On VAN VELDE: books—*Bram Van Velde,* exhibition catalogue, with an introduction by Edouard Loeb, Paris 1945; *Derrière Le Miroir; Bram Van Velde,* exhibition catalogue, Paris 1948; *Bilan d'Art Actuel* by Georges Duthuit, Paris 1954; *Bram Van Velde,* exhibition catalogue, with texts by Samuel Beckett and Goerges Duthuit, Paris 1957; *Dictionnaire de la Peinture Abstraite* by Michel Seuphor, Paris 1957; *Bram Van Velde,* exhibition catalogue, with text by Franz Meyer, Berne 1958; *Bram Van Velde* by Samuel Beckett, Georges Duthuit, and Jacques Putman, Paris 1958, New York 1959; *Bram Van Velde,* exhibition catalogue, with text by Samuel Beckett, Amsterdam 1959; *Tendances Contemporains* by Nello Ponente, Geneva 1960; *L'Analyse Photographique d'un Tableau de Bram Van Velde* by Jean Francois Baurel, Paris 1960; *L'Image et l'Instant* by Georges Duthuit, Paris 1961; *Bram van Velde* by Jacques Putman, Turin, Paris, and New York 1961: *Bram Van Velde* by Jacques Putman, Turin, Paris, and New York 1961; *Bram Van Velde,* exhibition catalogue, with text by Umbro Apollonio and Xavier Fourcade, Rome 1962; *Bram Van Velde: Catalogue Raisonné 1907–62*, Turin, Paris and New York 1962; *Bram Van Velde*, exhibition catalogue, with text by Jan van der Marck, New York 1964; *Bram Van Velde*, exhibition catalogue, with text by Franz Meyer, Cologne 1966; *Bram Van Velde*, exhibition catalogue, with texts by Luigi Malle, Franz Meyer, and Jacques Putman, Turin 1966; *Bram Van Velde: Paintings 1957–1967*, exhibition catalogue, with texts by Samuel Beckett and Franz Meyer, New York 1968; *Bram Van Velde: Das Graphische Werk*, exhibition catalogue, with text by Jacques Putman, Worpswede, West Germany 1969; *Bram moi Haas* by Hubert Lucot, Paris 1969; *Bram Van Velde*, exhibition catalogue, with texts by Jean Leymarie and others, Paris 1970; *Bram Van Velde*, exhibition catalogue, with texts by Peter F. Althaus and others, Basle 1971; *Bram Van Velde*, exhibition catalogue, with text by André du Bouchet, St.-Paul-de-Vence, France 1973; *Bram Van Velde*, exhibition catalogue, with text by Jan Leering, Eindhoven, Netherlands 1971; *Bram Van Velde: Oeuvre Lithographie 1923–1973*, exhibition catalogue with text by Rainer Michael Mason, Geneva 1974, as *Bram Van Velde: Les Lithographies 1923–1973*, Paris 1974; *Bram Van Velde: Restrospective 1908–1978*, exhibition catalogue, with text by Antonio Saura, Barcelona 1978; *Bram Van Velde: 1895–1981*, exhibition catalogue, with texts by Samuel Beckett, Georges Duthuit, and Pierre Alechinsky, New York 1982; *Bram Van Velde: Lithographies*, exhibition catalogue, with text by Rainer Michael Mason, Paris 1982; *Bram Van Velde*, exhibition catalogue with preface by Yves Peyre, Paris 1984.

Bram van Velde was already 12 years old at the time of his first confrontation with the World of Art. This came about when, as a boy from a poor Dutch family, he went to work for a firm of decorators. What he saw led him to try his own hand at making pictures, the earliest of which were attempts to register straightforward realism.

It was not until some time later when he left his Zoeterwoude home and moved to Worpswede coming in touch with the works of their artists (Paula Modersohn-Becker, in particular) that the formative period of this artistic development began. At first, paintings by the Expressionists fascinated him, although in his own work he preferred to reach out for the expressionist style while at the same time rejecting the aggressive tendencies and undertones of social change often pre-eminent in the works of these artists he had come to admire. A revolutionary spirit had not as yet become a part of his art make-up.

Bram van Velde's early experiments with his own form of Expressionism signalled the beginning of much that has come to be recognised as his painting style, even if this was like a ship in a storm often tossed hither and thither by forces of circumstance, twists of life pattern and situation conditions that were to impinge upon him and his art in future years.

At the start, Bram van Velde used heavy brush strokes rapidly applied in delineating manner to surround colour areas of bright and luminous character freely established on the canvas, tints which although never haphazard possessed a kind of random liberty. "I have nothing in my pocket," he said, "How shall I look for what I seek?"

Bram van Velde left Worpswede for Paris in 1944. In the French capital he maintained his familiar fashion of painting, except that her contact with Fauvism and Cubism had their effect. From the impacts of both of these he found himself able to insert extra elements into his work, flashes of intensified colour and the introduction of unfamiliar contours, heralding a new and personal association with abstraction. This was a period of great activity for him as a painter.

Eight years later in Mallorca the pace slackened. He was able to relax on the Spanish island. His workload as artist became less exhausting, and he was at liberty to assess everything he had achieved as an artist up to that time, seeking—and finding—a synthesis that combined the essences of his early art experiments in Worpswede with the experiences and their effects that he had acquired in Paris. This contemplative period was brought to an abrupt end with the outbreak of the Spanish Civil War which drove the painter back to Paris. Once back in France, he became involved in the production of a series of huge tempera paintings, finding himself torn away from the amalgam of Worpswede peace and Paris experimentation he felt he had carefully gained during his Spanish sojourn and projected into a temperamental world of pain, anguish, protest and realisation of the physical and psychological emptiness of human sorrow.

The years of World War II for Bram van Velde broke his spirit. As they drew to a close, he felt robbed of all bodily and spiritual energies. He felt incapable of going on painting. Desperately short of food, full of depression, he could not summon up the necessary vigour to put brush to canvas. Mind, imagination, inspiration and the will to create—all seemed lost. It was not until some time later that the first glimmers of what had been his vivid artistic instinct once more reasserted itself. For the artist, it was like the sensation of rebirth. For those who remembered him and his pictures, the products of the new era were a source of amazement.

Suddenly, in the mid-forties, his pictures became resonant with happiness. Plein-d'esprit and rich, seeming kindled with a lurch towards 'abstraction' that had nothing to do with grief, suffering and despair. A key date for this revival and change came in 1945 when Pierre Loeb opened the Galerie 'Mai' and was able to include works by the 50-year-old Bram van Velde in the gallery's first exhibition. Then, in 1948 and 1952, he was exhibited at the Paris Galerie Maeght and received plaudits (written texts) from Samuel Beckett and Georges Duthuit. Throughout this renaissance, the quality of his painting became steadily invigorated. The aggression he had earlier spurned was now pressed into service in an uncompromising fashion fresh zest to joy and tragedy alike.

A grand retrospective of his paintings was organised by Franz Meier at the Berne Kunsthalle in 1958, to be repeated by Willem Sandberg at Amsterdam's Stedelijk Museum a year later. This was followed by exhibitions at the Knoedler galleries in Paris and New York with Knoedler also organising museum exhibitions for him in Minneapolis, San Francisco and Colorado Springs. Bram van Velde had acquired his international reputation as an artist of consequence, and this assessment of his qualities continued to confirm itself and was sustained in Cologne, Turin and Oslo, and so on . . . and so on . . .

In 1969, Bram van Velde from a pinacle of success could still write: "My life does not hang from any doctrine or theory. Life itself must provide my home"

—Sheldon Williams

VASARELY, Victor.

French. Born in Pecs, Hungary, 9 April 1908; emigrated to France 1930: naturalized, 1959. Educated at State School, Budapest, until 1925; studied at the Academy of Painting, Budapest, 1925–27, and at the Bauhaus School, Budapest, 1929–30. Married Claire Spinner in 1930; sons: André and Jean-Pierre (Yvaral). Worked as a graphic artist, Agence Havas, Paris, and Editions Draeger Freres, Montrouge, 1930–39. Independent graphic artist, since 1930: produced first paintings, 1944; first architectural integrations, from 1954; Yellow Manifesto, Kinetic works, films and writings, from 1955; inauguration of Vasarely Didactic Museum, Gordes Chateau, Vaucluse, 1970; Vasarely Foundation, Aix-en-Provence, 1971; Vasarely Museum, Pecs, Hungary, 1976; Vasarely Center, New York, 1978; Centre Vasarely, Oslo, 1982. Recipient: Gold Medal, *International Biennale of Graphics*, Fredrikstad, Norway, 1974; Plastic Arts Medal, Académie d'Architecture, Paris, 1975; André Bello Grand Sash of Honor, Caracas, 1977; Der Kaiserring Art Prize, Goslar, 1978; Certificate of Distinction, New York University, 1978; Medal of the Order of the Flag of the Republic, Budapest, 1978; Gold Centenary Medal, Bruckmann Verlag, Munich, 1978. D.H.: Cleveland State University, 1977. Honorary Corresponding Member, Institute of Nuclear Engineers, London. 1977; Honorary President, France-Hungary Association, 1977. Member, 1965, and Officier, 1985, Ordre des Arts et des Lettres, France; Chevalier, 1970, and Officier, 1981, Legion d'Honneur, France; Officier, 1978, and Commandeur, 1984, Ordre du Merite, France; Officier du Merite Culturel, Monaco, 1980. Address: "Les Devens", 84220 Gordes, France.

Individual Exhibitions:

1930	Kovacs Akos Gallery, Budapest
1933	Ernst Museum, Budapest
1944	Galerie Denise René, Paris
1946	Galerie Denise René, Paris
1949	Galerie Denise René, Paris
1950	Arne Bruun Rasmussen Gallery, Copenhagen
1952	Galerie Denise René, Paris
	Samlaren Gallery, Stockholm
1954	Palais des Beaux-Arts, Brussels
	A.P.I.A.W., Liège, Belgium
1955	Galerie Denise René, Paris
1956	Blanche Gallery, Stockholm
	Galerie der Spiegel, Cologne
1958	Rose Fried Gallery, New York
	Galleria del Grattacielo, Milan
	Museo de Bellas Artes, Buenos Aires
	Museum of Modern Art, Montevideo
1959	Galerie der Spiegel, Cologne
	Galerie Denise René, Paris
	Museum of Fine Arts, Caracas
1960	Galerie Denise René, Paris
	Palais des Beaux-Arts, Brussels
1961	Galerie der Spiegel, Cologne
	Galleria Lorenzelli, Milan
	Galerie Le Point Cardinal, Paris
	Artek Gallery, Helsinki
	World House Galleries, New York
	Hanover Gallery, London
1962	Galerie Le Point Cardinal, Paris
	Artek Gallery, Helsinki
	Kaare Bernsten Gallery, Oslo
	Pace Gallery, Boston
1963	Taft Museum, Cincinnati
	Musée des Arts Décoratifs, Paris
	Kunstkabinett Klihm, Munich
	Kestner-Gesellschaft, Hannover
1964	Académie des Beaux-Arts, Paris
	Kunsthalle, Dusseldorf
	Pace Gallery, New York
	Galerie Le Point Cardinal, Paris
	Kunsthalle, Berne
	Hybler Gallery, Copenhagen
	Brook Street Gallery, London
	Haus am Waldsee, Berlin
	Gemeentemuseum, The Hague
	Galerie Renée Ziegler, Zurich
1965	Hanover Gallery, London
	Galleria Deposito, Genoa
	Galerie Handschin, Basle
	Galerie Müller, Stuttgart
	Pace Gallery, New York
1966	Sidney Janis Gallery, New York
	Hayden Gallery, Massachusetts Institute of Technology, Cambridge
	Brook Street Gallery, London
	Overbeck-Gesellschaft, Lübeck
	Gallery D, Prague
	Galerie Denise René, Paris
	Aura Krognoshuset, Lund, Sweden
	l'Armitiere, Rouen
	Galerie Aktuell, Berne
	Galerie der Spiegel, Cologne
1967	Musée des Arts Décoratifs, Paris
	De Cordova Museum, Lincoln, Massachusetts (graphics retrospective; toured the United States)
	Muzeum V, Moste, Czechoslovakia
	Gallery D, Prague
	Stedelijk Museum, Amsterdam
	Galerie Hans Meyer, Esslingen, West Germany
1968	Sidney Janis Gallery, New York
	Galerie Pryzmat, Cracow

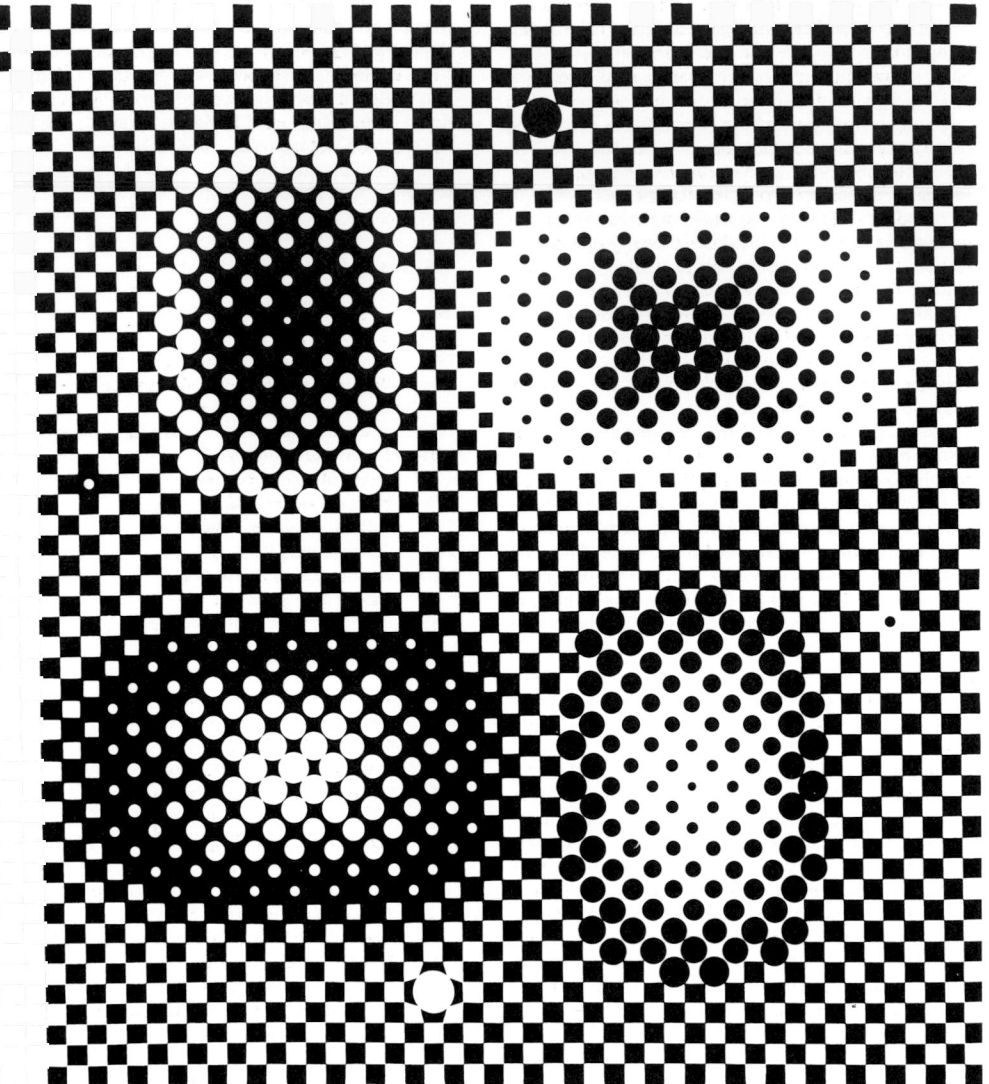

Victor Vasarely: *Metagalaxy*, **1961**

Galerija Suvremene, Zagreb
Galleria del Leone, Venice
Galerie Claude Nouel, Rouen
1969 Centre de Culture, Neuchâtel, Switzerland
Galeria Rene Metras, Barcelona
Gimpel and Hanover Galerie, Zurich
Museum of Fine Arts, Pecs, Hungary
Galerie Engelberts, Geneva
Galerie Les Contards, Lacost, France
Galerie Denise René, Paris
Palace of Fine Arts, Budapest
French Institute, Budapest
1970 Galerie Veranneman, Brussels
Hungarian Institute, Paris
Knoll International, Paris
Barney Weinger Gallery, New York
Musée d'Art Moderne de la Ville, Paris (films on Vasarely)
Vision Nouvelle, Paris
1971 Galerie Suzanne Egloff, Basle
Galerie Denise René, Paris
Stratford Art Association, Ontario
Kunsthalle, Cologne
Chateau de Vacoeuil, France
Galerie Hans Mayer, Dusseldorf
Galerie Veranneman, Brussels
Minami Gallery, Tokyo
Zellweger Building, Zurich
1972 Glenbow Albert Art Gallery, Calgary (retrospective; toured Canada)
Galerie Municipale Marie-Therese Douet, Montreuil, France (toured France)
Sidney Janis Gallery, New York
Denise René Gallery, New York

Galerie Argos, Nantes, France
Galerie Charles Kriwin, Brussels
Galerie Maurel, Nimes, France
Philadelphia Museum of Art
Museum of Ludwigshafen-am-Rhein, West Germany (toured Germany, Switzerland and the Netherlands)
Galerie Formes Nouvelles, Lyons
Galerie Semiha Huber, Zurich
Galerie Schöttenring, Vienna
1973 Gallery Moos, Toronto
Galerie Veranneman, Brussels
Galerie Philippe Reichenbach, Paris
Galerie Gulliver, Paris
Ateliers d'Art Plastiques, Dieppe, France
Musée de Meaux, France
Galerie Denise René Rive Gauche, Paris
Galerie Denise René Rive Droite, Paris (retrospective)
Galerie des Arcades, Biot, France
Galerie Moser, Graz, Austria
Museo de Arte Mderno, Mexico City
1974 Goodman Gallery, Johannesburg
Galerie Semiha Huber, Zurich
Galleria Annunciata, Milan
Minami Gallery, Tokyo
French Embassy, Dakar, Senegal
Heller Gallery, London
Galerie M-L Jeanneret, Geneva
Groupe Manouchian Sports Complex, Aubervilliers, France
Tour des Echevins, Luxeuil-les-Bains, France
L'Abbaye de Gard, Acquigny, France
Galleria La Borgogna, Rome

1975 Casino-Kursaal, Ostend, Belgium
Sala della Cultura, Modena, Italy
Chateau de Cujan, Cher, France
Galeria Theo, Madrid
Galerie Bel'Art, Stockholm
Musée du Bastion Saint-André, Ramparts d'Antibes, France
Teheran Gallery, Teheran
1976 Tel-Aviv Museum
Kunstmuseum, Dusseldorf
Galerie Denise René Rive Gauche, Paris
1977 Musée Postal, Paris
Kulturforum, Bonn
Galerie des Arcades, Biot, France
Galerie Mathilde, Amsterdam
Galerie Bel'Art, Stockholm
French Institute, Stockholm
Galerie Nordenhake, Malmo, Sweden
Museo de Arte Contemporaneo, Caracas
1978 Vasarely Center, New York (opening exhibition)
Modern Art Museum, Mönchengladbach, West Germany
Städtisches Museum, Goslar, West Germany
Hilliard Collection, Munich
Centre Culturel Jacques Prévert, Villeparisis (with Yvaral)
Galerie Inard, Paris
Vasarely Center, New York
Palm Springs Desert Museum, California
1979 Phoenix Art Museum, Arizona
Chateau de Rocheshouart, Limousin, France
Centre Culturel, Villeparisis, France (with Yvaral)
Fondation Vasarely, Aix-en-Provence
Chateau de Sedieres, Correze, France
1980 Fondation Vasarely, Aix-en-Provence
Fundacao Gulbenkian, Lisbon
Konsthalle, Malmo, Sweden
Galleri Homansbyen, Oslo
Galerie Holtman, Hannover
Junior Galerie, Vienna
Chateau-de-Val, Bort-les-Orgues, France
Galleria Planetario, Trieste
Ecole des Ingenieurs, Bienne, Switzerland
Young Gallery, San Jose, California
Reading Public Museum, Pennsylvania
Nanteshi Gallery, Tokyo
1981 Royal Palace Gallery, Budapest
Badisches Landesmuseum, Karlsruhe
Jazz Academy, Budapest (toured Hungary)
Midland Center of the Arts, Michigan
Hotel de Ville, Montelimar, France
Chateau de Vassiviere, Creuse, France
1982 Vasarely Center, New York
Musee des Beaux-Arts, Chateauroux, France
Centre Vasarely, Oslo
Galeria Freites, Caracas, Venezuela
Hotel de Ville, Lucerne, Switzerland
1983 Vasarely Center, New York
Societe Hongroise de Secours Mutuel, Paris
Aktion Museum, Mistelbach, Austria
Galerie des Arcades de Blot, Alpes Maritimes, France (with Yvaral)
Museum of Karcag, Hungary
Centre Vasarely, Museum of Fine Arts, Budapest
Vasarely Center, New York
1984 Hotel de Ville, Villeurbanne, France (retrospective)
Musee de Tauroentum, St. Cyr sur Mer, France
Town Hall, Leinfelden, West Germany
Artcurial, Munich (travelled to Dusseldorf)
1985 Palais des Papes, Avignon, France
Institut Francais, Budapest
Galeria S. Dubrownik, Smobor, Yugoslavia
Hotel de Ville, Villeurbanne, France
Espace Jacques Prevert, Aulnay-sous-Bois, France
Chapelle Belloin, France
Galerie du Quesne, Castillon du Gard, France
1986 Galerie der Stadt Esslingen, Neckar, West Germany
Maison de la Lithographie, Paris
Musee National des Beaux-Arts, Algiers
Kunstkreis Sudliche Vergstrasse, Kraichgau, West Germany
Alliance Francaise, Bangkok
Heimatmuseum, Gablitzhalle, Austria
Espace Belleville, France

Galerie Schemes, Lille, France
Maison Alexandre Dumas, Marly-le-Roi, France
Abbaye St. Germain, Auxerre, France
Galerie Lahumiere, Paris

Selected Group Exhibitions:

1929	*Muhely*, Museum of Applied Arts, Budapest
1947	*1st Salon des Realities Nouvelles*, Musee d'Art Moderne, Paris
1949	*Abstract Painting*, Betty Parsons' Gallery, New York
1953	*Younger European Painters*, Guggenheim Museum, New York
1958	*50 Years of Modern Art*, at *Exposition Internationale (World's Fair)*, Brussels
1961	*Le Mouvement*, Stedelijk Museum, Amsterdam
1964	*Painting and Sculpture of a Decade 1954–64*, Tate Gallery, London
1967	*Dada 1916–66*, Galleria Nazionale d'Arte Moderna, Rome
1970	*Collections Etzold*, Kolnischer Kunstverein, Cologne
1973	*The Non-Objective World 1914–55*, Annely Juda Fine Art, London (travelled to Austin, Texas)

Collections:

Centre Georges Pompidou, Paris; Tate Gallery, London; Stedelijk Museum, Amsterdam: Musée des Beaux-Arts, Brussels; Nationalgalerie, West Berlin; Israel Museum, Jerusalem; Power Gallery of Contemporary Art, Sydney; Musée d'Art Contemporain, Montreal: Museum of Modern Art, New York; Art Institute of Chicago.

Documentation of Vasarely's life and work is principally housed at the Fondation Vasarely, Aix-en-Provence: the Musée Vasarely, Vaucluse, France; the Vasarely Museum, Pecs; and the Vasarely Center, New York.

Publications:

By VASARELY: books and pamphlets—*La Forme-Couleur integrée dans la Cité par la Technique des Revetements Muraux*, Paris 1959; *Kassak-Vasarely* album of serigraphs, with an introduction by Denise René and Jean Cassou, Paris 1961; *Vasarely: Morphemes*, album of engravings with text by Imre Pan, Paris 1966; *Notes, Reflexions de Vasarely*, Paris 1964; *The Notebook of Vasarely*, Oxford 1964; *Discours de la Methode de Descartes accompagne du Discours de la Methode de Vasarely*, with a preface by Otto Hahn, Paris 1969; *Plasti-Cité*, edited by Michel Ragon, Paris 1970; *Victor-Vasarely—Notes brutes*, with a foreword by Bruno Alfiere, Venice 1970; *Folklore Planetaire—Farbwelt*, Munich 1973; *Réponses á Vasarely*, Munich and Paris 1974; *Vasarely Inconnu*, Neuchátel, Switzerland 1977; *Victor Vasarely Faabstadt/City Polychrome*, with a commentary by Eugen Gomringer, Munich 1977; *Vasarely*, Paris 1978; *Reflets*, portfolio of 4 prints, with poems by Maurice Bruzeau Paris 1979; *Vasarely Plasticien*, with William Desmond, Paris 1979; *Gea*, Paris 1982.

On VASARELY: books—*Vasarely* by Dewasne, Paris 1952; *Vasarely*, exhibition catalogue with text by Carlo Belloli, Milan 1961; *Victor Vasarely*, exhibition catalogue, with text by Wieland Schmied, Hannover 1963; *Arts Plastiques du 20e. Siecle: Vasarely*, Neuchatel, Switzerland 1965; *Vasarely* by Werner Spies, Stuttgart 1969; *Vasarely*, exhibition catalogue, with a preface by M. E. Rosta, Budapest 1969; *Vasarely II*, Neuchatel, Switzerland 1970; *Vasarely Analysen* by Axel Bruck, Hamburg 1970; *Victor Vasarely* by Werner Spies, Paris, Cologne and New York 1971; *Gesprache mit Victor Vasarely* by Jean Louis Ferrier, Cologne 1971; *Vasarely*, exhibition catalogue, with a preface by Helmut R. Leppien, Cologne 1971; *Victor Vasarely*, exhibition catalogue, with a preface by Manfred Fath, Ludwigshafen, West Germany 1972; *Ateliers Aujourd hui: Vasarely* by Marc Hallain, Paris 1973; *J'Apprends à Peindre avec Vasarely*, Paris 1973; *Arts Plastiques du 20e. Siecle: Vasarely III*, with a preface by Marcel Joray, Neuchatel, Switzerland 1974; *Vasarely* by Marcel Joray, Neuchatel, Switzerland 1976; *Le Musée Imaginaire de Vasarely*, with a foreword by Otto Hahn, Paris 1978; *Vasarely 4*, Neuchatel, Switzerland 1979; *Vasarely, Connaissance d'un Art Moleculaire* by Bernard Dahhan, Paris 1979; *Colorier avec Vasarely*, Paris 1980.

From 1930 when he moved to Paris from Budapest, Victor Vasarely followed a course that, while it initially did not renounce realistic elements, always activated the painting surface to create its own illusions of space proper to itself, and finally to nothing beyond the confines of the picture frame. His employment as a commercial artist went hand in glove with a technical proficiency that became more and more self-centered. An early work of his pre-war period—"Chessboard" (1935)—is a forerunner of his development. It shows strength in conveying illusions of space where the surface seems to buckle and corrugate as the wavy lines swell and contract in width. His method of painting then was meticulous in its definition of form reflecting the ambivalence of Orphism and to a degree Surrealism.

In the 1940's following his first one-man show in Paris, Vasarely committed himself to a programmed system of picture making based on geometrical modules and variations in colours that went through permutations of considerable complexity. Organic forms of circles, squares, ellipses and rectangles were arranged in compositions of ordered movement and ambiguities in which colours and tonal balances set up visual tensions of alternately harmonious and disturbing elements. This calculated adjustment of solid and transparency of warm and cold hues, of stepping and breaking of linear direction was achieved with a disposition of effect harking back to the Bauhaus principles of sheer outline and immaculate profile in space, eschewing the serif and the decorative as unnecessary in terms of architectonic logic.

"Orion MC" (1963) is a typical example of Vasarely's concept. The rectangle offers a highly charged checkerboard design composed of 420 squares containing circles of different sizes alternating with ellipses also varied in size and placed on different axes relating to the picture edge. The whole picture presents a quivering screen of light intensity established by the tonal strength and juxtaposition of subtly animated areas. Nothing Vasarely does is uncomposed. In his refinement of mosaical permutations he has evolved striking effects from shades of five different colours placed in four different zones adjacent to each other. In 1959 he patented a system of "plastic unity" where he put together collages from single elements: round, oval, square, rhomboid and triangular, cut out from squares of distinctive colours and alternating them on squares of different grounds. This limitless potential and its versatility has lent itself to kinetic exploitation as well as in architectural projects as sculptures both freestanding and in relief.

Acknowledged as the originator of post-war Op Art, Vasarely had a noticeable influence on such artists as Bridget Riley without relinquishing his own authority in constructive geometric abstraction. His own belief that he had formulated a new urban folklore through a multiplicity of prototypes mechanically permutated was justified perhaps in its maturity, but its very consistency imposed an inevitable diminution in returns of aesthetic satisfaction.

—G. S. Whittet

VAUGHAN, Keith.
British. Born in Selsey Bill, Sussex, in 1912; moved with his family to London, 1916. Early education in Sussex; self-taught in art. Served as clerk and German interpreter, in the British Army, Wiltshire and Yorkshire, 1941–46. Painter: worked for Lintas Advertising Agency, while painting in his spare time, London, 1931–38; shared house with painter John Minton, St. John's Wood, London, 1946; worked on book and magazine illustrations, 1946; visited France and Italy, 1948–52; commissioned to paint mural for the Dome of Discovery, *Festival of Britain*, London, 1951; worked in studio in Hampstead, London, from 1952; spent holidays and weekends in his cottage in

Essex from 1965. Part-time Lecturer, Camberwell School of Art, London, 1946–48; Lecturer, Slade School of Fine Art, London 1959; Resident Painter, State University of Iowa, Iowa City, 1959. Honorary Fellow, Royal College of Art, 1964. C.B.E. (companion, Order of the British Empire), 1965. *Died (by suicide; in London) 4 November 1977.*

Individual Exhibitions:

1944	Reid and Lefevre Gallery, London
1946	Reid and Lefevre Gallery, London
1948	George Dix Gallery, New York
	Reid and Lefevre Gallery, London
1950	instituto de Arte Moderno, Paraguay
	Museo D'Arte Moderno, Buenos Aires
	Redfern Gallery, London
1951	Reid and Lefevre Gallery, London
1952	Hanover Gallery, London
	Reid and Lefevre Gallery, London
	Redfern Gallery, London
	Durlacher Brothers, New York
1953	Leicester Galleries, London
1955	Durlacher Brothers, New York
	Leicester Galleries, London
1956	Hatton Gallery, Newcastle upon Tyne
	Leicester Galleries, London
1957	Durlacher Brothers, New York
1958	Leicester Galleries, London
	West of England Academy, Bristol
1959	Leicester Galleries, London
	University of Iowa, Iowa City
1960	Bear Lane Gallery, Oxford
	Matthiesen Gallery, London
1962	Whitechapel Art Gallery, London (toured the U.K.)
	Matthiesen Gallery, London
1964	Marlborough Fine Art Gallery, London
1965	Bear Lane Gallery, Oxford
	Marlborough Fine Art Gallery, London
1966	Redfern Gallery, London
	Durlacher Brothers, New York
	Hambledon Gallery, Blandford, Dorset
1967	Tib Lane Gallery, Manchester
1968	Rex Evans Gallery, Los Angeles
	Marlborough Fine Art Gallery, London
1969	Mappin Gallery, Sheffield
	Hamet Gallery, London
	Tib Lane Gallery, Manchester
1970	Bear Lane Gallery, Oxford
	Hamet Gallery, London
	University of York
1971	Hambledon Gallery, Blandford, Dorset
	Park Square Gallery, Leeds
1973	Waddington Galleries, London
1974	Victor Waddington, London
1976	Compass Gallery, Glasgow
1977	Mappin Gallery, Sheffield
1979	Penwith Galleries, St. Ives, Cornwall (with Tony O'Malley)
1981	*Images of Man*, Geffrey Museum, London (travelled to City Museum and Art Gallery, Birmingham)
1985	Agnew Gallery, London
1987	Austin/Desmond Fine Art, Sunninghill, Berkshire
	New Grafton Gallery, London

Selected Group Exhibitions:

1943	*War Artists Exhibition*, National Gallery, London
1948	*Contemporary British Painting*, Belgrade
1950	*contemporary British Painting*, Pennsylvania Academy of Fine Arts, Philadelphia
1951	*21 Modern British Painters*, Vancouver Art Gallery
1953	*International Water-Color Exhibition*, Brooklyn Museum, New York
1960	*Guggenheim International Award Exhibition*, Guggenheim Museum, New York
1963	*Bienal*, Sao Paulo

Collections:

Tate Gallery London; Tel Aviv Museum; Calouste

Gulbenkian Foundation, Lisbon; Albright-Knox Art Gallery, Buffalo, New York; Wadsworth Atheneum, Hartford, Connecticut; Phillips Collection, Washington, D.C.; National Gallery of South Australia, Adelaide; National Gallery of New South Wales, Sydney; National Gallery of Victoria, Melbourne; Auckland Museum, New Zealand.

Publications:

By VAUGHAN: book—*Journals and Drawings 1939–1965*, London 1966; book illustrated—*Une Saison en Enfer* by Arthur Rimbaud; articles—foreword to *Keith Vaughan*, exhibition catalogue, London 1944; "Notes on Painting: August 1964," in *London Magazine*, October 1964; interview in *Conversations with Painters* by Noel Barber, London 1964.

On VAUGHAN: books—*The Changing Forms of Art* by Patrick Heron, London 1955; *Keith Vaughan*, exhibition catalogue, by David Thompson, London 1962; *Keith Vaughan: Images of Man*, exhibition catalogue, by John Nicholas Ball, London 1981; *Keith Vaughan: Paintings, Gouaches, Watercolours and Drawings 1936–1976*, exhibition catalogue with text by Robert Buhler, Sunninghill 1987; articles—"Keith Vaughan" by Benedict Nicolson in *The Observer* (London), 28 February 1960; "Keith Vaughan" by Bryan Robertson in *Studio International* (London), November 1964; "Keith Vaughan" by Anthony Carter in *Studio International* (London), January 1969; "Keith Vaughan" by Alan Ross in *London Magazine*, February 1978; "Trial of an Outsider" by C. Neve in *Country Life* (London), June 1981.

*   *   *

When major artists are "ahead of their time," they seem to carry their times along with them. Keith Vaughan felt at odds with his times; yet had he lived only a few years longer, the more open art scene and style of living would surely have provided a more sympathetic environment for his art, and "rediscovered" him with a major retrospective.

Self-taught while working during the 1930's in an advertising agency, and interested in ballet and photography, he illustrated his notable journal (1939–1977) during the 1939–1945 war with evocative but non-violent drawings and gouaches of soldiers off-duty; published in part in *London Magazine*, this led him to meet "neo-romantic" artists such as Sutherland, Craxton and Minton. Around 1952, De Stael's flattened and abstracted forms became an influence; around 1959, with his teaching visit to the United States, he created paintings that were even more abstracted, though their harlequin lozenges of colour scattered in space never quite lost a human presence.

But really—with the examples of Cézanne's, Matisse's and Picasso's bathers and acrobats foremost, particularly Matisse's—Vaughan's prime interest was always his own resolution of that classical Greek preoccupation, the young male body as of man's birthright, power, innate harmony and aspiration—a theme dormant in art of the time, or awkwardly described as "figures in landscape," yet parallel to ballet's basic language of lyrical repose, graceful movement, significant gesture, tensions, heroism and nobility. Realism, nostalgia for remembered times of beaches and bathing before the war with companions now dead, the resolution of his own tensions in society, and the vision of an ideal, Arcadian world, all add to the emotions of these paintings, whose technical search might be described as the monumental expression of a lyrical human line in the freest space.

It could be said that Vaughan paints like a dancer and a choreographer (indeed, as they themselves might like to paint); and that would indicate the wide range of mood, gesture, expression and theme inherent in Vaughan's work beyond its lyrical physicality. In retrospect, Vaughan's courage in maintaining his artistic interests at an unsympathetic time should be praised (and he was well aware of that difficult area between eroticism and beauty too); he would have suited large public commissions, major book illustration commissions, and theatrical design. But what he describes in his eloquent, intelligent *Journal* as the ". . . constant baffling mystery—the duality of I and myself . . ." indicates the strength and enduring validity of his beautiful and memorable paintings.

—Michael Shepherd

VAUTIER, Ben.

Swiss. Born of a Swiss-French father and Irish mother in Naples, 18 July 1935. Educated in Turkey, Egypt, and Greece until 1949; mainly self-taught in art. Married Annie Baricolla in 1964; children: Eva and Francois. Independent artist in Nice since the mid-1950's; began actions and happenings and established gallery, Laboratoire 32 (32 rue Tondutti-de-l'Escarène), later re-named Galerie Ben Doute de Tout, Nice, 1958; associated with Fluxus artists in Paris and Cologne, 1962–70; established Galerie Fenetre, Nice, 1971, and Galerie La Difference, Nice, in late 1970's. Recipient: D.A.A.D. scholarship to West Berlin, 1978. Agents: Galerie Daniel Templon, 30 rue Beaubourg, 75003 Paris; Galerie Bischofberger, Buhlstrasse 7, 8700 Kussnacht, Switzerland. Address: 103 Route de Saint-Pancrace, 06100 Nice, France.

Individual Exhibitions:

1960	Laboratoire 32, Nice
1964	Amstell 47, Amsterdam
1966	La Cédille Qui Sourit, Villefranche-sur-Mer, France
1970	Galerie de la Salle, Vence, France
	Galerie Yellow Now, Brussels
	Galerie Daniel Templon, Paris
	Galerie Hans Mayer, Dusseldorf
	Galerie René Block, West Berlin
	Galleria Artestudio, Macerata, Italy
1971	Galleria Sant'Andrea, Milan
	Galleria Il Punto, Turin
	Galerie Daniel Templon, Paris
	Galerie Bischofberger, Zurich
1972	Galerie Günter Sachs, Hamburg
	Galleria Lia Rumma, Naples
	Galerie Grafikmeyer, Karlsruhe, West Germany
	Galerie Daniel Templon, Paris
1973	International Cultureel Centrum, Antwerp
	Galerie Daniel Templon, Paris
	Art=Ben, Stedelijk Museum, Amsterdam
	Galerie Rudolf Zwirner, Cologne
	Galleria La Bertesca, Milan
	Neue Galerie, Aachen, West Germany
1974	Galeria Foksal, Warsaw
	Galerie Yellow Now, Liège, Belgium
	Neue Galerie, Aachen, West Germany
	Galerie Le Flux, Perpignan, France
1975	Galleria dei Mille, Bergamo, Italy
	Studio F22, Palazzolo. Italy
	Centro d'Informazione Alternativa, Rome
	John Gibson Gallery, New York
1976	Galerie HM, Brussels
	Kunsthandel Brinkman, Amsterdam
1977	Galleria l'Uomo e l'Arte, Brescia, Italy
	Galerie Baudoin Lebon, Paris
1978	Galleria Rinaldo Rotta, Genoa
	Galerie Ecart, Geneva
1979	Galleri Léger, Malmo, Sweden
	Berlin Inventory, DAAD-Galerie, West Berlin
1980	Musée d'Art Contemporain, Montreal
1981	*Ben Libre*. Musée d'Art et d'Industrie. St.-Etienne, France
	Galerie Daniel Templon, Paris
	Photos chez Stenope, Nice
	Galerie Ecart, Geneva
1981	Galerie Catherine Issert, St. Paul de Vence, France
	Galerie Grimaldi, Aix-en-Provence, France
	Musee d'Art et d'Industrie, St. Etienne, France
	Galerie Errata, Montpellier, France
1983	Galerie Beaubourg, Paris
	Galerie La Hune, Paris
	Galerie Donguy, Paris
	Galerie Chantal Crousel, Paris
	Galerie Durand-Dessert, Paris
	Galerie Mollet Vieiville, Paris
	Galerie Avant Premiere, Paris
	Galerie Templon, Paris
	Galerie Fournier, Paris
	Galerie Lara Vincy, Paris
	Galerie Creatis, Paris
	Galerie Durand, Paris
	Galerie Nez en l'Air, Nice
	Galerie Catherine Issert, St. Paul de Vence, France
1984	Galerie Jollenbeck, Cologne
	Galerie Ecart, Geneva
	Galerie R.Z.A., Dusseldorf
	Galerie Baudoin Lebon at *FIAC 84*, Grand Palais, Paris
1985	Galerie Baudoin Lebon, Paris
	Galerie Bilinelli, Brussels
	Galerie d'Art Contemporain, Nice
	Stadtgalerie, Erlangen, West Germany
1986	Museum Ingelstad, Sweden
	Sala Parpallo, Valencia, Spain
	Galerie Leger, Malmo, Sweden
	Galerie Daniel Templon, Paris
	Galerie Semiha Huber, Geneva
	Galerie Catherine Issert, St. Paul de Vence, France
	Maison des artistes, Genas (Lyon), France
	Galerie Schuppenhauer, Essen, West Germany
1987	Galerie Camomille, Brussels
	Musee de Calais, France
	Musee de Ceret, France
	Centre Regional d'Art Contemporain, Lebege, France

Selected Group Exhibitions:

1962	*Festival of Misfits*, Gallery One, London
1967	*Ecole de Nice*, Galerie de la Salle, Vence, France
1970	*Happening and Fluxus*, Kunstverein, Cologne
1973	*Contemporanea*, Parcheggio Villa Borghese, Rome
1977	*A Propos de Nice*, Centre Georges Pompidou, Paris
1979	*Fluxus*, Espace Lyonnais d'Art Contemporain, Lyons (toured Europe)
1982	*Art Vivant 60/80*, Stedelijk Museum, Amsterdam
1984	*L'Ecriture dans la Peinture*, Centre Nicois des Arts Plastiques, Nice
1987	*Berlinart 1961–87*, Museum of Modern Art, New York (travelled to San Francisco)

Publications:

By BEN: books and pamphlets—*L'Esthetique de Ben*, Nice 1960; *Programme de 7 Jours de Recherche*, Nice 1964; *Tout Programme Publik*, Nice 1965; *Tout Cedille Qui Sourit*, Nice 1966; *Galerie Ben Doute de Tout Presente*, Nice 1966; *Ben Dieu (L'Art C'est les Autres)*, Nice 1966; *Propositions pour un Livre et pour des Objets Divers*, Nice 1966; *Tout Rebus*, Nice 1966; *Tout Poesis*, Nice 1966; *J'Aime et J'Attaque no. 1*, 1967; *J'Aime et J'Attaque no. 2*, Nice 1968; *tout (Musique et Cinema)*, Nice 1968; *Programme pour la Table*, Nice 1968; *Tout Moi Ben Je Signe*, Nice 1969; *Reedition de Vieux Stencils de Ben*, Nice 1969; *Capitre Idees*, Nice 1970; *Chronique Touche a Tout de Ben No. 1*, Nice 1970; *A P'Art*, Nice 1977; *Reg'Art*, Nice 1978; *Bag'Art Bay'Art*, Nice 1979; *Manuscrit pour une Premiere Internationale Ethniste*, Nice 1986; *La Verite de A a Z*, Toulouse 1987.

On BEN: books—*Aktionen, Happenings und Demonstrationen seit 1965*, edited by Wolf Vostell, Hamburg 1970; *Catalogue de Films de Ben*. Paris 1971; *Mail Art: Communication à Distance, Concept*, edited by Jean-Mare Poinsot, Paris 1971: *Documenta 5: Befragung der Realitat*, exhibition catalogue, edited by Harald Szeeman and others, Kassel, West Germany 1972; *Art = Ben*, exhibition catalogue, with an introduction by Ad Petersen, Amsterdam 1973; *Ben Vautier; Berlin Inventory*, exhibition catalogue, West Berlin 1979; *Ben Libre*, exhibition catalogue, St. Etienne, France 1981; *Ben: Encore des Mots*, exhibition catalogue, Lyon 1986.

*   *   *

Ben (as he signs his works) could be called the correspondence art network's Duchamp. In performance and on film he sits, or swims, or lies face down on a busy sidewalk, elevating the activity to art by giving it a title and a framework, or de-elevating art by linking it with such common actions. The notion of de-elevating art would not even arise were it not for Ben's frequent references to the questionability of the art world, the making of art and the grip that art has on him and his life.

Ben's art relies on thoughts and words; his works often contain calligraphic oneliners reflecting his humorous, reflective attitude which fluctuates between negative and positive, sometimes in the same piece. One work shows the artist sitting on a chair with a sign on his lap which reads "Art is Useless." To the right is another message: "I sold that piece, and with the money I went on holiday for a week."

The artist is based in Nice, where he has operated a second hand record shop and maintained widespread contact with the international art scene by publishing small books, posters, brochures, and post cards. An associate of Fluxus and the nouveau realisme group, Ben has participated in Flux kits and produced memorable rubber stamp art, a medium he has used since 1949. Post cards are especially suitable for Ben's art since they function as a support for his calligraphic text and, as multiples, are able to reach a wide audience. Two of his cards, "Postman's Choice," 1965, and "Your thumb present now . . . ." 1966, are among the best known works in correspondence art.

As a participant in Mieko Shiomi's "Spatial Poem," a correspondence/response project, Ben contributed responses which reflect his philosophy about art and life and the ever changing balance between the two:

Spatial Poem No. 2 direction event. Ben Vautier was most likely in bed facing the ceiling in Nice.

Spatial Poem No. 3 falling event. After hesitating a great deal, Ben Vautier swallowed the thin piece of paper joined to the invitation letter.

Spatial Poem No. 4 shadow event. A)I found the SHADOW plastic sheet in the shadow of an envelope. B)I put the SHADOW plastic sheet 1. in the shadow of a tree 2. in the shadow of myself Ben 3. in the shadow of the moon—at night 4. in the shadow of a beautiful naked girl—my daughter 5. in the shadow of . . . Then I put it into a special file for Shiomi, and it is there in the shadow of all the documents concerning her.

Spatial Poem No. 9 disappearing event. I have come to the conclusion that my interest in art is slowly disappearing.

In September 1983, *Art News* magazine reported that Ben's Nice boutique, known as Galerie Ben Doute de Tout, is now enshrined in Paris' National Museum of Modern Art at the Centre Pompidou.

—Mary Stofflet

VEDOVA, Emilio.

Italian. Born in Venice, 9 August 1919. Educated at schools in Venice, until 1930; mainly self-taught in painting from 1935, but attended Silvio Pucci's Free School of Painting, Florence, 1939-40. Served with the Italian partisans, in northern Italy, 1944-45. Worked in a local factory, Venice, 1930-37. Independent painter, in Rome, Florence and Venice, from 1937: established studio at Dorsoduro alla Salute, Venice, 1957. Member, Corrente artists movement, Milan, 1942; founder-member, Nuova Secessione (Fronte Nuovo delle Arti), Venice, 1946; member, Gruppo degli Otto, Venice, 1952. Director, Summer Academy, Salzburg, Austria, 1965-70; Professor of Painting, Accademia di Belle Arti, Venice, from 1975. Recipient: La Colomba Prize, Venice, 1938; Volpi Prize, 1950, Drawing Prize, 1954, and Grand Prize for Painting, 1960, *Bienal de Sao Paulo*, Brazil; Guggenheim Foundation Prize for Italy, 1956; Premio Lissone, Milan, 1958; First Prize, *Drawing Biennale*, Rijeka, 1976. Agent: Galleria Giorgio Persano, Piazza Vittorio Veneto 9, 10124 Turin. Address: Dorsoduro 46, 30123 Venice, Italy.

Individual Exhibitions:

1942	Galleria Euro Romano, Genoa, Italy
1943	Galleria La Spiga e Corrente, Milan
1945	Galleria Venezia, Venice
	Piccola Galleria, Venice
	Galleria del Pioppo, Mantua, Italy
1946	Art Club, Rome
	Galleria Del Bosco, Turin
	Piccola Galleria Venezia, Venice
1947	Galleria del Cavallino, Venice
	Art Club, Rome
1951	Viviano Gallery, New York
1954	Museu de Arte Moderna, Rio de Janeiro
1956	Galerie Gunther Franke, Munich (retrospective)
1957	Galerie Springer, West Berlin
1958	Zacheta Palace Museum, Warsaw (retrospective; travelled to Poznan, 1959)
	Galerie Springer, West Berlin
1960	Galleria Blu, Milan (retrospective)
	Galleria Il Disegno, Milan (retrospective)
	Kunsthalle, Hamburg
	Kunstmuseum, Lucerne
1961	Palazzo della Gran Guardia, Verona, Italy (retrospective)
	Galleria Annunciata, Milan
	Galleri M59, Copenhagen
	Museo de Ateneo, Madrid (retrospective)
	Sala Gaspar, Barcelona
1962	Galleria Libreria Einaudi, Rome
	Arco Palais Galerie, Monaco
	Galleri Haghfeldt, Copenhagen
	Galerie Pierre, Stockholm
	Kunstverein, Freiburg, West Germany (retrospective)
1963	Galleria Marlborough, Rome
	Museu de Arte Moderna, Rio de Janeiro
1964	Staatliche Kunsthalle, Baden-Baden, West Germany (retrospective)
1965	Institute of Contemporary Art, Washington, D.C. (retrospective)
	Kunstlerhaus, Salzburg, Austria (retrospective)
1967	Hollaru Gallery, Prague (toured Czechoslovakia)
1968	Kunstlerhaus, Salzburg, Austria (retrospective; travelled to Ferrara, Italy)
1970	Galerie Rothe, Heidelberg, West Germany
1971	Forum Gallery, Zagreb, Yugoslavia
1972	Galleria Falchi, Milan
1973	Kunstmuseum, Dusseldorf
1974	Galleria Linea 70, Verona, Italy
1975	Teatro Romano, Aosta, Italy
	Castello Visconteo, Pavia, Italy (retrospective)
1976	Galleria Mariani, Ravenna, Italy
1978	Museo Castello, Portofino, Italy (retrospective)
1979	Sala Medievale di San Jacopo, Prato, Italy (retrospective; toured Australia)
1980	Galerie im Taxispalais, Innsbruck (toured Austria)
	Museo Carrillo Gil, Mexico City
	Galleria Planetario, Trieste, Italy
1981	Städtisches Museum, Leverkusen, West Germany
	Palazzo dei Congressi, San Marino
	Kunstverein, Braunschweig, West Germany
1982	Van Abbemuseum, Eindhoven, Netherlands
	Galleria d'Arte Moderna, Bologna, Italy
	Galerie Annemarie Verna, Zurich
	Mura Aureliana, Rome
1983	Galerie Annemarie Verna 2, Zurich
	Istituto Artistico Universitario, Venice
	Galleria Stevens, Padua, Italy
	Galerie Thomas Borgmann, Cologne
	Galerie Fred Jahn, Munich
	Studio Marconi, Milan
	Galerija Sebastian, Belgrade
	Galerie Neuendorf, Hamburg (travelled to Venice)
1984	Galleria Loza/Galleria Meduza, Capodistria, Yugoslavia
	Museo Correr, Venice
	Galleria San Marco, Rome
1985	Galerie Buchmann, Basle
	Galleria Giorgio Persano, Turin
	Museo del Castello, Rivoli, Italy
1986	Galleria Tornabuoni, Florence
	Staatsgalerie Moderner Kunst, Munich
	Galerie Fred Jahn, Munich

	Musée Ingres, Toulouse, France
	Städtisches Museum, Leverkusen, West Germany
	Galerie Ulysses, Vienna
	Kunsthalle, Darmstadt, West Germany
	Padiglione Arte Contemporanea, Milan
	Galerie Academia, Salzburg, Austria
	Galleria Niccoli, Parma, Italy
1987	Museum Wiener Secession, Vienna
	Kunstmuseum, Lucerne, Switzerland
	Galerie XPO, Hamburg
	Museo Gorizia, Grado, Italy
	Musée d'Art Contemporain, Nimes, France
	Musée d'Art Contemporain, St. Etienne, France
	Galerie Hannah Feldmann, Berne
1988	Galleria L'Isola, Rome (travelled to Bologna)
	Fondazione Villa Celle, Santomato, Italy (installation)
	Galerie Rothe, Frankfurt
	Künstlerhaus, Salzburg, Austria

Selected Group Exhibitions:

1947	*Fronte Nuovo*, Galleria Cairola, Milan
1948	*Arte Astratta in Italia*, Galleria di Roma, Rome
1950	*Biennale*, Venice (and 1954, 1960, 1978)
1955	*Documenta 1*, Museum Fridericianum, Kassel, West Germany (and *Documenta 2*, 1958, *Documenta 3*, 1964)
1958	*Vitalita nell'arte*, Palazzo Grassi, Venice (travelled to Amsterdam)
1967	*Expo 67*, Montreal
1972	*Immagine per la Citta*, Museo Civico, Genoa, Italy
1977	*International Survey of Drawing*, Art Gallery of Western Australia, Perth
1985	*The European Iceberg*, Art Gallery of Ontario, Toronto
1987	*Berlinart 1961-87*, Museum of Modern Art, New York (travelled to San Francisco)

Publications:

On VEDOVA: books—*Pittura Moderna Italiana* by G. Marchiori, Trieste 1946; *Emilio Vedova* by G. Marchiori, Venice 1951; *Pittura Italiana del Dopoguerra 1945-57* by T. Sauvage, Milan 1957; *Confessions of an Art Addict* by Peggy Guggenheim, New York 1960; *New Tendencies in Art* by Aldo Pellegrini, New York 1966; *Ultime tendenze nell'arte d'oggi* by Gillo Dorfles, Milan 1973; *Emilio Vedova: Grafica e didattica*, exhibition catalogue, Aosta 1975; *Maestri Contemporanei: Vedova* by Filiberto Menna, Milan 1982; *Vedova Compresenze*, exhibition catalogue, San Marino 1981; *Emilio Vedova 1935-1984*, edited by Germano Celant and Ida Gianelli, Milan 1984; *Vedova 1986*, edited by Carla Schultz Hoffman, Munich 1986; *Vedova und Salzburg*, Salzburg 1988.

*   *   *

As an artist of international renown in the field of *Informel* painting, Emilio Vedova embodies one of the greatest protagonists of twentieth century Italian art. At the beginning of his career in 1935 to 1936, while still a young man, he demonstrated an extraordinary command of expressive means in a series of architectonic drawings. His elegant style has a descriptive and dynamic urgency which has become his hallmark. Up to the beginning of the 1940s, his oil paintings were clearly influenced by Tintoretto, Goya, Daumier and by the Expressionist tradition, one of the most evident premises of Vedova's work—as in *Assassinio* (1941) and *Operaio* (1942). Vedova's expressive dynamism is also reflected in his involvement with anti-fascism and a number of social issues. He had belonged to Corrente, the group opposed to 'official' art during the 1930s. At the end of the war, he joined the Fronte Nuovo delle Arti in 1946, and took part in the debate between 'abstract' and 'realist' movements that raged through Italian art in those years. Vedova formed a close relationship with the abstract painters championed by Lionello Venturi, and between 1952 and 1954 the Gruppo degli Otto was formed.

For Vedova and other abstractionists who had been suppressed by Fascist cultural policies, abstraction

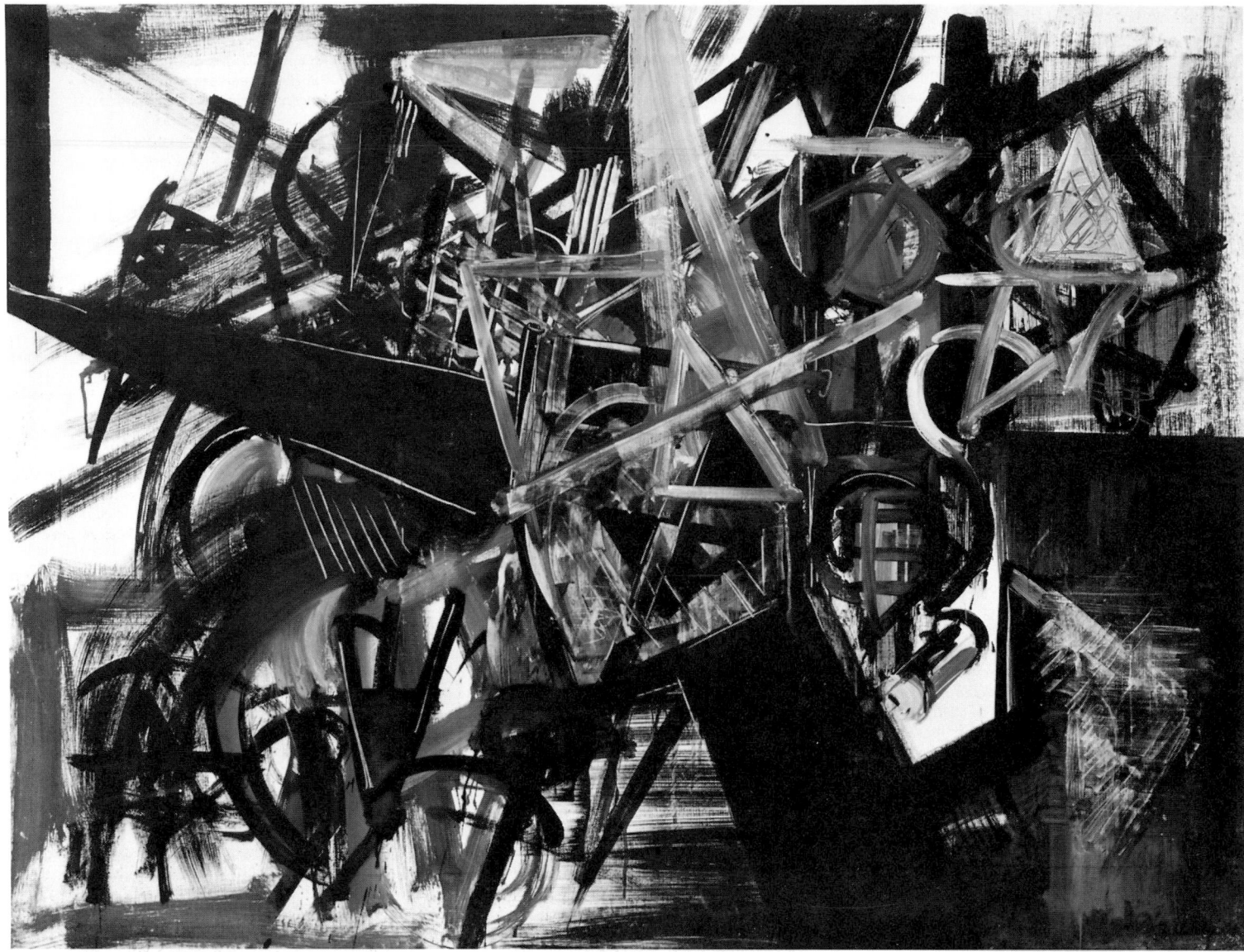

Emilio Vedova: *Image of Time* (*Barricade*), **1951** Courtesy Guggenheim Museum, New York

took as a starting point the reinterpretation of Picasso and Cubist figuration. The shifting and interpenetration of different planes is articulated, in Vedova's case, by irregular geometric modules building the figures into compact and rigid forms (Vedova himself was to speak of 'automatons' or 'machines'), as in *Cucitrice No. 1* (1946). Later on, his themes become more evocative, and the painted marks tend increasingly to signify rather than to represent. *Explosion* (1948) has relaxed from the earlier rigid style into a highly dynamic and forceful language. In this work, Vedova uses signals of energy, vectors of directions, forms in which the blacks defining them are accompanied by evanescent patches of white, the function of which is to underline their dynamic rhythm.

In the 1950s Vedova relinquished the geometry which he later confessed to have obsessed and inhibited him. In such works as *Immagine del Tempo n. 1 e 2* (1951), angularity is characterized by a more lyrical brushmark. Vedova's form of cubism had by now begun borrowing from the dynamic vocabulary of early futurism to combine with the fundamental expressionism that so deeply permeated his work with a sense of tragedy. His approach to painting now oscillated between substantiating signs as a body of ideograms, and liberating that gestural fluidity in which the range of colour was highly evocative besides functioning as structure. The resolution of these diametrically opposed features in Vedova's work is evident in *Ciclo della Protesta* and *Ciclo della Natura,* both of 1953. In each of these paintings, the resolution constitutes a highly dramatic event.

Throughout his long career, the actual gesture of painting has remained of paramount importance. The gesture disturbs the surface, signifying historical man's tragedy and loneliness, isolated and unable to control unconscious impulses. In 1962, Vedova wrote: "A materic sign will never give us access to a new dimension of a universe constantly being destroyed and re-aggregated." However, still understanding the limits of his artistic language, Vedova insists that "the sign affirms itself", and that his works are "full of structures." The gestural mark is the vehicle for the violence that destroys, but always within sight of a reconstruction. Vedova's negation is full of optimism.

In the multiple images of the 1970s, Vedova's negation destroys codified two-dimensionality where marks or signs virtually dismantle the space. The painting appears to fall apart, with surface planes expanding and combining freely, so that the picture becomes an event and visual process unfolding in front of the viewer's eyes. *Absudes Berliner Tagebuch* (1964) is a work of multiple images commemorating the erection of the Berlin Wall. The 'structures' of which Vedova speaks are also the structures of conscience. The work becomes an emblem of awakened conscience, an alarm ready to expose social injustice, and thus accentuates its role as communicable testimony.

After these multiple works Vedova returned to the single canvas, where he promotes the idea of the painting as a battleground. In the painting *Lacerazioni* (1977–78), Vedova's use of both negation and

affirmation is made clear by the function assigned to colours in relationship to the manner in which the paint is handled. Whereas the whites and yellows convey an aura of light and space, the reds are charged with violence. Vedova, however, balances this disruptive passion by conferring the role of regulator onto the viscous strength of his blacks. In only a few cases does Vedova yield to instinctive and informal gesture, as in *Da Dove* (1983).

Unlike Pollock, for instance, Vedova makes no attempt to match his own estangement from the world by means of an informal painting style. Through destructive and reconstructive valencies, he proclaims the world as worthy of reconquering.

—Giorgio Verzotti

VELICKOVIC, Vladimir.
Yugoslav. Born in Belgrade, 11 August 1935. Studied architecture at the University of Belgrade, 1954–60; self-taught in art, since 1960. Served as an engineer in Yugoslav Army, 1960–61. Married Maristella Matulic in 1962; children: Vuk and Marko. Independent painter, working in studio of Krsto Hegedusic in Zagreb, 1962–63, in Belgrade, 1964–66, and in Paris since 1966. Recipient: Painting Prize, *Biennale des*

Jeunes, Rijeka, 1962; Painting Prize, *October Salon,* Belgrade, 1963; Drawing Prize, *Yugoslav Triennale,* Sombor, 1963, 1966, 1975; Painting Prize, *Yugoslav Triennale,* Belgrade 1964; Painting Prize, *Biennale de Paris* 1965; Painting Prize, *Fantastique Poetique,* Sombor 1967; Painting Prize, Lignano, Italy, 1968; N. Petrovic Memorial Prize, Cacak, 1968, 1978; Prize, *International Drawings Exhibition,* Rijeka, Yugoslavia, 1970, 1974; Drawing Prize, *Internationale Grafikausstellung,* Vienna, 1970; Prize, *International Print Exhibition,* Ljubljana 1971, 1973, 1977; Painting Prize, *Momento Tangente Internazionale,* Gardone, Italy, 1971; Prize, *Yugoslav Painters 71,* Sombor, 1971; Print Prize, Belgrade Circle, 1972; Prize, *Print Biennale,* Tokyo, 1976; Painting Prize, *Bienal,* Sao Paulo, 1977; Painting Prize, 10 Anni della Galleria San Michele, Brescia, Italy, 1978; Graphics Prize, La Plume d'Or, Belgrade, 1979; Grand Prize, *Graphics Biennale,* Heidelberg, 1979, Prize, *Graphics Biennale,* Cracow, Poland 1980. Agents: Galerie du Dragon, 19 rue du Dragon, 75006 Paris France; Galerie Jan Krugier, 3 Place du Grand-Mezel, 1204 Geneva, Switzerland. Address: 7 Passage Ricaut, escalier 19/6, 75013 Paris France.

Individual Exhibitions:

1963	Museum of Modern Art, Belgrade
1964	Mala Galerija, Ljubliana, Yugoslavia
1965	Galerie Defacqz, Brussels
	Zygos Gallery, Athens
1967	*Peintures, dessins,* Galerie du Dragon, Paris
1968	Galleria Il Fante di Spade, Rome
	Galleria La Mutina, Modena, Italy
	Galleria Il Tempo, Bologna
	Dissegni 1965–1968, Galleria La Colonna, Como, Italy
1969	Museum of Modern Art, Belgrade
	Gallery of Contemporary Art, Zagreb
	Museum of Modern Art, Rijeka, Yugoslavia
1970	Musée d'Art Moderne de la Ville, Paris
	Galerie du Dragon, Paris
	Galerie T, Haarlem, Netherlands
	Galerie Jalmar, Amsterdam
	Hengelose Kunstzaal, Hengelo, Netherlands
1971	Galleria Vinciana, Milan
	Galleria San Michele, Brescia, Italy
	Art Gallery of Split, Yugoslavia
	Galleria Giulia, Rome
	Galleria Forni, Bologna
	Galleria Goethe, Bolzano, Italy
	Mala Galerija, Ljubljana, Yugoslavia
1972	Galleria Cartezius, Trieste
	Galleria Eidos, Milan
	Biennale, Venice
	Galerie Sebastian. Dubrovnik
	Maison de la Culture, Rennes, France
1973	Galerie du Dragon, Paris
	Galerie Herve Odermatt, Paris
	Galerie La Pochade, Paris
	Galerie T., Haarlem, Netherlands
	Graficki Kolektiv, Belgrade
	Galerie Richard Foncke, Ghent
	Galerie La Plage, Paris
1974	Galleria San Michele, Brescia, Italy
	Galerie T, Haarlem, Netherlands
	Galerie La Fleuve, Bordeaux
	Galleria Forni, Bologna
	Galleria Documenta, Turin
	Pryzmat Gallery, Cracow, Poland
	Galerie Sebastian, Dubrovnik
	Kunsthalle, Dusseldorf
1975	Galerie Arta, Geneva
	La Bijougalerie, Grenoble, France
	Galleri Futura, Stockholm
1976	Konsthall, Lund, Sweden
	Museum of Modern Art, Rijeka, Yugoslavia
	Galleria Visconti, Milan
	Konsthall, Gothenburg, Sweden
	Galeria Juana de Aizpuru, Seville
	Galleri Wallner, Malmo, Sweden
	Galleri Borjeson, Malmo, Sweden
	Kulturhuset, Stockholm

1977	Artcurial, Paris
	National Museum, Leskovac, Yugoslavia
	Galerie Hervé Odermatt, Paris
	Galerie La Hune, Paris
	Galleri Dierks, Aarhus, Denmark
	Bienal, Sao Paulo
	Galerie La Hune, at *FIAC 77,* Grand Palais, Paris
	Galleri Leger, Malmo, Sweden
1978	Student Cultural Centre, Belgrade
	Galerija Mladinska Knjiga, Ljubljana, Yugoslavia
1979	Gaerija Zagreb, Zagreb
	Galerie Miroir d'Encre, Brussels
	Galerie La Hune, Paris
	Galerie Albert Henri, Rennes, France
	Galerie 24, Novi Sad, Yugoslavia
	Salon de la Tribune des Jeunes, Novi Sad, Yugoslavia
	Galeria Ciento, Barcelona
	Galerie Larcos, Paris
1980	Galerie Una, Geneva
	Artcurial, Paris
	Galerie Jan Krugier, Geneva
	Galerie Krugier et Geofroy, Geneva
	Galerie Sebastian, Dubrovnik
	Galerie Collegium Artisticum, Sarajevo, Yugoslavia
	Galerie Jean-Marie Cupillard, Grenoble, France
	Galerija Nadezda Petrovic, Cacak, Yugoslavia
1981	Heni-Onstad Kunstsenter, Oslo
	Peintures et Dessins, Galerie Charles Kriwin, Brussels
1982	Galerie Presence Contemporaine, Aix-en-Provence, France
	Museo de Bellas Artes, Caracas
	Galerie Le Point, Monte Carlo
1983	Galerie Le Dessin, Paris
	Galerie de France, Paris
	Galerie Athanor, Marseille, France
1984	Galleri Kaj Forsblom, Helsinki
	Galleri Grafiart, Turku, Finland

	Galerie Jade, Colmar, France
	Stadtmuseum, Ratingen, West Germany
	Galerie Pierre Huber, Geneva
1985	Espace des Cordeliers, Chateauroux, France
	Galerie de l'Ancienne Poste, Calais, France
1986	Academy of Sciences and Arts, Belgrade
	Atrium Gallery, Belgrade
	Galerie BBL, Antwerp, Belgium
	Grand Palais, Paris
	Galerie Patrice Trigano, Paris

Selected Group Exhibitions:

1961	*Yugoslav Triennale,* Belgrade
1963	*Bienal,* Sao Paulo
1966	*Yugoslavia: Contemporary Trends,* Corcoran Gallery, Washington, D.C.
1968	*Contemporary Yugoslav Art,* Civic Center Museum, Philadelphia
1972	*Activite Artistique en France 1960–1972,* Grand Palais, Paris
1974	*Biennale of Prints,* National Museum of Modern Art, Tokyo
1978	*Arte Yugoslavo contemporaneo,* Fundacio Joan Miró, Barcelona (travelled to Madrid, Lisbon, London and Manchester)
1980	*20th Century Yugoslav Painting,* Museum of Modern Art, Belgrade
1984	*Ecriture dans la Peinture,* Villa Arson, Nice, France
1986	*Les Figurations,* Musee d'Art Moderne, Dunkirk, France

Collections:

Museum of Modern Art, Belgrade; Centre Georges Pompidou, Paris; Stedelijk Museum, Amsterdam; Kunstsammlung, Bochum, West Germany; Muzeum Sztuki, Lodz, Poland;

Vladimir Velickovic: *Cane No. 4,* **1970**

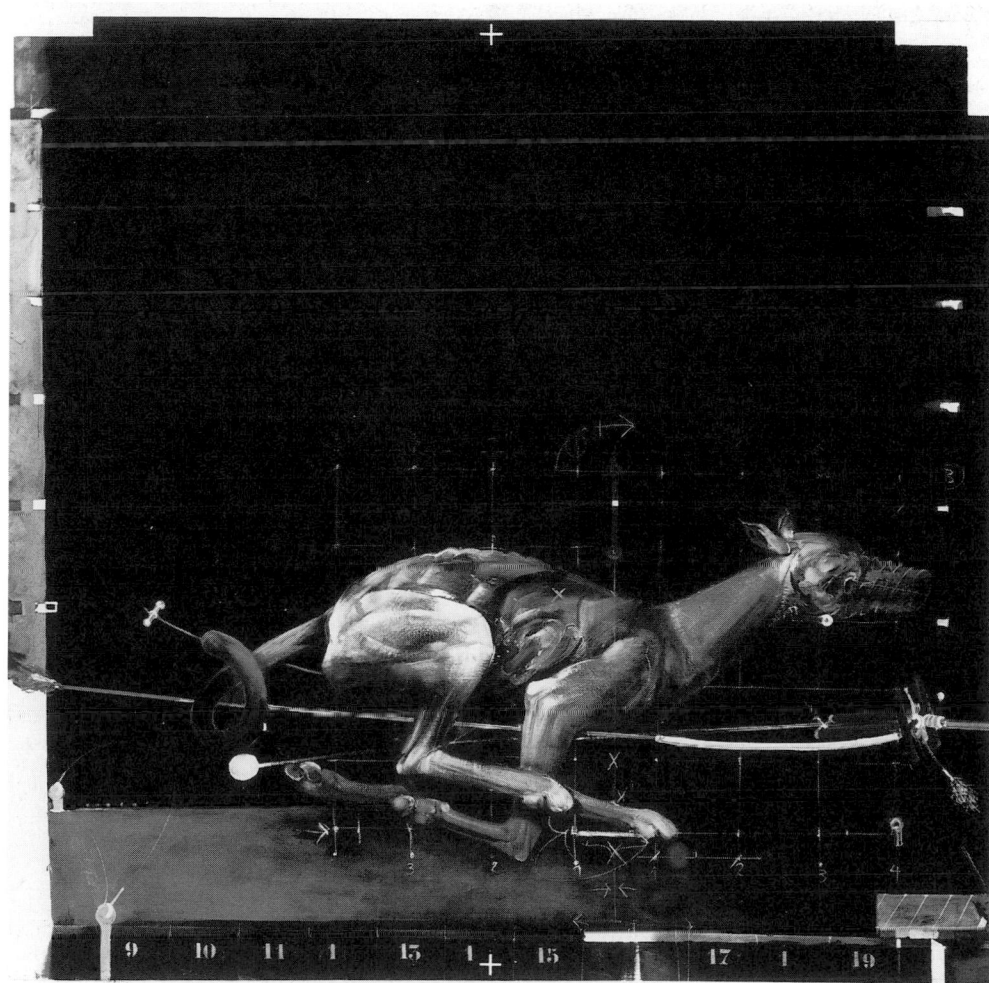

Museo Civico, Bologna; Museo Cantonal des Beaux-Arts, Lausanne, Switzerland; Museum voor Schone Kunsten, Ghent; Neue Galerie am Landesmuseum Joanneum, Graz, Austria; Museum of Modern Art, New York.

Publications:

On VELICKOVIC: books—*Velickovic: peintures, dessins,* exhibition catalogue, with text by M. Clarac-Serou, Paris 1967; *Velickovic; Dissegni 1965–1968,* exhibition catalogue, with text by I. Subotic, Como, Italy 1968: *Vladimir Velickovic: peintures, dessins 1968–1970,* exhibition catalogue, with text by Gérald Gassiot-Talabot, Paris 1970; *Velickovic,* exhibition catalogue, with text by Enrico Crispolti, Milan 1971; *Velickovic,* edited by Jean-Louis Ferrier, with texts by several authors, Paris 1976; *Vladimir Velickovic: essai sur le symbolisme artistique* by Marc Le Bot, Paris 1979; *Vladimir Velickovic: dessins et collages,* exhibition catalogue, with text by René Berger, Geneva 1980; *Vladimir Velickovic: peintures et dessins,* exhibition catalogue, with texts by Gérald Gassiot-Talabot, Jean-Pierre Faye, Alain Jouffroy and others, Brussels 1981; *Velickovic: dibujos 1958–1978/9: Veinte Anos de Agresividad* by Alain Jouffroy, Barcelona 1981; *Vladimir Velickovic,* exhibition catalogue with introduction by Marc Le Bot, Paris 1986; films—*Velickovic* by Pierre Desfons and Alain Jouffroy, 1973.

There are obvious comparisons to be made between Francis Bacon and Vladimir Velickovic, especially in the depiction of putrescent flesh, rotting or dissolving on human forms. Velickovic's paintings are less obviously autobiographic, although, in fact, the vivid images of injured, disintegrating children derive directly from memories of war-time Yugoslavia. These surrealistic nightmarish compositions, and the strange, fluid technique, would seem to derive from the Flemish masters, notably Bosch, and also Goya. Their pictorial directness is the result of an urgent need for personal exorcism and, just as important, for communication. Velickovic's brilliance as a draughtsman and painter enables him to register a disturbing imagination with extraordinary immediacy. No one seeing the work of this Yugoslav painter could ever claim indifference: the effect is either disgust, involvement, sympathy, or hatred. A more difficult-to-analyze aspect of Velickovic's work is its over sexuality, combined with a fascination for the mechanics of childbirth. Sexual allusions are already present in the paintings of mutilated children, where the positioning of the bodies, or irrational surrealistic details, permitted a wide range of interpretation. A series of paintings of reclining women, in 1972, illustrates the strange interplay of realism, sexuality, violence and nightmare in Velickovic's work; energetic images of women, with legs widespread, are alternately entitled "Birth" and "Aggression," the former suggesting the violent delivery of a screaming child, the latter showing rat-like creatures emerging from or entering the vagina. In a long series of works, rats became obsessive symbols of terror and attack, but at the same time Velickovic produced equally important, if less characteristic, images based on the famous photographs of movement by Muybridge. These paintings of running men and greyhounds develop a concern with movement already evident in the artist's earlier work and, whilst far less subjective or violent, they still convey a disturbing sense of menace.

—Charles Spencer

VENET, Bernar.

French. Born in Saint-Auban, 20 April 1941. Educated at Ecole Libre and Groupe Scolaire Paul Lapie, Saint-Auban, 1955–58; studied art at the La Villa Thiole, Nice, 1958–59. Served in the French Army, Algeria, 1961–62. Married Ella Bogval in 1971; sons: Alexander and Stephan. Worked as stage-decorator, Opera de Nice, 1959–61. Painter and "conceptual" artist, Nice, 1961–66, in New York,

since 1966. Agent: Galerie Daniel Templon, 30 rue Beaubourg, 75003 Paris, France. Address: 533 Canal Street, New York, New York 10013, U.S.A.

Individual Exhibitions:

1964	Galerie Ursula Girardon, Paris
1968	Judson Church Theatre, New York
1969	Newark College of Engineering, New Jersey
1970	O. K. Harris Gallery, New York
	Museum Haus Lange, Krefeld, West Germany
	Kunsthaus, Hamburg
	Studio Santandrea, Milan
	Denise René-Hans Mayer Editions, Dusseldorf
1971	Galerie Der Spiegel, Cologne
	X-One Gallery, Antwerp
	Galerie Daniel Templon, Paris
	Galleria Daniel Templon, Milan
1972	Galerie Bruno Bischofberger, Zurich
	Galerie Daniel Templon, Paris
	Galleria Daniel Templon, Milan
	New York Cultural Center (retrospective)
1973	Galerie Foksal, Warsaw
1974	Galleria La Seconda Scala, Rome
	Galerie Daniel Templon, Paris
	Galleria Daniel Templon, Milan
1975	Galerie Hetzler und Keller, Stuttgart
	Galleria Nuovi Strumenti, Brescia, Italy
	French Section, at the *Bienal,* Sao Paulo
	Galerie Daniel Templon, Paris
	Institute of Contemporary Arts, London
	Museu de Arte Moderna, Rio de Janeiro
1976	Dartmouth College, Hanover, New Hampshire
	Textural Criticism, La Jolla Museum of Contemporary Art, California
1977	Galerie Bruno Bischofberger, Zurich
	Musée d'Art et d'Industrie, Saint-Etienne, France
	Galerie Daniel Templon, Paris
	Galerie Gillespie-de Laage, Paris
	Henie-Onstad Kunstsenter, Oslo
	Galerie Denise René-Hans Mayer, Dusseldorf
1978	Special Project at PS 1, Long Island City, New York
	Galerie Denise René-Hans Mayer, Dusseldorf
1979	Arco Center for the Visual Arts, Los Angeles
	Hal Bromm Gallery, New York
	Galleria Civica d'Arte Moderna, Portofino, Italy
	Marianne Deson Gallery, Chicago
	Galerie Daniel Templon, Paris
1981	Galerie Denise René-Hans Mayer, Dusseldorf
	Galleria Unimedia, Genoa
	Galerie Artline, The Hague
	Galerie Daniel Templon, Paris
1982	Bonlow Gallery, New York
	Malinda Wyatt Gallery, Venice, California
1984	Musée Sainte-Croix, Poitiers, France
	Studio Marconi, Milan
	Marianne Deson Gallery, Chicago
	Centre d'Art Contemporain, Chateauroux, France
	Galerie Denise Rene/Hans Mayer, at *Art 84,* Basle
	Galerie ARCA, Marseille, France
	Galerie Jean-Jules Bertin, Lyon, France
	Musée d'Art Moderne, Villeneuve-d'Ascq, France
	Galerie Daniel Templon, Paris
1985	Galerie Denise Rene/Hans Mayer, Dusseldorf
	Musée Départemental des Vosges, Epinal, France
	Galerie Bernard Lucas, Nice, France
	Galerie Littmann, Basle
1986	Castelli Uptown, New York
	Galerie Elisabeth Frank, Brussels
	Daniel Templon Galerie Un, Paris
	Daniel Templon Galerie Deux, Paris
1987	Galerie Pierre Huber, Geneva
	Quadrat-Bottrop Moderne Galerie, Bottrop, West Germany
1988	Galerie Michèle Chomette, Paris

Selected Group Exhibitions:

1964	*Salon Comparaisons,* Musée d'Art Moderne de la Ville, Paris
1986	*Salon de la Jeune Peinture,* Musée d'Arte Moderne, Paris
1970	*Information,* Museum of Modern Art, New York
1975	*Tendencies of Contemporary Art,* Nordiyllands Kunstmuseum, Aalborg, Denmark (toured Denmark)
1977	*Documenta,* Kassel, West Germany
1979	*Construction and the Geometric Tradition,* Albright-Knox Art Gallery, Buffalo, New York (toured the United States)
1981	*Construction in Process in the Art of the 70's,* Muzeum Sztuki, Lodz, Poland
1983	*L'Art en France dans les Annees 60,* Musée d'Art et d'Industrie, St. Etienne, France
1985	*Livres d'Artistes,* Centre Georges Pompidou, Paris
1987	*Mathematik in der Kunst,* Wilhelm-Hack-Museum, Ludwigshafen, West Germany

Collections:

Centre National d'Art Contemporain, Paris; Kaiser-Wilhelm Museum, Krefeld, West Germany; Neue Galerie im Alten Kurhaus, Aachen, West Germany; Muzeum Sztuki, Lodz, Poland; Museum of Modern Art, New York; New York University; Akron Art Institute, Ohio; Georgia Museum of Art, Athens; Atlantic Richfield Company, Los Angeles; Santa Barbara Museum of Art, California.

Publications:

On VENET: books—*The Structure of Art* by Jack Burnham, New York 1970; *Bernar Venet,* exhibition catalogue, with text by Catherine Millet, Warsaw 1973; *Bernar Venet,* edited by Arthur Hubschmid, Paris and Zurich 1975; *La Linea Analitica dell'Arte Moderna* by Filiberto Menna, Turin 1975; *Dell'Informale alla Body-Art* by Lea Vergine, Turin 1976; *Bernar Venet: Textual Criticism,* exhibition catalogue, with text by Lawrence Alloway, La Jolla, California 1976; *Bernar Venet,* exhibition catalogue, with text by Bernard Ceysson, Saint-Etienne, France 1977; *A Propos de Nice,* exhibition catalogue, with text by Ben Vautier, Paris, 1977; *Biennale de Paris 1959–73,* exhibition catalogue, edited by Georges Boudaille, Tokyo 1978; *Bernar Venet,* exhibition catalogue, Portofino, Italy 1979; *Bernar Venet; Un cura di Bernar Venet,* Milan 1980; *Bernar Venet; Dessins 1963–1983,* exhibition catalogue with essay by Catherine Franklin, Poitiers 1983; *Bernar Venet,* exhibition catalogue with text by Bernard Ceysson, Epinal 1985.

Bernar Venet, born in France, worked in the late 1960's and 1970's on large photographic blow-ups of scientific equations. He then proceeded to use the look of scientific equations and diagrams in a painterly manner. He has also used segments of any number of texts, including weather reports, pages of stock market figures, and astrophysical and meteorological texts. Venet has made it his work to sell the look of contemporary science, yet in a distanced fashion. Venet has assisted in finishing the incomplete work of the scientists by presenting their work, in lieu of their own presentation, to the public. Many of his earlier projects included a number of presentations and lectures by prominent scientists. Venet's task was essentially to organize several hundred of these symposia.

Rather than repeating scientific work verbatim, Venet's canvases, such as "Calculation of the Diagonal of a Rectangle," 1966, and "Tracing of Two Complimentary Angles," 1977, expressed the look of science. Therefore, in a sense, they expressed the content of science, given the nature of belief associated with most of the contemporary sciences.

In Venet's work the contemporary need for science to hide research is revealed, and the contemporary utilization of art as decoration is proven. Perhaps the proof of art will work backwards on the contemporary mystery of science, by insisting on aesthetic reasoning along the way, reflectivity during construction. A painting on the wall, worthy of supra-scrutiny, is a misplaced aim. The scrutiny is held in the wrong area. The question is not to scrutinize the aesthetic work, but to examine the direction of the observing functions. Venet has been observing science and subjecting it, like a billboard, to the popular realm. We are supposed to be watching science, not art.

—John Robinson

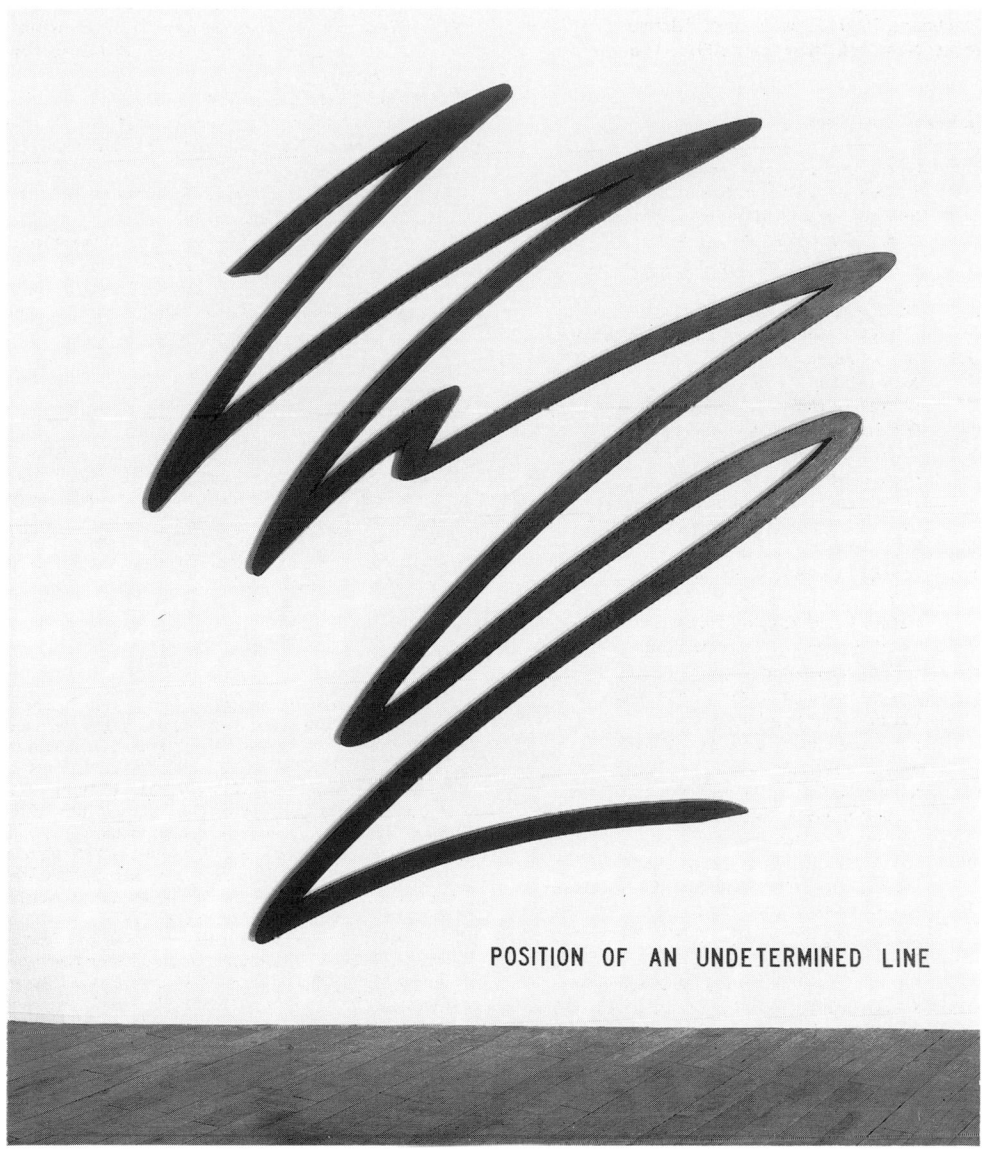

POSITION OF AN UNDETERMINED LINE

Bernar Venet: *Position of an Undetermined Line*, 1980

VIALLAT, Claude.

French. Born in Aubais, Le Gard, near Nimes, 18 May 1936. Studied under Descossis, Dezeuze, and Bessil, at the Ecole des Beaux-Arts, Montpellier, 1955–59; also studied at the Ecole des Beaux-Arts, Paris, 1962–63. Served in French Army, Constantine, Algeria, 1959–61. Married Henriette Pous in 1962; daughters: Claire and Isabelle. Painter: lived in Nice, 1964–67, Limoges, 1967–69, and in Marseilles, since 1969; Member, with Louis Cane, Marc Devade, Daniel Dezeuze, Andre Valensi and others, Groupe Supports Surfaces, Paris, 1969–71. Painting Instructor, Ecole des Beaux-Arts, Nice, 1964–67; Professor of Painting, Ecole des Beaux-Arts, Limoges, 1968–1969. Professor of Painting, Ecole des Beaux-Arts, Marseilles, from 1969. Agent: Galerie Daniel Templon, Paris. Address: c/o Galerie Daniel Templon, 30 rue Beaubourg, 75003 Paris, France.

Individual Exhibitions:

1966	Galerie A, Nice
1968	Galerie Jean Fournier, Paris
	Musée d'Art Moderne, Ceret, France
1971	Galerie Jean Fournier, Paris
1973	Galleria Daniel Templon, Milan
	Galerie Jean Fournier, Paris
1974	Galerie Delta, Brussels
	Musée d'Art et d'Industrie, St.-Etienne, France
	Chez Malabar et Cunegonde (Galerie Ben), Nice

	Galleria La Bertesca, Milan (with Dolla and Isnard)
	Maison de la Culture, Rennes (with Dezeuze and Saytour)
1975	Galerie Athanor, Marseilles (with Tony Grand)
	Galerie Jean Fournier, Paris
1976	Pierre Matisse Gallery, New York
	Von-der-Heydt Museum, Wuppertal, West Germany (with J. M. Meurice)
	Palais des Beaux-Arts Brussels
	Galerie A.16, Perpignan, France
1977	Galerie Jean Fournier, Paris
	Galerie C. M., St.-Etienne, France
	Galerie Sanguine, Collioure, France
	Galerie Athanor, Marseilles (with Jaccard and Pincemin)
1978	Galerie Arta, Geneva
	Maison de la Culture, Orleans, France
	Centre de Création Artistique, Senanque, France
	Galerie Athanor, Marseilles
	Traces, Musée d'Art et d'Histoire, Chambéry, France
1979	Galerie Wentzel, Hamburg
1980	Centre des Arts Plastiques Contemporains Bordeaux
	Neue Galerie, Aachen, West Germany
1981	Galerie L'Atelier, Nice, France
	Kamakura Gallery, Tokyo
	Ace Gallery, Venice, California
1982	Galerie Wentzel, Cologne
	Leo Castelli Gallery, New York
	Centre Georges Pompidou, Paris
1988	Institut Francais, Cologne

Selected Group Exhibitions:

1966	*Impact*, Musée d'Art Moderne, Ceret, France
1969	*Biennale*, Paris (and 1971)
1971	*Supports/Surfaces*, Théâtre de la Cité Universitaire, Paris (travelled to Nice)
1972	*Amsterdam-Paris-Dusseldorf*, Guggenheim Museum, New York
1973	*Regarder Ailleurs*, Entrepots Laine, Bordeaux
1975	*12 x 1: Europalia 75*, Palais des Beaux-Arts, Brussels
1977	*A Propos de Nice*, Centre Georges Pompidou, Paris
1978	*Espace/Nature*, Centre des Arts Plastiques Contemporains, Bordeaux
1980	*Die Neue Wilden*, Neue Galerie, Aachen, West Germany
1982	*Du Cubisme a nos Jours*, Musée Cantini, Marseille, France

Collections:

Musée d'Art et d'Industrie, St. Etienne, France: Fonds National d'Art Contemporain, Paris: Neue Galerie-Sammlung Ludwig, Aachen, West Germany.

Publications:

On VIALLAT: books—*Claude Viallat*, exhibition catalogue, with preface by Marcelin Pleynet, Paris 1971; *Art en France: Une Nouvelle Génération* by Jean Clair, Paris 1972; *L'Enseignment de la Peinture* by Marcelin Pleynet, Paris 1972; *Amsterdam-Paris-Dusseldorf*, exhibition catalogue, with texts by Blaise Gauthier, Cor Blok, and Jürgen Harton, New York 1972; *L'Art Actuel en France* by Anne Tronche and Hervé Gloaguen, Paris 1973; *Claude Viallat*, exhibition catalogue, with text by Jacques Lepage, St. Etienne, France 1974; *Claude Viallat: Traces*, exhibition catalogue, with texts by Dominque Fourcade and others, Chambéry, France 1978; *Claude Viallat*, exhibition catalogue, with text by Bernard Ceysson, Senanque, France 1978; *Claude Viallat*, exhibition catalogue, with texts by Jean-Louis Froment and Jean-Marie Poinsot, Bordeaux 1980.

There is one single form that Claude Viallat introduced into his painting in 1966 and never again abandoned—the form of a sponge soaked in colour that one presses onto the picture surface. However, when, by this means, an impression of wealth of colour and formal exuberance appears on his canvases, it is because he knew how to effect so many variations with this single motif that it invested entire rooms/spaces as endless ornamentation.

When Viallat began his work in 1966 a radical investigation into all painting was in progress in France. What had painting ever been until then, it was asked, other than a purveyor of illusions and false dreams, in the service of the art market, bourgeois society and its ideology? If one wanted a new beginning for painting, it had to be liberated from this traditional role. This discussion was perhaps successful in the sense that it made one think about the real origins of art. Viallat was one of the younger generation who tried to trace the origin of painting back to its handcraft beginnings, that beginning where the intention was to add a non-functional dimension to the merely functional object. But he also concluded that only where one expelled all content, any statement, every subjective expression from the work and replaced this on the canvas with unchanging neutral and anonymous forms, could one be sure that painting was concentrated only on the process of its becoming, and beyond that had no further significance. Indeed, at first, Viallat had in fact begun to work with the substance, the material grounds of painting, with rope, string, thread, which in tangled knots or composed nets call to mind the matrix of the canvas to be painted. He stressed the praxis of artistic work and not the ideas which it could generate. In so doing he set himself in opposition to the art of the Ecole de Paris and also to the new tendencies of conceptual art which came from America and which provided ideas about material and form.

In France people were looking for a new aesthetic

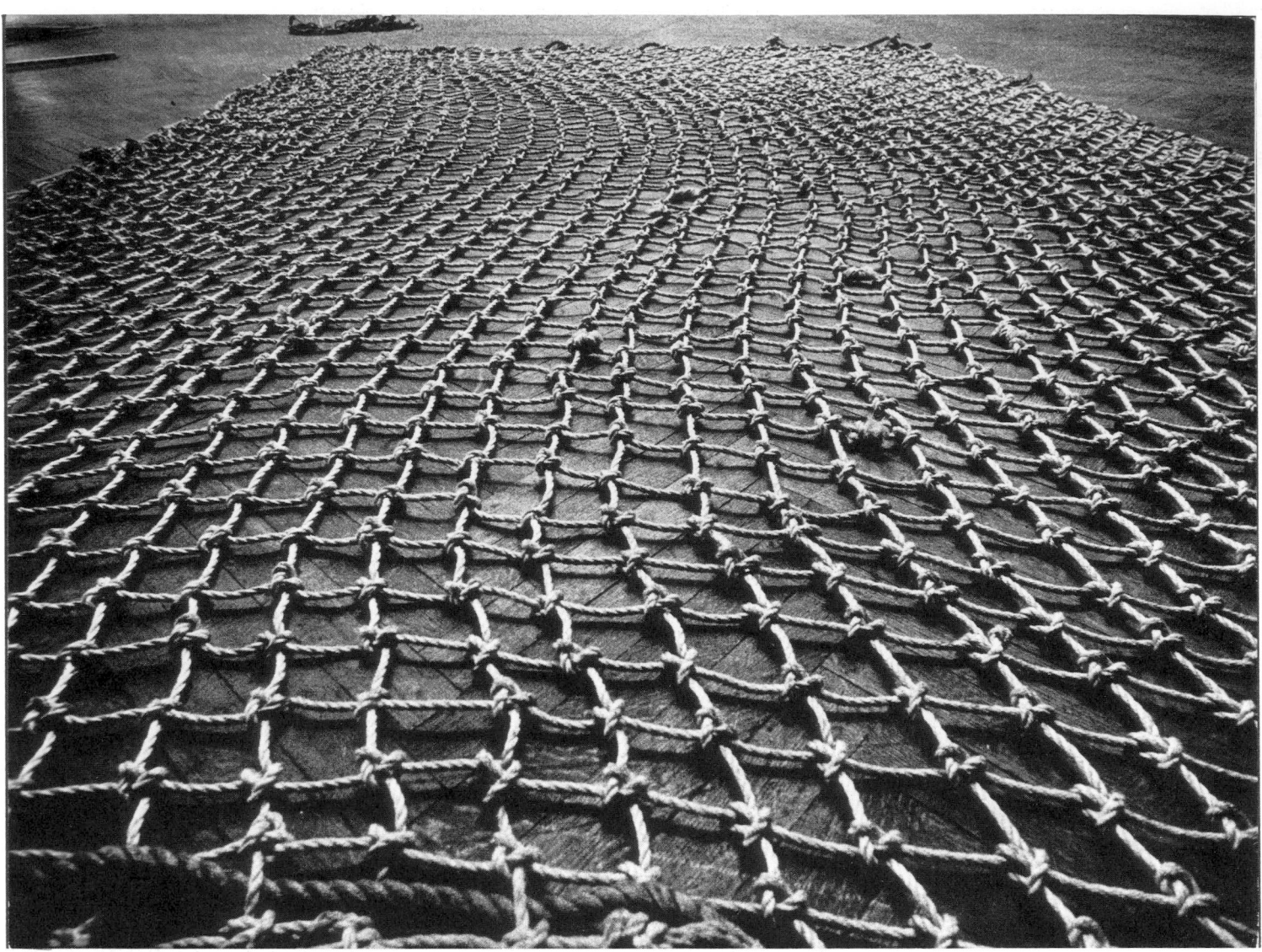

Claude Viallat: Installation at *Regarder Ailleurs* exhibition, Bordeaux, 1974

and for a new aesthetic ethic. Each had its theoretical basis in Marxism and in the structuralist critique of language. Painting was understood as a system of signs whose forms of expression, as long as they were taken over from tradition, were charged with specific connotations and meanings. Each artist who dealt with them had to be aware that he was more or less adapting himself to the fashion, the modern myths and current ideological thought structures. So Viallat set about making visible the mechanism of such a system of signs and submitting the signs themselves to criticism. He wanted to change fundamentally the basis, the material and economic suppositions of painting so as to renew the social function of the painter and of art. He subsequently restricted himself to large unframed canvases sewn together and including also found or already printed material, on which he carried out all the possible colour variations of his special form. A "necessary materialism" was involved, it was said, in which painting is an experimentation with the material means of art, a preoccupation with the real basis and not a communication of ideas.

Painting had become a metaphor for structural thought inasmuch as it accomplished in its forms the structures of a particular social situation. "In working we have to learn," Viallat wrote. "Everything develops its own organization: to reject it would be to exclude a reality." Everything has a special language, a particular discourse, as Michel Foucault has described it. That which has no power of language expresses itself in bodies and spaces, in lines, forms and colours. The object speaks for itself, and in that moment in which it enters into a relationship with the

artist's subject a corresponding composite of reality is expressed in concrete form. According to this interpretation there is no longer a difference, a separation, between subject and object, for they complement one another. In art it is important, Viallat wrote, that in working one learns from the object—or as Michel Foucault expressed it: the artist is through his body and his vision part of the visible world, and both form an inseparable essence.

Viallat wants the subject matter to intrude neither intellectually nor emotionally upon the visible but to engage with him in a process of gradual change. For that reason it is so essential in his work that with a theme which remains the same he should constantly search for fresh material, new contours and formats to whose peculiarities he has to readjust himself. From 1970 to 1971 Viallat was a member of the group Support/Surface, with which he was for a long time theoretically in agreement, but he left it when he was directing its attention less to the analysis of a situation than to direct political engagement. Art, to the group, meant intervening in historical development. Viallat's art stives for a value-free investigation of artistic means of expression, without hierarchy and differentiation between more or less "noble" activities. Everything is worthy of experience. Hence also the struggle against tasteful, academic painting and the restriction to one form, which can stand for all forms. Each impression is so similar to the next that it could be part of any picture, and in this dimension Viallat's painting also gains, over and above any theoretical, social-critical tendency, its ethical value.

—Marie Luise Syring

VIEIRA DA SILVA, Marie-Helene.

French. Born in Lisbon, Portugal, 13 June 1908; emigrated to France, 1928: naturalized, 1956. Studied drawing, under Emilia Santos Braga, in Lisbon, 1922–24; studied painting, under Armando Lucena, and sculpture, at the Academy of Fine Arts, Lisbon, 1924–27; studied painting, under Antoine Bourdelle, Académie de la Grande Chaumière, Paris, 1928–29; and engraving, under S. W. Hayter, Atelier 17, Paris. Married the painter Arpad Szenes in 1930 (died, 1985). Painter, illustrator, and fabric designer, Paris, 1929–39, Lisbon, 1939–40, Brazil, 1940–47, and again in Paris, since 1947. Recipient: Acquisition Prize, *Bienal*, Sao Paulo, 1953; Tapestry Prize, University of Basle, 1954; Grand International Prize, *Bienal*, Sao Paulo, 1961; Grand Prix des Arts, Paris, 1966; Grand Croix de Santiago da Espada, Lisbon, 1977; Medal of Honour, towns of Montargis and Montauban, France, 1983; Grand Prix Florence Gould, Académie des Beaux-Arts, Paris, 1986. Chevalier, 1960, and Commandeur, 1962, Ordre des Arts et Lettres, Paris; Member, Academy of Arts of Lisbon, 1970; Chevalier, Légion d'Honneur, Paris, 1979; Member, Académie des Sciences, des Arts et des Lettres, Paris, 1984. Address: c/o Guy Weelen, 8 Avenue Frochot, 75009 Paris, France.

Individual Exhibitions:

1933   Galerie Jeanne Bucher, Paris
1935   Galerie U.P., Lisbon
1936   Artist's Studio, Lisbon (with Arpad Szenes)
1937   Galerie Jeanne Bucher, Paris

1939   Galerie Jeanne Bucher, Paris
1942   Museu de Arte Moderna, Rio de Janeiro
1946   Galeria Askenazi, Rio de Janeiro
        Palacio Municipal, Belo Horizonte, Brazil
        Marian Willard Gallery, New York
1947   Galerie Jeanne Bucher, Paris
1949   Galerie Pierre, Paris
1950   Galerie Blanche, Stockholm
        Galerie La Hune, Paris
1951   Galerie Pierre, Paris
        Galerie Jeanne Bucher, Paris
1952   Galerie Dupont, Lille, France
1953   Redfern Gallery, London
        Cadby Birch Gallery, New York
1955   Stedelijk Museum, Amsterdam (with Germaine Richier)
        Galerie Pierre, Paris
1956   Saidenberg Gallery, New York
        Galerie Art Moderne, Basle
1957   Galerie de Perron, Geneva
        Hanover Gallery, London
        Galeria Portico, Lisbon
1958   Kestner-Gesellschaft, Hannover (retrospective, travelled to Bremen and Wuppertal, West Germany)
1960   Galerie Jeanne Bucher, Paris
1961   Phillips Art Gallery, Washington, D.C.
        Galerie Pierre Beres, Paris
        Kunsthalle, Mannheim
        Knoedler Gallery, New York
1963   Phillips Art Gallery, Washington, D.C.
        Knoedler Gallery, New York
        Galeria Gravura, Lisbon
        Bezalel Museum, Jerusalem
        Galerie Jeanne Bucher, Paris
1964   Galerie Alice Pauli, Lausanne
        Musée de Peinture et Sculpture, Grenoble (retrospective)
        Museo Civico, Turin (retrospective)
1965   Albert Loeb Gallery, New York
1966   Knoedler Gallery, New York
        Académie des Amateurs de Musique, Lisbon
1967   Galerie Jeanne Bucher, Paris
        Chateau de Ratilly, France (with Etienne Martin)
1969   Théâtre de la Comédie, Tours
        Musée d'Art Moderne, Paris (retrospective)
        Galerie Jeanne Bucher, Paris
        Galerie Jacob, Paris
1970   Museum Boymans-van Beuningen, Rotterdam (retrospective)
        Malerier 1935-1969, Kunstnernes Hus, Oslo
        Kunsthalle, Basle (retrospective)
        Fundacao Gulbenkian, Lisbon (retrospective)
        Galeria Sao Mamede, Lisbon
        Galerie 3, Lisbon
1971   Temperas, Lithographs, Gouaches et Serigraphies, Galerie Jeanne Bucher, Paris
        Galeria Zen, Porto, Portugal
        Paintings 1967-1971, Knoedler Gallery, New York
        Musée Fabre, Montpellier, France
1972   Galerie Regence, Brussels
        Musée Thomas Henry, Cherbourg
        Musée des Beaux-Arts, Rouen
        Museum Unterlinden, Colmar, France
1973   Centro Rizzoli, Milan
        Musée d'Art et d'Histoire, Orleans
1974   Galerie Artel, Geneva
        Gravuras e Litografias, Galeria Quadrum, Lisbon
1975   Institut Francais, Stockholm
        Helsinglands Museum, Hudiksvall, Sweden
        Saabskonstforening, Lingkoping, Sweden
        Konsthalle, Malmo, Sweden
        Galerie Monique Delcourt, Valenciennes, France
        Galerie Fremond, Paris
1976   Galerie Jeanne Bucher, Paris
        Maison des Arts et Loisirs, Sochaux, France
        Musée de Metz, France
        Musée d'Art Moderne, Paris (with Arpad Szenes)
1977   Musée de l'Etat, Luxembourg
        Galerie Kutter, Luxembourg
        Musée d'Art Moderne de la Ville, Paris
        Pinturas a Tempera, Fundacao Gulbenkian, Lisbon
        Galerie La Hune, Paris
        La Galerie, Nimes, France
1978   L'Art en Dreux, France

        Nordyjllands Kunstmuseum, Aalborg, Denmark (retrospective)
        Ty-Kan, Locronan, France
        Galerie Jeanne Bucher, Paris (with Louise Nevelson and Magdalena Abakanowicz)
1979   Musée des Beaux-Arts, Agen, France (toured France)
1980   Galeria Joan Prats, Barcelona
        Centre Culturel, Dakar, Senegal
1981   Musée de Cluny, France
        Bibliothèque Nationale, Paris
1982   Galerie Jeanne Bucher, Paris
        Galerie de l'Information, Tunis
1983   Musée Ingres, Montauban, France
        Museo de Bellas Artes, Bilbao, Spain
1984   Galeria EMI-Valentim de Carvalho, Lisbon
        Centre Culturel Francais, Rome
1985   Galeria III, Lisbon
1986   Galerie Jeanne Bucher, Paris
        Galeria Nasoni, Porto, Portugal (with Arpad Szenes)
        Artcurial, Paris

Selected Group Exhibitions:

1930   Salon des Surindépendants, Paris
1946   Salon des Réalités Nouvelles, Paris
1950   Biennale, Venice
1955   The New Decade, Museum of Modern Art, New York
1964   Painting and Sculpture of a Decade 1954-64, Tate Gallery, London
1971   Carnegie International, Pittsburgh
1973   L'Estampe Contemporaine, Bibliothèque Nationale, Paris
1976   Ratilly, Musée des Arts Décoratifs, Paris
1978   Portuguese Art since 1910, Royal Academy of Arts, London
1984   Biennale Internationale du Dessin, Clermont-Ferrand, France

Marie-Helène Vieira da Silva: *La Déchirure*, 1984

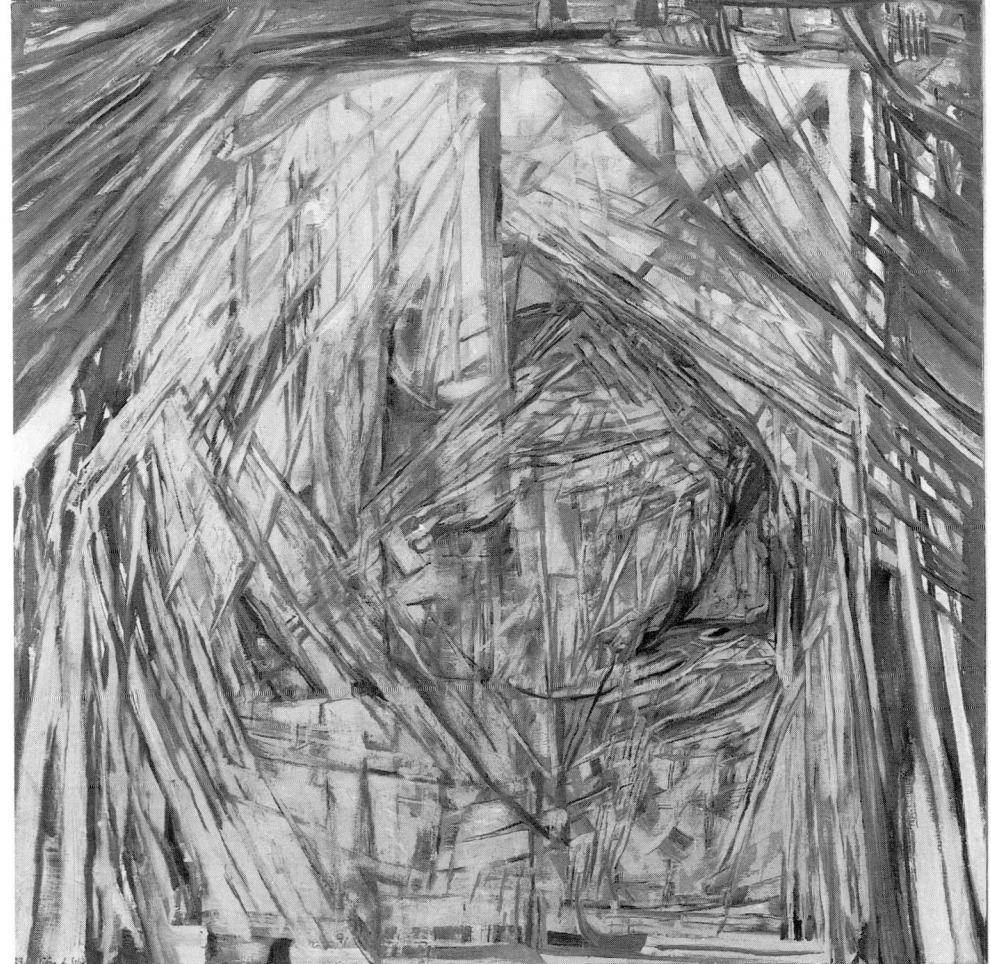

Collections:

Centre Georges Pompidou, Paris; Musée d'Art Moderne de la Ville, Paris; Tate Gallery, London; Stedelijk Museum, Amsterdam; Museum Folkwang, Essen; Kunsthaus, Zurich; Galleria d'Arte Moderna, Museo Civico, Turin; Museu de Arte Moderna, Rio de Janeiro; Museum of Modern Art, New York; Guggenheim Museum, New York.

Publications:

On VIEIRA DA SILVA: books—*Vieira da Silva* by Pierre Descargues, Paris 1949; *Le Musée de Poche: Vieira da Silva* by Rene de Solier, Paris 1956; *Vieira da Silva* by José Augusto Franca, Paris 1958; *Vieira da Silva* by Guy Weelen, Paris 1960; *Vieira da Silva*, exhibition catalogue, with text by Claude Esteban, Basle 1970; *Vieira da Silva: Malerier 1935–1969*, exhibition catalogue, with texts by Snorre Andersen and Guy Weelen, Oslo 1970; *Vieira da Silva*, exhibition catalogue, with texts by Joao Gaspar Simoes, Murilo Mendes and others, Lisbon 1970; *La Peinture de Vieira da Silva* by Dora Vallier, Paris 1971; *Vieira da Silva: Paintings 1967-1971*, exhibition catalogue, with text by John Rewald, New York 1971; *Vieira da Silva*, exhibition catalogue, with text by Georges Desmouliez, Montepellier, France 1971; *Vieira da Silva: Temperas, lithographies, gouaches et serigraphies*, exhibition catalogue, Paris 1971; *Vieira da Silva* by Guy Weelen, Paris 1973; *Vieira da Silva*, exhibition catalogue, with texts by René Char and John Rewald, Geneva 1974; *Vieira da Silva: Gravuras e Litografias*, exhibition catalogue, with text by Guy Weelen, Lisbon 1974; *Vieira da Silva: Les Estampes: Catalogue de l'Oeuvre Grave* by Guy Weelen, Paris 1976; *Vieira da Silva*, exhibition catalogue, with text by Jean-Francois Jaeger, Paris 1976; *L'Univers de Vieira da Silva* by Antoine Terrasse, Paris 1977; *Vieira da Silva: Pinturas a Tempera*, exhibition catalogue, with text by Agustina Bessa Luis, Lisbon 1977; *Vieira da Silva* by Jacques Lassaigne and Guy Weelen, Barcelona and Paris 1978; *L'Eclat de la Lumiere* by Anne Philipe, Paris 1979; *Longos dias tem cem anos: Presenca de Vieira da Silva* by Agustina Bessa Luis, Lisbon 1979; *Chemins d'approche: Vieira da Silva* by Dora Vallier, Paris 1982; *Vieira da Silva: Peintures* by Michel Butor, Paris 1983; *Vieira da Silva: Oeuvres sur Papier* by

Guy Weelen, Paris 1983; *Vieira da Silva e Arpad Szenes ou o Castelo Surrealista* by Mario Cesariny, Lisbon 1984.

The paintings of Vieira da Silva have a timeless modernity about them but it is still hard to realize that effectively her art career began as far back as 1919. To all familiar with the dramatis personae of the Ecole de Paris, although her transformation of architecture rendered upon canvas has been almost a permanent feature for so many years, each evidence of her extraordinary talent still seems paradoxically new.

It is true that as a young girl she once had ambitions to become a sculptor and even took a course under the tutelage of Despiau. But this shortlived enthusiasm cannot in any way explain the unusual and unique control she is able to exert on her canvases across the whole fabric of architectural conception.

Even a painting like the 1939 "Les Drapeaux" shows the same grasp of the building syndrome. The fluttering flags hang down like the tails of kites from windows, and there is no doubt that these are windows of huts set on stilts by some river people. The little squares of the "flags" and the rhodoid tiles on the roofs are repeated in the fabric between the posts and the relections in the water. Already the elaborate patterning of Vieira da Silva which sets such store on the heaving chessboards of tiled vistas of which she is so fond—already this central element in nearly all her later work is plainly evident. That it was subsequently to become thicker and more tantalising to the eye, taking on the form of a gigantic art crossword puzzle, was just a matter of time.

Vieira da Silva is the supreme manipulator of perspective. Cities, promenades, floods, night, time itself are all pressed into service to act as welcome excuse for stretch after stretch of mosaic-like detail; not carefully wrought *azulejos* of Portuguese mural artists, but mosaics that have been shaken by earth tremors or frozen into noble austerity for ever.

Architectural rectitude is only disturbed by the process of time and perhaps the incursion of decay. Looking at her pictures one realizes that she is deeply conscious of what age and weathering can do to her cherished subjects.

—Sheldon Williams

VILLALBA, Dario.

Spanish. Born in San Sebastian, 22 February 1939. Educated in Boston, Massachusetts, 1950-54; studied in the Department of Fine Arts, Harvard University, Cambridge, Massachusetts, 1957-58; studied painting in the studio of André Lhote, Paris, 1968, and at the Escuela de Bellas Arte de San Fernando, Madrid, 1958-62; studied literature and philosophy, University of Madrid, 1962-64. Independent artist, concentrating on painting, Madrid, from 1957; first plexiglass-encased figures, 1966; photographic figures in plexiglass, from 1972; canvases with photoemulsion, from 1973. Recipient: Critics prize, *Bienal of Ibiza*, Spain, 1973; International Prize, *Bienal*, Sao Paulo, 1973; International Prize, *Graphics Biennale*, Ljubljana, Yugoslavia, 1979. Agent: Galeria Vandres, Don Ramon de la Cruz 26, Madrid-1. Address: Fernandez de la Hoy 61, Madrid-3, Spain.

Individual Exhibitions:

1957	Sala Alfil, Madrid
1964	Weeden Gallery, Boston
	Galeria Biosca, Madrid
	Gallery 88, Miami
1966	Drian Galleries, London
	Pinturas 1966, Galeria El Bosco, Cronica de Palomares, Madrid
1970	Museo Espanol de Arte Contemporaneo, Madrid
	Galleria del Naviglio, Milan
	Galerie Defacqz, Brussels
	Spanish Pavilion, at the *Biennale*, Venice
1971	Musée d'Art et d'Histoire, Geneva
	Studio C, Brescia, Italy
1972	Deson-Zaks Gallery, Chicago
	Henry Mayer Gallery, Lausanne
	Cité Universitaire, Neuchâtel, Switzerland
1973	Espace Pierre Cardin, Paris
	Galleria del Naviglio, Milan
1974	Galeria Vandres, Madrid
	Kunstverein, Frankfurt
1975	Louisiana Museum, Humlebaek, Denmark
	Museum Boymans-van Beuningen, Rotterdam
	Museum Bochum, West Germany
1976	*Retrospective 1972-1976*, Palais des Beaux-Arts, Brussels
	Kunstverein, Heidelberg
1977	Kunstlerhaus, Vienna
	Galerie Gras, Vienna
1978	Galeria Juana Mordo, Madrid
	Galeria Vandres, Madrid
1980	Henie-Onstad Kunstsenter, Oslo
1981	Fondation Veranneman, Kruishoutem, Belgium
1982	Galleria del Naviglio, Milan
	Charles Cowles Gallery, New York
1983	Salas Pablo Picasso, Madrid

Selected Group Exhibitions:

1963	*Contemporary Spanish Painting*, D'Arcy Galleries, New York (toured the United States)
1965	*5 Spanish Painters*, at the *Bienal*, Sao Paulo
1970	*Testimonio 70*, Museo Espanol de Arte Contemporaneo, Madrid
1971	*Erotic Art in Spain Now*, Galeria Vandres, Madrid
1972	*Grands et Jeunes d'Aujourd'hui*, Grand Palais, Paris
1973	*Salon de Mai*, Musée d'Art Moderne, Paris
1975	*Biennale of Cagnes-sur-Mer*, France
1978	*La Materia*, Galeria Rayuela, Madrid
1980	*New Images from Spain*, Guggenheim Museum, New York
1983	*International Art Fair*, Chicago

Collections:

Musée des Beaux-Arts, Ostend, Belgium; Fondation Veranneman, Kruishoutem, Belgium; Musee Royal des Beaux-Arts, Brussels; Museo de Arte Contemporaneo, Seville; Louisiana Museum, Humlebaek, Denmark; Museum Boymans-van Beuningen, Rotterdam; Musee d'Art et d'Histoire, Geneva; Musée des Beaux-Arts, Lausanne; Museo de Arte Contemporaneo, Madrid; National Gallery of Australia, Canberra.

Publications:

By VILLALBA: book—*Grupo Quince*, 4 silkscreened objects, Milan 1973.

On VILLALBA: books—*Dario Villalba: Pinturas 1966*, exhibition catalogue, with text by Angel Crespo, Madrid 1966; *Nuevos Maestros de la Pintura Espanola* by Raul Chavarri, Madrid 1972; *Dario Villalba at the Deson-Zaks Gallery*, exhibition catalogue, with text by Franz Schulze, Chicago 1972; *Villalba*, exhibition catalogue, with texts by Pierre Restany and Giancarlo Politi, Madrid 1974; *Dario Villalba*, exhibition catalogue, with text by Peter Spielmann, Hans Gercke, Titia Berlage and Michael Fehr, Bochum, West Germany 1975; *Dario Villalba: Retrospective 1972-1976*, exhibition catalogue, with texts by Titia Berlage, René Micha, Luis Gonzalez Robles and others, Brussels 1976; *Europa-America: The Different Avant-Gardes* by Achille Bonito Oliva, Milan 1976; *Diccionario de Pintores Espanoles Contemporaneos* by Ignacio De Blas, Madrid 1976; *Kunst Kommt nicht von Konnen* by Hans-Jürgen Müller, Stuttgart 1977; *Dario Villalba*, exhibition catalogue, with text by Ole Henrik Moe, Oslo 1980; *Dario Villalba: Obra Reciente 1980-1983*, exhibition catalogue with text by Eugenio de Vicente, Madrid 1983.

*

Man with two coverings: one
his biological skin; the other his invention,
his own industry and web.

If our skin grew outward 30 cms. from
the organic one which encloses us and
crystallized, the magic of the solitary
man, circumscribed in a transparent projection
of his silhouette would be evoked.

Glass-skins invade creation forcing
man to live with industry in a state
of hibernation.

Pathological Toys for Adults.

Fragments of reality (scratches, scars,
bruises) blown-up though mass-
media photographic emulsions create
a neo-abstractionism.
Abstraction based on cold reality.

I do not participate. I only
choose.

My mind cannot forget what my
eyes have invented.

—Dario Villalba

*

Dario Villalba's plastic capsules got to London in 1968. They had already caused a considerable stir at the Venice *Biennale*. At that time they were so unexpected, such a novel experience, that too few people did more than step back and marvel at them. A bad reaction because what the artist wanted from his viewers was thought rather than emotion.

Above all, Villalba is a fighter for the acceptance of human rights. That his campaigns are waged through the artistic forms that he has chosen is our good fortune, but should in no way reduce the potencies of the many messages he wishes to deliver. Villalba's ideas about human rights are basic, certainly not the application of well thought-out laws and regulations. He wants proper understanding of pain and suffering, and he wants to throw out a lifeline to the hopeless.

Effectively his career in its most pertinent sense can be divided into three periods, all of which interrelate.

From 1966 to 1971 he made life-sized flesh-coloured figures which were enclosed in plexiglass and hand-rotated at variable speeds from a plexiglass superstructure.

A year later, using the same technique and materials, he switched from his earlier fluorescent-pink figures to blow-ups from press photos. The subjects in these works were also altered. By this time Villalba had turned his attention to the area of sociological problems—a worker in overalls beset with the difficulties of the class system; a youth in jeans and T-shirt glaring at the outside world and raising his clenched fist; the face of a woman, her eyes closed, at the point of death; a patient in a psychiatric ward, his protruding feet knotted together by the wet bed-sheet. Over these images where he felt it relevant, Villalba scrawled symbols as comments.

Since then he has still further expanded the process, reproducing the figures on emulsioned canvases. To emphasize his intention, sometimes the works appear in triptych form—first the feet, then the arm, then the head. or he takes disparate elements and welds them together in a near-abstract assemblage, making the blow-up technique of the press photograph create enlargements that turn the "screen" of the original newspaper photo into an independent patterning.

Villalba is operating on two levels. On one his "man" regards nature with imperturbable calm; on the other, the same man turns a look of cold and vitriolic hatred upon the cruelties of the social system.

For the viewer, the Villalba images are also bilateral. He looks at them, but they look back at him. And not just the faces. Feet and hands have become personalized. His presentation is at one and the same time fascinating and appalling.

Does an art public, or even a public at large, want

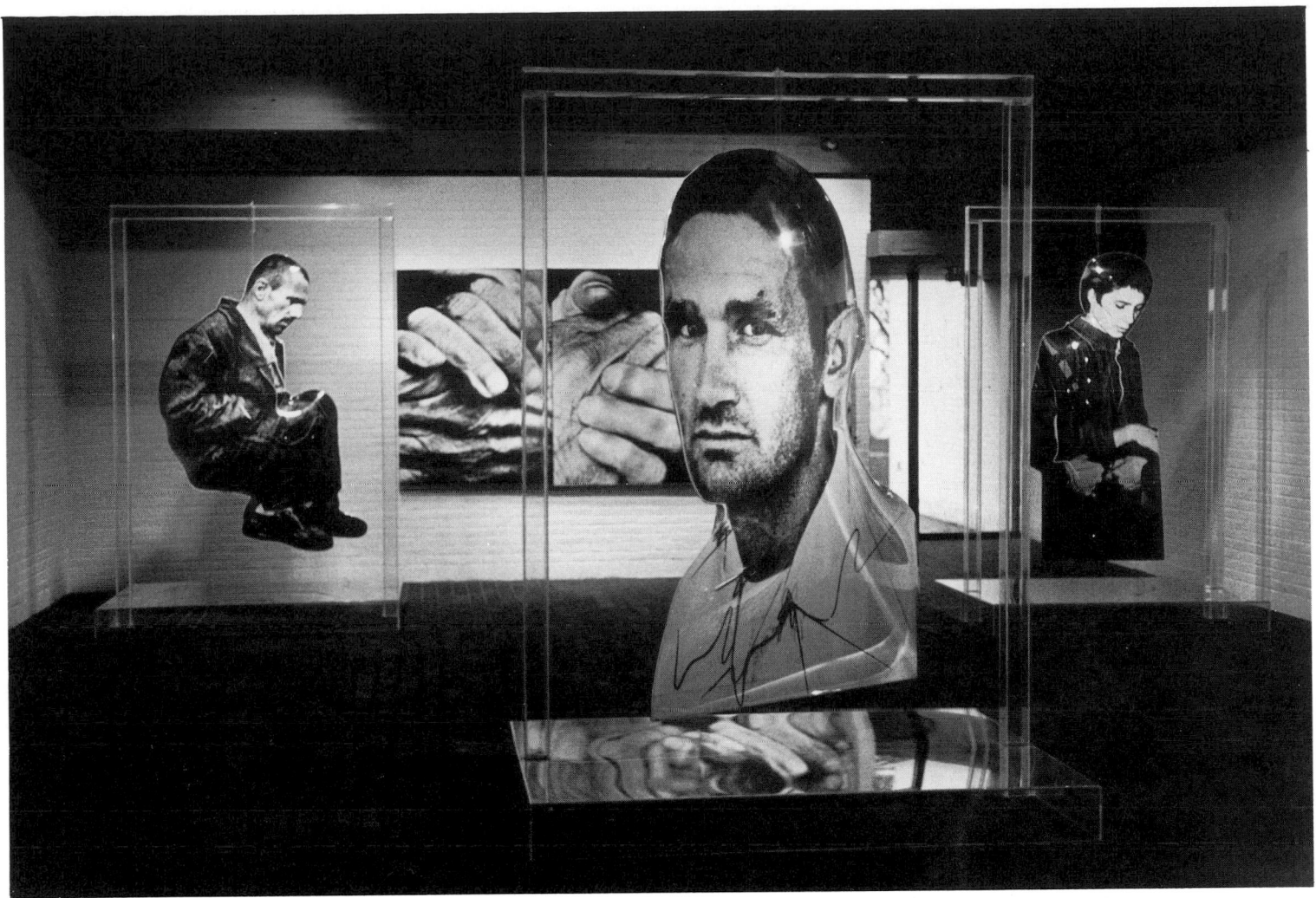

Dario Villalba: Exhibition at the Louisiana Museum, Humlebaek, Denmark, 1975

or require such aggressive preaching? The question is an academic one. So many frightening versions of the Temptation of Saint Anthony in no way deflected praise from those who appreciate good painting. Goya's etchings of the Horrors of War are a satchel of masterpieces. Now Villalba with great technical skill hangs up his plastic bags full of the Horrors of Man.

—Sheldon Williams

VILLEGLÉ, Jacques (Mahé) de la.
French. Born in Quimper, Finistere, 27 March 1926. Educated at secondary school in Vannes-Morbihan, 1934–43; studied at the Ecole des Beaux-Arts, Rennes, 1944–46; studied architecture at the Ecole Nationale Supérieure des Beaux-Arts, Nantes, 1947–49. Married Marie-Francoise de Faultrier in 1956; daughters: Valerie, Fabienne and Adeline. Worked as architectural draughtsman, Vannes, 1943–44; in St. Malo, 1946. Independent artist, writer and filmmaker, in Paris, since 1949; first decollaged poster assembly, 1949; collaborative works with Raymond Hains, 1950–53. Member, Nouveaux Realistes group of artists, Paris, 1960. Agent: Galerie Claudine Breguet, 10 passage Turquetil, 75011 Paris. Address: 15–17 rue au Maire, 75003 Paris, France.

Individual Exhibition:

1957 Galerie Colette Allendy, Paris (with Raymond Hains)
1959 Atelier Francois Dufrene, Paris
1963 Galerie J., Paris
1964 Galerie Ad Libitum, Antwerp
1967 Galerie Jacqueline Ranson, Paris
1971 Galerie Michael Werner, Cologne
Moderna Museet, Stockholm
1972 Galerie Der Spiegel, Cologne
Museum Haus Lange, Krefeld, West Germany
1974 *Temoin de Notre Temps*, Galerie Beaubourg, Paris
Galerie Semiha Huber, Zurich
Centre of Arts and Communication, Vaduz, Lichtenstein
1976 Studio Sant'Andrea, Milan
Galerie Alexandre de la Salle, St. Paul de Vence, France
Galerie Le Dessin, Paris
1978 *Ravisseur Ravi de la Réalité*, Musée des Jacobins, Morlaix, France
1979 Office d'Action Culturelle, Saint-Brieuc, France
1980 Galerie Beaubourg, Paris
Centre Noroit, Arras, France
1981 Galerie Convergence, Nantes, France
1982 Galerie J and J Donguy, Paris
Galerie Micheline Szwajcer, Antwerp
1985 Maison de la Culture Rennes, France
Espace Claudine Breguet, Paris
1986 Galerie Convergence, Nantes, France
Espace Claudine Breguet, Paris
1987 Galerie 44, Kaarst-Dusseldorf, West Germany
Galerie Reckermann, Cologne
Galerie Christian Laune, Montpellier, France
1988 Galerie d'Art Contemporain, Nice
Galerie Le Chanjour, Nice

Selected Group Exhibitions:

1959 *Biennale des Jeunes*, Musée d'Art Moderne de la Ville, Paris
1961 *The Art of Assemblage*, Museum of Modern Art, New York (toured the United States)
1965 *Pop Art, Nouveau Realisme*, Palais des Beaux-Arts, Brussels
1971 *Affiches Laceres*, Staatsgalerie, Stuttgart
1977 *Trois Villes*, Centre National d'Art Contemporain, Paris
1979 *Nouveau Realisme*, Freitags Galerie Imhof, Solothurn, Switzerland
1980 *Les Affichinistes*, Galerie Mathias Fels, Paris
1983 *Les Années 60*, Musée d'Art et d'Industrie, St. Etienne, France
1984 *Affiches*, Musée Départementale des Beaux-Arts, Valence, France
1987 *Les Nouveaux Realistes*, Musée des Beaux-Arts, Winterthur, Switzerland

Collections:

Centre Georges Pompidou, Paris; Reunion des Musée Nationaux (F.N.A.C.), Paris; Musée Cantini, Marseilles; Moderna Museet, Stockholm; Kaiser-Wilhelm Museum, Krefeld, West Germany; Hessiches Landesmuseum, Darmstadt; Von-der-Heydt Museum, Wuppertal, West Germany; Museum van Hedendaagse Kunst, Ghent; Museum Moderner Kunst, Vienna; Israel Museum, Jerusalem.

Publications:

By de la VILLEGLÉ: books—*Heperile Eclate*, with Raymond Hains and Camille Bryen, Paris 1953; *De Mathieu à Mahe*, Paris 1967; *Les Volantes du Ravisseur*, La Louvière,

Jacques de la Villeglé: *Rue Vieille du Temple*, 1980

Belgium 1974; *Lacere Anonyme*, Paris 1977; *Commemoration de la Loi du 29 Juillet 1881*, Paris 1981; *L'Innocence du Choix*, Nice 1982; *Urbi et Orbi*, Dijon 1986; *De la Manifestation Spontanée*, Cognac 1986; films—*Paris-Saint Brieuc*, 1952; *Etude aux allures*, with Raymond Hains, 1954.

On de la VILLEGLÉ: books—*Collage: Personalities, Concepts, Techniques* by Harriet Janis and Rudi Blesh, New York 1962; *Villegle*, exhibition catalogue, with text by Pierre Restany, Paris 1963; *Les Nouveaux Réalistes* by Pierre Restany, Pais 1968; *Pop Art et Cie* by Francois Pluchart, Paris 1971; *Villegle*, exhibition catalogue, with text by Otto Hahn, Stockholm 1971; *L'Art Actuel en France* by Anne Tronche, Paris 1974; *Villegle: Temoin de Notre Temps*, exhibition catalogue, with text by Pierre Restany, Paris 1974; *Les Pre-Voyants* by Alain Jouffroy, Brussels 1974; *Formalism and Historicity* by Benjamin H. D. Buchloh, Chicago 1977; *Villegle, Ravisseur Ravi de la Réalité*, exhibition catalogue, with text by Otto Hahn, Morlaix, France 1978; *Le retour de l'Hourloupe*, exhibition catalogue with text by Bernard Lamarche-Vadel, Rennes 1985; *Villeglé le chapardeur* by Jean-Phillipe Lemee, Nantes 1986; *1960: Les Nouveaux Realistes*, exhibition catalogue with text by Dieter Schwarz, Mannheim and Winterthur 1986; *Jacques Villeglé*, exhibition catalogue with text by Philippe Piquet, Montpellier 1987.

At the start of the 1950's, dislocating the square of cold abstracts which chastised emotion, the physiological and physical powers of the artist shifted position to the profit of an element of total chance which alone was becoming and could be productive. The artist, becoming "action-painter," then, to conclude the series and by reference to the street hoarding "automobile compressor," rejected on principle all conscious intervention, all hesitation and all conscious choice. As has been stated by the author of a general aesthetic, he opposed "learnt beauty, of which he is tired, the harsh and natural beauty which man finds fully equipped beneath his feet and which owes nothing to calculation or exertion."

The lacerations, traces of the gesture in its wild state, come out of anonymity. I would have liked to see them remain there.

If, after having torn down a fragment of a hoarding, the timidity of a certain fear disheartens me it sometimes happens that I unselfconsciously give it the necessary tear to make it stand out, being unable to completely repress the common taste for producing and creating falsities.

Falsities? No, let us recall that discussion between Arp and Mondrian. The latter opposed the artificiality of art to the naturalness of nature, I think, and Arp would not contradict me, that the impulsive gesture of the street is not opposed by that natural tendency to action which more or less everybody possesses. If my hand knows how to terminate the roughed-out gesture of an unknown person, to seek for glory on account of the fact would be inane. The appropriative and selective speculation of an object must not be lowered to the level of a studio procedure, as if to return to the game of dupes which the exercise of drawing and painting has become. "It tends toward the foolish glorification of the hand. The hand is the guilty party, and how can one accept being the slave of one's own hand? It is inadmissible that drawing and painting should today still be where writing was before Gutenberg" (André Breton).

It is regrettable to sign a poster—which the worker in paint, Fernand Léger, would have considered as "having become unusable"—but it remains true that by my label I facilitate its recognition and preserve it from destruction. Beauty is a tributary of bourgeois contingencies. Nevertheless, if I sign, would it not be natural for the successive purchasers or selectors to affix their signatures also, which would simply be resuming a Chinese custom whereby the collector was invited to add his mark beside that of the artist? In sharing my merit as inventor, they would with the same stroke diminish the importance of my imprint and would bring the laceration back to the anonymity of its point of departure.

The ensemble of lacerators, ravishers and collectors will therefore be called "Lacere Anonyme," and would it be to establish the facts of activity whose author would seem to be elusive that my goal would be restricted, or rather, would it be in reconstituting the work of a collective unconscious in personalising the "Lacere Anonyme"? Giambattista Vico did not act differently when he proved that Homer was not one single person but a collective being, a symbol of the Greek people, telling of its own history in national songs.

To endorse the secret of the creation of the lacerated work, I organized in June 1959 in the atelier of Francois Dufrene a series of soirees entitled "Lacere Anonyme." With this generic title each work acquires a specific character. By anonymous gestural aggression the poster become illegible becomes one of the most outstanding manifestations "of art made by everyone and not by one alone" of our time. When Caliban becomes a painter what happens to . . . OK? the professional and traditional painter and his craft?

—Jacques de la Villéglé

The so-called *affichistes* François Dufrène, Raymond Hains, Mimmo Rotella and Jacques Villéglé form a sort of subgroup of the group known as the Nouveaux Réalistes, since their works have a common starting point and are to some extent closely related, while the other artists in the group all tread very different paths. Along with Klein these four are also the Nouveaux Réalistes whose works, outwardly at least, most closely resemble the traditional canvas, which does not mean, however, that they are the 'painters' of the group.

Villéglé received his artistic training in Rennes, where he got to known Raymond Hains, an artist with whom he was frequently to work in the following years. While Hains was devoting his attention to photographic techniques, in 1947 Villéglé had already restricted his artistic activity to the collection of objects which he found near his home on the Breton coast: pieces of wire and other flotsam and jetsam washed up on the Atlantic coast, along with pamphlets and other fragments of printed material. He tells how in January 1947 Hains and he wandered through the Nantes docklands: during the course of that walk it became clear to him how impossible was the artistic transposition of lived reality in its entirety, with which he sought directly and objectively to confront the spectator.

Working with Hains in Paris in 1949, it was in *dé-*

collage that Villéglé found the medium for realising these ideas. The two artists worked together on their first poster abstracts. Such work was the logical consequence of the conversations revolving round the search for an alternative to the abstract art that was beginning to establish itself in Paris now the war was over. In opposition to painting, the aim of this poster abstract was to link up the avant-garde trends of the 1910s and 1920s which, in Europe, had come to an abrupt end. Not until many years later did Villéglé find a forefather for his historical researches in the person of the French Surrealist Leo Malet. Malet had coined the term *décollage* in 1938. For him *décollage* meant the tearing off of individual sections of poster in order to reveal parts of the underlying poster layers and to leave room for speculation concerning what was still concealed. It was a poetic street activity which was still fully in the service of the verbal text, and Malet did not go so far as to uproot the product of *décollage* from its immediate environment.

Hains and Villéglé removed the selected sections of poster from their backing and then mounted them on canvas; the canvas was used on account of its lightness and elasticity, not because of its association with the painted picture. In the process of mounting, the artists might in some cases introduce corrections into the selected poster section. Villéglé also mentions the 'coup de pouce' (finishing touch) which was often necessary in order to complete the insufficiently forceful works, but which was executed without destroying their overall anonymity.

Placarding, particularly that of small political placards, signifies, independently of any actual message carried by the placard, the act of occupying a public area. Under the clause 'Défense d'afficher', the bill that was passed in France on 29 July 1881, divides public areas into display-free zones and zones reserved for the display of advertising material (*emplacements réservés*); anyone who tears down such material is guilty of a criminal offence. The sticking up or pasting over, removal or defacement of posters and placards has correspondingly become a symbol of political struggle. In contrast to wall painting and graffiti, the defacement of the writing in the poster abstract follows no subjective-aesthetic rules. It signifies above all the adoption of an attitude, 'antidote contre toute propagande', and only as an ironic afterthought can it be understood in terms of a decorative design.

By their shabby appearance poster abstracts bear witness to life in certain Parisian quarters, and in his *Le flaneur aux palissades* Villéglé describes the differences between hoardings in the various quarters depending on the degree and nature of building and renovation work going on there. The transformation of the city and especially the erection of inaccessibly high large-format advertising hoardings could mean the end of the 'era' of the poster abstract.

The selection of an object, which becomes a work of art merely by grace of the artist's decision, takes us back to Marcel Duchamp's notion of the ready-made. There are however some fundamental differences between the poster abstract and the ready-made. Poster abstracts are closer from the outset to conventional art, since they assume the conventional form of a picture. They do not merely refer to the artistic context or, as the case may be, to themselves as autonomous works of art; they have besides this a representative function: they refer to the sections of poster that were not selected, to the permanent street exhibition, and thereby step beyond the closed world of art and into that of an anonymous public.

The tradition of artistic skill is replaced by a passive, receptive strolling around, in the course of which the stroller finds and selects posters. There is equally no clear intention in the mind of the artist engaged in tearing down and shredding posters: the spontaneous, unconsidered gesture takes the place of the premeditated composition. And even if certain gestures are deliberate, their significance is lost among the multitude of other gestures whereby the poster is built up. In this way the poster abstract denies essential elements which contribute towards the value of a work of art: craftsmanship, effort and time.

A new academic style could clearly develop out of the anonymous poster abstract. Bryen had already predicted: 'Anti-painting is becoming the painting of today and even in its freedom is adopting mannerisms and styles.' Villéglé had tried to avoid that by consistently assuming the role of sociological observer and abnegating the traditional one of the creative artist. He entitles his works with the place and date of the discovery and accords thematic importance to their timing. In 1982 he thus dedicated an exhibition to the *Présidentielles 81* (the 1981 Presidential Elections), following the progress of the various election candidates: "Je n'ai aucun parti pris sur les candidats, je suis presque un historien, qui prend les faits bruts" (I have no particular bias with regard to the candidates, I am virtually a historian, merely recording the bare facts). Through his writing, moreover, he has become the historian of what he calls the *Lacéré anonyme* (the anonymous slasher), the historian of the community of anonymous 'poster slashers', the discoverer and collector of their work.

—Dieter Schwarz

VISSER, Carel (Nicolaas).

Dutch. Born in Papendrecht, 3 May 1928. Studied architecture at the Technische Hogeschool, Delft, 1948–49; studied drawing and sculpture at the Koninklijke Academie voor Beeldende Kunsten, The Hague, 1949–51. Married Margareet Donker in 1953; sons: Harm and Geert Jan. Sculptor and graphic artist, Amsterdam, since 1952, and farmer, near Culemborg, since 1968. Visiting Professor, Washington University, St. Louis, 1962; Instructor, Koninklijke Academie voor Beeldende Kunsten, The Hague, 1958–62. Instructor, Atelier 63, Haarlem, since 1962. Recipient: Dutch Government travel stipend to Mexico, 1965; David Bright Award, *Biennale*, Venice, 1968; Museum of Western Art Prize, *International Print Biennale*, Tokyo, 1972; Dutch State Prize for Sculpture and Architecture, The Hague, 1972. Agents: Galerie Espace, Keizersgracht 548, Amsterdam; Art and Project, Prinsengracht 785, Amsterdam; and Galerie Paul Maenz, Schaafenstrasse 25, 5000 Cologne 1, West Germany. Address: Prinses Margrietstraat 2, 4023AD Rijswijk, Netherlands.

Individual Exhibitions:

1954	Kunsthandel Martinet, Amsterdam
1959	Steendrukkerij de Jong, Hilversum, Netherlands
	Neue Galerie Parnass-Jaehrling, Wuppertal, West Germany
1960	Stedelijk Museum, Amsterdam
	Gemeentemuseum, The Hague
1965	Galerie Espace, Amsterdam
1967	Municipal Museum, The Hague
1968	Galerie Espace, Amsterdam
1970	Galerie Espace, Amsterdam
1972	*Beelden 1969–1972*, Stedelijk Museum, Amsterdam (travelled to Gemeentemuseum, The Hague)
	Galerie Espace, Amsterdam
	Galerie Paul Maenz, Cologne
	Galerie Fenna de Vries, Rotterdam
	Sculptures, Beelden, Palais des Beaux-Arts, Brussels
1973	Form Meditation International, Amsterdam
	Lucy Milton Gallery, London
1974	Art and Project, Amsterdam
	Galerie Nouvelles Images, Ghent
	Galerie Nouvelles Images, The Hague
1975	Art and Project, Amsterdam
	Galerie Paul Maenz, Cologne
	Beelden, Tekeningen, Collages, Stedelijk Van Abbemuseum, Eindhoven, Netherlands
1976	Art and Project, Amsterdam
	Sperone-Westwater-Fischer, New York
1977	Art and Project, Amsterdam
	Galerie Konrad Fischer, Dusseldorf
	Galleria Primo Piano, Rome
	Kunsthalle, Dusseldorf
1978	*Sculptor's Work by Carel Visser: Sculpture Drawings, Prints and Jewelry 1952–1977*, Whitechapel Art Gallery, London (travelled to the Arnolfini Gallery, Bristol, and the Third Eye Centre, Glasgow)
	Papierbeelden, Stedelijk Museum, Amsterdam
1979	*Sculptures 1978–1979*, Groningen Museum, Netherlands
1981	Rijksmuseum Kröller-Müller, Otterlo, Netherlands
1982	Nigel Greenwood Gallery, London
1984	Groninger Museum, Groningen, Netherlands
	Art and Project, Amsterdam
	Galerie Plus-Kern, Brussels
1985	Institut Neerlandais, Paris
	Galerie Konrad Fischer, Dusseldorf
	Galerie Durand-Dessert, Paris
	Kasteel Wijlre, Netherlands
1986	Galerie Durand-Dessert, Paris
	Museum Boymans-van Beuningen, Rotterdam
	Art and Project, Amsterdam
	Galerie Fenna de Vries, Rotterdam
1987	Art and Project, Amsterdam

Selected Group Exhibitions:

1952	*Sonsbeek International Exhibition*, Sonsbeek Park, Arnhem, Netherlands
1958	*Biennale*, Venice, Italy
1961	*Carnegie International*, Pittsburgh
1969	*Biennale*, Paris
1972	*Amsterdam-Paris-Dusseldorf*, Guggenheim Museum, New York
1973	*Lof der Tekenkunst*, Stedelijk Van Abbemuseum, Eindhoven, Netherlands
1975	*Funkties van Tekeningen*, Rijksmuseum Kröller-Müller, Otterlo, Netherlands
1977	*Europe in the 70's*, Art Institute of Chicago (toured the United States)
1983	*De Statua*, Van Abbemuseum, Eindhoven, Netherlands
1986	*Geent op Bosch*, Museum Het Kruithuis, Den Bosch, Netherlands

Collections:

Stedelijk Museum, Amsterdam; Gemeentemuseum, The Hague; Rijksmuseum Kröller-Müller, Otterlo, Netherlands; Stedelijk Van Abbemuseum, Eindhoven, Netherlands; Tate Gallery, London.

Publications:

By VISSER: books—*Carel Visser*, exhibition catalogue, Amsterdam 1960; *Carel Visser: 10 Beelden*, exhibition catalogue, Otterlo, Netherlands 1981; articles—"Carel Visser in Gesprek met Jan Dibbets en Rudi H. Fuchs" in *Museumjournaal* (Amsterdam), February 1973; interview, with Ad Petersen, in *Carel Visser: Papierbeelden*, exhibition catalogue, Amsterdam, 1978.

On VISSER: books—*Art and Architecture in the Netherlands: Carel Visser* by Cor Blok, Amsterdam 1968; *34th Biennale di Venezia 1968: Olanda—Carel Visser*, exhibition catalogue, edited by R. W. D. Oxenaar, Hilversum, Netherlands 1968; *Amsterdam-Paris-Dusseldorf*, exhibition catalogue, with texts by Cor Blok, Blaise Gautier, and Jürgen Harten, New York 1972; *Carel Visser: Beelden*, exhibition catalogue, Brussels 1972; *Carel Visser: Beelden 1969–1972*, exhibition catalogue, Amsterdam 1972; *Lof der Tekenkunst*, exhibition catalogue, with text by Carel Blotkamp, Eindhoven, Netherlands 1973; *Carel Visser: Beelden, Tekeningen, Collages*, exhibition catalogue, with text by Rudi H. Fuchs, Eindhoven, Netherlands 1975; *Carel Visser: Papierbeelden*, exhibition catalogue, Amsterdam 1978; *Sculptor's Work by Carel Visser: Sculpture, Drawings, Prints and Jewelry 1952–1977*, exhibition catalogue, with texts by Nick Serota and Barbara Reise, London, 1978; *Carel Visser: Sculptures 1978–1979*, exhibition catalogue, with texts by Frans Haks and Carel Blotkamp, Groningen, Netherlands 1979; *Carel Visser: Beelden 1975–1985,* exhibition catalogue with text by Wim Beeren, Rotterdam 1986.

Carel Visser is undoubtedly the most important sculptor to come into prominence in the Netherlands since the Second World War. The great tradition of constructivism, as manifested in some of Mondrian's work and in the furniture and architecture of Gerrit Rietveld, is also present in Visser's art. Not that his work represents a mere continuation of *De Stijl:* that tradition, in combination with Visser's stern Calvinistic background, simply forms the basis for his struggle against the *Kubus* and helps to explain his preference for softer constructions.

Visser's first sculptures, done in steel around 1950, include the touching "Dying Horse" and many representations of birds. In 1954 or so he became strongly interested in the problems of vertical and horizontal symmetry. "Birds," for example, from 1954, is an almost abstract piece in which the top form mirrors the form beneath it, as a bird is reflected in the calm water over which it flies. In 1959 Visser produced "Great Auschwitz," another abstract work in which linear construction and spatial openness are brought together in a tension-filled relationship. In this respect, and because of the emotion-laden title, it is more than a spatial continuation of Mondrian's Pier + Ocean paintings from 1917.

The work Visser displayed at a 1972 exhibition in the Stedelijk Museum of Amsterdam represents a particularly important point in his development. His new material, thin, malleable plastic, is in strong contrast to the massive steel of his earlier work. The sculpture "Folded Tower" (1972) is made up of four folded plates, each of which is larger than the one below it: the tower literally sighs under its own weight. "Result With a Cube" (1970) is especially significant: here a plated steel cube is held together by leather cornerbands, while stretched out in front of it is a cross made up of six metal plates identical with those which make up the cube. Visser's battle with "the cube" is clearly apparent here.

In 1979 Visser surprised his audience with the small, strongly figurative and anecdotal objects he displayed in the Groningen Museum (South African ostrich eggs, for example, bound by leather straps to a Turkish walking stick). In 1981 he exhibited ten larger constructions in the Rijksmuseum Kröller-Müller, constructions which seemed to combine his drive towards figurative work and his battle against constructivist demands for summary and clarity. These works were made out of various kinds of simple materials drawn from Visser's own recent life in the country.

Visser is also famous as a draughtsman. Especially remarkable are his drawings from 1974: totally gray, graphite backgrounds which seem as if they were made of metal, and on which Visser has attached reproductions of such objects as avocados, fish, and labels of whisky bottles.

In his works from 1982 onwards, Visser exploits his newly discovered procedures. The sculptures seem to be objects of artistic recycling, a way of conserving those things and materials that have been left behind in the fields. His exhibition at the Art and Project Gallery, Amsterdam, in 1987 consisted of two farm transport vehicles serving as pedestals for the sculptures, creating a strong contrast with the architecture of the gallery itself. In some pieces, figurative imagery is dominant as in the cardboard portrayals of his old dog.

—A. F. Wagemans

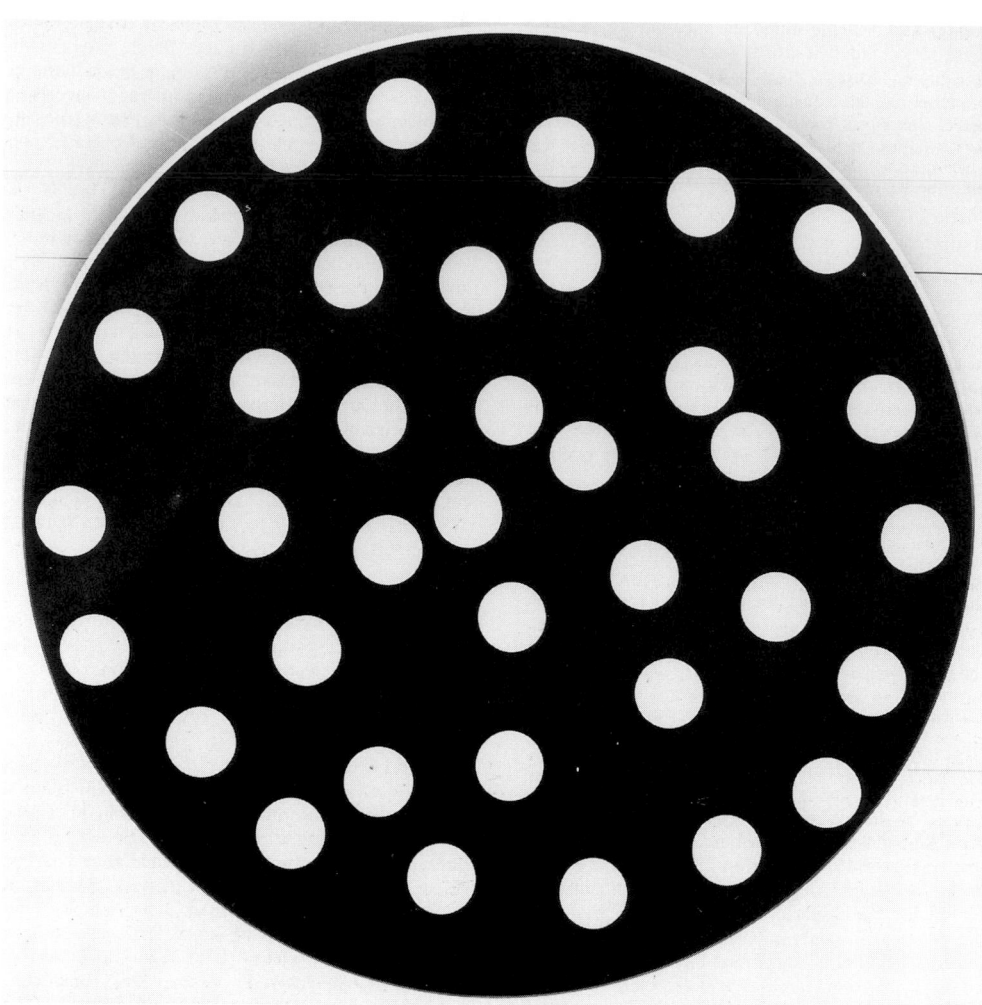

Gerhard Von Graevenitz: *Kinetic Object with White Disks,* 1965

von GRAEVENITZ, Gerhard.

German. Born in Schilde, Mark Brandenburg, 19 September 1934. Studied economics at the University of Frankfurt, 1955–56; studied art, under Ernst Geitlinger, Akademie der Schonen Künste, Munich, 1956–61: influenced by Josef Albers, Max Bill, and by Francois Morellet. Married Autje-Maria Ludwig in 1967; children: Julia and Moritz. Independent artist, concentrating on optical and kinetic works, in Munich, 1960–70, in Paris and Amsterdam, 1970 until his death in 1983: Founder-Member, Nouvelle Tendance group of artists, Paris, 1961–62. Instructor, Akademie der Schonen Künste, Kassel, 1969; Hochschule für Fernsehen und Film, Munich, 1970; and Akademie der Schonen Künste, Nuremberg, 1970; Guest-Professor, Kunstakademie, Hamburg, 1978. Editor, *Nota* magazine, Munich, 1960–61; Dutch Cocommissioner, *Biennale,* Venice, 1978; Concept and planner, *Pier Ocean* exhibition, Hayward Gallery, London, 1979–80. Agents: Galerie Reckermann, Albertusstrasse 16, 5000 Cologne 1, West Germany; Galerie Schoeller, Poststrasse 2, 4000 Dusseldorf, West Germany. *Died* (in an airplane crash in Switzerland) *in 1983.*

Individual Exhibitions:

1962	Galerie Roepcke, Wiesbaden, West Germany
1964	Galerie Wentdorf, Oldenburg, West Germany
1965	Op-Art Galerie, Esslingen, West Germany
	Galerie 123, Krefeld, West Germany
	Galerie Klihm, Munich
1966	Karl-Ernst-Osthaus Museum, Hagen, West Germany
	Galerie im Europa-Center, West Berlin
	Signals Gallery, London
1967	Galerie Klihm, Munich
1968	Museum Folkwang, Essen
	Galerie M. E. Thelen, Essen
	Galerie Ernst, Hannover
	Galerie Swart, Amsterdam
1970	Galerie Lichter, Frankfurt
	Galerie Klihm, Munich
1971	Galerie M, Bochum, West Germany
	Galerie Swart, Amsterdam
1972	Studio Marconi, Milan
	Galerie Swart, Amsterdam
1973	Lucy Milton Gallery, London
1974	Kunsthalle, Kiel (retrospective; toured Germany)
1976	Galerie Swart, Amsterdam
1977	Galerie Klihm, Munich
	Galerie M, Bochum, West Germany
	Stedelijk Museum, Amsterdam
1979	*Kinetische Objekten,* Stedelijk Van Abbemuseum, Eindhoven, Netherlands
1980	Galerie Reckermann, Cologne
	Cultureel Centrum, Tilburg, Netherlands
1983	Galerie Schoeller, Dusseldorf
1984	Rijksmuseum Kröller-Müller, Otterlo, Netherlands
1985	Wilhelm-Hack-Museum, Ludwigshafen, West Germany
1986	Kunsthalle, Bremen, West Germany
	Josef Albers Museum, Bottrop, West Germany

Selected Group Exhibitions:

1959	*Die neue Generation,* Kunstverein, Hannover
1964	*Nouvelle Tendance,* Musée des Arts Décoratifs, Paris
1966	*Directions in Kinetic Art,* Berkeley Museum, California
1968	*Documenta,* Kassel, West Germany
1970	*Biennale,* Venice
1973	*Kunst in Deutschland 1898–1973,* Kunsthalle, Hamburg
1979	*Zero: Bildvorstellung einer europaischen Avantgarde 1958–64,* Kunsthaus, Zurich (travelled to Antwerp)
1980	*Pier and Ocean,* Hayward Gallery, London
1985	*Kunst in der Bundesrepublik 1945–85,* Nationalgalerie, West Berlin

Collections:

Stedelijk Van Abbemuseum, Eindhoven, Netherlands; Gemeentemuseum, The Hague; Museum für Kunst und Gewerbe, Hamburg; Landesmuseum, Hannover; Städtische Galerie, Munich; Kunsthalle, Nuremberg; Westfälischer Landesmuseum, Münster, West Germany; Städtische Museum, Bochum, West Germany; Tate Gallery, London; University of California Art Museum, Berkeley.

Publications:

By von GRAEVENITZ: articles—"Statement" in *Kunstlicht-kunst*, exhibition catalogue, Eindhoven, Netherlands 1966; "Statement" in *Directions in Kinetic Art*, exhibition catalogue, Berkeley 1966; "Statement" in *Basically White*, exhibition catalogue, London 1974; statement in *To Do With Nature*, exhibition catalogue, Amsterdam 1978; statement in *Pier and Ocean*, catalogue, London 1980; text in *Schwarz*, exhibition catalogue, Dusseldorf 1981.

On von GRAEVENITZ: books—*Constructivism: Origins and Evolution* by George Rickey, New York 1967; *Gerhard von Graevenitz*, exhibition folder, with text by Hannah Weitemeier, Munich 1967; *Naissance de l'Art Cinetique* by Frank Popper, Paris 1967; *Gerhard von Graevenitz*, exhibition catalogue, with text by Dietrich Helms and Helmut Heissenbuttel, Hannover 1968; *Wesen und Kunst der Bewegung* by Gyorgy Kepes, Brussels 1969; *Deutsche Kunst: eine neue generation* by Rolf-Günter Dienst, Cologne 1970; *Deutsche Kunst der 60er Jahre: Malerei, Collage, Op-Art, Graphik* by Juliane Roh, Munich 1971; *Basically White*, exhibition catalogue, with texts by Carel Blotkamp and Lucy Milton, London 1974; *Gerhard von Graevenitz*, exhibition catalogue, with texts by Jens Christian Jensen and Heinz Spielmann, with an interview by Frans Haks, Kiel 1974; *Gerhard von Graevenitz: Kinetische Objekten*, exhibition catalogue, with texts by J. Bremer and C. Blotkamp, Eindhoven, Netherlands 1979; *Gerhard von Graevenitz*, exhibition catalogue with texts by R. Oxenaar, A. von Graevenitz, L. Gloser and others, Otterlo 1984.

My kinetic objects are visual objects. The elements are simple. The organization is non-hierarchic (no composition). The movement is not linear (no beginning, no end). The objects are structures: networks of connections, of elements or simple processes. Because the organization is open—as it has been developed in the theory of games—there is playfulness involved. The relation of my objects to reality is not that of copies, but rather of models, i.e., I try to make the objects so simple, so logical that they take on the character of models. My round objects with disks work according to a relatively simple principle. The disks are fixed at a point on the periphery, on axes which turn at random, sometimes clockwise, sometimes counter-clockwise, and are moved by an electric motor. As all disks move, the network changes continuously and therefore the path of each disk seems to be relatively complex, while the movement of the total circle cannot be seen. The number of possible situations is so great that a repetition is very improbable.

—Gerhard von Graevenitz (1965)

Gerhard von Graevenitz belonged to that new group of artists who at the beginning of the 1960's chose as themes previously little used mediums—light, movement, mechanics—and systematically, with wide and individual variations, developed early experiments—perhaps of Calder and Gabo—into a revolutionary art form. Characteristic of the movement, which was later labelled "Kineticism," was its internationalism. Whoever looks carefully, however, soon discovers in the international groups aspects of a thoroughly regional and individual kind. In the case of Gerhard von Graevenitz a fantasy presents itself, having a basis of sober calculation, yet not exhausting itself in it. The mechanics of his objects is simple, yet the same constellations of elements, light, movements in some of his objects should, according to the law of probability, only repeat themselves every 10–20,000 years—this means that during the expected life of an object it should never precisely repeat the pattern of the passing second. The incidence of chance is thereby largely eliminated.

Graevenitz never accepted the precision of a richly incidental mechanism as an end in itself. He agreed completely with Schiller-ian maxim about art being close to a game, and about man being never more himself than when he is at play.

Graevenitz arrived at results such as the kinetic objects by virtue of consistent development. In 1959 he began to model accurate structures in slight relief, without the aid of colour, in pure white, discovering, apart from the rhythm of structure, the ambivalence of concave and convex forms in the incidence of light. After accurate structures he then worked on structures with short lines the optical interactions of which preoccupied him. Next were the kinetic objects, which consistently followed the structural images of the time around 1960/61, built from small elements—chiefly squares and circles. In their place came circular discs with flat lamellae at changing angles to each other, flat discs as well as cruciform or triangular. With the introduction of single and multi-colored light falling from the changing constellation in small areas on the turning lamellae, there began that series of objects in which the optic play gained incalculable possibilities of variation and in front of which the spectator's imagination is attracted to associations other than the merely optical perception. They can work like a glimpse into the cosmos or the microscope, like signs of scientific experiment or metaphysical symbols.

In the late 1960's Graevenitz turned from complex programmes to simple ones again. He was more and more preoccupied with the irritation caused by the slight movement of plastic elements or by the light paths. On a wall in the Gemeentemuseum in The Hague in 1969 he carried out in monumental form an example for the modification of a surface relief by a constantly changing constellation. The conscious link with his chosen tradition is made visible in the arrangement of the room of the great Stijl architects, a link which to Graevenitz went back to the mathematically-based metaphysics of Pico della Mirandola or to the play with numbers in Mesopotamia. Graevenitz always protected himself from risk of being misunderstood by virtue of the admission of such references—and because the creative fantasy of his inventions always involved a return to the simplest starting points for new ideas.

—Heinz Spielmann

VON SCHLEGELL, David.

American. Born in St. Louis, 25 May 1920. Studied engineering at the University of Michigan, Ann Arbor, 1940–42; studied painting at the Art Students League, New York, 1945–48, and with his father, William von Schlegell, 1945–50. Served in United States Army Air Corps, 1943–44. Painter, 1950–61, and sculptor since 1961; now lives and works in Connecticut. Worked as an engineer, Douglas Aircraft, Long Beach, California, 1942–43, and in an architect's office, 1944–45. Taught privately, 1950–55; Visiting Lecturer in Sculpture, University of California at Santa Barbara, 1968; Instructor in Painting, School of Visual Arts, New York, 1968–69; Visiting Instructor in Sculpture, Cornell University, Ithaca, New York 1969–70. Director of Studies in Sculpture, Yale University, New Haven, Connecticut, since 1971. Recipient: First prize for Sculpture, Colman Award, Whitney Museum, New York, 1964; Purchase Prize, *Carnegie International*, Pittsburgh, 1967; National Endowment for the Arts Grant, 1969; St. Buttolph Award, Boston, 1969; Guggenheim Fellowship, 1974; Skowhegan School Medal for Sculpture, Maine, 1978; Pollock/Krasner Foundation Grant, New York, 1986. Agent: Pace Gallery, 32 East 57th Street, New York, New York 10022. Address: c/o Department of Art/Sculpture, Yale University, 180 York Street, New Haven, Connecticut 06520, U.S.A.

Individual Exhibitions:

1956	Swetzoff Gallery, Boston
1957	Poindexter Gallery, New York
1959	Swetzoff Gallery, Boston
1964	University of New Hampshire, Durham
	Stanhope Gallery, Boston
	Museum of Art, Ogunquit, Maine (with Jack Levine)
1965	Ward-Nasse Gallery, Boston
	Institute of Contemporary Art, Boston (three-person exhibition)
1966	Royal Marks Gallery, New York
1967	Royal Marks Gallery, New York
	New York University, New York (three-person exhibition)
1968	Brandeis University, Waltham, Massachusetts (retrospective)
1969	Obelisk Gallery, Boston
	Ward-Nasse Gallery, Boston
1970	Paula Cooper Gallery, New York
1971	Reese Palley Gallery, New York
1972	Reese Palley Gallery, New York
1974	Pace Gallery, New York
1975	Pace Gallery, New York
1976	Pace Gallery, New York
	Institute of Contemporary Art, Boston
1977	Pace Gallery, New York
1981	Pace Gallery, New York

Selected Group Exhibitions:

1957	*Whitney Annual*, Whitney Museum, New York (and 1964, 1968)
1963	*New England Sculpture Today*, Boston
	5 New England Sculptors, Wadsworth Atheneum, Hartford, Connecticut
1965	*World's Fair*, New York
1966	*Primary Structures*, Jewish Museum, New York
1967	*Innovations*, Art Institute of Chicago
	Carnegie International, Pittsburgh
1971	*Sculpture for New Spaces*, Walker Art Center, Minneapolis
	Sculpture in the Park, Van Saun Park, Paramus, New Jersey
	International Biennale of outdoor Sculpture, Middelheim Museum, Antwerp

Collections:

Whitney Museum, New York; Massachusetts Institute of Technology, Cambridge; University of Massachusetts, Amherst; Addison Gallery of American Art, Andover, Massachusetts; Rhode Island School of Design, Providence; Aldrich Museum of Contemporary Art, Ridgefield, Connecticut; Carnegie Institute, Pittsburgh.

Publications:

By VON SCHLEGELL: article—"The Artist Speaks: David von Schlegell" in *Art in America* (New York), May/June 1968.

On VON SCHLEGELL: article—"David von Schlegell" by Dennis Adrian in *Artforum* (New York), December 1965.

In 1961, after he had spent over a decade painting full-time, David Von Schlegell turned his attention to sculpture. Using his previous experience in boat building design, engineering, Air Force piloting, and working for an architect, he bases his sculpture on the possibilities inherent in the materials and construction methods used in engineering structures including aircraft and boats. Von Schlegell's materials are aluminum, stainless steel and wood, which he uses with great precision and skill to invent structures which push the limits of the material to create large yet fragile configurations which are arrived at intuitively and usually stress curved, irregular shapes. The process of design and construction is a complex one, done by Von Schlegell himself, and the resulting works are highly abstract and simplified forms.

Von Schlegell's intention is, as he stated in 1966, "to take hold of the invisible feelings one has toward form, space and motion and to make them visible." His works seem poised in a position of imminent movement, as if about to walk or fly away. In his 1966 work "Radio-Controlled Sculpture," Von Schlegell built in a complicated electronic system which enabled the twisting aluminum, three-pronged form to literally waddle away in response to radio command. Like his other sculptures, this one conveys anthropomorphic associations, which are amplified by the quality of implied motion in a gestural interaction with the surrounding environment. Titles such as "Marina" (1965) and "Voyage of Ulysses" (1977) further attest to this allusionary content level. Untitled works also refer ultimately to man-made and/or organic entities and also to the four elements. "Untitled" (1965, aluminum), consisting of a pyramid cut by a long, narrow, twisting horizontal, suggests the energy of lightning hitting this ancient symbol of mysterious and enduring architecture. "Untitled" (1978) curves and folds sensuously in vertical motion to a sharp point, transforming the dynamics of sails and wings into a 20th century icon.

Von Schlegell's most successful works have been those which harmonize with their surrounding environments, creating a sense of organic continuity with Nature's phenomena. Some use polished aluminum surfaces to reflect and warp in changing patterns dictated by time and weather. Others, such as "Storm King Project" (1972), use open, lightweight forms in tune with the lay of the land, and hover on the edge between visibility and invisibility.

Von Schlegell developed his sculpture at a time when Minimalism was coming into vogue. His inclusion in the 1966 exhibition, *Primary Structures*, mixed him with a group of sculptors most of whom were far more formally oriented. (A notable exception is Tony Smith who is also mistakenly aligned with 1960's Minimalism.) Von Schlegell stresses the abstract elements of his work, speaking against references to "some other object." Yet he often uses the word "intuitive" and speaks of a concern to make invisible feelings visible. His statements reflect a desire to avert readings which are too literal and to keep them on the level of ideas. Considering this factor, along with the underlying content visible in the sculptures themselves, and adding also Von Schlegell's previous painting in an Abstract Expressionist vein, the true nature of his work is best understood as arising out of the ideas promulgated in Abstract Expressionist painting during the 1940's and 50's.

During the early 1960's Von Schlegell stopped using wood, feeling that it aroused too many organic connotations. In recent works he has returned to wood to create horizontal configurations which are magnificently crafted and admit the loveliness of the medium as well as allusions to the sea and its crafts. At this point in time and with a large body of work behind him, Von Schlegell seems to feel freer to allow his referential content to surface. He has never been either a formalist or a depictor of specifics, and he continues to use his materials and his language of abstract forms to shape distilled visions which communicate the correspondence inherent in the nature of our industrial environment.

—Barbara Cavaliere

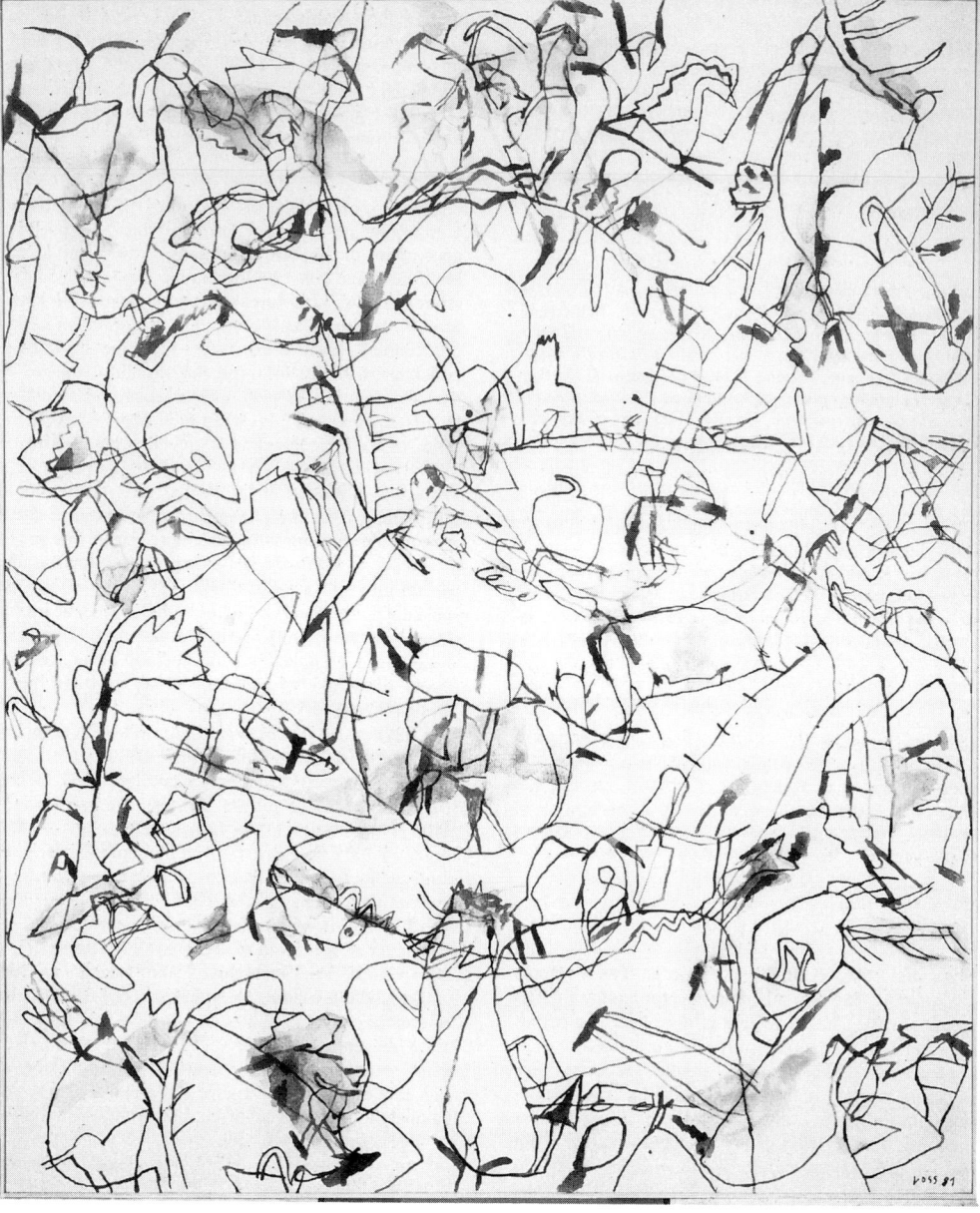

Jan Voss: *Untitled*, 1981

Kunstakademie, Hamburg, 1966–67. Agents: Galerie Lelong, 13/14 Rue de Teheran, 75008 Paris, France; Galerie Nothelfer, Uhlandstrasse 184, 1000 Berlin 12 (West), Germany; Galerie Moderne, Skoletorvet, 8600 Silkeborg, Denmark; Galerie Academia, Residenz, 5010 Salzburg, Austria; Galerie Satani, 4–2–6 Ginza, Chuo-ku, Tokyo, Japan. Address: 34 rue Dombasle, 75015 Paris, France.

Individual Exhibitions:

1963	Galerie Bayer, Mainz
1964	Galerie du Fleuve, Paris
1965	Galerie Lucien Durand, Paris
	Galleri Birch, Copenhagen
1966	Galerie Mathias Fels, Paris
	Lefebre Gallery, New York
1967	Galleria del Naviglio, Milan
1968	Galerie Brusberg, Hannover
1969	Galleri Birch, Copenhagen
1970	Galerie Van de Loo, Munich
1971	Lefebre Gallery, New York
	Galleria Del Naviglio, Milan
1972	Galerie Lucien Durand, Paris
1974	Galerie Brusberg, Hannover
	Galerie Buchholz, Munich
1975	Galerie Lucien Durand, Paris
	Goethe Institut, Paris
1976	Galleri Birch, Copenhagen
1977	Galerie C, Paris
1978	Musée d'Art Moderne de la Ville, Paris (retrospective)
	Galerie Le Dessin, Paris
	Galerie Nothelfer, West Berlin
1979	Galerie Van de Loo, Munich
	Centre Culturel, Toulouse
1980	Galerie Le Dessin, Paris
	Leopold-Hoesch Museum, Duren, West Germany
	Galerie Linssen, Bonn
1981	Kunstverein, Pforzheim, West Germany
	Landesmuseum, Oldenburg, West Germany
	Art Front Gallery, Tokyo
	Galerie Adrien Maeght, Paris
1982	Galeria Maeght, Barcelona
	Randers Museum, Denmark
	Museum van Hedendaagse Kunst, Utrecht
	Galerie Convergence, Nantes, France
	Galerie Bel'Art, Stockholm
	Centre Culturel, Bretigny-sur-Orge, France
1983	Galerie Satani, Tokyo
	Galerie Academia, Salzburg, Austria
	Galerie Grafica, Tokyo
	Artotheque, Lyon, France
	Museum van Hedendaagse Kunst, Ghent, Belgium
1984	Galerie Moderne, Silkeborg, Denmark
	Galerie Ulysses, Vienna
	Galerie Quaresso, Munich

VOSS, Jan.

German. Born in Hamburg, 9 October 1936. Studied at the Kunstakademie, Munich, 1955–60. Independent artist, Paris, since 1960. Painting instructor,

Galerie Satani, Tokyo
Galerie Grafica, Tokyo
1985 Manus Presse, Stuttgart
Galerie Beaumont, Luxembourg
Galerie Wentzel, Cologne
Galerie Satani, Tokyo
Galerie Grafica, Tokyo
1986 Galerie Nothelfer, West Berlin
Galerie Academia, Salzburg, Austria
Herstand Gallery, New York
1987 Maison de la Culture, La Rochelle, France
Les Cordeliers, Chateauroux, France
Galerie Laune, Nimes, France
Galerie Satani, Tokyo
1988 Galerie Wentzel, Cologne

Selected Group Exhibitions:

1962 *Donner à Voir*, Galerie Creuze, Paris
1963 *Biennale de Paris*, Musée d'Art Moderne de la Ville, Paris
1965 *Le Merveilleux Moderne*, Konsthall, Lund, Sweden
1967 *La Bande Dessinee et la Figuration Narrative*, Musée des Arts Decoratifs, Paris
1970 *Distances*, Musée d'Art Moderne de la Ville, Paris
1972 *German Contemporary Art*, National Museum of Modern Art, Tokyo (travelled to Kyoto)
1977 *Mythologies Quotidiennes 2*, Musée d'Art Moderne de la Ville, Paris
1981 *Phoenix*, Alte Oper, Frankfurt
1984 *Ecriture dans la Peinture*, Villa Arson, Nice
1986 *Kunst Heute in Frankreich*, Sammlung Ludwig, Aachen, West Germany

Collections:

Musée d'Art Moderne de la Ville de Paris; Centre National d'Art Contemporain, Paris; Centre Georges Pompidou, Paris; Musée Cantini, Marseilles; Moderna Museet, Stockholm; Goteborgs Kunstmuseum, Sweden; Städtisches Museum, Bonn; Sammlung Ludwig-Städtische Galerie, Aachen, West Germany; Stadtische Galerie im Lenbachhaus, Munich; Museum of Modern Art, New York.

Publications:

By VOSS: articles—"Entretien avec Jan Voss," with Bernard Lamerche-Vadel, in *Artistes* (Paris), October/November 1981; "Jan Voss—Interview," with Anne Dagbert, in *Art Press* (Paris), November 1981.

On VOSS: books—*Positionen* by Rolf-Günter Dienst, Cologne 1968; *Deutsche Kunst eine neue Generation II* by Rolf-Günter Dienst, Cologne 1970; *Deutsche Kunst der 60er Jahre* by Juliane Roh, Munich 1971; *Jan Voss*, exhibition catalogue, with text by Yves Michaud, Paris 1981; *Le Seismographe Lunatique: Jan Voss, Oeuvre Graphique 1964-1982*, exhibition catalogue with text be Anne Tronche, Paris 1982; *Jan Voss: un voyage ideal*, exhibition catalogue with essay by Katsuhiro Yamaguchi, Tokyo 1983; *Jan Voss—le presque parfait*, exhibition catalogue with text by Daniel Dobbels, Silkeborg 1984; *Trajet de Jan Voss* by Bernard Noel, Marseilles and West Berlin 1985.

Within view

Perhaps he had placed his hand against a rock and in outlining it with the help of a bit of charred wood had drawn its shape. Perhaps in this way he had recorded the beginning of history. His hand had then continued to grasp everything in sight: animals and gods, men and landscapes, objects, constructions, forms, ideas . . . .

He should never again stop taking possession of the world by marking/signing it, and we pursue this outline which connects prehistory to our decade and we observe it already overtaking us and vanishing in the vertiginous infinity like the condensation trail of an aircraft which has crossed the sound barrier.

—Jan Voss

Jan Voss has lived in Paris since 1960. Educated at a

time when lyrical abstraction dominated the art schools in Germany, he sought primarily a manner of expression personal to himself and as different as possible from the aimless poesy of this tendency. From the very first he was interested in writing as a painter's gesture, not in that which it could, unwilled and uncontrolled, set free in the layers of the unconscious but in that which it can contribute to painting in its role of go-between.

In the works from the beginning of the 1960's Voss had already given it the task of making a direct statement, less by direct legibility than by the fact that painting can on the whole be conceived as writing. These pictures from 1961 and 1962 recall picture stories put together from pure and simple pictograms which are so close to scrawl that the anecdote as such finally remains incomprehensible. During the 1960's both elements became more precise: both the individual signs and the writing role of the painterly gesture. The pictures became clearer in their expression, had something to say, serve communication. The latter is indeed one of the themes around which Jan Voss's entire work will soon revolve: which sign at what time and for whom is suitable for communication?

The scrawl hardens. The picture ground and signs are from then on more radically separated from each other. The individual pictograms take on firm outlines, become discernible and recognizable and therefore even interchangeable from picture to picture. Finally Jan Voss's pictures are peopled by a number of more or less naively drawn figures and objects which are arranged across a broad unorganized area in a kind of fictional running narrative.

A synthesis of all these works was perhaps reached in 1968 in the picture which he called "Reading for Everyone." It is a challenge to the viewer to read the picture like a book and to regard the painting as a multiplicity of languages, symbols and stereotypes--and an invitation to remain conscious and critical in relation to these languages and not to surrender to them in admiration, as with secret scripts that one does not understand. What Voss was making especially visible in this instance was a critique of political emblems and ideology related symbols: from the Mao bible to Ché Guevara, they serve the individual only to adopt a political code like a fashion and not as more effective communication from man to man.

In this way Voss's work enters completely into the painterly tendencies of the 1960's in Paris, which built on a structuralist critique of language and which above all did not remain uninfluenced by Michel Foucault's writing. Instead of investigating the contents of knowledge, Foucault has begun to analyze critically the discourses, the languages of our knowledge. He had shown that we are all dependent on that discourse into which, according to our era and environment, we are born, and that it is therefore necessary above all to be vigilant in relation to the languages and forms of expression which we employ in science, literature and art so that we understand their full significance.

In 1965 and 1967 Jan Voss exhibited occasionally with painters who belonged to the so-called "Figuration Narrative." I believe, however, that he aimed less at a confrontation between figuration, or the power of the figurative picture, and abstract painting than at the preservation of a critical attitude in relation to all languages of art. Consequently, he has also, in recent years, tended towards a painting of "indecision." From the beginning of the 1970's he gave up the previously discovered language patterns in favour of imaginary signs which he arranged uniformly across empty surfaces like elementary particles. These required only to be connected with an endless line in order to arrive at current works. The world of the pictogram seemed too constricting, too didactic and too little concerned with the real problems of painting. He retained the character of the element, but it was now bound up in a kind of linear labyrinth. Even colour was banished from the plane surface back to the line. The line is led across the surface unsteadily, sometimes hesitatingly, sometimes with wilful naivete, forms a foyer here and there in which archaic figure like images take shape without ever becoming

articulate forms. The line plays around them and itself; Voss liberates it from the individual object so that it may belong to all possible objects. It flies from one motif to the next; it crosses through, draws paths, horizons, mountains, in order immediately to destroy them.

Voss's pictures are thus a virtuoso example of structures which came from crossed lines. He shows without describing that one can speak neither of abstraction nor of the genesis of a picture: he has now reached an intermediate stage of landscapes without contour and distances without perspectives. He materializes a non-concentric thought, one that moves in many centres at once, that lies across the picture surface like a vibrating network which always remains incomplete and open. His pictures arise from moments of distraction—as he himself says, they arise unpremeditated from a balance between the will and the accidental, between reason and unreason.

—Marie Luise Syring

VOSTELL, Wolf.

German. Born in Leverkusen, near Cologne, 14 October 1932. Studied lithography in a printing works, Cologne, 1950-53; studied painting and typography at the Werkkunstschule, Wuppertal, 1954; studied painting, graphics and anatomy, under A. M. Cassandre, Ecole des Beaux-Arts, Paris, 1955-57; and at the Kunstakademie, Dusseldorf, 1957-58. Married Mercedes Guarado Olivenza in 1958; sons: Santiago David and Rafael Isaac. Independent artist in Paris, 1954-57, 1958-59, Dusseldorf, 1957-59, Cologne and Wuppertal, 1959-70, and in West Berlin, since 1971; and Malpartida, Spain, since 1975; produced first "décollages," Paris, 1954; first street happenings, Paris, 1958; first sculpture-actions, with cement "blockages," Cologne, 1969. Layout artist, *Neue Illustrierte*, Cologne, 1961-62; Founder-Editor, *Décoll-age*, Frankfurt, 1962-69; Founder, with George Maciunas, Jean-Pierre Wilhelm, Nam June Paik and others, Fluxus movement, Cologne, 1962-66; Founder, Happening-Archiv, West Berlin 1971; Co-Founder, Aktionen der Avantgarde (A.D.A.) foundation, West Berlin, 1973; Founder, Museo Vostell, Malpartida, Spain, 1976. Instructor in Typography, Werkkunstschule, Wuppertal, 1959-60. Agents: Galerie Van de Loo, Maximilianstrasse 27, 8000 Munich 22, West Germany; Galeria Punto, Baron de Carcer 37, Valencia, Spain. Addresses: Museo Vostell, Malpartida de Caceres (Caceres), Spain; and Giesebrechtstrasse 12, 1000 Berlin 12, West Germany.

Individual Exhibitions:

1950 Salon Educacion y Descanos, Caceres, Spain
1960 Galeria Sala Lux, Caceres, Spain
1961 Galerie Le Soleil dans la Tête, Paris
Galerie Haro Lauhus, Cologne
1962 Galerie Monet, Amsterdam
1963 Smolin Gallery, New York
Galerie Parnass, Wuppertal, West Germany
1964 Galerie Loehr, Frankfurt
1965 Galerie René Block, West Berlin
Studio F, Ulm, West Germany
1966 Something Else Gallery, New York
Verwischungen, Happening-Notationen 1961-66, Kölnischer Kunstverein, Cologne
1967 Galerie Tobies and Silex, Cologne
Galerie René Block, West Berlin
Museum of Contemporary Art, Chicago (with Allan Kaprow)
1968 Galerie Hake, Cologne
1969 Institut Dr. Gasch, Wiesbaden
Galerie Rolf Kuhn, Aachen, West Germany
Galerie Van de Loo, Munich

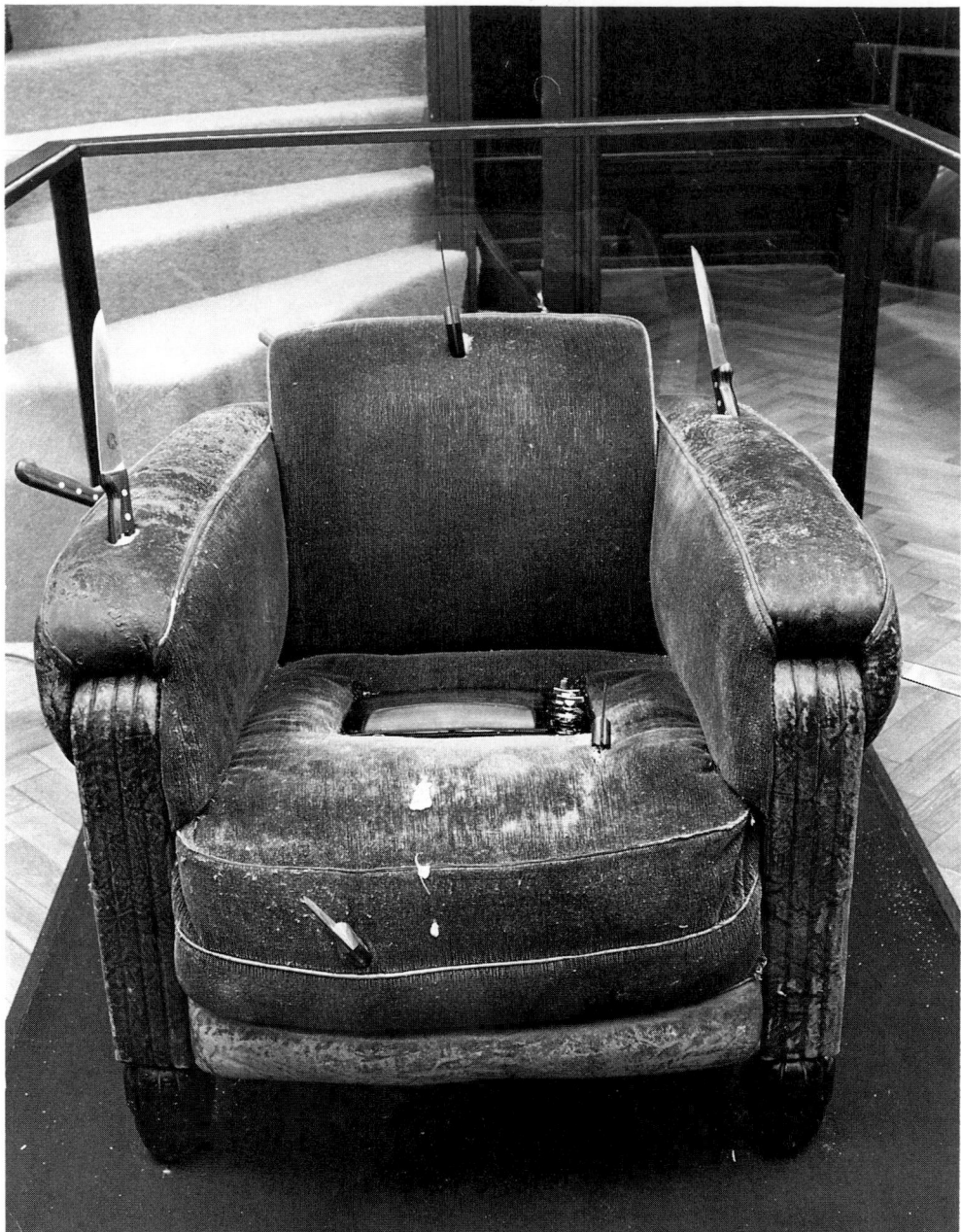

Wolf Vostell: *New Yorker Chair,* 1976

1970   Galerie Art Intermedia, Cologne
        Atelier NW 8, Beindersheim, West Germany
        Elektronisch, Galerie Rolf Kuh, Aachen, West Germany
        Galerie Inge Baecker, Bochum, West Germany
        Galerie René Block, West Berlin
1971   Galerie Bama, Paris
        Galerie Catacombe, Basle
        Galerie Press, Konstanz, West Germany
        Galerie Kerlikowsky und Kneiding, Munich
        Galerie Inge Baecker, Bochum, West Germany
        Galerie Hausdewell, Baden-Baden, West Germany
        Galerie Hausdewell, Hamburg
        Galerie René Block, West Berlin
        Galerie Kolczynski, Stuttgart
1972   Galerie Argelander, Bonn
        Rheinisches Landesmuseum, Bonn
        Galerie Art in Progress, Zurich
        Kunstverein, Freiburg
        Galerie Van de Loo, Munich
1973   Goethe Institut, Marseilles
        Galleria La Bertesca, Milan
        Galerie Paramedia, West Berlin
        Galerie Van de Loo, Munich
        Galerie Ingo Kummel, Dusseldorf
1974   Galerie Bama, Paris
        La Sala Vincon, Barcelona

        Galleria La Bertesca, Milan
        Galleria Multiphla, Milan
        Nuovi Strumenti, Brescia, Italy
        Deutsches Kulturinstitut, Madrid
        Kunsthalle, Bremen, West Germany
1975   *Environments/Happenings 1958–1974,* Musée d'Art Moderne de la Ville, Paris
        Galerie Van de Loo, Munich
        Retrospektive 1958–1974, Nationalgalerie, West Berlin
        Galleria Bocchi, Parma
        Galleria Bozzi, Turin
        Galleria Incontri, Rome
        Galleria Area, Florence
        Galerie Andre, West Berlin
        Galleria Multiphla, Milan
        Galerie Bama, Paris
        Galerie Carsta Zellermayer, West Berlin
        Galerie Inge Baecker, Bochum, West Germany
1976   Galerija Teatru-Studio, Warsaw
        Städtisches Museum, Wiesbaden
        Kunsthalle, Nuremberg
        Galerie Pool, Graz, Austria
        Galerie Kausch, Kassel, West Germany
        Museo Vostell, Malpartida de Caceres, Spain (inaugural exhibitions)
        Kunststation Faber, Fulda, West Germany

        Galerie Andre, West Berlin
        German Institute, Barcelona
1977   Galerie Kausch, Kassel, West Germany
1978   Anja Kunstsenter, Abenra, Denmark
        Museo de Arte Contemporaneo, Madrid
        Universitat Essen, Wset Germany
1979   Kunstlerkongress-Halle, Stuttgart
        Fundacion Joan Miro, Barcelona
        Fundacao Gulbenkian, Lisbon (retrospective)
        Museu Nacional de Soares Dos Reis, Porto, Portugal
        Museo Vostell, Malpartida de Caceres, Spain
        Galerie Ars Viva, West BErlin
1980   Galleria Il Centro, Naples, Italy
        Monte Video, Wuppertal, West Germany
        Galerie Inge Baecker, Bochum, West Germany
        Museo Vostell, Malpartida de Caceres, Spain
        Kunstverein, Braunschweig, West Germany
        Los Angeles Institute of Contemporary Art
1981   Galerie Ars Viva, West Berlin
        Fluxus Zug, Rail Stations in Dortmund, Aachen, Cologne, Dusseldorf and other cities in West Germany
1982   Gesellschaft für neue Kunst, Bremen, West Germany
        Kunstverein, Uelzen, West Germany
        Museo Vostell, Malpartida de Caceres, Spain
        Centre Culturel du Marais, Paris
        Musee de Calais, France
        DAAD-Galerie, West Berlin
1983   Palais des Beaux-Arts, Charleroi, Belgium
        Centro de Arte y Comunicacion, Buenos Aires
        Galerie Bama, Paris
        Nationalgalerie, West Berlin
1984   Galerie Armstorfer, Salzburg, Austria
        Galeria Punto, Valencia Spain
        Sala Parpallo, Valencia, Spain
1985   Galerie Inge Baecker, Cologne
        Galerie Wewerka, West Berlin
        Galerie Muda, Hamburg
        Espace Nord, Liege, Belgium
        Musée d'Art Moderne, Strasbourg, France

Selected Group Exhibitions:

1961   *Salon Comparaisons,* Musée d'Art Moderne, Paris
1962   *Schrift und Bild 1,* Kunsthalle, Baden-Baden, West Germany
1967   *Pictures to Be Read—Poetry to Be Seen,* Museum of Contemporary Art, Chicago
1968   *Von der Collage zur Assemblage,* Institut für Moderne Kunst, Nuremberg
1969   *Art by Telephone,* Museum of Contemporary Art, Chicago
1970   *Happening und Fluxus,* Kölnischer Kunstverein, Cologne
1973   *Contemporanea,* Parcheggio Villa Borghese, Rome
1977   *Documenta,* Kassel, West Germany
1980   *Forms of Realism Today,* Musee d'Art Contemporain, Montreal
1982   *20 Jahre Fluxus 1962–82,* Stadtisches Museum, Wiesbaden, West Germany

Collections:

Museum am Ostwall, Dortmund, West Germany; Neuer Berliner Kunstverein, West Berlin; Berlinische Galerie, West Berlin; Nationalgalerie, West Berlin; Neue Galerie, Aachen, West Germany; Kunstmuseum, Hannover; Bundesministerium des Innern, Bonn; Gesamthochschule, Wuppertal, West Germany; Bibliothèque Nationale, Paris.

Publications:

By VOSTELL: books and pamphlets—*Tombeau de Pierre Larousse,* with poems by Francois Dufrene, Wuppertal, West Germany 1961; *Happenings, Fluxus, Pop Art, Nouveau Realisme,* editor, with Jürgen Becker, Reinbek, West Germany 1965; *24 Stunden,* Itzehoe, West Germany 1965; *Wolf Vostell: Berlin and Phenomena,* New York 1966; *Wolf Vostell: Dokumentation,* edited by René Block, West Berlin 1968; *Vostell 1: Eine Dokumentation 1954–69,* with additional text by Sidney Simon, West Berlin 1969; *Miss Vietnam and Texts of Other Happenings*, San Francisco 1969; *Pop Architektur—Concept Art*, editor, with Dick Higgins, Dusseldorf 1969; *Wolf Vostell: Happening und Lebe*, Neuwied and West Berlin 1970; *Aktionen, Happenings und Demonstrationen seit 1965: Ein dokumentation von Wolf Vostell*, Reinbek, West Germany 1970; *Vostell: Betonierungen*, Hinwil, West Germany 1970; *Wolf Vostell: Elektronisch*, exhibition catalogue, Aachen, West Germany 1970; *Fantastic Architecture*, editor, with Dick Higgins, New York 1971; *T.O.T. (Technological Oak Tree): 310 Ideen*, Hinwil, West Germany 1973; *Wolf Vostell: Happenings Calvario*, Genoa 1973; *Vostell: Fandango*, Milan 1975; *Vostell: Zyklus Extremadura*, with interview by Maria Luisa Borras, Munich 1975; *Wolf Vostell: 10 Happeinings Knozerte 1954–1973*, Milan 1976; *Derriére l'arbre (Duchamp no ha comprendido a Rembrandt . . .): Un Video-Happening de Vostell*, Barcelona 1976; *Vostell: Projekte und Ideen meiner Medienkonzeption zu Hamlet*, Cologne 1979; *Shakespeare-Hamlet*, Cologne 1979; articles—*De-coll/ages: Bulletin aktueller ideen* (Frankfurt), nos. 1 7, 1962 69; *Postversandroman*, with Peter Faecke (Neuwied), no. 1–11, 1970–72; films—*Sun in Your Head, 1 and 2*, 1963; *Chasseur à Reaction*, 1967; *20 Juillet 1944 Aix la Chapelle*, 1967; *Notstandbordstein*, 1967; *21 Projecteurs*, 1967; *Brotvermessung*, 1969; *Circulation Bloquee*, 1969; *Vietnam 1967–71*, 1971; *Desastres*, 1972; *T.O.T.*, 1972.

On VOSTELL: books—*Postface and Jefferson's Birthday* by Dick Higgins, New York 1964; *A Primer of Happenings and Time-Space Art* by Al Hansen, New York 1965; *Assemblages, Environment and Happenings* by Allan Kaprow, New York 1976; *Pop Art* by Lucy R. Lippard, New York and Washington, D.C. 1966; *Collage: Personalities, Concepts, Techniques* by Harriet Janis and Rudi Blesh, New York, Philadelphia and London 1967; *Pop und die Folgen* by Heinz Ohff, Dusseldorf 1968; *Vostell Soziologisch* by Rainer Wick, Bonn 1969, *Wolf Vostell. Retrospektive 1958–1974*, exhibition catalogue, with text by Jorn Merket, West Berlin 1975; *Wolf Vostell: Environments/Happenings 1958–1974*, exhibition catalogue, with text by Suzanne Page, Paris 1975; *Vostell: Heuwagen*, with text by Christa Schwens, Essen 1978; *Vostell*, exhibition catalogue, with texts by Santiago Amon, Simon Marchan and Jürgen Schilling, Madrid 1978; *Vostell 1968–1979*, exhibition catalogue, with texts by Francesco Vicens, Santiago Amon and Eberhard Roters, Barcelona 1979; *Wolf Vostell: Decollagen, Verwischungen, Schichtenbilder, Bleibüder 1955–1979*, exhibition catalogue, with interview by Jürgen Schilling, Braunschweig, West Germany 1980; *LAICA-Los Angeles, Ars Viva-Berlin: Vostell*, exhibition catalogue, with text by Robert L. Smith, Los Angeles 1980; *Vostell und Berlin: Leben und Werk 1971–1981*, exhibition catalogue, with text by Wieland Schmied, West Berlin 1982; *Wolf Vostell: Estampes et Affiches*, exhibition catalogue, with text by Francoise Woimant and Anne Moeglin-Delcroix, Paris 1982; *Wolf Vostell: environment, video, peintures, dessins 1977–85*, exhibition catalogue with texts by Michael Marschall, Nadine Lehni and Michel Giroud, Strasbourg 1986.

In order to survive all the madness and craziness of daily life in a nuclear era, I have made my artwork more and more research to express more and more freedom in whatever I am doing. Art as an expression of individual freedom is the only illusion that I have developed from my work—much better than accomplishing a style, satisfying a market, or looking for a happy ending as an artist integrated with society.

The intelligence and the nervous system of the artist has to develop as far as it can; therefore, creative systems and also creative craftsmanship has to be rich and complex as it can be on all levels, far away from nature and trivial fantasy. I feel that my obligation is to concretize that which nature cannot but nature speaks through me, and I am therefore life *and* art at the same time. Every man an artwork means that before making art the artist must be complex. Anyone becomes an artist only through his work, but anyone can be an artwork through nature.

—Wolf Vostell

One of Wolf Vostell's best known Happenings was a crash between a car and a railway engine, which certainly had its intended effect of shocking and infuriating the average German consumer. And all Vostell's work is in a sense a single great composition, since it all arises from the basic idea of shocking his audience out of their normal complacency into a new critical and aesthetic awareness of the everyday world of technology and politics. Like Duchamp with his "Ready-mades," Vostell seizes and isolates a piece of reality and proclaims it to be a work of art. But instead of mystifying it by isolating it in a gallery stripped of its normal associations, Vostell leaves it in its normal environment, while looking at it afresh, not with the casual glance of everyday life, but with the critical and aesthetic awareness usually brought to art.

Vostell's early work was the production, alteration and destruction of images using the technique he called dé-coll/age, the opposite of the building up process of collage, since it involves tearing of posters or other printed matter. He took the word from a French newspaper headline in September 1954 which announced a plane crashing immediately after its *dé-collage*, which in this context merely means "take-off," though the general idea of "unsticking" fused with the violent event and the artistic meaning of collage to give the idea of torn posters on boardings, the resulting picture becoming a document of the violent action of tearing. The tearing away of various superimposed layers of posters on a hoarding means that bits of different posters are left, fragments of words or pictures or colours which may give each other new meaning, which however can be altered by further tearing, revealing new components.

Such pictorial dé-coll/ages already include not only the ideas of constant change and openness, but also the idea of action. So it was a short step to widen the meaning from torn posters on hoardings to actual real events, to be "torn," open actions of his dé-coll/age demonstrations. In Paris in the late 1950's Vostell collaborated with A. M. Cassandre, and the first of his demonstrations took its inspiration and its title from Cassandre's book *Das Theater ist auf der Strasse* (The Theatre Is in the Street). Vostell's demonstrations differed from the early American happenings not only in taking place out in the open in the streets, but also in relying much less on chance by giving precise instructions for action. These demonstrations had clearly defined objectives, and Vostell's aggressive attitude means that no one is allowed to be a mere passive spectator, but is involved as an actor in whatever is going on. In his TV dé-coll/ages, for instance, the viewer is unsettled by deliberately faulty pictures or sets tuned out of focus, or smeared with paint or bashed in and riddled with bullet holes.

Vostell works out illustrated "scores" with detailed instructions for his demonstrations and happenings, though without excluding chance events: "A primary characteristic of my work and that of my colleagues is that the Happening includes whatever noise, movement, object, color or psychology enters into the total work of art. Because of this I assert that people and life are art." This total work of art in which the public are performers is intended to arouse their critical and aesthetic awareness so that they "learn to live and experience in the psychological reality of their surroundings." They are to be involved in a total work of art which both arouses their sensuous and aesthetic responses and also has an intellectual impact which leads to each developing a new way of seeing, a consciousness both of himself and of his own body and of the ways in which his life is conditioned by the technological world.

From 1962 Vostell began to call his works Happenings and he became closely associated with the Fluxus movement, with such events as the group *24 Hour Happening* at Wuppertal in 1965 or Vostell's own most ambitious happening *In Ulm, round Ulm and round about Ulm* of 1964. He has called the events of May 1968 in Paris "the greatest Happening of all" because unrest supported by artistic means here moved into direct political action and the overthrow of de Gaulle. Unlike Duchamp's ready-mades, the materials Vostell selects for his happenings are not random objects but central achetypal elements of our machine age such as television, trains and cars. And unlike the futurist worship of the car as an object of beauty he emphasizes its destructive potential, seeing in the passing car "the accident too driving by." One instruction in his earliest demonstration was to make sculpture out of crashed cars by fixing the remains to the spot where the accident occurred, and the old tendency to simply clear up the mess and thrust it out of mind has indeed now given way in some countries to putting up photographs of some of the worst accidents as a grim warning. Vostell's work, whatever its creative limitations, always presents a challenge, both to extend artistic reality to all sorts of everyday events and to approach these with a new critical and aesthetic awareness.

—Konstantin Bazarov

VOULKOS, Peter.

American. Born in Bozeman, Montana, 29 January 1924. Educated at Montana State College, Bozeman, 1946–51, B.S. 1951: California College of Arts and Crafts, 1951–52, M.F.A. 1952. Served as B52 Rear Gunner, Army Air Corps, in the Pacific, 1942–45. Independent sculptor, since 1952: lives and works in Oakland, California. Taught at Archie Bray Foundation, Helena, Montana, and Black Mountain College, Beria, North Carolina, 1952–54; Otis Art Institute, Los Angeles, 1954–59; and Greenwich House Pottery, New York, Summer 1961. Instructor, 1959–63, and Professor, 1963–85, University of California, Berkeley. Recipient: Gold Medal, *International Ceramic Exhibition*, Cannes, 1955; Sculpture Prize, *Biennale*, Paris, 1959; Sculpture Prize, San Francisco, 1967; National Endowment for the Arts grant, Washington, D.C., 1976, 1986; Creative Arts Medal, Brandeis University, Waltham, Massachusetts, 1982; Guggenheim Fellowship, New York, 1984; Gold Medal, American Crafts Council, 1986. Honorary Doctorates: California College of Arts and Crafts, Oakland, 1974; Otis Art Institute, 1982. Agent: Braunstein Gallery, 254 Sutter Street, San Francisco, California 94108. Address: 951 62nd Street, Oakland, California 94608, U.S.A.

Individual Exhibitions:

1956	Felix Landau Gallery, Los Angeles
1957	University of Southern California, Los Angeles
1958	Felix Landau Gallery, Los Angeles
	Pasadena Art Museum, California
1961	Museum of Modern Art, New York
	Bonnier Gallery, New York
1964	Gallery Unlimited, San Francisco
	Primus-Stuart Gallery, Los Angeles
1965	David Stuart Gallery, Los Angeles
1968	Quay Gallery, San Francisco
1969	David Stuart Gallery, Los Angeles
1974	Quay Gallery, San Francisco
1975	Kansas City Art Institute
	Helen Drutt Gallery, Philadelphia
	Braunstein/Quay Gallery, New York
1976	Yaw Gallery, Bloomfield Hills, Michigan
	Detroit Institute of Art
	Exhibit A Gallery, Evanston, Illinois
1978	Braunstein/Quay Gallery, San Francisco
	San Francisco Museum of Modern Art (retrospective)
1979	Exhibit A Gallery, Chicago
1981	Jacksonville Art Museum, Florida
	Exhibit A Gallery, Chicago
	Thomas Segal Gallery, Boston
	Charles Cowles Gallery, New York
1982	Braunstein Gallery, San Francisco
1983	Point View Art Center, Tokyo (travelled to Nagoya and Kyoto)
	Charles Cowles Gallery, New York
1984	Magnolia Editions, Oakland, California
	University of Iowa, Ames
	Exhibit A Gallery, Chicago
	Braunstein Gallery, San Francisco
1985	Exhibit A Gallery, Chicago
1986	Braunstein Gallery, San Francisco
1987	Braunstein Gallery, San Francisco

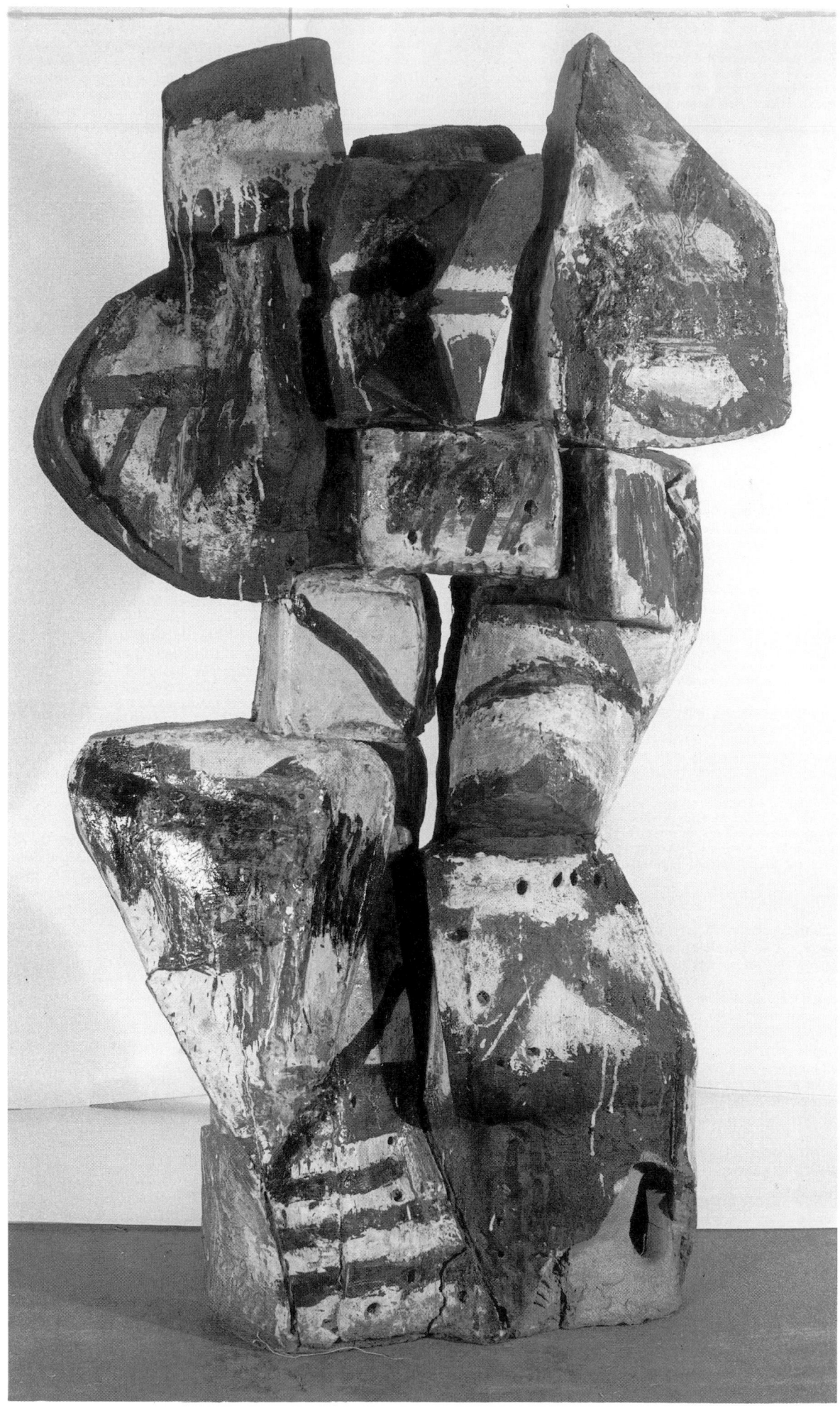

Peter Voulkos: *Untitled*, 1959

Selected Group Exhibitions:

Collections:

Museum of Modern Art, New York; Museum of Contemporary Crafts, New York; Baltimore Museum of Art; San Francisco Museum of Modern Art; Oakland Museum, California; Los Angeles County Museum of Art; Norton Simon Museum, Pasadena, California; Portland Art Museum, Oregon; Den Permanente, Copenhagen.

Publications:

On VOULKOS: books—*Objects: U.S.A.* by Lee Nordness, London 1970; *Peter Voulkos: A Dialogue with Clay* by Rose Slivka, Boston 1978; articles—"Los Angeles Letter" by M. Leopold in *Art International* (Lugano), Summer 1973; "The Art of Peter Voulkos" by Hal Fischer in *Artforum* (New York), November 1978; "Peter Voulkos: Ceramics that Transcend Art" by Thomas Albright in *San Francisco Chronicle,* 27 March 1984.

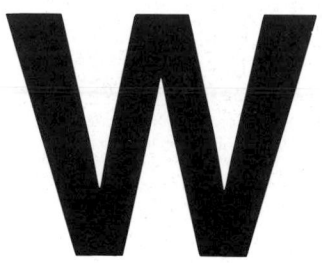

WADE, Robert (Shrope).

American. Born in Austin, Texas, 6 January 1943. Studied at the University of Texas at Austin, 1961–65, M.F.A. in Painting, 1965; University of California at Berkeley, 1965–66, M.A. in Painting, 1966. Married Susan Elaine Immel in 1966; daughter: Christine. Lives and works in Dallas: engaged in automobile customizing and hot-rod esthetics, 1957–62. Member, Advisory Committee, Texas Commission on the Arts and Humanities, 1975–78. Taught at McLennan College, Waco, Texas, 1966-70; Artist-in-Residence, Northwood Institute, Cedar Hill, Texas, 1970–72; Director, Northwood Experimental Art Institute, Dallas, 1972–73; Assistant Professor of Art, North Texas State University, Denton, 1973-77. Recipient: National Endowment for the Arts Grants, 1973 and 1974. Agent: Elaine Horwitch Galleries, Santa Fe, New Mexico. Address: c/o Elaine Horwitch Galleries, 129 West Palace Avenue, Santa Fe, New Mexico 87501, U.S.A.

Individual Exhibitions:

1967	Baylor University, Waco, Texas
1970	Chapman Kelley Gallery, Dallas
1971	Chapman Kelley Gallery, Dallas
	Kornblee Gallery, New York
1972	Smither Gallery, Dallas
	Temple University, Philadelphia (with Bladen)
1973	Baylor University, Waco
	University of St. Thomas, Houston
	Austin College, Sherman, Texas
	University of California at San Diego
1974	University of Texas at El Paso
	Kornblee Gallery, New York
1975	Delahunty Gallery, Dallas
	Laguna Gloria Art Museum, Austin, Texas
1976	Kornblee Gallery, New York
1978	Janus Gallery, Los Angeles
1984	Cultural Activities Center, Temple, Texas

Selected Group Exhibitions:

1966	*Annual Exhibition,* Dallas Museum of Fine Arts
1969	*Biennial,* New Orleans Museum of Art
	Biennial, Whitney Museum, New York
1972	*Painting and Sculpture Today,* Indianapolis Museum of Art
1974	*12 Texans,* Contemporary Arts Museum, Houston
1975	*5 Artists,* North Texas State University, Denton
	Texas Tough, White Museum, San Antonio, Texas
1976	*Photo Process as Medium,* Rutgers University, New Brunswick, New Jersey
1977	*Maps,* Museum of Modern Art, New York
1983	*Showdown,* Alternative Museum, New York

Collections:

Chase Manhattan Bank, New York; Illinois Bell Telephone Company, Chicago; Oklahoma Art Center, Oklahoma City; Witte Museum, San Antonio, Texas; Mountainview College, Dallas; Longview Museum, Longview, Texas; Centre Georges Pompidou, Paris; Groningen Museum, Netherlands.

Publications:

By WADE: article—"Visions of the City" in *D Magazine* (Dallas), October 1975.

On WADE: book—*Photo Process as Media,* exhibition catalogue, by Rosanne Truxes, New Brunswick, New Jersey 1976; articles—"Houston-Dallas Axis" by Janet Kutner in *Art in America* (New York), September/October 1972; "The Young Texans" by Jan Butterfield in *Arts Magazine* (New York), March 1973; "Contemporary Art in Texas" by Henry Hopkins in *Artnews* (New York), May 1973; "The ABC's of the Oak Cliff Four" by Josie Rabyor in *Southwest Art* (Austin, Texas), September 1973; "Texas Map" by Charlotte Moser in the *Houston Post,* October 1973; "Kick That Art Off Your Boots" by Josie Rabyor in *D Magazine* (Dallas), February 1975; "Texas" by Jane Kutner in *Artnews* (New York), Summer 1975; "Texas Ball and Chain Cult—112 Greene" by Mona da Vinci in *Soho Weekly News* (New York), September 1975.

*

At the beginning of his career Robert Wade was linked with the loosely-associated group of "Oak Cliff" artists, all of whom lived or worked in the same area of Dallas; they included such diverse members as Jim Roche (sculptor and conceptual artist) and Jack Mims (allegorical figurative painter who works in monumental scale). Although there are no formal resemblances among any of these artists, they do share similarities in approach and allusion, most noticeably in a proudly wry celebration of the state in which they all live. Wade is particularly drawn to the peccadillos for which Texas is (rightly or wrongly) known: a massive sense of both space and architectural size, and an undercurrent of cultivated violence and rawness which deliberately harks back to the early days of the American West.

Although this emphasis is overwhelmingly obvious, it would be the most popular of clichés to let it rest there. For Wade's work demonstrates a conceptual edge that takes it beyond regionalism, one which is frequently missed—or perhaps deliberately ignored—by many critics. For instance, national attention in America was first drawn to Wade's "Jumbo U.S. Map," a project that makes a cultural, rather than an aesthetic or political, statement. It is a work that is exactly what it says it is, an enormous recreation of the United States executed in earth, plywood, concrete and water and located just beside one of Dallas' busiest freeways. This project has had a precedent. The "Map of Texas," which, when completed in 1973, measured 40' x 40'. Although both the U.S. and Texas Maps are undoubtedly the most physically ambitious, other, smaller works are more important, and rely more heavily on a mixture of laden content and innovative form.

These are Wade's photo-emulsions on canvas, which operate as images frozen in time, frequently forcing the view to confront scenes of potential or actual violence. For Wade is at his best when he gives situations form—takes it, in effect, out of the *realm* of situation and makes it imagery. The best known of this series is entitled "Criminal Wall," in which we see large photos-on-canvas, loosely tacked to the wall, of such infamous and anti-heroic characters as Lee Harvey Oswald, Bonnie and Clyde, John Wesley Harding, and Pancho Villa, all "death-bed" portraits. They are all presented without comment, and are all the more powerful for that. In others, such as his series of postcard images, accompanied by texts from grade school textbooks, interior and landscape scenes are more complex, nostalgic, not self-consciously violent in the least but somehow sinister in their evocation of a past. This is true as well in his autobiographical work, which incorporated images of inanimate objects as well as human subjects—a piece which he terms "photographic projections on paper." Wade's obsessional sense of scale is much in evidence in this work, as it measures 30 feet long and 16 feet high, and requires fifteen hours of projection: yet there is also an idiosyncratic quality to this work, and to others, a calculated irony that stops short of exuberance.

—Jane Bell

WAGEMAKER, Jaap.

Dutch. Born Adriaan Barend in Haarlem, 6 January 1906; later adopted name Janus, then Jaap. Studied decorative arts, School voor Bouwkunde, Versierende Kunsten en Kunstambachten, Haarlem, 1920; mainly self-taught in painting. Married in 1943 (divorced, 1951): subsequently married Didi van der Meer. Painter: lived and worked in Haarlem, 1922–27, in Paris, 1927–45, and in Amsterdam, 1945–72; influenced by work of Alberto Burri and Antoni Tapies, from 1955; produced assemblage paintings, from 1960. Recipient: Premio Marzotto, Milan, 1960; Talensprijs, Amsterdam, 1962; Association Internationale des Critiques d'Art Prize, Section Pays-Bas, Luxembourg, 1965; Order van Oranje-Nassau, The Hague, 1966; Staatsprijs voor Beeldende Kunsten en Architectuur, The Hague, 1966; Gold Medal, *Biennale d'Arte Premio del Fiorino,* Florence, 1969. *Died (in Amsterdam) 28 January 1972.*

Individual Exhibitions:

1937	Kunsthandel de Schakel, Rotterdam (with Loots)
1948	Kunstzaal Eekman, Velp, Netherlands (with Fred Sieger)
1949	International Cultureel Centrum, Amsterdam (with J. L. Muler and Mark Kolthoff)
1955	Havezathe Hagen, Doetinchem, Netherlands
	Galerie Le Canard, Amsterdam
1955	Kunstcentrum 't Venster, Rotterdam
1957	Galerie C.C.C., Schiedam, Netherlands
	Stedelijk Museum, Amsterdam
1958	Galerie Gunar, Dusseldorf
1959	Markisches Museum, Witten, West Germany
	Städtische Kunsthalle, Recklinghausen, West Germany (with Jaap Mooy)
	Galerie Gunar, Dusseldorf

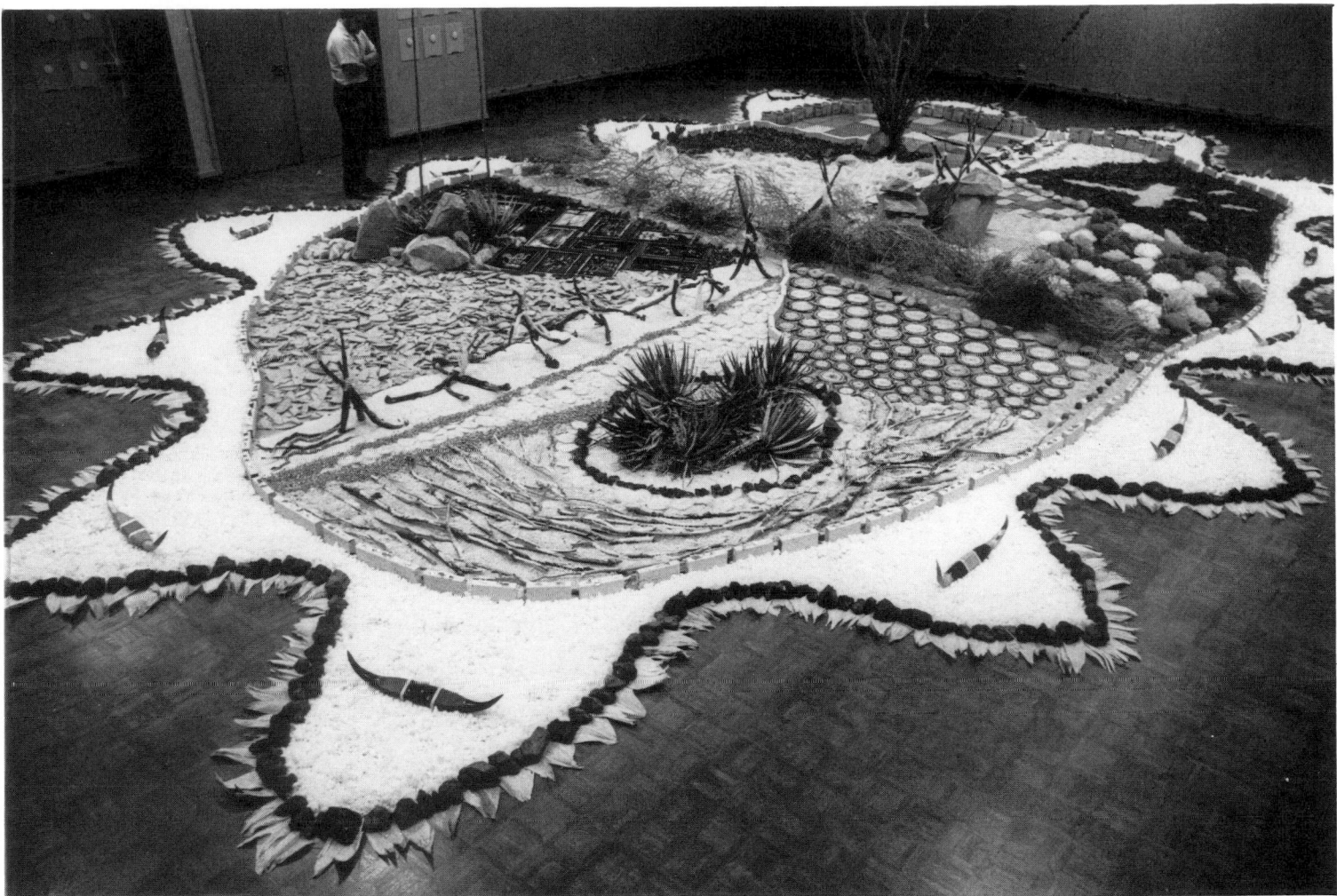

Robert Wade: *El Paso*, 1974

1960	Galerie Orez, The Hague

1960 Galerie Orez, The Hague
Kunstring, Rotterdam
Galerie de Boog, Willemstadt, Curacoa, Dutch Antilles (travelled Cultureel Centrum, Aruba)
Galerie Gunar, Dusseldorf (with Gust Romijn)
1961 Galerie 20, Arnhem, Netherlands
1962 Ulmer Museum, Ulm, West Germany (with Dahmen and Cimiotti)
Galerie Aujourd'hui, Brussels (with Kees van Bohemen and J. J. Schoonhoven)
1963 Kunstzaal de Mangelgang, Groningen, Netherlands
Marlborough New London Gallery (with Woty Werner and Hans Jaenisch)
1964 Galerie Cauberg, Walkenburg, Netherlands
Galerie Magdalene Sothmann, Amsterdam
1965 Haags Gemeentemuseum, The Hague
Groninger Museum, Groningen, Netherlands
1966 Galerie Delta, Rotterdam
Bilder, Städtische Kunstgalerie, Bochum, West Germany
Galerie Magdalene Sothmann, Amsterdam
1967 Stedelijk Museum, Amsterdam
1969 Galerie Rg., Curacao, Dutch Antilles
Galerie Fellson, Ijmulden, Netherlands
Galerie Magdalene Sothmann, Amsterdam
1970 Galerie Wijngaard, Groningen
Cultureel Centrum, Venlo, Netherlands
Galerie Willy Schoots, Eindhoven, Netherlands
Galerie Felix, Maastricht, Netherlands
Galerie Nouvelles Images, The Hague
1971 Drienerhoord T.H. Twente, Enschede, Netherlands
1972 *Bilder—Materialbilder,* Kunsthalle, Bremen, West Germany
Overbeck-Gesellschaft, Lübeck
1973 De Zonnewijzer, Eindhoven, Netherlands
1975 Kunstenaarscentrum, Bergen, Netherlands

Selected Group Exhibitions:

1925 *Bloemstillevens*, Frans Halsmuseum, Haarlem
1928 *Kunst zij ons Doel*, Frans Halsmuseum, Haarlem (and regularly until 1940)
1932 *Kennemer Kunstenaars Kring*, Hotel de Prins, Velsen, Netherlands
1945 *Kunst in Vrijheid*, Rijksmuseum, Amsterdam
1959 *Niederlandische Kunst seit 1945*, Westfälischer Kunstverein, Münster, West Germany
1961 *Trends in Dutch Painting since Van Gogh*, National Gallery of Victoria, Melbourne (toured Australia)
1969 *Dutch Art Today,* Smithsonian Institution, Washington, D.C.
1971 *Europalia '71,* Palais des Beaux-Arts, Brussels
1972 *Kunst van 20th eeuw,* Museum Boymans-van Beuningen, Rotterdam

Collections:

Stedelijk Museum, Amsterdam; Museum Boymans-van Beuningen, Rotterdam; Haags Gemeentemuseum, The Hague; Stedelijk van Abbemuseum, Eindhoven, Netherlands; Städtische Kunstgalerie, Bochum, West Germany; Kunsthalle, Bremen, West Germany; Kunsthalle, Dusseldorf; Städtisches Museum Schloss Morsbroich, Leverkusen, West Germany; National Gallery of Victoria, Melbourne; Museum of Modern Art, New York.

Publications:

On WAGEMAKER: books—*The Art of Assemblage* by William C. Seitz, New York 1961; *Jaap Wagemaker's Informal Art* by C. Doleman, Amsterdam 1963; *Jaap Wagemaker,* exhibition folder, London 1963; *Jaap Wagemaker: Bilder,* exhibition catalogue, with text by Albert Schulze Vellinghausen, Bochum, West Germany 1966; *Jaap Wagemaker,* exhibition catalogue, with text by Jan Wolkers, Rotterdam 1966; *Jaap Wagemaker: Bilder—Material Bilder,* exhibition catalogue, with texts by Günter Busch and Albert Schulze Vellinghausen, Bremen, West Germany 1972; *Jaap Wagemaker* by A. M. Hammacher, Didi Wagemaker and others, Amsterdam 1975.

*

One of the outstanding Dutch artists of his generation, Jaap Wagemaker bridged an inherited Nordic mythological paganism with the instincts of a mystic. Basic to an understanding of his career is the interest in African art, which dates from the time he developed away from the tachisme of the Cobra Group and the romantic expressionism of his early work. He was to create one of the finest collections of African sculpture, from which he learned the qualities of non-subjective drama and tension.

A slow-starter, and a slow worker, Wagemaker waited until his 49th year before holding a one-man show, but he soon emerged as a unique talent, earning a recognition outside his native land. Stylistically he can be linked to the movement of *matière* painting which swept through Europe, notably the Italian and Spanish schools, in the post-war period. Wagemaker never displayed the violence or bitter wit or the decorative playfulness which marks many painters in this group. He always retained the vigorous earthiness of his Dutch background, allied to a poetic inventiveness and an unfailing elegance.

His work most impressively conveys a sense of meditation, despite the heaviness of his chosen technique. This consisted of a surface composed of synthetic paint and fine sand, into which he would embody stones, shells, pieces of slate, wood, nails, tubing and miscellaneous oddments. Despite the seeming nihilism of choice, or even assemblage, there is nothing of Dadaist shock, or calculated satire, in his work. His images of a primaeval, physical world emerge as formal, sensitive messages; it is the world of *Genesis,* elementary, primitive, unoccupied by man, or, possibly, a world long after man has disappeared. It is also a private world, where the artist exposes his vision but makes no effort to impose it. Here one finds an analogy with the African art he understood so well; there is no polite effort to establish a dialogue, to reduce poetic insight to the level of conversation. The African carvings, like Wagemaker's lunar-landscapes, speak of natural forces which cannot be fed to computers or reduced to scientific formulas. Nevertheless, Wagemaker's best paintings have a marked positivism; the meaning may be obscure, but there is nothing hesitant or left unstated.

—Charles Spencer

WALKER, John.

British. Born in Birmingham, 12 November 1939. Studied at Birmingham College of Art, 1956–60, and Académie de la Grande Chaumière, Paris, 1961–63. Painter and graphic artist, in London, 1964–70, in New York, since 1970, and in Melbourne, Australia, since 1980. Professor of Painting and Drawing, Cooper Union, New York, 1974–75; Visiting Professor, Yale University, New Haven, Connecticut, 1975–77; Artist-in-Residence, St. Catherines College, Oxford, 1977–78; Painting Tutor, Royal College of Art, London, 1974–78; Visiting Artist, Columbia University, New York, 1974–78; Artist-in-Residence, Prahran Technical College, Melbourne, 1980; Dean, Victoria College of the Arts, Melbourne, 1982–86. Recipient: Drawing Prize, Arts Council of Great Britain, 1960; Edwin Abbey travel scholarship, 1960; First Prize, National Young Artists Drawing Competition, *London,* 1960; Purchase Award, Arts Council, 1967; Gregory Fellowship, University of Leeds, 1967–69; Theodoron Award, 1969; Harkness Fellowship, 1970–72; First Prize, *International Prize Biennale,* Bradford, Yorkshire, 1974; First Prize, *John Moores Exhibition,* Liverpool, 1976; Guggenheim Fellowship, 1981. Agent: Nigel Greenwood Inc., 4 New Burlington Street, London W1, England; and Knoedler Gallery, 19 East 70th Street, New York, New York, U.S.A.

Individual Exhibitions:

1967	Axiom Gallery, London
1968	Park Square Gallery, Leeds
	Axiom Gallery, London
	Hayward Gallery, London
1969	City Art Gallery, Leeds
1970	Nigel Greenwood Inc., London
1971	Reese Palley Gallery, New York
1972	British Pavilion at the *Biennale,* Venice
	Reese Palley Gallery, New York
	Studio la Città, Verona
	Ikon Gallery, Birmingham
	Galerie Rolf Ricke, Cologne
1973	Nigel Greenwood Inc., London (2 shows)
	Kunstverein, Hamburg
	Städtisches Museum, Bochum, West Germany
	Cunningham Ward Gallery, New York
	Park Square Gallery, Leeds
1974	Museum of Modern Art, New York
	Galerie Swart, Amsterdam
1975	Nigel Greenwood Inc., London
	Cunningham Ward Gallery, New York
1976	Galerie Marguerite Lamy, Paris
	Cunningham Ward Gallery, New York
	Reed College, Portland, Oregon
1977	Powell Street Gallery, Melbourne
1978	Cunningham Ward Gallery, New York
	Phillips Collection, Washington, D.C. (toured the United States)
	Museum of Modern Art, New York
	Art Gallery of New South Wales, Sydney
	Nigel Greenwood Inc., London

John Walker: *Labyrinth IV,* 1980

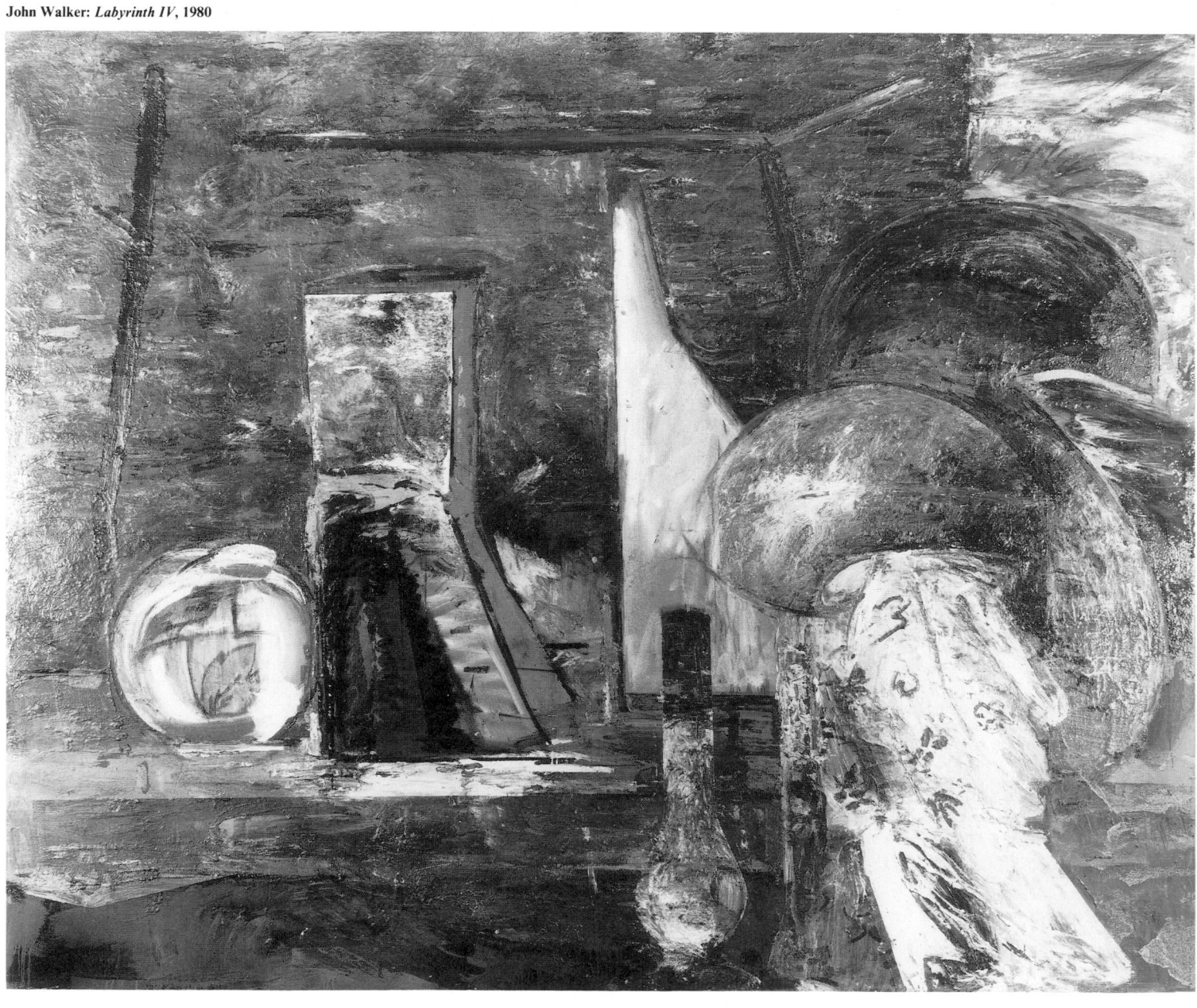

1979 University of Massachusetts, Amherst (travelled to
Brown University, Providence, Rhode Island, and
Brandeis University, Waltham, Massachusetts)
Powell Street Gallery, Melbourne
1980 Nigel Greenwood Inc., London (2 shows)
Betty Cunningham Gallery, New York
1981 *Drawings*, National Art Gallery, Wellington, New
Zealand (travelled to Robert McDougall Art Gal-
lery, Christchurch, Dunedin Public Art Gallery,
and the City Art Gallery, Auckland)
Nigel Greenwood Inc., London
Theo Waddington Gallery, London
1982 Phillips Collection, Washington, D.C. (travelled to
J. B. Speed Art Museum, Louisville, Kentucky)
1983 Madeleine Carter Gallery, Brookline, Massachusetts
M. Knoedler and Company, New York
1984 M. Knoedler and Company, New York
1985 Hayward Gallery, London (travelled to Ediburgh and
Birmingham)
Tate Gallery, London
M. Knoedler, Zurich
1986 M. Knoedler and Company, New York
John Walker, at the *Adelaide Festival of Arts*, South
Australia
1987 L. A. Louver Gallery, Venice, California
National Gallery of Victoria, Melbourne
Pamela Auchincloss Gallery, Santa Barbara, Califor-
nia
M. Knoedler and Company, New York

Selected Group Exhibitions:

1965 *John Moores Exhibition*, Walker Art Gallery, Liverpool (and 1974, 1976)
1968 *New British Painting and Sculpture*, University of
California, Los Angeles
1970 *Contemporary Art in Britain*, National Museum of
Modern Art, Tokyo
1973 *Towards Painting*, Tate Gallery, London
1975 *Color as Language*, Museum of Modern Art, New
York (toured South America)
1977 *25 Years of British Painting*, Royal Academy of Art,
London
1978 *Critic's Choice*, Institute of Contemporary Arts,
London
1982 *Aspects of British Art Today*, Metropolitan Art Museum, Tokyo
1984 *The British Art Show*, City Art Gallery, Birmingham
(and Ikon Gallery, Birmingham; travelled to Edinburgh, Sheffield, Southampton)
1987 *British Art 1900-80: The Modern Movement*, Royal
Academy, London (travelled to Stuttgart)

Collections:

Arts Council of Great Britain, London; Tate Gallery, London; Victoria and Albert Museum, London; City Art Gallery,
Leeds; Scottish National Gallery of Modern Art, Edinburgh;
Ulster Museum, Belfast; Museum am Ostwall, Dortmund,
West Germany; Museum of Modern Art, New York; Guggenheim Museum, New York; National Gallery of Art, Washington, D.C.

Publications:

By WALKER: article—"John Walker on His Painting: From
a Conversation with Tim Hilton," in *Studio International*
(London), June 1972.

On WALKER: books—*Contemporary Art in Britain*, exhibition catalogue, with text by Andrew Causey, Tokyo 1970;
36th Venice Biennale: British Pavilion—John Walker, exhibition catalogue, with text by John Elderfield, London 1972;
Color as Language, exhibition catalogue, with text by Kynaston McShine, New York 1975; *Arte Inglese Oggi*, exhibition
catalogue, with text by Norbert Lynton and others, Milan
1976; *John Walker*, exhibition catalogue, with text by Andrew
Forge, Washington, D.C. 1978; *Critic's Choice*, exhibition
catalogue, with text by John McEwen, London 1978; *Drawings 1981: John Walker*, exhibition catalogue, with text by
Anne Kirker, Wellington, New Zealand 1981; *John Walker*,
exhibition catalogue, with text by Jack B. Flam, Washington,
D.C. 1982; *John Walker: Paintings from the Alba and Ocea-

nia Series 1979-1984*, exhibition catalogue with introduction
by Dore Ashton, London 1985; *John Walker: Prints 1976-
84*, exhibition catalogue with text by Memory Holloway, London 1985; *John Walker: Salsipuedes Suite*, exhibition
catalogue with text by Ted Gott, Melbourne 1987.

There is something powerfully disciplined about John
Walker's ambitions as a painter. Conventional (in the
strict modernist sense of the word), Walker's work
has developed slowly over the last 15 years, re-
working given sets of forms and spatial schemes bit
by bit, slowly re-investing them with new expressive
power. The tightness of this process of transformation, its reliance on narrow formal re-invention (or
adjustment) rather than borrowing and re-working a
broad-school of forms, forces criticism very much
into a descriptive, defensive position. Although literary claims have been made for Walker's powerful
shapes, Walker's art is more at home within modernist historicism—Manet, Cézanne, Matisse, Pollock.
The artist's job is to find his place within that history,
to enter into a dialogue with—to measure himself
against—the best work of the past. As a modern
equivalent of l'art pour l'art this assumes a kind of
assertiveness against the modern world. Walker has
talked about the "monastic" challenge of being an
artist.

Walker's development can be divided into three
phases. A period of geometric abstraction, which introduces the awkward shapes (the lozenges, the
pinched-in figures) that reappear in all his work.
Here the shapes free-float in an atmospheric, non-
illusionist space. A period of cubist collage, represented by the monumental "Juggernauts" series,
which introduces into a "built" architectural space
tentative figure-ground relations. The shapes here are
jagged and the surface rough, ugly, which is to become a strong feature of the later work. And a period
of "illusionistic" picture building, represented by the
"Numinous" balcony series (a motif borrowed from
Matisse and Cézanne), the "Labyrinths" series, and
the recent drawings, which introduce a quasi-
figurative or fictive space.

This new work makes explicit what has been—in
varying degrees—the basis of Walker's art: the tension between our awareness of paintings as containers
and windows.

The key to this explicitness is Walker's self-
conscious re-working of elements from certain modernist (and proto-modernist) works such as
Velasquez's "Las Meninas," which, as a paradigm
for the artifice of picture making, becomes the perfect
model for Walker's own concerns. In Walker's latest
drawings, based on "Las Meninas," the re-worked
forms of the painting reappear within the work as a
mirror image. Walker's figure of the artist (the dwarf
in "Las Meninas") looks across at a screen/canvas
containing its own image. The depth of space that
Walker introduced into the "Labyrinths" is here given
a further illusionistic opening out.

This opening out—the transformation of shapes into
what might be called images—may not, in any crucial
sense, represent a change in outlook (an opening onto
the world), but it undoubtedly brings with it an increased sense of esprit or quirkiness, something that
seems to be at the basis of Walker's search for shapes
that "irritate" the eye, that remain in the memory
long after the details of the painting have been forgotten.

—John Roberts

WALL, Brian.

British. Born in London, 5 September 1931. Studied
at Luton College of Art, Bedfordshire, 1949-50.
Sculptor: worked as glass-blower, 1945-50; moved to
Paris, 1952, to London, 1953, and to St. Ives, Cornwall, 1955, where he worked as an assistant to Bar-

bara Hepworth, 1955-58; visited New York, 1969,
and spent several months of each year in California,
1969-73. Lecturer, Ealing College of Art, London,
1961-62; Principal Lecturer, Central School of Arts
and Design, London, 1962-72. Visiting Lecturer,
1969-73, Lecturer, 1973-75, and since 1975, Assistant Professor, University of California, Berkeley.
Agent: Braunstein/Quay Gallery, 560 Sutter Street,
San Francisco, California 94102. Address: 52 Prince-
dale Road, London W11, England.

Individual Exhibitions:

1958 Drian Gallery, London
1959 Woodstock Gallery, London
1960 AIA Gallery, London (with Joe Tilson and Anthony
Benjamin)
1961 Drian Gallery, London
1962 Grabowski Gallery, London (with Anthony Benjamin)
1963 Manchester City Art Gallery
1964 Grabowski Gallery, London
1966 Grosvenor Gallery, London
1967 Arnolfini Gallery, Bristol
1968 Grosvenor Gallery, London
1971 William Sawyer Gallery, San Francisco
1973 San Jose State University Art Gallery, California
1974 Quay Gallery, San Francisco
St. Mary's College, Morago, California
1976 Braunstein/Quay Gallery, San Francisco
Dootson/Calderhead Gallery, Seattle
University of Nevada, Las Vegas
1981 Max Hutchinson Gallery, New York
1982 Seattle Art Museum, Washington
1983 San Francisco Museum of Modern Art

Selected Group Exhibitions:

1958 *Contemporary British Sculpture*, Arts Council Gallery, London
1961 *Biennale*, Paris
1963 *British Art Today*, San Francisco Museum of Art
(toured the United States)
1965 *Sculpture in the 60's*, Tate Gallery, London
1966 *Sculpture 1960-1966*, Battersea Park, London
1971 *6 x 6 x 6*, Richmond Art Center, California
1975 *Bay Area Sculpture*, James Willis Gallery, San Francisco
1976 *American Sculptors*, University of Texas, Dallas
1979 *Apsects of Abstract*, Crocker Art Museum, Sacramento, California
1982 *One Hundred Years of California Sculpture*, Oakland
Museum, California

Collections:

Tate Gallery, London; Contemporary Art Society, London;
Arts Council of Great Britain, London; Whitworth Art Gal-
lery, Manchester; Penwyth Society, St. Ives, Cornwall; Mu-
seum of Art, Dublin; Billy Rose Sculpture Garden,
Jerusalem; University of California at Berkeley; Oakland
Museum, California; Gallery of New South Wales, Sydney.

Publications:

By WALL: articles—statement in *Architectural Design* (London), May 1959; statement in *Brian Wall*, exhibition catalogue, Bristol 1967; statement in *Sculpture International*
(Oxford), October 1969

On WALL: book—*Brian Wall*, exhibition catalogue with texts
by Peter Selz and George W. Neubert, Seattle 1982;
articles—"Brian Wall: Sculpture of Simplicity" by Charles
Spencer in *Studio International* (London), March 1966;
"London Show Offers Brian Wall Sculpture" by Charles
Spencer in *New York Times International Edition*, 30 April
1966; "Sculpture To See All At Once" by Christopher Andreae in *Christian Science Monitor* (Boston), 30 November
1966; "Question and Artist: Brian Wall" by G. S. Whittet in
Sculpture International (Oxford), October 1969; "Unusual
Art in San Francisco" by Thomas Albright in the *San Fran-
cisco Chronicle*, 7 January 1974; "Monumental Sculpture"

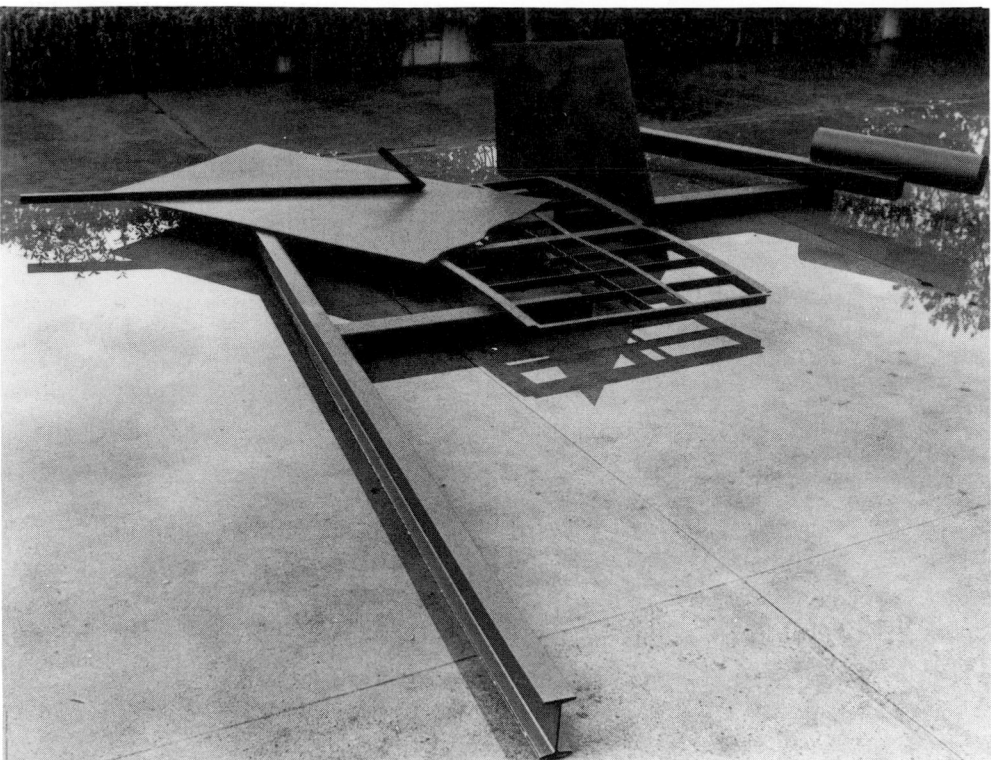

Brian Wall: *Kingfisher,* **1974**

by Thomas Albright in the *San Francisco Chronicle,* 16 January 1974; "The Fitness of Form" by Robert McDonald in *Artweek* (Oakland, California), February 1976.

A sculptor of outstanding qualities, Brian Wall has never found his true niche in the post-war British sculptural scene. Like Caro he is a teacher of special qualifications, and in Britain and America has exerted considerable influence on younger generations. His character and work are somewhat paradoxical, typically romantic in the English sense, yet preferring to condition intuitive, gestural elements within a severe discipline. Younger than Caro and Adams (his closest English colleagues), Wall has in some sense been more radical, working on large, simple steel structures when Caro was still involved in Richier-like symbols of the human form.

Wall is virtually self-taught, having taken part-time courses in art whilst serving in the Royal Air Force. A six-month stay in Paris made a decisive impression, notably admiration for Mondrian which led to detailed study of the Russian Constructivists, the Dutch de Stijl and Moholy-Nagy. The second major step in his development was a move to St. Ives, where he first worked in restaurants. Acquaintance with the local art colony led to an introduction to the late Barbara Hepworth, who engaged him as an assistant.

By 1956 he had digested all these various influences and trained himself to work in stone, wood, plaster and metal. His work at this time was distinctly Mondrianesque (painted wood boxes), but he soon switched to metal. The ethics and aims of de Stijl have remained pre-eminent in Wall's career, hence his insistence on large-scale, and his preference for public sculpture. His strength lies in an assured capacity to handle monumental proportions without over-complicating the design, retaining an impressive sense of power and drama. The sculptures are variations on a few limited shapes—flat panels, square or circular, tubular arms, four-sided boxes; this limited vocabulary is juggled with syntactic ingenuity, never reduced to the decorative or comforting. He has never favoured colour in sculpture, preferring black or white to emphasize the shapes, to stress their simplicity.

—Charles Spencer

WALTHER, Franz Erhard.

German. Born in Fulda, 22 July 1939. Studied at the Hochschule für Bildende Künste, Frankfurt, 1959–61, and the Kunstakademie, Dusseldorf, 1962–64. Married Johanna Friess in 1964; sons: Moritz and Lehmann. Worked in soap factory, Dusseldorf, 1966–67, and in bakery, New York, 1967–69. Independent artist, Dusseldorf, 1965–67, New York 1967–71, and in Hamburg, since 1971. Professor, Hochschule für Bildenden Künste, Hamburg, since 1970. Recipient: Gunter Fruhtrunk Prize, Munich, 1986. Agents: Reinhard Onnasch, Fasanenstrasse 47, 1000 Berlin 15 (West); Galerie Achim Kubinski, Olgastrasse 109, 7000 Stuttgart 1. Address: c/o Hochschule für Bildende Künste, Lerchenfeld 2, 2000 Hamburg 76, West Germany.

Individual Exhibitions:

1966	Neue Galerie, Aachen, West Germany
1967	Galerie Heiner Friedrich, Munich
	Staatliche Kunstakademie, Dusseldorf
1968	Galerie Rudolf Zwirner, Cologne
1969	Galerie Heiner Friedrich, Munich
	Galerie Rudolf Zwirner, Cologne
	Galerie Neuendorf, Hamburg
	Studio F, Ulm, West Germany
	Museum Haus Lange, Krefeld, West Germany
	Kunsthalle, Dusseldorf
	Museum of Modern Art, New York
1970	Kunstverein, Hamburg
1971	Hessisches Landesmuseum, Darmstadt
	Galerie Heiner Friedrich, Cologne
	Kunstverein, Frankfurt
	Galerie Heiner Friedrich, Munich
1972	Kunsthalle, Tübingen
	Videogalerie Gerry Schum, Dusseldorf
	Museum Haus Lange, Krefeld, West Germany
	Kaiser-Wilhelm-Museum, Krefeld, West Germany
	Stedelihk Van Abbemuseum, Eindhoven, Netherlands
1973	Vanier College, Montreal
	Kabinett für Aktuelle Kunst, Bremerhaven, West Germany
	Kunstverein, Freiburg
	Hessisches Landesmuseum, Darmstadt

	Galerie Heiner Friedrich, Munich (2 exhibitions)
1974	Kaiser-Wilhelm-Museum, Krefeld, West Germany
	Galerie Klein, Bonn
1975	Galerie Repassage, Warsaw
	Kabinett für Aktuelle Kunst, Bremerhaven, West Germany
1976	*Diagramme zum 1. Werksatz,* Kunstraum, Munich
	Städtisches Museum, Bonn
	Kunstverein, Frankfurt
1977	Kunsthalle, Baden-Baden, West Germany
	Heiner Friedrich Gallery, New York
	Wallraf-Richartz Museum, Cologne
	German Pavilion, at the *Bienal,* Sao Paulo
	Centro de Arte y Comunicacion, Buenos Aires
	Galerie Heiner Friedrich, Cologne
1978	*Arbeiten 1954–1963 aus der Sammlung Seng,* Städtisches Museum, Fulda, West Germany
	Kabinett für Aktuelle Kunst, Bremerhaven, West Germany
	Hessisches Landesmuseum, Darmstadt
1979	Stadtische Galerie im Lenbachhaus, Munich
1980	*Gegensatzpaare und Unterscheidungen im Werk,* Kunstverein, St. Gallen, Switzerland
	Arbeiten 1969–1963, Kunstmuseum, Bonn
1981	*Handlung Werk,* Nationalgalerie, West Berlin
	Produzentgalerie, Hamburg
1982	*Werkzeichnungen,* Museum Haus Lange, Krefeld, West Germany
	Galerie Klein, Bonn
	Badischer Kunstverein, Karlsruhe
	Kunstraum, Munich
	Galerie Schiessel, Munich
	Galerie Kubinski, Stuttgart
	Kunsthalle, Wilhelmshaven, West Germany
	Galerie Carinthia, Klagenfurt, Austria
	Overbeckgesellschaft, Lübeck
	Galerie Edition E, Munich
	Galerie Schiessel, Munich
	Kunsthalle, Wilhelmshaven, West Germany
	Galerie Carinthia, Klagenfurt, Austria
1983	Galerie Schöttle, Munich (with A. Oehlen)
	Ausstellungsraum Fettstrasse, Hamburg
1984	Raum für Kunst, Hamburg
	Galerie Haderek, Stuttgart
	Kabinett für Aktuelle Kunst, Bremerhaven, West Germany
	Galerie Onnasch, West Berlin
	Galerie Lock, St. Gallen, Switzerland
	Van Abbemuseum, Eindhoven, Netherlands
	Ulmer Museum, Ulm, West Germany
1985	Wilhelm-Hack-Museum, Ludwigshafen, West Germany
	Institut für moderne Kunst, Nuremberg, West Germany
	Galerie Reckermann, Cologne
	Ausstellungsraum, Fulda, West Germany
	Galerie Maria Wilkens/Dorit Jacobs, Cologne
	Galerie Loehrl, Mönchengladbach, West Germany
	Kunstverein, Bremerhaven, West Germany
	Städtische Galerie, Nordhorn, West Germany
1986	Galerie Carinthia, Klagenfurt, Austria
	Kunstverein, Braunschweig, West Germany
	Kunstverein, Frankfurt
	Galerie Achim Kubinski, Stuttgart
	Galerie Tilly Haderek, Stuttgart
	Gutenbergstrasse 62, Stuttgart
	Galerie Annette Gmeiner, Kirchzarten, West Germany
	Galerie Desluis, The Hague
1987	Galerie Edition E, Munich
	Galerie Schiessel, Munich
	Galerie Hufkens-de Lathuy, Brussels
	Kunsthalle, Winterthur, Switzerland
	Galerie Onnasch, West Berlin

Selected Group Exhibitions:

1969	*When Attitudes Become Form,* Kunsthalle, Berne (toured Europe)
1972	*Documenta 5,* Museum Fridericianum, Kassel, West Germany (and *Documenta 7,* 1982; *Documenta 8,* 1987)
1974	*Projekt 74,* Kunsthalle, Cologne

Collections:

Nationalgalerie, West Berlin; Kunsthalle, Hamburg; Kunstmuseum, Bonn; Kunstmuseum, Dusseldorf; City of Frankfurt; Wallraf-Richartz Museum/Museum Ludwig, Cologne; Kaiser-Wilhelm Museum, Krefeld, West Germany; Hessisches Landesmuseum, Darmstadt; Staatsgalerie, Stuttgart; Stedelijk Van Abbemuseum, Eindhoven, Netherlands.

Publications:

By WALTHER: books—*Leihobjekte*, Aachen, West Germany, 1966; *Information*, Dusseldorf 1967; *Objekte, Benutzen*, with photos by Barbara Brown, Cologne and New York 1968; *Tagebuch: Museum of Modern Art, New York, 28 December 1969 bis 1 Marz 1970*, Cologne 1971; *Prozessmaterial*, Cologne and Darmstadt 1971; *Proportionen*, with Ingrid Krupka, Cologne 1971; *Frank Erhard Walther: Werkmonographie, Arbeiten 1955-1963, Material zum 1, Werksatz 1963-1969*, edited by Gotz Adriani, with an interview by Ursula Meyer, texts by others, Cologne 1972; *Franz Erhard Walther: Werksatz*, Montreal 1973; *Franz Erhard Walther: Zeitbezogen/Raumbezogen/Personenbezogen/Handlungsbezogen*, Munich 1979; *Franz Erhard Walther: Hauptworte/Werkbegriffe*, Hannover 1981; *Franz Erhard Walther: 40 Sockel*, with an interview by Michael Lingner, Munich 1982; *Franz Erhard Walther: 30 x Werkbau*, Munich 1982; *Franz Erhard Walther: 2 Arbeiten—35 Werke*, Wilhelmshaven, West Germany 1982; *Organon: Feldbuch*, Klagenfurt 1983; *Franz Erhard Walther*, with Michael Lingner, Klagenfurt 1985; *Organon 2*, Klagenfurt 1987; *Gelenke im Raum*, Stuttgart 1987; *Franz Erhard Walther: Wortwerke*, Klagenfurt 1987.

On WALTHER: books—*Deutsche Kunst der 60er Jahre* by Jurgen Morschel, Munich 1972; *Franz Erhard Walther: Fruhe Arbeiten 1955-1963*, exhibition catalogue, with text by Paul Wember, Krefeld, West Germany 1972; *Bis Heute* by Karin Thomas, Cologne 1972; *Franz Erhard Walther*, exhibition catalogue, with texts by Argibald Buys, Oda den Boer, Wies Leering, and Jerven Ober, Eindhoven, Netherlands 1972; *Objekte Kunst* by Karin Thomas, Cologne 1972; *Geschichte der Collage* by Herta Wescher and Karin Thomas, Cologne 1974; *Franz Erhard Walther: Diagramme zum 1, Werksatz*, exhibition catalogue, with texts by Hermann Kern and Carl Vogel, Munich 1976; *Franz Erhard Walther: 2, Werksatz: Skulpturen, Zeichnungen*, exhibition catalogue, with texts by Evelyn Weiss and Dieter Ronte, and an interview by Georg Jappe, Cologne 1977; *International Biennale Sao Paulo: Franz Erhard Walther*, exhibition catalogue, with texts by Gotz Adriani and Carl Vogel, Cologne 1977; *Kunstlerlexicon von 1945 bis zur Gegenwart* by Karin Thomas and Gerd de Vries, Cologne 1977; *Franz Erhard Walther: Arbeiten 1954-1963 aus der Sammlung Seng*, exhibition catalogue, with texts by Gilbert Seng and Carl Vogel, Fulda, West Germany 1978; *Strukturen Zeitgenossische Kunst* by Ingrid Burgbacher-Krupka, Stuttgart 1979; *Franz Erhard Walther: Gegenstazpaare und Unterscheidungen im Werk*, exhibition catalogue, with text by Dietrich Helms, St. Gallen, Switzerland 1980; *Franz Erhard Walther: Arbeiten 1969-1963*, exhibition catalogue, with texts by Dirk Stemmler, Gisbert Seng and Karl Otto Gotz, Bonn 1980; *Franz Erhard Walther: Handlung Werk*, exhibition catalogue, with text by Michael Pauseback, West Berlin 1981; *Franz Erhard Walther*, exhibition catalogue, with text by Dietrich Helms, Hamburg 1981; *Franz Erhard Walther: Werkzeichnungen*, with a foreword by Gerhard Storck and Marianne Stockebrand, Krefeld, West Germany 1982; *Der Walther-Raum in der Hamburger Kunsthalle*, with text by Achim Lipp, Hamburg 1983; *Franz Erhard Walther: Words 1978-1984*, exhibition catalogue with text by Rudi Fuchs, Eindhoven 1984; *Der 1, Werksatz (1963-69) von Franz Erhard Walther*, with text by Barbara Grotkamp-Schepers, Darmstadt 1985; *Franz Erhard Walther: gesehen gehort gedacht*, with text by Gisbert Seng, Fulda 1985; *Franz Erhard Walther—Ort und Richtung angeben: Zeichnungen 1957-1984*, with texts by Gottfried Boehm, Marianne Stockebrand and Rudi Fuchs, Klagenfurt 1985; *Franz Erhard Walther*, exhibition catalogue by Kurt Muenger, Winterthur 1987.

From the very beginning I had an interest in work processes. In any event the emphasis on process is stronger than that on form. 1958-59: quantities of drawings arise from processes: movements like writing from the top to the bottom or from left to right. Superimpositions, coverings—yet readable as a process. The formlessness of these works had for me the character of a manifesto. From 1960 to 1963 there were extensive work composites resulting from material processes. Material and process—the material process—become decisive for the work. Material is not used for something but is itself the subject. At the same time I worked with extremely simple forms without using hierarchies and meanings. "Meaninglessness" was a challenge to oneself to construct meanings in one's activity. Therein lay the invitation to spontaneous action. This motive of operation and then action as an element of the work became the main theme. The determinant basic idea was to construct a work from action. These works originated in 1963. Action is a form of work. The operative has to answer for the work. He is involved not only optically but also with the whole body. All abilities are required. It is a total performance. Man could construct works in other, more extensive ways than were previously possible. Naturally then several people also appear in the development of the work. That is complex construction.

In the alternative work concept there are central concepts such as place, time, space, interior-exterior, body, field, direction, construction, among others, and the possibility to alter historic significance. And thereby a new concept of material has become necessary. For example language, body, space, place, action are material like wood and stone to the traditional sculptor. Spaces, performance areas, action areas, concepts and methods of work should be found which extend the dimensions of earlier means of expression.

—Franz Erhard Walther

Franz Erhard Walther: *Drei Saulen Gelb*, 1985

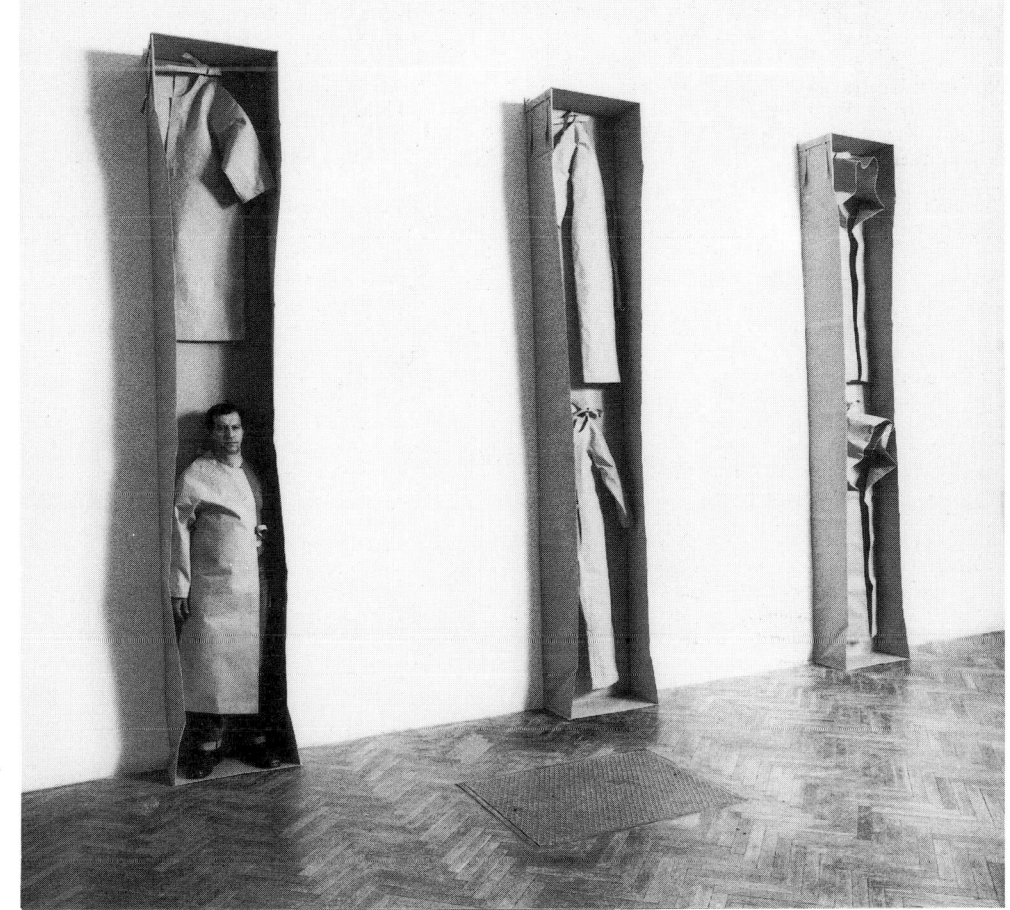

WARHOL, Andy.

American. Born in McKeesport, Pennsylvania, 6 August 1928. Studied at Carnegie Institute of Technology, Pittsburgh, 1945-49. Worked as illustrator for *Glamour Magazine*, New York, 1949-50, and as a commercial artist, New York, 1950-57. Independent artist, New York, 1957 until his death in 1987: concentrated on making paintings derived from strip comics and advertisements, 1960-61; first silkscreen paintings, 1962; first films, mainly with Paul Morrissey, 1963. Editor, *Inter/View* magazine, New York. Recipient: Art Directors Club of New York Medal for shoe advertisements, 1957; 6th Film Culture Award, New York, 1964; *Los Angeles Film Festival* Award, 1964. Died (in New York) 22 February 1987.

Individual Exhibitions:

1952   Hugo Gallery, New York

1956   Bodley Gallery, New York (and 1957, 1958, 1959)

1962   Ferus Gallery, Los Angeles
       Stable Gallery, New York

1963   Ferus Gallery, New York

1964   Leo Castelli Gallery, New York
       Stable Gallery, New York
       Galerie Sonnabend, Paris

1965   Leo Castelli Gallery, New York

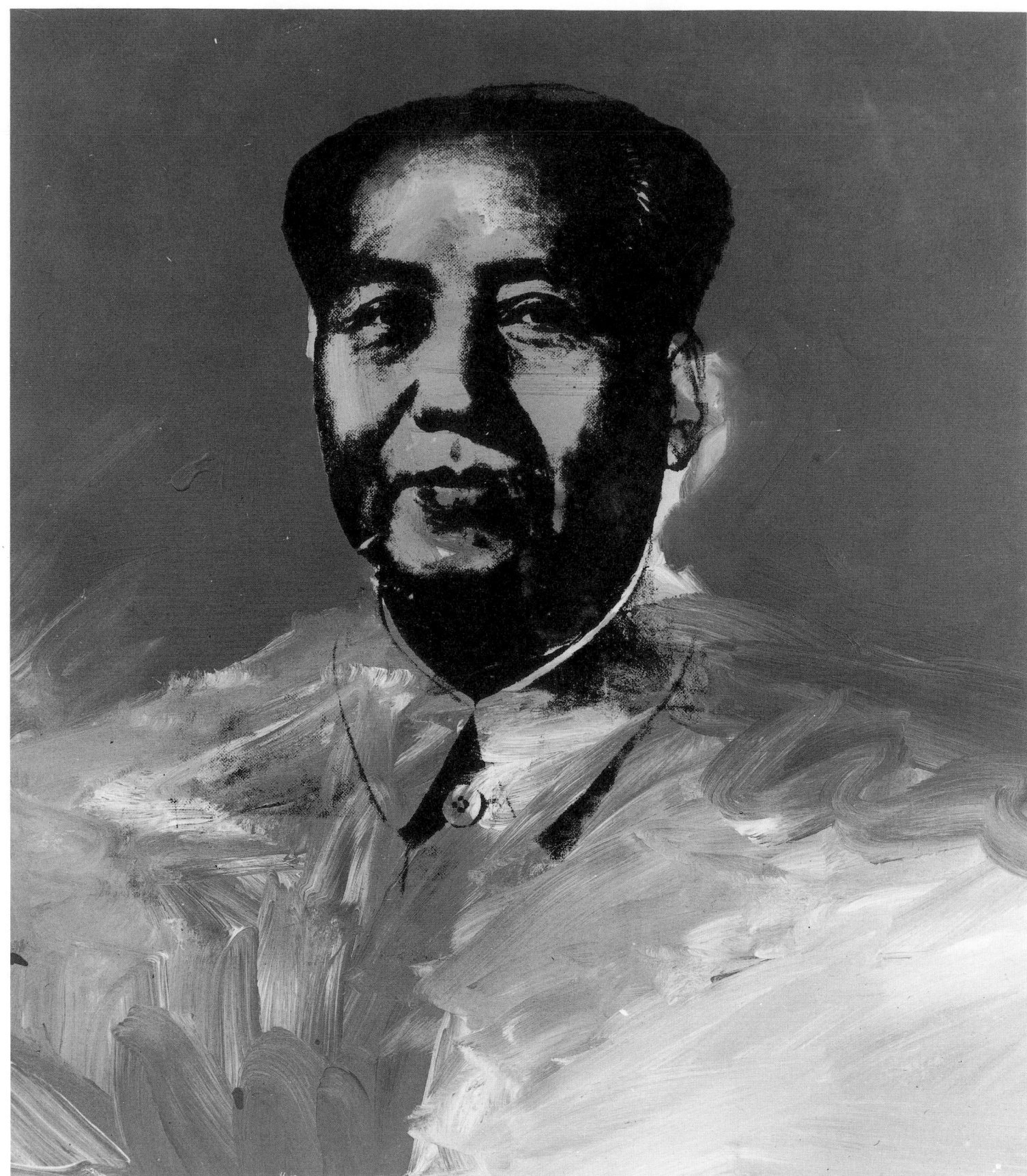

Andy Warhol: *Mao Tse-Tung*, 1970

Galerie Sonnabend, Paris
Galerie Rubbers, Buenos Aires
Galerie M. E. Thelen, Essen
Gian Enzo Sperone Arte Moderna, Milan
Institute of Contemporary Art, Philadelphia
Galerie Buren, Stockholm
Jerrold Morris International Gallery, Toronto
Gian Enzo Sperone Arte Moderna, Turin
1966   Galerie M. E. Thelen, Essen
Gian Enzo Sperone Arte Moderna, Milan
Institute of Contemporary Art, Boston
Contemporary Arts Center, Cincinnati, Ohio
Galerie Hans Neuendorf, Hamburg
Ferus Gallery, Los Angeles
Leo Castelli Gallery, New York
1957   Galerie Rudolf Zwirner, Cologne
Galerie Sonnabend, Paris
1968   Galerie Rudolf Zwirner, Cologne
Stedelijk Museum, Amsterdam
Galerie der Spiegel, Cologne
Rowan Gallery, London
Galerie Heiner Friedrich, Munich
Kunsternes, Oslo
Moderna Museet, Stockholm
1969   Neue Nationalgalerie der Staatlichen Museen Preussischer Kulturbesitz, West Berlin
Irvin Blum Gallery, Los Angeles
Leo Castelli Gallery, New York
1970   Galerie Folker Skulima, West Berlin
Museum of Contemporary Art, Chicago
Stedelijk van Abbemuseum, Eindhoven, Netherlands
Musée d'Art Moderne de la Ville, Paris
Pasadena Museum of Art, California (toured the Untied States and Europe)
1971   Galerie Bruno Bischofberger, Zurich
Gotham Book Mart Gallery, New York
Institute of Contemporary Arts, London
Musée d'Art Moderne, Paris
1972   Castelli Downtown Gallery, New York
Multiples Gallery, New York
1973   Margo Leavin Gallery, Los Angeles
1974   Mayor Gallery, London
Musée Galliera, Paris
1975   Baltimore Museum of Art
1976   Wurttembergischer Kunstverein, Stuttgart (travelled to Kunsthalle, Dusseldorf)
1980   *Andy Warhol: Photos*, Lisson Gallery, London
1981   *Portrait Screenprints 1965–1980*, Gloucestershire College of Arts and Technology, Cheltenham, England
1982   Galerie Schellmann und Kluser, Munich
Stadtische Galerie im Lenbachhaus, Munich
Galerie Daniel Templon, Paris
1983   Fraenkel Gallery, San Francisco
American Museum of Natural History, New York
Museum of Natural History, Cleveland, Ohio
1984   Scottsdale Center for the Arts, Arizona
Edition Schellmann und Kluser, Munich
Flow Ace Gallery, Los Angeles
Judith Goldberg Gallery, New York
Galerie Kammer, Hamburg
Galerie Schellmann und Kluser, Munich
1985   Museo di Capodimonte, Naples, Italy
1986   Galerie Daniel Templon, Paris
Edition Schellmann, Munich
Anthony D'Offay Gallery, London
1987   Galerie Bernd Kluser, Munich
Galerie Thaddaeus Ropac, Salzburg, Austria
Robert Miller Gallery, New York
Waddington Galleries, London
Kunstverein, Hamburg
1988   Galerie Bernd Kluser, Munich

Selected Group Exhibitions:

1956   *Recent Drawings USA*, Museum of Modern Art, New York
1962   *New Paintings of Common Objects*, Pasadena Museum of Art, California
1964   *American Pop Art*, Stedelijk Museum, Amsterdam
1966   *11 Pop Artists: The New Image*, Galerie M. E. Thelen, Essen, West Germany

1968   *Documenta 4*, Museum Fridericianum, Kassel, West Germany
1970   *De Giotto à Warhol*, Musée d'Art Moderne de la Ville, Paris
1977   *Paris-New York*, Centre Georges Pompidou, Paris
1981   *A New Spirit in Painting*, Royal Academy of Arts, London
1983   *Modern Art in the West*, Metropolitan Art Museum, Tokyo
1985   *Painterly Visions 1940–84*, Guggenheim Museum, New York

Collections:

Museum of Modern Art, New York; Whitney Museum, New York; Coreoran Gallery of Art, Washington, D.C.; Walker Art Center, Minneapolis; County Museum of Art, Los Angeles; Norton Simon Museum of Art, Pasadena, California; Art Gallery of Ontario, Toronto; Tate Gallery, London; Moderna Museet, Stockholm.

Publications:

By WARHOL: books—*Andy Warhol's Index Book*, New York 1967; *A: A Novel*, New York 1968; *Andy Warhol: Transcript of David Bailey's ATV Documentary*, London 1972; *A to B and Back Again*, London and New York 1975; *Ladies and Gentlemen*, Milan 1975; *Andy Warhol: Photographs*, portfolio of 12 photos, New York and Zurich 1980; *Popism: The Warhol 60s*, with Pat Hackett, New York 1980, London 1981; *Andy Warhol: Schweizer Portraits*, with text by George J. Dolezal, Thun 1982, *Andy Warhol's Children's Book*, Zurich 1983; *America*, New York 1985; articles—"My Favorite Superstar: Notes of My Epic, Chelsea Girls," interview with Gerard Malanga in *Arts* (New York), February 1967; "Andy Warhol Tapes Roman Polanski" in *Inter/View* (New York), November 1973; "Andy Warhol: Interview" in *Photo* (Paris), May 1979; "Warhol: Mon Carnet Mondain" in *Photo* (Paris), March 1980; films—*Kiss*, 1973; *Tarzan and Jane Regained Sort Of*, 1963; *Dance Movie*, also known as *Roller Skate*, 1963; *Haircut*, 1963; *Eat*, 1964; *Blow Job*, 1963–64; *Batman Dracula*, 1964; *Empire*, 1964, *Henry Geldzahler*, 1964; *Soap Opera*, also known as *The Lester Persky*, 1964; *Couch*, 1964; *Shoulder*, 1964; *Mario Banana*, 1964; *Harlot*, 1964; *13 Most Beautiful Women*, 1964–65; *13 Most Beautiful Boys*, 1964–65; *30 Fantastics and 50 Personalities*, 1964–66; *Ivy and John*, 1965; *Suicide*, 1965; *Screen Test I*, 1965; *Screen Test 2*, 1965; *The Life of Juanita Castro*, 1965; *Drunk*, 1965; *Horse*, 1965; *Poor Little Rich Girl*, 1965; *Vinyl*, 1965; *Bitch*, 1965; *Restaurant*, 1965; *Kitchen*, 1965; *Prison*, 1965; *Face*, 1965; *Afternoon*, 1965; *Beauty 2*, 1965; *Space*, 1965; *Outer and Inner Space*, 1965; *My Hustler*, 1965; *Camp*, 1965; *Paul Swan*, 1965; *Hedy*, also known as *Hedy the Shoplifter* and *The 14 Year Old Girl*, 1965; *The Closet*, 1965; *More Milk, Evette*, also known as *Lana Turner*, 1965; *Lupe*, 1965; *Bufferin*, also known as *Gerard Malanga Reads Poetry*, 1966; *Eating Too Fast*, 1966; *The Velvet Underground*, 1966; *Chelsea Girls*, 1966;****also known as *Four Stars*, 1966–67; *International Velvet*, segment of****, 1967; *Alan and Dickin*, segment of****, 1967; *Imitation of Christ*, segment of ****, 1967; *Gerard Has His Hair Removed with Nair*, segment of ****, 1967; *Alan and Apple*, segment of ****, 1967; *Bike Boy*, 1967; *Nude Restaurant*, 1967; *Lonesome Cowboys*, 1967; *Blue Movie*, 1969; *Schraff's Commercial*, 1969.

On WARHOL: books—*The Painter and the Photograph: From Delacroix to Warhol* by Van Deren Coke, Albuquerque, New Mexico, 1964, 1972; *Andy Warhol* by John Coplans, Pasadena, California 1970; *Andy Warhol* by Rainer Crone, London 1970; *The Autobiography and Sex Life of Andy Warhol* by John Wilcock, New York 1971; *Andy Warhol: Films and Paintings* by Peter Gidal, New York 1971; *Voglio essere una macchina: la fotografia di Andy Warhol* by Paolo Barozzi, Milan 1979; *Andy Warhol: Works 1962–1986*, exhibition catalogue with texts by William Mille, Stuart Morgan, David Hockney and others, Salzburg 1986; *Andy Warhol: Reversal Series*, exhibition catalolgue, London 1987; *Andy Warhol Photographs*, exhibition catalogue with text by Stephen Koch, New York 1987.

At a time when enigma is one of the most sought after of aesthetic virtues, Andy Warhol has achieved the difficult feat of remaining the most enigmatic artist of all. Since he first became known at the beginning of the Pop Art boom in the early 1960's, critics and public have argued about him, dismissed him, rein-

stated him again, endlessly questioned him and in the absence of any useful statement by the artist himself, declared themselves baffled by the bland success of his art.

Yet, of all post-war artists, Warhol made the most obvious breaks from past traditions and displayed the most single-minded consistency. His art can be seen for what it is only by stepping aside from our current assumptions about art and understanding the logic of his point of view.

The Pop Art movement started as a reaction against the success and high seriousness of Abstract Expressionism. As Roy Lichtenstein said, "We wanted to paint pictures so outrageous and ugly that no one would want to buy them." So the chosen subject matter was figurative (heresy!), commercial (but it's not Art) and frequently humorous (please don't laugh in the art gallery). But within two or three years, the Pop Artists found that they were as successful as their predecessors, and, what is more, that it was nice to be rich. As overdrafts disappeared though, so did invention and humour, and most of the artists settled down into comfortable lives making innumerable versions of their successful styles. But not Warhol.

Warhol was a much more sophisticated and analytical thinker than most artists, whose imaginations usually terminate at the end of their paint-brushes. He was aware of the pressure of success, of the danger of becoming an institution, but where most artists react to this by trying to fight it, Warhol decided to make success and being an institution his art form. Art had been manipulated by the art-world, the critics, dealers and collectors long enough; now Warhol was going to use them as his canvas.

His first successful work consisted of sculpture in the form of Campbell's Soup Cans and Brillo Boxes, and screenprinted paintings of contemporary icons from Elvis Presley to Jackie Kennedy, which he made with the assistance of the helpers in his Factory, as his large studio was called. These works immediately raised two important questions: did it matter that the works were not unique? and did it matter that Warhol himself had not actually made them? The critics and dealers, who were riding on the wave of newness and originality that they themselves had created, had to go along with the artist and the collectors dutifully followed.

Was his work, then, the huge confidence risk that the general public suspects all "modern art" to be? Yes, and No. Yes, because Warhol was deliberately attacking all the sacred shibboleths of art, and No, because the art itself was undeniably "good" and highly influential. The effect of Warhol pointing to commercial art as a source of visual energy and his use of violent colour overlays in his screenprints can be seen in every art college, every fashion magazine in the Western world. In purely visual terms he affected the language of art more than anyone else of his generation.

The critics would have been content to leave it at that, but Warhol was after bigger game. For one thing he realized the business potential of his painting method. Rich collectors would pay many times more for Warhol portraits of their wives than for conventional ones, even though the portrait would often be no more than a blow-up photograph screenprinted by a member of the Factory. Indeed it was the very casualness of Warhol that made his work so attractive and chic. For those with a more "concerned" view of the world he produced a series of paintings of electric chairs and wanted men. All of this work is handsome to look at and in his usual startling colour combinations, and Warhol had no lack of clients.

The Factory now became increasingly improtant and the work produced there became simply the means to its existence. To explain this next stage one must consider Warhol's personality or, to be exact, his lack of it. His nature was that of a vacuum, a void. He never made the earnest statements about his work that most artists are prone to, and apparently conversed entirely on trivialities. He condemned nothing and seemed to find any odd manifestation of human behaviour fascinating.

Because of this personality, he drew to his studio an

assortment of would be actors, failed poets, and all those, especially on the sexual fringes like transvestites, whose dreams were beyond the limits understood by normal society. "I dream, and others see my dreams," says an artist in a Cabell novel, which Warhol changes to "they dream, and I make their dreams visible."

When people are allowed to act as they wish, to be what they want to be, they create a "lifestyle," and it was to fashioning the lifestyle of the group that formed around him that Warhol now turned his attention. This he did, not by giving the lead for them to follow, but by pointing out what they were doing. He filmed them continuously, in little dramas where a man could act out the fantasy of being Jean Harlow or a woman could be high priestess and whore at the same time. He did this in a style that was deliberately rough and amateur, which left in all the mistakes, ended when the film ran out and which reflected exactly the street language and stoned lifestyle of its characters.

Early examples of this genre such as *My Hustler* were no more than home movies, but with *Chelsea Girls* came commercial success. The verbal obscenity of his characters fitted exactly the so-called "permissive society," and his works became notorious and fashionable for their sexual frankness. Warhol, who was never one to pass up a good thing, began to turn out full length films such as *Trash* and *Flesh,* and achieved the unique feat of making art films highly commercial.

Warhol's style of filmmaking has had a huge effect on the commercial cinema. While the whole weight of European "new wave" movies had failed to change Hollywood techniques, he succeeded single-handed. The casual styles of acting now fashionable, the type of wandering camera movement, the passages of apparently trivial conversation, all derive from Warhol.

To be a major influence on contemporary painting and film might have been enough for most artists, but Warhol was not yet finished. The lifestyle that he had allowed to grow around him was now becoming fashionable outside his circle. The most revolutionary aspect of this was the effect on sexual roles. At a time when the gamine mini-skirted look was de rigeur, Warhol reintroduced The Woman, via a return to 30's glamour. But the femininity did not mean weakness, for all Warhol's women are much stronger than his men; it was Jean Harlow, but without a patriarchal Clark Gable to subdue her.

Men were encouraged to express their femininity too. At the centre of the fashion were Warhol's "superstars," transvestites like Holly Woodlawn and Jackie Curtis, who had the effect of making bisexuality acceptable. This fashion has operated most strongly in the pop-rock world. There would have been no "glitter" without Warhol. Mick Jagger would have remained a blues shouter, David Bowie would not have happened at all, and it could be argued that the ubiquitous glamorous soul acts would never have happened.

Warhol opened a night-club for the "beautiful people" called The Exploding Plastic Inevitable, inventing the projected light show for it and managed the house band which was called The Velvet Underground. This band became one of the most influential in rock music, restoring in songs such as Heroin and White Light/White Heat a cutting, a poetical edge to a music that was fast drowning in the soft cotton wool of flower power.

As the influence of the lifestyle spread, Warhol changed the focus of his interests, putting out a gossip magazine called *Andy Warhol's Interview* which again furthered the effects of his ideas.

From painter to gossip magazine publisher is a big step, but in terms of Warhol's output a consistent and logical one. To consider his paintings by themselves, as most critics do, is to miss the point. Warhol's subject is society, which he manipulated in actuality as a painter manipulates his paint and for the same purpose; to create, to comment upon and to illustrate.

—Alastair Mackintosh

WATTS, Robert Marshall.

American. Born in Burlington, Iowa, 14 June 1923. Studied mechanical engineering at University of Louisville, Kentucky, 1942–44; also studied at the Art Students League, New York, 1946–48, and Columbia University, New York, 1951. Served in the United States Naval Reserve, 1942–46. Independent artist active in sculpture, performance, film and video, since 1953. Member of the Fluxus Group in new York in the early 1960's. Taught at the Institute of Applied Arts and Sciences. Brooklyn, New York, 1951–52. Professor of Art, Rutgers University, New Brunswick, New Jersey, 1953–84 (Resident Artist in Film and Mixed Media, 1964–82). Carnegie Corporation Visual Artist, University of California, 1968. Recipient: Research Council Grants, 1961–75, Faculty Fellowship, 1971, F.A.S.P. Grants, 1975, 1982, and CID Grant, 1978, Rutgers University; Experimental Workshop Award, Carnegie Corporation, 1964; Creative Artists Public Service Grant, New York State Council on the Arts, 1975; National Endowment for the Arts Fellowship, Washington, D.C., 1976. Agent: Francesco Conn, Vicolo Quadrelli 7, 37121 Verona, Italy. Address: R.D. 3, Bangor, Pennsylvania 18013, U.S.A.

Individual Exhibitions:

1960	Grand Central Moderns, New York
1966	Bianchini Gallery, New York
	Ricke Gallery, Kassel, West Germany
1970	Ricke Gallery, Cologne
1971	Apple Gallery, New York
1973	La Bertesca, Milan
	Galerie Baecker, Bochum, West Germany

Robert Watts: *System with Chrome Sphere*, 1986

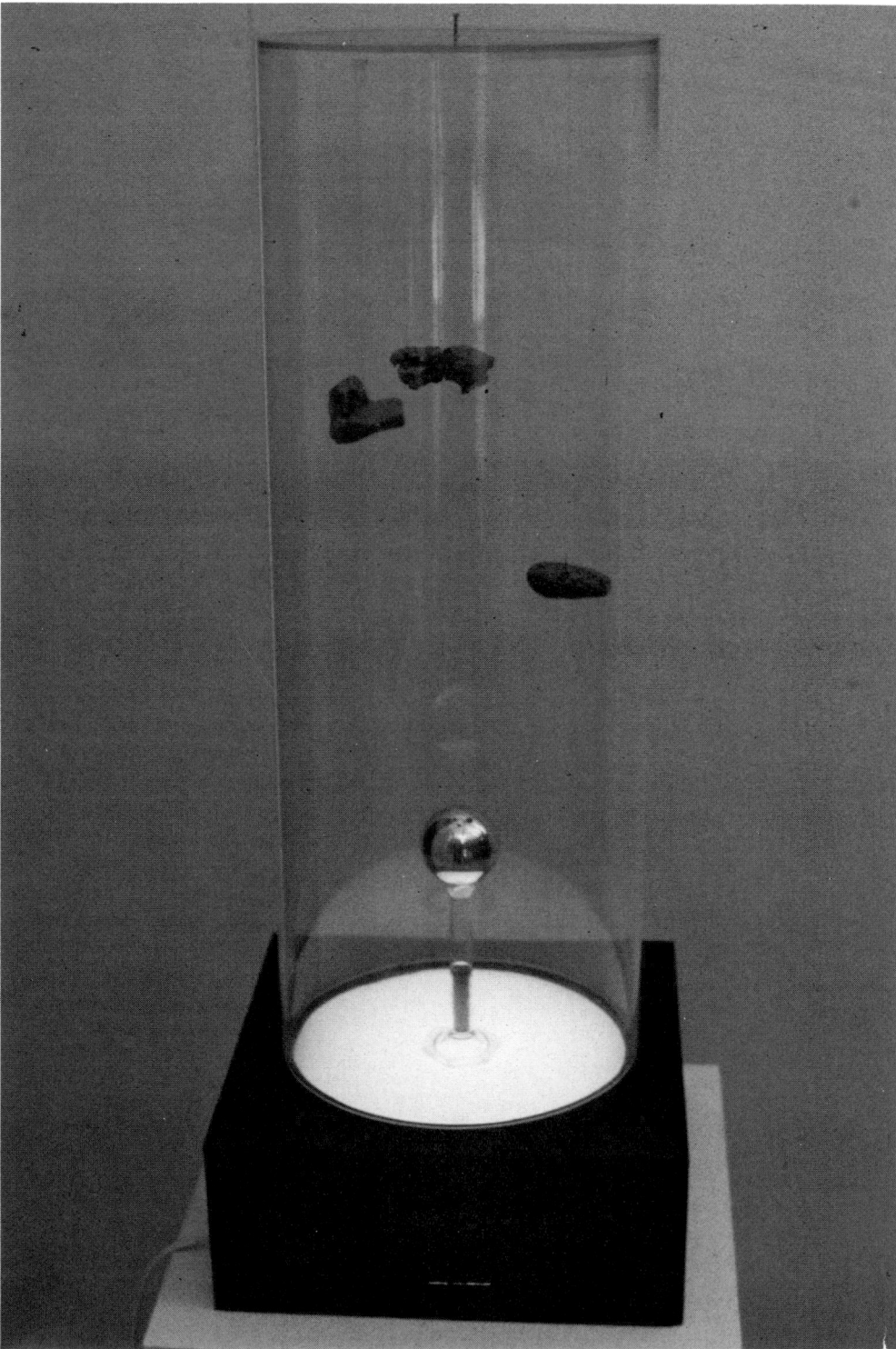

1974 Multhipla, Milan
1975 Multhipla, Milan
1976 René Block Gallery, New York
1977 Studio Morra, Naples
1978 Felius Gallery, Washington, D.C.
1982 Galleria d'Arte, Verona, Italy

Performances:

Magic Kazoo, New York City and New Jersey, 1960; *Yam Festival,* with George Brecht, in the United States and by international mail, 1962; *Yam Lecture,* with George Brecht, New York, 1963; *Yam Day,* with George Brecht, Hardware Poets Playhouse, New York, 1963; *Cake,* Kornblee Gallery, New York, 1964; *Monday Night Letter,* Cafe au Go Go, New York, 1964-65; *Performance Work/Fluxus/Body Covering,* Museum of Contemporary Crafts, New York, 1967; *Superstar,* University of California, Santa Cruz, 1969; *Communication in a Noisy Environment,* Automation House, New York, 1970; *Fluxyear/Gemini/74,* Onnasch Gallery, New York, 1974; *Performance Works for Audience,* Centro d'Informazione Alternativa, Rome, 1975; *Flux-Harpsichord Konzert,* Akademie der Kunste, West Berlin, 1976; *Oraculum,* Studio Morra, Naples, 1977; *FLuxus Concert,* Musee d'Art Contemporain, Montreal, 1980.

Selected Group Exhibitions:

1960 *New Forms, New Media,* Martha Jackson Gallery, New York
1961 *Assemblage,* Museum of Modern Art, New York
1968 *The Machine,* Museum of Modern Art, New York
1970 *Happening und Fluxus,* Kunstverein, Cologne (toured Europe)
1972 *Documenta 5,* Museum Fridericianum, Kassel, West Germany
1974 *Artists' Stamps,* Simon Fraser University, Burnaby, British Columbia
1979 *Re-Visions,* Whitney Museum, New York
1981 *Fluxus, etc.,* Cranbrook Academy of Art, Bloomfield Hills, Michigan
1985 *Festival of Fantastics,* Roskilde, Denmark
1987 *Made in USA,* University of California, Berkeley

Collections:

Albright-Knox Art Gallery, Buffalo, New York; Chrysler Art Museum, Provincetown, Massachusetts; Art Institute of Chicago; Museum of Fine Arts, Houston; Fort Worth Art Center, Texas; Los Angeles County Museum of Art; Moderna Museet, Stockholm.

Publications:

By WATTS: book—*Newspaper,* with George Brecht, New York 1963; *Postage Stamps,* New York 1963; *Fluxpost Postage Stamps,* New York 1965; *Event Cards Fluxus,* New York 1965; *The Arts on Campus,* edited by Margaret Mahoney, New York 1970; *Proposals for Art Education,* New York 1970; *S.O.S.,* 2 vols., New York 1977; *The Book As An Event,* Bangor 1978; *Notes and Sketches 1964-66,* Asolo 1979.

On WATTS: books—*AQ 16: Fluxus* by Silke Paul and Harve Wurz, Antibes 1977; *The Museum of Drawers* by Herbert Distel, Zurich 1978; *Fluxus* by Harry Rule, Amsterdam 1979; *Blam: The Explosion of Pop, Minimalism and Performance 1958-64* by Barbara Haskell, New York 1984; articles—in the *Institute of Contemporary Arts Bulletin* (London), January 1967; "Transformations from Nature" by Letty Eisenhauer in *Art and Artists* (London), November 1973.

From 1946 to 1958 I was a painter mainly in the tradition of abstract expressionism and geometric art. In 1957 I began working on pieces involving electric light, with random circuitry, incandescent wire, plants and fish. One day in July 1958 I stopped painting.

During the early '60s I exhibited works of an electro-mechanical nature guided by random or quasi-random circuits. At the same time I became interested in 16mm and 8mm film, photography, tape machines—and then I met Fluxus in 1963.

In 1960 I had produced my first event of 48 hours duration which moved from New York City to the Jersey shore, utilizing students as the primary participants, but acquiring others along the way. In a sense, Fluxus came at a time of consolidation of my ideas about art and art process; it was an exploratory forum for ideas and energy which eventually had an effect on all the arts.

Since 1970 I have continued to explore methods and attitudes toward art utilizing my knowledge and experience with past art and archaeology, esoteric information, science and technology, natural phenomena, and print technology. I work with concepts first and methods secondarily, chosen to suit the thought at hand.

—Robert Watts

WEGMAN, William.

American. Born in Holyoke, Massachusetts, 12 February 1942. Educated at Massachusetts College of Art, Boston, B.F.A. 1965; University of Illinois, Urbana, 1965-67, M.F.A. 1967. Married to Gayle Wegman; son: Man Ray. Artist and freelance photographer, California and New York. Instructor, University of Wisconsin at Wausau, 1967, and at Waukesha, 1968-69; Assistant Professor, University of Wisconsin, Madison, 1969-70; Lecturer, 1970-71, and Visiting Artist, 1978, California State University at Long Beach. Recipient: Guggenheim Fellowship, 1975; National Endowment for the Arts Grant, 1975-77, 1982; Creative Artists Public Service Grant, 1979. Agent: Holly Solomon Gallery, 724 Fifth Avenue, New York, New York 10019. Address: 27 Thames Street, New York, New York 10004, U.S.A.

Individual Exhibitions:

1971 Galerie Sonnabend, Paris
        Pomona College, California
1972 Sonnabend Gallery, New York
        Galerie Ernst, Hannover
        Situation, London
        Galerie Konrad Fischer, Dusseldorf
        Courtney Sale Gallery, Dallas
1973 Galerie Sonnabend, Paris
        Texas Gallery, Houston
        Los Angeles County Museum of Art
        Francoise Lambert and Claire Copley Gallery, Los Angeles
1974 Modern Art Agency, Naples
        Galerie D. Brussels
        Galeria Toselli, Milan
        112 Green Street Gallery, New York
        Texas Gallery, Houston
1975 Mayor Gallery, London
        Galleria Alessandra Castelli, Milan
        Galerie Konrad Fischer, Dusseldorf
1976 The Kitchen, New York
1977 Sonnabend Gallery, New York
        Bruno Soletti Gallery, Milan
1978 Rosamund Felsen Gallery, Los Angeles
        Robert Cumming/William Wegman, California Institute of Technology, Pasadena
1979 Holly Solomon Gallery, New York
        Arnolfini Gallery, Bristol
        Galerie Konrad Fischer, Dusseldorf
        Otis Art Institute, Los Angeles
        William Wegman: Retrospective, Fine Arts Galleries, University of Wisconsin at Milwaukee
1980 *William Wegman: Selected Works 1970-1979,* University of Colorado Art Galleries, Boulder (travelled to the Aspen Center for Visual Arts, Colorado)

1981 Clarence Kennedy Gallery, Cambridge, Massachusetts (with William Van Dyke and Olivia Parker)
1982 Dart Gallery, Chicago
1983 Walker Art Center, Minneapolis
        12 Duke Street Gallery, London
        Contemporary Arts Center, Cincinnati, Ohio
        Corcoran Gallery of Art, Washington, D.C.
1984 Mackenzie Art Gallery, Regina, Saskatchewan
        University of Miami, Coral Gables
1985 Albright College, Reading, Pennsylvania
1986 Daniel Wolf Gallery, New York
1988 San Francisco Museum of Modern Art

Selected Group Exhibitions:

1969 *Places and Process,* Edmonton Art Gallery, Alberta
1971 *Prospect '71,* Dusseldorf
1973 *Whitney Annual,* Whitney Museum, New York
1977 *Photography as an Art Form,* Ringling Museum of Art, Sarasota, Florida
1978 *23 Photographers,* Walker Art Gallery, Liverpool
1979 *The Altered Photograph,* Project Studio 1, Long Island City, Queens, New York
1980 *The Photograph Transformed,* Touchstone Gallery, New York
1983 *Subjective Vision,* High Museum of Art, Atlanta, Georgia
1987 *Photography and Art 1946-86,* Los Angeles County Museum of Art

Collections:

Whitney Museum, New York; Museum of Modern Art, New York; Ed Ruscha Collection, Los Angeles; International Museum of Photography at George Eastman House, Rochester, New York.

Publications:

By WEGMAN: book—*Man's Best Friend,* New York 1983; articles—"Shocked and Outraged" in *Avalanche* (New York), Winter 1971.

On WEGMAN: books—*Wegman's World,* exhibition catalogue with texts by Lisa Lyon and Kim Levin, Minneapolis 1983; *Photography and Art 1946-1986,* exhibition catalogue with essays by Andy Grundberg and Kathleen M. Gauss, Los Angeles 1987; articles—"Photography" by Ben Lifson in the *Village Voice* (New York), 9 April 1978; "Everything You Wanted to Know about William Wegman but Didn't Dare Ask" by Stuart Morgan in *Arnolfini Review* (Bristol), May/June 1979; "William Wegman" by Ian Walker in *Art Monthly* (London), no. 27, 1979; "William Wegman: Altered Photographs" in *Domus* (Milan), July 1979.

"I like to subvert the familiar, but not to put it down, or make fun of it." Wegman thus adequately described the intent and nuance of his photographs, video and films, and unpretentious graphic art; that is, until the early 1980s and the death of Man Ray, his 80 pound Weimaraner companion, with whom he had made of his domestic vaudeville and other spoof images. The dog had in a sense become Wegman's persona and allowed him the fragile, deliberately ephemeral attitude in a wide spectrum of theme. Although Wegman's recent works are still characterized by such burlesque fun (Wegman is said to have genuine disdain for "art"), there is now a more Surreal and emblematic quality in the elegantly produced Polaroid form which has come to distinguish his work.

Wegman states that he became annoyed with the utterly subjective nuance of modernity, and so was then led to jokes through the need to have his communication "complete itself." His primary metaphor formed around the rational absurdity of the joke structure; and perhaps his major role is to have brought into "high" art, the casual fun of public entertainment. (His critics have often chided him in just this regard—his "lightness" of tone.) And so there came about a long-standing attack upon artistic sincerity itself through Wegman's use of autobiographic subject matter, an improvisational spontaneity, and a humor often centered about the nature of our reality-perception. Prevalent also throughout his work has been the theme of incapacity and the thwartedness of failure. No doubt vital to his evolution has been his continuing acquaintance with his one-time studio-mate John Baldessari, and as well the appearance in 1963 at the Pasadena Museum of Art, of the first large exhibition of the works of Marcel Duchamp.

With the present decade, Wegman has used a large format Polaroid image which perhaps contradicts the self-effacing anti-mastery so important to his statement. The easy accessibility of his earlier work ("I didn't want them to be compared to paintings, and get involved in scale, and size, and 'wall' power") has thus been lost. The recent work often exudes a commercialized air through the long use of such tableaux-like imagery in the advertising world. Wegman has e.g., focused upon a female body builder as model in order to explore sexual role cliches; and in another lengthy exploration, has used a small child to present the poignance and strangeness of the child/adult interface.

—Joshua Kind

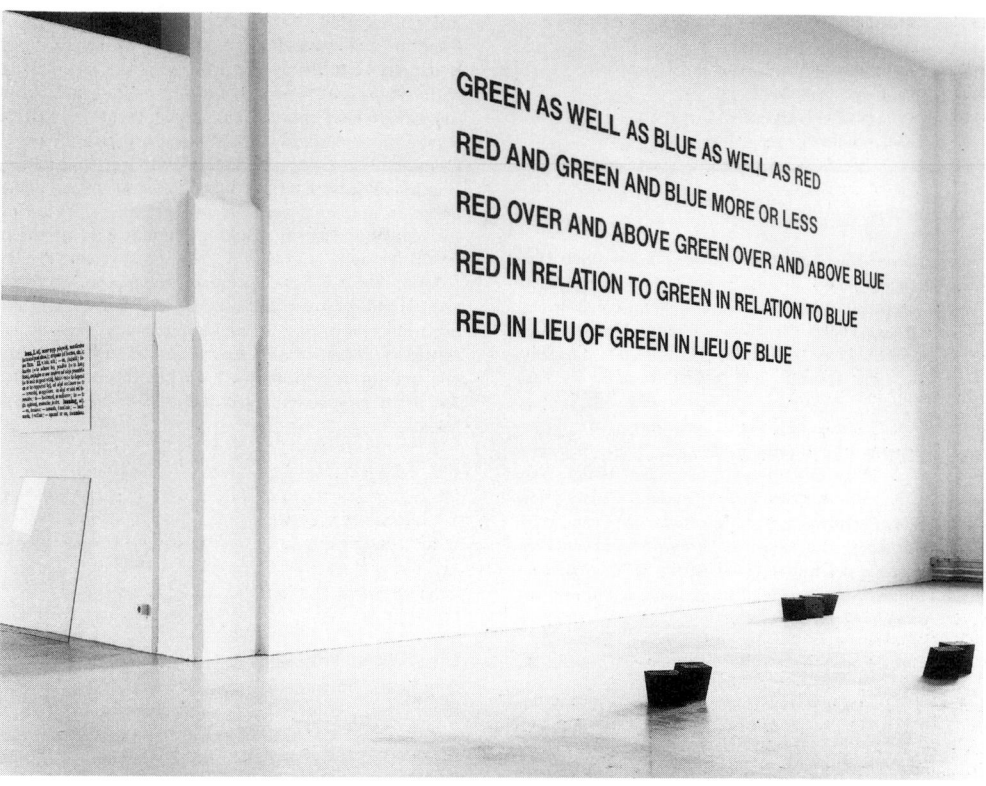

Lawrence Weiner: Installation in the Anton Herbert Collection, Ghent, 1982

WEINER, Lawrence.

American. Born in the Bronx, New York, 10 February 1940. Educated at Stuyvesant High School, New York; self-taught as an artist. Independent artist known for conceptual works incorporating verbal elements: lives and works in New York. Recipient: Deutscher Akademische Austauschdienst (DAAD) Award, 1975-76; National Endowment for the Arts Fellowship, Washington, D.C. 1977, 1985; American Exhibition Prize, Art Institute of Chicago, 1979. Agent: Leo Castelli, 420 West Broadway, New York, New York 10012. Address: 13 Bleecker Street, New York, New York 10012, U.S.A.

Individual Exhibitions:

1964	Seth Siegelaub Gallery, New York
1965	Seth Siegelaub Gallery, New York
1968	Seth Siegelaub Gallery, New York
1969	Konrad Fischer Galerie, Dusseldorf
	Nova Scotia College of Art and Design, Halifax
	Wide White Space Gallery, Antwerp
	Galleria Sperone, Turin
1970	Konrad Fischer Galerie, Dusseldorf
	Galleria Sperone, Turin
	Galerie Folker Skulima, Berlin
	Art & Project Gallery, Amsterdam
	Galerie Yvon Lambert, Paris
	Gegenverker, Aachen, West Germany
1971	Galerie Yvon Lambert, Paris
	Nova Scotia College of Art and Design, Halifax
	Leo Castelli Gallery, New York
1972	Jack Wendler Gallery, London
	Galleria Toselli, Milan
	Wide White Space Gallery, Antwerp
	Leo Castelli Gallery, New York
	Konrad Fischer Galerie, Dusseldorf
	Galleria Sperone, Turin
	Westfälischer Kunstverein, Münster, West Germany
	California Institute of the Arts, Los Angeles
1973	Project Inc., Cambridge, Massachusetts
	Städtisches Museum, Mönchenglabach, West Germany
	Jack Wendler Gallery, London
	Wide White Space Gallery, Brussels
	Galleria Sperone, Turin
	Modern Art Agency, Naples
	Kabinett für Aktuelle Kunst, Bremerhaven, West Germany
1974	Max Protetch Gallery, Washington, D.C.
	Rolf Preisig Gallery, Basle
	Galleria Toselli, Milan

	Gentofte Kommunes Kunstbibliotek, Hellerup, Denmark
	Galerie Yvon Lambert, Paris
	Leo Castelli Gallery, New York
	Claire Copley Gallery, Los Angeles
	Barbara Cusack Gallery, Houston
1975	Konrad Fischer Galerie, Dusseldorf
	Kabinett für Aktuelle Kunst, Bremerhaven, West Germany
	Galleria Sperone, Turin
	Rolf Preisig Gallery, Basel
1976	Van Abbemuseum, Eindhoven, Netherlands
	Institute for Contemporary Arts, London
	Robert Self Gallery, Newcastle upon Tyne
	Institute for Art and Urban Resources, New York
	Kunsthalle, Basle
	The Kitchen, New York
	Rüdiger Schöttle Galerie, Munich
1977	CEAC, Toronto
	Galerie Yvon Lambert, Paris
	Salle Patino, Centre d'Art Contemporain, Geneva
	Konrad Fischer Galerie, Dusseldorf
	Claire Copley Gallery, Los Angeles
	Laguna Gloria Art Museum, Austin, Texas
	Wide White Space Gallery, Antwerp
1978	Renaissance Society, University of Chicago
	INK, Halle für Internationale Neue Kunst, Zurich
1979	Galleria Francoise Lambert, Milan
	Leo Castelli Gallery, New York
	Nova Scotia College of Art and Design, Halifax
	Galerija Foksal PSP, Warsaw
	Saman Gallery, Genoa
	Art & Project Gallery, Amsterdam
	Rüdiger Schöttle Galerie, Munich
1980	Museum of Contemporary Art, Chicago
	Van Abbemuseum, Eindhoven, Netherlands
	Centre d'Art Contemporain, Geneva
	Anthony d'Offay Gallery, London
	Galerija Akumulatory 2, Poznan, Poland
	Leo Castelli Gallery, New York
	Art and Project, Amsterdam
1981	A Space, Toronto
	Leo Castelli Gallery, New York
	David Bellman Gallery, Toronto
	Kabinett für Aktuelle Kunst, Bremerhaven, West Germany
	P.S. 1, New York
	Konrad Fischer Galerie, Dusseldorf

1982	GEWAD, Ghent, Belgium
	Galerie Media, Neuchatel, Switzerland
	The Movies, Amsterdam
1983	Nordjyllands Kunstmuseum, Aalborg, Denmark (with Albert Merz)
	Bleecker Street Cinema, New York
	Kunsthalle, Berne
	Galerie Micheline Swaczer, Antwerp
	Nova Scotia College of Art and Design, Halifax
1984	David Bellman Gallery, Toronto
	Ohio State University, Columbus
	University of Cincinnati, Ohio
	Galerie Daniel Templon, Paris
	Espace Lyonnais d'Art Contemporain, Lyon, France
	TTL, BRT and NOS Teletekst, Belgium (television broadcast)
1985	Art and Project Plancius Straat Gallery, Amsterdam
	Art and Project Prinsegracht Gallery, Amsterdam
	Galerie Konrad Fischer, Dusseldorf
	Galerie Daniel Templon, Paris
	Le Coin du Miroir, Dijon, France
	City Thoughts, Amsterdam
	ARC/Musee d'Art Moderne de la Ville, Paris
	Musee St. Pierre d'Art Contemporain, Lyon, France
1986	State University of New York, Old Westbury
	Pier Art Centre, Stromness, Orkney Islands
	Fruitmarket Gallery, Edinburgh
	AIR Gallery, London (travelled to Derry, Northern Ireland)
	Anthony D'Offay Gallery, London
	Galerie Micheline Szwajcer, Antwerp
	Art Gallery of New South Wales, Sydney
	Marian Goodman Gallery, New York
	Leo Castelli Gallery, New York
1987	Galerie Daniel Templon, Paris
	Le Magasin Centre d'Art Contemporain, Grenoble, France

Selected Group Exhibitions:

1969	*When Attitude Becomes Form*, Kunsthalle, Bern
1971	*6th Guggenheim International Exhibition*, Guggenheim Museum, New York
1972	*Documenta 5*, Museum Fridericianum, Kassel, West Germany (and *Documenta 7*, 1982)
1973	*Prospekt '74*, Kunsthalle, Dusseldorf

1974 *Some Recent American Art*, City of Auckland Art Gallery, New Zealand
1979 *American Exhibition*, Art Institute of Chicago
1981 *Westkunst*, Cologne
1983 *When Words Become Works*, Minneapolis College of Art and Design, Minnesota
1985 *Artists' Books*, Centre Georges Pompidou, Paris
1987 *Comic Iconoclasm*, Institute of Contemporary Arts, London

Collections:

Centre Georges Pompidou, Paris; Stedelijk Museum, Amsterdam; Museum van Hedendaagse Kunst te Gent, Ghent, Belgium; Städtisches Museum, Mönchengladbach, West Germany; Van Abbemuseum, Eindhoven, Netherlands; British Museum, London; Museum of Modern Art, New York; Art Gallery of Ontario, Toronto; Nova Scotia College of Art and Design, Halifax; National Gallery of Australia, Canberra.

Publications:

By WEINER: books—*Statements*, New York 1968; *Traces*, Turin 1970; *Art & Project/Lawrence Weiner*, Amsterdam 1971; *10 Works*, Paris 1971; *Flowed*, Halifax, Nova Scotia 1971; *Causality: Affected and/or Effected*, New York 1971; *Having Been Done at/Having Been Done to*, Turin 1972; *A Primer*, Kassel 1972; *Green as Well as Blue as Well as Red*, London 1972; *Within Forward Motion*, Bremerhaven, West Germany 1973; *Within a Reasonable Doubt*, Milan 1973; *Once Upon a Time*, Milan 1973; *Having from Time to Time a Relation to*, Amsterdam 1973; *Towards a Reasonable End*, Bremerhaven, West Germany 1975; *Relative to Hanging*, Ringkobing, Denmark 1975; *Various Manners with Various Things*, London 1976; *Art & Project*, Amsterdam 1976; *On the Rocks*, Lund, Sweden 1976; *Pertaining to a Structure*, London 1977; *Coming and Going*, Geneva 1977; *In Relation to Probable Use*, Chicago 1978; *Regarding Inscriptions (of a Sort)*, Basle 1978; *With a Touch of Pink*, Bremerhaven, West Germany 1978; *Works*, New York 1978; *Hard Light*, with Edward Ruscha, Los Angeles 1978; *The Level of Water*, Ghent, Belgium 1978; *With a Probability of Being Seen*, Warsaw 1979; *Concerning 20 Works*, London 1980; *Passage to the North*, New York 1981; *Red/As Well as Green/As Well as Yellow/As Well as Blue*, with Albert Mertz, Aalborg 1983; *Sculpture*, with interview by Suzanne Page, Paris 1985; recordings—*7*, Paris 1972; *Having Been Done At*, Rome 1973; *Nothing to Lose/Niets aan Verloren*, Eindhoven, Netherlands, 1976; *Having Been Built on Sand with Another Base (Basis) in Fact*, Munich 1978; films and videos—*Beached*, 1970; *Broken off*, 1971; *To and Fro and Fro and To and Fro and Fro and To*, 1972; *Shifted from Side to Side*, 1972; *A First Quarter*, 1973; *Affected and/or Effected*, 1974; *Done To*, 1975; *A Second Quarter*, 1975; *Do You Believe in Water?*, 1976; *Green As Well As Blue As Well As Red*, 1976; *A Bit of Matter and a Little Bit More*, 1976; *For Example Decorated*, 1977; *Altered to Suit*, 1979; *There But For*, 1980; *Passage to the North*, 1981; *Plowmans Lunch*, 1982.

On WEINER: books—*Lawrence Weiner: Eine Ausstellung*, exhibition catalogue with essay by Klaus Honnef, Aachen 1971; *Lawrence Weiner: Jahresgabe 1972*, exhibition catalogue with introduction by Klaus Honnef, Munster 1973; *Lawrence Weiner, 8-30 Juni 1974*, exhibition catalogue with essay by Jane Pedersen, Hellerup 1974; *Lawrence Weiner*, exhibition catalogue with commentary by Rudi H. Fuchs, Basle 1978; *Lawrence Weiner: Mounds + Smooth Cairns*, exhibition catalogue with text by Edward Leffingwell, Columbus, Ohio 1984; *Lawrence Weiner: Above Beyond Below*, exhibition catalogue with essays by Erlend Brown and Mark Francis, Edinburgh 1986; *Lawrence Weiner: Posters, November 1965-April 1986*, edited by Benjamin H. D. Buchloh, Halifax, Nova Scotia 1986.

Art is not a metaphor upon the relationships of human beings to objects and objects to objects in relation to human beings but a representation of an empirical existing fact.

It does not tell the potential and capabilities of an object (material) but presents a reality concerning that relationship.

Constant placation of previous aesthetics consumes present resources to the extent that as the needs and desires of a present aesthetic make themselves felt (even when the basis is in a previous aesthetic) the resources have been exhausted.

There are very few material relationships of human beings to objects that at various (some) stages have not required various (some) forms of human being to human being relationships.

The utilization of media presents these various relationships at the moment of the presentation of what in essence is a material relationship. The utilization of media as both presentation and representation seems to require no justification other than the presentation itself.

The artists' reality is no different from any other reality. It is the content that gives the perceptions and observations of an artist (within the presentation/art) a use factor within the society.

The acceptance of the need for this distancing (in fact the need itself) by a society for its art to function has led to the misconception that art and artists are apart from society unless they do not function as art and artists.

The obvious change in the relationship of art to a culture is perhaps that the explanation (not needed justification) of the existence of art has been allied to the concept of production.

This reading while obviating some form of social unease is not in fact the case: art is in relation to its society a service industry.

—Lawrence Weiner

WELCH, Roger.
American. Born in Westfield, New Jersey, 10 February 1946. Educated at Westfield Senior High School, New Jersey, 1961-64; National Music Camp, Interlochen, Michigan, Summers 1963, 1964 and 1965; studied at York Junior College, Pennsylvania, 1964-65, Miami University, Oxford, Ohio, 1965-69, B.F.A. 1969, School of the Art Institute of Chicago, 1969-71, and with the Whitney Independent Study Program, New York, 1970-71. Multi-media artist: lives and works in New York. Recipient: Ford Foundation Scholarship, 1970; New York State Council on the Arts Grant, 1973; National Endowment for the Arts Grants, 1974, 1980. Agents: Ted Greenwald Gallery, 184 Mott Street, New York, New York 10013; Elizabeth Galasso Fine Arts, 191 Main Street, Ossining, New York 10562. Address: 87 East Houston Street, New York, New York 10012, U.S.A.

Individual Exhibitions:

1971   112 Greene Street, New York
         98 Greene Street Loft, New York
1972   98 Greene Street Loft, New York
         Galerie 20, Amsterdam
         Sonnabend Gallery, New York
1973   Galerie Konrad Fischer, Dusseldorf
         Galerie Sonnabend, Paris
         Nova Scotia College of Art, Halifax
         John Gibson Gallery, New York
1974   University of Rhode Island, Kingston
         Milwaukee Art Center
1975   Galleria Forma, Genoa
         Galerie Gérald Piltzer, Paris
         Stefanotty Gallery, New York
1977   Albright-Knox Art Gallery, Buffalo, New York
1980   Museo de Arte Moderno, Mexico City
1981   Museo Nacional, Havana
         Museo de Bellas Artes, Carcas
1982   Whitney Museum, New York
1984   Miami University, Oxford, Ohio (retrospective)
1986   Ted Greenwald Gallery, New York
         Elizabeth Galasso Fine Arts, Ossining, New York
1987   Ted Greenwald Gallery, New York

Selected Group Exhibitions:

1972   *Documenta*, Kassel, West Germany
1973   *20 Conceptual Artists*, Galerie Kriwin, Brussels
1974   *Projekt '74*, Wallraf-Richartz Museum, Cologne
1975   *Camera Art*, Lund Konsthall, Sweden
1977   *Words*, Whitney Museum, New York
         Video Art, Museo de Arte Moderno, Mexico City
1981   *Alternatives in Retrospect 1969-75*, New Museum, New York
1983   *Urban Pulses: The Artist and the City*, Pittsburgh Plan for Art, Pennsylvania
1985   *Prozess und Konstruktion 1985*, Landeshauptstadt Museum, Munich
1987   *Photography and Art 1946-86*, Los Angeles County Museum of Art

Collections:

Georgia Museum of Art, University of Georgia, Athens; Milwaukee Art Center; Wallraf-Richartz Museum, Cologne; Museum Haus Lange, Krefeld, West Germany; Lund Konsthall, Sweden; Museo Rufino Tamayo, Mexico City; Museo de Bellas Artes, Caracas, Venezuela; Museum of Modern Art, New York; Chase Manhattan Bank, New York.

Publications:

By WELCH: statement in *Roger Welch*, exhibition catalogue, Milwaukee 1975; statement in *Unbuilt America*, New York 1976; statement in *The Individual in a Social World*, New York 1977; statement in *The Big Jewish Book*, New York 1978; essay in *Alternatives in Retrospect 1969-75*, exhibition catalogue, New York 1981.

On WELCH: books—*Four Artists and the Map*, exhibition catalogue, by Roberta Smith, Kansas City 1980; *A Decade of New Art*, exhibition catalogue with text by Linda Cathcart, New York 1984; *Das Automobil in der Kunst 1886-1986*, exhibition catalogue with essay by Reimar Zeller, Munich 1986; *Photography and Art 1946-86*, exhibition catalogue with text by Andy Grundberg, Los Angeles 1987; articles—"Story Art" by Margarethe Jochimsen in *Magazin Kunst* (Mainz, West Germany), September 1974; "The Post-Perceptual Portrait" by Amy Goldwin in *Art in America* (New York), January/February 1975; "After Photography" by Douglas Davis in the *Village Voice* (New York), no. 14, 1981.

Roger Welch is a multi-media artist who uses film, photographs, video, drawings, diagrams, texts and various sculptural objects in multiple combinations in his environmental installations. Since 1969-70 Welch has been using real persons and events as the bases for his investigations into the nature of our perceptions as they are sifted and shifted by the passage of time. Welch's work begins with things personally experienced and/or experienced by people around him, and he expands his themes out of the purely autobiographical and biographical realms into iconic statements of the more generally recognizable social and cultural environment which shapes the typically American experience. Welch selects and organizes various visual and verbal elements of his subject matter to make interrelated and open-ended environments, making the viewer into an active participant who, by filling in meanings by association and by making choices as to how and when to take in the parts of the multi-layered work, finds possibilities for fresh and vital insights into situations which are usually either buried in half-forgotten memories or simply ingested at face value.

In 1970 Welch began examining his own memory. First, he wrote down what he was able to recall about his own experiences at Miami University in Ohio. Subsequently, he returned to that place and photographed sites which he had mentioned in his writings. In this manner Welch had created a sequence in which memory became cause, the trigger which determined the structure of present experiencing of things past. During the same period Welch began collaborating with friends and family. In graphic works of 1971 he juxtaposed older and newer photographs of members of various generations of his family and had those who were still alive write their memories of the events pictured under each photograph. In the film *Welch* (1972), he edited from old 16mm home

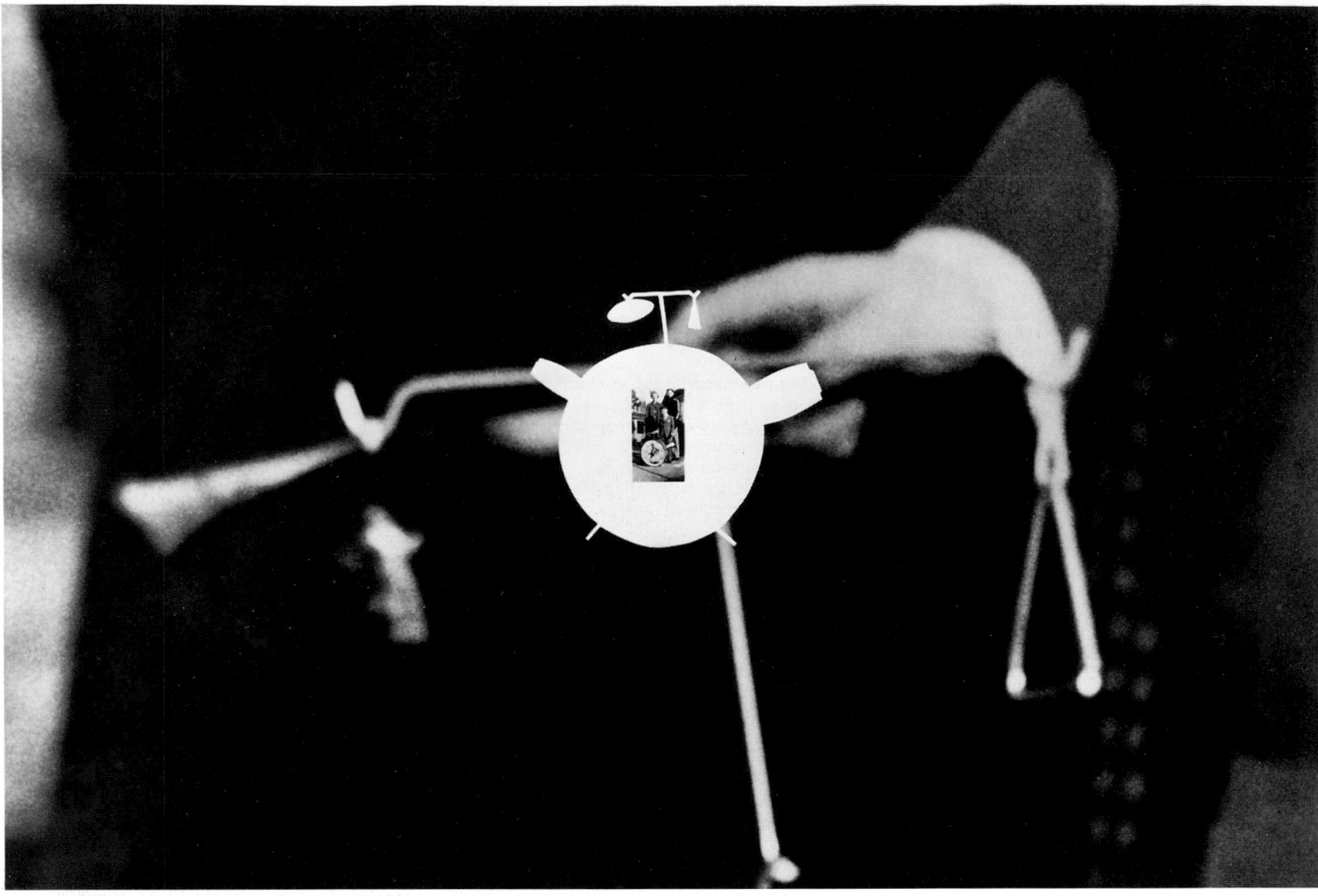

Roger Welch: *Self-Portrait*, 1987

movies made from 1926 to 1972 and covering five generations of his family. In the accompanying audiotape, his father, mother, brother, brother's son and himself comment spontaneously as they watch the movies together. Past events, rearranged by the artist, are given revitalization and continuation from a new perspective and vantage point. Old and new are both experienced candidly and immediately as past and present are occurring simultaneously for the participants and for the viewers alike. In a related series of works, Welch conducted interviews with persons all born before 1890, discussing with them their recollections of their childhood home towns. Out of their descriptions, Welch constructed maps, visualizations of their almost-faded memories which make tangible that which is nearly lost from present perception. One of the most memorable of Welch's collaboration with older people is his 1976 "Alton Carter, Plains, Georgia, Memory Map," a reconstruction of Plains based on discussions with Jimmy Carter's 88-year-old uncle, Alton. Beginning with a personal collaborative effort, the artist interprets the mythology communicated by a person who has experienced a chunk of history through his own perspective and personality.

During the mid-70's Welch became involved with the American sports figure, a heroic myth of another sort. In a work such as "Preliminaries" (1976), Welch studies the different human traits underlying the image of the boxer, too often perceived as a uni-dimensional figure only out for blood and glory. In "Niagara Falls Project—Roger Woodward" (1975), Welch combined Panavision film of the trip to the great falls with videotaped interview of a man who, at age seven, had gone over the falls, to weave a fascinating narrative of experience and memory on another kind of heroic/mythic style. As in many of his works, portraiture and landscape are combined

through various media to convey the extraordinary element in ordinary people and places.

In his sculptural installation titled "Drive In" (1980), recently remade as "Drive In: Second Feature" (1982), Welch explores an American phenomenon highly popular during the 1950's which has already become a part of the nostalgic past. The work is composed of a full-scale model of a 1958 Cadillac Eldorado made from twigs and branches tied together and of a series of "Coming Attractions Trailers" of 1950's movies interdispersed with clips taken from old drive-in intermission ads for junk food and time-left-to-the-next show. Welch himself describes it as "the product of an archaeological expedition into contemporary America," and the effect of the work is that of a half-ironic, half-reverent look at the near-past gone primitive. As you view promos for Hollywood efforts such as "Raw Wind in Eden," "The Time Machine," "Shane" and "Invaders from Mars," sending flickering light through Welch's painstakingly hand-made Caddy of twigs and branches, you realize the rapidity which now makes what was only recently stylish into a relic of nostalgia for the museum. Welch is continuing to dig into the American experience with an intuitive wit and studious understanding which promises that he will continue to unearth many more memories to be perceived as never before.

—Barbara Cavaliere

WESELER, Günter.
German. Born in Allenstein, 2 March 1930. Studied

architecture at the Technische Hochschule, Braunschweig, 1953–58, Dip. Arch. 1958. Married in 1958 (separated 1970); son: Justin. Independent artist, in Braunschweig, 1953–62, in Dusseldorf since 1962: first kinetic "moving pictures," 1953–58; "hair pictures," 1962–65; "breathing music" performance, Radio Bremen, 1964; "breathing objects," since 1966. Agents: Galerie Redmann, Fasanenstrasse 30, 1000 Berlin 15 (West); Galerie Hunermann, im Ratinger Tor, 4000 Dusseldorf. Address: Bonifatiusstrasse 57, 400 Dusseldorf-Lorick, West Germany.

Individual Exhibitions:

1960	Galerie Utermann, Dortmund, West Germany
1961	Galerie Appel, Frankfurt
1962	Galerie am Bohlweg, Braunschweig, West Germany
1966	Kunsthalle, Dusseldorf
1967	Kunstverein, Hannover
	Haus Ruhnau, Essen
1968	Galerie Art Intermedia, Cologne
	Galerie Gunar, Dusseldorf
1969	Städtisches Museum, Leverkusen, West Germany
	Kunstmuseum, Lucerne
	Die Insel, Hamburg
1970	Kunstverein, Göttingen, West Germany
	Edinburgh Art College
	Galeria Iven Spence, Ibiza, Spain
1971	Eat-Art Galerie, Dusseldorf
1972	Galerie Magers, Bonn
	Museum, Atheneum, Helsinki
1973	Turku Museum, Finland
1974	Musée d'Art Contemporain, Montreal
	Werke 1964–1974, Kunstverein für Rheinland und Westfalen, Dusseldorf
	Landesmuseum, Wiesbaden, West Germany
1975	Electric Gallery, Toronto

Selected Group Exhibitions:

Collections:

Kunstmuseum, Dusseldorf; Kulturministerium Nordrhein Westfalen, Dusseldorf; Kunsthalle, Bremen, West Germany; Städtisches Museum Schloss Morsbroich, Leverkusen, West Germany; Kaiser-Wilhelm Museum, Krefeld, West Germany; Institut für Auslandbeziehungen, Stuttgart; Landesmuseum, Wiesbaden, West Germany; Städtische Sammlung, Wolfsburg, West Germany; Stadtische Sammlung, Recklinghausen, West Germany; Power Gallery of Contemporary Art, Sydney.

Publications:

By WESELER: books—*Der optische Klan*, playscript, Mainz 1970; *Atemobjekte: Gunter Weseler*, Friedberg-Bruchenbrucken 1986; films—*Räume*, 1970; *Weseler, atmende Welt*, 1974.

On WESELER: books—*Raume und Environments*, Opladen, West Germany 1969; *Dusseldorfer Szene*, exhibition catalogue, with text by Jean-Christophe Ammann, Lucerne 1969; *Kunstszene Dusseldorf*, exhibition catalogue, with text by Gerhard Storck, Helsinki 1972; *Strategy—Get Arts*, exhibition catalogue, edited by Richard Demarco, Edinburgh 1970; *Bis Heute* by Karin Thomas, Cologne 1971; *Deutsche Kunst der 60er Jahr* by Jürgen Morschel, Munich 1972; *Kunstpraxis—Heute*, by Karin Thomas, Cologne 1972; *Günter Weseler: Werke 1964-1974*, exhibition catalogue, with texts by Karl Heinz Hering, Gerhard Storck, Helga Meister and others, Dusseldorf 1974; *Gunter Weseler* by Gerhard Storck and Manfred de la Motte, Bonn 1977.

The preoccupation with breathing as an artistic element was, from the beginning, an expression of a virtually neurotic sensitiveness in breathing. This coincided in those days with my conviction of the possibility to control artificially all organic processes in the body by means of chemicals, drugs, etc., and thus my inclination to influence myself by taking them in order to balance all imperfections of my own nature at will.

Hence arose (certainly based on the subconscious but as an expression of my personality) technically produced organisms whose fascination lay in breathing, in the sequence, in the pauses, in the slowness, alternating with quick phases, which no human abdomen can actually achieve.

The work with the breathing objects, the changing of relationships with respect to position, location and situation soon showed me that their character could be completely transformed, that the objects became essential symbolic figures for certain life-situations or certain fears. I noted those experiences as follows: "Actually the lattice of the crib was meant as a protection so that nobody would sit down on the reclining, breathing being . . . but at the same time I discovered that the object suddenly assumed an entirely different character: something disproportionately threatening, violent emanated from it . . . " It was the discovery that breathing objects can significantly change according to their location.

Objects which are comparatively abstract, perhaps "submarine" in the centre of the wall, appear winged when sitting on an edge; and, easily frightened, they may soon fly away again. In the corner or angle they are domestically hidden, sometimes in ambush; squatting on a log they become parasites; on the human body, possibly on the throat, they can spread terror like a malignant tumor.

This does not limit their ambiguity but gives them enigma, since a component appears which contradicts the character produced by the motion itself. The original "general metaphors of organic life" now become metaphors of parasitic growth or of the captive sufferer (in the cage) or of violent usurper (crib) and so on. The objects, the location, the room become part of a message. The breathing objects offered me the possibility to formulate a variety of environmental experiences and problems in an artistic manner.

Whereas the earlier breath-objects essentially subsisted on the contrast between artificiality and naturalness, also in the confrontation of the object with its surroundings, so to speak with its civilized environ-

Günther Weseler: *Open Mandala*, 1985

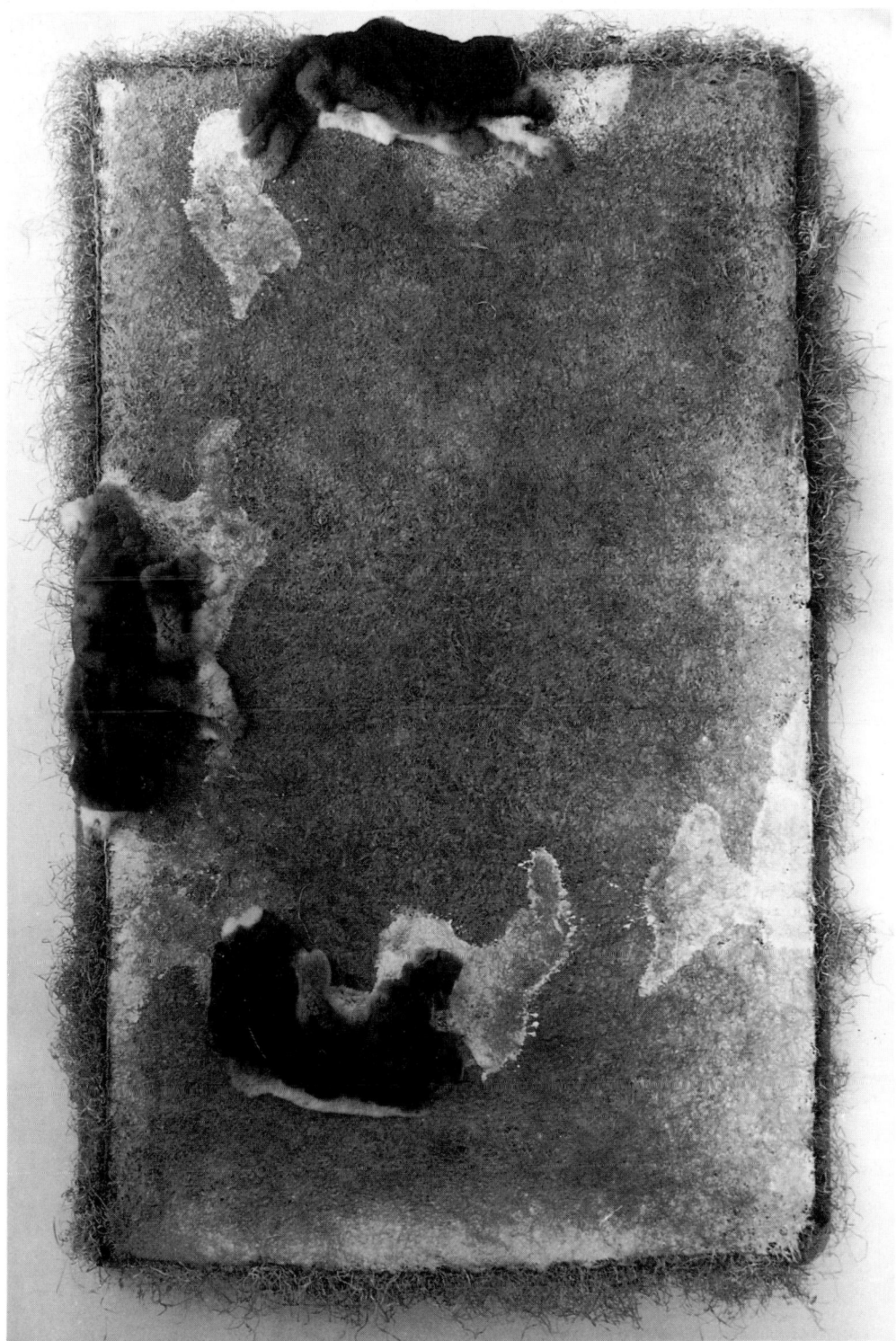

ment, recent years have brought about a distinct change toward the organic as towards the harmonic.

The tendency toward the integration of breath-objects into *mandala*-like forms has recently grown symptomatic of a harmonization and a certain re-orientation. The employment of breath-objects in *mandala*-structures corresponds to an important shift of meaning: the movement must no longer be seen as organic and animal-like but is placed in a context in which it must be understood in terms of magic and transcendence.

—Gunter Weseler

Born in Allenstein, east Prussia, in 1930 (his mother was an artist of local fame and also a pianist), Günter Weseler grew up in north Friesland/Schleswig-Holstein. His first occupation was as a farmer. He went on to train as a radio technician, studied architecture at the technical college in Braunschweig, and finally opted for the liberal arts. As a painter, Weseler tried his hand at a variety of styles that were then current, from Tachism to serial art, while, from 1962 to 1966, he also worked as an architect in Düsseldorf, where he has since lived. An increasing interest in kinetics and in musical structures brought him together with the young, experiment-crazy composer Dieter Schönbach, who was soon taking down his scores in 'graphic—painterly' fashion just as Weseler began 'composing' his pictures. Together they later produced (1964–68) 'breath music' and 'action music', predominantly for Radio Bremen, and also, in 1968 and 1971, musical theatre projects in 'breathing auditoria' in Kiel, Münster and Cologne.

Breath as a phenomenon of life fascinated Weseler increasingly; an illness which led to an 'almost neurotic respiratory disorder', since 'every physical effort made one aware of breathing', played its part in this. Around the same time Weseler gave up painting completely and began to make models out of monocoloured lumps of wax and hairs. These models, however, lacked dynamic energy, so Weseler then began experimenting with 'breathing balloons', which filled up rhythmically with compressed air and then collapsed again. What was important to him was the way objects are articulated and the way they move. His next experiment involved covering small motors with animal hides and controlling the speed and rhythm of the machines' movement with pulleys and levers. Under the guise of nature, kinetics imitated organic processes and obtained fascinating and magical effects: spherical fur-covered objects suddenly turned out to be apparently living fabulous beings that moved mysteriously and 'breathed'. Depending on position and context—we may be dealing with a bird cage, a child's bed, a cushion, or a necklace—Weseler's creations called up a multitude of other associations, including social and political ones. The addition of sound effects was provided by tape recordings. Four stuffed lion skins induced panic when they suddenly began breathing. A steel helmet complete with bullet hole moved in a macabre way.

Weseler soon began working along similar lines with foam. He made window dummies which spewed an unappetising grey-green substance due to a chemical reaction involving the combination and expansion of certain elements under the effects of heat. He also produced 'breathing walls' out of synthetic materials, as a stage set for the Cologne Opera House, for example, and increasingly vast artificial landscapes, abstract and organic at the same time, or 'post-human landscapes' with scorched trees, craters and spiny objects which breathed and rattled, or—in Edinburgh in 1970—a nauseating 'Breathing Banquet'. In 1984 Weseler designed a gently breathing 'Tidal Lake' which simulated the ebb and flow of the tide.

Since 1983 Weseler has been using grass mats for his work, making them himself by growing corn seeds on glass plates and a layer of plain-coloured humus. After a couple of months this process produces strong, naturally woven mats which gradually turn yellow. The artist then places his 'breathing objects' on top of them—fauna on top of flora—art thereby becoming one with nature.

During his investigations into breathing Weseler came across a number of ancient breathing therapies and also esoteric breathing techniques which contain possibilities for heightened physical and mental awareness, as in the case of Zen Buddhism and Tantra Yoga for example. This led him to integrate 'breathing objects' in closed structures that are inspired by Indian mandalas. "The use of breathing objects in mandala structures corresponds to an essential switch in meaning: the movement is no longer simply visible in an organic—animal sense; it exists now in a context in which it is to be understood in a magical, transcendental sense" (Weseler).

It is in this sense that one should interpret the stamp with which Weseler signs his catalogues and letters: "Weseler creates a new world—the new species."

—Werner Schulze-Reimpell

WESSELMANN, Tom.

American. Born in Cincinnati, Ohio, 23 February 1931. Educated at Hiram College, Ohio; The University of Cincinnati, Ohio, B.A. in Psychology; Art Academy of Cincinnati, Ohio; and, under Nicholas Marsicano, Cooper Union, New York. Married Claire Wesselmann in 1963; daughter: Jenny Claire. Painter. Agent: Sidney Janis Gallery, 110 West 57th Street, New York, New York 10019. Address: R.D. 1, Box 36, Long Eddy, New York 12760, U.S.A.

Individual Exhibitions:

1961	Tanager Gallery, New York
1962	Green Gallery, New York
1964	Green Gallery, New York
1965	Green Gallery, New York
1966	Sidney Janis Gallery, New York
	Galerie Ileana Sonnabend, Paris
1967	Galleria Gian Enzo Sperone, Turin
1968	Sidney Janis Gallery, New York
	Dayton's Gallery 12, Minneapolis (toured the United States)
1970	Sidney Janis Gallery, New York
	Early Still-Lifes 1962-1964, Newport Harbor Art Museum, Balboa, California (toured the United States)
1971	Jack Glenn Gallery, Corona del Mar, California
1972	Sidney Janis Gallery, New York
	Rosa Esman Gallery, New York
	Galerie Aronowitsch, Stockholm
1973	Multiples Gallery, Los Angeles
1974	Sidney Janis Gallery, New York
	Galerie des 4 Mouvements, Paris
	The Early Years: Collages 1959-62, Ohio University, Athens (toured the United States)
1976	Sidney Janis Gallery, New York
1979	Sidney Janis Gallery, New York
1981	Hokin Gallery, Bay Harbor Islands, Florida
	Hokin Gallery, Chicago
1982	Sidney Janis Gallery, New York
1985	Sidney Janis Gallery, New York
1987	Sidney Janis Gallery, New York

Selected Group Exhibitions:

1962	*Recent Painting U.S.A.: The Figure*, Museum of Modern Art, New York
1963	*Pop Goes the Easel*, Contemporary Arts Museum, Houston
1965	*Young America 1965*, Whitney Museum, New York
1966	*Art in a Mirror*, Museum of Modern Art, New York (toured the United States)
1967	*Bienal*, Sao Paulo
1968	*Documenta*, Kassel, West Germany
1974	*American Pop Art*, Whitney Museum, New York
1976	*Illusions of Reality*, Art Gallery of New South Wales, Sydney
1977	*The Dada/Surrealist Heritage*, Clark Art Institute, Williamstown, Massachusetts
1983	*Why New York?*, Futura Gallery, Stockholm

Collections:

Museum of Modern Art, New York; Whitney Museum, New York; Albright-Knox Art Gallery, Buffalo, New York; Worcester Art Museum, Massachusetts; Philadelphia Museum of Art; Cincinnati Art Museum, Ohio; Walker Art Center, Minneapolis; Minneapolis Institute of Arts; Dallas Museum of Fine Arts; Wallraf-Richartz Museum, Cologne.

Publications:

On WESSELMANN: books—*Pop Art* by Rolf Günter Dienst, Wiesbaden, West Germany, 1965; *Pop Art* by John Rublowsky, New York 1965; *Pop Art* by Lucy R. Lippard, New York 1966; *Pop Art and After* by Mario Amaya, New York 1966; *Pop Art U.S.A.* by Alberto Boatto, Milan and Rome 1967; *New York: The New Art Scene* by Ugo Mulas and Alan Solomon, New York 1967; *Art in the Age of Risk* by Nicolas Calas, New York 1968; articles—"Tom Wesselmann at Tanager" in *Arts Magazine* (New York), February 1962; "Tom Wesselmann at Green Gallery" by Jill Johnston in *Artnews* (New York), November 1962; "New Realists in New York" by Sonya Rodikoff, "Dada Then and Now" by Barbara Rose, and "Le Nouveau Realisme á la Coquete de New York" by Pierre Restany in *Art International* (Lugano, Switzerland), January 1973; "Symposium on Pop Art—Special Supplement" by Henry Geldzahler in *Arts Magazine* (New York), April 1963; "Tom Wesselmann" in *Time* (New York), February 1964; "Tom Wesselmann at Green Gallery" by Jill Johnston in *Artnews* (New York), April 1964; "The Honest Nude—Wesselmann" by Gene R. Swenson in *Art and Artists* (London), May 1966; "Tom Wesselmann and the Gates of Horn" by J. A. Abramson in *Arts Magazine* (New York), May 1966; "Paris: Wesselmann et le Nu Américain" by Jean-Louis Ferrier in *La Quinzaine* (Paris), November 1966; "Eros Presumptive" by Lucy Lippard in *Minimal Art: A Critical Anthology*, edited by Gregory Battock, New York 1968; "Images: Tom Wesselmann at Janis" in *Arts Magazine* (New York), February 1968; "Reviews: Tom Wesselmann" in *Arts Magazine* (New York), December 1972; "Reviews: Tom Wesselmann" by Carter Ratcliff in *Artforum* (New York), January 1973; "De Kinderen Kunner er 'n Joutje Van" by Tonni Burgering in *Rotterdam Nieuwsblad*, June 1973; "Art: Reading a Monumental Still Life" by John Perreault in the *Village Voice* (New York), May 1974.

If Tom Wesselmann does not tire, "The Great American Nude" will reach a thousand. This glamorous creation (*Max-Factorized*, Jean-Louis Ferrier has called her) continues her anonymous course across canvas after canvas, in and out of mixed-media setups, in paint, in plastic, or in any material that takes the artist's fancy. Only her personal number distinguishes her from her sisters, nearly all smiling broadly and seductively, most of them equipped with super-nubile nipples that look like erotic buttons.

And so many bathrooms . . . ! So many bathers . . . !

But it would be very wrong to think that Wesselmann never escapes from this centrally-heated eau-de-toilette inflated world of pulchritude. In her way, The Great American Nude is but one more adjunct to the late 20th-century living style. Her bosom may be bare, but her boudoir has a cassette and electric clock, her bathroom is rich with plumbing and generally a comfortable WC. And there are times when she is absent. A peep through the window shows photoch-

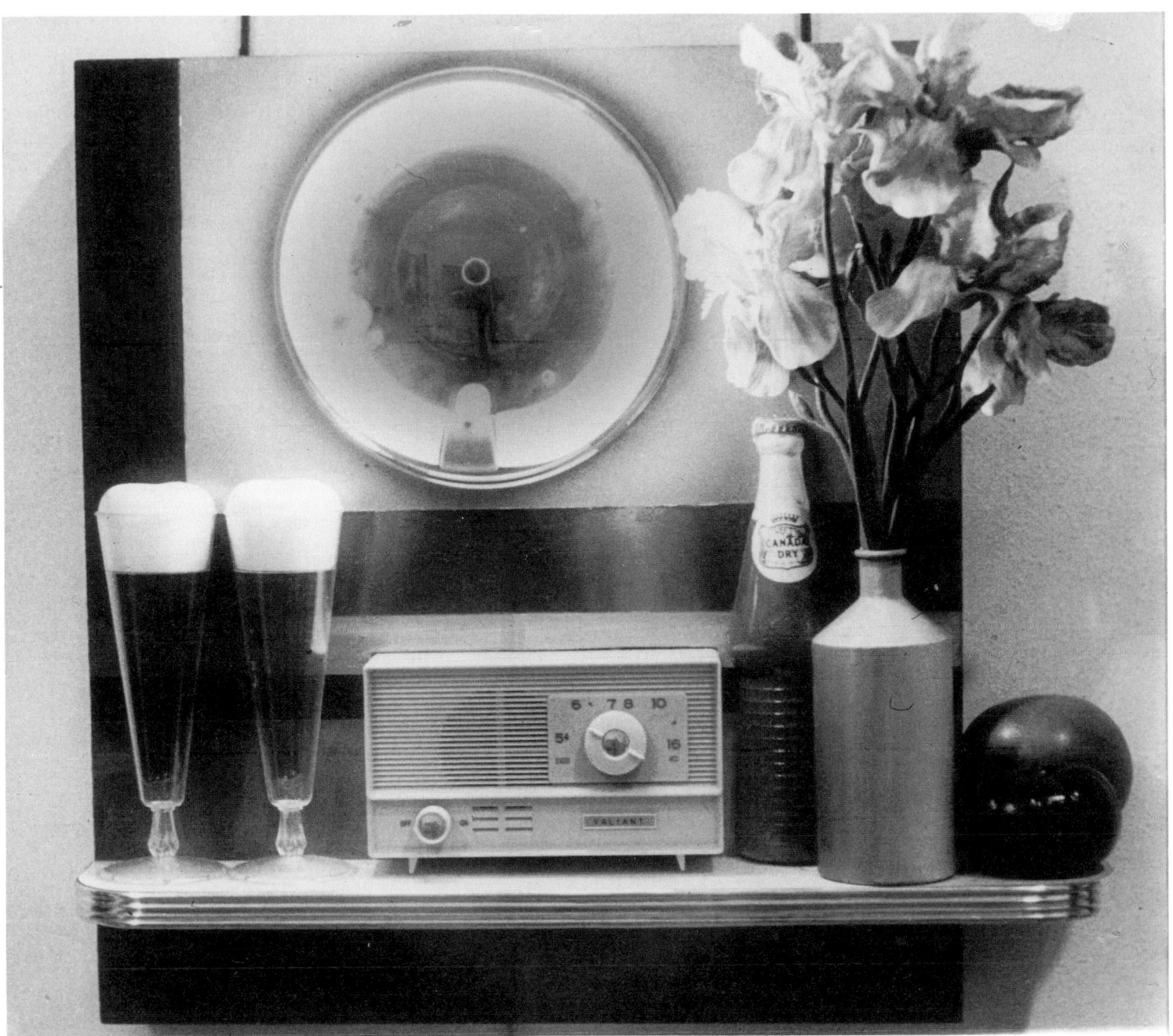

Tom Wesselman: *Still Life No. 39*, 1964

romatic pictures hanging on the wall above a table laid with bottle of beer and can of soda. All these appurtenances can be painted (sometimes in over-lifescale) or they can "be themselves" like Marcel Duchamp's *ready-mades*, although recruited for practical rather than surrealist purposes.

Wesselmann, supremely conscious of the mixed up world of modern times, knows full well (he is a Bachelor of Arts—Psychology) that contemporary life is based upon privately preserved classical myths in surprisingly easy concert with technical development. His girls are 20th century versions of so many sweethearts out of the past. But they live in a world of NOW. They are posed against a background that includes automobiles and TV. Their kitchens may be teeming with gadgetry, but the easy-to-serve snacks come from the supermarket and require a minimum of housewifery attention. A cardboard plate will suffice. Drinks are handy. Whoever heard of washing-up! The dishwasher will see to everything.

Lest such a coca-cola paradise be written off as trite, imagine what any other artist would make of this menu of canned lotus out of the refrigerator. Wesselmann is adept. He is able to flavour his irony with just the right amount of saccharine.

—Sheldon Williams

WESTERIK, Co.

Dutch. Born Jakobus Westerik in The Hague, 2 March 1924. Studied art, under Han van Dam, Rein Draijer, Henk Meyer, Willem Rozendaal and Willem Schrofer, Koninklijke Akademie van Beeldende Kunsten, The Hague, 1942–47. Married the painter Hens M. de Jong in 1948 (divorced, 1980); daughters: Christine, Victoria and Sophie; married gallery-director Fenna de Vries, in 1970; sons: Willem and Maurits. Painter, establishing own studio, The Hague, 1946–76, in Rotterdam, since 1971. Member, Haagsche Kunstkring artists' association, The Hague, 1946–57; Verve artists' group, The Hague, 1951–57; Pulchri Studio society of painters, The Hague, 1952. Instructor, International School, and Deutsche Schule, Scheveningen, 1953–58; Vrije Academie, The Hague, 1955–58; Koninklijke Academie van Beeldende Kunsten, The Hague, 1958–71; Ateliers 63, Haarlem, 1969–70. Recipient: Jacob Marisprijs, The Hague, 1951, 1955, 1961; Dutch Government Grant for Painting, 1953, 1954; Silver Medal, *Bienal*, Sao Paulo, 1965; Rembrandt Prize, Leiden, 1966; Dutch State Prize for Art and Architecture, 1970; Zuid-Holland Cultural Council Prize, 1987. Agent: Galerie Fenna de Vries, Rotterdam. Address: Eendrachtsplein 18, 3012 LA Rotterdam, Netherlands.

Individual Exhibitions:

1956   Museum Hofwijck, Voorburg, Netherlands
1964   Gemeentemuseum, The Hague (travelled to Vishal, Haarlem and Van Abbemuseum, Eindhoven, Netherlands)
1966   Stedelijk Museum de Lakenhal, Leiden
1968   Galerie 20, Amsterdam
        Galerie Fenna de Vries, Rotterdam
        Museum Boymans-van Beuningen, Rotterdam
1971   Galerie Fenna de Vries, Rotterdam
        Stedelijk Museum, Amsterdam (travelled to the Groninger Museum, Groningen: Palais des Beaux-Arts, Brussels)
        Galerie Escape, Amsterdam
1973   Galerie Fenna de Vries, Rotterdam
1974   Palais des Beaux-Arts, Brussels
1976   Galerie Fenna de Vries, Rotterdam
1977   Lens Fine Art, Antwerp
1978   Galerie Fenna de Vries, Rotterdam
1979   Stedelijk Museum, Amsterdam
1980   Galerie Fenna de Vries, Rotterdam
1981   Museum Boymans-van Beuningen, Rotterdam
1982   Galerie Fenna de Vries, Rotterdam
1983   Staatliche Kunsthalle, West Berlin (travelled to Saarbrucken and The Hague)

Co Westerik: *Self Portrait with Open Mouth*, 1985

dividual trying and longing for another person, or thrown back at his own. His painting is convincingly humanistic and his pictures never degenerate into mere storytelling or anecdote.

Undoubtedly his best known paintings are *Fishwoman* (1951), *Schoolteacher and Child* (1961), *Cut by Grass*(1966). The last mentioned piece shows some fingers sliding through green grass. One is meanly cut by a green leaf that leaves its mark like a razorblade. The picture however has psychological impact that by far outreaches the absurdity of the event itself. One feels, here as well as in most of Westerik's paintings, a continuous hidden struggle between individuals, their lack of power and immediacy that feeds feelings of shame. On top of this, eroticism and religiosity by all means find their way through the surface. Westerik's great quality is that he always visualizes, never moralizes. The refinement of his thematic procedure corresponds with a very detailed, multi-layered painting process.

Apart from his painting, Westerik has built up a very large oeuvre of drawings and watercolors. Most of these drawings are autonomous, only part of these can be considered as preliminary studies to the paintings.

During the last two decades all his work gained in popularity, including the graphic work. In an extensive catalogue (Municipal Museum, The Hague, 1984) it is justly stated that this too deserves an autonomous status. Etching and lithography are Westerik's favourite techniques. His imagery is intimate and just as detailed and complex as his painting. The editions usually are very limited and even the prints differ.

—A. F. Wagemans

Selected Group Exhibitions:

1945   *Parade der Debutanten*, Lange Vijverberg, The Hague
1951   *Verve*, Kunstzaal Esher Surrey, The Hague
1954   *Irish Exhibition of Living Art*, National College of Art, Dublin
1962   *Biennale*, Venice
1964   *Carnegie International*, Pittsburgh
1966   *Tokyo International Exhibition of Art*, Keio Department Store, Tokyo
1969   *Haager Kunstler in Helmhaus*, Zurich
1974   *Verve 1951-1957*, Gemeentemuseum, The Hague
1982   *Arte come Arte*, at the *Biennale*, Venice
1985   *Nouvelle Biennale*, Paris

Collections:

Gemeentemuseum, The Hague; Museum Boymans-van Beuningen, Rotterdam; Centraal Museum, Utrecht; Frans Halsmuseum, Haarlem; Stedelijk Museum, Amsterdam; Museum Het Princessehof, Leeuwarden; Groninger Museum voor Stadt en Lande, Groningen; Gemeentemuseum, Arnhem; Museum De Lakenahl, Leiden; Stedelijk Museum, Arnhem.

Publications:

On WESTERIK: books—*Domino Book 2: Co Westerik—42*

tekeningen, etsen en litho's, with text by R. W. D. Oxenaar, Amsterdam 1961; *Co Westerik*, exhibition catalogue, with text by R. W. D. Oxenaar, The Hague 1964; *Co Westerik: Tekeningen, Grafiek, Aquarellen uit de verzameling C. Kuijman*, exhibition catalogue, with an introduction by H. R. Hoetink, Rotterdam 1968; *Co Westerik*, exhibition catalogue, with text by Wim Beeren, Amsterdam 1971; *Westerik: Drawings, Watercolours and Prints*, with text by J. L. Locher and H. R. Hoetink, Vlaardingen 1971, Amsterdam and Antwerp 1979; *Verve 1951-1957*, exhibition catalogue, with text by John Sillevis, The Hague 1974; *Co Westerik*, exhibition catalogue, with texts by R. W. D. Oxenaar and Carel Blotkamp, Brussels 1974; *Co Westerik* by W. Meewis, Schelderode, Netherlands 1979; *Co Westerik*, documentary report, by C. Withoff, Groningen, Netherlands 1979; *Co Westerik, Painter* by W. A. L. Beeren, Venlo, Netherlands 1981; *Co Westerik*, exhibition catalogue with texts by M. Eberle and J. Locher, West Berlin 1983.

Within the context of the dutch art-climate the painter Co Westerik without any doubt is a certain and constant factor. Although he never belonged to any group, although he has never been exemplary for any direction or tendency, through the years he nevertheless has held a position that is merely reflected by his work being part of all the major dutch museum collections, and countless private collections as well. Westerik's work is figurative and realistic, and miles away from the mainstreams of dutch constructivism and expressionism. Westerik's works deal with the human condition, the psychology pertaining to the in-

WESTERMANN, H(orace) C(lifford).

American. Born in Los Angeles, California, 11 December 1922. Studied at the Art Institute of Chicago, with Paul Weighardt, 1947-54. Served in the United States Marine Corps, 1942-45. Married Joanna Beall in 1959. Travelled widely in the Orient, and worked as an acrobat, logger, carpenter and mason. Thereafter a full-time artist. Recipient: Campana Prize, Art Institute of Chicago, 1964; National Endowment for the Arts Grant, 1967; Tamarind Fellowship, 1968; *Bienal* Prize, Sao Paulo, 1973. Agent: Xavier Fourcade Inc., 36 East 57th Street, New York, New York 10021, U.S.A. *Died in 1981.*

Individual Exhibitions:

1957   Allan Frumkin Gallery, Chicago
1961   Allan Frumkin Gallery, New York
1962   Dilexi Gallery, Los Angeles
       Allan Frumkin Gallery, Chicago
1963   Dilexi Gallery, San Francisco
       Allan Frumkin Gallery, New York
1965   Allan Frumkin Gallery, New York
1966   Nelson Museum, Kansas City, Missouri
1967   Allan Frumkin Gallery, Chicago
       Allan Frumkin Gallery, New York
1968   Los Angeles County Museum of Art (retrospective)
       Allan Frumkin Gallery, New York
1969   Museum of Contemporary Art, Chicago (retrospective)
1970   Allan Frumkin Gallery, New York
1971   Allan Frumkin Gallery, New York
       Galerie Thomas Borgmann, Cologne
1974   James Corcoran Gallery, Los Angeles
       Smithsonian Institution, Washington, D.C.
       Allan Frumkin Gallery, New York
1976   Allan Frumkin Gallery, Chicago

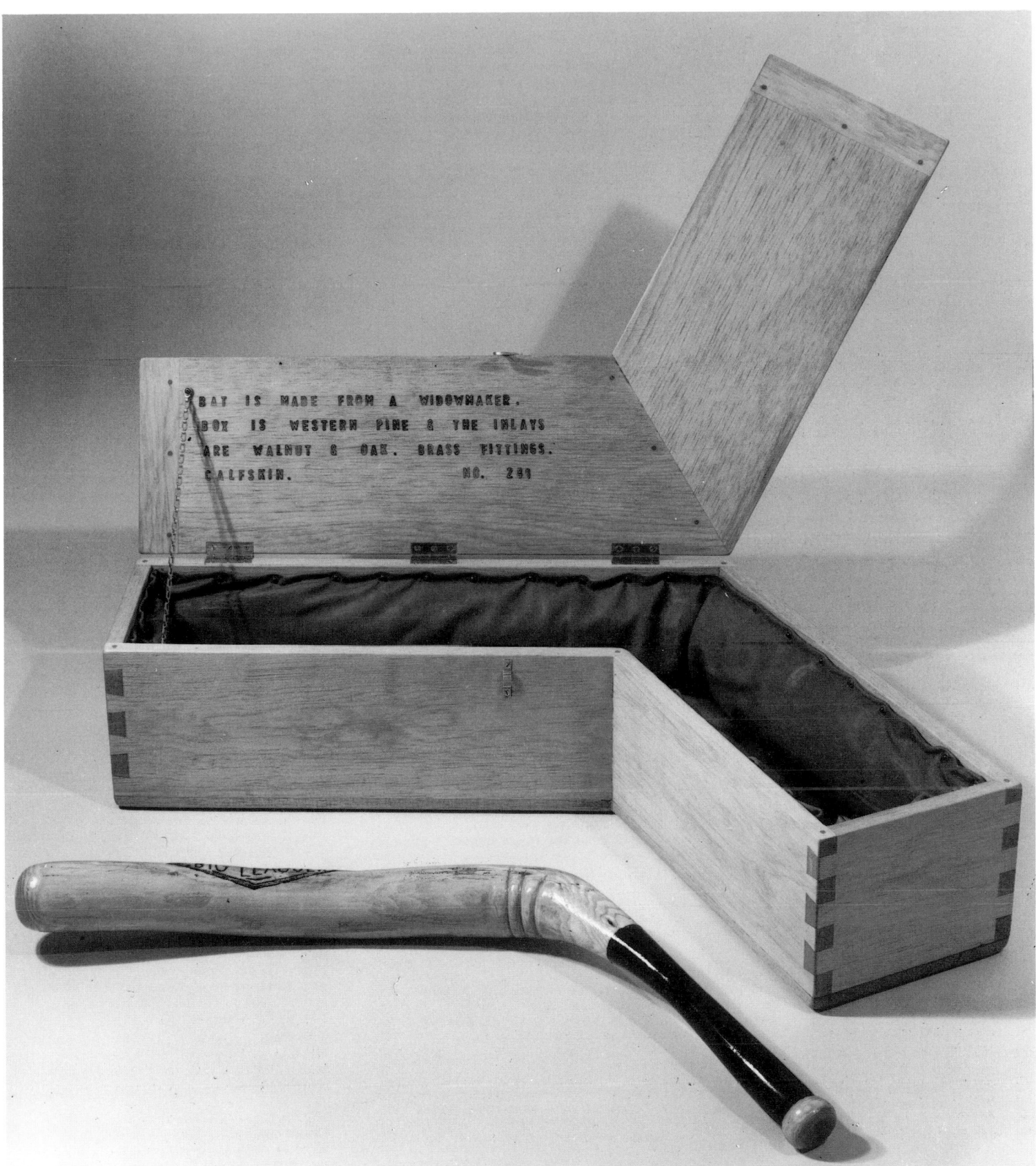

H. C. Westermann: *Big Leaguer,* 1978

1977 John Berggruen Gallery, San Francisco
1978 Whitney Museum, New York (retrospective; travelled to the New Orleans Museum of Art; Des Moines Art Center, Iowa; Seattle Art Museum; and the San Francisco Museum of Modern Art, 1978–79)
1980 Serpentine Gallery, London (retrospective)
1987 Art Institute of Chicago

Selected Group Exhibitions:

1960 *Surrealist Art*, Museum of Modern Art, New York
1964 *New Realism*, Gemeentemuseum, The Hague
1967 *American Sculpture of the 60's*, Los Angeles County Museum of Art
1968 *Documenta*, Kassel, West Germany (and 1972)
1973 *Bienal*, Sao Paulo
1974 *71st American Exhibition*, Art Institute of Chicago
1975 *Masterworks in Wood: The 20th Century*, Portland Art Museum, Oregon
1976 *200 Years of American Sculpture*, Whitney Museum, New York
1980 *One Major New Work Each*, Xavier Fourcade Inc., New York
1981 *Group Sculpture Show*, Xavier Fourcade Inc., New York

Collections:

Whitney Museum, New York; Wadsworth Atheneum, Hartford, Connecticut; Museum of Contemporary Art, Chicago; Art Institute of Chicago; Indiana University Art Museum, Bloomington; Des Moines Art Center, Iowa; Walker Art Center, Minneapolis; Los Angeles County Museum of Art; Norton Simon Art Museum, Pasadena, California; Seattle Art Museum.

Publications:

On WESTERMANN: books—*H. C. Westermann*, exhibition catalogue, by Max Kozloff, Los Angeles 1968; *Documenta 5*, exhibition catalogue, Kassel, West Germany 1972; *After Surrealism: Metaphors and Similes*, exhibition catalogue, by L. J. Ahlander, Sarasota, Florida 1972; *Fantastic Images* by Franz Schulze, Chicago 1972; *H. C. Westermann*, exhibition catalogue, by Barbara Haskell, New York 1978; *H. C. Westermann*, exhibition catalogue, by Dennis Adrian, London 1980; *H. C. Westermann: Selections from the Alan and Dorothy Press Collection*, exhibition catalogue with text by Neal Benezra, Chicago 1987.

I'm not being facetious at all—I think an artist should have very good feet!
—H. C. Westermann (1977)

H. C. Westermann was, I suppose, a sculptor. At least he worked in three dimensions and utilized such materials as wood and metal. But his work defies description. Comic strips in the round? Surrealistic statements of satire and disgust? Assemblages of hand-crafted components? His sculptures are, as the saying goes, beautifully crafted with lots of cunning detail. Quirky in the extreme and loaded with wry commentary—verbal as well as visual: here there be messages.

Westermann was from Chicago, a curious American city set on a lake which is notable for its importance as a railroad center, its slaughter houses, its grain exchange and its modern architecture. It also boasts a great art museum. Somehow all these things have helped to produce a very odd group of artists much given to the creation of a new-surrealist art involving outrageous eroticism and comic strips. Think of a marriage between George Crumb and Hieronymous Bosch. Very little of this kind of thing has come out of New York or San Francisco or Los Angeles, and one wonders what has caused it to flower in the Windy City.

Westermann fits in here but with a slight difference—his production of objects which are sculptural in implication rather than two-dimensional like comics, and the extreme fastidiousness with which he executed them. Part of their startling impressiveness is due to the beauty of their manufacture. Try to imagine a lollipop made by Hepplewhite. This "contradiction" between subject matter and technique is part of Westermann's surrealist displacement. Another contributing factor is his sly combining of images with words so that puns are put. Another is the air of fun fair about his work—things like openings to peak through, tiny doors or drawers to open, mirrors, models, abound. This in connection with the formal presentation of material so skillfully worked as to constitute a "subject" in itself.

All of it ending as a form of craziness that redefines sanity.

—Ralph Pomeroy

WHEELER, Doug.

American. Born in Globe, Arizona, 29 December 1939. Studied at Santa Monica City College, California, 1958–59; University of California at Los Angeles, 1960–64; B.F.A. Married Nancy Lee Harrison in 1965 (divorced, 1969). Instructor in Creative Studies, University of California at Santa Barbara, since 1978. Recipient: New Talent Award from the Los Angeles County Museum of Art, 1966; National Endowment for the Arts Grant, 1968, 1977; Guggenheim Fellowship, 1971. Agents: Riko Mizuno Gallery, 669 La Cienga, West Hollywood, California; Galleria Salvatore Ala, Via Mameli 3, 20129 Milan, Italy; Salvatore Ala Gallery, 32 West 20th Street, New York, New York 10011. Address: 2623 Main Street, Santa Monica, California 90405, U.S.A.

Individual Exhibitions:

1968 Pasadena Museum of Art, California
1969 Ace Gallery, Los Angeles
     Fort Worth Art Center, Texas (with Robert Irwin)
1970 Artist's Studio, Venice, California
     Tate Gallery, London (with Larry Bell and Robert Irwin)
1974 Riko Mizuno Gallery, Los Angeles
1975 Galleria Salvatore Ala, Milan

Selected Group Exhibitions:

1969 *Prospectus '69*, Kunsthalle, Dusseldorf
     Kompas IV, Stedelijk Museum, Eindhoven, Netherlands
1973 *3D into 2D*, New York Cultural Center (toured the United States)
1974 *American Exhibition*, Art Institute of Chicago
1975 *4 from 5, California*, School of Visual Arts, New York (travelled to the Corcoran Gallery of Art, Washington, D.C.)
1976 *Biennale*, Venice

Collections:

Art Institute of Chicago; Stedelijk Museum, Amsterdam.

Publications:

On WHEELER: books—*Doug Wheeler*, exhibition catalogue, by John Coplans, Pasadena, California 1968; *Wheeler/Irwin*, exhibition catalogue, by Jane Livingston, Los Angeles 1969; *Larry Bell, Robert Irwin, Doug Wheeler*, exhibition catalogue, by Michael Compton, London 1970; articles—"Place in the Sun" in *Time* (New York), 30 August 1968; "Doug Wheeler—Light Paintings" by John Coplans in *Artforum* (New York), March 1970; "Doug Wheeler—Exhibitions at Ace Gallery" by Peter Plagens in *Artforum* (New York), May 1970; "Exhibition at Ace Gallery" by Jo-

seph E. Young in *Art International* (Lugano, Switzerland), no. 3, 1970; "Exhibition at Riko Mizuno Gallery" by Melinda Wortz in *Artweek* (Oakland, California), April 1974; "Doug Wheeler—Riko Mizuno Gallery" by Peter Plagens in *Artforum* (New York), September 1974.

WHITMAN, Robert.

American. Born in New York City in 1935. Studied at Rutgers University, New Brunswick, New Jersey, 1953–57, B.A. 1957; also studied at Columbia University, New York. Performance artist: lives and works in New York. Agent: Bykert Gallery, New York. Address: c/o Bykert Gallery, 484 Broome Street, New York, New York 10013, U.S.A.

Individual Exhibitions:

1959 Hansa Gallery, New York
     Reuben Gallery, New York
     Rutgers University, New Brunswick, New Jersey
1963 9 Great Jones Street, New York (with Walter De Maria)
1967 Pace Gallery, New York
1968 Jewish Museum, New York
     Museum of Contemporary Art, Chicago
1973 Museum of Modern Art, New York
1974 Bykert Gallery, New York
     Galleria L'Attico, Rome
1975 Bykert Downtown Gallery, New York
1976 *Theatre Works 1960–1976*, Dia Art Foundation, New York
1979 Hudson River Museum, Yonkers, New York
1980 *Outdoor Performance Work*, Snug Harbor, Staten Island, New York

Selected Group Exhibitions:

1960 *New Forms—New Media*, Martha Jackson Gallery, New York
1962 *Environments, Situations and Spaces*, Martha Jackson Gallery, New York
1964 *6 Artists*, Sidney Janis Gallery, New York
1965 *11 from the Reuben Gallery*, Guggenheim Museum, New York
1966 *Erotic Art*, Sidney Janis Gallery, New York
1967 *Projected Art*, Finch College, New York
1968 *6 Artists, 6 Exhibitions*, Walker Art Center, Minneapolis
1969 *String and Rope*, Sidney Janis Gallery, New York
1971 *Art and Technology*, Los Angeles County Museum of Art
1974 *Projected Images*, Walker Art Center, Minneapolis

Collections:

Museum of Contemporary Art, Chicago; Jewish Museum, New York

Publications:

On WHITMAN: book—*Assemblages, Environments and Happenings* by Allan Kaprow, New York 1969; articles—"Whitman Room" in *Arts and Architecture* (Los Angeles), June 1964; "7 New Artists at Janis" by Sidney Tillim in *Arts Magazine* (New York), September 1964; "Pearstein, Jagger, Whitman, Gutman" by G. Brown in *Arts Magazine* (New York), September 1967; "Mother Turn Off the Picture" by Otto Piene in *Artscanada* (Toronto), June 1968; "Magic Theatre, Une Exposition á Kansas City" by S. Bann in *Oeil* (Paris), August September 1968; "A Planned Coincidence" by Dore Ashton in *Art in America* (New York), September/October 1969; "Some Thoughts on 'Art and Technology'" by Jane Livingston in *Studio International* (London), June 1971; "Corporate Art" by Jack Burnham in *Artforum* (New York), October 1971; "Bob Whitman and Things . . ." by George Segal in *Art and Artists* (London), November 1972.

Robert Whitman is a master of visual theatre-presentational performance which cohered in terms of imagery, rather than language or narrative. He was once regarded as a sometime visual artist, who had exhibited his paintings and sculptures, but had, unlike, say, Oldenburg and Rauschenberg, abandoned those crafts to concentrate exclusively on theater; his wilful concentration was, at the time, seen as a measure of serious purpose.

His masterpiece a decade ago was *Prune Flat* (1965), which was then curiously spelled "Prune. Flat." It opens with the image of a movie projector (implicitly announcing that one theme was cinematic images) and then shows a grapefruit (that nearly fills the screen) being cut by a knife. After other images, a tomato appears, which is also cut, black egg-like objects pouring out; and when the tomato sequence is repeated, two young women dressed in white smocks and white kerchiefs in front of the screen, the filmed blade cutting through them. As the film shows the two women walking down the street, one slightly behind the other, so the same two women walk across the stage, at a perpendicular angle to their images on the screen, but in the same formation. Later in the piece, the image of a woman undressing and showering is projected directly on the full length body of one of the women performers; but once the film shuts off, the woman who appears to be undressed is suddenly revealed to be definitely besmocked. The subject of *Prune Flat* is, of course, the perceptual discrepancies between filmed image and theatrical presence, and it differs from the other mixed-means pieces not only in its precise control but in its visual beauty.

Whitman staged other mixed-means pieces at the time, including the spectacularly scaled *Two Holes of the Water* (1966): but these tended to be diffuse and temporally flaccid. I have heard of earlier pieces of his, but did not see them until a retrospective was presented in the spring of 1976. The best innovation in *American Moon* (1960) was the positioning of the audience, which is divided into groups of ten, each assigned to a cubicle within a circular structure that looks into the performance area. In other words, that is "theatre-in-the-ground" with the audience subdivided by partitions. Translucent cloth screens separated each audience from the stage before them, and film is at times projected from behind on these individual screens, so that each section sees a different part of the movie. Once the curtains are raised, the climax of the piece is a cellophane structure that is blown up from an unheard source, the plastic filling the centerspace. Two performers walk through it. As a man is suspended in a swing above the space, the piece closes. *American Moon* struck me as the best of the other works in the retrospective, which included *Flower* (1963), *Nighttime Sky* (1965), *Salad P.N.* (1974), in addition to a new work, *Light Touch* (1976). Though each of the others has stunning particulars, it is still *Prune Flat* that remains the most extraordinary of Whitman's theatrical pieces.

His work has always been uneven, and always exploratory. His forte is evocative, memorable imagery; his recurring failings include a leaden sense of theatrical time and sado-masochistic undertones.

Though I have already seen *Prune Flat* perhaps a dozen times, I would gladly see it again.

—Richard Kostelanetz

WIELAND, Joyce.

Canadian. Born in Toronto in 1931. Studied under Carl Schaeffer, Doris McCarthy, and Bob Ross, Central Technical School, Toronto. Married the artist Michael Snow, *q.v.* Painter, film-maker, and maker of quilts: lives and works in Toronto: worked for Graphic Associates, Toronto, 1956–58; lived in New York, 1963–70. Recipient: Canada Council Grants, 1966, 1968; Toronto Arts Award, 1987. Agent: Isaacs Gallery, 179 John Street, Toronto, Ontario

M5T 1X3. Address: 497 Queen Street East, Toronto, Ontario M5A 1V1, Canada.

Individual Exhibitions:

1959	Isaacs Gallery, Toronto (with Gordon Rayner)
1964	Isaacs Gallery, Toronto
1967	National Gallery of Canada, Ottawa
1968	Vancouver Art Gallery (retrospective)
1971	*True Patriot Love*, National Gallery of Canada, Ottawa
1978	National Gallery of Canada, Ottawa
1979	Pauline McGibbon Art Centre, TOronto
1981	Isaacs Gallery, Toronto
1982	Forest City Gallery, London, Ontario
	Yajima/Galerie, Montreal
1983	Isaacs Gallery, Toronto
1985	Concordia University, Montreal
1987	Art Gallery of Ontario, Toronto
	Confederation Art Gallery, Charlottetown, Prince Edward Island
1988	Beaverbrook Art Gallery, Fredericton, New Brunswick
	Mackenzie Art Gallery, Regina, Saskatchewan
	Canada House Gallery, London

Selected Group Exhibitions:

1968	*Biennale of Canadian Painters*, National Gallery of Canada, Ottawa
1970	*8 Artists from Canada*, Tel Aviv Museum
1971	*49th Parallels: New Canadian Art*, Ringling Museum of Art, Sarasota, Florida
1972	*Toronto Painting 1953–1965*, National Gallery of Canada, Ottawa
1976	*Une Histoire du Cinéma*, Musée National d'Art Moderne, Paris
1977	*Canadian Tapestries 77*, Art Gallery of Ontario, Toronto
1981	*Twentieth Century Canadian Painting*, National Museum of Modern Art, Tokyo
1982	*Contemporary Outdoor Sculpture*, Guild of All Arts, Toronto
1983	*New Perceptions: Portraits*, Harbourfront Community Gallery, Toronto
1984	*Toronto Painting 84*, Art Gallery of Ontario, Toronto

Collections:

National Gallery of Canada, Ottawa; Art Gallery of Ontario, Toronto; Montreal Museum of Fine Arts; Winnipeg Art Gallery; Norman Mackenzie Art Gallery, Regina, Saskatchewan; Edmonton Art Gallery, Alberta; Vancouver Art Gallery; Museum of Modern Art, New York; Philadelphia Museum of Art; Royal Belgian Film Archives, Brussels.

Publications:

By WIELAND: article—interview, with Pierre Theberge, in *True Patriot Love*, exhibition catalogue, Ottawa 1971; films—*Larry's Recent Behaviour*, 1963; *Patriotism* (Parts 1 and 2), 1964; *Peggy's Blue Skylight*, 1964; *Barbara's Blindness*, with Betty Ferguson, 1965; *Water Sark*, 1965; *1933*, 1967; *Hand Tinting*, 1967; *Sailboat*, 1967; *Catfood*, 1968; *Rat Life and Diet in North America*, 1968; *La Raison avant la Passion*, 1969; *Dripping Water*, with Michael Snow, 1969; *Pierre Vallières*, 1972; *Solidarity*, 1973; *The Far Shore*, 1976; *A and B in Ontario*, 1984; *Birds at Sunrise*, 1985.

On WIELAND: books—*True Patriot Love*, exhibition catalogue, Ottawa 1971; *Contemporary Canadian Painting* by William Withrow, Toronto 1972; *A Concise History of Canadian Painting* by Dennis Reid, Toronto 1973; *Joyce Wieland*, exhibition catalogue with texts by Lucy Lippard, Marie Fleming and Lauren Rabinowitz, Toronto 1987; articles—"Joyce Wieland at the Isaacs Gallery" by David Donnell in *Canadian Art* (Ottawa), March/April 1964; "Joyce Wieland Retrospective, Vancouver Art Gallery: by Marguerite Pinney in *Artscanada* (Toronto), June 1968; "There Is Only One Joyce" by P. Adams Sitney in *Artscanada* (Toronto), April 1970; "True Patriot Love" by Harry Malcolmson in *Canadian Forum* (Toronto), June 1971; "True Patriot Love: The Films of Joyce Wieland" by Regina Cornwell in *Artforum*

(New York), September 1971; "Wieland: An Epiphany of North" by Hugo McPherson in *Artscanada* (Toronto), August/September 1971; "True Patriot Love: The Work of Joyce Wieland" by D. Magidson and J. Wright in *Art and Artists* (London), October 1973.

Unlike most other artist members of Toronto's art community in her generation, most of whom attended the Ontario College of Art, Joyce Wieland was a graduate of the art course at Central Technical School. More important for her later development was her experimentation with film at Graphic Associates, where she worked from 1956 to 1958 as an animator. Much of Wieland's later work either uses filmic elements (as in her sequential painting referring to an unfolding of a succession of things in film strips) or is in film. It is as a movie-maker that she has secured her international reputation today, especially for her major feature film, *The Far Shore* (completed in 1976).

In her early stained paintings and collages of the late 1950's and early 1960's, Wieland often used sexual imagery, as in "Time Machine Series." By 1965 the form of her work had changed to framed or boxed constructions and serial paintings. The plastic *collages* of 1965 were stuffed and quilted movies called "home totems."

In her domestic art works she has tried to discover and explore her femininity. In the late 1960's, seeking a place for feminine work within the dominating male aesthetic, she pioneered the use of the quilt medium traditionally associated with women as a fine art form. Her quilts can hang on the wall or be used on a bed. In quilts she was able to express her spirited nationalism (she is a "cultural activist") and her love of nature. In one quilt the insert hidden under a flap reads, "Down with U.S. Imperialist Technology." Elsewhere she may examine Canadian history.

The quilt is also a vehicle for her ecological concerns. In her "Water Quilt" there is a message under the 64 cushions with their 64 embroidered flaps of the Arctic flowers—the text is from James Laxer's ecological and political study, *The Energy Poker Game*. In 109 "Views of Canada" and "Arctic Day" she examines Canada and the much-disputed ecological area of the Canadian Arctic.

From 1977 on, in Wieland's drawings in coloured pencil, she explored stories of love and catalysm, landscape and light, "drawing together all the things I care about in one place." The paintings which developed in this period, culminating with *The Artist on Fire* (1983), explored in rich colour the artist's self-image and ideals. Today, after a retrospective in 1987 at the Art Gallery of Ontario (1987), Wieland has gone back to the freedom of her early abstractions and combined it with her basic themes of growth, nature, love and life.

—Joan Murray

WILEY, William T.

American. Born in Bedford, Indiana, 21 October 1937. Educated at Columbia High School, Richland, Washington, 1952–56; studied at the San Francisco Art Institute, B.F.A. 1961, M.F.A. 1962. Independent artist incorporating verbal humor in paintings, sculpture and prints, since 1960: lives and works in California. Associate Professor, University of California at Davis, 1962–73; Instructor, San Francisco Art Institute, 1963, 1966–67; Art Instructor, University of Nevada, Reno, 1967; Art Instructor, Washington State College, Pullman, 1967; Art Instructor, University of California at Berkeley, 1967; Instructor, School of Visual Arts, New York, 1968; Art Instructor, University of Colorado, Boulder, 1968. Recipient: Painting Prize, San Francisco Art Institute, 1959; First Prize, *San Francisco Art Institute Festival*, 1960; Fletcher Award, California School of Fine

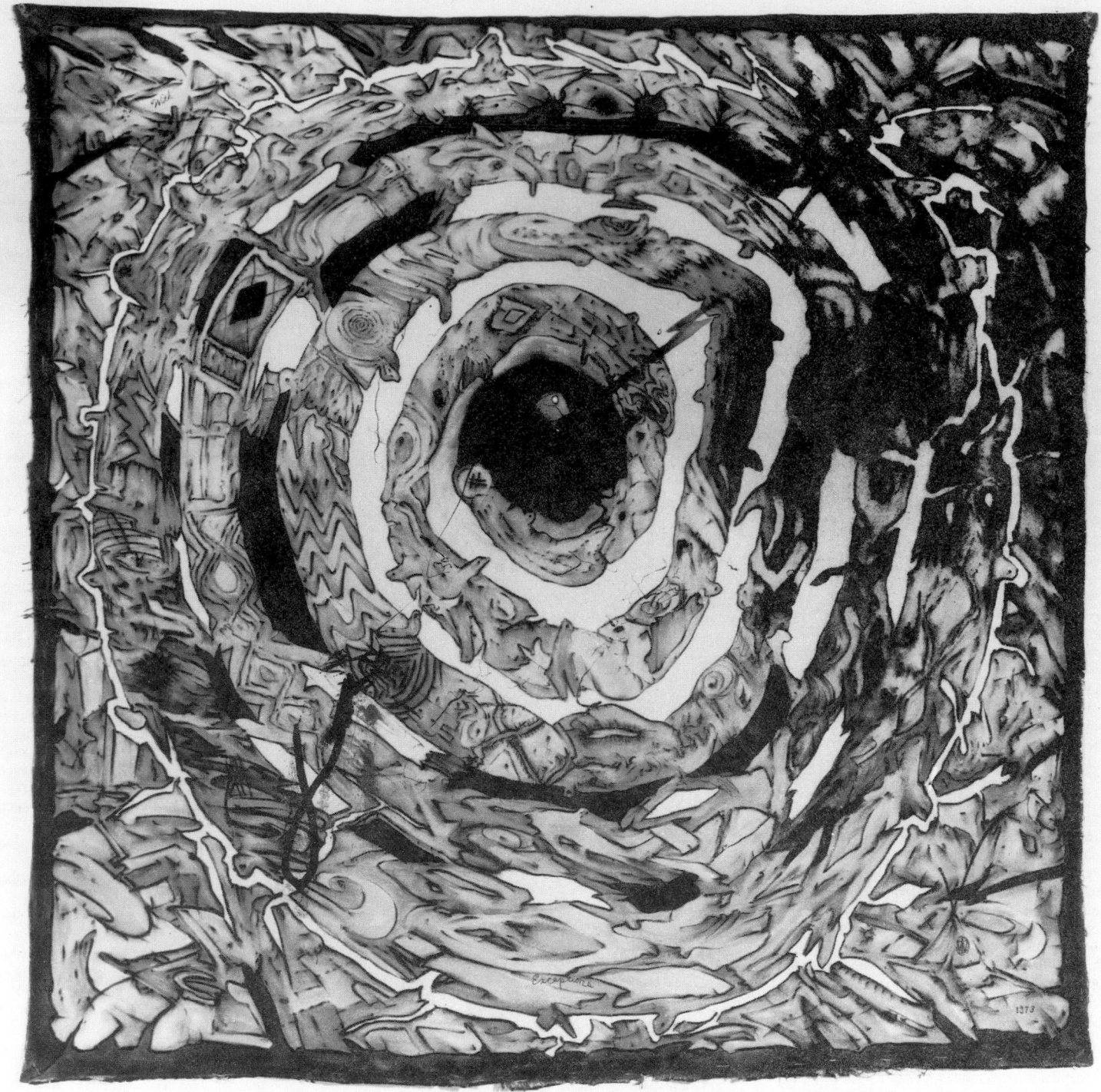

William T. Wiley: *With Few Exceptions,* **1973**

Arts, 1960; First Prize, Painting, *Oakland Annual,* 1960; New Talent Award, *Art in America,* 1961; Painting Prize, *65th Annual Exhibition,* Art Institute of Chicago, 1962; Sculpture Prize, Los Angeles County Museum of Art, 1962; Creative Arts Institute Award, University of California at Davis, 1968; Purchase Prize, Whitney Museum, New York, 1968; Nealie Sullivan Award, San Francisco Art Institute, 1968; Bartels Prize, *72nd American Exhibition,* Art Institute of Chicago, 1976; Traveling Grant to Australia, Australian Arts Council, 1980. Agent: Wanda Hansen, 615 Main Street, Sausalito, California 95965. Address: P.O. Box 609, Forest Knolls, California 94933, U.S.A.

Individual Exhibitions:

1960	Staempfli Gallery, New York
	San Francisco Museum of Art
1962	Staempfli Gallery, New York

1964	Staempfli Gallery, New York
1965	Lanyon Gallery, Palo Alto, California
1967	Mills College, Oakland, California
1968	Hansen Fuller Gallery, San Francisco
	Allan Frumkin Gallery, New York
1969	Hansen Fuller Gallery, San Francisco
	Allan Frumkin Gallery, Chicago
1970	Allan Frumkin Gallery, New York
	Keel Over, Madison Art Center, Wisconsin
1971	Hansen Fuller Gallery, San Francisco
	Manolides Gallery, Seattle (with Robert Arneson)
	Studio Marconi, Milan
	Corcoran Gallery, Washington, D.C. (travelled to the University Art Museum, University of California at Berkeley and the Art Institute of Chicago)
1972	Hansen Fuller Gallery, San Francisco
	Allan Frumkin Gallery, Chicago
	James Manolides Gallery, Seattle
	Margo Leavin Gallery, Los Angeles
	Galleria Odyssia, Rome

	Galerie Richard Foncke, Ghent
1973	Allan Frumkin Gallery, New York
	Van Abbemuseum, Eindhoven, Netherlands
1974	Hansen Fuller Gallery, San Francisco
	Allan Frumkin Gallery, Chicago
	Utah Fine Arts Museum, Salt Lake City
1975	Hansen Fuller Gallery, San Francisco
	3 One-Man Shows: William T. Wiley, Dorothy Hood, Armando Morales, University of Texas at Austin
1976	Allan Frumkin Gallery, New York
	Project Room, Museum of Modern Art, New York
1977	Galerie Paul Facchetti, Paris
	New Publications, Landfall Press Gallery, Chicago
	Suite of Daze, Art Institute of Chicago
1978	Hansen Fuller Gallery, San Francisco
	Myra Morgan Gallery, Shawnee Mission, Kansas
	Delahunty Gallery, Dallas, Texas
1979	*Graphics 1967–1979,* Allan Frumkin Gallery, New York and Chicago
	Prints, Baltimore Museum of Art (retrospective)
1980	Hansen Fuller Goldeen, San Francisco

Prints, Illinois State University, Normal
Prints and Sculpture, San Jose Museum of Art, California
Cornish Institute of Allied Arts Gallery, Seattle
Glen Hanson Gallery, Minneapolis
Realities Gallery, Melbourne (travelled to the Institute of Modern Art, Brisbane)
Redding Museum, Redding, California
1981 Allan Frumkin Gallery, New York
Emily Carr College of Art, Vancouver
Florida State University, Tallahassee (travelled to Florida International University, Miami, and the University of South Florida, Tampa)
Wiley Territory, Walker Art Center, Minneapolis (travelled to Dallas; Denver; Des Moines; San Francisco; Phoenix)
1983 Hansen Fuller Gallery, San Francisco
Allan Frumkin Gallery, New York
1985 Alberta College of Art, Calgary (Travelled to Chicago)
1986 *Steal Witness for the Time Being*, Newport Harbor Art Museum, Newport Beach, California (travelled to Palm Springs; Boise; Seattle; San Francisco)
Moore College, Philadelphia (travelled to New York)
Fulkler Goldeen Gallery, San Francisco
Hammarskjold Plaza Sculpture Garden, New York
Marsha Mateyka Gallery, Washington, D.C.
1987 *What Is Not Music*, Galerie Grita Insam, Vienna (travelled to Frankfurt)
L.A. Louver Gallery, Venice, California

Performance: *Over Evident Falls*, with Steve Reich, Sacramento, California, 1968.

Selected Group Exhibitions:

1973 *Extraordinary Realities*, Whitney Museum, New York
1974 *Surrealität-Bildrealität 1924-1974*, Städtische Kunst-Kunsthalle, Dusseldorf
1976 *3 From California*, Dalhousie Art Gallery, Halifax, Nova Scotia
1977 *Artists' Maps*, Philadelphia College of Art
1978 *Aesthetics of Graffiti*, San Francisco Museum of Modern Art
1979 *The 1970's: New American Painting*, New Museum, New York (toured Eastern Europe through 1981)
1981 *8 Funny Artists*, Institute for Art and Urban Resources, New York
1983 *Minimalism to Expressionism*, Whitney Museum, New York
1985 *Content: A Contemporary Focus 1974-84*, Hirshhorn Museum, Washington, D.C.
1987 *Bay Area Drawing*, Richmond Art Center, California

Collections:

San Francisco Museum of Modern Art; University Art Museum, University of California at Berkeley; Oakland Museum, California; Museum of Modern Art, New York; Whitney Museum, New York; Art Institute of Chicago; Fort Worth Art Center, Texas; Des Moines Art Center, Iowa; University of Kansas Art Museum, Lawrence; Van Abbemuseum, Eindhoven, Netherlands.

Publications:

By WILEY: films—*The Great Blondino*, San Francisco 1967; *Man's Nature*, San Francisco 1971.

On WILEY: books (exhibition catalogues) *Funk* by Peter Selz, Berkeley 1967; *Wizdumb*, with introduction by Brenda Richardson, berkeley 1971; *William T. Wiley: Retrospective*, with introduction by J. Leering, Eindhoven 1973; *Wiley Territory*, with texts by Graham Beal and John Perreault, Minneapolis 1979; *William T. Wiley*, with essays by Beth Coffelt, Matthew Kangas, John Perreault and others, Tallahassee 1981; *Steal Witness for the Time Being*, with introduction by Albert Stewart, North Haven 1984; *William T. Wiley: Recent Paintings and Watercolors*, with essay by Sarah McFadden,

Philadelphia and New York 1986; *What Is Not Music*, with texts by Peter Weiermair and Ben Marks, Frankfurt and Vienna 1987.

Hunger . . . For A Statement
Driven? By Something? I (We)
Don't Understand? We (I) Praise
Sing Dance Deny And Die In
The Face. Make? Pictures
Of Living, Dying, Becoming.
Knowledge Cannot Seem To Help
Much, Nor Suffering . . .
What Is Not Food?

—William T. Wiley

The surrealist elements that run through William Wiley's paintings and constructions are tempered by a kind of zany, dude dadaism and beguiling lyricism. A look at his work reveals an honest love of the land and a genuine child-like interest in minutia. This quality in turn is reflected in Wiley's style. In his two-dimensional works there are unmistakable references to comic strips, coloring books and children's book illustrations. Applied to the adult world of landscape painting, mysticism and ecology they create an off-balanced, fresh quality that is part of Wiley's distinction.

He seems very much a California artist but one who's been as they say, around. Any naivete he may display is strictly *faux*. His work abounds in visual and verbal puns. Yes, verbal. He is an artist much given to words. He likes to write all over his work—to include passages from logs, or notebooks, or fragments from letters to or from friends. He belongs to a kind of circle of like-minded fellow artists and there are constant cross-references to the work, lives, personalities, etc., of the circle.

Wiley's draughtsmanship is very fine with live, strong, *interesting* line, a little like those picture puzzles where you are supposed to locate and identify various hidden images. This incorporation of commonplace, popular material is somewhat related to Pop art—in the way, say, of relating to such things as Andy Warhol's color-me-by-numbers paintings. But Wiley's interests and direction are far more consciously "artistic" in technique than the products of most Pop artists. It can even be said that, in the end, his work has elegance.

This is related to the lyricism I spoke of and goes along with a gentleness and whimsy characteristic of much of Wiley's output. He likes to draw imaginary maps, to make charts and give directions. Besides orthodox painting on canvas he often introduces the third dimension incorporating feathers, rope, sticks, string, branches, etc., suggestive of American Indian artifacts, of camping trips, of cowboys-and-Indians. There are echoes of fetishism and secret rites, of poetry and religion, of children's games in his work and its success lies in the imaginative synthesis he has made from such complex and various subject matter. His work suggests that of a man deeply sympathetic to the American Far West and to the development of twentieth century art—a kind of pioneer who's read Proust.

—Ralph Pomeroy

WILLATS, Stephen.

British. Born in London, 17 August 1943. Studied, under Roy Ascott, at Ealing College of Art, 1952. Married Felicity Oliver in 1974; sons (from previous marriage): Justin and Nicholas. Founder, *Control* magazine, London, 1965; Founder, Centre for Behavioural Art, London, 1972-74. Lecturer, Ipswich School of Art, Suffolk, 1965-67, and Nottingham College of Art, 1968-72; Part-time Lecturer in Sculpture, Hornsey College of Art, London, 1969-

71. Agents: Lisson Gallery, 68 Bell Street, London NWI; Rudiger Schöttle, Martiusstrasse 7, 8000 Munich 40, West Germany. Address: 5 London Mews, London W2, England.

Individual Exhibitions:

1964 Chester Beatty Research Institute, London
1968 Museum of Modern Art, Oxford
1971 *Man from the 21st Century*, Nottingham
1972 *Social Resource Project for Tennis Clubs*, Nottingham
West London Social Resource Project, London
Oxford Insight Development Project, Oxford
1973 Gallery House, London
Edinburgh Social Model Construction Project, Edinburgh
1974 Gallery December, Münster, West Germany
1975 Galleria Banco, Brescia, Italy
The Gallery, London (toured the U.K.)
1976 Midland Group Gallery, Nottingham
Lisson Gallery, London
Stampa Gallery, Basle
1977 *From a Coded World*, London
Attitudes within 4 Relationships, Southhampton Art Gallery
1978 *Contained Living*, Museum of Modern Art, Oxford
Questions about Ourselves, Lisson Gallery, London
1979 *Concerning Our Present Way of Living*, Whitechapel Art Gallery, London
The Lurky Place, Galerie Schweinabraden, East Berlin
Berlin Wall Drawings, Rudiger Schöttle Galerie, Munich
4 Professionals, Lisson Gallery, London
1980 *Concerning Our Present Way of Living*, Stedelijk van Abbemuseum, Eindhoven, Netherlands
4 Inseln in Berlin, Nationalgalerie, Berlin
1981 *4 Inseln in Berlin*, Gothe Institute, London
Mens en Omgeving, De Beyerd Centrum, Breda, Netherlands
1982 *Meta Filter and Related Works* Tate Gallery, London
The New Reality, Orchard Gallery, Londonderry, Northern Ireland
1983 *Angst in den Strasse*, Galerie Rudiger Schottle, Munich
Inside the Night, Lisson Gallery, London
Under Cover, Arnolfini Gallery, Bristol
1984 *Means of Escape*, Rochdale Art Gallery, Lancashire
Another City, Riverside Studios, London
1985 *Doppelganger*, Lisson Gallery, London
Double Crossing, Galerie Ralph Wernicke, Stuttgart
1986 *City of Concrete*, Ikon Gallery, Birmingham
Grusse vom modernen Lebe, Stadtische Galerie, Regensburg, West Germany
Groeten uit het moderne leven, Museum van Hedendaagse Kunst, Utrecht, Netherlands
Concepts and Models, Institute of Contemporary Arts, London
Vier Huizen in Den Haag, Gemeentemuseum, The Hague
Striking Back, Mappin Art Gallery, Sheffield, Yorkshire
Fragments of Modern Living, Galerie Tanja Grunert, Cologne
1987 *Contemporary Living*, Museum van Hedendaagse Kunst, Ghent, Belgium
Concepts and Projects Bookworks, Nigel Greenwood Books, London
Between Objects and People, Leeds City Art Gallery, Yorkshire

Selected Group Exhibitions:

1966 *Kunst Licht/Kunst*, Stedelijk van Abbemuseum, Eindhoven, Netherlands
1967 *Light and Movement*, Herbert Art Gallery, Coventry (toured the U.K.)
1970 *Kinetic Art*, Hayward Gallery, London
1972 *Cognition Control*, Midland Group Gallery, Nottingham (toured the U.K.)
1975 *Codes and Structures*, Royal College of Art, London

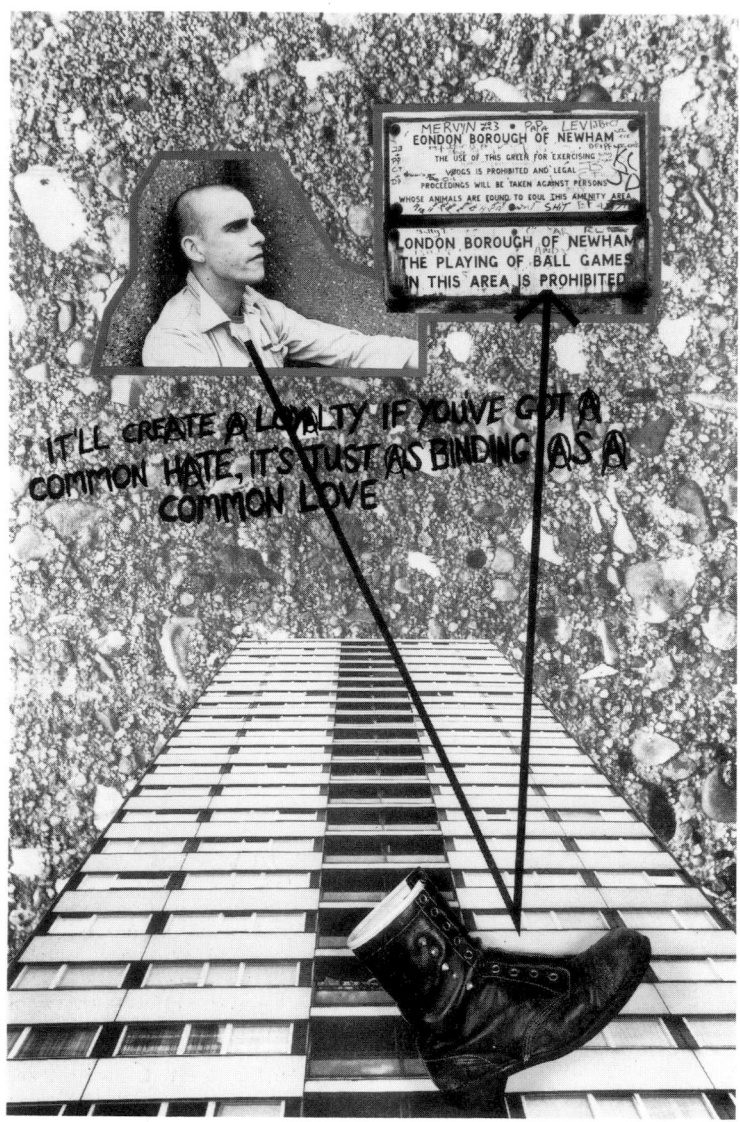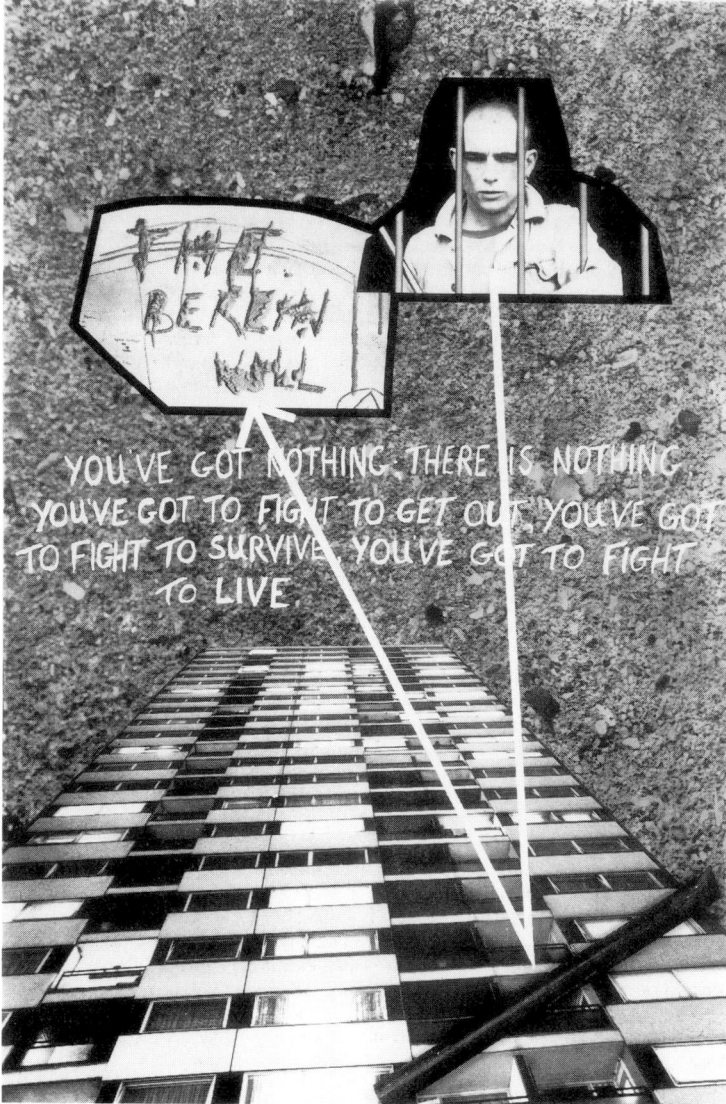

Stephen Willats: *Every Day and Every Night*, **1984**

1977   *Social Criticism and Art Practice,* San Francisco Art
        Institute
1980   *Artist and Camera,* Mappin Art Gallery, Sheffield
1983   *The Sculpture Show,* Hayward Gallery, London
1985   *The British Show,* Art Gallery of New South Wales,
        Sydney
1987   *Art and Craft in the Twentieth Century,* Laing Art
        Gallery, Newcastel-upon-Tyne

Collections:

Tate Gallery, London; Arts Council of Great Britain, London; British Council, London; City Art Gallery, Southhampton; Gallery of Modern Art, Edinburgh; Stedelijk van Abbemuseum, Eindhoven, Netherlands; De Beyerd Museum, Breda, Netherlands.

Publications:

By WILLATS: books—*Art and Social Function,* London 1976; *Ich Lebe in Einem Betonklotz,* Cologne 1980; *Cha Cha Cha,* London 1982; *Intervention and Audience: A Synopsis,* London 1984; *Doppelganger,* London 1985; *Intervention and Audience,* London 1986; articles—statement in *Control No. 2* (London), 1966; statement in *Studio International* (London), February 1967; statement in *Control No. 3* (London), 1968; statement in *Structure No. 1* (London), October 1968; statement in *Art and Artists* (London), January 1969; "Behavioural Nets and Life Structures" in *The Paper* (Trent Polytechnic, Nottingham), 1971; statement in *Platform* (Nottingham), 1972; "West London Social Resource Project" in *Studio International* (London), January 1973; "Art and Social Function" in *Art and Artists* (London), June 1973; "The Edinburgh Project" in *Art and Artists* (London), January 1974; "Meta Filter" in *Art and Artists* (London), November 1974; "Meta Filter" in *Flash Art* (Milan), November 1974; "The West London Social Resource Project" in *Leonardo* (Oxford), 1974; "Meta Filter" in *Studio International* (London), September 1975; "A State of Agreement" and "A Survey of Distance Models of Art" in *Control No. 9* (London), 1975; "Book as Interactive Tool: The Modelling Book" in *Artists' Bookworks,* exhibition catalogue, London 1975; "Social Codes and Behaviour Parameters: An Area of Concern for Art" in *Life Codes and Behaviour Parameters,* Nottingham 1976; "Art Work as a Social Model" in *Studio International* (London), March/April 1976; "From a Coded Word" in *Studio International* (London), vol. 194, 1978; "Working with the Work of Art" in *Art Monthly* (London), April 1979; "Contained Reality" in *Art Monthly* (London), April 1979; "Contained Reality" in *Art Monthly* (London), no. 3, 1980; "Kultureller Druck" and "West Berlin als Kulturelles Symbol" in *Stephen Willats,* exhibition catalogue, Berlin 1980; "Doppelganger," interview with Antonia Payne, in *Studio International* (London), no. 1011, 1985.

On WILLATS: books—*Un Certain Art Anglais,* exhibition catalogue with text by Sandy Nairne and others, Paris 1979; *Stephen Willats: Leben in vorgegebenen Grenzen/4 Inseln in Berlin,* exhibiton catalogue with essay by Arno Hoffmann, West Berlin 1980; *The Artist as Photographer* by Marina Vaizey, London 1982; *New Art,* exhibition catalogue by Michael Compton, London 1983; *The British Show,* exhibition catalogue with texts by Richard Francis and others, Sydney 1985; *Stephen Willats,* exhibition catalogue with texts by Michael Archer and Manfred Schmalriede, London 1986.

MEANS OF ESCAPE

Throughout my work I present two states of social consciousness that are in continual cultural opposition.

There is an institutional, authoritatively mapped out social consciousness, its ramifications affect everyone, and in my work it is contrasted with a social consciousness of self-organization that expresses mutuality and personal creativity. For I see that within every person there is the potential of creative self expression, but that this is inhibited and repressed by the authoritative determinism that underpins the physical and social composition of the everyday world. Counter consciousness is the creative response of people to express their own sensibility and psychology. The presentation of these two different, and culturally opposed ways of perceiving reality, has directed both my working procedure and the visual composition of each work. The concept of self organization is not only symbolically represented in my work, but the actual process of its internalization by the audience involves them in acts of cognitive self-organization, for they construct their own means of escape.

Symbols

It is a fundamental part of my working procedure to search for and identify symbols that are residual in the culture and which will powerfully represent, to an audience, the two opposed states of consciousness I have just described. First I look for obvious symbols of the deterministic, object-based consciousness, and then I uncover balancing expressions of people's self organization and statements of self identity. My starting point is the physical manifestations of our culture's institutional idealizations and self projections.

Contexts

At the same time as I am searching to identify symbols that represent the object-based consciousness I am revealing simultaneous, and contrasting, expressions of counter consciousness. The symbols of counter consciousness that I see as a counter balance revolve around self-organized contexts that have been established by people as a vehicle for their own expressions of creativity. Such contexts are not only hard to identify but are difficult to access as, by their very nature, they exist undercover in the inaccessible, forgotten corners of society, often directly repressed and usually alienated from their surroundings.

However, the establishing of a context or capsule is still dependent on the dominant culture, for it has to co-exist, being reliant on it as a source of material. Here lies the really creative act, which requires objects from the dominant culture, with their attendant pre-determined function, to be transformed into an agent for manifesting the counter consciousness. The set determinism given to the object by the dominant culture is broken by it being appropriated by the creators of the counter consciousness, becoming an agent for their self-organization.

Objects

Different objects have particular importance to different groups of creators of counter consciousness, and in each of my works about particular people I identify those objects that are central to them personally. These identified objects actually become part of my work so as to confront the audience with the reality they are viewing. Objects that are central to the audience's world are symbolically mirrored in the actual objects that have been incorporated into my work.

Audience

My works present the audience with a layer of references by depicting the same reality through various media forms. Each layer of references sets up disparate cues so that there is not a pre-formed, legislated, single view, but instead the disparate references are self-connected by the audience to create their own model. The audience make their own journey, their own transformations, between the cues associated with each state of consciousness; from the day to the night, the housing estate to the wasteland, from the conscious to the unconscious. My organization of the layout of the references from which the work's symbolic world is formed I consider essentially a parallel process to the audience's process of de-constructing and internalizing those disparate references into a coherent model. Thus to active, self-organization required from the audience in their cognitive relationship with a work is in itself a creative act, an expression of counter consciousness, and in this way the ideology that is its governing force is externalized. The work is the audience's means of escape.
—Stephen Willats

Stephen Willats' work is based on a critique of the isolated and elitist art practice of the 1950's and 60's and the specialist society that engendered such art. Noting the imbalance between theory and practice in much modernist art, he has tried to correct this by being especially concerned with the theory which underlies and informs his work, publishing articles and pamphlets and editing a magazine *Control* which is a forum for theoretical discussion on contemporary art. By making use of advances made in the technological and social science fields, which have begun to allow greater interaction between previously unrelated so-

cial groups, he has aimed to reach an audience not normally concerned with art, at the same time enabling them to understand the conditioning by which a manipulative society extends its controls. To reach an audience unused to according art proper attention, he had to develop ways in which to change the artist/art work/spectator relationship—away from an idea of art as commodity and decoration to one in which it is seen as a resource to be used by the whole community in a co-operative effort towards tolerance and understanding. These ideas have informed his work since the mid-1960's.

Initially the work of the late 60's and early 70's was seen as part of the Kinetic Art movement, and in so far as it made use of light and electronic systems this may have seemed appropriate, but the similarity is seen as superficial if we look at the methods and underlying meaning of such works as the "Visual Meta Language Simulation" of January 1972. This simulates the process by which separate decision-making organizations can co-operate to their mutual benefit with the minimum of antagonism. It consists of a Problem Display Box on which incomplete patterns are illuminated and two Decision Boxes on which the remainder of the pattern appears. Each Decision Box is worked by one participant. Although initially motivated by competition, the winning operator is progressively handicapped until only cooperation between operators enables completion of the game. The work enacts symbolically a decision-making process based on a system in which each unit is given equal information and effectiveness as opposed to the current pyramidal model in which information and decision-making is the prerogative of a few.

Other areas of Stephen Willats' work have had a more immediate social relevance, such as the series of Projects from 1965 in Ipswich, London, Notingham, Oxford and Edinburgh. One of the most successful was the West London Social Resource Project of 1972. This aimed to allow normally unrelated social groups to arrive at common models of their environment based on need. Four social groups were selected from areas of West London which were near enough to be visited by one another but seen as distinctly separate neighbourhoods. Using door to door techniques participants were gathered and a manual distributed. In the manual were a series of questions to be answered and tasks to be performed, the results of which were shown each day on display boards in the local library. As the complexity of the decision-making in the manual increased, so the participation between separate social groups developed. In this way people were enabled to rethink traditional ideas about their environment and to replace them with an "adaptive, self-organizing, evolutionary" social structure in which competition was replaced by cooperation. The documentation is now available in the library of Osterley used during the project and is discussed at length in Stephen Willats' book *Art and Social Function*, 1976.

"Meta Filter" 1973-75 is a direct development of the projects. It is a machine on which two participants symbolically enact the movement away from an individual, coded view of the world towards areas of common agreement. Working through a series of slides and using a thesaurus to describe the states represented, the operator, given the object of agreement attempts to understand the responses of his/her partner, to break through his restrictive perceptions to mutual understanding. The work breaks with traditional art practice; participation is not confined to an elite, for the images and language used are open to everyone. At the same time the work criticizes contemporary social divisions while offering a possible alternative.

The active participation of the spectator is necessary too for the works which take the form of panels with photographs and written descriptions. "Person A" of June 1974 is a series of six large and 12 smaller panels and a form to aid viewing. The spectator is asked to choose the most fitting description of the photograph in terms of behaviour states, attitudes etc., and is then directed to another photograph to continue the process. A narrative is built up which

starts to affect responses to later panels; not only does the viewer posit how "Person A" might behave in a particular situation, but also by bringing his unique set of experiences to bear on the work he starts to comprehend how his own attitudes are achieved through a coded system which may well disguise or distort the real meaning of behaviour. The concept of relativism is used positively in this work, for though the primary meaning is constant, the process by which it is understood will depend on the experiences brought to bear.

Other panel works such as "Perceptions of a Married Couple" of June 1975, and "Attitudes Within Four Relationships" of March 1976 are more complex, making use of two or more people and presenting a more contextualised situation. The reading of these works depends on a relationship between the coded panel and the process by which the spectator decodes and then encodes the information to attain understanding.

In Stephen Willats' work the artist becomes an active instigator of social change as opposed to a passive mirror of current ideology. His work breaks out of the isolated context of much contemporary art to reach a wider audience and the artist attains a more meaningful position in society.

—Jane Kelly

WILLENBECHER, John.

American. Born in Macungie, Pennsylvania, 5 May 1936. Educated at Mercerburg Academy, Pennsylvania, 1950–54; studied art history at Brown University, Providence, Rhode Island, 1954–58, B.A. 1958; Institute of Fine Arts, New York University, 1958–61. Independent artist, since 1962. Instructor in Painting, Philadelphia College of Art, 1972–73; Artist in Residence, Dartmouth College, Hanover, New Hampshire, 1977. Member, New York City Art Commission, since 1980. Recipient: MacDowell Colony Fellowship, New Hampshire, 1974; National Endowment for the Arts grant, 1977. Lives and works in New York. Address: 145 West Broadway, New York, New York 10013, U.S.A.

Individual Exhibitions:

1963	Feigen/Herbert Gallery, Los Angeles
	Feigen/Herbert Gallery, New York
1964	Richard Feigen Gallery, Chicago
1965	Richard Feigen Gallery, New York
1966	Richard Feigen Gallery, New York
1967	Richard Feigen Gallery, Chicago
1970	Richard Feigen Gallery, Chicago
1971	Lambert 910 Gallery, New York
1973	A. M. Sachs Gallery, New York
1975	A. M. Sachs Gallery, New York
	Bell Gallery, Brown University, Providence, Rhode Island
	Everson Museum, Syracuse, New York
1976	Alberta College of Art, Calgary
	Olympia Gallery, Philadelphia
	Arts Club of Chicago
1977	Hamilton Gallery, New York
	University of Massachusetts Art Gallery, Amherst
	Wright State University Art Gallery, Dayton, Ohio
	Jaffe-Friede Gallery, Dartmouth College, Hanover, New Hampshire
1978	Fine Arts Center, University of Rhode Island, Kingston
1979	*Day and Night*, Hamilton Gallery, New York (with Janet Stayton)
	John Willenbecher 1970–1978, Allentown Art Museum, Pennsylvania (travelled to the Neuberger Museum, State University of New York at Purchase)
	Dart Gallery, Chicago

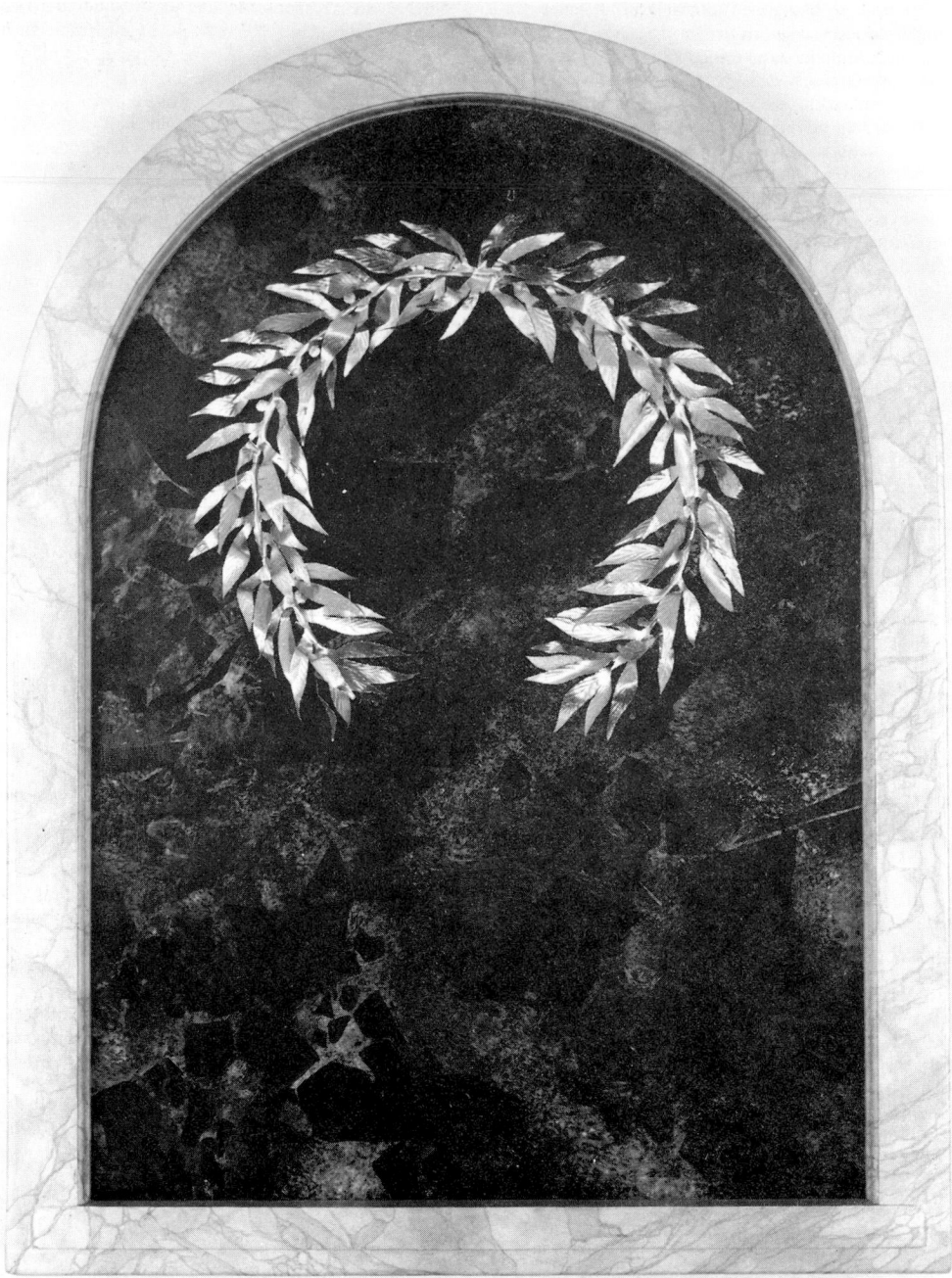

John Willenbecher: *Laureate* (*black*), 1982

1980   *Capriccios and Grottos*, Hamilton Gallery, New York
1981   *Susan Hall/John Willenbecher*, Hamilton Gallery, New York
1982   Hamilton Gallery, New York
1986   New York Academy of Sciences, New York

Selected Group Exhibitions:

1965   *Current Art*, Institute of Contemporary Art, Philadelphia
1967   *Contemporary American Painting and Sculpture*, Whitney Museum, New York
1968   *Annual Exhibition of Sculpture*, Whitney Museum, New York
1975   *Art in Boxes*, Monique Knowlton Gallery, New York
1977   *Contemporary Tableaux/Constructions*, University of California at Santa Barbara
1978   *Galaxies*, Taft Museum, Cincinnati, Ohio
1980   *Marking Black*, Bronx Museum of the Arts, New York
1984   *El Arte Narrativo*, Museo Rufino Tamayo, Mexico City
1986   *Olympus Revisited*, Summit Art Center, New Jersey

1987   *Faux Arts: Surface and Simulated Materials*, La Jolla Museum of Contemporary Art, California

Collections:

Guggenheim Museum, New York; Metropolitan Museum of Art, New York; Whitney Museum, New York; Chase Manhattan Bank Collection, New York; ATT Corporation Collection, New York; Neuberger Museum, State University of New York at Purchase; Museum of Art, Rhode Island School of Design, Providence; Hirshhorn Museum and Sculpture Garden, Washington, D.C.; Art Institute of Chicago; Centre Georges Pompidou, Paris.

Publications:

On WILLENBECHER: books—*John Willenbecher*, exhibition catalogue, with an essay by Ronald Onorato, Syracuse, New York 1975; *John Willenbecher*, exhibition catalogue, Philadelphia 1976; *The Commonplace Books of John Willenbecher*, Dayton, Ohio 1977; *John Willenbecher 1970-1978*, exhibition catalogue, with an essay by Jean-Louis Bourgeois, Allentown, Pennsylvania and Purchase, New York 1979; articles—"John Willenbecher" by Diane Waldman in *Artnews* (New York), February 1967; "John Willenbecher" by Max Kozloff in *Artforum* (New York), March 1975; "Through the Labyrinth: The Art of John Willenbecher" in *Art International* (Lugano, Switzerland), 20 March 1975; "John Willenbecher: Pyramids, Spheres and Labyrinths" by William Wilson in *Arts Magazine* (New York), March 1975; "The Modern Maze" by Ronald Onorato in *Art International* (Lugano, Switzerland), April/May 1976; "Janet Kardon Interviews Some Modern Maze-Makers" in *Art International* (Lugano, Switzerland), April/May 1976; "John Willenbecher" by Paul Gardner in *Arts Magazine* (New York), November 1977; "John Willenbecher's Burning Tetrahedron" by J. Kirk T. Varnedoe in *Arts Magazine* (New York), December 1978; "John Willenbecher" by Ronny Cohen in *Artforum* (New York), April 1982; "John Willenbecher and the Riddle of Grandeur" by Dan Cameron in *Arts Magazine* (New York), September 1983.

John Willenbecher's artworks have remarkably strong iconic presence. Based on archetypal forms like the circle, square and arch, his two-and-three dimensional objects impress as richly elegant but emotive objects.

Though trained as an art historian, Willenbecher preferred the active role of making art to the passive role of studying it. In 1963 he exhibited several examples from his early series of black boxes, filled with orderly, compartmentalized arrangements of simple forms—like balls—behind glass. The theme of this series was "unknown games of chance," and the sleek and autonomous/mechanistic look of the forms reflected the then dominant Pop and Minimalism sensibilities.

Willenbecher continued to make boxes through the middle 1960's and varied the colors—"Gold and White" (1964)—and the inside contents which mostly consisted of globes and balls. Some of them even lit up. And his boxes should be viewed within the context, then, of the period's fascination with this form found also in versions, say, by Joseph Cornell, Louise Nevelson, Richard Artschwager. By the late 1960's the circle and square, the forms emphasized in the boxes, were joined by the arch. Based on "found" wooden window frames, the arches were used as the support for different mixed mediums constructed paintings.

In the late 1960's, also, he began to investigate the labyrinth. He explored both the formal and thematic aspects of this clear, but deliberately convoluted structure in many of the works through the middle 1970's. Fraught with architectural associations and psychological sensations, involving traps and enclosures, the labyrinth served as the subject of both constructed relief objects and the 2-dimensional paintings. In "The Ladder and the Labyrinth" (1970) he centered a circular shaped labyrinth from which extended a small ladder on a rectangular ground; in "Labyrinth 23.IX.72" (1972), he painted a circular labyrinth around a sphere and centered these motifs on arch-shaped masonite. The labyrinth paintings, in turn, were the source for a group of painted triptychs which consisted of schematic renderings of enclosed structures—arch within square, circle within arch—from 1974-75. Maze-like configurations also appear in another major series of works: the cenotaphs. With arched frames on which various geometric motifs were painted, the cenotaphs also contained a built-out shelf section on the lower edge upon which three-dimensional objects like spheres, tetrahedrons and even ladders were placed. Measuring about chest size, these works bring to mind the memorial function of the cenotaphs which inspired them. The group made in homage to Etienne-Louis Boullée, the 18th century Neo-classical visionary architect, in 1974 are among the most moving.

Shelves also appear in the lower edges of the constructions in the next important series named after *Das Lied ven der Erde* of Gustav Mahler, 1975-1977. In 1977 he emphasized the circle, square and the ladder in a group of large-scale, floor constructions directly inspired by designs of Dürer and Goethe. The recent works find Willenbecher returning to the contained and specific relief pieces of the cenotaph group. The series "Laureate" (1980-81) consists of arch-shaped wooden frames that each encase a masonite support, painted to simulate marble; a circle in the form of a gold-leaf wreath adorns each surface. A tribute to creativity, the "Laureate" pictures reveal renewed interests in fine-tuning the pictorial qualities and turning them towards symbolic ends.

—Ronny Cohen

WILSON, Robert M. (Byrd Hoffman).

American. Born in Waco, Texas, 4 October 1941. Studied painting with George McNeil, Paris, 1962; studied architecture at the Pratt Institute, New York, 1962–65, B.F.A. 1965; served apprenticeship in architecture to Paolo Soleri, Phoenix, Arizona, 1965–66. Performance artist, New York, since 1966: directed theatre pieces with patients at Goldwater Memorial Hospital, New York, 1967–68; taught awareness classes, New Jersey Art Center, 1968–69, and movement classes for children, Bedford-Stuyvesant, Brooklyn, New York, 1968–69; Artistic Director, Byrd Hoffman Foundation, New York, since 1970. Recipient: Award for Best Foreign Play, Syndicat de la Critique Dramatique et Musicale, Paris, 1970; Drama Desk Award, for direction, New York, 1971; Obie Special Citation Award, for direction, New York, 1974; Lumen Award for Design, New York, 1977; Guggenheim Fellowship, 1980; Rockefeller Foundation Award, New York, 1981; Skowhegan Drawing Medal, Maine, 1987. Agent: Paula Cooper Gallery, 155 Wooster Street, New York, New York 10012. Address: 325 Spring Street, New York, New York 10013, U.S.A.

Individual Exhibitions:

1966	Byrd Hoffman Studio, New York
1967	*Theatre/Activity*, Bleecker Street Cinema, New York
1968	Grailville School, Loveland, Ohio
	ByrdwoMAN, Byrd Hoffman Studio, New York
1969	*The King of Spain*, Anderson Theatre, New York
	The Life and Times of Sigmund Freud, Brooklyn Academy of Music, New York
1970	*Deafman Glance*, University Theatre, Iowa City, Iowa (toured Europe and the United States)
1971	*Program Prologue Now: Overture for a Deafman*, Espace Pierre Cardin, Paris
	Willard Gallery, New York (with Ann Wilson)
1972	*Overture*, Byrd Hoffman Studio, New York (toured France and Iran)
	KA MOUNTAIN AND GUARDenia TERRACE, Haft Tan Mountain, Shiraz, Iran
1973	*King lyre and lady in the wasteland*, Byrd Hoffman Studio, New York
	The Life and Times of Joseph Stalin, Det Ny Teater, Copenhagen, and Brooklyn Academy of Music, New York
1974	*A MAD MAN A GIANT A MAD DOG A MAD URGE A MAD FACE*, John F. Kennedy Center, Washington, D.C. (toured the United States)
	Musée Galliera, Paris (with Christopher Knowles)
	Prologue to a Letter for Queen Victoria, Spoleto, Italy
	A Letter for Queen Victoria, Municipal Theatre, La Rochelle, France (toured France, Switzerland and the United States)
1975	*The $ Value of Man*, Brooklyn Academy of Music, New York
	Einstein on the Beach, New York
1977	Multiples/Marian Goodman Gallery, New York
1978	Paul Cooper Gallery, New York
1979	Galerie Zwinger, Cologne
	Multiples/Marian Goodman Gallery, New York
1980	Contemporary Arts Center, Cincinnati, Ohio
	State University of New York at Purchase
1981	*Medea*, Washington Project for the Arts, Washington, D.C.
1982	Marian Goodman Gallery, New York
	Galerie le Dessin, Paris

	Galerie Annemarie Verna, Zurich
	Stadtische Museum im Lenbachhaus, Munich
	Galerie Fred Jahn, Munich
	Franz Morat Institut, Freiburg, West Germany
1983	Pavillon des Arts, Paris
	Galerie Brinkman, Amsterdam
	Museum Boymans-van Beuningen, Rotterdam
	Produzentgalerie, Hamburg
	Festival Mondial du Theatre, Nancy, France
	Gallery Ueda, Tokyo
	Sogetsu School, Tokyo
	Castelli-Feigen-Corcoran Gallery, New York
	Rhode Island School of Design, Providence
1984	Paula Cooper Gallery, New York
	Otis Art Institute, Los Angeles
	Jones Troyer Gallery, Washington, D.C.
	Walker Art Center, Minneapolis
	Museo di Folklore, Rome
	Centre d'Art Contemporain, Marseille, France
	Kunstverein, Cologne
1985	Galleria Franca Mancini, Pesaro, Italy
	Kammerspiele, Munich
	Institute of Contemporary Art, Boston
1986	University of Iowa, Iowa City
	Kemo Gallery, Albuquerque, New Mexico
	Theater in der Kunsthalle, Hamburg
	Laguna Gloria Museum, Austin, Texas (retrospective)
	Grey Art Gallery, New York University
	Lehman College, Bronx, New York
	Carnegie-Mellon University, Pittsburgh
	Kuhlenschmidt Gallery, Los Angeles
	Alpha Gallery, Boston
	Rhona Hoffman Gallery, Chicago
1987	Paula Cooper Gallery, New York

Selected Group Exhibitions:

1965	*World's Fair*, New York
1972	*Overture*, Musee Galliera, Paris
1980	*Further Furniture*, Marian Goodman Gallery, New York
1981	*Other Realities*, Contemporary Arts Museum, Houston
1982	*American Drawings of the Seventies*, Louisiana Museum, Humlebaek, Denmark (travelled to Basle, Munich and Ludwigshafen)
1983	*Art and Dance 1890–1980*, State University of New York, Purchase
1984	*Survey of Contemporary Painting and Sculpture*, Museum of Modern Art, New York
1985	*High Style*, Whitney Museum, New York
1986	*The Painter and the Theatre in the Twentieth Century*, Schirn Kunsthalle, Frankfurt

Collections:

Museum of Modern Art, New York; Centre Georges Pompidou, Paris; Australian National Gallery, Canberra; Fonds d'Art Contemporain, Paris; Kunstmuseum, Berne; Museum of Fine Arts, Houston; Museum Boymans-van Beuningen, Rotterdam; Museum of Fine Arts, Boston; Rhode Island School of Design, Providence.

Publications:

By WILSON: books—*The King of Spain in New American Plays*, New York 1970; *Two Conversations with Edwin Denby*, New York 1973; *A Letter for Queen Victoria*, Paris 1974; *Einstein on the Beach*, with Philip Glass, New York 1976; *I Was Sitting On My Patio This Guy Appeared I Thought I Was Hallucinating*, New York 1978; *Death Destruction and Detroit*, New York 1978, West Berlin 1979; *The Golden Windows*, Munich 1982; *The Civil Wars: A Tree Is Best Measured When It Is Down* (Rotterdam section), Amsterdam and Paris 1983; *The Civil Wars: A Tree Is Best Measured When It Is Down* (Cologne section), Frankfurt 1984; *The Civil Wars: A Tree Is Best Measured When It Is Down* (Rome section), Rome 1984; *The Civil Wars: Drawings, Models and Documentation*, Los Angeles 1984; *The Civil Wars: A Tree Is Best Measured When It Is Down* (Act III Scene E; Act IV Scene A, and Epilogue), with Heiner Muller, Cambridge, Massachusetts 1985.

On WILSON: books—*Il Teatro di Robert Wilson* by Franco Quadri, Venice 1976; *The Theater of Visions: Robert Wilson* by Stephan Brecht, Frankfurt 1979; *American Alternative Theater* by Theodore Shank, New York 1982; *Robert Wilson: The Theater of Images* by Craig Nelson, New York 1984; *New Works on Paper 3* by Bernice Rose, New York 1985; *The President of Paradise: A Traveller's Account of the Civil Wars* by Janny Donker, Amsterdam 1985; *Robert Wilson: Die lithographischen Zyklen 1984–1986 (Medea, Parsifal, Alceste)* by Fred Jahn, Munich 1986.

Robert Wilson's most noted project has been his collaboration with composer Philip Glass on *Einstein on the Beach*. Wilson's interest, like that of Gertrude Stein, is in the use of components of syntax and sound to create a new form of language. In *Einstein on the Beach*, as part of the splicing of language, he combined both understood and senseless words and phrases. Because of Wilson's language, sets, and movement patterning, each of his works have a complex world of colorful and inane artistic principles.

Wilson generally chooses performers from the world at large, paralleling the casting of non-trained performers in a number of post-modern dance productions. The movements in the plays are generally influenced by both Andy deGroat's choreography and Wilson's own background in movement sensitization. The emphasis on internal movement, rather than dancerly, external and linear movements, is an aspect that ties Wilson's work to a theatrical, rather than dance, evolution. There has always been the suggestion though, that Wilson's work is actually silent, visual dance, as well as silent, visual opera.

The sense of allowing time to slip by, but very slowly, during Wilson's dream-like performances, is his special talent. *The Life and Times of Joseph Stalin* was a 12 hour play, *Deafman Glance* was 7 hours in duration, and *Ka Mountain*, performed in Iran, 7 days and 7 nights. Rather than a Western expansionism of space, he has chosen an Eastern withdrawing of Western, linear time. As Wilson's performances continue over long periods of time, audiences begin to lose the feeling of directionality.

Wilson has chosen several 20th century aspects of scale: delayed time, disoriented language and, finally, the inclusion of quantity. *The Life and Times of Joseph Stalin* had a complete cast of 148 performers. The performance of *Ka Mountain* included 17 directors, 9 authors, and a cast of 79. Wilson described the 7-day festival as a sort of family which existed throughout the course of time, a type of performance without end. There is the sense here that art-making reaches a scale of proportion akin to other 20th century mass activities. There has also been evidence, and he uses both conventionally trained and non-conventionally trained performers now, that life in the 20th century will go on as a very intricate, well-defined, necessary and habitually organic performance.

—John Robinson

WINNER, Gerd.

German. Born in Braunschweig, 8 October 1936. Studied art, under W. Volkert, Hochschule für Bildende Künste, West Berlin, 1956–62; and at the Suomen Taide-Akatemian Konki, Helsinki (West German Study Scholarship), 1959–62. Married to Ingmar Reuter. Graphic artist and printmaker: lived and worked in West Berlin, 1963–70, London 1970–72, New York, 1972–78, and in Braunschweig, since 1978. Recipient: Kunstpreis für Graphik, Wolfsburg, 1969; British Council travel scholarship, to work at Kelpra Studio, London, 1970; Deutscher Kritikerpreis für Bildende Kunst, West Berlin, 1972; 2 prizes, *International Biennale*, Cracow, 1972; Graphics Prize, *Biennale*, Lugano, Switzerland, 1972; Graphics Prize, *Print Biennale*, Ljubljana, 1973;

Graphics Prize, World Graphics Competition, San Francisco, 1973; Graphics Prize, *International Biennale*, Cracow, 1974; Arts Council Prize, *International Print Biennale*, Bradford, Yorkshire, 1982. Agent: Galerie Mikro, Carmerstrasse 1, Berlin. Address: Finkenherd 10, 3300 Braunschweig, West Germany.

Individual Exhibitions:

1960	Galerie Fenestra, Helsinki
1965	Galerie Mikro, West Berlin
	Galerie im Hailing, Goeppingen, Switzerland
	Galerie Sous Sol, Giessen, Switzerland
1966	Galerie für Grafikfreunde, Frankfurt
	Werkstaat Schnoor, Bremen, West Germany
	Städtisches Museum, Braunschweig, West Germany
1967	Galerie Gerda Bassenge, West Berlin
	Museum am Ostwall, Dortmund, West Germany
	Galerie C. D. Rothe, Wolfsburg, West Germany
	Schloss Wolfsburg, West Germany
1968	Galerie Mikro, West Berlin
	Galerie Nos, Duisburg, West Germany
	Werkstaat Schnoor, Bremen, West Germany
	Kunstkreis, Hameln, West Germany
	Galerie im Schinkelsaal, West Berlin
1969	Galerie Sous Sol, Giessen, Switzerland
	Galerie Wildeshausen, Wildeshausen, Switzerland
	Galerie Dr. Hartmann, Stuckvilla, Munich
	Galerie am Rhein, Cologne
1970	Overbeck-Gesellschaft, Lübeck
	Galerie Querschnitt, Braunschweig, West Germany
	Tilson: Siebdruck + Winner: Workshop, Haus am Waldsee, West Berlin (with Joe Tilson)
1971	Galerie M. E. Thelen, Cologne
	Staatliche Graphische Sammlung, Munich
	Kunstverein, Wolfsburg, West Germany (with Joe Tilson)
1972	Herzog-Anton-Ulrich Museum, Braunschweig, West Germany
	Galerie Schmucking, Braunschweig, West Germany
	Galerie 2000, West Berlin
1973	Marlborough Graphics, London
	Siebdruck, Kunstverein, Cologne
	Galerie Schmucking, Braunschweig, West Germany
	Institut für Moderne Kunst, Nuremberg
	Wentzel Galerie, Hamburg
	Galerie M. E. Thelen, Cologne
1974	Galerie Stangl, Munich
	Galerie Domberger, Reutlingen, West Germany
	Galerie Craven, Paris
	Galerie Schmucking, Basle
	Bundesministerium für Raumordnung, Bauwesen und Stadtebau, Bonn
	Arnolfini Gallery, Bristol
	Galleri Dierks, Aarhus, Denmark
	Konstmuseum, Aarhus, Denmark
	Galerie Wentzel, Hamburg
	Galerie 2000, West Berlin
1975	Kunsthalle, Bremen, West Germany
	Galerie M. E. Thelen, Cologne
1981	*Gerd Winner and Kelpra Studio*, Drumcroon Art Centre, Wigan, Lancashire
1982	University of Regina, Saskatchewan
1983	Riverside Studios, Hammersmith, London

Selected Group Exhibitions:

1961	*Grosse Berliner Kunstausstellung*, Messehallen, West Berlin (and regularly 1962–69)
1967	*20 Jahre Internationale Graphik*, Kunstverein, Wolfsburg, West Germany
1970	*International Print Biennale*, City Museum and Art Gallery, Bradford, Yorkshire
1971	*Biennale*, Musée d'Art Moderne, Paris
1974	*Print Biennale*, National Museum of Modern Art, Tokyo
1977	*Documenta*, Kassel, West Germany
1982	*Big Prints*, Southampton Art Gallery (toured the U.K.)

Collections:

Nationalgalerie, West Berlin; Kupferstichkabinett, West Berlin; Neue Galerie Sammlung Ludwig, Aachen, West Germany; Wallraf-Richartz-Museum, Cologne; Muzeum Sztuki, Lodz, Poland; Narodni Museum, Warsaw; Musée d'Art et d'Histoire, Geneva; Victoria and Albert Museum, London; Museum of Modern Art, New York; University of Iowa, Iowa City.

Publications:

By WINNER: book—*London Dockland*, West Berlin 1972; film—*Hommage à la France II*, 1969.

On WINNER: books—*Tilson: Siebdruck + Winner: Workshop*, exhibition catalogue, West Berlin 1970; *Gerd Winner*, exhibition catalogue, with text by Pat Gilmour, London 1973; *Gerd Winner: Siebdruck*, exhibition catalogue with text by Wulf Herzogenrath, Cologne 1973; *Gerd Winner and Kelpra Studio*, exhibition catalogue, with texts by R. C. Hopkinson and A. R. Taylor, Wigan, Lancashire 1981; *Gerd Winner: Paintings and Graphics 1970–1980* by Pat Gilmour, London 1981; *Gerd Winner*, exhibition catalogue, with texts by Carol A. Phillips and Maija Bismanis, Regina, Saskatchewan 1982.

In the catalogue to his 1975 Bremen Kunsthalle exhibition, Gerd Winner can be paraphrased as saying that to have people in a picture immediately imposes on that picture an interpretation, an explanation, a type of identity that it would never have acquired without people. Winner's work noticeably excludes the human figure. This makes his pictures, mostly urban landscapes, that much more haunting, for they are places where one would expect to see a figure from time to time, even if only a stray dog.

Because of his concern with photographic realism in his printmaking and his obsession with the more seamy areas of the city landscape, his series of e.g., the London dockland, the London underground or the canyons formed by New York City streets, his avoidance of human life could ultimately tend towards the depressing if it weren't for his non-descriptive use of colour. This is what takes Winner's work beyond a mere photo-realist or "pop" approach; it is his technical ability as a printmaker that keeps him from being completely typecast as one who makes "statements about deserted streets." The use of colour in his printmaking, particularly his work consequent to working with Chris Prater of Kelpra Studio, London, where he was invited by the British Council in 1970, tends to be pearly, giving an iridescent glitter to surfaces normally bereft of such delicacy.

—Victoria Keller

WINNEWISSER, Rolf.

Swiss. Born in Niedergosgoen, 5 June 1949. Educated in Lucerne, until 1965; studied graphics and design at the Kunstgewerbeschule, Lucerne, 1966–71. Served as music corps drummer in the Swiss Army, 1969. Worked as designer, Olten, 1971–72; as technical assistant on alphabetization project, Tillaberi region, River Niger, Africa, 1972–74. Independent artist, in Lucerne, since 1974; also worked in Zurich and Gambia, 1978–80, in New York, 1981–82, in Schongau, 1982–84, and in London, 1987–88. Drawing Instructor, Kunstgewerbeschule, Zurich, 1976–80, and since 1982. Recipient: Vordemberge-Gildewart Award, Rapperswil, 1984. Agent: Galerie und Edition Stahli, Bahnhof Enge, Postfach, 8027 Zurich. Address: P.O. Box 345, 6000 Lucerne 7, Switzerland.

Individual Exhibitions:

1972	Galerie Stahli, Lucerne
1973	Galerie Stahli, Lucerne
1975	Galerie Elisabeth Kaufmann, Olten, Switzerland
	Galerie Stahli, Zurich (with Aldo Walker)
1976	Galerie Meier, Geneva (with Martin Disler)
	Galerie Elisabeth Kaufmann, Olten, Switzerland (with Martin Disler)
	Galerie Stahli, Zurich (with Martin Disler)
1977	Galerie Elisabeth Kaufmann, Basle
1978	Galerie Stahli, Zurich
1979	Kunsthalle, Basle
1980	Studio d'Arte Cannaviello, Milan (with Martin Disler)
1981	Galerie Camomille, Brussels
	Galerie Stahli, Zurich
1982	Kunstverein, Mannheim (with Aldo Walker)
	Galerie Stahli, Zurich
1983	Kunsthalle Waaghaus, Winterthur, Switzerland
1985	Galerie Anton Meier, Geneva
	Galerie Biederberg, Amsterdam
	Galerie Stahli, Zurich
1986	Galerie Pro(s)art, Lucerne

Selected Group Exhibitions:

1972	*Giovane Arte Svizzera*, Rotonda della Besana, Milan
1973	*Biennale*, Musée d'Art Moderne de la Ville, Paris
1974	*Profile 10*, Städtisches Museum, Bochum, West Germany
1975	*Beryll Cristallo*, Kunstmuseum, Lucerne
1976	*Landscapes*, Mint Museum of Art, Charlotte, North Carolina
1980	*Aperto '80*, at the *Biennale*, Venice
1981	*Schweizer Kunst '70–'80*, Kunstmuseum, Lucerne (travelled to Bologna, Genoa, Bonn and Graz)
1983	*Eight Portfolios*, Nigel Greenwood Gallery, London
1984	*Bluten des Eigensinns*, Kunstverein, Munich
1987	*Malen, Schreiben-Schreiben malen*, Kunstmuseum, Solothurn, Switzerland

Collections:

Kunstmuseum, Lucerne; Kunstmuseum, Aarau, Switzerland; Kunthaus, Zurich.

Publications:

By WINNEWISSER: books—*Aus dem Logbuch Ikons*, Zurich 1982; *Immer Wieder Zuruck*, Rome 1984; *Nil*, with texts by Theo Kneubuhler and Karl Sauter, Lucerne 1986; *Prossima volta in due volupta*, edited by Stephan Banz, Lucerne 1986; articles—"Der Geraumte Weg oder das schrecklich Personliche in Beobachtungen über das andere" in *Kunst-Bulletin* (Berne), no. 7-8, 1976; "Zeichen in Bewegung ohne Titel: Fortlaufend" in *Sondern* (Berlin/Basle), no. 1, 1976; "Uberquerungen" in *Sondern* (Berlin/Basle), no. 2, 1977; "Arabesken einer Reise nach Seltsam" in *Innerschweizer Blatter* (Lucerne), February 1978; "Split Horizon" in *Oboe* (San Francisco), no. 5, 1981.

On WINNEWISSER: books—*Kunst: 28 Schweizer* by Theo Kneubuhler, Lucerne 1972; *Rolf Winnewisser*, exhibition catalogue, with text by Theo Kneubuhler, Lucerne 1973; *An Annual of New Art and Artists* by Willem Sandberg, Amsterdam 1973; *Rolf Winnewisser*, exhibition catalogue, with texts by Jean-Christophe Ammann and Theo Kneubuhler, Basle 1979; *Rolf Winnewisser*, exhibition catalogue, Geneva 1985.

Unplanned meeting of lines, a line meets, intersects another line, annullable at that point when "formulatable" wishes can be shaped out of the vantage point of pictorial plane into which flowing, unflagging signs can flee and a monochrome, with lines winding around an acrobatic sensation, pattern for thought and sensation, where words fail in the sense of following a trail, of wanting to make a language out of the image spoken by the image itself. Deviations between what is conceivable and what is still imaginable. Whereby

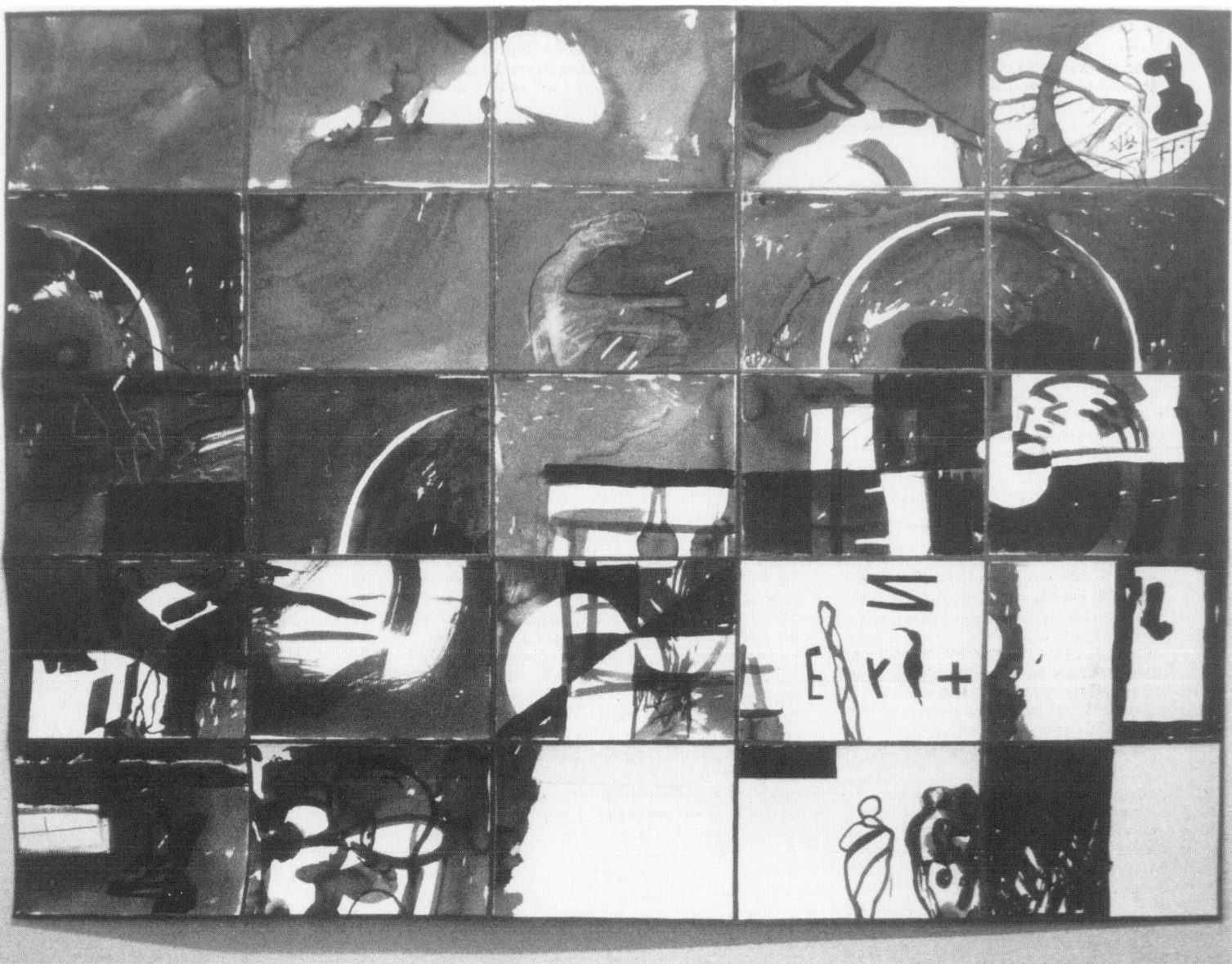

Rolf Winnewisser: *Map*, 1986

the image as image no longer works, is not longer able to give for consideration designs of a sign system to current, present-day dissected, dissectable opaque, disintegrating reality and imagination, forgotten in the image state: far from me, in me.

Things, thoughts, reflections, held outwards, turned inside out, there broken and breaking other things, expanding, fanning out, suffocating and making them breathe, domain between image and intent, image as sediment, residue of this activity, an incessant flowing, breaking and being broken of the within and the outermost, the innermost and the uttered.

Because it has to begin somewhere, where was I again when I forgot the image, when I forgot to speak of the image and disappointed by the image as expectation, by the expectation as image of what has already been, meanings running away to prevent signs from catching up with them, under way from image to image, through images. Things thought in the light of the representable and the non-representable movements between mind, mental signs in their brokenness, formulas of inconclusiveness, and the inconclusiveness of a formula, things existential in the light of acting and failing to act, the mistakes, the inconclusiveness of experience, the realities of appearance, embodied signs, when signs flow from their significance, contaminations held and released again.

—Rolf Winnewisser

WINSOR, Jacqueline.

American. Born in Newfoundland, Canada, 20 October 1941. Educated at Yale Summer School of Art and Music, New Haven, Connecticut, 1964; Massachusetts College of Art, Boston, 1965, B.F.A. 1965; Rutgers University, New Brunswick, New Jersey, 1967, M.F.A. 1967. Independent artist, New York, since 1967. Art and Ceramics Instructor, Douglass College, New Brunswick, New Jersey, 1967; Art Instructor, Middlesex County College, Edison, New Jersey, and Newark State Teacher's College, New Jersey, 1968–69; Ceramics Instructor, Mills College of Education, Oakland, California, 1968, 1971; Graphics Instructor, Loyola University, New Orleans, Summer 1969; Ceramics Instructor, Greenwich House Pottery School, New York, 1969–72; Sculpture Instructor, School of Visual Arts, New York, Spring 1971 and 1975; Art Instructor, Hunter College, New York, 1972–75. Recipient: Creative Artists' Public Service Program Award, 1973; New York State Council of the Arts Grant, 1973–74; Mather Award, Art Institute of Chicago, 1974; National Endowment for the Arts Grant, 1974, 1977, 1984; Louis Comfort Tiffany Foundation Award, 1977; Guggenheim Fellowship, 1978; Creative Artist's Award, Brandeis University, Waltham, Massachusetts, 1979. Agent: Paula Cooper Gallery, 155 Wooster Street, New York, New York 10012. Address: 141 Canal Street, New York, New York 10002, U.S.A.

Individual Exhibitions:

1968	Douglass College Gallery, New Brunswick, New Jersey
1971	Nova Scotia College of Art and Design, Halifax
1973	Paula Cooper Gallery, New York
1976	Paula Cooper Gallery, New York
	Contemporary Arts Center, Cincinnati, Ohio
	Portland Center for Visual Arts, Oregon
1977	Museum of Modern Art, San Francisco
1978	Wadsworth Atheneum, Hartford
1979	Museum of Modern Art, New York
	Art Gallery of Ontario, Toronto
	Fort Worth Art Museum, Texas
1981	Virginia Museum of Fine Arts, Richmond
1982	Paula Cooper Gallery, New York
	Akron Art Museum, Ohio
1983	Massachusetts Institute of Technology, Cambridge (with Barry Ledoux)
	Paula Cooper Gallery, New York
1985	Margarete Roeder Fine Arts, New York (with Richard Deacon)
1986	Paula Cooper Gallery, New York

Selected Group Exhibitions:

1969	*American Abstract Artists*, Riverside Museum, New York

1972 *American Women Artists*, Kunsthaus, Hamburg
1975 *The Condition of Sculpture*, Hayward Gallery, London
1976 *The Liberation: 14 American Artists*, Aarhus Museum of Art, Denmark (toured Europe)
1977 *Biennial*, Whitney Museum, New York
1978 *Fading Bounds in Sculpture*, Stedelijk Museum, Amsterdam
1979 *The Decade in Review*, Whitney Museum, New York
1982 *Currents: A New Mannerism*, Jacksonville Art Museum, Florida (travelled to Tampa, Florida)
1985 *Tranformations in Sculpture*, Guggenheim Museum, New York
1987 *The Success of Failure*, Laumeier Sculpture Park, St. Louis (travelled to Middlebury, Vermont; Tucson, Arizona)

Collections:

Museum of Modern Art, New York; Whitney Museum, New York; Detroit Institute of Arts; Musée d'Arte Moderne, Paris; Australian National Gallery, Canberra.

Publications:

By WINSOR: book—*Jackie Winsor: Sculpture*, exhibition catalogue, text with Ellen Phelan, Cincinnati, Ohio 1976; articles—"An Interview with Jackie Winsor," with Liza Bear, in *Avalanche* (New York), Spring 1972; interview in "Artists Now Living in New York" in *Criteria* (Vancouver), November 1977; statement in *Jackie Winsor*, exhibition catalogue (New York), 1979.

On WINSOR: books—*26 Women Artists*, exhibition catalogue, by Lucy Lippard, Ridgefield, Connecticut 1971; *12 Statements Beyond the 60's*, exhibition catalogue, by Frank Kolbert, Detroit 1972; *4 Young Americans*, exhibition catalogue, by Mario Amaya, New York 1973; *8th Biennale de Paris*, exhibition catalogue, by Georges Boudaille, Paris 1973; *A Response to the Environment*, exhibition catalogue, by Jeffrey Wechsler, New Brunswick, New Jersey 1975; *The Condition of Sculpture*, exhibition catalogue, by William Tucker, London 1975; *The Liberation: 14 Women Artists*, exhibition catalogue, Aarhus and Copenhagen, 1976; *Ideas in Sculpture 1965-77*, exhibition catalogue, essay by Anne Rorimer, Chicago 1977; *A View of a Decade*, exhibition catalogue, essay by Robert Pincus-Witten, Chicago 1977; *Strata: Nancy Graves/Eva Hesse/Michelle Stuart/Jackie Winsor*, exhibition catalogue, with an essay by Lucy Lippard, Vancouver 1977; *12 From Rutgers*, exhibition catalogue, by Jeffrey Wechsler, New Brunswick, New Jersey 1977; *Matrix 38*, exhibition catalogue, with an essay by Andrea Miller-Keller, Hartford 1978; *Jackie Winsor*, exhibition catalogue, with an essay by Ellen Johnson, New York 1979; *Born in Boston*, exhibition catalogue, Lincoln, Massachusetts 1979; articles—"Jackie Winsor: Doing It the Hard Way" by Claire C. Kelly in *Artweek* (Oakland, California), 15 January 1977; "Winsor Built" by Roberta Smith in *Art in America* (New York), January/February 1977; "Winsor Knots: The Sculpture of Jack Winsor" by Robert Pincus-Witten in *Arts Magazine* (New York), June 1977; "Art: Jackie Winsor" by David Bourdon in *Vogue* (New York), February 1979; "Raw Magic" by Mark Stevens in *Newsweek* (New York), 26 February 1979; "Jackie Winsor: Eloquence of a 'Yankee Pioneer'" by John Gruen in *Artnews* (New York), March 1979; "Jackie Winsor" by Ellen Johnson in *Parachute* (Montreal), Winter 1979; "Jackie Winsor" by Badanna Zack in *Artmagazine* (Toronto), September/October 1979; "Jackie Winsor and Post Minimalism" by Alan Barkley in *Vanguard* (Vancouver), September 1979.

Winsor's particular success is best seen in her '70s production, the moment in her career when her artistic temperament matched perfectly with the evolving Minimalist idiom to achieve an authentic significance. The nature of her art in its use of primary structures such as cube, sphere, and grid, but extended into a metaphorical position through emphasis upon process, material, and craft, has been labelled second wave Minimalism.

While the very forcefully delineated hand-made aura of this work was perhaps parallel to the feminist art of that time, Winsor typically chose manufactured materials and worked towards weight and density, if not as well a fragile poignance. She said of those works: "The overall element I seek is self-

containment. My aim is that the pieces not intrude on you, but that they give one time to come to them." Humbling in their often ritual-like craft repetitiveness, there may also be an essentially masochistic quality in the numbing anti-ego self-effacement implied in such work—aptly felt in the phrase "confessional formalism." (S. Westfall). Hundreds of the artist's hours are implied in the wrapping together, for instance, of the four logs of *Bound Square* (1972). Likewise in *Exploded Piece* (1980-82), a steel-reinforced concrete cube (with Winsor's signature small opening on each face presenting a view of the impacted interior space), was blown apart in order to be carefully, even lovingly reconstructed. This motif of tender repair on materials monstrous in either scale or industrial redolence is reminiscent of Grosvenor's approach in the last decade. He also comes to mind in an assessment of Winsor's pace of production: the unhurried appearance of their art betokens more than merely a private, meditative and personal aim. Both artists, among others, are at play with a puritanical American strain, testing the metaphysical implications of weight, idea, and silence within materials divided between the natural and industrial.

If there has been a selflessness in Winsor's art, it is also found in her persistent disinclination to reveal any details of her personal life; and as well in the control which she demands over the dispersal of her still small oeuvre by insisting that her of course obliging buyers sign a contract which permits Winsor to exercise exhibition and reproduction controls, and receive a percentage of the future sales of the works. In her recent sculptures, while still based upon weight, density, and aperture leading to a cubic interior, and as before constructed from industrial materials, it appears that Winsor's privacy of vision has attempted a more public self. The plaster board cubes are bevel-edged, and pastel hued, and the interior space is mirrored; and just so, a concrete, two-ton sphere is blue toned. For the moment, Winsor relinquished the tragic stance of the previous decade and more, and evinces a curious paradoxical decorous air.

—Joshua Kind

WODICZKO, Krzysztof.

Polish. Born in Warsaw, 16 April 1943. Studied industrial design, Academy of Fine Arts, Warsaw, 1962-68, MFA 1968. Worked as an industrial designer, Warsaw, 1969-77. Independent artist, living in Toronto and New York, since 1977. Instructor in design, Warsaw Polytechnic, 1969-77; Visiting Professor in Design, Nova Scotia College of Art and Design, Halifax, 1977-79; Part-time Professor of Drawing, Guelph University, Ontario, 1979; Part-time Professor in Design, Ontario College of Art, Toronto, 1979; Assistant Professor in Photography and Studio Art, Nova Scotia College of Art and Design, Halifax, 1980-81; Associate Professor of Design, New York Institute of Technology, Old Westbury and Columbus Circle, since 1983; Guest Professor, Cooper Union School of Art, New York, 1987; Visiting Professor in Photography, California Institute of the Arts, Valencia, 1988. Artist-in-Residence: University of Illinois, Urbana, 1975; York University, Toronto, 1976; A Space, Toronto, 1976; Nova Scotia College of Art and Design, Halifax, 1976, 1977; Artists Space, New York, 1977; South Australian School of Art, Adelaide, 1981-82. Agent: Hal Bromm Gallery, 90 West Broadway, New York, New York 10007. Address: 199 East 7th Street, Apt. 2D, New York, New York 10009, U.S.A.

Individual Exhibitions:

1970 Gallery Wspolczesna, Warsaw
1972 Gallery Wspolczesna, Warsaw
1973 Gallery Akumulatory 2, Warsaw
     Gallery Foksal, Warsaw

1974 Gallery Foksal, Warsaw
1975 Gallery Akumulatory 2, Warsaw
     Gallery Foksal, Warsaw
     N.A.M.E. Gallery, Chicago
     University of Illinois, Urbana
1976 Gallery Akumulatory 2, Warsaw
     Gallery Foksal, Warsaw
     Gallery St. Petri, Lund, Sweden
     Vehicule, Montreal
     A Space, Toronto
1977 Gallery Akumulatory 2, Warsaw
     Gallery Foksal, Warsaw
     Project Studio One, New York
     A Space, Toronto
     York University, Toronto
     Eye Level, Halifax, Nova Scotia
     Hal Bromm Gallery, New York
1978 Artists Space, New York
     Hal Bromm Gallery, New York
1979 Eye Level, Halifax, Nova Scotia
     Galerie Optica, Montreal
     Gallery 76, Toronto
1980 Hal Bromm Gallery, New York
1981 Eye Level, Halifax, Nova Scotia
     Great George Street Gallery, Charlottetown, Prince Edward Island
     Franklin Furnace, New York
     Artspace, Peterborough, Ontario
1982 South Australian School of Art, Adelaide
1983 Ydessa Gallery, Toronto
1984 Hal Bromm Gallery, New York
1985 State University of New York, Purchase
     Ydessa Gallery, Toronto
     Canada House, London
     Robert McLaughlin Gallery, Oshawa, Ontario
     Orchard Gallery, Derry, Northern Ireland
1986 49th Parallel Gallery, New York
     Gallery Foksal, Warsaw
1987 Massachusetts Institute of Technology, Cambridge
     Hal Bromm Gallery, New York
1988 Clocktower, New York
     La Jolla Museum of Contemporary Art, California

Selected Group Exhibitions:

1969 *Biennale de Paris*, Musee d'Art Moderne, Paris (and 1975)
1977 *Documenta 6*, Museum Fridericianum, Kassel, West Germany (and *Documenta 8*, 1987)
1979 *Biennale of Sydney*, Art Gallery of New South Wales (and 1982)
1983 *Presence Polonaise*, Centre Georges Pompidou, Paris
     Kunstler aus Kanada, Kunstverein, Stuttgart
1984 *Body Politic*, Tower Gallery, New York
1985 *Alles und Noch Viel Mehr*, Kunstmuseum, Berne
1986 *42nd Biennale*, Venice
     Expanding Commitment, Maryland Institute of Art, Baltimore
1987 *Poetic Injury*, Alternative Museum, New York

Collections:

National Gallery of Canada, Ottawa; Art Bank, Toronto; Mininstry of External Affairs, Ottawa; Muzeum Sztuki, Lodz; Gallery Foksal, Warsaw; National Museum, Poznan; Chase Manhattan Bank, New York; La Jolla Museum of Contemporary Art, California.

Publications:

By WODICZKO: books—*On Line*, Guelph, Ontario 1976; *Projection*, Halifax, Nova Scotia 1979; *Poetics of Authority, Vehicles, Line, Images of Propaganda, Public Architecture*, with essay by Alisa Maxwell, Adelaide 1982; *Homeless Vehicle Project, Homeless Conversations*, with Rudolph Luria, New York 1988.

On WODICZKO: books—*Krzysztof Wodiczko: Line*, exhibition catalogue, Warsaw 1976; *Krzysztof Wodiczko: References*, exhibition catalogue, Warsaw 1977; *Expanding Commitment: Diverse Approaches to Socially Concerned*

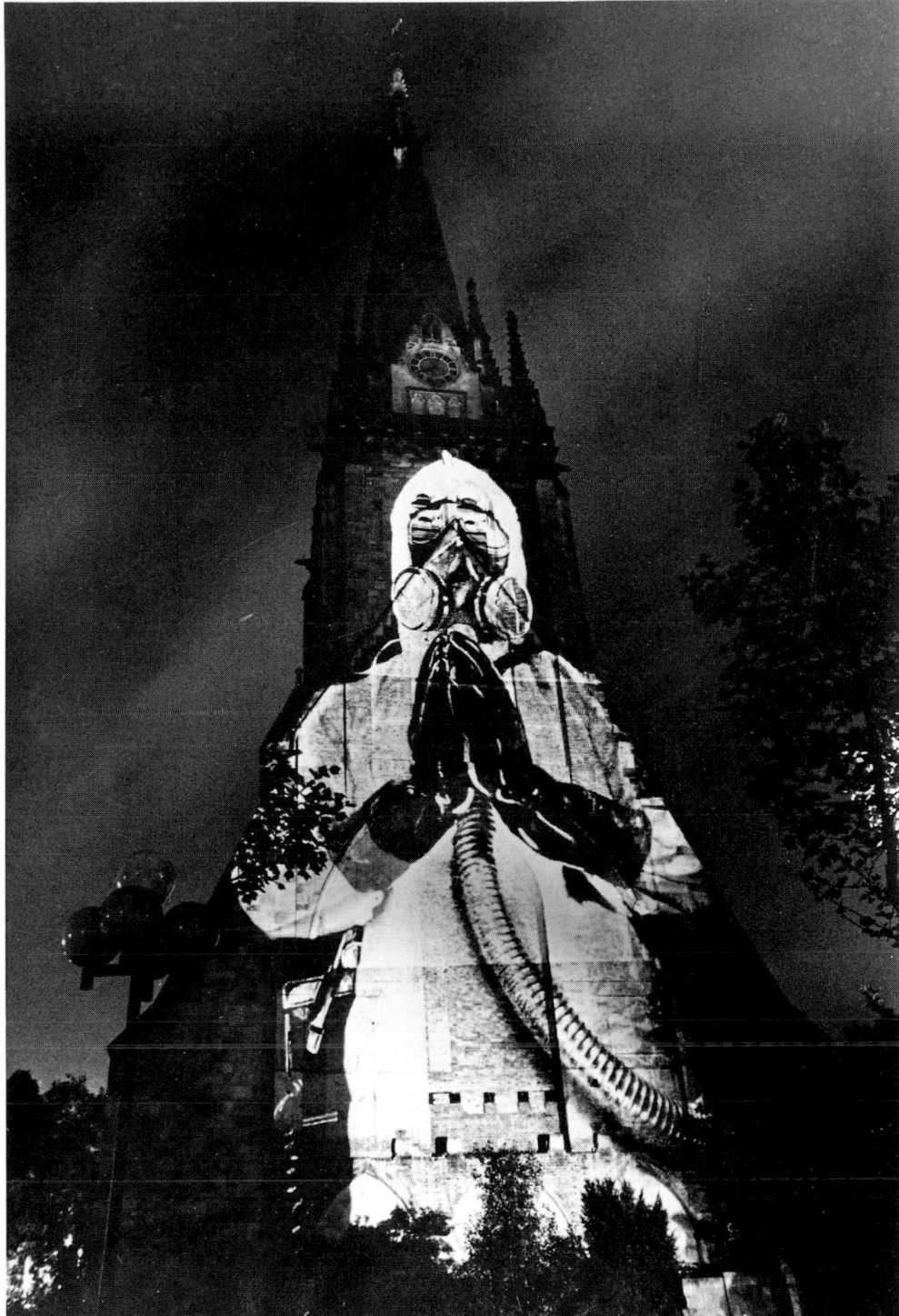

Krzysztof Wodiczko: *City Projection*, Kassel, West Germany, 1987

1966	Richard Feigen Gallery, New York
1968	Ad Libitum Gallery, Antwerp
1969	Jewish Museum, New York
1970	Richard Feigen Gallery, New York
1973	Rasdall Gallery, Lexington, Kentucky
1974	J.H. Duffy Gallery, New York
1976	University of Kentucky, Lexington
1980	Lexington Arts Council Gallery, Kentucky
1984	Northern Kentucky University, Frankfort

Selected Group Exhibitions:

1965	*The New Generation*, Whitechapel Gallery, London *Biennale*, Paris
1966	*International Exhibition*, Sonsbeek Park, Arnhem, Netherlands
	Primary Structures, Jewish Museum, New York
1968	*British Artists: 6 Painters, 6 Sculptors*, Museum of Modern Art, New York
1970	*British Sculpture of the 60's*, Institute of Contemporary Arts, London
1971	*Der Geist Surrealismus*,Baukunst, Cologne
1974	*Artists Choose Artists*, Tweed Museum, Duluth, Minnesota
1976	*National Sculpture Exhibition*, Athens, Georgia (travelled)
1985	*Midwest Sculpture Invitational*, Indianapolis, Indiana

Collections:

Arts Council of Great Britain, London; British Council, London; Peter Stuyvesant Foundation, London: Tate Gallery, London; North Jersey Cultural Council, Paramus, New Jersey; Nagaoka Museum of Art, Japan; Fort Worth Art Museum, Texas; Cincinnati Bell Collection, Ohio.

Publications:

On WOODHAM; books—*The New Generation.* exhibition catalogue, by Ian Dunlop, London 1976; *Jonge Engelse Bildhowers*, exhibition catalogue, by Christopher Finch, Amsterdam 1967; *The New Sculpture* by Udo Kultermann, New York 1968; *Form and Structure* by Teruo Fujieda, Tokyo 1971; articles—"Colour in Sculpture" by Jasia Reichardt in *Quadrum* (Brussels), no. 18, 1965; "Caro und die junge englische skulptur" by Jean-Christophe Ammann in *Werk* (Berne), vol.54, 1967; "Stage" in *Art and Artists* (London), Summer 1970; "Art: Sculpture Beside a Lake" by Hilton Kramer in the *New York Times*, 16 June 1974.

My originally recognized contribution to the dialogue amongst artists attracted to the presentation of experience in sculpture through the formal management of space, surface and colour, and our challenges to the de-sensitizing protocols of pedestal presentation, the convention of time, continues to motivate my work. I am fascinated by the expressive versatility of geometry and its propensity for organization. The mutuality of material and function.

This persistent engagement has drawn me into the realization of a variety of sets, systems, monoliths, arrangements and multiples. *Rotating Cube* is my latest example of the latter. This work, close to human scale, is intended to invite structural analysis. Each recognized cube re-orients the apparent attitude of the work (and the viewer).

—Derrick Woodham

There are striking similarities between the work that Derrick Woodham first exhibited in 1963 and his more recent pieces. Edges are clear and sharp, the surfaces are smooth, colors are muted but vibrant and volume is described with great precision. Woodham was a pioneer of what at the time was referred to as "minimal" sculpture, and it is hardly surprising that he has remained faithful to certain of the tenets he originated and exploited at the start of his career.

Photography, exhibition catalogue, Baltimore 1986; *42nd Venice Biennale, Canadian Pavilion: Krzysztof Wodiczko and Melvin Charney,* with essay by Diana Nemiroff, Ottawa 1986; *Counter-Monuments: Krzysztof Wodiczko's Public Projections,* exhibition catalogue, Cambridge, Massachusetts 1987.

WOODHAM, Derrick.

British. Born in Blackburn, Lancashire, 5 November 1940. Studied at South East Essex Technical College and School of Art, 1957-60, Hornsey College of Art London, 1960-62, and the Royal College of Art, London, with Meadows, Clatworthy, Brown, Dalwood and Atkins, 1962-65. Married Irene Janusaityte in 1966; children: Anele and Alexandra. Independent sculptor, since 1965. Part-time Instructor, Royal College of Art, 1965-68; Instructor, Philadelphia College of Art, 1968-70; Associate Professor, School of Art, University of Iowa, Iowa City, 1970-73; Assistant Professor, Department of Art, University of Kentucky, Lexington, 1973-80; Professor and Director of The School of Art, University of Cincinnati, Ohio, since 1980. Junior Member, Fine Arts Advisory Panel, Arts Council of Great Britain, 1966-68. Recipient: Walter Neurath Prize for Drawing, Royal College of Art, 1964; Peter Stuyvesant Award, 1965; Group Prize, Prix de la Ville de Paris, 1965; North Jersey Cultural Council Purchase Award, Van Saun Park, Paramus, New Jersey, 1974; University of Kentucky Research Council Grants, 1974-76. Address: 1910 Bluebell Drive, Cincinnati, Ohio 45224, U.S.A.

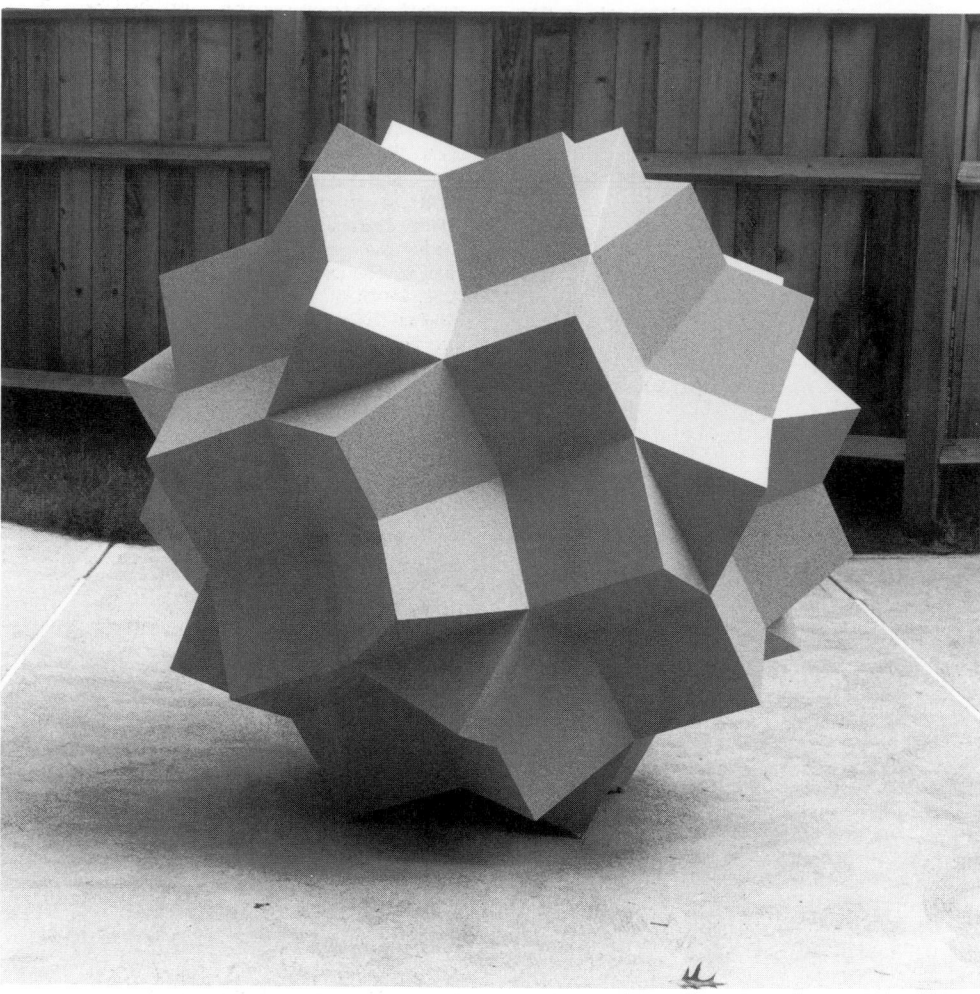

Derrick Woodham: *Rotating Cube,* 1986

an issue implies a separate identity for color that simply does not exist in the work as perceived.

With physically most prepossessing results, Woodham has doggedly stuck to the notion that quite apart from the formidable range of expression he can cull with his sculpture, it should not be divorced from principles of volume. Many of his peers, on both sides of the Atlantic, now take their cues from abstract painting and try to "draw" in space using flat planes of the now orthodox and ubiquitous brown corten steel. Woodham has reached far more meaningful levels of dialogue by surrounding and containing space and exploring it from the inside out. Yet there is nothing at all "fat" about Woodham's work. It is spare and lean.

"Fields" consists of a four-layered grid of twelve narrow girders stacked horizontally in a lattice formation. Each girder is monochrome and the colors vary from white through yellow, purple and grey to black. This piece operates on the viewer with great immediacy and the clear, sensational impact of a complex and provocative statement. Woodham's intellectual grasp of his vocation is prodigious, but even rarer is his ability to create a unique visual vocabulary that is well-defined, self-sufficient, spontaneous and universal.

—Michael Alistair Findlay

WOODROW, Bill.
British. Born in Henley, Oxfordshire, 1 November 1948. Studied at Winchester School of Art, Hampshire, 1967–68; Saint Martin's School of Art, London, 1968–71; Chelsea School of Art, London, 1972. Independent sculptor, London, since 1972. Agent: Lisson Gallery, 67 Lisson Street, London NW1 5DA. Address: 44 Camberwell Grove, London SE5 8RE, England.

Individual Exhibitions:

1972	Whitechapel Art Gallery, London
1979	Kunstlerhaus, Hamburg
1980	The Gallery, Acre Lane, South London
1981	LYC Gallery, Banks, Cumbria
	New 57 Gallery, Edinburgh
	Galerie Wittenbrink, Regensburg, West Germany
1982	Lisson Gallery, London
	Stuttgarter Kunstausstellungen, Stuttgart
	Galerie Eric Fabre, Paris
	St. Paul's Gallery, Leeds, Yorkshire
	Ray Hughes Gallery, Brisbane, Queensland
	Galerie 't Venster, Rotterdam
	Galerie Michele Lachowsky, Antwerp, Belgium
1983	Galleria Toselli, Milan
	Museum van Hedendaagse Kunst, Ghent, Belgium
	Lisson Gallery, London
1984	Mercer Union, Toronto
	Musee de Toulon, France
	Galerie Paul Maenz, Cologne
1985	Kunsthalle, Basle
	Barbara Gladstone Gallery, New York
	Donald Young Gallery, Chicago
	La Jolla Museum of Contemporary Art, California (travelled to Berkeley)
1986	Galleri Nordenhake, Malmo, Sweden
	Galerie Paul Maenz, Cologne
	Butler Gallery, Kilkenny, Ireland
	Fruitmarket Gallery, Edinburgh
	Mattress Factory, Pittsburgh
1987	Kunstverein, Munich
	Lisson Gallery, London
	Cornerhouse Gallery, Manchester, Lancashire
	Barbara Gladstone Gallery, New York
1988	Galerie Paul Maenz, Cologne

What is surprising, however, is that all of his subsequent work up to and including his more recent sculpture exemplifies a position of ideology and practice that continues to place him at the vanguard of contemporary art.

In the decade during which sculptors nurtured on Henry Moore capitulated by the dozens to the seductive embraces of technology and the fugitive dogmas of conceptualism, Woodham firmly followed a course dedicated to constantly testing the limits of expression that can be encompassed by the sculpture as object (rather than the sculpture as light, electricity, sound, printed word or invisible idea). As a teacher he has sponsored, encouraged and designed multi-media activities of radical dimensions and vital innovation. In 1972 at the University of Iowa he orchestrated a series of events that explored totally new directions for live performance possibilities. Such activities feed, rather than replace, Woodham's inspiration to create object-sculpture. These investigations suggest to him related stratagems that he anchors in solid materials. A major work of his, dated 1975 and titled "Arrangements with a Modular Group," consists of 86 units, square or oblong in shape and varying in length from six inches to eight feet. The material is Masonite, painted white. These units are arranged by the artist according to the space available. Specific preliminary settings are modified and not all the pieces need be used. The final appearance may vary from a seemingly random placement to a stacking system that looks almost symmetrical.

Although more recent work is predominantly rectilinear and contains no traces of the rounded, somewhat biomorphic, shapes of his early pieces, the human element in his work still assumes great importance. The scale of the sculpture, indoor or outdoor, is geared to stretch our normal ways of seeing. The gallery work must be explored perimetrically and looked down, into and across, much as one would have to examine a shallow valley from a hilltop. The outdoor work, three or four times human height, invites close inspection while towering above the viewer. Viewing his work makes one very conscious of one's own body scale, size and relative immobility.

His permanently installed outdoor commissions are very successful despite (or perhaps on account of) the fact that they do not self-consciously make the acquaintance of their sites. They do not suggest overtly that they have been custom-designed for the particular setting. Most of them have been erected in rural environments and they uncompromisingly resist blending into the landscape. Their severe angles and proportions are not mitigated by monochromes quite at odds with nature's friendly mix. Woodham does not try to adapt or design to accommodate a particular site because the strength of the work is implicit, not a product of its decorative suitability. Color is a very vital element in this work, and were his forms less stimulating he would still hold a very important position as a colorist. Most modern sculpture is either self-colored, the natural wood or steel exposed in a raw or rusted state or else flagrantly "painted on" with color applied so that it is impossible to eradicate the notion that two layers exist, a "skin" of paint over a quite differently colored solid. Woodham challenges both conventions by using the methods of the latter to confound the former. With the exception of "Gates," 1974, a huge outdoor work utilizing interlocking segments of identical timber frameworks, none of his colors are endemic to the materials, yet they appear so because the color is applied in such a skillful, controlled manner and the surface is so smooth and pure that the predominant sensation is that the color is completely through the material. Though they are carefully mixed and often very subtle (salmon, mauve, turquoise) the colors really seem to be *in* not *on* the sculpture. Woodham achieves a fusion of such density that even to speak of the color of his work as

Selected Group Exhibitions:

1971   *Art as an Idea in England*, Centro de Arte y Comun-
        icacion, Buenos Aires
1972   *Platform '72*, Museum of Modern Art, Oxford
1981   *British Sculpture in the 20th Century*, Whitechapel
        Art Gallery, London
1982   *Lecons des Choses*, Kunsthalle, Berne (travelled to
        Chambery and Chalon-sur-Saone, France)
1983   *Edges and Shadows: Sculpture in Britain*, Hayward
        Gallery/Serpentine Gallery, London
1984   *An International Survey of Recent Painting and
        Sculpture*, Museum of Modern Art, New York
1985   *Space Invaders*, Norman Mackenzie Art Gallery,
        Regina, Saskatchewan
1986   *Nine Artists from Britain*, Louisiana Museum,
        Humlebaek, Denmark
1987   *A Quiet Revolution: British Sculpture Since 1965*,
        San Francisco Museum of Modern Art (travelled
        to Newport Beach, California; Washington, D.C.;
        Buffalo, New York
1988   *Graven Images*, Harris Museum and Art Gallery,
        Preston, Lancashire

Collections:

Tate Gallery, London; Imperial War Museum, London;
Leeds City Art Gallery, Yorkshire; Scottish National Gallery
of Modern Art, Edinburgh; Kunsthaus, Zurich; Moderna
Museet, Stockholm; Museum Boymans-van Beuningen, Rot-
terdam; National Gallery of Canada, Ottawa; Musee d'Art
Contemporain, Montreal; La Jolla Museum of Contemporary
Art, California.

Publications:

On WOODROW: books—*Objects and Sculpture*, exhibition
catalogue with text by Iwona Blaszczyk, London and Bristol
1981; *Lecons des Choses*, exhibition catalogue with text by
Catherine Ferbos, Berne 1982; *Englische Plastik Heute*, exhibition catalogue with essay by Michael Newman, Lucerne
1982; *Bill Woodrow*, exhibition catalogue edited by Jean-
Christophe Ammann, Basle 1985; *Bill Woodrow*, exhibition
catalogue with essay by Lynne Cooke, Edinburgh 1986; *Bill
Woodrow*, exhibition catalogue with essay by Lynne Cooke,
Munich 1987; *A Quiet Revolution: British Sculpture Since
1965*, with texts by Lynne Cooke, Mary Jane Jacob and others, London 1987.

WUNDERLICH, Paul.

German. Born in Eberswalde, near Berlin, now in
East Germany, 10 May 1927. Educated at High
School in Eutin until 1946; studied art, under Willi
Titze and Willem Grimm, Landeskunstschule, and
Hochschule für Bildende Künste, Hamburg 1947–51;
studied printing techniques with Desjobert, Paris,
1961–62. Served in the German Army, 1943–45:
prisoner-of-war 1945. Married the photographer
Karin Székessy (see *Contemporary Photographers*) in
1972; children: Oliver, Natascha and Laura. Painter,
printmaker and sculptor, Hamburg, 1952–60 and
since 1963, in Paris and Italy, 1961–63. Freelance
instructor in graphics and printmaking, 1960–63;
Professor of Graphics, Hochschule für Bildende
Künste, Hamburg, 1963–67. Recipient: Cultural Circle bursary, Hamburg, 1951; Stipendium des Kulturkreises, Hamburg, 1955; Deutsche Kunstpreis der
Jugend für Grafik, 1960; M. S. Collins Prize, Philadelphia, 1962; Cultural Forum Prize, Tokyo, 1964;
Premio Marzotto, Milan, 1967; Graphic Art Prize,
Kamakura Museum, Tokyo, 1968; Gold Medal, Florence, 1970; Gold Medal, Oslo, 1973; Medal, Cracow, 1975; Gold Medal, *Graphics Biennale*,
Listowell, Ireland, 1978; Graphics Prize, Taiwan,
1984; Kunstpreis des Landes Scheswig Holstein,
West Germany, 1986. Agents: Galerie Levy, Magde-
lenstrasse 26, 20000 Hamburg 13; Redfern Gallery
20 Cork Street, London W1, England. Address:
Hayn Strasse 2, Eppendorf, 2000 Hamburg 20, West
Germany.

Individual Exhibitions;

1949   Overbeck-Gesellschaft, Lübeck
1955   Kunstlerklub Die Insel, Hamburg

Bill Woodrow: *Empty Grate*, 1987

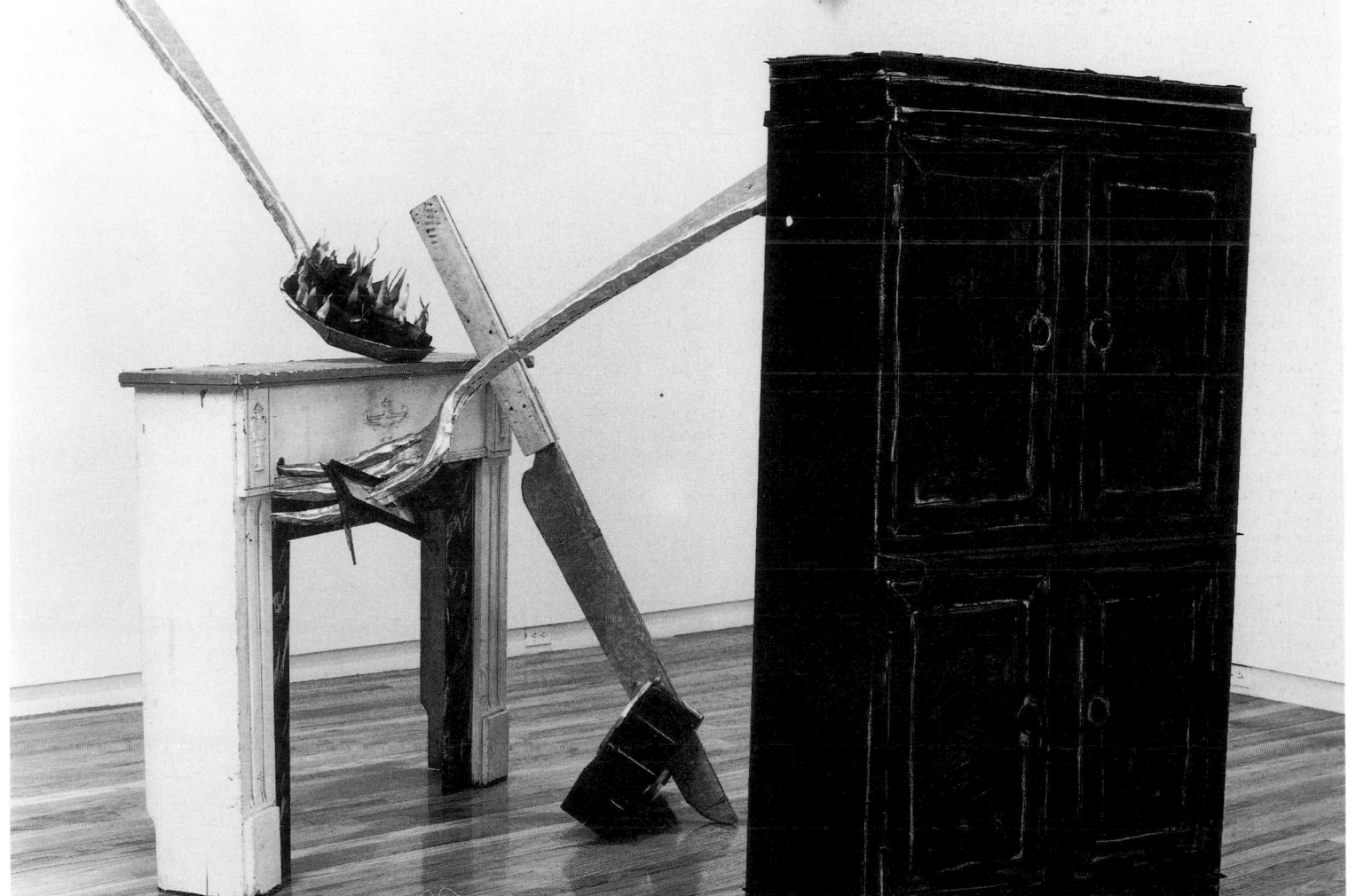

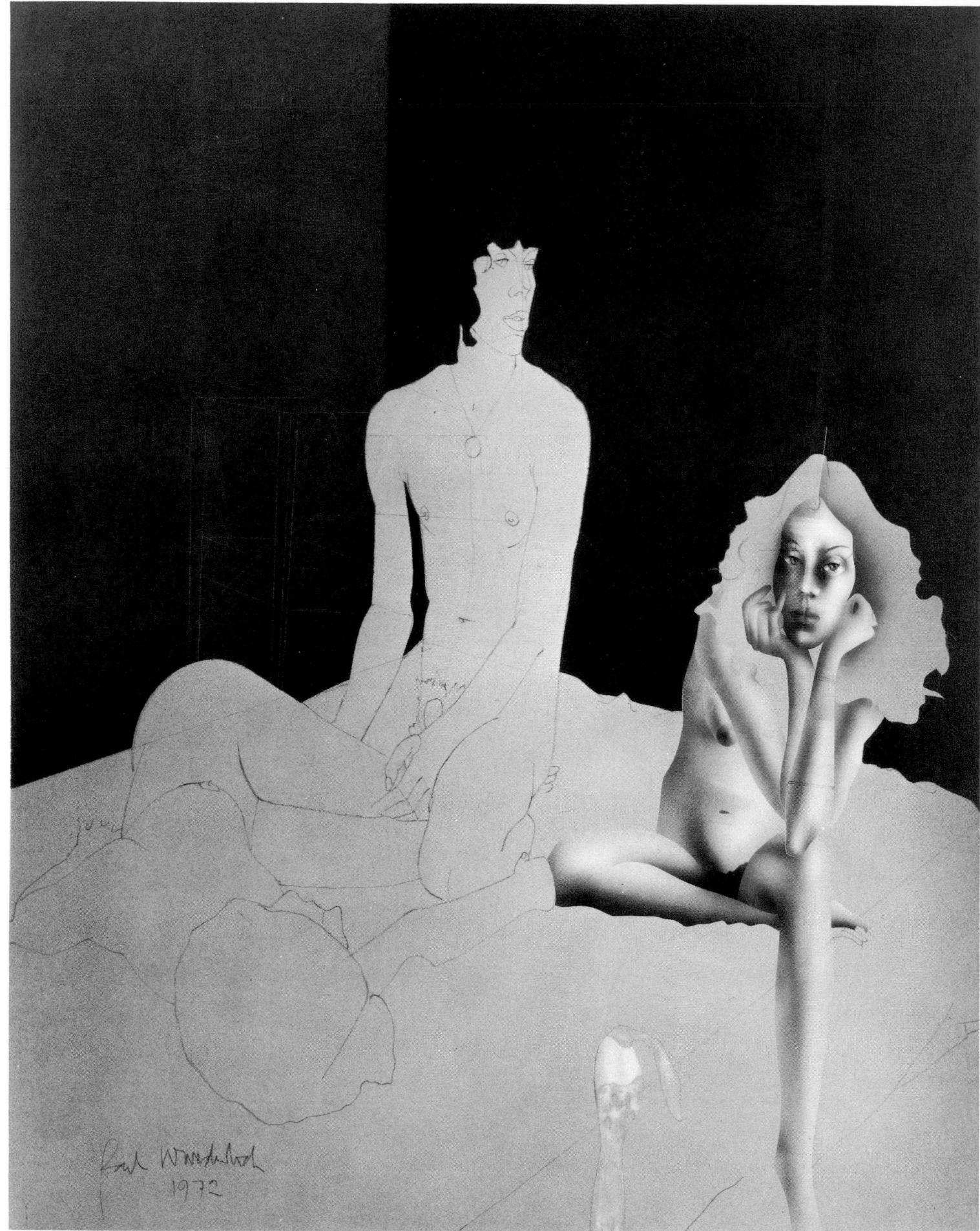

Paul Wunderlich: *Georg, Ulrike und Daniela II*, 1972

1958 Galerie Nebelung, Dusseldorf
      Orangerie, Eutin, West Germany
1960 Dragonerstall, Hamburg
1961 Galerie die Insel, Worpswede, West Germany
      Galerie Niepel, Dusseldorf
1962 Galerie Brusberg, Hannover
      Galerie Diogenes, West Berlin
      Galerie Brockstedt, Hamburg
1963 Galerie Sydow, Frankfurt
      Galerie Niedlich, Stuttgart
      Print Club, Philadelphia
      San Francisco Museum of Art
      Galerie Rothe, Heidelberg
      Galerie Niepel, Dusseldorf
      Miami Museum of Art
      Eric Locke Gallery, San Francisco
1964 *Olbilder*, Galerie Van de Loo, Munich
      Galerie Brechbuhl, Grenchen, Switzerland
1965 Galleria Arco, Rome
      Musee des Beaux-Arts, Mons, Belgium
      Galerie Hausdewell, Baden-Baden, West Germany
      Galerie Niepel, Dusseldorf
      Pfalzgalerie, Kaiserslautern, West Germany
      Galerie Wilbrand, Münster, West Germany
1966 Kubus-Ausstellung, Hannover
      Europa-Center, West Berlin
      Kunstverein, Dusseldorf
      Städtische Galerie, Bochum, West Germany
      Galerie Brusberg, Hannover
      Kunsthalle, Mannheim
1967 Overbeck-Gesellschaft, Lübeck
      Gallerie Dierks, Aarhus, Denmark
      Galerie Wolfgang Ketterer, Munich
      Galerie Toni Gerber, Berne
      Lithographs 1949–1967, Auckland City Art Gallery, New Zealand
1968 *Paintings, Sculpture, Drawings, Graphics*, Redfern Gallery, London
      Galerie Passepartout, Copenhagen
      Kunstverein, Wolfsburg, West Germany
      Galerie Brusberg, Hannover
      Gemalde/Zeichnungen/Graphik/Plastik, Badischer Kunstverein, Karlsruhe
      Galeric d'Eendt, Amsterdam
1969 Associated American Artists Gallery, New York
      Minneapolis Institute of Arts
      Perls Galleries, Los Angeles
      Phoenix Gallery, Berkeley, California
      Kovler Gallery, Chicago
1970 Galerie Brusberg, Hannover
      Recent Paintings, Drawings and Sculpture, Staempfli Gallery, New York
      Kunsthalle, REcklinghausen, West Germany
      Kunsthalle, Gelsenkirchen, West Germany
      Museum for Moderner Konst, Gothenburg, Sweden
      Galleri Leger, Copenhagen
1971 Galleri Aronowitsch, Stockholm
      Amos Andersonin Taidemuseo, Helsinki
      Perls Galleries, Los Angeles
      Kestner-Gesellschaft, Hannover
1972 Galleria Schwarz, Mulan
      Galerie Berggruen, Paris
      Galerie André-Francois Petit, Paris
      Galleria La Bussola, Turin
1973 *Recent Oils, Gouaches and Drawings*, Staempfli Gallery, New York
      Redfern Gallery, London
      Galerie Levy, Hamburg
      Retrospektive der Jahre 1958 bis 1973, Baukunst, Cologne
1974 Tokyo Gallery
      Galerie Art Contacts, Paris
      Graphischen, Radierungen, Lithographien, Plastische Werk, Kunsthalle, Kiel
1975 Wilhelm-Lehmbruck-Museum, Duisburg, West Germany
      Kunstverein, Augsburg, West Germany
      Galerie Cour Saint-Pierre, Geneva
      Galerie Orangerie, Cologne
1976 Fondation Veranneman, Kruishoutem, Belgium
      Galerie Octave Negru, Paris
      Galleri Uddenberg, Gothenburg, Sweden
      Galerie Berggruen, Paris
1977 Redfern Gallery, London

      Gouaches, Tekeningen, Litho's en Beeldhounnerken, Centrum voor Kunst en Cultuur, Ghent
1979 Galerie Veranneman, at *FIAC 79*, Paris
1980 Seibu Art Museum, Tokyo
      Kunsthalle, Kiel
      Redfern Gallery, London
1981 Seibu Museum of Art, Tokyo
      Staempfli Gallery, New York
      Von Informel zur Figuration: Bilder, Objekte, Druckgraphik seit 1957, Baukunst, Cologne
1983 Fondation Veranneman, Kruishoutem, Belgium
1985 Le Bateau Lavoir, Paris
      Sonet Galerie, Stockholm
1987 Kloster Gisma, Holstein, West Germany (retrospective)
      Museum Schloss Gottorf, Schleswig, West Germany (graphics retrospective)
      Redfern Gallery, London

Selected Group Exhibitions:

1955 *Farbige Grafik*, Kestner-Gesellschaft, Hannover
1962 *16 German Artists*, Corcoran Gallery, Washington, D.C.
1964 *Documenta* Kassel, West Germany
1966 *Phantastische Figuration*, Haus am Waldsee, West Berlin
1968 *Europaische Druckgraphik der Gegenwart*, Gemeentemuseum, The Hague
1970 *Malerei nach Fotografie*, Stadtmuseum, Munich
1972 *After Surrealism*, Ringling Museum of Art, Sarasota, Florida
1976 *Les Espaces Insolites*, Palais du Congres, Strasbourg
1987 *Zauber der Medusa*, Museum Moderner Kunst, Vienna

Collections:

Museum Boymans-van Beuningen, Rotterdam; Kunstverein, Darmstadt; Städtische Galerie, Bochum, West Germany; Museum of Modern Art, New York; San Francisco Museum of Modern Art; Miami Museum of Art.

Publications:

On WUNDERLICH: books—*Paul Wunderlich: Olbilder*, exhibition catalogue, Munich 1964; *Paul Wunderlich: Lithographs 1949–1967*, exhibition catalogue, with text by Edouard Roditi, Auckland 1967; *Paul Wunderlich:Gemalde/Zeichnungen/Graphik/Plastik*, exhibition catalogue, with text by G. Bussmann, Karlsruhe 1968; *Paul Wunderlich: Paintings, Sculpture, Drawings, Graphics*, exhibition catalogue, with texts by Frank Whitford and Wieland Schmied, London 1968; *Paul Wunderlich: Recent Paintings, Drawings and Sculpture*, exhibition catalogue, with text by George W. Staempfli, New York 1970; *Paul Wunderlich: Catalogue Raisonne de l'Oeuvre Graphique 1949–1971* by Max Bense, Hanns Theodor Flemming, Frank Whitford and others, West Berlin 1971; *Paul Wunderlich*, exhibition catalogue, with text by José Pierre, Paris 1972; *Paul Wunderlich: Recent Oils, Gouaches and Drawings*, exhibition folder, with text by George W. Staempfli, New York 1973; *Paul Wunderlich: Retrospektive der Jahre 1958 bis 1973*, exhibition catalogue, with text by Max Bense, Cologne 1973; *Paul Wunderlich: Skizzen 1966*, with text by Max Bense, Offenbach 1974; *Paul Wunderlich: Graphischen, Radierungen, Lithographien, Plastische Werk*, exhibition catalogue, with texts by Jens Christian Jensen, Johann Schlick and Eberhard Freitag, Kiel 1974; *Paul Wunderlich: Gouaches, Tekeningen, Litho's en Beeldhouwwerken*, exhibition catalogue, Ghent 1977; *Paul Wunderlich und Karin Szekessy: Corresppondenzen*, with an introduction by Fritz J. Raddaz, Hamburg 1977; *Paul Wunderlich* by Octave Negru, Paris 1979; *Paul Wunderlich: Werkverzeichnis* by Jens Christian Jensen, Offenbach 1979; *Paul Wunderlich*, exhibition catalogue, with text by Jens Christian Jensen,Tokyo 1980; *Paul Wunderlich:Von Informel zur Figuration: Bilder, Objekte, Druckgraphik seit 1957*, exhibition folder, with text by Jens Christian Jensen, Cologne 1981; *Paul Wunderlich: Werkverzeichnis der Lithografien*, Offenbach 1981; *Paul Wunderlich: Metamorphosen*, with text by H. Hollander, Dortmund 1985; *Paul Wunderlich*, exhibition catalogue, Holstein 1987; *Paul Wunderlich: Skulpturen und Objekte* by Heinz Spielmann, Offenbach 1987.

Paul Wunderlich's pictures are frequently associated with the tradition of surrealism. While this historical aspect may appear understandable in view of the imagination and fantasy in his art, the work can be described just as well if not more accurately as an analysis of political involvement, sense of reality, Eros, violence, space—that is, of direct experiences related to the present. Wunderlich has painted portraits, paraphrases of older masters, illustrations to the *Song of Solomon* and to Joyce; he has modelled sculptures and conceived useful objects which are not exhausted by use; he is a perfectionist in his craft—in the name of perfect form; he keeps his distance but is always available for practical help; he is very articulate but refrains almost entirely from comment on his pictures. This diversity serves him, however, as a stimulus to the style with which he makes each idea and each problem his own.

Apart from some graphic works Wundcrlich's oeuvre begins in 1959. Two series of lithographs at this time show two essential qualities which would always preoccupy him: the oppressed human being,susceptible to violence, whose worth is visible precisely in his destruction, and Eros as an essential human quality which Wunderlich shows as an aesthetic quality. The two series which, seen from today, appear as a key to Wunderlich's art, excited attention when they were shown in a small gallery: the first (the cycle "20 July 1944") translated the concrete political event, the assassination of the men involved in the revolt against Hitler, into a general interpretation of human sorrow; the other (the cycle "qui s'explique") became the occasion for a demonstration of anti-constitutional bigotry. The punishment of the artist for "pornography" brought his into public view, although he shuns rather than seeks publicity. The event has in no way influenced the development of his work.

In the early 1960's Wunderlich next varied the poetic, macabre, erotic themes with graphic works ("Francois Villon," "Leda," "Kleine Anatomie," among others), and then around 1964 he began an essential phase in his painting. Wunderlich strives for a painterly line away from traditional peinture by frequent use of the spray gun. The stimulus for his pictures is artificial reality, whether it be the artistic photographs of his wife Karin Szekessy or pictures by kindred spirits (Runge, the Fontainebleau school, Leonardo, Ingres, David, and later on Dürer and Manet). The pictures and coloured lithographs to the *Song of Solomon* may count as an initial high point in Wunderlich's art, soon followed by a second in the paraphrases of Dürer. It is not only concern for style and form, perfection of craft and execution that links Wunderlich to Dürer; in similar fashion, Wunderlich soon became a representative abroad of the art of his native land, mainly in Western Europe, Japan and the United States.

To the themes which are to him already classical, he added, in the 1970's, portraits in which he can demonstrate in exemplary fashion his relationship to reality. Sculpture to him is a further medium—there has not been since Max Ernst any comparable sculptural work carried out by a German painter. Wunderlich's useful objects are also sculpture that more clearly bewitches reality.

—Heinz Spielmann

WYETH, Andrew (Newell).
American. Born in Chadds Ford, Pennsylvania, 12 July 1917. Educated by private tutors; studied art with his father, N. C. Wyeth. Married Betsy Merle James in 1940; children: Nicholas and James. Painter: lives and works in Chadds Ford. Recipient: Dana Watercolor Medal. *Pennsylvania Academy Annual*, Philadelphia, 1947; Award of Merit, American Academy of Arts and Letters, 1947; Second Prize,

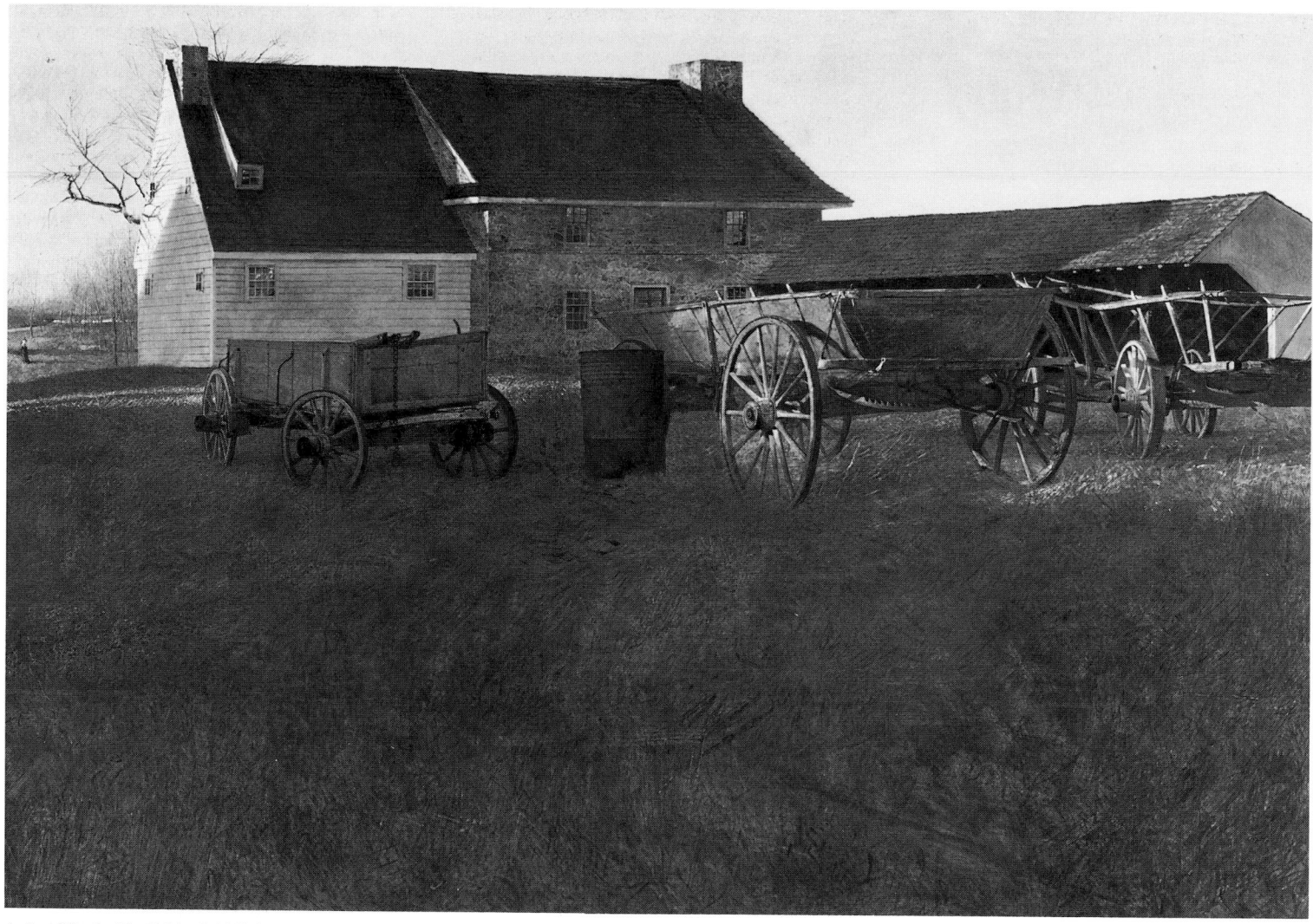

Andrew Wyeth: *Marsh Mawk*, 1964 Courtesy Terra Museum of American Art, Chicago

Painting in the United States, Carnegie Institute, Pittsburgh, 1948; Popular Prize, *Carnegie International*, Pittsburgh, 1958; Presidential Medal of Freedom, 1963; Annual Award, with James Johnson Sweeney, *Art in America*, 1963. D.F.A.: Harvard University, Cambridge, Massachusetts, 1955; Colby College, Waterville, Maine, 1955; Swarthmore College, Pennsylvania, 1958. Member, National Institute of Arts and Letters. Agent: Coe Kerr Gallery Inc., 49 East 82nd Street, New York 10028. Address: Chadds Ford, Pennsylvania 19317,U.S.A.

Individual Exhibitions:

1937	Macbeth Gallery, New York
1938	Macbeth Gallery, New York
	Doll and Richards, Boston
1939	Macbeth Gallery, New York
1940	Doll and Richards, Boston
1941	Macbeth Gallery, New York
1942	Doll and Richards, Boston
1943	Macbeth Gallery, New York
1944	Doll and Richards, Boston
1945	Macbeth Gallery, New York
1946	Doll and Richards, Boston
1948	Macbeth Gallery, New York
1950	Macbeth Gallery, New York
1951	Currier Gallery of Art, Manchester, New Hampshire (retrospective)
	William A. Farnsworth Library and Art Museum, Rockland, Maine (retrospective)
1952	Macbeth Gallery, New York
1953	M. Knoedler and Co., New York
1956	M. H. de Young Memorial Museum, San Francisco (retrospective)

	Santa Barbara Museum of Art, California (retrospective)
1957	Delaware Art Center, Wilmington (retrospective)
1958	M. Knoedler and Co., New York
1960	Charles Hayden Memorial Library, Massachusetts Institute of Technology, Cambridge (retrospective)
1962	Albright-Knox Art Gallery, Buffalo, New York (retrospective)
1963	Fogg Art Museum, Harvard University, Cambridge, Massachusetts (retrospective; toured the United States)
	University of Arizona Art Museum, Tucson
1966	Pennsylvania Academy of Fine Arts, Philadelphia (retrospective; toured the United States)
1970	Musuem of Fine Arts, Boston
1974	National Museum of Modern Art, Tokyo (retrospective)
	Lefevre Gallery, London
	National Museum of Modern Art, Kyoto, Japan
1976	Metropolitan Museum of Art, New York (retrospective)
1981	Station Gallery, Greenville, Connecticut
	Delaware Art Museum, Wilmington
	Brandywine River Museum, Chadds Ford, Pennsylvania
	Greenville County Museum of Art, South Carolina
	Galerie Claude Bernard, Paris
1982	Virginia Art Museum, Richmond
1983	Fort Lauderdale Museum of Art, Florida
	Brooks Museum of Art, Memphis, Tennessee
	Portland Museum of Art, Maine
1984	Brandywine River Museum, Chadds Ford, Pennsylvania
	Funabashi Gallery, Tokyo
	Gallery Iida, Tokyo
1985	Canton Art Institute, Ohio

1987	National Gallery of Art, Washington, D.C.
	Museum of Fine Arts, Boston
1988	Houston Museum of Fine Arts, Texas
	Los Angeles County Museum of Art
	Fine Arts Museum, San Francisco
	Detroit Institute of Arts, Michigan

Selected Group Exhibitions:

1938	*Pennsylvania Academy Annual*, Philadelphia (and frequently until 1963)
1943	*American Realists and Magic Realists*, Museum of Modern Art, New York
1947	*Painting in the United States*, Carnegie Institute, Pittsburgh (and 1948, 1949)
1950	*Carnegie International*, Pittsburgh (and 1952, 1958, 1961, 1964)
1959	*American Painting and Sculpture*, Moscow
1963	*Dunn International*, Beaverbrook Art Gallery, Fredericton, New Brunswick (travelled to the Tate Gallery, London)
1964	*Between the Fairs: 25 Years of American Art 1939-64*, Whitney Museum, New York
1965	*N. C. Wyeth and the Brandywine Tradition*, William Penn Memorial Museum, Harrisburg, Pennsylvania
1971	*The Brandywine Heritage*, Brandywine River Museum, Chadds Ford, Pennsylvania
1974	*10 Americans*, Andrew Crispo Gallery, New York

Collections:

Brandywine River Museum, Chadds Ford, Pennsylvania; Metropolitan Museum of Art, New York; Museum of Modern Art, New York; Museum of Fine Arts, Boston; Wadsworth Atheneum, Hartford, Connecticut; Currier Gallery of Art, Manchester, New Hampshire; Philadelphia Museum of Art; North Carolina Museum of Art, Raleigh; Art Institute of Chicago; Museum of Fine Arts, Houston.

Publications:

By WYETH: article—"Andrew Wyeth", interview, with George Plimpton and Donald Stewart, in *Horizon* (New York), September 1961.

On WYETH: books—*The Brandywine Tradition* by Henry C. Pitz, Boston 1969; *Andrew Wyeth from Public and Private Collections*, exhibition catalogue with introduction by M. J. Albacete, Canton, Ohio 1985; *Andrew Wyeth: The Helga Pictures* by John Wilmerding, New York 1987; articles— "Andrew Wyeth" by Lloyd Goodrich in *Art in America* (New York), October 1955; "Andrew Wyeth" by Henry C. Pitz in *American Artist* (New York), November 1958; "Andrew Wyeth" by Eliot Clark in *Studio* (London), December 1960; "The Four Seasons: Dry-Brush Drawings by Andrew Wyeth" by Lloyd Goodrich in *Art in America* (New York), no. 2, 1962; "New Light in Andrew Wyeth" by James W. Fosburgh in *Artnews* (New York), November 1962; "The Drawings of Andrew Wyeth" by Agnes Morgan in *American Artist* (New York), September 1963; "Andrew Wyeth" by E. P. Richardson in the *Atlantic* (Boston), June 1964; "Andrew Wyeth" by Brian O'Doherty in *Show* (New York), May 1965; article in *Current Biography*, New York 1981.

*   *   *

Not many artists in the 20th century, like their 16th century predecessors, have made good by staying home. Andrew Wyeth, born in Chadds Fork, Pennsylvania, is one such exception; his address in 1988 is still Chadds Ford. In more ways than one his fixed place of residence is symptomatic of his art. His father, N. C. Wyeth, was the pupil of Howard Pyle in that sleepy village and set up his own studio as an illustrator of the historical and romantic episodes of the Union's days of glory and struggle. Andrew, born and brought up in a home where art belonged, had no need to sever family ties to develop his own brand of imagery. His father taught him the techniques; his attitudes grew undisturbed by the pressures of the past or the competitions of the present among young artists in the cities. Pennsylvania alternated with summer sojourns in Maine and between the two localities the younger Wyeth's art grew along the parallel media of water-colour and tempera.

In water-colour the format is usually small and the landscape is the favorite motive. Often it is in the winter fields under snow where the gradual thawing presents a bonus to the artist in the metamorphosis in the changing colour of the ground and the melting tracery of frost-etched foliage.

In 1937–38 Wyeth held his first one-man shows in Boston and in New York. Since then he has exhibited all over the United States and abroad with success without ever failing, once the sterling character of his work became recognized for its consistency and unadulterated painterly quality. Never engaged in the equivocal dialogue of contemporary viability of experiment and discovery, Wyeth's accomplishments have been the seemingly archaic devotion to the search for perfection within a chosen system of conventions owing most to the native American tradition and its personal interpretation by a mind unswayed by art politics of any kind. This concentration of means and directions endows his paintings with the airless atmosphere of a studio where each brush stroke is meditated and deliberated before it takes its place in the canvas with the irrevocable logic of a segment in a jigsaw puzzle.

Sometimes there is a hint of contrived symbolism as in the picture of "Young America," the much exhibited painting of 1950. In this panel the young man rides his bicycle across the open pasture land. He wears a sundowner hat, one side clipped up by a quasi-military badge, and above his head flies a bright tricolour burgee from the long strut rising from the front hub. This mood of adolescent nostalgia for the pioneering past and the battles of adventurous frontiers seems dated now, but it is at one with the somewhat naive innocence of a genre tied firmly to sentiment and homebound associations.

In less allusive interiors and landscapes without figures Wyeth works in a restricted palette. His realism is of a totally composed scene in which every inch of surface plays its integral part towards the final impression. Its radical compass is short but magnetic. One can share the artist's serious passion in a reconstruction dictated by retinal plotting, leaving not only the memorable image but also a superlative material equivalent.

—G. S. Whittet

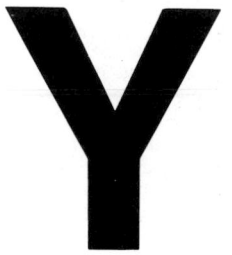

Y

YAMADA, Masaaki.

Japanese. Born in Tokyo in 1930. Studied with the artist Saburo Hasegawa, Tokyo, 1953; studied at Tokyo University, 1954. Independent painter, Tokyo, since 1954. Agent: Satani Gallery, Asahi Building 11 BF, 2-6, 4-chome, Ginza, Chuo-ku, Tokyo 104. Address: 1-3-16 Hikari-cho, Kokubunji, Tokyo 185, Japan.

Individual Exhibitions:

1958	Kyobunkan Gallery, Tokyo
1960	Yoseido Gallery, Tokyo (and 1962, 1963)
1964	Nantenshi Gallery, Tokyo
1965	Tsubaki Kindai Gallery, Tokyo
1966	Muramatsu Gallery, Tokyo
1968	Gallery Cristal, Tokyo
1978	Koh Gallery, Tokyo
1979	Satani Gallery, Tokyo (and 1980, 1981, 1982)
1982	Kasahara Gallery, Osaka, Japan
1983	Inoue Gallery, Tokyo
	Satani Gallery, Tokyo (and 1984, 1985)
1985	Gallery Yonetsu, Tokyo (twice)
1986	Inoue Gallery, Tokyo
	Satani Gallery, Tokyo (and 1987, 1988)
	Gallery Yonetsu, Tokyo (and 1987)
1988	Galerie Springer, West Berlin

Selected Group Exhibitions:

1949	*Yomiuri Independent Show*, Tokyo Metropolitan Museum of Art (and regularly until 1953)
1950	*Jiyu Bijutsu-ka Kyokai Association Show*, Tokyo Metropolitan Museum of Art (and regularly until 1956)
1963	*4th Ecole de Tokyo Exhibition*, Jewish Center Hall, Los Angeles
1969	*9th Contemporary Art Exhibition of Japan*, Tokyo Metropolitan Museum of Art
1972	*Modern Japanese Graphic Art*, Institute of Contemporary Arts, London
1974	*Japan: Tradition und Gegenwart*, Stadtische Kunsthalle, Dusseldorf
1980	*Variations on Planar Painting*, Fukuoka Art Museum, Japan
1984	*Contemporary Art: Tokyo/Paris*, Galerie Denise Rene, Paris
1985	*Japanese Contemporary Paintings*, Museum of Modern Art, New Delhi
1987	*19th Bienal de Sao Paulo*, Brazil

Collections:

National Museum of Modern Art, Tokyo; Museum of Modern Art, Toyama; Miyagi Museum of Art; Museum of Modern Art, Shiga; Museum of Modern Art, Saitama; Kitakyushu Municipal Museum of Art; Seibu Museum, Tokyo; Ohara Museum, Kurashiki; Seibu Museum, Karuizawa; Takamatsu Municipal Museum of Art.

Publications:

On YAMADA: books—*Japan: Tradition und Gegenwart*, exhibition catalogue with texts by Jurgen Harten and Joseph Love, Dusselforf 1974; *Masaaki Yamada's Paintings 1950-1980*, exhibition catalogue with text by Takashi Hayami, Tokyo 1981; *Masaaki Yamada: Works 1985-86*, exhibition catalogue edited by the Satani Gallery, Tokyo 1986; *Yamada: Paintings of the Late 1950s*, exhibition catalogue with essay by Tazmi Shinoda, Tokyo 1986; *19th Bienal Internacional de Sao Paulo: Japan*, exhibition catalogue with text by Yoshiaki Tono, Sao Paulo 1987.

In my work during the mid-1960s, paintings were examined within certain constraints as a condensation of an autonomous structure expressed by the act of painting. The opposition to color is seen in the merging of material and method and includes the brushstrokes and use of repressed color. The objective quality, which interacts with form and content through the use of things like crosses and stripes, is looked at from a position that lies in opposition to the real world, as I sought to indicate the fundamental meaning that paintings establish. The restraint, however, cannot be traced to silence. My later works reflect a shift toward previously anticipated colors and stratified forms; selecting a certain point in the midst of the endless flow of time tells where I was at a given time. A compelling feeling of diversity is incorporated in the paintings.

—Masaaki Yamada

Ever since the 1950s, Masaaki Yamada's paintings have been the best example that shows the intellectual essence of the abstract paintings in Japan. Surprisingly enough, his marvelous achievements have not been shared with a lot of people in the art circles in Japan until the 1970s. He has remained aloof from any other artist or movement, creating high-standard substantial paintings by himself which miraculously corresponded with those of some modernist painters in America.

Yamada was born in Tokyo in 1930 and studied at Tokyo University. He studied painting with Saburo Hasegawa, one of the pioneering abstractionists in prewar Japan. However, Yamada's existent canvases retain no evidences that he made paintings under the major influence of Hasegawa. It is notable that he kept apart from any influence of not only the Japanese abstract painters in the prewar period, but also his contemporary abstractionists in Japan in the postwar era which, in a sense, was strongly affected by the idea of the *Informel* movement advocated and introduced to Japan by the French critic/painter Michel Tapié. The ideas of *Informel* and Action Painting in the United States in the '40s and '50s rapidly assimilated into Japanese avant-garde art, and evolved into the Dadaistic movement in 1960s.

Yamada stood detached and was making his analytic paintings with great subtlety which many other Japanese contemporaries were apt to ignore. He stuck to painting and explored the pictorial heritage of Cubism and Cézanne all by himself.

Early in the 1950s, he started still lifes with very limited information of Cézanne and Giorgio Morandi, but soon decomposed the subjects in analytic manner which he acquired instinctively from Cubist methodology. The surface of his painting attained the pictorial unity with flat, decomposed and geometric forms. It was 1956 when he destroyed every simplistic geometric form and began the intricate mosaic painting with numerous small broken planes. But in order to maintain stability of the painted surface, he took the constructive direction in 1957 instead of destructive. His paintings in 1958 consisted of squares and rectangles that looked like nested boxes with different colors, most of which could be regarded as the similitudes of the canvas shapes. Those works remind us of paintings by Josef Albers, but it was not until 1965 that Yamada actually saw the works by the modernist painter. Probably Yamada's idea had the affinity with not so much Albers's as Ad Reinhardt's.

The vertical and lateral elements which were introduced to stabilize the picture developed in the first half of the 1960s into the paintings of the lateral stripes in various colors. The paintings with crossed lines followed from 1965 to 1967, which actually consisted of four painted square planes in monochrome arranged at right angles, leaving the ground in a different color in the shape of the narrowest crossed lines.

From 1968 to 1973 his canvases resumed stripes, but only in two colors with the thinner surface. Next six years until 1978 was replaced by the paintings of checkered-flag pattern, retaining the thinly painted surface in two colors of adjacent values. It has been pointed out that in this period Yamada allowed his paintings to approach nearest to 'objecthood', naturally with the great affinity to the Minimalist paintings.

Liberation of free-hand drawings began in 1979 and developed into the splendid variety of strokes and colors in the paintings in the 1980s. In the first half of the eighties, his canvases retained the segmentations by square lines, limiting his free-hand drawing lines in each division with the ground of subtle but rather restrained colors. However, since 1985, the segmenting square lines have reduced to the scattering crosses, and lavish drawings in rich colors spread over the canvas, making the painting an optical ravishment. It should not be overlooked that Yamada's exuberant works have been accomplished with the excellent texture and soft-hued, creamy colors, and they could be only possible through the Japanese sensibility.

—Tazmi Shinoda

YAMAGUCHI, Takeo.

Japanese. Born in Seoul, Korea, 23 November 1902. Studied at the Tokyo School of Art, 1922-27; also studied in France, 1927-31. Independent painter, working in Seoul, 1931-45, and in Tokyo, 1945 until

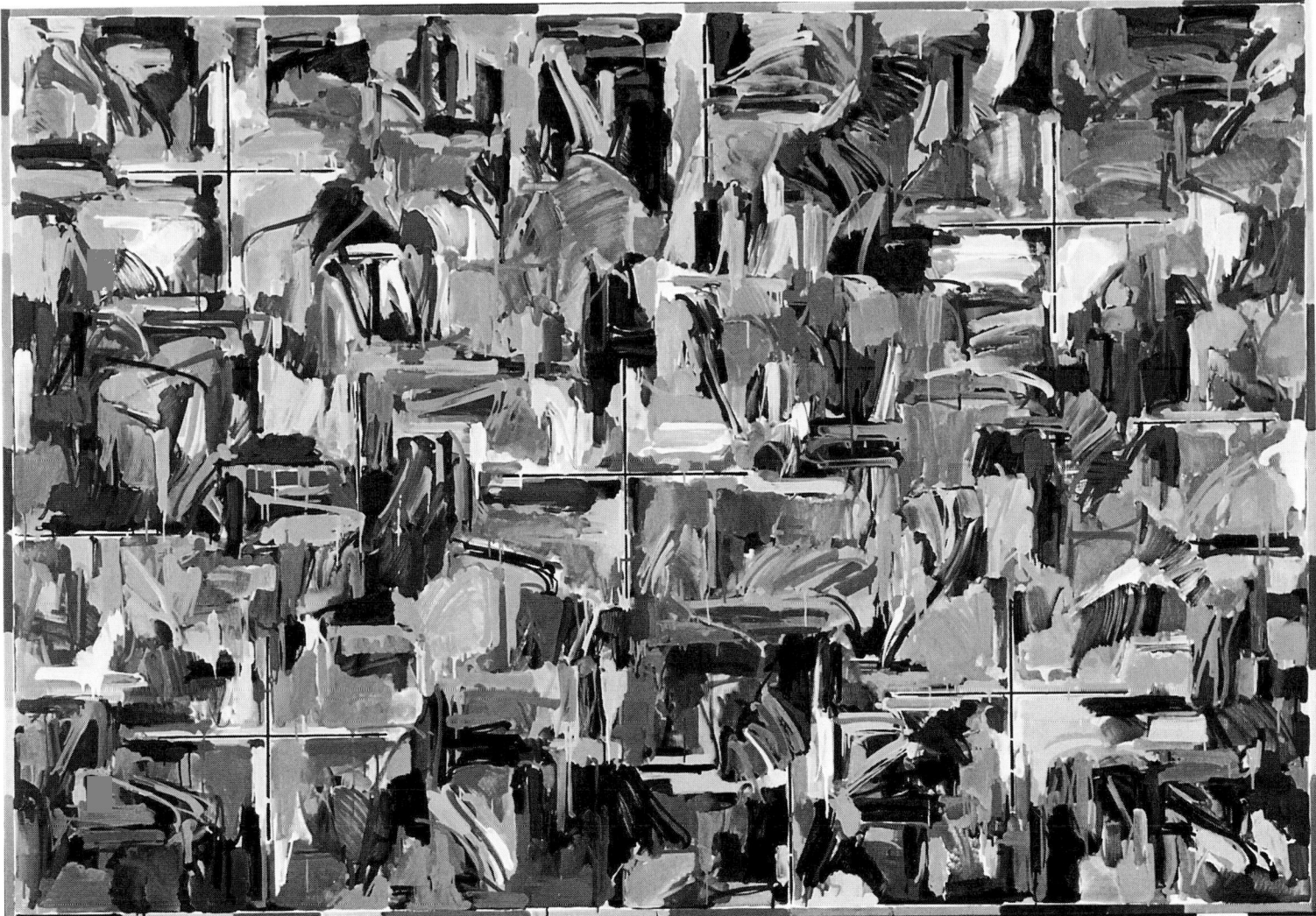

Masaaki Yamada: *Work E. 277, 1987*

his death in 1983: associated with the Nikka group of artists, Tokyo, from 1938. Professor, Musashino Art College, Tokyo, 1954-74. From 1974, Honorary Instructor, Tama Art College, Tokyo. Recipient: First Prize, *Contemporary Japanese Art Exhibition*, Tokyo, 1954; Guggenheim International Award, 1958. *Died (in Tokyo) in 1983*.

Individual Exhibitions:

1939	Seijusha, Tokyo
1961	Minami Gallery, Tokyo
1965	Minami Gallery, Tokyo
1968	Musashino Art College, Tokyo
	Minami Gallery, Tokyo
1969	Nihonbashi Gallery, New York
1972	Minami Gallery, Tokyo
1975	Minami Gallery, Tokyo
1980	National Museum of Modern Art, Tokyo (retrospective; with Masakazu Horiuti)

Selected Group Exhibitions:

1954	*Annual Exhibition*, American Artists Society, New York
	Contemporary Japanese Art, Tokyo
1955	*Bienal*, Sao Paulo
1956	*Biennale*, Venice
1963	*Bienal*, Sao Paulo
1965	*New Japanese Painting and Sculpture*, travelling exhibition (toured the United States)
	Modern Japanese Painting, Kunsthaus, Zurich
1970	*Expo*, Museum of Fine Arts, Osaka, Japan

Collections:

National Museum of Modern Art, Tokyo; Ohara Museum of Art, Kurashiki, Japan; Museum of Modern Art, Kamakura, Japan; Museum of Contemporary Art, Nagaoka, Japan; Museum of Modern Art, New York; Guggenheim Museum, New York.

Publications:

By YAMAGUCHI: article—"Various Confessions: Why I Use the Color Brown" in *Geijutsu Shincho* (Tokyo), October 1976.

On YAMAGUCHI: book—*Yamaguchi/Horiuti*, exhibition catalogue, with an essay by Tamon Miki, Tokyo 1980; articles— "From Wandering: Opened His Eyes to Abstract Painting" by S. Miyake in *Bijutsu Techo* (Tokyo), 1958; "The Art of Takeo Yamaguchi: The Unworldly Spirit and its Forms" by T. Uemura in *Mizue* (Tokyo), 1968.

*

Takeo Yamaguchi, a Japanese painter born in Seoul in Korea in 1902, was one of the leading figures in the country who plowed their way of abstraction through the postwar period up to the end of 1970s.

He left his home in Seoul for Tokyo in 1921 to study at the Tokyo School of Fine Art, the former institute of the Tokyo University of Fine Art, in which he enrolled in 1922 and took a classic training for five years. Soon after graduation in 1927, he went to France, counting on a Japanese expressionist painter in Paris, Yuzo Saeki, and stayed in and around Paris until 1930. He frequently visited the atelier of Ossip Zadkine, but there is no evident influence from the artist or other contemporary painters, for example, Picasso, Braque, Leger, Klee, Soutine, Picabia and Lipchitz, whose works Yamaguchi came to admire.

He settled in his home in Seoul again in 1931, where he was due to succeed his wealthy family business, farming and forestry. In that year, he sent the Nika Exhibition in Tokyo ten paintings, two of which were accepted. He continued, while engaging himself in the family business with tenant farmers working in the vast paddy field, to send his works to the exhibition every year until Japan's participation in the World War II in 1941 made it impossible for him to continue shipping paintings. Most of his paintings in this early stage were those in which a dozen of slow, small daubs or quick, narrow brushstrokes in yellow, blue, red, green and black were sporadically strewed over white backgrounds. (*Pond* (1936), *Garden A* (1936))

He was drafted into the army in 1945, but the war ended in that year, forcing him to abandon all the property in Seoul and be repatriated to Japan. He settled in Tokyo, resumed painting for Nika Exhibition, and became one of the important members of the group.

A new stage opened up when he introduced thick and dark, mostly black backgrounds into his postwar abstract paintings with a few oval shapes or distorted strips in yellow, white, red or brown pigment flatly overlayed with a painting knife. (*Shape* (1952)).

It is noteworthy that after 1953 he had limited his colors in a single work to only two, either yellow ochre with black or Venetian red with black. The artist had recollected that the yellow ochre reflected the characteristic color in China; on the other hand, the red, the color in Korea. And these peculiar colors as well as the limitation of colors to two had never changed until his death in 1983.

Up to the last half of the 1950s he made his own paintings with a thick, multi-layered surface consisting of black background with clear-cut, extended series of bands in red or yellow, many of them cornered almost at right angles, sometimes curved in boomerang shape, sometimes with an isolated circle like an island, as if the bands were making flat circuit-ways on dark cosmic space. (*Composition* (1955), *Yellow Shape* (1955)).

Around 1958, the bands in red or yellow began to spread over so that they assumed large quasi-geometric color-fields, putting aside the black background to the outer edges. He advanced the development to such a degree that there were no distinctions between subject and background, and from 1966 the color-field either in yellow ochre or red had begun to dominate over the surface with an impressively small corner area in black, or with a rift painted in black. (*Red Eye* (1959), *Red* (1971), *Track* (1975)).

His paintings in his last 15 years could be associated with color-field painting in Minimalism, but the texture and the color, reminding us of the muddy field, the clay house walls or the earthenware in his birthplace, definitely differ with those in Minimalist painting.

He had been a professor at the Musashino College of Fine Art in Tokyo from 1954 to 1974. He was selected as a Japanese artist for the third São Paolo Biennial in 1955, the 7th in 1963, and the 28th Venetian Biennial in 1956.

—Tazmi Shinoda

YOKOMI, Richard (Koji).

American. Born in Denver, Colorado, 12 March 1944. Studied at the Chouinard Art Institute, Los Angeles, 1962–65, B.A. 1965. Married Shigemi Susie Sasaki. Painter: lives and works in Los Angeles. Agents: Nicholas Wilder Gallery. 8225 Santa Monica Boulevard, Los Angeles, California 90046; and Felicity Samuel Gallery, 16 Savile Row, London WIXIAE, England. Address: 3666 Division Street, Los Angeles, California 90065, U.S.A.

Individual Exhibitions:

1969	Nicholas Wilder Gallery, Los Angeles
1970	Joseph Helman Gallery, St. Louis
1971	Jill Kornblee Gallery, New York
	Galerie Neuendorf, Cologne
1972	Nicholas Wilder Gallery, Los Angeles
1973	Felicity Samuel Gallery, London
1974	Nicholas Wilder Gallery, Los Angeles
1975	Seder/Creigh Gallery, Coronado, California

Selected Group Exhibitions:

1971   *Color and Scale*, Oakland Museum of Art, California
1972   *U.S.A. West Coast*, Galerie Neuendorf, Cologne
Southern California Attitudes 1972, Pasadena Museum of Art, California
1974   *15 Abstract Artists*, Santa Barbara Museum of Art, California
1975   *Current Concerns*, Los Angeles Institute of Contemporary Art
1976   *Painting and Sculpture in California: The Modern Era*, San Francisco Museum of Modern Art (travelled to the Smithsonian Institution, Washington, D.C., 1977)

Collections:

Norton Simon Museum of Art, Pasadena, California.

Publications:

On YOKOMI: articles—"Los Angeles: Richard Yokomi, Nicholas Wilder Gallery" by Peter Plagens in *Artforum* (New York, September/October 1974.

YOSHIDA, Kenji.

Japanese. Born in Osaka, 24 May 1924. Studied pedagogy, University of Osaka, 1939–44; studied with Stanley Hayter, Atelier 17, Paris, 1964–72; also influenced by the painter Hayashi Kiyoshi and the Spanish sculptor Apel-Les Fenosa. Served as an Ensign Second Class in the Japanese Marine Corps, 1943–44. Married Hiroko Uehara in 1973; daughter: Kiyoko. Teacher in Osaka, 1945–51, and Tokyo, 1952–64. Full-time artist, living and working in Paris, since 1964. Recipient: Norwegian Government Grant, Oslo, 1966. Agent: Galerie Hexagramme, 67b rue des Saints-Peres, 75006 Paris. Address: 49 rue de la Procession, 75015 Paris, France.

Individual Exhibitions:

1957	Muramatsu Gallery, Tokyo
1958	Muramatsu Gallery, Tokyo
1959	Muramatsu Gallery, Tokyo
1960	Muramatsu Gallery, Tokyo
1964	Takegawa Gallery, Tokyo
1966	Galerie Hammerlund, Oslo
1968	Museum of Japanese Art, Haifa, Israel
1971	Galerie St.-Johann, Saarbrucken, West Germany
1972	Linz Museum, Austria
1973	Seibu Gallery, Tokyo
1974	Galerie Modern-Art, Vienna
1976	Fuji Yoshi Gallery, Tokyo
1977	Galerie L'Estampille, Brussels
	Galerie Point W, Gallard, France
1979	Galerie Aujourd'hui, Geneva
1982	Atelier Alma, Lyon, France
	Ecole de Francais, Geneva
1983	Gallery Art-Houre, Tokyo
	Gallery Beni, Kyoto, Japan
	Gallery Taiken, Osaka, Japan
1984	Galerie Galise, Thonon, France
1986	Galerie Galise, Thonon, France
1987	Galerie Galise, at *FIAC 87*, Grank Palais, Paris

Selected Group Exhibitions:

1965   *Graphics Biennale*, Moderna Galerija, Ljubljana, Yugoslavia
1966   *Graphics Biennale*, Modern Museum, Cracow, Poland
Nordisk Grafik Union, Kunstforening, Oslo
1967   *Graphics Biennale*, Kunstverein, Grenchen, Switzerland
1968   *Wiener Sezession Grafika*, Wiener Sezession, Vienna
1970   *Print International*, Kunstverein, Frechen, West Germany
1974   *Graphik Klein-Plastik*, Kunstlerhaus, Vienna
1976   *Exposition International*, Maison de la Culture, Berck-Piage, France
1984   *Actu, Art 84*, Galerie Galise, Thonon, France (and 1985, 1986, 1987)
1986   *Contemporary Art:Japan/Denmark*, Konstmuseum, Copenhagen

Collections:

Bibliotheque Nationale, Paris; Ministere des Affaires Culturelles, Paris; Bibliotheque Royale, Brussels; Museum Louviers, France; Museum of Modern Art, Norrkoping, Sweden; Kunst pa Arbeidsplassen, Oslo; Bergen Art Association, Norway; Kunstverein, Frechen, West Germany; Museum of Modern Art, Skopje, Yugoslavia; Museum of Japanese Art, Haifa, Israel.

Kenji Yoshida: *La Vie*, 1980

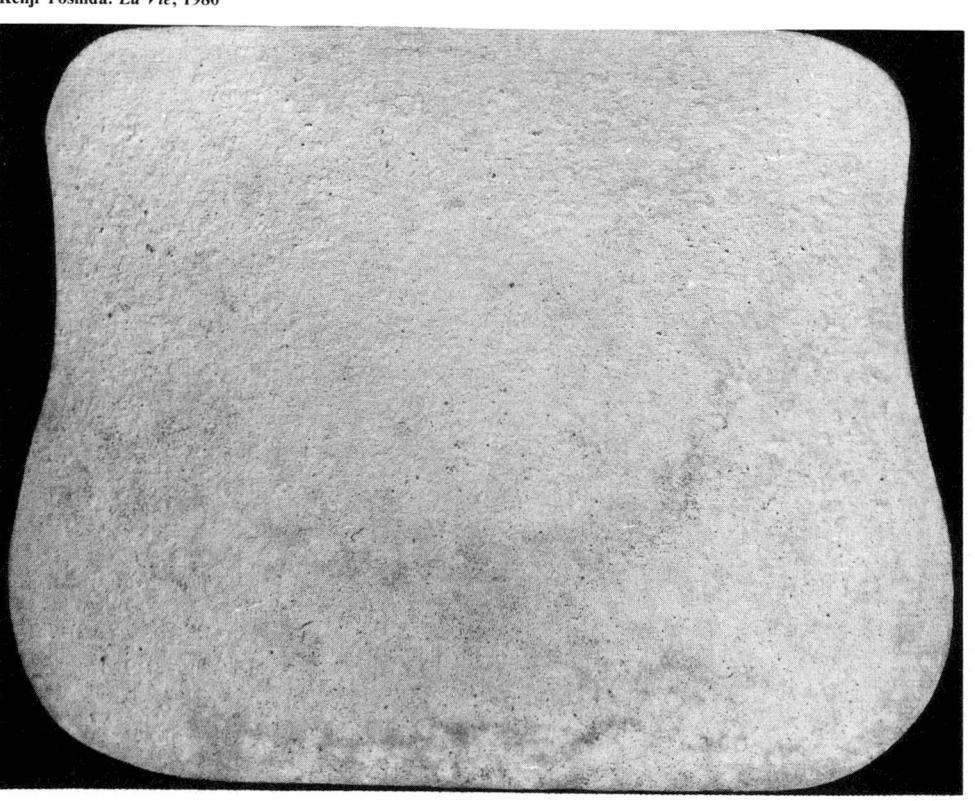

Publications:

On YOSHIDA: book—*Kenji Yoshida: La Vie,* exhibition catalogue with texts by Tadashi Fukuda, Joseph Paul Schneider and others, Thonon 1986; article—"My Friend Yoshida" by Uehara Kaza in *Sansai* (Tokyo), January 1974.

I was born in a farmhouse. I was brought up surrounded by sun, water, earth and men who knew how to work. So then I knew that man can not live without nature and can do nothing without nature . . . nature which runs according to laws on the cosmos that all things obey.

The movement of the cosmos is equal to the movement of life on a smaller scale.

The ancients called it "the voice of God".

The voice makes itself heard in nature and within me. It exists in all things.

When man moves with this voice in harmony with the movement of the cosmos, peace will come.

Therefore, we must have an attitude of moderation towards all things and all men.

I took part in the Second World War, and I found myself facing death and I saw the horrors of war. So, I had to think.

What is life? What is peace? Happily, I survived. I looked for the point of harmony of the voice within myself.

I think that it is my mission, and it is hard for me.

It is difficult to explain the spirit of Japan to a European. So I must say it on canvas.

One can only judge one's own feelings—isn't that right?

—Kenji Yoshida

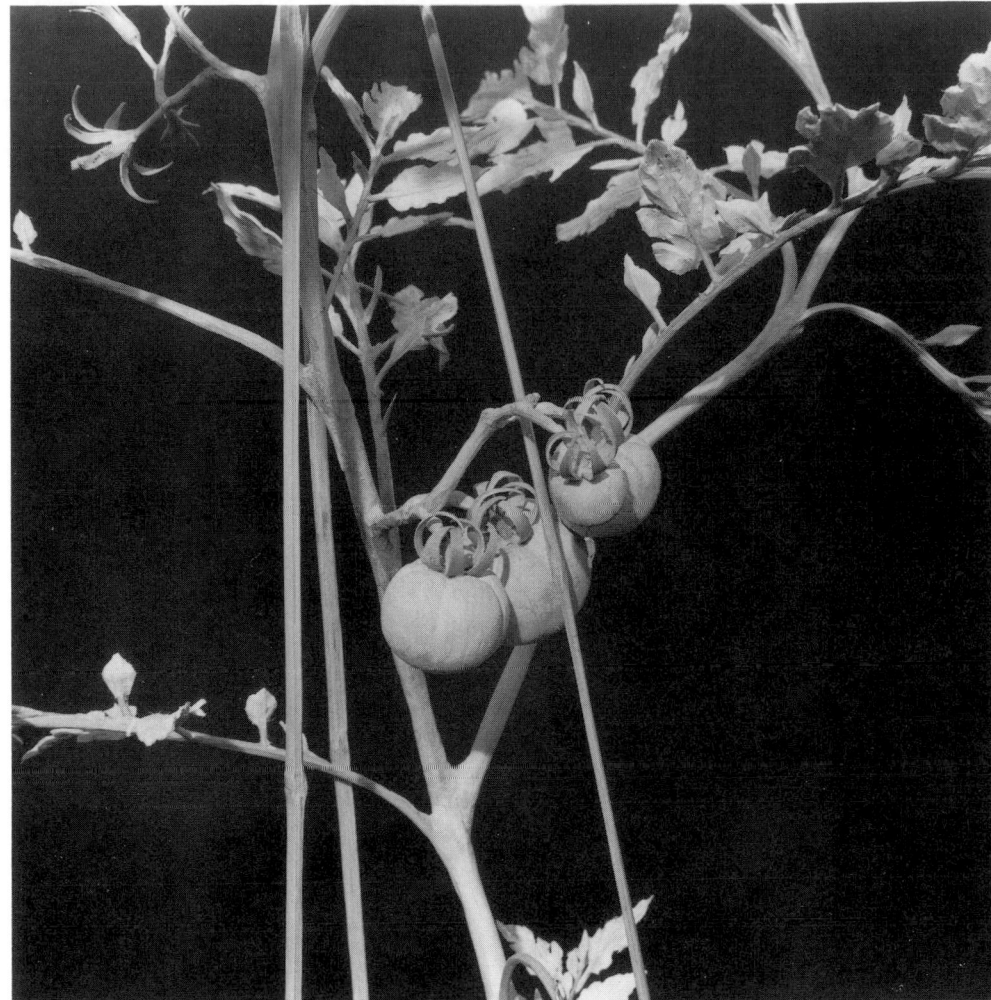

Fumio Yoshimura: *Tomato,* 1987

YOSHIMURA, Fumio.

Japanese. Born in Kamakura, 22 February 1926. Studied at Tokyo National University of Art, 1941–49, M.F.A. 1949. Served as Cadet in Japanese Imperial Army, 1945. Married Yoshiko Oshima in 1951 (died, 1963); married the American writer Kate Millett in 1965 (divorced, 1986); married Carol Ann Watkinson in 1987. Independent artist, Tokyo, 1950–61, and in New York since 1962: first realist wood sculptures, 1970. Taught kite-making at Brookfield Craft Center, Connecticut during summers, 1965–70; Assistant Professor, Dartmouth College, Hanover, New Hampshire, since 1982. Recipient: Faculty Research Grant, Dartmouth College, 1984, 1985. Addresses: 5 East Third Street, New York, New York 10003; R.R. 1, Box 139, Academy Road, Thetford, Vermont 05075, U.S.A.

Individual Exhibitions:

1950	Maramatsu Gallery, Tokyo (and yearly until 1958)
1970	Pennsylvania Academy of Fine Arts, Philadelphia
1971	Wichita Art Museum, Kansas
1972	Marian Locks Gallery, Philadelphia
1973	Nancy Hoffman Gallery, New York
1974	Galerie Arneson, Copenhagen
1975	Galeriet, Lund, Sweden
1976	Squibb Gallery, Princeton, New Jersey
	Nancy Hoffman Gallery, New York
1977	Marian Locks Gallery, Philadelphia
1978	Norton Gallery of Art, West Palm Beach, Florida
1979	Amherst College, Massachusetts
	Nancy Hoffmen Gallery, New York
1981	Beaumont and May Gallery, Dartmouth College, Hanover, New Hampshire
1983	Nancy Hoffman Gallery, New York
1984	Mitchell Museum, Mount Vernon, Illinois
1985	Atlantic Center of the Arts, New Smyrna Beach, Florida
1986	Windsor House, Vermont
1987	Temple Gallery, Philadelphia

Selected Group Exhibitions:

1968	*Made with Paper,* Museum of Contemporary Crafts, New York
1973	*Made with Wood,* Dartmouth College, Hanover, New Hampshire
1974	*New/Photo Realism,* Wadsworth Atheneum, Hartford, Connecticut
1976	*Object as Poet,* Renwick Gallery, Smithsonian Institution, Washington, D.C.
1979	*Illusion and Material,* Paterson College, Wayne, New Jersey
1981	*Katachi,* Albuquerque Museum of Art, New Mexico
1982	*Contemporary Realism,* Pennsylvania Academy of Fine Arts, Philadelphia
1983	*Materials and Illusion/Unlikely Materials,* Taft Museum, Cincinnati, Ohio
1985	*Fine Woodwork,* Filbrook Art Museum, Tulsa, Oklahoma
1987	*Four Wood Sculptors,* Kansas City Art Institute, Missouri

Collections:

Albright Knox Gallery, Buffalo, New York; Pennsylvania Academy of Fine Art, Philadelphia; Philadelphia Museum of Art; Taft Museum, Cincinnati, Ohio; Go Vett-Brewster Gallery, New Plymouth, New Zealand; Power Gallery of Contemporary Art, Sydney, Australia; Albuquerque Museum of Art, New Mexico; Delaware Art Museum, Wilmington; Mississippi Museum of Art, Jackson; Norton Gallery of Art, West Palm Beach, Florida.

Publications:

On YOSHIMURA: books—*New/Photo Realism,* exhibition catalogue, by Jack Cowart, Hartford, Connecticut, 1974; *Su-per Realism: A Critical Anthology,* edited by Gregory Battcock, New York 1975; *Super Realism* by Edward Lucie Smith, Oxford 1977; *Superrealist Painting and Sculpture* by Christine Lindsey, New York 1980; *Masters of Wood Sculpture* by Nicholas Rourkes, New York 1980; *Wood Working: The New Wave* by Dona Z. Meilach, New York 1981; *Poetry of the Physical,* exhibition catalogue by Paul Smith, New York 1986.

*

In 1970 Fumio Yoshimura began making illusionistic wooden sculptures using the forms of real objects covering a range of subjects from bicycles to tomato plants. Yoshimura had been a painter from around 1948, but it is for his sculpture that he became known.

Yoshimura turns readymade and organic forms into hand made simulations. The element of imitation is co-existent with an element of removal in his finely crafted, smooth wooden substitutes for the real thing. The works are both accurate to their models and modified by the translation into natural, untreated wood. (He prefers linden spruce and pine.) Yoshimura shows considerable involvement with literal depiction, but he is more concerned with close approximation than with scrupulously accurate reduplication down to the last details. This factor, along with the neutralizing colorlessness and smooth graining of the wood, place the appearance of reality at a distance. "I'm reproducing a ghost," Yoshimura has noted, and the sculptures have a disembodied quality achieved through the materials and the handmade craftsmanship which both imitate the original subject/object and simultaneously place it within a new level of artificiality.

"Motorcycle" (1973), "Typewriter" (1975), "Bicycle with Parking Meter" (1978) originate from precise working drawings, are made a part at a time and are assembled like the industrial objects they represent. The finished works are sensuously organic, solid yet soft wood, removed from the mobility and use of their models, and turned into three-dimensional objects of contemplation. There is an element of irony in Yoshimura's reversal process, a Zen-like move from the subjective particular to the objective general. He questions perception and the real nature of literal presence.

Yoshimura's work has obvious likenesses with Jasper Johns, George Segal and Claes Oldenburg. Yet, he remains closer to the literal than any of these artists, and he avoids the rough-edged wistfulness of Segal and the flamboyant Pop comedy of Oldenburg. Yoshimura's kind of Realism differs also from the deceptive mimicry central to the work of Duane Hanson or the Photo-Realists. Yoshimura reverses the Duchampian idea of the readymade, transforming it into the hand-crafted artifact. Illusionism is tempered; both organic forms and hard, metal, working objects are slowly and deliberately crafted into sleek, smooth, naturally grained presences, apparitions hovering in suspended animation on the border between becoming and being.

—Barbara Cavaliere

YOUNG, Peter (Ford).

American. Born in Pittsburgh, Pennsylvania, 2 January 1940. Studied at Chouinard Art Institute, Los Angeles, 1957; Pomona College, Claremont, California, 1958–60; Art Students League, New York, 1960; New York University, 1961–63, B.A. 1963. Influenced by Dynaton Group (Lee Mullican, Onslow Ford and Wolfgang Paalen). Independent painter practicing a formal abstraction rooted in study of primitive design and mysticism: lived and worked in New York, 1960–70, in Bisbee, Arizona, since 1970. Visiting Artist, Oberlin College, Ohio, 1970; Pima College, Tucson, Arizona, 1976. Agents: Leo Castelli, 420 West Broadway, New York, New York 10012; and Oil and Steel Gallery, 157 Chambers Street, New York, New York 10012. Address: Box 715, Bisbee, Arizona 85603, U.S.A.

Individual Exhibitions:

1968	Nicholas Wilder Gallery, Los Angeles
	Galerie Ricke, Cologne
1969	*Peter Young/David Diao*, Leo Castelli Gallery, New York
1970	Goldowsky Gallery, New York
1972	Galerie Ricke, Cologne
	Goldowsky Gallery, New York
	Greenberg Gallery, St. Louis
1974	Goldowsky Gallery, New York
1975	Texas Gallery, Houston
1980	Cochise Fine Arts, Bisbee, Arizona
1981	Leo Castelli Gallery, New York

Selected Group Exhibitions:

1967	*Painting Annual*, Whitney Museum, New York
1968	*Documenta 4*, Kassel, West Germany
1969	*31st Biennial*, Corcoran Gallery, Washington, D.C.
	9 Young Artists, Guggenheim Museum, New York
	The Development of Modernist Painting: Jackson Pollock to Present, Steinberg Art Gallery, Washington University, St. Louis
	One Tendency of Contemporary Art, Kunstmart, Cologne
1971	*6 Painters*, Albright-Knox Gallery, Buffalo, New York
1972	*Painting: New Options*, Walker Art Center, Minneapolis, Minnesota
1974	*8 Artists*, Art Museum of South Texas, Corpus Christi

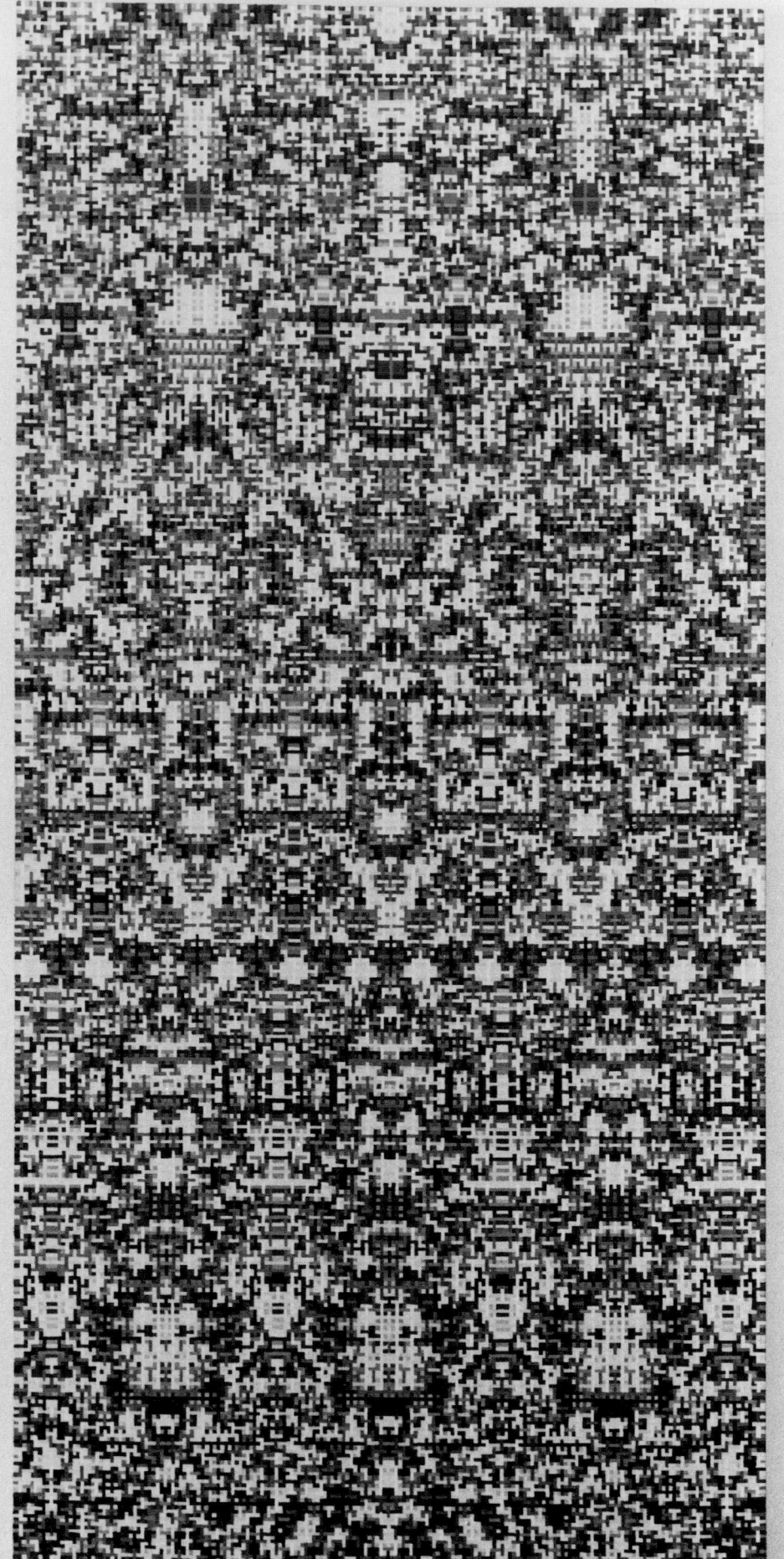

Peter Young: *Linear Weave Painting No. 14*, 1980

Collections:

Museum of Modern Art, New York: Whitney Museum, New York: Guggenheim Museum, New York: Albright-Knox Gallery, Buffalo, New York; Allen Art Museum, Oberlin College, Ohio.

Publications:

By YOUNG: articles—"Artists on Their Art" in *Art International* (Lugano, Switzerland), March 1968; "Peter Young" in *Art Now* (New York), vol. 1, no. 5, 1969.

On YOUNG: Books—*The Triumph of American Painting* by Irving Sandler, New York 1970; *The Twentieth Century (American Painting Vol. 2)* by Barbara Rose. Cleveland 1971; *Introduction to 6 Painters*, exhibition catalogue, by James Wood, Buffalo, New York 1971; articles—"Gallery Without Walls" by Barbara Rose in *Art in America* (New York). March 1968; "David Diao, Peter Young, R. Pettibone" by J. R. Baker in *Arts Magazine* (New York), March 1969; "Diao and Young at Castelli" by Dore Ashton in *Studio International* (London) April 1969; review by Emily Wasserman in *Artforum* (New York), May 1969; "Presenting Peter Young" in *Art in America* (New York), 1969; "Notes on American Painting of the '60s" by Walter Bannard in *Artforum* (New York), January 1970; "New Informalists" by Carter Ratcliff in *Artnews* (New York), February 1970; "Color Abstractionism" by Willis Domingo in *Arts Magazine* (New York), December 1970; "The Spectrum of Monochrome" by Lawrence Alloway in *Arts Magazine* (New York), December 1970; "Peter Young: A Chronology of the Works" by Ellen Johnson in *Artforum* (New York), April 1971; "Materiality and Painterliness" by Gregoire Muller in *Arts Magazine* (New York), September 1971; review by Hayden Herra in *Artnews* (New York), November 1974.

The very greatest art is the "art" of perfecting one's Self.

—Peter Young

Peter Young's involvement with painting began in the early '60's when there seemed to be a preference for coolness and linear abstraction, a reaction fostered by young artists who felt antagonized by the decadence of such late Abstract Expressionists as Bannard, Poons, Stella and Martin—an insistence on "doing the next thing." This became the theoretical enemy of Young.

Young's work has always been involved with a rich sense of history; primitive design, and American Indian and African art are important influences. Although his early work (1963–65) seemed to respond to the linear grid work of his contemporaries, he was to develop a "dot" technique derived from Seurat.

The "dot₆ technique, applied in acrylic, is basically an all-over type of composition which has an edge and corner-to-corner continuity related to the formal aspects of Jackson Pollock's work. The dots are irregular, applied with the tip of a brush; the dots may be marbleized, chained or connected, clustered or fully saturated into the canvas. The dot patterns may suggest constellations or star clusters. An analogy to heavenly bodies is not inconsistent with Young's own rather mystical approach to the mid-60's work. At that time he was concerned with the investigation of light and color on large fields. Working from a white background he developed a series of color studies which achieved the primal light and became the hallmark of his work.

Young is a color painter and considers color to be the one constant in a long series of stylistic experiments from 1965 to 1969. "There are many color painters in my generation who have worked from a mathematical process. My early painting was very pale and white. This had a lot to do with living in New York, having a lot of artificial lighting, and a sort of psychedelic yogic insistence of lightness," he states. His work established a serial format of color composition which was provocative in the midst of work he felt was lacking in warmth and a sense of life.

At the peak of his popularity in 1969, Young left New York to live in a remote Indian village in Costa Rica, then in Utah and New Mexico. Back in New York in early 1970 his work showed a loosening of the dot patterning and a more intense color palette.

After a trip to Morocco and Spain in 1972, a further bread occurred in his work. He began to fold his canvas when it was wet, producing a totemic two-column figural arrangement a la Rorschach. Already the ground of his dot painting had changed from white base to patchwork color base. In these folded works the figural element takes over and is defined not as a nuance but as sculptural form. The over-painting in these folded works was applied with the Pollock splash and drip method.

At some point in the folding process Young began to fold the canvas diagonally as well as vertically. The diagonal folds produce a mandala image. "When I began to fold the canvas I was aware that the sense of lightness I was once working for was not as important," he says. The color of these mandala paintings is deep and thick, recalling tantric manuscripts. The imagery of his paintings in fully integrated with the animation of moving forms. The busy surface of the circular shape is punctuated with hand over-painting and some splash and drip work.

Now in the mandala works there is still an all-over patterning and dotting. "The essence of these works is the centrality and decentrality of the image in various states of focus. The symbol is not specific to Indian culture but to all religious art of the world."

Mysticism and art are unified concepts in a chronology of Young's work. The use of hallucinogens was an additive for Young but only tangential to his belief in universal imagery and the importance of the artist's development of his own decorative motifs.

—Adina Wingate

YOUNGERMAN, Jack.

American. Born in Louisville, Kentucky, 25 March 1926. Studied at the University of North Carolina, Chapel Hill (United States Navy Training Program), 1944–46, and University of Missouri, Columbia, 1947, B.A. 1947; studied at the Académie des Beaux-Arts, Paris, 1947–48. Married Delphine Seyrig in 1950; son: Duncan. Painter and sculptor; lived in Europe, 1947–56; has lived and worked in New York since 1956; designed stage sets for Jean-Louis Barrault's production of *Histoire de Vasco*, Paris, 1956, and *Deathwatch* by Jean Genet, New York, 1958. Artist-in-Residence, Worcester Art Museum, Massachusetts, 1965; Instructor, Yale University, New Haven, Connecticut, 1974–75, and Hunter College, New York, 1981–82. Instructor, New York University, since 1982. Recipient: New Talent Award, *Art in America*, New York, 1959; National Endowment for the Arts Award, 1972; Guggenheim Fellowship, 1976. Agent: Washburn Gallery, New York. Address: c/o Washburn Gallery, 42 East 57th Street, New York, New York 10022, U.S.A.

Individual Exhibitions:

1951	Galerie Arnaud, Paris
1958	Betty Parsons Gallery, New York
1960	Betty Parsons Gallery, New York
1960	Betty Parsons Gallery, New York
1961	Betty Parsons Gallery, New York
1962	Galerie Lawrence, Paris
1963	Galleria dell'Ariete, Milan
	Everett Ellin Gallery, Los Angeles
1964	Betty Parsons Gallery, New York
1965	Betty Parsons Gallery, New York
	Worcester Art Museum, Massachusetts
1966	Massachusetts Institute of Technology, Cambridge
	Galerie Maeght, Paris
1967	Betty Parsons Gallery, New York
1968	Betty Parsons Gallery, New York
	Phillips Collection, Washington, D.C.
1971	Pace Gallery, New York
	J. L. Hudson Gallery, Detroit
1972	Pace Gallery, New York
	Center for the Visual Arts, Portland, Oregon
	Seattle Art Museum
1973	Arts Club of Chicago
	Galerie Denise René, Paris
	Pace Gallery, New York
	Galerie Denise René/Hans Mayer, Dusseldorf
1974	Fendrick Gallery, Washington, D.C.
	Kingpitcher Gallery, Pittsburgh
1975	Pace Gallery, New York
1976	Parrish Museum, Southampton, New York
1977	Tampa Bay Museum, Florida
1978	Truman Gallery, New York
1981	Washburn Gallery, New York
1982	Washburn Gallery, New York
1983	Alex Rosenberg Gallery, New York
1985	Washburn Gallery, New York
1986	Guggenheim Museum, New York

Selected Group Exhibitions:

1950	*Les Mains Ebouies*, Galerie Maeght, Paris
1959	*16 Americans*, Museum of Modern Art, New York
1961	*Abstract Expressionists and Imagists*, Guggenheim Museum, New York
1964	*American Drawings*, Guggenheim Museum, New York
1966	*Systemic Painting*, Guggenheim Museum, New York
1976	*Abstract Expressionists and Imagists*, University of Texas at Austin
1979	*Americans in Paris: The 50's*, California State University at Northridge
1981	*Contemporary Americans*, Guggenheim Museum, New York
1984	*The Folding Image*, National Gallery of Art, Washington, D.C.
1985	*Transformations in Sculpture*, Guggenheim Museum, New York

Collections:

Guggenheim Museum, New York; Whitney Museum, New York; Museum of Modern Art, New York; Albright-Knox Art Gallery, Buffalo, New York; Worcester Art Museum, Massachusetts; Hirshhorn Museum, Washington, D.C.; Phillips Collection, Washington, D.C.; Corcoran Gallery, Washington, D.C.; Carnegie Institute, Pittsburgh; Art Institute of Chicago.

Publications:

By YOUNGERMAN: article—"Interview with Jack Youngerman," with Barbara Rose, in *Artforum* (New York), January 1966.

On YOUNGERMAN: books—*Systemic Painting*, exhibition catalogue, by Lawrence Alloway, New York 1966; *Constructivism: Origins and Evolution* by George Rickey, New York 1967; *American Art since 1900: A Critical History* by Barbara Rose, New York 1967; *The Joys and Sorrows of Recent American Art* by A. S. Weller, Urbana, Illinois 1968; *Jack Youngerman*, exhibition catalogue with text by Diane Waldman, New York 1986.

Jack Youngerman's career has involved a continuing absorption with the formal and even psychological possibilities inherent in leaf-like form and flat and brilliantly-hued pictorial pattern. Impersonal and banal forms marked the work of many chromatic and hard-edged abstract artists of the 1960's; in strong contrast Youngerman, both then and to the present, has worked in distinctly natural-referent form. The form and color precedents of Arp and Matisse may easily be cited; yet perhaps more to the point might be the strong American symbolist precedents for such undulant and rhapsodic nature-focused art—for instance, Dove, O'Keeffe, Burchfield, and, with Gorky, the surrealist strain in American modernism. It is as if Youngerman would wish the clarity and rationalist force of the Constructivist tradition— with which he initially became conversant during his long European stay, 1947–1956—and yet also wish to imbue it with an irrepressible rhythm of nature. The emphatic urgency of Youngerman's painting and sculpture has been referred to by the artist: "We are immersed in the powerful and autonomous images of the world before these forms are possessed and diminished by names and uses—the name preempting the form. Painting involves the restoring of the image to that original primacy."

After some heavy-textured, expressionist work in the mid-1950's, Youngerman was, by the end of the decade, a post-painterly abstract artist. His images, already restricted to one or two colors, featured flat and sharp-edged forms which resolved themselves into landscape panorama. While he has restricted the internal shape and pattern of his work to natural reference, he has continuously attempted variance by his manipulation of the ground shape and the concomitant ordering of his forms in their positioning on these grounds. In 1967 he produced symmetrical works, with butterfly-like shapes on diamond shaped canvases— forms clearly influenced by beetle and fish patterning. His exhibition in 1971 featured circular, elliptical canvases. And in the following year, Youngerman detached his floral emblems from their ground and produced shaped canvases, at times in several sections whose edges conformed to the flaring-edged forms. He has also exhibited stainless steel sculpture (1971), and wooden cut-outs (1972), and all white fiberglass and resin three-dimensional sculpture (1976). A recent exhibition (1978) involved the use of folding screens on which he painted his signature shapes.

Youngerman's art has been marked by an almost heroic poignance because of his insistence upon a duality—clear abstractionist idealism yet linked with the resonance of an older subjective translation of nature into pattern. If this has been a detriment for the critical acceptance of his work—the restrictiveness of his form world—it may as well have operated to deny the artist access to larger, more current, views of the mechanico-metabolic confrontation.

—Joshua Kind

YUNKERS, Adja.

American. Born in Riga, Latvia, 15 July 1900; lived in Germany, 1919-22, Havana, 1924-27, Paris, 1927-38, and Stockholm, 1939-47; emigrated to the United States in 1947; subsequently naturalized. Educated at the Art Academy of Petrograd, 1914-17. Married the art critic Dore Ashton in 1952; daughters: Alexandra and Marina. Independent graphic artist, also active as a painter, magazine editor and interior designer: lived and worked in New York, 1947 until his death in 1983. Taught at the New School for Social Research, New York, 1947-56; summer sessions at the University of New Mexico, 1948-49; Cooper Union, New York, 1956-67; Barnard College, New York, 1967-69, Visiting Artist, Academy of Art, Honolulu, 1964; Visiting Critic, Columbia University, New York, 1967-69. Recipient: Guggenheim Fellowship, 1949, 1954; Ford Foundation Grant, 1960; Gold Medal, *2nd International Print Biennial,* Norway, 1974, Agent: C D S Gallery, 13 East 75th Street, New York, New York 10021. *Died* (in New York City), *24 December 1983.*

Individual Exhibitions:

1922-46	Maria Kunde, Hamburg
	Galleri Moderne, Stockholm
	Galleri Per, Oslo
	Galleri Tokanten, Copenhagen
1947-54	Henry Kleeman Gallery, New York
	Grace Borgenicht Gallery, New York
	Corcoran Gallery, Washington, D.C.
	Art Alliance, Philadelphia
	Art Institute of Chicago
	Colorado Springs Fine Arts Center
	San Francisco Museum of Art
	Buchholtz Galeria, Madrid
1955	Galerie d'Art Moderne, Basle
	Studio Paul Facchetti, Paris
	Galleria Numero, Florence
	Zwemmer Gallery, London
	Konstmuseum, Gothenburg, Sweden
	Grace Borgenicht Gallery, New York

1957-59	Los Angeles County Museum of Art
	Rose Fried Gallery, New York
	André Emmerich Gallery, New York
	Howard Wise Gallery, Cleveland
	Instituto de Arte Contemporaneo, Lima
1960	Baltimore Museum of Art
1962-65	Honolulu Academy of Art
	Feigen Gallery, Detroit
	Malmquist and Wood Gallery, Cleveland
1966	Museum Boymans-van-Boyningen, Rotterdam (organized exhibition)
1968	Rose Fried Gallery, New York
1969	Utah Museum of Art, Salt Lake City
1970	Estudio Actual, Caracas
1972	Whitney Museum, New York
	Estudio Actual, Caracas
1973	Hayden Gallery, Massachusetts Institute of Technology, Cambridge
	Lantern Gallery, Ann Arbor, Michigan
	Mazalow Gallery, Toronto
	Imprint Gallery, San Francisco
	Smith-Andersen Gallery, Palo Alto, California
1974	*Bienal Internacional de Arte Grafica y Arte Seriado,* Segovia, Spain
	Norwegian International Print Biennale, Frederikstad
	3rd International Exhibit of Graphic Art, Frechen, Germany
	Zabriskie Gallery, New York
	Estudio Actual, Caracas
	Lantern Gallery, Ann Arbor, Michigan
	Langsam Gallery, South Yarra, Australia
	Carpenter Center for the Visual Arts, Harvard University, Cambridge, Massachusetts
	Phoenix Art Museum, Arizona
1975	Museo do Arte Moderno, Chapultepec, Mexico
	Smith-Andersen Gallery, San Francisco
	Smith-Andersen Gallery, Palo Alto, California
	Nielsen Gallery, Boston
	Impressions Workshop, Boston
	Zabriskie Gallery, New York
	Kent State University, Ohio
1976	Simsar Gallery, Ann Arbor, Michigan
	Estudio Actual, Caracas
	Fairweather Hardin Gallery, Chicago
	Daedal Fine Arts Gallery, Baltimore
1977	Estudio Actual, Caracas
	Nielsen Gallery, Boston
	City Hall Gallery, Boston
	Impressions Workshop, Boston
	Simsar Gallery, Ann Arbor, Michigan
1978-80	Allrich Gallery, San Francisco
	Galeria Juan Martin, Mexico
	Philadelphia College of Art
	Museo de Bellas Artes, Caracas
	Smith-Andersen Gallery, Palo Alto, California
	Nielsen Gallery, Boston
	Simsar Gallery, Ann Arbor, Michigan
	Impressions Gallery, Boston
	Estudio Actual, Caracas
1981	Nielsen Gallery, Boston
1982	C D S Gallery, New York
1983	Galleria L'Isola, Rome

Selected Group Exhibitions:

1949	*Master Prints of the MOMA Collection,* Museum of Modern Art, New York
1950	*50 Years of American Painting,* Paris
1969	*The First Generation,* Museum of Modern Art, New York
1970	*L'Art Vivant aux Etats Unis,* Fondation Maeght, St.-Paul-de-Vence, France

Collections:

Museum of Modern Art, New York; Guggenheim Museum, New York; Corcoran Gallery, Washington, D.C.; Hirshhorn Museum, Smithsonian Institution, Washington, D.C.; Philadelphia Museum of Art; Museum of Fine Arts, Boston; Walker Arts Center, Minneapolis; Stadtmuseum, Hamburg; Goteborgs Konstmuseum, Sweden; Museo de Bellas Artes, Caracas.

Publications:

By YUNKERS: magazines edited and published—*Creation* (Stockholm), 1942; *Ars* (Stockholm), 1942; *Prints in the Desert* (Albuquerque, New Mexico), 1949; books illustrated—*5 Love Poems for Marie-Jose* by Octavio Paz, New York 1969; *Blanco* by Octavio Paz, New York 1974.

On YUNKERS: books—*Rio Grande Portfolios* by John Leeper, New York 1952; *Yunkers,* exhibition catalogue, by Grohman and Westholm, Gothenburg, Sweden 1955; *Perspectives, El Arte Moderno en los Estados Unidos* by William Lieberman, Barcelona 1955; *The New American Art, Western World, Volume 3* by Howard Devree, New York 1959; *Adja Yunkers,* exhibition catalogue, by Breeskin and Sawyers, Baltimore 1960; *American Art of Our Century* by John Baur, New York 1961; *50 Years of American Art 1916-1966* by Edward Henning, Cleveland 1966; *Amerikanse Skilderinen Collage* by Van Den Branden, Rotterdam 1966; *Drawings of the Masters: 20th Century Drawings* by Una Johnson, New York 1968; *Yunkers,* exhibition catalogue, by Edward Henning, Salt Lake City, Utah 1969; *Yunkers: American Graphic Artists of the 20th Century #7* by Una Johnson, New York 1969; *L'Art Vivant aux États Unis,* exhibition catalogue, by Dore Ashton, St.-Paul-de-Vence, France 1970; *Yunkers,* exhibition catalogue, by Nico Calas. New York 1972.

From the age of 18 in Germany Adja Yunkers was involved in art as his most intensive activity whether as printmaker, lecturer, interior decorator, magazine editor or painter. Best known as a graphic artist, he reflected in his prints of the 1940's something of the anguish of those years when he was in Sweden physically remote but mentally concerned with the struggles going on in mainland Europe and the Far East. Expressionist in figuration, his most poignant images echoed the harrowing sorrow of the woman as mother, wife and lover projecting something of the strong emotions of Munch and his German followers, distortions heightening the mood of strong feelings associated with the human form though this gradually came to assume less descriptive affinities and to rely more on the forcefully accented contour lines and masses.

After his move to the United States in 1947 Yunkers exploited the potential capacity of the print to emulate painting by expanding in size and colour ranges—he created one tour de force in a polyptych measuring 3 ft. 3 ins by 14 feet wide employing no fewer than 56 colours. From the self-contained area of the paper on which the impression from woodcut, silk screen and other multiple media made their effects, Yunkers proceeded to the revealing experiments with collage and the folding canvas to disrupt the even surface of his support. In one such work, "Folded Canvas I" of 1970, the mauve ground of one side is folded to form an asymmetrical pattern contrasting with the raw textures of the weave, the whole supported on a field of blue. "Yellow Form" (1971) is a collage where blue and mauve also predominate.

While in earlier prints gestural elements gave their emotional appeal, in his later works the shaped outlines in their encounters and association of linear contact produced lyrical suggestions of lovers in generous ovoid and rhythmic curves. Yunkers set himself the almost impossible task of commanding an emotional return from an investment in abstract forms that by themselves seem arbitrary without apparent correlation to the straight confines of the support. Yet such is his mastery of assembling a minimum of motives in telling relationships of outline and colour that he evokes a sense of classical economy and serene calm through such a simple means as the placing of what resembles a torn vertical strip laid across a roughly executed rectangular mass on the dark ground of the picture frame. Abstract as the works are in appearance there is also about them a strong presence of surrealist juxtaposition.

Almost defying analysis in conventional critical terms, Yunkers found the wave length of emotional communication by the mystic amalgam of surface delineation of shapes that nevertheless imply unidentified corporeal entities in space, inspiring an acceptive mood by emotively tuned harmonies of colour.

—G. S. Whittet

Adja Yunkers: *Aegean III*, **1967** Courtesy Whitney Museum, New York

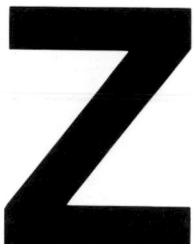

ZAPPETTINI, Gianfranco.

Italian. Born in Genoa, 16 June 1939. Studied at the Accademia di Belle Arti, Carrara. Married Gabrielle Gonfiantini in 1963; daughter: Martina. Painter: lives and works in Genoa. Address: via Aurelia 116, 16043 Chiavari, Italy.

Individual Exhibitions:

1962	Galleria Belle Arti, Genoa
1963	Galleria Pescetto, Albisola, Italy
1964	Galleria Ferrari, Verona
	Galleria 2000, Bologna
1965	Galleria La Polena, Genoa
1966	Galleria L'Arco, Macerata, Italy
1967	Galleria Vismara, Milan
	Galerie Du Disque Rouge, Brussels
1968	Galleria del Cavallino, Venice
1969	Galleria Il Punto, Turin
1971	Galleria Peccolo, Livorno
	Galleria pourquoi pas, Genoa
1972	Galerie Loehr, Frankfurt
	Galleria La Polena, Genoa
1973	Centro d'Arte Santelmo, Salo, Italy
1974	Galleria la Polena, Genoa
	Galleria La Piramide, Florence
	Galleria Vinciana, Milan
	Galleria Peccolo, Livorno
	Galerie December, Münster, West Germany
1975	Westfälischer Kunstverein, Münster, West Germany
	Galerie Karsten Greve, Cologne
1976	Galleria La Seconda Scala, Rome
	Galerie Peccolo, Cologne
1977	Studio Soldano, Milan
	Galleria La Bertesca, Genoa
1978	International Cultureel Centrum, Antwerp
	Galerie Peccolo, Cologne
	Galerie Artline, The Hague
	Galleria Eremitani, Padua

Selected Group Exhibitions:

1969	*Nove Tendencije 4*, Zagreb
1970	*Multiples*, Whitechapel Art Gallery, London
1971	*Triennale*, Delhi, India
	Concrete Art, Westfälischer Kunstverein, Münster, West Germany
1973	*Tempi du Percezione*, Casa della Cultura, Livorno
1974	*Geplante Malerei*, Westfälischer Kunstverein, Münster, West Germany
1975	*Pittura*, Palazzo Ducale, Genoa
1976	*A proposito della Pittura*, Stedelijk Museum, Amsterdam
1977	*Documenta*, Kassel, West Germany
1978	*Abstraction Analytique*, Centre Georges Pompidou, Paris

Collections:

Westfälischer Kunstverein, Münster, West Germany.

Publications:

By ZAPPETTINI: articles—"Ricerca di una Dimensione" in *Gala* (Milan), September 1974: "Per una Pittura Analitica" in *Data* (Milan), Winter 1974 and *Kunstforum* (Mainz, West Germany), October/November 1974; statement in *Gianfranco Zappettini*, exhibition catalogue, Münster, West Germany 1975; statement in *Gianfranco Zappettini*, exhibition catalogue. Antwerp 1978.

On ZAPPETTINI: book—*Gianfranco Zappettini*, exhibition catalogue, by Klaus Honnef, Münster, West Germany, 1975: article—"Gianfranco Zappettini" by Klaus Honnef in *Kunstforum* (Mainz, West Germany), October/November 1974.

The course followed by Gianfranco Zappettini in more than ten years of work might be called the "recovery of meaning," and to an extent it reflects a wider change of cultural direction than simply one of those that we are passing through at present. Zappettini started from a strictly, rigorously analytical painting, in which all the materials and other "ingredients" of pictorial work were subjected to a test both operational and conceptual. "Think in terms of painting," was his motto. The reduction of the metaphorical level to an absolute zero was obtained through an intent metonymic process, which always restrained the elements used to the same level of (non-) meaning. The "outside," the "world," anything "other than the picture" was never to be incorporated in the work; the process was vital, political, social. And this kind of process came into being by his painting exactly according to the autonomous instruments of painting, with no concession to Meaning but reinforcing the materiality of the source of Meaning.

Zappettini then moved on to a manner of painting which, while still retaining some elements typical of analysis (the breaking down of the support, for instance), nevertheless involved a more open attitude towards the world, its colours, its emotions and feelings, its power of evoking memories. But it is only in the past few years that Zappettini has completed the full, complete recovery, almost to the point of iconism, figuration, "pictorial reconciliation" (and not only pictorial) with the world.

This change has also had a great personal effect on him: he has gone to live in the country, on the Ligurian coast, where he has developed personal taste for "minor" painting, with little innovatory quotient but a high level of technique and craftsmanship. One might say that his investigation of "the painter's trade" is still going on, but with other, quite different means. The brush stroke is free, harking back to the Fauves and Impressionists (it might even be better to say, to Barbizon); the subjects are ordinary, everyday, slightly ironic, deliberately "common." In this way Zappettini displays the historicity of painting, reviving methods and processes typical to its still "heroic" past.

Most recently his work has been enriched by another aspect and other themes, always drawn from the outpouring of meaning, of metaphor, of the desire to narrate, to tell of himself. His painting has become more spectacular than ever; it has become theatrical, depicting scenes from films (with well-known actors quite recognizable) or historic scenes with famous people in them; this is the world of the Public, of kitsch, of the Myth of the Masses. With a special effect of alienation he puts himself into the scene, in poses sometimes deliberately ironic (no problem in identifying these), as if he were required to "introduce" and "present" what is going on around him, as if in one of his personal circuses. The return of the Subject (since that is basically what we are looking at) is thus completed, after an analytical period composed of total, anonymity, the disappearance of the "I" in the work processes—but it is a Subject which, despite all its bodily and concrete appearance, cannot but remain confined in the world of images, of icons, of phantasms.

—Massimo Carboni

ZORIO, Gilberto.

Italian. Born in Andorno Micca, Italy, 21 September 1944. Studied painting at the Accademia di Belle Arti, Turin, 1963-70. Lives and works in Turin. Lecturer, Liceo Artistica, Turin, since 1971. Agent: Galleria Christian Stein, Piazza San Carlo 206, 10121 Turin. Address: Via Gorizia 149, 10137 Turin, Italy.

Individual Exhibitions:

1967	Galleria Sperone, Turin
1968	Centro Calautti, Salerna, Italy
1969	Galerie Ileana Sonnabend, Paris
	Galleria Sperone, Turin
1970	Galleria Toselli, Milan
1971	Galleria Flori, Florence
	Galleria Sperone, Turin
	Modern Art Agency, Naples
	Palazzo Taverna, Rome
1973	Galleria Sperone, Turin
	Galerie MTL, Brussels
1974	Galleria Toselli, Milan
	Galleria Sperone, Turin
1975	Galleria dell'Ariete, Milan
1976	Kunstmuseum, Lucerne
	Galleria Schema, Florence
	Studio de Ambrogi Cavellini, Milan
1977	Galleria del Tritone, Biella, Italy
	Studio G 7, Bologna, Italy
	Studio Cesare Manzo, Pescara, Italy
1978	Galleria Cavellini, Brescia, Italy
	Galerie Albert Baronian, Brussels
	Galerie Eric Fabre, Paris
	Galerie t'Venster, Rotterdam
	Galleria del Tritone, Biella, Italy
	Studio Carlo Grossetti, Milan
	Galleria Cavellini, Milan
	Salone Annunciata, Milan
1979	Galleria Christian Stein, Turin
	Jean and Karen Bernier, Athens
	Stedelijk Museum, Amsterdam
	Galleria Emilio Mazzoli, Modena, Italy

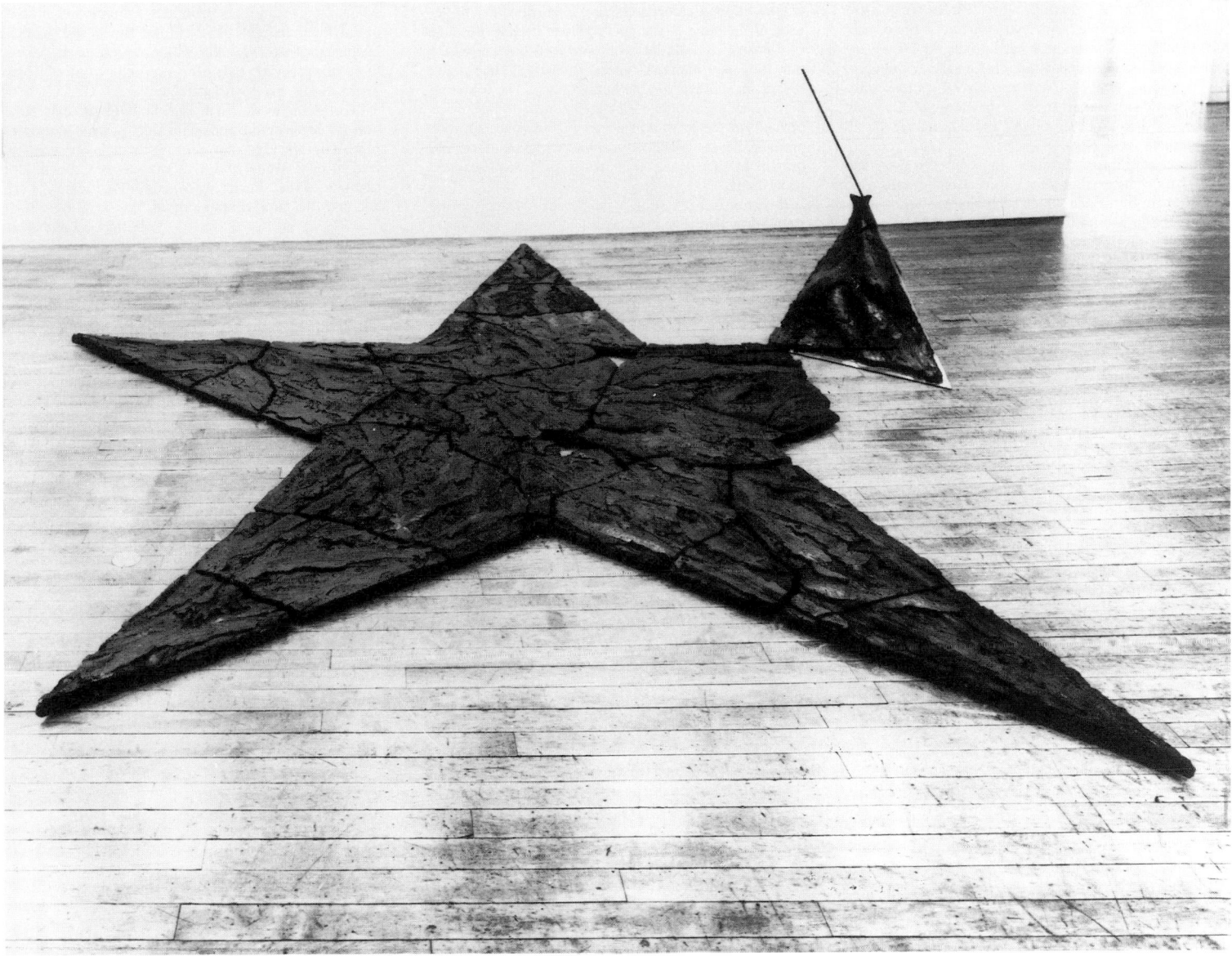

Gilberto Zorio: *Star (to purify words)*, 1980

1980	Galleria de Crescenzo, Rome
	Galerie Eric Fabre, Paris
	Studio G 7, Bologna, Italy
	Galerie Albert Baronian, Brussels
	Galerie Walter Storms, Munich (with Marco Gastini and Giuseppe Spagnulo)
1981	Galleria Salvatore Ala, Milan
	Galerie Meyer-Hahn, Dusseldorf
	Galerie Rudiger Schöttle, Munich
	Sonnabend Gallery, New York
	Galleria de Crescenzo, Rome
	Galerie Appel und Fertsch, Frankfurt
1982	Galleria Cavellini, Brescia, Italy
1092	Galleria Christian Stein, Turin
	Pinacoteca Comunale, Ravenna, Italy
1983	Galerie Mueller-Roth, Stuttgart
	Forum Kunst, Rottweil, West Germany
	Galerie Walter Storms, Munich
	Center of Contemporary Art, Syracuse, Italy
1984	Galérie au Fond de la Cour a Droite, Chagny, France
	Galerie Albert Baronian, Brussels
	Galleria Plurima, Udine, Italy
1985	Galleria Civica d'Arte, Modena, Italy
	Kunstverein, Stuttgart
1986	Galleria Christian Stein, Turin
	Centre d'Art Contemporain, Geneva
	Jean Bernier Gallery, Athens
	Centre Georges Pompidou, Paris
1987	Galleria Christian Stein, Turin

Selected Group Exhibitions:

1969	*When Attitudes Become Form*, Kunstahalle, Berne (travelled to the Museum Haus Lange, Krefeld, West Germany, and the Institute of Contemporary Arts, London)
1970	*Biennial*, Metropolitan Museum of Art, Tokyo (toured Japan)
1971	*Biennale de Paris*, Parc Floral, Paris
1972	*Documenta*, Kassel, West Germany
1974	*Projekt 74*, Kunsthalle, Cologne
1978	*Biennale*, Venice
1981	*Identité Italienne: L'Art en Italie depuis 1959*, Centre Georges Pompidou, Paris
1982	*Italian Art Now: An American Perspective*, Guggenheim Museum, New York
1984	*International Survey of Recent Painting and Sculpture*, Museum of Modern Art, New York
1986	*Hommage a Beuys*, Stadtische Museum im Lenbachhaus, Munich

Collections:

Galleria Nazionale d'Arte Moderna, Rome: Rijksmuseum Kröler-Müller, Otterlo, Netherlands: Stedelijk Museum, Amsterdam: Stedelijk van Abbemuseum, Eindhoven, Netherlands; Museum van Hedendaagse Kunst, Ghent; Kunstmuseum, Lucerne; Staatsgalerie, Stuttgart; Guggenheim Museum, New York.

Publications:

By ZORIO: article—"Gilberto Zorio" in *Data* (Milan), Summer 1978.

On ZORIO: books—*Gilberto Zorio*, exhibition catalogue, by Tommaso Trini, Turin 1967; *Arte Povera* by Germano Celant, Milan 1969; *Europe/America:The Different Avant Gardes* by Achille Bonito Oliva, Milan 1976; *Gilberto Zorio*, exhibition catalogue, by Jean-Christophe Ammann, Ugo Castagnotto and Werner Lippert, Lucerne 1976; *Avantguardia di Massa* by Maurizio Calvesi; Milan 1978; *Schema Informazione: Politic-Art*. Florence 1978: *Gilberto Zorio*, exhibition catalogue, by Jean-Christophe Ammann, Amsterdam 1979; *Gilberto Zorio*, exhibition catalogue with essay by Werner Lippert, Frankfurt 1981; articles—"Primary Energy and the Micro-Emotive Artists" by Piero Gilardi in *Arts Magazine* (New York). September/October 1968: "Gilberto Zorio: Corpo di Energia: by Jole de Sanna in *Date* (Milan), April 1972; "La Stella di Zorio" by Mirella Bandini in *Data* (Milan), December 1976: "Zorio's Star" by Mirella Bandini *Data* (Milan), December/January 1976/77; "Gilberto Zorio" by G. S. Brizio in *D'Ars* (Milan), July 1979; "Gilberto Zorio" by Flamino Gualdoni in *G7 Studio* (Bologna), June 1981.

Energy, tension, purification: these, essentially, are the concerns which govern Gilberto Zorio's aesthetic. His works are experiments in which he investigates the principles of change in time and space, in the elements of the atmosphere and physical phenomena, and in chemical reactions. In "Pieces of Lead" (1968), for example, two lead containers filled with chlorine and chloridic acid have produced crystalline salts on the copper bands which join the containers. In "Curtain" (1967), Zorio has placed a cloth saturated with salt water over a structure of Dalmine tubes, so that a border of salt appears as the liquid evaporates.

These works are designed to show physical and chemical changes, but also to direct our attention to the element of time in which such changes take place. In still other works the process of change itself becomes the subject-matter. This is the case, for example, with "Rose/Blue/Rose" (1967), in which the color of cobalt chlorite changes according to the degree of moisture in the air produced by the presence of viewers. A little later he produced objects which may be used to print words such as "Hate" and "Radical Fluidity" on the human body. The intention here is to use words to evoke images. "Hate" was printed on the artist's forehead on one occasion; on another, it was scratched on a wall with a hatchet; and on still another occasion the word itself was modelled in terracotta.

In his search for archetypal images which can be transformed into new vistas and produce new energies, Zorio sometimes chooses a figure such as a star and constructs it out of elements which are in themselves significant—a javelin, for example, or a laser or an incandescent nickel. Like the acids, metals, leather and even the skin which he had used before, these now become part of the repertory out of which Zorio makes his poetic statements.

In all of his work, then, it is the dynamic manipulation of energy and change which plays a dominant role. The tensions and energies which are released lead to pure archetypal symbols—as is the case, for example, with "Purifying Words." Purification itself becomes the final aesthetic goal.

—Roberto G. Lambarelli

NOTES ON ADVISERS AND CONTRIBUTORS

ABADIE, Daniel. Essayist. Curator at the Centre Georges Pompidou, Paris, since 1975; Editor of *Art/Cahiers*, Paris, since 1980. Curator, Centre National d'Art Contemporain, Paris, 1969–74; Professor, Ecole des Beaux-Arts, St.-Etienne, France, 1979–80. Author of *Bryen Abhomme; Hyperréalisme; Hélion; Klee;* and *Simonds.* **Essays:** Eddy; Moser; Stämpfli.

ALBRECHT, Dietrich (Albrecht D.). Essayist. Freelance artist and writer; Founder-Editor, Reflektion Press, Stuttgart. **Essay:** Muehl.

ALLOWAY, Lawrence. Essayist. Professor at the State University of New York at Stony Brook, since 1968. Deputy Director, Institute of Contemporary Arts, London, 1957–60; Curator, Guggenheim Museum, New York, 1962–66; Chairman, Division of Fine Arts, School of Visual Arts, New York, 1967–68. Art Editor, *The Nation*, 1968–81; Contributing Editor, *Artforum*, 1972–76. Author of *Nine Abstract Artists*, 1954; *Ettore Colla*, 1960; *The Metalization of a Dream*, 1963; *The Venice Biennale 1895-1968*, 1969; *Violent America: The Movies 1946–64*, 1970; *American Pop Art*, 1974; *Topics in American Art since 1945*, 1975. **Essay:** Sonfist.

AMMANN, Jean-Christophe. Adviser and essayist. Director of the Museum für Moderne Kunst, Frankfurt, from 1989. Director, Kunstmuseum, Lucerne, 1969–77, and Kunsthalle, Basle, 1978–88. Author of *Von Hodler zur Antiform*, with Harald Szeemann, 1968; *Louis Moilliet: Das Gesamtwerk*, 1972. **Essays:** Buthe; Erro.

ANDRAS, Ban. Essayist. Editor of *Elet es Irodalom* weekly art magazine, and art critic of *Magyar Nemzet* newspaper, Budapest. Author of *A fenykep kulturaja*, 1983; *Video*, with Beke Laszlo, 1983; *Fotoelmeleti szoveggyujtemeny*, with Beke Laszlo, 1984. **Essay:** Lupas.

BARKER, Carrie. Essayist. Freelance writer and journalist, London. **Essays:** Antonakos; Bernd and Hilla Becher; James Bishop; Bourgeois; Daphnis; Douglas Davis; De Rivera; Diehl; Robert Graham; Richard Hunt; Kushner; Lobdell; Merkin; Posen; Savelli; Sonnier; Stevenson.

BARRETT, D. C. Essayist. Reader in Philosophy at the University of Warwick, Coventry. Author of *Art*, 1970; *An Introduction to Optical Art*, 1971; *Michael Farrell: A Monograph*, 1979; *Paintings, Objects, Installations 1963-80: Peter Sedgley*, 1980; and editor of *Collected Papers on Aesthetics*, 1965, and *Ludwig*

Wittgenstein, 1966. **Essays:** Baer; Baskin; Buren; Coleman; Colombo; Le Brocquy; Lijn; Riley; Steele.

BAZAROV, Konstantin. Essayist. Freelance writer and researcher, London; also, professional geologist-zoologist. Author of *Landscape Painting*, 1981. **Essays:** Clark; Indiana; Johns; Latham; Le Parc; Mack; Matta; Metzger; Neizvestny; Olitski; Picasso; Piene; Rauschenberg; Rivers; David Smith; Takis; Vostell.

BELL, Jane. Essayist. Contributing Editor. *New York Arts Journal*, since 1974; Editorial Associate, *Artnews*, since 1978; Associate Director, International Network for the Arts, since 1979; and Senior Editor, *The Art Economist*, since 1981—all New York. Associate Editor, *Art Express*, 1980–81. **Essays:** Agnetti; Askevold; Beckley; Le Gac; Ossorio; Wade.

BENINCASA, Carmine. Essayist. Art Critic for *Corriere della Serra* since 1977; also, teacher of art history in the Faculty of Architecture at the University of Rome, and Adviser to the Italian Ministry of Culture and Environment. Author of *Sul Manierismo, Come Dentro ad Uno Specchio*, 1978; *Architettura come Dis-Identita: Le Teoria delle Catastrofi in Architettura*, 1979; *Paul Klee*, 1979; *Paul Klee*, 1981; *Il Labirinto dei Sabba, L'Architettura di Riema Pietila*, 1980; *Oskar Kokoschka*, 1981; *Roland Barthes*, 1981; *André Masson*, 1981; *Antoni Tapies*, 1982; *Portale, Alle Soglie del Sapere*, 1980; *Babilonia in Fiamme*, 1978; *L'Altra-Scena*, 1979. **Essay:** Parmiggiani.

BERGER, Maurice. Essayist. Visiting Assistant Professor, and Special Projects Curator of the Karl and Bertha Leubsdorf Art Gallery, Hunter College, City University of New York. Contributor to *Artforum, Arts Magazine, New Observations,* and *Artistes*. **Essays:** Andre; Bartlett; Gottlieb; Mason; Robert Morris; Serra; Shapiro.

BEX, Florent. Essayist. Director, International Cultureel Centrum, Antwerp (has organized more than 200 exhibitions of contemporary art). Administrator of La Jeune Peinture Belge; Vice-President, Belgian Association of Art Critics; Member, International Committee for Museums and Collections of Modern Art (CIMAM). **Essay:** Romberg.

BOHN, Willard. Essayist. Assistant Professor of French, Illinois State University at Normal, since 1981. Assistant Professor of French and Comparative Literature, Brandeis University, Waltham, Massachusetts, 1972–74; Research Associate in Comparative Literature, University of California, Berkeley, 1974–79; Lecturer in French, University of California at Santa Cruz, 1979–81. Frequent contributor to *The Art Bulletin, Arts Magazine,* and the *Journal of Aesthetics and Art Criticism.* Author of *Apollinaire et*

l'homme sans visage: creation et evolution d'un motif moderne, 1983, editor of *A quelle heure un train partira-t-il pour Paris?* by Apollinaire, 1982. **Essays:** Delvaux; Man Ray.

BOJKO, Szymon. Adviser and essayist. Freelance art critic and art historian, Warsaw, since 1975. Editor of *Projekt* (visual arts and design review), 1969–74; Editor-in-chief, *Polish Art Review*, 1972; Consultant to the Gmurzynska Gallery, Cologne, 1973–80; Visiting Lecturer, School of Art and Design, Lodz, 1976–79. Author of *Polish Poster Art: Its Origins and Development to 1939*, 1971; *The Polish Poster Today*, 1972; *New Graphic Design in Revolutionary Russia*, 1972; *Rot Schlägt Weiss*, 1975. **Essays:** Anuskiewicz; Cieslewicz; Lenica; Paschke; Stankiewicz; Tomaszewski.

BONITO OLIVA, Achille. Essayist. Freelance art critic, Rome. Professor, School of Architecture, Rome, since 1971; Editorial Staff Member, *Avanti*, Rome, since 1978. Author of *Il territorio magico*, 1971; *L'ideologia del traditore*, 1976; *Vita di Marcel Duchamp*, 1976; *Le avanguardie diverse*, 1976; *Passo dello strabismo*, 1978; *La transavanguardia italiana*, 1980; *La transavanguardia internazionale*, 1982. **Essay:** Jaccard.

BORDEAUX, Jean-Luc. Essayist. Professor of Art History, California State University at Northridge, since 1972 (Director of the Fine Arts Gallery, 1972–80). Visiting Curator, Department of Paintings, Musée du Louvre, Paris, 1979. Author of *Francois Le Moyne and His Generation*, 1983. **Essays:** Cooper; Lippold; McCoy.

BOURDON, David. Essayist. Art Critic for *The Village Voice*, New York. **Essay:** Christo.

BROWN, David. Essayist. Assistant Keeper of Modern Collections at the Tate Gallery, London (has written numerous catalogues for exhibitions at the Tate); also a doctor of veterinary medicine and surgery. **Essay:** Long.

BURROUGHS, William S. Essayist. Novelist and social critic. Author of *Junkie*, 1953; *The Naked Lunch*, 1959; *The Soft Machine*, 1961; *The Ticket That Exploded*, 1962; *Dead Fingers Talk*, 1963; *Nova Express*, 1964; *The Wild Boys*, 1971; *Exterminator*, 1973; *Short Novels*, 1978; *Blade Runner: A Movie*, 1979; *Port of Saints*, 1980; *Cities of the Red Night*, 1981; etc. **Essay:** Gysin.

CARBONI, Massimo. Essayist. Art critic, Livorno, since 1978. Sometime Lecturer, Faculty of Architecture, University of Rome. **Essays:** Boeyen; Burri; Cane; Gastini; Jaudon; Ryman; Zappettini.

CATALANO, Gary. Essayist. Freelance writer and critic, Melbourne. author of *Remembering the Rural Life* (verse), 1978; *The Years of Hope: Australian Art and Criticism 1959-1968*, 1981; *Heaven of Rags* (verse), 1982; *The Bandaged Image: A Study of Australian Artists' Books* 1982. **Essay:** Booth.

CAVALIERE, Barbara. Essayist. Contributing Editor, *Arts Magazine*, New York, since 1976. Helena Rubenstein Fellow, Whitney Museum, New York, 1975; Fellow in Art Criticism, National Endowment for the Arts, 1980. Author of the exhibition catalogue, *William Baziotes: A Retrospective*, 1978. **Essays:** Africano; Beal; Blume; Burden; Cornell; D'Arcangelo; Diebenkorn; Evergood; Ferrara; Foulkes; Gertsch; Glarner; Goings; Greene; Haacke; Hanson; Bryan Hunt; Lester Johnson; Kaprow; Kelly; Krasner; Le Va; Les Levine; Marden; Agnes Martin; McCracken; Morley; Nesbitt; Nonas; Pollock; Pousette-Dart; Rothko; Sandback; Simonds; Thek; Tillim; Truitt; Tuttle; Van Buren; Von Schlegell; Welch; Yoshimura.

COHEN, Ronny. Essayist. Editorial Associate, *Artnews*, New York. Reviewer for *Artforum*, New York. Author of *Thomas McKnight's World*, 1987; *Charles Ginnever*, 1987. **Essays:** Benglis; Bladen; Bolotowsky; Campus; Nancy Graves; Hamilton; Hicks; Ray Johnson; Kirili; Elizabeth Murray; Sugarman; Willenbecher.

COMPTON, Michael. Essayist. Director of Museum Services at the Tate Gallery, London. Author of numerous books and exhibition catalogues on contemporary art, including *Optical and Kinetic Art*, 1967; *Auguste Rodin: The Kiss*, 1967; *Pop Art*, 1970; *Art as a Thought Process*, 1974; *Art since 1945*, 1976; *Some Notes on the Work of Richard Long*, 1978; *Mark Boyle's Journey to the Surface of the Earth*, 1978; *Looking at Pictures in the Tate Gallery*, 1979; *Towards a New Art*, with others, 1980; *Howard Hodgkin's Indian Leaves*, 1982. **Essays:** Charlton; Hoyland; Milow.

COOKE, Lynne. Essayist. Lecturer in the History of Art, University College, University of London, since 1978. **Essays:** Armitage; Davies; Flanagan; Head; King; William Tucker.

CORTRIGHT, Barbara. Essayist. Art Critic for the *Scottsdale Progress*, Arizona. Contributing Editor, *Artspace*. **Essays:** Clarke; Cuevas; De Andrea.

CRICHTON, Fenella. Essayist. Art critic, London. **Essay:** Hill.

DAY, Melvin N. Adviser and essayist. Freelance writer and art historian, Wellington, New Zealand. Lecturer in Art History, University of London Extension, 1964-68; Director, National Art Gallery of New Zealand, 1968-78; Government Art Historian, New Zealand Department of Internal Affairs, 1978-87. Author of *Nicholas Chevalier, Artist*, 1980. **Essay:** Bullmore.

DORFLES, Gillo. Essayist. University Professor in Aesthetics, since 1965 (has taught at the universities of Milan, Cagliari, and Florence; also served as Director of the Institute of Fine Arts, University of Cagliari, 1970-75). Author of *Discorso tecnico delle arti*, 1951; *Barocco nell'architettura moderna*, 1952; *Bosch*, 1953; *L'architettura moderna*, 1954; *Dürer*, 1958; *Constantes tecnicas de las artes*, 1958; *Il divenire delle arti*, 1959; *Ultime tendenze dell'arte*

d'oggi, 1961; *Simbolo comunicazione consumo*, 1962; *Il disegno industriale e la sua estetica*, 1963; *Nuovi riti, nuovi miti*, 1965; *L'estetica del mito*, 1967; *Il Kitsch*, 1968; *Artificio e natura*, 1968; *Le Oscillazioni del gusto*, 1970; *Introduzione al disegno industriale*, 1972; *Sentido e Insenzatez en el Arte de Hoy*, 1973; *Dal significato alle scelte*, 1973; *Czlowiek zwielokrontniony*, 1973; *Mythes et rites d'aujourd'hui*, 1975; *Il devenire della critica*, 1976; *La Body Art*, 1978; *Mode e Modi*, 1979; *L'intervallo perduto*, 1980. **Essays:** Baj; Capogrossi; Chiari; Miró; Spagnulo.

ELLIS, Mary. Essayist. Freelance critic and lecturer at the Tate Gallery, London. **Essays:** Atkinson; Deacon; Dimitrijevic; Fulton; Guston; Law; Nash; Rothenberg.

EMANUEL, Muriel. Essayist. Freelance researcher, editor and writer, London. Editor of *Israel: A Survey and Bibliography*, 1971; *Contemporary Architects*, 1980. **Essays:** Neustein; Schad.

FELIX, Zdenek. Essayist. Curator at the Museum Folkwang, Essen. **Essays:** Nordman; Palermo; Raetz.

FINDLAY, Michael Alastair. Essayist. Art writer and artist's agent, New York. **Essay:** Woodham.

FORGE, Andrew. Essayist. Dean of the School of Art, Yale University, New Haven, Connecticut. Senior Lecturer, Slade School, London, 1950-64; Head of the Department of Fine Art, Goldsmith's College, London, 1964-70. Trustee, Tate Gallery, 1964-71, 1972-74, and National Gallery, London, 1966-72. President, London Group, 1964-71. Author of *Klee*, 1953; *Vermeer*, 1954; *Soutine*, 1965; *Rauschenberg*, 1972; *Monet at Giverny*, with C. Joyes, 1975; and editor of *The Townsend Journals*, 1976. **Essay:** Stephenson.

FOURNET, Claude. Essayist. Art critic, Paris. **Essay:** Aubertin.

FRASER, Alison. Essayist. Director, Victorian College of the Arts Gallery, Melbourne, since 1979. Education Officer, Art Gallery of New South Wales, Sydney, 1974-76; Art Education Consultant, Visual Arts Board, Australia Council, Sydney, 1978-79. Author of *History of Australian Art* (slide kit with text), 1981; and co-ordinator of *Tertiary Visual Arts Education in Australia*, 1980. **Essay:** John Davis.

FRIEDMAN, B. H. Essayist. Trustee, Whitney Museum of American Art, New York, since 1961, and of the Fine Arts Work Center, Provincetown, Massachusetts, since 1968; also, Member, Advisory Council of the College of Arts and Sciences and of the Herbert F. Johnson Museum, Cornell University, Ithaca, New York; Member, Fiction Collective, since 1973. Author of the biographies *Jackson Pollock: Energy Made Visible*, 1972, and *Gertrude Vanderbilt Whitney*, 1978; has edited written or contributed to various art monographs, including *School of New York*, 1959; *Robert Goodnough*, with Barbara Guest, 1962; *Lee Krasner*, 1965; *Alfonso Ossorio*, 1973; *Salvatore Scarpitta*, 1977; and *Myron Stout*, 1979; also a novelist and short story writer. **Essays:** Copley; Scarpitta.

FRIEDMAN, Kenneth S. Essayist. Artist and writer, New York. Consultant Editor, University of Michigan Research Press, since 1978; Director, Institute for Advance Studies in Contemporary Art

and Architecture, New York, since 1979. **Essay:** Kocman.

FRITSCH, Gerolf. Essayist. Professor of German Language and Literature, Chur, Switzerland. Author of *Die deutsche Ballade zwischen Herders naturaler Theorie und später Industriegesellschaft*, 1976; *Das deutsche Naturgedicht: Der fiktionale Text im Kommunikationsprozess*, 1978. **Essays:** Eggenschwiler; Giacometti.

GALE, Peggy. Essayist. Independent curator and critic, specializing in contemporary media and installation works, Toronto. Assistant Film and Video Officer, Canada Council, Ottawa, 1974; Video-Film Director, Art Metropole, Toronto, 1975-79; Executive Director, A Space, Toronto, 1979-81. Editor of *Video by Artists*, 1976; *Performance by Artists*, 1979; and *Museums by Artists*. 1983. **Essay:** General Idea.

GAZZERO, Edda. Essayist. Freelance art critic. Genoa. **Essay:** Costa.

GLOWEN, Ron. Essayist. Freelance art critic, Washington, since 1975. Contributing Editor, *Artweek*, Oakland, California, since 1976; Visual Arts Critic, *The Herald*, Everett, Washington, since 1978. **Essays:** Boyle; Bruce; Morris Graves; Kienholz; Raffael; Tobey.

GLUSBERG, Jorge. Adviser and essayist. Director, Centro de Arte y Communicacion, Buenos Aires. Author of *Towards a Topological Architecture*, with Clorindo Testa, 1977; *The Rhetoric of Latin American Art*, 1978; *Socio-Semiotic of Architecture*, 1978; *Myths and Magic of Fire, Gold and art*, 1978; *From Incan Habitat to the Lima of the Future*, 1979; *The Theory and Criticism of Architecture*, 1979. **Essays:** Benedit; Grippo; Maler; Uriburu.

GOLEAS, Janet. Essayist. Artist-in-Residence at the Sierra Nevada Museum of Art, and Fine Arts Instructor, University of Nevada, Reno, since 1980. **Essays:** Allen; Ronald Davis; Flavin; Grooms; Holland; Jensen.

GRANATH, Olle. Essayist. Freelance writer and art critic, Stockholm. Has written several books on contemporary Swedish art. **Essay:** Dietmann.

HARITHAS, James. Essayist. Art critic. Formerly: Curator, DeCordova Museum, Lincoln, Massachusetts. Director, Corcoran Gallery, Washington, D.C. **Essay:** Jimenez.

HIGGINS, Dick. Essayist and entrant. See his own entry. **Essay:** Knowles.

HOLLOWAY, John H. Essayist. British Co-Editor of *Leonardo* (international art journal), since 1971; also, Senior Lecturer in Chemistry, University of Leicester, since 1978. **Essay:** Albers.

HONNEF, Klaus. Adviser and essayist. Curator for Changing Exhibitions and the Photographic Collection, Rheinisches Landesmuseum, Bonn; also, Professor of the Theory of Photography at the University of Kassel. Director, Westfälischer Kunstverein, Münster, West Germany, 1970-74. Author of *20 Deutsche*, 1971; *Concept Art*, 1971; Gerhard Richter, 1976; *Wilhelm Schürman*, 1979 and editor of *Verkehrskultur*, 1974, and *Lichtbildnisse*, 1982. **Essays:** Darboven; Gaul; Krieg; Ruthenbeck.

JOHNSTON, Jill. Essayist. Author and art critic. Formerly, Columnist for *The Village Voice,* New York; contributor to various art journals. Author of *Marmalade Me; Lesbian Nation;* etc. **Essay:** Cage.

KARLSTROM, Paul J. Essayist. West Coast Director, Archives of American Art/Smithsonian Institution (based at the M. H. de Young Memorial Museum, San Francisco), since 1973. Assistant Curator, Grunwald Center for the Graphic Arts, University of California at Los Angeles, 1967–70; Instructor of Art History, California State University at Northridge, 1972–73; Guest Curator, Hirshhorn Museum and Sculpture Garden, Washington, D.C., 1977. Author of the monograph *Louis M. Eilshemius,* 1978, and of the catalogues, *Americans Abroad: Painters of the Victorian Era,* 1975; *The United States and the Impressionist Era,* 1979; and *Venice Panorama: Views of Venice in the Graphic Arts from the Late 15th Through the 18th Centuries,* 1979. **Essays:** Bechtle; Kauffman; McLaughlin; Oliveira; Valentine.

KELLER, Victoria. Essayist. Exhibitions Administrator, 369 Gallery, Edinburgh. **Essays:** Artschwager; Broodthaers; Francis; McLean; Nutt; Penck; Polke; Tinguely; Tworkov; Winner.

KELLY, Jane. Essayist. Art critic, London. **Essay:** Willats.

KEPINSKA, Alicja. Essayist. Professor, Academy of Visual Arts, Poznan, Poland. Author of *Jan Piotr Norblin: A Monograph,* 1978; *The New Polish Art 1945–1978,* 1981; *Element and Myth* (on action painting), 1983; *Ecology of Art,* 1988. **Essays:** Berdyszak; Brzozowski; Dibbets; Fischl; Fisher; Kruger; Merz; Opalka; Stazewski.

KIND, Joshua. Essayist. Professor of Art History, Northern Illinois University, DeKalb, since 1969. Instructor in Art History, Northwestern University, Evanston, Illinois, 1959–62; Instructor in the Humanities, University of Chicago, 1962–65; Visiting Professorial Lecturer, School of the Art Institute of Chicago, 1964–76; Assistant Professor of Humanities, Illinois Institute of Technology, Chicago, 1965–69. Author of *Rouault,* 1969; *Naive Painting in Illinois 1830–1976,* 1976; *Geometry as Abstract Art: The Lipschultz Collection,* 1980; and *The Geometric Impulse: The Florsheim Collection,* 1981. **Essays:** Albright; Baldessari; Bengston; Breer; Brooks; Close; Cottingham; Ferrer; Gilliam; Gorchov; Gordy; Grossman; Grosvenor; Irwin; Jenney; Judd; Lane; Robert and Sylvia Mangold; McGarrell; Catherine Murphy; Poons; Samaras; Sarkisian; Saul; Schnabel; Shields; Wegman; Winsor; Youngerman.

KINGSLEY, April. Essayist. Instructor, School of Visual Arts, New York, since 1973; Director, The Sculpture Center, New York, since 1980. Curatorial Assistant, Museum of Modern Art, New York, 1969–71; Associate Curator, Pasadena Art Museum, California, 1971–72. Secretary, American Section, International Art Critics Association, since 1978; Member, Board of Advisers, New York Feminist Art Institute, since 1978, and *Women's Art Journal,* since 1979. Author of numerous books/catalogues: *Frank Stella,* 1970; *Romare Bearden,* 1971; *Rafael Ferrer,* 1972; *Budd Hopkins,* 1973; *The Magic Circle,* 1977; *Cape Cod as an Art Colony,* 1977; *Victor Candell,* 1978; *Rudolf Baranik,* 1978; *David Shapiro/ Christopher Wilmarth,* 1978; *Michael Loew,* 1979; *Richard Hunt,* 1979; *Robert Motherwell,* 1980; *Nassos Daphnis,* 1980; *Melvin Edwards,* 1981; and *Alternative Realities,* 1981. **Essay:** Motherwell.

KLEIN, Mason. Essayist. Freelance writer, New York. Formerly, lecturer at Hunter College, and Brooklyn College, New York. Contributor to *Arts Magazine* and *New Observations.* **Essays:** Acconci; Anderson; Snow.

KONTOVA, Helena. Essayist. Co-Editor of *Flash Art,* Milan, since 1977. Assistant Curator, National Gallery, Prague, 1976–77. Editor of *The International Trans-Avantgarde,* with Achille Bonito Oliva, 1982; and *Jiri Kolar,* 1982. **Essays:** Abramovic; Collins; Knizák; Pane.

KOSTELANETZ, Richard. Essayist. Poet, critic, cultural historian; Co-Founder, Assembling Press, and proprietor, The Future Press, Co-Editor, *Precisely,* and Contributing Editor, *The Humanist* and *Performing Arts Journal.* Author of several books of verse, two novels, several collections of short stories, and critical works including *The Theatre of Mixed-Means,* 1968; *The End of Intelligent Writing,* 1974; and *Twenties in the Sixties,* 1978; *John Cage Conversing,* 1987; also editor of numerous collections and anthologies. **Essays:** Higgins; Whitman.

KULTERMANN, Udo. Essayist. Ruth and Norman Moore Professor of Architecture, Washington University, St. Louis. Director, City Art Museum, Leverkusen, West Germany, 1959–64; Architecture Commission Member, Venice Biennale, 1979–82; Member of the National Humanities Faculty, Georgia, 1986–88. Author of numerous critical works, including: *Architecture of Today,* 1958; *Dynamische Architektur,* 1969; *New Japanese Architecture,* 1960, 1967; *New Architecture in Africa,* 1963; *New Architecture in the World,* 1965–1976; *History of Art History,* 1966, 1981; *The New Sculpture,* 1969, 1977; *The New Painting,* 1969, 1977; *Art and Life: The Function of Intermedia,* 1970; *New Realism,* 1972; *Architecture in the Seventies,* 1980; *Contemporary Architecture in Eastern Europe,* 1985. **Essays:** Butterfield; Deem; Jonas; Jorn; Kanovitz; Messager; Roehr; Rosenbach; Schneemann.

LAMBARELLI, Roberto G. Essayist. Art critic: Contributor to *Flash Art,* Milan, since 1977, and *Segno,* since 1978; Editor of *AMP* since 1982. Author of *Maurizio Corona,* 1982; *Pier Luigi Meneghello,* 1982; and *Razionale Decorativo,* exhibition catalogue, 1981. **Essays:** Afro; Anselmo; Battaglia; Boetti; Carrino; Castellani; Ceroli; Cucchi; de Dominicis; Greco; Griffa; Kounellis; Mauri; Nagasawa; Novelli; Paolini; Pistoletto; Trotta; Zorio.

LANCER, Sharon. Essayist. Freelance art writer and exhibition organizer, London. Curator of the Ben Uri Gallery, London. **Essay:** Gilbert and George.

LaROSE, Elise. Essayist. Freelance art writer for *Arts Magazine, New Art Examiner,* and *Art Express.* **Essays:** Kuehn; Schapiro; Spero.

LEARMONT, Lavinia. Essayist. Freelance writer and artist, London. **Essays:** Dine; Finlay; Marisol; Roszak; Sedgley; Sutherland.

LIQUOIS, Dominique. Essayist. Freelance art writer and researcher, Paris. Formerly worked with the Galerie Chantal Crousel, Paris, the Galeria Yvan Martin, Mexico City, and the Centre Beaubourg, Paris. **Essays:** Berni; Cragg; Holzer; Kosice.

LIVINGSTONE, Marco. Essayist. Freelance writer and art historian, London. Formerly, Deputy Director of the Museum of Modern Art, Oxford. Author of the exhibition catalogues: *Sheer Magic by Allen Jones,* 1979; *David Hockney,* 1981; *Patrick Caulfield: Paintings 1963–1981,* 1981; *Peter Phillips Retrovision,* 1982. **Essay:** Barker.

LYNTON, Norbert. Essayist. Professor of the History of Art, University of Sussex, Brighton, since 1975. Senior Lecturer, then Head of the Department of Art History, Chelsea School of Art, London, 1961–70; London Correspondent, *Art International,* 1961–66; Art Critic, *The Guardian,* London, 1965–70; Director of Exhibitions, Arts Council of Great Britain, 1970–75. Author of *Kenneth Armitage,* 1962; *Paul Klee,* 1964; *The Modern World,* 1968; *The Story of Modern Art,* 1980. **Essay:** Moon.

MACKINTOSH, Alastair. (died, 1987). Essayist. Formerly, freelance writer and teacher, London; also, Visual Arts Officer, Scottish Arts Council, Edinburgh. Author of *Symbolism and Art Nouveau,* 1975. **Essays:** Bell; Beuys; Brisley; Di Suvero; Filliou; Laing; Medalla; Neagu; Price; Saura; Schöffer; Segal; Warhol.

MARECHAL-WORKMAN, Andrée. Essayist. Curator, Berkeley Art Center, and Instructor, University of California, Berkeley. Curator, Center for Visual Arts, Oakland, California, 1977–80; Creative Growth Gallery, Oakland, California, 1984–86. Author of the catalogues, *The Siegriests: A Family of Artists and Their Work,* 1980; *Robert DeNiro: Recent Paintings and Drawings,* 1981; *Chris Ranes: A Survey of Recent Paintings,* 1983. **Essays:** Connor; Ramos; Tapies; Thiebaud.

MARTIN, Henry. Essayist. Editorial Associate, *Art International,* Lugano, Switzerland, since 1968; Milan Correspondent for *Artnews,* New York, since 1980. Author of *Arman,* 1972; *Adami,* with Hubert Damish, 1974; *Renato Mambor's Evidenziatore,* 1975; *Fragments of a Possible Apocalypse,* with Gianfranco Baruchello, 1978; *An Introduction to George Brecht's "Book of the Tumbler on Fire,"* 1978; *Notes on the Work of Teodosio Magnoni,* 1980; *Gianfranco Baruchello,* 1982. **Essays:** Arman; Baruchello; Brecht; Fahlstrom; Gnoli; Hendricks; Nannucci; Télémaque.

MAURICE, Carine. Essayist. Freelance contributor to the *London Review of the Arts,* and Consultant to L. S. Graphics, London, since 1982. **Essays:** Caulfield; Davie; Green; Jones; Kitaj; Monro; Tom Phillips; Procktor; Steinberg.

McCANN, Cecile N. Editor/Publisher of *Artweek,* Oakland, California, since 1970. **Essays:** Abakanowicz; Arneson.

McINTYRE, Arthur. Adviser and essayist. Sydney Art Critic, *The Age,* Melbourne, since 1980. Lecturer in Design and Composition, University of New South Wales, since 1979; Lecturer in Australian Art History, Rollins College Australia Programme, since 1980. Art Critic, *The Australian,* 1977–78; contributor to *Art and Australia,* 1975–87. Author of *Australian Art of the 70s,* 1980; *Resurgence and Redefinition: Australian Contemporary Drawing,* 1988. **Essays:** Coleing; Drysdale; Nolan; Parr.

MENEGUZZO, Marco. Essayist. Teacher of Art History at the Istituto Statale d'Arte, Villa Reale, Monza, Italy, since 1978. Contributor to numerous magazines, including *Flash Art, Segno, D'Ars Agency,* etc. Author of *Il Moviemento Arte Concreta,* 1981; *Michelangelo,* 1981; *Leonardo: Disegni,* 1982; *Fausto Melotti: La Dimensione del Disegno,* with F. Gualdoni, 1981; *Schifano,* 1982. **Essays:** Nigro; Olivieri.

MESSER, Thomas. Essayist. Director of the Guggenheim Museum, New York, since 1961. Director, Institute of Contemporary Art, Boston, 1957–61; President, The MacDowell colony, 1977–78. Author of *Edward Munch,* 1973. **Essays:** Kolar; Soto.

METKEN, Günter. Essayist. Freelance writer on contemporary art and photography, Paris. Author of numerous exhibition catalogues. **Essay:** Lang.

MIKI, Tamon. Essayist. Art critic, Tokyo. **Essay:** Kudo.

MOORE, Alan. Essayist. Art critic, New York. **Essay:** Scanga.

MOORE, Barbara. Essayist. Administrative Director, Archives of Experimental Art, New York. Formerly, Editor-in-Chief of Something Else Press, New York. **Essay:** Miralda.

MORRIS, Lynda. Essayist. Curator, Norwich School of Art Gallery, Norfolk, England. Formerly, Curator at the Nigel Greenwood Gallery, London, and the Midland Group Gallery, Nottingham. **Essay:** Lamelas.

MURRAY, Joan. Adviser and essayist. Director of the Robert McLaughlin Gallery, Oshawa, Ontario, since 1974. Curator of Canadian Art, Art Gallery of Ontario, Toronto, 1969–74. Author of *Letters Home: William Blair Bruce 1859–1906*, 1982; *Kurelek's Vision of Canada*, 1983; *The Best of the Group of Seven*, 1984; *The Best of Tom Thomson*, 1986; *The Best Contemporary Canadian Art*, 1987. **Essays:** Carr-Harris; Curnoe; Meredith; Prent; Tousignant; Wieland.

MUSSA, Italo. Essayist. Art critic, Rome, since 1970; Director of the Centro di Cultura Ausoni, Rome. Contributor to *Flash Art*, *Segno* and *L'Avanti*. Author of *L'Ipperrealismo, il vero piu vero del vero*, 1974; *Victor Vasarely*, 1975; *Il Gruppo N e la situazione dei gruppi in Europa negli anni '60*, 1976; *Wilhelm von Gloeden: Photographs*, 1979; *Carlo Maria Mariani, Pictor Philosophus*, 1980; *L'Inattualita dell'arte*, 1982; *Arnaldo Pomodoro at the Belvedere Fort*, 1986; *La Peinture de l'Avenir*, 1987. **Essays:** Calzolari; Castelli; Nicola De Maria; Lupertz; Ontani; Pisani; Salle; Twombly; Uncini.

NARAHARA, Yusuke. Essayist. Freelance art critic, Tokyo. Author of *Man-Made Nature*, 1971; *Contemporary Sculpture*, 1977; and *Akira Baba's Work*, 1980. **Essays:** Matsuzawa; Suga.

NASGAARD, Roald. Essayist. Chief Curator, Art Gallery of Ontario, Toronto, since 1978 (Curator of Contemporary Art, 1975–78). Lecturer 1971–74, and Assistant Professor, 1974–75, Department of Fine Art, University of Guelph, Ontario. Contributing Editor, *Arts Magazine*, New York, 1974–75; Secretary-General, International Association of Art Critics (Canada), 1976–78. Author of the exhibition catalogues, *Ron Martin: World Paintings*, 1976; *Peter Kolisnyk*, 1977; *Structures for Behavior*, 1978; *Garry Neill Kennedy: Recent Work*, 1979; *Yves Gaucher: A 15 Year Perspective*, 1979; *The Mystic North: Symbolist Landscape Painting*, 1984; *Gerhard Richter: Retrospective*, 1988. **Essays:** Favro; Gaucher; Ron Martin; Molinari; Richter.

NEWMAN, Michael. Essayist. Freelance art critic and historian, London. **Essay:** Coleman.

NORTH, Percy. Essayist. Freelance art critic and writer, Atlanta, Georgia; Lecturer, Emory University, Atlanta, since 1987. Formerly, instructor at the University of Minnesota, George Mason University, and James Madison University. Author of the exhibition catalogues: *Hudson D. Walker*, 1977; *Max Weber: American Modern*, 1982; *Into the Melting Pot*, 1984; *Gene Davis: Child and Man*, 1985; *Visions of an Inner Life: Will Henry Stevens*, 1988. **Essays:** Bertoia; Gene Davis; Liberman.

OSBORNE, Harold. (died, 1987). Essayist. Editor, *British Journal of Aesthetics*, 1960–78; Vice-President, International Committee for Aesthetics, 1976–87; President, British Society of Aesthetics, 1982–87. Author of *Foundations of the Philosophy of Value*, 1933; *Christ and the Early Church*, 1934; *Indians of the Andes*, 1952; *Bolivia: A Land Divided*, 1954, 3rd ed. 1964; *Aesthetics and Criticism*, 1955; *Aesthetics and Art Theory*, 1968; *South American Mythology*, 1968; *The Art of Appreciation*, 1970; *The Oxford Companion to Art*, 1970; *The Oxford Companion to the Decorative Arts*, 1975; *Abstraction and Artifice in 20th Century Art*, 1979; *The Oxford Companion to 20th Century Art*, 1981. **Essays:** Appel; Bazaine; Chamberlain; Dubuffet; Esteve; Gerstner; Marca-Relli; Meadows; Morellet; Munari.

PAPARONI, Demetrio. Essayist. Director, Centro d'Arte Contemporanea, Siracusa, Italy, since 1981. Author of numerous exhibition catalogues, including *L'Annunciazione di Antonello*, 1979; *Aljofre barroco*, 1981; *L'Altra Anatomia*, 1981; *Thinking of Europe*, 1982; and *In virtu del possesso delle mani*, 1982. **Essays:** Baselitz; Fetting; Paladino; Schifano; Tatafiore; Van Elk.

PARMESANI, Loredana. Essayist. Contributor to *Flash Art* and to other Italian art magazines since 1979. Has organized various exhibitions, including *La frase e il discorso*, Cortina d'Ampezzo, 1981, and *Registrazione di Frequenze*, Bologna, 1982. Author of *Nuova Immagine*, 1980; and *Baj: I grandi quadri*, 1982. **Essays:** Cavaliere; Pascali; Tadini.

POMEROY, Ralph. Essayist. Associate Director, Forum Gallery, New York, since 1979; Contributing Editor, *Arts Magazine*, New York, since 1981. Member, Editorial Staff, *Artnews*, New York, 1963–68, and *Art and Artists*, London, 1966–73. Author of *Stills and Movies*, 1961; *The Canaries as They Are*, 1965; *In the Financial District*, 1968; *Stamos*, 1974; *The Ice Cream Connection*, 1975; *First Things First*, 1977. **Essays:** Balthus; Bearden; Calder; Estes; Hall; Held; John Koch; Mitchell; Morandi; Noguchi; Noland; O'Keeffe; Pearlstein; Reinhardt; Richard Smith; Tony Smith; Stamos; Turnbull; Westermann; Wiley.

POPPER, Frank. Adviser and essayist. Director of the Fine Arts Department since 1970, and Professor of Aesthetics and of the Science of Art since 1975, University of Paris VIII (Assistant Professor, 1969–70; Reader, 1970–75). Author of *Naissance de l'Art Cinétique*, 1967, 1970; *Origins and Development of Kinetic Art*, 1968; *L'Arte Cinetica*, 1970; *Le Déclin de l'Objet*, 1975; *Art-Action and Participation*, 1975; *Agam*, 1976, 3rd ed. 1982; *L'Artiste et la Créativité Aujourd'hui*, 1980. **Essays:** Agam; Boto; Cruz-Diez; Demarco; Kowalski.

RICKEY, George. Essayist and entrant. See his own entry. **Essay:** Baertling.

ROBERTS, John. Essayist. Freelance writer, London; regular contributor to various art magazines. **Essays:** Brus; Burgin; Craig-Martin; Hesse; Walker.

ROBINSON, John. Essayist. Editor, Archives of American Art, San Francisco office; Lecturer, California College of Arts and Crafts, Dominican College, and Holy Names College. Contributor to *Artforum*, *Artweek*, *San Francisco Review of Books*, and *Flash Art*. **Essays:** Borofsky; DeForest; Newton

Harrison; Hockney; Kaltenbach; LeWitt; Robert Smithson; Venet; Wilson.

ROBINSON, Marlee. Essayist. Personal assistant to Eduardo Paolozzi, and Lecturer at the Tate Gallery, London, since 1977. **Essays:** Buckley; Chicago; Page.

SCHIPPER, Merle. Essayist. Freelance art critic and exhibition organizer, Los Angeles. Contributing Editor, *Artweek*, Oakland, since 1983, and columnist, *Artscene*, Los Angeles, since 1987. Los Angeles Correspondent, *Artnews*, New York, 1985–87. Author of *Americans in Paris: the 50s*, 1979; *Abstract Painting and Sculpture in America 1927–44*, with others, 1983; *Jean Helion: Abstraktion und Mythen des Altags*, with others, 1984; *Susan Rankaitis*, 1988. **Essays:** Moses; Ruppersberg.

SCHULZE-REIMPELL, Werner. Essayist. Freelance journalist, West Germany, since 1977. Chief Editor of the theatre monthly *Die Deutsche Bühne* 1972–77. Author of *Structure and Development of the Theatre in the Federal Republic of Germany*, 1973, 1977. **Essays:** Grutzke; Schult; Schultze; Weseler.

SCHWARZ, Dieter. Essayist. Assistant Curator, Kunstmuseum, Winterthur, Switzerland, since 1985. Author of *Auf der Bogen Bahn: Studien zum literarische Werk von Dieter Roth*, 1981; *Camille Graeser: Zeichnungen*, 1986. Editor of *John Armleder*, 1987; *Andre Thomkins: Gesammelte Anagramme*, 1987. **Essays:** Armleder; Gosewitz; Hains; Roth; Villegle.

SELZ, Peter. Adviser and essayist. Professor of the History of Art, University of California, Berkeley, since 1965 (Director of the University Art Museum, 1965–73). Head, Graduate Program, Institute of Design, Chicago, 1949–55; Chairman of the Art Department, Pomona College, Claremont, California, 1955–58; Curator, Department of Painting and Sculpture Exhibitions, Museum of Modern Art, New York, 1958–65. Author of *German Expressionist Painting*, 1957; *New Images of Man*, 1959; *Art Nouveau*, 1960; *The Work of Jean Dubuffet*, 1962; *Emil Nolde*, 1963; *Max Beckmann*, 1964; *Ferdinand Hodler*, 1972; *Sam Francis*, 1975, 1982; *Art in Our Times: A Visual History*, 1981; *Art in a Turbulent Era*, 1985; *Chillida*, 1986. **Essay:** Denes.

SHEPHERD, Michael. Essayist. Art Critic of the *Sunday Telegraph*, London, since 1971; Consultant, *Art Review*, London, since 1975; Art Critic, *What's On in London*, since 1978; Postgraduate Thesis Tutor, Royal Academy of Arts, London, since 1979; London Correspondent, *Artmagazine*, Toronto since 1980. Author of *Barbara Hepworth*, 1963. **Essays:** Abrahams; Andrews; Burra; Tindle; Vaughan.

SHINODA, Tazmi. Adviser and essayist. Freelance art critic and art historian, Kanagawa, Japan. Member, Association Internationale des Critiques d' Art, since 1986. Co-author of *The Dictionary of Contemporary Art*, 1984. **Essays:** Kawara; Kitatsuji; Kusama; Nakazato; Niizuma; Onosato; Saito; Yamada; Yamaguchi.

SINZ, Dagmar. Essayist. Parisian Correspondent for Cultural Events, *Neue Zürcher Zeitung*, Zurich, since 1980, and for Saarlandischer Rundfunk/Radio Saarbrucken, West Germany, since 1981; Art Critic, *Artis*, Konstanz, West Germany, since 1977. **Essays:** Dado; Penalba; Anne and Patrick Poirier.

SMITH, Katharine. Essayist. Freelance art critic, Denver. Formerly, Colorado Editor, *Artspace* magazine. Author of numerous exhibition catalogues for museums and art centers in the western United States. **Essays:** Pepper; Ross.

SPENCER, Charles. Essayist. Freelance writer, and lecturer at various British art schools for the British Council. Formerly: Editor, *Art and Artists*, London; Art Critic for the London *Daily Mail* and the European Edition of the *New York Times*; Editor, Editions Alecto, London; and Principal Lecturer, Croydon College, Surrey. Author of *Erté*, 1970, 1981; *A Decade of Printmaking*, 1972; *The Aesthetic Movement*, 1972; *Leon Bakst*, 1973; *Cecil Beaton: Stage and Film Designs*, 1975; *The World of Serge Diaghilev*, 1978. **Essays:** Botero; Boyd; Butler; Canogar; Cascella; Chadwick; Chillida; Cohen; Consagra; Cremonini; Domela; Dorazio; Efrat; Frost; Genoves; Grau Garriga; Hilton; Hodgkin; Hoflehner; Ipousteguy; Kenny; Kossoff; Leverett; Lundquist; Morlotti; Partridge; Pasmore; Perilli; Piché; Arnaldo/Gio Pomodoro; Radice; Rotella; Sandle; William Scott; Shahn; Tajiri; Tilson; Velickovic; Wagemaker; Wall.

SPIELMANN, Heinz. Adviser and essayist. Director of the Landesmuseum Schleswig-Holstein, West Germany, since 1986. Professor at the University of Munster, since 1984. Chief Curator, Museum für Kunst und Gewerbe, Hamburg, 1960-85. Editor of *Das Fruhe Plakat in Europa und den USA*, 3 vols., 1969-75; *Oskar Kokoschka*, 4 vols., 1972-76; *Spektrum der Kunst*, 1974, 1987; *Oskar Kokoschka, Briefe*, 4 vols., 1984-88; *Die Japanische Photographie*, 1985. **Essays:** Bill; Janssen; Kokoschka; Nagel; Schumacher; von Graevenitz; Wunderlich.

STANISLAWSKI, Ryszard. Essayist. Freelance art critic and historian of contemporary art, Warsaw. Author of *Constructivism in Poland 1923-36*, 1973; etc. **Essay:** Kantor.

STOFFLET, Mary. Essayist. Curator of Education, San Diego Museum of Art, California, since 1985. Assistant Curator of Exhibitions and Cultural Programs, San Francisco International Airport, 1982-84; Instructor in Art History, Oakland Museum, California, 1977-83; Associate Editor, *Images and Issues*, Los Angeles, 1979-82; Editor, Western Association of Art Museums *Newsletter*, 1974-77. Author of *Women Artists: Sculpture*, with Karen Petersen, 1980; *Dr. Seuss from Then to Now*, 1986. **Essays:** Antin; Isabel Bishop; Cadmus; Hare; Katz; Ellen Lanyon; Leslie; Marilyn Levine; Maciunas; Marioni; Shiomi; Vautier.

SYRING, Marie Luise. Essayist. Art Critic, Paris, since 1976. Parisian Correspondent for *Du*, Zurich, and Contributing Editor, *Kunstforum*, Cologne. **Essays:** Gerz; Honegger; Viallat; Voss.

THOMAS, Daniel. Essayist. Senior Curator of Australian Art, Australian National Gallery, Canberra, since 1978. Curator of Australian Art, Art Gallery of New South Wales, Sydney, 1958-77. Author of *Outlines of Australian Art: The Joseph Brown Collection*, 1973, 1980. **Essays:** Albert Tucker; Unsworth.

TONO, Yoshiaki. Essayist. Art Critic, Tokyo; Professor, Tama University of Art; Guest Curator, Seibu Museum of Art, Tokyo, and Toyama Museum of Modern Art, Tokyo. Author of *Artists in Grotta*, 1957, 1965; *After Pollock*, 1965; *Diaries in the U.S.A.*, 1968; *Marcel Duchamp*, 1977; *Jasper Johns and/or*, 1979; *The Betrayed Regard*, 1980; *The Ambiguous Water*, 1980; *Chatting with Artists*, 1984; *Mrs. Robinson and Contemporary Art*, 1986. **Essays:** Arakawa; Ay-O; Kawaguchi; Kuwayama; Miki; Sekine; Sugai; Takamatsu.

TRINI, Tommaso. Adviser. Art critic and historian, Milan. Formerly, Editor of *Data*, Milan. Author of numerous works on 20th century art.

VAIZEY, Marina (Lady Vaizey). Advisor. Art Critic, *The Sunday Times*, London, since 1974. Art Critic, *The Financial Times*, London, 1970-74. Member of the Arts Panel, 1973-78, Member, 1976-78, and Chairman of Arts Films, 1976-78, Arts Council of Great Britain. Author of *100 Masterpieces of Art*, 1979; *Andrew Wyeth*, 1980; and *The Artist as Photographer*, 1982.

van HAAREN, H.J.A.M. Essayist. Art Critic, Rotterdam. **Essay:** van Munster.

VARIA, Radu. Essayist. Art critic, Paris and New York. Director of the International Committee of the *Biennale de Paris* in the 1970's, and Director of the International Section of the *Sao Paulo Bienal* in 1973; assisted Salvador Dali in the founding of the Dali Museum in Figueras, 1974. Has organized numerous exhibitions, particularly of the work of Horia Damian. **Essay:** Dali.

VENTURI, Luca. Freelance art critic, Milan. **Essay:** Turcato.

VERZOTTI, Giorgio. Essayist. Temporary Exhibitions Curator, Pinacoteca di Brera, Milan, since 1983; contributor to *Flash Art*, Milan, since 1979. Author of *Paesaggio Metropolitano*, 1982; and the exhibition catalogues: *Imago*, 1983; *In Labirinto*, 1983; *John Armleder/Alberto Garutti*, 1987; *Lucio Fontana*, 1987; *Presi per incantamento*, 1988. **Essays:** Bertrand; Chia; Clemente; Devade; Dias; Fabro; Immendorff; Kapoor; Mosset; Opie; Penone; Tremlett; Trockel; Vedova.

von ZITZEWITZ, Monika. Essayist. Cultural Correspondent in Italy for *Die Welt*, Bonn, since 1965. Author of *Auch so ist der Ivan*, 1953; *Verzaubert in Florenz*, 1962; *Golf von Neapel*, 1974, 1978; *Florenz und die Toskana*, 1979, 1980; *Toskana und Umbrien*, 1981. **Essays:** Guttuso; Manzù; Marini; Melotti.

WAGEMANS, A. F. Essayist. Instructor in Art Theory, State Academy, Amsterdam, since 1987. Assistant Curator, Rijksmuseum Kroller-Muller, Otterlo, 1980-81; Curator, Bonnefantenmuseum, Maastricht, 1982-84. **Essays:** Boezem; Botschuyver; Dahn; D'Armagnac; Dekkers; Dokoupil; Engels; Fernhout; Gijzen; Pyke Koch; Rajlich; Schoonhoven; Van der Heyden; Van Koningsbruggen; Visser; Westerik.

WEIL, John A. Essayist. Professor of Chemistry, University of Saskatchewan, Saskatoon, since 1971. **Essay:** Albers.

WHITTET, G. S. Essayist. Art critic and consultant, London. Assistant Editor, 1946-50, Managing Editor, 1950-58, and Editor, 1958-64, *The Studio*, London, and Editor, *Studio International*, 1964-66; London Art Correspondent, *Le Monde*, Paris, 1969-72; London Editor, *Pictures on Exhibit*, New York, 1972-80. Author of *Bouquet*, 1949; *London* (in the series "Art Centres of the World"), 1967; *Scotland Explored*, 1969; *Lovers in Art*, 1972. **Essays:** Antes; Boshier; Bury; Calderara; Cesar; Colville; Dahmen; Dewasne; Duchamp; Fraser; Freud; Goeritz; Hartigan; Hayter; Heiliger; Hepworth; Huxley; Jenkins; Jorn; Kricke; Peter Lanyon; Lichtenstein; Lipton; Manessier; Kenneth Martin; Mathieu; Mesens; Moore; Negret; Nevelson; Newman; Nicholson; Oldenburg; Paolozzi; Peter Phillips; Piper; Prassinos; Rickey; Rosenquist; Scanavino; Soulages; Frank Stella; Still; Sutton; Tal-Coat; Vasarely; Wyeth, Yunkers.

WILKIN, Karen. Essayist. Freelance curator and art critic, New York, since 1978. Chief Curator, The Edmonton Art Gallery, 1971-78. Author of *Modern Painting in Canada*, with Terry Fenton, 1978; *David Smith: The Formative Years*, 1981; *Jack Bush*, 1983; *Frankenthaler on Paper*, 1985; *Stuart Davis*, 1987. **Essays:** Bannard; Bush; Caro; Dzubas; Frankenthaler; Robert Murray; Tim Scott.

WILLIAMS, Sheldon. Essayist. English Correspondent of *L'Arte Naive*, Italy, since 1970; Artistic Adviser to RONA, London, since 1977. Editor, *Art Illustrated*, 1969-71. Author of *Situation Humaine*, 1967; *Verlon*, 1969; *A Background to Sfumato*, 1969; *Voodoo and the Art of Haiti*, 1971; *20th Century British Naive and Primitive Artists*, with Eric Lister, 1975; editor of *RONABOOK*, 1978, and *A Quiet Thunder*, 1978. **Essays:** Adami, Alechinsky; Arroyo; Auerbach; Bacon; Bayer; Bellmer; Berlewi; Biederman; Blake; Bontecou; Brauer; Bravo; Castillo; Chagall; Chryssa; Corneille; Crippa; Ad Dekkers; De Kooning; Ernst; Fangor; Fontana; Frink; Fruhtrunk; Fuchs; Furnival; Golub; Goodnough; Hajdu; Hartung; Helion; Hrdlicka; Hundertwasser; Iannone; Jacquet; Kalinowski, William King; Klapheck; Kothe; Krushenick; Lam; Lardera; Lenk; Lindner; Lindstrom; Lohse; Magritte; Masson; McWilliam; Michaux; Millares; Molinier; Monory; Mundy; Nitsch; Oiticica; Meret Oppenheim; Paik; Panamarenko; Pignon; Rainer; Raynaud; Raysse; Rebeyrolle; Rinke; Riopelle; Ruckriem; Ruscha; Saint-Phalle; Self; Seuphor; Sonderborg; Sorge; Spoerri; Tamayo; Titus-Carmel; Trevelyan; Trouille; Uecker; Van Amen; Van Velde; Vieira da Silva; Villalba; Wesselman.

WINGATE, Adina. Essayist. Development Consultant, Arizona Historical Society, Tucson, since 1980. Art Critic, *Arizona Daily Star*, Tucson, 1973-76; Public Information and Program Director, Tucson Museum of Art, 1976-79; Senior Curator, La Jolla Museum of Contemporary Art, California, 1979-80. **Essay:** Peter Young.

ZACHAREA, Chryssa. Essayist. Freelance writer and researcher, London. **Essay:** Louw.